2020
Harris
Connecticut
Manufacturers Directory

Exclusive Provider of
Dun & Bradstreet Library Solutions

 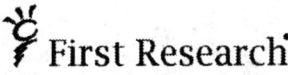 

Published February 2020 next update February 2021

WARNING: Purchasers and users of this directory may not use this directory to compile mailing lists, other marketing aids and other types of data, which are sold or otherwise provided to third parties. Such use is wrongful, illegal and a violation of the federal copyright laws.

CAUTION: Because of the many thousands of establishment listings contained in this directory and the possibilities of both human and mechanical error in processing this information, Harris InfoSource cannot assume liability for the correctness of the listings or information on which they are based. Hence, no information contained in this work should be relied upon in any instance where there is a possibility of any loss or damage as a consequence of any error or omission in this volume.

Publisher
Mergent Inc.
444 Madison Ave
New York, NY 10022

©Mergent Inc All Rights Reserved
2020 Mergent Business Press
ISSN 1080-2614
ISBN 978-1-64141-601-6

TABLE OF CONTENTS

Summary of Contents & Explanatory Notes 4
User's Guide to Listings 6

Geographic Section
County/City Cross-Reference Index 9
Firms Listed by Location 11

Standard Industrial Classification (SIC) Section
SIC Alphabetical Index 367
SIC Numerical Index 369
Firms Listed by SIC 371

Alphabetic Section
Firms Listed by Firm Name 473

Product Section
Product Index 601
Firms Listed by Product Category 619

SUMMARY OF CONTENTS

Number of Companies 10,698
Number of Decision Makers 18,536
Minimum Number of Employees 1

EXPLANATORY NOTES

How to Cross-Reference in This Directory

Sequential Entry Numbers. Each establishment in the Geographic Section is numbered sequentially (G-0000). The number assigned to each establishment is referred to as its "entry number." To make cross-referencing easier, each listing in the Geographic, SIC, Alphabetic and Product Sections includes the establishment's entry number. To facilitate locating an entry in the Geographic Section, the entry numbers for the first listing on the left page and the last listing on the right page are printed at the top of the page next to the city name.

Source Suggestions Welcome

Although all known sources were used to compile this directory, it is possible that companies were inadvertently omitted. Your assistance in calling attention to such omissions would be greatly appreciated. A special form on the facing page will help you in the reporting process.

Analysis

Every effort has been made to contact all firms to verify their information. The one exception to this rule is the annual sales figure, which is considered by many companies to be confidential information. Therefore, estimated sales have been calculated by multiplying the nationwide average sales per employee for the firm's major SIC/NAICS code by the firm's number of employees. Nationwide averages for sales per employee by SIC/NAICS codes are provided by the U.S. Department of Commerce and are updated annually. All sales—sales (est)—have been estimated by this method. The exceptions are parent companies (PA), division headquarters (DH) and headquarter locations (HQ) which may include an actual corporate sales figure—sales (corporate-wide) if available.

Types of Companies

Descriptive and statistical data are included for companies in the entire state. These comprise manufacturers, machine shops, fabricators, assemblers and printers. Also identified are corporate offices in the state.

Employment Data

The employment figure shown in the Geographic Section includes male and female employees and embraces all levels of the company: administrative, clerical, sales and maintenance. This figure is for the facility listed and does not include other plants or offices. It should be recognized that these figures represent an approximate year-round average. These employment figures are broken into codes A through G and used in the Product and SIC Sections to further help you in qualifying a company. Be sure to check the footnotes on the bottom of pages for the code breakdowns.

Standard Industrial Classification (SIC)

The Standard Industrial Classification (SIC) system used in this directory was developed by the federal government for use in classifying establishments by the type of activity they are engaged in. The SIC classifications used in this directory are from the 1987 edition published by the U.S. Government's Office of Management and Budget. The SIC system separates all activities into broad industrial divisions (e.g., manufacturing, mining, retail trade). It further subdivides each division. The range of manufacturing industry classes extends from two-digit codes (major industry group) to four-digit codes (product).

For example:

Industry Breakdown	Code	Industry, Product, etc.
*Major industry group	20	Food and kindred products
Industry group	203	Canned and frozen foods
*Industry	2033	Fruits and vegetables, etc.

*Classifications used in this directory

Only two-digit and four-digit codes are used in this directory.

Arrangement

1. The **Geographic Section** contains complete in-depth corporate data. This section is sorted by cities listed in alphabetical order and companies listed alphabetically within each city. A County/City Index for referencing cities within counties precedes this section.

> IMPORTANT NOTICE: It is a violation of both federal and state law to transmit an unsolicited advertisement to a facsimile machine. Any user of this product that violates such laws may be subject to civil and criminal penalties, which may exceed $500 for each transmission of an unsolicited facsimile. Harris InfoSource provides fax numbers for lawful purposes only and expressly forbids the use of these numbers in any unlawful manner.

2. The **Standard Industrial Classification (SIC) Section** lists companies under approximately 500 four-digit SIC codes. An alphabetical and a numerical index precedes this section. A company can be listed under several codes. The codes are in numerical order with companies listed alphabetically under each code.

3. The **Alphabetic Section** lists all companies with their full physical or mailing addresses and telephone number.

4. The **Product Section** lists companies under unique Harris categories. An index preceding this section lists all product categories in alphabetical order. Companies can be listed under several categories.

USER'S GUIDE TO LISTINGS

GEOGRAPHIC SECTION

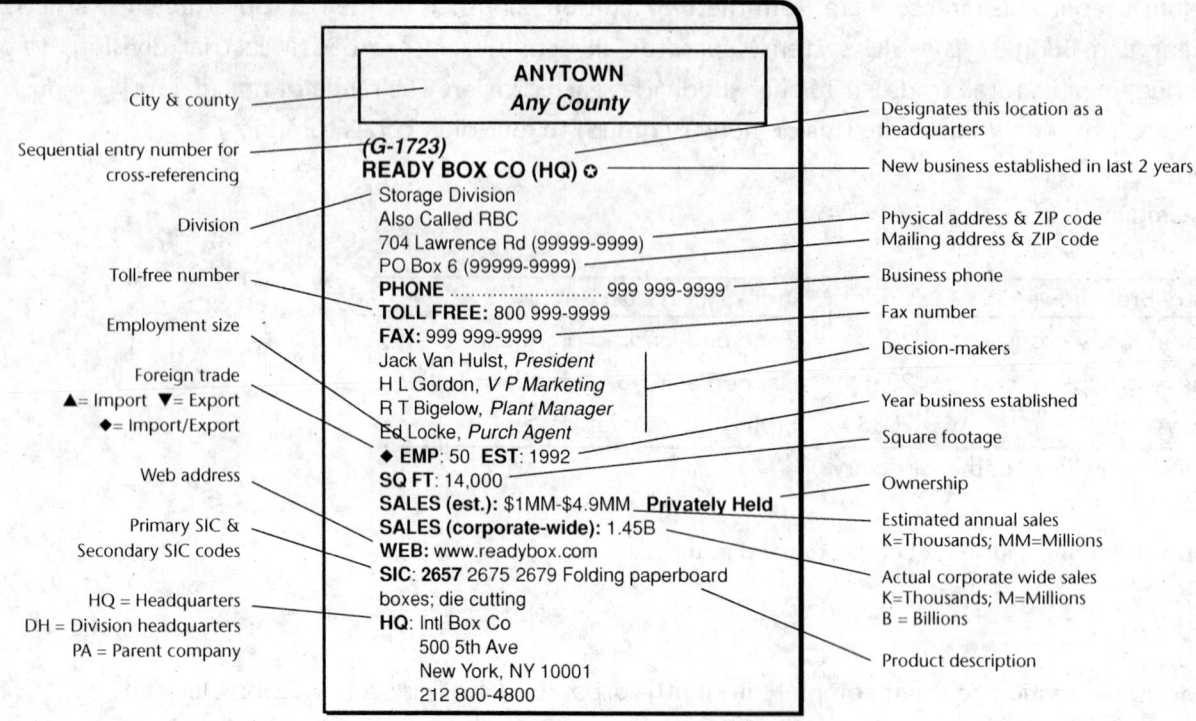

SIC SECTION

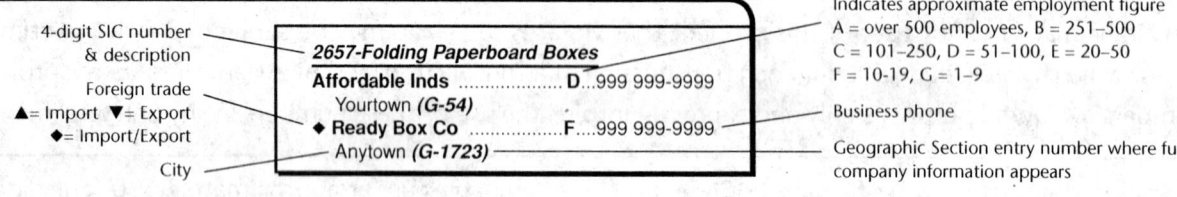

ALPHABETIC SECTION

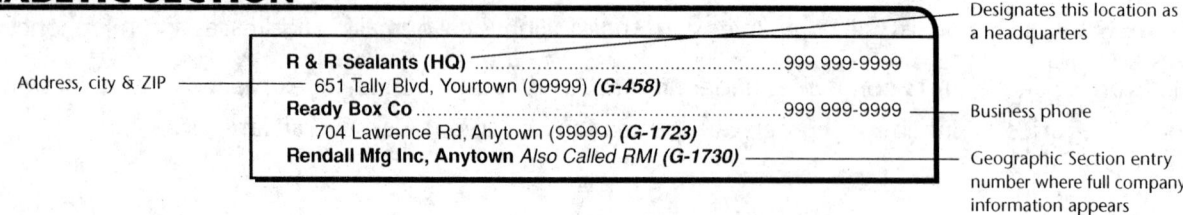

PRODUCT SECTION

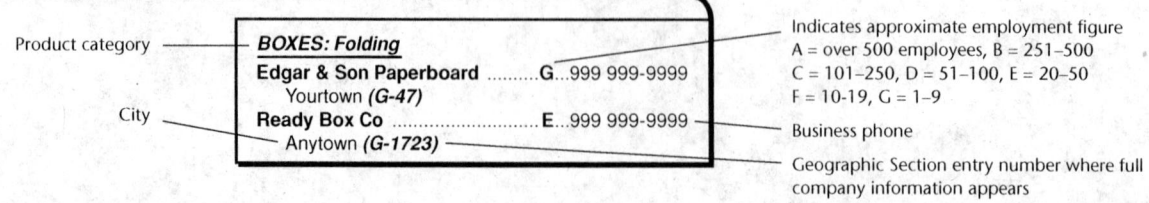

GEOGRAPHIC SECTION
Companies sorted by city in alphabetical order
In-depth company data listed

STANDARD INDUSTRIAL CLASSIFICATIONS
Alphabetical index of classifcation descriptions
Numerical index of classifcation descriptions
Companies sorted by SIC product groupings

ALPHABETIC SECTION
Company listings in alphabetical order

PRODUCT INDEX
Product categories listed in alphabetical order

PRODUCT SECTION
Companies sorted by product and manufacturing service classifications

Connecticut
County Map

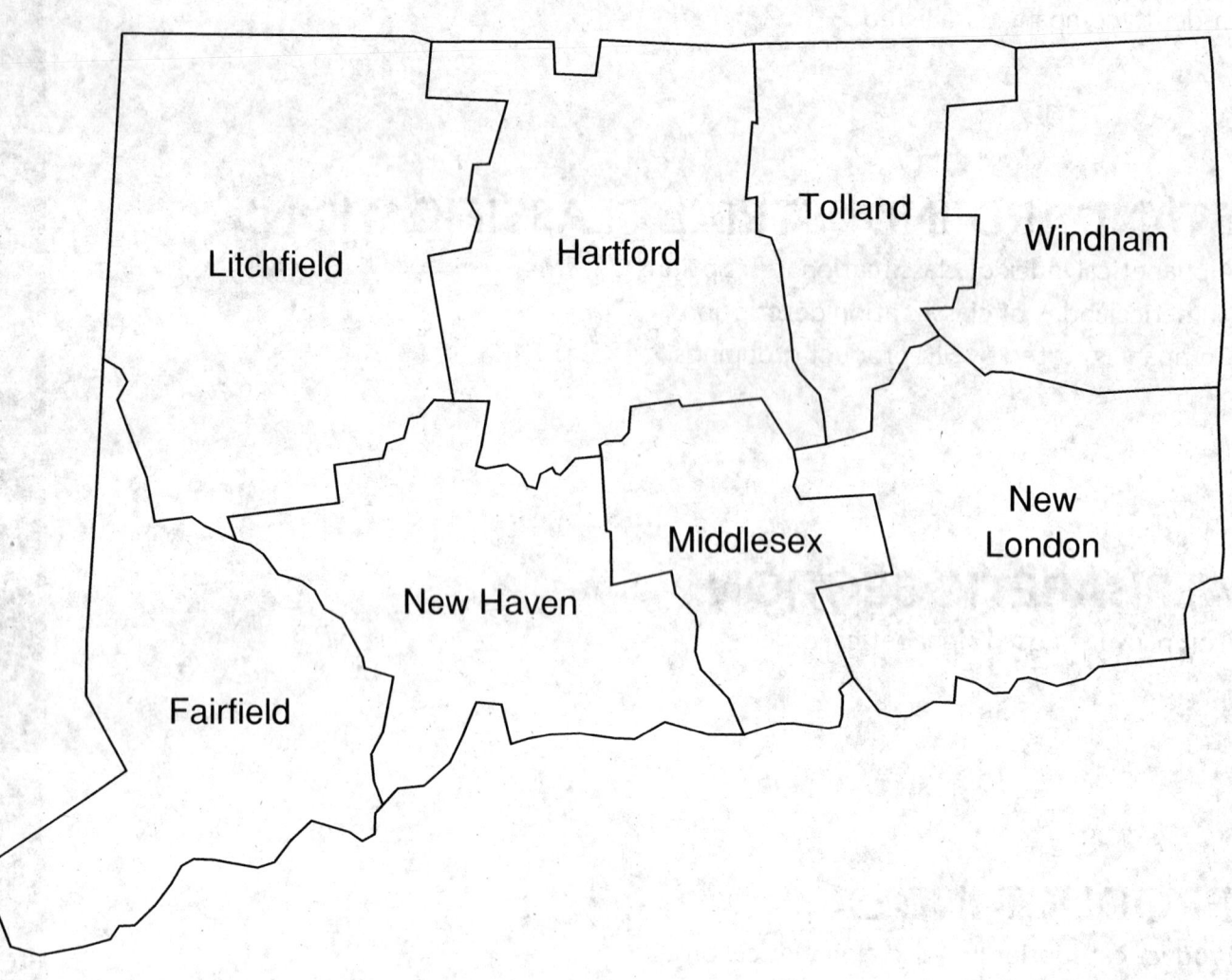

COUNTY/CITY CROSS-REFERENCE INDEX

Fairfield
City	Entry #
Bethel	(G-254)
Bridgeport	(G-678)
Brookfield	(G-1154)
Cos Cob	(G-1622)
Danbury	(G-1726)
Darien	(G-2007)
Easton	(G-2546)
Fairfield	(G-2740)
Georgetown	(G-2998)
Greenwich	(G-3116)
Hawleyville	(G-3744)
Monroe	(G-4690)
New Canaan	(G-5086)
New Fairfield	(G-5160)
Newtown	(G-5726)
Norwalk	(G-6056)
Old Greenwich	(G-6468)
Redding	(G-7087)
Ridgefield	(G-7113)
Riverside	(G-7189)
Sandy Hook	(G-7299)
Shelton	(G-7385)
Sherman	(G-7590)
Southport	(G-7998)
Stamford	(G-8048)
Stevenson	(G-8520)
Stratford	(G-8562)
Trumbull	(G-8994)
West Redding	(G-9969)
Weston	(G-10016)
Westport	(G-10048)
Wilton	(G-10262)

Hartford
City	Entry #
Avon	(G-71)
Berlin	(G-150)
Bloomfield	(G-378)
Bristol	(G-949)
Broad Brook	(G-1143)
Burlington	(G-1260)
Canton	(G-1303)
Collinsville	(G-1588)
East Berlin	(G-2162)
East Glastonbury	(G-2185)
East Granby	(G-2186)
East Hartford	(G-2286)
East Hartland	(G-2403)
East Windsor	(G-2478)
Enfield	(G-2610)
Farmington	(G-2873)
Glastonbury	(G-3002)
Granby	(G-3106)
Hartford	(G-3541)
Kensington	(G-3802)
Manchester	(G-3970)
Marion	(G-4117)
Marlborough	(G-4118)
Milldale	(G-4683)
New Britain	(G-4931)
Newington	(G-5614)
North Granby	(G-5880)
Plainville	(G-6758)
Plantsville	(G-6880)
Poquonock	(G-6948)
Rocky Hill	(G-7217)
Simsbury	(G-7608)
South Glastonbury	(G-7679)
South Windsor	(G-7696)
Southington	(G-7887)
Suffield	(G-8714)
Tariffville	(G-8743)
Unionville	(G-9110)
Weatogue	(G-9755)
West Granby	(G-9766)
West Hartford	(G-9768)
West Simsbury	(G-9971)
West Suffield	(G-9985)
Wethersfield	(G-10179)
Windsor	(G-10350)
Windsor Locks	(G-10467)
Windsorville	(G-10503)

Litchfield
City	Entry #
Bantam	(G-123)
Bethlehem	(G-366)
Bridgewater	(G-945)
Canaan	(G-1280)
Colebrook	(G-1584)
Cornwall	(G-1616)
Cornwall Bridge	(G-1617)
East Canaan	(G-2180)
Falls Village	(G-2869)
Gaylordsville	(G-2990)
Goshen	(G-3095)
Harwinton	(G-3717)
Kent	(G-3821)
Lakeside	(G-3841)
Lakeville	(G-3842)
Litchfield	(G-3884)
Morris	(G-4785)
New Hartford	(G-5184)
New Milford	(G-5499)
New Preston	(G-5611)
Norfolk	(G-5822)
Northfield	(G-6042)
Oakville	(G-6448)
Pine Meadow	(G-6733)
Pleasant Valley	(G-6920)
Plymouth	(G-6928)
Riverton	(G-7206)
Roxbury	(G-7275)
Salisbury	(G-7294)
Sharon	(G-7376)
South Kent	(G-7683)
Terryville	(G-8746)
Thomaston	(G-8778)
Torrington	(G-8884)
Warren	(G-9406)
Washington	(G-9411)
Washington Depot	(G-9416)
Watertown	(G-9678)
West Cornwall	(G-9761)
Winchester Center	(G-10343)
Winsted	(G-10504)
Woodbury	(G-10622)

Middlesex
City	Entry #
Centerbrook	(G-1329)
Chester	(G-1462)
Clinton	(G-1488)
Cobalt	(G-1537)
Cromwell	(G-1684)
Deep River	(G-2081)
Durham	(G-2135)
East Haddam	(G-2235)
East Hampton	(G-2251)
Essex	(G-2710)
Haddam	(G-3403)
Higganum	(G-3759)
Ivoryton	(G-3782)
Killingworth	(G-3828)
Middlefield	(G-4298)
Middletown	(G-4311)
Moodus	(G-4771)
Old Saybrook	(G-6522)
Portland	(G-6949)
Rockfall	(G-7210)
Westbrook	(G-9989)

New Haven
City	Entry #
Ansonia	(G-17)
Beacon Falls	(G-129)
Bethany	(G-234)
Branford	(G-534)
Cheshire	(G-1344)
Derby	(G-2107)
East Haven	(G-2406)
Guilford	(G-3321)
Hamden	(G-3408)
Madison	(G-3907)
Meriden	(G-4134)
Middlebury	(G-4271)
Milford	(G-4435)
Naugatuck	(G-4854)
New Haven	(G-5215)
North Branford	(G-5829)
North Haven	(G-5893)
Northford	(G-6043)
Orange	(G-6578)
Oxford	(G-6637)
Prospect	(G-6992)
Seymour	(G-7334)
Southbury	(G-7840)
Wallingford	(G-9192)
Waterbury	(G-9420)
West Haven	(G-9878)
Wolcott	(G-10548)
Woodbridge	(G-10594)
Yalesville	(G-10694)

New London
City	Entry #
Baltic	(G-118)
Bozrah	(G-522)
Colchester	(G-1538)
East Lyme	(G-2462)
Gales Ferry	(G-2980)
Gilman	(G-3000)
Griswold	(G-3263)
Groton	(G-3269)
Jewett City	(G-3791)
Lebanon	(G-3846)
Ledyard	(G-3867)
Lisbon	(G-3881)
Lyme	(G-3903)
Mashantucket	(G-4132)
Montville	(G-4768)
Mystic	(G-4794)
New London	(G-5455)
Niantic	(G-5801)
North Franklin	(G-5869)
North Stonington	(G-6018)
Norwich	(G-6405)
Oakdale	(G-6441)
Old Lyme	(G-6486)
Pawcatuck	(G-6703)
Preston	(G-6981)
Quaker Hill	(G-7082)
Salem	(G-7287)
South Lyme	(G-7685)
Stonington	(G-8521)
Taftville	(G-8740)
Uncasville	(G-9096)
Voluntown	(G-9187)
Waterford	(G-9638)
Yantic	(G-10695)

Tolland
City	Entry #
Amston	(G-2)
Andover	(G-6)
Bolton	(G-504)
Columbia	(G-1604)
Coventry	(G-1644)
Ellington	(G-2569)
Hebron	(G-3745)
Mansfield Center	(G-4111)
Somers	(G-7653)
Somersville	(G-7678)
Stafford Springs	(G-8015)
Storrs	(G-8543)
Storrs Mansfield	(G-8552)
Tolland	(G-8845)
Union	(G-9109)
Vernon	(G-9129)
Vernon Rockville	(G-9158)
Willington	(G-10243)

Windham
City	Entry #
Abington	(G-1)
Ashford	(G-57)
Brooklyn	(G-1243)
Canterbury	(G-1295)
Central Village	(G-1335)
Chaplin	(G-1338)
Danielson	(G-1985)
Dayville	(G-2053)
East Killingly	(G-2461)
Eastford	(G-2534)
Fabyan	(G-2739)
Hampton	(G-3534)
Moosup	(G-4777)
North Grosvenordale	(G-5883)
North Windham	(G-6033)
Plainfield	(G-6737)
Pomfret	(G-6931)
Pomfret Center	(G-6937)
Putnam	(G-7028)
Scotland	(G-7332)
South Windham	(G-7687)
Sterling	(G-8507)
Thompson	(G-8828)
Wauregan	(G-9752)
Willimantic	(G-10219)
Windham	(G-10345)
Woodstock	(G-10657)
Woodstock Valley	(G-10691)

GEOGRAPHIC SECTION

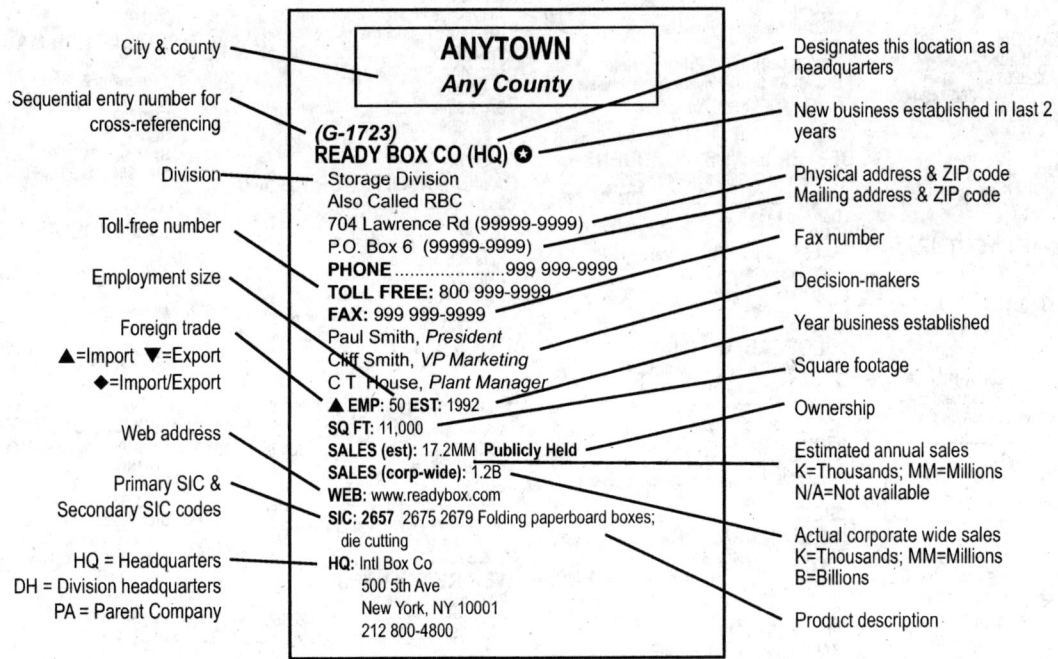

- *See footnotes for symbols and codes identification.*
- This section is in alphabetical order by city.
- Companies are sorted alphabetically under their respective cities.
- To locate cities within a county refer to the County/City Cross Reference Index.

IMPORTANT NOTICE: It is a violation of both federal and state law to transmit an unsolicited advertisement to a facsimile machine. Any user of this product that violates such laws may be subject to civil and criminal penalties which may exceed $500 for each transmission of an unsolicited facsimile. Harris InfoSource provides fax numbers for lawful purposes only and expressly forbids the use of these numbers in any unlawful manner.

Abington
Windham County

(G-1)
NCA INC
500 Hampton Rd (06230)
PHONE.................................860 974-2310
Richard G Whipple, *President*
Nicola Dabica, *Treasurer*
EMP: 6
SQ FT: 5,000
SALES: 1.3MM Privately Held
WEB: www.can.com
SIC: 2298 Cable, fiber

Amston
Tolland County

(G-2)
CARBON TOOLS INC
409 Church St (06231-1605)
PHONE.................................860 228-9383
Joseph Gore Jr, *President*
Janice Gore, *Corp Secy*
EMP: 2
SQ FT: 3,600
SALES: 250K Privately Held
SIC: 3624 Electrodes, thermal & electrolytic uses: carbon, graphite

(G-3)
JON MINARD LIGHTING
283 Hope Valley Rd (06231-1312)
PHONE.................................860 228-9069
Jonathan Minard, *Principal*

EMP: 2
SALES (est): 165.5K Privately Held
SIC: 3648 Lighting equipment

(G-4)
MYLO INDUSTRIES LLC
49 Northam Rd (06231-1315)
PHONE.................................860 228-1192
Jeffrey D Schwarz, *Manager*
EMP: 2 EST: 2001
SALES (est): 111.2K Privately Held
SIC: 3999 Manufacturing industries

(G-5)
PAW PATTERNS LLC
157 Cannon Dr (06231-1345)
PHONE.................................401 338-4723
Stefanie Paull, *Principal*
EMP: 2
SALES (est): 106.5K Privately Held
SIC: 3543 Industrial patterns

Andover
Tolland County

(G-6)
AMERICAN DREAM UNLIMITED LLC
212 Gilead Rd (06232-1603)
PHONE.................................860 742-5055
Brian Fufini,
EMP: 7
SALES: 98K Privately Held
SIC: 3845 Endoscopic equipment, electromedical

(G-7)
FINEST ENGRAVING LLC
5 Bunker Hill Rd (06232-1334)
PHONE.................................860 742-7579
Barry Boyle,
EMP: 4
SALES: 165K Privately Held
WEB: www.finestengraving.com
SIC: 7389 3469 Engraving service; metal stampings

(G-8)
GAGNE & GAGNE CO
3 Lindholms Cor (06232)
P.O. Box 357 (06232-0357)
PHONE.................................860 742-5038
Ray Gagne, *Owner*
EMP: 1
SALES (est): 116.9K Privately Held
SIC: 2431 3442 Doors, wood; window frames, wood; window screens, wood frame; metal doors, sash & trim

(G-9)
HI TEMP ELECTRIC COMPANY
102 Hendee Rd (06232-1010)
P.O. Box 802947, Santa Clarita CA (91380-2947)
PHONE.................................661 259-9225
EMP: 27
SALES (est): 3.6MM Privately Held
SIC: 5063 3297 Whol Electrical Equipment Mfg Nonclay Refractories

(G-10)
JIM N I LLC
36 Oak Farms Rd (06232-1424)
P.O. Box 156 (06232-0156)
PHONE.................................860 646-5155
EMP: 2 EST: 1984

SALES: 50K Privately Held
SIC: 1521 2421 Single-Family House Construction

(G-11)
JOE KAULBACK
Also Called: Kdc Mobile Mix
405 Route 6 (06232-1319)
P.O. Box 27 (06232-0027)
PHONE.................................860 742-0434
Joe Kaulback, *Owner*
EMP: 1 EST: 2001
SALES (est): 88.6K Privately Held
SIC: 3273 Ready-mixed concrete

(G-12)
LEE & SONS WOODWORKERS
475 Lake Rd (06232-1323)
PHONE.................................860 742-7707
Paul Leger, *Owner*
EMP: 2
SALES (est): 153.8K Privately Held
SIC: 2431 Millwork

(G-13)
MARY CARROLL
22 Bailey Rd (06232-1005)
PHONE.................................860 543-0750
Mary Carroll, *Principal*
EMP: 1
SALES (est): 77.4K Privately Held
SIC: 2741 Miscellaneous publishing

(G-14)
MONAS MONOGRAMS
902 East St (06232-1418)
PHONE.................................860 463-9530
Mona Garray, *Owner*
EMP: 1

(PA)=Parent Co (HQ)=Headquarters (DH)=Div Headquarters
✪ = New Business established in last 2 years

2020 Harris Connecticut
Manufacturers Directory

Andover - Tolland County (G-15)

SALES (est): 94.1K **Privately Held**
SIC: 2395 Embroidery products, except schiffli machine

(G-15)
MTM CORPORATION
643 Route 6 (06232-1320)
P.O. Box 268 (06232-0268)
PHONE..................860 742-9600
William Thurston Jr, *President*
EMP: 9
SQ FT: 12,000
SALES (est): 1.6MM **Privately Held**
SIC: 3728 Aircraft parts & equipment

(G-16)
RICHARD G SWARTWOUT JR
Also Called: New England Woodturners
627 Route 6 (06232-1320)
P.O. Box 455 (06232-0455)
PHONE..................860 377-2321
Richard Swartwout, *Owner*
EMP: 1
SALES (est): 107.9K **Privately Held**
WEB: www.newenglandwoodturners.com
SIC: 2439 Structural wood members

Ansonia
New Haven County

(G-17)
AERO-MED MOLDING TECHNOLOGIES (PA)
50 Westfield Ave (06401-1121)
PHONE..................203 735-2331
Lawrence Saffran, *President*
Richard Carpentiere, *Engineer*
EMP: 10
SQ FT: 30,000
SALES (est): 2MM **Privately Held**
WEB: www.aeromedmolding.com
SIC: 3089 Injection molding of plastics

(G-18)
AMERICAN PRECISION MFG LLC
26 Beaver St Ste 1 (06401-3250)
PHONE..................203 734-1800
Leigh Dawid, *President*
EMP: 24
SQ FT: 30,000
SALES: 2MM **Privately Held**
WEB: www.ap-mfg.com
SIC: 3599 Machine shop, jobbing & repair

(G-19)
AMERICAN VETERAN TEXTILE LLC
674 Main St Fl 2 (06401-2311)
PHONE..................203 583-0576
Yusuf Arslan, *Mng Member*
Resit Akcam, *Mng Member*
Nehmet Pehlivan, *Mng Member*
EMP: 3
SALES (est): 200.5K **Privately Held**
SIC: 2273 Bathmats & sets, textile

(G-20)
ANSONIA PLASTICS LLC
Also Called: Npi Medical
401 Birmingham Blvd (06401-1035)
PHONE..................203 736-5200
Randy Ahlm, *President*
William Ball, *Project Mgr*
Edmond Meyer, *CFO*
Edmund Meyer, *CFO*
Dan Singer, *Sales Executive*
EMP: 80
SALES (est): 24.9MM **Privately Held**
SIC: 3086 Plastics foam products

(G-21)
ARROW PRINTERS INC
311 Main St (06401-2301)
PHONE..................203 734-7272
David Conti, *President*
Daniel Conti Jr, *Vice Pres*
EMP: 2 EST: 1970
SQ FT: 12,000
SALES: 290K **Privately Held**
SIC: 2752 Commercial printing, offset

(G-22)
ARTISAN HAND TOOLS INC
4 Hershey Dr (06401-2312)
PHONE..................203 308-2063
Michael Bousquet, *President*
EMP: 2
SALES (est): 150K **Privately Held**
SIC: 3423 Screw drivers, pliers, chisels, etc. (hand tools)

(G-23)
BETTER LAWNS & GARDENS
1 Chestnut St Bldg 5 (06401-2300)
PHONE..................203 735-5296
Danielle Minerly, *Owner*
EMP: 2
SALES (est): 289.2K **Privately Held**
SIC: 3423 Garden & farm tools, including shovels

(G-24)
BOUDREAU VASILIKI
Also Called: Sykies Diagnostics
16 Reservoir Dr (06401-2863)
PHONE..................203 734-6754
Vasiliki Boudreau, *Owner*
EMP: 1
SALES (est): 62K **Privately Held**
SIC: 3829 Ultrasonic testing equipment

(G-25)
BUESTAN USA LLC
5 Dorel Ter (06401-3347)
PHONE..................203 954-8889
Patricio Silva,
Samira Silva,
EMP: 2 EST: 2013
SALES (est): 96.6K **Privately Held**
SIC: 3143 3144 3149 3111 Men's footwear, except athletic; women's footwear, except athletic; footwear, except rubber; leather tanning & finishing; mechanical rubber goods; fabricated rubber products

(G-26)
C B S CONTRACTORS INC
Also Called: CBS Contractors
1 Riverside Dr Ste D (06401-1255)
PHONE..................203 734-8015
Angelo Giordano, *President*
EMP: 10
SALES (est): 1.1MM **Privately Held**
SIC: 1711 3444 Warm air heating & air conditioning contractor; sheet metalwork

(G-27)
CASTLE BEVERAGES INC
105 Myrtle Ave (06401-2099)
PHONE..................203 732-0883
Kenneth Dworkin, *President*
David Pantalone, *Vice Pres*
EMP: 9
SQ FT: 96,000
SALES (est): 989K **Privately Held**
SIC: 2086 Carbonated beverages, nonalcoholic: bottled & canned

(G-28)
CENTRAL MARBLE & GRANITE LLC
22 Maple St (06401-1230)
PHONE..................203 734-4644
Naomi King,
Richard P Smeland Jr,
EMP: 4
SQ FT: 12,000
SALES (est): 466.2K **Privately Held**
SIC: 2493 3281 Marbleboard (stone face hard board); curbing, granite or stone

(G-29)
COBAL-USA ALTRNATIVE FUELS LLC
40 James St (06401-1961)
PHONE..................203 751-1974
Petr Lisa, *Principal*
EMP: 3
SALES (est): 167K **Privately Held**
SIC: 2869 Fuels

(G-30)
CONNECTICUT METAL INDUSTRIES
1 Riverside Dr Ste G (06401-1255)
P.O. Box 234, Monroe (06468-0234)
PHONE..................203 736-0790
Tom Mele, *Principal*
◆ EMP: 4
SALES (est): 323.1K **Privately Held**
SIC: 3999 Manufacturing industries

(G-31)
DAWID MANUFACTURING INC
26 Beaver St (06401-3250)
PHONE..................203 734-1800
Leigh Dawid, *President*
Karen Dawid, *Treasurer*
EMP: 8
SQ FT: 4,000
SALES (est): 600K **Privately Held**
SIC: 3599 5088 Machine shop, jobbing & repair; marine supplies

(G-32)
DIVERSIFIED MANUFACT
1 Riverside Dr Ste H (06401-1255)
PHONE..................203 734-0379
Kazimierz Bialczak, *President*
EMP: 8
SALES (est): 790.9K **Privately Held**
SIC: 3999 Manufacturing industries

(G-33)
EVER READY PRESS
78 Clifton Ave (06401-2227)
PHONE..................203 734-5157
Frank Halpin, *Owner*
EMP: 3
SQ FT: 3,750
SALES (est): 232.5K **Privately Held**
WEB: www.everreadypress.com
SIC: 2759 Screen printing

(G-34)
FARREL CORPORATION (DH)
Also Called: Farrel Pomini
1 Farrel Blvd (06401-1256)
PHONE..................203 736-5500
Mark Meulbroek, *CEO*
Michael Melotto, *Purchasing*
Paul M Zepp, *CFO*
Peng Ye, *Sales Staff*
James L Burns, *Admin Sec*
◆ EMP: 91
SQ FT: 60,000
SALES (est): 76.1MM
SALES (corp-wide): 360.4K **Privately Held**
WEB: www.farrel.com
SIC: 3559 1011 3089 Rubber working machinery, including tires; plastics working machinery; iron ore pelletizing; extruded finished plastic products
HQ: Harburg-Freudenberger Maschinenbau Gmbh
Seevestr. 1
Hamburg 21079
407 717-90

(G-35)
FUEL FIRST
575 Main St (06401-2310)
PHONE..................203 735-5097
Brad Badel, *Owner*
EMP: 4 EST: 2009
SALES (est): 313.3K **Privately Held**
SIC: 2869 Fuels

(G-36)
GARRETT & CO MFG LLC
16 Ells St (06401-3009)
PHONE..................203 494-0935
Tgarrett Mnging,
EMP: 1
SALES (est): 83.3K **Privately Held**
SIC: 3999 Manufacturing industries

(G-37)
GROHE MANUFACTURING
26 Beaver St Ste 2 (06401-3250)
PHONE..................203 516-5536
Christian Grohe, *Owner*
EMP: 3 EST: 2011

SALES (est): 285K **Privately Held**
SIC: 3999 Barber & beauty shop equipment

(G-38)
HATA HI-TECH MACHINING LLC
Also Called: Hht
1 Riverside Dr Ste E (06401-1255)
PHONE..................203 333-9139
EMP: 28
SQ FT: 13,000
SALES: 3.7MM **Privately Held**
SIC: 3541 Mfg Machine Tools-Cutting

(G-39)
INDEPENDENT METALWORX INC
4 Hershey Dr Ste 1a (06401-2312)
PHONE..................203 520-4089
Michael Bousquet, *President*
EMP: 5
SALES (est): 291.6K **Privately Held**
SIC: 3499 Fabricated metal products

(G-40)
IPG (US) HOLDINGS INC
4 Hershey Dr (06401-2312)
PHONE..................813 621-8410
EMP: 2
SALES (corp-wide): 1B **Privately Held**
SIC: 2672 Tape, pressure sensitive: made from purchased materials
HQ: Ipg (Us) Holdings Inc.
100 Paramount Dr Ste 300
Sarasota FL 34232
941 727-5788

(G-41)
JAY TEE CORP
Also Called: Rubber Fabricators
7 Pin Oak Ln (06401-2731)
PHONE..................203 732-5215
Thomas J McQueeney, *President*
EMP: 2
SQ FT: 4,000
SALES: 130K **Privately Held**
WEB: www.rubberfabricators.com
SIC: 3069 Weather strip, sponge rubber

(G-42)
JEFFREY MINGOLLELLO BACKHOE SR
33 N Coe Ln (06401-2817)
PHONE..................203 735-5458
Jefferey Mingolello, *Owner*
EMP: 1
SALES (est): 92.4K **Privately Held**
SIC: 3446 1711 Architectural metalwork; plumbing, heating, air-conditioning contractors

(G-43)
JUMP4FUN USA LLC
96 Garden St (06401-3127)
PHONE..................203 735-3702
John Lepeska, *Mng Member*
EMP: 1 EST: 2007
SALES (est): 64.7K **Privately Held**
SIC: 3069 Balloons, advertising & toy: rubber

(G-44)
KENSCO INC (PA)
Also Called: Tub's & Stuff Plumbing Supply
41 Clifton Ave (06401-2203)
P.O. Box 43 (06401-0043)
PHONE..................203 734-8827
Kenneth R Shortell, *President*
Yvette Shortell, *Vice Pres*
EMP: 12
SQ FT: 10,000
SALES (est): 1.5MM **Privately Held**
SIC: 3431 3089 5074 5999 Bathtubs: enameled iron, cast iron or pressed metal; tubs, plastic (containers); plumbing & hydronic heating supplies; plumbing & heating supplies; bathroom fixtures, equipment & supplies

(G-45)
NEW ENGLAND CSTM CONCRETE
112 Pershing Dr Ste 5 (06401-2254)
PHONE..................203 924-2142
EMP: 2

GEOGRAPHIC SECTION

Avon - Hartford County (G-76)

SALES (est): 91.3K **Privately Held**
SIC: **3272** Concrete products

(G-46)
PRO COUNTERS NEW ENGLAND LLC
1 Chestnut St (06401-2300)
PHONE....................203 347-8663
Camilla Resende, *Manager*
J V Nogueira,
Rafael Resende,
EMP: 7
SALES: 700K **Privately Held**
SIC: **2541** Counter & sink tops

(G-47)
PUMP TECHNOLOGY INCORPORATED
Also Called: Homa Pump Technology
390 Birmingham Blvd (06401-1032)
PHONE....................203 736-8890
Chris Terranova, *President*
Henry Hubli, *Chairman*
James Engleman, *Regional Mgr*
Juliet Stautner, *Vice Pres*
Dan Regan, *Engineer*
◆ EMP: 20
SQ FT: 38,500
SALES (est): 5.6MM **Privately Held**
WEB: www.grinder-pumps.com
SIC: **5084** 3561 Pumps & pumping equipment; pumps, domestic: water or sump

(G-48)
QUALITY WOODWORKS LLC
1 Riverside Dr (06401-1228)
PHONE....................203 736-9200
Jack Zansardino, *President*
Jack Zanfardino,
EMP: 3
SQ FT: 2,000
SALES (est): 467.7K **Privately Held**
SIC: **2434** Wood kitchen cabinets

(G-49)
ROYAL WOODCRAFT INC
1 Riverside Dr (06401-1228)
PHONE....................203 847-3461
Dominick Mudugno, *President*
EMP: 12
SALES (est): 1.8MM **Privately Held**
WEB: www.royalwoodcraft.com
SIC: **5211** 2434 Cabinets, kitchen; bathroom fixtures, equipment & supplies; vanities, bathroom: wood

(G-50)
SEEMS INC
Also Called: 3 Brothers EMB & Screen Prtg
26 East St (06401-3121)
PHONE....................203 284-0259
Joseph Seymour, *President*
Stuart Brenner, *Vice Pres*
EMP: 12
SQ FT: 8,000
SALES (est): 956.6K **Privately Held**
SIC: **5941** 2396 2395 Sporting goods & bicycle shops; screen printing on fabric articles; emblems, embroidered

(G-51)
SOBER TOUCH SENSORING LLC
182 N State St (06401-3043)
PHONE....................203 540-2486
Lakesha Stines,
EMP: 1
SALES (est): 56K **Privately Held**
SIC: **3629** Inverters, nonrotating: electrical

(G-52)
STELRAY PLASTIC PRODUCTS INC
50 Westfield Ave (06401-1121)
PHONE....................203 735-2331
Mortimer Saffran, *Ch of Bd*
Lawrence David Saffran, *President*
Robert Bowns, *Mfg Mgr*
Jennifer Spaulding, *Accounting Mgr*
Sandeep Singh, *Supervisor*
▲ EMP: 48
SQ FT: 15,000
SALES (est): 8.6MM **Privately Held**
WEB: www.stelray.com
SIC: **3089** 5031 Injection molding of plastics; molding, all materials

(G-53)
TRI STATE EMBROIDERY LLC
26 East St (06401-3121)
PHONE....................203 732-7636
EMP: 2
SALES (est): 102.8K **Privately Held**
SIC: **2395** 5949 5131 Pleating/Stitching Services Ret Sewing Supplies/Fabrics Whol Piece Goods/Notions

(G-54)
TRI-STATE EMB SCREEN PRTG LLC
26 East St (06401-3121)
PHONE....................203 732-7636
EMP: 2 EST: 2009
SALES (est): 160K **Privately Held**
SIC: **2752** Lithographic Commercial Printing

(G-55)
VALLEY INDEPENDENT SENTINEL
158 Main St (06401-1836)
PHONE....................203 446-2335
Eugene Driscoll, *Manager*
EMP: 3 EST: 2009
SALES (est): 122.2K **Privately Held**
SIC: **2711** Newspapers, publishing & printing

(G-56)
VP PRINTING
2 N Westwood Rd (06401-1227)
PHONE....................203 736-1756
Lisa Spinelli, *Principal*
EMP: 2 EST: 2009
SALES (est): 125.9K **Privately Held**
SIC: **2759** Commercial printing

Ashford
Windham County

(G-57)
BIOFIBERS CAPITAL GROUP LLC
14 Amidon Dr (06278-2003)
PHONE....................203 561-6133
Timothy Dowding, *Mng Member*
Eric Metz,
Richard Parnas,
EMP: 5
SALES (est): 164K **Privately Held**
SIC: **2493** 7389 Particleboard products;

(G-58)
COUNTRY TOOL & DIE INC
278 Pumpkin Hill Rd (06278-1711)
PHONE....................860 429-7325
Richard Barry, *President*
Jan Barry, *Treasurer*
EMP: 1
SALES (est): 136.1K **Privately Held**
SIC: **3544** Special dies & tools

(G-59)
DEPERCIO WOODWORKING LLC
136 Moon Rd (06278-1200)
PHONE....................860 477-1051
Bruce Depercio, *Principal*
EMP: 2
SALES (est): 65.4K **Privately Held**
SIC: **2431** Millwork

(G-60)
E & M MACHINE
358 Westford Rd (06278-2525)
PHONE....................860 429-2427
Edward Polnik, *Owner*
EMP: 1
SALES: 30K **Privately Held**
SIC: **3599** Machine shop, jobbing & repair

(G-61)
EVANGELICAL CHRISTIAN CENTER (PA)
Also Called: Evangelical Baptist Center
574 Ashford Center Rd (06278-1721)
PHONE....................860 429-0856
Alexander Henkel, *CEO*
Rev Vitaly Korchevsky, *President*
Harry Lubanasky, *Treasurer*
Peter Pleshko, *Director*
Bill Smirnoff, *Director*
EMP: 4
SALES (est): 356.5K **Privately Held**
SIC: **8661** 8361 7032 2721 Assembly of God Church; home for the aged; recreational camps; periodicals: publishing & printing; radio broadcasting stations

(G-62)
EVANGELICAL CHRISTIAN CENTER
Slavic Missionary Publication
574 Ashfor Center Rd (06278)
P.O. Box 103 (06278-0103)
PHONE....................860 429-0856
Basilio Sapoval, *Pastor*
EMP: 1
SALES (corp-wide): 356.5K **Privately Held**
SIC: **2721** Magazines: publishing only, not printed on site
PA: Evangelical Christian Center Inc
574 Ashford Center Rd
Ashford CT 06278
860 429-0856

(G-63)
PITH PRODUCTS LLC
39 Nott Hwy Unit 1 (06278-1341)
PHONE....................860 487-4859
Louis Albert,
Lance J Bouchard,
EMP: 16
SALES (est): 2.8MM **Privately Held**
WEB: www.pithproducts.com
SIC: **2449** Rectangular boxes & crates, wood

(G-64)
RIENDEAU & SONS LOGGING LLC
109 Supina Rd (06278-2226)
PHONE....................860 429-7919
Karl Riendeau,
EMP: 1
SALES (est): 150K **Privately Held**
SIC: **2411** Logging camps & contractors

(G-65)
RIVERS EDGE SUGAR HOUSE
326 Mansfield Rd (06278-1414)
PHONE....................860 429-1510
Bill Prulyx, *Owner*
EMP: 3
SALES (est): 177.8K **Privately Held**
WEB: www.riversedgesugarhouse.com
SIC: **2099** Maple syrup

(G-66)
SHAYNA BS & PICKLE LLC
627 Westford Rd (06278-2420)
PHONE....................860 428-3835
Christine Reed, *Principal*
EMP: 2 EST: 2008
SALES (est): 128.3K **Privately Held**
SIC: **2051** Bakery: wholesale or wholesale/retail combined

(G-67)
WALKER INDUSTRIES LLC
464 Zaicek Rd (06278-1044)
PHONE....................860 455-3554
Thomas Walker,
EMP: 3
SALES: 500K **Privately Held**
SIC: **2421** Sawmills & planing mills, general

(G-68)
WALKER WOODWORKING LLC
18 Cotswold Dr (06278-1503)
PHONE....................860 429-2644
John Walker, *Principal*
EMP: 2

SALES (est): 120K **Privately Held**
SIC: **2431** Millwork

(G-69)
WESTFORD HILL DISTILLERS LLC
196 Chatey Rd (06278-1007)
PHONE....................860 429-0464
Louis Chatey, *Mng Member*
Margaret Chatey,
EMP: 6
SALES: 300K **Privately Held**
SIC: **2085** Distilled & blended liquors

(G-70)
WRAITH INDUSTRIES LLC (PA)
Also Called: Trophy Shop, The
9 Hillside Rd (06278-2204)
PHONE....................860 454-4003
Allen Armstrong,
Adam Armstrong,
Kathy Armstrong,
EMP: 1
SALES (est): 337.5K **Privately Held**
SIC: **3999** Manufacturing industries

Avon
Hartford County

(G-71)
ABBEY AESTHETICS LLC
135 Cold Spring Rd (06001-4054)
PHONE....................860 242-0497
Rainerio J Reyes, *Principal*
EMP: 4 EST: 2009
SALES (est): 206.3K **Privately Held**
SIC: **3845** Laser systems & equipment, medical

(G-72)
ADVANCED HEARING SOLUTIONS LLC
Also Called: Advance Affrdale Hring Sltions
47 W Main St (06001-4706)
PHONE....................860 674-8558
Rich Stokes, *Mng Member*
Anne Byrnes, *Mng Member*
EMP: 10
SALES (est): 835.9K **Privately Held**
WEB: www.advancedhearingsolutions.com
SIC: **3842** Hearing aids

(G-73)
AIR SOLUTIONS EAST LLC
41 Brian Ln (06001-3530)
PHONE....................860 883-4700
Lawrence Kushner,
EMP: 1
SQ FT: 10,000
SALES (est): 136.7K **Privately Held**
SIC: **3585** Refrigeration & heating equipment

(G-74)
ALEXIS AEROSPACE INDS LLP
94 Bronson Rd (06001-2930)
PHONE....................860 673-6801
EMP: 1
SALES (est): 55K **Privately Held**
SIC: **3999** Manufacturing industries

(G-75)
ALTARE PUBLISHING INC
79 Westbury (06001-3172)
PHONE....................860 490-6144
EMP: 2 EST: 2015
SALES (est): 80.1K **Privately Held**
SIC: **2741** Miscellaneous publishing

(G-76)
ARTFUL FRAMER LLC
195 W Main St Ste 15 (06001-3685)
PHONE....................860 678-1321
Elizabeth Evanick,
EMP: 4
SQ FT: 1,600
SALES (est): 306.8K **Privately Held**
SIC: **5999** 2499 3499 Art dealers; picture & mirror frames, wood; picture frames, metal

Avon - Hartford County (G-77)

(G-77)
BALL SUPPLY CORPORATION
52 Old Mill Rd (06001-4022)
P.O. Box 303, Riverside NJ (08075-0303)
PHONE.................................860 673-3364
Rudy Presutti, *President*
Barbara Presutti, *Corp Secy*
Leon Petersen, *Vice Pres*
EMP: 4 EST: 1996
SALES: 780K Privately Held
SIC: 3399 Steel balls

(G-78)
BOSTON SCIENTIFIC CORPORATION
85 Bridgewater Dr (06001-4400)
PHONE.................................860 673-2500
Alexander Galati, *Principal*
EMP: 341
SALES (corp-wide): 9.8B Publicly Held
SIC: 3841 Surgical & medical instruments
PA: Boston Scientific Corporation
     300 Boston Scientific Way
     Marlborough MA 01752
     508 683-4000

(G-79)
CRAFTY CREATIONS
55 Sunnybrook Dr (06001-2529)
PHONE.................................860 673-6225
Dorthoria Shaw, *Owner*
EMP: 1
SALES (est): 45.3K Privately Held
SIC: 5945 3944 Arts & crafts supplies; craft & hobby kits & sets

(G-80)
FASTSIGNS
11 E Main St (06001-3803)
PHONE.................................860 470-7936
Joel Miller, *Principal*
EMP: 1 EST: 2018
SALES (est): 74K Privately Held
SIC: 3993 Signs & advertising specialties

(G-81)
FLAGMAN OF AMERICA LLP
22 E Main St (06001-3801)
P.O. Box 440 (06001-0440)
PHONE.................................860 678-0275
Annette Dimesky, *Managing Prtnr*
David Dimesky, *Managing Prtnr*
James Walz, *Managing Prtnr*
EMP: 8
SQ FT: 1,900
SALES (est): 1.1MM Privately Held
WEB: www.flagman.com
SIC: 5999 2399 Flags; flags, fabric

(G-82)
GENERAL DYNAMICS ORDNANCE
Also Called: Simunition Operations
65 Sandscreen Rd (06001-2222)
P.O. Box 576 (06001-0576)
PHONE.................................860 404-0162
Brian Berger, *Branch Mgr*
EMP: 10
SALES (corp-wide): 36.1B Publicly Held
SIC: 3482 8741 Small arms ammunition; management services
HQ: General Dynamics Ordnance And Tactical Systems, Inc.
     11399 16th Ct N Ste 200
     Saint Petersburg FL 33716
     727 578-8100

(G-83)
HARTFORD COURANT COMPANY
80 Darling Dr (06001-4217)
PHONE.................................860 678-1330
Bonnie Phillips, *Manager*
EMP: 7
SQ FT: 500
SALES (corp-wide): 1B Publicly Held
WEB: www.courantnie.com
SIC: 2711 Newspapers: publishing only, not printed on site
HQ: The Hartford Courant Company Llc
     285 Broad St
     Hartford CT 06115
     860 241-6200

(G-84)
HIGHER CONSCIOUSNESS LLC
10 Templeton Ct (06001-3950)
PHONE.................................310 977-7541
Robert Tolk,
Ernest Rudyak,
EMP: 2
SALES (est): 120K Privately Held
SIC: 2741 7389 Miscellaneous publishing;

(G-85)
IDEVICES LLC
50 Tower Ln (06001-4228)
PHONE.................................860 352-5252
Mike Daigle, *COO*
Jennifer Gutierrez, *Vice Pres*
Jonathan Wilson, *Project Mgr*
Jim Millis, *Engineer*
Kelley McIntyre, *CFO*
▲ EMP: 25
SALES (est): 7.8MM
SALES (corp-wide): 4.4B Publicly Held
SIC: 3625 Timing devices, electronic
PA: Hubbell Incorporated
     40 Waterview Dr
     Shelton CT 06484
     475 882-4000

(G-86)
K2STEAM
5 Delbon Ln (06001-3422)
PHONE.................................860 251-9824
Keith Lee, *Principal*
EMP: 1
SALES (est): 44.8K Privately Held
SIC: 5632 3961 Costume jewelry; costume jewelry

(G-87)
L G ASSOCIATES
2 Farmstead Ln (06001-3936)
PHONE.................................860 677-7167
Linda Goodman, *Principal*
EMP: 2
SALES (est): 153K Privately Held
SIC: 3537 Forklift trucks

(G-88)
LEECO INC
5 Alexandra Ln (06001-2210)
PHONE.................................860 404-8876
EMP: 4
SALES (est): 224.3K Privately Held
SIC: 3545 Machine tool accessories

(G-89)
LEGERE GROUP LTD
Also Called: Legere Woodworking
80 Darling Dr (06001-4217)
P.O. Box 1527 (06001-1527)
PHONE.................................860 674-0392
Craig Froh, *CEO*
Ronald Legere, *President*
Bill Bruneau, *Vice Pres*
William Bruneau, *Vice Pres*
Francis Legere, *Vice Pres*
EMP: 125
SQ FT: 144,000
SALES (est): 28MM Privately Held
WEB: www.legeregroup.com
SIC: 2434 2431 3442 2499 Wood kitchen cabinets; millwork; metal doors, sash & trim; decorative wood & woodwork

(G-90)
LITTLE BLUE BOOK
302 W Main St Ste 206 (06001-3681)
PHONE.................................860 409-7000
Doug Walton, *Director*
EMP: 1
SALES (est): 36.6K Privately Held
SIC: 2731 Book publishing

(G-91)
LIVE AND DREAM GREEN LLC
Also Called: L D G
4 Orchard Farms Ln (06001-3265)
PHONE.................................860 670-0870
Kristin Webster, *Mng Member*
Greg Webster,
EMP: 2
SALES: 175K Privately Held
WEB: www.resnackit.com
SIC: 2393 7389 Flour bags, fabric: made from purchased materials;

(G-92)
MARK TOOL CO
88 Tamara Cir (06001-2233)
PHONE.................................860 673-5039
Jeannette Manaresi, *President*
EMP: 2
SALES (est): 107.7K Privately Held
SIC: 3312 Tool & die steel & alloys

(G-93)
MINUTEMAN PRESS
195 W Main St Ste E (06001-3685)
PHONE.................................860 674-8700
Katie Sanford, *Manager*
EMP: 2
SALES (est): 162.6K Privately Held
SIC: 2752 Commercial printing, lithographic

(G-94)
MOGO REHAB INCORPORATED
193 W Avon Rd (06001-3508)
PHONE.................................860 673-5324
Richard K Wagner, *CEO*
Mary P Wagner, *Director*
EMP: 2
SALES (est): 86K Privately Held
WEB: www.mogorehab.com
SIC: 3452 Bolts, nuts, rivets & washers

(G-95)
NATURAL NUTMEG LLC
53 Mountain View Ave (06001-3813)
PHONE.................................860 206-9500
Chris Hindman, *Principal*
EMP: 3
SALES (est): 230K Privately Held
SIC: 2721 Magazines: publishing & printing

(G-96)
OFS FITEL LLC
Also Called: Ofs Specialty Photonics Div
55 Darling Dr (06001-4273)
PHONE.................................860 678-0371
Jane Cercena, *Vice Pres*
EMP: 350 Privately Held
SIC: 3357 Nonferrous wiredrawing & insulating
HQ: Ofs Fitel Llc
     2000 Northeast Expy
     Norcross GA 30071
     888 342-3743

(G-97)
OLDCASTLE INFRASTRUCTURE INC
Also Called: Rotondo Precast
151 Old Farms Rd (06001-2253)
PHONE.................................860 673-3291
Joel Dickinson, *General Mgr*
Ronald Hoinsky, *Safety Mgr*
EMP: 23
SALES (corp-wide): 30.6B Privately Held
WEB: www.oldcastle-precast.com
SIC: 3272 Concrete products
HQ: Oldcastle Infrastructure, Inc.
     7000 Cntl Prkaway Ste 800
     Atlanta GA 30328
     470 602-2000

(G-98)
ORAFOL AMERICAS INC
120 Darling Dr (06001-4217)
PHONE.................................860 676-7100
Steve Scott, *President*
Riccardo Plenzich, *Regional Mgr*
Mike Egan, *Business Mgr*
Joseph Lupone, *COO*
David Knight, *Vice Pres*
EMP: 143
SALES (corp-wide): 661.1MM Privately Held
WEB: www.reflexite.com
SIC: 3081 5162 3827 Vinyl film & sheet; plastics film; plastics products; lenses, optical: all types except ophthalmic
HQ: Orafol Americas Inc.
     1100 Oracal Pkwy
     Black Creek GA 31308
     912 851-5000

(G-99)
PETRINI ART & FRAME LLC (PA)
35 E Main St (06001-3845)
PHONE.................................860 677-2747
Elizabeth Petrini, *Mng Member*
Joe Petrini, *Mng Member*
EMP: 5
SALES (est): 433.3K Privately Held
SIC: 7999 2499 Art gallery, commercial; picture & mirror frames, wood

(G-100)
PINKE&BROWN PUBLISHING LLP
35 E Main St Ste 373 (06001-3845)
PHONE.................................860 798-9858
Cynthia Dokas-Whipple, *Principal*
EMP: 1
SALES (est): 52.7K Privately Held
SIC: 2741 Miscellaneous publishing

(G-101)
PUBLISHING DIRECTIONS LLC
Also Called: Book Mktg Works
50 Lovely St (06001-3138)
P.O. Box 715 (06001-0715)
PHONE.................................860 673-7650
Brian Jud, *Mng Member*
EMP: 3
SALES: 120K Privately Held
SIC: 2741 Miscellaneous publishing

(G-102)
R R DONNELLEY & SONS COMPANY
60 Security Dr (06001-4226)
PHONE.................................860 773-6140
Steve Policks, *Manager*
EMP: 50
SALES (corp-wide): 6.8B Publicly Held
WEB: www.rrdonnelley.com
SIC: 2759 2752 Advertising literature: printing; newspapers: printing; commercial printing, lithographic
PA: R. R. Donnelley & Sons Company
     35 W Wacker Dr
     Chicago IL 60601
     312 326-8000

(G-103)
REAC READY LLC (PA)
1 Darling Dr (06001-4277)
PHONE.................................860 760-8886
Eddie Brady White, *Mng Member*
EMP: 2
SALES (est): 326.5K Privately Held
SIC: 1389 8742 Construction, repair & dismantling services; training & development consultant

(G-104)
READYDOCK INC
46 W Avon Rd Ste 302 (06001-3679)
PHONE.................................860 523-9980
David Engelhardt, *President*
EMP: 3 EST: 2012
SALES (est): 306.1K Privately Held
SIC: 3999 3448 Dock equipment & supplies, industrial; docks: prefabricated metal

(G-105)
RIVER DOG PRINTS LLC
50 Forge Dr (06001-3206)
PHONE.................................860 276-1578
Cynthia Thomas, *Principal*
EMP: 2
SALES (est): 163.8K Privately Held
SIC: 2752 Commercial printing, offset

(G-106)
RMI CORPORATION
20 Tower Ln (06001-4212)
PHONE.................................860 680-7368
EMP: 2
SALES (est): 90K Privately Held
SIC: 3674 Semiconductors & related devices

(G-107)
RUSSIAN FLARE LLC
24 Brentwood Dr (06001-3409)
PHONE.................................860 404-1781
Nikolay Synkov, *Principal*
EMP: 2
SALES (est): 85.2K Privately Held
SIC: 2899 Flares

GEOGRAPHIC SECTION
Beacon Falls - New Haven County (G-136)

(G-108)
S&A PUZZLE LLC
468 Lovely St (06001-2333)
PHONE..................860 675-0477
William S Wilkey, *Principal*
EMP: 1
SALES (est): 51K **Privately Held**
SIC: 3944 Puzzles

(G-109)
SDI SYSTEMS DEVELOPMENT
13 Francis St (06001-3615)
PHONE..................860 967-5464
Andrew Chellman,
EMP: 1
SALES (est): 63.3K **Privately Held**
SIC: 2657 Folding paperboard boxes

(G-110)
SERVICETUNE INC
107 Cider Brook Rd (06001-2850)
PHONE..................860 284-4445
David Putt, *President*
EMP: 6
SQ FT: 1,000
SALES (est): 500K **Privately Held**
SIC: 7372 Application computer software

(G-111)
SHARI M ROTH MD
100 Simsbury Rd Ste 210 (06001-3793)
PHONE..................860 676-2525
Shari Roth, *Owner*
EMP: 4
SALES (est): 265.8K **Privately Held**
SIC: 3851 Protectors, eye

(G-112)
SILVER LITTLE SHOP INC
23 E Main St (06001-3805)
P.O. Box 100 (06001-0100)
PHONE..................860 678-1976
Richard E Parker, *President*
D C Thompson, *Vice Pres*
M J Parker, *Admin Sec*
EMP: 4
SQ FT: 288
SALES (est): 647.3K **Privately Held**
WEB: www.littlesilvershop.com
SIC: 3911 5944 Jewelry, precious metal; jewelry, precious stones & precious metals

(G-113)
SITEONE LANDSCAPE SUPPLY LLC
15 Industrial Dr (06001-2252)
PHONE..................860 673-6912
Matthew Clement, *Branch Mgr*
EMP: 2
SALES (corp-wide): 2.1B **Publicly Held**
WEB: www.johndeerelandscapes.com
SIC: 2875 Fertilizers, mixing only
HQ: Siteone Landscape Supply, Llc
    300 Colonial Center Pkwy # 600
    Roswell GA 30076
    770 255-2100

(G-114)
SONS OF UN VTRANS OF CIVIL WAR
4 Raven Cir (06001-3317)
PHONE..................816 241-5353
EMP: 2
SALES (est): 72.6K **Privately Held**
SIC: 3993 Signs & advertising specialties

(G-115)
SPIRIT OF HARTFORD LLC
45 Crocus Ln (06001-4547)
PHONE..................860 404-1776
Kay Olsen,
▲ EMP: 2
SALES: 850K **Privately Held**
WEB: www.foursquarerum.com
SIC: 2085 5921 Distilled & blended liquors; liquor stores

(G-116)
SVL LLC
369 W Main St Ste 4d (06001-3675)
PHONE..................860 819-9929
Michael James Hull,
EMP: 4

SALES (est): 72.6K **Privately Held**
SIC: 0781 1794 4959 3271 Landscape services; excavation work; snowplowing; blocks, concrete: landscape or retaining wall; mowing services, lawn

(G-117)
TREND OFFSET PRINTING SVCS INC
60 Security Dr (06001-4226)
PHONE..................860 773-6140
EMP: 1
SALES (corp-wide): 337.5MM **Privately Held**
SIC: 2752 Commercial printing, offset
PA: Trend Offset Printing Services, Inc.
    3701 Catalina St
    Los Alamitos CA 90720
    562 598-2446

Baltic
New London County

(G-118)
AMGRAPH PACKAGING INC
90 Paper Mill Rd (06330-1436)
PHONE..................860 822-2000
Kenneth L Fontaine, *CEO*
Michael Devlin, *Vice Pres*
Michael Drab, *Vice Pres*
Robert Guertin, *Vice Pres*
Desmond P O'Grady, *Treasurer*
▲ EMP: 125
SQ FT: 75,000
SALES (est): 66.4MM **Privately Held**
SIC: 2671 2759 2752 2673 Paper coated or laminated for packaging; waxed paper: made from purchased material; plastic film, coated or laminated for packaging; commercial printing; commercial printing, lithographic; bags: plastic, laminated & coated

(G-119)
FAILLE PRECISION MACHINING
118 W Main St (06330-1077)
P.O. Box 606 (06330-0606)
PHONE..................860 822-1964
Alfred Faille, *Owner*
EMP: 4
SALES (est): 486K **Privately Held**
SIC: 3728 3599 Military aircraft equipment & armament; machine & other job shop work

(G-120)
J & D EMBROIDERING CO
26 Bushnell Hollow Rd A (06330-1364)
PHONE..................860 822-9777
Debbie McKenzie, *Owner*
EMP: 4 EST: 1973
SQ FT: 2,500
SALES (est): 255.9K **Privately Held**
SIC: 2395 2396 Embroidery & art needlework; screen printing on fabric articles

(G-121)
NUTMEG WIRE
14 Main St (06330-1443)
P.O. Box 719 (06330-0719)
PHONE..................860 822-8616
Fred Stackpole, *President*
Sharon Stackpole, *Admin Sec*
EMP: 10
SQ FT: 15,400
SALES (est): 1.3MM **Privately Held**
SIC: 3315 Wire products, ferrous/iron: made in wiredrawing plants

(G-122)
THIRTY TWO SIGNS
220 Main St (06330-1329)
PHONE..................860 822-1132
Thomas Abele, *Principal*
EMP: 2
SALES (est): 180.6K **Privately Held**
SIC: 3993 Signs & advertising specialties

Bantam
Litchfield County

(G-123)
BANTAM SHEET METAL
1160 Bantam Rd (06750-1406)
P.O. Box 310 (06750-0310)
PHONE..................860 567-9690
EMP: 4
SALES (est): 306.4K **Privately Held**
SIC: 3444 Sheet Metalwork, Nsk

(G-124)
METALCRAFT LLC
607 Bantam Rd Ste D (06750-1635)
PHONE..................860 361-6767
Daniel V Bates,
Jason W Buchta,
EMP: 1 EST: 2011
SALES (est): 213.6K **Privately Held**
SIC: 3446 5031 3499 Stairs, staircases, stair treads: prefabricated metal; structural assemblies, prefabricated: wood; aerosol valves, metal

(G-125)
NEW STAR MOLD INC
607 Bantam Rd Ste B (06750-1635)
P.O. Box 614 (06750-0614)
PHONE..................860 567-7760
Michael Chal, *President*
Catherine Kennedy, *Vice Pres*
▲ EMP: 1
SALES (est): 220.1K **Privately Held**
SIC: 3089 Injection molded finished plastic products; injection molding of plastics

(G-126)
NORTHWEST NEWS SERVICE
33 Trumbull St (06750)
PHONE..................860 567-4150
Michael Eriksen, *Principal*
EMP: 1
SALES (est): 93.9K **Privately Held**
SIC: 2711 Newspapers, publishing & printing

(G-127)
PRECISION EXPLOSIVES INC
28 Countryside Ln (06750-1317)
PHONE..................860 567-4952
J W Jankowski, *President*
EMP: 1 EST: 1994
SALES (est): 9.4K **Privately Held**
SIC: 2892 Explosives

(G-128)
WHITEBECK JOHN
Also Called: Bantam Manufacturing Company
931 Bantam Rd (06750-1606)
P.O. Box 48 (06750-0048)
PHONE..................860 567-1398
John Whitbeck, *Owner*
Richard Sheldon, *Partner*
Judy Elliott, *Principal*
EMP: 2
SQ FT: 3,000
SALES (est): 173.6K **Privately Held**
SIC: 3469 Metal stampings

Beacon Falls
New Haven County

(G-129)
ANSONIA STL FABRICATION CO INC
164 Pines Bridge Rd (06403-1018)
P.O. Box 175 (06403-0175)
PHONE..................203 888-4509
Bart Hogestyn, *President*
Debra Hogestyn, *Director*
William Hogestyn, *Director*
▲ EMP: 20
SQ FT: 11,000
SALES (est): 3.3MM **Privately Held**
WEB: www.ansoniasteel.com
SIC: 7692 3444 3441 Welding repair; sheet metalwork; fabricated structural metal

(G-130)
APEX TOOL & CUTTER CO INC
59 Old Turnpike Rd (06403-1310)
P.O. Box 188 (06403-0188)
PHONE..................203 888-8970
Jim Norton, *President*
George Norton, *Treasurer*
Joseph Norton, *Admin Sec*
EMP: 4 EST: 1997
SALES: 300K **Privately Held**
SIC: 3599 Machine shop, jobbing & repair

(G-131)
BETKOSKI BROTHERS LLC
332 Bethany Rd (06403-1404)
PHONE..................203 723-8262
Peter Betkoski,
EMP: 5
SQ FT: 2,063
SALES (est): 632.8K **Privately Held**
SIC: 2951 Asphalt & asphaltic paving mixtures (not from refineries)

(G-132)
COMMON SENSE ENGINEERED PDTS
164 Pines Bridge Rd (06403-1018)
P.O. Box 193 (06403-0193)
PHONE..................203 888-8695
Debbie Hogeston, *Partner*
EMP: 3
SALES (est): 410.7K **Privately Held**
SIC: 2653 Boxes, solid fiber: made from purchased materials

(G-133)
CONKLIN-SHERMAN COMPANY INCTHE
59 Old Turnpike Rd (06403-1310)
P.O. Box 188 (06403-0188)
PHONE..................203 881-0190
Bernadette Norton, *President*
Janice Kopchik, *Vice Pres*
Debra Lindsay, *Admin Sec*
EMP: 3 EST: 1950
SQ FT: 800
SALES (est): 459.9K **Privately Held**
WEB: www.conklin-sherman.com
SIC: 3671 Electron tubes

(G-134)
GMQ PUBLISHING
375 Bethany Rd (06403-1405)
PHONE..................203 558-6142
EMP: 1
SALES (est): 37.5K **Privately Held**
SIC: 2741 Miscellaneous publishing

(G-135)
GOLDENROD CORPORATION
25 Lancaster Dr (06403-1049)
P.O. Box 95 (06403-0095)
PHONE..................203 723-4400
Alessio Pretto, *CEO*
John Pretto, *President*
Stephen Pretto, *Vice Pres*
David Sullivan, *Vice Pres*
Judith Pretto, *Treasurer*
▲ EMP: 35
SQ FT: 30,000
SALES: 14.3MM **Privately Held**
WEB: www.goldrod.com
SIC: 5084 3554 3545 8711 Industrial machine parts; paper industries machinery; machine tool accessories; engineering services

(G-136)
INDUSTRIAL FLAME CUTTING INC
45 Lancaster Dr (06403-1049)
P.O. Box 277 (06403-0277)
PHONE..................203 723-4897
Michael Wassel, *President*
William Heiden, *Vice Pres*
Catherine Wassel, *Treasurer*
Cathy Wassel, *Treasurer*
EMP: 6
SQ FT: 10,000
SALES: 1.5MM **Privately Held**
SIC: 3312 Structural shapes & pilings, steel

Beacon Falls - New Haven County (G-137)

(G-137)
KNAPP CONTAINER INC
17 Old Turnpike Rd (06403-1310)
PHONE.....................203 888-0511
George A Meder Jr, *President*
EMP: 4
SQ FT: 40,000
SALES (est): 551.9K **Privately Held**
SIC: 2653 Boxes, corrugated: made from purchased materials

(G-138)
KORZON SCREEN PRINTING LLC
53a Lancaster Dr (06403-1049)
PHONE.....................203 729-1090
Edward S Korzon,
Gary Korzon,
EMP: 1
SALES (est): 116.1K **Privately Held**
SIC: 2759 Screen printing

(G-139)
KORZON SILK SCREENING
49 Rimmon Hill Rd (06403-1029)
PHONE.....................203 888-3273
Edward Korzon, *Owner*
EMP: 1
SALES (est): 61.6K **Privately Held**
SIC: 2759 Screen printing

(G-140)
LIBERTY SCREEN PRINT CO LLC
141 S Main St (06403-1469)
PHONE.....................203 632-5449
Monica Maglaris,
EMP: 16
SQ FT: 10,000
SALES (est): 750K **Privately Held**
SIC: 2752 2759 Commercial printing, lithographic; screen printing

(G-141)
M I R INC
103 Breault Rd (06403-1033)
PHONE.....................203 888-2541
EMP: 10 EST: 1971
SQ FT: 30,500
SALES (est): 100.3K **Privately Held**
SIC: 3559 Rebuild Rubber & Plastic Equipment

(G-142)
MAGNA STEEL SALES INC
2 Alliance Cir (06403-1054)
PHONE.....................203 888-0300
Edward Mulligan, *President*
Patricia Mavlouganes, *Admin Sec*
EMP: 15
SQ FT: 27,000
SALES (est): 2MM **Privately Held**
WEB: www.magnasteel.com
SIC: 3441 5051 Fabricated structural metal; steel

(G-143)
METAL WORKS NORTH
141 S Main St (06403-1469)
PHONE.....................203 723-9075
Thomas Kassery, *Owner*
EMP: 1
SALES (est): 91.4K **Privately Held**
SIC: 2842 Metal polish

(G-144)
MOVE BOOKS LLC
10 N Main St Apt S103 (06403-1135)
P.O. Box 183 (06403-0183)
PHONE.....................203 709-0490
Eileen Robinson,
EMP: 1 EST: 2011
SALES (est): 81.3K **Privately Held**
WEB: www.move-books.com
SIC: 2741 Miscellaneous publishing

(G-145)
O & G INDUSTRIES INC
105 Breault Rd (06403-1283)
PHONE.....................203 881-5192
EMP: 147
SALES (corp-wide): 538MM **Privately Held**
SIC: 3999 Atomizers, toiletry

PA: O & G Industries, Inc.
112 Wall St
Torrington CT 06790
860 489-9261

(G-146)
O & G INDUSTRIES INC
Railroad Ave Ext (06403)
PHONE.....................203 729-4529
William Stanley, *Branch Mgr*
EMP: 10
SALES (corp-wide): 538MM **Privately Held**
WEB: www.ogind.com
SIC: 3281 1542 Stone, quarrying & processing of own stone products; commercial & office building, new construction
PA: O & G Industries, Inc.
112 Wall St
Torrington CT 06790
860 489-9261

(G-147)
SIGNS BY FLACH
59 Old Turnpike Rd (06403-1310)
PHONE.....................203 881-0272
Mark Flach, *Owner*
EMP: 1
SQ FT: 1,800
SALES (est): 100K **Privately Held**
WEB: www.flashsigns.com
SIC: 3993 Signs & advertising specialties

(G-148)
TRADEWINDS
274 Bethany Rd (06403-1402)
P.O. Box 2158, Bristol (06011-2158)
PHONE.....................203 723-6966
Kim Ashley, *Principal*
▲ EMP: 4
SALES (est): 186.9K **Privately Held**
SIC: 2711 Newspapers

(G-149)
TRICO WELDING COMPANY LLC
84 Feldspar Ave (06403-1439)
PHONE.....................203 720-3782
Lou Poeta,
EMP: 3
SQ FT: 1,200
SALES (est): 462.1K **Privately Held**
SIC: 7692 Welding repair

Berlin
Hartford County

(G-150)
ADVANCED WINDOW SYSTEMS LLC
71 Deming Rd (06037-1512)
PHONE.....................800 841-6544
Joseph Lavoie, *Mng Member*
EMP: 15 EST: 1997
SQ FT: 12,000
SALES (est): 1.6MM **Privately Held**
SIC: 3442 5031 Window & door frames; doors & windows

(G-151)
AEROCESS INC
500 Four Rod Rd Ste 110 (06037-2282)
P.O. Box 4139, Wallingford (06492-1489)
PHONE.....................860 357-2451
William Winakor, *President*
Arthur Donorfrio, *Treasurer*
Ken Labieniec, *Admin Sec*
EMP: 12
SQ FT: 8,000
SALES (est): 880K **Privately Held**
WEB: www.aerocess.com
SIC: 3365 5088 3769 Aerospace castings, aluminum; marine crafts & supplies; guided missile & space vehicle parts & auxiliary equipment

(G-152)
AFFORDABLE CABINETS
208 Beckley Rd (06037-2506)
PHONE.....................860 919-5204
EMP: 2 EST: 2013
SALES (est): 172.6K **Privately Held**
SIC: 2434 Wood kitchen cabinets

(G-153)
ALDEN TOOL COMPANY INC
199 New Park Dr (06037-3738)
PHONE.....................860 828-3556
Charles Muravnick, *President*
Kathleen Muravnick, *Vice Pres*
EMP: 30
SQ FT: 20,000
SALES (est): 5.4MM **Privately Held**
WEB: www.aldentool.com
SIC: 3545 Cutting tools for machine tools

(G-154)
ALL FIVE TOOL CO INC
Also Called: North Amercn Spring TI Co Div
169 White Oak Dr (06037-1638)
PHONE.....................860 583-1693
Joseph B Panella, *President*
▲ EMP: 30 EST: 1967
SQ FT: 18,000
SALES (est): 2.9MM
SALES (corp-wide): 6MM **Privately Held**
WEB: www.all5tool.com
SIC: 3544 3545 Special dies & tools; gauges (machine tool accessories)
PA: Sirois Tool Company, Inc.
169 White Oak Dr
Berlin CT 06037
860 828-5327

(G-155)
AMCO PRECISION TOOLS INC (PA)
Also Called: Aerospace
921 Farmington Ave (06037-2218)
P.O. Box 442 (06037-0442)
PHONE.....................860 828-5640
Aldo Zovich, *President*
Richard Zovich, *CFO*
Theresa Zovich, *Admin Sec*
EMP: 32 EST: 1966
SQ FT: 17,000
SALES (est): 5.5MM **Privately Held**
WEB: www.amcoprecision.com
SIC: 3845 3721 Medical cleaning equipment, ultrasonic; aircraft

(G-156)
AMERICAN EMBROIDERY
83 Vivian Dr (06037-1531)
PHONE.....................860 829-8586
Lisa Mariano, *Owner*
EMP: 1
SALES (est): 90.3K **Privately Held**
SIC: 2395 Embroidery products, except schiffli machine; embroidery & art needlework

(G-157)
AMERICAN SILK SCREENING LLC
386 Deming Rd (06037-1521)
PHONE.....................860 828-5486
EMP: 3 EST: 2008
SALES (est): 396.5K **Privately Held**
SIC: 2759 Commercial Printing

(G-158)
AMITY PRINTING & COPY CTR LLC
947 Farmington Ave (06037-2218)
PHONE.....................860 828-0202
Brian Prytko, *President*
EMP: 1
SALES (est): 95K **Privately Held**
SIC: 2759 2752 Letterpress printing; commercial printing, offset

(G-159)
ANDY RAKOWICZ
Also Called: A R Tool
600 Four Rod Rd Ste 4 (06037-3665)
PHONE.....................860 828-1620
Andy Rakowicz, *Owner*
EMP: 3
SQ FT: 3,000
SALES (est): 170K **Privately Held**
SIC: 3599 Machine shop, jobbing & repair

(G-160)
ASSA ABLOY ACCSS & EDRSS HRDWR
Also Called: Corbin Russwin Arch Hdwr
225 Episcopal Rd (06037-1524)
P.O. Box 4004 (06037-0512)
PHONE.....................860 225-7411
Martin Huddart, *President*
John R Carlson, *Principal*
Mike Mortillaro, *Principal*
John C Davenport, *Treasurer*
John F Hannon, *Admin Sec*
◆ EMP: 500
SQ FT: 1,000,000
SALES (est): 98.2MM
SALES (corp-wide): 9.3B **Privately Held**
SIC: 3429 Door locks, bolts & checks; locks or lock sets
PA: Assa Abloy Ab
Klarabergsviadukten 90
Stockholm 111 6
850 648-500

(G-161)
ASTRO INDUSTRIES INC
819 Farmington Ave Unit A (06037-1306)
P.O. Box 149 (06037-0149)
PHONE.....................860 828-6304
Edward Kasabucki, *President*
Joe Corallo, *Principal*
Kristin Kasbucki, *Purchasing*
Theresa Tierpack, *Info Tech Dir*
EMP: 6 EST: 1979
SQ FT: 3,600
SALES (est): 51K **Privately Held**
SIC: 3544 3469 Jigs & fixtures; machine parts, stamped or pressed metal

(G-162)
BEES KNEES ZIPPER WAX LLC
3 Canoe Birch Ct (06037-4088)
PHONE.....................203 521-5727
Linda Mendonca, *Principal*
EMP: 5
SALES (est): 367.9K **Privately Held**
SIC: 3965 Zipper

(G-163)
BERLIN INDUSTRIES LLC
84 Bernard Rd (06037-2019)
P.O. Box 7353 (06037-7353)
PHONE.....................860 819-9997
Jennie Scofield, *CEO*
Steven Biella Jr,
EMP: 3
SALES (est): 340.6K **Privately Held**
SIC: 1611 3271 0782 4212 Highway & street construction; blocks, concrete: landscape or retaining wall; mowing services, lawn; mulching services, lawn; seeding services, lawn; spraying services, lawn; furniture moving, local: without storage

(G-164)
BODYCOTE THERMAL PROC INC
675 Christian Ln (06037-1425)
PHONE.....................860 225-7691
Marty Haran, *General Mgr*
Mike Sakelakos, *Branch Mgr*
EMP: 40
SALES (corp-wide): 935.8MM **Privately Held**
SIC: 3398 Metal heat treating
HQ: Bodycote Thermal Processing, Inc.
12700 Park Central Dr # 700
Dallas TX 75251
214 904-2420

(G-165)
BOMAR MACHINE LLC
600 Four Rod Rd Ste 7 (06037-3665)
PHONE.....................860 505-7299
Marek Szkotak, *Owner*
EMP: 3
SALES (est): 369.2K **Privately Held**
SIC: 3599 Machine shop, jobbing & repair

(G-166)
BUDNEY AEROSPACE INC
131 New Park Dr (06037-3740)
PHONE.....................860 828-0585
Kevin M Budney, *President*
Lisa Budney, *Vice Pres*

GEOGRAPHIC SECTION

Berlin - Hartford County (G-198)

Tony Biondo, *Opers Staff*
Roman Napierkowski, *Manager*
Richard V Newcombe, *Admin Sec*
EMP: 75
SALES (est): 10.2MM **Privately Held**
SIC: 3728 Aircraft assemblies, subassemblies & parts

(G-167)
BUDNEY OVERHAUL & REPAIR LTD
131 New Park Dr (06037-3740)
PHONE................................860 828-0585
Kevin M Budney, *President*
Puzio Walter, *General Mgr*
Lisa Budney, *Vice Pres*
Richard Newcombe, *CFO*
Richard V Newcombe, *Admin Sec*
▲ **EMP:** 160
SQ FT: 37,500
SALES (est): 30.3MM **Privately Held**
WEB: www.budneyoverhaul.com
SIC: 3599 Machine shop, jobbing & repair

(G-168)
CAMBRIDGE SPECIALTY CO INC
588 Four Rod Rd (06037-2280)
PHONE................................860 828-3579
Peter M Campanelli, *President*
Mark Labbe, *Vice Pres*
Seth Rutkowski, *Mfg Mgr*
Jack Fager, *Purchasing*
Eric Frick, *Purchasing*
EMP: 76 **EST:** 1951
SQ FT: 27,500
SALES (est): 18.3MM **Privately Held**
SIC: 3423 3728 3724 3714 Mechanics' hand tools; aircraft parts & equipment; aircraft engines & engine parts; motor vehicle parts & accessories; special dies, tools, jigs & fixtures

(G-169)
CENTRAL CONNECTICUT WATERJET
194 Christian Ln Ste A (06037-1449)
PHONE................................860 828-3877
Brian Lerose, *Principal*
EMP: 2 **EST:** 2010
SALES (est): 197.6K **Privately Held**
SIC: 3599 Machine shop, jobbing & repair

(G-170)
CO-OP JIG BORING JIG GRINDING
1152 Worthington Rdg (06037-3206)
PHONE................................860 828-9882
Fred Lewchik, *Owner*
Fred R Lewchik, *Owner*
EMP: 2 **EST:** 1969
SALES (est): 166.5K **Privately Held**
SIC: 3541 3599 Jig boring & grinding machines; crankshafts & camshafts, machining

(G-171)
COCCOMO BROTHERS DRILLING LLC
1897 Berlin Tpke (06037-3615)
PHONE................................860 828-1632
Thomas Coccomo, *Managing Prtnr*
Michael Coccomo,
Paul Coccomo,
EMP: 12
SQ FT: 5,000
SALES (est): 1MM **Privately Held**
SIC: 1411 Limestone, dimension-quarrying

(G-172)
COMPLETE SHEET METAL LLC
500 Four Rod Rd Ste 122 (06037-2282)
PHONE................................860 310-5447
Jeffrey Michaud, *Principal*
EMP: 2
SALES (est): 210K **Privately Held**
SIC: 3444 Sheet metalwork

(G-173)
COMPUTER EXPRESS LLC
365 New Britain Rd Ste D (06037-1366)
PHONE................................860 829-1310
Michael Psillas, *CEO*
▲ **EMP:** 14
SQ FT: 8,500
SALES (est): 3.9MM **Privately Held**
WEB: www.computerexpressct.com
SIC: 3577 Computer peripheral equipment

(G-174)
CT AMATEUR JAI ALAI LLC
500 Four Rod Rd Ste 119 (06037-2282)
PHONE................................860 357-2544
Matthew R Didomizio, *Principal*
EMP: 2
SALES (est): 139.3K **Privately Held**
SIC: 3949 Sporting & athletic goods

(G-175)
DAV-CO FINISHING LLC
1082 Farmington Ave (06037-5202)
PHONE................................860 828-5552
David Audette, *Mng Member*
EMP: 5
SALES (est): 598.3K **Privately Held**
SIC: 7389 3471 Finishing services; plating of metals or formed products

(G-176)
DELMAR PRODUCTS INC
Also Called: D'Andrea USA
400 Christian Ln (06037-1424)
P.O. Box 504 (06037-0504)
PHONE................................860 828-6501
John Di Mugno Jr, *President*
James Innes, *Manager*
Gale Chaplin, *Admin Sec*
▲ **EMP:** 18 **EST:** 1966
SQ FT: 32,500
SALES (est): 8.3MM **Privately Held**
WEB: www.delmarproducts.com
SIC: 5162 3089 Plastics sheets & rods; laminating of plastic

(G-177)
EMBROIDERY WORKS
1083 Farmington Ave (06037-2292)
PHONE................................800 681-0805
Craig Drezek, *Partner*
Richard Drezek, *Partner*
EMP: 2
SQ FT: 1,000
SALES (est): 90K **Privately Held**
WEB: www.embworks.com
SIC: 2395 Embroidery products, except schiffli machine

(G-178)
ERECTION & WELDING CONTRS LLC
190 New Park Dr (06037-3741)
PHONE................................860 828-9353
EMP: 1
SALES (est): 57K **Privately Held**
SIC: 7692 5082 Welding Repair Whol Construction/Mining Equipment

(G-179)
FOCUS TECHNOLOGIES INC
600 Four Rod Rd Ste 5 (06037-3665)
PHONE................................860 829-8998
EMP: 7
SALES (est): 754.8K **Privately Held**
SIC: 3599 Machine shop, jobbing & repair

(G-180)
FORREST MACHINE INC
236 Christian Ln (06037-1420)
PHONE................................860 563-1796
David Forrest, *President*
EMP: 54 **EST:** 1973
SQ FT: 17,250
SALES (est): 4.8MM **Privately Held**
WEB: www.forrestmachine.com
SIC: 3469 3728 Machine parts, stamped or pressed metal; aircraft parts & equipment

(G-181)
FOUR TWENTY INDUSTRIES LLC
314 Deming Rd (06037-1519)
PHONE................................860 818-3334
David Edelson, *Principal*
EMP: 3
SALES (est): 137.4K **Privately Held**
SIC: 3999 Manufacturing industries

(G-182)
FSB INC
Also Called: Fsb North America
24 New Park Dr (06037-3741)
PHONE................................203 404-4700
John Bergstrom, *President*
William S Ferguson, *Vice Pres*
▲ **EMP:** 11
SALES (est): 2.2MM **Privately Held**
WEB: www.fsbusa.com
SIC: 3429 Locks or lock sets

(G-183)
G A MALS WOODWORKING
77 Willow Brook Dr (06037-1533)
PHONE................................860 828-8702
Gerald A Mals, *Owner*
EMP: 1
SALES (est): 82.8K **Privately Held**
SIC: 2511 Wood household furniture

(G-184)
GRACE MACHINE COMPANY LLC
46 Woodlawn Rd Ste A (06037-1544)
PHONE................................860 828-8789
Kazimierz Perzan, *Mng Member*
Grace Perzan,
EMP: 10
SQ FT: 5,500
SALES (est): 990K **Privately Held**
SIC: 3599 Machine shop, jobbing & repair

(G-185)
GUEST CO
24 New Park Dr (06037-3741)
PHONE................................203 235-4421
EMP: 2
SALES (est): 88.3K **Privately Held**
SIC: 3699 Electrical equipment & supplies

(G-186)
H & W MACHINE LLC
37 Willow Brook Dr (06037-1533)
PHONE................................860 828-7679
Walter Sewerniak, *President*
EMP: 8
SALES (est): 1.1MM **Privately Held**
SIC: 3599 Machine shop, jobbing & repair

(G-187)
HEART INDUSTRIAL UNIONS LLC
870a Four Rod Rd (06037-3630)
PHONE................................800 769-0503
Scott Tremblay, *Principal*
EMP: 2
SALES (est): 210.7K **Privately Held**
SIC: 2452 Prefabricated wood buildings

(G-188)
HOSOKAWA MICRON INTL INC
Also Called: Hosokawa Polymer Systems Div
63 Fuller Way (06037-1540)
PHONE................................860 828-0541
Robert Voorhees, *President*
EMP: 20 **Privately Held**
WEB: www.hosokawa.com
SIC: 3089 Plastic hardware & building products
HQ: Hosokawa Micron International Inc.
10 Chatham Rd
Summit NJ 07901
908 273-6360

(G-189)
HOT SPOT STOVES & MECH LLC
4 Lower Ln (06037-2236)
PHONE................................860 829-7283
Jesse Dube, *Principal*
EMP: 1
SALES (est): 140.9K **Privately Held**
SIC: 3433 Stoves, wood & coal burning

(G-190)
INNER ARMOUR BLACK LLC
83 White Oak Dr (06037-1638)
PHONE................................860 656-7720
Diane Lagace, *Vice Pres*
EMP: 1
SALES (est): 130K **Privately Held**
SIC: 2023 Dietary supplements, dairy & non-dairy based

(G-191)
KENNEDY GUSTAFSON AND COLE INC
Also Called: Kgc
100 White Oak Dr (06037-1635)
PHONE................................860 828-2594
Edward Charles Cole, *President*
Roberts T Cole, *Vice Pres*
Pierre Joseph Roy, *Vice Pres*
Ryan Cole, *Sales Engr*
Edward Cole, *Executive*
EMP: 30
SQ FT: 25,000
SALES (est): 8.8MM **Privately Held**
SIC: 3564 Exhaust fans: industrial or commercial; dust or fume collecting equipment, industrial

(G-192)
KENSINGTON GLASS AND FRMNG CO
124 Woodlawn Rd (06037-1536)
PHONE................................860 828-9428
Frank Carfora Jr, *President*
Frank Carfora Sr, *Treasurer*
Mary Sue Hermann, *Admin Sec*
Jennifer L Carfora, *Asst Sec*
EMP: 8 **EST:** 1976
SQ FT: 2,400
SALES (est): 750K **Privately Held**
SIC: 2499 5719 1793 Picture & mirror frames, wood; mirrors; pictures, wall; glass & glazing work

(G-193)
LED LIGHTING SOLUTIONS LLC
169 Circlewood Dr (06037-3323)
PHONE................................860 770-6023
Thomas Desantos,
EMP: 1
SALES (est): 1MM **Privately Held**
SIC: 3646 7389 Commercial indusl & institutional electric lighting fixtures;

(G-194)
LIBERTY PRODUCTS INC
598 Deming Rd (06037-1606)
PHONE................................860 829-2122
▲ **EMP:** 2
SQ FT: 5,000
SALES (est): 200K **Privately Held**
SIC: 3841 Mfg Surgical/Medical Instruments

(G-195)
LISAS CLOVER HILL QUILTS LLC
27 Webster Square Rd (06037-2326)
PHONE................................860 828-9325
Lisa Salonia, *Owner*
James Salonia, *Co-Owner*
Jim Salonia, *Manager*
EMP: 1
SALES (est): 188.9K **Privately Held**
SIC: 2258 Fabric finishing, warp knit

(G-196)
LLC DOW GAGE
169 White Oak Dr 6037 (06037-1638)
PHONE................................860 828-5327
Scott Brotherton, *Manager*
EMP: 35 **EST:** 1946
SQ FT: 24,000
SALES: 400K **Privately Held**
SIC: 3545 Gauges (machine tool accessories)

(G-197)
LLC DOW GAGE
169 White Oak Dr (06037-1638)
PHONE................................860 828-5327
Scott Brotherton, *Manager*
Alan E Ortner,
EMP: 35
SALES: 7MM **Privately Held**
SIC: 3674 Strain gages, solid state

(G-198)
LORENCE SIGN WORKS LLC
Also Called: Lorence Signworks
55 Willow Brook Dr (06037-1533)
PHONE................................860 829-9999
Michelle Lorence, *Partner*
Paul Lorence, *Vice Pres*
EMP: 4

SALES (est): 499.2K **Privately Held**
SIC: **3993** 5046 Signs & advertising specialties; signs, electrical

(G-199)
MC KINNEY PRODUCTS COMPANY
225 Episcopal Rd 1 (06037-1524)
PHONE..................................800 346-7707
Thanasis Molokotos, *President*
Jeffrey A Mereschuk, *Admin Sec*
◆ EMP: 219
SQ FT: 200,000
SALES (est): 39.2MM
SALES (corp-wide): 9.3B **Privately Held**
SIC: **3429** Manufactured hardware (general)
HQ: Assa, Inc.
   110 Sargent Dr
   New Haven CT 06511
   203 624-5225

(G-200)
MIDSUN SPECIALTY PRODUCTS INC
Also Called: Tommy Tape
378 Four Rod Rd (06037-2257)
P.O. Box 864, Southington (06489-0864)
PHONE..................................860 378-0111
Mark C Hatje, *CEO*
Robert F Vojtila, *Ch of Bd*
Michael Ossowski, *Vice Pres*
Theodore Vaccaro, *VP Sales*
Terese Escoto, *Sales Staff*
▲ EMP: 34
SQ FT: 16,600
SALES (est): 6.7MM **Privately Held**
WEB: www.midsunspecialtyproducts.com
SIC: **3069** Rubber tape
PA: Midsun Group, Inc.
   135 Redstone St
   Southington CT 06489

(G-201)
MKB MACHINE & TOOL MFG
600 Four Rod Rd Ste 3 (06037-3665)
PHONE..................................860 828-5728
Gene Kozlowski, *Principal*
EMP: 3
SALES (est): 376K **Privately Held**
SIC: **3599** Machine shop, jobbing & repair

(G-202)
NALBOR MFG
872 Four Rod Rd Ste C (06037-3677)
P.O. Box 217 (06037-0217)
PHONE..................................860 828-7676
Jack Borkowski, *Partner*
EMP: 2
SALES (est): 217.1K **Privately Held**
SIC: **3728** Aircraft parts & equipment

(G-203)
NIRO COMPANIES LLC
100 Harding St (06037-5301)
PHONE..................................860 982-5645
Anthony M Niro II,
Nicholas J Niro,
Pietro A Niro,
EMP: 3
SALES (est): 91.3K **Privately Held**
SIC: **3471** Cleaning, polishing & finishing

(G-204)
OKAY INDUSTRIES INC
Also Called: Okay Medical Products Mfg
245 New Park Dr (06037-3740)
PHONE..................................860 225-8707
EMP: 6
SALES (corp-wide): 31.7MM **Privately Held**
SIC: **3469** 3542 Stamping metal for the trade; machine tools, metal forming type
PA: Okay Industries, Inc
   200 Ellis St
   New Britain CT 06051
   860 225-8707

(G-205)
OVL MANUFACTURING INC LLC
49 Cambridge Hts (06037-2310)
PHONE..................................860 829-0271
Craig Ogrin, *President*
Alfred Lassen, *Admin Sec*
EMP: 6

SALES (est): 96.7K **Privately Held**
SIC: **3444** 3441 Pipe, sheet metal; fabricated structural metal

(G-206)
PIONEER PRECISION PRODUCTS (PA)
2311 Chamberlain Hwy (06037-3964)
P.O. Box 396 (06037-0396)
PHONE..................................860 828-5838
Marian Rozycki, *President*
John Kumitis, *Commissioner*
Teresa Rozycki, *Admin Sec*
EMP: 12
SQ FT: 15,000
SALES (est): 1.5MM **Privately Held**
SIC: **3599** Machine shop, jobbing & repair

(G-207)
POINT MACHINE COMPANY
588 Four Rod Rd (06037-2280)
P.O. Box 188 (06037-0188)
PHONE..................................860 828-6901
Peter M Campanelli, *Principal*
Peter Campanelli, *CFO*
EMP: 48
SALES (est): 6.3MM **Privately Held**
SIC: **3724** Aircraft engines & engine parts

(G-208)
PRECISION METALS AND PLAS
758 Four Rod Rd (06037-3628)
PHONE..................................860 559-8843
EMP: 2
SALES (est): 102.4K **Privately Held**
SIC: **3599** Industrial machinery

(G-209)
PRECISION MILL LLC
872 Four Rod Rd Ste B (06037-3677)
PHONE..................................860 357-4729
Derek Kiczuk, *Principal*
EMP: 1
SALES (est): 83.5K **Privately Held**
SIC: **2431** Millwork

(G-210)
PRECISION PUNCH + TOOLING CORP (PA)
304 Christian Ln (06037-1420)
PHONE..................................860 229-9902
Kevin Gregoire, *President*
Dennis Glynn, *Treasurer*
EMP: 66
SQ FT: 44,000
SALES (est): 11.8MM **Privately Held**
WEB: www.ppunch.com
SIC: **3544** Punches, forming & stamping; industrial molds; special dies & tools

(G-211)
PRECISION PUNCH + TOOLING CORP
Eastern Industries
304 Christian Ln (06037-1420)
P.O. Box 7087 (06037-7087)
PHONE..................................860 225-4159
Kevin Gregoire, *Vice Pres*
EMP: 9
SALES (corp-wide): 11.8MM **Privately Held**
SIC: **3545** Gauges (machine tool accessories)
PA: Precision Punch + Tooling Corporation
   304 Christian Ln
   Berlin CT 06037
   860 229-9902

(G-212)
PRO TOOL AND DESIGN INC
230 Deming Rd (06037-1517)
PHONE..................................860 828-4667
Michael Bosse, *President*
Albert Gallnot, *Vice Pres*
EMP: 10
SQ FT: 2,500
SALES (est): 614.5K **Privately Held**
SIC: **3599** Machine shop, jobbing & repair

(G-213)
PYC DEBORRING LLC F/K/A C &
500 Four Rod Rd Ste 114 (06037-2282)
PHONE..................................860 828-6806
Krzysztof Pyc, *Principal*
EMP: 3

SALES (est): 439.4K **Privately Held**
SIC: **3559** Metal finishing equipment for plating, etc.

(G-214)
RACEWORKS INC
Also Called: Race Works
55 Willow Brook Dr (06037-1533)
PHONE..................................860 829-1312
John Ruggiero, *President*
Edward Flempkrf J, *Vice Pres*
EMP: 2
SQ FT: 3,600
SALES (est): 297K **Privately Held**
WEB: www.raceworks.com
SIC: **3711** Cars, armored, assembly of

(G-215)
RED BARN RADIATOR CO
54 Fuller Way (06037-1540)
PHONE..................................860 829-2060
Gail Spada, *President*
EMP: 2
SALES (est): 73.4K **Privately Held**
SIC: **3433** Heating equipment, except electric

(G-216)
RES-TECH CORPORATION
Also Called: Restech Plastic Molding
114 New Park Dr (06037-3741)
PHONE..................................860 828-1504
Don Caske, *Manager*
EMP: 60 **Privately Held**
SIC: **3089** Injection molded finished plastic products; injection molding of plastics
HQ: Res-Tech Corporation
   34 Tower St
   Hudson MA 01749
   978 567-1000

(G-217)
ROYAL MACHINE AND TOOL CORP
4 Willow Brook Dr (06037-1534)
P.O. Box Y (06037-0505)
PHONE..................................860 828-6555
Richard Ruscio, *President*
Joseph Dibattista, *Exec VP*
Frank Biello, *QC Mgr*
William Caco, *Engineer*
John Darling, *Engineer*
EMP: 49 EST: 1952
SQ FT: 25,000
SALES (est): 9.2MM **Privately Held**
WEB: www.royalworkholding.com
SIC: **3545** 5084 3544 Chucks: drill, lathe or magnetic (machine tool accessories); tools & accessories for machine tools; industrial machinery & equipment; special dies, tools, jigs & fixtures

(G-218)
SAINDON CRANE SERVICE
1830 Berlin Tpke (06037-3616)
PHONE..................................860 505-7245
Richard Martel, *Principal*
EMP: 2 EST: 2012
SALES (est): 146.7K **Privately Held**
SIC: **3625** Crane & hoist controls, including metal mill

(G-219)
SIGMAWEAR
202 New Britain Rd (06037-5304)
PHONE..................................860 924-2908
Brian Teske, *Principal*
EMP: 2
SALES (est): 148.9K **Privately Held**
SIC: **2759** Commercial printing

(G-220)
SIROIS TOOL COMPANY INC (PA)
169 White Oak Dr (06037-1638)
PHONE..................................860 828-5327
Alan E Ortner, *President*
Marc Begin, *President*
Bruce Northrup, *Vice Pres*
Scott Horton, *Prdtn Mgr*
Barry Labarge, *Prdtn Mgr*
EMP: 52
SQ FT: 20,000

SALES: 6MM **Privately Held**
WEB: www.siroistool.com
SIC: **3544** 3545 3542 3599 Jigs & fixtures; gauges (machine tool accessories); machine tools, metal forming type; machine shop, jobbing & repair

(G-221)
SPACE ELECTRONICS LLC
81 Fuller Way (06037-1540)
PHONE..................................860 829-0001
Kurt Wiener, *Principal*
Daniel Otlowski, *Exec VP*
Brandon Rathdun, *Exec VP*
Blair James, *Engineer*
Brandon Rathbun, *Engineer*
EMP: 22
SQ FT: 23,000
SALES (est): 6.3MM **Privately Held**
WEB: www.space-electronics.com
SIC: **3825** 3545 Electrical power measuring equipment; balancing machines (machine tool accessories)

(G-222)
SPOT-ON SIGN SOLUTIONS INC
67 Burgundy Dr (06037-1800)
PHONE..................................860 584-9008
Michael McAdam, *Principal*
EMP: 1 EST: 2016
SALES (est): 46K **Privately Held**
SIC: **3993** Signs & advertising specialties

(G-223)
STAXX CONSTRUCTION SVCS LLC
84 Bernard Rd (06037-2019)
PHONE..................................860 259-5003
Jennie L Scofield,
EMP: 2
SALES (est): 50K **Privately Held**
SIC: **1389** Construction, repair & dismantling services

(G-224)
STEELWRIST INC
576 Christian Ln (06037-1426)
PHONE..................................225 936-1111
Stefan Stockhaus, *President*
Erik Hedenryd, *Treasurer*
EMP: 4
SALES (est): 194.2K **Privately Held**
SIC: **3531** Construction machinery attachments

(G-225)
TIGHITCO INC
Aerostructures Group
245 Old Brickyard Ln (06037-1423)
PHONE..................................860 828-0298
Brandi Durity, *General Mgr*
Tawne Castorina, *Vice Pres*
Nancy Castorina, *Sales Staff*
Debbie Mlinek, *Supervisor*
EMP: 130
SALES (corp-wide): 1.6B **Privately Held**
SIC: **3369** Titanium castings, except die-casting
HQ: Tighitco Inc.
   1375 Sboard Indus Blvd Nw
   Atlanta GA 30318

(G-226)
TOMZ CORPORATION
47 Episcopal Rd (06037-1522)
PHONE..................................860 829-0670
Zbig Matulaniec, *CEO*
Tom Barwinski, *President*
Tom Matulaniec, *Vice Pres*
Mike Fries, *Engineer*
Dmitriy Mikhaylichenko, *Engineer*
EMP: 130
SQ FT: 55,000
SALES (est): 24.5MM **Privately Held**
WEB: www.tomz.com
SIC: **3451** Screw machine products

(G-227)
TRI-STAR INDUSTRIES INC
101 Massirio Dr (06037-2311)
PHONE..................................860 828-7570
Andrew Nowakowski, *Vice Pres*
EMP: 35
SQ FT: 27,300

SALES: 8.8MM
SALES (corp-wide): 185.9MM **Privately Held**
WEB: www.tristar-inserts.com
SIC: 3451 Screw machine products
HQ: Mw Industries, Inc.
    9501 Tech Blvd Ste 401
    Rosemont IL 60018
    847 349-5760

(G-228)
TRIGILA CONSTRUCTION INC
30 And A Half Ripple Ct (06037)
PHONE..................................860 828-8444
Thomas Trigila, *President*
Tina Trigila, *Vice Pres*
EMP: 20
SALES (est): 1.9MM **Privately Held**
SIC: 2452 1521 Prefabricated wood buildings; general remodeling, single-family houses

(G-229)
VAS INTEGRATED LLC
600 Four Rod Rd Ste 9 (06037-3665)
PHONE..................................860 748-4058
Chris Parzych, *President*
Jim Cox, *CFO*
EMP: 9 EST: 2011
SALES (est): 1.4MM **Privately Held**
SIC: 3498 Manifolds, pipe: fabricated from purchased pipe

(G-230)
VINTAGE SHEET METAL FABG
44 Washington Ave Ste 7 (06037-2290)
P.O. Box 7392 (06037-7392)
PHONE..................................860 595-8423
EMP: 2
SALES (est): 145.1K **Privately Held**
SIC: 3499 Fabricated metal products

(G-231)
VISUAL SOFTWARE SYSTEMS LLC
32 Maryann Ct (06037-3708)
P.O. Box 7144, Kensington (06037-7144)
PHONE..................................860 829-1223
Richard D Brown II, *Principal*
EMP: 2
SALES (est): 35.3K **Privately Held**
SIC: 7372 Prepackaged software

(G-232)
VITAL SIGNS & GRAPHIC LLC
873 Farmington Ave Ste B (06037-2291)
PHONE..................................860 829-7446
Kathy Naple, *Mng Member*
Robert Marut,
EMP: 2
SQ FT: 1,100
SALES: 200K **Privately Held**
SIC: 3993 Signs & advertising specialties

(G-233)
YALE SECURITY INC
Also Called: Yale Commercial Locks & Hdwr
225 Episcopal Rd (06037-1524)
P.O. Box 4004 (06037-0512)
PHONE..................................865 986-7511
Jan Mc Kenzie, *Mktg Dir*
Dick Krajewski, *Manager*
EMP: 350
SQ FT: 2,300
SALES (corp-wide): 9.3B **Privately Held**
SIC: 3429 Locks or lock sets
HQ: Assa Abloy Accessories And Door Controls Group, Inc.
    1902 Airport Rd
    Monroe NC 28110
    704 283-2101

Bethany
New Haven County

(G-234)
AFCON PRODUCTS INC
35 Sargent Dr (06524-3135)
PHONE..................................203 393-9301
John Mark Chayka, *President*
James Chayka, *Vice Pres*
Helen Plante, *Purchasing*
Kathy Kovacs, *Manager*

EMP: 15
SQ FT: 10,000
SALES (est): 2.9MM **Privately Held**
SIC: 3621 3563 7629 7699 Generating apparatus & parts, electrical; air & gas compressors; generator repair; industrial equipment services; compressor repair

(G-235)
BRENDA JUBIN
Also Called: Boswell's
199 Wooding Hill Rd (06524-3144)
PHONE..................................203 393-2366
Brenda Jubin, *Owner*
EMP: 2
SALES (est): 98.2K **Privately Held**
SIC: 2791 Typesetting

(G-236)
BULLIE INDUSTRIES LLC
21 Tollgate Rd (06524-3095)
PHONE..................................203 393-9763
Brian Laubstein, *Principal*
EMP: 1
SALES (est): 55.1K **Privately Held**
SIC: 3999 Manufacturing industries

(G-237)
CARDIOPHOTONICS LLC
14 Lacey Rd (06524-3021)
PHONE..................................203 645-6077
Thomas Wood, *Principal*
EMP: 2
SALES (est): 88.3K **Privately Held**
SIC: 3661 Fiber optics communications equipment

(G-238)
COLOR ITE REFINISHING CO
Also Called: Colorite Refinishing
868 Carrington Rd (06524-3121)
PHONE..................................203 393-0240
Edward Spagnolo, *Owner*
EMP: 2
SALES: 250K **Privately Held**
WEB: www.color-ite.com
SIC: 3471 7532 Plating & polishing; paint shop, automotive

(G-239)
CONNECTICUT ANALYTICAL CORP
696 Amity Rd Ste 13 (06524-3006)
PHONE..................................203 393-9666
Joseph Bango, *General Mgr*
Joseph J Bango Jr, *Principal*
Joseph J Bango Sr, *Treasurer*
EMP: 11
SALES (est): 1.1MM **Privately Held**
WEB: www.ctanalytical.com
SIC: 3812 5169 8731 8711 Search & navigation equipment; industrial gases; electronic research; engineering services; analytical instruments

(G-240)
EYE-CON FOODS LLC
7 Green Hill Rd (06524-3324)
PHONE..................................203 752-7525
Conley Taylor,
EMP: 1
SALES (est): 39.6K **Privately Held**
SIC: 3999 Manufacturing industries

(G-241)
FAIRFIELD COUNTY MILLWORK
20 Sargent Dr (06524-3136)
PHONE..................................203 393-9751
John Ianin, *President*
Mandy Ianri, *Admin Sec*
EMP: 16
SQ FT: 20,000
SALES (est): 2.5MM **Privately Held**
WEB: www.fcmillwork.com
SIC: 2431 Millwork

(G-242)
FREEZER HILL MULCH COMPANY LLC
845 Carrington Rd (06524)
P.O. Box 1318, Naugatuck (06770-1318)
PHONE..................................203 758-3725
Theron Simons, *Mng Member*
EMP: 3

SALES (est): 360.8K **Privately Held**
SIC: 2499 Mulch, wood & bark

(G-243)
GAVIN WELDING LLC
290 Bear Hill Rd (06524-3249)
PHONE..................................203 393-9707
Charles W Gavin, *Manager*
EMP: 1
SALES (est): 64.8K **Privately Held**
SIC: 7692 Welding repair

(G-244)
HERITAGE NEWSPRINT LLC
68 Anthony Ct (06524-3202)
PHONE..................................203 393-0567
Hugo Kranz Jr, *President*
EMP: 1
SALES (est): 100.5K **Privately Held**
SIC: 2611 Pulp manufactured from waste or recycled paper

(G-245)
LATICRETE INTERNATIONAL INC
91 Amity Rd (06524-3423)
PHONE..................................203 393-0010
EMP: 2
SALES (corp-wide): 165MM **Privately Held**
SIC: 2891 2899 Epoxy adhesives; chemical preparations
PA: Laticrete International, Inc.
    1 Laticrete Park N
    Bethany CT 06524
    203 393-0010

(G-246)
LATICRETE SUPERCAP LLC
91 Amity Rd (06524-3423)
PHONE..................................203 393-4558
Edward Metcalf, *President*
EMP: 3 EST: 2017
SALES (est): 131.5K **Privately Held**
SIC: 3823 Moisture meters, industrial process type

(G-247)
LIBBY POWER SYSTEMS LLC (PA)
35 Sargent Dr (06524-3135)
P.O. Box 854, Cheshire (06410-0854)
PHONE..................................203 393-1239
John Chayka, *President*
Kathy Kovacs, *Manager*
EMP: 2
SQ FT: 10,000
SALES: 1MM **Privately Held**
WEB: www.afconproducts.com
SIC: 3621 Motors & generators

(G-248)
PLASTIC ASSEMBLY SYSTEMS LLC
Also Called: Pas
19 Sargent Dr (06524-3135)
PHONE..................................203 393-0639
Eric Gregorich, *Vice Pres*
Kurt Fugal, *Mng Member*
Paul J Mauro,
EMP: 15
SQ FT: 9,000
SALES: 3MM **Privately Held**
WEB: www.heatstaking.com
SIC: 3432 Plastic plumbing fixture fittings, assembly

(G-249)
RESTOPEDIC INC
695 Amity Rd (06524-3026)
PHONE..................................203 393-1520
Joseph Da Silva, *President*
Joe Soares, *Corp Secy*
▲ EMP: 8
SQ FT: 18,000
SALES (est): 1.3MM **Privately Held**
SIC: 2515 Mattresses, innerspring or box spring

(G-250)
SUPER CELL INDUSTRIES INC
229 Hatfield Hill Rd (06524-3511)
PHONE..................................203 393-1335
Susan A Purcell, *Principal*
EMP: 2

SALES (est): 108.5K **Privately Held**
SIC: 3999 Manufacturing industries

(G-251)
TUTORS & COMPUTERS INC
36 Perkins Rd (06524-3108)
PHONE..................................203 393-3006
Gary Schulman, *President*
EMP: 2
SALES (est): 210.5K **Privately Held**
WEB: www.tutorsandcomputers.com
SIC: 5734 7372 7371 8243 Computer & software stores; prepackaged software; computer software systems analysis & design, custom; data processing schools; cash registers

(G-252)
WILD LEAF PRESS INC
12 Fatima Dr (06524-3214)
PHONE..................................203 415-5309
R William Hunter, *Director*
EMP: 2
SALES: 1.2K **Privately Held**
SIC: 2731 Book publishing

(G-253)
WOODWORKING PLUS LLC
375 Bethmour Rd (06524-3358)
PHONE..................................203 393-1967
John J Migliaro Jr, *Manager*
EMP: 3
SALES (est): 450K **Privately Held**
SIC: 2431 Millwork

Bethel
Fairfield County

(G-254)
227 GREENWOOD LLC
52 Sunset Hill Rd (06801-2919)
PHONE..................................203 798-9716
Michael Rizzo, *Principal*
EMP: 2
SALES (est): 70.7K **Privately Held**
SIC: 2499 Wood products

(G-255)
A WILD QUILTER
6 Taylor Ave (06801-2412)
PHONE..................................203 744-3405
Alexa C Wild, *Owner*
EMP: 1
SALES (est): 92.2K **Privately Held**
SIC: 2221 Comforters & quilts, manmade fiber & silk

(G-256)
ACADEMY MARBLE & GRANITE LLC (PA)
101 Wooster St Ste C (06801-1867)
PHONE..................................203 791-2956
Sinan Sepicin, *Mng Member*
▲ EMP: 4
SALES (est): 1.2MM **Privately Held**
SIC: 1411 Granite dimension stone

(G-257)
ALL PHASE DUMPSTERS LLC
30 Wolfpits Rd (06801-2950)
PHONE..................................203 778-9104
Valerie Gauthier, *Principal*
EMP: 4
SALES (est): 315.4K **Privately Held**
SIC: 3443 Dumpsters, garbage

(G-258)
ART SCREEN
Also Called: Artscreen
12 Francis J Clarke Cir (06801-2850)
PHONE..................................203 744-1991
William J Fischl, *Partner*
Olga Fischl, *Partner*
William Fischl, *Partner*
EMP: 2
SQ FT: 3,600
SALES (est): 279.3K **Privately Held**
SIC: 2759 2396 Screen printing; automotive & apparel trimmings

(G-259)
ARTECH PACKAGING LLC
Also Called: Artech Lubricants
18 Taylor Ave Ste 2 (06801-2435)
PHONE..................845 858-8558
Thomas Arkins,
◆ EMP: 4
SALES (est): 538K Privately Held
SIC: 2992 5172 Lubricating oils & greases; lubricating oils & greases

(G-260)
B & R MACHINE WORKS INC
23 Henry St (06801-2405)
PHONE..................203 798-0595
Bela Zagyi, President
Yavette Zagyi, Vice Pres
EMP: 7
SQ FT: 6,500
SALES (est): 958.5K Privately Held
SIC: 3599 Machine shop, jobbing & repair

(G-261)
BARZETTI WELDING LLC
Also Called: Barzettis Fabricating & Wldg
143 Grassy Plain St (06801-2806)
PHONE..................203 748-3200
David Barzetti, Mng Member
Carla Barzetti, Mng Member
Nicholas Barzetti,
EMP: 2
SQ FT: 5,000
SALES (est): 381K Privately Held
SIC: 3441 7692 3444 Fabricated structural metal; welding repair; sheet metalwork

(G-262)
BETHEL MAIL SERVICE
Also Called: Bethel Mail Service Center
211 Greenwood Ave Ste 2 (06801-2146)
PHONE..................203 730-1399
Silvia Duff, Owner
Silvia Guss, Owner
EMP: 17
SALES (est): 1.2MM Privately Held
SIC: 2542 Mail racks & lock boxes, postal service: except wood

(G-263)
BETHEL PRINTING & GRAPHICS
81 Greenwood Ave Ste 10 (06801-2553)
PHONE..................203 748-7034
Tom Omasta, President
Edward Hannan, Vice Pres
EMP: 6
SQ FT: 2,000
SALES (est): 811.6K Privately Held
SIC: 2752 Commercial printing, offset

(G-264)
BETHEL SAND & GRAVEL CO
2 Maple Avenue Ext (06801-1507)
P.O. Box 185 (06801-0185)
PHONE..................203 743-4469
Mary Nazzaro, Partner
EMP: 8 EST: 1956
SQ FT: 7,000
SALES (est): 642.1K Privately Held
SIC: 1442 Construction sand & gravel

(G-265)
BIOMASS INDUSTRIES INC
30 Henry St (06801-2441)
PHONE..................203 207-9958
Douglas D Griffin, Principal
EMP: 1 EST: 2010
SALES (est): 49K Privately Held
SIC: 3999 Manufacturing industries

(G-266)
BLACKSTONE INDUSTRIES LLC
Also Called: Foredom Electric Co
16 Stony Hill Rd (06801-1031)
PHONE..................203 792-8622
Richard Milici, President
Rob Horton, Executive
▲ EMP: 60 EST: 1984
SQ FT: 38,000
SALES (est): 14MM Privately Held
WEB: www.blackstoneind.com
SIC: 3546 3425 Power-driven handtools; saw blades for hand or power saws

(G-267)
BURNDY LLC
Also Called: Framatone Connectors USA
185 Grassy Plain St (06801-2899)
PHONE..................203 792-1115
Michelle Pemberton, Sales Staff
Ben Himes, Branch Mgr
EMP: 70
SALES (corp-wide): 4.4B Publicly Held
WEB: www.fciconnect.com
SIC: 3678 3643 Electronic connectors; current-carrying wiring devices
HQ: Burndy Llc
    47 E Industrial Park Dr
    Manchester NH 03109

(G-268)
CAPITOL ELECTRONICS INC
11 Francis J Clarke Cir (06801-2872)
PHONE..................203 744-3300
Richard Warren, President
Jamie Musulin, Accounts Mgr
EMP: 10 EST: 1997
SQ FT: 7,000
SALES: 1MM Privately Held
SIC: 3613 Switchgear & switchgear accessories

(G-269)
CFM TEST & BALANCE CORP
14 Depot Pl Ste 2 (06801-2540)
PHONE..................203 778-1900
Robert Wade, President
EMP: 4 EST: 1972
SALES (est): 310K Privately Held
SIC: 3821 5411 Balances, laboratory; grocery stores

(G-270)
CHIARA PUBLICATIONS
211 Greenwood Ave 22186 (06801-2124)
PHONE..................203 797-1905
Mario Chiara, Owner
EMP: 1 EST: 1999
SALES (est): 50K Privately Held
SIC: 2741 Miscellaneous publishing

(G-271)
CHROMATICS INC
19 Francis J Clarke Cir (06801-2847)
PHONE..................203 743-6868
Stephen Newlin, Principal
▲ EMP: 16
SQ FT: 10,000
SALES (est): 3.4MM Publicly Held
WEB: www.colorant-chromatics.com
SIC: 2819 Industrial inorganic chemicals
HQ: Colorant Chromatics Ag
    Gotthardstrasse 28
    Zug ZG 6302
    417 410-101

(G-272)
CLEAR SITE THE HEATED WIPER
4 Paul St (06801-1712)
PHONE..................203 790-2100
Matt Kornhaas, Vice Pres
Timothy Prunty, Vice Pres
Patrick Schulz, Vice Pres
Mark Jacobs, CFO
Charles E King Jr, Mng Member
EMP: 10
SQ FT: 1,500
SALES (est): 537.8K Privately Held
SIC: 3545 Milling cutters

(G-273)
CONNECTICUT COINING INC
10 Trowbridge Dr (06801-2858)
PHONE..................203 743-3861
Gregory J Marciano, President
Lisa Pittman, Purch Mgr
Marlene Gaberel, Sales Staff
Patricia R Gershwin, Admin Sec
Elise Marciano, Admin Sec
EMP: 55 EST: 1963
SQ FT: 8,500
SALES (est): 10MM Privately Held
WEB: www.ctcoining.com
SIC: 3599 3671 Machine shop, jobbing & repair; electron tubes

(G-274)
CROWN HOUSE PUBLISHING CO LLC
Also Called: Seminar Services
6 Trowbridge Dr Ste 5 (06801-2882)
PHONE..................203 778-1300
Mark Tracten,
▲ EMP: 2
SALES (est): 174.2K Privately Held
SIC: 2731 Books: publishing only

(G-275)
CUDZILO ENTERPRISES INC
Also Called: Tibby's Electric Motor Service
40 Taylor Ave (06801-2450)
PHONE..................203 748-4694
Gregory Cudzilo, President
Chris Cudzilo, Vice Pres
EMP: 3 EST: 1977
SQ FT: 7,000
SALES (est): 266.8K Privately Held
SIC: 7694 5065 5063 Electric motor repair; electronic parts; motors, electric; electrical supplies

(G-276)
D R S DESIGNS
Also Called: Lasting Impressions
217 Greenwood Ave (06801-2113)
PHONE..................203 744-2858
William Wichman, Owner
Louise Wichman, Bookkeeper
EMP: 6 EST: 1948
SQ FT: 2,000
SALES (est): 549.9K Privately Held
WEB: www.drs-designs.com
SIC: 3953 5945 Embossing seals & hand stamps; hobby, toy & game shops

(G-277)
DAILY FARE LLC
13 Durant Ave (06801-1906)
PHONE..................203 743-7300
Robin Grubard, Principal
EMP: 5 EST: 2008
SALES (est): 263.8K Privately Held
SIC: 2711 Newspapers, publishing & printing

(G-278)
DANBURY STAIRS CORPORATION
25 Francis J Clarke Cir # 1 (06801-2873)
PHONE..................203 743-5567
EMP: 2 EST: 2011
SALES (est): 132.5K Privately Held
SIC: 2431 Millwork

(G-279)
DCG-PMI INC
Also Called: Dcg Precision Manufacturing
9 Trowbridge Dr (06801-2858)
PHONE..................203 743-5525
Gerald Palanzo, CEO
Paul Sullivan, CFO
EMP: 49 EST: 1943
SQ FT: 33,000
SALES (est): 11.6MM Privately Held
WEB: www.dcgprecision.com
SIC: 3499 3841 Machine bases, metal; surgical & medical instruments

(G-280)
DEL-TRON PRECISION INC
5 Trowbridge Dr Ste 1 (06801-2869)
PHONE..................203 778-2727
Ralph A McIntosh Jr, President
Edward Keane, Vice Pres
Katherine Keane, Vice Pres
William Schule, Engineer
Emil Melvin, Sales Executive
EMP: 50 EST: 1975
SQ FT: 28,000
SALES (est): 13.2MM Privately Held
SIC: 3562 5084 3568 Roller bearings & parts; industrial machinery & equipment; power transmission equipment

(G-281)
DMB PUBLISHING LLC
5 Kingswood Dr (06801-1861)
PHONE..................203 798-9231
Donna Benevento Fluegel, President
EMP: 1 EST: 2012
SALES (est): 41.3K Privately Held
SIC: 2741 Miscellaneous publishing

(G-282)
DR MIKES ICE CREAM INC
Also Called: Dr Mike's Ice Cream Shop
158 Greenwood Ave (06801-2530)
PHONE..................203 792-4388
Robert Allison, President
EMP: 2
SQ FT: 400
SALES (est): 204.6K Privately Held
WEB: www.culinarymenus.com
SIC: 2024 Ice cream & frozen desserts

(G-283)
DUNE DENIM LLC
6 Meadow Ln (06801-1130)
PHONE..................203 241-5409
April Damraksa, Manager
EMP: 1
SALES (est): 101.7K Privately Held
SIC: 2211 Denims

(G-284)
DURACELL COMPANY (HQ)
14 Research Dr (06801-1040)
PHONE..................203 796-4000
Ron Rabinowitz, CEO
Paul Schacht, Vice Pres
Perry Peiffer, Opers Staff
Gail Searels, Buyer
Linda Jacobsen, Purchasing
EMP: 21
SALES (est): 5.5MM
SALES (corp-wide): 225.3B Publicly Held
SIC: 3691 Alkaline cell storage batteries
PA: Berkshire Hathaway Inc.
    3555 Farnam St Ste 1140
    Omaha NE 68131
    402 346-1400

(G-285)
DURACELL COMPANY
Duracell USA
Berkshire Corporate Bldg (06801)
PHONE..................203 796-4000
Ed Degrand, Vice Pres
EMP: 580
SALES (corp-wide): 225.3B Publicly Held
SIC: 3691 Storage batteries
HQ: The Duracell Company
    14 Research Dr
    Bethel CT 06801
    203 796-4000

(G-286)
DURACELL MANUFACTURING INC
15 Research Dr (06801)
PHONE..................203 796-4000
EMP: 6
SALES (est): 185.8K Privately Held
SIC: 3691 Mfg Storage Batteries

(G-287)
DURACELL MANUFACTURING LLC
14 Research Dr (06801-1040)
PHONE..................203 796-4000
Mark Leckie, President
EMP: 250
SALES (est): 407.7K
SALES (corp-wide): 225.3B Publicly Held
SIC: 3692 Dry cell batteries, single or multiple cell
PA: Berkshire Hathaway Inc.
    3555 Farnam St Ste 1140
    Omaha NE 68131
    402 346-1400

(G-288)
DURACELL US HOLDING LLC (HQ)
14 Research Dr (06801-1040)
PHONE..................203 796-4000
Laura Becker, President
EMP: 10
SALES (est): 29.1MM
SALES (corp-wide): 225.3B Publicly Held
SIC: 3691 Alkaline cell storage batteries

GEOGRAPHIC SECTION
Bethel - Fairfield County (G-319)

PA: Berkshire Hathaway Inc.
3555 Farnam St Ste 1140
Omaha NE 68131
402 346-1400

(G-289)
DURACELL US OPERATIONS INC
14 Research Dr (06801-1040)
PHONE.................................203 796-4000
Angelo Pantaleo, *CEO*
EMP: 1
SALES (est): 399.3K
SALES (corp-wide): 225.3B **Publicly Held**
SIC: 3691 Alkaline cell storage batteries
HQ: The Duracell Company
14 Research Dr
Bethel CT 06801
203 796-4000

(G-290)
DYNAXA LLC
211 Greenwood Ave Ste 2 (06801-2146)
PHONE.................................203 300-5237
Stephen P Griffing, *Principal*
EMP: 2
SALES (est): 153.5K **Privately Held**
SIC: 2097 Manufactured ice

(G-291)
EAST COAST SIGN AND SUPPLY INC
11 Francis J Clarke Cir (06801-2872)
PHONE.................................203 791-8326
Richard Carroll, *President*
Madeline Carroll, *Vice Pres*
EMP: 6
SQ FT: 1,800
SALES (est): 839.5K **Privately Held**
WEB: www.eastcoastsign.net
SIC: 3993 5084 Signs, not made in custom sign painting shops; safety equipment

(G-292)
EATON AEROSPACE LLC
15 Durant Ave (06801-1901)
PHONE.................................203 796-6000
Mel Drummond, *Manager*
EMP: 45 **Privately Held**
SIC: 3679 3812 3643 3829 Electronic switches; acceleration indicators & systems components, aerospace; current-carrying wiring devices; pressure transducers
HQ: Eaton Aerospace Llc
1000 Eaton Blvd
Cleveland OH 44122
216 523-5000

(G-293)
EATON CORPORATION
15 Durant Ave (06801-1901)
PHONE.................................203 796-6000
Jeremy Betsold, *Engineer*
Anthony D'Ostilio, *Engineer*
Mark Walter, *Project Engr*
Michael J Dodd, *Manager*
EMP: 20 **Privately Held**
WEB: www.eaton.com
SIC: 3643 Current-carrying wiring devices
HQ: Eaton Corporation
1000 Eaton Blvd
Cleveland OH 44122
440 523-5000

(G-294)
ELC ACQUISITION CORPORATION
6 Trowbridge Dr (06801-2881)
PHONE.................................203 743-4059
Bob McClernon, *President*
EMP: 5
SALES (est): 365K **Privately Held**
SIC: 3648 Lighting equipment

(G-295)
ELECTRO-LITE CORPORATION
6 Trowbridge Dr (06801-2881)
PHONE.................................203 743-4059
Dr Joshua Friedman, *CEO*
Allan Brooks, *Senior VP*
Lisa Quillinan, *Mfg Spvr*
EMP: 10
SQ FT: 6,750
SALES (est): 1.8MM **Privately Held**
WEB: www.electro-lite.com
SIC: 5049 3641 Optical goods; electric lamps

(G-296)
ELECTRONIC DESIGN LAB INC
23 Francis J Clarke Cir 1b (06801-2861)
PHONE.................................203 790-0500
Fax: 203 938-3663
EMP: 9 **EST:** 1971
SQ FT: 1,500
SALES: 900K **Privately Held**
SIC: 7371 8711 8731 3672 Computer Programming Svc Engineering Services Coml Physical Research Mfg Printed Circuit Brds

(G-297)
ESDRAS STEEL FABRICATION
9 Francis J Clarke Cir (06801-2845)
PHONE.................................203 917-3053
Antonia Martinez, *Principal*
EMP: 3
SALES (est): 266.6K **Privately Held**
SIC: 3441 Building components, structural steel

(G-298)
EVANS FABRICATION
Also Called: Awnings Are US
184 Grassy Plain St (06801-2807)
PHONE.................................203 791-9517
Karl Verner, *Owner*
EMP: 2
SALES: 150K **Privately Held**
SIC: 2394 3446 Awnings, fabric: made from purchased materials; stairs, staircases, stair treads: prefabricated metal

(G-299)
FALLS FUEL LLC
5 Laughlin Rd (06801-1127)
PHONE.................................203 744-3835
Ed Archer, *Principal*
EMP: 3
SALES (est): 176K **Privately Held**
SIC: 2869 Fuels

(G-300)
FOCAL METALS
11 Trowbridge Dr (06801-2858)
PHONE.................................203 743-4443
Richard Varnum, *Principal*
EMP: 1 **EST:** 2016
SALES (est): 86.9K **Privately Held**
SIC: 2434 5021 5211 Wood kitchen cabinets; furniture; counter tops

(G-301)
FOCUS MEDICAL LLC
Also Called: Naturalase
23 Francis J Clarke Cir (06801-2861)
PHONE.................................203 730-8885
John B Lee Jr, *CEO*
Osmonnie Erat,
EMP: 8
SQ FT: 4,000
SALES (est): 1.7MM **Privately Held**
WEB: www.focusmedical.com
SIC: 3845 Laser systems & equipment, medical

(G-302)
FREDS AUTO MACHINE
151 Grassy Plain St C2 (06801-2866)
PHONE.................................203 744-2950
Alfred D Linck, *Owner*
EMP: 1
SQ FT: 1,600
SALES (est): 142.5K **Privately Held**
SIC: 3559 5531 Automotive related machinery; automotive parts

(G-303)
GILLETTE COMPANY
14 Research Dr (06801-1040)
PHONE.................................203 796-4000
EMP: 4
SALES (corp-wide): 67.6B **Publicly Held**
SIC: 3421 2844 3951 2899 Razor blades & razors; toilet preparations; pens & mechanical pencils; correction fluid
HQ: The Gillette Company
1 Gillette Park
Boston MA 02127
617 421-7000

(G-304)
GRECO INDUSTRIES INC
14 Trowbridge Dr (06801-2858)
PHONE.................................203 798-7804
Hugo Greco, *President*
Enrico Greco, *Vice Pres*
Michael Greco, *Vice Pres*
EMP: 7
SQ FT: 2,800
SALES: 500K **Privately Held**
SIC: 3499 Trophies, metal, except silver

(G-305)
GREENWORKS WOODWORKING
72 Turkey Plain Rd (06801-2841)
PHONE.................................203 886-8573
EMP: 1
SALES (est): 54.1K **Privately Held**
SIC: 2431 Millwork

(G-306)
GREGORY WOODWORKS LLC
6 Sympaug Park Rd (06801-2838)
PHONE.................................203 794-0726
Devin P Gregory,
EMP: 9
SALES (est): 932.7K **Privately Held**
SIC: 2521 2541 Cabinets, office: wood; cabinets, lockers & shelving

(G-307)
H G STEINMETZ MACHINE WORKS
2 Turnage Ln (06801-2853)
PHONE.................................203 794-1880
William Michelotti, *President*
Robert Muldoon, *Vice Pres*
EMP: 12
SQ FT: 15,000
SALES (est): 1.8MM **Privately Held**
WEB: www.steinmetzmachine.com
SIC: 3599 3499 7699 7692 Machine shop, jobbing & repair; strapping, metal; industrial machinery & equipment repair; welding repair

(G-308)
HIS VINEYARD INC
2 Vail Rd (06801-1138)
PHONE.................................203 790-1600
Keri Lynne Baldelli, *Principal*
EMP: 3
SALES (est): 163.9K **Privately Held**
SIC: 2084 Wines, brandy & brandy spirits

(G-309)
HOME SWEETER HM KIT & BATH LLC
8 Topstone Dr (06801-2624)
PHONE.................................203 948-6482
Joseph Edelmann, *Principal*
EMP: 2
SALES (est): 103.2K **Privately Held**
SIC: 3261 2511 Bathroom accessories/fittings, vitreous china or earthenware; kitchen & dining room furniture

(G-310)
IMPRINT PRINTING
17 Francis J Clarke Cir (06801-2847)
PHONE.................................203 794-1092
William Jones, *Principal*
Michael Sexton, *Opers Staff*
EMP: 2 **EST:** 2008
SALES (est): 146.7K **Privately Held**
SIC: 2752 Commercial printing, offset

(G-311)
INSULATED WIRE INC
Iw Microwave Products Division
2c Park Lawn Dr (06801-1042)
PHONE.................................203 791-1999
John Morelli, *President*
EMP: 11
SALES (corp-wide): 9.7MM **Privately Held**
SIC: 3357 Nonferrous wiredrawing & insulating
PA: Insulated Wire Inc.
960 Sylvan Ave
Bayport NY 11705
631 472-4070

(G-312)
INTERSURFACE DYNAMICS INC
Also Called: Polypolish Products Div
21 Francis J Clarke Cir (06801-2847)
P.O. Box 181 (06801-0181)
PHONE.................................203 778-9995
Jonathon J Wolk, *President*
Walter Wolk Jr, *Vice Pres*
▲ **EMP:** 14
SQ FT: 20,000
SALES (est): 3.1MM **Privately Held**
WEB: www.isurface.com
SIC: 2899 Chemical preparations

(G-313)
IR INDUSTRIES INC
21 Francis J Clarke Cir (06801-2847)
PHONE.................................203 790-8273
Eric Rothstein, *President*
Patricia Borza, *Vice Pres*
▲ **EMP:** 15
SQ FT: 25,000
SALES (est): 1.5MM **Privately Held**
SIC: 3069 5113 Tape, pressure sensitive: rubber; shipping supplies

(G-314)
J & B SERVICE COMPANY LLC
12 Trowbridge Dr (06801-2858)
P.O. Box 879 (06801-0879)
PHONE.................................203 743-9357
Richard D Jennings IV,
EMP: 8
SQ FT: 1,200
SALES (est): 690K **Privately Held**
SIC: 3822 1711 Hydronic pressure or temperature controls; hardware for environmental regulators; warm air heating & air conditioning contractor

(G-315)
J J CONCRETE FOUNDATIONS
15 Stony Hill Rd (06801-1030)
PHONE.................................203 798-8310
Rui M Ribeiro, *Principal*
EMP: 3
SALES (est): 411.3K **Privately Held**
SIC: 2515 1771 Foundations & platforms; concrete work; concrete pumping

(G-316)
JOHN J PAWLOSKI LUMBER INC
4 Pleasantview Ter (06801-2321)
PHONE.................................203 794-0737
Richard Pawloski, *President*
EMP: 3
SQ FT: 100
SALES (est): 199.6K **Privately Held**
SIC: 2421 Sawmills & planing mills, general

(G-317)
JORDAN WOODWORKS
24 Wolfpits Rd (06801-2921)
PHONE.................................203 512-3581
Joanna Worrell, *Principal*
EMP: 2 **EST:** 2008
SALES (est): 118.8K **Privately Held**
SIC: 2431 Millwork

(G-318)
KELLER PRODUCTS INC
26 Old Hawleyville Rd (06801-3111)
PHONE.................................203 794-0075
Arthur Keller, *President*
Will Keller, *Vice Pres*
EMP: 2
SQ FT: 1,800
SALES: 200K **Privately Held**
SIC: 3599 Machine shop, jobbing & repair

(G-319)
KELLOGG HARDWOODS INC
11 Diamond Ave (06801-1802)
PHONE.................................203 797-1992
Allen G Kellogg, *CEO*
Allen A Kellogg, *President*
Cheryl A Kellogg, *Admin Sec*
EMP: 3

Bethel - Fairfield County (G-320)

SALES (est): 593.4K **Privately Held**
WEB: www.kellogghardwoods.com
SIC: 2426 Hardwood dimension & flooring mills

(G-320)
KINETIC INSTRUMENTS INC
17 Berkshire Blvd (06801-1095)
PHONE 203 743-0080
William J Becker, *President*
EMP: 20
SQ FT: 5,000
SALES (est): 3.3MM **Privately Held**
WEB: www.kineticinc.com
SIC: 3843 Dental equipment

(G-321)
LEADING EDGE CONCEPTS INC
15 Berkshire Blvd Ste A (06801-1052)
PHONE 203 797-1200
Addison Unangst, *President*
Carolyn Mc Grath, *Vice Pres*
Rosemarie Unangst, *Admin Sec*
EMP: 7
SQ FT: 6,300
SALES (est): 1MM **Privately Held**
WEB: www.leadingedgeconcepts.com
SIC: 3728 Aircraft propellers & associated equipment

(G-322)
LEFFERTS BROTHERS VINTAGE MACH
20 Henry St (06801-2417)
PHONE 203 205-0500
Mark J Lefferts, *Principal*
EMP: 1
SALES (est): 67.1K **Privately Held**
SIC: 3541 Machine tools, metal cutting type

(G-323)
LORENCO INDUSTRIES INC
25 Henry St (06801-2405)
PHONE 203 743-6962
Jay Cugini, *President*
Loren Cugini, *Vice Pres*
EMP: 10
SQ FT: 6,500
SALES (est): 1.6MM **Privately Held**
WEB: www.loren.bc.ca
SIC: 2759 Screen printing

(G-324)
LOWBROW
103 Greenwood Ave (06801-2571)
PHONE 203 518-4189
Brian Dicrescenzo, *President*
EMP: 2
SALES (est): 92.3K **Privately Held**
SIC: 2752 Commercial printing, lithographic

(G-325)
MCFIGS BEYOND SIGNS LLC
61 Quaker Ridge Rd (06801-1253)
PHONE 203 792-4057
Daniel Figueroa,
EMP: 2
SALES (est): 176.1K **Privately Held**
SIC: 3993 Signs & advertising specialties

(G-326)
MEMRY CORPORATION (HQ)
Also Called: Saes Memry
3 Berkshire Blvd (06801-1037)
PHONE 203 739-1100
Dean Tulumaris, *CEO*
Nicola Dibartolomeo, *President*
Philippe Poncet, *President*
John Schosser, *Vice Pres*
Tim Wilson, *Opers Staff*
EMP: 150
SQ FT: 37,500
SALES (est): 66.4MM
SALES (corp-wide): 60.2MM **Privately Held**
WEB: www.memry.com
SIC: 3841 Surgical & medical instruments
PA: Saes Getters Spa
 Viale Italia 77
 Lainate MI 20020
 029 317-81

(G-327)
MEMRY CORPORATION
8 Berkshire Blvd (06801-1001)
PHONE 203 739-1146
EMP: 3
SALES (corp-wide): 60.2MM **Privately Held**
SIC: 3841 Surgical & medical instruments
HQ: Memry Corporation
 3 Berkshire Blvd
 Bethel CT 06801
 203 739-1100

(G-328)
MONO CRETE STEP CO OF CT LLC
12 Trowbridge Dr (06801-2858)
P.O. Box 74 (06801-0074)
PHONE 203 748-8419
Shawn Mc Loughlin, *Principal*
Chip McLoughin,
EMP: 10
SQ FT: 19,000
SALES (est): 1.3MM **Privately Held**
SIC: 3272 3446 Steps, prefabricated concrete; burial vaults, concrete or precast terrazzo; railings, prefabricated metal

(G-329)
MORRISTOWN STAR STRUCK LLC
8 Francis J Clarke Cir (06801-2850)
P.O. Box 308 (06801-0308)
PHONE 203 778-4925
Wesley Lang, *Principal*
Ricardo Rago, *COO*
Rose McCallum, *Manager*
Keith Sessler,
▲ **EMP:** 31
SQ FT: 20,000
SALES (est): 12.5MM **Privately Held**
SIC: 3873 Watches & parts, except crystals & jewels

(G-330)
NUTMEG ENERGY SAVERS
35 Hickok Ave (06801-1497)
PHONE 203 733-0147
Marain Bainis, *Owner*
EMP: 2
SALES (est): 117K **Privately Held**
SIC: 3825 Integrating electricity meters

(G-331)
PARAMA CORP
7 Trowbridge Dr (06801-2858)
PHONE 203 790-8155
Aloyzas Petrikas, *President*
EMP: 15 **EST:** 1978
SQ FT: 13,500
SALES (est): 384.1K **Privately Held**
SIC: 7692 Brazing

(G-332)
PRECISION MANUFACTURING LLC
Also Called: Precision Mfg Tool & TI Design
153 Gracty Plain St A12 (06801)
PHONE 203 790-4663
Edmond Yammine, *President*
EMP: 4
SQ FT: 2,400
SALES (est): 431.1K **Privately Held**
SIC: 3599 Machine shop, jobbing & repair

(G-333)
PRINT B2B LLC
3 Hillcrest Rd (06801-1210)
PHONE 203 744-5435
Joseph McCabe, *Principal*
EMP: 2 **EST:** 2016
SALES (est): 101.5K **Privately Held**
SIC: 2752 Commercial printing, lithographic

(G-334)
PRINT PROMOTIONS INC
Also Called: Super Coups
50 Oak Ridge Rd (06801-1151)
PHONE 203 778-2672
Elsa Cutting, *President*
Robert Cutting, *Vice Pres*
▲ **EMP:** 2
SALES (est): 120K **Privately Held**
WEB: www.supercoups.biz
SIC: 2752 Commercial printing, lithographic

(G-335)
RIBEIRO WOODWORKING LLC
19 Putnam Park Rd (06801-2220)
PHONE 203 942-5838
Marcelo Ribeiro, *Principal*
EMP: 2
SALES (est): 87.4K **Privately Held**
SIC: 2431 Millwork

(G-336)
RR DESIGN
13 Hearthstone Dr (06801-1208)
PHONE 203 792-3419
Richard Osiecki, *Owner*
EMP: 4
SALES (est): 15K **Privately Held**
SIC: 3999 Wreaths, artificial

(G-337)
SANDVIK WIRE AND HTG TECH CORP
119 Wooster St (06801-1837)
P.O. Box 281 (06801-0281)
PHONE 203 744-1440
Lars Erricson, *Branch Mgr*
EMP: 100
SALES (corp-wide): 11.1B **Privately Held**
SIC: 3357 3316 3312 3621 Nonferrous wiredrawing & insulating; cold finishing of steel shapes; wire products, steel or iron; motors & generators; industrial furnaces & ovens; steel wire & related products
HQ: Sandvik Wire And Heating Technology Corporation
 119 Wooster St
 Bethel CT 06801

(G-338)
SANDVIK WIRE AND HTG TECH CORP (DH)
Also Called: Sandvik Heating Technogy USA
119 Wooster St (06801-1837)
PHONE 203 744-1440
Parag Satpute, *CEO*
Nicklas Nilsson, *Ch of Bd*
Phil Yu, *President*
John Stowe, *General Mgr*
John Hilson, *Engrg Mgr*
▲ **EMP:** 82
SALES (est): 32.8MM
SALES (corp-wide): 11.1B **Privately Held**
WEB: www.kanthal.com
SIC: 3316 3357 Cold finishing of steel shapes; nonferrous wiredrawing & insulating
HQ: Sandvik, Inc.
 17-02 Nevins Rd
 Fair Lawn NJ 07410
 201 794-5000

(G-339)
SCENE 1 ARTS LLC
10 Library Pl (06801-9210)
P.O. Box 909 (06801-0909)
PHONE 203 748-0899
EMP: 1
SALES (est): 37.5K **Privately Held**
SIC: 2741 Miscellaneous publishing

(G-340)
SCREEN DESIGNS
81 Codfish Hill Rd (06801-3303)
PHONE 203 797-9806
Mark White, *Owner*
EMP: 1
SALES (est): 128.4K **Privately Held**
WEB: www.screendesignsinc.com
SIC: 2759 2396 Screen printing; screen printing on fabric articles

(G-341)
SEAL KING SEALCOATING
11 Old Town Rd (06801-3110)
PHONE 203 871-1423
Joseph Piatnik, *Principal*
EMP: 2
SALES (est): 90.7K **Privately Held**
SIC: 2952 Asphalt felts & coatings

(G-342)
SILVER TOUCH
211 Greenwood Ave Ste 6 (06801-2131)
PHONE 203 778-1778
Lorraine Schrameck, *President*
EMP: 2
SALES: 151K **Privately Held**
SIC: 3914 Silverware, sterling silver

(G-343)
SOCIETY FOR EXPRMNTAL MCHANICS
7 School St (06801-1855)
PHONE 203 790-6373
Kristen Zimmerman, *Exec Dir*
Thomas Proulx, *Director*
EMP: 6
SQ FT: 1,600
SALES: 1MM **Privately Held**
WEB: www.sem1.com
SIC: 8621 2721 2731 Engineering association; scientific membership association; trade journals: publishing only, not printed on site; book publishing

(G-344)
SOCIETY PLASTICS ENGINEERS INC (PA)
Also Called: S P E
6 Berkshire Blvd Ste 306 (06801-1065)
PHONE 203 740-5422
Susan Oderwald, *Exec Dir*
EMP: 27
SQ FT: 12,000
SALES: 3.6MM **Privately Held**
WEB: www.4spe.org
SIC: 8621 2721 7389 2731 Engineering association; trade journals: publishing only, not printed on site; advertising, promotional & trade show services; book publishing

(G-345)
SOLAR DATA SYSTEMS INC
23 Francis J Clarke Cir (06801-2861)
PHONE 203 702-7189
Guy Thouin, *CEO*
Steve Cheung, *General Mgr*
Peter Scarola, *Manager*
EMP: 12 **EST:** 2010
SALES (est): 2.4MM
SALES (corp-wide): 4.9B **Privately Held**
SIC: 3825 Power measuring equipment, electrical
HQ: Solare Datensysteme Gmbh
 Fuhrmannstr. 9
 Geislingen 72351
 742 894-1820

(G-346)
SPEEDI SIGN
3 Reservoir St (06801-2322)
PHONE 203 431-0836
EMP: 2
SALES (est): 80.6K **Privately Held**
SIC: 2759 Publication printing

(G-347)
SQUARE CREAMERY LLC
7 P T Barnum Sq (06801-1838)
PHONE 203 456-3490
Segundo Sanchez, *Principal*
EMP: 4 **EST:** 2013
SALES (est): 194.3K **Privately Held**
SIC: 2021 Creamery butter

(G-348)
SUMMIT STAIR CO INC
101 Wooster St (06801-1847)
PHONE 203 778-2251
Al Curesky, *President*
EMP: 12
SALES (est): 1.7MM **Privately Held**
SIC: 2431 Staircases & stairs, wood

(G-349)
SUMNER COMMUNICATIONS INC
24 Stony Hill Rd Ste 5 (06801-1166)
PHONE 203 748-2050
Jeff Dwight, *Publisher*
Scott Sumner, *COO*
Amber Lautier, *Sales Mgr*
Dan Trombetto, *Wholesale*
Meaghan Brophy, *Manager*

GEOGRAPHIC SECTION

Bloomfield - Hartford County (G-380)

EMP: 20
SQ FT: 5,000
SALES (est): 3.8MM **Privately Held**
WEB: www.sumnercom.com
SIC: 2721 Magazines: publishing only, not printed on site

(G-350)
SUZANNE RAMLJAK
22 Rockwell Rd (06801-1607)
PHONE..................203 792-5599
Suzanne Ramljak, *Owner*
EMP: 1
SALES (est): 52.3K **Privately Held**
SIC: 2721 Periodicals

(G-351)
SWING RITE GOLF
3 Ridge Rd (06801-1143)
PHONE..................203 748-4985
Tim Belansky, *Owner*
EMP: 1 **EST:** 1993
SALES (est): 80.6K **Privately Held**
SIC: 3949 Golf equipment

(G-352)
THORN INDUSTRIES LLC
81 Milwaukee Ave Apt 3 (06801-2256)
PHONE..................845 531-7767
Joseph Hansen, *Principal*
EMP: 1
SALES (est): 43.6K **Privately Held**
SIC: 3999 Manufacturing industries

(G-353)
TIBBYS ELECTRIC MOTOR SERVICE
40 Taylor Ave (06801-2450)
PHONE..................203 748-4694
Greg Cudzilo, *President*
Chris Cudzilo, *Vice Pres*
EMP: 4
SALES: 300K **Privately Held**
SIC: 7694 Electric motor repair

(G-354)
TRAJAN SCIENTIFIC AMERICAS INC
Also Called: Trajan Scientific and Medical
21 Berkshire Blvd (06801-1037)
PHONE..................203 830-4910
Robert Wagner, *Branch Mgr*
EMP: 5 **Privately Held**
SIC: 3826 Analytical instruments
HQ: Trajan Scientific Americas Inc.
1421 W Wells Branch Pkwy # 108
Pflugerville TX 78660
512 837-7190

(G-355)
TRI STAR GRAPHICS
274 Greenwood Ave (06801-2424)
P.O. Box 698 (06801-0698)
PHONE..................203 748-4792
James Hansen, *Owner*
EMP: 3
SALES (est): 208.3K **Privately Held**
SIC: 7389 3552 Printed circuitry graphic layout; embroidery machines

(G-356)
TRINE ACCESS TECHNOLOGY INC
2 Park Lawn Dr (06801-1042)
PHONE..................203 730-1756
Fred Schildwachter III, *Ch of Bd*
William Schildwachter, *Ch of Bd*
Betsy Schildwachter, *Vice Pres*
▲ **EMP:** 19
SQ FT: 12,000
SALES (est): 4MM **Privately Held**
WEB: www.trineonline.com
SIC: 3699 Electrical equipment & supplies

(G-357)
UNDERGROUND SYSTEMS INC (PA)
Also Called: USI
3a Trowbridge Dr (06801-2858)
PHONE..................203 792-3444
Paul A Alex, *Ch of Bd*
James Shattuck, *Director*
EMP: 45
SQ FT: 12,000
SALES (est): 16.4MM **Privately Held**
WEB: www.usi-power.com
SIC: 5063 3823 Cable conduit; temperature instruments: industrial process type

(G-358)
UNIMATION
102 Wooster St Ste 4a (06801-1862)
PHONE..................203 792-3412
Ben Clark, *Owner*
EMP: 4
SALES (est): 220K **Privately Held**
SIC: 3535 Robotic conveyors

(G-359)
UNIVERSITY HLTH PUBG GROUP LLC
6 Trowbridge Dr Ste 1 (06801-2882)
PHONE..................203 791-0101
EMP: 7
SALES (est): 350K **Privately Held**
SIC: 2741 Misc Publishing

(G-360)
V & V WOODWORKING LLC
107 Wooster St (06801-1837)
PHONE..................203 740-9494
Carlos M Veloso,
EMP: 4
SALES (est): 357.7K **Privately Held**
SIC: 2431 Millwork

(G-361)
VANDERBILT CHEMICALS LLC
Also Called: Bethel Division
31 Taylor Ave (06801-2411)
PHONE..................203 744-3900
John Eshelman, *Principal*
Jim Fernandez, *Purch Mgr*
Paul Bork, *Engineer*
Bryan Lutz, *Engineer*
Joe D'Antonio, *Manager*
EMP: 42
SQ FT: 40,000
SALES (corp-wide): 272.5MM **Privately Held**
SIC: 2891 2819 2869 Adhesives & sealants; industrial inorganic chemicals; industrial organic chemicals
HQ: Vanderbilt Chemicals, Llc
30 Winfield St
Norwalk CT 06855
203 295-2141

(G-362)
VARNUM ENTERPRISES LLC
Also Called: Danbury Sheet Metal
11 Trowbridge Dr (06801-2858)
PHONE..................203 743-4443
Richard C Varnum,
EMP: 12 **EST:** 1944
SQ FT: 14,000
SALES (est): 2.4MM **Privately Held**
WEB: www.dsmfab.com
SIC: 3441 3699 Fabricated structural metal; laser welding, drilling & cutting equipment

(G-363)
VECTOR CONTROLS LLC (PA)
Also Called: Vector Contrls & Automtn Group
17 Francis J Clarke Cir (06801-2847)
PHONE..................203 749-0883
Blake S Bonnabeau,
Markus Benzenhofer,
Rolf Schweizer,
▲ **EMP:** 10
SALES (est): 3.5MM **Privately Held**
SIC: 3585 Refrigeration & heating equipment

(G-364)
VITTA CORPORATION
7 Trowbridge Dr Ste 2 (06801-2864)
PHONE..................203 790-8155
Aloyzas Petrikas, *President*
Paul Petrikas, *Admin Sec*
▼ **EMP:** 20
SQ FT: 20,000
SALES (est): 5MM **Privately Held**
WEB: www.vitta.com
SIC: 3443 Weldments

(G-365)
WESTROCK RKT COMPANY
Also Called: WESTROCK RKT COMPANY
2 Research Dr (06801-1040)
PHONE..................203 739-0318
Aj Knapp, *Manager*
EMP: 12
SALES (corp-wide): 16.2B **Publicly Held**
WEB: www.rocktenn.com
SIC: 2653 Corrugated & solid fiber boxes
HQ: Westrock Rkt, Llc
1000 Abernathy Rd Ste 125
Atlanta GA 30328
770 448-2193

Bethlehem
Litchfield County

(G-366)
AIR VALVES LLC
78 Thomson Rd (06751-2019)
PHONE..................203 266-7175
Leonard J Assard, *Principal*
EMP: 2 **EST:** 2009
SALES (est): 220.1K **Privately Held**
SIC: 3592 Valves

(G-367)
CANFIELD ELECTRIC
151 Hickory Ln (06751-2311)
PHONE..................203 266-5290
Boyd E Canfield Jr, *Owner*
EMP: 2
SQ FT: 2,800
SALES (est): 188K **Privately Held**
SIC: 7694 Electric motor repair

(G-368)
CORTS CUSTOM WOODWORKING
154 Town Line Hwy S (06751-1800)
PHONE..................203 266-0146
Cortland S Heyniger, *Principal*
EMP: 1
SALES (est): 59.1K **Privately Held**
SIC: 2499 Decorative wood & woodwork

(G-369)
EAGLE ELECTRIC SERVICE LLC
145 Flanders Rd (06751-2208)
PHONE..................860 868-9898
EMP: 16
SALES (est): 1.1MM **Privately Held**
SIC: 3699 Mfg Electrical Equipment/Supplies

(G-370)
EAST SPRING OBSOLETE AUTO
60 Woodland Rd (06751-1512)
PHONE..................203 266-5488
William Petitgean, *Owner*
EMP: 1 **EST:** 1996
SALES (est): 55.1K **Privately Held**
SIC: 3089 Automotive parts, plastic

(G-371)
GRIFFIN GREEN
190 Hard Hill Rd N (06751-1519)
PHONE..................203 266-5727
Kevin Griffin, *Principal*
EMP: 3
SALES (est): 188.4K **Privately Held**
SIC: 2431 Millwork

(G-372)
HERFF JONES LLC
39 Terrell Farm Rd (06751-1407)
PHONE..................203 266-7170
Maureen Hawthorne, *Branch Mgr*
EMP: 8
SALES (corp-wide): 1.1B **Privately Held**
SIC: 2752 Commercial printing, lithographic
HQ: Herff Jones, Llc
4501 W 62nd St
Indianapolis IN 46268
800 419-5462

(G-373)
KACERGUIS FARMS INC
78 Crane Hollow Rd (06751-1920)
PHONE..................203 405-1202
James Kucerguis, *President*
Theresa Kacerguis, *Corp Secy*
Matthew Kacerguis, *Vice Pres*
Vincent Kacerguis, *Vice Pres*
EMP: 4
SALES (est): 400K **Privately Held**
SIC: 1442 Common sand mining; gravel mining

(G-374)
LEVEL WOODWORKS
7 White Birch Ln (06751-1120)
PHONE..................203 266-7153
Joseph Leveille, *Owner*
EMP: 1
SALES (est): 54.1K **Privately Held**
SIC: 2431 Millwork

(G-375)
PLASTIC SOLUTIONS LLC
263 Hickory Ln (06751-2313)
PHONE..................203 266-5675
Joseph A Humenik, *Principal*
EMP: 3
SALES (est): 248.7K **Privately Held**
SIC: 3089 Injection molding of plastics

(G-376)
PRO FORM PRINTED BUS SOLUTIONS
246 Magnolia Hill Rd (06751-1811)
PHONE..................203 266-5302
Craig Haven, *Owner*
EMP: 1
SALES (est): 77.7K **Privately Held**
SIC: 2396 Screen printing on fabric articles

(G-377)
WOODY MOSCH CABINET MAKERS
23 Wood Creek Rd (06751-1706)
PHONE..................203 266-7619
Woody Mosch, *Owner*
EMP: 1
SALES (est): 58K **Privately Held**
SIC: 2511 Wood household furniture

Bloomfield
Hartford County

(G-378)
A A GENTLE HOUSE WASHING
11 Harvest Ln (06002-1171)
PHONE..................860 243-8800
Richard Whinnem, *Owner*
Kimberly Whinnem, *Co-Owner*
EMP: 2
SALES (est): 128.1K **Privately Held**
SIC: 3635 Household vacuum cleaners

(G-379)
AAA FIRE AND SAFETY INC (PA)
67 Old Windsor Rd (06002-1416)
P.O. Box 151, East Hampton (06424-0151)
PHONE..................860 267-1965
Peter Freund, *Principal*
EMP: 2
SALES: 275K **Privately Held**
SIC: 3569 Firefighting apparatus & related equipment

(G-380)
ADVANCED DEF SLUTIONS TECH LLC
23 Britton Dr (06002-3616)
P.O. Box 66 (06002-0066)
PHONE..................860 243-1122
Steven Smith,
EMP: 4
SALES (est): 559.7K
SALES (corp-wide): 20MM **Privately Held**
SIC: 2295 3728 Coated fabrics, not rubberized; aircraft parts & equipment
PA: Swift Textile Metalizing Llc
23 Britton Dr
Bloomfield CT 06002
860 243-1122

Bloomfield - Hartford County (G-381)   **GEOGRAPHIC SECTION**

(G-381)
ADVANCED WELDING & REPAIR INC
51 Old Windsor Rd (06002-1416)
PHONE......................860 242-0400
Robert Clark, *President*
EMP: 2
SALES: 60K **Privately Held**
SIC: 7692 Welding repair

(G-382)
AEROSPACE ALLOYS INC
11 Britton Dr (06002-3616)
PHONE......................860 882-0019
Christopher D Allinson, *President*
Robert Allinson, *President*
Richard M Allinson, *Treasurer*
EMP: 76
SQ FT: 30,000
SALES (est): 66.4MM **Privately Held**
WEB: www.aalloys.com
SIC: 5051 3449 7389 Sheets, metal; plates, metal; bars, metal; tubing, metal; miscellaneous metalwork; design services

(G-383)
AMERICAN PREFAB WOOD PDTS CO
1217 Blue Hills Ave (06002-1955)
PHONE......................860 242-5468
Allen Gaudet, *President*
EMP: 7 EST: 1976
SALES (est): 747.4K **Privately Held**
WEB: www.americanpre-fab.com
SIC: 2452 Prefabricated buildings, wood

(G-384)
AMERICAN STEEL FABRICATORS INC (PA)
105 Old Windsor Rd (06002-1433)
PHONE......................860 243-5005
Ted Kensah, *President*
Mary Kensah, *Admin Sec*
EMP: 1
SQ FT: 2,500
SALES (est): 224.1K **Privately Held**
SIC: 7692 Welding repair

(G-385)
ANDERSEN LABORATORIES INC
45 Old Iron Ore Rd (06002-1423)
PHONE......................860 286-9090
Lewis Springer, *Principal*
EMP: 2
SALES (est): 107.4K **Privately Held**
SIC: 3569 General industrial machinery

(G-386)
APPLE HOMECARE INNOVATIONS LLC
15 Beaudry Ln Ste 2 (06002-1175)
PHONE......................860 940-5005
EMP: 2
SALES (est): 85.9K **Privately Held**
SIC: 3571 Mfg Electronic Computers

(G-387)
AQUA BLASTING CORP
2 Northwood Dr (06002-1911)
PHONE......................860 242-8855
Victoria Stavola, *President*
Craig Stavola, *Vice Pres*
EMP: 12
SQ FT: 12,000
SALES: 1.4MM **Privately Held**
WEB: www.aquablasting.com
SIC: 3398 3471 7699 Shot peening (treating steel to reduce fatigue); cleaning, polishing & finishing; sand blasting of metal parts; engine repair & replacement, non-automotive

(G-388)
ARBON EQUIPMENT CORPORATION
29 Griffin Rd S (06002-1351)
PHONE......................410 796-5902
Jeff Friedrich, *Branch Mgr*
EMP: 3
SALES (corp-wide): 779.4MM **Privately Held**
SIC: 2431 Millwork

HQ: Arbon Equipment Corporation
    8900 N Arbon Dr
    Milwaukee WI 53223
    414 355-2600

(G-389)
ARMOR BOX COMPANY LLC
29 Woods Rd (06002-1120)
PHONE......................860 242-9981
Michael Swan,
Laurel Swan,
EMP: 5
SQ FT: 3,000
SALES: 200K **Privately Held**
WEB: www.armorbox.com
SIC: 3161 3089 Cases, carrying; casein products

(G-390)
ARTEFFECTS INCORPORATED
Also Called: Artfx Signs
27 Britton Dr (06002-3616)
P.O. Box 804 (06002-0804)
PHONE......................860 242-0031
Lawrin Rosen, *President*
Mel Cornette, *Corp Secy*
Paula Hansen, *Manager*
Melissa Boehm, *Director*
EMP: 26
SQ FT: 14,000
SALES (est): 4.9MM **Privately Held**
WEB: www.artfxsigns.com
SIC: 3993 7336 Signs, not made in custom sign painting shops; graphic arts & related design

(G-391)
ASCEND ELEVATOR INC
Also Called: Cemcolift Elevator Systems
212 W Newberry Rd (06002-5305)
PHONE......................215 703-0358
Enery Wilcox, *President*
Walter J Herrmann, *Principal*
S Choi, *Vice Pres*
H Moon, *Vice Pres*
◆ EMP: 205 EST: 1999
SQ FT: 265,000
SALES (est): 30.2MM
SALES (corp-wide): 66.5B **Publicly Held**
WEB: www.cemcolift.com
SIC: 3534 Elevators & equipment
PA: United Technologies Corporation
    10 Farm Springs Rd
    Farmington CT 06032
    860 728-7000

(G-392)
BASS PLATING COMPANY
82 Old Windsor Rd (06002-1417)
PHONE......................860 243-2557
Rocco Mastrobattista, *President*
Peter Mastrobattista, *Vice Pres*
Linda Tassone, *Office Mgr*
EMP: 33 EST: 1956
SQ FT: 32,000
SALES (est): 4.5MM **Privately Held**
SIC: 3471 Electroplating of metals or formed products; anodizing (plating) of metals or formed products

(G-393)
BAY STATE ELEVATOR COMPANY INC
105 W Ddley Town Rd Ste H (06002)
PHONE......................860 243-9030
Sal Morassi, *Superintendent*
Peter Kalousdian, *Sales Staff*
Shari Racht, *Representative*
EMP: 12
SALES (corp-wide): 15.1MM **Privately Held**
SIC: 1796 3534 Elevator installation & conversion; elevators & equipment
PA: Bay State Elevator Company, Inc.
    275 Silver St
    Agawam MA 01001
    413 786-7000

(G-394)
BECON INCORPORATED (PA)
522 Cottage Grove Rd (06002-3111)
PHONE......................860 243-1428
Michael G Economos, *President*
James Schleicher, *General Mgr*
Gary A Laurito, *Corp Secy*
Sovann Meach, *Assistant VP*

David Archilla, *Vice Pres*
▲ EMP: 80
SQ FT: 65,000
SALES (est): 31.5MM **Privately Held**
WEB: www.beconinc.com
SIC: 3511 Turbines & turbine generator sets

(G-395)
BIRKEN MANUFACTURING COMPANY
3 Old Windsor Rd (06002-1397)
PHONE......................860 242-2211
Gary Greenberg, *President*
Gary Connolly, *General Mgr*
Brian Poegel, *General Mgr*
Robert Yoo, *General Mgr*
Adam Greenberg, *Principal*
EMP: 92 EST: 1943
SQ FT: 80,000
SALES (est): 36MM **Privately Held**
WEB: www.birken.net
SIC: 3724 3728 Aircraft engines & engine parts; aircraft parts & equipment

(G-396)
BLASTECH OVERHAUL & REPAIR
86 W Dudley Town Rd (06002-1347)
PHONE......................860 243-8811
Jeffrey D Wolpert, *President*
Karl D Wolpert, *Treasurer*
Abigail Saunders, *Manager*
EMP: 14
SQ FT: 15,000
SALES (est): 2.4MM **Privately Held**
WEB: www.blastechusa.com
SIC: 3511 Turbines & turbine generator sets & parts

(G-397)
BLOOMFIELD CENTER VOLUNTEE
18 Wintonbury Ave (06002-2416)
PHONE......................860 242-1779
William Riley, *Manager*
EMP: 2
SALES (est): 150K **Privately Held**
SIC: 3711 Fire department vehicles (motor vehicles), assembly of

(G-398)
BLOOMFIELD WOOD & MELAMINE INC
1 Griffin Rd S (06002-1351)
PHONE......................860 243-3226
Eddie Leshem, *President*
Steven Leshem, *Vice Pres*
Jerry Leshem, *Admin Sec*
EMP: 10
SALES (est): 790K **Privately Held**
SIC: 2521 5072 Wood office furniture; furniture hardware

(G-399)
BRICO LLC
6c Northwood Dr (06002-1911)
PHONE......................860 242-7068
Blake Johnson, *Manager*
EMP: 3
SALES (est): 270K **Privately Held**
SIC: 2851 Lead-in-oil paints

(G-400)
BRICO INC
185 W Newberry Rd (06002-1330)
PHONE......................203 693-0323
EMP: 1 EST: 1970
SALES: 50K **Privately Held**
SIC: 2951 3299 5961 Driveway Sealer

(G-401)
CATHOLIC TRANSCRIPT INC
Also Called: Catholic Transcript Online
467 Bloomfield Ave (06002-2903)
PHONE......................860 286-2828
Henry Mansell, *President*
David Liptak, *Principal*
Jane Lachapelle, *Business Mgr*
EMP: 11
SQ FT: 5,000
SALES (est): 713.9K **Privately Held**
WEB: www.catholictranscript.org
SIC: 2711 Newspapers: publishing only, not printed on site

(G-402)
CHILDRENS MEDICAL GROUP (PA)
6 Northwestern Dr Ste 101 (06002-3416)
PHONE......................860 242-8330
Dr Lee Hoffman, *Partner*
David L Brown, *Partner*
Lee I Hoffman, *Partner*
Harry C Weinerman, *Partner*
Bernadette Canning, *Office Mgr*
EMP: 35
SALES (est): 3.7MM **Privately Held**
SIC: 8011 2326 Pediatrician; men's & boys' work clothing

(G-403)
CLASSIC IMAGES INC
16 Walts Hl (06002-1202)
P.O. Box 7314 (06002-7314)
PHONE......................860 243-8365
David O Sullivan, *President*
EMP: 3
SALES (est): 330K **Privately Held**
SIC: 2678 Stationery products

(G-404)
COHERENT INC
Also Called: Coherent Bloomfield
1280 Blue Hills Ave Ste A (06002-5317)
PHONE......................860 243-9557
Leon Newmes, *President*
Ed Clapp, *General Mgr*
Kerri Carle, *Buyer*
Alissa Karp, *Buyer*
Paulo Lopes, *Research*
EMP: 48
SALES (corp-wide): 1.9B **Publicly Held**
SIC: 3699 3845 Outboard motors, electric; laser systems & equipment, medical
PA: Coherent, Inc.
    5100 Patrick Henry Dr
    Santa Clara CA 95054
    408 764-4000

(G-405)
COHERENT-DEOS LLC
1280 Blue Hills Ave Ste A (06002-5317)
PHONE......................860 243-9557
Leon Newman,
Eric R Mueller,
David Stone,
▲ EMP: 180
SQ FT: 50,000
SALES (est): 22.7MM
SALES (corp-wide): 1.9B **Publicly Held**
SIC: 3699 Laser systems & equipment
PA: Coherent, Inc.
    5100 Patrick Henry Dr
    Santa Clara CA 95054
    408 764-4000

(G-406)
DERING-NEY INC
353 Woodland Ave (06002-1386)
PHONE......................847 932-6782
Jim Ryan, *COO*
EMP: 2
SALES (est): 119.2K **Privately Held**
SIC: 3643 Current-carrying wiring devices

(G-407)
DERINGER-NEY INC (PA)
353 Woodland Ave (06002-1386)
PHONE......................860 242-2281
Rod Lamm, *CEO*
Keith Kowalski, *COO*
Gregory Demko, *Engineer*
Brett Utter, *Finance Dir*
Sherman Ponder, *Manager*
▼ EMP: 175 EST: 1950
SQ FT: 100,000
SALES (est): 109.3MM **Privately Held**
WEB: www.deringerney.com
SIC: 3469 3542 3316 3452 Metal stampings; machine tools, metal forming type; cold finishing of steel shapes; bolts, nuts, rivets & washers; contacts, electrical

(G-408)
DUCTCO LLC
13 Britton Dr (06002-3616)
PHONE......................860 243-0350
Peter Molin, *President*
Jay Schneider, *Supervisor*
EMP: 32
SQ FT: 4,000

▲ = Import ▼ = Export
◆ = Import/Export

GEOGRAPHIC SECTION

Bloomfield - Hartford County (G-433)

SALES: 6MM **Privately Held**
SIC: 3444 Sheet metal specialties, not stamped

(G-409)
ENGINEERED BUILDING PDTS INC
18 Southwood Dr (06002-1952)
PHONE 860 243-1110
Joel Smith, *President*
Theresa J Demorais, *Treasurer*
EMP: 28
SALES: 14.2MM **Privately Held**
WEB: www.ebpfab.com
SIC: 1791 3446 3449 3444 Structural steel erection; architectural metalwork; miscellaneous metalwork; sheet metalwork; prefabricated metal buildings; fabricated structural metal

(G-410)
FAXON ENGINEERING COMPANY INC (PA)
17 Britton Dr (06002-3616)
P.O. Box 330337, West Hartford (06133-0337)
PHONE 860 236-4266
John Newton Clark, *President*
Jennifer Osborne, *General Mgr*
Robert J Granoth Sr, *Regional Mgr*
Daniel Laiho, *QC Mgr*
Jim Burns, *Engineer*
EMP: 14 EST: 1946
SQ FT: 10,000
SALES (est): 4.3MM **Privately Held**
WEB: www.faxonengineering.com
SIC: 8711 5084 3492 5085 Consulting engineer; hydraulic systems equipment & supplies; pneumatic tools & equipment; hose & tube fittings & assemblies, hydraulic/pneumatic; hose & tube couplings, hydraulic/pneumatic; industrial fittings; hydraulic equipment repair

(G-411)
FLEMMING LLC
9 Jonathan Pl (06002-1739)
P.O. Box 167 (06002-0167)
PHONE 818 746-6495
Ruth Flemming,
EMP: 1
SALES (est): 97.8K **Privately Held**
SIC: 5137 2038 2329 Women's & children's clothing; soups, frozen; men's & boys' sportswear & athletic clothing; shirt & slack suits: men's, youths' & boys'

(G-412)
FLORAL GREENS
31 Revere Dr Apt 1 (06002-2651)
P.O. Box 937 (06002-0937)
PHONE 860 995-8772
Dawn A Harden, *Principal*
EMP: 2
SALES (est): 99.6K **Privately Held**
SIC: 2741 Miscellaneous publishing

(G-413)
FMI CHEMICAL INC
4 Northwood Dr (06002-1911)
PHONE 860 243-3222
Harry M Fine, *President*
Christopher McCluskey, *Engineer*
Nancy Daigle, *CFO*
Marie Morgan, *Administration*
▼ EMP: 11
SQ FT: 12,000
SALES: 4.9MM **Privately Held**
WEB: www.fmipaint.com
SIC: 2822 Silicone rubbers

(G-414)
FOILMARK INC
Also Called: ITW Foilmark
40 E Newberry Rd (06002-1441)
PHONE 860 243-0343
EMP: 15
SALES (corp-wide): 14.7B **Publicly Held**
SIC: 3497 3549 3544 Metal foil & leaf; metalworking machinery; special dies, tools, jigs & fixtures
HQ: Foilmark, Inc.
5 Malcolm Hoyt Dr
Newburyport MA 01950

(G-415)
GROTE & WEIGEL INC (PA)
76 Granby St (06002-3512)
PHONE 860 242-8528
Michael J Greiner, *President*
▲ EMP: 50
SQ FT: 20,000
SALES (est): 6.3MM **Privately Held**
WEB: www.groteandweigel.com
SIC: 2013 2011 Sausages & other prepared meats; meat packing plants

(G-416)
GUHRING INC
121 W Ddley Town Rd Ste C (06002)
PHONE 860 216-5948
Debbie Wentworth, *Manager*
EMP: 135
SALES (corp-wide): 1.3B **Privately Held**
SIC: 3545 Cutting tools for machine tools
HQ: Guhring, Inc.
1445 Commerce Ave
Brookfield WI 53045
262 784-6730

(G-417)
HARTFORD AIRCRAFT PRODUCTS
94 Old Poquonock Rd (06002-1427)
PHONE 860 242-8228
James P Griffin, *President*
Susan M Griffin, *Vice Pres*
EMP: 24
SQ FT: 13,000
SALES (est): 4.3MM **Privately Held**
SIC: 3429 3812 Aircraft hardware; search & navigation equipment

(G-418)
HARTFORD INDUSTRIAL FINSHG CO
25 Northwood Dr (06002-1908)
P.O. Box 313 (06002-0313)
PHONE 860 243-2040
Frederick C Hillier Jr, *President*
John J Ferguson, *Vice Pres*
Jeannie Ferguson, *Admin Sec*
EMP: 3 EST: 1947
SQ FT: 13,500
SALES (est): 271.1K **Privately Held**
SIC: 3479 Enameling, including porcelain, of metal products; lacquering of metal products

(G-419)
HERMELL PRODUCTS INC
9 Britton Dr (06002-3616)
P.O. Box 7345 (06002-7345)
PHONE 860 242-6550
Ronald Pollack, *President*
Michelle Gladden, *General Mgr*
Dan Aitchison, *VP Bus Dvlpt*
Lynn Polaski, *Sales Mgr*
Allie McConnell, *Marketing Staff*
▲ EMP: 38
SQ FT: 23,000
SALES (est): 7.4MM **Privately Held**
WEB: www.hermell.com
SIC: 3842 Bandages & dressings

(G-420)
HISCO PUMP INCORPORATED (PA)
4 Mosey Dr (06002-3531)
PHONE 860 243-2705
Joseph Montineri, *President*
Roy Sjolund, *Vice Pres*
Quenton Wheeler, *Traffic Mgr*
Jennifer Guliano, *Accounting Mgr*
Joey Montineri, *Sales Mgr*
▲ EMP: 23
SQ FT: 54,000
SALES (est): 11.2MM **Privately Held**
SIC: 3429 3561 7699 Pumps & pumping equipment; pumps & pumping equipment; pumps & pumping equipment repair

(G-421)
INDEPENDENT EXPLOSIVES
103 Old Windsor Rd (06002-1438)
PHONE 860 243-0137
Skip Sibley, *President*
David Whiteside, *Manager*
EMP: 2

SALES (est): 98.9K **Privately Held**
SIC: 2892 Explosives

(G-422)
INQUIRING NEWS
51 Gilbert Ave (06002-3824)
PHONE 860 983-7587
EMP: 4 EST: 2013
SALES (est): 223K **Privately Held**
SIC: 2711 Newspapers, publishing & printing

(G-423)
INTERNATIONAL TURBINE SYSTEMS
131 W Dudley Town Rd (06002-5328)
PHONE 860 761-0358
Steve Lamond, *President*
EMP: 2 EST: 2014
SALES (est): 238.2K **Privately Held**
SIC: 3511 Turbines & turbine generator sets

(G-424)
ITW HLOGRAPHIC SPECIALTY FILMS
40 E Newberry Rd (06002-1441)
PHONE 860 243-0343
Jerome Scharr, *President*
▲ EMP: 2
SALES (est): 195.7K **Privately Held**
SIC: 3479 Metal coating & allied service

(G-425)
JACOBS VEHICLE SYSTEMS INC
Also Called: Jake Brake
22 E Dudley Town Rd (06002-1440)
PHONE 860 243-5222
Sergio Sgarbi, *President*
Dennis Gallagher, *President*
William Wang, *General Mgr*
Joao John Cullen, *Vice Pres*
Sam Fabian, *Vice Pres*
◆ EMP: 420
SALES (est): 125.7MM
SALES (corp-wide): 1.1B **Publicly Held**
WEB: www.jakebrake.com
SIC: 3519 Engines, diesel & semi-diesel or dual-fuel
PA: Altra Industrial Motion Corp.
300 Granite St Ste 201
Braintree MA 02184
781 917-0600

(G-426)
JAMES & CO LLC
2 Wyndemere Rd (06002-1715)
PHONE 860 897-6242
Keith James,
EMP: 1
SALES (est): 41K **Privately Held**
SIC: 1389 Construction, repair & dismantling services

(G-427)
JAMES L HOWARD AND COMPANY INC
10 Britton Dr (06002-3617)
PHONE 860 242-3581
Fred Rotondo Jr, *President*
Steven Eppler, *Vice Pres*
EMP: 30 EST: 1841
SQ FT: 18,300
SALES (est): 5.2MM **Privately Held**
WEB: www.jameslhowardco.com
SIC: 3429 3743 Keys, locks & related hardware; railroad equipment

(G-428)
JOHNSON GAGE COMPANY
534 Cottage Grove Rd (06002-3093)
PHONE 860 242-5541
Lowell C Johnson, *President*
Matthew Woods, *General Mgr*
Jim Speck, *Regional Mgr*
Johnson Gage, *Personnel*
Karen Broehl, *Accounts Mgr*
▼ EMP: 37 EST: 1922
SQ FT: 15,000

SALES (est): 7.4MM **Privately Held**
WEB: www.johnsongage.com
SIC: 3545 8711 3823 Precision tools, machinists'; machine tool design; industrial instrmnts msrmnt display/control process variable

(G-429)
JUNGLE BREW LLC
125 Duncaster Rd (06002-1253)
PHONE 860 335-4941
William Kaufman,
Jasden Mendez,
EMP: 1 EST: 2016
SALES (est): 39.6K **Privately Held**
SIC: 3999 Manufacturing industries

(G-430)
KAMAN AEROSPACE CORPORATION (DH)
1332 Blue Hills Ave (06002-5302)
PHONE 860 242-4461
Neal J Keating, *Ch of Bd*
Gregory Steiner, *President*
Alphonse J Lariviere Jr, *Division Pres*
James C Larwood Jr, *Division Pres*
Gerald C Ricketts, *Division Pres*
◆ EMP: 750
SQ FT: 185,000
SALES (est): 265.6MM
SALES (corp-wide): 1.8B **Publicly Held**
WEB: www.kamanaero.com
SIC: 3721 3728 Aircraft; aircraft parts & equipment

(G-431)
KAMAN AEROSPACE CORPORATION
Kaman Cmpsites-Connecticut Div
30 Old Windsor Rd (06002-1414)
PHONE 860 242-4461
EMP: 34
SALES (corp-wide): 1.8B **Publicly Held**
SIC: 3721 3728 5085 Helicopters; aircraft parts & equipment; roto-blades for helicopters; flaps, aircraft wing; wing assemblies & parts, aircraft; bearings
HQ: Kaman Aerospace Corporation
1332 Blue Hills Ave
Bloomfield CT 06002
860 242-4461

(G-432)
KAMAN AEROSPACE CORPORATION
Air Vehicles & Mro Division
30 Old Windsor Rd (06002-1414)
P.O. Box 2 (06002)
PHONE 860 242-4461
Salvatore Bordonaro, *Manager*
EMP: 83
SALES (corp-wide): 1.8B **Publicly Held**
WEB: www.kamanaero.com
SIC: 3728 3721 3724 Airframe assemblies, except for guided missiles; aircraft; aircraft engines & engine parts
HQ: Kaman Aerospace Corporation
1332 Blue Hills Ave
Bloomfield CT 06002
860 242-4461

(G-433)
KAMAN AEROSPACE GROUP INC (HQ)
1332 Blue Hills Ave (06002-5302)
PHONE 860 243-7100
Richard R Barnhart, *President*
Gregory L Steiner, *President*
James C Larwood Jr, *Division Pres*
Dennis Elwood, *Vice Pres*
Richard C Forsberg, *Vice Pres*
◆ EMP: 14
SQ FT: 40,000
SALES: 702MM
SALES (corp-wide): 1.8B **Publicly Held**
SIC: 3721 3724 3728 3769 Aircraft; aircraft engines & engine parts; aircraft parts & equipment; guided missile & space vehicle parts & auxiliary equipment
PA: Kaman Corporation
1332 Blue Hills Ave
Bloomfield CT 06002
860 243-7100

Bloomfield - Hartford County (G-434)

(G-434)
KAMAN CORPORATION (PA)
1332 Blue Hills Ave (06002-5302)
PHONE 860 243-7100
Neal J Keating, *Ch of Bd*
John Blanchard, *District Mgr*
Shawn G Lisle, *Senior VP*
Paul M Villani, *Senior VP*
Robert D Starr, *CFO*
EMP: 60
SQ FT: 103,041
SALES: 1.8B **Publicly Held**
WEB: www.kaman.com
SIC: 3721 3728 5085 Helicopters; aircraft parts & equipment; roto-blades for helicopters; flaps, aircraft wing; wing assemblies & parts, aircraft; bearings

(G-435)
KAMATICS CORPORATION (DH)
1330 Blue Hills Ave (06002-5303)
PHONE 860 243-9704
Neal J Keating, *CEO*
Robert G Paterson, *President*
Steven J Smidler, *Exec VP*
Gregory L Steiner, *Exec VP*
Ronald M Galla, *Senior VP*
EMP: 50
SQ FT: 140,000
SALES (est): 94MM
SALES (corp-wide): 1.8B **Publicly Held**
WEB: www.kamatics.com
SIC: 3451 3562 3724 3728 Screw machine products; ball & roller bearings; aircraft engines & engine parts; aircraft parts & equipment

(G-436)
KAMATICS CORPORATION
1331 Blue Hills Ave (06002-1304)
PHONE 860 243-7230
Glen Gauvin, *General Mgr*
EMP: 5
SALES (corp-wide): 1.8B **Publicly Held**
SIC: 3562 Ball & roller bearings
HQ: Kamatics Corporation
1330 Blue Hills Ave
Bloomfield CT 06002
860 243-9704

(G-437)
KATAHDIN PRINTING
23 Old Windsor Rd Ste D (06002-5313)
PHONE 860 461-7037
Michelle Gilbert, *Manager*
EMP: 2
SALES (est): 101.5K **Privately Held**
SIC: 2752 Commercial printing, lithographic

(G-438)
KENNETH LEROUX
Also Called: Alrite Manufacturing Company
105 Filley St Unit C (06002-1852)
PHONE 860 769-9800
Ken Larue, *Owner*
EMP: 4
SQ FT: 1,200
SALES: 480K **Privately Held**
SIC: 3599 Machine shop, jobbing & repair

(G-439)
KOOL INK LLC
Also Called: Sir Speedy
21 Old Windsor Rd Ste B (06002-1362)
PHONE 860 242-0303
Diane Muska, *Executive*
Mark Jacobs,
EMP: 13
SQ FT: 5,000
SALES (est): 2.1MM **Privately Held**
WEB: www.sirspeedy.cc
SIC: 2752 2791 2789 2759 Commercial printing, lithographic; typesetting; bookbinding & related work; commercial printing

(G-440)
LENSES ONLY LLC
812 Park Ave (06002-2417)
PHONE 860 769-2020
Steven Abbate, *Mng Member*
Thomas Gonthier,
EMP: 12

SALES (est): 3MM **Privately Held**
SIC: 3841 3851 Bronchoscopes, except electromedical; eyeglasses, lenses & frames

(G-441)
LEPPERT/NUTMEG INC
113 W Dudley Town Rd (06002-1379)
PHONE 860 243-1737
Brian Scott, *President*
Bob Slossar, *Purch Mgr*
William Hartnet, *Finance Dir*
EMP: 30
SQ FT: 20,000
SALES (est): 8.1MM **Privately Held**
WEB: www.leppert-nutmeg.com
SIC: 7629 7694 5084 Electrical equipment repair services; electric motor repair; compressors, except air conditioning; pumps & pumping equipment; controlling instruments & accessories

(G-442)
LESRO INDUSTRIES INC
1 Griffin Rd S (06002-1351)
PHONE 800 275-7545
Adam Leshem, *CEO*
Jerry Leshem, *President*
Ed Leshem, *Treasurer*
Dan O'Malley, *Sales Mgr*
Cindi McGee, *Accounts Mgr*
◆ **EMP:** 100 **EST:** 1973
SQ FT: 120,000
SALES (est): 20.6MM **Privately Held**
WEB: www.lesro.com
SIC: 2521 Wood office furniture

(G-443)
LIQUIDPISTON INC
1292a Blue Hills Ave (06002-1301)
PHONE 860 838-2677
James Norrod, *CEO*
Alexander Shkolnik, *President*
Nikolay Shkolnik, *Vice Pres*
David Habiger, *Director*
▲ **EMP:** 11
SQ FT: 6,000
SALES (est): 2.3MM **Privately Held**
WEB: www.liquidpiston.com
SIC: 3519 Internal combustion engines

(G-444)
LUMENTUM OPERATIONS LLC
45 Griffin Rd S (06002-1353)
PHONE 408 546-5483
EMP: 10
SALES (corp-wide): 1.5B **Publicly Held**
SIC: 3669 Emergency alarms
HQ: Lumentum Operations Llc
400 N Mccarthy Blvd
Milpitas CA 95035
408 546-5483

(G-445)
MINARIK CORPORATION
Also Called: Minarik Automation & Control
1 Vision Way (06002-5321)
P.O. Box 723 (06002-0723)
PHONE 860 687-5000
Steven J Smidler, *President*
Gary J Haseley, *Senior VP*
Kyle Ahlfinger, *Vice Pres*
Roger S Jorgensen, *Vice Pres*
Robert D Starr, *Treasurer*
▲ **EMP:** 250
SQ FT: 90,000
SALES (est): 45.4MM
SALES (corp-wide): 781.2MM **Privately Held**
WEB: www.minarikdrives.com
SIC: 3625 Relays & industrial controls
PA: Ruby Industrial Technologies, Llc
1 Vision Way
Bloomfield CT 06002
860 687-5000

(G-446)
MOORES SAWMILL INC
171 Mountain Ave (06002-1694)
PHONE 860 242-3003
Donald Moore, *President*
Douglas Moores, *Corp Secy*
EMP: 3

SALES (est): 160K **Privately Held**
SIC: 2421 5211 Sawmills & planing mills, general; lumber & other building materials

(G-447)
MOSLEY HOSIERY AND SOCKS LLC
71 Prospect St (06002-3038)
PHONE 860 690-9227
Deena Mosley, *Principal*
EMP: 2
SALES (est): 73.4K **Privately Held**
SIC: 2252 Socks

(G-448)
MOUNTAIN OCARINAS
323 Tunxis Ave (06002-1211)
PHONE 860 242-6626
Karl Ahrens, *President*
▲ **EMP:** 2
SALES (est): 120K **Privately Held**
WEB: www.mountainocarinas.com
SIC: 3931 Ocarinas

(G-449)
NEWMAN INFORMATION SYSTEMS
Also Called: Nis
37 Jerome Ave (06002-2487)
PHONE 860 286-0540
Scott Newman, *President*
EMP: 1
SQ FT: 500
SALES (est): 67.3K **Privately Held**
SIC: 7372 Business oriented computer software

(G-450)
NIAGARA BOTTLING LLC
380 Woodland Ave (06002-1342)
PHONE 909 226-7353
EMP: 6 **EST:** 2017
SALES (est): 479.1K **Privately Held**
SIC: 2086 Bottled & canned soft drinks

(G-451)
NORTHAST LGHTNING PRTCTION LLC
10 Peters Rd (06002-1333)
PHONE 860 243-0010
James G Barnard,
EMP: 15
SQ FT: 4,800
SALES: 2MM **Privately Held**
SIC: 3643 Lightning protection equipment

(G-452)
NORTHEAST CABINETRY LLC
111 W Dudley Town Rd (06002-1361)
PHONE 860 216-0781
EMP: 1 **EST:** 2011
SALES (est): 69K **Privately Held**
SIC: 3553 Mfg Woodworking Machinery

(G-453)
O/D DOMINION SOFTWARE LLC
21 High Wood Rd (06002-2113)
PHONE 860 904-9261
Brendan Sayers, *Principal*
EMP: 2
SALES (est): 55K **Privately Held**
SIC: 7372 Prepackaged software

(G-454)
OLD CAMBRIDGE PRODUCTS CORP
244 Woodland Ave (06002-5318)
PHONE 860 243-1761
William Oneill, *Principal*
EMP: 3
SALES (est): 169.6K **Privately Held**
SIC: 3643 Current-carrying wiring devices

(G-455)
ONLY QUEENS LLC
21 Barry Cir (06002-1967)
PHONE 860 888-4413
Kamari Arti,
EMP: 1
SALES (est): 32.7K **Privately Held**
SIC: 7372 7389 Application computer software;

(G-456)
OTIS ELEVATOR COMPANY
212 W Newberry Rd (06002-5305)
PHONE 860 242-3632
Bruce Lerner, *Principal*
Troy Chicoine, *Senior Engr*
Tom Vaccaro, *Manager*
Mr Jeffrey Costley, *Manager*
EMP: 300
SQ FT: 116,000
SALES (corp-wide): 66.5B **Publicly Held**
WEB: www.otis.com
SIC: 5084 1796 3534 Elevators; elevator installation & conversion; elevators & moving stairways
HQ: Otis Elevator Company
1 Carrier Pl
Farmington CT 06032
860 674-3000

(G-457)
P M HILL
60 Loeffler Rd (06002-2279)
PHONE 860 242-2915
EMP: 2
SALES (est): 86.3K **Privately Held**
SIC: 2759 Commercial printing

(G-458)
P&G METAL COMPONENTS CORP
98 Filley St (06002-1874)
PHONE 860 243-2220
Andrew Ponkow, *President*
EMP: 19
SQ FT: 27,500
SALES: 900K **Privately Held**
SIC: 3469 3471 3563 4961 Stamping metal for the trade; plating & polishing; air & gas compressors including vacuum pumps; steam & air-conditioning supply; shot peening (treating steel to reduce fatigue); die sets for metal stamping (presses)

(G-459)
P/A INDUSTRIES INC (PA)
522 Cottage Grove Rd B (06002-3111)
PHONE 860 243-8306
Edward Morris, *President*
Jerome Edward Finn, *Principal*
Mark Beiner, *Regional Mgr*
Gary Eschner, *Materials Mgr*
Chris Crider, *Chief Engr*
◆ **EMP:** 50 **EST:** 1953
SQ FT: 30,000
SALES: 15MM **Privately Held**
WEB: www.pa.com
SIC: 3549 3625 Coiling machinery; relays & industrial controls

(G-460)
PAP PRODUCTS LLC
14 Griffin Rd S (06002-1350)
PHONE 860 242-0415
Pasquale Attenello, *Principal*
EMP: 2
SALES (est): 136.7K **Privately Held**
SIC: 3751 Motorcycles, bicycles & parts

(G-461)
PAXXUS INC
Also Called: Rollprint Packaging
16 Southwood Dr (06002-1952)
PHONE 860 242-0663
Tom Sheridan, *Manager*
EMP: 24
SQ FT: 28,000
SALES (corp-wide): 56.2MM **Privately Held**
WEB: www.rollprint.com
SIC: 3086 2671 Packaging & shipping materials, foamed plastic; packaging paper & plastics film, coated & laminated
PA: Paxxus, Inc.
320 S Stewart Ave
Addison IL 60101
630 628-1700

(G-462)
PDS ENGINEERING & CNSTR INC
107 Old Windsor Rd (06002-1400)
PHONE 860 242-8586
Ronald Jodice, *President*

▲ = Import ▼ = Export
◆ = Import/Export

Frank Borawski, *Partner*
Karl Johnson, *Superintendent*
William Jodice, *Vice Pres*
Randy Becker, *Project Mgr*
EMP: 46
SQ FT: 13,000
SALES (est): 21.9MM **Privately Held**
WEB: www.pdsec.com
SIC: 1541 1542 3441 Industrial buildings, new construction; commercial & office building, new construction; building components, structural steel

(G-463)
PEPPERIDGE FARM INCORPORATED
1414 Blue Hills Ave (06002-1348)
PHONE..................860 286-6400
Mike Vallen, *Plant Mgr*
Jay Gould, *Manager*
EMP: 250
SALES (corp-wide): 8.1B **Publicly Held**
WEB: www.pepperidgefarm.com
SIC: 5461 2052 2099 2053 Bakeries; cookies; bread crumbs, not made in bakeries; frozen bakery products, except bread
HQ: Pepperidge Farm, Incorporated
595 Westport Ave
Norwalk CT 06851
203 846-7000

(G-464)
PHOENIX SHEET METAL LLC
16 Joyce St (06002-3317)
PHONE..................860 478-4579
James F Thomas, *Principal*
EMP: 1
SALES (est): 76.7K **Privately Held**
SIC: 3444 Sheet metalwork

(G-465)
PIONEER OPTICS COMPANY INC
35 Griffin Rd S (06002-1351)
PHONE..................860 286-0071
Ron Hille, *President*
Edward Hille, *QC Mgr*
Kathy Heggland, *Manager*
EMP: 14
SQ FT: 8,000
SALES: 4MM **Privately Held**
WEB: www.pioneeroptics.com
SIC: 3845 3229 Laser systems & equipment, medical; fiber optics strands

(G-466)
PMD SCIENTIFIC INC
105 W Ddley Town Rd Ste F (06002)
PHONE..................860 242-8177
Igor Abramovich, *President*
EMP: 7
SQ FT: 2,300
SALES: 1.5MM **Privately Held**
WEB: www.pmdsci.com
SIC: 3829 Geophysical & meteorological testing equipment

(G-467)
POINT LIGHTING CORPORATION
61-65 W Dudley Town Rd (06002)
P.O. Box 686, Simsbury (06070-0686)
PHONE..................860 243-0600
Michael J Callahan, *President*
Christine Breton, *Vice Pres*
Robert Malley, *Vice Pres*
Ryan Pape, *Vice Pres*
Meghan Pugliese, *Admin Sec*
EMP: 32
SQ FT: 48,000
SALES (est): 4.2MM **Privately Held**
WEB: www.pointlighting.com
SIC: 3648 5063 Outdoor lighting equipment; airport lighting fixtures: runway approach, taxi or ramp; lighting fixtures, commercial & industrial

(G-468)
POSITIVE VENTURES LLC
Also Called: Positive Pos
244 Woodland Ave (06002-5318)
PHONE..................860 499-0599
Daniel Fite, *Mng Member*
EMP: 5

SALES: 1.2MM **Privately Held**
SIC: 8748 3578 Telecommunications consultant; point-of-sale devices

(G-469)
PRATT WHTNEY MSUREMENT SYSTEMS
66 Douglas St (06002-3619)
PHONE..................860 286-8181
David N Stelly, *President*
Dane Mattran, *Engineer*
Daniel J Tycz, *CFO*
Kerrie Stelly, *Office Mgr*
▲ **EMP:** 24
SQ FT: 20,000
SALES (est): 6MM **Privately Held**
WEB: www.prattandwhitney.com
SIC: 3829 Measuring & controlling devices

(G-470)
PROSTHETIC AND ORTHOTIC
45 Wintonbury Ave (06002-2470)
PHONE..................860 904-2419
EMP: 2
SALES (est): 107.3K **Privately Held**
SIC: 3842 Limbs, artificial

(G-471)
QUALITY BEAD CRAFT INC
25 Northwood Dr (06002-1908)
P.O. Box 712 (06002-0712)
PHONE..................860 242-2167
John J Ferguson, *President*
Frederick Hillier, *Vice Pres*
EMP: 12
SQ FT: 13,500
SALES (est): 1.3MM **Privately Held**
WEB: www.qualitybead.com
SIC: 3999 Beads, unassembled

(G-472)
R&D DYNAMICS CORPORATION
49 W Dudley Town Rd (06002-1316)
PHONE..................860 726-1204
Giridhari L Agrawal, *President*
Sunil Agrawal, *Vice Pres*
Alexander Nelson, *Engineer*
Kirty Patel, *Engineer*
Ian Power, *Engineer*
EMP: 45
SALES (est): 10.1MM **Privately Held**
WEB: www.rddynamics.com
SIC: 8711 3511 Designing: ship, boat, machine & product; turbines & turbine generator sets

(G-473)
RAYGINN MFG LLC
109 W Ddley Town Rd Ste J (06002)
PHONE..................860 243-2257
Donald Coffin, *Mng Member*
EMP: 2
SALES (est): 326.1K **Privately Held**
SIC: 3531 Construction machinery

(G-474)
RED BULL LLC
460 Woodland Ave (06002-1342)
PHONE..................860 519-1018
EMP: 5 **EST:** 2015
SALES (est): 377.4K **Privately Held**
SIC: 2086 Bottled & canned soft drinks

(G-475)
RED DOOR INDUSTRIES
96 Old Windsor Rd (06002-1418)
PHONE..................860 243-1960
David Upton, *Owner*
EMP: 1
SQ FT: 960
SALES (est): 70.5K **Privately Held**
SIC: 3999 Manufacturing industries

(G-476)
REILLY FOAM CORP
16 Britton Dr (06002-3617)
PHONE..................860 243-8200
Mark S Burns, *Branch Mgr*
EMP: 30
SALES (corp-wide): 33.5MM **Privately Held**
SIC: 3069 3086 Foam rubber; plastics foam products

PA: Reilly Foam Corp.
751 5th Ave
King Of Prussia PA 19406
610 834-1900

(G-477)
RKP PRINTING SERVICES LLC
79 W Eggleston St (06002-3248)
PHONE..................860 242-0131
Robert K Palmer, *Principal*
EMP: 1 **EST:** 2009
SALES: 220K **Privately Held**
SIC: 2752 Commercial printing, lithographic

(G-478)
ROMCO CONTRACTORS INC
12 E Newberry Rd (06002-1404)
PHONE..................860 243-8872
Keith Lacourciere, *President*
Steve Hansen, *Vice Pres*
EMP: 11
SQ FT: 4,000
SALES (est): 1.1MM **Privately Held**
WEB: www.romcocontractors.com
SIC: 3441 Fabricated structural metal

(G-479)
RUBY AUTOMATION LLC (HQ)
Also Called: Kaman Automation, Inc.
1 Vision Way (06002-5321)
PHONE..................860 687-5000
Steven J Smidler, *President*
Gary J Haseley, *Senior VP*
Gary Haseley, *Vice Pres*
Roger S Jorgensen, *Vice Pres*
Roger Jorgensen, *Vice Pres*
EMP: 175
SALES (est): 68.5MM
SALES (corp-wide): 781.2MM **Privately Held**
SIC: 3491 5085 Industrial valves; industrial supplies
PA: Ruby Industrial Technologies, Llc
1 Vision Way
Bloomfield CT 06002
860 687-5000

(G-480)
RUBY FLUID POWER LLC (HQ)
Also Called: Kaman Fluid Power, LLC
1 Vision Way (06002-5321)
PHONE..................860 243-7100
Neal Keating,
James Coogan,
Richard Forsberg,
Ronald M Galla,
Patricia Goldenberg,
EMP: 25
SALES (est): 10.4MM
SALES (corp-wide): 781.2MM **Privately Held**
SIC: 3492 Hose & tube fittings & assemblies, hydraulic/pneumatic
PA: Ruby Industrial Technologies, Llc
1 Vision Way
Bloomfield CT 06002
860 687-5000

(G-481)
RUBY INDUSTRIAL TECH LLC (PA)
1 Vision Way (06002-5321)
PHONE..................860 687-5000
Neal J Keating, *CEO*
Steven J Smidler, *President*
Thomas A Weihsmann, *Vice Pres*
Carl A Conlon, *Controller*
Richard Kandetzki, *Director*
▲ **EMP:** 100
SQ FT: 5,000
SALES (est): 781.2MM **Privately Held**
SIC: 3491 5085 Industrial valves; industrial supplies

(G-482)
RUNWAY LIQUIDATION LLC
Also Called: Bcbg
3033 W Jefferson St (06002)
PHONE..................302 998-0551
EMP: 2
SALES (corp-wide): 570.1MM **Privately Held**
SIC: 2335 Women's, juniors' & misses' dresses

HQ: Runway Liquidation, Llc
2761 Fruitland Ave
Vernon CA 90058
323 589-2224

(G-483)
SAKLAX MANUFACTURING COMPANY
1346 Blue Hills Ave Ste B (06002-5310)
PHONE..................860 242-2538
Dhru Bhut, *President*
Bita Bhut, *President*
Dayalal Bhut, *Vice Pres*
Kusum Bhut, *Vice Pres*
Bhanji Bhut, *Treasurer*
EMP: 6
SQ FT: 3,200
SALES: 2MM **Privately Held**
SIC: 3728 Aircraft parts & equipment

(G-484)
SALAMANDER DESIGNS LTD
811 Blue Hills Ave (06002-3709)
PHONE..................860 761-9500
Salvatore Carrabba, *President*
Scott Srolis, *Vice Pres*
Mario Pacheco, *Production*
Kerry Hall, *Human Resources*
Michael Benedietto, *Natl Sales Mgr*
◆ **EMP:** 22
SQ FT: 85,000
SALES (est): 6MM **Privately Held**
WEB: www.salamanderdesigns.com
SIC: 2511 2514 2521 Wood household furniture; metal household furniture; wood office furniture

(G-485)
SALTWATER USA LLC
Also Called: Hatchway Corals
214 Cottage Grove Rd (06002-3210)
PHONE..................860 899-9240
Alexis Vasquez,
EMP: 1
SALES (est): 68.3K **Privately Held**
SIC: 3089 Plastics products

(G-486)
SECURITIES SOFTWARE & CON
705 Bloomfield Ave (06002-2479)
PHONE..................860 242-7887
EMP: 2 **EST:** 2006
SALES (est): 120K **Privately Held**
SIC: 7372 Prepackaged Software Services

(G-487)
SNAPLOK SYSTEMS LLC
24 Tobey Rd (06002-3522)
PHONE..................888 570-5407
David Kresge,
EMP: 2
SQ FT: 6,500
SALES (est): 104.7K **Privately Held**
SIC: 3272 Fireplace & chimney material: concrete

(G-488)
SOUND CONSTRUCTION & ENGRG CO
522 Cottage Grove Rd H (06002-3111)
PHONE..................860 242-2109
Michael G Economos, *President*
David Archilla, *Vice Pres*
George Economos, *Vice Pres*
Gary Laurito, *CFO*
EMP: 40
SQ FT: 80,000
SALES: 7.2MM
SALES (corp-wide): 31.5MM **Privately Held**
WEB: www.beconinc.com
SIC: 3625 Relays & industrial controls
PA: Becon Incorporated
522 Cottage Grove Rd
Bloomfield CT 06002
860 243-1428

(G-489)
SUBIMODS LLC
9 Old Windsor Rd Ste B (06002-1390)
PHONE..................860 291-0015
Joseph Miller III, *Principal*
EMP: 8
SALES (est): 549.8K **Privately Held**
SIC: 3465 Body parts, automobile: stamped metal

Bloomfield - Hartford County (G-490)

(G-490)
SWIFT TEXTILE METALIZING LLC (PA)
23 Britton Dr (06002-3616)
P.O. Box 66 (06002-0066)
PHONE..................................860 243-1122
Steven Sigmon, *CEO*
Richard Lenhardt, *CFO*
Wendy Benanti, *Office Mgr*
Jeff Rydel, *Info Tech Mgr*
Bryan Wyrebek, *Technology*
▲ **EMP:** 65 **EST:** 1955
SQ FT: 35,000
SALES: 20MM **Privately Held**
WEB: www.swift-textile.com
SIC: 2295 2297 2257 2221 Metallizing of fabrics; nonwoven fabrics; weft knit fabric mills; broadwoven fabric mills, manmade

(G-491)
THOMAS HOOKER BREWING CO LLC
16 Tobey Rd Rear (06002-3522)
PHONE..................................860 242-3111
Lisa Bielawski, *Sales Dir*
Curt Cameron,
▲ **EMP:** 31
SQ FT: 11,500
SALES: 2.6MM **Privately Held**
WEB: www.thomashookerbeer.com
SIC: 2082 Beer (alcoholic beverage)

(G-492)
TIMELESS STONE INC
21b E Dudley Town Rd (06002-1409)
PHONE..................................860 242-3300
Graziela Trabach, *President*
Norman Godard, *Vice Pres*
EMP: 2
SQ FT: 5,000
SALES (est): 213.1K **Privately Held**
SIC: 3281 Granite, cut & shaped

(G-493)
TRIPLE D TRANSPORTATION INC
129 W Dudley Town Rd (06002-1379)
PHONE..................................860 243-5057
Raymond Dufresne, *President*
Lawrence Dufresne, *Corp Secy*
Charles Dufresne, *Vice Pres*
EMP: 4
SQ FT: 8,500
SALES (est): 599.9K **Privately Held**
SIC: 3711 Road oilers (motor vehicles), assembly of

(G-494)
TRIUMPH GROUP INC
1395 Blue Hills Ave (06002-1309)
PHONE..................................860 726-9378
Thomas Holzthum, *Exec VP*
Richard Brauer, *Research*
Tom Holzthum, *Branch Mgr*
Troy Mullens, *Administration*
EMP: 8 **Publicly Held**
WEB: www.triumphgrp.com
SIC: 3728 Aircraft parts & equipment
PA: Triumph Group, Inc.
   899 Cassatt Rd Ste 210
   Berwyn PA 19312

(G-495)
TURBINE CONTROLS INC (PA)
5 Old Windsor Rd (06002-1311)
PHONE..................................860 242-0448
Glen Greenberg, *President*
Jeff Faszcza, *President*
Miriam Greenberg, *Admin Sec*
EMP: 97
SQ FT: 35,000
SALES: 28.5MM **Privately Held**
WEB: www.turbine-controls.com
SIC: 3541 4581 Milling machines; aircraft maintenance & repair services

(G-496)
UNIVERSAL FOAM PRODUCTS LLC
101 W Dudley Town Rd (06002-1319)
P.O. Box 421, Ellington (06029-0421)
PHONE..................................860 216-3015
Daniel Ekstrom,
◆ **EMP:** 12 **EST:** 2014
SQ FT: 25,000
SALES: 3.5MM **Privately Held**
SIC: 3069 3086 Latex, foamed; packaging & shipping materials, foamed plastic

(G-497)
VAN COTT ROWE & SMITH
60 Hoskins Rd (06002-1164)
PHONE..................................860 242-0707
C Smith, *Principal*
EMP: 1
SALES (est): 48.5K **Privately Held**
SIC: 2741 Miscellaneous publishing

(G-498)
VIAVI SOLUTIONS INC
45 Griffin Rd S (06002-1353)
PHONE..................................860 243-6600
Chris Lawson, *Manager*
EMP: 2
SALES (corp-wide): 1.1B **Publicly Held**
WEB: www.jdsuniphase.com
SIC: 3674 Modules, solid state
PA: Viavi Solutions Inc.
   6001 America Center Dr # 6
   San Jose CA 95002
   408 404-3600

(G-499)
WALLACE SERVICES GROUP LLC
6 Biltmore Park (06002-2141)
PHONE..................................860 350-2992
Mark Rosen, *Manager*
EMP: 1
SALES (est): 88.3K **Privately Held**
SIC: 2761 Manifold business forms

(G-500)
WAYPOINT DISTILLERY
410 Woodland Ave (06002-1342)
PHONE..................................860 519-5390
EMP: 5 **EST:** 2015
SALES (est): 329.8K **Privately Held**
SIC: 2085 Distilled & blended liquors

(G-501)
WIRETEK INC
48 E Newberry Rd (06002-1404)
PHONE..................................860 242-9473
Kuldeep Singh Sandhu, *President*
Parminder Singh Sandhu, *Vice Pres*
Deepika K Narwan, *Director*
Sarbjeet S Narwan, *Director*
EMP: 10
SQ FT: 10,000
SALES (est): 1.7MM **Privately Held**
WEB: www.wiretek.com
SIC: 3357 3315 Nonferrous wiredrawing & insulating; wire & fabricated wire products

(G-502)
WRITERS PRESS LLC
1010 Kensington Park (06002)
PHONE..................................860 242-9271
William L Newell, *Owner*
EMP: 1
SALES (est): 59.1K **Privately Held**
SIC: 2731 Book publishing

(G-503)
YANKEE DELIVERY SYSTEM
1 Flyer Row (06002-1401)
PHONE..................................860 243-1056
Donald L Gorman, *President*
EMP: 1
SALES (est): 101.9K **Privately Held**
SIC: 4212 2711 2741 Local trucking, without storage; newspapers, publishing & printing; miscellaneous publishing

Bolton
Tolland County

(G-504)
ABLE COIL AND ELECTRONICS CO
25 Howard Rd (06043-7428)
P.O. Box 9127 (06043-9127)
PHONE..................................860 646-5686
Steven K Rockfeller, *President*
Lynn Johnson, *Purch Mgr*
Tom Revall, *CFO*
Ed Gambacorta, *Manager*
Paul Asvestas, *Info Tech Mgr*
▼ **EMP:** 30
SQ FT: 25,000
SALES (est): 6.4MM **Privately Held**
WEB: www.ablecoil.com
SIC: 3677 3679 3089 3676 Filtration devices, electronic; solenoids for electronic applications; injection molding of plastics; electronic resistors; transformers, except electric

(G-505)
BARRE PRECISION PRODUCTS INC
Also Called: Moran Tool & Die
199 Hopriver Rd (06043-7443)
PHONE..................................860 647-1913
Ted Moran, *President*
Kim Briggs, *Treasurer*
Joyce Fraietta, *Admin Sec*
EMP: 3
SQ FT: 5,000
SALES: 76.3K **Privately Held**
WEB: www.morantool.com
SIC: 3599 Machine shop, jobbing & repair

(G-506)
BREAKAWAY BREW HAUS LLC
5 Steel Crossing Rd (06043-7622)
PHONE..................................860 647-9811
Matthew Soucy, *Principal*
EMP: 4 **EST:** 2016
SALES (est): 75.4K **Privately Held**
SIC: 2082 Malt beverages

(G-507)
BUDGET OIL
271 Hopriver Rd (06043-7411)
PHONE..................................860 649-1527
Charles J Minicucci Jr, *Principal*
EMP: 2
SALES (est): 120.2K **Privately Held**
SIC: 1381 Service well drilling

(G-508)
CARLYLE JOHNSON MACHINE CO LLC (PA)
Also Called: Cjmco
291 Boston Tpke (06043-7252)
P.O. Box 9546 (06043-9546)
PHONE..................................860 643-1531
Michael Gamache, *President*
Donald Kennet, *Vice Pres*
Gerry Staves, *Production*
Wessell Amy, *Purchasing*
Tom Thiffault, *Marketing Staff*
▼ **EMP:** 46
SQ FT: 40,000
SALES (est): 9.3MM **Privately Held**
WEB: www.cjmco.com
SIC: 3568 3625 3566 5063 Clutches, except vehicular; brakes, electromagnetic; speed changers (power transmission equipment), except auto; torque converters, except automotive; transformers & transmission equipment; valves & fittings

(G-509)
FISH FAMILY FARM INC
20 Dimock Ln (06043-7220)
PHONE..................................860 646-9745
Donald W Fish, *President*
Sharon Fish, *Vice Pres*
EMP: 2
SALES: 100K **Privately Held**
SIC: 0241 2024 5451 Milk production; ice cream & frozen desserts; ice cream (packaged)

(G-510)
HART STAMP & SEAL LLC
22 Westridge Dr (06043-7516)
PHONE..................................860 474-5382
Kelly Shorey,
EMP: 1 **EST:** 2014
SALES (est): 95.2K **Privately Held**
SIC: 3953 7389 Marking devices;

(G-511)
HATHAWAY SAND & GRAVEL LLC
10 Quarry Rd (06043-7315)
PHONE..................................860 647-7772
Rosemary J Hathaway, *Principal*
EMP: 2
SALES (est): 66K **Privately Held**
SIC: 1442 Construction sand & gravel

(G-512)
JLP MACHINE COMPANY
115 Cidermill Rd (06043-7213)
PHONE..................................860 649-5730
Jose Tinilla, *Owner*
EMP: 2
SALES (est): 214.1K **Privately Held**
SIC: 3599 Machine & other job shop work

(G-513)
LARCO MACHINES CO INC
239 Hopriver Rd (06043-7411)
PHONE..................................860 647-9769
Loren H Gouchoe, *President*
Bernard Gouchoe, *Vice Pres*
EMP: 3 **EST:** 1960
SALES: 150K **Privately Held**
SIC: 3599 Machine shop, jobbing & repair

(G-514)
LEADER MANAGEMENT CORP
282 Hebron Rd (06043-7830)
PHONE..................................860 643-4445
William J Rady, *President*
Christine Roche, *Principal*
Carol J Rady, *Vice Pres*
EMP: 2
SQ FT: 450
SALES (est): 201.9K **Privately Held**
SIC: 3161 7389 Traveling bags;

(G-515)
M D WELDING & FABRICATING LLC
112 French Rd (06043-7706)
P.O. Box 154, Dover Foxcroft ME (04426-0154)
PHONE..................................860 643-2448
Michael Doyon,
EMP: 1
SALES (est): 189.1K **Privately Held**
SIC: 7692 Welding repair

(G-516)
MIDNIGHT READER
11 Green Hill Dr (06043-7805)
PHONE..................................860 643-4220
Melissa Scheffey, *Owner*
EMP: 1
SALES (est): 67.6K **Privately Held**
SIC: 2731 Books: publishing only

(G-517)
MUNSONS CANDY KITCHEN INC (PA)
Also Called: Munson's Chocolates
174 Hopriver Rd (06043-7444)
PHONE..................................860 649-4332
Robert Munson, *President*
Josephine Munson, *Treasurer*
EMP: 50 **EST:** 1946
SQ FT: 32,000
SALES (est): 11.2MM **Privately Held**
WEB: www.munsonschocolates.com
SIC: 5947 5441 2066 2064 Gift, novelty & souvenir shop; candy; chocolate & cocoa products; candy & other confectionery products

(G-518)
RUBBERHOUSE
29 Mount Sumner Dr (06043-7231)
PHONE..................................860 646-3012
David Maidment, *President*
EMP: 1
SALES: 250K **Privately Held**
WEB: www.rubberhouse.com
SIC: 3069 7389 Hard rubber & molded rubber products

(G-519)
SIGNATURE SIGNWORKS LLC
10 Garth Ln (06043-7304)
PHONE..................................860 646-4598
Christopher Morianos, *Principal*
EMP: 2
SALES (est): 130.1K **Privately Held**
SIC: 5099 3993 Signs, except electric; signs & advertising specialties

▲ = Import ▼ = Export ◆ = Import/Export

GEOGRAPHIC SECTION

Branford - New Haven County (G-549)

(G-520)
SIMONIZ USA INC (PA)
201 Boston Tpke (06043-7203)
PHONE..................................860 646-0172
William M Gorra, *President*
Christine Brunette-Gorra, *Vice Pres*
Christine Gorra, *Vice Pres*
William Hibbard, *Plant Mgr*
Mark Kershaw, *CFO*
▲ **EMP:** 132
SQ FT: 30,000
SALES: 34.2MM **Privately Held**
WEB: www.simonizusa.com
SIC: 2842 2841 Cleaning or polishing preparations; detergents, synthetic organic or inorganic alkaline

(G-521)
W H PREUSS SONS INCORPORATED
228 Boston Tpke (06043-7204)
PHONE..................................860 643-9492
N James Preuss, *President*
Sharon Preuss, *Vice Pres*
Norman J Preuss, *Treasurer*
Eleanor H Preuss, *Admin Sec*
EMP: 7
SQ FT: 18,000
SALES (est): 1.1MM **Privately Held**
SIC: 5261 5722 7699 7629 Lawnmowers & tractors; lawn & garden equipment; electric household appliances; lawn mower repair shop; electrical household appliance repair; awnings, fabric: made from purchased materials

Bozrah
New London County

(G-522)
ADELMAN SAND & GRAVEL INC
34 Bozrah St (06334-1304)
PHONE..................................860 889-3394
Linda Adelman, *President*
Seymour Adelman, *Principal*
Linda Perry, *Bookkeeper*
Wesley Hyde, *Admin Sec*
EMP: 25 **EST:** 1950
SALES (est): 6.1MM **Privately Held**
SIC: 5032 1442 Sand, construction; gravel; construction sand & gravel

(G-523)
AEN ASPHALT INC
34 Bozrah St (06334-1304)
PHONE..................................860 885-0500
Linda Adelman, *President*
Ellen Adelman, *Admin Sec*
EMP: 4
SALES (est): 715.3K **Privately Held**
SIC: 2951 Asphalt & asphaltic paving mixtures (not from refineries)

(G-524)
ELECTRO MECH SPECIALISTS LLC
6 Commerce Park Rd (06334-1122)
PHONE..................................860 887-2613
Donna Laparre, *President*
Mervin Laparre II, *COO*
Merv Laparre, *Vice Pres*
Charles St Germain, *Manager*
David R Weller, *Info Tech Mgr*
EMP: 8
SQ FT: 20,000
SALES (est): 2.2MM **Privately Held**
SIC: 3699 Electrical equipment & supplies

(G-525)
FLOWE MANUFACTURING
12 Stockhouse Rd (06334-1120)
PHONE..................................860 859-1573
Jeremiah Lowe, *Principal*
EMP: 1 **EST:** 2017
SALES (est): 48K **Privately Held**
SIC: 3999 Manufacturing industries

(G-526)
LABRADOR PRESS LLC
107 Bashon Hill Rd (06334-1225)
PHONE..................................860 887-0567
Eliza Gager, *Principal*
EMP: 1
SALES (est): 55.8K **Privately Held**
SIC: 2741 Miscellaneous publishing

(G-527)
MAGIC INDUSTRIES INC
140 Bozrah St (06334-1405)
P.O. Box 158 (06334-0158)
PHONE..................................860 949-8380
Michael Krasun, *CEO*
EMP: 10
SALES (est): 560.5K **Privately Held**
SIC: 3229 3446 Glass furnishings & accessories; architectural metalwork

(G-528)
MARTY GILMAN INCORPORATED
Also Called: Gilman Gear
1 Commerce Park Rd (06334-1122)
P.O. Box 97 (06334-0097)
PHONE..................................860 889-7334
Shirley Gilman, *Chairman*
EMP: 7
SALES (est): 694.5K
SALES (corp-wide): 6.3MM **Privately Held**
SIC: 3949 Sporting & athletic goods
PA: Marty Gilman, Incorporated
    30 Gilman Rd
    Gilman CT 06336
    860 889-7334

(G-529)
NEW ENGLAND CRRAGE IMPORTS LLC
279 Bozrah St (06334-1401)
PHONE..................................860 889-6467
Peter Von Halem, *Principal*
EMP: 2 **EST:** 2015
SALES (est): 126K **Privately Held**
SIC: 3799 Transportation equipment

(G-530)
NGRAVER COMPANY
Also Called: Phillips, R J Associates
67 Wawecus Hill Rd (06334-1529)
PHONE..................................860 823-1533
Ray J Phillips, *Partner*
Brian J Phillips, *Partner*
Abby Mouat, *Technology*
EMP: 3 **EST:** 1955
SALES (est): 250K **Privately Held**
WEB: www.ngraver.com
SIC: 3423 5961 Engravers' tools, hand; mail order house, order taking office only

(G-531)
PERFORMANCE SHEET METAL
57 Bishop Rd (06334-1504)
PHONE..................................860 889-0550
William Roberts, *Owner*
EMP: 1
SALES (est): 99K **Privately Held**
SIC: 3443 Ducting, metal plate

(G-532)
SMITH FRAME & MOULDING LLC
112 Stockhouse Rd (06334-1137)
PHONE..................................860 389-8871
Luke Smith,
EMP: 2
SALES (est): 160.2K **Privately Held**
SIC: 2499 Decorative wood & woodwork

(G-533)
TIMBERS EDGE WOODWORKING
24 Goshen Rd (06334-1205)
PHONE..................................860 836-7328
Karen Martin, *Principal*
EMP: 1
SALES (est): 54.1K **Privately Held**
SIC: 2431 Millwork

Branford
New Haven County

(G-534)
A GREY SOIREE LLC
65 Parish Farm Rd (06405-6026)
PHONE..................................203 530-0277
Jacqueline Cusano, *Principal*
EMP: 2
SALES (est): 149.4K **Privately Held**
SIC: 2752 Commercial printing, lithographic

(G-535)
AAR RESULTS LLC
80 S Montowese St (06405-5222)
PHONE..................................203 627-2193
Antonia Ragozzino,
EMP: 1
SALES (est): 34.6K **Privately Held**
SIC: 8742 7319 2741 Marketing consulting services; advertising;

(G-536)
ACE BEAUTY SUPPLY INC
937 W Main St (06405-3431)
P.O. Box 303, Monroe (06468-0303)
PHONE..................................203 488-2416
Leslie Denford, *Manager*
EMP: 4
SALES (corp-wide): 24.6MM **Privately Held**
WEB: www.acebeautysupply.com
SIC: 3999 5087 Barber & beauty shop equipment; service establishment equipment
PA: Ace Beauty Supply Inc
    578 Pepper St
    Monroe CT
    203 268-6447

(G-537)
AEROMICS INC
11000 Cedar Ave Ste 270 (06405)
PHONE..................................216 772-1004
Marc Pelletier, *CEO*
Walter Boron, *Ch of Bd*
John Foster, *Principal*
Frederick Jones, *Principal*
Peter Longo, *Principal*
EMP: 7
SALES (est): 584.6K **Privately Held**
SIC: 2834 Pharmaceutical preparations

(G-538)
AIRBORNE INDUSTRIES INC
6 Sycamore Way Ste 2 (06405-6528)
PHONE..................................203 315-0200
Anthony Gentile, *President*
Jenny Gentile, *Vice Pres*
EMP: 10 **EST:** 1963
SQ FT: 15,000
SALES: 3MM **Privately Held**
WEB: www.airborneindustries.com
SIC: 3728 2399 Aircraft body assemblies & parts; military insignia, textile

(G-539)
AK INTERACTIVE USA LLC
122 Monticello Dr (06405-4165)
PHONE..................................845 313-9380
Kristin Irwin, *Principal*
EMP: 1
SALES (est): 46.2K **Privately Held**
SIC: 3999 Manufacturing industries

(G-540)
ALACRITY SEMICONDUCTORS INC
4 Pin Oak Dr Ste B (06405-6506)
PHONE..................................475 325-8435
James Lin, *President*
Francesco Annetta, *COO*
EMP: 3 **EST:** 2014
SALES (est): 224.3K **Privately Held**
SIC: 3674 8731 Integrated circuits, semiconductor networks, etc.; microcircuits, integrated (semiconductor); energy research; electronic research

(G-541)
ALL PANEL SYSTEMS LLC
9 Baldwin Dr Unit 1 (06405-6501)
P.O. Box 804 (06405-0804)
PHONE..................................203 208-3142
Venance Lafrancois, *COO*
Joe Criscuolo, *CFO*
Philip P Delise, *Mng Member*
▲ **EMP:** 67 **EST:** 2009
SQ FT: 39,000
SALES: 25.4MM **Privately Held**
SIC: 3441 Fabricated structural metal

(G-542)
AMERICAN CATATECH INC
Also Called: American Catalytic Tech
209 Montowese St Ste 3 (06405-3868)
PHONE..................................203 483-6692
EMP: 4
SQ FT: 600
SALES: 500K **Privately Held**
WEB: www.americancatalytic.com
SIC: 3567 Industrial furnaces & ovens

(G-543)
AMERICAN POLYFILM INC (PA)
Also Called: API
15 Baldwin Dr (06405-6501)
PHONE..................................203 483-9797
Victor J Cassella, *President*
Matthew V Cassella, *Vice Pres*
Paul C Cassella, *Vice Pres*
Larysa Olenska, *Treasurer*
Paul Cassella, *Sales Staff*
EMP: 8
SQ FT: 10,000
SALES: 3.6MM **Privately Held**
WEB: www.apiusa.com
SIC: 3081 Unsupported plastics film & sheet

(G-544)
ANCERA INC
15 Commercial St (06405-2801)
PHONE..................................203 819-2322
Arjun Duraisamy Ganesan, *Mng Member*
Hur Koser,
James Byron, *Commercial*
EMP: 9 **EST:** 2012
SALES (est): 1MM **Privately Held**
SIC: 7371 3821 Custom computer programming services; laboratory measuring apparatus

(G-545)
ANCHOR SCIENCE LLC
37 Victoria Dr (06405-3127)
PHONE..................................203 231-6181
Ewa S Kirkor,
EMP: 3
SALES (est): 203.3K **Privately Held**
WEB: www.anchorscience.com
SIC: 8748 3829 Business consulting; measuring & controlling devices

(G-546)
APACHE MILL
491 Main St (06405-3505)
PHONE..................................401 597-5580
EMP: 2 **EST:** 2018
SALES (est): 96.4K **Privately Held**
SIC: 3069 Fabricated rubber products

(G-547)
ARTES MAGAZINE LLC
242 Greens Farm Rd (06405-5913)
PHONE..................................203 530-9811
EMP: 2
SALES (est): 120K **Privately Held**
SIC: 2721 Periodicals-Publishing/Printing

(G-548)
ASSOCIATED CHEMICALS & ABR INC
Also Called: A C A
31 Business Park Dr Ste 3 (06405-6502)
PHONE..................................203 481-7235
John F Offredi, *President*
Christine T Offredi, *Admin Sec*
EMP: 4
SQ FT: 23,000
SALES (est): 1MM **Privately Held**
WEB: www.acaabrasives.com
SIC: 5085 3291 Abrasives; abrasive products

(G-549)
ATLAS INDUSTRIAL SERVICES LLC
30 Ne Industrial Rd (06405-2845)
PHONE..................................203 315-4538
Michael C Picard, *Mng Member*
EMP: 45
SQ FT: 20,000
SALES: 12MM **Privately Held**
SIC: 3444 1611 Guard rails, highway: sheet metal; guardrail construction, highways

Branford - New Haven County (G-550) GEOGRAPHIC SECTION

(G-550)
AUTAC INCORPORATED (PA)
25 Thompson Rd (06405-2842)
P.O. Box 306, North Branford (06471-0306)
PHONE.................................203 481-3444
Marie Burkle, *CEO*
EMP: 9
SQ FT: 12,000
SALES (est): 1.9MM **Privately Held**
WEB: www.autacusa.com
SIC: 3357 5063 Automotive wire & cable, except ignition sets: nonferrous; wire & cable; power wire & cable; building wire & cable; control & signal wire & cable, including coaxial

(G-551)
AUTAC INCORPORATED
25 Thompson Rd (06405-2842)
PHONE.................................203 481-3444
Scott Higgins, *Director*
EMP: 15
SALES (corp-wide): 1.9MM **Privately Held**
WEB: www.autacusa.com
SIC: 3621 Coils, for electric motors or generators
PA: Autac, Incorporated
    25 Thompson Rd
    Branford CT 06405
    203 481-3444

(G-552)
AXIOMX INC
688 E Main St (06405-2971)
PHONE.................................203 208-1034
Christopher McLeod, *President*
Dong Wang, *Production*
Felicity Acca, *Research*
Diane Buhr, *Research*
Meghan Kelly, *Research*
EMP: 28
SALES (est): 2MM
SALES (corp-wide): 312.7MM **Privately Held**
SIC: 2836 Biological products, except diagnostic
PA: Abcam Plc
    Discovery Drive
    Cambridge CAMBS CB2 0
    122 369-6000

(G-553)
AXIS WOOD WORKS LLC
41 Yowago Ave (06405-5526)
PHONE.................................203 481-4946
Mark Lillie,
EMP: 1
SALES (est): 79.6K **Privately Held**
SIC: 2434 Wood kitchen cabinets

(G-554)
B & B VENTURES LTD LBLTY CO
Also Called: Willoughby's Coffee & Tea
550 E Main St Ste 27 (06405-2948)
PHONE.................................203 481-1700
Bob Williams, *Mng Member*
Lubna Sparks, *Manager*
▲ EMP: 20
SQ FT: 250,000
SALES (est): 2.4MM **Privately Held**
WEB: www.willoughbyscoffee.com
SIC: 2095 Coffee roasting (except by wholesale grocers)

(G-555)
BAKERS ARCHITECTURAL WDWKG LLC
184 N Main St (06405-3021)
PHONE.................................203 483-3173
Greg Baker,
EMP: 1
SALES (est): 88.5K **Privately Held**
SIC: 3553 Woodworking machinery

(G-556)
BARLO MANUFACTURING
4 Beaver Rd Ste 1 (06405-3495)
PHONE.................................203 481-3426
Barbara Barcsansky, *Owner*
EMP: 5
SQ FT: 5,000
SALES: 450K **Privately Held**
SIC: 3599 Machine shop, jobbing & repair

(G-557)
BECKLEY INC
Also Called: Bud's Bait Box
4 Sybil Ave (06405-5315)
PHONE.................................203 488-1019
William Beckley, *President*
Hal Beckley, *Vice Pres*
EMP: 6
SQ FT: 1,400
SALES (est): 662.6K **Privately Held**
SIC: 5941 5421 3949 5812 Bait & tackle; fish markets; sporting & athletic goods; delicatessen (eating places)

(G-558)
BETTER PALLETS INC
10 Corbin Cir (06405-6105)
PHONE.................................203 230-9549
S Gordon Demetre, *Principal*
EMP: 3 EST: 2010
SALES (est): 164.1K **Privately Held**
SIC: 2448 Pallets, wood & wood with metal

(G-559)
BICK PUBLISHING HOUSE
16 Marion Rd (06405-4213)
PHONE.................................203 208-5253
Dale Carlson, *Owner*
EMP: 1 EST: 1993
SALES (est): 63K **Privately Held**
WEB: www.bickpubhouse.com
SIC: 2731 Books: publishing only

(G-560)
BIG PURPLE CUPCAKE LLC
6 Conifer Dr (06405-3258)
PHONE.................................203 483-8738
Regina F Criscuolo, *Owner*
EMP: 4 EST: 2013
SALES (est): 168.3K **Privately Held**
SIC: 2051 Bread, cake & related products

(G-561)
BLAKESLEE PRESTRESS INC (PA)
At Mc Dermott Rd Rr 139 (06405)
P.O. Box 510 (06405-0510)
PHONE.................................203 315-7090
R W Vine, *Ch of Bd*
Mario J Bertolini, *President*
Robert J Vitelli, *Senior VP*
Vincent A Gambardella, *Vice Pres*
Robert Vitelli, *Vice Pres*
▲ EMP: 251
SQ FT: 165,000
SALES (est): 51.3MM **Privately Held**
SIC: 3272 Prestressed concrete products; ties, railroad: concrete

(G-562)
BRANFORD AUTO & MARINE CENTER
Also Called: Branford Auto & Marine Cover
28 N Main St (06405-3022)
PHONE.................................203 481-6572
Robert Carbone, *Owner*
EMP: 1
SALES (est): 68K **Privately Held**
WEB: www.branfordautomarine.com
SIC: 7532 2394 Upholstery & trim shop, automotive; tops (canvas or plastic), installation or repair: automotive; canvas boat seats

(G-563)
BRANFORD OPEN MRI & DIAGNOSTIC
1208 Main St (06405-3787)
PHONE.................................203 481-7800
EMP: 3
SALES (est): 268.1K **Privately Held**
SIC: 2835 8011 Mfg Diagnostic Substances Medical Doctor's Office

(G-564)
BRASH ENGINES INC
34 Averill Pl (06405-3801)
PHONE.................................203 843-0757
Michael J Brookman, *Principal*
EMP: 2
SALES (est): 217.4K **Privately Held**
SIC: 3519 Internal combustion engines

(G-565)
BRITELITE PROMOTIONS
1008 Main St Ste 1 (06405-3773)
PHONE.................................203 481-5755
Bob Intravia, *Sales Staff*
Rob Montravia, *Mng Member*
EMP: 3
SALES (est): 423.3K **Privately Held**
WEB: www.britelitepromotions.com
SIC: 7319 2759 Advertising; screen printing

(G-566)
BURNS WALTON
Also Called: Alphabet Publishing
29 Milo Dr (06405-6133)
PHONE.................................203 422-5222
Walton Burns, *Owner*
EMP: 3
SALES (est): 45.4K **Privately Held**
SIC: 2741 2731 Miscellaneous publishing; books: publishing only; textbooks: publishing only, not printed on site

(G-567)
C P I COMPUTER CENTER INC
Also Called: Computer Playscapes
1245 Main St (06405-3739)
P.O. Box 659 (06405-0659)
PHONE.................................203 483-8505
David Chew, *President*
Lai Chew, *Admin Sec*
EMP: 1
SALES (est): 120.2K **Privately Held**
WEB: www.ct-medical.com
SIC: 7372 Prepackaged software

(G-568)
CAS MEDICAL SYSTEMS INC
32 Park Dr E (06405-6516)
PHONE.................................203 488-1957
EMP: 1
SALES (corp-wide): 22.9MM **Publicly Held**
SIC: 3841 Business Services
PA: Cas Medical Systems, Inc.
    44 E Industrial Rd
    Branford CT 06405
    203 488-6056

(G-569)
CAS MEDICAL SYSTEMS INC
Also Called: Casmed
32 E Industrial Rd (06405-6532)
PHONE.................................203 315-6953
EMP: 6
SALES (corp-wide): 3.7B **Publicly Held**
SIC: 3841 Blood pressure apparatus
HQ: Cas Medical Systems, Inc.
    44 E Industrial Rd
    Branford CT 06405
    203 488-6056

(G-570)
CAS MEDICAL SYSTEMS INC (HQ)
44 E Industrial Rd (06405-6554)
PHONE.................................203 488-6056
Thomas Patton, *President*
Jeffery Baird, *CFO*
Paul Benni, *Security Dir*
EMP: 76
SQ FT: 24,000
SALES: 21.9MM
SALES (corp-wide): 3.7B **Publicly Held**
WEB: www.casmed.com
SIC: 3841 Diagnostic apparatus, medical; blood pressure apparatus
PA: Edwards Lifesciences Corp
    1 Edwards Way
    Irvine CA 92614
    949 250-2500

(G-571)
CD SOLUTIONS INC
420 E Main St Ste 16 (06405-2942)
PHONE.................................203 481-5895
David Pfrommer, *President*
EMP: 20
SALES (est): 894.5K **Privately Held**
SIC: 7372 4226 Prepackaged software; document & office records storage

(G-572)
CELLDEX THERAPEUTICS INC
688 E Main St Ste 1 (06405-2971)
PHONE.................................203 864-5771
Larry Ellberger, *Chairman*
EMP: 1
SALES (corp-wide): 9.5MM **Publicly Held**
SIC: 2834 Pharmaceutical preparations
PA: Celldex Therapeutics, Inc.
    53 Frontage Rd Ste 220
    Hampton NJ 08827
    908 200-7500

(G-573)
CERRITO FURNITURE INDS INC
Also Called: Cerritos Upholstery Concepts
7 Venice St (06405-3111)
PHONE.................................203 481-2580
Ronald Cerrito, *President*
Robert Cerrito, *Admin Sec*
EMP: 16 EST: 1976
SQ FT: 7,000
SALES (est): 1.5MM **Privately Held**
WEB: www.cerritofurniture.com
SIC: 2512 5712 Upholstered household furniture; furniture stores

(G-574)
COASTLINE PRINTING
11 Briarwood Ln (06405-4301)
PHONE.................................203 481-2744
Kenneth Palmieri, *Principal*
EMP: 2
SALES (est): 161K **Privately Held**
SIC: 2752 Commercial printing, lithographic

(G-575)
COMPRHNSIVE PRSTHETIC SVCS LLC
21 Business Park Dr (06405-2935)
PHONE.................................203 315-1400
John Zenie, *Mng Member*
EMP: 4
SALES: 1MM **Privately Held**
WEB: www.cpsbranford.com
SIC: 3842 Grafts, artificial: for surgery

(G-576)
CONNECTICUT PARENT MAGAZINE
420 E Main St Ste 18 (06405-2942)
PHONE.................................203 483-1700
Joel Macclaren, *Principal*
Lauren Piscitelle, *Accounts Exec*
EMP: 10
SALES (est): 780K **Privately Held**
SIC: 2731 Book publishing

(G-577)
CRYSTAL JOURNEY CANDLES LLC
69 N Branford Rd (06405-2810)
PHONE.................................203 433-4735
Cosmo Coriglianao, *Owner*
Agnes Coriglianao,
▲ EMP: 20
SQ FT: 5,000
SALES (est): 1.9MM **Privately Held**
WEB: www.crystaljourneycandles.com
SIC: 3999 5947 Candles; gift, novelty & souvenir shop

(G-578)
CYGNUS MEDICAL LLC
965 W Main St Ste 2 (06405-3454)
PHONE.................................800 990-7489
Kelley Roche, *Sales Staff*
Walter L Maquire Jr,
▲ EMP: 8
SALES: 920K **Privately Held**
WEB: www.cygnusmedical.com
SIC: 3841 Surgical & medical instruments

(G-579)
DIFFERENTIAL PRESSURE PLUS
67 N Branford Rd Ste 4 (06405-2852)
PHONE.................................203 481-2545
Joe Gordon, *Manager*
EMP: 7
SALES (est): 913.8K **Privately Held**
SIC: 3823 Industrial instrmnts msrmnt display/control process variable

GEOGRAPHIC SECTION

Branford - New Haven County (G-609)

(G-580)
DOLTRONICS LLC
65-4 N Branford Rd (06405-2861)
PHONE.................................203 488-8766
Chris Abbatello, *Sales Executive*
Christopher Abbatello,
EMP: 21
SQ FT: 3,500
SALES (est): 3.3MM **Privately Held**
WEB: www.doltronics.com
SIC: 8731 3679 Electronic research; electronic circuits

(G-581)
DUNNOTTAR PUBLISHING LLC
3 Lakeview Ter (06405-4012)
PHONE.................................203 488-0350
EMP: 1
SALES (est): 37.5K **Privately Held**
SIC: 2741 Miscellaneous publishing

(G-582)
DUTCH WHARF BOAT YARD & MARINA
70 Maple St (06405-3582)
PHONE.................................203 488-9000
Paul Jacques, *Vice Pres*
EMP: 18
SQ FT: 5,000
SALES (est): 2.7MM **Privately Held**
SIC: 3732 Boat building & repairing

(G-583)
E S CUSTOM MACHINING
195 N Main St Apt A (06405-3063)
PHONE.................................203 481-8653
Edward Schwall, *Owner*
EMP: 1
SALES (est): 120.2K **Privately Held**
SIC: 3599 Machine shop, jobbing & repair

(G-584)
E-SKYLIGHT INC
66 N Main St (06405-3032)
P.O. Box 830 (06405-0830)
PHONE.................................203 208-1351
Caitlin O'Neill, *President*
Kari Freund, *Manager*
EMP: 5 **Privately Held**
SIC: 1761 3444 Skylight installation; skylights, sheet metal
PA: E-Skylight, Inc.
66 N Main St
Branford CT 06405

(G-585)
ECLIPSE SYSTEMS INC
14 Commercial St Ub (06405-2801)
P.O. Box 82, Guilford (06437-0082)
PHONE.................................203 483-0665
William J Carroll, *President*
Nancy H Carroll, *Vice Pres*
EMP: 5
SQ FT: 6,000
SALES: 624.9K
SALES (corp-wide): 28MM **Privately Held**
WEB: www.eclipsesystems.com
SIC: 3845 Magnetic resonance imaging device, nuclear
HQ: Bc Technical, Inc.
7172 S Airport Rd
West Jordan UT 84084

(G-586)
EHRLICH & COMPANY
3 Wellsweep Rd (06405-6140)
PHONE.................................203 481-1999
David Mahon, *President*
Kent Dasjardins, *Admin Sec*
EMP: 3
SALES (est): 504.1K **Privately Held**
WEB: www.boxxbizz.com
SIC: 2652 Setup paperboard boxes

(G-587)
ELDORADO USA INC
322 E Main St Ste 2 (06405-3136)
PHONE.................................203 208-2282
Robert B Davidson, *President*
Breanna Richardson, *Principal*
Marcos Paletta Camara, *Treasurer*
Edwin Velazquez, *Accounts Mgr*
▲ **EMP:** 5

SALES: 105.4MM **Privately Held**
SIC: 2611 Pulp mills

(G-588)
ELM CITY PTTERN FNDRY WRKS INC
14 Griffing Pond Rd (06405-6407)
PHONE.................................203 481-2518
Helen Burkhardt, *President*
Francis X Conlon, *Director*
EMP: 8 **EST:** 1949
SQ FT: 5,000
SALES (est): 670K **Privately Held**
SIC: 3369 Nonferrous foundries

(G-589)
ENHANCED MFG SOLUTIONS LLC
33 Business Park Dr Ste 4 (06405-2973)
PHONE.................................203 488-5796
Stephen Giardina, *Principal*
▲ **EMP:** 12
SQ FT: 2,100
SALES (est): 2.5MM **Privately Held**
SIC: 3672 Printed circuit boards

(G-590)
ESSEX PUBLISHING CO
130 Montowese St Ste B (06405-3841)
PHONE.................................314 627-0300
EMP: 2
SALES (est): 100.8K **Privately Held**
SIC: 2741 Miscellaneous publishing

(G-591)
EVOTEC (US) INC
33 Business Park Dr # 6 (06405-2973)
PHONE.................................650 228-1400
Werner Lanthaler, *President*
EMP: 28
SALES (corp-wide): 429.7MM **Privately Held**
SIC: 2836 2834 Biological products, except diagnostic; pharmaceutical preparations
HQ: Evotec (Us) Inc.
303b College Rd E
Princeton NJ 08540

(G-592)
EXHIBITEASE LLC
1204 Main St Unit 207 (06405-3787)
PHONE.................................203 481-0792
Bonnie O'Malley,
EMP: 1
SALES (est): 90K **Privately Held**
SIC: 7336 3993 2759 5199 Graphic arts & related design; signs & advertising specialties; commercial printing; art goods & supplies

(G-593)
FABRIQUE LTD
28 School St (06405-3328)
PHONE.................................203 481-5400
Francine Farkas Sears, *President*
▲ **EMP:** 12
SALES (est): 15.5MM **Privately Held**
SIC: 3161 Cases, carrying

(G-594)
FITZGERALD & WOOD INC
85 Rogers St Ste 3 (06405-3674)
PHONE.................................203 488-2553
Thomas J Shanley, *President*
Susan Shanley, *Manager*
EMP: 8 **EST:** 1924
SQ FT: 3,000
SALES: 500K **Privately Held**
SIC: 3432 Plumbing fixture fittings & trim

(G-595)
FLOODMASTER LLC
27 Business Park Dr (06405-2925)
PHONE.................................203 488-4477
Steven E Schicker,
EMP: 1
SALES (est): 130.3K
SALES (corp-wide): 10.8MM **Privately Held**
SIC: 3643 3823 Current-carrying wiring devices; liquid level instruments, industrial process type

PA: Madison Company
27 Business Park Dr
Branford CT 06405
203 488-4477

(G-596)
FRANK DRAGO CUSTOM MAPPING
94 Ivy St Fl 1 (06405-3714)
PHONE.................................203 483-7594
Frank Drago, *Owner*
EMP: 1
SALES (est): 71K **Privately Held**
SIC: 7336 2741 Chart & graph design; maps: publishing & printing

(G-597)
FREETHINK TECHNOLOGIES INC
35 Ne Industrial Rd # 201 (06405-6802)
PHONE.................................860 237-5800
Kenneth C Waterman, *CEO*
K Waterman, *President*
Ken Waterman, *President*
Mark Kastan, *Vice Pres*
Butch Waterman, *CFO*
EMP: 19
SALES (est): 316.3K **Privately Held**
SIC: 7372 8732 Prepackaged software; research services, except laboratory

(G-598)
FREVVO INC
500 E Main St Ste 330 (06405-2937)
PHONE.................................203 208-3117
Ashish Desphande, *CEO*
Leandro D Costa, *President*
Leandro Dacosta, *President*
Nancy Esposito, *COO*
Eric Pias, *Vice Pres*
EMP: 11
SALES (est): 829.4K **Privately Held**
SIC: 7372 Business oriented computer software

(G-599)
FYC APPAREL GROUP LLC (PA)
Also Called: Allison Taylor
30 Thompson Rd (06405-2842)
P.O. Box 812 (06405-0812)
PHONE.................................203 481-2420
John Warfel, *Vice Pres*
Maia Chiat,
Sunny Leigh,
Kathe Sherman,
▲ **EMP:** 100
SQ FT: 42,000
SALES (est): 69.8MM **Privately Held**
WEB: www.akdesigns.net
SIC: 2331 2335 2337 5651 Women's & misses' blouses & shirts; women's, juniors' & misses' dresses; women's & misses' suits & skirts; family clothing stores

(G-600)
GLOBE ENVIRONMENTAL CORP
131 Commercial Pkwy 1b (06405-2536)
P.O. Box 235 (06405-0235)
PHONE.................................203 481-5586
Lorraine Saputo, *Vice Pres*
Richard True, *Vice Pres*
Charles S Blaha, *CFO*
EMP: 11
SALES (est): 1.9MM **Privately Held**
SIC: 2899 Water treating compounds

(G-601)
GREG ROBBINS AND ASSOCIATES
15 Park Pl (06405-7726)
PHONE.................................888 699-8876
Gregory Robbins, *Principal*
EMP: 3
SALES (est): 155.2K **Privately Held**
SIC: 2024 Ice cream & frozen desserts

(G-602)
HAESCHE MACHINE REPAIR SERVICE
422 Shore Dr (06405-6229)
PHONE.................................203 488-7271
Joe Haesche, *Owner*
Gale Haesche, *Co-Owner*
EMP: 2

SALES: 15K **Privately Held**
SIC: 7699 3545 Industrial machinery & equipment repair; cams (machine tool accessories)

(G-603)
HARCOSEMCO LLC
186 Cedar St (06405-6011)
P.O. Box 10 (06405-0010)
PHONE.................................203 483-3700
Raymond Laubenthal, *CEO*
Michael Milardo, *President*
Gregory Rufus, *Corp Secy*
Jennifer Viglione, *Production*
Lester Allen, *Engineer*
EMP: 137 **EST:** 1951
SQ FT: 1,200
SALES (est): 44.7MM
SALES (corp-wide): 3.8B **Publicly Held**
WEB: www.harcolabs.com
SIC: 3829 Aircraft & motor vehicle measurement equipment
HQ: Transdigm, Inc.
4223 Monticello Blvd
Cleveland OH 44121

(G-604)
HENRY W ZUWALICK & SONS INC
36 Zuwallack Ln (06405-3332)
PHONE.................................203 488-3821
Jack E Zuwalick, *President*
David R Zuwalick, *Vice Pres*
EMP: 2
SALES (est): 259K **Privately Held**
SIC: 2421 Sawmills & planing mills, general

(G-605)
HOFFMANN-LA ROCHE INC
15 Commercial St (06405-2801)
PHONE.................................203 871-2303
John Waterhouse, *Branch Mgr*
EMP: 608
SALES (corp-wide): 57.2B **Privately Held**
SIC: 2834 Pharmaceutical preparations
HQ: Hoffmann-La Roche Inc.
150 Clove Rd Ste 88th
Little Falls NJ 07424
973 890-2268

(G-606)
HOTCHKISS PUBLISHING
17 Frank St (06405-4608)
PHONE.................................203 430-6289
EMP: 2
SALES (est): 50K **Privately Held**
SIC: 2741 Miscellaneous publishing

(G-607)
HOUSTON WEBER SYSTEMS INC
31 Business Park Dr Ste 3 (06405-2977)
PHONE.................................203 481-0115
Via Weber, *President*
Charles Weber, *Vice Pres*
Carol Weber, *Admin Sec*
EMP: 8 **EST:** 1958
SQ FT: 13,000
SALES: 560K **Privately Held**
SIC: 3494 3599 Valves & pipe fittings; machine shop, jobbing & repair

(G-608)
HOWMET CORPORATION
Howmet Trbine Cmpnents Coating
4 Commercial St (06405-2801)
PHONE.................................203 481-3451
John Schilbe, *Manager*
EMP: 331
SALES (corp-wide): 14B **Publicly Held**
SIC: 3324 Commercial investment castings, ferrous
HQ: Howmet Corporation
1 Misco Dr
Whitehall MI 49461
231 894-5686

(G-609)
ISKRA JOHN
Also Called: Spark Manufacturing
2 Research Dr Ste 8 (06405-2859)
PHONE.................................203 488-5402
John Iskra, *Owner*
EMP: 1 **EST:** 1997

(G-610)
IVY BIOMEDICAL SYSTEMS INC
11 Business Park Dr # 10 (06405-2959)
PHONE.................................203 481-4183
James W Biondi, *President*
Sara Dean, *General Mgr*
Zack Curello, *Vice Pres*
Richard Kosmala, *Vice Pres*
Christopher Sheridan, *Vice Pres*
▲ **EMP:** 47
SQ FT: 14,700
SALES (est): 9.5MM **Privately Held**
WEB: www.ivybiomedical.com
SIC: 3845 Patient monitoring apparatus

(G-611)
J + J BRANFORD INC (PA)
Also Called: Joe's Paint Center
145 N Mn St (06405)
PHONE.................................203 488-5637
Joseph R Pagliaro, *President*
EMP: 4
SALES (est): 815K **Privately Held**
SIC: 2851 Paints & allied products

(G-612)
JENKINS SOFTWARE ASSOC LLC
60 Averill Pl (06405-3801)
PHONE.................................203 483-8386
David Jenkins, *Principal*
EMP: 2
SALES (est): 98.5K **Privately Held**
SIC: 7372 Prepackaged software

(G-613)
JOHN P SMITH CO
20 Baldwin Dr (06405-6501)
PHONE.................................203 488-7226
Fax: 203 483-5405
EMP: 1 **EST:** 2011
SALES (est): 60K **Privately Held**
SIC: 3496 Mfg Misc Fabricated Wire Products

(G-614)
K & G GRAPHICS
540 E Main St Ste 7 (06405-2946)
PHONE.................................203 481-4884
Roger Guay, *Partner*
Romualdis A Kaminskas Jr, *Partner*
EMP: 2 **EST:** 1976
SALES (est): 180K **Privately Held**
WEB: www.kggraphics.com
SIC: 2752 Commercial printing, offset

(G-615)
K&D PRINT LLC
33 Beechwood Rd (06405-3200)
P.O. Box 250 (06405-0250)
PHONE.................................203 483-1199
EMP: 2
SALES (est): 137.9K **Privately Held**
SIC: 2752 Lithographic Commercial Printing

(G-616)
KELSEY BOAT YARD
1 Paynes Pt (06405-4717)
PHONE.................................203 488-9567
Edwin R Kelsey III, *Owner*
EMP: 1
SALES (est): 99.4K **Privately Held**
SIC: 4493 3732 Boat yards, storage & incidental repair; boat building & repairing

(G-617)
KINETIC INNVTIVE STING SYS LLC
Also Called: Kiss
26 N Main St Ofc Bldg (06405-3059)
P.O. Box 935 (06405-0935)
PHONE.................................203 488-1758
Susan Farricielli,
EMP: 1
SQ FT: 1,000
SALES (est): 142.1K **Privately Held**
SIC: 3842 Wheelchairs

(G-618)
LEFT HANDED HOLSTERS
8 7th Ave (06405-5424)
PHONE.................................203 488-9654
Paul Maresca, *Principal*
EMP: 1
SALES (est): 49.1K **Privately Held**
SIC: 3199 Holsters, leather.

(G-619)
LQ MECHATRONICS INC
2 Sycamore Way (06405-6551)
PHONE.................................203 433-4430
Hans-Elmar Kessler, *President*
Tammy Wright, *Principal*
▲ **EMP:** 9
SQ FT: 2,000
SALES (est): 1.8MM
SALES (corp-wide): 55.4MM **Privately Held**
SIC: 3823 3824 3679 Industrial instrmnts msrmnt display/control process variable; electromechanical counters; harness assemblies for electronic use: wire or cable
PA: Lq Mechatronik-Systeme Gmbh
Carl-Benz-Str. 6
Besigheim 74354
714 396-830

(G-620)
M S B INTERNATIONAL LTD
Also Called: New York City Blouse Co
30 Thompson Rd (06405-2842)
PHONE.................................203 466-6525
Noor Hasso, *Manager*
EMP: 2 **Privately Held**
SIC: 4222 2384 2341 2337 Refrigerated warehousing & storage; robes & dressing gowns; women's & children's underwear; women's & misses' suits & coats; women's, juniors' & misses' dresses; women's & misses' blouses & shirts
PA: M S B International, Ltd.
1412 Broadway Rm 1210
New York NY 10018

(G-621)
MADISON COMPANY (PA)
27 Business Park Dr (06405-2954)
PHONE.................................203 488-4477
Steven Schickler, *President*
Donna Dotson, *Vice Pres*
Eileen Revoir, *Sales Staff*
Resha Patel, *Info Tech Mgr*
Robert Wawrzeniak, *Director*
EMP: 45 **EST:** 1959
SQ FT: 20,000
SALES (est): 10.8MM **Privately Held**
SIC: 3613 3823 Switchgear & switchboard apparatus; liquid level instruments, industrial process type

(G-622)
MADISON POLYMERIC ENGRG INC
Also Called: M P E
965 W Main St Ste 2 (06405-3454)
PHONE.................................203 488-4554
Walter L Maguire Jr, *President*
Robert Hojnacki, *Vice Pres*
John Dacier, *Plant Mgr*
Gary Stevens, *Sales Engr*
Audie Jackson, *Manager*
EMP: 45
SQ FT: 50,000
SALES (est): 10.4MM **Privately Held**
WEB: www.madpoly.com
SIC: 3086 Plastics foam products

(G-623)
MAKE A CANDLE
11 Rose St (06405-7719)
PHONE.................................203 871-8426
Shelby Zoccano, *Principal*
EMP: 1 **EST:** 2017
SALES (est): 39.6K **Privately Held**
SIC: 3999 Candles

(G-624)
MARINE FABRICATORS
145 S Montowese St (06405-5268)
PHONE.................................203 488-7093
Joseph Kolodej, *Owner*
EMP: 1
SALES (est): 150K **Privately Held**
SIC: 3429 5551 3732 3444 Marine hardware; boat dealers; boat building & repairing; sheet metalwork

(G-625)
MEDICAL LASER SYSTEMS INC
20 Baldwin Dr (06405-6501)
PHONE.................................203 481-2395
Brian Richardson, *President*
EMP: 1
SQ FT: 10,000
SALES (est): 113.9K **Privately Held**
WEB: www.medicallasersystems.com
SIC: 3699 Laser systems & equipment

(G-626)
MIAMI BAY BEVERAGE COMPANY LLC
Also Called: Trimino
7 Sycamore Way Unit 3 (06405-6523)
PHONE.................................203 453-0090
Peter J Dacey, *CEO*
Casey P Hoban, *COO*
Robert J Leary, *Director*
EMP: 10
SQ FT: 1,200
SALES (est): 850K **Privately Held**
SIC: 5499 2086 Beverage stores; carbonated beverages, nonalcoholic: bottled & canned

(G-627)
MOLD THREADS INC
21 W End Ave (06405-4549)
PHONE.................................203 483-1420
Bruce Argetsinger, *President*
EMP: 4
SQ FT: 10,000
SALES (est): 947.3K **Privately Held**
WEB: www.moldthreads.com
SIC: 3089 3544 Injection molding of plastics; forms (molds), for foundry & plastics working machinery

(G-628)
NATIONAL EDUC SUPPT TRUST US
1204 Main St Ste 535 (06405-3787)
PHONE.................................860 420-8008
Mary L McKenna, *Vice Pres*
Jacob S Bronstein,
EMP: 2
SALES (est): 79.6K **Privately Held**
SIC: 7372 Educational computer software

(G-629)
NEW ENGLAND COMPUTER SVCS INC
Also Called: Necs
322 E Main St (06405-3136)
PHONE.................................475 221-8200
Christopher Anatra, *President*
Tony Vlahos, *Engineer*
Michael Hubbard, *Software Dev*
EMP: 22 **EST:** 1990
SALES (est): 2.1MM **Privately Held**
SIC: 7372 Application computer software; business oriented computer software

(G-630)
OUT ON A LIMB
51 Mill Plain Rd (06405-2749)
PHONE.................................203 315-8977
Dylan Ward, *Principal*
EMP: 2
SALES (est): 160.7K **Privately Held**
SIC: 3842 Limbs, artificial

(G-631)
PAPER ALLIANCE LLC
45 Ne Industrial Rd (06405-6801)
PHONE.................................203 315-3116
Paula Nancuso, *Vice Pres*
Michael Siegel, *Mng Member*
EMP: 4 **EST:** 2011
SALES (est): 522.9K
SALES (corp-wide): 74.6MM **Privately Held**
SIC: 2631 Container board
HQ: Evergreen Fibres, Inc.
45 Ne Industrial Rd
Branford CT 06405

(G-632)
PAULS LEATHER CO
7 Bryan Rd (06405-4503)
PHONE.................................203 871-7238
EMP: 2
SALES (est): 121.9K **Privately Held**
SIC: 3199 Leather goods

(G-633)
PAULS WIRE ROPE & SLING INC
4 Indian Neck Ave (06405-4616)
PHONE.................................203 481-3469
Paul Cianciola Jr, *President*
Dale Cianciola, *Admin Sec*
EMP: 10
SQ FT: 1,000
SALES (est): 1.4MM **Privately Held**
SIC: 3496 Slings, lifting: made from purchased wire

(G-634)
PEXAGON TECHNOLOGY INC
14 Business Park Dr Ste E (06405-2909)
PHONE.................................203 458-3364
Brian R Campbell, *President*
Albert Conte, *Vice Pres*
Susan Campbell, *Treasurer*
Tommy Fair, *Sales Mgr*
John Russo, *Mktg Dir*
◆ **EMP:** 30
SQ FT: 10,000
SALES (est): 7MM **Privately Held**
WEB: www.pexagontech.com
SIC: 3572 Computer storage devices

(G-635)
PHOENIXSONGS BIOLOGICALS INC
33 Business Park Dr 1a (06405-2973)
PHONE.................................203 433-4329
Richard Malavarca, *President*
Marsha Roach, *Exec VP*
Lola Reid, *Officer*
EMP: 4 **EST:** 2012
SQ FT: 4,500
SALES (est): 576.5K **Privately Held**
SIC: 2836 Biological products, except diagnostic

(G-636)
PPK INC
41 Montoya Dr (06405-2516)
PHONE.................................203 376-9180
Gale Morrison, *Principal*
EMP: 3
SALES (est): 327.8K **Privately Held**
SIC: 2421 Building & structural materials, wood

(G-637)
PRATT-READ CORPORATION (PA)
Also Called: Cornwall & Patterson Div
193 Turtle Bay Dr (06405-4903)
PHONE.................................860 625-3620
Harwood B Comstock, *Ch of Bd*
Gordon Christie, *CFO*
EMP: 15 **EST:** 1798
SQ FT: 120,000
SALES (est): 6.2MM **Privately Held**
WEB: www.hexkeys.com
SIC: 3469 Metal stampings

(G-638)
PROTEOWISE INC
34 Bryan Rd (06405-4504)
PHONE.................................203 430-4187
Erik Gunther, *CEO*
Mikhail Kostylev, *Principal*
Stephen Strittmatter, *Principal*
EMP: 3
SALES (est): 128K **Privately Held**
SIC: 3821 Laboratory apparatus & furniture

(G-639)
PSJ SOFTWARE LLC
60 Jerimoth Dr (06405-2226)
PHONE.................................203 315-1523
EMP: 2
SALES (est): 87.7K **Privately Held**
SIC: 7372 Prepackaged Software Services

GEOGRAPHIC SECTION
Branford - New Haven County (G-671)

(G-640)
REBORN HOUSE
204 Damascus Rd (06405-6109)
PHONE 203 216-9874
Rachel Kalman, *Principal*
EMP: 1
SALES (est): 63.7K **Privately Held**
SIC: 2512 7641 Upholstered household furniture; antique furniture repair & restoration

(G-641)
RESPOND SYSTEMS
20 Baldwin Dr (06405-6501)
PHONE 203 481-2810
Donald E Hudson, *President*
Dave Lantieri, *Engineer*
Doreen O Hudson, *Director*
EMP: 10 **EST:** 1981
SALES (est): 880K **Privately Held**
WEB: www.respondsystems.com
SIC: 3845 8041 Laser systems & equipment, medical; offices & clinics of chiropractors

(G-642)
ROBIN REED LTD LLC
175 E Main St (06405-3734)
PHONE 203 481-6378
Philip Schilke, *Principal*
EMP: 2 **EST:** 2007
SALES (est): 225.5K **Privately Held**
SIC: 3648 Lighting equipment

(G-643)
ROBINSON TAPE & LABEL INC
32 Park Dr E Ste 1 (06405-6524)
PHONE 203 481-5581
Edward A Pepe, *President*
Dennis Smith, *Vice Pres*
Dawn Sterns, *Shareholder*
Beth Kinney, *Administration*
EMP: 20
SQ FT: 11,000
SALES (est): 5MM **Privately Held**
WEB: www.robinsontapeandlabel.com
SIC: 2672 Labels (unprinted), gummed: made from purchased materials

(G-644)
ROSTRA TOOL COMPANY
Also Called: Sargent Quality Tools
30 E Industrial Rd (06405-6507)
PHONE 203 488-8665
Michael Sunter, *President*
Richard A Steiner, *President*
Pat Tropeano, *Vice Pres*
▲ **EMP:** 44
SQ FT: 22,000
SALES (est): 8.9MM **Privately Held**
WEB: www.rostratool.com
SIC: 3423 Hand & edge tools
PA: Rostra Technologies, Inc
2519 Dana Dr
Laurinburg NC 28352

(G-645)
S & V SCREEN PRINTING
288 E Main St Apt 4 (06405-3129)
PHONE 203 208-3112
Ralph Spaduzzi, *Principal*
EMP: 2 **EST:** 2008
SALES (est): 123.2K **Privately Held**
SIC: 2759 Screen printing

(G-646)
SANTORINI BREEZE LLC
374 E Main St (06405-2938)
PHONE 203 640-3431
Konstantinos Sousoulas,
EMP: 6 **EST:** 2016
SALES (est): 485.6K **Privately Held**
SIC: 2037 Frozen fruits & vegetables

(G-647)
SAPHLUX INC
4 Pin Oak Dr (06405-6506)
PHONE 475 221-8981
EMP: 6 **EST:** 2014
SQ FT: 8,000
SALES: 100K **Privately Held**
SIC: 3674 Wafers (semiconductor devices)

(G-648)
SCENIC ROUTE CANDLE CO LLC
67 S Montowese St (06405-5221)
PHONE 203 606-7300
Erica Rice, *Principal*
EMP: 2
SALES (est): 64.5K **Privately Held**
SIC: 3999 Candles

(G-649)
SEABUZZ BOATWORKS
15 Swift St (06405-4528)
PHONE 203 483-4576
EMP: 2
SALES (est): 212.7K **Privately Held**
SIC: 3732 Boat building & repairing

(G-650)
SEMCO INSTRUMENTS INC (DH)
Also Called: Harcosemco
186 Cedar St (06405-6011)
PHONE 661 257-2000
Vincent Sandoval, *CEO*
Michael G Moore, *President*
Deanne Davis, *Senior Buyer*
Matthew Pitcher, *Buyer*
EMP: 177
SQ FT: 38,000
SALES (est): 65.3MM
SALES (corp-wide): 3.8B **Publicly Held**
WEB: www.semcoinstruments.com
SIC: 3829 Thermometers & temperature sensors

(G-651)
SEMCO INSTRUMENTS INC
Also Called: Harcosemco
186 Cedar St (06405-6011)
PHONE 661 362-6117
Theresa V Von Szilassy, *Manager*
EMP: 3
SALES (corp-wide): 3.8B **Publicly Held**
WEB: www.semcoinstruments.com
SIC: 3829 Measuring & controlling devices
HQ: Semco Instruments, Inc.
186 Cedar St
Branford CT 06405
661 257-2000

(G-652)
SIGNS BY AUTOGRAFIX
7 Svea Ave (06405-3724)
PHONE 203 481-6502
John Miller, *Owner*
Heidi Miller, *Co-Owner*
EMP: 4
SQ FT: 3,000
SALES: 350K **Privately Held**
SIC: 3993 Signs, not made in custom sign painting shops

(G-653)
SMOOTHIE KING
847 W Main St Ste 3 (06405-3456)
PHONE 203 208-4098
EMP: 1 **EST:** 2016
SALES (est): 23.9K **Privately Held**
SIC: 5499 2024 Beverage stores; ice cream & frozen desserts

(G-654)
SOUTHERN NENG ULTRAVIOLET INC
Also Called: Southern Neng Ultraviolet Co
55029 E Main St (06405)
PHONE 203 483-5810
Ronald Paolella, *President*
Jean Farricilli, *Admin Sec*
EMP: 6 **EST:** 1980
SQ FT: 5,000
SALES (est): 993.8K **Privately Held**
SIC: 3641 Electric lamps & parts for specialized applications; ultraviolet lamps

(G-655)
STAMLER PUBLISHING COMPANY
Also Called: Highway Vehicle/Safety Report
178 Thimble Island Rd (06405-5727)
P.O. Box 3367 (06405-1967)
PHONE 203 488-9808
S Paul Stamler, *President*
EMP: 4
SQ FT: 1,000
SALES (est): 328.3K **Privately Held**
SIC: 2741 2731 Miscellaneous publishing; book publishing

(G-656)
STATEWIDE SHEET METAL LLC
92 Sunny Meadow Rd (06405-4007)
P.O. Box 110120, Trumbull (06611-0120)
PHONE 203 315-1159
Mark Miller, *Principal*
EMP: 2 **EST:** 2001
SALES (est): 290.8K **Privately Held**
SIC: 3444 Sheet metal specialties, not stamped

(G-657)
STERLING MATERIALS LLC
17 Tanglewood Dr (06405-3355)
PHONE 203 315-6619
Suzanne Hopkins, *Principal*
EMP: 5 **EST:** 2011
SALES (est): 363.7K **Privately Held**
SIC: 3273 Ready-mixed concrete

(G-658)
STONY CREEK LIQUOR LLC
Also Called: Stony Creek Package Store
3 Thimble Island Rd (06405-5720)
P.O. Box 3145 (06405-1745)
PHONE 203 488-3318
Laura Richter,
EMP: 2
SALES: 650K **Privately Held**
SIC: 5921 7372 Liquor stores; application computer software

(G-659)
STONY CREEK QUARRY CORPORATION
7 Business Park Dr Ste A (06405-2926)
PHONE 203 483-3904
Doug Anderson, *President*
Bill Gaunt, *Treasurer*
William E Gaunt Jr, *Treasurer*
EMP: 9
SALES (est): 750K **Privately Held**
SIC: 1411 Granite, dimension-quarrying

(G-660)
TANGEN BIOSCIENCES INC
780r E Main St Ste 1 (06405)
PHONE 203 433-4045
John Nobile, *CEO*
Richard Carroll, *Vice Pres*
Brian Chirico, *Vice Pres*
John Davidson, *Vice Pres*
EMP: 2
SQ FT: 2,700
SALES (est): 245.6K **Privately Held**
SIC: 3841 Diagnostic apparatus, medical

(G-661)
TECHNOSOFT SOLUTIONS INC
87 Florence Rd Unit 1a (06405-4247)
P.O. Box 4668, New York NY (10163-4668)
PHONE 203 676-8299
Anis Siddiqy, *President*
John Chandler, *Vice Pres*
Jorgen Dahl, *Software Engr*
EMP: 25
SALES (est): 1MM **Privately Held**
SIC: 7371 7372 Computer software systems analysis & design, custom; computer software development & applications; computer software writing services; business oriented computer software

(G-662)
TEK-MOTIVE INC
171 Turtle Bay Dr (06405-4902)
PHONE 203 468-2224
Ronald Moalli, *CEO*
Thomas Moalli, *President*
Carol Maolli, *Vice Pres*
Angela R Moalli, *Vice Pres*
Richard Moalli, *Vice Pres*
EMP: 65
SALES (est): 18.3MM **Privately Held**
SIC: 5013 3714 3499 Automotive supplies & parts; motor vehicle brake systems & parts; friction material, made from powdered metal

(G-663)
THIMBLE ISLAND BREWING COMPANY
16 Business Park Dr (06405-2924)
PHONE 203 208-2827
Justin Gargano, *President*
EMP: 25 **EST:** 2011
SALES (est): 312.9K **Privately Held**
SIC: 5813 2082 Bars & lounges; near beer

(G-664)
TOTAL CONCEPT TOOL INC
2 Research Dr Ste 1 (06405-2858)
PHONE 203 483-1130
Albert Mirto, *President*
Jennifer Mirto, *Vice Pres*
EMP: 8
SALES (est): 1MM **Privately Held**
SIC: 3544 3599 Special dies & tools; machine shop, jobbing & repair

(G-665)
VERTICAL DEVELOPMENT LLC
20 Commercial St (06405-2801)
PHONE 203 208-0806
Christopher Jardine, *Mng Member*
EMP: 1
SALES (est): 110K **Privately Held**
SIC: 2591 Blinds vertical

(G-666)
VIBRASCIENCE INC
186 N Main St (06405-3021)
PHONE 203 483-6113
Joe Fattore, *President*
Martha Fattore, *Admin Sec*
EMP: 5
SQ FT: 2,500
SALES (est): 1MM **Privately Held**
WEB: www.vibrasciences.com
SIC: 3086 5033 5065 Insulation or cushioning material, foamed plastic; insulation materials; sound equipment, electronic

(G-667)
VOLPE CABLE CORPORATION
201 Linden Ave (06405-5123)
PHONE 203 623-1818
Frank Volpe, *CEO*
Dennis Flanders, *Sales Dir*
▲ **EMP:** 115
SALES (est): 21.3MM **Privately Held**
WEB: www.ezform.com
SIC: 3357 Coaxial cable, nonferrous

(G-668)
WALLINGFORD INDUSTRIES INC
31 Business Park Dr Ste 3 (06405-2977)
PHONE 203 481-0359
Charles Weber Jr, *President*
Vincea Weber, *Vice Pres*
Carol Weber, *Admin Sec*
EMP: 10 **EST:** 1947
SQ FT: 15,000
SALES (est): 1.7MM **Privately Held**
SIC: 3599 Machine & other job shop work

(G-669)
WALLINGFORD PRTG BUS FORMS INC
758 E Main St (06405-2918)
PHONE 203 481-1911
Jennifer Bright, *President*
Thomas Bright, *Vice Pres*
EMP: 10
SQ FT: 5,500
SALES (est): 1.3MM **Privately Held**
WEB: www.wallprint.com
SIC: 2761 5111 2759 Manifold business forms; printing & writing paper; commercial printing

(G-670)
WEB CHARITY LLC
36 Park Dr E (06405-6522)
PHONE 203 481-7600
EMP: 2 **EST:** 2001
SALES (est): 160K **Privately Held**
SIC: 7372 Prepackaged Software Services

(G-671)
WEST ROCK ART GLASS INC
11 Sycamore Way Ste 106 (06405-6553)
PHONE 203 488-8225

Roger Gandelman, *Owner*
EMP: 2
SALES (est): 200K **Privately Held**
SIC: 3229 Pressed & blown glass

(G-672)
WEZENSKI WOODWORKING
214 Crosswoods Rd (06405-5802)
PHONE...................203 488-3255
Paul Wezenski, *Principal*
EMP: 3
SALES (est): 241.7K **Privately Held**
SIC: 2431 Millwork

(G-673)
WFS EARTH MATERIALSI LLC
11 Business Park Dr (06405-2958)
PHONE...................203 488-2055
Douglas Anderson, *Mng Member*
EMP: 5
SQ FT: 2,500
SALES (est): 1.5MM **Privately Held**
SIC: 1442 Sand mining

(G-674)
WILLIAMS WALTER OVRHD DOOR LLC
10 Vineyard Rd (06405-6246)
PHONE...................203 488-8620
Glen K Newell, *President*
EMP: 3
SALES: 360K **Privately Held**
SIC: 5211 3699 Doors, wood or metal, except storm; door opening & closing devices, electrical

(G-675)
WILSON ARMS COMPANY
97 Leetes Island Rd 101 (06405-3308)
PHONE...................203 488-7297
Hugo E Vivero, *President*
EMP: 18 **EST:** 1954
SQ FT: 15,000
SALES (est): 5MM **Privately Held**
SIC: 3484 Rifles or rifle parts, 30 mm. & below

(G-676)
WINDOW PDTS AWNGS BLIND SHADE
11 Business Park Dr (06405-2958)
PHONE...................203 481-9772
Blake Cramer, *President*
Robert Blake Cramer, *Corp Secy*
Genny Proto, *Materials Mgr*
Mark Lyon, *Controller*
Mark Harris, *Manager*
EMP: 4
SALES (est): 519.2K **Privately Held**
WEB: www.windowproductsct.com
SIC: 5999 5719 5023 2394 Awnings; window furnishings; venetian blinds; vertical blinds; window shades; vertical blinds; canvas awnings & canopies

(G-677)
XCEL FUEL
501 Main St (06405-3526)
PHONE...................203 481-4510
EMP: 4
SALES (est): 203.9K **Privately Held**
SIC: 2869 Fuels

Bridgeport
Fairfield County

(G-678)
24 HOURS DESIGN & PRINT
195 Garden Dr (06606-4427)
PHONE...................347 350-4484
Francine Louis, *Principal*
EMP: 2
SALES (est): 83.9K **Privately Held**
SIC: 2752 Commercial printing, lithographic

(G-679)
A & S PHARMACEUTICAL CORP
480 Barnum Ave Ste 3 (06608-2459)
P.O. Box 2005 (06608-0005)
PHONE...................203 368-2538
Arnold Lewis, *Ch of Bd*
Seth Lewis, *Treasurer*
◆ **EMP:** 50 **EST:** 1971
SQ FT: 40,000
SALES (est): 7.6MM **Privately Held**
SIC: 2834 Pharmaceutical preparations

(G-680)
A J R INC
Also Called: Interface Technology
67 Poland St (06605-3266)
PHONE...................203 384-0400
John Vaughan, *President*
Joe Saja, *Opers Mgr*
Lidia Sotomayor, *Admin Asst*
EMP: 10
SQ FT: 14,000
SALES (est): 1.8MM **Privately Held**
SIC: 3357 Coaxial cable, nonferrous

(G-681)
ACCUMOLD TECHNOLOGIES INC
52 Carroll Ave (06607-2317)
PHONE...................203 384-9256
Joseph Fiorini, *President*
Ted Deandrade, *Admin Sec*
EMP: 6
SQ FT: 5,000
SALES (est): 680K **Privately Held**
SIC: 3089 Injection molded finished plastic products; molding primary plastic

(G-682)
ACSON TOOL COMPANY
62 Carroll Ave (06607-2317)
PHONE...................203 334-8050
David Deandrade, *President*
Antro Deandrade, *Vice Pres*
EMP: 11 **EST:** 1951
SALES (est): 1.3MM **Privately Held**
SIC: 3544 Dies, plastics forming; special dies & tools

(G-683)
ADAM BISSON
15 Janet Cir Unit A (06606-2661)
PHONE...................203 861-8271
Adam Bisson, *Administration*
EMP: 2
SALES (est): 88.3K **Privately Held**
SIC: 3669 Communications equipment

(G-684)
ADVANCE HEAT TREATING CO
147 West Ave (06604)
PHONE...................203 380-8898
EMP: 3
SQ FT: 1,250
SALES (est): 208.7K **Privately Held**
SIC: 3398 Metal heat treating

(G-685)
ALLOY ENGINEERING CO INC (PA)
304 Seaview Ave (06607-2434)
PHONE...................203 366-5253
Kris Lorch, *President*
Fred Lorch, *Vice Pres*
Ken Popadic, *Traffic Dir*
▲ **EMP:** 42 **EST:** 1958
SQ FT: 28,800
SALES (est): 4.3MM **Privately Held**
WEB: www.thermowells.com
SIC: 3822 3823 Auto controls regulating residntl & coml environmt & applncs; industrial instrmnts msrmnt display/control process variable

(G-686)
ALLOY ENGINEERING CO INC
224 Dekalb Ave (06607)
PHONE...................203 366-5253
Kris Lorch, *Branch Mgr*
EMP: 2
SALES (corp-wide): 4.3MM **Privately Held**
SIC: 3822 Auto controls regulating residntl & coml environmt & applncs
PA: Alloy Engineering Co., Inc.
304 Seaview Ave
Bridgeport CT 06607
203 366-5253

(G-687)
ALPHA-CORE CORP
915 Pembroke St (06608-2406)
PHONE...................203 335-6805
EMP: 2
SALES (est): 88.3K **Privately Held**
SIC: 3612 Transformers, except electric

(G-688)
ALTERNATIVE PROSTHETIC SVCS
Also Called: A P S
191 Bennett St (06605-2902)
PHONE...................203 367-1212
Michael Curtin, *President*
EMP: 3
SALES (est): 450K **Privately Held**
SIC: 3842 Prosthetic appliances

(G-689)
ALUMINUM FINISHING COMPANY INC
1575 Railroad Ave (06605-2031)
P.O. Box 3379 (06605-0379)
PHONE...................203 333-1690
Edward Sivri, *President*
EMP: 26
SALES: 2.5MM **Privately Held**
SIC: 3471 Anodizing (plating) of metals or formed products

(G-690)
AMERICAN AUTOMATION
540 Barnum Ave (06608-2447)
PHONE...................203 556-7839
Brian Sutherland,
EMP: 2
SALES (est): 85.2K **Privately Held**
SIC: 3541 Machine tool replacement & repair parts, metal cutting types

(G-691)
AMERICAN FNSHG SPECIALISTS INC
40 Cowles St (06607-2101)
PHONE...................203 367-0663
Tim Calahan, *President*
EMP: 6
SALES (est): 733.1K **Privately Held**
SIC: 3599 Machine shop, jobbing & repair

(G-692)
AMERICAN HYDROGEN NORTHEAST
520 Savoy St (06606-4125)
PHONE...................203 449-4614
Roy E McAlister, *Principal*
Daniel J Valentine, *Treasurer*
EMP: 40
SALES (est): 1.7MM **Privately Held**
SIC: 3999 Manufacturing industries

(G-693)
AMERICAN MARKETING GROUP INC
Also Called: Small Black Dog
51 Crescent Ave (06608-2249)
PHONE...................203 367-2378
Eugene Haba Jr, *President*
Eugene Haba Sr, *Treasurer*
EMP: 5
SQ FT: 4,000
SALES (est): 480K **Privately Held**
SIC: 8742 2393 Management consulting services; canvas bags

(G-694)
AMERICAN MOLDED PRODUCTS INC
130 Front St (06605-5109)
PHONE...................203 333-0183
Mehmed Ramic, *President*
Paul Cipriono Taulo, *Vice Pres*
EMP: 10
SQ FT: 4,800
SALES (est): 1.3MM **Privately Held**
WEB: www.americanmoldedproducts.com
SIC: 3089 3544 Injection molding of plastics; industrial molds

(G-695)
AMERICAN-DIGITAL LLC
Also Called: Fedex Authorized Ship Center
135 Clarence St (06608-2227)
PHONE...................203 838-0148
Larry Kaminski,
EMP: 4
SALES (est): 215.9K **Privately Held**
SIC: 4783 3695 5113 7371 Packing goods for shipping; computer software tape & disks: blank, rigid & floppy; shipping supplies; computer software development; software training, computer

(G-696)
AMODEX PRODUCTS INC
1354 State St (06605-2003)
P.O. Box 3332 (06605-0332)
PHONE...................203 335-1255
Sylvia Fatse, *President*
Beverlee F Dacey, *Vice Pres*
Peter Dacey, *Opers Staff*
Nicolas Dacey, *Info Tech Dir*
James Fatse, *Admin Sec*
EMP: 30 **EST:** 1957
SQ FT: 1,500
SALES (est): 6.8MM **Privately Held**
SIC: 2842 2844 2841 Stain removers; cosmetic preparations; soap: granulated, liquid, cake, flaked or chip

(G-697)
APEX CSTM CABINETRY WDWKG LLC
50 Lansing Pl (06606-2908)
PHONE...................203 396-0496
Oral McDonald, *Owner*
EMP: 1
SALES (est): 65.6K **Privately Held**
SIC: 2431 Millwork

(G-698)
APPAREL SOLUTIONS INCORPORATED
Also Called: Asi - A Soft Idea
67 Poland St Ste 4 (06605-3266)
PHONE...................203 226-8600
Claudia Vargish, *President*
Ed Steinglass, *CFO*
▲ **EMP:** 2
SALES (est): 265K **Privately Held**
SIC: 2231 Blankets & blanketings: wool or similar fibers

(G-699)
ARCADE TECHNOLOGY LLC
Also Called: A R C O
38 Union Ave (06607-2336)
PHONE...................203 366-3871
Steve Pepe, *Mng Member*
William Rhone,
EMP: 50
SQ FT: 45,000
SALES: 5.6MM **Privately Held**
SIC: 3469 3644 3599 3544 Stamping metal for the trade; electric outlet, switch & fuse boxes; outlet boxes (electric wiring devices); electric conduits & fittings; electrical discharge machining (EDM); special dies, tools, jigs & fixtures

(G-700)
ARCHITECTURAL STONE GROUP LLC
9 Island Brook Ave (06606-5113)
PHONE...................203 494-5451
Tom Astram, *Principal*
EMP: 6
SALES (est): 397.8K **Privately Held**
SIC: 3281 Cut stone & stone products

(G-701)
AREPAS LA ORQUIDEA
1163 E Main St (06608-1620)
PHONE...................203 275-8478
EMP: 1
SALES (est): 10.2K **Privately Held**
SIC: 3421 Table & food cutlery, including butchers'

(G-702)
ART CRAFT SIGNS
1697 Barnum Ave (06610-3210)
PHONE...................203 212-3980
EMP: 1 **EST:** 2010

GEOGRAPHIC SECTION
Bridgeport - Fairfield County (G-732)

SALES (est): 78.1K **Privately Held**
SIC: 3993 Signs & advertising specialties

(G-703)
ARTIST AND CRAFTSMAN
1001 Main St (06604-4200)
PHONE.................................203 330-0459
Steve Kenney, *Principal*
EMP: 1
SALES (est): 43K **Privately Held**
SIC: 5945 5231 3229 Arts & crafts supplies; paint & painting supplies; art, decorative & novelty glassware

(G-704)
ARTISTA STUDIO MONUMENT
500 Bostwick Ave (06605-2440)
PHONE.................................203 333-9224
James V Bria, *Principal*
EMP: 5 EST: 2016
SALES (est): 82.2K **Privately Held**
SIC: 5999 3272 Monuments, finished to custom order; monuments & grave markers, except terrazo

(G-705)
AUDUBON COPY SHPPE OF FIRFIELD
540 Barnum Ave Ste 4 (06608-2461)
PHONE.................................203 259-4311
Robert Love, *President*
Linda Love, *Vice Pres*
EMP: 5
SQ FT: 1,800
SALES (est): 636K **Privately Held**
SIC: 2752 7334 2741 Commercial printing, offset; photocopying & duplicating services; miscellaneous publishing

(G-706)
B & C SAND & GRAVEL COMPANY
412 Housatonic Ave (06604-3326)
PHONE.................................203 335-6640
Edward T Burns, *Owner*
EMP: 5
SALES (est): 525.5K **Privately Held**
SIC: 1442 Construction sand & gravel

(G-707)
B & E JUICES INC
Also Called: Snapple Juices
550 Knowlton St (06608-1816)
PHONE.................................203 333-1802
Robert Clyne, *President*
Rene Ferellec, *Vice Pres*
Anita Allen, *Manager*
EMP: 20
SQ FT: 40,000
SALES (est): 6.7MM **Privately Held**
SIC: 2086 Bottled & canned soft drinks

(G-708)
BCT-042 LLC
42 Dean Pl (06610-1639)
PHONE.................................203 331-0008
EMP: 2
SALES (est): 83.9K **Privately Held**
SIC: 2752 Commercial printing, lithographic

(G-709)
BECKSON MANUFACTURING INC (PA)
165 Holland Ave (06605-2136)
P.O. Box 3336 (06605-0336)
PHONE.................................203 366-3644
Frank Sbeckerer, *President*
Eloise Beckerer, *Vice Pres*
Frank S Beckerer Jr, *Treasurer*
◆ EMP: 30
SQ FT: 15,000
SALES (est): 8.3MM **Privately Held**
WEB: www.becksonmfg.com
SIC: 3561 3429 3083 Pumps & pumping equipment; marine hardware; laminated plastics plate & sheet

(G-710)
BEN BAENA & SON
Also Called: Baena Ben & Matthew
218 Charles St (06606-5661)
PHONE.................................203 334-8568
Matthew Baena, *Partner*
Irene Baena Robinson, *Partner*

EMP: 6 EST: 1947
SQ FT: 2,400
SALES: 700K **Privately Held**
SIC: 2591 7641 Drapery hardware & blinds & shades; reupholstery

(G-711)
BEYOND FOREVER CABINETRY LLC
10 Gurdon St (06606-5029)
PHONE.................................203 427-7968
EMP: 1
SALES (est): 53.7K **Privately Held**
SIC: 2434 Wood kitchen cabinets

(G-712)
BIG CITY STRING CO
820 Queen St (06606-3216)
P.O. Box 6366 (06606-0366)
PHONE.................................203 371-8117
Leo Brogan, *Owner*
EMP: 1
SALES (est): 103K **Privately Held**
SIC: 3931 Musical instruments

(G-713)
BL PRINTING SHOP
Also Called: Dart Products Screen Printing
3442 Fairfield Ave (06605-3226)
PHONE.................................203 334-7779
Richard L Testani, *President*
Lisa Santos, *President*
Michelle Testani, *Vice Pres*
EMP: 3 EST: 1972
SQ FT: 5,000
SALES (est): 200K **Privately Held**
SIC: 2759 Screen printing

(G-714)
BLACK ROCK TECH GROUP LLC
211 State St Ste 203 (06604-4824)
PHONE.................................203 916-7200
Chris Davis, *Director*
John East,
EMP: 12
SQ FT: 3,000
SALES (est): 4.4MM **Privately Held**
SIC: 3571 Electronic computers

(G-715)
BOLT CUSTOM & MFG LLC
307 Remington St (06610-2212)
PHONE.................................203 685-1840
Michael Banda, *Owner*
EMP: 1
SALES (est): 39.6K **Privately Held**
SIC: 3999 Manufacturing industries

(G-716)
BONNEY-GEE CUISINES
957 Platt St (06606-3762)
PHONE.................................203 372-3385
Clinton Jerome Gee Sr, *Owner*
EMP: 2
SALES (est): 10K **Privately Held**
SIC: 2099 Food preparations

(G-717)
BOSTON ENDO-SURGICAL TECH LLC
Also Called: Pep Be-St
1146 Barnum Ave (06610-2705)
PHONE.................................203 336-6479
Alan M Huffenus, *CEO*
Kenneth Lisk, *President*
EMP: 98 EST: 2012
SALES (est): 2.4MM
SALES (corp-wide): 770.6MM **Publicly Held**
SIC: 3841 5047 Surgical & medical instruments; surgical equipment & supplies
HQ: Precision Engineered Products Llc
110 Frank Mossberg Dr
Attleboro MA 02703
508 226-5600

(G-718)
BRI METAL WORKS INC
105 Island Brook Ave (06610-5132)
P.O. Box 5540 (06610-0540)
PHONE.................................203 368-1649
Jeffrey Mc Cathron, *President*
Joseph Mc Cathron, *Chairman*
Shirley Mc Cathron, *Treasurer*

Patricia Mc Cathron, *Admin Sec*
EMP: 6
SQ FT: 67,000
SALES (est): 799K **Privately Held**
SIC: 3441 7699 Fabricated structural metal; boiler repair shop

(G-719)
BRIDGEPORT BOATWORK INC (PA)
837 Seaview Ave (06607-1607)
PHONE.................................860 536-9651
Harry Boardsen, *President*
Melissa Howard, *Bookkeeper*
EMP: 5
SQ FT: 50,000
SALES: 5MM **Privately Held**
SIC: 3731 Shipbuilding & repairing

(G-720)
BRIDGEPORT DENTAL LLC
633 Clinton Ave (06605-1711)
PHONE.................................203 384-2261
Michael Caserta, *President*
EMP: 2
SALES (est): 257.9K **Privately Held**
SIC: 3843 8021 Enamels, dentists'; dental clinics & offices

(G-721)
BRIDGEPORT INSULATED WIRE CO (PA)
51 Brookfield Ave (06610-3004)
P.O. Box 5217 (06610-0217)
PHONE.................................203 333-3191
Christopher Pelletier, *CEO*
Ronald A Pelletier, *Chairman*
Milton L Cohn, *Admin Sec*
EMP: 30
SQ FT: 16,000
SALES (est): 5.6MM **Privately Held**
SIC: 3357 3496 3315 Nonferrous wire-drawing & insulating; miscellaneous fabricated wire products; steel wire & related products

(G-722)
BRIDGEPORT PROC & MFG LLC
155 Davenport St (06607)
PHONE.................................203 612-7733
Moises R Prieto, *Mng Member*
Christopher J Taylor, *Manager*
EMP: 6
SALES (est): 235.9K **Privately Held**
SIC: 3999 Barber & beauty shop equipment

(G-723)
BRIDGEPORT TL & STAMPING CORP
35 Burr Ct (06605-2204)
PHONE.................................203 336-2501
Julius Kish, *President*
Rolf Schmidt, *Vice Pres*
Sharon Kish, *Admin Sec*
Darlene Kish, *Asst Sec*
EMP: 21 EST: 1939
SQ FT: 14,000
SALES (est): 3.8MM **Privately Held**
SIC: 3469 3544 Stamping metal for the trade; special dies & tools

(G-724)
BRODY PRINTING COMPANY INC
265 Central Ave (06607-2495)
PHONE.................................203 384-9313
Karen Brody Collett, *CEO*
Preseo Bonacci, *President*
EMP: 18 EST: 1971
SQ FT: 13,500
SALES (est): 3.3MM **Privately Held**
WEB: www.brodyprinting.com
SIC: 2752 Commercial printing, offset

(G-725)
BUDDY-MENTOR INC
155 Brewster St Apt 4b (06605-3109)
PHONE.................................203 258-3871
EMP: 2 EST: 2018
SALES (est): 73.4K **Privately Held**
SIC: 3483 Ammunition, except for small arms

(G-726)
BUSWELL MANUFACTURING CO INC
229 Merriam St (06604-2915)
PHONE.................................203 334-6069
Norman Buecher, *President*
Mildred Fitch, *Vice Pres*
Lisa Chormanski, *Office Mgr*
Chris Minotti, *Manager*
EMP: 10
SQ FT: 9,000
SALES: 1.8MM **Privately Held**
WEB: www.buswellmfg.com
SIC: 3562 3599 Ball bearings & parts; machine shop, jobbing & repair

(G-727)
BYRNE WOODWORKING INC
170 Herbert St (06604-2903)
PHONE.................................203 953-3205
Frank Byrne, *Principal*
EMP: 4
SALES (est): 486K **Privately Held**
SIC: 2431 Millwork

(G-728)
CALZONE LTD (PA)
Also Called: Calzone Case Company
225 Black Rock Ave (06605-1204)
PHONE.................................203 367-5766
Joseph Edward Calzone III, *President*
Donald Sessions, *General Mgr*
Joseph E Calzone Jr, *Corp Secy*
Vincent James Calzone, *Vice Pres*
Stephen Bajda, *Controller*
▲ EMP: 50 EST: 1979
SQ FT: 26,000
SALES (est): 19.5MM **Privately Held**
WEB: www.calzonecase.com
SIC: 3161 Cases, carrying; musical instrument cases

(G-729)
CARDINAL SHEHAN CENTER INC
1494 Main St (06604-3600)
PHONE.................................203 336-4468
Fletcher Thompson, *CFO*
Toni Boyd, *Finance*
Terrance O'Connor, *Director*
Christine Bianchi, *Program Dir*
Dj Ellis, *Program Dir*
EMP: 30
SALES: 1.7MM **Privately Held**
WEB: www.shehancenter.org
SIC: 3999 Education aids, devices & supplies

(G-730)
CARISMO PRODUCTIONS
150 Scofield Ave (06605-2925)
PHONE.................................203 334-8469
EMP: 2 EST: 2016
SALES (est): 86K **Privately Held**
SIC: 3724 Aircraft Engines And Engine Parts

(G-731)
CASCO PRODUCTS CORPORATION (HQ)
1000 Lafayette Blvd # 100 (06604-4725)
PHONE.................................203 922-3200
Scott Brown, *General Mgr*
Robert Andrea, *Vice Pres*
Mike Dietz, *Vice Pres*
Chris Rountos, *Engrg Dir*
James Langelotti, *Treasurer*
▲ EMP: 15
SQ FT: 168,000
SALES (est): 22.9MM
SALES (corp-wide): 8.2B **Publicly Held**
WEB: www.cascoglobal.com
SIC: 3714 Motor vehicle electrical equipment
PA: Amphenol Corporation
358 Hall Ave
Wallingford CT 06492
203 265-8900

(G-732)
CEDAR WOODWORKING
65 Hawley Ave (06606-5035)
PHONE.................................203 335-4108
Kal Dager, *Owner*
EMP: 2

Bridgeport - Fairfield County (G-733)

SALES (est): 214.9K **Privately Held**
SIC: 2431 Millwork

(G-733)
CHRISTOPOULOS DESIGNS INC
195 Dewey St (06605-2114)
PHONE....................203 576-1110
George Christopoulos, *President*
Nicholas Daniolos, *Treasurer*
EMP: 10
SQ FT: 10,000
SALES: 1.4MM **Privately Held**
WEB: www.christopoulosdesigns.com
SIC: 2511 2517 2434 End tables: wood; television cabinets, wood; vanities, bathroom: wood

(G-734)
CITY CEMENT BLOCK-DEL CORP INC
83 North Ave (06606-5120)
PHONE....................203 334-0702
Russell F Delvento, *President*
Stephen V Delvento Sr, *Vice Pres*
Robert F Delvento Sr, *Admin Sec*
EMP: 6 **EST:** 1880
SQ FT: 15,000
SALES (est): 561.1K
SALES (corp-wide): 2MM **Privately Held**
SIC: 3271 Blocks, concrete or cinder: standard
PA: Delvento, Inc.
   83 North Ave
   Bridgeport CT 06606
   203 371-7279

(G-735)
CJS EMBROIDERY LLC
119 Lee Ave (06605-1561)
PHONE....................203 650-9066
Carmelo Jiminez, *President*
EMP: 1
SALES (est): 61.3K **Privately Held**
SIC: 2395 Embroidery & art needlework

(G-736)
CLIFFSIDE ENTERTAINMENT LLC
1355 Fairfield Ave (06605-1712)
PHONE....................203 290-7484
Sheron Rose, *Principal*
Anthony Burnett, *Principal*
EMP: 1
SALES (est): 42.8K **Privately Held**
SIC: 7929 5947 7372 6321 Entertainers & entertainment groups; trading cards: baseball or other sports, entertainment, etc.; home entertainment computer software; mutual accident & health associations;

(G-737)
COASTAL PALLET CORPORATION
135 E Washington Ave (06604-3607)
PHONE....................203 333-1892
Peter Standish, *President*
EMP: 25
SQ FT: 15,000
SALES: 3MM **Privately Held**
WEB: www.coastalpallet.com
SIC: 2448 2441 Pallets, wood; nailed wood boxes & shook

(G-738)
COMEX MACHINERY
Also Called: Industrial Prcision Components
145 Front St (06606-5108)
PHONE....................203 334-2196
Paul Huber, *President*
Theodore Jeffries, *Vice Pres*
EMP: 5
SQ FT: 20,000
SALES (est): 90.3K **Privately Held**
SIC: 3545 3523 Tools & accessories for machine tools; farm machinery & equipment

(G-739)
CONNECTICUT ANODIZING FINSHG
128 Logan St (06607-1930)
PHONE....................203 367-1765
Victor Sinko II, *President*
EMP: 21
SQ FT: 24,000
SALES (est): 2.8MM **Privately Held**
SIC: 3471 Finishing, metals or formed products; anodizing (plating) of metals or formed products

(G-740)
CT MOLDINGS INC
308 Bishop Ave (06610-3055)
PHONE....................203 612-4922
Dariusz A Franek, *President*
Ryszard Klos, *President*
EMP: 2
SQ FT: 12,000
SALES: 100K **Privately Held**
SIC: 3299 2431 3442 3465 Moldings, architectural: plaster of paris; moldings & baseboards, ornamental & trim; moldings & trim, except automobile: metal; moldings or trim, automobile: stamped metal

(G-741)
D ROTONDI LLC
Also Called: Bread Empire
480 Barnum Ave Ste 4 (06608-2459)
PHONE....................505 427-3233
Paola Rotondi, *CEO*
Dominic Rotondi, *COO*
EMP: 2 **EST:** 2014
SQ FT: 2,000
SALES: 15K **Privately Held**
SIC: 5149 2051 Bakery products; bread, cake & related products

(G-742)
DAYBRAKE DONUTS INC
941 Madison Ave (06606-5218)
PHONE....................203 368-4962
Thomas Devaulinius, *President*
EMP: 12
SALES (est): 1.1MM **Privately Held**
SIC: 2051 5812 Doughnuts, except frozen; coffee shop

(G-743)
DECORATOR SERVICES INC
25 Wells St Ste 1 (06604-2800)
PHONE....................203 384-8144
Charles Musante, *President*
Frances Musante, *Admin Sec*
EMP: 22
SQ FT: 9,500
SALES (est): 1.8MM **Privately Held**
SIC: 2391 2591 Draperies, plastic & textile: from purchased materials; blinds vertical

(G-744)
DELCON INDUSTRIES
480 Barnum Ave Ste 4 (06608-2459)
PHONE....................203 540-5757
EMP: 2
SALES (est): 95.7K **Privately Held**
SIC: 3999 Manufacturing industries

(G-745)
DELCON INDUSTRIES LLC
560 N Washington Ave # 4 (06604-2900)
PHONE....................203 331-9720
Ronald Delmonico, *Principal*
EMP: 3
SALES (est): 200.6K **Privately Held**
SIC: 3999 Manufacturing industries

(G-746)
DELTA-RAY CORP
805 Housatonic Ave (06604-2807)
PHONE....................203 367-6910
John Ray, *President*
John M Ray, *President*
Pablo Casiano, *Engineer*
EMP: 1
SQ FT: 12,000
SALES (est): 130K **Privately Held**
SIC: 3599 Machine shop, jobbing & repair

(G-747)
DELTA-RAY INDUSTRIES INC
805 Housatonic Ave (06604-2807)
PHONE....................203 367-9903
John M Ray, *President*
Slawek Karpinski, *Engineer*
EMP: 10
SALES (est): 2.4MM **Privately Held**
SIC: 3728 Research & dev by manuf., aircraft parts & auxiliary equip

(G-748)
DELVENTO INC (PA)
Also Called: Henderson Trumbull Supply Co
83 North Ave (06606-5120)
PHONE....................203 371-7279
Robert F Delvento Sr, *President*
Stephen Polifka, *Vice Pres*
Arlene Delvento, *Treasurer*
Russell Delvento, *Admin Sec*
EMP: 12
SQ FT: 45,000
SALES (est): 2MM **Privately Held**
SIC: 5211 5031 3271 Lumber & other building materials; building materials, exterior; building materials, interior; concrete block & brick

(G-749)
DEVAR INC
706 Bostwick Ave (06605-2396)
PHONE....................203 368-6751
A James Ruscito, *President*
Marianne Ruscito, *Treasurer*
Anthony J Ruscito, *Director*
EMP: 30
SQ FT: 33,000
SALES (est): 5.6MM **Privately Held**
WEB: www.devarinc.com
SIC: 3625 5084 3823 Electric controls & control accessories, industrial; industrial machinery & equipment; industrial instrmnts msrmnt display/control process variable

(G-750)
DEYULIO SAUSAGE COMPANY LLC
1501 State St (06605-2010)
PHONE....................203 348-1863
Lauren Oxer, *Principal*
Michael Taylor, *Sales Mgr*
Jennifer Oxer, *Manager*
Nicholas J Deyulio,
EMP: 10
SQ FT: 700
SALES (est): 909.6K **Privately Held**
SIC: 2013 Sausages & other prepared meats

(G-751)
DIAMOND HRDWD FLRS OF FAIRFLD
40 Hillside Ave (06604-1446)
PHONE....................203 650-9192
Melitsa Paetropoulos, *Principal*
EMP: 1 **EST:** 2008
SALES (est): 74.1K **Privately Held**
SIC: 2426 1771 1752 Flooring, hardwood; flooring contractor; floor laying & floor work

(G-752)
DIGITAL CHAMELEON LLC
55 Hawley Ave (06606-5035)
PHONE....................203 354-4111
Keith Eschert, *Principal*
EMP: 2
SALES (est): 272.6K **Privately Held**
SIC: 2759 Promotional printing

(G-753)
DIGITAL COPY LLC
3076 Fairfield Ave (06605-3218)
PHONE....................203 540-5181
EMP: 2
SALES (est): 62.9K **Privately Held**
SIC: 7334 2759 Photocopying & duplicating services; publication printing

(G-754)
DJS MOBILE MARINE & POWER EQP
141 Wilmot Ave (06607-1835)
PHONE....................203 331-9010
Dave Ellis, *Owner*
EMP: 1
SALES (est): 135.6K **Privately Held**
WEB: www.djsmarine.com
SIC: 3089 Plastic boats & other marine equipment

(G-755)
DLPUBLSHERS MYSTRYNTRTNMENTLLC
390 Charles St Apt 216 (06606-5677)
PHONE....................203 556-4893
Deshawn Harper,
EMP: 2
SALES (est): 78.8K **Privately Held**
SIC: 2741 7929 7389 Miscellaneous publishing; entertainment service;

(G-756)
DRS NAVAL POWER SYSTEMS INC
141 North Ave (06606-5120)
PHONE....................203 366-5211
Shaune Miller, *Purch Agent*
EMP: 300
SALES (corp-wide): 9.2B **Privately Held**
SIC: 3621 Generators & sets, electric
HQ: Drs Naval Power Systems, Inc
   4265 N 30th St
   Milwaukee WI 53216
   414 875-4314

(G-757)
DRS NAVAL POWER SYSTEMS INC
206 Island Brook Ave (06606-5118)
PHONE....................203 366-5211
Gene Frohman, *President*
Rodney Holt, *Branch Mgr*
EMP: 40
SALES (corp-wide): 9.2B **Privately Held**
WEB: www.engineeredsupport.com
SIC: 3621 Generators & sets, electric
HQ: Drs Naval Power Systems, Inc
   4265 N 30th St
   Milwaukee WI 53216
   414 875-4314

(G-758)
DUPONT DE NEMOURS INC
615 Asylum St (06610-2127)
PHONE....................203 330-6755
EMP: 1
SALES (corp-wide): 85.9B **Publicly Held**
SIC: 2879 Agricultural chemicals
PA: Dupont De Nemours, Inc.
   974 Centre Rd
   Wilmington DE 19805
   302 774-1000

(G-759)
E&S AUTOMOTIVE OPERATIONS LLC
425 Boston Ave (06610-1701)
PHONE....................203 332-4555
Harry Gill, *Owner*
EMP: 3
SALES (est): 312.7K **Privately Held**
SIC: 2869 Fuels

(G-760)
EDCO INDUSTRIES INC
203 Dekalb Ave (06607-2492)
PHONE....................203 333-8982
John Thomas Szalan, *President*
Anne Marie Szalan, *Vice Pres*
▲ **EMP:** 16 **EST:** 1969
SQ FT: 13,500
SALES (est): 2.8MM **Privately Held**
SIC: 3089 5162 Injection molding of plastics; plastics materials

(G-761)
ELECTRICAL MAINTENANCE SVC CO
Also Called: E M S
143 Bennett St (06605-2902)
PHONE....................203 333-6163
David Goodfellow, *President*
R Scott Goodfellow, *Vice Pres*
Johnny Mastri, *Sales Staff*
EMP: 4 **EST:** 1923
SQ FT: 26,000
SALES: 1MM **Privately Held**
WEB: www.electricmaintenance.com
SIC: 5063 7694 5075 Motors, electric; electric motor repair; warm air heating equipment & supplies

GEOGRAPHIC SECTION

(G-762)
EMJ CONTRACTING LLC
695 Beechwood Ave (06605-1664)
PHONE....................475 449-7725
Shenida Westfield,
EMP: 5
SALES (est): 315.1K **Privately Held**
SIC: 1542 3589 Commercial & office building contractors; commercial cleaning equipment

(G-763)
ENGINEERS WELDING LLC
425 Kossuth St (06608-2240)
PHONE....................203 334-2492
Trevor Smith,
Alex Smith,
Kai Smith,
▲ **EMP:** 3
SQ FT: 6,000
SALES: 1.5MM **Privately Held**
SIC: 1799 3441 Welding on site; building components, structural steel

(G-764)
EXCEPTIONAL SCRATCH GAMES LLC
348 Harmony St (06606-3831)
PHONE....................203 526-8696
Pierre Jolicoeur, *Partner*
▼ **EMP:** 2
SALES (est): 90.6K **Privately Held**
SIC: 2796 Platemaking services

(G-765)
EXECUTIVE OFFICE SERVICES INC
2085 Madison Ave (06606-3234)
PHONE....................203 373-1333
Ben Carrara, *Vice Pres*
EMP: 22
SALES (est): 2.8MM **Privately Held**
SIC: 2752 2791 2759 Commercial printing, lithographic; typesetting; commercial printing

(G-766)
EXTRA FUEL
540 Boston Ave (06610-1705)
PHONE....................203 330-0613
Yasmin Mazick, *Principal*
EMP: 3
SALES (est): 243.2K **Privately Held**
SIC: 2869 Fuels

(G-767)
EXTREME FOAM INSULATIONS LLC
47 Scofield Ave (06605-2926)
PHONE....................203 522-2207
Martin Rodriguez, *President*
EMP: 2
SALES (est): 77.4K **Privately Held**
SIC: 3086 Insulation or cushioning material, foamed plastic

(G-768)
FAYERWEATHER PRESS LLC
2 Seabright Ave (06605-3460)
PHONE....................203 367-1601
Bruce Williams, *Principal*
EMP: 1
SALES (est): 44.1K **Privately Held**
SIC: 2741 Miscellaneous publishing

(G-769)
FEROLETO STEEL COMPANY INC (DH)
300 Scofield Ave (06605-2931)
P.O. Box 3344 (06605-0344)
PHONE....................203 366-3263
Robert Siitonen, *President*
Bob Siitonen, *Principal*
Jim Hillas, *Senior VP*
Ronald Penaiti, *Senior VP*
Michael Pierson, *Vice Pres*
▲ **EMP:** 78
SQ FT: 200,000
SALES (est): 12.6MM **Privately Held**
WEB: www.feroletosteel.com
SIC: 3316 Cold-rolled strip or wire; sheet, steel, cold-rolled: from purchased hot-rolled

HQ: Toyota Tsusho America, Inc.
805 3rd Ave Fl 17
New York NY 10022
212 355-3600

(G-770)
FLUTED PARTITION INC (PA)
850 Union Ave (06607-1137)
PHONE....................203 368-2548
Arthur M Vietze Jr, *President*
Rudolph Neidermeir, *Chairman*
Robert Neidermeir, *Vice Pres*
John Rainieri, *Financial Exec*
EMP: 125
SQ FT: 120,000
SALES (est): 20.9MM **Privately Held**
WEB: www.flutedpartition.com
SIC: 2671 2653 2631 Packaging paper & plastics film, coated & laminated; partitions, corrugated: made from purchased materials; paperboard mills

(G-771)
FLUTED PARTITION INC
Cell Pack Div
850 Union Ave (06607-1137)
PHONE....................203 334-3500
Robert Niedermeier, *President*
Rudy Niedermeier, *Manager*
EMP: 11
SALES (corp-wide): 20.9MM **Privately Held**
WEB: www.flutedpartition.com
SIC: 2653 Partitions, corrugated: made from purchased materials
PA: Fluted Partition, Inc.
850 Union Ave
Bridgeport CT 06607
203 368-2548

(G-772)
FRUTA JUICE BAR LLC
295 Fairfield Ave (06604-4207)
PHONE....................203 690-9168
Christopher Jarrin, *Principal*
EMP: 9 **EST:** 2012
SALES (est): 767.8K **Privately Held**
SIC: 2037 Fruit juices

(G-773)
FULCRUM PROMOTIONS & PRINTING
75 Wheeler Ave Apt 102 (06606-5611)
PHONE....................203 909-6362
Gia Marie Vacca, *Principal*
EMP: 4
SALES (est): 263.6K **Privately Held**
SIC: 2752 Commercial printing, lithographic

(G-774)
GENERAL ELECTRIC COMPANY
1285 Boston Ave (06610-2693)
PHONE....................203 396-1572
Bill O'Brien, *Plant Mgr*
Bob Landa, *Design Engr*
EMP: 100
SALES (corp-wide): 121.6B **Publicly Held**
SIC: 3625 Relays & industrial controls
PA: General Electric Company
41 Farnsworth St
Boston MA 02210
617 443-3000

(G-775)
GENERAL SHEET METAL WORKS INC
120 Silliman Ave (06605-2185)
PHONE....................203 333-6111
Jeffrey D Cibulas, *President*
EMP: 10 **EST:** 1916
SQ FT: 6,500
SALES: 780K **Privately Held**
SIC: 3444 1761 Ducts, sheet metal; roofing, siding & sheet metal work

(G-776)
GLOBAL SCENIC SERVICES INC
46 Brookfield Ave (06610-3005)
PHONE....................203 334-2130
Warren Katz, *President*
James Malski, *Acting Pres*
John Cashman, *Project Mgr*
Seth Gist, *Manager*
Emily Williams, *Manager*
▲ **EMP:** 46
SQ FT: 40,000
SALES (est): 7MM **Privately Held**
WEB: www.globalscenicservices.com
SIC: 3999 Theatrical scenery

(G-777)
GOLDEN HILL CSTM CABINETRY LLC
315 Harral Ave (06604-3102)
PHONE....................203 366-2222
Sergio Posada, *Principal*
EMP: 2 **EST:** 2007
SALES (est): 255.8K **Privately Held**
SIC: 2434 Wood kitchen cabinets

(G-778)
GRAFIK PRINT SHOPP
378 Granfield Ave (06610-2305)
PHONE....................203 335-0777
EMP: 2
SALES (est): 150K **Privately Held**
SIC: 2752 Lithographic Commercial Printing

(G-779)
GRANT MANUFACTURING & MCH CO
90 Silliman Ave (06605-2127)
P.O. Box 3345 (06605-0345)
PHONE....................203 366-4557
Bruce W Mc Naughton, *Ch of Bd*
EMP: 20 **EST:** 1904
SQ FT: 22,000
SALES (est): 2.9MM **Privately Held**
SIC: 3542 Machine tools, metal forming type

(G-780)
GRIFFITH COMPANY
239 Asylum St (06610-2103)
PHONE....................203 333-5557
Gary Griffith, *President*
Emma Griffith, *Corp Secy*
EMP: 5 **EST:** 1936
SQ FT: 30,000
SALES (est): 915K **Privately Held**
SIC: 2842 5087 Specialty cleaning, polishes & sanitation goods; cleaning & maintenance equipment & supplies

(G-781)
HARRISON ENTERPRISE LLC
Also Called: Philip Cups
237 Asylum St (06610-2103)
PHONE....................914 665-8348
Richard Harrison,
Roxanne Gittens,
EMP: 4
SALES (est): 599.2K **Privately Held**
WEB: www.harrisonenterprise.com
SIC: 2679 Cups, pressed & molded pulp: made from purchased material

(G-782)
HARRY THOMMEN COMPANY
Also Called: Thommen, Harry Co
3404 Fairfield Ave (06605-3225)
PHONE....................203 333-3637
Jeffrey Thommen, *President*
EMP: 4
SQ FT: 2,500
SALES (est): 561.5K **Privately Held**
SIC: 7692 3498 Welding repair; tube fabricating (contract bending & shaping)

(G-783)
HAWIE MANUFACTURING COMPANY
Also Called: So-Lo Marine Division
73 River St (06604-2920)
PHONE....................203 366-4303
Robert L Hawie, *President*
Mary Ellen Cicero, *Office Mgr*
Ann Hawie, *Admin Sec*
EMP: 2 **EST:** 1897
SQ FT: 100,000
SALES: 2MM **Privately Held**
WEB: www.hawiemfg.com
SIC: 3965 2389 Buckles & buckle parts; garters

(G-784)
HISPANIC ENTERPRISES INC
Also Called: Emtec Metal Products
200 Cogswell St (06610-1941)
PHONE....................203 588-9334
Winston A Malcolm, *President*
EMP: 20
SQ FT: 12,500
SALES (est): 2.3MM **Privately Held**
SIC: 3444 Sheet metal specialties, not stamped; coal chutes, prefabricated sheet metal

(G-785)
HONEY CELL INC (PA)
850 Union Ave (06607-1137)
PHONE....................203 925-1818
Rudolph Niedermeier, *President*
Arthur Vietze Jr, *Vice Pres*
William Vietze, *Vice Pres*
Robert Niedermeier, *Treasurer*
EMP: 4
SALES: 13.9MM **Privately Held**
SIC: 2679 Building, insulating & packaging paper

(G-786)
HOPE KIT CBINETS STONE SUP LLC (PA)
1901 Commerce Dr (06605-2226)
PHONE....................203 610-6147
Sung Young,
Ren Wu Zheng,
▲ **EMP:** 4
SALES (est): 800.6K **Privately Held**
SIC: 2434 Wood kitchen cabinets

(G-787)
HORBERG INDUSTRIES INC
19 Staples St (06604-2202)
P.O. Box 6273 (06606-0273)
PHONE....................203 334-9444
Robert C Leety, *President*
Carlos Laracuente, *Sales Executive*
Anita Stabler, *Executive Asst*
EMP: 10 **EST:** 1935
SQ FT: 10,000
SALES (est): 1.7MM **Privately Held**
WEB: www.horberg.com
SIC: 3452 Dowel pins, metal

(G-788)
HUB INDUSTRIES
209 Center St (06604-3314)
PHONE....................203 803-8836
Leigh Scott, *Principal*
EMP: 1
SALES (est): 74.6K **Privately Held**
SIC: 3999 Manufacturing industries

(G-789)
HUBBELL TECHNICAL CTR
1613 State St (06605)
PHONE....................203 337-3333
Jeff Snyder, *Sales Mgr*
EMP: 2
SALES (est): 88.3K **Privately Held**
SIC: 3643 Current-carrying wiring devices

(G-790)
IDENTIFICATION PRODUCTS CORP
104 Silliman Ave (06605-2140)
P.O. Box 320307 (06605)
PHONE....................203 331-0931
Hugh F McCann, *Branch Mgr*
EMP: 1
SALES (corp-wide): 7.4MM **Privately Held**
SIC: 2759 3479 2671 Flexographic printing; name plates: engraved, etched, etc.; packaging paper & plastics film, coated & laminated
PA: Identification Products Corp
104 Silliman Ave
Bridgeport CT 06605
203 334-5969

(G-791)
IDENTIFICATION PRODUCTS CORP
1073 State St (06605-1504)
PHONE....................203 334-5969
Hugh F McCann, *Manager*
EMP: 10

Bridgeport - Fairfield County (G-792)

SALES (corp-wide): 7.4MM **Privately Held**
SIC: 2759 3479 2671 Flexographic printing; name plates: engraved, etched, etc.; packaging paper & plastics film, coated & laminated
PA: Identification Products Corp
104 Silliman Ave
Bridgeport CT 06605
203 334-5969

(G-792)
INNOVATIVE ARC TUBES CORP
Also Called: I T C
1240 Central Ave (06607-1065)
PHONE..................................203 333-1031
Vijay Mehan, *President*
Ramesh Mehan, *Chairman*
Renee Mehan, *Treasurer*
▲ **EMP:** 25
SQ FT: 30,000
SALES: 3MM
SALES (corp-wide): 10MM **Privately Held**
WEB: www.itc-1.com
SIC: 3646 Commercial indusl & institutional electric lighting fixtures
PA: Innovative Technologies Corp.
1020 Woodman Dr Ste 100
Dayton OH 45432
937 252-2145

(G-793)
INTEGRATED PRINT SOLUTIONS INC
Also Called: Everett Print
35 Benham Ave Ste 2 (06605-1436)
PHONE..................................203 330-0200
Philip Palmieri, *President*
Elizabeth Alesevich, *Marketing Mgr*
▲ **EMP:** 11
SQ FT: 40,000
SALES (est): 2.1MM **Privately Held**
SIC: 2759 Screen printing

(G-794)
IS CABINETRY LLC
141 Arcadia Ave (06604-1504)
PHONE..................................203 583-5857
Isaias C Saguilan, *Principal*
EMP: 1
SALES (est): 59K **Privately Held**
SIC: 2434 Wood kitchen cabinets

(G-795)
J & S FASHION
762 Boston Ave (06610-2027)
PHONE..................................203 572-0154
Stephanie Wynter, *Owner*
EMP: 1
SALES (est): 46.5K **Privately Held**
SIC: 2299 Jute & flax textile products

(G-796)
J J BOX CO INC
25 Admiral St (06605-1808)
PHONE..................................203 367-1211
James Garamella, *President*
EMP: 9
SQ FT: 10,000
SALES: 1.4MM **Privately Held**
SIC: 2448 Pallets, wood

(G-797)
J&R SIGNS
172 Dover St (06610-2207)
PHONE..................................203 551-0781
Jaime Pons, *Principal*
EMP: 1
SALES (est): 53.4K **Privately Held**
SIC: 3993 Signs & advertising specialties

(G-798)
J&T INDUSTRIES LLC
876 Huntington Rd (06610)
PHONE..................................203 375-8424
Joseph Piacentini, *Principal*
EMP: 1
SALES (est): 54.7K **Privately Held**
SIC: 3999 Manufacturing industries

(G-799)
JAMES IPPOLITO & CO CONN INC
1069 Conn Ave Ste 16 (06607-1228)
PHONE..................................203 366-3840
Gerald V Cavallo, *President*
EMP: 40 **EST:** 1995
SQ FT: 25,000
SALES (est): 7MM **Privately Held**
WEB: www.chinooksports.com
SIC: 3429 Aircraft hardware

(G-800)
JAMES J LICARI (PA)
Also Called: Licari Woodworking
300 N Washington Ave (06604-2810)
PHONE..................................203 333-5000
James Licari, *Owner*
EMP: 5
SALES: 600K **Privately Held**
SIC: 2431 Woodwork, interior & ornamental

(G-801)
JASK WOODWORKING INC
209 Center St (06604-3314)
PHONE..................................954 766-7105
Suzy Zolotov, *Principal*
EMP: 1
SALES (est): 54.1K **Privately Held**
SIC: 2431 Millwork

(G-802)
JC TURN MFG
86 Willow St (06610-3221)
PHONE..................................203 366-6164
Jeff Syganowski, *Owner*
EMP: 1
SALES (est): 114.4K **Privately Held**
SIC: 2426 Turnings, furniture: wood

(G-803)
JERRYS PRINTING & GRAPHICS LLC
1183 Broad St (06604-4172)
PHONE..................................203 384-0015
Scott G Fisher, *President*
Barbara Fisher,
Ernest Fisher,
EMP: 3
SQ FT: 1,200
SALES: 150K **Privately Held**
SIC: 2752 7334 2791 2789 Commercial printing, offset; photocopying & duplicating services; typesetting; bookbinding & related work

(G-804)
JET CORPORATION
146 Davis Ave (06605-2557)
PHONE..................................203 334-3317
Jose E Tamayo, *President*
Jose L Tamayo, *Vice Pres*
EMP: 11
SALES (est): 1.8MM **Privately Held**
WEB: www.jetcorp.com
SIC: 3365 3566 Aluminum foundries; gears, power transmission, except automotive

(G-805)
JGF HARDWOOD FLOOR
40 Quarry St Apt C (06606-4334)
PHONE..................................203 650-9192
Jonhon Ferreiza, *Principal*
EMP: 1
SALES (est): 71.4K **Privately Held**
SIC: 2426 1771 1752 Flooring, hardwood; flooring contractor; floor laying & floor work

(G-806)
JJK WOODWORKING LLC
230 5th St (06607-1082)
PHONE..................................203 224-0139
Jacek Siciak, *Principal*
EMP: 1 **EST:** 2017
SALES (est): 54.1K **Privately Held**
SIC: 2431 Millwork

(G-807)
JOBO ENTERPRIZES LLC
608 N Summerfield Ave (06610-2551)
PHONE..................................203 367-7517
Jonathan Dubose Jr, *Principal*
EMP: 2
SALES (est): 108.7K **Privately Held**
SIC: 3931 Guitars & parts, electric & non-electric

(G-808)
JOHN JUNE CUSTOM CABINETRY LLC
541 Fairfield Ave (06604-3904)
PHONE..................................203 334-1720
John June,
EMP: 8
SALES (est): 826.6K **Privately Held**
SIC: 2434 Wood kitchen cabinets

(G-809)
JOHN MEZES & SONS INC
Also Called: Mezes J & Sons
322 Dewey St (06605-2143)
PHONE..................................203 255-6841
John R Mezes, *President*
James Mezes, *Corp Secy*
Robert A Mezes, *Vice Pres*
EMP: 6 **EST:** 1932
SQ FT: 13,000
SALES (est): 710K **Privately Held**
SIC: 7532 3713 Body shop, automotive; truck painting & lettering; truck & bus bodies

(G-810)
JOZEF CUSTOM IRONWORKS INC
Also Called: Aesthetic Blacksmithing
250 Smith St (06607-2219)
PHONE..................................203 384-6363
Erik Witkowski, *CEO*
Jozef Witkowski, *President*
Lidia Botero, *General Mgr*
Victor Botero, *Technology*
▲ **EMP:** 16 **EST:** 1994
SQ FT: 40,000
SALES (est): 2.7MM **Privately Held**
WEB: www.jozef.net
SIC: 3446 Architectural metalwork

(G-811)
JUANOS GLASS LLC
56 Davis Ave (06605-2505)
PHONE..................................203 449-5378
Juan Munoz,
EMP: 1
SALES (est): 75.4K **Privately Held**
SIC: 3211 Construction glass

(G-812)
KAFA GROUP LLC
800 Union Ave (06607-1422)
PHONE..................................475 275-0090
Steve McKenzie, *President*
Nicole McKenzie, *Vice Pres*
EMP: 8
SQ FT: 1,200
SALES (est): 819.4K **Privately Held**
SIC: 1389 1542 1541 Construction, repair & dismantling services; commercial & office building, new construction; industrial buildings, new construction

(G-813)
KASTEN INC
Also Called: Dakota Life Sciences
304 Bishop Ave (06610-3050)
P.O. Box 3540, Silver Springs NV (89429-3540)
PHONE..................................702 860-2407
Jose Delgado, *CEO*
EMP: 2
SALES (est): 74.4K **Privately Held**
SIC: 2834 Pharmaceutical preparations

(G-814)
KB SERVICES
1 Bostwick Ave (06605-2435)
P.O. Box 3523 (06605-0523)
PHONE..................................203 243-3594
Kevin Blagys, *Owner*
EMP: 1
SALES: 10K **Privately Held**
SIC: 3545 8748 Calipers & dividers; business consulting

(G-815)
KERIGANS FUEL INC
258 Dekalb Ave (06607-2417)
PHONE..................................203 334-3646
James W Kerigan, *President*
EMP: 4
SALES (est): 641.5K **Privately Held**
SIC: 3433 Heaters, swimming pool: oil or gas

(G-816)
KEYSTONE RV COMPANY
2660 North Ave (06604-2355)
PHONE..................................203 367-9847
Stephen Holmes, *General Mgr*
Michael McGuire, *Sales Mgr*
P A Giorgio, *Manager*
Jason Clark, *Manager*
Ryan Spaeth, *Manager*
EMP: 150
SALES (corp-wide): 7.8B **Publicly Held**
WEB: www.keystonerv.com
SIC: 3792 Travel trailers & campers
HQ: Keystone Rv Company
2642 Hackberry Dr
Goshen IN 46526

(G-817)
KEYTAG1
955 Conn Ave Ste 1306 (06607-1200)
PHONE..................................203 873-0749
Stan Barski, *President*
EMP: 1
SQ FT: 1,000
SALES: 400K **Privately Held**
SIC: 3089 Identification cards, plastic

(G-818)
KITCHEN CAB RESURFACING LLC
136 Merriam St (06604-2912)
PHONE..................................203 334-2857
James Svab, *President*
EMP: 10
SALES (est): 929K **Privately Held**
WEB: www.kcrct.com
SIC: 2434 Wood kitchen cabinets

(G-819)
KITCHENMAX LLC
198 Knowlton St (06608-2107)
PHONE..................................203 330-5041
Marcin Bogucki, *Owner*
Julius Janusz, *Principal*
EMP: 4
SALES (est): 581.4K **Privately Held**
SIC: 5712 2434 Cabinet work, custom; wood kitchen cabinets

(G-820)
L P MACADAMS COMPANY INC
50 Austin St (06604-5437)
P.O. Box 5540 (06610-0540)
PHONE..................................203 366-3647
D Paul Macadams, *CEO*
Lawrence P Macadams, *President*
Kay Macadams, *Vice Pres*
▲ **EMP:** 85
SQ FT: 150,000
SALES (est): 11.8MM **Privately Held**
WEB: www.lpmacadams.com
SIC: 2759 7331 4225 2752 Imprinting; direct mail advertising services; general warehousing & storage; commercial printing, lithographic

(G-821)
LACEY MANUFACTURING CO LLC
1146 Barnum Ave (06610-2794)
PHONE..................................203 336-7427
Ken Lisk, *President*
Robert Warner,
▲ **EMP:** 310
SQ FT: 100,000
SALES (est): 75MM
SALES (corp-wide): 770.6MM **Publicly Held**
WEB: www.laceymfg.com
SIC: 3841 3089 Surgical instruments & apparatus; injection molding of plastics
HQ: Precision Engineered Products Llc
110 Frank Mossberg Dr
Attleboro MA 02703
508 226-5600

GEOGRAPHIC SECTION
Bridgeport - Fairfield County (G-854)

(G-822)
LAKE GRINDING COMPANY
231 Asylum St (06610-2103)
PHONE..................203 336-3767
Marion Lake, *President*
Marian Crichton Lake, *Director*
Nancy Johnson, *Admin Sec*
EMP: 3
SQ FT: 1,500
SALES (est): 257.6K **Privately Held**
SIC: 3471 Finishing, metals or formed products

(G-823)
LATE NITE PRINTING CO
97 Travis Dr (06606-1628)
PHONE..................203 374-9287
Emilio Torres, *Principal*
EMP: 2 **EST:** 2007
SALES (est): 120.9K **Privately Held**
SIC: 2752 Commercial printing, offset

(G-824)
LEONARD F BROOKS (PA)
Also Called: A & B Ice Co
199 Asylum St (06610-2103)
PHONE..................203 335-4934
Leonard F Brooks, *Owner*
EMP: 5
SQ FT: 5,600
SALES (est): 600K **Privately Held**
SIC: 2097 Manufactured ice

(G-825)
LINDQIST HISTORICAL GUIDES INC
119 Midland St (06605-3543)
PHONE..................203 335-8568
Brian Lindquist, *Principal*
EMP: 2
SALES (est): 107.9K **Privately Held**
SIC: 2741 Miscellaneous publishing

(G-826)
LUCILLE PICCIRILLO
Also Called: Micalizzi Ice Cream
712 Madison Ave (06606-5511)
PHONE..................203 366-2353
Lucille Piccirillo, *Owner*
EMP: 2 **EST:** 1965
SALES (est): 130.1K **Privately Held**
SIC: 2024 2038 Ice cream & ice milk; ices, flavored (frozen dessert); frozen specialties

(G-827)
M & O CORPORATION
164 Alex St (06607-1905)
PHONE..................203 367-4292
Emilio Espejo, *President*
Alan M Decaprio, *Vice Pres*
Robert H Oetjen, *Shareholder*
Scott Cole, *Administration*
EMP: 35 **EST:** 1976
SQ FT: 8,000
SALES: 2.9MM **Privately Held**
WEB: www.mocorp.net
SIC: 1711 3444 Warm air heating & air conditioning contractor; ducts, sheet metal

(G-828)
MAPS AND MORE
226 Sampson St (06606-4949)
PHONE..................203 335-0556
William Stone, *Owner*
EMP: 2
SALES (est): 149K **Privately Held**
SIC: 2899

(G-829)
MARDINI POWER STATION
1267 Fairfield Ave (06605-1119)
PHONE..................203 576-8951
Eric Arar, *Manager*
EMP: 2
SALES (est): 137.7K **Privately Held**
SIC: 3589 Car washing machinery

(G-830)
MARKAL FINISHING CO INC
400 Bostwick Ave (06605-2407)
PHONE..................203 384-8219
Craig Sander, *President*
Christine Royer, *Corp Secy*
Jason Sanden, *Vice Pres*
EMP: 44 **EST:** 1961
SQ FT: 40,000
SALES (est): 7.4MM **Privately Held**
SIC: 2672 Coated & laminated paper

(G-831)
MARS ARCHITECTURAL MILLWORK
55 Randall Ave Ste A (06606-5701)
PHONE..................203 579-2632
Richard Marsilio, *President*
Kara Marsilio, *Vice Pres*
EMP: 4
SQ FT: 8,000
SALES (est): 338.8K **Privately Held**
SIC: 2431 Millwork

(G-832)
MASTER CRAFT KITCHENS
2397 E Main St (06610-1802)
PHONE..................203 366-1461
Joao Ferreira, *Principal*
EMP: 1
SALES (est): 87.8K **Privately Held**
SIC: 2434 5031 Wood kitchen cabinets; kitchen cabinets

(G-833)
MASTRIANI GOURMET FOOD LLC
570 Barnum Ave (06608-2446)
PHONE..................203 368-9556
Ralph Mastriani, *Principal*
Althea Paris,
EMP: 3
SALES (est): 199K **Privately Held**
SIC: 2099 Pasta, uncooked: packaged with other ingredients

(G-834)
MBS WEB CREATIONS
432 Indian Ave (06606-3905)
PHONE..................203 521-0642
Michael B Stone, *Owner*
EMP: 1
SALES (est): 64.6K **Privately Held**
SIC: 2241 Webbing, braids & belting

(G-835)
MCLODESIGNSCOM
1138 Hancock Ave (06605-1611)
PHONE..................203 296-1400
EMP: 2
SALES (est): 113.9K **Privately Held**
SIC: 2759 Commercial printing

(G-836)
MEDELCO INC
54 Washburn St (06605-1848)
PHONE..................203 275-8070
Elaine Robinson, *President*
▲ **EMP:** 5
SQ FT: 76,000
SALES (est): 1MM **Privately Held**
WEB: www.medelcoinc.com
SIC: 3559 3229 3632 Jewelers' machines; pressed & blown glass; refrigerators, mechanical & absorption: household

(G-837)
MESSIAH DEVELOPMENT LLC
210 Congress St (06604-4007)
PHONE..................203 368-2405
Collin Vice, *Mng Member*
EMP: 7
SALES (est): 539.4K **Privately Held**
SIC: 3271 Concrete block & brick

(G-838)
MILESTONE GRAPHICS
434 Grand St (06604-3213)
PHONE..................203 218-4528
James Reed, *Manager*
EMP: 2 **EST:** 2017
SALES (est): 83.9K **Privately Held**
SIC: 2752 Commercial printing, lithographic

(G-839)
MILL MANUFACTURING INC
105 Willow St (06610-3220)
PHONE..................203 367-9572
Karl E Ostberg, *President*
EMP: 8
SQ FT: 2,000
SALES (est): 1.1MM **Privately Held**
SIC: 3599 Machine shop, jobbing & repair

(G-840)
MJ METAL INC
225 Howard Ave (06605-1825)
PHONE..................203 334-3484
Jeffrey Dreyer, *President*
George Dreyer, *Vice Pres*
Sandy Noerenberg, *Comptroller*
▲ **EMP:** 20
SQ FT: 32,000
SALES (est): 5.1MM **Privately Held**
SIC: 5093 4953 3341 Ferrous metal scrap & waste; refuse systems; secondary nonferrous metals

(G-841)
ML INDUSTRIES
312 Cambridge St (06606-1806)
PHONE..................203 820-4922
Tim Minor, *Principal*
EMP: 1
SALES (est): 39.6K **Privately Held**
SIC: 3999 Manufacturing industries

(G-842)
MOHAWK TOOL AND DIE MFG CO INC
25 Wells St Ste 4 (06604-2800)
PHONE..................203 367-2181
Vincent A Bonazzo, *President*
Lucy R Bonazzo, *Admin Sec*
▲ **EMP:** 13 **EST:** 1946
SQ FT: 8,000
SALES (est): 2MM **Privately Held**
SIC: 3544 3089 Forms (molds), for foundry & plastics working machinery; injection molding of plastics

(G-843)
MOORE TOOL COMPANY INC (HQ)
800 Union Ave (06607-1422)
PHONE..................203 366-3224
Newman Marsilius III, *President*
Newman M Marsilius, *Vice Pres*
Kathie Dennis, *Purch Mgr*
Sebastian Zawadzki, *Engineer*
◆ **EMP:** 63
SQ FT: 334,113
SALES (est): 23.8MM
SALES (corp-wide): 65.8MM **Privately Held**
SIC: 3541 3544 3545 Machine tools, metal cutting: exotic (explosive, etc.); dies & die holders for metal cutting, forming, die casting; gauges (machine tool accessories)
PA: Pmt Group, Inc.
    800 Union Ave
    Bridgeport CT 06607
    203 367-8675

(G-844)
MTJ MANUFACTURING INC
127 Wilmot Ave (06610-1835)
PHONE..................203 334-4939
Mark Carpenter, *President*
EMP: 6
SALES (est): 889.8K **Privately Held**
WEB: www.mtjmanufacturing.com
SIC: 3441 Fabricated structural metal

(G-845)
MUGGERS MARROW LLC
150 Shelton St (06608-1522)
PHONE..................203 548-9566
Maurice Jenkins, *CEO*
EMP: 1
SALES (est): 47.9K **Privately Held**
SIC: 2035 7389 Seasonings, meat sauces (except tomato & dry);

(G-846)
NEONWORKS
125 Front St (06606-5108)
PHONE..................203 335-6366
Howard Bujese, *Owner*
EMP: 1
SALES: 80K **Privately Held**
SIC: 3993 Signs & advertising specialties

(G-847)
NES SPORTS LLC
456 Ruth St (06606-3360)
PHONE..................765 532-2178
Ned Eric Simerlein, *Principal*
EMP: 2
SALES (est): 109.9K **Privately Held**
SIC: 3949 Sporting & athletic goods

(G-848)
NEUROHYDRATE LLC
4637 Main St Unit 5 (06606-1838)
PHONE..................203 799-7900
Justin Higgins,
Hamid Sami,
EMP: 5
SQ FT: 4,500
SALES (est): 129.5K **Privately Held**
SIC: 2834 Drugs acting on the central nervous system & sense organs; syrups, pharmaceutical; vitamin preparations

(G-849)
NEW ENGLAND GRINDING AND MA
30 Radel St (06607-2113)
PHONE..................203 333-1885
Walter Jacques,
EMP: 4
SQ FT: 30,000
SALES (est): 561.6K **Privately Held**
SIC: 3599 Machine shop, jobbing & repair

(G-850)
NEW RESOURCES GROUP INC
955 Conn Ave Ste 1211 (06607-1246)
P.O. Box 320049, Fairfield (06825-0049)
PHONE..................203 366-1000
William Wales, *President*
Annamari Wales, *Admin Sec*
▲ **EMP:** 4
SQ FT: 7,500
SALES: 1MM **Privately Held**
WEB: www.nrgideas.com
SIC: 3088 8748 5074 Plastics plumbing fixtures; energy conservation consultant; plumbing fittings & supplies

(G-851)
NNTECHNOLOGY MOORE SYSTEMS LLC
800 Union Ave (06607-1422)
P.O. Box 1381 (06601-1381)
PHONE..................203 366-3224
Lucio Imbimblo, *Electrical Engi*
Ranae Wright, *Administration*
EMP: 4
SALES (corp-wide): 65.8MM **Privately Held**
SIC: 3827 Optical instruments & lenses
HQ: Moore Nanotechnology Systems Llc
    230 Old Homestead Hwy
    Swanzey NH 03446
    603 352-3030

(G-852)
NOLAN WOODWORKING LLC
187 Monroe St (06605-2747)
PHONE..................203 258-1538
Gene Nolan, *Principal*
EMP: 2
SALES (est): 65.4K **Privately Held**
SIC: 2431 Millwork

(G-853)
NOLLYSOURCE ENTERTAINMENT LLC
1455 Penboke Ln (06608)
PHONE..................347 264-6655
Akinbiyi Epega, *Mng Member*
EMP: 1 **EST:** 2009
SALES (est): 34.7K **Privately Held**
SIC: 7929 3651 3931 7812 Entertainers & entertainment groups; music distribution apparatus; musical instruments; music video production; musical instruments parts & accessories; book music publishing & printing

(G-854)
O & G INDUSTRIES INC
240 Bostwick Ave (06605-2434)
P.O. Box 907, Torrington (06790-0907)
PHONE..................203 366-4586
John Leverty, *Branch Mgr*

Bridgeport - Fairfield County (G-855)   GEOGRAPHIC SECTION

John Legarza, *Executive*
EMP: 50
SALES (corp-wide): 538MM **Privately Held**
WEB: www.ogind.com
SIC: 3273 1771 1794 2951 Ready-mixed concrete; blacktop (asphalt) work; excavation & grading, building construction; asphalt paving mixtures & blocks; commercial & office building, new construction
PA: O & G Industries, Inc.
112 Wall St
Torrington CT 06790
860 489-9261

(G-855)
OCEAN RIGGING LLC
1 Bostwick Ave (06605-2435)
PHONE.................................800 624-2101
Ian Williams,
Rick Granville,
EMP: 6
SALES (est): 740.8K **Privately Held**
SIC: 3731 Marine rigging

(G-856)
ONTRA STONE CONCEPTS LLC
541 Central Ave (06607-1714)
PHONE.................................203 371-8225
Badia J Ontra,
EMP: 2
SALES (est): 59.5K **Privately Held**
SIC: 3281 Building stone products; dimension stone for buildings

(G-857)
ORISHA ORACLE INC
59 Regent St (06606-2332)
PHONE.................................203 612-8989
Sherwaine Mathurin, *Principal*
EMP: 4
SALES (est): 93.7K **Privately Held**
SIC: 7372 Prepackaged software

(G-858)
P & S MANUFACTURING LLC
225 Wheeler Ave (06606-5668)
PHONE.................................203 685-2256
Luis Pelaez, *Mng Member*
EMP: 1
SALES: 100K **Privately Held**
SIC: 3721 8711 Aircraft; mechanical engineering

(G-859)
PALMIERI INDUSTRIES INC
Also Called: Ctr
118 Burr Ct Ste 1 (06605-2210)
PHONE.................................203 384-6020
Jospeh A Palmieri Jr, *President*
Robert Kellerman, *Vice Pres*
Dan Bresnahan, *Project Mgr*
Tim Firla, *Project Mgr*
Tom Finnucan, *Opers Mgr*
EMP: 70
SALES (est): 15.8MM **Privately Held**
WEB: www.cctank.com
SIC: 1389 Lease tanks, oil field: erecting, cleaning & repairing

(G-860)
PANBOUD PIERROT
240 William St (06608-2194)
PHONE.................................203 296-4806
EMP: 2
SALES (est): 99.3K **Privately Held**
SIC: 3571 Mfg Electronic Computers

(G-861)
PANEL PRO TECHNOLOGY
104 Silliman Ave (06605-2140)
PHONE.................................203 333-0083
EMP: 2
SALES: 80K **Privately Held**
SIC: 3353 Mfg Aluminum Sheet/Foil

(G-862)
PARK CITY PACKAGING INC
1069 Conn Ave Ste 22 (06607-1228)
PHONE.................................203 579-1965
Steve Jicanda, *Manager*
EMP: 15

SALES (corp-wide): 9MM **Privately Held**
WEB: www.thepackcenter.com
SIC: 4783 2653 5199 8734 Packing goods for shipping; boxes, corrugated: made from purchased materials; packaging materials; pollution testing
PA: Park City Packaging, Inc.
480 Sniffens Ln
Stratford CT 06615
203 378-7384

(G-863)
PARK DISTRIBUTORIES INC (PA)
Also Called: Universal Relay Company
347 Railroad Ave (06604-5424)
P.O. Box 1020 (06601-1020)
PHONE.................................203 579-2140
Alan Goodman, *President*
Rick Depaulis, *Principal*
Larry Depaulis, *Vice Pres*
Bill Miller, *Vice Pres*
Ricard Depaulis, *CFO*
EMP: 9 **EST:** 1966
SQ FT: 16,000
SALES (est): 3.1MM **Privately Held**
WEB: www.parkdistributors.com
SIC: 3625 5065 Relays & industrial controls; electronic parts

(G-864)
PARK DISTRIBUTORIES INC
Also Called: Electronic Finishing Company
347 Railroad Ave (06604-5424)
P.O. Box 1020 (06601-1020)
PHONE.................................203 366-7200
Allan Goodman, *Manager*
EMP: 18
SALES (corp-wide): 3.1MM **Privately Held**
WEB: www.parkdistributors.com
SIC: 3625 3679 Relays & industrial controls; electronic circuits
PA: Park Distributories Inc.
347 Railroad Ave
Bridgeport CT 06604
203 579-2140

(G-865)
PARK DISTRIBUTORIES INC
Also Called: Universal Relays
347 Railroad Ave (06604-5424)
P.O. Box 1020 (06601-1020)
PHONE.................................203 366-7200
Alan J Goodman, *Branch Mgr*
EMP: 15
SALES (corp-wide): 3.1MM **Privately Held**
WEB: www.parkdistributors.com
SIC: 5065 3625 Electronic parts; relays & industrial controls
PA: Park Distributories Inc.
347 Railroad Ave
Bridgeport CT 06604
203 579-2140

(G-866)
PATALANOS WOODWORKING LLC
53 Arthur St (06605-3120)
PHONE.................................203 612-7537
Donna Demattia, *Principal*
EMP: 1
SALES (est): 84.5K **Privately Held**
SIC: 2431 Millwork

(G-867)
PATTY MOMMYS
578 Boston Ave (06610-1705)
PHONE.................................203 330-8575
Patty Mommys, *Principal*
EMP: 1
SALES (est): 94.8K **Privately Held**
SIC: 3421 Table & food cutlery, including butchers'

(G-868)
PEQUONNOCK IRONWORKS INC
621 Knowlton St (06608-1536)
P.O. Box 6280 (06606-0280)
PHONE.................................203 336-2178
EMP: 15 **EST:** 1997
SALES (est): 1.8MM **Privately Held**
SIC: 3446 3312 Mfg Architectural Metalwork Blast Furnace-Steel Works

(G-869)
PEQUOT
1000 Lafayette Blvd # 1100 (06604-4710)
PHONE.................................800 620-1492
Christopher Duffy- Acevedo, *CEO*
Christopher Duffy-Acevedo, *CEO*
Stefanie Breitung Duffy, *CFO*
EMP: 5
SQ FT: 500
SALES (est): 2.5MM **Privately Held**
SIC: 3674 5074 1711 7382 Semiconductors & related devices; plumbing & hydronic heating supplies; heating equipment (hydronic); plumbing, heating, air-conditioning contractors; protective devices, security; turbines & turbine generator sets

(G-870)
PEREY TURNSTILES INC
308 Bishop Ave (06610-3055)
PHONE.................................203 333-9400
M Edmund Hendrickson, *President*
Jeanne Hendrickson, *Treasurer*
EMP: 24 **EST:** 1999
SQ FT: 15,000
SALES (est): 8MM **Privately Held**
WEB: www.turnstile.com
SIC: 3829 Turnstiles, equipped with counting mechanisms

(G-871)
PHILLIPS FUEL SYSTEMS
109 Holland Ave (06605-2136)
PHONE.................................203 908-3323
Rodolfo Garcia, *Principal*
George Seganos, *Materials Mgr*
EMP: 6
SALES (est): 616.7K **Privately Held**
SIC: 3714 Filters: oil, fuel & air, motor vehicle

(G-872)
PHILLIPS PUMP LLC
Also Called: Phillips Pumps
661 Lindley St (06606-5045)
P.O. Box 320742, Fairfield (06825-0742)
PHONE.................................203 576-6688
Patrick Crossin,
EMP: 10
SQ FT: 3,800
SALES: 2MM **Privately Held**
SIC: 3561 Pumps & pumping equipment

(G-873)
PIECES OF PUZZLE DAYCARE
160 Wake St (06610-2338)
PHONE.................................203 916-8332
Danaisha Lawrence, *Principal*
EMP: 1
SALES (est): 41K **Privately Held**
SIC: 3944 Puzzles

(G-874)
PLASTIC FACTORY LLC
678 Howard Ave (06605-1916)
P.O. Box 3111 (06605-0111)
PHONE.................................203 908-3468
Amelia Clark, *Sales Staff*
Robert J Carbone,
Barbara C Carbone,
EMP: 4
SALES (est): 697.3K **Privately Held**
SIC: 3081 3082 Plastic film & sheet; tubes, unsupported plastic; rods, unsupported plastic

(G-875)
PMT GROUP INC (PA)
800 Union Ave (06607-1422)
PHONE.................................203 367-8675
Newman M Marsilius III, *President*
Armand Luzi, *Vice Pres*
◆ **EMP:** 110
SQ FT: 218,000
SALES (est): 65.8MM **Privately Held**
WEB: www.producto.com
SIC: 3541 3545 3544 Machine tools, metal cutting: exotic (explosive, etc.); machine tool attachments & accessories; special dies, tools, jigs & fixtures; special dies & tools; industrial molds

(G-876)
POPLAR TOOL & MFG CO INC
420 Poplar St (06605-1644)
PHONE.................................203 333-4369
David Conroy, *President*
Rudolf Divjak, *Vice Pres*
EMP: 6 **EST:** 1951
SQ FT: 4,200
SALES (est): 450K **Privately Held**
SIC: 3599 Machine shop, jobbing & repair

(G-877)
POST PUBLISHING COMPANY
410 State St (06604-4501)
PHONE.................................203 333-0161
Paul Barbetta, *Principal*
Robert Laska, *Principal*
Kaarn Lynch, *Consultant*
EMP: 1
SALES (est): 69.4K **Privately Held**
SIC: 2711 Newspapers, publishing & printing

(G-878)
PRECISION ENGINEERED PDTS LLC
Also Called: Boston Endo-Surgical Tech
1146 Barnum Ave (06610-2705)
PHONE.................................203 336-6479
Alan M Huffenus, *CEO*
EMP: 7
SALES (corp-wide): 770.6MM **Publicly Held**
SIC: 3841 5047 Surgical & medical instruments; surgical equipment & supplies
HQ: Precision Engineered Products Llc
110 Frank Mossberg Dr
Attleboro MA 02703
508 226-5600

(G-879)
PRIMA DONA LLC
Also Called: Donavita International
80 Bywatyr Ln (06605-3158)
PHONE.................................203 820-9327
Donna J Gaspero,
EMP: 1
SALES (est): 30.5K **Privately Held**
SIC: 5699 3161 Leather garments; traveling bags

(G-880)
PRIME RESOURCES CORP
Also Called: Prime Line
1100 Boston Ave Bldg 1 (06610-2658)
PHONE.................................203 331-9100
Jeff Lederer, *President*
David Mercado, *Vice Pres*
Nelson Frey, *Prdtn Mgr*
Eileen Ferreira, *Purch Dir*
Michael Wiskind, *Finance Dir*
◆ **EMP:** 500
SQ FT: 128,000
SALES (est): 87.8MM
SALES (corp-wide): 3.7B **Privately Held**
WEB: www.primeworld.com
SIC: 3993 2759 Signs & advertising specialties; promotional printing
PA: Broder Bros., Co.
6 Neshaminy Interplex Dr
Trevose PA 19053
215 291-0300

(G-881)
PRINT & POST SERVICES
1 Seaview Ave (06607-2400)
PHONE.................................203 336-0055
Gary Grossman, *Owner*
EMP: 6
SQ FT: 3,000
SALES (est): 421.1K **Privately Held**
SIC: 2759 Commercial printing

(G-882)
PRODUCTO CORPORATION (HQ)
Also Called: Producto Machine Company, The
800 Union Ave (06607-1422)
PHONE.................................203 366-3224
Newman M Marsilius III, *CEO*
Joanne Clark, *Vice Pres*
Maynard Cotter, *Vice Pres*
Jon Krchnavy, *Vice Pres*
Newman Marsilius Jr, *Vice Pres*
EMP: 10

GEOGRAPHIC SECTION — Bridgeport - Fairfield County (G-912)

SALES (est): 37.3MM
SALES (corp-wide): 65.8MM **Privately Held**
WEB: www.ringprecision.com
SIC: 3541 3545 3544 Machine tools, metal cutting type; machine tool accessories; special dies, tools, jigs & fixtures
PA: Pmt Group, Inc.
800 Union Ave
Bridgeport CT 06607
203 367-8675

(G-883)
QUALITY STAIRS INC
70 Logan St (06607-1930)
PHONE.................................203 367-8390
Lee Pereira, *President*
Jason Pereira, *Vice Pres*
Manuel Pereira, *Vice Pres*
Vicki Perez, *Bookkeeper*
Geomar Pereira, *Admin Sec*
EMP: 20
SQ FT: 8,000
SALES (est): 3.4MM **Privately Held**
SIC: 2431 3446 Staircases & stairs, wood; stairs, staircases, stair treads: prefabricated metal

(G-884)
RADER INDUSTRIES INC
115 Island Brook Ave (06606-5132)
PHONE.................................203 334-6739
Sonia Halapin, *President*
Brian Halapin, *Corp Secy*
Donald S Halapin Jr, *Vice Pres*
EMP: 4
SQ FT: 10,000
SALES (est): 737.6K **Privately Held**
SIC: 3444 3471 7699 Forming machine work, sheet metal; chromium plating of metals or formed products; metal reshaping & replating services

(G-885)
RAND INNOVATIONS LLC
Also Called: Rand Brands
3389 Fairfield Ave (06605-3228)
PHONE.................................475 282-4643
James A Randel, *Mng Member*
Danny Devlin, *Director*
Mark Simonetti,
EMP: 11
SALES (est): 1.5MM **Privately Held**
SIC: 8733 2899 Physical research, non-commercial; corrosion preventive lubricant

(G-886)
RAYFLEX COMPANY INC
1061 Howard Ave (06605-1970)
PHONE.................................203 336-2173
Gregory Marcantonio, *President*
EMP: 4 EST: 1937
SQ FT: 4,000
SALES (est): 360K **Privately Held**
SIC: 3599 Machine shop, jobbing & repair

(G-887)
READY4 PRINT LLC
2051 Main St (06604-2721)
PHONE.................................203 345-0376
Sean Reeves,
Todd Reaves,
EMP: 3
SALES (est): 338K **Privately Held**
SIC: 2752 Calendar & card printing, lithographic

(G-888)
RELIABLE PLATING & POLSG CO
80 Bishop Ave (06607-1541)
PHONE.................................203 366-5261
Joseph D Bourdeau, *Ch of Bd*
James Bourdeau, *President*
Lynn Myers, *Treasurer*
EMP: 35 EST: 1956
SQ FT: 225,000
SALES (est): 3.6MM **Privately Held**
SIC: 3471 Finishing, metals or formed products; anodizing (plating) of metals or formed products; plating of metals or formed products; polishing, metals or formed products

(G-889)
REMESAS EXPRESS
1213 North Ave (06604-2713)
PHONE.................................203 330-1444
Orlando Gonzales, *Principal*
EMP: 1
SALES (est): 64.2K **Privately Held**
SIC: 2741 Miscellaneous publishing

(G-890)
RICCO VISHNU
Also Called: Rich Snob Fashions
79 Sage Ave (06610-3061)
PHONE.................................203 449-0124
Raheem Nixon, *Owner*
EMP: 7
SALES (est): 181.7K **Privately Held**
SIC: 2389 Apparel & accessories

(G-891)
RIVETING SYSTEMS USA LLC
Also Called: Grant Riveters USA
90 Silliman Ave (06605-2127)
PHONE.................................203 366-4557
Bruce W McNaughton, *Principal*
EMP: 6
SALES (est): 239.9K **Privately Held**
SIC: 3542 Machine tools, metal forming type

(G-892)
ROTAIR AEROSPACE CORPORATION
964 Crescent Ave (06607-1066)
PHONE.................................203 576-6545
Wesley Harrington, *President*
Christine Kudravy, *Vice Pres*
Wayne Walberg, *IT/INT Sup*
EMP: 46 EST: 1975
SQ FT: 80,000
SALES (est): 11.5MM **Privately Held**
WEB: www.rotair.com
SIC: 3728 Aircraft parts & equipment

(G-893)
ROYALTEES LLC
1645 Chopsey Hill Rd (06606-1935)
PHONE.................................203 767-2808
EMP: 2 EST: 2018
SALES (est): 104.5K **Privately Held**
SIC: 2759 Screen printing

(G-894)
SANGUINARIA PUBLISHING INC
85 Ferris St (06605-3138)
PHONE.................................203 576-9168
Noel Furie, *Owner*
Betsy Beaven, *Partner*
Selma Miriam, *Partner*
EMP: 2
SQ FT: 144
SALES (est): 97.2K **Privately Held**
SIC: 2731 Books: publishing only

(G-895)
SANTA ENERGY CORPORATION
154 Admiral St (06605-1807)
P.O. Box 1141 (06601-1141)
PHONE.................................800 937-2682
Donald F Santa, *Admin Sec*
EMP: 2
SALES (est): 65.5K **Privately Held**
SIC: 1389 1311 Oil field services; crude petroleum & natural gas

(G-896)
SASSONE LABWEAR LLC
Also Called: Labwear.com
480 Barnum Ave Ste 5 (06608-2459)
PHONE.................................860 666-4484
Robert Sassone, *Mng Member*
EMP: 5
SALES (est): 1.5MM **Privately Held**
SIC: 2326 2311 Medical & hospital uniforms, men's; men's & boys' suits & coats

(G-897)
SAVETIME CORPORATION
2710 North Ave Ste 105b (06604-2352)
PHONE.................................203 382-2991
Donna Buckenmaier, *President*
Erwin Theodore Buckenmaier, *Chairman*
Robert Zuklie, *Vice Pres*
EMP: 14
SQ FT: 6,100

SALES (est): 1.1MM **Privately Held**
WEB: www.rainhandler.com
SIC: 3089 1761 Gutters (glass fiber reinforced), fiberglass or plastic; roofing, siding & sheet metal work

(G-898)
SCHWERDTLE STAMP COMPANY
41 Benham Ave (06605-1419)
P.O. Box 1461 (06601-1461)
PHONE.................................203 330-2750
Katherine Saint, *President*
John Schwerdtle Jr, *Treasurer*
Stephen Francis, *Controller*
Phillip Kocsis, *Marketing Staff*
Erika McCarthy, *Admin Sec*
EMP: 35 EST: 1879
SQ FT: 14,000
SALES (est): 6.3MM **Privately Held**
WEB: www.schwerdtle.com
SIC: 3953 7336 Marking devices; graphic arts & related design

(G-899)
SEAVIEW PLASTIC RECYCLING INC
938 Crescent Ave (06607-1024)
PHONE.................................203 367-0070
Joseph Cirillo, *President*
Jay Cirillo, *Manager*
EMP: 4
SQ FT: 58,724
SALES (est): 427.1K **Privately Held**
SIC: 4953 2821 5169 Recycling, waste materials; plastics materials & resins; synthetic resins, rubber & plastic materials

(G-900)
SERVICE DEPT
30 Unquowa Hill St (06604-2149)
PHONE.................................203 335-1491
Steven J Leckrone, *Principal*
EMP: 1
SALES (est): 117.7K **Privately Held**
WEB: www.krellonline.com
SIC: 3651 Audio electronic systems

(G-901)
SHARPAC LLC
Also Called: Sharpac Cutter Grinding & Sls
114 Miles St (06607-2111)
PHONE.................................203 384-0568
Kevin Foley, *Partner*
Brian Foley, *Partner*
EMP: 5
SQ FT: 3,000
SALES (est): 565.8K **Privately Held**
SIC: 3599 Machine shop, jobbing & repair

(G-902)
SIEMPRE LLC
3360 Fairfield Ave (06605-3225)
PHONE.................................203 873-0303
Patricia Dente, *Principal*
EMP: 1
SALES (corp-wide): 78.8K **Privately Held**
SIC: 3645 Residential lighting fixtures
PA: Siempre, Llc
2007 Bridgeport Ave
Milford CT

(G-903)
SIGN CENTER LTD LIABILITY CO
140 North Ave (06606-5140)
PHONE.................................203 549-9820
EMP: 1
SALES (est): 85K **Privately Held**
SIC: 3993 Mfg Signs/Advertising Specialties

(G-904)
SIGN FAST
3841 Main St (06606-2813)
PHONE.................................203 549-8500
Nelson Lima, *Principal*
EMP: 2 EST: 2010
SALES (est): 133.1K **Privately Held**
SIC: 3993 Signs & advertising specialties

(G-905)
SIGN MAINTENANCE SERVICE CO
Also Called: Smsc Flags and Flagpoles
24 Wallace St (06604-2733)
P.O. Box 508 (06601-0508)
PHONE.................................203 336-1051
Leonard Morano, *President*
Duke Morano, *Vice Pres*
EMP: 3
SQ FT: 5,000
SALES (est): 400K **Privately Held**
SIC: 3993 7699 Neon signs; aircraft & heavy equipment repair services

(G-906)
SIGNMAN SIGNS LLC
775 Wood Ave (06604-2124)
PHONE.................................203 296-2846
Sandro Pizzicarola, *Principal*
EMP: 2
SALES (est): 113.3K **Privately Held**
SIC: 3993 Signs & advertising specialties

(G-907)
SIKORSKY AIRCRAFT CORPORATION
1201 South Ave (06604-5246)
PHONE.................................203 384-7532
Robert Brady, *Manager*
EMP: 500 **Publicly Held**
WEB: www.sikorsky.com
SIC: 3721 Helicopters
HQ: Sikorsky Aircraft Corporation
6900 Main St
Stratford CT 06614

(G-908)
SIKORSKY AIRCRAFT CORPORATION
1210 South Ave (06604-5243)
PHONE.................................203 386-4000
Edgar Baker, *Branch Mgr*
EMP: 138 **Publicly Held**
SIC: 3721 Aircraft
HQ: Sikorsky Aircraft Corporation
6900 Main St
Stratford CT 06614

(G-909)
SINGLE LOAD LLC
2056 Main St (06604-2720)
PHONE.................................860 944-7507
Vincent Bryant, *President*
Jack Cook, *Business Mgr*
EMP: 9 EST: 2012
SALES (est): 550K **Privately Held**
SIC: 3559 7389 Tobacco products machinery;

(G-910)
SMOKE & PRINT UNIVERSE
4106 Main St (06606-2301)
PHONE.................................203 540-5151
Syedbuali Naqvi, *Principal*
EMP: 4
SALES (est): 284.9K **Privately Held**
SIC: 2752 Commercial printing, lithographic

(G-911)
SPEC PLATING INC
740 Seaview Ave (06607-1606)
PHONE.................................203 366-3638
Geoffrey Scott, *President*
Steve Balgach, *QC Mgr*
EMP: 14
SQ FT: 10,000
SALES (est): 1.4MM **Privately Held**
SIC: 3471 Electroplating of metals or formed products

(G-912)
SPFM CORP
Also Called: Spray Market, The
330 Pine St (06605-2318)
PHONE.................................203 900-0005
Martin Baum, *Manager*
EMP: 2
SALES (corp-wide): 500K **Privately Held**
SIC: 3563 Air & gas compressors
PA: Spfm Corp.
162 2nd Ave
Brooklyn NY 11215
718 788-6800

(G-913)
STERLING CUSTOM CABINETRY LLC
323 North Ave (06606-5125)
PHONE..................203 335-5151
Charles Marsilio,
Salvatore K Dinardo,
EMP: 8
SALES (est): 72K Privately Held
SIC: 2434 Wood kitchen cabinets

(G-914)
STONE WORKSHOP LLC
1108 Railroad Ave (06605-1835)
PHONE..................203 362-1144
Mario Muralles,
Daniel Manetta,
▲ EMP: 7
SQ FT: 12,000
SALES (est): 940.5K Privately Held
SIC: 3281 Granite, cut & shaped

(G-915)
SUAREZ SERVICES LLC
47 Cityview Ave (06606-2518)
PHONE..................203 895-0465
Luis A Suarez Suarez, *Principal*
Nancy Suarez, *Manager*
EMP: 1
SALES (est): 86K Privately Held
SIC: 2842 7389 Specialty cleaning preparations;

(G-916)
SUNNYSIDE FAB & WELDING INC
1146 E Main St (06608-1619)
PHONE..................203 378-9515
Thomas Krasniewicz, *President*
EMP: 1
SALES (est): 49K Privately Held
SIC: 7692 Welding repair

(G-917)
SUPERIOR FUEL CO
154 Admiral St (06605-1807)
PHONE..................203 337-1213
Bart Liquigli, *President*
EMP: 3
SALES (est): 149.4K Privately Held
SIC: 2869 Fuels

(G-918)
SWAGNIFICENT ENT LLC
Also Called: Ricco Vishnu Brew House
79 Sage Ave (06610-3061)
PHONE..................203 449-0124
Raheem Nixon,
EMP: 7
SALES: 400K Privately Held
SIC: 2082 5813 Malt beverages; bars & lounges

(G-919)
TACHWA ENTERPRISES INC
805 Housatonic Ave (06604-2807)
PHONE..................203 367-9903
Andrew Wilks, *Principal*
EMP: 2
SALES (est): 86K Privately Held
SIC: 3728 Aircraft parts & equipment

(G-920)
TAR LLC
2209 Main St (06606-5330)
PHONE..................203 449-4520
Thomas A Romano, *Principal*
EMP: 2
SALES (est): 100.5K Privately Held
SIC: 2865 Tar

(G-921)
TEA-RRIFIC ICE CREAM LLC
480 Barnum Ave Ste 3 (06608-2459)
PHONE..................203 354-9805
Mario Leite,
Robert Jakobi,
Kunal Kohli,
Souvannee Leite,
Sharone Sapir,
EMP: 2
SALES (est): 158.4K Privately Held
SIC: 2024 Ice cream, bulk

(G-922)
TEE SQUARES
672 Lakeside Dr (06604-1954)
PHONE..................844 669-8337
Christopher Banks, *Principal*
EMP: 2
SALES (est): 149.9K Privately Held
SIC: 2759 Screen printing

(G-923)
TEES PLUS
850 Main St Fl 6 (06604-4917)
PHONE..................800 782-8337
▲ EMP: 13
SALES: 38.7K Privately Held
SIC: 2759 Commercial Printing

(G-924)
THOMAS DELSPINA FINE FRAMES
67 Poland St (06605-3266)
PHONE..................203 256-8628
Thomas Delspina, *Owner*
EMP: 2
SALES (est): 350K Privately Held
SIC: 2499 Picture frame molding, finished

(G-925)
THOMMEN INDUSTRIES LLC
450 Lake Ave (06605-3517)
PHONE..................203 332-7999
David Thommen, *Principal*
EMP: 2
SALES (est): 94.1K Privately Held
SIC: 3999 Manufacturing industries

(G-926)
TOM VOYTEK
186 Bradley St (06610-2008)
PHONE..................203 367-3991
Tom C Voytek, *Owner*
EMP: 1
SALES (est): 52.8K Privately Held
SIC: 2211 Slip cover fabrics, cotton

(G-927)
TONYS SMOKE SHOP OUTLET LLC
2738 Main St (06606-5382)
PHONE..................203 367-8558
Antoine Mohigel,
EMP: 2
SALES (est): 191.9K Privately Held
SIC: 3999 Cigarette & cigar products & accessories

(G-928)
TOP SHEFT CABINETRY
955 Connecticut Ave (06607-1224)
PHONE..................203 345-0000
EMP: 2 EST: 2008
SALES (est): 134.1K Privately Held
SIC: 2434 Wood kitchen cabinets

(G-929)
TRADITIONAL BATH AND TILE
435 Dogwood Dr (06606-1407)
P.O. Box 9366 (06601-9366)
PHONE..................347 539-2088
Leroy R Thomas Sr, *Owner*
EMP: 1
SALES (est): 63.9K Privately Held
SIC: 3272 Roofing tile & slabs, concrete

(G-930)
UNGER ENTERPRISES LLC
425 Asylum St (06610-2105)
PHONE..................203 366-4884
Rote Charles, *Vice Pres*
Peter Lupoli, *Vice Pres*
Bob Camp, *Project Mgr*
Charles Perry, *Prdtn Mgr*
Ken Paolini, *Purch Agent*
◆ EMP: 125 EST: 1975
SQ FT: 70,000
SALES (est): 29.6MM Privately Held
WEB: www.ungerglobal.com
SIC: 3423 Hand & edge tools

(G-931)
UNGER INDUSTRIAL LLC
425 Asylum St (06610-2105)
PHONE..................203 336-3344
Dane Unger,
EMP: 9
SALES (est): 1.3MM Privately Held
SIC: 3429 Manufactured hardware (general)

(G-932)
US HIGHWAY PRODUCTS INC
Also Called: American Fiber Technologies
500 Bostwick Ave (06605-2440)
PHONE..................203 336-0332
EMP: 15
SQ FT: 18,000
SALES (est): 1MM Privately Held
SIC: 3993 5085 Mfg Signs/Advertising Specialties Whol Industrial Supplies

(G-933)
VALLEY CONTAINER INC
850 Union Ave (06607-1137)
PHONE..................203 368-6546
Arthur Vietze Jr, *CEO*
Rudolph Neidermeir, *Ch of Bd*
Robert Neidermeir, *President*
Robert Vietze, *Vice Pres*
Dave Law, *Plant Mgr*
▲ EMP: 45
SQ FT: 120,000
SALES: 16.8MM Privately Held
WEB: www.valleycontainer.com
SIC: 2679 7319 Corrugated paper: made from purchased material; display advertising service

(G-934)
VINEGAR SYNDROME LLC
100 Congress St (06604-4046)
PHONE..................212 722-9755
Joe Rubin, *Principal*
EMP: 3 EST: 2013
SALES (est): 218.9K Privately Held
SIC: 2099 Vinegar

(G-935)
WASTE TO GREEN FUEL LLC
1376 Chopsey Hill Rd (06606-2422)
PHONE..................203 536-5855
EMP: 4
SALES (est): 358K Privately Held
SIC: 2869 Fuels

(G-936)
WHITE BRONZE LLC
60 Wordin Ave (06605-1530)
PHONE..................214 605-7352
Elizabeth Kang, *Principal*
EMP: 1
SALES (est): 54.9K Privately Held
SIC: 3462 Iron & steel forgings

(G-937)
WILHELM GDALE ELZABETH DESIGNS
333 Vincellette St # 37 (06606-2253)
PHONE..................203 371-8787
Elizabeth Wilhelm-Goodale, *Owner*
EMP: 1
SALES: 75K Privately Held
SIC: 8299 2299 3961 0782 Floral arrangement instruction; acoustic felts; bracelets, except precious metal; garden services

(G-938)
WINDCHECK LLC
110 Chapel St (06604-4020)
PHONE..................203 332-7639
Ann Hannah, *Owner*
Chris Gill, *Partner*
EMP: 2
SALES (est): 152.5K Privately Held
WEB: www.windcheckis.com
SIC: 2731 Book publishing

(G-939)
WINDOW TINTING & SIGNS INC
68 Elizabeth St (06610-3219)
PHONE..................203 336-5539
Bill Kovak, *President*
EMP: 3
SALES (est): 85.4K Privately Held
SIC: 7549 3993 Glass tinting, automotive; signs & advertising specialties

(G-940)
WOODWORKERS HEAVEN INC
955 Conn Ave Ste 4106 (06607-1222)
PHONE..................203 333-2778
John W Eskew, *President*
EMP: 10
SQ FT: 5,000
SALES: 1MM Privately Held
SIC: 2511 Wood household furniture

(G-941)
YANKEE METALS LLC
76 Knowlton St (06608-2105)
PHONE..................203 612-7470
Leonard D Strocchia,
EMP: 4
SALES (est): 624.6K Privately Held
SIC: 3441 Fabricated structural metal

(G-942)
YANKEE PLAK CO INC
Also Called: Yankee Photo Service
240 Alice St (06606-5675)
PHONE..................203 333-3168
Joseph Abruzzo Jr, *President*
Melanie Abruzzo, *Vice Pres*
EMP: 20
SQ FT: 12,000
SALES (est): 1.9MM Privately Held
WEB: www.yankeeplak.com
SIC: 7384 3993 Photofinish laboratories; signs & advertising specialties

(G-943)
YARD STICK DECORE
145 Hart St # 1 (06606-5048)
PHONE..................203 330-0360
Joe Costa, *Mng Member*
EMP: 10
SALES (est): 70.5K Privately Held
SIC: 2391 Curtains & draperies

(G-944)
YOGUEZ WOODWORKING LLC
22 Colorado Ave (06605-1718)
PHONE..................203 943-6956
Jorge Yoguez, *Principal*
EMP: 1
SALES (est): 168.9K Privately Held
SIC: 2431 Trim, wood

Bridgewater
Litchfield County

(G-945)
BTF LLC
236 Henry Sanford Rd (06752-1224)
PHONE..................860 354-8926
Patrick Trowbridge, *Principal*
EMP: 1
SALES (est): 54.1K Privately Held
SIC: 2389 Men's miscellaneous accessories

(G-946)
LINE X OF WESTERN CONNECTICUT
26 New Milford Rd E (06752-1137)
PHONE..................860 355-6997
EMP: 2
SALES (est): 120K Privately Held
SIC: 2821 Mfg Plastic Materials/Resins

(G-947)
TOWN OF BRIDGEWATER
Also Called: Townhall Bridgewater Selectman
44 Main St (06752)
P.O. Box 216 (06752-0216)
PHONE..................860 354-5250
William Stuart, *Manager*
EMP: 19 Privately Held
WEB: www.bridgewatertownhall.org
SIC: 9121 2711 Town council; newspapers
PA: Town Of Bridgewater
44 Main St S
Bridgewater CT 06752
860 354-2731

(G-948)
WATCHDOG WELDING LLC
26 New Milford Rd (06752-1137)
PHONE..................860 355-9549
Leslie Thompson, *Owner*

GEOGRAPHIC SECTION
Bristol - Hartford County (G-976)

EMP: 1
SALES (est): 103.2K Privately Held
SIC: 7692 Welding repair

Bristol
Hartford County

(G-949)
A & D COMPONENTS INC
33 Stafford Ave Ste 2 (06010-4699)
PHONE...............................860 582-9541
Harold Etherington, *President*
Rita McKenzie, *Corp Secy*
Nora Etherington, *Vice Pres*
EMP: 8
SQ FT: 25,000
SALES (est): 1.2MM Privately Held
WEB: www.adcomponents.com
SIC: 3469 Stamping metal for the trade

(G-950)
A & E ENGRAVING SERVICE
37 Main St (06010-6596)
PHONE...............................860 582-6503
John Kucinskas Sr, *Partner*
Andrew Grande, *Partner*
Ernest Grande, *Partner*
EMP: 2
SQ FT: 450
SALES (est): 258.1K Privately Held
SIC: 3479 5999 3555 Engraving jewelry silverware, or metal; trophies & plaques; printing trades machinery

(G-951)
A C MANUFACTURING
87 Mine Rd (06010-2411)
PHONE...............................860 314-8225
Andre Cloutier, *Executive*
EMP: 1
SALES (est): 86K Privately Held
SIC: 3999 Manufacturing industries

(G-952)
A EMERGENCY ROOTER SERVICE
116 Kilmartin Ave (06010-7119)
PHONE...............................860 582-3612
EMP: 1
SALES (est): 76.6K Privately Held
SIC: 1711 2842 Plumbing/Heating/Air Cond Contractor Mfg Polish/Sanitation Goods

(G-953)
ABEK LLC
492 Birch St (06010-7837)
PHONE...............................860 314-3905
Alex N Beavers, *CEO*
John B Thomson Jr, *Chairman*
Robert C Magee, *Vice Chairman*
Patrick Mazzeo, *Vice Pres*
Jeffry Peterson, *Vice Pres*
▲ EMP: 11 EST: 1976
SQ FT: 12,500
SALES (est): 1.9MM
SALES (corp-wide): 19.8B Publicly Held
SIC: 3562 Ball bearings & parts
PA: Danaher Corporation
    2200 Penn Ave Nw Ste 800w
    Washington DC 20037
    202 828-0850

(G-954)
ACCURATE CENTERLESS GRINDING
43 Deer Park Rd (06010-2893)
PHONE...............................860 747-9794
Rod Laddie, *Owner*
EMP: 1
SQ FT: 2,000
SALES: 300K Privately Held
SIC: 3599 Grinding castings for the trade

(G-955)
ACE FINISHING CO LLC
225 Terryville Rd (06010-4010)
P.O. Box 1213 (06011-1213)
PHONE...............................860 582-4600
Nick E Phillips,
Antoni Phillips,
Edward A Phillips,
EMP: 5

SALES (est): 511.6K Privately Held
SIC: 2396 3542 Fabric printing & stamping; die casting & extruding machines

(G-956)
ACT ROBOTS INC
95 Wooster Ct (06010-6777)
PHONE...............................860 314-1557
Richard Morgan, *President*
Mark Zamaria, *Corp Secy*
Katarina Zamaria, *Manager*
EMP: 9 EST: 1996
SQ FT: 12,000
SALES (est): 2.1MM Privately Held
WEB: www.actrobots.com
SIC: 8711 3569 Industrial engineers; robots, assembly line: industrial & commercial

(G-957)
ADK PRESSURE EQUIPMENT CORP (DH)
745 Clark Ave (06010-4068)
PHONE...............................860 585-0050
William F Steinen, *Ch of Bd*
William F Steinen Jr, *President*
G Menninga, *Vice Pres*
Thomas Keenan, *Treasurer*
EMP: 6
SALES (est): 754K
SALES (corp-wide): 15.3MM Privately Held
SIC: 3564 Blowers & fans
HQ: Mcintire Company
    745 Clark Ave
    Bristol CT 06010
    860 585-8559

(G-958)
ADOR INC
210 Redstone Hill Rd # 5 (06010-7796)
PHONE...............................860 583-2367
Chang Lieh Hsieh, *Principal*
Pam Sokolosky, *Vice Pres*
▲ EMP: 3
SALES: 100K Privately Held
SIC: 3429 Manufactured hardware (general)

(G-959)
ADVANCED SCREEN PRINTING LLC
75 Seneca Rd (06010-7139)
PHONE...............................860 845-8337
Joseph Bochicchio, *Principal*
EMP: 2
SALES (est): 110.3K Privately Held
SIC: 2752 Commercial printing, lithographic

(G-960)
AFFORDABLE CONVEYORS SVCS LLC
144 W Washington St (06010-5444)
P.O. Box 2252 (06011-2252)
PHONE...............................860 582-1800
Philip J Robotham,
Karen Tibbals, *Admin Sec*
EMP: 10
SALES (est): 2MM Privately Held
WEB: www.affordableconveyor.com
SIC: 3535 Conveyors & conveying equipment

(G-961)
ALLGREENIT LLC
123 Farmington Ave # 162 (06010-4200)
PHONE...............................860 516-4948
Patrick Ouellette, *Sales Dir*
Peter Stevenson,
Bobbi Shafer, *Admin Asst*
EMP: 3
SALES (est): 492.7K Privately Held
SIC: 3433 Solar heaters & collectors

(G-962)
ALLOY WELDING & MFG CO INC
233 Riverside Ave (06010-6319)
PHONE...............................860 582-3638
Alfred L Frechette, *President*
Darren Frechette, *General Mgr*
Alfred Frechette, *Vice Pres*
Edith Frechette, *Vice Pres*
Ken Nelson, *Sales Mgr*
EMP: 15

SQ FT: 14,000
SALES (est): 3.5MM Privately Held
SIC: 3441 1799 Fabricated structural metal; welding on site

(G-963)
APPLE VALLEY CANDLE COMPANY
25 Ingraham Pl (06010-4109)
PHONE...............................860 940-1176
EMP: 2
SALES (est): 78K Privately Held
SIC: 3999 Mfg Misc Products

(G-964)
APPSTRACT IDEAS
81 Martin Rd (06010-4020)
PHONE...............................860 857-1123
Donald McKeith, *Owner*
Jonathan Bimler,
Leo Carroll,
EMP: 3
SALES (est): 150K Privately Held
SIC: 7372 Prepackaged software

(G-965)
ARM MEDICAL DEVICES INC
190 Dino Rd (06010-7888)
PHONE...............................860 583-5165
Anthony Calderoni, *President*
EMP: 1
SALES (est): 126.7K Privately Held
SIC: 3841 Surgical & medical instruments

(G-966)
ARROW MANUFACTURING COMPANY
16 Jeannette St (06010-7000)
PHONE...............................860 589-3900
Thomas E Selnau, *President*
William R Selnau, *Vice Pres*
Laurie Angers, *Safety Mgr*
Ray Girardin, *QC Mgr*
Paula Green, *Bookkeeper*
EMP: 27 EST: 1951
SQ FT: 40,000
SALES (est): 5MM Privately Held
WEB: www.arrowmfg.com
SIC: 3469 3493 3496 Stamping metal for the trade; steel springs, except wire; miscellaneous fabricated wire products

(G-967)
ARTHUR G RUSSELL COMPANY INC
750 Clark Ave (06010-4065)
P.O. Box 237 (06011-0237)
PHONE...............................860 583-4109
Robert J Ensminger, *CEO*
Mark Burzynski, *President*
William Mis, *Vice Pres*
Don Palaia, *Vice Pres*
Jim Maloney, *Project Mgr*
◆ EMP: 85
SQ FT: 80,000
SALES (est): 32.2MM Privately Held
WEB: www.arthurgrussell.com
SIC: 3569 Assembly machines, non-metalworking

(G-968)
ATLANTIC PRECISION SPRING INC
125 Ronzo Rd (06010-8620)
PHONE...............................860 583-1864
Neil Fries, *President*
Brian J Fries, *Vice Pres*
Michael J Fries, *Vice Pres*
Terry Fries, *Admin Sec*
EMP: 32 EST: 1958
SQ FT: 15,000
SALES (est): 7.9MM Privately Held
WEB: www.aps-ct.com
SIC: 3493 3495 3469 Flat springs, sheet or strip stock; wire springs; metal stampings

(G-969)
B & P PLATING EQUIPMENT LLC
74 Broderick Rd (06010-7736)
PHONE...............................860 589-5799
Ronald Landrette, *Mng Member*
EMP: 10
SQ FT: 10,000

SALES (est): 1.1MM Privately Held
SIC: 3471 3544 Plating of metals or formed products; special dies & tools

(G-970)
B & R STAIR
1 Glenn St (06010-7311)
PHONE...............................860 582-6584
EMP: 1 EST: 1986
SALES (est): 97K Privately Held
SIC: 1521 2431 Single-Family House Construction Mfg Millwork

(G-971)
B&T SCREW MACHINE CO INC
571 Broad St (06010-6662)
P.O. Box 431 (06011-0431)
PHONE...............................860 314-4410
Theresa Gokey, *President*
Jessica Schroder, *Opers Staff*
EMP: 12
SQ FT: 20,000
SALES (est): 2.4MM Privately Held
SIC: 3451 Screw machine products

(G-972)
BARLOW METAL STAMPING INC
2 Barlow St (06010-4001)
P.O. Box 1397 (06011-1397)
PHONE...............................860 583-1387
Peter Gaughan, *Ch of Bd*
Terry Gaughan, *President*
Norman Lazerow, *Vice Pres*
Sandy Gaughan, *Technology*
EMP: 20
SQ FT: 15,600
SALES (est): 4MM Privately Held
WEB: www.barlowmetalstamping.com
SIC: 3469 Stamping metal for the trade

(G-973)
BARNES GROUP INC (PA)
123 Main St (06010-6376)
PHONE...............................860 583-7070
Thomas O Barnes, *Ch of Bd*
Patrick J Dempsey, *President*
Norbert Scheid, *President*
Michael A Beck, *Senior VP*
Dawn N Edwards, *Senior VP*
▲ EMP: 277
SALES: 1.5B Publicly Held
WEB: www.barnesgroupinc.com
SIC: 3724 3495 3469 Aircraft engines & engine parts; precision springs; stamping metal for the trade

(G-974)
BARNES GROUP INC
Associated Spring
18 Main St (06010-6581)
PHONE...............................860 582-9581
Paulo Coit, *Branch Mgr*
Mike McGinty, *Manager*
Scott Litchfield, *MIS Dir*
Eric Norton, *MIS Staff*
EMP: 100
SALES (corp-wide): 1.5B Publicly Held
WEB: www.barnesgroupinc.com
SIC: 3469 3495 Metal stampings; wire springs
PA: Barnes Group Inc.
    123 Main St
    Bristol CT 06010
    860 583-7070

(G-975)
BARNES GROUP INC
Also Called: Barnes Aerospace W Chester Div
123 Main St (06010-6376)
PHONE...............................513 759-3503
Rick Barnhart, *General Mgr*
EMP: 3700
SALES (corp-wide): 1.5B Publicly Held
WEB: www.barnesgroupinc.com
SIC: 3724 Aircraft engines & engine parts
PA: Barnes Group Inc.
    123 Main St
    Bristol CT 06010
    860 583-7070

(G-976)
BARON & YOUNG CO INC
400 Middle St Ste 13 (06010-8405)
PHONE...............................860 589-3235

Bristol - Hartford County (G-977)

Donald Baron, *President*
Dennis Dutkiewicz, *Vice Pres*
Patricia Baron, *Admin Sec*
EMP: 9
SQ FT: 10,080
SALES (est): 900K **Privately Held**
SIC: 3471 3479 Buffing for the trade; polishing, metals or formed products; lacquering of metal products

(G-977)
BASS PRODUCTS LLC
435 Lake Ave (06010-7332)
P.O. Box 1359 (06011-1359)
PHONE 860 585-7923
Tony Sposato, *General Mgr*
Craig Verneau, *Engineer*
Jack Warhola, *Finance Mgr*
Kevin Warhola, *Info Tech Mgr*
Matthew Benson, *Technical Staff*
EMP: 9
SQ FT: 17,000
SALES (est): 1.5MM **Privately Held**
WEB: www.bassproducts.com
SIC: 3613 Power circuit breakers

(G-978)
BAUER INC
175 Century Dr (06010-7482)
PHONE 860 583-9100
Lou Auletta Jr, *President*
Andy Novotny, *Principal*
Thomas Gilchrist, *Vice Pres*
Rob Michell, *Vice Pres*
Jeff Broomhead, *Project Engr*
▲ **EMP:** 58
SQ FT: 38,000
SALES (est): 17.6MM **Privately Held**
WEB: www.bauerct.com
SIC: 3829 Aircraft & motor vehicle measurement equipment

(G-979)
BEEKLEY MEDICAL
1 Prestige Ln (06010-7468)
PHONE 860 583-4700
Ayn Laplant, *President*
Paul Mathews, *Business Mgr*
Tony Main, *Traffic Mgr*
Beth Kyle, *Research*
Sally Calcaterra, *Accounts Mgr*
EMP: 1 **EST:** 2017
SALES (est): 46.5K
SALES (corp-wide): 16.6MM **Privately Held**
SIC: 3841 Surgical & medical instruments
PA: Beekley Corporation
    1 Prestige Ln
    Bristol CT 06010
    860 583-4700

(G-980)
BELMONT CORPORATION
Also Called: Village Cabinets
60 Crystal Pond Pl (06010-7475)
PHONE 860 589-5700
David T Clark, *CEO*
Bruce L Clark, *President*
Robert L Boutot, *Exec VP*
EMP: 45
SQ FT: 41,000
SALES (est): 5.6MM **Privately Held**
WEB: www.villagecabinets.com
SIC: 2434 2521 2517 Wood kitchen cabinets; wood office furniture; wood television & radio cabinets

(G-981)
BES CU INC
400 Middle St (06010-8405)
PHONE 860 582-8660
Ed O'Hannessian, *CEO*
Jay Rasmus, *President*
Karen Cunningham, *Vice Pres*
EMP: 7
SQ FT: 3,500
SALES (est): 500K **Privately Held**
SIC: 3496 Miscellaneous fabricated wire products

(G-982)
BETTER MOLDED PRODUCTS INC (PA)
95 Valley St Ste 2 (06010-4985)
P.O. Box 2141 (06011-2141)
PHONE 860 589-0066
Roy Izzo, *President*
EMP: 170
SQ FT: 60,000
SALES (est): 21.6MM **Privately Held**
WEB: www.bettermolded.com
SIC: 3089 3544 Injection molding of plastics; special dies, tools, jigs & fixtures

(G-983)
BHS
Also Called: Bristol Hydraulic Scaffolding
43 Seminary St (06010-9116)
PHONE 860 585-0125
Jean Marc Lacroix, *Owner*
EMP: 7
SALES (est): 538.7K **Privately Held**
SIC: 3446 1521 Scaffolds, mobile or stationary: metal; single-family housing construction

(G-984)
BM PUBLISHING LLC
557 Pine St (06010-6919)
PHONE 860 778-1583
Bobby Garcia, *Principal*
EMP: 1
SALES (est): 52.2K **Privately Held**
SIC: 2741 Miscellaneous publishing

(G-985)
BOWDEN ENGINEERING CO
88 Jeannette St (06010-7036)
PHONE 860 583-9585
James Bowden, *Owner*
Melvin Bowden, *Owner*
EMP: 1
SQ FT: 700
SALES (est): 73.9K **Privately Held**
SIC: 3469 Machine parts, stamped or pressed metal

(G-986)
BRADLEY GUN SIGHT CO INC
300 Riverside Ave (06010-6320)
PHONE 860 589-0531
Donald E Day Sr, *Ch of Bd*
Peter A Day, *Admin Sec*
EMP: 1 **EST:** 1965
SALES (est): 138.6K **Privately Held**
SIC: 3827 Sighting & fire control equipment, optical

(G-987)
BRISTOL ADULT RESOURCE CTR INC
97 Peck Ln (06010-6163)
PHONE 860 583-8721
Ronnie Cassin, *Branch Mgr*
EMP: 50
SALES (corp-wide): 7.5MM **Privately Held**
SIC: 2621 Bristols
PA: Bristol Adult Resource Center, Inc.
    195 Maltby St
    Bristol CT 06010
    860 261-5592

(G-988)
BRISTOL BLISS LLC
229 Fall Mountain Rd (06010-5910)
PHONE 203 704-0952
Mary Brown, *Principal*
EMP: 1
SALES (est): 100.4K **Privately Held**
SIC: 2621 Paper mills

(G-989)
BRISTOL INSTRUMENT GEARS INC
164 Central St Ste 1 (06010-6778)
P.O. Box 9248 (06011-9248)
PHONE 860 583-1395
James Carros, *President*
David Carros, *Vice Pres*
Alex Carros, *Opers-Prdtn-Mfg*
Rosemary P Carros, *Credit Mgr*
EMP: 15 **EST:** 1951
SQ FT: 20,000
SALES (est): 2.4MM **Privately Held**
WEB: www.bristolgears.com
SIC: 3462 Iron & steel forgings

(G-990)
BRISTOL NITRO SOFTBALL CORP
104 Driftwood Rd (06010-2590)
PHONE 860 940-1924
Barrett Cretella, *Founder*
EMP: 1
SALES (est): 57.5K **Privately Held**
SIC: 2621 Bristols

(G-991)
BRISTOL PLAZA
576 Farmington Ave (06010-3933)
PHONE 617 553-1820
EMP: 1
SALES (est): 57.5K **Privately Held**
SIC: 2621 Bristols

(G-992)
BRISTOL SIGNART INC
550 Broad St (06010-6664)
P.O. Box 9081 (06011-9081)
PHONE 860 582-2577
Francis Blethen, *President*
Mark Blethen, *Admin Sec*
EMP: 3
SQ FT: 2,500
SALES: 180K **Privately Held**
SIC: 3993 Signs & advertising specialties

(G-993)
BRISTOL TOOL & DIE COMPANY
550 Broad St Ste 13 (06010-6677)
PHONE 860 582-2577
Carl Guenther, *President*
EMP: 20 **EST:** 1965
SQ FT: 5,000
SALES (est): 3.1MM **Privately Held**
SIC: 3469 3599 3544 Stamping metal for the trade; machine & other job shop work; special dies & tools

(G-994)
BRISTOL TOOL WORKS LLC
61 E Main St (06010-7060)
PHONE 860 585-7302
Richard E Lacey, *President*
EMP: 2 **EST:** 1999
SALES (est): 202.5K **Privately Held**
SIC: 3451 Screw machine products

(G-995)
BVC PUBLISHING
103 Harrison St (06010-5173)
PHONE 860 202-0704
EMP: 2
SALES (est): 103.7K **Privately Held**
SIC: 2741 Miscellaneous publishing

(G-996)
CACO PRINT PRODUCTIONS LLC
132 Riverside Ave (06010-6311)
PHONE 860 583-1223
William Lozito, *Owner*
EMP: 2 **EST:** 2012
SALES (est): 204.2K **Privately Held**
SIC: 2752 Commercial printing, offset

(G-997)
CADENTIA LLC
Also Called: Wiperbooties
136 Rockwell Ave (06010-5942)
PHONE 860 995-0173
Patrick Nelligan,
EMP: 3 **EST:** 2010
SALES (est): 282K **Privately Held**
SIC: 5013 5015 7372 Motor vehicle supplies & new parts; automotive parts & supplies, used; application computer software

(G-998)
CAMBRDGE FINE WDWKG RENOVATION ◆
803 Wolcott St (06010-5918)
PHONE 860 583-7561
EMP: 1 **EST:** 2019
SALES (est): 54.1K **Privately Held**
SIC: 2431 Millwork

(G-999)
CANDLES FOR A CAUSE USA
30 Summer St Apt 2 (06010-5056)
PHONE 860 912-3946
Jonathan Mendonca, *Principal*
EMP: 1
SALES (est): 39.6K **Privately Held**
SIC: 3999 Candles

(G-1000)
CENTURY SPRING MFG CO INC
100 Wooster Ct (06010-6731)
P.O. Box 301 (06011-0301)
PHONE 860 582-3344
Walter Waseleski, *CEO*
William J Waseleski, *President*
Theresa Waseleski, *Admin Sec*
Jessica Baril, *Assistant*
EMP: 25 **EST:** 1975
SQ FT: 14,000
SALES (est): 5.8MM **Privately Held**
WEB: www.centuryspringmfg.com
SIC: 3495 3493 3469 Mechanical springs, precision; steel springs, except wire; metal stampings

(G-1001)
CLASSIC COIL COMPANY INC
205 Century Dr (06010-7486)
PHONE 860 583-7600
Rudolf Zeidler, *CEO*
James E Dowman, *President*
Nancy Matute, *Purchasing*
Richard Bisaillon, *CFO*
Heather Bauer, *Controller*
▲ **EMP:** 100 **EST:** 1976
SQ FT: 25,000
SALES (est): 29.7MM **Privately Held**
WEB: www.classic-coil.com
SIC: 3677 Coil windings, electronic

(G-1002)
CLASSIC TRIM LLC
70 Maple Ave (06010-2656)
PHONE 860 543-9102
Roxanne Forcier, *Owner*
Margaret Shumbo, *Principal*
EMP: 2
SALES (est): 126.1K **Privately Held**
WEB: www.classicsofttrim.com
SIC: 3423 Carpenters' hand tools, except saws: levels, chisels, etc.

(G-1003)
CMI SPECIALTY PRODUCTS INC
105 Redstone Hill Rd (06010-7799)
PHONE 860 585-0409
Joseph A Bozzuto, *President*
▲ **EMP:** 10
SQ FT: 2,100
SALES (est): 2.2MM **Privately Held**
WEB: www.cmispecialty.com
SIC: 3312 3353 Rods, iron & steel: made in steel mills; aluminum sheet & strip

(G-1004)
COMMUNITY ACPNCTURE BRSTOL LLC
25 Newell Rd (06010-5100)
PHONE 860 833-9330
Robert G Robles, *Principal*
EMP: 1 **EST:** 2015
SALES (est): 98K **Privately Held**
SIC: 2621 Bristols

(G-1005)
COMPUMAIL CORP
135 Cross St (06010-7434)
PHONE 860 583-1906
EMP: 1 **Privately Held**
SIC: 2752 Commercial printing, offset
PA: Compumail Corp
    298 Captain Lewis Dr
    Southington CT 06489

(G-1006)
CONNECTICUT TOOL & CUTTER CO
280 Redstone Hill Rd # 1 (06010-8624)
P.O. Box 368, Plainville (06062-0368)
PHONE 860 314-1740
Alfonse Skudlarek Sr, *President*
Caroline Skudlarek, *Vice Pres*
Dennis Shields, *QC Mgr*
Cindy Vincent, *Office Mgr*
EMP: 20 **EST:** 1970
SQ FT: 16,900
SALES: 3.6MM **Privately Held**
SIC: 3541 Machine tools, metal cutting: exotic (explosive, etc.)

Bristol - Hartford County

(G-1007)
CONVEYCO TECHNOLOGIES INC (PA)
47 Commerce Dr (06010-8608)
P.O. Box 1000 (06011-1000)
PHONE..................860 589-8215
Raymond Cocozza, *President*
Jim Benevides, *Principal*
Terry McAlister, *Project Mgr*
Doug Cartona, *Manager*
Chris Benevides, *Executive*
EMP: 23
SQ FT: 15,000
SALES (est): 10.4MM **Privately Held**
WEB: www.conveyco.com
SIC: 5084 3625 Materials handling machinery; conveyor systems; control equipment, electric

(G-1008)
CP SOLAR THERMAL LLC
210 Century Dr (06010-7477)
PHONE..................860 877-2238
Thomas Etter, *Mng Member*
EMP: 3
SALES (est): 174.3K **Privately Held**
SIC: 3433 Heating equipment, except electric

(G-1009)
CT CONVEYOR LLC
320 Terryville Rd (06010-4012)
PHONE..................860 637-2926
Louis Labelle, *Mng Member*
EMP: 6
SQ FT: 1,000
SALES: 310K **Privately Held**
SIC: 3535 Conveyors & conveying equipment

(G-1010)
CURTIS PRODUCTS LLC
70 Halcyon Dr (06010-7464)
PHONE..................203 754-4155
Ronald Weintraub, *Mng Member*
EMP: 18 **EST:** 1950
SALES: 3.9MM **Privately Held**
WEB: www.curtisproducts.net
SIC: 3451 Screw machine products

(G-1011)
DACRUZ MANUFACTURING INC
100 Broderick Rd (06010-7724)
PHONE..................860 584-5315
Victor P Dacruz, *President*
Chelsea E Castor, *Vice Pres*
Parrish Castor, *Production*
Michael Boudreau, *Purch Mgr*
Betty Dacruz, *CFO*
EMP: 43
SQ FT: 33,000
SALES: 6MM **Privately Held**
WEB: www.cmscrew.com
SIC: 3451 Screw machine products

(G-1012)
DAY FRED A CO LLC
Also Called: F A D C O
11 Commerce Dr (06010-8608)
PHONE..................860 589-0531
Randy Mencil,
EMP: 4
SQ FT: 9,200
SALES (est): 611.7K **Privately Held**
SIC: 3451 Screw machine products

(G-1013)
DBA NE SHEET METAL
385 King St (06010-5279)
PHONE..................860 584-0362
Diane Boudreau, *Principal*
EMP: 2 **EST:** 2008
SALES (est): 131.4K **Privately Held**
SIC: 3444 Sheet metalwork

(G-1014)
DEKA ENTERPRISES
200 Central St (06010-6716)
PHONE..................860 582-6976
Dennis Martin, *Owner*
EMP: 1 **EST:** 2000
SALES (est): 94.1K **Privately Held**
SIC: 3495 Wire springs

(G-1015)
DEXON TECH LLC
550 Broad St Unit H (06010-6664)
PHONE..................860 584-1442
Derek D Dworak, *Owner*
EMP: 1
SALES: 200K **Privately Held**
SIC: 3999 Manufacturing industries

(G-1016)
DI VENERE CO
35 Wooster Ct Ste 1 (06010-6785)
PHONE..................860 582-0208
Tom Di Venere Jr, *Owner*
EMP: 1
SALES (est): 134.9K **Privately Held**
SIC: 2431 Woodwork, interior & ornamental

(G-1017)
DI-COR INDUSTRIES INC
139 Center St (06010-5074)
P.O. Box 3128 (06011-3128)
PHONE..................860 585-5583
Harry Vassiliou, *President*
Tom Vassiliou, *Treasurer*
▼ **EMP:** 15
SQ FT: 24,000
SALES (est): 3.8MM **Privately Held**
SIC: 3441 2542 5021 Fabricated structural metal; racks, merchandise display or storage: except wood; racks

(G-1018)
DOUBLETREE
42 Century Dr (06010-4779)
PHONE..................860 589-7766
Lynn Dell, *Owner*
EMP: 12
SALES (est): 2.4MM **Privately Held**
SIC: 2621 Bristols

(G-1019)
DRAPERIES PLUS
31 Ridgecrest Ln (06010-2910)
PHONE..................860 589-3634
William Foley, *Owner*
EMP: 1
SALES (est): 87.6K **Privately Held**
SIC: 2391 5714 Draperies, plastic & textile: from purchased materials; draperies

(G-1020)
DRM ASSOCIATES LLC
21 Yale Dr (06010-2301)
PHONE..................860 583-7744
Daniel Messler,
EMP: 2
SALES (est): 170.5K **Privately Held**
SIC: 3312 Structural shapes & pilings, steel

(G-1021)
DT MANUFACTURING LLC
550 Broad St Unit P (06010-6664)
PHONE..................860 384-8449
Dariusz Trojanowski, *Principal*
EMP: 1
SALES (est): 71.2K **Privately Held**
SIC: 3999 Manufacturing industries

(G-1022)
DYNAMIC COATING SOLUTIONS LLC
26 Columbus Ave (06010-4407)
PHONE..................860 321-7483
EMP: 2
SALES (est): 69.9K **Privately Held**
SIC: 3479 Coating/Engraving Service

(G-1023)
DYNAMIC MANUFACTURING COMPANY
Also Called: Dymco
95 Valley St Ste 5 (06010-4985)
P.O. Box 1880 (06011-1880)
PHONE..................860 589-2751
John Beckwith, *President*
Brian Beckwith, *Vice Pres*
Rosemary Beckwith, *Vice Pres*
Lori Ann Jones, *Admin Sec*
▼ **EMP:** 5
SQ FT: 15,000

SALES: 750K **Privately Held**
WEB: www.dymco.com
SIC: 3493 3469 Coiled flat springs; flat springs, sheet or strip stock; torsion bar springs; metal stampings

(G-1024)
E P M CO INC
Also Called: Precision Swiss Screw Machine
147 Terryville Rd (06010-4010)
P.O. Box 207, Pequabuck (06781-0207)
PHONE..................860 589-3233
Donna Patnode, *President*
EMP: 3 **EST:** 2001
SALES (est): 194.8K **Privately Held**
SIC: 3451 Screw machine products

(G-1025)
EARTH LOVING STITCHES
60 Leominster Rd (06010-4337)
PHONE..................405 833-9343
EMP: 1
SALES (est): 31.2K **Privately Held**
SIC: 2395 Embroidery & art needlework

(G-1026)
EMME CONTROLS LLC
32 Valley St Fl C (06010-4991)
P.O. Box 2251 (06011-2251)
PHONE..................503 793-3792
Jon Brodeur, *CEO*
David Cohen, *President*
Kim Wilson, *Sales Staff*
EMP: 8 **EST:** 2015
SQ FT: 12,000
SALES (est): 472.1K **Privately Held**
SIC: 3822 Air flow controllers, air conditioning & refrigeration

(G-1027)
EMME E2MS LLC
32 Valley St Fl C (06010-4991)
P.O. Box 2251 (06011-2251)
PHONE..................860 845-8810
Jonathan Brodeur, *CEO*
EMP: 10
SQ FT: 10,000
SALES (est): 1.4MM **Privately Held**
SIC: 3822 Limit controls, residential & commercial heating types

(G-1028)
EMPCO INC (PA)
Also Called: Empco Prcision Swiss Screw Mch
147 Terryville Rd (06010-4010)
P.O. Box 207, Pequabuck (06781-0207)
PHONE..................860 589-3233
Henry Patnode, *President*
EMP: 8 **EST:** 1969
SQ FT: 1,000
SALES (est): 874.5K **Privately Held**
SIC: 3599 Machine shop, jobbing & repair

(G-1029)
ENFLO CORPORATION (PA)
315 Lake Ave (06010-7397)
P.O. Box 490 (06011-0490)
PHONE..................860 589-0014
Myron A Rudner, *President*
Robert E Dalton, *Vice Pres*
Karl Forsander, *Vice Pres*
Jonathan Stanek, *CFO*
Tasha Brown, *Sales Staff*
▲ **EMP:** 39 **EST:** 1955
SQ FT: 25,000
SALES (est): 4MM **Privately Held**
WEB: www.enflo.com
SIC: 2821 Plastics materials & resins

(G-1030)
EQUIPMENT WORKS
542 Jerome Ave (06010-2666)
PHONE..................860 585-9686
James Bialobrzeski, *Owner*
EMP: 2
SALES (est): 229.2K **Privately Held**
SIC: 3441 Fabricated structural metal

(G-1031)
ETHERINGTON BROTHERS INC
Also Called: E B Buffing
33 Stafford Ave Ste 2 (06010-4699)
PHONE..................860 585-5624
Nora Etherington, *President*
Harold Etherington, *Vice Pres*

EMP: 8
SALES (est): 815.9K **Privately Held**
SIC: 3471 Polishing, metals or formed products

(G-1032)
EWALD INSTRUMENTS CORP
95 Wooster Ct Ste 3 (06010-6777)
P.O. Box 398, Goshen (06756-0398)
PHONE..................860 491-9042
Richard Vreeland, *President*
Susan Vreeland, *Corp Secy*
EMP: 12 **EST:** 1954
SQ FT: 14,000
SALES (est): 2MM **Privately Held**
WEB: www.ewaldinstruments.com
SIC: 3545 3625 7699 Cutting tools for machine tools; resistance welder controls; welding equipment repair

(G-1033)
EXCEL SPRING & STAMPING LLC
61 E Main St Ste 2 (06010-7060)
PHONE..................860 585-1495
John Sandstrom,
EMP: 9
SQ FT: 7,500
SALES (est): 1.2MM **Privately Held**
SIC: 3469 3495 3496 3493 Perforated metal, stamped; precision springs; cages, wire; coiled flat springs

(G-1034)
FAD TOOL COMPANY LLC
95 Valley St Ste 7 (06010-4985)
P.O. Box 1117 (06011-1117)
PHONE..................860 582-7890
David Scott, *President*
Rick Miner, *Controller*
EMP: 40
SQ FT: 3,500
SALES (est): 6.1MM **Privately Held**
WEB: www.fadtool.com
SIC: 3544 Special dies & tools

(G-1035)
FARMINGTON MTAL FBRICATION LLC
26 Lewis St (06010-3640)
PHONE..................860 402-5148
John Cunningham, *Principal*
EMP: 1
SALES (est): 54.3K **Privately Held**
SIC: 3499 Fabricated metal products

(G-1036)
FARMINGTON MTAL FBRICATION LLC
139 Center St Ste 2001 (06010-5082)
P.O. Box 260, Unionville (06085-0260)
PHONE..................860 404-7415
John Cunningham, *Mng Member*
Carol Cunningham,
EMP: 6
SALES (est): 840.7K **Privately Held**
SIC: 3498 Fabricated pipe & fittings

(G-1037)
FASTSIGNS
1290 Farmington Ave (06010-4701)
PHONE..................860 583-8000
Fax: 860 314-0505
EMP: 4
SALES (est): 150K **Privately Held**
SIC: 3993 Signsadv Specs

(G-1038)
FINAL LIQUID COATING LLC
134 Mcintosh Dr (06010-3021)
PHONE..................860 585-5625
Jeremy Nightingale, *Principal*
EMP: 2
SALES (est): 117.4K **Privately Held**
SIC: 3479 Metal coating & allied service

(G-1039)
FIRESTONE BUILDING PDTS CO LLC
780 James P Casey Rd # 4 (06010-8537)
PHONE..................860 584-4516
William Probert, *Manager*
EMP: 60 **Privately Held**
WEB: www.bfis.com

Bristol - Hartford County (G-1040)

SIC: 5531 7534 5014 2952 Automotive tires; tire retreading & repair shops; tires & tubes; asphalt felts & coatings; asphalt paving mixtures & blocks
HQ: Firestone Building Products Company, Llc
200 4th Ave S
Nashville TN 37201

(G-1040)
FLEXCO
95 Rossi Dr (06010-2622)
PHONE.................................860 583-0219
Jay Larranaga, *Owner*
EMP: 2
SALES (est): 120K **Privately Held**
SIC: 8711 3599 8742 Engineering services; custom machinery; automation & robotics consultant

(G-1041)
FOUR STAR MANUFACTURING CO
400 Riverside Ave (06010-8807)
PHONE.................................860 583-1614
Edward Plonski, *President*
Gary Plonski, *Vice Pres*
Florence Plonski, *Admin Sec*
EMP: 25 **EST:** 1961
SQ FT: 18,000
SALES (est): 3.7MM **Privately Held**
SIC: 3469 Stamping metal for the trade

(G-1042)
FOURSLIDE SPRING STAMPING INC
87 Cross St (06010-7434)
P.O. Box 839 (06011-0839)
PHONE.................................860 583-1688
Bryan Funk, *President*
Bruce Klimkoski, *QC Mgr*
Judy Schmidt, *Financial Exec*
Jim Richards, *Mktg Dir*
Arthur P Funk, *CIO*
EMP: 25 **EST:** 1962
SQ FT: 20,000
SALES (est): 6MM **Privately Held**
WEB: www.fourslide.com
SIC: 3493 3469 3495 Flat springs, sheet or strip stock; metal stampings; wire springs

(G-1043)
FUTURE MANUFACTURING INC
75 Center St (06010-4979)
P.O. Box 23 (06011-0023)
PHONE.................................860 584-0685
Denis Boroski, *President*
EMP: 30
SQ FT: 10,000
SALES: 1.5MM **Privately Held**
WEB: www.futuremfg.com
SIC: 3677 Electronic coils, transformers & other inductors

(G-1044)
G A INDUSTRIES
630 Emmett St Unit 1 (06010-7793)
PHONE.................................860 261-5484
EMP: 3
SALES (est): 242K **Privately Held**
SIC: 3999 Manufacturing industries

(G-1045)
GARRETT PRINTING & GRAPHICS
331 Riverside Ave (06010-8810)
PHONE.................................860 589-6710
Greg Kowalczyk, *President*
Holley Kowalczyk, *Vice Pres*
Kris Hart, *Prdtn Mgr*
Morgan Leduc, *Sales Mgr*
EMP: 6 **EST:** 1900
SQ FT: 5,000
SALES (est): 944.9K **Privately Held**
SIC: 2752 5699 7336 5043 Commercial printing, offset; business forms, lithographed; posters, lithographed; T-shirts, custom printed; commercial art & graphic design; printing apparatus, photographic

(G-1046)
GMN USA LLC
181 Business Park Dr (06010-8628)
PHONE.................................800 686-1679
Gary P Quirion, *President*
Jeffrey Lepage, *Accountant*
Don Loveless, *Sales Mgr*
Graham Peers, *Manager*
▲ **EMP:** 14 **EST:** 1998
SQ FT: 27,815
SALES: 5MM
SALES (corp-wide): 109.5MM **Privately Held**
WEB: www.gmnusa.com
SIC: 3541 Machine tools, metal cutting type
HQ: Gmn Paul Muller Industrie Gmbh & Co. Kg
AuBere Bayreuther Str. 230
Nurnberg 90411
911 569-10

(G-1047)
HARRIS SECURITY LLC
34 4th St (06010-5341)
P.O. Box 838 (06011-0838)
PHONE.................................860 583-6637
Mark Harris, *Principal*
EMP: 2 **EST:** 2018
SALES (est): 88.3K **Privately Held**
SIC: 3669 Communications equipment

(G-1048)
HERBALIFE DISTRIBUTOR
607 King St (06010-4478)
PHONE.................................860 584-9721
Robin Plourde, *Principal*
EMP: 1
SALES (est): 39.5K **Privately Held**
SIC: 2023 Dry, condensed, evaporated dairy products

(G-1049)
HRF FASTENER SYSTEMS INC
70 Horizon Dr (06010-7473)
PHONE.................................860 589-0750
Robert R Rohrs, *President*
Marsha Rohrs, *Admin Sec*
EMP: 30 **EST:** 1970
SQ FT: 5,000
SALES (est): 6.5MM **Privately Held**
SIC: 3441 3546 Fabricated structural metal; power-driven handtools

(G-1050)
IDEX HEALTH & SCIENCE LLC
Also Called: Eastern Plastics
110 Halcyon Dr (06010-7487)
PHONE.................................860 314-2880
Noy Xayavong, *Buyer*
Art Bauer, *Engineer*
Daniel Rodriguez, *Engineer*
Daniel Czarnecki, *Design Engr*
Phil Anderson, *Manager*
EMP: 124
SALES (corp-wide): 2.4B **Publicly Held**
SIC: 3821 3089 3494 3823 Laboratory apparatus & furniture; plastic processing; valves & pipe fittings; industrial instrmnts msrmnt display/control process variable; analytical instruments
HQ: Idex Health & Science Llc
600 Park Ct
Rohnert Park CA 94928
707 588-2000

(G-1051)
INSIGHT PLUS TECHNOLOGY LLC
191 Redstone Hill Rd (06010-7773)
PHONE.................................860 930-4763
Thomas J Holtz, *Principal*
EMP: 4 **EST:** 2017
SALES (est): 609.9K **Privately Held**
SIC: 3651 7382 3699 Household audio & video equipment; protective devices, security; security devices

(G-1052)
JARVIS PRECISION POLISHING
190 Century Dr (06010-7491)
PHONE.................................860 589-5822
Wallace F Jarvis, *President*
EMP: 10
SALES (est): 842.1K **Privately Held**
SIC: 3471 Electroplating & plating; cleaning, polishing & finishing

(G-1053)
JEANANN STAGNITA
44 Rita Dr (06010-2103)
PHONE.................................860 516-4655
Jeanann Stagnita, *Principal*
EMP: 2 **EST:** 2009
SALES (est): 111.2K **Privately Held**
SIC: 2759 Commercial printing

(G-1054)
JEFFREY MORGAN
Also Called: Exper-Tees
61 E Main St Ste 1 (06010-7060)
PHONE.................................860 583-2567
Jeffrey Morgan, *Owner*
EMP: 1
SQ FT: 2,500
SALES (est): 120K **Privately Held**
SIC: 2759 5699 2395 Screen printing; T-shirts, custom printed; sports apparel; pleating & stitching

(G-1055)
JOVEK TOOL AND DIE
474 Birch St (06010-7837)
PHONE.................................860 261-5020
Joseph Longo, *Principal*
EMP: 8
SALES: 1.7MM **Privately Held**
SIC: 3544 Special dies & tools

(G-1056)
KBJ MANUFACTURING INC
137 Stafford Ave (06010-4613)
PHONE.................................860 585-7257
Kenneth Beeler Jr, *President*
Kenneth Beeler Sr, *Vice Pres*
EMP: 5
SQ FT: 3,000
SALES (est): 700K **Privately Held**
SIC: 3599 Machine shop, jobbing & repair

(G-1057)
KILL SHOT PRECISION LLC
43 Elm St (06010-6334)
PHONE.................................860 681-3162
Zachary Duffany,
EMP: 2
SALES (est): 73.4K **Privately Held**
SIC: 3484 Guns (firearms) or gun parts, 30 mm. & below

(G-1058)
KLEAN AIR SUPPLIES INC
32 Valley St (06010-4991)
P.O. Box 638 (06011-0638)
PHONE.................................860 583-1589
Michelle Lussier, *CEO*
Hitul Patel, *President*
Sebastian Russo, *Manager*
▲ **EMP:** 2
SQ FT: 2,000
SALES: 500K **Privately Held**
SIC: 5169 3069 Specialty cleaning & sanitation preparations; mats or matting, rubber

(G-1059)
KRIS SQUIRES PRINTING & P
21 Lexington St (06010-3648)
PHONE.................................860 582-0782
Kris Squires, *Principal*
EMP: 2
SALES (est): 281.9K **Privately Held**
SIC: 2752 Commercial printing, lithographic

(G-1060)
LAB SECURITY SYSTEMS CORP
Also Called: L A B
700 Emmett St (06010-7714)
PHONE.................................860 589-6037
Robert A Labbe, *President*
Gerald Roraback Jr, *Vice Pres*
Richard Labbe, *Admin Sec*
▲ **EMP:** 45 **EST:** 1957
SQ FT: 36,000
SALES (est): 6.5MM **Privately Held**
WEB: www.lockpins.com
SIC: 3429 3452 Keys, locks & related hardware; bolts, nuts, rivets & washers

(G-1061)
LANGLAIS COMPUTER CONS LLC
67 Posa Dr (06010-5477)
PHONE.................................860 589-0093
Mark Langlais, *Mng Member*
EMP: 1
SALES (est): 75K **Privately Held**
WEB: www.cncsw.com
SIC: 7372 Prepackaged software

(G-1062)
LEE SPRING COMPANY LLC
245 Lake Ave (06010-7398)
P.O. Box 1038 (06011-1038)
PHONE.................................860 584-0991
Marcel Ouellette, *Plant Mgr*
EMP: 28
SALES (corp-wide): 40.6MM **Privately Held**
WEB: www.leespring.com
SIC: 3495 3493 5085 3315 Mechanical springs, precision; steel springs, except wire; springs; wire & fabricated wire products
HQ: Lee Spring Company Llc
140 58th St Ste 3c
Brooklyn NY 11220
888 777-4647

(G-1063)
LEFORA PUBLISHING LLC
18 Chimney Crest Ln (06010-7971)
PHONE.................................860 845-8445
Dawn L Leger, *Principal*
Brian Ruby, *Vice Pres*
Richard Low, *Gnrl Med Prac*
EMP: 1
SALES (est): 60.6K **Privately Held**
SIC: 2741 Miscellaneous publishing

(G-1064)
LP HOMETOWN PIZZA LLC
90 Burlington Ave (06010-4201)
PHONE.................................860 589-1208
Lumbardh Pacuku, *Principal*
EMP: 3
SALES (est): 92.7K **Privately Held**
SIC: 2621 Bristols

(G-1065)
MACKSON MFG CO INC
139 Center St Ste 2002 (06010-5082)
PHONE.................................860 589-4035
Raymond J Macklosky, *President*
EMP: 12 **EST:** 1962
SQ FT: 10,000
SALES (est): 1.6MM **Privately Held**
SIC: 3451 Screw machine products

(G-1066)
MACNEILL ALTRNTIVE CNCEPTS LLC
47 Colony St (06010-6147)
PHONE.................................860 877-3968
John Macneill,
EMP: 1
SALES (est): 20K **Privately Held**
SIC: 3677 Coupling transformers

(G-1067)
MAGNIFICAT MOTHER OF DIV MRCY
12 Pleasant St (06010-6253)
PHONE.................................860 584-8803
Gloria Brophy, *Principal*
EMP: 1 **EST:** 2010
SALES (est): 88.5K **Privately Held**
SIC: 2621 Bristols

(G-1068)
MARK NICOLETTI
Also Called: Mk Manufacturing
33 Stafford Ave Ste 2 (06010-4699)
P.O. Box 3213 (06011-3213)
PHONE.................................860 582-5645
Mark Nicoletti, *Owner*
EMP: 1
SALES (est): 92K **Privately Held**
SIC: 3495 3493 3469 Wire springs; steel springs, except wire; metal stampings

GEOGRAPHIC SECTION — Bristol - Hartford County

(G-1069)
MARTIN CABINET INC
500 Broad St (06010)
PHONE 860 747-5769
Dan Chamberland, *Principal*
EMP: 60
SALES (corp-wide): 6.8MM **Privately Held**
WEB: www.cabinet-mart.com
SIC: 2434 Vanities, bathroom: wood
PA: Martin Cabinet Inc
 336 S Washington St Ste 2
 Plainville CT 06062
 860 747-5769

(G-1070)
MCINTIRE COMPANY (HQ)
Also Called: Western Progress
745 Clark Ave (06010-4068)
PHONE 860 585-8559
William F Steinen, *Chairman*
Thomas R Keenan, *Vice Pres*
John J Delaney Jr, *Admin Sec*
▲ **EMP:** 15
SQ FT: 12,000
SALES (est): 17.2MM
SALES (corp-wide): 15.3MM **Privately Held**
WEB: www.mcintireco.com
SIC: 3564 3993 3842 3634 Blowers & fans; signs & advertising specialties; surgical appliances & supplies; electric housewares & fans; heating equipment, except electric
PA: Wm. Steinen Mfg. Co.
 29 E Halsey Rd
 Parsippany NJ 07054
 973 887-6400

(G-1071)
MIDCONN PRECISION MFG LLC
190 Century Dr Ste 9 (06010-7491)
PHONE 860 584-1340
Brent Tanguay,
EMP: 6
SALES (est): 336.6K **Privately Held**
SIC: 3469 Machine parts, stamped or pressed metal

(G-1072)
MINUTEMAN PRESS OF BRISTOL
98 Farmington Ave (06010-4218)
PHONE 860 589-1100
EMP: 4 **EST:** 2011
SALES (est): 456.5K **Privately Held**
SIC: 2752 Commercial printing, lithographic

(G-1073)
MONOPOL CORPORATION
394 Riverside Ave (06010-6320)
P.O. Box 3056 (06011-3056)
PHONE 860 583-3852
Wesley Woisna, *President*
Lucy Woisna, *Admin Sec*
EMP: 10
SQ FT: 6,000
SALES: 450K **Privately Held**
WEB: www.monopol-colors.ch
SIC: 3841 Surgical & medical instruments

(G-1074)
MORIN CORPORATION (DH)
Also Called: Morin East
685 Middle St (06010-8441)
P.O. Box 3028 (06011-3028)
PHONE 860 584-0900
Russell Shiels, *President*
Doug Matthews, *Regional Mgr*
Ilhan Eser, *Vice Pres*
George McDuffee, *Vice Pres*
Denise Signore, *Purchasing*
▲ **EMP:** 60
SALES (est): 27.1MM **Privately Held**
WEB: www.kingspanpanels.us
SIC: 3448 Prefabricated metal buildings
HQ: Kingspan-Medusa Inc.
 726 Summerhill Dr
 Deland FL 32724
 386 626-6789

(G-1075)
MOTOR CONNECTIONS
225 Terryville Rd (06010-4010)
PHONE 860 583-3407
EMP: 1
SALES (est): 84K **Privately Held**
SIC: 3711 Auto Remanufacturers

(G-1076)
MULTI-CABLE CORP
37 Horizon Dr (06010-7480)
P.O. Box 797 (06011-0797)
PHONE 860 589-9035
Patrick Joyce, *President*
Grant Campbell, *President*
Guy Campbell, *Chairman*
Emily S Joyce, *Admin Sec*
Amy Campbell, *Representative*
EMP: 15
SQ FT: 15,000
SALES (est): 3.8MM **Privately Held**
WEB: www.multicable.com
SIC: 3357 Nonferrous wiredrawing & insulating

(G-1077)
NATIONWIDE CNVYOR SPCLISTS LLC
340 Maple Ave (06010-2631)
P.O. Box 1118 (06011-1118)
PHONE 860 582-9816
Richard J Bugryn,
Richard Bugryn,
EMP: 6
SALES (est): 948.3K **Privately Held**
SIC: 3535 Passenger baggage belt loaders

(G-1078)
NELSON TOOL & MACHINE CO INC
675 Emmett St (06010-7715)
PHONE 860 589-8004
David Florian, *Principal*
EMP: 3
SALES (est): 230K **Privately Held**
SIC: 3728 Aircraft parts & equipment

(G-1079)
NORTH CONTROLS COMPANY LLC
75 Julia Rd (06010-8010)
PHONE 860 584-8364
John Colin North,
EMP: 1 **EST:** 2000
SALES: 60K **Privately Held**
SIC: 3823 Combustion control instruments

(G-1080)
NORTHEAST TOOL DIST LLC
280 Morningside Dr E (06010-4548)
PHONE 860 973-1455
EMP: 2 **EST:** 2014
SALES (est): 120.2K **Privately Held**
SIC: 3599 Industrial machinery

(G-1081)
NOVO PRECISION LLC
150 Dolphin Rd (06010-8041)
PHONE 860 583-0517
Butch Hermann, *Plant Mgr*
William B Hazard,
◆ **EMP:** 22
SQ FT: 14,000
SALES (est): 6.2MM **Privately Held**
WEB: www.wirestraighteners.com
SIC: 3496 5084 Miscellaneous fabricated wire products; industrial machinery & equipment

(G-1082)
OFS COMPANIES
180 Pondview Ln (06010-3085)
PHONE 860 678-6574
Kevin Bouchard, *Development*
EMP: 2
SALES (est): 90.8K **Privately Held**
SIC: 3357 Nonferrous wiredrawing & insulating

(G-1083)
OSCAR JOBS
Also Called: Reliable Spring Company
165 Riverside Ave (06010-6322)
P.O. Box 1952 (06011-1952)
PHONE 860 583-7834
Oscar Jobs, *Owner*
EMP: 8
SQ FT: 15,000
SALES (est): 1MM **Privately Held**
WEB: www.reliablespring.net
SIC: 3469 3493 3495 Stamping metal for the trade; steel springs, except wire; wire springs

(G-1084)
P-Q CONTROLS INC (PA)
95 Dolphin Rd (06010-8000)
PHONE 860 583-6994
Douglas D Schumann, *President*
Bart Matthew Guthrie, *Vice Pres*
To Cheung, *Engineer*
Jake Mockler, *Engineer*
Chase Monroe, *Engineer*
▲ **EMP:** 41
SQ FT: 20,000
SALES (est): 6.7MM **Privately Held**
WEB: www.pqcontrols.com
SIC: 3625 Control equipment, electric

(G-1085)
PALMISANO PRINTING LLC
319 Queen St (06010-6358)
P.O. Box 372 (06011-0372)
PHONE 860 582-6883
Philip Palmisano, *Mng Member*
EMP: 5
SQ FT: 1,200
SALES (est): 688.8K **Privately Held**
WEB: www.palmisanoprinting.com
SIC: 2752 2791 2789 Commercial printing, offset; typesetting; bookbinding & related work

(G-1086)
PATRIOT MANUFACTURING LLC
Also Called: Bluewater Designs
205 Cross St (06010-7434)
PHONE 860 506-2213
Edward Borkoski, *President*
Debbie Macdonald, *Office Mgr*
EMP: 3 **EST:** 1946
SQ FT: 5,000
SALES (est): 525.5K **Privately Held**
WEB: www.bluewaterdesigns.com
SIC: 3469 3544 Stamping metal for the trade; special dies, tools, jigs & fixtures; special dies & tools

(G-1087)
PATTISON SIGN GROUP INC
2074 Perkins St (06010-2323)
PHONE 860 583-3000
Joan Pelletier, *Manager*
EMP: 7
SALES (corp-wide): 19B **Privately Held**
WEB: www.pattisonsign.com
SIC: 3993 Electric signs
HQ: Pattison Sign Group Inc.
 520 W Summit Hill Dr # 702
 Knoxville TN 37902
 865 693-1105

(G-1088)
PATWIL LLC
Also Called: Amstep Products
190 Century Dr Ste 102 (06010-7491)
PHONE 860 589-9085
Pat Will, *Mng Member*
EMP: 8 **EST:** 1911
SQ FT: 6,400
SALES (est): 1.4MM **Privately Held**
WEB: www.amstep.com
SIC: 3446 Stairs, staircases, stair treads: prefabricated metal

(G-1089)
PBN LLC
200 Central St (06010-6716)
PHONE 860 582-9111
Michael Brault, *Vice Pres*
Robert Nadeau, *Vice Pres*
Orlando Sarria, *Project Engr*
James Gustavson, *Senior Engr*
Gianna Lukcso, *Accounting Mgr*
EMP: 2
SALES (est): 343.6K **Privately Held**
WEB: www.ultimateniti.com
SIC: 3843 Dental metal

(G-1090)
PEPIN STEEL AND IRON WORKS LLC
47 Old Waterbury Rd (06010-5915)
PHONE 860 582-1852
Allan Pepin, *Mng Member*
Kathy Pepin, *Mng Member*
EMP: 6
SQ FT: 17,000
SALES (est): 2.1MM **Privately Held**
WEB: www.pepinsteel.com
SIC: 5051 3441 Steel; fabricated structural metal

(G-1091)
PLAINVILLE MACHINE & TL CO INC
65 Ronzo Rd (06010-8621)
PHONE 860 589-5595
Lawrence M Frey, *President*
Henry R Frey Jr, *Vice Pres*
EMP: 15 **EST:** 1965
SQ FT: 9,000
SALES (est): 2.8MM **Privately Held**
WEB: www.plainvillemachinetool.com
SIC: 3544 Special dies & tools

(G-1092)
PLANIT MANUFACTURING LLC
515 Broad St Unit D (06010-6693)
PHONE 203 641-6055
Samuel Slivinski,
James O'Regan,
EMP: 2
SALES (est): 141.6K **Privately Held**
SIC: 5084 7699 3443 Industrial machinery & equipment; industrial machinery & equipment repair; metal parts

(G-1093)
PLYMOUTH SPRING COMPANY INC
281 Lake Ave (06010-7322)
P.O. Box 1358 (06011-1358)
PHONE 860 584-0594
Richard Rubenstein, *President*
Lea Rubenstein, *Vice Pres*
Joseph Vanasse, *Foreman/Supr*
Jack Haber, *Treasurer*
Diane Gagnon, *Controller*
EMP: 63 **EST:** 1958
SQ FT: 40,000
SALES (est): 16.1MM **Privately Held**
WEB: www.plymouthspring.com
SIC: 3495 Instrument springs, precision

(G-1094)
PQ OPTICS
63 Saw Mill Rd (06010-2457)
P.O. Box 332, Farmington (06034-0332)
PHONE 860 582-2636
Michael W Masailo, *Principal*
EMP: 1
SALES (est): 58K **Privately Held**
SIC: 3229 Optical glass

(G-1095)
PRECISION CUT-OFF SERVICE INC
625 Emmett St (06010-7792)
PHONE 860 582-7521
Paul Ruch, *President*
Sara R Stadler, *Director*
EMP: 4
SQ FT: 7,200
SALES (est): 605.6K **Privately Held**
WEB: www.pcscuts.com
SIC: 7389 3599 Metal cutting services; machine shop, jobbing & repair

(G-1096)
PRECISION DEBURRING INC
139 Center St Ste 5002 (06010-5086)
PHONE 860 583-4662
Fax: 860 589-8658
EMP: 4
SQ FT: 2,200
SALES (est): 320K **Privately Held**
SIC: 3541 3471 Mfg Machine Tools-Cutting Plating/Polishing Service

(G-1097)
PRECISION EXPRESS MFG LLC
630 Emmett St Unit 3 (06010-7793)
PHONE 860 584-2627
Alban Bebri, *Principal*
EMP: 10
SALES (est): 1.3MM **Privately Held**
SIC: 3999 Manufacturing industries

(PA)=Parent Co (HQ)=Headquarters (DH)=Div Headquarters
✪ = New Business established in last 2 years

(G-1098)
PRINTING SERVICES INC
889 Farmington Ave Ste A (06010-3945)
PHONE..................................860 584-9598
Robert Masi, *President*
Cheryl Masi, *Corp Secy*
EMP: 2
SQ FT: 900
SALES (est): 240.4K **Privately Held**
SIC: 2752 Commercial printing, offset

(G-1099)
QUALITY COILS INCORPORATED (PA)
748 Middle St (06010-8417)
P.O. Box 1480 (06011-1480)
PHONE..................................860 584-0927
Keith A Gibson, *President*
Gary A Gibson, *Vice Pres*
Jason Vallee, *Plant Mgr*
Carol Hawkins, *Prdtn Mgr*
Mike Thiem, *Prdtn Mgr*
EMP: 120 **EST:** 1965
SQ FT: 30,000
SALES (est): 34.5MM **Privately Held**
WEB: www.qualitycoils.com
SIC: 3677 Coil windings, electronic; electronic transformers

(G-1100)
QUALITY WELDING LLC
61 E Main St Bldg C (06010-7060)
PHONE..................................860 585-1121
Peter Fortier, *Project Mgr*
Celeste Walters, *Human Res Mgr*
Samuel Walters, *Mng Member*
EMP: 9
SQ FT: 1,800
SALES (est): 1.2MM **Privately Held**
WEB: www.qualityweldingllc.com
SIC: 7692 Welding repair

(G-1101)
QUALITY WIRE EDM INC
329 Redstone Hill Rd (06010-7741)
PHONE..................................860 583-9867
Jeffrey Rimcoski, *President*
EMP: 9
SQ FT: 2,000
SALES (est): 1.2MM **Privately Held**
SIC: 3599 3544 Electrical discharge machining (EDM); special dies & tools

(G-1102)
R & R CORRUGATED CONTAINER INC
360 Minor St (06010-8543)
P.O. Box 399, Terryville (06786-0399)
PHONE..................................860 584-1194
Robert J Braverman, *President*
Roger Rainville, *Accounts Exec*
EMP: 58
SQ FT: 32,000
SALES (est): 14.4MM **Privately Held**
SIC: 2653 Boxes, corrugated: made from purchased materials

(G-1103)
RADCLIFF WIRE INC
97 Ronzo Rd (06010-8619)
P.O. Box 603 (06011-0603)
PHONE..................................312 876-1754
Jean Radcliff, *CEO*
Charlie Radcliff, *President*
Donald F Radcliff, *Treasurer*
Kathy Sweetman, *Bookkeeper*
Scott Kirkpatrick, *VP Sales*
▲ **EMP:** 36 **EST:** 1959
SQ FT: 25,000
SALES (est): 9.3MM **Privately Held**
WEB: www.radcliffwire.com
SIC: 3357 3315 3496 Nonferrous wire-drawing & insulating; wire, ferrous/iron; miscellaneous fabricated wire products

(G-1104)
REED & STEFANOW MACHINE TL CO
165 Riverside Ave (06010-6322)
P.O. Box 1952 (06011-1952)
PHONE..................................860 583-7834
Joseph S Reed, *President*
Alice Reed, *Treasurer*
▲ **EMP:** 13 **EST:** 1972
SQ FT: 2,000

SALES (est): 2.2MM **Privately Held**
SIC: 3599 Machine shop, jobbing & repair

(G-1105)
RELIABLE SCALES & SYSTEMS LLC
150 Village St (06010-8035)
PHONE..................................860 380-0600
Edwin C Hollenbeck Jr,
EMP: 3
SALES (est): 305K **Privately Held**
SIC: 3596 Scales & balances, except laboratory

(G-1106)
REM TOOL & DIE LLC
550 Broad St (06010-6664)
PHONE..................................860 582-7559
Raymond L Renouf,
Ricky Renouf,
EMP: 2
SQ FT: 3,500
SALES (est): 100K **Privately Held**
SIC: 3544 Special dies & tools

(G-1107)
RGD TECHNOLOGIES CORP
Also Called: New Tech Replacement Part Co
50 Emmett St (06010-6623)
P.O. Box 9308 (06011-9308)
PHONE..................................860 589-0756
Robert G Dabkowski, *President*
Debra D Martin, *Corp Secy*
Cynthia D Policki, *Vice Pres*
▲ **EMP:** 60
SQ FT: 200,000
SALES (est): 11.4MM **Privately Held**
WEB: www.rgdtech.com
SIC: 3451 Screw machine products

(G-1108)
RICHARD DAHLEN
Also Called: R & R McHy & Rebuilding Co
350 Riverside Ave (06010-6320)
P.O. Box 52, Torrington (06790-0052)
PHONE..................................860 584-8226
Richard Dahlen, *Owner*
EMP: 7 **EST:** 1973
SQ FT: 13,000
SALES (est): 721.7K **Privately Held**
SIC: 3599 5084 3542 Machine shop, jobbing & repair; industrial machinery & equipment; machine tools, metal forming type

(G-1109)
RIOPEL INDUSTRIES
31 Dipietro Ln (06010-7843)
PHONE..................................860 384-9610
Dennis Sirianni, *Principal*
EMP: 2
SALES (est): 85.2K **Privately Held**
SIC: 3999 Manufacturing industries

(G-1110)
RJ 15 INC
115 Cross St (06010-7434)
PHONE..................................860 585-0111
Joseph E Palfini, *President*
Margaret J Palfini, *Admin Sec*
EMP: 17
SQ FT: 14,500
SALES (est): 4.5MM **Privately Held**
WEB: www.rayjurgen.com
SIC: 3713 Truck & bus bodies

(G-1111)
RONALD BOTTINO
Also Called: C & R Printing
381 Riverside Ave (06010-8810)
P.O. Box 9035 (06011-9035)
PHONE..................................860 585-9505
Chris Bottino, *Owner*
Ronald Bottino, *Owner*
EMP: 5
SQ FT: 3,000
SALES (est): 613.2K **Privately Held**
SIC: 2752 Commercial printing, offset

(G-1112)
ROSTRA VERNATHERM LLC
Also Called: Bilbe Controls
106 Enterprise Dr (06010-8403)
P.O. Box 3060 (06011-3060)
PHONE..................................860 582-6776
Kevin Lamb, *General Mgr*

Douglas Banks, *Opers Staff*
Carah Conlon, *Purch Mgr*
James Agard, *Engineer*
Alberto Medina, *Engineer*
▲ **EMP:** 31
SALES (est): 9.8MM **Privately Held**
WEB: www.rostravernatherm.com
SIC: 3491 Industrial valves

(G-1113)
ROWLEY SPRING & STAMPING CORP
210 Redstone Hill Rd # 2 (06010-7796)
PHONE..................................860 582-8175
John Dellalana, *President*
Barbara Tomcak, *Prdtn Mgr*
William R Joyce, *Treasurer*
Ted Sobota, *CIO*
Darlene B Krammer, *Director*
EMP: 160 **EST:** 1954
SQ FT: 150,000
SALES (est): 35.2MM **Privately Held**
WEB: www.rowleyspring.com
SIC: 3495 3621 3496 3493 Mechanical springs, precision; motors & generators; miscellaneous fabricated wire products; steel springs, except wire; metal stampings

(G-1114)
ROYAL SCREW MACHINE PDTS CO
409 Lake Ave (06010-7330)
P.O. Box 1325, Waterbury (06721-1325)
PHONE..................................860 845-8920
Thomas H Derwin, *President*
Rory Derwin, *Info Tech Mgr*
Jason Derwin, *Information Mgr*
Lee Agostine, *Admin Sec*
EMP: 25 **EST:** 1940
SQ FT: 20,000
SALES (est): 5.4MM **Privately Held**
WEB: www.royalscrew.com
SIC: 3451 Screw machine products

(G-1115)
RUNWAY LIQUIDATION LLC
Also Called: Bcbg
112 S 42nd St (06010)
PHONE..................................202 466-2050
EMP: 2
SALES (corp-wide): 570.1MM **Privately Held**
SIC: 2335 Women's, juniors' & misses' dresses
HQ: Runway Liquidation, Llc
2761 Fruitland Ave
Vernon CA 90058
323 589-2224

(G-1116)
SCOTTS METAL FINISHING LLC
Also Called: Scott Metal Finishing
310 Birch St (06010-7800)
P.O. Box 9091 (06011-9091)
PHONE..................................860 589-3778
James Barnes, *President*
Scott Barnes, *Vice Pres*
EMP: 15
SALES: 1MM **Privately Held**
WEB: www.scottmetalfinishing.com
SIC: 3471 5051 Finishing, metals or formed products; metals service centers & offices

(G-1117)
SIGN SOLUTIONS INC
1290 Farmington Ave (06010-4701)
PHONE..................................860 583-8000
EMP: 2
SALES (est): 137.1K **Privately Held**
SIC: 3993 Mfg Signs/Advertising Specialties

(G-1118)
SMART FOODS OF BRISTOL
63 Middle St (06010-5202)
PHONE..................................860 582-8882
EMP: 1
SALES (est): 57.5K **Privately Held**
SIC: 2621 Paper Mill

(G-1119)
SOMERS MANUFACTURING INC
165 Riverside Ave (06010-6322)

Joe Fazzina, *President*
EMP: 5 **EST:** 1965
SQ FT: 5,000
SALES (est): 370K **Privately Held**
SIC: 3599 7692 3544 Machine shop, jobbing & repair; welding repair; special dies, tools, jigs & fixtures

(G-1120)
SOMERS TOOL & WELD SHOP
165 Riverside Ave (06010-6322)
PHONE..................................860 314-1075
Joe Fazzina, *Owner*
EMP: 2
SALES (est): 112.3K **Privately Held**
SIC: 3469 Machine parts, stamped or pressed metal

(G-1121)
SPRINGFIELD SPRING CORPORATION
24 Dell Manor Dr (06010-7436)
PHONE..................................860 584-6560
Malissa Vyce, *Engineer*
Dave Reno, *Manager*
EMP: 13
SALES (corp-wide): 9.2MM **Privately Held**
WEB: www.springfieldspring.com
SIC: 3495 Wire springs
PA: Springfield Spring Corporation
311 Shaker Rd
East Longmeadow MA 01028
413 525-6837

(G-1122)
SSI MANUFACTURING TECH CORP
675 Emmett St (06010-7715)
PHONE..................................860 589-8004
Gary Hutchison, *President*
Keith K Blethen, *Vice Pres*
Bob Peterson, *Vice Pres*
Peterson Robert, *Vice Pres*
Adam Wankier, *Vice Pres*
EMP: 36
SQ FT: 14,000
SALES (est): 8.1MM **Privately Held**
WEB: www.ssimanufacturing.com
SIC: 3599 Machine shop, jobbing & repair

(G-1123)
STATE OF CONNECTICUT EDUC
431 Minor St (06010-2269)
PHONE..................................860 584-8433
EMP: 1 **EST:** 2014
SALES (est): 95K **Privately Held**
SIC: 2621 Paper Mill

(G-1124)
SUTTERS MILL
1142 Hill St (06010-2256)
PHONE..................................860 585-5333
EMP: 2 **EST:** 2011
SALES (est): 120K **Privately Held**
SIC: 2431 Mfg Millwork

(G-1125)
TAILLON AUTO TOP COMPANY
334 West St Ste 1 (06010-4998)
PHONE..................................860 583-5525
Ray Taillon, *Owner*
EMP: 2
SQ FT: 5,000
SALES (est): 110.1K **Privately Held**
SIC: 2399 7532 Seat covers, automobile; tops (canvas or plastic), installation or repair: automotive

(G-1126)
TECK WELDING & FABRICATION LLC
52 Carmelo Rd (06010-2616)
PHONE..................................860 584-1264
Thomas Kosiba, *Manager*
EMP: 1
SALES (est): 49.5K **Privately Held**
SIC: 7692 Welding repair

(G-1127)
THEIS PRECISION STEEL USA INC (HQ)
300 Broad St (06010-6600)
PHONE..................................860 589-5511
Robert W Garthwait Jr, *President*

GEOGRAPHIC SECTION

Brookfield - Fairfield County (G-1157)

David Elliott, *COO*
David Elliot, *Vice Pres*
Thaddeus M Sendzimir, *Vice Pres*
Keith Doolittle, *Engineer*
◆ **EMP:** 215
SQ FT: 350,000
SALES (est): 96.4MM
SALES (corp-wide): 62.8MM **Privately Held**
WEB: www.theis-usa.com
SIC: 3316 Cold finishing of steel shapes
PA: Tps Acquisition, Llc
 151 Sharon Rd
 Waterbury CT 06705
 860 589-5511

(G-1128)
THOMPSON AEROSPACE LLC
Also Called: Precision Threaded Products
220 Business Park Dr (06010-8629)
PHONE.................860 516-0472
R Paul Nichols, *President*
Sharon Newton, *General Mgr*
EMP: 16
SQ FT: 16,500
SALES (est): 3.2MM **Privately Held**
WEB: www.ptp-inc.com
SIC: 3728 Aircraft parts & equipment

(G-1129)
TO GIVE IS BETTER
139 Center St Ste 5007 (06010-5086)
PHONE.................860 261-5443
Philip Dubois, *President*
EMP: 6
SALES (est): 316.4K **Privately Held**
SIC: 2261 Screen printing of cotton broad-woven fabrics

(G-1130)
TOLLMAN SPRING COMPANY INC
560 Birch St (06010)
PHONE.................860 583-4856
Chris Zink, *Branch Mgr*
EMP: 4
SALES (corp-wide): 12.5MM **Privately Held**
WEB: www.tollmanspring.com
SIC: 3493 Steel springs, except wire
PA: Spring Tollman Company Incorporated
 91 Enterprise Dr
 Bristol CT 06010
 860 583-1326

(G-1131)
TOP NOTCH MANUFACTURING CO
130 Enterprise Dr (06010-7493)
PHONE.................860 583-2080
Brian Czajkowski, *Owner*
EMP: 2 **EST:** 1979
SALES (est): 197.1K **Privately Held**
SIC: 3599 Machine shop, jobbing & repair

(G-1132)
TRIPLE A SPRING LTD PARTNR
Also Called: Colonial Spring Company
95 Valley St Ste 1 (06010-4985)
P.O. Box 1079 (06011-1079)
PHONE.................860 589-3231
William Lathrop, *Managing Prtnr*
EMP: 25 **EST:** 1946
SQ FT: 33,000
SALES (est): 5.3MM **Privately Held**
WEB: www.colonialspringco.com
SIC: 3493 Steel springs, except wire

(G-1133)
ULTIMATE COMPANIES INC (PA)
200 Central St (06010-6716)
PHONE.................860 582-9111
Nancy J Brault, *President*
Michael Brault, *Vice Pres*
EMP: 2
SALES (est): 236.2K **Privately Held**
SIC: 3843 Dental equipment & supplies

(G-1134)
ULTIMATE WIREFORMS INC
200 Central St (06010-6716)
PHONE.................860 582-9111
Paul Blanchette, *President*
Tom Cameron, *General Mgr*
Robert Nadeau, *Vice Pres*
Alan J Bednaz, *VP Opers*
Bruce Keevers, *QC Mgr*
EMP: 53
SALES (est): 7.5MM **Privately Held**
WEB: www.ultimateluresaver.com
SIC: 3841 8021 3843 3496 Surgical & medical instruments; offices & clinics of dentists; dental equipment & supplies; miscellaneous fabricated wire products

(G-1135)
VINTAGE BOAT RESTORATIONS LLC
201 Terryville Rd Ste 1 (06010-9606)
PHONE.................860 582-0774
James Murdock Jr, *Mng Member*
Gail Murdock, *Manager*
EMP: 3
SALES (est): 351.3K **Privately Held**
SIC: 3732 Boats, fiberglass: building & repairing

(G-1136)
W M G AND SONS INC
8 Summerberry Rd (06010-2958)
PHONE.................860 584-0143
William M Ghio, *President*
EMP: 5
SALES (est): 547.8K **Privately Held**
SIC: 1389 Construction, repair & dismantling services

(G-1137)
WESTFALIA INC
625 Middle St (06010-8415)
P.O. Box 9529 (06011-9529)
PHONE.................860 314-2920
Stefan Hauk, *President*
Robert E Crumb, *Vice Pres*
Marc Gaudioso, *Finance Dir*
Michael Mussatto, *Manager*
Curtis Titus, *Admin Sec*
▲ **EMP:** 26
SQ FT: 35,000
SALES (est): 9.2MM
SALES (corp-wide): 581.2MM **Privately Held**
WEB: www.westfalia.com
SIC: 3714 Camshafts, motor vehicle
HQ: Westfalia Metallschlauchtechnik Verwaltungs-Gmbh
 Konigsallee 4
 Hilchenbach
 273 328-3100

(G-1138)
WHITMAN CONTROLS LLC
201 Dolphin Rd (06010-8000)
PHONE.................800 233-4401
Richard Sexton, *Mng Member*
William Brame,
EMP: 13
SQ FT: 10,000
SALES (est): 565.6K **Privately Held**
SIC: 3822 Auto controls regulating residntl & coml environmt & applncs

(G-1139)
WIKI COMMUNITY LLC
35 Drayla Dr (06010-7738)
PHONE.................860 582-3489
Christopher Russo, *Principal*
EMP: 2
SALES (est): 113.5K **Privately Held**
SIC: 2752 Commercial printing, lithographic

(G-1140)
WILDSIDE FABRICATION LLC
625 N Main St (06010-1801)
PHONE.................860 585-0514
Robert Cochran, *Mng Member*
EMP: 1
SALES (est): 59K **Privately Held**
SIC: 3999 Manufacturing industries

(G-1141)
WOODWORK SPECIALTIES INC
123 New St (06010-5353)
PHONE.................860 583-4848
Clement Letourneau, *President*
EMP: 4
SALES (est): 429.8K **Privately Held**
SIC: 2431 Millwork

(G-1142)
YARD WELDING AND REPAIR LLC
96 Chestnut St (06010-6281)
PHONE.................860 402-8321
Stephenie Thibeault, *Principal*
EMP: 2
SALES (est): 70.4K **Privately Held**
SIC: 7692 7389 Welding repair;

Broad Brook
Hartford County

(G-1143)
ACE ENERGY LLC
152 Broad Brook Rd (06016-9685)
PHONE.................860 623-3308
Catherine Ann Schantz, *Principal*
EMP: 2 **EST:** 2018
SALES (est): 125.5K **Privately Held**
SIC: 1382 Oil & gas exploration services

(G-1144)
BASEMENT SCREEN PRINTING
11 Lindsay Ln (06016-9786)
PHONE.................860 462-9103
Steven Berardi, *Principal*
EMP: 2 **EST:** 2017
SALES (est): 88.6K **Privately Held**
SIC: 2759 Screen printing

(G-1145)
BROMLEY INDUSTRIES
4 Plantation Rd (06016-9548)
PHONE.................860 370-9566
Daniel Bromley, *Principal*
EMP: 2
SALES (est): 116.6K **Privately Held**
SIC: 3999 Manufacturing industries

(G-1146)
DATA COLLECTION DISPERSAL INC
Also Called: D C D
42 Skinner Rd (06016-9694)
P.O. Box 149 (06016-0149)
PHONE.................860 623-7364
Micheal Ceppegelli, *President*
John Ceppegelli, *CFO*
EMP: 6
SALES: 350K **Privately Held**
SIC: 8711 3699 Electrical or electronic engineering; electrical equipment & supplies

(G-1147)
DC & D INC
42 Skinner Rd (06016-9694)
PHONE.................860 623-2941
Michael Ceppetelli, *President*
EMP: 5
SALES (est): 572.2K **Privately Held**
SIC: 3699 8711 Electrical equipment & supplies; engineering services

(G-1148)
DOUBLE H ACRES LLC
47 Broad Brook Rd (06016-9618)
P.O. Box 307 (06016-0307)
PHONE.................860 250-3311
Herbert W Holden, *Principal*
EMP: 2
SALES (est): 169.3K **Privately Held**
SIC: 3523 Cattle feeding, handling & watering equipment

(G-1149)
ELENA DIECK
7 Eastwood Dr (06016-9670)
PHONE.................860 623-9872
Elena Dieck, *Owner*
EMP: 1
SALES (est): 41.1K **Privately Held**
SIC: 8999 2851 Art related services; colors in oil, except artists'

(G-1150)
HARTFORD TONER & CARTRIDGE INC (PA)
6 Wapping Rd (06016-9717)
PHONE.................860 292-1280
John Collins, *CEO*
Catherine Collins, *President*
Tim Golubeff, *Manager*
Joseph Mason, *Real Est Agnt*
EMP: 4
SQ FT: 6,000
SALES (est): 1MM **Privately Held**
WEB: www.hartfordtoner.com
SIC: 2759 5111 5085 5734 Laser printing; printing & writing paper; ink, printers'; printers & plotters: computers

(G-1151)
LATELIER BADE LLC
6 Old Ellington Rd (06016-9734)
P.O. Box 104 (06016-0104)
PHONE.................860 623-4661
Hans-Heinrich Bade, *President*
EMP: 1
SALES (est): 101.9K **Privately Held**
SIC: 3523 Tobacco curers

(G-1152)
RYAN INDUSTRIES LLC
95 Rye St (06016-9555)
P.O. Box 306 (06016-0306)
PHONE.................860 716-0226
Steve Dearborn, *Principal*
EMP: 2
SALES (est): 187.3K **Privately Held**
SIC: 3999 Manufacturing industries

(G-1153)
STROUTS WOODWORKING
Also Called: Strout Custom Millwork
45 Plantation Rd (06016-9551)
PHONE.................860 623-8445
Ken Strouts, *Owner*
Cynthia Strouts, *Co-Owner*
EMP: 4
SALES (est): 292K **Privately Held**
SIC: 2499 Decorative wood & woodwork

Brookfield
Fairfield County

(G-1154)
3T LIGHTING INC
Also Called: Nessen Lighting
20 Pocono Rd (06804-3303)
P.O. Box 165 (06804-0165)
PHONE.................203 775-1805
Hsiaoching Yu, *Officer*
EMP: 7
SALES (est): 1.2MM **Privately Held**
SIC: 3645 3646 Residential lighting fixtures; commercial indusl & institutional electric lighting fixtures

(G-1155)
AB ELECTRONICS INC
61 Commerce Dr (06804-3405)
PHONE.................203 740-2793
Armando Bernardo, *President*
Maria Bernardo, *Vice Pres*
EMP: 35
SQ FT: 13,000
SALES (est): 10.8MM **Privately Held**
WEB: www.abelectronicsinc.com
SIC: 3672 3679 8711 Printed circuit boards; electronic circuits; electrical or electronic engineering

(G-1156)
ACCESSION MEDIA
51 Prange Rd (06804-1061)
PHONE.................203 702-4951
Joshua Katinger, *President*
EMP: 1
SALES (est): 37.5K **Privately Held**
SIC: 2741 Miscellaneous publishing

(G-1157)
AJ TUCK COMPANY
32 Tucks Rd (06804-1814)
P.O. Box 215 (06804-0215)
PHONE.................203 775-1234
Alvin J Tuck IV, *Ch of Bd*
Lois Hunt, *Vice Pres*
Linda Pendergast, *Shareholder*
EMP: 20 **EST:** 1917
SQ FT: 8,000
SALES (est): 3.8MM **Privately Held**
WEB: www.ajtuckco.com
SIC: 3599 Machine & other job shop work

Brookfield - Fairfield County (G-1158)

(G-1158)
ALL CELL RECOVERY LLC
19 Logging Trail Ln (06804-1345)
PHONE.................................203 948-2566
Michael Cordisco, *Principal*
EMP: 1
SALES (est): 114.3K **Privately Held**
SIC: 3841 Surgical & medical instruments

(G-1159)
APB ASSOCIATES LLC
Also Called: AlphaGraphics
35 Obtuse Rocks Rd (06804-3228)
PHONE.................................203 740-9792
Andrew Paul Boschetto,
Andrew Boschetto,
EMP: 1
SALES (est): 500K **Privately Held**
SIC: 2752 Commercial printing, lithographic

(G-1160)
AQUATIC TECHNOLOGIES INC
81 Whisconier Rd (06804-3815)
PHONE.................................203 770-6791
Shaun Monastero, *Principal*
EMP: 2
SALES (est): 191.5K **Privately Held**
SIC: 2369 Bathing suits & swimwear: girls', children's & infants'

(G-1161)
ASTRALITE INC
20 Pocono Rd (06804)
P.O. Box 91 (06804-0091)
PHONE.................................203 775-0172
Robert Yu, *President*
Richard Yu, *Web Dvlpr*
▲ EMP: 6 EST: 2000
SQ FT: 23,988
SALES (est): 1.3MM **Privately Held**
WEB: www.astralitelighting.com
SIC: 3648 Lighting equipment

(G-1162)
BOB THE BAKER LLC
594 Federal Rd (06804-2008)
P.O. Box 281 (06804-0281)
PHONE.................................203 775-1032
Frank R Labarbera, *Principal*
EMP: 10
SALES (est): 1MM **Privately Held**
SIC: 2052 Cookies & crackers

(G-1163)
BOLTPRINTINGCOM
20 Old Grays Bridge Rd (06804-2623)
PHONE.................................203 885-0571
Lana Corsano, *Owner*
Orellana Sully, *Graphic Designe*
▼ EMP: 2
SALES (est): 120K **Privately Held**
SIC: 2752 Commercial printing, lithographic

(G-1164)
BRIDGEWATER CHOCOLATE LLC
559 Federal Rd (06804-2017)
PHONE.................................203 775-2286
Jennifer Burgdeffor, *General Mgr*
Bhavna Gursahaney, *Manager*
Mia Landegren, *Technology*
Erik Landegren,
Andrew Blauner,
▲ EMP: 8
SQ FT: 4,800
SALES (est): 784.1K **Privately Held**
WEB: www.bridgewaterchocolate.com
SIC: 5441 2064 Candy; candy & other confectionery products

(G-1165)
BROOKFELD MDCL/SRGICAL SUP INC
Also Called: Brookfield Phrm Compounding
60 Old New Milford Rd (06804-2430)
PHONE.................................203 775-0862
James Cangelosi, *President*
Diane Cangelosi, *Corp Secy*
EMP: 10 EST: 1988
SALES: 1.2MM **Privately Held**
SIC: 2834 Druggists' preparations (pharmaceuticals)

(G-1166)
BROOKFIELD STAINLESS LLC
12 Allen Rd (06804-1602)
PHONE.................................203 987-6773
Darren Hill,
EMP: 2
SALES (est): 109.9K **Privately Held**
SIC: 3312 Stainless steel

(G-1167)
C & E ELECTRIC
31 Old Route 7 Ste 5 (06804-1714)
PHONE.................................203 546-7255
Ernest Belmont, *President*
EMP: 2 EST: 2011
SALES (est): 153.2K **Privately Held**
SIC: 3699 1731 Electrical equipment & supplies; electrical work

(G-1168)
CARRIER ACCESS - TRIN NETWORKS
61 Commerce Dr (06804-3405)
PHONE.................................203 778-8222
EMP: 3 EST: 2014
SALES (est): 117.7K **Privately Held**
SIC: 3661 Telephone & telegraph apparatus

(G-1169)
CHANNEL SOURCES LLC
Also Called: Channel Sources Company
246 Federal Rd Ste A12-1 (06804-2635)
PHONE.................................203 775-6464
Randy Hujar, *COO*
Paul Hertz, *Vice Pres*
Diane Daudelin, *Sales Executive*
Tom Fitzsimmons, *Mng Member*
Ted Allen, *Bd of Directors*
EMP: 13
SALES (est): 1.4MM **Privately Held**
WEB: www.channelsources.com
SIC: 7372 Business oriented computer software

(G-1170)
CHANNEL SOURCES DIST CO LLC
246 Federal Rd Ste A12-1 (06804-2635)
PHONE.................................203 775-6464
Thomas T Fitzsimons,
EMP: 2
SALES (est): 169.4K **Privately Held**
SIC: 7372 Prepackaged software

(G-1171)
CHESTNUT SHELL
819 Federal Rd (06804-1806)
PHONE.................................203 775-5067
Jarnail Dhaliwal, *Owner*
EMP: 2 EST: 2008
SALES (est): 176.8K **Privately Held**
SIC: 3578 Automatic teller machines (ATM)

(G-1172)
CLARK POWER SYSTEMS INC
7 Premium Point Ln (06804-2108)
PHONE.................................203 775-8444
Richard Clark, *President*
EMP: 1
SALES (est): 246.9K **Privately Held**
SIC: 3699 Electrical equipment & supplies

(G-1173)
COL-LAR ENTERPRISES INC
Also Called: Col Lar Enterprises
4 Chelsea Ct (06804-2704)
PHONE.................................860 799-6970
EMP: 1 **Privately Held**
SIC: 3944 Games, toys & children's vehicles
PA: Col-Lar Enterprises, Inc.
   37 S End Plz
   New Milford CT 06776

(G-1174)
COLIN HARRISON LLC
16 Cove Rd (06804-1302)
PHONE.................................203 775-5035
Colin G Harrison,
EMP: 2
SALES (est): 157.9K **Privately Held**
SIC: 3651 Compact disk players

(G-1175)
CREATIVE PLAYTHINGS LTD
559a Federal Rd Ste 4 (06804-2044)
PHONE.................................203 748-7206
Dan Ciccarelli, *Branch Mgr*
EMP: 1
SALES (corp-wide): 41MM **Privately Held**
SIC: 3949 Playground equipment
PA: Creative Playthings, Ltd.
   33 Loring Dr
   Framingham MA 01702
   508 620-0900

(G-1176)
CULTEC INC
878 Federal Rd (06804-1830)
P.O. Box 280 (06804-0280)
PHONE.................................203 775-4416
Robert Ditullio Sr, *CEO*
Gina Carolan, *President*
Robert Ditullio Jr, *Vice Pres*
Chris Ditullio, *CFO*
▼ EMP: 15
SQ FT: 12,000
SALES (est): 3.1MM **Privately Held**
WEB: www.cultec.com
SIC: 3089 Washers, plastic

(G-1177)
DAVE ROSS
Also Called: Brookfield Tractor Prfmce Eqp
92 S Lake Shore Dr (06804-1429)
PHONE.................................203 775-4327
Dave Ross, *Owner*
EMP: 4
SALES (est): 200K **Privately Held**
SIC: 3648 Outdoor lighting equipment

(G-1178)
DEFEO MANUFACTURAING
115 Commerce Dr (06804-3400)
PHONE.................................203 775-1950
Artie Defeo, *Principal*
EMP: 2
SALES (est): 149.7K **Privately Held**
SIC: 3714 Motor vehicle parts & accessories

(G-1179)
DEFEO MANUFACTURING
559 Federal Rd (06804-2017)
PHONE.................................203 775-0254
EMP: 2
SALES (est): 87.2K **Privately Held**
SIC: 3714 Motor Vehicle Parts And Accessories

(G-1180)
DEFEO MANUFACTURING INC
57 Commerce Dr (06804-3405)
PHONE.................................203 775-0254
EMP: 1
SALES (est): 55.6K **Privately Held**
SIC: 3714 Motor vehicle parts & accessories

(G-1181)
DEFEO MANUFACTURING INC
115 Commerce Dr (06804-3400)
PHONE.................................203 775-0254
Arturo De Feo, *President*
Anthony De Feo, *Vice Pres*
Danielle Tryjada, *Manager*
◆ EMP: 29
SQ FT: 14,000
SALES (est): 5.9MM **Privately Held**
WEB: www.defeomfg.com
SIC: 3714 Transmission housings or parts, motor vehicle

(G-1182)
DESIGNS & SIGNS
20 Beverly Dr (06804-2519)
PHONE.................................203 775-0152
Daniel McKee, *Owner*
EMP: 1
SALES (est): 121.7K **Privately Held**
SIC: 7336 3993 Commercial art & illustration; silk screen design; electric signs; neon signs

(G-1183)
DI GRAZIA VINEYARDS LTD
Also Called: Digrazia Vineyards & Winery
131 Tower Rd (06804-3654)
PHONE.................................203 775-1616
Paul Di Grazia, *President*
Barbara Di Grazia, *Vice Pres*
EMP: 3
SQ FT: 676
SALES (est): 646.4K **Privately Held**
WEB: www.digrazia.com
SIC: 5182 2084 Wine; wines, brandy & brandy spirits

(G-1184)
DOW CHEMICAL COMPANY
9 Meadowview Dr (06804-1810)
P.O. Box 896 (06804-0896)
PHONE.................................203 740-7510
EMP: 1
SALES (corp-wide): 57B **Publicly Held**
SIC: 2821 Mfg Plastic Materials/Resins
PA: The Dow Chemical Company
   2030 Dow Ctr
   Midland MI 48642
   989 636-1000

(G-1185)
DSAENCORE LLC (PA)
50 Pocono Rd (06804-3303)
PHONE.................................203 740-4200
Steve Friedman, *CEO*
Terry Algier, *Vice Pres*
Terri Winchell, *Vice Pres*
Rudolph Kraus,
EMP: 60
SQ FT: 30,000
SALES (est): 8MM **Privately Held**
SIC: 3679 Power supplies, all types: static

(G-1186)
EASTERN PRECAST COMPANY INC
1 Commerce Dr (06804)
P.O. Box 5133 (06804-5133)
PHONE.................................203 775-0230
Richard G Ditullio Sr, *President*
Richard G Ditullio Jr, *Exec VP*
John J Ditullio, *Treasurer*
Judith H Ditullio, *Admin Sec*
Judith Ditullio, *Admin Sec*
EMP: 21
SQ FT: 3,000
SALES (est): 3.4MM **Privately Held**
WEB: www.easternprecast.com
SIC: 3272 Concrete products, precast; septic tanks, concrete

(G-1187)
EF LEE PUBLISHING LLC
44 Whisconier Rd (06804-3810)
PHONE.................................203 546-7148
Daryl Janney, *Principal*
EMP: 1
SALES (est): 50K **Privately Held**
SIC: 2741 Miscellaneous publishing

(G-1188)
FIRST PAPERMILL LLC
2 Old New Milford Rd 1f (06804-2426)
PHONE.................................203 740-1991
Dennis J Ramey, *Principal*
EMP: 1
SALES (est): 71.5K **Privately Held**
SIC: 2621 Paper mills

(G-1189)
FWT4 LLC
12 Jason Ct (06804-3034)
PHONE.................................203 775-7087
Dr Robert Aledort, *Manager*
EMP: 2
SALES (est): 119.4K **Privately Held**
SIC: 3441 Fabricated structural metal

(G-1190)
GENIE SHELF
16 S Lake Shore Dr (06804-1430)
PHONE.................................203 241-7523
EMP: 1
SALES (est): 46.2K **Privately Held**
SIC: 2511 Wood household furniture

Brookfield - Fairfield County

(G-1191)
GK MECHANICAL SYSTEMS LLC
934 Federal Rd Ste 1b (06804-1143)
PHONE....................203 775-4970
Keith Overthrow, *VP Opers*
Mike Dravis, *Project Engr*
Mike Sleet, *CTO*
Michael Barnes,
Steve Fournier,
EMP: 8
SQ FT: 4,500
SALES (est): 3.5MM **Privately Held**
SIC: 3429 Keys, locks & related hardware

(G-1192)
GLOBAL SHIELD SOLUTIONS LLC
Also Called: SD Labs
22 Westview Ln (06804-3465)
PHONE....................860 983-3566
Francis J Catapano, *CEO*
EMP: 1
SALES (est): 174.9K **Privately Held**
SIC: 2842 Specialty cleaning, polishes & sanitation goods

(G-1193)
GORDON ENGINEERING CORP
67 Del Mar Dr (06804-2494)
PHONE....................203 775-4501
Steven Weighart, *President*
Barb Baldino, *Sales Staff*
EMP: 16 **EST:** 1971
SQ FT: 3,000
SALES: 1MM **Privately Held**
WEB: www.gordoneng.com
SIC: 3823 3842 Industrial process control instruments; surgical appliances & supplies

(G-1194)
GORDON PRODUCTS INCORPORATED
67 Del Mar Dr (06804-2401)
PHONE....................203 775-4501
Steven Weighart, *President*
Debbie Rabito, *Prdtn Mgr*
EMP: 25
SQ FT: 14,000
SALES (est): 3.6MM **Privately Held**
WEB: www.gordonproducts.com
SIC: 3625 3674 3643 Electric controls & control accessories, industrial; semiconductors & related devices; current-carrying wiring devices

(G-1195)
GREENWAY INDUSTRIES INC
150 Laurel Hill Rd (06804-1022)
PHONE....................203 885-1059
EMP: 2
SALES (est): 108.6K **Privately Held**
SIC: 3999 Manufacturing industries

(G-1196)
IMAGES FINE PRINT
594 Federal Rd Ste 5 (06804-2008)
PHONE....................203 482-1695
EMP: 2 **EST:** 2018
SALES (est): 83.9K **Privately Held**
SIC: 2752 Commercial printing, lithographic

(G-1197)
IMPERIAL ELCTRNIC ASSEMBLY INC
Also Called: I E A
1000 Federal Rd (06804-1123)
PHONE....................203 740-8425
Tony Conte, *President*
Edward O'Donnell, *Vice Pres*
Sandy Connolly, *Purchasing*
Tom Vrba, *Purchasing*
Heather White, *Engineer*
▲ **EMP:** 93
SQ FT: 45,000
SALES (est): 34.3MM **Privately Held**
WEB: www.impea.com
SIC: 3679 Electronic circuits

(G-1198)
INTERSPACE INDUSTRIES LLC
72 Grays Bridge Rd Ste 1c (06804-2638)
PHONE....................203.814-1879
David Humphrys, *Principal*
EMP: 1
SALES (est): 44.7K **Privately Held**
SIC: 3999 Manufacturing industries

(G-1199)
JENRAY PRODUCTS INC
4 Production Dr (06804-1156)
PHONE....................914 375-5596
Raymond D'Urso, *President*
▲ **EMP:** 26 **EST:** 1999
SALES (est): 3.5MM **Privately Held**
SIC: 3999 Sprays, artificial & preserved

(G-1200)
JK ANTENNAS INC
72 Grays Bridge Rd Ste D (06804-2632)
PHONE....................845 228-8700
Ken Garg, *President*
Charlisa Garg, *Vice Pres*
Ann Garg, *Director*
EMP: 5
SALES (est): 278.2K **Privately Held**
SIC: 3663 Antennas, transmitting & communications

(G-1201)
LA PIETRA THINSTONE VENEER
Also Called: La Pietra Custom Marble & Gran
1106 Federal Rd (06804-1122)
P.O. Box 5149 (06804-5149)
PHONE....................203 775-6162
Fabio Figueiredo, *President*
EMP: 3
SALES (est): 99.6K **Privately Held**
SIC: 3281 5211 Marble, building: cut & shaped; tile, ceramic

(G-1202)
LETOUT & BLISS LLC
246 Federal Rd (06804-2647)
PHONE....................203 775-3548
Fax: 203 775-3902
EMP: 2 **EST:** 2004
SALES (est): 160K **Privately Held**
SIC: 7372 Prepackaged Software Services

(G-1203)
LIGHTHOUSE MAPS
20 Obtuse Rocks Rd (06804-3227)
P.O. Box 217 (06804-0217)
PHONE....................203 981-1090
Gary Owens,
EMP: 2
SALES: 180K **Privately Held**
SIC: 2721 7011 Magazines: publishing only, not printed on site; hotels & motels

(G-1204)
MCMULLIN MANUFACTURING CORP
70 Pocono Rd (06804-3303)
P.O. Box 780 (06804-0780)
PHONE....................203 740-3360
Timothy McMullin, *President*
Kevin J McMullin, *Vice Pres*
Kevin McMullin, *Vice Pres*
Marlys J McMullin, *Director*
EMP: 31
SQ FT: 12,800
SALES (est): 5.9MM **Privately Held**
WEB: www.mcmullinmfg.com
SIC: 3469 3444 Stamping metal for the trade; sheet metalwork

(G-1205)
MICHAEL LAZORCHAK
35 Mist Hill Dr (06804-1611)
PHONE....................203 775-0608
Michael Lazorchak, *Owner*
EMP: 2
SALES (est): 101.3K **Privately Held**
SIC: 2754 Announcements: gravure printing

(G-1206)
MILLBROOK PRESS INC
2 Old New Milford Rd 2e (06804-2413)
PHONE....................203 740-2220
David Allen, *President*
EMP: 46
SALES (est): 4.8MM **Privately Held**
SIC: 2731 Books: publishing only

(G-1207)
MIST HILL PROPERTY MAINT LLC
32 Mist Hill Dr (06804-1621)
PHONE....................203 648-7434
Kyle Embree,
EMP: 2
SQ FT: 25,000
SALES (est): 129.8K **Privately Held**
SIC: 2879 1794 5083 0782 Insecticides & pesticides; excavation & grading, building construction; landscaping equipment; garden maintenance services

(G-1208)
MOONLIGHTING LLC
4 Jackson Dr (06804-1608)
PHONE....................203 740-8964
David Morin, *Principal*
EMP: 4
SALES (est): 256.2K **Privately Held**
SIC: 3648 Lighting equipment

(G-1209)
NITCH TO STITCH LLC
419 Federal Rd (06804-2037)
PHONE....................203 948-9921
Scott Mitchell, *Manager*
EMP: 1
SALES (est): 51.9K **Privately Held**
SIC: 2395 Embroidery & art needlework

(G-1210)
PAPER AND PROSE PUBLISHING LLC
9 Willow Run (06804-3744)
PHONE....................203 775-8228
Julie Kerton, *Principal*
EMP: 1
SALES (est): 52.4K **Privately Held**
SIC: 2741 Miscellaneous publishing

(G-1211)
PHOTRONICS INC (PA)
15 Secor Rd (06804-3937)
P.O. Box 5226 (06804-5226)
PHONE....................203 775-9000
Peter S Kirlin, *CEO*
Constantine S Macricostas, *Ch of Bd*
Richelle E Burr, *Vice Pres*
Christopher J Progler, *Vice Pres*
Rust Jay, *Traffic Mgr*
EMP: 277
SALES: 535.2MM **Publicly Held**
WEB: www.photronics.com
SIC: 3674 Integrated circuits, semiconductor networks, etc.; light sensitive devices; light sensitive devices, solid state

(G-1212)
PHOTRONICS INC
15 Secor Rd (06804-3937)
PHONE....................203 740-5669
Steve Haff, *Manager*
EMP: 150
SALES (corp-wide): 535.2MM **Publicly Held**
WEB: www.photronics.com
SIC: 3674 Light sensitive devices
PA: Photronics, Inc.
15 Secor Rd
Brookfield CT 06804
203 775-9000

(G-1213)
PHOTRONICS TEXAS INC
15 Secor Rd (06804-3937)
PHONE....................203 546-3039
Sean T Smith, *Principal*
Dan Pullen, *Engineer*
Maria Nunez, *Manager*
EMP: 4
SALES (est): 255.4K
SALES (corp-wide): 535.2MM **Publicly Held**
SIC: 3674 Semiconductors & related devices
PA: Photronics, Inc.
15 Secor Rd
Brookfield CT 06804
203 775-9000

(G-1214)
PHOTRONICS TEXAS I LLC
15 Secor Rd (06804-3937)
PHONE....................203 775-9000
Constantine S Macricostas, *Chairman*
EMP: 4
SALES (est): 139K
SALES (corp-wide): 535.2MM **Publicly Held**
SIC: 3674 Semiconductors & related devices
PA: Photronics, Inc.
15 Secor Rd
Brookfield CT 06804
203 775-9000

(G-1215)
PRECISION PLASTIC FAB
5d Del Mar Dr (06804)
PHONE....................203 775-7047
John Clayton, *Owner*
EMP: 3
SALES (est): 377K **Privately Held**
SIC: 3089 Plastic processing

(G-1216)
PREDCISION PLASTICS INC
150 Laurel Hill Rd (06804-1022)
PHONE....................203 775-7047
Oscar Kress, *Owner*
EMP: 2
SALES (est): 88.9K **Privately Held**
SIC: 3089 Plastics products

(G-1217)
R LANGE WELDING-FABRICATION
114 Candlewood Lake Rd (06804-2227)
PHONE....................203 994-5516
EMP: 1 **EST:** 2017
SALES (est): 28.1K **Privately Held**
SIC: 7692 Welding repair

(G-1218)
REVIVE BEAUTY AND WELLNESS LLC
Also Called: Art of Perfection
2 Old New Milford Rd 3d (06804-2426)
PHONE....................860 921-4952
EMP: 2
SQ FT: 1,200
SALES: 100K **Privately Held**
SIC: 2844 5999 Mfg Toilet Preparations Ret Misc Merchandise

(G-1219)
ROTHSTEIN ASSOCIATES INC
Also Called: Rothstein Ctlg On Distr Recvry
4 Arapaho Rd (06804-3104)
PHONE....................203 740-7400
Philip J Rothstein, *President*
Carla Rothstein, *Vice Pres*
Glyn Davis, *Chief Mktg Ofcr*
EMP: 8
SQ FT: 1,500
SALES (est): 402.9K **Privately Held**
WEB: www.rothstein.com
SIC: 8742 2731 Management consulting services; books: publishing only

(G-1220)
RUNWAY LIQUIDATION LLC
Also Called: Bcbg
2812 N Univisity Dr (06804)
PHONE....................202 544-1900
EMP: 2
SALES (corp-wide): 570.1MM **Privately Held**
SIC: 2335 Women's, juniors' & misses' dresses
HQ: Runway Liquidation, Llc
2761 Fruitland Ave
Vernon CA 90058
323 589-2224

(G-1221)
SAUGATUCK TREE & LOGGING LLC
117 Whisconier Rd (06804-3436)
PHONE....................203 470-9195
Derek A Smith, *Branch Mgr*
EMP: 4

SALES (corp-wide): 1.2MM **Privately Held**
WEB: www.saugreen.com
SIC: **1629** 2411 Land clearing contractor; logging
PA: Saugatuck Tree & Logging, Llc
 309 S Main St
 Newtown CT 06470
 203 304-1326

(G-1222)
SAVANT PUBLISHING LLC
1 Deer Trail Dr (06804-3910)
PHONE..................................203 740-9850
Charles Tupper, *Principal*
EMP: 1 EST: 2012
SALES (est): 63.2K **Privately Held**
SIC: **2741** Miscellaneous publishing

(G-1223)
SIBTECH INC
115 Commerce Dr Ste A (06804-3400)
PHONE..................................203 775-5677
Joseph Backer, *CEO*
Dr Victor Sidorov, *Vice Pres*
EMP: 2
SQ FT: 3,000
SALES: 750K **Privately Held**
WEB: www.sibtech.com
SIC: **8733** 2759 Biotechnical research, noncommercial; commercial printing

(G-1224)
SOFTWARE GALLERY INC
Also Called: Tsg Web Plus
86 Ironworks Hill Rd (06804-1227)
PHONE..................................203 775-0520
Malin Zergiebel, *President*
EMP: 1
SALES (est): 75K **Privately Held**
WEB: www.thesoftwaregallery.com
SIC: **7372** Prepackaged software

(G-1225)
SPEEDI SIGN LLC
770 Federal Rd (06804-2026)
PHONE..................................203 775-0700
James A Myles, *Mng Member*
EMP: 3
SQ FT: 1,400
SALES (est): 272.9K **Privately Held**
SIC: **3993** Signs, not made in custom sign painting shops

(G-1226)
SPRUCE IT UP WOODWORKING LLC
1 Richards Rd (06804-1215)
P.O. Box 561 (06804-0561)
PHONE..................................203 740-7975
Victor Oricchio, *Principal*
EMP: 1
SALES (est): 59.5K **Privately Held**
SIC: **2431** Millwork

(G-1227)
STAR WOODS CABINET
132 Federal Rd (06804-2545)
PHONE..................................203 546-8688
Arly De Almeida Barros, *Principal*
EMP: 2
SALES (est): 155.9K **Privately Held**
SIC: **2434** Wood kitchen cabinets

(G-1228)
TARGET FLAVORS INC
7 Del Mar Dr (06804-2401)
PHONE..................................203 775-4727
John Maclean, *President*
Bill McLean, *General Mgr*
John S Maclean Jr, *Vice Pres*
William Maclean, *Vice Pres*
Mike Malone, *Technical Staff*
▲ EMP: 12
SQ FT: 25,000
SALES (est): 2.7MM **Privately Held**
WEB: www.targetflavors.com
SIC: **2087** Concentrates, flavoring (except drink)

(G-1229)
TECHNIPOWER SYSTEMS INC (HQ)
57 Commerce Dr (06804-3405)
PHONE..................................203 748-7001

EMP: 8
SQ FT: 15,000
SALES (est): 3.2MM
SALES (corp-wide): 10.4MM **Privately Held**
SIC: **3621** Manufacturing Of Motors And Generators
PA: Technipower Llc
 3900 Coral Ridge Dr
 Coral Springs FL 33071
 203 748-7001

(G-1230)
THOMAS J HUNT INC
317 Federal Rd Ste A (06804-2428)
PHONE..................................203 775-5050
Jim Torrisi, *Sales Associate*
Thomas J Hunt, *Branch Mgr*
Sonia Lopes, *Associate*
EMP: 1
SALES (corp-wide): 5.1MM **Privately Held**
WEB: www.thecreativebath.com
SIC: **3432** 5074 5251 5722 Plumbing fixture fittings & trim; plumbing fittings & supplies; pumps & pumping equipment; air conditioning room units, self-contained
PA: Thomas J. Hunt, Inc.
 28 Finance Dr
 Danbury CT 06810
 203 748-2635

(G-1231)
TOPPAN PHOTOMASKS INC
246 Federal Rd Ste C22 (06804-2647)
PHONE..................................203 775-9001
Michael G Hadsell, *Branch Mgr*
EMP: 49 **Privately Held**
SIC: **3559** Semiconductor manufacturing machinery
HQ: Toppan Photomasks, Inc.
 131 E Old Settlers Blvd
 Round Rock TX 78664
 512 310-6500

(G-1232)
TORNOS TECHNOLOGIES US CORP
70 Pocono Rd (06804-3303)
PHONE..................................203 775-4319
Thomas Dierks, *Branch Mgr*
EMP: 1
SALES (corp-wide): 1.7MM **Privately Held**
SIC: **3541** Screw machines, automatic
PA: Tornos Technologies Us Corp
 840 Parkview Blvd
 Lombard IL 60018
 630 812-2040

(G-1233)
TRIANJA TECHNOLOGIES INC
15 Secor Rd (06804-3937)
PHONE..................................203 775-9000
EMP: 2
SALES (est): 97.1K **Privately Held**
SIC: **3674** Semiconductors & related devices

(G-1234)
UNIVERSAL VOLTRONICS CORP
57 Commerce Dr (06804-3405)
PHONE..................................203 740-8555
Tom Kell, *CEO*
William T Carney, *President*
Rosa Feliciano, *Accountant*
Bert Yost, *Technical Staff*
EMP: 40
SQ FT: 22,000
SALES (est): 6.9MM **Privately Held**
WEB: www.voltronics.com
SIC: **3612** Specialty transformers

(G-1235)
UNLIMITED SIGNS DESIGNS & GRAP
72 Grays Bridge Rd Ste F (06804-2632)
PHONE..................................203 546-7267
Marian Goldstein, *Owner*
Michael Goldstein, *Co-Owner*
EMP: 5
SALES (est): 467.3K **Privately Held**
SIC: **7336** 3993 Graphic arts & related design; electric signs; neon signs; letters for signs, metal

(G-1236)
VALIDUS DC SYSTEMS LLC
50 Pocono Rd (06804-3303)
PHONE..................................203 448-3600
Rudy Kraus, *CEO*
Ronald Croce, *COO*
Frank Catapano, *Vice Pres*
Al Dei Maggi, *Vice Pres*
Larry Hess,
EMP: 14
SQ FT: 29,000
SALES (est): 111.7MM **Privately Held**
SIC: **3679** Static power supply converters for electronic applications

(G-1237)
VISION DESIGNS LLC
1120 Federal Rd Ste 2 (06804-1122)
PHONE..................................203 778-9898
Scott D Johnson, *Managing Prtnr*
Dan Lombardo, *Partner*
Tom Seeley, *Partner*
Lenny Margiotta, *Vice Pres*
EMP: 15
SALES (est): 2.2MM **Privately Held**
WEB: www.visiondesignsct.com
SIC: **2759** 5099 Screen printing; signs, except electric

(G-1238)
VISION KITCHENS AND MLLWK LLC
3 Production Dr Ste 4 (06804-1148)
PHONE..................................203 775-0604
Rob Masciarelli, *Principal*
EMP: 1
SALES (est): 57.2K **Privately Held**
SIC: **2431** Millwork

(G-1239)
WENTWORTH LABORATORIES INC (PA)
1087 Federal Rd Ste 4 (06804-1145)
PHONE..................................203 775-0448
Arthur Evans, *Ch of Bd*
Stephen AA Evans, *President*
Stephen Evans, *President*
Robert Bollo, *Vice Pres*
Sue Murphy, *Production*
EMP: 57
SQ FT: 25,000
SALES (est): 16.1MM **Privately Held**
WEB: www.wentworthlabs.com
SIC: **3825** Instruments to measure electricity

(G-1240)
WENTWORTH LABORATORIES INC
500 Federal Rd (06804-2019)
P.O. Box 320 (06804-0320)
PHONE..................................203 775-9311
EMP: 4
SALES (corp-wide): 25.1MM **Privately Held**
SIC: **3825** 3826 3823 Mfg Electrical Measuring Instruments Mfg Analytical Instruments Mfg Process Control Instruments
PA: Wentworth Laboratories, Inc.
 1087 Federal Rd Ste 4
 Brookfield CT 06804
 203 775-0448

(G-1241)
WHALEN STICKS LLC
518 Federal Rd (06804-2019)
PHONE..................................203 546-8515
Barry Whalen, *Mng Member*
EMP: 1
SALES (est): 84K **Privately Held**
SIC: **3949** Baseball equipment & supplies, general

(G-1242)
YANKEE PENNYSAVER INC
246 Federal Rd Ste D15 (06804-2649)
PHONE..................................203 775-9122
Susan Blumenthal, *President*
Steven Silver, *Vice Pres*
John Effinger, *Art Dir*
John Benusis, *Fmly & Gen Dent*
EMP: 23

SALES (est): 1MM **Privately Held**
WEB: www.ctpennysaver.com
SIC: **2711** Newspapers, publishing & printing

Brooklyn
Windham County

(G-1243)
101 BUSINESS SOLUTIONS LLC
128 Fitzgerald Rd (06234-1409)
PHONE..................................860 774-6904
Carmel A Osterlund,
EMP: 2
SALES (est): 392K **Privately Held**
SIC: **2759** Screen printing

(G-1244)
A F M ENGINEERING CORP
24 Woodward Rd (06234-1425)
PHONE..................................860 774-7518
Steven A Gilman, *President*
Lee Gilman, *Corp Secy*
EMP: 5
SQ FT: 6,600
SALES (est): 500K **Privately Held**
WEB: www.afmengineering.com
SIC: **3569** 5084 Assembly machines, non-metalworking; industrial machinery & equipment

(G-1245)
AD LABEL INC
59 N Society Rd (06234-2313)
PHONE..................................860 779-0513
Richard Baril, *President*
Robert Benson, *Vice Pres*
EMP: 7 EST: 1981
SQ FT: 3,200
SALES (est): 1.3MM **Privately Held**
SIC: **2759** Labels & seals: printing

(G-1246)
BARRETTE MECHANICAL
36 Bush Hill Rd (06234-1400)
PHONE..................................860 774-0499
Bruce Barrette, *Principal*
EMP: 3
SALES (est): 195K **Privately Held**
SIC: **3999** Barrettes

(G-1247)
GRAVELINES AMERCN MARTIAL ARTS
12 Providence Rd (06234-1819)
PHONE..................................860 753-1402
Joseph Graveline, *Principal*
EMP: 2
SALES (est): 173.1K **Privately Held**
SIC: **2752** Commercial printing, lithographic

(G-1248)
JMJP LLC
18 Suzanne Ln (06234-2530)
PHONE..................................888 737-7577
John Pepper,
EMP: 2
SALES (est): 85.5K **Privately Held**
SIC: **7372** Prepackaged software

(G-1249)
MONOGRAMIT LLC
9 S Main St (06234-3400)
PHONE..................................860 779-0694
Georgia Ludovici, *Owner*
EMP: 3
SALES: 95K **Privately Held**
SIC: **2395** Embroidery products, except schiffli machine

(G-1250)
MSR WELDING SERVICE
158 Providence Rd (06234-1820)
PHONE..................................860 234-9949
Matthew Robert, *Principal*
EMP: 1
SALES (est): 38.9K **Privately Held**
SIC: **7692** Welding repair

▲ = Import ▼=Export
◆ =Import/Export

GEOGRAPHIC SECTION

(G-1251)
NATIONAL PICTURE FRAME INC
9 Whitebrook Dr (06234-1564)
PHONE...................860 774-5668
Diane Clarkin, *President*
Matthew Clarkin, *Treasurer*
EMP: 5
SALES (est): 283.7K Privately Held
SIC: 5999 3231 3499 5023 Art, picture frames & decorations; picture frames, ready made; framed mirrors; picture frames, metal; mirrors & pictures, framed & unframed

(G-1252)
POST PATTERN
100 Tatnic Rd (06234-1622)
PHONE...................860 774-7911
Mark Luzio, *Principal*
EMP: 2
SALES (est): 215.4K Privately Held
SIC: 3543 Industrial patterns

(G-1253)
QUIET CORNER PRINTING LLC ✪
200 Bailey Woods Rd (06234-2404)
PHONE...................860 753-0420
Jonathan Sands, *Mng Member*
EMP: 2 EST: 2019
SALES (est): 83.9K Privately Held
SIC: 2752 Commercial printing, lithographic

(G-1254)
SIGFRIDSON WOOD PRODUCTS LLC
125 Fitzgerald Rd (06234-1411)
PHONE...................860 774-2075
Kenneth Sigfridson,
Andrew Sigfridson,
EMP: 7
SQ FT: 20,000
SALES: 2MM Privately Held
WEB: www.sigfridson.com
SIC: 2421 Sawmills & planing mills, general

(G-1255)
SIGNS OF AMERICA
59 N Society Rd (06234-2313)
PHONE...................860 412-0054
Richard Healy, *Principal*
EMP: 1
SALES (est): 53.7K Privately Held
SIC: 3993 Signs & advertising specialties

(G-1256)
TAILORED KITCHENS BY ANN-MORIN
33 Grand View Ter (06234-2030)
PHONE...................860 428-2397
Ann Morin, *Owner*
EMP: 1
SALES: 10K Privately Held
SIC: 2514 Kitchen cabinets: metal

(G-1257)
UNINSRED ALTTUDE CNNECTION INC
Also Called: Peregrine Manufacturing
330 Day St (06234-1517)
PHONE...................860 333-1461
David Singer, *President*
Colleen Malone, *Accounts Mgr*
EMP: 3
SQ FT: 3,000
SALES (est): 208.2K Privately Held
SIC: 2393 Bags & containers, except sleeping bags: textile

(G-1258)
VINEYARD AT FOXRUN
580 Pomfret Rd (06234-1527)
PHONE...................860 779-0230
John Cordes, *Owner*
EMP: 1
SALES: 2K Privately Held
SIC: 2084 Wines, brandy & brandy spirits

(G-1259)
WOLD TOOL ENGINEERING INC
7 Commonway Dr (06234-1839)
PHONE...................860 564-8338
EMP: 7 EST: 1945
SQ FT: 3,600
SALES: 500K Privately Held
SIC: 3451 Mfg Screw Machine Products

Burlington
Hartford County

(G-1260)
ASSOC STUCCO
31 Wood Creek Rd (06013-1920)
PHONE...................860 221-5791
Andrcej Dyl, *Owner*
EMP: 1
SALES (est): 83.7K Privately Held
SIC: 3299 Stucco

(G-1261)
BROWN LARKIN & CO LLC
63 Black Walnut Ln (06013-2205)
PHONE...................860 280-8858
Richard M Larkin,
EMP: 1
SQ FT: 5,000
SALES (est): 400K Privately Held
SIC: 8742 7379 3841 3569 Management consulting services; computer related consulting services; surgical & medical instruments; assembly machines, non-metalworking

(G-1262)
BURLINGTON GOLF CENTER INC
Also Called: Hogan's Cider Mill
522 Spielman Hwy (06013-1609)
PHONE...................860 675-7320
Theresa C Dunlop, *President*
Chet Dunlop, *Admin Sec*
▲ EMP: 4
SALES (est): 440.1K Privately Held
SIC: 7999 2099 Golf driving range; golf professionals; cider, nonalcoholic

(G-1263)
CEM GROUP LLC (DH)
Also Called: Chand Eisenmann Metallurgical
258 Spielman Hwy Ste 7 (06013-1723)
PHONE...................860 675-5000
Mark Eisenmann,
EMP: 10
SQ FT: 10,000
SALES (est): 2.5MM
SALES (corp-wide): 170.1MM Privately Held
WEB: www.chandeisenmann.com
SIC: 3449 Miscellaneous metalwork
HQ: Porvair Filtration Group, Inc.
   301 Business Ln
   Ashland VA 23005
   804 550-1600

(G-1264)
CK IMAGING AND EMBROIDERY
3 Northridge Dr (06013-1553)
PHONE...................716 984-1957
Christopher Shaffer, *Principal*
EMP: 1
SALES (est): 57.8K Privately Held
SIC: 2395 Embroidery products, except schiffli machine

(G-1265)
CRESCENT MNFACTURING OPERATING
700 George Wash Tpke (06013-1718)
P.O. Box 1350 (06013-0350)
PHONE...................860 673-1921
Richard Hrinak,
Joanne Gates,
Richard V Gates,
Richard Green,
James Speck,
EMP: 34 EST: 1960
SQ FT: 18,000
SALES: 1,000K Privately Held
WEB: www.crescentmanufacturing.com
SIC: 3452 Screws, metal

(G-1266)
E R HINMAN & SONS INC
Also Called: Hinman Lumber
77 Milford St (06013-1722)
PHONE...................860 673-9170
Julia Hinman, *CEO*
Michael J Hinman, *President*
Paul Hinman, *Vice Pres*
EMP: 8 EST: 1915
SQ FT: 5,000
SALES (est): 1.2MM Privately Held
SIC: 2421 2426 Lumber: rough, sawed or planed; hardwood dimension & flooring mills

(G-1267)
ENERGY SAVING PRODUCTS AND SLS
713 George Washington Tpk (06013-1718)
P.O. Box 2037 (06013-1037)
PHONE...................860 675-6443
Richard Lamothe, *President*
Susan Lamothe, *Vice Pres*
EMP: 50
SQ FT: 30,000
SALES (est): 6.8MM Privately Held
SIC: 3579 Forms handling equipment

(G-1268)
ETRON LLC
9 Hunters Xing (06013-1536)
P.O. Box 1113 (06013-0113)
PHONE...................860 673-0121
Nathan W Howard, *Partner*
EMP: 2
SALES (est): 70K Privately Held
WEB: www.etron-llc.com
SIC: 8748 3699 Business consulting; electrical equipment & supplies

(G-1269)
GYPSUM SYSTEMS LLC
11 Hinman Meadow Rd (06013-1739)
P.O. Box 2022 (06013-1022)
PHONE...................860 470-3916
Nicole Rodrigue, *Principal*
EMP: 2
SALES (est): 129.9K Privately Held
SIC: 3599 Industrial machinery

(G-1270)
INK 13 LLC
9 Deerfield Trce (06013-1514)
PHONE...................860 921-6910
Paul Costanzo, *Principal*
EMP: 2
SALES (est): 160.4K Privately Held
SIC: 2759 Screen printing

(G-1271)
JACOB DAVID POPPEL
35 Gilbert Ln (06013-2114)
PHONE...................860 904-3749
Jacob Poppel, *Owner*
EMP: 1
SALES (est): 56.4K Privately Held
SIC: 3443 1799 Weldments; ornamental metal work

(G-1272)
MARK RAMPONI PRINTING
28 Covey Rd (06013-1316)
PHONE...................860 673-5507
Mark Ramponi, *Principal*
EMP: 2
SALES (est): 139.5K Privately Held
SIC: 2752 Commercial printing, lithographic

(G-1273)
METALAST INTERNATIONAL IN
12 Stanwich Ln (06013-2000)
PHONE...................860 673-1725
EMP: 1
SALES (est): 60.1K Privately Held
SIC: 2869 Industrial organic chemicals

(G-1274)
MILLER FUEL LLC
28 Monce Rd (06013-2539)
P.O. Box 1506 (06013-0506)
PHONE...................860 675-6121
Michael J Miller, *President*
EMP: 7
SALES (est): 896.5K Privately Held
SIC: 2869 Fuels

(G-1275)
NELSON PUBLISHING
479 Spielman Hwy (06013-1607)
PHONE...................860 404-5292
Sue Nelson, *Principal*
EMP: 2
SALES (est): 86.7K Privately Held
SIC: 2741 Miscellaneous publishing

(G-1276)
TARGET MACHINES INC
713 George Wash Tpke (06013-1718)
PHONE...................860 675-1539
Richard Lamothe, *President*
Susan Lamothe, *Corp Secy*
EMP: 6
SALES (est): 660K Privately Held
WEB: www.targetmachines.com
SIC: 3599 7389 Machine shop, jobbing & repair;

(G-1277)
TYNE PLASTICS LLC (PA)
252 Spielman Hwy Ste B (06013-1753)
PHONE...................860 673-7100
Wendy L Carrafa,
EMP: 4
SALES (est): 2.7MM Privately Held
WEB: www.tyne.com
SIC: 2821 Plastics materials & resins

(G-1278)
W R HARTIGAN & SON INC
10 Spielman Hwy (06013-1909)
PHONE...................860 673-9203
Gerald H Mullen, *President*
Alice I Hartigan, *Corp Secy*
Bryan Mullen, *Vice Pres*
EMP: 6 EST: 1869
SQ FT: 6,500
SALES (est): 200K Privately Held
SIC: 2541 2441 2499 7371 Display fixtures, wood; cases, wood; plugs, wood; computer software development & applications; computer peripheral equipment

(G-1279)
WASHBURN DESIGN LLC
148 Jerome Ave (06013-2433)
PHONE...................860 675-3215
Steve Washburn,
Ben Washburn,
Marie Washburn,
EMP: 2
SALES (est): 220K Privately Held
SIC: 3312 Tool & die steel

Canaan
Litchfield County

(G-1280)
AD COMM INK
325 Ashley Falls Rd (06018-2040)
PHONE...................860 824-7565
Mary Einfeldt, *Owner*
EMP: 2
SALES (est): 125.5K Privately Held
SIC: 3479 Etching & engraving

(G-1281)
BECTON DICKINSON AND COMPANY
Grace Way Rr 7 (06018)
P.O. Box 749 (06018-0749)
PHONE...................860 824-5487
Todd Zeller, *Manager*
EMP: 400
SALES (corp-wide): 15.9B Publicly Held
SIC: 3841 3842 Hypodermic needles & syringes; surgical appliances & supplies
PA: Becton, Dickinson And Company
   1 Becton Dr
   Franklin Lakes NJ 07417
   201 847-6800

(G-1282)
BONSAL AMERICAN INC
43 Clayton Rd (06018-2153)
P.O. Box 996 (06018-0996)
PHONE...................860 824-7733

George Sperry, *Vice Pres*
EMP: 8
SALES (corp-wide): 30.6B **Privately Held**
WEB: www.bonsalamerican.com
SIC: 3272 Concrete products
HQ: Bonsal American, Inc.
625 Griffith Rd Ste 100
Charlotte NC 28217
704 525-1621

(G-1283)
BONSAL AMERICAN INC
43 Clayton Rd (06018-2153)
PHONE..................860 824-7733
EMP: 20
SQ FT: 2,000
SALES (corp-wide): 23.5B **Privately Held**
SIC: 3273 3272 3255 Mfg Ready-Mixed Concrete Mfg Concrete Products Mfg Clay Refractories
HQ: Bonsal American, Inc.
8201 Arrowridge Blvd
Charlotte NC 28217
704 525-1621

(G-1284)
CENTURY ACQUISITION
49 Clayton Rd (06018-2153)
P.O. Box 485 (06018-0485)
PHONE..................518 758-7229
Brendan Clemente, *Owner*
EMP: 9
SALES (est): 1.3MM **Privately Held**
SIC: 3273 Ready-mixed concrete

(G-1285)
COUNTRY LOG HOMES
77 Clayton Rd (06018-2153)
PHONE..................413 229-8084
EMP: 2
SALES (est): 112.9K **Privately Held**
SIC: 2452 Log cabins, prefabricated, wood

(G-1286)
HITBRO REALTY LLC
78 High St (06018-2535)
PHONE..................860 824-1370
Timothy A Hitchcock, *Principal*
EMP: 4
SALES (est): 333.1K **Privately Held**
SIC: 2869 Fuels

(G-1287)
JACQUIER WELDING
213 Daisy Hill Rd (06018-2119)
PHONE..................860 824-4182
Lisa Jacquier, *Principal*
EMP: 1
SALES (est): 119.8K **Privately Held**
SIC: 7692 Welding repair

(G-1288)
JILL GHI
Also Called: Ghi Sign Service
532 Ashley Falls Rd (06018-2017)
P.O. Box 45 (06018-0045)
PHONE..................860 824-7123
Jill Ghi, *Principal*
Gary Rovelto, *Prdtn Mgr*
Philip J Ghi, *Asst Treas*
EMP: 3 **EST:** 1955
SQ FT: 1,000
SALES: 150K **Privately Held**
WEB: www.ghisign.com
SIC: 3993 Signs, not made in custom sign painting shops; electric signs

(G-1289)
MINTEQ INTERNATIONAL INC
Also Called: Mineral Technology
30 Daisy Hill Rd (06018-2115)
P.O. Box 667 (06018-0667)
PHONE..................860 824-5435
Mark Lambert, *Principal*
EMP: 130 **Publicly Held**
WEB: www.minteq.com
SIC: 2851 3823 3624 Paints & allied products; industrial instrmnts msrmnt display/control process variable; carbon & graphite products
HQ: Minteq International Inc.
35 Highland Ave
Bethlehem PA 18017

(G-1290)
PATRICK BARRETT DBA LUCKY DUCK
79 Old Turnpike Rd (06018-2232)
PHONE..................347 703-3984
EMP: 2 **EST:** 2011
SALES (est): 93.5K **Privately Held**
SIC: 2741 Miscellaneous publishing

(G-1291)
SANDRI PRODUCTS
24 Sand Rd (06018-2424)
PHONE..................860 824-0001
Lawrence J Sandri, *Owner*
EMP: 1
SALES (est): 50.4K **Privately Held**
SIC: 3955 Print cartridges for laser & other computer printers

(G-1292)
SPECIALTY MINERALS INC
30 Daisy Hill Rd (06018-2115)
P.O. Box 667 (06018-0667)
PHONE..................860 824-5435
Mark Lambert, *Branch Mgr*
EMP: 130 **Publicly Held**
WEB: www.specialtyminerals.com
SIC: 3297 2819 1422 Nonclay refractories; industrial inorganic chemicals; crushed & broken limestone
HQ: Specialty Minerals Inc.
622 3rd Ave Fl 38
New York NY 10017
212 878-1800

(G-1293)
TALLON LUMBER INC
2 Tallon Dr (06018)
P.O. Box 1058 (06018-1058)
PHONE..................860 824-0733
James A Tallon, *President*
Brion Tallon, *Vice Pres*
EMP: 26
SQ FT: 1,200
SALES (est): 4.3MM **Privately Held**
WEB: www.tallonlumber.com
SIC: 2421 2426 Lumber: rough, sawed or planed; flooring, hardwood

(G-1294)
TRANSDUCER PRODUCTS INC
4 Gandolfo Dr (06018-2431)
PHONE..................860 824-1002
John Titherington, *Manager*
EMP: 2 **EST:** 1963
SQ FT: 7,500
SALES (est): 311.4K **Privately Held**
SIC: 3679 Electronic crystals

Canterbury
Windham County

(G-1295)
BRAD KETTLE
Also Called: Brad's Logging
4 Howe Rd (06331-1919)
PHONE..................860 546-9929
Brad Kettle, *Principal*
EMP: 3
SALES (est): 266.8K **Privately Held**
SIC: 2411 Logging

(G-1296)
BROOK BURGIS ALPACAS LLC
44 N Canterbury Rd (06331-1231)
PHONE..................203 605-0588
Alisa Mierzejewski, *Principal*
EMP: 2 **EST:** 2008
SALES (est): 124.4K **Privately Held**
SIC: 2231 Alpacas, mohair: woven

(G-1297)
CANTERBURY MACHINERY RND LLC
22 N Society Rd (06331-1216)
PHONE..................860 546-5000
Chris Johnson, *Owner*
EMP: 1
SALES (est): 165.5K **Privately Held**
SIC: 3531 Construction machinery

(G-1298)
DAVCO SYSTEMS
383 Brooklyn Rd (06331-1139)
PHONE..................860 546-9681
David Norell, *Owner*
EMP: 1
SALES (est): 48.4K **Privately Held**
SIC: 7692 Welding repair

(G-1299)
J D & ASSOCIATES
115 John Brook Rd (06331-1624)
PHONE..................860 546-2112
James F Ennis III, *Managing Prtnr*
Dorothy Ennis, *Managing Prtnr*
EMP: 3 **EST:** 1987
SALES (est): 200.1K **Privately Held**
SIC: 3542 Press brakes

(G-1300)
MAURICES COUNTRY MEAT MKT LLC
155 Gooseneck Hill Rd (06331-1800)
PHONE..................860 546-9588
Harold Levesque,
Paul Levesque,
Linda Mazur,
EMP: 3
SQ FT: 100,000
SALES (est): 209.3K **Privately Held**
SIC: 2011 2013 Meat packing plants; sausages & other prepared meats

(G-1301)
ROYS FAMILY POOLS & BILLIARDS
7 Plainfield Rd (06331-1931)
PHONE..................860 546-0608
Mary Roy, *Owner*
Joseph Roy, *Co-Owner*
EMP: 1
SALES (est): 11.6K **Privately Held**
SIC: 3949 Billiard & pool equipment & supplies, general

(G-1302)
THOMAS LORD CABINET MAKER
68 N Society Rd (06331-1218)
PHONE..................860 546-9283
Thomas Lord, *Owner*
EMP: 1
SALES (est): 44.6K **Privately Held**
SIC: 2511 Wood household furniture

Canton
Hartford County

(G-1303)
ALEXIS AEROSPACE INDS LLC
Also Called: A A I
200 Smith Way (06019-2489)
P.O. Box 173, Terryville (06786-0173)
PHONE..................860 516-4602
Frederick A Sundberg,
EMP: 5
SQ FT: 3,000
SALES: 250K **Privately Held**
SIC: 3728 Aircraft parts & equipment

(G-1304)
ARC AND HAMMER
514 Cherry Brook Rd (06019-4518)
P.O. Box 62, Canton Center (06020-0062)
PHONE..................860 605-0344
Valued Customer, *Owner*
EMP: 2
SALES (est): 206.3K **Privately Held**
SIC: 3446 Architectural metalwork

(G-1305)
ARTIC OIL
321 Albany Tpke (06019-2528)
PHONE..................860 693-6925
EMP: 2 **EST:** 2012
SALES (est): 90.9K **Privately Held**
SIC: 1389 Oil & gas field services

(G-1306)
BAHRES WELDING
248 Albany Tpke (06019-2521)
P.O. Box 91 (06019-0091)
PHONE..................860 693-4950
Howard Bahre, *Owner*
EMP: 1
SALES (est): 113.5K **Privately Held**
SIC: 7692 Welding repair

(G-1307)
BREWERY LEGITIMUS LLC
24 Shingel Miil Dr Canton (06019)
PHONE..................860 810-8894
Christopher Sayer, *Mng Member*
Christina Sayer,
EMP: 2 **EST:** 2015
SALES: 68K **Privately Held**
SIC: 2082 Beer (alcoholic beverage)

(G-1308)
CABINET RESOURCES CT INC
180 Cherry Brook Rd (06019-4510)
PHONE..................860 352-2030
William G Trevethan, *President*
Jonathan L Fein, *Admin Sec*
EMP: 3
SALES (est): 810K **Privately Held**
SIC: 2434 Wood kitchen cabinets

(G-1309)
CAS-KEL MANUFACTURING CO INC
292 Albany Tpke (06019-2521)
P.O. Box 467 (06019-0467)
PHONE..................860 693-8704
Richard Caserta, *President*
Mary Caserta, *Admin Sec*
EMP: 5 **EST:** 1971
SQ FT: 6,800
SALES (est): 784.7K **Privately Held**
SIC: 7389 3544 Hand tool designers; special dies & tools; jigs & fixtures

(G-1310)
CLUB RESOURCE INC
10 Andrew Dr (06019-5000)
PHONE..................317 225-6940
Scott Smith, *President*
EMP: 2
SALES (est): 205.5K **Privately Held**
SIC: 7997 7374 7372 Membership sports & recreation clubs; computer graphics service; application computer software

(G-1311)
COLLINSVILLE SCREEN/EMBROIDERY
35 Secret Lake Rd (06019-2627)
PHONE..................860 693-2601
Linda Cournoyer, *Owner*
EMP: 2
SALES (est): 77.4K **Privately Held**
SIC: 2759 Screen printing

(G-1312)
DELTA ELEVATOR SERVICE CORP (DH)
Also Called: Otis Elevator Company
1 Farm Springs Rd (06019)
PHONE..................860 676-6152
Randy Wilclx, *President*
Chris Gouyd, *Manager*
EMP: 20
SALES (est): 6MM
SALES (corp-wide): 66.5B **Publicly Held**
SIC: 3625 Control equipment, electric

(G-1313)
DON POMASKI (PA)
Also Called: Pomaski Tool & Mfg Co
2 Highfields Dr (06019-2439)
PHONE..................860 693-4469
Don Pomaski, *Owner*
EMP: 1
SALES (est): 227.2K **Privately Held**
SIC: 3599 Machine shop, jobbing & repair

(G-1314)
F M ASSOCIATES
17 Blueberry Ln (06019-4502)
PHONE..................860 693-2263
Mark Amoroso, *Owner*
EMP: 2

GEOGRAPHIC SECTION

SALES: 200K **Privately Held**
SIC: 3369 Nonferrous foundries

(G-1315)
FINISHING TOUCH WOODCRAFT
3 Noja Trl (06019-2154)
PHONE..................860 916-2642
Robert J Donovan Jr, *Principal*
EMP: 2
SALES (est): 143.7K **Privately Held**
SIC: 2511 Wood household furniture

(G-1316)
JOSEPH GARRITY
Also Called: Canton Sign Shop
5 Old Albany Tpke (06019-2620)
P.O. Box 8 (06019-0008)
PHONE..................860 693-2134
Joseph Garrity, *Owner*
EMP: 1
SALES: 131.2K **Privately Held**
SIC: 3993 Signs, not made in custom sign painting shops

(G-1317)
LIFE WARMER INC
336 E Hill Rd (06019-2119)
PHONE..................860 204-1711
John Pettini, *President*
EMP: 1
SALES (est): 174.3K **Privately Held**
SIC: 3841 Surgical & medical instruments

(G-1318)
MICRO TRAINING ASSOCIATES INC
320 Albany Tpke (06019-2540)
P.O. Box 328 (06019-0328)
PHONE..................860 693-7740
Marilyn W Jones, *President*
EMP: 10
SQ FT: 2,000
SALES (est): 979.9K **Privately Held**
WEB: www.microtrain.com
SIC: 7372 Educational computer software

(G-1319)
MJ TOOL MFG
359 E Hill Rd (06019-2150)
PHONE..................860 352-2688
Brian Jaeggi, *Owner*
EMP: 2
SALES: 200K **Privately Held**
SIC: 3599 Machine shop, jobbing & repair; machine & other job shop work

(G-1320)
NORTH CANTON CUSTOM WDWKG
760 Cherry Brook Rd (06019-5015)
PHONE..................508 451-5826
Thomas Affsa, *Principal*
EMP: 1
SALES (est): 54.1K **Privately Held**
SIC: 2431 Millwork

(G-1321)
NORTHERN FABRICATION
382 Cherry Brook Rd (06019-4513)
PHONE..................860 693-0635
Richard Leavitt, *Owner*
EMP: 1 EST: 1999
SALES (est): 128K **Privately Held**
WEB: www.northernfabrication.com
SIC: 3441 Fabricated structural metal

(G-1322)
OBI LASER PRODUCTS
45 Bristol Dr (06019-2237)
PHONE..................860 305-0038
Robert Obrien, *Owner*
EMP: 1
SALES: 80K **Privately Held**
SIC: 3549 Metalworking machinery

(G-1323)
OWH LLC
Also Called: Whitehawk Construction Svcs
50 Albany Tpke (06019-2516)
PHONE..................860 693-9464
EMP: 22
SQ FT: 3,500
SALES (est): 1.4MM **Privately Held**
SIC: 1751 1795 2431 1742 Carpentry work; demolition, buildings & other structures; millwork; plastering, drywall & insulation

(G-1324)
PATTAGANSETT PUBLISHING INC
176 Morgan Rd (06019-2034)
P.O. Box 602 (06019-0602)
PHONE..................860 693-6156
Carol G York, *Principal*
EMP: 1
SALES (est): 52.8K **Privately Held**
SIC: 2741 Miscellaneous publishing

(G-1325)
PRECISION WOODCRAFT INC
Also Called: Precision Woodcraft ME
16 Cheryl Dr (06019-2232)
PHONE..................860 693-3641
David Byrne, *President*
Lauwrina Byrne, *Admin Sec*
EMP: 6
SQ FT: 5,000
SALES (est): 560K **Privately Held**
SIC: 2431 Interior & ornamental woodwork & trim

(G-1326)
ST PIERRE BOX AND LUMBER CO
66 Lovely St (06019-2630)
PHONE..................860 413-9813
John St Pierre, *President*
John Flattery, *Vice Pres*
Douglas Kress, *Vice Pres*
EMP: 5 EST: 1953
SQ FT: 13,000
SALES (est): 625.8K **Privately Held**
SIC: 2441 2448 5211 2449 Boxes, wood; pallets, wood; lumber products; rectangular boxes & crates, wood

(G-1327)
VETERINARY MEDICAL ASSOCIATES
Also Called: Roaring Brook Veterenary Hosp
60 Lovely St (06019-2630)
P.O. Box 330 (06019-0330)
PHONE..................860 693-0214
Peter Berk, *President*
Tim Burns, *Partner*
Dan Benner, *Manager*
EMP: 4
SALES (est): 830.3K **Privately Held**
SIC: 2835 0742 Veterinary diagnostic substances; animal hospital services, pets & other animal specialties

(G-1328)
VISUAL POLYMER TECH LLC
34 Westwood Dr (06019-4500)
PHONE..................603 488-5263
Gregory Caldwell, *Principal*
EMP: 2
SALES (est): 77.4K **Privately Held**
SIC: 3087 Custom compound purchased resins

Centerbrook
Middlesex County

(G-1329)
APCO PRODUCTS
6 Essex Industrial Park (06409)
P.O. Box 236, Essex (06426-0236)
PHONE..................860 767-2108
Morton Reich, *President*
EMP: 25
SQ FT: 30,000
SALES (est): 4.9MM **Privately Held**
SIC: 3496 Miscellaneous fabricated wire products

(G-1330)
KIRKHILL AIRCRAFT PARTS CO
Also Called: Kapco Valtec
1 Industrial Park Rd (06409-1020)
PHONE..................860 581-5701
Debra Melson, *Branch Mgr*
EMP: 50
SALES (corp-wide): 141MM **Privately Held**
SIC: 5088 3728 Aircraft & parts; aircraft parts & equipment
PA: Kirkhill Aircraft Parts Co.
3120 Enterprise St
Brea CA 92821
323 216-9136

(G-1331)
ONE LOOK SIGN COMPANY
17 Industrial Park Rd # 7 (06409-1062)
PHONE..................860 581-8574
EMP: 2 EST: 2018
SALES (est): 98.6K **Privately Held**
SIC: 3993 Electric signs

(G-1332)
QUALITY CARE DRG/CNTRBROOK LLC
33 Main St (06409-1083)
P.O. Box 540, Higganum (06441-0540)
PHONE..................860 767-0206
Richard Allen Olson, *Mng Member*
Mark G McKenna,
EMP: 7
SALES (est): 985.3K **Privately Held**
SIC: 2834 Druggists' preparations (pharmaceuticals)

(G-1333)
RED ROCKET SITE 2
47 Industrial Park Rd (06409-1020)
PHONE..................860 581-8019
EMP: 3
SALES (est): 296.2K **Privately Held**
SIC: 3577 Printers & plotters

(G-1334)
TOWER LABORATORIES LTD (PA)
Also Called: Tower Brands
8 Industrial Park Rd (06409-1019)
P.O. Box 306 (06409-0306)
PHONE..................860 767-2127
Norman Needleman, *President*
E Cook Rand, *Admin Sec*
◆ EMP: 95
SQ FT: 38,000
SALES (est): 30.4MM **Privately Held**
SIC: 2834 Effervescent salts; laxatives; tablets, pharmaceutical

Central Village
Windham County

(G-1335)
ARNIO WELDING LLC
12 Water St (06332-3255)
P.O. Box 443 (06332-0443)
PHONE..................860 564-7696
Brian Arnio, *Mng Member*
EMP: 10
SQ FT: 20,994
SALES: 500K **Privately Held**
SIC: 1799 3312 Welding on site; rails, steel or iron

(G-1336)
BEAR HANDS BREWING COMPANY
13 Palmer Ct (06332-3227)
PHONE..................860 576-5374
Matthew Trant, *Principal*
EMP: 3
SALES (est): 74.5K **Privately Held**
SIC: 2082 Malt beverages

(G-1337)
GUY RAVENELLE
Also Called: Ravco Wood Products
71 Black Hill Rd (06332)
P.O. Box 532 (06332-0532)
PHONE..................860 564-3200
Guy Ravenelle, *Owner*
EMP: 6
SALES: 150K **Privately Held**
SIC: 2448 Wood pallets & skids

Chaplin
Windham County

(G-1338)
DANIEL K ROGERS
Also Called: Rogers Fiber Optics
25 Nutmeg Ln (06235-2232)
PHONE..................860 455-0530
Daniel K Rogers, *Owner*
EMP: 1
SALES (est): 101.2K **Privately Held**
SIC: 3661 Fiber optics communications equipment

(G-1339)
DYLANS DUMPSTERS LLC
84 Scotland Rd (06235-4615)
PHONE..................860 455-9924
Jacques Desautels,
EMP: 1
SALES: 50K **Privately Held**
SIC: 3443 Dumpsters, garbage

(G-1340)
HAMMER TRANSPORT LLC
9 Mansure Rd (06235-2508)
PHONE..................860 338-0667
Richard W Laferriere Jr,
EMP: 2 EST: 2011
SALES: 80K **Privately Held**
SIC: 3743 Freight cars & equipment

(G-1341)
SIGNATURE PET MEMORIALS
187 Federal Rd (06235-2113)
PHONE..................860 455-0118
Peter Kegler, *Owner*
EMP: 2
SALES (est): 46.1K **Privately Held**
SIC: 3281 3272 Monument or burial stone, cut & shaped; stone, cast concrete

(G-1342)
SPRAGUE LOGGING LLC
138 Bujak Rd (06235-2109)
PHONE..................860 455-9768
EMP: 2
SALES (est): 89.8K **Privately Held**
SIC: 2411 Logging

(G-1343)
TRANSPORTABLE LLC
851 Phoenixville Rd (06235-2217)
PHONE..................860 455-9208
Jerome Calchera, *President*
EMP: 1 EST: 2015
SALES (est): 62.3K **Privately Held**
SIC: 2511 Lawn furniture: wood

Cheshire
New Haven County

(G-1344)
A B & F SHEET METAL
Also Called: AB&f Sheet Metal Products
327 Sandbank Rd (06410-1506)
PHONE..................203 272-9340
Milford Armstrong, *Owner*
EMP: 7
SQ FT: 4,500
SALES (est): 915.6K **Privately Held**
SIC: 3444 Sheet metalwork

(G-1345)
A MATTER OF STYLE LLC
Also Called: A Matter Style Kitchens Baths
680 S Main St Ste 201 (06410-3190)
PHONE..................203 272-1337
John Ricci, *Owner*
Robbin H Ricci, *Mng Member*
EMP: 2
SALES (est): 212.3K
SALES (corp-wide): 1.3MM **Privately Held**
WEB: www.ricciconstructiongroup.com
SIC: 2434 5031 Wood kitchen cabinets; kitchen cabinets

Cheshire - New Haven County (G-1346)

PA: Ricci Construction Group Inc
680 S Main St Ste 301
Cheshire CT 06410
203 272-4323

(G-1346)
ACCURATUS OPTICS TECH LLC
130 Rockview Dr (06410-3636)
PHONE..........................213 344-9397
Guan Cao, *Principal*
EMP: 1
SALES (est): 53.3K **Privately Held**
SIC: 3229 Optical glass

(G-1347)
ACE INDUSTRIAL LLC
108 Victoria Dr (06410-7126)
PHONE..........................203 272-7675
Howard Gladstone, *Principal*
EMP: 2
SALES (est): 119.1K **Privately Held**
SIC: 3599 Industrial machinery

(G-1348)
AI-TEK INSTRUMENTS LLC
152 Knotter Dr (06410-1136)
P.O. Box 748 (06410-0748)
PHONE..........................203 271-6927
Peter Sandore,
David Elliott,
Leonard Mecca,
▼ **EMP:** 38
SQ FT: 18,000
SALES (est): 8.2MM **Privately Held**
WEB: www.aitekinstruments.com
SIC: 3829 Measuring & controlling devices

(G-1349)
AIS GLOBAL HOLDINGS LLC
Also Called: Atlantic Inertial Systems
250 Knotter Dr (06410-1137)
PHONE..........................203 250-3500
Christopher Holmes, *Mng Member*
David Oldham,
EMP: 800
SALES (est): 30.7MM
SALES (corp-wide): 66.5B **Publicly Held**
SIC: 3812 Gyroscopes; navigational systems & instruments
HQ: Goodrich Corporation
2730 W Tyvola Rd 4
Charlotte NC 28217
704 423-7000

(G-1350)
ALL TECH SIGN & CRANE SERVICE
128 Blacks Rd Ste A (06410-1679)
PHONE..........................203 272-2207
Ken Jackie, *Principal*
EMP: 1
SALES (est): 112.1K **Privately Held**
SIC: 3993 Signs & advertising specialties

(G-1351)
AMERICAN RUBBER STAMP COMPANY
Also Called: American Mailing Depot
35 Judson Ct (06410-2837)
PHONE..........................203 755-1135
Vincent Lentini, *President*
Elizabeth Lentini, *Treasurer*
Bryan Lentini, *Admin Sec*
EMP: 3 **EST:** 1944
SQ FT: 2,200
SALES: 195K **Privately Held**
SIC: 3953 3479 7331 Date stamps, hand; rubber or metal; seal presses, notary & hand; stationery embossers, personal; stencils, painting & marking; name plates: engraved, etched, etc.; mailing service

(G-1352)
ANACONDA UNIVERSAL ASSOC LLC
76 Belridge Rd (06410-2101)
P.O. Box 219, Milldale (06467-0219)
PHONE..........................203 699-9344
Carole Moran, *President*
Charles Moran, *Vice Pres*
▲ **EMP:** 2
SALES (est): 181.9K **Privately Held**
SIC: 3599 Flexible metal hose, tubing & bellows

(G-1353)
APEX MACHINE TOOL COMPANY INC
500 Knotter Dr (06410)
PHONE..........................860 677-2884
Dominick A Pagano, *President*
Glenn L Purple, *Admin Sec*
EMP: 99 **EST:** 1944
SQ FT: 44,008
SALES (est): 16MM **Privately Held**
WEB: www.apexmachinetool.com
SIC: 3544 3545 3546 3089 Jigs & fixtures; precision tools, machinists'; power-driven handtools; injection molded finished plastic products; designing: ship, boat, machine & product
HQ: Edac Technologies Llc
5 Mckee Pl
Cheshire CT 06410
203 806-2090

(G-1354)
APEX MACHINE TOOL COMPANY INC
Also Called: Edac Technologies
5 Mckee Pl (06410-1119)
PHONE..........................203 806-2090
Dominick A Pagano, *President*
EMP: 2
SALES (est): 682.7K **Privately Held**
SIC: 7692 3812 Welding repair; aircraft/aerospace flight instruments & guidance systems

(G-1355)
AQUACOMFORT SOLUTIONS LLC
15 Burton Dr (06410-1205)
PHONE..........................407 831-1941
EMP: 9
SALES (corp-wide): 3MM **Privately Held**
SIC: 3648 Swimming pool lighting fixtures
PA: Aquacomfort Solutions Llc
950 Sunshine Ln
Altamonte Springs FL 32714
407 831-1941

(G-1356)
ATLANTIC INERTIAL SYSTEMS INC (DH)
Also Called: Goodrich Sensors and Integrate
250 Knotter Dr (06410-1137)
PHONE..........................203 250-3500
Justin Robert Keppy, *President*
Zenon Melnyk, *General Mgr*
Richard S Caswell, *Vice Pres*
Kevin Swain, *Manager*
Susan Crowley, *Info Tech Mgr*
▲ **EMP:** 490 **EST:** 2000
SQ FT: 70,000
SALES (est): 110.8MM
SALES (corp-wide): 66.5B **Publicly Held**
WEB: www.condorpacific.com
SIC: 3812 Gyroscopes; navigational systems & instruments
HQ: Goodrich Corporation
2730 W Tyvola Rd 4
Charlotte NC 28217
704 423-7000

(G-1357)
ATLANTIC INERTIAL SYSTEMS INC
Also Called: Cheshire Division
250 Knotter Dr (06410-1137)
PHONE..........................203 250-3500
Robert Nead, *Branch Mgr*
EMP: 600
SALES (corp-wide): 66.5B **Publicly Held**
SIC: 3812 3845 Gyroscopes; electromedical equipment
HQ: Atlantic Inertial Systems Inc.
250 Knotter Dr
Cheshire CT 06410
203 250-3500

(G-1358)
AUTOMATED MAILING SERVICES LLC
1687 Reinhard Rd (06410-1222)
PHONE..........................203 439-2763
Mark Zanelli,
EMP: 8
SQ FT: 10,000

SALES (est): 931K **Privately Held**
SIC: 7331 2752 Mailing service; promotional printing, lithographic

(G-1359)
AZTEC WOODWORKING
384 Moss Farms Rd (06410-1961)
PHONE..........................203 272-3814
Edward Lucas, *Principal*
EMP: 2
SALES (est): 199.4K **Privately Held**
SIC: 2431 Millwork

(G-1360)
BARKER ADVG SPECIALTY CO INC (PA)
Also Called: Barker Specialty Co
27 Realty Dr (06410-1656)
PHONE..........................203 272-2222
Gerald Barker, *CEO*
Herbert Barker, *President*
Gloria Barker, *Vice Pres*
Steven E Barker, *Vice Pres*
Darlene J Bowen, *Treasurer*
▲ **EMP:** 64
SQ FT: 50,000
SALES (est): 23.3MM **Privately Held**
SIC: 7389 7336 2741 Subscription fulfillment services: magazine, newspaper, etc.; silk screen design; catalogs: publishing & printing

(G-1361)
BOVANO INDUSTRIES INCORPORATED
Also Called: Bovano of Cheshire
830 S Main St Ofc A (06410-3474)
PHONE..........................203 272-3208
James A Flood, *President*
David Flood, *Vice Pres*
Kevin Flood, *Opers Mgr*
EMP: 15
SQ FT: 17,000
SALES (est): 1.8MM **Privately Held**
SIC: 3231 5947 3229 Enameled glass; gift shop; pressed & blown glass

(G-1362)
BRASS CITY SIGNS LLC
1662 Musso View Ave (06410-1043)
PHONE..........................860 628-2046
Steve Pedbereznak, *Principal*
EMP: 1
SALES (est): 81.2K **Privately Held**
SIC: 3993 Signs & advertising specialties

(G-1363)
BRIAN SAFA
80 Royalwood Ct (06410-2242)
PHONE..........................203 271-3499
Brian Safa, *Principal*
EMP: 3 **EST:** 2010
SALES (est): 247.8K **Privately Held**
SIC: 2869 Industrial organic chemicals

(G-1364)
BRIMATCO CORPORATION
1486 Highland Ave Ste 10 (06410-1200)
P.O. Box 88 (06410-0088)
PHONE..........................203 272-0044
James Dacunto, *President*
Mark Dacunto, *Vice Pres*
EMP: 3
SQ FT: 4,000
SALES (est): 513.1K **Privately Held**
WEB: www.brimatco.com
SIC: 3423 Wrenches, hand tools

(G-1365)
BUNTING & LYON INC
615 Broad Swamp Rd (06410-2918)
PHONE..........................203 272-4623
Peter Bunting, *President*
EMP: 6
SALES (est): 480K **Privately Held**
WEB: www.buntingandlyon.com
SIC: 2731 8748 7361 Books: publishing only; educational consultant; teachers' agency

(G-1366)
CARTEN CONTROLS INC
604 W Johnson Ave (06410-4500)
PHONE..........................203 699-2100
Hidet S Kataoka, *CEO*

Hiroshi Ogawa, *CEO*
Kenji Yamamoto, *President*
Monty L Botkin, *Vice Pres*
▲ **EMP:** 15
SQ FT: 65,000
SALES (est): 3.8MM **Privately Held**
SIC: 3592 3494 Valves; valves & pipe fittings

(G-1367)
CARTEN-FUJIKIN INCORPORATED
604 W Johnson Ave (06410-4500)
PHONE..........................203 699-2134
Seamus Sweeney, *General Mgr*
▲ **EMP:** 8
SALES (est): 770K **Privately Held**
SIC: 3674 Microcircuits, integrated (semiconductor)

(G-1368)
CASTLE SYSTEMS INC
125 Commerce Ct Ste 4 (06410-1243)
PHONE..........................203 250-3140
Paul Casavina, *President*
Rony Itzhaki, *Vice Pres*
Stan Johnson, *Vice Pres*
Sarah Pisani, *Opers Mgr*
James Rock, *Admin Sec*
EMP: 4
SQ FT: 2,700
SALES: 800K **Privately Held**
SIC: 7373 3571 Computer integrated systems design; electronic computers

(G-1369)
CHESHIRE MANUFACTURING CO INC
312 E Johnson Ave Ste 1 (06410-1297)
PHONE..........................203 272-3586
Joseph Whitright Jr, *President*
Dora Whitright, *Corp Secy*
EMP: 7 **EST:** 1957
SQ FT: 6,500
SALES (est): 687.5K **Privately Held**
SIC: 3714 3469 7692 Motor vehicle parts & accessories; metal stampings; welding repair

(G-1370)
CINTAS CORPORATION
10 Diana Ct (06410-1206)
PHONE..........................203 272-2036
Thomas Vega, *President*
EMP: 10
SALES (corp-wide): 6.8B **Publicly Held**
SIC: 2326 Work uniforms
PA: Cintas Corporation
6800 Cintas Blvd
Cincinnati OH 45262
513 459-1200

(G-1371)
COLD BREW COFFEE COMPANY LLC
27 E Ridge Ct (06410-1236)
PHONE..........................860 250-4410
Gary Riccini, *Principal*
EMP: 3
SALES (est): 75.4K **Privately Held**
SIC: 2082 Malt beverages

(G-1372)
CONNECTICUT PRESS
36 Wildlife Ct (06410-2958)
PHONE..........................203 257-6020
Malia J Peter, *Principal*
EMP: 1
SALES (est): 37.5K **Privately Held**
SIC: 2741 Miscellaneous publishing

(G-1373)
CONNSTEM INC
505 Highland Ave (06410-2253)
PHONE..........................203 558-4671
Noel Richard, *President*
EMP: 2
SALES: 80K **Privately Held**
SIC: 2869 Industrial organic chemicals

(G-1374)
CONSOLDTED INDS ACQSITION CORP
677 Mixville Rd (06410-3836)
PHONE..........................203 272-5371

GEOGRAPHIC SECTION

Cheshire - New Haven County (G-1400)

John David Wilbur, *President*
Drew Papio, *Vice Pres*
Benjamin Mark Palazzo, *Admin Sec*
▲ **EMP:** 100
SQ FT: 87,000
SALES: 30MM **Privately Held**
SIC: 3462 3369 Aircraft forgings, ferrous; aerospace castings, nonferrous: except aluminum

(G-1375)
CORD-MATE INC
705 Wallingford Rd (06410-2914)
PHONE..................................203 272-8415
Robert Wilowski Jr, *President*
Sammi Pryer, *Cust Mgr*
EMP: 2
SALES (est): 210K **Privately Held**
SIC: 3669 Emergency alarms

(G-1376)
CREATIVE DIMENSIONS INC
345 Mccausland Ct (06410-1278)
PHONE..................................203 250-6500
Joel P Roy, *President*
Bill Violette, *Vice Pres*
Adam Glasz, *Project Mgr*
Don Roche, *Prdtn Mgr*
John Stifel, *Foreman/Supr*
▲ **EMP:** 37
SQ FT: 48,000
SALES (est): 7.6MM **Privately Held**
WEB: www.creative-dimensions.com
SIC: 3993 2541 Electric signs; wood partitions & fixtures

(G-1377)
CUMMINS - ALLISON CORP
Also Called: Cummins Allison
125 Commerce Ct Ste 6 (06410-1243)
PHONE..................................203 794-9200
Tom Mack, *Manager*
EMP: 8
SALES (corp-wide): 390.1MM **Privately Held**
WEB: www.gsb.com
SIC: 5046 5087 3519 Commercial equipment; shredders, industrial & commercial; internal combustion engines
PA: Cummins-Allison Corp
  852 Feehanville Dr
  Mount Prospect IL 60056
  800 786-5528

(G-1378)
CUPRAK ENTERPRISES LLC
Also Called: Connecticut Java User Group
150 N Timber Ln (06410-3941)
PHONE..................................203 376-8789
Ryan Cuprak, *Principal*
EMP: 2
SALES (est): 160K **Privately Held**
SIC: 7371 7372 Computer software development; business oriented computer software; utility computer software

(G-1379)
DALTON ENTERPRISES INC (PA)
131 Willow St (06410-2732)
PHONE..................................203 272-3221
John A Dalton, *President*
Barbara Alberino, *Vice Pres*
Ernest Hallbach, *Vice Pres*
Matt Urban, *Traffic Mgr*
Darlene Stabile, *Manager*
▼ **EMP:** 100
SALES (est): 42.8MM **Privately Held**
WEB: www.latexite.com
SIC: 3272 Paving materials, prefabricated concrete

(G-1380)
DANJON MANUFACTURING CORP
1075 S Main St (06410-3414)
P.O. Box 212 (06410-0212)
PHONE..................................203 272-7258
Eugene Johnson, *President*
Lorraine Johnson, *Vice Pres*
EMP: 11
SQ FT: 4,000
SALES (est): 853.9K **Privately Held**
WEB: www.danjon.com
SIC: 3545 Machine tool attachments & accessories; drills (machine tool accessories)

(G-1381)
DB PRESS LLC
14 Bradford Dr (06410-3520)
PHONE..................................203 699-9510
Elaine Dacey, *Principal*
EMP: 2
SALES (est): 100.7K **Privately Held**
SIC: 2741 Miscellaneous publishing

(G-1382)
DP FOODS L L C
152 Knotter Dr (06410-1136)
P.O. Box 748 (06410-0748)
PHONE..................................203 271-6212
Peter Sandore, *Principal*
EMP: 2
SALES (est): 60K **Privately Held**
SIC: 2099 Food preparations

(G-1383)
EDAC TECHNOLOGIES LLC (HQ)
5 Mckee Pl (06410-1119)
PHONE..................................203 806-2090
Terry Bruni, *President*
Kenneth Cook, *Opers Staff*
Mike Debolt, *CFO*
John Smith, *Program Mgr*
Kevin Mrozinski, *Manager*
EMP: 223
SQ FT: 19,200
SALES (est): 95.1MM **Privately Held**
WEB: www.edactechnologies.com
SIC: 3769 3541 3724 Guided missile & space vehicle parts & auxiliary equipment; machine tools, metal cutting type; aircraft engines & engine parts

(G-1384)
ELECTRO-TECH INC
Also Called: E T I
408 Sandbank Rd (06410-1544)
PHONE..................................203 271-1976
Jerry F Camarota, *President*
Charles W Terry, *Vice Pres*
Kurt Puleo, *QC Mgr*
Carol Terry, *Treasurer*
April Terry, *Human Res Mgr*
EMP: 50
SQ FT: 10,000
SALES (est): 8.9MM **Privately Held**
WEB: www.eti-electrotech.com
SIC: 3451 3679 3678 Screw machine products; electronic circuits; electronic connectors

(G-1385)
ENGINEERED POLYMERS INDS INC
726 S Main St (06410-3472)
PHONE..................................203 272-2233
Len Azzaro, *Principal*
▲ **EMP:** 5 EST: 2015
SALES (est): 219.3K
SALES (corp-wide): 65.5MM **Privately Held**
SIC: 2821 Plastics materials & resins
PA: Osterman & Company, Inc.
  726 S Main St
  Cheshire CT 06410
  203 272-2233

(G-1386)
ERICKSON METALS CORPORATION (PA)
25 Knotter Dr (06410-1133)
PHONE..................................203 272-2918
Richard H Erickson, *President*
Michael Varney, *General Mgr*
James A Basta Jr, *Vice Pres*
Jeffrey L Schaschl, *CFO*
Sherlynn Erickson, *Director*
▲ **EMP:** 36 EST: 1972
SQ FT: 40,000
SALES (est): 39.3MM **Privately Held**
SIC: 5051 3355 3444 Aluminum bars, rods, ingots, sheets, pipes, plates, etc.; sheets, metal; strip, metal; aluminum rolling & drawing; sheet metalwork

(G-1387)
EVERLAST PRODUCTS LLC
150 Knotter Dr (06410-1136)
P.O. Box 748 (06410-0748)
PHONE..................................203 250-7111
Anthony Tremaglio, *Partner*
Leonard Mecca, *Partner*
EMP: 3
SQ FT: 5,000
SALES (est): 181.4K **Privately Held**
SIC: 3625 3643 Relays & industrial controls; current-carrying wiring devices

(G-1388)
FIBER MOUNTAIN INC
Also Called: F M
700 W Johnson Ave Ste 100 (06410-1197)
PHONE..................................203 806-4040
M H Raza, *CEO*
Michael Lagana, *Vice Pres*
Aristito Lorenzo, *Vice Pres*
Bill Miller, *Vice Pres*
David Stone, *Vice Pres*
EMP: 40
SALES (est): 2.4MM **Privately Held**
SIC: 3674 Semiconductor circuit networks

(G-1389)
FIMOR NORTH AMERICA INC (HQ)
Also Called: Harkness Industries, Inc.
50 Grandview Ct (06410-1261)
P.O. Box 764 (06410-0764)
PHONE..................................203 272-3219
Manuel Zuckerman, *President*
Robert P Williams, *Vice Pres*
Nancy P Williams, *Executive*
David Corbin, *Admin Sec*
EMP: 24
SQ FT: 30,000
SALES (est): 3.9MM
SALES (corp-wide): 8.4MM **Privately Held**
WEB: www.harknessindustries.com
SIC: 3089 2821 Injection molding of plastics; plastics materials & resins
PA: Fimor
  210 Rue Du Polygone
  Le Mans 72100
  243 400-095

(G-1390)
FIMOR NORTH AMERICA INC
30 Grandview Ct (06410-1261)
PHONE..................................941 921-5138
EMP: 2
SALES (corp-wide): 8.4MM **Privately Held**
SIC: 3089 2821 Injection molding of plastics; plastics materials & resins
HQ: Fimor North America, Inc.
  50 Grandview Ct
  Cheshire CT 06410
  203 272-3219

(G-1391)
G SCHOEPFER INC
460 Cook Hill Rd (06410-3707)
PHONE..................................203 250-7794
James Schoepfer, *President*
David Pagado, *Principal*
Dave Pagno, *Admin Sec*
Mary Schoepfer, *Admin Sec*
EMP: 12
SQ FT: 4,000
SALES (est): 1.2MM **Privately Held**
SIC: 3229 Pressed & blown glass

(G-1392)
GEOSONICS INC
416 Highland Ave Ste D (06410-2527)
PHONE..................................203 271-2504
Mohamad Sharif, *Vice Pres*
Susan Shepley, *Manager*
Mike Donahue, *Manager*
Chuck Jaworski, *Manager*
Todd Pester, *Manager*
EMP: 10
SALES (corp-wide): 5.5MM **Privately Held**
SIC: 1382 Seismograph surveys
PA: Geosonics, Inc.
  359 Northgate Dr Ste 200
  Warrendale PA 15086
  724 934-2900

(G-1393)
GORILLA SIGNS & WRAPS
182 Sandbank Rd (06410-1521)
PHONE..................................203 439-8838
EMP: 1
SALES (est): 46K **Privately Held**
SIC: 3993 Signs & advertising specialties

(G-1394)
GRAPHICS PRESS LLC
1161 Sperry Rd (06410-3747)
P.O. Box 430 (06410-0430)
PHONE..................................203 272-9187
Gregory Mayer, *Controller*
Edward Tufte, *Mng Member*
EMP: 7
SALES (est): 1MM **Privately Held**
SIC: 2731 Books: publishing only

(G-1395)
GROS-ITE INDUSTRIES INC
5 Mckee Pl (06410-1119)
PHONE..................................800 242-1790
Dominic Pagano, *President*
Glenn L Purple, *Admin Sec*
EMP: 1
SALES (est): 196.1K **Privately Held**
SIC: 3991 Hair pencils (artists' brushes)

(G-1396)
HI-TECH FABRICATING INC
30 Knotter Dr (06410-1122)
PHONE..................................203 284-0894
John Berges, *President*
Kevin Sook, *Vice Pres*
EMP: 24
SQ FT: 18,000
SALES (est): 3.4MM **Privately Held**
WEB: www.hitechfab.com
SIC: 3444 3469 3443 2396 Sheet metalwork; metal stampings; fabricated plate work (boiler shop); automotive & apparel trimmings

(G-1397)
HYLIE PRODUCTS INCORPORATED
30 Grandview Ct (06410-1261)
PHONE..................................203 439-8786
Deanne C Gauya, *CEO*
Ruji Gomes, *President*
John C Gauya, *Vice Pres*
Joe Ferreira, *Engineer*
EMP: 16 EST: 1951
SQ FT: 10,000
SALES (est): 3.1MM **Privately Held**
WEB: www.hylie.com
SIC: 3469 Perforated metal, stamped; stamping metal for the trade

(G-1398)
IMAGINE SOFTWARE LLC
60 Frances Ct (06410-2600)
PHONE..................................203 271-0252
Andrew A Magioncalda, *Principal*
EMP: 2
SALES (est): 76.8K **Privately Held**
SIC: 7372 Prepackaged software

(G-1399)
INDIA WEEKLY CO
328 Industrial Ave (06410-1501)
PHONE..................................203 699-8419
Shivesh Kumar, *Principal*
EMP: 5
SALES (est): 192.1K **Privately Held**
SIC: 2711 Newspapers, publishing & printing

(G-1400)
INDUSTRIAL HEATER CORP
30 Knotter Dr (06410-1122)
PHONE..................................203 250-0500
Thomas A McGwire Jr, *President*
Ted McGwire, *President*
James Czarzasty, *VP Sales*
Robert Evans, *Sales Staff*
Dona Nappi, *Office Mgr*
▼ **EMP:** 80 EST: 1921
SALES (est): 19.3MM **Privately Held**
WEB: www.industrialheater.com
SIC: 3567 Heating units & devices, industrial: electric

(PA)=Parent Co (HQ)=Headquarters (DH)=Div Headquarters
✪ = New Business established in last 2 years

Cheshire - New Haven County (G-1401)

(G-1401)
JOHN CANNING & CO LTD
150 Commerce Ct (06410-1253)
PHONE..................203 272-9868
John Canning, *President*
Sarah Canning, *Vice Pres*
David Riccio, *Vice Pres*
Marcie Clifford, *Project Mgr*
Marcie Rengifo, *Project Mgr*
EMP: 25
SQ FT: 7,500
SALES (est): 3.1MM **Privately Held**
WEB: www.canning-studios.com
SIC: 1721 3299 1741 8999 Commercial painting; ornamental & architectural plaster work; masonry & other stonework; art restoration

(G-1402)
KANINE KNITS
877 Marion Rd (06410-3837)
PHONE..................203 272-8548
Margaret Gaffney, *Owner*
EMP: 1
SALES (est): 47.3K **Privately Held**
SIC: 5949 7389 2741 Patterns: sewing, knitting & needlework; ; patterns, paper: publishing & printing

(G-1403)
KOVIL MANUFACTURING LLC
Also Called: Masterman & Kovil
1486 Highland Ave Ste 2 (06410-1200)
PHONE..................203 699-9425
Vilmos Kovacs, *President*
Frank Kovacs, *Vice Pres*
Katalin Kovacs, *Treasurer*
EMP: 5
SQ FT: 1,000
SALES: 250K **Privately Held**
WEB: www.kovil.com
SIC: 3599 Machine shop, jobbing & repair

(G-1404)
LAMINATED GLASS SOLUTIONS LLC
270 Oregon Rd (06410-1866)
PHONE..................203 250-1025
Peter Greenwood, *Manager*
EMP: 1
SALES (est): 39.7K **Privately Held**
SIC: 3211 Laminated glass

(G-1405)
LANE CONSTRUCTION CORPORATION (DH)
90 Fieldstone Ct (06410-1212)
PHONE..................203 235-3351
James Hughes, *President*
Thomas R Larson, *President*
Tom Larson, *President*
Dominic Barilla, *Superintendent*
Tom Glaser, *Superintendent*
EMP: 250
SQ FT: 90,000
SALES: 847.8MM
SALES (corp-wide): 18K **Privately Held**
WEB: www.laneconstruct.com
SIC: 1622 1611 1629 3272 Highway construction, elevated; bridge construction; airport runway construction; subway construction; dam construction; power plant construction; building materials, except block or brick: concrete; paving materials
HQ: Lane Industries Incorporated
90 Fieldstone Ct
Cheshire CT 06410
203 235-3351

(G-1406)
LANE INDUSTRIES INCORPORATED (DH)
90 Fieldstone Ct (06410-1212)
PHONE..................203 235-3351
Robert Alger, *Ch of Bd*
Mark Schiller, *President*
Mike Cote, *Exec VP*
Kirk Junco, *Exec VP*
David Benton, *Vice Pres*
EMP: 7
SQ FT: 18,000
SALES: 856.8MM
SALES (corp-wide): 18K **Privately Held**
SIC: 1629 5032 1622 3272 Subway construction; dam construction; power plant construction; paving materials; highway construction, elevated; bridge construction; building materials, except block or brick: concrete; airport runway construction
HQ: Salini-Impregilo Us Holdings, Inc.
90 Fieldstone Ct
Cheshire CT 06410
203 439-2900

(G-1407)
LOGOD SOFTWEAR INC
500 Cornwall Ave Ste 3 (06410-2641)
PHONE..................203 272-4883
EMP: 40
SQ FT: 12,000
SALES: 5MM **Privately Held**
SIC: 5961 2759 3993 2396 Ret Mail-Order House Commercial Printing Mfg Signs/Ad Specialties Mfg Auto/Apparel Trim Pleating/Stitching Svcs

(G-1408)
LOU-JAN TOOL & DIE INC
161 E Johnson Ave (06410-1209)
P.O. Box 148 (06410-0148)
PHONE..................203 272-3536
Reita Jannetty, *President*
Louis Jannetty Jr, *Vice Pres*
EMP: 15
SQ FT: 12,000
SALES (est): 800K **Privately Held**
WEB: www.lou-jan.com
SIC: 3544 3542 Special dies & tools; machine tools, metal forming type

(G-1409)
LUCERION LLC
10 Teds Ct (06410-3584)
PHONE..................203 699-8136
Madan Anant,
EMP: 1
SALES (est): 68.8K **Privately Held**
SIC: 2835 In vitro diagnostics

(G-1410)
M K M ENTERPRISES INC
758 Jarvis St (06410-1522)
PHONE..................203 250-7937
Michael Krasnovsky, *President*
Doreen Krasnovsky, *Admin Sec*
EMP: 4
SQ FT: 2,800
SALES (est): 683.4K **Privately Held**
SIC: 7539 3599 Machine shop, automotive; machine shop, jobbing & repair

(G-1411)
MARION MANUFACTURING COMPANY
1675 Reinhard Rd (06410-1222)
PHONE..................203 272-5376
Mary L Cramer, *President*
Douglas Johnson, *Vice Pres*
David Dubois, *Plant Mgr*
Nancy Zawerton, *Sales Staff*
Toni Cardinale, *Manager*
▼ EMP: 24
SQ FT: 28,000
SALES (est): 7MM **Privately Held**
WEB: www.marionmfg.com
SIC: 3469 Stamping metal for the trade

(G-1412)
MC GUIRE MANUFACTURING CO INC
60 Grandview Ct (06410-1261)
P.O. Box 746 (06410-0746)
PHONE..................203 699-1801
Ken Byrant, *Ch of Bd*
T Michael McRoberts, *President*
Leah Davenport, *VP Mktg*
▲ EMP: 87
SQ FT: 13,500
SALES (est): 15.6MM
SALES (corp-wide): 9.7MM **Privately Held**
WEB: www.mcguiremfg.com
SIC: 3432 Plumbing fixture fittings & trim
PA: Bead Industries, Inc.
11 Cascade Blvd
Milford CT 06460
203 301-0270

(G-1413)
MCMELLON ASSOCIATES LLC
510 Cornwall Ave Ste 4 (06410-2602)
PHONE..................203 272-5859
Art McMellon,
EMP: 3
SQ FT: 13,000
SALES (est): 396.8K **Privately Held**
SIC: 5712 3429 7699 Cabinet work, custom; furniture builders' & other household hardware; antique repair & restoration, except furniture, automobiles

(G-1414)
MEADOW WOODWORKING LLC
22 Cedar Ln (06410-2208)
PHONE..................203 213-3332
Thomas Slack, *Owner*
EMP: 2 EST: 2012
SALES (est): 222.9K **Privately Held**
SIC: 2431 Millwork

(G-1415)
MEMORY LANE QUILTERS LLC
330 Towpath Ln (06410-3356)
PHONE..................203 272-1010
EMP: 2
SALES (est): 74.5K **Privately Held**
SIC: 2395 Pleating/Stitching Services

(G-1416)
MICROTECH INC
1425 Highland Ave (06410-1233)
PHONE..................203 272-3234
James A McGregor III, *President*
Flavio Montiero, *Vice Pres*
Nick Petinero, *Safety Mgr*
Jennifer Danard, *Human Res Mgr*
Silva Marco, *Manager*
EMP: 83
SQ FT: 36,000
SALES (est): 13.3MM **Privately Held**
SIC: 3678 3679 3677 3663 Electronic connectors; waveguides & fittings; microwave components; electronic coils, transformers & other inductors; radio & TV communications equipment

(G-1417)
NANTUCKET BLONDE LLC
131 Paulney Rd (06410-2711)
PHONE..................203 415-1522
Hanna Calcagni, *Mng Member*
EMP: 2
SALES (est): 67.3K **Privately Held**
SIC: 2033 Barbecue sauce: packaged in cans, jars, etc.

(G-1418)
NEMTEC INC
B 8 Trackside (06410)
P.O. Box 1103 (06410-5103)
PHONE..................203 272-0788
Joe Silva, *President*
EMP: 3
SQ FT: 2,000
SALES (est): 484.7K **Privately Held**
WEB: www.nemtec.com
SIC: 3541 7699 Machine tool replacement & repair parts, metal cutting types; industrial equipment services

(G-1419)
NESOLA SCARVES LLC
309 Old Lane Rd (06410-3727)
PHONE..................203 288-5058
Lois Goglia,
EMP: 2
SALES (est): 130K **Privately Held**
SIC: 2392 5136 7929 7389 Scarves: table, dresser, etc., from purchased materials; men's & boys' hats, scarves & gloves; country music groups or artists;

(G-1420)
NEW DESIGNZ INC
Also Called: Ndz Performance
278 Sanbank Rd (06410)
PHONE..................860 384-1809
Antonin Blazek, *Vice Pres*
EMP: 18
SALES: 1.2MM **Privately Held**
SIC: 3484 Guns (firearms) or gun parts, 30 mm. & below

(G-1421)
NEW ENGLAND PRESS PARTS LLC
124 Belridge Rd (06410-2101)
PHONE..................203 623-7533
Mike Votto, *Owner*
EMP: 1
SALES (est): 71.1K **Privately Held**
SIC: 2741 Miscellaneous publishing

(G-1422)
NEWMARK INC
182 Sandbank Rd (06410-1521)
PHONE..................203 272-1158
EMP: 2
SALES (est): 86.6K **Privately Held**
SIC: 3841 Mfg Surgical/Medical Instruments

(G-1423)
NUTMEG UTILITY PRODUCTS INC (PA)
1755 Highland Ave (06410-1289)
P.O. Box 723 (06410-0723)
PHONE..................203 250-8802
Jeannine Lavallee, *CEO*
Theresa Lavallee, *President*
EMP: 35
SALES (est): 3.9MM **Privately Held**
WEB: www.nutmegutility.com
SIC: 3825 3669 3661 Instruments to measure electricity; emergency alarms; burglar alarm apparatus, electric; fire alarm apparatus, electric; telephone & telegraph apparatus

(G-1424)
OGS TECHNOLOGIES INC
Also Called: Waterbury Button Company
1855 Peck Ln (06410-4411)
PHONE..................203 271-9055
Michael L Salamone, *President*
Salvatore Geraci, *Exec VP*
Chris Keenan, *Manager*
▲ EMP: 45
SQ FT: 40,000
SALES: 7.3MM **Privately Held**
WEB: www.waterburybutton.com
SIC: 3993 3965 Signs & advertising specialties; buttons & parts

(G-1425)
OSLO SWITCH INC
Also Called: Oslo Switches
30 Diana Ct (06410-1206)
PHONE..................203 272-2794
Joseph Martinecz, *President*
Elizabeth Martinez, *Vice Pres*
Thomas Martinez, *Vice Pres*
Donald Lunt, *Treasurer*
Flo Sengstacken, *Sales Staff*
EMP: 31
SQ FT: 30,000
SALES (est): 4.8MM **Privately Held**
WEB: www.osloswitch.com
SIC: 3613 3825 3643 3429 Switches, electric power except snap, push button, etc.; indicating instruments, electric; current-carrying wiring devices; manufactured hardware (general)

(G-1426)
OSTERMAN & COMPANY INC (PA)
Also Called: Osterman Trading Div
726 S Main St (06410-3472)
PHONE..................203 272-2233
James O Dwyer, *Ch of Bd*
John Dwyer, *President*
Jennifer Vestergaard, *CFO*
Lucia De Medal, *Regl Sales Mgr*
Andrew Gorman, *Sales Staff*
◆ EMP: 55
SQ FT: 10,000
SALES (est): 65.5MM **Privately Held**
WEB: www.reeves.com
SIC: 2821 Plastics materials & resins

GEOGRAPHIC SECTION
Cheshire - New Haven County (G-1458)

(G-1427)
OSTERMAN & COMPANY INC
Also Called: Engineered Polymer Industries
726 S Main St (06410-3472)
PHONE..................................203 272-2233
Paul Dikan, *Manager*
EMP: 40
SALES (corp-wide): 65.5MM **Privately Held**
WEB: www.reeves.com
SIC: 2821 Polycarbonate resins
PA: Osterman & Company, Inc.
  726 S Main St
  Cheshire CT 06410
  203 272-2233

(G-1428)
PELEGANOS STAINED GLASS STUDIO
83 Saint Joseph St (06410-4408)
PHONE..................................203 272-8067
Stella Pelegano, *Owner*
EMP: 1
SALES (est): 48.5K **Privately Held**
SIC: 3231 1799 Stained glass: made from purchased glass; sandblasting of building exteriors

(G-1429)
PLASTICRETE
210 Realty Dr (06410-1676)
PHONE..................................203 250-6700
EMP: 2
SALES (est): 126.9K **Privately Held**
SIC: 3272 Mfg Concrete Products

(G-1430)
POLYMOLD CORP
Also Called: Poly Mold Inc Building 1
951 S Meriden Rd (06410-1843)
PHONE..................................203 272-2622
Michael Chernik, *President*
Olga Chernik, *Treasurer*
EMP: 12
SQ FT: 13,000
SALES (est): 2.5MM **Privately Held**
SIC: 3089 Injection molding of plastics

(G-1431)
POWER FUELS LLC
143 Main St (06410-2408)
PHONE..................................203 699-0099
Michael Monnerat, *Principal*
EMP: 3
SALES (est): 190.4K **Privately Held**
SIC: 2869 Fuels

(G-1432)
PRIVY PINE PRODUCTS
180 Brentwood Dr (06410-3440)
PHONE..................................203 272-6169
Michael Burwick, *Owner*
EMP: 2
SALES (est): 165.9K **Privately Held**
WEB: www.privypine.com
SIC: 2434 Vanities, bathroom: wood

(G-1433)
QUINNIPIAC VALLEY ALPACAS
30 Homestead Pl (06410-2633)
PHONE..................................203 271-0773
EMP: 2
SALES (est): 73.4K **Privately Held**
SIC: 2231 Alpacas, mohair: woven

(G-1434)
R & R PALLET CORP
120 Schoolhouse Rd (06410-1293)
PHONE..................................203 272-2784
Joseph Rizzo Jr, *President*
EMP: 12
SQ FT: 16,000
SALES (est): 1.9MM **Privately Held**
WEB: www.rr-products.com
SIC: 2448 Pallets, wood

(G-1435)
RAND MACHINE & FABRICATION CO
1486 Highland Ave Ste 2 (06410-1200)
PHONE..................................203 272-1352
Donald J Ranaudo, *President*
Tom Saath, *Owner*
Connie Ranaudo, *Vice Pres*
EMP: 10
SQ FT: 4,000
SALES (est): 1.9MM **Privately Held**
WEB: www.randmachineco.com
SIC: 3599 Machine shop, jobbing & repair

(G-1436)
RAND NEWCO LLC
151 Moss Farms Rd (06410-1987)
PHONE..................................203 699-9125
Cliff Perdion, *Principal*
EMP: 2
SALES (est): 188.4K **Privately Held**
SIC: 3131 Rands

(G-1437)
RAND SHEAVES & PULLEYS LLC
1486 Highland Ave (06410-1200)
PHONE..................................203 272-1352
Donald J Ranaudo, *Mng Member*
EMP: 9
SALES (est): 780K **Privately Held**
SIC: 3599 Machine shop, jobbing & repair

(G-1438)
RAYMOND J BYKOWSKI
Also Called: Dried Materials Unlimited
1685 Reinhard Rd (06410-1222)
PHONE..................................203 271-2385
Raymond J Bykowski, *Owner*
EMP: 3
SQ FT: 13,000
SALES: 690K **Privately Held**
SIC: 3999 5193 Flowers, artificial & preserved; florists' supplies

(G-1439)
RIFF COMPANY INC
1484 Highland Ave Ste 7 (06410-1268)
PHONE..................................203 272-4899
Daniel McCormick, *President*
Donna Mc Cormick, *Admin Sec*
◆ EMP: 5
SQ FT: 5,500
SALES (est): 712.1K **Privately Held**
WEB: www.riff-co.com
SIC: 3599 Machine shop, jobbing & repair

(G-1440)
ROBERT AUDETTE (PA)
Also Called: MGA Emblem Co
1732 S Main St (06410-3539)
PHONE..................................203 872-3119
Robert Audette, *Owner*
▲ EMP: 5
SALES (est): 282.4K **Privately Held**
SIC: 3999 3479 2759 2395 Badges, metal: policemen, firemen, etc.; military insignia; engraving jewelry silverware, or metal; commercial printing; pleating & stitching; engraving service

(G-1441)
SALIN-MPREGILO US HOLDINGS INC (DH)
90 Fieldstone Ct (06410-1212)
PHONE..................................203 439-2900
Micheal M Cote, *Vice Pres*
Lauralee Heckman, *Comms Mgr*
Komran Aghazadeh, *Sr Project Mgr*
Gianfranco Catrini, *Admin Sec*
Heather Hess, *Clerk*
EMP: 0
SALES (est): 2.2MM
SALES (corp-wide): 18K **Privately Held**
SIC: 6719 1629 1622 1611 Investment holding companies, except banks; subway construction; dam construction; power plant construction; highway construction, elevated; bridge construction; airport runway construction; building materials, except block or brick: concrete; paving materials
HQ: Salini Impregilo Spa
  Via Dei Missaglia 97
  Milano MI 20142
  024 442-2111

(G-1442)
SAVIN ROCK SOFTWARE LLC
129 Crescent Cir (06410-3652)
PHONE..................................203 272-5039
Karen Ann Pesapane, *Principal*
EMP: 2
SALES (est): 105.9K **Privately Held**
SIC: 7372 Prepackaged software

(G-1443)
SCRIPTURE RESEARCH & PUBG CO
Also Called: SCRIPTURAL RESEARCH PUBG CO
344 E Johnson Ave Ste 4 (06410-1208)
P.O. Box 725, New Britain (06050-0725)
PHONE..................................203 272-1780
Joseph Poulin, *Administration*
EMP: 2
SALES (est): 71.3K **Privately Held**
SIC: 2741 2752 2731 2721 Miscellaneous publishing; commercial printing, lithographic; book publishing; periodicals

(G-1444)
SHARP RACING ENTERPRISES
Also Called: R & R Fabricaton
128 Blacks Rd (06410-1679)
PHONE..................................203 699-1191
Melinda Rotondo, *Partner*
EMP: 2
SALES (est): 242.3K **Privately Held**
SIC: 3711 Automobile assembly, including specialty automobiles

(G-1445)
SHILOH SOFTWARE INC
718 Cortland Cir (06410-2938)
PHONE..................................203 272-8456
Barbara Walkup, *Principal*
EMP: 5
SALES (est): 517.7K **Privately Held**
SIC: 7372 7379 Prepackaged software; data processing consultant

(G-1446)
SIGNS BY MB
202 Mixville Rd (06410-1906)
PHONE..................................203 710-9948
Michael Barszczewski, *Principal*
EMP: 1
SALES (est): 46K **Privately Held**
SIC: 3993 Signs & advertising specialties

(G-1447)
SKY MFG COMPANY
268 Sandbank Rd (06410-1537)
PHONE..................................203 439-7016
Atousa Jalayer, *President*
EMP: 5 EST: 1966
SQ FT: 4,000
SALES (est): 772.6K **Privately Held**
SIC: 3728 Aircraft parts & equipment

(G-1448)
SNAPWIRE INNOVATIONS LLC
125 Commerce Ct Ste 11 (06410-1243)
PHONE..................................203 806-4773
EMP: 5
SALES: 22MM **Privately Held**
SIC: 3559 Mfg Misc Industry Machinery

(G-1449)
SOFTWARE BY DESIGN LLC
15 Kelly Ct (06410-4227)
PHONE..................................203 271-1061
Peter Sparago, *Owner*
EMP: 1
SALES (est): 74.8K **Privately Held**
WEB: www.sparago.com
SIC: 7372 Business oriented computer software

(G-1450)
SON OF A STITCH LLC
78 George Ave (06410-2501)
PHONE..................................203 272-2548
Karen Demers, *Principal*
EMP: 1
SALES (est): 61.4K **Privately Held**
SIC: 2395 Embroidery & art needlework

(G-1451)
SPECIAL VHCL DEVELOPMENTS INC
337 Blacks Rd (06410-1695)
PHONE..................................203 272-7928
William Mitchell, *President*
EMP: 4
SQ FT: 6,000
SALES: 600K **Privately Held**
SIC: 3711 Motor vehicles & car bodies

(G-1452)
SPECTRUM VIRTUAL LLC
55 Realty Dr Ste 315 (06410-4600)
PHONE..................................203 303-7540
Jonathan Reeves, *Principal*
Charles Baudinet, *Principal*
Randy Geary, *VP Bus Dvlpt*
Mario Dinatale, *CIO*
Darren Reeves, *CTO*
EMP: 6
SALES (est): 381.9K **Privately Held**
SIC: 3577 7374 Data conversion equipment, media-to-media: computer; data processing & preparation

(G-1453)
SPLINTERS WOODWORKING LLC
40 Copper Valley Ct (06410-1761)
PHONE..................................203 272-1314
EMP: 1
SALES (est): 126.8K **Privately Held**
SIC: 2431 Mfg Millwork

(G-1454)
SUPERIOR PRODUCTS DISTRS INC
Also Called: Rex Precast Systems
210 Realty Dr (06410-1676)
PHONE..................................203 250-6700
Fax: 203 250-6707
EMP: 12
SALES (corp-wide): 85.6MM **Privately Held**
SIC: 5074 3272 Whol Plumbing Equipment/Supplies Mfg Concrete Products
PA: Superior Products Distributors, Inc.
  1403 Meriden Waterbury Rd
  Milldale CT 06467
  860 621-3621

(G-1455)
THOMSON ARPAX MECHATRONICS LLC
7 Mckee Pl (06410-1119)
PHONE..................................516 883-8000
Gerald Ford, *Executive*
EMP: 2
SALES (est): 88.3K **Privately Held**
SIC: 3621 Motors & generators

(G-1456)
TJL INDUSTRIES LLC
19 Willow St (06410-2731)
P.O. Box 837 (06410-0837)
PHONE..................................203 250-2187
Tod J Lorenzen, *Principal*
EMP: 3 EST: 2010
SALES (est): 266.7K **Privately Held**
SIC: 3999 Manufacturing industries

(G-1457)
WANHO MANUFACTURING LLC
154 Knotter Dr (06410-1136)
PHONE..................................203 759-3744
Johanna Mendoza, *Production*
Kristine Boisits, *Human Res Mgr*
David R Elliott, *Mng Member*
Eric Lester,
John Williamson,
▲ EMP: 25
SQ FT: 50,000
SALES (est): 26.5MM
SALES (corp-wide): 50MM **Privately Held**
WEB: www.wanho.com
SIC: 5065 3443 Electronic parts; cable trays, metal plate
PA: Us Capital Resources, Llc
  137 Mattatuck Heights Rd
  Waterbury CT 06705
  203 759-3744

(G-1458)
WEIDNER PUBLICATION GROUP
490 Cornwall Ave (06410-2650)
PHONE..................................203 272-2463
Sharon Weidner, *Principal*
EMP: 1 EST: 2011
SALES (est): 63.2K **Privately Held**
SIC: 2741 Miscellaneous publishing

(G-1459)
WOOD CREATIONS & GRAPHICS LLC
41 Willow St (06410-2731)
PHONE..............................203 271-3568
Richard Watson, *Owner*
EMP: 1
SALES: 10K **Privately Held**
SIC: 2499 Decorative wood & woodwork

(G-1460)
WTF MFG CO LLC
523 W Main St (06410-2422)
PHONE..............................860 387-7472
Laurie Mallette, *Owner*
EMP: 2
SALES (est): 73.4K **Privately Held**
SIC: 3999 Manufacturing industries

(G-1461)
ZOSSIMA PRESS
366 S Brooksvale Rd (06410-3515)
PHONE..............................203 687-9385
Robert Trexler, *Principal*
EMP: 2
SALES: 86K **Privately Held**
SIC: 2741 Miscellaneous publishing

Chester
Middlesex County

(G-1462)
AEROCISION LLC
12a Inspiration Ln (06412-1366)
PHONE..............................860 526-9700
Andrew Gibson, *CEO*
Dan Collins, *General Mgr*
Timothy Wallace, *Materials Mgr*
Sean Morrissey, *Production*
Michele Larson, *Purch Mgr*
EMP: 70
SQ FT: 40,000
SALES: 20MM
SALES (corp-wide): 177.9K **Privately Held**
WEB: www.pyeandhogan.com
SIC: 3728 Aircraft parts & equipment
HQ: Bromford Industries Limited
    1 Bromford Gate
    Birmingham W MIDLANDS B24 8
    121 683-6200

(G-1463)
ASCENTECH LLC
127 Goose Hill Rd (06412-1260)
PHONE..............................860 526-8903
Randy Allinson,
EMP: 2 **EST:** 1999
SALES (est): 301.3K **Privately Held**
SIC: 3699 Electrical equipment & supplies

(G-1464)
BLACKWOLD INC
Also Called: Greenwald Industries
212 Middlesex Ave (06412-1273)
PHONE..............................860 526-0800
Leonard F Leganza, *CEO*
Leonard Samela, *President*
Paul Cloutier, *Plant Mgr*
Alan Stanwix, *Plant Mgr*
Jeff Carlson, *Materials Mgr*
▲ **EMP:** 80
SQ FT: 140,000
SALES (est): 16.5MM
SALES (corp-wide): 234.2MM **Publicly Held**
WEB: www.greenwaldindustries.com
SIC: 3581 3578 Mechanisms for coin-operated machines; calculating & accounting equipment
PA: The Eastern Company
    112 Bridge St
    Naugatuck CT 06770
    203 729-2255

(G-1465)
BO-DYN BOBSLED PROJECT INC
51 Winthrop Rd (06412-1036)
P.O. Box 4337, Waterbury (06704-0337)
PHONE..............................860 526-9504
Phil Kurtze, *Exec Dir*
EMP: 1
SALES: 84.4K **Privately Held**
SIC: 3949 Bobsleds

(G-1466)
CHAKANA SKY ALPACAS
36a Turkey Hill Rd (06412-1132)
PHONE..............................860 204-1646
William Bernhart, *Principal*
EMP: 2 **EST:** 2016
SALES (est): 100K **Privately Held**
SIC: 2231 Alpacas, mohair: woven

(G-1467)
CHAPCO INC (PA)
10 Denlar Dr (06412-1208)
P.O. Box 378 (06412-0378)
PHONE..............................860 526-9535
Robert Weinstein, *Principal*
▲ **EMP:** 70
SQ FT: 22,000
SALES (est): 18MM **Privately Held**
WEB: www.chapcoinc.com
SIC: 3444 3599 Sheet metal specialties, not stamped; machine shop, jobbing & repair

(G-1468)
CONQUIP SYSTEMS LLC
78 Turkey Hill Rd (06412-1132)
PHONE..............................860 526-7883
Katherine Beaulieu, *Owner*
EMP: 4
SALES (est): 443.1K **Privately Held**
SIC: 3423 Ironworkers' hand tools

(G-1469)
DENLAR FIRE PROTECTION LLC
20 Denlar Dr (06412-1208)
PHONE..............................860 526-9846
Bryan Weinstein, *President*
EMP: 2
SALES: 200K **Privately Held**
SIC: 3444 Hoods, range: sheet metal

(G-1470)
EAST COAST PRECISION MFG
221 Middlesex Ave (06412-1221)
PHONE..............................860 322-4624
Mark Rohlfs, *Principal*
EMP: 3 **EST:** 2013
SALES (est): 206.5K **Privately Held**
SIC: 3999 Manufacturing industries

(G-1471)
EASTERN COMPANY
Greenwald Industries, Inc Del
212 Middlesex Ave (06412-1273)
PHONE..............................860 526-0800
Leonard Samela, *President*
EMP: 90
SALES (corp-wide): 234.2MM **Publicly Held**
WEB: www.easterncompany.com
SIC: 3581 Mechanisms for coin-operated machines
PA: The Eastern Company
    112 Bridge St
    Naugatuck CT 06770
    203 729-2255

(G-1472)
EMS INTERNATIONAL INC
Also Called: Essex Motorsports Int'l
244 Middlesex Ave (06412-1248)
PHONE..............................860 526-2060
Fax: 860 526-1527
▲ **EMP:** 3
SQ FT: 6,000
SALES (est): 520K **Privately Held**
SIC: 5521 5571 5531 7532 Ret Used Automobiles Ret Motorcycles Ret Auto/Home Supplies Auto Body Repair/Paint

(G-1473)
GARY D KRYSZAT
Also Called: Pattaconk Millwork
194 Middlesex Ave (06412-1219)
P.O. Box 216 (06412-0216)
PHONE..............................860 526-3145
Gary D Kryszat, *Owner*
EMP: 2
SQ FT: 7,000
SALES (est): 243.6K **Privately Held**
SIC: 5211 2431 5031 Millwork & lumber; millwork; millwork

(G-1474)
GRAYCON DEFENSE INDUSTRIES LLC
71 Goose Hill Rd (06412-1228)
PHONE..............................860 339-2505
Derek Walden, *Owner*
EMP: 1
SALES (est): 60.5K **Privately Held**
SIC: 3449 7389 Miscellaneous metalwork;

(G-1475)
NEW ENGLAND FINE WOODWORKING
37 Castle View Dr (06412-1230)
PHONE..............................860 526-5799
David Strobel, *Manager*
EMP: 3
SALES (est): 231.7K **Privately Held**
SIC: 2431 Millwork

(G-1476)
NUPAL LLC
49 Parkers Point Rd (06412-1206)
PHONE..............................860 227-7964
Benjamin Otfinoski,
EMP: 2
SALES (est): 106.5K **Privately Held**
SIC: 7372 Prepackaged software

(G-1477)
PAGODA TIMBER FRAMES
8 Butter Jones Rd (06412-1031)
PHONE..............................860 526-3077
William Cadley, *Owner*
EMP: 1
SALES (est): 81.9K **Privately Held**
SIC: 2431 Moldings, wood: unfinished & prefinished; panel work, wood; brackets, wood; floor baseboards, wood

(G-1478)
PAMELA GORDONDUPONT MS CCCA
38 Gilbert Hill Rd (06412-1306)
PHONE..............................860 526-8686
Pamela Gordondupont, *Principal*
EMP: 2
SALES (est): 137.3K **Privately Held**
SIC: 2879 Agricultural chemicals

(G-1479)
PDQ INC
65 Airport Industrial Rd (06412-1061)
PHONE..............................860 322-4412
Charles Gill, *Branch Mgr*
EMP: 1
SALES (corp-wide): 4.7MM **Privately Held**
SIC: 3599 Machine shop, jobbing and repair
PA: Pdq, Inc.
    24 Evans Rd
    Rocky Hill CT 06067
    860 529-9051

(G-1480)
PURIFICATION TECHNOLOGIES LLC (DH)
67 Winthrop Rd (06412-1036)
PHONE..............................860 526-7801
Gerald A Richard, *President*
James Lusis, *CFO*
James F Lusis, *Treasurer*
◆ **EMP:** 14
SQ FT: 32,000
SALES: 8.4MM
SALES (corp-wide): 1.4B **Publicly Held**
WEB: www.purificationtech.com
SIC: 2911 2899 Solvents; chemical preparations
HQ: Vwr Corporation
    Radnor Corp Ctr 1 200
    Radnor PA 19087
    610 386-1700

(G-1481)
RICHARD BATCHELDER
61 Winthrop Rd (06412-1036)
PHONE..............................860 526-1614
Richard Batchelder, *Principal*
EMP: 2
SALES (est): 92.8K **Privately Held**
SIC: 3999 Airplane models, except toy

(G-1482)
ROTO-FRANK OF AMERICA INC
Also Called: Roto Hardware Systems
14 Inspiration Ln (06412-1366)
PHONE..............................860 526-4996
Greg Koch, *President*
Chrissostomos Dimou, *President*
Patrick Donnelly, *Business Mgr*
Debra Wallis, *Corp Secy*
Charly Pachiodo, *QC Mgr*
◆ **EMP:** 100 **EST:** 1979
SQ FT: 64,000
SALES (est): 19.7MM
SALES (corp-wide): 750.8MM **Privately Held**
WEB: www.roto-frank.com
SIC: 2591 Window blinds
PA: Roto Frank Holding Ag
    Wilhelm-Frank-Platz 1
    Leinfelden-Echterdingen 70771
    711 759-80

(G-1483)
SAMSARA FITNESS LLC
Also Called: Trueform Runner
10 Denlar Dr (06412-1208)
PHONE..............................860 895-8533
Jocelyn Coutant, *Sales Mgr*
Jeff Vernon,
EMP: 11
SALES (est): 420.5K **Privately Held**
SIC: 3949 Treadmills

(G-1484)
SHARP CANVAS
22 Denlar Dr Apt D (06412-1290)
P.O. Box 576 (06412-0576)
PHONE..............................860 526-2302
Matthew Sharp, *Owner*
EMP: 1 **EST:** 1997
SALES (est): 81.2K **Privately Held**
SIC: 2394 Canvas & related products

(G-1485)
WHELEN ENGINEERING COMPANY INC (PA)
51 Winthrop Rd (06412-1036)
PHONE..............................860 526-9504
John Olson, *President*
Alex Stepinski, *Division Mgr*
Christine Angersola, *Editor*
George Whelen IV, *Exec VP*
Charles Andrus, *Vice Pres*
◆ **EMP:** 291 **EST:** 1952
SQ FT: 90,000
SALES (est): 186.3MM **Privately Held**
SIC: 3647 3646 3671 3651 Automotive lighting fixtures; aircraft lighting fixtures; commercial indusl & institutional electric lighting fixtures; electron tubes; household audio & video equipment; lighting equipment; electric lamps

(G-1486)
WHELEN ENGINEERING COMPANY INC
Also Called: Austin Electronics
Rr 145 (06412)
PHONE..............................860 526-9504
John Olson, *Branch Mgr*
EMP: 18
SALES (corp-wide): 186.3MM **Privately Held**
SIC: 3646 Commercial indusl & institutional electric lighting fixtures
PA: Whelen Engineering Company, Inc.
    51 Winthrop Rd
    Chester CT 06412
    860 526-9504

(G-1487)
WINDSORS & WOODWORK LLC
12 Brooks Ln (06412-1137)
PHONE..............................860 526-4092
Joseph Carl, *Manager*
EMP: 2
SALES (est): 174.2K **Privately Held**
SIC: 2431 Millwork

Clinton
Middlesex County

(G-1488)
A & L WELDING SERVICE
14 Old Mill Rd Trlr 45 (06413-1768)
PHONE..........................860 664-1700
Alan Browne, *Owner*
EMP: 3
SQ FT: 4,000
SALES: 100K **Privately Held**
SIC: 7699 7692 Welding equipment repair; automotive welding

(G-1489)
A DANCING THREAD
23 Riverside Dr Apt A13 (06413-2615)
PHONE..........................860 669-9094
Catherine Beckstein, *Principal*
EMP: 1
SALES (est): 67.6K **Privately Held**
SIC: 2395 Embroidery & art needlework

(G-1490)
ACK PRECISION MACHINE CO
6 Old Post Rd (06413-1806)
P.O. Box 221 (06413-0221)
PHONE..........................860 664-0789
Mark Clapp, *Owner*
EMP: 1
SALES: 120K **Privately Held**
SIC: 3599 7692 Machine shop, jobbing & repair; welding repair

(G-1491)
ARRIGONI DISTRIBUTORS LTD LLC
Also Called: Arrigoni Design
41 Commerce St (06413-2054)
PHONE..........................860 669-6637
Ann Arrigoni, *Mng Member*
Ann B Arrigoni,
Chelso Arrigoni,
EMP: 2
SQ FT: 3,000
SALES: 750K **Privately Held**
WEB: www.arrigonidesign.com
SIC: 3732 Yachts, building & repairing

(G-1492)
BAUSCH ADVANCED TECH INC (PA)
115 Nod Rd (06413-1058)
PHONE..........................860 669-7380
Oliver Bausch, *President*
James Smith, *General Mgr*
Bernd Stroeter, *Vice Pres*
Purdum Jessica, *Department Mgr*
Adamiec Christine, *Info Tech Mgr*
▲ **EMP:** 49
SALES (est): 11.6MM **Privately Held**
WEB: www.bascotech.com
SIC: 3559 Sewing machines & hat & zipper making machinery

(G-1493)
CHAMARD VINEYARDS INC
115 Cow Hill Rd (06413-1346)
PHONE..........................860 664-0299
William R Chaney, *President*
Carolyn Chaney, *Corp Secy*
Matthew R Prosser, *Director*
EMP: 2
SALES (est): 76.5K **Privately Held**
SIC: 0172 2084 Grapes; wines

(G-1494)
CLINTON INSTRUMENT COMPANY
295 E Main St (06413-2232)
PHONE..........................860 669-7548
Marianne Clinton Szreders, *President*
Donna Langley, *Vice Pres*
EMP: 23
SQ FT: 15,000
SALES (est): 5.8MM **Privately Held**
WEB: www.clintoninstrument.com
SIC: 3823 3825 3829 Industrial instrmnts msrmnt display/control process variable; instruments to measure electricity; measuring & controlling devices

(G-1495)
COLD STONE CREAMERY (PA)
7 Glenwood Rd Unit F (06413-1712)
PHONE..........................860 669-7025
Christopher Anatra, *Owner*
EMP: 9
SALES (est): 383.3K **Privately Held**
SIC: 5812 5451 2024 Ice cream stands or dairy bars; ice cream (packaged); ice cream & frozen desserts

(G-1496)
CONNECTCUT SHRELINE DEVELOPERS
10 Long Hill Rd (06413-1824)
PHONE..........................860 669-4424
Warren Shoemac, *President*
EMP: 4
SALES: 1.5MM **Privately Held**
SIC: 1389 1522 Construction, repair & dismantling services; residential construction

(G-1497)
CONNELLY 3 PUBG GROUP INC
10 W Main St Fl 2 (06413-2030)
P.O. Box 920 (06413-0920)
PHONE..........................860 664-4988
Rick Connelly, *President*
Sean Connelly, *Vice Pres*
Sandra Nicholas, *Vice Pres*
Darylle Connelly, *Shareholder*
EMP: 5
SALES: 1.4MM **Privately Held**
WEB: www.c3pg.com
SIC: 2741 Miscellaneous publishing

(G-1498)
CONOPCO INC
Unilever Home & Personal Care
1 John St (06413-1753)
PHONE..........................860 669-8601
Donald Wilbur, *Manager*
EMP: 325
SALES (corp-wide): 58.3B **Privately Held**
SIC: 2844 Face creams or lotions
HQ: Conopco, Inc.
700 Sylvan Ave
Englewood Cliffs NJ 07632
201 894-7760

(G-1499)
CUSTOM COVERS
20 Riverside Dr (06413-2625)
P.O. Box 424 (06413-0424)
PHONE..........................860 669-4169
Barbara Whiting, *Owner*
EMP: 9
SQ FT: 600
SALES (est): 502.7K **Privately Held**
SIC: 2394 Liners & covers, fabric: made from purchased materials

(G-1500)
DEARBORN DEUCE LLC
28 Cream Pot Rd (06413-1405)
PHONE..........................860 669-3232
Mike Hochberg, *Principal*
EMP: 1
SALES (est): 94.7K **Privately Held**
SIC: 3714 Motor vehicle parts & accessories

(G-1501)
EASTERN COMPANY
Also Called: Argo Ems
1 Heritage Park Rd (06413-1836)
PHONE..........................860 669-2233
John Hughes III, *Branch Mgr*
EMP: 24
SALES (corp-wide): 234.2MM **Publicly Held**
SIC: 3672 Printed circuit boards
PA: The Eastern Company
112 Bridge St
Naugatuck CT 06770
203 729-2255

(G-1502)
EMI INC
4 Heritage Park Rd (06413-1836)
PHONE..........................860 669-1199
Sean Donkin, *President*
EMP: 8
SALES (est): 920K **Privately Held**
SIC: 3556 Mixers, commercial, food

(G-1503)
FLEA MARKET MUSIC INC
22 Pratt Rd (06413-1923)
PHONE..........................860 664-1669
Jim Beloff, *President*
EMP: 2
SALES: 500K **Privately Held**
SIC: 2731 Book music: publishing only, not printed on site

(G-1504)
FRAMING AND PRINTING SOLU
11 Davis Farm Rd (06413-1374)
PHONE..........................860 664-9679
EMP: 2
SALES (est): 83.9K **Privately Held**
SIC: 2752 Commercial printing, lithographic

(G-1505)
GLORIAN PUBLISHING INC
455 Boston Post Rd Ste 9 (06413)
P.O. Box 110225, Brooklyn NY (11211-0225)
PHONE..........................844 945-6742
Glorianna Peter, *Principal*
Suzanne Kuczun, *Vice Pres*
EMP: 2
SALES: 181.1K **Privately Held**
SIC: 2741 Miscellaneous publishing

(G-1506)
GREENSCAPE OF CLINTON LLC
13 Janes Ln (06413-1220)
PHONE..........................860 669-1880
Diane Byrne, *Principal*
Frank Byrne,
EMP: 7
SALES (est): 927.4K **Privately Held**
SIC: 3524 0782 Lawn & garden equipment; lawn & garden services

(G-1507)
HELANDER PRODUCTS INC
Also Called: Tiny-Clutch
26 Knollwood Dr (06413-1606)
P.O. Box 247 (06413-0247)
PHONE..........................860 669-7953
Gordon Helander, *President*
Helander Andrew, *Vice Pres*
Andrew Helander, *Treasurer*
EMP: 10 **EST:** 1964
SQ FT: 5,000
SALES: 680K **Privately Held**
WEB: www.helanderproducts.com
SIC: 3568 5084 Clutches, except vehicular; industrial machinery & equipment

(G-1508)
INDIKON BOATWORKS
11 Bright Hill Dr (06413-1801)
PHONE..........................860 395-8297
Todd Berman, *Administration*
EMP: 2 **EST:** 2016
SALES (est): 72.7K **Privately Held**
SIC: 3732 Boat building & repairing

(G-1509)
INTEGRATED CHEMICAL & EQP CORP
Also Called: IC&e
22 Jefferson Cir (06413-1518)
PHONE..........................860 664-3951
Michael Gosselin, *President*
EMP: 2
SALES (est): 157.1K **Privately Held**
SIC: 2819 5169 Peroxides, hydrogen peroxide; organic chemicals, synthetic

(G-1510)
KENYON INTERNATIONAL INC
11 Heritage Park Rd (06413-1836)
PHONE..........................860 664-4906
EMP: 2
SALES (est): 88.3K **Privately Held**
SIC: 3631 Household Cooking Equipment, Nsk

(G-1511)
KENYON INTERNATIONAL INC
8 Heritage Park Rd (06413-1836)
P.O. Box 925 (06413-0925)
PHONE..........................860 664-4906
Phillip Williams, *President*
Mike Reischmann, *Vice Pres*
Rhonda Hooper,
◆ **EMP:** 33
SQ FT: 24,000
SALES (est): 8.8MM **Privately Held**
WEB: www.kenyonappliances.com
SIC: 3631 Barbecues, grills & braziers (outdoor cooking)

(G-1512)
LABRADOR PUBLISHING LLC
24 W Main St Ste 330 (06413-2053)
PHONE..........................860 552-2564
Christine Baker, *Principal*
EMP: 1
SALES (est): 37.5K **Privately Held**
SIC: 2741 Miscellaneous publishing

(G-1513)
LIGHTICIANS INC
80 Waterside Ln (06413-2141)
PHONE..........................203 494-2542
Timothy Duff, *President*
EMP: 2
SALES (est): 145.7K **Privately Held**
SIC: 3612 Lighting transformers, fluorescent

(G-1514)
MALLACE INDUSTRIES CORP
Also Called: Iconotech
2 Heritage Park Rd (06413-1836)
PHONE..........................800 521-0194
EMP: 2 **EST:** 2017
SALES (est): 171.7K **Privately Held**
SIC: 2759 Commercial printing

(G-1515)
NAVTEC RIGGING SOLUTIONS INC
37 Stanton Rd (06413-2733)
PHONE..........................203 458-3163
Allen E Goddu, *President*
William Carson, *Vice Pres*
▲ **EMP:** 47
SQ FT: 62,000
SALES (est): 8.6MM **Privately Held**
SIC: 3731 3594 3492 Marine rigging; fluid power pumps & motors; control valves, fluid power: hydraulic & pneumatic

(G-1516)
NINE WEST HOLDINGS INC
Also Called: Kasper
20 Killingworth Tpke # 125 (06413-1377)
PHONE..........................860 669-3799
EMP: 8
SALES (corp-wide): 2.2B **Privately Held**
SIC: 2337 Mfg Women's/Misses' Suits/Coats
HQ: Nine West Holdings, Inc.
180 Rittenhouse Cir
Bristol PA 10018
215 785-4000

(G-1517)
ONSITE SERVICES INC
23 Meadow Rd (06413-2211)
PHONE..........................860 669-3988
Kathleen Miller, *President*
David Miller, *Vice Pres*
Jonathan Miller, *Vice Pres*
EMP: 12
SALES (est): 1.8MM **Privately Held**
WEB: www.onsiteservices.com
SIC: 3669 Pedestrian traffic control equipment

(G-1518)
PREFERRED FOAM PRODUCTS INC
140 Killingworth Tpke (06413-1325)
P.O. Box 942 (06413-0942)
PHONE..........................860 669-3626
Louis Chioccio, *President*
Mark Richards, *Treasurer*
▲ **EMP:** 6
SQ FT: 28,000
SALES (est): 1.2MM **Privately Held**
WEB: www.prefoam.com
SIC: 3086 5162 Plastics foam products; plastics materials & basic shapes

Clinton - Middlesex County (G-1519)

(G-1519)
R E S WOODWORKING LLC
22 Nod Pl (06413-1612)
PHONE..................860 664-9663
Raymond Swan,
Amy Fwan,
Raymond Fwan,
EMP: 1 **EST:** 2000
SQ FT: 4,200
SALES (est): 177.2K **Privately Held**
WEB: www.reswoodworking.com
SIC: 2431 Millwork

(G-1520)
REGIONAL INDUSTRIES LLC
41 Commerce St (06413-2054)
PHONE..................860 227-3627
EMP: 2
SALES (est): 167.7K **Privately Held**
SIC: 3999 Manufacturing industries

(G-1521)
RIVER MILL CO
43 River Rd (06413-1049)
PHONE..................860 669-5915
Michael Simmons, *Owner*
EMP: 15
SQ FT: 4,000
SALES (est): 1.1MM **Privately Held**
SIC: 2599 2431 5031 Cabinets, factory; door frames, wood; window frames, wood; lumber: rough, dressed & finished

(G-1522)
SCHIESS JOHN
100 Cow Hill Rd (06413-1341)
PHONE..................860 664-0336
John-Wn Schiess, *Executive*
EMP: 2
SALES (est): 88.9K **Privately Held**
SIC: 3446 Architectural metalwork

(G-1523)
SEA HOUSE PRESS LLC
155 Shore Rd (06413-2346)
PHONE..................860 552-4141
EMP: 1 **EST:** 2018
SALES (est): 37.5K **Privately Held**
SIC: 2741 Miscellaneous publishing

(G-1524)
SHIRT SHARK
87 W Main St (06413-1622)
PHONE..................860 552-4197
Trishe Doyle, *Owner*
EMP: 2
SALES (est): 108.2K **Privately Held**
SIC: 2759 Screen printing

(G-1525)
SHORELINE STAIR & MILLWORK CO
10 Robin Ln (06413-2214)
PHONE..................860 669-9591
Brian Faucher, *President*
EMP: 2
SALES (est): 227.2K **Privately Held**
SIC: 3446 Stairs, staircases, stair treads: prefabricated metal

(G-1526)
SIGN OF OUR TIMES
232 E Main St (06413-2230)
PHONE..................860 669-4318
John R Pryor, *Owner*
EMP: 2
SALES (est): 144.1K **Privately Held**
SIC: 3993 Signs, not made in custom sign painting shops

(G-1527)
SPARKLERS
307 E Main St (06413-2222)
PHONE..................860 669-5110
Claire Tracy, *Owner*
EMP: 2
SALES (est): 152.1K **Privately Held**
WEB: www.sparklers.com
SIC: 2899 Fireworks

(G-1528)
SPECIALTY SIGN SERVICES LLC
24 W Main St (06413-2053)
PHONE..................860 391-3291
Patricia Desantis, *Manager*
EMP: 1
SALES (est): 98.4K **Privately Held**
SIC: 3993 Signs & advertising specialties

(G-1529)
TECHNIQUE PRINTERS INC
36 Old Post Rd (06413-1812)
PHONE..................860 669-2516
Peter Hubbard, *President*
Thomas Snelgrove, *Vice Pres*
EMP: 7
SQ FT: 2,300
SALES (est): 811K **Privately Held**
SIC: 2752 7331 Commercial printing, offset; mailing service

(G-1530)
TOTAL MACHINE CO
6 Walkley Ml (06413-1070)
PHONE..................203 481-8780
EMP: 2
SQ FT: 1,000
SALES (est): 400K **Privately Held**
SIC: 3599 3545 Mfg Industrial Machinery Mfg Machine Tool Accessories

(G-1531)
TOWER LABORATORIES LTD
7 Heritage Park Rd (06413-1836)
PHONE..................860 669-7078
Robin Fey, *Branch Mgr*
EMP: 40
SALES (corp-wide): 30.4MM **Privately Held**
SIC: 2834 Pharmaceutical preparations
PA: Tower Laboratories, Ltd.
  8 Industrial Park Rd
  Centerbrook CT 06409
  860 767-2127

(G-1532)
TOWN PRIDE
201 Cow Hill Rd (06413-1175)
P.O. Box 8 (06413-0008)
PHONE..................860 664-0448
Christine Elder, *Mng Member*
EMP: 1
SALES (est): 101.3K **Privately Held**
SIC: 2759 2395 Screen printing; embroidery & art needlework

(G-1533)
ULTRA CLEAN EQUIPMENT INC
112 Nod Rd Ste 9 (06413-1009)
PHONE..................860 669-1354
Bill Clorite, *President*
Deborah Coe, *Office Mgr*
Christine Clorite, *Admin Sec*
EMP: 8
SALES (est): 760K **Privately Held**
WEB: www.ultracleanequip.com
SIC: 3699 Cleaning equipment, ultrasonic, except medical & dental

(G-1534)
WILLIAMS OIL COMPANY
1 Walnut Hill Rd (06413-1303)
PHONE..................860 664-9587
Don Fowler, *Owner*
EMP: 2
SALES (est): 98.8K **Privately Held**
SIC: 1389 Oil field services

(G-1535)
WOODWORKERS
7 Oakwood Ln (06413-1355)
PHONE..................860 669-9113
EMP: 2
SALES (est): 120K **Privately Held**
SIC: 2431 Millwork

(G-1536)
WOODYS WOODEN WONDERS LLC
80 Olde Orchard Rd (06413-1107)
PHONE..................860 669-5221
Robert W H Wilkins, *Owner*
EMP: 1
SALES: 119.1K **Privately Held**
SIC: 2499 Kitchen, bathroom & household ware: wood

Cobalt
Middlesex County

(G-1537)
COZY PANTS LLC
6 Stagecoach Run (06414-8012)
PHONE..................860 267-7507
Jessica Grant,
Elaine Grant,
EMP: 2
SALES (est): 135.1K **Privately Held**
SIC: 2253 Pants, slacks or trousers, knit

Colchester
New London County

(G-1538)
A TELLING TIME LIMITED CB
244 Upton Rd Ste 4 (06415-2748)
PHONE..................877 486-7865
Craig Hester, *President*
Kristine Vanraalte, *Corp Secy*
EMP: 2
SALES (est): 160K **Privately Held**
SIC: 3873 Watches, clocks, watchcases & parts

(G-1539)
ALTERNATIVE FUEL & ENERGY LLC
31 Halls Hill Rd (06415-1402)
PHONE..................860 537-5345
Bruce Hayn, *Administration*
EMP: 3
SALES (est): 87.4K **Privately Held**
SIC: 2869 Fuels

(G-1540)
ARTISTIC HARDWOOD FLOORS CT
92 Pinebrook Rd (06415-2411)
PHONE..................860 537-5334
Wayne Patterson, *Principal*
EMP: 2
SALES (est): 278.5K **Privately Held**
SIC: 2426 1771 1752 Flooring, hardwood; flooring contractor; floor laying & floor work

(G-1541)
AVALANCHE DOWNHILL RACING INC
12 Davidson Rd (06415-1600)
PHONE..................860 537-4306
Craig Seekins, *President*
▲ **EMP:** 4
SALES (est): 405.7K **Privately Held**
WEB: www.avalanchedownhillracing.com
SIC: 3751 5941 Bicycles & related parts; sporting goods & bicycle shops

(G-1542)
B T WELDING
121 Van Cedarfield Rd (06415-1629)
PHONE..................860 537-6197
Bernard Tkatzuk, *Owner*
EMP: 1
SALES (est): 43K **Privately Held**
SIC: 7692 Welding repair

(G-1543)
BOBS SANDBOX
109 Westchester Rd (06415-2421)
PHONE..................860 267-4530
EMP: 1
SALES (est): 64K **Privately Held**
SIC: 3589 Mfg Service Industry Machinery

(G-1544)
CAREFREE BUILDING CO INC (PA)
Also Called: Carefree Small Buildings
48 Westchester Rd (06415-2420)
PHONE..................860 267-7600
Norman Gustafson, *President*
Todd Gustafson, *Vice Pres*
Brian Marvin, *Vice Pres*
Reynold Marvin, *Treasurer*
Rick Nowsch, *Director*
EMP: 18
SQ FT: 20,000
SALES (est): 3.2MM **Privately Held**
WEB: www.carefreebuildings.com
SIC: 2452 2511 Prefabricated buildings, wood; lawn furniture: wood

(G-1545)
CHRISTOPHER ANNELLI
Also Called: Annelli Paving
448 New London Rd (06415-1827)
PHONE..................860 537-4397
Christopher Annelli, *Owner*
EMP: 6
SALES (est): 711K **Privately Held**
SIC: 1771 2951 Blacktop (asphalt) work; asphalt paving mixtures & blocks

(G-1546)
COMPETITIVE EDGE COATINGS LLC
164 Bull Hill Rd (06415-2602)
PHONE..................860 267-6255
Christopher J Scutnik, *Principal*
EMP: 2
SALES (est): 130K **Privately Held**
SIC: 3479 Metal coating & allied service

(G-1547)
DREAM CABINETS LLC
25 Pickeral Dr (06415-2335)
PHONE..................860 301-5625
Zbigniew Majka, *Principal*
EMP: 2 **EST:** 2011
SALES (est): 220.8K **Privately Held**
SIC: 2434 Wood kitchen cabinets

(G-1548)
E6S INDUSTRIES LLC
38 Scott Hill Rd (06415-2027)
PHONE..................512 920-3671
Aaron Spearin, *Principal*
EMP: 2 **EST:** 2015
SALES (est): 55.9K **Privately Held**
SIC: 3999 Manufacturing industries

(G-1549)
EAGLE MANUFACTURING CO INC
13 Homonick Rd (06415-1911)
P.O. Box 186 (06415-0186)
PHONE..................860 537-3759
Clifton O'Donal, *President*
Jerry Risley, *Controller*
Geri Risley, *Financial Exec*
EMP: 15
SQ FT: 10,000
SALES (est): 3.7MM **Privately Held**
SIC: 3441 Fabricated structural metal

(G-1550)
ESSEX WOOD PRODUCTS INC
Also Called: Ewp
75 Mill St (06415-1263)
P.O. Box 513 (06415-0513)
PHONE..................860 537-3451
Stephen Lloyd Schwartz, *President*
Michael Pasternak, *Vice Pres*
EMP: 30
SQ FT: 20,000
SALES (est): 3.1MM **Privately Held**
WEB: www.ssww.com
SIC: 3944 2499 Craft & hobby kits & sets; novelties, wood fiber

(G-1551)
FINISHING SOLUTIONS LLC
28 Jurach Rd (06415-2106)
PHONE..................860 705-8231
EMP: 3
SALES (est): 268.4K **Privately Held**
SIC: 2499 Mfg Wood Products

(G-1552)
GRANITE GROUP WHOLESALERS LLC
Also Called: Granite Group, The
464 S Main St Ste 1 (06415-1548)
PHONE..................860 537-7600
Matt Tallman, *Sales Associate*
Robert Tellegrini, *Manager*
EMP: 9

GEOGRAPHIC SECTION
Colebrook - Litchfield County (G-1587)

SALES (corp-wide): 181.6MM **Privately Held**
SIC: 5999 5074 3432 Plumbing & heating supplies; plumbing & hydronic heating supplies; plumbing fixture fittings & trim
PA: The Granite Group Wholesalers Llc
6 Storrs St
Concord NH 03301
603 224-1901

(G-1553)
HEAD EAST WOODWORKING
90 Davidson Rd (06415-1644)
PHONE 860 537-2072
EMP: 1 **EST:** 2017
SALES (est): 56.7K **Privately Held**
SIC: 2431 Millwork

(G-1554)
HNAT MOLD & DIE INC
14 Scott Hill Rd (06415-2025)
P.O. Box 249, Bozrah (06334-0249)
PHONE 860 537-0573
Joseph Hnat, *President*
EMP: 1
SALES (est): 148.8K **Privately Held**
SIC: 3544 Special dies & tools

(G-1555)
INTERNATIONAL CORDAGE EAST LTD
Also Called: Baynets Safety Systems
226 Upton Rd (06415-2712)
PHONE 860 873-5000
Robert T Martin, *President*
Edward A Ritz, *Vice Pres*
Brian Stevenson, *Vice Pres*
Mary Martin, *Admin Sec*
◆ **EMP:** 70
SQ FT: 25,000
SALES (est): 15.5MM **Privately Held**
SIC: 2298 Cargo nets; nets, rope

(G-1556)
INTRICUT
199 Upton Rd (06415-2712)
PHONE 860 537-7766
Martin Jenkins, *Owner*
EMP: 2
SALES (est): 146.5K **Privately Held**
SIC: 3599 Machine shop, jobbing & repair

(G-1557)
MONTANAS BOARD SPORTS
32 Bruce Cir (06415-1011)
PHONE 860 537-2927
Debra Powley, *Mng Member*
EMP: 6
SALES (est): 284K **Privately Held**
SIC: 5611 3949 Clothing, men's & boys': everyday, except suits & sportswear; sporting & athletic goods

(G-1558)
NANTZ WOODCRAFT
608 Westchester Rd (06415-2240)
PHONE 860 267-8853
Mark Nantz, *Owner*
EMP: 1
SALES (est): 56K **Privately Held**
SIC: 2499 Wood products

(G-1559)
NEW ENGLAND SOFT SERVE
56 School Rd (06415-1729)
P.O. Box 689 (06415-0689)
PHONE 860 537-5459
David Dander, *Owner*
EMP: 1
SALES (est): 65.5K **Privately Held**
SIC: 2024 Ice cream & ice milk

(G-1560)
NORTON PAPER MILL LLC
167 Marvin Rd (06415-1915)
PHONE 860 861-9701
N Wasniewski, *Bd of Directors*
EMP: 2
SALES (est): 103.6K **Privately Held**
SIC: 2621 Paper mills

(G-1561)
NOVA ELECTRONICS
36 Dr Foote Rd Ste A (06415-1523)
PHONE 860 537-3471
Stephen Hanley, *President*
EMP: 2
SALES (est): 167.6K **Privately Held**
SIC: 3648 Lighting equipment

(G-1562)
PATHWAY LIGHTING SOURCE
226 Upton Rd (06415-2712)
PHONE 860 537-0600
Todd Guertin, *Owner*
EMP: 2
SALES (est): 140.3K **Privately Held**
SIC: 3648 Lighting equipment

(G-1563)
PEREGRINE TECHNICAL SVCS LLC
Also Called: Parachute Indust Engrg Consult
87 Brookstone Dr (06415-2241)
PHONE 813 469-9355
David L Singer, *Mng Member*
EMP: 1
SALES: 80K **Privately Held**
SIC: 3429 8711 Parachute hardware; consulting engineer

(G-1564)
PERSONALLY YOURS
83 Oconnell Rd (06415-1727)
PHONE 860 537-2248
Christine Farrick, *Owner*
EMP: 2
SALES (est): 62.7K **Privately Held**
SIC: 2395 Embroidery & art needlework

(G-1565)
PHRACTION MANAGEMENT LLC
288 Old Hebron Rd (06415-2723)
PHONE 860 531-9590
Jason Stollman, *CIO*
EMP: 3
SALES: 500K **Privately Held**
SIC: 6282 7372 Investment advisory service; application computer software

(G-1566)
PLAY-IT PRODUCTIONS INC
167b Lebanon Ave (06415-1225)
PHONE 212 695-6530
Terri Tyler, *Vice Pres*
Sergio Sandino, *Art Dir*
EMP: 10
SALES (est): 1.8MM **Privately Held**
WEB: www.play-itproductions.net
SIC: 2752 7336 7812 7819 Commercial printing, lithographic; graphic arts & related design; audio-visual program production; video tape or disk reproduction

(G-1567)
PODSKOCH PRESS
36 Waterhole Rd (06415-2323)
PHONE 860 267-2442
Martin Podskoch, *Owner*
Lynn Podskoch, *Co-Owner*
EMP: 2
SALES (est): 87.3K **Privately Held**
SIC: 2741 Miscellaneous publishing

(G-1568)
PRO KART RACING KARTS
483 Lebanon Ave (06415-2126)
PHONE 860 537-6900
Rory West,
EMP: 1
SALES (est): 138.8K **Privately Held**
WEB: www.prokarts.com
SIC: 3799 Go-carts, except children's

(G-1569)
Q ALPHA INC
Also Called: Glastonbury Southern Gage Div
87 Upton Rd (06415-2712)
P.O. Box 531 (06415-0531)
PHONE 860 357-7340
Richard Jones, *Vice Pres*
Jim Klein, *Manager*
Erica Gootkin, *Assistant*
EMP: 24
SQ FT: 25,000
SALES (corp-wide): 33.9MM **Privately Held**
SIC: 3545 Gauges (machine tool accessories)

PA: Alpha Q, Inc.
87 Upton Rd
Colchester CT 06415
860 537-4681

(G-1570)
QUICK PRINT
48 Main St (06415-1529)
PHONE 860 425-5580
Bryan Lawson, *Principal*
EMP: 2
SALES (est): 162.5K **Privately Held**
SIC: 2752 Commercial printing, offset

(G-1571)
RED ROSE DESSERTS
125 Lebanon Ave (06415-1226)
PHONE 860 603-2670
Jacqueline Sirois, *Owner*
Rianna Merray, *Regional Mgr*
EMP: 5
SALES: 135K **Privately Held**
SIC: 2051 Bread, cake & related products

(G-1572)
REDCO INDUSTRIES LLC
15 Sashel Ln (06415-2055)
PHONE 860 537-2664
Robert D'Atri, *Principal*
EMP: 2
SALES (est): 136.3K **Privately Held**
SIC: 3999 Manufacturing industries

(G-1573)
RETECH USA LLC
12 Esther Ln (06415-1777)
PHONE 860 531-9653
Gary Bell, *Opers Mgr*
Nicole Golubeff,
EMP: 2
SALES (est): 30K **Privately Held**
SIC: 3572 Computer storage devices

(G-1574)
S & S WORLDWIDE INC
75 Mill St (06415-1263)
P.O. Box 513 (06415-0513)
PHONE 860 537-3451
Stephen L Schwartz, *CEO*
Adam L Schwartz, *President*
Hy J Schwartz, *President*
Allen Dyer, *COO*
Audrey Bis, *Vice Pres*
◆ **EMP:** 235 **EST:** 1906
SQ FT: 200,000
SALES (est): 221.8MM **Privately Held**
WEB: www.ssww.com
SIC: 5199 5049 3944 Art goods; school supplies; games, toys & children's vehicles

(G-1575)
SHAEFFER PLASTIC MFG CORP
523 Old Hartford Rd (06415-2717)
PHONE 860 537-5524
Robert J Shaeffer, *President*
EMP: 3
SQ FT: 3,000
SALES: 300K **Privately Held**
SIC: 3089 Molding primary plastic

(G-1576)
SHAMROCK SHEET METAL
23 Briarwood Dr (06415-1831)
PHONE 860 537-4282
Daniel Cavanaugh, *Principal*
EMP: 8
SALES (est): 390K **Privately Held**
SIC: 3449 Miscellaneous metalwork

(G-1577)
SKYDOG KITES LLC
220 Westchester Rd (06415-2423)
PHONE 860 365-0600
J D Christianson, *Mng Member*
▲ **EMP:** 3
SALES (est): 329.7K **Privately Held**
SIC: 3944 Kites

(G-1578)
SWEET COUNTRY ROADS LLC
180 Mcdonald Rd (06415-1940)
PHONE 860 537-0069
Charlotte Abbott,
EMP: 3

SALES (est): 149.5K **Privately Held**
SIC: 2033 Jams, jellies & preserves: packaged in cans, jars, etc.

(G-1579)
TORQ INDUSTRIES LLC
38 Skinner Rd (06415-2214)
PHONE 860 537-8539
Raymond Camire, *Principal*
EMP: 1 **EST:** 2010
SALES (est): 47.4K **Privately Held**
SIC: 3999 Manufacturing industries

(G-1580)
VITAL SIGNS LLC
56 Stoneridge Rd (06415-2347)
PHONE 860 365-0897
Richard J Dadona, *Manager*
EMP: 1
SALES (est): 78.9K **Privately Held**
SIC: 3993 Signs & advertising specialties

(G-1581)
WESTCHESTER PET VACCINES
111 Loomis Rd Ste 1 (06415-2337)
PHONE 860 267-4554
Lewis D Kimball Jr, *President*
EMP: 3
SALES (est): 298.3K **Privately Held**
SIC: 2836 Vaccines

(G-1582)
WILLIAM CLARK WELDING INC
248 Boretz Rd (06415-1026)
PHONE 860 537-0122
William Clark, *Principal*
EMP: 1
SALES (est): 52.4K **Privately Held**
SIC: 7692 Welding repair

(G-1583)
WORLD WIDE GAMES INC
10 Mill St (06415)
PHONE 860 537-3451
Edna K Schwartz, *Ch of Bd*
Stephen L Schwartz, *President*
Michael Pasternak, *Vice Pres*
EMP: 1 **EST:** 1953
SQ FT: 5,000
SALES (est): 89.3K **Privately Held**
WEB: www.ssww.com
SIC: 3944 5961 Structural toy sets; novelty merchandise, mail order

Colebrook
Litchfield County

(G-1584)
CAM INDUSTRIES
8 Millbrook Rd (06021-3916)
PHONE 860 738-8338
Craig M Maiolo, *Principal*
EMP: 2
SALES (est): 232.2K **Privately Held**
SIC: 3999 Manufacturing industries

(G-1585)
NORTHWEST CONNECTICUT MFG CO
95 Beech Hill Rd (06021-3606)
PHONE 860 379-1553
Louis Fasano Jr, *President*
Jane Fasano, *Admin Sec*
EMP: 8 **EST:** 1974
SQ FT: 5,200
SALES (est): 760K **Privately Held**
SIC: 3599 Machine shop, jobbing & repair

(G-1586)
SANDY BROOK MANUFACTURING LLC
12 Riverton Rd (06021-4309)
PHONE 860 205-4438
Paul Madore, *Principal*
EMP: 1
SALES (est): 39.6K **Privately Held**
SIC: 3999 Manufacturing industries

(G-1587)
SPERA COTTAGE CRAFTERS
Also Called: Dave's Storage Train
65 Stillman Hill Rd (06021-3902)
PHONE 860 738-2391

Robin Denaro, *Principal*
EMP: 2
SALES (est): 130K **Privately Held**
SIC: 3944 Craft & hobby kits & sets

Collinsville
Hartford County

(G-1588)
BF ENTERPRISES LLC
241 Wright Rd (06019-3754)
PHONE..................860 693-8953
Matthew Calabro, *Principal*
EMP: 2
SALES (est): 81.6K **Privately Held**
SIC: 3011 Tires & inner tubes

(G-1589)
BLUMEN LADEN ARTIFICIAL FLOWER
41 Bridge St (06019-3301)
PHONE..................860 693-8600
Ann Wincze, *Owner*
EMP: 2
SALES (est): 144.5K **Privately Held**
SIC: 3999 Artificial flower arrangements

(G-1590)
CAROL ACKERMAN DESIGNS
107 Main St (06019-3134)
PHONE..................860 693-1013
Carol Ackerman, *Owner*
EMP: 3
SQ FT: 820
SALES (est): 500K **Privately Held**
WEB: www.carolackerman.com
SIC: 3911 Jewelry, precious metal

(G-1591)
COLLINSVILLE SCREEN PRINTING
30 Depot St (06019-4113)
P.O. Box 154 (06022-0154)
PHONE..................860 693-2601
Linda Cournoyer, *Owner*
EMP: 2
SALES (est): 191K **Privately Held**
SIC: 2759 Screen printing

(G-1592)
CONNECTICUT VALLEY PACKG LLC
20 Country Ln (06019-3406)
PHONE..................860 693-0776
William Ross, *Owner*
EMP: 1
SALES (est): 84.7K **Privately Held**
SIC: 3089 Plastics products

(G-1593)
DON POMASKI
10 Front St (06019-3181)
PHONE..................860 693-4469
Don Pomaski, *Principal*
EMP: 1 **Privately Held**
SIC: 3699 Teaching machines & aids, electronic
PA: Don Pomaski
2 Highfields Dr
Canton CT 06019

(G-1594)
EMILIE COHEN
Also Called: Connecticut School Jewelry Art
51 Bridge St (06019-3302)
P.O. Box 118, New Hartford (06057-0118)
PHONE..................860 693-9427
Emilie Cohen, *Owner*
EMP: 2
SALES (est): 111K **Privately Held**
SIC: 3911 Jewelry, precious metal

(G-1595)
KELYNIAM GLOBAL INC
97 River Rd Ste A (06019-3246)
PHONE..................800 280-8192
Tennyson Anthony, *CEO*
Chris Breault, *COO*
Christopher Breault, *Vice Pres*
Nicholas Breault, *Vice Pres*
Nick Breault, *Vice Pres*
EMP: 17
SQ FT: 7,000
SALES (est): 3.1MM **Privately Held**
SIC: 3842 Surgical appliances & supplies

(G-1596)
KOSTER KEUNEN MANUFACTURING
13 Sweetheart Mountain Rd (06019-3425)
PHONE..................860 693-1295
EMP: 1
SALES (est): 44.7K **Privately Held**
SIC: 3999 Manufacturing industries

(G-1597)
LEDGEWOOD PUBLICATIONS
3 Mountain Laurel Ct (06019-3727)
PHONE..................860 693-9055
EMP: 2
SALES (est): 100K **Privately Held**
SIC: 2759 Commercial Printing

(G-1598)
ON-SITE WELDING LLC
106 Dunne Ave (06019-3322)
PHONE..................860 662-6332
David Hyde, *Principal*
EMP: 1
SALES (est): 55.8K **Privately Held**
SIC: 7692 Welding repair

(G-1599)
PELCHS WELDING & REPAIR
Also Called: Pelchs Auto Repair
40 Ramp Rd (06019)
P.O. Box 444, Canton (06019-0444)
PHONE..................860 693-6328
Terry Pelczar, *Owner*
EMP: 1
SALES (est): 98K **Privately Held**
SIC: 1799 7692 Welding on site; welding repair

(G-1600)
PRECISION CANVAS LLC
20 Collins Rd (06019-3318)
PHONE..................860 693-2353
Mark E Lowell Esq, *Administration*
EMP: 2
SALES (est): 73.4K **Privately Held**
SIC: 2211 Canvas

(G-1601)
PURITAN INDUSTRIES INC
122 Powder Mill Rd (06019-3502)
P.O. Box 186 (06022-0186)
PHONE..................860 693-0791
Andrew P Papanek, *President*
▲ EMP: 20
SQ FT: 10,000
SALES (est): 3MM **Privately Held**
SIC: 3559 Sewing machines & attachments, industrial

(G-1602)
ROBERT DOWNEY LOGGING
31 Wright Rd (06019-3743)
PHONE..................860 693-2914
Robert Downey, *Owner*
EMP: 1
SALES (est): 123.8K **Privately Held**
SIC: 2411 Logging camps & contractors

(G-1603)
SINISH WORKS
20 Dyer Ave (06019-3004)
PHONE..................860 693-0073
David Sinish, *Owner*
EMP: 2
SALES (est): 144K **Privately Held**
SIC: 2789 Map mounting

Columbia
Tolland County

(G-1604)
COLUMBIA MANUFACTURING INC
165 Route 66 E (06237-1223)
P.O. Box 368 (06237-0368)
PHONE..................860 228-2259
Kimberly Bell, *President*
Lupoli Nick, *General Mgr*
Kathryn Conlon, *Vice Pres*
Kim Bell, *Export Mgr*
Emmanuel Quiles, *Mfg Spvr*
▲ EMP: 99
SQ FT: 100,000
SALES (est): 30.9MM **Privately Held**
SIC: 3724 5088 Pumps, aircraft engine; starting vibrators, aircraft engine; turbo-superchargers, aircraft; exhaust systems, aircraft; transportation equipment & supplies

(G-1605)
GRAND VIEW STABLE LLC
42 Pine St (06237-1516)
PHONE..................860 228-3791
Rochelle L Drisco, *Manager*
EMP: 2
SALES (est): 146.2K **Privately Held**
SIC: 3199 Riding crops

(G-1606)
HAWK INTEGRATED PLASTICS LLC
1 Commerce Dr (06237-1231)
PHONE..................860 337-0310
Dana Schnabel, *Engineer*
Sharon Espinosa, *Office Mgr*
Joseph Bak, *Mng Member*
EMP: 12 EST: 2000
SQ FT: 12,500
SALES (est): 2.4MM **Privately Held**
WEB: www.hawkiplas.com
SIC: 3089 Injection molding of plastics

(G-1607)
LEARNERS DIMENSION
7 Lakeview Dr (06237-1004)
PHONE..................860 228-1236
K Butler, *Owner*
EMP: 1
SALES (est): 58.9K **Privately Held**
SIC: 8748 2741 Business consulting; miscellaneous publishing

(G-1608)
MME PUBLISHING LLC
15 Homestead Ln (06237-1346)
PHONE..................860 228-1369
Margaret M Earnest, *Principal*
EMP: 1
SALES (est): 55.8K **Privately Held**
SIC: 2741 Miscellaneous publishing

(G-1609)
MY DENIM QUEEN
23 Yeomans Rd (06237-1534)
PHONE..................860 729-1142
Ellen Clark, *Principal*
EMP: 1 EST: 2016
SALES (est): 46.5K **Privately Held**
SIC: 2211 Denims

(G-1610)
OLD HOUSE WOODCRAFT LLC
77 Johnson Rd (06237-1215)
PHONE..................860 228-2174
Daniel W Clark, *Principal*
EMP: 2
SALES (est): 114K **Privately Held**
SIC: 2511 Wood household furniture

(G-1611)
RM LANDCLEARING & LOGGING LLC
10 Pine St (06237-1516)
PHONE..................860 228-1499
EMP: 2
SALES (est): 174.5K **Privately Held**
SIC: 2411 Logging

(G-1612)
RTI TECHNOLOGIES LLC (PA)
32 Lake Rd (06237-1314)
PHONE..................860 306-4772
Avner J Bawabe, *President*
EMP: 1
SALES (est): 100K **Privately Held**
SIC: 3728 Military aircraft equipment & armament

(G-1613)
THORNVIEW CUSTOM CABINETS
186 Pine St (06237-1522)
PHONE..................860 228-5054
James E Thorn, *Principal*
EMP: 2
SALES (est): 129.2K **Privately Held**
SIC: 2434 Wood kitchen cabinets

(G-1614)
US PRODUCT MECHANIZATION CO
Also Called: Promec
21 Route 87 (06237-1023)
PHONE..................860 450-1139
Christopher H Ramm, *President*
EMP: 1
SALES: 400K **Privately Held**
SIC: 3542 3599 Swaging machines; swage blocks

(G-1615)
WH ROSE INC
9 Route 66 E (06237-1235)
PHONE..................860 228-8258
Lisa Rose, *President*
William Rose, *Corp Secy*
Daniel J Marriott, *Vice Pres*
Christopher Rose, *Vice Pres*
EMP: 27
SALES (est): 4.1MM **Privately Held**
WEB: www.whroseinc.com
SIC: 5013 7539 7692 Truck parts & accessories; front end repair, automotive; frame & front end repair services; automotive welding

Cornwall
Litchfield County

(G-1616)
CLOVER HILL FOREST LLC
20 Hurlburt Pl (06753)
PHONE..................860 672-0394
Gary Ocain,
EMP: 6
SALES (est): 616.7K **Privately Held**
SIC: 2411 Logging

Cornwall Bridge
Litchfield County

(G-1617)
DAVID COLBERT
76 Warren Hill Rd (06754-1302)
PHONE..................860 672-0064
David Colbert, *Owner*
EMP: 1
SALES (est): 66.6K **Privately Held**
WEB: www.davidcolbert.com
SIC: 3299 Architectural sculptures: gypsum, clay, papier mache, etc.

(G-1618)
ORCHARD PRESS
78 Popple Swamp Rd (06754-1138)
PHONE..................860 672-4273
Matthew Collins, *Owner*
EMP: 2
SALES: 100K **Privately Held**
SIC: 2731 Book publishing

(G-1619)
SILVER HILL WOODWORKS LLC
150 Kent Rd S (06754-1210)
PHONE..................860 318-1887
Andrew Lundeen,
EMP: 1
SALES (est): 54.1K **Privately Held**
SIC: 2431 Millwork

(G-1620)
STATIC SAFE PRODUCTS COMPANY
8 Cook Rd (06754-1320)
P.O. Box 5346, Milford (06460-0705)
PHONE..................203 937-6391
David F Greco, *President*
EMP: 10
SALES (est): 850.3K **Privately Held**
SIC: 2522 Office furniture, except wood

Coventry - Tolland County (G-1655)

(G-1621)
STRAWBERRY RIDGE VINEYARD INC
Also Called: Vineyard At Strawberry Ridge
23 Strawbery Ridge Rd (06754)
PHONE..................860 868-0730
Nick Belarge, *Manager*
Lance M Newton, *Manager*
EMP: 4
SALES (est): 141.2K **Privately Held**
SIC: 2084 0172 Wines; grapes

Cos Cob
Fairfield County

(G-1622)
ALBIN MANUFACTURING CORP
143 River Rd (06807-2539)
PHONE..................203 661-4341
EMP: 2
SALES (est): 190K **Privately Held**
SIC: 3732 Manufacturing

(G-1623)
ALBIN MARINE INC
143 River Rd (06807-2539)
P.O. Box 73 (06807-0073)
PHONE..................203 661-4341
Fax: 203 661-6040
EMP: 1
SQ FT: 3,000
SALES (est): 120K **Privately Held**
SIC: 3732 Boatbuilding/Repairing

(G-1624)
ARNITEX LLC
Also Called: Jagtar
110 Orchard St (06807-2010)
PHONE..................203 869-1406
Bruno Garros, *Owner*
▲ EMP: 3
SALES (est): 425.2K **Privately Held**
SIC: 2211 8711 Card roll fabrics, cotton; building construction consultant

(G-1625)
BEELIGHTFUL CANDLE LLC
222 Cognewaugh Rd (06807-1507)
PHONE..................203 912-7122
Olivia Holt, *Principal*
EMP: 1
SALES (est): 43.6K **Privately Held**
SIC: 3999 Candles

(G-1626)
CHICKEN SOUP FOR SOUL LLC
132 E Putnam Ave Ste 20 (06807-2724)
P.O. Box 700 (06807-0369)
PHONE..................203 861-4000
William J Rouhana Jr, *CEO*
EMP: 50
SALES (est): 1.7MM **Privately Held**
SIC: 2741 Miscellaneous publishing

(G-1627)
CHICKEN SOUP FOR SOUL ENTRMT I (HQ)
132 E Putnam Ave Fl 2w (06807-2744)
PHONE..................855 398-0443
William J Rouhana Jr, *Ch of Bd*
Scott W Seaton, *Vice Ch Bd*
Elana B Sofko, *COO*
Christopher Mitchell, *CFO*
EMP: 6
SQ FT: 6,000
SALES: 26.8MM **Publicly Held**
SIC: 2741 Miscellaneous publishing
PA: Chicken Soup For The Soul Productions, Llc
132 E Putnam Ave Ste 20
Cos Cob CT 06807
855 398-0443

(G-1628)
CHICKEN SOUP FOR SOUL PUBG LLC
132 E Putnam Ave (06807-2744)
PHONE..................203 861-4000
William J Rouhana Jr, *Principal*
Daniel Pess, *CFO*
Nancy Autio, *Director*
EMP: 1
SALES (est): 85.4K **Privately Held**
SIC: 2741 Miscellaneous publishing

(G-1629)
CHICKEN SOUP FOR THE SOUL (PA)
132 E Putnam Ave Ste 20 (06807-2724)
PHONE..................855 398-0443
William J Rouhana Jr, *CEO*
EMP: 2
SALES (est): 26.8MM **Publicly Held**
SIC: 2741 Miscellaneous publishing

(G-1630)
COMPLIMENTARY HEALING
45 Valleywood Rd (06807-2330)
PHONE..................203 622-1697
Valerie Free, *Owner*
EMP: 1 EST: 2016
SALES (est): 47.5K **Privately Held**
SIC: 2741 Miscellaneous publishing

(G-1631)
DOONEY WOODWORKS LLC
105 River Rd (06807-2554)
PHONE..................203 340-9770
Peter Dewart Dooney, *Mng Member*
EMP: 1 EST: 2010
SALES (est): 111K **Privately Held**
SIC: 2431 Millwork

(G-1632)
GTRPET SMF LLC
10 Mead Ave Unit B (06807-2706)
PHONE..................203 661-1229
Ajmal Khan,
Alexander Khan,
▲ EMP: 7
SALES (est): 845.6K **Privately Held**
WEB: www.gtrpet.com
SIC: 3565 Packaging machinery

(G-1633)
HELEN GRACE
Also Called: Town Planner
25 Dartmouth Rd (06807-1713)
PHONE..................203 661-1927
Helen Grace, *Principal*
EMP: 1
SALES (est): 41.1K **Privately Held**
SIC: 2741 Miscellaneous publishing

(G-1634)
INTERNATIONAL ELEVATOR CORP
97 Valley Rd (06807-2209)
PHONE..................203 302-1023
Grant Gyesky, *President*
EMP: 5
SALES (est): 419.2K **Privately Held**
SIC: 3534 Elevators & equipment

(G-1635)
JJ GRECO CARTING LLC
40 Gregory Rd (06807-1609)
PHONE..................203 661-4947
Jeffrey J Greco, *Principal*
EMP: 2 EST: 2011
SALES (est): 197.2K **Privately Held**
SIC: 2599 Carts, restaurant equipment

(G-1636)
KWANT ELEMENTS INTL LLC
464 Valley Rd (06807-1626)
PHONE..................203 625-5553
Peter Janis, *Principal*
EMP: 3
SALES (est): 260.2K **Privately Held**
SIC: 2819 Industrial inorganic chemicals

(G-1637)
MEAD MONOGRAMMING
9 Mead Ave (06807-2705)
PHONE..................203 618-0701
Jane Flinn, *CEO*
EMP: 2
SALES (est): 58.2K **Privately Held**
SIC: 2395 Emblems, embroidered

(G-1638)
MILLBROOK DISTILLERY LLC
687 River Rd (06807-1908)
PHONE..................203 637-2231
EMP: 3
SALES (est): 130.6K **Privately Held**
SIC: 2085 Distilled & blended liquors

(G-1639)
PERRY INDUSTRIES LLC
41 Sundance Dr (06807-1809)
PHONE..................203 505-5187
Robert Perry, *Principal*
EMP: 1
SALES (est): 39.6K **Privately Held**
SIC: 3999 Manufacturing industries

(G-1640)
RIVERSIDE SEAT COVER INC
Also Called: Riverside Boat Covers Cushions
535 E Putnam Ave (06807-2506)
PHONE..................203 661-7893
Stan Krupnik, *President*
EMP: 1
SQ FT: 800
SALES (est): 124.6K **Privately Held**
SIC: 2392 Boat cushions; slipcovers: made of fabric, plastic etc.

(G-1641)
SEAN MECESERY
Also Called: Cos Cob T V & Video
5 Strickland Rd (06807-2736)
PHONE..................203 869-2277
Sean Mecesery, *Owner*
Chris Booth, *Project Mgr*
EMP: 5
SQ FT: 2,000
SALES (est): 699K **Privately Held**
SIC: 3679 7622 Electronic circuits; radio repair shop; television repair shop

(G-1642)
SWIZZLES OF GREENWHICH
207 E Putnam Ave (06807-2734)
PHONE..................917 662-0080
Nicole Cornelio, *Principal*
EMP: 4
SALES (est): 243.9K **Privately Held**
SIC: 2026 Yogurt

(G-1643)
WAGNER INSTRUMENTS INC
88 River Rd (06807-2516)
PHONE..................203 869-9681
William Wagner, *Principal*
EMP: 2
SALES (est): 178.9K **Privately Held**
SIC: 3826 Analytical instruments

Coventry
Tolland County

(G-1644)
AURAS ORACLE
830 Boston Tpke (06238-1377)
PHONE..................860 308-0893
Sharon Vitiello, *Principal*
EMP: 2 EST: 2017
SALES (est): 56.5K **Privately Held**
SIC: 7372 Prepackaged software

(G-1645)
BLACKBIRD MANUFACTURING AND DE
112 Gardner Tavern Ln (06238-6101)
PHONE..................860 331-3477
William Piotroski, *Principal*
EMP: 3 EST: 2010
SALES (est): 253.8K **Privately Held**
SIC: 3999 Manufacturing industries

(G-1646)
BNE PUBLISHING INC
3050 Main St (06238-1625)
PHONE..................860 498-0032
EMP: 1
SALES (est): 41.3K **Privately Held**
SIC: 2741 Miscellaneous publishing

(G-1647)
BOLTON HILL INDUSTRIES INC (PA)
Also Called: Bolton Hill Industries-Marine
65 Cedar Swamp Rd (06238)
PHONE..................860 742-0311
Lawrence Giglio, *President*
EMP: 2
SQ FT: 3,000
SALES (est): 280.3K **Privately Held**
SIC: 2541 2521 2511 Cabinets, except refrigerated: show, display, etc.: wood; wood office furniture; wood household furniture

(G-1648)
BRANDON NICHOLAS EZA PUBG
3050 Main St (06238-1625)
PHONE..................860 498-0032
Megan Eza, *Principal*
EMP: 2
SALES (est): 50K **Privately Held**
SIC: 2741 Miscellaneous publishing

(G-1649)
CHARLES BOGGINI COMPANY LLC
Also Called: Cbc Co
733 Bread And Milk St (06238-1014)
PHONE..................860 742-2652
Glen Boggini, *Partner*
Jane Boggini, *Partner*
Evan Boggini, *Opers Staff*
Marie Oliphant, *Office Mgr*
David Boggini, *Mng Member*
◆ EMP: 6
SQ FT: 13,000
SALES (est): 889.5K **Privately Held**
WEB: www.bogginicola.com
SIC: 2087 Extracts, flavoring

(G-1650)
CUSTOM CARPENTRY UNLIMITED
Also Called: James Hunt
82 Woodbridge Rd (06238-1530)
PHONE..................860 742-8932
James Hunt, *Owner*
EMP: 1
SALES (est): 84.3K **Privately Held**
SIC: 2431 Millwork

(G-1651)
CUVEE 59
3718 South St (06238-1451)
PHONE..................707 259-0559
Tina Masquelier, *President*
EMP: 1
SALES (est): 40.9K **Privately Held**
SIC: 2399 Fabricated textile products

(G-1652)
DESIATO SAND & GRAVEL
245 Brigham Rd (06238-1703)
PHONE..................860 742-7573
Phil Desiato, *Principal*
EMP: 2 EST: 2001
SALES (est): 110K **Privately Held**
SIC: 1442 Construction sand & gravel

(G-1653)
ECOSYSTEM CONSULTING SVC INC
30 Mason St (06238-3121)
P.O. Box 370 (06238-0370)
PHONE..................860 742-0744
Robert Kortmann, *President*
Mary S Kortmann, *Vice Pres*
EMP: 5
SQ FT: 6,600
SALES: 574.5K **Privately Held**
WEB: www.ecosystemconsulting.com
SIC: 3589 1623 8748 Sewage & water treatment equipment; water & sewer line construction; environmental consultant

(G-1654)
FOWLER D J LOG LAND CLEARING
150 Plains Rd (06238-3420)
PHONE..................860 742-5842
Daniel J Fowler, *Principal*
EMP: 2
SALES (est): 124.2K **Privately Held**
SIC: 2411 Logging camps & contractors

(G-1655)
IMAGE WORKS SIGN & GRAPH
200 Brewster St (06238-1407)
PHONE..................860 569-7446
EMP: 2

Coventry - Tolland County (G-1656)

SALES (est): 72.6K **Privately Held**
SIC: **3993** Signs & advertising specialties

(G-1656)
IN-MOTION LLC
55 Pine Knoll Rd (06238)
PHONE.................................860 742-3612
James E Wieloch Jr, *Mng Member*
EMP: 1
SALES (est): 167.7K **Privately Held**
SIC: **5063** 3625 Motor controls, starters & relays; electric; relays & industrial controls

(G-1657)
JC EMBROIDERY
2508 Boston Tpke (06238-1003)
PHONE.................................860 742-8686
EMP: 1
SALES (est): 34.4K **Privately Held**
SIC: **2395** Embroidery & art needlework

(G-1658)
JERRY FREEMAN PENNYWHISTLES
500 Flanders Rd (06238-3434)
PHONE.................................860 498-0014
Jerry Freeman, *Owner*
EMP: 1 EST: 2009
SALES (est): 59.6K **Privately Held**
SIC: **3931** Guitars & parts, electric & non-electric

(G-1659)
KARL STETSON ASSOCIATES LLC
Also Called: Holometrology
2060 South St (06238-2441)
PHONE.................................860 742-8414
Karl Stetson, *President*
EMP: 3
SALES: 100K **Privately Held**
SIC: **3827** Optical instruments & lenses

(G-1660)
LEGNO BLDRS & FINE WDWKG LLC
35 Ross Ave (06238-2428)
PHONE.................................860 282-0091
Michael Betti, *Principal*
EMP: 2
SALES (est): 75.6K **Privately Held**
SIC: **2431** Millwork

(G-1661)
LILY FORCE INDUSTRIES
65 Cedar Swamp Ext (06238-1024)
PHONE.................................860 729-2458
EMP: 1
SALES (est): 47.3K **Privately Held**
SIC: **3999** Manufacturing industries

(G-1662)
M & S PRODUCTS
24 Brigham Tavern Rd Ext (06238-1316)
PHONE.................................860 742-5141
Michael Carroll, *Owner*
Srah Carroll, *Co-Owner*
EMP: 2
SALES (est): 174.6K **Privately Held**
SIC: **3599** Machine shop, jobbing & repair

(G-1663)
MIKE SADLAK
Also Called: Sadlak Innovative Design
712 Bread Milk St Unit A6 (06238-1093)
P.O. Box 207 (06238-0207)
PHONE.................................860 742-0227
Mike Sadlak, *Owner*
John Barrett, *Sales Staff*
EMP: 7
SQ FT: 3,000
SALES (est): 302.5K **Privately Held**
SIC: **3949** 8711 3484 Snow skiing equipment & supplies, except skis; engineering services; rifles or rifle parts, 30 mm. & below

(G-1664)
NATIONAL RIBBON LLC
1159 Main St (06238-3115)
P.O. Box 268 (06238-0268)
PHONE.................................860 742-6966
William Wilde, *Mng Member*
Lois Pepin,
Pamela Wilde,
EMP: 4
SQ FT: 4,000
SALES (est): 525.8K **Privately Held**
WEB: www.nationalribbon.com
SIC: **2241** Ribbons

(G-1665)
NEW ENGLAND HONING LLC
151 Barnsbee Ln (06238-1681)
PHONE.................................860 712-6094
George Lankton III, *Principal*
EMP: 2 EST: 2010
SALES (est): 173K **Privately Held**
SIC: **3599** Grinding castings for the trade

(G-1666)
NEW LINE USA INC
247 Brigham Tavern Rd (06238-1312)
PHONE.................................860 498-0347
Ilan Bartov, *President*
EMP: 3
SQ FT: 3,000
SALES: 700K **Privately Held**
WEB: www.newlineusa.com
SIC: **3699** Security control equipment & systems

(G-1667)
OMONDI WOODWORKING
2690 Boston Tpke (06238-1007)
PHONE.................................860 513-2292
EMP: 1
SALES (est): 54.1K **Privately Held**
SIC: **2431** Millwork

(G-1668)
PRECISION WELDING SERVICES LLC
30 Babcock Hill Road Ext (06238-3405)
PHONE.................................860 268-0580
Douglas A French, *Principal*
EMP: 1
SALES (est): 43.3K **Privately Held**
SIC: **7692** Welding repair

(G-1669)
PRINTED PRFMCE INNOVATIONS LLC
362 S River Rd (06238-1509)
PHONE.................................860 942-7338
Slade Culp,
EMP: 1
SALES (est): 110K **Privately Held**
SIC: **3679** Electronic circuits

(G-1670)
PRIVATEER DIVERS LLC
425 Geraldine Dr (06238-1333)
PHONE.................................860 742-2699
Eric D Simon, *Principal*
EMP: 2
SALES (est): 154.9K **Privately Held**
SIC: **3999** Manufacturing industries

(G-1671)
RG WOODWORKING LLC
327 Dunn Rd (06238-1163)
PHONE.................................860 742-0397
Rejean Giguere,
EMP: 1
SALES: 55K **Privately Held**
SIC: **2431** Millwork

(G-1672)
ROUND HILL ALPACAS LLC
56 Round Hill Rd (06238-1657)
PHONE.................................860 742-5195
Randall R Hall, *Principal*
EMP: 2 EST: 2012
SALES (est): 168.8K **Privately Held**
SIC: **2231** Alpacas, mohair: woven

(G-1673)
SADLAK INDUSTRIES LLC
712 Bread And Milk St A9 (06238-1093)
P.O. Box 207 (06238-0207)
PHONE.................................860 742-0227
Michael W Sadlak,
John Barrett,
EMP: 25
SALES: 3MM **Privately Held**
SIC: **3541** 3949 Machine tool replacement & repair parts, metal cutting types; targets, archery & rifle shooting

(G-1674)
SADLAK MANUFACTURING LLC
712 Bread And Milk St # 7 (06238-1093)
PHONE.................................860 742-0227
Michael Sadlak, *Mng Member*
John Barret,
EMP: 25
SALES (est): 812.7K **Privately Held**
SIC: **3999** Manufacturing industries

(G-1675)
SOUND OF FURY PUBLISHING LLC
600 Hop River Rd (06238-3262)
PHONE.................................860 803-0651
Leonard Bosh Jr, *Principal*
EMP: 1
SALES (est): 71.8K **Privately Held**
SIC: **2741** Miscellaneous publishing

(G-1676)
SPOOKY SIGNS AND HOLIDAY CREAT
23 Leslie Ln (06238-2348)
PHONE.................................860 742-2805
Beth Roop, *Principal*
EMP: 1 EST: 2011
SALES (est): 97.9K **Privately Held**
SIC: **3993** Signs & advertising specialties

(G-1677)
STYLE WOODWORKING
199 Nathan Hale Rd (06238-3238)
PHONE.................................860 944-7179
Glenn Ferrari, *Owner*
EMP: 1
SALES (est): 100K **Privately Held**
SIC: **2431** Millwork

(G-1678)
SUM MACHINE & TOOL CO INC
156 Mark Dr (06238-1124)
PHONE.................................860 742-6827
Donald Morris, *President*
Diana Morris, *Treasurer*
EMP: 4 EST: 1966
SQ FT: 5,000
SALES (est): 260K **Privately Held**
SIC: **3599** Machine shop, jobbing & repair

(G-1679)
SWAGECO LLC
112 Gardner Tavern Ln (06238-6101)
PHONE.................................860 331-3477
William Piotroski,
EMP: 2
SALES (est): 201K **Privately Held**
SIC: **3599** Custom machinery; machine shop, jobbing & repair; swage blocks

(G-1680)
SWIFT SCIENTIFIC LLC
89 S River Rd (06238-1510)
PHONE.................................860 498-8577
Owen Swift, *President*
EMP: 1
SALES: 300K **Privately Held**
SIC: **3826** 7389 Laser scientific & engineering instruments;

(G-1681)
TELEFLEX INCORPORATED
1295 Main St (06238-3117)
P.O. Box 219 (06238-0219)
PHONE.................................860 742-8821
James Olson, *Technical Mgr*
Paul Jacovich, *Manager*
Debra Masso, *Manager*
EMP: 22
SALES (corp-wide): 2.4B **Publicly Held**
WEB: www.teleflex.com
SIC: **3842** Surgical appliances & supplies
PA: Teleflex Incorporated
550 E Swedesford Rd # 400
Wayne PA 19087
610 225-6800

(G-1682)
WHISPERING WINDS ANIMAL
178 Nathan Hale Rd (06238-3227)
PHONE.................................860 796-8098
Carmen Ligato, *Principal*
Brenda Stoeke,
EMP: 2

SALES (est): 120K **Privately Held**
SIC: **2015** Egg processing

(G-1683)
WHITE DOVE WOODWORKING LLC
117 Eastview Dr (06238-1678)
PHONE.................................860 268-4426
Raymond Riddell, *Principal*
EMP: 1 EST: 2010
SALES (est): 103.4K **Privately Held**
SIC: **2431** Millwork

Cromwell
Middlesex County

(G-1684)
ACCURATE MOLD COMPANY INC
64 Nooks Hill Rd (06416-1563)
PHONE.................................860 301-1988
Nelson Dion Jr, *President*
Judith R Dion, *Director*
EMP: 3
SQ FT: 3,500
SALES (est): 389.7K **Privately Held**
SIC: **3089** Injection molding of plastics

(G-1685)
ACTIMUS INC
189 Coles Rd (06416-1144)
PHONE.................................617 438-9968
Ramanath Reddy Ajjagottu, *President*
EMP: 60
SALES: 1.5MM **Privately Held**
SIC: **2834** 7389 Pharmaceutical preparations;

(G-1686)
ALBRAYCO TECHNOLOGIES INC
38 River Rd (06416-2325)
PHONE.................................860 635-3369
Allan Aylward, *President*
EMP: 8
SQ FT: 6,500
SALES: 750K **Privately Held**
SIC: **3826** Laser scientific & engineering instruments

(G-1687)
APOGEE CORPORATION
Also Called: Impact Plastics
154 West St Ste C (06416-4400)
PHONE.................................860 632-3550
Steven Ryan, *Manager*
EMP: 57
SALES (corp-wide): 10MM **Privately Held**
WEB: www.impactplastics-ct.com
SIC: **3081** Unsupported plastics film & sheet
PA: Apogee Corporation
5 Highland Dr
Putnam CT 06260
860 963-1976

(G-1688)
ARCHAMBAULT GROUP LLC
9 Greenway Dr (06416-2570)
PHONE.................................860 635-4006
Donna Archambault, *Mng Member*
EMP: 2
SALES (est): 167.8K **Privately Held**
SIC: **3993** Advertising artwork

(G-1689)
ATI NEW ENGLAND
14 Alcap Rdg (06416-1002)
PHONE.................................860 358-9698
Christopher Darby, *Principal*
EMP: 2
SALES (est): 128.1K **Privately Held**
SIC: **3312** Stainless steel

(G-1690)
ATLANTIC VENT & EQP CO INC
125 Sebethe Dr (06416-1033)
PHONE.................................860 635-1300
Martin F Cosker, *President*
Thomas Cosker, *President*
Keith Hellstrom, *Vice Pres*
Joe Angello, *Project Mgr*
Chris Corwel, *Manager*

GEOGRAPHIC SECTION

Cromwell - Middlesex County (G-1722)

EMP: 40
SQ FT: 27,113
SALES (est): 7.3MM **Privately Held**
WEB: www.atlanticventilating.com
SIC: 1711 3564 3444 Ventilation & duct work contractor; blowers & fans; sheet metalwork

(G-1691)
BEMAT TEC LLC
114 West St (06416-1902)
PHONE 860 632-0049
Brian Matyka, *Owner*
EMP: 3
SALES: 200K **Privately Held**
SIC: 7694 Rebuilding motors, except automotive

(G-1692)
BIOLOGICAL INDUSTRIES
100 Sebethe Dr Ste A3 (06416-1037)
PHONE 860 316-5197
Tanya Potcova, *Principal*
EMP: 3
SALES (est): 173.1K **Privately Held**
SIC: 3999 Manufacturing industries

(G-1693)
BOB VESS BUILDING LLC
605 Main St (06416-1433)
PHONE 860 729-2536
Bob Vess,
EMP: 4
SALES (est): 337.3K **Privately Held**
SIC: 3949 Sporting & athletic goods

(G-1694)
CAREY MANUFACTURING CO INC (PA)
Also Called: Amatom Electronic Hardwares
5 Pasco Hill Rd Unit A (06416-1012)
PHONE 860 829-1803
John L Carey, *President*
Laure Carey, *Vice Pres*
Raymond Bedard, *Controller*
▲ **EMP:** 30
SQ FT: 25,000
SALES (est): 7.8MM **Privately Held**
WEB: www.amatom.com
SIC: 3699 Electrical equipment & supplies

(G-1695)
CAREY MANUFACTURING CO INC
Also Called: Amatom Electronic Hardware
5 Pasco Hill Rd Unit B (06416-1012)
PHONE 860 829-1803
John L Carey, *President*
EMP: 40
SALES (corp-wide): 7.8MM **Privately Held**
SIC: 3699 Electrical equipment & supplies
PA: Carey Manufacturing Company, Inc.
   5 Pasco Hill Rd Unit A
   Cromwell CT 06416
   860 829-1803

(G-1696)
COFFEE NEWS
271 Main St (06416-2304)
PHONE 860 613-0796
EMP: 1
SALES (est): 55.6K **Privately Held**
SIC: 2711 Newspapers-Publishing/Printing

(G-1697)
CRRC LLC
Also Called: Ripley
46 Nooks Hill Rd (06416-1562)
PHONE 860 635-2200
Kenneth Mac Cormac, *President*
David Leith, *Prdtn Mgr*
Dominic Nanci, *Opers Staff*
Barbara Aiello, *Purchasing*
Steve Parkinson, *Engineer*
EMP: 100
SALES (corp-wide): 22.9MM **Privately Held**
WEB: www.capewell.com
SIC: 3429 3423 3634 Parachute hardware; hand & edge tools; blowers, portable, electric
PA: Crrc, Llc
   105 Nutmeg Rd S
   South Windsor CT 06074
   877 684-6464

(G-1698)
CT FINE WOODWORKING
211 Shunpike Rd Ste 4 (06416-1105)
PHONE 860 613-0856
Ernie Lacore, *Owner*
EMP: 2 **EST:** 2012
SALES (est): 278.4K **Privately Held**
SIC: 2431 Millwork

(G-1699)
DANE MILLETTE
Also Called: Dynamic Print Management
15 Robertson Rd (06416-1045)
PHONE 860 635-6383
Dane Millette, *Owner*
EMP: 1 **EST:** 1997
SALES (est): 59.5K **Privately Held**
SIC: 2752 Commercial printing, lithographic

(G-1700)
DEEP RIVER DISTILLERS LLC
10 Bellaire Mnr (06416-2105)
PHONE 860 788-6061
EMP: 2
SALES (est): 70.4K **Privately Held**
SIC: 2085 Distilled & blended liquors

(G-1701)
FUSION ONE INDUSTRIES INC
6 Sydney Ln (06416-1135)
PHONE 860 992-4377
Joe Kobos, *President*
EMP: 1
SALES: 35K **Privately Held**
SIC: 3751 Motorcycles & related parts

(G-1702)
GKN ARSPACE SVCS STRCTURES LLC
1000 Corporate Row (06416-2074)
PHONE 860 613-0236
David Olchowski, *CEO*
Alex Cassarino, *Engineer*
Megan Voelker, *Engineer*
Colleen Mulryan, *Human Res Mgr*
Lori Rece, *Sales Mgr*
EMP: 135
SQ FT: 28,500
SALES (est): 39MM
SALES (corp-wide): 11B **Privately Held**
SIC: 3724 Aircraft engines & engine parts
HQ: Gkn Limited
   Po Box 4128
   Redditch WORCS
   152 751-7715

(G-1703)
HANGER PRSTHETCS & ORTHO INC
10 Countyline Dr (06416-1175)
PHONE 860 667-5300
Dennis Huysman, *Branch Mgr*
EMP: 7
SALES (corp-wide): 1B **Publicly Held**
SIC: 3842 Surgical appliances & supplies
HQ: Hanger Prosthetics & Orthotics, Inc.
   10910 Domain Dr Ste 300
   Austin TX 78758
   512 777-3800

(G-1704)
HEW PUBLISHING LLC ✪
5 Redwood Ct (06416-1735)
PHONE 860 514-2045
Brian J Wilcox, *Principal*
EMP: 1 **EST:** 2019
SALES (est): 37.5K **Privately Held**
SIC: 2741 Miscellaneous publishing

(G-1705)
HORTON BRASSES INC
49 Nooks Hill Rd (06416-1561)
P.O. Box 95 (06416-0095)
PHONE 860 635-4400
Orion Henderson, *President*
▲ **EMP:** 9
SQ FT: 21,440
SALES: 2MM **Privately Held**
WEB: www.horton-brasses.com
SIC: 3429 Cabinet hardware; furniture hardware

(G-1706)
LITURGICAL PUBLICATIONS INC
5 Progress Dr (06416-1096)
PHONE 860 635-9560
Don Samuels, *Purch Mgr*
Oliver Marcantonio, *Marketing Staff*
Patrick Reinhard, *Manager*
EMP: 1
SALES (corp-wide): 103.5MM **Privately Held**
WEB: www.mylpi.com
SIC: 2721 2752 Periodicals; commercial printing, lithographic
PA: Liturgical Publications, Inc.
   2875 S James Dr
   New Berlin WI 53151
   262 785-1188

(G-1707)
MALLERY LUMBER INC
162 West St (06416-4404)
PHONE 860 632-3505
EMP: 2 **EST:** 2010
SALES (est): 190K **Privately Held**
SIC: 2421 5031 Hardwood Sawmill Kilns And Wholesaler Of Lumber

(G-1708)
NEW ENGLAND MACHINING LLC
18 Senator Dr (06416-1658)
PHONE 860 301-9434
EMP: 2
SALES (est): 205.3K **Privately Held**
SIC: 3599 Machine shop, jobbing & repair

(G-1709)
NORTH STAR COMPUTING SVCS LLC
288 Skyview Dr (06416-1874)
P.O. Box 22 (06416-0022)
PHONE 860 635-7117
Eric J Seamon, *Principal*
EMP: 1 **EST:** 2008
SALES (est): 81.3K **Privately Held**
SIC: 7372 Prepackaged software

(G-1710)
NORTHEAST PRINTING NETWOR
135 Sebethe Dr 8 (06416-1033)
PHONE 860 788-3572
Ken Paradis, *Principal*
EMP: 2
SALES (est): 244.9K **Privately Held**
SIC: 2752 Commercial printing, offset

(G-1711)
NORTHEAST QUALITY SERVICES LLC
14 Alcap Rdg (06416-1002)
PHONE 860 632-7242
Ralph Coppola, *President*
Bill Hutchinson, *Sales Staff*
▲ **EMP:** 50
SQ FT: 60,000
SALES (est): 11.7MM **Privately Held**
WEB: www.northeastquality.com
SIC: 3599 Machine shop, jobbing & repair

(G-1712)
NUTRIVENTUS INC
8 Elm Rd (06416-2146)
PHONE 860 990-9324
Carey Ramm, *President*
EMP: 1
SALES (est): 43.6K **Privately Held**
SIC: 2099 Food preparations

(G-1713)
ONE SOURCE PRINT AND PROMO LLC
150 Salem Dr (06416-1239)
PHONE 860 635-3257
John Hunter, *Principal*
EMP: 4
SALES (est): 360.5K **Privately Held**
SIC: 2752 Commercial printing, offset

(G-1714)
R & K COOKIES LLC
9 Smith Farm Rd (06416-2492)
PHONE 860 613-2893
Prashant Dave, *Principal*
EMP: 4
SALES (est): 203.5K **Privately Held**
SIC: 2052 Cookies

(G-1715)
RIPLEY TOOLS LLC (PA)
46 Nooks Hill Rd (06416-1562)
PHONE 860 635-2200
Richard Potash, *Warehouse Mgr*
Craig Tooker, *Opers Staff*
Brian Bourgoin, *Engineer*
Richard Brooks, *Sales Staff*
Robert G McCreary III,
EMP: 27
SALES (est): 4.9MM **Privately Held**
SIC: 3643 5063 4841 Current-carrying wiring devices; wiring devices; cable & other pay television services

(G-1716)
RUNWAY LIQUIDATION LLC
Also Called: Bcbg
2510 E 15th St (06416)
PHONE 202 865-3311
EMP: 2
SALES (corp-wide): 570.1MM **Privately Held**
SIC: 2335 Women's, juniors' & misses' dresses
HQ: Runway Liquidation, Llc
   2761 Fruitland Ave
   Vernon CA 90054
   323 589-2224

(G-1717)
RWK TOOL INC
200 Corporate Row (06416-2029)
PHONE 860 635-0116
William Buggie, *President*
Kenneth Buggie, *Vice Pres*
Robert V Buggie, *Director*
Donna Buggie, *Admin Sec*
EMP: 22 **EST:** 1978
SQ FT: 49,000
SALES (est): 3MM **Privately Held**
SIC: 3599 Machine shop, jobbing & repair

(G-1718)
SERGE & FRIENDS LLC
34 Winthrop Blvd (06416-1259)
PHONE 860 526-3882
Serg Pavlov, *Mng Member*
EMP: 2
SALES (est): 192.1K **Privately Held**
SIC: 2211 Canvas

(G-1719)
SIGN BY GREUBEL
1100 Corporate Row (06416-2082)
PHONE 860 632-2573
Duane Greubel, *Owner*
EMP: 1
SALES (est): 113.9K **Privately Held**
SIC: 3993 Signs & advertising specialties

(G-1720)
SUPERIOR PLAS EXTRUSION CO INC
154 West St (06416-4400)
PHONE 860 234-1864
EMP: 3
SALES (est): 274.2K
SALES (corp-wide): 12.6MM **Privately Held**
SIC: 3081 Plastic film & sheet
PA: Superior Plastics Extrusion Company, Inc.
   5 Highland Dr
   Putnam CT 06260
   860 963-1976

(G-1721)
TRAXX SOFTWARE LLC
1 Pleasant St (06416-2323)
PHONE 860 632-8712
Felix Rodriguez, *Principal*
EMP: 2
SALES (est): 97.9K **Privately Held**
SIC: 7372 Prepackaged software

(G-1722)
TRUE INSPIRATION LLC
20 Timber Hill Rd (06416-2259)
PHONE 860 635-7941
Sherry Boutin, *Principal*

Cromwell - Middlesex County (G-1723)

EMP: 2
SALES (est): 136.8K **Privately Held**
SIC: **2759** Commercial printing

(G-1723)
UNIQUE EXTRUSIONS INCORPORATED
10 Countyline Dr (06416-1175)
PHONE 860 632-1314
Robert M Tabshey, *President*
John Rankin, *General Mgr*
Lauren Dalal, *Corp Secy*
Tami N Tabshey, *Vice Pres*
Kathy Ross, *Treasurer*
▲ EMP: 25
SQ FT: 5,600
SALES (est): 10MM **Privately Held**
WEB: www.uniqueextrusions.com
SIC: **3354** Aluminum extruded products

(G-1724)
WHAT A LIFE LLC
Also Called: Up In Smoke
136 Berlin Rd Ste 118 (06416-2600)
PHONE 860 632-1962
Anthony J Tine,
EMP: 1
SQ FT: 1,200
SALES (est): 79K **Privately Held**
SIC: **5812** 2121 Coffee shop; cigars

(G-1725)
XEROX SERVICES
73 Court St (06416-1655)
PHONE 860 883-8377
Jorge Rovirosa, *Principal*
EMP: 1
SALES (est): 82.6K **Privately Held**
SIC: **3861** Photographic equipment & supplies

Danbury
Fairfield County

(G-1726)
A GUIDEPOSTS CHURCH CORP (PA)
Also Called: Peale Ctr For Christn Living
39 Old Ridgebury Rd # 27 (06810-5103)
PHONE 203 749-0203
John F Temple, *President*
Brian Porter, *President*
Heather Dennis, *Vice Pres*
Pablo Diaz, *Vice Pres*
Rocco Martino, *Vice Pres*
EMP: 430
SQ FT: 120,000
SALES (est): 31.6MM **Privately Held**
SIC: **8661** 2721 2731 Churches, temples & shrines; magazines: publishing only, not printed on site; books: publishing only

(G-1727)
A PAPISH INCORPORATED (PA)
Also Called: Papish, Leo & Company
21 Taylor St (06810-6922)
P.O. Box 67 (06813-0067)
PHONE 203 744-0323
Stephen Papish, *President*
Harriet Papish, *Corp Secy*
EMP: 40 EST: 1900
SQ FT: 13,000
SALES (est): 2.5MM **Privately Held**
SIC: **3568** Bearings, plain

(G-1728)
ABB ENTERPRISE SOFTWARE INC
24 Commerce Dr (06810-4131)
PHONE 203 790-8588
Tishore Sundararajan, *Manager*
EMP: 76
SALES (corp-wide): 36.4B **Privately Held**
SIC: **3612** Transformers, except electric
HQ: Abb Inc.
    305 Gregson Dr
    Cary NC 27511

(G-1729)
ABB ENTERPRISE SOFTWARE INC
A B B Control
152 Deer Hill Ave Ste 304 (06810-7766)
PHONE 203 798-6210
E Santacana, *Vice Pres*
EMP: 25
SALES (corp-wide): 36.4B **Privately Held**
WEB: www.elsterelectricity.com
SIC: **3625** Motor controls, electric
HQ: Abb Inc.
    305 Gregson Dr
    Cary NC 27511

(G-1730)
ACCUTROL LLC
21 Commerce Dr (06810-4131)
PHONE 203 445-9991
Fred George, *Principal*
O'Rourke Brian, *VP Engrg*
EMP: 31
SALES (est): 5.4MM **Privately Held**
SIC: **3599** Air intake filters, internal combustion engine, except auto

(G-1731)
ACUREN INSPECTION INC (HQ)
Also Called: Hellier
30 Main St Ste 402 (06810-3004)
PHONE 203 702-8740
Peter Scannell, *President*
Peter O Scannell, *President*
John P Lockwood, *Vice Pres*
Joby Suarez, *Marketing Staff*
Jim Gustafson, *Manager*
EMP: 532 EST: 1976
SQ FT: 30,000
SALES (est): 1.4B
SALES (corp-wide): 1.7B **Privately Held**
WEB: www.hellierndt.com
SIC: **1389** 8071 Testing, measuring, surveying & analysis services; testing laboratories
PA: Rockwood Service Corporation
    43 Arch St
    Greenwich CT 06830
    203 869-6734

(G-1732)
ADVANCED TECHNOLOGY MTLS INC (DH)
7 Commerce Dr (06810-4131)
PHONE 203 794-1100
Bertrand Loy, *President*
Tim Carlson, *Exec VP*
Dan Sharkey, *Exec VP*
Christian F Kramer, *Senior VP*
Mario Philips, *Senior VP*
▲ EMP: 1
SALES (est): 238.4K
SALES (corp-wide): 1.5B **Publicly Held**
SIC: **3674** Semiconductors & related devices
HQ: Entegris Professional Solutions, Inc.
    7 Commerce Dr
    Danbury CT 06810
    203 794-1100

(G-1733)
AIRGAS USA LLC
50 Mill Plain Rd (06811-5140)
PHONE 203 792-1834
Andrew Cichocki, *Branch Mgr*
EMP: 227
SALES (corp-wide): 125.9MM **Privately Held**
SIC: **5084** 5085 5169 2813 Welding machinery & equipment; welding supplies; chemicals & allied products; industrial gases
HQ: Airgas Usa, Llc
    259 N Radnor Chester Rd
    Radnor PA 19087
    610 687-5253

(G-1734)
AJ WOOD WORK LLC
17 South Ave Apt A (06810-8013)
PHONE 203 826-9851
Alesandro G Bourguignon, *Owner*
EMP: 2
SALES (est): 146.3K **Privately Held**
SIC: **2431** Millwork

(G-1735)
ALL STAR WELDING & DEM LLC
Also Called: Allstar Welding and Demolition
50 Shelter Rock Rd (06810-7089)
PHONE 203 948-0528
John Pasquence, *Owner*
EMP: 2
SALES (est): 374K **Privately Held**
SIC: **1799** 5093 3715 3446 Welding on site; metal scrap & waste materials; truck trailers; architectural metalwork; fabricated structural metal; wrecking & demolition work

(G-1736)
ALL TECH AUTO/TRUCK ELECTRIC
36 Kenosia Ave Ste B (06810-7392)
PHONE 203 790-8990
Joe Fiore, *President*
Bill Williams, *Vice Pres*
EMP: 4
SQ FT: 3,600
SALES (est): 664.9K **Privately Held**
SIC: **3694** 7538 3714 Engine electrical equipment; ignition apparatus & distributors; alternators, automotive; generators, automotive & aircraft; general automotive repair shops; motor vehicle electrical equipment

(G-1737)
ALLIED SINTERINGS INCORPORATED
29 Briar Ridge Rd (06810-7248)
PHONE 203 743-7502
Mark Foster, *President*
Diana Foster, *Admin Sec*
Natalie Garrick, *Assistant*
EMP: 32 EST: 1959
SQ FT: 15,000
SALES (est): 7.3MM **Privately Held**
WEB: www.alliedsinterings.com
SIC: **3399** Powder, metal

(G-1738)
ALTERNATE ENERGY FUTURES
3121 Avalon Valley Dr (06810-4051)
PHONE 917 745-7097
Brian Kirk,
Steve Miller,
Kevin Richardson,
EMP: 5
SALES (est): 380K **Privately Held**
SIC: **1311** 7389 Crude petroleum & natural gas;

(G-1739)
AMPHENOL CORPORATION
Also Called: Amphenol Rf
4 Old Newtown Rd Ste 2 (06810-6221)
PHONE 203 743-9272
Mark Cunningham, *General Mgr*
Dennis Nesterov, *Business Mgr*
Sam Kom, *Mfg Staff*
Bo Chen, *Purch Agent*
Vickie Hills, *Buyer*
EMP: 150
SALES (corp-wide): 8.2B **Publicly Held**
WEB: www.amphenolrf.com
SIC: **3678** Electronic connectors
PA: Amphenol Corporation
    358 Hall Ave
    Wallingford CT 06492
    203 265-8900

(G-1740)
ANDECO SOFTWARE LLC
14 South St Unit 9 (06810-8152)
PHONE 225 229-2491
Paul Therrien, *Principal*
EMP: 2
SALES (est): 81.5K **Privately Held**
SIC: **7372** Prepackaged software

(G-1741)
APPLIED ADVERTISING INC
71 Newtown Rd Ste 5 (06810-6251)
PHONE 860 640-0800
Jason D Bergeron, *President*
Denise Guzman, *CFO*
EMP: 10

SALES (est): 1.5MM **Privately Held**
WEB: www.appliedadvertisinginc.com
SIC: **3993** 7319 7311 Electric signs; transit advertising services; advertising consultant

(G-1742)
APPLIED LASER SOLUTIONS INC
28 Commerce Dr (06810-4131)
P.O. Box 1217 (06813-1217)
PHONE 203 739-0179
Edward Standke, *President*
Michele Standke, *Admin Sec*
EMP: 8
SQ FT: 22,000
SALES (est): 1.6MM **Privately Held**
WEB: www.appliedlasersolutions.net
SIC: **3441** Fabricated structural metal

(G-1743)
ARABIC BREAD BAKERY
13 Well Ave Fl 2 (06810-6301)
PHONE 203 743-4743
Nuhad Haddah, *Partner*
Eli Haddad, *Partner*
EMP: 2
SALES (est): 163.7K **Privately Held**
WEB: www.shamra.com
SIC: **2051** Bread, all types (white, wheat, rye, etc): fresh or frozen

(G-1744)
ARMOR ALL/STP PRODUCTS COMPANY (DH)
44 Old Ridgebury Rd # 300 (06810-5107)
PHONE 203 205-2900
Guy J Andrysick, *President*
Nathan Fagre, *Vice Pres*
◆ EMP: 5
SALES (est): 1.2MM
SALES (corp-wide): 3.1B **Publicly Held**
SIC: **5172** 2842 Fuel oil; automobile polish

(G-1745)
ARMOR ALL/STP PRODUCTS COMPANY
Global Auto Care, The
44 Old Ridgebury Rd (06810-5107)
PHONE 203 205-2900
EMP: 2
SALES (corp-wide): 3.1B **Publicly Held**
SIC: **2842** Automobile polish
HQ: The Armor All/Stp Products Company
    44 Old Ridgebury Rd # 300
    Danbury CT 06810
    203 205-2900

(G-1746)
ARMORED AUTOGROUP INC (DH)
Also Called: Armored Auto Group
44 Old Ridgebury Rd # 300 (06810-5107)
PHONE 203 205-2900
Michael Klein, *CEO*
David P Lundstedt, *Ch of Bd*
Guy J Andrysick, *President*
Michael K Bauersfeld, *Exec VP*
J Andrew Bolt, *CFO*
◆ EMP: 60
SQ FT: 18,819
SALES: 298.1MM
SALES (corp-wide): 3.1B **Publicly Held**
SIC: **3714** Motor vehicle parts & accessories

(G-1747)
ARMORED AUTOGROUP PARENT INC (DH)
44 Old Ridgebury Rd # 300 (06810-5107)
PHONE 203 205-2900
Michael Klein, *CEO*
Andy Bolt, *CFO*
EMP: 7 EST: 2010
SALES (est): 149.1K
SALES (corp-wide): 3.1B **Publicly Held**
SIC: **2842** 2911 2899 Automobile polish; fuel additives; chemical preparations

(G-1748)
ARMORED AUTOGROUP SALES INC
44 Old Ridgebury Rd # 300 (06810-5107)
PHONE 203 205-2900

Heather Clefisch, *President*
EMP: 182 **EST:** 2010
SALES (est): 81K
SALES (corp-wide): 3.1B **Publicly Held**
SIC: 3714 Motor vehicle parts & accessories
HQ: Armored Autogroup Inc.
 44 Old Ridgebury Rd # 300
 Danbury CT 06810

(G-1749)
BAGELMAN III INC
40 1/2 Padanaram Rd (06811-4840)
PHONE..............................203 792-0030
Mark L Froehlich, *President*
Valerie Froehlich, *Vice Pres*
EMP: 10
SQ FT: 2,800
SALES (est): 272.3K **Privately Held**
SIC: 5812 2052 Delicatessen (eating places); bakery products, dry

(G-1750)
BEDOUKIAN RESEARCH INC (PA)
6 Commerce Dr (06810-4131)
PHONE..............................203 830-4000
Robert H Bedoukian, *President*
Izzy Heller, *General Mgr*
Ben Silidjian, *Opers Mgr*
Michael Cuan, *Production*
Caryn Hasseltine, *Human Res Mgr*
▲ **EMP:** 42
SQ FT: 44,000
SALES (est): 17.4MM **Privately Held**
WEB: www.bedoukian.com
SIC: 2844 2869 2879 Concentrates, perfume; flavors or flavoring materials, synthetic; insecticides & pesticides

(G-1751)
BEGELL HOUSE INC
50 North St (06810-5664)
PHONE..............................203 456-6161
Yelena Shafeyeva, *President*
Vivian Wang, *President*
Vicky Lipowski, *Vice Pres*
Harpal Gill, *Sales Mgr*
Lolly Madden, *Marketing Staff*
EMP: 10
SALES (est): 1.2MM **Privately Held**
SIC: 2731 Books: publishing only

(G-1752)
BELIMO AIRCONTROLS (USA) INC (HQ)
Also Called: Belimo Air Controls USA
33 Turner Rd (06810-5101)
P.O. Box 2928 (06813-2928)
PHONE..............................800 543-9038
Alexander Van Der Weerd, *President*
David Hauser, *Engineer*
David Liss, *Engineer*
John Coppola, *CFO*
Robert Greco, *Controller*
◆ **EMP:** 115
SQ FT: 44,000
SALES (est): 68.8MM
SALES (corp-wide): 646.4MM **Privately Held**
SIC: 3822 5075 3625 Refrigeration/air-conditioning defrost controls; humidifiers, except portable; relays & industrial controls
PA: Belimo Holding Ag
 Brunnenbachstrasse 1
 Hinwil ZH
 438 436-111

(G-1753)
BELIMO AUTOMATION AG
33 Turner Rd (06810-5101)
PHONE..............................203 749-3319
Andreas Steiner, *President*
Alan Bolduc, *Manager*
Steve Rybka, *Manager*
Brent Kidd, *Technical Staff*
Beat Trutmann, *Admin Sec*
▲ **EMP:** 13
SALES (est): 2.3MM **Privately Held**
SIC: 3822 Refrigeration/air-conditioning defrost controls

(G-1754)
BELIMO CUSTOMIZATION USA INC
33 Turner Rd (06810-5101)
PHONE..............................203 791-9915
Lars Van Der Haegen, *President*
Philip Alesi, *Production*
Beat Trutmann, *Admin Sec*
▲ **EMP:** 5
SALES (est): 1.2MM
SALES (corp-wide): 646.4MM **Privately Held**
SIC: 3822 5075 3625 Refrigeration/air-conditioning defrost controls; humidifiers, except portable; relays & industrial controls
HQ: Belimo Aircontrols (Usa), Inc.
 33 Turner Rd
 Danbury CT 06810
 800 543-9038

(G-1755)
BELLE IMPRESSION PUBG INC
404 Larson Dr (06810-7371)
PHONE..............................203 826-5426
Lindsay Janet, *Principal*
EMP: 2 **EST:** 2013
SALES (est): 111.3K **Privately Held**
SIC: 2741 Miscellaneous publishing

(G-1756)
BEST IN BACKYARDS (PA)
66 Sugar Hollow Rd (06810-7530)
PHONE..............................203 917-4381
Frank Piper, *President*
EMP: 1
SALES (est): 158.2K **Privately Held**
SIC: 3496 Grilles & grillework, woven wire

(G-1757)
BLACK PLTNUM MNS ESSNTIALS LLC
47 Rocky Glen Rd (06810-8003)
PHONE..............................203 501-3768
Carleen Cole, *President*
EMP: 1 **EST:** 2012
SALES (est): 57.1K **Privately Held**
SIC: 2844 Lotions, shaving; perfumes, natural or synthetic; shampoos, rinses, conditioners: hair; bath salts

(G-1758)
BLUE PRINT
42 White St (06810-6640)
PHONE..............................203 948-3883
Marvin Shepard, *Principal*
EMP: 2
SALES (est): 167.8K **Privately Held**
SIC: 2752 Commercial printing, lithographic

(G-1759)
BRANSON ULTRASONICS CORP (DH)
41 Eagle Rd Ste 1 (06810-4179)
P.O. Box 1961 (06813-1961)
PHONE..............................203 796-0400
E Joe Dillon, *President*
Jon Piasecki, *President*
Robert Tibbetts, *Vice Pres*
Louis Testa, *Engineer*
Nitin Phadnis, *Manager*
▲ **EMP:** 275 **EST:** 1965
SQ FT: 200,000
SALES (est): 170.5MM
SALES (corp-wide): 17.4B **Publicly Held**
WEB: www.bransonic.com
SIC: 3699 3548 3541 Welding machines & equipment, ultrasonic; cleaning equipment, ultrasonic, except medical & dental; welding apparatus; machine tools, metal cutting type
HQ: Emerson Electric (U.S.) Holding Corporation
 850 Library Ave Ste 204c
 Saint Louis MO 63136
 314 553-2000

(G-1760)
C N C ROUTER TECHNOLOGIES
4 Barnard Dr (06810-8401)
PHONE..............................203 744-6651
Bill Lounsbury, *Owner*
Jill Lounsberg, *Owner*
EMP: 5
SALES (est): 260K **Privately Held**
SIC: 2499 Decorative wood & woodwork

(G-1761)
CAM2 TECHNOLOGIES LLC
6 Finance Dr (06810-4132)
PHONE..............................203 456-3025
Craig Markleski, *Principal*
EMP: 4
SALES (est): 635.6K **Privately Held**
SIC: 3826 Infrared analytical instruments; analytical optical instruments

(G-1762)
CANDLEWOOD STARS INC
Also Called: Mega Resveratrol
60 Newtown Rd Ste 32 (06810-6257)
PHONE..............................203 994-8826
Doron Efrat, *President*
EMP: 7
SALES (est): 500K **Privately Held**
SIC: 2833 Medicinals & botanicals

(G-1763)
CAPITAL DESIGN & ENGRG INC
Also Called: Cde
35 Eagle Rd Ste 2 (06810-4177)
PHONE..............................203 798-6027
Len Staib, *President*
Mike Staib, *Treasurer*
Anita J Staib, *Director*
Scott Staib, *Admin Sec*
EMP: 5
SQ FT: 4,200
SALES (est): 800K **Privately Held**
WEB: www.cdeinc.net
SIC: 3599 Machine shop, jobbing & repair

(G-1764)
CECI PRINTER LLC
19 Germantown Rd Fl 2 (06810-5013)
PHONE..............................203 994-6314
Celia C Galarza, *Principal*
EMP: 2 **EST:** 2018
SALES (est): 100.1K **Privately Held**
SIC: 2752 Commercial printing, lithographic

(G-1765)
CELB LLC
11 Mountainville Ave (06810-7931)
PHONE..............................203 739-0157
Carlos Brasil, *Manager*
EMP: 3
SALES (est): 136.9K **Privately Held**
SIC: 0781 3647 7389 Landscape services; parking lights, automotive;

(G-1766)
CHEM-TRON PNTG PWDR CATING INC
92 Taylor St (06810-6986)
PHONE..............................203 743-5131
Michael Showah, *President*
EMP: 4
SALES (est): 376.4K **Privately Held**
SIC: 3479 Coating of metals & formed products

(G-1767)
CHEMICAL-ELECTRIC CORPORATION
Also Called: Chem-Tron
92 Taylor St (06810-6947)
P.O. Box 303 (06813-0303)
PHONE..............................203 743-5131
Samuel P Showah, *President*
Michael Showah, *Vice Pres*
EMP: 5 **EST:** 1965
SQ FT: 9,000
SALES (est): 577.2K **Privately Held**
SIC: 3471 Anodizing (plating) of metals or formed products

(G-1768)
CIFC EARLY LRNG PROGRAMS/WIC
80 Main St (06810-7832)
PHONE..............................203 206-6341
EMP: 1
SALES (est): 57.5K **Privately Held**
SIC: 2621 Bristols

(G-1769)
CLICROI LLC
13 Caldwell Ter (06810-5193)
PHONE..............................203 599-1237
Nelson Merchan, *President*
EMP: 1 **EST:** 2006
SQ FT: 100
SALES: 350K **Privately Held**
SIC: 2759 Advertising literature: printing

(G-1770)
CLOUD CAP TECHNOLOGY INC
Also Called: Isr Systems
100 Wooster Hts (06810-7509)
PHONE..............................541 308-1089
EMP: 8
SALES (corp-wide): 66.5B **Publicly Held**
SIC: 8711 3812 Consulting engineer; search & navigation equipment
HQ: Cloud Cap Technology, Inc.
 202 Wasco Loop Ste 103
 Hood River OR 97031
 541 387-2120

(G-1771)
COMMUNICATION NETWORKS LLC
3 Corporate Dr (06810-4166)
PHONE..............................203 796-5300
Andrew Acquarulo, *President*
George J Lichtblau, *Chairman*
Tony Lau, *Regional Mgr*
Jaiprakash Vappala, *Regional Mgr*
Peggy Hayes, *Vice Pres*
▲ **EMP:** 48
SALES (est): 15.9MM **Privately Held**
SIC: 3661 Fiber optics communications equipment

(G-1772)
COMUNIDADE NEWS
4 Laurel St (06810-5321)
PHONE..............................203 730-0175
Bremo Damada, *Director*
Lucio Salsa, *Director*
EMP: 4
SALES (est): 125.3K **Privately Held**
SIC: 2711 Newspapers, publishing & printing

(G-1773)
CONOPTICS INC
19 Eagle Rd (06810-4127)
PHONE..............................203 743-3349
Ronald Pizzo, *President*
Richard Kocka, *Exec VP*
Chay Wong, *Purch Dir*
Charles Dooley, *Senior Engr*
EMP: 15 **EST:** 1981
SQ FT: 9,000
SALES (est): 3MM **Privately Held**
WEB: www.conoptics.com
SIC: 3827 Optical instruments & apparatus

(G-1774)
COOPER MARKETING GROUP INC
41 Eagle Rd Ste 2 (06810-8802)
PHONE..............................203 797-9386
David Cooper, *President*
EMP: 6
SQ FT: 4,000
SALES: 1.5MM **Privately Held**
SIC: 2053 Frozen bakery products, except bread

(G-1775)
CORPORATE AIRCRAFT SVCS LLC
38 Maplewood Dr (06811-4211)
PHONE..............................203 730-2024
Arthur Jack Stockman, *President*
EMP: 1
SALES (est): 110.4K **Privately Held**
SIC: 3721 Autogiros

(G-1776)
CORPORATE FLIGHT MGT INC
53 Miry Brook Rd (06810-7408)
PHONE..............................203 826-9224
David Lucas, *Exec VP*
Annette Morton, *Vice Pres*
EMP: 2

SALES (corp-wide): 70MM **Privately Held**
SIC: 3812 Aircraft/aerospace flight instruments & guidance systems
PA: Corporate Flight Management, Inc.
808 Blue Angel Way
Smyrna TN 37167
615 220-1761

(G-1777)
COUPON MAGAZINE PUBLISHERS INC
31 Corn Tassle Rd (06811-3208)
PHONE 561 676-6498
Michael Tagliafer, *Director*
EMP: 1
SALES (est): 37.5K **Privately Held**
SIC: 2741 Miscellaneous publishing

(G-1778)
CTR WELDING
39 Padanaram Rd (06811-3701)
PHONE 704 473-1587
Rick Kaufman, *Principal*
EMP: 5
SALES (est): 89.2K **Privately Held**
SIC: 7692 Welding repair

(G-1779)
CUSTOM ART SGNS LLC
34 Tamarack Ave (06811)
PHONE 203 837-7674
Aileen S Passaretti, *Principal*
EMP: 1 EST: 2007
SALES (est): 76.7K **Privately Held**
SIC: 3993 Signs & advertising specialties

(G-1780)
CUSTOM DESIGN SERVICE CORP
6 Ohehyahtah Pl (06810-7668)
P.O. Box 518 (06813-0518)
PHONE 203 748-1105
Suzanne Vetter, *President*
Sheila Vetter, *Treasurer*
EMP: 4
SALES: 1MM **Privately Held**
WEB: www.cdscorp.us
SIC: 3672 Printed circuit boards

(G-1781)
CZITEK LLC
4 Ford Ln (06811-4614)
PHONE 888 326-8186
David W Schiering, *Mng Member*
EMP: 9
SALES (est): 732.7K **Privately Held**
SIC: 3826 Mass spectroscopy instrumentation

(G-1782)
DANBURY GRASSROOTS TENNIS INC
196 Main St (06810-6602)
P.O. Box 2912 (06813-2912)
PHONE 203 797-0500
Carl Bailey, *President*
Arthur Goldblatt, *Corp Secy*
EMP: 2
SALES: 398.2K **Privately Held**
SIC: 7999 3949 Tennis courts, outdoor/indoor: non-membership; tennis professional; tennis equipment & supplies

(G-1783)
DANBURY MEDI-CAR SERVICE INC
14 Walnut St (06811-4821)
PHONE 203 748-3433
Victor De Simone, *President*
Angelo De Simone, *Corp Secy*
Joseph De Simone, *Vice Pres*
Joseph D Simone, *Vice Pres*
EMP: 6
SQ FT: 2,500
SALES: 132K **Privately Held**
SIC: 4119 3842 Ambulance service; surgical appliances & supplies

(G-1784)
DANBURY METAL FINISHING INC
124 West St (06810-6360)
P.O. Box 1175 (06813-1175)
PHONE 203 748-5044
Warren Levy, *President*
Elizabeth Levy, *Corp Secy*
EMP: 6
SQ FT: 2,500
SALES (est): 651.1K **Privately Held**
SIC: 3471 Electroplating of metals or formed products

(G-1785)
DANBURY ORTHO
2 Riverview Dr (06810-6268)
PHONE 203 797-1500
EMP: 3 EST: 2017
SALES (est): 293.8K **Privately Held**
SIC: 3842 Surgical appliances & supplies

(G-1786)
DANBURY POWERSPORTS INC
41 Lake Avenue Ext (06811-5247)
PHONE 203 791-1310
Frank Chamberlain, *President*
Teresa Hearty, *Manager*
EMP: 13 EST: 1998
SALES (est): 3.3MM **Privately Held**
WEB: www.danburypowersports.com
SIC: 5571 3799 Motorcycles; all terrain vehicles (ATV)

(G-1787)
DANBURY SQUARE BOX COMPANY
1a Broad St (06810-6204)
PHONE 203 744-4611
Chris Ann Allen, *President*
Michael Allen, *Vice Pres*
EMP: 22 EST: 1906
SQ FT: 37,000
SALES: 5.5MM **Privately Held**
SIC: 2653 Boxes, corrugated: made from purchased materials

(G-1788)
DANBURY WELDING LLC
26 New St Apt 1 (06810-6520)
PHONE 203 482-9306
Joselito Yunga, *Principal*
EMP: 1
SALES (est): 26.3K **Privately Held**
SIC: 7692 Welding repair

(G-1789)
DAVIS TREE & LOGGING LLC
57 North St Ste 209 (06810-5627)
PHONE 203 938-2153
Peter Davis,
EMP: 27
SQ FT: 10,000
SALES (est): 1.9MM **Privately Held**
SIC: 0783 2411 0782 Ornamental shrub & tree services; logging; lawn & garden services

(G-1790)
DEFABRICATIONS LLC
39 Rockwood Ln (06811-2718)
PHONE 203 791-1407
Paul Defabritis, *Manager*
EMP: 2
SALES (est): 204.8K **Privately Held**
SIC: 3399 Primary metal products

(G-1791)
DEFENSE CMMNICATIONS SOLUTIONS
11 Autumn Dr (06811-2725)
P.O. Box 3145 (06813-3145)
PHONE 203 947-6283
Colleen Moles, *Owner*
EMP: 2
SALES (est): 102.4K **Privately Held**
SIC: 3679 Electronic components

(G-1792)
DELCOM PRODUCTS INC
45 Backus Ave (06810-7328)
PHONE 914 934-5170
Doug Lovett, *Principal*
EMP: 8
SALES (est): 1MM **Privately Held**
WEB: www.delcom-eng.com
SIC: 8711 3674 Electrical or electronic engineering; solid state electronic devices

(G-1793)
DESIGNS IN STITCHES EMBROIDERY
11 Frandon Dr (06811-3117)
PHONE 203 730-1013
Margaret Williams, *Owner*
EMP: 1
SALES (est): 61K **Privately Held**
SIC: 2395 Embroidery products, except schiffli machine

(G-1794)
DFS IN-HOME SERVICES
15 Great Pasture Rd (06810-8127)
PHONE 845 405-6464
Roman Abreu, *Principal*
EMP: 4
SALES (est): 210.2K **Privately Held**
SIC: 3089 5033 Gutters (glass fiber reinforced), fiberglass or plastic; roofing & siding materials

(G-1795)
DIBA INDUSTRIES INC (HQ)
4 Precision Rd (06810-7317)
PHONE 203 744-0773
Charles E Dubois, *CEO*
Timothy O'Sullivan, *President*
John Cronin, *General Mgr*
Chris Becker, *Business Mgr*
Mick Pearson, *VP Opers*
EMP: 103
SQ FT: 36,000
SALES (est): 19.8MM
SALES (corp-wide): 1.5B **Privately Held**
WEB: www.dibaind.com
SIC: 3823 3498 3083 Fluidic devices, circuits & systems for process control; fabricated pipe & fittings; laminated plastics plate & sheet
PA: Halma Public Limited Company
Misbourne Court
Amersham BUCKS HP7 0
149 472-1111

(G-1796)
DIVERSIFIED PRINTING SOLUTIONS
128 E Liberty St (06810-6767)
PHONE 203 826-7198
EMP: 3 EST: 2015
SALES (est): 107.2K **Privately Held**
SIC: 2759 Commercial printing

(G-1797)
DMT SOLUTIONS GLOBAL CORP
Also Called: Bluecrest
37 Executive Dr (06810-4147)
PHONE 203 233-6231
Grant Miller, *President*
EMP: 1300
SALES (est): 440MM **Privately Held**
SIC: 7372 Prepackaged software

(G-1798)
DOCTORS OF OPTOMETRY
7 Backus Ave (06810-7422)
PHONE 203 743-9897
Ivan Wong, *Principal*
EMP: 3
SALES (est): 59.5K **Privately Held**
SIC: 8042 5048 3827 Offices & clinics of optometrists; contact lenses; optical instruments & lenses

(G-1799)
DRS LEONARDO INC
21 South St Nn (06810-8147)
PHONE 203 798-3172
Elias C David, *Engineer*
Paul Naiden, *Engineer*
EMP: 28
SALES (corp-wide): 9.2B **Privately Held**
SIC: 3812 Search & navigation equipment
HQ: Leonardo Drs, Inc.
2345 Crystal Dr Ste 1000
Arlington VA 22202
703 416-8000

(G-1800)
DRS NAVAL POWER SYSTEMS INC
21 South St (06810-8147)
PHONE 203 798-3000
Mark Newmann, *Branch Mgr*
Bill Theobald, *Manager*
EMP: 478
SALES (corp-wide): 9.2B **Privately Held**
SIC: 3812 Nautical instruments
HQ: Drs Naval Power Systems, Inc
4265 N 30th St
Milwaukee WI 53216
414 875-4314

(G-1801)
DRS NAVAL POWER SYSTEMS INC
21 South St (06810-8147)
PHONE 203 798-3000
Mark Newmann, *Branch Mgr*
EMP: 478
SALES (corp-wide): 9.2B **Privately Held**
SIC: 3823 Nuclear reactor controls
HQ: Drs Naval Power Systems, Inc
4265 N 30th St
Milwaukee WI 53216
414 875-4314

(G-1802)
DRUG IMPRMENT DTCTION SVCS LLC
Also Called: Streetime Technologies
71 Newtown Rd (06810-6258)
PHONE 203 616-3735
Christopher Crucilla, *CEO*
EMP: 5
SALES (est): 1.3MM **Privately Held**
WEB: www.passpoint.org
SIC: 4813 7372 7389 ; ; application computer software;

(G-1803)
ECONOMY PRINTING & COPY CENTER (PA)
128 E Liberty St Ste 4 (06810-6682)
PHONE 203 792-5610
Paul Dewitt, *Owner*
EMP: 3 EST: 1973
SQ FT: 600
SALES (est): 989.6K **Privately Held**
SIC: 2752 7334 Commercial printing, offset; photocopying & duplicating services

(G-1804)
EDUCATIONAL REFERENCE PUBLISHI
13 Lindencrest Dr (06811-4217)
PHONE 203 797-1517
Doris Castagno, *Principal*
EMP: 1
SALES (est): 66.6K **Privately Held**
SIC: 2741 Miscellaneous publishing

(G-1805)
EMC FUN FACTORY INC
7 Backus Ave (06810-7422)
PHONE 914 837-2899
EMP: 2
SALES (est): 85.9K **Privately Held**
SIC: 3572 Computer storage devices

(G-1806)
EMHART TEKNOLOGIES LLC
Heli-Coil Co
4 Shelter Rock Rd (06810)
PHONE 877 364-2781
John Huntley, *Branch Mgr*
EMP: 5
SALES (corp-wide): 13.9B **Publicly Held**
SIC: 3559 Semiconductor manufacturing machinery
HQ: Emhart Teknologies Llc
480 Myrtle St
New Britain CT 06053
800 783-6427

(G-1807)
EMHART TEKNOLOGIES LLC
Emhart Fastening Teknologies
Shelter Rock (06810)
PHONE 203 790-5000
John Carvalho, *Branch Mgr*
EMP: 30
SALES (corp-wide): 13.9B **Publicly Held**
WEB: www.helicoil.com
SIC: 3541 Machine tools, metal cutting type

GEOGRAPHIC SECTION   Danbury - Fairfield County (G-1833)

HQ: Emhart Teknologies Llc
480 Myrtle St
New Britain CT 06053
800 783-6427

(G-1808)
EMHART TEKNOLOGIES LLC
Also Called: Stanley Engineered Fastening
4 Shelter Rock Ln (06810-8159)
PHONE..................877 364-2781
Ricardo Gonzales, *Branch Mgr*
EMP: 2
SALES (corp-wide): 13.9B **Publicly Held**
SIC: 7389 3442 Metal cutting services; rolling doors for industrial buildings or warehouses, metal
HQ: Emhart Teknologies Llc
480 Myrtle St
New Britain CT 06053
800 783-6427

(G-1809)
EMOSYN AMERICA INC
7 Commerce Dr (06810-4131)
PHONE..................203 794-1100
Nick Wood, *President*
EMP: 40
SALES (est): 2.3MM
SALES (corp-wide): 5.3B **Publicly Held**
SIC: 3674 Semiconductors & related devices
HQ: Silicon Storage Technology, Inc.
1020 Kifer Rd
Sunnyvale CA 94086
408 735-9110

(G-1810)
ENDO GRAPHICS INC
41 Kenosia Ave Ste 102 (06810-7360)
PHONE..................203 778-1557
EMP: 6
SQ FT: 2,500
SALES (est): 1.2MM **Privately Held**
SIC: 2796 Pre-Press Graphic

(G-1811)
ENERGY USA INCORPORATED (HQ)
83 Wooster Hts (06810-7548)
PHONE..................203 791-2222
Aki Tsuji, *CEO*
Junichi Hirokawa, *CFO*
EMP: 2
SQ FT: 5,600
SALES (est): 1.2MM **Privately Held**
WEB: www.marubeni.com
SIC: 1094 8742 Uranium-radium-vanadium ores; industrial consultant

(G-1812)
ENS MICROWAVE LLC
37 Ironwood Dr (06811-2703)
PHONE..................203 241-1888
Kristen Schretzenmayer, *Principal*
EMP: 2
SALES (est): 158.3K **Privately Held**
SIC: 3679 Electronic components

(G-1813)
ENS MICROWAVE LLC
14 Commerce Dr (06810-4198)
PHONE..................203 794-7940
Kristen Schretzenmayer, *Mng Member*
EMP: 3
SALES (est): 384.1K **Privately Held**
SIC: 3679 Microwave components

(G-1814)
ENTEGRIS INC
7 Commerce Dr (06810-4131)
PHONE..................800 766-2681
Tom Baum, *Vice Pres*
Mark Deloughy, *Manager*
EMP: 424
SALES (corp-wide): 1.5B **Publicly Held**
SIC: 3089 Plastic processing
PA: Entegris, Inc.
129 Concord Rd
Billerica MA 01821
978 436-6500

(G-1815)
ENTEGRIS PROF SOLUTIONS INC (HQ)
Also Called: Atmi, Inc.
7 Commerce Dr (06810-4131)
PHONE..................203 794-1100
Douglas A Neugold, *Ch of Bd*
Ellen T Harmon, *President*
Brian Horos, *President*
Lawrence H Dubois, *Senior VP*
Kathleen G Minicieli, *Senior VP*
◆ **EMP:** 105
SQ FT: 31,000
SALES (est): 185.7MM
SALES (corp-wide): 1.5B **Publicly Held**
WEB: www.atmi.com
SIC: 3674 Thin film circuits
PA: Entegris, Inc.
129 Concord Rd
Billerica MA 01821
978 436-6500

(G-1816)
ERINCO MARKETING
7 Olympic Dr (06810-8216)
PHONE..................203 545-4550
Kathleen Demacarty, *Owner*
EMP: 1
SALES (est): 43.4K **Privately Held**
SIC: 2731 Book publishing

(G-1817)
ETHAN ALLEN INTERIORS INC (PA)
25 Lake Avenue Ext (06811-5286)
PHONE..................203 743-8000
M Farooq Kathwari, *Ch of Bd*
Kathy Bliss, *Senior VP*
Daniel M Grow, *Senior VP*
Tracy Paccione, *Senior VP*
Holly Tedesco, *Senior VP*
EMP: 268
SQ FT: 144,000
SALES (est): 746.6MM **Publicly Held**
WEB: www.ethanallen.com
SIC: 2512 5712 Upholstered household furniture; furniture stores; wood bedroom furniture

(G-1818)
ETHAN ALLEN RETAIL INC (HQ)
25 Lake Avenue Ext (06811-5286)
P.O. Box 1966 (06813-1966)
PHONE..................203 743-8000
Farooq Kathwari, *Ch of Bd*
Ed Teplitz, *Exec VP*
Corey Whitely, *Exec VP*
John Derrett, *Vice Pres*
Cliff Good, *Vice Pres*
◆ **EMP:** 300
SQ FT: 144,000
SALES (est): 610.2MM
SALES (corp-wide): 746.6MM **Publicly Held**
WEB: www.smyrna.ethanallen.com
SIC: 5712 5719 5713 5231 Furniture stores; bedding (sheets, blankets, spreads & pillows); lighting fixtures; carpets; rugs; wallpaper; carpets & rugs
PA: Ethan Allen Interiors Inc.
25 Lake Avenue Ext
Danbury CT 06811
203 743-8000

(G-1819)
ETHAN ALLEN RETAIL INC
25 Lake Avenue Ext (06811-5286)
P.O. Box 1966 (06813-1966)
PHONE..................203 743-8600
M Kathwari, *Manager*
EMP: 325
SALES (corp-wide): 746.6MM **Publicly Held**
WEB: www.smyrna.ethanallen.com
SIC: 5712 2512 5021 5023 Furniture stores; upholstered household furniture; household furniture; home furnishings
HQ: Ethan Allen Retail, Inc.
25 Lake Avenue Ext
Danbury CT 06811
203 743-8000

(G-1820)
EXPRESSWAY LUBE CENTERS
Also Called: Lubrication Management
225 White St (06810-6827)
PHONE..................203 744-2511
Don Daseliva, *Manager*
Vito Vontana, *Manager*
EMP: 10
SALES (est): 616.6K **Privately Held**
WEB: www.lubricationmanagement.com
SIC: 3599 3714 Oil filters, internal combustion engine, except automotive; motor vehicle parts & accessories

(G-1821)
FAG BEARINGS LLC (DH)
200 Park Ave (06810-7553)
PHONE..................203 790-5474
Dieter Kuetemeier, *President*
Nobert Broger, *Vice Pres*
Richard Lutringer, *Admin Sec*
◆ **EMP:** 100
SQ FT: 27,000
SALES (est): 51.7MM
SALES (corp-wide): 68.1B **Privately Held**
SIC: 3562 Ball bearings & parts; roller bearings & parts
HQ: F'ag Holding Corporation
200 Park Ave
Danbury CT 06810
203 790-5474

(G-1822)
FAG HOLDING CORPORATION (DH)
200 Park Ave (06810-7553)
PHONE..................203 790-5474
Claus Bauer, *President*
John Hess, *Info Tech Dir*
◆ **EMP:** 11
SQ FT: 27,000
SALES (est): 96.4MM
SALES (corp-wide): 68.1B **Privately Held**
SIC: 3562 Ball bearings & parts
HQ: Schaeffler Schweinfurt Beteiligungs Gmbh
Georg-Schafer-Str. 30
Schweinfurt 97421
972 191-0

(G-1823)
FAIRFIELD PROCESSING CORP (PA)
88 Rose Hill Ave (06810-5495)
P.O. Box 1157 (06813-1157)
PHONE..................203 744-2090
Roy Young, *Ch of Bd*
Nancy Sasso, *COO*
Jordan Young, *Exec VP*
Amy D'Alessandro, *Vice Pres*
Anthony Parker, *Opers Staff*
▲ **EMP:** 150
SQ FT: 100,000
SALES (est): 64.6MM **Privately Held**
WEB: www.poly-fil.com
SIC: 2824 Polyester fibers

(G-1824)
FEDERAL PRISON INDUSTRIES
Also Called: Unicor
Rr 37 (06811)
PHONE..................203 743-6471
David Gold, *Superintendent*
EMP: 17 **Publicly Held**
WEB: www.unicor.gov
SIC: 3315 9223 Cable, steel: insulated or armored; correctional institutions;
HQ: Federal Prison Industries, Inc
320 1st,St Nw
Washington DC 20534
202 305-3500

(G-1825)
FINELINE ARCHITECHTURAL WDWKG
1 Mannions Ln (06810-8156)
PHONE..................914 426-2648
EMP: 1
SALES (est): 54.1K **Privately Held**
SIC: 2431 Millwork

(G-1826)
FLAGSHIP CONVERTERS INC
205 Shelter Rock Rd (06810-7049)
PHONE..................203 792-0034
Frank E Gustafson, *President*
E Michael Davies, *Vice Pres*
Allan Wolfe, *Vice Pres*
James McAvoy, *CFO*
▲ **EMP:** 57
SQ FT: 95,000
SALES (est): 10.1MM **Privately Held**
WEB: www.flagshipconverters.com
SIC: 3089 2671 7389 3081 Laminating of plastic; packaging paper & plastics film, coated & laminated; laminating service; unsupported plastics film & sheet

(G-1827)
FLYING ACES PRESS LLC
25 Sunrise Rd (06810-4150)
PHONE..................203 791-1172
Thayer Syme, *Principal*
EMP: 2
SALES (est): 102.7K **Privately Held**
SIC: 2741 Miscellaneous publishing

(G-1828)
FOLEYS PUMP SERVICE INC
30 Miry Brook Rd (06810-7410)
PHONE..................203 792-2236
James J Foley, *President*
Will Freeborn, *Opers Mgr*
Jeanette Passarella, *Opers Mgr*
Paul Czap, *Manager*
EMP: 26
SALES (est): 4.1MM **Privately Held**
WEB: www.foleyspump.com
SIC: 3561 1799 Pumps & pumping equipment; petroleum storage tank installation, underground

(G-1829)
FRAM GROUP OPERATIONS LLC
39 Old Ridgebury Rd (06810-5103)
PHONE..................203 830-7800
Don Nelson, *President*
Joseph Pace, *Engineer*
Dmitri Sedov, *Engineer*
Prior Doug, *Senior Engr*
Bradley Maitre, *Finance Mgr*
▼ **EMP:** 27
SALES (est): 9.3MM **Privately Held**
SIC: 3714 Motor vehicle parts & accessories

(G-1830)
FRUITBUD JUICE LLC
131 West St (06810-6376)
P.O. Box 766 (06813-0766)
PHONE..................203 790-8200
Fax: 203 791-2875
EMP: 30
SALES (est): 4.4MM **Privately Held**
SIC: 2037 2033 Frozen Fruits And Vegetables, Nsk

(G-1831)
G P TOOL CO INC
59 James St (06810-6196)
PHONE..................203 744-0310
David Parille, *President*
Mark Parille, *Vice Pres*
EMP: 13 **EST:** 1947
SQ FT: 8,000
SALES (est): 2MM **Privately Held**
SIC: 3544 Special dies & tools; jigs & fixtures

(G-1832)
GAR ELECTRO FORMING
3 Commerce Dr (06810-4131)
PHONE..................203 885-1105
Russell Richter, *Vice Pres*
EMP: 2 **EST:** 2009
SALES (est): 149.2K **Privately Held**
SIC: 3471 Electroplating of metals or formed products

(G-1833)
GOLDWORKS
5 Locust Ave (06810-6103)
PHONE..................203 743-9668
Emilio De Grazia, *Owner*
EMP: 3 **EST:** 1978
SQ FT: 300
SALES (est): 213.5K **Privately Held**
SIC: 3911 5944 7631 Jewelry, precious metal; jewelry stores; jewelry repair services

Danbury - Fairfield County (G-1834) — GEOGRAPHIC SECTION

(G-1834)
GOODRICH CORPORATION
Goodrich Arospc Flight Systems
100 Wooster Hts (06810-7509)
PHONE.................................505 345-9031
Steve Baluzy, *Business Mgr*
Charles Laxson, *Exec VP*
Gregory Beach, *Vice Pres*
Andreas Nonnenmacher, *Vice Pres*
Brenda Roberts, *Senior Buyer*
EMP: 460
SALES (corp-wide): 66.5B **Publicly Held**
WEB: www.bfgoodrich.com
SIC: 3679 8711 Electronic circuits; aviation &/or aeronautical engineering
HQ: Goodrich Corporation
2730 W Tyvola Rd 4
Charlotte NC 28217
704 423-7000

(G-1835)
GOODRICH CORPORATION
Goodrich Optical Space Systems
100 Wooster Hts (06810-7509)
PHONE.................................203 797-5000
Tom Bergeon, *President*
Liliana Sokolov, *Managing Dir*
Aaron Turner, *Managing Dir*
EMP: 500
SALES (corp-wide): 66.5B **Publicly Held**
WEB: www.bfgoodrich.com
SIC: 3728 Aircraft parts & equipment
HQ: Goodrich Corporation
2730 W Tyvola Rd 4
Charlotte NC 28217
704 423-7000

(G-1836)
GORILLA SEALCOATING LLC
38 Balmforth Ave Apt 3 (06810-3901)
PHONE.................................475 218-3506
Edwin Zorrilla, *Principal*
EMP: 1
SALES (est): 57.5K **Privately Held**
SIC: 2952 Asphalt felts & coatings

(G-1837)
GRANTA USA LTD
62 E Starrs Plain Rd (06810-8319)
PHONE.................................440 207-6051
REA Hederman, *President*
▲ **EMP:** 10
SALES (est): 660K **Privately Held**
WEB: www.granta.com
SIC: 2721 Magazines: publishing only, not printed on site

(G-1838)
GROLIER OVERSEAS INCORPORATED (DH)
90 Sherman Tpke (06816-0002)
PHONE.................................203 797-3500
Richard Robinson, *CEO*
Edward J Russo, *President*
▲ **EMP:** 1
SALES (est): 164.5K
SALES (corp-wide): 1.6B **Publicly Held**
SIC: 2731 Books: publishing only
HQ: Scholastic Inc.
557 Broadway Lbby 1
New York NY 10012
212 343-6100

(G-1839)
GS THERMAL SOLUTIONS INC
144 Old Brookfield Rd C (06811-4071)
PHONE.................................475 289-4625
Rick Depalma, *President*
EMP: 8
SALES (est): 118.4K **Privately Held**
SIC: 3645 Garden, patio, walkway & yard lighting fixtures: electric

(G-1840)
GUY MONTANARI
Also Called: Montanari Repair
82 Payne Rd (06810-4108)
PHONE.................................203 791-0642
Guy Montanari, *Owner*
EMP: 2
SQ FT: 1,965
SALES (est): 131K **Privately Held**
SIC: 7699 7692 Aircraft & heavy equipment repair services; welding repair

(G-1841)
HAMAR LASER INSTRUMENTS INC
5 Ye Olde Rd (06810-7322)
PHONE.................................203 730-4600
Roderick M Hamar, *President*
Martin Hamar, *Chairman*
Anne Hamar, *Vice Pres*
Roderick Hamar, *Vice Pres*
Anne Hamer, *VP Finance*
EMP: 20
SQ FT: 12,000
SALES (est): 8.4MM **Privately Held**
WEB: www.hamarlaser.com
SIC: 5084 3699 Measuring & testing equipment, electrical; laser systems & equipment

(G-1842)
HAT TRICK GRAPHICS LLC
Also Called: Infinity Printing
87 Sand Pit Rd Ste 1 (06810-4043)
PHONE.................................203 748-1128
Tom Tannone,
EMP: 4
SQ FT: 3,000
SALES (est): 450K **Privately Held**
WEB: www.infinitypcd.com
SIC: 2752 2759 Commercial printing, offset; commercial printing

(G-1843)
HI-TEMP PRODUCTS CORP
88 Taylor St (06810-6923)
PHONE.................................203 744-3025
Tony Silva, *President*
Lucy Silva, *Office Mgr*
▲ **EMP:** 6
SQ FT: 9,600
SALES (est): 1.2MM **Privately Held**
SIC: 3433 Burners, furnaces, boilers & stokers

(G-1844)
HIGH VOLTAGE OUTSOURCING LLC
Also Called: Hvo
1 Corporate Dr (06810-4130)
PHONE.................................203 456-3101
Mariano Moran, *Branch Mgr*
EMP: 6
SALES (corp-wide): 524.8K **Privately Held**
SIC: 3629 8711 8748 Power conversion units, a.c. to d.c.: static-electric; electrical or electronic engineering; systems engineering consultant, ex. computer or professional
PA: High Voltage Outsourcing Llc
115 Chambers Rd
Danbury CT
203 730-2415

(G-1845)
HOLOGIC INC
36 Apple Ridge Rd (06810-7301)
PHONE.................................203 790-1188
Bill Healy, *Vice Pres*
EMP: 195
SALES (corp-wide): 3.2B **Publicly Held**
WEB: www.hologic.com
SIC: 3844 3841 X-ray apparatus & tubes; surgical & medical instruments
PA: Hologic, Inc.
250 Campus Dr
Marlborough MA 01752
508 263-2900

(G-1846)
HUNT ARCHITECTURAL WDWKG INC
5 Robinson Ave (06810)
PHONE.................................203 947-1137
Richard Hunt, *CEO*
EMP: 1 **EST:** 2006
SALES (est): 11.1K **Privately Held**
SIC: 2431 Millwork

(G-1847)
I TECH SERVICES INC (PA)
Also Called: Mobile Asset Solutions
39 Old Ridgebury Rd D1-1 (06810-5103)
PHONE.................................800 559-8991
Dawn Giobbie, *President*
Ed Ignarra, *Managing Dir*
EMP: 5
SALES (est): 322.2K **Privately Held**
SIC: 7382 4899 7375 3663 Protective devices, security; data communication services; information retrieval services;

(G-1848)
ILL INK GRAPHIC & PRTG SVCS
258 Main St (06810-6644)
PHONE.................................203 748-0711
Jose Velez, *Owner*
EMP: 1
SALES (est): 127.1K **Privately Held**
SIC: 2752 Commercial printing, lithographic

(G-1849)
INDUSTRIAL ELECTRIC MOTORS
85 Shelter Rock Rd (06810-7043)
PHONE.................................203 743-9611
George Lahoud, *President*
Darlene Lahoud, *Admin Sec*
EMP: 4
SQ FT: 13,000
SALES (est): 1MM **Privately Held**
SIC: 5063 7694 5999 Motors, electric; electric motor repair; motors, electric

(G-1850)
INFORMA MEDIA INC
252 Great Plain Rd (06811-3152)
PHONE.................................203 885-1045
Steven Krejci, *Branch Mgr*
EMP: 1
SALES (corp-wide): 3B **Privately Held**
SIC: 2721 Magazines: publishing only, not printed on site
HQ: Informa Media, Inc.
605 3rd Ave Fl 22
New York NY 10158
212 204-4200

(G-1851)
IOVINO BROS SPORTING GOODS
2 Lee Mac Ave Ste 2 # 2 (06810-6999)
PHONE.................................203 790-5966
Stephen Kaplanis, *President*
Rob Gurry, *Sales Staff*
Greg Newkirk, *Sales Staff*
Kimberly Kaplanis, *Admin Sec*
EMP: 3
SQ FT: 5,000
SALES (est): 457.4K **Privately Held**
SIC: 2759 5941 Screen printing; sporting goods & bicycle shops

(G-1852)
ISAAC INDUSTRIES
108 Stadley Rough Rd (06811-3290)
PHONE.................................203 778-3239
Jan Angrave, *Owner*
EMP: 3
SALES (est): 190.3K **Privately Held**
SIC: 3999 Manufacturing industries

(G-1853)
ISR (NTLLGNCE SRVLLANCE RECONN
100 Wooster Hts (06810-7509)
PHONE.................................203 797-5000
Marshall O Larsen, *Principal*
EMP: 3
SALES (est): 299.2K **Privately Held**
SIC: 3728 Aircraft parts & equipment

(G-1854)
ITHACO SPACE SYSTEMS INC
100 Wooster Hts (06810-7509)
PHONE.................................607 272-7640
Thomas C Bergeron, *Chairman*
EMP: 60 **EST:** 1996
SALES (est): 5.3MM
SALES (corp-wide): 66.5B **Publicly Held**
WEB: www.bfgoodrich.com
SIC: 3728 Aircraft parts & equipment
HQ: Goodrich Corporation
2730 W Tyvola Rd 4
Charlotte NC 28217
704 423-7000

(G-1855)
J AND R SHELTER ROCK ROAD LLC
2 Old Shelter Rock Rd (06810-7057)
PHONE.................................203 739-0697
Sam Singh, *Principal*
EMP: 2
SALES (est): 118K **Privately Held**
SIC: 1389 Oil & gas field services

(G-1856)
J-TECK USA INC
50 Miry Brook Rd (06810-7411)
P.O. Box 1209, Soddy Daisy TN (37384-1209)
PHONE.................................203 791-2121
Fred Macaluso, *President*
▲ **EMP:** 4
SALES (est): 613.9K
SALES (corp-wide): 6.9B **Publicly Held**
SIC: 3555 Printing trades machinery
PA: Dover Corporation
3005 Highland Pkwy # 200
Downers Grove IL 60515
630 541-1540

(G-1857)
JAMES P SMITH
156 Long Ridge Rd (06810-8461)
PHONE.................................203 744-1031
James Smith, *Manager*
EMP: 2
SALES (est): 62.3K **Privately Held**
SIC: 2033 Canned fruits & specialties

(G-1858)
JCM INDUSTRIES
2 Westwood Dr (06811-4239)
PHONE.................................203 748-1806
EMP: 1
SALES (est): 39.6K **Privately Held**
SIC: 3999 Manufacturing industries

(G-1859)
JEDCONTROL CORP
4 Mill Plain Rd (06810-5141)
PHONE.................................914 328-8593
Jim Duffy, *President*
Joyce Duffy, *Corp Secy*
EMP: 2
SALES: 300K **Privately Held**
SIC: 3824 Liquid meters

(G-1860)
JEFF OSBORNE INDUSTRIES
3 Sunset Rdg (06811-5120)
PHONE.................................203 794-0863
Jeffrey A Osborne, *Principal*
EMP: 2
SALES (est): 117.8K **Privately Held**
SIC: 3999 Manufacturing industries

(G-1861)
JEWELRY DESIGNS INC
86 Mill Plain Rd (06811-5140)
PHONE.................................203 797-0389
Robert Underhill, *President*
Steven Lopes, *Info Tech Mgr*
Karen Olson Underhill, *Director*
▲ **EMP:** 33
SQ FT: 7,500
SALES (est): 3.7MM **Privately Held**
WEB: www.jewelrydesigns.com
SIC: 5944 3911 Jewelry, precious stones & precious metals; jewelry, precious metal

(G-1862)
JIMS WELDING SERVICE LLC
18 Finance Dr (06810-4132)
PHONE.................................203 744-2982
James E Beckman, *Owner*
EMP: 3
SQ FT: 2,000
SALES (est): 627.5K **Privately Held**
SIC: 7692 Welding repair

(G-1863)
JOSEPH MERRITT & COMPANY INC
Also Called: Merritt, Joseph & Company
4c Chrstpher Columbus Ave (06810-7352)
PHONE.................................203 743-6734
Tony Texeira, *Branch Mgr*
EMP: 7
SQ FT: 10,000

SALES (corp-wide): 31.9MM **Privately Held**
SIC: 2752 5049 2789 Commercial printing, offset; engineers' equipment & supplies; bookbinding & related work
PA: Joseph Merritt & Company Incorporated
650 Franklin Ave Ste 3
Hartford CT 06114
860 296-2500

(G-1864)
JOVIL UNIVERSAL LLC
10 Precision Rd (06810-7317)
PHONE..................................203 792-6700
Keith Fredlund, *President*
Jeff Fairchild, *General Mgr*
EMP: 25 EST: 2014
SQ FT: 24,000
SALES (est): 4.7MM **Privately Held**
SIC: 3549 5084 Coil winding machines for springs; industrial machinery & equipment

(G-1865)
JOY CAROLE CREATIONS INC
Also Called: Pyramid Productions
42 Mill Plain Rd (06811-5140)
PHONE..................................203 794-1401
Fax: 203 740-4495
▲ **EMP:** 4
SQ FT: 5,000
SALES (est): 210K **Privately Held**
SIC: 2771 Mfg Greeting Cards

(G-1866)
JUAN GALLEGOS
Also Called: Colonial Wood Turning
29 Benson Dr (06810-7212)
PHONE..................................203 744-0575
Juan Gallegos, *Owner*
EMP: 2
SALES: 145K **Privately Held**
SIC: 2426 2499 Turnings, furniture: wood; carved & turned wood

(G-1867)
JW GALLAS ROD CO
7 Mirijo Rd (06811-3825)
PHONE..................................203 790-4188
John W Gallas, *Owner*
EMP: 1
SALES (est): 46.7K **Privately Held**
SIC: 3949 Rods & rod parts, fishing

(G-1868)
KIMCHUK INCORPORATED (PA)
1 Corporate Dr Ste 1 # 1 (06810-4139)
PHONE..................................203 790-7800
Jim Marquis, *President*
William Kimbell, *President*
James A Marquis, *Vice Pres*
Denise Jurasek, *Materials Mgr*
Annabelle Almeida, *Production*
EMP: 15
SQ FT: 10,000
SALES (est): 41.5MM **Privately Held**
WEB: www.kimchuk.com
SIC: 3625 7389 3312 7371 Control equipment, electric; design, commercial & industrial; sheet or strip, steel, cold-rolled: own hot-rolled; custom computer programming services; computer integrated systems design

(G-1869)
KIMCHUK INCORPORATED
4 Finance Dr (06810-4191)
PHONE..................................203 798-0799
Jim Maquis, *President*
EMP: 125
SALES (corp-wide): 41.5MM **Privately Held**
SIC: 3571 Electronic computers
PA: Kimchuk, Incorporated
1 Corporate Dr Ste 1 # 1
Danbury CT 06810
203 790-7800

(G-1870)
KINGSWOOD KITCHENS CO INC
70 Beaver St (06810-5497)
PHONE..................................203 792-8700
Henry Blevio, *President*
Richard Rausch, *Shareholder*
EMP: 75
SQ FT: 75,000
SALES (est): 9.1MM **Privately Held**
WEB: www.kingswoodkitchens.com
SIC: 2434 Vanities, bathroom: wood

(G-1871)
KOMPUTATION COMPUTER SERVICES
5 Windaway Rd (06810-7235)
PHONE..................................203 744-3652
Mitchell B Kuperman, *Principal*
EMP: 2
SALES (est): 92K **Privately Held**
SIC: 7372 Prepackaged software

(G-1872)
LESSER EVIL
18 Finance Dr (06810-4132)
PHONE..................................203 529-3555
Andrew Strife, *President*
EMP: 3 EST: 2015
SALES (est): 287.6K **Privately Held**
SIC: 2099 Food preparations

(G-1873)
LIBERTY GARAGE INC
51 Sugar Hollow Rd Ste 1 (06810-7532)
PHONE..................................203 778-0222
Anthony Sigillito, *Principal*
EMP: 4
SALES (est): 535.8K **Privately Held**
SIC: 2599 Cabinets, factory

(G-1874)
LIGHT ROCK SPRING WATER CO
Also Called: Light Rock Beverage
9 Balmforth Ave (06810-5908)
PHONE..................................203 743-2251
George Antous, *President*
Morris Antous, *Corp Secy*
Frederick Antous, *Vice Pres*
EMP: 15 EST: 1905
SQ FT: 7,500
SALES (est): 2.7MM **Privately Held**
SIC: 2086 Soft drinks: packaged in cans, bottles, etc.

(G-1875)
LO STOCCO MOTORS
19 Chestnut St (06810-6816)
PHONE..................................203 797-9618
Joe Lo Stocco, *Owner*
EMP: 6
SALES (est): 412.9K **Privately Held**
SIC: 3713 5531 7538 Garbage, refuse truck bodies; truck equipment & parts; truck engine repair, except industrial

(G-1876)
LORAD CORPORATION
Also Called: Lorad Medical Systems
36 Apple Ridge Rd (06810-7301)
P.O. Box 1946 (06813-1946)
PHONE..................................203 790-5544
Raymond Calvo, *Vice Pres*
▲ **EMP:** 200
SQ FT: 63,500
SALES (est): 38.2MM
SALES (corp-wide): 3.2B **Publicly Held**
WEB: www.hologic.com
SIC: 3844 3841 Radiographic X-ray apparatus & tubes; biopsy instruments & equipment
PA: Hologic, Inc.
250 Campus Dr
Marlborough MA 01752
508 263-2900

(G-1877)
LOSTOCCO REFUSE SERVICE LLC
Also Called: Lostocco Services
79 Beaver Brook Rd (06810-6211)
P.O. Box 964 (06813-0964)
PHONE..................................203 748-9296
Joseph Lostocco,
EMP: 20
SQ FT: 6,000
SALES (est): 4.2MM **Privately Held**
SIC: 4953 7692 3444 Rubbish collection & disposal; welding repair; sheet metalwork

(G-1878)
M & M PRECAST CORP
39 Padanaram Rd (06811-3701)
PHONE..................................203 743-5559
Robert Kaufman, *President*
Todd Kaufman, *Admin Sec*
EMP: 18
SQ FT: 5,000
SALES (est): 3MM **Privately Held**
SIC: 3272 Septic tanks, concrete; concrete products, precast

(G-1879)
MANNKIND CORPORATION
Also Called: Mannkind Biopharm
1 Casper St (06810-6903)
PHONE..................................203 798-8000
Larry Belenchia, *Project Mgr*
Art Bailey, *Research*
Yin Liu, *Research*
Mike Walton, *Research*
Edwin Amoro, *Engineer*
EMP: 1
SALES (corp-wide): 27.8MM **Publicly Held**
SIC: 2834 Pharmaceutical preparations
PA: Mannkind Corporation
30930 Russell Ranch Rd # 300
Westlake Village CA 91362
818 661-5000

(G-1880)
MAPLEGATE MEDIA GROUP INC
1503 Sienna Dr (06810-7156)
PHONE..................................203 826-7557
Sharon E Warner, *President*
EMP: 22
SALES (est): 3.4MM **Privately Held**
WEB: www.maplegatemedia.com
SIC: 2721 Magazines: publishing & printing; magazines: publishing only, not printed on site

(G-1881)
MCM STAMPING CORPORATION
66 Beaver Brook Rd (06810-6298)
PHONE..................................203 792-3080
Arlene Mc Mullin, *President*
Kathy Timm, *Admin Sec*
EMP: 25 EST: 1970
SQ FT: 10,000
SALES (est): 4MM **Privately Held**
SIC: 3469 Stamping metal for the trade

(G-1882)
MEGA SOUND AND LIGHT LLC
36 Mill Plain Rd Ste 312 (06811-5114)
PHONE..................................203 743-4200
Ran Artsi,
Al Gellman,
Ran Nizin,
▲ **EMP:** 7
SQ FT: 3,000
SALES: 5.5MM **Privately Held**
WEB: www.mega-sound.com
SIC: 5112 5111 3951 2621 Pens &/or pencils; printing & writing paper; pens & mechanical pencils; stationery, envelope & tablet papers

(G-1883)
MGI USA INC
23 Forest Ave (06810-5706)
PHONE..................................203 312-1200
EMP: 6
SQ FT: 3,500
SALES (est): 473K
SALES (corp-wide): 0 **Privately Held**
SIC: 3111 Leather Tanning/Finishing
PA: Jiangsu Maydiang Leather Goods Co., Ltd.
Meidiyang Rd., Zhaoshi Industrial Zone, Meili Town
Changshu
512 523-8137

(G-1884)
MICHAEL KORS
7 Backus Ave Ste H102 (06810-7422)
PHONE..................................203 748-4300
EMP: 1
SALES (est): 42.5K **Privately Held**
SIC: 2389 Apparel & accessories

(G-1885)
MINUTEMAN PRESS
12 Mill Plain Rd Ste 1 (06811-5135)
PHONE..................................973 748-7160
Sam Shin, *Owner*
EMP: 2
SALES (est): 205.6K **Privately Held**
SIC: 2752 Commercial printing, lithographic

(G-1886)
MINUTEMAN PRESS OF DANBURY
12 Mill Plain Rd Ste 10 (06811-5135)
PHONE..................................203 743-6755
Tom Wilson, *Partner*
EMP: 9
SQ FT: 2,450
SALES (est): 1.5MM **Privately Held**
WEB: www.minutemandanbury.com
SIC: 2752 Commercial printing, lithographic

(G-1887)
MM CANDLES
119 Carol St (06810-8312)
PHONE..................................203 205-0180
Monica Mueller, *Principal*
EMP: 1
SALES (est): 39.6K **Privately Held**
SIC: 3999 Candles

(G-1888)
MOHAWK INDUSTRIES INC
4 Nabby Rd (06811-3258)
PHONE..................................203 739-0260
Bill Bitting, *Branch Mgr*
EMP: 156
SALES (corp-wide): 9.9B **Publicly Held**
SIC: 2273 3253 Finishers of tufted carpets & rugs; smyrna carpets & rugs, machine woven; ceramic wall & floor tile
PA: Mohawk Industries, Inc.
160 S Industrial Blvd
Calhoun GA 30701
706 629-7721

(G-1889)
MULCH FERRIS PRODUCTS LLC
6 Plumtrees Rd (06810-7023)
PHONE..................................203 790-1155
Percy Ferris, *Mng Member*
EMP: 3
SALES (est): 391.1K **Privately Held**
SIC: 2499 Mulch or sawdust products, wood

(G-1890)
MWB TOY COMPANY LLC
Also Called: Luke's Toy Factory
128 E Liberty St (06810-6767)
PHONE..................................212 598-4500
James Barber, *Mng Member*
EMP: 3
SQ FT: 1,500
SALES (est): 234.6K **Privately Held**
SIC: 3944 Automobiles & trucks, toy

(G-1891)
NEW MACHINE PRODUCTS LLC
81 Beaver Brook Rd Ste B (06810-6297)
PHONE..................................203 790-5520
Joseph Basilva,
Barry Neumann,
EMP: 3
SQ FT: 3,000
SALES: 400K **Privately Held**
SIC: 3599 Machine shop, jobbing & repair

(G-1892)
NEWS TIMES
333 Main St (06810-5818)
PHONE..................................203 744-5100
Nicole London, *President*
Mark F Lukas, *Publisher*
Jacqueline Smith, *Principal*
Ralph Hohman, *Editor*
Teresa Rousseau, *Editor*
EMP: 4
SALES (est): 370.6K **Privately Held**
SIC: 2711 Newspapers, publishing & printing

Danbury - Fairfield County (G-1893)

(G-1893)
NORDIC AMERICAN SMOKELESS INC
100 Mill Plain Rd Ste 115 (06811-5189)
PHONE 203 207-9977
Darren Quinn, *President*
EMP: 12
SALES (est): 1.1MM **Privately Held**
SIC: 2131 Chewing & smoking tobacco

(G-1894)
NORTHEAST WATERJET SVCS LLC
24 Finance Dr (06810-4132)
P.O. Box 919, Brookfield (06804-0919)
PHONE 203 794-0766
Robert A Ellis, *Principal*
EMP: 1
SALES (est): 122.3K **Privately Held**
SIC: 3599 Machine shop, jobbing & repair

(G-1895)
NORTHERN COMFORT MECH LLC
178 Osborne St (06810-6052)
PHONE 203 456-5163
David Da Silva, *Mng Member*
EMP: 4
SALES (est): 83K **Privately Held**
SIC: 1711 3444 Heating & air conditioning contractors; sheet metalwork

(G-1896)
NOVY INTERNATIONAL INC
6 Abbott St (06810-5310)
PHONE 203 743-7720
George Novy, *President*
EMP: 5
SALES (est): 766.1K **Privately Held**
WEB: www.novyinternational.com
SIC: 3585 Heating equipment, complete

(G-1897)
O & G INDUSTRIES INC
9 Segar St (06810-6324)
PHONE 203 748-5694
Drew Oneglia, *Branch Mgr*
EMP: 21
SALES (corp-wide): 538MM **Privately Held**
WEB: www.ogind.com
SIC: 3273 1542 Ready-mixed concrete; commercial & office building, new construction
PA: O & G Industries, Inc.
    112 Wall St
    Torrington CT 06790
    860 489-9261

(G-1898)
OLDE TYME GRAPHICS
4 Starr Rd (06810-4018)
PHONE 203 748-3360
David Carvalho, *Owner*
EMP: 2
SALES (est): 73.2K **Privately Held**
SIC: 2759 Commercial printing

(G-1899)
ON LINE BUILDING SYSTEMS LLC
Also Called: Integ Systems
22 Shelter Rock Ln Unit 4 (06810-8268)
PHONE 203 798-1194
James Spinner, *Principal*
Pamela Spinner, *Corp Secy*
Judy Kuhn,
Stanley Plato,
EMP: 9
SALES (est): 640K **Privately Held**
WEB: www.integsystems.com
SIC: 7389 5063 7629 1731 Design, commercial & industrial; electrical apparatus & equipment; storage batteries, industrial; electrical equipment repair services; computer power conditioning; standby or emergency power specialization; current-carrying wiring devices

(G-1900)
PARKING LT STRPNG & ASPHLT SGN
4 Liberty Ave (06810-8141)
P.O. Box 354 (06813-0354)
PHONE 203 648-6323
Jose Palmeira, *Administration*
EMP: 1
SALES (est): 46K **Privately Held**
SIC: 3993 Signs & advertising specialties

(G-1901)
PARTS CUTTER CNC
78 Triangle St (06810-6977)
PHONE 203 947-4407
Stephen Williams, *Principal*
EMP: 2
SALES (est): 192.9K **Privately Held**
SIC: 3599 Machine shop, jobbing & repair

(G-1902)
PAUL DEWITT
Also Called: Economy Printing
128 E Liberty St Ste 4 (06810-6767)
PHONE 203 792-5610
Paul Dewitt, *Owner*
EMP: 15
SALES (est): 1.5MM **Privately Held**
SIC: 2752 2796 2791 2789 Commercial printing, offset; platemaking services; typesetting; bookbinding & related work; commercial printing

(G-1903)
PAULAS BAKERY
Also Called: International Bky Waterberry
54 Liberty St Ste 1 (06810-3225)
PHONE 203 743-9000
Jose Teixeira, *Owner*
Paula Teixeira, *Co-Owner*
EMP: 1
SALES (est): 42K **Privately Held**
SIC: 2051 Bread, cake & related products

(G-1904)
PERFEX MANUFACTURING
30 Commerce Dr (06810-4131)
PHONE 203 739-0930
Jules Drabkin, *Principal*
EMP: 2 EST: 2009
SALES (est): 91.7K **Privately Held**
SIC: 3999 Manufacturing industries

(G-1905)
PEROSPHERE INC
20 Kenosia Ave (06810-7357)
PHONE 203 885-1111
Solomon S Steiner PHD, *CEO*
EMP: 12
SALES (est): 2.7MM **Privately Held**
SIC: 2834 7389 Pharmaceutical preparations;

(G-1906)
PEROSPHERE TECHNOLOGIES INC
108 Mill Plain Rd Ste 301 (06811-1501)
PHONE 475 218-4600
Sasha Bakhru, *President*
Stefan Zappe, *Exec VP*
EMP: 3
SALES (est): 369.7K **Privately Held**
SIC: 3841 Diagnostic apparatus, medical

(G-1907)
PHARMACEUTICAL DISCOVERY CORP
1 Casper St (06810-6903)
PHONE 203 796-3425
David Thompson, *Principal*
EMP: 3
SALES (est): 175.3K **Privately Held**
SIC: 2834 Pharmaceutical preparations

(G-1908)
PINE BUSH PUBLISHING LLC
33 Crestview Ln (06810-7162)
PHONE 203 570-3523
Philip Defreese Brown,
EMP: 2 EST: 2013
SALES (est): 91.9K **Privately Held**
SIC: 2741 Miscellaneous publishing

(G-1909)
PMC ENGINEERING LLC
Also Called: P.M.c
11 Old Sugar Hollow Rd (06810-7517)
PHONE 203 792-8686
Robert P Knowles, *President*
Ray Bartko, *Engineer*
Andrea Preftes, *Accounting Mgr*
Jim Errickson, *Manager*
Mark Knowles, *Technology*
EMP: 31 EST: 1963
SQ FT: 24,000
SALES: 6MM **Privately Held**
WEB: www.pmc1.com
SIC: 3823 Pressure measurement instruments, industrial

(G-1910)
POWER UP ELECTRIC
48 Pembroke Rd (06811-2956)
PHONE 203 312-0601
Martin F Johnson, *Principal*
EMP: 2
SALES (est): 193.7K **Privately Held**
SIC: 3699 1731 Electrical equipment & supplies; electrical work

(G-1911)
PPG INDUSTRIES INC
Also Called: PPG Painters Supply
211 White St (06810-6826)
PHONE 203 744-4977
Joseph Renda, *Manager*
EMP: 4
SALES (corp-wide): 15.3B **Publicly Held**
WEB: www.painterssupply.com
SIC: 2851 Paints & allied products
PA: Ppg Industries, Inc.
    1 Ppg Pl
    Pittsburgh PA 15272
    412 434-3131

(G-1912)
PRAXAIR INC
10 Riverview Dr (06810-6268)
PHONE 800 772-9247
Bob Law, *Engineer*
Mike Barr, *Manager*
Rajasekhar Inturi, *Software Dev*
EMP: 80 **Privately Held**
SIC: 3842 Respiratory protection equipment, personal
HQ: Praxair, Inc.
    10 Riverview Dr
    Danbury CT 06810
    203 837-2000

(G-1913)
PRAXAIR INC (HQ)
10 Riverview Dr (06810-6268)
PHONE 203 837-2000
Stephen F Angel, *Ch of Bd*
Fabricio Nunes, *Counsel*
Steve Bogard, *Vice Pres*
Elizabeth T Hirsch, *Vice Pres*
Riva Krut, *Vice Pres*
◆ EMP: 400
SALES: 11.4B **Privately Held**
SIC: 2813 3569 3471 3479 Industrial gases; gas producers (machinery); plating of metals or formed products; coating of metals & formed products

(G-1914)
PRAXAIR DISTRIBUTION INC (DH)
10 Riverview Dr (06810-6268)
PHONE 203 837-2000
Dick Marini, *President*
James Baughman, *Vice Pres*
Barney Patel, *Opers Mgr*
Lisa Hurley, *Treasurer*
Myron Stewart, *Accounts Mgr*
▲ EMP: 15
SALES (est): 664.9MM **Privately Held**
WEB: www.parxair.com
SIC: 2813 5084 5999 Industrial gases; carbon dioxide; dry ice, carbon dioxide (solid); oxygen, compressed or liquefied; welding machinery & equipment; welding supplies
HQ: Praxair, Inc.
    10 Riverview Dr
    Danbury CT 06810
    203 837-2000

(G-1915)
PRAXAIR DISTRIBUTION INC
55 Old Ridgebury Rd (06810-5121)
PHONE 203 837-2162
Franco Mazzali, *Managing Dir*
Don Blanchat, *Branch Mgr*
EMP: 18 **Privately Held**
SIC: 2813 Industrial gases
HQ: Praxair Distribution, Inc.
    10 Riverview Dr
    Danbury CT 06810
    203 837-2000

(G-1916)
PRAXAIR SURFACE TECH INC
39 Old Ridgebury Rd (06810-5103)
PHONE 203 837-2000
EMP: 2
SALES (corp-wide): 11.4B **Privately Held**
SIC: 3479 Coating/Engraving Service
HQ: Praxair Surface Technologies, Inc.
    1500 Polco St
    Indianapolis IN 46222
    317 240-2500

(G-1917)
PRECISION POWDERS LLC
9 Flintlock Dr (06811-3618)
PHONE 203 748-7879
Frank Mooney,
EMP: 2
SALES (est): 160K **Privately Held**
SIC: 3356 Titanium

(G-1918)
PREFERRED UTILITIES MFG CORP (HQ)
Also Called: Preferred Instruments
31-35 South St (06810-8147)
PHONE 203 743-6741
David G Bohn, *President*
David H Paddock, *Corp Secy*
Charles A White III, *Exec VP*
Darrel Scribner, *Vice Pres*
Gilbert Sy, *Vice Pres*
EMP: 60 EST: 1920
SQ FT: 44,000
SALES (est): 25.2MM **Privately Held**
WEB: www.preferred-mfg.com
SIC: 3829 3433 3561 8711 Measuring & controlling devices; gas burners, industrial; oil burners, domestic or industrial; industrial pumps & parts; designing: ship, boat, machine & product; industrial furnaces & ovens; machine tool accessories
PA: Pumc Holding Corporation
    31-35 South St
    Danbury CT 06810
    203 743-6741

(G-1919)
PRESTONE PRODUCTS CORPORATION
55 Federal Rd (06810-4001)
PHONE 203 731-7880
Steven Clancy, *President*
EMP: 39
SALES (corp-wide): 3.2MM **Privately Held**
SIC: 2899 Antifreeze compounds
HQ: Prestone Products Corporation
    6250 N River Rd Ste 6000
    Rosemont IL 60018

(G-1920)
PROCESS AUTOMTN SOLUTIONS INC (HQ)
107 Mill Plain Rd Ste 301 (06811-6100)
PHONE 203 207-9917
Ricardo De La Cierva, *Exec VP*
Rick De La Cierva, *Exec VP*
EMP: 21
SQ FT: 2,400
SALES: 38MM
SALES (corp-wide): 947.9MM **Privately Held**
WEB: www.gap5.com
SIC: 7373 7379 3822 Systems integration services; computer related consulting services; building services monitoring controls, automatic
PA: Ats Automation Tooling Systems Inc
    730 Fountain St Suite 2b
    Cambridge ON N3H 4
    519 653-6500

GEOGRAPHIC SECTION
Danbury - Fairfield County (G-1948)

(G-1921)
PUMC HOLDING CORPORATION (PA)
31-35 South St (06810-8147)
PHONE..................203 743-6741
Robert G Bohn, *Ch of Bd*
David G Bohn, *President*
David H Paddock, *Corp Secy*
Jeff Eichenwald, *Sales Engr*
Cindy Robertson, *Shareholder*
EMP: 42
SQ FT: 44,000
SALES (est): 25.2MM **Privately Held**
SIC: 3433 8711 Gas burners, industrial; oil burners, domestic or industrial; designing: ship, boat, machine & product

(G-1922)
PUSHPIN PRESS
209 Long Ridge Rd (06810-8412)
PHONE..................203 797-8691
EMP: 1
SALES (est): 37.5K **Privately Held**
SIC: 2741 Miscellaneous publishing

(G-1923)
QUALITY KITCHEN CORP DELAWARE
131 West St Ste 1 (06810-6372)
PHONE..................203 744-2000
Albert J Salame, *President*
Peter Bliss, *Vice Pres*
Mary Lou Lytle, *Manager*
EMP: 4
SQ FT: 40,000
SALES (est): 473.5K **Privately Held**
WEB: www.royalkitchens-ny.com
SIC: 2037 Fruit juice concentrates, frozen

(G-1924)
QUALITY TANK SERVICE LP
16 Driftway Rd (06811-5102)
PHONE..................203 792-9373
Al Morrell, *Partner*
Leanthony Morrell, *Partner*
EMP: 2
SALES: 50K **Privately Held**
SIC: 3443 Fuel tanks (oil, gas, etc.): metal plate

(G-1925)
QUARRY STONE & GRAVEL LLC
4 Ridgewood St (06811-4550)
PHONE..................203 770-2664
Robert Kovacs,
EMP: 2
SALES (est): 147.2K **Privately Held**
SIC: 1422 Cement rock, crushed & broken-quarrying

(G-1926)
R D WOODWORK LLC
29 Morris St (06810-5428)
PHONE..................203 947-9550
Rafael Damasceno, *Principal*
EMP: 2
SALES (est): 140.2K **Privately Held**
SIC: 2431 Millwork

(G-1927)
RCSI PUBLISHING
114 Westville Ave (06810-5362)
PHONE..................203 917-4223
Matthew Sowers, *Principal*
EMP: 1
SALES (est): 37.5K **Privately Held**
SIC: 2741 Miscellaneous publishing

(G-1928)
RENNER STAIRS
92 Sand Pit Rd (06810-4033)
PHONE..................203 743-2452
David Renner, *Principal*
EMP: 1
SALES (est): 71.1K **Privately Held**
SIC: 1799 2431 Special trade contractors; staircases, stairs & railings

(G-1929)
RINCO ULTRASONICS USA INC
87 Sand Pit Rd Ste 1b (06810-4043)
PHONE..................203 744-4500
J Michael Goodson, *CEO*
Anthony Hern, *Admin Sec*
▲ EMP: 5
SALES (est): 1MM
SALES (corp-wide): 54.7MM **Privately Held**
SIC: 3699 Generators, ultrasonic
HQ: Crest Ultrasonics Corp.
18 Graphics Dr
Ewing NJ 08628
609 883-4000

(G-1930)
RK MANUFACTURING CORP CONN
34 Executive Dr Ste 2 (06810-4190)
PHONE..................203 797-8700
Donna Krebs, *President*
Richard Ponton, *VP Opers*
Josh Hubbard, *Project Engr*
Jonathan Richards, *Project Engr*
Jodi Dipreta, *Human Resources*
EMP: 83
SQ FT: 42,000
SALES (est): 15.4MM **Privately Held**
SIC: 3599 Machine shop, jobbing & repair

(G-1931)
RSA CORP
36 Old Sherman Tpke (06810-4124)
PHONE..................203 790-8100
Jan S Anthony, *President*
Stephanie Weber, *Vice Pres*
▲ EMP: 25
SQ FT: 20,000
SALES: 10.7MM **Privately Held**
WEB: www.rsachem.com
SIC: 2869 Plasticizers, organic: cyclic & acyclic

(G-1932)
SANDVIK PUBG INTERACTIVE INC (PA)
83 Wooster Hts Ste 208 (06810-7549)
PHONE..................203 205-0188
Marius Sandvik, *President*
Robert Israel, *Corp Secy*
Linda Fletcher, *Accounting Mgr*
▲ EMP: 17
SALES (est): 5.7MM **Privately Held**
SIC: 2741 Miscellaneous publishing

(G-1933)
SANDVIKS INC (PA)
83 Wooster Hts Ste 110 (06810-7552)
PHONE..................866 984-0188
Marius Sandvik, *President*
Robert Israel, *Treasurer*
Andrena Carroll Gerace, *Human Res Mgr*
EMP: 6 EST: 2010
SALES (est): 6.7MM **Privately Held**
SIC: 3542 Machine tools, metal forming type

(G-1934)
SANTOTO LLC
Also Called: Danbury Aviation
Danbury Municipal (06810)
P.O. Box 267, New Canaan (06840-0267)
PHONE..................203 984-2540
Andre Bohy,
Santo Silvestro,
EMP: 4
SALES (est): 335.2K **Privately Held**
SIC: 3721 Aircraft

(G-1935)
SCANTUBE INC
22 Shelter Rock Ln # 24 (06810-8268)
PHONE..................203 743-0908
Robert Paltauf, *Managing Dir*
▲ EMP: 3
SALES (est): 497.3K **Privately Held**
WEB: www.scantube.com
SIC: 3498 Tube fabricating (contract bending & shaping)

(G-1936)
SCHAEFFLER AEROSPACE USA CORP (DH)
Also Called: Barden Corporation, The
200 Park Ave (06810-7553)
P.O. Box 2449 (06813-2449)
PHONE..................203 744-2211
Peter J Enright, *CEO*
Edward Silver, *General Mgr*
Robert Hillstrom, *Vice Pres*
Michael Palanzo, *Purch Mgr*
Gail Bardelli, *Engineer*
▲ EMP: 400 EST: 1942
SQ FT: 192,000
SALES (est): 111.3MM
SALES (corp-wide): 68.1B **Privately Held**
SIC: 3562 3469 3842 3089 Ball bearings & parts; machine parts, stamped or pressed metal; surgical appliances & supplies; injection molded finished plastic products; steel balls
HQ: Schaeffler Group Usa Inc.
308 Springhill Farm Rd
Fort Mill SC 29715
803 548-8500

(G-1937)
SCHAEFFLER GROUP USA INC
200 Park Ave (06810-7553)
PHONE..................203 790-5474
Chris McAndrew, *President*
Anthony Tamburro, *Materials Mgr*
EMP: 342
SALES (corp-wide): 68.1B **Privately Held**
SIC: 3562 Roller bearings & parts
HQ: Schaeffler Group Usa Inc.
308 Springhill Farm Rd
Fort Mill SC 29715
803 548-8500

(G-1938)
SCHOLASTIC INC (DH)
90 Old Sherman Tpke (06810-4124)
PHONE..................212 343-6100
Barry Jones, *President*
Sara Boak, *Editor*
Alfred C Bier Jr, *Vice Pres*
P Charnsak, *Vice Pres*
Michael Pitcher, *Facilities Mgr*
▲ EMP: 3 EST: 1895
SQ FT: 300,000
SALES (est): 2.7MM
SALES (corp-wide): 1.6B **Publicly Held**
WEB: www.grolier.com
SIC: 5192 2741 2731 Books; periodicals; miscellaneous publishing; book publishing
HQ: Scholastic Library Publishing, Inc.
90 Sherman Tpke
Danbury CT 06816
203 797-3500

(G-1939)
SCHOLASTIC LIBRARY PUBG INC (HQ)
90 Sherman Tpke (06816-0002)
P.O. Box 3765, Jefferson City MO (65102-3765)
PHONE..................203 797-3500
Dominique D'Hinnin, *Ch of Bd*
Arnaud Lagardere, *Ch of Bd*
Dick Robinson, *President*
David M Arganbright, *President*
Celia Lee, *Editor*
▲ EMP: 790 EST: 1988
SQ FT: 300,836
SALES (est): 335.9MM
SALES (corp-wide): 1.6B **Publicly Held**
WEB: www.grolier.com
SIC: 2731 5963 5192 2721 Books: publishing only; textbooks: publishing only, not printed on site; encyclopedias, house-to-house; encyclopedias & publications, direct sales; books; magazines: publishing only; books, magazines: publishing only, not printed on site; statistical reports (periodicals): publishing only; books, mail order (except book clubs); magazines, mail order; computer software development
PA: Scholastic Corporation
557 Broadway Lbby 1
New York NY 10012
212 343-6100

(G-1940)
SCHOLASTIC LIBRARY PUBG INC
90 Old Sherman Tpke (06810-4124)
P.O. Box 1737 (06816-1737)
PHONE..................573 632-1762
EMP: 13
SALES (corp-wide): 1.6B **Publicly Held**
WEB: www.grolier.com
SIC: 8231 2731 Libraries; book publishing
HQ: Scholastic Library Publishing, Inc.
90 Sherman Tpke
Danbury CT 06816
203 797-3500

(G-1941)
SCHWING BIOSET TECHNOLOGIES
98 Mill Plain Rd Ste A (06811-6101)
PHONE..................203 744-2100
Thomas Anderson, *President*
EMP: 50
SALES (est): 4MM
SALES (corp-wide): 3B **Privately Held**
WEB: www.schwing.com
SIC: 3592 Pistons & piston rings
HQ: Schwing America, Inc.
5900 Centerville Rd
Saint Paul MN 55127
651 429-0999

(G-1942)
SEALED AIR CORPORATION
10 Old Sherman Tpke (06810-4159)
PHONE..................203 791-3648
Randy Gouveia, *Vice Pres*
EMP: 120
SALES (corp-wide): 4.7B **Publicly Held**
WEB: www.sealedair.com
SIC: 3086 2671 Packaging & shipping materials, foamed plastic; packaging paper & plastics film, coated & laminated
PA: Sealed Air Corporation
2415 Cascade Pointe Blvd
Charlotte NC 28208
980 221-3235

(G-1943)
SELECT WOODWORKING LLC
11 Farm St (06811-4612)
PHONE..................203 743-1159
Chester Andrews III, *Principal*
EMP: 2
SALES (est): 147.6K **Privately Held**
SIC: 2431 Millwork

(G-1944)
SHARI GOODSTEIN ROSSI
81 Kenosia Ave (06810-7361)
PHONE..................914 485-1600
EMP: 2 EST: 2018
SALES (est): 86K **Privately Held**
SIC: 3728 Aircraft parts & equipment

(G-1945)
SHELTER ROCK WINERY
5 Shelter Rock Rd (06810-7052)
P.O. Box 5204, Brookfield (06804-5204)
PHONE..................203 948-8235
EMP: 2 EST: 2018
SALES (est): 158.6K **Privately Held**
SIC: 2084 Wines

(G-1946)
SI GROUP USA (USAA) LLC (DH)
Also Called: Addivant Usa, LLC
4 Mountainview Ter (06810-4116)
PHONE..................203 702-6140
John Steitz, *CEO*
Peter R Smith, *President*
Paul Trimble, *Vice Pres*
Patrick Weinberg, *CFO*
Jeff Kennel, *Treasurer*
◆ EMP: 150
SALES (est): 84.1MM **Privately Held**
SIC: 2869 2822 Antioxidants, rubber processing: cyclic or acyclic; ethylene-propylene rubbers, EPDM polymers
HQ: Si Group Usa Holdings (Usha) Corp.
4 Mountainview Ter
Danbury CT 06810
203 702-6140

(G-1947)
SI GROUP USA HLDINGS USHA CORP (HQ)
Also Called: Addivant USA Holdings Corp.
4 Mountainview Ter (06810-4116)
PHONE..................203 702-6140
Peter R Smith, *CEO*
◆ EMP: 29
SALES (est): 1.1B **Privately Held**
SIC: 2869 Antioxidants, rubber processing: cyclic or acyclic

(G-1948)
SIGMUND SOFTWARE LLC
83 Wooster Hts Ste 210 (06810-7549)
PHONE..................800 448-6975

Danbury - Fairfield County (G-1949)

Angelyn Spada, *Human Resources*
Jennifer Forys, *Accounts Mgr*
Joseph Santoro,
Marcus Sharpe,
EMP: 18
SALES (est): 2.7MM **Privately Held**
SIC: 7372 Prepackaged software

(G-1949)
SIGN A RAMA
Also Called: Sign-A-Rama
35 Eagle Rd (06810-4187)
PHONE.....................203 792-4091
Robert Morris, *President*
EMP: 7
SQ FT: 1,250
SALES (est): 400K **Privately Held**
SIC: 3993 Signs & advertising specialties

(G-1950)
SIGN LANGUAGE LLC
71 Newtown Rd Ste 6 (06810-6258)
PHONE.....................203 778-2250
Ira Rubinstein, *Mng Member*
Joyce Rubinstein, *Mng Member*
EMP: 3
SALES: 190K **Privately Held**
WEB: www.signlanguagesigns.com
SIC: 3993 Electric signs

(G-1951)
SIGNATURE 22 PAINTING
4 Driftway Rd Unit C2 (06811-5173)
PHONE.....................914 450-9780
Mary Anne Lichodolik, *Principal*
EMP: 2
SALES (est): 97.6K **Privately Held**
SIC: 2752 Commercial printing, lithographic

(G-1952)
SIMMONDS PRECISION PDTS INC
Also Called: UTC Aerospace Systems
100 Wooster Hts (06810-7509)
PHONE.....................203 797-5000
Justin Robert Keppy, *CEO*
Dwayne Baker, *Senior Buyer*
Eric Hansell, *Engineer*
Thomas Heydenburg, *Engineer*
Linda Kelly, *Accountant*
EMP: 36
SALES (corp-wide): 66.5B **Publicly Held**
SIC: 3829 3694 3724 3728 Aircraft & motor vehicle measurement equipment; ignition systems, high frequency; aircraft engines & engine parts; aircraft parts & equipment
HQ: Simmonds Precision Products, Inc.
100 Panton Rd
Vergennes VT 05491
802 877-4000

(G-1953)
SINGERS WELDING WORKS
44 Payne Rd (06810-4108)
PHONE.....................203 743-9353
Bernie Singer, *Owner*
EMP: 1
SALES (est): 33K **Privately Held**
SIC: 7692 Welding repair

(G-1954)
SOVIPE FOOD DISTRIBUTORS LLC
87 E Liberty St (06810-3237)
PHONE.....................203 648-2781
John C Pinto, *Principal*
EMP: 3
SALES (est): 86K **Privately Held**
SIC: 2099 Food preparations

(G-1955)
SPECTRUM BRANDS INC
Armored Autogroup
44 Old Autogbury Rd # 300 (06810-5107)
PHONE.....................203 205-2900
Guy J Andrysick, *Exec VP*
Josh Lew, *Director*
EMP: 8
SALES (corp-wide): 3.1B **Publicly Held**
SIC: 3714 Motor vehicle parts & accessories
HQ: Spectrum Brands, Inc.
3001 Deming Way
Middleton WI 53562
608 275-3340

(G-1956)
STERZINGERS WELDING LLC
28 Alan Rd (06810-8302)
PHONE.....................203 685-1575
Richard Sterzinger, *Principal*
EMP: 1
SALES (est): 92K **Privately Held**
SIC: 7692 Welding repair

(G-1957)
STP PRODUCTS MANUFACTURING CO (DH)
44 Old Ridgebury Rd # 300 (06810-5107)
PHONE.....................203 205-2900
Guy Andrysic, *President*
▼ **EMP:** 16 **EST:** 1994
SALES (est): 7.3MM
SALES (corp-wide): 3.1B **Publicly Held**
WEB: www.clorox.com
SIC: 2911 Oils, fuel

(G-1958)
T J RUSSELL ELECTRIC LLC
15 Connecticut Ave (06810-7601)
PHONE.....................203 791-8950
Todd J Russell, *Administration*
EMP: 2
SALES (est): 183.4K **Privately Held**
SIC: 3699 1731 Electrical equipment & supplies; electrical work

(G-1959)
TALK N FIX CT INC
7 Backus Ave Fl 2 (06810-7422)
PHONE.....................203 790-8905
Melissa Eigen, *Principal*
EMP: 1 **EST:** 2013
SALES (est): 72.1K **Privately Held**
SIC: 7629 3541 Electrical repair shops; machine tool replacement & repair parts, metal cutting types

(G-1960)
TARRY MEDICAL PRODUCTS INC
Also Called: Tarry Manufacturing
22 Shelter Rock Ln Unit 7 (06810-8268)
PHONE.....................203 794-1438
Scott Bell, *President*
Don Mortifoglio, *Vice Pres*
George Quatropanni, *Vice Pres*
Suzanne Anderson, *QC Mgr*
EMP: 15
SQ FT: 4,500
SALES (est): 3.3MM **Privately Held**
WEB: www.tarrymfg.com
SIC: 3841 5047 Surgical & medical instruments; medical & hospital equipment

(G-1961)
TECH AIR NORTHERN CAL LLC (PA)
Also Called: Alliance Welding Supplies
50 Mill Plain Rd (06811-5140)
PHONE.....................203 792-1834
Renee Harper, *Principal*
Myles Dempsey, *Principal*
EMP: 2
SALES (est): 4.8MM **Privately Held**
SIC: 2813 Industrial gases

(G-1962)
TEKTRONIX
100 Wooster Hts (06810-7509)
PHONE.....................203 730-2730
Jose Riojas, *President*
EMP: 2
SALES (est): 299.1K **Privately Held**
SIC: 3825 Instruments to measure electricity

(G-1963)
TOPEX INC
10 Precision Rd Fl 2 (06810-7317)
PHONE.....................203 748-5918
Anthony Pellegrino, *CEO*
John Brenna, *President*
EMP: 10

SALES: 3MM **Privately Held**
SIC: 3844 3679 X-ray apparatus & tubes; electronic loads & power supplies

(G-1964)
TP CYCLE & ENGINEERING INC
Also Called: T P Engineering
4 Finance Dr (06810-4191)
PHONE.....................203 744-4960
Thomas A Pirone, *President*
EMP: 25
SQ FT: 63,000
SALES (est): 4.9MM **Privately Held**
WEB: www.tpeng.com
SIC: 3599 8711 Machine shop, jobbing & repair; consulting engineer

(G-1965)
TRADES INDUSTRIES
20 Mountainville Ave (06810-7932)
PHONE.....................203 297-5648
EMP: 1
SALES (est): 39.6K **Privately Held**
SIC: 3999 Manufacturing industries

(G-1966)
TRIANGLE INDUSTRIES LLC
64 Triangle St Ste 1 (06810-6930)
PHONE.....................203 297-6255
Ross Rizzo, *Manager*
EMP: 1
SALES (est): 56.1K **Privately Held**
SIC: 3999 Manufacturing industries

(G-1967)
TRIBUNA NEWSPAPER LLC
32 Farview Ave 3 (06810-5533)
PHONE.....................203 730-0457
Celia Becelar,
Emmanuela Leaf,
EMP: 4
SALES (est): 326.8K **Privately Held**
SIC: 2711 Newspapers: publishing only, not printed on site

(G-1968)
TROPAX PRECISION MANUFACTURING
10 Precision Rd (06810-7317)
PHONE.....................203 794-0733
Bruno Tropeano, *President*
Elio Tropeano, *Corp Secy*
Mike Tropeano, *Vice Pres*
Keith Fredlund, *Manager*
EMP: 10
SQ FT: 6,000
SALES (est): 1.2MM **Privately Held**
SIC: 3599 Machine shop, jobbing & repair

(G-1969)
UNITEC
4 Larson Dr (06810-5132)
PHONE.....................203 778-0400
Albert Coccaro, *Owner*
EMP: 2
SALES (est): 120K **Privately Held**
SIC: 3714 Motor vehicle parts & accessories

(G-1970)
VANGUARD PRODUCTS CORPORATION
87 Newtown Rd (06810-4199)
PHONE.....................203 744-7265
Robert C Benn Sr, *Ch of Bd*
Robert C Benn Jr, *President*
Lisa Golino, *Purchasing*
Mark S Hansen, *Sales Mgr*
Merima Trako, *Program Mgr*
▲ **EMP:** 75 **EST:** 1965
SQ FT: 51,000
SALES (est): 16MM **Privately Held**
WEB: www.vanguardproducts.com
SIC: 3053 3061 Gaskets, all materials; mechanical rubber goods

(G-1971)
VERAS TRATTORIA
33 Mill Plain Rd Ste 400 (06811-7102)
PHONE.....................203 798-7800
EMP: 1
SALES (est): 80.3K **Privately Held**
SIC: 3421 Mfg Cutlery

(G-1972)
VILLARINA PASTA & FINE FOODS (PA)
22 Shelter Rock Ln Unit 4 (06810-8268)
PHONE.....................203 917-4463
Joseph Filc, *President*
Joseph M Filc, *President*
Joseph W Filc, *Vice Pres*
EMP: 7
SALES: 1.2MM **Privately Held**
SIC: 2098 2038 Macaroni & spaghetti; frozen specialties

(G-1973)
VISUAL IMPACT LLC
Also Called: Memory Lane Collections
12 Finance Dr (06810-4132)
PHONE.....................203 790-9650
William McCann,
EMP: 6
SALES: 575K **Privately Held**
SIC: 2759 Commercial printing

(G-1974)
VRD CUSTOMS LTD
50 Beaver Brook Rd Ste 1 (06810-6287)
PHONE.....................475 329-5184
EMP: 2
SALES (est): 73.2K **Privately Held**
SIC: 2759 Wrappers: printing; advertising literature: printing; posters, including billboards: printing

(G-1975)
WARMUP INC
52 Federal Rd Ste 1b (06810-6162)
PHONE.....................203 791-0072
Charles Mathias, *President*
Zoe Bean, *Human Res Mgr*
Maria Ciccia, *Sales Staff*
Martha Henry, *Sales Staff*
Keith Knorps, *Sales Staff*
▲ **EMP:** 10
SALES (est): 2.1MM **Privately Held**
SIC: 3567 Heating units & devices, industrial: electric

(G-1976)
WATER WORKS
60 Backus Ave (06810-7329)
PHONE.....................203 546-6000
Jennifer Cortes, *General Mgr*
Shanon McAvoy, *Manager*
◆ **EMP:** 5
SALES (est): 310K **Privately Held**
WEB: www.thewwwbeds.com
SIC: 3261 Bathroom accessories/fittings, vitreous china or earthenware

(G-1977)
WE STRING IT
89 Hayestown Rd (06811-4970)
PHONE.....................203 512-4513
EMP: 2
SALES (est): 109K **Privately Held**
SIC: 3949 Sporting & athletic goods

(G-1978)
WESCONN STAIRS INC
Also Called: A-1 Stairs By Wesconn Stairs
2 Mill Plain Rd (06811-5141)
P.O. Box 2148 (06813-2148)
PHONE.....................203 792-7367
Danna Mackey, *President*
EMP: 7 **EST:** 1974
SQ FT: 3,500
SALES (est): 1MM **Privately Held**
SIC: 2431 Staircases & stairs, wood

(G-1979)
WESTCHESTER PUBG SVCS LLC (PA)
Also Called: Westchester Book Group
4 Old Newtown Rd (06810-4200)
PHONE.....................203 791-0080
Dennis J Pistone, *CEO*
Susan Baker, *Director*
Tyler M Carey, *Director*
Terry Colosimo, *Director*
Michael Jon Jensen, *Director*
EMP: 8
SALES (est): 1.1MM **Privately Held**
SIC: 2791 Hand composition typesetting; typesetting, computer controlled

(G-1980)
WESTCHSTER BK/RNSFORD TYPE INC
4 Old Newtown Rd (06810-4200)
PHONE.....................203 791-0080
Dennis J Pistone, *President*
Nancy Rainsford-Pistone, *Vice Pres*
EMP: 104
SALES (est): 15.1MM **Privately Held**
SIC: 2791 Typesetting

(G-1981)
WESTCONN ORTHOPEDIC LABORATORY
52 Federal Rd Ste 2 (06810-6162)
PHONE.....................203 743-4420
Robert Foster, *President*
Elizabeth Foster, *Corp Secy*
EMP: 4
SQ FT: 1,000
SALES (est): 240K **Privately Held**
SIC: 3842 Orthopedic appliances

(G-1982)
WILBUR SIGNS
32 Concord Rd (06810-6349)
PHONE.....................203 313-4950
EMP: 1 **EST:** 2018
SALES (est): 46K **Privately Held**
SIC: 3993 Signs & advertising specialties

(G-1983)
WORLD LINK IMPORTS-EXPORTS
14 Chelsea Dr (06811-4464)
PHONE.....................203 792-0281
Victor Handal, *President*
Kathe Menick Townsend, *Vice Pres*
▲ **EMP:** 2
SQ FT: 800
SALES (est): 311.5K **Privately Held**
SIC: 3088 Plastics plumbing fixtures

(G-1984)
YARMOUTH MATERIALS INC
28 Shelter Rock Rd Ste 2 (06810-7461)
PHONE.....................203 739-0524
Michael Shea, *President*
▲ **EMP:** 1 **EST:** 2000
SQ FT: 1,200
SALES (est): 195.6K **Privately Held**
SIC: 2819 Inorganic metal compounds or salts

Danielson
Windham County

(G-1985)
A&D ENTERPRISES
16 Basley Rd (06239-2009)
PHONE.....................860 779-9025
Andrew C Stadig, *Owner*
EMP: 1
SALES (est): 56.6K **Privately Held**
SIC: 2421 Sawmills & planing mills, general

(G-1986)
ABERDEEN MFG
90 Wauregan Rd (06239-3712)
PHONE.....................860 774-9679
Tammy Joly, *Principal*
EMP: 1
SALES (est): 58K **Privately Held**
SIC: 3999 Manufacturing industries

(G-1987)
BROOKLYN SAND & GRAVEL LLC
42 Junior Ave (06239-4217)
PHONE.....................860 779-3980
Wayne L Jolley,
EMP: 4
SALES (est): 284K **Privately Held**
SIC: 1442 Construction sand & gravel

(G-1988)
DANIEL RICHARDSON
Also Called: Nutmeg Woodworking
482 Westcott Rd (06239-3202)
PHONE.....................860 774-3675
Daniel Richardson, *Owner*
EMP: 1
SALES (est): 77K **Privately Held**
SIC: 1751 2512 2511 Cabinet building & installation; upholstered household furniture; wood household furniture

(G-1989)
DENNIS SAVELA
Also Called: Independent Machine
35 Margaret Henry Rd (06239-3905)
PHONE.....................860 774-3963
Fax: 860 774-3963
EMP: 1 **EST:** 1995
SALES (est): 86K **Privately Held**
SIC: 7539 3541 Automotive Repair Mfg Machine Tools-Cutting

(G-1990)
DOUGLAS M GAGNON
Also Called: Gagnon Sign Studio
666 Upper Maple St (06239-1439)
PHONE.....................860 779-2255
Douglas M Gagnon, *Owner*
EMP: 1
SQ FT: 1,000
SALES (est): 120K **Privately Held**
WEB: www.doughaldeman.com
SIC: 3993 7389 Signs, not made in custom sign painting shops; electric signs; sign painting & lettering shop

(G-1991)
EAST COAST PULLING PARTS LLC
80 Tillinghast Rd (06239-3918)
PHONE.....................860 234-4285
Peter Barbeau, *Manager*
EMP: 2
SALES (est): 116.3K **Privately Held**
WEB: www.eastcoastpullingparts.com
SIC: 1389 Construction, repair & dismantling services

(G-1992)
GAMBREL ACRES
195 Terwilleger Rd (06239-3423)
PHONE.....................860 774-3047
Gordon Brennan, *Owner*
EMP: 1
SALES (est): 147.5K **Privately Held**
SIC: 2541 Cabinets, lockers & shelving

(G-1993)
HUTCHINSON PRECISION SS INC
39 Wauregan Rd (06239-3714)
PHONE.....................860 779-0300
Paul Fortier, *Vice Pres*
James Basque, *Controller*
▼ **EMP:** 180 **EST:** 1957
SQ FT: 51,000
SALES (est): 44.4MM
SALES (corp-wide): 8.4B **Publicly Held**
WEB: www.nnbr.com
SIC: 3069 Molded rubber products
HQ: Hutchinson
 2 Rue Balzac
 Paris 8e Arrondissement 75008
 140 748-300

(G-1994)
INS SREEN PRINTING & AIR
150 Main St (06239-2821)
PHONE.....................860 779-0566
EMP: 2
SALES (est): 131.1K **Privately Held**
SIC: 2752 Lithographic Commercial Printing

(G-1995)
JOLLEY PRECAST INC
463 Putnam Rd (06239-2041)
PHONE.....................860 774-9066
Clarence Jolley, *President*
David Jolley, *Vice Pres*
Eleanor Jolley, *Vice Pres*
Stacie Jolley, *Bookkeeper*
Duane Hipp, *Regl Sales Mgr*
EMP: 21
SQ FT: 1,080
SALES (est): 3.6MM **Privately Held**
SIC: 3272 5074 Septic tanks, concrete; covers, catch basin: concrete; steps, prefabricated concrete; pipes & fittings, plastic

(G-1996)
KAIBRY SCREEN PRINTING
17 Colleen St (06239-3301)
PHONE.....................860 774-0234
Ken Saucier, *Owner*
EMP: 1
SALES (est): 67.6K **Privately Held**
SIC: 2759 5699 Screen printing; T-shirts, custom printed

(G-1997)
MAGIC SIGNS
75 Connecticut Mills Ave (06239-1600)
PHONE.....................860 457-8940
EMP: 1
SALES (est): 61.3K **Privately Held**
SIC: 3993 Signs & advertising specialties

(G-1998)
MARC JOHNSON
16 Depot Rd (06239-2019)
PHONE.....................860 774-3315
Marc Johnson, *Principal*
EMP: 5
SALES (est): 538.5K **Privately Held**
SIC: 3161 Luggage

(G-1999)
NOVO NORDISK PHARMACEUTICALS
31 King St (06239-4120)
PHONE.....................860 779-2668
Glen Jensen, *Principal*
Chad Henry, *Opers Dir*
EMP: 2 **EST:** 2010
SALES (est): 118K **Privately Held**
SIC: 2834 Pharmaceutical preparations

(G-2000)
PELLETIER MILLWRIGHTS LLC
161 Moosup Pond Rd (06239-2015)
PHONE.....................860 564-8936
Debra Pelletier,
Marc Pelletier,
EMP: 5
SALES (est): 600.4K **Privately Held**
SIC: 2041 Flour & other grain mill products

(G-2001)
SEISMIC MONITORING SVCS LLC
70 Black Rock Ave (06239-4102)
PHONE.....................860 753-6363
Charles A Berube Jr, *President*
EMP: 2
SALES (est): 100.2K **Privately Held**
SIC: 1382 Seismograph surveys

(G-2002)
SIRI MANUFACTURING COMPANY
90 Wauregan Rd (06239-3712)
PHONE.....................860 236-5901
Roger Bond, *President*
Robert Bond, *Co-President*
Craig Bond, *Manager*
Tammy Joly, *Director*
Ruth Bond, *Admin Sec*
▲ **EMP:** 23
SQ FT: 100,000
SALES (est): 5.8MM **Privately Held**
WEB: www.siriwire.com
SIC: 3315 Wire & fabricated wire products

(G-2003)
SPIROL INTERNATIONAL CORP (HQ)
30 Rock Ave (06239-1434)
PHONE.....................860 774-8571
William R Hunt, *President*
Tammy Manning, *General Mgr*
Jeffrey F Koehl, *Chairman*
Hans H Koehl, *Chairman*
James C Shaw, *Chairman*
▲ **EMP:** 150
SQ FT: 120,000
SALES (est): 69.1MM **Privately Held**
WEB: www.spirol.com
SIC: 3452 3499 3469 3053 Pins; nuts, metal; washers; shims, metal; stamping metal for the trade; gaskets, all materials; fasteners, industrial: nuts, bolts, screws, etc.; copper foundries

PA: Spirol International Holding Corporation
 30 Rock Ave
 Danielson CT 06239
 860 774-8571

(G-2004)
SPIROL INTL HOLDG CORP (PA)
30 Rock Ave (06239-1425)
PHONE.....................860 774-8571
Jeffrey F Koehl, *CEO*
Christie Jones, *General Mgr*
Hans Koehl, *Chairman*
▲ **EMP:** 150 **EST:** 1979
SQ FT: 100,000
SALES (est): 69.1MM **Privately Held**
SIC: 3452 3499 3469 Pins; nuts, metal; washers, shims, metal; stamping metal for the trade

(G-2005)
UP TOP SCREEN PRINTING ✪
106 Main St (06239-2820)
PHONE.....................860 412-9798
EMP: 2 **EST:** 2019
SALES (est): 73.2K **Privately Held**
SIC: 2759 Letterpress & screen printing

(G-2006)
VEGWARE US INC
90 Wauregan Rd (06239-3712)
PHONE.....................860 779-7970
Robert A Bond, *President*
Craig A Bond, *Vice Pres*
▲ **EMP:** 8 **EST:** 2008
SALES (est): 969.7K **Privately Held**
SIC: 2836 Biological products, except diagnostic

Darien
Fairfield County

(G-2007)
BELLA PIETRA LLC
110 Post Rd Ste A (06820-2931)
PHONE.....................203 655-1322
Vincent A Sciarretta,
EMP: 1
SALES (est): 222.1K **Privately Held**
SIC: 3272 5999 Art marble, concrete; monuments & tombstones

(G-2008)
BERWICK INDUSTRIES LLC
366 Post Rd (06820-3605)
PHONE.....................475 228-5822
Paul Adinolfi,
EMP: 1
SALES (est): 44.3K **Privately Held**
SIC: 3944 Electronic games & toys

(G-2009)
BLINDS DEPT
366 Post Rd (06820-3605)
PHONE.....................203 655-3378
Paul Lewis, *Owner*
EMP: 2
SALES (est): 105.3K **Privately Held**
SIC: 2591 Drapery hardware & blinds & shades

(G-2010)
CECELIA NEW YORK LLC
23 Chestnut St (06820-4209)
PHONE.....................917 392-4536
Ashley N Cole, *Principal*
EMP: 6
SQ FT: 530
SALES (est): 594.7K **Privately Held**
SIC: 3144 Boots, canvas or leather: women's

(G-2011)
CHAPIN PACKAGING LLC
Also Called: Chapin Printing Group
1078 Post Rd Ste 1 (06820-5424)
PHONE.....................203 202-2747
Trask Pfeifle,
EMP: 8
SALES (est): 534.1K **Privately Held**
SIC: 7389 2789 Printers' services: folding, collating; bookbinding & related work

(G-2012)
CHECK IT DARIEN LLC
40 Fairfield Ave (06820-4213)
PHONE.....................................203 655-2036
Patrick Rogers, *Mng Member*
EMP: 2
SALES (est): 181.2K **Privately Held**
SIC: 3699 Security devices

(G-2013)
CJ CERAMICS AND MORE LLC
11 Homewood Ln (06820-6109)
PHONE.....................................203 246-2798
Cynthia J Shaw, *Principal*
EMP: 1
SALES (est): 45.4K **Privately Held**
SIC: 3269 Pottery products

(G-2014)
COMPLEAT ANGLER
Also Called: Tca
541 Post Rd (06820-3609)
PHONE.....................................203 655-9400
Michael Vaughn, *Owner*
Scott Bennett, *Principal*
Bob Boland, *Principal*
Todd Fedele, *Principal*
EMP: 1
SALES (est): 97K **Privately Held**
SIC: 3949 5091 5199 Fishing equipment; fishing tackle; bait, fishing

(G-2015)
CORPORATE CARTRIDGE
145 Raymond St (06820-4907)
PHONE.....................................203 655-7197
John Keena, *Partner*
Peter Keena, *Partner*
EMP: 2
SALES (est): 126.5K **Privately Held**
SIC: 2893 Duplicating ink

(G-2016)
CYTOGEL PHARMA LLC (PA)
3 Thorndal Cir (06820-5434)
PHONE.....................................203 662-6617
C Dean Maglaris, *CEO*
C Dean Marglaris,
EMP: 2
SALES (est): 268.1K **Privately Held**
SIC: 2834 Druggists' preparations (pharmaceuticals)

(G-2017)
DARIEN DOUGHNUT LLC
364 Heights Rd (06820)
PHONE.....................................203 656-2805
Philip Santomassi, *President*
EMP: 3
SALES (est): 92.2K **Privately Held**
SIC: 5461 2051 Doughnuts; doughnuts, except frozen

(G-2018)
DARIEN LAWN MOWER REPAIR
126 Post Rd (06820-2911)
PHONE.....................................203 656-1869
Theodore J Olsen, *Owner*
EMP: 1
SQ FT: 2,000
SALES (est): 90K **Privately Held**
SIC: 5261 7699 3546 Lawnmowers & tractors; lawn mower repair shop; saws & sawing equipment

(G-2019)
DARIEN TECHNOLOGY FOUNDATION I
5 Brook St Ste G (06820-4504)
PHONE.....................................203 655-5099
Ward Glassmeyer, *Principal*
EMP: 2
SALES (est): 554.1K **Privately Held**
SIC: 7372 Prepackaged software

(G-2020)
DATACOMM MANAGEMENT SVCS LLC
245 Noroton Ave (06820-4222)
PHONE.....................................203 858-9846
Jacqueline Conetta,
EMP: 1
SALES (est): 123.9K **Privately Held**
SIC: 3669 7389 Intercommunication systems, electric;

(G-2021)
DIORIO PRINTING SERVICE
14 Center St (06820-4501)
P.O. Box 1794 (06820-1794)
PHONE.....................................203 656-0557
Marc D'Iorio, *Owner*
EMP: 1
SQ FT: 1,200
SALES (est): 325K **Privately Held**
SIC: 2752 Commercial printing, offset

(G-2022)
DP2 LLC HEAD
25 Old Kings Hwy N (06820-4608)
PHONE.....................................203 655-0747
Peter Dan Winkle,
EMP: 12
SALES (est): 679K **Privately Held**
SIC: 3433 3585 Space heaters, except electric; air conditioning equipment, complete

(G-2023)
EXECUTIVE PRINTING DARIEN LLC
1082 Post Rd (06820-5441)
PHONE.....................................203 655-4691
J Trask Pfeifle, *Mng Member*
EMP: 6
SALES (est): 879.3K **Privately Held**
SIC: 2752 Commercial printing, offset

(G-2024)
FERGTECH INC
28 Thorndal Cir Ste 1 (06820-5429)
PHONE.....................................203 656-1139
Bruce Ferguson, *Branch Mgr*
EMP: 6
SALES (corp-wide): 1.9MM **Privately Held**
SIC: 7372 Application computer software
PA: Fergtech Inc
    19 Wilson Ridge Rd
    Darien CT 06820
    203 656-1139

(G-2025)
FERGTECH INC (PA)
19 Wilson Ridge Rd (06820-5133)
PHONE.....................................203 656-1139
Bruce S Ferguson, *President*
EMP: 6
SQ FT: 4,000
SALES (est): 1.9MM **Privately Held**
WEB: www.fergtech.com
SIC: 7372 7371 Business oriented computer software; computer software development & applications

(G-2026)
FLAVRZ ORGANIC BEVERAGES LLC
25 Hamilton Ln (06820-2810)
PHONE.....................................203 716-8082
Valli Stavros-Baker, *President*
Steven E Baker, *Mng Member*
EMP: 3
SALES (est): 219.7K **Privately Held**
SIC: 2087 Beverage bases, concentrates, syrups, powders & mixes

(G-2027)
HAY ISLAND HOLDING CORPORATION (PA)
20 Thorndal Cir (06820-5421)
PHONE.....................................203 656-8000
William T Ziegler, *President*
Helen Z Benjamin, *Vice Pres*
Cynthia Brighton, *Vice Pres*
John Haley, *Vice Pres*
Peter Ziegler, *Vice Pres*
◆ **EMP:** 160
SQ FT: 7,200
SALES (est): 582.9MM **Privately Held**
SIC: 5194 2131 Tobacco & tobacco products; chewing tobacco; snuff

(G-2028)
HEATHERWREATH PARTNERS LP
282 Noroton Ave (06820-4223)
PHONE.....................................203 662-1084
Christopher Krantz, *Principal*
EMP: 2
SALES (est): 100.8K **Privately Held**
SIC: 3999 Wreaths, artificial

(G-2029)
JOY FOOD COMPANY
138 Goodwives River Rd (06820-5807)
PHONE.....................................917 549-6240
Tom Arrix, *CEO*
EMP: 2
SALES (est): 62.3K **Privately Held**
SIC: 2047 Dog food

(G-2030)
JVCART LLC
10 Birch Rd (06820-2901)
PHONE.....................................917 497-8791
Janette Van Campenhout, *Manager*
EMP: 1
SALES (est): 54.1K **Privately Held**
SIC: 3993 Advertising artwork

(G-2031)
LIFE STUDY FLLWSHIP FOUNDATION
90 Heights Rd (06820-4129)
PHONE.....................................203 655-1436
Michael Keane, *CEO*
John J Keane Jr, *Vice Pres*
EMP: 26
SQ FT: 10,000
SALES: 1.3MM **Privately Held**
WEB: www.lifestudyfellowship.org
SIC: 2731 7331 2741 Books: publishing only; pamphlets: publishing only, not printed on site; direct mail advertising services; miscellaneous publishing

(G-2032)
LITTLE BLUE INSITE LLC
9 Old Kings Hwy S Fl 4 (06820-4505)
PHONE.....................................203 202-7690
Gregory F Mulligan, *Principal*
EMP: 1
SALES (est): 50.6K **Privately Held**
SIC: 2731 Book publishing

(G-2033)
NEW ENGLAND BPHRMCUTICALS CORP
10 Five Mile River Rd (06820-6230)
PHONE.....................................917 992-4250
Jeffery M Hudson Jr, *President*
EMP: 2
SALES (est): 74.4K **Privately Held**
SIC: 2834 Pharmaceutical preparations

(G-2034)
NOROTON PUBLISHING CO
100 Heights Rd (06820-4129)
PHONE.....................................203 655-1436
Ted Lumbberg, *Owner*
EMP: 1 **EST:** 2011
SALES (est): 44K **Privately Held**
SIC: 2741 Miscellaneous publishing

(G-2035)
NTECO INC
10 Center St (06820-4500)
PHONE.....................................203 656-1154
Kevin Ohara, *Director*
EMP: 30 **EST:** 2013
SALES (est): 1.4MM **Privately Held**
SIC: 3272 Tanks, concrete

(G-2036)
O-LIMINATOR LLC
137 Hollow Tree Ridge Rd (06820-5045)
PHONE.....................................800 608-9541
William Y Bogle, *Branch Mgr*
EMP: 1 **Privately Held**
SIC: 2074 Cottonseed oil, deodorized
PA: O-Liminator Llc
    902 S Randall Rd Ste C240
    Saint Charles IL 60174

(G-2037)
PEARTREE POINT SOFTWARE LLC
45 Edgerton St (06820-4124)
PHONE.....................................203 940-1069
James Backus, *Principal*
EMP: 2
SALES (est): 94.3K **Privately Held**
SIC: 7372 Prepackaged software

(G-2038)
PETROGLYPH ENERGY INC (PA)
1 Thorndal Cir Ste 3 (06820-5425)
PHONE.....................................208 685-7600
Paul Powell, *President*
William C Glynn, *President*
Michael E Rich, *President*
Rich Beath, *Vice Pres*
Marshall Murrin, *Vice Pres*
EMP: 1 **EST:** 1997
SALES (est): 7.6MM **Privately Held**
SIC: 1311 Crude petroleum production; natural gas production

(G-2039)
PHOTON PARTNERS LLC
366 Hollow Tree Ridge Rd (06820-3218)
PHONE.....................................203 807-3623
Joshua Gonnella, *Principal*
EMP: 2
SALES (est): 93.5K **Privately Held**
SIC: 3661 Fiber optics communications equipment

(G-2040)
PURPLE HEART INDUSTRIES LLC
25 Salt Box Ln (06820-5232)
PHONE.....................................203 655-5039
John R Tibbetts, *Principal*
EMP: 1
SALES (est): 64.4K **Privately Held**
SIC: 3999 Manufacturing industries

(G-2041)
RICHTER ELECTRIC INC
27 Middlesex Rd (06820-3732)
P.O. Box 2638 (06820-8638)
PHONE.....................................203 667-4644
Albert Richter, *Branch Mgr*
EMP: 1
SALES (corp-wide): 2.4MM **Privately Held**
SIC: 1731 3699 General electrical contractor; electrical equipment & supplies
PA: Richter Electric Inc
    3220 N Pontiac Dr
    Janesville WI 53545
    608 752-0456

(G-2042)
ROSEVILLE DESIGNS LLC (PA)
3 Cliff Ave (06820-4915)
PHONE.....................................203 858-5744
Alexandra M Shannan,
EMP: 1
SALES (est): 167.8K **Privately Held**
SIC: 2754 Stationery & invitation printing, gravure

(G-2043)
SAW MILL CAPITAL LLC
137 Hollow Tree Ridge Rd # 303 (06820-5045)
PHONE.....................................203 662-0573
EMP: 2
SALES (est): 100K **Privately Held**
SIC: 2421 Sawmills And Planing Mills, General

(G-2044)
SEWARD GROUP LLC
6 Oakshade Ave (06820-3711)
PHONE.....................................203 357-1900
Drew Kirby, *Manager*
EMP: 2
SALES (est): 140.5K **Privately Held**
SIC: 3469 Furniture components, porcelain enameled

(G-2045)
SMOKEY MOUNTAIN CHEW INC (PA)
1 Center St Fl 2 (06820-4503)
PHONE.....................................203 656-1088
David Savoca, *President*
EMP: 3
SQ FT: 2,500
SALES (est): 23.8MM **Privately Held**
WEB: www.smokeysnuff.com
SIC: 2131 Chewing & smoking tobacco

GEOGRAPHIC SECTION
Dayville - Windham County (G-2072)

(G-2046)
TELLUS TECHNOLOGY INC (PA)
10 Corbin Dr Ste 210 (06820-5403)
PHONE..............................646 265-7960
Sanford Ewing, *CEO*
Kenneth Hamby, *President*
James Kelly, *Chairman*
Cosmin Negulescu, *Vice Pres*
EMP: 4
SALES (est): 324.2K **Privately Held**
SIC: 3069 Reclaimed rubber (reworked by manufacturing processes)

(G-2047)
TOPS MANUFACTURING CO INC (PA)
83 Salisbury Rd (06820-2225)
PHONE..............................203 655-9367
Mitchell A Himmel, *President*
Patricia Himmel, *Vice Pres*
▲ **EMP:** 4 **EST:** 1964
SALES (est): 1.3MM **Privately Held**
SIC: 3089 3469 3229 Kitchenware, plastic; metal stampings; pressed & blown glass

(G-2048)
UBM LLC
Also Called: Cliggott Publishing
330 Post Rd Fl 2 (06820-3600)
PHONE..............................203 662-6501
Gary Marshal, *CEO*
EMP: 5
SALES (corp-wide): 1.3B **Privately Held**
WEB: www.cmp.com
SIC: 2721 2741 2731 8748 Periodicals; miscellaneous publishing; book publishing; publishing consultant
HQ: Ubm, Llc
1983 Marcus Ave Ste 250
New Hyde Park NY 11042
516 562-7800

(G-2049)
UNIWORLD BUS PUBLICATIONS INC
35 Kensett Ln (06820-2438)
PHONE..............................201 384-4900
Michael Shimkin, *Ch of Bd*
Barbara Fiorito, *CFO*
EMP: 7
SALES (est): 275K **Privately Held**
WEB: www.uniworldbp.com
SIC: 7372 7389 Publishers' computer software;

(G-2050)
US BARRICADES LLC
30 Old Kings Hwy S Ste 10 (06820-4519)
P.O. Box 2261 (06820-0261)
PHONE..............................203 883-8660
Tina Winter,
EMP: 2
SALES: 168K **Privately Held**
SIC: 3446 Fences or posts, ornamental iron or steel

(G-2051)
WHITE BRIDGE LIQUORS INC
Also Called: White Bride Wines
284 Tokeneke Rd Ste 3 (06820-4800)
PHONE..............................203 655-0658
Michael Interlandi, *President*
Jill Interlandi, *Admin Sec*
EMP: 3
SQ FT: 2,400
SALES (est): 580K **Privately Held**
WEB: www.winebargains.com
SIC: 5921 2086 Liquor stores; bottled & canned soft drinks

(G-2052)
ZIGA MEDIA LLC
5 Overbrook Ln (06820-2819)
PHONE..............................203 656-0076
Laura Livingston, *Prdtn Dir*
Charles J Ziga, *Mng Member*
▲ **EMP:** 3
SALES (est): 267.7K **Privately Held**
WEB: www.newyorklandmarks.com
SIC: 2752 2731 2741 Calendars, lithographed; books: publishing only; miscellaneous publishing

---

Dayville
Windham County

(G-2053)
ALL STATES ASPHALT INC
Also Called: Killingly Asphalt Products
127 Attwaugan Crossing Rd (06241-1601)
PHONE..............................860 774-7550
Todd Larkin, *Branch Mgr*
EMP: 6
SALES (corp-wide): 202.2MM **Privately Held**
WEB: www.allstatesasphalt.com
SIC: 2951 Asphalt paving mixtures & blocks
PA: All States Asphalt, Inc.
325 Amherst Rd
Sunderland MA 01375
413 665-7021

(G-2054)
BOLLORE INC
60 Louisa Viens Dr (06241-1106)
P.O. Box 530 (06241-0530)
PHONE..............................860 774-2930
Steve Brunetti, *President*
Bernard Jean-Luc, *General Mgr*
Xavier Cys, *Opers Staff*
Rob Caron, *Engineer*
Tracy Lefebvre, *Human Res Mgr*
▲ **EMP:** 80
SQ FT: 62,000
SALES (est): 20.5MM **Privately Held**
WEB: www.bolloreinc.com
SIC: 2671 Plastic film, coated or laminated for packaging
HQ: Bollore
Odet
Ergue-Gaberic 29500
298 667-200

(G-2055)
BOUDREAUS WELDING CO INC
1029 N Main St (06241-2170)
P.O. Box 339 (06241-0339)
PHONE..............................860 774-2771
Ronald Jussaume, *President*
Julie Jussaume, *Vice Pres*
Monique Jussaume, *Admin Sec*
Randall Jussaume, *Admin Sec*
EMP: 25 **EST:** 1957
SQ FT: 20,600
SALES (est): 2.4MM **Privately Held**
SIC: 3446 3312 Railings, bannisters, guards, etc.: made from metal pipe; railings, prefabricated metal; stairs, staircases, stair treads: prefabricated metal; structural & rail mill products

(G-2056)
CABINET MAKER
119 Soap St (06241-1611)
PHONE..............................860 933-0272
EMP: 1
SALES (est): 53.7K **Privately Held**
SIC: 2434 Wood kitchen cabinets

(G-2057)
CENTRAL ELECTRIC INC
364 Putnam Pike (06241-1621)
P.O. Box 34 (06241-0034)
PHONE..............................860 774-3054
EMP: 3 **EST:** 1996
SQ FT: 3,000
SALES (est): 250K **Privately Held**
SIC: 7694 Electric Motor Repair Services

(G-2058)
COLTS PLASTICS COMPANY INC
969 N Main St (06241-2123)
P.O. Box 429 (06241-0429)
PHONE..............................860 774-2277
Charles W Bentley Jr, *President*
Mark Egan, *Vice Pres*
Pat Garrity, *Vice Pres*
Patrick Garrity, *Vice Pres*
Chris Lepine, *Engineer*
▲ **EMP:** 125 **EST:** 1936
SQ FT: 80,000
SALES (est): 24.7MM **Privately Held**
WEB: www.coltsplastics.com
SIC: 3089 Jars, plastic; caps, plastic

(G-2059)
COUNTRYSIDE CRAFTS
517 Chestnut Hill Rd (06241-1705)
PHONE..............................860 774-0446
Ann Labelle, *Owner*
EMP: 1 **EST:** 1985
SALES (est): 48K **Privately Held**
SIC: 3999 Flowers, artificial & preserved

(G-2060)
CUSTOM PLASTIC DISTRS INC
Also Called: C P D
364 Putnam Pike (06241-1621)
P.O. Box 672, Putnam (06260-0672)
PHONE..............................860 779-5833
Daniel P Roy Jr, *President*
Patricia M Roy, *Treasurer*
▲ **EMP:** 1
SQ FT: 1,000
SALES (est): 161.2K **Privately Held**
WEB: www.accessfloorgrommets.com
SIC: 2298 Cable, fiber

(G-2061)
FERRON MOLD AND TOOL LLC
154 Louisa Viens Dr (06241-1133)
P.O. Box 144 (06241-0144)
PHONE..............................860 774-5555
Norman Ferron, *Partner*
Beverly Ferron, *Partner*
EMP: 8
SQ FT: 6,500
SALES (est): 1.4MM **Privately Held**
SIC: 3544 Industrial molds; special dies & tools

(G-2062)
FILMX TECHNOLOGIES
20 Louisa Viens Dr (06241-1106)
PHONE..............................860 779-3403
Donald Romine, *President*
Patricia Roy, *Human Res Mgr*
◆ **EMP:** 5
SALES (est): 551K **Privately Held**
SIC: 3081 Unsupported plastics film & sheet

(G-2063)
FRITO-LAY NORTH AMERICA INC
1886 Upper Maple St (06241-1555)
PHONE..............................860 412-1000
Kevin Richardson, *Opers Staff*
Bob Shrek, *Manager*
EMP: 600
SALES (corp-wide): 64.6B **Publicly Held**
WEB: www.fritolay.com
SIC: 2096 Potato chips & similar snacks
HQ: Frito-Lay North America, Inc.
7701 Legacy Dr
Plano TX 75024

(G-2064)
MIYOSHI AMERICA INC (HQ)
110 Louisa Viens Dr (06241-1132)
PHONE..............................860 779-3990
Kaoru Takagi, *President*
Taizo Miyoshi, *Chairman*
▲ **EMP:** 67
SQ FT: 82,000
SALES (est): 21.1MM **Privately Held**
WEB: www.us-cosm.com
SIC: 2844 5169 Cosmetic preparations; chemicals & allied products

(G-2065)
MIYOSHI AMERICA INC
313 Lake Rd (06241-1551)
P.O. Box 859 (06241-0859)
PHONE..............................860 779-3990
Kaoru Takagi, *President*
EMP: 11 **Privately Held**
SIC: 3295 5169 2844 Minerals, ground or otherwise treated; chemicals & allied products; toilet preparations
HQ: Miyoshi America, Inc.
110 Louisa Viens Dr
Dayville CT 06241
860 779-3990

(G-2066)
MIYOSHI AMERICA INC
90 Louisa Viens Dr (06241-1106)
P.O. Box 859 (06241-0859)
PHONE..............................860 779-3990
Kaoru Takagi, *President*
EMP: 6 **Privately Held**
SIC: 3295 5169 2844 Minerals, ground or otherwise treated; chemicals & allied products; toilet preparations
HQ: Miyoshi America, Inc.
110 Louisa Viens Dr
Dayville CT 06241
860 779-3990

(G-2067)
NORTHEAST FOODS INC
Also Called: Automatic Rolls of New England
328 Lake Rd (06241-1537)
PHONE..............................860 779-1117
John Denitti, *Engineer*
Fred Sexton, *Branch Mgr*
Kevin Ferra, *Technician*
EMP: 100
SALES (corp-wide): 335.5MM **Privately Held**
SIC: 2051 Bakery: wholesale or wholesale/retail combined
PA: Northeast Foods, Inc.
601 S Caroline St
Baltimore MD 21231
410 276-7254

(G-2068)
PACKRAT SOFTWARE
5 Conrad Park (06241-2141)
PHONE..............................860 774-1538
EMP: 2
SALES (est): 94.2K **Privately Held**
SIC: 7372 Prepackaged software

(G-2069)
PEPSI-COLA BTLG OF WRCSTER INC
Also Called: Pepsico
135 Louisa Viens Dr (06241-1105)
P.O. Box 736 (06241-0736)
PHONE..............................860 774-4007
Tim Brown, *Branch Mgr*
EMP: 30
SALES (corp-wide): 16.5MM **Privately Held**
WEB: www.pepsiworcester.com
SIC: 2086 Carbonated soft drinks, bottled & canned
PA: Pepsi-Cola Bottling Co., Of Worcester, Inc.
90 Industrial Dr
Holden MA 01520
508 829-6551

(G-2070)
PLASTICS COLOR CORP INC
349 Lake Rd (06241-1551)
PHONE..............................800 922-9936
Raymond Lachapelle, *Principal*
EMP: 2
SALES (est): 81.8K **Privately Held**
SIC: 2821 Plastics materials & resins

(G-2071)
PUTNAM PLASTICS CORPORATION
40 Louisa Viens Dr (06241-1106)
PHONE..............................860 774-1559
Jim Dandeneau, *CEO*
James Binch, *President*
Lawrence Acquarulo Jr, *Co-CEO*
Paul Bergstrom, *Purchasing*
William Appling, *Engineer*
EMP: 150
SQ FT: 40,000
SALES (est): 30.8MM **Privately Held**
WEB: www.putnamplastics.com
SIC: 3082 Tubes, unsupported plastic

(G-2072)
ROL-VAC LIMITED PARTNERSHIP
207 Tracy Rd (06241-1123)
P.O. Box 777 (06241-0777)
PHONE..............................860 928-9929
Ron Jones, *General Ptnr*
▲ **EMP:** 12 **EST:** 1998
SQ FT: 45,000
SALES (est): 292.5K **Privately Held**
WEB: www.rolvac.com
SIC: 2671 Packaging paper & plastics film, coated & laminated

Dayville - Windham County (G-2073)

(G-2073)
SLATER HILL TOOL
134 Slater Hill Rd (06241-1911)
PHONE..................................860 377-5503
Josh Nason, *Owner*
EMP: 1
SALES: 90K **Privately Held**
SIC: 3599 Machine shop, jobbing & repair

(G-2074)
SPECIALIZED MARKETING INTL INC
Also Called: SMI
505 Hartford Pike (06241-2119)
PHONE..................................860 779-3264
Vickie Washburn, *President*
Josh Washburn, *Vice Pres*
EMP: 2
SQ FT: 100
SALES: 550K **Privately Held**
WEB: www.smi-gripfast.com
SIC: 3429 3089 Metal fasteners; hardware, plastic

(G-2075)
SYMBOL MATTRESS OF NEW ENGLAND
312 Lake Rd (06241-1537)
P.O. Box 6689, Richmond VA (23230-0689)
PHONE..................................860 779-3112
Gordon Wallace, *CEO*
Charles Neal, *President*
Ronald Clevenger, *Vice Pres*
EMP: 450
SALES (est): 26.2MM
SALES (corp-wide): 106.8MM **Privately Held**
WEB: www.symbolmattress.com
SIC: 2515 Mattresses & foundations
PA: Eastern Sleep Products Company
4901 Fitzhugh Ave
Richmond VA 23230
804 254-1711

(G-2076)
UNIVERSITY OPTICS LLC
Also Called: University Opticians
791 Hartford Pike (06241-1715)
P.O. Box 450, Wasco IL (60183-0450)
PHONE..................................860 779-6123
Aarlan Acepo,
EMP: 3
SALES (est): 329.2K **Privately Held**
SIC: 3851 Eyeglasses, lenses & frames

(G-2077)
WEB INDUSTRIES
312 Lake Rd (06241-1537)
PHONE..................................860 779-3403
EMP: 1
SALES (est): 57.9K **Privately Held**
SIC: 3999 Manufacturing industries

(G-2078)
WEB INDUSTRIES HARTFORD INC (HQ)
20 Louisa Viens Dr (06241-1106)
PHONE..................................860 779-3197
Robert Fulton, *Ch of Bd*
Donald Romine, *President*
Steve Sherburne, *Controller*
James Hanrahan, *Admin Sec*
▲ **EMP:** 32 **EST:** 1982
SQ FT: 40,000
SALES: 4.7MM
SALES (corp-wide): 117.8MM **Privately Held**
WEB: www.primastrip.com
SIC: 3082 5162 Unsupported plastics profile shapes; plastics film
PA: Web Industries Inc.
700 Nickerson Rd Ste 250
Marlborough MA 01752
508 898-2988

(G-2079)
WEB INDUSTRIES INC
Also Called: Engineering Division
154 Louisa Viens Dr (06241-1133)
PHONE..................................860 779-3403
Ed Martins, *QC Mgr*
Tom E Mc Gurl, *Branch Mgr*
Tom McGurl, *Manager*
EMP: 2

SALES (corp-wide): 117.8MM **Privately Held**
SIC: 2621 2297 3441 Paper mills; nonwoven fabrics; fabricated structural metal
PA: Web Industries Inc.
700 Nickerson Rd Ste 250
Marlborough MA 01752
508 898-2988

(G-2080)
WHATEVER WELDING LLC
510 Putnam Pike (06241-1110)
PHONE..................................860 779-7703
Cynthia Church,
EMP: 1
SALES (est): 40.5K **Privately Held**
SIC: 7692 Welding repair

Deep River
Middlesex County

(G-2081)
A 2 Z SCREEN PRINTING LLC
500 Main St Ste 4 (06417-2000)
PHONE..................................860 526-9684
EMP: 1
SQ FT: 2,000
SALES (corp-wide): 210K **Privately Held**
SIC: 2759 Promotional Products
PA: A 2 Z Screen Printing, L.L.C.
6 Pine Lake Rd
Ivoryton CT 06442

(G-2082)
ABSTRACT TOOL INC
500 Main St Ste 15 (06417-2000)
PHONE..................................860 526-4635
Ken Hallden, *President*
Glenn Guggenheim, *Vice Pres*
Janet Hallden, *Treasurer*
Diane Guggenheim, *Admin Sec*
EMP: 10
SQ FT: 6,000
SALES (est): 660K **Privately Held**
SIC: 3599 Machine shop, jobbing & repair

(G-2083)
ANTHONY DA RE WELDING
118 Stevenstown Rd (06417-1560)
PHONE..................................860 526-2659
Anthony D Da RE, *Owner*
EMP: 1 **EST:** 2013
SALES (est): 48K **Privately Held**
SIC: 7692 Welding repair

(G-2084)
APS ROBOTICS & INTEGRATION LLC
500 Main St Ste 9 (06417-2000)
P.O. Box 245 (06417-0245)
PHONE..................................860 526-1040
Charles M Chadwick,
EMP: 3 **EST:** 1997
SQ FT: 5,000
SALES: 250K **Privately Held**
SIC: 3599 Machine shop, jobbing & repair; custom machinery

(G-2085)
BELL AND HOWELL LLC
6 Winter Ave (06417-1813)
PHONE..................................860 526-9561
EMP: 27 **Privately Held**
SIC: 3579 Paper handling machines
PA: Bell And Howell, Llc
3791 S Alston Ave
Durham NC 27713

(G-2086)
CHESTER BOATWORKS
444 Main St (06417-2034)
PHONE..................................860 526-2227
Gil Bartlett, *Owner*
EMP: 3 **EST:** 2014
SALES (est): 263.3K **Privately Held**
SIC: 3732 Boats, fiberglass: building & repairing

(G-2087)
CT SIGN SERVICE LLC
500 Industrial Park Rd (06417-1698)
PHONE..................................860 322-3954
John R Morrison III, *President*

EMP: 2
SALES (est): 71.8K **Privately Held**
SIC: 3993 Signs & advertising specialties

(G-2088)
ESSEX OLIVE OIL COMPANY LLC
39 Winthrop Rd (06417-1654)
PHONE..................................860 526-2205
Heather Olson, *Principal*
EMP: 3
SALES (est): 100.5K **Privately Held**
SIC: 2079 Olive oil

(G-2089)
FLEXO LABEL SOLUTIONS LLC
500 Main St Ste 6 (06417-2000)
PHONE..................................860 243-9300
Rod Milligan, *Owner*
EMP: 9
SALES (est): 1.4MM **Privately Held**
SIC: 2679 Labels, paper: made from purchased material

(G-2090)
G & R WELDING
537 Winthrop Rd (06417-1510)
PHONE..................................860 526-3353
Ronald E Larsen, *Owner*
EMP: 1
SALES: 80K **Privately Held**
SIC: 1799 3444 Welding on site; sheet metalwork

(G-2091)
GROVE SYSTEMS INC
572 Route 148 (06419-1107)
PHONE..................................860 663-2555
Jennifer Luzietti, *President*
EMP: 4
SALES (est): 984.1K **Privately Held**
WEB: www.grovesystems.com
SIC: 3822 Temperature controls, automatic

(G-2092)
HUNTER INDUSTRIES
17 Everett Ln (06417-1570)
PHONE..................................860 961-9646
Tom Marmelstein, *Principal*
EMP: 1
SALES (est): 54.5K **Privately Held**
SIC: 3523 Farm machinery & equipment

(G-2093)
INTERPRO LLC
Also Called: Interpro Rapid Technology
630 Industrial Park Rd (06417-1600)
PHONE..................................860 526-5869
Tiffany Batchelder, *Project Mgr*
Kevin Dyer,
EMP: 15
SQ FT: 7,500
SALES: 2MM **Privately Held**
SIC: 3555 Printing trades machinery

(G-2094)
INVENTEC PRFMCE CHEM USA LLC
500 Main St Ste 18 (06417-2000)
P.O. Box 989 (06417-0989)
PHONE..................................860 526-8300
Jean-Noel Poirier, *CEO*
David Reitz, *CFO*
Leigh Gesick, *Director*
Tina Williams, *Executive*
EMP: 20
SQ FT: 12,000
SALES (est): 3.9MM
SALES (corp-wide): 12.6MM **Privately Held**
SIC: 2899 Fluxes: brazing, soldering, galvanizing & welding
PA: Dehon
4 Rue De La Croix Faubin
Paris 11e Arrondissement
143 987-584

(G-2095)
MY FAIR LADY
246 Main St (06417-2024)
PHONE..................................860 322-4542
EMP: 2
SALES (est): 83.1K **Privately Held**
SIC: 5137 2389 Women's & children's clothing; apparel & accessories

(G-2096)
NEW ENGLAND MACHINE CO LLC
10 Spring St (06417-1811)
PHONE..................................860 526-7844
Paul Simoneau,
EMP: 1
SQ FT: 1,500
SALES (est): 173K **Privately Held**
SIC: 3569 Assembly machines, non-metalworking

(G-2097)
OLD LYME GOURMET COMPANY
Also Called: Deep River Snacks
16 Grove St (06417-1711)
P.O. Box 1127 (06417-1127)
PHONE..................................860 434-7347
Jim Golberg, *CEO*
Lee Whiting, *Vice Pres*
Rachel Barker, *Regl Sales Mgr*
Mark Maillett, *Regl Sales Mgr*
James Ostling, *Sales Staff*
▼ **EMP:** 28
SQ FT: 4,000
SALES (est): 13.2MM **Privately Held**
SIC: 5149 2096 Health foods; potato chips & other potato-based snacks
PA: Arca Continental, S.A.B. De C.V.
Av. San Jeronimo No. 813 Poniente
Monterrey N.L. 64640

(G-2098)
PARASON MACHINE INC
1000 Industrial Park Rd (06417)
P.O. Box 292 (06417-0292)
PHONE..................................860 526-3565
Charles Paradis, *President*
Janice Paradis, *Vice Pres*
EMP: 18
SQ FT: 10,000
SALES (est): 2.5MM **Privately Held**
WEB: www.parasonmachine.com
SIC: 3599 Machine shop, jobbing & repair; custom machinery

(G-2099)
SCHAEFER MACHINE COMPANY INC
200 Commercial Dr (06417-1682)
PHONE..................................860 526-4000
Robert C Gammons, *President*
Virginia Gammons, *Admin Sec*
▼ **EMP:** 6
SQ FT: 10,000
SALES (est): 1.3MM **Privately Held**
SIC: 3569 Assembly machines, non-metalworking

(G-2100)
SILGAN PLASTICS LLC
38 Bridge St (06417-1731)
P.O. Box 405 (06417)
PHONE..................................860 526-6300
Steve Monahan, *Engineer*
Jim Worthington, *Senior Engr*
Jim Leardi, *Manager*
Dave McLaughlin, *Supervisor*
Rosemary Grispino, *Executive*
EMP: 170
SALES (corp-wide): 4.4B **Publicly Held**
WEB: www.silganplastics.com
SIC: 3089 Plastic containers, except foam
HQ: Silgan Plastics Llc
14515 North Outer 40 Rd # 210
Chesterfield MO 63017
800 274-5426

(G-2101)
SNIBBETTS INC
58 Warsaw St (06417-1631)
PHONE..................................860 526-5536
Donald F Stebbins, *Principal*
EMP: 2
SALES (est): 124.8K **Privately Held**
SIC: 3648 Lighting equipment

(G-2102)
SOUND VIEW PLASTICS LLC
500 Main St Ste 25a (06417-2000)
PHONE..................................860 322-4139
Ronald Bodeau,
EMP: 2 **EST:** 2017
SALES (est): 88.9K **Privately Held**
SIC: 3089 Plastic processing

GEOGRAPHIC SECTION

Derby - New Haven County (G-2132)

(G-2103)
SWPC PLASTICS LLC
Also Called: Tri Town Precision Plastics
12 Bridge St (06417-1704)
PHONE.................................860 526-3200
Jeffrey Buchanan, *CFO*
James Debney, *Mng Member*
EMP: 112
SALES (est): 36.7MM
SALES (corp-wide): 638.2MM **Publicly Held**
SIC: 3089 Injection molding of plastics
HQ: American Outdoor Brands Sales Company
2100 Roosevelt Ave
Springfield MA 01104
413 781-8300

(G-2104)
TOWNSEND JOHN
Also Called: Absnavigator.com
132 Hemlock Dr (06417-1646)
PHONE.................................860 526-3896
John Townsend, *Owner*
EMP: 1
SALES: 100K **Privately Held**
WEB: www.townsendbooks.com
SIC: 5942 2789 5932 Book stores; bookbinding & related work; rare books

(G-2105)
VALLEY PRESS NEW AREA PRTG CO
Also Called: New ERA Printing Co
169 Main St Ste 1 (06417-2099)
PHONE.................................860 526-5696
Marsha Orzech, *Partner*
Sirgen Orzech, *Partner*
EMP: 2 EST: 1874
SQ FT: 821
SALES (est): 234.7K **Privately Held**
SIC: 2752 Commercial printing, offset

(G-2106)
WINTHROP CONSTRUCTION LLC
10 Woodbury Rd (06417-1602)
PHONE.................................860 322-4562
Nicholas Olson,
EMP: 1 EST: 2014
SALES (est): 163.4K **Privately Held**
SIC: 1521 2491 1771 1794 Single-family housing construction; piles, foundation & marine construction: treated wood; curb construction; excavation & grading, building construction; highway & street construction; airport runway construction

Derby
New Haven County

(G-2107)
ABSOLUTE COUNTERTOPS LLC
38 Commerce St (06418-2006)
P.O. Box 7, Shelton (06484-0007)
PHONE.................................203 395-8259
Keith Cagle, *Mng Member*
EMP: 1
SQ FT: 1,500
SALES (est): 688.5K **Privately Held**
SIC: 2541 Wood partitions & fixtures

(G-2108)
ALLEN OF ANSONIA STAMPS
16 Laurel Ave (06418-2121)
PHONE.................................203 736-2222
Ray Allen, *Owner*
Melissa Gilreath, *Exec Dir*
EMP: 1
SALES (est): 59K **Privately Held**
SIC: 3953 Marking devices

(G-2109)
BEARD CONCRETE CO DERBY INC
37 Main St (06418-1932)
P.O. Box 590, Milford (06460-0590)
PHONE.................................203 735-4641
James Beard, *Vice Pres*
EMP: 13
SALES (corp-wide): 1.1MM **Privately Held**
SIC: 3241 5211 Cement, hydraulic; masonry materials & supplies
PA: Beard Concrete Co. Of Derby, Inc.
127 Boston Post Rd
Milford CT 06460
203 874-2533

(G-2110)
BP COUNTERTOP DESIGN CO LLC
101 Elizabeth St Ste 1 (06418-1835)
PHONE.................................203 732-1620
EMP: 5
SQ FT: 7,000
SALES (est): 360K **Privately Held**
SIC: 2434 2541 Mfg Wood Kitchen Cabinets Mfg Wood Partitions/Fixtures

(G-2111)
DERBY DISCOUNT LIQUOR
441 Roosevelt Dr (06418-1034)
PHONE.................................203 732-0666
Jay Patel, *Owner*
EMP: 3
SALES (est): 330K **Privately Held**
SIC: 5921 2086 Liquor stores; bottled & canned soft drinks

(G-2112)
EARTH ENGINEERED SYSTEMS
630 Hawthorne Ave (06418-1022)
P.O. Box 159, East Haddam (06423-0159)
PHONE.................................203 231-4614
Jim Lindner, *Owner*
EMP: 3
SALES (est): 163.3K **Privately Held**
SIC: 3567 Industrial furnaces & ovens

(G-2113)
EMPIRE TOOL LLC
259 Roosevelt Dr (06418-1653)
PHONE.................................203 735-7467
Joe Sender,
Mark Banyacski,
EMP: 3
SALES (est): 240K **Privately Held**
SIC: 3089 Injection molding of plastics

(G-2114)
GORDON RUBBER AND PKG CO INC
10 Cemetery Ave (06418-1604)
P.O. Box 298 (06418-0298)
PHONE.................................203 735-7441
John A Mazur, *President*
EMP: 33 EST: 1948
SQ FT: 20,000
SALES (est): 6.4MM **Privately Held**
SIC: 3069 5085 3544 Molded rubber products; rubber goods, mechanical; special dies, tools, jigs & fixtures

(G-2115)
HESSEL INDUSTRIES INC
95 Roosevelt Dr (06418-1648)
PHONE.................................203 736-2317
Willie Krutoholow, *President*
EMP: 4 EST: 1960
SQ FT: 10,000
SALES (est): 592.6K **Privately Held**
WEB: www.hesselsindustries.com
SIC: 3496 3469 3452 Miscellaneous fabricated wire products; metal stampings; bolts, nuts, rivets & washers

(G-2116)
IDA INTERNATIONAL INC
200 Roosevelt Dr (06418-1625)
P.O. Box 284 (06418-0284)
PHONE.................................203 736-9249
Norman M Harbinson, *President*
Thomas Harbinson, *Principal*
Aldi Bylyku, *Project Mgr*
Mike Potkay, *Technology*
Robin Moscato, *Administration*
EMP: 45
SQ FT: 124,581
SALES (est): 10.6MM **Privately Held**
WEB: www.ida-intl.com
SIC: 3446 Architectural metalwork

(G-2117)
INFANTE COATINGS LLC
142 New Haven Ave (06418-2112)
PHONE.................................203 252-6370
Jeremy Infante, *Principal*
EMP: 1
SALES (est): 44.4K **Privately Held**
SIC: 3479 Metal coating & allied service

(G-2118)
LAWRENCE MC CONNEY
Also Called: Mc Conney's Farm
795 Roosevelt Dr (06418-1041)
PHONE.................................203 735-1133
Lawernce Mc Conney, *Owner*
EMP: 2
SALES (est): 95.4K **Privately Held**
SIC: 2099 Food preparations

(G-2119)
M & B ENTERPRISE LLC
Also Called: Wholesale Poster Frames
155 New Haven Ave (06418-2161)
PHONE.................................203 298-9781
Michael J Klein,
Basile Tzovolos,
EMP: 12 EST: 2004
SQ FT: 20,000
SALES: 1.5MM **Privately Held**
SIC: 3499 Picture frames, metal

(G-2120)
ON TIME SCREEN PRINTING & EMBR
155 New Haven Ave (06418-2161)
PHONE.................................203 874-4581
Michael J Klein, *Owner*
EMP: 15
SALES (est): 1.4MM **Privately Held**
SIC: 2399 2759 Banners, pennants & flags; screen printing

(G-2121)
PB&J DESIGN INC
251 Roosevelt Dr (06418-1665)
PHONE.................................203 332-4433
Daniele Disorbo, *Vice Pres*
EMP: 2
SQ FT: 1,500
SALES (est): 206.8K **Privately Held**
WEB: www.pbjlicensing.com
SIC: 7336 3999 7311 Graphic arts & related design; package design; novelties, bric-a-brac & hobby kits; advertising consultant

(G-2122)
PETER TASI
Also Called: P T Tool & Machine
10 Francis St (06418-1506)
PHONE.................................203 732-6540
Peter Tasi, *Owner*
EMP: 3
SALES (est): 410.1K **Privately Held**
WEB: www.pttool.com
SIC: 3599 Machine shop, jobbing & repair

(G-2123)
RELPROG LLC
174 Hawthorne Ave (06418-1152)
PHONE.................................203 734-7000
Jorge, *Principal*
EMP: 1 EST: 2012
SALES (est): 56.6K **Privately Held**
SIC: 7372 Prepackaged software

(G-2124)
RSS ENTERPRISES LLC
Also Called: City Stitchers
101 Elizabeth St Ste 7 (06418-1835)
PHONE.................................203 736-6220
Ron Bartone, *Owner*
EMP: 5
SALES (est): 443.7K **Privately Held**
SIC: 2395 Embroidery products, except schiffli machine

(G-2125)
RUBBER SUPPLIES COMPANY INC
1 Park Ave Ste 1 # 1 (06418-1650)
P.O. Box 378 (06418-0378)
PHONE.................................203 736-9995
Edward Manion Jr, *President*
Michael Manion, *Treasurer*
EMP: 3
SQ FT: 11,000
SALES (est): 636.8K **Privately Held**
WEB: www.list-link.net
SIC: 3053 Gaskets, all materials

(G-2126)
SIGNS UNLIMITED INC
2 Francis St (06418-1552)
PHONE.................................203 734-7446
Allan Esposito, *President*
EMP: 5
SQ FT: 13,000
SALES (est): 810.3K **Privately Held**
SIC: 3993 3089 7389 Signs & advertising specialties; awnings, fiberglass & plastic combination; sign painting & lettering shop

(G-2127)
STARSTATUS PUBLISHING
195 Caroline St (06418-1923)
PHONE.................................877 453-9532
EMP: 1
SALES (est): 37.5K **Privately Held**
SIC: 2741 Misc Publishing

(G-2128)
TASSELS
17 Cedric Ave (06418-1008)
PHONE.................................203 231-0973
Keren Richi, *Partner*
Kim Tucci, *Partner*
EMP: 2 EST: 1958
SALES (est): 163.6K **Privately Held**
SIC: 2211 7641 5714 Draperies & drapery fabrics, cotton; slip cover fabrics, cotton; reupholstery; drapery & upholstery stores; slip covers

(G-2129)
VALLEY PUBLISHING COMPANY INC
Also Called: Valley Times
7 Francis St (06418-1597)
PHONE.................................203 735-6696
Blaze A Garbatini, *President*
Irene Garbatini, *Corp Secy*
Romolo Garbatini, *Vice Pres*
EMP: 10
SALES (est): 928.4K **Privately Held**
WEB: www.thevalleytimes.com
SIC: 2711 Newspapers: publishing only, not printed on site

(G-2130)
WEIMANN BROTHERS MFG CO
247 Roosevelt Dr (06418-1626)
P.O. Box 333 (06418-0333)
PHONE.................................203 735-3311
James A Fair Sr, *President*
Jeff Fair, *Vice Pres*
James A Fair Jr, *Treasurer*
Marion Neville, *Admin Sec*
EMP: 15
SQ FT: 12,000
SALES (est): 2.5MM **Privately Held**
SIC: 3469 3544 Stamping metal for the trade; special dies & tools

(G-2131)
WHALLEY GLASS COMPANY (PA)
Also Called: Curved Glass Distributors
72 Chapel St (06418-2130)
PHONE.................................203 735-9388
Mark S Vece, *President*
Corinne V Cacopardo, *Vice Pres*
Blaise L Vece, *Treasurer*
Joyce Gaul, *Admin Sec*
▲ EMP: 100
SQ FT: 50,000
SALES (est): 2.7MM **Privately Held**
SIC: 3229 5023 Glass furnishings & accessories; glassware

(G-2132)
WILSON ANCHOR BOLT SLEEVE
259 Roosevelt Dr (06418-1653)
PHONE.................................203 516-5260
Theresa Somo Passander, *Principal*
EMP: 4
SALES (est): 256.1K **Privately Held**
SIC: 3452 Bolts, nuts, rivets & washers

Derby - New Haven County (G-2133)

(G-2133)
YANKEE SCREEN PRINTING
15 Kings Ct (06418-2241)
PHONE.................203 924-9926
Daniel L Blackwell, *Owner*
EMP: 3
SQ FT: 3,500
SALES (est): 192.3K **Privately Held**
SIC: 2759 2752 2262 5699 Screen printing; commercial printing, lithographic; finishing plants, manmade fiber & silk fabrics; T-shirts, custom printed

(G-2134)
YOUNG FLAN LLC
Also Called: Avenue Awards
155 New Haven Ave (06418-2161)
PHONE.................203 878-0084
Bret W Riley,
EMP: 2
SALES (est): 204.4K **Privately Held**
SIC: 3993 5699 2399 5999 Signs & advertising specialties; T-shirts, custom printed; banners, made from fabric; banners

Durham
Middlesex County

(G-2135)
ADVANCED SEMICONDUCTOR
30 Ozick Dr (06422-1022)
PHONE.................860 349-1121
EMP: 2
SALES (est): 90K **Privately Held**
SIC: 3674 Semiconductors & related devices

(G-2136)
ALEXANDER AND MASON
151r Main St (06422-2105)
PHONE.................860 349-0496
Alex Passavant, *Principal*
EMP: 2
SALES (est): 83.9K **Privately Held**
SIC: 2752 Commercial printing, lithographic

(G-2137)
APPLIED DIAMOND COATINGS LLC
30 Ozick Dr (06422-1022)
PHONE.................860 349-3133
John J Ozycz,
EMP: 4
SALES (est): 360K **Privately Held**
SIC: 3312 Coated or plated products

(G-2138)
ARROW ENGRAVING & SIGN LLC
9 Commerce Cir Unit E (06422-1020)
PHONE.................860 349-1788
Mark Driudahl, *Principal*
EMP: 1
SALES (est): 67.6K **Privately Held**
SIC: 3993 Signs & advertising specialties

(G-2139)
ASCT LLC
30 Ozick Dr (06422-1022)
PHONE.................860 349-1121
Tom Ozycz,
John Ozycz,
▲ **EMP:** 3
SQ FT: 7,000
SALES (est): 684.9K **Privately Held**
WEB: www.asct.com
SIC: 3674 Semiconductors & related devices

(G-2140)
CAMEO EMBROIDERY
34 School House Ln (06422-3607)
PHONE.................860 301-3123
EMP: 1 **EST:** 2017
SALES (est): 31.2K **Privately Held**
SIC: 2395 Embroidery & art needlework

(G-2141)
CHAPMAN MANUFACTURING COMPANY
471 New Haven Rd (06422-2514)
P.O. Box 250 (06422-0250)
PHONE.................860 349-9228
William Le Vee, *President*
Tracy Camassar, *General Mgr*
Carmella Kowalski, *Principal*
Doris Le Vee, *Vice Pres*
Jason Camassar, *Info Tech Mgr*
EMP: 10
SQ FT: 1,200
SALES (est): 1.3MM **Privately Held**
WEB: www.chapmanmfg.com
SIC: 5251 3423 Tools; screw drivers, pliers, chisels, etc. (hand tools)

(G-2142)
CHEMOTEX PROTECTIVE COATINGS (PA)
15 Commerce Cir (06422-1002)
PHONE.................860 349-0144
Kevin Wise, *President*
EMP: 11
SQ FT: 10,000
SALES (est): 1.1MM **Privately Held**
WEB: www.cpc-corp.com
SIC: 2899 Chemical preparations

(G-2143)
CLAREMONT SALES CORPORATION
35 Winsome Rd (06422-1315)
P.O. Box 430 (06422-0430)
PHONE.................860 349-4499
Keith Williams, *President*
Dave Coutts, *Treasurer*
David Coutts, *Admin Sec*
▼ **EMP:** 30
SQ FT: 32,000
SALES (est): 8.2MM **Privately Held**
WEB: www.claremontcorporation.com
SIC: 3086 2221 Insulation or cushioning material, foamed plastic; fiberglass fabrics; glass broadwoven fabrics

(G-2144)
DANCHAK WOODWORKS LLC
339 Oxbow Rd (06422-1814)
PHONE.................860 346-6057
Michael M Danchak, *Principal*
EMP: 2
SALES (est): 161.1K **Privately Held**
SIC: 2431 Millwork

(G-2145)
DIRT GUY TOPSOIL
601 Guilford Rd (06422-3308)
PHONE.................860 303-0500
John Mitchell, *Owner*
EMP: 1
SALES (est): 89.7K **Privately Held**
SIC: 3524 Lawn & garden equipment

(G-2146)
DURHAM MANUFACTURING COMPANY (PA)
201 Main St (06422-2108)
P.O. Box 230 (06422-0230)
PHONE.................860 349-3427
Richard Patterson, *CEO*
Francis Korn, *Senior VP*
John Patterson, *Vice Pres*
John Gowac, *CFO*
◆ **EMP:** 99 **EST:** 1922
SQ FT: 120,000
SALES (est): 55MM **Privately Held**
WEB: www.durhammfg.com
SIC: 3469 2542 2522 2514 Boxes, stamped metal; partitions & fixtures, except wood; office furniture, except wood; metal household furniture

(G-2147)
GLENN CURTIS (PA)
Also Called: Curtis Studio
105 Oak Ter (06422-1507)
PHONE.................860 349-8679
Glenn Curtis, *Owner*
EMP: 6 **EST:** 1975
SQ FT: 5,000
SALES (est): 420.7K **Privately Held**
SIC: 7221 2759 7334 Photographer, still or video; commercial printing; photocopying & duplicating services

(G-2148)
GRAPHITE DIE MOLD INC
18 Airline Rd (06422-1000)
PHONE.................860 349-4444
Don Klas, *President*
Don Ozycz, *General Mgr*
▲ **EMP:** 5 **EST:** 1977
SQ FT: 60,000
SALES (est): 1.3MM
SALES (corp-wide): 1.3B **Privately Held**
WEB: www.graphitediemold.com
SIC: 3624 Carbon & graphite products
HQ: Morgan Advanced Materials And Technology, Inc.
441 Hall Ave
Saint Marys PA 15857

(G-2149)
HOBSON AND MOTZER INCORPORATED (PA)
30 Airline Rd (06422-1000)
PHONE.................860 349-1756
Frank W Dworak, *President*
James O'Brien, *Vice Pres*
Donald Zak, *Vice Pres*
Alicia Jacobsen, *Human Res Mgr*
Ted Depaola, *Sales Staff*
EMP: 113 **EST:** 1912
SQ FT: 52,000
SALES (est): 26MM **Privately Held**
WEB: www.hobsonmotzer.com
SIC: 3469 3544 Stamping metal for the trade; special dies & tools

(G-2150)
KENNETH INDUSTRIAL PDTS INC
35 Winsome Rd (06422-1315)
P.O. Box 430 (06422-0430)
PHONE.................860 349-7454
Keith Williams, *President*
Christopher Darby, *Vice Pres*
Greg Williams, *Treasurer*
John Capodicasa, *Sales Staff*
Jose Hernandez, *Info Tech Mgr*
EMP: 2
SQ FT: 35,000
SALES (est): 3.6MM **Privately Held**
WEB: www.kennind.com
SIC: 5084 3053 Industrial machinery & equipment; gaskets & sealing devices

(G-2151)
MACWORKS LLC
230 Parmelee Hill Rd (06422-2609)
PHONE.................860 377-1371
Gerald Zigmont, *Principal*
EMP: 2 **EST:** 2008
SALES (est): 169.8K **Privately Held**
SIC: 3571 Electronic computers

(G-2152)
MATCHBOX USA
62 Saw Mill Rd (06422-2602)
PHONE.................860 349-1655
Charles Mack, *Owner*
EMP: 1
SALES (est): 68.1K **Privately Held**
WEB: www.charliemackonline.com
SIC: 2721 Periodicals

(G-2153)
MEDIAGRAPHICSCOM INC
9 Commerce Cir (06422-1020)
PHONE.................203 404-7233
James Greenwood, *President*
EMP: 11
SALES (est): 977.8K **Privately Held**
WEB: www.featherliteexhibits.com
SIC: 5963 2759 Direct sales, telemarketing; commercial printing

(G-2154)
PRAXAIR DISTRIBUTION INC
89 Commerce Cir (06422-1002)
PHONE.................860 349-0305
Ron Caselino, *General Mgr*
EMP: 42 **Privately Held**
SIC: 2813 Industrial gases
HQ: Praxair Distribution, Inc.
10 Riverview Dr
Danbury CT 06810
203 837-2000

(G-2155)
ROSEMARIE QUERNS
Also Called: Anything Goes
66 Middlefield Rd (06422-1220)
PHONE.................860 349-3315
Rosemarie Querns, *Owner*
EMP: 1
SALES (est): 59.7K **Privately Held**
SIC: 2759 Screen printing

(G-2156)
SIGMA ENGINEERING TECH LLC
19 Old Powder Hill Rd (06422-1030)
PHONE.................508 243-2888
Richard Rothstein,
EMP: 2
SALES (est): 62.5K **Privately Held**
SIC: 3999 Manufacturing industries

(G-2157)
SPIN SHOP
36 Commerce Cir (06422-1001)
PHONE.................860 349-1298
Tim Pulcifer, *Owner*
EMP: 2
SALES (est): 276K **Privately Held**
SIC: 3599 Machine shop, jobbing & repair

(G-2158)
TECHNICAL MANUFACTURING CORP
Also Called: T M C
645 New Haven Rd (06422-2512)
P.O. Box 306 (06422-0306)
PHONE.................860 349-1735
Mary Lou Bonito, *President*
Marylou Bonito, *President*
Fred Bonito, *Vice Pres*
Tony Calabrese, *VP Opers*
Catherine Bender, *Production*
EMP: 30
SQ FT: 70,000
SALES (est): 6.3MM **Privately Held**
SIC: 3672 3679 Printed circuit boards; harness assemblies for electronic use: wire or cable

(G-2159)
THERMAL FLUIDICS
42 Ozick Dr Ste 5 (06422-1029)
PHONE.................860 740-4880
EMP: 2
SALES (est): 70.8K **Privately Held**
SIC: 5063 3699 Electrical apparatus & equipment; electrical equipment & supplies

(G-2160)
TRANSFORMER TECHNOLOGY INC
60 Commerce Cir (06422-1001)
P.O. Box 436 (06422-0436)
PHONE.................860 349-1061
Bruce M Gueble Jr, *President*
Suzanne M Gueble, *Treasurer*
▲ **EMP:** 12
SQ FT: 20,000
SALES (est): 2MM **Privately Held**
SIC: 3679 3612 Power supplies, all types: static; power transformers, electric

(G-2161)
WELDER REPAIR & RENTAL SVC INC
37 Commerce Cir (06422-1002)
P.O. Box 659 (06422-0659)
PHONE.................203 238-9284
Bruce J Dowd, *Owner*
EMP: 4 **EST:** 1979
SQ FT: 16,000
SALES (est): 404.9K **Privately Held**
SIC: 7692 7359 Welding repair; equipment rental & leasing

East Berlin
Hartford County

(G-2162)
ASI SIGN SYSTEMS INC
100 Clark Dr (06023-1172)
PHONE.................................860 828-3331
Doden Hoff, *Manager*
EMP: 8
SALES (corp-wide): 20.7MM **Privately Held**
SIC: 3993 Signs & advertising specialties
PA: Asi Sign Systems, Inc.
   8181 Jetstar Dr Ste 110
   Irving TX 75063
   214 352-9140

(G-2163)
B & S MACHINE INC
54 Clark Dr Ste B (06023-1150)
PHONE.................................860 829-0813
Enzo Boccaccio, *President*
Maria Boccaccio, *Corp Secy*
EMP: 2
SQ FT: 1,800
SALES: 50K **Privately Held**
SIC: 3599 Machine shop, jobbing & repair

(G-2164)
BARETTA PROVISION INC
172 Commerce St (06023-1105)
P.O. Box 344 (06023-0344)
PHONE.................................860 828-0802
William Baretta Jr, *President*
Carol Baretta, *Admin Sec*
EMP: 10
SQ FT: 10,000
SALES (est): 2.6MM **Privately Held**
WEB: www.barettaprovision.com
SIC: 5147 2013 Meats, fresh; sausages & related products, from purchased meat

(G-2165)
DEBURRING HOUSE INC
230 Berlin St (06023-1032)
PHONE.................................860 828-0889
David Durity, *Vice Pres*
Steven Cyr, *Vice Pres*
Kevin Cyr, *Admin Sec*
EMP: 50
SQ FT: 10,000
SALES (est): 5.8MM **Privately Held**
WEB: www.deburringhouse.com
SIC: 3471 3484 3724 Buffing for the trade; cleaning, polishing & finishing; tumbling (cleaning & polishing) of machine parts; small arms; aircraft engines & engine parts

(G-2166)
EDRO CORPORATION
Also Called: Dynawash
37 Commerce St (06023-1106)
P.O. Box 308 (06023-0308)
PHONE.................................860 828-0311
Barbara Kirejczyk, *Ch of Bd*
Edward S Kirejczyk III, *President*
Edward S Kirejczyk Jr, *President*
Caroline Wojcicki, *Vice Pres*
Ed Kirejczyk, *VP Sales*
▲ **EMP:** 34
SQ FT: 45,000
SALES (est): 8.4MM **Privately Held**
WEB: www.edrodynawash.com
SIC: 3582 Washing machines, laundry: commercial, incl. coin-operated

(G-2167)
FENN LLC
80 Clark Dr Unit 5d (06023-1157)
PHONE.................................860 259-6600
David Somers, *CEO*
Ryan Cutter, *President*
Mike Geiger, *Sales Mgr*
Kevin Campion, *Accounts Mgr*
Weylin Trombley, *Sales Staff*
▲ **EMP:** 30
SQ FT: 22,000
SALES (est): 4.9MM
SALES (corp-wide): 24MM **Privately Held**
SIC: 3542 Rebuilt machine tools, metal forming types
PA: Quality Products, Inc.
   1 Air Cargo Pkwy E
   Swanton OH 43558
   614 228-0185

(G-2168)
FINISHERS TECHNOLOGY CORP
Also Called: Kelsey Mfg Division
319 Main St (06023)
PHONE.................................860 829-1000
EMP: 18
SQ FT: 14,500
SALES (est): 229.9K **Privately Held**
SIC: 3541 5084 Mfg Machine Tools-Cutting Whol Industrial Equipment

(G-2169)
FLETCHER-TERRY COMPANY LLC (PA)
91 Clark Dr (06023-1104)
PHONE.................................860 828-3400
John Peterson, *President*
Blair Tomalonis, *President*
Brian M Johnson,
◆ **EMP:** 90
SALES (est): 21.9MM **Privately Held**
SIC: 3423 3541 6512 3549 Hand & edge tools; machine tools, metal cutting type; nonresidential building operators; metalworking machinery; machine tool accessories

(G-2170)
HEISE INDUSTRIES INC (PA)
196 Commerce St (06023-1105)
PHONE.................................860 828-6538
Brooks B Heise Sr, *CEO*
Brooks B Heise Jr, *President*
Henry Vogel, *Vice Pres*
Michael Cesario, *Treasurer*
Carol Obrien, *Controller*
EMP: 60 **EST:** 1965
SQ FT: 25,000
SALES (est): 11.2MM
SALES (corp-wide): 10.1MM **Privately Held**
WEB: www.heiseindustries.com
SIC: 3544 Forms (molds), for foundry & plastics working machinery

(G-2171)
K & K PRECISION MANUFACTURING
54 Clark Dr Ste F (06023-1150)
PHONE.................................860 828-7681
Peter Kiss, *President*
Darlene Kiss, *Vice Pres*
EMP: 3
SALES: 220K **Privately Held**
SIC: 3599 Machine shop, jobbing & repair

(G-2172)
PALMER MANUFACTURING CO LLC
134 Commerce St (06023-1105)
PHONE.................................860 828-0344
EMP: 2
SALES (corp-wide): 368.2MM **Privately Held**
SIC: 3724 Aircraft engines & engine parts
HQ: Palmer Manufacturing Co., Llc.
   243 Medford St
   Malden MA 02148
   781 321-0480

(G-2173)
PARADIGM PRCISION HOLDINGS LLC
Also Called: Berlin Operations
134 Commerce St (06023-1105)
PHONE.................................860 829-3663
Lester Karolek, *Branch Mgr*
EMP: 70
SALES (corp-wide): 368.2MM **Privately Held**
SIC: 3545 Machine tool accessories
HQ: Paradigm Precision Holdings, Llc
   404 W Guadalupe Rd
   Tempe AZ 85283

(G-2174)
PRECISION GRAPHICS INC
10 Clark Dr (06023-1103)
P.O. Box 248 (06023-0248)
PHONE.................................860 828-6561
Burton Johnson, *President*
Eric Johnson, *Vice Pres*
Ross Johnson, *Vice Pres*
Karen Johnson, *Admin Sec*
EMP: 25
SQ FT: 13,000
SALES (est): 4.9MM **Privately Held**
WEB: www.frontpanels.com
SIC: 3613 3993 Control panels, electric; name plates: except engraved, etched, etc.: metal

(G-2175)
S D & D INC
Also Called: Sign Design & Display
99 Clark Dr 1 (06023-1104)
PHONE.................................860 357-2603
Mario Leuzzi, *President*
EMP: 15
SQ FT: 7,000
SALES (est): 1.9MM **Privately Held**
WEB: www.sdd.com
SIC: 3993 Displays & cutouts, window & lobby

(G-2176)
SMS MACHINE INC
54 Clark Dr Ste A (06023-1150)
PHONE.................................860 829-0813
Scott Steele, *President*
Sandra Steele, *Admin Sec*
EMP: 4
SQ FT: 2,000
SALES (est): 620.4K **Privately Held**
WEB: www.smsmachine.com
SIC: 2821 3471 Plastics materials & resins; cleaning, polishing & finishing

(G-2177)
SRE BRISTOL 322 PARK ST LLC
129 Ice Pond Ln (06023-1019)
PHONE.................................860 348-0198
Krzysztof Soltan, *Principal*
EMP: 1
SALES (est): 77K **Privately Held**
SIC: 2621 Paper mills

(G-2178)
T M INDUSTRIES INC
134 Commerce St (06023-1105)
P.O. Box 278 (06023-0278)
PHONE.................................860 828-0344
Rosemarie Fischer, *CEO*
Anthony Micacci, *President*
Lucia Micacci Bantle, *Principal*
Vincent Micacci, *Principal*
Lucille Micacci, *Chairman*
▲ **EMP:** 75
SQ FT: 70,000
SALES (est): 9.7MM **Privately Held**
WEB: www.tmindustries.com
SIC: 3599 Machine shop, jobbing & repair

(G-2179)
WAD INC
Also Called: Asi Modulex
100 Clark Dr (06023-1172)
P.O. Box 504 (06023-0504)
PHONE.................................860 828-3331
William Dodenhoff, *President*
Cindy Dodenhoff, *Vice Pres*
EMP: 25
SQ FT: 9,000
SALES (est): 3.5MM **Privately Held**
SIC: 3993 1799 Signs, not made in custom sign painting shops; sign installation & maintenance

East Canaan
Litchfield County

(G-2180)
ALLYNDALE CORPORATION
40 Allyndale Rd (06024)
P.O. Box 265 (06024-0265)
PHONE.................................860 824-7959
Louis C Allyn II, *President*
Brian Allyn, *General Mgr*
Steven Allyn, *Vice Pres*
Leonard Allyn, *Treasurer*
EMP: 15
SQ FT: 450
SALES (est): 3.6MM **Privately Held**
SIC: 1422 Agricultural limestone, ground

(G-2181)
CANAAN CUSTOM MACHINE
351 Norfolk Rd (06024-2608)
PHONE.................................860 824-0674
David Woodruff, *Owner*
W St Michael Del Monte, *Office Mgr*
EMP: 1
SALES (est): 50K **Privately Held**
SIC: 3599 Machine shop, jobbing & repair

(G-2182)
LAND OF NOD WINERY LLC
99 Lower Rd (06024-2624)
PHONE.................................860 824-5225
William S Adam, *Principal*
EMP: 7
SALES (est): 404.1K **Privately Held**
SIC: 2084 Wines

(G-2183)
LAURELBROOK NTRAL RSOURCES LLC
12 Casey Hill Rd (06024-2638)
P.O. Box 431, Norfolk (06058-0431)
PHONE.................................860 824-5843
Robert Jacquie,
James Jacquier,
EMP: 19 **EST:** 1926
SALES (est): 2.5MM **Privately Held**
SIC: 1442 Common sand mining; gravel mining

(G-2184)
WILLIAM LINKOVICH
Also Called: East Canaan Equipment Repair
41 Trescott Hill Rd (06024-2612)
PHONE.................................860 824-0298
William F Linkovich, *Owner*
EMP: 1
SALES (est): 60K **Privately Held**
SIC: 7699 7692 7629 Agricultural equipment repair services; farm machinery repair; aircraft & heavy equipment repair services; construction equipment repair; welding repair; electrical repair shops

East Glastonbury
Hartford County

(G-2185)
QUALITY NAME PLATE INC
Also Called: Qnp Technologies
22 Fisher Hill Rd (06025)
P.O. Box 308 (06025-0308)
PHONE.................................860 633-9495
Craig O Garneau, *President*
Barry B Ralston, *Vice Pres*
Barry Ralston, *Vice Pres*
Andrew Adams, *Engineer*
▲ **EMP:** 95 **EST:** 1946
SQ FT: 40,000
SALES (est): 20.4MM **Privately Held**
WEB: www.qnp.com
SIC: 3625 3613 2759 3083 Relays & industrial controls; switchgear & switchboard apparatus; screen printing; laminated plastics plate & sheet; automotive & apparel trimmings; packaging paper & plastics film, coated & laminated

East Granby
Hartford County

(G-2186)
ACCELERON INC
21 Lordship Rd Ste 1 (06026-9589)
PHONE.................................860 651-9333
Donald Montano, *CEO*
Rory Montano, *President*
Donald Christensen, *Vice Pres*
Lance Montano, *Vice Pres*
Jeffrey Burrows, *Mfg Staff*
EMP: 46 **EST:** 1974
SQ FT: 60,000
SALES (est): 10.3MM **Privately Held**
WEB: www.acceleron-enbeam.com
SIC: 3629 Electronic generation equipment

East Granby - Hartford County (G-2187)

(G-2187)
AD EMBROIDERY LLC
186 Hartford Ave (06026-9520)
PHONE.................................860 653-9553
Louis Zimmer, *Owner*
EMP: 1
SALES (est): 62.3K **Privately Held**
SIC: 5949 2395 Sewing, needlework & piece goods; embroidery & art needlework

(G-2188)
AMERICAN CLADDING TECHNOLOGIES
15 International Dr (06026-9718)
PHONE.................................860 413-3098
Scott Poeppel, *Vice Pres*
Matt Rossi, *Prdtn Mgr*
EMP: 3
SALES (est): 297.2K **Privately Held**
SIC: 3444 Sheet metalwork

(G-2189)
AMERICAN SOLUTION FOR BUSINESS
88 Kimberly Rd (06026-9540)
PHONE.................................860 413-9415
L Bickerstaff, *Principal*
EMP: 2
SALES (est): 127.3K **Privately Held**
SIC: 2759 Commercial printing

(G-2190)
APPLETON GRP LLC
Also Called: Egs Electrcl Grp Nelson Heat T
2 Connecticut South Dr (06026-9738)
PHONE.................................860 653-1603
Lynn Avers, *Manager*
EMP: 40
SALES (corp-wide): 17.4B **Publicly Held**
SIC: 3823 Industrial instrmnts msrmnt display/control process variable
HQ: Appleton Grp Llc
   9377 W Higgins Rd
   Rosemont IL 60018
   847 268-6000

(G-2191)
BARNES GROUP INC
Also Called: Aerospace Wndsor Airmotive Div
7 Connecticut South Dr (06026-9738)
PHONE.................................860 653-5531
Roy Goldsmith, *Principal*
EMP: 1
SALES (corp-wide): 1.5B **Publicly Held**
SIC: 3724 Aircraft engines & engine parts
PA: Barnes Group Inc.
   123 Main St
   Bristol CT 06010
   860 583-7070

(G-2192)
BRIGNOLE DISTILLERY LLC
Also Called: Brignole Vineyards
103 Hartford Ave (06026-9518)
PHONE.................................860 653-9463
Timothy Brignole, *Mng Member*
EMP: 2
SALES (est): 170.8K **Privately Held**
SIC: 2084 Wines

(G-2193)
BROOME & CO LLC
62 Turkey Hills Rd (06026-9572)
PHONE.................................860 653-2106
Christopher Broome,
EMP: 5
SALES (est): 519.6K **Privately Held**
SIC: 3931 Organs, all types: pipe, reed, hand, electronic, etc.

(G-2194)
BUG UMBRELLA GAZEBO LLC
48 Wynding Hills Rd (06026-9631)
PHONE.................................860 651-0030
Thomas Derlinga, *President*
Roxanne R Durlinga, *Vice Pres*
▲ **EMP:** 2
SALES (est): 118.3K **Privately Held**
WEB: www.bugumbrella.com
SIC: 3999 5699 Garden umbrellas; umbrellas

(G-2195)
BURKE PRECISION MACHINE CO INC
7 Hatchett Hill Rd (06026-9526)
P.O. Box 329 (06026-0329)
PHONE.................................860 408-1394
Peter Burke, *President*
Lisa Percy, *Office Mgr*
EMP: 9
SQ FT: 10,000
SALES (est): 1.1MM **Privately Held**
WEB: www.burkeprecision.com
SIC: 3599 Machine shop, jobbing & repair

(G-2196)
CBS MANUFACTURING COMPANY
35 Kripes Rd (06026-9644)
PHONE.................................860 653-8100
John James Lawton, *CEO*
Clifford James Lawton, *President*
Kevin Lawton, *General Mgr*
Robert Bruce Lawton, *Vice Pres*
Vince Klezos, *Engineer*
EMP: 39 **EST:** 1972
SQ FT: 16,000
SALES (est): 8MM **Privately Held**
WEB: www.cbsmfg.com
SIC: 3724 3728 Aircraft engines & engine parts; aircraft parts & equipment

(G-2197)
COLOR CRAFT LTD
Also Called: Createx Colors
14 Airport Park Rd (06026-9523)
P.O. Box 120 (06026-0120)
PHONE.................................800 509-6563
Vincent H Kennedy, *President*
Craig Kenndey, *Treasurer*
EMP: 13 **EST:** 1980
SQ FT: 10,000
SALES (est): 2.2MM **Privately Held**
WEB: www.autoaircolors.com
SIC: 3952 5199 5198 5961 Artists' materials, except pencils & leads; artists' materials; paints; arts & crafts equipment & supplies, mail order; paint

(G-2198)
COMMAND CORPORATION
59 Rainbow Rd (06026-9763)
P.O. Box 832 (06026-0832)
PHONE.................................800 851-6012
Robert Bazyk, *President*
John Bazyk, *Sales Staff*
EMP: 14
SQ FT: 1,150
SALES (est): 2.2MM **Privately Held**
WEB: www.commandco.com
SIC: 3699 1731 Security control equipment & systems; closed circuit television installation

(G-2199)
COMPUTER COMPONENTS INC
Also Called: Relays Unlimited
18 Kripes Rd (06026-9645)
P.O. Box 1378 (06026-1378)
PHONE.................................860 653-9909
Gary Flor, *President*
Bob Welner, *General Mgr*
EMP: 15 **EST:** 1959
SQ FT: 6,000
SALES (est): 1.8MM **Privately Held**
WEB: www.relays-unlimited.com
SIC: 3625 Relays, for electronic use

(G-2200)
COORSTEK INC
Also Called: Coorstek East Granby
10 Airport Park Rd (06026-9523)
PHONE.................................860 653-8071
Roman Czarniecki, *Engineer*
Roger Burleson, *Manager*
Derek Freeman, *Supervisor*
Janis Hunter, *Admin Sec*
EMP: 25
SALES (corp-wide): 407.6MM **Privately Held**
SIC: 3264 Porcelain electrical supplies
HQ: Coorstek, Inc.
   14143 Denver West Pkwy # 400
   Lakewood CO 80401
   303 271-7000

(G-2201)
DAS DISTRIBUTION INC
66e Floydville Rd (06026-9132)
PHONE.................................860 844-3058
Gary John Galka, *Principal*
EMP: 1
SALES (corp-wide): 774.3K **Privately Held**
SIC: 5084 3625 Cement making machinery; actuators, industrial
PA: Das Distribution Inc
   17 Connecticut South Dr D
   East Granby CT
   860 844-3058

(G-2202)
DAYTON BAG & BURLAP CO
10 Hazelwood Rd Ste A5 (06026-9670)
PHONE.................................860 653-8191
Mark Lundin, *Manager*
EMP: 3
SALES (corp-wide): 45.3MM **Privately Held**
SIC: 2393 5085 Textile bags; industrial supplies
PA: The Dayton Bag & Burlap Co
   322 Davis Ave
   Dayton OH 45403
   937 258-8000

(G-2203)
ENERGY BEAM SCIENCES INC
Also Called: Labpulse Medical
29 Kripes Rd Ste B (06026-9669)
PHONE.................................860 653-0411
Michael Nesta, *President*
Gary Braga, *Materials Mgr*
Paul Kenney, *Treasurer*
Cindy McMurray, *Asst Controller*
Mike Whittley, *Admin Sec*
EMP: 17
SQ FT: 18,000
SALES (est): 4.3MM **Privately Held**
WEB: www.ebsciences.com
SIC: 3826 Analytical instruments

(G-2204)
EXPRESS SOFTWARE PRODUCTION
99 Newgate Rd (06026-9545)
PHONE.................................860 844-0085
John Erbland, *Owner*
EMP: 2
SALES (est): 171K **Privately Held**
SIC: 7372 Business oriented computer software

(G-2205)
FUNKHOUSER INDUSTRIAL PRODUCTS
10 Hazelwood Rd Ste 3b (06026-9670)
P.O. Box 1153 (06026-1153)
PHONE.................................860 653-1972
Robert Funkhouser III, *President*
Kimberly Minch, *Vice Pres*
EMP: 3
SQ FT: 4,800
SALES: 800K **Privately Held**
SIC: 3492 Hose & tube fittings & assemblies, hydraulic/pneumatic

(G-2206)
GALASSO MATERIALS LLC
60 S Main St (06026-9550)
P.O. Box 1776 (06026-0676)
PHONE.................................860 527-1825
Timoth McAvoy,
Emil J Galasso,
Martin A Galasso,
Craig C Timpson,
EMP: 160
SQ FT: 7,000
SALES (est): 38.6MM **Privately Held**
WEB: www.galassomaterials.com
SIC: 1499 1429 1442 Asphalt mining & bituminous stone quarrying; grits mining (crushed stone); construction sand & gravel

(G-2207)
GULFSTREAM AEROSPACE CORP
95 Old County Rd (06026-9754)
PHONE.................................912 965-3000
Scott McDougall, *Branch Mgr*
EMP: 3
SALES (corp-wide): 36.1B **Publicly Held**
SIC: 3721 Aircraft
HQ: Gulfstream Aerospace Corporation
   500 Gulfstream Rd
   Savannah GA 31408
   912 965-3000

(G-2208)
J D PRECISION MACHINE INC
1 School St (06026-9770)
P.O. Box 27 (06026-0027)
PHONE.................................860 653-7787
John Damotta, *President*
Joseph Damotta, *Corp Secy*
EMP: 2
SALES (est): 66.5K **Privately Held**
SIC: 3469 Machine parts, stamped or pressed metal

(G-2209)
JOINING TECHNOLOGIES INC
17 Connecticut South Dr B (06026-9671)
PHONE.................................860 653-0111
David Hudson, *President*
Greg Miller, *General Mgr*
Michael Francoeur, *Chairman*
Gary Francoeur, *Vice Pres*
Scott Poeppel, *Vice Pres*
EMP: 75
SQ FT: 27,578
SALES: 14MM **Privately Held**
WEB: www.joiningtech.com
SIC: 7692 Welding repair

(G-2210)
MAGNATECH LLC
Also Called: Magnatech Dsd Co, The
6 Kripes Rd (06026-9645)
P.O. Box 260 (06026-0260)
PHONE.................................860 653-2573
Yuchi Liu, *Electrical Engi*
John G Emmerson, *Mng Member*
▼ **EMP:** 54
SQ FT: 24,000
SALES (est): 14.4MM **Privately Held**
SIC: 3548 3699 Welding apparatus; electrical welding equipment

(G-2211)
MARK V LABORATORY INC
18 Kripes Rd (06026-9645)
P.O. Box 540 (06026-0540)
PHONE.................................860 653-7201
Norman Villeneuve, *President*
Mark Villeneuve, *Vice Pres*
Karen Cox, *Marketing Staff*
Karen Swanson, *Marketing Staff*
Mark Vanata, *Executive*
EMP: 4
SQ FT: 10,000
SALES (est): 832.2K **Privately Held**
WEB: www.markvlab.com
SIC: 3821 Laboratory apparatus & furniture

(G-2212)
MB AEROSPACE
99 Rainbow Rd (06026-9400)
PHONE.................................860 653-0569
William Kircher, *COO*
Bill Evans, *Vice Pres*
Scott Truehart, *Foreman/Supr*
Gary Natale, *Production*
Robin Gamble, *Manager*
EMP: 4
SALES (est): 335K **Privately Held**
SIC: 3721 Aircraft

(G-2213)
MCGILL AIRFLOW LLC
99 Rainbow Rd Ste E (06026-9400)
PHONE.................................860 653-8001
Scott Schuck, *Mng Member*
EMP: 2
SALES (corp-wide): 67.7MM **Privately Held**
WEB: www.mcgillairflow.com
SIC: 3444 Ducts, sheet metal
HQ: Mcgill Airflow Llc
   1 Mission Park
   Groveport OH 43125
   614 829-1200

(G-2214)
MP SYSTEMS INC
34 Bradley Park Rd (06026-9789)
PHONE..................................860 687-3460
Bradley Morris, *President*
Graham Noake, *President*
EMP: 12
SALES (est): 3.3MM **Privately Held**
SIC: 3443 5078 Heat exchangers: coolers (after, inter), condensers, etc.; beverage coolers
PA: Morris Group, Inc.
910 Day Hill Rd
Windsor CT 06095

(G-2215)
NATIONAL CONVEYORS COMPANY INC
33 Nicholson Rd Ste 2 (06026-9304)
PHONE..................................860 653-0374
Donald B Brant Jr, *CEO*
Arnold Serenkin, *President*
James Dumaine-Savage, *Vice Pres*
Brian Smith, *Vice Pres*
Melia L Garrity, *VP Sales*
▲ **EMP:** 25 **EST:** 1933
SQ FT: 17,500
SALES (est): 6.5MM **Privately Held**
WEB: www.nationalconveyors.com
SIC: 3535 Conveyors & conveying equipment

(G-2216)
NEL GROUP LLC (PA)
32 Rainbow Rd (06026-9761)
PHONE..................................860 413-9042
Timothy Snelgrove, *Mng Member*
EMP: 2
SALES: 6MM **Privately Held**
SIC: 2066 5149 5441 5199 Chocolate; chocolate; candy, nut & confectionery stores; gifts & novelties; gift shop; novelties & giftware, including trophies

(G-2217)
NEWGATE DESIGNS CO
101 Newgate Rd (06026-9545)
PHONE..................................860 653-6991
Theresa Case, *Owner*
Luther Case, *Co-Owner*
EMP: 2
SALES (est): 170.4K **Privately Held**
SIC: 3556 Slicers, commercial, food

(G-2218)
NEWGATE INSTRUMENTS LLC
17 Connecticut South Dr B (06026-9671)
PHONE..................................860 784-1968
David Hudson,
EMP: 2
SALES (est): 104.2K **Privately Held**
SIC: 3822 Building services monitoring controls, automatic

(G-2219)
NIDEC AMERICA CORPORATION
16 International Dr (06026-9718)
PHONE..................................860 653-2144
EMP: 10 **Privately Held**
SIC: 3564 Blowers & fans
HQ: Nidec America Corporation
50 Braintree Hill Park # 110
Braintree MA 02184
781 848-0970

(G-2220)
NUFERN
7 Airport Park Rd (06026-9523)
PHONE..................................860 408-5000
Martin Seifert, *President*
Bryce Samson, *Vice Pres*
Dr Kanishka Tankala, *Vice Pres*
Jeff Wojtkiewicz, *Vice Pres*
Dawn Heller, *Purchasing*
▲ **EMP:** 68
SQ FT: 57,000
SALES (est): 11.6MM
SALES (corp-wide): 1.9B **Publicly Held**
WEB: www.nufern.com
SIC: 3229 Fiber optics strands
PA: Coherent, Inc.
5100 Patrick Henry Dr
Santa Clara CA 95054
408 764-4000

(G-2221)
OSHKOSH CORPORATION
35 Nicholson Rd (06026)
P.O. Box 1126 (06026-1126)
PHONE..................................860 653-5548
Bruce Anderson, *Manager*
EMP: 18
SALES (corp-wide): 7.7B **Publicly Held**
WEB: www.oshkoshtruck.com
SIC: 3711 Motor vehicles & car bodies
PA: Oshkosh Corporation
1917 Four Wheel Dr
Oshkosh WI 54902
920 502-3000

(G-2222)
OVENTROP CORP
29 Kripes Rd (06026-9669)
P.O. Box 789 (06026-0789)
PHONE..................................860 413-9173
Joe Walsh, *CEO*
Milind Pawar, *Marketing Staff*
Sigmund Michel, *Director*
▲ **EMP:** 26
SALES (est): 5MM
SALES (corp-wide): 272.2MM **Privately Held**
SIC: 3491 Process control regulator valves
HQ: Oventrop Gmbh & Co.Kg.
Paul-Oventrop-Str. 1
Olsberg 59939
296 282-0

(G-2223)
OVERHAUL SUPPORT SERVICES LLC
18 Connecticut South Dr (06026-9738)
PHONE..................................860 653-1980
Dave McManus, *Mfg Mgr*
David Dulude, *Branch Mgr*
EMP: 4
SQ FT: 15,820 **Privately Held**
WEB: www.overhaulsupportservices.com
SIC: 3728 Aircraft parts & equipment
PA: Overhaul Support Services, Llc
5 Connecticut South Dr
East Granby CT 06026

(G-2224)
OVERHAUL SUPPORT SERVICES LLC (PA)
5 Connecticut South Dr (06026-9738)
PHONE..................................860 264-2101
Ken O'Connor, *Vice Pres*
Brett Gillespie, *Prdtn Mgr*
Debbie Mlinek, *Safety Mgr*
Ana Langevin, *Purchasing*
Jack Dempsey, *Human Res Mgr*
EMP: 47
SQ FT: 10,000
SALES (est): 9.9MM **Privately Held**
SIC: 3728 Aircraft parts & equipment

(G-2225)
PHYSICAL FITNESS CONSULTANTS
169 Newgate Rd (06026-9545)
PHONE..................................860 653-4655
EMP: 1 **EST:** 1980
SALES (est): 60.8K **Privately Held**
SIC: 3949 Mfg Sporting/Athletic Goods

(G-2226)
R G L INC
121 Rainbow Rd (06026-9795)
P.O. Box 1051 (06026-1051)
PHONE..................................860 653-7254
Rocco G Lapenta, *President*
EMP: 46
SQ FT: 6,000
SALES (est): 3.4MM **Privately Held**
SIC: 2731 2721 2741 Books: publishing only; periodicals: publishing only; racing forms & programs: publishing only, not printing

(G-2227)
RIMARK MANUFACTURING LLC
6 Talcott Range Dr (06026-9567)
PHONE..................................860 924-6222
Matthew Ritchie,
EMP: 2
SALES (est): 121.9K **Privately Held**
SIC: 3724 Aircraft engines & engine parts

(G-2228)
RSCC WIRE & CABLE LLC (DH)
20 Bradley Park Rd (06026-9789)
PHONE..................................860 653-8300
Gary J Gagnon, *Vice Pres*
Mike St Jean, *Engineer*
Frederick Schwelm Jr, *Mng Member*
R C Gluth,
Wayne Yakich,
▲ **EMP:** 263
SQ FT: 140,000
SALES (est): 143.5MM
SALES (corp-wide): 225.3B **Publicly Held**
SIC: 3357 3315 Nonferrous wiredrawing & insulating; cable, steel: insulated or armored
HQ: Marmon Holdings, Inc.
181 W Madison St Ste 2600
Chicago IL 60602
312 372-9500

(G-2229)
SIGNS PLUS INC (PA)
3 Turkey Hills Rd (06026-9564)
P.O. Box 560 (06026-0560)
PHONE..................................860 653-0547
Christopher Aubin, *President*
Barbara A Aubin, *Admin Sec*
Barbara Aubin, *Admin Sec*
EMP: 7
SQ FT: 3,000
SALES (est): 853.6K **Privately Held**
SIC: 3993 Signs, not made in custom sign painting shops

(G-2230)
SIMULATIONS LLC
133 Hartford Ave Ste 3 (06026-9138)
PHONE..................................860 978-0772
Jeffrey Kezerian, *Owner*
EMP: 5
SALES (est): 356.4K **Privately Held**
SIC: 7389 8711 3489 Design services; engineering services; flame throwers (ordnance)

(G-2231)
SPECIALTY STEEL TREATING INC
Also Called: Heat Treating
12 Kripes Rd (06026-9645)
PHONE..................................860 653-0061
Dennis Kollmorgen, *Principal*
Ryan Kollmorgen, *QC Mgr*
EMP: 40
SALES (corp-wide): 49.4MM **Privately Held**
WEB: www.sstfraser.com
SIC: 3398 Metal heat treating
PA: Specialty Steel Treating, Inc.
34501 Commerce
Fraser MI 48026
586 293-5355

(G-2232)
TILCON CONNECTICUT INC
60 S Main St (06026-9550)
P.O. Box 578 (06026-0578)
PHONE..................................860 844-7000
Don Penepent, *Manager*
EMP: 20
SALES (corp-wide): 30.6B **Privately Held**
WEB: www.tilconct.com
SIC: 5032 3273 Stone, crushed or broken; sand, construction; gravel; cement; ready-mixed concrete
HQ: Tilcon Connecticut Inc.
642 Black Rock Ave
New Britain CT 06052
860 224-6010

(G-2233)
UNITED TECHNOLOGIES CORP
200 Signature Way (06026-2510)
PHONE..................................860 292-3270
Scott E Ashton, *Manager*
EMP: 14
SALES (corp-wide): 66.5B **Publicly Held**
SIC: 3534 4581 Elevators & moving stairways; airports, flying fields & services
PA: United Technologies Corporation
10 Farm Springs Rd
Farmington CT 06032
860 728-7000

(G-2234)
X L COLOR CORP
3 Turkey Hills Rd (06026-9564)
PHONE..................................860 653-9705
Phil Staron, *Manager*
EMP: 1 **EST:** 2010
SALES (est): 87K **Privately Held**
SIC: 3993 Signs & advertising specialties

East Haddam
Middlesex County

(G-2235)
ALL PHASE HTG COOLG CONTR LLC
500 Tater Hill Rd (06423-1636)
P.O. Box 577, Moodus (06469-0577)
PHONE..................................860 873-9680
Maryjane Fay,
EMP: 3
SALES (est): 250K **Privately Held**
SIC: 3585 Heating & air conditioning combination units

(G-2236)
BEST MANAGEMENT PRODUCTS INC
Also Called: Best Manager Products
9 Matthews Dr Unit A1-A2 (06423-1350)
PHONE..................................860 434-0277
Judith H Duran, *Principal*
EMP: 4
SALES (est): 695.8K **Privately Held**
SIC: 3589 Water treatment equipment, industrial

(G-2237)
C SHERMAN JOHNSON COMPANY
Also Called: Johnson Marine
1 Matthews Dr (06423-1350)
P.O. Box L (06423-0296)
PHONE..................................860 873-8697
Burton Johnson, *CEO*
Curtiss Johnson III, *President*
Elsie Johnson, *Admin Sec*
◆ **EMP:** 14
SQ FT: 5,200
SALES (est): 3.1MM **Privately Held**
WEB: www.csjohnson.com
SIC: 3429 Marine hardware

(G-2238)
CENTER ROAD SOFTWARE LLC
1 Acorn Dr (06423-1468)
PHONE..................................860 402-2767
Frank A Darrow,
EMP: 2
SALES (est): 104.2K **Privately Held**
SIC: 7372 Prepackaged software

(G-2239)
CNC MACHINE TL SPECIALIST LLC
55 Warner Rd (06423-1546)
P.O. Box 155 (06423-0155)
PHONE..................................860 873-1816
Steve Davis, *Owner*
Nic Damuck, *Consultant*
EMP: 2
SALES (est): 145.7K **Privately Held**
SIC: 7629 3599 Tool repair, electric; machine shop, jobbing & repair

(G-2240)
CUSTOM HOUSE LLC
8 Matthews Dr Ste 3 (06423-1350)
PHONE..................................860 873-1259
Robert Finch, *President*
EMP: 10
SALES (est): 1.4MM **Privately Held**
SIC: 3315 5731 Cable, steel: insulated or armored; radio, television & electronic stores

(G-2241)
EPIC PUBLISHING SERVICES LLC
Also Called: Fleur
1c Honey Hill Rd (06423-1708)
P.O. Box 182, Hadlyme (06439-0182)
PHONE..................................860 204-7450

East Haddam - Middlesex County (G-2242) GEOGRAPHIC SECTION

Wendy Vincent,
EMP: 1
SALES (est): 52.2K **Privately Held**
SIC: 2711 2731 6512 6794 Newspapers: publishing only, not printed on site; book clubs: publishing only, not printed on site; property operation, retail establishment; performance rights, publishing & licensing;

(G-2242)
GAME ON LLC
112 Shanaghans Rd (06423-1443)
PHONE 860 608-8931
Irene M Haines, *Principal*
EMP: 2
SALES (est): 120.5K **Privately Held**
SIC: 3944 Games, toys & children's vehicles

(G-2243)
INK LLC
107 Hemlock Valley Rd (06423-1415)
PHONE 860 581-0026
Jeffrey Lilly, *Principal*
EMP: 2
SALES (est): 88.5K **Privately Held**
SIC: 2741 Miscellaneous publishing

(G-2244)
MARK CAPPITELLAS HND-CUT WDEN
58 Schulman Veslak Rd (06423-1206)
PHONE 860 818-4334
EMP: 2
SALES (est): 64.6K **Privately Held**
SIC: 3944 Puzzles

(G-2245)
MARK G CAPPITELLA (PA)
Also Called: Mgc's Cstm Made Wooden
31 Bogue Ln (06423-1442)
PHONE 860 873-3093
Mark Cappitella, *Owner*
EMP: 3
SQ FT: 2,300
SALES: 150K **Privately Held**
WEB: www.ctrivervalley.com
SIC: 3944 Games, toys & children's vehicles

(G-2246)
NGS POWER LLC
385 Town St (06423-1366)
PHONE 860 873-0100
Manfred Roth, *Branch Mgr*
EMP: 1
SALES (corp-wide): 227.3K **Privately Held**
SIC: 3731 Ferryboats, building & repairing
PA: Ngs Power, Llc
25 Falls Rd
Moodus CT 06469
860 873-0100

(G-2247)
PENNYCORNER PRESS
382 Town St (06423-1371)
PHONE 860 873-3545
Glyle Kranz, *Principal*
EMP: 1
SALES (est): 37.5K **Privately Held**
SIC: 2741 Miscellaneous publishing

(G-2248)
PINE RIDGE GRAVEL LLC
24 Mount Parnassus Rd (06423-1475)
PHONE 860 873-2500
EMP: 3
SALES (est): 180K **Privately Held**
SIC: 1442 Construction Sand/Gravel

(G-2249)
TEX ELM INC
136 Town St (06423-1423)
PHONE 860 873-9715
Luella A Lyman, *President*
Emmett J Lyman, *Treasurer*
William B Harmon, *Clerk*
EMP: 15
SQ FT: 10,000
SALES (est): 1.1MM **Privately Held**
WEB: www.texas-relocation.org
SIC: 2759 Engraving

(G-2250)
WESTIE CABINETRY LLC
15 Main St (06423-1303)
PHONE 860 873-8953
Raymond Pelletier, *Principal*
EMP: 1
SALES (est): 86.8K **Privately Held**
SIC: 2434 Wood kitchen cabinets

East Hampton
Middlesex County

(G-2251)
4 D TECHNOLOGY CORPORATION
91 Daniel St (06424-1806)
PHONE 860 365-0420
James Wyant, *Branch Mgr*
Jack Latchinian, *Manager*
EMP: 3
SALES (corp-wide): 324.5MM **Publicly Held**
SIC: 3827 Optical test & inspection equipment
HQ: 4d Technology Corporation
3280 E Hmshre Loop Ste 14
Tucson AZ 85706
520 294-5600

(G-2252)
AMERICA EXTRACT CORPORATION
31 E High St (06424-1021)
PHONE 860 267-4444
Edward Jackowitz, *President*
EMP: 16
SQ FT: 65,000
SALES (est): 1MM **Privately Held**
SIC: 2087 Extracts, flavoring

(G-2253)
AMERICAN DISTILLING INC (PA)
31 E High St (06424-1021)
P.O. Box 319 (06424-0319)
PHONE 860 267-4444
Edward C Jackowitz, *President*
Kevin R Jackowitz, *Vice Pres*
George Perham, *Lab Dir*
Bryan E Jackowitz, *Admin Sec*
▼ **EMP:** 75
SQ FT: 65,000
SALES (est): 15.9MM **Privately Held**
SIC: 2085 2833 2844 2087 Distillers' dried grains & solubles & alcohol; botanical products, medicinal: ground, graded or milled; perfumes & colognes; flavoring extracts & syrups

(G-2254)
AMERICAN POWDERCOATING LLC
12 Summit St Ste 1 (06424-1242)
P.O. Box 338 (06424-0338)
PHONE 860 267-8870
Mark Mukon,
EMP: 4
SALES (est): 83K **Privately Held**
SIC: 3479 Coating of metals & formed products; coating of metals with plastic or resins; coating of metals with silicon; coating or wrapping steel pipe

(G-2255)
AMERICAN PRECISION MOLD INC
58 E High St (06424-1052)
P.O. Box 22 (06424-0022)
PHONE 860 267-1356
Richard Erlandson, *President*
EMP: 4
SQ FT: 3,000
SALES (est): 570.6K **Privately Held**
SIC: 3544 Industrial molds

(G-2256)
BERRY GLOBAL INC
44o Niles St (06424-1111)
PHONE 413 529-7602
R Jones, *Manager*
EMP: 2 **Publicly Held**
SIC: 3089 3081 Bottle caps, molded plastic; unsupported plastics film & sheet
HQ: Berry Global, Inc.
101 Oakley St
Evansville IN 47710
812 424-2904

(G-2257)
BEVIN BROS MANUFACTURING CO
Also Called: Bevin Bells
17 Watrous St (06424-1234)
P.O. Box 60 (06424-0060)
PHONE 860 267-4431
Stanley R Bevin, *President*
Alison Bevinlove, *Vice Pres*
EMP: 40
SALES (est): 7.1MM **Privately Held**
WEB: www.bevinbells.com
SIC: 3699 Bells, electric

(G-2258)
BOULE LLC
258 Injun Hollow Rd (06424-3022)
PHONE 860 267-8343
Donald Boule, *Mng Member*
EMP: 1
SALES: 170K **Privately Held**
SIC: 2434 Wood kitchen cabinets

(G-2259)
BRIAN REYNOLDS
Also Called: Clean Cut Logging
177 Hog Hill Rd (06424-1867)
PHONE 860 267-2021
Brian Reynolds, *Owner*
EMP: 2
SALES (est): 112.9K **Privately Held**
SIC: 2411 1629 Logging; land clearing contractor

(G-2260)
CENTRAL CT SNOW LLC
85 Middletown Ave (06424-1732)
P.O. Box 271, East Haddam (06423-0271)
PHONE 860 467-3107
Patricia Phillippi,
Christopher Phillippi,
EMP: 4
SALES (est): 298.5K **Privately Held**
SIC: 4959 7389 3271 0782 Snowplowing; ; blocks, concrete: landscape or retaining wall; landscape contractors; landscape services; landscape planning services

(G-2261)
CHATHAM DRAPERY CO INC
59 Edgerton St (06424-1614)
PHONE 860 267-7767
Craig Odell, *President*
EMP: 2
SQ FT: 1,800
SALES: 300K **Privately Held**
SIC: 2391 Draperies, plastic & textile: from purchased materials

(G-2262)
GREYWALL INC
Also Called: Absolute Metrology Services
144 Bear Swamp Rd (06424-1601)
PHONE 860 267-6177
Maria Robinson, *President*
Arthur Robinson, *Vice Pres*
EMP: 2
SALES (est): 118.6K **Privately Held**
SIC: 3229 8734 Pressed & blown glass; testing laboratories

(G-2263)
HARRY & HIOS WOODWORKING LLC
35 Stevenson Rd (06424-1534)
PHONE 860 267-1535
Harold H Wiley Jr, *Principal*
EMP: 2
SALES (est): 217.2K **Privately Held**
SIC: 2431 Millwork

(G-2264)
HUMPHREYS PHARMACAL INC
31 E High St (06424-1021)
P.O. Box 317 (06424-0317)
PHONE 860 267-8710
Tom Shultz, *President*
▼ **EMP:** 10 **EST:** 1854
SALES (est): 1MM
SALES (corp-wide): 4.9MM **Privately Held**
WEB: www.humphreysusa.com
SIC: 2834 Vitamin preparations
PA: Dickinson Brands Inc.
31 E High St
East Hampton CT 06424
860 267-2279

(G-2265)
INTEGRITY CYLINDER SALES LLC
17 Watrous St (06424-1234)
P.O. Box 60 (06424-0060)
PHONE 860 267-6667
Doug Dilla, *Mng Member*
Matthew Dedin,
Jeff True,
EMP: 3 **EST:** 2012
SALES: 89K **Privately Held**
SIC: 3479 Coating of metals & formed products

(G-2266)
JAMILAH HENNA CREATIONS
29 Peach Farm Rd (06424-1604)
PHONE 860 365-9542
Jamilah Zebarth, *Owner*
EMP: 1
SALES (est): 49K **Privately Held**
SIC: 2865 Color pigments, organic

(G-2267)
JOHNSON MILLWORK INC
222 Quarry Hill Rd (06424-3054)
PHONE 860 267-4693
Robert W Johnson, *President*
EMP: 3
SALES (est): 359.9K **Privately Held**
SIC: 2431 Millwork

(G-2268)
KITCHEN LIVING LLC
21 Main St (06424-1116)
PHONE 860 819-5847
Matthew Modglin, *Owner*
EMP: 2 **EST:** 2011
SALES (est): 160K **Privately Held**
SIC: 2434 Wood kitchen cabinets

(G-2269)
M S BICKFORD LLC
19 Crows Nest Ln (06424-3038)
PHONE 860 467-6937
Matthew Bickford, *Mng Member*
EMP: 1
SALES (est): 89K **Privately Held**
SIC: 3544 Special dies, tools, jigs & fixtures

(G-2270)
NAUTA ROLL CORPORATION
7 Whippoorwill Hollow Rd (06424-1830)
PHONE 860 267-2027
Robert Hilton, *President*
Cheryl Hilton, *Vice Pres*
Cheryl H Hilton, *Vice Pres*
EMP: 3
SQ FT: 6,000
SALES (est): 270K **Privately Held**
SIC: 3069 Rolls, solid or covered rubber

(G-2271)
NESCI ENTERPRISES INC
Also Called: Nesci Factory Store
12 Summit St (06424-1242)
P.O. Box 119 (06424-0119)
PHONE 860 267-2588
Ralph Nesci, *President*
Sandra Nesci, *Vice Pres*
EMP: 2
SQ FT: 24,000
SALES: 350K **Privately Held**
SIC: 3469 3425 5051 Boxes: tool, lunch, mail, etc.: stamped metal; saw blades & handsaws; welding machinery & equipment; steel; fabricated structural metal

(G-2272)
P&P LOGGING CO
38 Lakewood Rd (06424-1404)
PHONE 860 267-2176
Leo Paholsky, *Principal*
EMP: 2

GEOGRAPHIC SECTION   **East Hartford - Hartford County (G-2303)**

SALES (est): 120K **Privately Held**
SIC: 2411 Logging camps & contractors

(G-2273)
PETER CONRAD
3 Raymond Rd (06424-1339)
PHONE.................................860 673-3600
Peter Conrad, *Owner*
EMP: 1
SALES (est): 99.8K **Privately Held**
SIC: 2431 Staircases, stairs & railings

(G-2274)
POST & BEAM HOMES INC
4 Sexton Hill Rd (06424-1817)
PHONE.................................860 267-2060
Natale Malatesta, *President*
EMP: 3
SALES (est): 415.2K **Privately Held**
WEB: www.postandbeamhomes.com
SIC: 2452 1521 Log cabins, prefabricated, wood; new construction, single-family houses

(G-2275)
PRO GAS INSTALLATION & SVC LLC
176 Tartia Rd (06424-1639)
PHONE.................................860 982-1370
Ronald R Trapp, *Principal*
EMP: 1
SALES: 110K **Privately Held**
SIC: 1389 7389 Gas field services;

(G-2276)
PSI PLUS INC
17 Watrous St (06424-1234)
P.O. Box 147 (06424-0147)
PHONE.................................860 267-6667
Douglas Dilla, *President*
Stanley R Bevin, *Director*
EMP: 15
SQ FT: 14,000
SALES: 875K **Privately Held**
SIC: 3443 Cylinders, pressure: metal plate

(G-2277)
RICCIO ARTIFACTS
18 Abbey Rd (06424-2101)
PHONE.................................860 267-6023
Daniel Riccio, *Owner*
EMP: 1
SALES (est): 50.6K **Privately Held**
SIC: 5932 3299 Art objects, antique; architectural sculptures: gypsum, clay, papier mache, etc.

(G-2278)
RICHARD WALKER
Also Called: Rick's Sugar Shack
69 Collie Brook Rd (06424-1642)
PHONE.................................860 267-7117
Richard Walker, *Owner*
EMP: 1
SALES (est): 51.9K **Privately Held**
SIC: 2099 Maple syrup

(G-2279)
SHM WELDING AND REPAIR LLC
328 Moodus Rd (06424-1840)
PHONE.................................860 267-4012
Sean McLean, *Principal*
EMP: 1
SALES (est): 36.7K **Privately Held**
SIC: 7692 Welding repair

(G-2280)
STICKLER MACHINE COMPANY LLC
4 N Main St Ste 1 (06424-1048)
PHONE.................................860 267-8246
EMP: 4
SQ FT: 3,500
SALES (est): 27K **Privately Held**
SIC: 3599 Machine Shop

(G-2281)
T N DICKINSON COMPANY
Also Called: Dickinson's Cosmetics
31 E High St (06424-1021)
PHONE.................................860 267-2279
Edward C Jackowitz, *President*
Bryan E Jackowitz, *Corp Secy*
Kevin R Jackowitz, *Vice Pres*
EMP: 10

SALES (est): 1.1MM **Privately Held**
SIC: 2844 5122 Toilet preparations; toiletries; perfumes

(G-2282)
TURNKEY SOFTWARE LLC
18 Quiet Woods Rd (06424-1811)
PHONE.................................860 604-0837
Meredith Jirowetz, *Principal*
EMP: 2
SALES (est): 140.4K **Privately Held**
SIC: 7372 Prepackaged software

(G-2283)
VENTURE TOOL AND MANUFACTURING
12 Summit St (06424-1242)
P.O. Box 343 (06424-0343)
PHONE.................................860 267-9647
Daniel Woodis, *President*
Gary Woodis, *Corp Secy*
EMP: 3
SALES (est): 100K **Privately Held**
SIC: 3599 Machine shop, jobbing & repair

(G-2284)
YANKEE MINERAL & GEM CO
22 E Hayes Rd (06424-1717)
PHONE.................................860 267-0167
Ted Johnson, *Principal*
EMP: 2
SALES (est): 124.7K **Privately Held**
SIC: 3915 Jewelers' materials & lapidary work

(G-2285)
ZATORSKI COATING COMPANY INC
77 Wopowog Rd (06424-1674)
PHONE.................................860 267-9889
Diane A Zatorski, *President*
Diane Achenbach-Zatorski, *President*
Raymond Zatorski, *Admin Sec*
EMP: 14
SALES (est): 1.8MM **Privately Held**
SIC: 3554 Coating & finishing machinery, paper

East Hartford
Hartford County

(G-2286)
ACTUALMEDS CORPORATION
222 Pitkin St Ste 107 (06108-3261)
PHONE.................................888 838-9053
Patricia Meisner, *CEO*
Ann Marie Biernacki, *Vice Pres*
John Wagner, *VP Bus Dvlpt*
EMP: 5
SALES (est): 315.3K **Privately Held**
SIC: 7372 Application computer software

(G-2287)
ADAPTIVE OPTICS ASSOCIATES INC
Also Called: Aoa Xinetics
121 Prestige Park Cir (06108-1908)
PHONE.................................860 282-4401
Rick Little, *Manager*
EMP: 18 **Publicly Held**
WEB: www.adaptiveoptics.org
SIC: 3827 Optical elements & assemblies, except ophthalmic
HQ: Adaptive Optics Associates, Inc.
    115 Jackson Rd
    Devens MA 01434
    978 757-9600

(G-2288)
AERO COMPONENT SERVICES LLC
781 Goodwin St (06108-1202)
PHONE.................................860 291-0417
Kirk Morris, *Mng Member*
EMP: 5
SQ FT: 3,000
SALES (est): 605K **Privately Held**
SIC: 3724 Aircraft engines & engine parts

(G-2289)
AIR BORN COATINGS
52 Village St (06108-3904)
PHONE.................................860 684-6762
Matt Hartzog, *President*
EMP: 1
SALES (est): 47.2K **Privately Held**
SIC: 2851 Paints & allied products

(G-2290)
AMERICAN RAILWAY TECHNOLOGIES
61 Alna Ln Ste 1 (06108-1160)
P.O. Box 312, Glastonbury (06033-0312)
PHONE.................................860 291-1170
Donald Schucht, *President*
EMP: 5
SQ FT: 5,000
SALES (est): 526.4K **Privately Held**
WEB: www.americanrailwaytechnologies.com
SIC: 3571 1731 Electronic computers; electrical work

(G-2291)
ANDHER MFG LLC
24 Emely St (06108-3917)
PHONE.................................860 874-8816
Andrzej Herman, *Principal*
EMP: 2
SALES (est): 135.7K **Privately Held**
SIC: 3999 Manufacturing industries

(G-2292)
ARDENT INC (PA)
Also Called: Ardent Displays & Packaging
95 Leggett St (06108-1167)
PHONE.................................860 528-6000
Donald Budnick, *President*
Matthew Pope, *Vice Pres*
Megan Arcari, *Buyer*
Jake Thibault, *Natl Sales Mgr*
Steve Wurtzel, *Marketing Staff*
▲ EMP: 27
SQ FT: 55,000
SALES (est): 6.1MM **Privately Held**
WEB: www.ardentdisplays.com
SIC: 2542 5046 Fixtures: display, office or store: except wood; display equipment, except refrigerated

(G-2293)
ARTHUR J HURLEY COMPANY
60 Meadow St (06108-3218)
PHONE.................................860 257-5505
Arthur J Hurley, *Principal*
EMP: 2
SALES (est): 112.5K **Privately Held**
SIC: 3699 Electrical equipment & supplies

(G-2294)
ASTRO WELDING INC
11 Oakland Ave (06108-4016)
PHONE.................................860 289-6272
George Bakogiorgas, *Owner*
EMP: 2
SALES (est): 50.4K **Privately Held**
SIC: 7692 Welding repair

(G-2295)
ATI LADISH MACHINING INC (DH)
Also Called: ATI Forged Products
311 Prestige Park Rd (06108-1928)
PHONE.................................860 688-3688
John Delaney, *President*
Jeff Cebula, *General Mgr*
John S Minich, *Principal*
Dale G Reid, *Exec VP*
Susan Campbell, *Vice Pres*
EMP: 51 EST: 1946
SQ FT: 40,000
SALES (est): 17.6MM **Publicly Held**
WEB: www.stowemachine.com
SIC: 3724 Aircraft engines & engine parts
HQ: Ati Ladish Llc
    5481 S Packard Ave
    Cudahy WI 53110
    414 747-2611

(G-2296)
ATI LADISH MACHINING INC
Also Called: East Hartford Operations
311 Prestige Park Rd (06108-1928)
PHONE.................................860 688-3688

Richard Cleary, *Branch Mgr*
Erika Pafford, *Manager*
EMP: 100 **Publicly Held**
SIC: 3724 Aircraft engines & engine parts
HQ: Ati Ladish Machining, Inc.
    311 Prestige Park Rd
    East Hartford CT 06108
    860 688-3688

(G-2297)
BENETTIERIS STUDIO
115 Main St (06118-3212)
PHONE.................................860 568-3590
Connie Desoma, *President*
EMP: 1
SALES (est): 69.2K **Privately Held**
SIC: 2759 Commercial printing

(G-2298)
BESSETTE HOLDINGS INC
Also Called: Connecticut Die Cutting Svc
95 Leggett St (06108-1167)
PHONE.................................860 289-6000
Ken Besset, *Principal*
Gary R Bessette, *Vice Pres*
Raymond J Gruzas, *Treasurer*
Donald Budnick, *Mng Member*
Carmen Bessette, *Admin Sec*
EMP: 35
SQ FT: 25,000
SALES (est): 5.8MM **Privately Held**
WEB: www.connecticutdiecutting.com
SIC: 3544 3469 3423 Dies, steel rule; stamping metal for the trade; cutting dies, except metal cutting

(G-2299)
BF SERVICES LLC
44 Maplewood Ave (06108-4022)
PHONE.................................860 289-6929
William Foran, *Owner*
EMP: 1 EST: 1995
SALES (est): 130K **Privately Held**
SIC: 3011 Tires & inner tubes

(G-2300)
BRESCIAS PRINTING SERVICES INC
66 Connecticut Blvd (06108-3013)
PHONE.................................860 528-4254
William G Brescia, *President*
William Brescia, *President*
Laura Bolduc, *Associate*
EMP: 7
SQ FT: 5,000
SALES (est): 1MM **Privately Held**
WEB: www.brescias.com
SIC: 2752 7334 2791 7331 Commercial printing, offset; photocopying & duplicating services; typesetting; mailing service

(G-2301)
BURNSIDE SUPERMARKET LLC
Also Called: Connecticut Dist Svcs Ltd
1150 Burnside Ave (06108-1508)
PHONE.................................860 291-9965
Dereck Singh,
▲ EMP: 5 EST: 2010
SQ FT: 11,026
SALES (est): 378.4K **Privately Held**
SIC: 2099 5411 Sandwiches, assembled & packaged: for wholesale market; supermarkets

(G-2302)
CARDINAL HEALTH 414 LLC
131 Hartland St Ste 8 (06108-3229)
PHONE.................................860 291-9135
Arshad Mehmood, *Principal*
EMP: 9
SALES (corp-wide): 145.5B **Publicly Held**
SIC: 2835 2834 Radioactive diagnostic substances; pharmaceutical preparations
HQ: Cardinal Health 414, Llc
    7000 Cardinal Pl
    Dublin OH 43017
    614 757-5000

(G-2303)
CENTRAL CONNECTICUT COATING
52 Village St (06108-3904)
PHONE.................................860 528-8281
Gene Schaeffer, *President*
EMP: 11

(PA)=Parent Co (HQ)=Headquarters (DH)=Div Headquarters
✪ = New Business established in last 2 years

2020 Harris Connecticut
Manufacturers Directory

87

East Hartford - Hartford County (G-2304)

SALES (est): 1.6MM **Privately Held**
SIC: 3479 Coating of metals & formed products

(G-2304)
CENTRITEC SEALS LLC
222 Pitkin St Ste 104 (06108-3261)
PHONE.................................860 594-7183
Douglas Rode,
EMP: 3
SALES (est): 207.9K **Privately Held**
SIC: 3399 Iron ore recovery from open hearth slag

(G-2305)
CIRCUIT CELLAR INC
Also Called: C C I
111 Founders Plz Ste 904 (06108-3212)
P.O. Box 417, Chase City VA (23924-0417)
PHONE.................................860 289-0800
Steven Ciarcia, *President*
Kim Hopkins, *Advt Staff*
C Abate, *Manager*
Kc Prescott, *Art Dir*
EMP: 17
SQ FT: 19,000
SALES (est): 2MM **Privately Held**
WEB: www.circuitcellar.com
SIC: 2721 Magazines: publishing only, not printed on site

(G-2306)
CLARCOR ENG MBL SOLUTIONS LLC (DH)
Also Called: Parker
60 Prestige Park Rd (06108-1919)
PHONE.................................860 920-4200
Christopher Conway, *CEO*
Stephen S Langin, *CFO*
◆ EMP: 58
SQ FT: 571,000
SALES (est): 127.9MM
SALES (corp-wide): 14.3B **Publicly Held**
SIC: 3492 3714 Control valves, fluid power: hydraulic & pneumatic; fuel systems & parts, motor vehicle
HQ: Clarcor Inc.
 840 Crescent Centre Dr # 600
 Franklin TN 37067
 615 771-3100

(G-2307)
COCA-COLA BOTTLING
475 Main St (06118)
PHONE.................................800 241-2653
EMP: 2
SALES (est): 62.3K **Privately Held**
SIC: 2086 Bottled & canned soft drinks

(G-2308)
COMPANY OF COCA-COLA BOTTLING
471 Main St 471 # 471 (06118-1402)
PHONE.................................860 569-0037
Jody Lemay, *Branch Mgr*
EMP: 58 **Privately Held**
WEB: www.coke.com
SIC: 2086 Bottled & canned soft drinks
HQ: Coca-Cola Bottling Company Of Southeastern New England, Inc.
 150 Waterford Parkway S
 Waterford CT 06385
 860 443-2816

(G-2309)
CONGRESS CATERING INC
Also Called: Congress Rotisserie
53 Cherry St (06108-3922)
PHONE.................................860 291-8182
Lou Miazga, *President*
EMP: 20
SALES (est): 753.4K **Privately Held**
SIC: 5812 5813 4212 2051 American restaurant; carry-out only (except pizza) restaurant; caterers; drinking places; delivery service, vehicular; bakery: wholesale or wholesale/retail combined; franchises, selling or licensing

(G-2310)
COVALENT COATING TECH LLC
222 Pitkin St (06108-3261)
PHONE.................................860 214-6452
Orville Dialey, *Principal*
EMP: 3

SALES (est): 30K **Privately Held**
SIC: 3479 Coating of metals & formed products

(G-2311)
CT DRIVE-SHAFT SERVICE LLC
77 Cherry St (06108-2053)
PHONE.................................860 289-6459
Christopher Dewitt, *Principal*
EMP: 2 EST: 2014
SALES (est): 170.9K **Privately Held**
SIC: 3714 Motor vehicle parts & accessories

(G-2312)
DECO PRODUCTS INC
34 Nelson St Ste C (06108-3930)
P.O. Box 482, Bloomfield (06002-0482)
PHONE.................................860 528-4304
Gary A Dellorso, *President*
Shirley Dellorso, *Shareholder*
EMP: 4 EST: 1965
SQ FT: 2,400
SALES (est): 150K **Privately Held**
SIC: 3451 Screw machine products

(G-2313)
DEMUSZ MFG CO INC
303 Burnham St (06108-1183)
PHONE.................................860 528-9845
Waldemar Demusz, *President*
Wieslaw Demusz, *Vice Pres*
Alexander Demusz, *Engineer*
Roma Demusz, *VP Finance*
Judy Snarski, *Sales Staff*
EMP: 27
SQ FT: 12,000
SALES (est): 5.2MM **Privately Held**
WEB: www.demusz.com
SIC: 3724 Aircraft engines & engine parts

(G-2314)
DIGNIFIED ENDINGS LLC
15 Stanley St (06108-1662)
PHONE.................................860 291-0575
David Hurovite, *Principal*
Michelle Hurovite,
EMP: 65
SQ FT: 2,400
SALES (est): 4.3MM **Privately Held**
SIC: 3995 7261 Burial caskets; funeral service & crematories

(G-2315)
DRUM CRANE AND RIGGING LLC
324 Governor St (06108-3925)
PHONE.................................860 837-4517
Daniel Drummond, *Mng Member*
EMP: 1
SALES (est): 79.9K **Privately Held**
SIC: 3531 Backhoes, tractors, cranes, plows & similar equipment

(G-2316)
DUNN PAPER HOLDINGS INC
2 Forbes St (06108-3727)
PHONE.................................860 289-7496
Chris Fedler, *Plant Mgr*
EMP: 85
SALES (corp-wide): 139.6MM **Privately Held**
SIC: 2621 Towels, tissues & napkins: paper & stock
PA: Dunn Paper Holdings, Inc.
 218 Riverview St
 Port Huron MI 48060
 810 984-5521

(G-2317)
DUNN PAPER LLC
2 Forbes St (06108-3727)
PHONE.................................860 466-4141
James Dickerson,
EMP: 80
SALES (est): 13.8MM **Privately Held**
SIC: 2676 Sanitary paper products

(G-2318)
EASTERN TECHNOLOGY CORPORATION
42 Nelson St (06108-3907)
PHONE.................................860 528-9821
David Freidman, *President*
Carol Freidman, *Owner*

EMP: 7
SQ FT: 30,000
SALES (est): 400K **Privately Held**
WEB: www.easterntech.com
SIC: 3829 Aircraft & motor vehicle measurement equipment

(G-2319)
EBL PRODUCTS INC
22 Prestige Park Cir (06108-1917)
PHONE.................................860 290-3737
Joseph Zarrelli, *President*
Andrew Tremblay, *President*
EMP: 13
SALES (est): 1.8MM **Privately Held**
WEB: www.eblproducts.com
SIC: 3679 Piezoelectric crystals

(G-2320)
ELEMETAL DIRECT USA LLC
210 Roberts St Ste B (06108-3609)
PHONE.................................860 290-1701
EMP: 1 EST: 2015
SALES (est): 80.8K **Privately Held**
SIC: 3339 Precious metals

(G-2321)
ELJEN CORPORATION
125 Mckee St (06108-4018)
PHONE.................................860 610-0426
Joseph Glasser, *CEO*
Melissa Sanchez, *Office Mgr*
EMP: 28
SALES (corp-wide): 24.7MM **Privately Held**
SIC: 3259 Clay sewer & drainage pipe & tile
PA: Eljen Corporation
 10 N Main St Ste 216
 West Hartford CT
 860 232-0077

(G-2322)
EMR GLOBAL INC
265 Prestige Park Rd (06108-1939)
PHONE.................................203 452-8166
William Rudolph, *President*
Mark Mascheck, *Vice Pres*
Brian McHugh, *Treasurer*
EMP: 4
SALES (est): 282.6K **Privately Held**
SIC: 3053 Packing materials

(G-2323)
ENDOTO CORP
43 Franklin St (06108-1723)
PHONE.................................860 289-8033
Guy J Bolduc, *President*
▲ EMP: 3
SALES (est): 568.4K **Privately Held**
SIC: 3669 Emergency alarms

(G-2324)
ENDURO WHEELCHAIR COMPANY
750 Tolland St (06108-2727)
PHONE.................................860 289-0374
Kenneth J Messier, *Principal*
EMP: 3 EST: 2010
SALES (est): 185.4K **Privately Held**
SIC: 3842 Wheelchairs

(G-2325)
FLUOROPOLYMER RESOURCES INC
99 E River Dr (06108-3288)
PHONE.................................860 291-9521
Kevin F Buchanan, *President*
Julie A Buchanan, *Vice Pres*
EMP: 2
SALES (est): 333.7K
SALES (corp-wide): 157.5MM **Privately Held**
SIC: 2822 Ethylene-propylene rubbers, EPDM polymers
PA: Prime Materials Recovery Inc.
 99 E River Dr
 East Hartford CT 06108
 860 622-7626

(G-2326)
FLUOROPOLYMER RESOURCES LLC (PA)
99 Erver Dr Rvrview Sq Ii Riverview (06108)
P.O. Box 875, Old Lyme (06371-0875)
PHONE.................................860 423-7622
Kevin F Buchanan, *President*
Julie A Buchanan, *Vice Pres*
Mike Wilosko, *Vice Pres*
John Ieronimo, *Controller*
Denise Coyle, *Sales Mgr*
EMP: 7
SQ FT: 2,000
SALES (est): 8MM **Privately Held**
WEB: www.friusa.net
SIC: 3089 Injection molding of plastics

(G-2327)
FM INDUSTRIES LLC (PA)
166 Prestige Park Rd (06108)
PHONE.................................860 610-0340
Oliver Mueller, *Mng Member*
▲ EMP: 2
SALES (est): 1.4MM **Privately Held**
SIC: 2531 Assembly hall furniture

(G-2328)
FMI PAINT & CHEMICAL INC
14 Eastern Park Rd (06108-1105)
PHONE.................................860 218-2210
Harry Fine, *President*
EMP: 12
SQ FT: 10,000
SALES (est): 1.5MM **Privately Held**
SIC: 2851 Paints & paint additives; lacquers, varnishes, enamels & other coatings

(G-2329)
G W ELLIOT INC
95 Rene Ct (06108-1338)
PHONE.................................860 528-6143
Gordon Elliott, *President*
Lawrence Elliott, *Admin Sec*
EMP: 1 EST: 1966
SQ FT: 800
SALES (est): 130K **Privately Held**
SIC: 5941 3489 3484 Firearms; guns or gun parts, over 30 mm.; small arms

(G-2330)
GARDEN OF LIGHT INC (PA)
Also Called: Garden Light Natural Foods Mkt
127 Park Ave Ste 100 (06108-4012)
PHONE.................................860 895-6622
Michael Smulders, *President*
David Pescatello, *Maintence Staff*
EMP: 80
SQ FT: 110,000
SALES: 20MM **Privately Held**
SIC: 2043 Oatmeal: prepared as cereal breakfast food

(G-2331)
GOONG
798 Silver Ln (06118-1228)
PHONE.................................860 216-3041
Numi Hwang, *Principal*
EMP: 4
SALES (est): 357.4K **Privately Held**
SIC: 3421 Table & food cutlery, including butchers'

(G-2332)
GREENWOOD SUB LLC
162 Governor St (06108-2144)
PHONE.................................860 291-8833
EMP: 1
SALES (est): 41.5K **Privately Held**
SIC: 2499 Wood products

(G-2333)
HOODLUM SKATEBOARD COMPANY LLC
609 Oak St (06118-3042)
PHONE.................................860 690-6201
John Joseph Cassandra Jr, *Principal*
EMP: 2
SALES (est): 128K **Privately Held**
SIC: 3949 Skateboards

GEOGRAPHIC SECTION
East Hartford - Hartford County (G-2361)

(G-2334)
HORST ENGRG DE MEXICO LLC
36 Cedar St (06108-2003)
PHONE 860 289-8209
Scott Livingston,
EMP: 35
SQ FT: 18,000
SALES (est): 3.6MM **Privately Held**
SIC: 3452 3451 3724 Bolts, nuts, rivets & washers; screw machine products; aircraft engines & engine parts

(G-2335)
HYDRO HONING LABORATORIES INC (PA)
Also Called: Peening Technologies Conn
8 Eastern Park Rd (06108-1105)
P.O. Box 280306 (06128-0306)
PHONE 860 289-4328
Thomas Beach, *President*
Walter Beach Jr, *Treasurer*
Dorothy Bogan, *Office Mgr*
Richard Brooks, *Admin Sec*
EMP: 45 **EST:** 1966
SQ FT: 24,000
SALES (est): 4.6MM **Privately Held**
WEB: www.hydro-honing.com
SIC: 3398 Shot peening (treating steel to reduce fatigue)

(G-2336)
IAE INTERNATIONAL AERO ENGS AG
400 Main St Ms121-10 (06108-0968)
PHONE 860 565-1773
Jon Beatty, *President*
Rick Deurloo, *Senior VP*
Jim Guiliano, *Senior VP*
Steve Burrill, *Vice Pres*
John Green, *Vice Pres*
EMP: 150
SQ FT: 34,900
SALES (est): 52.8MM
SALES (corp-wide): 66.5B **Publicly Held**
WEB: www.iaev2500.com
SIC: 3724 Aircraft engines & engine parts
PA: United Technologies Corporation
10 Farm Springs Rd
Farmington CT 06032
860 728-7000

(G-2337)
IMAGE INSIGHT INC
87 Church St (06108-3720)
PHONE 860 528-9806
Eric Rubenstein, *President*
Gordon Drukier, *Vice Pres*
EMP: 3
SALES (est): 382.9K **Privately Held**
SIC: 3829 Measuring & controlling devices

(G-2338)
IMPERMIA COATINGS LLC
222 Pitkin St (06108-3261)
PHONE 413 356-0077
EMP: 1
SALES: 100K **Privately Held**
SIC: 2851 Mfg Paints/Allied Products

(G-2339)
IN DA CUT MUSIC
108 Jessica Dr (06118-2424)
PHONE 860 895-9445
EMP: 2
SALES (est): 81.4K **Privately Held**
SIC: 3599 Industrial machinery

(G-2340)
INTERNATIONAL AERO ENGINES LLC
Also Called: Iae
400 Main St (06108-0968)
PHONE 860 565-5515
Karen C McCusker, *Vice Pres*
EMP: 37
SALES (est): 26.4MM
SALES (corp-wide): 66.5B **Publicly Held**
SIC: 3724 Aircraft engines & engine parts
PA: United Technologies Corporation
10 Farm Springs Rd
Farmington CT 06032
860 728-7000

(G-2341)
INTLAERO BETA CORP
400 Main St (06108-0968)
PHONE 317 821-2000
David J Avery, *Principal*
EMP: 3
SALES (est): 279.5K **Privately Held**
SIC: 3724 Aircraft engines & engine parts

(G-2342)
KEITERBENNETT PUBLISHERS LLC
118 Oxford Dr (06118-2643)
PHONE 860 308-2666
Erwin Hurst, *Principal*
EMP: 2
SALES (est): 123.6K **Privately Held**
SIC: 2741 Miscellaneous publishing

(G-2343)
MARENA INDUSTRIES INC
Also Called: Marena Machinery Sales Div
433 School St (06108-1162)
PHONE 860 528-9701
Teodoro Marena, *President*
John Salisbury, *Superintendent*
Fran Marena, *Admin Sec*
EMP: 15
SQ FT: 19,000
SALES (est): 3.2MM **Privately Held**
WEB: www.championsaw.com
SIC: 3545 3541 Cutting tools for machine tools; gauges (machine tool accessories); grinding machines, metalworking

(G-2344)
MCMULLAN WALL COVERINGS
105 Huckleberry Rd (06118-3546)
PHONE 860 569-6260
Kenny McMullan, *Principal*
EMP: 1
SALES (est): 111.1K **Privately Held**
SIC: 2621 Paper mills

(G-2345)
MIDWOOD QUARRY AND CNSTR INC (PA)
Also Called: Better Stones & Garden
200 Tolland St (06108-2414)
PHONE 860 289-1414
William Smallwood, *President*
▲ **EMP:** 10
SQ FT: 11,000
SALES (est): 3.3MM **Privately Held**
SIC: 5211 5032 5261 1442 Masonry materials & supplies; brick; brick, stone & related material; masons' materials; brick, except refractory; nurseries & garden centers; construction sand & gravel; dimension stone

(G-2346)
NEW ENGLAND CHROME PLATING
63 Thomas St (06108-2056)
PHONE 860 528-7176
David Malinguaggio, *President*
Peter Brown, *General Mgr*
Dean Malinguaggio, *Vice Pres*
EMP: 6
SQ FT: 6,800
SALES (est): 846.7K **Privately Held**
WEB: www.newenglandchrome.com
SIC: 3471 Chromium plating of metals or formed products; plating of metals or formed products

(G-2347)
NEXT LEVEL PUBLISHING LLC
46 Leverich Dr (06108-1431)
PHONE 860 282-2428
Brian Klock, *Principal*
EMP: 1 **EST:** 2014
SALES (est): 48.2K **Privately Held**
SIC: 2741 Miscellaneous publishing

(G-2348)
NORTHROP GRUMMAN CORPORATION
121 Prestige Park Cir (06108-1908)
PHONE 860 282-4461
Mark Voris, *Engineer*
Benjamin Tuxbury, *Software Engr*
EMP: 80 **Publicly Held**
SIC: 3812 Search & navigation equipment
PA: Northrop Grumman Corporation
2980 Fairview Park Dr
Falls Church VA 22042

(G-2349)
OLDE BURNSIDE BREWING CO LLC
780 Tolland St (06108-2727)
PHONE 860 528-2200
▲ **EMP:** 8
SALES (est): 718.2K **Privately Held**
SIC: 2097 Mfg Ice

(G-2350)
OPEN SCIENCE PUBLISHING LLC
41 Applegate Ln Apt 217 (06118-1215)
PHONE 860 568-4675
Joseph Martel, *Principal*
EMP: 1
SALES (est): 37.5K **Privately Held**
SIC: 2741 Miscellaneous publishing

(G-2351)
PARKER-HANNIFIN CORPORATION
60 Prestige Park Rd (06108-1919)
PHONE 860 920-4231
EMP: 2
SALES (corp-wide): 14.3B **Publicly Held**
SIC: 3594 Fluid power pumps & motors
PA: Parker-Hannifin Corporation
6035 Parkland Blvd
Cleveland OH 44124
216 896-3000

(G-2352)
PARTS FEEDERS INC
22 John St (06108-2054)
PHONE 860 528-9579
James Llamas, *President*
EMP: 2
SALES (est): 118.1K **Privately Held**
SIC: 3569 General industrial machinery

(G-2353)
PEENING TECHNOLOGIES EQP LLC
8 Eastern Park Rd (06108-1105)
PHONE 860 289-4328
Thomas Beach,
Walter Beach Jr,
Richard Brooks,
EMP: 50
SALES (est): 5MM **Privately Held**
SIC: 3398 Shot peening (treating steel to reduce fatigue)

(G-2354)
PEENING TECHNOLOGIES EQP LLC
261 Burnham St (06108-1131)
PHONE 860 289-4328
Walter A Beach Jr,
Thomas A Beach,
Richard E Brooks,
EMP: 2
SALES (est): 81.4K **Privately Held**
SIC: 3599 Machine shop, jobbing & repair

(G-2355)
PICTURE THIS HARTFORD INC
Also Called: Hartford Fine Art & Framing Co
80 Pitkin St (06108-3318)
PHONE 860 528-1409
William Plage, *President*
Lauren Plage, *Vice Pres*
EMP: 7
SQ FT: 9,500
SALES (est): 887.1K **Privately Held**
WEB: www.hartfordfineart.com
SIC: 3993 5719 3999 Advertising artwork; pictures & mirrors; pictures, wall; framed artwork

(G-2356)
POPCORN MOVIE POSTER CO LLC
1 Cherry St (06108-3922)
P.O. Box 1121, Glastonbury (06033-6121)
PHONE 860 610-0000
David Graveen,
Annette Daniels,
EMP: 14
SQ FT: 4,500
SALES (est): 1.9MM **Privately Held**
SIC: 2759 Poster & decal printing & engraving

(G-2357)
PRATT & WHITNEY COMPANY INC (HQ)
Also Called: Middletown Engine Center
400 Main St (06108-0968)
PHONE 860 565-4321
Maria Della Posta, *President*
Laura Austin, *General Mgr*
Michael Mahonski, *General Mgr*
Buddy Remington, *General Mgr*
Todd Shields, *General Mgr*
EMP: 130 **EST:** 1986
SALES (est): 117.8MM
SALES (corp-wide): 66.5B **Publicly Held**
SIC: 3724 Aircraft engines & engine parts
PA: United Technologies Corporation
10 Farm Springs Rd
Farmington CT 06032
860 728-7000

(G-2358)
PRATT & WHITNEY ENG SVCS INC
126 Silver Ln Apt 19 (06118-1013)
PHONE 860 610-2631
Beach Eric, *Engineer*
Trinks Steven, *Design Engr*
Eskridge Joshua, *Human Res Mgr*
Hopkins Jeff, *Accounts Exec*
McFadden Kim, *Accounts Exec*
EMP: 212
SALES (corp-wide): 66.5B **Publicly Held**
SIC: 3724 Research & development on aircraft engines & parts
HQ: Pratt & Whitney Engine Services, Inc.
1525 Midway Park Rd
Bridgeport WV 26330
304 842-5421

(G-2359)
PRATT & WHITNEY ENGINE SVCS
Also Called: Pratt Whtney Cstmer Trning Ctr
400 Main St Ste 1 (06118-1888)
PHONE 860 565-4321
Lisa Madsen, *Business Mgr*
Ardell J Anderson, *Vice Pres*
Ivan Rojas, *Electrical Engi*
Joseph Oconnell, *HR Admin*
Brian Lammers, *Manager*
EMP: 27
SALES (corp-wide): 66.5B **Publicly Held**
SIC: 3724 Aircraft engines & engine parts
HQ: Pratt & Whitney Engine Services, Inc.
1525 Midway Park Rd
Bridgeport WV 26330
304 842-5421

(G-2360)
PRATT & WHITNEY SERVICES INC
400 Main St (06108-0968)
PHONE 860 565-5489
Paul Adams, *President*
EMP: 24 **EST:** 2007
SALES (est): 3.8MM
SALES (corp-wide): 66.5B **Publicly Held**
SIC: 3724 Aircraft engines & engine parts
PA: United Technologies Corporation
10 Farm Springs Rd
Farmington CT 06032
860 728-7000

(G-2361)
PRECISION OPTICAL CO
351 Burnham St (06108-1159)
P.O. Box 280023 (06128-0023)
PHONE 860 289-6023
Richard J Welch, *President*
Dan O'Brien, *Vice Pres*
Annemarie O'Brien, *Treasurer*
Dan O' Brein, *VP Sales*
Doreen Dias, *Manager*
EMP: 47
SQ FT: 8,000

East Hartford - Hartford County (G-2362) — GEOGRAPHIC SECTION

SALES: 5MM
SALES (corp-wide): 1.4MM Privately Held
WEB: www.precision-optical-co.com
SIC: 3851 5048 Eyeglasses, lenses & frames; ophthalmic goods
HQ: Perferx Optical Co., Inc.
  25 Downing Three Park
  Pittsfield MA 01201
  413 358-9020

(G-2362)
R AND K INDUSTRIES
24 Arbutus St (06108-2901)
PHONE 860 289-3879
EMP: 2 **EST:** 2010
SALES (est): 77K Privately Held
SIC: 3999 Mfg Misc Products

(G-2363)
REGIONAL STAIRS LLC
183 Prestige Park Rd (06108-1923)
PHONE 860 290-1242
Jake Strecevko,
Andrew Dobranski,
EMP: 5
SQ FT: 5,000
SALES (est): 1MM Privately Held
WEB: www.regionalstairs.com
SIC: 2499 Stepladders, wood

(G-2364)
REID INTERIORS
Also Called: B & C Upholstery
200 Burnside Ave (06108-2308)
PHONE 860 569-1240
Helen Reid, *Partner*
Robert F Reid, *Partner*
EMP: 2 **EST:** 1961
SALES (est): 269.1K Privately Held
SIC: 5131 5714 5231 2512 Piece goods & other fabrics; upholstery materials; draperies; slip covers; wallpaper; upholstered household furniture

(G-2365)
REPUBLIC SYSTEMS INC
222 Pitkin St Ste 117 (06108-3261)
PHONE 860 291-8832
Robert Hughes, *President*
EMP: 1
SALES (est): 68.2K Privately Held
SIC: 7371 7372 Computer software development; software programming applications; prepackaged software; application computer software

(G-2366)
RITE-WAY ELECTRIC MOTORS INC
27 Franklin St (06108-1723)
P.O. Box 281069 (06128-1069)
PHONE 860 528-8890
Wendel A Ridley, *President*
EMP: 2 **EST:** 1969
SQ FT: 4,000
SALES (est): 219.3K Privately Held
SIC: 7694 5063 Electric motor repair; motors, electric

(G-2367)
RSL FIBER SYSTEMS LLC
473 Silver Ln (06118-1152)
PHONE 860 282-4930
Giovanni Tomasi, *CTO*
Giovanni P Tomasi,
EMP: 13 **EST:** 2001
SALES: 2.2MM Privately Held
SIC: 3648 Lighting equipment

(G-2368)
RYKAM LLC
Also Called: Sign Stop
657 Main St (06108-3320)
PHONE 860 721-1411
Jeffrey M Conklin,
Cynthia Conklin,
EMP: 2 **EST:** 2010
SALES: 60K Privately Held
SIC: 3993 Signs & advertising specialties

(G-2369)
SCARLETHREAD LLC
34 Laraia Ave (06108-2731)
PHONE 860 528-0667
Emma Weatherington,
Mark Weatherington,
EMP: 2
SALES (est): 94.6K Privately Held
SIC: 2221 Dress fabrics, manmade fiber & silk

(G-2370)
SEALPRO LLC
721 Burnham St (06108-1307)
PHONE 860 289-0804
David Lombardo, *Owner*
EMP: 4
SALES (est): 480.5K Privately Held
SIC: 2891 Sealants

(G-2371)
SIGN STOP INC
657 Main St (06108-3320)
PHONE 860 721-1411
John Oudheusden, *President*
EMP: 3
SQ FT: 1,900
SALES (est): 190K Privately Held
SIC: 3993 Signs, not made in custom sign painting shops

(G-2372)
SKYLINE INDUSTRIES LLC
362 Tolland St (06108-2445)
PHONE 860 209-8013
Ronald J Walker, *Principal*
EMP: 2
SALES (est): 111.8K Privately Held
SIC: 3999 Manufacturing industries

(G-2373)
SMART SIGNS LLC
470 Burnside Ave (06108-2406)
PHONE 860 656-5257
Brenda Barrera-Calderon, *Principal*
EMP: 1 **EST:** 2014
SALES (est): 46K Privately Held
SIC: 3993 Signs & advertising specialties

(G-2374)
SMARTER SEALANTS LLC
14 Eastern Park Rd (06108-1105)
PHONE 860 218-2210
▲ **EMP:** 4
SALES (est): 240K Privately Held
SIC: 2891 Mfg Adhesives/Sealants

(G-2375)
SOCCER N MORE
525 Burnside Ave (06108-3574)
PHONE 860 282-0224
Bill Moore, *President*
EMP: 2 **EST:** 2010
SALES (est): 203.3K Privately Held
SIC: 3949 Soccer equipment & supplies

(G-2376)
STAMPT BY J
9 Glenn Rd (06118-2112)
PHONE 860 995-3292
Jalen French, *Principal*
EMP: 2
SALES (est): 77.1K Privately Held
SIC: 3953 Marking devices

(G-2377)
STANDARD WELDING COMPANY INC
212 Prospect St (06108-1653)
PHONE 860 528-9628
Richard Ashlaw, *President*
Clifford Wayner, *Treasurer*
EMP: 9
SQ FT: 7,000
SALES (est): 560.7K Privately Held
SIC: 7692 7549 7513 Welding repair; trailer maintenance; truck rental & leasing, no drivers

(G-2378)
STP BINDERY SERVICES INC
265 Prestige Park Rd # 2 (06108-1939)
PHONE 860 528-1430
Steven Pensiero, *President*
EMP: 30
SQ FT: 25,000
SALES (est): 4.2MM Privately Held
SIC: 2789 Binding only: books, pamphlets, magazines, etc.

(G-2379)
STRYKER CORPORATION
155 Founders Plz (06108-8313)
PHONE 860 528-1111
Vince Morgera, *Branch Mgr*
EMP: 11
SALES (corp-wide): 13.6B Publicly Held
SIC: 3841 Surgical & medical instruments
PA: Stryker Corporation
  2825 Airview Blvd
  Portage MI 49002
  269 385-2600

(G-2380)
SUEZ WTS SERVICES USA INC
405 School St (06108-1135)
PHONE 860 291-9660
Lyman B Dickerson, *President*
EMP: 26
SALES (corp-wide): 94.7MM Privately Held
WEB: www.ecolochem.com
SIC: 3589 2899 Water treatment equipment, industrial; water treating compounds
HQ: Suez Wts Services Usa, Inc.
  4545 Patent Rd
  Norfolk VA 23502
  757 855-9000

(G-2381)
SURE INDUSTRIES INC
122 Park Ave Ste C (06108-4045)
PHONE 860 289-2522
Reese Korman, *Principal*
Mark Peters, *Principal*
Prasad Grandhi, *Recruiter*
EMP: 6
SALES (est): 684.6K Privately Held
SIC: 3713 Truck cabs for motor vehicles

(G-2382)
TAYLOR COMMUNICATIONS INC
800 Connecticut Blvd (06108-7303)
PHONE 860 290-6851
Thomas Bareline, *Branch Mgr*
EMP: 11
SALES (corp-wide): 2.8B Privately Held
WEB: www.stdreg.com
SIC: 2761 Manifold business forms
HQ: Taylor Communications, Inc.
  1725 Roe Crest Dr
  North Mankato MN 56003
  507 625-2828

(G-2383)
THEBEAMER LLC
87 Church St (06108-3720)
PHONE 860 212-5071
Peter Solomon, *CEO*
EMP: 17 **EST:** 2014
SQ FT: 400
SALES (est): 200K Privately Held
SIC: 7372 Educational computer software

(G-2384)
THERESAS COLORFUL CREATIONS
15 Myrtle St (06108-2331)
PHONE 860 726-6909
Theresa Biscette, *Principal*
EMP: 1
SALES (est): 39.6K Privately Held
SIC: 3999 Candles

(G-2385)
THREAD ROLLING INC
41 Cedar St (06108-2051)
PHONE 860 528-1515
Steve Livingston, *President*
EMP: 10
SQ FT: 7,000
SALES: 600K
SALES (corp-wide): 22.3MM Privately Held
WEB: www.threadrolling.com
SIC: 3452 Screws, metal
PA: Horst Engineering & Manufacturing Co
  36 Cedar St
  East Hartford CT 06108
  860 289-8209

(G-2386)
TOTAL COMMUNICATIONS INC (PA)
333 Burnham St (06108-1183)
PHONE 860 282-9999
Richard Lennon, *President*
Linda Lennon, *Admin Sec*
EMP: 100
SQ FT: 24,000
SALES: 20.9MM Privately Held
SIC: 3661 5065 7629 Telephone & telegraph apparatus; telephone equipment; telephone set repair

(G-2387)
UNAS GRINDING CORPORATION
28 Cherry St (06108-2010)
P.O. Box 280535 (06128-0535)
PHONE 860 289-1538
John Orzech, *President*
George Wasilefsky, *General Mgr*
Greg Endrelunas, *Vice Pres*
Normand Drapeau, *Manager*
Kyle Endrelunas, *Manager*
EMP: 30 **EST:** 1952
SQ FT: 18,500
SALES (est): 4.6MM Privately Held
WEB: www.unasgrinding.com
SIC: 3599 Grinding castings for the trade; machine shop, jobbing & repair

(G-2388)
UNITED METAL SOLUTIONS
Also Called: United Steel Inc.
164 School St (06108-1867)
PHONE 860 610-4026
Ken Corneau, *CEO*
EMP: 2
SALES (est): 86.6K Privately Held
SIC: 3441 3446 3449 Fabricated structural metal; architectural metalwork; stairs, fire escapes, balconies, railings & ladders; bannisters, made from metal pipe; miscellaneous metalwork

(G-2389)
UNITED STEEL INC
164 School St (06108-1867)
PHONE 860 289-2323
Keith Corneau, *President*
Glen Corneau, *Vice Pres*
John Gagas, *Vice Pres*
Skip Henderson, *Safety Dir*
Joshua Messier, *Project Mgr*
EMP: 150 **EST:** 1979
SQ FT: 122,500
SALES (est): 67.8MM Privately Held
WEB: www.unitedsteel.com
SIC: 3441 3443 3446 3444 Fabricated structural metal; fabricated plate work (boiler shop); ornamental metalwork; sheet metalwork; structural steel erection; welding repair

(G-2390)
UNITED TECH ADVNCED PRJCTS INC
411 Silver Ln (06118-1127)
PHONE 860 610-7159
Jason Chua, *President*
EMP: 1
SALES (est): 54.6K
SALES (corp-wide): 66.5B Publicly Held
SIC: 3724 3534 3585 Aircraft engines & engine parts; elevators & moving stairways; refrigeration & heating equipment
PA: United Technologies Corporation
  10 Farm Springs Rd
  Farmington CT 06032
  860 728-7000

(G-2391)
UNITED TECHNOLOGIES CORP
Also Called: Pratt & Whitney
400 Main St (06118-1873)
PHONE 860 565-4321
Jon Forrest, *General Mgr*
Polis Vrionides, *General Mgr*
Qwandrell Banks, *Project Mgr*
Shyla Aker, *Purch Mgr*
Deborah Mattia, *Buyer*
EMP: 5
SALES (corp-wide): 66.5B Publicly Held
WEB: www.utc.com
SIC: 3724 Aircraft engines & engine parts

▲ = Import ▼ = Export
◆ = Import/Export

GEOGRAPHIC SECTION
East Haven - New Haven County (G-2421)

PA: United Technologies Corporation
10 Farm Springs Rd
Farmington CT 06032
860 728-7000

(G-2392)
UNITED TECHNOLOGIES CORP
400 Main St (06108-0968)
PHONE..................860 565-7622
Rick Silva, *President*
EMP: 214
SALES (corp-wide): 66.5B **Publicly Held**
WEB: www.utc.com
SIC: 3585 Refrigeration & heating equipment
PA: United Technologies Corporation
10 Farm Springs Rd
Farmington CT 06032
860 728-7000

(G-2393)
UNITED TECHNOLOGIES CORP
Also Called: Pratt & Whitney
400 Main St (06108-0968)
PHONE..................860 565-4321
Rick Silva, *President*
EMP: 100
SALES (corp-wide): 66.5B **Publicly Held**
SIC: 3724 Aircraft engines & engine parts
PA: United Technologies Corporation
10 Farm Springs Rd
Farmington CT 06032
860 728-7000

(G-2394)
UNITED TECHNOLOGIES CORP
Also Called: Pratt Whitney-Spare Parts Div
400 Main St (06118-1873)
PHONE..................860 565-4321
William Pursell, *Manager*
EMP: 6
SALES (corp-wide): 66.5B **Publicly Held**
WEB: www.utc.com
SIC: 3724 Aircraft engines & engine parts
PA: United Technologies Corporation
10 Farm Springs Rd
Farmington CT 06032
860 728-7000

(G-2395)
UNITED TECHNOLOGIES CORP
Also Called: Utrc
411 Silver Ln (06118-1127)
PHONE..................860 610-7000
Leslie Doody, *Branch Mgr*
EMP: 500
SALES (corp-wide): 66.5B **Publicly Held**
SIC: 3699 Security devices; security control equipment & systems
PA: United Technologies Corporation
10 Farm Springs Rd
Farmington CT 06032
860 728-7000

(G-2396)
UNITED TECHNOLOGIES CORP
Also Called: Pratt & Whitneys Repair &
400 Main St (06108-0968)
PHONE..................860 557-3333
EMP: 77
SALES (corp-wide): 66.5B **Publicly Held**
SIC: 3728 Aircraft body assemblies & parts
PA: United Technologies Corporation
10 Farm Springs Rd
Farmington CT 06032
860 728-7000

(G-2397)
UNITED THREAD ROLLING LLC
25 Rosenthal St (06108-3429)
PHONE..................860 290-9349
EMP: 3
SALES (est): 156K **Privately Held**
SIC: 3452 Bolts, nuts, rivets & washers

(G-2398)
UNITED-BIM INC
1111 Main St (06108-2241)
PHONE..................860 289-1100
Chirag B Thaker, *President*
EMP: 5

SALES (est): 123.7K **Privately Held**
SIC: 8712 1521 1522 1542 Architectural engineering; single-family housing construction; residential construction; commercial & office building contractors; manufacturing industries

(G-2399)
VACUMET CORP
300 Prestige Park Rd (06108-1924)
PHONE..................860 731-0860
John Calabrese, *Manager*
EMP: 2 **EST:** 2018
SALES (est): 77.4K **Privately Held**
SIC: 3081 Unsupported plastics film & sheet

(G-2400)
VIDEO OUTLET
775 Silver Ln (06118-1256)
PHONE..................860 568-7473
Don Haridat, *Principal*
EMP: 3 **EST:** 2007
SALES (est): 103.2K **Privately Held**
SIC: 7841 5099 3695 Video disk/tape rental to the general public; video & audio equipment; magnetic & optical recording media

(G-2401)
WEB SAVVY MARKETERS LLC
222 Pitkin St Ste 5 (06108-3265)
PHONE..................860 432-8756
Elizabeth Devine,
Carolyn Griswold,
EMP: 3
SALES (est): 407.8K **Privately Held**
SIC: 7311 8742 2741 Advertising consultant; marketing consulting services;

(G-2402)
YUSH SIGN DISPLAY CO INC
42 Thomas St (06108-2060)
PHONE..................860 289-1819
Herbert W Glick, *President*
Gail Glick, *Corp Secy*
EMP: 4
SQ FT: 3,300
SALES: 328K **Privately Held**
SIC: 7389 2759 7336 5046 Sign painting & lettering shop; lettering service; screen printing; graphic arts & related design; signs, electrical; signs & advertising specialties; electric signs

East Hartland
Hartford County

(G-2403)
J AND K LOGGING
26 Westwoods Rd (06027-1410)
PHONE..................860 653-6165
EMP: 2
SALES (est): 81.7K **Privately Held**
SIC: 2411 Logging

(G-2404)
PATRIOT WOODWORKING LLC
261 South Rd (06027-1603)
PHONE..................860 653-4349
Wade N Raabe, *Manager*
EMP: 2
SALES (est): 192.6K **Privately Held**
SIC: 2431 Millwork

(G-2405)
TR LANDWORKS LLC
36 Kensington Acres Rd (06027-1110)
PHONE..................860 402-6177
Theodore R Donofrio Jr,
EMP: 8
SALES (est): 699.8K **Privately Held**
SIC: 2411 Timber, cut at logging camp

East Haven
New Haven County

(G-2406)
A B C PRINTING INC
Also Called: A B C Printing & Mailing
875 Foxon Rd (06513-1837)
PHONE..................203 468-1245
Salvatore L Vadala, *President*
Salvatore A Vadala Jr, *Vice Pres*
Randy Carmona, *Graphic Designe*
Josh Coyne, *Graphic Designe*
Renee Domian, *Graphic Designe*
EMP: 10
SQ FT: 3,200
SALES: 400K **Privately Held**
SIC: 2752 Commercial printing, offset

(G-2407)
ACTION MEDIA INC
12 Baer Cir (06512-4166)
P.O. Box 120483 (06512-0483)
PHONE..................203 466-5535
Sam Shindler, *President*
Carla Marino, *Corp Secy*
Frank Marino, *Vice Pres*
EMP: 5
SQ FT: 4,000
SALES (est): 1.2MM **Privately Held**
SIC: 5065 2741 Electronic parts & equipment; miscellaneous publishing

(G-2408)
ALTON ENTERPRISES INC
Also Called: Alton Truck & Trailer
37 Panagrosi St (06512-4144)
PHONE..................203 469-9719
Frank Cofrancesco Jr, *President*
EMP: 3
SALES (est): 205.1K **Privately Held**
SIC: 7532 3713 Body shop, automotive; truck bodies (motor vehicles)

(G-2409)
AMERICAN IRON WORKS
49 Old Town Hwy (06512-4523)
PHONE..................203 469-6117
Anthony Maresca, *Owner*
Eileen Maresca, *Co-Owner*
EMP: 2
SALES (est): 87K **Privately Held**
SIC: 3446 Architectural metalwork

(G-2410)
ANGELOS ALUMINUM
55 Thompson St Apt 14g (06513-1942)
PHONE..................203 469-3117
Angelo Tammaro, *Principal*
EMP: 2
SALES (est): 178.9K **Privately Held**
SIC: 3334 Primary aluminum

(G-2411)
ANTARES AEROSPACE INDS LLC
90 Cosey Beach Ave (06512-4964)
PHONE..................203 903-7531
Deyanira Pacheco, *Principal*
EMP: 2
SALES (est): 102.9K **Privately Held**
SIC: 3721 Aircraft

(G-2412)
ASSOCIATED X-RAY CORP (PA)
Also Called: Advanced Control Systems Div
246 Dodge Ave (06512-3305)
P.O. Box 120559 (06512-0559)
PHONE..................203 466-2446
Gary Johnson, *President*
EMP: 15
SQ FT: 23,000
SALES (est): 3.2MM **Privately Held**
WEB: www.axrcorp.com
SIC: 5047 3844 X-ray machines & tubes; X-ray apparatus & tubes

(G-2413)
BARDELL PRINTING CORP
Also Called: Bardell Office Sty & Sups
42 Michael St (06513-1811)
PHONE..................203 469-2441
Frank Gambardella, *President*
Adeline Gambardella, *Vice Pres*

Anthony Gambardella, *Vice Pres*
Gary Gambardella, *CFO*
EMP: 7 **EST:** 1978
SQ FT: 6,000
SALES (est): 1MM **Privately Held**
SIC: 2759 Commercial printing

(G-2414)
BIG PRINTS LLC
15 Baer Cir Ste 2 (06512-4100)
PHONE..................203 469-1100
Mark Azzolina, *Mng Member*
Bob Garbo,
EMP: 3
SALES: 180K **Privately Held**
WEB: www.bigprintsct.com
SIC: 3993 Signs & advertising specialties

(G-2415)
CHADBOURNE WOODSHOP
190 Short Beach Rd (06512-3529)
PHONE..................203 468-4715
Paul Charbourne,
EMP: 1
SALES (est): 77.3K **Privately Held**
SIC: 2411 Wooden logs

(G-2416)
CIRILLO MANUFACTURING GROUP
34 Panagrosi St (06512-4143)
PHONE..................203 484-5010
Bob Cirillo, *President*
Joanne Cirillo, *Admin Sec*
EMP: 4
SALES (est): 580.3K **Privately Held**
SIC: 3599 3441 Machine shop, jobbing & repair; fabricated structural metal

(G-2417)
CLAYTON OFFROAD MANUFACTURER
99 Commerce St (06512-4146)
PHONE..................475 238-8251
Clayton Walters, *Principal*
EMP: 4 **EST:** 2013
SALES (est): 509.8K **Privately Held**
SIC: 3714 Motor vehicle parts & accessories

(G-2418)
CLEAN HOLDINGS LLC
47 Redfield Ave (06512-4122)
P.O. Box 120587 (06512-0587)
PHONE..................203 466-3365
Doreen Savran, *Managing Prtnr*
Connie Gates, *Accounts Mgr*
▲ **EMP:** 1
SALES (est): 146.8K **Privately Held**
SIC: 3089 Tissue dispensers, plastic

(G-2419)
COMPUTER XPRESS LLC
16 River Rd (06512-1223)
PHONE..................203 469-6107
Stephen Castiglione, *President*
EMP: 2
SALES (est): 99.1K **Privately Held**
SIC: 2741 Miscellaneous publishing

(G-2420)
CREATIVE STONE LLC
Also Called: Creative Stone & Tile
42 Vista Dr (06512-3433)
PHONE..................203 624-1882
Keith D Kronberg,
Andrew Donsiglio,
EMP: 10 **EST:** 1998
SALES (est): 1.2MM **Privately Held**
WEB: www.creativestonetile.com
SIC: 3281 Table tops, marble

(G-2421)
DUNBAR COMMERCIAL ENTERPRISES
372 Cosey Beach Ave (06512-4616)
P.O. Box 5176, Hamden (06518-0176)
PHONE..................203 469-7575
Louis W Palmieri, *President*
EMP: 2
SALES (est): 208.3K **Privately Held**
SIC: 3541 5085 Grinding machines, metalworking; industrial supplies; bearings

East Haven - New Haven County (G-2422)

(G-2422) EAST SHORE WIRE ROPE
5 Old Bradley St (06512-2344)
P.O. Box 308, North Haven (06473-0308)
PHONE.................................203 469-5204
Gary Lipkvich, *Owner*
EMP: 7
SALES: 950K **Privately Held**
SIC: 3462 Iron & steel forgings

(G-2423) EDAL INDUSTRIES INC
51 Commerce St (06512-4113)
PHONE.................................203 467-2591
Andrew Esposito, *President*
Pat Lauria, *Vice Pres*
▲ EMP: 23 EST: 1958
SQ FT: 14,000
SALES (est): 3.7MM **Privately Held**
SIC: 3679 3674 Rectifiers, electronic; semiconductors & related devices

(G-2424) EPIC PRINTING COMPNY INC
699 Silver Sands Rd (06512-4635)
P.O. Box 120084 (06512-0084)
PHONE.................................203 469-3988
Jeffrey Pine, *President*
EMP: 1 EST: 1984
SALES (est): 134.4K **Privately Held**
SIC: 2759 Commercial printing

(G-2425) F J WEIDNER INC
34 Tyler Street Ext (06512-3033)
PHONE.................................203 469-4202
John Weidner, *President*
Randy Weidner, *Corp Secy*
EMP: 4
SQ FT: 2,200
SALES (est): 405.5K **Privately Held**
WEB: www.zero-altitude-flight.com
SIC: 3544 3479 Jigs & fixtures; engraving jewelry silverware, or metal

(G-2426) FAC WOODWORKING LLC
67 Wood Ter (06513-1308)
PHONE.................................203 469-1900
Frank A Capuano Jr, *Principal*
EMP: 2 EST: 2007
SALES (est): 125.7K **Privately Held**
SIC: 2431 Millwork

(G-2427) FERRUCCI SERVICES
46 Gene St (06513-2709)
P.O. Box 120387 (06512-0387)
PHONE.................................203 468-2319
Lucien Ferrucci, *Principal*
EMP: 1
SALES (est): 127.4K **Privately Held**
SIC: 2879 Agricultural chemicals

(G-2428) FERRUCCI SIGNS
641 Main St (06512-2088)
PHONE.................................203 469-0043
Ernie Ferrucci, *Owner*
EMP: 1
SALES (est): 73.9K **Privately Held**
SIC: 3993 7532 Signs & advertising specialties; truck painting & lettering

(G-2429) FORSA TEAM SPORTS LLC
920 Foxon Rd Ste 1 (06513-1868)
PHONE.................................203 466-2890
Jeffrey A Forsa, *President*
EMP: 2
SALES (est): 198.6K **Privately Held**
SIC: 5941 2759 2395 Sporting goods & bicycle shops; screen printing; embroidery products, except schiffli machine

(G-2430) FOXON PARK BEVERAGES INC
103 Foxon Blvd (06513-1871)
PHONE.................................203 467-7874
Anthony M Naclerio, *President*
Jay Brancati, *COO*
Raymond Naclerio, *Admin Sec*
EMP: 8
SQ FT: 6,500
SALES (est): 1MM **Privately Held**
WEB: www.foxonpark.com
SIC: 2086 Soft drinks: packaged in cans, bottles, etc.

(G-2431) FUCHS LUBRICANTS CO
Also Called: Fuchs Northeast Division
281 Silver Sands Rd (06512-4140)
PHONE.................................203 469-2336
Cris Licursi, *Branch Mgr*
EMP: 24
SQ FT: 35,000
SALES (corp-wide): 2.9B **Privately Held**
WEB: www.fuchs.com
SIC: 2992 5172 Cutting oils, blending: made from purchased materials; rust arresting compounds, animal or vegetable oil base; lubricating oils & greases
HQ: Fuchs Lubricants Co.
17050 Lathrop Ave
Harvey IL 60426
708 333-8901

(G-2432) FYC APPAREL GROUP LLC
Donno Ricco
158 Commerce St (06512-4145)
PHONE.................................203 466-6525
Maia Chiatt, *President*
EMP: 30 **Privately Held**
WEB: www.akdesigns.net
SIC: 2331 Women's & misses' blouses & shirts
PA: Fyc Apparel Group, Llc
30 Thompson Rd
Branford CT 06405

(G-2433) GRAPHICA SIGN STUDIOS
140 Hunt Ln 2 (06512-1104)
PHONE.................................203 619-2255
EMP: 1 EST: 2011
SALES (est): 76.1K **Privately Held**
SIC: 3993 Signs & advertising specialties

(G-2434) HIGGINS SFTWR CONSULTING LLC
20 Hunt Ln (06512-1102)
PHONE.................................203 468-2350
William M Higgins, *Principal*
EMP: 2
SALES (est): 93.5K **Privately Held**
SIC: 7372 Prepackaged software

(G-2435) ICC WIRE HARNESS MFG LLC
46 Hobson St (06512-4628)
PHONE.................................203 469-8481
EMP: 1 EST: 2008
SALES (est): 53K **Privately Held**
SIC: 3999 Mfg Misc Products

(G-2436) KAPCOM LLC
86 John St (06512-2612)
PHONE.................................203 891-5112
David Kaplan, *Partner*
EMP: 4
SALES (est): 324.5K **Privately Held**
SIC: 3823 7812 Digital displays of process variables; motion picture & video production

(G-2437) LENOX STRATEGIES LLC
28 Ozone Rd (06512-3401)
P.O. Box 120271 (06512-0271)
PHONE.................................203 927-0871
Joseph Zullo, *Principal*
EMP: 2
SALES (est): 160.2K **Privately Held**
SIC: 3585 Refrigeration & heating equipment

(G-2438) LF ENGINEERING CO INC
Also Called: Lf Engineering Co.
17 Jeffrey Rd (06513-1252)
PHONE.................................860 526-4759
William Greeley, *Vice Pres*
EMP: 2
SALES (est): 224.8K **Privately Held**
WEB: www.lfengineering.com
SIC: 3663 Radio & TV communications equipment

(G-2439) LOOKERS EMBROIDERY
15 Wheelbarrow Ln (06513-2003)
PHONE.................................203 468-7262
Brett Scott, *Owner*
EMP: 2
SALES (est): 150K **Privately Held**
SIC: 2395 Embroidery & art needlework

(G-2440) M&M METAL FABRICATION LLC
105 Foxon Rd (06513-2014)
PHONE.................................203 889-6468
Jonathan H McGuire, *Principal*
EMP: 2
SALES (est): 104.9K **Privately Held**
SIC: 3499 Fabricated metal products

(G-2441) MACKENZIE MCH & MAR WORKS INC
36 Morgan Ter (06512-4501)
PHONE.................................203 777-3479
Kenneth Mackenzie Jr, *President*
Dana Mackenzie, *Vice Pres*
EMP: 6
SQ FT: 7,500
SALES (est): 852.9K **Privately Held**
WEB: www.mackenziemachine.com
SIC: 3599 7692 7378 Machine shop, jobbing & repair; welding repair; computer maintenance & repair

(G-2442) MILBAR LABS INC
20 Commerce St (06512-4145)
PHONE.................................203 467-1577
Mary Ann Emswiler, *CEO*
Susan S Lamar, *Treasurer*
Edward A Zelinsky, *Admin Sec*
▲ EMP: 15
SQ FT: 36,000
SALES (est): 4.4MM
SALES (corp-wide): 8.4MM **Privately Held**
SIC: 2844 Cosmetic preparations
PA: Dermatologic Cosmetic Laboratories Ltd.
20 Commerce St
East Haven CT 06512
800 552-5060

(G-2443) NATIONAL SCREW MANUFACTURING
259 Commerce St (06512-4147)
PHONE.................................203 469-7109
Cahrles Hirsch, *President*
William Feingold, *Vice Pres*
Joan Hirsch, *Admin Sec*
EMP: 12 EST: 1970
SALES (est): 1.1MM **Privately Held**
SIC: 3541 Boring mills

(G-2444) NEW HAVEN COMPANIES INC
41 Washington Ave (06512-3768)
PHONE.................................203 469-6421
EMP: 15
SALES (corp-wide): 59.8MM **Privately Held**
SIC: 2299 3625 5012 3537 Pads, fiber: henequen, sisal, istle; control equipment, electric; automobiles & other motor vehicles; industrial trucks & tractors; canvas & related products; carpets & rugs
PA: The New Haven Companies Inc
4820 Suthpoint Dr Ste 102
Fredericksburg VA 22407
540 898-2354

(G-2445) OEM DESIGN SERVICES LLC
34 Panagrosi St (06512-4143)
P.O. Box 120206 (06512-0206)
PHONE.................................203 467-5993
Michael Kaczynski,
Christine Kaczynski,
EMP: 9
SQ FT: 4,000
SALES (est): 400K **Privately Held**
SIC: 7699 3577 Industrial machinery & equipment repair; input/output equipment, computer

(G-2446) PATRICK ODONOGHUE
8 Wood Ter (06513-1307)
PHONE.................................203 467-4041
Patrick O Donoghue, *Principal*
EMP: 1
SALES (est): 82.5K **Privately Held**
SIC: 2431 Door frames, wood

(G-2447) POINT VIEW DISPLAYS LLC
200 Morgan Ave (06512-4519)
PHONE.................................203 468-0887
Cynthia Sedelmeyer,
EMP: 4
SALES: 700K **Privately Held**
WEB: www.pointviewdisplays.com
SIC: 3993 Signs & advertising specialties

(G-2448) PSD INC
80 Caroline Rd (06512-4651)
PHONE.................................860 305-6346
EMP: 3 EST: 2017
SALES (est): 251.4K **Privately Held**
SIC: 2759 Commercial printing

(G-2449) S&V SCREENPRINTING & EMBROIDER
121 Vista Dr (06512-3437)
PHONE.................................203 468-7538
Ralph Spaduzzi, *Principal*
EMP: 2
SALES (est): 122.6K **Privately Held**
SIC: 2395 Embroidery & art needlework

(G-2450) SABAR GRAPHICS LLC (PA)
Also Called: Minuteman Press
330 Main St (06512-2920)
P.O. Box 120541 (06512-0541)
PHONE.................................203 467-3016
Ronald S Burlakoff, *Mng Member*
Sandra T Burlakoff,
EMP: 4
SALES (est): 833K **Privately Held**
SIC: 2752 Commercial printing, lithographic

(G-2451) SCHOENROCK MARINE DOOR SYSTEMS
29 Massachusetts Ave (06512-2621)
PHONE.................................203 600-8370
Katherine Shine, *President*
EMP: 1
SALES (est): 56.4K **Privately Held**
SIC: 3442 Hangar doors, metal

(G-2452) SHORELINE METAL SERVICES LLC
250 Dodge Ave (06512-3360)
PHONE.................................203 466-7372
Jennifer Tower,
Mark Tower,
EMP: 8
SQ FT: 10,000
SALES (est): 1MM **Privately Held**
SIC: 3444 Sheet metalwork

(G-2453) SIMKINS INDUSTRIES
317 Foxon Rd Ste 3 (06513-2038)
PHONE.................................203 787-7171
EMP: 3 EST: 2010
SALES (est): 160K **Privately Held**
SIC: 3999 Mfg Misc Products

(G-2454) SPECIAL EVENTS SCREEN PRTG LLC
35 Washington Ave (06512-3768)
PHONE.................................203 468-5453
Scott Seward, *Mng Member*
EMP: 5
SALES: 300K **Privately Held**
SIC: 2759 Screen printing

GEOGRAPHIC SECTION

East Windsor - Hartford County (G-2483)

(G-2455)
THERMATOOL CORP (HQ)
31 Commerce St (06512-4172)
PHONE..................203 468-4100
Michael A Nallen, *President*
Elizabeth Baleck, *Regional Mgr*
Michael Didonato, *Business Mgr*
Ray Cagganello, *Plant Mgr*
Christopher Mallick, *Mfg Mgr*
◆ EMP: 65
SQ FT: 75,000
SALES (est): 18.4MM
SALES (corp-wide): 1B **Privately Held**
WEB: www.thermatool.com
SIC: 3599 Machine shop, jobbing & repair
PA: Rowan Technologies, Inc.
10 Indel Ave
Rancocas NJ 08073
609 267-9000

(G-2456)
THOMSON REUTERS CORPORATION
250 Dodge Ave (06512-3360)
PHONE..................203 466-5055
Estim Pop Lazarov, *Branch Mgr*
EMP: 15
SALES (corp-wide): 10.6B **Publicly Held**
SIC: 2741 Miscellaneous publishing
HQ: Thomson Reuters Corporation
3 Times Sq
New York NY 10036
646 223-4000

(G-2457)
TOTAL FAB LLC
140 Commerce St (06512-4145)
PHONE..................475 238-8176
Fred Moore Jr, *Mng Member*
EMP: 10
SQ FT: 3,500
SALES (est): 1.2MM **Privately Held**
SIC: 3441 7692 Fabricated structural metal; welding repair

(G-2458)
UNIVERSAL COMPONENT CORP
193 Silver Sands Rd (06512-4124)
PHONE..................203 481-8787
Tom Mort, *President*
John Jacksics, *Technical Staff*
Pam Onofrio, *Administration*
EMP: 25
SALES (est): 3.4MM **Privately Held**
SIC: 2439 Trusses, except roof: laminated lumber

(G-2459)
W J SAVAGE CO INC
Also Called: Savage Saws
31 Commerce St (06512-4113)
PHONE..................203 468-4100
Charles Corallo, *President*
Jimmy E Manar, *Treasurer*
EMP: 1 EST: 1885
SQ FT: 62,000
SALES (est): 148.5K
SALES (corp-wide): 1B **Privately Held**
WEB: www.savagesaws.com
SIC: 3541 3423 3556 3546 Saws, power (metalworking machinery); stonecutters' hand tools; meat, poultry & seafood processing machinery; power-driven hand-tools; machine tool accessories
HQ: Indel, Inc.
10 Indel Ave
Rancocas NJ 08073
609 267-9000

(G-2460)
WORK N GEAR LLC
Also Called: Work'n Gear 8014
52 Frontage Rd (06512-2103)
PHONE..................203 467-1156
Maria Olivaspas, *Manager*
EMP: 6
SALES (corp-wide): 46.1MM **Privately Held**
WEB: www.workngear.com
SIC: 5699 2759 Uniforms; screen printing
PA: Work 'n Gear, Llc
2300 Crown Colony Dr # 301
Quincy MA 02169
781 746-0100

East Killingly
Windham County

(G-2461)
NORTHEAST WIND ENERGY
225 Bear Hill Rd (06243)
PHONE..................860 779-2179
EMP: 1
SALES (est): 110K **Privately Held**
SIC: 3511 Fabricate Wind Turbine Generators

East Lyme
New London County

(G-2462)
ACE SAILMAKERS
3 Colton Rd (06333-1453)
PHONE..................860 739-5999
Dave Pelissier, *Principal*
EMP: 4
SALES (est): 238.1K **Privately Held**
SIC: 2394 Sails: made from purchased materials

(G-2463)
BAREMORE CANVAS LLC
157 Chesterfield Rd (06333-1243)
PHONE..................860 691-1402
Tracy Baremore, *Manager*
EMP: 1
SALES (est): 49.5K **Privately Held**
SIC: 2211 Canvas

(G-2464)
BIRK MANUFACTURING INC
14 Capitol Dr (06333-1452)
PHONE..................800 531-2070
Norman Birk, *President*
Scott Phelps, *Engineer*
▲ EMP: 95
SQ FT: 32,000
SALES (est): 10.8MM **Privately Held**
WEB: www.birkmfg.com
SIC: 3567 Heating units & devices, industrial: electric

(G-2465)
FIVES N AMERCN COMBUSTN INC
287 Boston Post Rd (06333-1554)
P.O. Box 160 (06333-0160)
PHONE..................860 739-3466
Ted Jablkowski, *Regional Mgr*
Philip Daigle, *Sales Executive*
EMP: 3
SALES (corp-wide): 871.2K **Privately Held**
SIC: 3433 Heating equipment, except electric
HQ: Fives North American Combustion, Inc.
4455 E 71st St
Cleveland OH 44105
216 271-6000

(G-2466)
HAYES SERVICES LLC
15 Colton Rd (06333-1436)
P.O. Box 365 (06333-0365)
PHONE..................860 739-2273
Kurt J Hayes, *CEO*
EMP: 7
SALES (est): 438.4K **Privately Held**
SIC: 0781 3443 4959 Landscape services; dumpsters, garbage; snowplowing

(G-2467)
J POMFRET& ASSOC INC
39 Plants Dam Rd (06333-1428)
PHONE..................860 691-2149
John A Pomfret, *President*
EMP: 1
SALES (est): 150K **Privately Held**
SIC: 3089 Molding primary plastic

(G-2468)
MISSION BMDICAL SCIENTIFIC INC
99 Arbor Xing (06333-1170)
PHONE..................860 941-8896
Francis Swenson, *Principal*
Franis Swenson, *Principal*
EMP: 1
SALES (est): 75.1K **Privately Held**
SIC: 3829 Thermometers & temperature sensors

(G-2469)
OPTIMIZED MICRO DEVICES LLC
184 Chesterfield Rd (06333-1238)
PHONE..................860 447-2142
David S Madole,
Roberta J Madole,
EMP: 2
SALES (est): 270K **Privately Held**
WEB: www.omd3.com
SIC: 3577 Computer peripheral equipment

(G-2470)
PAW PRINT PANTRY LLC (PA)
33 Gurley Rd (06333-1713)
PHONE..................860 447-8442
Jennifer Mohr, *Owner*
EMP: 3 EST: 2013
SALES (est): 782.3K **Privately Held**
SIC: 2752 Commercial printing, lithographic

(G-2471)
PRE -CLINICAL SAFETY INC
69 Quarry Dock Rd (06333)
PHONE..................860 739-9797
Ricardo Ochoa, *President*
EMP: 4
SALES (est): 305.8K **Privately Held**
SIC: 2834 Druggists' preparations (pharmaceuticals)

(G-2472)
Q LABTECH LLC
94 Arbor Xing (06333-1171)
PHONE..................860 501-9119
Weimin Qian, *Administration*
EMP: 2
SALES (est): 116.3K **Privately Held**
SIC: 2899 Chemical preparations

(G-2473)
R-D MFG INC
6 Colton Rd (06333-1435)
PHONE..................860 739-3986
Louis N Tashash, *President*
Nancy A Tashash, *Corp Secy*
Connelly Richard, *Vice Pres*
EMP: 12
SQ FT: 13,000
SALES (est): 2.4MM **Privately Held**
WEB: www.rdmfginc.com
SIC: 3444 Sheet metal specialties, not stamped

(G-2474)
ROMARK PRINTING SERVICE
39 Webster Rd (06333-1630)
PHONE..................860 691-0626
Alan Fanelli, *Owner*
EMP: 2
SQ FT: 2,500
SALES (est): 140K **Privately Held**
SIC: 2752 Commercial printing, offset

(G-2475)
SK SYSTEMS
231 Boston Post Rd # 16 (06333-1633)
PHONE..................860 691-0366
Sarjit Rattan, *Owner*
EMP: 1
SALES (est): 67K **Privately Held**
SIC: 7336 2791 Commercial art & graphic design; typographic composition, for the printing trade

(G-2476)
STUMP GRINDING PLUS
19 Heritage Rd (06333-1107)
PHONE..................860 884-6962
Leonard Sherrill, *Owner*
EMP: 2
SALES (est): 128.2K **Privately Held**
SIC: 3599 Grinding castings for the trade

(G-2477)
ULITTLESTITCH
451 Boston Post Rd (06333-1404)
PHONE..................860 857-4066
Hanna Christena, *Principal*
EMP: 1
SALES (est): 31.2K **Privately Held**
SIC: 2395 Embroidery & art needlework

East Windsor
Hartford County

(G-2478)
A HARDIMAN MACHINE CO INC
94 Newberry Rd (06088-9544)
PHONE..................860 623-8133
John Gould, *President*
Suzanne J Barstis, *Vice Pres*
EMP: 8
SALES (est): 647.5K **Privately Held**
SIC: 3599 Machine shop, jobbing & repair

(G-2479)
AEROCOR INC
59 Newberry Rd (06088-9631)
PHONE..................860 281-9274
Marc Corallo, *Principal*
Daniel Corallo, *Principal*
Erica Poulin, *Principal*
EMP: 12
SALES (est): 789.9K **Privately Held**
SIC: 3444 Sheet metalwork

(G-2480)
ALS BEVERAGE COMPANY INC
13 Revay Rd (06088-9688)
PHONE..................860 627-7003
Gerald E Martin, *President*
Marjorie Feldman, *President*
EMP: 20 EST: 1955
SQ FT: 11,000
SALES (est): 4.2MM
SALES (corp-wide): 24.2MM **Privately Held**
WEB: www.fallonreynolds.com
SIC: 2086 2095 Carbonated beverages, nonalcoholic: bottled & canned; roasted coffee
PA: Al's Holding Inc
13 Revay Rd
East Windsor CT 06088
860 627-7003

(G-2481)
ALS HOLDING INC (PA)
Also Called: Al's Beverage Company
13 Revay Rd (06088-9688)
PHONE..................860 627-7003
Marjorie Feldman, *CEO*
Jerry Martin, *President*
EMP: 1
SALES (est): 24.2MM **Privately Held**
SIC: 5149 5078 2086 Beverages, except coffee & tea; refrigerated beverage dispensers; carbonated beverages, nonalcoholic: bottled & canned; soft drinks: packaged in cans, bottles, etc.

(G-2482)
AUTOMOTIVE MACHINE
55 Newberry Rd (06088-9631)
PHONE..................860 627-9244
Dave Miller, *Owner*
EMP: 2
SALES (est): 238.6K **Privately Held**
SIC: 3519 Gas engine rebuilding

(G-2483)
AVALON ADVANCED TECH REPR INC
Also Called: Avatar
59 Newberry Rd (06088-9631)
PHONE..................860 254-5442
Vinod Franklin, *CEO*
Donald Ball, *President*
EMP: 24
SALES (est): 4.9MM **Privately Held**
SIC: 3728 Aircraft parts & equipment

East Windsor - Hartford County (G-2484)

(G-2484)
BLUE BELL MATTRESS COMPANY LLC
Also Called: King Koil Northeast
24 Thompson Rd (06088-9698)
PHONE..................................860 292-6372
Mark J Kolovson, *Ch of Bd*
Derek Ritzel, *President*
Steve Buyer, *Vice Pres*
Steven D Byer, *Vice Pres*
◆ **EMP:** 220
SQ FT: 100,000
SALES (est): 36.9MM **Privately Held**
SIC: 2515 Mattresses, innerspring or box spring; box springs, assembled

(G-2485)
BOEING COMPANY
1 Hartfield Blvd Ste 112 (06088-9582)
PHONE..................................860 627-9393
George Buswell, *Manager*
EMP: 6
SALES (corp-wide): 101.1B **Publicly Held**
SIC: 3812 Search & navigation equipment
PA: The Boeing Company
100 N Riverside Plz
Chicago IL 60606
312 544-2000

(G-2486)
BROOK BROAD BREWING LLC
122 Prospect Hill Rd (06088-9546)
PHONE..................................860 623-1000
Robert Muska, *Owner*
EMP: 14 **EST:** 2015
SALES (est): 2MM **Privately Held**
SIC: 2082 Malt beverages

(G-2487)
CA INC
160 Bridge St Ste 300 (06088)
PHONE..................................800 225-5224
Art Cartier, *Manager*
EMP: 45
SALES (corp-wide): 20.8B **Publicly Held**
WEB: www.cai.com
SIC: 7372 8742 Business oriented computer software; management consulting services
HQ: Ca, Inc.
520 Madison Ave
New York NY 10022
800 225-5224

(G-2488)
CANDLE THREADS
33 S Main St (06088-9744)
PHONE..................................860 292-1667
Megan E Piorek, *President*
EMP: 1
SALES (est): 80.6K **Privately Held**
SIC: 3999 Candles

(G-2489)
DRI-AIR INDUSTRIES INC
16 Thompson Rd (06088-9696)
P.O. Box 1020 (06088-1020)
PHONE..................................860 627-5110
Charles F Sears Jr, *President*
Jo-Ann Macfarlane, *Purchasing*
Steve Corcoran, *Natl Sales Mgr*
Herb Wischow, *Sales Mgr*
Jim Poglitsch, *Manager*
EMP: 23
SQ FT: 20,000
SALES (est): 7MM **Privately Held**
WEB: www.dri-air.com
SIC: 3567 3537 Driers & redriers, industrial process; industrial trucks & tractors

(G-2490)
EDAC TECHNOLOGIES LLC
68 Prospect Hill Rd (06088-9667)
PHONE..................................860 789-2511
EMP: 10 **Privately Held**
SIC: 3769 3541 3724 Guided missile & space vehicle parts & auxiliary equipment; machine tools, metal cutting type; aircraft engines & engine parts
HQ: Edac Technologies Llc
5 Mckee Pl
Cheshire CT 06410
203 806-2090

(G-2491)
ENGELHARD SURFACE TECHNOLOGIES
12 Thompson Rd (06088-9696)
PHONE..................................860 623-9901
Frank Gerlando, *Principal*
Tom Weber, *Safety Mgr*
Tony Cummings, *Facilities Mgr*
Bill Wood, *Engineer*
Jeremy Linamen, *Manager*
EMP: 2
SALES (est): 179.1K **Privately Held**
SIC: 3339 Primary nonferrous metals

(G-2492)
ESSEL DENTAL
44 S Main St Ste 14 (06088-1702)
PHONE..................................860 254-6955
Dr Rakesh Kumar, *Principal*
EMP: 3 **EST:** 2015
SALES (est): 240.6K **Privately Held**
SIC: 6324 3843 8021 Dental insurance; drills, dental; dental clinic

(G-2493)
FSM PLASTICOID MFG INC
32 North Rd (06088-9607)
P.O. Box 1036, Ada MI (49301-1036)
PHONE..................................860 623-1361
David Facchini, *President*
▲ **EMP:** 17
SALES (est): 2.5MM **Privately Held**
SIC: 3089 Injection molding of plastics

(G-2494)
GJG SIGNS DIGITAL SIGNS
250 S Main St (06088-9752)
PHONE..................................413 627-1852
EMP: 2
SALES (est): 72.6K **Privately Held**
SIC: 3993 Signs & advertising specialties

(G-2495)
HERITAGE CUSTOM PRODUCTS LLC
8 Thompson Rd Ste 6 (06088-6902)
PHONE..................................860 292-1979
EMP: 2
SALES: 90K **Privately Held**
SIC: 3724 Mfg Aircraft Engines/Parts

(G-2496)
HERMTECH INC
8 Thompson Rd Ste 9 (06088-6902)
PHONE..................................860 758-7528
John Griffin, *President*
Kevin Griffin, *Director*
EMP: 4 **EST:** 2011
SQ FT: 2,000
SALES: 90K **Privately Held**
SIC: 3812 Acceleration indicators & systems components, aerospace

(G-2497)
HOFFMAN TOWING & TRANSPORT
219 Scantic Rd (06088-9755)
PHONE..................................860 627-0405
Anthony Hoffman, *President*
EMP: 1
SALES (est): 182K **Privately Held**
SIC: 3799 Transportation equipment

(G-2498)
HOMELAND FUNDRAISING
Also Called: Kelleher Marketing
38 Borrup Rd (06088-9605)
PHONE..................................860 386-6698
Kevin Kelleher, *Owner*
EMP: 7
SQ FT: 2,300
SALES: 525K **Privately Held**
WEB: www.homelandfundraising.com
SIC: 3949 Sporting & athletic goods

(G-2499)
INTEGRATED PACKG SYSTEMS INC
256 Main St Ste D (06088-9558)
PHONE..................................860 623-2623
Lee Kelting, *President*
Carl Fossum, *Admin Sec*
EMP: 5
SQ FT: 2,000
SALES (est): 950.4K **Privately Held**
WEB: www.intpacsys.com
SIC: 3565 7629 Packaging machinery; electrical repair shops

(G-2500)
JMF GROUP LLC
Also Called: Al's Beverage Company
13 Revay Rd (06088-9688)
PHONE..................................860 627-7003
Toll Free:..................................888 -
Marjorie Feldman, *President*
EMP: 55
SALES (est): 7.4MM **Privately Held**
SIC: 2087 5149 Beverage bases, concentrates, syrups, powders & mixes; groceries & related products

(G-2501)
K F MACHINING
36 Newberry Rd (06088-9544)
PHONE..................................860 292-6466
EMP: 3
SQ FT: 1,000
SALES (est): 100K **Privately Held**
SIC: 3999 Mfg Misc Products

(G-2502)
K L & P WELDING
8 Thompson Rd (06088-9683)
PHONE..................................860 986-2518
John Favre, *President*
EMP: 1 **EST:** 2015
SALES (est): 89.8K **Privately Held**
SIC: 7692 Welding repair

(G-2503)
K T I TURBO-TECH INC
3 Thompson Rd (06088-9695)
P.O. Box 658 (06088-0658)
PHONE..................................860 623-2511
Howard Orr, *Principal*
John Minges, *Admin Sec*
EMP: 16
SALES (est): 342K
SALES (corp-wide): 2.4MM **Privately Held**
SIC: 7692 Welding repair
HQ: Kti Inc
3 Thompson Rd
East Windsor CT 06088
860 623-2511

(G-2504)
KIN-THERM INC
Also Called: K T I
3 Thompson Rd (06088-9695)
P.O. Box 658 (06088-0658)
PHONE..................................860 623-2511
Howard Orr, *President*
Warren H Reid Jr, *Vice Pres*
John Minges, *Admin Sec*
EMP: 15
SQ FT: 30,000
SALES (est): 986.4K
SALES (corp-wide): 2.4MM **Privately Held**
WEB: www.ktiinc.com
SIC: 7692 Welding repair
HQ: Kti Inc
3 Thompson Rd
East Windsor CT 06088
860 623-2511

(G-2505)
KINETIC TOOL CO INC
5 Craftsman Rd Ste 7 (06088-9617)
PHONE..................................860 627-5882
Jonathan Cherpak, *President*
EMP: 13
SQ FT: 4,000
SALES (est): 1.4MM **Privately Held**
SIC: 3545 Cutting tools for machine tools

(G-2506)
KTI BI-METALLIX INC
Also Called: Bi-Metalix
3 Thompson Rd (06088-9695)
P.O. Box 658 (06088-0658)
PHONE..................................860 623-2511
Howard Orr, *President*
Wasseluk Steve, *CTO*
John Minges, *Admin Sec*
EMP: 17
SQ FT: 30,000
SALES (est): 1MM
SALES (corp-wide): 2.4MM **Privately Held**
SIC: 7692 Welding repair
HQ: Kti Inc
3 Thompson Rd
East Windsor CT 06088
860 623-2511

(G-2507)
KTI INC (HQ)
Also Called: K T I Kin Therm
3 Thompson Rd (06088-9695)
P.O. Box 658 (06088-0658)
PHONE..................................860 623-2511
Eric Welker, *General Mgr*
Howard Orr, *Chairman*
EMP: 18
SQ FT: 30,000
SALES (est): 2.4MM **Privately Held**
SIC: 7692 Welding repair
PA: Applied Energy Corporation
33 East St Ste 4
Winchester MA
781 756-1216

(G-2508)
LIQUID SUN
10 S Main St (06088-9739)
PHONE..................................860 254-5757
EMP: 1
SALES (corp-wide): 340.5K **Privately Held**
SIC: 3999 Hydroponic equipment
PA: Liquid Sun
8 Lynwood Ave
Holyoke MA 01040
413 539-6875

(G-2509)
MAK INDUSTRIES LLC
40 Tromley Rd (06088-9647)
PHONE..................................860 623-4911
Paul Desroches, *Principal*
EMP: 1 **EST:** 2001
SALES (est): 63.5K **Privately Held**
WEB: www.mako-ind.com
SIC: 3999 Manufacturing industries

(G-2510)
MAX ANALYTICAL TECH INC
32 North Rd (06088-9607)
P.O. Box 390 (06088-0390)
PHONE..................................989 772-5088
Lester H Keepper, *President*
Bruce K Gartner, *Corp Secy*
Martin Spartz, *CTO*
EMP: 35
SQ FT: 6,000
SALES: 3MM **Privately Held**
WEB: www.pati-air.com
SIC: 8748 3826 Environmental consultant; analytical instruments

(G-2511)
METAL IMPROVEMENT COMPANY LLC
Curtiss-Wright Surface Tech
12 Thompson Rd (06088-9696)
PHONE..................................860 523-9901
EMP: 70
SALES (corp-wide): 2.4B **Publicly Held**
SIC: 3398 Shot peening (treating steel to reduce fatigue)
HQ: Metal Improvement Company, Llc
80 E Rte 4 Ste 310
Paramus NJ 07652
201 843-7800

(G-2512)
MLS ACQ INC
32 North Rd (06088-9607)
P.O. Box 390 (06088-0390)
PHONE..................................860 386-6878
John Stack, *CEO*
EMP: 10
SALES (est): 327.7K **Privately Held**
SIC: 3999 Manufacturing industries

(G-2513)
NOBLE FIRE BRICK COMPANY INC (PA)
Also Called: Noble Industrial Furnace Co
40 Woolam Rd (06088-9707)
PHONE..................................860 623-9256
Raymond G Noble, *President*

▲ = Import ▼=Export
◆ =Import/Export

Raymond Dan Noble, *Vice Pres*
Jennifer Fahey, *Office Mgr*
EMP: 5
SQ FT: 14,000
SALES (est): 668.6K **Privately Held**
SIC: 3567 Industrial furnaces & ovens

(G-2514)
PLASTICOID MANUFACTURING INC
Also Called: P M I
32 North Rd Rear (06088-9607)
P.O. Box 450 (06088-0450)
PHONE.................................860 623-1361
Jonathan Shoham, *President*
Robert Shoham, *President*
Daniel Shoham, *Vice Pres*
▲ **EMP:** 25
SQ FT: 16,200
SALES (est): 3.7MM **Privately Held**
WEB: www.plasticoidmfg.com
SIC: 3089 Injection molding of plastics

(G-2515)
R&R TOOL & DIE LLC
94 Newberry Rd (06088-9544)
PHONE.................................860 627-9197
Rolland Cote III,
EMP: 8
SQ FT: 2,000
SALES: 300K **Privately Held**
SIC: 3545 3544 Diamond cutting tools for turning, boring, burnishing, etc.; industrial molds

(G-2516)
ROTO-DIE COMPANY INC
Also Called: Preston Engravers
7d Pasco Dr (06088-1707)
PHONE.................................860 292-7030
Naomi Hamad, *Principal*
EMP: 10
SALES (corp-wide): 190.8MM **Privately Held**
WEB: www.rotometrics.com
SIC: 3944 2759 3544 Games, toys & children's vehicles; commercial printing; special dies, tools, jigs & fixtures
PA: Roto-Die Company, Inc.
   800 Howerton Ln
   Eureka MO 63025
   636 587-3600

(G-2517)
S A IT GRIND
2 North Rd (06088-9516)
PHONE.................................860 903-1455
EMP: 2 **EST:** 2008
SALES (est): 130K **Privately Held**
SIC: 3599 Mfg Industrial Machinery

(G-2518)
SIFCO APPLIED SRFC CNCEPTS LLC
Sifco Selective Plating Div
22 Thompson Rd Ste 2 (06088-9616)
PHONE.................................860 623-6006
David Parmenter, *Sales/Mktg Mgr*
EMP: 5
SALES (corp-wide): 7.6MM **Privately Held**
WEB: www.sifco.com
SIC: 3471 Electroplating & plating
PA: Sifco Applied Surface Concepts, Llc
   5708 E Schaaf Rd
   Cleveland OH 44131
   216 524-0099

(G-2519)
SPECIALTY PAPER MFG LLC
7b Pasco Dr (06088-1713)
PHONE.................................860 654-8044
Vincent P Sica, *Mng Member*
Greer Enterprises,
Ralph Tropeano,
EMP: 2
SALES (est): 63.9K **Privately Held**
SIC: 3999 Reconstituted wood products

(G-2520)
SPECIALTY PRINTING LLC
15 Thompson Rd (06088-9697)
PHONE.................................860 654-1850
William Bailey,
EMP: 10

SALES (est): 700K
SALES (corp-wide): 52.5MM **Privately Held**
SIC: 2752 Commercial printing, lithographic
PA: Specialty Printing, Llc
   4 Thompson Rd
   East Windsor CT 06088
   860 623-8870

(G-2521)
SPECIALTY PRINTING LLC (PA)
Also Called: S P
4 Thompson Rd (06088-9626)
PHONE.................................860 623-8870
Fred Bailey, *Vice Pres*
Tom Costella, *Vice Pres*
Roger Reed, *Vice Pres*
Anil Selby, *Vice Pres*
Alex Bellamy, *Production*
EMP: 100 **EST:** 1977
SQ FT: 40,000
SALES (est): 52.5MM **Privately Held**
WEB: www.specialtyprinting.net
SIC: 2679 2759 2672 Labels, paper: made from purchased material; labels & seals: printing; coated & laminated paper

(G-2522)
STACY B GOFF
Also Called: Stace Welding
100 Newberry Rd (06088-9544)
PHONE.................................860 623-2547
Stacy B Goff, *Owner*
EMP: 5
SQ FT: 10,000
SALES: 275K **Privately Held**
SIC: 3599 Machine & other job shop work

(G-2523)
STAKE COMPANY LLC
22 Thompson Rd Ste 7 (06088-9616)
P.O. Box 528 (06088-0528)
PHONE.................................860 623-2700
Donna Charette,
EMP: 4
SALES: 256K **Privately Held**
SIC: 2426 Lumber, hardwood dimension

(G-2524)
SUOMINEN US HOLDING INC (HQ)
1 Hartfield Blvd Ste 101 (06088-9500)
PHONE.................................860 386-8001
Lynn Hotchkiss, *Accountant*
John Bigos, *Director*
John M Bigos, *Director*
▼ **EMP:** 15
SALES (est): 139.5MM
SALES (corp-wide): 493.5MM **Privately Held**
SIC: 2297 Nonwoven fabrics
PA: Suominen Oyj
   Karvaamokuja 2b
   Helsinki 00380
   102 143-00

(G-2525)
SWEDES JEWELERS INC
98 Bridge St (06088-9679)
P.O. Box 598 (06088-0598)
PHONE.................................860 623-3916
Elaine S Ward, *President*
Alice Szwed, *Vice Pres*
Robert F Szwed, *Treasurer*
Stanley A Szwed Jr, *Admin Sec*
EMP: 8
SQ FT: 1,200
SALES (est): 953.6K **Privately Held**
WEB: www.swedesjewelers.com
SIC: 5944 7631 3911 Jewelry, precious stones & precious metals; jewelry repair services; jewelry, precious metal

(G-2526)
TAYLOR ENERGY
152 Broad Brook Rd (06088)
PHONE.................................860 623-3309
Mark Taylor, *Manager*
EMP: 2
SALES (est): 188.1K **Privately Held**
SIC: 1389 Oil consultants

(G-2527)
TITANIUM METALS CORPORATION
Also Called: Timet
7 Craftsman Rd (06088-9685)
PHONE.................................860 627-7051
Phil Macvain, *Manager*
EMP: 13
SQ FT: 22,000
SALES (corp-wide): 225.3B **Publicly Held**
WEB: www.timet.com
SIC: 3356 5051 Nonferrous rolling & drawing; metals service centers & offices
HQ: Titanium Metals Corporation
   4832 Richmond Rd Ste 100
   Warrensville Heights OH 44128
   610 968-1300

(G-2528)
TRENTO GROUP LLC
Also Called: Plastech Manufacturing
32 North Rd (06088-9607)
P.O. Box 997 (06088-0997)
PHONE.................................860 623-1361
Emanuele Mangiafico,
EMP: 3
SALES (est): 177.4K **Privately Held**
SIC: 3089 Injection molding of plastics

(G-2529)
VOYTEKS INC
7 Thompson Rd (06088-9614)
P.O. Box 479, Suffield (06078-0479)
PHONE.................................860 967-6558
Wojciech Skoczylas, *President*
EMP: 3
SALES (est): 232.4K **Privately Held**
SIC: 3599 Machine & other job shop work

(G-2530)
W B MASON CO INC
43 North Rd (06088-9523)
PHONE.................................888 926-2766
EMP: 145
SALES (corp-wide): 773MM **Privately Held**
SIC: 5943 5712 2752 Office forms & supplies; office furniture; commercial printing, lithographic
PA: W. B. Mason Co., Inc.
   59 Center St
   Brockton MA 02301
   781 794-8800

(G-2531)
WADSWORTH PRESS
182 Main St (06088-9519)
P.O. Box 407 (06088-0407)
PHONE.................................860 623-3820
Edward Bednarz, *Owner*
Paul Romanelli, *Manager*
EMP: 2
SQ FT: 4,000
SALES (est): 148.8K **Privately Held**
SIC: 2759 Envelopes: printing; letterpress printing; periodicals: printing; tickets: printing

(G-2532)
WEBBERS TRUCK SERVICE INC
27 Depot Hill Rd (06088)
P.O. Box 702 (06088-0702)
PHONE.................................860 623-4554
Hartson Webber, *President*
EMP: 13
SQ FT: 2,500
SALES (est): 2.3MM **Privately Held**
SIC: 3715 Truck trailers

(G-2533)
WINDSOR LOCKS NONWOVENS INC (DH)
Also Called: Suominen Nonwoven
1 Hartfield Blvd Ste 101 (06088-9500)
PHONE.................................860 292-5600
Nina Kopola, *CEO*
Petri Rolig, *Vice Pres*
John Bigos, *Finance*
◆ **EMP:** 30
SQ FT: 312,000
SALES (est): 67.9MM
SALES (corp-wide): 493.5MM **Privately Held**
SIC: 2297 Nonwoven fabrics
HQ: Suominen Us Holding, Inc.
   1 Hartfield Blvd Ste 101
   East Windsor CT 06088
   860 386-8001

Eastford
Windham County

(G-2534)
ANDERT INC
39 Boston Tpke (06242)
P.O. Box 372 (06242-0372)
PHONE.................................860 974-3893
Michael Andert, *President*
▲ **EMP:** 5
SQ FT: 5,000
SALES (est): 885.4K **Privately Held**
SIC: 3441 Fabricated structural metal

(G-2535)
DREAM CONSTRUCTION & WDWKG
28 Hall Rd (06242-9303)
PHONE.................................774 573-0495
Jason Stoneback, *Principal*
EMP: 1
SALES (est): 54.1K **Privately Held**
SIC: 2431 Millwork

(G-2536)
INDUSTRIAL PALLET LLC
27 Chaplin Rd (06242-9439)
P.O. Box 389 (06242-0389)
PHONE.................................860 974-0093
Joe O'Brien,
Randy Therrien,
▲ **EMP:** 46
SQ FT: 51,000
SALES (est): 6.7MM **Privately Held**
WEB: www.industrialpallet.com
SIC: 2448 Pallets, wood

(G-2537)
MT LEBANON JOINERY
89 John Perry Rd (06242-9464)
P.O. Box 7 (06242-0007)
PHONE.................................860 974-0896
Stephen Bell, *Principal*
EMP: 1
SALES (est): 137.4K **Privately Held**
SIC: 2431 Millwork

(G-2538)
NORTHEAST LOGGING INC
153 Pomfret Rd (06242-9421)
PHONE.................................860 974-2959
Bruce E Souza, *President*
EMP: 2
SALES: 130K **Privately Held**
SIC: 2411 Logging

(G-2539)
PUTNAM WELDING & EQP REPR INC
144 Eastford Rd (06242)
P.O. Box 114 (06242-0114)
PHONE.................................860 974-0292
Henry Becker, *President*
William Becker, *Admin Sec*
EMP: 4
SQ FT: 7,220
SALES (est): 521.5K **Privately Held**
SIC: 1794 3441 Excavation & grading, building construction; fabricated structural metal

(G-2540)
R&J HARVESTING LLC
54 Hartford Tpke (06242-9414)
PHONE.................................860 974-1323
Richard E Labbe,
Lucinda Labbe,
Richard Labbe,
EMP: 2 **EST:** 1998
SALES: 375K **Privately Held**
SIC: 2411 Logging camps & contractors; timber, cut at logging camp

(G-2541)
S S FABRICATIONS INC
82 County Rd (06242-7700)
P.O. Box 37 (06242-0037)
PHONE.................................860 974-1910

Eastford - Windham County (G-2542)

David Buchholz Jr, *President*
EMP: 8 **EST:** 1976
SQ FT: 3,000
SALES (est): 245.2K **Privately Held**
SIC: 7692 3599 Welding repair; machine shop, jobbing & repair

(G-2542)
SAFIN WLDG & FABRICATION LLC
278 Eastford Rd (06242-9756)
PHONE.................................860 974-3831
Mark W Safin, *Principal*
EMP: 2
SALES (est): 140K **Privately Held**
SIC: 7692 Welding repair

(G-2543)
STEPHEN SMITH
Also Called: Steve H Smith Cabinetmaker
226 Old Colony Rd (06242-9401)
PHONE.................................405 420-2226
Stephen Smith, *Owner*
EMP: 1
SALES (est): 51.4K **Privately Held**
SIC: 2392 Household furnishings

(G-2544)
WHITCRAFT LLC (PA)
76 County Rd (06242-7700)
P.O. Box 128 (06242-0128)
PHONE.................................860 974-0786
Colin Cooper, *CEO*
Jeff Paul, *President*
Steve Ruggiero, *VP Opers*
Larry Benson, *Purchasing*
Tammy Eckard, *Controller*
▲ **EMP:** 151 **EST:** 1960
SQ FT: 63,200
SALES (est): 96.3MM **Privately Held**
WEB: www.whitcraft.com
SIC: 3443 3444 3728 Weldments; sheet metalwork; aircraft parts & equipment

(G-2545)
WHITCRAFT SCRBOROUGH/TEMPE LLC (HQ)
76 County Rd (06242-7700)
PHONE.................................860 974-0786
Colin Cooper, *CEO*
EMP: 200
SALES (est): 5MM
SALES (corp-wide): 96.3MM **Privately Held**
SIC: 3728 3443 3444 Aircraft parts & equipment; weldments; sheet metalwork
PA: Whitcraft Llc
76 County Rd
Eastford CT 06242
860 974-0786

Easton
Fairfield County

(G-2546)
ARNOLD TRAUTH
85 Asmara Way (06612-2101)
PHONE.................................203 371-5624
Arnold Trauth, *Administration*
EMP: 1
SALES (est): 39.7K **Privately Held**
SIC: 3253 Ceramic wall & floor tile

(G-2547)
BLACKROCK MEDIA INC
112 Far Horizon Dr (06612-1900)
PHONE.................................203 374-0369
David J Schuldt, *President*
EMP: 1
SALES (est): 60.1K **Privately Held**
SIC: 7372 8742 7379 7371 Business oriented computer software; management consulting services; computer related consulting services; computer software development & applications

(G-2548)
CAT TALES PRESS INC
61 Hall Rd (06612-1731)
PHONE.................................203 268-3505
Stacy Lytwyn Maxwell, *Principal*
EMP: 2
SALES (est): 121.6K **Privately Held**
SIC: 2741 Miscellaneous publishing

(G-2549)
EAST COAST NAME PLATES INC
884 Black Rock Tpke (06612-1102)
PHONE.................................203 261-4347
Martin Rohde, *President*
Nancy Rohde, *Admin Sec*
EMP: 2
SALES (est): 197.3K **Privately Held**
SIC: 2759 3993 2752 Poster & decal printing & engraving; signs & advertising specialties; commercial printing, lithographic

(G-2550)
EASTON BREWING COMPANY LLC
53 Ridgeway Rd (06612-1717)
PHONE.................................203 921-7263
John Cavallero, *Principal*
EMP: 3
SALES (est): 75K **Privately Held**
SIC: 2082 Beer (alcoholic beverage)

(G-2551)
ECCLES-LEHMAN INC
Also Called: Eccles Carleton
44 Sanford Dr (06612-1423)
PHONE.................................203 268-0605
Rosemarie Lehman, *President*
Rosemary Lehman, *President*
EMP: 5
SQ FT: 6,000
SALES (est): 340K **Privately Held**
SIC: 2759 2752 5943 2796 Engraving; commercial printing, offset; stationery stores; platemaking services; typesetting; bookbinding & related work

(G-2552)
FAIRFIELD MARKETING GROUP INC (PA)
830 Sport Hill Rd (06612-1241)
PHONE.................................203 261-0884
Pamela Washchilla, *Treasurer*
Ed Washchilla Sr, *Officer*
Jason Miller, *Officer*
EMP: 12
SALES (est): 2.2MM **Privately Held**
WEB: www.fairfieldmarketing.com
SIC: 8742 8743 7331 2791 Marketing consulting services; sales promotion; direct mail advertising services; typesetting; commercial printing; commercial printing, lithographic

(G-2553)
FIELDSTONE CNSULTING GROUP LLC
50 Fieldstone Dr (06612-1016)
PHONE.................................203 610-5592
Paul Seo, *CEO*
EMP: 1
SALES (est): 61.2K **Privately Held**
SIC: 8748 7372 7379 8742 Business consulting; systems analysis & engineering consulting services; business oriented computer software; computer related consulting services; human resource consulting services

(G-2554)
FOUR WINDS INC
45 Kellers Farm Rd (06612-1341)
P.O. Box 435 (06612-0435)
PHONE.................................203 445-0733
David Dellenbaugh, *President*
EMP: 2 **EST:** 1995
SALES (est): 115.8K **Privately Held**
WEB: www.speedandsmarts.com
SIC: 2741 Newsletter publishing

(G-2555)
G F E
11 Birch Dr (06612-2244)
PHONE.................................203 371-7334
EMP: 2
SALES (est): 190K **Privately Held**
SIC: 3826 Manufactures Delivery Systems

(G-2556)
HENRY THAYER COMPANY
Also Called: Thayers Natural Remedies
65 Adams Rd (06612-1355)
PHONE.................................203 226-0940
Karen Clarke, *CEO*
John Reppucci, *Vice Pres*
Helen Kaufman, *Treasurer*
Betsy Streck, *Relations*
EMP: 3
SQ FT: 3,500
SALES (est): 511.1K **Privately Held**
WEB: www.thayers.com
SIC: 2834 Lozenges, pharmaceutical; cough medicines; cold remedies

(G-2557)
INSIGHT ENTERPRISES INC
78 Gate Ridge Rd (06612-1838)
PHONE.................................203 374-2013
Jason Cavanaugh, *Branch Mgr*
EMP: 3 **Publicly Held**
SIC: 7372 Prepackaged software
PA: Insight Enterprises, Inc.
6820 S Harl Ave
Tempe AZ 85283

(G-2558)
K4 INDUSTRIES LLC
15 Adirondack Trl (06612-2051)
PHONE.................................203 459-4992
Lucian Leszczynski, *Principal*
EMP: 2 **EST:** 2018
SALES (est): 102.9K **Privately Held**
SIC: 3999 Manufacturing industries

(G-2559)
MODEAN INDUSTRIES INC
15 Lucielle Dr (06612-1819)
P.O. Box 275 (06612-0275)
PHONE.................................203 371-6625
Dean Azzam, *President*
Haney Azzam, *Chairman*
EMP: 3
SALES (est): 900K **Privately Held**
WEB: www.modeanindustries.com
SIC: 3567 Industrial furnaces & ovens

(G-2560)
PAUL D WOLFF
77 Mile Common Rd (06612-1551)
PHONE.................................203 319-7242
Paul D Wolff, *Principal*
EMP: 1
SALES (est): 59.6K **Privately Held**
WEB: www.pcwolff.com
SIC: 2731 Book publishing

(G-2561)
POLARIS MANAGEMENT INC
30 Silver Hill Rd (06612-1114)
PHONE.................................203 261-6399
Robert G George, *President*
Matthew Simpson, *Vice Pres*
EMP: 4
SALES (est): 208.7K **Privately Held**
SIC: 3621 Generating apparatus & parts, electrical

(G-2562)
PRECISION SERVICING
242 Everett Rd (06612-1258)
PHONE.................................203 650-1392
Jeffrey Bento, *Principal*
EMP: 2 **EST:** 2010
SALES (est): 124.2K **Privately Held**
SIC: 1389 Roustabout service

(G-2563)
RAMBLING DOG PUBLICATIONS LLC
229 Mile Common Rd (06612-1547)
PHONE.................................203 254-9230
Bonnie Kreitler, *Principal*
EMP: 2
SALES (est): 127.1K **Privately Held**
SIC: 2741 Miscellaneous publishing

(G-2564)
ROCKET BOOKS INC
34 Ridgeway Rd (06612-1718)
PHONE.................................203 372-1818
Steven Loo, *President*
▲ **EMP:** 5
SALES (est): 400.7K **Privately Held**
WEB: www.rocketbooks.com
SIC: 2731 Books: publishing & printing

(G-2565)
SAVOUR INSTANT LLC
41 Flat Rock Rd (06612-1703)
PHONE.................................203 374-4599
Allen Sullivan, *Principal*
EMP: 2
SALES (est): 100.1K **Privately Held**
SIC: 2752 Commercial printing, lithographic

(G-2566)
SHARPLINE CABINETRY LLC
533 Sport Hill Rd (06612-1715)
PHONE.................................203 261-8454
Michelle Mauro, *Manager*
EMP: 1 **EST:** 2017
SALES (est): 58.9K **Privately Held**
SIC: 2434 Wood kitchen cabinets

(G-2567)
TOWN OF VERNON
366 Sport Hill Rd (06612-1714)
PHONE.................................203 268-7200
Gary Simone, *Director*
EMP: 2 **Privately Held**
WEB: www.vernonctpolice.com
SIC: 9512 2531 Recreational program administration, government; picnic tables or benches, park
PA: Town Of Vernon
14 Park Pl
Vernon CT 06066
860 870-3690

(G-2568)
TWO BSSES & A HRMONCA PRDCTNS
135 Mile Common Rd (06612-1507)
PHONE.................................203 259-5916
Matthew Pagliaro, *Owner*
EMP: 1
SALES (est): 82.2K **Privately Held**
SIC: 3931 Harmonicas

Ellington
Tolland County

(G-2569)
A CHANGE OF SCENERY
9 Benjamin Rd (06029-2128)
PHONE.................................860 872-4435
Joann Cleary, *Owner*
EMP: 1
SALES (est): 64.8K **Privately Held**
SIC: 2391 Curtains & draperies

(G-2570)
ACCU-TIME SYSTEMS INC (DH)
Also Called: A T S
420 Somers Rd (06029-2629)
PHONE.................................860 870-5000
James McHale, *CEO*
David Hopkins, *Senior VP*
Phillip SIS, *Opers Staff*
Stephanie Smith, *Buyer*
Lisa Gladysz, *CFO*
▲ **EMP:** 36
SQ FT: 23,500
SALES (est): 16.7MM **Privately Held**
WEB: www.accu-time.com
SIC: 3579 3873 Time clocks & time recording devices; watches, clocks, watchcases & parts
HQ: Amano Usa Holdings, Inc.
140 Harrison Ave
Roseland NJ 07068
973 403-1900

(G-2571)
ACTION PACKAGING SYSTEMS INC (PA)
372 Somers Rd (06029)
PHONE.................................860 222-9510
Douglas E Rice, *President*
Gordon E Rice, *Vice Pres*
▲ **EMP:** 5
SALES (est): 1MM **Privately Held**
WEB: www.actionpkg.com
SIC: 2631 Boxboard

GEOGRAPHIC SECTION
Ellington - Tolland County (G-2603)

(G-2572)
ADVANCE MOLD MFG INC
15 Teaberry Ridge Rd (06029-2726)
PHONE..................860 783-5024
Doug Schneider, *President*
EMP: 4
SALES (est): 296.1K **Privately Held**
SIC: 3089 Molding primary plastic

(G-2573)
ADVANCED MACHINE TECHNOLOGY
5 Industrial Dr (06029-2632)
P.O. Box 95 (06029-0095)
PHONE..................860 872-2664
Gary Hublard, *President*
Dorothy Hublard, *Admin Sec*
EMP: 3
SQ FT: 2,000
SALES (est): 390.9K **Privately Held**
SIC: 3599 Machine shop, jobbing & repair

(G-2574)
ALL STEEL LLC
240 Crystal Lake Rd (06029-3406)
PHONE..................860 871-6023
Eben J Holmes, *Mng Member*
EMP: 3
SALES (est): 279.2K **Privately Held**
SIC: 3334 Pigs, aluminum

(G-2575)
ANKLEAID LLC
7 Jonathan Dr (06029-3886)
P.O. Box 675 (06029-0675)
PHONE..................860 305-5178
Kj Camera, *Senior VP*
Ron Mirek, *Sales Staff*
Scott McKay,
EMP: 2
SALES (est): 194.1K **Privately Held**
SIC: 3841 Surgical & medical instruments

(G-2576)
ARROW DIVERSIFIED TOOLING INC
17 Pinney St (06029-3812)
P.O. Box 508 (06029-0508)
PHONE..................860 872-9072
David Trench, *President*
EMP: 22
SQ FT: 13,000
SALES: 3.3MM **Privately Held**
WEB: www.arrowdiversified.com
SIC: 3544 3363 3542 3543 Special dies & tools; aluminum die-castings; machine tools, metal forming type; industrial patterns; aircraft parts & equipment

(G-2577)
ART SIGNS
Also Called: Signs By Art Vassilopoulos
8 Middle Butcher Rd (06029-4155)
PHONE..................860 871-8361
Art Vassilopoulos, *Owner*
EMP: 1
SALES (est): 57.5K **Privately Held**
SIC: 3993 Signs, not made in custom sign painting shops

(G-2578)
BILLS MACHINE SHOP
2 Pinnacle Rd (06029-3509)
PHONE..................860 875-6607
EMP: 2
SALES (est): 80.1K **Privately Held**
SIC: 3599 Machine shop, jobbing & repair

(G-2579)
BRYMILL CORPORATION (PA)
Also Called: Brymill Cryogenic Sys
105 Windermere Ave Ste 3b (06029-3858)
PHONE..................860 875-2460
M Gail Bryne, *President*
Claudio Russo, *General Mgr*
Sheryl Thibeault, *General Mgr*
Mike Bryne, *Vice Pres*
EMP: 10 EST: 1966
SQ FT: 10,000
SALES (est): 1.1MM **Privately Held**
WEB: www.brymill.com
SIC: 3842 Surgical appliances & supplies

(G-2580)
CASCADES FINE PAPERS
265 Windsorville Rd (06029-3820)
PHONE..................860 870-7600
David Elovich, *Principal*
EMP: 2
SALES (est): 112.1K **Privately Held**
SIC: 3585 Soda fountain & beverage dispensing equipment & parts

(G-2581)
CLEMSON SHEETMETAL LLC
24 Ladd Rd (06029-3103)
P.O. Box 224 (06029-0224)
PHONE..................860 721-7906
Alan Clemson, *Owner*
EMP: 2
SALES (est): 246.9K **Privately Held**
SIC: 3444 Sheet metalwork

(G-2582)
CONNECTICUT AXLE SERVICE LLC
94 Muddy Brook Rd (06029-2117)
PHONE..................860 872-3858
Peter C Hany Jr, *Principal*
EMP: 1
SALES (est): 152.6K **Privately Held**
WEB: www.ctaxleservice.com
SIC: 3714 Motor vehicle parts & accessories

(G-2583)
COUNTRY PURE FOODS INC
58 West Rd (06029-4200)
PHONE..................330 753-2293
Kim Wilford, *Manager*
EMP: 106 **Privately Held**
WEB: www.countrypurefoods.com
SIC: 2033 Canned fruits & specialties
PA: Country Pure Foods, Inc.
222 W Main St Ste 401
Akron OH 44308

(G-2584)
COUNTRY SIDE SHEET METAL
Also Called: Countryside Sheet Metal
182 Jobs Hill Rd (06029-2208)
PHONE..................860 872-5729
Walter Stutz Jr, *Owner*
EMP: 1
SALES (est): 94.4K **Privately Held**
SIC: 1761 3444 Sheet metalwork; sheet metalwork

(G-2585)
CRYSTAL LABELS CO
116 Stafford Rd (06029-2835)
PHONE..................860 870-8627
Walter Albee, *Manager*
EMP: 2
SALES (est): 104.6K **Privately Held**
SIC: 2759 Commercial printing

(G-2586)
DESIGN IDEA PRINTING
344 Somers Rd (06029)
P.O. Box 2215, Vernon Rockville (06066-1615)
PHONE..................860 896-0103
David Pinkham, *Owner*
Irene Pinkham, *Owner*
EMP: 3
SALES (est): 254.1K **Privately Held**
SIC: 2752 Commercial printing, offset

(G-2587)
DYMOTEK CORPORATION
7 Main St (06029-3317)
PHONE..................860 875-2868
Steven R Trueb, *President*
Thomas W Trueb, *Vice Pres*
Nick Nettleton, *Engineer*
◆ **EMP:** 50
SQ FT: 35,000
SALES (est): 18.5MM **Privately Held**
WEB: www.dymotek.net
SIC: 3089 Injection molding of plastics

(G-2588)
ELLIGNTON ENERGY INC
263 Crystal Lake Rd (06029-3409)
PHONE..................860 872-9276
EMP: 2
SALES (est): 99.1K **Privately Held**
SIC: 1382 Oil & gas exploration services

(G-2589)
ELLINGTON PRINTERY INC
Also Called: Med Print
25 West Rd Ste B (06029-4260)
P.O. Box 219 (06029-0219)
PHONE..................860 875-3310
Carol White, *President*
EMP: 7
SQ FT: 2,000
SALES (est): 950.2K **Privately Held**
SIC: 2752 Commercial printing, offset

(G-2590)
FORTIS SOLUTIONS GROUP LLC
374 Somers Rd (06029-2628)
PHONE..................860 872-6311
EMP: 40 **Privately Held**
SIC: 5131 5113 5084 2671 Labels; ribbons; boxes & containers; processing & packaging equipment; packaging paper & plastics film, coated & laminated; corrugated & solid fiber boxes
PA: Fortis Solutions Group, Llc
2505 Hawkeye Ct
Virginia Beach VA 23452

(G-2591)
H & D ORNAMENTAL IRON WORKS
295 Somers Rd (06029-3428)
P.O. Box 162 (06029-0162)
PHONE..................860 871-1708
Bruno Starbuck, *Owner*
EMP: 1
SALES (est): 71.6K **Privately Held**
SIC: 1799 3446 Welding on site; stairs, staircases, stair treads: prefabricated metal

(G-2592)
HIGHLAND MEDICAL PRODUCTS INC
24 Highland Ave (06029-3794)
PHONE..................860 454-0625
Carter Lonsberry, *President*
EMP: 1
SALES (est): 85.3K **Privately Held**
SIC: 3841 Medical instruments & equipment, blood & bone work; bone plates & screws

(G-2593)
JOVIAN TECHNOLOGIES
115 West Rd Apt 206 (06029-3778)
PHONE..................860 896-1539
Marcel Villani, *Owner*
EMP: 1
SALES: 100K **Privately Held**
SIC: 3829 Measuring & controlling devices

(G-2594)
MAYARC INDUSTRIES INC
54 Minor Hill Rd (06029-3107)
PHONE..................860 871-1872
Matthew Minor, *President*
Mark Minor, *Principal*
EMP: 7
SALES (est): 380K **Privately Held**
WEB: www.midiaclick.net
SIC: 3441 Fabricated structural metal

(G-2595)
MERRILL INDUSTRIES INC
26 Village St (06029-3815)
P.O. Box 150 (06029-0150)
PHONE..................860 871-1888
Merrill Lieberman, *President*
Bernard Lieberman, *Vice Pres*
EMP: 38
SQ FT: 80,000
SALES (est): 8.2MM **Privately Held**
SIC: 2653 2441 3086 Boxes, corrugated: made from purchased materials; boxes, wood; plastics foam products

(G-2596)
MERRILL INDUSTRIES LLC
26 Village St (06029-3815)
P.O. Box 150 (06029-0150)
PHONE..................860 871-1888
Albert Gardiner, *Vice Pres*
Richard Cobuzzi, *Comptroller*
EMP: 25
SQ FT: 82,000
SALES (est): 5.2MM **Privately Held**
SIC: 2653 Boxes, corrugated: made from purchased materials

(G-2597)
NATURAL COUNTRY FARMS INC
Also Called: Country Pure Foods
58 West Rd (06029-4200)
PHONE..................860 872-8346
Bernie Garow, *Manager*
EMP: 100
SQ FT: 80,000 **Privately Held**
WEB: www.countrypure.com
SIC: 4222 2086 2033 Warehousing, cold storage or refrigerated; bottled & canned soft drinks; canned fruits & specialties
HQ: Natural Country Farms, Inc.
681 W Waterloo Rd
Akron OH 44314
330 753-2293

(G-2598)
RICE PACKAGING INC
356 Somers Rd (06029-2628)
PHONE..................860 870-7057
William A Rice, *Ch of Bd*
Clifford Rice, *President*
Ranee O'Neill, *Manager*
▲ **EMP:** 100 EST: 1964
SQ FT: 95,000
SALES (est): 27.3MM **Privately Held**
WEB: www.ricepackaging.com
SIC: 2657 2653 2652 2631 Folding paperboard boxes; corrugated & solid fiber boxes; setup paperboard boxes; paperboard mills

(G-2599)
SHAWS PUMP COMPANY INC
37 Windermere Ave (06029-3840)
PHONE..................860 872-6891
George Shaw, *President*
Joanne Shaw, *Corp Secy*
EMP: 4
SALES: 120K **Privately Held**
SIC: 3589 Sewage & water treatment equipment

(G-2600)
SJM PROPERTIES INC
164 Maple St (06029-3330)
PHONE..................860 979-0060
Stanley E Matczak, *President*
Stanley Matczak, *President*
Joseph Matczak, *Vice Pres*
EMP: 9
SQ FT: 12,000
SALES (est): 793.1K **Privately Held**
WEB: www.sjmproperties.com
SIC: 3545 Balancing machines (machine tool accessories)

(G-2601)
SPORTS DEPARTMENT LLC
18 Brookfield Dr (06029-2102)
PHONE..................860 872-0873
Kevin F Hayes, *Principal*
EMP: 2
SALES (est): 104.5K **Privately Held**
SIC: 2711 Newspapers

(G-2602)
SPRINGBROOK WOODCRAFTERS LLC
469 Somers Rd (06029-2521)
PHONE..................860 870-7303
Alan Vogel, *Principal*
EMP: 2
SALES (est): 120K **Privately Held**
SIC: 2511 Wood household furniture

(G-2603)
SUGAR CREEK VINEYARD LLC
20 Wheelock Rd (06029-2721)
PHONE..................860 454-4219
Robert J Dwyer, *Principal*
EMP: 2
SALES (est): 117.3K **Privately Held**
SIC: 2084 Wines

Ellington - Tolland County (G-2604)

(G-2604)
SYN-MAR PRODUCTS INC
5 Nutmeg Dr (06029-3899)
P.O. Box 333 (06029-0333)
PHONE..................................860 872-8505
Tim Hill, *President*
Ken Hill, *Marketing Staff*
EMP: 16
SALES (est): 3.3MM **Privately Held**
WEB: www.syn-marproducts.com
SIC: 3088 3261 Tubs (bath, shower & laundry), plastic; sinks, vitreous china

(G-2605)
T & R SPECIALTIES LLC
20 Ridgeview Dr (06029-3634)
PHONE..................................860 870-9684
Richard Willis, *President*
Beverly Swanson, *Manager*
EMP: 2
SALES (est): 97.2K **Privately Held**
SIC: 2024 Ice cream & frozen desserts

(G-2606)
THE AROUND THE WORLDS AROUND
126 Windermere Ave (06029-3856)
PHONE..................................860 871-7241
Stephen Schirra, *Principal*
EMP: 2
SALES (est): 69.2K **Privately Held**
SIC: 2711 Newspapers

(G-2607)
TOY PALLET
11 Rothe Ln (06029-3847)
PHONE..................................860 803-9838
Benjamin Priest, *Principal*
EMP: 3 **EST:** 2011
SALES (est): 248.8K **Privately Held**
SIC: 2448 Pallets, wood & wood with metal

(G-2608)
TRANS-TEK INC
10 Industrial Dr (06029-2632)
P.O. Box 338 (06029-0338)
PHONE..................................860 872-8351
Nancy Hamilton, *President*
James Donovan, *Engineer*
Daniel Mertzlufft, *Director*
James L Waters, *Admin Sec*
EMP: 25
SQ FT: 14,000
SALES (est): 5.8MM **Privately Held**
WEB: www.transtekinc.com
SIC: 3825 3669 3829 Transducers for volts, amperes, watts, vars, frequency, etc.; signaling apparatus, electric; measuring & controlling devices

(G-2609)
YELLOWFIN HOLDINGS INC
Yellowfin Distribution
160 West Rd (06029-3723)
P.O. Box 83 (06029-0083)
PHONE..................................866 341-0979
Joseph Teixeira, *Manager*
EMP: 46 **Privately Held**
SIC: 3577 Bar code (magnetic ink) printers
PA: Yellowfin Holdings, Inc.
26 Main St
Ellington CT 06029

Enfield
Hartford County

(G-2610)
A KICK IN CROCHET
2 Guild St (06082-5920)
PHONE..................................413 210-7890
Marla Deschenes, *Principal*
EMP: 2 **EST:** 2017
SALES (est): 83.2K **Privately Held**
SIC: 2399 Hand woven & crocheted products

(G-2611)
ABBEY PRINTING
920 Enfield St Ste B (06082-3673)
PHONE..................................860 745-0122
Kathleen McCabe, *Principal*
EMP: 2 **EST:** 2017
SALES (est): 92.3K **Privately Held**
SIC: 2752 Commercial printing, offset

(G-2612)
ADAMCZYK ENTERPRISES INC
Also Called: Enfield Collision
3 Palomba Dr (06082-3823)
P.O. Box 1143 (06083-1143)
PHONE..................................860 745-9830
Robert P Adamczyk, *President*
Thomas Adamczyk, *Admin Sec*
EMP: 9
SALES (est): 331.4K **Privately Held**
SIC: 3549 Assembly machines, including robotic

(G-2613)
ADVANCE IMAGES LLC
Also Called: Instant Imprints
16 Grand View Dr (06082-5554)
PHONE..................................860 749-1166
Donald Boulette,
EMP: 2
SALES (est): 130K **Privately Held**
SIC: 2752 Commercial printing, lithographic

(G-2614)
AMBER FOOD SALES
10 Misty Meadow Rd (06082-3943)
PHONE..................................860 749-7272
Diane Bellon, *Principal*
EMP: 2
SALES (est): 133.9K **Privately Held**
SIC: 2099 Food preparations

(G-2615)
ANDERSON DAVID C & ASSOC LLC (PA)
Also Called: Anderson Group
9 Moody Rd Ste 1 (06082-3120)
PHONE..................................860 749-7547
Chris Anderson, *Vice Pres*
David C Anderson,
Christopher Anderson,
EMP: 10
SQ FT: 7,200
SALES (est): 1.4MM **Privately Held**
SIC: 3089 8742 7389 8748 Plastic processing; industrial & labor consulting services; auction, appraisal & exchange services; business consulting

(G-2616)
ATLANTIC WOODCRAFT INC
Also Called: B&C Kitchen and Bath
199 Moody Rd (06082-3209)
PHONE..................................860 749-4887
Michael St Germain, *President*
Genevieve St Germain, *Admin Sec*
EMP: 15
SALES (est): 3.3MM **Privately Held**
SIC: 3423 2431 Edge tools for woodworking: augers, bits, gimlets, etc.; millwork

(G-2617)
BENETEC INC
99 Phoenix Ave (06082-4439)
PHONE..................................860 745-4455
Gerald Kaye, *President*
Chuck Gatto, *Manager*
EMP: 1
SALES (est): 81.1K **Privately Held**
WEB: www.benetecusa.com
SIC: 3541 Machine tools, metal cutting type

(G-2618)
BETTER LETTERS SIGNS
11 Camelot Dr (06082-5347)
PHONE..................................860 749-7235
Tracy Garrity, *Owner*
EMP: 1
SALES (est): 84.5K **Privately Held**
SIC: 3993 Signs & advertising specialties

(G-2619)
C J MACSATA LLC
115 Cottage Rd (06082-2208)
PHONE..................................860 623-6755
Charles Macsata, *Principal*
EMP: 2
SALES (est): 113.7K **Privately Held**
SIC: 2759 Screen printing

(G-2620)
CANDLE THREADS
20 Gem Grv (06082-5607)
PHONE..................................860 490-5890
Megan Piorek, *Owner*
EMP: 2
SALES (est): 144.4K **Privately Held**
SIC: 3999 Candles

(G-2621)
CARRIS REELS CONNECTICUT INC
11 Randolph St (06082-4724)
P.O. Box 1104 (06083-1104)
PHONE..................................860 749-8308
Dave Ferraro, *President*
David Ferraro, *Vice Pres*
Steve Sabourin, *Plant Mgr*
Frank Donovan, *Maint Spvr*
David Fitz-Gerald, *CFO*
▲ **EMP:** 64 **EST:** 1868
SQ FT: 116,640
SALES (est): 9.2MM **Privately Held**
WEB: www.carris.net
SIC: 2499 Spools, reels & pulleys: wood
PA: Carris Financial Corp.
49 Main St
Proctor VT 05765

(G-2622)
CHAINMAIL & MORE LLC
54 Hazard Ave Ste 175 (06082-3845)
PHONE..................................860 741-2965
Gregory J Benway, *Partner*
Natalie Bander-Heiden, *Partner*
EMP: 2
SALES (est): 60K **Privately Held**
WEB: www.sblades.com
SIC: 3911 Jewelry, precious metal

(G-2623)
CIRTEC MEDICAL CORP
99 Print Shop Rd (06082-3211)
PHONE..................................860 814-3973
Krystal Olko, *Buyer*
EMP: 120
SALES (corp-wide): 53.4MM **Privately Held**
SIC: 3841 Surgical & medical instruments
PA: Cirtec Medical Corp.
9200 Xylon Ave N
Brooklyn Park MN 55445
763 493-8556

(G-2624)
CJ AVIATION SERVICES LLC
4 Lovely Dr (06082-5925)
PHONE..................................860 741-6499
Yumi Tetreault, *Principal*
EMP: 2
SALES (est): 124.6K **Privately Held**
SIC: 3721 Aircraft

(G-2625)
CLASSIC CABINETS
44 N Maple St (06082-4615)
PHONE..................................860 749-9743
Roman Polaski, *Owner*
EMP: 1
SALES (est): 100K **Privately Held**
SIC: 2434 Wood kitchen cabinets

(G-2626)
CMI TIME MANAGEMENT LLC
89 Phoenix Ave (06082-4439)
PHONE..................................800 722-6654
James S Bianco, *CEO*
EMP: 2 **EST:** 2008
SALES (est): 126.1K
SALES (corp-wide): 11.3MM **Privately Held**
SIC: 3829 Measuring & controlling devices
PA: Control Module, Inc.
89 Phoenix Ave
Enfield CT 06082
860 745-2433

(G-2627)
CNC ENGINEERING INC
19 Bacon Rd (06082-2301)
PHONE..................................860 749-1780
Gary Caravella, *President*
Patrick Harrington, *Vice Pres*
Gene Burr, *Engineer*
Gus Mingesz, *Engineer*
Justin Caravella, *Sales Engr*
EMP: 32
SQ FT: 15,000
SALES (est): 13MM **Privately Held**
WEB: www.cnc1.com
SIC: 7699 7371 3541 Industrial machinery & equipment repair; computer software development; machine tools, metal cutting type

(G-2628)
COLLINS COMPOST
11 Powder Hill Rd (06082-5212)
PHONE..................................860 749-3416
Jack Collins, *Principal*
EMP: 3 **EST:** 1998
SALES (est): 219.7K **Privately Held**
SIC: 2875 Compost

(G-2629)
COLONIAL IRON SHOP INC
15 Dust House Rd (06082-4650)
P.O. Box 1116 (06083-1116)
PHONE..................................860 763-0659
Anthony Leno, *President*
Daniel Swenson, *Vice Pres*
EMP: 4
SQ FT: 6,000
SALES (est): 750K **Privately Held**
SIC: 3441 1791 Fabricated structural metal; structural steel erection

(G-2630)
COMPANY OF COCA-COLA BOTTLING
100 Print Shop Rd (06082)
PHONE..................................860 814-4241
EMP: 1 **Privately Held**
SIC: 2086 Bottled & canned soft drinks
HQ: Coca-Cola Bottling Company Of Southeastern New England, Inc.
150 Waterford Parkway S
Waterford CT 06385
860 443-2816

(G-2631)
COMVAC SYSTEMS INC
3 Peerless Way Ste U (06082-2388)
PHONE..................................860 265-3658
Daniel W Lawrence, *Principal*
Daniel Lawrence, *Principal*
▲ **EMP:** 3
SALES (est): 442.2K **Privately Held**
SIC: 3563 Vacuum pumps, except laboratory

(G-2632)
CONCEPT WOODWORKS LLC
30 Oakwood St (06082-2717)
PHONE..................................860 746-4271
Jeffrey Palladino, *Principal*
EMP: 1
SALES (est): 59.5K **Privately Held**
SIC: 2431 Millwork

(G-2633)
CONVAL INC
96 Phoenix Ave (06082-4408)
PHONE..................................860 749-0761
Frank A Siver, *Principal*
Gene McNamara, *Regional Mgr*
Mike Hendrick, *Vice Pres*
Marc Holly, *Engineer*
Philip Worrell, *Engineer*
▲ **EMP:** 105
SALES (est): 23MM **Privately Held**
WEB: www.conval.com
SIC: 3491 Industrial valves

(G-2634)
CUSTOM PRINTING & COPY INC (PA)
16 Debra St (06082-5031)
P.O. Box 280745, East Hartford (06128-0745)
PHONE..................................860 290-6890
Martin Madeux, *President*
Bedilea Bodo, *Vice Pres*
EMP: 11
SQ FT: 1,200
SALES (est): 1.4MM **Privately Held**
WEB: www.customprintingct.com
SIC: 2752 7334 Commercial printing, offset; photocopying & duplicating services

GEOGRAPHIC SECTION

Enfield - Hartford County (G-2663)

(G-2635)
DANGELO WOODCRAFT LLC
32 Fairview Ave (06082-4366)
PHONE.....................860 402-7175
Nicholas D'Angelo, *Principal*
EMP: 2
SALES (est): 55.2K **Privately Held**
SIC: 2499 Wood products

(G-2636)
DAVINCI TECHNOLOGIES INC
1 Corporate Rd (06082-6402)
PHONE.....................860 265-3388
Daniel Orefice, *President*
Claudio Orefice, *Vice Pres*
EMP: 2
SQ FT: 1,000
SALES (est): 529.2K **Privately Held**
SIC: 3555 Printing trades machinery

(G-2637)
EAST LONGMEADOW BUSINESS SVCS
Also Called: Priority Press
25 Lake Dr (06082-2336)
PHONE.....................413 525-6111
Patricia Mance, *President*
Eric Mance, *President*
EMP: 5
SALES: 450K **Privately Held**
WEB: www.prioritypress.com
SIC: 2752 7334 Commercial printing, offset; photocopying & duplicating services

(G-2638)
EASTERN METAL TREATING INC
28 Bacon Rd (06082-2302)
PHONE.....................860 763-4311
Maureen R Lyman, *President*
Lawrence C Lyman, *Director*
EMP: 10
SQ FT: 20,000
SALES (est): 1.5MM **Privately Held**
SIC: 3398 Metal heat treating

(G-2639)
ENFIELD PRINTING COMPANY
Also Called: Minuteman Press
1 Anngina Dr (06082-3222)
PHONE.....................860 745-3600
Michael Weber, *President*
Lindsey Weber, *Admin Sec*
EMP: 2
SALES (est): 260K **Privately Held**
SIC: 2752 Commercial printing, lithographic

(G-2640)
ENFIELD TRANSIT MIX INC
84 Broadbrook Rd (06082-5303)
P.O. Box 376 (06083-0376)
PHONE.....................860 763-0864
Zigmund Kertenis Jr, *President*
EMP: 16
SALES (est): 3MM **Privately Held**
SIC: 3273 Ready-mixed concrete

(G-2641)
EPPENDORF INC (DH)
175 Freshwater Blvd (06082-4444)
PHONE.....................732 287-1200
Lisa Kendzlic, *CEO*
William Dunne, *Vice Pres*
Dr Lee Eppstein, *Vice Pres*
Mary St John, *Buyer*
Martin Axelsson, *Engineer*
▲ **EMP:** 350 **EST:** 1946
SQ FT: 243,000
SALES (est): 67.1MM
SALES (corp-wide): 177.9K **Privately Held**
WEB: www.nbsc.com
SIC: 3821 Laboratory equipment: fume hoods, distillation racks, etc.; shakers & stirrers; sterilizers; chemical laboratory apparatus

(G-2642)
EPPENDORF HOLDING INC (DH)
175 Freshwater Blvd (06082-4444)
PHONE.....................860 253-3417
Martin Farb, *CEO*
Christian Jaaks, *CFO*
Klaus U Theidmann, *Admin Sec*
▲ **EMP:** 25
SALES (est): 62MM
SALES (corp-wide): 177.9K **Privately Held**
SIC: 3821 Shakers & stirrers
HQ: Eppendorf Ag
    Barkhausenweg 1
    Hamburg 22339
    405 380-10

(G-2643)
EPPENDORF MANUFACTURING CORP
175 Freshwater Blvd (06082-4444)
PHONE.....................860 253-3400
Kirti Patel, *CEO*
Mary Bombardier, *Purch Mgr*
Mary Stjohn, *Buyer*
Perry Aschenbrand, *Controller*
◆ **EMP:** 170
SALES (est): 37MM
SALES (corp-wide): 177.9K **Privately Held**
SIC: 3841 Surgical & medical instruments
HQ: Eppendorf Ag
    Barkhausenweg 1
    Hamburg 22339
    405 380-10

(G-2644)
EVSE LLC
89 Phoenix Ave (06082-4439)
PHONE.....................860 745-2433
James S Bianco, *Principal*
EMP: 3
SALES (est): 178.9K
SALES (corp-wide): 11.3MM **Privately Held**
SIC: 3699 Electrical equipment & supplies
PA: Control Module, Inc.
    89 Phoenix Ave
    Enfield CT 06082
    860 745-2433

(G-2645)
FAIR WEATHER LOGGING LLC
33 School St (06082-4726)
PHONE.....................860 394-8217
Adam Krajewski, *Principal*
EMP: 2
SALES (est): 81.7K **Privately Held**
SIC: 2411 Logging

(G-2646)
FALCON PRESS
13 Rockland Dr (06082-5815)
P.O. Box 142 (06083-0142)
PHONE.....................860 763-2293
Peter Sarno, *Owner*
EMP: 3
SQ FT: 5,800
SALES: 200K **Privately Held**
SIC: 2759 2789 2752 Screen printing; bookbinding & related work; commercial printing, lithographic

(G-2647)
FLEET MANAGEMENT LLC
89 Phoenix Ave (06082-4439)
PHONE.....................800 722-6654
James Bianco,
EMP: 3
SALES (est): 169.2K
SALES (corp-wide): 11.3MM **Privately Held**
SIC: 3823 Industrial instrmnts msrmnt display/control process variable
PA: Control Module, Inc.
    89 Phoenix Ave
    Enfield CT 06082
    860 745-2433

(G-2648)
HASSON SHEET METAL LLC
36 Ridge Rd (06082-3027)
PHONE.....................860 698-6951
Michael J Hasson, *Manager*
EMP: 1
SALES (est): 134.8K **Privately Held**
SIC: 3444 Sheet metalwork

(G-2649)
HIGH GRADE FINISHING CO LLC
Also Called: High Grade Furnishing
6 Print Shop Rd (06082-3212)
PHONE.....................860 749-8883
Valarie Ainsworth, *Vice Pres*
Russell Ainsworth,
EMP: 3 **EST:** 1959
SQ FT: 5,400
SALES: 140K **Privately Held**
SIC: 3479 7641 Painting of metal products; reupholstery & furniture repair

(G-2650)
HIGH-TECH CONVERSIONS INC (PA)
1699 King St Ste 104 (06082-6052)
PHONE.....................860 265-2633
Claudio Orefice, *President*
Subhra Roy, *General Mgr*
Kristin Carr, *Project Mgr*
Tony Roncalli, *Mfg Staff*
▲ **EMP:** 1
SALES (est): 2.9MM **Privately Held**
WEB: www.high-techconversions.com
SIC: 5169 2842 Sanitation preparations; dusting cloths, chemically treated

(G-2651)
I Q TECHNOLOGY LLC
9 Moody Rd Ste 18 (06082-3120)
PHONE.....................860 749-7255
Peter Hasiuk,
EMP: 12
SQ FT: 10,000
SALES: 2MM **Privately Held**
WEB: www.iqtechnology.com
SIC: 3555 Printing trades machinery

(G-2652)
INTEGRAL TECHNOLOGIES INC (DH)
120 Post Rd (06082-5690)
PHONE.....................860 741-2281
Gottfried Keusters, *President*
Paul Lettieri, *Admin Sec*
▲ **EMP:** 6
SQ FT: 75,000
SALES: 6.8MM
SALES (corp-wide): 101.5K **Privately Held**
SIC: 3699 3599 8731 Electron beam metal cutting, forming or welding machines; machine & other job shop work; industrial laboratory, except testing
HQ: Ptr Strahltechnik Gmbh
    Am Erlenbruch 9
    Langensenbold 63505
    618 420-550

(G-2653)
JANIK SAUSAGE CO INC
136 Hazard Ave (06082-4520)
P.O. Box 751 (06083-0751)
PHONE.....................860 749-4661
Diane Prokop, *President*
Raymond Prokop, *Vice Pres*
EMP: 3
SQ FT: 1,900
SALES (est): 242K **Privately Held**
SIC: 2013 Sausages & related products, from purchased meat; sausages from purchased meat; prepared pork products from purchased pork

(G-2654)
KENNETH ALLEVO
Also Called: Industrial Scale Service
18 Hudson St (06082-5950)
PHONE.....................860 745-0740
Kenneth Allevo, *Owner*
EMP: 1 **EST:** 1978
SALES (est): 134.5K **Privately Held**
SIC: 5046 3596 Scales, except laboratory; scales & balances, except laboratory

(G-2655)
LEGO SYSTEMS INC (DH)
Also Called: Lego Brand Retail
555 Taylor Rd (06082-2372)
PHONE.....................860 749-2291
Soren Torp Laursen, *President*
Rachel Wendt, *General Mgr*
Katherine Deurloo, *Project Mgr*
Chad Ketterling, *Store Mgr*
Robert Bishop, *Opers Staff*
◆ **EMP:** 1350
SQ FT: 1,000,000
SALES (est): 559.6MM
SALES (corp-wide): 1.6B **Privately Held**
SIC: 3944 5092 Erector sets, toy; structural toy sets; blocks, toy; toys & hobby goods & supplies
HQ: Lego A/S
    Astvej 1
    Billund 7190
    795 060-70

(G-2656)
MACALA TOOL INC
7 Moody Rd Bldg 5 (06082-3123)
P.O. Box 765, Vernon (06066-0765)
PHONE.....................860 763-2580
Ian Macala, *President*
EMP: 5
SQ FT: 2,000
SALES: 250K **Privately Held**
SIC: 3599 Machine shop, jobbing & repair

(G-2657)
MAGNUM INDUSTRIES
6 Harrison Ave (06082-2915)
PHONE.....................860 490-9513
Walter Zawrotny, *Principal*
EMP: 2 **EST:** 2009
SALES (est): 105.3K **Privately Held**
SIC: 3999 Manufacturing industries

(G-2658)
MELVIN MAYO
Also Called: Acad24 / A-Nusign
46 Sword Ave (06082-1849)
PHONE.....................802 698-7635
Melvin Mayo, *Owner*
EMP: 1
SALES (est): 49.8K **Privately Held**
SIC: 3993 7389 7336 Signs & advertising specialties; drafting service, except temporary help; commercial art & graphic design

(G-2659)
MFG SERVICE CO
10 Dust House Rd (06082)
PHONE.....................860 749-8316
Mike Assimus, *Owner*
EMP: 1
SALES (est): 54K **Privately Held**
SIC: 3999 Manufacturing industries

(G-2660)
MICHAEL HURLBURT
155 Pearl St (06082-3543)
PHONE.....................860 745-0681
Micahel Hurlburt, *Owner*
EMP: 1
SALES (est): 61.8K **Privately Held**
SIC: 3253 Ceramic wall & floor tile

(G-2661)
MKR SIGN COMPANY
3 Peerless Way Ste V (06082-2388)
PHONE.....................860 265-7996
Darlene A Reedy, *Principal*
EMP: 2 **EST:** 2013
SALES (est): 121.3K **Privately Held**
SIC: 3993 Signs & advertising specialties

(G-2662)
MOST EXCLLENT CMICS CLLCTIBLES
481 Enfield St (06082-2426)
PHONE.....................860 741-0113
Mason Allen, *Owner*
EMP: 1
SQ FT: 2,000
SALES (est): 85.8K **Privately Held**
SIC: 2721 3944 Comic books: publishing & printing; electronic games & toys

(G-2663)
MRND LLC
75 Hazard Ave Ste 1 (06082-3866)
PHONE.....................860 749-0256
Larry Vertefeuille, *Manager*
EMP: 7
SQ FT: 6,000
SALES (corp-wide): 2.5MM **Privately Held**
WEB: www.mrnd.com
SIC: 3444 Sheet metalwork

Enfield - Hartford County (G-2664)   GEOGRAPHIC SECTION

PA: Mrnd Llc
4418 Louisburg Rd
Raleigh NC
919 862-8480

(G-2664)
MSC FILTRATION TECH INC
Also Called: M S C
198 Freshwater Blvd (06082-4455)
PHONE..............................860 745-7475
Michael Assimus, *President*
▼ **EMP:** 10 **EST:** 1962
SQ FT: 6,800
SALES (est): 4.8MM **Privately Held**
WEB: www.mscliquidfiltration.com
SIC: 5085 3569 3561 5084 Filters, industrial; filters; pumps & pumping equipment; pumps & pumping equipment

(G-2665)
NANCY DIGHELLO
Also Called: Ellen and Crafts
4 Welch Dr (06082-5133)
PHONE..............................860 763-4294
Nancy Dighello, *Owner*
Luis Dighello, *Co-Owner*
EMP: 2
SALES (est): 68.6K **Privately Held**
SIC: 3944 5944 Craft & hobby kits & sets; jewelry stores

(G-2666)
NANCY R MARRYAT
63 Post Rd (06082-5696)
PHONE..............................860 749-2632
David Marryat, *Principal*
EMP: 1
SALES (est): 76.3K **Privately Held**
SIC: 2431 Millwork

(G-2667)
NEW BRITAIN HEAT TREATING CORP
5 Grant Ave (06082-3611)
PHONE..............................860 223-0684
Daniel Audet, *President*
Joan Litteral, *Manager*
Diane Audet, *Admin Sec*
EMP: 15
SALES: 1.1MM **Privately Held**
SIC: 3398 Metal heat treating

(G-2668)
NEW BRNSWICK SCIENTIFIC OF DEL
175 Freshwater Blvd (06082-4444)
PHONE..............................732 287-1200
David Freedman, *CEO*
EMP: 1
SALES (est): 76.2K
SALES (corp-wide): 177.9K **Privately Held**
WEB: www.nbsc.com
SIC: 3632 Household refrigerators & freezers
HQ: Eppendorf, Inc.
175 Freshwater Blvd
Enfield CT 06082
732 287-1200

(G-2669)
NEW ENGLAND PRINTING LLC
1 Anngina Dr (06082-3222)
PHONE..............................860 745-3600
Lindsey Weber, *Principal*
Gail Weber, *Principal*
EMP: 6
SALES (est): 182.6K **Privately Held**
SIC: 2759 Commercial printing

(G-2670)
NORTHEAST MFG CO LLC
3 Peerless Way Ste D (06082-2388)
PHONE..............................860 763-4000
Curtis St Germain,
Donald Jodoin Jr,
EMP: 2
SALES (est): 253.9K **Privately Held**
SIC: 3721 Airplanes, fixed or rotary wing

(G-2671)
NORWICH PRINTING CO INC
1 Anngina Dr (06082-3222)
PHONE..............................860 745-3600
EMP: 2
SALES (est): 83.9K **Privately Held**
SIC: 2752 Commercial printing, lithographic

(G-2672)
OLYMPIA SALES INC
Also Called: Enfield Stationers
215 Moody Rd Ste 3 (06082-3230)
P.O. Box 1800 (06083-1800)
PHONE..............................860 749-0751
Arthur O'Hara, *CEO*
Thomas O'Hara, *President*
Sue Smith, *Human Resources*
◆ **EMP:** 60 **EST:** 1966
SQ FT: 90,000
SALES (est): 8.7MM **Privately Held**
WEB: www.olympiaosi.com
SIC: 5112 5961 7389 2771 Greeting cards; mail order house; fund raising organizations; greeting cards

(G-2673)
ONPOINT CONNECTIONS
780 Enfield St (06082-2914)
PHONE..............................860 253-0489
Christy Peterson, *Principal*
Craig Stanek, *Manager*
EMP: 2
SALES (est): 136.1K **Privately Held**
SIC: 3211 1799 Window glass, clear & colored; glass tinting, architectural or automotive; batteries, automotive & truck; automobile & truck equipment & parts; automotive accessories; speed shops, including race car supplies

(G-2674)
P & M INVESTMENTS LLC
Also Called: Minuteman Press
1 Anngina Dr (06082-3222)
PHONE..............................860 745-3600
Paul Mazzaccaro,
EMP: 3
SALES (est): 411.7K **Privately Held**
SIC: 2752 Commercial printing, lithographic

(G-2675)
PAGANI PUBLISHING
47 Bernardino Ave (06082-1843)
P.O. Box 3351 (06083-3351)
PHONE..............................860 614-0303
EMP: 2 **EST:** 2017
SALES (est): 82.3K **Privately Held**
SIC: 2741 Miscellaneous publishing

(G-2676)
PETER HOELZEL
31 Taft Ln (06082-5223)
PHONE..............................860 749-4070
Peter Hoelzel, *CEO*
EMP: 2 **EST:** 2017
SALES (est): 85.2K **Privately Held**
SIC: 3542 Machine tools, metal forming type

(G-2677)
PHOENIX POULTRY CORPORATION
8 Wheeler Dr (06082-2227)
PHONE..............................413 732-1433
EMP: 20
SQ FT: 12,000
SALES (est): 2.4MM **Privately Held**
SIC: 2015 Poultry Processing

(G-2678)
POLYMERIC CONVERTING LLC
5 Old Depot Hill Rd (06082-6040)
PHONE..............................860 623-1335
Frank Magnani,
Alan Gervais,
▲ **EMP:** 20
SQ FT: 56,000
SALES (est): 4.6MM **Privately Held**
SIC: 2671 3089 Plastic film, coated or laminated for packaging; laminating of plastic

(G-2679)
POWDER HILL SAND & GRAVEL LLC (PA)
38 Post Office Rd (06082-5626)
P.O. Box 3282 (06083-3282)
PHONE..............................860 741-7274

Mark Spazzarini,
Edward Spazzarini,
EMP: 2
SQ FT: 1,000
SALES (est): 1.1MM **Privately Held**
WEB: www.powder-hill.com
SIC: 5211 1442 5032 1429 Sand & gravel; construction sand & gravel; stone, crushed or broken; boulder, crushed & broken-quarrying

(G-2680)
PREFERRED DISPLAY INC
215 Moody Rd Ste 1 (06082-3230)
PHONE..............................860 372-4653
Christian Slolorzano, *Branch Mgr*
EMP: 1 **Privately Held**
SIC: 2844 Cosmetic preparations
PA: Preferred Display, Inc.
78 Edwin Rd
South Windsor CT 06074

(G-2681)
PROGRESS MACHINING CO
15a Dust House Rd (06082-4650)
P.O. Box 839 (06083-0839)
PHONE..............................860 763-1752
Carl Wittenzellner, *Owner*
EMP: 2
SALES (est): 196.8K **Privately Held**
SIC: 3599 Machine shop, jobbing & repair

(G-2682)
PTI INDUSTRIES INC
5 Pearson Way (06082-2655)
PHONE..............................860 698-9266
Reed Todd, *Branch Mgr*
EMP: 2
SALES (corp-wide): 39.1MM **Privately Held**
SIC: 3479 Coating of metals & formed products
HQ: Pti Industries, Inc.
2 Peerless Way
Enfield CT 06082
800 318-8438

(G-2683)
PTI INDUSTRIES INC (HQ)
Also Called: P T I
2 Peerless Way (06082-2371)
PHONE..............................800 318-8438
Ronald Lalli, *CEO*
Harley Delude, *President*
Ed Moreau, *Facilities Mgr*
Eric Payette, *Facilities Mgr*
Spencer Roy, *QA Dir*
EMP: 42
SQ FT: 19,000
SALES (est): 6.1MM
SALES (corp-wide): 39.1MM **Privately Held**
WEB: www.ptiwebsite.com
SIC: 3479 8734 Coating of metals & formed products; coating, rust preventive; bonderizing of metal or metal products; metallurgical testing laboratory
PA: Iss 2, Llc
10070 Daniels Interstate
Fort Myers FL 33913
239 244-2244

(G-2684)
PULVER PRECISION LLC
38 Bacon Rd (06082-2302)
PHONE..............................860 763-0763
Brian Pulver,
EMP: 4
SALES (est): 552.4K **Privately Held**
SIC: 3599 Machine shop, jobbing & repair

(G-2685)
QG PRINTING II CORP
96 Phoenix Ave (06082-4408)
PHONE..............................860 741-0150
Ron Amarante, *Sales Staff*
EMP: 519
SALES (corp-wide): 4.1B **Publicly Held**
WEB: www.qwdys.com
SIC: 2752 Commercial printing, offset
HQ: Qg Printing Ii Corp.
N61w23044 Harrys Way
Sussex WI 53089

(G-2686)
R K S SECURITY LLC
4 Cleveland St (06082-5308)
PHONE..............................860 749-4106
Richard Sylvester, *Owner*
EMP: 2
SALES: 120K **Privately Held**
SIC: 3699 Security devices

(G-2687)
RELIABLE WELDING & SPEED LLC
85 North St (06082-3933)
PHONE..............................860 749-3977
Brad Hietala, *Mng Member*
Linda Hietala,
EMP: 6
SQ FT: 2,500
SALES (est): 800K **Privately Held**
SIC: 7692 5531 3444 3441 Welding repair; speed shops, including race car supplies; truck equipment & parts; sheet metalwork; fabricated structural metal

(G-2688)
RUNWAY LIQUIDATION LLC
Also Called: Bcbg
3802 A Britton Plz (06082)
PHONE..............................561 391-3334
EMP: 2
SALES (corp-wide): 570.1MM **Privately Held**
SIC: 2335 Women's, juniors' & misses' dresses
HQ: Runway Liquidation, Llc
2761 Fruitland Ave
Vernon CA 90058
323 589-2224

(G-2689)
SCHRADER BELLOWS
80 Shaker Rd (06082-3106)
PHONE..............................860 749-2215
EMP: 25
SALES (est): 895.4K **Privately Held**
SIC: 2796 Platemaking Services

(G-2690)
SCREENING INK LLC
39 Celtic Ct (06082-5778)
PHONE..............................860 212-0475
Brett Silva, *Principal*
EMP: 3
SALES (est): 224.6K **Privately Held**
SIC: 3952 Ink, drawing: black & colored

(G-2691)
SENIOR OPERATIONS LLC
Also Called: Senior Aerospace Connecticut
4 Peerless Way (06082-2371)
PHONE..............................860 741-2546
Michael Lang, *CEO*
David Squires, *President*
Ken Bernier, *QC Mgr*
Jeffrey Audet, *Engineer*
Donald Caravella, *Engineer*
EMP: 95 **EST:** 1992
SQ FT: 55,000
SALES (est): 22.2MM **Privately Held**
WEB: www.sterlingmachineco.com
SIC: 3728 Aircraft parts & equipment

(G-2692)
SENIOR OPERATIONS LLC
Also Called: Sterling Machine Division
4 Peerless Way (06082-2371)
PHONE..............................860 741-2546
Robert Segal, *CEO*
EMP: 80
SALES (corp-wide): 1.3B **Privately Held**
SIC: 3599 Hose, flexible metallic; tubing, flexible metallic; bellows, industrial: metal
HQ: Senior Operations Llc
300 E Devon Ave
Bartlett IL 60103
630 372-3500

(G-2693)
SEVEN STITCHES SCREEN PRNTNG ⊙
9 Moody Rd Unit C-13 (06082-3131)
PHONE..............................860 749-1166
EMP: 2 **EST:** 2019

GEOGRAPHIC SECTION

Essex - Middlesex County (G-2722)

SALES (est): 83.9K **Privately Held**
SIC: 2752 Commercial printing, lithographic

(G-2694)
SIGN A RAMA
Also Called: Sign-A-Rama
3 Peerless Way Ste V (06082-2388)
PHONE.................................860 265-7996
Mike Reedy, *Manager*
EMP: 2 EST: 2010
SALES (est): 177.8K **Privately Held**
SIC: 3993 Signs & advertising specialties

(G-2695)
SIGN FACTORY
Also Called: Little John's Sign Factory
25 Dust House Rd (06082-4650)
PHONE.................................860 763-1085
Little John, *Owner*
EMP: 10
SQ FT: 7,000
SALES (est): 782.8K **Privately Held**
SIC: 3993 Signs & advertising specialties

(G-2696)
SIGNS BY SCAVOTTO
5 Whitewood St (06082-2718)
PHONE.................................860 745-5629
Charles Scavotto, *Owner*
EMP: 1
SALES (est): 94.5K **Privately Held**
SIC: 3993 Signs & advertising specialties

(G-2697)
SIMPSON STRONG-TIE COMPANY INC
7 Pearson Way (06082-2655)
PHONE.................................860 741-8923
John Adkins, *Manager*
EMP: 16
SALES (corp-wide): 1B **Publicly Held**
SIC: 3449 Miscellaneous metalwork
HQ: Simpson Strong-Tie Company Inc.
5956 W Las Positas Blvd
Pleasanton CA 94588
925 560-9000

(G-2698)
STONEWALL CABINETRY LLC
3 Peerless Way (06082-2387)
PHONE.................................860 803-7595
Kenneth M Sylvain, *Principal*
EMP: 2 EST: 2011
SALES (est): 113.2K **Privately Held**
SIC: 2434 Wood kitchen cabinets

(G-2699)
STR HOLDINGS INC (PA)
1559 King St (06082-5844)
PHONE.................................860 272-4235
Robert S Yorgensen, *Ch of Bd*
EMP: 19
SQ FT: 69,500
SALES: 10.8MM **Publicly Held**
WEB: www.strus.com
SIC: 3081 Unsupported plastics film & sheet

(G-2700)
SWEETHEART FLUTE COMPANY LLC
32 S Maple St (06082-4653)
PHONE.................................860 749-8514
Ralph Sweet,
Walter D Sweet,
EMP: 3
SALES (est): 333.7K **Privately Held**
WEB: www.sweetheartflute.com
SIC: 3931 5736 Flutes & parts; musical instrument stores

(G-2701)
TILCON CONNECTICUT INC
245 Shaker Rd (06082-2327)
PHONE.................................860 224-6010
Tim Marti, *Manager*
EMP: 1
SALES (corp-wide): 30.6B **Privately Held**
WEB: www.tilconct.com
SIC: 3273 Ready-mixed concrete
HQ: Tilcon Connecticut Inc.
642 Black Rock Ave
New Britain CT 06052
860 224-6010

(G-2702)
TURNING STONE SAND & GRAV LLC
128 Moody Rd (06082-3202)
PHONE.................................413 519-1560
Anna L Lincoln, *Principal*
EMP: 3
SALES (est): 92K **Privately Held**
SIC: 1442 Construction sand & gravel

(G-2703)
U S GLASS DISTRIBUTORS INC
7 Niblick Rd (06082-4431)
PHONE.................................860 741-3658
Mark S Vece, *President*
Corinne Cacopardo, *Vice Pres*
Blaise Vece, *Treasurer*
▲ EMP: 20
SQ FT: 28,000
SALES (est): 6.6MM **Privately Held**
SIC: 5039 3231 Glass construction materials; products of purchased glass

(G-2704)
VERICO TECHNOLOGY LLC (HQ)
230 Shaker Rd (06082-2385)
PHONE.................................800 492-7286
Yuval Dubois, *President*
Rebecca Itkin Duffy, *CFO*
▲ EMP: 45
SQ FT: 11,500
SALES (est): 112.4MM **Privately Held**
WEB: www.presstek.com
SIC: 3577 3861 3555 Magnetic ink & optical scanning devices; graphic arts plates, sensitized; printing plates

(G-2705)
WEST SHORE METALS LLC
28 W Shore Dr (06082-2223)
PHONE.................................860 749-8013
Bruce Bouchard, *Principal*
EMP: 4
SALES (est): 199.1K **Privately Held**
SIC: 3469 Metal stampings

(G-2706)
WHOLE DONUT
920 Enfield St Ste A (06082-3673)
PHONE.................................860 745-3041
John Algiere, *President*
Joseph Algiere, *Vice Pres*
Nancy Algiere, *Treasurer*
Catherine Algiere, *Admin Sec*
EMP: 18
SQ FT: 2,000
SALES (est): 685.5K **Privately Held**
SIC: 5461 5812 2051 Doughnuts; coffee shop; doughnuts, except frozen

(G-2707)
WINTERS GROUP
150 Hazard Ave Ste C1 (06082-4587)
PHONE.................................860 749-3317
Betsy Winters, *Principal*
Janet Connolly, *Sales Staff*
EMP: 2
SALES (est): 208.1K **Privately Held**
SIC: 2431 Window frames, wood

(G-2708)
WORLD CORD SETS INC
210 Moody Rd (06082-3206)
P.O. Box 1111 (06083-1111)
PHONE.................................860 763-2100
Edward C Smith, *President*
Ed Smith, *Info Tech Mgr*
▲ EMP: 8
SALES (est): 1.4MM **Privately Held**
WEB: www.worldcordsets.com
SIC: 3699 3643 Appliance cords for household electrical equipment; current-carrying wiring devices

(G-2709)
YANKEE CASTING CO INC
243 Shaker Rd (06082-2327)
P.O. Box 813 (06083-0813)
PHONE.................................860 749-6171
Mark Vecchiarelli, *President*
Timothy Vecchiarelli, *Corp Secy*
Brian Vecchiarelli, *Vice Pres*
Kevin Vecchiarelli, *Vice Pres*
EMP: 55 EST: 1961
SQ FT: 51,000
SALES: 5.3MM **Privately Held**
WEB: www.yankeecasting.com
SIC: 3369 Castings, except die-castings, precision; magnesium & magnes.-base alloy castings, exc. die-casting

Essex
Middlesex County

(G-2710)
ACTIVE INTEREST MEDIA INC
10 Bokum Rd (06426-1500)
PHONE.................................860 767-3200
John Atzinger, *Editor*
EMP: 1
SALES (corp-wide): 113.1MM **Privately Held**
SIC: 2721 Magazines: publishing only, not printed on site
PA: Active Interest Media, Inc.
300 Continental Blvd # 650
El Segundo CA 90245
310 356-4100

(G-2711)
AMERICAN WIND CAPITAL CO LLC (HQ)
2 Essex Sq Unit 7 (06426-1177)
PHONE.................................860 767-1579
Charles Hinckley, *CEO*
Andrew J Hinckley, *Vice Pres*
EMP: 5 EST: 2009
SALES (est): 2MM
SALES (corp-wide): 137.8MM **Publicly Held**
SIC: 6799 3511 Investors; steam turbine generator set units, complete
PA: Hannon Armstrong Sustainable Infrastructure Capital, Inc.
1906 Towne Centre Blvd
Annapolis MD 21401
410 571-9860

(G-2712)
BELL POWER SYSTEMS LLC
Also Called: John Deere Authorized Dealer
34 Plains Rd (06426-1501)
P.O. Box 980 (06426-0980)
PHONE.................................860 767-7502
Michael J Hucovski,
▲ EMP: 60 EST: 2012
SALES: 11.4MM **Privately Held**
SIC: 3519 5082 Diesel, semi-diesel or duel-fuel engines, including marine; construction & mining machinery

(G-2713)
BROCKWAY FERRY CORPORATION (PA)
Also Called: Leather Man Limited
59 Plains Rd (06426-1504)
P.O. Box 57 (06426-0057)
PHONE.................................860 767-8231
W Cecil Lyon, *President*
Cecil Lyon, *Chancellor*
Tina Beaulac, *Sales Staff*
Linda B Lyon, *Admin Sec*
◆ EMP: 4 EST: 1967
SQ FT: 15,000
SALES (est): 597.6K **Privately Held**
WEB: www.leathermanlimited.com
SIC: 3199 2241 3172 Leather belting & strapping; beltings, woven or braided; personal leather goods

(G-2714)
CONNECTICUT SIGN SERVICE LLC
25 Saybrook Rd Ste 6 (06426)
P.O. Box 645, Old Saybrook (06475-0645)
PHONE.................................860 767-7446
Arlene Fernandes,
John Morrison,
EMP: 5
SALES (est): 900K **Privately Held**
WEB: www.ctsign.com
SIC: 2499 3993 Signboards, wood; signs & advertising specialties

(G-2715)
DINGHY PRO LLC
46 Plains Rd Ste 10 (06426-1550)
PHONE.................................860 767-1596
Jeffrey Going, *Partner*
Christopher Going, *Partner*
EMP: 1 EST: 2011
SALES (est): 112.6K **Privately Held**
SIC: 3732 Tenders (small motor craft), building & repairing

(G-2716)
EAGLE SIGNS LLC
50 West Ave (06426-1163)
PHONE.................................860 227-1959
EMP: 1 EST: 2008
SALES (est): 60K **Privately Held**
SIC: 3993 Mfg Signs/Advertising Specialties

(G-2717)
ESSEX CONCRETE PRODUCTS INC
141 Westbrook Rd (06426-1512)
PHONE.................................860 767-1768
Robert Vitari, *President*
Ruth Vitari, *Admin Sec*
EMP: 10 EST: 1958
SQ FT: 5,000
SALES (est): 1.6MM **Privately Held**
SIC: 3273 3272 Ready-mixed concrete; concrete products, precast

(G-2718)
HI-REL GROUP LLC
16 Plains Rd (06426-1501)
PHONE.................................860 767-9031
William Hubbard, *President*
EMP: 7 EST: 2013
SALES (est): 973.6K
SALES (corp-wide): 67.1MM **Privately Held**
SIC: 3674 Hybrid integrated circuits
PA: Hermetic Solutions Group Inc.
4000 State Route 66 # 310
Tinton Falls NJ 07753
732 722-8780

(G-2719)
HI-REL PRODUCTS LLC
16 Plains Rd (06426-1501)
PHONE.................................860 767-9031
William Hubbard, *President*
EMP: 40 EST: 2013
SQ FT: 16,500
SALES: 6.2MM
SALES (corp-wide): 67.1MM **Privately Held**
WEB: www.hi-rel.net
SIC: 3674 Hybrid integrated circuits
PA: Hermetic Solutions Group Inc.
4000 State Route 66 # 310
Tinton Falls NJ 07753
732 722-8780

(G-2720)
JACKSON CORRUGATED CONT CORP
45 River Rd (06426-1302)
PHONE.................................860 767-3373
William P Herlihy, *President*
Paula Bingham, *Admin Sec*
EMP: 40 EST: 1949
SQ FT: 60,000
SALES (est): 7.1MM **Privately Held**
WEB: www.jacksonbox.com
SIC: 2653 Boxes, corrugated: made from purchased materials

(G-2721)
JB FILTRATION LLC
18 River Road Dr (06426-1377)
P.O. Box 793 (06426-0793)
PHONE.................................860 333-7962
Matthew F Winkler IV, *Mng Member*
Judith B Winkler, *Mng Member*
EMP: 3
SALES: 1.3MM **Privately Held**
SIC: 3677 Filtration devices, electronic

(G-2722)
JYL LLP
Also Called: Essex Mail Mart
12 Plains Rd (06426-1501)
PHONE.................................860 767-7733
Kevin Brewer, *Managing Prtnr*
EMP: 3
SQ FT: 1,200

Essex - Middlesex County (G-2723)

SALES: 300K **Privately Held**
SIC: 7389 4822 5943 7334 Packaging & labeling services; mailing & messenger services; mailbox rental & related service; facsimile transmission services; office forms & supplies; photocopying & duplicating services; advertising novelties

(G-2723)
LEE COMPANY
55 Bokum Rd (06426-1506)
PHONE.....................860 399-6281
Steve Hanssen, *Senior Buyer*
Dave Schweitzer, *Chief Engr*
Joseph Blazevich, *Engineer*
Robert Lee, *Branch Mgr*
Judith Piner, *Manager*
EMP: 120
SALES (corp-wide): 207.5MM **Privately Held**
WEB: www.eeco.com
SIC: 3823 Fluidic devices, circuits & systems for process control
PA: The Lee Company
  2 Pettipaug Rd
  Westbrook CT 06498
  860 399-6281

(G-2724)
LIGHTING EDGE INC
50 West Ave Ste 4 (06426-1163)
P.O. Box 925 (06426-0925)
PHONE.....................860 767-8968
William Barber, *President*
Scott Thompson, *Admin Sec*
EMP: 5
SQ FT: 8,000
SALES: 540K **Privately Held**
WEB: www.lightingedge.com
SIC: 3646 5063 Commercial indusl & institutional electric lighting fixtures; electrical apparatus & equipment

(G-2725)
LIMB-IT-LESS LOGGING LLC
182 Saybrook Rd (06426-1414)
PHONE.....................860 227-0987
Andrew Clark, *CEO*
EMP: 3
SALES (est): 132.5K **Privately Held**
WEB: www.limbitlesslogging.com
SIC: 2411 Logging

(G-2726)
MOBIUS PRESS
Also Called: Present Perfect
23 Eagle Ridge Dr (06426-1330)
P.O. Box 555 (06426-0555)
PHONE.....................860 767-0880
Lawrence D Athey, *Owner*
Lawrence H Athey, *Owner*
Sherri Athey, *Owner*
EMP: 2
SALES: 100K **Privately Held**
WEB: www.giftelan.com
SIC: 2731 Book publishing

(G-2727)
MUD RIVER SERVICES
37 Bokum Rd (06426-1506)
PHONE.....................860 767-0592
Thomas J Macwhinney, *Owner*
EMP: 1
SALES (est): 141K **Privately Held**
SIC: 1542 2411 1629 Nonresidential construction; logging; land clearing contractor

(G-2728)
NEW ENGLAND JOINERY WORKS INC
19 Bokum Rd (06426-1506)
PHONE.....................860 767-3377
Matthew Ouellette, *President*
Peter Leffingwell, *Admin Sec*
EMP: 5
SQ FT: 8,600
SALES (est): 1MM **Privately Held**
SIC: 2431 2499 Millwork; decorative wood & woodwork

(G-2729)
PETES PRINT SHOP
46 Plains Rd (06426-1549)
PHONE.....................860 581-8043
EMP: 2

SALES (est): 80.6K **Privately Held**
SIC: 2752 Commercial printing, lithographic

(G-2730)
PLANES ROAD ASSOC LLC
38 Plains Rd (06426-1501)
PHONE.....................860 469-3200
Stokes Ken, *Vice Pres*
Ethan B Goller, *Manager*
EMP: 2
SALES (est): 103.4K **Privately Held**
SIC: 2759 Commercial printing

(G-2731)
PROCTOR WOODWORKS LLC
53 Grandview Ter (06426-1004)
PHONE.....................860 767-9881
Brian D Proctor, *Principal*
EMP: 2
SALES (est): 274.8K **Privately Held**
SIC: 2431 Millwork

(G-2732)
RIVER VALLEY STAIRS LLC
21 Main St (06426-1135)
PHONE.....................860 767-7561
EMP: 2 **EST:** 2004
SALES (est): 100K **Privately Held**
SIC: 3446 Mfg Architectural Metalwork

(G-2733)
SMITH HILL OF DELAWARE INC
34 Plains Rd (06426-1501)
P.O. Box 980 (06426-0980)
PHONE.....................860 767-7502
Martin A Bell, *President*
John Jackson, *Area Mgr*
Bob Jones, *Area Mgr*
Bill Rockelmann, *Area Mgr*
Jerry Stewart, *COO*
▲ **EMP:** 32
SQ FT: 52,000
SALES (est): 5.3MM **Privately Held**
WEB: www.bellpower.com
SIC: 3519 Internal combustion engines

(G-2734)
SMITH TIA CUSTM STATNARY PHOT
7 Hudson Ln (06426-1315)
PHONE.....................860 767-1976
Tia Smith, *Owner*
EMP: 1
SALES (est): 79.1K **Privately Held**
SIC: 2621 Stationery, envelope & tablet papers

(G-2735)
SOUNDINGS PUBLICATIONS LLC
Also Called: Woodshop News Magazine
10 Bokum Rd (06426-1500)
PHONE.....................860 767-8227
Glen Mallory, *Supervisor*
Dominion Enterprises,
EMP: 22
SALES (est): 2.8MM **Privately Held**
WEB: www.soundingspub.com
SIC: 2721 Magazines: publishing only, not printed on site

(G-2736)
UNITED TECHNOLOGIES CORP
10 Curiosity Ln (06426-1356)
PHONE.....................860 767-9592
Richard Gilliland, *Branch Mgr*
EMP: 268
SALES (corp-wide): 66.5B **Publicly Held**
SIC: 3585 Refrigeration & heating equipment
PA: United Technologies Corporation
  10 Farm Springs Rd
  Farmington CT 06032
  860 728-7000

(G-2737)
WEEKEND KITCHEN
16 Main St (06426-1118)
PHONE.....................860 767-1010
Nancy Smith, *Owner*
EMP: 2
SALES (est): 155.1K **Privately Held**
SIC: 3229 Cooking utensils, glass or glass ceramic

(G-2738)
WINTHROP TOOL LLC
55 Plains Rd (06426-1504)
PHONE.....................860 526-9079
Frederick J Malcarne,
EMP: 7
SQ FT: 2,500
SALES (est): 800K **Privately Held**
WEB: www.tmarksman.com
SIC: 3599 3544 Machine shop, jobbing & repair; special dies, tools, jigs & fixtures

Fabyan
Windham County

(G-2739)
SCOTS LANDING
929 Riverside Dr (06245)
PHONE.....................860 923-0437
EMP: 3
SALES (est): 207K **Privately Held**
SIC: 3826 Mfg Analytical Instruments

Fairfield
Fairfield County

(G-2740)
200 MILL PLAIN ROAD LLC
1411 Cross Hwy (06824-1706)
PHONE.....................203 254-0113
Terrence Keegan, *Principal*
EMP: 3
SALES (est): 76.2K **Privately Held**
SIC: 2711 Newspapers

(G-2741)
AB CUSTOM CABINETRY LLC
10 Vermont Ave (06824-5343)
PHONE.....................203 367-5047
Andres Almanza, *Principal*
EMP: 1
SALES (est): 66K **Privately Held**
SIC: 2434 Wood kitchen cabinets

(G-2742)
AB CUSTOM WOODWORK LLC
238 Roseville Ter (06824-4131)
PHONE.....................203 334-7882
Artur Bogusiewicz, *Manager*
EMP: 2 **EST:** 2011
SALES (est): 209.4K **Privately Held**
SIC: 2431 Millwork

(G-2743)
ACME UNITED CORPORATION (PA)
55 Walls Dr Ste 201 (06824-5163)
PHONE.....................203 254-6060
Walter C Johnsen, *Ch of Bd*
Brian S Olschan, *President*
Lisa Apostol, *Vice Pres*
John Sullivan, *Vice Pres*
Al Peterson, *Purchasing*
◆ **EMP:** 245
SQ FT: 15,400
SALES: 137.3MM **Publicly Held**
WEB: www.acmeunited.com
SIC: 3421 2499 3842 3579 Scissors, hand; shears, hand; rulers & rules, wood; first aid, snake bite & burn kits; pencil sharpeners; erasers: rubber or rubber & abrasive combined; tape measures

(G-2744)
ADVANCED GOLF NUTRITION LLC
536 Hemlock Dr (06824-1855)
PHONE.....................203 554-9120
Gerard Mullally, *Mng Member*
Gerard Mullally, *Mng Member*
EMP: 2
SALES: 200K **Privately Held**
SIC: 3999 5149 Barber & beauty shop equipment; health foods

(G-2745)
ADVANCED PHOTONICS INTL INC
96 Lamplighter Ln (06825-2321)
PHONE.....................203 259-0437

Dorothy Zweibaum, *President*
Frederic Zweibaum, *Vice Pres*
EMP: 3
SALES (est): 314.2K **Privately Held**
WEB: www.advancedphotonicsintl.com
SIC: 3699 3827 Laser systems & equipment; optical instruments & lenses

(G-2746)
AJK PUBLISHING
296 Partridge Ln (06824-2916)
PHONE.....................203 259-8026
Alice J Katz, *Owner*
EMP: 1
SALES (est): 50.9K **Privately Held**
SIC: 2731 Books: publishing only

(G-2747)
ARCAT INC
173 Sherman St (06824-5823)
PHONE.....................203 929-9444
F P Jannott, *President*
Don Mahlmeister, *District Mgr*
Leslie L Jannott, *Vice Pres*
Carla Nash, *Mktg Dir*
Roger Johnson, *Manager*
EMP: 8
SQ FT: 1,600
SALES (est): 958.6K **Privately Held**
WEB: www.arcat.com
SIC: 2752 2741 Publication printing, lithographic; miscellaneous publishing

(G-2748)
ARCHITECTURAL DOOR CORP
Also Called: Garage Door Center
75 N Pine Creek Rd (06824-4919)
PHONE.....................203 255-3033
Gary Zacchia, *CEO*
EMP: 2
SALES (est): 946.4K **Privately Held**
SIC: 2431 Millwork

(G-2749)
ASPETUCK BREW LAB LLC
167 Woods End Rd (06824-3043)
PHONE.....................203 256-1902
Peter P I Cowles, *Owner*
EMP: 1 **EST:** 2014
SALES (est): 84.2K **Privately Held**
SIC: 2082 Malt beverages

(G-2750)
BABCOCK & KING INCORPORATED (PA)
750 Commerce Dr (06825-5519)
PHONE.....................203 336-7989
David S Babcock, *President*
Mary K Babcock, *Chairman*
Brian Feidt, *Treasurer*
EMP: 7
SALES (est): 1MM **Privately Held**
SIC: 2891 5032 Cement, except linoleum & tile; concrete mixtures

(G-2751)
BDG EMBROIDERY
206 Romanock Rd (06825-7234)
PHONE.....................203 258-0175
Kathleen Reale, *Principal*
EMP: 1
SALES (est): 60.6K **Privately Held**
SIC: 2395 Embroidery & art needlework

(G-2752)
BEEHIVE HEAT TREATING SVCS INC
373 Katona Dr (06824-4047)
PHONE.....................203 866-1635
Barry Brown, *President*
Hector Martinez, *Vice Pres*
EMP: 8
SALES (est): 629.4K **Privately Held**
SIC: 3398 Metal heat treating

(G-2753)
BENCH PRESS 3 LLC
340 Joan Dr (06824-2237)
PHONE.....................203 848-5545
Jeffrey Pressman, *Principal*
EMP: 2
SALES (est): 128.5K **Privately Held**
SIC: 2741 Miscellaneous publishing

▲ = Import ▼=Export
◆ =Import/Export

GEOGRAPHIC SECTION
Fairfield - Fairfield County (G-2787)

(G-2754)
BG MACHINERY SERVICES LLC
66 Lola St (06825-1341)
PHONE.................................203 374-4732
Donald Grant,
EMP: 1 EST: 2009
SALES (est): 112.9K Privately Held
SIC: 3559 Optical lens machinery

(G-2755)
BIENNIX CORP
2490 Black Rock Tpke # 354 (06825-2400)
PHONE.................................203 254-1727
Clifford R Ennico, President
EMP: 1
SALES (est): 109K Privately Held
WEB: www.cliffennico.com
SIC: 2731 Book publishing

(G-2756)
CALMARE THERAPEUTICS INC (PA)
1375 Kings Hwy Ste 400 (06824-5380)
PHONE.................................203 368-6044
Peter Brennan, Ch of Bd
Conrad F Mir, President
Thomas P Richtarich, CFO
Stephen J D'Amato, Chief Mktg Ofcr
Donna Mays, Info Tech Mgr
EMP: 7
SQ FT: 2,700
SALES: 1.1MM Publicly Held
WEB: www.competitivetech.net
SIC: 3841 Surgical & medical instruments

(G-2757)
CAMARRO RESEARCH
345 Carroll Rd (06824-3071)
PHONE.................................203 254-1755
Kenneth Camarro, Owner
Theresa Camarro, Principal
EMP: 1
SALES: 150K Privately Held
SIC: 2721 8742 Trade journals: publishing only, not printed on site; business consultant

(G-2758)
CAREM ASSOC
178 Autumn Ridge Rd (06825-1002)
PHONE.................................203 372-6788
Stephen Balgach, Owner
EMP: 1
SALES (est): 92.4K Privately Held
SIC: 3053 Gaskets, packing & sealing devices

(G-2759)
CHARLES W SIMMONS
Also Called: Casting Development Associates
640 Unquowa Rd (06824-5034)
PHONE.................................203 254-3388
Charles Simmons, Owner
EMP: 1
SALES (est): 109.7K Privately Held
SIC: 3365 Aluminum foundries

(G-2760)
CHEMLOID CHEMICALS INC
399 N Benson Rd (06824-5131)
PHONE.................................203 255-7495
EMP: 1
SALES: 2MM Privately Held
SIC: 2843 Mfg Surface Active Agents

(G-2761)
CIMBALI USA INC
418 Meadow St Ste 203 (06824-5365)
PHONE.................................203 254-6046
Erwin Pas, President
Assaad Benabid, Vice Pres
Darcy Simonis, Admin Sec
▲ EMP: 5
SQ FT: 2,500
SALES: 500K
SALES (corp-wide): 531.1K Privately Held
WEB: www.cimbali.com
SIC: 3556 Beverage machinery
HQ: Gruppo Cimbali Spa
  Via Manzoni 0017
  Binasco MI 20082
  029 004-91

(G-2762)
CIRCLE PUBLISHING LLC
1525 Kings Hwy (06824-5321)
PHONE.................................516 459-5016
Bruce Kerner, Principal
EMP: 2
SALES (est): 62.9K Privately Held
SIC: 2711 Newspapers

(G-2763)
CLARKTRON PRODUCTS INC
1525 Kings Hwy Ste 7 (06824-5321)
PHONE.................................203 333-6517
William F Mason Jr, President
EMP: 8 EST: 1950
SQ FT: 5,000
SALES (est): 1.1MM Privately Held
WEB: www.clarktron.com
SIC: 3625 Electric controls & control accessories, industrial

(G-2764)
CLEAN AIR GROUP INC
Also Called: Atmosair
418 Meadow St Ste 204 (06824-5365)
PHONE.................................203 335-3700
Steve Levine, President
Carlos Gendron, Vice Pres
Ryota Aratani, Opers Staff
Tony Abate, Purch Agent
Michael Herz, CFO
EMP: 21
SQ FT: 1,500
SALES (est): 2.4MM Privately Held
SIC: 3564 Air purification equipment

(G-2765)
COASTAL SEAFOODS INC (PA)
35 Brentwood Ave Ste 4 (06824-5443)
P.O. Box 455, Ridgefield (06877-0455)
PHONE.................................203 431-0453
Robert Iseley, President
Linda Iseley, Corp Secy
EMP: 12
SQ FT: 5,000
SALES (est): 1.3MM Privately Held
SIC: 2092 5146 Crabcakes, frozen; crab meat, fresh: packaged in nonsealed containers; crabmeat, frozen; seafoods

(G-2766)
CONNECTICUT GREENSTAR INC
1157 Melville Ave (06825-2057)
P.O. Box 921, Los Olivos CA (93441-0921)
PHONE.................................203 368-1522
Val Luca, President
Olga Luca, Admin Sec
▲ EMP: 3
SALES (est): 210K Privately Held
SIC: 3429 Door opening & closing devices, except electrical

(G-2767)
CONNECTICUT TRADE COMPANY INC
1157 Melville Ave (06825-2057)
P.O. Box 921, Los Olivos CA (93441-0921)
PHONE.................................203 368-0398
Val Luca, President
▲ EMP: 3
SALES: 5MM Privately Held
SIC: 3429 7389 Door opening & closing devices, except electrical;

(G-2768)
CONVEXITY SCIENTIFIC LLC
418 Meadow St (06824-5364)
PHONE.................................949 637-1216
Ralph Mng, Principal
Ralph Finger, Mng Member
James Benjamin,
EMP: 3
SALES (est): 95.3K Privately Held
SIC: 3841 Inhalators, surgical & medical

(G-2769)
CORREIA WOOD WORKS LLC
79 Parkwood Rd (06824-7632)
PHONE.................................203 515-7670
Luciano G Correia, Manager
EMP: 1
SALES (est): 93.3K Privately Held
SIC: 2431 Millwork

(G-2770)
CUSTOM UPHOLSTERY WORKSHOP
10 Greenfield St (06824-4803)
PHONE.................................203 367-4231
John Hayes, Owner
EMP: 6
SQ FT: 3,000
SALES (est): 260.8K Privately Held
SIC: 7641 7389 2591 Reupholstery; interior decorating; window blinds; window shades

(G-2771)
DAYSPRING COMMUNICATIONS LLC
1220 Unquowa Rd W (06824-2809)
PHONE.................................336 775-2059
EMP: 2
SALES (est): 56.5K Privately Held
SIC: 7372 Prepackaged software

(G-2772)
DBEBZ APPAREL LLC
432 Old Post Rd (06824-6645)
PHONE.................................203 254-7356
David J Bebon, Mng Member
▲ EMP: 1
SALES (est): 109.7K Privately Held
SIC: 2326 Work apparel, except uniforms

(G-2773)
DEMATTIA CHARITABLE FOUND
163 Mistywood Ln (06824-1619)
PHONE.................................203 254-1558
Constance Mattia, Director
EMP: 2
SALES (est): 209.8K Privately Held
SIC: 2515 Foundations & platforms

(G-2774)
DIRECT SALES LLC (PA)
440 Sky Top Dr (06825-1219)
PHONE.................................203 371-2373
Anthony Reis,
EMP: 5
SQ FT: 8,200
SALES (est): 531.9K Privately Held
SIC: 3272 Building materials, except block or brick: concrete

(G-2775)
DOGWOOD PUBLISHING LLC
117 Deepwood Rd (06824-2213)
PHONE.................................203 292-3815
Joelle Fleming, Principal
EMP: 1
SALES (est): 39.4K Privately Held
SIC: 2741 Miscellaneous publishing

(G-2776)
DOMESTIC KITCHENS INC
515 Commerce Dr (06825-5541)
PHONE.................................203 368-1651
Pasquale Staltaro, President
Frank Staltaro, Corp Secy
EMP: 27
SALES (est): 4.2MM Privately Held
SIC: 2434 Wood kitchen cabinets

(G-2777)
DRONE IMAGING LLC
195 Wood House Rd (06824-1823)
PHONE.................................203 256-1151
Jeffrey Bloch, Principal
EMP: 2 EST: 2014
SALES (est): 108.7K Privately Held
SIC: 3721 Motorized aircraft

(G-2778)
EARLY ADVANTAGE LLC
426 Mine Hill Rd (06824-2151)
PHONE.................................203 259-6480
David Ward, Mng Member
▲ EMP: 10
SALES (est): 1.2MM Privately Held
WEB: www.early-advantage.com
SIC: 2731 Book publishing

(G-2779)
EDS PERFECT POLISHING
256 Pratt St (06824-6485)
PHONE.................................203 259-5187
Edwin Agosto, Principal
EMP: 1 EST: 2001
SALES (est): 100.9K Privately Held
SIC: 3471 Polishing, metals or formed products

(G-2780)
ELINCO INTERNATIONAL INC (PA)
1525 Kings Hwy (06824-5321)
PHONE.................................203 275-8885
Thomas McLaughlin, President
Greg Gilbert, Accounts Mgr
Brad Starr, Accounts Mgr
EMP: 2
SQ FT: 8,000
SALES (est): 403.6K Privately Held
SIC: 3621 5063 Motors & generators; motors, electric

(G-2781)
EMC CORPORATION
2150 Post Rd Fl 5 (06824-5669)
PHONE.................................203 418-4500
Raymond Banks, Partner
Dave Sheehan, General Mgr
EMP: 65
SALES (corp-wide): 90.6B Publicly Held
SIC: 3572 Computer storage devices
HQ: Emc Corporation
  176 South St
  Hopkinton MA 01748
  508 435-1000

(G-2782)
EMC7 LLC
149 Brookview Ave (06825-1867)
PHONE.................................203 429-4355
Rebecca Ryan, Principal
Curt Kibbe, Principal
David Orloff, Principal
EMP: 4
SALES (est): 170.2K Privately Held
SIC: 3572 Computer storage devices

(G-2783)
EXCLUSIVE DENIM
64 Grasmere Ave (06824-6136)
PHONE.................................203 549-9844
Daisy Lima, Principal
EMP: 2
SALES (est): 108.3K Privately Held
SIC: 2211 Denims

(G-2784)
FAIRFIELD BACKHOE LLC
1055 Old Academy Rd (06824-2051)
PHONE.................................203 247-4007
EMP: 2
SALES (est): 210K Privately Held
SIC: 3531 Mfg Construction Machinery

(G-2785)
FAIRFIELD POOL & EQUIPMENT CO (PA)
278 Meadow St (06824-5353)
PHONE.................................203 334-3600
Jeromy Luem, President
EMP: 6
SQ FT: 11,000
SALES (est): 1.9MM Privately Held
WEB: www.fairfieldpool.com
SIC: 3949 5999 1799 Swimming pools, except plastic; swimming pools, hot tubs & sauna equipment & supplies; swimming pools, above ground; swimming pool construction

(G-2786)
FOCUS NOW SOLUTIONS LLC
Also Called: Nootelligence
1140 Post Rd (06824-6020)
PHONE.................................203 247-9038
Ian O'Connell, Mng Member
Tyler Debussy,
Parjer Klingerman,
EMP: 3
SALES (est): 239.2K Privately Held
SIC: 2087 Beverage bases, concentrates, syrups, powders & mixes

(G-2787)
FREEDOM GRAFIX LLC
457 Castle Ave (06825-5446)
PHONE.................................815 900-6189
Timothy S Sturtevant, CEO
EMP: 1

Fairfield - Fairfield County (G-2788)

GEOGRAPHIC SECTION

SALES (est): 79.5K **Privately Held**
SIC: 3861 Photocopy machines

(G-2788)
FRESCOBENE FOODS LLC
185 Red Oak Rd (06824-1898)
PHONE.....................203 610-4688
Lisa Maute, *CEO*
Ann Riffice, *Principal*
EMP: 3
SALES (est): 206.1K **Privately Held**
SIC: 2099 Food preparations

(G-2789)
GARDEN GLASS LLC
578 Stratfield Rd (06825-1850)
PHONE.....................203 330-8789
Adelle Valovich, *Principal*
EMP: 2
SALES (est): 81K **Privately Held**
SIC: 3231 Art glass: made from purchased glass

(G-2790)
GE ENRGY PWR CNVERSION USA INC
3135 Eon Tpke (06828)
PHONE.....................203 373-2211
EMP: 3
SALES (corp-wide): 121.6B **Publicly Held**
SIC: 3629 Power conversion units, a.c. to d.c.: static-electric
HQ: Ge Energy Power Conversion Usa Inc.
100 E Kensinger Dr # 500
Cranberry Township PA 16066
412 967-0765

(G-2791)
GE TRANSPORTATION PARTS LLC
3135 Easton Tpke (06828-0002)
P.O. Box 60320, Fort Myers FL (33906-6320)
PHONE.....................816 650-6171
Eric Vorndran, *Engineer*
EMP: 8 EST: 2001
SALES (est): 386.8K
SALES (corp-wide): 121.6B **Publicly Held**
SIC: 3511 Turbines & turbine generator sets
PA: General Electric Company
41 Farnsworth St
Boston MA 02210
617 443-3000

(G-2792)
GRAYBARK ENTERPRISES LLC
20 Governors Ln (06824-2106)
PHONE.....................203 255-4503
Mark Grayson,
EMP: 9
SALES (est): 439.6K **Privately Held**
SIC: 7372 Prepackaged software

(G-2793)
HEALING ARTS PRESS LLC
432 Lockwood Rd (06825-2649)
PHONE.....................203 374-2084
Alan B Felman, *Principal*
EMP: 1
SALES (est): 58.2K **Privately Held**
SIC: 2741 Miscellaneous publishing

(G-2794)
HOOKED ON FISHING CHARTERS
15 Verna Hill Rd (06824-2157)
PHONE.....................203 257-3431
Rick A Dayhuff, *Principal*
EMP: 2
SALES (est): 113.9K **Privately Held**
SIC: 2399 Fishing nets

(G-2795)
INITIAL REACTION LLC
303 Linwood Ave Ste 3 (06824-4900)
PHONE.....................203 255-1200
Diane M Mirabile, *Partner*
EMP: 2
SALES (est): 225.5K **Privately Held**
WEB: www.initialreaction.net
SIC: 3961 Jewelry apparel, non-precious metals

(G-2796)
INTERNATIONAL CNSTR PDTS RES
750 Commerce Dr (06825-5519)
PHONE.....................203 336-7900
David Babcock, *President*
Mary Babcock, *Admin Sec*
EMP: 1
SALES (est): 97.2K
SALES (corp-wide): 1MM **Privately Held**
SIC: 2899 Concrete curing & hardening compounds
PA: Babcock & King, Incorporated
750 Commerce Dr
Fairfield CT 06825
203 336-7989

(G-2797)
IPC SYSTEMS INC
Also Called: IPC Information Systems
777 Commerce Dr Ste 100 (06825-5500)
PHONE.....................860 271-4100
Susan Mergenthaler, *COO*
Tim Bachmann, *Senior Engr*
Peter Gyurko, *Branch Mgr*
Tammy Negralle, *Manager*
Robin Zachariewicz, *Manager*
EMP: 135
SALES (corp-wide): 587.5MM **Privately Held**
SIC: 3661 Telephone & telegraph apparatus
PA: I.P.C. Systems, Inc.
3 2nd St Fl Plz10
Jersey City NJ 07311
201 253-2000

(G-2798)
IRONIC CHEMICALS LLC
252 Old Oaks Rd (06825-1932)
PHONE.....................646 352-2692
Scott Banta,
Alan West,
EMP: 2
SALES (est): 94K **Privately Held**
SIC: 2869 Industrial organic chemicals

(G-2799)
JAKSY 2 LLC
Also Called: Cold Stone Creamery
2323 Black Rock Tpke (06825-3220)
PHONE.....................203 371-4111
Syed Usman, *Mng Member*
EMP: 5
SALES (est): 92.3K **Privately Held**
SIC: 5812 2024 Ice cream stands or dairy bars; ice cream & frozen desserts

(G-2800)
JEAN ELTON STUDIOS LLC
1305 Round Hill Rd (06824-7329)
PHONE.....................917 287-0480
William Barker, *Principal*
Lois Barker,
EMP: 2 EST: 1973
SALES (est): 88.5K **Privately Held**
WEB: www.jeanelton.com
SIC: 3269 Art & ornamental ware, pottery

(G-2801)
JESSICA HOWARD CERAMICS
457 Wilson St (06825-1427)
PHONE.....................646 295-4778
Jessica Howard, *Principal*
EMP: 2
SALES (est): 57.1K **Privately Held**
SIC: 3269 Pottery products

(G-2802)
JK MOTORSPORTS
500 Grasmere Ave (06824-6146)
PHONE.....................203 255-9120
Jerome Kozera, *Principal*
EMP: 4
SALES (est): 270K **Privately Held**
SIC: 3714 Motor vehicle parts & accessories

(G-2803)
JOLEN CREAM BLEACH CORP
25 Walls Dr (06824-5156)
P.O. Box 458 (06824-0458)
PHONE.....................203 259-8779
Evelyn Kossak, *President*
Melissa Flores, *Publications*
EMP: 15 EST: 1964
SQ FT: 8,000
SALES (est): 1.5MM **Privately Held**
SIC: 2844 Face creams or lotions

(G-2804)
JUDITH BENNETT (PA)
Also Called: Red Coach Sand & Stone
27 Noyes Rd (06824-3842)
PHONE.....................203 255-6363
Judith Bennett, *Owner*
EMP: 3
SALES (est): 207.1K **Privately Held**
SIC: 4212 1442 Dump truck haulage; sand mining; gravel mining

(G-2805)
KATONA BAKERY LLC
1189 Post Rd Ste 3b (06824-6046)
PHONE.....................203 337-5349
Ken Kleban,
EMP: 22
SALES (est): 727.4K **Privately Held**
SIC: 2051 Bread, cake & related products

(G-2806)
KITTY GUERRILLA FILMS
25 Brett Rd (06824-1718)
PHONE.....................203 259-8395
John E David, *Principal*
EMP: 1
SALES (est): 70.5K **Privately Held**
SIC: 3861 Motion picture film

(G-2807)
KYUNG PAE SERVICING CO LLC
1910 Black Rock Tpke (06825-3543)
PHONE.....................203 394-7472
Son Mee, *Administration*
EMP: 2
SALES (est): 83.6K **Privately Held**
SIC: 1389 Roustabout service

(G-2808)
L R K COMMUNICATIONS INC
Also Called: American Litho
96 Toll House Ln (06825-1030)
PHONE.....................203 372-1456
Lionel Ketchian, *President*
Lionel R Ketchian, *President*
Barbara E Ketchian, *Corp Secy*
Glen L Ketchian, *Vice Pres*
EMP: 4
SQ FT: 1,000
SALES (est): 497.9K **Privately Held**
WEB: www.lrkcommunications.com
SIC: 2759 Commercial printing

(G-2809)
LAURA SPECTOR RUSTIC DESIGN
786 Westport Tpke (06824-1639)
PHONE.....................203 254-3952
Laura Spector, *Owner*
EMP: 1
SALES (est): 61.5K **Privately Held**
WEB: www.lauraspectorrusticdesign.com
SIC: 2392 Household furnishings

(G-2810)
LIFETIME ACRYLIC SIGNS INC
593 Cascade Dr (06825-2300)
PHONE.....................203 255-6751
Joel Bernstein, *President*
EMP: 8 EST: 1957
SQ FT: 8,000
SALES (est): 591K **Privately Held**
SIC: 3993 Letters for signs, metal

(G-2811)
LITTLE KING PRESS
15 May St (06825-7439)
PHONE.....................203 981-2324
Ryan Santangelo, *Principal*
EMP: 2 EST: 2011
SALES (est): 89K **Privately Held**
SIC: 2741 Miscellaneous publishing

(G-2812)
MANGLADESH LLC
172 Forest Ave (06824-6572)
PHONE.....................203 299-0697
Haley Elegant, *Mng Member*
EMP: 1
SQ FT: 1,000
SALES (est): 609.4K **Privately Held**
SIC: 5621 2339 7389 Ready-to-wear apparel, women's; bathing suits: women's, misses' & juniors'; beachwear: women's, misses' & juniors'; apparel designers, commercial

(G-2813)
MEDICAL INDUSTRIES AMERICA LLC
1735 Post Rd Ste 6 (06824-5700)
PHONE.....................203 254-8080
Patricia A Richard,
EMP: 1
SALES (est): 94.8K **Privately Held**
SIC: 3842 Orthopedic appliances

(G-2814)
MET TECH INC
1901 Post Rd (06824-5721)
PHONE.....................203 254-9319
Thomas Quick, *President*
Thomas Qucik, *President*
EMP: 3 EST: 1993
SALES (est): 500K **Privately Held**
WEB: www.mettech.com
SIC: 3449 Miscellaneous metalwork

(G-2815)
MICKEY HERBST
Also Called: Quality Printing & Graphics
32 Laurel St (06825-4218)
PHONE.....................203 993-5879
Ryan Zygmont, *Owner*
EMP: 5
SALES (est): 234K **Privately Held**
SIC: 2759 Commercial printing

(G-2816)
MODERN ELECTRONIC FAX & CMPT
Also Called: Modern Elec Fax & Computers
65 Milton St (06825-6921)
PHONE.....................203 292-6520
Naresh Doshi, *President*
EMP: 5
SQ FT: 2,000
SALES (est): 729.3K **Privately Held**
WEB: www.mecdot.com
SIC: 3571 7373 1731 7378 Electronic computers; systems integration services; local area network (LAN) systems integrator; electrical work; computer installation; computer maintenance & repair; electronic equipment repair

(G-2817)
MOHICAN VALLEY CONCRETE CORP
195 Ardmore St (06824-6127)
PHONE.....................203 254-7133
Mark Greenawalt, *CEO*
Thomas Greenawalt II, *Vice Pres*
Donna Sedgewick, *Treasurer*
Thomas Greenawalt Sr, *Shareholder*
EMP: 20
SQ FT: 2,700
SALES (est): 3.9MM **Privately Held**
WEB: www.mohicanvalley.com
SIC: 3273 Ready-mixed concrete

(G-2818)
MOHICAN VLY SAND & GRAV CORP
195 Ardmore St (06824-6127)
PHONE.....................203 254-7133
Mark Greenawalt Jr, *President*
Donna Sedgewick, *Corp Secy*
Thomas Greenawalt Jr, *Vice Pres*
Thomas Greenawalt Sr, *Shareholder*
EMP: 15
SQ FT: 2,500
SALES (est): 5MM **Privately Held**
SIC: 3273 Ready-mixed concrete

(G-2819)
MOMENTIVE PRFMCE MTLS USA INC
385 Lockwood Rd (06825-2650)
PHONE.....................203 240-5543
Beatriz C Blanco, *Principal*
EMP: 2
SALES (est): 190K **Privately Held**
SIC: 2865 Chemical indicators

Fairfield - Fairfield County

(G-2820)
MOTIV TECHNOLOGY INC
145 Ridgeview Ave (06825-3327)
PHONE..................203 371-7011
EMP: 2
SALES (est): 164.2K Privately Held
SIC: 3842 Mfg Surgical Appliances/Supplies

(G-2821)
MUSIC TOGETHER FAIRFIELD CHILD
76 Walbin Ct (06824-2975)
PHONE..................203 256-1656
Jacqueline Jacobs, *Director*
EMP: 3
SALES (est): 207.6K Privately Held
WEB: www.mtfcinfo.com
SIC: 8299 2741 Music school; miscellaneous publishing

(G-2822)
NCI WOODWORKING LLC LLC
230 Hollydale Rd (06824-2228)
PHONE..................203 391-1614
Charles Ferreira, *Principal*
EMP: 2
SALES (est): 72K Privately Held
SIC: 2431 Millwork

(G-2823)
OCCUPTNAL TRVL MDCINE SUPS LLC
2490 Black Rock Tpke (06825-2400)
PHONE..................866 206-4496
David Maffei, *Principal*
EMP: 2
SALES (est): 89K Privately Held
SIC: 2761 Manifold business forms

(G-2824)
ONE KID LLC
160 Carter Henry Dr (06824-5701)
PHONE..................203 254-9978
Eric Autard, *Branch Mgr*
EMP: 1
SALES (corp-wide): 342.8K Privately Held
SIC: 2369 5137 5641 Girls' & children's outerwear; children's goods; children's & infants' wear stores
PA: One Kid Llc
    188 Compo Rd S
    Westport CT 06880
    203 254-9978

(G-2825)
OPAL MANNING COMPANY INC
Also Called: Manning International
195 Grovers Ave (06824)
PHONE..................203 292-6981
Gerald Manning, *President*
Darryl Manning, *Vice Pres*
EMP: 2 EST: 1940
SALES (est): 349.3K Privately Held
SIC: 5094 3299 3915 Precious stones (gems); synthetic stones, for gem stones & industrial use; jewel cutting, drilling, polishing, recutting or setting

(G-2826)
PARISH ASSOCIATES INC
1383 Kings Hwy (06824-5312)
P.O. Box 2543, Bridgeport (06608-0543)
PHONE..................203 335-4100
Paul C Zec, *President*
▲ EMP: 5
SQ FT: 3,600
SALES (est): 613.3K Privately Held
SIC: 2511 Wood lawn & garden furniture

(G-2827)
PETER ARCH WOODWORKING LLC
611 Church Hill Rd (06825-1372)
PHONE..................203 374-9977
Piotr A Karpiel, *Manager*
EMP: 1
SALES (est): 129.2K Privately Held
SIC: 2431 Woodwork, interior & ornamental

(G-2828)
PINNACLE PRESS LLC
1700 Post Rd (06824-5795)
PHONE..................203 254-1947
Christopher Fairchild, *Principal*
EMP: 2 EST: 2013
SALES (est): 202.7K Privately Held
SIC: 2741 Miscellaneous publishing

(G-2829)
PLASTICS TECHNIQUES
160 Castle Ave (06825-5430)
PHONE..................203 335-8048
Fred Hull Jr, *Owner*
Carol Hull, *Manager*
EMP: 2
SALES (est): 35K Privately Held
SIC: 3089 Molding primary plastic

(G-2830)
POLSTER INDUSTRIES LLC
115 Verna Hill Rd (06824-2162)
PHONE..................203 521-8517
Patrick Polster, *Principal*
EMP: 2
SALES (est): 148.4K Privately Held
SIC: 3999 Manufacturing industries

(G-2831)
POWER STRATEGIES LLC
2384 Redding Rd (06824-1760)
PHONE..................203 254-9926
J Norman Allen, *Principal*
EMP: 3
SALES (est): 176.1K Privately Held
SIC: 3621 Motors & generators

(G-2832)
PROTIVITI INC
401 Fairfield Woods Rd (06825-2744)
PHONE..................203 371-5542
EMP: 1
SALES (est): 39.7K Privately Held
SIC: 3251 Brick & structural clay tile

(G-2833)
RBC LINEAR PRECISION PDTS INC
60 Round Hill Rd (06825-5172)
PHONE..................203 255-1511
EMP: 4
SALES (est): 347K
SALES (corp-wide): 702.5MM Publicly Held
SIC: 3562 Ball & roller bearings
PA: Rbc Bearings Incorporated
    102 Willenbrock Rd
    Oxford CT 06478
    203 267-7001

(G-2834)
RC BIGELOW INC (PA)
Also Called: Bigelow Tea
201 Black Rock Tpke (06825-5512)
PHONE..................888 244-3569
David C Bigelow, *Ch of Bd*
Cindi Bigelow, *President*
Cynthia Bigelow, *Co-President*
Lori Bigelow, *Co-President*
Eunice Bigelow, *Co-COB*
◆ EMP: 170 EST: 1945
SQ FT: 113,000
SALES (est): 94.8MM Privately Held
WEB: www.rcbigelow.com
SIC: 2099 Tea blending

(G-2835)
RESULTS-BASED OUTSOURCING INC
2490 Blck Rock Tpke # 344 (06825-2400)
PHONE..................203 635-7600
Mary Ellen Schloth, *Chairman*
EMP: 2
SALES (est): 70.6K Privately Held
SIC: 7372 Business oriented computer software

(G-2836)
RICHARD SADOWSKI
Also Called: Acme Railing Company
290 Euclid Ave (06825-1750)
PHONE..................203 372-2151
Richard Sadowski, *Owner*
EMP: 1 EST: 1973
SALES (est): 112.2K Privately Held
SIC: 1799 3446 3444 Ornamental metal work; architectural metalwork; sheet metalwork

(G-2837)
RIVERSIDE BAKING COMPANY LLC
1891 Post Rd (06824-5742)
PHONE..................203 451-0331
Richard Schneider, *Principal*
EMP: 4
SALES (est): 99.1K Privately Held
SIC: 2051 Bread, cake & related products

(G-2838)
ROSEMARY HALLGARTEN INC
116 Sherman St (06824-5822)
PHONE..................203 259-1003
Rosemary Hallgarten, *President*
Erin Delottie, *Business Mgr*
EMP: 1 EST: 1999
SALES (est): 107.1K Privately Held
SIC: 2273 Carpets & rugs

(G-2839)
ROTOUNDERWORLD LLC
2490 Black Rock Tpke (06825-2400)
PHONE..................202 236-7103
Matthew Kelley,
EMP: 1
SALES: 150K Privately Held
SIC: 2741 4832 7371 7389 Miscellaneous publishing; sports; computer software development & applications;

(G-2840)
SABON INDUSTRIES INC
150 Jennie Ln (06824-1914)
PHONE..................203 255-8880
Leslie N Wilder, *President*
Leslie Wilder, *Owner*
EMP: 6
SQ FT: 6,000
SALES (est): 550K Privately Held
WEB: www.sabonindustries.com
SIC: 2522 Office furniture, except wood

(G-2841)
SALLIE GAWRON
Also Called: Caseysediblescom
105 Blaine St (06824-5805)
PHONE..................203 258-9851
Sallie Gawron, *Principal*
EMP: 1
SALES (est): 49K Privately Held
SIC: 2844 Toilet preparations

(G-2842)
SANCO ENERGY
41 Riders Ln (06824-1940)
PHONE..................203 259-5914
EMP: 12
SALES (est): 637.5K Privately Held
SIC: 2869 Ethanol Manufacturing

(G-2843)
SCAP MOTORS INC
Also Called: Jeep
421 Tunxis Hill Rd (06824-4413)
PHONE..................203 384-0005
Geza Scap, *President*
Peter Kirby, *Business Mgr*
Julie Scap, *Treasurer*
Rick Hecker, *Sales Mgr*
Vid Sentocnik, *Manager*
EMP: 150
SQ FT: 58,000
SALES (est): 62.9MM Privately Held
SIC: 5511 3724 Automobiles, new & used; aircraft engines & engine parts

(G-2844)
SCHINDLER COMBUSTION LLC
159 Tahmore Dr (06825-2513)
PHONE..................203 371-5068
Edmund G Schindler,
EMP: 3 EST: 2015
SALES (est): 288.3K Privately Held
SIC: 3433 Heating equipment, except electric

(G-2845)
SCRAPEITRX LLC
363 Hemlock Rd (06824-1857)
PHONE..................203 918-8323
David Harvey,
EMP: 2 EST: 2017
SALES (est): 51.8K Privately Held
SIC: 3999 Manufacturing industries

(G-2846)
SHELDON AUTOMOTIVE ENTERPRISES
273 Wheeler Park Ave (06825-1180)
PHONE..................203 372-4948
EMP: 19
SALES: 3.6MM Privately Held
SIC: 5169 2992 Mfg Lubricating Oils/Greases Whol Chemicals/Products

(G-2847)
SHELDON WOODWORKS
895 Galloping Hill Rd (06824-7128)
PHONE..................203 260-2703
EMP: 2
SALES (est): 85.2K Privately Held
SIC: 2431 Millwork

(G-2848)
SIXFURLONGS LLC
382 Round Hill Rd (06824-5116)
PHONE..................203 255-8553
John Short, *Principal*
EMP: 4
SALES (est): 239.3K Privately Held
SIC: 2721 7313 Magazines: publishing only, not printed on site; magazine advertising representative

(G-2849)
SNREVIEW
197 Fairchild Ave (06825-4856)
PHONE..................203 366-5991
Joseph Conlin, *Owner*
EMP: 1
SALES (est): 81.1K Privately Held
SIC: 2721 Periodicals

(G-2850)
SPECIALTY METLS SMLTERS & RFNE
2490 Black Rock Tpke (06825-2400)
PHONE..................203 366-2500
Daniel Fried, *Mng Member*
EMP: 2
SQ FT: 3,500
SALES (est): 238.3K Privately Held
SIC: 3339 Gold refining (primary)

(G-2851)
SUNNY DAES OF FAIRFIELD
2505 Black Rock Tpke # 4 (06825-2408)
PHONE..................203 372-3058
Sergio Keskin, *Principal*
EMP: 2
SALES (est): 151.9K Privately Held
SIC: 2024 Ice cream & frozen desserts

(G-2852)
SYRVER LLC
Also Called: Syrver.com
501 Kings Hwy E Ste 201 (06825-4870)
PHONE..................203 598-5810
Peter Clayton,
EMP: 1 EST: 2016
SALES: 100K Privately Held
SIC: 7372 Application computer software

(G-2853)
TECHNISONIC RESEARCH INC
328 Commerce Dr (06825-5560)
PHONE..................203 368-3600
Kenneth Thompson, *President*
Joseph Di Blasi, *Vice Pres*
Tony Ruiz, *Sales Staff*
EMP: 9
SQ FT: 3,000
SALES (est): 2MM Privately Held
SIC: 3829 Ultrasonic testing equipment

(G-2854)
TECHNOLOGY INTEGRATORS INC
136 Szost Dr (06824-4059)
PHONE..................203 333-7185
Paul Mazzo, *President*

Fairfield - Fairfield County (G-2855)

EMP: 2
SALES: 160K **Privately Held**
SIC: **3825** Network analyzers

(G-2855)
THINK BIG PUBLICATIONS LLC
44 Moody Ave (06825-1925)
PHONE..................................203 685-4957
Brett Ingram, *Principal*
EMP: 1
SALES (est): 75.2K **Privately Held**
SIC: **2741** Miscellaneous publishing

(G-2856)
THOR AUDIO
315 Palamar Dr (06825-2539)
PHONE..................................203 373-9264
Paul Marks, *Owner*
EMP: 2
SALES (est): 151.1K **Privately Held**
SIC: **3651** Household audio equipment

(G-2857)
TINPLEX CORPORATION
210 Stillson Rd (06825-3227)
PHONE..................................203 335-8217
Colin Williams, *Branch Mgr*
EMP: 2
SALES (corp-wide): 804.4K **Privately Held**
WEB: www.tinplex.com
SIC: **3312** Tinplate
PA: Tinplex Corporation
1501 Loveridge Rd Ste 10a
Pittsburg CA 94565
925 427-7500

(G-2858)
TRICYCLE HILL LLC
461 Riverside Dr (06824-6962)
PHONE..................................203 895-2217
Geertrui Van De Heyning, *Principal*
EMP: 2
SALES (est): 120.2K **Privately Held**
SIC: **3944** Tricycles

(G-2859)
TWELVE BEVERAGE LLC
Also Called: O Beverages
1552 Post Rd (06824-5935)
P.O. Box 727, Millbrook NY (12545-0727)
PHONE..................................203 256-8100
Edward Slade, *Mng Member*
EMP: 1
SALES (est): 56.6K **Privately Held**
SIC: **5499** 2086 Beverage stores; carbonated beverages, nonalcoholic: bottled & canned

(G-2860)
UNCLE WILEYS INC
1220 Post Rd Ste 2 (06824-6027)
PHONE..................................203 256-9313
Wiley Mullins, *President*
Greg Hill, *Admin Sec*
EMP: 16 EST: 1992
SQ FT: 6,000
SALES (est): 2.4MM **Privately Held**
WEB: www.unclewileys.com
SIC: **2099** Seasonings & spices

(G-2861)
UNIVERSAL THREAD GRINDING CO
30 Chambers St (06825-5594)
PHONE..................................203 336-1849
William H Everett Jr, *President*
Carl Linley, *Treasurer*
EMP: 15 EST: 1947
SQ FT: 10,000
SALES (est): 2.7MM **Privately Held**
WEB: www.universal-thread.com
SIC: **3452** Screws, metal

(G-2862)
UPS AUTHORIZED RETAILER
857 Post Rd (06824-6041)
PHONE..................................203 256-9991
Ketsly Gedeon, *Principal*
EMP: 3
SALES (est): 425.4K **Privately Held**
SIC: **7389** 2759 Mailbox rental & related service; notary publics; commercial printing

(G-2863)
VENU MAGAZINE LLC
840 Reef Rd (06824-6540)
PHONE..................................203 259-2075
Tracey Alison Thomas, *Principal*
Tracey Thomas, *Vice Pres*
▲ EMP: 3
SALES (est): 195.7K **Privately Held**
SIC: **2721** Magazines: publishing only, not printed on site

(G-2864)
VERSA PRINTS
136 Papermill Ln (06824-5012)
PHONE..................................203 256-2342
EMP: 2
SALES (est): 230.4K **Privately Held**
SIC: **2752** Lithographic Commercial Printing

(G-2865)
VOICE EXPRESS CORP
1525 Kings Hwy Ste 1 (06824-5321)
PHONE..................................203 221-7799
Geoffrey Stern, *President*
Rick Rubin, *Vice Pres*
▲ EMP: 3
SQ FT: 1,000
SALES: 1.5MM **Privately Held**
WEB: www.voice-express.com
SIC: **3669** Intercommunication systems, electric

(G-2866)
WAYNE WOODWORKS
1680 Cross Hwy (06824-1707)
PHONE..................................203 362-8084
Ronald Wayne, *Principal*
EMP: 2
SALES (est): 148.7K **Privately Held**
SIC: **2431** Millwork

(G-2867)
WDL SOFTWARE LLC
131 Vesper St (06825-4334)
PHONE..................................203 366-8640
Angelo J Deleon,
EMP: 2
SALES (est): 126.8K **Privately Held**
SIC: **7372** Prepackaged software

(G-2868)
YUMELISH FOOD LLC
90 Harvester Rd (06825-1125)
PHONE..................................203 522-6933
Lisa Boyne, *President*
EMP: 1
SALES (est): 67.7K **Privately Held**
SIC: **2099** Dips, except cheese & sour cream based

Falls Village
Litchfield County

(G-2869)
CROSSROADS DELI & FUEL LLC
123 Johnson Rd (06031-1618)
PHONE..................................860 824-8474
Michael Hodgkins, *Principal*
EMP: 6
SALES (est): 823.7K **Privately Held**
SIC: **2869** Fuels

(G-2870)
GABRIEL INC
Rr 126 (06031)
PHONE..................................860 824-1412
Gabriel Seymour, *President*
Catryna Seymour, *Vice Pres*
Whitney Seymour Jr, *Admin Sec*
EMP: 2
SALES (est): 168K **Privately Held**
SIC: **3911** 3961 Jewelry, precious metal; costume jewelry

(G-2871)
HAMILTONBOOKCOM LLC
147 Route 7 S (06031-1603)
P.O. Box 5007 (06031-5007)
PHONE..................................860 824-0275
John J Tuozzolo, *Principal*
EMP: 3

SALES (est): 179.1K **Privately Held**
SIC: **2711** Newspapers, publishing & printing

(G-2872)
SNOOGS & WILDE LLC
25 Main St (06031-1307)
PHONE..................................860 824-9865
Sarah Martinez,
EMP: 1
SALES (est): 74.8K **Privately Held**
SIC: **2759** Souvenir cards: printing

Farmington
Hartford County

(G-2873)
16 CASE LLC
16 Case St (06032-3401)
PHONE..................................860 995-0555
Bianca Ouchana, *Owner*
EMP: 1
SALES (est): 63.5K **Privately Held**
SIC: **3523** Farm machinery & equipment

(G-2874)
5W LLC
222 Main St Ste 251 (06032-3623)
PHONE..................................860 751-9209
Jennifer A Diederich, *Fmly & Gen Dent*
EMP: 1
SALES (est): 78K **Privately Held**
SIC: **3844** X-ray apparatus & tubes

(G-2875)
ACK INDUSTRIES LLC
7 Belgravia Ter (06032-1550)
PHONE..................................860 677-0056
Carol T Ficks, *Manager*
EMP: 1
SALES (est): 69.8K **Privately Held**
SIC: **3999** Manufacturing industries

(G-2876)
AGENCYPORT SOFTWARE CORP
Also Called: Sword-Agencyport
190 Farmington Ave (06032-1713)
PHONE..................................860 674-6135
EMP: 3
SALES (corp-wide): 21MM **Privately Held**
SIC: **7372** Operating systems computer software
HQ: Agencyport Software Corporation
22 Boston Wharf Rd 10
Boston MA 02210
866 539-6623

(G-2877)
ANAPO PLASTICS CORP
222 Main St 214 (06032-3623)
PHONE..................................860 874-8174
Carmelo Piraneo, *President*
EMP: 3
SALES (est): 319.6K **Privately Held**
SIC: **2821** Plastics materials & resins

(G-2878)
ARK INNOVATIONS LLC
Also Called: Mirror Go Round
4a Farmington Chase Cres (06032-3132)
PHONE..................................860 674-8800
David J Abrahamian, *Mng Member*
EMP: 1
SALES (est): 73.7K **Privately Held**
SIC: **8743** 3231 Sales promotion; framed mirrors

(G-2879)
ASSOCIATED WELDING PROCESS
Also Called: Associated Welding & Radiator
1091 Farmington Ave (06032-1464)
PHONE..................................860 677-0671
J P Lavigne, *Owner*
EMP: 1
SALES (est): 66K **Privately Held**
SIC: **7692** 7539 Automotive welding; radiator repair shop, automotive

(G-2880)
AVITUS ORTHOPAEDICS INC
400 Farmington Ave R2826 (06032-1913)
PHONE..................................860 637-9922
Neil Shah, *President*
EMP: 10
SALES (est): 1.3MM **Privately Held**
SIC: **3842** Orthopedic appliances

(G-2881)
BACTANA CORP
Also Called: Bactana Animal Health
400 Farmington Ave (06032-1913)
PHONE..................................203 716-1230
John Kallassy, *President*
EMP: 2
SALES (est): 90K **Privately Held**
SIC: **2836** 2023 2048 Veterinary biological products; dietary supplements, dairy & non-dairy based; feed supplements

(G-2882)
BARNES GROUP INC
Barnes Aerospace
80 Scott Swamp Rd (06032-2847)
PHONE..................................860 298-7740
Joel Rafaniello, *Vice Pres*
Gregory Milzcik, *Manager*
Robert Dutton, *Manager*
Jeff Cormier, *Analyst*
EMP: 8
SALES (corp-wide): 1.5B **Publicly Held**
WEB: www.barnesgroupinc.com
SIC: **3495** 3469 Wire springs; metal stampings
PA: Barnes Group Inc.
123 Main St
Bristol CT 06010
860 583-7070

(G-2883)
BEAN COUNTERS
1730 New Britain Ave (06032-3191)
PHONE..................................860 404-2930
Joe Tine, *Principal*
EMP: 1
SALES (est): 91.1K **Privately Held**
SIC: **3131** Counters

(G-2884)
BIOARRAY GENETICS INC
400 Farmington Ave (06032-1913)
PHONE..................................508 577-0205
Marcia V Fournier, *CEO*
EMP: 3
SALES (est): 182.9K **Privately Held**
SIC: **2835** In vitro & in vivo diagnostic substances

(G-2885)
BREACH INTELLIGENCE INC
Also Called: Polarity
6 S Ridge Rd (06032-3021)
PHONE..................................844 312-7001
Paul Battista, *CEO*
Edmund Dorsey, *Treasurer*
Joseph Rivela, *Admin Sec*
EMP: 20
SALES (est): 171.6K **Privately Held**
SIC: **7372** Application computer software

(G-2886)
BROADCASTMED INC
Also Called: Or-Live, Inc.
195 Farmington Ave (06032-1700)
PHONE..................................860 953-2900
Ross J Joel, *CEO*
Peter Gailey, *President*
Joslyn Builders, *Vice Pres*
Richard Meyer, *CFO*
Denise Callan, *Producer*
EMP: 22
SQ FT: 5,000
SALES: 5.1MM **Privately Held**
SIC: **2741**

(G-2887)
CARRIER CORPORATION
426 Colt Hwy (06032-2587)
PHONE..................................860 728-7000
Allen Johnson, *Principal*
Bryan Mitchell, *Advt Staff*
Maria Campanello, *Manager*
Jared Greczyn, *Manager*
Kara Rademacher, *Supervisor*
EMP: 4

GEOGRAPHIC SECTION
Farmington - Hartford County (G-2916)

SALES (corp-wide): 66.5B Publicly Held
SIC: 3585 Air conditioning equipment, complete
HQ: Carrier Corporation
13995 Pasteur Blvd
Palm Beach Gardens FL 33418
800 379-6484

(G-2888) CISCO SYSTEMS INC
50 Stanford Dr (06032-2474)
PHONE.................860 284-5500
Tim Jahrling, Sales Staff
Dave Chalfon, Branch Mgr
Mike Saviano, Manager
Bob Williston, Executive
EMP: 691
SALES (corp-wide): 51.9B Publicly Held
WEB: www.cisco.com
SIC: 3577 Data conversion equipment, media-to-media: computer
PA: Cisco Systems, Inc.
170 W Tasman Dr
San Jose CA 95134
408 526-4000

(G-2889) CLASSIC SCHOOL UNIFORMS LTD
15 Salisbury Way (06032-1439)
P.O. Box 883 (06034-0883)
PHONE.................860 677-7207
Stephen Viola, President
EMP: 2
SALES (est): 190K Privately Held
SIC: 2389 Uniforms & vestments

(G-2890) COMPUTER SOFTWARE EDUC SE
19 Salisbury Way (06032-1439)
PHONE.................860 677-4527
M Srinath, Owner
EMP: 2
SALES (est): 105.1K Privately Held
SIC: 7372 Prepackaged software

(G-2891) CONNECTCUT SPRING STMPING CORP
Also Called: Connecticut Spring & Stamping
48 Spring Ln (06032-3140)
PHONE.................860 677-1341
William Stevenson, President
Shawn Gibbons, President
Steve Dicke, Vice Pres
David Fischler, Vice Pres
Chuck Thomas, Vice Pres
▲ EMP: 500 EST: 1939
SQ FT: 150,000
SALES (est): 123.6MM Privately Held
SIC: 3469 3495 3493 Stamping metal for the trade; machine parts, stamped or pressed metal; wire springs; precision springs; steel springs, except wire

(G-2892) CONNECTICUT CONCRETE FORM INC
168 Brickyard Rd (06032-1202)
PHONE.................860 674-1314
Richard N Dahle, President
EMP: 18
SQ FT: 12,000
SALES (est): 3.4MM Privately Held
SIC: 3271 Blocks, concrete or cinder: standard

(G-2893) COROTEC CORP
145 Hyde Rd (06032-2846)
PHONE.................860 678-0038
Bruce D Stobbe, President
Steve Easterday, Treasurer
Ronald Seaman, VP Sales
Larry Krupnick, Admin Sec
EMP: 13
SQ FT: 16,000
SALES (est): 2.8MM
SALES (corp-wide): 1B Privately Held
WEB: www.corotec.com
SIC: 3613 Control panels, electric

HQ: Indel, Inc.
10 Indel Ave
Rancocas NJ 08073
609 267-9000

(G-2894) CT THERMOGRAPHY LLC
2 Forest Park Dr (06032-1445)
PHONE.................860 415-1150
EMP: 2
SALES (est): 73.2K Privately Held
SIC: 2759 Thermography

(G-2895) CT TOOL & MANUFACTURING LLC
4 Right Ln (06032-3148)
PHONE.................860 846-0800
EMP: 1
SALES (est): 54.1K Privately Held
SIC: 3541 Machine tools, metal cutting type

(G-2896) DATA MANAGEMENT INC
557 New Britain Ave (06032)
PHONE.................800 243-1969
EMP: 2 EST: 2012
SALES (est): 160K Privately Held
SIC: 2752 Lithographic Commercial Printing

(G-2897) DAYON MANUFACTURING INC
1820 New Britain Ave (06032-3114)
P.O. Box 588 (06034-0588)
PHONE.................860 677-8561
Leslie R Dayon, President
Rose Dayon Sonstroem, Vice Pres
Bozena Grabek, Plant Mgr
Kim Sonstroem, Treasurer
▲ EMP: 32 EST: 1957
SQ FT: 17,000
SALES (est): 5.6MM Privately Held
WEB: www.dayonmfg.com
SIC: 3495 3493 Precision springs; steel springs, except wire

(G-2898) DUNDEE HOLDING INC (DH)
36 Spring Ln (06032-3140)
PHONE.................860 677-1376
EMP: 8
SALES (est): 24MM Privately Held
SIC: 3324 3599 Steel Investment Foundry Mfg Industrial Machinery
HQ: Doncasters 456 Limited
Millennium Court
Burton-On-Trent STAFFS
133 286-4900

(G-2899) DUNNING SAND & GRAVEL COMPANY
105 Brickyard Rd (06032-1236)
PHONE.................860 677-1616
Benjamin Dunning, President
EMP: 12
SQ FT: 900
SALES (est): 4.6MM Privately Held
WEB: www.dunningsand.com
SIC: 1442 Common sand mining

(G-2900) DYADIC INNOVATIONS LLC
400 Farmington Ave R1844 (06032-1913)
P.O. Box 340, Willington (06279-0340)
PHONE.................630 738-4113
Ruth Lucas,
EMP: 2
SALES (est): 165.3K Privately Held
SIC: 3825 Instruments to measure electricity

(G-2901) EAST COAST PACKAGING LLC (PA)
210 Main St Unit 1182 (06034-7047)
P.O. Box 1182 (06034-1182)
PHONE.................860 675-8500
Laura Lachance, Mng Member
Michael Lachance,
EMP: 3
SQ FT: 5,000

SALES (est): 1.1MM Privately Held
WEB: www.eastcoastpkg.com
SIC: 2752 7389 Commercial printing, offset; packaging & labeling services

(G-2902) EBM-PAPST INC (DH)
100 Hyde Rd (06032-2835)
PHONE.................860 674-1515
Robert Sobolewski, CEO
Gerhard Sturm, Ch of Bd
William T John, Senior VP
Bill Aston, Opers Staff
Hogan Eng, Engineer
▲ EMP: 300 EST: 1981
SALES (est): 155.7MM
SALES (corp-wide): 958.9MM Privately Held
WEB: www.ebm.com
SIC: 5084 3564 Fans, industrial; blowers & fans

(G-2903) EDMUNDS MANUFACTURING COMPANY (PA)
Also Called: Edmunds Gages
45 Spring Ln (06032-3139)
P.O. Box 385 (06034-0385)
PHONE.................860 677-2813
Robert F Edmunds Sr, Ch of Bd
Robert F Edmunds Jr, Chairman
Robert F Edmunds III, Vice Pres
Gary A Hutchinson, Engineer
Scott Sokolik, Engineer
EMP: 100
SQ FT: 43,000
SALES (est): 13.6MM Privately Held
WEB: www.edmundsgages.com
SIC: 3829 3545 Measuring & controlling devices; machine tool accessories

(G-2904) FARMINGTON DISPLAYS INC
Also Called: F D I
21 Hyde Rd Ste 2 (06032-2859)
PHONE.................860 677-2497
Sabastian Ditomosso, President
Robert Ditommaso, General Mgr
Maria Fabrizi, Corp Secy
Paul F Ditomaso Jr, Vice Pres
Salvatore Ditomaso, Vice Pres
▲ EMP: 45
SQ FT: 130,000
SALES (est): 7.6MM Privately Held
WEB: www.fdi-group.com
SIC: 3993 Displays & cutouts, window & lobby

(G-2905) FARMINGTON MACHINE TOOLS LLC
81 Spring Ln (06032-3139)
PHONE.................860 676-7736
Tomasz Zieba,
EMP: 2
SALES (est): 224.5K Privately Held
SIC: 3541 Machine tools, metal cutting type

(G-2906) FIRST AIRWAY LLC
6 Hartfield Ln (06032-3169)
PHONE.................860 679-9285
EMP: 2
SALES (est): 172.6K Privately Held
SIC: 3841 Surgical & medical instruments

(G-2907) FOR CHILDREN WITH LOVE PUBLIC
290 Mountain Spring Rd (06032-1617)
PHONE.................860 940-9878
Catherine Gibson, Principal
EMP: 2 EST: 2017
SALES (est): 65.4K Privately Held
SIC: 2741 Miscellaneous publishing

(G-2908) FORMATRON LTD
21 Hyde Rd (06032-2859)
PHONE.................860 676-0227
Salvatore Ditommaso, President
Paul Ditommaso Jr, Principal
EMP: 18
SQ FT: 25,000

SALES (est): 2.6MM Privately Held
WEB: www.formatron.com
SIC: 2541 3999 Store & office display cases & fixtures; furniture, barber & beauty shop

(G-2909) FREDERICKS JF AERO LLC
25 Spring Ln (06032-3128)
PHONE.................860 677-2646
Robert Mongell, Mng Member
Jerry Sirois,
▼ EMP: 92
SQ FT: 25,000
SALES (est): 21.9MM
SALES (corp-wide): 19.7MM Privately Held
WEB: www.jfftool.com
SIC: 3724 Aircraft engines & engine parts
PA: Wentworth Manufacturing Llc
1102 Windham Rd
South Windham CT 06266
860 423-4575

(G-2910) FREQUENCY THERAPEUTICS INC
400 Farmington Ave (06032-1913)
PHONE.................978 436-0704
David L Lucchino, President
EMP: 26
SALES (corp-wide): 471.6K Publicly Held
SIC: 2834 Pharmaceutical preparations
PA: Frequency Therapeutics, Inc.
19 Presidential Way Fl 2
Woburn MA 01801
866 389-1970

(G-2911) FUEL LAB
20 Burnt Hill Rd (06032-2039)
PHONE.................860 677-4987
Shashi Bansal, Owner
EMP: 5 EST: 2011
SALES (est): 266.5K Privately Held
SIC: 2869 Fuels

(G-2912) GA REMANUFACTURING LLC
298 Scott Swamp Rd (06032-3116)
PHONE.................860 404-5186
Anthony Aniello, Principal
EMP: 1
SALES (est): 52.5K Privately Held
SIC: 3999 Manufacturing industries

(G-2913) GLOBAL PUBLICATIONS & MKTG LLC
222 Main St Ste 156 (06032-3623)
PHONE.................860 676-9109
Robert F Strano, Principal
Robert Strano, Principal
EMP: 2
SALES (est): 103K Privately Held
SIC: 2741 Miscellaneous publishing

(G-2914) GRIGEREK CO
11 Oakland Ave (06032-1720)
PHONE.................860 677-2560
Donald J Grigerek, Principal
EMP: 2
SALES (est): 159.9K Privately Held
SIC: 3641 Electric lamps

(G-2915) GROS-ITE PRECISION SPINDLE
21 Spring Ln (06032-3128)
PHONE.................860 679-7490
EMP: 1
SALES (est): 89.7K Privately Held
SIC: 3552 Textile machinery

(G-2916) IBNR LLC
190 Farmington Ave (06032-1713)
PHONE.................860 676-8600
Michael McCarthy, General Mgr
Thomas Byrne, COO
Vincent J Dowling Jr, Mng Member
EMP: 2
SALES (est): 134K Privately Held
SIC: 2721 Periodicals: publishing only

Farmington - Hartford County (G-2917)

(G-2917)
INNOVATION GROUP
76 Batterson Park Rd (06032-2571)
PHONE..........................860 674-2900
Euan King, *CEO*
Chris Benecick, *Exec VP*
Mitch Letho, *Exec VP*
Andrew Peet, *Exec VP*
Karen Sullivan, *Exec VP*
EMP: 22
SALES (est): 4.3MM **Privately Held**
SIC: **7372** 7371 Business oriented computer software; computer software systems analysis & design, custom
HQ: The Innovation Group Limited
Yarmouth House
Fareham HANTS
148 989-8300

(G-2918)
INNOVATIONCOOPERATIVE3D LLC
400 Farmington Ave (06032-1913)
PHONE..........................860 540-4172
Roger Laflamme, *CEO*
EMP: 2
SALES (est): 79.9K **Privately Held**
SIC: **3586** Measuring & dispensing pumps

(G-2919)
INTEGRITY MANUFACTURING LLC
1451 New Britain Ave # 1 (06032-3348)
PHONE..........................860 678-1599
James Gadoury, *Mng Member*
EMP: 6
SQ FT: 3,200
SALES (est): 679.2K **Privately Held**
SIC: **3423** Hand & edge tools

(G-2920)
JOHN PECORA
Also Called: John Pecora Photography
21 Hyde Rd Ste 4 (06032-2859)
PHONE..........................860 677-9323
John Pecora, *Owner*
EMP: 6
SQ FT: 7,000
SALES (est): 629.3K **Privately Held**
WEB: www.autograph.com
SIC: **7336** 7335 7221 3861 Commercial art & graphic design; photographic studio, commercial; photographer, still or video; photographic equipment & supplies; typesetting

(G-2921)
JOSEPH HANNOUSH FAMILY INC
Also Called: Hannoush Jewelers
500 Westfarms Mall (06032-2615)
PHONE..........................860 561-4651
Sultana Hannoush, *President*
Souad Hannoush, *Vice Pres*
Sharvel Hannoush, *Treasurer*
EMP: 10
SALES (est): 1.2MM **Privately Held**
SIC: **5944** 3911 7631 Jewelry, precious stones & precious metals; jewelry, precious metal; jewelry repair services

(G-2922)
KIP INC
Also Called: Norgren
72 Spring Ln (06032-3140)
PHONE..........................860 677-0272
Nick Testanero, *President*
Nicholas Testanero, *President*
Gary Fett, *Vice Pres*
James Etter, *Treasurer*
Donald McMahan, *Admin Sec*
▲ EMP: 189
SALES (est): 53.4K
SALES (corp-wide): 2.4B **Privately Held**
SIC: **3491** Solenoid valves
HQ: Norgren Limited
Blenheim Way
Lichfield STAFFS WS13
154 326-5000

(G-2923)
LAMBDAVISION INCORPORATED
400 Farmington Ave Mc6409 (06032-1913)
PHONE..........................860 486-6593
Nicole Wagner, *CEO*
Mark Van Allen, *President*
EMP: 3
SALES (est): 269.9K **Privately Held**
SIC: **3841** Surgical & medical instruments

(G-2924)
LATIN AMERICAN HOLDING INC (DH)
1 Carrier Pl (06032-2562)
PHONE..........................860 674-3000
Robert Galli, *Director*
EMP: 1 EST: 1990
SALES (est): 430.6K
SALES (corp-wide): 66.5B **Publicly Held**
SIC: **3585** Refrigeration & heating equipment
HQ: Carrier Corporation
13995 Pasteur Blvd
Palm Beach Gardens FL 33418
800 379-6484

(G-2925)
LIPID GENOMICS INC
400 Farmington Ave R1718 (06032-1913)
PHONE..........................443 465-3495
Annabelle Rodriguez-Oquendo, *President*
Eric Oquendo, *Business Mgr*
Debora Wilder, *Accountant*
EMP: 4 EST: 2014
SALES (est): 351.9K **Privately Held**
SIC: **2834** Proprietary drug products

(G-2926)
LITHOGRAPHICS INC
55 Spring Ln (06032-3139)
P.O. Box 767 (06034-0767)
PHONE..........................860 678-1660
Judith A Wilson, *President*
Thomas R Smith, *Vice Pres*
Glenn H Wilson, *Treasurer*
Twyla Lambert, *Sales Staff*
Karen Swain, *Manager*
EMP: 54
SQ FT: 31,800
SALES (est): 9.4MM **Privately Held**
WEB: www.litholand.com
SIC: **2752** Commercial printing, offset

(G-2927)
LITTLE APPLE LLC
5 Blackberry Rdg (06032-2072)
PHONE..........................860 404-2833
EMP: 2
SALES (est): 93K **Privately Held**
SIC: **3571** Mfg Electronic Computers

(G-2928)
MICROSOFT CORPORATION
74 Batterson Park Rd # 100 (06032-2591)
PHONE..........................860 678-3100
Anissa Battaglino, *Manager*
EMP: 45
SQ FT: 14,000
SALES (corp-wide): 125.8B **Publicly Held**
WEB: www.microsoft.com
SIC: **7372** Application computer software
PA: Microsoft Corporation
1 Microsoft Way
Redmond WA 98052
425 882-8080

(G-2929)
MICROTECHNOLOGIES INC
Also Called: Temperature Guard
128 Garden St (06032-2254)
P.O. Box 8126, Berlin (06037-8126)
PHONE..........................860 517-8314
Frank Geissler Jr, *President*
Stephen Geissler, *Admin Sec*
EMP: 2
SQ FT: 1,500
SALES (est): 1.1MM **Privately Held**
WEB: www.temperatureguard.com
SIC: **3823** 3829 Temperature measurement instruments, industrial; thermometers & temperature sensors

(G-2930)
MOBILE SENSE TECHNOLOGIES INC
400 Farmington Ave # 2858 (06032-1913)
PHONE..........................203 914-5375
Justin Chickles, *CEO*
Ki Chon, *Vice Pres*
EMP: 5
SALES (est): 399.4K **Privately Held**
SIC: **3845** Cardiographs; electrocardiographs; respiratory analysis equipment, electromedical

(G-2931)
MOTT CORPORATION (PA)
84 Spring Ln (06032-3142)
PHONE..........................860 793-6333
Boris F Levin, *CEO*
David Allen, *Vice Pres*
Thomas Fahey, *Vice Pres*
Peter Munk, *Project Mgr*
Michael Owsiany, *Project Mgr*
▲ EMP: 189 EST: 1959
SQ FT: 50,000
SALES (est): 58.4MM **Privately Held**
WEB: www.mottcorp.com
SIC: **3569** Filters

(G-2932)
MOTT CORPORATION
75 Spring Ln (06032-3139)
PHONE..........................800 289-6688
Roger Klene, *Manager*
EMP: 180
SQ FT: 36,000
SALES (est): 18.2MM
SALES (corp-wide): 58.4MM **Privately Held**
WEB: www.mottcorp.com
SIC: **3312** Tool & die steel & alloys
PA: Mott Corporation
84 Spring Ln
Farmington CT 06032
860 793-6333

(G-2933)
NATIONAL INTEGRATED INDS INC (PA)
Also Called: American Electro Products
322 Main St (06032-2961)
P.O. Box 4129, Waterbury (06704-0129)
PHONE..........................860 677-7995
Dennis M Burke, *President*
Sue Gerchy, *Engineer*
EMP: 135
SQ FT: 100,000
SALES (est): 15MM **Privately Held**
SIC: **3471** 3312 Electroplating & plating; electroplating of metals or formed products; plating of metals or formed products; tool & die steel & alloys

(G-2934)
NATURAL POLYMER DEVICES INC
400 Farmington Ave Mc6409 (06032-1913)
PHONE..........................860 679-7894
Mark Van Allen, *President*
EMP: 3
SALES (est): 184.2K **Privately Held**
SIC: **3841** Surgical & medical instruments

(G-2935)
NELSON STUD WELDING INC
36 Spring Ln (06032-3140)
PHONE..........................800 635-9353
Ken Caratelli, *President*
EMP: 2
SALES (corp-wide): 13.9B **Publicly Held**
SIC: **3452** 3548 Bolts, nuts, rivets & washers; welding apparatus
HQ: Nelson Stud Welding, Inc.
7900 W Ridge Rd
Elyria OH 44035
440 329-0400

(G-2936)
NEW ENGLAND AIRFOIL PDTS INC
36 Spring Ln (06032-3140)
PHONE..........................860 677-1376
Stefano Rosa Uliana, *President*
EMP: 25
SQ FT: 100,000
SALES (est): 2.1MM
SALES (corp-wide): 359K **Privately Held**
SIC: **3721** 3724 3795 Aircraft; aircraft engines & engine parts; tanks & tank components
HQ: Pietro Rosa T.B.M. Srl
Via Francesco Petrarca 7
Maniago PN 33085
042 771-503

(G-2937)
NEW ENGLAND SHOULDER ELBOW SOC
Also Called: Neses
232 Farmington Ave (06030-0001)
PHONE..........................860 679-6600
Jon JP Warner, *President*
Tally Lassiter, *Director*
Ben Banister, *Instructor*
EMP: 3
SALES (est): 124.5K **Privately Held**
SIC: **3842** Surgical appliances & supplies

(G-2938)
NORGREN INC
Also Called: IMI Precision Engineering
72 Spring Ln (06032-3140)
P.O. Box 468 (06034-0468)
PHONE..........................860 677-0272
Nick Testanero, *Branch Mgr*
EMP: 200
SALES (corp-wide): 2.4B **Privately Held**
WEB: www.norgren.com
SIC: **3492** Control valves, fluid power: hydraulic & pneumatic
HQ: Norgren, Inc.
5400 S Delaware St
Littleton CO 80120
303 794-5000

(G-2939)
NORTH AMERICAN ELEV SVCS CO (DH)
Also Called: Delta Elevator Service
1 Farm Springs Rd (06032-2572)
PHONE..........................860 676-6000
Micheal Hartigan, *President*
Kent Brittan, *Vice Pres*
Kathie Johnson, *Administration*
EMP: 20
SALES (est): 6MM
SALES (corp-wide): 66.5B **Publicly Held**
SIC: **7699** 3625 Elevators: inspection, service & repair; control equipment, electric
HQ: Otis Elevator Company
1 Carrier Pl
Farmington CT 06032
860 674-3000

(G-2940)
NORTHEAST PANEL CO LLC
325 Main St Ste 3 (06032-2977)
PHONE..........................860 678-9078
Bert Rompre, *Principal*
EMP: 5
SALES (est): 430K **Privately Held**
SIC: **3444** Metal roofing & roof drainage equipment

(G-2941)
ORAL FLUID DYNAMICS LLC
400 Farmington Ave R1844 (06032-1913)
PHONE..........................860 561-5036
J Robert Kelly DDS, *Manager*
J Robert Kelly DDS PHD, *Manager*
EMP: 4
SALES: 240K **Privately Held**
SIC: **3841** Surgical & medical instruments

(G-2942)
OTIS ELEVATOR COMPANY (HQ)
1 Carrier Pl (06032-2562)
PHONE..........................860 674-3000
Judith F Marks, *President*
Mario Abajo, *President*
Todd M Bluedorn, *President*
Bruno Grob, *President*
Angelo J Messina, *President*
◆ EMP: 277
SQ FT: 200,000
SALES (est): 9.3B
SALES (corp-wide): 66.5B **Publicly Held**
WEB: www.otis.com
SIC: **3534** 7699 1796 Elevators & equipment; miscellaneous building item repair services; elevator installation & conversion

Farmington - Hartford County (G-2969)

PA: United Technologies Corporation
10 Farm Springs Rd
Farmington CT 06032
860 728-7000

(G-2943)
OTIS ELEVATOR COMPANY
5 Farm Springs Rd (06032-2575)
PHONE 860 290-3318
EMP: 8
SALES (corp-wide): 66.5B Publicly Held
SIC: 3534 Elevators & equipment
HQ: Otis Elevator Company
1 Carrier Pl
Farmington CT 06032
860 674-3000

(G-2944)
PACIFIC ENGINEERING INC
24 Colton St (06032-2321)
P.O. Box 145 (06034-0145)
PHONE 860 677-0795
Robert Sposato, President
Maureen Sposato, Treasurer
EMP: 2
SALES (est): 160K Privately Held
WEB: www.pewaxes.com
SIC: 2842 7371 8711 Furniture polish or wax; computer software systems analysis & design, custom; consulting engineer

(G-2945)
PANELOC CORPORATION
142 Brickyard Rd (06032-1202)
P.O. Box 547 (06034-0547)
PHONE 860 677-6711
Courtney Crocker III, President
Michele Anstett, Purch Mgr
Liza Rioux, Director
Sarah Horner, Admin Sec
EMP: 32
SQ FT: 13,000
SALES (est): 5.3MM Privately Held
SIC: 3429 3965 Aircraft hardware; fasteners

(G-2946)
PAR MANUFACTURING INC
Also Called: Par Thread Grinding
1824 New Britain Ave (06032-3114)
PHONE 860 677-1797
Ken Dimauro, President
John Vasellina Jr, President
Sal Dimauro, Vice Pres
EMP: 8 EST: 1951
SQ FT: 5,000
SALES (est): 580K Privately Held
WEB: www.parmfg.com
SIC: 3599 Machine shop, jobbing & repair

(G-2947)
PARK AVENUE SECURITIES
197 Scott Swamp Rd (06032-3149)
PHONE 860 677-2600
Bob Worgaftik, Principal
Richard Gribinas, Manager
Stephanie Schwartz, Analyst
EMP: 2 EST: 2016
SALES (est): 87.2K Privately Held
SIC: 3714 Motor vehicle parts & accessories

(G-2948)
PERFORMANCE FABRICATION
799 New Britain Ave (06032-2166)
PHONE 860 678-8070
Adam Pakutaa, Owner
EMP: 1
SALES (est): 60.6K Privately Held
SIC: 3496 Miscellaneous fabricated wire products

(G-2949)
POLYMER RESOURCES LTD (PA)
656 New Britain Ave (06032-2146)
PHONE 203 324-3737
Leslie M Klein, Ch of Bd
William R Feldman, President
Robert Borrello, Vice Pres
William Galla, Vice Pres
Stephanie Vollono, Controller
▲ EMP: 60
SALES (est): 25.6MM Privately Held
WEB: www.polymerresources.com
SIC: 2821 Plastics materials & resins

(G-2950)
POST MORTEM SERVICES LLC
82 Knollwood Rd (06032-1029)
PHONE 860 675-1103
Paul Marduson, Owner
EMP: 4
SALES (est): 267.6K Privately Held
SIC: 3444 Mail (post office) collection or storage boxes, sheet metal

(G-2951)
PROGRESSIVE STAMPING CO DE INC
36 Spring Ln (06032-3140)
PHONE 248 299-7100
Doug Shantz, General Mgr
▲ EMP: 45
SQ FT: 65,000
SALES (est): 4.5MM
SALES (corp-wide): 3.4B Privately Held
WEB: www.progressivestamping.com
SIC: 3465 3452 Automotive stampings; bolts, nuts, rivets & washers
HQ: Fastentech, Inc.
8500 Normandale Lake Blvd
Minneapolis MN 55437
952 921-2090

(G-2952)
RAYM-CO INC
62 Spring Ln (06032-3140)
PHONE 860 678-8292
Sarah Artibani, President
Karen Motta, General Mgr
Brandon Artibani, Vice Pres
Earl Reilly, Opers Mgr
EMP: 43 EST: 1980
SQ FT: 35,000
SALES: 4.3MM Privately Held
SIC: 3599 Machine shop, jobbing & repair

(G-2953)
RBK LATHE LLC
1451 New Britain Ave # 1 (06032-3343)
PHONE 860 321-7243
Robert Kozikowski,
EMP: 2
SALES (est): 282.3K Privately Held
SIC: 3541 Lathes

(G-2954)
RECON TACTICAL LLC
30 Lakeshore Dr Apt B2 (06032-1223)
PHONE 860 677-8202
Scott X Augeri,
EMP: 1
SQ FT: 100
SALES: 250K Privately Held
SIC: 5699 3443 Military goods & regalia; nuclear reactors, military or industrial

(G-2955)
SAAR CORPORATION
81 Spring Ln (06032-3139)
PHONE 860 674-9440
Mariusz Saar, President
Krystyna Saar, Vice Pres
Luke Saar, Vice Pres
Angela Gladding, Office Mgr
EMP: 13
SQ FT: 8,000
SALES (est): 3.1MM Privately Held
WEB: www.saarmed.com
SIC: 3841 3724 Surgical & medical instruments; aircraft engines & engine parts

(G-2956)
SHOCK SOCK INC LLC
409 Colt Hwy (06032-2535)
PHONE 860 680-7252
James M Manning, Principal
EMP: 4
SALES (est): 345.9K Privately Held
SIC: 2252 Socks

(G-2957)
SIKORSKY AIRCRAFT CORPORATION
9 Farm Springs Rd Ste 3 (06032-2576)
P.O. Box 766, Windsor (06095-0766)
PHONE 610 644-4430
Eugene Buckley, President
EMP: 25 Publicly Held
WEB: www.sikorsky.com
SIC: 3721 Helicopters
HQ: Sikorsky Aircraft Corporation
6900 Main St
Stratford CT 06614

(G-2958)
SODEXO INC
263 Farmington Ave (06032-1956)
PHONE 860 679-2803
Michael Lando, President
EMP: 28
SALES (corp-wide): 133.3MM Privately Held
SIC: 5963 2099 Food services, direct sales; food preparations
HQ: Sodexo, Inc.
9801 Washingtonian Blvd # 416
Gaithersburg MD 20878
301 987-4000

(G-2959)
STANLEY BLACK & DECKER INC
65 Spot Swamp Rd (06032)
PHONE 860 225-5111
Vito Spinelli, Engineer
John F Lundgren, Branch Mgr
EMP: 11
SALES (corp-wide): 13.9B Publicly Held
WEB: www.stanleyworks.com
SIC: 3423 Hand & edge tools
PA: Stanley Black & Decker, Inc.
1000 Stanley Dr
New Britain CT 06053
860 225-5111

(G-2960)
STANLEY BLACK & DECKER INC
Also Called: Stanley Access Technologies
65 Scott Swamp Rd (06032-2803)
PHONE 860 677-2861
Martin Amarell, Plant Mgr
EMP: 250
SALES (corp-wide): 13.9B Publicly Held
SIC: 5031 1751 7699 3699 Doors; window & door installation & erection; door & window repair; electrical equipment & supplies
PA: Stanley Black & Decker, Inc.
1000 Stanley Dr
New Britain CT 06053
860 225-5111

(G-2961)
SUMMIT BIRCH HILL
271 Main St (06032-2982)
PHONE 860 677-2763
EMP: 2
SALES (est): 159.7K Privately Held
SIC: 1389 Oil/Gas Field Services

(G-2962)
SYSTEMATIC AUTOMATION INC
20 Executive Dr (06032-2838)
PHONE 310 218-3361
Joseph J Gilberti, President
Justin Gilberti, General Mgr
Maria Gilberti, Vice Pres
Marty Zaccardo, Technology
EMP: 40
SQ FT: 40,000
SALES (est): 6.8MM Privately Held
SIC: 8711 3552 3555 2396 Designing: ship, boat, machine & product; silk screens for textile industry; printing trades machinery; automotive & apparel trimmings

(G-2963)
TAYLOR COML FOODSERVICE INC
Taylor Company
3 Farm Glen Blvd Ste 301 (06032-1981)
P.O. Box 410, Rockton IL (61072-0410)
PHONE 336 245-6400
Clark Wangaard, President
Larry Vondran, Data Proc Exec
Melissa McCormick, Director
Allan Stabenow, Director
EMP: 627
SQ FT: 100,000
SALES (corp-wide): 2.7B Publicly Held
WEB: www.ccr.carrier.com
SIC: 3556 Ice cream manufacturing machinery
HQ: Taylor Commercial Foodservice Inc.
750 N Blackhawk Blvd
Rockton IL 61072
815 624-8333

(G-2964)
THERMATOOL MILL SYST
15 Michael Dr (06032-1146)
PHONE 203 468-4178
Anthony Rigoglioso, Manager
EMP: 1
SALES (est): 54.1K Privately Held
SIC: 3548 Welding apparatus

(G-2965)
TRANE US INC
135 South Rd Ste 1 (06032-2570)
P.O. Box 977 (06034-0977)
PHONE 860 470-3901
Kevin McNamara, Branch Mgr
EMP: 60 Privately Held
SIC: 3585 Refrigeration & heating equipment
HQ: Trane U.S. Inc.
3600 Pammel Creek Rd
La Crosse WI 54601
608 787-2000

(G-2966)
TRINITY POLYMERS LLC
39 Robin Rd (06032-2510)
PHONE 860 321-7209
Nathan Deangelis, Principal
Jason Weaver, Supervisor
EMP: 2 EST: 2016
SALES (est): 108.3K Privately Held
SIC: 3089 Plastics products

(G-2967)
TRUMPF INC (DH)
111 Hyde Rd (06032-2851)
P.O. Box 105 (06034-0105)
PHONE 860 255-6000
Nicola Leibinger-Kammuller, Ch of Bd
Peter Hoecklin, President
Christof Lehner, General Mgr
Yessica Chavez, Regional Mgr
Robert Leahy, Regional Mgr
◆ EMP: 277 EST: 1969
SQ FT: 160,000
SALES (est): 206.9MM
SALES (corp-wide): 4.2B Privately Held
WEB: www.us.trumpf.com
SIC: 3542 3423 3546 Sheet metalworking machines; hand & edge tools; power-driven handtools
HQ: Trumpf International Beteiligungs-Gmbh
Johann-Maus-Str. 2
Ditzingen 71254
715 630-30

(G-2968)
TRUMPF INC
1 Johnson Ave (06032-2842)
PHONE 860 255-6000
Rolf Biekert, CEO
Jeff Curtis, Engineer
Paul Vetre, Engineer
Sheila Lamothe, Marketing Mgr
EMP: 500
SALES (corp-wide): 4.2B Privately Held
SIC: 3542 3423 3546 Sheet metalworking machines; hand & edge tools; power-driven handtools
HQ: Trumpf, Inc.
111 Hyde Rd
Farmington CT 06032
860 255-6000

(G-2969)
TRUMPF PHOTONICS INC
111 Hyde Rd (06032-2834)
PHONE 860 255-6000
Nicola Leibinger-Kammuller, CEO
Heinz-Jurgen Prokop, CEO
Christian Schmitz, CEO
Lars Grunert, CFO
Peter Leibinger, CTO
EMP: 8
SALES (est): 1.2MM Privately Held
SIC: 3444 Sheet metalwork

Farmington - Hartford County (G-2970)

(G-2970)
TRYCYCLE DATA SYSTEMS US INC
400 Farmington Ave # 1844 (06032-1913)
PHONE.................................860 558-1148
Kenneth House, *President*
John Macbeth, *President*
EMP: 4
SALES (est): 98.3K
SALES (corp-wide): 1.7MM Privately Held
SIC: 7372 Prepackaged software
PA: Trycycle Data Systems Inc
 1296 Carling Ave Suite 300
 Ottawa ON K1Z 7
 613 274-0001

(G-2971)
TURBINE TECHNOLOGIES INC (PA)
126 Hyde Rd (06032-2866)
P.O. Box 1267 (06034-1267)
PHONE.................................860 678-1642
Tyler J Burke, *President*
John A Guyette, *COO*
Brittany M Bowie, *Vice Pres*
John Guyette, *Vice Pres*
Justin H Lamprey, *Vice Pres*
EMP: 80
SALES: 20MM Privately Held
WEB: www.omegact.com
SIC: 3724 3714 Aircraft engines & engine parts; motor vehicle parts & accessories

(G-2972)
UNITED TECHNOLOGIES CORP (PA)
Also Called: UTC
10 Farm Springs Rd (06032-2577)
PHONE.................................860 728-7000
Robert K Ortberg, *CEO*
Gregory J Hayes, *Ch of Bd*
David L Gitlin, *President*
Robert F Leduc, *President*
Judith F Marks, *President*
▼ EMP: 430 EST: 1934
SALES: 66.5B Publicly Held
WEB: www.utc.com
SIC: 3724 3585 3721 3534 Aircraft engines & engine parts; research & development on aircraft engines & parts; refrigeration & heating equipment; aircraft; elevators & equipment; escalators; passenger & freight; emergency alarms; electrical equipment & supplies; security devices; security control equipment & systems

(G-2973)
UNITED TECHNOLOGIES CORP
Also Called: UTC Climate Controls & SEC
9 Farm Springs Rd Ste 3 (06032-2576)
PHONE.................................954 485-6501
William Brown, *President*
Steven McDaniel, *District Mgr*
Scott Sullivan, *Sales Mgr*
Danny Loggins, *Sales Staff*
Lorraine Smith, *Sales Staff*
EMP: 500
SALES (corp-wide): 66.5B Publicly Held
SIC: 3699 3669 Security devices; security control equipment & systems; fire detection systems, electric
PA: United Technologies Corporation
 10 Farm Springs Rd
 Farmington CT 06032
 860 728-7000

(G-2974)
UTC FIRE SEC AMERICAS CORP INC
Also Called: Edwards Detection & Alarm
30 Batterson Park Rd # 100 (06032-2545)
PHONE.................................941 739-4200
EMP: 2
SALES (corp-wide): 66.5B Publicly Held
SIC: 3669 5065 Burglar alarm apparatus, electric; electronic parts & equipment
HQ: Utc Fire & Security Americas Corporation, Inc.
 8985 Town Center Pkwy
 Lakewood Ranch FL 34202

(G-2975)
VICHEM INC
16 Evergreen Trl (06032-2145)
P.O. Box 184, Unionville (06085-0184)
PHONE.................................860 677-8133
David Ehler, *President*
Steve Wakefield, *Vice Pres*
EMP: 2
SQ FT: 2,400
SALES (est): 179.1K Privately Held
SIC: 2899 Chemical preparations

(G-2976)
VICTORY CONTROLS LLC
222 Main St Ste 261 (06032-3623)
PHONE.................................860 930-6226
EMP: 1
SALES (corp-wide): 250K Privately Held
SIC: 3625 Mfg Relays/Industrial Controls
PA: Victory Controls, Llc
 27819 Smyth Dr
 Valencia CA
 860 930-6226

(G-2977)
WATERLOGIC USA INC
8 Two Mile Rd Ste 200 (06032-2559)
PHONE.................................866 917-7873
Casey Taylor, *CEO*
EMP: 2
SALES (est): 79.9K Privately Held
SIC: 3585 5078 1711 Coolers, milk & water: electric; drinking water coolers, mechanical; refrigeration contractor

(G-2978)
WESTROCK RKT COMPANY
33 Skyview Dr (06032)
PHONE.................................860 284-9820
Karen Habig, *Branch Mgr*
EMP: 161
SALES (corp-wide): 16.2B Publicly Held
WEB: www.rocktenn.com
SIC: 2653 2652 2631 Hampers, solid fiber: made from purchased materials; boxes, corrugated: made from purchased materials; filing boxes, paperboard: made from purchased materials; container board; container, packaging & boxboard
HQ: Westrock Rkt, Llc
 1000 Abernathy Rd Ste 125
 Atlanta GA 30328
 770 448-2193

(G-2979)
ZERO HAZARD LLC
38 Pembroke Hl (06032-1461)
P.O. Box 767 (06034-0767)
PHONE.................................860 561-9879
Carlos M Rosales, *Principal*
EMP: 8
SALES (est): 539.1K Privately Held
SIC: 3292 Asbestos products

Gales Ferry
New London County

(G-2980)
AMERICAN INDUSTRIES
2 Chapman Ln (06335-1200)
PHONE.................................860 381-5083
EMP: 1 EST: 2017
SALES (est): 39.6K Privately Held
SIC: 3999 Manufacturing industries

(G-2981)
B&R SAND AND GRAVEL
1358 Baldwin Hill Rd (06335-1856)
PHONE.................................860 464-5099
EMP: 5 EST: 2016
SALES (est): 481.8K Privately Held
SIC: 3273 Ready-mixed concrete

(G-2982)
CALVIN BROWN
Also Called: Cal Brown Paving
259 Gallup Hill Rd (06339-2010)
PHONE.................................860 536-6178
Calvin Brown, *Owner*
EMP: 5
SALES (est): 191.8K Privately Held
WEB: www.calvinbrown.com
SIC: 3531 Pavers

(G-2983)
FINN-ADDICT MANUFACTURING LLC
940 Long Cove Rd Trlr 2 (06335-1951)
PHONE.................................860 464-2053
Steven McGahan, *Principal*
EMP: 1
SALES (est): 47.5K Privately Held
SIC: 3999 Manufacturing industries

(G-2984)
JONES FIRE SPRINKLER CO LLC
1360 Baldwin Hill Rd (06335-1856)
P.O. Box 1023, Groton (06340-1023)
PHONE.................................860 464-7284
Eva Mae Jones,
EMP: 1
SALES (est): 171.4K Privately Held
SIC: 3569 Sprinkler systems, fire: automatic

(G-2985)
KAPPA SAILS LLC
25 Whippoorwill Dr (06335-2029)
PHONE.................................860 399-8899
Clark Basset, *President*
Kathryn Bassett,
EMP: 6
SALES (est): 514.7K Privately Held
WEB: www.kappasails.com
SIC: 2394 Sails: made from purchased materials

(G-2986)
KLA KEMP LLC
34 Osprey Dr (06335-2016)
PHONE.................................860 464-6746
Karen Anderson-Kemp, *Principal*
EMP: 2
SALES (est): 173.5K Privately Held
SIC: 3825 Instruments to measure electricity

(G-2987)
STONINGTON SERVICES LLC (PA)
Also Called: Brand Services
39 Kings Hwy Ste 1 (06335-1535)
PHONE.................................860 464-1991
Roy Noss, *General Mgr*
Jami Allyn, *Vice Pres*
John Mancuso, *Facilities Mgr*
Jo-Ann Chiangi, *Mng Member*
John Coughlin, *Manager*
EMP: 50
SQ FT: 4,400
SALES (est): 9.6MM Privately Held
SIC: 8742 3442 Management consulting services; maintenance management consultant; fire doors, metal

(G-2988)
TOWN OF LEDYARD
Also Called: Town of Medyard, The
889 Colonel Ledyard Hwy (06339-1102)
PHONE.................................860 464-9060
Steve Maslin, *Branch Mgr*
EMP: 1 Privately Held
SIC: 3531 Road construction & maintenance machinery
PA: Town Of Ledyard
 741 Colonel Ledyard Hwy
 Ledyard CT 06339
 860 464-8740

(G-2989)
TRINSEO LLC
1761 Route 12 Bldg 21 (06335-1213)
PHONE.................................860 447-7298
Celso Goncalves, *CFO*
EMP: 20 Publicly Held
SIC: 2821 Plastics materials & resins
HQ: Trinseo Llc
 1000 Chesterbrook Blvd # 300
 Berwyn PA 19312

Gaylordsville
Litchfield County

(G-2990)
CANDLEWOOD TOOL & MACHINE SHOP
24 Martha Ln (06755-1501)
PHONE.................................860 355-1892
George Christophersen, *President*
James Jacques, *Vice Pres*
Amy Jacques, *Treasurer*
Joan B Christophersen, *Admin Sec*
EMP: 10
SQ FT: 5,300
SALES: 1MM Privately Held
SIC: 3599 3544 Machine shop, jobbing & repair; special dies & tools

(G-2991)
CONWAY HARDWOOD PRODUCTS LLC
Also Called: Conway, Jeremiah
37 Gaylord Rd (06755-1518)
PHONE.................................860 355-4030
Jeremiah C Conway, *Mng Member*
Mike Artese, *Manager*
▲ EMP: 25
SQ FT: 9,000
SALES (est): 3MM Privately Held
SIC: 2426 2434 2431 5211 Flooring, hardwood; wood kitchen cabinets; moldings, wood: unfinished & prefinished; doors, wood; lumber products

(G-2992)
GAIA CHEMICAL CORPORATION
23 George Washington Plz (06755)
PHONE.................................860 355-2730
A Kodylinsky, *Director*
EMP: 4
SALES (est): 262.9K Privately Held
SIC: 2834 Pharmaceutical preparations

(G-2993)
GENESIS D T P
36 Cedar Hill Rd (06755-1510)
PHONE.................................860 350-2827
Mark Lederman, *Owner*
EMP: 1
SALES (est): 810K Privately Held
WEB: www.genesysdtp.com
SIC: 7372 Publishers' computer software

(G-2994)
MECO PRECISION INDUSTRIES INC
523 River Rd (06755-1418)
PHONE.................................860 210-1801
Jeff Mandel, *President*
Suzanne Mandel, *Admin Sec*
EMP: 3
SALES (est): 150.5K Privately Held
SIC: 7389 2759 Engraving service; engraving

(G-2995)
MICRO SOURCE DISCOVERY SYSTEMS
11 George Washington Plz (06755)
PHONE.................................860 350-8078
John Devlin, *President*
Mary Ortner, *Vice Pres*
EMP: 7
SQ FT: 2,000
SALES (est): 1.1MM Privately Held
WEB: www.msdiscovery.com
SIC: 2834 Pharmaceutical preparations

(G-2996)
ROBERT SCHWARTZ
6 Buckingham Ln (06755-1321)
PHONE.................................203 515-8162
Robert Schwartz, *Owner*
EMP: 1
SALES (est): 84.5K Privately Held
SIC: 7692 Welding repair

(G-2997)
WILLIAM MARTIN
Also Called: Northville Horseshoe Supply
157 Gaylord Rd (06755-1520)
PHONE.................................860 355-1919

GEOGRAPHIC SECTION

Glastonbury - Hartford County (G-3026)

William Martin, *Owner*
EMP: 4
SQ FT: 3,500
SALES: 550K **Privately Held**
SIC: 5191 3462 Equestrian equipment; horseshoes

Georgetown
Fairfield County

(G-2998)
GEORGETOWN MACHINE
16 Sunset Hill Rd (06829)
PHONE..................203 544-8422
Richard Johnson, *Owner*
EMP: 1
SALES (est): 69K **Privately Held**
SIC: 3599 Machine shop, jobbing & repair

(G-2999)
TRASSIG CORP
65 Redding Rd Unit 874 (06829-7735)
P.O. Box 874 (06829-0874)
PHONE..................203 659-0456
Khalid Gourad, *President*
▲ **EMP:** 5 **EST:** 2007
SALES: 1MM **Privately Held**
SIC: 3949 Playground equipment

Gilman
New London County

(G-3000)
GILMAN CORPORATION
1 Polly Ln (06336)
P.O. Box 68 (06336-0068)
PHONE..................860 887-7080
Richard Gilman, *CEO*
Elizabeth Gilman, *President*
George Warner, *MIS Dir*
▼ **EMP:** 30
SQ FT: 32,000
SALES (est): 7MM **Privately Held**
WEB: www.gilmancorp.com
SIC: 3086 3949 Plastics foam products; sporting & athletic goods

(G-3001)
MARTY GILMAN INCORPORATED (PA)
Also Called: Gilman Gear
30 Gilman Rd (06336-1006)
P.O. Box 97 (06336-0097)
PHONE..................860 889-7334
Shirley Gilman, *Ch of Bd*
Neil Gilman, *President*
Nadine Parker, *Controller*
Geoffrey Gilman, *Admin Sec*
EMP: 55 **EST:** 1929
SQ FT: 20,000
SALES (est): 6.3MM **Privately Held**
WEB: www.magipotholders.com
SIC: 3949 Sporting & athletic goods

Glastonbury
Hartford County

(G-3002)
ABILITY PRSTHTICS ORTHTICS LLC
52 National Dr Ste 2 (06033-4369)
PHONE..................860 571-8979
Lisa Hewett, *Owner*
EMP: 2
SQ FT: 2,800
SALES (est): 205.1K **Privately Held**
SIC: 3842 Orthopedic appliances

(G-3003)
ACTIVE INTERNET TECH LLC
Also Called: Finalsite
655 Winding Brook Dr # 100 (06033-4337)
PHONE..................800 592-2469
Connie Cavallo, *Project Mgr*
Mike Hartzler, *Project Mgr*
Laurie Murphy, *Project Mgr*
Nathan Provost, *Controller*
Sergio Villareal, *Accounts Mgr*
EMP: 123
SALES (est): 21.1MM **Privately Held**
SIC: 7371 7372 Computer software development; educational computer software

(G-3004)
AGILE COMPUTER SYSTEMS
57 Littel Acres Rd (06033-3609)
P.O. Box 170, South Glastonbury (06073-0170)
PHONE..................860 633-7807
Jeff Giroux, *Owner*
EMP: 5
SALES (est): 513.4K **Privately Held**
WEB: www.agilecomputer.com
SIC: 7373 7372 Computer integrated systems design; prepackaged software

(G-3005)
AIRFLO INSTRUMENT COMPANY
53 Addison Rd (06033-1601)
P.O. Box 192 (06033-0192)
PHONE..................860 633-9455
William Lajewski, *President*
Anthony Coiro, *Shareholder*
EMP: 5 **EST:** 1948
SQ FT: 7,500
SALES (est): 490.7K **Privately Held**
SIC: 3648 3829 3812 3625 Airport lighting fixtures: runway approach, taxi or ramp; meteorological instruments; navigational systems & instruments; flow actuated electrical switches

(G-3006)
AM MANUFACTURING LLC
278 Oakwood Dr Ste 6 (06033-5019)
PHONE..................860 573-1987
Michael Karwowski, *Mng Member*
EMP: 4
SALES (est): 401.1K **Privately Held**
SIC: 3599 Machine shop, jobbing & repair

(G-3007)
ARCHITECTURAL OUTDOOR LIGHTING
199 Worthington Rd (06033-1374)
PHONE..................860 659-5795
Christina Carnevale, *Principal*
EMP: 2
SALES (est): 127.5K **Privately Held**
WEB: www.aol-llc.com
SIC: 3648 Outdoor lighting equipment

(G-3008)
ARRAY TECHNOLOGIES INC
21 Sequin Dr (06033-2443)
PHONE..................860 657-8086
David Loos, *CEO*
David Pirie, *President*
EMP: 5
SQ FT: 1,551
SALES (est): 927.7K **Privately Held**
WEB: www.arraytechnologies.com
SIC: 7372 Prepackaged software

(G-3009)
AZTECH ENGINEERING LLC
365 Weir St (06033-3520)
PHONE..................860 659-8892
Ron Gagnon,
EMP: 5
SQ FT: 2,700
SALES (est): 420K **Privately Held**
SIC: 8711 3571 Electrical or electronic engineering; mechanical engineering; electronic computers

(G-3010)
B DOUGLASS CUSTOM MLLWK LLC
80 Great Swamp Rd (06033-1315)
PHONE..................860 338-9305
Bradford Douglass,
EMP: 1
SALES (est): 91.6K **Privately Held**
SIC: 2431 Millwork

(G-3011)
BAGEL BOYS INC (PA)
85 Nutmeg Ln (06033-2314)
PHONE..................860 657-4400
Wes Becher, *President*
Michael Bellobuono, *Vice Pres*
EMP: 14
SALES (est): 2.4MM **Privately Held**
SIC: 2051 Bagels, fresh or frozen

(G-3012)
BARCO INDUSTRIES NEW ENGLAND
224 Eastern Blvd (06033-4310)
PHONE..................860 798-8258
EMP: 1
SALES (est): 39.6K **Privately Held**
SIC: 3999 Manufacturing industries

(G-3013)
BEDARD PUZZLES
382 Great Swamp Rd (06033-1426)
PHONE..................860 657-3781
EMP: 2
SALES (est): 60K **Privately Held**
SIC: 3944 Mfg Games/Toys

(G-3014)
BIOMED HEALTH INC
70 Oakwood Dr Ste 8 (06033-2459)
P.O. Box 911 (06033-0911)
PHONE..................860 657-2258
M E Sherman, *President*
Generosa Mendez, *Corp Secy*
EMP: 12
SALES (est): 1.9MM **Privately Held**
WEB: www.biomed-health.com
SIC: 2833 2834 Vitamins, natural or synthetic: bulk, uncompounded; pharmaceutical preparations

(G-3015)
BIZ WIZ PRINT & COPY CTR LLC
2341 Main St (06033-2211)
PHONE..................860 633-7446
Kelly Dotson, *Branch Mgr*
EMP: 5
SALES (est): 356.3K **Privately Held**
SIC: 7334 5099 2759 Photocopying & duplicating services; signs, except electric; commercial printing
PA: Biz Wiz Print & Copy Center L.L.C.
781 Cromwell Ave Ste E
Rocky Hill CT 06067

(G-3016)
BRITISH PRECISION INC
20 Sequin Dr (06033-2475)
PHONE..................860 633-3343
Ralph Naylor, *President*
Jason Naylor, *General Mgr*
Mary Naylor, *Treasurer*
EMP: 30
SQ FT: 11,000
SALES (est): 5.2MM **Privately Held**
WEB: www.britishprecision.com
SIC: 3599 Machine shop, jobbing & repair

(G-3017)
C & W MANUFACTURING CO INC
74 Eastern Blvd (06033-4304)
PHONE..................860 633-4631
Myles Covey, *President*
Scott Miller, *Vice Pres*
EMP: 20
SQ FT: 19,000
SALES (est): 2.3MM **Privately Held**
SIC: 3599 3841 3728 Machine shop, jobbing & repair; surgical & medical instruments; aircraft parts & equipment

(G-3018)
CAMERON INTERNATIONAL CORP
Also Called: Measurement Systems
256 Oakwood Dr Ste 1 (06033-2465)
PHONE..................860 633-0277
Kim Giansianti, *Manager*
EMP: 10 **Publicly Held**
SIC: 1389 Oil field services
HQ: Cameron International Corporation
4646 W Sam Houston Pkwy N
Houston TX 77041

(G-3019)
CARA C ANDREOLI
Also Called: Nutrition Matters
41 Mockingbird Ln (06033-1754)
PHONE..................860 888-6553
Cara Andreoli, *Principal*
EMP: 1 **EST:** 2015
SALES (est): 62.1K **Privately Held**
SIC: 2741 5065 7389 Miscellaneous publishing; electronic parts & equipment;

(G-3020)
CHEN-MAN FOODS LLC
110 Cedar Ridge Dr (06033-1816)
PHONE..................860 659-9549
John Cheney, *Principal*
EMP: 2
SALES (est): 139.2K **Privately Held**
SIC: 2099 Food preparations

(G-3021)
COMPOSICLEAN LLC
75 Hope Ln (06033-1702)
PHONE..................860 432-0067
▼ **EMP:** 1
SALES (est): 119.7K **Privately Held**
SIC: 3471 Vehicle - Wash / Wax / Detailing Products

(G-3022)
CONARD CORPORATION
101 Commerce St (06033-2312)
P.O. Box 676 (06033-0676)
PHONE..................860 659-0591
William J Fox, *President*
Craig Bernick, *Engineer*
Tom Odea, *Engineer*
▲ **EMP:** 23 **EST:** 1965
SQ FT: 12,000
SALES (est): 3.9MM **Privately Held**
WEB: www.conardcorp.com
SIC: 3479 Etching on metals

(G-3023)
CONNECTICUT ADVANCED PRODUCTS
41c New London Tpke (06033-4206)
PHONE..................860 659-2260
Jeffrey Kretzmer, *President*
Cynthia Kretzmer, *Vice Pres*
EMP: 4
SQ FT: 1,500
SALES (est): 429.3K **Privately Held**
WEB: www.capcad.com
SIC: 3728 5599 5088 5961 Aircraft parts & equipment; aircraft instruments, equipment or parts; aircraft equipment & supplies; catalog sales

(G-3024)
CONNECTICUT CABINET DISTRS LLC
27 Kreiger Ln (06033-2390)
P.O. Box 802, Portland (06480-0802)
PHONE..................860 508-6240
Greg Slocum,
Dave Nyren,
EMP: 2
SALES (est): 437.4K **Privately Held**
SIC: 2434 Wood kitchen cabinets

(G-3025)
CUSSON SASH COMPANY
128 Addison Rd (06033-1605)
PHONE..................860 659-0354
Walter Cusson, *President*
Richard Cusson, *Corp Secy*
Charles Cusson, *Vice Pres*
Howard Rath, *Vice Pres*
EMP: 5 **EST:** 1946
SQ FT: 10,000
SALES (est): 570K **Privately Held**
WEB: www.cussonssash.com
SIC: 3442 1521 1751 5211 Casements, aluminum; sash, door or window: metal; screen & storm doors & windows; general remodeling, single-family houses; window & door (prefabricated) installation; doors, storm: wood or metal; windows, storm: wood or metal; screens, door & window; metal doors, sash & trim; doors, combination, screen-storm; windows; trim, sheet metal

(G-3026)
CUSTOM CABINET & EUROPEAN
2934 Main St (06033-1027)
PHONE..................860 430-9396
EMP: 1
SALES (est): 97.8K **Privately Held**
SIC: 2434 Wood kitchen cabinets

Glastonbury - Hartford County (G-3027) — GEOGRAPHIC SECTION

(G-3027)
D CELLO ENTERPRISES LLC
Also Called: Proforma/Graphicworks
98 Newell Ln (06033-3716)
PHONE..................................860 659-0844
Debra C Smith,
EMP: 2
SALES: 400K Privately Held
SIC: 2752 2761 7312 2759 Commercial printing, lithographic; manifold business forms; outdoor advertising services; commercial printing;

(G-3028)
DYTHNAM INDUSTRIES LLC
529 Thompson St (06033-4030)
PHONE..................................860 480-7980
Samet Dy, Owner
EMP: 1
SALES (est): 46.2K Privately Held
SIC: 3999 Manufacturing industries

(G-3029)
EAST HARTFORD LAMINATION CO
Also Called: Ehl Kitchens
110 Commerce St (06033-2369)
P.O. Box 22 (06033-0022)
PHONE..................................860 633-4637
Mario Disomma, Owner
EMP: 4 EST: 1967
SQ FT: 10,000
SALES (est): 410K Privately Held
WEB: www.ehlkitchens.com
SIC: 2541 5211 2434 Sink tops, plastic laminated; table or counter tops, plastic laminated; cabinets, kitchen; wood kitchen cabinets

(G-3030)
EASTERN CONN HLTH NETWRK
Also Called: Glastonbury Dianostic Center
628 Hebron Ave Ste 104b (06033-5007)
PHONE..................................860 652-3182
Peter Karl, President
EMP: 5 EST: 1998
SALES (est): 243.2K Privately Held
SIC: 8011 8099 3829 Radiologist; health & allied services; medical diagnostic systems, nuclear

(G-3031)
EDAC ND INC
Also Called: Flanagan Brothers, Inc
81 National Dr (06033-1211)
P.O. Box 396 (06033-0396)
PHONE..................................860 633-9474
Terry Bruni, CEO
EMP: 100
SQ FT: 55,000
SALES (est): 19.1MM Privately Held
WEB: www.fillc.com
SIC: 3728 3812 3721 Aircraft assemblies, subassemblies & parts; search & navigation equipment; aircraft
HQ: Edac Technologies Llc
5 Mckee Pl
Cheshire CT 06410
203 806-2090

(G-3032)
EDWARD TOMKIEVICH
Also Called: Glastonbury Cabinets
65 Griswold St (06033-1005)
PHONE..................................860 633-5811
Edward Tomkievich, Owner
EMP: 6
SALES (est): 350K Privately Held
SIC: 1521 1542 5712 1542 Single-family housing construction; commercial & office building, new construction; cabinet work, custom; wood partitions & fixtures; wood kitchen cabinets

(G-3033)
ELITE WOODWORKING LLC
23 Chestnut Hill Rd (06033-4146)
PHONE..................................860 655-7806
Wade Cassells, Principal
EMP: 2
SALES (est): 144.2K Privately Held
SIC: 2431 Millwork

(G-3034)
EMPIRE PRINTING SYSTEMS LLC
Also Called: Signal Graphics Printing
63 Hebron Ave Ste C (06033-2078)
PHONE..................................860 633-3333
Phillip Bombart,
Maydie Bombart,
▲ EMP: 5
SQ FT: 2,080
SALES: 660K Privately Held
SIC: 2752 Commercial printing, offset

(G-3035)
ENGINE ALLIANCE LLC
124 Hebron Ave Ste 200 (06033-2063)
PHONE..................................860 565-2239
Dean Athans, President
Chip Blankenship, President
Jonathan Lynch, General Mgr
Melissa Argiro, Info Tech Mgr
Bernard Zimmerman, Officer
EMP: 400
SALES: 26.1MM
SALES (corp-wide): 66.5B Publicly Held
SIC: 3724 Aircraft engines & engine parts
PA: United Technologies Corporation
10 Farm Springs Rd
Farmington CT 06032
860 728-7000

(G-3036)
FLANAGAN BROTHERS INC
25 Mill St (06033-1209)
PHONE..................................860 633-3558
EMP: 4
SALES (corp-wide): 146.8MM Privately Held
SIC: 3728 Mfg Aircraft Assemblies Sub-assemblies & Parts
HQ: Flanagan Brothers, Inc.
25 Mill St
Glastonbury CT 06033
860 633-9474

(G-3037)
FREEDOM TECHNOLOGIES LLC
80 Timrod Trl (06033-1937)
P.O. Box 117, East Glastonbury (06025-0117)
PHONE..................................860 633-0452
Mary Ellen Gatti, President
Suzanne Gatti,
Victor Gatti,
EMP: 8
SQ FT: 5,000
SALES: 3MM Privately Held
WEB: www.freedomlaser.com
SIC: 3661 Telephone & telegraph apparatus

(G-3038)
GAC INC
Also Called: New England Traffic Solutions
160 Oak St Ste 412 (06033-2376)
PHONE..................................860 633-1768
Amy Vecchiarino, President
Claudio Vecchiarino, Vice Pres
Kevin Cramer, Technician
EMP: 5
SQ FT: 16,000
SALES (est): 1MM Privately Held
SIC: 3669 Transportation signaling devices

(G-3039)
GENERAL ELECTRO COMPONENTS
Also Called: Line Electric
122 Naubuc Ave Ste A7 (06033-4226)
PHONE..................................860 659-3573
Bill Harris, President
Billy D Harris, Director
◆ EMP: 8
SQ FT: 5,000
SALES (est): 943K Privately Held
WEB: www.lineelectric.com
SIC: 3679 3625 3613 Electronic circuits; solenoids for electronic applications; relays, for electronic use; switchgear & switchboard apparatus

(G-3040)
GLASTONBURY CITIZEN INC
87 Nutmeg Ln (06033-2353)
P.O. Box 373 (06033-0373)
PHONE..................................860 633-4691
Jane Hallas, President
Jason Baran, Editor
Marian Hallas, Corp Secy
James Hallas, Vice Pres
EMP: 25
SQ FT: 3,200
SALES (est): 1.4MM Privately Held
WEB: www.glcitizen.com
SIC: 2711 Job printing & newspaper publishing combined; newspapers: publishing only, not printed on site

(G-3041)
GLASTONBURY FIRE TRAINING CTR
87 Orchard St (06033-2491)
PHONE..................................860 633-3429
Jim Hallas, Owner
EMP: 2
SALES (est): 123K Privately Held
SIC: 3711 Fire department vehicles (motor vehicles), assembly of

(G-3042)
GRAPHIC IDENTITY LLC
Also Called: Graphik Identities
36 Kreiger Ln Ste G (06033-2368)
PHONE..................................860 657-9755
Kurt Knobel, President
Karin Knobel, Vice Pres
EMP: 2
SALES (est): 209.6K Privately Held
SIC: 3993 Signs & advertising specialties

(G-3043)
GREEN LEAF FOODS LLC
703 Hebron Ave (06033-5000)
PHONE..................................860 657-4404
Brian Whitney, Principal
EMP: 2
SALES (est): 71.8K Privately Held
SIC: 2099 Food preparations

(G-3044)
GUILLEMOT KAYAKS
10 Ash Swamp Rd (06033)
PHONE..................................860 659-8847
Nick Schade, Owner
EMP: 1
SALES (est): 105.9K Privately Held
WEB: www.guillemot-kayaks.com
SIC: 3732 Boat building & repairing

(G-3045)
HABCO INDUSTRIES LLC
172 Oak St (06033-2318)
PHONE..................................860 682-6800
Brian Montnari, CEO
Scott Brown, Vice Pres
Jeff Kretzmer, Vice Pres
James Maynard, Vice Pres
Nick Zandonella, Vice Pres
EMP: 32 EST: 2013
SQ FT: 50,000
SALES: 8.6MM Privately Held
SIC: 3824 3825 3829 Fluid meters & counting devices; instruments to measure electricity; measuring & controlling devices

(G-3046)
HARPERS INVITATIONS
22 Kreiger Ln Ste 18 (06033-2371)
PHONE..................................860 257-4615
Marie Harper, Owner
EMP: 1
SALES (est): 121.8K Privately Held
SIC: 2678 Stationery products

(G-3047)
HARPOON ACQUISITION CORP
455 Winding Brook Dr (06033-4315)
PHONE..................................860 815-5736
Louis Hernandez Jr, CEO
EMP: 1700
SALES (est): 43.4MM
SALES (corp-wide): 5.8B Publicly Held
SIC: 7372 7373 Business oriented computer software; systems integration services
PA: Fiserv, Inc.
255 Fiserv Dr
Brookfield WI 53045
262 879-5000

(G-3048)
HARTFORD MARATHON FOUNDATION
41 Sequin Dr Ste 1 (06033-5041)
PHONE..................................860 652-8866
Elizabeth Shluger, President
EMP: 4
SALES: 2.7MM Privately Held
WEB: www.hartfordmarathon.com
SIC: 7941 2721 Sports field or stadium operator, promoting sports events; periodicals

(G-3049)
HIGHWAY SAFETY CORP (PA)
Also Called: CONNECTICUT GALVANIZING
239 Commerce St Ste C (06033-2448)
P.O. Box 358 (06033-0358)
PHONE..................................860 659-4330
W Patric Gregory, CEO
Robert West, CFO
Bob West, Human Res Mgr
Jean Naan, Accounts Mgr
▼ EMP: 100
SQ FT: 83,000
SALES: 50.4MM Privately Held
SIC: 3444 3479 Guard rails, highway: sheet metal; galvanizing of iron, steel or end-formed products

(G-3050)
HORIZON SOFTWARE INC
148 Eastern Blvd Ste 208 (06033-4321)
P.O. Box 735 (06033-0735)
PHONE..................................860 633-2090
Thomas Riley, Owner
EMP: 5
SALES (est): 421.2K Privately Held
SIC: 7372 Prepackaged software

(G-3051)
INTERNTNL BAR CODE SYSTMS
160 Oak St Ste 1a (06033-2336)
PHONE..................................860 659-9660
Joseph Mizla, President
Diana Bogue, Office Mgr
Ed Bogue, Manager
Denise Mizla, Admin Sec
▼ EMP: 5
SQ FT: 4,000
SALES (est): 1.2MM Privately Held
WEB: www.interbar.com
SIC: 5045 3577 Computer software; computer peripheral equipment; bar code (magnetic ink) printers

(G-3052)
JEM PRECISION GRINDING INC
35 Nutmeg Ln (06033-2363)
PHONE..................................860 633-0152
Michael Pare, President
Ronald Bourbau, Vice Pres
EMP: 4
SQ FT: 7,000
SALES (est): 582.7K Privately Held
SIC: 3599 Grinding castings for the trade

(G-3053)
KDE INSTRUMENTATION
20 Coltsfoot Cir (06033-1312)
PHONE..................................860 657-2744
Donald T Eberhardt, Partner
Kathleen A Eberhardt, Partner
EMP: 2
SALES: 90K Privately Held
SIC: 5084 7699 3823 Controlling instruments & accessories; indicating instruments & accessories; recording instruments & accessories; measuring & testing equipment, electrical; precision instrument repair; industrial instrmnts msrmnt display/control process variable

(G-3054)
KEEPER PRESS LLC
218 Conestoga Way (06033-3360)
PHONE..................................860 810-9626
Kelli Twelves, Manager
EMP: 1
SALES (est): 56.9K Privately Held
SIC: 2741 Miscellaneous publishing

▲ = Import ▼ = Export ◆ = Import/Export

GEOGRAPHIC SECTION
Glastonbury - Hartford County (G-3084)

(G-3055)
KENT BILLINGS LLC
320 Spring Street Ext (06033-1240)
PHONE..................................860 659-1104
Kent Billings, *Managing Prtnr*
EMP: 3
SALES: 200K **Privately Held**
SIC: 3999 Barber & beauty shop equipment

(G-3056)
KINDERMA LLC
55 Village Pl (06033-1677)
PHONE..................................860 796-5503
David Thompson,
Todd Calder,
EMP: 5
SALES (est): 282.8K **Privately Held**
SIC: 2834 Dermatologicals

(G-3057)
MAURER & SHEPHERD JOYNERS
122 Naubuc Ave Ste B4 (06033-4271)
PHONE..................................860 633-2383
Galen Shepherd, *President*
Donna Shepherd, *Vice Pres*
EMP: 10 **EST:** 1973
SQ FT: 3,000
SALES (est): 1.2MM **Privately Held**
SIC: 2431 Woodwork, interior & ornamental

(G-3058)
MEPP TOOL CO INC
81 Commerce St (06033-2312)
P.O. Box 97, South Windsor (06074-0097)
PHONE..................................860 289-8230
Edward Pacholski, *President*
EMP: 4
SQ FT: 6,600
SALES: 461K **Privately Held**
SIC: 3599 Machine shop, jobbing & repair

(G-3059)
MINUTEMAN PRESS
63 Hebron Ave Ste B (06033-2078)
PHONE..................................860 266-4154
EMP: 2
SALES (est): 83.9K **Privately Held**
SIC: 2752 Commercial printing, lithographic

(G-3060)
MISSION CRITICAL SOFTWARE
146 Shagbark Rd (06033-1738)
PHONE..................................860 748-6946
Brad Hurley, *Principal*
EMP: 2 **EST:** 2011
SALES (est): 128K **Privately Held**
SIC: 7372 Prepackaged software

(G-3061)
MITCHELL MACHINE SCREW COMPANY
167 Oak St (06033-2319)
P.O. Box 43 (06033-0043)
PHONE..................................860 633-7713
Mitchell Paul Koziol, *President*
Laura Koziol, *Corp Secy*
Janet Koziol, *Vice Pres*
EMP: 4 **EST:** 1954
SQ FT: 3,600
SALES: 200K **Privately Held**
SIC: 3451 Screw machine products

(G-3062)
NAP BROTHERS PARLOR FRAME INC
122 Naubuc Ave Ste B3 (06033-4291)
PHONE..................................860 633-9998
Stephen Napoletano, *President*
Mike Napoletano, *Vice Pres*
EMP: 10 **EST:** 1948
SQ FT: 25,000
SALES (est): 1.4MM **Privately Held**
SIC: 2511 5712 Wood household furniture; furniture stores

(G-3063)
NEW ENGLAND BORING CONTRACTORS
129 Kreiger Ln Ste A (06033-2392)
PHONE..................................860 633-4649
Steven Preli, *President*
Edward Preli, *Vice Pres*
Janis Preli, *Treasurer*
EMP: 18
SQ FT: 6,000
SALES (est): 4MM **Privately Held**
WEB: www.newenglandboring.com
SIC: 1481 Test boring for nonmetallic minerals

(G-3064)
NEXT DOOR CREATIONS LLC
Also Called: Oliver Poons Children's Brand
15 Conestoga Way (06033-3303)
PHONE..................................860 933-0366
Lauryn Wendus, *Owner*
EMP: 1 **EST:** 2015
SALES (est): 70.6K **Privately Held**
SIC: 2731 3942 Books: publishing only; stuffed toys, including animals

(G-3065)
NORTHEAST CIRCUIT TECH LLC
112 Sherwood Dr (06033-3724)
PHONE..................................860 633-1967
George R Willis, *Principal*
EMP: 7
SALES (est): 883.4K **Privately Held**
SIC: 3672 Printed circuit boards

(G-3066)
OPEN SOLUTIONS LLC (HQ)
455 Winding Brook Dr # 101 (06033-4351)
PHONE..................................860 815-5000
Stephen J Cameron, *President*
Mike Reiskis, *President*
Sam Boggs, *Exec VP*
Wayne Ginn, *Senior VP*
Ken Boin, *Vice Pres*
EMP: 200
SQ FT: 66,000
SALES (est): 2MM
SALES (corp-wide): 5.8B **Publicly Held**
WEB: www.imagicsystems.com
SIC: 7372 7373 Business oriented computer software; systems integration services
PA: Fiserv, Inc.
   255 Fiserv Dr
   Brookfield WI 53045
   262 879-5000

(G-3067)
PARMACO LLC
111 Warner Ct (06033-5011)
PHONE..................................860 573-7118
Paul Marchinetti,
EMP: 3
SALES: 1.8MM **Privately Held**
SIC: 3629 Electronic generation equipment

(G-3068)
PARTNER IN PUBLISHING LLC
947 Neipsic Rd (06033-2503)
PHONE..................................860 430-9440
Susan Brusch, *Project Mgr*
Ryan Einarson, *Project Mgr*
Maegan Kimball, *Project Mgr*
Lisa March, *Mng Member*
Meg Cameron, *Sr Project Mgr*
EMP: 2 **EST:** 2011
SALES (est): 223.3K **Privately Held**
SIC: 2741 Miscellaneous publishing

(G-3069)
PEOPLE MEETING LLC (PA)
15 Conestoga Way (06033-3303)
PHONE..................................860 933-0366
Lauryn Wendus,
EMP: 1
SALES (est): 71.5K **Privately Held**
SIC: 7372 7389 Prepackaged software;

(G-3070)
PHOENIX WELDING
122 Naubuc Ave Ste A3 (06033-4294)
PHONE..................................860 657-9481
Ray Secondo, *Owner*
EMP: 1
SALES (est): 45K **Privately Held**
SIC: 7692 Welding repair

(G-3071)
PINTO MANUFACTURING LLC
122 Naubuc Ave Ste A6 (06033-4298)
PHONE..................................860 659-9543
Robert Pinto, *Owner*
EMP: 8
SQ FT: 3,000
SALES (est): 938.5K **Privately Held**
WEB: www.pintodesigns.com
SIC: 3599 Machine shop, jobbing & repair

(G-3072)
PLASTICS AND CONCEPTS CONN INC
101 Laurel Trl (06033-4055)
PHONE..................................860 657-9655
Kathleen Harris, *President*
Tom Harris, *Vice Pres*
Harold Harris, *Admin Sec*
EMP: 11
SQ FT: 3,000
SALES: 100K **Privately Held**
WEB: www.plasticsandconcepts.com
SIC: 3089 3498 Injection molding of plastics; tube fabricating (contract bending & shaping)

(G-3073)
PREMIER CUSTOM CABINETRY
22 Kreiger Ln (06033-2371)
PHONE..................................860 659-1863
Paul Burrows, *Owner*
EMP: 1
SQ FT: 1,800
SALES (est): 60.9K **Privately Held**
SIC: 2541 Cabinets, except refrigerated: show, display, etc.: wood

(G-3074)
PRINT HOUSE LLC
22 Kreiger Ln Ste 6 (06033-2371)
PHONE..................................860 652-0803
Laura Danaher, *Manager*
EMP: 4
SALES (est): 481.5K **Privately Held**
SIC: 2752 Commercial printing, lithographic

(G-3075)
PROJECTS INC
65 Sequin Dr (06033-2484)
P.O. Box 190 (06033-0190)
PHONE..................................860 633-4615
Adelle Kenyon, *Ch of Bd*
F Michael Kenyon, *President*
Edwin Rodriguez, *Opers Mgr*
John Bannon, *Mfg Spvr*
Alicia Corson, *Production*
EMP: 102
SQ FT: 36,000
SALES (est): 41.6MM **Privately Held**
WEB: www.projectsinc.com
SIC: 3829 3599 7699 3823 Thermocouples; thermometers & temperature sensors; machine shop, jobbing & repair; precision instrument repair; industrial instrmnts msrmnt display/control process variable

(G-3076)
PROLINK INC
148 Eastern Blvd Ste 104 (06033-4368)
PHONE..................................860 659-5928
Bruce Brigham, *President*
Gene Vanpatten, *Sales Dir*
Thomas Wrinkle, *Software Dev*
Barbara Brigham, *Admin Sec*
EMP: 6
SQ FT: 3,000
SALES (est): 786.9K **Privately Held**
WEB: www.prolinksoftware.com
SIC: 7372 Educational computer software

(G-3077)
PW POWER SYSTEMS LLC (HQ)
Also Called: Pw Power Systems, Inc.
628 Hebron Ave Ste 400 (06033-5018)
PHONE..................................860 368-5900
Moraith Macrae, *President*
Paul Coderre, *General Mgr*
Eric Albrecht, *Counsel*
Maurice Gabbidon, *Project Mgr*
Joseph Jaworski, *Project Mgr*
◆ **EMP:** 43
SQ FT: 120,000
SALES (est): 54.6MM **Privately Held**
WEB: www.utc.com
SIC: 3612 Transformers, except electric

(G-3078)
R & M ASSOCIATES INC
Also Called: Close To Home
277 Hebron Ave (06033-2116)
PHONE..................................860 633-0721
Ronald Gattinella, *President*
Marc Gattinella, *Principal*
Marilyn Gattinella, *Vice Pres*
EMP: 13 **EST:** 1982
SQ FT: 5,700
SALES (est): 1.1MM **Privately Held**
SIC: 5949 2591 Fabric stores piece goods; drapery hardware & blinds & shades

(G-3079)
RECOGNITION INC
77 Kreiger Ln Ste 810 (06033-2383)
PHONE..................................860 659-8629
Jeff Lederman, *President*
EMP: 6
SQ FT: 3,000
SALES (est): 1.4MM **Privately Held**
WEB: www.recognition.net
SIC: 5199 3499 3089 Gifts & novelties; foam rubber; novelties & giftware, including trophies; engraving of plastic

(G-3080)
SAINTS WOODWORKING LLC
111 Forest Ln (06033-3917)
PHONE..................................860 657-4733
Robert Saint-Amant,
EMP: 1
SALES (est): 92K **Privately Held**
SIC: 1799 2499 Special trade contractors; decorative wood & woodwork

(G-3081)
SAS INSTITUTE INC
95 Glastonbury Blvd # 301 (06033-4447)
PHONE..................................860 633-4119
Linda Admin, *Branch Mgr*
EMP: 30
SALES (corp-wide): 3B **Privately Held**
WEB: www.sas.com
SIC: 7372 Application computer software; business oriented computer software; educational computer software
PA: Sas Institute Inc.
   100 Sas Campus Dr
   Cary NC 27513
   919 677-8000

(G-3082)
SCHULZ CONSULTING LLC
160 Oak St Ste 1b (06033-2336)
P.O. Box 438 (06033-0438)
PHONE..................................860 657-4497
Wayne Schulz, *Executive*
EMP: 3
SALES (est): 214K **Privately Held**
SIC: 7379 7372 Computer related consulting services; prepackaged software

(G-3083)
SPECTRUM MARKING MATERIALS LLC
128 Addison Rd (06033-1605)
P.O. Box 1762, Block Island RI (02807-1762)
PHONE..................................860 533-9533
David Morrison,
Lucinda Morrison,
EMP: 2
SQ FT: 3,000
SALES (est): 294.8K **Privately Held**
WEB: www.spectrummarking.com
SIC: 3089 5162 Plastic hardware & building products; plastics materials

(G-3084)
SURFACE PLATE CO
23 Pearl St (06033-1013)
P.O. Box 135, Middle Haddam (06456-0135)
PHONE..................................860 652-8905
David Baribault, *President*
Walter Baribault, *Vice Pres*
EMP: 3 **EST:** 1989
SALES (est): 195.6K **Privately Held**
SIC: 3281 Granite, cut & shaped

Glastonbury - Hartford County (G-3085)

(G-3085)
SWAHN ENGRAVING LLC
1207 Main St (06033-3123)
PHONE..................................860 657-4709
Bryan L Swahn,
Bryan Swahn,
EMP: 2
SALES (est): 182.8K **Privately Held**
WEB: www.swahnengraving.com
SIC: 5999 3993 Trophies & plaques; signs & advertising specialties

(G-3086)
THOUGHTVENTIONS UNLIMITED LLC
40 Nutmeg Ln (06033-2314)
P.O. Box 1310 (06033-6310)
PHONE..................................860 657-9014
Stephen Bates,
EMP: 1
SQ FT: 3,000
SALES (est): 165K **Privately Held**
WEB: www.tvu.com
SIC: 3567 8733 Electrical furnaces, ovens & heating devices, exc. induction; non-commercial research organizations

(G-3087)
TIMKEN COMPANY
701 Hebron Ave Ste 2 (06033-2489)
PHONE..................................860 652-4630
Raymond Buckno, *Manager*
EMP: 11
SQ FT: 2,000
SALES (corp-wide): 3.5B **Publicly Held**
SIC: 3562 Ball & roller bearings
PA: The Timken Company
  4500 Mount Pleasant St Nw
  North Canton OH 44720
  234 262-3000

(G-3088)
TITUS TECHNOLOGICAL LABS
77 Kreiger Ln Ste 914 (06033-2370)
P.O. Box 1232 (06033-6232)
PHONE..................................860 633-5472
Lawrence L Titus, *Owner*
EMP: 2
SQ FT: 800
SALES: 70K **Privately Held**
WEB: www.tituslabs.com
SIC: 3663 Radio broadcasting & communications equipment

(G-3089)
TRAVERS & CO LLC
Also Called: Travers Macintosh Consulting
311 Woodhaven Rd (06033-1921)
PHONE..................................860 633-8586
Jeffrey Travers, *President*
EMP: 3
SALES: 500K **Privately Held**
WEB: www.traversco.com
SIC: 7379 7372 Computer related consulting services; prepackaged software; business oriented computer software

(G-3090)
TSHIRTS ETC INC
74 Kreiger Ln Ste 1 (06033-2377)
P.O. Box 995 (06033-0995)
PHONE..................................860 657-3551
Paul Bowler, *President*
Debra Bowler, *Vice Pres*
Stacey Fagan, *Manager*
Ernest Richardson, *Manager*
EMP: 7
SQ FT: 2,700
SALES (est): 674.2K **Privately Held**
WEB: www.tseink.com
SIC: 7299 2396 Stitching, custom; screen printing on fabric articles

(G-3091)
TURBINE KINETICS INC
60 Sequin Dr Ste 2 (06033-5042)
PHONE..................................860 633-8520
Mike Siegel, *CEO*
Bryan Peters, *Senior VP*
Matthew Levasseur, *Engineer*
Tim Williams, *Engineer*
EMP: 11
SALES (est): 3.9MM **Publicly Held**
SIC: 3724 Aircraft engines & engine parts

HQ: Heico Aerospace Holdings Corp.
  3000 Taft St
  Hollywood FL 33021
  954 987-4000

(G-3092)
TVU GOLD COATING SERVICES
40 Nutmeg Ln (06033-2314)
PHONE..................................860 657-2666
EMP: 2
SALES (est): 121.2K **Privately Held**
SIC: 3567 Industrial furnaces & ovens

(G-3093)
VINEYARD THIMBLE
808 Thompson St (06033-4003)
PHONE..................................860 416-5115
EMP: 2
SALES (est): 75.9K **Privately Held**
SIC: 2084 Wines

(G-3094)
WALKER PRODUCTS INCORPORATED
80 Commerce St Ste C (06033-2385)
PHONE..................................860 659-3781
Bernadine A Brock, *President*
Charles Y Brock Jr, *Admin Sec*
▲ EMP: 14
SQ FT: 25,000
SALES (est): 3.4MM **Privately Held**
SIC: 2675 Die-cut paper & board

Goshen
Litchfield County

(G-3095)
ANSTETT LUMBER CO
182 East St N (06756-1117)
P.O. Box 211 (06756-0211)
PHONE..................................860 491-3225
Roger Anstett, *Owner*
EMP: 1
SALES (est): 113.4K **Privately Held**
SIC: 2421 5031 Lumber: rough, sawed or planed; lumber: rough, dressed & finished

(G-3096)
CHICORY BLUE PRESS INC
795 East St N (06756-1130)
PHONE..................................860 491-2271
Sondra Zeidenstein, *President*
EMP: 1 EST: 2001
SALES (est): 68.4K **Privately Held**
WEB: www.chicorybluepress.com
SIC: 2731 Books: publishing only

(G-3097)
COUNTRY LOG HOMES INC
27 Rockwall Ct (06756-1714)
PHONE..................................413 229-8084
Ivan Chassie, *President*
Doreen Chassie, *Corp Secy*
EMP: 12
SQ FT: 12,000
SALES (est): 1.7MM **Privately Held**
WEB: www.countryloghomes.com
SIC: 2452 1521 Log cabins, prefabricated, wood; single-family housing construction

(G-3098)
DESJARDINS WOODWORKING INC
211 East St N (06756-1120)
PHONE..................................860 491-9972
Peter E Desjardins, *President*
EMP: 6
SALES (est): 520K **Privately Held**
SIC: 2499 Decorative wood & woodwork

(G-3099)
JUDY LOW
Also Called: Newspaper
192 5 1/2 Mile Rd (06756-1025)
PHONE..................................860 491-9101
Judy Low, *Owner*
EMP: 1
SALES (est): 40.3K **Privately Held**
SIC: 2711 Newspapers

(G-3100)
KORNER KARE
175 North St (06756-1204)
P.O. Box 291 (06756-0291)
PHONE..................................860 491-3731
Jim Korner, *Owner*
Antonette Korner, *Partner*
EMP: 4
SALES (est): 228.3K **Privately Held**
SIC: 2842 Specialty cleaning preparations

(G-3101)
L & L MECHANICAL LLC
28 Pie Hill Rd (06756-2024)
PHONE..................................860 491-4007
Lisa Lillis,
Charles Lillis,
EMP: 11
SALES (est): 1.1MM **Privately Held**
SIC: 3443 1711 Ducting, metal plate; ventilation & duct work contractor

(G-3102)
LAKE HOUSE BREWING COMPANY LLC
287 W Hyerdale Dr (06756-1704)
PHONE..................................917 620-6636
Eric S McKay,
J Patrick Murtaugh,
EMP: 2
SALES (est): 126.4K **Privately Held**
SIC: 2041 Corn grits & flakes, for brewers' use

(G-3103)
MIRANDA VINEYARD LLC
42 Ives Rd (06756-2118)
PHONE..................................860 491-9906
Manuel D Miranda, *Principal*
EMP: 4
SALES (est): 326.7K **Privately Held**
SIC: 2084 Wines

(G-3104)
SOFTWARE CNSLTING RSOURCES INC
9 Valcove Ct (06756-1913)
PHONE..................................860 491-2689
Stanley J Detwiler, *Owner*
Amanda Canon, *Partner*
EMP: 3
SALES (est): 220.4K **Privately Held**
WEB: www.scrinc.net
SIC: 7372 Prepackaged software

(G-3105)
YIELD INDUSTRIES LLC
209 Milton Rd (06756-1626)
PHONE..................................860 307-8202
Craig Bothroyd, *Principal*
EMP: 1 EST: 2016
SALES (est): 50.5K **Privately Held**
SIC: 3999 Manufacturing industries

Granby
Hartford County

(G-3106)
ARROW CONCRETE PRODUCTS INC (PA)
560 Salmon Brook St (06035-1100)
PHONE..................................860 653-5063
Kurt A Burkhart, *President*
Ronald Burkhart Sr, *Vice Pres*
Susan Burkhart, *Vice Pres*
Jon Maxwell, *Plant Mgr*
Bruce Ellis, *Sales Staff*
▲ EMP: 32 EST: 1953
SALES (est): 14.4MM **Privately Held**
WEB: www.arrow-concrete.com
SIC: 3272 Septic tanks, concrete; covers, catch basin: concrete; manhole covers or frames, concrete

(G-3107)
GAMMA VENTURES INC
11 Rondure Rd (06035-1223)
PHONE..................................860 653-2613
Glidden Doman, *President*
EMP: 1

SALES (est): 84.9K **Privately Held**
SIC: 3621 3724 Windmills, electric generating; turbines, aircraft type

(G-3108)
GRASS ROOTS CREAMERY
4 Park Pl (06035-2300)
PHONE..................................860 653-6303
Elizabeth Florian, *Principal*
EMP: 6
SALES (est): 169.6K **Privately Held**
SIC: 2021 Creamery butter

(G-3109)
KALLAI DESIGNS
1 Granby Farms Rd (06035-2024)
PHONE..................................860 653-6786
Rose Jones, *Owner*
EMP: 1
SALES (est): 67.4K **Privately Held**
SIC: 2335 Wedding gowns & dresses

(G-3110)
KRYSTAL INC LLC
Also Called: Krystal Restaurant
9a Bank St (06035-2303)
P.O. Box 14 (06035-0014)
PHONE..................................860 844-1267
Arun Lillaney, *President*
Ron Lira, *General Mgr*
EMP: 7
SQ FT: 2,500
SALES: 1.2MM **Privately Held**
SIC: 5812 5731 2085 American restaurant; video recorders, players, disc players & accessories; neutral spirits, except fruit

(G-3111)
KWIK KERB MASTERS LLC
45 Old Stagecoach Rd (06035-1503)
PHONE..................................860 653-8102
Kenneth L Agans, *Principal*
EMP: 2
SALES (est): 94.8K **Privately Held**
SIC: 3281 Curbing, paving & walkway stone

(G-3112)
MONARCH PLASTIC LLC
514r Salmon Brook St (06035-1425)
PHONE..................................860 653-2000
Michael Guarco Jr,
EMP: 10
SQ FT: 10,000
SALES (est): 1.3MM **Privately Held**
SIC: 3084 3089 Plastics pipe; fittings for pipe, plastic

(G-3113)
SHERWOOD EQUINE LLC
2 Hayfield Ln (06035-2923)
PHONE..................................860 653-3599
Jacklyn Stupienski, *Principal*
EMP: 2 EST: 2016
SALES (est): 65.4K **Privately Held**
SIC: 2499 Wood products

(G-3114)
SINGULARITY SPACE SYSTEMS LLC
Also Called: SSS
33 Wolcott Dr (06035-1320)
PHONE..................................860 713-3626
William Hosack, *CEO*
EMP: 4 EST: 2014
SALES (est): 190.3K **Privately Held**
SIC: 3761 4789 3823 Space vehicles, complete; space flight operations, except government; infrared instruments, industrial process type

(G-3115)
STITCHES BY ME
10 Hartford Ave (06035-2304)
P.O. Box 236 (06035-0236)
PHONE..................................860 653-9701
Tracy Gemme, *Partner*
Janet Gemme, *Partner*
EMP: 2
SALES (est): 88K **Privately Held**
SIC: 2395 Embroidery products, except schiffli machine

Greenwich
Fairfield County

(G-3116)
ACUREN INSPECTION INC
43 Arch St (06830-6512)
PHONE..................................203 869-6734
Peter Scannell, *Branch Mgr*
EMP: 52
SALES (corp-wide): 1.7B **Privately Held**
SIC: 1389 Testing, measuring, surveying & analysis services
HQ: Acuren Inspection, Inc.
30 Main St Ste 402
Danbury CT 06810
203 702-8740

(G-3117)
ALPHACOM INC
Also Called: Archstreet Designs
84 Havemeyer Pl (06830)
PHONE..................................203 637-7006
Christopher Bubbers, *President*
Veena Virmani, *Vice Pres*
EMP: 2
SQ FT: 950
SALES (est): 99.4K **Privately Held**
WEB: www.archstreet.com
SIC: 7336 7379 2791 Graphic arts & related design; computer related consulting services; typesetting

(G-3118)
AMCI CAPITAL LP
600 Steamboat Rd Ste 3 (06830-7149)
PHONE..................................203 625-9200
Kathleen Hayes, *Principal*
Miklos Salamon,
EMP: 1
SALES (est): 91.8K **Privately Held**
SIC: 1081 Metal mining services

(G-3119)
AMERICAN MARINE INC
40 High St (06830-5959)
PHONE..................................914 763-5367
Lou Dell, *President*
▲ **EMP:** 1
SALES (est): 120K **Privately Held**
SIC: 3824 Water meters

(G-3120)
AMERICAN METALS COAL INTL INC (HQ)
Also Called: A M C I
475 Steamboat Rd Fl 2nd (06830-7144)
PHONE..................................203 625-9200
Fritz Kundrun, *CEO*
Harris Antoniou, *CEO*
Hans J Mende, *President*
Thomas Buerger, *CFO*
Mike Walker, *Treasurer*
▲ **EMP:** 13
SQ FT: 3,720
SALES (est): 26.7MM **Privately Held**
WEB: www.amcigroup.com
SIC: 5052 5051 1222 6512 Coal; coke; steel; bituminous coal-underground mining; commercial & industrial building operation

(G-3121)
APRICOT HOME LLC
15 Sheffield Way (06831-3725)
PHONE..................................203 552-1791
Abby Pillari, *Mng Member*
▲ **EMP:** 7
SALES (est): 355.7K **Privately Held**
SIC: 2273 Carpets & rugs

(G-3122)
APTUIT GLOBAL LLC (PA)
2 Greenwich Office Park (06831-5148)
PHONE..................................203 660-6000
John Fikre, *Agent*
EMP: 3
SALES (est): 1MM **Privately Held**
SIC: 8731 2834 Biological research; powders, pharmaceutical

(G-3123)
ARTICRAFTS
3 Sound View Ter (06830-6430)
PHONE..................................203 618-1715
Lisa Bologna, *Owner*
EMP: 1
SALES (est): 86.2K **Privately Held**
WEB: www.preservedflorals.net
SIC: 3999 Flowers, artificial & preserved

(G-3124)
ASHA
9 Pecksland Rd (06831-3710)
PHONE..................................203 253-0146
Ashley Dodgen-Mccormick, *President*
EMP: 2
SALES (est): 88.3K **Privately Held**
SIC: 3911 Jewelry apparel

(G-3125)
ATLAS AGI HOLDINGS LLC
Also Called: Agi-Shorewood U.S.
100 Northfield St (06830-4618)
PHONE..................................203 622-9138
Larry Hall, *Asst Controller*
Andrew M Bursky, *Mng Member*
Andrew Bursky, *Mng Member*
Timothy J Fazio, *Mng Member*
Troy Schirk, *Info Tech Dir*
▼ **EMP:** 3860 **EST:** 2010
SALES (est): 228.8MM **Privately Held**
SIC: 2671 Packaging paper & plastics film, coated & laminated

(G-3126)
AXELS CUSTOM WOODWORKING LLC
45 Rodwell Ave (06830-6170)
PHONE..................................203 869-1317
James Decarlo, *Principal*
EMP: 4
SALES (est): 247.6K **Privately Held**
SIC: 2431 Millwork

(G-3127)
B H SHOE HOLDINGS INC (HQ)
124 W Putnam Ave Ste 1 (06830-5317)
PHONE..................................203 661-2424
James Issler, *President*
Marc Hamburg, *Vice Pres*
J Scott Bohling, *Admin Sec*
◆ **EMP:** 50
SALES (est): 372.6MM
SALES (corp-wide): 225.3B **Publicly Held**
SIC: 3143 Men's footwear, except athletic
PA: Berkshire Hathaway Inc.
3555 Farnam St Ste 1140
Omaha NE 68131
402 346-1400

(G-3128)
BACK COUNTRY GRAPHICS
1147 King St (06831-3246)
PHONE..................................203 531-5878
Andre Dedekam, *Owner*
EMP: 2
SALES (est): 120K **Privately Held**
SIC: 2752 Commercial printing, offset

(G-3129)
BAOBAB ASSET MANAGEMENT LLC
2 Greenwich Office Park # 300 (06831-5155)
PHONE..................................203 340-5700
Russell Fryer, *Mng Member*
EMP: 3
SALES (est): 922.3K **Privately Held**
SIC: 1021 Copper ores

(G-3130)
BAXTER BROS INC
Also Called: Baxter Investment Management
1030 E Putnam Ave (06830)
PHONE..................................203 637-4559
William J Baxter Jr, *President*
Jamie Gioia, *Manager*
John Baxter, *Director*
EMP: 5
SQ FT: 2,000
SALES (est): 675.9K **Privately Held**
SIC: 2721 6282 Periodicals: publishing only; investment advisory service

(G-3131)
BAYER CLOTHING GROUP INC (PA)
Also Called: Hyde Clothes Div
503 Riversville Rd (06831-2914)
PHONE..................................203 661-4140
Robert Bayer, *President*
Philip P Looby, *COO*
Kathy Jo Corry, *Purch Mgr*
▼ **EMP:** 59 **EST:** 1951
SQ FT: 40,000
SALES (est): 45.3MM **Privately Held**
SIC: 2311 2337 2325 Suits, men's & boys': made from purchased materials; tailored dress & sport coats: men's & boys'; suits: women's, misses' & juniors'; slacks, dress: men's, youths' & boys'

(G-3132)
BELVOIR PUBLICATIONS ✪
75 Holly Hill Ln (06830-6098)
PHONE..................................203 422-7300
EMP: 1 **EST:** 2019
SALES (est): 37.5K **Privately Held**
SIC: 2741 Miscellaneous publishing

(G-3133)
BIGS PUBLISHING LLC
22 Round Hill Club Rd (06831-3326)
PHONE..................................203 249-1059
Benjamin Carpenter,
EMP: 1
SALES (est): 45.2K **Privately Held**
SIC: 2731 Books: publishing & printing

(G-3134)
BLAUNER BOOKS
19 Field Point Dr (06831-7013)
PHONE..................................203 222-6042
EMP: 1
SALES (est): 67K **Privately Held**
SIC: 2731 Books-Publishing/Printing

(G-3135)
BLUE SKY STUDIOS INC
Also Called: Blue Sky/Vifx
1 American Ln Ste 301 (06831-2563)
PHONE..................................203 992-6000
Robert Cohen, *Ch of Bd*
Brian Keane, *CFO*
EMP: 200 **EST:** 1987
SALES (est): 24.5MM
SALES (corp-wide): 90.2B **Publicly Held**
WEB: www.blueskystudios.com
SIC: 7372 7812 Prepackaged software; motion picture & video production
HQ: Fox Entertainment Group, Llc
1211 Ave Of The Americas
New York NY 10036
212 852-7000

(G-3136)
BRANT INDUSTRIES INC (PA)
Also Called: White Birch Paper Company
80 Field Point Rd Ste 3 (06830-6416)
PHONE..................................203 661-3344
Peter M Brant, *CEO*
Christopher Brant, *President*
Bruno Antonios, *Senior VP*
Jean Blais, *Senior VP*
Russell Lowder, *Senior VP*
◆ **EMP:** 18
SQ FT: 4,500
SALES (est): 257.7MM **Privately Held**
SIC: 2621 Paper mills

(G-3137)
BRIDGWELL RSOURCES HOLDINGS LLC (HQ)
1 Sound Shore Dr Ste 302 (06830-7251)
PHONE..................................203 622-9138
Andrew M Bursky, *President*
Daniel E Cromie,
Timothy J Fazio,
Edward J Fletcher,
Jacob D Hudson,
EMP: 6
SALES (est): 174.6MM
SALES (corp-wide): 2.9B **Privately Held**
SIC: 5031 2491 5039 5153 Paneling, wood; wood products, creosoted; prefabricated structures; grain & field beans
PA: Atlas Holdings, Llc
100 Northfield St
Greenwich CT 06830
203 622-9138

(G-3138)
BRYNWOOD PARTNERS V LTD PARTNR (PA)
8 Sound Shore Dr Ste 265 (06830-7264)
PHONE..................................203 622-1790
Hendrik J Hartong Jr, *Partner*
Kevin C Hartnett, *Partner*
Ian B Mactaggart, *Partner*
Robert Sperry, *Partner*
EMP: 5
SALES (est): 86.6MM **Privately Held**
SIC: 6282 1751 3442 5031 Investment advice; window & door installation & erection; metal doors; metal doors, sash & trim; aluminum extruded products

(G-3139)
BUISSON JEWELERS INC
200 Railroad Ave Ste 201 (06830-6384)
PHONE..................................203 869-8895
Joel Buisson, *President*
Yves Buisson, *Admin Sec*
EMP: 8
SALES (est): 980K **Privately Held**
SIC: 5944 3961 Jewelry, precious stones & precious metals; costume jewelry

(G-3140)
CAPRICORN INVESTORS II LP
30 E Elm St (06830-6529)
PHONE..................................203 861-6600
Herbert Winokur Jr, *General Ptnr*
James M Better, *General Ptnr*
Nathaniel A Gregory, *General Ptnr*
Dudley C Mecum, *General Ptnr*
EMP: 5953
SALES (est): 3.3MM **Privately Held**
WEB: www.capricornholdings.com
SIC: 2676 5461 6794 Diapers, paper (disposable); bakeries; patent owners & lessors

(G-3141)
CAPRICORN INVESTORS III LP (PA)
30 E Elm St (06830-6529)
PHONE..................................203 861-6600
Herbert Winiker, *Partner*
Dudley Micum, *Partner*
James Petter, *Partner*
▼ **EMP:** 10
SALES (est): 13.1MM **Privately Held**
SIC: 5812 6794 3556 5046 Eating places; patent owners & lessors; food products machinery; commercial equipment; short-term business credit

(G-3142)
CASTRO INDUSTRIES LLC
12 Joshua Ln (06830-3928)
PHONE..................................203 249-9268
Lindsay Shea, *Principal*
EMP: 2
SALES (est): 78.9K **Privately Held**
SIC: 3999 Manufacturing industries

(G-3143)
CHRISTOPHER PEACOCK HOMES
2 Dearfield Dr Ste 1 (06831-5301)
PHONE..................................203 862-9333
Christopher L Peacock, *Owner*
EMP: 1
SALES (est): 152.1K **Privately Held**
SIC: 2434 Wood kitchen cabinets

(G-3144)
CONNECTICUT IRON WORKS INC
59 Davenport Ave (06830-7105)
PHONE..................................203 869-0657
Albert Margenot, *President*
John R Margenot, *Vice Pres*
EMP: 8 **EST:** 1921
SQ FT: 8,800
SALES: 750K **Privately Held**
SIC: 3441 3446 Fabricated structural metal; ornamental metalwork

Greenwich - Fairfield County (G-3145)

(G-3145)
COSS SYSTEMS INC
8 Fairview Ter (06831-4151)
PHONE................................800 961-0288
Antonia Spitver, *Principal*
EMP: 2
SALES (est): 79.3K **Privately Held**
SIC: 7372 Prepackaged software

(G-3146)
COUPONZ DIRECT LLC
25 Lewis St Ste 303 (06830-5537)
PHONE................................212 655-9615
Penny Oloughnane,
EMP: 3
SALES (est): 71.1K **Privately Held**
SIC: 7372 Prepackaged software

(G-3147)
CP APN INC
599 W Putnam Ave (06830-6005)
PHONE................................330 682-3000
Scott A Dahnke, *President*
EMP: 1
SALES (est): 4.5MM
SALES (corp-wide): 7.8B **Publicly Held**
SIC: 2047 Dog food
HQ: Nu Pet Company
1 Strawberry Ln
Orrville OH 44667
330 682-3000

(G-3148)
CUSTOM FOOD PDTS HOLDINGS LLC
411 W Putnam Ave (06830-6261)
PHONE................................310 637-0900
Ervin J Hickerson, *President*
EMP: 55
SALES (est): 16.3MM **Privately Held**
SIC: 2013 Prepared beef products from purchased beef
PA: Contrarian Capital Management Llc
411 W Putnam Ave Ste 425
Greenwich CT 06830

(G-3149)
DELANY & LONG LTD
41 Chestnut St (06830-5969)
PHONE................................203 532-0010
Jack Flynn, *President*
EMP: 3
SALES (est): 290K **Privately Held**
SIC: 3441 Fabricated structural metal

(G-3150)
DELFIN MARKETING INC
500 W Putnam Ave Ste 400 (06830-6096)
PHONE................................203 554-2707
Aki Immonen, *Principal*
Heikki Meriranta, *Engineer*
EMP: 8
SALES (est): 723.1K
SALES (corp-wide): 511.1K **Privately Held**
SIC: 3841 Surgical & medical instruments
PA: Delfin Technologies Oy
Microkatu 1
Kuopio 70210
509 111-199

(G-3151)
DEMANE GOLF INC
35 Chapel St (06831-5108)
PHONE................................203 531-9126
Richard Demane, *President*
Margarette Demane, *Treasurer*
Rene Demane, *Admin Sec*
EMP: 2 EST: 1950
SALES (est): 294.5K **Privately Held**
WEB: www.demanegolf.com
SIC: 3949 7699 5941 Golf equipment; golf club & equipment repair; golf goods & equipment

(G-3152)
DESROSIER OF GREENWICH INC
Also Called: Lighthouse Technology Partners
103 Mason St (06830-6605)
PHONE................................203 661-2334
Brian Desrosier, *President*
Jon Gould, *General Mgr*
EMP: 15
SQ FT: 8,000
SALES (est): 1.3MM **Privately Held**
WEB: www.computersupercenter.com
SIC: 7372 7371 7373 Business oriented computer software; computer software development; systems software development services

(G-3153)
DITRIORICHARD
21 Grey Rock Dr (06831-4218)
PHONE................................203 531-0625
Richard Ditrio, *Principal*
EMP: 2
SALES (est): 74.4K **Privately Held**
SIC: 2821 Plastics materials & resins

(G-3154)
DOCTORS CLOTHES
67 Church St (06830-5624)
PHONE................................203 485-0494
Chuck Paulk, *Owner*
EMP: 2
SALES (est): 101.8K **Privately Held**
SIC: 2326 Medical & hospital uniforms, men's

(G-3155)
DOONEY WOODWORKS LLC
55 Conyers Farm Dr (06831-2736)
PHONE................................203 869-5457
EMP: 2 EST: 2010
SALES (est): 252.8K **Privately Held**
SIC: 2431 Millwork

(G-3156)
EASY GRAPHICS INC
Also Called: Minuteman Press
31 Saint Roch Ave Ste 1 (06830-6775)
PHONE................................203 622-0001
David Goldvug, *President*
▲ EMP: 3
SQ FT: 1,100
SALES (est): 572.5K **Privately Held**
SIC: 2752 Commercial printing, lithographic

(G-3157)
EDWARD FLEUR FNCL EDUCATN CORP
Also Called: Pass Perfect Associates
176 Bedford Rd (06831-2536)
PHONE................................203 629-9333
EMP: 2
SQ FT: 2,000
SALES (est): 3.5MM **Privately Held**
SIC: 2731 Publishes Exam Preparation Material

(G-3158)
FAIRFIELD COUNTY LOOK
6 Wyckham Hill Ln (06831-3049)
PHONE................................203 869-0077
Elaine Ubina, *Principal*
EMP: 3
SALES (est): 312.7K **Privately Held**
SIC: 2721 Magazines: publishing only, not printed on site

(G-3159)
FINCH PAPER HOLDINGS LLC (PA)
1 Sound Shore Dr Ste 302 (06830-7251)
PHONE................................203 622-9138
Sam Astor, *Manager*
Vishal Seernani, *Associate*
David Shi, *Associate*
EMP: 1
SALES (est): 83.7MM **Privately Held**
SIC: 2621 Paper mills

(G-3160)
FINE PETS LLC
229 Stanwich Rd (06830-3501)
PHONE................................203 833-1517
Janette Souliere,
EMP: 5
SALES: 100K **Privately Held**
SIC: 2047 Dog & cat food

(G-3161)
FISHER FOOTWEAR LLC
777 W Putnam Ave (06830-5091)
PHONE................................203 302-2800
Marc Fisher, *CEO*
Roger Ho, *Vice Pres*
▲ EMP: 10
SQ FT: 45,000
SALES (est): 1.2MM **Privately Held**
SIC: 3143 3144 Men's footwear, except athletic; women's footwear, except athletic

(G-3162)
FISHER SIGERSON MORRISON LLC
777 W Putnam Ave (06830-5091)
PHONE................................203 302-2800
Marc Fisher, *Mng Member*
Richard Daderline,
Miranda Morrison,
Kari Sigerson,
▲ EMP: 30
SQ FT: 1,600
SALES: 4.6MM
SALES (corp-wide): 120.9MM **Privately Held**
SIC: 3144 Women's footwear, except athletic
PA: Marc Fisher Llc
777 W Putnam Ave
Greenwich CT 06830
203 302-2800

(G-3163)
FLANGE LOCK LLC
57 Old Post Rd No 2 Ste 3 (06830-6786)
PHONE................................203 861-9400
Arnold Frumin, *Mng Member*
EMP: 6
SALES (est): 457.9K **Privately Held**
SIC: 3462 Flange, valve & pipe fitting forgings, ferrous

(G-3164)
FMP PRODUCTS
100 Melrose Ave Ste 206 (06830-6277)
PHONE................................203 422-0686
Thomas Friedlander, *Principal*
EMP: 4
SALES: 50K **Privately Held**
SIC: 3821 Laboratory apparatus & furniture

(G-3165)
FRESHIANA LLC
375 Greenwich Ave Apt 6 (06830-6545)
PHONE................................800 301-8071
John Stewart, *Principal*
EMP: 3
SALES (est): 76.2K **Privately Held**
SIC: 2711 Newspapers

(G-3166)
GATEWAY HELICOPTER SERVICE
Also Called: Gateway Helicopters
34 Bedford Rd (06831-2533)
PHONE................................203 531-4395
Mark Palozzo, *Owner*
EMP: 2
SALES (est): 92K **Privately Held**
SIC: 3721 Aircraft

(G-3167)
GLOVEWHISPERER INC
22 Hartford Ave (06830-5935)
PHONE................................203 487-8997
EMP: 2
SALES (est): 174.8K **Privately Held**
SIC: 3949 Sporting & athletic goods

(G-3168)
GRADUATION SOLUTIONS LLC
Also Called: Graduation Source
200 Pemberwick Rd (06831-4236)
PHONE................................914 934-5991
Jessie Alexander, *Mng Member*
Matthew Gordon, *Mng Member*
◆ EMP: 30
SQ FT: 3,600
SALES: 6.1MM **Privately Held**
SIC: 2384 Robes & dressing gowns

(G-3169)
GRAFFEAST INC
25 Sherwood Pl (06830-5606)
PHONE................................203 622-1622
Christine Hauck, *President*
EMP: 1
SALES (est): 42.5K **Privately Held**
SIC: 7336 3993 Graphic arts & related design; advertising artwork

(G-3170)
GRANOLA BAR
41 Greenwich Ave (06830-5510)
PHONE................................914 763-6320
EMP: 1 EST: 2017
SALES (est): 56.3K **Privately Held**
SIC: 2043 Granola & muesli, except bars & clusters

(G-3171)
GREAT AMERICAN PUBLISHING SOC
219 Pemberwick Rd (06831-4225)
PHONE................................203 531-9300
EMP: 1
SALES (est): 37.5K **Privately Held**
SIC: 2741 Misc Publishing

(G-3172)
GREEN RAY LED INTL LLC (PA)
115 E Putnam Ave Ste 3 (06830-5643)
PHONE................................203 485-1435
Tony Allan, *President*
Rey Norat, *CFO*
EMP: 5
SALES (est): 11.2MM **Privately Held**
SIC: 3646 Commercial indusl & institutional electric lighting fixtures

(G-3173)
GREENWICH CARBON LLC
500 W Putnam Ave Ste 400 (06830-6096)
PHONE................................203 531-7064
Anne Carley, *Mng Member*
Suhas Kundapoor, *Mng Member*
EMP: 3
SALES (est): 221.4K **Privately Held**
SIC: 3624 Carbon specialties for electrical use

(G-3174)
GREENWICH FREE PRESS LLC
21 Lincoln Ave (06830-5749)
PHONE................................203 622-1731
Leslie Yager, *Principal*
EMP: 1
SALES (est): 65.1K **Privately Held**
SIC: 2741 Miscellaneous publishing

(G-3175)
GREENWICH SENTINEL
28 Bruce Park Ave (06830-2728)
PHONE................................203 883-1430
Beth Barhydt, *Owner*
EMP: 4 EST: 2017
SALES (est): 169.6K **Privately Held**
SIC: 2711 Newspapers, publishing & printing

(G-3176)
HARRIER TECHNOLOGIES INC
67 Holly Hill Ln Ste 301 (06830-6072)
PHONE................................203 625-9700
Lee H Miller, *Chairman*
EMP: 2
SALES (est): 290K **Privately Held**
SIC: 3561 Pumps & pumping equipment

(G-3177)
HH BROWN SHOE COMPANY INC (DH)
Also Called: Cove Shoe Company Division
124 W Putnam Ave Ste 1a (06830-5317)
PHONE................................203 661-2424
J E Issler, *CEO*
Francis C Rooney Jr, *Ch of Bd*
James Issler, *President*
J Scott Bohling, *Exec VP*
◆ EMP: 50 EST: 1927
SQ FT: 13,000
SALES (est): 298.5MM
SALES (corp-wide): 225.3B **Publicly Held**
WEB: www.coveshoe.com
SIC: 3143 3144 Work shoes, men's; boots, dress or casual: men's; women's footwear, except athletic

Greenwich - Fairfield County (G-3209)

(G-3178)
IDA PUBLISHING CO INC
Also Called: Total Food Service
282 Railroad Ave Ste 4 (06830-6382)
P.O. Box 2507 (06836-2507)
PHONE 203 661-9090
Leslie Klashman, *President*
Michael Scinto, *Director*
EMP: 6
SALES (est): 909.4K Privately Held
SIC: 2721 Trade journals: publishing only, not printed on site

(G-3179)
IMPACT NUTRACEUTICALS LLC
401 Riversville Rd (06831-3230)
PHONE 203 493-4268
Joseph E Magaro Jr, *Principal*
EMP: 2 EST: 2011
SALES (est): 141.9K Privately Held
SIC: 1321 Natural gas liquids

(G-3180)
INDUSTRIAL FORREST PRODUCTS LL
21 Stanwich Rd (06830-4840)
PHONE 203 863-9486
EMP: 3
SALES (est): 185.2K Privately Held
SIC: 2411 Logging

(G-3181)
INKA INC
Also Called: Vital Eyes
390 Lake Ave (06830-3850)
PHONE 212 475-2180
Inka Doerrig, *President*
EMP: 1
SALES (est): 140K Privately Held
WEB: www.pearl-ice.com
SIC: 3842 Cosmetic restorations

(G-3182)
INTERSTATE + LAKELAND LBR CORP
184 S Water St (06830-6849)
PHONE 203 531-8050
Sheldon Kahan, *Owner*
Damian Kane, *Sales Staff*
EMP: 15
SALES (corp-wide): 24.8MM Privately Held
SIC: 2421 Box lumber
PA: Interstate + Lakeland Lumber Corporation
   247 Mill St
   Greenwich CT 06830
   203 531-8885

(G-3183)
JACOBSEN WOODWORKING CO INC
3 Oak St W (06830-6885)
P.O. Box 4422 (06831-0408)
PHONE 203 531-9050
EMP: 3
SALES (est): 223.3K Privately Held
SIC: 2431 Millwork

(G-3184)
JOHN M KRISKEY CARPENTRY
129 N Water St (06830-5816)
PHONE 203 531-0194
John Kriskey, *Partner*
Scott Kriskey, *Partner*
EMP: 3
SALES (est): 288.9K Privately Held
SIC: 2499 2541 2434 2431 Decorative wood & woodwork; wood partitions & fixtures; wood kitchen cabinets; millwork

(G-3185)
JUICE PRESS LLC
360 Greenwich Ave (06830-6522)
PHONE 212 777-0034
EMP: 1
SALES (corp-wide): 3.1MM Privately Held
SIC: 2033 Fruit juices: fresh
PA: The Juice Press Llc
   375 Hudson St Frnt A
   New York NY 10014
   212 777-0034

(G-3186)
KAREN CALLAN DESIGNS INC
30 Field Point Dr (06830-7014)
PHONE 203 762-9914
Karen Callan, *President*
Noel Konrad, *Office Mgr*
EMP: 7
SQ FT: 2,200
SALES (est): 750K Privately Held
WEB: www.karencallan.com
SIC: 7389 2387 Design services; apparel belts

(G-3187)
KENNETH FINN
Also Called: Gemini Group
422 W Lyon Farm Dr (06831-4359)
PHONE 914 764-4938
Kenneth Finn, *Owner*
EMP: 5
SALES (est): 60K Privately Held
SIC: 8742 7372 Marketing consulting services; publishers' computer software

(G-3188)
KENNY KALIPERSHAD
12 Wessels Pl (06830-6923)
PHONE 917 345-5038
Kenny Kalipershad, *Principal*
EMP: 2
SALES (est): 83.9K Privately Held
SIC: 2752 Commercial printing, lithographic

(G-3189)
LAUNELL INC
Also Called: Launell Group, The
24 Spring St Unit 2 (06830-6129)
P.O. Box 254, Old Greenwich (06870-0254)
PHONE 203 340-2150
Steven Rubin, *President*
Jean Rubin, *Vice Pres*
▲ EMP: 2
SQ FT: 400
SALES: 10MM Privately Held
SIC: 2389 Men's miscellaneous accessories

(G-3190)
LENOX34 LLC
66 Milbank Ave (06830-5740)
PHONE 203 869-6909
Bonita Copp, *Principal*
EMP: 2
SALES (est): 152.2K Privately Held
SIC: 3585 Refrigeration & heating equipment

(G-3191)
LGL GROUP INC
140 Greenwich Ave Ste 4 (06830-6560)
PHONE 407 298-2000
Jeremiah Healy, *CEO*
EMP: 3
SALES (est): 265.9K Privately Held
SIC: 2672 Coated & laminated paper

(G-3192)
LONGVIEW HOLDING CORPORATION (HQ)
43 Arch St (06830-6512)
PHONE 203 869-6734
Peter O Scannell, *President*
Harald B Findlay, *Vice Pres*
John P Lockwood, *CFO*
Margaret O'Brien, *Asst Sec*
EMP: 7
SQ FT: 3,500
SALES (est): 223.5MM
SALES (corp-wide): 1.7B Privately Held
WEB: www.rockwoodservice.com
SIC: 6719 1389 Personal holding companies, except banks; testing, measuring, surveying & analysis services
PA: Rockwood Service Corporation
   43 Arch St
   Greenwich CT 06830
   203 869-6734

(G-3193)
LU LU HOLDINGS LLC
55 Lewis St (06830-5528)
PHONE 203 861-1988
Jody Pennette, *Mng Member*
Andrew Rolse,
EMP: 25
SALES: 2.7MM Privately Held
SIC: 5812 4212 7372 Chinese restaurant; delivery service, vehicular; application computer software

(G-3194)
LUXURY BRAND NETWORK LLC
35 Anderson Rd (06830-6704)
PHONE 203 930-2703
Marshall Cooper, *CEO*
EMP: 2
SALES (est): 99.4K Privately Held
SIC: 2741

(G-3195)
LYNCH CORP
140 Greenwich Ave Ste 3 (06830-6560)
PHONE 203 452-3007
Ralph Papitto, *Principal*
Dick Robinson, *Manager*
EMP: 3
SALES (est): 314.3K Privately Held
SIC: 3559 Special industry machinery

(G-3196)
MADONNA BLACK BUDDIST LLC
32 Greenwich Ave 3 (06830-5503)
PHONE 203 589-9796
Morrissa Hammie, *CEO*
EMP: 1
SALES (est): 43.9K Privately Held
SIC: 7389 8999 7929 2911 Cosmetic kits, assembling & packaging; fund raising organizations; music arranging & composing; entertainers & entertainment groups; fractionation products of crude petroleum, hydrocarbons

(G-3197)
MAINE POWER EXPRESS LLC
485 W Putnam Ave (06830-6060)
PHONE 203 661-0055
Joseph Cotter, *Mng Member*
EMP: 3
SALES (est): 95.3K Privately Held
SIC: 1382 8731 Oil & gas exploration services; energy research

(G-3198)
MALIA MILLS SWIM WEAR
16 Greenwich Ave (06830-5503)
PHONE 203 622-3137
Malia Mills, *Principal*
EMP: 1
SALES (est): 50.2K Privately Held
SIC: 2253 Bathing suits & swimwear, knit

(G-3199)
MARMOT MOUNTAIN LLC
165 Greenwich Ave (06830-6515)
PHONE 203 869-0162
EMP: 4
SALES (corp-wide): 8.6B Publicly Held
SIC: 2329 Men's & boys' sportswear & athletic clothing
HQ: Marmot Mountain, Llc
   5789 State Farm Dr # 100
   Rohnert Park CA 94928
   707 544-4590

(G-3200)
MBF HOLDINGS LLC
777 W Putnam Ave (06830-5091)
PHONE 203 302-2812
Roger Ho, *VP Finance*
Marc Fisher, *Mng Member*
▲ EMP: 10
SQ FT: 70,000
SALES: 100MM Privately Held
SIC: 3143 Men's footwear, except athletic

(G-3201)
MED OPPORTUNITY PARTNERS LLC (PA)
1 Roger Dr (06831-3323)
PHONE 203 622-1333
Robert S Vaters, *General Ptnr*
James A Breckenridge, *General Ptnr*
Vicente Trelles, *General Ptnr*
EMP: 8
SALES (est): 23.9MM Privately Held
WEB: www.medopportunity.com
SIC: 6799 2869 Venture capital companies; industrial organic chemicals

(G-3202)
MERCURIA ENERGY TRADING INC
33 Benedict Pl Ste 1 (06830-5323)
PHONE 203 413-3355
Joseph Donner, *Branch Mgr*
Scot Lilly, *Officer*
EMP: 8 Privately Held
SIC: 1381 Drilling oil & gas wells
HQ: Mercuria Energy Trading, Inc.
   20 Greenway Plz Ste 650
   Houston TX 77046

(G-3203)
MILLBRAE ENERGY LLC (PA)
500 W Putnam Ave Ste 400 (06830-6096)
PHONE 203 742-2800
Stewart Mills Reid, *CEO*
Robert E King Jr, *President*
Charles R Boyce, *COO*
Ryburn McCullough, *Senior VP*
Gary A Watson, *Senior VP*
EMP: 10
SALES (est): 960.3K Privately Held
SIC: 1381 Directional drilling oil & gas wells

(G-3204)
MODA LLC
777 W Putnam Ave Ste 10 (06830-5014)
PHONE 203 302-2800
Marc B Fisher,
EMP: 2
SALES (est): 38MM Privately Held
SIC: 3144 3021 Women's footwear, except athletic; rubber & plastics footwear

(G-3205)
MODERN CLASSICS
1049 North St (06831-2701)
PHONE 203 422-2862
John Johnston,
Jerry Heckett,
EMP: 2
SQ FT: 800
SALES (est): 236.4K Privately Held
SIC: 2434 Wood kitchen cabinets

(G-3206)
MONOGRAM STUDIO GREENWICH CT
222 Pemberwick Rd (06831-4236)
PHONE 203 428-5700
Dancia Rose, *Owner*
EMP: 1
SALES (est): 133.6K Privately Held
SIC: 3552 Embroidery machines

(G-3207)
MUNK PACK INC
222 Railroad Ave Ste 2 (06830-2711)
PHONE 203 769-5005
Michelle Leutzinger, *CEO*
Tobias Glienke, *President*
EMP: 10
SALES: 361.9K Privately Held
SIC: 2043 Oatmeal: prepared as cereal breakfast food

(G-3208)
NEW ENGLAND FILTER COMPANY INC (PA)
21 S Water St Ste 2a (06830-6822)
P.O. Box 31111 (06831-0811)
PHONE 203 531-0500
Thomas H James, *President*
William James, *Vice Pres*
Diane James, *Treasurer*
Joan James, *Admin Sec*
▼ EMP: 6
SALES (est): 707.6K Privately Held
SIC: 3677 Filtration devices, electronic

(G-3209)
NEXTEC APPLICATIONS INC (PA)
Also Called: Epic By Nextec
11 Turner Dr (06831-4415)
P.O. Box 150, Bonsall CA (92003-0150)
PHONE 203 661-1484

Greenwich - Fairfield County (G-3210)

Peter Santoro, *Ch of Bd*
Bill McCabe, *Co-CEO*
Jamie Henderson, *Opers Staff*
▲ **EMP:** 4
SALES (est): 1.1MM **Privately Held**
WEB: www.nextec.com
SIC: 2262 2295 2221 Chemical coating or treating; manmade broadwoven fabrics; coated fabrics, not rubberized; broadwoven fabric mills, manmade

(G-3210)
NORFOLK INDUSTRIES LLC
Also Called: Husky Meadows Farm
21 Deer Park Dr (06830-4602)
PHONE.................................860 618-8822
Tracy Hayhurst,
EMP: 6
SALES (est): 200.3K **Privately Held**
SIC: 3999 Atomizers, toiletry

(G-3211)
NOVANGLUS PUBLISHING LLC
16 Dingletown Rd (06830-3537)
PHONE.................................203 885-7476
Michelle Peacock, *Principal*
EMP: 2 **EST:** 2011
SALES (est): 107.5K **Privately Held**
SIC: 2741 Miscellaneous publishing

(G-3212)
ONCOSYNERGY INC
380 Greenwich Ave (06830-6523)
PHONE.................................617 755-9156
Shawn Carbonell, *CEO*
EMP: 3
SALES (est): 290.2K **Privately Held**
SIC: 2836 Biological products, except diagnostic

(G-3213)
PAPER MILL GRAPHIX INC
Also Called: Papaer Mill Graphix
2 Armonk St (06830-5803)
P.O. Box 320534, Fairfield (06825-0534)
PHONE.................................203 531-5904
Sonny Mehta, *President*
Kammi Mehta, *Manager*
EMP: 20
SQ FT: 5,000
SALES (est): 2.4MM **Privately Held**
WEB: www.paper-mill.com
SIC: 7334 2752 7336 3993 Photocopying & duplicating services; commercial printing, offset; graphic arts & related design; signs & advertising specialties; typesetting; bookbinding & related work

(G-3214)
PASS PERFECT LLC
176 Bedford Rd (06831-2536)
PHONE.................................203 629-9333
Edward Fleur, *President*
EMP: 1
SALES (est): 33.3K
SALES (corp-wide): 117.7K **Privately Held**
SIC: 2731 Textbooks: publishing only, not printed on site
PA: Cerifi, Llc
590 Madison Ave Fl 41
New York NY 10022
212 835-2000

(G-3215)
PIGEONHOLE PRESS LLC
368 Davis Ave (06830-7135)
PHONE.................................203 629-5754
Melisse Shapiro, *Principal*
EMP: 1 **EST:** 2010
SALES (est): 82.8K **Privately Held**
SIC: 2741 Miscellaneous publishing

(G-3216)
PINNACLE AEROSPACE MFG LLC
361 Field Point Rd (06830-7054)
PHONE.................................203 258-3398
Deb Husti, *Principal*
EMP: 15
SALES (est): 1MM **Privately Held**
SIC: 3724 Aircraft engines & engine parts

(G-3217)
POOF-ALEX HOLDINGS LLC (PA)
Also Called: Slinky
10 Glenville St Ste 1 (06831-3680)
PHONE.................................203 930-7711
Kristen Park, *Personnel*
John Belniak,
Michael Cornell,
EMP: 9
SALES (est): 11.7MM **Privately Held**
SIC: 3944 Blocks, toy

(G-3218)
PRINTING HOUSE THE INC
11 Carissa Ln (06830-3117)
PHONE.................................203 869-1767
Carlo V Dorazio, *President*
EMP: 2
SALES (est): 13.1K **Privately Held**
SIC: 2759 Commercial printing

(G-3219)
PUPPY HUGGER
Also Called: Hugger Design
121 North St (06830-4722)
PHONE.................................203 661-4858
Elaine Doran, *Managing Prtnr*
Judy McAuliff, *Managing Prtnr*
EMP: 8
SALES (est): 513.7K **Privately Held**
SIC: 2399 Horse & pet accessories, textile

(G-3220)
QUEBECOR WORLD (USA) INC
340 Pemberwick Rd (06831-4240)
PHONE.................................203 532-4200
EMP: 2 **EST:** 2013
SALES (est): 130K **Privately Held**
SIC: 2752 Lithographic Commercial Printing

(G-3221)
R VAN LOAN CUSTOM FRAMING LLC
115 Mason St Ste 6 (06830-6630)
PHONE.................................203 422-2881
Robert Van Loan, *Principal*
EMP: 2
SALES (est): 89K **Privately Held**
SIC: 3999 Framed artwork

(G-3222)
RAY GREEN CORP
115 E Putnam Ave Ste 1 (06830-5643)
PHONE.................................707 544-2662
EMP: 13
SALES (est): 1.8MM **Privately Held**
SIC: 3674 Mfg Semiconductors/Related Devices

(G-3223)
REGENERATIVE MEDICINE LLC (PA)
Also Called: Regen Med
68 Doubling Rd (06830-4047)
PHONE.................................203 629-1438
Michael P Tierney, *CEO*
EMP: 2
SALES (est): 77K **Privately Held**
SIC: 8082 7372 7389 Home health care services; prepackaged software;

(G-3224)
REGISTRANT JAMES TRIPPE
137 Valley Dr (06831-5208)
PHONE.................................203 517-7567
Jocelyn Audet, *Principal*
EMP: 1
SALES (est): 37.5K **Privately Held**
SIC: 2741 Miscellaneous publishing

(G-3225)
REMOTE TECHNOLOGIES INC (PA)
57 Old Mill Rd (06831-3344)
P.O. Box 1185 (06836-1185)
PHONE.................................203 661-2798
Cheryl Makrinos, *President*
EMP: 4
SQ FT: 300
SALES (est): 733K **Privately Held**
WEB: www.remotetechnologies.com
SIC: 3844 X-ray apparatus & tubes

(G-3226)
RHINO ENERGY HOLDINGS LLC
411 W Putnam Ave Ste 125 (06830-6294)
PHONE.................................203 862-7000
Arthur Amron, *Mng Member*
EMP: 860
SALES (est): 11.3MM **Privately Held**
SIC: 1222 1221 Bituminous coal-underground mining; bituminous coal surface mining
PA: Wexford Capital, L.P.
411 W Putnam Ave Ste 125
Greenwich CT 06830

(G-3227)
RITCH HERALD & LINDA
10 Fort Hill Ln (06830-3719)
PHONE.................................203 661-8634
Herald Ritch, *Principal*
EMP: 3
SALES (est): 118K **Privately Held**
SIC: 2711 Newspapers, publishing & printing

(G-3228)
RJTB GROUP LLC
253 Mill St (06830-5806)
PHONE.................................203 531-7216
Ana Bangay, *CFO*
Thomas Butkiewicz,
EMP: 4
SQ FT: 400
SALES (est): 8MM **Privately Held**
SIC: 2844 Toilet preparations

(G-3229)
RJTB INITIATIVES INC
253 Mill St (06830-5806)
PHONE.................................203 531-7216
Ana Bangay, *CFO*
Thomas Butkiewicz,
EMP: 2
SQ FT: 400
SALES (est): 81.8K **Privately Held**
SIC: 2844 Toilet preparations

(G-3230)
ROCKWOOD SERVICE CORPORATION (PA)
43 Arch St (06830-6512)
PHONE.................................203 869-6734
Peter Scannell, *President*
Don Thomas, *Opers Mgr*
Tim Hauck, *Opers Staff*
John Lockwood, *Treasurer*
Dennis Nolan, *Human Res Dir*
EMP: 9
SALES (est): 1.7B **Privately Held**
SIC: 1389 Testing, measuring, surveying & analysis services

(G-3231)
SASC LLC (PA)
Also Called: Sangari Active Science
44 Amogerone Crossway (06830-9993)
PHONE.................................203 846-2274
Eric Johnson, *CEO*
Dan Toberman, *Regional Mgr*
Tom Pence, *Exec VP*
Tom Laster, *Senior VP*
Benjamin Reynolds, *Production*
EMP: 9
SALES (est): 2MM **Privately Held**
SIC: 2731 Book publishing

(G-3232)
SAXONY WOOD PRODUCTS INC
18 Beech St (06830-5945)
PHONE.................................203 869-3717
John Giagnorio, *President*
EMP: 5 **EST:** 1955
SQ FT: 5,000
SALES (est): 401.2K **Privately Held**
SIC: 2431 Millwork

(G-3233)
SDA LABORATORIES INC
280 Railroad Ave Ste 207 (06830-6338)
PHONE.................................203 861-0005
Sheldon Davis, *President*
EMP: 8
SQ FT: 1,200
SALES (est): 1.1MM **Privately Held**
SIC: 2834 Vitamin preparations

(G-3234)
SILKSCREENING PLUS INC
175 Hamilton Ave (06830-6166)
PHONE.................................203 622-6909
Stacey Naughton, *President*
EMP: 1
SQ FT: 700
SALES (est): 125K **Privately Held**
SIC: 7336 2395 Silk screen design; embroidery products, except schiffli machine

(G-3235)
SILVERSMITH INC
392 W Putnam Ave (06830-6215)
PHONE.................................203 869-4244
Mark Fakundiny, *President*
Jennifer Fakundiny, *Vice Pres*
EMP: 3
SQ FT: 2,000
SALES (est): 307.1K **Privately Held**
SIC: 3471 3479 5944 3914 Polishing, metals or formed products; plating of metals or formed products; engraving jewelry silverware, or metal; silverware; silverware & plated ware; jewelry, precious metal

(G-3236)
SIMON PEARCE US INC
125 E Putnam Ave (06830-5612)
PHONE.................................203 861-0780
Nancy Defillippo, *Branch Mgr*
EMP: 6
SALES (corp-wide): 64.2MM **Privately Held**
WEB: www.simonpearce.com
SIC: 3229 Pressed & blown glass
PA: Simon Pearce U.S., Inc.
109 Park Rd
Windsor VT 05089
802 674-6280

(G-3237)
SJS INDUSTRIES LLC
21 Wilshire Rd (06831-2723)
PHONE.................................203 552-3001
Steven Simes, *Principal*
EMP: 1
SALES (est): 57.8K **Privately Held**
SIC: 3999 Manufacturing industries

(G-3238)
SKAARSHIP APIARIES LLC
50 Hunting Ridge Rd (06831-3134)
PHONE.................................860 805-9398
Fredrick Krumeich,
EMP: 1
SALES (est): 39.5K **Privately Held**
SIC: 2099 Honey, strained & bottled

(G-3239)
SONITOR TECHNOLOGIES INC
37 Brookside Dr (06830-6422)
PHONE.................................727 466-4557
Arvid Gomez, *President*
Erik Fausa Olsen, *CFO*
Debbie Parrish, *Manager*
Jim Laurance, *Technical Staff*
EMP: 6 **EST:** 2005
SALES (est): 965.4K **Privately Held**
SIC: 3663 Mobile communication equipment
PA: Sonitor Ips Holding As
Drammensveien 288
Oslo 0283

(G-3240)
SOUNDVIEW PAPER MILLS LLC (DH)
1 Sound Shore Dr Ste 203 (06830-7251)
PHONE.................................201 796-4000
George Wurtz, *CEO*
Karl Meyers, *President*
Tim Crawford, *Senior VP*
John McLean, *Vice Pres*
Kimberly Knotts, *CFO*
EMP: 7 **EST:** 2012
SALES (est): 477.6MM
SALES (corp-wide): 2.9B **Privately Held**
SIC: 2676 Sanitary paper products
HQ: Soundview Paper Holdings Llc
1 Market St
Elmwood Park NJ 07407
201 796-4000

GEOGRAPHIC SECTION
Groton - New London County (G-3273)

(G-3241)
STELLA PRESS LLC
58 Brookridge Dr (06830-4830)
PHONE.....................203 661-2735
Irving Schwartz, *Principal*
EMP: 3 EST: 2016
SALES (est): 81.4K **Privately Held**
SIC: 2711 Newspapers

(G-3242)
STUDENT EMPLOYMENT SFTWR LLC
107 Maple Ave (06830-5621)
PHONE.....................203 485-9417
James H Hohorst, *Principal*
EMP: 2
SALES (est): 164.9K **Privately Held**
SIC: 7372 Application computer software

(G-3243)
TEED OFF PUBLISHING INC
48 Nicholas Ave (06831-4924)
PHONE.....................561 266-0872
EMP: 4 EST: 2009
SALES (est): 277.5K **Privately Held**
SIC: 2741 Misc Publishing

(G-3244)
TIME AVIATION LLC
75 Holly Hill Ln Ste 100 (06830-2917)
PHONE.....................203 496-5716
Erick Fukuda,
EMP: 1
SALES (est): 60K **Privately Held**
SIC: 3724 Aircraft engines & engine parts

(G-3245)
TIMER DIGEST PUBLISHING INC
268 Round Hill Rd (06831-3359)
P.O. Box 1688 (06836-1688)
PHONE.....................203 629-2589
Jim Schmidt, *President*
EMP: 5
SALES (est): 429.1K **Privately Held**
WEB: www.timerdigest.com
SIC: 2721 6282 Magazines: publishing only, not printed on site; investment advisory service

(G-3246)
TMS INTERNATIONAL LLC
165 W Putnam Ave (06830-5222)
PHONE.....................203 629-8383
EMP: 3 **Privately Held**
SIC: 3312 Blast furnaces & steel mills
HQ: Tms International, Llc
2835 E Carson St Fl 2
Glassport PA 15203
412 678-6141

(G-3247)
TONTINE PARTNERS L P
55 Railroad Ave Fl 3 (06830-6378)
PHONE.....................203 769-2000
Anthony Garofalo, *Bd of Directors*
EMP: 2
SALES (est): 152.8K **Privately Held**
SIC: 3272 Cast stone, concrete

(G-3248)
TRI-STATE LED INC
255 Mill St (06830-5806)
PHONE.....................203 813-3791
Ron Young, *President*
Chris Anastasi, *Regional Mgr*
Todd Cormier, *Regional Mgr*
Mike Forlivio, *Regional Mgr*
Carrie Kaltwasser, *Regional Mgr*
EMP: 14 EST: 2010
SALES (est): 3.5MM
SALES (corp-wide): 99.9MM **Publicly Held**
SIC: 3646 Commercial indusl & institutional electric lighting fixtures
PA: Revolution Lighting Technologies, Inc.
177 Broad St Fl 12
Stamford CT 06901
203 504-1111

(G-3249)
TRICYCLE GRANOLA LLC
27 Meadow Wood Dr (06830-7023)
PHONE.....................203 861-1740
Joseph A Profaci, *Principal*
EMP: 1
SALES (est): 73K **Privately Held**
SIC: 3944 Tricycles

(G-3250)
TURNSTONE INC
Also Called: AlphaGraphics
154 Prospect St (06830-6130)
PHONE.....................203 625-0000
Karen Brinker, *President*
EMP: 15
SALES (est): 2.2MM **Privately Held**
SIC: 2752 Commercial printing, lithographic

(G-3251)
UNICORN PHARMACEUTICALS INC
181 Milbank Ave Ste W (06830-6616)
PHONE.....................973 699-3843
Frederic Huser, *CEO*
EMP: 1
SALES (est): 47.2K **Privately Held**
SIC: 2834 Drugs acting on the gastrointestinal or genitourinary system

(G-3252)
UST
100 W Putnam Ave (06830-5361)
PHONE.....................203 661-1100
Vincent Gierer, *Chairman*
EMP: 15
SALES (est): 2.2MM **Privately Held**
SIC: 2141 Tobacco stemming & redrying

(G-3253)
VCS GROUP LLC
Vincent Camuto LLC-Mens
411 W Putnam Ave Fl 2 (06830-6261)
PHONE.....................203 413-6500
Alex Delcielo, *Branch Mgr*
EMP: 3 **Privately Held**
SIC: 3143 Dress shoes, men's
HQ: Vcs Group Llc
411 W Putnam Ave Ste 210
Greenwich CT 06830
203 413-6500

(G-3254)
VERTICAL MANAGEMENT LLC
110 Patterson Ave (06830-4622)
PHONE.....................203 422-2547
Tad Haley, *Manager*
EMP: 2
SALES (est): 135K **Privately Held**
SIC: 2591 Blinds vertical

(G-3255)
W2W PARTNERS LLC
Also Called: Organic Project The
125 Greenwich Ave Ste 3 (06830-5527)
PHONE.....................781 424-7824
Thyme Sullivan, *Mng Member*
Denielle Finkelstein, *Mng Member*
EMP: 4
SALES (est): 357.7K **Privately Held**
SIC: 2676 Feminine hygiene paper products

(G-3256)
WEI WEI FASHIONS INC
58 Washington Ave (06830-5748)
PHONE.....................646 322-2599
Elizabeth WEI, *Principal*
EMP: 2
SALES (est): 190K **Privately Held**
SIC: 2369 Bathing suits & swimwear: girls', children's & infants'

(G-3257)
WESTCHESTER INDUSTRIES INC
485 W Putnam Ave (06830-6060)
PHONE.....................203 661-0055
Joe Cotter, *Ch of Bd*
EMP: 18
SALES (est): 3.6MM **Privately Held**
SIC: 2951 1611 Asphalt & asphaltic paving mixtures (not from refineries); highway & street paving contractor

(G-3258)
WEXFORD CAPITAL LP (PA)
411 W Putnam Ave Ste 125 (06830-6294)
PHONE.....................203 862-7000
Joseph Jacobs, *President*
Robert Holtz, *Partner*
Charles Davidson, *Chairman*
Paul Jacobi, *Vice Pres*
John Pontius, *Vice Pres*
EMP: 97
SALES (est): 111.3MM **Privately Held**
SIC: 8741 6282 1221 1222 Management services; investment advice; bituminous coal surface mining; bituminous coal-underground mining

(G-3259)
WIDE HORIZONS CO INC
18 Huckleberry Ln (06831-3341)
PHONE.....................203 661-9252
Kathleen Rotzies, *President*
EMP: 2
SALES (est): 85.2K **Privately Held**
SIC: 3999 7699 Sprays, artificial & preserved; blacksmith shop

(G-3260)
WIZARDS NUTS HOLDINGS LLC (PA)
100 Northfield St (06830-4618)
PHONE.....................708 483-1315
Timothy Fazio, *Mng Member*
Jacob Hudson, *Mng Member*
EMP: 60
SALES (est): 56.2MM **Privately Held**
SIC: 6719 5411 2068 Investment holding companies, except banks; grocery stores; salted & roasted nuts & seeds

(G-3261)
WOOD SERVICES LLC
1 Sound Shore Dr Ste 203 (06830-7251)
PHONE.....................203 983-5752
Ed Sletcher, *Principal*
EMP: 1
SALES (est): 112.9K **Privately Held**
SIC: 2499 Decorative wood & woodwork

(G-3262)
XMI CORPORATION
140 Greenwich Ave (06830-6556)
PHONE.....................800 838-0424
Elizabeth Pulitzer, *Manager*
EMP: 3
SALES (est): 154.6K
SALES (corp-wide): 6.8MM **Privately Held**
WEB: www.xmi.com
SIC: 2323 Men's & boys' neckwear
PA: Xmi Corporation
8296 Commerce Pkwy Ste 2
Chippewa Falls WI 54729
715 723-1999

Griswold
New London County

(G-3263)
DANTE LTD LIABILITY COMPANY
633 Plainfield Rd (06351-1025)
PHONE.....................860 376-0204
Dante Grassi,
EMP: 1
SALES (est): 103.8K **Privately Held**
SIC: 2431 Millwork

(G-3264)
FLATLAND ALPACAS
285 Sam Chikan Rd (06351-8909)
PHONE.....................860 376-4658
EMP: 2
SALES (est): 139.9K **Privately Held**
SIC: 2231 Alpacas, mohair: woven

(G-3265)
GRACIE MAES KITCHEN LLC
383 Bethel Rd (06351-8802)
PHONE.....................860 885-8250
Jennifer Chominski,
Betty Kubica,
EMP: 5
SALES (est): 277.9K **Privately Held**
SIC: 2051 Bakery: wholesale or wholesale/retail combined

(G-3266)
JANES CUSTOM CANVAS LLC
201 Slater Ave (06351-2525)
PHONE.....................860 376-6778
Jane Delaney, *Principal*
EMP: 1
SALES (est): 65K **Privately Held**
SIC: 2211 Canvas

(G-3267)
MAPLE PRINT SERVICES INC
92 Osga Ln (06351-8832)
PHONE.....................860 381-5470
Michael D Johnson, *Principal*
EMP: 2 EST: 2013
SALES (est): 135.8K **Privately Held**
SIC: 2752 Commercial printing, offset

(G-3268)
TIRED MOMMY CANDLES
52 Bergendahl Dr (06351-2602)
PHONE.....................860 407-2002
L Nicole, *Principal*
EMP: 1
SALES (est): 39.6K **Privately Held**
SIC: 3999 Candles

Groton
New London County

(G-3269)
210 INNOVATIONS
210 Leonard Dr (06340-5334)
PHONE.....................860 445-0210
James Marquis, *Partner*
▲ **EMP:** 6
SALES (est): 515K **Privately Held**
SIC: 3999 Manufacturing industries

(G-3270)
ALGONQUIAN FREE PRESS LLC
230 Crosswinds Dr (06340-4878)
PHONE.....................860 572-4811
Karen J Hatcher, *Principal*
EMP: 1
SALES (est): 50.9K **Privately Held**
SIC: 2741 Miscellaneous publishing

(G-3271)
APPLIED PHYSICAL SCIENCES CORP (HQ)
475 Bridge St Ste 100 (06340-3780)
PHONE.....................860 448-3253
Charles N Corrado Jr, *President*
David Horne, *CFO*
Julie P Aslaksen, *Admin Sec*
EMP: 79
SQ FT: 20,000
SALES (est): 29.6MM
SALES (corp-wide): 36.1B **Publicly Held**
WEB: www.aphysci.com
SIC: 8711 3669 Consulting engineer; intercommunication systems, electric
PA: General Dynamics Corporation
11011 Sunset Hills Rd
Reston VA 20190
703 876-3000

(G-3272)
BOSPHORUS BOOKS
3 Ridge Rd (06340-8927)
P.O. Box 3452 (06340-8205)
PHONE.....................860 536-2540
EMP: 1
SALES (est): 47K **Privately Held**
SIC: 2731 5192 Books-Publishing/Printing Whol Books/Newspapers

(G-3273)
BRAIN INSTITUTE OF AMERICA LLC
93 Shennecossett Rd (06340-5115)
PHONE.....................860 967-5937
Brian Adams, *President*
EMP: 3
SQ FT: 50
SALES (est): 34.7K **Privately Held**
SIC: 8731 2741 Biological research; biotechnical research, commercial; commercial research laboratory; medical research, commercial;

(G-3274)
BRIDGEPORT BOATWORK INC
145 Pearl St (06340-5773)
PHONE.................................860 536-9651
Harry Boardsen, *President*
EMP: 1
SALES (corp-wide): 5MM **Privately Held**
SIC: 3731 Shipbuilding & repairing
PA: Bridgeport Boatwork, Inc
  837 Seaview Ave
  Bridgeport CT 06607
  860 536-9651

(G-3275)
CASE PATTERNS INC
Also Called: Case Patterns & Wood Products
257 South Rd (06340-4611)
P.O. Box 666 (06340-0666)
PHONE.................................860 445-6722
James Case, *President*
Carol Case, *Vice Pres*
EMP: 3 **EST:** 1975
SQ FT: 3,500
SALES: 350K **Privately Held**
SIC: 3543 3999 Industrial patterns; models, general, except toy

(G-3276)
CASHON
Also Called: Alue Optics
350 W Shore Ave (06340-8843)
PHONE.................................786 325-4144
John X Watson, *Principal*
EMP: 3
SALES (est): 224.3K **Privately Held**
SIC: 3851 Glasses, sun or glare

(G-3277)
CATELECTRIC CORP (PA)
33 Island Cir S (06340-8823)
PHONE.................................860 912-0800
Robert M Furek, *CEO*
Peter D Pappas, *President*
EMP: 3
SQ FT: 400
SALES (est): 432.9K **Privately Held**
WEB: www.catelectric.biz
SIC: 3567

(G-3278)
COMMANDTECH LLC
404 Thames St Ste C (06340-3962)
PHONE.................................860 857-8502
Igor Boris,
EMP: 3
SALES (est): 151.1K **Privately Held**
SIC: 4731 2731 Freight forwarding; books: publishing only

(G-3279)
COMPONENTS FOR MFG LLC
26 High St (06340-5752)
PHONE.................................860 572-1671
Tracey Jacey, *Branch Mgr*
EMP: 3
SALES (corp-wide): 1.4MM **Privately Held**
SIC: 3999 Barber & beauty shop equipment
PA: Components For Manufacturing Llc
  800 Flanders Rd Unit 3-5
  Mystic CT 06355
  860 245-5326

(G-3280)
CONNECTICUT MACHINE & MARINE
266 Bridge St Ste 4 (06340-3739)
PHONE.................................860 446-8286
Michael Ziobron, *President*
EMP: 1
SQ FT: 3,000
SALES (est): 213.9K **Privately Held**
SIC: 3599 Machine shop, jobbing & repair

(G-3281)
CUSTOM MARINE CANVAS LLC
Also Called: Hood Sailmakers
71 Marsh Rd (06340-5619)
PHONE.................................860 572-9547
Katharine Bradford,
EMP: 6
SQ FT: 3,000
SALES: 330K **Privately Held**
SIC: 2211 2394 Canvas; canvas & related products

(G-3282)
DONCASTERS INC
Also Called: Doncasters Precision Castings-
835 Poquonnock Rd (06340-4537)
PHONE.................................860 446-4803
Bruce Ebright, *Manager*
Richard Brown, *Manager*
EMP: 84
SALES (corp-wide): 3.4B **Privately Held**
SIC: 3356 3369 3324 Nonferrous rolling & drawing; nonferrous foundries; steel investment foundries
HQ: Doncasters Inc.
  835 Poquonnock Rd
  Groton CT 06340

(G-3283)
DONCASTERS INC (DH)
835 Poquonnock Rd (06340-4537)
P.O. Box 1146 (06340-1146)
PHONE.................................860 449-1603
David Smoot, *CEO*
Christian Garcia, *General Mgr*
Steve Conrad, *Opers Staff*
Dan Davis, *Opers Staff*
Alex Ragone, *Purch Mgr*
◆ **EMP:** 60
SQ FT: 100,000
SALES (est): 135.1MM
SALES (corp-wide): 3.4B **Privately Held**
SIC: 3356 3728 7699 3511 Titanium; aircraft parts & equipment; aircraft propellers & associated equipment; aircraft & heavy equipment repair services; turbines & turbine generator sets & parts
HQ: Doncasters Group Limited
  Millennium Court
  Burton-On-Trent STAFFS
  133 286-4900

(G-3284)
DONCASTERS US HLDINGS 2018 INC
835 Poquonnock Rd (06340-4537)
PHONE.................................860 677-1376
Ian Molyneux, *President*
Duncan Hinks, *Treasurer*
EMP: 10
SALES (est): 390.1K **Privately Held**
SIC: 3324 Aerospace investment castings, ferrous

(G-3285)
ELECTRIC BOAT CORPORATION
210 Mitchell St (06340-4046)
P.O. Box 949 (06340-0949)
PHONE.................................860 433-0503
Ellen Mathews, *Principal*
Philip Kiley, *Senior Buyer*
Scott Fermeglia, *Engineer*
Bob Hevey, *Engineer*
Taylor Peterson, *Engineer*
EMP: 91
SALES (corp-wide): 36.1B **Publicly Held**
SIC: 3731 Submarines, building & repairing
HQ: Electric Boat Corporation
  75 Eastern Point Rd
  Groton CT 06340

(G-3286)
ELECTRIC BOAT CORPORATION
Also Called: Electric Boat Fairwater Div
75 Eastern Point Rd (06340-4905)
PHONE.................................860 433-3000
Susan Williams, *Branch Mgr*
EMP: 91
SALES (corp-wide): 36.1B **Publicly Held**
SIC: 3731 8711 Submarines, building & repairing; engineering services
HQ: Electric Boat Corporation
  75 Eastern Point Rd
  Groton CT 06340

(G-3287)
ELECTRIC BOAT CORPORATION (HQ)
Also Called: General Dynamics Electric Boat
75 Eastern Point Rd (06340-4905)
P.O. Box 1327 (06340-1327)
PHONE.................................860 433-3000
John P Casey, *President*
Craig Sipe, *General Mgr*
Lew Clark, *Editor*
Paul Ramsey, *Editor*
Greg Haines, *Division VP*
◆ **EMP:** 6399
SQ FT: 2,600,000
SALES (est): 2.4B
SALES (corp-wide): 36.1B **Publicly Held**
WEB: www.gdeb.com
SIC: 3731 8711 Submarines, building & repairing; engineering services
PA: General Dynamics Corporation
  11011 Sunset Hills Rd
  Reston VA 20190
  703 876-3000

(G-3288)
FINE FOOD SERVICES INC
Also Called: Paul's Pasta Shop
223 Thames St (06340-3955)
PHONE.................................860 445-5276
Paul Fidrych, *President*
Dorothy P Fidrych, *Principal*
Edward J Planeta Jr, *Principal*
Edward J Planeta, *Senior VP*
Paul T Fidrych, *Treasurer*
EMP: 24
SQ FT: 2,000
SALES (est): 1.8MM **Privately Held**
WEB: www.paulspasta.com
SIC: 2099 5812 Pasta, uncooked: packaged with other ingredients; eating places

(G-3289)
GOLD STAR DENTAL
491 Gold Star Hwy Ste 300 (06340-6226)
PHONE.................................860 445-1330
EMP: 2
SALES (est): 86.6K **Privately Held**
SIC: 3843 Gold, dental

(G-3290)
H & M SYSTEMS
34 Pegasus Dr (06340-2410)
PHONE.................................860 445-2347
Howard Martin, *Principal*
EMP: 2
SALES (est): 95.9K **Privately Held**
SIC: 2899 Chemical preparations

(G-3291)
HBI BOAT LLC
145 Pearl St (06340-5773)
PHONE.................................860 536-7776
William Reed,
EMP: 4
SALES: 82K **Privately Held**
SIC: 3732 Boat building & repairing

(G-3292)
KINGSNAKE PUBLISHING LLC
149 Buckeye Rd (06340-3031)
PHONE.................................860 865-0307
Amanda Balser, *Principal*
EMP: 1
SALES (est): 52.1K **Privately Held**
SIC: 2741 Miscellaneous publishing

(G-3293)
KONGSBERG DGTAL SIMULATION INC
170 Leonard Dr (06340-5320)
P.O. Box 180, West Mystic (06388-0180)
PHONE.................................860 405-2300
Geir Haoy, *President*
Erich Stritzel, *President*
Herbert Taylor, *General Mgr*
David Meers, *Vice Pres*
Norman Sousa, *Info Tech Mgr*
▲ **EMP:** 18
SQ FT: 10,000
SALES (est): 3.4MM
SALES (corp-wide): 1.7B **Privately Held**
WEB: www.navpac.com
SIC: 3824 Controls, revolution & timing instruments
HQ: Kongsberg Maritime As
  Strandpromenaden 50
  Horten 3183

(G-3294)
LAND SEA AIR INC
108 Fort Hill Rd (06340-4335)
PHONE.................................860 448-9004
EMP: 2
SALES (est): 73.4K **Privately Held**
SIC: 3429 Mfg Hardware

(G-3295)
LARRYS AUTO MACHINE LLC
Also Called: Larry's Auto Machine & Supply
175 Leonard Dr (06340-5320)
PHONE.................................860 449-9112
Gary Espinosa,
EMP: 3
SQ FT: 2,000
SALES (est): 492.5K **Privately Held**
SIC: 3599 Machine shop, jobbing & repair

(G-3296)
LBI INC
Also Called: Legnos Boat Industries
973 North Rd (06340-3219)
PHONE.................................860 446-8058
Peter J Legnos, *President*
EMP: 18
SALES: 2.9MM **Privately Held**
WEB: www.lbifiberglass.com
SIC: 5085 5088 3732 Industrial supplies; marine supplies; boats, fiberglass: building & repairing

(G-3297)
LEGNOS MEDICAL INC
973 North Rd (06340-3272)
PHONE.................................860 446-8058
Peter J Legnos, *President*
EMP: 10
SALES (est): 399.6K **Privately Held**
SIC: 3845 Ultrasonic medical equipment, except cleaning

(G-3298)
LUTHER FENCE INC
145 Leonard Dr Unit A (06340-5342)
PHONE.................................860 445-5660
Jon Luther, *Principal*
EMP: 2 **EST:** 2015
SALES (est): 66.8K **Privately Held**
SIC: 2499 Wood products

(G-3299)
LYNNE MARSHALL
118 Pearl St (06340-5733)
P.O. Box 9247 (06340-9247)
PHONE.................................860 245-3645
Lynne Marshall, *Owner*
EMP: 1
SALES (est): 61.6K **Privately Held**
SIC: 3842 Surgical appliances & supplies

(G-3300)
NEW ENGLAND INFO DISTRICTS
Also Called: Neid Printing
15 Chicago Ave (06340-4907)
PHONE.................................860 446-1906
Glen Allvord, *President*
Marjorie Allvord, *Corp Secy*
Omar Allvord, *Vice Pres*
EMP: 2
SQ FT: 2,200
SALES (est): 181.6K **Privately Held**
SIC: 2752 Commercial printing, offset

(G-3301)
NOANK CONTROLS LLC (PA)
195 Leonard Dr Unit 6 (06340-5341)
P.O. Box 278, West Mystic (06388-0278)
PHONE.................................860 449-6776
Andrew Tubbs,
▼ **EMP:** 2
SQ FT: 2,000
SALES (est): 285K **Privately Held**
WEB: www.noankcontrols.com
SIC: 3625 3491 Switches, electric power; industrial valves

(G-3302)
OUTER LIGHT BREWING CO LLC
266 Bridge St Ste 1 (06340-3739)
PHONE.................................475 201-9972
Matthew Ferrucci,
Tom Drejer,
EMP: 3
SALES: 500K **Privately Held**
SIC: 2082 Malt beverage products

GEOGRAPHIC SECTION

Guilford - New Haven County (G-3332)

(G-3303)
PAW TO PRESS
224 Thames St (06340-3914)
PHONE.................303 709-2807
Joshua Germain, *Principal*
EMP: 1
SALES (est): 37.5K Privately Held
SIC: 2741 Miscellaneous publishing

(G-3304)
PCC STRUCTURALS GROTON (DH)
839 Poquonnock Rd (06340-4537)
PHONE.................860 405-3700
William C McCormick, *Ch of Bd*
Joseph B Cox, *President*
James Serreira, *Controller*
▲ EMP: 175 EST: 1990
SALES (est): 301MM
SALES (corp-wide): 225.3B Publicly Held
SIC: 3364 Nonferrous die-castings except aluminum
HQ: Wyman-Gordon Company
   244 Worcester St
   North Grafton MA 01536
   508 839-8252

(G-3305)
PEL ASSOCIATES LLC (PA)
187 Ledgewood Rd Apt 407 (06340-6627)
PHONE.................860 446-9921
Morton L Wallach, *Owner*
EMP: 4 EST: 1990
SQ FT: 2,000
SALES (est): 729K Privately Held
WEB: www.pelassociates.com
SIC: 3089 Plastic processing

(G-3306)
PFIZER INC
445 Eastern Point Rd (06340)
PHONE.................860 441-4000
John Goggin, *Principal*
Craig Barrila, *Vice Pres*
Justin McCarthy, *Vice Pres*
Yangzhen Ciringh, *Research*
David Resetar, *Business Anlyst*
EMP: 1
SALES (corp-wide): 53.6B Publicly Held
WEB: www.pfizer.com
SIC: 2833 2834 8731 Medicinals & botanicals; pharmaceutical preparations; commercial physical research
PA: Pfizer Inc.
   235 E 42nd St
   New York NY 10017
   212 733-2323

(G-3307)
PFIZER INC
156a Eastern Point Rd (06340-4950)
PHONE.................860 389-7509
Matthew Parsons, *Director*
EMP: 2
SALES (corp-wide): 53.6B Publicly Held
SIC: 2834 Pharmaceutical preparations
PA: Pfizer Inc.
   235 E 42nd St
   New York NY 10017
   212 733-2323

(G-3308)
PFIZER INC
100 Eastern Point Rd (06340-4950)
PHONE.................860 441-4100
Gerardo Ortiz, *General Mgr*
Nancy Walsh-Sayles, *General Mgr*
Lori Siller, *Purchasing*
Cheryl Tow-Keogh, *QC Mgr*
Iasson Mustakis, *Research*
EMP: 146
SALES (corp-wide): 53.6B Publicly Held
WEB: www.pfizer.com
SIC: 2834 Pharmaceutical preparations
PA: Pfizer Inc.
   235 E 42nd St
   New York NY 10017
   212 733-2323

(G-3309)
PIPER
63 Elderberry Rd (06340-2542)
PHONE.................860 405-1495
J Piper, *COO*
EMP: 2

SALES (est): 90.8K Privately Held
SIC: 3317 Steel pipe & tubes

(G-3310)
PRESS ON SANDWICH CRAFTERS
136 Mitchell St (06340-4021)
PHONE.................860 694-9882
Jody Davies, *Principal*
EMP: 1
SALES (est): 37.5K Privately Held
SIC: 2741 Miscellaneous publishing

(G-3311)
R & B APPAREL PLUS LLC
78 Plaza Ct (06340-4223)
PHONE.................860 333-1757
Connie Flynn, *Finance*
Amy Henon, *Sales Executive*
Richard P Bernardo, *Mng Member*
Patricia Jullarine,
EMP: 4
SQ FT: 1,000
SALES (est): 522.6K Privately Held
SIC: 2759 7389 5199 Screen printing; embroidering of advertising on shirts, etc.; advertising specialties

(G-3312)
SKYLINE VET PHARMA INC
37 Skyline Dr (06340-5427)
PHONE.................860 625-0424
Serge Martinod, *CEO*
George Murphy, *Vice Pres*
EMP: 3
SALES (est): 123.2K Privately Held
SIC: 2834 Veterinary pharmaceutical preparations

(G-3313)
SPICER PLUS INC (PA)
Also Called: Spicer Advanced Gas
36 Thames St (06340-3629)
P.O. Box 903 (06340-0903)
PHONE.................860 445-2436
Larry Chesler, *President*
John P Holstein, *Vice Pres*
EMP: 1
SQ FT: 2,000
SALES (est): 16.4MM Privately Held
WEB: www.spicergas.com
SIC: 5541 1321 5984 5411 Filling stations, gasoline; propane (natural) production; liquefied petroleum gas, delivered to customers' premises; convenience stores, independent

(G-3314)
SYSTAMEDIC INC
1084 Shennecossett Rd (06340-6061)
PHONE.................860 912-6101
Robert A Volkmann, *President*
EMP: 4
SALES (est): 291.4K Privately Held
SIC: 2834 Pharmaceutical preparations

(G-3315)
THAYERMAHAN INC
120b Leonard Dr (06340-5336)
PHONE.................860 785-9994
Michael Connor, *CEO*
Richard Hines, *CFO*
EMP: 19
SALES (est): 3.6MM Privately Held
SIC: 3812 Sonar systems & equipment

(G-3316)
UNITED STATES DEPT OF NAVY
Also Called: D L A Disposition Services
33 Grayback Ave Bldg 33 (06349)
P.O. Box 12 (06349-5012)
PHONE.................860 694-3524
Michael Efstathiou, *Director*
EMP: 6 Publicly Held
SIC: 3812 Defense systems & equipment
HQ: United States Department Of The Navy
   1200 Navy Pentagon
   Washington DC 20350

(G-3317)
WEISS SLEEP SHOP INC
Also Called: Weiss Sleep Shop Outlet
740 Long Hill Rd (06340-4273)
PHONE.................860 445-1219
Gregory Weiss, *President*
Michael Rocchetti, *Vice Pres*

EMP: 4
SALES (est): 800K Privately Held
SIC: 5712 2512 Mattresses; beds & accessories; living room furniture: upholstered on wood frames

(G-3318)
WELLES MACHINE SHOP
61 Wells St (06340)
PHONE.................860 536-8398
Peter Welles, *Owner*
EMP: 1
SALES (est): 131.2K Privately Held
SIC: 3599 Machine shop, jobbing & repair

(G-3319)
WILD BILLS ACTION SPORTS LLC
93 Marsh Rd (06340-5656)
PHONE.................860 536-6648
William Pagel,
EMP: 3
SQ FT: 800
SALES (est): 92.7K Privately Held
SIC: 5941 2395 5699 7999 Bait & tackle; embroidery & art needlework; sports apparel; beach & water sports equipment rental & services

(G-3320)
YOURMEMBERSHIPCOM INC
Also Called: Your Membership.com
541 Eastern Point Rd (06340-5158)
PHONE.................860 271-7241
EMP: 7
SALES (corp-wide): 2.2B Privately Held
SIC: 7372 Prepackaged software
HQ: Yourmembership.Com, Inc.
   9620 Exec Ctr N 200
   Saint Petersburg FL 33702
   727 827-0046

Guilford
New Haven County

(G-3321)
ACOUSTIC MUSIC
Also Called: Acousticmusic.org
1238 Boston Post Rd (06437-2465)
PHONE.................203 458-2525
Brian Wolfe, *Manager*
EMP: 1
SALES (est): 62.1K Privately Held
SIC: 5736 3931 String instruments; guitars & parts, electric & nonelectric

(G-3322)
ADVANCE DEVELOPMENT & MFG
325 Soundview Rd (06437-2970)
P.O. Box 396 (06437-0396)
PHONE.................203 453-4325
John F Fisher, *President*
Robert Fisher, *Chairman*
EMP: 10 EST: 1956
SQ FT: 12,000
SALES (est): 2.2MM Privately Held
SIC: 3599 Machine shop, jobbing & repair

(G-3323)
ALARMCO
1 Bailey Dr (06437-2376)
PHONE.................203 458-2646
Ron Cook, *Owner*
EMP: 2
SALES (est): 208.7K Privately Held
WEB: www.messagerepeaters.com
SIC: 3651 Audio electronic systems

(G-3324)
ALGONQUIN INDUSTRIES INC (HQ)
129 Soundview Rd (06437-2943)
PHONE.................203 453-4348
Kamesh Chivukula, *President*
John Bielot, *Administration*
◆ EMP: 54
SQ FT: 104,000

SALES (est): 18.9MM
SALES (corp-wide): 400MM Privately Held
WEB: www.reawire.com
SIC: 3357 Nonferrous wiredrawing & insulating
PA: Rea Magnet Wire Company, Inc.
   3400 E Coliseum Blvd # 200
   Fort Wayne IN 46805
   260 421-7321

(G-3325)
AMERICAN MELODY RECORDS
102 Wheeler Path (06437-1206)
P.O. Box 270 (06437-0270)
PHONE.................203 457-0881
Phillip Rosenthal, *Owner*
EMP: 2
SALES (est): 125.8K Privately Held
WEB: www.americanmelody.com
SIC: 7389 3652 Music recording producer; master records or tapes, preparation of

(G-3326)
APRIL ROSE DESIGNS
69 Boston St (06437-2802)
PHONE.................203 453-1797
Diane Gourlie, *Owner*
EMP: 2
SALES (est): 85K Privately Held
SIC: 2353 5621 Hats, caps & millinery; women's clothing stores

(G-3327)
BECKM LLC
Also Called: Teleflight Stair System
131 Nut Plains Rd (06437-2135)
PHONE.................203 458-3800
Richard D Walston, *CEO*
Marie Walston, *Manager*
Teleflight Stair, *Master*
EMP: 1 EST: 2011
SALES (est): 111K Privately Held
SIC: 3446 Stairs, staircases, stair treads: prefabricated metal

(G-3328)
BILLS BOAT REPAIR LLC
44 Williamsburg Cir (06437-2017)
PHONE.................203 804-8801
William R Johnson Jr, *Manager*
EMP: 2
SALES (est): 149.7K Privately Held
SIC: 3732 Boat building & repairing

(G-3329)
BIO-MED DEVICES INC
Also Called: Bmd
61 Soundview Rd (06437-2937)
PHONE.................203 458-0202
Dean J Bennett Jr, *Ch of Bd*
Dean J Bennett III, *President*
Brian Arnone, *Controller*
Doris A Bennett, *Admin Sec*
▼ EMP: 67
SQ FT: 20,000
SALES (est): 14.1MM Privately Held
WEB: www.biomeddevices.com
SIC: 3845 3841 Electromedical equipment; surgical & medical instruments

(G-3330)
BMR ASSOCIATES
45 Water St C (06437-2861)
P.O. Box 428, Madison (06443-0428)
PHONE.................203 453-1796
Darrell Ripley, *Owner*
EMP: 3
SALES (est): 293.3K Privately Held
SIC: 5085 3429 Bearings; manufactured hardware (general)

(G-3331)
BOOMERANG STUDIO
178 Denison Dr (06437-2482)
PHONE.................203 689-5155
EMP: 1
SALES (est): 47K Privately Held
SIC: 3949 Boomerangs

(G-3332)
BREAKFAST WOODWORKS INC
135 Leetes Island Rd (06437-3027)
PHONE.................203 458-8888
Louis Mackall, *President*
Ken Field, *Vice Pres*

Guilford - New Haven County (G-3333) — GEOGRAPHIC SECTION

EMP: 6
SQ FT: 9,000
SALES: 1.1MM **Privately Held**
WEB: www.breakfastwoodworks.com
SIC: 2431 Millwork

(G-3333)
BROOK & WHITTLE HOLDING CORP (PA)
20 Carter Dr (06437-2125)
PHONE..................203 483-5602
Stephen T Stewart, *CEO*
EMP: 0
SALES (est): 7.8MM **Privately Held**
SIC: 6719 2741 Investment holding companies, except banks; catalogs: publishing & printing

(G-3334)
BROOK & WHITTLE LIMITED (HQ)
20 Carter Dr (06437-2125)
P.O. Box 409, North Branford (06471-0409)
PHONE..................203 483-5602
Simon Grimes, *Vice Pres*
Richard Marsie, *Plant Mgr*
Bob Bovee, *Prdtn Mgr*
Gary Sullivan, *Purchasing*
Laura Cain, *QC Mgr*
▲ EMP: 130
SALES (est): 39.1MM
SALES (corp-wide): 7.8MM **Privately Held**
WEB: www.bwhittle.com
SIC: 2754 Commercial printing, gravure
PA: Brook & Whittle Holding Corp.
    20 Carter Dr
    Guilford CT 06437
    203 483-5602

(G-3335)
BRUSHFOIL LLC
1 Shoreline Dr Ste 6 (06437-2978)
PHONE..................203 453-7403
Fax: 203 453-7408
EMP: 12
SALES (est): 4.7MM
SALES (corp-wide): 267.2MM **Privately Held**
SIC: 3081 Unsupported Plastics Film And Sheet, Nsk
HQ: Transilwrap Company, Inc.
    127 Turningstone Ct
    Greenville SC 60067
    864 269-4690

(G-3336)
BUTTERFLY NETWORK INC (PA)
530 Old Whitfield St (06437-3441)
PHONE..................855 296-6188
Michael Rothberg, *President*
Alexander Magary, *President*
Jaime Zahorian, *Research*
James Beach, *Engineer*
David Grosjean, *Engineer*
EMP: 34
SALES (est): 5.6MM **Privately Held**
SIC: 8733 3841 Medical research; surgical & medical instruments

(G-3337)
CARIBE HOUSE PRESS LLC
109 Bittersweet Cir (06437-1431)
PHONE..................812 320-5303
Catherine Adele Berry,
EMP: 1
SALES (est): 37.5K **Privately Held**
SIC: 2741 Miscellaneous publishing

(G-3338)
CARLS CLOSETS LLC
118 Williams Dr (06437-1401)
PHONE..................203 457-9401
Carl Iaccarino Jr, *Executive*
EMP: 1
SALES (est): 153K **Privately Held**
SIC: 3553 Cabinet makers' machinery

(G-3339)
COMPETITION ENGINEERING INC
80 Carter Dr (06437-2125)
PHONE..................203 453-5200
Richard B Moroso, *President*
Pamela Kiss, *Admin Sec*
EMP: 140
SQ FT: 70,000
SALES (est): 8MM
SALES (corp-wide): 38MM **Privately Held**
WEB: www.competitionengineering.com
SIC: 3714 Motor vehicle parts & accessories
PA: Moroso Performance Products, Inc.
    80 Carter Dr
    Guilford CT 06437
    203 453-6571

(G-3340)
CONNECTICUT LAW BOOK CO INC
39 Chaffinch Island Rd (06437-3244)
P.O. Box 575 (06437-0575)
PHONE..................203 458-8000
Eugene Oleary, *President*
EMP: 15
SALES (est): 1.4MM **Privately Held**
WEB: www.lawreporter.com
SIC: 2731 Book publishing

(G-3341)
COOPERSURGICAL INC
Also Called: Lifeglobal Group, The
393 Soundview Rd (06437-2970)
PHONE..................203 453-1700
Monica Mezezi, *Manager*
EMP: 40
SALES (corp-wide): 2.5B **Publicly Held**
SIC: 2836 Biological products, except diagnostic
HQ: Coopersurgical, Inc.
    95 Corporate Dr
    Trumbull CT 06611

(G-3342)
D & C INDUSTRIES
282 Stepstone Hill Rd (06437-2041)
PHONE..................203 453-4424
D Carlson, *Owner*
EMP: 2
SALES (est): 152.6K **Privately Held**
SIC: 3999 Manufacturing industries

(G-3343)
DAYBREAK NUCLEAR & MED SYSTEMS
50 Denison Dr (06437-2344)
PHONE..................203 453-3299
Jeanne Bortolot, *President*
Victor Bortolot, *Vice Pres*
EMP: 2
SALES (est): 350K **Privately Held**
SIC: 3829 Medical diagnostic systems, nuclear

(G-3344)
DEFIBTECH LLC (PA)
741 Boston Post Rd # 201 (06437-2714)
PHONE..................866 333-4248
Robert Reinhardt, *CEO*
Glenn W Laub, *CEO*
Dina Bell-Svenningse, *Buyer*
Scott Lindsay, *QC Mgr*
Scott Smallshaw, *Info Tech Mgr*
EMP: 57
SQ FT: 10,850
SALES (est): 24.4MM **Privately Held**
WEB: www.defibtech.com
SIC: 3845 Defibrillator

(G-3345)
DIGITAL IMAGINING & PACKAGING
761 Goose Ln (06437-2114)
PHONE..................203 458-3509
Matthew Pittorie, *Principal*
EMP: 2
SALES (est): 83.9K **Privately Held**
SIC: 2752 Commercial printing, lithographic

(G-3346)
DONALI SYSTEMS INTEGRATION INC
128 Tanner Marsh Rd (06437-2203)
PHONE..................860 715-5432
Donald Ludington, *President*
EMP: 3
SALES (est): 395.8K **Privately Held**
SIC: 3699 7389 Security control equipment & systems;

(G-3347)
DONNIN PUBLISHING INC
Also Called: The Real Estate Book
800 Village Walk (06437-2762)
PHONE..................203 453-8866
Robert Schmidt, *President*
Glen Ramsteck, *Vice Pres*
EMP: 3
SQ FT: 350
SALES (est): 1.5MM **Privately Held**
SIC: 2721 Magazines: publishing only, not printed on site

(G-3348)
DUNELAND PRESS
3 Rockland Rd (06437-1137)
PHONE..................860 535-0362
EMP: 1 EST: 2011
SALES (est): 53.5K **Privately Held**
SIC: 2741 Miscellaneous publishing

(G-3349)
EAGLE ALLOYS
2514 Boston Post Rd 6c (06437-1338)
PHONE..................203 453-9910
Walter Schrader, *Owner*
EMP: 1
SALES (est): 112.1K **Privately Held**
SIC: 3843 Dental materials

(G-3350)
EASTWOODS ARMS LLC
37 Orcutt Dr (06437-2221)
PHONE..................203 615-3476
Jonathan Caviola, *Principal*
EMP: 1
SALES (est): 45.6K **Privately Held**
SIC: 2499 Wood products

(G-3351)
ENTERPLAY LLC
800 Village Walk Ste 307 (06437-2762)
PHONE..................203 458-1128
Dean E Irwin, *Mng Member*
▲ EMP: 10 EST: 2007
SALES (est): 770K **Privately Held**
SIC: 3944 Electronic games & toys

(G-3352)
FITZHUGH ELECTRICAL CORP
Also Called: Timco Instruments Div
361 Long Hill Rd (06437-1827)
P.O. Box 100, Rockville RI (02873-0100)
PHONE..................203 453-3171
James T Fitzhugh, *President*
EMP: 5
SALES (est): 39.7K **Privately Held**
SIC: 3825 Electron tube test equipment

(G-3353)
FLEXXRAY LLC
320 Soundview Dr (06437-2973)
PHONE..................203 689-5435
EMP: 1
SALES (corp-wide): 2.8MM **Privately Held**
SIC: 3861 X-ray film
PA: Flexxray Llc
    3751 New York Ave Ste 130
    Arlington TX 76014
    817 453-3539

(G-3354)
GENX INTERNATIONAL INC (PA)
Also Called: Life Global
393 Soundview Rd (06437-2970)
PHONE..................203 453-1700
Fax: 203 453-1769
EMP: 30 EST: 1996
SQ FT: 18,000
SALES (est): 4MM **Privately Held**
SIC: 2836 Mfg Biological Products

(G-3355)
GEORGE SCHMITT & CO INC (PA)
251 Boston Post Rd (06437-2904)
P.O. Box 448 (06437-0448)
PHONE..................203 453-4334
William Gunther, *CEO*
◆ EMP: 59 EST: 1874
SQ FT: 48,000
SALES (est): 19.9MM **Privately Held**
WEB: www.georgeschmitt.com
SIC: 2759 Commercial printing

(G-3356)
GEORGE SCHMITT & CO INC
Also Called: George Schmithet and Company
251 Boston Post Rd (06437-2904)
PHONE..................203 453-4334
Gunther William, *President*
EMP: 5
SALES (corp-wide): 19.9MM **Privately Held**
SIC: 2759 Labels & seals: printing
PA: George Schmitt & Co., Inc.
    251 Boston Post Rd
    Guilford CT 06437
    203 453-4334

(G-3357)
GUILFORD LOGGING
484 Goose Ln (06437-2101)
PHONE..................203 453-5190
Kenneth Carrho, *Owner*
EMP: 1
SALES (est): 69.4K **Privately Held**
SIC: 2411 Logging camps & contractors

(G-3358)
GUILFORD PRINTING INC
Also Called: Guilford Printworks
74 Wildrose Ave (06437-2544)
PHONE..................203 453-5585
Charles Havrda, *President*
Marlene Havrda, *Corp Secy*
EMP: 2
SQ FT: 3,000
SALES (est): 200K **Privately Held**
SIC: 2752 Commercial printing, offset

(G-3359)
HABANERO SOFTWARE INCORPORATED
281 Durham Rd (06437-2088)
PHONE..................203 453-5458
Frank Vincent Russello Jr, *Principal*
EMP: 2
SALES (est): 113.9K **Privately Held**
SIC: 7372 Prepackaged software

(G-3360)
HIRAM ROCK PUBLISHING LLC
359 Willow Rd (06437-1754)
PHONE..................203 453-0440
John F Curran III,
EMP: 1
SALES (est): 37.5K **Privately Held**
SIC: 2741 Miscellaneous publishing

(G-3361)
IMAGE PROCESSING
251 Boston Post Rd (06437-2904)
PHONE..................203 488-3252
Steve Cushman, *President*
EMP: 50
SQ FT: 25,000
SALES (est): 3.6MM **Privately Held**
SIC: 7336 2791 Graphic arts & related design; typesetting

(G-3362)
INTERNATIONAL COMM SVCS INC
Also Called: Ics
2 Burgis Ln (06437-2286)
PHONE..................401 580-8888
Steven Lee, *President*
EMP: 3
SALES: 1.5MM **Privately Held**
SIC: 2759 Commercial printing

(G-3363)
JAMES KINGSLEY
Also Called: Lee Rail Embroidery
1250 Boston Post Rd Ste 5 (06437-2451)
PHONE..................203 458-6626
James Kingsley, *Owner*
EMP: 1
SALES (est): 53.7K **Privately Held**
SIC: 5947 5949 2395 Gift shop; needlework goods & supplies; embroidery products, except schiffli machine

GEOGRAPHIC SECTION
Guilford - New Haven County (G-3395)

(G-3364)
JONAS LIEPONIS
461 Vineyard Point Rd (06437-3245)
PHONE............................203 458-6912
Jonas Lieponis, *Principal*
EMP: 2
SALES (est): 65.5K **Privately Held**
SIC: 1389 Oil & gas field services

(G-3365)
KENDALL SVENGALIS
Also Called: New England Lawpress
3 Rockland Rd (06437-1137)
PHONE............................860 535-0362
Kendall Svengalis, *Owner*
Ellen Svengalis, *Principal*
EMP: 2
SALES: 100K **Privately Held**
WEB: www.rilawpress.com
SIC: 2731 Books: publishing only

(G-3366)
LAM THERAPEUTICS INC
530 Old Whitfield St (06437-3441)
PHONE............................203 458-7100
Marylens Hernandez, *Research*
Wes Conard, *Marketing Staff*
Henri Lichenstein, *Officer*
Elizabeth Whayland, *Admin Sec*
EMP: 12
SALES (est): 1.9MM **Privately Held**
SIC: 2835 In vivo diagnostics

(G-3367)
LEWMAR INC (DH)
Also Called: Lewmar Marine
351 New Whitfield St (06437-3400)
PHONE............................203 458-6200
Peter Tierney, *CEO*
Harcourt Schutz, *General Mgr*
Stacy Richards, *Business Mgr*
Kevin Donahue, *COO*
Monica Gilhuly, *Accountant*
▲ EMP: 20
SQ FT: 2,500
SALES (est): 4.1MM
SALES (corp-wide): 72.1MM **Privately Held**
WEB: www.lewmarusa.com
SIC: 3423 3429 3714 Axes & hatchets; manufactured hardware (general); motor vehicle steering systems & parts
HQ: Lewmar Limited
Southmoor Lane
Havant HANTS PO9 1
239 247-1841

(G-3368)
LION HEART INDUSTRIES LLC
1809 Little Meadow Rd (06437-1623)
P.O. Box 436 (06437-0436)
PHONE............................203 376-2212
Ronald G Johnson,
EMP: 1
SALES (est): 68.2K **Privately Held**
SIC: 3999 Manufacturing industries

(G-3369)
LIONHEART MILITARIA LLC
2458 Boston Post Rd Ste 5 (06437-1398)
PHONE............................203 800-5759
Peter Leonardo,
EMP: 1 EST: 2017
SALES (est): 54.9K **Privately Held**
SIC: 3484 Guns (firearms) or gun parts, 30 mm. & below

(G-3370)
MARKET76 INC
58 Boston St (06437-2801)
PHONE............................866 808-5491
Michael Adkins, *COO*
EMP: 2
SALES (est): 167K **Privately Held**
SIC: 7372 Business oriented computer software

(G-3371)
MATTHEW FISEL ND
20 Dunk Rock Rd (06437-2509)
PHONE............................203 453-0122
Matthew Fisel, *Principal*
EMP: 3 EST: 2010
SALES (est): 196.4K **Privately Held**
SIC: 3221 Medicine bottles, glass

(G-3372)
MCBOOKS PRESS INC
246 Goose Ln Ste 200 (06437-2186)
PHONE............................607 272-2114
Alexander Skutt, *President*
Panda Musgrove, *Publisher*
▲ EMP: 5
SALES (est): 1.2MM
SALES (corp-wide): 293.8MM **Privately Held**
WEB: www.mcbooks.com
SIC: 2731 Books: publishing only
PA: The Rowman & Littlefield Publishing Group Inc
4501 Forbes Blvd Ste 200
Lanham MD 20706
301 459-3366

(G-3373)
MCDOWELL GROUP INC
107 River St (06437-2620)
PHONE............................203 494-4120
Tod Hart, *President*
EMP: 1
SALES (est): 46.6K **Privately Held**
SIC: 3433 Heating equipment, except electric

(G-3374)
ME2HEALTH LLC
253 Village Pond Rd (06437-2001)
PHONE............................203 208-8927
Dave Hutten,
EMP: 1
SALES (est): 38.9K **Privately Held**
SIC: 7372 Business oriented computer software

(G-3375)
MEDPRICERCOM INC
Also Called: Government Sourcing Group
2346 Boston Post Rd Ste 2 (06437-4367)
PHONE............................203 453-4554
Lester Grant, *Director*
EMP: 1
SALES (est): 1.6MM **Privately Held**
SIC: 7372 7374 7389 Prepackaged software; data processing & preparation;

(G-3376)
MOROSO PERFORMANCE PDTS INC (PA)
80 Carter Dr (06437-2116)
PHONE............................203 453-6571
Richard B Moroso, *President*
Gary Burkel, *Opers Dir*
James Knudsen, *Buyer*
Phil Tulli, *QC Mgr*
John Galayda, *Engineer*
▲ EMP: 190
SQ FT: 70,000
SALES (est): 38MM **Privately Held**
WEB: www.moroso.com
SIC: 3714 Motor vehicle engines & parts

(G-3377)
MORRIS COMMUNICATIONS CO LLC
Also Called: Globe Pequot Press
246 Goose Ln Ste 200 (06437-2186)
P.O. Box 480 (06437-0480)
PHONE............................203 458-4500
Scott Watrous, *General Mgr*
David Legere, *Editor*
Ellen Urban, *Editor*
Lynn Zelem, *Production*
Bounthavy Soukthideth, *Human Res Mgr*
EMP: 90 **Privately Held**
WEB: www.morris.com
SIC: 2711 Newspapers
HQ: Morris Communications Company Llc
725 Broad St
Augusta GA 30901
706 724-0851

(G-3378)
MUSICA RUSSICA INC
310 Glenwood Dr (06437-2233)
PHONE............................203 458-3225
EMP: 1 EST: 2010
SALES (est): 56K **Privately Held**
SIC: 2741 Misc Publishing

(G-3379)
NEW ENGLAND FOREST PRODUCTS
564 Great Hill Rd (06437-3629)
PHONE............................203 457-0314
Samuel Bartlett, *President*
EMP: 2
SQ FT: 4,000
SALES (est): 276.3K **Privately Held**
WEB: www.newenglandforestproducts.com
SIC: 2421 Sawmills & planing mills, general

(G-3380)
NORTHSTAR BIOSCIENCES LLC
2514 Boston Post Rd 4r (06437-1338)
PHONE............................203 689-5399
Mike Vitagliano, *COO*
EMP: 3
SALES (est): 162K **Privately Held**
SIC: 2834 Pharmaceutical preparations

(G-3381)
OMICRONWORLD ENTERTAINMENT LLC
Also Called: Fahren Heit Book
29 Horseshoe Rd (06437-2961)
PHONE............................203 453-5700
Jason Marthi, *Manager*
EMP: 2
SALES: 20K **Privately Held**
SIC: 2731 Book publishing

(G-3382)
PASSION ENGINEERING LLC
579 Lake Dr (06437-1161)
PHONE............................203 204-3090
David Fennell,
EMP: 1
SALES (est): 90.1K **Privately Held**
SIC: 3441 3593 Fabricated structural metal; fluid power actuators, hydraulic or pneumatic

(G-3383)
PEACEFUL DAILY INC
800 Village Walk Ste 103 (06437-2762)
PHONE............................203 909-2961
Sandra Corso, *CEO*
EMP: 6
SALES (est): 445.8K **Privately Held**
SIC: 2711 Newspapers, publishing & printing

(G-3384)
PRIME BUSINESS SERVICES
40 Stillmeadow Dr (06437-2018)
P.O. Box 1436 (06437-0536)
PHONE............................203 453-1627
Laura Remmers, *Partner*
Glenn Remmers, *Partner*
EMP: 2
SALES (est): 200K **Privately Held**
SIC: 8611 7372 7371 Business associations; prepackaged software; computer software systems analysis & design, custom

(G-3385)
RAM TECHNOLOGIES LLC
29 Soundview Rd Ste 12 (06437-2997)
PHONE............................203 453-3916
Richard Mentelos, *President*
Nancy Degray, *Mfg Staff*
Susan Senter, *CFO*
▲ EMP: 10 EST: 1992
SQ FT: 3,000
SALES (est): 4MM **Privately Held**
SIC: 3845 Electromedical apparatus

(G-3386)
REA MAGNET WIRE COMPANY INC
Algonquin Industries Division
129 Soundview Rd (06437-2972)
PHONE............................203 738-6100
Kamesh Chivukula, *President*
EMP: 90
SQ FT: 104,000
SALES (corp-wide): 400MM **Privately Held**
WEB: www.reawire.com
SIC: 3357 Nonferrous wiredrawing & insulating
PA: Rea Magnet Wire Company, Inc.
3400 E Coliseum Blvd # 200
Fort Wayne IN 46805
260 421-7321

(G-3387)
RYALL RBERT ARCHTCTRAL IR WRKS
1352 Little Meadow Rd (06437-1659)
PHONE............................203 458-1356
Robert Ryall, *Owner*
EMP: 1
SALES (est): 65K **Privately Held**
WEB: www.cybertermlife.com
SIC: 3446 Architectural metalwork

(G-3388)
SAYBROOK PRESS INCORPORATED
39 Chaffinch Island Rd (06437-3244)
P.O. Box 575 (06437-0575)
PHONE............................203 458-3637
Eugene O Leary, *President*
Jean Oleary, *Treasurer*
EMP: 15
SALES (est): 926.3K **Privately Held**
SIC: 2791 2789 2759 Typesetting; bookbinding & repairing: trade, edition, library, etc.; commercial printing

(G-3389)
SFN LLC
340 Boston St (06437-2811)
PHONE............................203 314-8436
EMP: 2
SALES (est): 139.3K **Privately Held**
SIC: 3949 Sporting & athletic goods

(G-3390)
SHORELINE DRONE SOLUTIONS
151 Flat Iron Rd (06437-1415)
PHONE............................347 239-5636
Edward Bermudez, *Principal*
EMP: 2
SALES (est): 86K **Privately Held**
SIC: 3721 Motorized aircraft

(G-3391)
SHORELINE SEGWAY INC
1310 Boston Post Rd Ste 5 (06437-2480)
PHONE............................203 453-6036
Richard Petrillo, *Owner*
EMP: 2
SALES (est): 94.9K **Privately Held**
SIC: 2311 Tuxedos: made from purchased materials

(G-3392)
SOLAR GENERATIONS LLC
741 Podunk Rd (06437-2217)
PHONE............................203 453-3920
Daphne Byrne, *Mng Member*
▲ EMP: 3
SALES (est): 350K **Privately Held**
SIC: 3823 Thermal conductivity instruments, industrial process type

(G-3393)
STEVEN VANDERMAELEN LLC
709 County Rd (06437-1036)
PHONE............................203 457-0143
Steven H Vandermaelen,
EMP: 1
SALES (est): 90.4K **Privately Held**
SIC: 2434 2431 Wood kitchen cabinets; staircases & stairs, wood

(G-3394)
STEVENSON PROTOTYPE
77 Fair St (06437-2601)
PHONE............................203 245-0278
Peter Stevenson, *Owner*
EMP: 1
SALES (est): 64.1K **Privately Held**
SIC: 3999 Models, general, except toy

(G-3395)
STONESLIDE MEDIA LLC
4 Elm St (06437-1029)
PHONE............................203 464-3471
Jonathan Weisberg,
EMP: 2
SALES (est): 68.8K **Privately Held**
SIC: 2731 Book publishing

Guilford - New Haven County (G-3396)   GEOGRAPHIC SECTION

(G-3396)
T KEEFE AND SONS
1790 Little Meadow Rd (06437-1620)
PHONE..................................203 457-0267
Thomas Keefe, *Partner*
Jason Keefe, *Partner*
Regina Keefe, *Partner*
EMP: 3
SALES (est): 472.9K **Privately Held**
SIC: 3441 Building components, structural steel

(G-3397)
TABAR DESIGNS
71 Whitfield St Ste 204 (06437-2610)
PHONE..................................203 453-8868
Scott Tabar, *Owner*
EMP: 1
SALES: 66K **Privately Held**
SIC: 3911 Jewelry, precious metal

(G-3398)
TACTICAL COMMUNICATIONS INC
29 Soundview Rd (06437-2910)
PHONE..................................203 453-2389
David Moffat, *President*
Beth F Moffat, *Admin Sec*
Glen Hawley, *Technician*
EMP: 10
SQ FT: 5,000
SALES (est): 720K **Privately Held**
WEB: www.taccomm.com
SIC: 7622 3663 Radio repair shop; radio broadcasting & communications equipment

(G-3399)
TAKE CAKE LLC
2458 Boston Post Rd Ste 2 (06437-1398)
PHONE..................................203 453-1896
Nancy Purcell, *Owner*
EMP: 8
SQ FT: 1,200
SALES (est): 410K **Privately Held**
WEB: www.originaltakethecake.com
SIC: 2051 Pastries, e.g. danish: except frozen; cakes, pies & pastries

(G-3400)
UP WITH PAPER
34 York St Ste 3 (06437-2473)
PHONE..................................203 453-3300
Monika Brandrup, *General Mgr*
Brandrup Monika, *Vice Pres*
EMP: 6
SALES (est): 616K **Privately Held**
SIC: 2621 Greeting card paper

(G-3401)
WALSTON INC
131 Nut Plains Rd (06437-2135)
PHONE..................................203 453-5929
Richard Walston, *President*
Marie Walston, *Vice Pres*
EMP: 9
SQ FT: 4,500
SALES (est): 1.1MM **Privately Held**
SIC: 2431 Staircases & stairs, wood

(G-3402)
ZUSE INC
727 Boston Post Rd Ste 1 (06437-2793)
PHONE..................................203 458-3295
Ted Zuse, *President*
Skip Zuse, *Vice Pres*
Thatcher Zuse, *Shareholder*
EMP: 11
SQ FT: 6,000
SALES (est): 1.2MM **Privately Held**
SIC: 2396 2395 Screen printing on fabric articles; pleating & stitching

Haddam
Middlesex County

(G-3403)
CONNECTICUT BRACE AND LIMB LLC
59 Timms Hill Rd (06438-1042)
PHONE..................................860 740-2154
David A Knapp, *Principal*
EMP: 2
SALES (est): 121.1K **Privately Held**
SIC: 3842 Limbs, artificial

(G-3404)
ENERGY TECH LLC
63 Church Hill Rd (06438-1124)
PHONE..................................860 345-3993
Joseph L Brasky,
Diane Brasky,
EMP: 6
SALES (est): 949.5K **Privately Held**
WEB: www.energytech-brasky.com
SIC: 3825 Radar testing instruments, electric

(G-3405)
JOE SALAFIA WOODWORKING LLC
152 Old Cart Rd (06438-1245)
PHONE..................................860 345-8657
Joseph J Salafia, *Principal*
EMP: 1
SALES (est): 73.4K **Privately Held**
SIC: 2431 Millwork

(G-3406)
K J WELDING
116 Filley Rd (06438-1206)
PHONE..................................860 345-8743
Ken Pellegrini, *President*
EMP: 1
SALES: 120K **Privately Held**
SIC: 7692 3441 Welding repair; fabricated structural metal

(G-3407)
MOONLIGHT MEDIA LLC
Also Called: Koolart USA
95 Bridge Rd Bldg 4b (06438-1354)
PHONE..................................860 345-3595
Valerie Cox,
Kristopher Cox,
EMP: 6 EST: 1996
SQ FT: 5,600
SALES (est): 250K **Privately Held**
WEB: www.storesign.com
SIC: 2759 Commercial printing

Hamden
New Haven County

(G-3408)
A & C CONNECTION INSPECTION
30 Overlook Dr (06514-1139)
PHONE..................................203 287-8504
David Beedle, *Principal*
EMP: 2
SALES (est): 197.8K **Privately Held**
SIC: 7699 5084 1389 Sewer cleaning & rodding; industrial machinery & equipment; pipe testing, oil field service

(G-3409)
A & K RAILROAD MATERIALS INC
200 Benton St (06517-3907)
PHONE..................................203 495-8790
Ronald Johnson, *Manager*
EMP: 6
SALES (corp-wide): 150.1MM **Privately Held**
WEB: www.akrailroad.com
SIC: 3531 5211 5088 Laying equipment, rail; lumber products; railroad equipment & supplies
PA: A & K Railroad Materials, Inc.
1505 S Redwood Rd
Salt Lake City UT 84104
801 974-5484

(G-3410)
ABBOTT PRINTING COMPANY INC
912 Dixwell Ave (06514-5014)
PHONE..................................203 562-5562
Nancy B Mellone, *President*
David Mellone, *Vice Pres*
EMP: 5
SQ FT: 5,000
SALES (est): 696.8K **Privately Held**
SIC: 2752 Commercial printing, offset

(G-3411)
ACCUWIND INC
1068 Sherman Ave (06514-1337)
PHONE..................................203 287-9697
Mark Bishop, *President*
EMP: 2 EST: 1979
SALES (est): 382.4K **Privately Held**
WEB: www.accuwind.com
SIC: 7694 Electric motor repair

(G-3412)
ADVANCED PRODUCT SOLUTIONS LLC
555 Sherman Ave Unit C16 (06514-1152)
PHONE..................................203 745-4225
Rick Palmeri, *Partner*
Jim Beveridge, *Partner*
EMP: 6
SQ FT: 3,000
SALES: 350K **Privately Held**
SIC: 3672 5063 Printed circuit boards; electronic wire & cable

(G-3413)
ALPHAGRAPHICS LLC
24 Rossotto Dr (06514-1335)
PHONE..................................203 230-0018
Jerry Kenney, *Vice Pres*
EMP: 4 EST: 2010
SALES (est): 428.4K **Privately Held**
SIC: 2752 Commercial printing, lithographic

(G-3414)
AMERICAN METASEAL OF CONN
Also Called: Packaging Displays
336 Putnam Ave (06517-2744)
P.O. Box 4124 (06514-0124)
PHONE..................................203 787-0281
Timothy Pagnam, *President*
Julia Pagnam, *Vice Pres*
EMP: 2
SQ FT: 4,200
SALES (est): 205.5K **Privately Held**
SIC: 2499 3479 3411 3089 Rollers, wood; coating of metals & formed products; tin cans; plastic containers, except foam; lighting equipment; coated fabrics, not rubberized

(G-3415)
AMPHENOL CORPORATION
Amphenol Spctr-Strip Oprations
720 Sherman Ave (06514-1146)
P.O. Box 4340 (06514-0340)
PHONE..................................203 287-2272
Eric Juntwait, *General Mgr*
Dennis Lynn, *Controller*
Denise Masulli, *Human Res Mgr*
Kathy Pickering, *Marketing Mgr*
Mark Pierson, *Maintence Staff*
EMP: 72
SALES (corp-wide): 8.2B **Publicly Held**
SIC: 3678 Electronic connectors
PA: Amphenol Corporation
358 Hall Ave
Wallingford CT 06492
203 265-8900

(G-3416)
B-P PRODUCTS INC
100 Sanford St (06514-1775)
PHONE..................................203 288-0200
Dorothy R Podgwaite, *CEO*
Michael J Podgwaite, *President*
Bruce Giannetti, *Administration*
EMP: 28
SQ FT: 32,000
SALES: 2.3MM **Privately Held**
WEB: www.b-pproducts.com
SIC: 2657 2675 2679 2631 Folding paperboard boxes; die-cut paper & board; paper products, converted; boxboard; dies, steel rule; commercial printing

(G-3417)
BAR-PLATE MANUFACTURING CO
1180 Sherman Ave (06514-1300)
P.O. Box 185470 (06518-0470)
PHONE..................................203 397-0033
Brian Garrity, *President*
▲ EMP: 10 EST: 1985
SQ FT: 17,000
SALES: 973.4K
SALES (corp-wide): 360.9MM **Privately Held**
WEB: www.barplate.com
SIC: 3554 Die cutting & stamping machinery, paper converting
PA: R.A.F. Industries, Inc.
165 Township Line Rd # 2100
Jenkintown PA 19046
215 572-0738

(G-3418)
BEVERAGE PUBLICATIONS INC
Also Called: Connecticut Beverage Journal
2508 Whitney Ave Apt N (06518-3042)
P.O. Box 185159 (06518-0159)
PHONE..................................203 288-3375
Gerald Slone, *President*
EMP: 3 EST: 1949
SQ FT: 2,000
SALES (est): 357.6K **Privately Held**
WEB: www.ctbeveragejournal.com
SIC: 2721 Magazines: publishing only, not printed on site

(G-3419)
BLACK CROW PRESS LLC
85 Spring Garden St (06517-1913)
P.O. Box 185626 (06518-0626)
PHONE..................................203 281-1034
Kathy M Umbricht Straka, *Principal*
EMP: 1
SALES (est): 41.3K **Privately Held**
SIC: 2741 Miscellaneous publishing

(G-3420)
BURT PROCESS EQUIPMENT INC (PA)
100 Overlook Dr (06514-1139)
P.O. Box 185100 (06518-0100)
PHONE..................................203 287-1985
Stephen J Burt, *President*
Steve Burt, *Principal*
Alan L Speckhart, *Vice Pres*
Alan Speckhart, *Vice Pres*
Edward Simpson, *Mfg Staff*
EMP: 21
SQ FT: 29,000
SALES (est): 27.8MM **Privately Held**
WEB: www.burtprocess.com
SIC: 5085 3432 Industrial fittings; plumbing fixture fittings & trim

(G-3421)
CABIN WOODWORKS
280 Forest Street Ext (06518-2715)
PHONE..................................203 410-1073
EMP: 1
SALES (est): 54.1K **Privately Held**
SIC: 2431 Millwork

(G-3422)
CAMPO ENTERPRISES
1 Gallagher Rd (06517-3171)
PHONE..................................203 776-0664
Tina Silkoff, *Principal*
EMP: 2
SALES (est): 86.6K **Privately Held**
SIC: 3841 Surgical & medical instruments

(G-3423)
CAN STRAPS LLC
127 Woodlawn St (06517-1341)
PHONE..................................203 281-7333
Robert F Roscow, *Mng Member*
EMP: 1
SALES (est): 138K **Privately Held**
SIC: 3199 Mill strapping for textile mills, leather

(G-3424)
CARLTON INDUSTRIES CORP
33 Rossotto Dr (06514-1336)
PHONE..................................203 288-5605
Brad Carlton, *President*
Weston See, *Vice Pres*
Beverly Kempa, *Purch Agent*
Donna Conklin, *Buyer*
Susan Stone, *Purchasing*
◆ EMP: 49
SQ FT: 27,000

SALES (est): 11.8MM **Privately Held**
WEB: www.carltonindustriesonline.com
SIC: 3672 Printed circuit boards

(G-3425)
CAROGEN CORPORATION
295 Washington Ave (06518-3025)
PHONE..................203 606-8796
Bijan Almassian, *Principal*
Valerian Nakaar, *Vice Pres*
Joseph Rininger, *Vice Pres*
EMP: 2
SALES (est): 202.1K **Privately Held**
SIC: 2834 Druggists' preparations (pharmaceuticals)

(G-3426)
CARRANO RAILINGS
1130 Sherman Ave (06514-1363)
PHONE..................203 248-7245
EMP: 1 EST: 2016
SALES (est): 58.6K **Privately Held**
SIC: 7692 Welding repair

(G-3427)
CENTURY SIGN LLC
2666 State St (06517-2232)
PHONE..................203 230-9000
Bill Lynch,
EMP: 3
SQ FT: 3,600
SALES (est): 386K **Privately Held**
SIC: 3993 7389 Electric signs; sign painting & lettering shop

(G-3428)
CHARLES K WHITE
Also Called: Metal Perfection
2259 State St (06517-3723)
PHONE..................203 631-2540
Charles K White, *Owner*
EMP: 2
SALES (est): 148.5K **Privately Held**
SIC: 2842 Metal polish

(G-3429)
COLUMBIA MAT & UPHOLSTERING CO
Also Called: Columbia Mattress Co
824 Dixwell Ave (06514-5098)
P.O. Box 1022, North Branford (06471-2022)
PHONE..................203 789-1213
David Oliverio, *President*
Susan Oliverio, *Vice Pres*
EMP: 6 EST: 1921
SQ FT: 15,000
SALES (est): 619.6K **Privately Held**
WEB: www.columbiamattressuph.com
SIC: 7641 2514 2515 Upholstery work; metal household furniture; mattresses & bedsprings

(G-3430)
CONCRETE CORING CO CONN INC
34 Raccio Park Rd Ste 2 (06514-1366)
PHONE..................203 287-8400
Thomas V Martucci, *President*
Arlene Martucci, *Admin Sec*
EMP: 4
SQ FT: 3,600
SALES (est): 457.6K **Privately Held**
SIC: 1771 1381 Concrete work; service well drilling

(G-3431)
CONNECTICUT STUCCO LLC
82 Leo Rd (06517-2629)
PHONE..................203 237-9500
Walder Ewer Ramos, *Principal*
EMP: 1
SALES (est): 192K **Privately Held**
SIC: 3299 Stucco

(G-3432)
COPPERWORKS INC (PA)
277 Still Hill Rd (06518-1828)
PHONE..................203 248-3516
Robert R Banti, *President*
Madelyn Banti, *Vice Pres*
EMP: 2
SQ FT: 168

SALES: 401.8K **Privately Held**
SIC: 1761 3444 Sheet metalwork; sheet metalwork

(G-3433)
COPY STOP INC
Also Called: Printing Store, The
2371 Whitney Ave (06518-3206)
PHONE..................203 288-6401
Joyce Curran, *President*
Robert Curran, *Vice Pres*
Margaret Curran, *Treasurer*
Christopher Curran, *Director*
Jacob Curran, *Director*
EMP: 4 EST: 1974
SQ FT: 6,000
SALES (est): 39.9K **Privately Held**
SIC: 2752 5943 2791 Commercial printing, offset; office forms & supplies; typesetting

(G-3434)
CROWN MOLDING ETC LLC
148 Gillies Rd (06517-2116)
PHONE..................203 287-9424
Jefrey B Agli, *Principal*
EMP: 3
SALES (est): 216.8K **Privately Held**
SIC: 3089 Molding primary plastic

(G-3435)
CT PRINTS
3000 Whitney Ave (06518-2353)
PHONE..................203 281-6996
Mike Ross, *Owner*
EMP: 2
SALES (est): 134.7K **Privately Held**
SIC: 2752 Commercial printing, lithographic

(G-3436)
CUSTOM & PRECISION PDTS INC
2893 State St Rear (06517-1712)
P.O. Box 5446 (06518-0446)
PHONE..................203 281-0818
Diamante Dente, *President*
Gregory Dente, *Admin Sec*
EMP: 9
SQ FT: 12,000
SALES (est): 1.4MM **Privately Held**
WEB: www.injection-moldings.com
SIC: 3444 Sheet metalwork

(G-3437)
CYCLONE MICROSYSTEMS INC
25 Marne St (06514-3610)
PHONE..................203 786-5536
Joel Zackin, *President*
George Tafuto, *Opers Mgr*
Scott Coulter, *Engineer*
Szeming Leung, *Human Res Dir*
EMP: 38
SALES (est): 7.3MM **Privately Held**
WEB: www.cyclone.com
SIC: 3571 3672 Personal computers (microcomputers); printed circuit boards

(G-3438)
CYCLONE PCIE SYSTEMS LLC
25 Marne St (06514-3610)
PHONE..................203 786-5536
George Tafuto,
EMP: 5
SQ FT: 4,000
SALES (est): 210.9K **Privately Held**
SIC: 3577 Input/output equipment, computer

(G-3439)
DAILY IMPRESSIONS LLC
Also Called: Janitorial Commercial Gen Svc
60 Village Cir (06514-3342)
PHONE..................203 508-5305
Tommie Shields, *Mng Member*
EMP: 4
SALES: 50K **Privately Held**
SIC: 2711 Newspapers, publishing & printing

(G-3440)
DUCTWORX UNLIMITED LLC
62 Crestway (06514-1141)
PHONE..................203 535-1425
Kevin Lynch, *Manager*
EMP: 2

SALES (est): 123.9K **Privately Held**
SIC: 3585 Heating equipment, complete

(G-3441)
DUROL COMPANY
2580 State St (06517-3009)
P.O. Box 4141 (06514-0141)
PHONE..................203 288-3383
Cynthia Civitello, *President*
Carol D Newman, *Vice Pres*
EMP: 15 EST: 1962
SQ FT: 9,000
SALES (est): 2.6MM **Privately Held**
WEB: www.durol.com
SIC: 3599 Machine shop, jobbing & repair

(G-3442)
ELECTRONIC SPC CONN INC
19 Hamden Park Dr (06517-3151)
PHONE..................203 288-1707
William Kovacs, *President*
Duc Huu Nguyen, *Vice Pres*
Nicole Foster, *Office Mgr*
EMP: 24
SQ FT: 12,500
SALES (est): 4.7MM **Privately Held**
SIC: 3672 Printed circuit boards

(G-3443)
ELM CITY CHEESE COMPANY INC
2240 State St (06517-3798)
PHONE..................203 865-5768
Marjorie Weinstein-Kowal, *President*
Suzanne Weinstein, *Admin Sec*
EMP: 10 EST: 1896
SQ FT: 12,000
SALES (est): 1.5MM **Privately Held**
SIC: 2022 Natural cheese

(G-3444)
ELM CITY MFG JEWELERS INC
29 Marne St (06514)
PHONE..................203 248-2195
Anthony Cuomo, *President*
Marianne Cuomo, *Treasurer*
Rosemarie Cuomo, *Admin Sec*
EMP: 6 EST: 1927
SQ FT: 2,000
SALES (est): 670.5K **Privately Held**
SIC: 3911 5094 5944 Jewelry, precious metal; jewelry; jewelry, precious stones & precious metals

(G-3445)
EMBROIDERY WORLD INC
62 Bagley Ave (06514-4102)
PHONE..................203 281-7303
Robert Vincent Karpel, *President*
Donna Karpel, *Treasurer*
EMP: 2
SQ FT: 1,200
SALES: 100K **Privately Held**
SIC: 2395 7336 Embroidery & art needlework; silk screen design

(G-3446)
EXTREME TECH PROS LLC
10 Collins St (06514-4051)
PHONE..................203 903-3050
Sebastian A McCall,
EMP: 1
SALES (est): 57.1K **Privately Held**
SIC: 3679 Loads, electronic

(G-3447)
FARMINGTON RIVER HOLDINGS LLC
Also Called: Earmark
1125 Dixwell Ave (06514-4735)
PHONE..................203 777-2130
Andrew Cowell, *Mng Member*
EMP: 5
SQ FT: 11,000
SALES (est): 334.9K **Privately Held**
SIC: 3669 Intercommunication systems, electric

(G-3448)
FIRST PLACE USA LLC
1349 Dixwell Ave Ste 1 (06514-4124)
PHONE..................203 777-5510
Howard Gutkin,
Debbie Graf, *Graphic Designe*
Carol Gutkin,

EMP: 6
SQ FT: 5,000
SALES (est): 773.9K **Privately Held**
WEB: www.firstplaceusa.com
SIC: 5099 3953 Rubber stamps; signs, except electric; marking devices

(G-3449)
FURS BY PREZIOSO LTD
Also Called: Prezioso Furs
2969 Whitney Ave Ste 201 (06518-2556)
PHONE..................203 230-2930
Tom Prezioso, *President*
EMP: 3
SQ FT: 2,800
SALES (est): 344.2K **Privately Held**
SIC: 2221 Fur-type fabrics, manmade fiber

(G-3450)
GABBRO FORGE AND WELDING LLC
93 Quaker Rd (06517-3625)
PHONE..................617 699-0031
Daniel McColgan, *Principal*
EMP: 1
SALES (est): 30.3K **Privately Held**
SIC: 7692 Welding repair

(G-3451)
GIULIANO CONSTRUCTION LLC
730 Still Hill Rd (06518-1165)
PHONE..................203 230-3094
Pat Giuliano, *Mng Member*
EMP: 1
SALES (est): 157.1K **Privately Held**
SIC: 5211 2452 Prefabricated buildings; modular homes, prefabricated, wood

(G-3452)
GOLDSLAGER CONVEYOR COMPANY
73 Fernwood Rd (06517-2915)
P.O. Box 6326 (06517-0326)
PHONE..................203 795-9886
Bruce Goldslager, *CEO*
Ralph Gould, *Shareholder*
Sharon Goldslager, *Admin Sec*
EMP: 3
SALES (est): 557.4K **Privately Held**
SIC: 3535 Conveyors & conveying equipment

(G-3453)
GRAND PUBLICATIONS LLC
95 Brooksvale Ave (06518-1203)
PHONE..................203 288-5721
Michele Hoffnung, *Principal*
EMP: 1
SALES (est): 37.5K **Privately Held**
SIC: 2741 Miscellaneous publishing

(G-3454)
GUTKIN ENTERPRISES LLC
Also Called: First Place USA
1349 Dixwell Ave Ste 1 (06514-4124)
PHONE..................203 777-5510
Carol Gutkin, *CFO*
Howard Gutkin,
EMP: 6
SALES (est): 544.3K **Privately Held**
SIC: 3999 3953 Plaques, picture, laminated; pads, inking & stamping

(G-3455)
HAMDEN GRINDING
555 Sherman Ave Ste 11 (06514-1154)
PHONE..................203 288-2906
Joe Nuzzo, *Owner*
EMP: 5
SALES (est): 190K **Privately Held**
SIC: 3999 Custom pulverizing & grinding of plastic materials

(G-3456)
HAMDEN JOURNAL LLC
99 Burke St (06514-4819)
P.O. Box 187101 (06518-7019)
PHONE..................203 668-6307
Shala Latorraca, *Sales Staff*
EMP: 3
SALES (est): 189.9K **Privately Held**
SIC: 2711 Newspapers, publishing & printing

Hamden - New Haven County (G-3457) GEOGRAPHIC SECTION

(G-3457)
HAMDEN METAL SERVICE COMPANY
2 Broadway (06518-2629)
PHONE.....................203 281-1522
Jay Hirsch, *President*
Edward Hirsch III, *Vice Pres*
Martha Hirsch, *Admin Sec*
EMP: 15 EST: 1976
SALES (est): 2.1MM **Privately Held**
WEB: www.hamdenmetal.com
SIC: **3315** 3357 Wire, ferrous/iron; building wire & cable, nonferrous

(G-3458)
HAMDEN PRESS INC
1054 Dixwell Ave (06514-4912)
PHONE.....................203 624-0554
Phillip Costanzo, *President*
Jerome Constanzo, *Treasurer*
Robert Costanzo, *Admin Sec*
EMP: 3
SQ FT: 2,700
SALES (est): 326.7K **Privately Held**
SIC: **2752** Photo-offset printing

(G-3459)
HAMDEN SHEET METAL INC
1079 Dixwell Ave (06514-4718)
PHONE.....................203 776-1472
Michael Soufrine, *President*
Samford Soufrine, *Vice Pres*
Wayne Soufrine, *Vice Pres*
Betty Soufrine, *Admin Sec*
EMP: 4
SQ FT: 5,000
SALES: 200K **Privately Held**
SIC: **3444** 1711 1799 Sheet metalwork; warm air heating & air conditioning contractor; welding on site

(G-3460)
HAMDEN SPORTS CENTER INC
2858 Whitney Ave (06518-2554)
PHONE.....................203 248-9898
Robert Bush, *President*
Dan Bush, *Vice Pres*
EMP: 3
SALES (est): 248.2K **Privately Held**
SIC: **3949** Sporting & athletic goods

(G-3461)
HAWKLINE PRESS
50 Ives St (06518-2202)
PHONE.....................203 248-4615
EMP: 1
SALES (est): 37.5K **Privately Held**
SIC: **2741** Miscellaneous publishing

(G-3462)
HEALTHPER INC
24 Guenevere Ct (06518-1148)
PHONE.....................203 506-0957
David Lenihan, *Principal*
EMP: 1
SALES (corp-wide): 1MM **Privately Held**
SIC: **7372** Application computer software
PA: Healthper, Inc.
    124 Brookstone Dr
    Princeton NJ 08540
    888 257-1804

(G-3463)
HERRICK & COWELL COMPANY INC
839 Sherman Ave (06514-1132)
P.O. Box 4332 (06514-0332)
PHONE.....................203 288-2578
EMP: 9 EST: 1874
SQ FT: 16,000
SALES (est): 1.1MM **Privately Held**
SIC: **3599** 3549 Mfg Industrial Machinery Mfg Metalworking Machinery

(G-3464)
HPI MANUFACTURING INC
375 Morse St (06517-3133)
PHONE.....................203 777-5395
Glenn M Ayer, *Principal*
EMP: 4 EST: 2016
SALES (est): 344.8K **Privately Held**
SIC: **3999** Manufacturing industries

(G-3465)
INSULPANE CONNECTICUT INC
Also Called: Solar Seal of Connecticut
30 Edmund St (06517-3914)
PHONE.....................800 922-3248
Paul Cody, *CEO*
Frederick Federico Sr, *Principal*
Frederick Federico Jr, *Vice Pres*
Beth Lesniak, *Vice Pres*
Rick Shaw, *Vice Pres*
▲ EMP: 62
SQ FT: 12,000
SALES (est): 10.5MM
SALES (corp-wide): 462.1MM **Privately Held**
SIC: **3211** 3469 Insulating glass, sealed units; architectural panels or parts, porcelain enameled
PA: Grey Mountain Partners, Llc
    1470 Walnut St Ste 400
    Boulder CO 80302
    303 449-5692

(G-3466)
J&A WOODWORKING CO INC
90 Chatterton Way (06518-1115)
PHONE.....................203 287-1915
John Christina, *President*
Angela Christina, *Vice Pres*
EMP: 2
SALES (est): 307.7K **Privately Held**
SIC: **1531** 1521 2434 Operative builders; general remodeling, single-family houses; wood kitchen cabinets

(G-3467)
JEFFREY GOLD
Also Called: Laser Body Solutions
2440 Whitney Ave Ste 6 (06518-3268)
PHONE.....................203 281-5737
Jeffrey Gold, *Owner*
Vicki Gold, *Co-Owner*
EMP: 7
SALES (est): 1MM **Privately Held**
WEB: www.laserbody.com
SIC: **3845** 8011 Laser systems & equipment, medical; ophthalmologist

(G-3468)
JFD TUBE & COIL PRODUCTS INC
7 Hamden Park Dr (06517-3151)
P.O. Box 6309 (06517-0309)
PHONE.....................203 288-6941
Diane Orlowski, *Corp Secy*
Daniel Orlowski, *Vice Pres*
Thomas Orlowski, *Vice Pres*
EMP: 34
SQ FT: 14,200
SALES (est): 7.3MM **Privately Held**
WEB: www.jfdcoil.com
SIC: **3443** 3498 Heat exchangers, condensers & components; weldments; coils, pipe; fabricated from purchased pipe; pipe sections fabricated from purchased pipe

(G-3469)
JOSEPH A CNTE MFG JEWELERS INC
2582 Whitney Ave (06518-3032)
PHONE.....................203 248-9853
Joseph A Conte, *President*
EMP: 4
SALES (est): 423K **Privately Held**
SIC: **3911** 5944 Jewelry, precious metal; jewelry stores

(G-3470)
KTT ENTERPRISES LLC
15 Marne St (06514)
PHONE.....................203 288-7883
Richard J Coffey, *Mng Member*
Nancy J Coffey,
▲ EMP: 5
SQ FT: 15,000
SALES: 1MM **Privately Held**
WEB: www.kttenterprises.com
SIC: **3069** Latex, foamed

(G-3471)
LANDINO SIGNS LLC
15 Corporate Ridge Rd # 11 (06514-1138)
PHONE.....................203 248-5437
John Landino, *Mng Member*
EMP: 1
SQ FT: 1,000
SALES (est): 87.8K **Privately Held**
SIC: **7389** 3993 Sign painting & lettering shop; signs & advertising specialties

(G-3472)
LEED - HIMMEL INDUSTRIES INC
75 Leeder Hill Dr (06517-2731)
PHONE.....................203 288-8484
Howard B Goldfarb, *President*
Larry Himmel, *Exec VP*
Shadi Goldslager, *Credit Mgr*
Nancy Chovitz, *Human Res Mgr*
Adam Stern, *Chief Mktg Ofcr*
EMP: 70 EST: 1945
SQ FT: 120,000
SALES (est): 24.5MM **Privately Held**
WEB: www.leed-himmel.com
SIC: **3446** Architectural metalwork

(G-3473)
LEGAL AFFAIRS INC
Also Called: LEGAL AFFAIRS MAGAZINE
115 Blake Rd (06517-3405)
PHONE.....................203 865-2520
Lincoln Caplan, *President*
EMP: 9
SALES (est): 0 **Privately Held**
WEB: www.legalaffairs.com
SIC: **2721** Periodicals

(G-3474)
LESS PAY OIL LLC
78 Linden Ave (06518-2821)
PHONE.....................203 230-2568
Allan E Selmquist, *Principal*
EMP: 2
SALES (est): 222.8K **Privately Held**
SIC: **1311** Crude petroleum & natural gas

(G-3475)
LIGHT SPEED LLC
653 Gaylord Mountain Rd (06518-1007)
PHONE.....................203 248-8550
Brenda H O Neal, *Managing Prtnr*
Carlton L O Neal, *Managing Prtnr*
Carlton L Oneal, *Partner*
Branda O Neal, *Partner*
EMP: 2
SQ FT: 2,000
SALES (est): 166.3K **Privately Held**
WEB: www.lightspeedu.com
SIC: **8748** 7372 Business consulting; prepackaged software

(G-3476)
LOCKING FILTER LLC
151 Sandquist Cir (06514-2650)
PHONE.....................203 691-1221
EMP: 2
SALES (est): 130K **Privately Held**
SIC: **3569** Mfg General Industrial Machinery

(G-3477)
LONE WOLFE PRINTING LLC
740 Mix Ave Unit 102 (06514-2279)
PHONE.....................203 444-5131
Robert Musial, *Principal*
EMP: 2
SALES (est): 121.6K **Privately Held**
SIC: **2752** Commercial printing, lithographic

(G-3478)
M G M INSTRUMENTS INC (PA)
925 Sherman Ave (06514-1171)
PHONE.....................203 248-4008
George Mismas, *President*
Murray Dennis, *Mfg Mgr*
Steve Meyer, *QC Mgr*
Janice Mismas, *Treasurer*
Kris Schied, *Financial Exec*
EMP: 30
SQ FT: 12,000
SALES (est): 3MM **Privately Held**
WEB: www.mgminstruments.com
SIC: **3841** Diagnostic apparatus, medical

(G-3479)
MATHWORD PRESS LLC
97 Fennbrook Dr (06517-1607)
PHONE.....................203 288-8114
Marianne Prokop,
EMP: 1 EST: 2011
SALES (est): 48.5K **Privately Held**
SIC: **2741** Miscellaneous publishing

(G-3480)
MEDIA ONE LLC
44 Hawley Rd (06517-2128)
PHONE.....................203 745-5825
Saad Mobarak, *CEO*
Muhd Molla, *President*
EMP: 50
SALES (est): 1.7MM **Privately Held**
SIC: **3559** Sewing machines & attachments, industrial

(G-3481)
MERRITT EXTRUDER CORP
15 Marne St (06514)
PHONE.....................203 230-8100
Lucien D Yokana, *Ch of Bd*
Alexander Guthrie, *President*
Thomas J Oravits, *Vice Pres*
Mark Roland, *Controller*
Charles Jaffin, *Admin Sec*
EMP: 50
SQ FT: 45,000
SALES (est): 9.8MM **Privately Held**
WEB: www.merrittdavis.com
SIC: **3559** 3089 3549 3542 Fiber optics strand coating machinery; extruded finished plastic products; metalworking machinery; machine tools, metal forming type

(G-3482)
MEYER WIRE & CABLE COMPANY LLC
1072 Sherman Ave (06514-1337)
PHONE.....................203 281-0817
Karen Meyer,
Brian Meyer,
EMP: 21
SQ FT: 2,000
SALES (est): 3.7MM **Privately Held**
SIC: **3496** Miscellaneous fabricated wire products

(G-3483)
MINUTE MAN PRESS
Also Called: Minuteman Press
5 Hamden Park Dr (06517-3150)
PHONE.....................203 891-6251
EMP: 4
SALES (est): 234.6K **Privately Held**
SIC: **2752** Commercial printing, lithographic

(G-3484)
MOON CUTTER CO INC
2969 State St (06517-1712)
PHONE.....................203 288-9249
Eleanor Moon, *President*
Charles Moon, *Vice Pres*
Matt Rome, *Engineer*
Lenore Capasso, *Asst Sec*
EMP: 45
SQ FT: 54,000
SALES (est): 7MM **Privately Held**
SIC: **3541** 3545 Machine tools, metal cutting type; machine tool accessories

(G-3485)
MR CONNECTICUT LEATHER INC
30 Rossotto Dr (06514-1335)
PHONE.....................203 230-2166
George Peet, *Principal*
EMP: 1
SALES (est): 65.8K **Privately Held**
SIC: **3199** Leather goods

(G-3486)
MT CARMEL WOODWORK LLC
770 Evergreen Ave (06518-2309)
PHONE.....................203 230-8377
William Wilson, *Principal*
EMP: 2
SALES (est): 109.2K **Privately Held**
SIC: **2431** Millwork

(G-3487)
NDR LIUZZI INC
Also Called: Liuzzi Cheese
86 Rossotto Dr (06514-1335)
PHONE.....................203 287-8477

Nicola Liuzzi, *President*
▲ **EMP:** 48
SALES (est): 4.7MM **Privately Held**
SIC: 2022 5143 Cheese, natural & processed; cheese

(G-3488)
NEW ENGLAND CNC INC
46 Manila Ave (06514-4107)
PHONE....................203 288-8241
Ronald Krutz, *Vice Pres*
EMP: 15
SALES (est): 1.7MM **Privately Held**
SIC: 3599 Machine shop, jobbing & repair

(G-3489)
NEW ENGLAND ORTHO NEURO LLC
2080 Whitney Ave Ste 290 (06518-3604)
PHONE....................203 200-7228
James Yue, *Principal*
EMP: 3
SALES (est): 168.2K **Privately Held**
SIC: 2813 Neon

(G-3490)
NEW ENGLAND THEATRE CONFERENCE
215 Knob Hill Dr (06518-2431)
PHONE....................203 288-8680
J Juliano, *Manager*
EMP: 2
SALES (est): 62.9K **Privately Held**
SIC: 2711 Newspapers

(G-3491)
NEW HAVEN SIGN CO
264 Morse St (06517-3130)
P.O. Box 4187 (06514-0187)
PHONE....................203 891-5710
Peter Deyo, *President*
EMP: 2
SALES (est): 79.3K **Privately Held**
SIC: 3993 Signs & advertising specialties

(G-3492)
ORIGINAL MATERIALS INDS LLC
94 Squire Ln (06518-1418)
P.O. Box 185862 (06518-0862)
PHONE....................203 535-1192
Thomas Aitkenhead, *Owner*
EMP: 2
SALES (est): 110.1K **Privately Held**
SIC: 3999 Manufacturing industries

(G-3493)
PACE CHIROPRACTIC WELLNESS CTR
3154 Whitney Ave (06518-2321)
PHONE....................203 281-9635
Michael Pace, *Principal*
EMP: 1
SALES (est): 49.1K **Privately Held**
SIC: 3131 Footwear cut stock

(G-3494)
PARKWAY PRINTERS INC
60 Connolly Pkwy (06514-2593)
PHONE....................203 281-6773
George Di Battista, *President*
William Olsen, *Corp Secy*
EMP: 2
SQ FT: 2,500
SALES (est): 137.7K **Privately Held**
SIC: 2752 2759 Commercial printing, offset; invitations: printing

(G-3495)
PARVA INDUSTRIES INC
2974 Whitney Ave (06518-2339)
PHONE....................203 248-5553
Armand Audette, *Principal*
EMP: 1
SALES (est): 57.9K **Privately Held**
SIC: 3999 Manufacturing industries

(G-3496)
PAUL DRINGOLI
Also Called: Yankee Woodcraft
3569 Whitney Ave (06518-1919)
PHONE....................203 248-0281
Paul Dringoli, *Owner*
EMP: 2

SALES: 50K **Privately Held**
WEB: www.yankeewoodcraft.com
SIC: 2499 2511 Picture & mirror frames, wood; wood household furniture

(G-3497)
POROBOND PRODUCTS LLC
80 Sanford St (06514-1707)
P.O. Box 5, North Haven (06473-0005)
PHONE....................203 234-7747
Wayne Paulsen,
◆ **EMP:** 10
SQ FT: 25,000
SALES (est): 1.5MM **Privately Held**
SIC: 3443 Heat exchangers, condensers & components

(G-3498)
PUSHING ENVELOPE LLC
2315 Whitney Ave (06518-3529)
PHONE....................203 745-0988
Ellen Swirsky,
Susan Margolis,
EMP: 2
SALES: 20K **Privately Held**
SIC: 2759 Invitations: printing

(G-3499)
QUEENIE INDUSTRIES LLC
50 Harrison Dr (06514-2800)
PHONE....................917 848-4490
Esther Rockson, *Mng Member*
EMP: 1
SALES (est): 39.6K **Privately Held**
SIC: 3999 Manufacturing industries

(G-3500)
QUINNIPIAC VALLEY TIMES
2301 State St (06517-3721)
PHONE....................203 675-9483
Fred Nevin, *Principal*
EMP: 3
SALES (est): 114.3K **Privately Held**
SIC: 2711 Newspapers

(G-3501)
RAYMON TOOL LLC
79 Rossotto Dr (06514-1336)
PHONE....................203 248-2199
Vincent Palumbo, *Mng Member*
Paul Derenzo,
EMP: 12 **EST:** 1997
SQ FT: 10,000
SALES (est): 2.5MM **Privately Held**
WEB: www.raymontool.com
SIC: 3542 Machine tools, metal forming type

(G-3502)
RAZZBERRY INC
2228 Shepard Ave (06518-1509)
PHONE....................510 495-5366
Alexandra Sweeney, *CEO*
Alexandra Barton-Sweeney, *CEO*
EMP: 2 **EST:** 2016
SALES (est): 86.6K **Privately Held**
SIC: 3845 Automated blood & body fluid analyzers, except laboratory

(G-3503)
RAZZBERRY OPERATING CO INC
2228 Shepard Ave (06518-1509)
PHONE....................510 495-5366
Alexandra Barton-Sweeney, *CEO*
Mildred Amis, *Administration*
EMP: 2 **EST:** 2016
SALES (est): 104.8K **Privately Held**
SIC: 3845 Electromedical equipment

(G-3504)
RECORD PRODUCTS AMERICA INC
Also Called: R P A
700 Sherman Ave (06514-1360)
PHONE....................203 248-6371
Robert Roczynski, *President*
▲ **EMP:** 14
SQ FT: 13,000
SALES (est): 4.5MM **Privately Held**
WEB: www.recordproducts.com
SIC: 5084 3469 Industrial machinery & equipment; machine parts, stamped or pressed metal

(G-3505)
RHODE ISLAND BEVERAGE JOURNAL
2508 Whitney Ave (06518-3040)
PHONE....................203 288-3375
Gerald Slone, *Principal*
EMP: 3
SALES (est): 176.7K **Privately Held**
SIC: 2711 Newspapers, publishing & printing

(G-3506)
ROLLINS PRINTING INCORPORATED
3281 Whitney Ave (06518-1923)
PHONE....................203 248-3200
Carl F De Rosa, *President*
Patricia De Rosa, *Admin Sec*
EMP: 6
SQ FT: 5,000
SALES (est): 750K **Privately Held**
WEB: www.rollinsprintingusa.com
SIC: 2752 Commercial printing, offset

(G-3507)
SATIN STYLE LLC
331 Deerfield Dr (06518-1753)
PHONE....................203 287-5466
EMP: 2 **EST:** 2007
SALES (est): 102.1K **Privately Held**
SIC: 2221 Manmade Broadwoven Fabric Mill

(G-3508)
SCREEN TEK PRINTING CO INC
130 Welton St (06517-3930)
PHONE....................203 248-6248
Robert Mastriano, *President*
Paul Mastriano, *Vice Pres*
EMP: 3
SQ FT: 6,000
SALES: 1.1MM **Privately Held**
WEB: www.screentek.net
SIC: 2752 Commercial printing, lithographic

(G-3509)
SECONDARY OPERATIONS INC
46 Manila Ave (06514-4107)
PHONE....................203 288-8241
Lawrence Carrignan, *President*
Ronald Krutz, *Vice Pres*
EMP: 10 **EST:** 1960
SQ FT: 6,600
SALES (est): 910K **Privately Held**
WEB: www.secondaryoperations.com
SIC: 3599 3541 Machine shop, jobbing & repair; machine tools, metal cutting type

(G-3510)
SKICO MANUFACTURING CO LLC
3 Industrial Cir (06517-3153)
PHONE....................203 230-1305
Daniel D Skibitcky, *Partner*
Tom Skibitcky, *Partner*
Dan Skibitcky,
EMP: 9
SQ FT: 7,200
SALES (est): 788.3K **Privately Held**
SIC: 3599 3545 3544 7699 Machine shop, jobbing & repair; crankshafts & camshafts, machining; precision tools, machinists'; special dies & tools; aircraft & heavy equipment repair services

(G-3511)
SPECIALIST SENSOR
47 Park Ave (06517-1839)
PHONE....................203 287-9699
Samuel Agulian, *Executive*
EMP: 2
SALES (est): 213.4K **Privately Held**
SIC: 3829 Measuring & controlling devices

(G-3512)
SPECIALTY WIRE & CORD SETS
Also Called: SWC
1 Gallagher Rd (06517-3171)
PHONE....................203 498-2932
Lynn Campo, *President*
Liborio Campo, *Vice Pres*
EMP: 18
SQ FT: 12,000

SALES: 2.2MM **Privately Held**
WEB: www.specialtywire.com
SIC: 3351 Wire, copper & copper alloy

(G-3513)
STN LAUNDRY SYSTEMS LLC
844 W Woods Rd (06518-1725)
PHONE....................203 887-8986
David Lemieux, *Principal*
EMP: 2
SALES (est): 160K **Privately Held**
SIC: 3582 Commercial laundry equipment

(G-3514)
STRAIGHT STITCHES
198 Sandquist Cir (06514-2649)
PHONE....................203 804-0409
Kathy Abbott, *Principal*
EMP: 1
SALES (est): 65.8K **Privately Held**
SIC: 2395 Embroidery & art needlework

(G-3515)
SUPERIOR PRINTING INK CO INC
750 Sherman Ave (06514-1191)
PHONE....................203 281-1921
Andrew Anselmo, *Branch Mgr*
EMP: 45
SQ FT: 5,200
SALES (corp-wide): 151.6MM **Privately Held**
SIC: 2893 Printing ink
PA: Superior Printing Ink Co Inc
   100 North St
   Teterboro NJ 07608
   201 478-5600

(G-3516)
SUTTON MIX AVENUE LLC
760 Mix Ave Apt 1s (06514-2210)
PHONE....................203 288-8482
Annette Dimassa, *Manager*
EMP: 2
SALES (est): 282.1K **Privately Held**
SIC: 3273 Ready-mixed concrete

(G-3517)
TACHWA ENTERPRISES INC
4 Industrial Cir (06517-3152)
PHONE....................203 691-5772
James White Jr, *President*
Andrew Wilkes, *Vice Pres*
EMP: 7
SQ FT: 7,200
SALES (est): 1.5MM **Privately Held**
WEB: www.tachwa.com
SIC: 3728 Aircraft assemblies, subassemblies & parts

(G-3518)
THREE POETS PUBLISHING CO LLC
900 Mix Ave U64 (06514-5142)
P.O. Box 4489 (06514-0489)
PHONE....................203 248-0200
Ana Kyle, *Principal*
EMP: 1
SALES (est): 55.8K **Privately Held**
SIC: 2741 Miscellaneous publishing

(G-3519)
TL WOODWORKING
299 Welton St (06517-3900)
PHONE....................203 787-9661
Thomas Leary, *Principal*
EMP: 4 **EST:** 2011
SALES (est): 304.2K **Privately Held**
SIC: 2431 Millwork

(G-3520)
TLC MEDIA LLC
900 Mix Ave Apt 22 (06514-5107)
PHONE....................203 980-1361
EMP: 6
SALES (est): 229.3K **Privately Held**
SIC: 2711 Newspapers

(G-3521)
TO THE TENTH INC
60 Connolly Pkwy 15b-101 (06514-2593)
PHONE....................203 248-9437
Mark Zikaras, *President*
Robert Browning, *President*
Mark William Zikaras, *Director*

Hamden - New Haven County

EMP: 2
SQ FT: 2,000
SALES: 250K **Privately Held**
SIC: 3599 Electrical discharge machining (EDM)

(G-3522)
TOMTEC INC
1000 Sherman Ave (06514-1358)
PHONE.................................203 281-6790
Tom Astle, *CEO*
Gade Ajeigbe, *CEO*
Joan Astle, *Corp Secy*
Ted Miller, *Technology*
John Daddio, *Software Engr*
▲ EMP: 68
SQ FT: 70,000
SALES (est): 11.9MM **Privately Held**
WEB: www.tomtec.com
SIC: 3845 3826 3821 Electromedical apparatus; analytical instruments; laboratory apparatus & furniture

(G-3523)
TRANSACT TECHNOLOGIES INC (PA)
2319 Whitney Ave Ste 3b (06518-3534)
PHONE.................................203 859-6800
Bart C Shuldman, *Ch of Bd*
Lindsay Nix, *COO*
David Block, *Senior VP*
Donald E Brooks, *Senior VP*
Tracey S Chernay, *Senior VP*
EMP: 123
SQ FT: 11,100
SALES: 54.5MM **Publicly Held**
WEB: www.transact-tech.com
SIC: 3577 7378 Computers & plotters; printers, computer; computer peripheral equipment repair & maintenance

(G-3524)
TUDOR HOUSE FURNITURE CO INC
929 Sherman Ave (06514-1150)
PHONE.................................203 288-8451
Harold Margolies, *President*
EMP: 28 EST: 1963
SQ FT: 20,000
SALES (est): 4.1MM **Privately Held**
SIC: 2512 2511 Living room furniture: upholstered on wood frames; wood household furniture

(G-3525)
ULTRAMATIC WEST
87 Beechwood Ave (06514-2913)
PHONE.................................203 745-4688
Richard Golia, *Owner*
EMP: 3
SQ FT: 1,000
SALES: 350K **Privately Held**
SIC: 3552 Embroidery machines

(G-3526)
W AND G MACHINE COMPANY INC
4 Hamden Park Dr (06517-3149)
P.O. Box 6187 (06517-0187)
PHONE.................................203 288-8772
Jay Kroopnick, *President*
Dan Duhamel, *Production*
Gene Borysewicz, *VP Engrg*
Robin Kroopnick, *Treasurer*
Sheree A Napolitan, *Admin Sec*
EMP: 36 EST: 1952
SQ FT: 12,000
SALES (est): 8.1MM **Privately Held**
SIC: 3728 Aircraft parts & equipment

(G-3527)
WARNER PRECISION MACHINING & F
875 Shepard Ave (06514-1356)
PHONE.................................203 281-3660
J Warner, *Principal*
EMP: 2
SALES (est): 169.7K **Privately Held**
SIC: 3599 Machine shop, jobbing & repair

(G-3528)
WATTS
11 Quarry Ln (06518-1771)
PHONE.................................203 230-8582
Alfred Watts, *Principal*
EMP: 2
SALES (est): 187K **Privately Held**
SIC: 3491 Industrial valves

(G-3529)
WESTFORT CONSTRUCTION CORP
3000 Whitney Ave (06518-2353)
PHONE.................................860 833-7970
Erica Morizio, *Principal*
EMP: 3
SALES (est): 148.1K **Privately Held**
SIC: 2952 7389 Mastic roofing composition;

(G-3530)
WILDCAT FUEL SYSTEMS CONN LLC
36 Vantage Rd (06514-2805)
PHONE.................................203 627-4310
Pasqualino Digregorio, *Principal*
EMP: 1
SALES (est): 75.4K **Privately Held**
SIC: 2869 Fuels

(G-3531)
WORTH PROPERTIES LLC
27 Spring Glen Ter (06517-1534)
PHONE.................................203 281-1792
Joseph Reagan, *Owner*
EMP: 1
SALES (est): 93.7K **Privately Held**
SIC: 3524 Lawnmowers, residential: hand or power

(G-3532)
YACHT SPECIALTY PRODUCTS
86 Birchwood Dr (06518-1160)
PHONE.................................203 565-5598
Francis A McGurk,
EMP: 1
SALES: 200K **Privately Held**
SIC: 3429 Marine hardware

(G-3533)
Z&Z INDUSTRIES LLC
30 Glen Ridge Rd (06518-5360)
PHONE.................................203 230-9533
Ming Zhao, *Principal*
▲ EMP: 1
SALES (est): 67K **Privately Held**
SIC: 3999 Manufacturing industries

Hampton
Windham County

(G-3534)
BURELL BROS INC
Rr 97 (06247)
PHONE.................................860 455-9681
Frances Burell, *President*
Francis Burell, *President*
John Burell, *Vice Pres*
Carol Burell, *Admin Sec*
EMP: 7
SQ FT: 10,000
SALES (est): 957.4K **Privately Held**
SIC: 2421 Sawmills & planing mills, general

(G-3535)
CHARLES PIKE & SONS
311 Providence Tpke (06247-1433)
PHONE.................................860 455-9968
Charles Pike, *Owner*
Virginia Pike, *Co-Owner*
EMP: 4
SALES (est): 150K **Privately Held**
SIC: 2421 Sawmills & planing mills, general

(G-3536)
JUSKHAS WP CO
632 Brook Rd (06247-1508)
PHONE.................................860 455-0502
William Juskhas, *Owner*
EMP: 1
SALES (est): 122K **Privately Held**
SIC: 3545 Cutting tools for machine tools

(G-3537)
LUCKY ENOUGH CANVAS
453 Brook St (06247-2104)
PHONE.................................860 455-6994
Jacob Schneider, *Manager*
EMP: 1
SALES (est): 46.5K **Privately Held**
SIC: 2211 Canvas

(G-3538)
NEW ENGLAND CTR FOR HRING RHAB
Also Called: N E C H E A R
354 Hartford Tpke (06247-1320)
PHONE.................................860 455-1404
Diane Brackett, *Director*
EMP: 6
SALES (est): 836.2K **Privately Held**
SIC: 3842 8099 Hearing aids; blood related health services

(G-3539)
RAINBOW FOREST LOG & FIREWD
88 Old Canterbury Rd (06247-1610)
PHONE.................................860 455-1023
Jody Charron, *Owner*
EMP: 1
SALES (est): 80.4K **Privately Held**
SIC: 2411 5989 Logging camps & contractors; wood (fuel)

(G-3540)
TROWBRIDGE FOREST PRODUCTS LLC (PA)
136 Lewis Rd (06247-1207)
PHONE.................................860 455-9931
John Trowbridge, *Owner*
EMP: 1
SALES (est): 166.3K **Privately Held**
SIC: 2411 Logging

Hartford
Hartford County

(G-3541)
90 ARCH ST LLC
41 Crossroads Plz Ste 220 (06117-2402)
PHONE.................................860 881-2063
Filippos Milios, *Principal*
EMP: 2 EST: 2011
SALES (est): 117.1K **Privately Held**
SIC: 3312 Stainless steel

(G-3542)
A & P COAT APRON & LIN SUP INC
Also Called: Unitex Textile Rental Service
420 Ledyard St (06114-3207)
PHONE.................................914 840-3200
Raymond Neal, *Plant Mgr*
Raymon Neal, *Branch Mgr*
EMP: 60
SALES (corp-wide): 70.3MM **Privately Held**
WEB: www.rent-a-uniform.com
SIC: 2299 7213 7218 Textile mill waste & remnant processing; uniform supply; industrial launderers
PA: A & P Coat, Apron, & Linen Supply, Inc.
565 Taxter Rd Ste 620
Elmsford NY 10523
914 840-3200

(G-3543)
A G RUSSELL COMPANY INC
60 George St (06114-2915)
P.O. Box 1685 (06144-1685)
PHONE.................................860 247-9093
Francis Fertera, *President*
Leroy Lowe, *Vice Pres*
Douglas Lowe, *Treasurer*
EMP: 5
SQ FT: 3,900
SALES: 425K **Privately Held**
WEB: www.stampitmarkit.com
SIC: 3469 3953 3542 Metal stampings; printing dies, rubber or plastic, for marking machines; marking machines

(G-3544)
ABRANTES BAKERY & PASTRY SHOP
1851 Park St (06106-2121)
PHONE.................................860 232-1464
Anthony Abrantes, *President*
EMP: 1
SALES: 31K **Privately Held**
SIC: 5461 2051 Bakeries; bread, cake & related products

(G-3545)
ACE TECHNICAL PLASTICS INC
122 Park Ave J (06108-4036)
P.O. Box 4519 (06147-4519)
PHONE.................................860 278-2444
Bob Stevenson, *Principal*
EMP: 6
SALES (est): 812K **Privately Held**
SIC: 3089 Injection molding of plastics

(G-3546)
ACTION STEEL LLC
55 Airport Rd Ste 104 (06114-2031)
PHONE.................................860 216-6595
Liza Bonadies, *President*
EMP: 1
SALES (est): 98.9K **Privately Held**
SIC: 3499 Fabricated metal products

(G-3547)
ADAMSAHERN SIGN SOLUTIONS INC
30 Arbor St Unit 208 (06106-1238)
PHONE.................................860 523-8835
Diane Ahern, *President*
Chris Adams, *Admin Sec*
EMP: 14
SALES (est): 700K **Privately Held**
SIC: 3993 1799 Electric signs; signs, not made in custom sign painting shops; sign installation & maintenance

(G-3548)
AEROSPACE METALS INC
Also Called: Suisman & Blumenthal
239 W Service Rd (06120-1205)
PHONE.................................860 522-3123
Paul Haveson, *President*
Michael Suisman, *Principal*
Robert Kaseta, *CFO*
EMP: 112
SQ FT: 225,000
SALES (est): 13.2MM **Privately Held**
WEB: www.mtlm.com
SIC: 3356 Titanium
HQ: Metal Management, Inc.
200 W Madison St Ste 3600
Chicago IL 60606
312 645-0700

(G-3549)
AFC INDUSTRIES LLC
80 Weston St (06120-1504)
PHONE.................................860 246-7411
Matthew Currey,
EMP: 1
SALES (est): 87.4K **Privately Held**
SIC: 3462 Chains, forged steel

(G-3550)
ALBERT KEMPERLE INC
141 Locust St (06114-1504)
PHONE.................................860 727-0933
Ronald Kemperle, *President*
EMP: 19
SALES (corp-wide): 163.8MM **Privately Held**
SIC: 2851 Paints & allied products
PA: Albert Kemperle, Inc.
8400 New Horizons Blvd
Amityville NY 11701
631 841-1241

(G-3551)
ALM MEDIA LLC
Also Called: The Connecticut Law Tribune
201 Ann Uccello St Fl 4 (06103-2000)
PHONE.................................860 527-7900
Jeffrey Forte, *Branch Mgr*
EMP: 22
SALES (corp-wide): 181.8MM **Privately Held**
WEB: www.alm.com
SIC: 2711 Newspapers

HQ: Alm Media, Llc
150 E 42nd St
New York NY 10017
212 457-9400

(G-3552)
AQUASTONE GRAPHIX LLC
Also Called: Aquastone Graphix Arts & Print
1477 Park St Ste 8 (06106-2237)
PHONE.................................860 206-4935
Dyshann Anderson, *Mng Member*
EMP: 2
SQ FT: 500
SALES (est): 74K **Privately Held**
SIC: 7374 7389 2759 2721 Computer graphics service; design services; publication printing; periodicals: publishing & printing; stationery & invitation printing, gravure; graphic arts & related design

(G-3553)
AQUILINE DRONES LLC
750 Main St Ste 319 (06103-2706)
PHONE.................................860 361-7958
Barry Alexander, *Mng Member*
EMP: 15
SALES: 5K **Privately Held**
SIC: 3721 Non-motorized & lighter-than-air aircraft

(G-3554)
AUSTIN ORGANS INCORPORATED
156 Woodland St (06105-1284)
P.O. Box 355, Chester (06412-0355)
PHONE.................................860 522-8293
Richard G Taylor, *CEO*
Michael B Fazio, *President*
EMP: 25 **EST:** 1893
SQ FT: 35,000
SALES (est): 3.4MM **Privately Held**
WEB: www.austinorgans.com
SIC: 3931 Organs, all types: pipe, reed, hand, electronic, etc.; organ parts & materials

(G-3555)
BARCLAY-DAVIS ENTERPRISES LLC
306 Sigourney St 2s (06105-1334)
PHONE.................................860 578-9563
Donna Barclay-Davis, *Principal*
EMP: 1
SALES (est): 31.7K **Privately Held**
SIC: 7299 8322 2842 7991 Diet center, without medical staff; outreach program; specialty cleaning preparations; athletic club & gymnasiums, membership

(G-3556)
BLUE EARTH COMPOST INC
3580 Main St Ste 10 (06120-1100)
PHONE.................................860 508-7114
Alex Williams, *President*
Alexander Williams, *Opers Staff*
Sam King, *Marketing Staff*
EMP: 1
SALES (est): 196K **Privately Held**
SIC: 2875 Compost

(G-3557)
BLUSH BY LONDON
2 Fraser Pl Unit 2a (06105-1457)
PHONE.................................860 610-9891
Shavonne Mason, *Owner*
EMP: 2
SALES (est): 87K **Privately Held**
SIC: 2339 Women's & misses' outerwear

(G-3558)
BOTANICA CHACHITAS
Also Called: Chachitas Chango
831 Park St (06106-2352)
PHONE.................................860 247-5103
Rosa Juan, *Owner*
EMP: 2
SQ FT: 4,000
SALES (est): 171.2K **Privately Held**
SIC: 2833 7841 Medicinals & botanicals; video tape rental

(G-3559)
BRIAN DAIGLE
158 Beacon St (06105-2913)
PHONE.................................860 263-7831

Sergio Garcia, *Owner*
EMP: 1
SALES (est): 54.1K **Privately Held**
SIC: 2431 Millwork

(G-3560)
CABLE ELECTRONICS INC
221 Newfield Ave Ste 2 (06106-3662)
P.O. Box 330326, West Hartford (06133-0326)
PHONE.................................860 953-0300
David H Farrah, *President*
Florence Farrah, *Vice Pres*
EMP: 5
SQ FT: 3,500
SALES (est): 555.1K **Privately Held**
SIC: 3679 5084 7622 Electronic circuits; industrial machinery & equipment; radio & television repair

(G-3561)
CAPITOL PRINTING CO INC
Also Called: Minuteman Press
52 Pratt St (06103-1601)
PHONE.................................860 522-1547
Joel Steinman, *President*
Steve Weber, *Vice Pres*
Amy Steinman, *Director*
Gail Weber, *Director*
EMP: 8
SQ FT: 1,500
SALES (est): 1.3MM **Privately Held**
SIC: 2752 Commercial printing, lithographic

(G-3562)
CAPITOL SAUSAGE & PROVS INC
101 Reserve Rd Bldg 14 (06114-1608)
PHONE.................................860 527-5510
William Driscoll, *President*
Sandra Driscoll, *Admin Sec*
EMP: 7
SQ FT: 10,000
SALES (est): 959.1K **Privately Held**
SIC: 2013 5149 Sausages & other prepared meats

(G-3563)
CARPET PRODUCTS
218 Murphy Rd (06114-2107)
PHONE.................................860 278-6160
Michael Cosgrove, *Manager*
EMP: 1
SALES (est): 84.5K **Privately Held**
SIC: 5713 5023 3272 2426 Carpets; floor coverings; floor tile, precast terrazzo; flooring, hardwood

(G-3564)
CAT LLC
819 N Mountain Rd (06111-1414)
PHONE.................................860 953-1807
Daniel Bourget,
▼ **EMP:** 4
SALES (est): 464.9K **Privately Held**
WEB: www.billetcats.com
SIC: 3751 Motorcycle accessories

(G-3565)
CELESTE INDUSTRIES CORPORATION
30 High St (06103)
PHONE.................................860 278-9800
Michael E Moran, *Principal*
EMP: 1
SALES (est): 62K
SALES (corp-wide): 14.7B **Publicly Held**
SIC: 3089 Injection molded finished plastic products
PA: Illinois Tool Works Inc.
155 Harlem Ave
Glenview IL 60025
847 724-7500

(G-3566)
CHOWDER POT OF HARTFORD LLC
165 Brainard Rd (06114-2102)
PHONE.................................860 244-3311
Dennis Longo,
EMP: 1 **EST:** 2017
SQ FT: 30,000
SALES (est): 55.5K **Privately Held**
SIC: 2099 Food preparations

(G-3567)
CITY SIGN
1811 Park St (06106-2121)
PHONE.................................860 232-4803
Martin Glennie, *Mng Member*
Carol Glennie, *Mng Member*
EMP: 4 **EST:** 1977
SQ FT: 8,400
SALES (est): 455.1K **Privately Held**
SIC: 3993 Signs & advertising specialties

(G-3568)
CITY WELDING
84 Wellington St (06106-2952)
PHONE.................................860 951-4714
Frank Serrao, *Owner*
EMP: 3
SALES (est): 200K **Privately Held**
SIC: 7692 Welding repair

(G-3569)
CONNECTCUT HSPNIC YELLOW PAGES
2074 Park St Ste 2 (06106-2055)
PHONE.................................860 560-8713
Hector Torres, *President*
Angel Funtes, *Principal*
▲ **EMP:** 10
SALES (est): 879.9K **Privately Held**
SIC: 2741 Telephone & other directory publishing

(G-3570)
COPELAND LATASHA
Also Called: Catera, The
354 Woodland St (06112-2149)
PHONE.................................860 728-8289
Latasha Copeland, *Owner*
EMP: 1
SALES (est): 57.3K **Privately Held**
SIC: 2599 5149 Food wagons, restaurant; food gift baskets

(G-3571)
CORE FILTRATION LLC
30 Arbor St Ste 210b (06106-1232)
PHONE.................................860 904-6640
Blair T Scoble, *President*
EMP: 1
SALES (est): 154.2K **Privately Held**
SIC: 3589 Water filters & softeners, household type

(G-3572)
COURANT SPECIALTY PRODUCTS INC
285 Broad St (06115-3785)
PHONE.................................860 241-3795
Stephen D Carver, *President*
Richard S Feeney, *Vice Pres*
David P Eldersveld, *Admin Sec*
EMP: 30
SALES (est): 120.6K
SALES (corp-wide): 2.7B **Publicly Held**
WEB: www.tribune.com
SIC: 2711 Newspapers, publishing & printing
HQ: Tribune Media Company
515 N State St Ste 2400
Chicago IL 60654
312 222-3394

(G-3573)
CT PRINTS & MORE LLC
100 Margarita Dr (06106-3766)
PHONE.................................860 604-5694
Carmelo Castro,
EMP: 2
SALES (est): 119.2K **Privately Held**
SIC: 2752 Commercial printing, lithographic

(G-3574)
CTV PIPING AND STRUCTURAL
407 Goff Rd (06109-2411)
PHONE.................................860 257-3027
Thomas Varughese, *Owner*
EMP: 1
SALES (est): 82.9K **Privately Held**
SIC: 3494 Line strainers, for use in piping systems

(G-3575)
DAMALIAS CANDLE AND BODY BAR
3580 Main St (06120-1121)
PHONE.................................860 725-2168
Damalia Thomas, *Principal*
EMP: 1
SALES (est): 44.7K **Privately Held**
SIC: 3999 Candles

(G-3576)
DAS STATE OF CT
18-20 Trinity St (06106-1600)
PHONE.................................860 566-4718
EMP: 2
SALES (est): 83.9K **Privately Held**
SIC: 2752 Commercial printing, lithographic

(G-3577)
DE MUERTE USA LLC
73 Morningside St W (06112-1142)
PHONE.................................860 331-7085
Kevin Dumont, *Principal*
Josh Jenkins, *Principal*
EMP: 3
SALES (est): 139.8K **Privately Held**
SIC: 2389 Men's miscellaneous accessories

(G-3578)
DLZ ARCHITECTURAL MILL WORK
510 Ledyard St (06114-3213)
PHONE.................................860 883-7562
David L Zavarella, *President*
EMP: 4
SALES (est): 246K **Privately Held**
SIC: 2431 Millwork

(G-3579)
DMJC PRINTING LLC
579 New Britain Ave (06106-4059)
PHONE.................................860 502-4882
Rudy Cerpa, *Principal*
EMP: 2
SALES (est): 185.1K **Privately Held**
SIC: 2752 Commercial printing, lithographic

(G-3580)
DRINKING WATER DIV
410 Capitol Ave (06106-1367)
PHONE.................................860 509-7333
Gerald Iwan, *Exec Dir*
EMP: 1
SALES (est): 60K **Privately Held**
SIC: 2086 Water, pasteurized: packaged in cans, bottles, etc.

(G-3581)
EBK PICTURE FRAMING & GALLERY
30 Bartholomew Ave (06106-2201)
PHONE.................................860 523-9384
Eric Benkiki,
EMP: 2
SALES: 250K **Privately Held**
SIC: 2499 Picture & mirror frames, wood

(G-3582)
ECONOMY CANVAS CO
Also Called: Economy Canvas
115 Hamilton St (06106-3010)
PHONE.................................860 289-5281
Donald Moulton, *Owner*
EMP: 2
SALES (est): 180.6K **Privately Held**
WEB: www.economycanvas.net
SIC: 2394 5999 Awnings, fabric: made from purchased materials; canvas products

(G-3583)
EDI LANDSCAPE LLC
32 Belmont St (06106-2905)
PHONE.................................860 216-6871
Joan M Davidson, *Partner*
Kimberly Colapietro, *Mng Member*
Susan Mercer, *Administration*
EMP: 15
SQ FT: 1,200

SALES: 3.2MM **Privately Held**
WEB: www.winterberrygarden.com
SIC: **0781** 0721 0783 3446 Landscape services; planting services; planting services, ornamental tree; fences or posts, ornamental iron or steel

(G-3584)
EL PASO PROD OIL GAS TEXAS LP
490 Capitol Ave (06106-1354)
PHONE 860 293-1990
Tom Starr, *Manager*
EMP: 11 **Publicly Held**
SIC: **1382** 1311 Oil & gas exploration services; crude petroleum production; natural gas production
HQ: El Paso Production Oil & Gas Texas, L.P.
1001 Louisiana St
Houston TX 77002
713 997-1000

(G-3585)
ENVIRONMANTAL SYSTEMS COR
18 Jansen Ct (06110-1913)
PHONE 860 953-5167
Donald McCurdy, *Principal*
EMP: 10
SALES (est): 2.4MM **Privately Held**
SIC: **3569** Liquid automation machinery & equipment

(G-3586)
EXPRESS LAB SERVICE
286 Silas Deane Hwy (06109-1735)
PHONE 860 571-0355
John Kupper, *President*
EMP: 2
SALES (est): 150.8K **Privately Held**
SIC: **2741** Miscellaneous publishing

(G-3587)
FASTSIGNS
942 Main St (06103-1214)
PHONE 860 969-3030
EMP: 1
SALES (est): 49.7K **Privately Held**
SIC: **3993** Signs & advertising specialties

(G-3588)
FEDEX OFFICE & PRINT SVCS INC
544 Farmington Ave (06105-3049)
PHONE 860 233-8245
EMP: 18
SALES (corp-wide): 69.6B **Publicly Held**
WEB: www.kinkos.com
SIC: **7334** 2759 Photocopying & duplicating services; commercial printing
HQ: Fedex Office And Print Services, Inc.
7900 Legacy Dr
Plano TX 75024
800 463-3339

(G-3589)
FIDELUX LIGHTING LLC (HQ)
100 Great Meadow Rd # 600 (06109-2355)
PHONE 860 436-5000
Suzanne Templeton, *Office Mgr*
Jay Jayanthan,
▲ EMP: 12
SALES (est): 4MM
SALES (corp-wide): 5.6MM **Privately Held**
SIC: **3674** 3648 7371 Solar cells; lighting equipment; computer software development & applications
PA: Prime Ae Group
100 Great Meadow Rd # 600
Wethersfield CT 06109
203 269-2993

(G-3590)
FLY OR DIE NATION LLC
166 Cleveland Ave (06120-1049)
PHONE 860 218-3547
Aaron Lewis, *Principal*
EMP: 2 EST: 2016
SALES (est): 89.4K **Privately Held**
SIC: **3544** Special dies & tools

(G-3591)
FOCUS SIGN AWNING
83 Meadow St Ste G (06114-1526)
PHONE 860 890-6577
Jorge Rivas, *Principal*
EMP: 1
SALES (est): 82.6K **Privately Held**
SIC: **3993** Signs & advertising specialties

(G-3592)
FOSTER GRANDPARENT PROGRAM
30 Laurel St Ste 3 (06106-1362)
PHONE 860 525-5437
Laura Green, *Exec Dir*
EMP: 2
SALES (est): 62.3K **Privately Held**
SIC: **2051** Bread, cake & related products

(G-3593)
G & R ENTERPRISES INCORPORATED
Also Called: Heritage Printers
101 Kinsley St (06103-1813)
PHONE 860 549-6120
Ron Miller, *President*
J Duff Miller, *Vice Pres*
EMP: 3
SQ FT: 1,200
SALES (est): 500K **Privately Held**
SIC: **2759** 7334 2791 2789 Commercial printing; photocopying & duplicating services; typesetting; bookbinding & related work; commercial printing, lithographic

(G-3594)
G H BERLIN OIL COMPANY
155 W Service Rd (06120-1503)
PHONE 800 426-7754
David Waltz, *Director*
EMP: 1
SALES (est): 112.5K **Privately Held**
SIC: **2911** 5541 Petroleum refining; gasoline service stations

(G-3595)
G W P INC
Also Called: Warehouse Dept
141 South St Ste E (06110-1963)
PHONE 860 953-1153
EMP: 3 EST: 2010
SALES (est): 110.7K **Privately Held**
SIC: **7538** 3714 General automotive repair shops; windshield wiper systems, motor vehicle

(G-3596)
G&K SERVICES LLC
Also Called: G K Services
96 Murphy Rd (06114-2103)
PHONE 860 856-4400
EMP: 7
SALES (corp-wide): 6.8B **Publicly Held**
SIC: **2326** Men's & boys' work clothing
HQ: G&K Services, Llc
6800 Cintas Blvd
Mason OH 45040
952 912-5500

(G-3597)
GABRIELS WOODWORKING LLC
158 Beacon St (06105-2913)
PHONE 860 263-7831
Sergio G Garcia, *Owner*
EMP: 1
SALES (est): 72.2K **Privately Held**
SIC: **2431** Millwork

(G-3598)
GAMUT PUBLISHING
Also Called: Southside Media
563 Franklin Ave (06114-3019)
PHONE 860 296-6128
Jon Harden, *Owner*
EMP: 20
SALES (est): 840.5K **Privately Held**
SIC: **2711** 2721 2731 Newspapers; periodicals; book publishing

(G-3599)
GG SPORTSWEAR INC
241 Ledyard St Ste B10 (06114-2029)
PHONE 860 296-4441
Roberto Giansiracusa, *President*
George Marinelli, *Treasurer*
Gina Karavetsos, *Controller*
Inez Giansiracusa, *Admin Sec*
EMP: 30
SQ FT: 14,000
SALES (est): 3MM **Privately Held**
SIC: **2329** 2339 5136 5137 Men's & boys' sportswear & athletic clothing; sportswear, women's; sportswear, men's & boys'; sportswear, women's & children's; embroidery products, except schiffli machine

(G-3600)
GIMA LLC
Also Called: Gimasport
241 Ledyard St Ste B10 (06114-2029)
PHONE 860 296-4441
Roberto Giansiracusa, *Principal*
George Marinelli, *Principal*
Gina Karavetsos, *Controller*
EMP: 20
SQ FT: 20,000
SALES (est): 2.3MM **Privately Held**
WEB: www.gimasport.com
SIC: **2329** 5136 Men's & boys' sportswear & athletic clothing; gloves, men's & boys'

(G-3601)
GOVERNMENT SURPLUS SALES INC
Also Called: Government Sales
69 Francis Ave (06106-2102)
PHONE 860 247-7787
Eric L Schweitzer, *President*
David H Schweitzer, *Vice Pres*
EMP: 7
SQ FT: 15,000
SALES: 1.3MM **Privately Held**
WEB: www.aviationhelmets.com
SIC: **3469** 5571 Helmets, steel; motorcycle parts & accessories

(G-3602)
GREEN EGG DESIGN LLC
750 Main St Ste 506 (06103-2709)
PHONE 860 541-5411
Samuel McGee,
EMP: 3
SALES (est): 121.7K **Privately Held**
SIC: **3085** Plastics bottles

(G-3603)
H & K INDUSTRIES LLC
200 Nutmeg Ln Apt 119 (06118-1225)
PHONE 857 237-3944
Rosetta Kebreau, *Principal*
EMP: 1
SALES (est): 39.6K **Privately Held**
SIC: **3999** Manufacturing industries

(G-3604)
HANGER PRSTHETCS & ORTHO INC
282 Washington St 1b (06106-3322)
PHONE 860 545-9050
James Fezio, *Manager*
EMP: 10
SALES (corp-wide): 1B **Publicly Held**
SIC: **3842** Surgical appliances & supplies
HQ: Hanger Prosthetics & Orthotics, Inc.
10910 Domain Dr Ste 300
Austin TX 78758
512 777-3800

(G-3605)
HARTFORD ARTISANS WEAVING CTR
42 Woodland St (06105-2329)
PHONE 860 727-5727
Claudia Spaulding, *Treasurer*
Kitty Glass, *Exec Dir*
EMP: 3 EST: 2008
SALES: 194.1K **Privately Held**
WEB: www.weavingcenter.org
SIC: **8299** 2221 Arts & crafts schools; specialty broadwoven fabrics, including twisted weaves

(G-3606)
HARTFORD AVIATION GROUP INC (PA)
1 Gold St Apt 18a (06103-2931)
PHONE 860 549-0096
Carl Merz, *President*
Eric Hoffman, *Manager*
Diane Tyszka, *Admin Sec*
EMP: 6
SQ FT: 2,000
SALES (est): 1.2MM **Privately Held**
SIC: **7359** 3724 Equipment rental & leasing; airfoils, aircraft engine

(G-3607)
HARTFORD BUSINESS SUPPLY INC
Also Called: Printers
1718 Park St (06106-2132)
PHONE 860 233-2138
Susan Falotico, *President*
Daniel J Falotico, *Vice Pres*
Carole Becker, *Sales Staff*
EMP: 26
SQ FT: 12,050
SALES: 3.1MM **Privately Held**
SIC: **2752** 5943 Commercial printing, offset; office forms & supplies

(G-3608)
HARTFORD COURANT COMPANY LLC (HQ)
285 Broad St (06115-3785)
PHONE 860 241-6200
Rick Daniels, *CEO*
William Heider, *President*
Nancy Schoeffler, *Editor*
Mary Lou Stoneburner, *Vice Pres*
Andrea Pape, *Prdtn Dir*
EMP: 700 EST: 1764
SQ FT: 293,792
SALES: 115.6MM
SALES (corp-wide): 1B **Publicly Held**
WEB: www.courantnie.com
SIC: **2711** Newspapers, publishing & printing
PA: Tribune Publishing Company
160 N Stetson Ave
Chicago IL 60601
312 222-9100

(G-3609)
HARTFORD COURANT COMPANY LLC
Also Called: Hartford Courant South BR Off
121 Wawarme Ave (06114-1507)
PHONE 860 525-5555
George Sassano, *Branch Mgr*
EMP: 15
SALES (corp-wide): 1B **Publicly Held**
SIC: **2711** Newspapers: publishing only, not printed on site
HQ: The Hartford Courant Company Llc
285 Broad St
Hartford CT 06115
860 241-6200

(G-3610)
HARTFORD CPL CO-OP INC
75 Airport Rd (06114-2004)
PHONE 860 296-5636
William Galatis, *Ch of Bd*
William Ghio, *Treasurer*
Thomas Brazel, *Admin Sec*
EMP: 110
SALES (est): 17.4MM **Privately Held**
SIC: **2051** Doughnuts, except frozen

(G-3611)
HARTFORD FLAVOR COMPANY LLC
30 Arbor St Unit 107 (06106-1238)
PHONE 860 604-9767
Tom Dubay, *Manager*
Lelaneia Dubay,
EMP: 5
SALES (est): 209.9K **Privately Held**
SIC: **2085** Distilled & blended liquors

(G-3612)
HARTFORD JET CENTER LLC
20 Lindbergh Dr (06114-2132)
PHONE 860 548-9334
Arian Prevalla,
Robert J Morande,
EMP: 7 EST: 2015
SALES (est): 138.6K **Privately Held**
SIC: **3721** Aircraft

GEOGRAPHIC SECTION
Hartford - Hartford County (G-3644)

(G-3613)
HARTFORD PRINTS LLC
42 1/2 Pratt St (06103-1601)
PHONE..................860 578-8447
Rory Gale, *Creative Dir*
Aurelia D Gale,
EMP: 2
SALES (est): 101.5K **Privately Held**
SIC: 2752 Commercial printing, lithographic

(G-3614)
HOG RIVER MUSIC
1800 Albany Ave (06105-1005)
PHONE..................860 523-1820
James Sellers, *Mng Member*
Robert Black, *Mng Member*
Garry Knoble, *Mng Member*
EMP: 2
SALES (est): 110K **Privately Held**
WEB: www.hogriver.com
SIC: 2741 Music, sheet: publishing & printing

(G-3615)
HYDROCHEMICAL TECHNIQUES INC
Also Called: Hydroclean Rstrtn Clng Systms
253 Locust St (06114-2008)
P.O. Box 2078 (06145-2078)
PHONE..................860 527-6350
Thomas Rudder, *President*
Linda Clerget, *Corp Secy*
C Scott Rudder, *Vice Pres*
Chris Penny, *Finance Mgr*
EMP: 3
SQ FT: 2,300
SALES (est): 439.5K **Privately Held**
SIC: 2842 5169 Cleaning or polishing preparations; chemicals & allied products

(G-3616)
I3 ENGINEERING SCIENCES LLC
1 Linden Pl Apt 300 (06106-1744)
PHONE..................908 625-2347
Joanne McFadden, *Principal*
EMP: 2
SALES (est): 85.2K **Privately Held**
SIC: 8711 2741 Engineering services; technical manual & paper publishing

(G-3617)
INFORMATION BUILDERS INC
100 Pearl St Fl 14 (06103-4500)
PHONE..................860 249-7229
EMP: 12
SALES (corp-wide): 176MM **Privately Held**
SIC: 7372 Prepackaged Software Services
PA: Information Builders, Inc.
2 Penn Plz Fl 28
New York NY 10121
212 736-4433

(G-3618)
INTERNTONAL MBL GRAN ENTPS INC
110 Airport Rd (06114-2005)
PHONE..................860 296-0741
Adrian R Costa, *President*
Brian Costa, *Sales Mgr*
EMP: 6
SALES (est): 646.4K **Privately Held**
SIC: 3281 1752 1522 Cut stone & stone products; floor laying & floor work; residential construction

(G-3619)
J C PUBLISHING LLC
132 Adams St (06112-1802)
PHONE..................860 525-7226
Jerome T Clapton, *Owner*
EMP: 2
SALES (est): 106.6K **Privately Held**
SIC: 2741 Miscellaneous publishing

(G-3620)
JOSEPH MERRITT & COMPANY INC (PA)
650 Franklin Ave Ste 3 (06114-3091)
PHONE..................860 296-2500
Edward W Perry, *President*
Jessica Grant, *Exec VP*
Patrick Freer, *Vice Pres*
Craig Perry, *Vice Pres*
Jessica Perez, *Project Mgr*
EMP: 40
SQ FT: 24,000
SALES (est): 31.9MM **Privately Held**
WEB: www.Merrittgraphics.com
SIC: 8748 2752 7331 7374 Communications consulting; commercial printing, offset; direct mail advertising services; computer graphics service; document & office record destruction

(G-3621)
JWC STEEL CO LLC
540 Ledyard St (06114)
PHONE..................860 296-5517
Andrew Jarosz,
EMP: 35
SALES (est): 980.3K **Privately Held**
SIC: 1791 3441 Structural steel erection; fabricated structural metal

(G-3622)
K & L WELDING LLC
87 Campfield Ave (06114-1836)
PHONE..................860 970-2390
Kelvin Myles, *Owner*
EMP: 1
SALES (est): 49.8K **Privately Held**
SIC: 7692 Welding repair

(G-3623)
L & P GATE COMPANY INC
83 Meadow St (06114-1526)
PHONE..................860 296-8009
Bolivar Jimenez, *President*
EMP: 6
SQ FT: 1,800
SALES (est): 1MM **Privately Held**
SIC: 3548 Welding apparatus

(G-3624)
L A VISION LLC
112 S Whitney St Ste 1 (06105-4125)
PHONE..................860 523-0339
Liza Azinheira, *Mng Member*
EMP: 1
SALES (est): 154.5K **Privately Held**
SIC: 3851 Eyeglasses, lenses & frames

(G-3625)
LANDMARK SIGN SERVICE LLC
111 Amherst St (06106-4513)
PHONE..................860 206-0643
Raymond Santa, *Mng Member*
EMP: 1
SALES: 100K **Privately Held**
SIC: 3993 Signs & advertising specialties

(G-3626)
LAWES INTERNATIONAL GROUP LLC
Also Called: Stacy Lawes International
1465 Albany Ave Fl 2 (06112-2110)
PHONE..................860 808-4981
Stacy Lawes, *CEO*
EMP: 1 EST: 2015
SQ FT: 400
SALES (est): 60K **Privately Held**
SIC: 2384 2325 2321 2335 Dressing gowns, men's & women's: from purchased materials; trousers, dress (separate): men's, youths' & boys'; men's & boys' dress shirts; bridal & formal gowns; gowns, formal

(G-3627)
LENSES ONLY
42 Pratt St (06103-1601)
PHONE..................860 278-2020
EMP: 2
SALES (est): 101.7K **Privately Held**
SIC: 3851 Ophthalmic goods

(G-3628)
LINE-X OF HARTFORD
192 Ledyard St (06114-2006)
PHONE..................860 216-6180
EMP: 2
SALES (est): 69.9K **Privately Held**
SIC: 3479 Metal coating & allied service

(G-3629)
LIVING WORD IMPRINTS LLC
450 Homestead Ave (06112-2127)
PHONE..................860 882-1679
Herman Todd, *Mng Member*
EMP: 2
SALES (est): 331.9K **Privately Held**
SIC: 2759 Screen printing

(G-3630)
LOAVES & FISHES MINISTRIES
646 Prospect Ave (06105-4203)
PHONE..................860 524-1730
Alyce Hild, *Exec Dir*
EMP: 4
SALES: 256.5K **Privately Held**
SIC: 2099 Ready-to-eat meals, salads & sandwiches

(G-3631)
MAGNANI PRESS INCORPORATED
120 New Park Ave (06106-2185)
PHONE..................860 236-2802
EMP: 5
SQ FT: 5,000
SALES (est): 460K **Privately Held**
SIC: 2752 2791 Lithographic Commercial Printing Typesetting Services

(G-3632)
MALTA FOOD PANTRY INC
19 Woodland St Ste 37 (06105-2335)
PHONE..................860 725-0944
Scott Muryasz, *Principal*
EMP: 3
SALES (est): 196.9K **Privately Held**
SIC: 2099 Food preparations

(G-3633)
MANCHESTER TL & DESIGN ADP LLC
Also Called: ADP Rivet
465 Ledyard St (06114-3211)
PHONE..................860 296-6541
Joe Derosie, *COO*
Michelle Bucholz, *Project Mgr*
Peter Depaola, *Mng Member*
EMP: 7 EST: 1951
SQ FT: 12,000
SALES (est): 1.1MM **Privately Held**
WEB: www.adprivet.com
SIC: 3965 3599 Fasteners; custom machinery

(G-3634)
MARK KAROTKIN
17 Grassmere Ave (06110-1216)
PHONE..................860 202-7821
Mark Karotkin, *Owner*
EMP: 4
SALES: 500K **Privately Held**
SIC: 3715 Truck trailers

(G-3635)
MARMON ENGNERED WIRE CABLE LLC
280 Trumbull St Fl 23 (06103-3599)
PHONE..................860 653-8300
Dennis Chalk, *President*
EMP: 2
SALES (est): 70.8K **Privately Held**
SIC: 5063 3999 Wire & cable; atomizers, toiletry

(G-3636)
MASSACHUSETTS ENVELOPE CO INC
General Business Envelope Co
10 Midland St (06120-1118)
P.O. Box 750 (06142-0750)
PHONE..................860 727-9100
Emilie Camarco, *Div Sub Head*
Doug Smith, *CFO*
Bruce Newell, *Sales Staff*
Thomas Cummings, *Business Anlyst*
Maralyn Dolan, *Business Anlyst*
EMP: 30
SQ FT: 34,000
SALES (corp-wide): 12.1MM **Privately Held**
WEB: www.massenvplus.com
SIC: 2754 2752 5112 Commercial printing, gravure; commercial printing, lithographic; envelopes
PA: Massachusetts Envelope Company, Inc.
30 Cobble Hill Rd
Somerville MA 02143
617 623-8000

(G-3637)
MATRIXX PRODUCTIONS
232 Farmington Ave (06105-3519)
PHONE..................860 218-5565
EMP: 1
SALES (est): 68K **Privately Held**
SIC: 3663 Mfg Radio/Tv Communication Equipment

(G-3638)
MERRILL CORPORATION
100 Pearl St Fl 14 (06103-4500)
PHONE..................860 249-7220
Summa Josepha, *Manager*
EMP: 87
SALES (corp-wide): 566.6MM **Privately Held**
WEB: www.merrillcorp.com
SIC: 2759 Commercial printing
PA: Merrill Corporation
1 Merrill Cir
Saint Paul MN 55108
651 646-4501

(G-3639)
MERRITT SIGN
143 Quaker Ln S (06119-1635)
PHONE..................860 233-3557
Travis Cook, *Principal*
EMP: 2
SALES (est): 154.9K **Privately Held**
SIC: 3993 Signs, not made in custom sign painting shops

(G-3640)
METAL INDUSTRIES INC
806r Wethersfield Ave (06114-3197)
PHONE..................860 296-6228
Vincent M Zito, *President*
EMP: 5
SQ FT: 8,000
SALES (est): 1MM **Privately Held**
SIC: 7692 3599 Welding repair; machine shop, jobbing & repair

(G-3641)
METALLIZING SERVICE CO INC (PA)
11 Cody St (06110-1949)
PHONE..................860 953-1144
David S Gollob, *President*
Rona B Gollob, *Vice Pres*
EMP: 43
SQ FT: 14,000
SALES (est): 7.4MM **Privately Held**
WEB: www.mscplasma.com
SIC: 3479 Coating of metals & formed products; painting, coating & hot dipping

(G-3642)
MICHAEL SHORTELL
Also Called: Shortell Framing
30 Arbor St Ste 2 (06106-1215)
PHONE..................860 236-4787
Michael Shortell, *Owner*
EMP: 1
SQ FT: 3,000
SALES: 175K **Privately Held**
SIC: 2499 5932 Picture & mirror frames, wood; art objects, antique

(G-3643)
MINH LONG FINE PORCELAIN
635 New Park Ave (06110-1329)
PHONE..................860 586-8755
EMP: 2 EST: 2010
SALES (est): 114.6K **Privately Held**
SIC: 3469 Porcelain enameled products & utensils

(G-3644)
MINUTEMAN PRESS
52 Pratt St (06103-1601)
PHONE..................860 646-0601
EMP: 2
SALES (est): 83.9K **Privately Held**
SIC: 2752 Comm Prtg Litho

Hartford - Hartford County (G-3645)

(G-3645)
MODERN PASTRY SHOP INC
422 Franklin Ave (06114-2518)
PHONE 860 296-7628
Carmelo Sardelli, *President*
EMP: 25
SQ FT: 4,000
SALES (est): 1.2MM **Privately Held**
WEB: www.modernpastryshop.com
SIC: 5461 2052 2051 Cakes; pastries; cookies & crackers; bread, cake & related products

(G-3646)
MOZZICATO PASTRY & BAKE SHOP
Also Called: Mozzict-De Psqale Bky Pstry Sp
329 Franklin Ave (06114-1851)
PHONE 860 296-0426
Luigi Mozzicato, *President*
Gisella Mozzicato, *Corp Secy*
EMP: 28
SQ FT: 25,000
SALES (est): 1.4MM **Privately Held**
WEB: www.mozzicato.com
SIC: 5461 5149 2099 2052 Cakes; bakery products; food preparations; cookies & crackers; bread, cake & related products; ice cream & frozen desserts

(G-3647)
MWK PUBLISHING LLC
2446 Albany Ave Ste 3 (06117-2522)
PHONE 860 675-6067
EMP: 2
SALES (est): 93K **Privately Held**
SIC: 2741 Misc Publishing

(G-3648)
NANOCAP TECHNOLOGIES LLC (PA)
17 Morningcrest Dr (06117-2906)
PHONE 860 521-9743
Arthur S Kesten, *President*
Jack N Blechner, *President*
EMP: 3
SALES (est): 776.4K **Privately Held**
SIC: 3585 Air conditioning units, complete: domestic or industrial; humidifiers & dehumidifiers

(G-3649)
NELSON APOSTLE INC
11 Sherman St (06110-1914)
P.O. Box 330147, West Hartford (06133-0147)
PHONE 860 953-4633
William Lyth, *President*
EMP: 6
SQ FT: 5,000
SALES (est): 540K **Privately Held**
SIC: 3545 7699 5085 Cutting tools for machine tools; knife, saw & tool sharpening & repair; tools

(G-3650)
NEW ENGLAND FOAM PRODUCTS LLC (PA)
760 Windsor St (06120-1918)
P.O. Box 583, Windsor (06095-0583)
PHONE 860 524-0121
Nicholas Elia, *General Mgr*
Krisandra Elia, *Controller*
Chris Elia, *Marketing Mgr*
Tammy Nefoam, *Office Mgr*
Anthony D Elia,
EMP: 49
SQ FT: 80,000
SALES (est): 11.3MM **Privately Held**
WEB: NewEnglandFoam.com
SIC: 3069 3086 Foam rubber; plastics foam products

(G-3651)
NEW ENGLAND ORTHOTIC & PROST
100 Retreat Ave Ste 805 (06106-2528)
PHONE 860 967-0877
EMP: 2
SALES (corp-wide): 28.1MM **Privately Held**
SIC: 3842 Prosthetic appliances

PA: New England Orthotic And Prosthetic Systems, Llc
16 Commercial St
Branford CT 06405
203 483-8488

(G-3652)
NEW KING OF HARTFORD
102 Weston St (06120-1504)
PHONE 860 241-0664
John Crispina, *Manager*
EMP: 1
SALES (est): 67.2K **Privately Held**
SIC: 3421 Table & food cutlery, including butchers'

(G-3653)
NEW MASS MEDIA INC
Also Called: Hartford Advocate
285 Broad St (06115-3785)
PHONE 860 241-3617
Josh Mamis, *Publisher*
EMP: 50
SALES (est): 2MM **Privately Held**
SIC: 2711 Newspapers, publishing & printing

(G-3654)
NIELSEN/SESSIONS
770 Wethersfield Ave (06114-3106)
PHONE 860 522-8145
EMP: 2
SALES (est): 73.4K **Privately Held**
SIC: 3429 Manufactured hardware (general)

(G-3655)
NORTHEAST MINORITY NEWS INC
3580 Main St Ste 1 (06120-1131)
P.O. Box 4159 (06147-4159)
PHONE 860 249-6065
Eugene Monroe, *President*
EMP: 4
SALES (est): 50K **Privately Held**
SIC: 2711 Newspapers, publishing & printing

(G-3656)
NORTHEND AGENTS LLC
150 Trumbull St Fl 4 (06103-2446)
P.O. Box 2308 (06146-2308)
PHONE 860 244-2445
Sasha Allen Walton, *Principal*
EMP: 3
SALES (est): 132.7K **Privately Held**
SIC: 2711 Newspapers: publishing only, not printed on site

(G-3657)
NRG CONNECTICUT LLC
Also Called: Jewish Ledger
36 Woodland St Ste 1 (06105-2328)
PHONE 860 231-2424
N Richard Greenfield, *Principal*
Joan Gaffin, *Accounts Exec*
EMP: 25 EST: 1929
SQ FT: 2,000
SALES (est): 1.4MM **Privately Held**
WEB: www.jewishledger.com
SIC: 2711 8661 Newspapers, publishing & printing; religious organizations

(G-3658)
NUBRIDAL
655 Garden St Apt 3 (06112-2067)
PHONE 860 768-5745
Dani Martin, *Owner*
EMP: 1
SALES (est): 10K **Privately Held**
SIC: 2335 Bridal & formal gowns

(G-3659)
ONE PIECE OF PUZZLE LLC
122 Grant St (06106-4109)
PHONE 860 919-6956
Jennifer Krom, *Principal*
EMP: 1
SALES (est): 59.2K **Privately Held**
SIC: 3944 Puzzles

(G-3660)
PAOLETTI FENCE COMPANY INC
241 Ledyard St Ste B8 (06114-2029)
PHONE 860 296-0396

Fax: 860 296-0396
EMP: 4
SQ FT: 6,000
SALES (est): 380K **Privately Held**
SIC: 1799 3312 Fencing Contractor & Mfg Wrought Iron Fences

(G-3661)
PARENT ENGAGEMENT TRACKER LLC
126 Yale St (06106-4525)
PHONE 860 209-5522
Arcineagas Milly, *President*
Lillian Arciniegas,
John Patterson,
EMP: 1
SALES (est): 57.1K **Privately Held**
SIC: 7372 Application computer software

(G-3662)
PATRICIA BEAVERS
Also Called: Pnb Designs
48 Beacon St (06105-4101)
PHONE 860 233-4071
Patricia Beavers, *Principal*
EMP: 1
SALES (est): 46.3K **Privately Held**
SIC: 3171 Women's handbags & purses

(G-3663)
PERMATEX INC (PA)
Also Called: Permatex, Inc./ A Division ITW
10 Columbus Blvd Ste 1 (06106-2069)
PHONE 860 543-7500
Harry Blake, *President*
Andy Robinson, *General Mgr*
Wayne Gibson, *Buyer*
Felix L Rodriguez, *Director*
◆ EMP: 50
SQ FT: 19,424
SALES (est): 71MM **Privately Held**
WEB: www.notouch.com
SIC: 2891 2899 2992 Adhesives; chemical preparations; lubricating oils & greases

(G-3664)
PISTRITTO MARBLE IMPORTS INC
97 Airport Rd (06114-2004)
PHONE 860 296-5263
Joseph Pistritto, *CEO*
Sabrina Pistritto, *Vice Pres*
Luciano Pistritto, *Treasurer*
Mariella Pistritto, *Sales Staff*
▲ EMP: 5
SQ FT: 7,000
SALES (est): 741.3K **Privately Held**
WEB: www.pistrittomarble.com
SIC: 3281 5999 5032 Marble, building: cut & shaped; granite, cut & shaped; monuments & tombstones; marble building stone

(G-3665)
PLAINVILLE ELECTRO PLATING CO
21 Forest Hills Dr (06117-1112)
PHONE 860 525-5328
Jerry Glassman, *Owner*
EMP: 5
SALES (est): 465.6K **Privately Held**
SIC: 3471 Finishing, metals or formed products

(G-3666)
PLASTONICS INC
230 Locust St (06114-2081)
PHONE 860 249-5455
Robert B Zimmerli Jr, *President*
Brian Zimmerli, *Sales Executive*
EMP: 28
SQ FT: 32,000
SALES (est): 4.6MM **Privately Held**
WEB: www.plastonics.com
SIC: 3479 Coating of metals with plastic or resins; coating of metals & formed products

(G-3667)
POPPYS LLC
Also Called: Emilee's Italian Ice
260 Steele Rd (06117-2743)
PHONE 860 778-9044
Michele Tabora, *Sales Staff*

Christopher L Tabora,
Janet Davis,
EMP: 15
SQ FT: 3,000
SALES (est): 680K **Privately Held**
SIC: 2024 Dairy based frozen desserts

(G-3668)
PPG INDUSTRIES INC
Also Called: PPG 9431
292 Murphy Rd (06114-2107)
PHONE 860 522-9544
Mike King, *Manager*
EMP: 5
SALES (corp-wide): 15.3B **Publicly Held**
WEB: www.ppg.com
SIC: 2851 Paints & allied products
PA: Ppg Industries, Inc.
1 Ppg Pl
Pittsburgh PA 15272
412 434-3131

(G-3669)
PRESS HARTFORD
187 Allyn St (06103-1403)
PHONE 860 216-6538
EMP: 1
SALES (est): 37.5K **Privately Held**
SIC: 2741 Miscellaneous publishing

(G-3670)
PYNE-DAVIDSON COMPANY
237 Weston St (06120-1209)
PHONE 860 522-9106
Harry H Davidson, *CEO*
Daniel J Davidson, *President*
Jeff Milliard, *Vice Pres*
Diane Davidson, *Admin Sec*
EMP: 28
SQ FT: 12,500
SALES (est): 4MM **Privately Held**
WEB: www.pyne-davidson.com
SIC: 2752 Commercial printing, offset

(G-3671)
QSR STEEL CORPORATION LLC
121 Elliott St E (06114-1515)
PHONE 860 548-0248
Rosalie Jukonski, *Controller*
David Rusconi,
Marc Mantia,
Glen Salamone,
EMP: 20
SALES (est): 6MM **Privately Held**
SIC: 3441 Building components, structural steel

(G-3672)
QUALITY ERECTORS LLC
300 Locust St (06114-2010)
PHONE 860 548-0248
Glenn Salamone, *Principal*
EMP: 2 EST: 2010
SALES (est): 136.1K **Privately Held**
SIC: 3441 Fabricated structural metal

(G-3673)
QUATUM INC
43 Maselli Rd (06111-5520)
PHONE 860 666-3464
Manuel Inacio, *President*
Maria J Inacio, *Treasurer*
EMP: 4
SQ FT: 2,400
SALES (est): 534.4K **Privately Held**
SIC: 3089 Molding primary plastic

(G-3674)
R L FISHER INC
Also Called: Rlf Homes
30 Bartholomew Ave (06106-2201)
PHONE 860 951-8110
Robin Fisher, *President*
Philip Sarrantonio, *Vice Pres*
EMP: 99
SQ FT: 36,000
SALES (est): 11.6MM **Privately Held**
WEB: www.rlfhome.com
SIC: 2391 2392 Curtains, window: made from purchased materials; draperies, plastic & textile: from purchased materials; household furnishings

▲ = Import ▼ = Export
◆ = Import/Export

Hartford - Hartford County (G-3707)

(G-3675)
RAMDIAL PARTS AND SERVICES LLC
18 Adelaide St (06114-1801)
PHONE 860 296-5175
Chunilall Ramdial, *Mng Member*
EMP: 3
SALES (est): 145.5K **Privately Held**
SIC: 2515 Mattresses & bedsprings

(G-3676)
RELIABLE ELECTRIC MOTOR INC
285 Murphy Rd (06114-2111)
PHONE 860 522-2257
Brian Langille, *President*
EMP: 12
SQ FT: 15,000
SALES (est): 5MM **Privately Held**
WEB: www.reliableelectricmotor.com
SIC: 5063 7694 Motors, electric; electric motor repair

(G-3677)
RENAISSANCE CRAFTSMEN LLC
263 Simsbury Rd (06117-1453)
P.O. Box 370063, West Hartford (06137-0063)
PHONE 860 916-3583
Ihor Budzinski, *Owner*
EMP: 1
SALES: 20K **Privately Held**
SIC: 2499 Wood products

(G-3678)
RESERVED MAGAZINE
99 Pratt St (06103-1607)
PHONE 860 560-9120
EMP: 2
SALES (est): 82.8K **Privately Held**
SIC: 2721 Periodicals

(G-3679)
ROBERT DINUCCI
469 Mountain Rd (06117-1820)
PHONE 860 561-3730
Robert-Wn-Daei Dinucci, *Principal*
EMP: 1 EST: 2017
SALES (est): 47.2K **Privately Held**
SIC: 2841 Soap & other detergents

(G-3680)
ROCKING HORSE SALOON
181 Ann Uccello St (06103-2010)
PHONE 860 247-2566
Brian Richards, *Principal*
EMP: 2
SALES (est): 104.6K **Privately Held**
SIC: 3944 Rocking horses

(G-3681)
RODRIGUEZ RUIZ ROSA MARGARITA
Also Called: Sulas
336 Jefferson St (06106-2318)
PHONE 860 840-0344
Rosa Rodriguez, *Owner*
EMP: 1
SALES (est): 44K **Privately Held**
SIC: 3479 5632 7389 Engraving jewelry silverware, or metal; costume jewelry;

(G-3682)
ROSS ENTERPRISES
23 Edgewood St Apt 2s (06112-2396)
PHONE 860 308-2238
Michael Ross, *Principal*
EMP: 2
SALES (est): 91.6K **Privately Held**
SIC: 3069 Fabricated rubber products

(G-3683)
ROYAL WELDING LLC
50 Francis Ave Ste 4 (06106-2183)
PHONE 860 232-5255
David Pronovost, *Owner*
Francesco Formica, *Co-Owner*
Alicia Formica, *Admin Sec*
EMP: 4
SALES (est): 607.6K **Privately Held**
SIC: 3499 Fabricated metal products

(G-3684)
SEVERANCE FOODS INC
Also Called: Pan De Oro Brand
3478 Main St (06120-1138)
PHONE 860 724-7063
Richard Stevens, *President*
Kim Huynh, *Plant Mgr*
Leif Dana, *Director*
EMP: 45
SQ FT: 40,400
SALES (est): 9.5MM **Privately Held**
WEB: www.severancefoods.com
SIC: 2096 Tortilla chips

(G-3685)
SHEPARD STEEL CO INC (PA)
110 Meadow St (06114-1598)
PHONE 860 525-4446
George R Beckerman, *President*
Paul Socolosky, *Superintendent*
Brian Ritchie, *Exec VP*
Keith Wolf, *Vice Pres*
Norbert Kropiewnicki, *Project Mgr*
▲ EMP: 65
SQ FT: 100,000
SALES (est): 19.4MM **Privately Held**
WEB: www.shepardsteel.com
SIC: 3441 3446 Building components, structural steel; architectural metalwork

(G-3686)
SIDEBURNZ
87 Market Sq (06111-2912)
PHONE 860 667-1900
Kristan Trumbull, *Principal*
EMP: 2
SALES (est): 183.2K **Privately Held**
SIC: 3999 Barber & beauty shop equipment

(G-3687)
SIGN WIZARD
1 Union Pl (06103-1490)
PHONE 860 525-7729
Joseph Coppola, *Owner*
John Schmid, *Partner*
EMP: 4
SALES (est): 221.4K **Privately Held**
SIC: 3993 Signs & advertising specialties

(G-3688)
SIGNATURE GOLD
698 Park St (06106-4614)
PHONE 860 523-0385
Ki Hong Jang, *Principal*
EMP: 1 EST: 2007
SALES (est): 80.7K **Privately Held**
SIC: 3423 Jewelers' hand tools

(G-3689)
SISKIN AGENCY
33 Quincy Ln (06111-1022)
PHONE 860 561-2937
Sid Siskin, *Owner*
Rachael Welch, *Manager*
EMP: 2 EST: 1995
SALES (est): 99.1K **Privately Held**
SIC: 3999 Manufacturing industries

(G-3690)
SLEEP MANAGEMENT SOLUTIONS LLC (HQ)
20 Church St Ste 900 (06103-1248)
PHONE 888 497-5337
Sam Helmick, *CEO*
EMP: 10
SALES (est): 1.4MM **Privately Held**
SIC: 3841 8741 Diagnostic apparatus, medical; management services

(G-3691)
SPECIALTY SINTERED
3580 Main St Bldg 11 (06120-1121)
PHONE 860 263-8332
Rahul Gaiki, *Mng Member*
EMP: 2 EST: 2001
SALES (est): 88.9K **Privately Held**
SIC: 3089 Automotive parts, plastic

(G-3692)
STATE AWNING COMPANY
100 Cedar St (06106-1622)
P.O. Box 261010 (06126-1010)
PHONE 860 246-2575
James Fitzgerald, *President*
Susan Adams, *Corp Secy*
Patricia La Barron, *Vice Pres*
EMP: 8 EST: 1928
SQ FT: 10,000
SALES: 400K **Privately Held**
SIC: 2394 Awnings, fabric: made from purchased materials

(G-3693)
STEP BY STEP CNSELING SVCS LLC
3580 Main St (06120-1121)
PHONE 860 244-9836
EMP: 1
SALES (est): 39.6K **Privately Held**
SIC: 3999 Mfg Misc Products

(G-3694)
STONEGATE CAPITAL GROUP
100 Pearl St Fl 12 (06103-4511)
PHONE 860 899-1181
Allen Mendelson, *Principal*
EMP: 3 EST: 2009
SALES (est): 296.7K **Privately Held**
SIC: 3721 Aircraft

(G-3695)
SWING BY SWING GOLF INC
80 State House Sq # 158 (06123-7701)
PHONE 310 922-8023
Charles A Cox, *CEO*
James Reid Gorman, *CFO*
EMP: 7
SQ FT: 2,000
SALES (est): 362.6K **Privately Held**
SIC: 7372 Application computer software

(G-3696)
SYCAST INC
148 Bartholomew Ave (06106-2903)
PHONE 860 308-2122
Anhared Stowe, *CEO*
John W Stowe, *President*
EMP: 6
SALES (est): 885.5K **Privately Held**
SIC: 3369 Castings, except die-castings, precision

(G-3697)
TAB BROWN PUBLISHING LLC
49 Girard Ave (06105-2230)
PHONE 860 985-9621
Tina A Brown, *Principal*
EMP: 1
SALES (est): 58.9K **Privately Held**
SIC: 2741 Miscellaneous publishing

(G-3698)
TAX TRACKER LLC
380 Ranklin Ave (06114)
PHONE 860 296-8143
Gerald R Karp,
EMP: 1
SALES (est): 58.7K **Privately Held**
WEB: www.tax.cchgroup.com
SIC: 2741 Technical manual & paper publishing

(G-3699)
TECHNOLOGY GROUP LLC
280 Trumbull St Fl 24 (06103-3599)
PHONE 860 524-4400
Lawrence Davis, *Engineer*
David Modzelewski, *Manager*
Michael Brown, *Network Enginr*
Charlie Cipriani, *Sr Ntwrk Engine*
Mark Torello,
EMP: 2
SALES (est): 251.1K **Privately Held**
WEB: www.technologygroupllc.com
SIC: 7372 Prepackaged software

(G-3700)
TEES & MORE LLC
306 Murphy Rd (06114-2127)
PHONE 860 244-2224
Marco Venditti,
EMP: 9
SALES (est): 1MM **Privately Held**
WEB: www.teesandmore1.com
SIC: 2262 Screen printing: manmade fiber & silk broadwoven fabrics

(G-3701)
TEREX UTILITIES INC
Also Called: Hartford Division
61 Arrow Rd Ste 12 (06109-1357)
PHONE 860 436-3700
Tom Ofleherty, *Branch Mgr*
EMP: 5
SALES (corp-wide): 5.1B **Publicly Held**
SIC: 3531 Construction machinery
HQ: Terex Utilities, Inc.
12805 Sw 77th Pl
Tigard OR 97223
503 620-0611

(G-3702)
THE SMITH WORTHINGTON SAD CO
275 Homestead Ave (06112-2183)
PHONE 860 527-9117
Curtis C Hanks, *President*
Ruth Hanks, *Vice Pres*
▲ EMP: 6
SQ FT: 14,000
SALES (est): 1MM **Privately Held**
WEB: www.smithworthington.com
SIC: 3199 Equestrian related leather articles; harness or harness parts; saddles or parts

(G-3703)
THOMAS W RAFTERY INC
1055 Broad St (06106-2310)
PHONE 860 278-9870
Gary Rigoletti, *CEO*
Robert O'Connor, *President*
Irena D Santos, *VP Opers*
Johnny Castro, *Prdtn Mgr*
EMP: 45
SQ FT: 60,000
SALES (est): 7.7MM **Privately Held**
WEB: www.thomaswraftery.com
SIC: 2391 2392 5131 2591 Draperies, plastic & textile: from purchased materials; blankets, comforters & beddings; synthetic fabrics; drapery hardware & blinds & shades

(G-3704)
THREE SUNS LTD
157 Robin Rd (06119-1242)
PHONE 860 233-7658
John Flattery Jr, *President*
EMP: 4
SALES (est): 159.1K **Privately Held**
SIC: 2084 Wines

(G-3705)
TRANE US INC
485 Ledyard St (06114-3211)
PHONE 860 541-1721
Tim Chamberlain, *Branch Mgr*
EMP: 4 **Privately Held**
SIC: 3585 Refrigeration & heating equipment
HQ: Trane U.S. Inc.
3600 Pammel Creek Rd
La Crosse WI 54601
608 787-2000

(G-3706)
TRIUMPH CONSULTING
75 Tremont St (06105-3070)
PHONE 860 263-8335
Remila Triumph, *Principal*
EMP: 1
SALES (est): 76.5K **Privately Held**
SIC: 6531 3199 8322 8742 Real estate managers; leather garments; individual & family services; hospital & health services consultant

(G-3707)
TRUTH TRCKG EXPEDITED SVCS LLC
2015 Main St (06120-2316)
P.O. Box 2261 (06146-2261)
PHONE 860 306-5630
Akwan Shabazz,
Ahmad Compton,
Justin Marshall,
EMP: 4
SALES (est): 176.5K **Privately Held**
SIC: 3537 Trucks, tractors, loaders, carriers & similar equipment

Hartford - Hartford County (G-3708)

(G-3708)
UNITED STATES FIRE ARMS MFG CO
445 Ledyard St Ste 453 (06114-3211)
PHONE..................860 296-7441
EMP: 23
SALES (est): 1.7MM **Privately Held**
SIC: 3489 3484 3471 Mfg Ordnance/Accessories Mfg Small Arms Plating/Polishing Service

(G-3709)
UNITED TECH EMPLOYEE SAV PLAN
1 Financial Plz (06103-2608)
PHONE..................860 728-7000
EMP: 2
SALES (est): 110K **Privately Held**
SIC: 3585 Air conditioning, motor vehicle

(G-3710)
URISE LLC
Also Called: Urban Reach Institute
15 Lewis St Ste 302 (06103-2510)
PHONE..................860 833-3009
Alice Turner,
EMP: 1
SALES (est): 89.8K **Privately Held**
SIC: 7372 Educational computer software

(G-3711)
US FIREARMS MANUFACTURING CO
453 Ledyard St (06114-3211)
P.O. Box 1901 (06144-1901)
PHONE..................860 296-7441
EMP: 4
SALES (est): 501K **Privately Held**
SIC: 3484 Mfg Small Arms

(G-3712)
VALKYRIE INDUSTRIES
114 Waverly St (06112-1624)
PHONE..................860 518-5311
Shaneia Wylie, *Principal*
EMP: 2
SALES (est): 89.2K **Privately Held**
SIC: 3999 Manufacturing industries

(G-3713)
VIVAN TRUCKING LLC
67 E Morningside St (06112-1241)
PHONE..................573 486-2811
EMP: 2
SALES (est): 88.9K **Privately Held**
SIC: 3089 Plastics products

(G-3714)
WEST HARTFORD LOCK CO LLC
360 Prospect Ave (06105-4100)
PHONE..................860 236-0671
Eric Brown,
Maria Brown,
EMP: 18 EST: 1947
SQ FT: 3,000
SALES (est): 3MM **Privately Held**
WEB: www.westhartfordlock.com
SIC: 5999 5031 7699 3873 Architectural supplies; lumber, plywood & millwork; doors & windows; locksmith shop; watches, clocks, watchcases & parts

(G-3715)
WILD CARD GOLF LLC
394 Ledyard St (06114-3201)
PHONE..................860 296-1661
Mark Blair, *Principal*
◆ EMP: 2 EST: 2009
SALES (est): 133.3K **Privately Held**
SIC: 5091 3949 Golf equipment; golf equipment

(G-3716)
WILD CARD GOLF LLC
222 Murphy Rd (06114-2107)
PHONE..................860 296-1661
Mike Blair, *Mng Member*
▲ EMP: 3
SALES (est): 28.3K **Privately Held**
SIC: 3949 5091 Sporting & athletic goods; golf equipment

Harwinton
Litchfield County

(G-3717)
A & H TOOL WORKS
101 Rocky Rd E (06791-2911)
PHONE..................860 302-9284
David Baril, *Principal*
EMP: 2
SALES (est): 167K **Privately Held**
SIC: 3544 Special dies, tools, jigs & fixtures

(G-3718)
A+ PLUS APPLIANCE
352 Scoville Hill Rd (06791-1015)
PHONE..................860 878-9624
EMP: 1
SALES (est): 56K **Privately Held**
SIC: 3639 Household appliances

(G-3719)
ADVANCED RECEIVER RESEARCH
Also Called: Arr
535 Burlington Rd (06791-1505)
P.O. Box 1242, Burlington (06013-0242)
PHONE..................860 485-0310
Jay Rusgrove, *Owner*
EMP: 3
SQ FT: 3,000
SALES (est): 326.4K **Privately Held**
WEB: www.advancedreceiver.com
SIC: 3663 Amplifiers, RF power & IF

(G-3720)
ARCHERS ONLY LLC
194 Harmony Hill Rd (06791-2022)
PHONE..................860 689-0594
Joseph H Marzullo, *Principal*
EMP: 2
SALES (est): 113.6K **Privately Held**
SIC: 3949 Arrows, archery

(G-3721)
BABY KNITS AND MORE
Also Called: Knits For Baby
121 Delay Rd (06791-2507)
PHONE..................860 485-0146
Colleen Baldwin, *Owner*
EMP: 1 EST: 2010
SALES (est): 100K **Privately Held**
SIC: 5199 2254 5949 Knit goods; underwear, knit; knitting goods & supplies

(G-3722)
BRAZING WAY LLC
25 Highview Dr (06791-1917)
PHONE..................860 485-9337
Janice C Jankauskas, *Owner*
EMP: 1
SALES (est): 25K **Privately Held**
SIC: 7692 Brazing

(G-3723)
BRYAN HEAVENS LOGGING & FIREWO
50 Shingle Mill Rd (06791-2310)
PHONE..................860 485-1712
Gene A Heavens, *Manager*
EMP: 6
SALES (est): 449.6K **Privately Held**
SIC: 2411 Logging camps & contractors

(G-3724)
DAR MORE MFG CO
601 Hill Rd (06791-2623)
PHONE..................860 605-9164
Douglas Roy, *Principal*
EMP: 2
SALES (est): 171.4K **Privately Held**
SIC: 3999 Manufacturing industries

(G-3725)
DURSTIN MACHINE & MFG
57 Westleigh Dr (06791-1107)
PHONE..................860 485-1257
Michael Durstin, *President*
Elizabeth Durstin, *Admin Sec*
EMP: 4
SALES: 350K **Privately Held**
SIC: 3599 Custom machinery

(G-3726)
EASTERN ELECTRIC CNSTR CO
75 North Rd (06791-1902)
PHONE..................860 485-1100
Thomas Simko, *Principal*
David Pallanck, *Vice Pres*
EMP: 7 EST: 2010
SALES (est): 821.5K **Privately Held**
SIC: 3699 1731 1521 Electrical equipment & supplies; electrical work; single-family housing construction

(G-3727)
EASTSIDE ELECTRIC INC
178 Birge Park Rd (06791-1909)
PHONE..................860 485-0700
Gregory L Mele, *Principal*
Ed Zdancewicz, *Project Mgr*
EMP: 19
SALES (est): 3.6MM **Privately Held**
SIC: 3699 1731 Electrical equipment & supplies; electrical work

(G-3728)
FABCON INC
141 Terryville Rd (06791-2404)
P.O. Box 183 (06791-0183)
PHONE..................860 485-9019
Austin King, *President*
Michael Kosta, *General Mgr*
James King, *Admin Sec*
EMP: 1
SALES (est): 130K **Privately Held**
SIC: 3613 8748 Control panels, electric; business consulting

(G-3729)
FOX PRINT
48 Lake Harwinton Rd (06791-1202)
PHONE..................860 485-0429
Teresa Fox, *Partner*
Laeverett Cooper, *Partner*
EMP: 2
SALES: 70K **Privately Held**
SIC: 2752 Commercial printing, offset

(G-3730)
FRACTAL WATER LLC
18 Burlington Rd (06791-2001)
P.O. Box 71 (06791-0071)
PHONE..................888 897-6968
Jason Matozzo, *Principal*
EMP: 2
SALES (est): 190.7K **Privately Held**
SIC: 3589 Water treatment equipment, industrial

(G-3731)
FREEMANS NEWS SERVICE
75 Westleigh Dr (06791-1107)
PHONE..................860 485-1000
Tom Freeman, *Owner*
Tom Dudley, *Owner*
EMP: 2
SQ FT: 1,684
SALES (est): 66.5K **Privately Held**
SIC: 2711 Newspapers

(G-3732)
LITCHFIELD WINDSORS
10 Robinwood Ln (06791-2830)
PHONE..................860 485-1019
James Duda, *President*
EMP: 1
SALES (est): 61.6K **Privately Held**
SIC: 2499 Decorative wood & woodwork

(G-3733)
LUC-TARDIFF LOGGING
112 Valley Rd (06791-2602)
PHONE..................860 485-0693
Luc Tardiff, *Owner*
EMP: 1
SALES (est): 85.2K **Privately Held**
SIC: 2411 Logging camps & contractors

(G-3734)
MURPHY BOYZ PRTG & MKTG LLC
271 North Rd (06791-1402)
PHONE..................860 485-0607
EMP: 2 EST: 2012
SALES (est): 232K **Privately Held**
SIC: 2752 Lithographic Commercial Printing

(G-3735)
O & G INDUSTRIES INC
255 Lower Bogue Rd (06791-1626)
PHONE..................860 485-6600
Bob Oneglia, *Vice Pres*
Carol Lucia, *Associate*
EMP: 110
SALES (corp-wide): 538MM **Privately Held**
SIC: 3999 Atomizers, toiletry
PA: O & G Industries, Inc.
112 Wall St
Torrington CT 06790
860 489-9261

(G-3736)
PRECISION WIRE CUTTING
9 Windmill Rd (06791-1116)
PHONE..................860 485-1494
John Corey, *Owner*
EMP: 3
SQ FT: 1,500
SALES (est): 170K **Privately Held**
SIC: 3599 Machine shop, jobbing & repair

(G-3737)
RICHIES AUTOMOTIVE LLC
205 Birge Park Rd (06791-1908)
PHONE..................860 482-0667
Richard Girolimon, *Mng Member*
EMP: 1 EST: 2015
SALES (est): 86.9K **Privately Held**
SIC: 7538 7692 General automotive repair shops; automotive welding

(G-3738)
RONALD R ESCHNER
283 Terryville Rd (06791-2400)
PHONE..................860 485-9373
EMP: 1
SALES (est): 50.3K **Privately Held**
SIC: 7692 Welding Repair

(G-3739)
SPRING COMPUTERIZED INDS LLC
Also Called: Csi
93 Oakwood Dr (06791-1307)
PHONE..................860 605-9206
Elliot Cyr, *Owner*
Janice Syr -Ofc, *Manager*
EMP: 8
SQ FT: 1,500
SALES (est): 630K **Privately Held**
WEB: www.csi-springs.com
SIC: 3495 3493 Wire springs; steel springs, except wire

(G-3740)
STEVENSON GROUP CORPORATION
120 Wilson Pond Rd (06791-2815)
PHONE..................860 689-0011
John A Stevenson, *President*
Donna B Stevenson, *Vice Pres*
Melissa A Stevenson, *Treasurer*
EMP: 16
SALES (est): 1MM **Privately Held**
SIC: 1796 2541 Elevator installation & conversion; wood partitions & fixtures

(G-3741)
SUMMIT RIDGE PUBLISHING LLC
421 Hill Rd (06791-2619)
PHONE..................860 689-3463
Jan Prenoveau, *Principal*
EMP: 2 EST: 2009
SALES (est): 98.5K **Privately Held**
SIC: 2741 Miscellaneous publishing

(G-3742)
UNI MACHINE & MFG LLC
72 Orchard Hill Rd (06791-1621)
PHONE..................860 485-0643
Thomas Bronson,
Priscilla Bronson,
EMP: 2 EST: 1976
SALES (est): 75K **Privately Held**
SIC: 3315 Wire & fabricated wire products

(G-3743)
WINCHESTER WOODWORKING LLC
243 Woodchuck Ln (06791-1514)
PHONE..................860 485-0742
James P Charette, *Principal*
EMP: 2
SALES (est): 79.3K Privately Held
SIC: 2431 Woodwork, interior & ornamental

Hawleyville
Fairfield County

(G-3744)
MISSION ALLERGY INC
28 Hawleyville Rd (06440)
P.O. Box 45 (06440-0045)
PHONE..................203 364-1570
Jeffrey Miller, *President*
Janet Kerr, *General Mgr*
EMP: 6
SQ FT: 13,959
SALES (est): 1.1MM Privately Held
WEB: www.missionallergy.com
SIC: 3822 Auto controls regulating residntl & coml environmt & applncs

Hebron
Tolland County

(G-3745)
BENNETTSVILLE HOLDINGS LLC
Also Called: Bennettisville Printing
33 Pendleton Dr A (06248-1512)
PHONE..................860 444-9400
Victor Winogradow, *Mng Member*
Carol Winogradrow,
EMP: 85
SALES (est): 6.2MM Privately Held
SIC: 2396 Fabric printing & stamping

(G-3746)
COUNTRY CARPENTERS INC
326 Gilead St (06248-1347)
PHONE..................860 228-2276
Roger G Barrett Jr, *President*
Lois M Barrett, *Vice Pres*
Mark Coppinger, *Finance Mgr*
Barrett Leslie, *Sales Staff*
EMP: 8
SALES (est): 1.5MM Privately Held
WEB: www.carriagesheds.com
SIC: 2491 1521 2452 2439 Poles, posts & pilings: treated wood; single-family housing construction; prefabricated wood buildings; structural wood members

(G-3747)
DISTINCTIVE COATING LLC
42 Knollwood Dr (06248-1280)
P.O. Box 52 (06248-0052)
PHONE..................860 530-1233
Michael P Lawrence, *Manager*
EMP: 1
SALES (est): 68.8K Privately Held
SIC: 3479 Metal coating & allied service

(G-3748)
EVONIK TOCKHAUSEN LLC
25 Wildflower Dr (06248-1448)
PHONE..................860 530-1363
EMP: 2
SALES (est): 92.2K Privately Held
SIC: 2899 Chemical preparations

(G-3749)
FRONT LINE APPAREL GROUP LLC
Also Called: Front Line Group, The
33 Pendleton Dr (06248-1512)
PHONE..................860 859-3524
Ronald Levine, *CEO*
Victor Winogradow, *Vice Pres*
Lori Rapuano, *Controller*
EMP: 250
SQ FT: 75,000
SALES: 5MM Privately Held
SIC: 7349 0781 2311 Janitorial service, contract basis; landscape services; military uniforms, men's & youths': purchased materials

(G-3750)
IAMAW
249 East St (06248-1311)
PHONE..................860 228-0049
EMP: 1
SALES (est): 84.6K Privately Held
SIC: 3541 Vertical turning & boring machines (metalworking)

(G-3751)
INNOVATIVE SOFTWARE LLC
94 Country Ln (06248-1400)
PHONE..................860 228-4144
Fred W Knapp Jr, *Mng Member*
EMP: 5
SALES (est): 346.6K Privately Held
SIC: 7372 Prepackaged software

(G-3752)
JUMP 4 TEES
33 Scarboro Rd (06248-1339)
PHONE..................860 228-4813
EMP: 2
SALES (est): 97.9K Privately Held
SIC: 2759 Screen printing

(G-3753)
PRINTING SOLUTIONS GROUP LLC
210 Skinner Ln (06248-1349)
PHONE..................860 647-0317
Richard P Healy,
EMP: 2 EST: 2012
SALES (est): 136.1K Privately Held
SIC: 2752 Commercial printing, offset

(G-3754)
RADIATION SAFETY ASSOC INC
Also Called: Rsa Laboratories
19 Pendleton Dr (06248-1525)
P.O. Box 107 (06248-0107)
PHONE..................860 228-0721
Paul Steinmeyer, *President*
Tara Gadarowski, *Info Tech Mgr*
EMP: 6
SQ FT: 3,800
SALES (est): 1.1MM Privately Held
WEB: www.radpro.com
SIC: 8734 3829 Radiation laboratories; testing equipment: abrasion, shearing strength, etc.

(G-3755)
RECOR RUST SOLUTIONS
246 Wall St (06248-1328)
PHONE..................860 573-1942
Thomas Probulis, *Principal*
EMP: 2
SALES (est): 119.7K Privately Held
SIC: 2899 Chemical preparations

(G-3756)
RICK BULACH
Also Called: Blue Chip Tool
36 Cone Rd (06248-1306)
P.O. Box 203, East Glastonbury (06025-0203)
PHONE..................860 875-7999
Rick Bulach, *Owner*
EMP: 1
SALES (est): 100K Privately Held
SIC: 3599 Machine shop, jobbing & repair

(G-3757)
TEK ARMS INC
282 Jagger Ln (06248-1122)
PHONE..................860 748-6289
Mark Matheny, *Principal*
Alaina Matheny, *Officer*
EMP: 5
SALES (est): 355.1K Privately Held
SIC: 3489 Guns or gun parts, over 30 mm.; flame throwers (ordnance); guns, howitzers, mortars & related equipment; smoke generators (ordnance)

(G-3758)
WHITAKERS
58 Indian Field Rd (06248-1337)
PHONE..................860 228-3762
EMP: 2
SALES (est): 120K Privately Held
SIC: 3728 Mfg Aircraft Parts/Equipment

Higganum
Middlesex County

(G-3759)
APERTURE OPTICAL SCIENCES INC
23 Soobitsky Rd (06441-4476)
PHONE..................860 301-2589
Flemming Tinker, *Principal*
EMP: 3
SALES (est): 236.1K Privately Held
SIC: 3827 Optical instruments & lenses

(G-3760)
B&B LOGGING LLC
298 Brainard Hill Rd (06441-4070)
PHONE..................860 982-2425
Robert F Mesick Sr,
EMP: 3
SALES: 180K Privately Held
SIC: 2411 0851 Logging; forestry services

(G-3761)
BIZCARD XPRESS LLC
26 Killingworth Rd (06441-9995)
PHONE..................860 324-6840
Daniela M Morello, *Principal*
EMP: 3
SALES (est): 173.8K Privately Held
SIC: 2752 Commercial printing, lithographic

(G-3762)
BURDON ENTERPRISES LLC
20 Reisman Trl (06441-4360)
PHONE..................860 345-4882
Gayle Burdon, *Principal*
EMP: 8 EST: 1995
SALES (est): 443.2K Privately Held
SIC: 3446 Fences or posts, ornamental iron or steel

(G-3763)
FOXRUN DANES
17 Hickory Ln (06441-4569)
PHONE..................860 685-8784
Kathy Grasso, *Principal*
EMP: 2
SALES (est): 96.5K Privately Held
SIC: 3999 Pet supplies

(G-3764)
GEORGE SIMA
Also Called: Charles J Sima & Son
863 Killingworth Rd (06441-4464)
PHONE..................860 345-4660
George Sima, *Owner*
George G Sima, *Owner*
EMP: 1
SALES (est): 83K Privately Held
SIC: 1381 Drilling water intake wells

(G-3765)
HARLEY INDUSTRIES LLC
34 Foxglove Cir (06441-4383)
PHONE..................860 951-5727
Harlan Corriveau, *Mng Member*
EMP: 1
SALES (est): 39.6K Privately Held
SIC: 3999 Manufacturing industries

(G-3766)
KENYON LABORATORIES LLC
Also Called: Ken-Labs
12 Scovil Rd (06441-4218)
PHONE..................860 345-2097
Ron Denman,
Bobbie Kenyon,
EMP: 7
SQ FT: 17,000
SALES: 1MM Privately Held
WEB: www.ken-lab.com
SIC: 3861 Photographic equipment & supplies

(G-3767)
LAKEVIEW ENGINEERING & MFG LLC
420 Hidden Lake Rd (06441-4543)
PHONE..................860 490-2760
Philip Porriello, *Manager*
Cynthia Porriello,
EMP: 2
SALES (est): 123.2K Privately Held
WEB: www.lakeviewengineering.com
SIC: 8711 3554 Engineering services; paper industries machinery

(G-3768)
MANNAN 3D INNOVATIONS LLC
Also Called: M3di
35 Country Walk (06441-4400)
PHONE..................860 306-4203
Nasir Mannan, *Mng Member*
EMP: 1
SALES: 50K Privately Held
SIC: 7371 7372 3577 8711 Computer software development & applications; application computer software; optical scanning devices; mechanical engineering; office computer automation systems integration

(G-3769)
MORIARTYS DESKTOP PUBLISHING
39 Little Fawn Trl (06441-4361)
PHONE..................860 345-8063
EMP: 1
SALES (est): 51K Privately Held
SIC: 2741 Misc Publishing

(G-3770)
N EXCELLENCE WOOD INC
Also Called: Wood N Excellence Cab Refacing
323 Hidden Lake Rd (06441-4528)
PHONE..................860 345-2050
Paul Gregaitis, *President*
Karen Gregaitis, *Admin Sec*
EMP: 4
SALES (est): 363.4K Privately Held
WEB: www.woodnexcellence.com
SIC: 2434 Wood kitchen cabinets

(G-3771)
NEW ENGLAND PUBLISHING ASSOC (PA)
59 Parker Hill Rd (06441-4445)
P.O. Box 66066, Lawrenceville NJ (08648-6066)
PHONE..................860 345-7323
Elizabeth F Knappman, *President*
Edward Knappman, *Vice Pres*
EMP: 5
SALES: 1.2MM Privately Held
WEB: www.nepa.com
SIC: 7389 2731 8748 Authors' agents & brokers; books: publishing only; publishing consultant

(G-3772)
NUTMEG NATURALS LLC
67 Parker Hill Rd (06441-4445)
P.O. Box 685 (06441-0685)
PHONE..................860 554-1272
Jennifer L Knapp, *Principal*
EMP: 2
SALES (est): 129.7K Privately Held
SIC: 2844 Toilet preparations

(G-3773)
OH FUDGE AND MORE LLC
19 Larkspur Dr (06441-4385)
PHONE..................860 788-3839
Bridget Marshall, *President*
EMP: 2
SALES (est): 74.4K Privately Held
SIC: 2064 Fudge (candy)

(G-3774)
P J S SERVICES
135 Skunk Misery Rd (06441-4437)
PHONE..................860 345-4896
Paul Stankiewicz, *Principal*
EMP: 1 EST: 2008
SALES (est): 77.9K Privately Held
SIC: 1389 Oil field services

Higganum - Middlesex County (G-3775)

(G-3775)
PHILS WELDING
6 Soobitsky Rd (06441-4476)
PHONE.................................860 685-1713
Philip Powell, *Principal*
EMP: 2
SALES (est): 216.9K **Privately Held**
SIC: 7692 Welding repair

(G-3776)
PRO COATINGS LLC
47 Boulder Dell Rd (06441-4113)
PHONE.................................860 345-2107
Jason Potter, *Principal*
EMP: 1
SALES (est): 85.9K **Privately Held**
SIC: 3479 Metal coating & allied service

(G-3777)
PW PRECISION MACHINE LLC
12 Scovil Rd Unit B (06441-4218)
PHONE.................................203 889-8615
Philip Warner, *Principal*
EMP: 4
SALES (est): 139.1K **Privately Held**
SIC: 3599 Electrical discharge machining (EDM)

(G-3778)
SOJA WOODWORKING LLC
548 Killingworth Rd (06441-4310)
PHONE.................................860 345-3909
Bryan Soja, *Principal*
EMP: 4
SALES (est): 240.8K **Privately Held**
SIC: 2431 Millwork

(G-3779)
STANLEY BURR
46 Jackson Rd (06441-6402)
PHONE.................................860 345-3578
Stanley Burr, *Owner*
EMP: 1
SALES (est): 88.1K **Privately Held**
SIC: 2411 Logging

(G-3780)
TYLERVILLE TECHNOLOGIES LLC
67 Bartman Rd (06441-4416)
PHONE.................................860 798-0501
Richard T Thompson, *Mng Member*
EMP: 1
SALES (est): 100.7K **Privately Held**
SIC: 2869 Industrial organic chemicals

(G-3781)
VICTOR F LEANDRI
286 Killingworth Rd (06441-4306)
PHONE.................................860 345-8705
Victor F Leandri, *Owner*
EMP: 1
SALES (est): 58.8K **Privately Held**
SIC: 3669 Visual communication systems

Ivoryton
Middlesex County

(G-3782)
A 2 Z SCREEN PRINTING LLC (PA)
6 Pine Lake Rd (06442-1117)
PHONE.................................860 526-9684
John Steindl,
Linda Steindl,
EMP: 2 EST: 1976
SALES (est): 280.3K **Privately Held**
WEB: www.a2zscreenprinting.com
SIC: 2759 Screen printing; promotional printing

(G-3783)
BONNIEVIEW WOODWORK LLC
9 Westwood Rd (06442-1254)
PHONE.................................860 767-3299
Joseph Defelice, *Principal*
EMP: 2 EST: 2009
SALES (est): 140.9K **Privately Held**
SIC: 2431 Millwork

(G-3784)
BUSHY HILL NATURE CENTER
Also Called: Encarnation Center The
253 Bushy Hill Rd (06442)
P.O. Box 577 (06442-0577)
PHONE.................................860 767-2148
Peter Larom, *Exec Dir*
Erik Becker, *Director*
EMP: 3
SQ FT: 2,800
SALES: 250K **Privately Held**
WEB: www.bushyhill.org
SIC: 8211 2261 2399 Specialty education; screen printing of cotton broadwoven fabrics; flags, fabric

(G-3785)
ELM CITY DISTILLERY LLC
7 Read St (06442-1216)
PHONE.................................203 285-8830
Eric Kotowski, *Principal*
EMP: 2
SALES (est): 111.5K **Privately Held**
SIC: 2085 Distilled & blended liquors

(G-3786)
MOELLER INSTRUMENT COMPANY INC
126 Main St (06442-1102)
P.O. Box 668 (06442-0668)
PHONE.................................800 243-9310
Jeff Murtz, *President*
Darla Allen, *Purchasing*
Thomas Janet, *Executive*
Janet Thomas, *Executive*
Darcy Murtz, *Admin Sec*
EMP: 20
SQ FT: 5,000
SALES: 1.8MM **Privately Held**
WEB: www.moellerinstrument.com
SIC: 3823 Temperature measurement instruments, industrial; pressure measurement instruments, industrial

(G-3787)
NEW AIR TECHNOLOGIES INC
65 N Main St (06442-1010)
P.O. Box 486 (06442-0486)
PHONE.................................860 767-1542
John Carlson, *President*
EMP: 1
SQ FT: 3,500
SALES: 43K **Privately Held**
WEB: www.newairtech.com
SIC: 3822 8711 Air conditioning & refrigeration controls; heating & ventilation engineering

(G-3788)
ORTRONICS LEGRAND
14 Windermere Way (06442-1275)
PHONE.................................860 767-3515
Mike Hines, *Principal*
EMP: 3
SALES (est): 199.8K **Privately Held**
SIC: 3577 Computer peripheral equipment

(G-3789)
RICHARD RIGGIO AND SONS INC
Also Called: Innovative Designs
90 Pond Meadow Rd (06442-1156)
PHONE.................................860 767-0812
Gary R Riggio, *President*
Paul Riggio, *Treasurer*
Julie C Ladone, *Manager*
EMP: 38 EST: 1978
SQ FT: 12,000
SALES (est): 4.8MM **Privately Held**
SIC: 1521 2542 6552 New construction, single-family houses; counters or counter display cases: except wood; subdividers & developers

(G-3790)
THE L C DOANE COMPANY (PA)
110 Pond Meadow Rd (06442-1121)
PHONE.................................860 767-8295
Margaret P Eagan, *President*
Bill Psillos, *Vice Pres*
William Psillos, *Vice Pres*
Rose Sypher, *Purch Mgr*
Amy Sypher, *Purchasing*
EMP: 15 EST: 1947
SQ FT: 140,000
SALES (est): 14.2MM **Privately Held**
SIC: 3646 3647 Commercial indusl & institutional electric lighting fixtures; boat & ship lighting fixtures

Jewett City
New London County

(G-3791)
ANCHOR WOODWORKING LLC
494 Roode Rd (06351-1222)
PHONE.................................860 376-0795
EMP: 2 EST: 2011
SALES (est): 140K **Privately Held**
SIC: 2431 Mfg Millwork

(G-3792)
CLINT S CUSTOM WOODWORKIN
628 River Rd (06351-3230)
P.O. Box 250, Ledyard (06339-0250)
PHONE.................................860 887-1476
Clinton Babcock Jr, *Principal*
EMP: 8
SALES (est): 829.4K **Privately Held**
SIC: 2499 Decorative wood & woodwork

(G-3793)
DANTE LTD
633 Plainfield Rd (06351-1025)
PHONE.................................860 376-0204
Dante L Grassi, *President*
EMP: 5
SQ FT: 6,000
SALES: 1.5MM **Privately Held**
SIC: 2434 2431 2499 Wood kitchen cabinets; panel work, wood; kitchen, bathroom & household ware: wood

(G-3794)
DOCUMENT DYNAMICS LLC
178 Preston Rd (06351-2634)
PHONE.................................860 376-2944
Robert G Caffary Jr,
EMP: 4
SQ FT: 1,500
SALES (est): 340K **Privately Held**
SIC: 7371 7373 7372 Computer software development; computer software development & applications; value-added resellers, computer systems; prepackaged software

(G-3795)
GEER CONSTRUCTION CO INC
Also Called: Geer Sand & Gravel
852 Voluntown Rd (06351-3315)
PHONE.................................860 376-5321
H David Geer, *President*
Barbara Geer, *Vice Pres*
Richard B Geer, *Vice Pres*
Thomas D Geer, *Vice Pres*
EMP: 4
SALES (est): 693.4K **Privately Held**
WEB: www.geersfamilytree.com
SIC: 1442 0811 Sand mining; gravel mining; tree farm

(G-3796)
GRISWOLD MACHINE & FABRICATION
8 Sheldon Rd (06351-3622)
PHONE.................................860 376-9891
Richard Farina Jr, *Owner*
EMP: 4
SQ FT: 16,000
SALES: 220K **Privately Held**
SIC: 3599 Machine shop, jobbing & repair

(G-3797)
JULIE WAKELY ENTERPRISES LLC
31 Bushnell Rd (06351-2910)
PHONE.................................860 376-4515
Julie Wakely, *President*
EMP: 1
SALES (est): 57.9K **Privately Held**
SIC: 2741 Catalogs: publishing & printing

(G-3798)
K & D BUSINESS VENTURES LLC
39 1/2 Wedgewood Dr (06351-2439)
P.O. Box 199 (06351)
PHONE.................................860 237-1458
Michael Giacobbe, *Branch Mgr*
EMP: 3
SALES (corp-wide): 20K **Privately Held**
SIC: 3949 Rods & rod parts, fishing; fishing tackle, general; lures, fishing; artificial
PA: K & D Business Ventures, Llc
4322 Carrollwood Vlg Dr
Tampa FL 33618
321 474-5948

(G-3799)
MAPLE PRINT SERVICES INC
39 Wedgewood Dr (06351-2437)
PHONE.................................860 381-5470
Mike Johnson, *President*
EMP: 4
SALES (est): 179.8K **Privately Held**
SIC: 2752 Commercial printing, lithographic

(G-3800)
S TM EMBROIDERY LLC
290 Preston Rd (06351-2634)
PHONE.................................860 376-4537
Stanislaw Mieldzioc, *Principal*
EMP: 1
SALES (est): 85.4K **Privately Held**
SIC: 2395 Embroidery products, except schiffli machine; embroidery & art needlework

(G-3801)
SPECTRUM POWDERCOATING LLC
1131 Voluntown Rd (06351-1621)
PHONE.................................860 591-1034
Paul Romano, *Mng Member*
Thomas Grabino,
EMP: 2
SALES (est): 191.4K **Privately Held**
SIC: 2952 Coating compounds, tar

Kensington
Hartford County

(G-3802)
3RD HALF PRODUCTIONS
141 Carriage Dr (06037-2703)
PHONE.................................860 828-6929
Jim Casseo, *Owner*
EMP: 1
SALES (est): 79.8K **Privately Held**
SIC: 2396 Screen printing on fabric articles

(G-3803)
ACADEMY PRINTING SERVICE
Also Called: Austin Rubber Stamps
900 Farmington Ave Ste 2 (06037-2219)
PHONE.................................860 828-5549
Timothy J Mc Mullen, *Owner*
EMP: 3
SQ FT: 1,950
SALES (est): 276.6K **Privately Held**
SIC: 2752 5999 Commercial printing, offset; rubber stamps

(G-3804)
AEROCOMPOSITES INC
49 Cambridge Hts (06037-2310)
PHONE.................................860 829-6809
John Violette, *President*
Ernest Glastris, *Vice Pres*
Harrison Griswold, *Vice Pres*
EMP: 2
SALES (est): 235.8K **Privately Held**
SIC: 3728 Aircraft propellers & associated equipment

(G-3805)
ALINABAL INC
Also Called: Sterling Screw Machine Pdts
384 Christian Ln (06037-1424)
PHONE.................................860 828-9933
Larry Desimone, *Manager*
EMP: 16

SALES (corp-wide): 57MM **Privately Held**
WEB: www.dacoinstrument.com
SIC: 3451 Screw machine products
HQ: Alinabal, Inc.
28 Woodmont Rd
Milford CT 06460
203 877-3241

(G-3806)
BERLIN STEEL CONSTRUCTION CO (PA)
76 Depot Rd (06037-1439)
P.O. Box 428 (06037-0428)
PHONE..............................860 828-3531
Carl A Johnson, *President*
Rick Bailey, *Division Mgr*
David J Baffaro, *Principal*
Drew G Brown, *Exec VP*
Jim Hamby, *Vice Pres*
▲ **EMP:** 50
SQ FT: 62,500
SALES (est): 37.9MM **Privately Held**
WEB: www.berlinsteel.com
SIC: 1791 3441 Structural steel erection; iron work, structural; fabricated structural metal for bridges

(G-3807)
CIGAR WORLD
126 Mill St (06037-2319)
PHONE..............................860 828-7870
EMP: 1
SALES (est): 103K **Privately Held**
SIC: 3999 Mfg Misc Products

(G-3808)
D S MANUFACTURING CO
806 Four Rod Rd (06037-3630)
PHONE..............................860 829-0334
Dom Secondo, *Owner*
EMP: 2
SALES (est): 220.5K **Privately Held**
SIC: 3599 Machine shop, jobbing & repair

(G-3809)
DEVELLIS WOODWORKS LLC
763 Orchard Rd (06037-3526)
PHONE..............................203 610-4762
Marco Devellis, *Principal*
EMP: 1
SALES (est): 79.1K **Privately Held**
SIC: 2499 Wood products

(G-3810)
FIT TO A TEE CSTM SCREEN PRTG
95 Four Rod Rd (06037-2224)
PHONE..............................860 828-6632
Margaret C Farone, *Owner*
EMP: 1
SALES (est): 54.1K **Privately Held**
SIC: 2759 3993 Screen printing; signs & advertising specialties

(G-3811)
KENSINGTON WELDING & TRLR CO
1114 Farmington Ave (06037-2245)
PHONE..............................860 828-3564
Jerry Marcoux, *President*
EMP: 5 **EST:** 1947
SQ FT: 7,500
SALES (est): 710.6K **Privately Held**
SIC: 7692 3715 5013 Welding repair; truck trailers; trailer parts & accessories

(G-3812)
KENSINGTON WOODWORKING CO
430 New Britain Rd (06037-1323)
PHONE..............................860 828-4972
Antonino Campailla, *Owner*
EMP: 1 **EST:** 1941
SQ FT: 5,000
SALES (est): 78.8K **Privately Held**
SIC: 2511 5712 Bookcases, household; wood; furniture stores

(G-3813)
MEADOW MANUFACTURING INC
120 Old Brickyard Ln (06037-1437)
PHONE..............................860 357-3785
Mark Gregoretti, *President*
Patrick D Temme, *Principal*
Joshua A McPhail, *Vice Pres*
Heidi Pascucci, *Controller*
EMP: 15
SALES (est): 2.6MM **Privately Held**
SIC: 3545 Tools & accessories for machine tools

(G-3814)
MICHELE PAVISIC
Also Called: Kim Machine
37 Willow Brook Dr (06037-1533)
PHONE..............................860 876-2509
Michele Pavisic, *Owner*
EMP: 1
SALES (est): 81.1K **Privately Held**
SIC: 3599 Machine & other job shop work

(G-3815)
NETWORK EXPERT SFTWR SYSTEMS
110 E Shore Ave (06037)
PHONE..............................860 829-1427
David Staub, *President*
EMP: 1
SALES (est): 79.2K **Privately Held**
WEB: www.nessinc.com
SIC: 7372 Prepackaged software

(G-3816)
PARVA MFG GROUP INC
Also Called: PMG
101 Alling St (06037-2008)
PHONE..............................860 828-6285
Carolyn Audette, *President*
EMP: 1
SALES (est): 64.6K **Privately Held**
SIC: 3999 Identification badges & insignia

(G-3817)
PMR PERFORMANCE
114 Burnham St (06037-2212)
PHONE..............................860 828-8828
Philip Molski, *Owner*
EMP: 2
SQ FT: 2,000
SALES: 140K **Privately Held**
WEB: www.performansteam.com
SIC: 3519 Gas engine rebuilding

(G-3818)
ROTATING COMPOSITE TECH LLC
49 Cambridge Hts (06037-2310)
PHONE..............................860 829-6809
John Violette, *President*
Jacob Virkler, *Engineer*
Christopher Aliapoulios, *Webmaster*
EMP: 8 **EST:** 2007
SALES: 1.6MM **Privately Held**
SIC: 3728 Aircraft parts & equipment

(G-3819)
TELKE TOOL & DIE MFG CO
47 Cambridge Hts (06037-2310)
P.O. Box 97 (06037-0097)
PHONE..............................860 828-9955
Bruce Telke, *President*
Steve Telke, *Vice Pres*
Lynn Telke, *Treasurer*
EMP: 4 **EST:** 1950
SQ FT: 2,500
SALES: 150K **Privately Held**
SIC: 3544 3469 Special dies & tools; metal stampings

(G-3820)
WALSH PRINTS
143 Winding Meadow Dr (06037-2270)
PHONE..............................860 829-5566
EMP: 2
SALES (est): 129.4K **Privately Held**
SIC: 2752 Lithographic Commercial Printing

Kent
Litchfield County

(G-3821)
CHESNUT WOODWORKING
5 Fulling Ln (06757-1738)
PHONE..............................860 592-0383
EMP: 1
SALES (est): 63.6K **Privately Held**
SIC: 2431 Millwork

(G-3822)
INDIGO COAST INC
Also Called: Trailheads
17 Meadow St (06757-1329)
PHONE..............................860 592-0088
Stephanie Raftery, *President*
Ed Raftery, *Vice Pres*
Lorienne Cote, *Admin Sec*
▲ **EMP:** 8
SALES: 994K **Privately Held**
SIC: 2353 7389 Hats, caps & millinery; business services

(G-3823)
KENT FALLS BREWING COMPANY
33 Camps Rd (06757-1901)
PHONE..............................860 398-9645
Barry Labendz, *Founder*
EMP: 3
SALES (est): 68.6K **Privately Held**
SIC: 2082 Brewers' grain

(G-3824)
MODERN STITCH COMPANY
13 Railroad St (06757-1506)
P.O. Box 166 (06757-0166)
PHONE..............................860 927-5065
Sara Good, *Manager*
EMP: 1
SALES (est): 38.1K **Privately Held**
SIC: 2395 Embroidery & art needlework

(G-3825)
QUILTED LIZARD
19 South Rd (06757-1718)
PHONE..............................860 927-4296
Karen Eckmeier, *Owner*
EMP: 1
SALES (est): 55.8K **Privately Held**
SIC: 2395 Quilting & quilting supplies

(G-3826)
ST JOHNS BRIDGE LLC
25 Railroad St (06757)
P.O. Box 441 (06757-0441)
PHONE..............................860 927-3315
Gregory St John, *Personnel Exec*
Gregory Stjohn, *Mng Member*
EMP: 5
SALES (est): 497.8K **Privately Held**
WEB: www.stjohnsbridge.com
SIC: 1751 2541 2517 2511 Cabinet & finish carpentry; wood partitions & fixtures; wood television & radio cabinets; wood household furniture; wood kitchen cabinets; millwork

(G-3827)
WHEELER WOODWORKING
415 Kent Hollow Rd (06757-1911)
PHONE..............................860 355-1638
Bruce Wheeler, *Principal*
EMP: 2 **EST:** 2013
SALES (est): 120K **Privately Held**
SIC: 2431 Millwork

Killingworth
Middlesex County

(G-3828)
ANDERSON TECHNOLOGIES INC
243 Roast Meat Hill Rd (06419-2346)
P.O. Box 643, Guilford (06437-0643)
PHONE..............................860 663-2100
Andy Anderson, *President*
Lawrence Anderson, *Vice Pres*
◆ **EMP:** 4
SQ FT: 2,500
SALES (est): 722K **Privately Held**
SIC: 3564 5084 Blowers & fans; industrial machinery & equipment

(G-3829)
CHARLYS CUSTOM WOODWORKING
18 Rosemary Ln (06419-1458)
PHONE..............................860 227-2155
Charly Trentini, *Principal*
EMP: 1
SALES (est): 54.1K **Privately Held**
SIC: 2431 Millwork

(G-3830)
COASTAL GROUP INC
Also Called: Coastal Tooling
145 Chestnut Hill Rd (06419-1300)
PHONE..............................860 452-4148
Martha Springer, *CEO*
Jeff Springer, *President*
Shane Springer, *Director*
EMP: 3
SQ FT: 500
SALES: 100K **Privately Held**
SIC: 3545 Machine tool accessories

(G-3831)
CUSTOM WOODWORKING BY NORMAN
15 Goldfield Rd (06419-2419)
PHONE..............................860 663-3462
Paul Norman, *Principal*
EMP: 1
SALES (est): 190.6K **Privately Held**
SIC: 2431 Millwork

(G-3832)
EAST COAST PRECISION MFG LLC
63 Pond Meadow Rd (06419-1136)
P.O. Box 294, Boxford MA (01921-0294)
PHONE..............................978 887-5920
Chris Marchand, *Engineer*
Mark Rohlfs, *Associate Dir*
EMP: 4
SALES: 190K **Privately Held**
WEB: www.eastcoastmfg.com
SIC: 3082 Rods, unsupported plastic

(G-3833)
ENW PHARMA WRITING LLC
181 N Chestnut Hill Rd (06419-1002)
PHONE..............................860 663-0263
Eva N Wilford, *Principal*
EMP: 1 **EST:** 2013
SALES (est): 65.3K **Privately Held**
SIC: 2834 Pharmaceutical preparations

(G-3834)
GIDEON S FLEECE WOODWORKIN
42 Kenilworth Dr (06419-1266)
PHONE..............................860 663-2757
Robert Ferraro, *Principal*
EMP: 2
SALES (est): 111.7K **Privately Held**
SIC: 2431 Millwork

(G-3835)
ISLAND VIEW WOODWORKS LLC
259 Route 81 (06419-1244)
PHONE..............................203 494-1760
Robert Murphy, *Owner*
EMP: 2
SALES (est): 99.9K **Privately Held**
SIC: 2431 Millwork

(G-3836)
MARTIN MFG SERVICES LLC
96 Cow Hill Rd (06419-2402)
PHONE..............................860 663-1465
Paul J Martin, *Mng Member*
EMP: 4
SALES (est): 57.9K **Privately Held**
SIC: 3999 Manufacturing industries

(G-3837)
NEW ENGLAND TOOLING INC
145 Chestnut Hill Rd (06419-1300)
PHONE..............................800 866-5105
Shane Springer, *President*
Jeff Springer, *Vice Pres*
Gary Beeman, *Technical Staff*
Tom Bittner, *Technical Staff*
EMP: 10
SALES (est): 952.8K **Privately Held**
SIC: 3541 Machine tools, metal cutting type

Killingworth - Middlesex County (G-3838) — GEOGRAPHIC SECTION

(G-3838)
PYROTEK INCORPORATED
66 Lovers Ln (06419-1195)
PHONE 509 926-6212
Allan G Roy, *Branch Mgr*
EMP: 1
SALES (corp-wide): 565.8MM **Privately Held**
SIC: 3365 Aluminum foundries
PA: Pyrotek Incorporated
705 W 1st Ave
Spokane WA 99201
509 926-6212

(G-3839)
SEXTANT BTSLLC
166 Route 81 (06419-1481)
PHONE 203 500-3245
EMP: 3
SALES (est): 251.9K **Privately Held**
SIC: 3812 Sextants

(G-3840)
YANKEE PEDDLER
267 Route 81 (06419-1218)
PHONE 860 663-0526
Marie Azzaro, *Owner*
EMP: 2
SALES (est): 144.6K **Privately Held**
WEB: www.yankeepeddler.com
SIC: 2273 Carpets & rugs

Lakeside
Litchfield County

(G-3841)
BOB WORDEN
Also Called: Worden's Welding
53 Kenyon Rd (06758-1604)
PHONE 860 567-4722
Bob Worden, *Owner*
EMP: 1
SALES (est): 117.7K **Privately Held**
SIC: 3499 7692 Welding tips, heat resistant: metal; welding repair

Lakeville
Litchfield County

(G-3842)
BLUE MOON BINDERY LLC
206 Millerton Rd (06039-1445)
PHONE 860 435-9100
Nancy Baker, *Principal*
EMP: 2
SALES (est): 111.3K **Privately Held**
SIC: 2789 Bookbinding & related work

(G-3843)
GILBERT G FITCH
Also Called: Gilbert Fitch Woodworking
352 Millerton Rd (06039-1305)
PHONE 860 824-5832
Gilbert G Fitch, *Owner*
EMP: 1
SALES: 90K **Privately Held**
SIC: 2431 Exterior & ornamental woodwork & trim

(G-3844)
ILLINOIS TOOL WORKS INC
ITW Impro Lakeville Operations
14 Brook St (06039-1104)
P.O. Box 1570 (06039-1570)
PHONE 860 435-2574
Bill Thurston, *Manager*
EMP: 50
SQ FT: 20,000
SALES (corp-wide): 14.7B **Publicly Held**
SIC: 3089 Injection molding of plastics
PA: Illinois Tool Works Inc.
155 Harlem Ave
Glenview IL 60025
847 724-7500

(G-3845)
LAKEVILLE JOURNAL COMPANY LLC (PA)
Also Called: Lakeville Journal, The
33 Bissell St (06039)
P.O. Box 1688 (06039-1688)
PHONE 860 435-9873
Will Little, *President*
Cynthia Hochswender, *Editor*
EMP: 51
SQ FT: 10,000
SALES (est): 3.1MM **Privately Held**
WEB: www.lakevillejournal.com
SIC: 2711 Job printing & newspaper publishing combined

Lebanon
New London County

(G-3846)
ANN S DAVIS
Also Called: Recognition Products
754 Exeter Rd (06249-1735)
P.O. Box 1980 (06249-1980)
PHONE 860 642-7228
Ann S Davis, *Owner*
EMP: 10
SALES (est): 771.5K **Privately Held**
WEB: www.rproducts.com
SIC: 3999 3479 7389 Identification tags, except paper; name plates: engraved, etched, etc.; engraving service

(G-3847)
APPLIED MICROBIOLOGY SERVICES
7 Deepwood Dr (06249-2106)
PHONE 860 537-3118
Daniel S Feldman, *Principal*
EMP: 1
SALES (est): 82.7K **Privately Held**
WEB: www.appliedmicrobiologyservices.com
SIC: 2835 Microbiology & virology diagnostic products

(G-3848)
C AND B WELDING LLC
20 Hillside Dr (06249-1017)
PHONE 860 423-9047
Chris Pearl, *Owner*
EMP: 6
SALES (est): 224.4K **Privately Held**
SIC: 7692 Welding repair

(G-3849)
CALHOUN PRESS INC
205 Clarke Rd (06249-1635)
PHONE 860 202-0998
Laurence Carlson, *President*
EMP: 1 EST: 2016
SALES (est): 41.3K **Privately Held**
SIC: 2741 Miscellaneous publishing

(G-3850)
CENTRAL ELECTRIC MOTOR
1378 Exeter Rd (06249-2015)
PHONE 860 642-7421
Eric W Hesse, *Owner*
EMP: 1 EST: 1951
SALES (est): 45.7K **Privately Held**
SIC: 7694 5999 Electric motor repair; motors, electric

(G-3851)
CREATIVE CANVAS LLC
89 Madley Rd (06249-1820)
PHONE 860 559-8509
Bonnie D Pistritto, *Principal*
EMP: 1
SALES (est): 48.8K **Privately Held**
SIC: 2211 Canvas

(G-3852)
CUSTOM WOODWORKING
54 Pigeon Swamp Rd (06249-1333)
PHONE 860 456-4466
Albert A Siragusa, *Principal*
EMP: 2
SALES (est): 122.6K **Privately Held**
SIC: 2431 Millwork

(G-3853)
DENS SAND & GRAVEL
970 Goshen Hill Rd Ext (06249-2303)
PHONE 860 642-6478
EMP: 3
SALES (est): 166.4K **Privately Held**
SIC: 1442 Construction sand & gravel

(G-3854)
INDARS STAIRS LLC
39 W Town St (06249-1536)
P.O. Box 87, Willimantic (06226-0087)
PHONE 860 208-3826
Albert Manning, *Mng Member*
Kellie Monroe, *Manager*
EMP: 4
SALES: 730K **Privately Held**
SIC: 2431 Millwork

(G-3855)
JOE CHARRON
Also Called: Maple Slope Creations
43 Pigeon Swamp Rd (06249-1331)
PHONE 860 423-2805
Joe Charron, *Owner*
EMP: 1
SALES (est): 59.8K **Privately Held**
SIC: 2499 Decorative wood & woodwork

(G-3856)
JOHNSON MEADOWS LLC
779 Exeter Rd (06249-1708)
PHONE 860 642-0618
James W Jahoda,
EMP: 1
SALES (est): 66.5K **Privately Held**
SIC: 3842 Ear plugs

(G-3857)
LSR ELECTRONIC ASSEMBLY
99 Old Colchester Rd (06249-2338)
PHONE 860 642-6883
Lynn Russo, *Owner*
EMP: 1
SALES (est): 80.4K **Privately Held**
SIC: 3679 Electronic circuits

(G-3858)
MIRACLE INSTRUMENTS CO
1667 Exeter Rd (06249-1904)
PHONE 860 642-7745
John Ryan, *President*
EMP: 11
SQ FT: 3,000
SALES (est): 1.7MM **Privately Held**
WEB: www.miracleinstrument.com
SIC: 3545 3829 3699 Chucks: drill, lathe or magnetic (machine tool accessories); levels & tapes, surveying; door opening & closing devices, electrical

(G-3859)
NICHOLS FORESTRY & LOGGING LLC
151 Exeter Rd (06249-1323)
PHONE 860 642-4292
Scott Nichols, *Partner*
EMP: 2
SALES (est): 187.7K **Privately Held**
SIC: 2411 Logging

(G-3860)
PURVINS WOODCRAFT
333 Trumbull Hwy (06249-1435)
PHONE 860 456-1933
Mark Purvins, *Owner*
EMP: 1
SALES (est): 109.8K **Privately Held**
SIC: 2499 Novelties, wood fiber

(G-3861)
RED OAK STABLE LLC
4 Oliver Rd (06249-1618)
PHONE 860 642-4671
Eric Hoxie, *Owner*
EMP: 1
SALES (est): 125.6K **Privately Held**
SIC: 3462 Horseshoes

(G-3862)
SCOTTS COMPANY LLC
20 Industrial Rd (06249-1326)
P.O. Box 143 (06249-0143)
PHONE 860 642-7591
Darren Talbert, *Plant Mgr*
Anita Wood, *Facilities Mgr*
Todd Guzman, *Production*
Mark Kulling, *Manager*
Amanda Green, *Manager*
EMP: 70
SALES (corp-wide): 2.6B **Publicly Held**
WEB: www.scottscompany.com
SIC: 2875 Fertilizers, mixing only
HQ: The Scotts Company Llc
14111 Scottslawn Rd
Marysville OH 43040
937 644-0011

(G-3863)
STEVEN SABO
636 Trumbull Hwy (06249-1431)
PHONE 860 642-6031
Steven Sabo, *Principal*
EMP: 1 EST: 2001
SALES (est): 46.2K **Privately Held**
SIC: 7692 Welding repair

(G-3864)
TRI-COUNTY MOLD & MACHINE
Also Called: Tri-County Power Sled
1912 Exeter Rd (06249-1903)
PHONE 860 642-7033
John Strenkowski, *Partner*
Virginia Strenkowski, *Partner*
EMP: 2 EST: 1966
SALES: 75K **Privately Held**
SIC: 3599 5561 Machine shop, jobbing & repair; recreational vehicle parts & accessories

(G-3865)
TTPOCKETTOOLS LLC
266 Clubhouse Rd (06249-1612)
PHONE 860 642-6020
Todd Pannone, *Owner*
EMP: 1
SALES: 52K **Privately Held**
SIC: 5251 3423 Tools, hand; hand & edge tools

(G-3866)
WASTE RESOURCE RECOVERY INC (PA)
505 Exeter Rd (06249-1544)
PHONE 860 287-3332
Richard N Madrak, *President*
Richard Madrak, *President*
EMP: 3 EST: 2014
SQ FT: 5,000
SALES (est): 331.3K **Privately Held**
SIC: 2869 Fatty acid esters, aminos, etc.

Ledyard
New London County

(G-3867)
ARTHUR RODGERS
Also Called: Elite Electronics
7 Jessica Ln (06339-1452)
PHONE 860 967-4598
Arthur Rodgers, *Owner*
EMP: 1 EST: 2013
SALES (est): 53.6K **Privately Held**
SIC: 7629 3728 Electronic equipment repair; aircraft parts & equipment

(G-3868)
B & D LURES
11 Hillcrest Ave (06339-1019)
PHONE 860 861-6530
EMP: 1
SALES (est): 51.7K **Privately Held**
SIC: 3949 Lures, fishing: artificial

(G-3869)
BAA CREATIONS
13 Lambtown Rd (06339-1925)
PHONE 860 464-1339
Elizabeth Macleod, *Owner*
EMP: 3
SALES: 85K **Privately Held**
SIC: 2395 Appliqueing, for the trade

(G-3870)
CIMARRON MUSIC PRESS
79 Meeting House Ln (06339-1724)
PHONE 860 536-2185
EMP: 1

GEOGRAPHIC SECTION

Litchfield - Litchfield County (G-3902)

SALES (est): 37.5K **Privately Held**
SIC: 2741 Miscellaneous publishing

(G-3871)
CLINTON BABCOCK & SONS
Also Called: Clint's Cabinets
54 Silas Deane Rd (06339-1331)
PHONE..................................860 887-9166
Clinton Babcock, *Owner*
EMP: 2
SALES (est): 178.2K **Privately Held**
SIC: 2434 Wood kitchen cabinets

(G-3872)
FORTE RTS INC
Also Called: Forte Carbon Fiber Products
14 Lorenz Industrial Pkwy (06339-1946)
PHONE..................................860 464-5221
Anthony F Delima, *President*
Clint Rand, *Marketing Mgr*
▼ **EMP:** 8
SALES (est): 1.3MM **Privately Held**
WEB: www.fortecarbon.com
SIC: 3825 Spark plug testing equipment, electric

(G-3873)
GEM EMBROIDERY
227 Haley Rd (06339-1920)
PHONE..................................860 326-0676
Millie Burke, *Owner*
EMP: 1
SALES (est): 41.6K **Privately Held**
SIC: 2395 Embroidery & art needlework

(G-3874)
GRAND SLAM SIGNS
15 Tuckers Run (06339-1000)
PHONE..................................972 874-3658
EMP: 1
SALES (est): 46K **Privately Held**
SIC: 3993 Mfg Signs/Advertising Specialties

(G-3875)
JOHNSON CONTROLS INC
39 Route 2 (06339-1128)
PHONE..................................860 886-9021
Tom Oneil, *Manager*
EMP: 94 **Privately Held**
SIC: 2531 Seats, automobile
HQ: Johnson Controls, Inc.
   5757 N Green Bay Ave
   Milwaukee WI 53209
   414 524-1200

(G-3876)
LASTING LEGACY PUBLISHERS LLC
57 Coachman Pike (06339-1308)
PHONE..................................860 917-3545
Mary Jane Haddad, *Principal*
EMP: 2
SALES (est): 90.7K **Privately Held**
SIC: 2741 Miscellaneous publishing

(G-3877)
MANAGEMENT SOFTWARE INC
Also Called: MSI
547 Colonel Ledyard Hwy (06339-1611)
PHONE..................................860 536-5177
Frank Thompson, *President*
Margaret Thompson, *CFO*
EMP: 4
SALES (est): 340.8K **Privately Held**
WEB: www.managementsoftware.com
SIC: 7372 7379 7373 Business oriented computer software; computer related consulting services; computer related maintenance services; office computer automation systems integration

(G-3878)
MAUGLE SIERRA VINEYARDS LLC
825 Colonel Ledyard Hwy # 827 (06339-1207)
P.O. Box 220 (06339-0220)
PHONE..................................860 464-2987
Paul Maugle,
Betty Maugle,
EMP: 2
SALES (est): 196.6K **Privately Held**
SIC: 2084 Wines

(G-3879)
PEQUOT PRINTING LLC
1 Windward Ln (06339-1053)
PHONE..................................860 381-5193
Allan Thomas, *Principal*
EMP: 2
SALES (est): 106.4K **Privately Held**
SIC: 2752 Commercial printing, lithographic

(G-3880)
STONINGTON WOODWORKS LLC
272 Gallup Hill Rd (06339-2009)
PHONE..................................646 321-6412
Sean Wimpfheimer, *Principal*
EMP: 1
SALES (est): 54.1K **Privately Held**
SIC: 2431 Millwork

Lisbon
New London County

(G-3881)
JUST BREAKFAST & THINGS
15 River Rd (06351-3035)
PHONE..................................860 376-4040
Mary Thompson, *Owner*
EMP: 4
SALES (est): 264.5K **Privately Held**
SIC: 2038 Breakfasts, frozen & packaged

(G-3882)
OMNI MOLD SYSTEMS LLC
21 Kimball Heights Ln (06351-2833)
PHONE..................................888 666-4755
Gaston Cyr, *Principal*
EMP: 5
SALES (est): 606K **Privately Held**
SIC: 3544 Industrial molds

(G-3883)
SYMPHONYCS LLC
210 S Burnham Hwy (06351-3008)
PHONE..................................860 884-2308
Robert Mazarelli, *Principal*
EMP: 2
SALES (est): 99.2K **Privately Held**
SIC: 2731 8742 Books: publishing only; business consultant

Litchfield
Litchfield County

(G-3884)
BEARICUDA INC
Also Called: Bearicuda Bins
3 West St Ste 3e (06759-3501)
P.O. Box 56 (06759-0056)
PHONE..................................860 361-6860
Kevin Lacilla, *President*
EMP: 5 **EST:** 2008
SALES (est): 323.6K **Privately Held**
SIC: 3469 Garbage cans, stamped & pressed metal

(G-3885)
BRITISH W INDIES TRDG USA LLC (PA)
166 Town Farm Rd (06759)
PHONE..................................704 451-8400
Georgia Dunn,
EMP: 1 (**EST:** 2013
SALES (est): 129.4K **Privately Held**
SIC: 2082 Beer (alcoholic beverage)

(G-3886)
CONCRETE SUPPLEMENT CO
272 Norfolk Rd (06759-2517)
P.O. Box 501 (06759-0501)
PHONE..................................860 567-5556
Alan Landau, *President*
Christopher Krone, *Vice Pres*
EMP: 9
SQ FT: 36,000
SALES (est): 2.8MM **Privately Held**
WEB: www.consupco.com
SIC: 2899 Concrete curing & hardening compounds

(G-3887)
CUSTOM FURNITURE & DESIGN LLC
601 Bantam Rd (06759)
P.O. Box 1533 (06759-1533)
PHONE..................................860 567-3519
Mike Moskowitz, *Mng Member*
Michael Moskowitz, *Mng Member*
Robert Paradis,
EMP: 11
SQ FT: 6,000
SALES (est): 1.5MM **Privately Held**
SIC: 2434 2511 Wood kitchen cabinets; wood household furniture

(G-3888)
EAST COAST SHEET METAL LLC
141 Woodruff St (06759-3528)
PHONE..................................860 283-1126
Lisa Patchell, *Mng Member*
David Patchell, *Mng Member*
EMP: 19
SALES (est): 2MM **Privately Held**
SIC: 1711 3444 Heating & air conditioning contractors; sheet metalwork

(G-3889)
ENGINEERED COATINGS INC
272 Norfolk Rd (06759-2517)
P.O. Box 501 (06759-0501)
PHONE..................................860 567-5556
Jack Walnes, *President*
Alfred Matarese, *Vice Pres*
Richard Novak, *Vice Pres*
EMP: 32
SQ FT: 21,200
SALES (est): 3.1MM **Privately Held**
SIC: 3479 Coating of metals & formed products

(G-3890)
GRAPHIC PACKAGING INTL LLC
133 Goodhouse Rd (06759-2216)
PHONE..................................860 567-4196
Tom Binstadt, *Manager*
EMP: 3
SQ FT: 1,500 **Publicly Held**
SIC: 2631 Paperboard mills
HQ: Graphic Packaging International, Llc
   1500 Riveredge Pkwy # 100
   Atlanta GA 30328

(G-3891)
GREEN & SONS LLC
Also Called: Green and Sons
19 Little Pitch Rd (06759-4016)
PHONE..................................860 459-4049
Gregory M Green, *Mng Member*
Quentin S Green,
EMP: 2 **EST:** 2008
SALES (est): 246.4K **Privately Held**
SIC: 3531 Plows: construction, excavating & grading

(G-3892)
HAIGHT VINEYARD INC (PA)
29 Chestnut Hill Rd (06759-4101)
PHONE..................................860 567-4045
Sherman P Haight Jr, *President*
Robert Coe, *Admin Sec*
EMP: 6
SQ FT: 4,500
SALES (est): 647.3K **Privately Held**
SIC: 0172 2084 5921 Grapes; wines; wine

(G-3893)
JAMIESON LASER LLC
50 Thomaston Rd (06759)
P.O. Box 1531 (06759-1531)
PHONE..................................860 482-3375
Wolfgang Kesselring, *General Mgr*
Wolfgang Kesselring, *Mng Member*
▲ **EMP:** 5
SQ FT: 12,000
SALES: 500K **Privately Held**
SIC: 3699 Electrical equipment & supplies

(G-3894)
LITCHFIELD INTERNATIONAL INC
457 Bantam Rd Ste 12 (06759-3225)
PHONE..................................860 567-8824
C Stuart Hungerford, *President*

Kate Hungerford, *Vice Pres*
Sharon McGuire, *Sales Associate*
Fred Perrotti, *Agent*
Charles Hungerford, *Shareholder*
▲ **EMP:** 5
SQ FT: 4,000
SALES (est): 1MM **Privately Held**
SIC: 3317 Conduit: welded, lock joint or heavy riveted; pipes, wrought: welded, lock joint or heavy riveted

(G-3895)
MERLIN ASSOCIATES INC
Also Called: Airfax R
457 Bantam Rd Ste 5 (06759-3225)
P.O. Box 940, Fort Lauderdale FL (33302-0940)
PHONE..................................860 567-1620
Jim Williams, *President*
EMP: 3
SALES (est): 295.2K **Privately Held**
WEB: www.airtrading.com
SIC: 2721 Periodicals

(G-3896)
MURPHY BOYZ PRINTING MARK
110 Richards Rd (06759-3700)
PHONE..................................860 836-0829
EMP: 2
SALES (est): 83.9K **Privately Held**
SIC: 2752 Commercial printing, lithographic

(G-3897)
NJD ENTERPRISES
15 Bigos Rd (06759-2605)
PHONE..................................860 210-1113
Jennifer Despirito, *Owner*
EMP: 1
SALES (est): 37K **Privately Held**
SIC: 3999 Manufacturing industries

(G-3898)
PEPSI FOODS
Also Called: Pepsico
143 Northfield Rd (06759-3712)
P.O. Box 86 (06759-0086)
PHONE..................................860 567-5774
John Hula, *President*
EMP: 5
SALES (est): 225.8K **Privately Held**
SIC: 2086 Carbonated soft drinks, bottled & canned

(G-3899)
S-Y-M PRODUCTS COMPANY LLC
49 Clark Rd (06759-2826)
P.O. Box 1136 (06759-1136)
PHONE..................................203 329-2469
Daniel V Fowler, *General Mgr*
Daniel Fowler,
▼ **EMP:** 16
SALES (est): 1.6MM **Privately Held**
WEB: www.symproducts.com
SIC: 5047 3841 Medical equipment & supplies; surgical & medical instruments

(G-3900)
SPACE SWISS MANUFACTURING INC
428 Maple St (06759-2100)
PHONE..................................860 567-4341
EMP: 10 **EST:** 1963
SQ FT: 18,000
SALES (est): 720K **Privately Held**
SIC: 3451 Mfg Screw Machine Products

(G-3901)
SWEET PEET NORTH AMERICA INC
3 West St Ste 3 (06759-3501)
P.O. Box 56 (06759-0056)
PHONE..................................860 361-6444
EMP: 3
SALES (est): 160K **Privately Held**
SIC: 2499 Mfg Wood Products

(G-3902)
THOMAS F KYASKY
442 Milton Rd (06759-2112)
PHONE..................................860 567-4077
Thomas Kyasky, *Owner*
EMP: 2

Lyme - New London County (G-3903)

GEOGRAPHIC SECTION

SALES (est): 161.9K **Privately Held**
SIC: 2431 Millwork

Lyme
New London County

(G-3903)
CONNECTICUT COMPASS SERVICE
301 Grassy Hill Rd (06371-3300)
PHONE................................860 434-2019
Wayne S Kyder, *Owner*
EMP: 1
SALES (est): 70K **Privately Held**
SIC: 3829 Compasses, magnetic: portable type

(G-3904)
DEBRASONG PUBLISHING LLC
82-3 Mount Archer Rd (06371-3158)
PHONE................................413 204-4682
Debra L Alt, *Principal*
EMP: 3
SALES (est): 107.3K **Privately Held**
SIC: 2741 Miscellaneous publishing

(G-3905)
LIMBKEEPERS LLC
25 Joshuatown Rd (06371-3119)
PHONE................................860 304-3250
Deborah Vezan, *Principal*
EMP: 3 **EST:** 2013
SALES (est): 195.6K **Privately Held**
SIC: 3842 Surgical appliances & supplies

(G-3906)
SUNSET HILL VINEYARD
5 Elys Ferry Rd (06371-3406)
PHONE................................860 598-9427
Salvatore A Caruso, *Principal*
EMP: 3
SALES (est): 151.6K **Privately Held**
SIC: 2084 Wines, brandy & brandy spirits

Madison
New Haven County

(G-3907)
ARTCHRIST COM INC
Also Called: Sound View Press
70 Wall St Unit Rr (06443-3118)
PHONE................................203 245-2246
Thinrry Thrmann, *CEO*
Peter Hastings Falk, *President*
EMP: 1
SQ FT: 1,600
SALES (est): 94.5K **Privately Held**
WEB: www.falkart.com
SIC: 2731 Books: publishing only

(G-3908)
ARTEMIS PINE CANDLE CO LLC
182 Opening Hill Rd (06443-1952)
PHONE................................203 245-5170
Sarah Taylor, *Principal*
EMP: 1
SALES (est): 39.6K **Privately Held**
SIC: 3999 Candles

(G-3909)
ARTISTIC SIGN LANGUAGE LLC
114 Bradley Rd (06443-2666)
PHONE................................203 245-8213
Michelle Olds,
EMP: 1
SQ FT: 1,000
SALES (est): 100K **Privately Held**
WEB: www.artisticsignlanguage.com
SIC: 3993 Signs, not made in custom sign painting shops

(G-3910)
BEAUTYBRAIN BRACELET LLC
36 Kelsey Pl (06443-2800)
PHONE................................203 245-8913
Lisa Mazzol, *Owner*
EMP: 1
SALES (est): 51.5K **Privately Held**
SIC: 3911 Jewelry, precious metal

(G-3911)
BELLA CIAO
806 Green Hill Rd (06443-2404)
PHONE................................203 245-4433
Thomas Braun, *Partner*
Pamela Braun, *Partner*
EMP: 2 **EST:** 1998
SALES (est): 188.1K **Privately Held**
WEB: www.ciaobellastudio.com
SIC: 2771 Greeting cards

(G-3912)
BELLE INDUSTRIES LLC
13 Corinth Dr (06443-2222)
PHONE................................203 245-0382
Larry Papuga, *Principal*
EMP: 1 **EST:** 2015
SALES (est): 44.7K **Privately Held**
SIC: 3999 Manufacturing industries

(G-3913)
CLEANSOURCE INDUSTRIES
126 Green Hill Rd (06443-2152)
PHONE................................203 401-1535
EMP: 2
SALES (est): 86.9K **Privately Held**
SIC: 3999 Manufacturing industries

(G-3914)
CR-TEC ENGINEERING INC
15 Orchard Park Rd A20 (06443-2268)
PHONE................................203 318-9500
Charles W Lehberger, *President*
EMP: 4
SALES (est): 474.7K **Privately Held**
WEB: www.crtec.com
SIC: 3491 Valves, automatic control

(G-3915)
CRANIAL TECHNOLOGIES INC
1343 Boston Post Rd (06443-3481)
PHONE................................203 318-8739
Lynne Ball, *Branch Mgr*
EMP: 17 **Privately Held**
SIC: 3842 Orthopedic appliances
PA: Cranial Technologies, Inc.
1395 W Auto Dr
Tempe AZ 85284

(G-3916)
D P ENGINEERING INC
211 Summer Hill Rd (06443-1850)
PHONE................................203 421-7965
David Penniman, *President*
EMP: 2
SQ FT: 2,000
SALES (est): 200K **Privately Held**
WEB: www.polyhangers.com
SIC: 3589 5082 Asbestos removal equipment; general construction machinery & equipment

(G-3917)
DARLENE ANN MICONI
Also Called: Crossgrain Wood Products
615 Horse Pond Rd (06443-2082)
PHONE................................203 245-4127
Darlene Miconi, *Owner*
EMP: 1
SALES (est): 71.2K **Privately Held**
SIC: 3131 Footwear cut stock

(G-3918)
E M M INC
8 Bishop Ln (06443-3367)
PHONE................................203 245-0306
Herbert D'Alo, *President*
Melissa D'Alo, *Vice Pres*
Melissa Dalo, *Sales Mgr*
EMP: 20
SALES (est): 1.9MM **Privately Held**
SIC: 3841 Medical instruments & equipment, blood & bone work

(G-3919)
EDITORIAL DIRECTIONS INC
46 Brookview Ter (06443-2036)
PHONE................................203 245-2011
Bob Woods, *President*
EMP: 1
SALES (est): 85K **Privately Held**
SIC: 8999 2731 5311 Editorial service; book publishing; department stores

(G-3920)
FELK PUBLISHING LLC
15 Sheffield Ln (06443-1769)
PHONE................................203 421-3714
Elbert Patterson, *Principal*
EMP: 2
SALES (est): 67.6K **Privately Held**
SIC: 2741 Miscellaneous publishing

(G-3921)
FLUID SOLUTIONS LLC
18 Johns Path (06443-2081)
PHONE................................203 245-0708
Daniel Whelahan,
EMP: 2
SALES (est): 229.8K **Privately Held**
SIC: 3594 Fluid power pumps & motors

(G-3922)
GAISERTIM
11 Soundview Ave (06443-2709)
PHONE................................203 245-9276
EMP: 2
SALES (est): 85.9K **Privately Held**
SIC: 3572 Mfg Computer Storage Devices

(G-3923)
GRAYFIN SECURITY LLC
Also Called: Grayfin Micro
82 Bradley Rd (06443-2684)
P.O. Box 1333 (06443-1333)
PHONE................................203 800-6760
Benjamin Gray, *Mng Member*
EMP: 6 **EST:** 2012
SQ FT: 1,320
SALES: 1.5MM **Privately Held**
SIC: 7372 7373 7371 5065 Business oriented computer software; value-added resellers, computer systems; computer software systems analysis & design, custom; security control equipment & systems; burglar alarm maintenance & monitoring

(G-3924)
GRIFFITH & PARROTT
120 Acorn Rd (06443-3340)
PHONE................................203 245-7837
Anita Griffith, *Owner*
Robert Parrott, *Co-Owner*
EMP: 2
SALES (est): 53K **Privately Held**
SIC: 3269 Pottery products

(G-3925)
HARBOR PUBLICATIONS INC
Also Called: Mail-A-Map
1 Orchard Park Rd Ste 8 (06443-2272)
P.O. Box 883 (06443-0883)
PHONE................................203 245-8009
Matt Holmes, *President*
EMP: 4
SQ FT: 1,400
SALES: 1.3MM **Privately Held**
SIC: 2741 Maps: publishing & printing

(G-3926)
HAWKS NEST PUBLISHING LLC
194 Opening Hill Rd (06443-1952)
PHONE................................860 536-5868
EMP: 2
SALES (est): 120K **Privately Held**
SIC: 2741 Misc Publishing

(G-3927)
HEALTHY HARVEST INC
42 Godman Rd (06443-2033)
PHONE................................203 245-3786
David Roach, *President*
Russell Phillips, *Vice Pres*
EMP: 5
SQ FT: 5,000
SALES (est): 477.2K **Privately Held**
SIC: 2879 8732 Agricultural disinfectants; research services, except laboratory

(G-3928)
IMAGINE 8 LLC
26 Eagle Meadow Rd (06443-8123)
PHONE................................203 421-0905
Michael Mazzaferro,
◆ **EMP:** 4
SALES (est): 225.3K **Privately Held**
WEB: www.imagine8.com
SIC: 3944 Games, toys & children's vehicles

(G-3929)
IN O SCENTS OF MADISON
837 Boston Post Rd (06443-3103)
PHONE................................203 641-8910
Dyan Salemi, *President*
EMP: 2
SALES (est): 177.2K **Privately Held**
SIC: 2844 Toilet preparations

(G-3930)
INDEPENDENCE PARK
38 Sheffield Ln (06443-1770)
PHONE................................203 421-9396
Tom Burke, *President*
EMP: 3
SALES (est): 252.8K **Privately Held**
SIC: 3625 Relays & industrial controls

(G-3931)
INDUSTRIAL ANALYTICS CORP
1 Orchard Park Rd Ste 10 (06443-2272)
PHONE................................203 245-0380
Nicholas J Afragola, *President*
Ann Afragola, *Admin Sec*
EMP: 3
SALES: 1MM **Privately Held**
SIC: 3826 Analytical instruments

(G-3932)
JOSEPH L GENTILE ENTPS LLC
28 Lenore Dr (06443-8016)
PHONE................................203 421-5144
Joseph Gentile, *Mng Member*
EMP: 1
SALES (est): 94.9K **Privately Held**
SIC: 3841 Medical instruments & equipment, blood & bone work

(G-3933)
KC PUBLISHING
67 Flintlock Rd (06443-2426)
PHONE................................203 318-8544
Glenn Freiman, *Principal*
EMP: 1
SALES (est): 60.9K **Privately Held**
SIC: 2741 Miscellaneous publishing

(G-3934)
KIRCHOFF WOHLBERG INC
897 Boston Post Rd (06443-3155)
PHONE................................212 644-2020
Morris Kirchoff, *President*
Mary Jane Martin, *Vice Pres*
Ronald Zollshan, *Treasurer*
EMP: 13 **EST:** 1974
SQ FT: 8,000
SALES (est): 3MM **Privately Held**
WEB: www.kirchoffwohlberg.com
SIC: 2731 7389 Textbooks: publishing only, not printed on site; artists' agents & brokers

(G-3935)
KPB INDUSTRIES LLC
71 Deepwood Dr (06443-1764)
PHONE................................203 687-7943
Karen Buck, *Principal*
EMP: 2
SALES (est): 139.4K **Privately Held**
SIC: 3999 Manufacturing industries

(G-3936)
LASER ENGRAVED SERVICES
164b Horse Pond Rd (06443-2561)
PHONE................................203 779-5116
EMP: 2
SALES (est): 79.4K **Privately Held**
SIC: 2759 Publication printing

(G-3937)
MADD FIUSCH INDUSTRIES
1085 Durham Rd (06443-1855)
PHONE................................203 982-8306
EMP: 2 **EST:** 2017
SALES (est): 95.4K **Privately Held**
SIC: 3999 Manufacturing industries

(G-3938)
MADISON TSTG ACQSTION SVCS LLC
Also Called: Mtaas
899 Durham Rd (06443-1827)
PHONE................................203 421-9388
Barbara Paresi,
EMP: 2

SALES (est): 281K **Privately Held**
SIC: 3825 5084 Test equipment for electronic & electric measurement; measuring & testing equipment, electrical

(G-3939)
MENTAL CANVAS LLC
61 Hartford Ave (06443-2743)
PHONE..................................475 329-0515
Julie Dorsey,
EMP: 5
SALES (est): 179.1K **Privately Held**
SIC: 7372 Application computer software

(G-3940)
METRO NEIGHBORS PUBLISHING LLC
22 Esterly Farms Rd (06443-2278)
PHONE..................................203 494-3600
Michael D Perry, *Owner*
EMP: 1
SALES (est): 37.5K **Privately Held**
SIC: 2741 Miscellaneous publishing

(G-3941)
NEW PRECISION TECHNOLOGY LLC
Also Called: USI Education & Government Sls
98 Fort Path Rd Ste B (06443-2264)
PHONE..................................800 243-4565
Nicholas Gianacoplos, *Owner*
Sherri Montminy, *Principal*
Frederick Franco, *Info Tech Mgr*
EMP: 7
SQ FT: 14,000
SALES (est): 630K **Privately Held**
WEB: www.np-tek.com
SIC: 3083 Thermosetting laminates: rods, tubes, plates & sheet

(G-3942)
NO BUTTS BIN COMPANY INC
16 Birch Ln (06443-2535)
P.O. Box 1065 (06443-1065)
PHONE..................................203 245-5924
Martyn A Bright, *President*
Greg Burke, *General Mgr*
▲ EMP: 4
SQ FT: 5,000
SALES: 900K **Privately Held**
SIC: 3469 Ash trays, stamped metal

(G-3943)
ONCOARENDI THERAPEUTICS LLC
125 Devonshire Ln (06443-8124)
PHONE..................................609 571-0306
Stanislaw Pikul,
Adam Golebiowski,
EMP: 4 EST: 2014
SALES (est): 211.5K **Privately Held**
SIC: 2834 Pharmaceutical preparations

(G-3944)
ORIGINALS LLC
2096 Durham Rd (06443-8101)
PHONE..................................203 421-4867
Birch Bidwell, *Principal*
Sandra Olenik,
EMP: 1
SALES (est): 91K **Privately Held**
SIC: 7336 2731 Graphic arts & related design; textbooks: publishing only, not printed on site

(G-3945)
OUTDOOR INDUSTRIES LLC
80 Devonshire Ln (06443-1681)
P.O. Box 948 (06443-0948)
PHONE..................................203 350-2275
Mark Decillis, *Principal*
EMP: 2
SALES (est): 110.4K **Privately Held**
SIC: 3999 Manufacturing industries

(G-3946)
OZZ
33 Seaview Ave (06443-3207)
PHONE..................................203 318-5080
Christian Bardin, *Principal*
EMP: 1
SALES (est): 73.2K **Privately Held**
SIC: 2844 Toilet preparations

(G-3947)
PATTERN GENOMICS LLC
22 Alex Dr (06443-3477)
PHONE..................................203 779-5470
Daniel Fasulo, *Principal*
EMP: 2
SALES (est): 180.5K **Privately Held**
SIC: 3543 Industrial patterns

(G-3948)
PIONEER COATINGS & MFG LLC
188 Warpas Rd (06443-2024)
PHONE..................................203 421-6086
Kevin J Maclellan, *Principal*
EMP: 2
SALES (est): 100.5K **Privately Held**
SIC: 3479 Metal coating & allied service

(G-3949)
PUCUDA INC
Also Called: Leading Edge Safety Systems
14 New Rd (06443-2507)
P.O. Box 471 (06443-0471)
PHONE..................................860 526-8004
John Rexroad, *President*
Jason Lawlor, *Vice Pres*
Drew Bishop, *Graphic Designe*
Vanda Winakor,
◆ EMP: 15
SQ FT: 12,500
SALES: 5MM **Privately Held**
WEB: www.netting.com
SIC: 3089 Netting, plastic

(G-3950)
QUANTUM CIRCUITS INC
44 Northwood Rd (06443-1658)
PHONE..................................203 432-4289
Brian Pusch, *President*
EMP: 2 EST: 2016
SALES (est): 284.1K **Privately Held**
SIC: 3572 Computer storage devices

(G-3951)
RJ KACH LTD
21 Old Toll Rd (06443-8218)
P.O. Box 1401, Guilford (06437-0501)
PHONE..................................203 457-1349
Richard Kach, *Owner*
EMP: 2 EST: 1975
SALES (est): 120K **Privately Held**
SIC: 2514 Novelty furniture, household: metal

(G-3952)
ROCKLAND MUSIC LLC
130 Fort Path Rd Ste 11 (06443-2200)
PHONE..................................203 779-5299
EMP: 2
SALES (est): 131.8K **Privately Held**
SIC: 3271 Blocks, concrete: landscape or retaining wall

(G-3953)
RWT CORPORATION
Also Called: Welding Works
32 New Rd (06443-2507)
PHONE..................................203 245-2731
Ross E McCartney, *President*
Maria Teixeira, *Office Mgr*
Laurie McCartney, *Admin Sec*
EMP: 24
SQ FT: 22,000
SALES: 5MM **Privately Held**
SIC: 3441 3448 Fabricated structural metal; prefabricated metal components

(G-3954)
S-FRAME SOFTWARE LLC
7 Carmel Ct (06443-1790)
PHONE..................................203 421-8527
Marinos Stylianou, *Owner*
EMP: 2
SALES (est): 195.8K **Privately Held**
SIC: 7372 Prepackaged software

(G-3955)
SCOTT WOODFORD
817 Boston Post Rd (06443-3155)
PHONE..................................203 245-4266
Scott Woodford, *Principal*
EMP: 4
SALES (est): 348.1K **Privately Held**
SIC: 3843 Enamels, dentists'

(G-3956)
SHORE PUBLISHING LLC
724 Boston Post Rd (06443-3039)
P.O. Box 1010 (06443-1010)
PHONE..................................203 245-1877
Robyn Wolcott, *Publisher*
Lee Howard, *Editor*
Pem McNerney, *Editor*
Chris Negrini, *Editor*
Erin Shanley, *Editor*
EMP: 45 EST: 1994
SQ FT: 2,500
SALES (est): 2.6MM **Privately Held**
WEB: www.shorepublishing.com
SIC: 2711 Commercial printing & newspaper publishing combined; newspapers: publishing only, not printed on site

(G-3957)
SHORELINE VINE
724 Boston Post 105a (06443)
PHONE..................................203 779-5331
Dawn Schwab, *Principal*
EMP: 3
SALES (est): 237.9K **Privately Held**
SIC: 2079 Olive oil

(G-3958)
SOLUTHIN INC
30 Renees Way (06443-8130)
PHONE..................................860 424-1228
John Daniels, *President*
EMP: 2
SALES (est): 157.6K **Privately Held**
SIC: 3674 Semiconductors & related devices

(G-3959)
SOUTH PAINT AND SIGN CO
96 Robin Ridge Dr (06443-2003)
PHONE..................................203 245-7591
Alfred South, *Principal*
EMP: 2
SALES (est): 143.6K **Privately Held**
SIC: 3993 Signs & advertising specialties

(G-3960)
SPECTROGRAM CORPORATION
287 Boston Post Rd (06443-2938)
PHONE..................................203 245-2433
Herbert R Gram, *President*
Joan Friborg, *Vice Pres*
Geoffery A Gram, *Director*
EMP: 3
SQ FT: 6,000
SALES: 100K **Privately Held**
WEB: www.spectrogram.com
SIC: 3826 8731 3812 Environmental testing equipment; commercial physical research; search & navigation equipment

(G-3961)
SRIRRET AMERICA
20 Maplewood Ln (06443-2957)
P.O. Box 1338 (06443-1338)
PHONE..................................203 988-1852
McCrady Axon, *Owner*
EMP: 2
SALES (est): 20K **Privately Held**
WEB: www.shirret.com
SIC: 2273 Rugs, hand & machine made

(G-3962)
STEVENS PRINTING
289 Horse Pond Rd (06443-2402)
PHONE..................................203 245-3267
Robert Stevens, *Owner*
EMP: 2
SALES (est): 120K **Privately Held**
SIC: 2752 Commercial printing, lithographic

(G-3963)
TANGO MODEM LLC
303 Race Hill Rd (06443-1628)
PHONE..................................203 421-2245
Robert Allen, *Principal*
Michael Borsari, *Opers Staff*
Leonard Labuschagne, *Program Dir*
EMP: 5
SALES (est): 381.9K **Privately Held**
SIC: 3661 Modems

(G-3964)
TILLERMAN
28 Field Brook Rd (06443-2429)
PHONE..................................203 421-6643
EMP: 2 EST: 2014
SALES (est): 141.9K **Privately Held**
SIC: 3577 Computer peripheral equipment

(G-3965)
TWO EMS INC
782 Boston Post Rd Ste 2 (06443-3036)
PHONE..................................203 245-8211
Margaret M Sprague, *President*
Kent Sprague, *Vice Pres*
Paul David Sprague, *Admin Sec*
EMP: 2
SQ FT: 1,200
SALES (est): 203K **Privately Held**
WEB: www.two-ems.com
SIC: 2731 7334 4822 8743 Books: publishing & printing; pamphlets: publishing & printing; photocopying & duplicating services; facsimile transmission services; public relations services

(G-3966)
V CANNELLI CO LLC
120 Genesee Ln (06443-1678)
PHONE..................................203 421-4697
Victor Cannelli, *Principal*
EMP: 2
SALES (est): 136.2K **Privately Held**
SIC: 3423 Hand & edge tools

(G-3967)
VALENTINE CO LLC
60 Boston Post Rd (06443-2157)
PHONE..................................203 245-9145
Louisa Lobello,
EMP: 2
SALES (est): 152.8K **Privately Held**
SIC: 2273 Carpets, textile fiber

(G-3968)
WIRE ASSOCIATION INTL INC (PA)
Also Called: Wai
71 Bradley Rd Unit 9 (06443-2662)
P.O. Box 578, Guilford (06437-0578)
PHONE..................................203 453-2777
Brain Bouvier, *President*
David B Lavalley, *Treasurer*
Steven J Fetteroll, *Exec Dir*
EMP: 24
SQ FT: 7,000
SALES: 988.9K **Privately Held**
WEB: www.wirenet.org
SIC: 8621 2721 Professional membership organizations; magazines: publishing only, not printed on site

(G-3969)
WIRE JOURNAL INC
71 Bradley Rd Unit 9 (06443-2662)
P.O. Box 578, Guilford (06437-0578)
PHONE..................................203 453-2777
Sanford May, *Exec Dir*
EMP: 20
SQ FT: 10,000
SALES: 1.9MM
SALES (corp-wide): 988.9K **Privately Held**
WEB: www.wirenet.org
SIC: 2721 Magazines: publishing only, not printed on site
PA: The Wire Association International Inc
71 Bradley Rd Unit 9
Madison CT 06443
203 453-2777

Manchester
Hartford County

(G-3970)
1 WAY CUSTOM PRINT
61 Charter Oak St Apt D (06040-6286)
PHONE..................................860 712-0027
Chris Walker, *Principal*
EMP: 2 EST: 2015
SALES (est): 83.9K **Privately Held**
SIC: 2752 Commercial printing, lithographic

Manchester - Hartford County (G-3971) — GEOGRAPHIC SECTION

(G-3971)
3333 LLC
Also Called: Kaplan Tarps & Cargo Controls
42 Hilliard St (06042-3002)
PHONE..................860 643-1384
Nick Repay,
Justin Laraia,
EMP: 7
SQ FT: 12,000
SALES (est): 209.7K Privately Held
SIC: 7359 2394 3792 Tent & tarpaulin rental; canvas covers & drop cloths; liners & covers, fabric: made from purchased materials; convertible tops, canvas or boat: from purchased materials; pickup covers, canopies or caps

(G-3972)
A-1 SEAMLESS GUTTERS
406 Oakland St (06042-2193)
PHONE..................860 432-9118
Joe Cabral, Principal
EMP: 2 EST: 2007
SALES (est): 173.6K Privately Held
SIC: 3444 Gutters, sheet metal

(G-3973)
ABA-PGT EMPLOYEE MEDICAL TRUST
10 Gear Dr (06042-8907)
PHONE..................860 649-4591
Samuel Pierson, Principal
EMP: 2
SALES: 1.6MM Privately Held
SIC: 3089 Injection molding of plastics

(G-3974)
ABA-PGT INC (PA)
Also Called: A B A Tool & Die Div
10 Gear Dr (06042-8907)
PHONE..................860 649-4591
Samuel D Pierson, CEO
Michael J Rice, Corp Secy
Thomas R Peck, Vice Pres
Nancy Russo, Human Res Dir
EMP: 104 EST: 1944
SQ FT: 67,000
SALES (est): 30.5MM Privately Held
WEB: www.abapgt.com
SIC: 3089 3544 Injection molding of plastics; dies, plastics forming

(G-3975)
ABLE SCALE & EQUIPMENT CORP
10 Hilliard St (06042-3002)
P.O. Box 1292 (06045-1292)
PHONE..................860 646-6929
Randall Izikewicz, President
Robert Wetishefsky, Vice Pres
EMP: 4
SQ FT: 12,000
SALES: 400K Privately Held
SIC: 7699 3596 7359 Scale repair service; scales & balances, except laboratory, equipment rental & leasing

(G-3976)
ACCURATE BRAZING CORPORATION
4 Progress Dr (06042)
PHONE..................860 432-1840
Bob Sartori, Manager
Waleska Laureano, Assistant
EMP: 18
SALES (corp-wide): 3.1B Privately Held
SIC: 3398 Brazing (hardening) of metal
HQ: Accurate Brazing Corporation
36 Cote Ave Ste 5
Goffstown NH 03045

(G-3977)
ACMT INC
369 Progress Dr (06042-2296)
PHONE..................860 645-0592
Michael G Polo, President
Dan Polo, General Mgr
Paul Polo Sr, Vice Pres
Michael Cyr, Facilities Mgr
Bob Coulombe, Purchasing
EMP: 100
SQ FT: 48,000
SALES (est): 17.9MM Privately Held
WEB: www.acmtct.com
SIC: 3728 3061 3724 Aircraft parts & equipment; mechanical rubber goods; aircraft engines & engine parts

(G-3978)
ACTION INDUSTRIES
164 E Center St Ste 8 (06040-5241)
PHONE..................860 644-3020
George Hickey, Owner
EMP: 2 EST: 2010
SALES (est): 123.1K Privately Held
SIC: 3999 Manufacturing industries

(G-3979)
ADVANCE MOLD & MFG INC
Also Called: Vision Technical Molding
71 Utopia Rd (06042-2192)
PHONE..................860 432-5887
Douglas Schneider, President
Joseph Valade, Sales Staff
John Corraccio, Program Mgr
EMP: 150 EST: 1959
SQ FT: 28,500
SALES (est): 34.9MM
SALES (corp-wide): 26.2B Privately Held
WEB: www.advancemold.com
SIC: 3544 3089 Industrial molds; injection molding of plastics
HQ: Flextronics International Usa, Inc.
6201 America Center Dr
San Jose CA 95002

(G-3980)
ALLIED PRINTING SERVICES INC (PA)
1 Allied Way (06042-8933)
P.O. Box 850 (06045-0850)
PHONE..................860 643-1101
John G Sommers, President
Chuck Samar, Business Mgr
Bettina Sommers, Exec VP
Gerald Sommers, Exec VP
Mark Carter, Vice Pres
▲ EMP: 350 EST: 1950
SALES (est): 80.8MM Privately Held
SIC: 2396 2752 2759 2789 Automotive & apparel trimmings; commercial printing, offset; commercial printing; bookbinding & related work; typesetting

(G-3981)
ALLOY SPECIALTIES INCORPORATED
110 Batson Dr (06042-1694)
PHONE..................860 646-4587
Richard Ramondetta, President
Dennis P Dimauro, Vice Pres
Rob Siggia, Production
Jim Thurston, Purchasing
Steve Bissell, Engineer
EMP: 40
SQ FT: 14,500
SALES (est): 9MM Privately Held
WEB: www.alloysp.com
SIC: 3724 5051 Aircraft engines & engine parts; metals service centers & offices; steel

(G-3982)
AMERICAN BUS TELE & TECH LLC
Also Called: All Products Painting
1651 Tolland Tpke (06042-1639)
PHONE..................860 643-2200
Nancy Ferguson, Mng Member
Cliff Ferguson,
EMP: 5 EST: 1998
SQ FT: 6,000
SALES: 400K Privately Held
WEB: www.abtelephone.com
SIC: 5999 7389 3479 4226 Mobile telephones & equipment; telephone services; painting of metal products; special warehousing & storage

(G-3983)
AMERICAN REFACING CSTM CAB LLC
1 Mitchell Dr (06042-2394)
PHONE..................860 647-0868
George Warner,
EMP: 5
SQ FT: 1,800
SALES (est): 537.5K Privately Held
SIC: 2434 Wood kitchen cabinets

(G-3984)
ARM SCREEN PRINTING
307 E Center St (06040-5243)
PHONE..................860 649-6295
Alan Menasian, Owner
EMP: 1
SQ FT: 3,000
SALES: 250K Privately Held
SIC: 2759 Screen printing

(G-3985)
BAKELITE N SUMITOMO AMER INC (DH)
24 Mill St (06042-2316)
PHONE..................860 645-3851
Henny Van Dijk, President
Shintaro Ishiwata, Chairman
Kevin Provencher, Controller
Alan Houghton, Admin Sec
▲ EMP: 85 EST: 2002
SALES (est): 16MM Privately Held
WEB: www.sumitomobakelite.com
SIC: 2821 Plastics materials & resins

(G-3986)
BENEDICT M LAI
Also Called: Easy Powerful Innovations Co
125 N School St (06042-2028)
PHONE..................425 698-7267
Benedict Lai, Owner
EMP: 1
SALES (est): 63.3K Privately Held
SIC: 7372 8732 Educational computer software; educational research

(G-3987)
BRAVO LLC (PA)
Also Called: Bravo Pet Store
349 Wetherell St (06040-6349)
PHONE..................866 922-9222
David J Bogner,
EMP: 17
SALES (est): 5.6MM Privately Held
WEB: www.bravo.com
SIC: 2047 Dog food

(G-3988)
BREAD AND WINE PUBLISHING LLC
220 Charter Oak St (06040-6213)
PHONE..................860 649-3109
Frank Bausola,
EMP: 3
SQ FT: 1,500
SALES (est): 224.8K Privately Held
SIC: 2759 Commercial printing

(G-3989)
CAM GROUP LLC
130 Chapel Rd (06042-1625)
PHONE..................860 646-2378
Charles Joseph Angle,
EMP: 10
SQ FT: 2,000
SALES: 2.5MM Privately Held
WEB: www.camgroup.com
SIC: 3519 Jet propulsion engines

(G-3990)
CAMETOID TECHNOLOGIES INC
150 Colonial Rd (06042-2306)
P.O. Box 130 (06045-0130)
PHONE..................860 646-4667
John W Adams, President
Robert Sanderson, Vice Pres
Ray Berasi, Controller
Keith Kevorkian, Manager
Susanne Hilbert, Officer
EMP: 19
SQ FT: 18,000
SALES (est): 2.8MM Privately Held
WEB: www.cametoid.com
SIC: 3479 Coating of metals & formed products

(G-3991)
CARLOS WELDING AND FAB LLC
74 Bretton Rd (06042-3328)
PHONE..................860 647-8592
Carlos Diaz, Principal
EMP: 1
SALES (est): 30K Privately Held
SIC: 7692 Welding repair

(G-3992)
CARRIAGE HOUSE COMPANIES INC
42 Steeplechase Dr (06040-7067)
PHONE..................860 647-1909
EMP: 472
SALES (est): 15.4B Publicly Held
SIC: 2099 Mfg Syrups Mfg
HQ: The Carriage House Companies Inc
196 Newton St
Fredonia NY 14063
716 673-1000

(G-3993)
CERBERUS ENTERPRISE SFTWR LLC
Also Called: Insrcd
180 Porter St (06040-5440)
PHONE..................860 432-3861
Adam Shaw, Principal
EMP: 2
SALES (est): 115K Privately Held
SIC: 7372 Prepackaged software

(G-3994)
CHAMPLIN-PACKRITE INC
151 Batson Dr (06042-1624)
PHONE..................860 951-9217
Rory T Poole, President
Christine E Poole, Corp Secy
Larry Harrison, Purch Mgr
Sean T Poole, Director
EMP: 44
SQ FT: 75,000
SALES (est): 7.9MM Privately Held
SIC: 2441 2449 2653 3412 Packing cases, wood: nailed or lock corner; shipping cases, wood: nailed or lock corner; shipping cases & drums, wood: wire-bound & plywood; boxes, corrugated: made from purchased materials; metal barrels, drums & pails

(G-3995)
CHARLES J ANGELO MFG GROUP LLC
130 Chapel Rd (06042-1625)
PHONE..................860 646-2378
Charles J Angelo,
EMP: 10 EST: 2003
SQ FT: 12,000
SALES: 1.7MM Privately Held
SIC: 3544 Special dies, tools, jigs & fixtures

(G-3996)
CLAY FURNITURE INDUSTRIES INC
41 Chapel St (06042-3034)
PHONE..................860 643-7580
Julie Clay, President
Richard F Clay Jr, Vice Pres
EMP: 10
SQ FT: 15,000
SALES (est): 1.2MM Privately Held
WEB: www.clayfurniture.com
SIC: 2521 Cabinets, office: wood

(G-3997)
COMPOSITES INC
485 Middle Tpke E (06040-3735)
PHONE..................860 646-1698
Donald K Kuehl, President
Paul De Kanel, Director
Mary C Coughlin, Admin Sec
EMP: 1
SQ FT: 3,000
SALES (est): 169.9K Privately Held
SIC: 2295 2819 8732 Tape, varnished: plastic & other coated (except magnetic); boron compounds, not from mines; research services, except laboratory

(G-3998)
CONNECTCUT CRNIAL FCIAL IMGERY
483 Middle Tpke W Ste 102 (06040-3864)
PHONE..................860 643-2940
Joel Rosenlicht, Principal
EMP: 3

GEOGRAPHIC SECTION
Manchester - Hartford County (G-4029)

SALES (est): 302.4K **Privately Held**
SIC: 2844 Oral preparations

(G-3999)
CORGYN WOODWORKS
152 Hawthorne St (06042-3023)
PHONE....................860 402-8273
EMP: 1
SALES (est): 54.1K **Privately Held**
SIC: 2431 Millwork

(G-4000)
CREATIVE MOBILE SYSTEMS INC
189 Adams St (06042-1919)
P.O. Box 8198 (06040-0198)
PHONE....................860 649-6272
Dominic Acquarulo Jr, *President*
Edward Izzo, *President*
Richard Lumpkin, *Vice Pres*
Brian L Smith, *Vice Pres*
EMP: 6
SQ FT: 8,000
SALES (est): 1.2MM **Privately Held**
WEB: www.cmssystem.com
SIC: 3589 Food warming equipment, commercial

(G-4001)
CROCHETED BY BIANCA
7 Pine Hill St (06042-3111)
PHONE....................860 916-2925
EMP: 2
SALES (est): 104.2K **Privately Held**
SIC: 2399 Hand woven & crocheted products

(G-4002)
CUSTOM TS
194 Bucklnd Hills Dr 10 Ste 1018 (06042)
PHONE....................860 644-1514
EMP: 2
SALES (est): 73.2K **Privately Held**
SIC: 2759 Commercial Printing

(G-4003)
DAVID DEREWIANKA
459 Dennison Rdg (06040-6839)
PHONE....................860 649-1983
David Derewianka, *Principal*
EMP: 3
SALES (est): 114.3K **Privately Held**
SIC: 3451 Screw machine products

(G-4004)
DAWN ENTERPRISES LLC
275 Progress Dr Ste B (06042-2211)
PHONE....................860 646-8200
Sarah Anderson, *Sales Staff*
Richard Sheldon,
Mike Bergeron,
Chad Glucksman,
◆ EMP: 9 EST: 1978
SALES (est): 1.7MM **Privately Held**
WEB: www.godawn.com
SIC: 3272 Cast stone, concrete

(G-4005)
DEROSA PRINTING COMPANY INC
485 Middle Tpke E (06040-3735)
P.O. Box 1567 (06045-1567)
PHONE....................860 646-1698
Richard De Rosa, *President*
EMP: 15 EST: 1980
SQ FT: 7,000
SALES (est): 2.1MM **Privately Held**
SIC: 2752 7334 Commercial printing, offset; photocopying & duplicating services

(G-4006)
DESIGNS BY DIANA
14 Ensign St (06040-4806)
PHONE....................860 649-1812
Diana Burnham, *Principal*
EMP: 1
SALES (est): 92.8K **Privately Held**
SIC: 3961 Costume jewelry

(G-4007)
DEVRAJAN GOVENDER
190 John Olds Dr Apt 112 (06042-8818)
PHONE....................678 429-3408
Dev Govender, *Principal*
EMP: 2 EST: 2018

SALES (est): 85.9K **Privately Held**
SIC: 3571 Electronic computers

(G-4008)
DIAMOND BREWING SERVICE
52 Hilltop Dr (06042-3442)
PHONE....................860 508-0013
Theodore Bolduc, *Owner*
EMP: 2
SALES (est): 140K **Privately Held**
SIC: 3556 Brewers' & maltsters' machinery

(G-4009)
DIVINE TREASURE
404 Middle Tpke W (06040-3824)
PHONE....................860 643-2552
Diane Wagemann, *Owner*
EMP: 5
SALES (est): 566.1K **Privately Held**
SIC: 2066 Chocolate & cocoa products

(G-4010)
DONWELL COMPANY
130 Sheldon Rd (06042-2388)
P.O. Box 906 (06045-0906)
PHONE....................860 649-5374
Tracey B Sherman, *President*
Jeffrey Sherman, *Treasurer*
Dean A Sherman, *Director*
EMP: 44 EST: 1957
SQ FT: 23,000
SALES (est): 5.3MM **Privately Held**
WEB: www.donwell.com
SIC: 3479 Coating of metals with plastic or resins; coating of metals & formed products

(G-4011)
DREAMER SOFTWARE LLC
17 Mckinley St (06040-4813)
PHONE....................860 645-1240
Christopher A Walnum, *Manager*
EMP: 5
SALES (est): 348.3K **Privately Held**
SIC: 7372 Prepackaged software

(G-4012)
DSW INC
120 Slater St (06042-1648)
PHONE....................860 644-6200
EMP: 13
SALES (corp-wide): 3.1B **Publicly Held**
SIC: 5661 5139 3149 Custom & orthopedic shoes; boots; athletic shoes, except rubber or plastic
PA: Designer Brands Inc.
810 Dsw Dr
Columbus OH 43219
614 237-7100

(G-4013)
EA PATTEN CO LLC
303 Wetherell St (06040-6349)
PHONE....................860 649-2851
David W Pinette, *President*
Forest E Patten, *Chairman*
Kevin Dougan, *QC Mgr*
Guscyna Davila, *Controller*
Rauls Ramans, *Marketing Mgr*
▼ EMP: 95 EST: 1945
SQ FT: 40,000
SALES (est): 28.7MM **Privately Held**
WEB: www.eapatten.com
SIC: 3498 3599 Tube fabricating (contract bending & shaping); amusement park equipment

(G-4014)
ELITE ENGRAVING & AWARDS
71 Woodland St B (06042-3009)
PHONE....................860 643-7459
Barry Stearns, *Owner*
EMP: 1
SQ FT: 1,100
SALES (est): 73K **Privately Held**
SIC: 7389 3993 5999 Engraving service; signs & advertising specialties; trophies & plaques

(G-4015)
EMPIRE INDUSTRIES INC
180 Olcott St (06040-2647)
PHONE....................860 647-1431
Mark Schauster, *President*
John Feeney, *Vice Pres*
Richard Schauster, *Treasurer*

▲ EMP: 37
SQ FT: 55,000
SALES (est): 10.2MM **Privately Held**
WEB: www.copperguard.com
SIC: 3469 Metal stampings

(G-4016)
FASTSIGNS OF HARTFORD
1540 Pleasant Valley Rd D (06042-8760)
PHONE....................860 644-5700
Michael Melillo, *Owner*
EMP: 2
SALES (est): 268.7K **Privately Held**
SIC: 3993 Signs & advertising specialties

(G-4017)
FEDORA OPTICAL INC
236 N Main St (06042-2004)
PHONE....................860 646-3577
Peter Fedora, *President*
Dani Marie Fedora, *Vice Pres*
EMP: 3
SQ FT: 2,000
SALES (est): 364.4K **Privately Held**
SIC: 5995 3827 Opticians; contact lenses, prescription; lenses, optical: all types except ophthalmic

(G-4018)
FLUID DYNAMICS LLC (PA)
192 Sheldon Rd (06042-2319)
P.O. Box 2468 (06045-2468)
PHONE....................860 791-6325
Tom Plourde, *General Mgr*
Judd Cooper, *COO*
Krista Cooper, *Opers Mgr*
Jeremy Bride, *Sales Staff*
Russ Neale, *Sales Executive*
EMP: 5
SQ FT: 9,000
SALES (est): 2.4MM **Privately Held**
WEB: www.flddyn.com
SIC: 3492 5085 Hose & tube fittings & assemblies, hydraulic/pneumatic; hose, belting & packing; industrial fittings

(G-4019)
FOWLERS STEEL & WELDING
Also Called: Fowler's Steel Store
405 New State Rd (06042-1805)
PHONE....................860 647-7641
Wayne Fowler, *Owner*
EMP: 1
SQ FT: 2,000
SALES (est): 80K **Privately Held**
SIC: 7692 Welding repair

(G-4020)
FUSION CROSS-MEDIA LLC
520 Center St Manchester (06040)
PHONE....................860 647-8367
Zachary Schwartz, *Principal*
Joanne Coan, *Project Mgr*
EMP: 1
SALES (est): 108.2K **Privately Held**
SIC: 8742 7389 7336 7331 Marketing consulting services; design services; commercial art & graphic design; mailing service; commercial printing, lithographic

(G-4021)
GENERAL DIGITAL CORP
160 Chapel Rd (06042-8929)
PHONE....................860 645-2200
Bryan Gudrian, *Principal*
James Grant, *Sr Software Eng*
EMP: 2
SALES (est): 175.3K **Privately Held**
SIC: 3571 Electronic computers

(G-4022)
GLOBAL AMERICAN PUBLISHERS LLC
5 Orchard St (06040-5015)
PHONE....................860 432-7589
Mirza M Barlas, *Principal*
EMP: 1
SALES (est): 57.1K **Privately Held**
SIC: 2741 Miscellaneous publishing

(G-4023)
GREEN MANOR CORPORATION (PA)
Also Called: Journal Inquirer
306 Progress Dr (06042-9011)
PHONE....................860 643-8111
Neil H Ellis, *President*
Elizabeth Ellis, *Treasurer*
Rudy Rudewicz, *VP Finance*
Roseann Read, *Accounts Exec*
Deborah J Ellis, *Director*
EMP: 280 EST: 1950
SQ FT: 36,000
SALES (est): 34.8MM **Privately Held**
SIC: 2711 Commercial printing & newspaper publishing combined; newspapers, publishing & printing

(G-4024)
GUY LINDSAY
Also Called: Lindsay Total Graphics
307 E Center St (06040-5243)
PHONE....................860 646-7865
Guy Lindsay, *Owner*
EMP: 2
SALES (est): 100K **Privately Held**
SIC: 2791 Typesetting

(G-4025)
HARRIS ENTERPRISE CORP
Also Called: Harris Woodworking
80 Colonial Rd (06042-2310)
P.O. Box 266, Wallingford (06492-0266)
PHONE....................860 649-4663
David Harris, *President*
Robert Osborne, *CFO*
John Harris, *Admin Sec*
EMP: 40
SQ FT: 24,380
SALES (est): 4.9MM **Privately Held**
SIC: 5211 2499 2431 Lumber products; decorative wood & woodwork; millwork

(G-4026)
HARRIS WOOD PRODUCTS INC
35 Country Club Dr (06040-6601)
PHONE....................860 649-7936
David M Harris, *Principal*
EMP: 1
SALES (est): 61.2K **Privately Held**
SIC: 2493 Reconstituted wood products

(G-4027)
HHC LLC
Also Called: Hydrofera
340 Progress Dr (06042-2280)
PHONE....................860 456-0677
Tom Rallo,
Thomas Drury,
EMP: 20
SQ FT: 10,000
SALES (est): 4.5MM **Privately Held**
WEB: www.hydrofera.com
SIC: 3086 Plastics foam products

(G-4028)
HIGHLAND MANUFACTURING INC
5 Glen Rd Ste 4 (06040-6793)
PHONE....................860 646-5142
Christian Wqueen, *President*
John Whitney, *Treasurer*
EMP: 28
SQ FT: 16,000
SALES (est): 6MM **Privately Held**
SIC: 3545 3544 Gauges (machine tool accessories); special dies & tools

(G-4029)
HOSMER MOUNTAIN BTLG CO INC
Also Called: Hosmer Mountain Soda Shack
15 Spencer St (06040-8151)
PHONE....................860 643-6923
John Judivic, *Manager*
EMP: 1
SQ FT: 800
SALES (corp-wide): 526.1K **Privately Held**
SIC: 5499 2086 Soft drinks; water, pasteurized: packaged in cans, bottles, etc.
PA: Hosmer Mountain Bottling Co., Inc.
217 Mountain St
Willimantic CT
860 423-1555

Manchester - Hartford County (G-4030)

(G-4030)
HYDROFERA LLC
340 Progress Dr (06042-2280)
PHONE 860 456-0677
Tom Drury, *Principal*
EMP: 65
SALES (est): 103K Privately Held
SIC: 3086 Plastics foam products

(G-4031)
ILLINOIS TOOL WORKS INC
ITW Graphics
375 New State Rd (06042-1818)
PHONE 860 646-8153
Joe Tetrault, *Opers Staff*
Amy Velasquez, *Accounting Mgr*
Karl Kisselle, *Sales Mgr*
James Moore, *Technical Staff*
EMP: 145
SALES (corp-wide): 14.7B Publicly Held
SIC: 2672 Adhesive papers, labels or tapes; from purchased material
PA: Illinois Tool Works Inc.
155 Harlem Ave
Glenview IL 60025
847 724-7500

(G-4032)
INDEPENDENCE ENTERPRISES LLC
Also Called: Noble Army, The
235 Cougar Dr (06040-6383)
PHONE 774 549-8153
Travis Miller, *Manager*
EMP: 1
SALES (est): 56.4K Privately Held
SIC: 3482 Small arms ammunition

(G-4033)
INFORMATION TECH INTL CORP
440 Oakland St (06042-5102)
PHONE 860 648-2570
Clive Thomas, *President*
Kenneth Koos, *Admin Sec*
EMP: 7
SQ FT: 5,000
SALES (est): 370.9K Privately Held
SIC: 7372 7379 Prepackaged software; computer related consulting services

(G-4034)
ISWISS CORPORATION
161 Sanrico Dr (06042-2224)
PHONE 860 327-4200
Zivorad M Tomic, *President*
EMP: 2
SALES (est): 85.2K Privately Held
SIC: 3545 Collets (machine tool accessories)

(G-4035)
J & H MACHINE COMPANY LLC
31 Mitchell Dr (06042-2317)
PHONE 860 643-6096
Terry Culvey, *President*
Paul Inkel, *Exec VP*
EMP: 2
SALES (est): 252.6K Privately Held
SIC: 3324 Aerospace investment castings, ferrous

(G-4036)
J & L MACHINE CO INC
62 Batson Dr (06042-1657)
PHONE 860 649-3539
Marian Jusko, *President*
Joann Rund, *General Mgr*
Sean Keane, *QC Mgr*
Barbara Jusko, *Admin Sec*
EMP: 49
SQ FT: 30,000
SALES (est): 10.8MM Privately Held
WEB: www.jlmachineco.com
SIC: 3599 Machine shop, jobbing & repair

(G-4037)
J G TAGLIERI
825 Main St (06040-6006)
PHONE 860 645-1060
J Taglieri, *Owner*
EMP: 1
SALES (est): 59.8K Privately Held
SIC: 7641 2512 Upholstery work; upholstered household furniture

(G-4038)
JIM KEPHART WOODTURNING
85 Hilliard St (06042-7335)
PHONE 860 643-9431
Jim Kephart, *Owner*
EMP: 1 **EST:** 2000
SALES (est): 53K Privately Held
SIC: 2499 Carved & turned wood

(G-4039)
JIM PRESS HOME IMPROVEMENT
47 Dougherty St (06040-4941)
PHONE 860 416-4494
James Press, *Principal*
EMP: 1
SALES (est): 59K Privately Held
SIC: 2741 Miscellaneous publishing

(G-4040)
JOURNAL PUBLISHING COMPANY INC
Also Called: Journal Inquirer
306 Progress Dr (06042-9011)
P.O. Box 510 (06045-0510)
PHONE 860 646-0500
Elizabeth Ellis, *President*
EMP: 560
SQ FT: 36,000
SALES (est): 34.8MM Privately Held
SIC: 2711 Newspapers, publishing & printing
PA: Green Manor Corporation
306 Progress Dr
Manchester CT 06042
860 643-8111

(G-4041)
K & G CORP
Also Called: R T G
219 Adams St (06042-1985)
P.O. Box 8267 (06040-0267)
PHONE 860 643-1133
Kenneth Wolf, *President*
Gail Wolf, *Vice Pres*
EMP: 10 **EST:** 1955
SQ FT: 6,000
SALES (est): 1.1MM Privately Held
WEB: www.kgcorp.com
SIC: 3479 3251 Coating of metals & formed products; fireproofing tile, clay

(G-4042)
K&L ENTERPRISES
25 Raymond Rd (06040-4515)
PHONE 860 645-7257
K Reiss, *Principal*
EMP: 1
SALES (est): 75.9K Privately Held
SIC: 3531 Ballast distributors

(G-4043)
KAGE POLY PRODUCTS LLC
Also Called: Kage Co
96 Elm St (06040-5932)
PHONE 860 646-8228
William E Hayes, *Mng Member*
EMP: 1 **EST:** 1934
SQ FT: 5,000
SALES (est): 225K Privately Held
WEB: www.kageco.com
SIC: 2673 Plastic bags: made from purchased materials

(G-4044)
KENNETH R CARSON
34 Cole St (06042-3621)
PHONE 860 247-2707
Fax: 860 247-2707
EMP: 4
SALES (est): 250K Privately Held
SIC: 3911 Mfg Precious Metal Jewelry

(G-4045)
KENYON WOODWORKING
85 Hilliard St (06042-7335)
PHONE 860 432-4641
Robert M Kenyon III, *Owner*
EMP: 2
SALES (est): 257.5K Privately Held
SIC: 2431 Millwork

(G-4046)
L M GILL WELDING AND MFR LLC (PA)
Also Called: Bhs-Torin
1422 Tolland Tpke (06042-1636)
PHONE 860 647-9931
Richard A Brink, *President*
Gale Brink, *Admin Sec*
EMP: 14 **EST:** 1978
SALES (est): 8.3MM Privately Held
SIC: 3542 5084 3549 Spring winding & forming machines; industrial machinery & equipment; metalworking machinery

(G-4047)
L M GILL WELDING AND MFR LLC
Also Called: Lm Gill Welding & Mfg
1422 Tolland Tpke (06042-1636)
P.O. Box 8185 (06040-0185)
PHONE 860 647-9931
Gale Brink, *Admin Sec*
EMP: 20
SALES (corp-wide): 8.3MM Privately Held
SIC: 7692 3728 Welding repair; aircraft parts & equipment
PA: L M Gill Welding And Manufacturer Llc
1422 Tolland Tpke
Manchester CT 06042
860 647-9931

(G-4048)
LINGARD CABINET CO LLC
540 N Main St Ste 2 (06042-1998)
PHONE 860 647-9886
Dan Lingard,
Carol Lingard, *Admin Sec*
EMP: 3
SALES (est): 300K Privately Held
SIC: 2541 2431 5211 Cabinets, except refrigerated: show, display, etc.: wood; millwork; millwork & lumber

(G-4049)
LM GILL WELDING & MFG LLC
1422 Tolland Tpke (06042-1636)
PHONE 860 647-9931
Richard A Brink, *Owner*
Harry Saddack,
EMP: 21
SQ FT: 25,000
SALES (est): 3MM Privately Held
SIC: 7692 3728 3731 Welding repair; aircraft parts & equipment; commercial cargo ships, building & repairing; military ships, building & repairing; commercial passenger ships, building & repairing

(G-4050)
LYDALL INC (PA)
1 Colonial Rd (06042-2307)
P.O. Box 151 (06045-0151)
PHONE 860 646-1233
Marc T Giles, *Ch of Bd*
Dale G Barnhart, *President*
Diane Beaudoin, *President*
Robert Junker, *President*
David Glenn, *Vice Pres*
EMP: 50
SALES: 785.9MM Publicly Held
WEB: www.lydall.com
SIC: 2297 3053 2899 2631 Nonwoven fabrics; gaskets, all materials; insulating compounds; automobile board; filters: oil, fuel & air, motor vehicle; oil strainers, motor vehicle; filters, air: furnaces, air conditioning equipment, etc.

(G-4051)
LYDALL THERMAL ACOUSTICAL INC
1 Colonial Rd (06042-2307)
P.O. Box 151 (06045-0151)
PHONE 860 646-1233
Dale G Barnhart, *CEO*
Robert K Julian, *President*
William M Lachenmeyer, *Vice Pres*
James Laughlan, *Vice Pres*
Chad McDaniel, *Vice Pres*
EMP: 6
SALES (est): 1.8MM Privately Held
SIC: 2297 Nonwoven fabrics

(G-4052)
MANCHESTER MOLDING AND MFG CO
96 Sheldon Rd (06042-2399)
PHONE 860 643-2141
Allan Griffin, *President*
Joseph Nadeau, *Owner*
Joanne Scanlon, *Vice Pres*
EMP: 50
SQ FT: 27,500
SALES (est): 9.5MM Privately Held
SIC: 3089 3544 Injection molding of plastics; special dies & tools

(G-4053)
MANCHESTER PACKING COMPANY INC
Also Called: Bogner's
349 Wetherell St (06040-6349)
PHONE 860 646-5000
Robert E Bogner, *President*
Kurt Bogner, *Vice Pres*
David Bogner, *Admin Sec*
▲ **EMP:** 60
SQ FT: 19,000
SALES (est): 10.7MM Privately Held
WEB: www.manchestersilkworms.org
SIC: 2011 5147 5421 2013 Meat packing plants; meats, cured or smoked; meat markets, including freezer provisioners; sausages & other prepared meats

(G-4054)
MANDEE
194 Buckland Hills Dr (06042-8705)
PHONE 860 644-2128
David Faircloth, *COO*
Carmen Andrade, *Sales Staff*
Danielle Suto, *Branch Mgr*
Joe Hollywood, *CTO*
Robert Edmond, *Software Dev*
EMP: 2
SALES (est): 49.3K Privately Held
SIC: 5621 5137 2389 Women's clothing stores; women's & children's clothing; apparel & accessories

(G-4055)
MANUSCRITOS PUBLISHING LLC
9 Coughlin Rd (06040-6671)
PHONE 860 432-9519
EMP: 1
SALES (est): 37.5K Privately Held
SIC: 2741 Miscellaneous publishing

(G-4056)
MARK D TWEEDIE DDS
Also Called: Tweedie Dental Arts
566 Center St (06040-3919)
PHONE 860 649-0436
Lori Kula, *Manager*
Mark D Tweedie DDS,
EMP: 4
SQ FT: 3,000
SALES (est): 345.9K Privately Held
SIC: 8072 3843 Dental laboratories; dental equipment & supplies

(G-4057)
MINUTEMAN PRESS
757 Main St (06040-5102)
PHONE 860 646-0601
EMP: 2
SALES (est): 83.9K Privately Held
SIC: 2752 Commercial printing, lithographic

(G-4058)
NE WOOD WORKS LLC
79 Lockwood St (06042-2939)
PHONE 860 883-3106
Thomas Pritchard, *Principal*
EMP: 2 **EST:** 2008
SALES (est): 146.9K Privately Held
SIC: 2431 Millwork

(G-4059)
NETSOURCE INC (PA)
260 Progress Dr (06042-9001)
PHONE 860 649-6000
Thor Swanson, *President*
Rob Giannitti, *Vice Pres*
Shannon Spence, *Financial Exec*
Kevin Ladabouche, *Sales Mgr*

Ben Godin, *Accounts Mgr*
EMP: 55
SALES (est): 10.7MM **Privately Held**
WEB: www.netsource-inc.com
SIC: 3496 Miscellaneous fabricated wire products

(G-4060)
NEW DEAL LLC
194 Buckland Hills Dr # 2225 (06042-8705)
PHONE..........................860 648-9567
Diane Kuronya, *Principal*
EMP: 1
SALES (est): 61.8K **Privately Held**
SIC: 2389 Apparel & accessories

(G-4061)
NORTHEAST DOUBLE DISC GRIND LL
31 Mitchell Dr (06042-2317)
PHONE..........................860 643-6096
EMP: 2 **EST:** 2008
SALES (est): 128.8K **Privately Held**
SIC: 3599 Mfg Industrial Machinery

(G-4062)
NOVEL TEES SCREEN PRTG EMB LLC
81 Tolland Tpke (06042-1737)
PHONE..........................860 643-6008
Connie Vandermyn,
EMP: 10 **EST:** 2016
SALES (est): 479.6K **Privately Held**
SIC: 2759 Screen printing

(G-4063)
NOVEL-TEES UNLIMITED LLC
81 Tolland Tpke (06042-1737)
PHONE..........................860 643-6008
Chet Dimovski, *President*
EMP: 3
SALES: 200K **Privately Held**
SIC: 2759 Screen printing

(G-4064)
NZYMSYS INC
642 Hilliard St Ste 1208 (06042-2700)
P.O. Box 840, Glastonbury (06033-0840)
PHONE..........................877 729-4190
John Fantry, *Vice Pres*
David Bloom, *Manager*
EMP: 3 **EST:** 2008
SALES: 200K **Privately Held**
SIC: 2833 Medicinal chemicals

(G-4065)
OCONNELL INDUSTRIES INC
20 Tolland Tpke (06042-1763)
PHONE..........................860 508-7052
David O'Connell, *Principal*
EMP: 1
SALES (est): 47.6K **Privately Held**
SIC: 3999 Manufacturing industries

(G-4066)
PARADIGM MANCHESTER INC
Also Called: Paradigm Precision
203 Sheldon Rd Bldg 2 (06042-2318)
PHONE..........................860 646-4048
Tom Polo, *Manager*
EMP: 100
SQ FT: 17,000
SALES (corp-wide): 368.2MM **Privately Held**
WEB: www.dgtmfg.com
SIC: 3444 3728 Sheet metal specialties, not stamped; aircraft parts & equipment
HQ: Manchester Paradigm Inc
967 Parker St
Manchester CT 06042
860 646-4048

(G-4067)
PARADIGM MANCHESTER INC
Also Called: Paradigm Precision
186 Adams St S Bldg 3 (06040)
PHONE..........................860 646-4048
Howard Miller, *CEO*
EMP: 191
SQ FT: 59,000
SALES (corp-wide): 368.2MM **Privately Held**
WEB: www.dgtmfg.com
SIC: 3444 3728 Sheet metal specialties, not stamped; aircraft parts & equipment
HQ: Manchester Paradigm Inc
967 Parker St
Manchester CT 06042
860 646-4048

(G-4068)
PARADIGM MANCHESTER INC (DH)
Also Called: Paradigm Precision
967 Parker St (06042-2208)
PHONE..........................860 646-4048
Michael Grunza, *President*
James Donahu, *President*
William W Booth, *Vice Pres*
Steve Lindsey, *Vice Pres*
Rita Lei, *CFO*
▲ **EMP:** 500
SQ FT: 66,000
SALES (est): 172.7MM
SALES (corp-wide): 368.2MM **Privately Held**
WEB: www.dgtmfg.com
SIC: 3728 Aircraft assemblies, subassemblies & parts

(G-4069)
PARADIGM MANCHESTER INC
Also Called: Dynamic Gunver Technologies
255 Sheldon Rd Bldg 4 (06042-2322)
P.O. Box 240 (06045-0240)
PHONE..........................860 649-2888
Howard Miller, *Ch of Bd*
EMP: 247
SALES (corp-wide): 368.2MM **Privately Held**
WEB: www.dgtmfg.com
SIC: 3444 3462 3429 3398 Sheet metal specialties, not stamped; iron & steel forgings; manufactured hardware (general); metal heat treating; secondary nonferrous metals; cold finishing of steel shapes
HQ: Manchester Paradigm Inc
967 Parker St
Manchester CT 06042
860 646-4048

(G-4070)
PARADIGM MANCHESTER INC
151 Sheldon Rd (06042-2318)
PHONE..........................860 646-4048
Howard Miller, *Ch of Bd*
EMP: 7
SALES (corp-wide): 368.2MM **Privately Held**
WEB: www.dgtmfg.com
SIC: 3444 Sheet metal specialties, not stamped
HQ: Manchester Paradigm Inc
967 Parker St
Manchester CT 06042
860 646-4048

(G-4071)
PARADIGM PRCISION HOLDINGS LLC
967 Parker St (06042-2208)
PHONE..........................860 649-2888
EMP: 4
SALES (corp-wide): 368.2MM **Privately Held**
SIC: 3469 Machine parts, stamped or pressed metal
HQ: Paradigm Precision Holdings, Llc
404 W Guadalupe Rd
Tempe AZ 85283

(G-4072)
PARAGON TOOL COMPANY INC
121 Adams St S (06040)
P.O. Box 8168 (06040-0168)
PHONE..........................860 647-9935
Valdis Klavins, *President*
Mark Whitney, *General Mgr*
John Zemzars, *Vice Pres*
Lorraine Amaio, *Manager*
EMP: 8
SQ FT: 7,400
SALES (est): 1.4MM **Privately Held**
SIC: 3544 3728 Special dies & tools; aircraft parts & equipment

(G-4073)
PARAMOUNT MACHINE COMPANY INC
138 Sanrico Dr (06042-9008)
PHONE..........................860 643-5549
Andrew Djiounas, *CEO*
Nick Djiounas, *President*
Steve Djiounas, *Vice Pres*
Ken Alexander, *Mfg Spvr*
Leah Farren, *Purchasing*
EMP: 50 **EST:** 1976
SQ FT: 46,000
SALES: 5.4MM **Privately Held**
WEB: www.paramountmachineco.com
SIC: 3599 Machine shop, jobbing & repair

(G-4074)
PAS TECHNOLOGIES INC
Also Called: Bolton Aerospace
321 Progress Dr (06042-2296)
PHONE..........................860 649-2727
EMP: 26 **Privately Held**
SIC: 3728 Ailerons, aircraft
HQ: Pas Technologies Inc.
1234 Atlantic Ave
North Kansas City MO 64116

(G-4075)
PERISTERE LLC
Also Called: Recovery Zone
95 Hilliard St (06042-3001)
PHONE..........................860 783-5301
Bruce Peristere, *Mng Member*
EMP: 4
SALES (est): 383.7K **Privately Held**
SIC: 2221 2522 Blanketings, manmade fiber; upholstery, tapestry & wall covering fabrics; wallcases, office: except wood

(G-4076)
PRAXAIR SURFACE TECH INC
1366 Tolland Tpke (06042-8903)
PHONE..........................860 646-0700
John Whalen, *Manager*
EMP: 80 **Privately Held**
WEB: www.sermatech.com
SIC: 3479 3548 Coating of metals & formed products; coating, rust preventive; hot dip coating of metals or formed products; electric welding equipment
HQ: Praxair Surface Technologies, Inc.
1500 Polco St
Indianapolis IN 46222
317 240-2500

(G-4077)
QUANAH SCENTS LLC
147 Tonica Spring Trl (06040-6735)
PHONE..........................888 849-2016
Suzanne Tanguay, *President*
EMP: 1
SALES (est): 51.9K **Privately Held**
SIC: 2834 Lip balms

(G-4078)
R R DONNELLEY & SONS COMPANY
151 Redstone Rd (06042-8754)
PHONE..........................860 649-5570
Mark Angelson, *CEO*
EMP: 17
SALES (corp-wide): 6.8B **Publicly Held**
SIC: 2759 2752 2732 7331 Commercial printing; letterpress printing; commercial printing, offset; books: printing & binding; direct mail advertising services; graphic arts & related design; catalogs: gravure printing, not published on site
PA: R. R. Donnelley & Sons Company
35 W Wacker Dr
Chicago IL 60601
312 326-8000

(G-4079)
R WOODWORKING LARSON INC
192 Sheldon Rd (06042-2319)
PHONE..........................860 646-7904
Richard F Larson, *President*
Linda M Larson, *Admin Sec*
EMP: 20
SQ FT: 10,000
SALES (est): 1.6MM **Privately Held**
SIC: 2431 Millwork

(G-4080)
R&M SERVICE
1 Shady Ln (06042-1659)
PHONE..........................860 645-7771
Robert Mack, *Owner*
EMP: 1
SALES (est): 71.7K **Privately Held**
SIC: 1389 Oil field services

(G-4081)
RADIUS MILL WORK
Also Called: Radius Millworks
22 Olcott Dr (06040-2709)
P.O. Box 8092 (06040-0092)
PHONE..........................860 645-1036
EMP: 1
SALES (est): 110K **Privately Held**
SIC: 2431 Mfg Millwork

(G-4082)
RAINBOW GRAPHICS INC
118 Adams St S (06040)
PHONE..........................860 646-8997
Fred Cask, *President*
Lisa Evans, *Sales Staff*
EMP: 6
SQ FT: 5,000
SALES: 600K **Privately Held**
SIC: 2396 2759 2395 Fabric printing & stamping; commercial printing; embroidery products, except schiffli machine

(G-4083)
ROYAL ICE CREAM COMPANY INC (PA)
27 Warren St (06040-6500)
PHONE..........................860 649-5358
James S Orfitelli, *President*
Cynthia L Orfitelli, *Admin Sec*
▲ **EMP:** 11
SQ FT: 12,000
SALES (est): 1.7MM **Privately Held**
WEB: www.royalicecream.com
SIC: 2024 Ice cream & ice milk

(G-4084)
ROYAL ICE CREAM COMPANY INC
16 Warren St (06040-6534)
PHONE..........................860 649-5358
EMP: 1
SALES (corp-wide): 1.7MM **Privately Held**
SIC: 2024 Ice cream & ice milk
PA: The Royal Ice Cream Company Incorporated
27 Warren St
Manchester CT 06040
860 649-5358

(G-4085)
SATELLITE AEROSPACE INC
240 Chapel Rd (06042-1629)
P.O. Box 1077 (06045-1077)
PHONE..........................860 643-2771
Mark Knec, *President*
Frances Lynch, *Corp Secy*
Debbie Kurker, *Prdtn Mgr*
John Lynch, *Prdtn Mgr*
Mary Lozada, *QC Mgr*
EMP: 22 **EST:** 1975
SQ FT: 13,000
SALES (est): 4.7MM **Privately Held**
SIC: 3469 Stamping metal for the trade

(G-4086)
SAZACKS INC
Also Called: PIP Printing
520 Center St (06040-3936)
PHONE..........................860 647-8367
Larry Schwartz, *President*
Bernice Schwartz, *Vice Pres*
EMP: 5
SQ FT: 4,000
SALES (est): 1.1MM **Privately Held**
WEB: www.pipmanchester.com
SIC: 2752 7334 Commercial printing, offset; photocopying & duplicating services

(G-4087)
SCAN-OPTICS LLC
169 Progress Dr (06042-2242)
PHONE..........................860 645-7878
Thomas Rice, *CEO*
Jerry D Thomas, *President*

Manchester - Hartford County (G-4088)

Paul Yantus,
EMP: 99
SALES (est): 13MM **Privately Held**
SIC: 3577 Optical scanning devices

(G-4088)
SEMIOTICS LLC
Also Called: FASTSIGNS
1540 Pleasant Valley Rd D (06042-8760)
PHONE 860 644-5700
Michael Melillo, *Owner*
EMP: 4
SALES: 757.4K **Privately Held**
SIC: 3993 Signs & advertising specialties

(G-4089)
SIGNS OF ALL KINDS
227 Progress Dr Ste A (06042-2278)
PHONE 860 649-1989
John Prusak, *Owner*
EMP: 4
SALES (est): 485.6K **Privately Held**
SIC: 3993 Signs, not made in custom sign painting shops

(G-4090)
SPARTAN AEROSPACE LLC
41 Progress Dr (06042-2293)
PHONE 860 533-7500
Allan Lehrer, *President*
Jaime Miller, *Vice Pres*
Wayne Thibodeau, *Vice Pres*
Victoria Zita, *Purch Mgr*
Lionel Andujar, *QC Mgr*
EMP: 89
SQ FT: 69,000
SALES (est): 13.8MM **Privately Held**
SIC: 3724 3544 3469 3769 Aircraft engines & engine parts; special dies & tools; metal stampings; guided missile & space vehicle parts & auxiliary equipment

(G-4091)
SPECIALTY SHOP INC
18 Sanrico Dr (06042-2225)
PHONE 860 647-1477
Hector Alzugaray Jr, *President*
Manny Rodrigues, *Vice Pres*
Hector Alzugaray Sr, *Treasurer*
EMP: 7
SQ FT: 15,000
SALES (est): 1.2MM **Privately Held**
WEB: www.gacoast.com
SIC: 2434 2541 Wood kitchen cabinets; counter & sink tops

(G-4092)
SPENCER STREET INC
Also Called: Dunkin' Donuts
1205 Tolland Tpke (06042-1666)
PHONE 860 647-2955
Anna Mederios, *President*
EMP: 5
SALES (est): 199.6K **Privately Held**
SIC: 5461 2051 Doughnuts; doughnuts, except frozen

(G-4093)
ST PETER WOODWORKS
120 Waddell Rd (06040-4731)
PHONE 860 816-0455
EMP: 2
SALES (est): 166.7K **Privately Held**
SIC: 2431 Millwork

(G-4094)
STANDARD WASHER & MAT INC
299 Progress Dr (06042-2211)
P.O. Box 368 (06045-0368)
PHONE 860 643-5125
Carl Eckblom, *President*
Brian Eckblom, *Vice Pres*
Robyn Willmore, *Purch Mgr*
Linda Lestini, *Sales Mgr*
Richard Rosinald, *Supervisor*
EMP: 20
SQ FT: 15,000
SALES: 2.5MM **Privately Held**
WEB: www.standardwasher.com
SIC: 3069 3089 3053 Washers, rubber; washers, plastic; gaskets, all materials

(G-4095)
STEPHENS PIPE & STEEL LLC
776 N Main St (06042-1989)
PHONE 877 777-8721
Donna Shaw, *VP Finance*
Peggy Adams, *Sales Staff*
Debbie Bray, *Sales Staff*
Marty Dittes, *Sales Staff*
Tiffany Garner, *Sales Staff*
EMP: 10 **Privately Held**
SIC: 5051 3315 3523 Pipe & tubing, steel; chain link fencing; cattle feeding, handling & watering equipment
HQ: Stephens Pipe & Steel, Llc
2224 E Highway 619
Russell Springs KY 42642
270 866-3331

(G-4096)
STERLING JEWELERS INC
194 Bucklnd Hills Dr 10 (06042)
PHONE 860 644-7207
Jeff Majka, *Branch Mgr*
EMP: 6 **Privately Held**
SIC: 3423 Jewelers' hand tools
HQ: Sterling Jewelers Inc.
375 Ghent Rd
Fairlawn OH 44333
330 668-5000

(G-4097)
STETSON BREWING CO INC
22 Fleming Rd (06042-2918)
PHONE 860 643-0257
Christopher J Stetson, *Principal*
EMP: 3 **EST:** 1998
SALES (est): 125.4K **Privately Held**
SIC: 2082 Malt beverages

(G-4098)
STITCHERS HIDEAWAY LLC
172 Birch St (06040-5461)
PHONE 860 268-4741
Susan L Donnelly, *Principal*
EMP: 3
SALES (est): 140.2K **Privately Held**
SIC: 2395 Embroidery & art needlework

(G-4099)
SUNDANCE SIGNS LLC
118 Adams St (06042-1915)
PHONE 860 432-5760
Todd Odermatt, *Principal*
EMP: 1 **EST:** 2012
SALES (est): 107.4K **Privately Held**
SIC: 3993 Signs & advertising specialties

(G-4100)
TECHNICAL ENGINEERING
100 Chapel Rd (06042-1625)
PHONE 860 645-9401
Majed Noujaim, *Owner*
EMP: 2
SALES (est): 347.6K **Privately Held**
SIC: 3599 Machine shop, jobbing & repair

(G-4101)
TIM WELDER LLC
37 Cook St (06040-3717)
PHONE 860 646-1356
Timothy Lehan, *Principal*
EMP: 2
SALES (est): 243.1K **Privately Held**
SIC: 3548 Welding apparatus

(G-4102)
TIMKEN AROSPC DRV SYSTEMS LLC
586 Hilliard St (06042-2879)
PHONE 860 649-0000
Richard G Kyle, *President*
William R Burkhart, *Exec VP*
Christopher A Coughlin, *Exec VP*
Philip D Fracassa, *CFO*
Bruce Angell, *Program Mgr*
EMP: 120
SQ FT: 18,700
SALES (est): 49MM
SALES (corp-wide): 3.5B **Publicly Held**
SIC: 3724 3728 Aircraft engines & engine parts; aircraft body assemblies & parts
HQ: Mpb Corporation
7 Optical Ave
Keene NH 03431
603 352-0310

(G-4103)
TOWN FAIR TIRE CENTERS INC
328 Middle Tpke W (06040-3842)
PHONE 860 646-2807
William Rivera, *Manager*
EMP: 15
SALES (corp-wide): 288.7MM **Privately Held**
WEB: www.townfair.com
SIC: 3011 Tire & inner tube materials & related products; tires, cushion or solid rubber
PA: Town Fair Tire Centers, Inc.
460 Coe Ave
East Haven CT 06512
203 467-8600

(G-4104)
UNISON ENGINE COMPONENTS
171 Utopia Rd (06042-2199)
PHONE 860 647-5586
EMP: 2
SALES (corp-wide): 368.2MM **Privately Held**
SIC: 3728 Aircraft parts & equipment
HQ: Manchester Paradigm Inc
967 Parker St
Manchester CT 06042
860 646-4048

(G-4105)
VISION TECHNICAL MOLDING
20 Utopia Rd (06042-2191)
PHONE 860 783-5050
EMP: 4
SALES (est): 218.1K **Privately Held**
SIC: 3089 Injection molding of plastics

(G-4106)
WHITELEDGE INC
Also Called: C B Enterprises Division
134 Pine St (06040-5831)
PHONE 860 647-1883
Robert Blass, *President*
Pamela Blass, *Admin Sec*
EMP: 5
SQ FT: 5,500
SALES (est): 623K **Privately Held**
SIC: 3451 Screw machine products

(G-4107)
WILLIAM KORN INC
132 1/2 Pine St (06040)
P.O. Box 1022 (06045-1022)
PHONE 860 647-0284
Agusta Grube, *President*
Wallace Grube, *Vice Pres*
Steven Grube, *Admin Sec*
EMP: 2 **EST:** 1880
SALES: 150K **Privately Held**
SIC: 3953 Marking devices

(G-4108)
WILLIAMS PRINTING LLC
1131 Tolland Tpke 0-134 (06042-1679)
PHONE 860 813-1717
EMP: 1
SALES (est): 90.8K **Privately Held**
SIC: 2752 Commercial printing, lithographic

(G-4109)
WILLSON MANUFACTURING OF CONN
71 Batson Dr (06042-1657)
P.O. Box 8020 (06040-0020)
PHONE 860 643-8182
Donald Willson, *President*
EMP: 4
SALES: 300K **Privately Held**
SIC: 3599 Machine shop, jobbing & repair

(G-4110)
WINDHAM SAND AND STONE INC
60 Adams St S (06040-2604)
P.O. Box 133, Willimantic (06226-0133)
PHONE 860 643-5578
Fax: 860 423-0300
EMP: 100
SQ FT: 2,000
SALES (est): 12MM
SALES (corp-wide): 28.8MM **Privately Held**
SIC: 3273 Mfg Ready-Mixed Concrete
PA: Windham Materials Llc
79 Boston Post Rd
Willimantic CT 06226
860 456-4111

Mansfield Center
Tolland County

(G-4111)
AFFORDABLE WATER TRTMNT
498 Stafford Rd (06250-1425)
PHONE 860 423-3147
Douglas Lohman, *Owner*
EMP: 4
SALES (est): 548.4K **Privately Held**
SIC: 3589 Water treatment equipment, industrial

(G-4112)
BOMBADILS SPIRIT SHOP INC
135 Storrs Rd 8 (06250-1638)
PHONE 860 423-9661
Roger Gagne, *President*
EMP: 5
SALES (est): 310.5K **Privately Held**
SIC: 2086 Bottled & canned soft drinks

(G-4113)
EZEE FABRICATORS LLC
221 Wormwood Hill Rd (06250-1033)
PHONE 860 429-5664
George Jones, *Principal*
EMP: 2
SALES (est): 127.2K **Privately Held**
SIC: 3999 Manufacturing industries

(G-4114)
LITEIDEAS LLC (PA)
417 Mulberry Rd (06250-1021)
PHONE 860 213-8311
Todd Hodrinsky,
EMP: 2
SALES (est): 1.1MM **Privately Held**
SIC: 3674 Light emitting diodes

(G-4115)
PRECISION WELDING
15 Buckingham Rd (06250-1404)
PHONE 860 423-7772
Mario Sgarellino, *Principal*
EMP: 1
SALES (est): 39.3K **Privately Held**
SIC: 7692 Welding repair

(G-4116)
YANKEE WOODWORKS LLC
91 Pleasant Valley Rd (06250-1539)
PHONE 860 933-9882
Eric Lanka, *Principal*
EMP: 2
SALES (est): 184.4K **Privately Held**
SIC: 2431 Millwork

Marion
Hartford County

(G-4117)
NORTHEAST WOOD SALES
1146 Marion Ave (06444)
PHONE 860 621-9613
Martin Mc Carthy, *Principal*
EMP: 1
SALES (est): 108.8K **Privately Held**
SIC: 2499 Wood products

Marlborough
Hartford County

(G-4118)
A DOUGLAS THIBODEAU LLC
21 Portland Rd (06447-1302)
PHONE 860 295-9189
A Douglas Thibodeau,
EMP: 1
SALES: 150K **Privately Held**
SIC: 3826 Environmental testing equipment

(G-4119)
AMERICAN DISTILLING INC
380 N Main St (06447-1346)
P.O. Box 319, East Hampton (06424-0319)
PHONE 860 267-4444

GEOGRAPHIC SECTION

Matthew McArthur, *Exec Dir*
EMP: 5
SALES (est): 433.6K
SALES (corp-wide): 15.9MM **Privately Held**
SIC: 2085 2833 2844 2087 Distillers' dried grains & solubles & alcohol; botanical products, medicinal: ground, graded or milled; perfumes & colognes; flavoring extracts & syrups
PA: American Distilling Inc.
31 E High St
East Hampton CT 06424
860 267-4444

(G-4120)
ANIYAQ LLC
45 Hemlock Dr (06447-1018)
PHONE.................................860 531-2835
Todd Sun, *Partner*
Chris Norton, *Partner*
EMP: 2
SALES (est): 92.1K **Privately Held**
SIC: 7372 7389 Prepackaged software;

(G-4121)
BEDROCK OIL LLC
16 Parker Rd (06447-1208)
PHONE.................................860 295-8230
EMP: 2 **EST:** 2010
SALES (est): 114.4K **Privately Held**
SIC: 1382 Oil/Gas Exploration Services

(G-4122)
CONNECTICUT CANVAS WORKS
27 Standish Dr (06447-1005)
P.O. Box 358 (06447-0358)
PHONE.................................860 295-9924
Jim Macrina, *Owner*
Ann Macrina, *Owner*
EMP: 2
SALES (est): 132.4K **Privately Held**
SIC: 2394 Canvas & related products

(G-4123)
ESSENTIAL TRADING SYSTEMS CORP
Also Called: Etc
9 Austin Dr Ste 3 (06447-1375)
PHONE.................................860 295-8100
Gilbert M Smith, *CEO*
David Harding, *President*
Jeffrey Hasbargen, *Vice Pres*
▲ **EMP:** 14
SQ FT: 10,000
SALES (est): 1.4MM **Privately Held**
WEB: www.essentialtel.com
SIC: 3669 Visual communication systems

(G-4124)
HEARTWOOD CABINETRY
345 N Main St (06447-1315)
PHONE.................................860 295-0304
Patrick Hart, *Principal*
EMP: 8
SALES (est): 420K **Privately Held**
SIC: 2434 Wood kitchen cabinets

(G-4125)
MARLBOROUGH PLASTICS INC
350 N Main St (06447-1346)
PHONE.................................860 295-9124
Joseph J Asklar, *President*
Corrine Machowski, *Treasurer*
Todd Machowski, *Manager*
▲ **EMP:** 8 **EST:** 1933
SQ FT: 11,250
SALES (est): 1.5MM **Privately Held**
WEB: www.marlplastics.com
SIC: 3089 Injection molded finished plastic products; injection molding of plastics

(G-4126)
MASTERS PUBLISHING
52 Keirstead Cir (06447-1431)
PHONE.................................860 295-8454
EMP: 1
SALES (est): 44K **Privately Held**
SIC: 2741 Misc Publishing

(G-4127)
MPS PLASTICS INCORPORATED
351 N Main St (06447-1315)
P.O. Box 59 (06447-0059)
PHONE.................................860 295-1161
Knut Imshaug, *President*

Dave Nickolonko, *Vice Pres*
Mike Griffin, *Engineer*
▲ **EMP:** 27
SQ FT: 18,000
SALES (est): 4.6MM **Privately Held**
WEB: www.mpsplastics.com
SIC: 3089 Molding primary plastic; injection molding of plastics

(G-4128)
PFD STUDIOS
213 Flood Rd (06447-1545)
PHONE.................................860 295-8500
Paul Drexler, *Owner*
EMP: 3
SALES (est): 250K **Privately Held**
SIC: 3949 Billiard & pool equipment & supplies, general

(G-4129)
POWDER PUSHERS
49 S Main St (06447-1556)
PHONE.................................860 295-6406
Hope Rubera, *Principal*
EMP: 2
SALES (est): 85.2K **Privately Held**
SIC: 3545 Pushers

(G-4130)
REDLINE ELEMENTS LLC
70 Finley Hill Rd (06447-1002)
PHONE.................................860 305-0095
Melanie A Folcik,
EMP: 1
SALES (est): 78K **Privately Held**
SIC: 2819 Industrial inorganic chemicals

(G-4131)
YELLOW GIRL PRESS LLC
315 Jones Hollow Rd (06447-1036)
PHONE.................................860 819-0260
Kathleen Sands, *Principal*
EMP: 1
SALES (est): 60.1K **Privately Held**
SIC: 2741 Miscellaneous publishing

Mashantucket
New London County

(G-4132)
GUESS INC
455 Trolley Line Blvd # 780 (06338-3830)
PHONE.................................860 629-0835
EMP: 2
SALES (corp-wide): 2.6B **Publicly Held**
SIC: 2325 Men's & boys' trousers & slacks
PA: Guess , Inc.
1444 S Alameda St
Los Angeles CA 90021
213 765-3100

(G-4133)
UNDER ARMOUR INC
455 Trolley Line Blvd # 760 (06338-3830)
PHONE.................................860 237-6031
EMP: 2
SALES (corp-wide): 5.1B **Publicly Held**
SIC: 2329 Men's & boys' sportswear & athletic clothing
PA: Under Armour, Inc.
1020 Hull St Ste 300
Baltimore MD 21230
410 454-6428

Meriden
New Haven County

(G-4134)
3M COMPANY
400 Research Pkwy (06450-7172)
PHONE.................................203 237-5541
WEI Moline, *President*
Christine Wetzel, *Research*
Paul Moore, *Engineer*
Dian Zheng, *Senior Engr*
Matt Kachur, *Human Res Mgr*
EMP: 80
SALES (corp-wide): 32.7B **Publicly Held**
SIC: 3465 Automotive stampings

PA: 3m Company
3m Center
Saint Paul MN 55144
651 733-1110

(G-4135)
3M PURIFICATION INC (HQ)
400 Research Pkwy (06450-7172)
P.O. Box 1018 (06450-1018)
PHONE.................................203 237-5541
Inge Thulin, *Ch of Bd*
Mark G Kachur, *Ch of Bd*
Timothy B Carney, *President*
David Schaeffer, *General Mgr*
Raymond Ponden, *Opers Mgr*
▲ **EMP:** 300
SQ FT: 189,000
SALES (est): 454.4MM
SALES (corp-wide): 32.7B **Publicly Held**
WEB: www.cuno.com
SIC: 3589 3569 Water purification equipment, household type; filters; filters, general line: industrial; filters & strainers, pipeline
PA: 3m Company
3m Center
Saint Paul MN 55144
651 733-1110

(G-4136)
A & M AUTO MACHINE INC
711 E Main St (06450-6018)
PHONE.................................203 237-3502
Ernie Adduci, *President*
David Maniscalco, *Vice Pres*
EMP: 3
SQ FT: 2,200
SALES (est): 300K **Privately Held**
SIC: 3599 7539 7538 Machine & other job shop work; machine shop, automotive; engine rebuilding: automotive

(G-4137)
A AL HARDING
Also Called: Harding, A C Company
165 Eaton Ave (06451-2609)
P.O. Box 620 (06450-0620)
PHONE.................................203 238-1993
A Al Harding, *Owner*
EMP: 3
SALES (est): 300K **Privately Held**
SIC: 5033 2299 Fiberglass building materials; fibers, textile: recovery from textile mill waste & rags

(G-4138)
A G C INCORPORATED (PA)
106 Evansville Ave (06451-5135)
PHONE.................................203 235-3361
R Bruce Andrews, *President*
Walter Layman, *President*
Doris D Harms, *Principal*
Mike Kopjanski, *Purch Mgr*
Fred Annunziata, *Research*
EMP: 160
SQ FT: 110,000
SALES (est): 28.3MM **Privately Held**
WEB: www.agcincorporated.com
SIC: 3728 3444 3398 3053 Aircraft assemblies, subassemblies & parts; sheet metalwork; metal heat treating; gaskets, packing & sealing devices; paints & allied products

(G-4139)
ACCEL INTL HOLDINGS INC
508 N Colony St (06450-2246)
PHONE.................................203 237-2700
Anthony OH, *President*
Kyle Senk, *VP Sales*
Kyle Scott Senk, *Chief Mktg Ofcr*
Jodi Lynn OH, *Admin Sec*
▲ **EMP:** 30
SQ FT: 150,000
SALES (est): 11.6MM **Privately Held**
SIC: 3315 Wire & fabricated wire products

(G-4140)
ACME PRESS PRINTERS LLC
1147 Hanover Ave (06451-6206)
P.O. Box 1765 (06450-8865)
PHONE.................................203 237-2702
Matt Toman, *Owner*
William Eperson, *Accountant*
EMP: 2
SQ FT: 1,500

SALES (est): 203.5K **Privately Held**
SIC: 2752 Commercial printing, offset

(G-4141)
AEROSWISS LLC
20 Powers Dr (06451-5556)
PHONE.................................203 634-4545
John Daniel Gullo,
EMP: 19 **EST:** 2000
SQ FT: 1,000
SALES (est): 3.8MM **Privately Held**
WEB: www.aeroswiss.com
SIC: 3599 Machine shop, jobbing & repair

(G-4142)
AGC ACQUISITION LLC
106 Evansville Ave (06451-5135)
PHONE.................................203 639-7125
Doris D Harms, *President*
Michael Doolan, *Vice Pres*
Glenn Dalessandro, *CFO*
EMP: 112
SALES (est): 22.9MM **Privately Held**
SIC: 3724 Aircraft engines & engine parts

(G-4143)
ANNIES OIL CO
10 Cooper St (06450-5506)
PHONE.................................203 237-9276
Jeff Giacco, *Manager*
EMP: 2
SALES (est): 158K **Privately Held**
SIC: 2911 Jet fuels

(G-4144)
APERTURE OPTICAL SCIENCES INC
170 Pond View Dr (06450-7142)
PHONE.................................860 301-2372
Flemming Tinker, *President*
Kai Xin, *Principal*
Robert Savastano, *Mfg Staff*
Joann Fazekas, *Bookkeeper*
Jennifer Buell, *Human Res Mgr*
EMP: 4 **EST:** 2010
SALES: 380K **Privately Held**
SIC: 3827 Optical instruments & lenses

(G-4145)
APLICARE PRODUCTS LLC (HQ)
550 Research Pkwy (06450-7172)
PHONE.................................203 630-0500
Charlie Mills, *CEO*
EMP: 198
SQ FT: 55,416
SALES (est): 7.8MM
SALES (corp-wide): 5.7B **Privately Held**
SIC: 2834 3841 Antiseptics, medicinal; surgical instruments & apparatus
PA: Medline Industries, Inc.
3 Lakes Dr
Northfield IL 60093
847 949-5500

(G-4146)
ARKALON CHEMICAL TECH LLC
200 Carpenter Ave Ste 211 (06450-6107)
PHONE.................................352 505-8098
Joseph Malik, *COO*
Michael Mc-Geary,
▲ **EMP:** 1
SQ FT: 3,000
SALES (est): 600K **Privately Held**
SIC: 2834 Solutions, pharmaceutical

(G-4147)
B & G FORMING TECHNOLOGY INC
956 Old Colony Rd (06451-7921)
PHONE.................................203 235-2169
Elizabeth Gassman,
Arthur A Bell,
Louis Bell,
Garrett Gassman,
EMP: 4
SALES (est): 418K **Privately Held**
WEB: www.bgforming.com
SIC: 3469 Metal stampings

(G-4148)
BAR PLATING INC
30 Powers Dr Ste 7 (06451-5589)
PHONE.................................203 630-1046
Bruce Rogers, *President*

Meriden - New Haven County (G-4149)

Sarah Rogers, *Admin Sec*
EMP: 2
SQ FT: 2,400
SALES: 325K **Privately Held**
SIC: 3471 Electroplating of metals or formed products

(G-4149)
BENNICE MOLDING CO
184 Gravel St Apt 42 (06450-4661)
PHONE 203 440-2543
EMP: 3
SALES (est): 151.4K **Privately Held**
SIC: 3089 Mfg Plastic Products

(G-4150)
BRAND-NU LABORATORIES INC (PA)
Also Called: Biosolutions
377 Research Pkwy Ste 2 (06450-7155)
PHONE 203 235-7989
John J Gorman III, *President*
Carol A Shea, *Vice Pres*
Eric Tranquist, *Prdtn Mgr*
Giovanna Coppola, *Technical Staff*
Karis Greene, *Technical Staff*
◆ **EMP:** 35 **EST:** 1955
SQ FT: 80,000
SALES (est): 13MM **Privately Held**
WEB: www.brandnu.com
SIC: 2899 Chemical preparations

(G-4151)
BRAND-NU LABORATORIES INC
Also Called: Bio Solutions
290 Pratt St Ofc (06450-8603)
P.O. Box 895 (06450-0895)
PHONE 203 235-7989
EMP: 2
SALES (corp-wide): 13MM **Privately Held**
WEB: www.brandnu.com
SIC: 2899 Chemical preparations
PA: Brand-Nu Laboratories Incorporated
377 Research Pkwy Ste 2
Meriden CT 06450
203 235-7989

(G-4152)
BUSHWICK METALS LLC
130 Research Pkwy Ste 203 (06450-7152)
PHONE 203 630-2459
EMP: 4
SALES (corp-wide): 194.6B **Publicly Held**
SIC: 3312 5051 Blast Furnace-Steel Works Metals Service Center
HQ: Bushwick Metals, Llc
560 N Washington Ave # 2
Bridgeport CT 06484
203 576-1800

(G-4153)
C & S ENGINEERING INC
956 Old Colony Rd (06451-7921)
PHONE 203 235-5727
Alfred L Cavallo, *President*
Michael Cavallo, *Vice Pres*
EMP: 29
SQ FT: 20,000
SALES (est): 3.6MM **Privately Held**
WEB: www.csengineering.com
SIC: 3449 3562 3471 Miscellaneous metalwork; ball & roller bearings; plating & polishing

(G-4154)
CABLE MANAGEMENT LLC
290 Pratt St Ste 1108 (06450-8600)
P.O. Box 2719 (06450-1788)
PHONE 860 670-1890
Josue Loic Trudeau, *Owner*
Josh Loic Trudeau, *Owner*
Dan Cotnoir, *Plant Mgr*
▲ **EMP:** 30
SALES (est): 1.2MM **Privately Held**
SIC: 3569 Baling machines, for scrap metal, paper or similar material

(G-4155)
CAROB DESIGNS LLC
Also Called: Skyart Studio and Gallery
290 Pratt St Ofc (06450-8603)
PHONE 203 630-9171
Lori Rob,
Paula Caretti,
EMP: 2
SALES (est): 160K **Privately Held**
WEB: www.skyartstudio.com
SIC: 3599 Weather vanes

(G-4156)
CENTER BROACH & MACHINE CO
525 N Colony St (06450-2287)
P.O. Box 2 (06450-0002)
PHONE 203 235-6329
William Phillips IV, *Vice Pres*
EMP: 9
SQ FT: 13,000
SALES: 500K **Privately Held**
SIC: 3545 Broaches (machine tool accessories)

(G-4157)
CHERISE CPL LLC
57 S Broad St (06450-6544)
PHONE 203 238-3482
EMP: 3
SALES (est): 207.3K **Privately Held**
SIC: 2052 Bakery products, dry

(G-4158)
CKO WOODWORKING LLC
85 Tremont St (06450-2273)
PHONE 203 815-3092
EMP: 1
SALES (est): 54.1K **Privately Held**
SIC: 2431 Millwork

(G-4159)
CLEAN UP GROUP
82 Jodi Dr (06450-3569)
PHONE 203 668-8323
Maurice Langlois, *Owner*
Donna Langlois, *Co-Owner*
EMP: 3
SALES (est): 110K **Privately Held**
SIC: 2851 Removers & cleaners

(G-4160)
COLD PLASMA NECK
639 Research Pkwy (06450-7154)
PHONE 203 935-0300
Perri Cone MD, *Principal*
EMP: 2
SALES (est): 120K **Privately Held**
SIC: 2836 Plasmas

(G-4161)
CONNECTICUT CARPENTRY LLC
290 Pratt St Ofc (06450-8603)
PHONE 203 639-8585
Leo Dufour, *Owner*
EMP: 40
SALES: 1MM **Privately Held**
SIC: 2431 Millwork

(G-4162)
COUTURIER INO
Also Called: Ogle Specialty
5 Cross St (06451-3201)
PHONE 203 238-4555
Ino Couturier, *Owner*
EMP: 6
SALES (est): 350K **Privately Held**
SIC: 3599 Machine shop, jobbing & repair

(G-4163)
CRC CHROME CORPORATION
169 Pratt St R (06450-4250)
PHONE 203 630-1008
Frank Ciarcia, *President*
Michael Ciarcia, *Corp Secy*
EMP: 10
SQ FT: 8,000
SALES (est): 1.4MM **Privately Held**
WEB: www.crcchrome.com
SIC: 3471 Chromium plating of metals or formed products; electroplating of metals or formed products

(G-4164)
CUSTOM CHOCOLATE DESIGNS LLC
16 Welles Ter (06450-4357)
PHONE 203 886-6777
Rosa Luzunaris,
EMP: 2
SALES (est): 80.4K **Privately Held**
SIC: 2066 Chocolate

(G-4165)
D & F SCRUBS & GADGETS LLC
235 Hanover St (06451-5465)
PHONE 203 440-4666
Donnie Frasier, *Principal*
EMP: 2 **EST:** 2013
SALES (est): 120K **Privately Held**
SIC: 2844 Toilet preparations

(G-4166)
DI-EL TOOL & MANUFACTURING
69 Research Pkwy Ste 1 (06450-7178)
PHONE 203 235-2169
Arthur A Bell Jr, *President*
Louis Bell, *Vice Pres*
Arthur B Bell, *Admin Sec*
EMP: 4 **EST:** 1956
SQ FT: 7,000
SALES (est): 641.7K **Privately Held**
SIC: 3469 Metal stampings

(G-4167)
DRT AEROSPACE LLC
620 Research Pkwy (06450-7127)
PHONE 203 781-8020
Gary Van Gundy, *CEO*
EMP: 38 **Privately Held**
SIC: 3724 Aircraft engines & engine parts
HQ: Drt Aerospace, Llc
8694 Rite Track Way
West Chester OH 45069
937 298-7391

(G-4168)
EAST COAST INSULATION LLC
657 E Main St Apt A12 (06450-6034)
PHONE 302 685-3152
Christopher Blake,
EMP: 1
SALES (est): 114K **Privately Held**
SIC: 2899 Insulating compounds

(G-4169)
ENVIRONMENTAL MONITOR SERVICE
87 Gypsy Ln (06450-7927)
P.O. Box 4340, Yalesville (06492-7562)
PHONE 203 935-0102
James Cognetta, *President*
Robert Zembruski, *General Mgr*
Ann Cognetta, *Corp Secy*
▼ **EMP:** 7
SQ FT: 6,600
SALES (est): 858.5K **Privately Held**
WEB: www.emsct.com
SIC: 7699 3564 7389 Industrial equipment services; air purification equipment; air pollution measuring service

(G-4170)
FLAG STORE
Also Called: Flag Store of Conn The
186 Hall Ave (06450-7758)
PHONE 203 237-8791
Robert Salocski, *Owner*
EMP: 1
SALES (est): 260.4K **Privately Held**
WEB: www.flagstoreusa.com
SIC: 3993 5999 Signs & advertising specialties; banners, flags, decals & posters

(G-4171)
FORM-ALL PLASTICS CORPORATION
104 Gracey Ave (06451-2295)
PHONE 203 634-1137
Tim Jennings, *President*
EMP: 7 **EST:** 1963
SQ FT: 7,000
SALES (est): 1.4MM **Privately Held**
WEB: www.form-all.com
SIC: 3089 Trays, plastic

(G-4172)
HAYNES HYDROGEN LLC
48 Whitney Dr (06450-7224)
PHONE 203 605-2837
John Haynes, *Principal*
EMP: 2
SALES (est): 121.2K **Privately Held**
SIC: 2813 Hydrogen

(G-4173)
HINT PERIPHERALS CORP
46 Gracey Ave (06451-2249)
PHONE 203 634-4468
Oscar Gimenez, *President*
EMP: 9
SALES (est): 1.9MM **Privately Held**
WEB: www.hintperipherals.com
SIC: 3577 Computer peripheral equipment

(G-4174)
INK AND STITCH SOLUTIONS LLC
88 Laurel Hts (06451-5427)
PHONE 203 600-7161
Anibal Rodriguez, *Principal*
EMP: 1 **EST:** 2017
SALES (est): 58.1K **Privately Held**
SIC: 2395 Embroidery & art needlework

(G-4175)
INNOVATIVE INDUSTRIES LLC
290 Pratt St Unit 1321 (06450-8600)
PHONE 860 225-0000
Donald Bossey, *Principal*
EMP: 2
SALES (est): 132.3K **Privately Held**
SIC: 3999 Manufacturing industries

(G-4176)
J M COMPOUNDS INC
290 Pratt St Ofc (06450-8603)
PHONE 203 376-9854
John Guida, *President*
Mary Dunkovich, *Vice Pres*
EMP: 6
SQ FT: 3,000
SALES (est): 716.3K **Privately Held**
WEB: www.jmcompounds.com
SIC: 3471 Buffing for the trade

(G-4177)
J T FANTOZZI CO INC
95 Fair St (06451-2005)
PHONE 203 238-7018
John T Fantozzi, *President*
EMP: 3
SALES (est): 200K **Privately Held**
SIC: 7692 1799 Welding repair; welding on site

(G-4178)
JOHN L PRENTIS & CO INC
35 Pratt St (06450-4241)
P.O. Box 126 (06450-0126)
PHONE 203 634-1266
Bruce Burchsted, *President*
Suzana Burchsted, *Vice Pres*
Mike Glynn, *Prdtn Mgr*
EMP: 6
SQ FT: 3,000
SALES (est): 777.1K **Privately Held**
WEB: www.jlpgraphics.com
SIC: 5049 2752 7389 7384 Engineers' equipment & supplies; commercial printing, offset; laminating service; photograph enlarging; blueprinting service

(G-4179)
JOHNSON CONTROLS INC
71 Deerfield Ln (06450-7151)
PHONE 678 297-4040
EMP: 94 **Privately Held**
SIC: 2531 3714 3691 3822 Seats, automobile; motor vehicle body components & frame; instrument board assemblies, motor vehicle; lead acid batteries (storage batteries); building services monitoring controls, automatic; facilities support services
HQ: Johnson Controls, Inc.
5757 N Green Bay Ave
Milwaukee WI 53209
414 524-1200

(G-4180)
JONAL LABORATORIES INC
456 Center St (06450-3302)
P.O. Box 743 (06450-0743)
PHONE 203 634-4444
Marc Nemeth, *President*
Ken Keegan, *Exec VP*
Kenneth Keegan, *Exec VP*
Dan Clifford, *Vice Pres*
David Nemeth, *Vice Pres*

EMP: 60
SQ FT: 20,000
SALES (est): 12.6MM **Privately Held**
WEB: www.jonal.com
SIC: 8711 3069 Engineering services; custom compounding of rubber materials; molded rubber products

(G-4181)
JONAL LABS LOGISTICS LLC
468 Center St (06450)
PHONE...................203 634-4444
Ralph Bonczewski, *Engineer*
Haley Nemeth, *Mng Member*
EMP: 3 EST: 2016
SQ FT: 1,000
SALES (est): 127.7K **Privately Held**
SIC: 3728 Aircraft parts & equipment

(G-4182)
JOURNAL OF EXPERIMNTAL SCNDARY
234 Debbie Dr (06451-3695)
PHONE...................203 630-6508
Ravi Shamarao Dinakar, *Principal*
EMP: 2
SALES (est): 121.5K **Privately Held**
SIC: 2711 Newspapers, publishing & printing

(G-4183)
JRA INDUSTRIES LLC
159 Springdale Ave 1 (06451-2936)
PHONE...................475 343-0262
Abraham Nieves,
EMP: 1
SALES (est): 45.5K **Privately Held**
SIC: 3999 Manufacturing industries

(G-4184)
KNIGHT LITE NEON
Also Called: Knight Light Neon
763 Hanover Rd (06451-5208)
PHONE...................203 238-4423
Jim Blackall, *Owner*
EMP: 1
SALES (est): 76.9K **Privately Held**
SIC: 3993 Neon signs

(G-4185)
L SUZIO ASPHALT CO INC
975 Westfield Rd (06450-2553)
P.O. Box 748 (06450-0748)
PHONE...................203 237-8421
Leonardo C Suzio, *President*
Scott P Suzio, *Vice Pres*
Leonardo H Suzio, *Admin Sec*
EMP: 12 EST: 1957
SQ FT: 10,000
SALES (est): 1.8MM **Privately Held**
WEB: www.suzioyorkhill.com
SIC: 2951 Asphalt & asphaltic paving mixtures (not from refineries)

(G-4186)
LEGACY WOODWORKING LLC
912 Old Colony Rd (06451-7921)
PHONE...................203 440-9710
Steven Pelczar,
EMP: 4 EST: 2008
SALES: 1MM **Privately Held**
SIC: 2431 Millwork

(G-4187)
LJS HOUSE OF CANDLES
49 Old Gate Rd (06451-3662)
PHONE...................203 464-5742
Laura-Jean Stevener, *Principal*
EMP: 1
SALES (est): 39.6K **Privately Held**
SIC: 3999 Candles

(G-4188)
LOGAN STEEL INC (PA)
Also Called: Logan Sandblasting
119 Empire Ave (06450-1928)
PHONE...................203 235-0811
Howard A Lohmann Jr, *President*
Erik K Lohmann, *Corp Secy*
Gail Lohmann, *Corp Secy*
Sean Miller, *Sales Staff*
EMP: 30
SQ FT: 16,000
SALES (est): 21.3MM **Privately Held**
WEB: www.logansteelinc.com
SIC: 5051 3471 3441 Structural shapes, iron or steel; sand blasting of metal parts; fabricated structural metal

(G-4189)
LOUIE S WELDING
55 Cooper St (06451-5541)
PHONE...................203 634-0873
EMP: 1
SALES (est): 50K **Privately Held**
SIC: 7692 Welding Repair

(G-4190)
LYONS TOOL AND DIE COMPANY
185 Research Pkwy (06450-7124)
PHONE...................203 238-2689
William Lyons III, *CEO*
William Lyons IV, *President*
David Brown, *Vice Pres*
Gini Selvaggi, *Treasurer*
John Malek, *Manager*
EMP: 38 EST: 1951
SQ FT: 32,000
SALES (est): 8.9MM **Privately Held**
WEB: www.lyons.com
SIC: 3469 3544 3545 Stamping metal for the trade; special dies & tools; jigs & fixtures; gauges (machine tool accessories)

(G-4191)
MAINVILLE WELDING CO INC
55 Goffe St (06451-1899)
PHONE...................203 237-3103
Jack Mainville, *President*
Carmel Mainville, *Admin Sec*
EMP: 4
SQ FT: 4,500
SALES (est): 270K **Privately Held**
SIC: 7692 Welding repair

(G-4192)
MARK FAHEY
64 Nutmeg Dr Apt B (06451-2887)
PHONE...................203 686-0852
Mark Fahey, *Principal*
EMP: 2
SALES (est): 85.9K **Privately Held**
SIC: 3571 Electronic computers

(G-4193)
MEB ENTERPRISES INC
496 S Broad St (06450-6662)
PHONE...................203 599-0273
Maryellen Beaudreault, *President*
EMP: 8
SALES (est): 945.7K **Privately Held**
SIC: 2819 Elements

(G-4194)
MERIDEN AWNING & DECORATING CO
336 Hanover St (06451-5459)
PHONE...................203 634-0067
Alton Evarts, *President*
EMP: 4 EST: 1928
SALES: 900K **Privately Held**
SIC: 5999 2394 Awnings; awnings, fabric: made from purchased materials

(G-4195)
MERIDEN ELECTRONICS CORP
Also Called: Melco
1777 N Colony Rd (06450-1964)
P.O. Box 139 (06450-0139)
PHONE...................203 237-8811
Mark R Merliss, *President*
EMP: 4
SQ FT: 12,000
SALES (est): 130K **Privately Held**
SIC: 3812 Antennas, radar or communications

(G-4196)
MERIDEN FIRE MARSHALS OFFICE
142 E Main St (06450-5605)
PHONE...................203 630-4010
Robert Morpurgo, *Manager*
EMP: 2 EST: 2010
SALES (est): 149.2K **Privately Held**
SIC: 3711 Fire department vehicles (motor vehicles), assembly of

(G-4197)
MERIDEN MANUFACTURING INC
230 State Street Ext (06450-3205)
P.O. Box 694 (06450-0694)
PHONE...................203 237-7481
Lester Maloney, *Ch of Bd*
Lester G Maloney, *Ch of Bd*
Sharon M Fox, *President*
James Muller, *President*
Mike Falis, *Purch Mgr*
EMP: 86
SQ FT: 27,000
SALES (est): 18.7MM **Privately Held**
WEB: www.meridenmfg.com
SIC: 3469 3769 3812 Machine parts, stamped or pressed metal; guided missile & space vehicle parts & auxiliary equipment; search & navigation equipment

(G-4198)
MERIDEN PRECISION PLASTICS LLC
290 Pratt St Ste 18 (06450-8601)
PHONE...................203 235-3261
Fax: 203 237-8627
EMP: 9
SQ FT: 8,500
SALES (est): 780K **Privately Held**
SIC: 3089 Mfg Toilet Repair Parts

(G-4199)
MERL INC
1777 N Colony Rd (06450-1964)
P.O. Box 188 (06450-0188)
PHONE...................203 237-8811
Mark R Merliss, *President*
EMP: 9 EST: 1978
SQ FT: 12,000
SALES (est): 1MM **Privately Held**
SIC: 3694 3663 Generators, automotive & aircraft; radio & TV communications equipment

(G-4200)
MEURER INDUSTRIES
400 Research Pkwy (06450-7172)
PHONE...................303 279-8373
Don Bersell, *Project Mgr*
EMP: 2
SALES (est): 86.5K **Privately Held**
SIC: 3589 Water treatment equipment, industrial

(G-4201)
MID STATE ARC INC
Also Called: Powers Industries & Laserpro
20 Powers Dr (06451-5556)
PHONE...................203 238-9001
Pamela Smith, *Manager*
EMP: 50
SALES (corp-wide): 11.6MM **Privately Held**
SIC: 8322 3861 Social services for the handicapped; photographic equipment & supplies
PA: Midstate Arc Inc
200 Research Pkwy
Meriden CT 06450
203 237-9975

(G-4202)
MID STATE ASSEMBLY & PACKG INC
604 Pomeroy Ave (06450-4872)
PHONE...................203 634-8740
Daniel Nichols, *President*
▲ EMP: 6
SALES (est): 930.9K **Privately Held**
SIC: 2671 3569 7389 Packaging paper & plastics film, coated & laminated; assembly machines, non-metalworking; packaging & labeling services

(G-4203)
MILLER COMPANY
275 Pratt St (06450-4251)
PHONE...................203 235-4474
Michael Rodgers, *Principal*
Timo Strobel, *Vice Pres*
Claudia Groten, *CFO*
Claudia Baraglia, *Finance Mgr*
Thomas Schmidt, *Sales Staff*
▲ EMP: 35
SALES (est): 10.6MM
SALES (corp-wide): 472MM **Privately Held**
WEB: www.themillerco.com
SIC: 3351 Strip, copper & copper alloy
PA: Diehl Metall Stiftung & Co. Kg
Heinrich-Diehl-Str. 9
Rothenbach A.D.Pegnitz 90552
911 570-40

(G-4204)
MIRION TECH CANBERRA INC (HQ)
Also Called: Canberra Industries, Inc.
800 Research Pkwy (06450-7127)
PHONE...................203 238-2351
Jean Bernard Koehl, *CEO*
Jesse Tyler, *Senior Buyer*
Gregory Bogorodzki, *Engineer*
Shawn Googins, *Engineer*
David Petroka, *Engineer*
▲ EMP: 277
SQ FT: 170,000
SALES (est): 97.8MM **Privately Held**
SIC: 3829 4813 Nuclear radiation & testing apparatus; voice telephone communications

(G-4205)
MISFIT PRINTS LLC
161 State St Apt 315 (06450)
PHONE...................203 306-6322
EMP: 2
SALES (est): 83.9K **Privately Held**
SIC: 2752 Commercial printing, lithographic

(G-4206)
MISTER BS JERKY CO
25 Harness Dr (06450-6922)
PHONE...................203 631-2758
Daniel Baril, *Principal*
EMP: 3 EST: 2017
SALES (est): 104.3K **Privately Held**
SIC: 2013 Snack sticks, including jerky: from purchased meat

(G-4207)
MULTIPRINTS INC
Also Called: Barker Screen Printers
812 Old Colony Rd (06451-7929)
P.O. Box 834 (06450-0834)
PHONE...................203 235-4409
Amy J P Barker, *President*
Susan Dunphy, *Admin Sec*
EMP: 12
SQ FT: 12,000
SALES (est): 1.2MM **Privately Held**
WEB: www.multiprints.necoxmail.com
SIC: 2759 Screen printing

(G-4208)
NEW ENGLAND ORTHOTIC & PROST
61 Pomeroy Ave Unit 2a (06450-7483)
PHONE...................203 634-7566
EMP: 3
SALES (corp-wide): 28.1MM **Privately Held**
SIC: 3842 Limbs, artificial
PA: New England Orthotic And Prosthetic Systems, Llc
16 Commercial St
Branford CT 06405
203 483-8488

(G-4209)
NOACKS MEAT PRODUCTS
1112 E Main St (06450-4804)
PHONE...................203 235-7384
Joseph Herz, *President*
Herbert Harteux, *Vice Pres*
EMP: 5
SQ FT: 1,250
SALES (est): 500.5K **Privately Held**
WEB: www.noacks.com
SIC: 5421 5147 2011 Meat markets, including freezer provisioners; meats, fresh; meat packing plants

(G-4210)
NORTH EASTERN SCALE CORP
201 4th St (06451-7606)
PHONE...................203 634-7942
Catherine Martin, *President*
Cliff Martin, *Admin Sec*

Meriden - New Haven County (G-4211)

EMP: 5
SQ FT: 1,000
SALES (est): 380K **Privately Held**
SIC: 7699 3596 Industrial equipment services; industrial scales

(G-4211)
OLIVE FLAVORED
167 Cobblestone Ln (06450-6746)
PHONE 203 641-2086
Nicole Katynski, *Principal*
EMP: 1
SALES (est): 90.3K **Privately Held**
SIC: 2099 Food preparations

(G-4212)
OMERIN USA INC
Also Called: Qs Tehcnoligies Divison
95 Research Pkwy (06450-7124)
PHONE 475 343-3450
Aurelien Paumier, *President*
Xavier Omerin, *Director*
EMP: 30
SALES (est): 6MM **Privately Held**
SIC: 3357 Aluminum wire & cable
HQ: Omerin Sas
  Omerin Div Silisol & Div Principale
  Zone Industrielle
  Ambert 63600
  473 824-436

(G-4213)
OMNOMNOM JAMS AND JELLIES LLC
31 Orient St (06450-4504)
PHONE 203 630-6557
Melissa Manjoney, *Principal*
EMP: 2
SALES (est): 149.8K **Privately Held**
SIC: 2033 Jams, jellies & preserves: packaged in cans, jars, etc.

(G-4214)
ORBIT DESIGN LLC
290 Pratt St (06450-8600)
PHONE 203 393-0171
Ron Oren, *Mng Member*
Melba Oren,
EMP: 10
SQ FT: 4,000
SALES (est): 900K **Privately Held**
SIC: 3089 Injection molding of plastics

(G-4215)
PASTRY SHOP
31 Main St (06451)
PHONE 203 238-0483
Freddy Gillette, *Partner*
EMP: 4
SALES (est): 174.8K **Privately Held**
SIC: 2051 Bread, cake & related products

(G-4216)
PERFORMANCE CONNECTION SYSTEMS
599 W Main St (06451-2751)
P.O. Box 556, Marion (06444-0556)
PHONE 203 868-5517
John Keefe, *Owner*
EMP: 8
SALES (est): 602K **Privately Held**
WEB: www.keefeperformance.com
SIC: 3499 Welding tips, heat resistant: metal

(G-4217)
PERRICONE HYDROGEN WTR CO LLC
639 Research Pkwy (06450-7154)
PHONE 844 341-5941
Nicholas Perricone,
EMP: 2
SALES (est): 74.4K **Privately Held**
SIC: 2899 Distilled water

(G-4218)
POP GRAPHICS INC
38 Elm St (06450-5704)
PHONE 203 639-1441
Robert Laurencelle, *President*
EMP: 1
SALES (est): 113.5K **Privately Held**
WEB: www.pop-graphics.com
SIC: 3993 7319 Signs & advertising specialties; display advertising service

(G-4219)
PRECISION INTERFACE
40 Hampshire Rd (06450-5957)
PHONE 203 235-2718
Peter Arntsen, *Owner*
EMP: 1
SALES (est): 46.6K **Privately Held**
SIC: 3999 Manufacturing industries

(G-4220)
PRENTIS PRINTING SOLUTIONS INC
35 Pratt St (06450-4241)
P.O. Box 126 (06450-0126)
PHONE 203 634-1266
Bruce Burchsted, *Principal*
EMP: 4
SALES (est): 473.6K **Privately Held**
SIC: 2752 Commercial printing, offset

(G-4221)
PRODUCTION EQUIPMENT COMPANY
401 Liberty St (06450-4500)
PHONE 800 758-5697
Rebecca Davis, *President*
Roswell Davis Sr, *Treasurer*
Stephanie Jordan, *Admin Sec*
EMP: 25
SQ FT: 10,000
SALES (est): 6.3MM **Privately Held**
WEB: www.peco1938.com
SIC: 3536 3535 Cranes, overhead traveling; overhead conveyor systems

(G-4222)
PROFESSIONAL PRINT GRAPHICS
40 Edgewood Pl (06451-2928)
PHONE 203 686-0151
Gwen Rochette, *Principal*
EMP: 2
SALES (est): 117.9K **Privately Held**
SIC: 2752 Commercial printing, offset

(G-4223)
PROSERV SOFTWARE & SUPPORT LLC
69 Research Pkwy (06450-7124)
PHONE 866 833-8999
Virginia Knowlden, *President*
EMP: 2 **EST:** 2011
SALES (est): 160K **Privately Held**
SIC: 7372 Business oriented computer software

(G-4224)
PROTEIN SCIENCES CORPORATION (HQ)
1000 Research Pkwy (06450-7149)
PHONE 203 686-0800
Elaine O'Hara, *President*
Mireli Fino, *Vice Pres*
Chan Lee, *Vice Pres*
Douglas McCormack, *Vice Pres*
Mireli W Fino, *VP Mfg*
EMP: 89
SQ FT: 26,000
SALES (est): 22.2MM **Privately Held**
WEB: www.proteinsciences.com
SIC: 2834 2836 8733 Pharmaceutical preparations; vaccines; medical research

(G-4225)
PYRAMID TIME SYSTEMS LLC
45 Gracey Ave (06451-2284)
PHONE 203 238-0550
John Augustyn, *President*
George Bucci, *Vice Pres*
Bob Lennon, *Vice Pres*
Anne Galanto, *Purch Agent*
Virginia Hutnik, *Cust Mgr*
▲ **EMP:** 50 **EST:** 1969
SQ FT: 70,000
SALES (est): 13.2MM **Privately Held**
WEB: www.pyramidtech.com
SIC: 3579 3873 Time clocks & time recording devices; watches, clocks, watchcases & parts

(G-4226)
QUICK MACHINE SERVICES LLC
290 Pratt St Ste 4 (06450-8601)
PHONE 203 634-8822
Danny Demerchant,
EMP: 7
SQ FT: 5,600
SALES (est): 994.2K **Privately Held**
SIC: 3599 7699 Machine shop, jobbing & repair; industrial machinery & equipment repair

(G-4227)
RADIO FREQUENCY SYSTEMS INC (DH)
200 Pond View Dr (06450-7195)
PHONE 203 630-3311
William Bayne, *President*
Suzanne Kasai, *Business Mgr*
Sal N Betro, *Vice Pres*
Steve Hull, *Vice Pres*
Phillip Lobato, *Vice Pres*
◆ **EMP:** 30
SQ FT: 380,000
SALES (est): 266.9MM
SALES (corp-wide): 25.8B **Privately Held**
WEB: www.rfsworld.com
SIC: 3663 3661 5045 5065 Antennas, transmitting & communications; microwave communication equipment; telephone & telegraph apparatus; telephones & telephone apparatus; computers, peripherals & software; electronic parts & equipment; communication equipment

(G-4228)
RAGIS FABRICATIONS INC
250 Goodspeed Ave (06451-2718)
PHONE 203 237-0424
Andy Ragis, *President*
Suzanne Ragis, *Admin Sec*
EMP: 2
SALES (est): 80K **Privately Held**
SIC: 3544 Special dies, tools, jigs & fixtures

(G-4229)
RAGOZZINO FOODS INC (PA)
10 Ames Ave (06451-2912)
P.O. Box 116 (06450-0116)
PHONE 203 238-2553
Gloria A Ragozzino, *CEO*
Nancy Ragozzino, *President*
Susan Darin, *Vice Pres*
Ellen Sattler, *Vice Pres*
Gregory Kelly, *Controller*
EMP: 15
SQ FT: 71,000
SALES: 35.7MM **Privately Held**
SIC: 2038 2033 Frozen specialties; spaghetti & other pasta sauce: packaged in cans, jars, etc.

(G-4230)
RECORD-JOURNAL NEWSPAPER (PA)
Also Called: Town Times
500 S Broad St Ste 2 (06450-6643)
PHONE 203 235-1661
Eliot C White, *Owner*
Bryant Carpenter, *Editor*
Eric Cotton, *Editor*
Eric Heredia, *Editor*
Lawrence Olivia, *Editor*
▲ **EMP:** 175 **EST:** 1867
SALES (est): 49.4MM **Privately Held**
SIC: 2711 2752 Commercial printing & newspaper publishing combined; commercial printing, offset

(G-4231)
RFS AMERICAS
Also Called: Radio Frequency Systems
175 Corporate Ct (06450-7180)
PHONE 203 630-3311
◆ **EMP:** 4 **EST:** 2010
SALES (est): 449K **Privately Held**
SIC: 3663 Cable television equipment

(G-4232)
RGB WOODWORKING
730 Allen Ave (06451-3616)
PHONE 203 537-1177
Geoffrey Rabe, *Principal*
EMP: 1
SALES (est): 59.5K **Privately Held**
SIC: 2431 Millwork

(G-4233)
RICH PLASTIC PRODUCTS INC
57 High St (06450-5739)
PHONE 203 235-4241
Daniel J Rich, *President*
Denise Rivard, *Admin Sec*
EMP: 7
SQ FT: 10,000
SALES (est): 1.4MM **Privately Held**
WEB: www.richplastics.com
SIC: 3822 Thermostats & other environmental sensors

(G-4234)
RICIA MAINHARDT AGENCY
85 Lincoln St Apt 1 (06451-3181)
PHONE 718 434-1893
EMP: 2 **EST:** 2016
SALES (est): 75K **Privately Held**
SIC: 2741 Miscellaneous publishing

(G-4235)
RIVEAL TECHNOLOGIES LLC
74 Hillwood Ln (06450-6649)
P.O. Box 705 (06450-0705)
PHONE 203 935-0997
Raymond Rivera, *Co-Owner*
EMP: 1
SALES (est): 62.5K **Privately Held**
SIC: 3599 Machine shop, jobbing & repair

(G-4236)
S J PAPPAS INC
Also Called: Roy Tech
718 Old Colony Rd (06451-7930)
PHONE 203 237-7701
Kalliroy Pappas, *President*
Jack Pappas, *Treasurer*
Steven J Pappas, *Shareholder*
Stratos Pappas, *Admin Sec*
EMP: 8 **EST:** 1953
SQ FT: 27,000
SALES (est): 1.7MM **Privately Held**
WEB: www.sjpappas.com
SIC: 5031 5712 1751 2521 Kitchen cabinets; cabinet work, custom; cabinet building & installation; wood office furniture; vanities, bathroom: wood

(G-4237)
SAF INDUSTRIES LLC
Also Called: General Pneumatics
106 Evansville Ave (06451-5135)
PHONE 203 729-4900
EMP: 28
SALES (corp-wide): 23.6MM **Privately Held**
WEB: www.gpcvalves.com
SIC: 3491 3592 3559 3492 Process control regulator valves; pressure valves & regulators, industrial; solenoid valves; valves, nuclear; valves, aircraft; cryogenic machinery, industrial; fluid power valves for aircraft; control valves, fluid power: hydraulic & pneumatic; hose & tube fittings & assemblies, hydraulic/pneumatic; hose & tube couplings, hydraulic/pneumatic; couplings, except pressure & soil pipe; accumulators, aircraft propeller
HQ: Saf Industries Llc
  106 Evansville Ave
  Meriden CT 06451

(G-4238)
SAF INDUSTRIES LLC (HQ)
Also Called: Gar Kenyon Aerospace & Defense
106 Evansville Ave (06451-5135)
PHONE 203 729-4900
Shelly Anderson, *President*
Jonathan Fournier, *Vice Pres*
EMP: 28
SQ FT: 44,000
SALES (est): 5.6MM
SALES (corp-wide): 23.6MM **Privately Held**
WEB: www.garkenyon.com
SIC: 3728 3812 Aircraft assemblies, sub-assemblies & parts; acceleration indicators & systems components, aerospace
PA: Loar Group Inc.
  450 Lexington Ave Fl 31
  New York NY 10017
  212 210-9348

(G-4239)
SAFE-T-TANK CORP
25 Powers Dr (06451-5578)
PHONE..................203 237-6320
Sheila R Bartis, *President*
Peter A Bartis, *Vice Pres*
EMP: 5
SQ FT: 5,000
SALES (est): 1.1MM **Privately Held**
SIC: 3443 Fuel tanks (oil, gas, etc.): metal plate

(G-4240)
SAVAGE PRODUCTS LLC
Also Called: Manufacturing
197 Pratt St (06450-4250)
PHONE..................203 440-1766
Steven M Gervais,
EMP: 1
SALES (est): 100.6K **Privately Held**
SIC: 3542 Machine tools, metal forming type

(G-4241)
SHINER SIGNS INC
Also Called: Signage US
38 Elm St Ste 3 (06450-5704)
PHONE..................203 634-4331
Robert Laurencelle, *President*
Irwin Laurencelle, *Treasurer*
EMP: 20 EST: 1904
SQ FT: 10,000
SALES (est): 3.2MM **Privately Held**
WEB: www.signageus.com
SIC: 3993 Electric signs

(G-4242)
SO AND SEW PLUSHIES
104 Elm St (06450-5708)
PHONE..................860 916-2918
Jessy Hart, *Principal*
EMP: 3
SALES (est): 168.3K **Privately Held**
SIC: 3566 Speed changers, drives & gears

(G-4243)
SOUTHINGTON CITIZEN
Also Called: Record Journal, The
500 S Broad St Ste 1 (06450-6643)
PHONE..................860 620-5960
Elliot White, *President*
EMP: 6
SALES (est): 250K **Privately Held**
SIC: 2711 Newspapers, publishing & printing

(G-4244)
SOUTHWICK & MEISTER INC
Also Called: Innovative Systems
1455 N Colony Rd (06450-1979)
P.O. Box 725 (06450-0725)
PHONE..................203 237-0000
Robert A Meister, *President*
Ernest M Meister, *President*
Lynn M Papale, *Vice Pres*
Barbara Meister, *Admin Sec*
EMP: 105
SQ FT: 45,000
SALES (est): 19.1MM **Privately Held**
WEB: www.s-mcollets.com
SIC: 3545 Tools & accessories for machine tools

(G-4245)
SPACE CRAFT MFG INC ✪
620 Research Pkwy (06450-7127)
PHONE..................860 583-1387
EMP: 2 EST: 2019
SALES (est): 81.4K **Privately Held**
SIC: 3599 Industrial machinery

(G-4246)
STONEHOUSE FINE CAKES
61 N 1st St (06451-4018)
PHONE..................203 235-5091
Susan Stone, *Mng Member*
Armand Stone,
EMP: 10 EST: 1997
SALES (est): 550.8K **Privately Held**
WEB: www.cakelady.com
SIC: 2051 Bakery: wholesale or wholesale/retail combined

(G-4247)
SULZER PUMP SOLUTIONS US INC (PA)
140 Pond View Dr (06450-7142)
PHONE..................203 238-2700
John Everhart, *President*
Stefan Baumgaertner, *Vice Pres*
▲ EMP: 25
SALES (est): 16.1MM **Privately Held**
SIC: 3561 5251 5084 Industrial pumps & parts; pumps, domestic: water or sump; pumps & pumping equipment; pumps & pumping equipment

(G-4248)
SUZIO YORK HILL COMPANIES
975 Westfield Rd (06450-2553)
PHONE..................888 789-4626
EMP: 2
SALES (est): 75.3K **Privately Held**
SIC: 5032 3273 Asphalt mixture; ready-mixed concrete

(G-4249)
T D I ENTERPRISES LLC
22 Gypsy Ln (06451-7910)
PHONE..................203 630-1268
Tim Isyk, *Owner*
EMP: 5 EST: 1982
SALES (est): 410.2K **Privately Held**
SIC: 2951 Asphalt & asphaltic paving mixtures (not from refineries)

(G-4250)
T G INDUSTRIES INC
361 S Colony St Ste 1 (06451-6280)
PHONE..................203 235-3239
Anthony Gullo, *President*
Bob Kowalski, *Vice Pres*
Helen Gullo, *Admin Sec*
EMP: 15
SQ FT: 10,000
SALES (est): 2.4MM **Privately Held**
WEB: www.tgimachine.com
SIC: 3599 Machine shop, jobbing & repair

(G-4251)
TEAM DESTINATION INC
Also Called: Instant Imprints
477 S Broad St Ste 14 (06450-6660)
PHONE..................203 235-6000
Vandan Divatia, *President*
Deepan Divatia, *Vice Pres*
Rudra Divatia, *Admin Sec*
EMP: 3
SQ FT: 1,566
SALES (est): 330K **Privately Held**
SIC: 2752 5699 Commercial printing, lithographic; customized clothing & apparel

(G-4252)
TGS CABLES
290 Pratt St (06450-8600)
P.O. Box 7174 (06450-7637)
PHONE..................203 668-6568
James Tyrrel, *General Ptnr*
EMP: 4
SQ FT: 2,500
SALES (est): 260K **Privately Held**
SIC: 3679 Electronic circuits

(G-4253)
THE L SUZIO CONCRETE CO INC (PA)
975 Westfield Rd (06450-2553)
P.O. Box 748 (06450-0748)
PHONE..................203 238-8421
Leonardo H Suzio, *Vice Pres*
Cheryl Suzio, *Vice Pres*
Henry E Suzio, *Vice Pres*
Scott P Suzio, *Vice Pres*
Henrietta R Suzio, *Admin Sec*
EMP: 37 EST: 1898
SQ FT: 10,000
SALES (est): 5.4MM **Privately Held**
WEB: www.lsuzio.com
SIC: 3273 Ready-mixed concrete

(G-4254)
THOMPSON BRANDS LLC
80 S Vine St (06451-3823)
PHONE..................203 235-2541
William H Thompson, *Founder*
Bob Lis, *Plant Mgr*
Joann Giddix, *Buyer*
Kristen Sullivan, *QC Mgr*
Joseph Ciullo, *CFO*
▲ EMP: 85
SQ FT: 114,000
SALES (est): 15.4MM **Privately Held**
SIC: 2064 5441 2066 5145 Candy & other confectionery products; candy; chocolate & cocoa products; candy

(G-4255)
THOMPSON CANDY COMPANY
80 S Vine St (06451-3823)
PHONE..................203 235-2541
Jeffrey H White, *President*
William Walsh, *Vice Pres*
Allan E White, *Vice Pres*
Susan Giddix, *Purch Mgr*
Joanne Giddix, *Buyer*
EMP: 70
SQ FT: 114,000
SALES (est): 26.9K **Privately Held**
WEB: www.thompsoncandy.com
SIC: 2064 5441 Candy & other confectionery products; candy

(G-4256)
TIMS SIGN & LIGHTING SERVICE
38 Elm St Ste 2 (06450-5704)
PHONE..................203 634-8840
Timothy G Walsh, *Principal*
EMP: 8
SQ FT: 4,500
SALES (est): 950K **Privately Held**
SIC: 3993 1799 7389 Signs & advertising specialties; sign installation & maintenance; crane & aerial lift service

(G-4257)
TRAP ROCK RIDGE WELDING LLC
513 High Hill Rd (06450-7116)
PHONE..................203 213-7578
Matthew Lafayette, *Owner*
EMP: 1
SALES (est): 25K **Privately Held**
SIC: 7692 Welding repair

(G-4258)
UNIQUE GRAPHICS
905 Hanover Rd (06451-5212)
PHONE..................203 634-1932
Artie Coscuna, *Owner*
EMP: 1
SALES (est): 111.5K **Privately Held**
SIC: 2759 Screen printing

(G-4259)
UNITED OPHTHALMICS LLC
430 Smith St (06451)
PHONE..................203 745-8399
Gaston S Levesque, *Principal*
EMP: 3
SALES (est): 377.4K **Privately Held**
SIC: 3841 Eye examining instruments & apparatus

(G-4260)
UNIVERSAL BUILDING CONTRLS INC
170 Research Pkwy Ste 1 (06450-7144)
PHONE..................203 235-1530
Andrew Divicino, *President*
Leonard Corso, *Project Mgr*
Michael Poplawski, *Treasurer*
Diana Poplawski, *Admin Sec*
EMP: 13
SQ FT: 2,000
SALES (est): 3.1MM **Privately Held**
WEB: www.universalbuildingcontrols.com
SIC: 3491 3822 1731 7373 Automatic regulating & control valves; building services monitoring controls, automatic; energy management controls; office computer automation systems integration; plumbing, heating, air-conditioning contractors

(G-4261)
UPC LLC
170 Research Pkwy (06450-7144)
PHONE..................877 466-1137
Andy Divicino,
EMP: 4
SALES (est): 32.8K **Privately Held**
SIC: 3089 Plastic containers, except foam

(G-4262)
USA WOOD INCORPORATED
998 N Colony Rd (06450-2372)
PHONE..................203 238-4285
Dominick A Derobertis Jr, *President*
▲ EMP: 4
SALES (est): 380K **Privately Held**
SIC: 2511 Wood household furniture

(G-4263)
VERSIFI LLC
380 S Curtis St (06450-6654)
PHONE..................860 890-1982
EMP: 2 EST: 2016
SALES (est): 122.2K **Privately Held**
SIC: 2752 Commercial printing, lithographic

(G-4264)
VICTOR TOOL CO INC
290 Pratt St Ste 7 (06450-8601)
PHONE..................203 634-8113
David Victor, *President*
Travis Vumback, *Vice Pres*
EMP: 6
SQ FT: 9,500
SALES (est): 1.4MM **Privately Held**
SIC: 3544 3545 Special dies & tools; jigs & fixtures; gauges (machine tool accessories)

(G-4265)
W B MASON CO INC
194 Research Pkwy (06450-7125)
PHONE..................888 926-2766
EMP: 60
SALES (corp-wide): 773MM **Privately Held**
SIC: 5943 5712 2752 Ret Office Supplies Office Furniture And Printing Solutions
PA: W. B. Mason Co., Inc.
59 Center St
Brockton MA 02301
781 794-8800

(G-4266)
WASHER TECH INC
956 Old Colony Rd (06451-7921)
PHONE..................203 886-0054
Garret Gassman, *President*
Elizabeth Gassman, *Vice Pres*
Don Clark, *Treasurer*
Don N Clark, *Treasurer*
EMP: 4
SQ FT: 4,000
SALES (est): 440K **Privately Held**
SIC: 3469 Metal stampings

(G-4267)
WESS TOOL & DIE COMPANY INC
140 Research Pkwy Ste 2 (06450-7162)
PHONE..................203 237-5277
Robert Wisniewski, *President*
Richard Wisniewski, *Vice Pres*
Tim Wisniewski, *Administration*
EMP: 5 EST: 1960
SALES: 400K **Privately Held**
WEB: www.wesstoolanddie.com
SIC: 3544 Special dies & tools

(G-4268)
WILLIES WELDING INC
313 Spring St (06451-5318)
P.O. Box 1744 (06450-8844)
PHONE..................203 237-6235
William Davis Phillips Jr, *President*
Franklin Phillips, *Vice Pres*
Catherine Phillips, *Admin Sec*
EMP: 3
SQ FT: 8,400
SALES: 190K **Privately Held**
SIC: 7692 Welding repair

(G-4269)
WINSTANLEY INC
321 Research Pkwy (06450-8301)
PHONE..................203 238-6614
EMP: 2
SALES (est): 245.5K **Privately Held**
SIC: 3679 5065 Mfg Electronic Components Whol Electronic Parts/Equipment

Meriden - New Haven County

(G-4270)
YORK HILL TRAP ROCK QUARRY CO
975 Westfield Rd (06450-2553)
P.O. Box 748 (06450-0748)
PHONE 203 237-8421
Leonardo C Suzio, *President*
Cheryl Suzio, *Vice Pres*
Henry E Suzio, *Vice Pres*
Scott P Suzio, *Vice Pres*
EMP: 16
SQ FT: 16,000
SALES (est): 1.7MM **Privately Held**
SIC: 1429 Trap rock, crushed & broken-quarrying

Middlebury
New Haven County

(G-4271)
ACTION SCALE SERVICE
760 Whittemore Rd (06762-3005)
PHONE 203 577-6420
Rich Malyszko, *Principal*
EMP: 1
SALES (est): 134.4K **Privately Held**
SIC: 3596 Scales & balances, except laboratory

(G-4272)
AECC/PEARLMAN BUYING GROUP LLC
1255 Middlebury Rd (06762-2333)
P.O. Box 809 (06762-0809)
PHONE 203 598-3200
Norman S Drubner,
AP LLC,
EMP: 10
SALES (est): 1.6MM **Privately Held**
SIC: 3827 Optical instruments & lenses

(G-4273)
AMERICAN ROLLER COMPANY LLC
Also Called: Plasma Coatings
84 Turnpike Dr (06762-1819)
P.O. Box 10006, Waterbury (06725-0006)
PHONE 203 598-3100
Gary Carlo, *Plant Mgr*
EMP: 18
SALES (corp-wide): 102MM **Privately Held**
WEB: www.plasmacoatings.com
SIC: 3069 3479 Rubber rolls & roll coverings; coating of metals with plastic or resins
PA: American Roller Company, Llc
1440 13th Ave
Union Grove WI 53182
262 878-8665

(G-4274)
CAMPBELL PUBLICITY LLC
331 South St (06762-3523)
P.O. Box 5153, Westport (06881-5153)
PHONE 646 532-1512
Donnetra Campbell,
EMP: 1
SALES (est): 94.9K **Privately Held**
SIC: 2741 Miscellaneous publishing

(G-4275)
CISEN USA INC (PA)
4 Colonial Ct (06762-3344)
PHONE 203 706-9536
Xiulian Lu, *CEO*
EMP: 2
SALES (est): 273.4K **Privately Held**
SIC: 2834 Pills, pharmaceutical

(G-4276)
DAMBRUOSO STUDIOS LLC
67 Richardson Dr (06762-2121)
PHONE 203 758-9660
Samuel D'Ambruoso,
EMP: 1
SALES: 65K **Privately Held**
SIC: 8999 4725 2621 8742 Artist; tour operators; poster & art papers; management consulting services; marketing consulting services; business consulting

(G-4277)
DANCAR CORPORATION
145 N Benson Rd Unit 2 (06762-3214)
P.O. Box 888, Woodbury (06798-0888)
PHONE 203 598-0205
Daniel Carten, *President*
Donald D'Ateuil, *Vice Pres*
Virginia Garms, *Admin Sec*
▲ **EMP:** 2
SQ FT: 7,000
SALES (est): 230K **Privately Held**
SIC: 3494 Valves & pipe fittings

(G-4278)
DAVID CHRISTIAN CERAMICS LLC
35 George St (06762-2723)
PHONE 203 758-1532
David Santamaria, *Principal*
EMP: 1 **EST:** 2014
SALES (est): 51.9K **Privately Held**
SIC: 3269 Pottery products

(G-4279)
HOLNESS CABINETRY LLC
395 Shadduck Rd (06762-3621)
PHONE 203 598-0430
Gerald Holness, *Principal*
EMP: 1
SALES (est): 96.8K **Privately Held**
SIC: 2434 Wood kitchen cabinets

(G-4280)
JMS GRAPHICS INC
Also Called: Velocity Print Solution
850 Straits Tpke Ste 204 (06762-2843)
PHONE 203 598-7555
James Stiles, *CEO*
Mike Mello, *CFO*
EMP: 3
SQ FT: 300
SALES (est): 3.6MM
SALES (corp-wide): 34.3MM **Privately Held**
WEB: www.sm-pm.com
SIC: 2752 2759 Commercial printing, offset; commercial printing
PA: Shipmates/Printmates Holding Corp.
705 Corporation Park # 2
Scotia NY 12302
518 370-1158

(G-4281)
KATY INDUSTRIES INC
765 Straits Tpke Bldg 2 (06762-2853)
PHONE 314 656-4321
Jacob Saliba, *Principal*
EMP: 1 **EST:** 2008
SALES (est): 166.1K **Privately Held**
SIC: 3999 Manufacturing industries

(G-4282)
KLL AEROSPACE LLC
116 Breakneck Hill Rd (06762-1915)
PHONE 860 806-8858
Lei Zhang, *Principal*
EMP: 2
SALES (est): 86K **Privately Held**
SIC: 3721 Aircraft

(G-4283)
MAILOURINVITATIONSCOM
896 Middlebury Rd (06762-2403)
PHONE 203 758-1860
EMP: 2
SALES (est): 103.4K **Privately Held**
SIC: 2759 Commercial printing

(G-4284)
MIDDLBURY BEE-INTELLIGENCER-CT
2030 Straits Tpke (06762-1831)
P.O. Box 10 (06762-0010)
PHONE 203 577-6800
EMP: 6
SALES (est): 190.4K **Privately Held**
SIC: 2711 Job printing & newspaper publishing combined

(G-4285)
NEWMACK INC
209 Munson Rd (06762-1331)
P.O. Box 1168 (06762-1168)
PHONE 203 568-0443
Michael McDonald, *President*
EMP: 5
SALES (est): 604K **Privately Held**
SIC: 8731 3577 Computer (hardware) development; computer peripheral equipment

(G-4286)
O2 CONCEPTS LLC
199 Park Road Ext Ste B (06762-1833)
PHONE 877 867-4008
EMP: 2
SALES (corp-wide): 17.4MM **Privately Held**
SIC: 2813 Oxygen, compressed or liquefied
PA: O2 Concepts, Llc
6303 Waterford Blvd # 150
Oklahoma City OK 73118
877 867-4008

(G-4287)
PLASTI-COAT
80 Turnpike Dr Ste 4 (06762-1830)
PHONE 860 274-1234
EMP: 2
SALES (est): 69.9K **Privately Held**
SIC: 3479 Metal coating & allied service

(G-4288)
PROTOSHIELD
Also Called: Protoshield.com
140 Christian Rd (06762-2903)
PHONE 203 527-0321
David Stratton, *Partner*
Lucas Adler, *Partner*
EMP: 2 **EST:** 2012
SALES (est): 140K **Privately Held**
SIC: 7372 Prepackaged software

(G-4289)
ROLLER BEARING CO AMER INC
Pic Design
86 Benson Rd (06762-3215)
P.O. Box 1004 (06762-1004)
PHONE 203 758-8272
Michael J Hartnett, *President*
Andrew Frisbie, *General Mgr*
Darlene Svendberg, *General Mgr*
John Queenen, *VP Finance*
Canio Tortora, *VP Finance*
EMP: 50
SALES (corp-wide): 702.5MM **Publicly Held**
SIC: 3568 3566 3535 3462 Power transmission equipment; speed changers, drives & gears; conveyors & conveying equipment; iron & steel forgings; manufactured hardware (general)
HQ: Roller Bearing Company Of America, Inc.
102 Willenbrock Rd
Oxford CT 06478
203 267-7001

(G-4290)
SEARCHLIGHT LLC
271 Southford Rd (06762-2929)
PHONE 203 577-4400
Zakir Ali, *Principal*
EMP: 2
SALES (est): 88.3K **Privately Held**
SIC: 3648 Searchlights

(G-4291)
SEW BEAUTIFUL WIN TREATMENTS
203 Burr Hall Rd (06762-1404)
P.O. Box 216 (06762-0216)
PHONE 203 598-0544
Jeannie Sikora, *Owner*
EMP: 2
SALES (est): 133.8K **Privately Held**
SIC: 2391 Curtains & draperies

(G-4292)
SIR SPEEDY PRINTING
199 Park Road Ext Ste D (06762-1833)
PHONE 203 346-0716
Heather Boesch Wages, *Owner*
EMP: 20
SALES (est): 1.8MM **Privately Held**
SIC: 2752 Commercial printing, lithographic

(G-4293)
SOLUTION PUBLISHING
177 Falcon Crest Rd (06762-1526)
PHONE 203 758-9137
EMP: 1
SALES (est): 52.5K **Privately Held**
SIC: 2741 Miscellaneous publishing

(G-4294)
SPARROW INDUSTRIES
162 Old Watertown Rd (06762-1307)
PHONE 203 598-0034
Christopher B Evans, *Owner*
EMP: 2
SALES (est): 183.9K **Privately Held**
SIC: 3999 Manufacturing industries

(G-4295)
STRIDE INC
80 Turnpike Dr Ste 1 (06762-1830)
PHONE 203 758-8307
Roberta Nole, *President*
EMP: 13
SALES (est): 610.5K **Privately Held**
WEB: www.stride.com
SIC: 3842 Limbs, artificial

(G-4296)
SUGARPLUMS
93 Fenn Rd (06762-2516)
PHONE 860 426-9945
Lesley K Massey, *Owner*
EMP: 1
SALES (est): 96.6K **Privately Held**
SIC: 2754 Stationery & invitation printing, gravure

(G-4297)
TIMEX GROUP USA INC (HQ)
555 Christian Rd (06762-3206)
PHONE 203 346-5000
Paolo Marai, *CEO*
Jeff Grosberg, *Counsel*
Benjamin Abitbol, *Senior VP*
Robert Butler, *Senior VP*
Greg Miller, *Senior VP*
◆ **EMP:** 230 **EST:** 1857
SQ FT: 81,000
SALES (est): 486.5MM
SALES (corp-wide): 78.6MM **Privately Held**
SIC: 3873 Watches & parts, except crystals & jewels
PA: Timex Group B.V.
Herengracht 466
Amsterdam 1017
235 563-660

Middlefield
Middlesex County

(G-4298)
ADVANCED SHEETMETAL ASSOC LLC
52 Indstrial Pk Access Rd (06455-1263)
PHONE 860 349-1644
Joseph Cohn, *General Mgr*
Kevin Thibodeau, *Manager*
EMP: 20
SALES (est): 4.6MM **Privately Held**
SIC: 3444 Sheet metalwork

(G-4299)
AMERICAN RADIANT TECHNOLO
67 Indstrial Pk Access Rd (06455-1263)
PHONE 203 484-2888
EMP: 2
SALES (corp-wide): 223K **Privately Held**
SIC: 3433 Mfg Heating Equipment-Non-electric
PA: American Radiant Technolo
88 Parsonage Hill Rd
Northford CT 06472
203 484-2888

(G-4300)
COOPER-ATKINS CORPORATION (HQ)
33 Reeds Gap Rd (06455-1138)
PHONE 860 349-3473
Carol P Wallace, *President*

GEOGRAPHIC SECTION

Middletown - Middlesex County (G-4326)

Robert Nerbonne, *Treasurer*
Carol Duplessis, *Admin Sec*
▲ **EMP:** 115 **EST:** 1885
SQ FT: 40,000
SALES (est): 20.5MM
SALES (corp-wide): 17.4B **Publicly Held**
WEB: www.cooper-atkins.com
SIC: 3829 Thermometers, including digital; clinical; thermometers, liquid-in-glass & bimetal type
PA: Emerson Electric Co.
8000 West Florissant Ave
Saint Louis MO 63136
314 553-2000

(G-4301)
DAVID W LINTZ COMPANY
Also Called: David W Lintz Woodworking
24 West St (06455-1150)
PHONE 860 349-1392
EMP: 1
SQ FT: 2,000
SALES: 175K **Privately Held**
SIC: 2431 Mfg Millwork

(G-4302)
LYMAN FARM INCORPORATED
Also Called: Lyman Orchards
7 Lyman Rd (06455-1254)
PHONE 860 349-1793
Stephen Ciskowski, *President*
John Lyman Jr, *Treasurer*
Irene Corona, *Human Res Mgr*
Clif Radziunas, *Manager*
Craig Schatzlein, *Manager*
EMP: 250
SQ FT: 2,000
SALES (est): 16.9MM **Privately Held**
WEB: www.lymanorchards.com
SIC: 0175 2099 5431 7992 Apple orchard; peach orchard; pear orchard; cider, nonalcoholic; fruit stands or markets; public golf courses; golf goods & equipment; recreation center

(G-4303)
NEW ENGLAND SIGN CARVERS
25 Lyman Rd (06455-1254)
PHONE 860 349-1669
William Shaw, *Partner*
Steven Sutton, *Partner*
EMP: 2
SQ FT: 1,000
SALES: 100K **Privately Held**
WEB: www.nesigncarvers.com
SIC: 3993 Signs, not made in custom sign painting shops

(G-4304)
POWERHOLD INC
63 Old Indian Trl (06455-1248)
P.O. Box 447 (06455-0447)
PHONE 860 349-1044
Richard C Spooner, *CEO*
R Chadwick Spooner, *President*
Marilyn D Harris, *Corp Secy*
William T Spooner, *Vice Pres*
Will Spooner, *VP Mfg*
EMP: 24 **EST:** 1958
SQ FT: 14,900
SALES (est): 5.4MM **Privately Held**
WEB: www.powerholdinc.com
SIC: 3545 Cutting tools for machine tools; machine tool attachments & accessories; boring machine attachments (machine tool accessories); chucks: drill, lathe or magnetic (machine tool accessories)

(G-4305)
R E F MACHINE COMPANY INC
24 West St (06455-1150)
P.O. Box 54 (06455-0054)
PHONE 860 349-9344
Robert Fowler, *President*
Lorraine Fowler, *Vice Pres*
EMP: 4
SQ FT: 5,000
SALES: 700K **Privately Held**
SIC: 3599 Machine shop, jobbing & repair

(G-4306)
RAMAR-HALL INC
26 Old Indian Trl (06455-1200)
P.O. Box 218 (06455-0218)
PHONE 860 349-1081
David Ferraguto, *President*
Tom Varricchio, *Vice Pres*
Scott Condry, *VP Opers*
John Dockendorff, *Engineer*
EMP: 28 **EST:** 1956
SQ FT: 9,000
SALES (est): 7.2MM **Privately Held**
WEB: www.ramarhall.com
SIC: 3728 3544 3769 Aircraft parts & equipment; special dies & tools; jigs & fixtures; guided missile & space vehicle parts & auxiliary equipment

(G-4307)
TET MFG CO INC
Also Called: Tet Mfg Co/Machine Shop
2 Old Indian Trl (06455-1200)
PHONE 860 349-1004
Thomas H Cady Jr, *President*
Virginia F Cady, *Vice Pres*
John Scholten, *Plant Mgr*
Dennis Brault, *Director*
EMP: 22
SQ FT: 10,000
SALES (est): 3.8MM **Privately Held**
SIC: 3599 Machine shop, jobbing & repair

(G-4308)
TIMES PUBLISHING LLC
Also Called: Antiqueweb.com
491 Main St (06455-1205)
P.O. Box 333 (06455-0333)
PHONE 860 349-8532
Robert G Ahlgren, *President*
EMP: 8
SALES (est): 339.5K **Privately Held**
WEB: www.monkeytv.com
SIC: 2741 Miscellaneous publishing

(G-4309)
WEPCO PLASTICS INC
27 Indstrial Pk Access Rd (06455-1263)
P.O. Box 182 (06455-0182)
PHONE 860 349-3407
Waldo Parmelee Jr, *President*
David Parmelee, *Vice Pres*
Charles Daniels, *CFO*
EMP: 21
SQ FT: 10,350
SALES (est): 3.5MM **Privately Held**
WEB: www.wepcoplastics.com
SIC: 3089 3544 Injection molding of plastics; special dies, tools, jigs & fixtures

(G-4310)
ZYGO CORPORATION (HQ)
21 Laurel Brook Rd (06455-1291)
PHONE 860 347-8506
Gary K Willis, *President*
▲ **EMP:** 8 **EST:** 1970
SQ FT: 153,500
SALES (corp-wide): 141.3MM
SALES (corp-wide): 4.8B **Publicly Held**
WEB: www.zygo.com
SIC: 3827 Optical instruments & lenses
PA: Ametek, Inc
1100 Cassatt Rd
Berwyn PA 19312
610 647-2121

Middletown
Middlesex County

(G-4311)
2394 BERLIN TURNPIKE ASSOC LLC
955 Washington St (06457-2941)
PHONE 860 347-1624
Jim Valentine, *Owner*
EMP: 2
SALES (est): 151.8K **Privately Held**
WEB: www.ctbeverage.com
SIC: 7372 Prepackaged software

(G-4312)
AAA DISTRIBUTORS
46 Sisk St (06457-2375)
PHONE 860 346-0230
Doug Allen, *Owner*
EMP: 2 **EST:** 2014
SALES (est): 83.6K **Privately Held**
SIC: 5099 5092 3944 Durable goods; model kits; board games, puzzles & models, except electronic

(G-4313)
ADDITIVE MANUFACTURING NENG
1270 Newfield St (06457-1874)
PHONE 860 316-5946
EMP: 1 **EST:** 2016
SALES (est): 39.6K **Privately Held**
SIC: 3999 Manufacturing industries

(G-4314)
ALLSTATE FIRE SYSTEMS LLC
35 Phil Mack Dr (06457-1567)
PHONE 860 246-7711
Thomas O'Connor, *Mng Member*
Jeremiah O'Connor,
Jeremy S O'Connor,
Thomas M O'Connor,
EMP: 48
SALES (est): 4.4MM **Privately Held**
WEB: www.thesprink.com
SIC: 1711 3669 Sprinkler contractors; fire sprinkler system installation; fire alarm apparatus, electric
PA: Encore Holdings, Llc
70 Bacon St
Pawtucket RI 02860

(G-4315)
AMERICAN LIBRARY ASSOCIATION
Also Called: Choice Magazine
575 Main St Ste 300 (06457-2845)
PHONE 860 347-6933
Ervin E Rockwood, *Branch Mgr*
EMP: 25
SALES (corp-wide): 49MM **Privately Held**
WEB: www.alawash.org
SIC: 2721 Magazines: publishing only, not printed on site
PA: American Library Association
50 E Huron St
Chicago IL 60611
800 545-2433

(G-4316)
AMERICAN OVERHEAD RET DIV INC
1885 S Main St (06457-6149)
PHONE 860 876-4552
Michael Misenti, *President*
EMP: 4
SQ FT: 500
SALES (est): 168.9K **Privately Held**
SIC: 2431 3442 Garage doors, overhead: wood; garage doors, overhead: metal

(G-4317)
ARMETTA LLC
Also Called: Copar Industries
90 Industrial Park Rd (06457-1521)
PHONE 860 788-2369
Kimberley Ponticelli, *Accounting Mgr*
Antonia Armetta,
EMP: 29
SALES (est): 6.9MM **Privately Held**
SIC: 1411 Granite, dimension-quarrying

(G-4318)
ARP PUBLISHING INC
84 Mccormick Ln (06457-2076)
PHONE 888 503-6617
EMP: 1 **EST:** 2015
SALES (est): 40.1K **Privately Held**
SIC: 2741 Miscellaneous publishing

(G-4319)
AUBURN MANUFACTURING COMPANY
29 Stack St (06457-2274)
PHONE 860 346-6677
Gary Mittelman, *President*
Ronald Carta Jr, *Plant Mgr*
Robert L Mittelman, *Treasurer*
Mary Banker, *Bookkeeper*
Rob Mittelman, *Manager*
▲ **EMP:** 23
SQ FT: 40,000
SALES (est): 4.8MM **Privately Held**
WEB: www.auburn-mfg.com
SIC: 3053 5169 3069 Gasket materials; synthetic rubber; washers, rubber

(G-4320)
AUTOMATIC MACHINE PRODUCTS
40 Liberty St (06457-2724)
P.O. Box 548 (06457-0548)
PHONE 860 346-7064
John Houston, *President*
Catherine Houston, *Treasurer*
EMP: 6 **EST:** 1949
SQ FT: 4,200
SALES (est): 490K **Privately Held**
SIC: 3451 3599 Screw machine products; machine shop, jobbing & repair

(G-4321)
AZTEC INDUSTRIES LLC
Also Called: American Metalcrafters
695 High St (06457-2288)
PHONE 860 343-1960
Donna Noonan, *Mng Member*
Ken Pearson,
EMP: 50
SQ FT: 60,000
SALES (est): 9.8MM **Privately Held**
SIC: 3339 Primary nonferrous metals

(G-4322)
BALDWIN LAWN FURNITURE LLC
440 Middlefield St Ste 1 (06457-3551)
PHONE 860 347-1306
Max Baldwin, *Partner*
Sherry Baldwin, *Mng Member*
EMP: 18
SQ FT: 30,000
SALES (est): 900K **Privately Held**
WEB: www.baldwinfurniture.com
SIC: 2511 5021 Lawn furniture: wood; outdoor & lawn furniture

(G-4323)
BARCELLO DEVELOPMENT CO
160 Greenview Ter (06457-8741)
PHONE 860 635-7676
Rudolph Barcello, *President*
EMP: 2
SALES (est): 159.4K **Privately Held**
SIC: 2452 Prefabricated wood buildings

(G-4324)
BERGAN ARCHITECTURAL WDWKG INC
55 N Main St (06457-2228)
PHONE 860 346-0869
Richard Bergan, *President*
Maria Bergan, *Vice Pres*
EMP: 20 **EST:** 1976
SQ FT: 16,000
SALES (est): 3.6MM **Privately Held**
WEB: www.berganwood.com
SIC: 2431 2521 2435 2434 Millwork; wood office furniture; hardwood veneer & plywood; wood kitchen cabinets

(G-4325)
BIDWELL INDUSTRIAL GROUP INC (PA)
Also Called: Rapidprint
2055 S Main St (06457-6151)
PHONE 860 346-9283
Donald Bidwell, *CEO*
Donald Bidwell Jr, *Vice Pres*
Michael M Bidwell, *Vice Pres*
Susan Barton, *Sales Executive*
Michael Bidwell, *Officer*
EMP: 50 **EST:** 1969
SQ FT: 40,000
SALES (est): 11.7MM **Privately Held**
WEB: www.bidwellinc.com
SIC: 3824 3579 3089 3861 Electromechanical counters; duplicating machines; organizers for closets, drawers, etc.: plastic; photographic equipment & supplies; X-ray apparatus & tubes

(G-4326)
BOURDON FORGE CO INC
99 Tuttle Rd (06457-1827)
PHONE 860 632-2740
Peter Bourdon, *President*
Jeff Bourdon, *Vice Pres*
Jose Resto, *Safety Mgr*
Cashmir Manczuk, *Engineer*
Frank Majka, *Supervisor*
▲ **EMP:** 145

Middletown - Middlesex County (G-4327)

SQ FT: 50,000
SALES (est): 33.5MM **Privately Held**
WEB: www.bourdonforge.com
SIC: 3429 3462 Parachute hardware; aircraft hardware; iron & steel forgings

(G-4327)
BRINGS MACHINE PRODUCTS
50 Saint Johns St (06457-2252)
PHONE..................860 346-0350
Hans Brings, *Owner*
EMP: 2 EST: 1973
SQ FT: 1,400
SALES: 125K **Privately Held**
SIC: 3599 Machine shop, jobbing & repair

(G-4328)
BRUCE BURGESS
Also Called: B & R Enterprises
6303 Town Brooke (06457-6639)
PHONE..................860 510-9185
Bruce Burgess, *Owner*
EMP: 1
SALES: 10K **Privately Held**
SIC: 1389 Construction, repair & dismantling services

(G-4329)
BULL METAL PRODUCTS INC
Also Called: Bull Display
191 Saybrook Rd (06457-4714)
P.O. Box 738 (06457-0738)
PHONE..................860 346-9691
Steven Z Bull, *President*
Lawrence J Malone, *Admin Sec*
Lisa Newman, *Administration*
EMP: 40
SQ FT: 40,000
SALES (est): 7.5MM **Privately Held**
WEB: www.bullmetal.com
SIC: 2542 3444 Cabinets: show, display or storage: except wood; racks, merchandise display or storage: except wood; sheet metalwork

(G-4330)
CARL PERRY
Also Called: Inotec
91 Highview Ter (06457-2431)
PHONE..................860 834-4459
Carl Perry, *Owner*
EMP: 3
SALES (est): 341.6K **Privately Held**
SIC: 3812 Acceleration indicators & systems components, aerospace

(G-4331)
COMPAIR INC
422 Timber Ridge Rd (06457-7540)
PHONE..................860 635-8811
Clark Burton, *President*
Chris Dipentima, *Principal*
EMP: 2
SQ FT: 5,700
SALES (est): 190K **Privately Held**
SIC: 3429 Aircraft hardware

(G-4332)
CONTEMPORARY PRODUCTS LLC
2055 S Main St (06457-6151)
PHONE..................860 346-9283
Eleni Gabrysiak, *Controller*
Susan Barton, *Sales Staff*
Donald Bidwell Sr,
Robert T Johnson,
EMP: 25
SQ FT: 40,000
SALES (est): 1.6MM **Privately Held**
SIC: 3842 3491 5047 Respiratory protection equipment, personal; respirators; industrial valves; medical equipment & supplies

(G-4333)
CREWELDING
50 Walnut St (06457-3848)
PHONE..................855 204-7352
EMP: 1
SALES (est): 25K **Privately Held**
SIC: 7692 Welding repair

(G-4334)
CUSTOM WOODWORK ETC
789 Saybrook Rd (06457-4722)
PHONE..................860 638-1006
Bruce Ring, *Owner*
EMP: 1 EST: 2014
SALES: 65K **Privately Held**
SIC: 2431 1751 Millwork; cabinet & finish carpentry

(G-4335)
DANTES JEWELRY & REPAIR
Also Called: Dante's Jewelry and Repairs
871b Newfield St (06457-1815)
PHONE..................860 346-4779
Dante Gennaro, *Owner*
EMP: 1
SQ FT: 1,000
SALES: 33K **Privately Held**
SIC: 7631 3911 Jewelry repair services; jewelry, precious metal

(G-4336)
DISCO CHICK
170 Main St (06457-3466)
PHONE..................860 788-6203
Michael Boney, *President*
EMP: 3
SALES (est): 109.8K **Privately Held**
SIC: 2711 Newspapers, publishing & printing

(G-4337)
DU-LITE CORPORATION
171 River Rd (06457-3917)
PHONE..................860 347-2505
Walter Smith, *President*
Patrick Smith, *Treasurer*
Amy Strickland, *Manager*
EMP: 4 EST: 1985
SQ FT: 7,500
SALES: 1MM **Privately Held**
SIC: 2911 2841 Oils, lubricating; soap: granulated, liquid, cake, flaked or chip; detergents, synthetic organic or inorganic alkaline

(G-4338)
DUPONT
1075 Newfield St (06457-1817)
PHONE..................860 368-0766
EMP: 2
SALES (est): 74.4K **Privately Held**
SIC: 2879 Agricultural chemicals

(G-4339)
E-B MANUFACTURING COMPANY INC
825 Middle St (06457-1524)
PHONE..................860 632-8563
Edward A Billings, *President*
Andrew Downs, *Engineer*
Chris Webber, *Office Mgr*
Mark Billings, *Supervisor*
Linda H Billings, *Admin Sec*
EMP: 26
SQ FT: 15,000
SALES (est): 5.2MM **Privately Held**
WEB: www.ebmanufacturing.com
SIC: 3599 Machine shop, jobbing & repair

(G-4340)
ECUA EXPRESS
470 Main St (06457-2810)
PHONE..................860 344-1144
Carlos Dodoj, *Principal*
EMP: 2
SALES (est): 130.5K **Privately Held**
SIC: 2741 Miscellaneous publishing

(G-4341)
EDDINGER ASSOC LLC
Also Called: Agratoursim
278 Chamberlain Rd (06457-5542)
PHONE..................860 344-0508
Richard Eddinger, *Partner*
Barbara Eddinger, *Principal*
Joshua Eddinger,
EMP: 2
SALES (est): 230K **Privately Held**
SIC: 2441 Flats, wood: greenhouse

(G-4342)
EMILYS SWEET CONFECTIONS LLC
680 Ridge Rd (06457-5457)
PHONE..................860 301-2586
Emily D Andrea,
EMP: 1

SALES (est): 51.7K **Privately Held**
SIC: 2064 Candy & other confectionery products

(G-4343)
FASTSIGNS
182 Court St (06457-3302)
PHONE..................860 347-8569
EMP: 1
SALES (est): 46K **Privately Held**
SIC: 3993 Signs & advertising specialties

(G-4344)
FASTSIGNS
182 Court St (06457-3302)
PHONE..................860 347-8569
EMP: 1
SALES (est): 46K **Privately Held**
SIC: 3993 Signs And Advertising Specialties

(G-4345)
FIRST CHANCE INC
598 Washington St (06457-2513)
PHONE..................860 346-3663
Stephen Lapenta, *President*
Sarah S Lapenta, *Director*
EMP: 10 EST: 1980
SQ FT: 800
SALES (est): 780K **Privately Held**
SIC: 5499 2099 Health foods; food preparations; tofu, except frozen desserts

(G-4346)
GARBECK AIRFLOW INDUSTRIES
442 Arbutus St (06457-5121)
PHONE..................860 301-5032
Michael Garofalo, *Owner*
EMP: 3
SALES (est): 81.3K **Privately Held**
SIC: 3999 Manufacturing industries

(G-4347)
GODFREY MEMORIAL LIBRARY
134 Newfield St (06457-2534)
PHONE..................860 346-4375
Richard Black, *Director*
EMP: 5
SALES: 165.6K **Privately Held**
WEB: www.godfrey.org
SIC: 8231 2731 Public library; book publishing

(G-4348)
GORILLA GRAPHICS INC
52 N Main St (06457-2269)
PHONE..................860 704-8208
Geoff Konstan, *President*
Brian Konopka, *Finance Mgr*
Geoffrey Konstan, *Sales Executive*
Jack Huynh, *Info Tech Dir*
Courtney Grippo, *Executive*
EMP: 10
SQ FT: 13,000
SALES (est): 1MM **Privately Held**
WEB: www.gorillagraphics.com
SIC: 2269 Linen fabrics: dyeing, finishing & printing

(G-4349)
HABASIT ABT INC
150 Industrial Park Rd (06457-1521)
PHONE..................860 632-2211
Harry Cardillo, *CEO*
Andrew Arzamarski, *Research*
Byron Sitaras, *Engineer*
Chad Gibbs, *Controller*
Steve Venice, *Info Tech Mgr*
▲ EMP: 140
SQ FT: 78,000
SALES (est): 24.1MM
SALES (corp-wide): 708MM **Privately Held**
WEB: www.habasitabt.com
SIC: 3496 Conveyor belts
HQ: Habasit America, Inc.
805 Satellite Blvd Nw
Suwanee GA 30024
678 288-3600

(G-4350)
HABASIT AMERICA INC
150 Industrial Park Rd (06457-1521)
PHONE..................860 632-2211
Gary Peterson, *Branch Mgr*
EMP: 100
SALES (corp-wide): 708MM **Privately Held**
WEB: www.habasit.com
SIC: 3496 Miscellaneous fabricated wire products
HQ: Habasit America, Inc.
805 Satellite Blvd Nw
Suwanee GA 30024
678 288-3600

(G-4351)
HILVERSUM EMBROIDERY
85 Barbara Rd (06457-2466)
PHONE..................860 729-8532
Eric Hilversum, *Principal*
EMP: 1
SALES (est): 43K **Privately Held**
WEB: www.hilversumembroidery.com
SIC: 2395 Embroidery & art needlework

(G-4352)
HUNT PRINTING CO
675 Newfield St Apt 2 (06457-1844)
P.O. Box 4345, Hamden (06514-0345)
PHONE..................203 891-5778
Ashley Ragusa, *Owner*
EMP: 2
SALES (est): 151.4K **Privately Held**
SIC: 2759 Commercial printing

(G-4353)
HYDRO SERVICE & SUPPLIES INC
975 Middle St Ste K (06457-7572)
PHONE..................203 265-3995
Wes Robbins, *Vice Pres*
Richard Desrosiers, *Manager*
EMP: 9
SALES (corp-wide): 18.7MM **Privately Held**
SIC: 3589 7699 Water treatment equipment, industrial; industrial equipment services
PA: Hydro Service & Supplies, Inc.
513 United Dr
Durham NC 27713
919 544-3744

(G-4354)
HYPACK INC (PA)
56 Bradley St (06457-1513)
PHONE..................860 635-1500
Patrick Sanders, *President*
John D Marinuzzi, *VP Human Res*
Lourdes Evans, *Sales Staff*
Christine Hypack, *Sales Staff*
Brittany Danek, *Marketing Staff*
EMP: 15
SALES (est): 1.9MM **Privately Held**
WEB: www.hypack.com
SIC: 7372 Business oriented computer software

(G-4355)
IMAGE STAR LLC
35 Phil Mack Dr (06457-1567)
PHONE..................888 632-5515
Gerald P Crean III,
EMP: 2 EST: 2015
SALES (est): 141.1K **Privately Held**
SIC: 3555 3552 Printing presses; printing machinery, textile

(G-4356)
J ARNOLD MITTLEMAN
29 Stack St (06457-2265)
PHONE..................860 346-6562
J Arnold Mittleman, *Owner*
EMP: 22
SALES (est): 1MM **Privately Held**
SIC: 2284 Embroidery thread

(G-4357)
JARVIS PRODUCTS CORPORATION (HQ)
33 Anderson Rd (06457-4926)
PHONE..................860 347-7271
Vincent R Volpe, *President*
Michael Abdul, *Opers Mgr*
Penfield Jarvis, *Treasurer*
Robert Cornelius Danaher, *Admin Sec*
◆ EMP: 10
SQ FT: 54,800

SALES (est): 22.8MM
SALES (corp-wide): 23.6MM Privately Held
WEB: www.jarvisproducts.com
SIC: 3556 Meat, poultry & seafood processing machinery
PA: Penco Corporation
229 Buckingham St
Hartford CT
860 278-2345

(G-4358)
JJ PORTLAND NEWS LLC
264 Main St (06457)
PHONE.................................860 342-1432
EMP: 4
SALES (est): 213K Privately Held
SIC: 2711 Newspapers-Publishing/Printing

(G-4359)
KADOMAR KRAFTS
398 Wadsworth St (06457-4062)
PHONE.................................860 346-2000
Kenneth Nichols, Principal
EMP: 2 EST: 2011
SALES (est): 66.6K Privately Held
SIC: 2395 Quilted fabrics or cloth

(G-4360)
KAMAN AEROSPACE CORPORATION
Precision Products Division
217 Smith St (06457-8750)
PHONE.................................860 632-1000
Gerald C Ricketts, Manager
EMP: 234
SALES (corp-wide): 1.8B Publicly Held
WEB: www.kamanaero.com
SIC: 3489 3572 3823 Ordnance & accessories; computer storage devices; industrial instrmnts msrmnt display/control process variable
HQ: Kaman Aerospace Corporation
1332 Blue Hills Ave
Bloomfield CT 06002
860 242-4461

(G-4361)
KAMAN CORPORATION
217 Smith St (06457-8750)
PHONE.................................860 632-1000
EMP: 158
SALES (corp-wide): 1.8B Publicly Held
SIC: 3812 Acceleration indicators & systems components, aerospace
PA: Kaman Corporation
1332 Blue Hills Ave
Bloomfield CT 06002
860 243-7100

(G-4362)
KAMAN PRECISION PRODUCTS INC
217 Smith St (06457-8750)
PHONE.................................860 632-1000
EMP: 20
SALES (corp-wide): 1.8B Publicly Held
SIC: 3812 Acceleration indicators & systems components, aerospace
HQ: Kaman Precision Products, Inc.
6655 E Colonial Dr
Orlando FL 32807
407 282-1000

(G-4363)
KIRO BESPOKE LLC
23 Roberts St (06457-4637)
PHONE.................................203 981-4945
Ronald Sansone, CEO
EMP: 1 EST: 2016
SALES: 100K Privately Held
SIC: 2084 5182 5921 Wines; bottling wines & liquors; wine

(G-4364)
KIWANIS FNDTION MIDDLETOWN INC
340 Chamberlain Hill Rd (06457-7200)
PHONE.................................860 638-8135
David Darling, Principal
Lyn Baldoni, Vice Pres
EMP: 4
SALES: 82.2K Privately Held
SIC: 3732 Boat building & repairing

(G-4365)
KSE CABINETS
129 Highland Ave (06457-4189)
PHONE.................................860 754-7236
EMP: 2 EST: 2011
SALES (est): 141.4K Privately Held
SIC: 2434 Wood kitchen cabinets

(G-4366)
L&P AEROSPACE ACQUISITION LLC
Also Called: Pegasus Manufacturing
422 Timber Ridge Rd (06457-7540)
P.O. Box 501, East Berlin (06023-0501)
PHONE.................................860 635-8811
Chris Dipentima, President
Todd Dipentima, Vice Pres
Nicholas Zandonella, Materials Mgr
Art Rodgers, Facilities Mgr
EMP: 82
SALES (corp-wide): 4.2B Publicly Held
SIC: 3498 Tube fabricating (contract bending & shaping)
HQ: L&P Aerospace Acquisition Company, Llc
1 Leggett Rd
Carthage MO 64836
417 358-8131

(G-4367)
LABCO WELDING INC
129 Industrial Park Rd (06457-1520)
PHONE.................................860 632-2625
Vincent La Bella, President
Susan M La Bella, Admin Sec
EMP: 5
SQ FT: 15,000
SALES (est): 1MM Privately Held
WEB: www.labcowelding.com
SIC: 3444 3599 7692 Sheet metalwork; machine shop, jobbing & repair; welding repair

(G-4368)
LENZ ENTERPRISES LLC
180 Johnson St (06457-2247)
PHONE.................................860 961-2893
David Lenz, President
EMP: 1
SALES (est): 81.5K Privately Held
SIC: 2879 Agricultural chemicals

(G-4369)
LORD & HODGE INC
362 Industrial Park Rd # 4 (06457-1548)
P.O. Box 737 (06457-0737)
PHONE.................................860 632-7006
Gary Lord, President
EMP: 10
SQ FT: 9,000
SALES (est): 1.4MM Privately Held
WEB: www.lordandhodge.com
SIC: 3965 3069 3545 Fasteners, snap; grommets, rubber; vises, machine (machine tool accessories)

(G-4370)
LYMAN PRODUCTS CORPORATION (PA)
Also Called: Raytech Industries Div
475 Smith St (06457-1529)
PHONE.................................860 632-2020
Richard Ranzinger, President
Thomas Andersen, Vice Pres
Luke Fichthorn III, Treasurer
Karl Oberg, Controller
Edward W Wytrych, Admin Sec
◆ EMP: 100 EST: 1876
SQ FT: 100,000
SALES (est): 21.5MM Privately Held
WEB: www.lymanproducts.com
SIC: 3559 Ammunition & explosives, loading machinery; metal finishing equipment for plating, etc.

(G-4371)
LYMAN PRODUCTS CORPORATION
Raytech Industries
475 Smith St (06457-1529)
PHONE.................................860 632-2020
Miles Herrick, Branch Mgr
EMP: 20
SALES (corp-wide): 21.5MM Privately Held
SIC: 3559 Ammunition & explosives, loading machinery
PA: Lyman Products Corporation
475 Smith St
Middletown CT 06457
860 632-2020

(G-4372)
M DESIGN & PRINTING SVCS LLC
163 Newtown St (06457-4235)
PHONE.................................860 344-8289
Mario Maselli Jr, Principal
EMP: 2
SALES (est): 183.3K Privately Held
SIC: 2752 Commercial printing, lithographic

(G-4373)
MA & PA FUR LLC
746 Long Hill Rd (06457-5073)
P.O. Box 1094 (06457-1094)
PHONE.................................860 659-7766
Geoffrey C Saunders, Principal
EMP: 2
SALES (est): 104.2K Privately Held
SIC: 3999 Furs

(G-4374)
MACHINE REPAIR SERVICES LLC
142 Freeman Rd (06457-5706)
PHONE.................................860 729-7410
Bruce Clark, Owner
EMP: 1
SALES: 100K Privately Held
SIC: 3541 Machine tool replacement & repair parts, metal cutting types

(G-4375)
METAL IMPROVEMENT COMPANY LLC
20 Tuttle Pl Ste 6 (06457-1870)
PHONE.................................860 635-9994
Paul Dimatti, Manager
EMP: 25
SALES (corp-wide): 2.4B Publicly Held
SIC: 3398 Shot peening (treating steel to reduce fatigue)
HQ: Metal Improvement Company, Llc
80 E Rte 4 Ste 310
Paramus NJ 07652
201 843-7800

(G-4376)
MHQ INC
Also Called: Natick Auto Sales
750 Newfield St (06457-1869)
PHONE.................................888 242-1118
Michael Fratoni, Principal
EMP: 16 Privately Held
SIC: 5999 3711 Police supply stores; patrol wagons (motor vehicles); assembly of
PA: Mhq, Inc.
401 Elm St
Marlborough MA 01752

(G-4377)
MICROSPECIALITIES INC
430 Smith St (06457-1531)
PHONE.................................203 874-1832
Gaston Levesque, CEO
EMP: 10 EST: 1997
SQ FT: 5,200
SALES (est): 1.6MM Privately Held
WEB: www.microspecialties.com
SIC: 3841 Surgical knife blades & handles

(G-4378)
MIDDLESEX SHADES AND BLINDS ✪
386 Main St (06457-3360)
PHONE.................................860 346-7705
EMP: 1 EST: 2019
SALES (est): 57.3K Privately Held
SIC: 2591 Window blinds

(G-4379)
MIDDLETOWN PRINTING CO INC
Also Called: Minuteman Press
512 Main St (06457-2810)
PHONE.................................860 347-5700
Charlie Lazich, President
EMP: 10
SALES (est): 1.2MM Privately Held
SIC: 2752 Commercial printing, lithographic

(G-4380)
MIKES SIGN MAINTENANCE LLC
35 Sisk St (06457-2392)
PHONE.................................860 347-1462
Doren Perruccio,
EMP: 1
SALES: 51K Privately Held
SIC: 3993 Signs & advertising specialties

(G-4381)
MOHAWK MANUFACTURING COMPANY
1270 Newfield St (06457-1842)
PHONE.................................860 632-2345
William W Ferguson Jr, President
William P Ferguson, Vice Pres
Debra J Ferguson, Admin Sec
EMP: 18 EST: 1921
SQ FT: 32,000
SALES (est): 3.4MM Privately Held
WEB: www.mohawk-mfg.com
SIC: 3469 Stamping metal for the trade

(G-4382)
MORRIS WOODWORKING
75 Pease Ave (06457-2259)
PHONE.................................860 346-7500
Thomas Morris, Partner
Peter Westerberg, Partner
EMP: 2
SALES: 150K Privately Held
SIC: 2431 2541 2434 2531 Millwork; wood partitions & fixtures; wood kitchen cabinets; public building & related furniture; metal household furniture; wood household furniture

(G-4383)
NATIONAL WELDING LLC
27 Clinton Ave (06457-2703)
P.O. Box 452 (06457-0452)
PHONE.................................860 818-1240
Sebastiano Spada, Principal
EMP: 2 EST: 2014
SALES (est): 65K Privately Held
SIC: 7692 Welding repair

(G-4384)
NATS INC
Also Called: North American Technical Svcs
511 Centerpoint Dr (06457-7570)
PHONE.................................860 635-6820
Syed R Maswood, President
Awatef Gacem Maswood, Vice Pres
EMP: 11
SQ FT: 3,000
SALES (est): 1.7MM Privately Held
WEB: www.nats-usa.com
SIC: 8734 3822 3826 Radiation laboratories; auto controls regulating residntl & coml environmt & applncs; elemental analyzers

(G-4385)
NDC TECHNOLOGIES INC
Z-Mike Division
454 Smith St (06457-1531)
PHONE.................................860 635-2100
Marc Binette, Sales/Mktg Mgr
EMP: 4
SALES (corp-wide): 2B Privately Held
WEB: www.betalasermike.com
SIC: 7699 3823 Caliper, gauge & other machinists' instrument repair; industrial instrmnts msrmnt display/control process variable
HQ: Ndc Technologies, Inc.
5314 Irwindale Ave
Irwindale CA 91706
626 960-3300

(G-4386)
NICE T-SHIRT
180 Johnson St Ste 1 (06457-2247)
PHONE.................................860 349-0727
EMP: 2
SALES (est): 73.2K Privately Held
SIC: 2759 Commercial printing

Middletown - Middlesex County (G-4387)

(G-4387)
NORTHERN WOLF PRESS LLC
1189 Washington St E19 (06457-2948)
PHONE..................860 227-0135
Michael A Ramirez, *Principal*
EMP: 1
SALES (est): 45.9K **Privately Held**
SIC: 2741 Miscellaneous publishing

(G-4388)
NU VISION HOMES LLC
110 Court St (06457-3333)
PHONE..................860 209-8492
EMP: 1 **EST:** 2002
SALES: 80K **Privately Held**
SIC: 2452 Mfg Prefabricated Wood Buildings

(G-4389)
ORACLE CORPORATION
54 Shady Hill Ln (06457-1786)
PHONE..................860 632-8329
Nancy Marx, *Branch Mgr*
EMP: 302
SALES (corp-wide): 39.5B **Publicly Held**
SIC: 7372 Business oriented computer software
PA: Oracle Corporation
    500 Oracle Pkwy
    Redwood City CA 94065
    650 506-7000

(G-4390)
PASSPORT PUBLICATIONS OF
1099 Arbutus St (06457-5181)
PHONE..................631 736-6691
Thomas Maddaloni, *Principal*
EMP: 1 **EST:** 2015
SALES (est): 41.3K **Privately Held**
SIC: 2741 Miscellaneous publishing

(G-4391)
PEAKS PARROTS
749 Saybrook Rd Ste 2 (06457-4742)
PHONE..................860 316-2788
Edgar Hurle, *Principal*
EMP: 2
SALES (est): 85.5K **Privately Held**
SIC: 3999 Pet supplies

(G-4392)
PENCO CORPORATION
Also Called: Jarvis Products
33 Anderson Rd (06457-4901)
PHONE..................860 347-7271
Vincent Volpe, *President*
Daniel Burr, *Technician*
John Sadlowski, *Technician*
EMP: 130
SALES (corp-wide): 23.6MM **Privately Held**
SIC: 3556 Food products machinery
PA: Penco Corporation
    229 Buckingham St
    Hartford CT
    860 278-2345

(G-4393)
PLASTIC DESIGN INTL INC (PA)
Also Called: PDI
111 Industrial Park Rd (06457-1520)
PHONE..................860 632-2001
Donald A Bergeron, *President*
Yvonne Ledoux, *Vice Pres*
Suzette Gaudet, *Safety Mgr*
Kim Guillemin, *Purch Agent*
Roman Suski, *Engineer*
▲ **EMP:** 46 **EST:** 1977
SQ FT: 30,000
SALES: 5.9MM **Privately Held**
WEB: www.plasticdesign.com
SIC: 3089 3544 Injection molding of plastics; forms (molds), for foundry & plastics working machinery

(G-4394)
POLISH WELDING LLC
476 Long Hill Rd (06457-4917)
PHONE..................860 347-0368
David Blachura, *Principal*
EMP: 1
SALES (est): 40.8K **Privately Held**
SIC: 7692 Welding repair

(G-4395)
POWER-DYNE LLC
Also Called: Power-Dyne LLC/Bidwll Indstrl
2055 S Main St (06457-6151)
PHONE..................860 346-9283
Susan Barton, *Chief Mktg Ofcr*
Donald Bidwell Jr, *CIO*
EMP: 25
SQ FT: 40,000
SALES (est): 2.6MM **Privately Held**
SIC: 3423 3829 7699 Wrenches, hand tools; gauging instruments, thickness ultrasonic; hydraulic equipment repair

(G-4396)
PRATT & WHITNEY ENGINE SVCS
1 Aircraft Rd (06457-5723)
P.O. Box 611 (06457-0611)
PHONE..................860 344-4000
Robert Ouellette, *Fire Chief*
Roger Cherichoni, *Vice Pres*
Barry Brimmer, *Maint Spvr*
Grant Stanczuk, *Production*
Tracy Parks, *QC Mgr*
EMP: 500
SALES (corp-wide): 66.5B **Publicly Held**
SIC: 3728 3724 3714 Aircraft assemblies, subassemblies & parts; aircraft engines & engine parts; motor vehicle parts & accessories
HQ: Pratt & Whitney Engine Services, Inc.
    1525 Midway Park Rd
    Bridgeport WV 26330
    304 842-5421

(G-4397)
PRECISION SPEED MFG LLC
422 Timber Ridge Rd (06457-7540)
P.O. Box 501, East Berlin (06023-0501)
PHONE..................860 635-8811
Todd Dipentima,
Chris Dipentima,
Vincent Dipentima,
EMP: 30 **EST:** 2004
SQ FT: 21,000
SALES (est): 5.3MM **Privately Held**
WEB: www.precisionspeedmfg.com
SIC: 3724 3728 Aircraft engines & engine parts; aircraft parts & equipment

(G-4398)
PROTOTYPE PLASTIC MOLD CO INC
35 Industrial Park Pl (06457-1501)
PHONE..................860 632-2800
Victor De Jong, *President*
Victor Feldesy, *QC Mgr*
Brian Smith, *Manager*
Murray A Gerber, *Admin Sec*
EMP: 46
SQ FT: 27,000
SALES (est): 10.2MM **Privately Held**
WEB: www.prototypeplastic.net
SIC: 3089 3544 Injection molding of plastics; special dies, tools, jigs & fixtures

(G-4399)
QUEMERE INTERNATIONAL LLC
234 Middle St (06457-7517)
PHONE..................914 934-8366
Celine Quemere, *Owner*
EMP: 8 **EST:** 1999
SALES (est): 706K **Privately Held**
SIC: 3253 Ceramic wall & floor tile

(G-4400)
R AND B PRTECTIVE COATINGS LLC
29 Copper Beech Dr (06457-6161)
PHONE..................860 836-7854
Benny John Tavana, *President*
EMP: 2
SALES (est): 86.7K **Privately Held**
SIC: 3479 Metal coating & allied service

(G-4401)
RA SMYTHE LLC
439 Higby Rd (06457-2383)
PHONE..................860 398-5764
Catherine L Smythe, *Principal*
EMP: 4

SALES (est): 235.2K **Privately Held**
SIC: 3823 Industrial instrmnts msrmnt display/control process variable

(G-4402)
RAYCO METAL FINISHING INC
134 Mill St (06457-3749)
P.O. Box 177 (06457-0177)
PHONE..................860 347-7434
Louise Goldreich, *Ch of Bd*
Mark Goldreich, *Vice Pres*
George Goldreich, *Treasurer*
EMP: 18
SQ FT: 7,500
SALES: 1MM **Privately Held**
SIC: 3471 Electroplating of metals or formed products

(G-4403)
REAL-TIME ANALYZERS INC
362 Industrial Park Rd # 8 (06457-1548)
PHONE..................860 635-9800
Stuart Farquharson, *President*
David Hamblen, *Corp Secy*
Chetan Shende, *Research*
EMP: 8
SQ FT: 3,000
SALES (est): 1.6MM **Privately Held**
WEB: www.rta.biz
SIC: 3826 Mass spectroscopy instrumentation

(G-4404)
RELIANT SERVICES LLC
100 Saddle Hill Dr (06457-5806)
PHONE..................860 346-6107
Randall Root, *Principal*
EMP: 1
SALES (est): 43.4K **Privately Held**
SIC: 7692 7389 Welding repair; scrap steel cutting

(G-4405)
RISHA RISHI LLC
Also Called: West and Package
596 Washington St (06457-2513)
PHONE..................860 346-7645
Risha Rishi, *Owner*
EMP: 3
SALES (est): 207.3K **Privately Held**
SIC: 2631 Container, packaging & boxboard

(G-4406)
ROLLCORP LLC
9 Red Orange Rd (06457-4916)
PHONE..................860 347-5225
Michael John Antol, *President*
EMP: 1
SALES (est): 125K **Privately Held**
SIC: 3562 3471 Roller bearings & parts; chromium plating of metals or formed products

(G-4407)
SAM AUGERI & SONS SIGNS
695 High St Ste A (06457-2288)
PHONE..................860 346-1261
Michael Augeri, *Owner*
EMP: 1
SQ FT: 2,400
SALES: 100K **Privately Held**
SIC: 3993 5699 Signs & advertising specialties; T-shirts, custom printed

(G-4408)
SEA-LION AMERICA COMPANY
800 Plaza Middlesex 1 (06457-3475)
PHONE..................860 316-5563
Edward Kirejczyk III, *Principal*
Caroline Wojcicki, *Principal*
EMP: 2
SALES (est): 79.9K **Privately Held**
SIC: 3582 Commercial laundry equipment

(G-4409)
SECURITY SYSTEMS INC
1125 Middle St (06457-1526)
PHONE..................800 833-3211
David G Roman, *Principal*
EMP: 3
SALES (est): 142.3K **Privately Held**
SIC: 3699 Security control equipment & systems

(G-4410)
SERVOTECH INC
478 Timber Ridge Rd (06457-7540)
P.O. Box 388, Haddam (06438-0388)
PHONE..................860 632-0164
Michael Norman, *President*
Debra Norman, *Vice Pres*
EMP: 4
SALES (est): 632.4K **Privately Held**
WEB: www.servotechusa.com
SIC: 7378 7694 Computer maintenance & repair; motor repair services

(G-4411)
SHARON M STINSON
Also Called: Embroidery By Sharon
60 Ferry St Apt 2c (06457-6803)
PHONE..................860 218-7282
EMP: 1
SALES (est): 34.9K **Privately Held**
SIC: 2395 Pleating/Stitching Services

(G-4412)
SIGNATURE SIGNS
22 Green Briar Cir (06457-4907)
PHONE..................860 704-0397
Sabrina Bartels, *Owner*
EMP: 1
SALES (est): 48.1K **Privately Held**
SIC: 3993 Signs & advertising specialties

(G-4413)
SIGNMART LLC
471 Washington St (06457-2525)
PHONE..................860 347-7446
Carolyn Yuris, *Principal*
EMP: 2
SALES (est): 130K **Privately Held**
SIC: 3993 Signs & advertising specialties

(G-4414)
SIGNS ON DEMAND
777 Laurel Grove Rd (06457-4961)
PHONE..................860 346-1720
Denis O'Brien, *Principal*
EMP: 2
SALES (est): 155.6K **Privately Held**
SIC: 3993 Signs & advertising specialties

(G-4415)
SILICONE CASTING TECHNOLOGIES
9 Red Orange Rd (06457-4916)
PHONE..................860 347-5227
Michael J Antol, *Principal*
EMP: 3
SALES (est): 181.6K **Privately Held**
SIC: 3325 Alloy steel castings, except investment

(G-4416)
SIMPLY SOAP
86 Plumb Rd (06457-1922)
PHONE..................860 347-4174
EMP: 2 **EST:** 2013
SALES (est): 151.7K **Privately Held**
SIC: 2841 Soap & other detergents

(G-4417)
SKYLINE EXHIBITS & GRAPHICS
362 Industrial Park Rd # 6 (06457-1548)
PHONE..................860 635-2400
Larry Zollo, *President*
Lawrence J Zollo, *Principal*
Sal Randazzo, *Buyer*
EMP: 10
SQ FT: 12,500
SALES (est): 1.7MM **Privately Held**
WEB: www.skyline-ct.com
SIC: 2653 Display items, corrugated: made from purchased materials

(G-4418)
SMILE EXCHANGE LLC
839 Long Hill Rd Apt C (06457-5085)
PHONE..................860 342-0333
Nancy Lucas, *Manager*
EMP: 2
SALES (est): 94K **Privately Held**
SIC: 3581 Automatic vending machines

(G-4419)
SMILING DOG
77 Arbutus St (06457-5118)
PHONE..................860 344-0707

Kimberly Barcello, *Principal*
EMP: 3
SALES (est): 158.6K **Privately Held**
SIC: 2393 3961 2771 Textile bags; costume jewelry; greeting cards

(G-4420)
SOFTWARE SYSTEMS & SUPPORT LLC
194 Rising Trail Dr (06457-1663)
PHONE....................203 470-8482
John-Paul Lamb, *Principal*
John Lamb, *Principal*
EMP: 1
SALES (est): 43.5K **Privately Held**
SIC: 7372 Prepackaged software

(G-4421)
SOMERSET PLASTICS COMPANY
454 Timber Ridge Rd (06457-7540)
P.O. Box 8446, Berlin (06037-8446)
PHONE....................860 635-1601
Clifford F White Jr, *President*
Clifford White Jr, *President*
Lois White, *Vice Pres*
Kim White, *Admin Sec*
EMP: 20
SQ FT: 10,000
SALES: 2MM **Privately Held**
SIC: 3544 3089 Forms (molds), for foundry & plastics working machinery; injection molding of plastics

(G-4422)
SPERIAN PROTECTN INSTRUMENTATN
651 S Main St (06457-4252)
PHONE....................860 344-1079
Jerry Mc Gurkin,
Jeffrey Brown,
EMP: 146
SQ FT: 75,000
SALES (est): 14.7MM
SALES (corp-wide): 41.8B **Publicly Held**
WEB: www.posichek.com
SIC: 3829 3812 3823 Gas detectors; search & navigation equipment; industrial instrmnts msrmnt display/control process variable
HQ: Honeywell Analytics Inc.
  405 Barclay Blvd
  Lincolnshire IL 60069
  847 955-8200

(G-4423)
T & J MANUFACTURING LLP
Also Called: T&J Manufacturing
1385 Newfield St (06457-1819)
PHONE....................860 632-8655
Mark Jablonski, *Owner*
Chris Targanski, *Partner*
EMP: 25
SALES (est): 3.7MM **Privately Held**
SIC: 3599 Machine shop, jobbing & repair

(G-4424)
TD&S ACQUISITION LLC
Also Called: Little Honey's Bakery
180 Johnson St (06457-2247)
PHONE....................860 341-1001
Seth Lieberfarb, *Principal*
EMP: 2
SALES (est): 166.4K **Privately Held**
SIC: 6799 2051 Investors; cakes, bakery: except frozen

(G-4425)
TEST LOGIC INC
17 Kenneth Dooley Dr (06457-7530)
PHONE....................860 347-8378
Rod Gwillam, *President*
Kwok Wong, *Exec VP*
Skip Haskell, *Mfg Staff*
Amanda Hartwig, *Purchasing*
Rachel Woolley, *Executive Asst*
EMP: 14
SQ FT: 9,000
SALES (est): 3.7MM **Privately Held**
WEB: www.testlogic.com
SIC: 3825 Engine electrical test equipment

(G-4426)
THESE GUYS
32 Washington St Ste 5 (06457-2962)
PHONE....................860 344-0022
Jim Schmaltz, *Owner*
EMP: 1
SALES (est): 122.9K **Privately Held**
SIC: 2517 Home entertainment unit cabinets, wood

(G-4427)
TINNY CORPORATION
Also Called: Shelco Filters Division
100 Bradley St (06457-1513)
PHONE....................860 854-6121
Robert Leconche Jr, *President*
Debra A Leconche, *Vice Pres*
Darin Dockter, *Sales Dir*
Bruce Hafner, *Sales Dir*
▲ **EMP:** 25
SQ FT: 40,000
SALES (est): 7.4MM **Privately Held**
WEB: www.shelco.com
SIC: 3569 5074 5085 Filters, general line: industrial; plumbing & hydronic heating supplies; filters, industrial

(G-4428)
TRIUMPH MANUFACTURING CO INC
422 Timber Ridge Rd (06457-7540)
P.O. Box 501, East Berlin (06023-0501)
PHONE....................860 635-8811
Vincent Dipentima, *President*
Todd Dipentima, *Vice Pres*
Ivonne Garcia, *Buyer*
EMP: 15
SQ FT: 7,100
SALES (est): 1.8MM **Privately Held**
SIC: 3599 Machine shop, jobbing & repair

(G-4429)
WESLEYAN UNIVERSITY
Also Called: Wesleyan University Press
215 Long Ln (06457-4073)
PHONE....................860 685-7727
Suzanna Tempelton, *Manager*
EMP: 1
SALES (corp-wide): 231.5MM **Privately Held**
WEB: www.wesleyan.edu
SIC: 2732 8221 Textbooks: printing & binding, not publishing; university
PA: Wesleyan University
  45 Wyllys Ave
  Middletown CT 06459
  860 685-2000

(G-4430)
WESLEYAN UNIVERSITY
Also Called: Wes Press
110 Mount Vernon St (06457-3289)
PHONE....................860 685-2980
Suzanna Tamminen, *Director*
EMP: 8
SALES (corp-wide): 231.5MM **Privately Held**
WEB: www.wesleyan.edu
SIC: 2731 8221 Book publishing; university
PA: Wesleyan University
  45 Wyllys Ave
  Middletown CT 06459
  860 685-2000

(G-4431)
WET CROW INTERNET INC
515 Centerpoint Dr 703 (06457-7570)
PHONE....................860 919-0164
Thomas G Psillas, *President*
EMP: 1
SALES (est): 60K **Privately Held**
SIC: 3537 Platforms, cargo

(G-4432)
WM CORVO CONSULTANTS INC
769 Newfield St (06457-1846)
PHONE....................860 346-6500
Andrew Corvo, *Principal*
EMP: 2
SALES (est): 97.1K **Privately Held**
SIC: 2759 Publication printing

(G-4433)
WRITESTUFF CREATIVE SERVICES L
32 Andrew St (06457-4500)
PHONE....................860 343-1919
Patrick R Spadaccino, *Manager*
EMP: 1
SALES (est): 47.5K **Privately Held**
SIC: 2731 Book publishing

(G-4434)
YOUNGS COMMUNICATIONS INC
Also Called: Youngs Printing
182 Court St (06457-3357)
PHONE....................860 347-8567
Daniel Litwin, *President*
Georgia Chu, *Vice Pres*
EMP: 10
SQ FT: 12,000
SALES (est): 1.9MM **Privately Held**
SIC: 2752 Commercial printing, offset

Milford
New Haven County

(G-4435)
26 BEECHWOOD AVENUE LLC
34 Highwood Rd (06460-5331)
PHONE....................203 713-6425
Jack Levine, *Principal*
EMP: 1
SALES (est): 78.2K **Privately Held**
SIC: 2499 Wood products

(G-4436)
A L C INOVATORS INC
230 Pepes Farm Rd Ste C (06460-8611)
PHONE....................203 877-8526
Scott Brown, *President*
Carol Musante, *Admin Sec*
◆ **EMP:** 6
SQ FT: 4,800
SALES (est): 748K **Privately Held**
WEB: www.alc-innovators.com
SIC: 2047 2048 3999 Dog food; cat food; feed supplements; pet supplies

(G-4437)
ABBOTT ASSOCIATES INC
261a Pepes Farm Rd (06460-3671)
P.O. Box 5405 (06460-0706)
PHONE....................203 878-2370
John Winfield, *President*
EMP: 15 **EST:** 1968
SQ FT: 10,000
SALES (est): 2.7MM **Privately Held**
WEB: www.goabbott.com
SIC: 3841 Surgical & medical instruments

(G-4438)
ABET TECHNOLOGIES INC
168 Old Gate Ln (06460-3651)
PHONE....................203 540-9990
Zbigniew Drozdowicz, *CEO*
Allen Smith, *President*
Valerie Smith, *Director*
EMP: 5
SQ FT: 2,900
SALES: 1.6MM **Privately Held**
WEB: www.abet-technologies.com
SIC: 3827 Optical test & inspection equipment

(G-4439)
ACME PRESS INC
95 Erna Ave (06461-3119)
P.O. Box 344 (06460-0344)
PHONE....................203 334-8221
Bruce Riso, *President*
Tom Riso, *Vice Pres*
EMP: 3 **EST:** 1925
SQ FT: 1,500
SALES (est): 330K **Privately Held**
SIC: 2752 Commercial printing, offset

(G-4440)
ADEMCO INC
Also Called: ADI Global Distribution
121 Woodmont Rd (06460-2840)
PHONE....................203 877-2702
EMP: 9

SALES (corp-wide): 4.8B **Publicly Held**
SIC: 5063 3669 3822 Electrical apparatus & equipment; emergency alarms; auto controls regulating residntl & coml environmt & applncs
HQ: Ademco Inc.
  1985 Douglas Dr N
  Golden Valley MN 55422
  800 468-1502

(G-4441)
ADVANCED LINEN GROUP
215 Pepes Farm Rd (06460-3626)
P.O. Box 3608 (06460-0945)
PHONE....................203 877-3896
Joel B Gorkowski, *Principal*
EMP: 10
SALES (est): 1.3MM **Privately Held**
SIC: 2299 Crash, linen

(G-4442)
ADVANCED PRCSION CASTINGS CORP
120 Pullman Dr (06461-2058)
PHONE....................203 736-9452
George Taylor Middleton, *President*
George M Middleton, *Vice Pres*
Maryann Middleton, *Vice Pres*
EMP: 4
SALES (est): 531.6K **Privately Held**
SIC: 3363 Aluminum die-castings

(G-4443)
AFFORDABLE SIGN CO
467 Naugatuck Ave (06460-5048)
P.O. Box 5111 (06460-1511)
PHONE....................203 874-0875
Rick Ciesluk, *Owner*
EMP: 1
SALES (est): 70.8K **Privately Held**
SIC: 3993 2759 Signs, not made in custom sign painting shops; screen printing

(G-4444)
AIR-LOCK INCORPORATED
108 Gulf St (06460-4859)
PHONE....................203 878-4691
Michael H McCarthy, *President*
John W Bassick, *President*
Robert A Vincent, *Chairman*
Lois Hetherington, *Vice Pres*
David A Sweet, *Treasurer*
EMP: 25 **EST:** 1951
SQ FT: 27,000
SALES (est): 5.3MM
SALES (corp-wide): 68.7MM **Privately Held**
WEB: www.airlockinc.com
SIC: 3728 3429 Aircraft parts & equipment; manufactured hardware (general)
PA: David Clark Company Incorporated
  360 Franklin St
  Worcester MA 01604
  508 756-6216

(G-4445)
ALC SALES COMPANY LLC (PA)
230 Pepes Farm Rd Ste C (06460-8611)
PHONE....................203 877-8526
Scott Brown, *Mng Member*
Carol Reitenbach, *Admin Asst*
EMP: 3
SQ FT: 6,000
SALES (est): 512.9K **Privately Held**
SIC: 2048 Feed supplements

(G-4446)
ALCAT INCORPORATED
116 W Main St (06460-3310)
PHONE....................203 878-0648
James Edwards, *President*
▲ **EMP:** 32
SQ FT: 31,000
SALES: 4MM **Privately Held**
WEB: www.alcat.com
SIC: 3083 Plastic finished products, laminated

(G-4447)
ALFA NOBEL LLC
94 Utica St (06461-2347)
PHONE....................203 876-2823
EMP: 5
SQ FT: 11,770
SALES: 1.5MM **Privately Held**
SIC: 2676 Mfg Wet Wipes

Milford - New Haven County (G-4448)

(G-4448)
ALINABAL INC (HQ)
Also Called: Sterling Screw Machine Div
28 Woodmont Rd (06460-2872)
PHONE..................................203 877-3241
Samuel S Bergami Jr, *President*
Luigi Cazzaniga, *General Mgr*
Tom Crowley, *General Mgr*
Kevin Conlisk, *Vice Pres*
Paul Kelley, *Vice Pres*
▲ **EMP:** 243
SQ FT: 110,000
SALES (est): 33.2MM
SALES (corp-wide): 57MM **Privately Held**
WEB: www.dacoinstrument.com
SIC: 3469 3399 3625 3728 Metal stampings; laminating steel; electric controls & control accessories, industrial; aircraft parts & equipment; tie rods, motor vehicle; dies & die holders for metal cutting, forming, die casting
PA: Alinabal Holdings Corporation
28 Woodmont Rd
Milford CT 06460
203 877-3241

(G-4449)
ALINABAL HOLDINGS CORPORATION (PA)
28 Woodmont Rd (06460-2872)
PHONE..................................203 877-3241
Samuel Bergami, *President*
Janet Muller, *Buyer*
Robert Pentino, *Chief Engr*
Greg Humphries, *Project Engr*
Kevin M Conlisk, *CFO*
▲ **EMP:** 300
SQ FT: 147,000
SALES: 57MM **Privately Held**
WEB: www.alinabal.com
SIC: 3714 3577 3399 3469 Bearings, motor vehicle; printers, computer; laminating steel; metal stampings; mechanical & electromechanical counters & devices

(G-4450)
ALL STEEL FABRICATING INC
49 Higgins Dr (06460-2853)
PHONE..................................203 783-1860
Steven Czupi, *President*
Helen Czupi, *Admin Sec*
EMP: 2
SQ FT: 1,500
SALES (est): 140K **Privately Held**
SIC: 3444 Sheet metalwork

(G-4451)
ALSTROM POWER
55 Shelland St (06461-1773)
PHONE..................................203 783-1046
Curtis Morgan, *CEO*
EMP: 2
SALES (est): 230.7K **Privately Held**
SIC: 3634 Electric housewares & fans

(G-4452)
ANNA M CHISILENCO-RAHO
67 Cherry St Ste 2 (06460-8904)
PHONE..................................203 877-0377
Anna M Chisilenco-Raho, *Principal*
EMP: 8
SALES (est): 784.1K **Privately Held**
SIC: 3843 Enamels, dentists'

(G-4453)
ANRAY LITHOGRAPHERS
8 Parkway Ter (06461-1929)
PHONE..................................203 877-1000
Gary Sherrick, *Owner*
EMP: 7 **EST:** 2018
SALES (est): 94.4K **Privately Held**
SIC: 2752 Commercial printing, lithographic

(G-4454)
ARCHER SIGN SERVICE LLC
Also Called: Archer Signs
316 Boston Post Rd (06460-2527)
PHONE..................................203 882-8484
EMP: 4
SALES (est): 319.2K **Privately Held**
SIC: 1799 3993 Investor

(G-4455)
ARCHER SIGN SERVICE LLC
316 Boston Post Rd (06460-2527)
PHONE..................................203 377-5362
John Rawlinson, *Owner*
John Leary, *Partner*
Jack Rawlinson, *Partner*
EMP: 5
SQ FT: 1,300
SALES (est): 353.1K **Privately Held**
SIC: 7389 3993 Sign painting & lettering shop; signs & advertising specialties

(G-4456)
ARGYLE OPTICS LLC
28 Tower St (06460-3213)
PHONE..................................203 451-3320
Eric Stanley, *Principal*
EMP: 3 **EST:** 2010
SALES (est): 258.1K **Privately Held**
SIC: 3827 Optical instruments & lenses

(G-4457)
ARRAY SYSTEMS LLC
205 Research Dr Ste 4 (06460-8552)
PHONE..................................203 877-4625
Brian R Ouellette,
EMP: 2
SQ FT: 800
SALES (est): 549.8K **Privately Held**
SIC: 3829 Measuring & controlling devices

(G-4458)
ART Q TECH SIGNS
282 Woodmont Rd Ste J1 (06460-8548)
PHONE..................................203 874-6504
Fady Jalaf, *Owner*
EMP: 2
SALES (est): 260.7K **Privately Held**
SIC: 3993 Electric signs

(G-4459)
ARTHUR I PLATT INC
Also Called: Tool Clip
160 Rock Ln (06460-3853)
PHONE..................................203 874-0091
John W Szoke, *President*
Margaret Szoke, *Vice Pres*
EMP: 2 **EST:** 1931
SQ FT: 2,500
SALES (est): 328.5K **Privately Held**
WEB: www.arthuriplatt.com
SIC: 3545 5084 Tool holders; industrial machinery & equipment

(G-4460)
ATLANTECH MANUFACTURING CO INC (PA)
89 Eastern Steel Rd (06460-2861)
PHONE..................................203 500-6880
Jason K Blake, *Principal*
EMP: 1
SALES (est): 139.5K **Privately Held**
SIC: 3599 Machine shop, jobbing & repair

(G-4461)
ATLANTIC SENSORS & CONTRLS LLC
301 Brewster Rd (06460-3700)
PHONE..................................203 878-8118
Peter Terek,
EMP: 4
SALES (est): 627.5K **Privately Held**
SIC: 3829 Thermocouples

(G-4462)
AUDIOWORKS INC
260 Old Gate Ln (06460-8621)
PHONE..................................203 876-1133
Frank A Ventresca, *President*
EMP: 5
SQ FT: 5,600
SALES (est): 1MM **Privately Held**
WEB: www.audioworksct.com
SIC: 3651 Electronic kits for home assembly: radio, TV, phonograph

(G-4463)
B & A COMPANY INC
160 Wampus Ln (06460-4861)
PHONE..................................203 876-7527
Richard Schwarz, *President*
Ronald Schwartz, *Vice Pres*
EMP: 20

SALES (est): 3.8MM **Privately Held**
SIC: 3599 Machine shop, jobbing & repair

(G-4464)
B L C INVESTMENTS INC
Also Called: Gradar Metals
228a Rowe Ave (06461-3031)
PHONE..................................203 877-1888
Barry Chuba, *Vice Pres*
EMP: 4
SQ FT: 5,000 **Privately Held**
SIC: 3444 1799 Sheet metalwork; hydraulic equipment, installation & service

(G-4465)
BALDING PRECISION INC
61 Woodmont Rd (06460-2840)
PHONE..................................203 878-9135
Mike Goodman, *President*
EMP: 8
SQ FT: 5,000
SALES (est): 1.2MM **Privately Held**
SIC: 3599 Machine shop, jobbing & repair

(G-4466)
BEAD INDUSTRIES INC (PA)
Also Called: Bead Electronics
11 Cascade Blvd (06460-2849)
PHONE..................................203 301-0270
Jill Bryant Mayer, *CEO*
Jerry Weglinski, *Engineer*
James Balazsi, *Senior Engr*
David Brenton, *Design Engr*
Brenton David, *Design Engr*
◆ **EMP:** 50 **EST:** 1914
SQ FT: 75,000
SALES (est): 9.7MM **Privately Held**
WEB: www.beadindustries.com
SIC: 3432 3679 3678 3643 Plumbing fixture fittings & trim; electronic circuits; electronic connectors; current-carrying wiring devices; power transmission equipment; bolts, nuts, rivets & washers

(G-4467)
BEARD CONCRETE CO DERBY INC (PA)
Also Called: Beard Concrete Company
127 Boston Post Rd (06460-3104)
PHONE..................................203 874-2533
Robert Beard, *President*
James R Beard, *Vice Pres*
EMP: 4 **EST:** 1957
SQ FT: 9,600
SALES (est): 1.1MM **Privately Held**
SIC: 3273 Ready-mixed concrete

(G-4468)
BETZ TOOL COMPANY INC
70 Raton Rd Ste K (06461-1768)
PHONE..................................203 878-1187
George Betz, *President*
Sharon Betz, *Vice Pres*
EMP: 3
SQ FT: 2,400
SALES: 250K **Privately Held**
WEB: www.betztool.com
SIC: 3544 3089 Industrial molds; injection molding of plastics

(G-4469)
BIC CONSUMER PRODUCTS MFG CO
565 Bic Dr (06461-1769)
PHONE..................................203 783-2000
Mario Guevara, *President*
Ken Brannin, *Vice Pres*
Thomas M Kelleher, *Vice Pres*
James V Dipietro, *Treasurer*
Lisa Palladino, *Manager*
▲ **EMP:** 120
SALES (est): 18.3MM
SALES (corp-wide): 791.2MM **Privately Held**
WEB: www.biceveryday.com
SIC: 3951 2899 Ball point pens & parts; correction fluid
HQ: Bic Usa Inc.
1 Bic Way Ste 1 # 1
Shelton CT 06484
203 783-2000

(G-4470)
BIC CORPORATION
95 Settlers Ridge Rd (06460-3782)
PHONE..................................203 538-5028

EMP: 2
SALES (corp-wide): 791.2MM **Privately Held**
SIC: 3951 Ball point pens & parts
HQ: Bic Corporation
1 Bic Way Ste 1 # 1
Shelton CT 06484
203 783-2000

(G-4471)
BILL HOAGLAND
250 Pond Point Ave (06460-6750)
PHONE..................................203 877-0157
Kimberlea Hoagland, *Principal*
EMP: 2
SALES (est): 129.8K **Privately Held**
SIC: 3999 Magic equipment, supplies & props

(G-4472)
BLAHUT MACHINE CO
655 Plains Rd Unit I (06461-1736)
PHONE..................................203 878-3643
Laszo Blahut, *Owner*
EMP: 2
SQ FT: 2,000
SALES (est): 201.7K **Privately Held**
WEB: www.blahutmc.biz
SIC: 3599 Machine shop, jobbing & repair

(G-4473)
BLUE LILY COTTON LLC
91 Governors Ave (06460-3439)
P.O. Box 561 (06460-0561)
PHONE..................................860 869-7734
Suzan Zanbak,
EMP: 1
SALES (est): 46.2K **Privately Held**
SIC: 2391 Curtains & draperies

(G-4474)
BOJAK COMPANY
152 Old Gate Ln D (06460-3651)
PHONE..................................203 378-5086
Carl Johansson, *President*
EMP: 7
SALES (est): 1MM **Privately Held**
SIC: 3829 Fire detector systems, non-electric

(G-4475)
BOMAN PRECISION TECH INC
67 Erna Ave (06461-3118)
PHONE..................................203 415-8350
Allen Godman, *President*
Robert Godman, *Admin Sec*
EMP: 6
SQ FT: 5,000
SALES (est): 1MM **Privately Held**
WEB: www.bomantool.com
SIC: 3599 Machine shop, jobbing & repair

(G-4476)
BOOST OXYGEN LLC
92 Woodmont Rd (06460-2832)
PHONE..................................203 331-8100
Anne Steele, *Office Mgr*
Robert Neuner, *Mng Member*
Elle Westphal, *Manager*
EMP: 2
SALES (est): 326.7K **Privately Held**
WEB: www.boostoxygen.com
SIC: 2813 Oxygen, compressed or liquefied

(G-4477)
BUCKS SPUMONI COMPANY INC
Also Called: Buck's Ice Cream
229 Pepes Farm Rd (06460-3671)
PHONE..................................203 874-2007
Charles Buck Jr, *President*
Lois Gosselin, *Admin Sec*
EMP: 15
SQ FT: 14,000
SALES (est): 2.5MM **Privately Held**
SIC: 2024 Ice cream, bulk; spumoni

(G-4478)
CAAP CO INC
152 Pepes Farm Rd (06460-3670)
P.O. Box 2066, Shelton (06484-1066)
PHONE..................................203 877-0375
James F Moraveck, *President*
Christopher J Moraveck, *Vice Pres*
Charles Scheidler Jr, *Vice Pres*

▲ = Import ▼ = Export
◆ = Import/Export

Christine L Sledge, *Vice Pres*
Kim Loomis, *Bookkeeper*
▲ **EMP:** 20
SQ FT: 10,000
SALES (est): 4.9MM **Privately Held**
WEB: www.caapco.com
SIC: 2899 Waterproofing compounds

(G-4479)
CADCOM INC
110 Raton Rd (06461-1779)
PHONE.................................203 877-0640
Richard Meisenheimer, *President*
Daniel Meisenheimer, *Vice Pres*
Maria Sabina, *Controller*
EMP: 10
SQ FT: 3,500
SALES (est): 1.5MM **Privately Held**
WEB: www.spectrumct.com
SIC: 3451 Screw machine products

(G-4480)
CAM MANUFACTURING CO LLC
63 Whitney Ave (06460-5320)
PHONE.................................203 301-0153
Michael J Merenda, *Principal*
EMP: 2
SALES (est): 155.5K **Privately Held**
SIC: 3999 Manufacturing industries

(G-4481)
CAM MANUFACTURING LLC
187 Rock Ln (06460-3831)
PHONE.................................203 415-0411
EMP: 1
SALES (est): 56.8K **Privately Held**
SIC: 3999 Manufacturing industries

(G-4482)
CANEVARI PLASTICS INC
10 Furniture Row (06460-3607)
P.O. Box 464 (06460-0464)
PHONE.................................203 878-4319
George Canevari, *President*
Kevin Callahan, *Vice Pres*
Janice Canevari, *Admin Sec*
EMP: 9
SQ FT: 1,200
SALES (est): 1.8MM **Privately Held**
WEB: www.canevariplastics.com
SIC: 3089 Molding primary plastic; injection molding of plastics

(G-4483)
CARD CARRIER GAMES LLC
589 Bridgeport Ave # 17 (06460-4261)
PHONE.................................203 521-0291
EMP: 2
SALES (est): 78.3K **Privately Held**
SIC: 3944 5092 Electronic game machines, except coin-operated; video games

(G-4484)
CARDIOPULMONARY CORP
200 Cascade Blvd Ste B (06460-8515)
PHONE.................................203 877-1999
Dr James Biondi, *Ch of Bd*
Joseph McGuire, *Vice Pres*
John Loeb, *Engineer*
John Fanuko, *CFO*
Nick Snow, *CFO*
▲ **EMP:** 45
SQ FT: 25,000
SALES (est): 5.8MM **Privately Held**
WEB: www.cardiopulmonarycorp.com
SIC: 3842 Surgical appliances & supplies

(G-4485)
CARRUBBA INCORPORATED
70 Research Dr (06460-8523)
PHONE.................................203 878-0605
Duane Carrubba, *President*
▲ **EMP:** 55 **EST:** 1976
SQ FT: 15,000
SALES (est): 11MM **Privately Held**
WEB: www.carrubba.com
SIC: 2869 2844 2087 Perfumes, flavorings & food additives; toilet preparations; flavoring extracts & syrups

(G-4486)
CET INC
270 Rowe Ave Ste D (06461-3085)
PHONE.................................203 882-8057
John Breger, *President*

Janelle Stauffer, *Principal*
EMP: 8
SQ FT: 5,000
SALES (est): 1.1MM **Privately Held**
SIC: 3625 Control equipment, electric; controls for adjustable speed drives; electric controls & control accessories, industrial; industrial controls: push button, selector switches, pilot

(G-4487)
CHAD LABS CORPORATION
128 Research Dr Ste G (06460-8567)
PHONE.................................203 877-3891
Chaudhary M Ramzan, *President*
Nusrat Ramzan, *Vice Pres*
Haroon Ramzan, *Admin Sec*
EMP: 6
SQ FT: 5,000
SALES (est): 3MM **Privately Held**
WEB: www.chadlandrie.com
SIC: 8732 2899 Research services, except laboratory; ink or writing fluids

(G-4488)
CHARGE SOLUTIONS INC
Also Called: C S I
205 Research Dr Unit 1011 (06460-8531)
PHONE.................................203 871-7282
Marc Karpel, *President*
EMP: 4 **EST:** 2015
SALES (est): 1.5MM **Privately Held**
SIC: 3629 Battery chargers, rectifying or nonrotating

(G-4489)
CHARMED PRESS LLC
53 Jennifer Ln (06461-1733)
PHONE.................................203 877-3777
Ronnie Ann Ryan, *Manager*
EMP: 2
SALES (est): 101.4K **Privately Held**
SIC: 2741 Miscellaneous publishing

(G-4490)
COLD LLC
393 Naugatuck Ave (06460-5402)
PHONE.................................203 543-6861
Nick Cunliffe,
EMP: 1
SALES (est): 262.9K **Privately Held**
SIC: 3569 7389 Gas producers (machinery);

(G-4491)
COLONIAL COATINGS INC
66 Erna Ave (06461-3115)
PHONE.................................203 783-9933
Russell A Colon, *President*
Richard S Castorina, *Vice Pres*
Richard Castorina, *Vice Pres*
Patrick Rossomando, *Production*
Jessica Tobin, *Production*
EMP: 45
SQ FT: 17,000
SALES (est): 7.6MM **Privately Held**
WEB: www.colonialcoatings.com
SIC: 3479 3471 2851 Coating of metals & formed products; enameling, including porcelain, of metal products; painting of metal products; plating & polishing; paints & allied products

(G-4492)
COMFORTABLE ENVIRONMENTS
11 Terrell Dr (06460-2037)
PHONE.................................203 876-2140
Joshua Miller,
EMP: 6
SALES (est): 800K **Privately Held**
SIC: 3585 Heating & air conditioning combination units

(G-4493)
CONNECTICUT COMPUTER SVC INC
344 W Main St (06460-2561)
PHONE.................................860 276-1285
Toll Free:...................................888 -
Dolores Baker, *Manager*
EMP: 1

SALES (corp-wide): 21.6MM **Privately Held**
SIC: 7373 7372 Value-added resellers, computer systems; educational computer software
PA: Connecticut Computer Service, Inc.
101 E Summer St
Plantsville CT 06479
860 276-1285

(G-4494)
CONNECTICUT CUSTOM WOODWORK
15 Monroe St Apt B (06460-5710)
PHONE.................................203 231-0097
Roberto Cintron, *Principal*
EMP: 1
SALES (est): 54.1K **Privately Held**
SIC: 2431 Millwork

(G-4495)
CONNECTICUT DIESEL AND MARINE
287 Woodmont Rd (06460-2847)
PHONE.................................203 481-1010
Marla Walker, *Owner*
EMP: 3
SALES (est): 273.7K **Privately Held**
SIC: 3731 Cargo vessels, building & repairing

(G-4496)
CONNECTICUT FABRICATING CO INC
15 Warfield St (06461-2930)
PHONE.................................203 878-3465
Thomas Wirkus, *President*
Richard T Wirkus, *Vice Pres*
Rosemarie Wirkus, *Admin Sec*
EMP: 6
SQ FT: 2,600
SALES: 400K **Privately Held**
SIC: 3444 Sheet metalwork

(G-4497)
CONNECTICUT MCH TOOLING & CAST
93 Research Dr (06460-8525)
PHONE.................................203 874-8300
George Paulis Jr, *President*
Marolyn Paulis, *Treasurer*
EMP: 12
SQ FT: 8,000
SALES (est): 1.6MM **Privately Held**
SIC: 3599 Machine shop, jobbing & repair

(G-4498)
CONNECTICUT SCREEN PRINT
215 Research Dr Ste 1 (06460-8554)
PHONE.................................203 877-6655
John Crissey, *Owner*
EMP: 2
SALES (est): 250K **Privately Held**
SIC: 2396 2395 Screen printing on fabric articles; emblems, embroidered

(G-4499)
CONNECTICUT STONE SUPPLIES INC (PA)
138 Woodmont Rd (06460-2832)
PHONE.................................203 882-1000
Joseph Dellacroce, *President*
Craig Duddy, *Opers Mgr*
Lance Dellacroce, *Sales Dir*
Julie Spaziane, *Office Mgr*
Ed Mish, *Sr Project Mgr*
▲ **EMP:** 83
SALES (est): 11.6MM **Privately Held**
SIC: 3281 5032 1411 Paving blocks, cut stone; building stone; dimension stone

(G-4500)
CROWN CORK & SEAL USA INC
86 Victory Cres (06460-3222)
PHONE.................................203 877-4131
EMP: 1
SALES (corp-wide): 8.7B **Publicly Held**
SIC: 3411 Mfg Metal Cans
HQ: Crown Cork & Seal Usa, Inc.
770 Township Line Rd # 100
Yardley PA 19067
215 698-5100

(G-4501)
CT DUMPSTER LLC
32 Birch Ave (06460-5301)
PHONE.................................203 521-0779
Saulo Silva, *Principal*
EMP: 3
SALES (est): 147.8K **Privately Held**
SIC: 3443 Dumpsters, garbage

(G-4502)
CURRY PRINTING & COPY CTR LLC
878 Boston Post Rd (06460-3530)
PHONE.................................203 878-5767
Lorraine Moran,
Frank Moran,
EMP: 2
SQ FT: 2,300
SALES (est): 250K **Privately Held**
SIC: 2752 7334 Commercial printing, offset; photocopying & duplicating services

(G-4503)
CUSTOM STILES
18 Cleveland Ave (06460-4109)
PHONE.................................203 410-2370
Scott Furtado, *Principal*
EMP: 2
SALES (est): 184.4K **Privately Held**
SIC: 2434 Wood kitchen cabinets

(G-4504)
D & B TOOL CO LLC
83 Erna Ave (06461-3118)
PHONE.................................203 878-6026
John Butka, *Owner*
EMP: 8
SALES (est): 125K **Privately Held**
SIC: 3429 Aircraft hardware

(G-4505)
DATA SIGNAL CORPORATION
16 Higgins Dr (06460-2853)
PHONE.................................203 882-5393
Lynda Kilgore, *President*
Gerard Kilgore, *Admin Sec*
EMP: 20
SQ FT: 15,900
SALES (est): 3.5MM **Privately Held**
SIC: 3679 Harness assemblies for electronic use: wire or cable

(G-4506)
DEL ARBOUR LLC
152 Old Gate Ln (06460-3651)
PHONE.................................203 882-8501
Ruzdi Muaremi,
EMP: 10
SQ FT: 2,500
SALES: 750K **Privately Held**
WEB: www.delarbour.com
SIC: 2329 2339 5136 5137 Athletic (warmup, sweat & jogging) suits: men's & boys'; athletic clothing: women's, misses' & juniors'; sportswear, men's & boys'; sportswear, women's & children's; clothing, mail order (except women's); skating equipment

(G-4507)
DELLTECH INC
175 Buckingham Ave (06460-4842)
PHONE.................................203 878-8266
Tom Dellipoali, *President*
Dolores Dellipoali, *Admin Sec*
EMP: 3
SQ FT: 3,000
SALES: 380K **Privately Held**
SIC: 3599 Machine shop, jobbing & repair

(G-4508)
DEPAUL INDUSTRIES
6 Drexel Rd (06460-6832)
PHONE.................................203 882-1331
Paul Gulyas, *Owner*
EMP: 1
SALES (est): 104.1K **Privately Held**
SIC: 2759 Screen printing

(G-4509)
DESIGNERS RESOURCE
116 Research Dr Ste G (06460-8568)
PHONE.................................203 874-7731
Dennis Cooper, *Owner*
Danielle Lacey, *Manager*

EMP: 2
SQ FT: 4,000
SALES (est): 157.9K **Privately Held**
SIC: 2511 Wood household furniture

(G-4510)
DIMIDE INC
252 Depot Rd (06460-3807)
PHONE..................................203 668-9621
Michael Costen, *President*
EMP: 1
SALES (est): 56.4K **Privately Held**
SIC: 3429 Clamps, metal

(G-4511)
DIRTCIRCLE MEDIA LLC
141 Welchs Point Rd (06460-7368)
PHONE..................................860 532-0674
Jonathan Sandoval,
EMP: 2 EST: 2015
SALES (est): 74K **Privately Held**
SIC: 7372 7389 Publishers' computer software;

(G-4512)
DIZZY FISH MUSIC LLC
910 E Broadway (06460-6218)
PHONE..................................203 599-5700
Eric Herbst, *Mng Member*
EMP: 1
SALES (est): 30.5K **Privately Held**
SIC: 7929 3931 Entertainers & entertainment groups; recorders (musical instruments)

(G-4513)
DOCTOR WELD LLC
170 Eastern Pkwy (06460-4956)
PHONE..................................203 877-3433
Gary F Demezzo, *Principal*
EMP: 1 EST: 2009
SALES (est): 93.5K **Privately Held**
SIC: 7692 Welding repair

(G-4514)
DONGHIA INC (PA)
Also Called: Donghia Furniture and Textiles
500 Bic Dr Gate 1 Ste 200 1 Gate (06461)
PHONE..................................800 366-4442
Andrea Favaretto Rubelli, *CEO*
William Peterson, *CFO*
Allan Chernak, *Accounting Mgr*
Stephanie McGow, *Accountant*
Nicole Clark, *Sales Staff*
▲ EMP: 76
SQ FT: 30,000
SALES (est): 80.1MM **Privately Held**
WEB: www.donghia.com
SIC: 5198 5131 5021 2342 Wallcoverings; piece goods & other fabrics; furniture; corset accessories: clasps, stays, etc.

(G-4515)
DPC QUALITY PUMP SERVICE
544 Bridgeport Ave (06460-4202)
PHONE..................................203 874-6877
Dean Cyr, *Owner*
EMP: 3
SALES (est): 220K **Privately Held**
SIC: 3561 5084 5074 Pumps, domestic: water or sump; pumps & pumping equipment; water purification equipment

(G-4516)
DRILLING DYNAMICS LLC
336 Boston Post Rd (06460-2559)
PHONE..................................203 783-1395
Steve Selvaggi, *General Mgr*
John Hall,
▲ EMP: 2
SALES (est): 261K **Privately Held**
WEB: www.drillingdynamics.net
SIC: 3544 Special dies & tools

(G-4517)
DUMOND CHEMICALS INC
620 West Ave (06461-3013)
PHONE..................................609 655-7700
EMP: 1
SALES (est): 50.9K **Privately Held**
SIC: 2851 Paints & allied products

(G-4518)
DUMOND CHEMICALS INC
695 West Ave (06461-3003)
PHONE..................................609 655-7700
Mohamad Ajjan, *General Mgr*
EMP: 9
SALES (corp-wide): 1.3MM **Privately Held**
WEB: www.dumondchemicals.com
SIC: 2851 Paints & allied products
PA: Dumond Chemicals, Inc.
    1475 Phnxvlle Pike Ste 18
    West Chester PA 19380
    609 655-7700

(G-4519)
DUZ MANUFACTURING INC
87 Opal St (06461-3029)
PHONE..................................203 874-1032
Janusz Duz, *President*
Aneta Duz, *Vice Pres*
EMP: 5
SALES (est): 550K **Privately Held**
SIC: 3086 Plastics foam products

(G-4520)
E-Z SWITCH MANUFACTURING INC
463 Naugatuck Ave (06460-5048)
PHONE..................................203 874-7766
Elizabeth G Bradley, *President*
▲ EMP: 15
SALES (est): 1.7MM **Privately Held**
SIC: 3625 Industrial controls: push button, selector switches, pilot

(G-4521)
EASTERN MACHINE CO
655 Plains Rd Unit I (06461-1791)
PHONE..................................203 877-6308
Vincent Horvat, *Owner*
EMP: 2
SQ FT: 2,500
SALES (est): 100K **Privately Held**
SIC: 3599 Machine shop, jobbing & repair

(G-4522)
EASTERN MARBLE & GRANITE LLC
201 Buckingham Ave (06460-4842)
PHONE..................................203 882-8221
Michael Ballaro, *Mng Member*
▲ EMP: 10
SALES (est): 366K **Privately Held**
SIC: 3281 Marble, building: cut & shaped; granite, cut & shaped

(G-4523)
EASTERN METAL WORKS INC
333 Woodmont Rd (06460-2847)
PHONE..................................203 878-6995
Raymond J Weiner, *President*
Christopher J Weiner, *Corp Secy*
▼ EMP: 22
SQ FT: 15,000
SALES (est): 10MM **Privately Held**
WEB: www.easternmetalworks.com
SIC: 3449 3446 5051 Bars, concrete reinforcing: fabricated steel; architectural metalwork; railings, prefabricated metal; steel

(G-4524)
EASTERN TECH LLC
Also Called: Eastern Trading
55 Old Gate Ln (06460-3612)
PHONE..................................203 877-5386
Chris Chen, *Technical Staff*
Clement Liu,
Audrey Liu,
▲ EMP: 2 EST: 1996
SQ FT: 3,000
SALES (est): 333.9K **Privately Held**
SIC: 2899 Ink or writing fluids

(G-4525)
ECO PALLET WORLD LLC
5 Chapel St (06460-8027)
PHONE..................................203 343-9089
Marisol Jabat, *Mng Member*
EMP: 1 EST: 2017
SALES (est): 60.9K **Privately Held**
SIC: 3944 5947 Craft & hobby kits & sets; artcraft & carvings

(G-4526)
EDGEWELL PER CARE BRANDS LLC
10 Leighton Rd (06460-3552)
PHONE..................................203 882-2300
Joseph Lynch, *Branch Mgr*
EMP: 98
SALES (corp-wide): 2.2B **Publicly Held**
WEB: www.eveready.com
SIC: 3421 Razor blades & razors
HQ: Edgewell Personal Care Brands, Llc
    6 Research Dr
    Shelton CT 06484
    203 944-5500

(G-4527)
EDGEWELL PERSONAL CARE COMPANY
10 Leighton Rd (06460-3552)
PHONE..................................203 882-2308
Lisa Geronimo, *Business Mgr*
Terry Schulke, *Exec VP*
Carlos Texidor, *Opers Staff*
Jeffrey Garrant, *Senior Buyer*
Lucy Vano, *Senior Buyer*
EMP: 29
SALES (corp-wide): 2.2B **Publicly Held**
SIC: 3421 Razor blades & razors
PA: Edgewell Personal Care Company
    1350 Tmberlake Manor Pkwy
    Chesterfield MO 63017
    314 594-1900

(G-4528)
ELECTRODES INCORPORATED
160 Cascade Blvd (06460-2848)
PHONE..................................203 878-7400
Michael Dudas, *Manager*
EMP: 25
SALES (corp-wide): 23.3MM **Privately Held**
WEB: www.electrodes-inc.com
SIC: 3699 Electrical equipment & supplies
PA: Electrodes, Incorporated
    260a Quarry Rd
    Milford CT 06460
    954 803-4736

(G-4529)
EMPTY CUP MAGIC
46 Whalley Ave (06460-7865)
PHONE..................................203 874-1093
Robert Plaut, *Owner*
EMP: 1
SALES (est): 53.1K **Privately Held**
SIC: 3999 Magic equipment, supplies & props

(G-4530)
ENCORE SALES CORP
500 Bic Dr Ste 102 (06461-1777)
PHONE..................................203 301-4949
Paul Pennino, *President*
Susan Pennino, *Vice Pres*
EMP: 5
SALES (est): 400K **Privately Held**
WEB: www.encoresales.net
SIC: 5199 2399 2759 Advertising specialties; banners, pennants & flags; business forms: printing

(G-4531)
ENGINEERED INSERTS & SYSTEMS (PA)
Also Called: Eis
26 Quirk Rd (06460-3745)
P.O. Box 610, Watertown (06795-0610)
PHONE..................................203 301-3334
Teri Cook, *President*
Dave Turechek, *General Mgr*
EMP: 15
SALES (est): 2.1MM **Privately Held**
WEB: www.eisinserts.com
SIC: 3429 Metal fasteners

(G-4532)
ENGINUITY PLM LLC (HQ)
Also Called: IMS
440 Wheelers Farms Rd (06461-9133)
PHONE..................................203 218-7225
John P Sottery, *CEO*
Donald F Logan Jr, *COO*
EMP: 19
SQ FT: 6,600
SALES (est): 2.5MM
SALES (corp-wide): 1.8B **Privately Held**
SIC: 7372 7373 8734 8742 Application computer software; systems software development services; testing laboratories; management consulting services
PA: Dassault Systemes
    10 Rue Marcel Dassault
    Velizy Villacoublay 78140
    161 623-000

(G-4533)
EXCELLO TOOL ENGRG & MFG CO
37 Warfield St (06461-2930)
PHONE..................................203 878-4073
Michael Zahornacky Jr, *President*
Jeffrey Solomon, *General Mgr*
Jeff Solomon, *Vice Pres*
EMP: 25 EST: 1960
SALES (est): 4.4MM **Privately Held**
WEB: www.excellotool.com
SIC: 3599 Machine shop, jobbing & repair

(G-4534)
F S P RESEARCH INC
148 Research Dr Ste F (06460-8537)
PHONE..................................203 874-3417
Philip Sherwood, *President*
EMP: 1
SQ FT: 1,600
SALES (est): 100K **Privately Held**
WEB: www.fspresearch.com
SIC: 8742 8731 8734 2842 Industry specialist consultants; commercial research laboratory; product testing laboratories; polishing preparations & related products

(G-4535)
FASTSIGNS
1015 Bridgeport Ave (06460-3160)
PHONE..................................203 298-4075
Brian Reeves, *Owner*
EMP: 5 EST: 2008
SALES (est): 617.5K **Privately Held**
SIC: 3993 Signs & advertising specialties

(G-4536)
FERRARO CUSTOM WOODWORK LLC
29 Eastern Steel Rd (06460-2837)
PHONE..................................203 876-1280
Joseph Ferraro, *Owner*
EMP: 5
SALES (est): 575.9K **Privately Held**
SIC: 2431 Woodwork, interior & ornamental

(G-4537)
FLOWSERVE CORPORATION
408 Woodmont Rd (06460-3789)
PHONE..................................203 877-4252
Robert Emerling, *Office Mgr*
David Krupp, *Manager*
Michael Woods, *Manager*
EMP: 20
SALES (corp-wide): 3.8B **Publicly Held**
SIC: 3561 Pumps & pumping equipment
PA: Flowserve Corporation
    5215 N Ocnnor Blvd Ste 23 Connor
    Irving TX 75039
    972 443-6500

(G-4538)
FORCE3 PRO GEAR LLC
45 Banner Dr 1 (06460-2859)
PHONE..................................315 367-2331
James Evans, *Partner*
Cole Flowers, *Partner*
Michael Klein, *Partner*
Jason Klein, *General Ptnr*
Lisa Franco, *Comms Dir*
EMP: 4 EST: 2017
SALES (est): 146K **Privately Held**
SIC: 3949 Baseball, softball & cricket sports equipment

(G-4539)
GALAXY FUEL LLC
180 New Haven Ave (06460-4829)
PHONE..................................203 878-8173
Mustafa Bayram, *Principal*
EMP: 3
SALES (est): 204.1K **Privately Held**
SIC: 2869 Fuels

Milford - New Haven County

(G-4540)
GL AND V
612 Wheelers Farms Rd # 1 (06461-1673)
PHONE.....................203 876-5400
EMP: 2 **EST:** 2010
SALES (est): 130K **Privately Held**
SIC: 3569 Mfg General Industrial Machinery

(G-4541)
GRAMMAS HANDS LLC
655 West Ave (06461-3003)
PHONE.....................203 301-0791
Harlene Lebine, *President*
EMP: 2
SALES (est): 138.7K **Privately Held**
SIC: 3732 Tenders (small motor craft), building & repairing

(G-4542)
GRAPHIC IMAGE INC
561 Boston Post Rd (06460-2676)
PHONE.....................203 877-8787
Leigh Danenberg, *President*
Silvano Stasolla, *President*
Lynn Tedler, *Pub Rel Mgr*
Carole Norman, *Accounts Exec*
Jose Ortiz,
EMP: 25
SQ FT: 11,000
SALES: 3.5MM **Privately Held**
WEB: www.graphicimage.net
SIC: 2752 Commercial printing, offset

(G-4543)
GREGMANS INC
167 Cherry St (06460-3466)
PHONE.....................203 464-2530
Jeanne Stephan, *Principal*
EMP: 1 **EST:** 2010
SALES (est): 68.3K **Privately Held**
SIC: 3911 Jewelry apparel

(G-4544)
GRILLO SERVICES LLC
1183 Oronoque Rd (06461-1714)
PHONE.....................203 877-5070
John Michael Grillo, *President*
Lawrence Grillo, *Vice Pres*
Mark Mumich, *Administration*
EMP: 25
SALES (est): 1MM **Privately Held**
SIC: 2875 4213 4953 5191 Potting soil, mixed; contract haulers; dumps, operation of; recycling, waste materials; soil, potting & planting; top soil
PA: Grillo Organic Inc
1183 Oronoque Rd
Milford CT 06461

(G-4545)
GROTTI TOOL COMPANY
80 Erna Ave (06461-3115)
PHONE.....................203 877-5570
John Grotti, *Owner*
EMP: 1
SQ FT: 2,000
SALES (est): 95.2K **Privately Held**
SIC: 3599 Machine shop, jobbing & repair

(G-4546)
GYBENORTH INDUSTRIES LLC
Also Called: American Dry Stripping
80 Wampus Ln Ste 13 (06461-4856)
PHONE.....................203 876-9876
Roger F Van Brussel, *Principal*
Roger Vanbrussel,
EMP: 12
SALES (est): 919.4K **Privately Held**
SIC: 3479 3471 Aluminum coating of metal products; electroplating & plating

(G-4547)
HAYWARD TURNSTILES INC
160 Wampus Ln (06460-4861)
PHONE.....................203 877-7096
Richard Schwarz, *CEO*
Ronald B Schwarz, *President*
EMP: 6
SQ FT: 6,000
SALES (est): 1.2MM **Privately Held**
SIC: 3829 Turnstiles, equipped with counting mechanisms

(G-4548)
HI INDUSTRIES LLC
55 Oak Ridge Ln (06461-1892)
PHONE.....................203 783-1084
Mark Haba, *Principal*
EMP: 1
SALES (est): 54.7K **Privately Held**
SIC: 3999 Manufacturing industries

(G-4549)
HUBBELL WIRING DEVICE
185 Plains Rd (06461-2473)
P.O. Box 1000, Shelton (06484-1000)
PHONE.....................203 882-4800
Frank Allen, *Principal*
Kevin Mallory, *Treasurer*
Craig Soucy, *VP Finance*
Jeff Heib, *Sales Mgr*
Seth Kaplowitz, *Sales Staff*
◆ **EMP:** 15
SALES (est): 3.1MM
SALES (corp-wide): 4.4B **Publicly Held**
WEB: www.hubbell.com
SIC: 3643 Current-carrying wiring devices
PA: Hubbell Incorporated
40 Waterview Dr
Shelton CT 06484
475 882-4000

(G-4550)
I & J MACHINE TOOL COMPANY
230 Woodmont Rd Ste V (06460-2845)
PHONE.....................203 877-5376
Ivan Jukic, *Partner*
Jure Jukic, *Partner*
▼ **EMP:** 15
SQ FT: 7,200
SALES (est): 3.1MM **Privately Held**
SIC: 3728 3724 Aircraft body assemblies & parts; airframe assemblies, except for guided missiles; aircraft engines & engine parts

(G-4551)
IDEAS INC
Also Called: Connecticut Engravers
80a Rowe Ave (06461-3031)
PHONE.....................203 878-9686
Paul Mangels, *President*
Marcia Mangels, *Admin Sec*
EMP: 4
SQ FT: 2,000
SALES (est): 300K **Privately Held**
SIC: 2754 2759 Cards, except greeting; gravure printing; invitation & stationery printing & engraving

(G-4552)
IEMCT
Also Called: International Energy MGT
205 Research Dr Ste 8 (06460-2874)
PHONE.....................203 683-4382
EMP: 4 **EST:** 2007
SALES: 500K **Privately Held**
SIC: 3699 Mfg Electrical Equipment/Supplies

(G-4553)
IMPERIAL GRPHIC CMMNCTIONS INC
Also Called: Imperial Graphics
22 Way St (06460-4200)
PHONE.....................203 650-3478
David Emery, *President*
Robert Emery, *Vice Pres*
EMP: 23
SQ FT: 20,000
SALES (est): 5.7MM **Privately Held**
WEB: www.imperialgraphics.com
SIC: 2752 2789 2759 Commercial printing, offset; bookbinding & related work; commercial printing

(G-4554)
INDECO NORTH AMERICA INC
135 Research Dr (06460-2839)
PHONE.....................203 713-1030
Michael Fischer, *CEO*
Randolph P Hood, *CFO*
Annalisa Ugalde, *Director*
▲ **EMP:** 28
SQ FT: 77,000
SALES (est): 8.7MM
SALES (corp-wide): 35.1MM **Privately Held**
WEB: www.indeco-breakers.com
SIC: 3531 Backhoe mounted, hydraulically powered attachments
PA: Indeco Ind Spa
Viale Guglielmo Lindemann 10
Bari BA 70132
080 531-3340

(G-4555)
INDUSTRIAL COMPONENTS CT LLC
270 Rowe Ave (06461-3085)
PHONE.....................203 882-8201
Larry McGeehan, *Mng Member*
John O'Connell,
EMP: 2
SQ FT: 4,000
SALES: 1.5MM **Privately Held**
SIC: 5085 3494 Valves, pistons & fittings; steam fittings & specialties

(G-4556)
INNOVATIVE MECHANICS LLC
11 Wilshire Blvd (06460-4250)
PHONE.....................203 530-6071
Garrett Mancini, *Managing Prtnr*
James Mancini, *Managing Prtnr*
EMP: 2 **EST:** 2010
SALES (est): 218.7K **Privately Held**
SIC: 3599 Machine & other job shop work

(G-4557)
INTERFACE DEVICES INCORPORATED
Also Called: IDI
230 Depot Rd (06460-3813)
PHONE.....................203 878-4648
Mark Robinson, *President*
Mike Hotchkiss, *Vice Pres*
Roger Dennis, *Treasurer*
William Ivanoff, *Info Tech Dir*
EMP: 8
SQ FT: 10,000
SALES: 1.9MM **Privately Held**
WEB: www.interfacedevices.com
SIC: 3599 5084 Machine & other job shop work; industrial machinery & equipment

(G-4558)
J T TOOL CO INC
57 Buckingham Ave (06460-4840)
P.O. Box 484 (06460-0484)
PHONE.....................203 874-1234
Mark Tirita, *President*
EMP: 1 **EST:** 1962
SQ FT: 5,500
SALES (est): 186.6K **Privately Held**
WEB: www.jttoolco.com
SIC: 3469 3544 Stamping metal for the trade; special dies & tools

(G-4559)
JEAN MARIE PAPERY LLC
61 Shelter Cove Rd (06460-6548)
PHONE.....................203 877-4299
Jean Tupper, *Principal*
EMP: 1
SALES (est): 75K **Privately Held**
SIC: 2754 Commercial printing, gravure

(G-4560)
JOE PASSARELLI & CO
67 Andrews Ave (06460-5815)
PHONE.....................203 877-1434
Jo-Anne Urena, *Manager*
EMP: 3
SALES (est): 167.9K **Privately Held**
SIC: 1429 Grits mining (crushed stone)

(G-4561)
JOHN C GREEN
Also Called: Cord Industries
21 Roselle St (06461-3127)
PHONE.....................203 878-3781
John C Green, *Owner*
EMP: 2
SQ FT: 2,000
SALES (est): 210K **Privately Held**
WEB: www.cordindustries.com
SIC: 3452 Wood screws; rivets, metal; bolts, metal; nuts, metal

(G-4562)
JOHN RAWLINSON JOHN LEARY
316 Boston Post Rd (06460-2527)
PHONE.....................203 882-8484
John Rawlinson, *Partner*
John Leary, *Partner*
EMP: 5
SALES: 750K **Privately Held**
SIC: 3993 Electric signs

(G-4563)
KBC ELECTRONICS INC
273 Pepes Farm Rd (06460-3671)
PHONE.....................203 298-9654
Kue Choi, *Owner*
Cheryl Burke, *Materials Mgr*
EMP: 15
SQ FT: 7,500
SALES (est): 2.2MM **Privately Held**
WEB: www.kbcelectronics.com
SIC: 3679 3841 3842 Electronic circuits; surgical & medical instruments; surgical appliances & supplies

(G-4564)
KEVIN FIELD
321 Rock Ln (06460-3834)
PHONE.....................203 878-6339
Kevin Field, *Principal*
EMP: 2
SALES (est): 81.9K **Privately Held**
SIC: 1311 Crude petroleum & natural gas

(G-4565)
KILO AMPERE SWITCH CORPORATION
Also Called: K A Switch
230 Woodmont Rd Ste 27 (06460-2845)
PHONE.....................203 877-5994
Ann Impellitteri, *President*
Thomas Impellitteri, *Treasurer*
EMP: 4
SQ FT: 2,750
SALES: 330K **Privately Held**
WEB: www.kaswitch.com
SIC: 3613 Switchgear & switchboard apparatus

(G-4566)
LAC LANDSCAPING LLC
60 Country Ln (06461-1943)
PHONE.....................203 807-1067
Luis A Castro,
EMP: 10
SALES (est): 1.3MM **Privately Held**
SIC: 3714 Dump truck lifting mechanism

(G-4567)
LIGHT SOURCES INC
70 Cascade Blvd (06460-2848)
P.O. Box 3010 (06460-0810)
PHONE.....................203 799-7877
EMP: 101
SALES (corp-wide): 37.4MM **Privately Held**
SIC: 3645 Residential lighting fixtures
PA: Light Sources, Inc.
37 Robinson Blvd
Orange CT 06477
203 799-7877

(G-4568)
LINDA HOAGLAND
Also Called: Telic Manufacturing
19 Pine Knob Ter (06461-1635)
PHONE.....................203 878-7188
Linda Hoagland, *Owner*
EMP: 2
SQ FT: 800
SALES (est): 137.5K **Privately Held**
SIC: 3053 Gaskets & sealing devices

(G-4569)
LIVING MAGAZINE
162 Bridgeport Ave (06460-3935)
PHONE.....................203 283-5290
Suzanne Cahill, *President*
EMP: 3
SALES (est): 173.4K **Privately Held**
SIC: 2721 Periodicals

Milford - New Haven County

(G-4570)
LUBBERT SUPPLY COMPANY LLC
89 Eastern Steel Rd (06460-2861)
PHONE 203 690-1105
Annalisa Lubbert,
▲ EMP: 1
SALES (est): 168.9K **Privately Held**
SIC: **2394** 2399 2842 Liners & covers, fabric: made from purchased materials; belting & belt products; aprons, breast (harness); waxes for wood, leather & other materials

(G-4571)
LYON MANUFACTURING LLC
215 Research Dr Ste 4 (06460-8554)
PHONE 203 876-7386
Gary Lyon, *Owner*
EMP: 4
SQ FT: 1,600
SALES: 500K **Privately Held**
SIC: **3444** Sheet metal specialties, not stamped

(G-4572)
MADDOG LLC
33 Tall Pine Rd (06461-1951)
PHONE 203 878-0147
Michael Garvey,
EMP: 3
SALES (est): 166K **Privately Held**
SIC: **2431** Woodwork, interior & ornamental

(G-4573)
MAGNA STANDARD MFG CO INC
122 Cascade Blvd (06460-2848)
PHONE 203 874-0444
Carl G Swebilius, *President*
George Adams, *Vice Pres*
EMP: 6
SQ FT: 7,000
SALES: 1MM **Privately Held**
WEB: www.magnastandard.com
SIC: **3599** Machine shop, jobbing & repair

(G-4574)
MAILROOM FINANCE INC (DH)
Also Called: Neopost USA
478 Wheelers Farms Rd (06461-9105)
PHONE 203 301-3400
Dennis Lestrange, *President*
Carl Amacker, *Vice Pres*
Joseph Bonassar, *Admin Sec*
EMP: 2
SALES (est): 2.7MM
SALES (corp-wide): 38.4MM **Privately Held**
SIC: **3579** Mailing machines

(G-4575)
MCGUIRE MANUFACTURING CO INC
11 Cascade Blvd (06460-2849)
PHONE 203 301-0270
EMP: 2
SALES (est): 62.5K **Privately Held**
SIC: **3999** Manufacturing industries

(G-4576)
MDM PRODUCTS LLC
Also Called: Rhino Shelters
105 Woodmont Rd (06460-2840)
PHONE 203 877-7070
Michael Skoldberg,
Don Skoldberg,
◆ EMP: 11
SQ FT: 65,000
SALES (est): 2.1MM **Privately Held**
WEB: www.mdmproducts.org
SIC: **3448** 3089 Garages, portable: prefabricated metal; sponges, plastic

(G-4577)
MICHAEL MARTINETTO (PA)
Also Called: M Martinetto & Sons Cnstr
170 Walnut St (06461-2661)
PHONE 203 874-6114
Michael Martinetto, *Owner*
EMP: 4
SQ FT: 1,200
SALES (est): 1.2MM **Privately Held**
SIC: **1521** 2541 New construction, single-family houses; cabinets, except refrigerated: show, display, etc.: wood

(G-4578)
MIDGET LOUVER COMPANY INC
671 Naugatuck Ave (06461-4064)
PHONE 203 783-1444
Michael Vignola, *President*
Paul Creatore, *Principal*
Delores Creatore, *Admin Sec*
EMP: 8 EST: 1948
SQ FT: 3,300
SALES (est): 1.2MM **Privately Held**
WEB: www.midgetlouver.com
SIC: **3444** Sheet metalwork

(G-4579)
MILFORD FABRICATING CO INC
500 Bic Dr Bldg 2 (06461-1777)
PHONE 203 878-2476
EMP: 80
SQ FT: 60,000
SALES: 14.2MM **Privately Held**
WEB: www.milfabct.com
SIC: **3444** Sheet metal specialties, not stamped

(G-4580)
MILFORD METAL PRODUCTS INC
394 Oronoque Rd (06461-1711)
P.O. Box 2215 (06460-1115)
PHONE 203 878-0148
John Cunningham Jr, *President*
Susan Cunningham, *Admin Sec*
EMP: 2
SQ FT: 1,200
SALES: 200K **Privately Held**
SIC: **3599** 5046 Machine shop, jobbing & repair; commercial cooking & food service equipment

(G-4581)
MILFORD SMOKE JUNCTION LLC
487a Bridgeport Ave (06460-4162)
PHONE 203 301-9956
Kamrul Chowdhury,
EMP: 2
SALES (est): 167.3K **Privately Held**
SIC: **3999** Cigarette & cigar products & accessories

(G-4582)
MILLER MARINE CANVAS
282 Woodmont Rd Ste 36 (06460-8546)
PHONE 203 878-9291
Ivon J Miller Jr, *Owner*
EMP: 2
SALES (est): 125K **Privately Held**
SIC: **2394** Awnings, fabric: made from purchased materials

(G-4583)
MITCHELL WOODWORKING LLC
72 Maple St (06460-3463)
PHONE 203 878-4249
Lloyd A Mitchell, *Owner*
EMP: 2
SALES (est): 250K **Privately Held**
SIC: **2431** Millwork

(G-4584)
MORGAN WOODWORKS LLC
169 Clark St (06460-2596)
PHONE 203 913-2489
Richard Morgan, *Principal*
EMP: 2 EST: 2008
SALES (est): 164.3K **Privately Held**
SIC: **2431** Millwork

(G-4585)
MORNING STAR TOOL LLC
Also Called: D&B Tool Co.
83 Erna Ave (06461-3118)
PHONE 203 878-6026
Leon Tyrrell, *President*
Rebekah Butler, *Business Mgr*
Alan Vensel, *Plant Mgr*
EMP: 5
SALES (est): 289.5K **Privately Held**
SIC: **3724** 3429 3728 Aircraft engines & engine parts; aircraft hardware; military aircraft equipment & armament

(G-4586)
MRH TOOL LLC
124 Research Dr Ste A (06460-8571)
PHONE 203 878-3359
George Scobie,
EMP: 4
SALES: 200K **Privately Held**
SIC: **3545** 3599 Precision tools, machinists'; machine & other job shop work

(G-4587)
NEATO PRODUCTS LLC
37 Eastern Steel Rd (06460-2837)
PHONE 203 466-5170
John Blakeslee, *President*
EMP: 4
SQ FT: 20,000
SALES (est): 544.2K **Privately Held**
SIC: **2672** Adhesive papers, labels or tapes: from purchased material

(G-4588)
NEOPOST USA INC (DH)
478 Wheelers Farms Rd (06461-9105)
PHONE 203 301-3400
Dennis P Lestrange, *President*
Austin Maddox, *General Mgr*
Jim Owens, *General Mgr*
Jim Gray, *Business Mgr*
Jason Tyson, *Business Mgr*
▲ EMP: 250
SQ FT: 62,000
SALES: 339.7MM
SALES (corp-wide): 38.4MM **Privately Held**
WEB: www.neopostinc.com
SIC: **3579** 7359 7629 Postage meters; business machine & electronic equipment rental services; business machine repair, electric

(G-4589)
NEW ENGLAND STANDARD CORP
16 Honey St (06461-3122)
PHONE 203 876-7733
Bill Marston, *Branch Mgr*
EMP: 8
SALES (corp-wide): 3.1MM **Privately Held**
SIC: **2431** Garage doors, overhead: wood
PA: New England Standard Corporation
   323 Boston Post Rd
   Old Saybrook CT 06475
   860 388-0438

(G-4590)
NEW ENGLAND STONE INC
35 Higgins Dr (06460-2853)
PHONE 203 876-8606
John Tomlinson Jr, *President*
▲ EMP: 17
SQ FT: 14,000
SALES (est): 3.1MM **Privately Held**
WEB: www.newenglandstone.com
SIC: **1743** 3281 1799 5032 Tile installation, ceramic; marble, building: cut & shaped; kitchen & bathroom remodeling; limestone

(G-4591)
NEWHART PLASTICS INC
10 Furniture Row (06460-3607)
P.O. Box 3386 (06460-0942)
PHONE 203 877-5367
Frank A Canevari, *President*
Pamela Zimmerman, *Admin Sec*
EMP: 5
SQ FT: 12,000
SALES (est): 727.9K **Privately Held**
SIC: **3089** Thermoformed finished plastic products; injection molding of plastics

(G-4592)
NEWHART PRODUCTS INC
80 Collingsdale Dr (06461-3054)
P.O. Box 2231 (06460-1131)
PHONE 203 878-3546
Thomas N D'Aulizio, *President*
EMP: 29
SQ FT: 25,000
SALES (est): 10.2MM **Privately Held**
WEB: www.newhartproducts.com
SIC: **5051** 3544 Stampings, metal; special dies, tools, jigs & fixtures

(G-4593)
NOREASTER YACHTS INC
29 Roselle St (06461-3165)
PHONE 203 877-4339
Hugh Whitman Jr, *President*
Steven Whitman, *Vice Pres*
EMP: 3
SQ FT: 2,050
SALES: 500K **Privately Held**
WEB: www.noreasteryachts.com
SIC: **2221** Glass & fiberglass broadwoven fabrics

(G-4594)
NORTH SAILS GROUP LLC (DH)
Also Called: North Technology Group
125 Old Gate Ln Ste 7 (06460-3611)
PHONE 203 874-7548
Thomas A Whidden, *CEO*
Jay Hansen, *Exec VP*
Dan Neri, *Vice Pres*
Kelly Bailey, *Facilities Mgr*
Brian Engel, *Export Mgr*
◆ EMP: 70
SQ FT: 3,000
SALES (est): 83.4MM **Privately Held**
WEB: www.northsails.com
SIC: **2394** 2211 Sails: made from purchased materials; sail cloth
HQ: Tehnology North Group Llc
   125 Old Gate Ln Ste 7
   Milford CT 06460
   203 877-7621

(G-4595)
NORTHEAST ELECTRONICS CORP
455 Bic Dr (06461-1735)
PHONE 203 878-3511
Armand J Cantafio, *President*
Timothy A Cantafio, *Vice Pres*
Timothy Cantafio, *Vice Pres*
Frank Gaudiano, *Vice Pres*
John Short, *Vice Pres*
▲ EMP: 100 EST: 1961
SQ FT: 36,000
SALES (est): 18.3MM **Privately Held**
WEB: www.northeast.com
SIC: **3679** Hermetic seals for electronic equipment

(G-4596)
NUTMEG WOODWORKS LLC
36 Castle Ln (06460-7514)
PHONE 203 980-5700
Sandra J Felix, *Principal*
EMP: 2
SALES (est): 77.2K **Privately Held**
SIC: **2431** Millwork

(G-4597)
OEM SOURCES LLC
214 Broadway (06460-5858)
PHONE 203 283-5415
Thomas Bach, *President*
Tom Bach, *Vice Pres*
▲ EMP: 9
SALES (est): 1.4MM **Privately Held**
WEB: www.oemsources.com
SIC: **3542** 3462 3469 3451 Die casting machines; iron & steel forgings; metal stampings; spinning metal for the trade; screw machine products; packaging machinery

(G-4598)
ORANGE RESEARCH INC
140 Cascade Blvd (06460-2893)
PHONE 203 877-5657
Leslie Hoffman, *Ch of Bd*
Paul A Hoffman, *President*
Don Malizia, *General Mgr*
Mike Donovan, *Vice Pres*
Ed Wilson, *Mfg Mgr*
EMP: 53
SQ FT: 10,000

SALES (est): 13.7MM **Privately Held**
SIC: 3823 Pressure measurement instruments, industrial; pressure gauges, dial & digital; flow instruments, industrial process type; industrial process measurement equipment

(G-4599)
OSDA CONTRACT SERVICES INC
291 Pepes Farm Rd (06460-3671)
P.O. Box 3048 (06460-0848)
PHONE..................................203 878-2155
David H Ingraham, *President*
George Grom, *Vice Pres*
Frank Fonck, *Engineer*
EMP: 25
SQ FT: 14,000
SALES (est): 6.8MM **Privately Held**
WEB: www.osda.com
SIC: 3679 Electronic circuits

(G-4600)
OSDA INC
98 Quirk Rd (06460-3763)
P.O. Box 3048 (06460-0848)
PHONE..................................203 878-2155
David Ingraham, *Principal*
Mark Haskins, *Human Resources*
EMP: 5
SALES (est): 736.8K **Privately Held**
SIC: 3679 Electronic circuits

(G-4601)
OUTLAND ENGINEERING INC
167 Cherry St Pmb 280 (06460-3466)
PHONE..................................800 797-3709
Stewart Burton, *President*
Grace Burton, *Admin Sec*
▲ EMP: 19
SQ FT: 54,000
SALES (est): 2.3MM **Privately Held**
WEB: www.ac-safe.com
SIC: 3429 5075 Manufactured hardware (general); air conditioning & ventilation equipment & supplies

(G-4602)
P&P TOOL & DIE CORP
72 Erna Ave (06461-3115)
PHONE..................................203 874-2571
Gabor Pernyeszi, *President*
EMP: 3
SALES: 250K **Privately Held**
SIC: 3599 Machine shop, jobbing & repair

(G-4603)
PARIDISE FOODS LLC
828 New Haven Ave (06460-3675)
P.O. Box 5178 (06460-0709)
PHONE..................................203 283-3903
Hristos Paridis, *Principal*
EMP: 3 EST: 2010
SALES (est): 246.2K **Privately Held**
SIC: 2099 Food preparations

(G-4604)
PAUL PETRUSHONIS STAIND GLSS
400 Boston Post Rd (06460-2579)
PHONE..................................203 878-0163
Paul Petrushonis, *Owner*
EMP: 1
SALES (est): 86K **Privately Held**
SIC: 3211 5231 Flat glass; glass, leaded or stained

(G-4605)
PENNY PRESS INC
185 Plains Rd Ste 100e (06461-2480)
PHONE..................................203 866-6688
Vincent Petrecca, *Principal*
EMP: 20
SALES (corp-wide): 12.7MM **Privately Held**
SIC: 2721 Magazines: publishing only, not printed on site
PA: Penny Press, Inc.
6 Prowitt St
Norwalk CT 06855
203 866-6688

(G-4606)
PENNY PUBLICATIONS LLC
185 Plains Rd Ste 201e (06461-2474)
PHONE..................................203 866-6688
Peter Kanter, *Branch Mgr*
EMP: 29
SALES (corp-wide): 16MM **Privately Held**
SIC: 2741 Miscellaneous publishing
PA: Penny Publications Llc
6 Prowitt St
Norwalk CT 06855
203 866-6688

(G-4607)
PEREZ WELDING SERVICES LLC
25 Belfast St (06460-5502)
PHONE..................................203 876-1066
Juan Rafael Perez, *Principal*
EMP: 1 EST: 2009
SALES (est): 33.2K **Privately Held**
SIC: 7692 Welding repair

(G-4608)
PERFECT INFINITY INC
167 Cherry St Ste 145 (06460-3466)
PHONE..................................203 906-0442
Winston Phillips, *Principal*
Desiree Mullins, *Treasurer*
EMP: 5
SQ FT: 2,400
SALES (est): 305.8K **Privately Held**
SIC: 2899 Distilled water

(G-4609)
PLASTIC AND MET COMPONENTS CO
381 Bridgeport Ave (06460-4103)
P.O. Box 312 (06460-0312)
PHONE..................................203 877-2723
John Ciesla, *President*
Robert E Dwyer, *President*
Donald Hoover, *Vice Pres*
Bill Smith, *Sales Staff*
Linda Staehly, *Sales Staff*
EMP: 12 EST: 1970
SQ FT: 4,500
SALES (est): 1.4MM **Privately Held**
SIC: 5072 3452 5085 5251 Hardware; bolts, nuts, rivets & washers; fasteners, industrial: nuts, bolts, screws, etc.; hardware

(G-4610)
POPS DONUTS
587 New Haven Ave (06460-3619)
PHONE..................................203 876-1210
Gus Grigo Riabis, *President*
EMP: 5
SALES (est): 270K **Privately Held**
SIC: 2051 5461 Doughnuts, except frozen; doughnuts

(G-4611)
PRACTICAL AUTOMATION INC (HQ)
45 Woodmont Rd (06460-2883)
P.O. Box 3028 (06460-0828)
PHONE..................................203 882-5640
Samuel Bergami, *President*
Luigi Cazzaniga, *General Mgr*
Kevin M Conlisk, *Vice Pres*
Dave Petreycik, *Purch Mgr*
John Prokop, *Purchasing*
▲ EMP: 52
SQ FT: 35,000
SALES (est): 9.8MM
SALES (corp-wide): 57MM **Privately Held**
WEB: www.practicalautomation.com
SIC: 2759 Thermography
PA: Alinabal Holdings Corporation
28 Woodmont Rd
Milford CT 06460
203 877-3241

(G-4612)
PRECISION METAL PRODUCTS INC
307 Pepes Farm Rd (06460-8605)
PHONE..................................203 877-4258
William O'Brien, *President*
Joseph Martino, *Vice Pres*
EMP: 196
SQ FT: 36,000
SALES (est): 51.9MM **Privately Held**
WEB: www.pmpinc.biz
SIC: 3841 Surgical & medical instruments

(G-4613)
PRECISION SENSORS INC
340 Woodmont Rd (06460-3702)
P.O. Box 509 (06460-0509)
PHONE..................................203 877-2795
Robert D Reis, *Ch of Bd*
David A Reis, *President*
R Tim Straub, *Vice Pres*
Ann Patry, *Purchasing*
Roberto Nicolia, *Electrical Engi*
▼ EMP: 39 EST: 1962
SQ FT: 10,000
SALES (est): 6.5MM
SALES (corp-wide): 39.4MM **Privately Held**
SIC: 3823 Pressure measurement instruments, industrial
PA: United Electric Controls Company
180 Dexter Ave
Watertown MA 02472
617 923-6900

(G-4614)
PRECISION TOOL & COMPONENTS
195 Rock Ln (06460-3831)
PHONE..................................203 874-9215
Joseph Reilly, *President*
Michael Yevich, *Treasurer*
EMP: 5
SQ FT: 1,700
SALES: 450K **Privately Held**
SIC: 3599 Machine shop, jobbing & repair

(G-4615)
PREMIERE KITCHENS & WDWKG LLC
111 Pepes Farm Rd (06460-3671)
PHONE..................................203 882-1745
EMP: 1
SALES (est): 54.1K **Privately Held**
SIC: 2431 Millwork, Nsk

(G-4616)
PRESTIGE TOOL MFG LLC
154 Old Gate Ln (06460-3651)
P.O. Box 5241 (06460-0702)
PHONE..................................203 874-0360
Kenneth E Dugan,
Cindy Dugan,
EMP: 6
SQ FT: 6,600
SALES (est): 770K **Privately Held**
WEB: www.prestigetoolmfg.com
SIC: 3599 Machine shop, jobbing & repair

(G-4617)
PRINT SOURCE LTD
116a Research Dr Ste D (06460-2838)
P.O. Box 5214 (06460-0701)
PHONE..................................203 876-1822
Douglas Hecker, *President*
EMP: 3
SALES (est): 329.9K **Privately Held**
SIC: 2759 7336 Commercial printing; commercial art & graphic design; graphic arts & related design

(G-4618)
PROBATTER SPORTS LLC
49 Research Dr Ste 1 (06460-2864)
PHONE..................................203 874-2500
Mike Suba, *Vice Pres*
Timothy Oreilly, *Engineer*
Wesley Hurty, *Sales Staff*
Greg Battersby, *Mng Member*
EMP: 8
SALES (est): 1.1MM **Privately Held**
WEB: www.probatter.com
SIC: 3949 5941 Baseball, softball & cricket sports equipment; sporting goods & bicycle shops

(G-4619)
PUCKS PUTTERS & FUEL LLC
10 Robert Dennis Dr (06461-2267)
PHONE..................................203 877-5457
Steven Genova, *Branch Mgr*
EMP: 11
SALES (corp-wide): 871.9K **Privately Held**
SIC: 2869 Fuels
PA: Pucks Putters & Fuel Llc
784 River Rd
Shelton CT 06484
203 494-3952

(G-4620)
QTRAN INC
155 Hill St Ste 3 (06460-3192)
PHONE..................................203 367-8777
John Tremaine, *CEO*
Susan Cutler Tremaine, *President*
Jordan Nodelman, *Vice Pres*
Elizabeth Pisano, *Vice Pres*
Alex Fiorelli, *Opers Mgr*
▲ EMP: 40
SQ FT: 10,000
SALES (est): 12.2MM **Privately Held**
WEB: www.q-tran.com
SIC: 3679 3677 Electronic circuits; electronic coils, transformers & other inductors

(G-4621)
QUALEDI INC (PA)
121 W Main St Ste 4 (06460-9201)
PHONE..................................203 874-4334
Stephen Morocco, *President*
EMP: 5
SALES (est): 1.2MM **Privately Held**
WEB: www.qualedi.com
SIC: 7372 Prepackaged software

(G-4622)
R A TOOL CO
230 Woodmont Rd Ste Y (06460-2845)
PHONE..................................203 877-2998
Diane Andrews, *Owner*
EMP: 4
SQ FT: 1,800
SALES (est): 399K **Privately Held**
SIC: 3544 3469 Special dies & tools; metal stampings; machine parts, stamped or pressed metal

(G-4623)
RED MAT MEDIA INC
162 Bridgeport Ave (06460-3935)
PHONE..................................203 283-5290
Timothy Lyon, *Principal*
EMP: 1
SALES (est): 115.1K **Privately Held**
SIC: 2741 Miscellaneous publishing

(G-4624)
REL-TECH ELECTRONICS INC
215 Pepes Farm Rd (06460-3626)
P.O. Box 3111 (06460-0911)
PHONE..................................203 877-8770
Ralph L Palumbo, *President*
Noreen C Palumbo, *Admin Sec*
EMP: 85
SQ FT: 12,000
SALES (est): 9.6MM
SALES (corp-wide): 50.2MM **Publicly Held**
WEB: www.rel-tech.com
SIC: 3679 5063 Harness assemblies for electronic use: wire or cable; wire & cable
PA: Rf Industries, Ltd.
7610 Miramar Rd Ste 6000
San Diego CA 92126
858 549-6340

(G-4625)
RELIABLE TOOL & DIE INC
435 Woodmont Rd (06460-3703)
PHONE..................................203 877-3264
Russell J Vecsey, *President*
Agail Reese, *Admin Sec*
EMP: 26 EST: 1978
SQ FT: 27,000
SALES (est): 6MM **Privately Held**
WEB: www.reliabletooling.com
SIC: 3544 Special dies & tools

(G-4626)
RICHARD BREAULT
Also Called: Datex Microcomputer Service
117 North St (06460-3443)
P.O. Box 5094 (06460-1494)
PHONE..................................203 876-2707
Richard Breault, *Owner*
EMP: 3

Milford - New Haven County (G-4627)

SALES (est): 200.9K **Privately Held**
SIC: 7372 5045 Prepackaged software; computer software

(G-4627)
RICHARD MANUFACTURING CO INC
250 Rock Ln (06460-3853)
PHONE..................203 874-3617
James F Steponavich, *President*
Linda Sill, *Human Res Mgr*
EMP: 35 **EST**: 1957
SQ FT: 13,000
SALES (est): 8MM **Privately Held**
WEB: www.rmcoonline.com
SIC: 3728 Aircraft assemblies, subassemblies & parts

(G-4628)
RIDGE VIEW ASSOCIATES INC
Also Called: J Burdon Division
122 Cascade Blvd (06460-2848)
PHONE..................203 878-8560
William B Maley Jr, *President*
Peter Murray, *Opers Spvr*
▲ **EMP**: 70
SQ FT: 55,000
SALES (est): 14.5MM **Privately Held**
WEB: www.trans-liteinc.com
SIC: 3647 3546 Locomotive & railroad car lights; subway car lighting fixtures; streetcar lighting fixtures; drills & drilling tools

(G-4629)
RINGS WIRE INC (PA)
257 Depot Rd (06460-3804)
P.O. Box 3013 (06460-0813)
PHONE..................203 874-6719
Stanley Reiter, *President*
Howard J Reiter, *Vice Pres*
EMP: 45
SQ FT: 300,000
SALES (est): 2.4MM **Privately Held**
SIC: 3965 Fasteners, snap; buckles & buckle parts

(G-4630)
RITAS OF MILFORD
175 Boston Post Rd (06460-3104)
PHONE..................203 301-4490
Michael Guerino, *Owner*
EMP: 10
SALES (est): 491.3K **Privately Held**
SIC: 2024 Ice cream, bulk

(G-4631)
ROME FASTENER CORPORATION
257 Depot Rd (06460-3804)
P.O. Box 3013 (06460-0813)
PHONE..................203 874-6719
Stanley F Reiter, *President*
Howard J Reiter, *Vice Pres*
Marcia W Reiter, *Director*
▲ **EMP**: 50
SQ FT: 75,000
SALES (est): 5.7MM **Privately Held**
WEB: www.romefast.com
SIC: 3999 3965 Forms: display, dress & show; fasteners

(G-4632)
ROME FASTENER SALES CORP
257 Depot Rd (06460-3804)
P.O. Box 3013 (06460-0813)
PHONE..................203 874-6719
Stanley F Reiter, *Manager*
EMP: 16
SALES (corp-wide): 4MM **Privately Held**
SIC: 3965 Fasteners
PA: Rome Fastener Sales Corporation
246 W 38th St Rm 501
New York NY 10018
212 741-9779

(G-4633)
ROSS CUSTOM CABINETRY
179 Buckingham Ave (06460-4889)
PHONE..................203 913-2753
Richard Ross,
EMP: 2
SALES (est): 12.8K **Privately Held**
SIC: 2434 Wood kitchen cabinets

(G-4634)
ROSS MFG & DESIGN LLC
124 Research Dr Ste A (06460-8571)
PHONE..................203 878-0187
Christopher Ross, *Managing Prtnr*
Donald Ross, *Partner*
EMP: 12
SQ FT: 4,200
SALES (est): 998.7K **Privately Held**
SIC: 3599 Machine shop, jobbing & repair

(G-4635)
RUBBER LABELS USA LLC
500 Bic Dr Bldg 2 (06461-1777)
PHONE..................203 713-8059
Robert Vero, *Mng Member*
EMP: 5
SALES (est): 171.1K **Privately Held**
SIC: 2754 Labels: gravure printing

(G-4636)
RYDZ ENGINEERING
136 Research Dr Ste H (06460-8541)
PHONE..................203 878-5499
Kristopher Rydzewski, *President*
EMP: 2
SALES (est): 127.2K **Privately Held**
SIC: 7699 3599 Industrial machinery & equipment repair; machine shop, jobbing & repair

(G-4637)
S AND Z GRAPHICS LLC
Also Called: Minuteman Press
415 Boston Post Rd Ste 7 (06460-2578)
PHONE..................203 783-9675
Paul Kely, *Marketing Staff*
Kevin M Mola,
EMP: 4
SQ FT: 1,000
SALES (est): 715K **Privately Held**
WEB: www.ambyth.com
SIC: 2752 7336 Commercial printing, lithographic; commercial art & graphic design

(G-4638)
SANTEC CORPORATION
84 Old Gate Ln (06460-8622)
PHONE..................203 878-1379
Laura Lombardo, *Vice Pres*
Laurajane Uruza, *Vice Pres*
Vito J Lombardo, *Opers Mgr*
EMP: 12
SQ FT: 14,000
SALES (est): 3.5MM **Privately Held**
WEB: www.santec-corp.com
SIC: 3555 Printing trades machinery

(G-4639)
SCHICK MANUFACTURING INC (HQ)
Also Called: Schick-Wilkinson Sword
10 Leighton Rd (06460-3552)
PHONE..................203 882-2100
David Hatfield, *President*
Jacques Desjardins, *General Mgr*
Joseph Lynch, *Principal*
Daniel J Sescleifer, *Exec VP*
William C Fox, *Vice Pres*
◆ **EMP**: 55
SALES (est): 113.6MM
SALES (corp-wide): 2.2B **Publicly Held**
WEB: www.energizer.com
SIC: 3421 Razor blades & razors
PA: Edgewell Personal Care Company
1350 Tmberlake Manor Pkwy
Chesterfield MO 63017
314 594-1900

(G-4640)
SEASAW LLC
16 Fenway St N (06460-4545)
PHONE..................203 815-9022
Lee Seslar,
EMP: 1
SALES (est): 39.6K **Privately Held**
SIC: 3999 Manufacturing industries

(G-4641)
SEI II INC
60 Commerce Park Ste 1 (06460-3513)
PHONE..................203 877-8488
Jeffrey A Stein, *President*
Amanda Konieczny, *Engineer*
EMP: 10

GEOGRAPHIC SECTION

SQ FT: 2,000
SALES (est): 940K **Privately Held**
WEB: www.synectic.net
SIC: 8711 3841 Consulting engineer; surgical & medical instruments

(G-4642)
SHEETMETAL SYSTEMS INC
Also Called: Sheet Metal Systems
30 Stran Rd (06461-3008)
PHONE..................203 878-2633
Rick Frederick, *President*
Brad Frederick, *Vice Pres*
Ryan Frederick, *Vice Pres*
Judith Frederick, *Admin Sec*
EMP: 5
SQ FT: 10,000
SALES (est): 620K **Privately Held**
SIC: 1761 3444 Sheet metalwork; sheet metalwork

(G-4643)
SHOW MOTION INC
1034 Bridgeport Ave (06460-3167)
PHONE..................203 866-1866
William Mensching Sr, *President*
William Mensching, *President*
Michael Stevens, *Vice Pres*
William M Mensching, *Project Mgr*
▲ **EMP**: 50
SQ FT: 30,000
SALES (est): 7.3MM **Privately Held**
WEB: www.showmotion.com
SIC: 3999 3531 1799 Theatrical scenery; winches; rigging, theatrical

(G-4644)
SIGNCENTER LLC
333 Quarry Rd (06460-8574)
PHONE..................800 269-2130
Michael Oliveras, *Principal*
Jimmy Whitehill, *Production*
▲ **EMP**: 6
SALES (est): 895.5K **Privately Held**
SIC: 3993 Signs & advertising specialties

(G-4645)
SILICON INTEGRATION INC
241 Research Dr Ste 9 (06460-8560)
PHONE..................203 876-2844
Cary Cieciuch, *President*
Peter Bockiaro, *Opers Mgr*
Margret Lombardi, *Purch Mgr*
EMP: 20 **EST**: 1997
SQ FT: 4,000
SALES (est): 3.5MM **Privately Held**
WEB: www.siliconint.com
SIC: 8711 3672 Electrical or electronic engineering; circuit boards, television & radio printed

(G-4646)
SMART SIGNS PRO LLC
225 Research Dr Unit 13 (06460-8507)
PHONE..................203 684-9839
Kevin Barnctt,
EMP: 1
SALES (est): 46K **Privately Held**
SIC: 3993 Signs & advertising specialties

(G-4647)
SONITEK CORPORATION
84 Research Dr (06460-8523)
PHONE..................203 878-9321
Robert James Bishop, *President*
Cheryl Ann Bishop, *Corp Secy*
Harry Crease, *Vice Pres*
Paul Denton, *Design Engr*
Linda Pereira, *Office Mgr*
EMP: 30
SQ FT: 7,500
SALES (est): 7.8MM **Privately Held**
WEB: www.plasticassembly.com
SIC: 3548 3541 Welding apparatus; ultrasonic metal cutting machine tools

(G-4648)
SOURCEBOOKS INC
18 Cherry St Ste 1 (06460-3485)
PHONE..................203 876-9790
Mary Altman, *Editor*
Debra Werksman, *Manager*
EMP: 2

SALES (corp-wide): 61.9MM **Privately Held**
SIC: 2731 5199 Books: publishing only; gifts & novelties
PA: Sourcebooks, Llc.
1935 Brookdale Rd Ste 139
Naperville IL 60563
630 961-3900

(G-4649)
SOUTHPORT BREWING CO
33 New Haven Ave (06460-3308)
PHONE..................203 874-2337
William Dasilva, *Principal*
EMP: 35
SALES (est): 2.3MM **Privately Held**
SIC: 2082 5812 Beer (alcoholic beverage); eating places

(G-4650)
SPECIALTY TOOL COMPANY USA LLC
61 Erna Ave (06461-3118)
PHONE..................203 874-2009
Richard E Fisk, *Manager*
EMP: 13 **EST**: 1968
SQ FT: 5,000
SALES: 1.8MM **Privately Held**
SIC: 3724 Aircraft engines & engine parts

(G-4651)
SPECTRUM ASSOCIATES INC
440 New Haven Ave Ste 5 (06460-3629)
P.O. Box 470 (06460-0470)
PHONE..................203 878-4618
Richard Meisenheimer, *President*
Daniel Meisenheimer III, *Vice Pres*
Thomas Casolino, *Engineer*
Peter Jackson, *Engineer*
Casolino Thomas, *Engineer*
EMP: 10
SALES (est): 1.3MM **Privately Held**
SIC: 3643 5084 5085 Current-carrying wiring devices; hydraulic systems equipment & supplies; industrial supplies

(G-4652)
SPECTRUM PRESS
Also Called: Spectrum Graphix
354 Woodmont Rd Ste 15 (06460-3766)
PHONE..................203 878-9090
Peter J Bonaventure, *Partner*
Kim Bonaventure, *Partner*
EMP: 15
SQ FT: 8,000
SALES (est): 1.6MM **Privately Held**
WEB: www.spectrumgphix.com
SIC: 2752 Commercial printing, lithographic

(G-4653)
STERLING FORMS AND CMPT SUPS
Also Called: Sterling Printing & Graphics
326 W Main St Ste 106 (06460-2560)
PHONE..................203 876-7337
Richard Meyers, *Owner*
EMP: 3
SALES (est): 364.9K **Privately Held**
SIC: 7389 2754 Printing broker; business forms: gravure printing

(G-4654)
STEVENS MANUFACTURING CO INC
220 Rock Ln (06460-3853)
PHONE..................203 878-2328
Stephen Fogler, *President*
John Mathieu, *General Mgr*
Nick Reinke, *General Mgr*
Elizabeth Fogler, *Vice Pres*
Maria Acevedo, *QC Mgr*
▲ **EMP**: 32 **EST**: 1957
SQ FT: 34,000
SALES (est): 12.8MM **Privately Held**
WEB: www.stevensmfgco.com
SIC: 3599 Machine shop, jobbing & repair

(G-4655)
SUMMIT ORTHOPEDIC TECH INC
294 Quarry Rd (06460-2851)
PHONE..................203 693-2727
Adam Ferrell, *President*
Jason Blake, *COO*

Ron Dunn, *Vice Pres*
EMP: 45 **EST:** 2014
SALES (est): 5.1MM **Privately Held**
SIC: 3841 Surgical & medical instruments

(G-4656)
SUMMIT SCREW MACHINE CORP
49 Research Dr Ste 3 (06460-2864)
PHONE..................................203 693-2727
EMP: 3
SALES (est): 385.4K **Privately Held**
SIC: 3599 Machine shop, jobbing & repair

(G-4657)
SUN FARM CORPORATION
75 Woodmont Rd (06460-2840)
PHONE..................................203 882-8000
Linus Sun, *President*
Alexander S Sun, *President*
EMP: 7
SALES (est): 840K **Privately Held**
SIC: 3556 Mills, food

(G-4658)
SURGIQUEST INC
488 Wheelers Farms Rd # 3 (06461-5801)
PHONE..................................203 799-2400
Kourosh Azabarzin, *CEO*
Christine Antalik, *CFO*
Carlos Babini, *Sales Staff*
Chris Klecher, *Sales Staff*
EMP: 83
SALES (est): 11.6MM
SALES (corp-wide): 859.6MM **Publicly Held**
SIC: 3841 Surgical & medical instruments
PA: Conmed Corporation
525 French Rd
Utica NY 13502
315 797-8375

(G-4659)
SWIPE INK SCREEN PRINTING LLC
233 Research Dr Ste 5 (06460-8559)
PHONE..................................203 783-0468
EMP: 2
SALES (est): 110K **Privately Held**
SIC: 2752 Lithographic Commercial Printing

(G-4660)
SYNECTIC ENGINEERING INC
60 Commerce Park Ste 1 (06460-3513)
PHONE..................................203 877-8488
Adam Lehman, *President*
EMP: 18 **EST:** 2013
SALES (est): 3.2MM
SALES (corp-wide): 432.8MM **Privately Held**
SIC: 3841 Catheters; surgical stapling devices
HQ: Mack Molding Company, Inc.
608 Warm Brook Rd
Arlington VT 05250
802 375-2511

(G-4661)
SYNECTIX LLC
291 Pepes Farm Rd (06460-3671)
PHONE..................................203 283-0701
Suresh Eswar,
Shashi Alabur,
David Mazza,
▲ **EMP:** 2
SQ FT: 2,800
SALES: 972.4K **Privately Held**
SIC: 3661 PBX equipment, manual or automatic

(G-4662)
TEF LLC
65 Centennial Dr (06461-1662)
PHONE..................................203 878-9740
EMP: 2
SALES (est): 73.2K **Privately Held**
SIC: 2759 Commercial printing

(G-4663)
THOMAS SPRING CO OF CONNENICUT
29 Seemans Ln (06460-4338)
PHONE..................................203 874-7030
Peter Tessitore, *President*

Gerry Tessitore, *Vice Pres*
EMP: 8
SALES (est): 1MM **Privately Held**
SIC: 3495 Mechanical springs, precision

(G-4664)
THULE INC
40 Pepes Farm Rd (06460-3670)
PHONE..................................203 881-9600
Elan Motkin, *Manager*
EMP: 1 **Privately Held**
SIC: 3714 5021 Motor vehicle parts & accessories; furniture
HQ: Thule, Inc.
42 Silvermine Rd
Seymour CT 06483
203 881-9600

(G-4665)
TINSLEY GROUP-PS&W INC (HQ)
Also Called: Olympic STEel-Ps&w
1 Eastern Steel Rd (06460-2837)
PHONE..................................919 742-5832
Michael Siegal, *CEO*
David A Wolfort, *President*
Richard T Marabito, *CFO*
▲ **EMP:** 53
SQ FT: 70,000
SALES (est): 23.1MM
SALES (corp-wide): 1.3B **Publicly Held**
SIC: 3531 7692 3441 Construction machinery; welding repair; fabricated structural metal
PA: Olympic Steel, Inc.
22901 Millcreek Blvd # 650
Cleveland OH 44122
216 292-3800

(G-4666)
TOTAL COMMUNICATIONS INC
500 Bic Dr Bldg 2 (06461-1777)
PHONE..................................203 882-0088
John Gaudio, *Manager*
EMP: 47
SALES (corp-wide): 20.9MM **Privately Held**
SIC: 5065 7629 3661 Telephone equipment; sound equipment, electronic; telephone set repair; telephone & telegraph apparatus
PA: Total Communications, Inc.
333 Burnham St
East Hartford CT 06108
860 282-9999

(G-4667)
ULTIMATE INTERFACES CORP
96 Salem Walk (06460-7132)
PHONE..................................203 230-8184
Thomas F Arciuolo, *President*
Larry Ciccarelli, *Admin Sec*
EMP: 5
SALES (est): 136.8K **Privately Held**
WEB: www.ultimateinterfaces.com
SIC: 5731 7372 7389 Consumer electronic equipment; prepackaged software;

(G-4668)
UNITED ELECTRIC CONTROLS CO
Also Called: Precision Sensors
340 Woodmont Rd (06460-3702)
PHONE..................................203 877-2795
Jack Button, *President*
Derek Dewitt, *Engineer*
Timothy R Straub, *Manager*
EMP: 55
SQ FT: 6,372
SALES (corp-wide): 39.4MM **Privately Held**
WEB: www.ueonline.com
SIC: 3823 3674 3643 3625 Pressure measurement instruments, industrial; semiconductors & related devices; current-carrying wiring devices; relays & industrial controls
PA: United Electric Controls Company
180 Dexter Ave
Watertown MA 02472
617 923-6900

(G-4669)
UNIVERSE PUBLISHING CO LLC
167 Cherry St Ste 261 (06460-3466)
PHONE..................................203 283-5201

Ioana Crupenschi, *President*
EMP: 3
SQ FT: 1,000
SALES (est): 130.2K **Privately Held**
SIC: 2741 Miscellaneous publishing

(G-4670)
UP & DOWN OVERHEAD DOOR
181 Research Dr Ste 1 (06460-8549)
P.O. Box 3451 (06460-0943)
PHONE..................................203 876-8045
Dan De Sdusa, *Principal*
EMP: 2
SALES (est): 158.4K **Privately Held**
SIC: 2431 Garage doors, overhead: wood

(G-4671)
URBAN ANTIQUE RADIO
58 Naugatuck Ave (06460-6033)
PHONE..................................203 877-2409
Mike Urban, *Owner*
EMP: 1
SQ FT: 2,129
SALES (est): 74.9K **Privately Held**
SIC: 3634 7641 Personal electrical appliances; antique furniture repair & restoration

(G-4672)
VARSITY IMPRINTS
22 Roller Ter (06461-2643)
PHONE..................................203 354-4371
Richard Kurtzman, *Principal*
EMP: 3
SALES (est): 225.9K **Privately Held**
SIC: 2759 Screen printing

(G-4673)
VERTECH INC
181 Research Dr Ste 5 (06460-8556)
PHONE..................................203 876-1552
Yew-Tsung Chen, *President*
Doris Chen, *Treasurer*
EMP: 2
SQ FT: 1,600
SALES (est): 267K **Privately Held**
SIC: 3545 8748 2819 Precision measuring tools; business consulting; alkali metals: lithium, cesium, francium, rubidium

(G-4674)
VINCENT JEWELERS
23 New Haven Ave (06460-3308)
PHONE..................................203 882-8900
Vincent Hutter, *Owner*
EMP: 1
SQ FT: 1,000
SALES: 200K **Privately Held**
SIC: 5944 3471 Jewelry, precious stones & precious metals; gold plating

(G-4675)
VITAL HLTHCARE CMMNCATIONS LLC
661 West Ave Apt 16 (06461-3066)
PHONE..................................866 478-4825
Barry Belucia,
EMP: 4
SALES (est): 245K **Privately Held**
SIC: 8742 5047 3845 Hospital & health services consultant; patient monitoring equipment; patient monitoring apparatus

(G-4676)
VITRO TECHNOLOGY LTD
205 Research Dr Ste 12 (06460-8552)
PHONE..................................203 783-9566
George Davis, *President*
EMP: 6
SALES (est): 166.8K **Privately Held**
SIC: 3229 Glass fiber products

(G-4677)
W&R MANUFACTURING INC
230 Woodmont Rd Ste U (06460-2845)
P.O. Box 191, Stratford (06615-0191)
PHONE..................................203 877-5955
Elizabeth Butrymowicz, *President*
Rose Zimnoch, *Vice Pres*
EMP: 4
SQ FT: 3,500
SALES (est): 456K **Privately Held**
SIC: 3728 Aircraft parts & equipment

(G-4678)
WADE R MOORE
124 Research Dr Ste C (06460-8570)
PHONE..................................203 767-6146
Wade Moore, *Owner*
Moore Wade, *Design Engr*
EMP: 1
SALES (est): 86.4K **Privately Held**
SIC: 3399 Primary metal products

(G-4679)
WALNUT BEACH CREAMERY LLC
17 Broadway 19 (06460-6004)
PHONE..................................203 878-7738
Susan Patrick, *Mng Member*
EMP: 2
SALES (est): 181.4K **Privately Held**
SIC: 2024 Ice cream, bulk

(G-4680)
WILDE MANUFACTURING LLC
80 Wampus Ln Ste 4 (06460-4856)
P.O. Box 53 (06460-0053)
PHONE..................................203 693-3939
Frank Wilde, *Principal*
EMP: 1 **EST:** 2013
SALES (est): 188.6K **Privately Held**
SIC: 3599 Machine shop, jobbing & repair

(G-4681)
WINE WELL CHILLER COMP INC
301 Brewster Rd Ste 3 (06460-3700)
PHONE..................................203 878-2465
Anna Bell Fisher, *President*
James Fisher, *Chairman*
Robert Hewson, *Director*
EMP: 3
SQ FT: 2,000
SALES: 300K **Privately Held**
WEB: www.wine-well.com
SIC: 3585 Refrigeration equipment, complete

(G-4682)
XYLEM INC
94 Midwood Rd (06460-6657)
PHONE..................................203 521-4934
EMP: 2 **Publicly Held**
SIC: 3561 Pumps & pumping equipment
PA: Xylem Inc.
1 International Dr
Rye Brook NY 10573

Milldale
Hartford County

(G-4683)
CENTURY TOOL AND DESIGN INC
260 Canal St (06467)
P.O. Box 545 (06467-0545)
PHONE..................................860 621-6748
Michael Aldi, *President*
Ray Koontz, *Vice Pres*
Raymond Koontz, *Vice Pres*
Charles Maxfield, *Treasurer*
EMP: 14 **EST:** 1975
SQ FT: 5,000
SALES: 2MM **Privately Held**
WEB: www.centool.com
SIC: 3545 7389 Machine tool attachments & accessories; tool holders; design services

(G-4684)
JAY SONS SCREW MCH PDTS INC
197 Burritt St (06467)
P.O. Box 674 (06467-0674)
PHONE..................................860 621-0141
David Tellerico, *President*
John Spinello, *Vice Pres*
Joseph Tellerico III, *Admin Sec*
EMP: 18 **EST:** 1945
SQ FT: 12,000
SALES (est): 3.5MM **Privately Held**
WEB: www.jaysons.com
SIC: 3451 Screw machine products

Milldale - Hartford County (G-4685)

(G-4685)
MICRO INSERT INC
183 Clark St (06467)
P.O. Box 673 (06467-0673)
PHONE.................................860 621-5789
James Deangelo, *President*
Keith Smith, *Vice Pres*
Kenneth Nelson, *Treasurer*
Fred Douglas Smith, *Admin Sec*
EMP: 9
SQ FT: 15,000
SALES (est): 1.3MM **Privately Held**
SIC: 3545 Tool holders

(G-4686)
MID-STATE MANUFACTURING INC
1610 Mriden Waterburytpke (06467)
P.O. Box 585 (06467-0585)
PHONE.................................860 621-6855
Robert Pisko, *President*
Dennis Pisko, *Shareholder*
EMP: 15
SQ FT: 5,000
SALES: 1MM **Privately Held**
WEB: www.midstatemfg.com
SIC: 3544 3599 3545 3541 Special dies & tools; machine shop, jobbing & repair; machine tool accessories; machine tools, metal cutting type

(G-4687)
NATURALLY RELAXED LLC
183 Clark St (06467-6501)
PHONE.................................860 402-0613
Denise J Glabau, *Principal*
EMP: 2 **EST:** 2007
SALES (est): 174.4K **Privately Held**
SIC: 8049 2844 ; cosmetic preparations

(G-4688)
STEEL RULE DIE CORP AMERICA
289 Clark Street Ext (06467)
P.O. Box 546 (06467-0546)
PHONE.................................860 621-5284
Thomas Brandt, *President*
Theresa Brandt, *Vice Pres*
EMP: 5
SQ FT: 2,600
SALES (est): 270K **Privately Held**
SIC: 3544 Special dies & tools

(G-4689)
TOFF INDUSTRY INC
323 Clark St (06467-6503)
P.O. Box 579 (06467-0579)
PHONE.................................860 378-0532
Harold Toffey, *President*
Dori Tapineau, *Office Mgr*
▲ **EMP:** 7
SQ FT: 5,000
SALES (est): 1MM **Privately Held**
WEB: www.toffindustries.com
SIC: 2394 Awnings, fabric: made from purchased materials

Monroe
Fairfield County

(G-4690)
AAPI
593 M St (06468)
PHONE.................................203 268-2450
Bill Harris, *Principal*
EMP: 3
SALES (est): 211.4K **Privately Held**
SIC: 2721 Periodicals: publishing & printing

(G-4691)
ALL AMERICAN EMBROIDERY
92 Purdy Hill Rd (06468-2244)
PHONE.................................203 906-9656
EMP: 1
SALES (est): 39.5K **Privately Held**
SIC: 2395 Pleating & stitching

(G-4692)
AMERICAN HEAT TREATING INC
16 Commerce Dr (06468-2601)
PHONE.................................203 268-1750
Peter J Wolcott, *President*
Charles Polatsek, *Vice Pres*
John H Weiland, *Treasurer*
EMP: 45 **EST:** 1969
SQ FT: 32,000
SALES (est): 8.6MM **Privately Held**
SIC: 3398 Metal heat treating

(G-4693)
AMERICAN IMEX CORPORATION
57 Maryanne Dr (06468-3209)
PHONE.................................203 261-5200
Yogesh Mehrotra, *President*
Patrice Green, *Vice Pres*
EMP: 5
SALES (est): 500K **Privately Held**
WEB: www.imex-co.com
SIC: 3357 Aircraft wire & cable, nonferrous

(G-4694)
AXEL PLASTICS RES LABS INC
50 Cambridge Dr (06468-2661)
PHONE.................................718 672-8300
Franklin Bk Axel, *CEO*
Jake Axel, *President*
Barbara Axel, *Corp Secy*
◆ **EMP:** 32
SQ FT: 4,500
SALES (est): 9MM **Privately Held**
WEB: www.axelplast.com
SIC: 2821 2992 Plastics materials & resins; lubricating oils & greases

(G-4695)
B-SWEET LLC
444 Main St Ste C (06468-1112)
PHONE.................................203 452-0499
EMP: 4
SALES (est): 248.7K **Privately Held**
SIC: 2024 Mfg Ice Cream/Frozen Desert

(G-4696)
BAUER COMPRESSORS INC
Also Called: Bauer Compressor North East
60 Twin Brook Ter (06468-1808)
PHONE.................................203 445-9514
Tom Liscinski, *Manager*
EMP: 5
SALES (corp-wide): 65MM **Privately Held**
WEB: www.bauersf.com
PA: Bauer Compressors, Inc.
1328 Azalea Garden Rd
Norfolk VA 23502
757 855-6006
SIC: 3563 Air & gas compressors

(G-4697)
BEN BARRETT CANVAS SERVICE LLC
14 Patmar Ln (06468-1517)
PHONE.................................203 268-4315
Ben Barrett, *Owner*
EMP: 2 **EST:** 2017
SALES (est): 80K **Privately Held**
SIC: 2211 Canvas

(G-4698)
BIOMERICS LLC
Biomerics Nle
246 Main St Ste C (06468-1178)
PHONE.................................203 268-7238
Rich Rosselli, *President*
EMP: 60 **Privately Held**
SIC: 7389 2679 3479 3953 Engraving service; labels, paper: made from purchased material; name plates: engraved, etched, etc.; stencils, painting & marking; packaging paper & plastics film, coated & laminated
HQ: Biomerics, Llc
6030 W Harold Gatty Dr
Salt Lake City UT 84116

(G-4699)
BML TOOL & MFG CORP
67 Enterprise Dr (06468-2674)
PHONE.................................203 880-9485
Philip Battaglia, *President*
Vincent Battaglia, *Vice Pres*
EMP: 60
SQ FT: 38,000
SALES (est): 11MM **Privately Held**
WEB: www.boottrac.com
SIC: 3469 3544 Stamping metal for the trade; special dies, tools, jigs & fixtures

(G-4700)
BOBBEX INC
523 Pepper St Ste B (06468-2676)
PHONE.................................800 792-4449
Robert Ecsedy, *President*
Greg Ecsedy, *Vice Pres*
Betty K Ecsedy, *Director*
EMP: 3
SQ FT: 3,000
SALES (est): 564.4K **Privately Held**
WEB: www.bobbex.com
SIC: 2873 5261 Fertilizers: natural (organic), except compost; nurseries & garden centers

(G-4701)
BQ BUSINESS SOLUTIONS
93 Lazy Brook Rd (06468-3315)
P.O. Box 225 (06468-0225)
PHONE.................................203 268-3500
Brian McHugh, *Owner*
EMP: 2
SALES (est): 13.1K **Privately Held**
SIC: 2732 Book printing

(G-4702)
BUDRAD ENGINEERING CO LLC
26 Patmar Cir (06468-1545)
PHONE.................................203 452-7310
Radoslaw Szawiola,
EMP: 3
SALES (est): 330.4K **Privately Held**
WEB: www.budrad.com
SIC: 3599 Machine & other job shop work

(G-4703)
CHURCH HILL CLASSICS LTD
Also Called: Diplomaframe.com
594 Pepper St (06468-2672)
PHONE.................................800 477-9005
Lucie Voves, *President*
Joe Voves, *Vice Pres*
Robin Schultz, *Opers Staff*
Caroline Corbett, *Human Resources*
Judith Parillo, *Accounts Mgr*
▲ **EMP:** 70
SQ FT: 25,000
SALES (est): 10MM **Privately Held**
WEB: www.diplomaframe.com
SIC: 7699 2499 Picture framing, custom; picture frame molding, finished

(G-4704)
CONNECTICUT DIGITAL POST INC
66 Grindstone Ln (06468-1349)
PHONE.................................203 268-4554
Jeffery Roos, *President*
Robyn Szarka Roos, *Vice Pres*
EMP: 2
SALES (est): 108.3K **Privately Held**
SIC: 2741 Miscellaneous publishing

(G-4705)
CONNECTICUT PRECAST CORP
Also Called: CT Precast
555 Fan Hill Rd (06468-1336)
PHONE.................................203 268-8688
Stephen Domizio, *President*
George T Domizio, *Vice Pres*
Robert Guile, *Engineer*
EMP: 23 **EST:** 1952
SQ FT: 20,000
SALES (est): 5.3MM **Privately Held**
WEB: www.ctprecast.com
SIC: 3272 Septic tanks, concrete; manhole covers or frames, concrete; liquid catch basins, tanks & covers: concrete

(G-4706)
CORNELL-CARR CO INC
626 Main St (06468-2808)
P.O. Box 253 (06468-0253)
PHONE.................................203 261-2529
Anton S Cornell, *President*
Philip H Gangnath, *Vice Pres*
Philip Gangnath, *Treasurer*
Stan Szarek, *Treasurer*
Margaret Carr, *Shareholder*
▲ **EMP:** 35 **EST:** 1955
SQ FT: 22,000
SALES (est): 10.7MM **Privately Held**
WEB: www.cornell-carr.com
SIC: 3442 3647 3429 Metal doors; sash, door or window: metal; window & door frames; boat & ship lighting fixtures; marine hardware

(G-4707)
CREATIVE PRINTED PRODUCTS LLC
446 Main St Fl 1 (06468-1114)
PHONE.................................203 268-8980
EMP: 2 **EST:** 2012
SALES (est): 170.8K **Privately Held**
SIC: 2752 Commercial printing, lithographic

(G-4708)
CUSTOM CRFT KTCHNS BY RIZIO BR
8 Maple Dr (06468-1603)
PHONE.................................203 268-0271
Ralph Rizio, *President*
Mario E Rizio, *Vice Pres*
Millie B Rizio, *Treasurer*
Angelina Rizio, *Admin Sec*
EMP: 12
SQ FT: 18,000
SALES (est): 3MM **Privately Held**
WEB: www.enkeboll.com
SIC: 2541 1799 1751 Counter & sink tops; counter top installation; cabinet building & installation

(G-4709)
D R CHARLES ENVMTL CNSTR LLC
Also Called: D.R. Charles Envmtl Excav
189 Monroe Tpke (06468-2248)
PHONE.................................203 445-0412
David Charles,
EMP: 2
SALES (est): 540.6K **Privately Held**
SIC: 1794 2499 3531 8744 Excavation & grading, building construction; mulch, wood & bark; plows: construction, excavating & grading;

(G-4710)
DAVIDS LEGAL SIGNS
384 Hammertown Rd (06468-1335)
PHONE.................................203 268-8943
David Lafollette, *Owner*
EMP: 1
SALES (est): 86.5K **Privately Held**
SIC: 3993 Signs, not made in custom sign painting shops

(G-4711)
DP CUSTOM BOAT REPR DETAIL LLC
483 Monroe Tpke Ste 167 (06468-2364)
PHONE.................................203 536-3997
Cayenne Phaosoung, *Principal*
EMP: 1
SALES (est): 54.6K **Privately Held**
SIC: 3732 Boat building & repairing

(G-4712)
DRB WOODWORKS
285 Wheeler Rd (06468-1922)
PHONE.................................203 216-7071
Daniel R Birkes, *Administration*
EMP: 2
SALES (est): 79.2K **Privately Held**
SIC: 2431 Millwork

(G-4713)
DYNAMIC FLIGHT SYSTEMS
303 Stanley Rd (06468-1526)
PHONE.................................203 449-7211
Linda Harrington, *Owner*
EMP: 5
SALES (est): 1,000K **Privately Held**
SIC: 3728 Aircraft parts & equipment

(G-4714)
DYNAMIC PRINTING
91 Main St (06468-1630)
PHONE.................................203 459-8762
Pete Juleson, *Owner*
EMP: 2
SQ FT: 600
SALES (est): 203.2K **Privately Held**
SIC: 2621 Printing paper

▲ = Import ▼ = Export
◆ = Import/Export

GEOGRAPHIC SECTION
Monroe - Fairfield County (G-4749)

(G-4715)
ELIDAH INC
810 Main St Ste C (06468-2809)
PHONE.....................978 435-4324
Gloria Kolb, *CEO*
EMP: 1 EST: 2014
SALES (est): 85.4K Privately Held
SIC: 3841 7389 Surgical & medical instruments;

(G-4716)
ENTREES MADE EASY
100 Cross Hill Rd (06468-2318)
PHONE.....................203 261-5777
Cathy Hayden, *Principal*
EMP: 3
SALES (est): 165.4K Privately Held
SIC: 2099 Food preparations

(G-4717)
FDK CUSTOM CABINETRY LLC
25 Lanthorne Rd (06468-1728)
PHONE.....................203 459-9909
Fred D Kaempfer, *Owner*
EMP: 1
SALES (est): 62.1K Privately Held
SIC: 2434 Wood kitchen cabinets

(G-4718)
FSNB ENTERPRISES INC
Also Called: Minuteman Press
12 Woodacre Ln (06468-1125)
PHONE.....................203 254-1947
Frank V Giacalone, *President*
Frank Giacalone, *President*
EMP: 4
SQ FT: 3,500
SALES (est): 643.4K Privately Held
SIC: 2752 Commercial printing, lithographic

(G-4719)
IGNATOWSKI JOHN
Also Called: Superior Signs
232 Main St Ste D (06468-1171)
PHONE.....................203 452-9601
John Ignatowski, *Mng Member*
EMP: 2
SALES (est): 158.2K Privately Held
SIC: 3993 Signs & advertising specialties

(G-4720)
IMAGE ONE PRTG & GRAPHICS INC
838 Main St Ste L (06468-2834)
PHONE.....................203 459-1880
Edward Mathey, *President*
Marcel Leroux, *Admin Sec*
EMP: 3
SQ FT: 2,400
SALES (est): 307.1K Privately Held
SIC: 2759 Commercial printing

(G-4721)
INTECHS LLC
17 Bittersweet Cir (06468-2649)
PHONE.....................203 260-8109
Maureen Bruen,
EMP: 2 EST: 2014
SALES (est): 94.7K Privately Held
SIC: 7336 7371 7373 2741 Commercial art & graphic design; custom computer programming services; computer systems analysis & design; technical manual & paper publishing; data processing service

(G-4722)
J & S INDUSTRIES LLC
17 Enterprise Dr (06468-2662)
PHONE.....................203 220-8970
EMP: 1 EST: 2009
SALES (est): 62.5K Privately Held
SIC: 3999 Mfg Misc Products

(G-4723)
JURMAN METRICS INC
555 Hammertown Rd (06468-1310)
P.O. Box 223 (06468-0223)
PHONE.....................203 261-9388
David R Jurman, *President*
Rudolf Jurman, *Vice Pres*
Regina Vey, *Office Admin*
Jeannette Jurman, *Admin Sec*
EMP: 13
SQ FT: 5,000
SALES: 3.3MM Privately Held
WEB: www.jurmanmetrics.com
SIC: 3829 Measuring & controlling devices

(G-4724)
K L S CUSTOM WOOD WORKING
88 Twin Brook Ter (06468-1808)
PHONE.....................203 520-5193
EMP: 1
SALES (est): 54.1K Privately Held
SIC: 2431 Millwork

(G-4725)
KEN HASTEDT
Also Called: Prestige Welding & Fabrication
33 W Maiden Ln (06468-1206)
PHONE.....................203 268-6563
Ken Hastedt, *Owner*
EMP: 1
SALES (est): 71.5K Privately Held
SIC: 1799 7692 3446 3444 Welding on site; welding repair; architectural metalwork; sheet metalwork

(G-4726)
KIAGRAPHICS
189 Josies Ring Rd (06468-1457)
PHONE.....................203 261-4328
Nancy Kia, *Owner*
EMP: 1
SALES: 50K Privately Held
SIC: 7374 2791 Computer graphics service; typesetting, computer controlled

(G-4727)
LD ASSOC LLC
16 Georges Ln (06468-3136)
PHONE.....................203 452-9393
Leon Barnaby, *Vice Pres*
EMP: 5
SALES (est): 339.1K Privately Held
SIC: 3442 Screen & storm doors & windows

(G-4728)
LIGHTHOUSE COMMUNICATIONS
47 Flint Ridge Rd (06468-1211)
PHONE.....................203 445-9733
Steven Twig, *Owner*
EMP: 1
SALES (est): 118.9K Privately Held
SIC: 3699 Security devices

(G-4729)
M CUBED TECHNOLOGIES INC
921 Main St (06468-2811)
PHONE.....................203 452-2333
Randall Price Sr, *Branch Mgr*
EMP: 3
SALES (corp-wide): 1.3B Publicly Held
SIC: 3599 Machine shop, jobbing & repair
HQ: M Cubed Technologies, Inc.
31 Pecks Ln Ste 8
Newtown CT 06470
203 304-2940

(G-4730)
MACLEAN WOODWORKING LLC
696 Main St (06468-2838)
PHONE.....................203 452-8285
Joseph A Maclean, *Principal*
EMP: 2
SALES (est): 227.2K Privately Held
SIC: 2431 Millwork

(G-4731)
MAGCOR INC
14 Wrabel Cir (06468-2669)
PHONE.....................203 445-0302
John Torrielli, *President*
EMP: 4
SALES (est): 467.8K Privately Held
SIC: 3291 3541 Wheels, abrasive; grinding machines, metalworking

(G-4732)
MALTESE SERVICES LLC
27 Diane Dr (06468-1302)
PHONE.....................203 805-7669
Joshua Krize, *Principal*
EMP: 1
SALES (est): 87.1K Privately Held
SIC: 3524 Snowblowers & throwers, residential

(G-4733)
MARSCO SHEETMETAL LLC
474 Pepper St (06468-2673)
PHONE.....................203 459-2698
Scott Lapke, *Partner*
Mark Lapke, *Partner*
▲ EMP: 2
SQ FT: 2,000
SALES: 740K Privately Held
SIC: 3444 Sheet metalwork

(G-4734)
MC CANN BROS INC
Also Called: Mc Cann Brothers Baskets
490 Pepper St (06468-2673)
PHONE.....................203 335-8630
Fred Ryan, *President*
▲ EMP: 40
SQ FT: 45,000
SALES: 5.6MM Privately Held
WEB: www.mccannbaskets.com
SIC: 5193 5023 2499 3269 Artificial flowers; planters & flower pots; home furnishings, wicker, rattan or reed; market baskets, wood; flower pots, red earthenware

(G-4735)
MC HUGH BUSINESS FORMS
93 Lazy Brook Rd (06468-3315)
P.O. Box 225 (06468-0225)
PHONE.....................203 268-3500
Brian Mc Hugh, *Owner*
EMP: 2
SALES (est): 305.8K Privately Held
SIC: 2754 5943 Commercial printing, gravure; stationery stores

(G-4736)
MIDNIGHT PRINTING LLC
241 Monroe Tpke (06468-2248)
PHONE.....................203 257-3307
EMP: 2
SALES (est): 83.9K Privately Held
SIC: 2752 Commercial printing, lithographic

(G-4737)
MIKRON CORP MONROE
200 Main St Ste D (06468-1174)
PHONE.....................203 261-3100
Oskar Weder, *President*
EMP: 1
SALES: 95K
SALES (corp-wide): 316.6MM Privately Held
SIC: 3541 Machine tools, metal cutting type
HQ: Mikron Corp. Monroe
200 Main St Unit 2a
Monroe CT 06468
203 261-3100

(G-4738)
MIKRON CORP STRATFORD
600a Pepper St # 1 (06468-2663)
PHONE.....................203 261-3100
Paul Zumbuhl, *Principal*
Hans Leichti, *VP Mfg*
Allen Strang, *Controller*
▲ EMP: 1
SALES (est): 74.2K Privately Held
SIC: 3999 Manufacturing industries

(G-4739)
MOBILE WELDING REPAIR
639 Wheeler Rd (06468-3235)
PHONE.....................203 459-2744
Darren Klittnick, *Owner*
EMP: 1
SALES (est): 94.6K Privately Held
SIC: 7692 Welding repair

(G-4740)
MUMM ENGINEERING INC
57 Wells Rd (06468-1266)
PHONE.....................203 445-9777
EMP: 4
SALES (est): 280K Privately Held
SIC: 3577 Mfg Industrial Parts

(G-4741)
NEW AGE MOTORSPORTS LLC
Also Called: Uh Motor Sports
501 Pepper St (06468-2670)
PHONE.....................203 268-1999
Edward C Ostrosky, *Partner*
Christopher Ostrosky, *Partner*
Ed Ostrosky, *Partner*
EMP: 3
SALES: 500K Privately Held
WEB: www.newage-motorsports.com
SIC: 2519 5521 Fiberglass furniture, household; padded or plain; used car dealers

(G-4742)
NEW ENGLAND KITCHEN DESIGN CTR
401 Monroe Tpke Ste 4 (06468-2200)
PHONE.....................203 268-2626
F Scott Johnson, *President*
Nancy A Johnson, *Vice Pres*
EMP: 5
SALES (est): 676.7K Privately Held
WEB: www.newenglandkitchen.com
SIC: 2434 Wood kitchen cabinets

(G-4743)
NEW ENGLAND MATERIALS LLC
64 Cambridge Dr (06468-2661)
PHONE.....................203 261-5500
John Kimball, *Mng Member*
EMP: 3 EST: 2004
SALES (est): 512.9K Privately Held
SIC: 3281 Stone, quarrying & processing of own stone products

(G-4744)
NORTH AMERICA OVERLAND LLC
181 Hattertown Rd (06468-4217)
PHONE.....................203 658-3697
Michael Sandone, *Mng Member*
EMP: 1
SALES (est): 110.9K Privately Held
SIC: 3531 Construction machinery

(G-4745)
PEAK ANTENNAS
200 Main St Unit 3a (06468-1174)
PHONE.....................203 268-3688
Martin Dawson, *Principal*
EMP: 2
SALES (est): 164.4K Privately Held
SIC: 5731 3663 Antennas, satellite dish; antennas, transmitting & communications

(G-4746)
PEAK ANTENNAS LLC
200 Main St Unit 3a (06468-1174)
PHONE.....................203 268-3688
Martin Dawson, *Manager*
EMP: 3
SALES (est): 135.3K Privately Held
WEB: www.peakantennas.com
SIC: 5731 3663 Antennas; radio & TV communications equipment

(G-4747)
PRECISION ELECTRONIC ASSEMBLY
133 Bart Rd (06468-1108)
PHONE.....................203 452-1839
William Romaniello, *President*
EMP: 12
SQ FT: 5,000
SALES: 1MM Privately Held
SIC: 3679 3575 Harness assemblies for electronic use: wire or cable; keyboards, computer, office machine

(G-4748)
PRO-LOCK USA LLC
62 Church St (06468-1819)
PHONE.....................203 382-3428
Noel Mara, *Mng Member*
Neil Blair,
Susan Blair,
Susan F Mara,
EMP: 7
SALES (est): 460K Privately Held
SIC: 3429 Locks or lock sets

(G-4749)
PROLUME INC
525 Fan Hill Rd Ste E (06468-1346)
P.O. Box 444, Randolph VT (05060-0444)
PHONE.....................203 268-7778
Robert Johnstone, *Co-President*

Monroe - Fairfield County

James Carson, *Co-President*
EMP: 7
SQ FT: 4,000
SALES: 900K **Privately Held**
WEB: www.prolumeled.com
SIC: 3646 Commercial indusl & institutional electric lighting fixtures

(G-4750)
PROUDFOOT COMPANY INC
588 Pepper St (06468-2672)
P.O. Box 276 (06468-0276)
PHONE 203 459-0031
EMP: 14 **EST:** 1965
SQ FT: 1,800
SALES: 350K **Privately Held**
SIC: 3275 Mfg Gypsum Products

(G-4751)
S & J STUCCO LLC
454 Moose Hill Rd (06468-2449)
PHONE 203 260-1457
Stanislav Skripek, *Principal*
EMP: 1 **EST:** 2009
SALES (est): 88.5K **Privately Held**
SIC: 3299 Stucco

(G-4752)
SIGNWORKS STUDIOS LLC
86 Field Rock Rd (06468-1250)
PHONE 203 268-3993
Gary Boros,
EMP: 1
SALES (est): 161.4K **Privately Held**
SIC: 3993 Signs & advertising specialties

(G-4753)
STANCOR LP
Also Called: Stancor Pumps
515 Fan Hill Rd (06468-1336)
PHONE 203 268-7513
Bill Tipton, *CEO*
Laurent Recalt, *Engineer*
Andrew Reichlin, *Marketing Staff*
◆ **EMP:** 38
SQ FT: 18,000
SALES (est): 20.5MM
SALES (corp-wide): 27.3MM **Privately Held**
WEB: www.stancorpumps.com
SIC: 5084 3561 Pumps & pumping equipment; industrial pumps & parts
PA: Industrial Flow Solutions Holdings Llc
1 N Wacker Dr Ste 1920
Chicago IL 60606
312 750-1771

(G-4754)
TACK TRUNK
444 Main St Ste B (06468-1168)
PHONE 203 880-9972
John Haydostian, *Principal*
EMP: 1
SALES (est): 77K **Privately Held**
SIC: 3161 Trunks

(G-4755)
TAG PROMOTIONS INC
500 Purdy Hill Rd Ste 9 (06468-1661)
PHONE 800 909-4011
Chris Zinkel, *President*
▲ **EMP:** 4
SALES (est): 541.8K **Privately Held**
SIC: 3999 Advertising display products

(G-4756)
TASHUA LITHO
79 Old Newtown Rd (06468-1160)
PHONE 203 268-5561
Dewey Foito, *Partner*
EMP: 2
SALES (est): 161.1K **Privately Held**
SIC: 2752 Commercial printing, lithographic

(G-4757)
TECHNICAL CONSULTING
17 Westview Dr (06468-1621)
PHONE 203 268-8890
Stephen Kurimai, *Owner*
EMP: 1
SALES (est): 82K **Privately Held**
SIC: 3699 7379 Teaching machines & aids, electronic; computer related consulting services

(G-4758)
TEK-AIR SYSTEMS INC
600 Pepper St (06468-2671)
PHONE 203 791-1400
Arnold B Siemer, *Ch of Bd*
Joseph Colletti Jr, *President*
Roger Bailey, *Corp Secy*
John Lombardi, *Engineer*
▲ **EMP:** 45
SALES (est): 7.4MM **Privately Held**
WEB: www.tek-air.com
SIC: 3829 3823 3822 Measuring & controlling devices; industrial instrmnts msrmnt display/control process variable; auto controls regulating residntl & coml environmt & applncs

(G-4759)
TELENITY INC
755 Main St Ste 7 (06468-2830)
PHONE 203 445-2000
Ilhan Bagoren, *CEO*
Yogesh S Bijlani, *Vice Pres*
Serkan Elden, *Vice Pres*
Esref Ozulkulu, *Treasurer*
Anita Raina, *Admin Mgr*
EMP: 185 **EST:** 2000
SQ FT: 3,000
SALES (est): 13.4MM **Privately Held**
WEB: www.telenity.com
SIC: 7372 Application computer software
PA: I3g Llc
755 Main St Ste 7
Monroe CT 06468
203 445-2000

(G-4760)
THREE D PRINT LLC
31 Scenic Hill Ln (06468-1259)
PHONE 203 590-3463
Matthew Levinson, *Owner*
EMP: 2
SALES (est): 101.5K **Privately Held**
SIC: 2752 Commercial printing, lithographic

(G-4761)
TIDES BLACK GROUP LLC
8 Diane Dr (06468-1330)
PHONE 203 244-8433
Anthony Battaglia, *Principal*
EMP: 2 **EST:** 2012
SALES (est): 161.2K **Privately Held**
SIC: 3499 Strapping, metal

(G-4762)
TOTAL QUALITY & MFG ASSOC
76 Holly Pl (06468-1424)
PHONE 203 261-3074
Ronald Bunovsky, *President*
EMP: 2
SALES (est): 114.1K **Privately Held**
SIC: 3999 Manufacturing industries

(G-4763)
WAKE PUBLISHING
1318 Monroe Tpke (06468-1402)
PHONE 860 559-2787
EMP: 2
SALES (est): 45.4K **Privately Held**
SIC: 2741 Miscellaneous publishing

(G-4764)
WENGER NA INC (DH)
Also Called: Swiss Army Parfums
7 Victoria Dr (06468-1664)
PHONE 845 365-3500
Marc Eskridge, *COO*
◆ **EMP:** 2 **EST:** 1954
SQ FT: 38,500
SALES (est): 1.3MM
SALES (corp-wide): 302.4MM **Privately Held**
SIC: 5091 5094 2844 3873 Sporting & recreation goods; jewelry & precious stones; clocks, watches & parts; toilet preparations; watches, clocks, watchcases & parts; cutlery; hardware
HQ: Wenger S.A.
Route De Bale 63
Delemont JU 2800
324 213-900

(G-4765)
WHITE HILLS TOOL
8 Maple Dr (06468-1603)
PHONE 203 590-3143
Lou Havanich, *Owner*
EMP: 5
SALES: 125K **Privately Held**
SIC: 3545 7389 Precision tools, machinists'; grinding, precision: commercial or industrial

(G-4766)
WOLFE PROMOTIONAL SERVICES LLC
56 Far Horizon Dr (06468-1733)
PHONE 203 452-7692
David Wolfe, *Managing Prtnr*
EMP: 2
SALES: 500K **Privately Held**
WEB: www.wolfepromo.com
SIC: 8743 2759 Promotion service; commercial printing

(G-4767)
WOODWORKS OF CONNECTICUT LTD
83 Purdy Hill Rd (06468-2255)
PHONE 914 318-7970
John Borzilleri, *Principal*
EMP: 2
SALES (est): 122.8K **Privately Held**
SIC: 2431 Millwork

Montville
New London County

(G-4768)
ALL-TIME MANUFACTURING CO INC
Bridge St (06353)
P.O. Box 37 (06353-0037)
PHONE 860 848-9258
David Brodie, *President*
EMP: 18 **EST:** 1946
SQ FT: 36,000
SALES (est): 3.4MM **Privately Held**
WEB: www.alltimemfg.com
SIC: 3442 1751 3089 Storm doors or windows, metal; window & door (prefabricated) installation; window frames & sash, plastic

(G-4769)
CIAUDELLI PRODUCTIONS INC
Also Called: Rayvel
14 Bridge St (06353)
PHONE 860 848-0411
Joseph J Ciaudelli, *President*
Rosemary Ciaudelli, *Admin Sec*
EMP: 2
SQ FT: 1,000
SALES: 25K **Privately Held**
SIC: 5199 5947 5043 3827 Advertising specialties; novelties; photographic equipment & supplies; gratings, diffraction; optical alignment & display instruments; engineering services

(G-4770)
RAND-WHITNEY RECYCLING LLC
370 Route 163 (06353)
PHONE 860 848-1900
Robert Kraft, *President*
▲ **EMP:** 100
SALES (est): 31.6MM **Privately Held**
SIC: 2679 Paperboard products, converted
PA: Kraft Group Llc
1 Patriot Pl
Foxboro MA 02035

Moodus
Middlesex County

(G-4771)
BROWNELL & COMPANY INC (PA)
423 E Haddam Moodus Rd (06469)
P.O. Box 362 (06469-0362)
PHONE 860 873-8625
Anthony A Ferraz, *President*
Cynthia Stackowitz, *Admin Sec*
▲ **EMP:** 12 **EST:** 1844
SQ FT: 100,000
SALES (est): 1.6MM **Privately Held**
WEB: www.brownellco.com
SIC: 2298 Twine; cordage: abaca, sisal, henequen, hemp, jute or other fiber; cargo nets; nets, rope

(G-4772)
CARLSON WELDING & FABRICATION
58 Great Hillwood Rd (06469-1217)
PHONE 860 788-3569
Robert A Carlson, *Owner*
EMP: 1
SALES: 50K **Privately Held**
SIC: 7692 Welding repair

(G-4773)
CARLTON FORGE WORKS
37 Eli Chapman Rd (06469-1403)
PHONE 860 873-9730
EMP: 20
SALES (corp-wide): 210.8B **Publicly Held**
SIC: 3462 Mfg Iron/Steel Forgings
HQ: Carlton Forge Works
7743 Adams St
Paramount CA 90723
562 633-1131

(G-4774)
MP IMPRESSIONS LLC
25 Salls Rd (06469)
P.O. Box 419 (06469-0419)
PHONE 860 873-1797
Pamela Arabas,
EMP: 1
SALES: 220K **Privately Held**
SIC: 3552 Embroidery machines

(G-4775)
NGS POWER LLC (PA)
25 Falls Rd (06469-1265)
P.O. Box 452 (06469-0452)
PHONE 860 873-0100
Jared Mondelci,
EMP: 1
SALES (est): 227.3K **Privately Held**
SIC: 3621 Power generators

(G-4776)
SWIFT KATHRYN
Also Called: Pinnacl X
16 W Cove Rd (06469-1300)
PHONE 860 754-4150
Kathryn Swift, *Owner*
EMP: 2
SALES (est): 125.4K **Privately Held**
SIC: 3721 Research & development on aircraft by the manufacturer

Moosup
Windham County

(G-4777)
A & A WELDING LLC
256 Moosup Pond Rd (06354-1712)
PHONE 860 933-1284
Jeffrey Eno, *Principal*
EMP: 1 **EST:** 2017
SALES (est): 30K **Privately Held**
SIC: 7692 Welding repair

(G-4778)
DETOTEC NORTH AMERICA INC
363 Ekonk Hill Rd (06354-2215)
PHONE 860 230-0078
Timothy J O'Brien, *President*

GEOGRAPHIC SECTION

Martha M O'Brien, *Admin Sec*
EMP: 3
SALES (est): 326.5K **Privately Held**
SIC: 2298 Cordage & twine

(G-4779)
GRISWOLD LLC
Also Called: Griswold Rubber Company
1 River St (06354-1309)
P.O. Box 638 (06354-0638)
PHONE.................................860 564-3321
David Natorski, *CEO*
Jerald Esrick, *Admin Sec*
Steven Lain, *Administration*
▼ **EMP:** 60 **EST:** 1949
SQ FT: 200,000
SALES (est): 15.1MM
SALES (corp-wide): 879MM **Publicly Held**
WEB: www.griswoldrubber.com
SIC: 3069 Sponge rubber & sponge rubber products
PA: Rogers Corporation
     2225 W Chandler Blvd
     Chandler AZ 85224
     480 917-6000

(G-4780)
INNER OFFICE INC
49 Daggett St (06354-1236)
P.O. Box 847 (06354-0847)
PHONE.................................860 564-6777
Joy Johnson, *President*
EMP: 4
SALES (est): 360.7K **Privately Held**
WEB: www.inneroffice.com
SIC: 7372 7291 Prepackaged software; tax return preparation services

(G-4781)
LURE OF CRIPPLE CREEK
147 Ekonk Hill Rd (06354-2215)
PHONE.................................860 564-5799
Malvin Bates, *Owner*
EMP: 1
SALES (est): 94.9K **Privately Held**
SIC: 3949 Golf equipment

(G-4782)
SLIDE RULE GROUP LLC
25 Mortimer Rd (06354-1808)
PHONE.................................860 317-1624
Andrew Vaillencourt, *Principal*
EMP: 2
SALES (est): 114.7K **Privately Held**
SIC: 3829 Slide rules

(G-4783)
TYPEISRIGHT
Also Called: Type Is Right The
11 E Main St (06354)
PHONE.................................860 564-0537
Shirley Hattayer, *Owner*
EMP: 3
SALES (est): 218.4K **Privately Held**
SIC: 2752 Commercial printing, lithographic

(G-4784)
VAPORIZER LLC
245 Main St (06354-1249)
PHONE.................................860 564-7225
Gunther Bowerman, *Mng Member*
Neil Cohen, *Mng Member*
Joseph Ducci, *Mng Member*
Kerri Frenette,
◆ **EMP:** 20
SALES (est): 4MM
SALES (corp-wide): 787.2MM **Privately Held**
SIC: 2097 Manufactured ice
PA: American Rock Salt Company Llc
     3846 Retsof Rd
     Retsof NY 14539
     585 991-6878

Morris
Litchfield County

(G-4785)
AMERICAN BACKPLANE INC
355 Bantam Lake Rd (06763-1102)
PHONE.................................860 567-2360
Thomas L Zampini, *President*
Marie Zampini, *Admin Sec*
EMP: 35
SQ FT: 85,000
SALES (est): 6MM **Privately Held**
WEB: www.americanbackplane.com
SIC: 3672 Printed circuit boards

(G-4786)
APPLIED IMMUNOTHERAPEUTICS INC
433 W Morris Rd (06763-1006)
PHONE.................................203 247-3895
Ronald Burch, *President*
EMP: 2
SALES (est): 79.6K **Privately Held**
SIC: 2899 Gelatin: edible, technical, photographic or pharmaceutical

(G-4787)
BIRKETT WOODWORKING LLC
14 Benedict Rd (06763-1134)
PHONE.................................860 361-9142
Tobylynne C Birkett,
EMP: 3
SALES (est): 209.4K **Privately Held**
SIC: 2431 Millwork

(G-4788)
CYNFUL SCENTS
26 Isaiah Smith Ln N (06763-1510)
PHONE.................................860 866-7670
Cynthia Lavoie, *Principal*
EMP: 1 **EST:** 2010
SALES (est): 49K **Privately Held**
SIC: 3999 Candles

(G-4789)
GORDON WOODWORKING LLC
499 W Morris Rd (06763-1006)
PHONE.................................860 489-5445
Scott Gordon, *Principal*
EMP: 1
SALES (est): 54.1K **Privately Held**
SIC: 2431 Millwork

(G-4790)
MK MILLWORK LLC
234 Thomaston Rd (06763-1915)
PHONE.................................860 567-0173
Kurt Heneveld,
EMP: 1
SALES (est): 39.6K **Privately Held**
SIC: 3999 Manufacturing industries

(G-4791)
NINAS SIGNS
90 Curtiss Hill Rd (06763-1018)
PHONE.................................315 963-2531
EMP: 1 **EST:** 2014
SALES (est): 46K **Privately Held**
SIC: 3993 Mfg Signs/Advertising Specialties

(G-4792)
SUN CORP
27 Anderson Road Ext (06763-1910)
PHONE.................................860 567-0817
Edwin H Nearing III, *President*
EMP: 7
SQ FT: 3,000
SALES: 954K **Privately Held**
SIC: 3451 Screw machine products

(G-4793)
WILDER HILL FARMS
84 Platt Farm Rd (06763-1813)
PHONE.................................860 567-2459
Daniel Coutu, *Owner*
EMP: 2
SALES (est): 99K **Privately Held**
SIC: 0241 3999 Dairy farms; candles

Mystic
New London County

(G-4794)
3 ETHOS LLC
169 Long Wharf Rd (06355-3135)
PHONE.................................860 415-9191
Donald Trone,
EMP: 2

SALES (est): 166.6K **Privately Held**
SIC: 8331 2741 Job training & vocational rehabilitation services; miscellaneous publishing

(G-4795)
ACCESSWARE
93 High Meadow Ln (06355-1649)
PHONE.................................860 235-2982
Ralph D Waite, *Ch of Bd*
Robert J Kot, *President*
Arrowhead Ventures LLC, *Shareholder*
EMP: 1
SQ FT: 4,000
SALES (est): 110K **Privately Held**
WEB: www.accessware.org
SIC: 7372 Business oriented computer software

(G-4796)
ACME WIRE PRODUCTS CO INC
1 Broadway Ave (06355-2752)
P.O. Box 218 (06355-0218)
PHONE.................................860 572-0511
Mary P Fitzgerald, *President*
Michael A Planeta, *CFO*
Shelley Williams, *Data Proc Staff*
Edward Planeta Jr, *Admin Sec*
▲ **EMP:** 50
SQ FT: 73,000
SALES (est): 14.4MM **Privately Held**
WEB: www.acmewire.com
SIC: 3496 Miscellaneous fabricated wire products

(G-4797)
ALICIA CERSOSIMORATHBUN
Also Called: Print Media Specialist
84 Route 27 (06355-1226)
PHONE.................................401 345-7097
Alicia Cersosimorathbun, *Principal*
EMP: 4
SALES (est): 111.5K **Privately Held**
SIC: 7389 2761 Printing broker; design services; design, commercial & industrial; printers' services: folding, collating; computer forms, manifold or continuous

(G-4798)
ANGELAS ITALIAN ICE INC
16 Cottrell St (06355)
PHONE.................................860 536-9828
John Chiangi, *Principal*
EMP: 2
SALES (est): 98.9K **Privately Held**
SIC: 2024 Ice cream & frozen desserts

(G-4799)
AQUA MASSAGE INTERNATIONAL INC
Also Called: A M I
1101 Noank Ledyard Rd (06355-1318)
P.O. Box 808, Groton (06340-0808)
PHONE.................................860 536-3735
David Cote, *President*
Hilaire Cote, *Vice Pres*
▲ **EMP:** 17
SQ FT: 29,000
SALES (est): 2.5MM **Privately Held**
WEB: www.amiaqua.com
SIC: 3949 Exercise equipment

(G-4800)
AVIATION PRO PAGES LLC
3033 Gold Star Hwy (06355-1243)
PHONE.................................860 910-9336
David Breard,
EMP: 1
SALES (est): 73K **Privately Held**
SIC: 3728 7699 Aircraft parts & equipment; aircraft & heavy equipment repair services

(G-4801)
BLUE MOON PRINTING LLC
44 Washington St Ste 5 (06355-2839)
PHONE.................................860 245-0827
Debra Sminkey,
EMP: 2
SALES (est): 186.8K **Privately Held**
SIC: 2759 Screen printing

(G-4802)
BRAINARD BREWING LLC
129 Irving St (06355-2207)
PHONE.................................860 324-5213

Keith Brainard, *Principal*
EMP: 1
SALES (est): 72.9K **Privately Held**
SIC: 2082 Beer (alcoholic beverage)

(G-4803)
C J BRAND & SON
9 Overlook Ave (06355-2232)
PHONE.................................860 536-9266
Muriel Brand, *Owner*
Pam Green Brand, *Co-Owner*
Peter Grand, *Co-Owner*
EMP: 4
SALES (est): 210K **Privately Held**
SIC: 2434 1521 Wood kitchen cabinets; single-family housing construction

(G-4804)
CAPSTONE SOFTWARE LLC
851 River Rd (06355-1237)
PHONE.................................617 413-4444
Charles Case, *Owner*
EMP: 1 **EST:** 2010
SALES (est): 150K **Privately Held**
SIC: 7372 Prepackaged software

(G-4805)
CARLIN MFG KITCHENS TO GO
31 Masons Island Rd (06355-2938)
PHONE.................................413 519-2822
EMP: 2
SALES (est): 83.1K **Privately Held**
SIC: 3999 Manufacturing industries

(G-4806)
CARLOS LEE PUBLISHING
202 Noank Ledyard Rd (06355-1526)
PHONE.................................860 536-8450
Aisha Lee, *Principal*
EMP: 1 **EST:** 2018
SALES (est): 37.5K **Privately Held**
SIC: 2741 Miscellaneous publishing

(G-4807)
CLYDES CIDER MILL
Also Called: B S Clyde's Cider Mill
129 N Stonington Rd (06355-3608)
PHONE.................................860 536-3354
Harold Miner, *Owner*
EMP: 2
SALES (est): 176.5K **Privately Held**
SIC: 2099 Cider, nonalcoholic

(G-4808)
COMPANY OF CRAFTSMEN
43 W Main St (06355-2545)
PHONE.................................860 536-4189
Jack Steel, *Owner*
EMP: 3
SQ FT: 1,000
SALES (est): 203.4K **Privately Held**
SIC: 3269 3446 2499 5947 Art & ornamental ware, pottery; architectural metalwork, decorative wood & woodwork; artcraft & carvings

(G-4809)
COMPONENTS FOR MFG LLC (PA)
800 Flanders Rd Unit 3-5 (06355-1347)
PHONE.................................860 245-5326
Tracey Jacey, *Owner*
EMP: 9
SALES (est): 1.4MM **Privately Held**
SIC: 3999 Manufacturing industries

(G-4810)
CYGNAL PUBLISHING CO
116 Godfrey Rd (06355-1126)
PHONE.................................860 983-4757
Robin Waller, *Principal*
EMP: 1
SALES (est): 37.5K **Privately Held**
SIC: 2741 Miscellaneous publishing

(G-4811)
DEXTER & CO
3 Pearl St Ste 1 (06355-2550)
PHONE.................................860 536-9506
Thomas Dexter, *Owner*
EMP: 4 **EST:** 1975
SQ FT: 1,000

Mystic - New London County (G-4812) — GEOGRAPHIC SECTION

SALES: 225K **Privately Held**
SIC: 5944 3479 Jewelry, precious stones & precious metals; engraving jewelry silverware, or metal

(G-4812)
DOCKO INC
14 Holmes St Ste 5 (06355-2644)
P.O. Box 421 (06355-0421)
PHONE 860 572-8939
Keith Neilson, *President*
EMP: 5
SQ FT: 1,600
SALES (est): 671.3K **Privately Held**
WEB: www.docko.com
SIC: 8711 3999 4491 Marine engineering; dock equipment & supplies, industrial; docks, incl. buildings & facilities: operation & maintenance

(G-4813)
DURANT MACHINE INC (PA)
Also Called: Dur-Mate
664 Noank Rd (06355-2119)
PHONE 860 536-7698
Walter F Durant, *President*
Russell Holly, *Vice Pres*
EMP: 6
SQ FT: 3,000
SALES: 600K **Privately Held**
WEB: www.duramate.com
SIC: 7692 3593 Welding repair; fluid power actuators, hydraulic or pneumatic

(G-4814)
DURANT MACHINE INC
Broadway Ext (06355)
PHONE 860 572-8211
Russell Holly, *Manager*
EMP: 2
SALES (corp-wide): 600K **Privately Held**
WEB: www.duramate.com
SIC: 3545 Machine tool accessories
PA: Durant Machine, Inc
  664 Noank Rd
  Mystic CT 06355
  860 536-7698

(G-4815)
FISHERS ISLAND LEMONADE
8 Summit St (06355-2722)
PHONE 860 306-3189
EMP: 2
SALES (est): 62.3K **Privately Held**
SIC: 2086 Lemonade: packaged in cans, bottles, etc.

(G-4816)
FLAT HAMMOCK PRESS
5 Church St (06355-2601)
PHONE 860 572-2722
Stephen Jones, *Partner*
Greta Jones, *Business Mgr*
EMP: 2
SALES (est): 123.8K **Privately Held**
WEB: www.flathammockpress.com
SIC: 2741 Miscellaneous publishing

(G-4817)
FORMULA BOAT WORKS LLC
Also Called: Jim Hanson Building
565 Noank Ledyard Rd (06355-1518)
PHONE 860 536-9309
EMP: 1
SALES (est): 173.3K **Privately Held**
SIC: 3732 Boatbuilding/Repairing

(G-4818)
FRED REIN
4 Marjorie St (06355-3626)
PHONE 860 460-8086
Fred Rein, *Owner*
EMP: 2
SALES (est): 110K **Privately Held**
SIC: 1481 Nonmetallic mineral services

(G-4819)
GPK MFG LLC
178 Colonel Ledyard Hwy (06355-1144)
PHONE 860 536-2084
George P Korteweg, *President*
EMP: 1
SALES (est): 74K **Privately Held**
SIC: 3999 Manufacturing industries

(G-4820)
HAK INDUSTRIES LLC
56 Washington St (06355-2813)
PHONE 860 572-7305
Ann M Buonocore, *Manager*
EMP: 1
SALES (est): 60.7K **Privately Held**
SIC: 3999 Manufacturing industries

(G-4821)
HUBBELL PREMISE WIRING INC
23 Clara Dr Ste 103 (06355-1959)
PHONE 860 535-8326
Gary Amato, *Principal*
Bob Holder, *Sales Mgr*
Rafael Vale, *Sales Mgr*
Mike Lee, *Marketing Staff*
Joanne Rush, *Marketing Staff*
EMP: 12
SALES (est): 34.9K
SALES (corp-wide): 4.4B **Publicly Held**
WEB: www.hubbell-premise.com
SIC: 3661 Telephone & telegraph apparatus
PA: Hubbell Incorporated
  40 Waterview Dr
  Shelton CT 06484
  475 882-4000

(G-4822)
JENNINGS YACHT SERVICES
800 Flanders Rd (06355-1331)
P.O. Box 159, West Mystic (06388-0159)
PHONE 860 625-1368
Bill Jennings, *Owner*
EMP: 5
SQ FT: 800
SALES (est): 501.1K **Privately Held**
SIC: 3732 Yachts, building & repairing

(G-4823)
JOHNSON MARINE
16 Fort Rachel Pl (06355-2506)
PHONE 860 536-8026
Marine Johnson, *Principal*
EMP: 4
SALES (est): 206.2K **Privately Held**
SIC: 3519 Marine engines

(G-4824)
KATHLEEN PARKER OBEIRNE
Also Called: Lifescape Enterprises
32 New London Rd (06355-2347)
P.O. Box 218, West Mystic (06388-0218)
PHONE 860 536-7179
Kathleen O'Beirne, *Owner*
EMP: 1
SALES (est): 45.2K **Privately Held**
SIC: 8999 8748 2741 Writing for publication; business consulting; miscellaneous publishing

(G-4825)
LEE LOWE & STITCH LLC
60 Hyde Pond Ct (06355-1220)
PHONE 860 536-1392
Jessica Lowe, *Principal*
EMP: 1 EST: 2010
SALES (est): 47.9K **Privately Held**
SIC: 2395 Embroidery & art needlework

(G-4826)
LLC WOLFF WOODS
12 Ivy Rd (06355-3056)
PHONE 860 415-9089
Benjamin Field, *Principal*
EMP: 1
SALES (est): 41.5K **Privately Held**
SIC: 2499 Wood products

(G-4827)
M BARON COMPANY
26 Packer Ln (06355-2310)
P.O. Box 204, West Mystic (06388-0204)
PHONE 860 536-1594
Sara Baron, *Owner*
EMP: 1
SALES (est): 64K **Privately Held**
SIC: 2732 Book music: printing only, not published on site

(G-4828)
M FRIEDMAN COMPANY
25 Willow St (06355-2652)
PHONE 860 447-9935
Buddy Cage, *President*
Mike Friedman, *Vice Pres*
EMP: 2
SQ FT: 700
SALES: 200K **Privately Held**
SIC: 3731 4491 Shipbuilding & repairing; marine cargo handling

(G-4829)
MACRIS INDUSTRIES INC
8 Summit St (06355-2722)
PHONE 860 514-7003
Harrison Macris, *President*
EMP: 4
SALES (est): 426K **Privately Held**
SIC: 3648 Lighting equipment

(G-4830)
MADISON TECHNOLOGY INTL
Also Called: M T I
375 Allyn St Unit 1 (06355-1665)
PHONE 860 245-0245
George C Connolly, *President*
EMP: 6
SALES (est): 742.5K **Privately Held**
SIC: 3826 8731 Instruments measuring magnetic & electrical properties; electronic research

(G-4831)
McCLAVE PHILBRICK & GIBLIN
929 Flanders Rd (06355-1313)
PHONE 860 572-7710
Andrew Giblin, *Mng Member*
Benjamin Philbrick,
Edward McClave,
EMP: 5
SQ FT: 1,152
SALES (est): 692.1K **Privately Held**
SIC: 3732 Sailboats, building & repairing

(G-4832)
MEDTRONIC XOMED INC
950 Flanders Rd (06355-1314)
P.O. Box 334 (06355-0334)
PHONE 860 572-9586
Sean Casley, *Research*
Thomas Niemiec, *Engineer*
Cathy Perry, *Human Res Mgr*
AC Cogburn, *Sales Staff*
James T Treace, *Branch Mgr*
EMP: 50 **Privately Held**
SIC: 3841 Surgical & medical instruments
HQ: Medtronic Xomed, Inc.
  6743 Southpoint Dr N
  Jacksonville FL 32216

(G-4833)
MONSANTO MYSTIC RESEARCH
62 Maritime Dr (06355-1958)
PHONE 860 572-5200
EMP: 2
SALES (est): 74.4K **Privately Held**
SIC: 2879 Mfg Agricultural Chemicals

(G-4834)
MYSTIC KNOTWORK LLC
25 Cottrell St Ste 1 (06355-2668)
PHONE 860 889-3793
Jill Beaudoin, *Director*
Matthew Beaudoin,
EMP: 12
SALES: 585K **Privately Held**
SIC: 3961 Bracelets, except precious metal

(G-4835)
MYSTIC RIVER FOUNDRY LLC
2 Broadway Ave (06355-2702)
P.O. Box 121 (06355-0121)
PHONE 860 536-7634
Sharon E Hertxler, *Owner*
EMP: 3
SALES: 250K **Privately Held**
SIC: 3366 Copper foundries

(G-4836)
MYSTIC RIVER MAR SURVEYORS LLC
16 Whitehall Pond (06355-1954)
PHONE 860 857-1798
Dexter White,
EMP: 1

SALES (est): 128.4K **Privately Held**
SIC: 3731 7389 4499 Submarines, building & repairing; industrial & commercial equipment inspection service; ; marine surveyors

(G-4837)
MYSTIC STAINLESS & ALUM INC
23 Jackson Ave (06355-2824)
P.O. Box 282, West Mystic (06388-0282)
PHONE 860 536-2236
Charles Marques, *President*
Ann-Marie Pals, *Admin Sec*
EMP: 4
SALES: 469.8K **Privately Held**
WEB: www.mysticstainless.com
SIC: 3441 Fabricated structural metal

(G-4838)
ORION MANUFACTURING LLC
800 Flanders Rd Unit 4-8 (06355-1349)
PHONE 860 572-2921
Byron N Foote, *Founder*
Byron Foote,
Geoff Foote,
Scott Russotto,
EMP: 8
SQ FT: 6,000
SALES (est): 915.2K **Privately Held**
SIC: 2431 Millwork

(G-4839)
PERENNIAL ELEMENTS LLC
15 Mystic Hill Rd (06355-3071)
PHONE 860 536-8593
EMP: 3
SALES (est): 246.6K **Privately Held**
SIC: 2819 Mfg Industrial Inorganic Chemicals

(G-4840)
RAYTHEON COMPANY
11 Main St Ste 3 (06355-3654)
PHONE 860 446-4900
Jeffrey Mazurek, *Manager*
EMP: 25
SALES (corp-wide): 27B **Publicly Held**
SIC: 3812 Search & navigation equipment
PA: Raytheon Company
  870 Winter St
  Waltham MA 02451
  781 522-3000

(G-4841)
RECORD-JOURNAL NEWSPAPER
Also Called: Mystic River Press
15 Holmes St Ste 3 (06355-2659)
PHONE 860 536-9577
Peter Griggs, *Manager*
Mike Blais, *Manager*
EMP: 4
SALES (corp-wide): 49.4MM **Privately Held**
SIC: 2711 Job printing & newspaper publishing combined; commercial printing & newspaper publishing combined
PA: Record-Journal Newspaper
  500 S Broad St Ste 2
  Meriden CT 06450
  203 235-1661

(G-4842)
SCOTT WALLACE WOODWORKING
54 Boulder Ct (06355-1202)
PHONE 860 867-7229
EMP: 1 EST: 2017
SALES (est): 58K **Privately Held**
SIC: 2431 Millwork

(G-4843)
SCUTTLEBUTT
10 Cottrell St (06355-2604)
PHONE 860 572-3999
Roberta Brown, *Owner*
Alan Bushwack, *Owner*
EMP: 2
SALES: 68K **Privately Held**
WEB: www.scuttlebuttbrewing.com
SIC: 2395 Embroidery & art needlework

(G-4844)
SEAPORT MARINE INC
2 Washington St (06355-2696)
PHONE..................................860 536-9651
Malcolm Robertson, *President*
EMP: 28 **EST:** 1914
SQ FT: 65,000
SALES (est): 2.7MM **Privately Held**
SIC: 5551 3732 Marine supplies; motorized boat, building & repairing

(G-4845)
SHUTTERS & SAILS LLC
31 Water St (06355-2568)
PHONE..................................860 331-1510
EMP: 3 **EST:** 2015
SALES (est): 235.6K **Privately Held**
SIC: 3442 Shutters, door or window: metal

(G-4846)
SPEEDY PRINTING LLC
Also Called: Miss Speedy Printing Center
8 Forest Ave (06355-1008)
PHONE..................................860 445-8252
Brad Sandlin,
Laurel Sandlin,
EMP: 1 **EST:** 1973
SALES (est): 116K **Privately Held**
WEB: www.speedyskwikkopy.com
SIC: 2752 2791 2789 2759 Commercial printing, offset; typesetting; bookbinding & related work; commercial printing

(G-4847)
SWIFT INNOVATIONS LLC
800 Flanders Rd Bldg 5 (06355-1331)
PHONE..................................860 572-8322
Wade A Swift, *Principal*
EMP: 4
SALES (est): 413K **Privately Held**
SIC: 3441 Fabricated structural metal

(G-4848)
THOMAS S KLISE CO
42 Denison Ave (06355-2728)
PHONE..................................860 536-4200
Margaret Mary Klise, *President*
Elizabeth Klise, *Vice Pres*
EMP: 7
SQ FT: 10,000
SALES (est): 648.3K **Privately Held**
WEB: www.klise.com
SIC: 3999 Education aids, devices & supplies

(G-4849)
THOMAS TOWNSEND CUSTOM MARINE
Also Called: Custom Marine Woodworking
100 Essex St (06355-3315)
P.O. Box 403 (06355-0403)
PHONE..................................860 536-9800
Thomas Townsend, *Owner*
EMP: 1
SALES (est): 45.9K **Privately Held**
SIC: 2499 2431 Decorative wood & woodwork; millwork

(G-4850)
TRADE LABELS INC
28 Cottrell St Ste 28e (06355-2650)
P.O. Box 879, Stonington (06378-0879)
PHONE..................................860 535-4828
Lynn Rajewski, *General Mgr*
EMP: 3
SALES (est): 376.7K **Privately Held**
WEB: www.tradelabels.com
SIC: 2754 Labels: gravure printing

(G-4851)
VECTOR ENGINEERING INC
Also Called: Tylaska Marine Hardware
800 Flanders Rd Unit 1-4 (06355-1341)
PHONE..................................860 572-0422
Tim Tylaska, *President*
▼ **EMP:** 19 **EST:** 1993
SQ FT: 70,000
SALES: 1.5MM **Privately Held**
WEB: www.tylaska.com
SIC: 3429 8711 Manufactured hardware (general); engineering services

(G-4852)
VOICE GLANCE LLC
12 Roosevelt Ave (06355-2809)
PHONE..................................800 260-3025
Chandrasekhar Naik, *President*
Thomas Longo, *Vice Pres*
EMP: 15
SALES (est): 600K **Privately Held**
SIC: 7372 Business oriented computer software

(G-4853)
WATROUS BROTHERS MACHINE SHOP
137 Fishtown Rd (06355-2011)
PHONE..................................860 536-7014
Brian Watrous, *Owner*
EMP: 1
SQ FT: 1,240
SALES (est): 119.9K **Privately Held**
SIC: 3599 Machine shop, jobbing & repair

Naugatuck
New Haven County

(G-4854)
ADVANTAGE SHEET METAL MFG LLC
Also Called: Micro Matic
51 Elm St (06770-4157)
PHONE..................................203 720-0929
Tom Britton, *Opers Mgr*
Jon Hare, *Sls & Mktg Exec*
EMP: 46
SALES (est): 8MM **Privately Held**
SIC: 3444 Sheet metalwork

(G-4855)
AHEAD COMMUNICATIONS SYSTEMS
6 Rubber Ave (06770-4117)
PHONE..................................203 720-0227
Anton Kaeslin, *CEO*
Linda Pagona, *Finance*
EMP: 72
SALES (est): 5.1MM **Privately Held**
WEB: www.aheadcomusa.com
SIC: 3661 4812 4813 Telephones & telephone apparatus; radio telephone communication; telephone communication, except radio

(G-4856)
AIRGAS USA LLC
Also Called: Tech Air
120 Rado Dr (06770-2211)
PHONE..................................203 729-2159
Kevin Haley, *Manager*
EMP: 6
SALES (corp-wide): 125.9MM **Privately Held**
WEB: www.techair.com
SIC: 2813 Industrial gases
HQ: Airgas Usa, Llc
 259 N Radnor Chester Rd
 Radnor PA 19087
 610 687-5253

(G-4857)
ANDREWS ARBORICULTURE LLC
860 Andrew Mountain Rd (06770-3621)
PHONE..................................203 565-8570
Russell Andrew, *Principal*
EMP: 4 **EST:** 2009
SALES (est): 426.3K **Privately Held**
SIC: 2879 Plant hormones

(G-4858)
ANNE QUEEN WOODWORKING
74 Great Hill Rd (06770-2224)
PHONE..................................203 720-1781
Robert Madore, *Owner*
EMP: 12
SQ FT: 5,000
SALES (est): 1.7MM **Privately Held**
SIC: 2499 Decorative wood & woodwork

(G-4859)
ANOMATIC CORPORATION
50 Rado Dr Unit B (06770-2254)
PHONE..................................203 720-2367
Nick Sicilian, *Mfg Staff*
Mark Krin, *Branch Mgr*
EMP: 9
SALES (corp-wide): 632.4MM **Privately Held**
SIC: 3471 Anodizing (plating) of metals or formed products
HQ: Anomatic Corporation
 8880 Innvation Campus Way
 Johnstown OH 43031
 740 522-2203

(G-4860)
BALTASAR & SONS INC
186 Sheridan Dr (06770-2033)
PHONE..................................203 723-0425
Jack Baltasar, *President*
Arthur Aniceto, *Admin Sec*
EMP: 3
SQ FT: 4,300
SALES: 200K **Privately Held**
SIC: 2013 5812 Sausages & other prepared meats; eating places

(G-4861)
BAR INDUSTRIES LLC
68 Radnor Ave (06770-2006)
PHONE..................................203 729-4490
Robert F Schmidt, *Principal*
EMP: 2
SALES (est): 106.5K **Privately Held**
SIC: 3999 Manufacturing industries

(G-4862)
BLACK GOLD ENTERPRISES
531 N Main St (06770-3036)
PHONE..................................203 729-4444
EMP: 2
SALES (est): 200K **Privately Held**
SIC: 3578 Mfg Calculating Equipment

(G-4863)
BRASS CITY TECHNOLOGIES LLC (PA)
1344 New Haven Rd (06770-5038)
PHONE..................................203 723-7021
Frank Testa,
Joe Testa,
EMP: 3
SQ FT: 5,000
SALES (est): 250K **Privately Held**
WEB: www.brasscitytech.com
SIC: 3545 3451 Cutting tools for machine tools; screw machine products

(G-4864)
BUSINESS CARDS TOMORROW INC
Also Called: B C T
69 Raytkwich Rd (06770-2223)
PHONE..................................203 723-5858
Jim Redwanz, *Branch Mgr*
EMP: 6
SALES (corp-wide): 1.2MM **Privately Held**
SIC: 2752 Commercial printing, lithographic
PA: Business Cards Tomorrow, Inc.
 3000 Ne 30th Pl Fl 5
 Fort Lauderdale FL 33306
 954 563-1224

(G-4865)
CADI CO INC (PA)
Also Called: Cadi Company
60 Rado Dr (06770-2211)
P.O. Box 1127 (06770-1127)
PHONE..................................203 729-1111
Rocco Capozzi, *President*
Dana M Capozzi, *Vice Pres*
Gary Farrar, *Foreman/Supr*
Dana Capozzi, *Controller*
Peter Tatalias, *Admin Sec*
▲ **EMP:** 35
SQ FT: 33,000
SALES (est): 8.4MM **Privately Held**
WEB: www.cadicompany.com
SIC: 3548 Electrode holders, for electric welding apparatus; seam welding apparatus, electric; spot welding apparatus, electric

(G-4866)
CAG IMAGING
209 Great Hill Rd (06770-2029)
PHONE..................................203 632-5799
EMP: 2
SALES (est): 73.1K **Privately Held**
SIC: 2796 Platemaking services

(G-4867)
CAGNO ENTERPRISES LLC
Also Called: Nutmeg Printers
98 Morning Dove Rd (06770-4806)
PHONE..................................203 729-3883
James Cagno,
EMP: 1 **EST:** 2009
SALES (est): 112.9K **Privately Held**
SIC: 2732 7389 Book printing;

(G-4868)
CKS PACKAGING INC
10 Great Hill Rd (06770-2224)
P.O. Box 979 (06770-0979)
PHONE..................................203 729-0716
Bill Padgett, *Manager*
Sandra Piscatelli, *Manager*
EMP: 100
SALES (corp-wide): 496.3MM **Privately Held**
SIC: 3089 Plastic containers, except foam
PA: C.K.S. Packaging, Inc.
 350 Great Sw Pkwy
 Atlanta GA 30336
 404 691-8900

(G-4869)
COMPOSITE PANEL TECH CO
Also Called: CPT
112 Bridge St (06770-2903)
PHONE..................................203 729-2255
John Sullivan, *CFO*
EMP: 3 **EST:** 2014
SALES (est): 158.9K
SALES (corp-wide): 234.2MM **Publicly Held**
SIC: 4789 3713 Cargo loading & unloading services; truck cabs for motor vehicles
PA: The Eastern Company
 112 Bridge St
 Naugatuck CT 06770
 203 729-2255

(G-4870)
CON-TEC INC
41 Raytkwich Rd (06770-2223)
PHONE..................................203 723-8942
Craig Corbett, *President*
Nancy Barbino, *Office Mgr*
EMP: 12
SQ FT: 5,000
SALES (est): 1.8MM **Privately Held**
WEB: www.con-tecinc.com
SIC: 3599 Flexible metal hose, tubing & bellows

(G-4871)
CONCENTRIC TOOL MFG CO
360 Prospect St (06770-3196)
PHONE..................................203 723-8846
Klaus Babiarz, *Principal*
EMP: 2
SALES (est): 157.3K **Privately Held**
SIC: 3999 Manufacturing industries

(G-4872)
CONNECTICUT SIGN CRAFT INC
47 Cherry St (06770-4109)
PHONE..................................203 729-0706
David Dunn, *President*
Robert Nepe, *Vice Pres*
Bill Dunn, *Admin Sec*
EMP: 4
SQ FT: 2,500
SALES (est): 320K **Privately Held**
SIC: 3993 Electric signs; signs, not made in custom sign painting shops

(G-4873)
CONVERTER CONSULTANTS LLC
1058 Rubber Ave (06770-1501)
PHONE..................................203 729-1031
Alec Wargo,
Ilse Wargo,
EMP: 5
SQ FT: 4,000
SALES: 650K **Privately Held**
WEB: www.converterconsultants.com
SIC: 3568 Power transmission equipment

Naugatuck - New Haven County (G-4874) — GEOGRAPHIC SECTION

(G-4874)
CUSTOM CREATIONS LLC
89 Beebe St (06770-3916)
PHONE..................................203 522-2113
Justin P Williams, *Principal*
EMP: 2 **EST:** 2008
SALES (est): 97.2K **Privately Held**
SIC: 3999 Manufacturing industries

(G-4875)
DASH N LASH EXTENSIONS LLC
18 Davin Dr (06770-5207)
PHONE..................................203 726-2952
Dasharah Nixon, *Mng Member*
EMP: 1
SALES (est): 39.6K **Privately Held**
SIC: 3999 Hair & hair-based products

(G-4876)
DENTAL IMPLANT SERVICES LLC
10 Peppermill Ct (06770-2962)
PHONE..................................203 720-1873
Tasim Tasimi, *Mng Member*
EMP: 1
SALES (est): 109.2K **Privately Held**
SIC: 3842 Implants, surgical

(G-4877)
EAST COAST METAL HOSE INC
41 Raytkwich Rd (06770-2223)
P.O. Box 978 (06770-0978)
PHONE..................................203 723-7459
Lloyd Corbett, *President*
Michelle Baranoski, *Vice Pres*
▼ **EMP:** 7
SALES (est): 934.2K **Privately Held**
WEB: www.eastcoastmetalhose.com
SIC: 3599 Hose, flexible metallic

(G-4878)
EASTERN COMPANY (PA)
112 Bridge St (06770-2903)
P.O. Box 460 (06770-0460)
PHONE..................................203 729-2255
James A Mitarotonda, *Ch of Bd*
August M Vlak, *President*
Angelo Labbadia, *COO*
Angelo M Labbadia, *Vice Pres*
Carmen Mitcho, *Vice Pres*
EMP: 40 **EST:** 1912
SQ FT: 8,000
SALES: 234.2MM **Publicly Held**
WEB: www.easterncompany.com
SIC: 3452 3316 2439 3429 Bolts, nuts, rivets & washers; cold finishing of steel shapes; structural wood members; locks or lock sets

(G-4879)
ELECTRIC CABLE COMPOUNDS INC
108 Rado Dr (06770-2211)
PHONE..................................203 723-2590
Ida L Fridland, *CEO*
Eugene Fridland, *President*
◆ **EMP:** 60
SQ FT: 60,000
SALES: 55MM **Privately Held**
WEB: www.electriccablecompounds.com
SIC: 3087 Custom compound purchased resins

(G-4880)
FLABEG TECHNICAL GLASS US CORP
451 Church St (06770-2834)
PHONE..................................203 729-5227
Patrick McGinley, *President*
Marge Dowling, *General Mgr*
Michael Priga, *CFO*
▲ **EMP:** 35 **EST:** 1928
SQ FT: 50,000
SALES (est): 6.2MM
SALES (corp-wide): 177.9K **Privately Held**
WEB: www.flabeg.com
SIC: 3231 3229 3827 Products of purchased glass; optical glass; mirrors, optical
HQ: Flabeg Us Holding Inc.
1000 Church St
Naugatuck CT 06770

(G-4881)
FLABEG US HOLDING INC (DH)
1000 Church St (06770)
P.O. Box 71 (06770-0071)
PHONE..................................203 729-5227
Axel Buchholz, *President*
EMP: 1
SALES (est): 11.2MM
SALES (corp-wide): 177.9K **Privately Held**
SIC: 3229 3433 Optical glass; solar heaters & collectors
HQ: Flabeg Gmbh
Waldaustr. 13
Nurnberg 90441
911 964-560

(G-4882)
FREIHOFER CHARLES BAKING CO
1041 New Haven Rd (06770-4746)
PHONE..................................203 729-4545
Dennis Brown, *Manager*
EMP: 4
SALES (est): 197K **Privately Held**
SIC: 2051 Bread, cake & related products

(G-4883)
GARMAC SCREW MACHINE INC
70 Great Hill Rd (06770-2224)
P.O. Box 1338 (06770-1338)
PHONE..................................203 723-6911
Gerald Gardino, *President*
James Mac Burney, *Vice Pres*
Anthony Gardino, *Admin Sec*
EMP: 16
SQ FT: 5,000
SALES (est): 2.8MM **Privately Held**
SIC: 3451 Screw machine products

(G-4884)
GDC FEDERAL SYSTEMS INC
6 Rubber Ave (06770-4117)
PHONE..................................203 729-0271
EMP: 1
SALES (est): 61.5K
SALES (corp-wide): 14.8MM **Publicly Held**
SIC: 3661 Mfr Telephone Equipment
PA: General Datacomm Industries, Inc.
353 Christian St Ste 4
Oxford CT 06478
203 729-0271

(G-4885)
GRAPHIC PLUS
99 Evening Star Dr (06770-3547)
PHONE..................................203 723-8387
Lynn Gregory, *Owner*
EMP: 1
SALES (est): 108.2K **Privately Held**
SIC: 2752 Commercial printing, offset

(G-4886)
H BARBER & SONS INC
15 Raytkwich Rd (06770-2223)
PHONE..................................203 729-9000
John H Barber, *President*
James P Barber, *Vice Pres*
Chris Kelly, *Sls & Mktg Exec*
Thomas Chapman, *Marketing Staff*
◆ **EMP:** 20
SQ FT: 5,000
SALES (est): 6.4MM **Privately Held**
WEB: www.hbarber.com
SIC: 3531 Construction machinery

(G-4887)
HG TECH LLC
162 Spencer St (06770-4552)
PHONE..................................203 632-5946
Henry Garcia,
EMP: 4 **EST:** 2009
SALES (est): 250K **Privately Held**
SIC: 3571 Electronic computers

(G-4888)
HITEK ELECTRONICS LLC
27 Pleasant View St (06770-4020)
PHONE..................................203 982-4574
Samuel Olivera,
EMP: 2
SALES (est): 312.8K **Privately Held**
SIC: 3559 Electronic component making machinery

(G-4889)
HOWARD ENGINEERING LLC
687 Wooster St (06770-3135)
P.O. Box 6211, Wolcott (06716-0211)
PHONE..................................203 729-5213
Lesley H Swirski, *CEO*
Brian N Howard, *President*
Holley E Duffy, *Asst Sec*
EMP: 44 **EST:** 1956
SQ FT: 32,840
SALES (est): 8.4MM **Privately Held**
WEB: www.howardengineering.com
SIC: 3469 3452 Stamping metal for the trade; rivets, metal

(G-4890)
ILLINOIS TOOL WORKS INC
Also Called: ITW Nutmeg
29 Rado Dr (06770-2220)
PHONE..................................203 720-1676
EMP: 33
SQ FT: 24,470
SALES (corp-wide): 14.7B **Publicly Held**
SIC: 3965 3469 3444 Fasteners, buttons, needles & pins; metal stampings; sheet metalwork
PA: Illinois Tool Works Inc.
155 Harlem Ave
Glenview IL 60025
847 724-7500

(G-4891)
INNOVATIVE FUSION INC
60 Great Hill Rd (06770-2224)
PHONE..................................203 729-3873
Tim Perusse, *Info Tech Mgr*
Robert T Budnik,
Daniel Budnik, *Admin Sec*
▲ **EMP:** 40
SQ FT: 8,000
SALES (est): 3.9MM **Privately Held**
WEB: www.innovativefusion.com
SIC: 1799 3822 7692 Welding on site; liquid level controls, residential or commercial heating; welding repair

(G-4892)
ITW POWERTRAIN FASTENING
29 Rado Dr (06770-2220)
PHONE..................................203 720-1676
Jim Dara, *President*
EMP: 4
SALES (est): 78.2K **Privately Held**
SIC: 3965 Fasteners

(G-4893)
J H R SOFTWARE
82 Nicole Dr (06770-4891)
PHONE..................................203 723-4091
John Hope-Ross, *Owner*
EMP: 1
SALES (est): 63.5K **Privately Held**
SIC: 7372 Prepackaged software

(G-4894)
JACOBS LADDER
1395 New Haven Rd (06770-5017)
PHONE..................................203 833-2227
Gerald Sanford, *Principal*
EMP: 2
SALES (est): 88.9K **Privately Held**
SIC: 3446 Ladders, for permanent installation: metal

(G-4895)
JUDITH BENNETT
Also Called: Red Coach Sand & Gravel
1236 New Haven Rd (06770-5000)
PHONE..................................203 729-6548
Judith Bennett, *Manager*
EMP: 1
SALES (corp-wide): 207.1K **Privately Held**
SIC: 1442 Sand mining; gravel & pebble mining
PA: Judith Bennett
27 Noyes Rd
Fairfield CT 06824
203 255-6363

(G-4896)
K & E AUTO MACHINE L L C
Also Called: Mike's Engine Stand
628 Prospect St (06770-3120)
PHONE..................................203 723-7189
Michael Adomaitis,
EMP: 3
SALES (est): 283.4K **Privately Held**
SIC: 3599 Machine shop, jobbing & repair

(G-4897)
KAMMETAL INC (PA)
300 Great Hill Rd (06770-2000)
PHONE..................................718 722-9991
Samuel Kusack, *President*
Alastair Kusack, *Vice Pres*
EMP: 28
SALES (est): 8.1MM **Privately Held**
SIC: 3446 Architectural metalwork

(G-4898)
KEYPOINT FORENSICS LLC
505 N Main St 1440 (06770-9994)
PHONE..................................860 877-6586
Daniel Puckowski, *CEO*
EMP: 1
SALES (est): 32.7K **Privately Held**
SIC: 7372 Application computer software

(G-4899)
LANXESS SOLUTIONS US INC
400 Elm St (06770-4556)
P.O. Box 490 (06770-0490)
PHONE..................................203 723-2237
Richard Hooper, *Manager*
Susan V Bryan, *Manager*
EMP: 75
SALES (corp-wide): 8.2B **Privately Held**
WEB: www.cromptoncorp.com
SIC: 2879 Agricultural chemicals
HQ: Lanxess Solutions Us Inc.
2 Armstrong Rd Ste 101
Shelton CT 06484
203 573-2000

(G-4900)
LANXESS SOLUTIONS US INC
12 Spencer St (06770-4525)
PHONE..................................203 605-5746
EMP: 2
SALES (corp-wide): 8.2B **Privately Held**
SIC: 2869 Industrial organic chemicals
HQ: Lanxess Solutions Us Inc.
2 Armstrong Rd Ste 101
Shelton CT 06484
203 573-2000

(G-4901)
MIL-CON INC
22 Great Hill Rd (06770-2224)
PHONE..................................630 595-2366
Micheal Machura, *CEO*
Bernard C Machura, *Ch of Bd*
Doris Machura, *Corp Secy*
EMP: 60
SQ FT: 30,000
SALES: 12.5MM **Privately Held**
SIC: 5063 5065 3613 3679 Electrical supplies; electronic parts; switchgear & switchboard apparatus; electronic circuits

(G-4902)
MINI LLC
66 Church St (06770-4112)
PHONE..................................203 464-5495
Derrick Lee,
John Migliore,
EMP: 6
SALES (est): 152.3K **Privately Held**
SIC: 3572 Computer auxiliary storage units

(G-4903)
MJM MARGA LLC
28 Raytkwich Rd (06770-2222)
PHONE..................................203 729-0600
Mario Mazzettini, *Mng Member*
Joe Mazzettini,
EMP: 7
SALES (est): 993.1K **Privately Held**
SIC: 3469 Stamping metal for the trade

(G-4904)
MULTI-METAL MANUFACTURING INC
Also Called: Precision Electronic Hardware
550 Spring St (06770-1906)
PHONE..................................203 723-8887
Ralph Minervino, *President*
Patrick Guarino, *Vice Pres*
EMP: 28 **EST:** 1974
SQ FT: 31,000

SALES (est): 4.6MM **Privately Held**
WEB: www.multimetalmfg.com
SIC: 3451 Screw machine products

(G-4905)
NAUGATUCK ELEC INDUS SUP LLC
68 Radnor Ave (06770-2006)
PHONE..................................203 723-1082
Robert M Schmidt,
Robert F Schmidt,
EMP: 3
SALES: 250K **Privately Held**
SIC: 3699 Appliance cords for household electrical equipment

(G-4906)
NAUGATUCK RECOVERY INC (HQ)
300 Great Hill Rd (06770-2000)
PHONE..................................203 723-1122
Fax: 203 729-4977
▲ **EMP:** 35
SALES (est): 4.5MM
SALES (corp-wide): 7.8MM **Privately Held**
SIC: 3582 Mfg Commercial Laundry Equipment
PA: Lavatec Laundry Technology Gmbh
Wannenackerstr. 53
Heilbronn 74078
713 129-80

(G-4907)
NAUGATUCK STAIR COMPANY INC
51 Elm St (06770-4157)
P.O. Box 384 (06770-0384)
PHONE..................................203 729-7134
Henry Carrier, *President*
Ginette Carrier, *Vice Pres*
EMP: 16
SQ FT: 7,000
SALES (est): 2.1MM **Privately Held**
SIC: 2431 3446 Staircases & stairs, wood; stairs, staircases, stair treads: prefabricated metal

(G-4908)
PALLADINO WELDING
270 City Hill St (06770-3335)
PHONE..................................203 729-7542
Teclo Palladino, *Principal*
EMP: 1 **EST:** 2010
SALES (est): 46.6K **Privately Held**
SIC: 7692 Welding repair

(G-4909)
PASTANCH LLC
Also Called: New Christie Ventures
31 Sheridan Dr (06770-2034)
PHONE..................................203 720-9478
Fereidoun Farahani, *Vice Pres*
Patrick A Depaolo Sr,
Phyllis Depaolo,
EMP: 30
SQ FT: 52,000
SALES (est): 8MM **Privately Held**
SIC: 7359 2821 3089 Equipment rental & leasing; elastomers, nonvulcanizable (plastics); injection molding of plastics

(G-4910)
PHOENIX COMPANY OF CHICAGO INC (PA)
22 Great Hill Rd (06770-2224)
PHONE..................................630 595-2300
Bernard C Machura, *Ch of Bd*
Michael B Machura, *President*
Doris G Machura, *Corp Secy*
▲ **EMP:** 60 **EST:** 1969
SQ FT: 550,000
SALES: 16MM **Privately Held**
WEB: www.mil-coninc.com
SIC: 3678 5063 5065 Electronic connectors; electronic wire & cable; connectors, electronic

(G-4911)
PISANI STEEL FABRICATION INC
360 Prospect St Ste 1 (06770-3196)
P.O. Box 2612, Waterbury (06723-2612)
PHONE..................................203 720-0679
Joseph Pisani, *President*
Frank Pisani, *Vice Pres*
Maryjean Pisani, *Admin Sec*
EMP: 5
SQ FT: 10,000
SALES (est): 769.7K **Privately Held**
SIC: 3441 Building components, structural steel

(G-4912)
POST SIGN SPECIALISTS
25 Cedar St (06770-2801)
PHONE..................................203 723-8448
Joe Diaferio, *Owner*
EMP: 6
SQ FT: 5,000
SALES (est): 294.3K **Privately Held**
SIC: 1799 3993 Sign installation & maintenance; signs, not made in custom sign painting shops

(G-4913)
PRAXAIR INC
120 Rado Dr (06770-2211)
PHONE..................................203 720-2477
Dennis Reilley, *President*
EMP: 20 **Privately Held**
SIC: 2813 Industrial gases
HQ: Praxair, Inc.
10 Riverview Dr
Danbury CT 06810
203 837-2000

(G-4914)
QA WOODWORKING LLC
74 Great Hill Rd (06770-2224)
PHONE..................................203 720-1781
Robert Madore, *Principal*
EMP: 2
SALES (est): 193.4K **Privately Held**
SIC: 2431 Millwork

(G-4915)
QUALITY SHEET METAL INC
17 Clark Rd (06770-5097)
PHONE..................................203 729-2244
Lawrence H Torto Jr, *President*
EMP: 17 **EST:** 1976
SQ FT: 10,000
SALES (est): 3.3MM **Privately Held**
WEB: www.qualitysheetmetal.com
SIC: 3444 Sheet metal specialties, not stamped

(G-4916)
RELIABLE SILVER CORPORATION
302 Platts Mill Rd (06770-2036)
P.O. Box 750, Waterbury (06720-0750)
PHONE..................................203 574-7732
Arlo Ellison, *President*
Jamie Reding, *Sales Staff*
EMP: 11
SQ FT: 13,000
SALES (est): 3.1MM **Privately Held**
WEB: www.reliablesilver.com
SIC: 3339 Precious metals

(G-4917)
RONDO AMERICA INCORPORATED
Also Called: Rondo Packaging Systems
209 Great Hill Rd (06770-2096)
PHONE..................................203 723-5831
James M Simkins, *President*
Morton H Simkins, *Treasurer*
Stephanie Simkins, *Admin Sec*
EMP: 200 **EST:** 1949
SQ FT: 55,000
SALES (est): 37.4MM **Privately Held**
WEB: www.rondopackaging.com
SIC: 2652 3569 Setup paperboard boxes; assembly machines, non-metalworking
PA: Simkins Corporation
1636 Valley Rd
Jenkintown PA 19046
215 739-4033

(G-4918)
SEMCO TOOL MANUFACTURING CO
30 Naugatuck Dr (06770-2094)
PHONE..................................203 723-7411
Thomas Semeraro, *President*
Rose Semeraro, *Vice Pres*
EMP: 5
SQ FT: 10,000
SALES (est): 634.1K **Privately Held**
SIC: 3469 Metal stampings

(G-4919)
SOLUTIONS WITH INNOVATION LLC
60 Great Hill Rd (06770-2224)
PHONE..................................203 729-3873
Marlin Underwood, *Vice Pres*
EMP: 1
SALES (est): 77K **Privately Held**
SIC: 7692 Welding repair

(G-4920)
SOUTH END EXPRESS 2
921 New Haven Rd (06770-4719)
PHONE..................................203 720-2085
EMP: 1
SALES (est): 71K **Privately Held**
SIC: 2741 Misc Publishing

(G-4921)
SPECIALTY METALS AND FAB
51 Elm St (06770-4157)
PHONE..................................203 509-5028
EMP: 4
SALES (est): 433.6K **Privately Held**
SIC: 3499 Fabricated metal products

(G-4922)
SPERRY AUTOMATICS CO INC
1372 New Haven Rd (06770-5039)
P.O. Box 717 (06770-0717)
PHONE..................................203 729-4589
Charles A Pugliese, *President*
David A Pugliese, *Vice Pres*
Richard Pugliese, *Treasurer*
EMP: 20 **EST:** 1963
SQ FT: 12,000
SALES (est): 3.5MM **Privately Held**
WEB: www.sperryautomatics.com
SIC: 3451 5085 3541 Screw machine products; industrial supplies; machine tools, metal cutting type

(G-4923)
SWAMP YANKEE PRODUCTS LLC
43 General Patton Dr (06770-4703)
PHONE..................................203 720-1202
Jason Morse, *Principal*
EMP: 2
SALES (est): 111.9K **Privately Held**
SIC: 2099 Food preparations

(G-4924)
UNIMETAL SURFACE FINISHING LLC
Also Called: Donham Crafts
15 E Waterbury Rd (06770-2138)
P.O. Box 1187 (06770-1187)
PHONE..................................203 729-8244
Pat Hayden, *President*
Jim Murphy, *Manager*
EMP: 30
SALES (corp-wide): 22.7MM **Privately Held**
SIC: 3471 Electroplating of metals or formed products
PA: Unimetal Surface Finishing, Llc
135 S Main St
Thomaston CT 06787
860 283-0271

(G-4925)
UNITED AVIONICS INC
Also Called: Ua
38 Great Hill Rd (06770-2224)
PHONE..................................203 723-1404
Richard F Nicolari, *President*
Thomas D Bunk, *President*
Joseph Cardella Sr, *Vice Pres*
Louis Nicoletti, *Vice Pres*
William Nicoletti, *Vice Pres*
EMP: 48
SQ FT: 22,000
SALES (est): 10.5MM **Privately Held**
WEB: www.unitedavionicsinc.com
SIC: 3728 Aircraft parts & equipment

(G-4926)
VALLEY EYELET COMPANY
10 E Waterbury Rd (06770-2137)
P.O. Box 303 (06770-0303)
PHONE..................................203 729-4363
Joseph Pinto, *Owner*
EMP: 2 **EST:** 1979
SQ FT: 4,000
SALES (est): 147.6K **Privately Held**
SIC: 3965 Eyelets, metal: clothing, fabrics, boots or shoes

(G-4927)
VITEK
33 Sheridan Dr Ste 1 (06770-2039)
PHONE..................................203 351-1813
EMP: 2 **EST:** 2012
SALES (est): 152.4K **Privately Held**
SIC: 3479 Painting, coating & hot dipping

(G-4928)
VITEK RESEARCH CORPORATION
33 Sheridan Dr (06770-2039)
P.O. Box 315, Derby (06418-0315)
PHONE..................................203 735-1813
Robert Evans, *President*
EMP: 13 **EST:** 1968
SQ FT: 10,000
SALES: 1.1MM **Privately Held**
WEB: www.vitekres.com
SIC: 3479 8732 Coating of metals & formed products; business research service

(G-4929)
VIVAX MEDICAL CORPORATION
54 Great Hill Rd (06770-2253)
PHONE..................................203 729-0514
Mark Plaumann, *CEO*
Rick Swanson, *President*
Ronald Capone, *Vice Pres*
Susanne Tavares, *Vice Pres*
EMP: 17
SALES (est): 3.8MM **Privately Held**
WEB: www.vivaxmedical.com
SIC: 7352 3841 Medical equipment rental; medical instruments & equipment, blood & bone work

(G-4930)
YOCRUNCH CO LLC
141 Sheridan Dr Ste A (06770-2034)
PHONE..................................866 963-7862
Ralph Tschantz, *Vice Pres*
Bruce Markwell, *Purch Agent*
Anda Pitut, *Purch Agent*
Barbara Bennette, *Human Res Mgr*
Roy Hernandez, *Maintence Staff*
EMP: 1
SALES (est): 520.4K
SALES (corp-wide): 762.4MM **Privately Held**
SIC: 2026 Yogurt
PA: Danone
17 Boulevard Haussmann
Paris 9e Arrondissement 75009
149 485-000

New Britain
Hartford County

(G-4931)
A-1 MACHINING CO
235 John Downey Dr (06051-2905)
PHONE..................................860 223-6420
David S Bovenizer, *CEO*
Thomas Daily, *President*
Tom Stanger, *Engineer*
Van H MAI, *Admin Sec*
▼ **EMP:** 52
SQ FT: 36,800
SALES (est): 9.9MM
SALES (corp-wide): 56.8MM **Privately Held**
WEB: www.a1machining.com
SIC: 3724 3728 3621 Aircraft engines & engine parts; aircraft parts & equipment; power generators
PA: Lionheart Holdings Llc
54 Friends Ln Ste 125
Newtown PA 18940
215 283-8400

New Britain - Hartford County (G-4932) GEOGRAPHIC SECTION

(G-4932)
ACE BEAUTY SYSTEMS NEW BRITAIN
984 W Main St (06053-3487)
PHONE..........................860 224-2943
Maria Beard, *Principal*
EMP: 1
SALES (est): 33.7K **Privately Held**
SIC: 7231 5087 3999 Beauty shops; beauty salon & barber shop equipment & supplies; barber & beauty shop equipment

(G-4933)
ACE CABINET COMPANY
321 Ellis St Ste 18 (06051-3504)
PHONE..........................860 225-6111
EMP: 3 **EST:** 1981
SALES (est): 200K **Privately Held**
SIC: 2541 Mfg Wood Partitions/Fixtures

(G-4934)
ACME MONACO CORPORATION (PA)
75 Winchell Rd (06052-1097)
PHONE..........................860 224-1349
Michael J Karabin, *CEO*
Thomas Sebastian, *President*
Mark Jarrett, *General Mgr*
Lucas Karabin, *Exec VP*
Rebecca Karabin-Ahern, *Exec VP*
▲ **EMP:** 125
SQ FT: 37,520
SALES (est): 24.4MM **Privately Held**
WEB: www.acmemonaco.com
SIC: 3841 3843 3469 3493 Surgical & medical instruments; orthodontic appliances; stamping metal for the trade; steel springs, except wire; miscellaneous fabricated wire products; aluminum rolling & drawing

(G-4935)
ACR TECHNICAL SERVICES
27 Anise St (06053-2509)
P.O. Box 1892 (06050-1892)
PHONE..........................860 225-0572
Carlos Rosario, *Owner*
EMP: 1 **EST:** 1996
SALES (est): 90.8K **Privately Held**
SIC: 3585 Heating & air conditioning combination units

(G-4936)
ADAM Z GOLAS (PA)
Also Called: Zag Machine & Tool Co
99 John Downey Dr (06051-2916)
P.O. Box 1120 (06050-1120)
PHONE..........................860 224-7178
Adam Z Golas, *Owner*
EMP: 8
SQ FT: 50,000
SALES (est): 2.1MM **Privately Held**
SIC: 3547 Rolling mill machinery

(G-4937)
ADDITIVE EXPERTS LLC
1 Liberty Sq (06051-2637)
PHONE..........................860 351-3324
Geza Czako III, *Mng Member*
EMP: 5
SALES (est): 150.7K **Privately Held**
SIC: 3999 Manufacturing industries

(G-4938)
ADKINS PRINTING COMPANY
40 South St Ste 2 (06051-3574)
P.O. Box 2440 (06050-2440)
PHONE..........................800 228-9745
Scott Pechout, *President*
EMP: 21 **EST:** 1880
SQ FT: 18,000
SALES (est): 3.1MM **Privately Held**
SIC: 2752 5943 5112 2789 Commercial printing, offset; office forms & supplies; office supplies; bookbinding & related work

(G-4939)
ADVANCED POWDER COATING TECHNO
10 Harvard St (06051-3270)
PHONE..........................860 612-0631
J Jonathan Scalise, *Manager*
EMP: 2

SALES (est): 94.8K **Privately Held**
SIC: 3479 Metal coating & allied service

(G-4940)
AGE PLASTICS LLC
395 Brittany Farms Rd # 238 (06053-1100)
PHONE..........................860 502-0418
Ahmed Gomaa, *Owner*
Klaus Bendixen, *Co-Owner*
EMP: 2
SALES (est): 74.4K **Privately Held**
SIC: 2821 2824 5169 Silicone resins; polyethylene resins; vinyl fibers; nylon fibers; resins, synthetic rubber

(G-4941)
AK STUCCO LLC
47 Hatch St (06053-2534)
PHONE..........................860 832-9589
Alfred Kania, *Principal*
EMP: 4
SALES (est): 306.5K **Privately Held**
SIC: 3299 Stucco

(G-4942)
ALTASCI LLC
1 Hartford Sq Unit 230 (06052-1161)
PHONE..........................860 224-6668
Armen Paronyan, *CEO*
Jose Zavaleta, *Admin Sec*
EMP: 2 **EST:** 2013
SALES (est): 342.8K **Privately Held**
SIC: 2899 8069 ; drug addiction rehabilitation hospital

(G-4943)
ALVARIUM BEER COMPANY LLC
30 Biltmore St (06053-2133)
PHONE..........................860 306-3857
Christopher Degasero, *Principal*
Brain Bugnacki, *Co-Owner*
Chris Degasero, *Co-Owner*
Michael Larson, *Co-Owner*
EMP: 3
SALES (est): 125.5K **Privately Held**
SIC: 2082 5921 5963 Near beer; wine & beer; coffee, soda, beer, etc: house-to-house sales

(G-4944)
AMERICAN WLDG FABRICATION LLC
30 Precision Ct (06051-2911)
PHONE..........................860 918-2094
Patrick O Connell, *Principal*
Patrick O'Connell,
EMP: 1
SALES (est): 125.6K **Privately Held**
SIC: 7692 Welding repair

(G-4945)
AMMUNITION STOR COMPONENTS LLC
206 Newington Ave (06051-2130)
PHONE..........................860 225-3548
Paul Sliwinski, *VP Opers*
Barry Bergen, *Manager*
EMP: 8 **EST:** 2011
SALES (est): 1MM **Privately Held**
SIC: 3949 Sporting & athletic goods

(G-4946)
ATLAS METALLIZING INC
5 East St (06051-3609)
PHONE..........................860 827-9777
Elizabeth Mierkiewicz, *President*
Tom Mierkiewicz, *Vice Pres*
▲ **EMP:** 13
SQ FT: 16,000
SALES (est): 1.8MM **Privately Held**
WEB: www.atlasmetallizing.com
SIC: 3081 Plastic film & sheet

(G-4947)
AVERYS BEVERAGE LLC
520 Corbin Ave (06052-1606)
PHONE..........................860 224-0830
Rob Metz, *General Mgr*
EMP: 5
SALES (est): 520K **Privately Held**
WEB: www.averysoda.com
SIC: 2086 5963 Soft drinks: packaged in cans, bottles, etc.; bottled water delivery

(G-4948)
B & F DESIGN INCORPORATED
120 Production Ct (06051-2912)
PHONE..........................860 357-4317
Raymond F Forgione, *President*
Darius Szczepankowski, *Vice Pres*
Nancy E Tegge, *Admin Sec*
EMP: 50
SQ FT: 15,000
SALES (est): 9.2MM **Privately Held**
SIC: 8711 7389 3721 Designing: ship, boat, machine & product; hand tool designers; aircraft

(G-4949)
B & F MACHINE CO INC
145 Edgewood Ave (06051-4154)
PHONE..........................860 225-6349
Federico Bragoni, *President*
Carl Francalangia, *Vice Pres*
Robert Riccini, *Project Mgr*
George Kemzura, *Prdtn Mgr*
Brian Poulter, *Buyer*
▲ **EMP:** 100
SQ FT: 37,400
SALES (est): 32.2MM **Privately Held**
WEB: www.bfmachine.com
SIC: 3599 7692 Machine shop, jobbing & repair; welding repair

(G-4950)
BARILE PRINTERS LLC
43 Viets St (06053-3988)
P.O. Box 2628 (06050-2628)
PHONE..........................860 224-0127
Joseph Barile,
EMP: 6
SQ FT: 3,000
SALES: 500K **Privately Held**
SIC: 2752 5999 5099 Commercial printing, offset; alarm & safety equipment stores; firearms & ammunition, except sporting

(G-4951)
BLACK & DECKER (US) INC
Also Called: Stanley Black and Decker
700 Stanley Dr (06053-1679)
PHONE..........................860 225-5111
EMP: 7
SALES (corp-wide): 13.9B **Publicly Held**
SIC: 3546 3634 Power-driven handtools; electric household cooking appliances; electric household cooking utensils; electric household fans, heaters & humidifiers
HQ: Black & Decker (U.S.) Inc.
 1000 Stanley Dr
 New Britain CT 06053
 860 225-5111

(G-4952)
BLACK & DECKER (US) INC (HQ)
1000 Stanley Dr (06053-1675)
PHONE..........................860 225-5111
Nolan D Archibald, *President*
Charles E Fenton, *Senior VP*
Barbara B Lucas, *Senior VP*
Michael D Mangan, *Senior VP*
Mark M Rothleitner, *Senior VP*
◆ **EMP:** 3
SQ FT: 100,000
SALES (est): 1.3B
SALES (corp-wide): 13.9B **Publicly Held**
WEB: www.dewalt.com
SIC: 3546 3634 Power-driven handtools; electric household cooking appliances; electric household cooking utensils; electric household fans, heaters & humidifiers
PA: Stanley Black & Decker, Inc.
 1000 Stanley Dr
 New Britain CT 06053
 860 225-5111

(G-4953)
BRYT MANUFACTURING
23 John St (06051-2724)
PHONE..........................860 224-4772
Stanley Szylobryt, *Owner*
Matthew Szylobryt, *Partner*
EMP: 4
SQ FT: 3,500
SALES: 150K **Privately Held**
SIC: 3599 Machine shop, jobbing & repair

(G-4954)
CABINETS KWIK
1 Hartford Sq (06052-1161)
PHONE..........................860 538-5047
Joseph Materek, *President*
EMP: 2 **EST:** 2016
SALES (est): 157.6K **Privately Held**
SIC: 2434 Wood kitchen cabinets

(G-4955)
CARRIER MANUFACTURING INC
70a Saint Claire Ave (06051-1631)
PHONE..........................860 223-2264
Michael Carrier, *President*
EMP: 6
SQ FT: 3,000
SALES (est): 1MM **Privately Held**
SIC: 3369 Aerospace castings, nonferrous: except aluminum

(G-4956)
CASH TIME INDUSTRIES LLC
522 Church St (06051-2313)
PHONE..........................860 770-7192
Edgar Vazquez, *Principal*
EMP: 2
SALES (est): 76.3K **Privately Held**
SIC: 3999 Manufacturing industries

(G-4957)
CCC MEDIA LLC
1 Court St (06051-2262)
P.O. Box 1090 (06050-1090)
PHONE..........................860 225-4601
Michael Schroeder, *President*
Harry J Binder, *Principal*
EMP: 5 **EST:** 2014
SQ FT: 1,500
SALES (est): 163.6K **Privately Held**
SIC: 2711 Newspapers: publishing only, not printed on site

(G-4958)
CENTRAL CONN CMMUNICATIONS LLC
Also Called: New Britain Herald , The
1 Court St Fl 4 (06051-2259)
P.O. Box 1090 (06050-1090)
PHONE..........................860 225-4601
Janet Schroeder, *Controller*
Michael Schroeder,
EMP: 80
SALES: 950K **Privately Held**
SIC: 2711 Newspapers, publishing & printing

(G-4959)
CENTRAL PALLET & BOX
271 John Downey Dr (06051-2905)
PHONE..........................860 224-4416
Michael T Hannifan, *Owner*
EMP: 13
SQ FT: 12,000
SALES: 1.2MM **Privately Held**
SIC: 2448 Pallets, wood

(G-4960)
CHEF J R ME REST GROUP CORP
240 Newington Ave (06051-2128)
P.O. Box 310029, Newington (06131-0029)
PHONE..........................860 940-8038
Jeremy Smith, *Mng Member*
Lilla Darden, *Mng Member*
EMP: 2
SQ FT: 7,900
SALES (est): 155.3K **Privately Held**
SIC: 2051 5812 Bakery: wholesale or wholesale/retail combined; ethnic food restaurants

(G-4961)
CLASSIC INK
104 Country Club Rd (06053-1022)
PHONE..........................860 225-3652
Greg McNamara, *Partner*
Peter Boehnert, *Partner*
EMP: 2
SALES (est): 20K **Privately Held**
SIC: 2752 Commercial printing, lithographic

▲ = Import ▼=Export
◆ =Import/Export

GEOGRAPHIC SECTION
New Britain - Hartford County (G-4993)

(G-4962)
CONNECTICUT BASS GUIDE
891 Slater Rd (06053-1930)
PHONE.....................860 827-0787
EMP: 1
SALES (est): 46.6K **Privately Held**
SIC: 2731 Book publishing

(G-4963)
CONNECTICUT VALLEY BINDERY
1 Hartford Sq Ste 28w (06052-1179)
PHONE.....................860 229-7637
Kevin Hubert, *President*
Dan Valente, *Vice Pres*
Tracey Hubert, *Treasurer*
Tracy Hubert, *Treasurer*
▼ EMP: 30 EST: 1980
SQ FT: 37,598
SALES (est): 3.1MM **Privately Held**
WEB: www.connvalleybindery.com
SIC: 2789 Binding only: books, pamphlets, magazines, etc.

(G-4964)
CONSOLIDATED CONTAINER LP
90 Pleasant St (06051-2714)
PHONE.....................860 224-9381
Steve Macadam, *President*
EMP: 1
SALES (est): 148.6K
SALES (corp-wide): 14B **Publicly Held**
WEB: www.ccllc.com
SIC: 3085 Plastics bottles
HQ: Consolidated Container Company, Llc
    2500 Windy Ridge Pkwy Se # 1400
    Atlanta GA 30339
    678 742-4600

(G-4965)
CONTINENTAL MACHINE TL CO INC
533 John Downey Dr (06051-2435)
PHONE.....................860 223-2896
Tadeusz Malkowski, *President*
Wanda Malkowski, *Corp Secy*
EMP: 97 EST: 1983
SQ FT: 24,800
SALES (est): 16.8MM **Privately Held**
WEB: www.continentalmachinetool.com
SIC: 3599 3714 3728 3484 Machine shop, jobbing & repair; motor vehicle parts & accessories; aircraft parts & equipment; machine guns or machine gun parts, 30 mm. & below

(G-4966)
CONTORQ COMPONENTS LLC
433 John Downey Dr (06051-2909)
PHONE.....................860 225-3366
John McCarthy Jr, *President*
Amy Cilfone, *Office Mgr*
EMP: 11
SALES (est): 2.7MM **Privately Held**
SIC: 3452 Bolts, nuts, rivets & washers

(G-4967)
CORPORATE FORMS PRINTING
80 Kent Rd (06052-1920)
PHONE.....................800 840-9945
EMP: 2
SALES (est): 83.9K **Privately Held**
SIC: 2752 Commercial printing, lithographic

(G-4968)
CREED-MONARCH INC
1 Pucci Park (06051)
P.O. Box 550 (06050-0550)
PHONE.....................860 225-7884
Richard Creed, *President*
Deborah Boynton, *Corp Secy*
David Creed, *Vice Pres*
Don Creed, *Vice Pres*
Jim Lundebjerg, *Engineer*
▲ EMP: 275 EST: 1952
SQ FT: 150,000
SALES (est): 62.4MM **Privately Held**
WEB: www.creedmonarch.com
SIC: 3451 Screw machine products

(G-4969)
D B F INDUSTRIES INC
Also Called: DB&f Industries
145 Edgewood Ave (06051-4109)
PHONE.....................860 827-8283
Carl Francalangia, *President*
Federico Bragoni, *Vice Pres*
EMP: 40
SQ FT: 7,000
SALES (est): 1.5MM **Privately Held**
SIC: 7692 Brazing

(G-4970)
DA CUNHA WOODWORKS
45 Noble St (06051-2009)
PHONE.....................860 529-3889
Thomas Da Cunha, *Owner*
EMP: 1
SQ FT: 1,500
SALES (est): 250K **Privately Held**
SIC: 5722 2512 Kitchens, complete (sinks, cabinets, etc.); upholstered household furniture

(G-4971)
DAY MACHINE SYSTEMS INC
221 South St Bldg F2 (06051-3650)
P.O. Box 2667 (06050-2667)
PHONE.....................860 229-3440
Jim Kostin, *President*
Gary Goen, *Plant Mgr*
EMP: 13 EST: 1984
SQ FT: 14,500
SALES (est): 2MM **Privately Held**
SIC: 3451 3559 Screw machine products; automotive related machinery

(G-4972)
DEBURRING LABORATORIES INC
206 Newington Ave (06051-2130)
PHONE.....................860 829-6300
Douglas Narins, *President*
Nina Narins, *Admin Sec*
EMP: 40
SALES (est): 4.5MM **Privately Held**
SIC: 3541 3471 Deburring machines; plating & polishing

(G-4973)
DECKS R US
35 Carlton St Fl 2 (06053-3101)
PHONE.....................860 505-0726
Vasyl Dyakun, *Principal*
EMP: 3
SALES (est): 242.9K **Privately Held**
SIC: 2421 Building & structural materials, wood

(G-4974)
DEMAND PRO LLC
120 Dogwood Dr (06052-1140)
PHONE.....................860 438-8843
EMP: 1
SALES (est): 56K **Privately Held**
SIC: 3639 Household appliances

(G-4975)
DR STITCH SEAMSTRESS TO STARS
21 Arch St (06051-2514)
P.O. Box 752, Lansdowne PA (19050-0752)
PHONE.....................706 631-0859
Shahid Abdul-Jabbar, *Principal*
EMP: 1 EST: 2016
SALES (est): 40.1K **Privately Held**
SIC: 2395 Embroidery & art needlework

(G-4976)
DSO MANUFACTURING COMPANY INC
390 John Downey Dr (06051-2932)
PHONE.....................860 224-2641
Carl Bernard Deleo, *President*
Tina Joan Deleo, *Vice Pres*
Tina D Leo, *Vice Pres*
Tina Deleo, *Manager*
EMP: 25 EST: 1947
SQ FT: 35,000
SALES (est): 5.7MM **Privately Held**
WEB: www.dsomfg.com
SIC: 3599 Machine shop, jobbing & repair

(G-4977)
E R HITCHCOCK COMPANY
Also Called: Hitchcock Printers
191 John Downey Dr (06051-2945)
PHONE.....................860 229-2024
Edward R Young, *President*
Dane Baclaski, *Vice Pres*
Melissa Ramos, *Accounts Mgr*
Kathy Young, *Accounts Mgr*
Stephen Rejniak, *Sales Staff*
EMP: 33 EST: 1895
SQ FT: 22,000
SALES (est): 6.3MM **Privately Held**
SIC: 2752 2791 2789 Commercial printing, offset; typesetting; bookbinding & related work

(G-4978)
EAST SIDE CAR CLINIC CORP
Also Called: East Side Welding
1181 East St (06051-1651)
PHONE.....................860 223-2247
Robert Mankowski, *President*
Marian Mankowski, *President*
Jutta Mankowski, *Treasurer*
EMP: 2 EST: 1978
SQ FT: 2,000
SALES (est): 290.5K **Privately Held**
SIC: 7692 Automotive welding

(G-4979)
EDITORS ONLY
275 Batterson Dr (06053-1005)
PHONE.....................860 881-2300
William Dunkerley, *Partner*
EMP: 2
SALES (est): 99K **Privately Held**
WEB: www.publishinghelp.com
SIC: 8748 2721 Publishing consultant; periodicals

(G-4980)
EK-RIS CABLE COMPANY INC
503 Burritt St Apt 7 (06053-3627)
PHONE.....................860 223-4327
Gary J Robinson, *President*
Adriana Bravo, *Prdtn Mgr*
Charles Wusterbarth, *Treasurer*
Chuck Wusterbarth, *Sales Mgr*
Dolores M Robinson, *Admin Sec*
EMP: 45
SALES (est): 7.6MM **Privately Held**
WEB: www.ekriscable.com
SIC: 3643 Current-carrying wiring devices

(G-4981)
ELKA PRECISION
124 Pennsylvania Ave (06052-1164)
PHONE.....................860 526-1674
EMP: 1 EST: 2011
SALES (est): 98K **Privately Held**
SIC: 3425 Mfg Saw Blades/Handsaws

(G-4982)
EMDEPOINT CANDLES USA LLC
334 Lewis Rd (06053-1460)
PHONE.....................860 205-8400
Katarzyna Polewacz, *Principal*
EMP: 2
SALES (est): 75K **Privately Held**
SIC: 3999 Candles

(G-4983)
EMHART TEKNOLOGIES LLC (HQ)
Also Called: Stanley Engineered Fastening
480 Myrtle St (06053-4018)
PHONE.....................800 783-6427
Michael A Tyll, *President*
Ed Delterio, *Vice Pres*
Charles Fenton, *Vice Pres*
EMP: 10 EST: 1902
SALES (est): 588MM
SALES (corp-wide): 13.9B **Publicly Held**
WEB: www.helicoil.com
SIC: 8711 3541 Engineering services; machine tools, metal cutting type
PA: Stanley Black & Decker, Inc.
    1000 Stanley Dr
    New Britain CT 06053
    860 225-5111

(G-4984)
ENJET AERO NEW BRITAIN LLC
150 John Downey Dr (06052-2904)
PHONE.....................860 356-0330
Bruce Breckenridge, *CEO*
Christopher Ferraro, *CFO*
EMP: 134
SQ FT: 63,000
SALES (est): 4MM
SALES (corp-wide): 42.7MM **Privately Held**
SIC: 3728 Aircraft parts & equipment
PA: Enjet Aero, Llc
    9401 Indian Creek Pkwy
    Overland Park KS 66210
    913 717-7396

(G-4985)
ERA REPLICA AUTOMOBILES
24 Dewey St (06051)
PHONE.....................860 229-7968
EMP: 2
SALES (est): 126.6K **Privately Held**
SIC: 3714 Motor vehicle parts & accessories

(G-4986)
EVERYTHING 2 WHEELS LLC
230 South St (06051-3637)
PHONE.....................860 225-2453
Mark Furrow, *Principal*
EMP: 5
SALES (est): 476K **Privately Held**
SIC: 3312 Wheels

(G-4987)
EZ WELDING LLC
47 Saint Claire Ave (06051-1630)
PHONE.....................860 707-3099
Ernest Zygo, *Mng Member*
EMP: 1
SALES (est): 129.8K **Privately Held**
SIC: 7692 Welding repair

(G-4988)
EZ WELDING LLC
244 Garry Dr (06052-1106)
PHONE.....................860 707-3100
EMP: 8
SALES (est): 88.7K **Privately Held**
SIC: 7692 Welding repair

(G-4989)
FITNESS ELEMNET
267 Chapman St (06051-2439)
PHONE.....................860 670-2855
EMP: 3
SALES (est): 171.6K **Privately Held**
SIC: 2819 Elements

(G-4990)
FORCE AUTOMATION INC
100 Production Ct Ste 2 (06051-2914)
PHONE.....................860 622-1618
Lukasz Poplawski, *President*
Tomasz Bucior, *VP Opers*
EMP: 2
SALES (est): 93.7K **Privately Held**
SIC: 3549 Assembly machines, including robotic

(G-4991)
GEORGES AUTOMOTIVE MACHINE SP
158 Dwight St (06051-2333)
PHONE.....................860 223-6547
George Karlan, *Owner*
EMP: 2
SALES (est): 76.5K **Privately Held**
SIC: 3599 Machine shop, jobbing & repair

(G-4992)
GLOBAL PALLET SOLUTIONS LLC
271 John Downey Dr (06051-2905)
PHONE.....................860 826-5000
Michael T Hannifan, *Manager*
EMP: 3
SALES (est): 226.3K **Privately Held**
SIC: 2448 Pallets, wood & wood with metal

(G-4993)
GRIMCO INC
221 South St Unit G1 (06051-3650)
PHONE.....................800 542-9941

New Britain - Hartford County (G-4994)

Sarah Monestero, *Branch Mgr*
EMP: 5
SALES (corp-wide): 97.5MM **Privately Held**
WEB: www.grimco.com
SIC: 3081 Vinyl film & sheet
PA: Grimco, Inc.
11745 Sppngton Brracks Rd
Saint Louis MO 63127
636 305-0088

(G-4994)
GUIDA-SEIBERT DAIRY COMPANY (PA)
Also Called: Guida's Milk & Ice Cream
433 Park St (06051-2700)
P.O. Box 2110 (06050-2110)
PHONE...................860 224-2404
Pat Panko, *CEO*
Michael Young, *President*
Alex Bachelor, *Vice Pres*
Joel Clark, *Vice Pres*
James Guida, *Vice Pres*
EMP: 225
SQ FT: 70,000
SALES (est): 74.2MM **Privately Held**
WEB: www.supercow.com
SIC: 2026 2033 5143 5149 Milk processing (pasteurizing, homogenizing, bottling); fruit juices: packaged in cans, jars, etc.; dairy products, except dried or canned; juices

(G-4995)
HAJAN LLC
788 W Main St (06053-3856)
PHONE...................860 223-2005
Mukhtar Ahmed, *Principal*
EMP: 5
SALES (est): 484.9K **Privately Held**
SIC: 2869 Industrial organic chemicals

(G-4996)
HARDWARE CY SOAPS CANDLES LLC
14 Dorman Rd (06053-1404)
PHONE...................860 209-8494
Russell Garuti, *Principal*
EMP: 2
SALES (est): 52.8K **Privately Held**
SIC: 3999 Candles

(G-4997)
HSB AIRCRAFT COMPONENTS LLC
80 Production Ct (06051-2917)
P.O. Box 342, East Berlin (06023-0342)
PHONE...................860 505-7349
Henry Wasik, *Mng Member*
Henry W Wasik Jr,
EMP: 12
SQ FT: 5,000
SALES (est): 1.6MM **Privately Held**
SIC: 3724 Aircraft engines & engine parts

(G-4998)
INCURE INC
1 Hartford Sq Ste 16w (06052-1175)
P.O. Box 16 (06050-0016)
PHONE...................860 748-2979
William Tan, *President*
EMP: 3 **Privately Held**
SIC: 2891 3648 Adhesives & sealants; ultraviolet lamp fixtures

(G-4999)
INTEGRA-CAST INC
265 Newington Ave (06051-2129)
PHONE...................860 225-7600
David Arcesi, *President*
Lori Theriault, *Safety Dir*
Meghann Parkinson, *Program Dir*
Matt Smith, *Executive*
EMP: 62
SQ FT: 30,000
SALES (est): 11MM **Privately Held**
WEB: www.integracast.com
SIC: 3365 3599 3364 3324 Aerospace castings, aluminum; machine shop, jobbing & repair; nonferrous die-castings except aluminum; steel investment foundries

(G-5000)
INTEGRO LLC
30 Peter Ct (06051-3545)
PHONE...................860 832-8960
Tara Stewart, *President*
Jessica Otero, *Purchasing*
Paul Kish, *Engineer*
Kimberly Czarnecki, *Accountant*
Carmen Duffy, *Accountant*
▲ **EMP:** 40 **EST:** 1971
SQ FT: 4,000
SALES (est): 9.7MM **Privately Held**
WEB: www.integro-usa.com
SIC: 3648 Airport lighting fixtures: runway approach, taxi or ramp

(G-5001)
INTERNATIONAL AUTOMOBILE ENTPS (PA)
Also Called: ERA Replica Automobiles
608 E Main St Ste 612 (06051-2074)
PHONE...................860 224-0253
Philip R Gaudette, *President*
Thomas Portante, *Vice Pres*
Robert Putnam, *CFO*
Peter Portante, *Manager*
EMP: 13
SQ FT: 4,000
SALES (est): 2.1MM **Privately Held**
WEB: www.erareplicas.com
SIC: 3714 5531 Motor vehicle parts & accessories; automotive & home supply stores

(G-5002)
INTERNATIONAL AUTOMOBILE ENTPS
608 E Main St (06051-2074)
PHONE...................860 224-0253
Phillip Glenda, *Manager*
EMP: 15
SALES (corp-wide): 2.1MM **Privately Held**
WEB: www.erareplicas.com
SIC: 3714 Motor vehicle parts & accessories
PA: International Automobile Enterprises, Inc
608 E Main St Ste 612
New Britain CT 06051
860 224-0253

(G-5003)
IRWIN INDUSTRIAL TOOL COMPANY
700 Stanley Dr Fl 2 (06053-1679)
PHONE...................860 438-3460
EMP: 2
SALES (est): 92.9K
SALES (corp-wide): 13.9B **Publicly Held**
SIC: 3423 Hand & edge tools
PA: Stanley Black & Decker, Inc.
1000 Stanley Dr
New Britain CT 06053
860 225-5111

(G-5004)
ITS IN BAG LLC
15 Parkmore St (06051-3357)
PHONE...................860 229-6672
Leanne Valengavich, *Partner*
EMP: 1
SALES (est): 84.4K **Privately Held**
SIC: 3171 Handbags, women's

(G-5005)
J H METAL FINISHING INC (PA)
1146 East St (06051-1619)
PHONE...................860 223-6412
John Helenek Sr, *President*
Jeanne Helenek, *Admin Sec*
EMP: 5 **EST:** 1953
SQ FT: 7,200
SALES (est): 1.5MM **Privately Held**
SIC: 3471 Finishing, metals or formed products

(G-5006)
JAM INDUSTRIES LLC
226 Grove St (06053-3734)
PHONE...................860 225-8862
John A Morell, *Principal*
EMP: 2
SALES (est): 91.8K **Privately Held**
SIC: 3999 Manufacturing industries

(G-5007)
K & K BLACK OXIDE LLC
50 Peter Ct (06051-3545)
P.O. Box 1856 (06050-1856)
PHONE...................860 223-1805
Marilyn Jester, *Manager*
EMP: 3
SALES (est): 283.6K **Privately Held**
SIC: 3471 Plating of metals or formed products

(G-5008)
K AND R PRECISION GRINDING
39 John St (06051-2724)
PHONE...................860 505-8030
Marc W Begin, *Administration*
EMP: 8 **EST:** 2017
SALES (est): 836.5K **Privately Held**
SIC: 3999 Custom pulverizing & grinding of plastic materials

(G-5009)
KAYCANDLES
82 Judd Ave (06051-1726)
PHONE...................860 794-3763
EMP: 2 **EST:** 2013
SALES (est): 90K **Privately Held**
SIC: 3999 Candles

(G-5010)
LEOS KITCHEN & STAIR CORP
48 John St (06051-2725)
PHONE...................860 225-7363
Jean-Paul Ayotte, *President*
EMP: 8 **EST:** 1950
SQ FT: 2,000
SALES: 660K **Privately Held**
SIC: 2434 2541 2431 Wood kitchen cabinets; table or counter tops, plastic laminated; staircases & stairs, wood

(G-5011)
LINK MECHANICAL SERVICES INC
Also Called: Honeywell Authorized Dealer
34 Walnut St (06051-2511)
P.O. Box 364 (06050-0364)
PHONE...................860 826-5880
Christopher Link, *President*
Joanna Link, *Admin Sec*
EMP: 33
SQ FT: 30,000
SALES (est): 7.3MM **Privately Held**
WEB: www.linkmechinc.com
SIC: 1711 3444 Mechanical contractor; sheet metalwork

(G-5012)
MAKINO INC
Also Called: Global E.D.M. Supplies
255 Myrtle St (06053-4161)
PHONE...................860 223-0236
Thomas Kucharski, *Principal*
EMP: 12 **Privately Held**
SIC: 2675 Die-cut paper & board
HQ: Makino Inc.
7680 Innovation Way
Mason OH 45040
513 573-7200

(G-5013)
MARSAM METAL FINISHING CO
206 Newington Ave (06051-2130)
P.O. Box 1975 (06050-1975)
PHONE...................860 826-5489
Jonathan Scalise, *President*
EMP: 25
SALES (est): 3.6MM **Privately Held**
WEB: www.marsammetalfinishing.com
SIC: 3471 Plating of metals or formed products; anodizing (plating) of metals or formed products

(G-5014)
MARTIN ROSOLS INC
45 Grove St (06053-4198)
PHONE...................860 223-2707
Robert C Rosol, *Ch of Bd*
Karen M Rosol, *Vice Pres*
EMP: 25 **EST:** 1929
SQ FT: 85,000
SALES (est): 3.8MM **Privately Held**
WEB: www.martinrosols.com
SIC: 2011 5421 2013 Meat packing plants; food & freezer plans, meat; bologna from purchased meat

(G-5015)
METAL IMPROVEMENT COMPANY LLC
E/M Coatings Solutions
1 John Downey Dr (06051-2901)
PHONE...................860 224-9148
Tony Cummings, *Prdtn Mgr*
Tom Gambino, *Engineer*
Eric Altomare, *Manager*
Dale Minor, *Technical Staff*
EMP: 28
SQ FT: 10,000
SALES (corp-wide): 2.4B **Publicly Held**
SIC: 3398 Shot peening (treating steel to reduce fatigue)
HQ: Metal Improvement Company, Llc
80 E Rte 4 Ste 310
Paramus NJ 07652
201 843-7800

(G-5016)
METALFORM ACQUISITION LLC (PA)
Also Called: Metalform Company
555 John Downey Dr (06051-2435)
PHONE...................860 224-2630
Martin C McCarthy, *Ch of Bd*
John P McCarthy, *Principal*
EMP: 19
SQ FT: 15,000
SALES (est): 2.4MM **Privately Held**
WEB: www.metalformcompany.com
SIC: 3965 3469 3452 Fasteners, hooks & eyes; stamping metal for the trade; nuts, metal

(G-5017)
MICHAELS FINEST LLC
19 Vibberts Ave (06051-1640)
PHONE...................860 223-7671
A Michael Jones III, *Manager*
EMP: 1
SALES (est): 106.8K **Privately Held**
SIC: 3161 Clothing & apparel carrying cases

(G-5018)
MICRO CARE CORPORATION (PA)
Also Called: Micro Care Marketing Svcs Div
595 John Downey Dr (06051-2435)
PHONE...................860 827-0626
Christopher A Jones, *President*
Michael D Jones, *Vice Pres*
Jay S Tourigny, *Vice Pres*
Clarence P Clapp, *Treasurer*
John Farris, *Director*
▲ **EMP:** 15
SQ FT: 12,000
SALES (est): 5.4MM **Privately Held**
WEB: www.microcare.com
SIC: 2842 Specialty cleaning preparations

(G-5019)
NALCO WTR PRTRTMENT SLTONS LLC
255 Myrtle St (06053-4161)
PHONE...................860 224-4443
EMP: 2
SALES (corp-wide): 14.6B **Publicly Held**
SIC: 7699 3589 7389 Industrial equipment services; water treatment equipment, industrial;
HQ: Nalco Water Pretreatment Solutions, Llc
1601 W Diehl Rd
Naperville IL 60563
708 754-2550

(G-5020)
NCM EMBROIDERY & SPORTSWEAR
203 Oakland Ave (06053-2338)
PHONE...................860 223-1589
Nancy Mariano, *Owner*
EMP: 1 **EST:** 2010
SALES (est): 35.1K **Privately Held**
SIC: 2395 Lace, burnt-out, for the trade

New Britain - Hartford County (G-5050)

(G-5021)
NEW ENGLAND CABINET CO INC
580 E Main St (06051-2042)
PHONE 860 747-9995
Joel Salwocki, *President*
EMP: 12
SQ FT: 20,000
SALES (est): 1.8MM **Privately Held**
SIC: 2541 2431 Cabinets, except refrigerated: show, display, etc.: wood; millwork

(G-5022)
NEW ENGLAND TOOL & AUTOMTN INC
321 Ellis St Ste 17 (06051-3504)
PHONE 860 827-9389
Yola Noga, *President*
John Noga, *Vice Pres*
EMP: 5
SALES: 350K **Privately Held**
SIC: 3599 Machine shop, jobbing & repair

(G-5023)
NEW ENGLAND TRAVELING WIRE LLC
Also Called: Netw
162 Whiting St (06051-3132)
PHONE 860 223-6297
Vincent Savulis, *Mng Member*
EMP: 4
SALES (est): 330K **Privately Held**
SIC: 3599 Machine & other job shop work

(G-5024)
NORTHEAST STUCCO LLC
14 Beatty St (06051-1090)
PHONE 860 770-9343
Bolivar F Vizuete, *Owner*
EMP: 1
SALES (est): 51K **Privately Held**
SIC: 3299 Stucco

(G-5025)
NOVA MACHINING LLC
56 Saint Claire Ave (06051-1631)
PHONE 860 223-9323
Mariusz Wroblewski, *Principal*
EMP: 2 **EST:** 2011
SALES (est): 207.4K **Privately Held**
SIC: 3599 Machine shop, jobbing & repair

(G-5026)
ORCA INC
199 Whiting St (06051-3146)
PHONE 860 223-4180
Gregory P Goguen, *Principal*
Kathleen Goguen, *Admin Sec*
EMP: 30
SQ FT: 60,000
SALES (est): 6.7MM **Privately Held**
WEB: www.orca-mfg.com
SIC: 3466 Closures, stamped metal

(G-5027)
OXFORD INDUSTRIES CONN INC
Also Called: Oxford Polymers
221 South St Bldg H (06051-3627)
PHONE 860 225-3700
Nicholas L Defelice, *President*
David Gambardella, *CFO*
John Oconnor, *VP Sales*
Karen Defelice, *Director*
David Stolfi, *Director*
▲ **EMP:** 24 **EST:** 1980
SQ FT: 100,000
SALES (est): 9.2MM **Privately Held**
WEB: www.oxfordpolymers.com
SIC: 2821 Thermoplastic materials

(G-5028)
PAINT & POWDER WORKS LLC
35 M And S Ct (06051-2280)
PHONE 860 225-2019
Fred H Sillner, *Manager*
Frederick Sillner, *Manager*
EMP: 10
SALES (est): 1.1MM **Privately Held**
WEB: www.paintandpowderworks.com
SIC: 3479 Hot dip coating of metals or formed products

(G-5029)
PARK TOOL & GAGE CO INC
56 Saint Claire Ave (06051-1631)
P.O. Box 1495 (06050-1495)
PHONE 860 225-0187
Jack W Nielsen, *President*
Wes Nielsen, *Vice Pres*
J Wester Nielsen, *Director*
EMP: 2 **EST:** 1958
SQ FT: 25,000
SALES (est): 206.5K **Privately Held**
SIC: 3599 Machine shop, jobbing & repair

(G-5030)
PARKER-HANNIFIN CORPORATION
Also Called: Fluid Controls Division
95 Edgewood Ave (06051-4151)
P.O. Box 1450 (06050-1450)
PHONE 860 827-2300
Steve Sawczuk, *Purch Mgr*
Peter Lennon, *Engineer*
Michael Williams, *Engineer*
Michael Valenches, *Project Engr*
Larry Ryba, *Branch Mgr*
EMP: 250
SALES (corp-wide): 14.3B **Publicly Held**
WEB: www.parker.com
SIC: 3491 3492 Solenoid valves; fluid power valves & hose fittings
PA: Parker-Hannifin Corporation
6035 Parkland Blvd
Cleveland OH 44124
216 896-3000

(G-5031)
PEARSE BERTRAM LLC
595 John Downey Dr (06051-2435)
PHONE 860 612-9060
EMP: 2
SALES (est): 175.2K **Privately Held**
SIC: 3592 Mfg Carburetors/Pistons/Rings

(G-5032)
PETER PAUL ELECTRONICS CO INC
480 John Downey Dr (06051-2910)
P.O. Box 1180 (06050-1180)
PHONE 860 229-4884
Paul S Mangiafico, *President*
Michael Mangiafico II, *President*
Mark Mangiafico, *Vice Pres*
Shelly Cyr, *Marketing Staff*
Jan Carroll, *Clerk*
▲ **EMP:** 140 **EST:** 1947
SQ FT: 77,000
SALES (est): 34.9MM **Privately Held**
WEB: www.peterpaul.com
SIC: 3491 Solenoid valves

(G-5033)
POLAMER PRECISION INC
105 Alton Brooks Way (06053-3359)
PHONE 860 259-6200
Chris Galik, *President*
Andrew Dulnik, *Exec VP*
Joanna Lutrzykowski, *QC Mgr*
Mario Gioco, *CFO*
Marcin Wiktorek, *Supervisor*
EMP: 145
SQ FT: 3,200
SALES (est): 58.8MM **Privately Held**
WEB: www.polamer.us
SIC: 3728 Aircraft parts & equipment

(G-5034)
POLAR CORP
33 Columbus Blvd (06051-2243)
PHONE 860 225-6000
Val Zurawlew, *Vice Pres*
EMP: 2
SALES (est): 86K **Privately Held**
SIC: 3724 Aircraft engines & engine parts

(G-5035)
POLAR CORPORATION
59 High St Ste 11 (06051-2279)
PHONE 860 223-7891
Andrew Kowalski, *President*
Lou Melluzzo, *General Mgr*
Zeb Alves, *Mfg Mgr*
Alicja Pawelek, *Manager*
Kazimiera Zamojska Kowalski, *Admin Sec*
EMP: 25
SQ FT: 15,000
SALES (est): 6.4MM **Privately Held**
WEB: www.polaraircraft.com
SIC: 3724 3812 3728 Aircraft engines & engine parts; search & navigation equipment; aircraft parts & equipment

(G-5036)
PRECISION GRINDING COMPANY
33 Charles St (06051-2162)
PHONE 860 229-9652
James Weber, *President*
EMP: 12 **EST:** 1957
SQ FT: 4,000
SALES (est): 1.5MM **Privately Held**
SIC: 3599 Machine shop, jobbing & repair

(G-5037)
PRINT LAB LLC
125 Carlton St (06053-3103)
PHONE 860 410-6624
Jorge Robles, *Owner*
EMP: 2
SALES (est): 83.9K **Privately Held**
SIC: 2752 Commercial printing, lithographic

(G-5038)
PROMAN INC
60 Saint Claire Ave Ste 2 (06051-1665)
PHONE 860 827-8778
Ted Jastrzebski, *President*
EMP: 3
SALES: 250K **Privately Held**
SIC: 3599 3544 Machine shop, jobbing & repair; special dies, tools, jigs & fixtures

(G-5039)
R K MACHINE COMPANY LLC
Also Called: Rk Machine
200 Myrtle St (06053-4160)
P.O. Box 1958 (06050-1958)
PHONE 860 224-7545
Rishard Kanar,
EMP: 6
SQ FT: 1,600
SALES (est): 177.1K **Privately Held**
SIC: 3599 Machine shop, jobbing & repair

(G-5040)
RAM BELTING COMPANY INC
100 Production Ct Ste 3 (06051-2914)
PHONE 860 438-7029
Rocco A Montano, *President*
Joyce L Montano, *Vice Pres*
EMP: 5 **EST:** 1980
SQ FT: 5,200
SALES: 1MM **Privately Held**
WEB: www.rambelting.com
SIC: 3052 8611 Rubber & plastics hose & beltings; business associations

(G-5041)
RAYCO INC
206 Newington Ave Fl 2 (06051-2130)
PHONE 860 357-4693
Jose Fontanez, *President*
Judith Emanuelson, *Office Mgr*
EMP: 8 **EST:** 1951
SALES (est): 2MM **Privately Held**
SIC: 3471 Polishing, metals or formed products

(G-5042)
RICH PRODUCTS CORPORATION
263 Myrtle St (06053-4161)
PHONE 866 737-8884
EMP: 750
SALES (corp-wide): 3.8B **Privately Held**
SIC: 2053 Frozen bakery products, except bread
PA: Rich Products Corporation
1 Robert Rich Way
Buffalo NY 14213
716 878-8000

(G-5043)
RICH PRODUCTS CORPORATION
263 Myrtle St (06053-4161)
P.O. Box 649, Burlington NJ (08016-0649)
PHONE 800 356-7094
EMP: 750
SALES (corp-wide): 3.8B **Privately Held**
SIC: 2053 Frozen bakery products, except bread
PA: Rich Products Corporation
1 Robert Rich Way
Buffalo NY 14213
716 878-8000

(G-5044)
RICH PRODUCTS CORPORATION
1 Celebration Way (06053-1480)
PHONE 860 827-8000
Bill Gisel, *Branch Mgr*
EMP: 450
SALES (corp-wide): 3.8B **Privately Held**
SIC: 2024 5143 Ice cream & frozen desserts; frozen dairy desserts; ice cream & ices
PA: Rich Products Corporation
1 Robert Rich Way
Buffalo NY 14213
716 878-8000

(G-5045)
RICH PRODUCTS CORPORATION
Also Called: Mother's Kitchen
263 Myrtle St (06053-4161)
PHONE 609 589-3049
Admir Mumic, *Principal*
EMP: 173
SALES (corp-wide): 3.8B **Privately Held**
WEB: www.richs.com
SIC: 2092 Fresh or frozen packaged fish
PA: Rich Products Corporation
1 Robert Rich Way
Buffalo NY 14213
716 878-8000

(G-5046)
RK STUCCO LLC
29 Curtin Ave (06053-2991)
PHONE 860 331-1791
Radoslaw T Kopacz, *Principal*
EMP: 2
SALES (est): 124.5K **Privately Held**
SIC: 7299 1522 1389 1521 Handyman service; residential construction; construction, repair & dismantling services; patio & deck construction & repair

(G-5047)
ROMAN WOODWORKING
1181 East St (06051-1651)
PHONE 860 490-5989
Roman Szewczak, *Owner*
EMP: 4
SALES: 400K **Privately Held**
SIC: 2431 1799 Millwork; kitchen & bathroom remodeling

(G-5048)
ROSIE BLAKES CHOCOLATES LLC
200 Myrtle St (06053-4160)
PHONE 732 604-3327
Rosie Kruze, *CEO*
Blake Kruze,
EMP: 1
SALES (est): 90.9K **Privately Held**
SIC: 2066 5947 Chocolate; gift baskets

(G-5049)
ROSSITTO WELDING INC
395 Allen St (06053-3321)
PHONE 860 223-1598
Ronald Rossitto, *President*
Donna Rossitto, *Vice Pres*
EMP: 1
SALES (est): 107K **Privately Held**
SIC: 7692 Welding repair

(G-5050)
RP3 CANVAS LLC
105 Jubilee St (06051-2402)
PHONE 860 225-7140
Richard Potter, *Manager*
EMP: 1
SALES (est): 46.9K **Privately Held**
SIC: 2394 Canvas & related products

New Britain - Hartford County (G-5051)   GEOGRAPHIC SECTION

(G-5051)
S & F TOOLS LLC
551 Stanley St (06051-2732)
PHONE 860 224-6839
Sofio Salemi,
Frank Salemi,
Rina Salemi,
Sarina Salemi,
EMP: 2 EST: 2001
SALES (est): 281K Privately Held
SIC: 3599 Machine shop, jobbing & repair

(G-5052)
SALAMON INDUSTRIES LLC
250 John Downey Dr (06051-2906)
PHONE 860 612-8420
Andrew Salamon, Principal
EMP: 4
SALES (est): 277.1K Privately Held
SIC: 3599 Machine shop, jobbing & repair

(G-5053)
SEABOARD METAL FINISHING CO
Also Called: Seaboard Plating
410 John Downey Dr (06051-2910)
PHONE 203 933-1603
Steven D Tarantino, President
Karen A Tarantino, Corp Secy
EMP: 26
SQ FT: 25,000
SALES: 3.9MM Privately Held
WEB: www.seaboardmetalfin.com
SIC: 3471 Electroplating of metals or formed products; polishing, metals or formed products; finishing, metals or formed products

(G-5054)
SIR SPEEDY PRNTNG CTR OF N BRI
200 Main St (06051-2222)
PHONE 860 826-1798
Maria Bernacki, President
Mark H Bernacki, Vice Pres
Carlos Couto, Store Mgr
EMP: 4
SQ FT: 3,000
SALES (est): 330K Privately Held
SIC: 2752 Commercial printing, lithographic

(G-5055)
SKINNER VALVE DIVISION
95 Edgewood Ave (06051-4100)
PHONE 860 827-2300
Larry Ryba, Manager
EMP: 2
SALES (est): 228.4K Privately Held
SIC: 3592 Valves

(G-5056)
SNACK ELECTRONICS
180 Broad St (06053-4106)
PHONE 860 225-3714
Christopher Szypulski, Owner
EMP: 1
SALES (est): 114.7K Privately Held
SIC: 3571 Electronic computers

(G-5057)
SOUTHPACK LLC
1 Hartford Sq (06052-1161)
PHONE 860 224-2242
Lynn Mogielnicki,
Kurt Mogielnicki,
EMP: 25
SQ FT: 20,000
SALES (est): 4.8MM Privately Held
WEB: www.southpack.com
SIC: 3089 Blister or bubble formed packaging, plastic

(G-5058)
STAG ARMS LLC
515 John Downey Dr (06051-2435)
PHONE 860 229-9994
▲ EMP: 8
SALES (est): 1.7MM Privately Held
SIC: 3484 Mfg Small Arms

(G-5059)
STAG ARMS LLC
515 John Downey Dr (06051-2435)
PHONE 860 229-9994
Kalani Laker,
Jesse Tischauser,
EMP: 8
SALES (est): 365.7K Privately Held
SIC: 3484 Rifles or rifle parts, 30 mm. & below

(G-5060)
STANDARD MANUFACTURING CO LLC
100 Burritt St (06053-4004)
PHONE 860 225-6581
Louis Frutuoso, Principal
EMP: 2
SALES (est): 112.4K Privately Held
SIC: 3999 Manufacturing industries

(G-5061)
STANLEY BLACK & DECKER INC (PA)
1000 Stanley Dr (06051-1675)
P.O. Box 7000 (06050-7000)
PHONE 860 225-5111
George W Buckley, Ch of Bd
James M Loree, President
Jeffery D Ansell, President
John H Wyatt, President
Keith Eisenhut, Regional Mgr
EMP: 200
SALES: 13.9B Publicly Held
WEB: www.stanleyworks.com
SIC: 3429 3546 3423 3452 Builders' hardware; power-driven handtools; hand & edge tools; bolts, nuts, rivets & washers; security devices; door opening & closing devices, electrical

(G-5062)
STANLEY BLACK & DECKER INC
100 Curtis St (06052-1326)
P.O. Box 1308 (06050-1308)
PHONE 860 225-5111
Patrick Egan, Branch Mgr
EMP: 100
SALES (corp-wide): 13.9B Publicly Held
WEB: www.stanleyworks.com
SIC: 3429 Manufactured hardware (general)
PA: Stanley Black & Decker, Inc.
1000 Stanley Dr
New Britain CT 06053
860 225-5111

(G-5063)
STANLEY BLACK & DECKER INC
480 Myrtle St (06053-4018)
PHONE 860 225-5111
John Cooper, Principal
Yolanda Costantini, Vice Pres
Corinne Herzog, Vice Pres
Christine Cicchetti, Cust Mgr
Joe Voelker, Branch Mgr
EMP: 220
SALES (corp-wide): 13.9B Publicly Held
SIC: 3699 3429 Security devices; builders' hardware
PA: Stanley Black & Decker, Inc.
1000 Stanley Dr
New Britain CT 06053
860 225-5111

(G-5064)
STANLEY BLACK & DECKER INC
Stanley Tools
480 Myrtle St (06053-4018)
P.O. Box 1308 (06050-1308)
PHONE 860 225-5111
Dan Seabourne, Controller
Thomas E Mahoney, Branch Mgr
EMP: 46
SALES (corp-wide): 13.9B Publicly Held
WEB: www.stanleyworks.com
SIC: 3429 5085 3546 3423 Builders' hardware; industrial supplies; power-driven handtools; hand & edge tools
PA: Stanley Black & Decker, Inc.
1000 Stanley Dr
New Britain CT 06053
860 225-5111

(G-5065)
STANLEY FASTENING SYSTEMS LP
Also Called: Stanley-Bostitch
480 Myrtle St (06053-4018)
PHONE 860 225-5111
Bruce Behnke, President
Adam Leuenberger, Engineer
EMP: 5
SALES (corp-wide): 13.9B Publicly Held
SIC: 3579 Stapling machines (hand or power)
HQ: Stanley Fastening Systems Lp
2 Briggs Dr
East Greenwich RI 02818
401 884-2500

(G-5066)
STANLEY INDUSTRIAL & AUTO LLC
Also Called: Proto Industrial Tools
480 Myrtle St (06053-4018)
PHONE 800 800-8005
Kate White, Director
EMP: 46
SALES (corp-wide): 13.9B Publicly Held
SIC: 3429 Manufactured hardware (general)
HQ: Stanley Industrial & Automotive, Llc
505 N Cleveland Ave
Westerville OH 43082
614 755-7000

(G-5067)
SUMMIT PLASTICS LLC
100 Production Ct (06051-2914)
P.O. Box 65 (06050-0065)
PHONE 860 832-9730
Rob Casey, President
EMP: 2
SQ FT: 3,400
SALES (est): 360K Privately Held
WEB: www.summit-plastics.com
SIC: 3089 Molding primary plastic; injection molding of plastics

(G-5068)
SUPERB STEEL LLC
40 Harvard St (06051-2332)
PHONE 860 518-7281
Sabina Ostynska,
Tomasz Ostyski,
EMP: 6 EST: 2011
SALES (est): 895K Privately Held
SIC: 5051 7692 Steel; welding repair

(G-5069)
SUPERIOR MOLD CORP
206 South St (06051-3634)
PHONE 860 225-7654
EMP: 2
SALES (est): 94.6K Privately Held
SIC: 3544 Mfg Dies/Tools/Jigs/Fixtures

(G-5070)
SWISTRO WELDING
115 Paul Manafort Dr (06053-2142)
PHONE 860 978-3238
Thomas J Swistro, Principal
EMP: 1
SALES (est): 29.2K Privately Held
SIC: 7692 Welding repair

(G-5071)
SYLAG MANUFACTURING LLC
365 John Downey Dr Ste 2 (06051-2922)
PHONE 860 832-8772
Andy Lutkowski, Principal
EMP: 2 EST: 2007
SALES (est): 194.1K Privately Held
SIC: 3999 Manufacturing industries

(G-5072)
TDY INDUSTRIES LLC
Also Called: ATI Specialty Materials
33 John St Ste 39 (06051-2748)
PHONE 860 259-6346
EMP: 4 Publicly Held
SIC: 3724 Aircraft engines & engine parts
HQ: Tdy Industries, Llc
1000 Six Ppg Pl
Pittsburgh PA 15222
412 394-2800

(G-5073)
THERMAL ENERGY RESOURCE MFG &
312 Monroe St (06052-1628)
PHONE 860 225-8792
Shelby Ann Robertson,
EMP: 1
SALES (est): 48.3K Privately Held
SIC: 3999 Manufacturing industries

(G-5074)
TILCON CONNECTICUT INC (DH)
642 Black Rock Ave (06052-1037)
PHONE 860 224-6010
Carmine Abate, President
▲ EMP: 100
SQ FT: 2,000
SALES (est): 79.3MM
SALES (corp-wide): 30.6B Privately Held
WEB: www.tilconct.com
SIC: 5032 1611 3273 2951 Sand, construction; highway & street paving contractor; ready-mixed concrete; asphalt paving mixtures & blocks
HQ: Tilcon Inc.
301 Hartford Ave
Newington CT 06111
860 223-3651

(G-5075)
TOG MANUFACTURING COMPANY INC
1000 Stanley Dr (06053-1675)
PHONE 413 663-5753
Tedd Sellers, President
Travis Bolte, General Mgr
John Alibozek, COO
David Bialas, Engineer
Raymond K Guba, CFO
▲ EMP: 33
SQ FT: 28,000
SALES (est): 4.2MM
SALES (corp-wide): 188.9MM Privately Held
WEB: www.togmanufacturing.com
SIC: 3599 Machine shop, jobbing & repair
PA: Williams Industrial Services Group Inc.
100 Crescent Center Pkwy
Tucker GA 30084
770 879-4400

(G-5076)
TOP PRIORITY TOOL LLC
321 Ellis St Ste 8 (06051-3504)
PHONE 860 665-1012
Lawrence Ledoux,
EMP: 1
SALES: 150K Privately Held
SIC: 3646 3599 Commercial indusl & institutional electric lighting fixtures; machine & other job shop work

(G-5077)
ULTRA FOOD AND FUEL
788 W Main St (06053-3856)
PHONE 860 223-2005
Mukhtar Ahmed, Principal
EMP: 4 EST: 2010
SALES (est): 275.3K Privately Held
SIC: 2869 Fuels

(G-5078)
UNITED ENTERPRISES INC
264 Broad St (06053-4035)
P.O. Box 1236 (06050-1236)
PHONE 860 225-9955
Edward Angelo,
EMP: 3
SALES (est): 334.5K Privately Held
SIC: 4212 7389 2024 Moving services; laminating service; ice cream & frozen desserts

(G-5079)
UNITED PLASTICS TECHNOLOGIES
163 John Downey Dr (06051-2903)
PHONE 860 224-1110
Vincent Dicioccio Jr, President
Anthony Straska, Vice Pres
John Shurkus, Treasurer
EMP: 12
SQ FT: 28,000
SALES (est): 2MM Privately Held
SIC: 3089 Novelties, plastic

GEOGRAPHIC SECTION

New Canaan - Fairfield County (G-5110)

(G-5080)
VIKING KITCHEN CABINETS LLC (PA)
33-39 John St (06051)
PHONE..................860 223-7101
David J Trachten, *President*
Kathy Bujda, *Credit Mgr*
Michael-Kopman Fried,
EMP: 40 EST: 1997
SQ FT: 11,000
SALES (est): 31.3MM **Privately Held**
WEB: www.vikingkitchens.com
SIC: **5031** 5211 2541 2434 Kitchen cabinets; lumber & other building materials; wood partitions & fixtures; wood kitchen cabinets; home furnishings; hardware

(G-5081)
VINCENT MASONRY
Also Called: Vincent Masonry & Chimney
332 Barbour Rd (06053-1828)
PHONE..................860 836-5916
Vincenzo Santoro, *Principal*
EMP: 1 EST: 2008
SALES (est): 90.5K **Privately Held**
SIC: **3299** 1771 1741 Stucco; exterior concrete stucco contractor; chimney construction & maintenance

(G-5082)
WENTWORTH MANUFACTURING LLC
623 E Main St (06051-2032)
PHONE..................860 205-6437
Kevin McDermott,
EMP: 4
SALES (est): 950K **Privately Held**
SIC: **3724** Aircraft engines & engine parts

(G-5083)
WESTBROOK PRODUCTS LLC
623 E Main St (06051-2032)
PHONE..................860 205-6437
Kevin McDermott,
EMP: 3
SALES (est): 600K **Privately Held**
SIC: **3724** Aircraft engines & engine parts

(G-5084)
WINSLOW AUTOMATICS INC
23 Saint Claire Ave (06051-1630)
PHONE..................860 225-6321
Janusz Podlasek, *CEO*
Walter Borysewicz, *Vice Pres*
J George Podlasek, *Vice Pres*
Wendi P Scata, *Vice Pres*
Andy King, *Mfg Mgr*
EMP: 91
SQ FT: 70,000
SALES (est): 18.9MM **Privately Held**
WEB: www.winslowautomatics.com
SIC: **3841** 3724 3843 3743 Surgical & medical instruments; aircraft engines & engine parts; dental equipment & supplies; brakes, air & vacuum: railway

(G-5085)
ZACHMAN INDUSTRIES LLC
30 Alexander Rd (06053-1039)
PHONE..................860 337-2234
Denise Chapman, *Owner*
EMP: 1
SALES (est): 44.7K **Privately Held**
SIC: **3999** Manufacturing industries

New Canaan
Fairfield County

(G-5086)
ADVANTAGE COMMUNICATIONS LLC
43 Pine St (06840-5409)
P.O. Box 757 (06840-0757)
PHONE..................203 966-8390
Maria Crocitto,
EMP: 20 EST: 1997
SQ FT: 10,000
SALES (est): 1.6MM **Privately Held**
SIC: **2721** Trade journals: publishing & printing

(G-5087)
AMMONITE CORP
181 Mariomi Rd (06840-3314)
PHONE..................203 972-1130
G Warfield Hobbs, *President*
Robert T Edmundson, *Corp Secy*
EMP: 2
SALES (est): 234.5K **Privately Held**
SIC: **1382** 1311 Oil & gas exploration services; crude petroleum & natural gas production

(G-5088)
ARCHER-DANIELS-MIDLAND COMPANY
Also Called: ADM
49 Locust Ave Ste 104 (06840-4764)
PHONE..................203 966-4755
EMP: 1
SALES (corp-wide): 64.3B **Publicly Held**
WEB: www.admworld.com
SIC: **2041** Flour & other grain mill products
PA: Archer-Daniels-Midland Company
77 W Wacker Dr Ste 4600
Chicago IL 60601
312 634-8100

(G-5089)
BRIAN AND BRENDA BASINGER
521 Brookside Rd (06840-6924)
PHONE..................203 972-9407
Brian Basinger, *Administration*
EMP: 2
SALES (est): 62.9K **Privately Held**
SIC: **2711** Newspapers

(G-5090)
C D INDUSTRIES INC
10 Hill St (06840-4802)
PHONE..................203 966-4983
Antone Addesso, *Owner*
EMP: 1
SALES (est): 131.9K **Privately Held**
SIC: **3599** Machine shop, jobbing & repair

(G-5091)
CAFFEINE AND CARBURETORS
77 Pine St (06840-5409)
PHONE..................203 966-2704
Doug Zumbach, *Principal*
EMP: 2
SALES (est): 109.3K **Privately Held**
SIC: **3592** Carburetors

(G-5092)
CALANCA & ASSOC LLC
40 Conrad Rd (06840-6724)
PHONE..................203 972-6344
Anthony Calanca,
Patricia Calanca,
EMP: 1
SALES (est): 110K **Privately Held**
SIC: **3089** Clothes hangers, plastic

(G-5093)
CHARLES CLAY LTD
149 Cherry St (06840-5525)
PHONE..................203 662-0125
Gordon Smith, *President*
▲ EMP: 3
SALES (est): 92.8K **Privately Held**
SIC: **2396** Ribbons & bows, cut & sewed

(G-5094)
CHILDRENS PRESS
795 Carter St (06840-5025)
PHONE..................203 972-9404
Eve Hood, *Owner*
EMP: 1
SALES (est): 56.1K **Privately Held**
SIC: **2791** Photocomposition, for the printing trade

(G-5095)
CJ FIRST CANDLE
49 Locust Ave (06840-4764)
PHONE..................203 966-1300
Allison Jacobson, *CEO*
EMP: 2
SALES (est): 52.8K **Privately Held**
SIC: **3999** Candles

(G-5096)
CONNECTICUT DRONE SERVICES LLC
125 Forest St (06840-4708)
PHONE..................203 966-7016
Arthur Armand, *Principal*
EMP: 2
SALES (est): 86K **Privately Held**
SIC: **3721** Motorized aircraft

(G-5097)
CONTEK INTERNATIONAL CORP
93 Cherry St (06840)
PHONE..................203 972-3406
John J C Chen, *Principal*
EMP: 4
SALES (est): 123.5K **Privately Held**
SIC: **3577** Computer peripheral equipment

(G-5098)
CONTEK INTERNATIONAL CORP
Also Called: Century Products
60 Field Crest Rd (06840-6328)
PHONE..................203 972-7330
John Chen, *President*
Alice Chen, *Vice Pres*
▲ EMP: 15
SQ FT: 5,000
SALES (est): 1.8MM **Privately Held**
WEB: www.contek.net
SIC: **3577** Computer peripheral equipment

(G-5099)
CSC COCOA LLC
36 Grove St (06840-5329)
PHONE..................203 846-5611
Paul Farmer, *COO*
Andrew Reul, *CFO*
EMP: 5 EST: 2017
SALES (est): 139.9K **Privately Held**
SIC: **2066** Powdered cocoa

(G-5100)
CSC SUGAR LLC (PA)
Also Called: CSC El Paso
36 Grove St Ste 2 (06840-5329)
PHONE..................203 846-5610
Paul J Farmer, *President*
Francis X Claps, *CFO*
◆ EMP: 16
SQ FT: 5,000
SALES (est): 77.1MM **Privately Held**
SIC: **5159** 2062 2063 Sugar, raw; refined cane sugar from purchased raw sugar or syrup; liquid sugar from sugar beets

(G-5101)
DE VILLIERS INCORPORATED
Also Called: STS Special Technology & Svcs
194 Putnam Rd (06840-6808)
P.O. Box 1587 (06840-1587)
PHONE..................203 966-9645
Louriens Devilliers, *President*
Lourens De Villiers, *President*
Ruth De Villiers, *Treasurer*
EMP: 2
SALES (est): 210K **Privately Held**
WEB: www.businessbooksusa.com
SIC: **8742** 2731 5052 5182 Management consulting services; pamphlets: publishing only, not printed on site; coal & other minerals & ores; wine

(G-5102)
EASTERN INC
Also Called: Taroli Chris
95 Locust Ave (06840-4727)
PHONE..................203 563-9535
Chris Taroli, *Principal*
EMP: 9
SALES (est): 1.6MM **Privately Held**
SIC: **3441** Fabricated structural metal

(G-5103)
ENTERSPORT MANAGEMENT INC
128 Heather Dr (06840-5224)
P.O. Box 370665, Miami FL (33137-0665)
PHONE..................203 972-9090
Mark Fletcher, *President*
EMP: 3
SALES (est): 509.7K **Privately Held**
WEB: www.entersport.net
SIC: **7941** 2752 Sports promotion; commercial printing, lithographic

(G-5104)
EVERTIDE GAMES INC
459 Old Stamford Rd (06840-6612)
P.O. Box 4343, Stamford (06907-0343)
PHONE..................203 701-9145
Richard James, *President*
EMP: 1
SALES (est): 79.6K **Privately Held**
SIC: **2741** 7371 Miscellaneous publishing; computer software development & applications

(G-5105)
FREDERCKS JNNE LITERARARY AGCY
221 Benedict Hill Rd (06840-2913)
PHONE..................203 972-3011
Jeanne Fredericks, *President*
Wesley Fredericks, *Corp Secy*
EMP: 2 EST: 1997
SALES (est): 87.4K **Privately Held**
SIC: **2731** Book publishing

(G-5106)
GRANITE HILL EQUITY
280 New Norwalk Rd (06840-4921)
PHONE..................203 801-4396
A Dean Davis, *Manager*
EMP: 2
SALES (est): 151.6K **Privately Held**
WEB: www.granitehillequity.com
SIC: **3272** Cast stone, concrete

(G-5107)
GREEK ELEMENTS LLC
49 Journeys End Rd (06840-2414)
PHONE..................203 594-2022
Athanasios Damis, *Principal*
EMP: 3 EST: 2014
SALES (est): 157K **Privately Held**
SIC: **2819** Industrial inorganic chemicals

(G-5108)
GRIDIRON CAPITAL LLC (PA)
220 Elm St Fl 2 (06840-5322)
PHONE..................203 972-1100
Thomas A Burger, *Managing Prtnr*
Scott Harrison, *COO*
Donald E Cihak,
Timothy W Clark,
Eugene P Conese Jr,
EMP: 53
SALES (est): 309.1MM
SALES (corp-wide): 307.7MM **Privately Held**
WEB: www.gridironcapital.com
SIC: **2434** Wood kitchen cabinets

(G-5109)
HEARST CORPORATION
Also Called: New Canaan Advertiser
42 Vitti St (06840-4823)
P.O. Box 605 (06840-0605)
PHONE..................203 438-6544
V Donald Hersam, *Manager*
EMP: 40
SALES (corp-wide): 8.3B **Privately Held**
WEB: www.acorn-online.com
SIC: **2711** 2741 Newspapers, publishing & printing; miscellaneous publishing
PA: The Hearst Corporation
300 W 57th St Fl 42
New York NY 10019
212 649-2000

(G-5110)
HERSAM PUBLISHING COMPANY
Also Called: Darien Times
42 Vitti St (06840-4823)
P.O. Box 605 (06840-0605)
PHONE..................203 966-9541
Martin Hersam, *CEO*
Donald V Hersam Jr, *President*
V Hersham, *Publisher*
Eric Gatten, *Technology*
EMP: 300
SQ FT: 6,000
SALES (est): 11.7MM **Privately Held**
SIC: **2711** 2741 Commercial printing & newspaper publishing combined; miscellaneous publishing

New Canaan - Fairfield County (G-5111)

(G-5111)
INNOVANT INC
Also Called: Innovant Group
21 Locust Ave Ste 2d (06840-4735)
PHONE..................................203 594-7270
Mary Hudson, *Branch Mgr*
EMP: 1
SALES (corp-wide): 47.5MM **Privately Held**
SIC: 2521 Wood office furniture
PA: Innovant, Inc.
   37 W 20th St Ste 1101
   Islandia NY 11749
   212 929-4883

(G-5112)
JOR SERVICES LLC
4 Parting Brook Rd (06840-2827)
PHONE..................................203 594-7774
Joachim Roesler, *Principal*
EMP: 3
SALES (est): 300.3K **Privately Held**
SIC: 3089 Automotive parts, plastic

(G-5113)
K SMITH CUSTOM WOODWORKING LLC
33 Fitch Ln (06840-5052)
PHONE..................................203 981-4268
Kerry Smith, *Principal*
EMP: 2
SALES (est): 170.2K **Privately Held**
SIC: 2431 Millwork

(G-5114)
LFBW LLC
137 Llewellyn Dr (06840-4434)
PHONE..................................203 966-8499
Laura F Baldwin, *Principal*
▲ EMP: 1
SALES (est): 72K **Privately Held**
SIC: 3911 Jewelry, precious metal

(G-5115)
LITURGICAL PUBLICATIONS INC
Also Called: Parish Publishing
87 Lambert Rd (06840-3631)
PHONE..................................203 966-6470
Ken Pranger, *Manager*
EMP: 12
SALES (corp-wide): 103.5MM **Privately Held**
WEB: www.mylpi.com
SIC: 2721 2741 Periodicals; miscellaneous publishing
PA: Liturgical Publications, Inc.
   2875 S James Dr
   New Berlin WI 53151
   262 785-1188

(G-5116)
LOWENCORP PUBLISHING LLC
82 Puddin Hill Rd (06840-2325)
PHONE..................................203 966-3474
Alexander Lowen, *Principal*
EMP: 1
SALES (est): 57.8K **Privately Held**
SIC: 2741 Miscellaneous publishing

(G-5117)
MAGNELI MATERIALS LLC
33 Weeburn Dr (06840-5228)
P.O. Box 9 (06840-0009)
PHONE..................................203 644-8560
Robert Sterner, *Principal*
EMP: 5 EST: 2014
SALES (est): 362K **Privately Held**
SIC: 2816 Titanium dioxide, anatase or rutile (pigments)

(G-5118)
MB SPORT LLC (PA)
31 Grove St (06840-5324)
PHONE..................................203 966-1985
Alfred Lam, *Vice Pres*
Michael Buscher, *Mng Member*
Sonia Lamp, *Mng Member*
Joseph Bove, *Info Tech Dir*
▲ EMP: 19 EST: 1998
SQ FT: 5,500
SALES (est): 1.3MM **Privately Held**
WEB: www.mbsport.com
SIC: 2321 2337 Sport shirts, men's & boys': from purchased materials; women's & misses' suits & coats

(G-5119)
MECHANCAL ENGNERED SYSTEMS LLC
180 Jonathan Rd (06840-2116)
PHONE..................................203 400-4658
Matthew Farrell,
EMP: 7 EST: 2012
SQ FT: 2,000
SALES: 1.1MM **Privately Held**
SIC: 3564 3585 Turbo-blowers, industrial; refrigeration & heating equipment

(G-5120)
MEGASONICS INC
205 Benedict Hill Rd (06840-2913)
PHONE..................................203 966-3404
Chan Kob Chung, *President*
EMP: 3
SALES (est): 507.8K **Privately Held**
SIC: 3829 Measuring & controlling devices

(G-5121)
MR SKYLIGHT LLC
411 South Ave (06840-6316)
PHONE..................................203 966-6005
John A Cole, *Manager*
EMP: 3
SALES (est): 320.2K **Privately Held**
SIC: 3993 Signs & advertising specialties

(G-5122)
MRK FINE ARTS LLC
65 Locust Ave Ste 301 (06840-4753)
PHONE..................................203 972-3115
Christina Usher, *Production*
Rod Kosann,
Monica Kosann,
▲ EMP: 5
SALES (est): 683.8K **Privately Held**
SIC: 3911 Precious metal cases

(G-5123)
NEW CANAAN FORGE LLC (PA)
26 Burtis Ave (06840-5503)
PHONE..................................203 966-3858
Joseph Haas, *Mng Member*
EMP: 3
SQ FT: 3,235
SALES: 400K **Privately Held**
SIC: 7692 1791 Welding repair; structural steel erection

(G-5124)
NEW POLYMER SYSTEMS
4 Parting Brook Rd (06840-2827)
PHONE..................................203 594-7774
Joachim P Roesler, *Principal*
EMP: 2
SALES (est): 166.1K **Privately Held**
SIC: 3087 Custom compound purchased resins

(G-5125)
NEWSBANK INC
58 Pine St Ste 1 (06840-5426)
PHONE..................................203 966-1100
John McDowell, *Vice Pres*
EMP: 3
SALES (corp-wide): 77.3MM **Privately Held**
WEB: www.newsbank.com
SIC: 2741 Miscellaneous publishing
PA: Newsbank, Inc.
   5801 Pelican Bay Blvd
   Naples FL 34108
   800 762-8182

(G-5126)
NOVOGEN INC
262 Marvin Ridge Rd (06840-6909)
PHONE..................................203 972-5901
Reinhard Koenig, *President*
Warren Lancaster, *Exec VP*
Eve Langford-Smith, *VP Finance*
EMP: 10
SQ FT: 2,500
SALES (est): 1.3MM **Privately Held**
WEB: www.novogen.com
SIC: 2834 2023 Pharmaceutical preparations; dietary supplements, dairy & non-dairy based
PA: Kazia Therapeutics Limited
   Three International Twrs L 24 300
   Barangaroo Ave
   Sydney NSW

(G-5127)
OFFICE INSIGHT
24 East Ave (06840-5529)
PHONE..................................203 966-5008
Brad Powell, *Owner*
EMP: 2
SALES (est): 126K **Privately Held**
SIC: 2741 Miscellaneous publishing

(G-5128)
OOMPH LLC
5 Elm St (06840-5502)
PHONE..................................203 216-9848
Katherine Urban, *Opers Staff*
Jeffrey Johnston, *Marketing Mgr*
Patty Hopple,
Louise Brooks,
Amy Rice,
▼ EMP: 6
SALES (est): 1.1MM **Privately Held**
SIC: 2519 2511 Furniture, household: glass, fiberglass & plastic; fiberglass furniture, household: padded or plain; chairs, household, except upholstered: wood; bed frames, except water bed frames: wood

(G-5129)
PALADIN SOFTWARE INC
379 South Ave (06840-6314)
PHONE..................................203 966-0548
Neale C Hutcheson, *Principal*
EMP: 2 EST: 2001
SALES (est): 83.6K **Privately Held**
SIC: 7372 Prepackaged software

(G-5130)
PETER JAMES ASSOCIATES INC
296 Old Norwalk Rd (06840-6426)
P.O. Box 358 (06840-0358)
PHONE..................................203 972-1070
Gene Brissie, *President*
EMP: 1
SALES: 200K **Privately Held**
SIC: 2731 Book publishing

(G-5131)
POINTER PRESS
57 Holly Rd (06840-6407)
PHONE..................................650 269-3492
James Lavin, *Owner*
EMP: 2
SALES (est): 83.9K **Privately Held**
SIC: 2752 Commercial printing, lithographic

(G-5132)
POLLINATE NEWS
4 Holmewood Ln (06840-4102)
PHONE..................................203 801-9623
Haley Priebe, *Principal*
EMP: 2 EST: 2016
SALES (est): 62.9K **Privately Held**
SIC: 2711 Newspapers

(G-5133)
PRODUCT SPRING LLC
30 Butler Ln (06840-6817)
PHONE..................................203 966-6766
Christopher P Dooley, *Principal*
▲ EMP: 2
SALES (est): 223.4K **Privately Held**
SIC: 3999 Advertising display products

(G-5134)
PROOF AND WOOD VENTURES INC
365 West Rd (06840-3020)
PHONE..................................203 856-8680
David Schmier, *President*
EMP: 1
SALES: 500K **Privately Held**
SIC: 2084 Wines, brandy & brandy spirits

(G-5135)
PRS AIR ELITE
19 Gray Squirrel Dr (06840-6902)
PHONE..................................203 327-3500
EMP: 1 EST: 2018
SALES (est): 37.5K **Privately Held**
SIC: 2741 Miscellaneous publishing

(G-5136)
PUTU LLC
Also Called: Lolo Bags
48 Elm St (06840-5501)
PHONE..................................203 594-9700
Leila Roxo, *Office Mgr*
Bruce McLaire, *Mng Member*
▲ EMP: 3
SALES (est): 419.5K **Privately Held**
SIC: 3172 Cosmetic bags

(G-5137)
QUANTUM
192 Cross Ridge Rd (06840-2313)
PHONE..................................732 407-1200
EMP: 2
SALES (est): 85.9K **Privately Held**
SIC: 3572 Computer storage devices

(G-5138)
REEL TIME LLC
43 Green Meadow Ln (06840-6823)
PHONE..................................203 326-0664
Michael Carusi, *CEO*
EMP: 2
SALES (est): 83K **Privately Held**
SIC: 7372 Prepackaged software

(G-5139)
SARA CAMPBELL LTD
137 Elm St (06840-5405)
PHONE..................................203 966-5488
EMP: 1
SALES (corp-wide): 4.5MM **Privately Held**
SIC: 2337 Women's & misses' suits & coats
PA: Sara Campbell, Ltd.
   67 Kemble St Ste 4
   Boston MA 02119
   617 423-3134

(G-5140)
SEQUENT CONSULTING LLC
925 Oenoke Rdg (06840-2605)
PHONE..................................203 966-2340
Thomas Tesluk, *Principal*
EMP: 2
SALES (est): 200.2K **Privately Held**
SIC: 3571 3572 5045 Electronic computers; computer storage devices; computers, peripherals & software

(G-5141)
SERAPURE TECHNOLOGIES LLC
17 Autumn Ln (06840-6346)
PHONE..................................203 972-0481
Joan C Pehta,
EMP: 1
SALES (est): 94.3K **Privately Held**
SIC: 2836 Biological products, except diagnostic

(G-5142)
SLOGIC HOLDING CORP (PA)
36 Grove St (06840-5329)
PHONE..................................203 966-2800
James Kelly, *Sales Mgr*
Christa Spry, *Director*
EMP: 7 EST: 2016
SALES (est): 121.5MM **Privately Held**
SIC: 2394 5091 Tents: made from purchased materials; camping equipment & supplies

(G-5143)
SMYTH INK
128 Putnam Rd (06840-6806)
PHONE..................................203 801-4335
Peter Drakos, *Principal*
EMP: 2
SALES (est): 99K **Privately Held**
SIC: 2262 Printing: manmade fiber & silk broadwoven fabrics

(G-5144)
SONG BATH LLC
146 Old Kings Hwy (06840-6415)
PHONE..................................800 353-0313
Peter Nemiroff, *Principal*
▲ EMP: 3
SALES (est): 232.3K **Privately Held**
SIC: 2434 Wood kitchen cabinets

(G-5145)
SOUTHERN ALMNUM INTRMDTE HLDIN (PA)
130 Main St (06840-5509)
PHONE..................................870 234-8660
Allison Schultz, *CEO*
EMP: 2
SALES (est): 25MM **Privately Held**
SIC: 2514 Metal household furniture

(G-5146)
SPORTCO INC
Also Called: Techwear USA
75 Parish Rd (06840-4424)
PHONE..................................631 244-4513
Robert Novak, *President*
EMP: 1
SQ FT: 12,000
SALES (est): 50K **Privately Held**
WEB: www.techwearusa.com
SIC: 2321 Men's & boys' sports & polo shirts

(G-5147)
STEVENS INDUSTRIES INC
585 Old Stamford Rd (06840-6617)
PHONE..................................203 966-7555
Allen L Stevens, *President*
John McCown, *Vice Pres*
EMP: 25
SQ FT: 1,500
SALES (est): 952.3K **Privately Held**
SIC: 6512 4491 2311 2326 Nonresidential building operators; marine terminals; military uniforms, men's & youths': purchased materials; men's & boys' work clothing

(G-5148)
STRUCTURED SOLUTIONS II LLC
55 Saint Johns Pl Ste 201 (06840-4530)
PHONE..................................203 972-5717
Mark Noonan, *President*
Pat Green, *Manager*
Alexandria Lawer,
Hank Pohl,
▲ EMP: 6
SQ FT: 2,500
SALES (est): 1.1MM **Privately Held**
WEB: www.structuredsolutionsii.com
SIC: 3711 Snow plows (motor vehicles), assembly of

(G-5149)
SUPERNOVA DIAGNOSTICS INC
36 Richmond Hill Rd (06840-5301)
PHONE..................................301 792-4345
Neil J Campbell, *CEO*
Hans-Georg Eisenwiener, *Ch of Bd*
Dr Christopher M Ball, *Exec VP*
Dane Saglio, *CFO*
George W H Cautherley, *Director*
EMP: 7
SALES (est): 510K **Privately Held**
SIC: 3841 Diagnostic apparatus, medical

(G-5150)
TAYLORS LUGGAGE INC
8 Elm St (06840-5599)
PHONE..................................203 966-9961
Wendy Diamond, *President*
Helen Diamond, *Corp Secy*
Jules Aspesi,
EMP: 3
SQ FT: 700
SALES (est): 369.5K **Privately Held**
SIC: 5948 5699 5947 5944 Luggage, except footlockers & trunks; leather goods, except luggage & shoes; umbrellas; gift shop; clocks; watches; attache cases

(G-5151)
TENZINGBROOK SOFTWARE LLC
887 Weed St (06840-4034)
PHONE..................................203 918-4500
Steven Strom, *Principal*
EMP: 2
SALES (est): 118.5K **Privately Held**
SIC: 7372 Prepackaged software

(G-5152)
TESTING FOR TOXINS
159 Lost District Dr (06840-2008)
PHONE..................................203 972-6501
EMP: 2
SALES (est): 74.4K **Privately Held**
SIC: 2836 Biological Products, Except Diagnostic

(G-5153)
TODDLER TEAMS LLC
5 Southwood Dr (06840-6641)
PHONE..................................203 972-7713
Boyd Harden,
EMP: 1
SALES (est): 66K **Privately Held**
SIC: 3944 Baby carriages & restraint seats

(G-5154)
TRIPLE CLOVER PRODUCTS LLC
4 Smith Ridge Ln (06840-3217)
PHONE..................................475 558-9503
Joanne Grasso, *Mng Member*
Michael Kirby,
Tricia O'Connor,
EMP: 2
SALES (est): 250K **Privately Held**
SIC: 3423 7389 Hooks: bush, grass, baling, husking, etc.;

(G-5155)
UNIMIN LIME CORPORATION (DH)
258 Elm St (06840-5309)
PHONE..................................203 966-8880
Joseph Shapiro, *President*
EMP: 11
SALES (est): 14MM
SALES (corp-wide): 142.6MM **Publicly Held**
SIC: 1446 Industrial sand
HQ: Covia Holdings Corporation
3 Summit Park Dr Ste 700
Independence OH 44131
440 214-3284

(G-5156)
UNIVERSAL STORAGE CNTRS LLC
Also Called: U S C
146 Old Kings Hwy (06840-6415)
PHONE..................................203 966-3043
Peter Nemiroff, *President*
Diane Nemiroff, *Vice Pres*
▲ EMP: 2
SALES (est): 342.6K **Privately Held**
SIC: 3542 Metal container making machines: cans, etc.

(G-5157)
US CHEMICALS INC
280 Elm St (06840-5313)
PHONE..................................203 655-8878
H T Von Oehsen, *CEO*
Jennifer Hensel, *Accounts Exec*
EMP: 3
SALES (est): 202.1K **Privately Held**
SIC: 2911 5169 Solvents; acids

(G-5158)
WESTCHESTER FORGE INC
28 Benedict Hill Rd (06840-2903)
PHONE..................................914 584-2429
EMP: 3
SALES (est): 243.7K **Privately Held**
SIC: 2721 Periodicals

(G-5159)
WILLIS MILLS HOUSE LLC
1380 Ponus Rdg (06840-3426)
PHONE..................................917 287-3260
James Seuss, *Mng Member*
Stephen Skowron,
EMP: 2
SALES (est): 85.9K **Privately Held**
SIC: 2431 Millwork

New Fairfield
Fairfield County

(G-5160)
ALLTOP LTD
13 Colonial Rd (06812-5023)
PHONE..................................203 746-1509
Charles Sheridan, *President*
Stephen J Sheridan, *Director*
EMP: 2
SALES (est): 290K **Privately Held**
SIC: 5085 3053 Rubber goods, mechanical; gaskets, packing & sealing devices

(G-5161)
APPLE JOHN
1 Hickory Ln (06812-3213)
PHONE..................................203 746-3459
EMP: 2
SALES (est): 198.9K **Privately Held**
SIC: 3571 Mfg Electronic Computers

(G-5162)
BRADLEY WOODWORKING LLC
276 State Route 39 (06812-2404)
PHONE..................................203 746-8357
Marc B Bass, *Principal*
EMP: 2
SALES (est): 150.3K **Privately Held**
SIC: 2431 Millwork

(G-5163)
C3 MANUFACTURING LLC
3a Pheasant Dr (06812-2212)
PHONE..................................914 943-6877
William Marino, *Mng Member*
EMP: 2
SALES (est): 114.4K **Privately Held**
SIC: 3841 Surgical & medical instruments

(G-5164)
CABIN CRITTERS INC
3 Dunham Dr Ste A (06812-4055)
PHONE..................................203 778-4552
David Smith, *President*
▲ EMP: 4
SALES (est): 200K **Privately Held**
WEB: www.cabincrittersinc.com
SIC: 3942 Stuffed toys, including animals

(G-5165)
CANDLEWOOD BOAT RESTORATION
10 Meetinghouse Hill Cir (06812-2559)
PHONE..................................203 223-7893
Salvatore Gangi, *Principal*
EMP: 1
SALES (est): 41.5K **Privately Held**
SIC: 2499 Wood products

(G-5166)
CITIZEN NEWS
Candle Wood Cor Rm 39 (06812)
P.O. Box 8048 (06812-8048)
PHONE..................................203 746-4669
Ellen Burnett, *Owner*
EMP: 6
SALES: 362K **Privately Held**
SIC: 2711 Newspapers: publishing only, not printed on site

(G-5167)
DANIEL F CRAPA
17 Calverton Dr (06812-3705)
PHONE..................................203 746-5706
Daniel F Crapa, *Principal*
EMP: 2
SALES (est): 145.2K **Privately Held**
SIC: 2431 Millwork

(G-5168)
GLEASON GROUP INCORPORATED
5 Fox Hollow Rd (06812-2629)
PHONE..................................203 312-0683
Jerry Gleason, *President*
EMP: 1
SALES (est): 91.6K **Privately Held**
SIC: 5734 2678 8999 8748 Computer software & accessories; tablets & pads, book & writing: from purchased materials; writing for publication; publishing consultant

(G-5169)
INTEGRITY INDUSTRIES INC
1 Saw Mill Rd Ste 7 (06812-4045)
PHONE..................................203 312-9788
EMP: 6
SALES (corp-wide): 225.3B **Publicly Held**
SIC: 2841 Detergents, synthetic organic or inorganic alkaline
HQ: Integrity Delaware, Llc
2710 E Corral Ave
Kingsville TX 78363
361 595-5561

(G-5170)
JOSEPH MALAVENDA
Also Called: Cine Research Laboratory
15 Mill Pond Rd (06812-2103)
PHONE..................................203 746-4160
Joseph Malavenda, *Owner*
EMP: 1
SALES (est): 102.6K **Privately Held**
SIC: 2721 7819 Magazines: publishing only, not printed on site; video tape or disk reproduction

(G-5171)
MATRIX APPAREL GROUP LLC
29 Candlewood Dr (06812-5111)
PHONE..................................203 740-7837
James Mager, *Mng Member*
James K Mager, *Mng Member*
EMP: 3 EST: 2002
SQ FT: 2,500
SALES: 2.5MM **Privately Held**
SIC: 2389 Men's miscellaneous accessories

(G-5172)
NEW FAIRFIELD PRESS INC
3 Dunham Dr (06812-4055)
P.O. Box 8864 (06812-8864)
PHONE..................................203 746-2700
John Paul Parille, *President*
Arlene Pugliatti, *Vice Pres*
EMP: 15 EST: 1965
SQ FT: 5,000
SALES (est): 2.1MM **Privately Held**
WEB: www.nfpress.com
SIC: 2759 2752 Business forms: printing; commercial printing, lithographic

(G-5173)
PHOENIX WOODWORKING
141 Pine Hill Rd (06812-2214)
P.O. Box 397 (06812-0397)
PHONE..................................203 512-3521
Gary Gouveia, *Principal*
EMP: 2
SALES (est): 160.8K **Privately Held**
SIC: 2431 Interior & ornamental woodwork & trim

(G-5174)
PINPOINT THERMOGRAPHY LLC
32 Windmill Rd (06812-2915)
PHONE..................................203 546-8906
Steven Males, *Principal*
EMP: 2
SALES (est): 109.6K **Privately Held**
SIC: 2759 Thermography

(G-5175)
ROBERT J BALLAS
14 Jeremy Dr (06812-2110)
PHONE..................................203 746-0506
Robert Ballas, *Owner*
EMP: 2
SALES (est): 112.5K **Privately Held**
SIC: 3272 Concrete products

(G-5176)
STAR TECH INSTRUMENTS INC
3 State Route 39 (06812-4000)
P.O. Box 1822 (06812-1822)
PHONE..................................203 312-0767
William C Fricke, *President*
EMP: 4

SALES (est): 496.8K **Privately Held**
SIC: 3845 Laser systems & equipment, medical

(G-5177)
STORK N MORE
1 Penney Ln (06812-2829)
PHONE 203 746-7500
Fred Van Sauter, *Owner*
EMP: 1
SALES: 25K **Privately Held**
SIC: 2771 Greeting cards

(G-5178)
SWANHART WOODWORKING
5 Bayberry Ln (06812-2565)
PHONE 203 746-1184
Kenneth Swanhart, *Principal*
EMP: 4
SALES (est): 388.5K **Privately Held**
SIC: 2431 Millwork

(G-5179)
TOWN TRIBUNE LLC
10 Sleepy Hollow Rd (06812-5102)
PHONE 203 648-6085
Marylou Schirmer, *Principal*
Christy Thompson, *Exec Dir*
EMP: 4
SALES (est): 216.5K **Privately Held**
SIC: 2711 Newspapers

(G-5180)
TUNE DOOR INC
19 Joels Dr (06812-3123)
PHONE 914 713-0257
Thomas Garben, *President*
EMP: 1 **EST:** 2012
SALES: 10K **Privately Held**
SIC: 2741 Music, sheet: publishing & printing

(G-5181)
ULTIMATE HARDWOOD FLOORS
119 Shortwoods Rd (06812-2711)
PHONE 203 746-9692
Gary Peck, *Principal*
EMP: 2
SALES (est): 169.8K **Privately Held**
SIC: 2426 1771 1752 Flooring, hardwood; flooring contractor; floor laying & floor work

(G-5182)
VIDEO AUTOMATION SYSTEMS INC
13 Arrow Meadow Rd (06812-3901)
PHONE 203 312-0152
Thorsten Cook, *President*
EMP: 3 **EST:** 1976
SALES: 216.4K **Privately Held**
WEB: www.videoautomation.com
SIC: 3663 8748 Transmitting apparatus, radio or television; business consulting

(G-5183)
WESTERN CONN CRAFTSMEN LLC
246 Pine Hill Rd (06812-2209)
PHONE 203 312-8167
Anthony N Kaplanis, *Manager*
A Nicholas Kaplanis,
EMP: 5
SALES: 500K **Privately Held**
SIC: 2511 Unassembled or unfinished furniture, household: wood

New Hartford
Litchfield County

(G-5184)
ADVANCED PWR SYSTEMS INTL INC
18 Hemlock Dr (06057-2814)
PHONE 860 921-0009
Chris Wright, *COO*
EMP: 25
SQ FT: 3,000

SALES (est): 4.4MM **Privately Held**
WEB: www.fitchfuelcatalyst.com
SIC: 5084 2819 2899 2869 Engines & transportation equipment; engines & parts, air-cooled; engines & parts, diesel; engines, gasoline; catalysts, chemical; chemical preparations; industrial organic chemicals

(G-5185)
ALTRA INDUSTRIAL MOTION CORP
31 Industrial Park Rd (06057-2310)
PHONE 860 379-1673
Donald Beall, *Branch Mgr*
EMP: 6
SALES (corp-wide): 1.1B **Publicly Held**
SIC: 5085 3568 Power transmission equipment & apparatus; power transmission equipment
PA: Altra Industrial Motion Corp.
  300 Granite St Ste 201
  Braintree MA 02184
  781 917-0600

(G-5186)
BETX LLC
440 Cedar Ln (06057-2403)
PHONE 860 459-1681
Krish Dasgupta, *CEO*
EMP: 3
SALES (est): 86.5K **Privately Held**
SIC: 2741 7371 ; computer software development & applications

(G-5187)
CONNECTICUT VALLEY WINERY LLC
1480 Litchfield Tpke (06057-3210)
PHONE 860 489-9463
Anthony Ferraro,
EMP: 3
SALES: 147K **Privately Held**
SIC: 2084 Wines

(G-5188)
CTECH ADHESIVES
39 Maple Hollow Rd (06057-3020)
PHONE 860 482-5947
Wells Cunningham, *Principal*
EMP: 3
SALES (est): 206.4K **Privately Held**
SIC: 2891 Adhesives

(G-5189)
CUNNINGHAM TECH LLC (PA)
39 Maple Hollow Rd (06057-3020)
PHONE 860 738-8759
Wells Cunningham, *Owner*
Robin Cunningham,
EMP: 4
SALES: 200K **Privately Held**
SIC: 2891 Adhesives & sealants

(G-5190)
EXECUTIVE GREETINGS INC (HQ)
Also Called: Baldwin Cooke
120 Industrial Park Rd (06057-2308)
P.O. Box 3669, Mankato MN (56002-3669)
PHONE 860 379-9911
Dan RAO, *President*
Stephen D Roberts, *CFO*
▼ **EMP:** 450
SQ FT: 140,000
SALES (est): 49.1MM
SALES (corp-wide): 2.8B **Privately Held**
WEB: www.executivegreetings.com
SIC: 2741 5112 5199 2759 Miscellaneous publishing; greeting cards; business forms; gifts & novelties; commercial printing
PA: Taylor Corporation
  1725 Roe Crest Dr
  North Mankato MN 56003
  507 625-2828

(G-5191)
FENDER MUSICAL INSTRS CORP
37 Greenwoods Rd (06057-2207)
PHONE 860 379-7575
Bob Saunders, *Branch Mgr*
EMP: 6

SALES (corp-wide): 711.9MM **Privately Held**
SIC: 3931 Musical instruments
PA: Fender Musical Instruments Corporation
  17600 N Perimeter Dr # 100
  Scottsdale AZ 85255
  480 596-9690

(G-5192)
GLASSWORKS
790 Litchfield Tpke (06057-3310)
PHONE 860 673-1250
Mary Anne De Lorenzo, *Owner*
EMP: 2
SALES (est): 98K **Privately Held**
SIC: 3231 Products of purchased glass

(G-5193)
HITCHCOCK HOLDING COMPANY INC (DH)
31 Industrial Park Rd (06057-2310)
PHONE 860 738-0141
Robin Faccenda, *Ch of Bd*
Ron Coleman, *President*
EMP: 8
SQ FT: 110,000
SALES (est): 26.4MM
SALES (corp-wide): 182.4MM **Privately Held**
SIC: 5712 2511 6719 Furniture stores; wood household furniture; investment holding companies, except banks
HQ: Faccenda Investments Limited
  Willow Road
  Brackley NORTHANTS
  128 070-3641

(G-5194)
HURLEY MANUFACTURING COMPANY
37 Greenwoods Rd (06057-2207)
P.O. Box 366 (06057-0366)
PHONE 860 379-8506
David J Hurley, *President*
Thomas P Hurley, *Vice Pres*
EMP: 30 **EST:** 1945
SQ FT: 22,600
SALES (est): 5.8MM **Privately Held**
WEB: www.hurleyspring.com
SIC: 3493 3469 Steel springs, except wire; metal stampings

(G-5195)
IMPALED LONGBOARDS LLC
298 Niles Rd (06057-4230)
PHONE 860 379-1101
John Pierce, *Principal*
EMP: 2
SALES (est): 121.9K **Privately Held**
SIC: 3949 Skateboards

(G-5196)
INDEPENDENT WELDING & FABG
171 Dings Rd (06057-3013)
PHONE 860 605-4712
Devon Soucy, *Principal*
EMP: 1 **EST:** 2017
SALES (est): 25K **Privately Held**
SIC: 7692 Welding repair

(G-5197)
INERTIA DYNAMICS LLC
31 Industrial Park Rd (06057-2310)
PHONE 860 379-1252
Csceve Myquist,
▲ **EMP:** 110
SQ FT: 32,000
SALES (est): 20.8MM
SALES (corp-wide): 1.1B **Publicly Held**
WEB: www.inertiadynamics.com
SIC: 3625 3568 Brakes, electromagnetic; clutches, except vehicular
PA: Altra Industrial Motion Corp.
  300 Granite St Ste 201
  Braintree MA 02184
  781 917-0600

(G-5198)
INERTIA DYNAMICS INC
31 Industrial Park Rd (06057-2310)
P.O. Box 641, South Beloit IL (61080-0641)
PHONE 860 379-1252
Steve Nyquist, *Principal*

David Weed, *Purchasing*
Oliwer Janiec, *Engineer*
Adam Krukar, *Technician*
EMP: 18
SALES (est): 3.2MM **Privately Held**
SIC: 3465 Body parts, automobile: stamped metal

(G-5199)
INJECTECH ENGINEERING LLC (PA)
19 Pioneer Rd (06057-4235)
PHONE 860 379-9781
Kenneth Heyse, *Mng Member*
Robert Risbridger,
EMP: 7
SQ FT: 7,000
SALES (est): 1.8MM **Privately Held**
SIC: 3089 Injection molded finished plastic products

(G-5200)
KELLOG SPLITTERS INC
224 Bruning Rd (06057-2535)
PHONE 860 738-4986
Kelvin Smith, *Owner*
EMP: 2 **EST:** 2008
SALES (est): 100.5K **Privately Held**
SIC: 3999 Manufacturing industries

(G-5201)
L & M MANUFACTURING CO INC
37 Greenwoods Rd (06057-2207)
PHONE 860 379-2751
Maurice J La Brecque, *President*
Joseph J Mangiome, *Vice Pres*
EMP: 20
SQ FT: 24,000
SALES (est): 2.8MM **Privately Held**
WEB: www.lmmfg.com
SIC: 3452 Screws, metal; pins

(G-5202)
MISE EN PLACE WOOD WORKS INC
135 Whitbeck Rd (06057-3218)
PHONE 860 921-0208
Prescott Musler, *Principal*
EMP: 2
SALES (est): 72K **Privately Held**
SIC: 2431 Millwork

(G-5203)
NEW HARTFORD INDUSTRIAL PARK
Also Called: Hurley Manufacturing
37 Greenwoods Rd (06057-2207)
P.O. Box 366 (06057-0366)
PHONE 860 379-8506
David Hurley, *President*
Thomas Hurley, *Vice Pres*
EMP: 30
SQ FT: 30,000
SALES (est): 2.4MM **Privately Held**
WEB: www.hurleymfg.com
SIC: 3469 Metal stampings

(G-5204)
NEW HARTFORD WINE AND BEV LLC
516 Main St (06057-2126)
P.O. Box 18 (06057-0018)
PHONE 860 379-3764
Jason Bannerman,
Adam Burrows,
EMP: 5 **EST:** 1970
SALES (est): 514.9K **Privately Held**
SIC: 5921 2086 Liquor stores; bottled & canned soft drinks

(G-5205)
PAPAS MAPLE SYRUP
624 Niles Rd (06057-2412)
PHONE 860 379-0117
Barbara Marsh, *Principal*
EMP: 2
SALES (est): 62.3K **Privately Held**
SIC: 2099 Maple syrup

(G-5206)
PERRY TECHNOLOGY CORPORATION
120 Industrial Park Rd (06057-2308)
P.O. Box 21 (06057-0021)
PHONE 860 738-2525

▲ = Import ▼ = Export
◆ = Import/Export

Lansford Perry, *President*
Bernie Levesque, *Purch Agent*
Jan Almstedt, *Buyer*
Deana Dawson, *Buyer*
Jason Ferree, *Engineer*
EMP: 85 **EST:** 1938
SQ FT: 55,000
SALES (est): 28.5MM **Privately Held**
WEB: www.perrygear.com
SIC: 3545 3728 3568 3462 Machine tool accessories; gears, aircraft power transmission; power transmission equipment; iron & steel forgings; manufactured hardware (general)

(G-5207)
PROSPECT DESIGNS INC
11 Prospect St (06057-2223)
P.O. Box 62, Pine Meadow (06061-0062)
PHONE..........................860 379-7858
Ann Evans, *President*
Marshall Janes, *General Mgr*
EMP: 5
SQ FT: 2,000
SALES (est): 591.1K **Privately Held**
WEB: www.prospectdesigns.com
SIC: 3842 Technical aids for the handicapped

(G-5208)
R L TURICK CO INC
186 Main St (06057-2746)
PHONE..........................860 693-2230
David R Turick, *President*
Richard Turick, *Vice Pres*
▼ **EMP:** 7 **EST:** 1961
SQ FT: 3,200
SALES (est): 900K **Privately Held**
SIC: 3599 Machine shop, jobbing & repair

(G-5209)
RAMCO SYSTEMS CORPORATION
30 Kinsey Rd (06057-3308)
PHONE..........................860 496-0099
Parameswar Subramanian, *President*
EMP: 2
SALES (est): 92K **Privately Held**
SIC: 7372 Prepackaged software

(G-5210)
RIDGETOP PUBLISHING LLC
37 Richards Rd (06057-2817)
PHONE..........................860 489-9555
Barbara Henri, *Principal*
EMP: 1
SALES (est): 37.5K **Privately Held**
SIC: 2741 Miscellaneous publishing

(G-5211)
SCP MANAGEMENT LLC
Also Called: Syntac Coated Products
29 Industrial Park Rd (06057-2310)
PHONE..........................860 738-2600
Aaron Rutsky, *Vice Pres*
Curt Rutsky, *Mng Member*
▲ **EMP:** 45
SALES (est): 21.5MM **Privately Held**
SIC: 3312 Coated or plated products

(G-5212)
SHURTAPE SPECIALTY COATING LLC (DH)
29 Industrial Park Rd (06057-2310)
PHONE..........................860 738-2600
Curt Rutsky, *CEO*
Jay Hirschberg, *Sales Staff*
EMP: 50
SQ FT: 60,000
SALES (est): 7MM
SALES (corp-wide): 691.3MM **Privately Held**
SIC: 2891 Adhesives

(G-5213)
STATE WIDE WELDING SERVICE
110 Whitbeck Rd (06057-3216)
PHONE..........................860 489-2465
Paul Janco, *Owner*
EMP: 1
SALES (est): 53K **Privately Held**
SIC: 7692 Welding repair

(G-5214)
WAYNE HORN
308 Cedar Ln (06057-2907)
PHONE..........................860 491-3315
Wayne Horn, *Principal*
EMP: 3
SALES (est): 279.3K **Privately Held**
SIC: 2411 Logging camps & contractors

New Haven
New Haven County

(G-5215)
109 DESIGN LLC (PA)
55 Whitney Ave Fl 2 (06510-1301)
PHONE..........................203 941-1812
Sebastian Monzon, *Principal*
Levi Deluke, *Principal*
Ellen Su, *Principal*
Elliot Swart, *Director*
EMP: 3
SALES (est): 434.5K **Privately Held**
SIC: 3841 8711 Surgical & medical instruments; mechanical engineering

(G-5216)
90 RIVER STREET LLC
90 River St (06513-4382)
PHONE..........................203 772-4700
Marc Suraci,
EMP: 2
SALES (est): 340K **Privately Held**
SIC: 3629 Electrical industrial apparatus

(G-5217)
A D PERKINS COMPANY
43 Elm St (06510-2032)
PHONE..........................203 777-3456
Kirk Schroff, *President*
Nancy Schroff, *Corp Secy*
Jay Smilovich, *Vice Pres*
EMP: 9
SQ FT: 1,200
SALES (est): 200K **Privately Held**
WEB: www.adperkins.com
SIC: 3953 3993 7389 Embossing seals & hand stamps; advertising novelties; engraving service

(G-5218)
ACCUSTANDARD INC
125 Market St (06513-3031)
PHONE..........................203 786-5290
Amy Harvey, *President*
Michael Bolgar, *Chairman*
Matthew Bolgar, *Vice Pres*
Anke Gelbin, *Safety Mgr*
Eric Dzialo, *Mktg Dir*
EMP: 65
SQ FT: 34,000
SALES (est): 10.2MM **Privately Held**
WEB: www.accustandard.com
SIC: 8731 2869 Commercial physical research; industrial organic chemicals

(G-5219)
ACHILLION PHARMACEUTICALS INC
300 George St Ste 801 (06511-6656)
PHONE..........................203 624-7000
Milind S Deshpande, *President*
Joel Barrish, *Exec VP*
Martha Manning, *Exec VP*
Mingjun Huang, *Senior VP*
Laura Barrow, *Vice Pres*
EMP: 80
SQ FT: 38,632
SALES (est): 22.3MM **Privately Held**
WEB: www.achillion.com
SIC: 2834 8731 Druggists' preparations (pharmaceuticals); biotechnical research, commercial

(G-5220)
ALEXANDER STREET PRESS
110 Curtis Dr (06515-2308)
PHONE..........................203 389-6881
EMP: 2
SALES (est): 59.2K **Privately Held**
SIC: 2741 Miscellaneous publishing

(G-5221)
ALEXION PHARMA LLC (HQ)
100 College St (06510-3210)
PHONE..........................203 272-2596
Nikhil Jayaram, *Regional Mgr*
Nick Gurreri, *Vice Pres*
Todd Spalding, *Vice Pres*
Martine Zimmermann, *Vice Pres*
Patricia Bento, *Research*
EMP: 45 **EST:** 2015
SALES (est): 36.9MM **Publicly Held**
SIC: 2834 8733 Pharmaceutical preparations; medical research

(G-5222)
ALL PHASE STEEL WORKS LLC
57 Trumbull St (06510-1004)
PHONE..........................203 375-8881
Paul J Pinto, *Principal*
EMP: 55 **EST:** 2012
SQ FT: 30,000
SALES (est): 14.6MM **Privately Held**
SIC: 3441 1791 Building components, structural steel; building front installation metal

(G-5223)
ALLIANCE ENERGY LLC
Also Called: Connecticut Refining Co
Merritt Pkwy (06535)
P.O. Box 9545 (06535-0545)
PHONE..........................203 933-2511
Rich Hyland, *Manager*
EMP: 4
SALES (corp-wide): 12.6B **Publicly Held**
SIC: 1389 Construction, repair & dismantling services
HQ: Alliance Energy Llc
  800 South St Ste 500
  Waltham MA 02453

(G-5224)
ALLOY WELDING
85 Willow St (06511-2668)
PHONE..........................203 737-5609
Sandra Lee Talley, *Principal*
EMP: 1
SALES (est): 37.4K **Privately Held**
SIC: 7692 Welding repair

(G-5225)
ALVA HEALTH INC
157 Church St Fl 19 (06510-2100)
PHONE..........................832 515-8235
EMP: 1
SALES (est): 39K **Privately Held**
SIC: 7372 7389 Prepackaged software;

(G-5226)
ALVAREZ INDUSTRIES LLC (PA)
26 Brownell St Fl 3 (06511-4006)
PHONE..........................203 401-1152
Lenny Alvarez,
EMP: 1 **EST:** 2011
SALES (est): 262.6K **Privately Held**
SIC: 3499 Metal household articles

(G-5227)
AMERICAN GREENFUELS LLC
30 Waterfront St (06512-1713)
PHONE..........................203 672-9028
Mikulas Gasparik, *VP Opers*
Kevin Luddy, *CFO*
EMP: 11
SALES (est): 2.1MM
SALES (corp-wide): 177.9K **Privately Held**
SIC: 2869 Fuels
HQ: Kolmar Americas, Inc.
  10 Middle St Ph
  Bridgeport CT 06604
  203 873-2051

(G-5228)
AMERICAN IRON WORKS
17 Morris St (06519-2507)
PHONE..........................203 624-7360
Anthony Maresca, *Owner*
EMP: 2
SQ FT: 3,500
SALES (est): 206.3K **Privately Held**
SIC: 3446 Railings, prefabricated metal; stairs, staircases, stair treads: prefabricated metal

(G-5229)
AMERICAN SIGN INC
614 Ferry St (06513-2924)
PHONE..........................203 624-2991
David Lafo, *President*
EMP: 21 **EST:** 1979
SQ FT: 10,500
SALES (est): 2.4MM **Privately Held**
SIC: 7389 3993 3953 2394 Sign painting & lettering shop; signs & advertising specialties; marking devices; canvas & related products

(G-5230)
AMIUS PARTNERS LLC
180 E Rock Rd (06511-1326)
PHONE..........................203 526-5926
Bruce Benson, *Owner*
EMP: 5
SALES (est): 342.4K **Privately Held**
SIC: 3812 Defense systems & equipment

(G-5231)
ANDERSON TOOL COMPANY INC
85 Willow St Ste 3 (06511-2694)
PHONE..........................203 777-4153
David Christensen, *President*
Thomas Christensen, *Vice Pres*
Harold Christensen, *Shareholder*
EMP: 5 **EST:** 1957
SQ FT: 4,500
SALES: 335.2K **Privately Held**
SIC: 3544 7692 Special dies & tools; jigs & fixtures; welding repair

(G-5232)
APICELLAS BAKERY INC
365 Grand Ave (06513-3732)
PHONE..........................203 865-6204
Alphonse J Cimino, *President*
EMP: 20
SQ FT: 6,000
SALES: 1.7MM **Privately Held**
SIC: 5149 5461 2051 Bakery products; bread; bread, cake & related products

(G-5233)
ARROW LOCK MANUFACTURING CO
110 Sargent Dr (06511-5918)
PHONE..........................203 603-5959
Michael Matteo, *Purch Agent*
EMP: 2
SALES (est): 116.4K **Privately Held**
SIC: 3999 Manufacturing industries

(G-5234)
ARVINAS INC (PA)
Also Called: Protac
395 Winchester Ave (06511)
PHONE..........................203 535-1456
John Dombrosky, *CEO*
Timothy Shannon, *Ch of Bd*
John Houston, *President*
Angela Cacace, *Vice Pres*
John Grosso, *Vice Pres*
EMP: 14
SQ FT: 34,000
SALES: 7.5MM **Publicly Held**
SIC: 2834 8731 Pharmaceutical preparations; biotechnical research, commercial

(G-5235)
ASSA INC (HQ)
Also Called: Assa Abloy Inc.
110 Sargent Dr (06511-5918)
PHONE..........................203 624-5225
Thanasis Molokotos, *President*
Chris Johnson, *Sales Mgr*
Greg Buchtmann, *Manager*
◆ **EMP:** 400
SQ FT: 325,000
SALES (est): 2B
SALES (corp-wide): 9.3B **Privately Held**
WEB: www.assaabloy.com
SIC: 3429 3699 Keys, locks & related hardware; security control equipment & systems
PA: Assa Abloy Ab
  Klarabergsviadukten 90
  Stockholm 111 6
  850 648-500

New Haven - New Haven County (G-5236) — GEOGRAPHIC SECTION

(G-5236)
ASSA INC (DH)
Also Called: Assa High Security Locks
110 Sargent Dr (06511-5918)
P.O. Box 9453 (06534-0453)
PHONE.................................800 235-7482
Lance Berger, *Opers-Prdtn-Mfg*
Edmond Dorne, *Sales/Mktg Mgr*
Richard Eisen, *Director*
L Page Heslin, *Admin Sec*
▲ EMP: 4
SQ FT: 5,000
SALES: 7.5MM
SALES (corp-wide): 9.3B **Privately Held**
SIC: 3429 Locks or lock sets
HQ: Assa, Inc.
110 Sargent Dr
New Haven CT 06511
203 624-5225

(G-5237)
ATTICUS BAKERY LLC
Also Called: Chabaso Bakery
360 James St (06513-3013)
PHONE..................................203 562-9007
Charles J Negaro, *CEO*
Conor Quinn, *Sales Staff*
Colleen Carol, *Asst Mgr*
EMP: 110
SALES (est): 22.2MM **Privately Held**
WEB: www.chabaso.com
SIC: 2051 Bread, cake & related products

(G-5238)
AU NEW HAVEN LLC
30 Lenox St (06513-4419)
PHONE..................................203 468-0342
Rick Landau, *General Mgr*
Brian Lathrop, *VP Engrg*
Milton Berlinski, *Mng Member*
Stuart Press,
◆ EMP: 102
SQ FT: 65,000
SALES (est): 31.5MM **Privately Held**
WEB: www.uretek.com
SIC: 2295 Resin or plastic coated fabrics

(G-5239)
B AND G ENTERPRISE LLC (PA)
Also Called: New Haven Awning Co
178 Chapel St (06513-4209)
PHONE..................................203 562-7232
Dan Barnick, *Mng Member*
Tom Gumkowski, *Mng Member*
Blake Crmer, *Manager*
EMP: 4
SQ FT: 4,500
SALES (est): 343.2K **Privately Held**
WEB: www.nhawning.com
SIC: 2394 Awnings, fabric: made from purchased materials; canopies, fabric: made from purchased materials

(G-5240)
BARNES TECHNICAL PRODUCTS LLC
15 High St (06510-2304)
PHONE..................................203 931-8852
Aaron Frazier, *Engineer*
Russell Barnes, *Mng Member*
EMP: 7
SALES (est): 680K **Privately Held**
SIC: 3599 Machine shop, jobbing & repair

(G-5241)
BECAID LLC
Also Called: C8 Sciences
5 Science Park Ste 29 (06511-1967)
PHONE..................................203 915-6914
Ken Coleman, *Director*
Kenneth Coleman,
EMP: 8
SALES (est): 699.5K **Privately Held**
SIC: 7372 Educational computer software

(G-5242)
BENJI BILLIONAIRE
128 Carlisle St (06519-2302)
PHONE..................................203 361-7744
EMP: 1 EST: 2018
SALES (est): 42.5K **Privately Held**
SIC: 2389 Apparel & accessories

(G-5243)
BETHANY WELDING
793 Amity Rd (06524-3062)
PHONE..................................203 393-0002
Carolyn Crotia, *Principal*
EMP: 1
SALES (est): 38.8K **Privately Held**
SIC: 7692 Welding repair

(G-5244)
BEVERAGE BOSS LLC
226 Whalley Ave (06511-3206)
PHONE..................................203 865-2240
Arpan Patel, *Mng Member*
Ronak Patel,
Shailen Patel,
EMP: 2 EST: 2015
SALES (est): 31.8K **Privately Held**
SIC: 5499 7372 Beverage stores; application computer software

(G-5245)
BIOHAVEN PHARMACEUTICALS INC
215 Church St (06510-1803)
PHONE..................................203 404-0410
Robert Berman, *CEO*
Clifford Bechtold, *COO*
Kimberly Gentile, *Vice Pres*
Jim Engelhart, *CFO*
EMP: 65 EST: 2013
SALES (est): 676.3K
SALES (corp-wide): 1MM **Privately Held**
SIC: 2834 Pharmaceutical preparations
HQ: Biohaven Pharmaceutical Holding Company Ltd.
C/O Maples Corporate Services (Bvi) Limited
Road Town

(G-5246)
BIOHAVEN PHRM HOLDG CO LTD
Also Called: Biohaven Pharmaceuticals
215 Church St (06510-1803)
PHONE..................................203 404-0410
Vlad Coric, *CEO*
Declan Doogan, *Ch of Bd*
Alex Deboissiere, *Vice Pres*
Kimberly Gentile, *Vice Pres*
James Engelhart, *CFO*
EMP: 42
SQ FT: 4,240
SALES (est): 8.2MM **Privately Held**
SIC: 2834 Drugs acting on the central nervous system & sense organs

(G-5247)
BIOXCEL THERAPEUTICS INC
555 Long Wharf Dr (06511-6107)
PHONE..................................475 238-6837
Peter Mueller, *Ch of Bd*
Vimal Mehta, *President*
Richard Steinhart, *CFO*
Vincent O'Neill, *Chief Mktg Ofcr*
Frank Yocca, *Security Dir*
EMP: 15
SQ FT: 11,040
SALES (est): 864.1K
SALES (corp-wide): 3MM **Publicly Held**
SIC: 2834 Pharmaceutical preparations
PA: Bioxcel Corporation
780 E Main St
Branford CT 06405
203 433-4086

(G-5248)
BIRDTRACK PRESS
26 Mckinley Ave (06515-2732)
PHONE..................................203 389-7789
David Goodrich, *Owner*
EMP: 3 EST: 1990
SALES (est): 158.5K **Privately Held**
WEB: www.birdtrack.com
SIC: 2791 2731 Typesetting; book publishing

(G-5249)
BOLD WOOD INTERIORS LLC
138 Haven St (06513-3522)
PHONE..................................203 907-4077
Robert Bolduc, *Mng Member*
▲ EMP: 15
SQ FT: 8,500
SALES (est): 1MM **Privately Held**
WEB: www.boldwoodinteriors.com
SIC: 2521 Wood office furniture

(G-5250)
BOSTON MODEL BAKERY
Also Called: Lupi-Marchigiano Bakery
169 Washington Ave (06519-1618)
PHONE..................................203 562-9491
Peter Luppi, *President*
EMP: 20
SALES (est): 1.3MM **Privately Held**
SIC: 2051 Bread, cake & related products

(G-5251)
BROADSTRIPES LLC
129 Church St Ste 805 (06510-2005)
PHONE..................................203 350-9824
EMP: 3
SALES: 500K **Privately Held**
SIC: 3599 7371 Industrial machinery; computer software development & applications

(G-5252)
CALLE MARKET
155 Kimberly Ave (06519-2613)
PHONE..................................203 789-0632
Rafael Brito, *Owner*
EMP: 1
SALES (est): 64.1K **Privately Held**
SIC: 3421 Table & food cutlery, including butchers'

(G-5253)
CAPITAL CITIES COMMUNICATIONS
8 Elm St (06510-2006)
PHONE..................................203 784-8800
Hank Yaggi, *Principal*
EMP: 3
SALES (est): 111.8K **Privately Held**
SIC: 2711 Newspapers, publishing & printing

(G-5254)
CARESTREAM HEALTH MOLECULAR
Also Called: Carestream Molecular Imaging
4 Science Park (06511-1962)
PHONE..................................888 777-2072
Stephanie Chiang, *Principal*
Shahram Hejazi, *Principal*
Sindy Woodhams, *Principal*
Eric Ambrose, *Mfg Spvr*
Greg Holmes, *Opers Spvr*
EMP: 50
SALES (est): 1.3MM **Privately Held**
SIC: 3826 Analytical instruments

(G-5255)
CARIGENT THERAPEUTICS INC
5 Science Park Ste 10 (06511-1989)
PHONE..................................203 887-2873
Peter Fong, *Principal*
EMP: 3
SALES (est): 234.8K **Privately Held**
WEB: www.carigent.com
SIC: 2834 Pharmaceutical preparations

(G-5256)
CHIP IN A BOTTLE LLC
837 Whalley Ave Ste 1 (06515-1794)
PHONE..................................203 460-0665
Darrell Nurse, *Mng Member*
EMP: 3 EST: 2016
SQ FT: 1,400
SALES: 60K **Privately Held**
SIC: 2024 5441 2066 Ice cream & frozen desserts; confectionery; confectionery produced for direct sale on the premises; chocolate

(G-5257)
CHRISTMAS CREATIONS
395 Howard Ave (06519-2407)
PHONE..................................203 605-2464
Christina Suggs, *Principal*
EMP: 2 EST: 2011
SALES (est): 116.2K **Privately Held**
SIC: 3999 Candles

(G-5258)
COGSTATE INC (HQ)
195 Church St Ste 1004 (06510-4000)
PHONE..................................203 773-5010
Brad O Connor, *President*
Paula Van Berkum, *Receptionist*
EMP: 2
SALES: 100K **Privately Held**
SIC: 3625 Switches, electronic applications

(G-5259)
CONNECTCUT ACDEMY ARTS SCENCES
310 Prospect St (06511-2187)
P.O. Box 208211 (06520-8211)
PHONE..................................203 432-3113
Catherine Skinner, *Director*
EMP: 2
SALES: 40.1K **Privately Held**
SIC: 2731 Book publishing

(G-5260)
CONNECTICUT LAMINATING CO INC
162 James St (06513-3845)
PHONE..................................203 787-2184
Henry S Snow, *President*
Steven M Snow, *Vice Pres*
Sandra Snow, *Admin Sec*
▲ EMP: 100
SQ FT: 55,000
SALES (est): 11.3MM **Privately Held**
WEB: www.ctlaminating.com
SIC: 3089 Identification cards, plastic; laminating of plastic

(G-5261)
CONTINUITY CONTROL (PA)
59 Elm St Ste 300 (06510-2047)
PHONE..................................203 459-0155
Andy Greenawalt, *CEO*
Stephanie Wandell, *Mktg Dir*
Justin Cole, *Director*
Alexandra Ramin,
EMP: 1
SALES (est): 129.4K **Privately Held**
SIC: 7372 Prepackaged software

(G-5262)
CONTINUITY ENGINE INC
59 Elm St (06510-2047)
PHONE..................................203 907-4470
Andy Greenawalt, *CEO*
Noel May, *Mktg Dir*
EMP: 2
SALES (est): 209K **Privately Held**
SIC: 3599 Machine & other job shop work; machine shop, jobbing & repair

(G-5263)
CORBIN RUSSWIN
110 Sargent Dr (06511-5918)
PHONE..................................860 225-7411
Douglas Millikan, *Principal*
EMP: 9
SALES (est): 710.8K **Privately Held**
SIC: 3429 Keys, locks & related hardware; door locks, bolts & checks; locks or lock sets

(G-5264)
CORE SITE SERVICES LLC
470 James St Ste 7 (06513-3175)
PHONE..................................475 227-9026
Allen Page, *Principal*
Jazimine Salvodon, *Opers Staff*
EMP: 7
SALES (est): 620.3K **Privately Held**
SIC: 1794 1799 3281 Excavation work; grave excavation; curbing, paving & walkway stone

(G-5265)
COVIDIEN LP
Also Called: Surgical Devices
555 Long Wharf Dr Fl 4 (06511-6102)
PHONE..................................781 839-1722
Robert Bowdon, *Principal*
Daniel Liebrand, *Research*
Scott Riley, *Branch Mgr*
Tim Hightower, *Manager*
Luke Urtz, *Manager*
EMP: 430 **Privately Held**
SIC: 3841 Surgical & medical instruments

GEOGRAPHIC SECTION New Haven - New Haven County (G-5296)

HQ: Covidien Lp
710 Medtronic Pkwy
Minneapolis MN 55432
763 514-4000

(G-5266)
CUSTOM TEES PLUS
365 Whalley Ave (06511-3044)
PHONE...................................203 752-1071
William Gibbs, *Owner*
EMP: 25
SALES (est): 1.4MM **Privately Held**
SIC: 2759 Screen printing

(G-5267)
DOCUPRINT & IMAGING INC
Also Called: Docuprintnow
27 Whitney Ave (06510-1219)
PHONE...................................203 776-6000
Anthony Colasanto, *President*
EMP: 8 **EST:** 1972
SQ FT: 4,000
SALES (est): 1.4MM **Privately Held**
WEB: www.docuprintandimaging.com
SIC: 2752 Commercial printing, offset

(G-5268)
DOLLAR EXPRESS LLC
690 Washington Ave (06519-2014)
PHONE...................................203 495-9209
Camilo Castillano, *Principal*
EMP: 2
SALES (est): 119K **Privately Held**
SIC: 2741 Miscellaneous publishing

(G-5269)
DOW COVER COMPANY INCORPORATED
Also Called: Dcci
373 Lexington Ave (06513-4061)
PHONE...................................203 469-5394
Mark Steinhardt, *President*
Barry Konet, *Admin Sec*
▲ **EMP:** 68 **EST:** 1947
SQ FT: 38,000
SALES (est): 7.8MM **Privately Held**
WEB: www.dowcover.com
SIC: 2393 Textile bags

(G-5270)
DS SEWING INC
260 Wolcott St (06513-3834)
P.O. Box 8983 (06532-0983)
PHONE...................................203 773-1344
David Steinhard, *President*
Saul Steinhard, *Admin Sec*
EMP: 11
SQ FT: 11,000
SALES (est): 910.2K **Privately Held**
SIC: 7389 2399 Sewing contractor; lettering service; banners, made from fabric

(G-5271)
EAST ROCK BREWING COMPANY LLC
285 Nicoll St (06511-2625)
PHONE...................................203 530-3484
Tim Wilson, *Mng Member*
Christopher J Wilson,
Shaun M Wilson,
EMP: 3
SALES (est): 73.1K **Privately Held**
SIC: 2082 Beer (alcoholic beverage)

(G-5272)
EASTERN SALT COMPANY
400 Waterfront St (06512-1717)
PHONE...................................203 466-3761
Greg Baribault, *Transportation*
EMP: 2
SALES (est): 114.6K **Privately Held**
SIC: 2899 Salt

(G-5273)
EDSAN CHEMICAL COMPANY INC
150 Whittier Rd (06515-2474)
PHONE...................................203 624-3123
Susan Fewes, *President*
EMP: 110 **EST:** 1948
SQ FT: 10,000
SALES (est): 11.5MM **Privately Held**
SIC: 2842 5087 Specialty cleaning, polishes & sanitation goods; janitors' supplies

(G-5274)
ELECTRIX LLC
45 Spring St (06519-2340)
P.O. Box 9575 (06535-0575)
PHONE...................................203 776-5577
Haim Swisha, *Ch of Bd*
Daniel Swisha, *Vice Pres*
Gordon Swisha, *Vice Pres*
David Michaud, *Senior Buyer*
Armando Abrina, *Engineer*
▲ **EMP:** 54 **EST:** 1961
SQ FT: 84,000
SALES (est): 13.1MM **Privately Held**
WEB: www.electrix.com
SIC: 3648 Decorative area lighting fixtures; lighting fixtures, except electric: residential

(G-5275)
ELEVATION SELLS GROUP LLC
120 Curtis Dr (06515-2308)
PHONE...................................203 871-7172
David Murphy,
EMP: 1
SALES (est): 39.6K **Privately Held**
SIC: 3999 Manufacturing industries

(G-5276)
ELMAR FILTER CORPORATION
72 Blatchley Ave (06513-4249)
PHONE...................................203 624-1708
Julius Corniello, *President*
Benjamin Corniello, *Vice Pres*
EMP: 2
SQ FT: 15,000
SALES (est): 357.5K **Privately Held**
SIC: 3569 Filters, general line: industrial

(G-5277)
ETHER & INDUSTRIES LLC
40 Walnut St (06511-5029)
PHONE...................................475 224-0650
Erik Diggs, *Principal*
EMP: 1
SALES (est): 43.6K **Privately Held**
SIC: 3999 0781 7349 Barber & beauty shop equipment; landscape services; maid services, contract or fee basis

(G-5278)
F & L IRON WORK INC
105 Barclay St (06519-2032)
PHONE...................................203 777-0751
Lorraine Pizzola, *President*
Frank Pizzola, *Treasurer*
EMP: 5
SQ FT: 4,000
SALES (est): 789K **Privately Held**
SIC: 3446 Architectural metalwork

(G-5279)
F W WEBB COMPANY
Also Called: Johnson Contrls Authorized Dlr
650 Boulevard (06519-1810)
PHONE...................................203 865-6124
Michael Sewell, *Manager*
EMP: 10
SALES (corp-wide): 1B **Privately Held**
SIC: 3432 5074 5251 Plumbing fixture fittings & trim; plumbing fittings & supplies; hardware
PA: F. W. Webb Company
160 Middlesex Tpke
Bedford MA 01730
781 272-6600

(G-5280)
FAIR HAVEN GLASS
103 Clinton Ave (06513-3102)
PHONE...................................203 773-3040
Elizabeth Dunkle, *Owner*
EMP: 2
SALES (est): 74.3K **Privately Held**
SIC: 3229 Pressed & blown glass

(G-5281)
FAIRCLOUGH SAILMAKERS INC
620 Ella T Grasso Blvd (06519-1808)
PHONE...................................203 787-2322
Edward D Fairclough, *President*
Jud Miller, *Vice Pres*
Candice Haven, *Admin Sec*
EMP: 1
SQ FT: 7,200

SALES (est): 179.6K **Privately Held**
WEB: www.faircloughsailmakers.com
SIC: 2394 Sails: made from purchased materials

(G-5282)
FAIRFIELD MINUTEMAN
40 Sargent Dr (06511-6111)
PHONE...................................203 752-2711
Gretchen Webster, *Manager*
EMP: 2
SALES (est): 107K **Privately Held**
SIC: 2752 Commercial printing, offset

(G-5283)
FLO-TECH LLC (PA)
545 Long Wharf Dr Ste 602 (06511-5960)
PHONE...................................860 613-3333
Leo Bonetti, *CEO*
Steve Therrien, *COO*
Mike Assunto, *Vice Pres*
Scott Macgregor, *Vice Pres*
Arthur G Aery Jr, *CFO*
▲ **EMP:** 88
SALES (est): 80.3MM **Privately Held**
WEB: www.flotech.net
SIC: 5045 3577 Printers, computer; printers, computer

(G-5284)
G I PACKAGE STORE
282 Ferry St (06513-3803)
PHONE...................................203 624-4606
Michael Como, *Owner*
EMP: 2
SALES (est): 134.9K **Privately Held**
SIC: 5921 2086 Beer (packaged); hard liquor; bottled & canned soft drinks

(G-5285)
GELATO GIULIANA LLC
240 Sargent Dr Ste 9 (06511-6108)
PHONE...................................203 772-0607
Giuliana Maravalle,
EMP: 9
SALES (est): 1MM **Privately Held**
SIC: 2024 Dairy based frozen desserts

(G-5286)
GET GO IT PUBLISHING
69 Rock Creek Rd (06515-1207)
PHONE...................................203 772-9877
Gabrielle Salters, *Principal*
EMP: 1 **EST:** 2017
SALES (est): 37.5K **Privately Held**
SIC: 2741 Miscellaneous publishing

(G-5287)
GOODCOPY PRINTING CENTER INC
Also Called: Goodcopy Printing & Graphics
110 Hamilton St (06511-5813)
P.O. Box 8088 (06530-0088)
PHONE...................................203 624-0194
Louis Goldberg, *President*
Edith Goldberg, *Vice Pres*
Corey Greco, *Prdtn Mgr*
Dave Signore, *Prdtn Mgr*
Arleen Claudio-Gore, *Sales Staff*
EMP: 20
SQ FT: 10,000
SALES (est): 5MM **Privately Held**
WEB: www.goodcopy.com
SIC: 2752 Commercial printing, offset

(G-5288)
GRACIES KITCHENS INC
211 Food Terminal Plz (06511-5911)
PHONE...................................203 773-0795
Ralph Parillo, *President*
EMP: 10
SQ FT: 30,000
SALES: 1MM **Privately Held**
SIC: 5148 2099 5149 Fruits, fresh; vegetables, fresh; vegetables, peeled for the trade; sauces

(G-5289)
GRAND FISH MARKET LLC
353 Grand Ave (06513-3732)
PHONE...................................203 691-8904
Jose Cuapio, *Owner*
EMP: 1 **EST:** 2015

SALES (est): 74.1K **Privately Held**
SIC: 5421 2086 5148 Fish markets; carbonated beverages, nonalcoholic: bottled & canned; fresh fruits & vegetables

(G-5290)
GREENLEAF BFUELS NEW HAVEN LLC
100 Waterfront St (06512-1713)
PHONE...................................203 672-9028
Mark McCall, *Mng Member*
Augustus G Kellogg, *Manager*
EMP: 10
SALES (est): 3MM **Privately Held**
SIC: 2869 Industrial organic chemicals

(G-5291)
GREY WALL SOFTWARE LLC
Also Called: Veoci.com
195 Church St Fl 14 (06510-2009)
PHONE...................................203 782-5944
Drew Mazurek, *Partner*
Ken Moon, *Project Mgr*
Tamas Simon, *Engineer*
Vincent Jessel, *Accounts Exec*
Sukh Greywal, *Mng Member*
EMP: 15 **EST:** 2011
SQ FT: 5,600
SALES (est): 1.8MM **Privately Held**
SIC: 7372 Application computer software

(G-5292)
H KREVIT AND COMPANY INC
73 Welton St (06511-1523)
PHONE...................................203 772-3350
Thomas Ross, *President*
Donald Dechello, *Vice Pres*
Gary Gitlitz, *Sales Staff*
Roland R Guerin, *Sales Staff*
Carolyn Dechello, *Admin Sec*
EMP: 44
SQ FT: 45,000
SALES (est): 26.1MM **Privately Held**
WEB: www.hkrevit.com
SIC: 2869 2819 3589 Industrial organic chemicals; industrial inorganic chemicals; water treatment equipment, industrial

(G-5293)
HARTY PRESS INC
Also Called: Harty Integrated Solutions
25 James St (06513-4218)
P.O. Box 324 (06513-0324)
PHONE...................................203 562-5112
George Platt, *President*
Bill Nims, *Vice Pres*
Kevin Platt, *Vice Pres*
Angela Berger, *Project Mgr*
Michael Platt, *Treasurer*
EMP: 86 **EST:** 1957
SQ FT: 68,000
SALES (est): 25.1MM **Privately Held**
WEB: www.hartynet.com
SIC: 2752 Commercial printing, offset

(G-5294)
HARVARD BUSINESS SCHOOL PUBG
1050 State St Apt 202 (06511-2764)
PHONE...................................203 318-1234
EMP: 1 **EST:** 2017
SALES (est): 37.5K **Privately Held**
SIC: 2741 Miscellaneous publishing

(G-5295)
HEART HEALTH INC
1440 Whalley Ave (06515-1144)
PHONE...................................800 692-7753
Michael Kron, *CEO*
EMP: 1
SQ FT: 300
SALES: 400K **Privately Held**
SIC: 3845 Cardiographs

(G-5296)
HISPANIC COMMUNICATIONS LLC
Also Called: La Voz Hispana De Connecticut
51 Elm St (06510-2049)
PHONE...................................203 624-8007
Jeff Pipeling, *Accounts Exec*
Abelardo King, *Manager*
Norma R Reyes,
EMP: 8
SQ FT: 2,000

New Haven - New Haven County (G-5297)

SALES (est): 568.3K **Privately Held**
WEB: http://www.lavozhispanact.com
SIC: **2711** Newspapers: publishing only, not printed on site

(G-5297)
HPS INDUSTRIES LLC
33 Long Hill Ter (06515-1821)
PHONE.....................................203 915-5627
Harley P Saresky, *Principal*
EMP: 2 **EST:** 2008
SALES (est): 93.3K **Privately Held**
SIC: 3999 Manufacturing industries

(G-5298)
HUMMEL BROS INC
180 Sargent Dr (06511-5919)
PHONE.....................................203 787-4113
William F Hummel, *President*
Kurt Hummel, *Corp Secy*
Robert W Hummel Jr, *Vice Pres*
Mary Ellen Hummel, *CFO*
EMP: 70 **EST:** 1933
SQ FT: 42,000
SALES (est): 11.7MM **Privately Held**
WEB: http://www.hummelbros.com
SIC: 2099 2013 Food preparations; sausages from purchased meat

(G-5299)
IDEAL PRINTING CO INC
228 Food Terminal Plz (06511-5910)
P.O. Box 8488 (06531-0488)
PHONE.....................................203 777-7626
Jim Cohane, *President*
Rocco Candela, *Treasurer*
EMP: 7 **EST:** 1920
SQ FT: 7,920
SALES (est): 1.1MM **Privately Held**
SIC: 2759 2752 Letterpress printing; screen printing; commercial printing, off-set

(G-5300)
IMPRIMI FOTOS YA LLC
66 Lyon St (06511-4927)
PHONE.....................................860 628-1787
Bruce Seymour,
EMP: 1
SALES (est): 190K **Privately Held**
SIC: 7372 7389 Application computer software;

(G-5301)
INNOVATICX LLC
50 Fitch St (06515-1366)
PHONE.....................................203 836-3501
Daniel Szender,
Chen Ho Yin,
EMP: 2
SALES (est): 56.5K **Privately Held**
SIC: 7372 Application computer software

(G-5302)
INTERPACE DIAGNOSTICS CORP
2 Church St S Ste B-05b (06519-1717)
PHONE.....................................855 776-6419
Stephen J Sullivan, *Ch of Bd*
EMP: 2
SALES (est): 104.2K **Privately Held**
SIC: 3829 Medical diagnostic systems, nuclear

(G-5303)
JOHNSON GOODYER II INC
Also Called: Johnson-Goodyear
199 Terminal Ln (06519-1817)
PHONE.....................................203 777-3424
Kristopher J Kelly, *President*
Eugene Kelly, *Admin Sec*
EMP: 12
SQ FT: 3,500
SALES: 2MM **Privately Held**
WEB: http://www.johnson-goodyer.com
SIC: 3822 Temperature controls, automatic

(G-5304)
JOSHUA LLC (PA)
Also Called: Unicast Development Co.
90 Hamilton St (06515-5920)
PHONE.....................................203 624-0080
Chris Syvertsen, *General Mgr*
Christopher Syvertsen,
Tanya Cunningham,
Joshua H Meshiach,
Hs Paraclete,
EMP: 35
SQ FT: 8,600
SALES (est): 4.3MM **Privately Held**
WEB: http://www.unicastdev.com
SIC: 3542 2819 3297 3624 Machine tools, metal forming type; catalysts, chemical; nonclay refractories; carbon & graphite products

(G-5305)
JOURNAL REGISTER EAST
100 Gando Dr (06513-1049)
PHONE.....................................203 401-4004
EMP: 2
SALES (est): 62.9K **Privately Held**
SIC: 2711 Newspapers-Publishing/Printing

(G-5306)
K H CORNELL INTERNATIONAL INC
59 Amity Rd (06515-1407)
PHONE.....................................203 392-3660
K H Maeng, *President*
Emil Brown, *Manager*
EMP: 4
SQ FT: 1,500
SALES: 700K **Privately Held**
WEB: http://www.cornellkh.com
SIC: 3442 Metal doors, sash & trim

(G-5307)
KAUFMAN ENTERPRISES INC
Also Called: Yale Surgical Company
627 Chapel St 629 (06511-6992)
PHONE.....................................203 777-2396
Marie Kaufman, *President*
Edward Kaufman, *Treasurer*
EMP: 12 **EST:** 1899
SQ FT: 2,800
SALES (est): 1.6MM **Privately Held**
WEB: http://www.yalesurgical.com
SIC: 5999 3842 3149 3143 Orthopedic & prosthesis applications; orthopedic appliances; braces, orthopedic; orthopedic shoes, children's; orthopedic shoes, men's; orthopedic shoes, women's

(G-5308)
KENNETH M CHAMPLIN & ASSOC INC
85 Willow St Ste 6 (06511-2696)
PHONE.....................................203 562-8400
Kenneth Champlin, *President*
Kathryn Champlin, *Vice Pres*
EMP: 15
SQ FT: 6,000
SALES: 600K **Privately Held**
WEB: http://www.kmca.com
SIC: 8712 3299 Architectural engineering; architectural sculptures: gypsum, clay, papier mache, etc.

(G-5309)
KEYES ON KITES TATTOO GALLERY
869 Whalley Ave Fl 1 (06515-1728)
PHONE.....................................203 387-5397
Eric C Mikita, *Owner*
EMP: 1
SALES (est): 71K **Privately Held**
SIC: 3944 Kites

(G-5310)
KNB DESIGN LLC
91 Shelton Ave (06511-1811)
PHONE.....................................203 777-6661
Nir Bongart, *Principal*
EMP: 3
SALES (est): 359.8K **Privately Held**
SIC: 2434 Vanities, bathroom: wood

(G-5311)
KOLLTAN PHARMACEUTICALS INC (HQ)
300 George St Ste 530 (06511-6624)
PHONE.....................................203 773-3000
Gerald McMahon, *President*
Theresa M Lavallee, *Vice Pres*
Jane Henderson, *CFO*
Ronald A Peck, *Chief Mktg Ofcr*
Rich Gedrich, *Director*
EMP: 25
SALES (est): 1.9MM
SALES (corp-wide): 9.5MM **Publicly Held**
SIC: 2834 Pharmaceutical preparations
PA: Celldex Therapeutics, Inc.
53 Frontage Rd Ste 220
Hampton NJ 08827
908 200-7500

(G-5312)
KUEHNE NEW HAVEN LLC
71 Welton St (06511)
PHONE.....................................203 508-6703
William Paulin,
EMP: 23
SALES: 10MM **Privately Held**
SIC: 2812 2899 Chlorine, compressed or liquefied; sodium chloride, refined

(G-5313)
LA CAYEYANA DONIS BAKERY
188 Lamberton St (06519-2517)
PHONE.....................................203 789-8030
Martha Rodriguez, *Owner*
EMP: 1
SALES (est): 100.8K **Privately Held**
SIC: 2051 Bread, cake & related products

(G-5314)
LAFARGE NORTH AMERICA INC
410 Waterfront St (06512-1717)
PHONE.....................................203 468-6068
Gerald Muscad, *Manager*
EMP: 3
SALES (corp-wide): 27.6B **Privately Held**
WEB: http://www.lafargenorthamerica.com
SIC: 3241 5032 Cement, hydraulic; cement
HQ: Lafarge North America Inc.
8700 W Bryn Mawr Ave
Chicago IL 60631
773 372-1000

(G-5315)
LAMBERTI PACKING COMPANY
207 Food Terminal Plz # 207 (06511-5911)
PHONE.....................................203 562-0436
Joseph Kelley, *President*
Jean Lamberti, *Admin Sec*
EMP: 8
SALES (est): 932.1K **Privately Held**
SIC: 2013 Sausages from purchased meat

(G-5316)
LATINO MULTISERVICE LLC
552 Ferry St (06513-3053)
PHONE.....................................203 691-9715
David Banegas, *Owner*
EMP: 2
SALES (est): 137.5K **Privately Held**
SIC: 3663 Mobile communication equipment

(G-5317)
LAYDON INDUSTRIES LLC (PA)
51 Longhini Ln (06519-1820)
PHONE.....................................203 562-7283
Jeffrey E Laydon,
Kristy Leydon,
EMP: 51
SALES (est): 17.7MM **Privately Held**
WEB: http://www.laydonindustries.com
SIC: 1611 3271 1795 4213 Highway signs & guardrails; paving blocks, concrete; demolition, buildings & other structures; automobiles, transport & delivery; prefabricated structures

(G-5318)
LIBERATO ITALIAN ICES INC
139 Wooster St Ste 141 (06511-5709)
PHONE.....................................203 772-0381
Joann Dell'amura, *President*
Dolores Dell'amura, *Treasurer*
Leona Delcore, *Admin Sec*
EMP: 1
SQ FT: 3,000
SALES (est): 132.2K **Privately Held**
SIC: 2024 Ices, flavored (frozen dessert)

(G-5319)
LISA LEE CREATIONS INC
10 Selden St (06525-2218)
PHONE.....................................203 479-4462
EMP: 3 **EST:** 2010
SALES (est): 150K **Privately Held**
SIC: 3399 Mfg Primary Metal Products

(G-5320)
LONGHINI LLC
41 Longhini Ln (06519-1820)
PHONE.....................................212 219-1230
Richard Longhini Jr, *President*
David Kemp, *Mng Member*
EMP: 22
SQ FT: 7,500
SALES (est): 834.2K
SALES (corp-wide): 22.3MM **Privately Held**
SIC: 2013 Sausages & other prepared meats
PA: 3 Little Pigs, Llc
4223 1st Ave Fl 2
Brooklyn NY 11232
212 219-1230

(G-5321)
LOUIS RODRIGUZ
Also Called: Sofrito Ponce
145 Adeline St (06519-2037)
PHONE.....................................203 777-6937
Louie Rodriguz, *Owner*
EMP: 3
SALES (est): 244.7K **Privately Held**
SIC: 2032 Spanish foods: packaged in cans, jars, etc.

(G-5322)
LUCKEY LLC
184 Chapel St (06513)
PHONE.....................................203 285-3819
Nancy Bradley,
Dana M Peterson,
EMP: 10 **EST:** 2008
SALES (est): 1.2MM **Privately Held**
SIC: 3299 3446 2431 Architectural sculptures: gypsum, clay, papier mache, etc.; architectural metalwork; millwork

(G-5323)
LUPIS INC
169 Washington Ave (06519-1618)
PHONE.....................................203 562-9491
Peter P Lupi, *President*
Ellen Lupi, *Admin Sec*
EMP: 25 **EST:** 1935
SQ FT: 10,000
SALES (est): 3.1MM **Privately Held**
WEB: http://www.lupis.com
SIC: 2051 5461 Bread, all types (white, wheat, rye, etc): fresh or frozen; rolls, bread type: fresh or frozen; bakeries

(G-5324)
MAGER & GOUGELMAN INC
200 Orchard St Ste 305 (06511-5365)
PHONE.....................................203 773-1753
Henry Gougelman, *Manager*
EMP: 2
SALES (corp-wide): 855.4K **Privately Held**
WEB: http://www.artificial-eyes.com
SIC: 3851 Intraocular lenses
PA: Mager & Gougelman Inc
345 E 37th St Rm 316
New York NY 10016
212 661-3939

(G-5325)
MARINUS PHARMACEUTICALS INC
8 Mansion St (06512-3947)
PHONE.....................................484 801-4670
EMP: 1
SALES (corp-wide): 2.7MM **Publicly Held**
SIC: 2834 Pharmaceutical preparations
PA: Marinus Pharmaceuticals, Inc.
100 W Matsonford Rd # 304
Radnor PA 19087
267 440-4200

(G-5326)
MARYANN D LANGDON
Also Called: Able To Cane
178 E Rock Rd (06511-1326)
PHONE.....................................203 562-7161
Maryann D Langdon, *Principal*
EMP: 1
SALES (est): 71.3K **Privately Held**
SIC: 3471 Anodizing (plating) of metals or formed products

GEOGRAPHIC SECTION
New Haven - New Haven County (G-5357)

(G-5327)
MCVAC ENVIRONMENTAL SVCS INC
481 Grand Ave (06513-3800)
PHONE.....................203 497-1960
Serge Demers, *President*
Joseph Barraco, *CFO*
Charles Demers, *Admin Sec*
Florence Demers, *Admin Sec*
EMP: 44
SQ FT: 15,000
SALES (est): 13.3MM **Privately Held**
WEB: www.mcvacenvironmental.com
SIC: 4959 3561 1711 Environmental cleanup services; pumps & pumping equipment; heating & air conditioning contractors

(G-5328)
MECHA NOODLE BAR
201 Crown St (06510-2701)
PHONE.....................203 691-9671
Tony Pham, *President*
EMP: 5
SALES (est): 110.5K **Privately Held**
SIC: 2098 Noodles (e.g. egg, plain & water), dry

(G-5329)
MELINTA SUBSIDIARY CORP (HQ)
300 George St Ste 301 (06511-6663)
PHONE.....................203 624-5606
Eugene Sun, *CEO*
Mary T Szela, *Ch of Bd*
John Temperato, *President*
Lyn Baranowski, *Senior VP*
Peter Diroma, *Vice Pres*
EMP: 40
SQ FT: 27,000
SALES (est): 10.8MM
SALES (corp-wide): 96.4MM **Publicly Held**
WEB: www.rib-x.com
SIC: 2834 Pharmaceutical preparations
PA: Melinta Therapeutics, Inc.
  300 George St Ste 301
  New Haven CT 06511
  908 617-1309

(G-5330)
MELINTA THERAPEUTICS INC (PA)
300 George St Ste 301 (06511-6663)
PHONE.....................908 617-1309
Jennifer Sanfilippo, *CEO*
David Gill, *Ch of Bd*
EMP: 3 EST: 2008
SQ FT: 32,182
SALES: 96.4MM **Publicly Held**
SIC: 2834 Pharmaceutical preparations

(G-5331)
MILLER REBAR LLC
157 Church St Fl 19 (06510-2100)
PHONE.....................203 717-6645
Ivory Brewer,
EMP: 2
SALES (est): 538K **Privately Held**
SIC: 5051 3496 Reinforcement mesh, wire; concrete reinforcing bars; concrete reinforcing mesh & wire

(G-5332)
MILLERWALK PUBLISHING LLC
221 W Rock Ave (06515-2222)
PHONE.....................203 397-8926
Jon S Miller, *Principal*
EMP: 2
SALES (est): 123.9K **Privately Held**
SIC: 2741 Miscellaneous publishing

(G-5333)
MINIT PRINT INC
27 Whitney Ave (06510-1219)
PHONE.....................203 776-6000
Antonio Colasanto, *Principal*
EMP: 2
SALES (est): 285.6K **Privately Held**
SIC: 2752 Commercial printing, offset

(G-5334)
MLJ PUBLISHING RECORD CO LLC
385 Peck St (06513-2921)
PHONE.....................203 752-9021
Moses Johnson, *Principal*
EMP: 2
SALES (est): 110K **Privately Held**
SIC: 2741 Miscellaneous publishing

(G-5335)
MLK BUSINESS FORMS INC
25 James St (06513-4218)
P.O. Box 383 (06513-0383)
PHONE.....................203 624-6304
Gene Booth, *President*
Fred Levesh, *Vice Pres*
Craig Levesh, *Admin Sec*
EMP: 13
SQ FT: 12,500
SALES (est): 1.8MM **Privately Held**
SIC: 2759 2761 Business forms: printing; manifold business forms

(G-5336)
MONGILLO PRESS
16 Alfred St (06512-3927)
PHONE.....................203 467-1371
Kathryn Gyuina, *Owner*
EMP: 2 **Privately Held**
SIC: 2741 Art copy: publishing & printing

(G-5337)
MT CALVARY HOLY CHURCH
392 Legion Ave (06519-5522)
P.O. Box 7694 (06519-0694)
PHONE.....................203 785-1253
Daniel Bland, *Pastor*
EMP: 1
SALES (est): 120K **Privately Held**
SIC: 8661 7372 Miscellaneous denomination church; application computer software

(G-5338)
N KARPEL STUDIO LLC
Also Called: Karpel N Studio
87 Willow St Bldg A (06511-2627)
PHONE.....................203 782-9108
Nancy Karpel,
EMP: 1
SQ FT: 360
SALES (est): 100.5K **Privately Held**
SIC: 7631 3911 Jewelry repair services; jewelry, precious metal

(G-5339)
NAFFA INC
Also Called: Real Estate Valuation Magazine
315 Whitney Ave Ste 8 (06511-3715)
PHONE.....................203 562-3159
Henry S Harrison, *Principal*
Julie Harrison, *Admin Sec*
EMP: 2
SQ FT: 1,000
SALES (est): 216.6K **Privately Held**
WEB: www.revmag.com
SIC: 2721 6531 Magazines: publishing only, not printed on site; appraiser, real estate

(G-5340)
NETZ NEW HAVEN NORTON
66 Norton St (06511-4248)
PHONE.....................203 507-2108
Haven Norton, *Executive*
EMP: 2
SALES (est): 151.7K **Privately Held**
SIC: 3534 Elevators & equipment

(G-5341)
NEW AMRCAN POLITICAL PRESS INC
100 York St Apt 8o (06511-5613)
PHONE.....................860 747-2037
Charlotte Goldstein, *Principal*
EMP: 2
SALES (est): 130.1K **Privately Held**
SIC: 2741 Miscellaneous publishing

(G-5342)
NEW ENGLAND DERMATOLOGICAL
333 Cedar St (06510-3206)
PHONE.....................203 432-0092
Tania Phillips, *Principal*
EMP: 3 EST: 2017
SALES: 243.3K **Privately Held**
SIC: 2834 Dermatologicals

(G-5343)
NEW HAVEN CHLOR-ALKALI LLC
Also Called: H.krevit
73 Welton St (06511-1523)
PHONE.....................203 772-3350
Nalluru C Murthy, *Mng Member*
EMP: 70
SALES (est): 3.5MM **Privately Held**
SIC: 2819 Hydrofluoric acid

(G-5344)
NEW HAVEN GL & MIRROR CO LLC
Also Called: New Haven Glass and Mirror
40 Edgemere Rd (06512-1827)
PHONE.....................203 469-2440
Richard McCormack,
EMP: 6 EST: 2000
SALES (est): 1.1MM **Privately Held**
SIC: 1793 5719 2431 Glass & glazing work; mirrors; louver windows, glass, wood frame

(G-5345)
NEW HAVEN NATUROPATHIC CENTER
14 Judwin Ave (06515-2313)
PHONE.....................203 387-8661
Jennifer Botwick, *Principal*
EMP: 3
SALES (est): 285.6K **Privately Held**
SIC: 2834 Medicines, capsuled or ampuled

(G-5346)
NEW HAVEN REGISTER LLC
100 Gando Dr (06513-1014)
PHONE.....................203 789-5200
Kevin F Walsh, *President*
Al Santangelo, *Editor*
Thomas Rice, *Senior VP*
John Collins, *CFO*
Betsy Lemkin, *Sales Staff*
▲ EMP: 590 EST: 1915
SQ FT: 250,000
SALES (est): 32.7MM
SALES (corp-wide): 8.3B **Privately Held**
WEB: www.journalregister.com
SIC: 2711 2752 Commercial printing & newspaper publishing combined; commercial printing, lithographic
PA: The Hearst Corporation
  300 W 57th St Fl 42
  New York NY 10019
  212 649-2000

(G-5347)
NEW HAVEN RGSTER FRESH AIR FND
100 Gando Dr (06513-1049)
PHONE.....................800 925-2509
EMP: 3
SALES: 31.1K **Privately Held**
SIC: 2752 Commercial printing, lithographic

(G-5348)
NEW HAVEN SHEET METAL CO
42 Foxon St (06513-2320)
PHONE.....................203 468-0341
EMP: 6 EST: 1975
SQ FT: 5,000
SALES (est): 360K **Privately Held**
SIC: 3443 Mfg Fabricated Plate Work

(G-5349)
NEW WAVE SURGICAL CORP
555 Long Wharf Dr Fl 2 (06511-6102)
PHONE.....................954 796-4126
Andrew Widmark, *Ch of Bd*
R Alexander Gomez, *President*
Matt Sokany, *Vice Pres*
Michael Lpez, *Admin Sec*
▲ EMP: 45
SQ FT: 2,700
SALES (est): 11.3MM **Privately Held**
SIC: 3841 Surgical & medical instruments

(G-5350)
NIKLYN CORP
90 River St Ste A (06513-4382)
P.O. Box 268, Durham (06422-0268)
PHONE.....................860 440-6244
Tamara Defonzo, *CEO*
EMP: 1
SALES (est): 280.3K **Privately Held**
SIC: 3444 Sheet metalwork

(G-5351)
NOFET LLC
227 Church St Apt 5j (06510-1825)
P.O. Box 466, Shelton (06484-0466)
PHONE.....................203 848-9064
Idit Hoter-Ishay, *Owner*
Idit Hoter-Ishay, *Owner*
Ran Assaf,
EMP: 10 EST: 2013
SALES: 3MM **Privately Held**
SIC: 3691 7389 Batteries, rechargeable;

(G-5352)
NOLAN INDUSTRIES INC
67 Mill River St (06511-3907)
PHONE.....................203 865-8160
Mark Nolan, *President*
Dan Nolan, *Treasurer*
EMP: 4
SQ FT: 8,000
SALES (est): 477K **Privately Held**
SIC: 3599 Machine shop, jobbing & repair

(G-5353)
ONE STOP JAMACIA
117 Whalley Ave (06511-3220)
PHONE.....................203 507-2315
Suaneshia Toyloy, *Owner*
EMP: 1
SALES (est): 76.4K **Privately Held**
SIC: 3421 Table & food cutlery, including butchers'

(G-5354)
ONLINE JOURNALISM PROJECT INC
Also Called: NEW HAVEN INDEPENDENT
493 Central Ave (06515-2101)
PHONE.....................203 668-5790
Paul Bass, *Principal*
EMP: 1
SALES: 415.5K **Privately Held**
SIC: 2711 Newspapers, publishing & printing

(G-5355)
ONOFRIOS ULTIMATE FOODS INC
35 Wheeler St (06512-1632)
PHONE.....................203 469-4014
John Astarita, *Buyer*
Pat Palmieri, *Plant Engr*
Richard Onofrio, *Mng Member*
EMP: 10
SALES (est): 1.6MM **Privately Held**
SIC: 2033 2035 Spaghetti & other pasta sauce: packaged in cans, jars, etc.; tomato sauce: packaged in cans, jars, etc.; barbecue sauce: packaged in cans, jars, etc.; soy sauce

(G-5356)
ORGANIZATIONAL & DIVERSITY CON
66 Colony Rd (06511-2812)
PHONE.....................203 777-3324
Norm Davis, *Principal*
EMP: 2
SALES (est): 96.9K **Privately Held**
SIC: 2741 Miscellaneous publishing

(G-5357)
OVERSEAS MINISTRIES STUDY CTR
Also Called: OMSC
490 Prospect St Ste A (06511-2139)
PHONE.....................203 624-6672
Dr Charles W Forman, *Vice Pres*
R Mac Dougall, *Treasurer*
Mich Le Sigg, *Manager*
Thomas Hastings, *Exec Dir*
Nelson Jennings, *Director*
▲ EMP: 13
SQ FT: 11,600

New Haven - New Haven County (G-5358)   **GEOGRAPHIC SECTION**

SALES: 1.2MM **Privately Held**
WEB: www.omsc.org
SIC: 8299 2721 Educational service, non-degree granting: continuing educ.; periodicals: publishing only

(G-5358)
PEMKO MANUFACTURING CO
110 Sargent Dr (06511-5918)
PHONE...............................901 365-2160
EMP: 4
SALES (est): 121.1K **Privately Held**
SIC: 3429 Manufactured hardware (general)

(G-5359)
PENFIELD COMMUNICATIONS INC
Also Called: Inner City Newspaper Group
50 Fitch St (06515-1366)
P.O. Box 9431 (06534-0431)
PHONE...............................203 387-0354
John Thomas, *President*
EMP: 2
SQ FT: 1,500
SALES: 300K **Privately Held**
WEB: www.penfieldcomm.com
SIC: 2711 Newspapers: publishing only, not printed on site

(G-5360)
PEPSICO
150 Munson St (06511-3572)
PHONE...............................203 974-8912
Magdalena Mackay, *District Mgr*
Karl Fuchs, *Technician*
EMP: 10
SALES (est): 1.4MM **Privately Held**
SIC: 2086 Carbonated soft drinks, bottled & canned

(G-5361)
PFIZER INC
1 Howe St (06511-5473)
PHONE...............................203 401-0100
Subhashis Banerjee MD, *Manager*
EMP: 9
SALES (corp-wide): 53.6B **Publicly Held**
WEB: www.pfizer.com
SIC: 2834 Pharmaceutical preparations
PA: Pfizer Inc.
    235 E 42nd St
    New York NY 10017
    212 733-2323

(G-5362)
PGXHEALTHHOLDING INC (PA)
5 Science Park (06511-1966)
PHONE...............................203 786-3400
Kevin Rakin, *President*
Gerald F Vovis, *Exec VP*
EMP: 164
SQ FT: 72,000
SALES (est): 17.1MM **Privately Held**
WEB: www.genaissance.com
SIC: 2834 Pharmaceutical preparations

(G-5363)
PHOENIX PRESS INC
15 James St (06513-4253)
P.O. Box 347 (06513-0347)
PHONE...............................203 865-5555
Brian Driscoll, *President*
Troy Jasaitis, *Accounts Exec*
EMP: 30
SQ FT: 56,000
SALES (est): 3.5MM **Privately Held**
WEB: www.phoenixpressinc.com
SIC: 2752 2791 2789 Commercial printing, offset; typesetting; bookbinding & related work

(G-5364)
PHONE BOOTH INC
14 Kimberly Ave (06519-2412)
PHONE...............................203 859-5389
EMP: 2
SALES (est): 115.1K **Privately Held**
SIC: 2541 Store fixtures, wood

(G-5365)
PINNACLE TRAINING AND PUBL
470 Quinnipiac Ave (06513-4418)
PHONE...............................203 691-6221
Ron Moulton, *Principal*
EMP: 2 **EST:** 2011

SALES (est): 99.4K **Privately Held**
SIC: 2741 Miscellaneous publishing

(G-5366)
PIONEER POWER SOLUTIONS INC
Also Called: Harmonics Limited
900 Chapel St Fl 10 (06510-2806)
PHONE...............................203 782-4348
EMP: 2 **Publicly Held**
SIC: 3677 Electronic coils, transformers & other inductors
PA: Pioneer Power Solutions, Inc.
    400 Kelby St Ste 12
    Fort Lee NJ 07024

(G-5367)
PLATT BROTHERS REALTY II LLC
25 James St (06513-4218)
PHONE...............................203 562-5112
George Platt,
EMP: 3 **EST:** 1982
SALES: 60K **Privately Held**
SIC: 2759 Commercial printing

(G-5368)
PONY PATTERNS LLC
56 W Hills Rd (06515-1230)
PHONE...............................203 535-0347
Danielle Roberts, *Principal*
EMP: 2
SALES (est): 109.8K **Privately Held**
SIC: 3543 Industrial patterns

(G-5369)
PPG INDUSTRIES INC
Also Called: PPG Painters Supply
390 East St (06511-5018)
PHONE...............................203 562-5173
Don Bradford, *Branch Mgr*
EMP: 5
SALES (corp-wide): 15.3B **Publicly Held**
SIC: 2851 Paints & allied products
PA: Ppg Industries, Inc.
    1 Ppg Pl
    Pittsburgh PA 15272
    412 434-3131

(G-5370)
PRECIPIO INC
5 Science Park (06511-1966)
PHONE...............................203 907-2205
Bill Thomas, *Branch Mgr*
EMP: 1 **Publicly Held**
SIC: 3826 Analytical instruments
PA: Precipio, Inc.
    4 Science Park Ste 3
    New Haven CT 06511

(G-5371)
PRECIPIO INC (PA)
4 Science Park Ste 3 (06511-1962)
PHONE...............................402 452-5400
Samuel D Riccitelli, *Ch of Bd*
Paul Kinnon, *President*
Danielle Salka, *Opers Staff*
Ori Karev, *Officer*
▲ **EMP:** 37
SALES: 2.8MM **Publicly Held**
WEB: www.transgenomic.com
SIC: 8734 3826 8731 Testing laboratories; analytical instruments; biological research

(G-5372)
PRO BEVERAGE SALES LLC
5 Clinton Pl (06513)
PHONE...............................203 931-1029
Paul Labanara,
EMP: 1 **EST:** 1996
SALES (est): 120K **Privately Held**
SIC: 2086 Bottled & canned soft drinks

(G-5373)
QUANTUM CIRCUITS INC
25 Science Park Ste 203 (06511-1984)
PHONE...............................203 891-6216
Martin Mengwall, *CEO*
EMP: 18
SALES (est): 94.5K **Privately Held**
SIC: 3572 Computer storage devices

(G-5374)
R & F WELDING CO
51 Ructell Rd Ste 3 (06524)
PHONE...............................203 393-2851
Frank Pegnataro, *Partner*
Randy Pegnataro, *Partner*
EMP: 2
SQ FT: 2,500
SALES: 70K **Privately Held**
SIC: 7692 1799 Welding repair; welding on site

(G-5375)
RADIALL USA INC
104 John W Murphy Dr (06513-3504)
P.O. Box 510 (06513-0510)
PHONE...............................203 776-2813
Jolanda Meinen, *General Mgr*
Gary Ramadei, *Facilities Mgr*
Claude Brocheton, *Engineer*
Janice Martin, *Human Res Mgr*
Marion Rapp, *Sales Staff*
EMP: 190
SQ FT: 65,000
SALES (corp-wide): 160.1MM **Privately Held**
SIC: 3678 Electronic connectors
PA: Radiall Usa, Inc.
    8950 S 52nd St Ste 401
    Tempe AZ 85284
    480 682-9400

(G-5376)
RADX CLOUD
123 York St Apt 11a (06511-5626)
PHONE...............................909 910-7434
Aaron Abajian, *Principal*
Ann Nguyen, *Principal*
EMP: 2
SALES (est): 83.6K **Privately Held**
SIC: 3841 Diagnostic apparatus, medical

(G-5377)
REACTEL INC
315 Peck St Fl 3 (06513-2933)
PHONE...............................203 773-0135
John Jansen, *President*
Edward Choklakian, *Chairman*
George Conner, *Admin Sec*
EMP: 3
SQ FT: 2,000
SALES (est): 463.5K **Privately Held**
SIC: 3613 Metering panels, electric

(G-5378)
RENETX BIO INC
157 Church St Fl 19 (06510-2100)
PHONE...............................203 444-6642
Erika Smith, *CEO*
EMP: 5
SALES (est): 688.8K **Privately Held**
SIC: 2834 Pharmaceutical preparations

(G-5379)
REUSABLE GREENWORKS
192 Forbes Ave (06512-1613)
PHONE...............................203 745-3695
Peter Mastriano Jr, *Principal*
EMP: 2
SALES (est): 182.6K **Privately Held**
SIC: 2421 Building & structural materials, wood

(G-5380)
RITE WAY CLEANER
Also Called: Rite-Way Cleaners & Tailors
192 Dixwell Ave Ste 1 (06513-3470)
PHONE...............................203 789-9561
Elizabeth Hayes, *Owner*
Edward McCall, *Co-Owner*
EMP: 2
SALES: 150K **Privately Held**
SIC: 3582 7212 Drycleaning equipment & machinery, commercial; garment pressing & cleaners' agents

(G-5381)
RIVERA MARINA
Also Called: Amazing Strawberries
1290 Townsend Ave Apt 2 (06513-4502)
PHONE...............................917 676-4100
Marina Rivera, *Owner*
EMP: 1
SALES (est): 39.5K **Privately Held**
SIC: 2043 Rye: prepared as cereal breakfast food

(G-5382)
ROCKWOOD MANUFACTURING CO
100 Sargent Dr (06511-5918)
PHONE...............................800 582-2424
EMP: 2
SALES (est): 62.5K **Privately Held**
SIC: 3999 Manufacturing industries

(G-5383)
SAFETY TEK INC
28 Rockview Ter (06511-1656)
PHONE...............................203 785-1808
Robert D Friedman, *Principal*
Noah Ottenstein, *Research*
EMP: 3
SALES (est): 133.4K **Privately Held**
SIC: 3272 Concrete products

(G-5384)
SAGE MAGAZINE
205 Prospect St (06511-2106)
PHONE...............................347 452-3752
Jason Schwartz, *President*
EMP: 2
SALES (est): 76.1K **Privately Held**
SIC: 2721 Periodicals

(G-5385)
SAINT JOSEPHS WOOD PDTS LLC
80 Middletown Ave (06513-2101)
PHONE...............................203 787-5746
Andrew Anastasia Sr,
Barbara Anastasia,
EMP: 4
SALES (est): 315K **Privately Held**
SIC: 2499 Engraved wood products

(G-5386)
SALSA FRESCA NEW HAVEN
51 Broadway (06511-3411)
PHONE...............................301 675-6226
EMP: 2
SALES (est): 82.7K **Privately Held**
SIC: 2099 Dips, except cheese & sour cream based

(G-5387)
SAME DAY DUMPSTERS LLC
225 Quinnipiac Ave (06513-4574)
PHONE...............................203 676-1219
Fabricio Freitas, *Principal*
EMP: 3 **EST:** 2014
SALES (est): 159.5K **Privately Held**
SIC: 3443 Dumpsters, garbage

(G-5388)
SAMMI SLEEPING SYSTEMS LLC
5 Science Park (06511-1966)
PHONE...............................203 684-3131
Carlton Chen, *Mng Member*
Vivian Jiang, *Mng Member*
Allen Weng, *Mng Member*
EMP: 3
SALES (est): 91.1K **Privately Held**
SIC: 2392 5719 Cushions & pillows; bedding (sheets, blankets, spreads & pillows)

(G-5389)
SARGENT MANUFACTURING COMPANY
Also Called: Assa Abloy USA
100 Sargent Dr (06511-5943)
P.O. Box 9725 (06536-0915)
PHONE...............................203 562-2151
Thanasis Molokotos, *CEO*
David M Ambrosini, *Treasurer*
Jon Hulse, *Manager*
Jeffrey Mereschuk, *Admin Sec*
◆ **EMP:** 227
SQ FT: 344,000
SALES (est): 175.8MM
SALES (corp-wide): 9.3B **Privately Held**
SIC: 3429 Locks or lock sets; builders' hardware
HQ: Assa, Inc.
    110 Sargent Dr
    New Haven CT 06511
    203 624-5225

▲ = Import ▼ = Export
◆ = Import/Export

GEOGRAPHIC SECTION — New Haven - New Haven County (G-5421)

(G-5390)
SEC ELECTRICAL INC
30 Gando Dr (06513-1049)
PHONE...................203 562-5811
Robert C Davis, *President*
EMP: 17
SQ FT: 12,000
SALES (est): 4.6MM **Privately Held**
WEB: www.secelectricalinc.com
SIC: 5063 7694 Motors, electric; transformers, electric; generators; motor controls, starters & relays: electric; rewinding stators; motor repair services

(G-5391)
SECOND WIND MEDIA LIMITED
Also Called: Business New Haven
315 Front St (06513-3200)
PHONE...................203 781-3480
Michael Bingham, *President*
EMP: 10
SQ FT: 1,200
SALES (est): 912.8K **Privately Held**
WEB: www.conntact.com
SIC: 2711 Newspapers: publishing only, not printed on site

(G-5392)
SENSOR SWITCH INC (DH)
265 Church St Fl 15 (06510-7003)
PHONE...................203 265-2842
Vernon J Nagel, *President*
Brian Platner, *President*
Richard K Reece, *Exec VP*
Beverly Platner, *Vice Pres*
C Dan Smith, *Vice Pres*
EMP: 29
SQ FT: 36,000
SALES (est): 13.8MM
SALES (corp-wide): 3.6B **Publicly Held**
WEB: www.sensorswitch.com
SIC: 3812 3648 Infrared object detection equipment; lighting equipment

(G-5393)
SEPDX
291 Humphrey St Unit 1 (06511-3998)
PHONE...................803 479-6332
Melissa Davis, *Principal*
EMP: 1
SALES (est): 32.7K **Privately Held**
SIC: 7372 Application computer software

(G-5394)
SEPSISDX
291 Humphrey St Unit 1 (06511-3998)
PHONE...................856 359-5309
Melissa Davis, *Principal*
Ankur Kapadia, *Principal*
David Kaufman, *Principal*
Prashant Krishnakumar, *Principal*
Baichang Tan, *Associate*
EMP: 1
SALES (est): 32.7K **Privately Held**
SIC: 7372 Application computer software

(G-5395)
SIN FRNTRAS HSPNIC NEWSPPR LLC
266 Grand Ave (06513-3723)
PHONE...................203 691-5986
Alberto Bustos, *Principal*
EMP: 2
SALES (est): 67.3K **Privately Held**
SIC: 2711 Newspapers

(G-5396)
SMG WOODWORKING
425 W Rock Ave (06515-1775)
PHONE...................203 804-1029
EMP: 1
SALES (est): 54.1K **Privately Held**
SIC: 2431 Millwork

(G-5397)
SMM NEW ENGLAND CORPORATION
808 Washington Ave (06519-1825)
PHONE...................203 777-7445
Brian More, *Manager*
EMP: 12 **Privately Held**
SIC: 5051 3341 Metals service centers & offices; secondary nonferrous metals

HQ: Smm New England Corporation
234 Universal Dr
North Haven CT 06473
203 777-2591

(G-5398)
SOFT TISSUE REGENERATION INC
470 James St Ste 14 (06513-3175)
PHONE...................973 879-6367
Joseph Reilly, *President*
EMP: 2
SALES (est): 205.5K **Privately Held**
SIC: 3841 Surgical & medical instruments

(G-5399)
SOMETHING SWEET INC (PA)
724 Grand Ave (06511-5006)
P.O. Box 8238 (06530-0238)
PHONE...................203 603-9766
Greg Menke, *CEO*
Joseph Montesano, *Principal*
Brian Murray, *COO*
Mark Cohen, *CFO*
EMP: 30
SQ FT: 35,000
SALES (est): 17.2MM **Privately Held**
SIC: 2053 Cakes, bakery: frozen

(G-5400)
SOTO HOLDINGS INC
300 East St (06511-5801)
PHONE...................203 781-8020
John Soto, *President*
Azizul Quaderi, *Purch Agent*
Selvan Candron, *Manager*
Tim Evans, *Manager*
Adrienne Montano, *Admin Sec*
EMP: 43 EST: 1970
SQ FT: 44,000
SALES (est): 11.6MM **Privately Held**
WEB: www.space-craft.com
SIC: 3724 Aircraft engines & engine parts

(G-5401)
SOUTHERN NENG TELECOM CORP (HQ)
Also Called: AT&T
2 Science Park (06511-1963)
PHONE...................203 771-5200
William Blase, *President*
Michelle Macauda, *Vice Pres*
Donald McGregor, *CFO*
Joseph O'Brien, *Manager*
Buddy Robinson,
EMP: 300
SQ FT: 100,000
SALES (est): 2.2B
SALES (corp-wide): 170.7B **Publicly Held**
SIC: 4813 4812 5065 6159 Local & long distance telephone communications; local telephone communications; cellular telephone services; paging services; telephone equipment; machinery & equipment finance leasing; directories, telephone: publishing & printing; electronic mail
PA: At&T Inc.
208 S Akard St
Dallas TX 75202
210 821-4105

(G-5402)
STUART HARDWOOD CORP
Also Called: Stuart Xlan
32 Old Amity Rd (06524-3418)
PHONE...................203 376-0036
Stuart Paley, *President*
Diego Fernandez, *Admin Sec*
EMP: 6
SQ FT: 14,000
SALES (est): 900K **Privately Held**
SIC: 2421 Lumber: rough, sawed or planed

(G-5403)
SUNDAY PAPER
19 Colony Rd (06511-2811)
PHONE...................203 624-2520
Gretchen W Pritchard, *Owner*
EMP: 1
SALES (est): 90K **Privately Held**
SIC: 2731 Pamphlets: publishing only, not printed on site

(G-5404)
SUPERCOOL METALS LLC
5 Science Park Ste 2 (06511-1989)
PHONE...................203 823-9032
Evgenia Tekarsaaya, *Mng Member*
Evgenia Pekarskaya, *CTO*
Miriam Schroers,
EMP: 3
SALES (est): 214.5K **Privately Held**
SIC: 8731 3449 Commercial physical research; miscellaneous metalwork

(G-5405)
SUPERTYPE INC
1275 Chapel St Apt 15 (06511-4574)
PHONE...................216 816-8119
James Lorber Haynes, *Director*
EMP: 2
SALES (est): 98.5K **Privately Held**
SIC: 2791 Typesetting

(G-5406)
SURACI CORP
Also Called: Suraci Paint & Powder Coating
90 River St Ste 2 (06513-4382)
PHONE...................203 624-1345
Bruno F Suraci, *CEO*
Bruno Suraci Jr, *Founder*
EMP: 60
SALES (est): 6.7MM **Privately Held**
SIC: 3444 Sheet metalwork

(G-5407)
SURACI METAL FINISHING LLC
90 River St Ste 2 (06513-4382)
PHONE...................203 624-1345
Bruno F Suraci Jr, *CEO*
Marc Suraci, *COO*
EMP: 24
SQ FT: 26,000
SALES (est): 4MM **Privately Held**
WEB: www.suracicorp.com
SIC: 3471 Finishing, metals or formed products

(G-5408)
SWISS TACTICS INDUSTRIES LLC
157 Church St Fl 19 (06510-2100)
PHONE...................203 974-3427
Jose Dominguez,
EMP: 1
SALES (est): 55.1K **Privately Held**
SIC: 3999 Manufacturing industries

(G-5409)
SYMMETRY PRESS LLC
17 Pine St (06513-3237)
PHONE...................203 988-2329
Ken Schwarz, *Principal*
EMP: 1
SALES (est): 38.9K **Privately Held**
SIC: 2741 Miscellaneous publishing

(G-5410)
TASTY KALE LLC
65 Mckinley Ave (06515-2733)
PHONE...................203 560-9451
Laurence Brownstein,
Thomas Brophy,
EMP: 2
SQ FT: 300
SALES (est): 276.3K **Privately Held**
SIC: 3556 Dehydrating equipment, food processing

(G-5411)
TECHNICAL BRIEF
222 York St (06511-8925)
P.O. Box 208244 (06520-8244)
PHONE...................203 432-8188
EMP: 1 EST: 2010
SALES (est): 56K **Privately Held**
SIC: 2741 Misc Publishing

(G-5412)
TECHNOLUTIONS INC
234 Church St Fl 15 (06510-1800)
PHONE...................203 404-4835
Alexander Grant Clark, *CEO*
EMP: 35
SALES (est): 286.8K **Privately Held**
WEB: www.technolutions.com
SIC: 7372 Prepackaged software

(G-5413)
TELL ME PRESS LLC
98 Mansfield St (06511-3514)
PHONE...................203 562-4215
Lisa Clyde Nielsen, *Principal*
EMP: 2
SALES (est): 110.1K **Privately Held**
SIC: 2741 Miscellaneous publishing

(G-5414)
TFAC LLC
27 Whitney Ave (06510-1219)
PHONE...................203 776-6000
Anthony Colasanto, *Principal*
EMP: 2
SALES (est): 114.4K **Privately Held**
SIC: 2752 Commercial printing, lithographic

(G-5415)
TIPPING PT RESOURCES GROUP LLC
100 Waterfront St (06512-1713)
P.O. Box 8532 (06531-0532)
PHONE...................800 603-8902
Alfred Kovalik,
EMP: 5
SALES (est): 66K **Privately Held**
SIC: 4953 3532 Refuse systems; sedimentation machinery, mineral

(G-5416)
TOTAL INDUSTRIES LLC
81 Howard Ave (06519-2810)
PHONE...................203 624-0426
Gina D'Errico, *Principal*
EMP: 1
SALES (est): 59.8K **Privately Held**
SIC: 3999 Manufacturing industries

(G-5417)
TOTO LLC
27 Whitney Ave (06510-1219)
PHONE...................203 776-6000
Antonio Colasanto, *Mng Member*
EMP: 10
SALES: 400K **Privately Held**
SIC: 2752 Commercial printing, lithographic

(G-5418)
TRACK180 LLC
900 Chapel St Fl 10 (06510-2806)
P.O. Box 574, Old Saybrook (06475-0574)
PHONE...................203 605-3540
Drue Hontz, *CEO*
Smith Erik R, *Manager*
EMP: 6
SALES (est): 373.3K **Privately Held**
SIC: 2711 Newspapers

(G-5419)
TRACY S PRODUCTS
Also Called: Tracy's Products
300 Whalley Ave Ste 2 (06511-3142)
PHONE...................203 787-2013
Gussie O'Steele, *Mng Member*
EMP: 1
SALES (est): 108.6K **Privately Held**
SIC: 3999 5087 Hair & hair-based products; beauty parlor equipment & supplies

(G-5420)
TRANE INC
Also Called: Trane Supply
178 Wallace St (06511-5032)
PHONE...................860 437-6208
John Rosenboom, *Branch Mgr*
EMP: 100 **Privately Held**
SIC: 3585 Refrigeration & heating equipment
HQ: Trane Inc.
1 Centennial Ave Ste 101
Piscataway NJ 08854
732 652-7100

(G-5421)
TRELLEBORG CTD SYSTEMS US INC
Also Called: Uretek
30 Lenox St (06513-4419)
PHONE...................203 468-0342
Paolo Astarita, *Vice Pres*
Patrik Romberg, *Vice Pres*
Kurt Rutt, *Safety Mgr*

Steven Clow, *Mfg Staff*
Brian Lathrop, *VP Engrg*
EMP: 180
SALES (corp-wide): 3.7B **Privately Held**
SIC: 2295 Resin or plastic coated fabrics
HQ: Trelleborg Coated Systems Us, Inc.
715 Railroad Ave
Rutherfordton NC 28139
828 286-9126

(G-5422)
TREVI THERAPEUTICS INC
195 Church St Fl 14 (06510-2009)
PHONE..................................203 304-2499
David Meeker, *Ch of Bd*
Jennifer Good, *President*
Christopher Seiter, *CFO*
Yann Mazabraud, *Ch Credit Ofcr*
Thomas Sciascia, *Chief Mktg Ofcr*
EMP: 16
SQ FT: 5,600
SALES (est): 3.2MM **Privately Held**
SIC: 2834 Pharmaceutical preparations

(G-5423)
TRINITY MOBILE NETWORKS INC
770 Chapel St Ste 2 (06510-3101)
PHONE..................................301 332-6401
Tyler Reynolds, *CEO*
Stephen Hall, *Chief Engr*
EMP: 4
SALES (est): 204.7K **Privately Held**
SIC: 7372 Prepackaged software

(G-5424)
TYCO PRINTING & COPYING
262 Elm St (06511-4768)
PHONE..................................203 562-2679
Elanor Iannuzzi, *Vice Pres*
Vin Morrotti, *Accounts Mgr*
Dan Bellucci, *Manager*
EMP: 2
SALES (est): 216.8K **Privately Held**
SIC: 2759 5734 7334 Commercial printing; printers & plotters: computers; photocopying & duplicating services

(G-5425)
UNITED STATES SURGICAL CORP (HQ)
Also Called: U.s Surgical
555 Long Wharf Dr Fl 4 (06511-6102)
PHONE..................................203 845-1000
John W Kapples, *President*
Gregory Andrulonis, *Vice Pres*
▲ **EMP:** 1000
SALES (est): 160.9MM **Privately Held**
SIC: 3841 3845 3842 Surgical instruments & apparatus; surgical stapling devices; trocars; electromedical apparatus; ultrasonic scanning devices, medical; surgical appliances & supplies

(G-5426)
VESPOLI USA INC
385 Clinton Ave (06513-4812)
PHONE..................................203 773-0311
Michael Vespoli, *President*
Nancy P Vespoli, *Principal*
Walter Torres, *Opers Staff*
Jeff Border, *Sales Staff*
John Monaghan, *Manager*
◆ **EMP:** 45
SQ FT: 32,000
SALES (est): 8.1MM **Privately Held**
WEB: www.vespoli.com
SIC: 3732 5551 Boats, fiberglass: building & repairing; sails & equipment

(G-5427)
VILLANO J SIGN COMPANY LLC
414 East St (06511-5018)
PHONE..................................203 624-7550
Joseph Villano, *Owner*
Joseph P Villano, *Owner*
Phil Corso, *Principal*
Karyn Villano, *Office Mgr*
EMP: 6 **EST:** 1968
SQ FT: 5,000

SALES (est): 564.8K **Privately Held**
SIC: 7389 3993 7336 Sign painting & lettering shop; electric signs; letters for signs, metal; signs, not made in custom sign painting shops; graphic arts & related design

(G-5428)
VIOLA AUDIO LABORATORIES INC
446a Blake St Ste 220 (06515)
PHONE..................................203 772-0435
Paul Jayson, *President*
EMP: 9
SQ FT: 5,000
SALES (est): 1.5MM **Privately Held**
WEB: www.violalabs.com
SIC: 3651 Home entertainment equipment, electronic

(G-5429)
VISIONAGE
131 Cottage St (06511-2438)
PHONE..................................203 787-0037
Mark Potter, *Owner*
EMP: 2
SALES (est): 78.4K **Privately Held**
SIC: 3269 Pottery products

(G-5430)
WELLINKS INC
770 Chapel St Ste 2d (06510-3101)
PHONE..................................650 704-0714
Ellen Su, *CEO*
EMP: 3
SQ FT: 1,200
SALES (est): 261.9K **Privately Held**
SIC: 3842 Orthopedic appliances

(G-5431)
WHOLE G FOOD INTL DISTRS LLC
105 Hamilton St (06511-5828)
PHONE..................................203 848-2136
Andrea Corazzini, *Principal*
EMP: 2
SALES (est): 165.9K **Privately Held**
SIC: 2099 Food preparations

(G-5432)
WHOLE GERMAN BREADS LLC
85 Willow St (06511-2668)
PHONE..................................203 507-0663
Andrea Corazzini, *Mng Member*
EMP: 9
SALES (est): 1MM **Privately Held**
SIC: 2051 Bread, cake & related products

(G-5433)
WILES CHARLES PRESTON M D
291 Whitney Ave Ste 303 (06511-3764)
PHONE..................................203 562-7550
Charles P D, *Principal*
EMP: 2
SALES (est): 88.3K **Privately Held**
SIC: 3613 Switchgear & switchboard apparatus

(G-5434)
WINDSOR WOODWORKS
53 Chamberlain St (06512-1604)
PHONE..................................203 386-6975
EMP: 2 **EST:** 2009
SALES (est): 140K **Privately Held**
SIC: 2431 Mfg Millwork

(G-5435)
WING STC REVISION PROJECT
Also Called: Wings
120 High St Rm 607 (06511-8944)
PHONE..................................203 432-1753
John Morrison, *Director*
Milton Devane, *Director*
Stephen Parks, *Director*
Cathya W Stephenson, *Director*
Robert Wing, *Director*
EMP: 2
SALES (est): 141.7K **Privately Held**
SIC: 2752 Commercial printing, lithographic

(G-5436)
XIJET CORP
8 Lunar Dr Ste 3 (06525-2352)
PHONE..................................203 397-2800

Scott Snietka, *President*
Philip Black, *Vice Pres*
EMP: 10
SALES (est): 1.7MM **Privately Held**
WEB: www.xijet.com
SIC: 3577 7389 Printers, computer; printers' services: folding, collating

(G-5437)
XTREME DESIGNS LLC
192 Forbes Ave (06512-1613)
PHONE..................................203 773-9303
Treavor John Schatz,
EMP: 8
SALES (est): 855.9K **Privately Held**
SIC: 7336 2759 Graphic arts & related design; screen printing

(G-5438)
YAKKA LLC
24 Dixwell Ave (06511-3402)
PHONE..................................617 877-7553
Andrew Williams,
EMP: 2
SALES (est): 222K **Privately Held**
SIC: 5091 3949 7389 Fitness equipment & supplies; gymnasium equipment; dumbbells & other weightlifting equipment; gymnasium equipment;

(G-5439)
YALE ALUMNI PUBLICATIONS INC
149 York St Fl 2 (06511-8923)
PHONE..................................203 432-0645
J Weili Cheng, *Chairman*
EMP: 9
SALES (est): 1.9MM **Privately Held**
WEB: www.yalealumnimagazine.com
SIC: 2721 Magazines: publishing only, not printed on site

(G-5440)
YALE DAILY NEWS PUBLISHING CO
212 York St (06511-8925)
P.O. Box 209007 (06520-9007)
PHONE..................................203 432-2400
Kimberly Schramberg, *President*
EMP: 4
SQ FT: 5,000
SALES (est): 366.3K **Privately Held**
WEB: www.yaledailynews.com
SIC: 2711 2731 Newspapers, publishing & printing; book music: publishing only, not printed on site

(G-5441)
YALE LAW JOURNAL CO INC
Also Called: Yale Law Journal, The
127 Wall St Rm 452 (06511-8918)
P.O. Box 208215 (06520-8215)
PHONE..................................203 432-1666
Susan McDonald, *Treasurer*
EMP: 2
SALES: 1.9MM **Privately Held**
SIC: 2721 2711 Periodicals; newspapers, publishing & printing

(G-5442)
YALE PRINTING AND PUBG SVCS
344 Winchester Ave (06511-1918)
PHONE..................................203 432-6560
EMP: 2
SALES (est): 62.6K **Privately Held**
SIC: 2741 Miscellaneous publishing

(G-5443)
YALE UNIVERSITY (PA)
105 Wall St (06511-8917)
PHONE..................................203 432-2550
Richard C Levin, *President*
Timothy Nottoli, *Managing Dir*
Peter Salovey, *Principal*
James Vivian, *Editor*
John Geibel, *Vice Chairman*
▲ **EMP:** 50
SALES: 4.1B **Privately Held**
WEB: www.yale.edu
SIC: 8221 2731 2721 2741 University; book publishing; magazines: publishing & printing; catalogs: publishing & printing

(G-5444)
YALE UNIVERSITY
Also Called: Cira
135 College St Ste 200 (06510-2483)
PHONE..................................203 764-4333
Leif Mitchell, *Principal*
EMP: 55
SALES (corp-wide): 4.1B **Privately Held**
SIC: 8221 2731 2721 2741 University; book publishing; magazines: publishing & printing; catalogs: publishing & printing
PA: Yale University
105 Wall St
New Haven CT 06511
203 432-2550

(G-5445)
YALE UNIVERSITY
Also Called: Printing & Graphic Services
149 York St (06511-8923)
P.O. Box 208227 (06520-8227)
PHONE..................................203 432-2880
Joseph Maynard, *Branch Mgr*
Melissa Fournier, *Manager*
Peter Yacono, *Supervisor*
EMP: 7
SALES (corp-wide): 4.1B **Privately Held**
WEB: www.yale.edu
SIC: 2711 8221 Newspapers, publishing & printing; university
PA: Yale University
105 Wall St
New Haven CT 06511
203 432-2550

(G-5446)
YALE UNIVERSITY
Also Called: Computing and Media Center
333 Cedar St Ie90shm (06510-3206)
PHONE..................................203 737-1244
Susan Grajek, *Director*
EMP: 20
SALES (corp-wide): 4.1B **Privately Held**
WEB: www.yale.edu
SIC: 8221 2759 University; commercial printing
PA: Yale University
105 Wall St
New Haven CT 06511
203 432-2550

(G-5447)
YALE UNIVERSITY
Also Called: Kline Chemistry Laboratory
225 Prospect St Rm 1 (06511-8499)
PHONE..................................203 432-3916
Kerri Sancomb, *Production*
Joanne Bentley, *Manager*
EMP: 4
SALES (corp-wide): 4.1B **Privately Held**
WEB: www.yale.edu
SIC: 2869 8221 Laboratory chemicals, organic; university
PA: Yale University
105 Wall St
New Haven CT 06511
203 432-2550

(G-5448)
YALE UNIVERSITY
Also Called: Yale Daily News
202 York St (06511-4804)
P.O. Box 209007 (06520-9007)
PHONE..................................203 432-2424
Lewis York, *Branch Mgr*
EMP: 5
SALES (corp-wide): 4.1B **Privately Held**
WEB: www.yale.edu
SIC: 2621 8221 Catalog, magazine & newsprint papers; university
PA: Yale University
105 Wall St
New Haven CT 06511
203 432-2550

(G-5449)
YALE UNIVERSITY
Also Called: Marsh Botanical Garden
285 Mansfield St (06511)
PHONE..................................203 432-6320
Eric Warson, *Manager*
EMP: 4
SALES (corp-wide): 4.1B **Privately Held**
WEB: www.yale.edu
SIC: 2833 8221 Medicinals & botanicals; university

▲ = Import ▼ = Export
◆ = Import/Export

GEOGRAPHIC SECTION

New London - New London County (G-5476)

PA: Yale University
105 Wall St
New Haven CT 06511
203 432-2550

(G-5450)
YALE UNIVERSITY
Also Called: Yale Review, The
314 Prospect St (06511-2187)
P.O. Box 208243 (06520-8243)
PHONE..................203 432-0499
JD McClatchy, *Editor*
Susan Laity, *Editor*
Joel Silverman, *Dean*
Dana Jehan, *Opers Staff*
Jennifer Gargano, *Financial Analy*
EMP: 5
SALES (corp-wide): 4.1B **Privately Held**
WEB: www.yale.edu
SIC: 8221 2721 University; trade journals: publishing only, not printed on site
PA: Yale University
105 Wall St
New Haven CT 06511
203 432-2550

(G-5451)
YALE UNIVERSITY
Also Called: Yale Herald
305 Crown St (06511-6612)
PHONE..................203 432-7494
Alexis Peter, *Branch Mgr*
EMP: 5
SALES (corp-wide): 4.1B **Privately Held**
WEB: www.yale.edu
SIC: 2621 8221 Catalog, magazine & newsprint papers; university
PA: Yale University
105 Wall St
New Haven CT 06511
203 432-2550

(G-5452)
YALE-NEW HAVEN HLTH SVCS CORP
789 Howard Ave (06519-1300)
PHONE..................203 688-2100
Joe Zaccagnino, *President*
EMP: 100
SALES (corp-wide): 449.8MM **Privately Held**
WEB: www.yalenewhavenhealth.com
SIC: 8741 8011 2752 Hospital management; clinic, operated by physicians; commercial printing, lithographic
PA: Yale New Haven Health Services Corporation
789 Howard Ave
New Haven CT 06519
888 461-0106

(G-5453)
ZENELI PIZZERIA
138 Wooster St (06511-5710)
PHONE..................203 745-4194
EMP: 2
SALES (est): 62.3K **Privately Held**
SIC: 2041 Pizza dough, prepared

(G-5454)
ZENITH-OMNI HEARING CENTER (PA)
Also Called: Zenith Hearing Aid
111 Park St Ste 1k (06511-5472)
PHONE..................203 624-9857
David Mc Mahon, *President*
Richard Mc Mahon, *Owner*
Susan Mc Mahon, *Vice Pres*
EMP: 3
SQ FT: 1,000
SALES (est): 437.1K **Privately Held**
SIC: 3842 5999 7629 Hearing aids; hearing aids; hearing aid repair

New London
New London County

(G-5455)
A CAPELA DO SANTO ANTONIO INC
35 Henry St (06320-3311)
PHONE..................860 447-3329
Roberta Vincent, *Director*
Brenda Delgado, *Director*
Alfred Gonsalves, *Director*
EMP: 3
SALES (est): 130K **Privately Held**
SIC: 3961 Ornaments, costume, except precious metal & gems

(G-5456)
ASCON PRODUCTS CO
Also Called: Ascon Products Co, The
2 Ferry St (06320-6418)
PHONE..................860 439-1305
Susan Wronowski, *President*
Richard McMurray, *Vice Pres*
John Wronowski, *Admin Sec*
EMP: 4 **EST:** 1940
SALES (est): 494.2K **Privately Held**
SIC: 5023 3069 Floor coverings; flooring, rubber; tile or sheet

(G-5457)
BAYARD INC (DH)
Also Called: Creative Communications
1 Montauk Ave Ste 3 (06320-4967)
PHONE..................860 437-3012
Richard Johnson, *President*
Didier Remiot, *Director*
Guylene Dumais, *Admin Sec*
Lise Marie C Zanghetti, *Admin Sec*
EMP: 40
SALES (est): 18.1MM
SALES (corp-wide): 40K **Privately Held**
WEB: www.bayard-inc.com
SIC: 2759 Publication printing
HQ: Bayard Presse
18 Rue Barbes
Montrouge 92120
174 316-060

(G-5458)
BIOCLINICA INC
234 Bank St (06320-6070)
PHONE..................860 701-0082
Michaelene Hussey, *Manager*
Jesse Mazarelli, *Manager*
EMP: 6
SALES (corp-wide): 86.8MM **Privately Held**
SIC: 3821 Clinical laboratory instruments, except medical & dental
HQ: Bioclinica, Inc.
211 Carnegie Ctr
Princeton NJ 08540

(G-5459)
BRYAN DOUGHTY
Also Called: Bvd Press
975 Ocean Ave (06320-2910)
PHONE..................860 536-2185
Bryan Doughty, *Owner*
EMP: 1
SALES: 30K **Privately Held**
WEB: www.bvdpress.com
SIC: 2731 Book music: publishing & printing

(G-5460)
BUON APPETITO FROM ITALY LLC
15 Shaw St (06320-4939)
PHONE..................860 437-3668
Petrit Marku,
Sander Marku,
EMP: 8 **EST:** 2010
SALES (est): 381.6K **Privately Held**
SIC: 1389 Construction, repair & dismantling services

(G-5461)
CARWILD CORPORATION (PA)
3 State Pier Rd (06320-5817)
PHONE..................860 442-4914
Joel S Wildstein, *Ch of Bd*
Rebecca Wildstein, *Treasurer*
Heather Schryver, *Controller*
Thomas McDonald, *Director*
◆ **EMP:** 32
SQ FT: 40,000
SALES: 20MM **Privately Held**
WEB: www.carwild.com
SIC: 3842 3841 Surgical appliances & supplies; surgical & medical instruments

(G-5462)
CIMARRON MUSIC PRESS LLC
975 Ocean Ave (06320-2910)
PHONE..................860 859-3705
Lewis J Buckley, *Manager*
EMP: 2
SALES (est): 127.1K **Privately Held**
WEB: www.cimarronmusic.com
SIC: 2741 Miscellaneous publishing

(G-5463)
CLARK MANNER MARGUARITE
Also Called: Leon's Upholstery
601 Broad St (06320-2544)
PHONE..................860 444-7679
EMP: 7
SALES: 350K **Privately Held**
SIC: 2512 Mfg Upholstered Household Furniture

(G-5464)
CLEAN TECH INDUSTRIES LLC
16 Elm St (06320-5022)
PHONE..................860 447-1434
Tamara Beach, *Manager*
EMP: 2
SALES (est): 111.1K **Privately Held**
SIC: 3999 Manufacturing industries

(G-5465)
COPY CATS INC
458 Williams St Ste 1 (06320-5860)
PHONE..................860 442-8424
Marion Brick, *President*
Alan Terris, *Vice Pres*
Forrest Sklar, *CFO*
Jennifer Gualt, *Info Tech Dir*
Amy Conley, *Graphic Designe*
EMP: 17
SQ FT: 6,000
SALES (est): 3.7MM **Privately Held**
WEB: www.copycatsnl.com
SIC: 7334 2759 2672 Photocopying & duplicating services; commercial printing; coated & laminated paper

(G-5466)
DAY PUBLISHING COMPANY (HQ)
Also Called: Day, The
47 Eugene Oneill Dr (06320-6351)
P.O. Box 1231 (06320-1231)
PHONE..................860 701-4200
Gary Farrugia, *President*
Melissa Johnson, *Editor*
Bob Tousignant, *CFO*
Rebecca Angelastro, *Accounts Exec*
Lisa Brown, *Sales Staff*
EMP: 352
SQ FT: 20,000
SALES (est): 33.4MM **Privately Held**
WEB: www.marianireck.com
SIC: 2711 Commercial printing & newspaper publishing combined; newspapers, publishing & printing
PA: The Day Trust
47 Eugene Oneill Dr
New London CT 06320
860 442-2200

(G-5467)
DAY TRUST (PA)
47 Eugene Oneill Dr (06320-6351)
P.O. Box 1231 (06320-1231)
PHONE..................860 442-2200
Gary Farrugia, *President*
Richard Willis, *CFO*
EMP: 2
SQ FT: 12,000
SALES (est): 33.4MM **Privately Held**
SIC: 2711 Newspapers, publishing & printing

(G-5468)
DISTRIBUTORS OF STANDARD TILE
531 Broad St (06320-2517)
PHONE..................860 439-0627
Rebecca Pope, *Principal*
EMP: 1
SALES (corp-wide): 17.8MM **Privately**
SIC: 5211 5032 3253 1743 Lumber products; ceramic wall & floor tile; ceramic wall & floor tile; tile installation, ceramic

PA: Standard Tile Distributors Of New Haven, Inc.
105 Hamilton St
New Haven CT 06511
203 777-3637

(G-5469)
DJS CAMPUS KITCHEN LLC
405 Williams St (06320-5830)
PHONE..................860 439-1572
Daniel Mason, *Owner*
EMP: 2
SALES (est): 214.3K **Privately Held**
SIC: 2599 Food wagons, restaurant

(G-5470)
EPATH LEARNING INC
300 State St Ste 400 (06320-6115)
PHONE..................860 444-7900
Dudley Molina, *President*
Steve Morse, *Vice Pres*
Carol Wojtkun, *Vice Pres*
Donna Lord, *Production*
Erik Foberg, *VP Engrg*
EMP: 32
SQ FT: 3,457
SALES (est): 4MM **Privately Held**
WEB: www.epathcampus.com
SIC: 7372 Business oriented computer software

(G-5471)
FARRAR SAILS INC
6 Union St Ste 6 # 6 (06320-6107)
PHONE..................860 447-0382
Kevin Farrar, *President*
William Reed, *Corp Secy*
John Lucey, *Vice Pres*
EMP: 4
SQ FT: 12,000
SALES (est): 300K **Privately Held**
WEB: www.farrarsails.com
SIC: 2394 7699 Sails: made from purchased materials; nautical repair services

(G-5472)
FIRST AID BANDAGE CO INC
Also Called: Fabco Wrap
3 State Pier Rd (06320-5817)
PHONE..................860 443-8499
Joel S Wildstein, *President*
EMP: 15 **EST:** 1932
SQ FT: 4,000
SALES (est): 1.6MM **Privately Held**
WEB: www.fabco.net
SIC: 3842 5122 Adhesive tape & plasters, medicated or non-medicated; drugs, proprietaries & sundries

(G-5473)
HALTECH MANUFACTURING SVCS LLC
100 Blinman St (06320-5646)
PHONE..................860 625-0189
Michael J Hallisey, *Owner*
EMP: 1
SQ FT: 20,000
SALES: 100K **Privately Held**
SIC: 3491 Industrial valves

(G-5474)
JEWISH LEADER NEWSPAPER
28 Channing St (06320-5756)
PHONE..................860 442-7395
Jerome Fischer, *Exec Dir*
EMP: 3 **EST:** 2016
SALES (est): 74K **Privately Held**
SIC: 2711 Newspapers

(G-5475)
JOSHUA FRIEDMAN & CO LLC
49 Jay St (06320-5919)
PHONE..................860 439-1637
Joshua Friedman,
Elizabeth Friedman,
EMP: 10
SQ FT: 11,500
SALES: 800K **Privately Held**
SIC: 7641 2431 Furniture repair & maintenance; furniture refinishing; millwork

(G-5476)
LIFEPHARMS INC
143 Shaw St (06320-4930)
PHONE..................860 447-8583
E Edward Mena, *Partner*

(PA)=Parent Co (HQ)=Headquarters (DH)=Div Headquarters
◆ = New Business established in last 2 years

New London - New London County

(G-5477) (continued)
EMP: 2
SALES (est): 222K Privately Held
WEB: www.lifepharms.com
SIC: 2836 Biological products, except diagnostic

(G-5477)
LOCKHEED MARTIN CORPORATION
18 4th St (06320-6419)
PHONE.................................860 447-8553
EMP: 2 Publicly Held
SIC: 3812 Search & navigation equipment
PA: Lockheed Martin Corporation
6801 Rockledge Dr
Bethesda MD 20817

(G-5478)
MI GENTE EXPRESS
130 Bank St (06320-6002)
PHONE.................................860 447-2525
Bairon Cruz, *Principal*
EMP: 2
SALES (est): 110.4K Privately Held
SIC: 2741 Miscellaneous publishing

(G-5479)
MICHAELS DAIRY INC
11 Harbor Ln (06320-4324)
PHONE.................................860 443-7617
Michael Buscetto, *President*
Philomena Buscetto, *Vice Pres*
EMP: 12
SQ FT: 1,000
SALES (est): 510K Privately Held
SIC: 5812 2024 Ice cream stands or dairy bars; ice cream & ice milk

(G-5480)
MINDSCAPE INDUSTRIES
159 Hawthorne Dr (06320-4051)
PHONE.................................860 574-9308
EMP: 1
SALES (est): 42.8K Privately Held
SIC: 3999 Manufacturing industries

(G-5481)
NEW LONDON PRINTING CO LLC
Also Called: Minuteman Press
147 State St Ste 1 (06320-6353)
PHONE.................................860 701-9171
Gail Weber,
EMP: 4
SALES (est): 501K
SALES (corp-wide): 23.4MM Privately Held
SIC: 2752 Commercial printing, lithographic
PA: Minuteman Press International, Inc.
61 Executive Blvd
Farmingdale NY 11735
631 249-1370

(G-5482)
ORTRONICS INC (DH)
125 Eugene Oneill Ave # 140 (06320-6417)
PHONE.................................860 445-3900
Mark Panico, *President*
Halsey Cook, *President*
Doug Fikse, *President*
Jerry Mix, *President*
Larry Giles, *Partner*
▲ EMP: 60
SALES (est): 108.2MM
SALES (corp-wide): 21.2MM Privately Held
WEB: www.ortronics.com
SIC: 3577 3357 Computer peripheral equipment; communication wire
HQ: Legrand Holding, Inc.
60 Woodlawn St
West Hartford CT 06110
860 233-6251

(G-5483)
QDISCOVERY LLC (HQ)
Also Called: Forensicon
125 Eugene Oneill Dr # 140 (06320-6430)
PHONE.................................860 271-7080
Robert Polus, *President*
EMP: 28 EST: 2011
SALES (est): 5.5MM Privately Held
SIC: 7372 Business oriented computer software

(G-5484)
QUALITY PRINTERS INC
141 Shaw St (06320-4930)
P.O. Box 749 (06320-0749)
PHONE.................................860 443-2800
Faye Vathauer, *President*
Brenda Vathauer, *Vice Pres*
Chad Waterman, *Info Tech Mgr*
Frank Londregan, *Admin Sec*
EMP: 9
SQ FT: 4,800
SALES (est): 1.5MM Privately Held
WEB: www.qualityprintersct.com
SIC: 2752 Commercial printing, offset

(G-5485)
QUINN AND GELLAR MARKETING LLC
Also Called: Island Design
147 State St (06320-6353)
P.O. Box 456 (06320-0456)
PHONE.................................860 444-0448
Dave Gellar, *Mng Member*
Callie Manwaring, *Executive*
EMP: 6
SQ FT: 1,000
SALES (est): 494.6K Privately Held
WEB: www.promocountry.com
SIC: 7336 7334 3993 2796 Graphic arts & related design; photocopying & duplicating services; signs & advertising specialties; platemaking services; typesetting; commercial printing

(G-5486)
RBI INC
30 Plant St (06320-4420)
PHONE.................................860 444-0534
Frasier Reid, *President*
Lee Palombo, *Manager*
EMP: 2
SALES (est): 148.3K Privately Held
SIC: 2673 Plastic bags: made from purchased materials

(G-5487)
ROOFING SOLUTIONS
45 Bank St (06320-6001)
PHONE.................................860 444-0486
Daryl Ceccarelli, *Owner*
EMP: 2
SALES (est): 172.2K Privately Held
SIC: 2952 5033 Roofing materials; roofing & siding materials

(G-5488)
SHEFFIELD PHARMACEUTICALS LLC (PA)
170 Broad St (06320-5313)
PHONE.................................860 442-4451
Jeffrey Davis, *President*
Roland Hernandez, *Exec VP*
Ana De Oliveira, *Vice Pres*
Anthony Sollima, *Vice Pres*
James Congdon, *VP Opers*
◆ EMP: 135
SQ FT: 113,618
SALES (est): 35.4MM Privately Held
WEB: www.sheffield-labs.com
SIC: 2844 5122 Toothpastes or powders, dentifrices; pharmaceuticals

(G-5489)
SIGN A RAMA
Also Called: Sign-A-Rama
365 Broad St (06320-3726)
PHONE.................................860 443-9744
Bill Shaw, *Owner*
EMP: 5
SQ FT: 2,500
SALES (est): 240K Privately Held
SIC: 3993 Signs & advertising specialties

(G-5490)
STEPHEN A BESADE
11 Konomoc St (06320-3805)
P.O. Box 771, Waterford (06385-0771)
PHONE.................................860 443-6033
Stephan A Besade, *Owner*
EMP: 1 EST: 1998
SALES (est): 53.3K Privately Held
SIC: 3423 Hand & edge tools

(G-5491)
SWEETWATER BOATWORKS LLC
18 Smith St (06320-5514)
PHONE.................................860 984-5118
Kieran M Aday Jr,
EMP: 2
SALES (est): 209.2K Privately Held
SIC: 3732 Boats, fiberglass: building & repairing

(G-5492)
T L S DESIGN & MANUFACTURING
100 Blinman St (06320-5646)
PHONE.................................860 439-1414
Thomas L Smith II, *President*
EMP: 5
SQ FT: 6,600
SALES (est): 616.7K Privately Held
SIC: 3599 8711 Custom machinery; machine tool design

(G-5493)
THAMES SHIPYARD & REPAIR CO
50 Farnsworth St (06320-4104)
P.O. Box 791 (06320-0791)
PHONE.................................860 442-5349
John P Wronowski, *President*
Richard Macmurray, *Vice Pres*
Thomas Tyreseck, *Vice Pres*
Adam C Wronowski, *Vice Pres*
EMP: 100
SQ FT: 6,000
SALES (est): 19.1MM Privately Held
SIC: 3731 Shipbuilding & repairing

(G-5494)
TIMES COMMUNITY NEWS GROUP
47 Eugene Oneill Dr (06320-6306)
PHONE.................................860 437-1150
Howard Lee, *Principal*
EMP: 3
SALES (est): 138.8K Privately Held
SIC: 2711 Newspapers, publishing & printing

(G-5495)
TRANE US INC
571 Broad St (06320-2517)
PHONE.................................860 437-6208
Chuck Mrowka, *Branch Mgr*
EMP: 62 Privately Held
SIC: 3585 Refrigeration & heating equipment
HQ: Trane U.S. Inc.
3600 Pammel Creek Rd
La Crosse WI 54601
608 787-2000

(G-5496)
WEPA SPORTS LLC
39 W High St (06320-3518)
PHONE.................................203 971-9372
Robert Ortiz, *Principal*
EMP: 1
SALES (est): 67.7K Privately Held
SIC: 3949 2531 Track & field athletic equipment; bases, baseball; pads: football, basketball, soccer, lacrosse, etc.; balls: baseball, football, basketball, etc.; picnic tables or benches, park

(G-5497)
X OVER Y SYSTEMS
35 Neptune Ave (06320-2839)
PHONE.................................860 885-0034
Gloria Woerheide, *Owner*
EMP: 2 EST: 2001
SALES (est): 135.8K Privately Held
WEB: www.newlondoncountyguide.com
SIC: 7372 Prepackaged software

(G-5498)
ZOMBIE GANG SKATEBOARDS LLC
176 State St (06320-6319)
PHONE.................................860 367-2650
EMP: 2
SALES (est): 56.9K Privately Held
SIC: 3949 Mfg Sporting/Athletic Goods

New Milford
Litchfield County

(G-5499)
27 WEST MAIN STREET LLC
27 Main St (06776-2858)
PHONE.................................860 799-6494
Robert Miller, *Principal*
EMP: 1 EST: 2016
SALES (est): 54.6K Privately Held
SIC: 3993 Signs & advertising specialties

(G-5500)
3 STORY SOFTWARE LLC
63 Bridge St (06776-3527)
PHONE.................................203 530-3224
Darren Reid, *Mng Member*
EMP: 8 EST: 2007
SALES (est): 819.7K
SALES (corp-wide): 7.7B Privately Held
SIC: 7372 Prepackaged software
PA: Hays Plc
250 Euston Road
London NW1 2
207 383-2266

(G-5501)
450 WOODWORKING LLC
11 Heacock Ln (06776-3086)
PHONE.................................860 350-0525
Guy Scarcella, *Principal*
EMP:
SALES (est): 54.1K Privately Held
SIC: 2431 Millwork

(G-5502)
71 PICKETT DISTRICT ROAD LLC
71 Pickett District Rd (06776-4412)
PHONE.................................860 350-5964
Hector Reyes, *Technology*
Antonio Capanna Jr,
EMP: 3
SALES (est): 243.1K Privately Held
SIC: 3612 3677 3679 Line voltage regulators; electronic transformers; static power supply converters for electronic applications

(G-5503)
ALEXANDER HUSSEY
Also Called: New Milford Printing
221 Danbury Rd Ste D (06776-4354)
PHONE.................................860 354-0118
Alexander Hussey, *Owner*
EMP: 3
SQ FT: 1,500
SALES (est): 393.2K Privately Held
WEB: www.newmilfordprinting.com
SIC: 7334 2759 2789 2752 Photocopying & duplicating services; commercial printing; bookbinding & related work; commercial printing, lithographic

(G-5504)
ARKETTYPE
221 Danbury Rd Ste L (06776-4354)
PHONE.................................860 350-4007
Louisa Okell, *Owner*
Andrew Okell, *Vice Pres*
EMP: 2
SALES (est): 151.7K Privately Held
WEB: www.arkett.com
SIC: 2791 Typesetting

(G-5505)
ART METAL INDUSTRIES LLC
564 Danbury Rd 1 (06776-4318)
PHONE.................................203 733-3092
Yvonne Hermina-Biebel,
EMP: 2
SALES (est): 286K Privately Held
SIC: 3446 Ornamental metalwork

(G-5506)
ART METAL INDUSTRIES AMI
564 Danbury Rd (06776-4318)
PHONE.................................860 799-5575
EMP: 1
SALES (est): 54.2K Privately Held
SIC: 3999 Manufacturing industries

New Milford - Litchfield County (G-5538)

(G-5507)
ARTS OF STONE LLC
362 Danbury Rd (06776-4316)
PHONE..................860 355-9468
Jose Lima, *Mng Member*
EMP: 5
SALES (est): 310.6K **Privately Held**
SIC: **1743** 1411 1389 Marble installation, interior; dimension stone; construction, repair & dismantling services

(G-5508)
BALL & ROLLER BEARING CO LLC
46 Old State Rd Ste 4 (06776-4330)
PHONE..................860 355-4161
David Nohe, *President*
Mike Smith, *Mktg Dir*
EMP: 10
SALES (est): 1.7MM **Privately Held**
WEB: www.bandrb.com
SIC: **3568** 3562 3312 Bearings, plain; ball & roller bearings; blast furnaces & steel mills

(G-5509)
BARRON PRINT
11 Howland Rd (06776-2905)
PHONE..................860 355-9535
Shari Barron, *Principal*
EMP: 2
SALES (est): 193.9K **Privately Held**
SIC: **2752** Commercial printing, lithographic

(G-5510)
BELLA ALPACAS
155 Squash Hollow Rd (06776-5406)
PHONE..................860 946-3076
Salvatore Apicella, *Principal*
EMP: 2
SALES (est): 145.6K **Privately Held**
SIC: **2231** Alpacas, mohair: woven

(G-5511)
BLACK DOG FUEL LLC
148 Candlewood Mtn Rd (06776-5810)
PHONE..................860 489-0655
John Homrok, *Manager*
EMP: 1
SALES (est): 73.2K **Privately Held**
SIC: **2869** Fuels

(G-5512)
BOOK AUTOMATION INC
458 Danbury Rd Ste B10 (06776-4380)
PHONE..................860 354-7900
Manrico Caglioni, *President*
Giovanna Meratti, *Admin Sec*
▲ EMP: 4 EST: 1975
SQ FT: 3,000
SALES: 1.9MM
SALES (corp-wide): 4.6MM **Privately Held**
WEB: www.bookautomation.com
SIC: **2789** 3541 Binding only: books, pamphlets, magazines, etc.; machine tools, metal cutting type
PA: Cofint Sa
    Avenue Pasteur 3
    Luxembourg 2311

(G-5513)
CALCULATOR TRAINING
94 Buckingham Rd (06776-2235)
PHONE..................860 355-8255
T Patrick Burke, *Owner*
EMP: 3
SALES (est): 100K **Privately Held**
SIC: **2731** Textbooks: publishing & printing

(G-5514)
CANDLEWOOD MACHINE PDTS LLC
46 Old State Rd Ste 6 (06776-4330)
P.O. Box 262, Brookfield (06804-0262)
PHONE..................860 350-2211
EMP: 3
SQ FT: 1,000
SALES (est): 210K **Privately Held**
SIC: **3599** Machine Shop

(G-5515)
CAREERPATH MOBILE LLC
8 Wildlife Dr (06776-5235)
P.O. Box 34 (06776-0034)
PHONE..................203 512-2379
Richard Portelance, *Principal*
EMP: 2
SALES (est): 129.4K **Privately Held**
SIC: **7372** 7389 Educational computer software;

(G-5516)
CARLSON SHEET METAL
24 Bostwick Pl (06776-3510)
PHONE..................860 354-4660
Craig R Carlson, *Principal*
EMP: 3
SALES (est): 287.3K **Privately Held**
SIC: **3444** Sheet metalwork

(G-5517)
CEDAR ACCESSORIES
5 Old Town Park Rd (06776-4212)
PHONE..................860 350-6969
Sandra Cotter, *Owner*
EMP: 1
SALES (est): 168.1K **Privately Held**
SIC: **3553** Bandsaws, woodworking

(G-5518)
CENTER MASS LLC
94 Town Farm Rd (06776-3710)
PHONE..................860 350-0239
Jack Dever, *Principal*
Anna Lukasik, *Business Mgr*
EMP: 1
SALES (est): 95K **Privately Held**
SIC: **3541** 3559 3441 3499 Machine tools, metal cutting type; automotive related machinery; fabricated structural metal; machine bases, metal

(G-5519)
CHEMESSENCE INC
180 Sunny Valley Rd # 15 (06776-3393)
PHONE..................860 355-4108
Michael Lavelle, *President*
Robert Booth, *CFO*
Robert W Booth Jr, *Treasurer*
George Whitmeyer, *Sales Staff*
EMP: 4 EST: 1964
SQ FT: 4,000
SALES (est): 470.9K **Privately Held**
WEB: www.chemessence.com
SIC: **2844** Perfumes, natural or synthetic

(G-5520)
CLEARWATER TREATMENT SYSTEMS L
446 W Meetinghouse Rd (06776-4917)
PHONE..................860 799-0303
EMP: 2
SALES (est): 150K **Privately Held**
SIC: **7389** 5999 3589 1711 Business Services Ret Misc Merchandise Mfg Svc Industry Mach Plumbing/Heat/Ac Contr

(G-5521)
COL-LAR ENTERPRISES INC (PA)
37 S End Plz (06776-4243)
PHONE..................203 798-1786
Lawrence Prockter, *President*
Collen G Prockter, *Vice Pres*
▲ EMP: 11
SQ FT: 1,000
SALES (est): 2MM **Privately Held**
SIC: **3944** Games, toys & children's vehicles

(G-5522)
COMPART NORTH AMERICA INC
30 Bridge St Ste 2 (06776-3517)
PHONE..................860 799-5612
John Lynch, *Vice Pres*
Christof Mayer, *CTO*
EMP: 11
SALES: 1.8MM
SALES (corp-wide): 18.7MM **Privately Held**
SIC: **5045** 7372 8243 Computer software; prepackaged software; business oriented computer software; software training, computer
PA: Compart Ag
    Otto-Lilienthal-Str. 38
    Boblingen 71034
    703 162-050

(G-5523)
COMPUCISION LLC
29 S End Plz (06776-4235)
PHONE..................860 355-9790
George Blass,
Eve Sturdevant,
EMP: 4
SQ FT: 3,600
SALES (est): 688.7K **Privately Held**
SIC: **3599** Machine shop, jobbing & repair

(G-5524)
CREATE A CASTLE LLC
15 Glenbrook Dr (06776-3925)
P.O. Box 433, Bridgewater (06752-0433)
PHONE..................203 648-3553
Kevin Lane, *Mng Member*
Laurie Lane,
EMP: 2
SQ FT: 1,100
SALES (est): 95K **Privately Held**
SIC: **3089** Injection molded finished plastic products

(G-5525)
CRYSTAL FAIRFIELD TECH LLC
8 S End Plz (06776-4200)
PHONE..................860 354-2111
Andrew Timmerman,
Shaoping Wang,
▼ EMP: 11
SQ FT: 6,500
SALES (est): 1.5MM **Privately Held**
WEB: www.fairfieldcrystal.com
SIC: **3679** Electronic crystals

(G-5526)
D F & B PRECISION MFG INC
180 Sunny Valley Rd Ste 3 (06776-3361)
PHONE..................860 355-5663
Domenico Franciamore, *President*
Domingo Franciamore, *Vice Pres*
EMP: 6
SQ FT: 18,000
SALES (est): 862.6K **Privately Held**
SIC: **3599** Machine shop, jobbing & repair

(G-5527)
DAVIS SAWMILL
28 Squash Hollow Rd (06776-5403)
PHONE..................860 354-6008
Robert Davis, *Owner*
EMP: 1
SALES: 100K **Privately Held**
SIC: **5211** 2421 Lumber & other building materials; sawmills & planing mills, general

(G-5528)
DYNAMIC LASERS LLC
324 Candlewood Mtn Rd (06776-5802)
PHONE..................866 731-9610
EMP: 5 EST: 2011
SALES: 2MM **Privately Held**
SIC: **3845** Mfg Electromedical Equipment

(G-5529)
EAST BRANCH ENGRG & MFG INC
57 S End Plz (06776-4244)
PHONE..................860 355-9661
Paul Guidotti, *President*
Chris Guidotti, *Principal*
Linda Guidotti, *Admin Sec*
EMP: 16
SQ FT: 1,500
SALES (est): 2.5MM **Privately Held**
WEB: www.eastbrancheng.com
SIC: **3089** Injection molding of plastics

(G-5530)
EASTERN CONECTR SPECIALTY CORP
566 Danbury Rd Ste 3 (06776-4331)
P.O. Box 1957 (06776-1957)
PHONE..................860 355-8100
Michael J Nahom, *Owner*
Maria Noham, *Vice Pres*
Michelle Noham, *Treasurer*
EMP: 6
SQ FT: 2,500
SALES (est): 1.7MM **Privately Held**
WEB: www.easternconnector.com
SIC: **5065** 5063 3548 Electronic parts; electrical apparatus & equipment; arc welders, transformer-rectifier

(G-5531)
ELEMENTAL MERCURY LLC
22 Howland Rd (06776-2906)
PHONE..................860 355-9569
EMP: 2
SALES (est): 74.4K **Privately Held**
SIC: **2819** Elements

(G-5532)
FARRELL PRCSION MTALCRAFT CORP
192 Danbury Rd (06776-4311)
PHONE..................860 355-2651
Michael Tkacs, *President*
William Farrell, *Vice Pres*
Terrance Farrell, *Treasurer*
EMP: 40
SQ FT: 17,500
SALES (est): 8.8MM **Privately Held**
SIC: **3444** 3479 7692 Sheet metal specialties, not stamped; painting of metal products; welding repair

(G-5533)
FAT CITY SCREEN PRINTERS
180 Sunny Valley Rd Ste 9 (06776-3361)
PHONE..................860 354-4650
Laura Talbot, *Managing Prtnr*
EMP: 2
SQ FT: 1,500
SALES: 200K **Privately Held**
SIC: **2396** Screen printing on fabric articles

(G-5534)
FERNELLIE LLC
5 Church St (06776-3003)
PHONE..................860 799-7739
Elizabeth Martins, *Principal*
EMP: 1
SALES (est): 47.7K **Privately Held**
SIC: **2395** Embroidery & art needlework

(G-5535)
GEORGE USATY SONS HEAT
Also Called: Honeywell Authorized Dealer
67 Bonnie Vu Ln (06776-2651)
PHONE..................860 350-2622
George Usaty, *Owner*
Jennifer Usaty, *Co-Owner*
EMP: 1
SALES (est): 143.6K **Privately Held**
SIC: **3585** Heating & air conditioning combination units

(G-5536)
GLACIER COMPUTER LLC (PA)
46 Bridge St Ste 1 (06776-3531)
PHONE..................860 355-7552
Daniel Poisson, *Vice Pres*
Mary Ross Mistretta, *Accounts Mgr*
Ronald D'Ambrosio, *Mng Member*
Brian Wallace, *Info Tech Mgr*
EMP: 4
SQ FT: 2,500
SALES (est): 2.9MM **Privately Held**
WEB: www.glaciercomputer.com
SIC: **3571** Electronic computers

(G-5537)
GLIMMER OF LIGHT
56 Danbury Rd Ste 10 (06776-3415)
PHONE..................860 605-4086
EMP: 2
SALES (est): 73.4K **Privately Held**
SIC: **3483** Ammunition, except for small arms

(G-5538)
GO GREEN INDUSTRIES LLC
23 Meredith Ln (06776-3723)
PHONE..................914 772-0026
David Robles, *Principal*
EMP: 3
SALES (est): 127.4K **Privately Held**
SIC: **3999** Manufacturing industries

New Milford - Litchfield County (G-5539)

(G-5539)
GOAT BOY SOAP
1 Murphys Way (06776-3857)
PHONE 860 350-0676
Lisa M Agee, *Owner*
EMP: 1
SALES (est): 141.1K **Privately Held**
SIC: 2841 Soap & other detergents

(G-5540)
GP INDUSTRIES LTD LLC (PA)
106 Fort Hill Rd (06776-3331)
PHONE 860 350-5400
Bhupinder Singh,
Harinder Kaur,
Rittu Singh,
EMP: 2
SQ FT: 8,000
SALES: 25K **Privately Held**
SIC: 3089 Injection molded finished plastic products; injection molding of plastics

(G-5541)
GUARDIAN ENVMTL TECH INC
208 Sawyer Hill Rd (06776-2018)
P.O. Box 2344, New Preston (06777-0344)
PHONE 860 350-2200
William Litwin, *President*
Patricia Garland, *Marketing Staff*
James McKeon, *Technical Staff*
EMP: 18
SQ FT: 800
SALES (est): 2.4MM **Privately Held**
WEB: www.guardianenvironmental.com
SIC: 3589 3564 Water filters & softeners, household type; filters, air: furnaces, air conditioning equipment, etc.

(G-5542)
GULFSTREAM AEROSPACE CORP
142 Second Hill Rd (06776-3138)
PHONE 860 210-1469
EMP: 4
SALES (corp-wide): 36.1B **Publicly Held**
SIC: 3721 4581 Aircraft; aircraft maintenance & repair services
HQ: Gulfstream Aerospace Corporation
500 Gulfstream Rd
Savannah GA 31408
912 965-3000

(G-5543)
GWILLIAM COMPANY INC
46 Old State Rd (06776-4330)
PHONE 860 354-2884
David Nohe, *President*
Margaret Nohe, *Admin Sec*
▲ EMP: 12 EST: 1929
SALES (est): 3.2MM **Privately Held**
SIC: 3562 3568 Ball bearings & parts; roller bearings & parts; power transmission equipment

(G-5544)
H & S WOODWORKS L T D
161 Merryall Rd (06776-5226)
PHONE 914 391-3926
Howard Senior, *Principal*
EMP: 4 EST: 2009
SALES (est): 502.2K **Privately Held**
SIC: 2431 Millwork

(G-5545)
IMAGES UNLIMITED
38 Old State Rd (06776-4358)
PHONE 860 350-6608
Tina Ploos, *Partner*
Jeanne Fleckenstein, *Partner*
EMP: 2
SALES: 100K **Privately Held**
WEB: www.imagesultd.com
SIC: 2396 2759 Screen printing on fabric articles; screen printing

(G-5546)
INK WELL T-SHIRTS LLC
7 Mill Ln (06776-3619)
PHONE 860 355-3065
Catherine Hanley, *Principal*
EMP: 2
SALES (est): 105.5K **Privately Held**
SIC: 2752 Commercial printing, lithographic

(G-5547)
IT HELPS LLC
54 Boxwood Ln (06776-4673)
PHONE 860 799-8321
Weimin LI, *Principal*
Xueyan Dong, *Principal*
EMP: 5 EST: 2016
SALES (est): 115.2K **Privately Held**
SIC: 7372 Business oriented computer software

(G-5548)
J & J PRINTING CO
11 Howland Rd (06776-2905)
PHONE 860 355-9535
Shari Barron, *Owner*
EMP: 2
SQ FT: 3,000
SALES (est): 254.5K **Privately Held**
SIC: 2759 Commercial printing

(G-5549)
JB MUZE ENTERPRISES
Also Called: Fat City Sports
180 Sunny Valley Rd Ste 9 (06776-3361)
PHONE 860 355-5949
Jill Weiss, *Owner*
EMP: 4
SALES (est): 321.7K **Privately Held**
SIC: 2759 Screen printing

(G-5550)
JF GRANITE & MARBLE
190 Danbury Rd (06776-4311)
PHONE 860 355-4414
Franco A Feitosa, *Owner*
EMP: 1
SALES (est): 144.1K **Privately Held**
SIC: 1799 1411 Counter top installation; granite dimension stone

(G-5551)
JNT WELDING SERVICES LLC
32 New St (06776-3008)
PHONE 860 350-3957
Tito L Arana, *Principal*
EMP: 1
SALES (est): 45.3K **Privately Held**
SIC: 7692 Welding repair

(G-5552)
JOSEPH J MCFADDEN JR
Also Called: Quality Machine
87 Danbury Rd (06776-3413)
PHONE 860 354-6794
Joseph J McFadden Jr, *Owner*
Edwin Estinal, *Manager*
EMP: 6
SQ FT: 4,500
SALES (est): 466.8K **Privately Held**
SIC: 3599 Machine shop, jobbing & repair

(G-5553)
KARAS ENGINEERING CO INC
20 Old Route 7 Plz (06776-4339)
PHONE 860 355-3153
Denny Karas, *President*
Andrea Karas, *COO*
Shane Karas, *Engineer*
Lisa Karas, *Admin Sec*
EMP: 8
SQ FT: 5,000
SALES (est): 1.3MM **Privately Held**
WEB: www.karaseng.com
SIC: 3599 Machine shop, jobbing & repair

(G-5554)
KAT ART INC
Also Called: Katart Graphics
458 Danbury Rd Ste B17 (06776-4380)
PHONE 860 350-8016
Arthur Foote, *President*
Rick Rushka, *Manager*
EMP: 4
SQ FT: 6,000
SALES (est): 470K **Privately Held**
WEB: www.aroundnewmilford.com
SIC: 7336 7371 7338 2791 Graphic arts & related design; custom computer programming services; secretarial & court reporting; typesetting

(G-5555)
KILCOURSE SPECIALTY PRODUCTS
46 Old State Rd Ste 3 (06776-4330)
PHONE 860 210-2075
David Kilcourse, *Principal*
EMP: 6
SQ FT: 6,000
SALES (est): 968K **Privately Held**
SIC: 2591 7389 Blinds vertical; interior design services

(G-5556)
KIMBERLY-CLARK CORPORATION
58 Pickett District Rd (06776-4493)
PHONE 860 210-1602
Marvin Prewitt, *Warehouse Mgr*
Tom Condon, *Engineer*
Scott Hamylak, *Engineer*
Wayne Sanders, *Manager*
Daphy Mc Kay, *Technician*
EMP: 600
SALES (corp-wide): 18.4B **Publicly Held**
WEB: www.kimberly-clark.com
SIC: 2621 2676 Sanitary tissue paper; infant & baby paper products
PA: Kimberly-Clark Corporation
351 Phelps Dr
Irving TX 75038
972 281-1200

(G-5557)
LABLITE LLC
8 S Main St (06776-3508)
P.O. Box 1206 (06776-1206)
PHONE 860 355-8817
Randy Bell, *COO*
Curtis Read, *Executive*
EMP: 10
SQ FT: 1,400
SALES (est): 953.9K **Privately Held**
WEB: www.lablite.com
SIC: 7372 Application computer software

(G-5558)
LOCAL MEDIA GROUP INC
Also Called: Greater New Milford Spectrum
45 Main St (06776-2807)
PHONE 860 354-2273
Deborah Rose, *Principal*
EMP: 4
SALES (corp-wide): 1.5B **Privately Held**
WEB: www.ottaway.com
SIC: 2711 Newspapers: publishing only, not printed on site
HQ: Local Media Group, Inc.
40 Mulberry St
Middletown NY 10940
845 341-1100

(G-5559)
LUNDGREN ERIC WOODWORKING
Also Called: Lundgren Woodworking
89 Cherniske Rd (06776-4922)
PHONE 860 350-5153
Eric Lundgren, *Owner*
EMP: 2
SALES (est): 162.5K **Privately Held**
SIC: 1799 2499 Special trade contractors; decorative wood & woodwork

(G-5560)
MARBLE & GRANITE CREATIONS LLC
469 Danbury Rd Ste 4 (06776-4334)
PHONE 860 350-1306
Tony Haddad, *Owner*
EMP: 2
SALES (est): 110K
SALES (corp-wide): 569.5K **Privately Held**
SIC: 3281 Table tops, marble
PA: Marble & Granite Creations
493 Danbury Rd
New Milford CT 06776
860 350-1306

(G-5561)
MEDINSTILL LLC
201 Housatonic Ave (06776-5540)
PHONE 860 350-1900
Florent Arnoux, *Project Mgr*
Jean-Denis Giraudet,
Daniel Py,
EMP: 1
SALES (est): 47.2K **Privately Held**
SIC: 2834 Pharmaceutical preparations

(G-5562)
MF INDUSTRIES
5 Old Town Park Rd (06776-4212)
PHONE 860 355-8188
EMP: 2
SALES (est): 83K **Privately Held**
SIC: 3999 Mfg Misc Products

(G-5563)
MODELVISION INC
566 Danbury Rd Ste 4 (06776-4331)
PHONE 860 355-3884
David Spiegel, *President*
Laura Spiegel, *Corp Secy*
EMP: 7
SQ FT: 7,500
SALES (est): 829.3K **Privately Held**
SIC: 3999 Models, general, except toy

(G-5564)
NEELTRAN INC
71 Pickett District Rd (06776-4412)
PHONE 860 350-5964
Antonio Capanna Jr, *President*
Dave Franco, *Owner*
◆ EMP: 117
SQ FT: 45,000
SALES (est): 36.2MM **Privately Held**
WEB: www.neeltran.com
SIC: 3612 3677 3679 Line voltage regulators; electronic transformers; static power supply converters for electronic applications

(G-5565)
NEELTRAN INTERNATIONAL INC
71 Pickett District Rd (06776-4412)
PHONE 860 350-5964
Antonio Capanna Sr, *President*
EMP: 2
SALES (est): 106.9K **Privately Held**
SIC: 3612 Line voltage regulators

(G-5566)
NEW ENGLAND GRAPHICS MTLS LLC (PA)
312 Danbury Rd (06776-4335)
PHONE 860 210-2180
James J Hart Jr, *Partner*
Brian R Hart, *Partner*
EMP: 15
SALES (est): 2.7MM **Privately Held**
WEB: www.nege.com
SIC: 5084 3599 Printing trades machinery, equipment & supplies; machine shop, jobbing & repair

(G-5567)
NEW ENGLAND SIGNAL LLC
10 Bridge St (06776-3502)
PHONE 860 350-3212
Chris Gardner, *Principal*
EMP: 2
SALES (est): 181.2K **Privately Held**
SIC: 3993 Signs & advertising specialties

(G-5568)
NEW MILFORD BLOCK & SUPPLY
574 Danbury Rd (06776-4341)
PHONE 860 355-1101
Jay Montfort, *President*
John Montfort, *Admin Sec*
EMP: 15
SQ FT: 25,000
SALES (est): 2.3MM **Privately Held**
SIC: 3271 5032 5211 5039 Blocks, concrete or cinder: standard; concrete & cinder block; masons' materials; concrete & cinder block; masonry materials & supplies; glass construction materials; concrete products, precast

(G-5569)
NEW MILFORD COMMISSION
Also Called: New Milfrd Water Pollutn Cntrl
123 West St (06776-3540)
P.O. Box 178 (06776-0178)
PHONE 860 354-3758

GEOGRAPHIC SECTION — New Milford - Litchfield County (G-5602)

Ken Bailey, *Superintendent*
EMP: 11
SQ FT: 3,652
SALES (est): 1.3MM **Privately Held**
SIC: 3589 Sewage & water treatment equipment

(G-5570)
NEW MILFORD FARMS INC
60 Boardman Rd (06776-5516)
PHONE..................................860 210-0250
Walter Carey, *President*
EMP: 12
SALES (est): 1.4MM
SALES (corp-wide): 14.9B **Publicly Held**
WEB: www.garick.com
SIC: 2875 Compost
HQ: Garick, Llc
  13600 Broadway Ave Ste 1
  Cleveland OH 44125
  216 581-0100

(G-5571)
NEW MILFORD FOUNDRY & MCH CO
84 West St (06776-3538)
PHONE..................................860 354-5561
Daniel J Caldwell, *President*
EMP: 8
SQ FT: 5,000
SALES (est): 706.1K **Privately Held**
SIC: 1711 7692 Plumbing contractors; heating & air conditioning contractors; welding repair

(G-5572)
NEW MILFORD PRINT WORKS INC
481 Danbury Rd Ste 3 (06776-4353)
PHONE..................................860 799-0530
Douglas R Johnson, *President*
Nancy Johnson, *Assistant*
EMP: 1
SQ FT: 1,000
SALES (est): 147.4K **Privately Held**
SIC: 2752 Commercial printing, offset

(G-5573)
NIELSEN CONSULTING INC (PA)
Also Called: Viking Automation
186 Pickett District Rd (06776-4415)
PHONE..................................914 831-1681
Christian E Nielsen, *President*
EMP: 7
SALES (est): 1MM **Privately Held**
WEB: www.vikingautomation.com
SIC: 7373 8742 3549 Systems integration services; automation & robotics consultant; assembly machines, including robotic

(G-5574)
NORTEK GEAR AND MACHINE LLC
5 Old Town Park Rd 18 (06776-4212)
PHONE..................................860 355-5541
David O'Boyle,
EMP: 1
SQ FT: 1,000
SALES (est): 165K **Privately Held**
WEB: www.northerngear.com
SIC: 3541 Gear cutting & finishing machines

(G-5575)
NUTEK AEROSPACE CORP
180 Sunny Valley Rd Ste 2 (06776-3361)
PHONE..................................860 355-3169
Joseph Di Candido, *President*
Thomas Dicandido, *General Mgr*
Eloise Di Candido, *Treasurer*
EMP: 7
SQ FT: 7,000
SALES (est): 1.2MM **Privately Held**
WEB: www.nutekaerospace.com
SIC: 3592 Valves, aircraft

(G-5576)
O & G INDUSTRIES INC
271 Danbury Rd (06776-4313)
PHONE..................................860 354-4438
Bill Eayrs, *Branch Mgr*
EMP: 53
SQ FT: 7,485
SALES (corp-wide): 538MM **Privately Held**
WEB: www.ogind.com
SIC: 2951 1542 Asphalt paving mixtures & blocks; commercial & office building, new construction
PA: O & G Industries, Inc.
  112 Wall St
  Torrington CT 06790
  860 489-9261

(G-5577)
ODYSSEY INTERACTIVE LLC
126 Aspetuck Vlg (06776-5621)
PHONE..................................860 799-6088
Joseph G Durdock, *CEO*
EMP: 1
SALES (est): 58K **Privately Held**
SIC: 2741 Newsletter publishing

(G-5578)
OLIVE NUTMEG OIL ✪
25 Main St (06776-2807)
PHONE..................................860 354-7300
EMP: 3 **EST:** 2019
SALES (est): 91.3K **Privately Held**
SIC: 2079 Olive oil

(G-5579)
PARKER MEDICAL INC
5 Old Town Park Rd # 34 (06776-4212)
PHONE..................................860 350-3446
Darlene Adam, *Office Mgr*
Tony Szklany, *Manager*
EMP: 4
SALES (corp-wide): 6.4MM **Privately Held**
SIC: 3844 X-ray apparatus & tubes
PA: Parker Medical Inc.
  137 New Milford Rd E
  Bridgewater CT 06752
  860 350-4304

(G-5580)
PATRICIA POKE
Also Called: Patricias Presents
20 Maple Ln (06776-4021)
P.O. Box 1449 (06776-1449)
PHONE..................................860 354-4193
Patricia Poke, *Owner*
EMP: 6
SALES (est): 420.9K **Privately Held**
WEB: www.patriciaspresents.com
SIC: 3111 Accessory products, leather

(G-5581)
QUALITY MACHINE INC
87 Danbury Rd (06776-3413)
PHONE..................................860 354-6794
Joseph John McFadden Jr, *Principal*
EMP: 3
SALES (est): 260.6K **Privately Held**
SIC: 3599 Machine shop, jobbing & repair

(G-5582)
R C E MACHINE WORKS
39 Old Route 7 Plz (06776-4340)
PHONE..................................860 354-6976
Lloyd Riley, *Owner*
EMP: 1
SQ FT: 1,200
SALES (est): 122.2K **Privately Held**
SIC: 3599 Machine shop, jobbing & repair

(G-5583)
RAND WHITNEY
7 Nutmeg Dr (06776-4113)
PHONE..................................860 354-6063
Elmer Burkey, *Principal*
EMP: 3 **EST:** 2009
SALES (est): 215.2K **Privately Held**
SIC: 3131 Rands

(G-5584)
REXNORD LLC
14 Crescent Ln (06776-2135)
PHONE..................................860 355-0478
EMP: 1 **Publicly Held**
SIC: 3566 Mfg Speed Changers/Drives
HQ: Rexnord Llc
  3001 W Canal St
  Milwaukee WI 53208
  414 342-3131

(G-5585)
RISSOLO PRECISION SHEET METAL
22 Palomino Dr (06776-2228)
PHONE..................................860 355-1949
Ken Rissolo, *Owner*
EMP: 2
SALES (est): 230K **Privately Held**
SIC: 3444 Sheet metalwork

(G-5586)
ROLL-OFF BEST SERVICE LLC
36 S End Plz (06776-4243)
PHONE..................................860 350-2378
Donna Klzo,
Andrew Klzo,
EMP: 2
SALES (est): 140K **Privately Held**
SIC: 3443 Dumpsters, garbage

(G-5587)
RWS MARINE RESTORATION
26 Old Route 7 Plz (06776-4339)
PHONE..................................860 350-4977
Roger Standt, *Owner*
EMP: 1
SALES (est): 59K **Privately Held**
SIC: 3732 Boat building & repairing

(G-5588)
S M CHURYK IRON WORKS INC
Also Called: Churyk, Stefan M
539 Danbury Rd (06776-4304)
PHONE..................................860 355-1777
Stefan Churyk, *President*
Wayne Churyk, *Vice Pres*
EMP: 5
SQ FT: 10,000
SALES (est): 713.2K **Privately Held**
SIC: 3446 Fire escapes, metal; stairs, staircases, stair treads: prefabricated metal; railings, bannisters, guards, etc.: made from metal pipe

(G-5589)
SEGA READY MIX INCORPORATED (PA)
519 Danbury Rd (06776-4392)
PHONE..................................860 354-3969
Roderic Oneglia, *President*
EMP: 10
SQ FT: 8,000
SALES (est): 2MM **Privately Held**
SIC: 3273 Ready-mixed concrete

(G-5590)
SETMA INC
458 Danbury Rd Ste A2 (06776-4381)
PHONE..................................409 833-9797
Joseph Duchon, *President*
Pat Crawford, *Director*
Margaret Ross, *Admin Sec*
EMP: 4 **EST:** 1975
SQ FT: 2,000
SALES (est): 300K **Privately Held**
WEB: www.setma.com
SIC: 3599 Machine shop, jobbing & repair

(G-5591)
SPEDDING CO
315 Litchfield Rd (06776-2002)
PHONE..................................860 355-4076
Cheryl Bakewell, *Partner*
EMP: 2
SALES (est): 86.7K **Privately Held**
SIC: 2452 Prefabricated wood buildings

(G-5592)
TALMADGE & VALENTINE CO INC
85 Danbury Rd (06776-3413)
PHONE..................................860 350-3534
Jeff Talmadge, *President*
Gary Valentine, *Admin Sec*
EMP: 2
SALES: 120K **Privately Held**
SIC: 2448 Pallets, wood; skids, wood

(G-5593)
TED BOCCUZZI
Also Called: Ducksworth Antq Vintage & Cstm
64 Sunny Valley Ln (06776-3321)
PHONE..................................860 354-3799
Ted Boccuzzi, *Owner*
EMP: 1
SALES (est): 50.2K **Privately Held**
SIC: 7692 Welding repair

(G-5594)
TELEMARK SYSTEMS INC
42 Squire Hill Rd (06776-5013)
PHONE..................................860 355-8001
Jim Scheef, *President*
EMP: 1
SALES: 100K **Privately Held**
WEB: www.telemarksys.com
SIC: 7372 Prepackaged software

(G-5595)
TG FLOORS
Also Called: T and G Floors
63 Heacock Crossbrook Rd (06776-3027)
PHONE..................................860 355-5660
Tim Gribbin, *Owner*
EMP: 1
SALES (est): 77.8K **Privately Held**
SIC: 2426 Flooring, hardwood

(G-5596)
TIMBERCRAFT CSTM DVTAIL DRWERS
5 Old Town Park Rd (06776-4212)
PHONE..................................800 345-4930
James McGough, *President*
EMP: 1
SALES (est): 83.7K **Privately Held**
SIC: 2434 Wood kitchen cabinets

(G-5597)
TIMBERCRAFT LLC
70 S End Plz (06776-4245)
PHONE..................................860 355-5538
James McGough,
EMP: 5
SALES (est): 762.5K **Privately Held**
SIC: 3731 Trawlers, building & repairing

(G-5598)
TITO WELDING LLC
2 Tito Ln (06776-3661)
PHONE..................................860 354-1536
Vincent J Tito,
EMP: 1
SALES (est): 69.2K **Privately Held**
SIC: 7692 Welding repair

(G-5599)
TLC ULTRASOUND INC
143 West St Ste V (06776-3525)
PHONE..................................860 354-6333
Thomas Leveille, *President*
Joan F Leveille, *Admin Sec*
EMP: 5
SQ FT: 2,500
SALES (est): 1MM **Privately Held**
SIC: 3829 Ultrasonic testing equipment

(G-5600)
TOTAL REGISTER INC
180 Sunny Valley Rd Ste 1 (06776-3361)
PHONE..................................860 210-0465
Terence Gallagher, *President*
Daniel J Gallagher, *Vice Pres*
John Gallagher, *Vice Pres*
▲ **EMP:** 10
SALES (est): 870K **Privately Held**
WEB: www.totalregister.com
SIC: 3699 Laser systems & equipment

(G-5601)
TRI STATE CHOPPERS LLC
30 Old Route 7 Plz (06776-4340)
PHONE..................................860 210-1854
Carl J Lindstrom, *Manager*
EMP: 3
SALES (est): 329.5K **Privately Held**
SIC: 3751 Motorcycles & related parts

(G-5602)
TRUSOURCE PUBLICATIONS LLC
7 Elbo Dr (06776-5134)
PHONE..................................860 350-6477
EMP: 2
SALES (est): 115.7K **Privately Held**
SIC: 2741 Miscellaneous publishing

New Milford - Litchfield County (G-5603)   GEOGRAPHIC SECTION

(G-5603)
U-MARQ USA LLC
137 Danbury Rd (06776-3428)
PHONE.................................860 799-7800
Elisha Kaufman, CEO
William Salvador, Sales Mgr
◆ EMP: 1
SQ FT: 1,000
SALES (est): 118.4K Privately Held
SIC: 3479 Etching & engraving; engraving jewelry silverware, or metal; etching on metals

(G-5604)
UPPERCURVE LLC
143 West St Ste T (06776-3599)
PHONE.................................203 770-0223
Robert Pearce, Principal
EMP: 2
SALES (est): 176.3K Privately Held
SIC: 3843 Dental equipment

(G-5605)
VALLEY GOLF CENTER CT LLC
562 Danbury Rd (06776-4318)
P.O. Box 864, Brookfield (06804-0864)
PHONE.................................860 799-7605
Glenn Banning, Principal
EMP: 1
SALES (est): 122.5K Privately Held
SIC: 3949 7999 Driving ranges, golf, electronic; golf driving range

(G-5606)
VALLEY MARBLE AND SLATE CORP
15 Valmar Dr (06776-4388)
PHONE.................................860 354-3955
EMP: 2 EST: 2016
SALES (est): 62.6K Privately Held
SIC: 3281 Mfg Cut Stone/Products

(G-5607)
VINCENT JAJER
Also Called: Park Lane Cider Mill
4 Chestnut Land Rd (06776-2504)
PHONE.................................860 354-4747
Vincent Jajer, Owner
EMP: 1
SALES (est): 67.7K Privately Held
SIC: 2099 Cider, nonalcoholic

(G-5608)
WOODWORKING
89 Cherniske Rd (06776-4922)
PHONE.................................860 354-6757
Eric Lundgren, Principal
EMP: 2
SALES (est): 161.7K Privately Held
SIC: 2431 Millwork

(G-5609)
YORK STREET STUDIO INC
Also Called: Yorkstreet.com
143 West St Ste Y (06776-3525)
PHONE.................................203 266-9000
Linda Zelenko, CEO
Stephen Piscuskas, Vice Pres
EMP: 6
SALES (est): 1.4MM Privately Held
WEB: www.yorkstreet.com
SIC: 3429 3648 Furniture builders' & other household hardware; lighting equipment

(G-5610)
ZSIBA & SMOLOVER LTD
Also Called: Arts In Architecture
87 Danbury Rd (06776-3413)
PHONE.................................860 354-5221
Peter Zsiba, President
Maura B Smolover, Corp Secy
EMP: 2
SQ FT: 2,500
SALES (est): 199.6K Privately Held
SIC: 7389 3229 Design, commercial & industrial; glassware, art or decorative

New Preston
Litchfield County

(G-5611)
BUILT TO LAST FINE WDWKG LLC
61 Christian St (06777-1803)
PHONE.................................860 619-0119
Benjamin Bogie, Principal
EMP: 2
SALES (est): 128.4K Privately Held
SIC: 2431 Millwork

(G-5612)
D K SCHULMAN
239 New Milford Tpke (06777-1604)
P.O. Box 2325 (06777-0325)
PHONE.................................860 868-4300
Dana Schulman, Owner
EMP: 3
SALES (est): 338.4K Privately Held
SIC: 2621 Stationery, envelope & tablet papers

(G-5613)
STUDIO STEEL INC
159 New Milford Tpke (06777-1603)
PHONE.................................860 868-7305
Spencer Hardy, President
Matt Archer, Manager
EMP: 9
SQ FT: 10,000
SALES (est): 1.3MM Privately Held
WEB: www.studiosteel.com
SIC: 3648 Lighting equipment

Newington
Hartford County

(G-5614)
261 PASCONE PLACE LLC
261 Pascone Pl (06111-4524)
PHONE.................................860 666-7845
Nicholas Lococo, Principal
EMP: 2
SALES (est): 118.4K Privately Held
SIC: 3585 Soda fountain & beverage dispensing equipment & parts

(G-5615)
A J TOOL COMPANY INC
16 Progress Cir Bldg 2 (06111-5559)
PHONE.................................860 666-2883
Adelme Sirois, President
Jean Sirois, Vice Pres
EMP: 1
SQ FT: 2,600
SALES (est): 69.2K Privately Held
SIC: 3599 Machine shop, jobbing & repair

(G-5616)
A-1 CHROME AND POLISHING CORP
125 Stamm Rd (06111-3619)
PHONE.................................860 666-4593
Claudio Spada, President
Joseph Spada, Vice Pres
EMP: 14 EST: 1980
SQ FT: 2,400
SALES (est): 1.6MM Privately Held
WEB: www.a1chrome.com
SIC: 3471 Plating of metals or formed products

(G-5617)
ACCUPAULO HOLDING CORPORATION (PA)
Also Called: Accurate Threaded Products
280 Hartford Ave (06111-1501)
PHONE.................................860 666-5621
Jon Omichinski, President
Harold Etherington, President
Rita Mackenzie, General Mgr
EMP: 25
SQ FT: 20,000
SALES (est): 31.5MM Privately Held
SIC: 3769 3599 3724 Guided missile & space vehicle parts & auxiliary equipment; machine shop, jobbing & repair; aircraft engines & engine parts

(G-5618)
ACCURATE THREADED PRODUCTS CO
280 Hartford Ave (06111-1501)
PHONE.................................860 666-5621
Gary Fett, President
EMP: 40
SQ FT: 20,000
SALES (est): 800K Privately Held
SIC: 3599 Machine shop, jobbing & repair
PA: Atp Industries, Llc
75 Northwest Dr
Plainville CT 06062

(G-5619)
ADDAMO MANUFACTURING INC
360 Stamm Rd (06111-3627)
PHONE.................................860 667-2601
Sebastian Addamo, President
Paul Addamo, Vice Pres
Sevvy Addamo, Vice Pres
Lucy Addamo, Admin Sec
EMP: 7
SQ FT: 15,000
SALES (est): 1MM Privately Held
SIC: 3469 3599 Machine parts, stamped or pressed metal; machine shop, jobbing & repair

(G-5620)
ADMILL MACHINE CO
115 Pane Rd (06111-5522)
PHONE.................................860 667-3676
EMP: 2
SALES (est): 85.2K Privately Held
SIC: 3545 Mfg Machine Tool Accessories

(G-5621)
ADVANCED ADHESIVE SYSTEMS INC
Also Called: A A S
681 N Mountain Rd (06111-1349)
PHONE.................................860 953-4100
Robert Batson, CEO
Andy Batson, President
Carol Batson, Treasurer
EMP: 28
SALES (est): 6.9MM Privately Held
WEB: www.advancedadhesivesystems.com
SIC: 2891 Adhesives; sealants

(G-5622)
ADVANCED TORQUE PRODUCTS LLC
56 Budney Rd (06111-5132)
P.O. Box 7241, Berlin (06037-7241)
PHONE.................................860 828-1523
Dan Castle, Mng Member
George L Castle,
EMP: 8
SQ FT: 12,146
SALES (est): 1.6MM Privately Held
WEB: www.advancedtorque.com
SIC: 3545 Vises, machine (machine tool accessories)

(G-5623)
AIRFLOW TRUCK COMPANY
32 Old Musket Dr (06111-3428)
PHONE.................................860 666-1977
Robert J Sliwa, Owner
EMP: 1
SALES (est): 116K Privately Held
SIC: 3711 Motor vehicles & car bodies

(G-5624)
ALLIANCE GRAPHICS INC
16 Progress Cir Bldg 3 (06111-5545)
PHONE.................................860 666-7992
Mark Bruks, CEO
EMP: 10
SQ FT: 4,200
SALES (est): 1.9MM Privately Held
WEB: www.agink.com
SIC: 2752 7334 Commercial printing, offset; photocopying & duplicating services

(G-5625)
ALLIED MACHINING CO INC
Also Called: Allied Engineering
50 Progress Cir Ste 3 (06111-5547)
PHONE.................................860 665-1228
Katherine Jankowski, President
Peter Jankowski, Corp Secy
Chris Jankowski, Vice Pres
EMP: 9
SQ FT: 9,600
SALES (est): 2MM Privately Held
SIC: 3599 Machine shop, jobbing & repair

(G-5626)
AMERICAN TOOL & MFG CORP
125 Rockwell Rd (06111-5535)
PHONE.................................860 666-2255
Grzegorz Wolanin, CEO
EMP: 11
SQ FT: 6,000
SALES (est): 1.5MM Privately Held
SIC: 3599 Machine shop, jobbing & repair

(G-5627)
ANCHOR RUBBER PRODUCTS LLC
152 Rockwell Rd Ste C9 (06111-5554)
PHONE.................................860 667-2628
Michael Shannon, General Mgr
Mike Shannon, Manager
Robert Shannon,
▲ EMP: 6 EST: 1996
SQ FT: 5,000
SALES (est): 938.9K Privately Held
WEB: www.anchorrubber.com
SIC: 3069 Molded rubber products

(G-5628)
ANDVIC-PRECISION LLC
11 Woodmere Rd (06111-1344)
PHONE.................................860 836-7422
Yuri Alekseyko, Principal
Tania Alekseyko, Co-Owner
EMP: 2 EST: 2016
SALES (est): 119.3K Privately Held
SIC: 3599 Machine shop, jobbing & repair

(G-5629)
ATLAS STAMPING & MFG CORP
729 N Mountain Rd (06111-1424)
PHONE.................................860 757-3233
Kenneth Prigodich, President
EMP: 30
SQ FT: 13,500
SALES (est): 6MM Privately Held
WEB: www.asm.necoxmail.com
SIC: 3469 3544 Stamping metal for the trade; dies & die holders for metal cutting, forming, die casting

(G-5630)
B&N AEROSPACE INC
44 Rockwell Rd (06111-5526)
PHONE.................................860 665-0134
Dennis Blaszko, President
Walter Blaszko, Principal
Donna Blaszko, Corp Secy
Gary Klinsman Sr, Vice Pres
Gary Klinzmann, Vice Pres
EMP: 45
SQ FT: 15,000
SALES (est): 10MM Privately Held
WEB: www.bntool.com
SIC: 3728 Aircraft assemblies, subassemblies & parts

(G-5631)
BEACON GROUP INC (PA)
549 Cedar St (06111-1814)
PHONE.................................860 594-5200
Suresh Mirchandani, President
Karishma Mirchandani, Vice Pres
Robert Sarkisian, Vice Pres
Nishita Mirchandani, Human Resources
EMP: 135
SQ FT: 100,000
SALES (est): 23.4MM Privately Held
WEB: www.thebeacongroup.com
SIC: 3724 3812 3053 3714 Aircraft engines & engine parts; search & navigation equipment; gaskets, packing & sealing devices; motor vehicle parts & accessories

(G-5632)
BEACON INDUSTRIES INC
549 Cedar St (06111-1814)
PHONE.................................860 594-5200
Suresh Mirchandani, CEO
Richard Mitchell, Vice Pres
Robert S Sarkisian, Vice Pres
Leon Sorits, Engineer
Mietek Kostaniak, Technology

▲ = Import ▼=Export
◆ =Import/Export

▲ EMP: 122 EST: 1948
SQ FT: 300,000
SALES: 18MM
SALES (corp-wide): 23.4MM Privately Held
WEB: www.beacongp.com
SIC: 3728 Aircraft parts & equipment
PA: The Beacon Group Inc
549 Cedar St
Newington CT 06111
860 594-5200

(G-5633)
BEN & JERRYS HOMEMADE INC
120 Northwood Rd (06111-3152)
PHONE.................................203 488-9666
EMP: 3
SALES (corp-wide): 67.1B Privately Held
SIC: 2024 Mfg Ice Cream/Frozen Desert
HQ: Ben & Jerry's Homemade, Inc.
30 Community Dr Ste 1
South Burlington VT 05403
802 846-1500

(G-5634)
BRAMPTON TECHNOLOGY LTD
61 Maselli Rd (06111-5520)
PHONE.................................860 667-7689
Shaun Wheatley, Principal
EMP: 5 EST: 1996
SALES (est): 568.1K Privately Held
WEB: www.bramptontechnology.com
SIC: 3949 Golf equipment

(G-5635)
BRYKA SKYSTOCKS LLC
549 Cedar St (06111-1814)
PHONE.................................845 507-8200
Suresh Mirchandani,
Karishma Mirchandani,
EMP: 5
SQ FT: 1,700
SALES: 2MM Privately Held
SIC: 3728 Aircraft parts & equipment

(G-5636)
C & A MACHINE CO INC
49 Progress Cir (06111-5532)
PHONE.................................860 667-0605
Joe Milluzzo, President
Andre Senteio, QC Mgr
John Marut, Admin Sec
EMP: 43
SQ FT: 16,000
SALES: 10MM Privately Held
SIC: 3451 3599 Screw machine products; machine shop, jobbing & repair

(G-5637)
CATSKILL GRAN COUNTERTOPS INC
Also Called: Counters
156 Pane Rd Ste A (06111-5557)
PHONE.................................860 667-1555
Nicacio F Pinho, President
EMP: 12
SALES (est): 1.8MM Privately Held
SIC: 3131 Counters

(G-5638)
CEDA COMPANY INC
36 Holmes Rd (06111-1787)
PHONE.................................860 666-1593
Donald Morander, President
Derek Morander, Software Dev
EMP: 6
SQ FT: 8,750
SALES: 1MM Privately Held
WEB: www.cedacompany.com
SIC: 3541 8711 Jig boring & grinding machines; machine tool design

(G-5639)
CENTRAL CONNECTICUT SLS & MFG
37 Stanwell Rd (06111-4531)
PHONE.................................860 667-1411
Paul Campbell, President
Cindy Campbell, Principal
Richard Campbell, Vice Pres
EMP: 7
SQ FT: 6,000
SALES (est): 860.1K Privately Held
WEB: www.walbernprecision.com
SIC: 3599 Machine shop, jobbing & repair

(G-5640)
CHARTING ECONOMY
171 Market Sq Ste 213 (06111-2930)
PHONE.................................860 667-9909
Robert Williams, Owner
EMP: 1
SALES (est): 72.5K Privately Held
WEB: www.chartingtheeconomy.com
SIC: 2721 Magazines: publishing only, not printed on site

(G-5641)
COMPONENT TECHNOLOGIES INC (PA)
Also Called: CTI
68 Holmes Rd (06111-1708)
PHONE.................................860 667-1065
Fred Viggiano, President
Fred Viggiano Jr, President
Larry Hutnick, Vice Pres
EMP: 22
SQ FT: 24,000
SALES (est): 3.1MM Privately Held
WEB: www.componenttechnologiesinc.com
SIC: 3471 Plating of metals or formed products

(G-5642)
CONNECTICUT MFG SVCS LLC
631 Church St (06111-5503)
PHONE.................................860 667-8712
Harold Deschenes, Principal
EMP: 2
SALES (est): 106.2K Privately Held
SIC: 3999 Manufacturing industries

(G-5643)
CONVERTING MCHY ADHESIVES LLC
50 Sleepy Hollow Rd (06111-1034)
PHONE.................................860 561-0226
Vincent J Barresi, Principal
EMP: 4
SALES (est): 293.8K Privately Held
SIC: 2891 Adhesives

(G-5644)
CT THERMOGRAPHY LLC
70 Golf St (06111-3435)
PHONE.................................860 690-9202
April Beaman, Principal
EMP: 2
SALES (est): 80.6K Privately Held
SIC: 2759 Thermography

(G-5645)
CUSTOM METAL CRAFTERS INC
Also Called: Custom Metal Crafters CMC
815 N Mountain Rd (06111-1489)
PHONE.................................860 953-4210
Daniel F Bourget, President
Stephen Rosner, President
Jean Bourget, Chairman
Lynn M Clemente, Vice Pres
▲ EMP: 56
SQ FT: 55,000
SALES (est): 10.6MM Privately Held
WEB: www.custom-metal.com
SIC: 3364 3369 3363 Nonferrous die-castings except aluminum; nonferrous foundries; aluminum die-castings

(G-5646)
CYR WOODWORKING INC
139 Summit St (06111-1715)
PHONE.................................860 232-1991
Roderique Cyr, President
Lisa Salvini, Sales Executive
EMP: 7 EST: 1966
SALES (est): 900K Privately Held
WEB: www.cyrwoodworking.com
SIC: 2521 2434 Wood office furniture; wood kitchen cabinets

(G-5647)
DATA-GRAPHICS INC
240 Hartford Ave (06111-2077)
PHONE.................................860 667-0435
Andrew Mandell, President
Bruce Mandell, Vice Pres
Joyce Mandell, Admin Sec
▲ EMP: 74
SQ FT: 15,000

SALES (est): 22.6MM Privately Held
SIC: 2752 Commercial printing, lithographic

(G-5648)
DOWN HOME PUBLISHING
46 Dover Rd (06111-1014)
PHONE.................................860 521-6177
EMP: 1
SALES (est): 51.1K Privately Held
SIC: 2741 Miscellaneous publishing

(G-5649)
EDAC TECHNOLOGIES LLC
Edac Aero
275 Richard St (06111-5046)
PHONE.................................860 667-2134
Tom Mosdale, General Mgr
EMP: 120 Privately Held
WEB: www.edactechnologies.com
SIC: 3728 Aircraft parts & equipment
HQ: Edac Technologies Llc
5 Mckee Pl
Cheshire CT 06410
203 806-2090

(G-5650)
EDRIVE ACTUATORS INC
385 Stamm Rd (06111-3628)
PHONE.................................860 953-0588
Richard Swanson, President
James Haury, Vice Pres
EMP: 8
SQ FT: 3,600
SALES (est): 1.4MM
SALES (corp-wide): 2.7B Publicly Held
WEB: www.edriveactuators.com
SIC: 3545 Machine tool attachments & accessories
HQ: Joyce/Dayton Corp.
3300 S Dixie Dr Ste 101
Dayton OH 45439
937 294-6261

(G-5651)
ENVELOPES & MORE INC
124 Francis Ave (06111-1216)
PHONE.................................860 286-7570
Mike Sullivan, President
John Sullivan, President
Michael Sullivan, President
Tim Sullivan, Treasurer
EMP: 15
SALES: 2.5MM Privately Held
WEB: www.envmore.com
SIC: 2759 Envelopes: printing

(G-5652)
FINE PRINT NEW ENGLAND INC
711 N Mountain Rd (06111-1424)
PHONE.................................860 953-0660
James Weber Jr, President
EMP: 8
SQ FT: 7,200
SALES (est): 495K Privately Held
SIC: 2752 Commercial printing, lithographic

(G-5653)
FLOW RESOURCES INC (HQ)
Also Called: Wolf Colorprint
135 Day St Ste 1 (06111-1200)
PHONE.................................860 666-1200
John W Meier, CEO
Glenn Basale, Vice Pres
EMP: 25
SQ FT: 20,000
SALES (est): 4.7MM
SALES (corp-wide): 35MM Privately Held
WEB: www.wolfcolorprint.com
SIC: 2752 Commercial printing, offset
PA: J.S. Mccarthy Co., Inc.
15 Darin Dr
Augusta ME 04330
207 622-6241

(G-5654)
FRASAL TOOL CO INC
14 Foster St (06111-4906)
PHONE.................................860 666-3524
Frank Giangrave, President
Pierrette Giangrave, Corp Secy
Paul Giangrave, Vice Pres
▲ EMP: 10

SALES (est): 1.5MM Privately Held
WEB: www.frasaltool.com
SIC: 3599 3546 Machine shop, jobbing & repair; power-driven handtools

(G-5655)
GKN AEROSPACE NEWINGTON LLC
183 Louis St (06111)
PHONE.................................800 667-8502
EMP: 3
SALES (est): 180K Privately Held
SIC: 3724 Aircraft Engines And Engine Parts

(G-5656)
GKN AEROSPACE NEWINGTON LLC (DH)
183 Louis St (06111)
PHONE.................................860 667-8502
Jeffrey McDaniel, Plant Mgr
Anita Szahaj, Purch Mgr
Jon Ford, Engineer
Martin Thorden,
▲ EMP: 146
SQ FT: 43,000
SALES (est): 34.7MM
SALES (corp-wide): 11B Privately Held
SIC: 3724 3728 Aircraft engines & engine parts; aircraft parts & equipment
HQ: Gkn Aerospace Sweden Ab
Flygmotorvagen 1m
Trollhattan 461 3
520 940-00

(G-5657)
GRANITE LLC
116 Willard Ave (06111-1125)
PHONE.................................860 586-8132
Luiz C Ribeiro, Principal
EMP: 6
SALES (est): 455.9K Privately Held
SIC: 3281 Curbing, granite or stone

(G-5658)
HANGER PRSTHETCS & ORTHO INC
181 Patricia M Genova Dr (06111-1500)
PHONE.................................860 667-5370
Patricia Havens, Manager
EMP: 5
SALES (corp-wide): 1B Publicly Held
SIC: 3842 Surgical appliances & supplies
HQ: Hanger Prosthetics & Orthotics, Inc.
10910 Domain Dr Ste 300
Austin TX 78758
512 777-3800

(G-5659)
HI-TECH POLISHING INC
50 Progress Cir Ste 3 (06111-5547)
PHONE.................................860 665-1399
Pasquale Griffo, President
Frances Griffo, Vice Pres
EMP: 13
SQ FT: 1,600
SALES (est): 1.5MM Privately Held
SIC: 3471 Tumbling (cleaning & polishing) of machine parts

(G-5660)
IMAGE 360
2434 Berlin Tpke (06111-4121)
PHONE.................................860 667-8339
EMP: 2
SALES (est): 168.3K Privately Held
SIC: 3993 Signs & advertising specialties

(G-5661)
IMAGE INK INC
102 Pane Rd Ste A (06111-5561)
PHONE.................................860 665-9792
Jeff Gambino, President
Scott Skates, Vice Pres
EMP: 5
SQ FT: 2,200
SALES (est): 700.5K Privately Held
SIC: 2752 Commercial printing, lithographic

(G-5662)
INKWELL
18 Kinnear Ave (06111-3344)
P.O. Box 310075 (06131-0075)
PHONE.................................860 666-8312

Newington - Hartford County (G-5663)

Joyce Boncal, *Owner*
EMP: 2
SQ FT: 300
SALES: 270K **Privately Held**
SIC: 2752 Commercial printing, lithographic

(G-5663)
INTEGRAL INDUSTRIES INC
111 Holmes Rd (06111-1714)
PHONE 860 953-0686
Edward R Mascolo, *President*
Joann Mascolo, *Corp Secy*
Edward Mark Mascolo, *Vice Pres*
EMP: 17
SQ FT: 8,000
SALES (est): 4.6MM **Privately Held**
WEB: www.integralind.com
SIC: 3545 Precision tools, machinists'

(G-5664)
INTEGRATED SYSTEMS SOLUTIONS
25 Holly Dr (06111-2243)
PHONE 860 665-1600
EMP: 2 **EST:** 2010
SALES (est): 20.5K **Privately Held**
SIC: 3812 Aircraft/aerospace flight instruments & guidance systems

(G-5665)
INTELIUM SOFTWARE LLC
80 Forest Dr (06111-3117)
PHONE 860 667-4300
Rui Calado, *Principal*
EMP: 2
SALES (est): 121.7K **Privately Held**
SIC: 7372 Prepackaged software

(G-5666)
J OCONNOR LLC
Also Called: Connecticut Metalworks
309 Pane Rd Ste 1 (06111-5500)
PHONE 860 665-7702
Jim Oconnor, *Principal*
James O' Connor,
James O'Connor,
EMP: 15
SQ FT: 12,000
SALES (est): 2.4MM **Privately Held**
SIC: 3499 3444 Metal household articles; sheet metalwork

(G-5667)
JENSEN MACHINE CO
721 Russell Rd (06111-1527)
PHONE 860 666-5438
John Andrew Jensen Jr, *President*
Alice Jensen, *Treasurer*
Timothy Lewis, *Manager*
EMP: 9
SQ FT: 15,000
SALES: 1MM **Privately Held**
WEB: www.jensenmachine.com
SIC: 3599 Machine shop, jobbing & repair

(G-5668)
KANIA DARIUS
75 Rockwell Rd (06111-5564)
PHONE 860 667-4400
Darius Kania, *Principal*
EMP: 2
SALES (est): 107.4K **Privately Held**
SIC: 3599 Machine shop, jobbing & repair

(G-5669)
KELLOGG COMPANY
52 Hollow Tree Ln (06111)
PHONE 860 665-9920
EMP: 699
SALES (corp-wide): 13.5B **Publicly Held**
WEB: www.kelloggs.com
SIC: 2043 Cereal breakfast foods
PA: Kellogg Company
1 Kellogg Sq
Battle Creek MI 49017
269 961-2000

(G-5670)
KOHLER MIX SPECIALTIES LLC
100 Milk Ln (06111-2242)
PHONE 860 666-1511
Rachel A Gonzalez,
Midd McManus,
EMP: 132 **EST:** 2001
SQ FT: 70,000
SALES (est): 13.7MM **Publicly Held**
SIC: 2099 2038 2026 2023 Food preparations; frozen specialties; fluid milk; ice cream mix, unfrozen: liquid or dry
HQ: Dean Holding Company
2711 N Haskell Ave # 340
Dallas TX 75204
214 303-3400

(G-5671)
KRUTCH PACK LLC
56 Forest Dr (06111-3117)
PHONE 860 836-1745
Nathalie Inho, *Principal*
EMP: 1
SALES (est): 173.5K **Privately Held**
SIC: 5047 3842 2393 Orthopedic equipment & supplies; crutches & walkers; bags & containers, except sleeping bags; textile

(G-5672)
LYNN WELDING CO INC
75 Rockwell Rd Ste 1 (06111-5564)
PHONE 860 667-4400
Jan Kania, *President*
James Inglis Sr, *President*
Ricardo Kimball, *General Mgr*
Joseph Inglis, *Treasurer*
Regina Kania, *Admin Sec*
EMP: 13
SQ FT: 13,900
SALES (est): 2.4MM **Privately Held**
SIC: 3599 7692 Machine shop, jobbing & repair; welding repair

(G-5673)
M & R MANUFACTURING INC
Also Called: National Tool & CAM
111 Carr Ave (06111-4331)
PHONE 860 666-5066
Joseph Wieter, *President*
EMP: 6
SQ FT: 3,200
SALES (est): 894.5K **Privately Held**
SIC: 3544 3545 Jigs & fixtures; cutting tools for machine tools

(G-5674)
MACRISTY INDUSTRIES INC (PA)
610 N Mountain Rd (06111-1347)
PHONE 860 225-4637
Jeff Barlow, *President*
Jon Brad Barlow, *Asst Sec*
Kristin Barlow, *Asst Sec*
▲ **EMP:** 247
SQ FT: 150,000
SALES (est): 31MM **Privately Held**
WEB: www.macristyindustries.com
SIC: 3498 3432 3433 4226 Tube fabricating (contract bending & shaping); plumbing fixture fittings & trim; heating equipment, except electric; special warehousing & storage; general farms, primarily crop; nonresidential building operators

(G-5675)
MATIAS IMPORTING & DISTRG CORP
Also Called: Matias Importing & Distrg Co
135 Fenn Rd (06111-2250)
PHONE 860 666-5544
Ernest Matias, *President*
Mary L Matias, *Director*
▲ **EMP:** 3
SQ FT: 1,200
SALES (est): 250K **Privately Held**
SIC: 3443 7692 5181 5182 Fuel tanks (oil, gas, etc.): metal plate; welding repair; beer & other fermented malt liquors; wine

(G-5676)
MEGA MANUFACTURING LLC
115 Pane Rd (06111-5522)
PHONE 860 666-5555
EMP: 7
SALES (est): 300K **Privately Held**
SIC: 3599 Mfg Industrial Machinery

(G-5677)
MID-CONN TESTERS LLC
269 W Hill Rd (06111-1134)
PHONE 860 232-1943
James E Giansanti, *Principal*
EMP: 2 **EST:** 2012

SALES (est): 73.6K **Privately Held**
SIC: 1389 Testing, measuring, surveying & analysis services

(G-5678)
MINIATURE NUT & SCREW CORP
820 N Mountain Rd (06111-1415)
PHONE 860 953-4490
Pauline Smith, *President*
Keith Smith, *Vice Pres*
Mark Smith, *Vice Pres*
EMP: 6 **EST:** 1963
SQ FT: 10,000
SALES (est): 788.9K **Privately Held**
SIC: 3452 Bolts, nuts, rivets & washers

(G-5679)
MODERN ELEMENTS PRODUCTS LLC ◎
141 Superior Ave (06111-3952)
PHONE 860 667-4247
EMP: 2 **EST:** 2019
SALES (est): 74.4K **Privately Held**
SIC: 2819 Elements

(G-5680)
MTU AERO ENGINE DESIGN INC
Also Called: Edac Aero Components
275 Richard St (06111-5046)
PHONE 860 667-2134
Alain Derube, *President*
Thomas Seifert, *Controller*
▲ **EMP:** 1 **EST:** 2001
SALES (est): 419K **Privately Held**
SIC: 3728 Aircraft parts & equipment
HQ: Edac Technologies Llc
5 Mckee Pl
Cheshire CT 06410
203 806-2090

(G-5681)
MUIR ENVELOPE PLUS INC
Also Called: Muir Envelope Div
124 Francis Ave (06111-1216)
PHONE 860 953-6847
Paul Klett, *President*
Jack Muir, *Corp Secy*
EMP: 12
SQ FT: 40,000
SALES (est): 1.4MM **Privately Held**
SIC: 2759 2752 Commercial printing; commercial printing, lithographic

(G-5682)
N & B MANUFACTURING CO INC
215 Pascone Pl (06111-4524)
PHONE 860 667-3204
Miroslaw Boksz, *President*
Krzysztos Nowakowski, *Corp Secy*
Jesse Boksz, *Vice Pres*
EMP: 4
SQ FT: 7,000
SALES (est): 499.9K **Privately Held**
SIC: 3724 Aircraft engines & engine parts

(G-5683)
NATIONS RENT
2258 Berlin Tpke (06111-3202)
PHONE 860 665-1489
EMP: 2
SALES (est): 111.5K **Privately Held**
SIC: 3429 Mfg Hardware

(G-5684)
NCT INC
Also Called: Numerical Control Technology
20 Holmes Rd (06111-1708)
PHONE 860 666-8424
Volodmyr Drobockyi, *President*
Adam Jarzebowski, *President*
Elizabeth Jarzebowski, *Vice Pres*
Walter Jarzebowski, *Vice Pres*
EMP: 15
SQ FT: 12,500
SALES: 700K **Privately Held**
WEB: www.nctfrictionwelding.com
SIC: 7692 7629 7389 Welding repair; electronic equipment repair; grinding, precision: commercial or industrial

(G-5685)
NEW ENGLAND LIFT SYSTEMS LLC
714 N Mountain Rd (06111-1348)
PHONE 860 372-4040
EMP: 1 **EST:** 2016
SALES (est): 78.8K **Privately Held**
SIC: 3536 3625 Mfg Hoist/Crane/Monorail Mfg Relay/Indstl Control

(G-5686)
NEWINGTON MEAT CENTER
847 Main St (06111-2471)
PHONE 860 666-3431
Vito Lattarulo, *Partner*
EMP: 12
SQ FT: 1,000
SALES (est): 150K **Privately Held**
SIC: 5421 2013 Meat markets, including freezer provisioners; sausages & other prepared meats

(G-5687)
NOWAK PRODUCTS INC
101 Rockwell Rd (06111-5535)
PHONE 860 666-9685
Gary Nowak, *President*
Jay Giblin, *Corp Secy*
Florian Nowak, *Director*
EMP: 9
SQ FT: 20,000
SALES: 1.5MM **Privately Held**
WEB: www.nowakproducts.com
SIC: 3541 Machine tools, metal cutting type

(G-5688)
NUTMEG INDUSTRIES LLC
354 Main St Ste 5 (06111-2067)
PHONE 860 436-6553
Craig Hebert,
EMP: 1
SQ FT: 1,400
SALES: 890K **Privately Held**
SIC: 3999 Barber & beauty shop equipment

(G-5689)
OMAR COFFEE COMPANY
41 Commerce Ct (06111-2246)
PHONE 860 667-8889
Steve Costas, *Ch of Bd*
Diane C Bokron, *President*
George Cocola, *General Mgr*
Joann Lemnior, *Vice Pres*
Greg Dadinos, *Plant Mgr*
EMP: 50 **EST:** 1937
SQ FT: 30,000
SALES (est): 9.4MM **Privately Held**
WEB: www.omarcoffeecompany.com
SIC: 2095 5149 Coffee roasting (except by wholesale grocers); condiments; dairy products, dried or canned

(G-5690)
PAL CORPORATION
Also Called: Model Works
45 Maselli Rd (06111-5520)
PHONE 860 666-9211
Timothy Dostie, *President*
Julia R Dostie, *Vice Pres*
Alice Dostie, *Treasurer*
EMP: 6
SQ FT: 2,500
SALES (est): 568.3K **Privately Held**
SIC: 3599 Machine shop, jobbing & repair

(G-5691)
PALADIN COMMERCIAL PRTRS LLC
300 Hartford Ave (06111-1501)
PHONE 860 953-4900
William Saunders, *Owner*
Sean Coane, *Sales Staff*
George Feisthamel, *Program Mgr*
EMP: 27
SQ FT: 13,000
SALES (est): 5MM **Privately Held**
SIC: 2752 Commercial printing, offset

(G-5692)
PAPER STATION
29 E Cedar St (06111-2533)
PHONE 860 667-9087
Susan Davidoff, *Owner*

GEOGRAPHIC SECTION

Newington - Hartford County (G-5720)

EMP: 2
SALES (est): 243.7K Privately Held
SIC: 2759 Invitations: printing

(G-5693)
PAUL WELDING COMPANY INC
157 Kelsey St (06111-5419)
PHONE.................................860 229-9945
Michael Paul, *President*
Terese Seidl, *Corp Secy*
David Paul, *Vice Pres*
Jeffrey Paul, *Vice Pres*
Michael J Paul, *Director*
EMP: 8
SQ FT: 5,000
SALES: 500K Privately Held
SIC: 7692 Welding repair

(G-5694)
PCX AEROSTRUCTURES LLC
300 Fenn Rd (06111-2277)
PHONE.................................860 666-2471
EMP: 40
SALES (corp-wide): 100MM Privately Held
WEB: www.spx.com
SIC: 3441 Fabricated structural metal
PA: Pcx Aerostructures, Llc
    300 Fenn Rd
    Newington CT 06111
    860 666-2471

(G-5695)
PCX AEROSTRUCTURES LLC (PA)
300 Fenn Rd (06111-2277)
PHONE.................................860 666-2471
Jeff Frisby, *President*
Trevor Hartman, *Vice Pres*
Tim Fagan, *CFO*
▲ EMP: 200
SQ FT: 145,000
SALES: 100MM Privately Held
SIC: 3728 Aircraft assemblies, subassemblies & parts

(G-5696)
PROMISE PROPANE
110 Holmes Rd (06111-1713)
PHONE.................................860 685-0676
Justin Kovalcek, *Principal*
EMP: 3
SALES (est): 112.1K Privately Held
SIC: 1311 Crude petroleum & natural gas

(G-5697)
PRONTO PRINTER OF NEWINGTON
2406 Berlin Tpke (06111-4105)
PHONE.................................860 666-2245
Robert Sander, *President*
Holly H Sander, *Vice Pres*
EMP: 5
SQ FT: 2,700
SALES (est): 746.3K Privately Held
WEB: www.prontoprinterofnewington.com
SIC: 2752 Commercial printing, offset

(G-5698)
PROSPECT PRODUCTS INCORPORATED
43 Kelsey St (06111-5415)
PHONE.................................860 666-0323
Richard E Carlson, *President*
Jerry Johnson, *General Mgr*
Liza Bang, *Office Mgr*
EMP: 26 EST: 1950
SQ FT: 4,000
SALES (est): 18.9MM Privately Held
WEB: www.prospectproducts.com
SIC: 3559 3826 3089 Semiconductor manufacturing machinery; electrolytic conductivity instruments; injection molding of plastics

(G-5699)
RADICAL COMPUTING CORPORATION
705 N Mountain Rd A210 (06111-1432)
PHONE.................................860 953-0240
Timur Y Ruban, *President*
EMP: 5
SQ FT: 1,500

SALES (est): 328.8K Privately Held
WEB: www.radicalcomputing.com
SIC: 7372 Publishers' computer software

(G-5700)
RENO MACHINE COMPANY INC
170 Pane Rd Ste 1 (06111-5537)
PHONE.................................860 666-5641
Antonio Occhialini, *Ch of Bd*
Mark Occhialini, *President*
Art Santos, *Production*
David Occhialini, *Treasurer*
Denise Markiewicz, *Controller*
▲ EMP: 65 EST: 1956
SQ FT: 68,000
SALES (est): 13.3MM Privately Held
SIC: 3599 7692 3544 Machine shop, jobbing & repair; welding repair; special dies, tools, jigs & fixtures

(G-5701)
RICHARDS MACHINE TOOL CO INC
187 Stamm Rd (06111-3619)
PHONE.................................860 436-2938
Lillian Bartkowicz, *President*
Dorothy Bartkowicz Weber, *Vice Pres*
Stephen Weber, *VP Opers*
EMP: 12 EST: 1978
SQ FT: 7,000
SALES (est): 2.1MM Privately Held
SIC: 3599 3544 Machine shop, jobbing & repair; special dies & tools

(G-5702)
SACCUZZO COMPANY INC
149 Louis St (06111-4517)
PHONE.................................860 665-1101
Vincent Saccuzzo, *President*
Marco Saccuzzo, *Senior VP*
Vincenzo Saccuzzo, *Engineer*
▲ EMP: 7
SQ FT: 16,000
SALES (est): 1MM Privately Held
WEB: www.icaffe.com
SIC: 2095 5046 5149 Coffee roasting (except by wholesale grocers); coffee brewing equipment & supplies; flavourings & fragrances

(G-5703)
SCHUCO USA LLLP (HQ)
Also Called: Schuco International
240 Pane Rd (06111-5527)
PHONE.................................860 666-0505
Thomas Knobloch, *CEO*
Dirk U Hindrichs, *President*
Edgar Freind, *Partner*
Ilhan Demirag, *Opers Staff*
Dennis Hashagen, *Sales Staff*
◆ EMP: 56 EST: 1997
SQ FT: 90,000
SALES (est): 14.4MM
SALES (corp-wide): 1.1B Privately Held
WEB: www.schuco-usa.com
SIC: 2431 Windows, wood
PA: SchUco International Kg
    Karolinenstr. 1-15
    Bielefeld 33609
    521 783-0

(G-5704)
SHEPARD STEEL CO INC
55 Shepard Dr (06111-1159)
PHONE.................................860 525-4446
Allen Shilosky, *Branch Mgr*
EMP: 30
SALES (corp-wide): 19.4MM Privately Held
WEB: www.shepardsteel.com
SIC: 3316 3446 3441 Cold finishing of steel shapes; architectural metalwork; fabricated structural metal
PA: Shepard Steel Co. Inc.
    110 Meadow St
    Hartford CT 06114
    860 525-4446

(G-5705)
SIGNS NOW LLC
2434 Berlin Tpke Ste 14 (06111-4122)
PHONE.................................860 667-8339
Susan Hamilton, *Principal*
Randy Hamilton,
EMP: 6

SALES: 390K Privately Held
SIC: 3993 2759 Signs & advertising specialties; screen printing

(G-5706)
SOUSA CORP
565 Cedar St (06111-1814)
PHONE.................................860 523-9090
Norman W Sousa Jr, *President*
Kate Sousa, *Business Mgr*
EMP: 11
SQ FT: 37,000
SALES (est): 2.4MM Privately Held
SIC: 3398 3471 8734 Metal heat treating; plating & polishing; product testing laboratories

(G-5707)
SUMMIT PROMOTIONAL PRINTING LL
100 School House Rd (06111-4032)
PHONE.................................860 666-1605
Gilbert Valfer, *Principal*
EMP: 2
SALES (est): 150K Privately Held
SIC: 2752 Commercial printing, lithographic

(G-5708)
SYCHRON INC
683 N Mountain Rd (06111-1350)
PHONE.................................860 953-8157
EMP: 3
SALES (est): 153.4K Privately Held
SIC: 2861 Wood extract products

(G-5709)
SYNCHRON INC
683 N Mountain Rd Ste 2 (06111-1350)
PHONE.................................860 953-8157
Ewald Dickau, *President*
EMP: 2
SALES (est): 208.1K Privately Held
SIC: 2891 Adhesives

(G-5710)
TEAM WALBERN
Also Called: R & T Manufacturing
37 Stanwell Rd (06111-4531)
PHONE.................................860 667-7627
Paul Campbell, *Owner*
EMP: 1
SALES (est): 45.6K Privately Held
SIC: 3944 Games, toys & children's vehicles

(G-5711)
THE KEENEY MANUFACTURING CO (PA)
Also Called: Plumb Pak Medical
1170 Main St (06111-3098)
PHONE.................................603 239-6371
Robert S Holden, *CEO*
Jean Hanna Holden, *Chairman*
Marisa Bruno, *Exec Officer*
James H Holden, *Exec VP*
Edwin F Atkins, *Vice Pres*
▲ EMP: 200
SQ FT: 150,000
SALES: 132MM Privately Held
WEB: www.keeneymfg.com
SIC: 3432 5074 Plumbers' brass goods: drain cocks, faucets, spigots, etc.; plumbing fittings & supplies

(G-5712)
TILCON CONNECTICUT INC
301 Harford Ave Unit 301 (06111)
P.O. Box 310903 (06131-0903)
PHONE.................................860 756-8016
Tim Marti, *Manager*
EMP: 3
SALES (corp-wide): 30.6B Privately Held
WEB: www.tilconct.com
SIC: 1442 Sand mining; gravel & pebble mining
HQ: Tilcon Connecticut Inc.
    642 Black Rock Ave
    New Britain CT 06052
    860 224-6010

(G-5713)
TILCON INC (DH)
301 Hartford Ave (06111-1503)
P.O. Box 1357, New Britain (06050-1357)
PHONE.................................860 223-3651
Angelo Tomasso Jr, *Ch of Bd*
Joseph Abate, *President*
Joseph A Abate, *President*
James Ryan, *Senior VP*
Michael Carbone, *Vice Pres*
EMP: 300
SQ FT: 2,000
SALES (est): 494MM
SALES (corp-wide): 30.6B Privately Held
WEB: www.tilcon.com
SIC: 1611 5032 3273 2951 Highway & street paving contractor; sand, construction; gravel; stone, crushed or broken; ready-mixed concrete; asphalt paving mixtures & blocks
HQ: Crh Americas, Inc.
    900 Ashwood Pkwy Ste 600
    Atlanta GA 30338
    770 804-3363

(G-5714)
TRUSS MANUFACTURING INC
97 Stanwell Rd (06111-4531)
PHONE.................................860 665-0000
Lawrence Vernon, *President*
Aurelien Giguere, *Vice Pres*
EMP: 13
SQ FT: 8,000
SALES (est): 2.3MM Privately Held
WEB: www.trussmfg.com
SIC: 2439 Trusses, wooden roof

(G-5715)
U S STUCCO LLC
28 Costello Pl (06111-5146)
PHONE.................................860 667-1935
Beata Pszczola, *Principal*
EMP: 9
SALES (est): 792.8K Privately Held
SIC: 3299 Stucco

(G-5716)
U-SEALUSA LLC
56 Fenn Rd (06111-2212)
PHONE.................................860 667-0911
Ilran Kim,
EMP: 90 EST: 2011
SQ FT: 20,000
SALES (est): 8.9MM Privately Held
SIC: 3444 Gutters, sheet metal; metal roofing & roof drainage equipment; sheet metal specialties, not stamped

(G-5717)
UCI SALES GROUP LLC
22 Whiteside St (06111-3963)
PHONE.................................860 667-4766
S E Pike, *Principal*
EMP: 1
SALES (est): 97.7K Privately Held
SIC: 3999 Manufacturing industries

(G-5718)
UNITED TECHNOLOGIES CORP
25 Holly Dr (06111-2243)
PHONE.................................860 595-4114
James Goldblatt, *Branch Mgr*
Jim Donovan, *Technology*
EMP: 1
SALES (corp-wide): 66.5B Publicly Held
WEB: www.utc.com
SIC: 3812 Aircraft/aerospace flight instruments & guidance systems
PA: United Technologies Corporation
    10 Farm Springs Rd
    Farmington CT 06032
    860 728-7000

(G-5719)
VALLEY WOODWORKING LLC
22 Styles Ave (06111-3439)
PHONE.................................860 667-1241
Steven Courtemanche, *Manager*
EMP: 2
SALES (est): 143.3K Privately Held
SIC: 2431 Millwork

(G-5720)
VISIONPOINT LLC
152 Rockwell Rd Ste B6 (06111-5546)
PHONE.................................860 436-9673

Newington - Hartford County (G-5721) — GEOGRAPHIC SECTION

Artur Kapuscinski, *Engineer*
Kevin Lavoie, *Mng Member*
Arlene White, *Manager*
Lee Andy, *Technology*
Zofia Lavoie,
EMP: 28
SQ FT: 6,500
SALES: 7MM **Privately Held**
WEB: www.visionpointllc.com
SIC: 7371 7373 3669 3651 Custom computer programming services; systems integration services; visual communication systems; audio electronic systems

(G-5721)
VN MACHINE CO
57 Maselli Rd (06111-5520)
PHONE..................................860 666-8797
Lan Psam, *Owner*
EMP: 3
SQ FT: 2,000
SALES (est): 267K **Privately Held**
SIC: 3599 Machine shop, jobbing & repair

(G-5722)
WAYSIDE FENCE CO
56 Fenn Rd (06111-2212)
PHONE..................................860 594-1090
Douglas De Lorenzo, *Branch Mgr*
EMP: 1
SALES (corp-wide): 1.3MM **Privately Held**
SIC: 3089 1799 Fences, gates & accessories: plastic; fence construction
PA: Wayside Fence Co., Inc.
    63 3rd Ave
    Bay Shore NY 11706
    631 968-6828

(G-5723)
WEST HRTFORD STIRS CBINETS INC
17 Main St (06111-1314)
P.O. Box 330118, West Hartford (06133-0118)
PHONE..................................860 953-9151
Andre Letourneau, *President*
Terry Letourneau, *Office Mgr*
Dana Donovan, *Representative*
EMP: 85 **EST:** 1937
SQ FT: 68,000
SALES (est): 11.6MM **Privately Held**
SIC: 2431 2434 Staircases & stairs, wood; wood kitchen cabinets

(G-5724)
YANKEE FINISHING
700 N Mountain Rd Ste 3 (06111-1351)
PHONE..................................203 910-0645
David Simoneau, *Owner*
EMP: 2
SALES: 100K **Privately Held**
SIC: 2434 5031 Wood kitchen cabinets; kitchen cabinets

(G-5725)
ZAVARELLA WOODWORKING INC
48 Commerce Ct (06111-2246)
PHONE..................................860 666-6969
Bruno Zavarella, *President*
Jeff Smith, *Project Mgr*
Alex Zavarella, *Project Mgr*
EMP: 9
SALES (est): 1.9MM **Privately Held**
WEB: www.zavarellawoodworking.com
SIC: 2431 Millwork

Newtown
Fairfield County

(G-5726)
AMERICAN ALLOY WIRE CORP
1 Wire Rd (06470-1613)
P.O. Box 667, Sandy Hook (06482-0667)
PHONE..................................203 426-3133
William J McCarthy, *President*
James Dyke, *Vice Pres*
EMP: 4
SALES: 500K **Privately Held**
SIC: 3357 Nonferrous wiredrawing & insulating

(G-5727)
AMERICAN WIRE CORPORATION
1 Wire Rd (06470-1613)
P.O. Box 667, Sandy Hook (06482-0667)
PHONE..................................203 426-3133
William J McCarthy, *President*
William J Mc Carthy, *President*
William Dyke, *Vice Pres*
EMP: 15 **EST:** 1928
SQ FT: 40,000
SALES: 1.5MM **Privately Held**
SIC: 3357 Magnet wire, nonferrous

(G-5728)
ARROCHAR SOFTWARE LLC
45 Turkey Hill Rd (06470-2342)
PHONE..................................203 987-5412
James McFarland,
EMP: 1
SALES (est): 88.4K **Privately Held**
WEB: www.arrochar.com
SIC: 7372 Business oriented computer software

(G-5729)
BETLAN CORPORATION
31 Pecks Ln Ste 7 (06470-5312)
PHONE..................................203 270-7898
Thomas A Polchowski, *President*
EMP: 10
SQ FT: 6,000
SALES (est): 980K **Privately Held**
WEB: www.betlan.com
SIC: 3634 1711 Fans, exhaust & ventilating, electric: household; ventilation & duct work contractor

(G-5730)
CABINET AUTHORITY LLC
11 Overlook Dr (06470-1513)
PHONE..................................203 304-2010
Richard C Haylon, *Principal*
EMP: 2 **EST:** 2009
SALES (est): 215.9K **Privately Held**
SIC: 2434 Wood kitchen cabinets

(G-5731)
CAD/CAM DNTL STDIO MIL CTR INC
184 Mount Pleasant Rd (06470-1408)
PHONE..................................203 733-3069
Bernt Balke,
EMP: 3 **EST:** 2017
SALES (est): 83.9K **Privately Held**
SIC: 3999 Manufacturing industries

(G-5732)
CASCADES HOLDING US INC
Cascades Cntnrbard Pckg Nwtown
1 Edmund Rd (06470-1632)
PHONE..................................203 426-5871
Geoff Schiffenhaus, *Plant Mgr*
EMP: 61
SALES (corp-wide): 3.5B **Privately Held**
SIC: 2653 Corrugated & solid fiber boxes
HQ: Cascades Holding Us Inc.
    4001 Packard Rd
    Niagara Falls NY 14303
    716 285-3681

(G-5733)
CHASE MEDIA GROUP
31 Pecks Ln Ste 3 (06470-5312)
PHONE..................................914 962-3871
Dave Fitzmorris, *Manager*
EMP: 14
SALES (est): 619.6K **Privately Held**
SIC: 2711 Newspapers: publishing only, not printed on site

(G-5734)
CORE STUDIOS
Also Called: Corerepro
117 Mount Pleasant Rd (06470-1570)
PHONE..................................203 364-9594
Roy Schfeumanm, *Owner*
EMP: 1
SALES (est): 170K **Privately Held**
SIC: 7389 2759 Advertising, promotional & trade show services; commercial printing

(G-5735)
COUNTRY OIL LLC
3 Bentagrass Ln (06470-1916)
PHONE..................................203 270-6439
William Landgrebe, *Principal*
EMP: 2
SALES (est): 99.1K **Privately Held**
SIC: 1311 Crude petroleum & natural gas

(G-5736)
EDELMAN METALWORKS INC
36 Butterfield Rd (06470-1009)
PHONE..................................203 744-7331
David Edelman, *President*
Dana Edelman, *Vice Pres*
EMP: 6
SALES (est): 1MM **Privately Held**
SIC: 3446 Stairs, fire escapes, balconies, railings & ladders

(G-5737)
ESG WOODWORKING AND BLDG LLC
24 Park Ln (06470-2249)
PHONE..................................203 667-0811
Edward Geoghegan, *Administration*
EMP: 1 **EST:** 2016
SALES (est): 54.1K **Privately Held**
SIC: 2431 Millwork

(G-5738)
FLAGPOLE SOFTWARE LLC
19 Scudder Rd (06470-1769)
PHONE..................................203 426-5166
Philip Crevier,
EMP: 4
SALES: 400K **Privately Held**
SIC: 7372 Business oriented computer software

(G-5739)
FORECAST INTERNATIONAL INC
22 Commerce Rd Ste 1 (06470-1643)
PHONE..................................203 426-0800
Edward M Nebinger, *CEO*
Douglas A Nebinger, *President*
Margaret G Nebinger, *Vice Pres*
Monty Nebinger, *Vice Pres*
Marge Nebinger, *VP Finance*
EMP: 57
SQ FT: 15,600
SALES (est): 7.6MM **Privately Held**
WEB: www.forecastinternational.com
SIC: 2731 8742 Book publishing; management consulting services

(G-5740)
GRAPHICS SERVICES CORPORATION
153 S Main St (06470-2791)
P.O. Box 141, Hawleyville (06440-0141)
PHONE..................................203 270-7578
Jay Willie, *President*
EMP: 1
SALES (est): 139.5K **Privately Held**
SIC: 2621 Packaging paper

(G-5741)
GUYS BLIND
37 Mount Pleasant Rd (06470-1530)
PHONE..................................203 270-8977
EMP: 2
SALES (est): 158K **Privately Held**
SIC: 2591 Window blinds

(G-5742)
HELIUM PLUS INC
17 Pebble Rd (06470-2229)
PHONE..................................203 304-1880
Rose Mary Savo, *President*
EMP: 5
SALES (est): 682.1K **Privately Held**
SIC: 2813 Helium

(G-5743)
HILLTOP PUBLISHING LLC
10 The Old Rd (06470-1553)
PHONE..................................203 426-8834
Robert Potsus, *President*
EMP: 1
SALES (est): 78.8K **Privately Held**
SIC: 2741 Miscellaneous publishing

(G-5744)
HOMETOWN PUBLISHING LLC
87 S Main St Ste 13 (06470-2315)
PHONE..................................203 426-5252
Steven C Bigham, *Principal*
Kari Rustici, *Prdtn Mgr*
Lisa Bigham, *Office Mgr*
EMP: 2 **EST:** 2010
SALES (est): 157.1K **Privately Held**
SIC: 2741 Telephone & other directory publishing

(G-5745)
HOPEWELL HARMONY LLC
8 Hopewell Rd (06470-1821)
PHONE..................................203 222-2268
Leslie J Huston, *Principal*
EMP: 2
SALES (est): 108K **Privately Held**
SIC: 3999 Manufacturing industries

(G-5746)
HOPP COMPANIES INC
3 Simm Ln Ste 2 (06470-2393)
PHONE..................................800 889-8425
Robert Hopp, *President*
EMP: 12
SQ FT: 5,000
SALES (est): 2MM **Privately Held**
WEB: www.hoppcompanies.com
SIC: 3578 3086 Point-of-sale devices; plastics foam products

(G-5747)
HP HOOD LLC
153 S Main St (06470-2791)
PHONE..................................203 304-9151
Matthew J D Amico, *President*
EMP: 296
SALES (corp-wide): 2.2B **Privately Held**
SIC: 2026 Fluid milk
PA: Hp Hood Llc
    6 Kimball Ln Ste 400
    Lynnfield MA 01940
    617 887-8441

(G-5748)
HUBBELL INCORPORATED
14 Prospect Dr (06470-2338)
PHONE..................................203 426-2555
Michael O'Connor, *Vice Pres*
Julie Brown, *Buyer*
Robert Khansen, *Branch Mgr*
Jason Cauchon, *Maintence Staff*
EMP: 20
SALES (corp-wide): 4.4B **Publicly Held**
WEB: www.hubbell.com
SIC: 3643 Connectors & terminals for electrical devices
PA: Hubbell Incorporated
    40 Waterview Dr
    Shelton CT 06484
    475 882-4000

(G-5749)
HUMAN INTERESTS LLC
22 Whitewood Rd (06470-1561)
PHONE..................................203 270-9107
Joseph Michael James, *Principal*
EMP: 2
SALES (est): 114.7K **Privately Held**
SIC: 2252 Socks

(G-5750)
INSTANT WIN INNOVATIONS
32 Butterfield Rd (06470-1009)
PHONE..................................203 648-4499
Linda Geils, *Vice Pres*
Chris Barr, *VP Mktg*
EMP: 2 **EST:** 2016
SALES (est): 101.5K **Privately Held**
SIC: 2752 Commercial printing, lithographic

(G-5751)
JSR MICRO INC
3 Taunton Lake Dr (06470-1528)
PHONE..................................203 426-7794
Mark Dennen, *Manager*
EMP: 2 **Privately Held**
WEB: www.jsrmicro.com
SIC: 2869 Industrial organic chemicals
HQ: Jsr Micro, Inc.
    1280 N Mathilda Ave
    Sunnyvale CA 94089
    408 543-8800

GEOGRAPHIC SECTION
Newtown - Fairfield County (G-5783)

(G-5752)
L M T COMMUNICATIONS INC
Also Called: L M T Magazine
84 S Main St (06470-2356)
PHONE..................................203 426-4568
Judy Fishman, *President*
Kate Conetta, *Production*
Zhane Cardenas, *Sales Staff*
Susan Poitras, *Office Mgr*
Lauren Meehan, *Manager*
EMP: 11
SQ FT: 1,600
SALES: 1.2MM **Privately Held**
WEB: www.lmtcommunications.com
SIC: 2721 7389 Magazines: publishing only, not printed on site; trade journals: publishing only, not printed on site; trade show arrangement

(G-5753)
LAGNESE WOODWORKING
9 Pebble Rd (06470-2229)
PHONE..................................203 426-6434
Paul Lagnese, *Principal*
EMP: 2
SALES (est): 155K **Privately Held**
SIC: 2431 Millwork

(G-5754)
LENS
33 Currituck Rd (06470-1331)
PHONE..................................203 426-8833
Robert Bixby, *Principal*
EMP: 2
SALES (est): 77.4K **Privately Held**
SIC: 3851 Ophthalmic goods

(G-5755)
LOCTEC CORPORATION
15 Commerce Rd Ste 2 (06470-1633)
PHONE..................................203 364-1000
Victor Anderson, *President*
Steven Schoenfeld, *Vice Pres*
EMP: 50
SQ FT: 9,500
SALES: 4.5MM **Privately Held**
SIC: 5072 3429 Security devices, locks; furniture hardware; locks or lock sets; furniture hardware

(G-5756)
LONG FA INC
228 S Main St (06470-2764)
PHONE..................................203 270-3878
EMP: 2
SALES (est): 52.8K **Privately Held**
SIC: 3999 Manufacturing industries

(G-5757)
M CUBED TECHNOLOGIES INC (HQ)
31 Pecks Ln Ste 8 (06470-5312)
PHONE..................................203 304-2940
Randall Price Sr, *President*
Jai Singh, *Exec VP*
Mike Aghajanian, *Vice Pres*
Lori Capomolla, *Vice Pres*
Brian Farrell, *Opers Mgr*
▲ EMP: 45 EST: 1993
SQ FT: 110,000
SALES (est): 773.2K
SALES (corp-wide): 1.3B **Publicly Held**
WEB: www.mmmt.com
SIC: 3444 5051 3599 Sheet metalwork; metals service centers & offices; machine shop, jobbing & repair
PA: Ii-Vi Incorporated
    375 Saxonburg Blvd
    Saxonburg PA 16056
    724 352-4455

(G-5758)
M-SYSTEMS INC
12 Valley View Rd (06470-1922)
PHONE..................................203 270-8926
Manfred Schmidt, *President*
Betty Schmidt, *Admin Sec*
EMP: 2
SALES: 300K **Privately Held**
SIC: 3669 Traffic signals, electric

(G-5759)
MAINELY CUSTOM CARVING
9 Cobblestone Ln (06470-1779)
PHONE..................................203 426-8375
James Loring, *Owner*
EMP: 1
SALES (est): 70.7K **Privately Held**
SIC: 2752 Commercial printing, lithographic

(G-5760)
METIS MICROSYSTEMS LLC
48 Farrell Rd (06470-1201)
PHONE..................................203 512-8453
Azeez Bhavnagarwala,
EMP: 2
SALES (est): 90K **Privately Held**
SIC: 3674 Integrated circuits, semiconductor networks, etc.

(G-5761)
MINUTEMAN PRESS
123 S Main St Ste 210 (06470-5309)
PHONE..................................203 261-9569
Fred Flemming, *Manager*
EMP: 2
SALES (est): 196.1K **Privately Held**
SIC: 2752 Commercial printing, lithographic

(G-5762)
NATIONAL SHOOTING SPORTS FOUND
11 Mile Hill Rd Ste A (06470-2328)
PHONE..................................203 426-1320
Steve Sanetti, *President*
Bill Dunn, *Managing Dir*
Nancy Coburn, *Vice Pres*
John Smith, *Vice Pres*
Melanie Knox, *Marketing Staff*
EMP: 44
SQ FT: 20,000
SALES: 44MM **Privately Held**
WEB: www.nssf.org
SIC: 2721 8611 2741 Magazines: publishing only, not printed on site; trade associations; miscellaneous publishing

(G-5763)
NEW LEAF PHARMACEUTICAL
77 S Main St (06470-2388)
P.O. Box 735 (06470-0735)
PHONE..................................203 270-4167
Paul Carpenter, *CEO*
EMP: 17
SALES (est): 763.3K **Privately Held**
SIC: 2834 Proprietary drug products

(G-5764)
NEWTOWN SPORTS GROUP
15 Anthony Ridge Rd (06470-1344)
PHONE..................................508 341-1238
Robert Burbank, *Principal*
EMP: 3
SALES (est): 112K **Privately Held**
SIC: 2711 Newspapers

(G-5765)
NINA NAIL SPA
14 Church Hill Rd Ste A2 (06470-1640)
PHONE..................................203 270-0777
Suyoung Jang, *Principal*
EMP: 2
SALES (est): 174.6K **Privately Held**
SIC: 2844 Manicure preparations

(G-5766)
OLD CASTLE FOODS LLC
13 Old Castle Dr (06470-1783)
PHONE..................................203 426-1344
William Meier, *Principal*
EMP: 3 EST: 2012
SALES (est): 182.4K **Privately Held**
SIC: 2099 Food preparations

(G-5767)
PAGES OF YESTERYEAR
9 Old Hawleyville Rd (06470-1221)
PHONE..................................203 426-0864
John Renjilian, *Owner*
EMP: 1
SALES (est): 25K **Privately Held**
SIC: 5192 2711 Books; newspapers

(G-5768)
PARIOT SIGN COMPANY LLC
78 Main St (06470-2128)
PHONE..................................203 364-9009
Andrew Bryant, *Principal*
EMP: 2
SALES (est): 155.2K **Privately Held**
SIC: 3993 Signs & advertising specialties

(G-5769)
PARK GROUP SOLUTIONS LLC
8 Pecks Ln Ste A2 (06470-2396)
PHONE..................................203 459-8784
Amber Dodge, *Vice Pres*
Paul Crisci, *Mng Member*
EMP: 4
SALES (est): 755.2K **Privately Held**
SIC: 7311 8742 8748 8331 Advertising consultant; marketing consulting services; economic consultant; job training services; magazines: publishing & printing

(G-5770)
QSONICA LLC
Also Called: Sonicators
53 Church Hill Rd (06470-1614)
PHONE..................................203 426-0101
Lauren Soloff, *President*
Robert Soloff, *Vice Pres*
Steven A Bowen, *CFO*
Ronald Verrilli, *Admin Sec*
EMP: 8
SALES (est): 544.3K
SALES (corp-wide): 19.6MM **Publicly Held**
WEB: www.Sonicator.com
SIC: 3569 Liquid automation machinery & equipment
PA: Sonics & Materials, Inc.
    53 Church Hill Rd
    Newtown CT 06470
    203 270-4600

(G-5771)
QUALITY SCANNING SOLUTION
5 Ferris Rd (06470-1758)
PHONE..................................203 270-1833
Robert R Zupcoe, *Owner*
EMP: 1
SALES (est): 46.7K **Privately Held**
SIC: 7699 3699 Camera repair shop; laser systems & equipment

(G-5772)
QUIXPRESS CAR WASH
1 Simm Ln (06470-2307)
PHONE..................................203 364-9777
EMP: 1 EST: 2018
SALES (est): 37.5K **Privately Held**
SIC: 2741 Miscellaneous publishing

(G-5773)
R BOTSFORD CUSTOM WDWKG LLC
171 Brushy Hill Rd (06470-2514)
PHONE..................................203 994-5302
Ron Botsford, *President*
EMP: 2
SALES (est): 85.3K **Privately Held**
SIC: 2431 Millwork

(G-5774)
RAND-WHITNEY GROUP LLC
Also Called: Rand-Whitney Container Newtown
1 Edmund Rd (06470-1600)
P.O. Box 498 (06470-0498)
PHONE..................................203 426-5871
Dick Minton, *Manager*
EMP: 75 **Privately Held**
SIC: 2653 Boxes, corrugated: made from purchased materials; boxes, solid fiber: made from purchased materials
HQ: Rand-Whitney Group Llc
    1 Rand Whitney Way
    Worcester MA 01607
    508 791-2301

(G-5775)
RICE LAKE WEIGHING SYSTEMS INC
Also Called: Condec
3 Simm Ln Ste 2a (06470-2393)
PHONE..................................203 270-6012
Steve Parkman, *Branch Mgr*
EMP: 2
SALES (corp-wide): 129.5MM **Privately Held**
WEB: www.ishidaretail.com
SIC: 3596 Scales & balances, except laboratory

PA: Rice Lake Weighing Systems, Inc.
    230 W Coleman St
    Rice Lake WI 54868
    715 234-9171

(G-5776)
ROBERT LOUIS COMPANY INC
31 Shepard Hill Rd (06470-1936)
PHONE..................................203 270-1400
Robert Foege, *President*
EMP: 3
SALES (est): 270K **Privately Held**
SIC: 3949 Shooting equipment & supplies, general

(G-5777)
ROOSTER MALT COMPANY LLC
21 Plumtrees Rd (06470-1729)
PHONE..................................203 364-7612
James Tanner,
EMP: 1
SALES (est): 54.3K **Privately Held**
SIC: 3999 Manufacturing industries

(G-5778)
SAUGATUCK TREE & LOGGING LLC (PA)
Also Called: Smith Bros Woodland Mgmt LLC
309 S Main St (06470-2777)
PHONE..................................203 304-1326
Derek Smith,
Dwight Smith,
EMP: 3
SQ FT: 3,200
SALES (est): 1.2MM **Privately Held**
WEB: www.saugreen.com
SIC: 1629 2411 Land clearing contractor; logging

(G-5779)
SHOP SMART CENTRAL INC
Also Called: Chase Press
31 Pecks Ln (06470-5312)
PHONE..................................914 962-3871
Carla Chase, *President*
EMP: 7 EST: 2005
SALES (est): 659.4K **Privately Held**
SIC: 2741 Business service newsletters: publishing & printing

(G-5780)
SINOL USA INC
77 S Main St (06470-2388)
P.O. Box 735 (06470-0735)
PHONE..................................203 470-7404
Paul Carpenter, *CEO*
EMP: 10
SALES (est): 1.6MM **Privately Held**
WEB: www.sinolusa.com
SIC: 2834 Pharmaceutical preparations

(G-5781)
SONICS & MATERIALS INC (PA)
Also Called: Ultra Sonic Seal Co
53 Church Hill Rd (06470-1699)
PHONE..................................203 270-4600
Robert Soloff, *CEO*
Lauren H Soloff, *Vice Pres*
Lauren Soloff, *Vice Pres*
Dan Grise, *VP Opers*
Steven Bowen, *CFO*
▲ EMP: 75 EST: 1969
SQ FT: 44,000
SALES (est): 19.6MM **Publicly Held**
WEB: www.Sonics.com
SIC: 3548 3569 Welding apparatus; liquid automation machinery & equipment

(G-5782)
STANDARD PNEUMATIC PRODUCTS
31 Shepard Hill Rd (06470-1936)
PHONE..................................203 270-1400
Robert Foege, *President*
Jeanne Foege, *Corp Secy*
EMP: 3 EST: 1992
SQ FT: 2,600
SALES: 500K **Privately Held**
WEB: www.stdpneumatics.com
SIC: 3563 Air & gas compressors

(G-5783)
SWIVEL MACHINE WORKS INC
11 Monitor Hill Rd (06470-2242)
PHONE..................................203 270-6343

Newtown - Fairfield County (G-5784)

Glen Ekstrom, *President*
EMP: 3
SALES: 250K **Privately Held**
WEB: www.swivelmachine.com
SIC: **3949** 5941 Sporting & athletic goods; sporting goods & bicycle shops

(G-5784)
SYNCOTE CHEMICAL COMPANY INC
16 Greenbriar Ln (06470-2218)
PHONE 203 426-5526
George J Grosner, *President*
EMP: 2
SALES (est): 10K **Privately Held**
SIC: **3291** Abrasive products

(G-5785)
TAUNTON INC
Also Called: Taunton Press
63 S Main St (06470-2355)
P.O. Box 5506 (06470-0921)
PHONE 203 426-8171
Daniel R McCarthy, *CEO*
Andrea Roman, *Ch of Bd*
Timothy Rahr, *President*
Robina Lewis, *Marketing Staff*
Patrick McCombe, *Assoc Editor*
EMP: 844
SQ FT: 70,000
SALES (est): 76.7MM **Privately Held**
SIC: **2721** 2731 7812 5963 Magazines: publishing only, not printed on site; books: publishing only; video tape production; direct sales, telemarketing

(G-5786)
TAUNTON INTERACTIVE INC
63 S Main St (06470-2355)
PHONE 203 426-8171
Timothy Rahr, *President*
EMP: 1
SALES (est): 54.8K **Privately Held**
SIC: **2731** Books: publishing only

(G-5787)
TAUNTON PRESS INC
191 S Main St (06470-2733)
PHONE 203 426-8171
John Lively, *CEO*
EMP: 285
SALES (corp-wide): 72MM **Privately Held**
WEB: www.taunton.com
SIC: **2721** Magazines: publishing only, not printed on site
PA: The Taunton Press Inc
63 S Main St
Newtown CT 06470
203 426-8171

(G-5788)
TAUTON PRESS
52 Church Hill Rd (06470-1622)
PHONE 203 304-3000
Sue Roman, *Principal*
▲ EMP: 1
SALES (est): 133.6K **Privately Held**
SIC: **2721** Magazines: publishing only, not printed on site

(G-5789)
THE BEE PUBLISHING COMPANY (PA)
Also Called: Health Monitor
5 Church Hill Rd (06470-1605)
P.O. Box 5503 (06470-5503)
PHONE 203 426-8036
R Scudder Smith, *President*
Scott Baggett, *General Mgr*
Laura Beach, *Editor*
Helen Smith, *Vice Pres*
Kim Smith, *Controller*
▼ EMP: 50 EST: 1877
SQ FT: 20,000
SALES (est): 3.7MM **Privately Held**
WEB: www.thebee.com
SIC: **2711** Commercial printing & newspaper publishing combined

(G-5790)
THE BEE PUBLISHING COMPANY
17 Commerce Rd (06470-1607)
PHONE 203 426-0178

James Busby, *Manager*
EMP: 4
SALES (est): 251.9K
SALES (corp-wide): 3.7MM **Privately Held**
WEB: www.thebee.com
SIC: **2711** Newspapers: publishing only, not printed on site
PA: The Bee Publishing Company
5 Church Hill Rd
Newtown CT 06470
203 426-8036

(G-5791)
TIER ONE LLC
31 Pecks Ln Ste 1 (06470-5312)
PHONE 203 426-3030
Don Stankus, *Mfg Staff*
Terry Toth, *Engineer*
Ted Turiano, *Engineer*
Linda Iassogna, *CFO*
Stan Montefusco, *Human Resources*
EMP: 67
SQ FT: 35,000
SALES (est): 12.7MM **Privately Held**
WEB: www.tieronemachining.com
SIC: **3599** Machine shop, jobbing & repair

(G-5792)
TILLYS NATURAL BLEND LLC
32 Old Farm Hill Rd (06470-1146)
PHONE 203 270-8406
Giselle Graham, *Mng Member*
EMP: 1 EST: 2010
SALES (est): 85.8K **Privately Held**
SIC: **3199** 7389 Dog furnishings: collars, leashes, muzzles, etc.: leather;

(G-5793)
TRI-UNION SEAFOODS LLC
Also Called: Chicken of The Sea
16 Palestine Rd (06470-2525)
PHONE 203 426-1266
EMP: 1 **Privately Held**
SIC: **2091** 5146 Canned & cured fish & seafoods; fish & seafoods
HQ: Tri-Union Seafoods, Llc
2150 E Grand Ave
El Segundo CA 90245
858 558-9662

(G-5794)
TRIPLE A MANUFACTURING COMPANY
1 Brookwood Dr (06470-1842)
PHONE 203 743-9043
Louis Schulz, *President*
Alain Schulz, *Vice Pres*
Patrick Schulz, *Vice Pres*
Christiane Schulz, *Admin Sec*
▲ EMP: 2
SALES (est): 314.6K **Privately Held**
SIC: **3599** Machine shop, jobbing & repair

(G-5795)
TUDOR CONVERTED PRODUCTS INC (PA)
22 Main St Unit 1b (06470-2106)
PHONE 203 304-1875
Richard P Cuminale Jr, *President*
Debbie T Cuminale, *Admin Sec*
▲ EMP: 20
SQ FT: 34,000
SALES (est): 2.7MM **Privately Held**
SIC: **2679** Paper products, converted

(G-5796)
UTC FIRE SEC AMERICAS CORP INC
Fiber Options Division
16 Commerce Rd (06470-1607)
PHONE 203 426-1180
EMP: 120
SALES (corp-wide): 59.8B **Publicly Held**
SIC: **3669** 3827 Mfg Communications Equipment Mfg Optical Instruments/Lenses
HQ: Utc Fire & Security Americas Corporation, Inc.
8985 Town Center Pkwy
Lakewood Ranch FL 34202

(G-5797)
WILD RVER CSTM SCREEN PRTG LLC
3 Simm Ln Ste 2e1 (06470-2300)
PHONE 203 426-1500
Meredith Ledney,
EMP: 4
SALES: 200K **Privately Held**
SIC: **2752** Commercial printing, lithographic

(G-5798)
WILLOW WOODWORKING INC
36 Maltbie Rd (06470-2508)
PHONE 203 426-8200
Anatole Burkin, *Principal*
EMP: 2 EST: 2000
SALES (est): 175.5K **Privately Held**
SIC: **2431** Millwork

(G-5799)
WIND CORPORATION
Also Called: Wind Hardware & Engineering
30 Pecks Ln (06470-2361)
PHONE 203 778-1001
Patrick E Wind, *President*
Kevin Houlihan, *Vice Pres*
Matthews Brian, *Warehouse Mgr*
Dave Carlson, *Opers Staff*
Mike Gallo, *Engineer*
◆ EMP: 28
SQ FT: 60,000
SALES (est): 7.4MM **Privately Held**
WEB: www.windcorp.com
SIC: **3429** Manufactured hardware (general)

(G-5800)
ZEPHYR LOCK LLC
30 Pecks Ln (06470-2361)
PHONE 866 937-4971
Patrick Wind,
Kevin Houlihan,
▲ EMP: 12
SQ FT: 20,000
SALES (est): 1.3MM **Privately Held**
WEB: www.zephyrlock.com
SIC: **3429** Locks or lock sets

Niantic
New London County

(G-5801)
AT INDUSTRIES LLC
31 Greencliff Dr (06357-1523)
PHONE 860 739-6639
Adam McCaffery, *Principal*
EMP: 2
SALES (est): 98.6K **Privately Held**
SIC: **3599** Industrial machinery

(G-5802)
BUDGET WOODWORKER LLC
214 Pennsylvania Ave (06357-1910)
PHONE 860 468-5551
Benjamin Wright, *Principal*
EMP: 1 EST: 2017
SALES (est): 54.1K **Privately Held**
SIC: **2431** Millwork

(G-5803)
CHARLES MCDOUGAL
61 White Birch Cir (06357-1610)
PHONE 860 739-9952
Linda McDougal, *Principal*
EMP: 1
SALES (est): 55.9K **Privately Held**
SIC: **2731** Books: publishing only

(G-5804)
CSG AUTOMATION LLC
36 Industrial Park Rd (06357-1262)
PHONE 860 691-1885
Victor Abreu, *Mng Member*
EMP: 6 EST: 2015
SALES (est): 163.5K **Privately Held**
SIC: **5084** 3569 Industrial machinery & equipment; assembly machines, non-metalworking

(G-5805)
EAST LYME PUPPETRY PROJECT
11 Lake Avenue Ext (06357-2413)
PHONE 860 739-7225
Richard Waterman, *President*
EMP: 2
SALES (est): 57.8K **Privately Held**
SIC: **8699** 3999 Charitable organization; puppets & marionettes

(G-5806)
FOUR COLOR INC
10 Liberty Way Unit A8 (06357-1034)
PHONE 860 691-1782
William Argyle, *Owner*
EMP: 2
SALES (est): 245.7K **Privately Held**
WEB: www.fourcolorinc.com
SIC: **2759** 2791 Commercial printing; typesetting

(G-5807)
GBC MARKETING LLC
13 Saunders Dr (06357-2710)
PHONE 860 739-8760
Gary Burchsted Sr, *Owner*
EMP: 2
SALES (est): 90.7K **Privately Held**
SIC: **2653** Corrugated & solid fiber boxes

(G-5808)
HAYLONS MARKET LLC
157 W Main St Ste 1 (06357-1057)
PHONE 860 739-9509
David Haylon, *Principal*
EMP: 3 EST: 2015
SALES (est): 110K **Privately Held**
SIC: **2051** Bakery products, partially cooked (except frozen)

(G-5809)
HEATERS INC
11 Freedom Way Unit D5 (06357-1041)
PHONE 860 739-5477
Debra Thurlow, *President*
EMP: 5 EST: 1945
SQ FT: 5,000
SALES: 450K **Privately Held**
WEB: www.heatincorp.com
SIC: **2822** Silicone rubbers

(G-5810)
HMS PUBLICATIONS INC
2 Louise Dr (06357-1713)
P.O. Box 524 (06357-0524)
PHONE 860 739-3187
Harvey Snitkin, *President*
EMP: 1
SALES (est): 81.8K **Privately Held**
WEB: www.hmspublications.com
SIC: **2741** Miscellaneous publishing

(G-5811)
JAMMAR MFG CO INC
26 Industrial Park Rd (06357-1209)
P.O. Box 392, Uncasville (06382-0392)
PHONE 866 848-1113
James Bliss, *President*
Marian Bliss, *Admin Sec*
EMP: 5
SALES (est): 607.9K **Privately Held**
WEB: www.jammarmfg.com
SIC: **3949** Playground equipment

(G-5812)
JANUS MOTORSPORTS LLC
22 Park Pl (06357-2318)
PHONE 860 857-6041
Kendall Janus, *President*
EMP: 2
SALES (est): 204.3K **Privately Held**
SIC: **3714** Motor vehicle parts & accessories

(G-5813)
NIANTIC AWNING COMPANY
Also Called: Niantic Awning & Sunroom Co
193 Pennsylvania Ave (06357-1927)
PHONE 860 739-0161
Edwin Franklin, *President*
Karen Franklin, *Vice Pres*
EMP: 3 EST: 1995
SQ FT: 800

▲ = Import ▼ = Export
◆ = Import/Export

GEOGRAPHIC SECTION

SALES (est): 453.1K **Privately Held**
WEB: www.nianticawning.com
SIC: **2431** 2591 3444 3448 Awnings, blinds & shutters, wood; porch shades, wood slat; awnings & canopies; sunrooms, prefabricated metal

(G-5814)
NIANTIC TOOL INC
Also Called: Machine Shop
32 Industrial Park Rd (06357-1209)
P.O. Box 205, East Lyme (06333-0205)
PHONE..................860 739-2182
David Nelson, *President*
Robert W Nelson, *Vice Pres*
Joanne Nelson, *Admin Sec*
EMP: 6
SQ FT: 8,500
SALES: 839.9K **Privately Held**
WEB: www.nianticoolinc.com
SIC: **3599** Machine shop, jobbing & repair

(G-5815)
PAW PRINT PANTRY LLC
214 Flanders Rd Ste A (06357-1260)
PHONE..................860 447-8442
Jennifer Mohr, *Branch Mgr*
EMP: 9
SALES (corp-wide): 782.3K **Privately Held**
SIC: **2752** Commercial printing, lithographic
PA: Paw Print Pantry Llc
  33 Gurley Rd
  East Lyme CT 06333
  860 447-8442

(G-5816)
REMOTE SITE SERVICE LLC
46 Old Black Point Rd (06357-2833)
PHONE..................860 691-1911
Peter Caron, *Partner*
EMP: 2 EST: 1999
SALES (est): 166.4K **Privately Held**
SIC: **3441** Tower sections, radio & television transmission

(G-5817)
SIGN CRAFT LLC
5 Black Point Rd (06357-2364)
PHONE..................860 739-2863
John C Wilson,
Julie Wilson,
EMP: 2
SQ FT: 2,000
SALES (est): 270.8K **Privately Held**
WEB: www.signcraftsigns.com
SIC: **3993** 7929 Signs & advertising specialties; disc jockey service

(G-5818)
TREBLE CLEF MUSIC PRESS
14 N Washington Ave (06357-3212)
PHONE..................919 932-5455
EMP: 1
SALES (est): 37.5K **Privately Held**
SIC: **2741** Misc Publishing

(G-5819)
WATSON FABRICATION LLC
15 E Pattagansett Rd (06357-2313)
PHONE..................860 912-8778
Andrew Watson, *Principal*
EMP: 2
SALES (est): 80.7K **Privately Held**
SIC: **3999** Manufacturing industries

(G-5820)
WILD-FROYO LLC
16 Town Rd (06357-2718)
PHONE..................860 739-6124
William Wild, *Principal*
EMP: 1 EST: 2013
SALES (est): 63.2K **Privately Held**
SIC: **2024** Yogurt desserts, frozen

(G-5821)
ZZ POWDER COATING
13 Roxbury Ct (06357-1313)
PHONE..................860 917-7495
Zack Zurzuski, *Manager*
William Holland, *Executive*
EMP: 2
SALES (est): 155.4K **Privately Held**
SIC: **3479** Coating of metals & formed products

Norfolk
Litchfield County

(G-5822)
542 RUSTIC WOODWORKS
108 Sunset Ridge Rd (06058-1214)
PHONE..................860 387-8680
Peter Kelley, *Principal*
EMP: 2 EST: 2017
SALES (est): 85.2K **Privately Held**
SIC: **2431** Millwork

(G-5823)
CHRIS PETERSON WOODWORKS
44 Ashpohtag Rd (06058-1004)
PHONE..................860 542-0140
Chris Peterson, *Owner*
EMP: 1
SALES (est): 120K **Privately Held**
SIC: **2434** Wood kitchen cabinets

(G-5824)
KINGSLAND CO
7 Colebrook Rd (06058-1332)
P.O. Box 594 (06058-0594)
PHONE..................860 542-6981
Luke K Burke, *President*
Liane Burke, *Corp Secy*
Mark K Burke, *Vice Pres*
Matthew K Burke, *Vice Pres*
EMP: 8
SQ FT: 7,200
SALES (est): 1MM **Privately Held**
WEB: www.kingsland-shutters.com
SIC: **2431** Doors & door parts & trim, wood; windows & window parts & trim, wood; door shutters, wood

(G-5825)
LOUIS E ALLYN SONS INC
270 Ashpohtag Rd (06058-1007)
P.O. Box 217, East Canaan (06024-0217)
PHONE..................860 542-5741
Walter Allyn, *President*
Lisa Allen, *Manager*
EMP: 4
SALES (est): 251.4K **Privately Held**
SIC: **1381** Drilling oil & gas wells

(G-5826)
SOUTH NORFOLK LUMBER CO
1117 Litchfield Rd (06058-1362)
PHONE..................860 542-5650
Henry Gundlach, *Owner*
EMP: 2
SALES (est): 170K **Privately Held**
SIC: **2421** 5211 Sawmills & planing mills, general; planing mill products & lumber

(G-5827)
STITCHING ON MAPLE STUDIO
48 Maple Ave (06058-1102)
PHONE..................860 480-2793
EMP: 1 EST: 2017
SALES (est): 38.1K **Privately Held**
SIC: **2395** Embroidery & art needlework

(G-5828)
VINTAGE PERFORMANCE LLC
7 Terrace Vw (06058)
P.O. Box 200 (06058-0200)
PHONE..................860 542-5753
Carl Dudesh, *President*
EMP: 2
SALES (est): 139.7K **Privately Held**
WEB: www.vintageperformance.com
SIC: **3651** 8711 Audio electronic systems; electrical or electronic engineering

North Branford
New Haven County

(G-5829)
BEST BUILT CUSTOM STAIR BUILDI
2175 Maple Rd (06471-1577)
PHONE..................203 488-8031
Joel Parillo, *Principal*
EMP: 2
SALES (est): 147.4K **Privately Held**
SIC: **2431** Staircases & stairs, wood

(G-5830)
BRIAN BERLEPSCH
Also Called: Imposition Graphics
21 Commerce Dr Ste 2 (06471-3204)
PHONE..................203 484-9799
Brian Berlepsch, *Owner*
EMP: 4
SQ FT: 2,000
SALES (est): 220K **Privately Held**
SIC: **2752** Commercial printing, lithographic

(G-5831)
COASTLINE ENVIRONMENTAL LLC
12 Ridgetop Ln (06471-1477)
PHONE..................203 483-6898
Eric J Golia,
EMP: 3
SALES (est): 51.7K **Privately Held**
SIC: **8999** 7699 3089 Earth science services; septic tank cleaning service; toilets, portable chemical: plastic

(G-5832)
CONCORDIA LTD
Also Called: J B Silk Screen Printing
5 Enterprise Dr (06471-1324)
P.O. Box 130 (06471-0130)
PHONE..................203 483-0221
Rocco Esposito, *President*
Christopher Esposito, *Vice Pres*
EMP: 5
SQ FT: 4,000
SALES (est): 350K **Privately Held**
WEB: www.concordia-iye.org.uk
SIC: **2759** 2396 Screen printing; automotive & apparel trimmings

(G-5833)
CUTTER & DRILL PARTS LLC
31 Ciro Rd (06471-1521)
PHONE..................203 483-0876
Chris Mitrzyk, *Principal*
EMP: 2
SALES (est): 166.1K **Privately Held**
WEB: www.cutter-drill.com
SIC: **3111** Bookbinders' leather

(G-5834)
DEPENDABLE REPAIR INC
Also Called: Dependable Hydraulics
2110 Foxon Rd (06471-1511)
PHONE..................203 481-9706
Benedict Larosa, *Owner*
Tom Larosa, *Managing Dir*
EMP: 10
SALES (corp-wide): 4MM **Privately Held**
SIC: **7699** 3599 Hydraulic equipment repair; machine shop, jobbing & repair
PA: Dependable Repair, Inc.
  18 Ranick Dr W
  Amityville NY 11701
  631 842-0700

(G-5835)
DICON CONNECTIONS INC
33 Fowler Rd (06471-1519)
P.O. Box 190 (06471-0190)
PHONE..................203 481-8080
Jeffrey Williams, *President*
Timothy Williams, *Vice Pres*
Buzz Johnson, *Sales Staff*
EMP: 50
SQ FT: 18,000
SALES (est): 11.7MM **Privately Held**
WEB: www.diconconnections.com
SIC: **3643** Current-carrying wiring devices

(G-5836)
DWYER ALUMINUM MAST COMPANY
2 Commerce Dr Ste 1 (06471-1200)
PHONE..................203 484-0419
Robert Dwyer, *President*
Joy Sperrazza, *Manager*
Andrew Dwyer, *Admin Sec*
◆ EMP: 10
SQ FT: 10,500
SALES (est): 1.8MM **Privately Held**
WEB: www.dwyermast.com
SIC: **3365** 3429 Masts, cast aluminum; marine hardware

(G-5837)
DYNAMIC RACING TRANSM LLC
104-5 Enterprise Dr (06471)
PHONE..................203 315-0138
Harold Miller,
EMP: 4
SALES (est): 800K **Privately Held**
WEB: www.dynamicracingtrans.com
SIC: **3714** Transmissions, motor vehicle

(G-5838)
FARACE INDUSTRIES LLC
21 Ciro Rd (06471-1521)
PHONE..................203 315-1293
Thomas Farace, *Principal*
Karen Green, *Office Mgr*
EMP: 2
SALES (est): 118.6K **Privately Held**
SIC: **3999** Manufacturing industries

(G-5839)
GOODYFAB LLC
88 Totoket Rd (06471-1031)
PHONE..................203 927-3059
Matt Goodwin,
EMP: 5
SALES (est): 667.8K **Privately Held**
SIC: **3446** 7389 7692 Ornamental metalwork; metal slitting & shearing; welding repair

(G-5840)
HALL MACHINE SYSTEMS INC (HQ)
Also Called: Hall Industries
8c Commerce Dr (06471-1250)
P.O. Box 647, Branford (06405-0647)
PHONE..................203 481-4275
Robert Johnson, *President*
William Gurecki, *Vice Pres*
Douglas Hall, *Vice Pres*
Thomas McComiskey, *Vice Pres*
Dean Williams, *Vice Pres*
EMP: 9
SQ FT: 20,000
SALES (est): 2.1MM
SALES (corp-wide): 18MM **Privately Held**
SIC: **3549** 5084 Metalworking machinery; industrial machinery & equipment
PA: M.G.S. Manufacturing Inc.
  122 Otis St
  Rome NY 13441
  315 337-3350

(G-5841)
HALLS RENTAL SERVICE LLC
Also Called: D C Hall Rental Service
45 Cedar Lake Rd (06471-1247)
PHONE..................203 488-0383
David Hall, *Mng Member*
Catherine Hall,
EMP: 4
SALES: 290K **Privately Held**
SIC: **2531** Chairs, table & arm

(G-5842)
HARRISON FARM
95 North St (06471-1420)
PHONE..................203 488-7963
Dudley Harrison, *Partner*
Ethel Harrison, *Partner*
EMP: 2
SALES (est): 66.4K **Privately Held**
SIC: **0722** 2099 Fruit & tree nuts, machine harvesting services; food preparations

(G-5843)
HONEYWELL INTERNATIONAL INC
12 Clintonville Rd (06471)
PHONE..................203 484-7161
EMP: 657
SALES (corp-wide): 41.8B **Publicly Held**
WEB: www.honeywell.com
SIC: **3724** Aircraft engines & engine parts
PA: Honeywell International Inc.
  300 S Tryon St
  Charlotte NC 28202
  973 455-2000

North Branford - New Haven County (G-5844)

(G-5844)
HYDROGEN HIGHWAY LLC
242 Branford Rd (06471-1303)
PHONE..................203 871-1000
Terri S Alpert, *Manager*
EMP: 3
SALES (est): 146.1K **Privately Held**
SIC: 2813 Hydrogen

(G-5845)
INTERNATIONAL INSTRUMENTS DIV
344 Twin Lakes Rd (06471-1220)
PHONE..................203 481-3450
James Jamieson, *Principal*
EMP: 2
SALES (est): 123.4K **Privately Held**
SIC: 3825 Test equipment for electronic & electric measurement

(G-5846)
INTERNATIONAL PIPE & STL CORP
4 Enterprise Dr (06471-1354)
PHONE..................203 481-7102
W A Lalani, *President*
Sada Lalani, *Admin Sec*
▼ **EMP:** 10
SQ FT: 25,000
SALES (est): 1.9MM **Privately Held**
WEB: www.internationalpipe.net
SIC: 3446 5051 3496 3315 Architectural metalwork; pipe & tubing, steel; steel; miscellaneous fabricated wire products; steel wire & related products

(G-5847)
JCB PLASTICS LLC
437 Sea Hill Rd (06471-1413)
PHONE..................203 315-8154
Roman Jakubiec,
EMP: 1
SALES (est): 82.4K **Privately Held**
SIC: 2821 Molding compounds, plastics

(G-5848)
MFG DIRECTIONS
31 Ciro Rd (06471-1521)
PHONE..................203 483-0797
Chris Metric, *Principal*
EMP: 1
SALES (est): 85.2K **Privately Held**
SIC: 3999 Manufacturing industries

(G-5849)
MGS MANUFACTURING INC
Also Called: Mgs Group-Hall Industries The
8c Commerce Dr (06471-1250)
PHONE..................203 481-4275
EMP: 4
SALES (corp-wide): 18MM **Privately Held**
SIC: 3549 Metalworking machinery
PA: M.G.S. Manufacturing Inc.
    122 Otis St
    Rome NY 13441
    315 337-3350

(G-5850)
MGS MANUFACTURING INC
8 Commerce Dr (06471-1250)
PHONE..................203 484-9275
EMP: 3
SALES (corp-wide): 18MM **Privately Held**
SIC: 5051 3599 Metal wires, ties, cables & screening; amusement park equipment
PA: M.G.S. Manufacturing Inc.
    122 Otis St
    Rome NY 13441
    315 337-3350

(G-5851)
PENNSYLVANIA GLOBE GASLIGHT CO
300 Shaw Rd (06471-1061)
PHONE..................203 484-7749
Marcia Lafemina, *President*
Mark Lahner, *Vice Pres*
EMP: 20
SQ FT: 16,000
SALES (est): 4.7MM **Privately Held**
WEB: www.pennglobe.com
SIC: 3648 5063 Outdoor lighting equipment; lighting fixtures

(G-5852)
PRECISION X-RAY INC
15 Comm Dr Unit 1 (06471)
PHONE..................203 484-2011
Brian P Dermott, *President*
Michael Aiello CPA, *Vice Pres*
Donald Santacroce, *Treasurer*
▲ **EMP:** 15
SQ FT: 16,500
SALES (est): 3MM **Privately Held**
WEB: www.pxinc.com
SIC: 3844 X-ray apparatus & tubes

(G-5853)
PRIME TECHNOLOGY LLC
344 Twin Lakes Rd (06471-1220)
P.O. Box 185 (06471-0185)
PHONE..................203 481-5721
Raymon S Sterman, *Mng Member*
▲ **EMP:** 150
SQ FT: 38,000
SALES (est): 27.8MM **Privately Held**
WEB: www.primetechnology.com
SIC: 3676 3825 3823 3679 Electronic resistors; meters: electric, pocket, portable, panelboard, etc.; controllers for process variables, all types; power supplies, all types: static

(G-5854)
S A CANDELORA ENTERPRISES
Also Called: Taconic Wire
250 Totokel Rd (06471-1035)
PHONE..................203 484-2863
Angela Watrous, *President*
Salvatore Candelora, *Chairman*
Anthony Candelora, *Vice Pres*
Joseph Candelora, *Admin Sec*
◆ **EMP:** 19
SQ FT: 30,000
SALES (est): 5.8MM **Privately Held**
WEB: www.taconicwire.com
SIC: 3315 Wire, steel: insulated or armored

(G-5855)
SHORELINE COATINGS LLC
14 Commerce Dr Ste 1 (06471-1240)
PHONE..................203 213-3471
Trevor King, *Principal*
EMP: 4
SALES (est): 388.7K **Privately Held**
SIC: 3479 Coating of metals & formed products

(G-5856)
SISTER ACT PRINTING
229 Branford Rd Unit 455 (06471-1319)
PHONE..................203 481-7171
Lori Beaudreau, *Owner*
EMP: 2
SALES (est): 150.2K **Privately Held**
SIC: 2752 Commercial printing, offset

(G-5857)
SOPHIA SWIM WEAR LLC
115 Crossfield Rd (06471-1803)
PHONE..................203 481-9397
Josephine A Consiglio, *Principal*
EMP: 1
SALES (est): 66.2K **Privately Held**
SIC: 2253 Bathing suits & swimwear, knit

(G-5858)
SOURCE INC (PA)
101 Fowler Rd (06471-1556)
PHONE..................203 488-6400
Susan Domizi, *President*
◆ **EMP:** 9
SQ FT: 18,000
SALES (est): 848.3K **Privately Held**
WEB: www.4source.com
SIC: 2048 2099 Feed supplements; food preparations

(G-5859)
STREAMLINE PRESS
21 Commerce Dr Ste 2 (06471-3204)
PHONE..................203 484-9799
Brian Berlepsch, *Partner*
Holly Berlepsch, *Partner*
EMP: 6
SALES (est): 651.5K **Privately Held**
WEB: www.streamline-press.com
SIC: 2752 Commercial printing, offset

(G-5860)
STREAMLINE PRESS LLC
21 Commerce Dr Ste 2 (06471-3204)
PHONE..................203 484-9799
Elizabeth Detmers,
EMP: 4
SQ FT: 5,000
SALES (est): 230.5K **Privately Held**
SIC: 2752 Commercial printing, offset

(G-5861)
T WOODWARD STAIR BUILDING LLC
10 Bailey Dr (06471-1447)
PHONE..................860 664-0515
Woodward Tom, *Principal*
EMP: 3
SALES (est): 312.2K **Privately Held**
SIC: 3446 Stairs, staircases, stair treads: prefabricated metal

(G-5862)
TIM WELDING
107 W Pond Rd (06471-1587)
PHONE..................203 488-3486
Timothy Buravski, *Principal*
EMP: 6
SALES (est): 107.3K **Privately Held**
SIC: 7692 Welding repair

(G-5863)
TRANSMONDE USA INC
Also Called: Transmode USA
100 Shaw Rd (06471-1062)
PHONE..................203 484-1528
Carol Mansfield, *President*
Marcella Sheridan, *President*
Mark Tracey, *President*
Marcella Walten-Sherdon, *President*
James M Foley, *Vice Pres*
▲ **EMP:** 60
SALES (est): 8.3MM **Privately Held**
SIC: 2752 7331 Commercial printing, lithographic; direct mail advertising services

(G-5864)
TREAD WELL STAIR & MILLWO
26 Altieri Rd (06471-1424)
PHONE..................203 488-2146
Susan Sandar, *Owner*
EMP: 2
SALES (est): 96K **Privately Held**
SIC: 2431 Millwork

(G-5865)
WALSH CLAIM SERVICES
6 Enterprise Dr (06471-1354)
P.O. Box 439 (06471-0439)
PHONE..................203 481-0680
Kevin Walsh, *Owner*
EMP: 3
SALES (est): 434.8K **Privately Held**
SIC: 3553 Jointers, woodworking machines

(G-5866)
WALTS TROOPER FACTORY LLC
44 Circle Dr (06471-1313)
PHONE..................203 871-9254
Walter Vongher, *President*
EMP: 1 **EST:** 2017
SALES (est): 64.4K **Privately Held**
SIC: 3944 Electronic toys

(G-5867)
WEST END AUTO PARTS
797 Foxon Rd (06471-1107)
P.O. Box 151 (06471-0151)
PHONE..................203 453-9009
Roman Dzruba, *Owner*
EMP: 3
SALES (est): 259.6K **Privately Held**
SIC: 3694 Automotive electrical equipment

(G-5868)
WITKOWSKY JOHN
73 Branford Rd (06471-1323)
PHONE..................203 483-0152
Tiffanie Witkowsky, *Principal*
EMP: 3
SALES (est): 225.6K **Privately Held**
SIC: 2411 Logging

North Franklin
New London County

(G-5869)
ADVANCED FUEL CO LLC
126 Pleasure Hill Rd (06254-1007)
PHONE..................860 642-4817
Richard Williams, *Principal*
EMP: 3 **EST:** 2010
SALES (est): 245.3K **Privately Held**
SIC: 2869 Fuels

(G-5870)
ARICO ENGINEERING INC
841 Route 32 Ste 19 (06254-1132)
PHONE..................860 642-7040
John Arico, *President*
Mary Ann Arico, *Vice Pres*
EMP: 7
SQ FT: 5,000
SALES (est): 1.2MM **Privately Held**
WEB: www.aricoengineering.com
SIC: 3555 7699 Printing trade parts & attachments; industrial machinery & equipment repair

(G-5871)
BOSS SNOWPLOWS & ICE CONTROL
53 Lebanon Rd (06254-1803)
PHONE..................860 886-7081
Dave Dube, *Vice Pres*
EMP: 2 **EST:** 2015
SALES (est): 104.1K **Privately Held**
SIC: 3713 Truck & bus bodies

(G-5872)
CT WOODWORKING LLC
438 Route 32 (06254-1322)
PHONE..................860 884-9586
James B Crofts, *Principal*
EMP: 4 **EST:** 2008
SALES (est): 368K **Privately Held**
SIC: 2431 Millwork

(G-5873)
EXPRESS LANE FOODS
96 Route 32 (06254-1810)
PHONE..................860 889-2266
Rebecca Dalton, *Principal*
EMP: 2
SALES (est): 93.1K **Privately Held**
SIC: 2741 Miscellaneous publishing

(G-5874)
M & W SHEET METAL LLC
841 Route 32 Ste 7 (06254-1132)
PHONE..................860 642-7748
Paul Warbin, *Principal*
EMP: 2
SALES (est): 422.8K **Privately Held**
SIC: 3444 Sheet metal specialties, not stamped

(G-5875)
MILLER CASTINGS INC
30 Pautipaug Hill Rd (06254-1210)
PHONE..................860 822-9991
William Smith, *Branch Mgr*
EMP: 234
SALES (corp-wide): 76.1MM **Privately Held**
SIC: 3324 Steel investment foundries
PA: Miller Castings, Inc.
    2503 Pacific Park Dr
    Whittier CA 90601
    562 695-0461

(G-5876)
MOARK LLC (HQ)
28 Under The Mountain Rd (06254-1421)
PHONE..................951 332-3300
Craig Willardson,
▲ **EMP:** 28
SQ FT: 55,000
SALES (est): 507.7MM
SALES (corp-wide): 6.8B **Privately Held**
WEB: www.moarkllc.com
SIC: 5144 2048 0252 2015 Eggs; poultry feeds; chicken eggs; started pullet farm; poultry slaughtering & processing

▲ = Import ▼=Export
◆ =Import/Export

PA: Land O'lakes, Inc.
4001 Lexington Ave N
Arden Hills MN 55126
651 375-2222

(G-5877)
PRECISION MACHINE AND GEARS
21 Country Club Dr (06254-1202)
PHONE.............................860 822-6993
Michael Earling, *Owner*
EMP: 3 EST: 2001
SALES (est): 232.3K **Privately Held**
SIC: 3599 Machine shop, jobbing & repair

(G-5878)
QMDI PRESS
841 Route 32 Ste 19 (06254-1132)
PHONE.............................860 642-8074
EMP: 4
SALES (est): 66.5K **Privately Held**
SIC: 2741 Miscellaneous publishing

(G-5879)
U T Z
140 Route 32 (06254-1811)
PHONE.............................860 383-4266
Cory Gervais, *Manager*
EMP: 3
SALES (est): 143.3K **Privately Held**
SIC: 2096 Potato chips & similar snacks

North Granby
Hartford County

(G-5880)
AEROTEK WELDING CO INC
51 Loomis St (06060-1205)
PHONE.............................860 653-0120
Robert W Fusick, *President*
Elizabeth L Fusick, *Admin Sec*
EMP: 4
SQ FT: 1,200
SALES (est): 450K **Privately Held**
SIC: 7692 Welding repair

(G-5881)
SOLAR NEBULA LLC
7 Dara Ln (06060-1109)
PHONE.............................516 362-8048
Adela Victoria Korshin, *Mng Member*
EMP: 2
SALES (est): 137K **Privately Held**
SIC: 3728 Aircraft parts & equipment

(G-5882)
THOMAS CARR III
Also Called: T N T Logging
52 Cooley Rd (06060-1214)
PHONE.............................860 653-3431
Thomas Carr III, *Owner*
EMP: 1
SALES (est): 72.1K **Privately Held**
SIC: 2411 Logging camps & contractors

North Grosvenordale
Windham County

(G-5883)
AMERICAN WELDING SERVICE
214 Labby Rd (06255-1233)
PHONE.............................860 935-5314
Dave Marks, *Owner*
EMP: 1
SALES (est): 131.9K **Privately Held**
SIC: 7692 Welding repair

(G-5884)
FABYAN SUGAR SHACK LLC
384 Fabyan Rd (06255-1509)
PHONE.............................860 935-9281
Gary Durand,
EMP: 2
SALES (est): 60K **Privately Held**
SIC: 2099 Maple syrup

(G-5885)
FRENCH RIVER MTLS THOMPSON LLC
307 Reardon Rd (06255)
PHONE.............................860 450-9574
Harold Hopkins, *Owner*
EMP: 3
SALES (est): 262.9K **Privately Held**
SIC: 3281 Stone, quarrying & processing of own stone products

(G-5886)
G THOMAS AND SONS INC
573 Fabyan Rd (06255-1514)
P.O. Box 807 (06255-0807)
PHONE.............................860 935-5174
David Thomas, *President*
EMP: 3 EST: 1948
SALES (est): 700K **Privately Held**
SIC: 2221 Broadwoven fabric mills, man-made

(G-5887)
IRON CRAFT FABRICATING LLC
34 Corttiss Rd (06255-1102)
PHONE.............................860 923-9869
Lewis Bunker,
EMP: 6
SQ FT: 17,500
SALES (est): 1.1MM **Privately Held**
SIC: 3441 Fabricated structural metal

(G-5888)
LIBERTY GLASS AND MET INDS INC
339 Riverside Dr (06255-2160)
PHONE.............................860 923-3623
Donna Esposito, *President*
Edward Esposito Sr, *Vice Pres*
Daniel Marschat, *Admin Sec*
EMP: 32
SQ FT: 52,000
SALES (est): 3.6MM **Privately Held**
WEB: www.libertywindowsystems.com
SIC: 3229 3442 1793 5039 Glassware, industrial; sash, door or window: metal; glass & glazing work; glass construction materials

(G-5889)
LITTLE BITS MANUFACTURING INC
694 Riverside Dr (06255-2170)
P.O. Box 215 (06255-0215)
PHONE.............................860 923-2772
Charles T Skowron, *President*
EMP: 6 EST: 1966
SQ FT: 6,000
SALES (est): 396K **Privately Held**
SIC: 3089 Molding primary plastic

(G-5890)
LORIC TOOL INC
95 Gaumond Rd (06255-2011)
PHONE.............................860 928-0171
Ricky Smith, *President*
Lorraine Smith, *Admin Sec*
EMP: 10
SQ FT: 3,000
SALES (est): 810K **Privately Held**
SIC: 3599 Machine shop, jobbing & repair

(G-5891)
MODIFIED WELDING LLC
90 Rich Rd (06255-1302)
PHONE.............................860 428-3599
Donald F Dumas, *Principal*
EMP: 1
SALES (est): 88.9K **Privately Held**
SIC: 7692 Welding repair

(G-5892)
SUPERIOR BAKERY INC
Also Called: Kasanof Bread
72 Main St (06255-1712)
P.O. Box 898 (06255-0898)
PHONE.............................860 923-9555
Louis P Faucher, *President*
Michael Faucher, *Vice Pres*
Raymond P Faucher Sr, *Admin Sec*
EMP: 50
SQ FT: 30,000
SALES (est): 13.2MM **Privately Held**
SIC: 5149 2051 Bakery products; bread, cake & related products

North Haven
New Haven County

(G-5893)
687 STATE STREET ASSOC LLC
32 Windsor Rd E (06473-3050)
PHONE.............................203 915-8469
Paul H Kaplan, *Principal*
EMP: 2
SALES (est): 77.4K **Privately Held**
SIC: 3131 Quarters

(G-5894)
A & A MANUFACTURING CO INC
Polyclutch Division
457 State St (06473-3019)
PHONE.............................262 786-1500
EMP: 20
SALES (corp-wide): 2.3B **Privately Held**
SIC: 3495 Wire Springs, Nsk
HQ: Dynatect Manufacturing, Inc.
2300 S Calhoun Rd
New Berlin WI 53151
262 786-1500

(G-5895)
ACM WAREHOUSE & DISTRIBUTION
77 Sackett Point Rd (06473-3211)
PHONE.............................203 239-9557
Steve Andreucci, *Partner*
EMP: 3
SALES (est): 250K **Privately Held**
SIC: 2448 Wood pallets & skids

(G-5896)
ADVISOR
83 State St (06473-2208)
P.O. Box 460 (06473-0460)
PHONE.............................203 239-4121
Patricia Flagg, *Owner*
Jim Eberhardt, *Advisor*
Shirley Weidler, *Advisor*
EMP: 14 EST: 1965
SALES (est): 400K **Privately Held**
SIC: 2711 Newspapers: publishing only, not printed on site

(G-5897)
AER CONTROL SYSTEMS LLC
36 Nettleton Ave (06473-3619)
PHONE.............................203 772-4700
John Dixon, *President*
EMP: 6
SALES: 1.2MM **Privately Held**
WEB: www.aercontrolsystems.com
SIC: 3677 Filtration devices, electronic

(G-5898)
ALARM ONE
142 Maple Ave (06473-2606)
P.O. Box 307 (06473-0307)
PHONE.............................203 239-1714
Roger Bailey, *Owner*
EMP: 3
SALES (est): 323.6K **Privately Held**
SIC: 3669 5063 Burglar alarm apparatus, electric; burglar alarm systems

(G-5899)
ALDLAB CHEMICALS LLC
410 Sackett Point Rd (06473-3168)
P.O. Box 465, Branford (06405-0465)
PHONE.............................203 589-4934
EMP: 3
SALES (est): 143.6K **Privately Held**
SIC: 2813 Industrial gases

(G-5900)
AMENTOS GOLD BUYERS AND SECON
140 Washington Ave Ste 1d (06473-1712)
PHONE.............................203 691-1020
Paul Amento, *Owner*
EMP: 1
SALES (est): 43.8K **Privately Held**
SIC: 5999 3339 Miscellaneous retail stores; precious metals

(G-5901)
AMERICAN EAGLE EMBROIDERY LLC
201 State St (06473-2202)
PHONE.............................203 239-7906
Joel Frank,
Al Francisco,
Richard Signor,
EMP: 2 EST: 2007
SALES: 63K **Privately Held**
SIC: 5949 2395 Sewing, needlework & piece goods; embroidery & art needlework

(G-5902)
AMERICAN STITCH & PRINT INC
222 Elm St Ste 9 (06473-3260)
PHONE.............................203 239-5383
Alan V Golia, *President*
Vincent J Golia, *Director*
EMP: 9
SALES (est): 909.5K **Privately Held**
WEB: www.american-stitch.com
SIC: 2395 2759 Embroidery & art needlework; screen printing

(G-5903)
AMERICAN WOOD PRODUCTS
Also Called: Bar Co American
301 State St (06473-6104)
PHONE.............................203 248-4433
Valerie Galleuba, *CEO*
William Geremia, *General Mgr*
EMP: 7
SALES (est): 748.9K **Privately Held**
SIC: 2511 Wood household furniture

(G-5904)
ANDERSON STAIR & RAILING
348 Sackett Point Rd (06473-3103)
PHONE.............................203 288-0117
Art Anderson, *Owner*
EMP: 10
SALES (est): 852.6K **Privately Held**
SIC: 2431 Staircases, stairs & railings

(G-5905)
APIZZA GRANDE
630 Washington Ave Ste 1 (06473-1132)
PHONE.............................475 238-6928
Frederick Nuzzo, *Principal*
EMP: 1
SALES (est): 99.3K **Privately Held**
SIC: 3421 Table & food cutlery, including butchers'

(G-5906)
APPLE LEAF
56 Laydon Ave (06473-2740)
PHONE.............................203 988-7262
EMP: 2
SALES (est): 97.9K **Privately Held**
SIC: 3571 Mfg Electronic Computers

(G-5907)
APRICUS INC
370 State St Ste 2 (06473-3157)
PHONE.............................203 889-2667
EMP: 1
SALES (est): 39.6K **Privately Held**
SIC: 3999 Manufacturing industries

(G-5908)
AQUA DESIGN KITCHEN AND BATH S
222 Elm St Ste 1 (06473-3260)
PHONE.............................203 773-1649
Richard Decola Sr,
EMP: 1
SALES (est): 100.6K **Privately Held**
WEB: www.aquadesignshowroom.com
SIC: 2499 Kitchen, bathroom & household ware: wood

(G-5909)
AQUALOGIC INC
30 Devine St (06473-2236)
PHONE.............................203 248-8959
Nicholas Papa, *President*
Dorothy F Papa, *Corp Secy*
Lisa Papa, *Finance*
Maryann Papa, *Director*
EMP: 20
SQ FT: 6,000

North Haven - New Haven County (G-5910)

SALES (est): 4.4MM **Privately Held**
WEB: www.aqualogic.com
SIC: **3589** Water treatment equipment, industrial; sewage treatment equipment

(G-5910)
ASHKAAR PUBLISHERS LLC
325 Mansfield Rd (06473-1213)
PHONE..................................203 248-4804
Abbas Amanat, *Principal*
EMP: 1
SALES (est): 37.5K **Privately Held**
SIC: **2741** Miscellaneous publishing

(G-5911)
ATCO WIRE ROPE AND INDUS SUP
11 Leonardo Dr (06473-2528)
P.O. Box 580 (06473-0580)
PHONE..................................203 239-1632
Aniello Tagliamonte, *President*
Frances Tagliamonte, *Admin Sec*
EMP: 2
SQ FT: 5,000
SALES: 500K **Privately Held**
SIC: **3315** 2824 Wire & fabricated wire products; nylon fibers

(G-5912)
AVAYA INC
38 Brockett Farm Rd (06473-3546)
PHONE..................................203 234-9300
Ronald Coleman, *Manager*
EMP: 1 **Publicly Held**
WEB: www.avaya.com
SIC: **3661** Telephone & telegraph apparatus
HQ: Avaya Inc.
   4655 Great America Pkwy
   Santa Clara CA 95054
   908 953-6000

(G-5913)
BAY CRANE SERVICE CONN INC
37 Nettleton Ave (06473-3618)
PHONE..................................203 785-8000
Kenneth Bernardo, *President*
Joe Zils, *Manager*
EMP: 6
SALES (est): 990.2K **Privately Held**
SIC: **3531** Cranes

(G-5914)
BEYOND HOME IMPROVEMENT
30 Manor Dr (06473-3709)
PHONE..................................203 859-0113
Thomas Dechello, *Principal*
EMP: 1
SQ FT: 875
SALES (est): 80.5K **Privately Held**
SIC: **1799** 1721 7299 3589 Cleaning building exteriors; residential painting; home improvement & renovation contractor agency; high pressure cleaning equipment

(G-5915)
BONITO MANUFACTURING INC
Also Called: New England Clock
445 Washington Ave (06473-1320)
PHONE..................................203 234-8786
Fax: 203 248-6399
EMP: 61
SQ FT: 70,000
SALES (est): 6.9MM **Privately Held**
SIC: **2429** 7641 2522 2511 Barrels & barrel parts; reupholstery & furniture repair; office furniture, except wood; wood household furniture; wood kitchen cabinets; millwork & lumber

(G-5916)
C COWLES & COMPANY (PA)
Also Called: Hydrolevel Div
126 Bailey Rd (06473-2612)
PHONE..................................203 865-3117
Lawrence C Moon Jr, *President*
Richard Lyons, *Exec VP*
Robert Gaura, *CFO*
Russel Spector, *Controller*
Cherie Poer, *Personnel*
▲ EMP: 75
SQ FT: 170,000

SALES (est): 43.3MM **Privately Held**
WEB: www.ccowles.com
SIC: **3089** 3465 3443 3646 Injection molding of plastics; moldings or trim, automobile: stamped metal; boiler shop products: boilers, smokestacks, steel tanks; ceiling systems, luminous; fluorescent lighting fixtures, commercial

(G-5917)
C S M S-I P A
127 Washington Ave Ste 3 (06473-1715)
PHONE..................................203 562-7228
Alison Zebendon, *Opers Mgr*
Lisa Guerino, *Branch Mgr*
EMP: 9
SQ FT: 6,210
SALES (corp-wide): 2.7MM **Privately Held**
SIC: **8621** 8099 2711 Medical field-related associations; medical services organization; newspapers, publishing & printing
PA: C S M S-I P A
   6 Corporate Dr Ste 430
   Shelton CT 06484
   203 225-1291

(G-5918)
CARLIN COMBUSTION TECH INC
126 Bailey Rd (06473-2612)
PHONE..................................413 525-7700
EMP: 4
SALES (corp-wide): 43.3MM **Privately Held**
SIC: **3433** Heating equipment, except electric
HQ: Carlin Combustion Technology, Inc.
   126 Bailey Rd
   North Haven CT 06473

(G-5919)
CARLIN COMBUSTION TECH INC (HQ)
126 Bailey Rd (06473-2612)
PHONE..................................203 680-9401
Lawrence C Moon Jr, *President*
Richard Lyons, *Vice Pres*
Russell Spector, *Treasurer*
▲ EMP: 75
SALES (est): 15.5MM
SALES (corp-wide): 43.3MM **Privately Held**
SIC: **3433** Gas burners, industrial
PA: C. Cowles & Company
   126 Bailey Rd
   North Haven CT 06473
   203 865-3117

(G-5920)
CKO WOODWORKING
33 Laydon Ave (06473-2705)
PHONE..................................203 234-7156
Michael Benson, *Principal*
EMP: 2
SALES (est): 151.4K **Privately Held**
SIC: **2431** Millwork

(G-5921)
CLOPAY CORPORATION
285 State St Ste 4 (06473-2170)
PHONE..................................203 230-9116
Joel Eberlein, *Vice Pres*
EMP: 231
SALES (corp-wide): 1.5B **Publicly Held**
SIC: **3081** Plastic film & sheet
HQ: Clopay Corporation
   8585 Duke Blvd
   Mason OH 45040
   800 282-2260

(G-5922)
COLE S CREW MACHINE PRODUCTS
69 Dodge Ave (06473-1119)
PHONE..................................203 723-1418
David F Calabrese, *President*
Patricia Calabrese, *Admin Sec*
EMP: 22
SQ FT: 6,500
SALES (est): 3.5MM **Privately Held**
SIC: **3451** 3542 Screw machine products; thread rolling machines

(G-5923)
COMPOSITE MCHINING EXPERTS LLC
222 Universal Dr Bldg 1 (06473-3658)
PHONE..................................203 624-0664
Rose Tomaszewski, *General Mgr*
Frank Tomaszewski,
Rose Tomaszeski,
EMP: 5
SQ FT: 19,100
SALES (est): 266.2K **Privately Held**
SIC: **3429** Manufactured hardware (general)

(G-5924)
CONNECTICUT CONTAINER CORP (PA)
Also Called: Unicorr Group
455 Sackett Point Rd (06473-3199)
PHONE..................................203 248-2161
Harry A Perkins, *President*
Louis Ceruzzi, *Vice Pres*
Isabel Martins, *Accounts Mgr*
Linda Kafka, *Sales Staff*
Sarah Krinopol, *Sales Staff*
◆ EMP: 132 EST: 1946
SQ FT: 160,000
SALES (est): 121.1MM **Privately Held**
WEB: www.unicorr.com
SIC: **2653** 3993 3412 2631 Boxes, corrugated: made from purchased materials; signs & advertising specialties; metal barrels, drums & pails; paperboard mills

(G-5925)
CONNECTICUT VALLEY LITHO CLUB
190 Clintonville Rd (06473-2410)
PHONE..................................203 234-0536
Susan Mulqueen, *Principal*
EMP: 2 EST: 2010
SALES (est): 159.9K **Privately Held**
SIC: **2752** Commercial printing, offset

(G-5926)
CONTRACTORS STEEL SUPPLY
111 Quinnipiac Ave (06473-3623)
PHONE..................................203 782-1221
Paul Keil, *President*
Lisa Keil, *Treasurer*
Linda Keil, *Admin Sec*
EMP: 10
SQ FT: 7,000
SALES (est): 4.1MM **Privately Held**
SIC: **5051** 3441 Steel; fabricated structural metal

(G-5927)
COVIDIEN HOLDING INC
195 Mcdermott Rd (06473-3665)
PHONE..................................203 492-5000
Stan Malinowski, *Manager*
EMP: 5 **Privately Held**
SIC: **3841** Surgical & medical instruments
HQ: Covidien Holding Inc.
   710 Medtronic Pkwy
   Minneapolis MN 55432

(G-5928)
COVIDIEN LP
195 Mcdermott Rd (06473-3665)
PHONE..................................203 492-6332
Richard Kelly, *Superintendent*
Paul Landino, *Maint Spvr*
Mike Prescott, *Engineer*
Christine Morrissey, *Marketing Staff*
Sengkeo Kroeber, *Supervisor*
EMP: 430 **Privately Held**
SIC: **3841** Surgical & medical instruments
HQ: Covidien Lp
   710 Medtronic Pkwy
   Minneapolis MN 55432
   763 514-4000

(G-5929)
COVIDIEN LP
Also Called: Surgical Devices
60 Middletown Ave (06473-3908)
PHONE..................................203 492-5000
Armand Lacombe, *Project Mgr*
Dipino Rae, *Production*
Arthur Hislop, *Research*
Darlene Nebinger, *Engineer*
Chris Penna, *Engineer*
EMP: 521 **Privately Held**

SIC: **3841** Surgical & medical instruments
HQ: Covidien Lp
   710 Medtronic Pkwy
   Minneapolis MN 55432
   763 514-4000

(G-5930)
COWLES PRODUCTS COMPANY INC
126 Bailey Rd (06473-2612)
PHONE..................................203 865-3110
Lawrence Moon, *President*
Arturo Moreno, *Business Mgr*
Russell Spector, *VP Finance*
Sherri Helget, *Human Res Dir*
Barbara Gratchian, *Marketing Staff*
▲ EMP: 100
SALES (est): 14.5MM
SALES (corp-wide): 43MM **Privately Held**
WEB: www.ccowles.com
SIC: **3089** Extruded finished plastic products
PA: C. Cowles & Company
   126 Bailey Rd
   North Haven CT 06473
   203 865-3117

(G-5931)
COWLES STAMPING INC
126 Bailey Rd (06473-2612)
PHONE..................................203 865-3117
Lawrence C Moon Jr, *President*
Whyn Pelkey, *Engineer*
Robert Massa, *Director*
▲ EMP: 40
SQ FT: 64,000
SALES (est): 5.4MM
SALES (corp-wide): 43MM **Privately Held**
WEB: www.ccowles.com
SIC: **3469** Stamping metal for the trade
PA: C. Cowles & Company
   126 Bailey Rd
   North Haven CT 06473
   203 865-3117

(G-5932)
CRISCOLA DESIGN LLC
Also Called: Jeanne Crscola Crscola Design
1477 Ridge Rd (06473-3059)
PHONE..................................203 248-4285
Jeanne Criscola, *Principal*
EMP: 2
SALES (est): 151.3K **Privately Held**
WEB: www.criscoladesign.com
SIC: **7336** 7311 7371 2791 Commercial art & graphic design; advertising agencies; custom computer programming services; typesetting

(G-5933)
DSW INC
410 Universal Dr N (06473-3174)
PHONE..................................203 985-8241
EMP: 13
SALES (corp-wide): 3.1B **Publicly Held**
SIC: **5661** 5139 3149 Children's shoes; boots; athletic shoes, except rubber or plastic
PA: Designer Brands Inc.
   810 Dsw Dr
   Columbus OH 43219
   614 237-7100

(G-5934)
EAST SHRE WRE RPE/RGGNG SPPLY
78 Rebeschi Dr (06473-3934)
P.O. Box 308 (06473-0308)
PHONE..................................203 469-5204
Gary Lipkvich, *President*
Richard Lipkvich, *Vice Pres*
Wayne Lipkvich, *Treasurer*
EMP: 10
SQ FT: 10,000
SALES (est): 3.9MM **Privately Held**
SIC: **5051** 5072 2298 3496 Rope, wire (not insulated); cable, wire; chains; slings, rope; miscellaneous fabricated wire products

(G-5935)
ECOCHLOR INC
285 State St Ste 12 (06473-2170)
PHONE..................................203 915-4593

▲ = Import ▼=Export
◆ =Import/Export

GEOGRAPHIC SECTION

North Haven - New Haven County (G-5965)

Leif Melhus, *Engineer*
Pete Thompson, *Engineer*
EMP: 2
SALES (est): 188.5K **Privately Held**
SIC: 3589 Water treatment equipment, industrial

(G-5936)
ELM CITY MANUFACTURING LLC
Also Called: Atlantic Millwork
370 Sackett Point Rd (06473-3106)
PHONE...................203 248-1969
Paul McKechnie, *Vice Pres*
Mark Bolling, *Mng Member*
Paul W McKechnie,
EMP: 12
SQ FT: 13,000
SALES (est): 1.9MM **Privately Held**
SIC: 2499 Decorative wood & woodwork

(G-5937)
EPICUREAN FEAST MEDTRON O
195 Mcdermott Rd (06473-3665)
PHONE...................203 492-5000
EMP: 3
SALES (est): 95.3K **Privately Held**
SIC: 3845 Electromedical equipment

(G-5938)
ERIC SAPPER
Also Called: North Shore Door
55 Beach Ln (06473-4002)
PHONE...................203 239-6020
Eric Sapper, *Owner*
Joe Sapper, *Associate*
EMP: 1
SALES (est): 103.3K **Privately Held**
SIC: 1751 5211 3699 Garage door, installation or erection; lumber & other building materials; door opening & closing devices, electrical

(G-5939)
F D GRAVE & SON INC
85 State St Ste C (06473-2240)
P.O. Box 2085 (06473-8285)
PHONE...................203 239-9394
Frederick D Grave Jr, *President*
EMP: 8
SQ FT: 25,000
SALES (est): 982.5K **Privately Held**
SIC: 2121 Cigars

(G-5940)
FARMINGTON ENGINEERING INC
73 Defco Park Rd (06473-1135)
PHONE...................800 428-7584
Bob Adelson, *Principal*
▲ **EMP:** 7
SALES (est): 800.5K **Privately Held**
SIC: 3499 Drain plugs, magnetic

(G-5941)
FASTSIGNS
310 Washington Ave Ste 1 (06473-1315)
PHONE...................203 239-9090
Brian Homer, *Partner*
EMP: 2
SALES (est): 150K **Privately Held**
SIC: 3993 5999 7336 7532 Signs & advertising specialties; banners, flags, decals & posters; graphic arts & related design; truck painting & lettering

(G-5942)
FLIGHT SUPPORT INC
101 Sackett Point Rd (06473-3211)
P.O. Box 498 (06473-0498)
PHONE...................203 562-1415
Wayne Blake, *CEO*
Bernadette Blake, *Admin Sec*
EMP: 50
SQ FT: 17,200
SALES (est): 8.3MM **Privately Held**
WEB: www.flightsupport.net
SIC: 3728 Aircraft parts & equipment

(G-5943)
GREENWOOD INDUSTRIES INC
88 Leonardo Dr (06473-2527)
PHONE...................203 234-2041
Paul Gibson, *Bd of Directors*
EMP: 2

SALES (est): 228K **Privately Held**
SIC: 3999 Manufacturing industries

(G-5944)
GRIMES FIREARMS LLC
3132 Avalon Haven Dr (06473-1636)
PHONE...................203 843-2271
Christopher Grimes,
EMP: 1
SALES (est): 56.7K **Privately Held**
SIC: 3484 Guns (firearms) or gun parts, 30 mm. & below

(G-5945)
HANGER PRSTHETCS & ORTHO INC
260 State St (06473-2135)
PHONE...................203 230-0667
David Knatt, *Manager*
EMP: 5
SALES (corp-wide): 1B **Publicly Held**
SIC: 3842 Surgical appliances & supplies
HQ: Hanger Prosthetics & Orthotics, Inc.
  10910 Domain Dr Ste 300
  Austin TX 78758
  512 777-3800

(G-5946)
HYDROLEVEL COMPANY
126 Bailey Rd (06473-2612)
PHONE...................203 776-0473
Alan C Bennett, *Ch of Bd*
John Downs, *President*
Tim Van Leeuwen, *Engineer*
Russell Specter, *CFO*
T Richard Coss, *Treasurer*
▲ **EMP:** 10 **EST:** 1979
SQ FT: 5,000
SALES: 2MM
SALES (corp-wide): 43.3MM **Privately Held**
SIC: 3494 Valves & pipe fittings
PA: C. Cowles & Company
  126 Bailey Rd
  North Haven CT 06473
  203 865-3117

(G-5947)
INDEPENDENT REPAIR SERVICE
156 State St (06473-2207)
PHONE...................203 234-0218
Joseph Galati, *Owner*
◆ **EMP:** 3
SQ FT: 4,400
SALES (est): 450K **Privately Held**
SIC: 7699 3829 Scientific equipment repair service; nuclear radiation & testing apparatus

(G-5948)
INTELLGENT CLEARING NETWRK INC
110 Washington Ave (06473-1723)
PHONE...................203 972-0861
Gary Oakley, *CEO*
Brian Schulte, *President*
Rich Thibedeau, *Exec VP*
Ron Schulte, *Sr Software Eng*
EMP: 8
SALES (est): 533.6K **Privately Held**
SIC: 7372 Prepackaged software

(G-5949)
INTERACTIVE MARKETING CORP
Also Called: IMC Internet
399 Sackett Point Rd (06473-3105)
PHONE...................203 248-5324
Robert Caldarella, *President*
EMP: 7
SQ FT: 6,000
SALES (est): 1.2MM **Privately Held**
WEB: www.imcinternet.net
SIC: 3571 7373 Personal computers (microcomputers); local area network (LAN) systems integrator

(G-5950)
JAMES STENQVIST
18 Larson Dr (06473-1834)
PHONE...................203 339-6418
James Stenqvist, *Principal*
EMP: 1
SALES (est): 40.9K **Privately Held**
SIC: 2399 Fabricated textile products

(G-5951)
JENSEN INDUSTRIES INC (PA)
Also Called: Jensen Dental
50 Stillman Rd (06473-1622)
P.O. Box 514 (06473-0514)
PHONE...................203 285-1402
David J Stine, *President*
Peter Kouvaris, *Vice Pres*
Kevin Mahan, *Vice Pres*
Ray McTeague, *Opers Mgr*
Anthony M Schittina, *CFO*
▲ **EMP:** 60
SQ FT: 25,000
SALES (est): 30.8MM **Privately Held**
WEB: www.jensenindustries.com
SIC: 3843 Dental alloys for amalgams

(G-5952)
JESKEY LLC
Also Called: James Manufacturing
69 Dodge Ave (06473-1119)
PHONE...................203 772-6675
Adam Jeskey, *Mng Member*
EMP: 23 **EST:** 1946
SQ FT: 29,000
SALES (est): 2.7MM **Privately Held**
WEB: www.jamesscrew.com
SIC: 3451 Screw machine products

(G-5953)
JET PROCESS CORPORATION
57 Dodge Ave (06473-1119)
PHONE...................203 985-6000
Richard Hart, *Ch of Bd*
Bret Halpern, *Engineer*
Krista Hart, *Bookkeeper*
EMP: 8
SQ FT: 16,000
SALES (est): 1.1MM **Privately Held**
WEB: www.jetprocess.com
SIC: 3559 3479 8731 2851 Semiconductor manufacturing machinery; painting, coating & hot dipping; commercial physical research; paints & allied products

(G-5954)
JOHNSTONE COMPANY INC
222 Sackett Point Rd (06473-3160)
P.O. Box 472 (06473-0472)
PHONE...................203 239-5834
David R Johnstone Jr, *President*
Michael Johnstone, *Vice Pres*
Tonya Johnstone, *Admin Sec*
▼ **EMP:** 26 **EST:** 1941
SQ FT: 20,000
SALES (est): 9.8MM **Privately Held**
WEB: www.johnstonecompany.com
SIC: 3398 3559 3443 Metal heat treating; refinery, chemical processing & similar machinery; fabricated plate work (boiler shop)

(G-5955)
JOSEPH COHN SON TILE TRAZO LLC
50 Devine St (06473-2244)
PHONE...................203 772-2420
Louis Monico, *Mng Member*
Richard Monico,
Robert Monico,
EMP: 45 **EST:** 2011
SQ FT: 50,000
SALES: 2MM **Privately Held**
SIC: 1743 2273 Tile installation, ceramic; floor coverings, textile fiber

(G-5956)
KATHIES KITCHEN LLC
Also Called: Superseedz
50 Devine St (06473-2244)
PHONE...................203 407-0546
Joe Tellicio, *Principal*
Helen Barajas, *Opers Staff*
Kathie Telliccio, *Mng Member*
EMP: 2
SQ FT: 1,000
SALES: 1.2MM **Privately Held**
SIC: 2068 Seeds: dried, dehydrated, salted or roasted

(G-5957)
KB CUSTOM STAIR BUILDERS INC
101 Powdered Metal Rd # 1 (06473-3280)
PHONE...................203 234-0836

Kevin P Boyle, *President*
EMP: 6 **EST:** 2001
SALES: 500K **Privately Held**
SIC: 2431 Staircases & stairs, wood

(G-5958)
KOBUTA CHOPPERS LLC
439 Washington Ave (06473-1310)
PHONE...................203 234-6047
Steve Kobuta, *President*
EMP: 1
SALES (est): 60K **Privately Held**
SIC: 3751 Motorcycles & related parts

(G-5959)
LIBBYS ITALIAN PASTRY SHOP
310 Washington Ave (06473-1315)
PHONE...................203 234-2530
Guiseppina Dell Amura, *Principal*
EMP: 6
SALES (est): 116.2K **Privately Held**
SIC: 5812 5461 2024 Italian restaurant; bakeries; ice cream & frozen desserts

(G-5960)
M & J BUS CO
121 Quinnipiac Ave (06473-3623)
PHONE...................203 624-0836
Michael Beebe, *President*
EMP: 2
SALES (est): 92.1K **Privately Held**
SIC: 7519 5012 3711 Recreational vehicle rental; buses; buses, all types, assembly of

(G-5961)
MAVERICK ARMS INC
7 Grasso Ave (06473-3237)
PHONE...................203 230-5300
A Iver Mossberg Jr, *Principal*
EMP: 3
SALES (est): 227.2K **Privately Held**
SIC: 3484 Small arms

(G-5962)
MEDTRONIC INC
60 Middletown Ave (06473-3908)
PHONE...................203 492-5764
Holly Donahue, *Principal*
Tim Dwyer, *Project Mgr*
Danyel Racenet, *Research*
Scott Prior, *Engineer*
Emily V Gwynne, *Sales Staff*
EMP: 35 **Privately Held**
SIC: 3841 Surgical & medical instruments
HQ: Medtronic, Inc.
  710 Medtronic Pkwy
  Minneapolis MN 55432
  763 514-4000

(G-5963)
METAL MORPHOUS
222 Elm St Ste 11 (06473-3260)
PHONE...................203 239-0411
Renee B Randall, *Principal*
EMP: 2
SALES (est): 194K **Privately Held**
SIC: 3479 Coating of metals & formed products

(G-5964)
MILLTURN MANUFACTURING CO
1203 Ridge Rd (06473-4437)
PHONE...................203 248-1602
Rudy Krizan, *Owner*
EMP: 3
SQ FT: 1,500
SALES (est): 170K **Privately Held**
SIC: 3599 Machine shop, jobbing & repair

(G-5965)
MILLWOOD INC
33 Stiles Ln (06473-2133)
PHONE...................203 248-7902
Edwin Melendez, *Branch Mgr*
EMP: 17 **Privately Held**
SIC: 3565 5084 Packaging machinery; packaging machinery & equipment
PA: Millwood, Inc.
  3708 International Blvd
  Vienna OH 44473

North Haven - New Haven County

(G-5966)
MOSSBERG CORPORATION (PA)
7 Grasso Ave (06473-3259)
PHONE......................203 230-5300
Alan Iver Mossberg, *Ch of Bd*
Joseph Bartozzi, *Senior VP*
John Maclellan, *Vice Pres*
Dan Jean, *Plant Mgr*
Alain Leyva, *Project Mgr*
▲ **EMP:** 5
SQ FT: 80,000
SALES: 41.9MM **Privately Held**
SIC: 3484 Shotguns or shotgun parts, 30 mm. & below

(G-5967)
NEU SPCLTY ENGINEERED MTLS LLC
15 Corporate Dr (06473-3255)
PHONE......................203 239-9629
Mark Crist, *Vice Pres*
Isaac Deluca, *Vice Pres*
Giuseppe Di Salvo, *Vice Pres*
Michael A Garratt, *Vice Pres*
EMP: 12
SALES (est): 2.7MM **Publicly Held**
SIC: 2821 3087 5162 Thermoplastic materials; polyvinyl chloride resins (PVC); vinyl resins; custom compound purchased resins; resins; plastics basic shapes
PA: Polyone Corporation
33587 Walker Rd
Avon Lake OH 44012

(G-5968)
NORTH HILL WOODWORKING LLC
117 N Hill Rd (06473-3522)
PHONE......................203 985-0200
Antoinette McKeon, *Principal*
EMP: 1
SALES (est): 54.1K **Privately Held**
SIC: 2431 Millwork

(G-5969)
NOVA DENTAL LLC (PA)
41 Middletown Ave Ste 2 (06473-3940)
PHONE......................203 234-3900
Asma Ijaz, *Manager*
EMP: 4
SALES (est): 563.2K **Privately Held**
SIC: 3843 Dental equipment

(G-5970)
O F MOSSBERG & SONS INC (HQ)
7 Grasso Ave (06473-3237)
P.O. Box 497 (06473-0497)
PHONE......................203 230-5300
A Iver Mossberg Jr, *Ch of Bd*
Alan I Mossberg, *President*
Joseph H Bartozzi, *Senior VP*
John Maclellan, *Vice Pres*
Christopher Orlando, *Vice Pres*
▲ **EMP:** 160 **EST:** 1919
SQ FT: 80,000
SALES (est): 38MM **Privately Held**
WEB: www.mossberg.com
SIC: 3484 Shotguns or shotgun parts, 30 mm. & below

(G-5971)
OSKR INC
14a Buell St (06473-4311)
PHONE......................475 238-2634
Tony Lawlor, *President*
EMP: 8
SQ FT: 1,800
SALES: 2.4MM **Privately Held**
SIC: 3942 Stuffed toys, including animals

(G-5972)
PACTIV CORPORATION
458 Sackett Point Rd (06473-3111)
PHONE......................203 288-7722
Ed Sidlowsky, *Branch Mgr*
EMP: 45
SALES (corp-wide): 14.1MM **Privately Held**
WEB: www.pactiv.com
SIC: 2679 5199 Honeycomb core & board: made from purchased material; packaging materials
HQ: Pactiv Llc
1900 W Field Ct
Lake Forest IL 60045
847 482-2000

(G-5973)
PALLET GUYS LLC
102 Bailey Rd (06473-2611)
PHONE......................203 691-6716
David Schneider, *Principal*
EMP: 4
SALES (est): 222.1K **Privately Held**
SIC: 2448 Pallets, wood & wood with metal

(G-5974)
PARKER-HANNIFIN CORPORATION
Also Called: Advanced Products Operation
33 Defco Park Rd (06473-1129)
PHONE......................203 239-3341
Alexander Froning, *Engineer*
Robert Akumbak, *Project Engr*
Jim Randall, *Branch Mgr*
Willie Ortiz, *Manager*
EMP: 100
SALES (corp-wide): 14.3B **Publicly Held**
WEB: www.parker.com
SIC: 3053 Gaskets, all materials
PA: Parker-Hannifin Corporation
6035 Parkland Blvd
Cleveland OH 44124
216 896-3000

(G-5975)
PEPSI-COLA METRO BTLG CO INC
Also Called: Pepsico
27 Leonardo Dr (06473-2528)
P.O. Box 690 (06473-0690)
PHONE......................203 234-9014
Mat Karl, *Manager*
EMP: 115
SALES (corp-wide): 64.6B **Publicly Held**
WEB: www.pbg.com
SIC: 2086 5149 Soft drinks: packaged in cans, bottles, etc.; soft drinks
HQ: Pepsi-Cola Metropolitan Bottling Company, Inc.
1111 Westchester Ave
White Plains NY 10604
914 767-6000

(G-5976)
PLATT & LABONIA COMPANY LLC
70-80 Stoddard Ave (06473)
PHONE......................800 505-9099
Guy A Ferraiolo, *President*
EMP: 45 **EST:** 2015
SALES (est): 1.7MM **Privately Held**
SIC: 3441 Fabricated structural metal

(G-5977)
PLATT-LABONIA OF N HAVEN INC
Also Called: Craftline
70 Stoddard Ave (06473-2524)
P.O. Box 398 (06473-0398)
PHONE......................203 239-5681
Guy Ferraiolo, *President*
Vincent Labonia Jr, *President*
Elizabeth Labonia, *Vice Pres*
Peter Corrado, *Prdtn Mgr*
▲ **EMP:** 65 **EST:** 1953
SQ FT: 110,000
SALES (est): 11MM **Privately Held**
WEB: www.plattlabonia.com
SIC: 2542 3714 Cabinets: show, display or storage: except wood; motor vehicle parts & accessories

(G-5978)
PRATT & WHITNEY ENGINE SVCS
415 Washington Ave (06473)
PHONE......................203 934-2806
Bob Winer, *Branch Mgr*
EMP: 500
SALES (corp-wide): 66.5B **Publicly Held**
SIC: 3724 Aircraft engines & engine parts
HQ: Pratt & Whitney Engine Services, Inc.
1525 Midway Park Rd
Bridgeport WV 26330
304 842-5421

(G-5979)
PREFERRED MANUFACTURING CO
68 Old Broadway E (06473-1605)
P.O. Box 279 (06473-0279)
PHONE......................203 239-0727
Brian D Vanacore, *President*
EMP: 6
SQ FT: 13,000
SALES (est): 863.2K **Privately Held**
SIC: 3599 Machine shop, jobbing & repair

(G-5980)
PROFLOW INC
Also Called: Proflow Process Equipment
303 State St (06473-6104)
P.O. Box 748 (06473-0748)
PHONE......................203 230-4700
Kurt Uihlein, *President*
Brendan Rowley, *General Mgr*
William Iaai-Fit, *COO*
Lawrence Bee Jr, *Vice Pres*
Susan Sargeant, *Vice Pres*
EMP: 47
SQ FT: 18,000
SALES (est): 13.4MM **Privately Held**
SIC: 3823 5084 5251 3561 Industrial flow & liquid measuring instruments; pumps & pumping equipment; pumps & pumping equipment; pumps & pumping equipment; measuring & dispensing pumps

(G-5981)
PROSTAFF PRO SHOP
156 State St (06473-2207)
PHONE......................203 239-3835
Vic Marotta, *Owner*
EMP: 2
SALES (est): 95.3K **Privately Held**
SIC: 3629 Power conversion units, a.c. to d.c.: static-electric

(G-5982)
PROTEEM LLC
9 Wilson Ave (06473-1954)
PHONE......................203 787-2221
Mark Hogan,
EMP: 1
SALES (est): 104.2K **Privately Held**
SIC: 2824 Organic fibers, noncellulosic

(G-5983)
PURE CYCLE ENVIRONMENTAL LLC
30 Devine St (06473-2203)
PHONE......................203 230-3631
Nick Papa, *General Mgr*
EMP: 2
SALES (est): 85.2K **Privately Held**
SIC: 2834 Chlorination tablets & kits (water purification)

(G-5984)
Q-JET DSI INC
303 State St (06473-6104)
PHONE......................203 230-4700
Kurt Uihlein, *President*
EMP: 7
SALES (est): 578.3K **Privately Held**
WEB: www.q-jet.com
SIC: 3556 Dehydrating equipment, food processing

(G-5985)
QUAD/GRAPHICS INC
291 State St (06473-2131)
P.O. Box 860 (06473-0860)
PHONE......................203 288-2468
Marc Shapiro, *Branch Mgr*
EMP: 509
SALES (corp-wide): 4.1B **Publicly Held**
SIC: 2752 2754 3823 2721 Commercial printing, offset; commercial printing, gravure; controllers for process variables, all types; magazines: publishing & printing
PA: Quad/Graphics Inc.
N61w23044 Harrys Way
Sussex WI 53089
414 566-6000

(G-5986)
RC FABRICATION AND OFF RD LLC
96 Pond Hill Rd Unit 24 (06473-2894)
PHONE......................203 500-7071
Robert Carey, *Principal*
EMP: 1
SALES (est): 39.6K **Privately Held**
SIC: 3999 Manufacturing industries

(G-5987)
RELIANCE BUSINESS SYSTEMS INC
420 Sackett Point Rd # 8 (06473-3171)
PHONE......................203 281-4407
William K Rothfuss, *President*
Christine Nastri, *Admin Sec*
EMP: 5
SQ FT: 2,400
SALES (est): 807.7K **Privately Held**
SIC: 3861 Photocopy machines

(G-5988)
RUSSELL PARTITION CO INC
20 Dodge Ave (06473-1124)
PHONE......................203 239-5749
Jim Bango, *President*
EMP: 9 **EST:** 1969
SQ FT: 25,000
SALES (est): 2.6MM **Privately Held**
SIC: 2653 2631 Partitions, corrugated: made from purchased materials; paperboard mills

(G-5989)
S CAMEROTA & SONS INC
Also Called: Camerota Truck Parts
166 Universal Dr Unit 2 (06473-3630)
P.O. Box 1134, Enfield (06083-1134)
PHONE......................203 782-0360
Tom Antonioli, *General Mgr*
EMP: 6
SALES (corp-wide): 111MM **Privately Held**
WEB: www.camerota.com
SIC: 3714 5531 Motor vehicle parts & accessories; truck equipment & parts
PA: S. Camerota & Sons, Inc.
245 Shaker Rd
Enfield CT 06082
860 763-0896

(G-5990)
SAFT AMERICA INC
3 Powdered Metal Rd (06473-3209)
PHONE......................203 234-8333
Marty Waltemyer, *Materials Mgr*
Ivor Hay, *Marketing Staff*
David Cox, *Manager*
Sara Lopofsky, *Info Tech Mgr*
EMP: 35
SALES (corp-wide): 8.4B **Publicly Held**
SIC: 3691 Storage batteries
HQ: Saft America Inc
13575 Waterworks St
Jacksonville FL 32221
904 861-1501

(G-5991)
SCHWARTZ BODY COMPANY LLC
89 Stoddard Ave (06473-2526)
PHONE......................203 234-6046
Joseph Barnick,
EMP: 1
SALES: 500K **Privately Held**
SIC: 3713 Truck bodies (motor vehicles)

(G-5992)
SFC KOENIG LLC
73 Defco Park Rd (06473-1135)
PHONE......................203 245-1100
Jim Allen,
▲ **EMP:** 30
SQ FT: 9,800
SALES (est): 5.6MM
SALES (corp-wide): 2.4B **Publicly Held**
WEB: www.expanderplugs.com
SIC: 8742 3561 3594 Industry specialist consultants; pumps & pumping equipment; motors, pneumatic; motors: hydraulic, fluid power or air

GEOGRAPHIC SECTION

North Stonington - New London County (G-6024)

HQ: Sfc Koenig Ag
Lagerstrasse 8
Dietikon ZH 8953
447 434-600

(G-5993)
SIKORSKY AIRCRAFT CORPORATION
1 N Frontage Rd (06473)
PHONE..................516 228-2000
Kevin Doheny, *Manager*
EMP: 18 **Publicly Held**
WEB: www.sikorsky.com
SIC: 3721 Aircraft
HQ: Sikorsky Aircraft Corporation
6900 Main St
Stratford CT 06614

(G-5994)
SIROCCO SCREENPRINTS INC
376 State St (06473-3114)
PHONE..................203 288-3565
James Townsend, *President*
Adair Townsend, *Vice Pres*
EMP: 2
SALES: 150K **Privately Held**
SIC: 2759 Screen printing

(G-5995)
SOFTWARE STUDIOS LLC
26 Grandview Ter (06473-2043)
PHONE..................203 288-3997
Joshua Liebermann, *Owner*
EMP: 2 **EST:** 2011
SALES (est): 145K **Privately Held**
SIC: 7372 Prepackaged software

(G-5996)
SOLON MANUFACTURING
7 Grasso Ave (06473-3237)
PHONE..................203 230-5300
Rick Battis, *Principal*
EMP: 1
SALES (est): 165.6K **Privately Held**
SIC: 3999 Manufacturing industries

(G-5997)
SPARTAN INDUSTRIES LLC
58 Summer Ln (06473-3573)
PHONE..................203 464-8600
EMP: 2
SALES (est): 93.5K **Privately Held**
SIC: 3999 Manufacturing industries

(G-5998)
THE E J DAVIS COMPANY
10 Dodge Ave (06473-1140)
P.O. Box 326 (06473-0326)
PHONE..................203 239-5391
Gregory J Godbout, *President*
Evelyn Davis Edwards, *Treasurer*
Barbara D Godbout, *Admin Sec*
EMP: 30 **EST:** 1953
SQ FT: 62,000
SALES (est): 5MM **Privately Held**
WEB: www.ejdavis.com
SIC: 3296 3083 2672 Fiberglass insulation; laminated plastics plate & sheet; coated & laminated paper

(G-5999)
THOMAS KEEGAN & SONS INC (PA)
Also Called: Keegan Construction
75 Valley Service Rd (06473-1624)
PHONE..................203 239-9248
Terrence Keegan, *President*
Terrence J Keegan, *President*
Mary L Keegan, *Admin Sec*
EMP: 4
SQ FT: 4,600
SALES (est): 2.9MM **Privately Held**
SIC: 7359 4212 1794 1442 Equipment rental & leasing; local trucking, without storage; excavation work; construction sand & gravel; driveway, parking lot & blacktop contractors

(G-6000)
TRANQUIL PERSPECTIVES LLC
46 Blakeslee Ave (06473-1832)
PHONE..................860 919-9762
Phyllis V Pavlik, *Principal*
EMP: 2

SALES (est): 184.9K **Privately Held**
SIC: 3721 Research & development on aircraft by the manufacturer

(G-6001)
TRI STATE MAINTENANCE SVCS LLC
356 Old Maple Ave (06473-3248)
P.O. Box 180 (06473-0180)
PHONE..................203 691-1343
Thomas Giuliano,
EMP: 11 **EST:** 2006
SALES (est): 1.3MM **Privately Held**
SIC: 1389 1731 Construction, repair & dismantling services; general electrical contractor

(G-6002)
TWELVE PERCENT LLC
341 State St (06473-3112)
PHONE..................203 556-7024
EMP: 2
SALES (est): 62.3K **Privately Held**
SIC: 2084 Wines, brandy & brandy spirits

(G-6003)
TYCO INTERNATIONAL MGT CO LLC
195 Mcdermott Rd (06473-3665)
PHONE..................203 492-5000
Steve Toth, *Manager*
EMP: 2
SQ FT: 95,000 **Privately Held**
SIC: 3841 3842 Surgical & medical instruments; surgical appliances & supplies
HQ: Tyco International Management Company, Llc
9 Roszel Rd Ste 2
Princeton NJ 08540
609 720-4200

(G-6004)
U-TECH WIRE ROPE & SUPPLY LLC
222 Universal Dr Bldg 9 (06473-3659)
PHONE..................203 865-8885
Igor Ursini,
▲ **EMP:** 6
SQ FT: 8,000
SALES (est): 890K **Privately Held**
WEB: www.utechwirerope.com
SIC: 3496 Miscellaneous fabricated wire products

(G-6005)
ULBRICH OF GEORGIA INC
153 Washington Ave (06473-1710)
PHONE..................203 239-4481
EMP: 3
SALES (est): 139.4K **Privately Held**
SIC: 3495 Mfg Wire Springs

(G-6006)
ULBRICH SOLAR TECHNOLOGIES INC
153 Washington Ave (06473-1710)
PHONE..................203 239-4481
EMP: 2
SALES (est): 90.8K **Privately Held**
SIC: 3315 Steel wire & related products

(G-6007)
ULBRICH SOLAR WIRE LLC
153 Washington Ave (06473-1710)
PHONE..................203 239-4481
John J Cei, *Mng Member*
EMP: 11 **EST:** 2011
SALES (est): 4MM **Privately Held**
SIC: 3914 Stainless steel ware

(G-6008)
ULBRICH STAINLESS STEELS (PA)
153 Washington Ave (06473-1710)
P.O. Box 294 (06473-0294)
PHONE..................203 239-4481
Frederick C Ulbrich III, *CEO*
Cesar Medellin, *General Mgr*
John J Cei, *COO*
Rich Papeika, *Vice Pres*
Arnie Muniz, *Plant Mgr*
▲ **EMP:** 60 **EST:** 1924
SQ FT: 25,000

SALES (est): 224.5MM **Privately Held**
WEB: www.ulbrich.com
SIC: 3316 3356 5051 3341 Strip steel, cold-rolled: from purchased hot-rolled; nickel & nickel alloy: rolling, drawing or extruding; titanium & titanium alloy: rolling, drawing or extruding; strip, metal; secondary nonferrous metals; blast furnaces & steel mills

(G-6009)
UNIVERSAL METALWORKS LLC
5 Philip Pl (06473-1607)
PHONE..................203 239-6349
Steve Olajos, *Principal*
EMP: 2
SALES (est): 264.6K **Privately Held**
SIC: 3444 Sheet metalwork

(G-6010)
VALLEY SAND & GRAVEL CORP
400 N Frontage Rd (06473-3620)
PHONE..................203 562-3192
Bill Ladum, *Director*
EMP: 40
SALES (est): 2.4MM **Privately Held**
SIC: 1771 1442 Driveway, parking lot & blacktop contractors; construction sand & gravel

(G-6011)
VEROTEC INC
473 Washington Ave Unit E (06473-1310)
P.O. Box 469, Londonderry NH (03053-0469)
PHONE..................603 821-9921
Marc Harvey, *President*
Doreen Harvey, *General Mgr*
EMP: 5
SALES: 125K **Privately Held**
SIC: 3679 Electronic circuits

(G-6012)
VERTICAL STUDIOS LLC
18 Montowese Ave (06473-3615)
PHONE..................203 562-6542
Anthony Lavorgna, *Owner*
EMP: 1
SALES (est): 70.4K **Privately Held**
SIC: 2591 Blinds vertical

(G-6013)
VIOS SPORTS PLUS
117 Washington Ave Ste 6 (06473-1708)
PHONE..................203 234-7231
Mike Vio, *Principal*
EMP: 2
SALES (est): 212K **Privately Held**
SIC: 2759 Screen printing

(G-6014)
WINDOW MASTER REAL WD PDTS LLC
400 Sackett Point Rd (06473-3106)
PHONE..................203 230-2638
Carla Kling, *Manager*
Christian Kling,
EMP: 2
SQ FT: 13,000
SALES (est): 197.2K **Privately Held**
SIC: 2431 Millwork

(G-6015)
WMB INDUSTRIES LLC
62 Pool Rd (06473-2733)
PHONE..................203 927-2822
William M Bakutis, *Principal*
EMP: 3
SALES (est): 152.7K **Privately Held**
SIC: 3999 Manufacturing industries

(G-6016)
WOODMSTERS MLLWK RSTRATION LLC
119 Patten Rd (06473-2877)
PHONE..................203 745-3165
Eileen Condron, *Principal*
EMP: 2
SALES (est): 126.7K **Privately Held**
SIC: 2431 Millwork

(G-6017)
ZP COUTURE LLC
410 State St Rm 6 (06473-3149)
PHONE..................888 697-7239

Zeb Powell,
EMP: 4
SQ FT: 900
SALES (est): 291.3K **Privately Held**
SIC: 2731 7336 7389 Book publishing; commercial art & graphic design; graphic arts & related design; decoration service for special events

North Stonington
New London County

(G-6018)
ALEXIS HOMEMADE SCRUBS
25 Ella Wheeler Rd (06359-1708)
PHONE..................401 480-5074
EMP: 2 **EST:** 2012
SALES (est): 86.7K **Privately Held**
SIC: 2844 Toilet preparations

(G-6019)
AMERICAN KUHNE
75 Frontage Rd 201 (06359-1702)
PHONE..................401 326-6200
Marc Manville, *Engineer*
EMP: 2
SALES (est): 216K **Privately Held**
SIC: 3569 General industrial machinery

(G-6020)
BEEDE ELECTRICAL INSTR CO INC
75 Frontage Rd 106 (06359-1769)
PHONE..................603 753-6362
Walter Pelletier, *Ch of Bd*
Robert Janisch, *President*
David Curdie, *Treasurer*
Cathy Wagenrener, *Treasurer*
▲ **EMP:** 110
SALES (est): 20.2MM **Privately Held**
WEB: www.beede.com
SIC: 3694 Engine electrical equipment

(G-6021)
CAVEKRAFT WOODWORKING LLC ✪
155 Anna Farm Rd E (06359-1035)
PHONE..................860 230-4480
Laura L Mello,
EMP: 1 **EST:** 2019
SALES (est): 54.1K **Privately Held**
SIC: 2431 Millwork

(G-6022)
DYNAMIC BLDG ENRGY SLTIONS LLC (PA)
183 Provdnc New London (06359-1721)
PHONE..................860 599-1872
Julia Discuillo, *Principal*
Craig Olisky,
EMP: 10
SQ FT: 5,000
SALES: 2MM **Privately Held**
WEB: www.dynasys.org
SIC: 3599 3625 Oil filters, internal combustion engine, except automotive; gasoline filters, internal combustion engine, except auto; industrial controls: push button, selector switches, pilot

(G-6023)
EDWARDS WINES LLC
Also Called: Edwards, Jonathan Winery
74 Chester Maine Rd (06359-1303)
PHONE..................860 535-0202
Jonathan Edwards,
Karen Edwards,
Robert Edwards,
▲ **EMP:** 3
SALES (est): 220K **Privately Held**
SIC: 2084 Wines

(G-6024)
FARIA BEEDE INSTRUMENTS INC
Also Called: Faria Marine Instruments
75 Frontage Rd Ste 106 (06359-1711)
PHONE..................860 848-9271
Pam Meissner, *President*
Jason Blackburn, *Vice Pres*
Bill Randall, *Vice Pres*
Kevin Terry, *Vice Pres*

North Stonington - New London County (G-6025)

Cassie Daniels, *Senior Buyer*
▲ **EMP:** 165
SALES (est): 64.8MM **Privately Held**
WEB: www.faria-instruments.com
SIC: 3824 3825 3823 3643 Tachometer, centrifugal; speedometers; gauges for computing pressure temperature corrections; instruments to measure electricity; industrial instrmnts msrmnt display/control process variable; current-carrying wiring devices; switchgear & switchboard apparatus

(G-6025)
FISHER CONTROLS INTL LLC
95 Pendleton Hill Rd (06359)
PHONE 860 599-1140
John Wells, *Marketing Staff*
Bill Quernemoen, *Manager*
EMP: 170
SALES (corp-wide): 17.4B **Publicly Held**
WEB: www.emersonprocess.com/fisher
SIC: 3491 3494 Valves, automatic control; valves & pipe fittings
HQ: Fisher Controls International Llc
205 S Center St
Marshalltown IA 50158
641 754-3011

(G-6026)
G M WOODWORKING
490a Prov NI Tpke (06359)
PHONE 860 599-3781
Gary Marsh, *Owner*
EMP: 2
SQ FT: 1,000
SALES: 150K **Privately Held**
SIC: 2431 Millwork

(G-6027)
ISOPUR FLUID TECHNOLOGIES INC
183 Provi New Londo Tpke (06359)
PHONE 860 599-1872
Jason Lin, *CEO*
James V Gibbons, *General Mgr*
EMP: 10
SQ FT: 7,000
SALES: 1.3MM **Privately Held**
WEB: www.isopurfluid.com
SIC: 3569 Filters
PA: Dynamic Building & Energy Solutions Llc
183 Provdnc New London
North Stonington CT 06359

(G-6028)
JIM MURRAY WLDG & FABRICATION
294b Cossaduck Hill Rd (06359-1041)
PHONE 860 889-7777
Jim Murray, *Owner*
EMP: 1
SALES: 110K **Privately Held**
SIC: 7692 Welding repair

(G-6029)
MARSHALL PAPER TUBE
159 Babcock Rd (06359-1335)
PHONE 860 245-5536
EMP: 2 **EST:** 2010
SALES (est): 122.1K **Privately Held**
SIC: 2655 Fiber cans, drums & similar products

(G-6030)
MONTAUK PILOTS INC
90 Wintechog Hill Rd (06359-1215)
PHONE 860 535-3200
Bradley Glas, *President*
Clair Glas, *Principal*
EMP: 6
SALES (est): 346.4K **Privately Held**
SIC: 7999 3732 Fishing boats, party; operation; boat building & repairing

(G-6031)
PRESS ON SANDWICH CRAFTERS LLC
391 Norwich Westerly Rd (06359-9992)
PHONE 860 415-9906
Michael C Davies, *Principal*
EMP: 1
SALES (est): 59.5K **Privately Held**
SIC: 2741 Miscellaneous publishing

(G-6032)
WILKINSON TOOL & DIE CO
55 Stillman Rd (06359-1734)
PHONE 860 599-5821
Fax: 860 599-5821
EMP: 5 **EST:** 1978
SQ FT: 1,800
SALES: 1.2MM **Privately Held**
SIC: 3544 3089 Mfg Special Dies & Tools & Injection Molding Of Plastics

North Windham
Windham County

(G-6033)
ADAM FULLER WOODWORKING
143 S Brook Rd (06235)
PHONE 860 455-1296
Adam Fuller, *Owner*
EMP: 1
SALES (est): 65K **Privately Held**
SIC: 1521 2431 General remodeling, single-family houses; doors, wood; windows, wood; woodwork, interior & ornamental

(G-6034)
BOLDUCS MACHINE WORKS INC
207 Miller Rd (06235-2649)
PHONE 860 455-1232
John F Bolduc, *President*
Doreen L Bolduc, *Treasurer*
EMP: 4
SALES: 530K **Privately Held**
WEB: www.icegroup.com
SIC: 3724 Engine mount parts, aircraft

(G-6035)
BUILDERS CONCRETE EAST LLC
79 Boston Post Rd (06256-1302)
P.O. Box 133, Willimantic (06226-0133)
PHONE 860 456-4111
Kevin Jones, *QC Mgr*
Thomas Fricchione, *Sales Mgr*
Steven E Aiudi, *Mng Member*
Steve Aiudi, *Executive*
Harold Hopkins,
EMP: 25
SQ FT: 12,000
SALES (est): 6.1MM **Privately Held**
SIC: 3273 Ready-mixed concrete

(G-6036)
COLD RIVER LOGGING LLC
195 Tuckie Rd (06256-1317)
PHONE 860 334-9506
David J Labombard, *Principal*
EMP: 3
SALES (est): 108.7K **Privately Held**
SIC: 2411 Logging

(G-6037)
CONCRETE PRODUCTS
356 Tuckie Rd (06256-1329)
PHONE 860 423-4144
William Hamill, *President*
EMP: 6
SALES (est): 718.2K **Privately Held**
SIC: 3272 Concrete products, precast; septic tanks, concrete; tile, precast terrazzo or concrete

(G-6038)
HITECH CHROME PLTG & POLSG LC
30 Baker Rd (06256)
P.O. Box 204 (06256-0204)
PHONE 860 456-8070
Fabrizio Chiulli, *Managing Prtnr*
Lisa Krukoff, *Mng Member*
EMP: 4
SQ FT: 1,500
SALES: 176.1K **Privately Held**
SIC: 3471 Plating of metals or formed products

(G-6039)
MOTIVE INDUSTRIES LLC
356 Tuckie Rd (06256-1329)
PHONE 860 423-2064
Steven Gould,
EMP: 3
SALES (est): 266.6K **Privately Held**
SIC: 3999 Manufacturing industries

(G-6040)
UNITED ABRASIVES INC (PA)
185 Boston Post Rd (06256-1302)
PHONE 860 456-7131
Aris Marziali, *Ch of Bd*
Eric Marziali, *President*
Michael Smyth, *Plant Mgr*
Michael Smardon, *Opers Mgr*
Scott Lavallie, *Purch Agent*
◆ **EMP:** 280 **EST:** 1969
SQ FT: 300,000
SALES (est): 52.9MM **Privately Held**
SIC: 3291 3553 2296 Abrasive buffs, bricks, cloth, paper, stones, etc.; woodworking machinery; tire cord & fabrics

(G-6041)
WILLIAMS PRINTING GROUP LLC
387 Tuckie Rd Ste G (06256-1330)
P.O. Box 121201, Clermont FL (34712-1201)
PHONE 860 423-8779
L Franklin Williams Jr, *Principal*
EMP: 4
SALES (est): 386.5K **Privately Held**
SIC: 2752 Commercial printing, offset

Northfield
Litchfield County

(G-6042)
BARN BEAM CO OF NENG LLC
23 Old Northfield Rd (06778-2510)
PHONE 860 488-0317
David Dillon,
EMP: 1 **EST:** 2017
SALES (est): 39.6K **Privately Held**
SIC: 3999 Manufacturing industries

Northford
New Haven County

(G-6043)
BRASCO TECHNOLOGIES LLC
76 Woodland Dr (06472-1206)
PHONE 203 484-4291
David Winchell,
EMP: 3 **EST:** 1998
SQ FT: 1,000
SALES: 360K **Privately Held**
WEB: www.brascotech.com
SIC: 3589 Water treatment equipment, industrial

(G-6044)
CONSERV EPOXY LLC
49 Old Post Rd (06472-1035)
P.O. Box 454 (06472-0454)
PHONE 203 484-4123
Paul Marlowe, *Owner*
Cindi Marlowe,
EMP: 2
SALES (est): 258.5K **Privately Held**
SIC: 2891 Epoxy adhesives

(G-6045)
HONEYWELL INTERNATIONAL INC
12 Clintonville Rd (06472-1610)
PHONE 203 484-7161
Dan Corbett, *Marketing Mgr*
Andrew Nolan, *Branch Mgr*
Patrick Garvy, *Manager*
Robert Rex, *Manager*
EMP: 60
SALES (corp-wide): 41.8B **Publicly Held**
SIC: 3724 Aircraft engines & engine parts
PA: Honeywell International Inc.
300 S Tryon St
Charlotte NC 28202
973 455-2000

(G-6046)
HONEYWELL INTERNATIONAL INC
12 Clintonville Rd (06472-1610)
PHONE 203 484-7161
Mike Lynch, *President*
Paul Stone, *Branch Mgr*
EMP: 450
SALES (corp-wide): 41.8B **Publicly Held**
WEB: www.honeywell.com
SIC: 3724 Aircraft engines & engine parts
PA: Honeywell International Inc.
300 S Tryon St
Charlotte NC 28202
973 455-2000

(G-6047)
HONEYWELL INTERNATIONAL INC
12 Clintonville Rd (06472-1610)
PHONE 203 484-6202
Abraham William, *President*
EMP: 500
SALES (corp-wide): 41.8B **Publicly Held**
WEB: www.honeywell.com
SIC: 3724 Aircraft engines & engine parts
PA: Honeywell International Inc.
300 S Tryon St
Charlotte NC 28202
973 455-2000

(G-6048)
HONEYWELL INTERNATIONAL INC
1 Fire Lite Pl 4 (06472-1662)
PHONE 203 484-7161
Steven Chow, *Branch Mgr*
EMP: 48
SALES (corp-wide): 41.8B **Publicly Held**
SIC: 3724 Aircraft engines & engine parts
PA: Honeywell International Inc.
300 S Tryon St
Charlotte NC 28202
973 455-2000

(G-6049)
KEHL TECHNOLOGY & PRFMCE LLC
1831 Middletown Ave L6 (06472-1149)
PHONE 203 484-4808
Deborah Kehlenbach,
Ralph Kehlenbach,
EMP: 2
SALES (est): 400K **Privately Held**
SIC: 7539 3599 Machine shop, automotive; machine shop, jobbing & repair

(G-6050)
MB SPORTS TRAINING LLC
24 Fire Lite Pl (06472-1662)
PHONE 203 269-1410
Michael Brouchard, *President*
EMP: 2
SALES (est): 104.5K **Privately Held**
SIC: 3949 Team sports equipment

(G-6051)
NEW HAVEN SIGN COMPANY
1831 Middletown Ave (06472-1167)
P.O. Box 4187, Hamden (06514-0187)
PHONE 203 484-2777
Peter L Deyo, *Principal*
EMP: 3
SALES (est): 267.3K **Privately Held**
SIC: 3993 Signs & advertising specialties

(G-6052)
REFLECTED IMAGE
21 Westwind Dr (06472-1365)
PHONE 203 484-0760
Scott Du Little, *Owner*
EMP: 1
SALES (est): 70K **Privately Held**
WEB: www.reflectedimage.com
SIC: 3993 Signs, not made in custom sign painting shops

(G-6053)
SOLIDIFICATION PDTS INTL INC
524 Forest Rd (06472-1485)
P.O. Box 35 (06472-0035)
PHONE 203 484-9494
William Gannon, *President*
Bill Gannon, *President*
Paul Melaccio, *Manager*

▲ = Import ▼ = Export
◆ = Import/Export

Mari Ansaldo, *Admin Asst*
EMP: 7
SALES (est): 1MM **Privately Held**
SIC: 2843 2819 3999 Oils & greases; industrial inorganic chemicals; atomizers, toiletry

(G-6054)
SOLIDIFICATION PRODUCTS INTL
Also Called: Solidification Products Intl
215 Village St (06472-1405)
P.O. Box 35 (06472-0035)
PHONE.................................203 484-9494
William J Gannon Jr, *President*
EMP: 12
SALES (est): 2.2MM **Privately Held**
WEB: www.oilbarriers.com
SIC: 2819 Industrial inorganic chemicals

(G-6055)
SPECIALTY STAIRS LLC
58 Lanes Pond Rd (06472-1124)
PHONE.................................203 484-2557
Peter Spayd, *Owner*
EMP: 1
SALES (est): 98.8K **Privately Held**
SIC: 3446 Stairs, staircases, stair treads: prefabricated metal

Norwalk
Fairfield County

(G-6056)
420 SIGN DESIGN INC
25 Commerce St (06850-4111)
PHONE.................................203 852-1255
John Malagisi, *President*
Mary Malagisi, *Corp Secy*
EMP: 3 **EST:** 1996
SQ FT: 2,500
SALES (est): 499.3K **Privately Held**
WEB: www.signdesignct.com
SIC: 3993 Electric signs

(G-6057)
A TO Z SIGNS
607 Main Ave Ste 3p (06851-1058)
PHONE.................................203 840-0644
Raymond McClelland Jr, *President*
EMP: 2
SALES (est): 329.2K **Privately Held**
WEB: www.a-to-z-signs.com
SIC: 3993 Signs, not made in custom sign painting shops

(G-6058)
A WESTPORT WORDSMITH
101 Winfield St (06855-2116)
PHONE.................................203 354-7309
EMP: 2 **EST:** 2012
SALES (est): 150K **Privately Held**
SIC: 3579 Mfg Office Machines

(G-6059)
ABB FINANCE (USA) INC
501 Merritt 7 Ste 2 (06851-7001)
PHONE.................................919 856-2360
EMP: 4
SALES (est): 23.3K
SALES (corp-wide): 36.4B **Privately Held**
SIC: 3613 Switchgear & switchboard apparatus
PA: Abb Ltd
　Affolternstrasse 44
　ZUrich ZH 8050
　433 177-111

(G-6060)
AC SKIPS WELDING INC
50 Commerce St (06850-4141)
PHONE.................................203 838-2089
Alfred C Savage, *President*
Alfred Consavage, *Owner*
EMP: 1
SALES (est): 88.4K **Privately Held**
SIC: 7692 Welding repair

(G-6061)
ACCENT MAGAZINE
535 Connecticut Ave # 300 (06854-1713)
PHONE.................................203 853-6015
EMP: 2 **EST:** 2010
SALES (est): 95.1K **Privately Held**
SIC: 2721 Periodicals-Publishing/Printing

(G-6062)
ACCESS INTELLIGENCE
761 Main Ave Ste 2 (06851-1080)
PHONE.................................203 854-6730
EMP: 5
SALES (est): 497.6K **Privately Held**
SIC: 2721 Periodicals

(G-6063)
AG JEWELRY DESIGNS LLC
314 Wilson Ave (06854-4654)
PHONE.................................800 643-0978
Michael Soutar,
EMP: 2
SALES (corp-wide): 1MM **Privately Held**
SIC: 3911 5094 Jewelry, precious metal; jewelry & precious stones
PA: Ag Jewelry Designs Llc
　1 Stamford Plz
　Stamford CT 06901
　800 643-0978

(G-6064)
AIRPOT CORPORATION
35 Lois St (06851-4405)
PHONE.................................800 848-7681
Mark Gaberman, *President*
Barbara Cohen, *Principal*
Tom Lee, *Vice Pres*
Robert M Cohen, *Director*
▲ **EMP:** 26
SQ FT: 12,000
SALES (est): 5.7MM **Privately Held**
WEB: www.airpot.com
SIC: 3499 3714 3593 Machine bases, metal; motor vehicle parts & accessories; fluid power cylinders & actuators

(G-6065)
AJ CASEY LLC
Also Called: Beverly Feldman
597 Westport Ave C363 (06851-4440)
PHONE.................................203 226-5961
Anthony J Casey, *Mng Member*
▲ **EMP:** 7
SQ FT: 2,100
SALES: 6.8MM **Privately Held**
SIC: 3144 Dress shoes, women's

(G-6066)
ALTENERGY LLC
137 Rowayton Ave (06853-1413)
PHONE.................................203 299-1400
Russell M Stidolph,
EMP: 1
SALES (est): 135.9K **Privately Held**
SIC: 2282 Throwing & winding mills

(G-6067)
ALVARADO CUSTOM CABINETRY LLC
51 Midrocks Dr (06851-1623)
PHONE.................................203 831-0181
Carlos Alvarado, *Principal*
EMP: 12
SALES (est): 1.4MM **Privately Held**
SIC: 2431 Millwork

(G-6068)
AMBIANCE PAINTING LLC
67 Murray St (06851-3307)
PHONE.................................203 354-8689
Douglas Kitchen,
EMP: 13
SALES (est): 1.7MM **Privately Held**
WEB: www.ambiancepainting.com
SIC: 2679 Wallpaper

(G-6069)
AMY COE INC
20 Marshall St Ste 118 (06854-2281)
PHONE.................................203 227-9900
Amy Coe, *President*
Mark Coe, *Vice Pres*
EMP: 2 **EST:** 1993
SALES (est): 25.9K **Privately Held**
WEB: www.amycoe.com
SIC: 2211 Sheets, bedding & table cloths: cotton

(G-6070)
ANSA COMPANY INC
130 Water St (06854-3140)
PHONE.................................203 687-1664
Austin Iodice, *Manager*
EMP: 11
SQ FT: 34,000
SALES (corp-wide): 2.6MM **Privately Held**
SIC: 3085 Plastics bottles
PA: Ansa Company, Inc
　1200 S Main St
　Muskogee OK 74401
　918 687-1664

(G-6071)
APPLIED BIOSYSTEMS LLC
301 Merritt 7 Ste 23 (06851-1062)
PHONE.................................781 271-0045
Tony L White, *Principal*
EMP: 9
SALES (corp-wide): 24.3B **Publicly Held**
WEB: www.applera.com
SIC: 3826 Analytical instruments
HQ: Applied Biosystems, Llc
　5791 Van Allen Way
　Carlsbad CA 92008

(G-6072)
ARCTIME LLC
23 W Rocks Rd (06851-2927)
PHONE.................................203 321-5628
Peter Costandaki, *Principal*
EMP: 2
SALES (est): 168.2K **Privately Held**
SIC: 3366 Bronze foundry

(G-6073)
ARENSKY GROUP INC
12 Coventry Pl (06854-1301)
PHONE.................................203 919-1575
Gizeli R Donofrio, *President*
EMP: 6
SALES: 25K **Privately Held**
SIC: 5137 2341 Women's & children's lingerie & undergarments; women's & children's undergarments

(G-6074)
ARTISAN BREAD & PRODUCTS LLC
13 Dry Hill Rd (06851-4002)
PHONE.................................914 843-4401
Diego Perez,
EMP: 8
SALES (est): 607K **Privately Held**
SIC: 2051 Bakery: wholesale or wholesale/retail combined

(G-6075)
ARTISTIC IRON WORKS LLC
11 Reynolds St (06855-1014)
PHONE.................................203 838-9200
Maciej Jankowski, *Prdtn Mgr*
Edward Jankowski, *Mng Member*
Renata Singh, *Mng Member*
EMP: 9
SALES: 350K **Privately Held**
SIC: 3446 Gates, ornamental metal; railings, prefabricated metal; fences or posts, ornamental iron or steel

(G-6076)
ASEA BROWN BOVERI INC (DH)
Also Called: A B B Power Transmission
501 Merritt 7 (06851-7000)
PHONE.................................203 750-2200
Donald Aiken, *President*
J P Brett, *Senior VP*
Jeff Halsey, *Senior VP*
Han-Anders Nilsson, *Senior VP*
Julie Guarino, *Vice Pres*
EMP: 8 **EST:** 1978
SQ FT: 36,000
SALES (est): 456.4MM
SALES (corp-wide): 36.4B **Privately Held**
SIC: 3612 3613 5063 3511 Transformers, except electric; switchgear & switchboard apparatus; electrical apparatus & equipment; power transmission equipment, electric; switchgear; steam turbine generator set units, complete; gas turbines, mechanical drive; relays & industrial controls; engineering services; chemical engineering; petroleum engineering
HQ: Abb Holdings Inc.
　305 Gregson Dr
　Cary NC 27511
　919 856-2360

(G-6077)
ASPECTA
15 Oakwood Ave (06850-1365)
PHONE.................................855 400-7732
EMP: 1 **EST:** 2014
SALES (est): 83K **Privately Held**
SIC: 3253 Mfg Ceramic Wall/Floor Tile

(G-6078)
ASSOCIATES INC BEDFORD
401 Merritt 7 (06851-1000)
PHONE.................................203 846-0230
EMP: 2
SALES (est): 150K **Privately Held**
SIC: 3577 Computer peripheral equipment

(G-6079)
ASTROPHONIC CORP AMERICA
Also Called: Lion Cords Division
149 Woodward Ave (06854-4730)
PHONE.................................203 853-9300
Andrew Miller, *President*
William Miller, *Vice Pres*
▲ **EMP:** 2 **EST:** 1946
SQ FT: 25,000
SALES (est): 338.2K **Privately Held**
SIC: 5399 3699 Warehouse club stores; electrical equipment & supplies

(G-6080)
ATLANTIC GROUP CONNECTICUT LLC
501 Merritt 7 Ste 1 (06851-7001)
PHONE.................................203 847-0000
Roger Abramson, *CEO*
EMP: 1
SALES (est): 45.8K **Privately Held**
WEB: www.atlanticgroupct.com
SIC: 2521 Wood office furniture

(G-6081)
AUTO SUTURE COMPANY AUSTRALIA
150 Glover Ave (06850-1308)
PHONE.................................203 845-1000
EMP: 3
SALES (est): 17.1K **Publicly Held**
SIC: 3841 3842 Surgical And Medical Instruments
PA: Medtronic Public Limited Company
　20 Lower Hatch Street
　Dublin

(G-6082)
AUTO SUTURE COMPANY UK
150 Glover Ave (06850-1308)
PHONE.................................203 845-1000
EMP: 500
SALES (est): 16.7MM **Publicly Held**
SIC: 3841 3842 Surgical And Medical Instruments
PA: Medtronic Public Limited Company
　20 Lower Hatch Street
　Dublin

(G-6083)
AUTO SUTURE RUSSIA INC
150 Glover Ave (06850-1308)
PHONE.................................203 845-1000
EMP: 3
SALES (est): 138.1K **Publicly Held**
SIC: 3841 Surgical And Medical Instruments
PA: Medtronic Public Limited Company
　20 Lower Hatch Street
　Dublin

(G-6084)
AVARA PHARMACEUTICAL SVCS INC (HQ)
401 Merritt 7 (06851-1000)
PHONE.................................203 918-1659
Leonard Levi, *Ch of Bd*
Paul Larrat, *Dean*
Andy Glanville, *Exec VP*
Keith A Lyon, *CFO*
Bill Pasek, *Sales Staff*
EMP: 31

Norwalk - Fairfield County (G-6085)

SALES (est): 39.3MM
SALES (corp-wide): 39.8MM **Privately Held**
SIC: 2834 Pharmaceutical preparations
PA: Avara Us Holdings Llc
 101 Merritt 7
 Norwalk CT 06851
 203 655-1333

(G-6085)
AVARA US HOLDINGS LLC (PA)
101 Merritt 7 (06851-1059)
PHONE.................................203 655-1333
Timothy Tyson, *CEO*
James Scandura, *COO*
Keith Lyon, *CFO*
Donald Britt, *Officer*
Rick Mark, *Officer*
EMP: 0 EST: 2016
SALES (est): 39.8MM **Privately Held**
SIC: 6719 2834 Investment holding companies, except banks; druggists' preparations (pharmaceuticals)

(G-6086)
BARBARA GARELICK ENTERPRISES
Also Called: Dge
280 Richards Ave (06850-2726)
PHONE.................................203 855-9897
Barbara Garelick, *Owner*
EMP: 1
SALES (est): 500K **Privately Held**
WEB: www.bgeprint.com
SIC: 2759 Promotional printing

(G-6087)
BATTERS BOX
327 Main Ave Ste 2 (06851-6156)
PHONE.................................203 845-0212
Louis Chochos, *Principal*
EMP: 2
SALES (est): 146.6K **Privately Held**
SIC: 2299 Batting, wadding, padding & fillings

(G-6088)
BEIERSDORF INC
360 Dr Martin Luther King (06854-4648)
P.O. Box 5529 (06856)
PHONE.................................203 854-8000
Kathleen Shea, *Vice Pres*
EMP: 500
SALES (corp-wide): 11.8B **Privately Held**
WEB: www.bdfusa.com
SIC: 2844 5122 3842 2841 Face creams or lotions; antiseptics; bandages & dressings; stockinette, surgical; soap: granulated, liquid, cake, flaked or chip; tape, pressure sensitive: made from purchased materials
HQ: Beiersdorf, Inc.
 45 Danbury Rd
 Wilton CT 06897
 203 563-5800

(G-6089)
BELVOIR MEDIA GROUP LLC
535 Cnncticut Ave Ste 100 (06854)
PHONE.................................203 857-3128
Jared Max Hendler, *Principal*
EMP: 4
SALES (est): 238.4K **Privately Held**
SIC: 2721 Magazines: publishing only, not printed on site

(G-6090)
BELVOIR PUBLICATIONS INC (PA)
Also Called: Belvoir Media Group
800 Connecticut Ave 4w02 (06854-1628)
P.O. Box 5656 (06856-5656)
PHONE.................................203 857-3100
Robert Englander, *CEO*
Greg King, *Exec VP*
Ron Goldberg, *CFO*
Kerstin M McCall, *Manager*
Larry Canale, *Director*
EMP: 50
SQ FT: 11,000
SALES (est): 61.6MM **Privately Held**
WEB: www.belvoir.com
SIC: 2731 Book publishing

(G-6091)
BENDER MANAGEMENT INC
Also Called: Bender Showrooms
235 Westport Ave (06851-4310)
P.O. Box 857 (06852-0857)
PHONE.................................203 847-3865
David Bender, *President*
Stephen Fecteau, *Vice Pres*
James Narduzzo, *Vice Pres*
EMP: 7
SALES (est): 158.7K **Privately Held**
SIC: 1799 2499 Kitchen & bathroom remodeling; kitchen, bathroom & household ware: wood

(G-6092)
BIO MED PACKAGING SYSTEMS INC
100 Pearl St (06850-1629)
PHONE.................................203 846-1923
James B Brown, *President*
Janet Kaufman, *Vice Pres*
▼ EMP: 25
SQ FT: 50,000
SALES (est): 4MM **Privately Held**
SIC: 3842 Surgical appliances & supplies

(G-6093)
BITE TECH INC
20 Glover Ave Ste 1 (06850-1234)
PHONE.................................203 987-6898
Jeff Padovan, *CEO*
James Meyers, *Vice Pres*
▼ EMP: 27 EST: 1995
SQ FT: 3,500
SALES (est): 5.6MM **Privately Held**
SIC: 3069 Mouthpieces for pipes, cigarette holders, etc.: rubber

(G-6094)
BLUE LOTUS BRACELETS
175 Silvermine Ave (06850-1610)
PHONE.................................203 858-6526
Patty Robinson, *Principal*
EMP: 2
SALES (est): 83.3K **Privately Held**
SIC: 3961 Bracelets, except precious metal

(G-6095)
BMHS PRESS BOX
300 Highland Ave (06854-4029)
PHONE.................................203 810-4380
Robert Lamp, *Principal*
EMP: 1
SALES (est): 67.9K **Privately Held**
SIC: 2741 Miscellaneous publishing

(G-6096)
BOMBOO LLC
32 West Ave (06854-2224)
PHONE.................................475 731-0865
Armando Vargas,
EMP: 1
SALES: 8K **Privately Held**
SIC: 2131 Smoking tobacco

(G-6097)
BPI REPROGRAPHICS
Also Called: American Reprographics
87 Taylor Ave (06854-2038)
PHONE.................................203 866-5600
John P Schaberg, *President*
EMP: 10 EST: 1946
SQ FT: 6,000
SALES (est): 714.5K **Privately Held**
SIC: 7373 3861 7334 Computer-aided system services; photographic equipment & supplies; blueprinting service

(G-6098)
BR INDUSTRIES LLC
16 Lakewood Dr (06851-1021)
PHONE.................................203 216-3576
Francis Fanzilli, *Principal*
EMP: 2
SALES (est): 100.1K **Privately Held**
SIC: 3999 Manufacturing industries

(G-6099)
BREISLER PRCSION MACHINING LLC
31 Ingleside Ave (06850-2521)
PHONE.................................203 847-6614
Richard J Breisler, *Owner*
EMP: 2
SALES (est): 275.2K **Privately Held**
SIC: 3599 Machine shop, jobbing & repair

(G-6100)
BRUCE PARK SPORTS EMB LLC
20 Chatham Dr (06854-2528)
PHONE.................................203 853-4488
John Mackenzie, *Mng Member*
EMP: 3
SQ FT: 1,800
SALES (est): 257.4K **Privately Held**
SIC: 2395 Embroidery products, except schiffli machine; embroidery & art needlework

(G-6101)
BUCK SCIENTIFIC INC
58 Fort Point St (06855-1097)
PHONE.................................203 853-9444
Robert Anderson, *President*
Edward Nadeau, *Vice Pres*
John Mellor, *Prdtn Mgr*
Eric Anderson, *Admin Sec*
Theresa Perkins, *Contractor*
EMP: 55
SQ FT: 10,000
SALES (est): 11.6MM **Privately Held**
WEB: www.bucksci.com
SIC: 3826 3823 Analytical instruments; gas analyzing equipment; gas chromatographic instruments; densitometers, analytical; absorption analyzers: infrared, X-ray, etc.: industrial

(G-6102)
BUSINESS JOURNALS INC (PA)
Also Called: Travel Wear
50 Day St Fl 3 (06854-3100)
PHONE.................................203 853-6015
Renfrew M Brighton, *Ch of Bd*
Britton Jones, *President*
Alexandra D'Archangelo, *Director*
Coleman McCartan, *Director*
Nickie Milazzo,
EMP: 55
SQ FT: 20,000
SALES (est): 5.6MM **Privately Held**
WEB: www.breweryage.com
SIC: 2721 2741 Trade journals: publishing only, not printed on site; technical manuals: publishing only, not printed on site

(G-6103)
BUTTERFLY WINGS PUBG CO LLC
2 Wildmere Ln (06851-4118)
PHONE.................................203 642-4481
Jaime Troiano, *Mng Member*
EMP: 1
SALES (est): 37.5K **Privately Held**
SIC: 2741 Miscellaneous publishing

(G-6104)
C & D UPHOLSTERY
234 East Ave (06855-1934)
PHONE.................................203 838-1050
Christos Simoulidis, *Owner*
EMP: 2
SQ FT: 9,000
SALES (est): 74K **Privately Held**
SIC: 5949 2512 7641 Fabric stores piece goods; upholstered household furniture; reupholstery

(G-6105)
CALUMMA TECHNOLOGIES LLC
11 Bedford Ave Apt H3 (06850-3838)
PHONE.................................914 557-4562
Gabriel Nelson, *Owner*
EMP: 1
SALES (est): 40.7K **Privately Held**
SIC: 7372 7389 Application computer software;

(G-6106)
CANTATA MEDIA LLC
Also Called: Daily Voice
132b Water St (06854-3140)
P.O. Box 464 (06856-0464)
PHONE.................................203 951-9885
Sam Barron, *Editor*
Travis Hardman, *Mng Member*
EMP: 12

SALES (est): 227.1K **Privately Held**
SIC: 2711 7371 Newspapers; computer software development & applications

(G-6107)
CARLUCCI WELDING & FABRICATION
205 Wilson Ave (06854-5025)
PHONE.................................203 588-0746
Canio C Carlucci, *President*
EMP: 2 EST: 2015
SALES (est): 81.8K **Privately Held**
SIC: 7692 Welding repair

(G-6108)
CARNEGIE TOOL INC
25 Perry Ave Ste 12 (06850-1655)
PHONE.................................203 866-0744
Paul C Stratton, *President*
Phyllis Stratton, *Vice Pres*
EMP: 10
SALES (est): 1.4MM **Privately Held**
SIC: 3544 3599 Special dies & tools; machine & other job shop work

(G-6109)
CB SEATING ETC LLC (PA)
324 Strawberry Hill Ave (06851-4328)
PHONE.................................203 359-3880
Carol Bruno, *Principal*
EMP: 4
SALES (est): 767.1K **Privately Held**
SIC: 2511 5021 Chairs, household, except upholstered: wood; household furniture

(G-6110)
CEBAL AMERICAS (PA)
Also Called: Alcan Packaging
101 Merritt 7 Ste 2 (06851-1060)
PHONE.................................203 845-6356
Christel Bories, *CEO*
EMP: 7
SALES (est): 200MM **Privately Held**
WEB: www.cebalamerica.com
SIC: 3082 Tubes, unsupported plastic

(G-6111)
CELLMARK PULP & PAPER INC
80 Washington St Ste 1 (06854-3049)
PHONE.................................203 299-5050
Johan Rafstedt, *President*
Andreas Ceder, *Vice Pres*
EMP: 19
SALES (est): 4.8MM
SALES (corp-wide): 3.1B **Privately Held**
SIC: 2611 Pulp mills
HQ: Cellmark Ab
 Lilla Bommen 3c
 Goteborg 411 0
 311 900-07

(G-6112)
CHANNEL ALLOYS
301 Merritt 7 Ste 1 (06851-1051)
PHONE.................................203 975-1404
Chris Howard, *President*
▲ EMP: 5 EST: 2015
SALES (est): 228.4K **Privately Held**
SIC: 3316 2041 Bars, steel, cold finished, from purchased hot-rolled; flour & other grain mill products

(G-6113)
CHRISTIAN SCIENCE COMMITTEE ON
50 Washington St (06854-2710)
PHONE.................................203 866-1200
Richard Evans, *Principal*
EMP: 1 EST: 2017
SALES (est): 41.3K **Privately Held**
SIC: 2741 Miscellaneous publishing

(G-6114)
CHRISTOPHER CONDORS
Also Called: Condor Press
23 1st St Ste 1 (06855-2333)
PHONE.................................203 852-8181
Christopher Condors, *Owner*
EMP: 4 EST: 1992
SQ FT: 2,500
SALES: 200K **Privately Held**
SIC: 2759 Commercial printing

GEOGRAPHIC SECTION — Norwalk - Fairfield County

(G-6115)
CISCO SYSTEMS INC
383 Main Ave Ste 7 (06851-1544)
PHONE.....................203 229-2300
Jeff Distasio, *Regional Mgr*
Paul La Croix, *Engineer*
Mark King, *Marketing Mgr*
Greg Prindel, *Manager*
Gil Brouillette, *Manager*
EMP: 40
SALES (corp-wide): 51.9B **Publicly Held**
WEB: www.cisco.com
SIC: 3577 5045 Data conversion equipment, media-to-media: computer; computers, peripherals & software
PA: Cisco Systems, Inc.
170 W Tasman Dr
San Jose CA 95134
408 526-4000

(G-6116)
CLARKE DISTRIBUTION CORP
64 S Main St (06854-2934)
PHONE.....................203 838-9385
Thomas Clarke, *President*
EMP: 7
SQ FT: 14,894 **Privately Held**
SIC: 3639 5722 Major kitchen appliances, except refrigerators & stoves; electric household appliances, major
PA: Clarke Distribution Corporation
393 Fortune Blvd
Milford MA 01757

(G-6117)
COASTLINE FUEL INC
Also Called: J Furano Trucking
3 Van Zant St (06855-1700)
PHONE.....................203 846-3601
Stephen Cenatiempo Jr, *President*
Claire Furano, *Admin Sec*
EMP: 2
SALES (est): 140.8K **Privately Held**
SIC: 4212 2869 Local trucking, without storage; industrial organic chemicals

(G-6118)
COBRA GREEN LLC
50 N Water St (06854-2278)
PHONE.....................203 354-5000
Eugene A Gorab, *President*
EMP: 600
SALES (est): 14.3MM **Privately Held**
SIC: 8748 6799 7372 8721 Business consulting; venture capital companies; prepackaged software; accounting, auditing & bookkeeping

(G-6119)
COCCHIA NORWALK GRAPE CO
Also Called: Homemade Lbtons By Ccchia Sons
25 Ely Ave (06854-2995)
PHONE.....................203 855-7911
Fax: 203 866-4690
EMP: 10
SQ FT: 3,000
SALES (est): 620K **Privately Held**
SIC: 2084 5149 5084 Winery & Whol Wine Makers' Equipment & Brewery Products Machinery

(G-6120)
COLONIAL WOODWORKING INC
145 Water St (06854-3129)
PHONE.....................203 866-5844
Frank Carlucci, *President*
Nancy Carlucci, *Vice Pres*
Peter Carlucci, *Vice Pres*
Veronica Mahan, *Admin Sec*
EMP: 18 EST: 1975
SQ FT: 13,000
SALES (est): 1.6MM **Privately Held**
WEB: www.colonialwoodworking.com
SIC: 2431 Staircases & stairs, wood

(G-6121)
COLOR FILM MEDIA GROUP LLC (PA)
45 Keeler Ave (06854-2307)
PHONE.....................203 202-2929
J Bradford Lareau,
EMP: 8
SALES (est): 942.2K **Privately Held**
SIC: 3651 Compact disk players

(G-6122)
COMPUTER SUPPORT PEOPLE LLC
Also Called: Tcsp
16 River St Ste 1 (06850-3402)
P.O. Box 17186, Stamford (06907-7186)
PHONE.....................203 653-4643
Jorge Raigoza, *President*
EMP: 3 EST: 2007
SALES (est): 991K **Privately Held**
SIC: 5045 7373 7372 7376 Computers, peripherals & software; computer integrated systems design; systems integration services; local area network (LAN) systems integrator; value-added resellers, computer systems; prepackaged software; computer facilities management; computer maintenance & repair; computer related consulting services

(G-6123)
COMPUTER TECH EXPRESS LLC
95 New Canaan Ave (06850-2620)
PHONE.....................203 810-4932
Mohammad Ghazi, *Principal*
EMP: 5
SALES (est): 369.7K
SALES (corp-wide): 118.4K **Privately Held**
SIC: 7372 7379 Application computer software;
PA: Computer Tech Express Llc
912 Hope St
Stamford CT 06907
203 817-0100

(G-6124)
CONCORD INDUSTRIES INC
Also Called: Concord Distributing
19 Willard Rd (06851-4414)
PHONE.....................203 750-6060
Karen Muller Condron, *President*
▲ EMP: 45
SQ FT: 27,000
SALES (est): 5.7MM **Privately Held**
WEB: www.concordind.com
SIC: 3499 5199 3993 Novelties & giftware, including trophies; gifts & novelties; signs & advertising specialties

(G-6125)
CONCORD LITHO
9 Walnut Ave (06851-5102)
PHONE.....................203 866-9394
EMP: 2 EST: 2011
SALES (est): 110K **Privately Held**
SIC: 2752 Lithographic Commercial Printing

(G-6126)
CONN DEPT MOTOR VEHICLES
540 Main Ave (06851-1038)
PHONE.....................203 840-1993
Mollein Gray, *Principal*
EMP: 2
SALES (est): 113.6K **Privately Held**
SIC: 3469 Automobile license tags, stamped metal

(G-6127)
CONNECTICUT LEAF FILTER LLC
288 East Ave Apt 2 (06855-1902)
PHONE.....................203 857-0846
Michael A Kaplan, *Principal*
EMP: 2
SALES (est): 117.8K **Privately Held**
SIC: 3569 Filters

(G-6128)
CONNECTICUT TICK CONTROL LLC
15 Chapel St (06850-4113)
P.O. Box 1439 (06856-1439)
PHONE.....................203 855-7849
David Whitman,
Richard Whitman,
EMP: 17 EST: 1998
SALES (est): 1.8MM **Privately Held**
WEB: www.nixticks.org
SIC: 7342 2879 Pest control in structures; insecticides & pesticides

(G-6129)
COOK PRINT
35 Van Zant St (06855-1919)
PHONE.....................203 855-8785
William Cook, *Owner*
EMP: 3
SQ FT: 3,720
SALES (est): 179.9K **Privately Held**
SIC: 7336 5699 7299 2396 Silk screen design; T-shirts, custom printed; stitching services; automotive & apparel trimmings; pleating & stitching

(G-6130)
CORR/DIS INCORPORATED
Also Called: Fastserv/Northeast
38 Burchard Ln (06853-1105)
P.O. Box 125 (06853-0125)
PHONE.....................203 838-6075
Jeffrey Gerwig, *President*
Christopher Gerwig, *Vice Pres*
Norma Gerwig, *Treasurer*
EMP: 2
SALES (est): 250K **Privately Held**
WEB: www.fastservnortheast.com
SIC: 2653 3993 Display items, corrugated: made from purchased materials; displays & cutouts, window & lobby

(G-6131)
CPC CHILDRENSWEAR INC
6 Logan Pl (06853-1403)
P.O. Box 142 (06853-0142)
PHONE.....................203 286-6204
Ginger Drysdale, *CEO*
EMP: 2
SALES (est): 67K **Privately Held**
SIC: 2361 Girls' & children's dresses, blouses & shirts

(G-6132)
CRAIG KEATING
39 Fairfield Ave Rear D (06854-2179)
PHONE.....................203 852-0571
Craig Keating, *Principal*
EMP: 2
SALES (est): 56.5K **Privately Held**
SIC: 7372 Prepackaged software

(G-6133)
CRITERION INC
Also Called: Perfectsoftware
501 Merritt 7 Ste 1 (06851-7001)
PHONE.....................203 703-9000
Sunil Reddy, *CEO*
EMP: 25
SALES (est): 2.3MM **Privately Held**
SIC: 7372 Business oriented computer software

(G-6134)
DARK MOON METALS LLC
38 Creeping Hemlock Dr (06851-1029)
PHONE.....................203 858-3015
Jeffrey Santo,
Dana Cole,
EMP: 2 EST: 2012
SALES (est): 56.6K **Privately Held**
SIC: 7692 Welding repair

(G-6135)
DESIGNING ELEMENT
6 Barnum Ave (06851-4111)
PHONE.....................203 849-3076
Deborah Docimo, *Principal*
EMP: 3
SALES (est): 189.2K **Privately Held**
SIC: 2819 Elements

(G-6136)
DEVINE BROTHERS INCORPORATED
38 Commerce St (06850-4109)
P.O. Box 189 (06852-0189)
PHONE.....................203 866-4421
Tom Devine, *President*
Michael M Devine, *President*
Stephen C Devine, *Vice Pres*
Sean Devine, *Plant Mgr*
Wilfredo Torres, *Terminal Mgr*
EMP: 37 EST: 1918
SQ FT: 5,000
SALES (est): 9.8MM **Privately Held**
SIC: 5983 5032 5031 3273 Fuel oil dealers; concrete mixtures; building materials, exterior; building materials, interior; ready-mixed concrete; concrete & cinder block

(G-6137)
DIAGEO AMERICAS INC
801 Main Ave (06851-1127)
PHONE.....................203 229-2100
Deirdre Mahlan, *CEO*
James Thompson, *President*
Elizabeth Tong, *Vice Pres*
Corinn Williams, *Manager*
Gabriel Bisio, *Admin Sec*
EMP: 8
SALES (est): 658.4K
SALES (corp-wide): 16.3B **Privately Held**
SIC: 2084 Wines, brandy & brandy spirits
PA: Diageo Plc
Lakeside Drive Park Royal
London NW10
208 978-6000

(G-6138)
DIAGEO AMERICAS SUPPLY INC
801 Main Ave (06851-1127)
PHONE.....................203 229-2100
Paul Gallagher, *President*
Dan Russo, *Vice Pres*
Aren Korte, *CFO*
Claire Macintyre, *VP Human Res*
Gabriel Bisio, *Director*
◆ EMP: 4 EST: 2008
SALES (est): 806.5K **Privately Held**
SIC: 2084 Wines, brandy & brandy spirits

(G-6139)
DIAGEO INVESTMENT CORPORATION
801 Main Ave (06851-1127)
PHONE.....................203 229-2100
Michael Fernandez, *General Mgr*
Jeff Millstein, *Exec VP*
Scott Barnhart, *Vice Pres*
Harry Bigelow, *Vice Pres*
Gary Galanis, *Vice Pres*
◆ EMP: 12
SALES (est): 1.3MM
SALES (corp-wide): 16.3B **Privately Held**
SIC: 2082 Malt beverages
PA: Diageo Plc
Lakeside Drive Park Royal
London NW10
208 978-6000

(G-6140)
DIAGEO NORTH AMERICA INC (HQ)
801 Main Ave (06851-1127)
PHONE.....................203 229-2100
Ivan Menezes, *CEO*
Alberta Hawkins, *President*
Maggie Lapcewich, *President*
Larry Schwartz, *President*
Thomas Day, *Vice Pres*
◆ EMP: 3500
SALES (est): 2.6B
SALES (corp-wide): 16.3B **Privately Held**
SIC: 2084 2085 Wines, brandy & brandy spirits; cordials, alcoholic
PA: Diageo Plc
Lakeside Drive Park Royal
London NW10
208 978-6000

(G-6141)
DIAGEO PLC
Joseph E Seagram & Sons
801 Main Ave (06851-1127)
PHONE.....................203 229-2100
Edgar M Bronfman Jr, *President*
Jennifer Van Ness, *VP Mktg*
Cody Hickok, *Marketing Staff*
EMP: 100
SALES (corp-wide): 16.3B **Privately Held**
SIC: 2085 2084 Distilled & blended liquors; wines, brandy & brandy spirits
PA: Diageo Plc
Lakeside Drive Park Royal
London NW10
208 978-6000

Norwalk - Fairfield County (G-6142)

(G-6142)
DICKSON PRODUCT DEVELOPMENT
14 Perry Ave (06850-1623)
PHONE..................................203 846-2128
Maurice Bennett, *President*
Margaret Bennett, *Vice Pres*
EMP: 7
SQ FT: 6,000
SALES (est): 725.4K **Privately Held**
WEB: www.dicksonconsulting.biz
SIC: 3599 Machine shop, jobbing & repair

(G-6143)
DIIORIO WOODWORKS
Also Called: Dilorio Woodworks
304 Wilson Ave (06854-4631)
PHONE..................................203 855-1331
Rinaldi Diiorio, *Partner*
EMP: 1
SALES (est): 116.4K **Privately Held**
SIC: 2499 1751 Decorative wood & woodwork; carpentry work

(G-6144)
DIIORIOS CUSTOM WDWKG LLC
32 Triangle St (06855-1507)
PHONE..................................203 855-1635
Rinaldo Diiorio, *Principal*
EMP: 1
SALES (est): 50.5K **Privately Held**
SIC: 3952 Chalk: carpenters', blackboard, marking, tailors', etc.

(G-6145)
DOMINICS DECORATING INC
6 Allen Ct (06851-2306)
PHONE..................................203 838-1827
Michael Nardella, *President*
Peter Murphy, *Vice Pres*
EMP: 6
SQ FT: 4,000
SALES (est): 730.6K **Privately Held**
SIC: 2211 2231 2391 2392 Upholstery fabrics, cotton; draperies & drapery fabrics, cotton; slip cover fabrics, cotton; upholstery fabrics, wool; curtains & draperies; slip covers & pads

(G-6146)
DOONEY & BOURKE INC (PA)
1 Regent St (06855-1405)
P.O. Box 841 (06856-0841)
PHONE..................................203 853-7515
H Peter Dooney, *President*
Philip R Kinsley, *Vice Pres*
Frederick A Bourke Jr, *Treasurer*
Palmer Chiappetta, *Accountant*
▲ EMP: 38
SQ FT: 56,000
SALES (est): 26.1MM **Privately Held**
SIC: 3171 2387 3161 3172 Handbags, women's; apparel belts; suitcases; wardrobe bags (luggage); personal leather goods; women's footwear, except athletic

(G-6147)
DORADO TANKERS POOL INC
20 Glover Ave (06850-1219)
PHONE..................................203 662-2600
Mark La Monte, *President*
John Greenwood, *Admin Sec*
EMP: 20
SALES (est): 3.8MM **Privately Held**
SIC: 3731 Shipbuilding & repairing

(G-6148)
DOUGH GIRL BAKING CO LLC
50 Sammis St (06853-1516)
PHONE..................................203 838-9695
Laura Jayson, *Principal*
EMP: 2
SALES (est): 136.8K **Privately Held**
SIC: 2051 Bread, cake & related products

(G-6149)
DOUGLAS MOSS
Also Called: E Magazine
28 Knight St Ste 5 (06851-4719)
P.O. Box 5098, Westport (06881-5098)
PHONE..................................203 854-5559
EMP: 9
SALES (est): 510K **Privately Held**
SIC: 2721 Periodicals-Publishing/Printing

(G-6150)
DRAPERY CONSULTANTS
Also Called: Fasanella, Frank T
88 Old Saugatuck Rd (06855-2217)
PHONE..................................203 855-0454
Frank Fasanella, *Owner*
EMP: 1
SALES: 80K **Privately Held**
SIC: 2591 5211 Drapery hardware & blinds & shades; lumber & other building materials

(G-6151)
DULCE DOMUM LLC
Also Called: Cottages & Grdns Publications
40 Richards Ave Ste 4 (06854-2320)
PHONE..................................203 227-1400
Mary A Howatson,
EMP: 22
SQ FT: 3,225
SALES (est): 3MM **Privately Held**
WEB: www.cottages-gardens.com
SIC: 2721 Magazines: publishing & printing

(G-6152)
E-Z TOOLS INC
5 Poplar St (06855-2108)
PHONE..................................203 838-2102
Fax: 203 855-9965
EMP: 5
SALES: 100K **Privately Held**
SIC: 3423 Mfg Hand/Edge Tools

(G-6153)
EC HOLDINGS INC
2 Muller Ave (06851)
PHONE..................................203 846-1651
Daniel Kahn, *President*
EMP: 9
SQ FT: 40,000
SALES (est): 1.7MM **Privately Held**
SIC: 3613 5063 Circuit breakers, air; time switches, electrical switchgear apparatus; electrical apparatus & equipment

(G-6154)
ECOMETICS INC
19 Concord St (06854-3706)
P.O. Box 179 (06856-0179)
PHONE..................................203 853-7856
Mark Lowenstein, *President*
Michael Lowenstein, *Vice Pres*
Judith Lowenstein, *Admin Sec*
▲ EMP: 30
SQ FT: 25,000
SALES (est): 6.8MM **Privately Held**
SIC: 2844 Cosmetic preparations

(G-6155)
EDGE PRINTING
6 Bayberry Ln (06851-1602)
PHONE..................................609 707-4555
Ed Goobic, *Principal*
EMP: 2
SALES (est): 89.9K **Privately Held**
SIC: 2752 Commercial printing, lithographic

(G-6156)
ELEGANT DRYCLEANING
388 Westport Ave (06851-4423)
PHONE..................................203 849-1000
Jahnny Kim, *Owner*
EMP: 3
SALES (est): 99.2K **Privately Held**
SIC: 7216 3589 Cleaning & dyeing, except rugs; servicing machines, except dry cleaning, laundry: coin-oper.

(G-6157)
ELEMENT ONE LLC
1 N Water St Ste 100 (06854-2260)
PHONE..................................203 344-1553
Clayton H Fowler, *Principal*
EMP: 4
SALES (est): 338.2K **Privately Held**
SIC: 2819 Elements

(G-6158)
ETS-LINDGREN INC
Also Called: Ray Proof Shielding Systems
97 Richards Ave Apt A11 (06854-1640)
PHONE..................................203 838-4555
Kevin Baldwin, *Manager*
EMP: 1

SALES (corp-wide): 771.5MM **Publicly Held**
WEB: www.lindgrenfilters.com
SIC: 3825 Radio frequency measuring equipment
HQ: Ets-Lindgren Inc.
1301 Arrow Point Dr
Cedar Park TX 78613
512 531-6400

(G-6159)
EXQUISITE SURFACES INC
139 Woodward Ave (06854-4728)
PHONE..................................203 866-9100
Frank Nataf, *Branch Mgr*
EMP: 1
SALES (corp-wide): 7.8MM **Privately Held**
SIC: 1411 Dimension stone
PA: Exquisite Surfaces, Inc.
11817 Wicks St
Sun Valley CA 91352
818 767-2700

(G-6160)
FABRIC BTY INC
179 Westport Ave (06851-5207)
PHONE..................................203 845-7966
Linda Stewart, *President*
EMP: 2
SALES (est): 118.4K **Privately Held**
SIC: 2381 Fabric dress & work gloves

(G-6161)
FAIRFIELD WOOD WORKS
7 Lexington Ave (06854-4310)
PHONE..................................203 838-6883
Fax: 203 838-8493
EMP: 1 EST: 2011
SALES (est): 75K **Privately Held**
SIC: 2431 Mfg Millwork

(G-6162)
FC MEYER PACKAGING LLC (HQ)
108 Main St Ste 3 (06851-4640)
PHONE..................................203 847-8500
Steve Gilliand, *CFO*
Kenneth Schulman, *Mng Member*
Steven Schulman,
EMP: 60
SQ FT: 12,000
SALES (est): 42.4MM
SALES (corp-wide): 100.3MM **Privately Held**
SIC: 3086 Packaging & shipping materials, foamed plastic
PA: Mafcote, Inc.
108 Main St Ste 3
Norwalk CT 06851
203 847-8500

(G-6163)
FCA LLC
26 2nd St (06855-2316)
PHONE..................................203 857-0825
Frank C Arcamone Jr, *Principal*
EMP: 4
SALES (est): 283.7K **Privately Held**
SIC: 2448 Wood pallets & skids

(G-6164)
FIDUCIARYAI INC
13 N Main St (06854-2702)
PHONE..................................203 724-7571
Cynthia Steer, *President*
John Nawrocki, *COO*
EMP: 2 EST: 2017
SALES (est): 75K **Privately Held**
SIC: 7372 Prepackaged software

(G-6165)
FINANCIAL ACCNTING FOUNDATION (PA)
Also Called: Financial Accnting Stndards Bd
401 Merritt 7 Ste 5 (06851-1069)
P.O. Box 5116 (06856-5116)
PHONE..................................203 847-0700
Teresa S Polley, *President*
Robert Attmore, *Chairman*
Jack Brennan, *Chairman*
Leslie Seidman, *Chairman*
Mary P Crotty, *COO*
EMP: 165 EST: 1972
SQ FT: 60,000

SALES (est): 35.2MM **Privately Held**
SIC: 8621 2721 Accounting association; periodicals: publishing only

(G-6166)
FINE WOODWORKER
20 Fitch St (06855-1309)
PHONE..................................203 717-2444
EMP: 2
SALES (est): 85.2K **Privately Held**
SIC: 2431 Millwork

(G-6167)
FIRE PREVENTION SERVICES
13 Winfield St (06855-1307)
PHONE..................................203 866-6357
Andrew Delcarmine, *Owner*
Julio Delcarmine, *Co-Owner*
Andrew Carmine, *Vice Pres*
EMP: 10
SALES (est): 1.1MM **Privately Held**
SIC: 3999 Fire extinguishers, portable

(G-6168)
FIRST CLASS CUSTOM WOODWORKING
4 Wilton Ave (06851-4533)
PHONE..................................203 857-1000
EMP: 1
SALES (est): 54.1K **Privately Held**
SIC: 2431 Millwork

(G-6169)
FITZGERALD-NORWALK AWNING CO
Also Called: Norwalk Awning Company
131 Main St (06851-4628)
PHONE..................................203 847-5858
George H Genuario Jr, *President*
Carol Genuario, *Treasurer*
Gregory Genuario, *Admin Sec*
EMP: 7
SALES (est): 682.1K **Privately Held**
SIC: 2394 1799 Awnings, fabric: made from purchased materials; awning installation

(G-6170)
FLAT VERNACULAR
173 Ponus Ave (06850-1826)
PHONE..................................347 457-6227
EMP: 2 EST: 2015
SALES (est): 200.6K **Privately Held**
SIC: 2679 Wallpaper

(G-6171)
FORTIFIED HOLDINGS CORP
40 Richards Ave Ste 3 (06854-2320)
PHONE..................................203 594-1686
Brendan Reilly, *Principal*
EMP: 1
SALES (est): 75K **Privately Held**
SIC: 3524 Lawn & garden equipment

(G-6172)
G M F WOODWORKING LLC
22 Sunset Hill Ave (06851-5828)
PHONE..................................203 788-8979
George Farrington, *Principal*
EMP: 4
SALES (est): 192.2K **Privately Held**
SIC: 2431 Millwork

(G-6173)
G WOODCRAFT
11 Ruby St (06850-1614)
PHONE..................................203 846-4168
Gary Cimino, *Managing Prtnr*
EMP: 3
SALES (est): 279.6K **Privately Held**
SIC: 2521 Cabinets, office: wood

(G-6174)
GALASSIA PRESS LLC
17 Ponus Ave (06850-2609)
PHONE..................................203 846-9075
F Vance Fazzino, *Principal*
EMP: 1
SALES (est): 55.1K **Privately Held**
SIC: 2741 Miscellaneous publishing

(G-6175)
GATEWAY DIGITAL INC
16 Testa Pl (06854-4638)
PHONE..................................203 853-4929

▲ = Import ▼=Export
◆ =Import/Export

GEOGRAPHIC SECTION
Norwalk - Fairfield County (G-6204)

Van David Cudiner, *President*
Ray Compagna, *General Mgr*
Tom Steele, *Vice Pres*
Bill Bepko, *Accounts Exec*
Doug Edwards, *Accounts Exec*
EMP: 19
SQ FT: 13,000
SALES (est): 3MM Privately Held
WEB: www.gwayonline.com
SIC: 2796 2752 2791 2759 Color separations for printing; commercial printing, lithographic; typesetting; commercial printing

(G-6176)
GCN PUBLISHING INC
Also Called: Gcn Media Services
194 Main St Ste 2nw (06851-3502)
PHONE..................203 665-6211
Joanne Persico, *Principal*
Elaine Goncalves, *Accounts Exec*
EMP: 13
SALES (est): 1.1MM Privately Held
SIC: 2741

(G-6177)
GENERAL ELECTRIC COMPANY
901 Main Ave Ste 103 (06851-1187)
PHONE..................518 385-7164
Don Kesterson, *Engineer*
Matthew Laylock, *Engineer*
Mark Robson, *Sales Mgr*
Kurt Wildermuth, *Regl Sales Mgr*
David Kohl, *Sales Staff*
EMP: 65
SALES (corp-wide): 121.6B Publicly Held
SIC: 3825 Energy measuring equipment, electrical
PA: General Electric Company
   41 Farnsworth St
   Boston MA 02210
   617 443-3000

(G-6178)
GENERAL PACKAGING PRODUCTS INC
3 Valley View Rd Apt 9 (06851-1033)
PHONE..................203 846-1340
Peter D Schonberg, *President*
Anthony Lorenzo, *Admin Sec*
EMP: 9
SQ FT: 1,400
SALES (est): 1.4MM Privately Held
SIC: 3086 2653 2671 Packaging & shipping materials, foamed plastic; boxes, corrugated: made from purchased materials; boxes, solid fiber: made from purchased materials; plastic film, coated or laminated for packaging; thermoplastic coated paper for packaging

(G-6179)
GENVARIO AWNING CO
131 Main St (06851-4628)
PHONE..................203 847-5858
George Genvario, *CEO*
EMP: 4
SALES (est): 156.2K Privately Held
SIC: 2394 Canvas awnings & canopies

(G-6180)
GEORGIA-PACIFIC LLC
19 Meadow St (06854-4505)
PHONE..................203 866-9774
Jim Slay, *Principal*
EMP: 2
SALES (corp-wide): 40.6B Privately Held
SIC: 2676 Sanitary paper products
HQ: Georgia-Pacific Llc
   133 Peachtree St Nw
   Atlanta GA 30303
   404 652-4000

(G-6181)
GLOBENIX INC
9 Lois St (06851-4404)
PHONE..................203 740-7070
Young Chun, *President*
EMP: 7 EST: 2013
SQ FT: 1,000
SALES: 601.6K Privately Held
SIC: 5045 5049 3731 Communication equipment; optical goods; submersible marine robots, manned or unmanned

(G-6182)
GOLF GALAXY LLC
Also Called: Golfsmith
595 Connecticut Ave Ste 4 (06854-1734)
PHONE..................203 855-0500
Steve Partin, *Principal*
EMP: 5
SALES (corp-wide): 8.4B Publicly Held
SIC: 3949 5091 5941 Golf equipment; golf equipment; golf goods & equipment
HQ: Golf Galaxy, Llc
   345 Court St
   Coraopolis PA 15108

(G-6183)
GOTHAM CHEMICAL COMPANY INC
21 South St (06854-2602)
PHONE..................203 854-6644
Richard Zane Elkin, *President*
Ernest Elkin, *President*
Richard Elkin, *Vice Pres*
EMP: 100
SQ FT: 10,000
SALES (est): 17.4MM Privately Held
SIC: 2899 Water treating compounds

(G-6184)
GRANA PASTIFICIO LLC
23 Sachem St (06850-2516)
PHONE..................203 979-2828
Pasquale Pascarella,
EMP: 2 EST: 2015
SALES (est): 89.3K Privately Held
SIC: 2099 Pasta, uncooked: packaged with other ingredients

(G-6185)
GRAPES OF NORWALK
10 Cross St (06854-4613)
PHONE..................203 845-9640
EMP: 2
SALES (est): 89K Privately Held
SIC: 0172 2084 Grape Vineyard Mfg Wines/Brandy/Spirits

(G-6186)
GSC ORTHOTICS PROSTHETICS LLC
37 Hunt St (06853-1045)
PHONE..................203 857-0887
Gregory S Carford, *Principal*
EMP: 2
SALES (est): 108.9K Privately Held
SIC: 3842 Orthopedic appliances

(G-6187)
GUASA SALSA VZLA
9 Rainbow Rd (06854-2806)
PHONE..................203 981-7011
Maria Quiroga, *Principal*
EMP: 3
SALES (est): 139.1K Privately Held
SIC: 2099 Dips, except cheese & sour cream based

(G-6188)
GUINNESS AMERICA INC
801 Main Ave (06851-1127)
PHONE..................203 229-2100
Chuck Phillips, *Principal*
▼ **EMP:** 5
SALES (est): 325.3K
SALES (corp-wide): 16.3B Privately Held
SIC: 2082 Beer (alcoholic beverage)
PA: Diageo Plc
   Lakeside Drive Park Royal
   London NW10
   208 978-6000

(G-6189)
H J HOFFMAN COMPANY
25 Hanford Pl (06854-3017)
PHONE..................203 853-7740
David C Hoffman, *President*
Michael Hoffman, *Vice Pres*
EMP: 9
SQ FT: 4,000
SALES (est): 1.2MM Privately Held
WEB: www.hjhco.com
SIC: 7336 2395 Silk screen design; embroidery & art needlework

(G-6190)
H MUEHLSTEIN & CO INC
800 Connecticut Ave 5n01 (06854-1696)
PHONE..................800 257-3746
James W Duffy, *President*
Josh Luster, *Accounts Mgr*
Wilson Moya, *Manager*
George Philips, *Manager*
◆ **EMP:** 1
SALES (est): 204K Privately Held
SIC: 2899 Chemical preparations

(G-6191)
H&A DETAIL ON WHEELS
7 Testa Pl (06854-4613)
PHONE..................203 354-8845
EMP: 2 EST: 2007
SALES (est): 140K Privately Held
SIC: 3312 Blast Furnace-Steel Works

(G-6192)
HANNES PRECISION INDUSTRY INC
74 Fort Point St (06855-1210)
PHONE..................203 853-7276
Jean Schaer, *President*
EMP: 12
SALES (corp-wide): 700K Privately Held
SIC: 3999 Barber & beauty shop equipment
PA: Hannes Precision Industry Inc
   12 Pleasant St
   Norwalk CT
   203 853-7276

(G-6193)
HATCH AND BAILEY COMPANY (PA)
1 Meadow Street Ext (06854-4300)
PHONE..................203 866-5515
Michael Defelice, *General Mgr*
David Z Bailey, *Vice Pres*
Tony Bernardelli, *Sales Staff*
Peter Carlo, *Sales Staff*
Matt Destefano, *Sales Staff*
EMP: 25
SQ FT: 5,000
SALES (est): 20.8MM Privately Held
WEB: www.hatchandbailey.com
SIC: 5031 5032 5211 3271 Doors & windows; building materials, exterior; building blocks; door & window products; roofing material; masonry materials & supplies; blocks, concrete or cinder: standard

(G-6194)
HAWKEYE PRESS INC
8 Day St (06854-3020)
PHONE..................203 855-8580
Gerald Hauck, *President*
EMP: 2
SQ FT: 2,500
SALES (est): 255.5K Privately Held
SIC: 2759 Letterpress printing

(G-6195)
HAWTHRN SMTH MFG & CNSLTNG SRV
32 Hemlock Pl (06854-4331)
PHONE..................203 866-2227
Hawthorne Smith, *Principal*
EMP: 1
SALES (est): 69.8K Privately Held
SIC: 3599 Machine shop, jobbing & repair

(G-6196)
HB PUBLISHING & MARKETING
50 Washington St Fl 7 (06854-2751)
PHONE..................203 852-9200
Henry Berkowitz, *Principal*
EMP: 1
SALES (est): 71.5K Privately Held
SIC: 2741 Miscellaneous publishing

(G-6197)
HB PUBLISHING & MARKETING CO
4 Top Sail Rd (06853-1518)
PHONE..................203 852-1324
Henry Berkowitz, *Manager*
EMP: 1
SALES (est): 85.8K Privately Held
SIC: 2741 Miscellaneous publishing

(G-6198)
HEALTHPRIZE TECHNOLOGIES LLC
230 East Ave Ste 101 (06855-1927)
PHONE..................203 957-3400
John Monahan, *President*
Thomas Kottler, *Principal*
David Rector, *CFO*
Tom Kottler, *Mng Member*
Eric Simmerman, *CTO*
EMP: 2
SALES (est): 349.2K Privately Held
SIC: 7372 Business oriented computer software

(G-6199)
HEARST CORPORATION
Also Called: Greenwich Time
301 Merritt 7 Ste 1 (06851-1051)
PHONE..................203 625-4445
EMP: 25
SALES (corp-wide): 6.6B Privately Held
SIC: 2711 Newspapers-Publishing/Printing
PA: The Hearst Corporation
   300 W 57th St Fl 42
   New York NY 10019
   212 649-2000

(G-6200)
HICKS AND OTIS PRINTS INC
9 Wilton Ave (06851-4515)
PHONE..................203 846-2087
Harold Kaplan, *President*
Linwood Wade, *Vice Pres*
Steven Crovatto, *Admin Sec*
▲ **EMP:** 32 EST: 1939
SQ FT: 45,000
SALES (est): 5.8MM Privately Held
WEB: www.dorrie.com
SIC: 3083 3429 Plastic finished products, laminated; manufactured hardware (general)

(G-6201)
HOLLAND & SHERRY INC (PA)
Also Called: Elizabeth Eakins
5 Taft St (06854-4201)
PHONE..................212 628-1950
Elizabeth Eakins, *President*
Scott Lethbridge, *Vice Pres*
▲ **EMP:** 10
SALES (est): 1.9MM Privately Held
WEB: www.elizabetheakins.com
SIC: 2273 5713 5023 Carpets, hand & machine made; carpets; carpets

(G-6202)
HOLLY PRESS INC
8 College St (06851-4006)
PHONE..................203 846-1720
EMP: 3 EST: 1962
SQ FT: 1,500
SALES (est): 330K Privately Held
SIC: 2752 Commercial Offset Printers

(G-6203)
HVC LIZARD CHOCOLATE LLC
Also Called: Hvc Brands
13 Marshall St Ste 100 (06854-2300)
PHONE..................203 899-3075
James Walsh,
EMP: 15
SALES (est): 1.5MM Privately Held
SIC: 5149 2066 Chocolate; chocolate & cocoa products

(G-6204)
IHS HEROLD INC (DH)
200 Connecticut Ave Ste 8 (06854-1907)
PHONE..................203 857-0215
Christin Juneau, *CEO*
Gilbert Baliki, *Senior VP*
Lysle Brinker, *Vice Pres*
John Parry, *Vice Pres*
Donald Whelley, *CFO*
▼ **EMP:** 66
SQ FT: 16,000
SALES (est): 5.6MM Privately Held
WEB: www.herold.com
SIC: 3826 6282 8742 Analytical instruments; investment research; marketing consulting services
HQ: Ihs Global Inc.
   15 Inverness Way E
   Englewood CO 80112
   303 790-0600

Norwalk - Fairfield County (G-6205)

(G-6205)
INDUSTRIAL PRESS
32 Haviland St (06854-3005)
PHONE.................................203 838-4080
EMP: 1 EST: 2013
SALES (est): 49K Privately Held
SIC: 2741 Misc Publishing

(G-6206)
INDUSTRIAL PRESS INC
32 Haviland St 3 (06854-3005)
PHONE.................................212 889-6330
Michael A Backer, *Ch of Bd*
Alex Luchars, *President*
Judy Bass, *Editor*
Peter Burri, *CFO*
Doris Youngblood, *Manager*
▲ EMP: 11 EST: 1894
SQ FT: 3,400
SALES (est): 1.5MM Privately Held
WEB: www.industrialpress.com
SIC: 2731 Books: publishing only

(G-6207)
INFORMATION RESOURCES INC
383 Main Ave Ste 20 (06851-1582)
PHONE.................................203 845-6400
Samantha Desfrancesco, *Principal*
Joann Dickson, *Vice Pres*
EMP: 70
SALES (corp-wide): 364.2MM Privately Held
WEB: www.infores.com
SIC: 7372 8732 Prepackaged software; market analysis or research
PA: Information Resources, Inc
   150 N Clinton St
   Chicago IL 60661
   312 726-1221

(G-6208)
INSIGHT MEDIA LLC
Also Called: Microdisplay Report
3 Morgan Ave Ste 2 (06851-5018)
PHONE.................................203 831-8464
Chris Chinnock, *Mng Member*
EMP: 4 EST: 1998
SQ FT: 4,452
SALES (est): 295.1K Privately Held
WEB: www.mdreport.com
SIC: 2741 Technical papers: publishing & printing

(G-6209)
INSYS MICRO INC
40 Richards Ave Ste 3 (06854-2320)
PHONE.................................917 566-5045
Yuriy Kartoshkin, *President*
EMP: 7
SALES (est): 632.7K Privately Held
SIC: 3679 7373 Electronic components; computer integrated systems design

(G-6210)
INTERSTATE TAX CORPORATION
83 East Ave Ste 110 (06851-4902)
PHONE.................................203 854-0704
Carol Sheiber, *President*
Harvey Sheiber, *Treasurer*
EMP: 3
SALES (est): 304.7K Privately Held
WEB: www.interstatetaxcorp.com
SIC: 2721 Magazines: publishing only, not printed on site

(G-6211)
ISLAND NATION PRESS LLC
144 Rowayton Woods Dr (06854-3940)
PHONE.................................203 852-0028
Charlotte Allen, *Mng Member*
EMP: 1 EST: 1997
SALES (est): 57.6K Privately Held
WEB: www.charlottevaleallen.com
SIC: 2731 Book publishing

(G-6212)
ISLAND STYLE MAR CANVAS REPR
49 Myrtle Street Ext (06855-1456)
PHONE.................................707 338-8789
David Taylor, *Partner*
Devyn Pekera, *Partner*
EMP: 1
SALES (est): 87.4K Privately Held
SIC: 2211 2393 2394 Canvas; duffle bags, canvas: made from purchased materials; convertible tops, canvas or boat: from purchased materials; shades, canvas: made from purchased materials

(G-6213)
IZZI BS ALLERGY FREE LLC
Also Called: Izzi B'S Allergen Free Cupcake
22 Knight St (06851-4707)
PHONE.................................203 810-4378
Pamela G Nicholas, *Mng Member*
EMP: 4
SALES (est): 220K Privately Held
SIC: 2051 Cakes, bakery: except frozen

(G-6214)
J & E HIDALGO ENTERPRISES LLC
Also Called: Wolfpit Silencer Solutions
59 Wolfpit Ave (06851-4233)
PHONE.................................203 246-2252
Joseph Hidalgo,
Erika Hidalgo,
EMP: 2
SALES (est): 112.6K Privately Held
SIC: 3484 7389 Guns (firearms) or gun parts, 30 mm. & below;

(G-6215)
J G KURTZMAN
Also Called: J G Kurtman Sign Shop
97 Taylor Ave Ste 1 (06854-2098)
PHONE.................................203 838-7791
J G Kurtzman, *Owner*
EMP: 2
SALES: 100K Privately Held
WEB: www.kurtzmansigns.com
SIC: 3993 Signs, not made in custom sign painting shops

(G-6216)
JAIME M CAMACHO
Also Called: Sign-A-Rama
345 Main Ave (06851-1547)
PHONE.................................203 846-8221
Jamie M Camacho, *Owner*
EMP: 4
SQ FT: 1,400
SALES: 185K Privately Held
SIC: 3993 Signs & advertising specialties

(G-6217)
JAMES RIVER CORP
800 Connecticut Ave 4w01 (06854-1631)
PHONE.................................203 854-2328
EMP: 2 EST: 2011
SALES (est): 130K Privately Held
SIC: 2656 Mfg Sanitary Food Containers

(G-6218)
JARDEN CORPORATION
301 Merritt 7 Ste 5 (06851-1051)
PHONE.................................203 845-5300
James Lillie, *President*
EMP: 23
SALES (corp-wide): 8.6B Publicly Held
SIC: 3089 3634 Plastic containers, except foam; plastic kitchenware, tableware & houseware; electric housewares & fans; electric household cooking appliances; electric household cooking utensils; personal electrical appliances
HQ: Jarden Llc
   221 River St
   Hoboken NJ 07030

(G-6219)
JARED MANUFACTURING CO INC
25 Perry Ave (06850-1655)
P.O. Box 266 (06850)
PHONE.................................203 846-1732
Timothy C Frate, *President*
Tim Frate, *CFO*
EMP: 15
SQ FT: 11,000
SALES (est): 3.2MM Privately Held
WEB: www.jaredmfg.com
SIC: 3444 3599 3699 Sheet metal specialties, not stamped; machine shop, jobbing & repair; electrical equipment & supplies

(G-6220)
JASON KURTZMAN SIGNS
3 Devon Ave (06850-2905)
PHONE.................................203 847-4397
Jason Kurtzman, *Owner*
EMP: 1
SALES (est): 60.8K Privately Held
SIC: 7699 3993 Boat repair; signs & advertising specialties

(G-6221)
JENKINS SUGAR GROUP INC
16 S Main St Ste 202 (06854-2981)
PHONE.................................203 853-3000
Frank Jenkins, *President*
Eric Bergman, *Broker*
EMP: 10
SALES (est): 710.8K Privately Held
SIC: 2062 Cane sugar refining

(G-6222)
JK SIGN COMPANY
3 Devon Ave (06850-2905)
PHONE.................................203 544-7373
Jason Kurtzman, *Principal*
EMP: 1
SALES (est): 106.2K Privately Held
SIC: 3993 Signs & advertising specialties

(G-6223)
JKB DAIRA INC
22 S Smith St (06855-1018)
PHONE.................................203 642-4824
Yoichi Ota, *CEO*
Joan Brakeley, *President*
▲ EMP: 7
SQ FT: 4,800
SALES (est): 1.3MM Privately Held
WEB: www.jkbdaira.com
SIC: 3482 3484 Small arms ammunition; guns (firearms) or gun parts, 30 mm. & below

(G-6224)
JMP SOFTWARE
98 Spring Hill Ave (06850-2628)
PHONE.................................203 984-4096
Maurice N Picard, *Owner*
EMP: 2
SALES (est): 91.4K Privately Held
SIC: 7372 Business oriented computer software

(G-6225)
JUDITH LYNN CHARTERS LLC
29 Starlight Dr (06851-3425)
PHONE.................................203 246-6662
Frankie S Lanzo, *Mng Member*
EMP: 2
SALES (est): 122.3K Privately Held
SIC: 2399 Fishing nets

(G-6226)
K W GRIFFEN COMPANY
Also Called: Biomed Packing Systems
100 Pearl St (06850-1629)
PHONE.................................203 846-1923
James B Brown, *President*
Rosemary Brown, *Treasurer*
EMP: 40
SQ FT: 32,000
SALES (est): 7.1MM Privately Held
SIC: 3842 Surgical appliances & supplies; first aid, snake bite & burn kits

(G-6227)
KANDO APPS LLC
9 Country Club Rd (06851-5602)
PHONE.................................203 722-4359
Renato Erive, *Mng Member*
▲ EMP: 1
SALES (est): 63.8K Privately Held
SIC: 7372 7389 Application computer software;

(G-6228)
KARAVAS FASHIONS LTD
17 Wall St (06850-3413)
PHONE.................................203 866-4000
Stelios Paraskevas, *President*
Carol Paraskevas, *Admin Sec*
EMP: 10 EST: 1979
SALES (est): 1.2MM Privately Held
SIC: 3911 Jewelry, precious metal

(G-6229)
KIERA PUBLISHING INC
161 East Ave (06851-5710)
PHONE.................................203 838-5485
Anne I Treimanis, *Principal*
EMP: 2 EST: 2016
SALES (est): 59.2K Privately Held
SIC: 2741 Miscellaneous publishing

(G-6230)
LAJOIES AUTO WRECKING CO INC
Also Called: La Joies Auto Scrap & Recycl
40 Meadow St (06854-4599)
PHONE.................................203 870-0641
Donald L La Joie, *President*
James Murphy, *Treasurer*
EMP: 25
SQ FT: 3,750
SALES (est): 5.2MM Privately Held
WEB: www.lajoies.com
SIC: 5093 3341 Automotive wrecking for scrap; secondary nonferrous metals

(G-6231)
LASERMAN OF CONNECTICUT
168 East Ave (06851-5715)
PHONE.................................203 972-2887
Chris Tiefenthaler, *Owner*
EMP: 1
SALES (est): 80.6K Privately Held
WEB: www.lasermanct.com
SIC: 3861 7378 Toners, prepared photographic (not made in chemical plants); computer maintenance & repair

(G-6232)
LEEK BUILDING PRODUCTS INC
205 Wilson Ave Ste 3 (06854-5025)
PHONE.................................203 853-3883
William A Leek Jr, *President*
Martha K Leek, *Corp Secy*
▲ EMP: 20
SQ FT: 10,000
SALES (est): 4.3MM Privately Held
SIC: 3446 3444 3296 5211 Architectural metalwork; sheet metalwork; mineral wool; door & window products

(G-6233)
LEXO GROUP
241 New Canaan Ave (06850-1410)
PHONE.................................203 847-8293
George A Wood, *Owner*
EMP: 1
SALES (est): 42K Privately Held
SIC: 3299 Synthetic stones, for gem stones & industrial use

(G-6234)
LIVING ABROAD LLC
501 Westport Ave (06851-4411)
PHONE.................................203 221-1997
Micheal Cadden, *Partner*
EMP: 2
SALES: 250K Privately Held
WEB: www.livingabroad.com
SIC: 7372 Publishers' computer software

(G-6235)
LMJ DESIGNS INC
345 Wilson Ave Ste 1 (06854-4666)
PHONE.................................845 363-1120
John Taranto, *President*
EMP: 1
SALES (est): 147.2K Privately Held
SIC: 2262 Screen printing: manmade fiber & silk broadwoven fabrics

(G-6236)
LONZA WOOD PROTECTION
501 Merritt 7 (06851-7000)
PHONE.................................203 229-2900
Steven Wisnewski, *Principal*
EMP: 3 EST: 2013
SALES (est): 323.4K Privately Held
SIC: 2899 Chemical preparations

(G-6237)
LOOKOUT SOLUTIONS LLC
Also Called: Shelfgenie
7 Lookout Rd (06850-1035)
PHONE.................................203 750-0307
Alejandro Modica, *Principal*

▲ = Import ▼ = Export
◆ = Import/Export

GEOGRAPHIC SECTION
Norwalk - Fairfield County (G-6267)

EMP: 5 EST: 2009
SALES (est): 714.5K Privately Held
SIC: 2511 Wood household furniture

(G-6238)
LOREX PLASTICS CO INC
221 Wilson Ave (06854-5026)
PHONE.................203 286-0020
Ed Abdelnour, Owner
EMP: 7
SALES (est): 791.6K Privately Held
SIC: 3089 Injection molding of plastics

(G-6239)
LOTA WOODWORKING LLC
15 Styles Ln (06850-1817)
PHONE.................203 978-0277
EMP: 1
SALES (est): 54.1K Privately Held
SIC: 2431 Millwork, Nsk

(G-6240)
LUMIVISIONS ARCHITECTURAL ELEM
300 Wilson Ave Ste 202 (06854-4663)
PHONE.................203 529-3232
Thomas J St Denis, President
Roger Alwais, CFO
EMP: 5
SALES (est): 875.2K Privately Held
SIC: 2821 3645 3646 7349 Polycarbonate resins; residential lighting fixtures; commercial indusl & institutional electric lighting fixtures; lighting maintenance service

(G-6241)
M G SOLUTIONS
285 W Cedar St (06854-1804)
PHONE.................203 945-9615
Radha Mundra, Owner
Narottam Mundra, Co-Owner
EMP: 2 EST: 2014
SALES: 150K Privately Held
SIC: 7389 3423 Brokers' services; ; plumbers' hand tools

(G-6242)
M K M WOODWORKS LLC
20 Nostrum Rd (06850-3118)
PHONE.................203 838-5605
EMP: 1
SALES (est): 54.1K Privately Held
SIC: 2431 Millwork

(G-6243)
M2 TACTICAL SOLUTIONS LLC
12 Rainbow Rd (06851-2807)
PHONE.................203 247-3477
Matthew Mitchell,
EMP: 1
SALES (est): 73.7K Privately Held
SIC: 3484 5941 Guns (firearms) or gun parts, 30 mm. & below; firearms

(G-6244)
MAFCOTE INTERNATIONAL INC (HQ)
108 Main St Ste 3 (06851-4640)
PHONE.................203 644-1200
Steven A Schulnan, President
Miles Hisiger, Treasurer
EMP: 11
SALES (est): 1.8MM
SALES (corp-wide): 100.3MM Privately Held
WEB: www.mafcote.com
SIC: 2621 Paper mills
PA: Mafcote, Inc.
    108 Main St Ste 3
    Norwalk CT 06851
    203 847-8500

(G-6245)
MANGO DSP INC
Also Called: Mango Intllgent Vdeo Solutions
83 East Ave Ste 115 (06851-4902)
PHONE.................203 857-4008
Edward Czernik, President
EMP: 24
SQ FT: 2,554
SALES (est): 4.4MM
SALES (corp-wide): 1.7MM Privately Held
WEB: www.mangodsp.com
SIC: 3663 Digital encoders
PA: Mango D.S.P. Ltd
    250 Emek Haela
    Modiin-Maccabim-Reut 71779
    258 850-00

(G-6246)
MANUP LLC
345 Wilson Ave (06854-4666)
PHONE.................203 588-9861
Connor Prescott, Accounts Mgr
Brenna Rainone, Sales Staff
Butler Brandon, Manager
John Arrix,
George West,
EMP: 8
SQ FT: 14,500
SALES (est): 8MM Privately Held
SIC: 5941 7382 2353 3161 Specialty sport supplies; security systems services; hats, caps & millinery; luggage

(G-6247)
MARATHON WOOD WORK
Also Called: Marathon Speaker System
327 Main Ave Ste 2 (06851-6156)
PHONE.................203 847-2800
Louis Chochos, Owner
EMP: 1
SALES (est): 104.8K Privately Held
WEB: www.omegaloudspeakers.com
SIC: 3651 Speaker systems

(G-6248)
MARK MISERCOLA
105 Silvermine Ave (06850-2038)
PHONE.................423 323-0183
Mark Misercola, Owner
EMP: 2 EST: 2017
SALES (est): 85.9K Privately Held
SIC: 3571 Electronic computers

(G-6249)
MARYJANESFARM PUBLISHING GROUP
535 Cnncticut Ave Ste 100 (06854)
PHONE.................203 857-4880
EMP: 1
SALES (est): 59K Privately Held
SIC: 2741 Misc Publishing

(G-6250)
MAX PRODUCTIONS LLC
Also Called: Minuteman Press
167 Main St Ste 1 (06854-3757)
PHONE.................203 838-2795
Greg Duffey, Mng Member
Joe Brenneis,
EMP: 5
SQ FT: 1,800
SALES (est): 693.6K Privately Held
SIC: 2752 Commercial printing, lithographic

(G-6251)
MAYAN CORPORATION
79 Day St (06854-3733)
PHONE.................203 854-4711
Luis M Huerta, President
Ronald E Pair, Vice Pres
EMP: 15
SQ FT: 6,800
SALES: 1.4MM Privately Held
WEB: www.mayanet.net
SIC: 3172 Personal leather goods

(G-6252)
MBM SALES
Also Called: Bank Sails
40 Quintard Ave (06854-3735)
PHONE.................203 866-3674
Steven Benjaman, President
Park Benjiman, Treasurer
EMP: 12
SQ FT: 6,000
SALES (est): 750K Privately Held
SIC: 2394 Sails: made from purchased materials

(G-6253)
MEDIA VENTURES INC
200 Connecticut Ave # 23 (06854-1971)
PHONE.................203 852-6570
David Perssn, President
Donna L Perssn, Admin Sec
EMP: 24
SQ FT: 6,000
SALES (est): 2.4MM Privately Held
WEB: www.mediaventuresinc.com
SIC: 2741 2721 Miscellaneous publishing; periodicals

(G-6254)
MEDIANEWS GROUP INC
Also Called: Connecticut Post
301 Merritt 7 Ste 1 (06851-1051)
PHONE.................203 333-0161
Michael Daly, Editor
Eileen Fischer, Editor
Ron Darr, Senior VP
Lauren Corbo, Human Res Mgr
Robert Laska, Branch Mgr
EMP: 10
SALES (corp-wide): 4.2B Privately Held
SIC: 2711 Newspapers, publishing & printing
HQ: Medianews Group, Inc.
    101 W Colfax Ave Ste 1100
    Denver CO 80202

(G-6255)
MEDITECH LLC
2 Farm House Ln (06851-1400)
PHONE.................203 219-3688
Barry L Natale, President
Barry Natale, Manager
EMP: 1
SALES (est): 93.2K Privately Held
SIC: 5047 3842 Instruments, surgical & medical; surgical appliances & supplies

(G-6256)
METSA BOARD AMERICAS CORP
301 Merritt 7 Ste 2 (06851-1051)
PHONE.................203 229-0037
Lasse Wikstrom, CEO
Mika Paljakka, Ch of Bd
Jorma Sahlstedt, President
Paul Zelinsky, COO
Jerry Gallagher, Vice Pres
◆ EMP: 69
SQ FT: 12,000
SALES (est): 22.4MM
SALES (corp-wide): 2.2B Privately Held
SIC: 2631 Paperboard mills
PA: Metsa Board Oyj
    Revontulentie 6
    Espoo 02100
    104 611-

(G-6257)
MIAMI WABASH PAPER LLC (HQ)
108 Main St Ste 3 (06851-4640)
PHONE.................203 847-8500
Steven D Schulman,
Miles Hisiger,
Miles E Misiger,
Kenneth B Schulman,
EMP: 20
SQ FT: 12,000
SALES (est): 13.1MM
SALES (corp-wide): 100.3MM Privately Held
WEB: www.miamiwabashpaper.com
SIC: 2671 Paper coated or laminated for packaging
PA: Mafcote, Inc.
    108 Main St Ste 3
    Norwalk CT 06851
    203 847-8500

(G-6258)
MIKES WELDING
124 Lexington Ave (06854-4327)
PHONE.................203 855-9631
Michael Williams, Owner
Michael Wiilliams, Owner
EMP: 1 EST: 1993
SALES: 250K Privately Held
SIC: 7692 Welding repair

(G-6259)
MILLEN INDUSTRIES INC (PA)
108 Main St Ste 4 (06851-4640)
PHONE.................203 847-8500
Steven A Schulman, President
Miles E Hisiger, Vice Pres
Kenneth B Schulman, Vice Pres
Dan Legg, Sales Mgr
▲ EMP: 3
SQ FT: 11,000
SALES (est): 19.3MM Privately Held
WEB: www.millenindustries.com
SIC: 2652 2631 Setup paperboard boxes; folding boxboard

(G-6260)
MIMFORMS LLC
50 Washington St Fl 7 (06854-2751)
PHONE.................800 445-1245
Robert C Linke, Mng Member
◆ EMP: 6
SALES: 5MM Privately Held
SIC: 3443 Metal parts

(G-6261)
MINUTEMAN LAND SERVICES INC
377 Highland Ave (06854-3439)
PHONE.................203 854-4949
Jordan Grant, Principal
EMP: 2 EST: 2016
SALES (est): 110.1K Privately Held
SIC: 2752 Commercial printing, offset

(G-6262)
MK & T DESIGN & PRINT LLC
250 Westport Ave (06851-4158)
PHONE.................203 295-8211
Gregory Vasillo, Principal
EMP: 2 EST: 2016
SALES (est): 184.2K Privately Held
SIC: 2752 Commercial printing, lithographic

(G-6263)
MODERN DISTILLERY AGE
228 Silvermine Ave (06850-2032)
PHONE.................203 971-8710
Gregg Glaser, President
EMP: 3
SALES (est): 134.3K Privately Held
SIC: 2085 Distilled & blended liquors

(G-6264)
MODERN OBJECTS INC
5 River Dr (06855-2505)
PHONE.................203 378-5785
Michael Aguero, President
EMP: 4
SALES (est): 491.1K Privately Held
SIC: 2514 5023 Metal household furniture; decorative home furnishings & supplies

(G-6265)
MR SHOWER DOOR INC
651 Connecticut Ave Ste 1 (06854-1684)
PHONE.................203 838-3667
Tom Whitaker, Principal
EMP: 2
SALES (corp-wide): 2.6MM Privately Held
WEB: www.mrshowerdoor.com
SIC: 2541 Wood partitions & fixtures
PA: Mr. Shower Door, Inc.
    260 Hathaway Dr
    Stratford CT 06615
    203 838-3667

(G-6266)
MV LIGHTING
228 Newtown Ave (06851-2414)
PHONE.................203 856-3564
Anthony Depanfilis, Principal
EMP: 1
SALES (est): 120.1K Privately Held
SIC: 3648 Lighting equipment

(G-6267)
MY SLIDE LINES LLC
173 Main St (06851-3606)
PHONE.................203 324-1642
Michael Keating,
EMP: 5

Norwalk - Fairfield County (G-6268)

SALES (est): 502.1K **Privately Held**
SIC: **1389** Construction, repair & dismantling services

(G-6268)
NANO PET PRODUCTS LLC
Also Called: Dog Gone Smart
10 Hoyt St (06851-4605)
PHONE.................203 345-1330
Chris Onthank, *CEO*
▲ **EMP:** 3
SALES (est): 435.6K **Privately Held**
SIC: **3999** Pet supplies

(G-6269)
NC BRANDS LP
40 Richards Ave Ste 2 (06854-2320)
PHONE.................203 295-2300
Robert Kulperger, *CEO*
Mark Munford, *President*
Debra Gordon, *CFO*
EMP: 85
SQ FT: 3,500
SALES (est): 20.6MM
SALES (corp-wide): 3.2MM **Privately Held**
SIC: **2842** Specialty cleaning, polishes & sanitation goods
HQ: Bio-Lab, Inc.
1725 N Brown Rd
Lawrenceville GA 30043
678 502-4000

(G-6270)
NCI HOLDINGS INC (PA)
40 Richards Ave Ste 2 (06854-2320)
PHONE.................203 295-2300
Robert J Kulperger, *CEO*
Debbie Gordon, *Treasurer*
▲ **EMP:** 43
SALES (est): 21.7MM **Privately Held**
SIC: **2842** Specialty cleaning, polishes & sanitation goods

(G-6271)
NEASI-WEBER INTERNATIONAL
17 Little Fox Ln (06850-2317)
PHONE.................203 857-4404
Michael Brier, *Senior VP*
EMP: 3
SALES (est): 126.6K
SALES (corp-wide): 5.5MM **Privately Held**
WEB: www.nwintl.com
SIC: **7372** Prepackaged software
PA: Neasi-Weber International
25115 Ave Stnford Ste 220
Valencia CA 91355
818 895-6900

(G-6272)
NEW ENGLAND FIBERGLASS REPAIR (PA)
144 Water St (06854-3191)
PHONE.................203 866-1690
Bob Mills, *Owner*
EMP: 3
SALES (est): 314.2K **Privately Held**
SIC: **3732** Boats, fiberglass: building & repairing

(G-6273)
NEW ENGLAND QUARTZ CO
270 Main Ave (06851-6104)
PHONE.................203 846-9723
Wayne Lysobey, *Owner*
EMP: 2
SQ FT: 5,000
SALES (est): 120K **Privately Held**
SIC: **3851** 5047 Lens grinding, except prescription: ophthalmic; medical & hospital equipment

(G-6274)
NEW ENGLAND WOODWORKING
190 Fillow St (06850-2315)
PHONE.................203 505-0830
Curtis M Basdeo, *Owner*
EMP: 1
SALES (est): 54.1K **Privately Held**
SIC: **2431** Millwork

(G-6275)
NEW ENGLAND WOODWORKING LLC
1 Burlington Ct (06851-3001)
PHONE.................203 984-5032
EMP: 2
SALES (est): 120K **Privately Held**
SIC: **2431** Mfg Millwork

(G-6276)
NEWS 12 CONNECTICUT
28 Cross St (06851-4632)
PHONE.................203 849-1321
Charles F Dolan, *Principal*
Lori Golias, *Editor*
Sean McCabe, *Editor*
Frank Bruce, *Manager*
Adam Jenkins, *Asst Mgr*
EMP: 26
SALES (est): 1.3MM **Privately Held**
SIC: **2711** Newspapers, publishing & printing

(G-6277)
NEWSPAPER SPACE BUYERS
149 Rowayton Ave Ste 2 (06853-1460)
PHONE.................203 967-6452
Gerry Walsh, *Principal*
EMP: 5
SALES (est): 263.4K **Privately Held**
SIC: **2711** Newspapers

(G-6278)
NICHOLAS MELFI JR
Also Called: Norwalk Electric Mtrs & Pumps
41 Commerce St (06850-4110)
PHONE.................203 853-7235
Nicholas Melfi Jr, *Owner*
Gary Melfi, *Co-Owner*
EMP: 2 **EST:** 1946
SQ FT: 3,500
SALES (est): 455.9K **Privately Held**
SIC: **7694** 5999 3599 Electric motor repair; motors, electric; machine shop, jobbing & repair

(G-6279)
NOHTBOOK INC
597 Westport Ave B521 (06851-4440)
PHONE.................203 493-1633
Matthew Di Pasquale, *CEO*
Matthew Packer, *CFO*
EMP: 2
SALES (est): 86.6K **Privately Held**
SIC: **7372** Application computer software

(G-6280)
NORFIELD DATA PRODUCTS INC
Also Called: Cofmic Computers
181 Main St Ste 2 (06853-3624)
PHONE.................203 849-0292
Hasmukh Parikh, *President*
Richard C Miller, *Vice Pres*
David Podejko, *Senior Engr*
Richard Miller, *Software Engr*
Jayshree Parikh, *Admin Sec*
EMP: 10
SQ FT: 2,500
SALES (est): 1.1MM **Privately Held**
SIC: **7379** 7373 7372 3672 Computer related maintenance services; systems software development services; prepackaged software; printed circuit boards; nonferrous wiredrawing & insulating

(G-6281)
NORWALK RUTLEDGE PRINTING OFF
28 Cross St (06851-4632)
PHONE.................203 956-5967
EMP: 2
SALES (est): 73.2K **Privately Held**
SIC: **2759** Commercial printing

(G-6282)
NORWALK SIGN COMPANY INC
19 Fitch St (06855-1308)
PHONE.................203 838-1942
Anthony Masi, *President*
Carol Salvato, *Treasurer*
EMP: 2

SALES (est): 75K **Privately Held**
SIC: **7389** 3993 Lettering service; sign painting & lettering shop; signs & advertising specialties

(G-6283)
OASIS COFFEE CORP
327 Main Ave (06851-6156)
PHONE.................203 847-0554
Ralph Sandolo, *President*
Veronica Rondini, *Vice Pres*
Joseph Sandolo, *Vice Pres*
EMP: 20
SQ FT: 6,000
SALES (est): 2.5MM **Privately Held**
SIC: **2095** 2098 5461 Roasted coffee; macaroni & spaghetti; bread

(G-6284)
OMEGA ENGINEERING INC (HQ)
Also Called: Omegadyne
800 Connecticut Ave 5n01 (06854-1696)
P.O. Box 4047, Stamford (06907-0047)
PHONE.................203 359-1660
James R Dale, *President*
Michael Lopez, *General Mgr*
Dewana Harris, *Materials Mgr*
Suzanne Babic, *Purch Mgr*
Joseph Aiello, *Engineer*
◆ **EMP:** 233 **EST:** 1962
SALES (est): 138.4MM
SALES (corp-wide): 2B **Privately Held**
WEB: www.omega.com
SIC: **3823** 3575 3577 3433 Temperature measurement instruments, industrial; pH instruments, industrial process type; flow instruments, industrial process type; computer interface equipment for industrial process control; computer terminals, printers, computer; plotters, computer; heating equipment, except electric; environmental testing equipment; periodicals: printing
PA: Spectris Plc
Heritage House
Egham TW20
178 447-0470

(G-6285)
OMEGA ENGINEERING INC
Also Called: Newport Electronics
800 Cnncticut Ave Ste 5n1 (06854)
PHONE.................714 540-4914
Bill Keating, *General Mgr*
EMP: 70
SALES (corp-wide): 2B **Privately Held**
SIC: **3559** 3829 3822 3825 Electronic component making machinery; temperature sensors, except industrial process & aircraft; temperature controls, automatic; measuring instruments & meters, electric; switchgear & switchboard apparatus; pumps & pumping equipment
HQ: Omega Engineering, Inc.
800 Connecticut Ave 5n01
Norwalk CT 06854
203 359-1660

(G-6286)
OPERA GLASS NETWORKS LLC
597 Westport Ave C261 (06851-4440)
PHONE.................203 919-2777
Barry Goldberg, *Mng Member*
EMP: 1
SALES (est): 260K **Privately Held**
SIC: **7373** 3231 Local area network (LAN) systems integrator; products of purchased glass

(G-6287)
OVER MOON
35 Lenox Ave (06854-4022)
PHONE.................203 853-2498
Neville Peltz, *Owner*
EMP: 2
SALES (est): 81.8K **Privately Held**
SIC: **2679** Converted paper products

(G-6288)
PACO ASSENSIO WOODWORKING LLC
15 Meadow St (06854-4504)
PHONE.................203 536-2608
Francisco Paco Fernandez, *Principal*
EMP: 5

SALES (est): 471.7K **Privately Held**
SIC: **2431** Millwork

(G-6289)
PALM CANYON PICTURES
24 Crockett St (06853-1611)
PHONE.................203 853-1808
Peter Morrison, *Principal*
EMP: 1
SALES (est): 43.8K **Privately Held**
SIC: **2741** Miscellaneous publishing

(G-6290)
PALMERS ELC MTRS & PUMPS INC
40 Osborne Ave (06855-1021)
PHONE.................203 348-7378
Michael Vigneault, *President*
Carlton Brown, *Vice Pres*
Clive Hyde, *Vice Pres*
Lorraine Vigneault, *Treasurer*
Hunter Vigneault, *Master*
EMP: 7
SQ FT: 6,600
SALES: 1.2MM **Privately Held**
WEB: www.palmerselectric.com
SIC: **7694** 5063 5999 Electric motor repair; motors, electric; motors, electric

(G-6291)
PARMA 1901 USA INC
1 Selleck St Fl 2 (06855-1117)
PHONE.................203 855-1356
Luca Bertozzi, *President*
EMP: 1
SQ FT: 4,000
SALES (est): 39.5K **Privately Held**
SIC: **2099** Sandwiches, assembled & packaged: for wholesale market

(G-6292)
PDC INTERNATIONAL CORP (PA)
8 Sheehan Ave (06854-4659)
P.O. Box 492 (06856-0492)
PHONE.................203 853-1516
Neal Konstantin, *President*
Neal A Konstantin, *Principal*
Gary Tantimonico, *Vice Pres*
Dave Guzowski, *Engineer*
Anthony Caccamo, *Manager*
EMP: 55 **EST:** 1968
SQ FT: 19,000
SALES (est): 11.4MM **Privately Held**
WEB: www.pdc-corp.com
SIC: **3565** Packing & wrapping machinery

(G-6293)
PEACOCK CABINETRY
9 Bettswood Rd (06851-5103)
PHONE.................203 862-9333
Kathy Conroy, *Vice Pres*
Tim Gotsch, *Project Mgr*
Julie Sabbagh, *Technical Mgr*
Christopher L Peacock, *Manager*
Christopher Peacock, *Manager*
EMP: 4
SALES (est): 360K **Privately Held**
SIC: **2434** Wood kitchen cabinets

(G-6294)
PEACOCK MANUFACTURING CO LLC
9 Bettswood Rd (06851-5103)
PHONE.................203 388-4100
Christopher L Peacock, *Principal*
James Morton, *Exec VP*
EMP: 2 **EST:** 2009
SALES (est): 176.1K **Privately Held**
SIC: **3999** Barber & beauty shop equipment

(G-6295)
PENNY MARKETING LTD PARTNR (PA)
6 Prowitt St (06855-1204)
PHONE.................203 866-6688
Cathrine Cappelliri, *Partner*
EMP: 21
SALES (est): 1.2MM **Privately Held**
WEB: www.dellmagazines.com
SIC: **2721** Magazines: publishing only, not printed on site

▲ = Import ▼=Export
◆ =Import/Export

GEOGRAPHIC SECTION
Norwalk - Fairfield County (G-6326)

(G-6296)
PENNY PRESS INC (PA)
6 Prowitt St (06855-1220)
PHONE 203 866-6688
William E Kanter, *Ch of Bd*
Peter A Kanter, *President*
Selma Kanter, *Admin Sec*
EMP: 130
SQ FT: 20,000
SALES (est): 12.7MM **Privately Held**
WEB: www.pennypress.com
SIC: 2721 Magazines: publishing only, not printed on site

(G-6297)
PENNY PUBLICATIONS LLC (PA)
6 Prowitt St (06855-1204)
PHONE 203 866-6688
Peter Kanter,
EMP: 100
SALES (est): 16MM **Privately Held**
SIC: 2721 Magazines: publishing & printing

(G-6298)
PEPPERIDGE FARM INCORPORATED (HQ)
595 Westport Ave (06851-4413)
PHONE 203 846-7000
Irene Chang Britt, *President*
Tom Smith, *Senior VP*
Paul Amorello, *Vice Pres*
David Burke, *Vice Pres*
Graham Corneck, *Vice Pres*
◆ **EMP:** 700 **EST:** 1937
SQ FT: 71,000
SALES (est): 471.4MM
SALES (corp-wide): 8.1B **Publicly Held**
WEB: www.pepperidgefarm.com
SIC: 5461 2099 2053 5145 Bakeries; bread crumbs, not made in bakeries; frozen bakery products, except bread; pastries (danish): frozen; cakes, bakery: frozen; doughnuts, frozen; snack foods
PA: Campbell Soup Company
  1 Campbell Pl
  Camden NJ 08103
  856 342-4800

(G-6299)
PIC20 GROUP LLC
Also Called: Ranger Ready Repellents
155 Woodward Ave Ste 3 (06854-4731)
PHONE 203 957-3555
Chris L Fuentes, *President*
Ted Kespen, *COO*
EMP: 10 **EST:** 2016
SQ FT: 5,000
SALES: 700K **Privately Held**
SIC: 5191 5999 2879 Insecticides; pesticides; insecticides; insecticides & pesticides; pesticides, agricultural or household

(G-6300)
PILOT MACHINE DESIGNERS INC
32 Hemlock Pl (06854-4331)
PHONE 203 866-2227
James Cobb, *President*
EMP: 5
SQ FT: 4,800
SALES (est): 250K **Privately Held**
SIC: 3599 Custom machinery; machine shop, jobbing & repair

(G-6301)
PINK LEMON BLUE LIME LLC
64 Wall St (06850-3403)
PHONE 203 521-2364
Evelina Socha, *Principal*
EMP: 2
SALES (est): 225.5K **Privately Held**
SIC: 3274 Lime

(G-6302)
PIXELS 2 PRESS LLC
26 Pearl St Ste 8 (06850-1647)
PHONE 203 642-3740
Edward Belenski, *Principal*
EMP: 4
SALES (est): 300.1K **Privately Held**
SIC: 2741 Miscellaneous publishing

(G-6303)
PORTFOLIO ARTS GROUP LTD
Also Called: New York Graphic Society
129 Glover Ave (06850-1345)
PHONE 203 661-2400
Richard Fleischmann, *President*
EMP: 18 **EST:** 2007
SALES (est): 1.9MM **Privately Held**
SIC: 2741 Miscellaneous publishing

(G-6304)
PPG INDUSTRIES INC
Also Called: PPG Painters Supply
106 Main St (06851-4648)
PHONE 203 750-9553
Charles E Bunch, *Ch of Bd*
EMP: 3
SALES (corp-wide): 15.3B **Publicly Held**
SIC: 2851 Paints & allied products
PA: Ppg Industries, Inc.
  1 Ppg Pl
  Pittsburgh PA 15272
  412 434-3131

(G-6305)
PRICED RIGHT FUEL LLC
29 Golden Hill St (06854-2031)
PHONE 203 856-7031
Jaime Chetta, *Principal*
EMP: 3 **EST:** 2019
SALES (est): 166.9K **Privately Held**
SIC: 2869 Fuels

(G-6306)
PRINTERS OF CONNECTICUT INC
Also Called: Total Printing Center, The
89 Taylor Ave Fl 1 (06854-2038)
PHONE 203 852-0070
David Jaycox, *President*
EMP: 2
SQ FT: 4,000
SALES: 300K **Privately Held**
SIC: 2752 7334 Commercial printing, offset; photocopying & duplicating services

(G-6307)
PROFESSIONAL GRAPHICS INC
25 Perry Ave (06850-1655)
PHONE 203 846-4291
Thomas Bumbolow, *President*
Anthony Federici, *Vice Pres*
EMP: 12
SQ FT: 9,000
SALES (est): 1.9MM **Privately Held**
WEB: www.progi.net
SIC: 2752 2791 Commercial printing, offset; typesetting

(G-6308)
PROLASER PROLASER
83 N Main St (06854-2219)
PHONE 203 939-1750
EMP: 2
SALES (est): 85.9K **Privately Held**
SIC: 3577 Printers & plotters

(G-6309)
PROPELLER LLC
24 Meridian Rd (06853-1619)
PHONE 203 831-0877
EMP: 2
SALES (est): 188.9K **Privately Held**
SIC: 3366 Copper Foundry

(G-6310)
PUB GAMES PLUS
176 Main St Ste 2 (06851-3634)
PHONE 203 846-5991
Sara Fliess, *Owner*
EMP: 1
SALES (est): 61.2K **Privately Held**
SIC: 3944 Darts & dart games

(G-6311)
PUPPET PRESS
162 Strawberry Hill Ave (06851-5936)
PHONE 203 838-3665
Stanley Thompson, *Owner*
EMP: 1
SALES (est): 46K **Privately Held**
SIC: 2741 Miscellaneous publishing

(G-6312)
R F CASE
178 Flax Hill Rd Apt C101 (06854-2867)
PHONE 203 956-6348
Renwick Case, *Principal*
EMP: 2
SALES (est): 140.3K **Privately Held**
SIC: 2431 Millwork

(G-6313)
R F H COMPANY INC
79 Rockland Rd Ste 3 (06854-4628)
PHONE 203 853-2863
Pamela Falcone, *President*
Blake Billmeyer, *Vice Pres*
EMP: 10
SQ FT: 5,000
SALES (est): 643.9K **Privately Held**
WEB: www.rfhcompany.com
SIC: 2395 2396 Embroidery & art needlework; automotive & apparel trimmings

(G-6314)
RAFAEL CAKES & SUGAR LLC
77 N Main St 79 (06854-2219)
PHONE 203 642-4840
Rafael Ramirez, *President*
Kevin Leon, *Vice Pres*
EMP: 4 **EST:** 2012
SALES (est): 155K **Privately Held**
SIC: 5461 2051 Cakes; cakes, pies & pastries

(G-6315)
RAHZEL ENTERPRIZE LLC
15 Madison St Apt C8 (06854-2918)
PHONE 475 449-6561
Jeffery Moore, *Administration*
Jeffrey Moore,
EMP: 1
SALES (est): 75.5K **Privately Held**
SIC: 1799 1521 3271 1721 Home/office interiors finishing, furnishing & remodeling; kitchen & bathroom remodeling; general remodeling, single-family houses; blocks, concrete: landscape or retaining wall; commercial painting;

(G-6316)
RED 7 MEDIA LLC (HQ)
10 Norden Pl Ste 202 (06855-1445)
PHONE 203 853-2474
Kerry Smith, *President*
EMP: 38
SQ FT: 5,000
SALES (est): 2.7MM
SALES (corp-wide): 77.7MM **Privately Held**
WEB: www.red7media.com
SIC: 2721 Magazines: publishing & printing
PA: Access Intelligence Llc
  9211 Corporate Blvd Fl 4
  Rockville MD 20850
  301 354-2000

(G-6317)
RED BEARD PUBLISHING LLC
22 France St (06851-3819)
PHONE 203 847-1655
Matthew Morris, *Principal*
EMP: 1 **EST:** 2013
SALES (est): 52.5K **Privately Held**
SIC: 2741 Miscellaneous publishing

(G-6318)
REEDS INC
201 Merritt 7 (06851-1056)
PHONE 203 890-0557
John Bello, *CEO*
Stefan Freeman, *COO*
Norman E Snyder Jr, *COO*
Iris Snyder, *CFO*
Neal Cohane, *VP Sales*
◆ **EMP:** 22
SQ FT: 76,000
SALES (est): 38.1MM **Privately Held**
WEB: www.reedsgingerbrew.com
SIC: 2086 2064 2024 Soft drinks: packaged in cans, bottles, etc.; candy & other confectionery products; ice cream & ice milk

(G-6319)
RELOCATION INFORMATION SVC INC
Also Called: National Relocation & RE Mag
69 East Ave Ste 4 (06851-4904)
PHONE 203 855-1234
John Featherston, *President*
Darryl McPherson, *Exec VP*
Anne Kraft, *Senior VP*
John Scully, *Vice Pres*
Paul Purvis, *VP Sales*
EMP: 23
SALES (est): 3.5MM **Privately Held**
SIC: 2721 2741 8742 Magazines: publishing only, not printed on site; directories: publishing only, not printed on site; industry specialist consultants

(G-6320)
RELX INC
Reed Exhibitions
383 Main Ave Fl 3 (06851-1544)
PHONE 203 840-4800
Charlie Acquisto, *President*
Christine Flanagan, *Opers Mgr*
Jacqueline Boswick, *Sales/Mktg Mgr*
Joann Bottoni-Jepsen, *VP Human Res*
Larry Settembrini, *Sales Staff*
EMP: 4000
SQ FT: 238,000
SALES (corp-wide): 9.6B **Privately Held**
WEB: www.lexis-nexis.com
SIC: 2721 Periodicals
HQ: Relx Inc.
  230 Park Ave Ste 700
  New York NY 10169
  212 309-8100

(G-6321)
REMA DRI-VAC CORP
45 Ruby St (06850-1614)
P.O. Box 86 (06852-0086)
PHONE 203 847-2464
F W Petri, *President*
Barry Gunterson, *Vice Pres*
James J Reed Jr, *Vice Pres*
James Flynn, *Treasurer*
▲ **EMP:** 15
SQ FT: 9,300
SALES (est): 4MM **Privately Held**
WEB: www.remadrivac.com
SIC: 3582 5084 Drycleaning equipment & machinery, commercial; water pumps (industrial)

(G-6322)
RETINOGRAPHICS INC
9 Dock Rd (06854-4704)
PHONE 203 853-1735
William Eppler, *President*
EMP: 1
SALES (est): 104.1K **Privately Held**
SIC: 3841 Surgical & medical instruments

(G-6323)
REYES WELDING SVCS
46 Elmwood Ave (06854-2823)
PHONE 203 505-1111
Hever Reyes, *Principal*
EMP: 1
SALES (est): 35.3K **Privately Held**
SIC: 7692 Welding repair

(G-6324)
RINDLE LLC
3 Richards Ave (06854-2309)
PHONE 551 482-2037
Brian Faust, *Mng Member*
EMP: 5
SALES (est): 232.6K **Privately Held**
SIC: 7372 Application computer software

(G-6325)
RISING SIGN COMPANY INC
50 Commerce St Ste 1 (06850-4141)
PHONE 203 853-4155
EMP: 5
SQ FT: 2,500
SALES: 225K **Privately Held**
SIC: 3993 Mfg Signs

(G-6326)
ROBERT READY
11 Woodland Rd (06854-5012)
PHONE 203 853-0051

Norwalk - Fairfield County (G-6327)

Robert Ready, *Principal*
EMP: 1
SALES: (est): 106.3K **Privately Held**
WEB: www.robertready.com
SIC: 3273 Ready-mixed concrete

(G-6327)
ROBERT W BROSKA ENTERPRISES
Also Called: Prestige Tournament Supplies
11 Assisi Way (06851-3202)
PHONE..................203 846-0583
Robert W Broska, *Owner*
EMP: 2
SALES: 250K **Privately Held**
WEB: www.swb23.com
SIC: 3949 Golf equipment

(G-6328)
ROSS INDUSTRIES
15 Rolling Ln (06851-6018)
PHONE..................203 838-6180
Michael Ross, *Principal*
EMP: 1
SALES: (est): 76.6K **Privately Held**
SIC: 3999 Manufacturing industries

(G-6329)
ROWAYTON PRESS LLC
108 Witch Ln (06853-1128)
PHONE..................203 866-6646
Allan Cunningham, *Manager*
EMP: 1
SALES: (est): 72.9K **Privately Held**
SIC: 2741 Miscellaneous publishing

(G-6330)
ROYAL CONSUMER PRODUCTS LLC (HQ)
Also Called: Geographics Australia
108 Main St Ste 3 (06851-4640)
P.O. Box 25118 Network Pl, Chicago IL (60673-0001)
PHONE..................203 847-8500
Nona Nicau, *Accounts Mgr*
Baciu Irina, *Manager*
Steven A Schulman,
Steve Gilliland,
Kenneth B Schulman,
▲ EMP: 40
SQ FT: 1,000
SALES: (est): 16.9MM
SALES: (corp-wide): 100.3MM **Privately Held**
SIC: 2679 2621 Tags & labels, paper; gift wrap & novelties, paper; telegraph, teletype & adding machine paper; building, insulating & packaging paper; stationery, envelope & tablet papers
PA: Mafcote, Inc.
  108 Main St Ste 3
  Norwalk CT 06851
  203 847-8500

(G-6331)
RT VANDERBILT HOLDING CO INC (PA)
30 Winfield St (06855-1329)
PHONE..................203 295-2141
Hugh B Vanderbilt Jr, *Ch of Bd*
Randall L Johnson, *President*
Jim Faile, *General Mgr*
Stephen Turbak, *Counsel*
Paul R Vanderbilt, *Exec VP*
◆ EMP: 12
SALES: 272.5MM **Privately Held**
SIC: 5169 2869 2819 1499 Chemicals, industrial & heavy; laboratory chemicals, organic; industrial inorganic chemicals; talc mining; clays (common) quarrying

(G-6332)
RUCKUS MEDIA GROUP INC
55 Tory Hill Ln (06853-1137)
PHONE..................203 939-1409
Robert Richter, *CEO*
Ellen Coomaraswamy, *Office Mgr*
Richesh Ruchir, *CTO*
EMP: 2
SALES: (est): 250.6K **Privately Held**
SIC: 2741 Miscellaneous publishing

(G-6333)
RUIZ IMPRESS SCRN PRNTG &
430 Main Ave (06851-7004)
PHONE..................203 750-0050
Hugo Ruiz, *Owner*
EMP: 2
SALES: (est): 173K **Privately Held**
SIC: 2752 Commercial printing, lithographic

(G-6334)
RUIZ IMPRESSIONS SCREEN PRNTG
31 N Taylor Ave (06854-1407)
PHONE..................203 559-4865
Javier Flores, *Principal*
EMP: 2
SALES: (est): 186.4K **Privately Held**
SIC: 2752 Commercial printing, lithographic

(G-6335)
SACLA NORTH AMERICA INC
1 Selleck St Fl 2 (06855-1117)
PHONE..................203 855-1356
Laura Ronco, *President*
Alberto Bretti, *Vice Pres*
Antonio Valla, *Admin Sec*
EMP: 1
SALES: (est): 76.5K
SALES: (corp-wide): 636.7K **Privately Held**
SIC: 2032 Italian foods: packaged in cans, jars, etc.
HQ: F.Lli Sacla' S.P.A. In Forma Sviluppata
  Fratelli Sacla' Spa
  Piazza Giovanni Amendola 2
  Asti AT 14100
  014 139-71

(G-6336)
SAFE HARBOUR PRODUCTS INC
1 Selleck St Ste 3e (06855-1126)
PHONE..................203 295-8377
Adam Stolpen, *Principal*
EMP: 3
SALES: (est): 388.2K **Privately Held**
SIC: 2992 Lubricating oils & greases

(G-6337)
SAM & TY LLC (PA)
Also Called: Tailor Vintage
12 S Main St Ste 403 (06854-2980)
PHONE..................212 840-1871
Ashley Erhardt, *Prdtn Mgr*
Richard Rosenthal, *Mng Member*
Joy Rosenthal,
▲ EMP: 8
SALES: (est): 2.7MM **Privately Held**
SIC: 2396 Linings, apparel: made from purchased materials

(G-6338)
SEAFARER CANVAS
45 Calf Pasture Beach Rd (06855-2714)
PHONE..................203 939-1872
EMP: 1
SALES: (est): 46.5K **Privately Held**
SIC: 2211 Canvas

(G-6339)
SEAFARER CANVAS (PA)
144 Water St (06854-3191)
PHONE..................203 853-2624
William Ashley, *Principal*
William Tomasello, *Manager*
EMP: 10
SALES: (est): 1.1MM **Privately Held**
SIC: 2394 Canvas & related products

(G-6340)
SEBASTIAN KITCHEN CABINETS
4 Taft St Ste B1 (06854-4252)
PHONE..................203 853-4411
Sebastian Tornatore, *Owner*
EMP: 7
SQ FT: 5,000
SALES: (est): 604.8K **Privately Held**
WEB: www.sebastiancorealestate.com
SIC: 2434 Vanities, bathroom: wood

(G-6341)
SECOND LAC INC (PA)
401 Merritt 7 Ste 1 (06851-1069)
PHONE..................203 321-1221
James W Hart Jr, *Principal*
Douglas B Hart, *COO*
▲ EMP: 5
SALES: (est): 39.2MM **Privately Held**
SIC: 2221 2295 2394 2396 Broadwoven fabric mills, manmade; coated fabrics, not rubberized; canvas & related products; automotive & apparel trimmings

(G-6342)
SELECT PLASTICS LLC
219 Liberty Sq (06855-1029)
PHONE..................203 866-3767
Anthony G D'Andrea, *Mng Member*
EMP: 5
SQ FT: 6,000
SALES: (est): 716K **Privately Held**
WEB: www.selectplastics.com
SIC: 3089 Plastic containers, except foam

(G-6343)
SERVERS STORAGE NETWORKING LLC
25 Perry Ave (06850-1655)
PHONE..................203 433-0808
Justin Samuels,
EMP: 8
SALES: (est): 295.3K **Privately Held**
SIC: 3674 5065 Solid state electronic devices; electronic parts

(G-6344)
SHIBUMICOM INC
50 Washington St Ste 302e (06854-2792)
PHONE..................855 744-2864
Robert Nahmias, *CEO*
EMP: 10 EST: 2011
SQ FT: 6,000
SALES: (est): 789.8K **Privately Held**
SIC: 7372 7374 Business oriented computer software; data processing & preparation

(G-6345)
SHOW MANAGEMENT ASSOCIATES LLC
8 Knight St Ste 205 (06851-4720)
PHONE..................203 939-9901
Brian Vargas,
EMP: 7
SQ FT: 1,500
SALES: (est): 175K **Privately Held**
SIC: 7389 2721 Trade show arrangement; magazines: publishing & printing

(G-6346)
SIGGPAY INC
50 Water St Rear B (06854-3061)
PHONE..................203 957-8261
Brian Fuller, *CEO*
Carlyn Martino, *Vice Pres*
Shae Morris, *Vice Pres*
EMP: 5
SALES: (est): 6K **Privately Held**
SIC: 7372 Business oriented computer software

(G-6347)
SIGMA TANKERS INC
20 Glover Ave Ste 5 (06850-1234)
PHONE..................203 662-2600
Ben Ognibene, *CEO*
John Greenwood, *Principal*
Kathleen Haines, *CFO*
EMP: 16
SALES: (est): 3.5MM
SALES: (corp-wide): 1.1MM **Privately Held**
SIC: 1389 Oil field services
HQ: Heidmar Inc.
  383 Main Ave Ste 506
  Norwalk CT 06851

(G-6348)
SIGN SMARTS LLC (PA)
2 Fair St (06851)
PHONE..................203 854-0808
Walter Martinez, *Principal*
EMP: 1
SALES: (est): 145K **Privately Held**
SIC: 3993 Signs & advertising specialties

(G-6349)
SIGNS BY ANTHONY INC
19 Fitch St (06855-1308)
PHONE..................203 866-1744
Anthony Masi, *President*
EMP: 3
SALES: 90K **Privately Held**
SIC: 3993 Signs & advertising specialties

(G-6350)
SILVERMINE PRESS INC
4 Van Tassell Ct (06851-3504)
PHONE..................203 847-4368
Louis H Brehm, *President*
Helen Brehm, *Admin Sec*
EMP: 5 EST: 1947
SQ FT: 880
SALES: (est): 451.4K **Privately Held**
WEB: www.adeleart.com
SIC: 2759 Letterpress printing

(G-6351)
SIMPLY ORIGINALS LLC
14 Crest Rd (06853-1207)
PHONE..................203 273-3523
Renato Varas, *Principal*
EMP: 4
SALES: (est): 204.5K **Privately Held**
SIC: 2086 Carbonated beverages, nonalcoholic: bottled & canned

(G-6352)
SOUND CONTROL TECHNOLOGIES
Also Called: S C T
22 S Smith St (06855-1018)
PHONE..................203 854-5701
David Neaderland, *President*
Dan Julian, *Manager*
Leslie Ward, *Technical Staff*
▲ EMP: 7
SQ FT: 5,000
SALES: (est): 1.3MM **Privately Held**
WEB: www.soundcontrol.net
SIC: 3661 Telephones & telephone apparatus

(G-6353)
SPECTRUM MKTG CMMNICATIONS INC
30 Osborne Ave (06855-1710)
PHONE..................203 853-4585
Ravi Dhingra, *President*
Inni Dhingra, *Vice Pres*
EMP: 5
SQ FT: 2,000
SALES: (est): 530.6K **Privately Held**
WEB: www.spectrummarketing.com
SIC: 7336 2759 Graphic arts & related design; commercial printing

(G-6354)
SPRAY FOAM OUTLETS LLC
30 Muller Ave Unit 19 (06851)
P.O. Box 1182, New Canaan (06840-1182)
PHONE..................631 291-9355
Anthony Brezac, *COO*
EMP: 25
SQ FT: 5,000
SALES: 40MM **Privately Held**
SIC: 3531 Construction machinery

(G-6355)
STATHAM WOODWORK
38 Hemlock Pl (06854-4331)
PHONE..................203 831-0629
Gary Statham, *President*
Emily Statham, *Vice Pres*
Andrew Catron, *Project Mgr*
EMP: 7
SQ FT: 7,000
SALES: (est): 684.3K **Privately Held**
SIC: 2521 Cabinets, office: wood

(G-6356)
STEIN LABORATORIES LLC
46 Chestnut St (06854-3623)
P.O. Box 252, West Redding (06896-0252)
PHONE..................203 853-9500
Richard J Stein, *Principal*
Richard Stein, *Principal*
EMP: 1
SALES: (est): 100.5K **Privately Held**
SIC: 3443 8999 High vacuum coaters, metal plate; scientific consulting

▲ = Import ▼ = Export
◆ = Import/Export

GEOGRAPHIC SECTION — Norwalk - Fairfield County

(G-6357)
STEPPING STONES MBL & GRAN LLC (PA)
4 Taft St Ste D1 (06854-4280)
PHONE..................203 854-0552
Dale Hamman, *Mng Member*
EMP: 9
SALES (est): 1.2MM **Privately Held**
WEB: www.classicstones.com
SIC: 2493 Marbleboard (stone face hard board)

(G-6358)
STEVE S CUSTOM IRONWORKS LLC
176 Main St Rear Rear (06851-3635)
PHONE..................203 229-0612
Steve Stefanidis, *Owner*
EMP: 1
SALES (est): 171.3K **Privately Held**
SIC: 3446 Architectural metalwork

(G-6359)
SUCCESS PRINTING & MAILING INC
10 Pearl St (06850-1629)
PHONE..................203 847-1112
Robert Hurwitz, *President*
William Roos, *Vice Pres*
EMP: 12
SQ FT: 15,000
SALES (est): 2.6MM **Privately Held**
WEB: www.successprint.com
SIC: 2752 2796 7336 Commercial printing, offset; platemaking services; commercial art & graphic design

(G-6360)
SUR-SEAL HOLDING LLC (PA)
301 Merritt 7 (06851-1070)
PHONE..................203 625-0770
Tony Wright, *CFO*
James Sidwa,
EMP: 2
SALES (est): 40MM **Privately Held**
SIC: 3053 3069 6719 Gaskets, all materials; packing, rubber; molded rubber products; investment holding companies, except banks

(G-6361)
SWEDISH NEWS INC
Also Called: North Shannon
268 Fillow St (06850-2215)
P.O. Box 1710, New Canaan (06840-1710)
PHONE..................203 299-0380
Ulf Martensson, *CEO*
▲ EMP: 5
SALES (est): 407.7K **Privately Held**
SIC: 2711 Newspapers: publishing only, not printed on site

(G-6362)
TAM COMMUNICATIONS INC
Also Called: Road Bike
37 North Ave Ste 208 (06851-3827)
PHONE..................203 425-8777
John D Kanter, *President*
Marjorie Kleiman, *Editor*
Gail Kanter, *Vice Pres*
Matt Kopec, *Art Dir*
Chuck Queener, *Creative Dir*
EMP: 20
SALES (est): 2.5MM **Privately Held**
WEB: www.roadbike.com
SIC: 2721 2741 Magazines: publishing only, not printed on site; miscellaneous publishing

(G-6363)
TCC MULTI KARGO
349 Dr Mrtin L King Jr Dr (06854-4691)
PHONE..................203 803-1462
EMP: 4 EST: 2012
SALES (est): 268.3K **Privately Held**
SIC: 2448 Cargo containers, wood & metal combination

(G-6364)
TEAK LLC
215 Westport Ave (06851-4310)
PHONE..................203 845-0345
Virginia Hough Matchak, *Principal*
EMP: 2 EST: 2009

SALES (est): 163.6K **Privately Held**
SIC: 2499 Decorative wood & woodwork

(G-6365)
TECHNICAL REPRODUCTIONS INC
326 Main Ave (06851-6108)
PHONE..................203 849-9100
William R Boczer, *CEO*
Karyn Boczer, *President*
Amy Boczer, *Vice Pres*
Holly Boczer, *Vice Pres*
Patricia Boczer, *Shareholder*
EMP: 14 EST: 1971
SQ FT: 7,500
SALES (est): 1.5MM **Privately Held**
SIC: 5999 5049 5199 2752 Architectural supplies; engineers' equipment & supplies; architects' supplies (non-durable); commercial printing, offset; photo-offset printing; blueprinting service; laminating service

(G-6366)
THARAVADU COR
86 Washington St (06854-3077)
PHONE..................203 852-1213
▲ EMP: 1
SALES (est): 91K **Privately Held**
SIC: 3421 Mfg Cutlery

(G-6367)
THREE ACROSS LLC
6 Prowitt St (06855-1204)
PHONE..................203 866-6688
Peter Kanter,
EMP: 2 EST: 2001
SALES (est): 159.3K **Privately Held**
SIC: 3944 Puzzles

(G-6368)
TICK BOX TECHNOLOGY CORP
15 Chapel St (06850-4113)
P.O. Box 1439 (06856-1439)
PHONE..................203 852-7171
David Whitman, *President*
Richard Whitman, *Vice Pres*
EMP: 4
SALES (est): 442K **Privately Held**
SIC: 2879 Insecticides & pesticides

(G-6369)
TINY WOODSHOP
123 Stuart Ave (06850-3135)
PHONE..................203 866-6725
James Sanders Jr, *Principal*
EMP: 1
SALES (est): 53.7K **Privately Held**
SIC: 3942 Dolls & stuffed toys

(G-6370)
TITANIUM ELECTRIC LLC
15 Arbor Dr (06854-3407)
PHONE..................203 810-4050
Riccardo Arruzza, *Administration*
EMP: 2
SALES (est): 90.8K **Privately Held**
SIC: 3356 Titanium

(G-6371)
TM WARD CO OF CONNECTICUT LLC
5 Wilbur St (06854-4112)
PHONE..................203 866-9203
Jeffrey Sommer, *Mng Member*
EMP: 7
SALES (est): 1.4MM **Privately Held**
SIC: 2095 Coffee roasting (except by wholesale grocers)

(G-6372)
TOASTMASTERS INTERNATIONAL
10 Maher Dr (06850-2433)
PHONE..................203 847-5667
Charles Donen, *Branch Mgr*
EMP: 11
SALES (corp-wide): 31.3MM **Privately Held**
WEB: www.d70toastmasters.org
SIC: 8299 2721 Educational service, non-degree granting: continuing educ.; magazines: publishing only, not printed on site

PA: Toastmasters International
9127 S Jamaica St Ste 400
Englewood CO 80112
949 858-8255

(G-6373)
TOOL LOGISTICS II
46 Chestnut St (06854-3623)
PHONE..................203 855-9754
Cawthon Smith, *Owner*
EMP: 10
SALES (est): 800.7K **Privately Held**
SIC: 3599 3315 Machine shop, jobbing & repair; welded steel wire fabric

(G-6374)
TOPAZ ENTERPRISE SAND PUBG
304 Main Ave (06854-6167)
PHONE..................203 449-1903
Harry Francois, *Principal*
EMP: 6
SALES (est): 60.5K **Privately Held**
SIC: 2741 Miscellaneous publishing

(G-6375)
TOPAZ ENTERPRISES & PUBG LLC
26 Monroe St (06854-2948)
PHONE..................203 993-9051
Harry Francois, *Principal*
EMP: 1 EST: 2009
SALES (est): 68K **Privately Held**
SIC: 2741 Miscellaneous publishing

(G-6376)
TOWER OPTICAL COMPANY INC
275 East Ave Fl 2 (06855-1924)
P.O. Box 251 (06856-0251)
PHONE..................203 866-4535
Bonnie Rising, *President*
Gregory Rising, *Admin Sec*
EMP: 7
SQ FT: 4,000
SALES (est): 650K **Privately Held**
WEB: www.toweropticalco.com
SIC: 3827 5049 Binoculars; scientific & engineering equipment & supplies

(G-6377)
TRANE INC
145 Main St (06851-3709)
PHONE..................203 866-7115
EMP: 100 **Privately Held**
SIC: 3585 Air conditioning units, complete: domestic or industrial
HQ: Trane Inc.
1 Centennial Ave Ste 101
Piscataway NJ 08854
732 652-7100

(G-6378)
TUCCI LUMBER CO LLC
227 Wilson Ave (06854-5026)
PHONE..................203 956-6181
Peter Tucci, *Mng Member*
Sean Mathews,
Pablo Sandoval,
Amy Tucci,
Troy Tulowitzki,
EMP: 8
SQ FT: 10,300
SALES (est): 762.3K **Privately Held**
SIC: 3949 5941 Baseball equipment & supplies, general; baseball equipment

(G-6379)
TWENTY FIVE COMMERCE INC
Also Called: Cico
25 Commerce St (06854-4111)
P.O. Box 146 (06852-0146)
PHONE..................203 866-0540
Robert Slapin, *President*
EMP: 8 EST: 1924
SALES (est): 761.2K **Privately Held**
WEB: www.cico.com
SIC: 2097 Ice cubes

(G-6380)
VAL SCANSAROLI MAGAZINE CNSLTN
603 Foxboro Dr (06851-1149)
PHONE..................203 229-0256
Val Scansaroli,
EMP: 1

SALES (est): 67.7K **Privately Held**
SIC: 2721 Periodicals

(G-6381)
VALORE INC
Also Called: Grannick's Bitter Apple Co
2 Academy St (06850-4015)
PHONE..................203 854-4799
Valerie Cohen, *President*
Harrie J Grannick, *Vice Pres*
Jack Cohen, *Treasurer*
▲ EMP: 9
SQ FT: 50,000
SALES (est): 2MM **Privately Held**
SIC: 3999 Pet supplies

(G-6382)
VAN GELDERN MACHINE COMPANY
151 Rowayton Ave (06853-1433)
PHONE..................203 853-9402
Steven Van Geldern, *President*
Anne Van Geldern, *Vice Pres*
EMP: 2
SALES (est): 100K **Privately Held**
SIC: 3599 Machine shop, jobbing & repair

(G-6383)
VANDERBILT CHEMICALS LLC (HQ)
30 Winfield St (06855-1329)
P.O. Box 5150 (06856-5150)
PHONE..................203 295-2141
Roger Burtraw, *President*
Stephen Turbak, *Corp Secy*
Paul Graves, *Vice Pres*
Vncent Gatto, *Research*
Daniel Gershon, *Engineer*
◆ EMP: 67
SALES (est): 90.1MM
SALES (corp-wide): 272.5MM **Privately Held**
SIC: 2819 2869 5169 Industrial inorganic chemicals; industrial organic chemicals; chemicals & allied products
PA: R.T. Vanderbilt Holding Company, Inc.
30 Winfield St
Norwalk CT 06855
203 295-2141

(G-6384)
VANDERBILT MINERALS LLC (HQ)
33 Winfield St (06855)
P.O. Box 5150 (06856-5150)
PHONE..................203 295-2140
James Ian Begley, *President*
Jeffrey Brohel, *Corp Secy*
Peter Ciullo, *Treasurer*
Elizabeth Slaby, *Manager*
Matt Stewart, *Director*
◆ EMP: 20
SALES (est): 77.7MM
SALES (corp-wide): 272.5MM **Privately Held**
SIC: 1459 Bentonite mining
PA: R.T. Vanderbilt Holding Company, Inc.
30 Winfield St
Norwalk CT 06855
203 295-2141

(G-6385)
VENTUS TECHNOLOGIES LLC
10 Norden Pl Ste 8 (06855-1445)
PHONE..................203 642-2800
Keith Charette, *Mng Member*
Jerry Cuevas, *Technical Staff*
Joseph Sylvester, *Technical Staff*
Michael Kern, *Administration*
EMP: 10
SALES: 2.2MM **Privately Held**
SIC: 8731 3577 Computer (hardware) development; computer peripheral equipment

(G-6386)
VERSIMEDIA
117 Glover Ave (06850-1311)
PHONE..................203 604-8094
John Babina III, *President*
EMP: 2
SALES (est): 96.6K **Privately Held**
SIC: 2741 Miscellaneous publishing

(PA)=Parent Co (HQ)=Headquarters (DH)=Div Headquarters
✪ = New Business established in last 2 years

Norwalk - Fairfield County

(G-6387)
VESSELON INC
101 Merritt 7 Ste 300 (06851-1059)
PHONE..................203 989-0500
Clay Larsen, *CEO*
Rhodemann LI, *Exec VP*
EMP: 2
SALES (est): 164.9K **Privately Held**
SIC: 3845 Electromedical apparatus; ultrasonic medical equipment, except cleaning; ultrasonic scanning devices, medical

(G-6388)
VETO PRO PAC LLC
3 Morgan Ave Ste 4 (06851-5018)
P.O. Box 2072 (06852-2072)
PHONE..................203 847-0297
Roger Brouard, *Partner*
Chris Greco, *Marketing Mgr*
Ben Daily, *Manager*
Toni Nethers, *Manager*
▲ EMP: 3
SALES (est): 537K **Privately Held**
WEB: www.vetopropac.com
SIC: 3111 Bag leather

(G-6389)
VILLA RIDGE LLC
9 Ridge St (06854-3516)
PHONE..................303 330-9183
Bryan Rowe, *Principal*
EMP: 2
SALES (est): 81.2K **Privately Held**
SIC: 7372 4813 Prepackaged software;

(G-6390)
VISION MUSICAL INSTRUMENTS
20 Fitch St (06855-1309)
PHONE..................203 416-6359
EMP: 1
SALES (est): 41K **Privately Held**
SIC: 3931 Musical instruments

(G-6391)
VITAL STRETCH LLC
112 Main St (06851-4617)
PHONE..................203 847-4477
Melissa Goldring, *Mng Member*
EMP: 3
SALES: 300K **Privately Held**
SIC: 3542 Stretching machines

(G-6392)
W B MASON CO INC
151 Woodward Ave Ste 1 (06854-4721)
PHONE..................888 926-2766
EMP: 41
SALES (corp-wide): 773MM **Privately Held**
SIC: 5943 5712 2752 Office forms & supplies; office furniture; commercial printing, lithographic
PA: W. B. Mason Co., Inc.
59 Center St
Brockton MA 02301
781 794-8800

(G-6393)
WDSS CORPORATION
7 Old Well Ct (06855-2014)
PHONE..................203 854-5930
Wayne Nasution, *President*
EMP: 10 EST: 2009
SALES: 150K **Privately Held**
SIC: 3599 Industrial machinery

(G-6394)
WESPORT SIGNS
17 Linden St (06851-1506)
PHONE..................203 286-7710
Jeremias Refosco, *Principal*
EMP: 3
SALES (est): 158.7K **Privately Held**
SIC: 3993 Signs & advertising specialties

(G-6395)
WINCHESTER INTERCONNECT CORP (PA)
68 Water St (06854-3071)
PHONE..................203 741-5400
Kevin S Perhamus, *President*
Beth Beadle, *General Mgr*
Stephen Eccles, *General Mgr*
Roger Rawlins, *General Mgr*
Mac Robinson, *General Mgr*
EMP: 45
SALES (est): 400.7MM **Privately Held**
SIC: 3678 Electronic connectors

(G-6396)
WINDHOVER INFORMATION INC (DH)
Also Called: Windhver Rvw-Emerging Med Vent
383 Main Ave (06851-1543)
PHONE..................203 838-4401
Roger Longman, *President*
David Cassak, *Vice Pres*
▼ EMP: 30
SQ FT: 5,000
SALES (est): 4MM
SALES (corp-wide): 9.6B **Privately Held**
WEB: www.windhover.com
SIC: 2721 2731 7375 Magazines: publishing only, not printed on site; books: publishing only; data base information retrieval
HQ: Elsevier Inc.
230 Park Ave Fl 8
New York NY 10169
212 989-5800

(G-6397)
WMO INDUSTRIES LLC
58 Ponus Ave (06850-1920)
PHONE..................203 246-2366
William Odierno, *Principal*
EMP: 1 EST: 2016
SALES (est): 48.3K **Privately Held**
SIC: 3999 Manufacturing industries

(G-6398)
WOODHALL PRESS LLP
81 Old Saugatuck Rd (06855-2227)
PHONE..................203 428-1876
Christopher Madden, *Principal*
EMP: 1
SALES (est): 37.5K **Privately Held**
SIC: 2741 Miscellaneous publishing

(G-6399)
WOODWORKERS CLUB LLC
215 Westport Ave (06851-4310)
PHONE..................203 847-9663
John Matchack, *President*
Tom Matchak,
Virgina Matchak,
EMP: 3
SALES (est): 456K **Privately Held**
WEB: www.woodworkersclubnorwalk.com
SIC: 2431 Millwork

(G-6400)
WOOL SOLUTIONS INC
57 Cranbury Rd (06851-2616)
PHONE..................203 845-0921
Janice Byrne, *President*
Philip Byrne, *Vice Pres*
▲ EMP: 2
SALES (est): 390.9K **Privately Held**
SIC: 5023 2273 Carpets; axminster carpets

(G-6401)
XEROX CORPORATION (HQ)
201 Merritt 7 (06851-1056)
P.O. Box 4505 (06856-4505)
PHONE..................203 968-3000
Giovanni Visentin, *CEO*
Keith Cozza, *Ch of Bd*
Louis J Pastor, *Exec VP*
Stephen P Hoover, *Senior VP*
Brian Cannatelli, *Vice Pres*
EMP: 475
SALES: 9.8B
SALES (corp-wide): 405.1MM **Publicly Held**
WEB: www.xerox.com
SIC: 3577 3861 3579 7629 Computer peripheral equipment; photocopy machines; paper handling machines; business machine repair, electric; computer peripheral equipment repair & maintenance; data processing & preparation
PA: Xerox Holdings Corporation
201 Merritt 7
Norwalk CT 06851
203 968-3000

(G-6402)
XEROX HOLDINGS CORPORATION (PA)
201 Merritt 7 (06851-1056)
P.O. Box 4505 (06856-4505)
PHONE..................203 968-3000
Giovanni Visentin, *CEO*
Keith Cozza, *Ch of Bd*
Steven J Bandrowczak, *President*
Louis J Pastor, *Exec VP*
William F Osbourn Jr, *CFO*
EMP: 0
SALES (est): 405.1MM **Publicly Held**
SIC: 6719 3577 3861 3579 Investment holding companies, except banks; computer peripheral equipment; photocopy machines; paper handling machines; business machine repair, electric; computer peripheral equipment repair & maintenance

(G-6403)
XIAOHAO JIA
Also Called: Aki Computer
97 Taylor Ave Ste 2 (06854-2098)
PHONE..................:203 866-3120
Jia Xiaohao, *Owner*
EMP: 3
SALES (est): 240K **Privately Held**
SIC: 5065 3571 Electronic parts & equipment; electronic computers

(G-6404)
ZILLION GROUP INC
501 Merritt 7 (06851-7000)
PHONE..................203 810-5400
James R Boyle, *Ch of Bd*
William Van Wyck, *President*
Brent Wilkinson, *COO*
Gregg Tavolacci, *Opers Staff*
Andy Brooks, *CFO*
EMP: 18
SALES (est): 2.9MM **Privately Held**
SIC: 7372 Educational computer software

Norwich
New London County

(G-6405)
ALAN M CRANE
Also Called: Aef Supply
177 Maple St (06360-5410)
PHONE..................860 608-2788
Alan Crane, *Owner*
EMP: 1
SALES (est): 58.9K **Privately Held**
WEB: www.aefsupply.com
SIC: 2389 Apparel & accessories

(G-6406)
AP DISPOSITION LLC
387 N Main St (06360-3917)
PHONE..................860 889-1344
Paul Siefert,
James Brown,
Doreen Sylvistre,
▼ EMP: 55 EST: 2004
SALES (est): 5.7MM **Privately Held**
WEB: www.atlanticpackaginggroup.com
SIC: 2653 Boxes, corrugated: made from purchased materials

(G-6407)
AUTUMN COLORS
453 Scotland Rd (06360-9406)
PHONE..................860 822-6568
Thurston Lilbridge, *Owner*
EMP: 1
SALES (est): 77K **Privately Held**
SIC: 2421 Sawdust & shavings

(G-6408)
CAG IMAGING LLC
387 N Main St (06360-3917)
PHONE..................860 887-0836
Stuart Swan, *Principal*
Frank Fazenbaker, *Vice Pres*
EMP: 2
SALES (est): 115.5K **Privately Held**
SIC: 2752 3861 7335 Photo-offset printing; enlargers, photographic; color separation, photographic & movie film

(G-6409)
CHARLES RIVER LABORATORIES INC
Charles Rver Avian Vccine Svcs
1 Wisconsin Ave Ste 100 (06360-1515)
PHONE..................860 889-1389
Joan Johnson, *Human Res Mgr*
Landin Fox, *Marketing Mgr*
Kevin White, *Manager*
EMP: 35
SALES (corp-wide): 2.2B **Publicly Held**
SIC: 2836 Veterinary biological products
HQ: Charles River Laboratories, Inc.
251 Ballardvale St
Wilmington MA 01887
781 222-6000

(G-6410)
DERRICK MASON (PA)
Also Called: Sign-Grafx Group
2 Nelson St (06360-1336)
PHONE..................413 527-4282
Derrick Mason, *Owner*
Wife Mason, *Vice Pres*
EMP: 6
SQ FT: 3,800
SALES (est): 313.5K **Privately Held**
WEB: www.sign-grafx.com
SIC: 3993 5046 1799 Signs, not made in custom sign painting shops; signs, electrical; sign installation & maintenance

(G-6411)
DRAGON HOLLOW DESIGN LLC
Also Called: Dragon Hollow Promotions
230 Dunham St (06360-6134)
PHONE..................860 861-6200
Christopher Carter, *Principal*
Jennifer Smyth, *Principal*
EMP: 2
SALES (est): 82.4K **Privately Held**
SIC: 5999 3999 2399 7389 Trophies & plaques; buttons: Red Cross, union, identification; identification tags, except paper; identification badges & insignia; emblems, badges & insignia

(G-6412)
E B ASPHALT & LANDSCAPING LLC
60 Terminal Way (06360-6760)
PHONE..................860 639-1921
Rickie Emmons Jr, *Principal*
EMP: 10
SQ FT: 80,000
SALES: 1.5MM **Privately Held**
SIC: 2951 0781 Asphalt paving mixtures & blocks; landscape services

(G-6413)
FOUR COUNTY CATHOLIC NEWSPAPER
31 Perkins Ave (06360-3613)
PHONE..................860 886-1281
Michael Strammiello, *Exec Dir*
EMP: 1
SALES (est): 57.1K **Privately Held**
SIC: 2711 Newspapers

(G-6414)
GATEHOUSE MEDIA LLC
Norwich Bulletin, The
10 Railroad Ave (06360-5829)
PHONE..................860 886-0106
Nadine McBride, *Opers Staff*
Louvenia Brandt, *Sales Mgr*
Dan Graziano, *Adv Dir*
Sharon Brochu, *Advt Staff*
Ellen Lind, *Branch Mgr*
EMP: 150
SALES (corp-wide): 1.5B **Privately Held**
WEB: www.gatehousemedia.com
SIC: 2711 Newspapers, publishing & printing
HQ: Gatehouse Media, Llc
175 Sullys Trl Fl 3
Pittsford NY 14534
585 598-0030

(G-6415)
GATEHOUSE MEDIA CONN HOLDINGS
Also Called: Colchester Bulletin Bulletin
10 Railroad Ave (06360-5829)
PHONE..................860 887-9211

▲ = Import ▼ = Export
◆ = Import/Export

Michael E Reed, *Ch of Bd*
Kirk A Davis, *President*
Melinda Ajanik Sr, *Senior VP*
Polly Grunfeld Sack Sr, *Senior VP*
EMP: 39
SALES (est): 5.8MM
SALES (corp-wide): 1.5B **Privately Held**
SIC: 2711 Commercial printing & newspaper publishing combined; newspapers, publishing & printing
PA: New Media Investment Group Inc.
1345 Avenue Of The Americ
New York NY 10105
212 479-3160

(G-6416)
HIGGS ENERGY LLC
66 Franklin St (06360-5806)
P.O. Box 172 (06360-0172)
PHONE 860 213-5561
Eddie Oquendo,
EMP: 3
SALES (est): 121.7K **Privately Held**
SIC: 3812 Aircraft/aerospace flight instruments & guidance systems

(G-6417)
INCJET INC
31 Clinton Ave Ste 2 (06360-2165)
PHONE 860 823-3090
Marc Perkins, *President*
EMP: 13
SALES (est): 1.5MM
SALES (corp-wide): 2.6MM **Privately Held**
WEB: www.guntherintl.com
SIC: 3229 Stationers' glassware: inkwells, clip cups, etc.
PA: Inc.Jet Holding, Inc.
1 Winnenden Rd
Norwich CT 06360
860 823-1427

(G-6418)
J & M PLUMBING & CNSTR LLC
16 West St (06360-6120)
PHONE 860 319-3082
Michael Watkinson,
EMP: 12 **EST:** 2015
SALES (est): 825.5K **Privately Held**
SIC: 1389 1799 1711 Construction, repair & dismantling services; construction site cleanup; plumbing contractors

(G-6419)
JOHNSON CONTROLS INC
100 Winnenden Rd (06360-1574)
PHONE 860 887-7185
Dan Almeida, *Manager*
EMP: 1 **Privately Held**
SIC: 2531 3714 3691 3822 Seats, automobile; motor vehicle body components & frame; instrument board assemblies, motor vehicle; lead acid batteries (storage batteries); building services monitoring controls, automatic; facilities support services
HQ: Johnson Controls, Inc.
5757 N Green Bay Ave
Milwaukee WI 53209
414 524-1200

(G-6420)
KATHY POOLER
Also Called: Publications Plus
5 Melody Ln (06360-1717)
PHONE 860 889-2893
Kathy Pooler, *Owner*
EMP: 1
SALES: 70K **Privately Held**
WEB: www.publicationsplus.com
SIC: 2741 2752 Miscellaneous publishing; commercial printing, lithographic

(G-6421)
KONINKLIJKE PHILIPS ELEC NV
40 Wisconsin Ave (06360-1533)
PHONE 860 886-2621
Cliff Jackson, *General Mgr*
EMP: 12
SALES (corp-wide): 2.4MM **Privately Held**
SIC: 5999 3229 Electronic parts & equipment; glass lighting equipment parts
PA: Philips Koninklijke Electronics Nv
631 Airport Rd
Fall River MA 02720
508 646-3134

(G-6422)
LAUREL TOOL & MANUFACTURING
177 Franklin St (06360-4516)
PHONE 860 889-5354
Dennis Moran, *Owner*
EMP: 3
SALES (est): 216K **Privately Held**
SIC: 3544 Special dies & tools

(G-6423)
MILLS ON WHEELS
30 Forest St (06360-4953)
PHONE 860 705-2903
Malik Edwards, *Principal*
EMP: 2 **EST:** 2010
SALES (est): 136.9K **Privately Held**
SIC: 3312 Blast furnaces & steel mills

(G-6424)
NALAS ENGINEERING SERVICES
1 Winnenden Rd (06360-1513)
PHONE 860 861-3691
Jerry Salan, *CEO*
David AM Ende, *President*
Shilpa Amato, *Exec VP*
Kerri Salan, *Vice Pres*
EMP: 52
SALES (est): 1.8MM **Privately Held**
SIC: 2869 Industrial organic chemicals

(G-6425)
NORWICH PRINTING COMPANY INC
Also Called: Minuteman Press
595 W Main St Ste 2 (06360-5300)
PHONE 860 887-7468
Steve Weber, *President*
Gail Weber, *Vice Pres*
EMP: 10
SQ FT: 4,300
SALES (est): 1.3MM **Privately Held**
SIC: 7389 2789 Mailbox rental & related service; bookbinding & related work

(G-6426)
NUTRON MANUFACTURING INC
5 Wisconsin Ave (06360-1515)
P.O. Box 314, Waterford (06385-0314)
PHONE 860 887-4550
Jack Edward Feinberg, *President*
Mark L Favalora, *Vice Pres*
Joseph L Feinberg, *Treasurer*
Mark Feinberg, *Treasurer*
Michael J Feinberg, *Treasurer*
▲ **EMP:** 24
SQ FT: 95,000
SALES (est): 4.6MM **Privately Held**
WEB: www.nutron-mfg.com
SIC: 3646 Commercial indusl & institutional electric lighting fixtures

(G-6427)
ONE AND CO INC
Also Called: Eon Designs
154 N Main St (06360-5121)
PHONE 860 892-5180
Gordon Kyle, *President*
Mark Stasko, *Vice Pres*
EMP: 12
SQ FT: 16,000
SALES (est): 1.7MM **Privately Held**
WEB: www.eondesigns.com
SIC: 2522 2541 Office furniture, except wood; wood partitions & fixtures

(G-6428)
PRO FORMING SHEET METAL LLC
31 Connecticut Ave Ste 3 (06360-7511)
PHONE 860 886-9900
Tom Garbarino,
EMP: 2
SQ FT: 5,000
SALES (est): 180K **Privately Held**
SIC: 3444 Sheet metal specialties, not stamped

(G-6429)
ROSS CURTIS PRODUCT INC
Also Called: Ross Custom Switches
45 Church St (06360-5001)
PHONE 860 886-6800
Steven Ross Brenneisen, *President*
Thomas Monroe, *Vice Pres*
Heidi Fields Revocable Trust, *Shareholder*
EMP: 6
SALES (est): 750K **Privately Held**
WEB: www.rossswitches.com
SIC: 3944 Trains & equipment, toy: electric & mechanical

(G-6430)
SAINT VINCENT DE PAUL PLACE
120 Cliff St (06360-5155)
PHONE 860 889-7374
Jillian Corbin, *Director*
EMP: 8 **EST:** 1978
SALES: 1.1MM **Privately Held**
SIC: 8322 2759 Social service center; commercial printing

(G-6431)
SHEFFIELD PHARMACEUTICALS LLC
9 Wisconsin Ave (06360-1562)
PHONE 860 442-4451
Jeffrey Davis, *President*
EMP: 10
SALES (corp-wide): 35.4MM **Privately Held**
SIC: 2834 Pharmaceutical preparations
PA: Sheffield Pharmaceuticals, Llc
170 Broad St
New London CT 06320
860 442-4451

(G-6432)
SIGN PROFESSIONALS
303 W Main St (06360-5430)
PHONE 860 823-1122
Scott Lawrence, *Partner*
David McDowell, *Partner*
EMP: 4
SQ FT: 5,000
SALES (est): 350K **Privately Held**
SIC: 3993 Signs, not made in custom sign painting shops

(G-6433)
SYBA SYSTEMS LLC
20 Huntington Pl (06360-4415)
PHONE 401 829-0822
Edward Detoffol, *Principal*
EMP: 2 **EST:** 2008
SALES (est): 147.5K **Privately Held**
SIC: 3823 Industrial instrmnts msrmnt display/control process variable

(G-6434)
SYLVIA ENGINEERING WLDG & EQP
42 Case St (06360-2215)
P.O. Box 33, Bozrah (06334-0033)
PHONE 860 859-1791
Joseph Sylvia, *Principal*
EMP: 1
SALES: 125K **Privately Held**
SIC: 7692 Welding repair

(G-6435)
TAPPED APPLE WINERY
32 Perkins Ave (06360-3642)
PHONE 860 887-0727
John Wiedenheft, *Principal*
EMP: 2
SALES (est): 87.9K **Privately Held**
SIC: 3571 Wines

(G-6436)
TERRY BRICK
Also Called: Tlb Auto Machine
77 Clinton Ave (06360-2113)
PHONE 860 889-2232
Terry Brick, *Owner*
EMP: 1
SALES: 150K **Privately Held**
WEB: www.tlbautomachine.com
SIC: 3519 Gas engine rebuilding

(G-6437)
VERMONT PALLET & SKID SHOP
104 Baltic Rd (06360-9409)
P.O. Box 646, Baltic (06330-0646)
PHONE 860 822-6949
James Adams, *President*
Dave Renfahw, *Vice Pres*
Inez Urso, *Treasurer*
EMP: 9
SQ FT: 3,200
SALES (est): 605K **Privately Held**
SIC: 2448 2441 2449 Pallets, wood; skids, wood; boxes, wood; wood containers

(G-6438)
VIKING SUPPLY CO
31 Connecticut Ave (06360-1523)
PHONE 860 886-0220
John F Kindelan Jr, *President*
EMP: 2
SALES (est): 188.6K **Privately Held**
SIC: 3432 5074 Plumbing fixture fittings & trim; plumbing & hydronic heating supplies

(G-6439)
W B MASON CO INC
2 Consumers Ave (06360-7521)
PHONE 888 926-2766
EMP: 51
SALES (corp-wide): 773MM **Privately Held**
SIC: 5943 5712 2752 Office forms & supplies; office furniture; commercial printing, lithographic
PA: W. B. Mason Co., Inc.
59 Center St
Brockton MA 02301
781 794-8800

(G-6440)
XUARE LLC
471 N Main St (06360-3923)
PHONE 860 383-8863
Peter Obuchowski, *Principal*
EMP: 3
SQ FT: 4,000
SALES (est): 336K **Privately Held**
SIC: 3599 Machine shop, jobbing & repair

Oakdale
New London County

(G-6441)
BILLS SHEET METAL
1451 Old Colchester Rd (06370-1222)
PHONE 860 859-2821
William Thiel, *Owner*
EMP: 2
SALES (est): 187.2K **Privately Held**
SIC: 3444 Metal ventilating equipment

(G-6442)
ERASABLE IMAGES
450 Oxoboxo Dam Rd (06370-1225)
PHONE 860 367-4545
Scott Cook, *Owner*
EMP: 2 **EST:** 2008
SALES (est): 500.6K **Privately Held**
SIC: 3589 High pressure cleaning equipment

(G-6443)
INCORD LTD
430 Chapel Hill Rd (06370-1425)
PHONE 860 537-1414
EMP: 2
SALES (est): 174.5K **Privately Held**
SIC: 3999 Manufacturing industries

(G-6444)
LITTLE T QUARTER MIDGET CLUB
32 Georgia Rd (06370-1524)
PHONE 860 885-1376
EMP: 1
SALES (est): 49.1K **Privately Held**
SIC: 3131 Quarters

Oakdale - New London County (G-6445)

(G-6445)
NORTHMEN DEFENSE LLC
24 Old Colchester Rd Ext (06370-1031)
PHONE...................860 908-9308
Brent Walker, *Principal*
EMP: 5
SALES (est): 210.1K **Privately Held**
SIC: 3812 Defense systems & equipment

(G-6446)
RICHARDSON MACHINE
162 Connecticut Blvd (06370-1511)
PHONE...................860 859-1458
Fred Richardson, *Principal*
EMP: 2
SALES (est): 99.2K **Privately Held**
SIC: 3599 Machine shop, jobbing & repair

(G-6447)
T B MARBLE GRANITE LLC
1404 Hartfrd New Lndn Tpk (06370-1812)
PHONE...................860 443-0817
EMP: 2
SALES (est): 62.6K **Privately Held**
SIC: 3281 Cut stone & stone products

Oakville
Litchfield County

(G-6448)
A&R PLATING SERVICES LLC
147 Riverside St (06779-1537)
PHONE...................860 274-9562
Robert Rose, *President*
EMP: 1
SALES (est): 446.8K **Privately Held**
SIC: 3471 Plating of metals or formed products

(G-6449)
B T S GRAPHICS LLC
36 Zoar Ave Ste 2 (06779-1651)
P.O. Box 86 (06779-0086)
PHONE...................860 274-6422
Tom Taylor,
EMP: 6 EST: 1997
SALES (est): 560K **Privately Held**
SIC: 2759 Screen printing

(G-6450)
BANNER WORKS
Also Called: Banner & Awning Works
15 Rockland Ave (06779-1611)
P.O. Box 3115, Waterbury (06705-0115)
PHONE...................203 597-9999
Jennifer Nelson, *Owner*
EMP: 3
SALES (est): 136.1K **Privately Held**
SIC: 2399 Banners, made from fabric

(G-6451)
CABINET DREAMS LLC
158 Falls Ave (06779-1812)
PHONE...................203 558-4178
Jose Pinho, *Principal*
EMP: 1
SALES (est): 53.7K **Privately Held**
SIC: 2434 Wood kitchen cabinets

(G-6452)
FERRE FORM METAL PRODUCTS
25 Falls Ave (06779-1807)
P.O. Box 109, Waterbury (06720-0109)
PHONE...................860 274-3280
Thomas Boileau, *President*
Jeff Valentine, *Vice Pres*
EMP: 10
SQ FT: 5,900
SALES (est): 1.4MM **Privately Held**
SIC: 3469 Metal stampings

(G-6453)
GET BACK INC
27 Main St Ste 4 (06779-1703)
PHONE...................860 274-9991
Tim Burns, *President*
EMP: 2
SALES (est): 648.5K **Privately Held**
SIC: 5021 2511 2514 Furniture; wood household furniture; kitchen & dining room furniture; metal household furniture

(G-6454)
GUTTER FILTER NEW ENGLAND LLC
51 Ice House Rd (06779-1514)
P.O. Box 172 (06779-0172)
PHONE...................860 274-5943
EMP: 2 EST: 2008
SALES (est): 110K **Privately Held**
SIC: 3569 Mfg General Industrial Machinery

(G-6455)
JK SIGN & STAMP LLC
63 Capewell Ave (06779-2348)
PHONE...................860 729-3860
John Kobialka, *Principal*
EMP: 1 EST: 2017
SALES (est): 47.9K **Privately Held**
SIC: 3993 Signs & advertising specialties

(G-6456)
M T S TOOL LLC
27 Main St Ste 2 (06779-1703)
PHONE...................860 945-0875
Christopher McKenna,
Robert McCarthy,
EMP: 4
SQ FT: 1,000
SALES (est): 399.3K **Privately Held**
WEB: www.mtstool.com
SIC: 3545 Diamond cutting tools for turning, boring, burnishing, etc.

(G-6457)
NAUGATUCK EMERGENCY EQP LLC
54 Ridgeway Ave (06779-1435)
PHONE...................203 228-7117
Michael Granoth,
EMP: 1
SALES (est): 94.1K **Privately Held**
SIC: 3647 Vehicular lighting equipment

(G-6458)
PINHOS CABINETS
158 Falls Ave (06779-1812)
PHONE...................860 274-1740
Jose Pinho, *Owner*
EMP: 2
SALES (est): 187K **Privately Held**
SIC: 2434 Wood kitchen cabinets

(G-6459)
QUALITY AUTOMATICS INC (PA)
15 Mclennan Dr (06779-1428)
P.O. Box 11190, Waterbury (06703-0190)
PHONE...................860 945-4795
Stephen White, *President*
Robert Cermola, *Vice Pres*
EMP: 40
SQ FT: 25,000
SALES (est): 6.7MM **Privately Held**
WEB: www.qualityautomatics.com
SIC: 3451 Screw machine products

(G-6460)
RAMDY CORPORATION
40 Mclennan Dr (06779-1429)
P.O. Box 834, Watertown (06795-0834)
PHONE...................860 274-3713
Richard Jklipp, *President*
John Mendicino, *President*
Allen Thornberg, *President*
Mark Pavao, *Vice Pres*
Paul Thornberg, *Vice Pres*
EMP: 45
SQ FT: 10,000
SALES (est): 9MM **Privately Held**
SIC: 3541 Machine tools, metal cutting type

(G-6461)
RDL COATINGS LLC
28 Main St (06779-1704)
PHONE...................203 232-0411
Donna Lopez, *Principal*
EMP: 2
SALES (est): 85.2K **Privately Held**
SIC: 3479 Metal coating & allied service

(G-6462)
RINTEC CORPORATION
30 Mclennan Dr (06779-1429)
PHONE...................860 274-3697
Antonio F Rinaldi, *President*

Veronica S Rinaldi, *Vice Pres*
EMP: 10
SQ FT: 5,500
SALES (est): 930K **Privately Held**
SIC: 3544 Special dies & tools

(G-6463)
T & J SCREW MACHINE PDTS LLC
27 Main St (06779-1703)
PHONE...................860 417-3801
Anthony P Troisi, *Principal*
EMP: 3
SALES (est): 413K **Privately Held**
SIC: 3451 Screw machine products

(G-6464)
TPC REPLACEMENT WINDOW LLC
122 Capewell Ave (06779-2304)
PHONE...................860 274-6971
Thomas Pedro, *Mng Member*
EMP: 2 EST: 2007
SALES (est): 231.6K **Privately Held**
SIC: 2952 Asphalt felts & coatings

(G-6465)
TULALOO
72 Parkman St (06779-1345)
PHONE...................860 417-2587
Jessica Creter, *Principal*
EMP: 2
SALES (est): 175.5K **Privately Held**
SIC: 2754 Stationery & invitation printing, gravure

(G-6466)
UNIVERSAL BODY & EQP CO LLC
17 Di Nunzio Rd (06779-1407)
PHONE...................860 274-7541
Todd Richards, *Mng Member*
John Dufour,
Nick Nicol,
EMP: 16
SQ FT: 6,000
SALES (est): 3.3MM **Privately Held**
SIC: 3713 3711 Truck bodies (motor vehicles); snow plows (motor vehicles), assembly of

(G-6467)
WATERTOWN CANVAS AND AWNG LLC
98 Falls Ave (06779-1810)
PHONE...................860 274-0933
Fax: 860 274-8519
EMP: 5
SQ FT: 4,000
SALES (est): 330K **Privately Held**
SIC: 2394 Mfg Canvas/Related Products

Old Greenwich
Fairfield County

(G-6468)
BOXTREE ACCESSORIES INC
34 Lincoln Ave (06870-2211)
PHONE...................203 637-5794
John Graves, *President*
Louise Graves, *Vice Pres*
EMP: 2
SQ FT: 1,000
SALES: 1.5MM **Privately Held**
SIC: 2387 3915 3999 Apparel belts; jewelers' materials & lapidary work; handbag & pocketbook frames

(G-6469)
CLANOL SYSTEMS INC
Also Called: Colonial Print & Imaging
1374 E Putnam Ave (06870-1308)
P.O. Box 416, Riverside (06878-0416)
PHONE...................203 637-9909
Samantha Carter, *CEO*
Benjamin Carter, *President*
EMP: 5
SQ FT: 2,750
SALES (est): 607.5K **Privately Held**
SIC: 2759 2752 Letterpress printing; commercial printing, offset

(G-6470)
COSS SYSTEMS INC (NOT INC)
26 Arcadia Rd (06870-1721)
PHONE...................732 447-7724
Antonia Spitzer, *Principal*
EMP: 7
SALES (est): 436.6K **Privately Held**
SIC: 7372 Prepackaged software

(G-6471)
E G TECH SOLUTIONS LLC
6 Ledge Rd (06870-2320)
PHONE...................203 200-7047
A Ellenbogen, *Mng Member*
ARI Ellenbogen, *Mng Member*
EMP: 1 EST: 2009
SALES (est): 38.9K **Privately Held**
SIC: 7379 8748 3694 Computer related consulting services; systems engineering consultant, ex. computer or professional; automotive electrical equipment

(G-6472)
ELOT INC (PA)
Also Called: Elottery
51 Forest Ave Apt 117 (06870-1529)
PHONE...................203 388-1808
Edwin J McGuinn Jr, *President*
EMP: 4
SALES (est): 537.8K **Privately Held**
WEB: www.elottery.com
SIC: 3661 8741 Telephones & telephone apparatus; management services

(G-6473)
GREENWICH GOFER
56 Halsey Dr (06870-1225)
PHONE...................203 637-8425
Lisa Gapp Palmer, *Principal*
EMP: 3
SALES (est): 109K **Privately Held**
SIC: 2711 Newspapers, publishing & printing

(G-6474)
GRILL DADDY BRUSH COMPANY
29 Arcadia Rd (06870-1701)
PHONE...................888 840-7552
Michael A Wales, *President*
Grace L Wales, *Admin Sec*
▲ EMP: 30
SQ FT: 2,000
SALES: 10MM **Privately Held**
SIC: 2842 Cleaning or polishing preparations

(G-6475)
HONEYPOTZ INC
1465 E Putnam Ave Apt 604 (06870-1369)
PHONE...................203 542-7891
EMP: 2
SALES (est): 56.5K **Privately Held**
SIC: 7372 Prepackaged Software Services

(G-6476)
IGS-MED LLC
7 Ferris Dr (06870-1407)
PHONE...................203 698-0396
Salvatore Cioppa, *Mng Member*
Rosalia Donnina,
EMP: 2
SALES (est): 110.5K **Privately Held**
SIC: 7363 3731 Medical help service; cargo vessels, building & repairing

(G-6477)
INFINITE NUTRITION INC
3 Nimitz Pl (06870-1211)
PHONE...................203 940-1783
Matthew Weber, *President*
EMP: 2
SALES (est): 62.3K **Privately Held**
SIC: 2099 Food preparations

(G-6478)
JUDITH JACKSON INC
1535 E Putnam Ave Apt 406 (06870-1356)
PHONE...................203 698-3011
Judith Jackson, *President*
EMP: 3
SALES (est): 340.5K **Privately Held**
WEB: www.judithjackson.com
SIC: 2844 Cosmetic preparations

GEOGRAPHIC SECTION — Old Lyme - New London County

(G-6479)
MARCIA JEAN FABRIC AND CFT LLC
35 Lincoln Ave (06870-2210)
PHONE...................................203 273-1665
Leslie J Davis, *Principal*
EMP: 1 EST: 2013
SALES (est): 94.3K **Privately Held**
SIC: 2211 Jean fabrics

(G-6480)
NAVTECH SYSTEMS INC
322 Sound Beach Ave (06870-1931)
PHONE...................................203 661-7800
Sushil Advaney, *President*
EMP: 4
SALES (est): 246.7K **Privately Held**
WEB: www.navtechsys.com
SIC: 7372 Prepackaged software

(G-6481)
OPEN WATER DEVELOPMENT LLC
Also Called: Speakeasy Ai
14 Cove Ridge Ln (06870-1903)
PHONE...................................646 883-2062
Richard Simons,
EMP: 5
SALES (est): 117.2K **Privately Held**
SIC: 7372 Application computer software

(G-6482)
ORTHOTRACTION PADS LLC
3 Old Club House Rd (06870-2012)
P.O. Box 20 (06870-0020)
PHONE...................................203 698-0291
Elizabeth Ann Towne, *President*
EMP: 3 EST: 2007
SALES (est): 319.4K **Privately Held**
SIC: 5047 3843 Dental equipment & supplies; dental equipment & supplies

(G-6483)
RIVERSIDE AVIATION
8 Rocky Point Rd (06870-2314)
PHONE...................................203 637-4231
John Kukral, *President*
Karin Kukral, *Vice Pres*
▲ EMP: 2
SALES (est): 169.7K **Privately Held**
SIC: 3721 Airplanes, fixed or rotary wing

(G-6484)
SWEET PEAS BAKING COMPANY LLC
6 Highview Ave (06870-1704)
PHONE...................................203 637-4031
Katja Pita,
Rafael Pita,
EMP: 2
SALES (est): 135.8K **Privately Held**
SIC: 2051 Bakery: wholesale or wholesale/retail combined

(G-6485)
YORK MILLWORK LLC
210 Sound Beach Ave (06870-1600)
PHONE...................................203 698-3460
Nicholas Barile, *Manager*
EMP: 4
SALES (est): 386K **Privately Held**
SIC: 2431 Millwork

Old Lyme
New London County

(G-6486)
29 WYCHWOOD ROAD LLC
13 Whippoorwill Rd (06371-1437)
PHONE...................................860 434-8078
Shannon Benodetto, *Principal*
EMP: 1
SALES (est): 50.2K **Privately Held**
SIC: 2499 Wood products

(G-6487)
2SEAL LLC
6 Peppermint Rdg (06371-2803)
PHONE...................................860 227-6854
Joe Milazzo, *Mng Member*
EMP: 1
SALES (est): 130.1K **Privately Held**
SIC: 3442 Screen & storm doors & windows

(G-6488)
AERIAL IMAGING SOLUTIONS LLC
5 Myrica Way (06371-1874)
PHONE...................................860 434-3637
Donald Leroi, *Owner*
Don Leroi, *General Mgr*
EMP: 1
SALES (est): 50K **Privately Held**
SIC: 7379 3861 Computer related consulting services; aerial cameras

(G-6489)
ARTEMISIA INC
35 Sill Ln (06371-1132)
PHONE...................................917 797-7644
Rosemarie Padovano, *Principal*
EMP: 1
SALES (est): 73.4K **Privately Held**
SIC: 5719 2392 Bedding (sheets, blankets, spreads & pillows); cushions & pillows

(G-6490)
ASHLAWN FARM STORE (PA)
78 Bill Hill Rd (06371-3549)
PHONE...................................860 434-3636
Chip Dahlke, *Owner*
Carol Dahlke, *Co-Owner*
EMP: 1
SALES (est): 211.3K **Privately Held**
WEB: www.farmcoffee.com
SIC: 0191 2095 General farms, primarily crop; coffee roasting (except by wholesale grocers)

(G-6491)
BRUSHLINE DESIGN
4 Jadon Dr (06371-1420)
PHONE...................................860 434-5055
Sophie Marsh, *Owner*
EMP: 1 EST: 1992
SALES (est): 62K **Privately Held**
SIC: 3993 Signs & advertising specialties

(G-6492)
BUREAUS SUGAR HOUSE
Also Called: Maple Syrup
60 Rowland Rd (06371-1519)
PHONE...................................860 434-5787
Donald Bureau, *Owner*
EMP: 2
SALES (est): 79.8K **Privately Held**
SIC: 2099 Maple syrup

(G-6493)
BYRON LORD INC
18 Bailey Rd (06371-1701)
PHONE...................................203 287-9881
James Byron, *President*
George Byron, *Vice Pres*
Erna Byron, *Admin Sec*
EMP: 5 EST: 1978
SQ FT: 2,400
SALES: 1MM **Privately Held**
WEB: www.lordbyron.on.ca
SIC: 2396 2391 3545 Automotive trimmings, fabric; draperies, plastic & textile: from purchased materials; tool holders

(G-6494)
C J CUSHING WOODWORKING
4 Green Valley Lake Rd (06371-1524)
PHONE...................................860 848-2746
EMP: 1 EST: 2017
SALES (est): 54.1K **Privately Held**
SIC: 2431 Mfg Millwork

(G-6495)
CALLAWAY CARS INC
3 High St (06371-1529)
PHONE...................................860 434-9002
E Reeves Callaway III, *President*
Joanne Mercer, *Engineer*
Michael Zoner, *Admin Sec*
EMP: 18 EST: 1976
SQ FT: 10,000
SALES (est): 4.6MM
SALES (corp-wide): 6.2MM **Privately Held**
SIC: 3714 Motor vehicle engines & parts
PA: The Callaway Companies Inc
3 High St
Old Lyme CT 06371
860 434-9002

(G-6496)
CALLAWAY COMPANIES INC (PA)
3 High St (06371-1529)
PHONE...................................860 434-9002
E Reeves Callaway III, *President*
▲ EMP: 15
SQ FT: 16,300
SALES (est): 6.2MM **Privately Held**
SIC: 3714 8732 Motor vehicle engines & parts; research services, except laboratory

(G-6497)
CAN-AM TRADING & LOGISTICS LLC
2 Sands Dr (06371-1641)
P.O. Box 674 (06371-0674)
PHONE...................................860 961-9932
Patricia Laplatney,
EMP: 1 EST: 2014
SALES (est): 126.8K **Privately Held**
SIC: 2411 Logging

(G-6498)
CONNECTICUT SIGN SERVICE LLC
5 Chadwick Dr (06371-2106)
PHONE...................................860 391-9614
EMP: 1
SALES (est): 46K **Privately Held**
SIC: 3993 Signs & advertising specialties

(G-6499)
CUMMINS ENVIRO TECH INC
29 Mile Creek Rd (06371-1710)
PHONE...................................860 388-6377
Hansen Cummins, *President*
EMP: 12
SALES (est): 1.3MM **Privately Held**
WEB: www.cenvirotech.com
SIC: 8711 3519 Consulting engineer; internal combustion engines

(G-6500)
CUMMINS ENVIROTECH
61 Buttonball Rd (06371-1705)
PHONE...................................860 598-9564
Cummins Hansen, *President*
EMP: 1
SALES (est): 68.6K **Privately Held**
SIC: 8748 8711 1799 3519 Environmental consultant; engineering services; special trade contractors; internal combustion engines

(G-6501)
CUSHS HOMEGROWN LLC
4 Green Valley Lake Rd (06371-1524)
PHONE...................................860 739-7373
Elizabeth Cushing, *President*
James C Cushing, *Treasurer*
Christopher J Cushing, *Mng Member*
Phyllis P Cushing, *Admin Sec*
EMP: 4 EST: 2009
SALES (est): 135K **Privately Held**
SIC: 2032 Canned specialties

(G-6502)
CUSTOM DESIGN WOODWORKS LLC
10 Maywood Dr (06371-1523)
P.O. Box 376 (06371-0376)
PHONE...................................860 434-0515
Christopher Defiore, *Principal*
EMP: 4
SALES (est): 444.2K **Privately Held**
SIC: 2431 Millwork

(G-6503)
DAVID SHUCK
Also Called: Advanced Precast Concrete
Hatchetts Hill Rd (06371)
P.O. Box 492 (06371-0492)
PHONE...................................860 434-8562
David Shuck, *Owner*
EMP: 3
SALES (est): 342.8K **Privately Held**
SIC: 3272 Septic tanks, concrete

(G-6504)
DEEP RIVER LLC
1 Davis Rd W (06371-1414)
PHONE...................................860 388-9442
Dave Sistare,
Michael Knizeski,
Daniel Schuessler,
EMP: 2
SALES (est): 216.4K **Privately Held**
SIC: 7372 Business oriented computer software
PA: Appriss Inc.
9901 Linn Station Rd # 500
Louisville KY 40223

(G-6505)
DESIGN LABEL MANUFACTURING INC (PA)
12 Nottingham Dr (06371-1820)
PHONE...................................860 739-6266
Jeff Paul Dunphy, *President*
Paul Dunphy, *Chairman*
Kim D Eaton, *CFO*
Scott J Dunphy, *Shareholder*
Gene Toombs, *Shareholder*
EMP: 38 EST: 1963
SQ FT: 15,000
SALES (est): 7.1MM **Privately Held**
SIC: 2672 2759 Adhesive papers, labels or tapes: from purchased material; labels & seals: printing

(G-6506)
EAST DELTA RESOURCES CORP
76 Lyme St (06371-2363)
PHONE...................................860 434-7750
David Bikerman, *President*
EMP: 5
SALES: 1.3MM **Privately Held**
SIC: 1081 Metal mining exploration & development services

(G-6507)
ECOFLIK LLC
1 Old Bridge Rd (06371-1425)
P.O. Box 966 (06371-0999)
PHONE...................................860 460-4419
Duane W Buckingham, *Mng Member*
Samantha W Noonan,
EMP: 5
SALES (est): 1.2MM **Privately Held**
SIC: 3172 Cigarette & cigar cases

(G-6508)
FIBERQA LLC
10 Vista Dr (06371-5108)
PHONE...................................860 739-8044
Douglas Wilson, *COO*
Joe Salemi, *Vice Pres*
EMP: 2
SALES (est): 365.7K **Privately Held**
SIC: 3357 Fiber optic cable (insulated)

(G-6509)
FISHING INNOVATIONS LLC
2 Dogwood Dr (06371-2014)
PHONE...................................860 434-3974
Michael Warecke, *Manager*
EMP: 2
SALES (est): 96.6K **Privately Held**
SIC: 3949 Sporting & athletic goods

(G-6510)
GENERATORS ON DEMAND LLC
61-1 Buttonball Rd (06371-1761)
PHONE...................................860 662-4090
Ronald J Swaney,
EMP: 13
SALES (est): 2.1MM **Privately Held**
SIC: 3621 Motors & generators

(G-6511)
GRAPHIC MEMORIES BY MCKIE
Also Called: Barbara McKie
40 Bill Hill Rd (06371-3501)
PHONE...................................860 434-5222
Barbara A McKie, *Owner*
EMP: 1
SALES (est): 60K **Privately Held**
SIC: 2273 Art squares, textile fiber

Old Lyme - New London County

(G-6512)
HECKMAN CONSULTING LLC
21-3 Library Ln (06371-2358)
PHONE..................860 434-5877
John Heckman,
EMP: 2
SALES: 100K **Privately Held**
SIC: 7372 Business oriented computer software

(G-6513)
HIGH HOOK LURES LLC
25 Noyes Rd (06371-1658)
PHONE..................860 334-2324
Michael Mullen, *Principal*
EMP: 2
SALES (est): 68.9K **Privately Held**
SIC: 3949 Lures, fishing: artificial

(G-6514)
KEELING COMPANY INC
Also Called: Keeling's
107 Shore Dr (06371-1209)
PHONE..................860 349-0916
John Keeling, *President*
Avelina Broekstra, *Treasurer*
Pamela Keeling, *Admin Sec*
EMP: 4
SQ FT: 4,500
SALES (est): 422.9K **Privately Held**
WEB: www.keelinglamps.com
SIC: 3645 5719 Residential lighting fixtures; lamps & lamp shades

(G-6515)
NANCY LARSON PUBLISHERS INC
27 Talcott Farm Rd (06371-1474)
P.O. Box 688 (06371-0688)
PHONE..................860 434-0800
Nancy A Larson, *President*
Margaret Heisserer, *Editor*
Leann Harmon, *Marketing Staff*
Madon Dailey, *Manager*
Lynda Dasmann, *Consultant*
EMP: 30
SALES: 1.1MM **Privately Held**
SIC: 2741 Miscellaneous publishing

(G-6516)
NANCY LARSON PUBLISHERS HQ ⬥
120 Boston Post Rd (06371-1346)
PHONE..................860 598-9783
EMP: 1 EST: 2019
SALES (est): 37.5K **Privately Held**
SIC: 2741 Miscellaneous publishing

(G-6517)
PATRICIA SPRATT FOR HOME LLC
60 Lyme St (06371-2332)
PHONE..................860 434-9291
Patricia Spratt,
Emily Spratt,
John Patrick Spratt,
Lilliane Spratt,
Meredith Spratt,
EMP: 10
SQ FT: 1,000
SALES (est): 1MM **Privately Held**
WEB: www.patriciasprattforthehome.com
SIC: 2392 5131 Tablecloths & table settings; linen piece goods, woven

(G-6518)
RWS CO INC
41 Brockway Ferry Rd (06371-3002)
PHONE..................860 434-2961
Richard W Sutton, *President*
Wendolyn B Hill, *Treasurer*
Doug Eitelman, *Accounts Exec*
EMP: 2
SQ FT: 2,500
SALES (est): 247.2K **Privately Held**
SIC: 3565 3569 3541 Packaging machinery; assembly machines, non-metalworking; machine tools, metal cutting type

(G-6519)
STERLING INDUSTRIES LLC
41 Sterling Hill Rd (06371-3304)
PHONE..................860 434-6239
Jennifer Whitney Tiffany, *Owner*
EMP: 2
SALES (est): 133.1K **Privately Held**
SIC: 3999 Manufacturing industries

(G-6520)
TETRAFLO
100 Halls Rd (06371-1456)
PHONE..................860 575-0867
Mark Diebolt, *President*
EMP: 2
SALES (est): 69.9K **Privately Held**
SIC: 3479 Metal coating & allied service

(G-6521)
VIP ASSOCIATES LLC
16 Oak Tree Ln (06371-3639)
PHONE..................203 230-1878
Robert J Burke, *Owner*
EMP: 1
SALES (est): 73.4K **Privately Held**
SIC: 3999 Manufacturing industries

Old Saybrook
Middlesex County

(G-6522)
ALL-TEST PRO LLC (PA)
20 Research Pkwy Unit G&H (06475-4214)
P.O. Box 1139 (06475-5139)
PHONE..................860 399-4222
Tim Scully, *General Mgr*
Jorgen Bjorkman, *Treasurer*
Mike Schneider, *Regl Sales Mgr*
Howley Heather, *Mktg Coord*
Mike Bjorkman, *Marketing Staff*
◆ EMP: 10
SQ FT: 10,000
SALES: 3MM **Privately Held**
WEB: www.alltestpro.com
SIC: 3825 Test equipment for electronic & electric measurement

(G-6523)
BFF HOLDINGS INC (HQ)
Also Called: B L R
141 Mill Rock Rd E (06475-4217)
PHONE..................860 510-0100
Robert L Brady, *President*
Matthew Humphrey, *President*
Stephen Bruce, *Editor*
Ed Cromer, *Editor*
Brian E Gurnham, *COO*
EMP: 175
SQ FT: 75,000
SALES (est): 15.3MM **Privately Held**
WEB: www.blr.com
SIC: 2721 2731 7812 3652 Periodicals; book publishing; motion picture & video production; pre-recorded records & tapes; miscellaneous publishing

(G-6524)
BJM PUMPS LLC
123 Spencer Plain Rd # 1 (06475-4051)
P.O. Box 1138 (06475-5138)
PHONE..................860 399-5937
Ron Woodward, *President*
▲ EMP: 35
SALES: 6.7MM
SALES (corp-wide): 27.3MM **Privately Held**
SIC: 3561 5084 Industrial pumps & parts; industrial machinery & equipment
PA: Industrial Flow Solutions Holdings Llc
1 N Wacker Dr Ste 1920
Chicago IL 60606
312 750-1771

(G-6525)
BRANNKEY INC
137 Mill Rock Rd E (06475-4217)
PHONE..................860 510-0501
Anthony Carambot, *Branch Mgr*
EMP: 38
SALES (corp-wide): 10.6MM **Privately Held**
SIC: 3911 Jewelry, precious metal
PA: Brannkey Inc.
1385 Broadway Fl 14
New York NY 10018
212 371-1515

(G-6526)
BREWER YACHT YARDS INC
333 Boston Post Rd (06475)
PHONE..................860 399-5128
Jack Brewer, *President*
EMP: 9
SALES (corp-wide): 4.1MM **Privately Held**
SIC: 4493 3732 3731 Marinas; boat building & repairing; shipbuilding & repairing
PA: Brewer Yacht Yards Inc
155 E Boston Post Rd
Mamaroneck NY 10543
914 698-0295

(G-6527)
COMPUTER SGNS OLD SAYBROOK LLC
460 Boston Post Rd (06475-1550)
PHONE..................860 388-9773
Maura Vercillo, *General Ptnr*
Andrew J Vercillo,
Craig Rahemba, *Graphic Designe*
EMP: 5
SALES (est): 750K **Privately Held**
SIC: 3993 Signs, not made in custom sign painting shops

(G-6528)
CONDON LLC
33 Main St Ste P (06475-1532)
PHONE..................860 883-5416
Seth M Condon, *Mng Member*
EMP: 60
SQ FT: 800
SALES (est): 428K **Privately Held**
SIC: 6531 3711 Real estate agents & managers; snow plows (motor vehicles), assembly of

(G-6529)
CONNECTICUT VALLEY INDS LLC
8 Center Rd (06475-4012)
PHONE..................860 388-0822
Timothy P Johnson,
▲ EMP: 5
SQ FT: 10,000
SALES (est): 857.7K **Privately Held**
SIC: 3648 3613 Airport lighting fixtures: runway approach, taxi or ramp; control panels, electric

(G-6530)
CRYSTAL TOOL LLC
50 Connally Dr (06475-1162)
PHONE..................860 510-0113
Lisa Fitzsimmons,
Scott Fitzsimmons,
EMP: 4
SQ FT: 700
SALES (est): 485.5K **Privately Held**
WEB: www.crystaltool.com
SIC: 3629 Battery chargers, rectifying or nonrotating

(G-6531)
DLINE LLC
57 Fenwood Grove Rd (06475-3025)
P.O. Box 437 (06475-0437)
PHONE..................860 984-2076
Dmitry Kuzmin, *Principal*
EMP: 2
SALES (est): 172.7K **Privately Held**
SIC: 3714 Motor vehicle parts & accessories

(G-6532)
EATZY LLC
38 Pond Rd (06475-2137)
PHONE..................303 720-7532
Douglas Wrightsman,
EMP: 1
SALES (est): 41.7K **Privately Held**
SIC: 7372 Business oriented computer software

(G-6533)
EZFLOW LIMITED PARTNERSHIP (DH)
4 Business Park Rd (06475-4238)
P.O. Box 768 (06475-0768)
PHONE..................860 577-7064
Roy E Moore, *CEO*
Bryan Coppes, *Vice Pres*
James Bransfield, *Manager*
EMP: 50
SALES (est): 8.2MM
SALES (corp-wide): 1.3B **Publicly Held**
SIC: 3531 Construction machinery
HQ: Infiltrator Water Technologies, Llc
4 Business Park Rd
Old Saybrook CT 06475
860 577-7000

(G-6534)
FOUR COLOR INK LLC
2 Business Park Rd (06475-4206)
PHONE..................860 395-5471
Paul Ross,
William Argyle,
EMP: 3
SQ FT: 2,200
SALES (est): 200K **Privately Held**
SIC: 2796 Color separations for printing

(G-6535)
GREGS OUTBOARD SERVICE LLC
304 Boston Post Rd (06475-1561)
PHONE..................860 339-5139
Gregory Andrew Fiorelli, *Principal*
EMP: 2
SALES (est): 96.7K **Privately Held**
SIC: 3732 Non-motorized boat, building & repairing

(G-6536)
GUNWORKS INTERNATIONAL L L C
4 Center Rd (06475-4007)
P.O. Box 252 (06475-0252)
PHONE..................860 388-4591
Chris Gosselin, *Principal*
EMP: 3
SQ FT: 3,000
SALES (est): 183K **Privately Held**
SIC: 3484 5941 Guns (firearms) or gun parts, 30 mm. & below; sporting goods & bicycle shops

(G-6537)
H&H ENGINEERED SOLUTIONS INC
20 N Cove Rd (06475-2517)
PHONE..................860 575-0005
Wayne Hurd, *President*
Joanne Hurd, *CFO*
▼ EMP: 2
SALES (est): 232.5K **Privately Held**
SIC: 2299 Felts & felt products

(G-6538)
HANFORD CABINET & WDWKG CO
102 Ingham Hill Rd (06475-4115)
PHONE..................860 388-5055
Steve Hanford, *President*
Lane T Hanford, *Director*
EMP: 7 EST: 1969
SQ FT: 6,000
SALES (est): 862K **Privately Held**
WEB: www.hanfordcabinet.com
SIC: 2434 1521 Wood kitchen cabinets; single-family housing construction

(G-6539)
HEARTLAND PUBLICATIONS LLC
20 Research Pkwy Ste G (06475-4214)
PHONE..................860 388-3470
Clifton E Forrest, *Principal*
EMP: 1
SALES (est): 70K **Privately Held**
SIC: 2741 Miscellaneous publishing

(G-6540)
HERBS FARMSTEAD & GOODS
Also Called: Farmstead Goods
155 Ingham Hill Rd (06475-1109)
PHONE..................860 876-3670
Alicia Hernas, *Co-Owner*
Simon Hernas, *Co-Owner*
Carol McCoy, *Treasurer*
EMP: 3

▲ = Import ▼ = Export
◆ = Import/Export

GEOGRAPHIC SECTION
Old Saybrook - Middlesex County (G-6572)

SALES (est): 71.6K **Privately Held**
SIC: **0181** 2033 2035 5431 Ornamental nursery products; jams, jellies & preserves; packaged in cans, jars, etc.; cucumbers, pickles & pickle salting; fruit & vegetable markets; chicken eggs

(G-6541)
IBBITSON TREE SERVICE
5 Hilltop Dr (06475-1123)
PHONE..................................860 388-0624
Jennifer Ibbitson, *Owner*
EMP: 2
SALES (est): 140K **Privately Held**
SIC: **2411** Stumps, wood

(G-6542)
INK PUBLISHING LLC
71 Maple Ave (06475-2407)
PHONE..................................860 581-0026
Jeffery Lilly, *Principal*
EMP: 1
SALES (est): 37.5K **Privately Held**
SIC: **2741** Miscellaneous publishing

(G-6543)
IPC SYSTEMS INC
Also Called: IPC Information Systems
8 Custom Dr (06475-4008)
PHONE..................................203 339-7000
Antoine Verzilli, *Branch Mgr*
EMP: 15
SALES (corp-wide): 587.5MM **Privately Held**
SIC: **3661** Telephone & telegraph apparatus
PA: I.P.C. Systems, Inc.
3 2nd St Fl Plz10
Jersey City NJ 07311
201 253-2000

(G-6544)
IPT TECHNOLOGY
119 Ayers Point Rd (06475-4303)
PHONE..................................860 395-1083
Ingolf Janerus, *Owner*
EMP: 1
SALES (est): 62.9K **Privately Held**
SIC: **3423** Hand & edge tools

(G-6545)
ITERUM THERAPEUTICS INC
20 Research Pkwy (06475-4214)
PHONE..................................860 391-8349
Jeff Schaffnit, *Ch Credit Ofcr*
EMP: 4 EST: 2016
SALES (est): 284.4K **Privately Held**
SIC: **2834** Pharmaceutical preparations

(G-6546)
JAGER PROF GAS SVCS LLC
93 Elm St Apt E (06475-4142)
PHONE..................................860 388-3422
Michael D Jager,
EMP: 1
SALES (est): 170K **Privately Held**
SIC: **1382** Oil & gas exploration services

(G-6547)
JAKES REPAIR LLC
251 School House Rd (06475-1051)
PHONE..................................203 627-8603
Jason Pascale, *Mng Member*
EMP: 2 EST: 2016
SALES (est): 70K **Privately Held**
SIC: **7699** 7692 Professional instrument repair services; welding repair

(G-6548)
JFJ SERVICES LLC
17 Forest Glen Rd (06475-2605)
PHONE..................................860 395-1922
Beverly Johnson, *Owner*
EMP: 4
SALES (est): 337.9K **Privately Held**
SIC: **3589** Commercial cleaning equipment

(G-6549)
KELLY INDUSTRIES LLC
2 Center Rd (06475-4054)
PHONE..................................860 388-5666
Brian J Kelly,
Joy Kely,
EMP: 2
SQ FT: 4,800

SALES (est): 181K **Privately Held**
SIC: **3999** Dock equipment & supplies, industrial

(G-6550)
KNOLL INC
5 Connolly Dr (06475-1163)
PHONE..................................860 395-2093
EMP: 50
SALES (corp-wide): 887.5MM **Publicly Held**
SIC: **2521** Mfg Wood Office Furniture
PA: Knoll, Inc.
1235 Water St
East Greenville PA 18041
215 679-7991

(G-6551)
KONECKY & KONECKY LLC
72 Ayers Point Rd (06475-4301)
PHONE..................................860 388-0878
Sean Konecky, *President*
EMP: 1
SALES (est): 33.3K **Privately Held**
SIC: **2731** Book publishing

(G-6552)
LEONARD DONGWECK
23 School House Rd (06475-4043)
PHONE..................................860 388-0700
Lenard Dongweck, *Owner*
EMP: 2
SALES (est): 116.3K **Privately Held**
SIC: **2759** Engraving

(G-6553)
LIFTLINE CAPITAL LLC
Also Called: Stencil Ease
7 Center Rd W (06475-4053)
P.O. Box 1127 (06475-5127)
PHONE..................................860 395-0150
Milissa Brigante, *Office Mgr*
Stephanie Olmstead, *Art Dir*
James Randolph,
John Helm,
▼ EMP: 18
SQ FT: 30,000
SALES (est): 4.4MM **Privately Held**
WEB: www.stencilease.com
SIC: **2675** 3991 3953 Stencils & lettering materials: die-cut; paint brushes; stencils, painting & marking

(G-6554)
LIGHTHOUSE PRINTING LLC
315 Boston Post Rd Ste 3 (06475-1544)
P.O. Box 1158 (06475-5158)
PHONE..................................860 388-2677
Bill Dempsey, *Mng Member*
EMP: 4
SALES: 300K **Privately Held**
SIC: **2752** Commercial printing, lithographic

(G-6555)
MAHONEY MACHINE & FABRICATION
341 Boston Post Rd 2s (06475-1551)
PHONE..................................203 722-4771
John Mahoney, *Owner*
EMP: 1
SALES (est): 51.7K **Privately Held**
SIC: **3599** Machine shop, jobbing & repair

(G-6556)
METALPRO INC
50 School House Rd (06475-4029)
PHONE..................................860 388-1811
Thomas Wright, *President*
Elizabeth Wright, *Vice Pres*
EMP: 50
SQ FT: 45,000
SALES (est): 4.6MM **Privately Held**
SIC: **3599** Machine shop, jobbing & repair

(G-6557)
MJ MARTIN WOOD WORKING LLC
851 Middlesex Tpke (06475-1317)
PHONE..................................860 577-5311
EMP: 1
SALES (est): 79.4K **Privately Held**
SIC: **2434** Wood kitchen cabinets

(G-6558)
MOLDING TECHNOLOGIES LLC
304 Boston Post Rd Ste 1 (06475-1561)
PHONE..................................860 395-3230
William Stoner, *Owner*
EMP: 3
SQ FT: 5,000
SALES (est): 600K **Privately Held**
WEB: www.ttkbox.com
SIC: **3089** Injection molded finished plastic products; injection molding of plastics

(G-6559)
NEED FOR SPEED RACING
1383 Boston Post Rd 3 (06475-1700)
PHONE..................................860 388-1204
Robert Wilcox, *Owner*
EMP: 1 EST: 1992
SQ FT: 1,200
SALES (est): 320K **Privately Held**
SIC: **3751** Motorcycles, bicycles & parts

(G-6560)
NORTHEAST PUBLICATIONS LLC
5 Thompson Ln (06475-1630)
PHONE..................................860 399-4801
Philip H Thompson, *Manager*
Philip Thompson, *Manager*
EMP: 2
SALES (est): 128.5K **Privately Held**
SIC: **2741** Miscellaneous publishing

(G-6561)
NORTHSIDE MINIS LLC
27 Bellaire Dr (06475-2703)
PHONE..................................860 388-6871
Robert Preece, *Principal*
EMP: 2
SALES (est): 142.2K **Privately Held**
SIC: **3537** Trucks, tractors, loaders, carriers & similar equipment

(G-6562)
OCTAVO EDITIONS LLC
72 Ayers Point Rd (06475-4301)
PHONE..................................860 388-5772
Sean Konecky,
Sibylle Konecky,
EMP: 2
SALES (est): 100.9K **Privately Held**
SIC: **8748** 2731 Business consulting; book publishing

(G-6563)
PARAGON PRODUCTS INC
175 Elm St Ste 1 (06475-4109)
P.O. Box 747 (06475-0747)
PHONE..................................860 388-1363
John Schutz, *President*
John Contreras, *Executive*
EMP: 3
SQ FT: 5,000
SALES: 150K **Privately Held**
SIC: **3089** Injection molding of plastics

(G-6564)
PATHWAY LIGHTING PRODUCTS INC
Also Called: Pathway The Lighting Source
175 Elm St 5 (06475-4109)
P.O. Box 591 (06475-0591)
PHONE..................................860 388-6881
Frederick W Stark III, *President*
Jill Elizabeth Coan, *Corp Secy*
David Bradley, *Purch Mgr*
Johnna Maynard, *Purch Agent*
Kenton Baker, *Technical Mgr*
▲ EMP: 85
SALES (est): 12.7MM **Privately Held**
WEB: www.pathwaylighting.com
SIC: **3646** 3648 5063 Commercial indusl & institutional electric lighting fixtures; lighting equipment; electrical apparatus & equipment

(G-6565)
PAUL H GESSWEIN & COMPANY INC
40 River St (06475)
PHONE..................................860 388-0652
John Hoadley, *Manager*
EMP: 8

SALES (corp-wide): 593.1K **Privately Held**
SIC: **3281** Stone, quarrying & processing of own stone products
PA: Paul H. Gesswein & Company, Inc.
201 Hancock Ave
Bridgeport CT 06605
203 366-5400

(G-6566)
PINK FISH EMBROIDERY AND D
41 Great Hammock Rd (06475-2003)
PHONE..................................860 339-5083
Jennifer Kawecki, *Owner*
EMP: 1
SALES (est): 38.5K **Privately Held**
SIC: **2395** Embroidery & art needlework

(G-6567)
PRECISION SHTMTL FABRICATION
51 Donnelly Rd (06475-4101)
PHONE..................................860 388-4466
Steve Collier, *CFO*
EMP: 2
SALES (est): 198.4K **Privately Held**
SIC: **3444** Sheet metalwork

(G-6568)
PRIVATEER LTD
Also Called: Label One
5 Center Rd W (06475-4053)
PHONE..................................860 526-1837
Richard Wilczewski, *President*
Gregg Viebranz, *General Mgr*
EMP: 18
SQ FT: 10,000
SALES (est): 2.7MM **Privately Held**
WEB: www.privateerusa.com
SIC: **2759** Flexographic printing

(G-6569)
SOUND MANUFACTURING INC
1 Williams Ln (06475-4233)
PHONE..................................860 388-4466
Kelli Valleries, *CEO*
Marco Piacenti, *Production*
Laura Young, *Purch Mgr*
Glen Guidi, *Engineer*
Emily Rockwell, *Bookkeeper*
▲ EMP: 81
SALES (est): 16.6MM **Privately Held**
SIC: **3444** Sheet metalwork

(G-6570)
STAVOLA SIGNS
14 Riverside Ave (06475-1415)
PHONE..................................860 395-0897
John Stavola, *Owner*
EMP: 1
SALES (est): 51.1K **Privately Held**
SIC: **3993** Signs & advertising specialties

(G-6571)
STEVE CRYAN STUDIO
30 Howard St (06475-2429)
PHONE..................................860 388-5010
Steven Cryan, *Owner*
Lauren Cryan, *IT/INT Sup*
EMP: 1
SALES (est): 52.5K **Privately Held**
SIC: **3952** 8999 Water colors, artists'; artist

(G-6572)
TANTOR MEDIA INCORPORATED
6 Business Park Rd (06475-4238)
PHONE..................................860 395-1155
Kevin Colebank, *CEO*
Melanie Bodin, *Editor*
Kaitlin Johnstone, *Editor*
Amanda Currier, *Prdtn Mgr*
Hilary Eurich, *Production*
▼ EMP: 164
SALES (est): 18.3MM **Privately Held**
WEB: www.tantor.com
SIC: **2731** Books: publishing only; book music: publishing only, not printed on site
PA: Recorded Books, Inc.
270 Skipjack Rd
Prince Frederick MD 20678

Old Saybrook - Middlesex County (G-6573)

(G-6573)
TARGET CUSTOM MANUFACTURING CO
164 Old Boston Post Rd (06475-2230)
PHONE..................860 388-5848
Neil Gallagher, *President*
Christine Gallagher, *Vice Pres*
Vanessa Braig, *Admin Sec*
EMP: 9
SQ FT: 7,500
SALES (est): 1.1MM **Privately Held**
SIC: 3444 3469 Sheet metalwork; stamping metal for the trade

(G-6574)
VIGIRODA PRODUCTS LLC
6 Business Park Rd Ste 2 (06475-4238)
PHONE..................860 391-8457
James J Mokoski, *Branch Mgr*
EMP: 1 **Privately Held**
SIC: 3631 Barbecues, grills & braziers (outdoor cooking)
PA: Vigiroda Products, Llc
  38c New Britain Ave
  Rocky Hill CT

(G-6575)
VIJON STUDIOS INC
97a Spencer Plain Rd (06475-4001)
PHONE..................860 399-7440
Vincent F Yannone, *President*
EMP: 3
SALES (est): 184K **Privately Held**
SIC: 2515 Studio couches

(G-6576)
VIJON STUDIOS INC
Also Called: Vijon Stdios Stined GL Sup Ctr
97 Spencer Plain Rd Ste A (06475-4001)
PHONE..................860 399-7440
Vincent Yannone, *President*
EMP: 3
SALES: 150K **Privately Held**
SIC: 3231 5719 5231 5961 Stained glass; made from purchased glass; lamps & lamp shades; glass, leaded or stained; collectibles & antiques, mail order

(G-6577)
VITA PASTA INC
225 Elm St (06475-4135)
P.O. Box 523 (06475-0523)
PHONE..................860 395-1452
Richard Cersosimo, *President*
Luis A Castanho, *Vice Pres*
EMP: 7
SQ FT: 3,000
SALES (est): 400K **Privately Held**
WEB: www.nottapasta.com
SIC: 2099 5149 Pasta, uncooked: packaged with other ingredients; pasta & rice

Orange
New Haven County

(G-6578)
ACE SERVICING CO INC
340 Edward Ct (06477-2526)
PHONE..................203 795-1400
Christopher Prisco, *Principal*
EMP: 3 EST: 2016
SALES (est): 108.8K **Privately Held**
SIC: 1389 Roustabout service

(G-6579)
ADVANCED DECISIONS INC
350 Woodland Ln (06477-3038)
PHONE..................203 402-0603
Michael R Landino, *President*
Gary Felberbaum, *Treasurer*
EMP: 16
SALES (est): 1MM **Privately Held**
WEB: www.advanceddecisions.com
SIC: 7372 7379 Application computer software; computer hardware requirements analysis

(G-6580)
ALVAREZ INDUSTRIES LLC
312 Boston Post Rd (06477-3505)
P.O. Box 964 (06477-0964)
PHONE..................203 799-2356
Lenny Alvarez, *Branch Mgr*
EMP: 1
SALES (corp-wide): 262.6K **Privately Held**
SIC: 3499 Metal household articles
PA: Alvarez Industries Llc
  26 Brownell St Fl 3
  New Haven CT 06511
  203 401-1152

(G-6581)
AMERICAN SEAL AND ENGRG CO INC (DH)
Also Called: Ase
295 Indian River Rd (06477-3609)
PHONE..................203 789-8819
Thomas Kinisky, *President*
Joseph Kedues, *Vice Pres*
Todd Stockwell, *Engineer*
Terri Doughty, *Sales Staff*
Joe Kedves, *Sales Executive*
EMP: 40
SQ FT: 30,000
SALES: 5.3MM
SALES (corp-wide): 215.9MM **Privately Held**
WEB: www.ameriseal.com
SIC: 3053 Gaskets & sealing devices; gaskets, all materials

(G-6582)
ANH REFRACTORIES
55 Connair Rd (06477-3601)
PHONE..................203 795-0597
George Nassra, *Principal*
EMP: 2
SALES (est): 131.7K **Privately Held**
SIC: 3714 Rebuilding engines & transmissions, factory basis

(G-6583)
ARPIE KRISIE GEMS & JEWELRY
438 Taulman Rd (06477-3016)
P.O. Box 897 (06477-0897)
PHONE..................203 799-8927
Kriko Chaghatzbanian, *Owner*
EMP: 2
SALES (est): 124.3K **Privately Held**
SIC: 3911 7631 Jewelry, precious metal; jewelry repair services

(G-6584)
ATECH INDUSTRIES LLC
879 Robert Treat Ext (06477-1649)
PHONE..................203 887-4900
Michael Micheli, *Principal*
EMP: 6 EST: 2016
SALES (est): 458.9K **Privately Held**
SIC: 3999 Manufacturing industries

(G-6585)
BERNIES TOOL & FASTENER SVCS
269 S Lambert Rd (06477-3502)
PHONE..................203 466-5252
EMP: 2
SALES (est): 111.6K **Privately Held**
SIC: 3965 Fasteners

(G-6586)
BIMBO BAKERIES USA INC
Also Called: Best Foods Baking Co. Now.
284 Bull Hill Ln (06477-3211)
PHONE..................203 932-1000
John Payne, *Manager*
EMP: 58 **Privately Held**
WEB: www.englishmuffin.com
SIC: 2051 2052 Cakes, bakery: except frozen; pies, bakery: except frozen; cookies
HQ: Bimbo Bakeries Usa, Inc
  255 Business Center Dr # 200
  Horsham PA 19044
  215 347-5500

(G-6587)
BUTLER IRRIGATION
85 Grannis Rd (06477-1911)
PHONE..................203 877-2248
Greg Butler, *Owner*
EMP: 1
SALES (est): 114.1K **Privately Held**
SIC: 3432 Lawn hose nozzles & sprinklers

(G-6588)
BUTLER PROPERTY SVC
85 Grannis Rd (06477-1911)
PHONE..................203 530-4554
Greg Butler, *Owner*
EMP: 2 EST: 2017
SALES (est): 80.8K **Privately Held**
SIC: 3432 Plumbing fixture fittings & trim

(G-6589)
CBD101 LLC
284 Racebrook Rd (06477-3103)
PHONE..................203 273-9941
Thomas P Macre, *Manager*
EMP: 1
SALES (est): 39.6K **Privately Held**
SIC: 3999

(G-6590)
CEE ORANGE LLC
Also Called: Chef's Equipment
449 Boston Post Rd (06477-3509)
PHONE..................203 799-2665
Barbara Demartino, *Mng Member*
Michelle Demartino, *Mng Member*
EMP: 2
SALES (est): 375.4K **Privately Held**
SIC: 3469 Household cooking & kitchen utensils, metal; household cooking & kitchen utensils, porcelain enameled

(G-6591)
CHRIS & ZACK GOURMET FOODS
383 Boston Post Rd (06477)
PHONE..................203 912-7805
Nick Jhilal, *President*
EMP: 2 EST: 2010
SALES (est): 72.5K **Privately Held**
SIC: 2013 2053 Sausages & other prepared meats; cakes, bakery: frozen

(G-6592)
CHRIS & ZACK LLC
385 Boston Post Rd (06477-3507)
PHONE..................203 298-0742
Kam Jhilal, *Principal*
EMP: 3
SALES (est): 167.5K **Privately Held**
SIC: 2015 2022 Poultry slaughtering & processing; cheese, natural & processed

(G-6593)
CTI INDUSTRIES INC (HQ)
283 Indian River Rd (06477-3609)
PHONE..................203 795-0070
Perry Tallman, *President*
Jake Bajko, *Treasurer*
Peter Mace Tallman, *Admin Sec*
▲ EMP: 25
SQ FT: 22,000
SALES: 6.1MM
SALES (corp-wide): 21MM **Privately Held**
SIC: 3443 Fabricated plate work (boiler shop)
PA: Rocore Thermal Systems, Llc
  2401 Directors Row Ste R
  Indianapolis IN 46241
  317 227-2929

(G-6594)
CYRO INDUSTRIES
25 Executive Blvd 1 (06477-3659)
P.O. Box 425, Wallingford (06492-7050)
PHONE..................203 269-4481
Fax: 203 795-5800
EMP: 8 EST: 2007
SALES (est): 430K **Privately Held**
SIC: 3999 Mfg Misc Products

(G-6595)
DATAPREP INC
109 Boston Post Rd Ste 2 (06477-3235)
PHONE..................203 795-2095
Fax: 203 795-2096
EMP: 30
SQ FT: 1,500
SALES (corp-wide): 5.2MM **Privately Held**
SIC: 7372 7374 7371 Prepackaged Software Services Data Processing/Preparation Custom Computer Programing
PA: Dataprep Inc
  97 South St Ste 105
  West Hartford CT 06611
  860 728-5224

(G-6596)
DESIGN & PRINT INTERESTS LLC
719 Derby Ave (06477-1007)
PHONE..................203 494-9072
Lorraine Bellico, *Principal*
EMP: 2 EST: 2016
SALES (est): 83.9K **Privately Held**
SIC: 2752 Commercial printing, lithographic

(G-6597)
DOONEY & BOURKE
22 Marsh Hill Rd (06477-3611)
PHONE..................203 795-3131
Brain McCade, *Manager*
EMP: 1 EST: 2018
SALES (est): 49.1K **Privately Held**
SIC: 3171 Women's handbags & purses

(G-6598)
EMERSON ELECTRIC CO
58 Robinson Blvd Ste C (06477-3647)
PHONE..................203 891-1080
George Stuckey, *Manager*
EMP: 1
SALES (corp-wide): 17.4B **Publicly Held**
WEB: www.gotoemerson.com
SIC: 3823 Industrial instrmnts msrmnt display/control process variable
PA: Emerson Electric Co.
  8000 West Florissant Ave
  Saint Louis MO 63136
  314 553-2000

(G-6599)
EXPRESS CNTERTOPS KIT FLRG LLC
303 Boston Post Rd (06477-3520)
PHONE..................203 283-4909
Roger Mehta, *Branch Mgr*
EMP: 3
SALES (corp-wide): 5.2MM **Privately Held**
SIC: 3263 Kitchen articles, semivitreous earthenware
PA: Express Countertops, Kitchen & Flooring, Llc
  231 Weston St
  Hartford CT 06120
  860 247-1000

(G-6600)
F & W RENTALS INC
164 Boston Post Rd (06477-3234)
PHONE..................203 795-0591
Harold R Funk, *President*
Jenn Kellogg, *Parts Mgr*
EMP: 15
SQ FT: 15,000
SALES (est): 1.2MM **Privately Held**
SIC: 7692 5084 Welding repair; industrial machine parts

(G-6601)
FEDEX OFFICE & PRINT SVCS INC
400 Boston Post Rd Ste 1 (06477-3545)
PHONE..................203 799-2679
EMP: 17
SALES (corp-wide): 69.6B **Publicly Held**
WEB: www.kinkos.com
SIC: 7334 5943 2789 Photocopying & duplicating services; stationery stores; bookbinding & related work
HQ: Fedex Office And Print Services, Inc.
  7900 Legacy Dr
  Plano TX 75024
  800 463-3339

(G-6602)
FOX STEEL PRODUCTS LLC
312 Boston Post Rd (06477-3505)
P.O. Box 592 (06477-0592)
PHONE..................203 799-2356
Peter Cosentino, *Mng Member*
Jon Lundberg,
EMP: 10
SQ FT: 6,500

SALES (est): 1.9MM **Privately Held**
WEB: www.foxsteel.com
SIC: 5051 3441 Bars, metal; fabricated structural metal

(G-6603)
FOX STEEL SERVICES LLC
312 Boston Post Rd (06477-3505)
PHONE 203 799-2356
Peter Cosentino,
EMP: 2
SALES (est): 214K **Privately Held**
SIC: 5051 3441 Bars, metal; fabricated structural metal

(G-6604)
GAMERS THAT LIFT LLC
530 Ridge Rd (06477-2853)
PHONE 203 988-9211
Bryce Glassberg,
EMP: 1
SALES (est): 29.2K **Privately Held**
SIC: 7371 7372 Computer software development & applications; application computer software

(G-6605)
K&P WEAVER LLC
527 Carriage Dr (06477-2917)
PHONE 203 795-9024
Paula Weaver, *Mng Member*
Ken Weaver,
▲ **EMP:** 2
SALES (est): 220K **Privately Held**
SIC: 2329 2395 Baseball uniforms: men's, youths' & boys'; decorative & novelty stitching, for the trade

(G-6606)
KCO NUMET INC (PA)
235 Edison Rd (06477-3603)
PHONE 203 375-4995
Mark Roscio, *CEO*
Andrew Gale, *CEO*
Joseph Sartori, *COO*
Antonio Neto, *Vice Pres*
Scott Kokosa, *CFO*
EMP: 15
SQ FT: 40,000
SALES (est): 9MM **Privately Held**
SIC: 3519 6719 Jet propulsion engines; investment holding companies, except banks

(G-6607)
KEEPSAKE EMBROIDERY
46 Sunset Dr (06477-3013)
P.O. Box 809 (06477-0809)
PHONE 203 503-1725
EMP: 1
SALES (est): 54.1K **Privately Held**
SIC: 2395 Embroidery & art needlework

(G-6608)
KI INC
342 Cedarwood Dr (06477-1665)
PHONE 203 641-5492
Rondi D'Agostino, *President*
Anna Pinvoices, *Manager*
▲ **EMP:** 20
SALES (est): 1.3MM **Privately Held**
SIC: 3651 Amplifiers: radio, public address or musical instrument

(G-6609)
KRELL INDUSTRIES LLC
45 Connair Rd Ste 1 (06477-3681)
PHONE 203 298-4000
Rondi D'Agostino, *Mng Member*
EMP: 16
SQ FT: 10,000
SALES (est): 1.2MM **Privately Held**
SIC: 3651 Amplifiers: radio, public address or musical instrument

(G-6610)
LCD LIGHTING INC
Also Called: Voltarc
37 Robinson Blvd (06477-3623)
P.O. Box 948 (06477-0948)
PHONE 203 799-7877
Christian L Sauska, *CEO*
Bruce Kingsley, *Chief*
Susan Rocchio, *Human Res Dir*
Karl Platzer, *Sales Staff*
Graham Foster, *Manager*

▲ **EMP:** 110
SQ FT: 75,000
SALES (est): 21.3MM **Privately Held**
WEB: www.lcdl.com
SIC: 3641 3646 Electric lamps & parts for generalized applications; commercial indusl & institutional electric lighting fixtures

(G-6611)
LIGHT SOURCES INC (PA)
Also Called: L S I
37 Robinson Blvd (06477-3623)
P.O. Box 948 (06477-0948)
PHONE 203 799-7877
Christian Sauska, *President*
Arpad Pirovic, *Vice Pres*
Ula Kret, *Purchasing*
Anrui Zhu, *Electrical Engi*
Mohamed Maklad, *VP Finance*
▲ **EMP:** 129
SQ FT: 150,000
SALES (est): 37.4MM **Privately Held**
WEB: www.light-sources.com
SIC: 3641 Ultraviolet lamps; lamps, fluorescent, electric

(G-6612)
MARENNA AMUSEMENTS LLC
88 Marsh Hill Rd (06477-3625)
P.O. Box 788 (06477-0788)
PHONE 203 623-4386
George J Marenna Jr,
EMP: 10
SALES: 333K **Privately Held**
SIC: 3599 Carnival machines & equipment, amusement park

(G-6613)
MCWEENEY MARKETING GROUP INC
53 Robinson Blvd (06477-3623)
P.O. Box 989 (06477-0989)
PHONE 203 891-8100
George E McWeeney Jr, *President*
John Kelly, *Vice Pres*
George Mc Weeney, *Manager*
EMP: 9
SQ FT: 3,000
SALES (est): 966.6K **Privately Held**
WEB: www.mcweeneymarketing.com
SIC: 2759 5199 Commercial printing; advertising specialties

(G-6614)
NATURES FIRST INC (PA)
58 Robinson Blvd Ste C (06477-3647)
PHONE 203 795-8400
Harjit Singh, *President*
▼ **EMP:** 8
SQ FT: 12,000
SALES (est): 1MM **Privately Held**
WEB: www.naturesfirst.com
SIC: 2023 Dietary supplements, dairy & non-dairy based

(G-6615)
NAUTIGIRL MARINE CANVAS
598 High Ridge Rd (06477-1529)
PHONE 203 891-8558
Barbara Dolan-Lewis, *Principal*
EMP: 1 **EST:** 2015
SALES (est): 72.6K **Privately Held**
SIC: 2211 Canvas

(G-6616)
NOHHA INC
109 Cummings Dr (06477-1907)
PHONE 203 687-6741
EMP: 2
SALES (est): 137.5K **Privately Held**
SIC: 2499 Trophy bases, wood

(G-6617)
NORTH HAVEN EQP & LSG LLC
212 Argyle Rd (06477-2914)
P.O. Box 943 (06477-0943)
PHONE 203 795-9494
John Pritchard, *Manager*
EMP: 4 **EST:** 2001
SALES (est): 100K **Privately Held**
SIC: 3569 General industrial machinery

(G-6618)
NUMET MACHINING TECHNIQUES INC
235 Edison Rd (06477-3603)
PHONE 203 375-4995
Andrew Gale, *CEO*
Scott Kokosa, *CFO*
▲ **EMP:** 32
SQ FT: 40,000
SALES (est): 9MM **Privately Held**
WEB: www.numetmachining.com
SIC: 3724 Aircraft engines & engine parts
PA: Kco Numet, Inc.
  235 Edison Rd
  Orange CT 06477
  203 375-4995

(G-6619)
ORANGE CHEESE COMPANY
5 Hampton Close (06477-1934)
PHONE 917 603-4378
Hangyu Liu, *Principal*
EMP: 4
SALES (est): 191.7K **Privately Held**
SIC: 2022 2038 Natural cheese; cheese spreads, dips, pastes & other cheese products; processed cheese; spreads, cheese; snacks, including onion rings, cheese sticks, etc.

(G-6620)
ORANGE DEMOCRAT
297 Boston Post Rd (06477-3537)
PHONE 203 298-4575
EMP: 3 **EST:** 2009
SALES (est): 102.5K **Privately Held**
SIC: 2711 Newspapers, publishing & printing

(G-6621)
OWL KING PUBLISHING LLC
119 Kennedy Dr (06477-2631)
PHONE 203 530-6846
Ethan Rappaport, *Principal*
EMP: 2
SALES (est): 121.8K **Privately Held**
SIC: 2741 Miscellaneous publishing

(G-6622)
PEZ CANDY INC (HQ)
35 Prindle Hill Rd (06477-3616)
PHONE 203 795-0531
Christian Jegen, *CEO*
Steve Rowe, *Plant Mgr*
Brian Fry, *CFO*
Jeanine Santana, *Accounting Mgr*
Randy Duncan, *Sales Staff*
▲ **EMP:** 61 **EST:** 1953
SALES (est): 25.3MM
SALES (corp-wide): 355.8K **Privately Held**
WEB: www.pezcandyinc.com
SIC: 2064 Candy & other confectionery products
PA: Pez Inter Holding Ag
  C/O Globaltax Gmbh
  ZUrich ZH
  432 550-816

(G-6623)
PEZ MANUFACTURING CORP
35 Prindle Hill Rd (06477-3616)
PHONE 203 795-0531
Christian Jegen, *CEO*
Brian Fry, *CFO*
Peter Graf, *Admin Sec*
▲ **EMP:** 100 **EST:** 1973
SQ FT: 50,000
SALES (est): 14.3MM
SALES (corp-wide): 355.8K **Privately Held**
SIC: 2064 Candy & other confectionery products
HQ: Pez Candy, Inc.
  35 Prindle Hill Rd
  Orange CT 06477
  203 795-0531

(G-6624)
PIERCE-CORRELL CORPORATION
168 Christian Cir (06477-3023)
PHONE 203 799-1208
Charles Correll Jr, *President*
EMP: 2 **EST:** 1976

SQ FT: 6,500
SALES (est): 180K **Privately Held**
SIC: 3429 3537 Motor vehicle hardware; industrial trucks & tractors

(G-6625)
RESAVUE INC
Also Called: Resavue Exhibits
48 Grannis Rd (06477-1908)
PHONE 203 878-0944
John B Kelman, *CEO*
Christine Kelman, *Admin Sec*
◆ **EMP:** 10
SALES (est): 2.2MM **Privately Held**
WEB: www.resavue.com
SIC: 3577 7319 Graphic displays, except graphic terminals; display advertising service

(G-6626)
ROEBIC LABORATORIES INC (PA)
Also Called: Roetech
25 Connair Rd (06477-3601)
P.O. Box 927 (06477-0927)
PHONE 203 795-1283
Stuart J Bush, *CEO*
Derek J Bush, *President*
Hedy S Bush, *COO*
John Peters, *COO*
Steven Smith, *Vice Pres*
EMP: 5 **EST:** 1959
SQ FT: 30,000
SALES (est): 4MM **Privately Held**
WEB: www.roebic.com
SIC: 2842 Sanitation preparations

(G-6627)
SABOL INDUSTRIES LLC
349 W River Rd (06477-2741)
PHONE 203 430-6502
Frank W Sabol Jr, *Principal*
EMP: 2
SALES (est): 127.1K **Privately Held**
SIC: 3999 Manufacturing industries

(G-6628)
SALLY CONANT
Also Called: Orange Restoration Labs
454 Old Cellar Rd (06477-3707)
PHONE 203 878-3005
Sally Conant, *President*
EMP: 12
SALES (est): 78.8K **Privately Held**
WEB: www.gownrestoration.com
SIC: 2221 7212 7211 Apparel & outerwear fabric, manmade fiber or silk; garment pressing & cleaners' agents; power laundries, family & commercial

(G-6629)
SIGN A RAMA
Also Called: Sign-A-Rama
553 Boston Post Rd (06477-3331)
PHONE 203 795-5450
Barbara Metzger, *Partner*
David Metzger, *Mng Member*
EMP: 5
SALES (est): 368K **Privately Held**
SIC: 3993 Signs & advertising specialties

(G-6630)
SZOSTEK CUSTOM WOODWORKING LLC
366 Coachmans Ln (06477-2805)
PHONE 203 891-9127
Michael Szostek, *Principal*
EMP: 1 **EST:** 2010
SALES (est): 65.2K **Privately Held**
SIC: 2431 Millwork

(G-6631)
TOMTEC
607 Harborview Rd (06477-2031)
PHONE 203 795-5030
Fax: 203 248-5724
EMP: 3 **EST:** 2010
SALES (est): 259K **Privately Held**
SIC: 3841 Mfg Surgical/Medical Instruments

Orange - New Haven County

(G-6632)
VALLEY TOOL AND MFG LLC
22 Prindle Hill Rd (06477-3615)
P.O. Box 564 (06477-0564)
PHONE..................203 799-8800
Phillip C Freidman, *CEO*
Howard Turner, *President*
Cheryl Darin, *Senior Buyer*
Kathy Swoszowski, *Senior Buyer*
Kurt Maurer, *CFO*
EMP: 72 EST: 2017
SQ FT: 36,000
SALES: 12MM
SALES (corp-wide): 118.6MM **Privately Held**
SIC: 3728 Aircraft parts & equipment
PA: Harlow Aerostructures Llc
   1501 S Mclean Blvd
   Wichita KS 67213
   316 265-5268

(G-6633)
VITALE WOODWORKS LLC
842 Alling Rd (06477-1351)
PHONE..................203 387-3565
Philip Vitale, *Principal*
EMP: 1 EST: 2015
SALES (est): 55.1K **Privately Held**
SIC: 2499 Wood products

(G-6634)
WIRE DESIGN ORIGINALS
985 Garden Rd (06477-1014)
P.O. Box 1004 (06477-7004)
PHONE..................203 795-3783
Carol Bejnerowicz, *Owner*
EMP: 1 EST: 1999
SALES (est): 85.5K **Privately Held**
SIC: 3496 Miscellaneous fabricated wire products

(G-6635)
WOODBRIDGE TOWN NEWS
653 Orange Center Rd (06477-2400)
PHONE..................203 298-4399
EMP: 4
SALES (est): 157.1K **Privately Held**
SIC: 2711 Newspapers, publishing & printing

(G-6636)
WORK N GEAR LLC
Also Called: Work 'n Gear 8061
440 Boston Post Rd Ste A (06477-3538)
PHONE..................203 795-8998
Tamara Metatos, *Manager*
EMP: 5
SALES (corp-wide): 46.1MM **Privately Held**
WEB: www.workngear.com
SIC: 5699 2759 Uniforms; screen printing
PA: Work 'n Gear, Llc
   2300 Crown Colony Dr # 301
   Quincy MA 02169
   781 746-0100

Oxford
New Haven County

(G-6637)
ADVANCED BUSINESS GROUP
14 Douglas Rd (06478-1123)
PHONE..................203 881-9660
John Zybort, *Owner*
Maribeth Zybort, *Vice Pres*
EMP: 2
SALES (est): 150K **Privately Held**
SIC: 5734 3825 Computer & software stores; network analyzers

(G-6638)
ADVANCED MACHINE SERVICES LLC
55 Old State Rd (06478-1967)
PHONE..................203 888-6600
Christopher G Mackenzie, *Branch Mgr*
EMP: 2 **Privately Held**
SIC: 3552 5169 Spindles, textile; silicon lubricants
PA: Advanced Machine Services Llc
   2056 Thomaston Ave
   Waterbury CT 06704

(G-6639)
ADVANCED SONICS LLC
Also Called: Advanced Sonic Proc Systems
324 Christian St (06478-1023)
PHONE..................203 266-4440
David Hunicke, *Mng Member*
EMP: 7
SQ FT: 17,500
SALES (est): 1.3MM **Privately Held**
WEB: www.advancedsonics.com
SIC: 3629 7379 Electronic generation equipment; data processing consultant

(G-6640)
AEROTURN LLC
115 Hurley Rd Ste 2c (06478-1047)
PHONE..................203 262-8309
Robert R Hellman Jr,
EMP: 6
SALES (est): 998.2K **Privately Held**
WEB: www.aeroturn.com
SIC: 3699 Security devices

(G-6641)
ALL POWER MANUFACTURING CO (HQ)
1 Tribiology Ctr (06478-1035)
PHONE..................562 802-2640
Michael J Hartnett, *CEO*
▲ EMP: 130
SQ FT: 40,000
SALES (est): 22.1MM
SALES (corp-wide): 702.5MM **Publicly Held**
WEB: www.allpowermfg.com
SIC: 3728 2899 Aircraft assemblies, sub-assemblies & parts; chemical preparations
PA: Rbc Bearings Incorporated
   102 Willenbrock Rd
   Oxford CT 06478
   203 267-7001

(G-6642)
ALTERIO TRACTOR PULLING LLC
37 Cold Spring Dr (06478-1903)
PHONE..................203 305-9812
Matthew Alterio, *Principal*
EMP: 5
SALES (est): 310.7K **Privately Held**
SIC: 1389 Construction, repair & dismantling services

(G-6643)
APTEX CORP
6 Benson Rd (06478-1000)
PHONE..................203 743-6412
Ian Glen, *Principal*
EMP: 2
SALES (est): 80.3K **Privately Held**
SIC: 2899 Chemical preparations

(G-6644)
AUTOMATION CONTROLS
127 Hogs Back Rd (06478-1364)
PHONE..................203 888-9330
Rudy Danowski, *Owner*
EMP: 1
SALES (est): 85.7K **Privately Held**
SIC: 3625 Relays & industrial controls

(G-6645)
BALFOR INDUSTRIES INC
327 Riggs St (06478-1129)
PHONE..................203 828-6473
Richard Ballot, *President*
Felice Ballot, *Manager*
EMP: 15 EST: 1955
SQ FT: 17,500
SALES (est): 4.4MM **Privately Held**
WEB: www.cmail.cz
SIC: 3089 Molding primary plastic

(G-6646)
BOTANICAL ORIGINS LLC
341 Christian St (06478-1023)
PHONE..................203 267-6061
Devjani Mitra, *Principal*
EMP: 1
SALES (est): 83.2K **Privately Held**
SIC: 2833 Botanical products, medicinal: ground, graded or milled

(G-6647)
BRIGHTON & HOVE MOLD LTD
115 Hurley Rd Ste 2c (06478-1047)
PHONE..................203 264-3013
Robert Hellman Jr, *President*
Michael A Stoll, *CFO*
EMP: 6
SQ FT: 6,000
SALES (est): 805.9K **Privately Held**
SIC: 3089 5162 Injection molded finished plastic products; plastics products

(G-6648)
CAST GLOBAL MANUFACTURING CORP
Also Called: Met-Craft
66 Prokop Rd (06478-1107)
PHONE..................203 828-6147
Chung Hsuen Hu, *President*
EMP: 11
SALES (est): 1.4MM **Privately Held**
SIC: 3452 Bolts, nuts, rivets & washers

(G-6649)
CATACHEM INC
353 Christian St Ste 2 (06478-1053)
PHONE..................203 262-0330
Luis P Leon, *President*
David Templeton, *COO*
Angelo Guerrera, *Technician*
▲ EMP: 7
SQ FT: 3,500
SALES (est): 500K **Privately Held**
SIC: 3841 Diagnostic apparatus, medical

(G-6650)
CD RACING PRODUCTS
91 Willenbrock Rd Ste B3 (06478-1036)
PHONE..................203 264-7822
Michael Paquette, *Owner*
EMP: 3
SALES (est): 303.8K **Privately Held**
SIC: 3711 Motor vehicles & car bodies

(G-6651)
CHASSIS DYNAMICS INC
91 Willenbrock Rd Ste A1 (06478-1036)
PHONE..................203 262-6272
Robert Cuneo, *President*
EMP: 3 EST: 1974
SQ FT: 3,800
SALES (est): 220K **Privately Held**
SIC: 3711 Chassis, motor vehicle

(G-6652)
COLORGRAPHIX LLC
91 Willenbrock Rd Ste B5 (06478-1036)
P.O. Box 545, Southbury (06488-0545)
PHONE..................203 264-5212
Jeff Jones, *Mng Member*
EMP: 8
SQ FT: 4,500
SALES (est): 1MM **Privately Held**
WEB: www.colorgraphix.com
SIC: 2759 Screen printing

(G-6653)
CONSULTING ENGRG DEV SVCS INC
Also Called: C E D
3 Fox Hollow Rd (06478-3162)
PHONE..................203 828-6528
Steven G Meyer, *President*
Lisa Brayall, *QC Mgr*
David Keckley, *Info Tech Mgr*
Christopher Defusco, *Technology*
EMP: 55
SQ FT: 20,000
SALES (est): 15MM **Privately Held**
WEB: www.cedservicesinc.com
SIC: 3599 3469 Machine shop, jobbing & repair; machine parts, stamped or pressed metal

(G-6654)
COUNTRY SOAP SAMPLERS
156 Punkup Rd (06478-1750)
PHONE..................203 881-1986
Dawn Sotir, *Owner*
EMP: 1
SALES (est): 48.8K **Privately Held**
SIC: 2841 Soap & other detergents

(G-6655)
DEWEY J MANUFACTURING COMPANY
112 Willenbrock Rd (06478-1031)
PHONE..................203 264-3064
George Dewey, *President*
Brian Dewey, *Vice Pres*
EMP: 6
SQ FT: 2,500
SALES (est): 460K **Privately Held**
WEB: www.deweyrods.com
SIC: 3484 3949 Shotguns or shotgun parts, 30 mm. & below; sporting & athletic goods

(G-6656)
DIGITALDRUKER INC
Also Called: AlphaGraphics
11 Old Farm Rd (06478-1704)
PHONE..................203 888-6001
Robert J Talbot, *President*
Robert Talbot, *Principal*
EMP: 2
SALES (est): 189.8K **Privately Held**
SIC: 2752 Commercial printing, lithographic

(G-6657)
ENVAX PRODUCTS INC
349 Christian St (06478-1023)
PHONE..................203 264-8181
Michael Tarby, *President*
EMP: 3
SQ FT: 2,000
SALES (est): 542.5K **Privately Held**
SIC: 3567 Vacuum furnaces & ovens

(G-6658)
FLIGHT ENHANCEMENTS CORP
47 Oakcrest Rd (06478-1247)
PHONE..................912 257-0440
Robert Steven Takacs, *CEO*
EMP: 3
SALES (est): 179K **Privately Held**
SIC: 3728 Aircraft parts & equipment

(G-6659)
FRYER CORPORATION
43 Old State Road 67 (06478-1978)
P.O. Box 565 (06478-0565)
PHONE..................203 888-9944
Tracy Fryer, *President*
George Fryer, *Admin Sec*
EMP: 5 EST: 1952
SQ FT: 5,500
SALES (est): 500K **Privately Held**
SIC: 3599 Custom machinery

(G-6660)
GEN-EL-MEC ASSOCIATES INC
2 Fox Hollow Rd (06478-3161)
PHONE..................203 828-6566
Dean Contaxis, *President*
Theresa Contaxis, *Corp Secy*
Tom Villano, *Vice Pres*
EMP: 24 EST: 1961
SQ FT: 30,000
SALES (est): 4.4MM **Privately Held**
SIC: 3599 Machine shop, jobbing & repair

(G-6661)
GENERAL DATACOMM INC (HQ)
353 Christian St Ste 4 (06478-1053)
PHONE..................203 729-0271
Howard S Modlin, *President*
George Gray, *Vice Pres*
Jeff Turner, *Opers Staff*
Joe Autem, *CFO*
William G Henry, *CFO*
◆ EMP: 50
SQ FT: 360,000
SALES (est): 7.5MM
SALES (corp-wide): 12.9MM **Publicly Held**
SIC: 3661 1731 7629 Telephones & telephone apparatus; communications specialization; telecommunication equipment repair (except telephones)
PA: General Datacomm Industries, Inc.
   353 Christian St Ste 4
   Oxford CT 06478
   203 729-0271

▲ = Import ▼=Export
◆ =Import/Export

GEOGRAPHIC SECTION
Oxford - New Haven County (G-6693)

(G-6662)
GENERAL DATACOMM INDS INC (PA)
353 Christian St Ste 4 (06478-1053)
PHONE.....................203 729-0271
Howard S Modlin, *Ch of Bd*
George M Gray, *Vice Pres*
Mark Preston, *Engineer*
William G Henry, *CFO*
EMP: 25 **EST:** 1969
SQ FT: 360,000
SALES (est): 12.9MM **Publicly Held**
WEB: www.gdc.com
SIC: 3661 Multiplex equipment, telephone & telegraph

(G-6663)
GRAND EMBROIDERY INC
Also Called: Grand Imprints
225 Christian St (06478-1252)
PHONE.....................203 888-7484
Joseph Grandieri, *President*
Patricia Grandieri, *Vice Pres*
EMP: 11
SQ FT: 6,300
SALES (est): 838.3K **Privately Held**
WEB: www.grandembroidery.com
SIC: 2395 2269 Embroidery & art needlework; finishing plants

(G-6664)
HART TOOL & ENGINEERING
339 Christian St (06478-1023)
PHONE.....................203 264-9776
Gilbert Hart, *Owner*
EMP: 7 **EST:** 1975
SQ FT: 2,500
SALES (est): 811.3K **Privately Held**
SIC: 3545 Precision tools, machinists'

(G-6665)
HUSKY FUEL
62 Larkey Rd (06478-3149)
PHONE.....................203 783-0783
Robert James Hofmiller, *Principal*
EMP: 3
SALES (est): 88.3K **Privately Held**
SIC: 2869 Fuels

(G-6666)
HYDROTEC INC
115 Hurley Rd Ste 7a (06478-1037)
PHONE.....................203 264-6700
Kjell D Oloffsson, *President*
EMP: 5
SQ FT: 5,000
SALES (est): 1.3MM **Privately Held**
WEB: www.hydrotec-inc.com
SIC: 3621 Motors & generators

(G-6667)
INDUSTRIAL SENSOR VISION INTER
3 Morse Rd Ste 2a (06478-1059)
PHONE.....................203 592-8723
Brian D'Amico, *President*
EMP: 2
SALES (est): 124.3K **Privately Held**
SIC: 3861 Stands, camera & projector

(G-6668)
INSTANT REPLAY
83 Hawley Rd (06478-1017)
PHONE.....................203 264-1177
Mickey Weinstein, *Principal*
EMP: 2
SALES (est): 161K **Privately Held**
SIC: 2752 Commercial printing, lithographic

(G-6669)
IRON OXEN NETWORK COMM
51 Old Good Hill Rd (06478-1508)
PHONE.....................203 228-2556
John Seymour,
EMP: 2
SALES (est): 109.6K **Privately Held**
SIC: 1011 Iron ores

(G-6670)
JARDEN CORPORATION
288 Christian St Ste 11 (06478-1038)
PHONE.....................203 264-9717
EMP: 3

SALES (est): 180.3K **Privately Held**
SIC: 3089 Mfg Plastic Products

(G-6671)
KENNETH LYNCH & SONS INC
114 Willenbrock Rd (06478-1031)
PHONE.....................203 762-8363
Melody Sonntag, *Sales Mgr*
Timothy A Lynch, *Manager*
▲ **EMP:** 9 **EST:** 1946
SQ FT: 30,000
SALES (est): 1.4MM **Privately Held**
WEB: www.klynchandsons.com
SIC: 3446 3281 Architectural metalwork; stone, quarrying & processing of own stone products

(G-6672)
LEAD DOG PRODUCTION
235 Freeman Rd (06478-1783)
PHONE.....................203 732-4566
Wendy Cook, *Owner*
EMP: 2
SALES (est): 59.6K **Privately Held**
WEB: www.leaddogproductions.com
SIC: 2741 Music book & sheet music publishing

(G-6673)
LEWIS R MARTINO
328 Oxford Rd (06478-1617)
PHONE.....................203 463-4430
Lewis R Martino, *Principal*
EMP: 4
SALES (est): 189.5K **Privately Held**
SIC: 3433 Heating equipment, except electric

(G-6674)
MACTON CORPORATION
116 Willenbrock Rd (06478-1031)
PHONE.....................203 267-1500
Peter McGonagle, *President*
Steve Schumacher, *Vice Pres*
John C Shepherd, *Vice Pres*
Paul Spicer, *Vice Pres*
Thomas E Young Sr, *Vice Pres*
▼ **EMP:** 60
SQ FT: 27,000
SALES (est): 20MM **Privately Held**
WEB: www.macton.com
SIC: 3537 Industrial trucks & tractors

(G-6675)
MACTON OXFORD LLC
116 Willenbrock Rd (06478-1031)
PHONE.....................203 267-1500
David Perkins, *Principal*
EMP: 2
SALES (est): 205.9K **Privately Held**
SIC: 3599 Industrial machinery

(G-6676)
MARHALL BROWING INTL CORP
Also Called: Rovic
353 Christian St Ste 3 (06478-1053)
PHONE.....................203 264-2702
Donald Schoder, *President*
▲ **EMP:** 2
SALES (est): 82.9K **Privately Held**
SIC: 3873 Timers for industrial use, clockwork mechanism only

(G-6677)
MICROFAB COMPANY
339 Christian St (06478-1023)
PHONE.....................203 267-1000
Pawel Remiszewski, *Principal*
EMP: 2
SALES (est): 215.3K **Privately Held**
SIC: 3444 Sheet metalwork

(G-6678)
MODERN METAL FINISHING INC
110 Willenbrock Rd (06478-1031)
PHONE.....................203 267-1510
Russell Peterson, *President*
David Murelli, *Treasurer*
Bruno Perin, *Admin Sec*
EMP: 18
SQ FT: 6,300
SALES (est): 2.3MM **Privately Held**
WEB: www.mmfinc.com
SIC: 3479 Painting, coating & hot dipping; aluminum coating of metal products

(G-6679)
MORSE WATCHMANS INC
2 Morse Rd (06478-1040)
PHONE.....................203 264-1108
Manuel Pires, *President*
Joe Granitto, *General Mgr*
Fernando Pires, *Vice Pres*
W Schr Eyer, *Engineer*
Tim Purpura, *VP Sls/Mktg*
▲ **EMP:** 50
SQ FT: 20,000
SALES (est): 11MM **Privately Held**
WEB: www.morsewatchman.com
SIC: 3699 3577 Security control equipment & systems; computer peripheral equipment

(G-6680)
NAC INDUSTRIES INC
112 Hurley Rd (06478-1027)
PHONE.....................845 214-0659
Rowland Riccardi, *Principal*
EMP: 2
SALES (est): 197.1K **Privately Held**
SIC: 3999 Candles

(G-6681)
NASH SURGICAL SUPPLY CO INC
10 Tall Pines Dr (06478-1470)
PHONE.....................203 828-6098
Edward Buchsbaum, *President*
Mary Buchsbaum, *Treasurer*
EMP: 2
SQ FT: 650
SALES (est): 136.1K **Privately Held**
SIC: 3842 Limbs, artificial; braces, orthopedic

(G-6682)
NXTID INC
288 Christian St (06478-1038)
PHONE.....................203 266-2103
Gino M Pereira, *Principal*
Vincent Miceli, *Vice Pres*
Bonnie Bartosiak, *Controller*
EMP: 10
SALES (est): 1.9MM **Privately Held**
SIC: 7372 Prepackaged software

(G-6683)
OMNIPRINT LLC
160 Christian St (06478-1221)
PHONE.....................203 881-9013
Janine Taylor, *Mng Member*
Janine Moore, *Mng Member*
EMP: 1
SALES (est): 374.8K **Privately Held**
WEB: www.omniprint.com
SIC: 7389 7336 2759 2752 Printing broker; commercial art & illustration; commercial printing; commercial printing, lithographic

(G-6684)
OXFORD OUTDOOR SERVICES LLC
2 Little Valley Rd (06478-1187)
P.O. Box 544 (06478-0544)
PHONE.....................860 800-6260
Steven Gelineau,
EMP: 1
SALES (est): 101.4K **Privately Held**
SIC: 1795 2411 Wrecking & demolition work; timber, cut at logging camp

(G-6685)
OXFORD SCIENCE INC
178 Christian St (06478-1239)
PHONE.....................203 881-3115
Edward L Carver Jr, *President*
EMP: 18
SQ FT: 18,000
SALES (est): 3.3MM **Privately Held**
WEB: www.oxfordscienceinc.com
SIC: 3841 Surgical & medical instruments

(G-6686)
OXFORD SCIENCE CENTER LLC
Also Called: O S C
Iii One American Way (06478)
PHONE.....................203 751-1912
Tanya G Carver,
EMP: 4

SALES (est): 278.3K **Privately Held**
SIC: 3841 Surgical & medical instruments

(G-6687)
OXFORD WOODWORKING LLC
133 Moose Hill Rd (06478-6116)
PHONE.....................203 482-0982
Peter Johannsen, *Principal*
EMP: 1
SALES (est): 92K **Privately Held**
SIC: 2431 Millwork

(G-6688)
POWER TRANS CO INC
Also Called: Meritronics
315 Riggs St Ste 2 (06478-1176)
PHONE.....................203 881-0314
Paul Zaloumis, *President*
Shirley Zaloumis, *Vice Pres*
▼ **EMP:** 5
SQ FT: 7,000
SALES (est): 1.5MM **Privately Held**
SIC: 3612 3679 3672 Power transformers, electric; harness assemblies for electronic use: wire or cable; circuit boards, television & radio printed

(G-6689)
PRO SCIENTIFIC INC
99 Willenbrock Rd (06478-1032)
P.O. Box 448, Monroe (06468-0448)
PHONE.....................203 267-4600
Richard Yacko, *President*
Patricia Yacko, *Vice Pres*
Holly Yacko-Archibald, *Sales Dir*
Holly Yacko, *Sales Mgr*
Lynn Signoriello, *Manager*
EMP: 10
SALES (est): 2MM **Privately Held**
WEB: www.proscientific.com
SIC: 3556 Homogenizing machinery: dairy, fruit, vegetable

(G-6690)
R WAY SIGNS LLC
18 Bowers Hill Rd (06478-1527)
PHONE.....................203 888-9709
R Fredrick Kennett,
Therese R Fredrick,
EMP: 2 **EST:** 2001
SALES (est): 173.5K **Privately Held**
WEB: www.rwaysigns.com
SIC: 3993 Signs & advertising specialties

(G-6691)
RBC BEARINGS INCORPORATED (PA)
102 Willenbrock Rd (06478-1033)
PHONE.....................203 267-7001
Michael J Hartnett, *Ch of Bd*
Daniel A Bergeron, *COO*
Patrick S Bannon, *Vice Pres*
Patrick Bannon, *Vice Pres*
Richard Edwards, *Vice Pres*
EMP: 277 **EST:** 1919
SALES: 702.5MM **Publicly Held**
WEB: www.rbcbearings.com
SIC: 3562 Ball bearings & parts

(G-6692)
RBC PRCISION PDTS - BREMEN INC (DH)
102 Willenbrock Rd (06478-1033)
PHONE.....................203 267-7001
George Viering, *General Mgr*
▲ **EMP:** 42 **EST:** 1971
SQ FT: 50,000
SALES (est): 11.5MM
SALES (corp-wide): 702.5MM **Publicly Held**
SIC: 3452 Dowel pins, metal; pins
HQ: Roller Bearing Company Of America, Inc.
  102 Willenbrock Rd
  Oxford CT 06478
  203 267-7001

(G-6693)
ROLLER BEARING CO AMER INC (HQ)
Also Called: R B C
102 Willenbrock Rd (06478-1033)
PHONE.....................203 267-7001
Michael J Harnett, *Ch of Bd*
Thomas Williams, *Counsel*

Oxford - New Haven County (G-6694)

Michael S Gostomski, *Exec VP*
Richard J Edwards, *Vice Pres*
Christopher Thomas, *Vice Pres*
◆ **EMP:** 155 **EST:** 1934
SQ FT: 40,000
SALES (est): 507MM
SALES (corp-wide): 702.5MM **Publicly Held**
SIC: 3562 Roller bearings & parts
PA: Rbc Bearings Incorporated
102 Willenbrock Rd
Oxford CT 06478
203 267-7001

(G-6694)
ROLLER BEARING CO AMER INC
1 Tribiology Ctr (06478-1035)
PHONE 203 267-7001
Anthony Cavalieri, *Principal*
Michelle Peralta, *Engineer*
EMP: 20
SALES (est): 4.4MM
SALES (corp-wide): 702.5MM **Publicly Held**
SIC: 3562 Ball & roller bearings
PA: Rbc Bearings Incorporated
102 Willenbrock Rd
Oxford CT 06478
203 267-7001

(G-6695)
STIHL INCORPORATED
Also Called: Northeast Stihl
2 Patriot Way (06478-1274)
PHONE 203 929-8488
Nick Jiannas, *Branch Mgr*
EMP: 50
SALES (corp-wide): 4B **Privately Held**
WEB: www.stihlusa.com
SIC: 3546 5083 Power-driven handtools; farm & garden machinery
HQ: Stihl Incorporated
536 Viking Dr
Virginia Beach VA 23452
757 486-9100

(G-6696)
SUSAN MARTOVICH
Also Called: Ms Design CT
118 Bowers Hill Rd (06478-1757)
PHONE 203 881-1848
Susan Martovich, *President*
EMP: 4
SALES: 900K **Privately Held**
SIC: 3728 3446 Aircraft parts & equipment; architectural metalwork

(G-6697)
TEXTRON AVIATION INC
Also Called: Cessna Aircraft
288 Christian St (06478-1038)
PHONE 203 262-9366
EMP: 697
SALES (corp-wide): 13.9B **Publicly Held**
SIC: 3721 Aircraft
HQ: Textron Aviation Inc.
1 Cessna Blvd
Wichita KS 67215
316 517-6000

(G-6698)
VANGOR ENGINEERING CORPORATION
115 Hurley Rd Ste 7f (06478-1046)
PHONE 203 267-4377
Greg Van Gor, *President*
Greg Vangor, *President*
EMP: 4
SQ FT: 5,000
SALES: 500K **Privately Held**
SIC: 3549 Assembly machines, including robotic

(G-6699)
WALZ & KRENZER INC (PA)
Also Called: Mapeco Products
91 Willenbrock Rd Ste B4 (06478-1036)
PHONE 203 267-5712
Benjamin Rising, *President*
Tom Themel, *Vice Pres*
Tomislav Themel, *Vice Pres*
Steven Shepstone, *Director*
▲ **EMP:** 13
SQ FT: 3,750
SALES (est): 2.4MM **Privately Held**
WEB: www.wkdoors.com
SIC: 3429 Marine hardware

(G-6700)
WALZ & KRENZER INC
Also Called: Pilgrim Nuts
91 Willenbrock Rd Ste B4 (06478-1036)
PHONE 203 267-5712
Benjamin Rising, *President*
EMP: 9
SALES (est): 343.9K
SALES (corp-wide): 2.4MM **Privately Held**
WEB: www.wkdoors.com
SIC: 3443 Water tanks, metal plate
PA: Walz & Krenzer, Inc.
91 Willenbrock Rd Ste B4
Oxford CT 06478
203 267-5712

(G-6701)
ZACKIN PUBLICATIONS INC
Also Called: Alternative Energy Retailer
100 Willenbrock Rd (06478-1044)
P.O. Box 2180, Waterbury (06722-2180)
PHONE 203 262-4670
David Zackin, *President*
Paul M Zackin, *President*
Mark Delfranco, *Editor*
Jennifer Zackin, *Vice Pres*
Jeffrey Jacques, *Accounts Exec*
EMP: 24 **EST:** 1967
SQ FT: 2,000
SALES (est): 3.4MM **Privately Held**
WEB: www.zackin.com
SIC: 2721 Trade journals: publishing only, not printed on site

(G-6702)
ZANNI ANI ORGANIC SNACKS LLC
586 Oxford Rd (06478-1232)
PHONE 203 214-2360
Shonda Hunter-Feher,
Raymond Feher,
EMP: 2
SALES (est): 180.7K **Privately Held**
SIC: 2034 Fruits, freeze-dried

Pawcatuck
New London County

(G-6703)
AGJO PRINTING SERVICE
Also Called: Agio Printing Service
173 S Broad St (06379-1920)
PHONE 860 599-3143
Joseph Tasca, *Owner*
EMP: 2
SQ FT: 1,600
SALES (est): 120K **Privately Held**
SIC: 2752 2789 7334 3993 Commercial printing, offset; trade binding services; photocopying & duplicating services; signs & advertising specialties; sign painting & lettering shop

(G-6704)
CAMERON BORTZ
Also Called: Finest Kind Signs
256 S Broad St (06379-1999)
PHONE 860 599-0477
Cameron Bortz, *Owner*
EMP: 1
SQ FT: 1,600
SALES: 100K **Privately Held**
WEB: www.finestkindsigns.com
SIC: 3993 Signs, not made in custom sign painting shops

(G-6705)
CLEAN OCEAN TECHNOLOGY
113 Greenhaven Rd (06379-2090)
PHONE 401 212-8171
Christian Oates,
EMP: 1
SALES (est): 72.2K **Privately Held**
SIC: 1389 Oil consultants; oil field services

(G-6706)
CLEVER CLOVER LLC
72 Greenhaven Rd (06379-2029)
PHONE 860 501-2800
Debra J Widmer,
Matthew Maynard,
EMP: 2 **EST:** 2009
SALES (est): 113.5K **Privately Held**
SIC: 8742 2731 7389 8049 Training & development consultant; book publishing; ; physical therapist

(G-6707)
DAVIS-STANDARD LLC (HQ)
Also Called: Harrel
1 Extrusion Dr (06379-2327)
PHONE 860 599-1010
James Murphy, *President*
Charles Buckley, *Chairman*
Bob Preston, *Vice Chairman*
Robert Armstrong, *Vice Pres*
Kent Wang, *Engineer*
◆ **EMP:** 398
SALES (est): 161.7MM **Privately Held**
SIC: 3089 Extruded finished plastic products

(G-6708)
DAVIS-STANDARD HOLDINGS INC (PA)
Also Called: Egan, Sterling, Nrm, Brookes
1 Extrusion Dr (06379-2327)
PHONE 860 599-1010
James Murphy, *President*
Charles Buckley, *President*
Hassan Helmy, *Exec VP*
Mark Panozzo, *Exec VP*
Ernest Plasse, *Exec VP*
◆ **EMP:** 400
SQ FT: 170,000
SALES (est): 262.2MM **Privately Held**
WEB: www.davis-standard.com
SIC: 3559 Plastics working machinery

(G-6709)
DESCHENES & COOPER ARCHITECTUR
25 White Rock Bridge Rd (06379-1312)
P.O. Box 9222, Groton (06340-9222)
PHONE 860 599-2481
Brian Cooper, *President*
EMP: 8
SQ FT: 10,000
SALES (est): 928.6K **Privately Held**
SIC: 2431 1521 Doors, wood; general remodeling, single-family houses

(G-6710)
EMULSION APPAREL
Also Called: Emotion Printing
21 River Rd (06379)
PHONE 860 495-5792
EMP: 2 **EST:** 2013
SALES (est): 100K **Privately Held**
SIC: 5699 2759 Ret Misc Apparel/Accessories Commercial Printing

(G-6711)
FREEDOM PRESS
30 Sunrise Ave (06379-2006)
P.O. Box 1213 (06379-0213)
PHONE 860 599-5390
Jeffrey Tebbets, *Owner*
EMP: 3 **EST:** 2002
SALES (est): 123.9K **Privately Held**
WEB: www.freedompress.org
SIC: 2741 Miscellaneous publishing

(G-6712)
GENERAL DYNAMICS INFO TECH INC
100 Mechanic St (06379-2163)
PHONE 860 441-2400
Don Wood, *Mfg Staff*
Joseph M Marino, *Branch Mgr*
Joseph Marino, *Branch Mgr*
Vin Delmore, *Technical Staff*
EMP: 84
SQ FT: 10,000
SALES (corp-wide): 36.1B **Publicly Held**
SIC: 7379 8711 7373 3444 Computer related maintenance services; engineering services; computer integrated systems design; sheet metalwork
HQ: General Dynamics Information Technology, Inc.
3150 Frview Pk Dr Ste 100
Falls Church VA 22042
703 995-8700

(G-6713)
GUIDERA MARKETING SERVICES
Also Called: Fabricgraphics
21 Pawcatuck Ave (06379-2421)
P.O. Box 108, Stonington (06378-0108)
PHONE 860 599-8880
Timothy Guidera, *President*
Pamela Guidera, *Vice Pres*
EMP: 20
SQ FT: 2,500
SALES: 800K **Privately Held**
WEB: www.embroiderygiant.com
SIC: 2395 Embroidery & art needlework

(G-6714)
HI TECH PROFILES INC
185 S Broad St Ste 301 (06379-1997)
PHONE 401 377-2040
Sherry Quinlan, *Principal*
EMP: 2
SALES (est): 85.1K **Privately Held**
SIC: 3069 Fabricated rubber products

(G-6715)
HOMEWOOD CABINET CO INC
262 S Broad St (06379-1922)
PHONE 860 599-2441
James Varas, *President*
Michael Varas, *Vice Pres*
EMP: 3
SQ FT: 1,000
SALES (est): 351.6K **Privately Held**
SIC: 2434 5211 Wood kitchen cabinets; lumber & other building materials

(G-6716)
HS WELDING LLC
879 Stonington Rd (06379-1445)
PHONE 860 599-0372
Harold Stedman, *Principal*
EMP: 1 **EST:** 2016
SALES (est): 34.7K **Privately Held**
SIC: 7692 Welding repair

(G-6717)
INTERNATIONAL PRINTING ACCESS
Also Called: Teakflex Products
113 Liberty St (06379-1648)
PHONE 860 599-8005
Kenneth Clift, *Owner*
▲ **EMP:** 1 **EST:** 1995
SQ FT: 3,600
SALES: 100K **Privately Held**
WEB: www.teakflex.com
SIC: 2759 Commercial printing

(G-6718)
LEHVOSS NORTH AMERICA LLC
185 S Broad St Ste 2b (06379-1997)
PHONE 860 495-2046
Crystal Wang, *General Mgr*
Robert Healy, *Managing Dir*
Jim Meegan, *Business Mgr*
Meghan Moore, *Office Mgr*
Ted Sidoriak, *Manager*
▲ **EMP:** 10
SALES (est): 1.4MM
SALES (corp-wide): 247.5MM **Privately Held**
SIC: 3089 Thermoformed finished plastic products
PA: Lehmann & Voss & Co. Kg
Alsterufer 19
Hamburg 20354
404 419-70

(G-6719)
LILYWORK CERAMIC ORNAMENT LLC
42 Palmer St (06379-2136)
PHONE 215 859-8753
Esther Halferty, *Principal*
EMP: 2
SALES (est): 132K **Privately Held**
SIC: 3269 Pottery products

GEOGRAPHIC SECTION
Plainfield - Windham County (G-6750)

(G-6720)
MALACHITE PUBLISHING LLC
15 Croft Ct (06379-1233)
PHONE..........................860 495-5484
Terri Kenyon, *Principal*
EMP: 2 **EST:** 2014
SALES (est): 88K **Privately Held**
SIC: 2741 Miscellaneous publishing

(G-6721)
OLIVE CAPIZZANO OILS & VINEGAR
5 Coggswell St Ste 1 (06379-1672)
PHONE..........................860 495-2187
Stephen Capizzano, *Principal*
EMP: 5
SALES (est): 326.6K **Privately Held**
SIC: 2079 Olive oil

(G-6722)
PERFORMANCE COMPOUNDING INC
185 S Broad St Ste 2a (06379-1997)
PHONE..........................860 599-5616
Michael Valsamis, *CEO*
Dr Lefteris Valsamis, *General Mgr*
Hubertus Richert, *Admin Sec*
EMP: 6
SQ FT: 40,000
SALES (est): 1.5MM
SALES (corp-wide): 247.5MM **Privately Held**
WEB: www.performancecompounding.com
SIC: 3087 Custom compound purchased resins
PA: Lehmann & Voss & Co. Kg
Alsterufer 19
Hamburg 20354
404 419-70

(G-6723)
PRESCOTT CABINET CO
31 Buckingham St (06379-2524)
PHONE..........................860 495-0176
Gary Prescott, *Owner*
EMP: 8 **EST:** 1980
SQ FT: 6,000
SALES (est): 479.4K **Privately Held**
SIC: 2434 2431 5072 Wood kitchen cabinets; millwork; builders' hardware

(G-6724)
SAW MINERS MILL
153 N Anguilla Rd (06379-1267)
PHONE..........................860 599-5012
Randall Miner, *Owner*
EMP: 1
SALES (est): 90.4K **Privately Held**
SIC: 2421 Sawmills & planing mills, general

(G-6725)
STONINGTON PUBLICATIONS INC
12 Stillman Ave (06379-1612)
PHONE..........................860 599-2019
John V Durgin, *Principal*
John Durgin, *Principal*
EMP: 1
SALES (est): 56K **Privately Held**
SIC: 2741 Miscellaneous publishing

(G-6726)
THAVENET MACHINE COMPANY INC
12 Chase St Ste 14 (06379-2127)
PHONE..........................860 599-4495
Fax: 860 599-4495
EMP: 8
SQ FT: 4,000
SALES (est): 720K **Privately Held**
SIC: 3599 5084 Machine Shop & Whol Welding Supplies

(G-6727)
THREAD MILL PARTNERS LLC
12 River Rd (06379-2600)
PHONE..........................860 495-5319
EMP: 1 **EST:** 2016
SALES (est): 46.5K **Privately Held**
SIC: 2284 Thread mills

(G-6728)
TIGER FABRICATION LLC
12 Alice Ct Ste 3 (06379-1384)
PHONE..........................860 460-7600
John English, *Principal*
EMP: 2
SALES (est): 221K **Privately Held**
SIC: 3441 Fabricated structural metal

(G-6729)
TOM SANTOS PUBLISHING
107-3 Brookside Ln (06379-3908)
PHONE..........................860 599-5067
Tom Santos, *Principal*
EMP: 1
SALES (est): 37.5K **Privately Held**
SIC: 2741 Miscellaneous publishing

(G-6730)
VACCA ARCHITECTURAL WOODWORKIN
9 Coggswell St (06379-1626)
PHONE..........................860 599-3677
Annette Vacca,
EMP: 8
SQ FT: 6,958
SALES (est): 842.5K **Privately Held**
SIC: 2499 Decorative wood & woodwork

(G-6731)
WESCON CORP OF CONN
Elmata Ave (06379)
P.O. Box 296, Westerly RI (02891-0296)
PHONE..........................860 599-2500
Paul Lynch, *President*
Steven Lynch, *Corp Secy*
EMP: 8
SQ FT: 1,200
SALES (est): 1.2MM
SALES (corp-wide): 95.6MM **Privately Held**
WEB: www.wesconco.com
SIC: 2951 Asphalt & asphaltic paving mixtures (not from refineries)
PA: J.H. Lynch & Sons, Inc.
50 Lynch Pl
Cumberland RI 02864
401 333-4300

(G-6732)
WESTERLY SUN
99 Mechanic St Ste C (06379-2189)
PHONE..........................401 348-1000
David Lucey, *Publisher*
Bob Laux-Bachand, *Editor*
John Layton, *Sales Staff*
Kathy Enders, *Advt Staff*
Alex Walker, *Consultant*
EMP: 8 **EST:** 2015
SALES (est): 395.8K **Privately Held**
SIC: 2711 Newspapers, publishing & printing

Pine Meadow
Litchfield County

(G-6733)
CUNNINGHAM TECH LLC
Also Called: Ctech
10 Wickett St (06061)
PHONE..........................860 738-8759
Wells Cunningham, *Branch Mgr*
EMP: 2
SALES (est): 176.8K **Privately Held**
SIC: 2259 2891 Gloves & mittens, knit; adhesives & sealants
PA: Cunningham Tech Llc
39 Maple Hollow Rd
New Hartford CT 06057

(G-6734)
KOVACS TAMAS
Also Called: Ttm
63 Industrial Park Rd (06061)
P.O. Box 371, New Hartford (06057-0371)
PHONE..........................860 738-8976
Tamas Kovacs, *Owner*
EMP: 1
SQ FT: 10,000
SALES: 360K **Privately Held**
SIC: 3399 Brads: aluminum, brass or other nonferrous metal or wire

(G-6735)
M J BOLLER COMPANY
8 Wickett St (06061)
P.O. Box 112 (06061-0112)
PHONE..........................860 738-8073
Mike Boller, *Owner*
EMP: 1
SALES (est): 129.6K **Privately Held**
SIC: 3444 Sheet metalwork

(G-6736)
TRD SPECIALTIES INC
Also Called: T R D Specialities
8 Wickett St (06061-2039)
P.O. Box 80 (06061-0080)
PHONE..........................860 738-4505
Thomas Reading, *President*
Albert De Gaeta, *Treasurer*
▲ **EMP:** 8
SQ FT: 7,500
SALES (est): 1.2MM **Privately Held**
WEB: www.trdspecialties.com
SIC: 3399 Steel balls

Plainfield
Windham County

(G-6737)
AMTEC CORPORATION
30 Center Pkwy (06374-2051)
PHONE..........................860 230-0006
David E Fallon, *President*
Donna M Hunt, *Admin Sec*
EMP: 30
SQ FT: 15,000
SALES (est): 5.8MM **Privately Held**
WEB: www.amtecgrips.com
SIC: 3496 Woven wire products

(G-6738)
APCM MANUFACTURING LLC
Also Called: Adhesives Prepregs
1366 Norwich Rd (06374-1931)
P.O. Box 264 (06374-0264)
PHONE..........................860 564-7817
David L Young, *CEO*
Rj Young, *Marketing Mgr*
EMP: 3
SQ FT: 7,000
SALES (est): 556.9K **Privately Held**
WEB: www.prepregs.com
SIC: 2891 Adhesives

(G-6739)
ARS PRODUCTS LLC
43 Lathrop Road Ext (06374-1965)
P.O. Box 288 (06374-0288)
PHONE..........................860 564-0208
Theodore A Coppola,
EMP: 43
SALES (est): 953.6K **Privately Held**
WEB: www.arsproducts.com
SIC: 3825 Analog-digital converters, electronic instrumentation type

(G-6740)
ASAP MACHINE SP & FABRICATION
89 Mill Brook Rd (06374-1967)
PHONE..........................860 564-4114
Earl Starks, *Principal*
EMP: 7
SALES (est): 1.1MM **Privately Held**
SIC: 3599 Machine shop, jobbing & repair

(G-6741)
ATLANTIC COAST POLYMERS INC
12 East Pkwy (06374-2045)
P.O. Box 151 (06374-0151)
PHONE..........................860 564-5641
Stewart Siegele, *President*
EMP: 1
SQ FT: 8,475 **Privately Held**
SIC: 2899 Chemical preparations
PA: Atlantic Coast Polymers, Inc.
6207 Bee Caves Rd Ste 180
Austin TX

(G-6742)
B S T SYSTEMS INC
78 Plainfield Pike (06374-1700)
PHONE..........................860 564-4078
Kenneth P Avery, *President*
Thomas T Terjesen, *President*
Edward J Mulvey, *Director*
Michael A Solis, *Director*
▲ **EMP:** 55
SQ FT: 27,000
SALES (est): 13.6MM **Privately Held**
WEB: www.bstsys.com
SIC: 3692 3691 3629 Primary batteries, dry & wet; storage batteries; electronic generation equipment

(G-6743)
BAY STATE MACHINE INC
21 Center Pkwy (06374-2054)
PHONE..........................860 230-0054
Robert Stafford, *President*
Pamela Stafford, *Corp Secy*
EMP: 8 **EST:** 1970
SQ FT: 2,000
SALES: 500K **Privately Held**
SIC: 3599 Machine shop, jobbing & repair

(G-6744)
CLASSIC BRANDS LLC
55 Lathrop Road Ext (06374-1965)
PHONE..........................303 936-2444
EMP: 1
SALES (corp-wide): 6.5MM **Privately Held**
SIC: 2048 Prepared feeds
PA: Classic Brands, Llc
3600 S Yosemite St # 1000
Denver CO 80237
303 936-2444

(G-6745)
COLONIAL METAL DETECTORS
299 Gendron Rd (06374-1716)
PHONE..........................860 317-1284
Richard Oconnor, *Owner*
EMP: 2
SALES (est): 149.9K **Privately Held**
SIC: 3669 Metal detectors

(G-6746)
LATHROP STABLES LLC
427 Lathrop Rd (06374-2038)
PHONE..........................860 230-9949
Lori A Holbert, *Manager*
EMP: 1
SALES (est): 57.4K **Privately Held**
SIC: 2399 7999 Horse & pet accessories, textile; saddlehorse rental

(G-6747)
LINEMASTER SWITCH CORPORATION
16 Center Pkwy (06374-2051)
PHONE..........................860 564-7713
▲ **EMP:** 3
SALES (est): 364.4K **Privately Held**
SIC: 3679 Electronic switches

(G-6748)
MARTEL WOODWORKING CO
196 Black Hill Rd (06374-1445)
PHONE..........................860 564-1983
Richard Martel, *President*
Earl Martel, *Co-President*
EMP: 4
SALES (est): 490K **Privately Held**
SIC: 1751 2431 Cabinet & finish carpentry; millwork

(G-6749)
MERIDIAN OPERATIONS LLC
1414 Norwich Rd (06374-1931)
PHONE..........................860 564-8811
EMP: 10
SALES (est): 720K **Privately Held**
SIC: 3069 Mfg Fabricated Rubber Products

(G-6750)
PRO-MANUFACTURED PRODUCTS INC
29 Center Pkwy (06374-2054)
PHONE..........................860 564-2197
Ward E Walker, *President*
Kristin D Walker, *Treasurer*

Plainfield - Windham County (G-6751)   GEOGRAPHIC SECTION

EMP: 8
SQ FT: 5,250
SALES (est): 1.5MM **Privately Held**
WEB: www.pro-equine.com
SIC: 3451 Screw machine products

(G-6751)
RADECO OF CT INC
17 West Pkwy (06374-2048)
P.O. Box 1304, Forestdale MA (02644-0715)
PHONE..................................860 564-1220
Paul Lovendale, *President*
Keith Lovendale, *Vice Pres*
Brad Lovendale, *VP Sales*
Ann Lovendale, *Admin Sec*
▼ EMP: 12
SQ FT: 6,000
SALES: 1.6MM **Privately Held**
WEB: www.radecoinc.com
SIC: 3674 Radiation sensors

(G-6752)
SCOPE TECHNOLOGY INC
8 Center Pkwy (06374-2051)
PHONE..................................860 963-1141
Ronald Green, *President*
EMP: 10
SQ FT: 4,000
SALES (est): 968K **Privately Held**
WEB: www.scopetech.com
SIC: 3827 Magnifying instruments, optical

(G-6753)
SPA MACHINING CO
31 Center Pkwy (06374-2054)
P.O. Box 817, Moosup (06354-0817)
PHONE..................................860 564-9584
EMP: 1
SALES (est): 110K **Privately Held**
SIC: 3599 Mfg Industrial Machinery

(G-6754)
THELEMIC PRINTSHOP
13 West Pkwy (06374-2048)
PHONE..................................860 383-4014
Eric Ross, *President*
EMP: 4
SALES (est): 217.3K **Privately Held**
SIC: 2752 Commercial printing, lithographic

(G-6755)
THIRTY TWO SIGNS LLC
13 West Pkwy (06374-2048)
PHONE..................................860 564-0532
EMP: 1
SALES (est): 54.9K **Privately Held**
SIC: 3993 Signs & advertising specialties

(G-6756)
WESTMINSTER TOOL INC
5 East Pkwy (06374-2046)
PHONE..................................860 564-6966
Raymond S Coombs Jr, *President*
Paul L Szydlo, *Vice Pres*
Jason Eliasson, *Production*
Michael Belmont, *Sales Staff*
Nicholas Stein, *Manager*
▲ EMP: 30 EST: 1997
SQ FT: 4,500
SALES: 6MM **Privately Held**
WEB: www.westminstertool.com
SIC: 3599 Machine shop, jobbing & repair

(G-6757)
ZAMPELL REFRACTORIES INC
1370 Norwich Rd (06374-1931)
PHONE..................................860 564-2883
Steven Cotta, *Manager*
EMP: 12
SALES (corp-wide): 52.1MM **Privately Held**
WEB: www.zampellrefractories.com
SIC: 1711 3255 3296 Heating systems repair & maintenance; clay refractories; firebrick, clay; mineral wool
PA: Zampell Refractories, Inc.
3 Stanley Tucker Dr
Newburyport MA 01950
978 465-0055

Plainville
Hartford County

(G-6758)
A -LINE CUSTOM COUNTER TOP
7 Johnson Ave (06062-1115)
PHONE..................................860 747-1917
Steve Roux, *Owner*
EMP: 2
SALES (est): 115.4K **Privately Held**
SIC: 5211 5031 2434 Counter tops; kitchen cabinets; wood kitchen cabinets

(G-6759)
A AIUDI & SONS LLC (PA)
190 Camp St (06062-1612)
P.O. Box 279 (06062-0279)
PHONE..................................860 747-5534
Elmo Aiudi,
Alison Aiudi,
Christopher Aiudi,
Steven Aiudi,
Sandra Aiudi Divincenzo,
EMP: 9 EST: 1945
SQ FT: 3,000
SALES (est): 1.9MM **Privately Held**
SIC: 1771 3273 Concrete work; ready-mixed concrete

(G-6760)
A D GRINDING
54 Lewis St (06062-2049)
PHONE..................................860 747-6630
Anthony Loumbard, *President*
Dan Haag, *Admin Sec*
EMP: 13
SALES (est): 1.6MM **Privately Held**
SIC: 3599 Grinding castings for the trade

(G-6761)
A G M TOOL
15 Hultenius St (06062-2878)
PHONE..................................860 793-6808
Gregory Cajezckow, *Owner*
Gregory Cajezckowski, *Owner*
EMP: 1
SALES (est): 56K **Privately Held**
SIC: 3599 3544 Machine shop, jobbing & repair; special dies, tools, jigs & fixtures

(G-6762)
A2Z EMBROIDERY
433 East St (06062-3241)
PHONE..................................860 747-9849
Lisa Roberge, *Owner*
EMP: 1
SALES (est): 78.2K **Privately Held**
SIC: 2395 Embroidery & art needlework

(G-6763)
ABB ENTERPRISE SOFTWARE INC
Also Called: GE
41 Woodford Ave (06062-2372)
PHONE..................................860 747-7111
Gary Arnott, *General Mgr*
Steven Meiners, *General Mgr*
Scott P Parent, *General Mgr*
Thomas Henning, *Project Mgr*
Carlos Sanabria, *Project Mgr*
EMP: 900
SALES (corp-wide): 36.4B **Privately Held**
SIC: 3613 7361 3643 Switches, electric power except snap, push button, etc.; circuit breakers, air; power circuit breakers; employment agencies; current-carrying wiring devices
HQ: Abb Inc.
305 Gregson Dr
Cary NC 27511

(G-6764)
ACCU-MILL TECHNOLOGIES LLC
161 Woodford Ave Ste 39 (06062-2369)
PHONE..................................860 747-3921
Wojciech Wojtak, *Principal*
Artur Wojtak,
EMP: 3
SQ FT: 5,000
SALES (est): 400K **Privately Held**
SIC: 3365 7539 Aerospace castings, aluminum; machine shop, automotive

(G-6765)
ACCURATE BURRING COMPANY
161 Woodford Ave Ste 19 (06062-2368)
PHONE..................................860 747-8640
Robert Beaudoin, *Owner*
EMP: 12
SQ FT: 20,000
SALES (est): 1.1MM **Privately Held**
SIC: 3471 Finishing, metals or formed products; tumbling (cleaning & polishing) of machine parts

(G-6766)
ADMINISTRATIVE PUBLICATIONS IN
6 Highland Dr (06062-2603)
PHONE..................................860 747-6768
Arnold Ira Menchel, *Principal*
EMP: 1
SALES (est): 62.8K **Privately Held**
SIC: 2741 Telephone & other directory publishing

(G-6767)
AFFORDABLE FINE CABINETRY
143 Whiting St (06062-2825)
PHONE..................................860 919-5204
EMP: 2 EST: 2013
SALES (est): 154.4K **Privately Held**
SIC: 2434 Wood kitchen cabinets

(G-6768)
ALPHA PLATING AND FINISHING CO
169 W Main St (06062-1925)
P.O. Box 89 (06062-0089)
PHONE..................................860 747-5002
Rafael Bawabe, *President*
EMP: 12
SQ FT: 15,000
SALES (est): 960K **Privately Held**
SIC: 3471 Plating of metals or formed products; finishing, metals or formed products

(G-6769)
ALTO PRODUCTS CORP AL
Also Called: Plainville Special Tool
63 N Washington St (06062-1972)
P.O. Box 160 (06062-0160)
PHONE..................................860 747-2736
Rick Statchen, *Manager*
EMP: 38 **Privately Held**
WEB: www.altousa.com
SIC: 3469 3599 Stamping metal for the trade; machine shop, jobbing & repair
PA: Alto Products Corp. Al
1 Alto Way
Atmore AL 36502

(G-6770)
ANDYS AUTOMOTIVE MACHINE
48 Lewis St (06062-2049)
PHONE..................................860 793-2455
Andy Krawiec, *Owner*
EMP: 1 EST: 1978
SALES (est): 146.3K **Privately Held**
WEB: www.andysautomotivemachine.com
SIC: 7539 7694 Machine shop, automotive; rebuilding motors, except automotive

(G-6771)
APP POLONIA LLC
Also Called: App Polonia Trading
95 Metacomet Rd (06062-1424)
PHONE..................................860 747-3397
Eric I Izdebski,
EMP: 2
SALES: 300K **Privately Held**
WEB: www.apppolonia.com
SIC: 2911 5147 Diesel fuels; meats & meat products

(G-6772)
ATLANTIC PIPE CORPORATION
60 N Washington St (06062-1994)
PHONE..................................860 747-5557
Fax: 860 793-2477
EMP: 75 EST: 1962
SQ FT: 60,000
SALES (est): 8.5MM **Privately Held**
SIC: 3272 Mfg Concrete Products

(G-6773)
ATP INDUSTRIES LLC (PA)
75 Northwest Dr (06062-1101)
PHONE..................................860 479-5007
Gary Fett, *Mng Member*
Mariusz Saar,
EMP: 14
SQ FT: 20,000
SALES: 1MM **Privately Held**
SIC: 3541 3492 8711 3451 Vertical turning & boring machines (metalworking); fluid power valves & hose fittings; control valves, fluid power: hydraulic & pneumatic; mechanical engineering; screw machine products; bolts, nuts, rivets & washers

(G-6774)
B & L TOOL AND MACHINE COMPANY
76 Northwest Dr (06062-1164)
P.O. Box 308 (06062-0308)
PHONE..................................860 747-2721
Joseph Berarducci, *President*
Peter Berarducci, *Vice Pres*
EMP: 3 EST: 1948
SQ FT: 10,000
SALES (est): 400K **Privately Held**
SIC: 3544 3541 Special dies & tools; machine tools, metal cutting: exotic (explosive, etc.)

(G-6775)
BCT REPORTING LLC
55 Whiting St Ste 1a (06062-2262)
P.O. Box 1774, Bristol (06011-1774)
PHONE..................................860 302-1876
Brenda Lafleur, *Mng Member*
EMP: 6
SALES (est): 293.5K **Privately Held**
SIC: 2752 Commercial printing, lithographic

(G-6776)
BEADAZZLE
31 Lincoln St (06062-2625)
PHONE..................................860 747-5101
Laura Miller, *Owner*
EMP: 1
SALES (est): 60.9K **Privately Held**
WEB: www.beadazzle.com
SIC: 3961 Costume jewelry

(G-6777)
BONATI BROTHERS WELDING & FABR
26 S Canal St (06062-2722)
PHONE..................................860 582-5000
Jason Bonati, *Owner*
EMP: 1
SALES (est): 114.9K **Privately Held**
SIC: 7692 Welding repair

(G-6778)
BRIARWOOD PRINTING COMPANY INC
301 Farmington Ave (06062-1398)
PHONE..................................860 747-6805
David M Drew, *President*
Brian Kupchik, *Vice Pres*
EMP: 12 EST: 1960
SQ FT: 10,000
SALES (est): 2.1MM **Privately Held**
WEB: www.briarwoodprinting.com
SIC: 2752 Commercial printing, offset

(G-6779)
BRYCE GEAR INC
11 N Washington St (06062)
P.O. Box 406 (06062-0406)
PHONE..................................860 747-3341
Eric Sanderson, *President*
EMP: 1 EST: 1930
SQ FT: 1,800
SALES (est): 110K **Privately Held**
SIC: 3541 5084 Gear cutting & finishing machines; machine tools & metalworking machinery

(G-6780)
BURN TIME ENTERPRISES LLC
15 Cronk Rd Ste 1 (06062-1254)
PHONE..................................860 410-0747
Brian Martin, *Branch Mgr*
EMP: 1

SALES (corp-wide): 1.1MM **Privately Held**
SIC: **2448** Pallets, wood
PA: Burn Time Enterprises Llc
    500 Broad St
    Bristol CT 06010
    860 410-0747

(G-6781)
CABINET SPECIALTIES LLC
38 Neal Ct (06062-1606)
PHONE.................................860 747-4114
Henry Andrew Han Jr,
Brett Buchas,
EMP: 2
SQ FT: 2,400
SALES (est): 300K **Privately Held**
SIC: **2434** Wood kitchen cabinets

(G-6782)
CAD CAM MACHINE LLC
150 Robert Jackson Way (06062-2651)
PHONE.................................860 410-9788
Darek Tuczapski, *General Mgr*
Malgorzata Zbrzeski, *Technology*
EMP: 6
SQ FT: 8,775
SALES (est): 1MM **Privately Held**
SIC: **3599** Machine shop, jobbing & repair

(G-6783)
CANIDAE CORP
1975 Tandem Way (06062)
PHONE.................................860 539-5307
John Gordon, *President*
Scott Whipple, *Principal*
EMP: 2
SALES (est): 126.8K **Privately Held**
SIC: **2048** Canned pet food (except dog & cat)

(G-6784)
CAPITOL MACHINE INC PRECI
30 Hayden Ave Ste B (06062-2872)
PHONE.................................860 410-0758
Joseph Szabo, *Owner*
EMP: 3
SALES (est): 316.9K **Privately Held**
SIC: **3599** Machine shop, jobbing & repair

(G-6785)
CARLING TECHNOLOGIES INC (PA)
Also Called: Carlingswitch
60 Johnson Ave (06062-1181)
PHONE.................................860 793-9281
Richard W Sorenson, *President*
Jennifer Buddenhagen, *Exec VP*
Edward Rosenthal, *Exec VP*
Richard Sorenson Jr, *Exec VP*
Simon Cordner, *Vice Pres*
▲ EMP: 175 EST: 1920
SQ FT: 135,000
SALES (est): 34.8MM **Privately Held**
SIC: **3643** 3613 3612 Electric switches; power circuit breakers; transformers, except electric

(G-6786)
CELTIC STONEWORKS
174 Whiting St (06062-2845)
PHONE.................................860 846-0279
EMP: 2 EST: 2014
SALES (est): 158.3K **Privately Held**
SIC: **2434** Wood kitchen cabinets

(G-6787)
CHARLES MANUFACTURING CO
161 Woodford Ave (06062-2370)
PHONE.................................860 747-3550
EMP: 3 EST: 2015
SALES (est): 149.3K **Privately Held**
SIC: **3999** Manufacturing industries

(G-6788)
COMPU-SIGNS LLC
105 E Main St (06062-1992)
PHONE.................................860 747-1985
Vincent J Zavarella, *Mng Member*
EMP: 3
SALES (est): 246.9K **Privately Held**
SIC: **3993** Signs, not made in custom sign painting shops

(G-6789)
CONDOMDEPOT CO
186 Camp St (06062-1612)
PHONE.................................860 747-1338
John Fidi, *Principal*
Jennifer Amato, *Mktg Dir*
EMP: 3
SALES (est): 218K **Privately Held**
SIC: **2834** Druggists' preparations (pharmaceuticals)

(G-6790)
CONNECTICUT HONE INCORPORATED
9 Grace Ave (06062-2849)
P.O. Box 263 (06062-0263)
PHONE.................................860 747-3884
Bert Simard, *President*
Bertrand Simard, *President*
Douglas Simard, *Vice Pres*
Gregory Simard, *Vice Pres*
Doug Simard, *Opers Staff*
EMP: 7
SQ FT: 2,500
SALES (est): 724.7K **Privately Held**
SIC: **3599** Machine shop, jobbing & repair

(G-6791)
CONNECTICUT SOLID SURFACE LLC
361 East St (06062-3260)
PHONE.................................860 410-9800
Steven Roux, *Mng Member*
Raymond Roux, *Mng Member*
Jaclyn Roux,
EMP: 40
SQ FT: 36,000
SALES (est): 5.9MM **Privately Held**
WEB: www.ctsolidsurface.com
SIC: **2434** 2511 3281 Wood kitchen cabinets; wood household furniture; cut stone & stone products

(G-6792)
CONNECTICUT TOOL & MFG CO LLC
Also Called: CT Tool
35 Corp Ave (06062)
PHONE.................................860 846-0800
Sadik Lilaporia, *Engineer*
Collin Cooper, *Mng Member*
Evan Filacchione, *Manager*
▲ EMP: 70
SQ FT: 29,000
SALES (est): 26.4MM
SALES (corp-wide): 96.3MM **Privately Held**
WEB: www.cttool.com
SIC: **3728** Aircraft assemblies, subassemblies & parts; spinners, aircraft propeller
PA: Whitcraft Llc
    76 County Rd
    Eastford CT 06242
    860 974-0786

(G-6793)
COPY SIGNS LLC
105 E Main St (06062-1992)
PHONE.................................860 747-1985
Vincent Zavarella,
Vincent J Zavarella,
EMP: 2
SALES (est): 130K **Privately Held**
SIC: **3993** Signs & advertising specialties

(G-6794)
CUSTOM CHECKERING
46 Spring St (06062-3203)
PHONE.................................860 747-8035
Byron Shaples, *Owner*
EMP: 1
SALES (est): 69.1K **Privately Held**
SIC: **2426** Gun stocks, wood

(G-6795)
D & M SCREW MACHINE PDTS LLC
Also Called: Lowe Manufacturing
97 Forestville Ave (06062-2149)
PHONE.................................860 410-9781
Dennis Morin, *President*
Gerry Glass, *Sales Executive*
EMP: 5
SALES (est): 370K **Privately Held**
SIC: **3429** 3451 Manufactured hardware (general); screw machine products

(G-6796)
D & S PRECISION TURNING LLC
57 Brussel Ave (06062)
P.O. Box 82 (06062-0082)
PHONE.................................860 793-2640
Slawomier Zdunczyk,
EMP: 2 EST: 1996
SALES (est): 466.7K **Privately Held**
SIC: **3599** Machine shop, jobbing & repair

(G-6797)
DANIEL DECHAMPS
50 Corporate Ave (06062-1195)
PHONE.................................860 463-3105
Michael Reed, *Service Mgr*
EMP: 2
SALES (est): 87.9K **Privately Held**
SIC: **3599** Machine shop, jobbing & repair

(G-6798)
DELL ACQUISITION LLC
Also Called: Dell Manufacturing
35 Corporate Ave (06062-1194)
PHONE.................................860 677-8545
Joe Maisto, *Principal*
EMP: 40 EST: 2011
SALES: 6MM **Privately Held**
SIC: **3728** Aircraft parts & equipment

(G-6799)
DISPLAYCRAFT INC
335 S Washington St (06062-2729)
PHONE.................................860 747-9110
Richard Seigars, *President*
Rui Carvalho, *Exec VP*
Susan Seigars, *Vice Pres*
▲ EMP: 20
SQ FT: 80,000
SALES (est): 2.6MM **Privately Held**
WEB: www.displaycraft.com
SIC: **3993** 2542 Displays & cutouts, window & lobby; partitions & fixtures, except wood

(G-6800)
DR TEMPLEMAN COMPANY
1 Northwest Dr (06062-1340)
PHONE.................................860 747-2709
Richard Williams, *President*
Theresa Butler, *General Mgr*
Arthur Williams, *Vice Pres*
David Williams, *Vice Pres*
▼ EMP: 18 EST: 1938
SQ FT: 15,000
SALES (est): 3.6MM **Privately Held**
WEB: www.drtempleman.com
SIC: **3495** Mechanical springs, precision

(G-6801)
DSD DISTRIBUTOR LLC
27 E Maple St (06062-2312)
PHONE.................................860 378-4487
David Sanabria, *Principal*
EMP: 1
SALES (est): 72.5K **Privately Held**
SIC: **3429** Aircraft & marine hardware, inc. pulleys & similar items; aircraft hardware

(G-6802)
EASTERN BROACH INC
10 Sparks St (06062-2052)
PHONE.................................860 828-4800
Ivor Tarver, *President*
Patricia Tarver, *Corp Secy*
Robert Tarver, *Vice Pres*
Charles H Tarver, *Shareholder*
Malcolm Tarver, *Admin Sec*
EMP: 15
SQ FT: 6,000
SALES (est): 2.5MM **Privately Held**
WEB: www.easternbroach.com
SIC: **3545** 7699 Broaches (machine tool accessories); tool repair services

(G-6803)
EDGE TOOL LLC
163 Stillwell Dr (06062-2951)
PHONE.................................860 747-1820
Andrew J Edgerton, *Mng Member*
EMP: 2
SALES (est): 172.5K **Privately Held**
SIC: **3423** Hand & edge tools

(G-6804)
EDISON COATINGS INC
3 Northwest Dr (06062-1336)
PHONE.................................860 747-2220
Michael Edison, *President*
Leya Edison, *Vice Pres*
Chad Lausberg, *Engineer*
◆ EMP: 13
SQ FT: 20,000
SALES (est): 2.8MM **Privately Held**
WEB: www.edisoncoatings.com
SIC: **2891** Adhesives

(G-6805)
ELLIS MANUFACTURING LLC
161 Woodford Ave Ste 62 (06062-2374)
PHONE.................................865 518-0531
Robert Knowlton, *Principal*
EMP: 3
SALES (est): 164.8K **Privately Held**
SIC: **3999** Manufacturing industries

(G-6806)
ENGINERING COMPONENTS PDTS LLC
Also Called: Industrial Automation
35 Forshaw Ave (06062-2555)
PHONE.................................860 747-6222
Robert Reeve, *President*
John Nejfelt,
EMP: 5 EST: 1970
SQ FT: 11,000
SALES (est): 400K **Privately Held**
SIC: **3441** 3541 Fabricated structural metal; machine tools, metal cutting type

(G-6807)
EXECUTIVE PRESS INC
27 East St (06062-2308)
PHONE.................................860 793-0060
Robert Crago, *President*
John Crago, *President*
EMP: 3
SALES (est): 491.5K **Privately Held**
SIC: **2752** Commercial printing, offset

(G-6808)
FABTRON INCORPORATED
80 Farmington Valley Dr (06062-1193)
PHONE.................................860 410-1801
Garret J Maino, *President*
Joseph H Maino, *Vice Pres*
Jeffrey P Maino, *Treasurer*
EMP: 9
SQ FT: 31,000
SALES (est): 1.4MM **Privately Held**
WEB: www.fabtronusa.com
SIC: **1761** 7692 Sheet metalwork; welding repair

(G-6809)
FARMINGTON VALLEY WOODCRAFTS
119 Williams St (06062-1756)
PHONE.................................860 793-9034
David Kelsey, *Owner*
EMP: 1
SALES (est): 65.3K **Privately Held**
SIC: **2434** Wood kitchen cabinets

(G-6810)
FINE LINES CUSTOM CABINETRY &
16 Unionville Ave (06062-1128)
PHONE.................................860 729-6526
Justin Fink, *Owner*
EMP: 1
SALES (est): 54.1K **Privately Held**
SIC: **2431** Millwork

(G-6811)
FLEETWOOD INDUSTRIES INC
4 Northwest Dr (06062-1311)
P.O. Box 862 (06062-0862)
PHONE.................................860 747-6750
Harry G Raymond, *President*
Darren Raymond, *Vice Pres*
EMP: 6
SQ FT: 2,500
SALES (est): 1MM **Privately Held**
SIC: **3451** Screw machine products

Plainville - Hartford County (G-6812) — GEOGRAPHIC SECTION

(G-6812)
FONDA FABRICATING & WELDING CO
50 Milford Street Ext (06062-2494)
PHONE..........................860 793-0601
Edward J Zakowski, *President*
Vallarie A Zakowski, *Admin Sec*
EMP: 5 **EST:** 1981
SQ FT: 20,000
SALES (est): 420K **Privately Held**
SIC: 3444 7692 3479 Sheet metalwork; welding repair; painting of metal products

(G-6813)
FORESTVILLE MACHINE CO INC
355 S Washington St (06062-2742)
PHONE..........................860 747-6000
Jeffrey Paul Hamel, *President*
Peter Lionell Vigue, *Vice Pres*
▲ **EMP:** 45 **EST:** 1945
SQ FT: 28,000
SALES (est): 9MM **Privately Held**
WEB: www.forestvillemachine.com
SIC: 3451 Screw machine products

(G-6814)
GA MALS WOODWOORKING LLC
20 Ciccio Ct (06062-2701)
PHONE..........................860 747-4767
Gerald A Mals, *President*
EMP: 1
SALES (est): 125K **Privately Held**
SIC: 2426 Carvings, furniture: wood

(G-6815)
GEMS SENSORS INC (HQ)
Also Called: Gems Sensors & Controls
1 Cowles Rd (06062-1107)
PHONE..........................860 747-3000
Anne N De Greeg-Sasst, *President*
Muriel Bras-Jorge, *President*
Dalek Joe, *Opers Mgr*
Brenda Hall, *Senior Buyer*
Patricia Santoro, *Buyer*
▲ **EMP:** 325
SALES (est): 93.9MM
SALES (corp-wide): 6.4B **Publicly Held**
SIC: 3824 5084 3812 3625 Fluid meters & counting devices; industrial machinery & equipment; search & navigation equipment; relays & industrial controls; switchgear & switchboard apparatus
PA: Fortive Corporation
6920 Seaway Blvd
Everett WA 98203
425 446-5000

(G-6816)
GEMS SENSORS INC
1 Cowles Rd (06062-1107)
PHONE..........................800 378-1600
Tom Kepler, *Controller*
EMP: 12
SALES (corp-wide): 6.4B **Publicly Held**
SIC: 3829 5099 Measuring & controlling devices; firearms & ammunition, except sporting
HQ: Gems Sensors Inc.
1 Cowles Rd
Plainville CT 06062
860 747-3000

(G-6817)
GERDAU AMERISTEEL US INC
75 Neal Ct (06062-1622)
PHONE..........................860 351-9029
EMP: 5 **Privately Held**
SIC: 3312 Hot-rolled iron & steel products
HQ: Gerdau Ameristeel Us Inc.
4221 W Boy Scout Blvd # 600
Tampa FL 33607
813 286-8383

(G-6818)
GPA
10 Farmington Valley Dr # 5 (06062-1182)
PHONE..........................860 410-0624
Greg Kuns, *Principal*
EMP: 6
SALES (est): 317.6K **Privately Held**
SIC: 2711 Commercial printing & newspaper publishing combined

(G-6819)
GREGORY PENTA
Also Called: Penta Woodworking Shop
111 Laurel Ct (06062-2988)
PHONE..........................860 747-2681
Gregory Penta, *Owner*
Peter A Penta, *Partner*
EMP: 3
SQ FT: 4,000
SALES (est): 266.7K **Privately Held**
SIC: 1521 5211 2434 2431 General remodeling, single-family houses; lumber & other building materials; wood kitchen cabinets; millwork

(G-6820)
H & B WOODWORKING CO
105 E Main St (06062-1992)
PHONE..........................860 793-6991
Matthew Malley, *President*
EMP: 3
SALES (est): 397.6K **Privately Held**
SIC: 2434 Wood kitchen cabinets

(G-6821)
HARTFORD FIRE EQUIPMENT
394 East St (06062-3238)
P.O. Box 457 (06062-0457)
PHONE..........................860 747-2757
Jeff Wells, *President*
EMP: 30 **EST:** 1975
SALES (est): 630.7K **Privately Held**
SIC: 7349 1231 5063 Cleaning service, industrial or commercial; anthracite mining; electrical apparatus & equipment

(G-6822)
HILL INDUSTRIES LLC
15 N Washington St (06062-1995)
PHONE..........................860 747-6421
Sean Hill, *Owner*
EMP: 2
SQ FT: 4,000
SALES (est): 174.1K **Privately Held**
SIC: 3999 Manufacturing industries

(G-6823)
HYGRADE PRECISION TECH INC
329 Cooke St (06062-1448)
PHONE..........................860 747-5773
John A Salce, *CEO*
Richard J Cleary, *President*
Stephen Lsaltzman, *Admin Sec*
EMP: 28 **EST:** 1962
SQ FT: 40,000
SALES (est): 6.6MM **Privately Held**
WEB: www.hygrade.com
SIC: 3599 Machine shop, jobbing & repair

(G-6824)
INDUSTRIAL CNNCTONS SLTONS LLC
41 Woodford Ave (06062-2372)
PHONE..........................860 747-7677
EMP: 20
SALES (corp-wide): 36.4B **Privately Held**
SIC: 3613 Control panels, electric
HQ: Industrial Connections & Solutions Llc
4200 Wildwood Pkwy
Atlanta GA 30339
678 844-6000

(G-6825)
J & J STAIRS
230 S Washington St # 11 (06062-2761)
PHONE..........................860 793-8333
Jean Marquis, *Principal*
EMP: 2
SALES (est): 147.1K **Privately Held**
SIC: 1799 2431 Special trade contractors; staircases, stairs & railings

(G-6826)
J M SHEET METAL LLC
161 Woodford Ave Ste 11 (06062-2336)
PHONE..........................860 747-5537
Juan Marimon, *Mng Member*
EMP: 4 **EST:** 2001
SQ FT: 4,954
SALES (est): 575.7K **Privately Held**
SIC: 3444 Sheet metalwork

(G-6827)
J RO GROUNDING SYSTEMS INC (PA)
Also Called: J-Ro Tool & Die Co
161 Woodford Ave Ste 39 (06062-2369)
PHONE..........................860 747-2106
John Deleo, *CEO*
Rose Deleo, *Vice Pres*
EMP: 2
SQ FT: 2,500
SALES (est): 258.1K **Privately Held**
WEB: www.j-rotool.com
SIC: 3643 3699 3613 3429 Ground clamps (electric wiring devices); electrical equipment & supplies; switchgear & switchboard apparatus; manufactured hardware (general)

(G-6828)
J&P MFG LLC
125 Robert Jackson Way F (06062-2663)
PHONE..........................860 747-4790
Pawel Surowaniec, *Owner*
EMP: 4
SALES (est): 279K **Privately Held**
SIC: 3999 Manufacturing industries

(G-6829)
KEBERG LLC
45 Tyler Farms Rd (06062-1186)
PHONE..........................860 255-8135
Chris Freyberg,
EMP: 2
SALES (est): 300K **Privately Held**
WEB: www.keberg.com
SIC: 3469 Tile, floor or wall: stamped metal

(G-6830)
KEVCO
63 Bartlett St (06062-3122)
PHONE..........................860 747-4135
Kevin Blanchette, *Owner*
EMP: 1
SALES (est): 95.8K **Privately Held**
SIC: 3599 Amusement park equipment

(G-6831)
LAROSA MANUFACTURING LLC
15 Hultenius St (06062-2878)
PHONE..........................860 819-7066
Catherine Larosa,
EMP: 2
SALES (est): 193.4K **Privately Held**
SIC: 3544 Special dies, tools, jigs & fixtures

(G-6832)
LASSY TOOLS INC
96 Bohemia St (06062-2122)
P.O. Box G (06062-0956)
PHONE..........................860 747-2748
William Lassy, *President*
Dave Lassy, *Vice Pres*
Marc Lassy, *Vice Pres*
Lassy Marc, *Vice Pres*
Gail Sjogren, *Admin Sec*
EMP: 7 **EST:** 1938
SQ FT: 10,000
SALES: 800K **Privately Held**
WEB: www.lassytools.com
SIC: 3429 3544 Clamps, metal; special dies & tools; jigs & fixtures

(G-6833)
LITTLE ARTIST PAINT CO LLC
8 Race Ave (06062-2838)
PHONE..........................860 989-1996
Heather Bernier,
EMP: 1
SALES (est): 41K **Privately Held**
SIC: 3952 Tables, drawing, artists'

(G-6834)
LOGIC SEAL LLC
10 Sparks St (06062-2052)
PHONE..........................203 598-3400
Gary Rogers, *Prdtn Mgr*
Gregory Guay, *Mng Member*
EMP: 6 **EST:** 2011
SQ FT: 1,800
SALES (est): 1MM **Privately Held**
SIC: 3491 Automatic regulating & control valves

(G-6835)
LPG METAL CRAFTS LLC
54 Carol Dr (06062-3206)
PHONE..........................860 982-3573
Leonard Gale, *Mng Member*
EMP: 3
SALES (est): 260K **Privately Held**
SIC: 3446 Architectural metalwork

(G-6836)
M & A TURNING CO LLC
15 Hultenius St Ste 3a (06062-2878)
PHONE..........................860 793-2774
Jan Zajaczkowski,
EMP: 1
SALES (est): 169.6K **Privately Held**
SIC: 3599 Machine shop, jobbing & repair

(G-6837)
M & I INDUSTRIES INC
15 N Washington St (06062-1995)
P.O. Box 813 (06062-0813)
PHONE..........................860 747-6421
Ellis Ibbotson, *President*
Ann Ibbotson, *Corp Secy*
EMP: 2
SQ FT: 6,000
SALES (est): 334.3K **Privately Held**
SIC: 3643 3469 3648 Current taps, attachment plug & screw shell types; metal stampings; lighting equipment

(G-6838)
MARETRON LLP
60 Johnson Ave (06062-1181)
PHONE..........................602 861-1707
Saguaro Marine LLC, *Partner*
Mark Biegel, *Vice Pres*
▲ **EMP:** 14
SALES (est): 3.4MM **Privately Held**
SIC: 3531 Marine related equipment

(G-6839)
MARK DZIDZK
Also Called: Continental Marble & Granite
20k Hultenius St (06062-2848)
PHONE..........................860 793-2767
Mark Dzidzk, *Owner*
EMP: 20 **EST:** 1999
SALES (est): 1.8MM **Privately Held**
SIC: 3281 Building stone products

(G-6840)
MARTIN CABINET INC (PA)
336 S Washington St Ste 2 (06062-2752)
PHONE..........................860 747-5769
Jean Martin, *President*
Brian Martin, *Admin Sec*
EMP: 26 **EST:** 1971
SQ FT: 5,000
SALES (est): 6.8MM **Privately Held**
WEB: www.cabinet-mart.com
SIC: 2434 5211 Wood kitchen cabinets; cabinets, kitchen

(G-6841)
MASTER TOOL & MACHINE INC
13 Grace Ave (06062-2849)
PHONE..........................860 747-2581
Robert William Mastrianni, *President*
Alfred James Mastrianni, *Vice Pres*
EMP: 6
SQ FT: 2,000
SALES: 3.5MM **Privately Held**
SIC: 3599 Machine shop, jobbing & repair

(G-6842)
MASTER TOOL AND MACHINES LLC
13 Grace Ave (06062-2849)
PHONE..........................860 747-2581
Robert S Mastrianni, *President*
EMP: 1
SALES (est): 51.7K **Privately Held**
SIC: 3599 Machine shop, jobbing & repair

(G-6843)
MERCURY FUEL CO
301 East St (06062-3297)
PHONE..........................860 793-6602
EMP: 1
SALES (est): 80.8K **Privately Held**
SIC: 2869 Fuels

▲ = Import ▼ = Export
◆ = Import/Export

GEOGRAPHIC SECTION
Plainville - Hartford County (G-6874)

(G-6844)
MICRODYNE TECHNOLOGIES
64 Neal Ct (06062-1606)
PHONE..................860 747-9473
David J Sperduti, *Partner*
Alexander J Sperduti, *Partner*
EMP: 4
SQ FT: 3,200
SALES (est): 528.4K **Privately Held**
WEB: www.microdynetech.com
SIC: 3312 Wire products, steel or iron

(G-6845)
MODERN WOODCRAFTS LLC
72 Northwest Dr (06062-1164)
PHONE..................860 677-7371
Gerald L Pelletier, *Founder*
John Lapre, *Vice Pres*
Scott Thibodeau, *Plant Mgr*
Rob Cadrain, *Project Mgr*
Philip Shuman, *CFO*
EMP: 70
SQ FT: 65,000
SALES: 15MM **Privately Held**
WEB: www.modernwoodcrafts.com
SIC: 2541 2431 Wood partitions & fixtures; millwork

(G-6846)
NEW BRITAIN SAW TECH
161 Woodford Ave Ste 62a (06062-2374)
PHONE..................860 410-1077
Joseph Sazzino, *Owner*
EMP: 2
SALES: 90K **Privately Held**
SIC: 5085 3599 Industrial supplies; machine shop, jobbing & repair

(G-6847)
NICKSON INDUSTRIES INC
336 Woodford Ave (06062-2487)
PHONE..................860 747-1671
Ilan Ginga, *President*
Tasdelen Ozlem, *Controller*
▲ EMP: 48 EST: 1968
SQ FT: 100,000
SALES (est): 10.8MM
SALES (corp-wide): 30.1MM **Privately Held**
WEB: www.nickson.com
SIC: 3714 Motor vehicle parts & accessories
PA: Metapoint Partners, A Limited Partnership
    108 Beach St
    Manchester MA 01944
    978 531-1398

(G-6848)
NOBBY BEVERAGES INC
30 Hayden Ave Ste E (06062-2872)
P.O. Box 397 (06062-0397)
PHONE..................860 747-3888
Marie Bogdanski, *President*
Paul G Bogdanski, *Vice Pres*
Sarah Bogdanski-Bourdon, *Admin Sec*
▲ EMP: 2
SQ FT: 6,000
SALES: 300K **Privately Held**
SIC: 2087 Syrups, drink; beverage bases

(G-6849)
NORMIKE INDUSTRIES INC
1 Town Line Rd Ste 6 (06062-2750)
PHONE..................860 747-1110
Robert Ruck, *President*
Cynthia Ruck, *Corp Secy*
EMP: 2
SQ FT: 1,000
SALES: 235K **Privately Held**
SIC: 3599 Machine shop, jobbing & repair

(G-6850)
OLSON BROTHERS COMPANY
272 Camp St (06062-1612)
P.O. Box 188 (06062-0188)
PHONE..................860 747-6844
Robert R Carroll, *CEO*
Christopher Carroll, *President*
EMP: 16
SQ FT: 7,000
SALES (est): 1.9MM **Privately Held**
WEB: www.obcinc.net
SIC: 3451 Screw machine products

(G-6851)
PASTRANA UNLIMITED LLC
Also Called: Airbrush Studio's
131 Whiting St Ste 1 (06062-2877)
PHONE..................860 747-6633
Alan Pastrana, *Owner*
EMP: 1
SALES (est): 98.4K **Privately Held**
WEB: www.airbrushstudios.com
SIC: 3952 Easels, artists'

(G-6852)
PLAINVILLE PLATING COMPANY INC
21 Forestville Ave (06062-2159)
P.O. Box 219 (06062-0219)
PHONE..................860 747-1624
Gerald Glassman, *Ch of Bd*
Charles L Pratt, *President*
Roy Manzie, *Opers Staff*
Jay R Fienman, *Treasurer*
Richard Bochenek, *Director*
EMP: 60 EST: 1920
SQ FT: 23,000
SALES (est): 7.5MM **Privately Held**
WEB: www.plainvilleplating.com
SIC: 3471 Plating of metals or formed products

(G-6853)
PRALINES OF PLAINVILLE
107 New Britain Ave (06062-2073)
PHONE..................860 410-1151
Jim Scarfo, *Owner*
EMP: 4
SALES (est): 167.7K **Privately Held**
SIC: 2024 Ice cream, bulk

(G-6854)
PRINT INDIE LLC
56 Neal Ct Ste 2 (06062-1620)
PHONE..................860 986-9446
Lee Boucher, *Principal*
EMP: 2
SALES (est): 176.7K **Privately Held**
SIC: 2752 Commercial printing, offset

(G-6855)
R J BRASS INC
26 Ashford Rd (06062-1236)
PHONE..................860 793-2336
Richard Robinson, *President*
Joyce Robinson, *Vice Pres*
EMP: 10
SQ FT: 15,000
SALES (est): 700K **Privately Held**
SIC: 3471 Buffing for the trade; polishing, metals or formed products

(G-6856)
ROAD-FIT ENTERPRISES LLC
98 Whiting St (06062-2881)
PHONE..................860 371-5137
James A Cole,
EMP: 3
SALES (est): 120.5K **Privately Held**
SIC: 3949 Sporting & athletic goods

(G-6857)
ROLLING MOTION INDUSTRIES
75 Northwest Dr (06062-1101)
PHONE..................860 846-0530
EMP: 1
SALES (est): 39.6K **Privately Held**
SIC: 3999 Manufacturing industries

(G-6858)
ROMA TOOL & MACHINE CO
65 Robert Jackson Way (06062-2650)
PHONE..................860 793-2315
John Mikulski, *Owner*
EMP: 2
SQ FT: 5,000
SALES (est): 245.8K **Privately Held**
SIC: 3599 Machine shop, jobbing & repair

(G-6859)
ROZELLE SPECIALTY PROCESSES
123 Whiting St Ste G (06062-2889)
P.O. Box 5, Farmington (06034-0005)
PHONE..................860 793-9400
Pamela Ann Roberge, *Principal*
EMP: 2 EST: 2009

SALES (est): 170.8K **Privately Held**
SIC: 7692 Welding repair

(G-6860)
SCOTT A HEBERT
Also Called: Hebert Tool
230 East St (06062-2935)
PHONE..................860 990-0793
Scott A Hebert, *Owner*
EMP: 1 EST: 2017
SALES (est): 59K **Privately Held**
SIC: 3541 Machine tools, metal cutting type

(G-6861)
SHUSTER-METTLER CORP
Also Called: Shuster Machines
10 Sparks St (06062-2052)
P.O. Box 883, New Haven (06504-0883)
PHONE..................203 562-3178
Dennis Polio, *President*
Joyce Polio, *Vice Pres*
EMP: 30 EST: 1947
SQ FT: 20,000
SALES (est): 6.5MM **Privately Held**
SIC: 5084 3541 3315 3549 Industrial machinery & equipment; machine tools, metal cutting type; steel wire & related products; cutting & slitting machinery

(G-6862)
SIGN WIZ LLC
452 East St Ste 1r (06062-3406)
PHONE..................860 351-5368
EMP: 1
SALES (est): 46K **Privately Held**
SIC: 3993 Signs & advertising specialties

(G-6863)
STYLAIR LLC
161 Woodford Ave (06062-2370)
P.O. Box 7014 (06062-7014)
PHONE..................860 747-4588
Roger Kidwell,
Pelly Esposito,
EMP: 14
SQ FT: 8,000
SALES (est): 3.6MM **Privately Held**
WEB: www.stylair.com
SIC: 3564 3563 Blowers & fans; air & gas compressors

(G-6864)
SUPERIOR ELC HOLDG GROUP LLC (HQ)
1 Cowles Rd (06062-1107)
PHONE..................860 582-9561
Julian Watt, *COO*
Pam Metzer, *CFO*
Michael Miga, *Sales Dir*
Ted Gladis, *Marketing Mgr*
James Greeno, *Manager*
▲ EMP: 34
SQ FT: 27,000
SALES (est): 3.9MM
SALES (corp-wide): 19.8B **Publicly Held**
SIC: 3612 Transformers, except electric
PA: Danaher Corporation
    2200 Penn Ave Nw Ste 800w
    Washington DC 20037
    202 828-0850

(G-6865)
SYMAN MACHINE LLC
161 Woodford Ave Ste 5b (06062-2336)
PHONE..................860 747-8337
EMP: 3
SALES (est): 330K **Privately Held**
SIC: 3541 Mfg Machine Tools-Cutting

(G-6866)
T/A ENGINES
124 Hilltop Rd (06062-1027)
PHONE..................860 747-6713
Anthony Alteri, *Partner*
William H O'Sullivan, *Partner*
EMP: 2
SALES (est): 260K **Privately Held**
SIC: 3519 7549 Engines, diesel & semi-diesel or dual-fuel; high performance auto repair & service

(G-6867)
TACO FASTENERS INC
71 Northwest Dr (06062-1101)
P.O. Box 338 (06062-0338)
PHONE..................860 747-5597
Arnold Finn, *President*
Marguerite Finn, *Admin Sec*
EMP: 10
SQ FT: 10,000
SALES (est): 1.5MM **Privately Held**
SIC: 3469 3544 Stamping metal for the trade; special dies & tools

(G-6868)
TAG MANUFACTURING LLC
161 Woodford Ave Ste 49 (06062-2374)
PHONE..................860 479-5120
Nathan Collier, *Mfg Mgr*
David Florian, *Mng Member*
EMP: 2
SQ FT: 3,200
SALES (est): 64.4K **Privately Held**
SIC: 3721 3599 Aircraft; machine shop, jobbing & repair

(G-6869)
TETCO INC
4 Northwest Dr (06062-1311)
PHONE..................860 747-1280
Sandra T Simmons, *President*
Sandra Thibault, *President*
George Simmons, *Vice Pres*
EMP: 15
SQ FT: 14,000
SALES: 1MM **Privately Held**
SIC: 3541 Grinding machines, metalworking

(G-6870)
TOP FLIGHT MACHINE TOOL LLC
Also Called: Aircraft
90 Robert Jackson Way (06062-2650)
PHONE..................860 747-4726
Stanley Kusmider,
EMP: 9
SALES (est): 1.7MM **Privately Held**
SIC: 3599 Machine shop, jobbing & repair

(G-6871)
TRANSIT SYSTEMS INC
161 Woodford Ave Ste 34 (06062-2369)
PHONE..................860 747-3669
Jeffrey Yost, *President*
Walter J Lappen, *Treasurer*
Walter Lappen, *CTO*
Fred Weingarten, *Technology*
EMP: 7
SQ FT: 8,000
SALES (est): 1.2MM **Privately Held**
SIC: 3743 Interurban cars & car equipment

(G-6872)
TRUMPF INC
3 Johnson Ave (06062)
PHONE..................860 255-6000
Shelia Lamothe, *Manager*
EMP: 262
SALES (corp-wide): 4.2B **Privately Held**
SIC: 3542 3546 3423 Sheet metalworking machines; power-driven handtools; hand & edge tools
HQ: Trumpf, Inc.
    111 Hyde Rd
    Farmington CT 06032
    860 255-6000

(G-6873)
U S HAIRSPRING LLC
47 Reliance Rd (06062-1419)
PHONE..................860 747-9526
Rane Dayon,
EMP: 1
SQ FT: 1,000
SALES (est): 140.7K **Privately Held**
WEB: www.ushairspring.com
SIC: 3495 Clock springs, precision

(G-6874)
V B WOODWORKING LLC
13 Spring St (06062-3202)
PHONE..................860 747-0228
Vincent J Bartolucci, *Principal*
EMP: 2

Plainville - Hartford County (G-6875)

SALES (est): 124.1K **Privately Held**
SIC: **2431** Millwork

(G-6875)
VAB INC
49 Johnson Ave (06062-1155)
P.O. Box 349, New Hartford (06057-0349)
PHONE...............................860 793-0246
Victor Tomasso Sr, *President*
Victor F Tomasso, *Director*
EMP: 5
SALES (est): 356.3K **Privately Held**
WEB: www.vytas.net
SIC: **1382** Oil & gas exploration services

(G-6876)
WASHINGTON CONCRETE PRODUCTS
328 S Washington St (06062-2752)
P.O. Box 176 (06062-0176)
PHONE...............................860 747-5242
Richard M Sewell, *President*
Nancy Sewell, *Admin Sec*
EMP: 15
SQ FT: 15,000
SALES (est): 3.6MM **Privately Held**
WEB: www.paversrus.com
SIC: **5032** 5999 3446 3272 Concrete & cinder building products; concrete products, pre-cast; architectural metalwork; concrete products

(G-6877)
WIDEBAND SOLUTIONS INC
37 Northwest Dr (06062-1234)
PHONE...............................860 383-8918
Lonny Bowers, *President*
Andrew Chiang, *Vice Pres*
David Sulliven, *CIO*
Jun Yang, *CTO*
EMP: 3
SQ FT: 2,500
SALES (est): 727K **Privately Held**
WEB: www.widebandsolutions.com
SIC: **3845** Audiological equipment, electromedical

(G-6878)
WIRE SOLUTIONS LLC
138 Farmington Ave (06062-1733)
P.O. Box 75 (06062-0075)
PHONE...............................860 836-0787
Gary Valencis,
EMP: 1
SALES (est): 100K **Privately Held**
SIC: **3496** 3452 Miscellaneous fabricated wire products; pins

(G-6879)
ZEECO INC
80 Spring Ln (06062-1151)
PHONE...............................860 479-0999
EMP: 5 **Privately Held**
SIC: **3433** Gas burners, industrial
HQ: Zeeco, Inc.
22151 E 91st St S
Broken Arrow OK 74014
918 258-8551

Plantsville
Hartford County

(G-6880)
A&V TYPOGRAPHICS
36 Buckland St Unit 27 (06479-7605)
PHONE...............................860 276-9060
Anita Scaringe, *Owner*
EMP: 2
SALES: 100K **Privately Held**
SIC: **2791** 7338 Photocomposition, for the printing trade; secretarial & court reporting

(G-6881)
ACCUBEND LLC
1657 Mrden Wtrbury Tpke (06479)
P.O. Box 532 (06479-0532)
PHONE...............................860 378-0303
Ron Dehnel,
EMP: 3
SALES: 200K **Privately Held**
SIC: **3542** Bending machines

(G-6882)
ADVANCED GLASS DESIGN LLC
30 Deer Run (06479-1304)
PHONE...............................860 426-0401
William Seamon III,
EMP: 2
SALES (est): 99.9K **Privately Held**
SIC: **3231** Decorated glassware: chipped, engraved, etched, etc.

(G-6883)
ADVANCED HM AUDIO & VIDEO LLC
962 S Main St Apt 7 (06479-1699)
PHONE...............................860 621-0631
James Dobensky, *Owner*
EMP: 2
SQ FT: 1,000
SALES (est): 750K **Privately Held**
SIC: **3651** 7389 Audio electronic systems; personal service agents, brokers & bureaus

(G-6884)
AMERICAN METAL MASTERS LLC
Also Called: American Metal Master Mch Tl
141 Summer St (06479-1156)
PHONE...............................860 621-6911
Frank Carbone,
Doreen Sward,
EMP: 3
SQ FT: 7,000
SALES (est): 145.7K **Privately Held**
SIC: **3599** 3511 3492 Machine shop, jobbing & repair; turbines & turbine generator sets; control valves, aircraft: hydraulic & pneumatic

(G-6885)
ATHENS INDUSTRIES INC
220 West St (06479-1145)
P.O. Box 487, Southington (06489-0487)
PHONE...............................860 621-8957
Richard Emmings Sr, *President*
Jennifer Brush, *President*
Patty Osowecki, *Sales Mgr*
EMP: 9
SQ FT: 5,000
SALES (est): 1.7MM **Privately Held**
SIC: **3728** Aircraft assemblies, subassemblies & parts

(G-6886)
BERKSHIRE BALLOONS LLC
190 Tomlinson Ave Apt 12h (06479)
PHONE...............................203 250-8441
Robert Zirpolo, *Mng Member*
EMP: 1
SALES (est): 81K **Privately Held**
WEB: www.berkshireballoons.com
SIC: **7999** 3721 Hot air balloon rides; aircraft

(G-6887)
BUNNY DO LLC
634 Old Turnpike Rd (06479-1609)
PHONE...............................860 621-2365
Roberta Beaulieu, *Owner*
EMP: 1
SALES (est): 76.7K **Privately Held**
SIC: **3999** Hair, dressing of, for the trade

(G-6888)
CLINICAL DYNAMICS CONN LLC
1210 Mrden Waterbury Tpke (06479-2024)
PHONE...............................203 269-0090
Tom Danko, *Manager*
Joe Rebot,
EMP: 9
SALES (est): 1.1MM **Privately Held**
SIC: **3841** Surgical & medical instruments

(G-6889)
COPY-RITE INC
384 Old Turnpike Rd # 2 (06479-1566)
PHONE...............................203 272-6923
Jim Amato, *President*
EMP: 1
SALES (est): 200K **Privately Held**
SIC: **2752** Commercial printing, offset

(G-6890)
DEBURR CO
201 Atwater St (06479-1653)
P.O. Box 24 (06479-0024)
PHONE...............................860 621-6634
Ben Divalentino, *President*
Gino Brino, *Vice Pres*
EMP: 27
SQ FT: 6,500
SALES (est): 2.1MM **Privately Held**
WEB: www.deburr.com
SIC: **3471** Finishing, metals or formed products

(G-6891)
EAZY OIL LLC
415 Marion Ave (06479-1460)
PHONE...............................860 426-3184
Craig Henderson, *Principal*
EMP: 2 EST: 2016
SALES (est): 95.7K **Privately Held**
SIC: **1311** Crude petroleum production

(G-6892)
FORRATI MANUFACTURING & TL LLC
411 Summer St (06479-1122)
PHONE...............................860 426-1105
Mark Forauer, *Mng Member*
EMP: 7
SALES (est): 997.4K **Privately Held**
SIC: **3599** Machine shop, jobbing & repair

(G-6893)
FRANKS PERFORMANCE
131 W Main St (06479-1133)
PHONE...............................860 426-0439
Frank Lanzofa, *Owner*
EMP: 1
SALES (est): 81K **Privately Held**
SIC: **3714** Lubrication systems & parts, motor vehicle

(G-6894)
G M T MANUFACTURING CO INC
Also Called: Gmt Mfg
220 West St (06479-1145)
P.O. Box 324 (06479-0324)
PHONE...............................860 628-6757
Guy Touma, *President*
EMP: 8 EST: 1947
SQ FT: 11,000
SALES (est): 500K **Privately Held**
SIC: **3451** Screw machine products

(G-6895)
GRANITECH LLC
409 Canal St Ste 4 (06479-1751)
PHONE...............................860 620-1733
Brendan O'Connor,
Brendan O Connor,
EMP: 6
SALES (est): 641.4K **Privately Held**
SIC: **3281** Granite, cut & shaped

(G-6896)
INNOVATIVE COMPONENTS LLC
635 Old Turnpike Rd (06479-1608)
PHONE...............................860 621-7220
Michael Meade, *Mng Member*
EMP: 6
SQ FT: 3,200
SALES (est): 859K **Privately Held**
WEB: www.innovativecomponents.com
SIC: **3823** Industrial instrmnts msrmnt display/control process variable

(G-6897)
J J RYAN CORPORATION
Also Called: Rex Forge Div
355 Atwater St (06479-1653)
P.O. Box 39 (06479-0039)
PHONE...............................860 628-0393
Ronald Fontanella, *President*
Dimitri Sayegh, *CFO*
Mark Dudzinski, *Manager*
David Yates, *Director*
Joseph P Polzella, *Admin Sec*
EMP: 170 EST: 1975
SQ FT: 150,000
SALES (est): 43.2MM **Privately Held**
WEB: www.jjryanradio.com
SIC: **3312** 3423 3451 3462 Forgings, iron & steel; mechanics' hand tools; screw machine products; iron & steel forgings

(G-6898)
KC CRAFTS LLC
384 Old Turnpike Rd (06479-1566)
PHONE...............................860 426-9797
Normand Charette,
EMP: 6
SQ FT: 8,000
SALES (est): 830.5K **Privately Held**
WEB: www.kccrafts.com
SIC: **3625** Switches, electronic applications

(G-6899)
KITE BUSINESS SOLUTIONS LLC
95 Great Pine Path (06479-1347)
PHONE...............................860 302-0682
Kimberly A Therrien, *President*
EMP: 2 EST: 2011
SALES (est): 66.7K **Privately Held**
SIC: **3944** Kites

(G-6900)
KYLE C NILES
116 Mount Vernon Rd (06479-1218)
PHONE...............................860 637-7625
Kyle C Niles, *Principal*
EMP: 1
SALES (est): 46.1K **Privately Held**
SIC: **3993** Signs & advertising specialties

(G-6901)
LADRDEFENSE LLC
Also Called: Krav Maga Southington
243 Canal St (06479-1734)
PHONE...............................860 637-8488
Robert Rand, *Principal*
EMP: 3
SALES (est): 176.3K **Privately Held**
SIC: **3812** 7371 Defense systems & equipment; computer software development & applications

(G-6902)
MICHAEL PETRUZZI
39 Crescent St (06479-1614)
PHONE...............................860 621-7515
Michael Petruzzi, *Principal*
EMP: 1 EST: 2018
SALES (est): 56.4K **Privately Held**
SIC: **3449** Miscellaneous metalwork

(G-6903)
MILIARD CUSTOM WOODWORKS LLC
60 Hacienda Cir (06479-1912)
PHONE...............................860 621-5131
Fernand Miliard, *Principal*
EMP: 1 EST: 2013
SALES (est): 111K **Privately Held**
SIC: **2431** Millwork

(G-6904)
NATIONAL MAGNETIC SENSORS INC
141 Summer St Ste 3 (06479-1154)
P.O. Box 64 (06479-0064)
PHONE...............................860 621-6816
Robert J Bardoorian, *President*
Margaret Bardoorian, *Corp Secy*
Michael Bardoorian, *Vice Pres*
EMP: 6
SQ FT: 3,000
SALES (est): 510K **Privately Held**
WEB: www.nationalmagnetic.com
SIC: **3823** Industrial instrmnts msrmnt display/control process variable

(G-6905)
NEW ENGLAND WELDING SVCS LLC
47 West St (06479-1137)
PHONE...............................860 406-4030
Thomas Pattison,
EMP: 1
SALES: 116K **Privately Held**
SIC: **7692** Welding repair

GEOGRAPHIC SECTION

Pomfret - Windham County (G-6933)

(G-6906)
NORTHEAST FLUID TECHNOLOGY
161 Atwater St (06479-1644)
PHONE 860 620-0393
EMP: 2
SALES (est): 79.9K Privately Held
SIC: 3589 Water purification equipment, household type

(G-6907)
PELEGNOS STINED GL ART GALLERY
1241 Mrden Waterbury Tpke (06479-2011)
PHONE 860 621-2900
Stella Pelegano, *Principal*
EMP: 2
SALES (est): 185.5K Privately Held
SIC: 3479 5231 7999 8299 Etching & engraving; glass, leaded or stained; art gallery, commercial; arts & crafts schools

(G-6908)
PRECISION FIRE FABRICATION LLC
8 West St (06479-1141)
PHONE 203 706-0749
Brendan Cote,
EMP: 2 EST: 2017
SALES (est): 62.5K Privately Held
SIC: 3999 Manufacturing industries

(G-6909)
RM PRINTING
384 Old Turnpike Rd (06479-1566)
P.O. Box 485 (06479-0485)
PHONE 860 621-0498
Bill Trainor, *Partner*
James Mac Donald, *Partner*
EMP: 5 EST: 1977
SQ FT: 6,000
SALES: 390K Privately Held
WEB: www.rmprinting.com
SIC: 2752 Commercial printing, offset

(G-6910)
SAY IT WITH SIGNS
216 Summer St (06479-1119)
PHONE 860 621-6535
Cynthia Martel, *Principal*
EMP: 2
SALES (est): 155.5K Privately Held
SIC: 3993 Signs & advertising specialties

(G-6911)
SIGN PRO INC
60 Westfield Dr (06479-1753)
PHONE 860 229-1812
Peter Rappoccio, *President*
Keith Dubois, *General Mgr*
Chelseah Carroll, *Project Mgr*
Rob Mulcunry, *Prdtn Mgr*
Denise Sirios, *Sales Staff*
EMP: 15
SQ FT: 16,000
SALES (est): 349.2K Privately Held
WEB: www.signpro-usa.com
SIC: 3993 Signs, not made in custom sign painting shops

(G-6912)
SOUTHINGTON TOOL & MFG CORP
Also Called: Stmc
300 Atwater St (06479-1643)
P.O. Box 595, Southington (06489-0595)
PHONE 860 276-0021
Lynette Nadeau, *President*
Edward Kalat, *Principal*
Arthur Pfaff, *Sales Staff*
Andrea L Kalat, *Director*
EMP: 37
SQ FT: 25,000
SALES (est): 5MM Privately Held
WEB: www.stmc.com
SIC: 3841 3469 3495 Surgical stapling devices; stamping metal for the trade; wire springs

(G-6913)
SUPREME-LAKE MFG INC
455 Atwater St (06479-1666)
P.O. Box 19 (06479-0019)
PHONE 860 621-8911
Gary N Dobrindt, *President*
Richard L Fazzone, *General Mgr*
Dave Cano, *Vice Pres*
David A Cano, *Vice Pres*
Troy Fazzone, *Vice Pres*
▲ EMP: 85
SQ FT: 42,739
SALES (est): 35MM Privately Held
SIC: 3451 Screw machine products

(G-6914)
TIGER ENTERPRISES INC
379 Summer St (06479-1149)
PHONE 860 621-9155
Rex Florian, *President*
Lance Florian, *Treasurer*
EMP: 28
SQ FT: 30,000
SALES: 3.2MM Privately Held
WEB: www.tigerstamping.com
SIC: 3469 3496 3429 3423 Stamping metal for the trade; miscellaneous fabricated wire products; manufactured hardware (general); hand & edge tools

(G-6915)
TORREY S CRANE COMPANY
492 Summer St (06479-1123)
P.O. Box 374 (06479-0374)
PHONE 860 628-4778
David Baker, *President*
Barbara Baker, *Vice Pres*
▲ EMP: 25
SQ FT: 10,000
SALES (est): 4.9MM Privately Held
SIC: 3356 Solder: wire, bar, acid core, & rosin core

(G-6916)
TRAUMAWAY LLC
82 Parkview Dr (06479-1918)
PHONE 860 628-0706
James Cheyne, *Owner*
EMP: 2
SALES (est): 235.9K Privately Held
SIC: 3635 Household vacuum cleaners

(G-6917)
UNITED STATES CHEMICAL CORP
609 Old Turnpike Rd (06479-1664)
P.O. Box 293 (06479-0293)
PHONE 860 621-6831
Jim Rawn, *President*
David Govoni, *Exec VP*
Coral Rawn, *Admin Sec*
▲ EMP: 6
SQ FT: 6,000
SALES: 1.5MM Privately Held
SIC: 2899 2841 Metal treating compounds; detergents, synthetic organic or inorganic alkaline

(G-6918)
WELD TEC LLC
Also Called: Weld-TEC
245 Summer St (06479-1160)
P.O. Box 361 (06479-0361)
PHONE 860 628-5750
Christopher Gourley,
EMP: 2
SALES: 150K Privately Held
SIC: 7692 1798 3398 Welding repair; welding on site; metal heat treating

(G-6919)
Z & M WOODWORKING LLC
118 Old Mill Rd (06479-1435)
PHONE 860 378-0563
Zbigniew Cieslak, *Principal*
EMP: 2 EST: 2010
SALES (est): 186.9K Privately Held
SIC: 2431 Millwork

Pleasant Valley
Litchfield County

(G-6920)
AUTOBOND EASTERN
60 Lavander Rd (06063-1804)
PHONE 860 383-8962
John Gilmore, *President*
▲ EMP: 2 EST: 2008
SALES (est): 193.5K Privately Held
SIC: 2759 Commercial printing

(G-6921)
CENTURY WOODWORKING INC
40 River Rd (06063-3315)
P.O. Box 1097, Enfield (06083-1097)
PHONE 860 379-7538
Paul Richardson, *President*
Bradford W Hamel, *Treasurer*
Ellyn Hamel, *Office Mgr*
EMP: 19
SQ FT: 12,000
SALES (est): 3MM Privately Held
WEB: www.centurywoodworking.com
SIC: 2431 Millwork

(G-6922)
GOULET ENTERPRISES INC
Also Called: Goulet Printery
115 New Hartford Rd (06063-3350)
PHONE 860 379-0793
Paul Goulet, *President*
Barbara Goulet, *Corp Secy*
Dennis M Goulet, *Vice Pres*
Richard Goulet, *Asst Treas*
Cyril Goulet, *Asst Sec*
EMP: 16
SQ FT: 10,000
SALES (est): 2.3MM Privately Held
SIC: 2752 Commercial printing, offset

(G-6923)
JOSEPH REMBOCK
Also Called: Accurate Welding
7 Old County Rd (06063-3313)
PHONE 860 738-3981
Joseph Rembock, *Owner*
EMP: 2
SALES (est): 140K Privately Held
SIC: 3599 7692 Machine & other job shop work; welding repair

(G-6924)
LUIS RAIMUNDI
Also Called: Calabria Granite & Stone
64 Ratlum Rd (06063-1814)
PHONE 860 294-1468
Luis Raimundi, *Owner*
EMP: 1
SALES (est): 81.9K Privately Held
SIC: 3281 Curbing, granite or stone

(G-6925)
PLEASANT VALLEY FENCE CO INC
Also Called: Bazzano, J Cedar Products
Rr 181 (06063)
P.O. Box 153 (06063-0153)
PHONE 860 379-0088
Katherine Bazzano, *President*
Richard Bazzano, *Vice Pres*
Pat Bazzano, *Treasurer*
Pasquale Bazzano, *Admin Sec*
EMP: 12
SQ FT: 1,115
SALES (est): 1.6MM Privately Held
WEB: www.pleasantvalleyfence.com
SIC: 2499 3999 Fencing, wood; pet supplies

(G-6926)
STERLING ENGINEERING CORP
236 New Hartford Rd (06063-3345)
P.O. Box 559, Winsted (06098-0559)
PHONE 860 379-3366
John N Lavieri, *President*
Patricia L Minton, *Admin Sec*
▲ EMP: 105
SQ FT: 75,000
SALES (est): 17.6MM Publicly Held
WEB: www.sterlingeng.com
SIC: 3599 3769 Machine shop, jobbing & repair; guided missile & space vehicle parts & auxiliary equipment
PA: Air Industries Group
   1460 5th Ave
   Bay Shore NY 11706

(G-6927)
TRU HITCH INC
16 W West Hill Rd (06063-3221)
PHONE 860 379-7772
Martin Marola, *President*
Anthony Cuozzo, *Corp Secy*
EMP: 12
SQ FT: 13,000
SALES (est): 2.4MM Privately Held
SIC: 3714 Fifth wheel, motor vehicle

Plymouth
Litchfield County

(G-6928)
CT CRANE AND HOIST SERVICE LLC
19 Burr Rd (06782-2220)
PHONE 860 283-4320
George Frost, *President*
John Thomas Kerski,
Sandra Kerski,
EMP: 7
SALES (est): 458K Privately Held
WEB: www.ctcrane.com
SIC: 5084 3531 Cranes, industrial; hoists; backhoes, tractors, cranes, plows & similar equipment

(G-6929)
TECHNOLOGY IN CONTROLS INC
390 South St (06782-2422)
PHONE 860 283-8405
Ted Williams, *President*
EMP: 2 EST: 2008
SALES (est): 121.6K Privately Held
SIC: 3547 Rod mills (rolling mill equipment)

(G-6930)
WASP ARCHERY PRODUCTS INC
707 Main St (06782-2243)
P.O. Box 303 (06782-0303)
PHONE 860 283-0246
Richard C Maleski, *President*
Karen Maleski, *Admin Sec*
EMP: 5 EST: 1972
SQ FT: 11,000
SALES (est): 1.5MM Privately Held
WEB: www.wasparchery.com
SIC: 3949 Arrows, archery

Pomfret
Windham County

(G-6931)
FIBEROPTICS TECHNOLOGY INC (PA)
1 Quasset Rd (06258)
P.O. Box 286 (06258-0286)
PHONE 860 928-0443
Joan Loos, *Chairman*
Tim Chiou, *CFO*
Richard Griswold, *Treasurer*
Renfree Deborah, *Human Res Dir*
Robin Messier, *Sales Staff*
▲ EMP: 110 EST: 1977
SQ FT: 62,000
SALES (est): 17.6MM Privately Held
WEB: www.fiberoptix.com
SIC: 3357 Nonferrous wiredrawing & insulating

(G-6932)
FIBEROPTICS TECHNOLOGY INC
1 Fiber Rd (06258-8003)
PHONE 860 928-0443
August Loos, *Branch Mgr*
EMP: 100
SALES (corp-wide): 17.6MM Privately Held
WEB: www.fiberoptix.com
SIC: 3229 Glass fibers, textile
PA: Fiberoptics Technology, Inc.
   1 Quasset Rd
   Pomfret CT 06258
   860 928-0443

(G-6933)
LOOS & CO INC (PA)
Also Called: Wire Rope Div
16b Mashamoquet Rd (06258)
P.O. Box 98 (06258-0098)
PHONE 860 928-7981

Pomfret - Windham County (G-6934)

William Loos, *President*
Richard Griswold, *President*
Joseph Stagon, *General Mgr*
Russ Cox, *Vice Pres*
Alan Jaaskela, *VP Opers*
◆ **EMP:** 300 **EST:** 1989
SQ FT: 175,000
SALES: 60MM **Privately Held**
WEB: www.loosnaples.com
SIC: 3357 3315 5051 2298 Nonferrous wiredrawing & insulating; wire, ferrous/iron; cable, wire; cordage & twine

(G-6934)
LOOS & CO INC
Jewel Wire Company
Rr 101 (06258)
P.O. Box 282 (06258-0282)
PHONE.................860 928-6681
Samuel Dixon, *General Mgr*
EMP: 13
SALES (corp-wide): 60MM **Privately Held**
WEB: www.loosnaples.com
SIC: 3315 3991 Wire, ferrous/iron; brooms & brushes
PA: Loos & Co., Inc.
16b Mashamoquet Rd
Pomfret CT 06258
860 928-7981

(G-6935)
LOOS AND CO INC
1 Cable Rd (06258-8004)
PHONE.................304 445-7820
B Paddon, *Mfg Staff*
Anthony Rondeau, *Engineer*
Curt Schopfer, *Engineer*
Laura Taylor, *Admin Sec*
EMP: 1
SALES (est): 54.3K **Privately Held**
SIC: 3496 Miscellaneous fabricated wire products

(G-6936)
SHARPE HILL VINEYARD INC
108 Wade Rd (06258)
P.O. Box 1 (06258-0001)
PHONE.................860 974-3549
Steven Vollweiler, *President*
Catherine Vollweiler, *Co-President*
Jill R Vollweiler, *Treasurer*
EMP: 30
SQ FT: 11,000
SALES (est): 4.1MM **Privately Held**
WEB: www.sharpehill.com
SIC: 2084 5812 Wines; eating places

Pomfret Center
Windham County

(G-6937)
ARTWORK BY NORA LLC
239 Kearney Rd (06259-2239)
PHONE.................860 963-0723
Eleonora St Jean, *Mng Member*
EMP: 1
SALES (est): 100.9K **Privately Held**
SIC: 3993 Advertising artwork

(G-6938)
GRATTON CONCRETE SAWINGDRI
677 Hampton Rd (06259-2013)
PHONE.................860 974-9127
D Gratton, *Owner*
EMP: 2
SALES (est): 88.5K **Privately Held**
SIC: 3241 Cement, hydraulic

(G-6939)
HULL FOREST PRODUCTS INC
101 Hampton Rd (06259-1712)
PHONE.................860 974-0127
William Boston Hull, *CEO*
Jeffrey M Durst, *President*
Samuel I Hull, *Vice Pres*
David Foisy, *Mill Mgr*
Dave Foisy, *Manager*
◆ **EMP:** 42
SQ FT: 61,000
SALES (est): 23.2MM **Privately Held**
SIC: 5031 2421 2426 Lumber: rough, dressed & finished; paneling, wood; sawmills & planing mills, general; hardwood dimension & flooring mills

(G-6940)
JAKES JR LAWRENCE
Also Called: J & J Moulding
405 Brooklyn Rd (06259-2403)
PHONE.................860 974-3744
Lawrence Jakes Jr, *Owner*
EMP: 22
SALES (est): 1.2MM **Privately Held**
SIC: 2431 Moldings & baseboards, ornamental & trim; moldings, wood: unfinished & prefinished

(G-6941)
LLC GLASS HOUSE
Also Called: Glasshouse
50 Swedetown Rd (06259-1014)
PHONE.................860 974-1665
James Potrezeba,
EMP: 5
SALES (est): 524.1K **Privately Held**
SIC: 3448 Sunrooms, prefabricated metal; greenhouses: prefabricated metal

(G-6942)
MIKE FINERAN
Also Called: Fineran's Finishing
280 Hampton Rd (06259-1719)
PHONE.................860 974-3276
Michael Fineran, *Owner*
EMP: 1
SALES (est): 68.4K **Privately Held**
WEB: www.mikefeinbergcompany.com
SIC: 1741 3471 Marble masonry, exterior construction; decorative plating & finishing of formed products

(G-6943)
MTR PRECISION MACHINING INC
60a Bradley Rd (06259-1501)
PHONE.................860 928-9440
Michael E Gibeault, *President*
Thomas St Jean, *Vice Pres*
EMP: 4
SQ FT: 864
SALES (est): 218K **Privately Held**
SIC: 3599 Machine shop, jobbing & repair; machine & other job shop work

(G-6944)
NESTLE USA INC
151 Mashamoquet Rd (06259)
PHONE.................860 928-0082
Peter Argentine, *Branch Mgr*
EMP: 139
SALES (corp-wide): 92B **Privately Held**
WEB: www.nestleusa.com
SIC: 2023 Evaporated milk
HQ: Nestle Usa, Inc.
1812 N Moore St Ste 118
Rosslyn VA 22209
818 549-6000

(G-6945)
OLD WOOD WORKSHOP
193 Hampton Rd (06259-1712)
PHONE.................860 655-5259
Thomas M Campbell, *Owner*
EMP: 1
SALES (est): 111.5K **Privately Held**
WEB: www.oldwoodworkshop.com
SIC: 2499 Decorative wood & woodwork

(G-6946)
PROMOS & PRINTING
61 Wrights Crossing Rd (06259-2225)
PHONE.................860 481-9212
EMP: 2
SALES (est): 83.9K **Privately Held**
SIC: 2752 Commercial printing, lithographic

(G-6947)
TONMAR LLC
Also Called: Majilly
56 Babbitt Hill Rd (06259-1700)
PHONE.................860 974-3714
Tony Emilio,
Martha Emilio,
▲ **EMP:** 3
SALES: 990K **Privately Held**
WEB: www.majilly.com
SIC: 3269 Pottery cooking & kitchen articles; pottery household articles, except kitchen articles

Poquonock
Hartford County

(G-6948)
PREVENTATIVE MAINTENANCE CORP
55 Tunxis St (06064)
PHONE.................860 683-1180
Richard Rzasa, *President*
Pamela Rzasa, *Treasurer*
▲ **EMP:** 10
SQ FT: 3,000
SALES: 200K **Privately Held**
WEB: www.presat.com
SIC: 3471 Cleaning & descaling metal products

Portland
Middlesex County

(G-6949)
AMERICAN MACHINING TECH INC
141 Pickering St (06480-1961)
PHONE.................860 342-0005
Craig Gervais, *President*
Tracy Gervais, *Admin Sec*
EMP: 5
SQ FT: 2,500
SALES: 475K **Privately Held**
SIC: 3599 Machine shop, jobbing & repair

(G-6950)
ARRIGONI WINERY
209 Sand Hill Rd (06480-1774)
PHONE.................860 342-1999
Edward B Manner, *Principal*
EMP: 3
SALES (est): 248.3K **Privately Held**
SIC: 2084 Wines

(G-6951)
B & B EQUIPMENT LLC
80 Main St Ste D (06480-4825)
PHONE.................860 342-5773
Stephen J Bankowski,
Peter J Bankowski,
EMP: 8
SQ FT: 45,000
SALES (est): 1.2MM **Privately Held**
SIC: 3565 Packaging machinery

(G-6952)
BILL MARLOW
Also Called: Marlow Tool Co
228 Rose Hill Rd (06480-1086)
PHONE.................860 829-1712
EMP: 2
SALES (est): 158.2K **Privately Held**
SIC: 3599 Mfg Industrial Machinery

(G-6953)
BIMBO BAKERIES USA INC
9 Freedom Way (06480-1058)
PHONE.................860 691-1180
EMP: 23 **Privately Held**
SIC: 2051 Bakery: wholesale or wholesale/retail combined
HQ: Bimbo Bakeries Usa, Inc
255 Business Center Dr # 200
Horsham PA 19044
215 347-5500

(G-6954)
BROWNSTONE EXPLORATION
161 Brownstone Ave (06480-1855)
P.O. Box 208 (06480-0208)
PHONE.................860 866-0208
Deb Bensenhaver, *Human Resources*
Edward Hayes, *Mng Member*
Veonica Cuthill, *Executive Asst*
Sean Hayes,
▲ **EMP:** 1 **EST:** 2005
SALES (est): 375.8K **Privately Held**
SIC: 1382 Oil & gas exploration services

(G-6955)
CLONDALKIN PHARMA & HEALTHCARE
264 Freestone Ave (06480-1640)
PHONE.................860 342-1987
EMP: 27
SALES (corp-wide): 1.3B **Privately Held**
SIC: 2657 Mfg Folding Paperboard Boxes
HQ: Clondalkin Pharma & Healthcare, Inc
1072 Boulder Rd
Greensboro NC 46268
336 292-4555

(G-6956)
DEEP RIVER FUEL TERMINALS LLC
29 Myrtle Rd (06480-1643)
P.O. Box 32 (06480-0032)
PHONE.................860 342-4619
David J Daniels, *Principal*
EMP: 3
SALES (est): 350.5K **Privately Held**
SIC: 2869 Fuels

(G-6957)
DEL PRINTING LLC
42 Gospel Ln (06480-1714)
PHONE.................860 342-2959
Gary Del, *Mng Member*
Lisa Del,
EMP: 2 **EST:** 1986
SALES (est): 190K **Privately Held**
SIC: 2752 Commercial printing, offset

(G-6958)
DIMAURO OIL CO LLC
48 Gospel Ln (06480-1714)
P.O. Box 516 (06480-0516)
PHONE.................860 342-2969
Steven Dimauro,
EMP: 1
SALES (est): 142.6K **Privately Held**
SIC: 1389 Oil field services

(G-6959)
DURBIN MACHINE INC
101 Airline Ave (06480-1908)
P.O. Box 237, Bombay NY (12914-0237)
PHONE.................860 342-1602
Gil Durbin Jr, *President*
EMP: 5
SQ FT: 2,600
SALES: 250K **Privately Held**
SIC: 3599 Machine shop, jobbing & repair

(G-6960)
JANE STERRY
Also Called: Patches and Patchwork
216 Main St (06480-1861)
PHONE.................860 342-4567
Jane F Sterry, *Owner*
EMP: 1 **EST:** 1980
SQ FT: 500
SALES: 30K **Privately Held**
SIC: 2395 5949 7299 5947 Quilted fabrics or cloth; fabric stores piece goods; quilting materials & supplies; quilting for individuals; gift shop

(G-6961)
JARVIS AIRFOIL INC
528 Glastonbury Tpke (06480-1099)
PHONE.................860 342-5000
Wal Jarvis, *President*
Elaine Nichols, *Production*
Thomas Flanagan, *QC Mgr*
Greg Terwilliger, *QC Mgr*
Michael Hrubiec, *Engineer*
▲ **EMP:** 88 **EST:** 1954
SQ FT: 50,000
SALES (est): 16.3MM
SALES (corp-wide): 20.4MM **Privately Held**
WEB: www.jarvisairfoil.com
SIC: 3728 Aircraft assemblies, subassemblies & parts; blades, aircraft propeller: metal or wood
PA: Jarvis Group, Inc.
229 Buckingham St
Hartford CT
860 278-2353

GEOGRAPHIC SECTION

(G-6962)
JOSEPH ORGANEK
Also Called: Mold-Craft Plastics
151 Freestone Ave (06480-1641)
PHONE..................860 342-1906
Joseph Organek, *Owner*
EMP: 1
SQ FT: 170
SALES (est): 136.1K **Privately Held**
SIC: 3089 3544 Injection molding of plastics; special dies, tools, jigs & fixtures

(G-6963)
LA CHANCE CONTROLS
175 Penfield Hill Rd (06480-1352)
PHONE..................860 342-2212
Ronald Lachance, *Owner*
Ronald La Chance, *Owner*
EMP: 3
SALES (est): 400K **Privately Held**
SIC: 3613 Control panels, electric

(G-6964)
MAIL CORECRON
80 Main St (06480-1870)
PHONE..................860 342-1055
Stanley Hanson, *President*
EMP: 2 **EST:** 2011
SALES (est): 101.6K **Privately Held**
SIC: 3599 Industrial machinery

(G-6965)
MARKS CONSTRUCTION CO LLC (PA)
201 Marlborough St (06480-4634)
PHONE..................860 407-2391
Shaun Mark, *Mng Member*
EMP: 1
SQ FT: 1,000
SALES (est): 180K **Privately Held**
SIC: 7692 8742 1623 1791 Welding repair; construction project management consultant; oil & gas line & compressor station construction; iron work, structural

(G-6966)
NICHOLAS PRECISION PDTS LLC
136 Marlborough St Unit F (06480-4821)
PHONE..................518 428-8109
Tiffany Cunningham, *Vice Pres*
Jim Oslander,
EMP: 2
SALES (est): 12K **Privately Held**
SIC: 3559 Pharmaceutical machinery

(G-6967)
PERMANENT PRESS LLC
86 Appletree Ln (06480-1072)
PHONE..................860 788-6001
Stephanie J Gaudino, *Manager*
EMP: 1
SALES (est): 59.7K **Privately Held**
WEB: www.thepermanentpress.net
SIC: 2741 Miscellaneous publishing

(G-6968)
PORTLAND SLITTING CO INC
193 Pickering St (06480-1961)
PHONE..................860 342-1500
James Riotte, *President*
EMP: 3
SALES (est): 290K **Privately Held**
SIC: 3312 Stainless steel

(G-6969)
PRECISION PLASTIC PRODUCTS INC
151 Freestone Ave (06480-1641)
PHONE..................860 342-2233
Edward Organek Sr, *President*
Edward Organek Jr, *Vice Pres*
Rosemarie Organek, *Admin Sec*
▲ **EMP:** 14 **EST:** 1981
SQ FT: 17,000
SALES (est): 2.5MM **Privately Held**
SIC: 3089 Injection molding of plastics

(G-6970)
QUALITY WELDING SERVICE LLC
265 Brownstone Ave (06480-1803)
PHONE..................860 342-7202
James Vacca, *Mng Member*
Joy Vacca,
EMP: 3
SALES (est): 374.7K **Privately Held**
SIC: 7692 3548 Welding repair; welding apparatus

(G-6971)
REALEJO DONUTS INC
Also Called: Dunkin' Donuts
860 Portland Cobalt Rd (06480-1731)
PHONE..................860 342-5120
Frank Realejo, *President*
Joseph Realejo, *Owner*
EMP: 13
SALES (est): 600K **Privately Held**
SIC: 5461 2051 Doughnuts; doughnuts, except frozen

(G-6972)
REDIFOILS LLC
193 Pickering St (06480-1961)
PHONE..................860 342-1500
Ketan Patel, *Mng Member*
Tushar Patel,
▲ **EMP:** 10
SQ FT: 10,000
SALES (est): 3.3MM **Privately Held**
WEB: www.redifoilsllc.com
SIC: 3312 Sheet or strip, steel, cold-rolled: own hot-rolled

(G-6973)
RIVER VALLEY OIL SERVICE LLC
695 Portland Cobalt Rd (06480-1725)
P.O. Box 866, Middletown (06457-0866)
PHONE..................860 342-5670
John Dimauro, *Mng Member*
Michael Dimauro,
EMP: 3
SALES (est): 302.5K **Privately Held**
SIC: 1311 Crude petroleum & natural gas

(G-6974)
STANDARD-KNAPP INC
63 Pickering St (06480-1957)
PHONE..................860 342-1100
Robert Roiger, *CEO*
James Michael Weaver, *President*
Mark Jehinges, *COO*
Tara Bogucki, *Accountant*
Edward Bartus, *Marketing Mgr*
▲ **EMP:** 55 **EST:** 1893
SQ FT: 50,000
SALES (est): 21.4MM
SALES (corp-wide): 355.8K **Privately Held**
WEB: www.standard-knapp.com
SIC: 3565 Packaging machinery
PA: Eol Packaging Experts Gmbh
Industriestr. 11-13
Kirchlengern

(G-6975)
SUMMIT PLASTICS LLC
91 Main St (06480-1825)
PHONE..................860 740-4482
EMP: 2 **EST:** 2016
SALES (est): 75.2K **Privately Held**
SIC: 2821 Plastics materials & resins

(G-6976)
SUPERIOR CONCRETE PRODUCTS LLC
830 Portland Cobalt Rd (06480-1731)
P.O. Box 17 (06480-0017)
PHONE..................860 342-0186
Joseph Labbadia, *Partner*
William Buggie, *Partner*
EMP: 3 **EST:** 1952
SQ FT: 3,200
SALES (est): 505.8K **Privately Held**
SIC: 3272 Septic tanks, concrete; steps, prefabricated concrete

(G-6977)
TILCON CONNECTICUT INC
Also Called: Tilcon Bituminous Concrete
231 Airline Ave (06480-1926)
PHONE..................860 342-6157
Ben Norris, *Manager*
EMP: 4
SALES (corp-wide): 30.6B **Privately Held**
WEB: www.tilconct.com
SIC: 2951 Concrete, bituminous
HQ: Tilcon Connecticut Inc.
642 Black Rock Ave
New Britain CT 06052
860 224-6010

(G-6978)
TILCON CONNECTICUT INC
Also Called: Tilcon Connecticut Portland
Black Rock Ave (06480)
P.O. Box 311228, Newington (06131-1228)
PHONE..................860 342-1096
Joel Edman, *Manager*
EMP: 8
SALES (corp-wide): 30.6B **Privately Held**
WEB: www.tilconct.com
SIC: 3273 Ready-mixed concrete
HQ: Tilcon Connecticut Inc.
642 Black Rock Ave
New Britain CT 06052
860 224-6010

(G-6979)
TRANSPORTATION CONN DEPT
Also Called: Portland Connecticut Mch Sp
263 Freestone Ave (06480-1641)
PHONE..................860 342-5996
Peter Mrowka, *Manager*
EMP: 7 **Privately Held**
WEB: www.grotonnewlondonairport.com
SIC: 3599 9621 Machine shop, jobbing & repair; regulation, administration of transportation;
HQ: Connecticut Department Of Transportation
2800 Berlin Tpke
Newington CT 06111

(G-6980)
WS WELDING LLC
121 Rose Hill Rd (06480-1245)
PHONE..................860 262-0214
Matthew Dzialo-Evans, *Mng Member*
EMP: 1
SALES (est): 34K **Privately Held**
SIC: 7692 Welding repair

Preston
New London County

(G-6981)
ARLENE LEWIS
Also Called: Stampworks, The
22 School House Rd (06365-8422)
PHONE..................860 887-4265
Arlene Lewis, *Owner*
EMP: 1
SALES: 10K **Privately Held**
SIC: 3953 5999 Embossing seals & hand stamps; rubber stamps

(G-6982)
CHICKS SANDBLASTING
101 Pierce Rd (06365-8123)
PHONE..................860 334-0059
EMP: 2 **EST:** 2017
SALES (est): 97.2K **Privately Held**
SIC: 3471 Plating & polishing

(G-6983)
FINANCIAL PRTG SOLUTIONS LLC
21a River Rd (06365-8024)
PHONE..................860 886-9931
Stephen C Behrens, *Principal*
EMP: 4
SALES (est): 550.2K **Privately Held**
SIC: 2752 Commercial printing, lithographic

(G-6984)
HYTEK PLUMBING AND HEATING LLC
241 Krug Rd (06365-8004)
PHONE..................860 389-1122
Thomas Kaiser, *CEO*
EMP: 6
SALES (est): 250.1K **Privately Held**
SIC: 3494 Plumbing & heating valves

(G-6985)
KC SERVICING LLC
461 Route 164 (06365-8111)
PHONE..................860 822-9766
Casey McLaughlin, *Principal*
EMP: 2
SALES (est): 76.3K **Privately Held**
SIC: 1389 Oil & gas field services

(G-6986)
MCGUIRES OIL LLC
19 Burdick Rd (06365-8106)
PHONE..................860 889-2567
James McGuire, *Principal*
EMP: 2
SALES (est): 108.9K **Privately Held**
SIC: 1311 Crude petroleum & natural gas

(G-6987)
PIELA ELECTRIC INC
16 Halls Mill Rd (06365-8503)
PHONE..................860 889-8476
Joseph W Piela, *President*
Joanne Piela, *Treasurer*
Judith Piela Yasi, *Admin Sec*
EMP: 15
SQ FT: 50,000
SALES (est): 5.4MM **Privately Held**
WEB: www.pielaelectric.com
SIC: 5063 7694 Motors, electric; rewinding stators; electric motor repair

(G-6988)
PRESTON RIDGE VINEYARD LLC
26 Miller Rd (06365-8515)
PHONE..................860 383-4278
Stephen J Sawyer, *Principal*
EMP: 6
SALES (est): 600.7K **Privately Held**
SIC: 2084 Wines

(G-6989)
SWEET GRASS CREAMERY LLC
51 Mattern Rd (06365-8615)
PHONE..................860 887-8098
Edward Mattern, *Principal*
EMP: 2
SALES (est): 67.3K **Privately Held**
SIC: 2021 Creamery butter

(G-6990)
SWIFT INNOVATIONS LLC
166 Watson Rd (06365-8837)
P.O. Box 3174, Mashantucket (06338-3174)
PHONE..................860 710-2725
Wade Swift,
EMP: 1
SALES (est): 125.6K **Privately Held**
SIC: 3441 Fabricated structural metal

(G-6991)
WBCB VENTURES LLC
88 Hollowell Rd (06365-8709)
PHONE..................860 383-4203
William T Buckley, *Principal*
EMP: 2
SALES (est): 141.7K **Privately Held**
SIC: 3131 Quarters

Prospect
New Haven County

(G-6992)
ACE WLDING FBRCTION RSTORATION
47 Sherwood Dr (06712-1341)
PHONE..................203 758-3550
Benjamin Vitko, *Principal*
EMP: 1
SALES (est): 48.9K **Privately Held**
SIC: 3999 Manufacturing industries

(G-6993)
BEN ART MANUFACTURING CO INC
109 Waterbury Rd (06712-1295)
PHONE..................203 758-4435
Benny A Paventy, *President*
Albert M Paventy, *Vice Pres*
Robert Paventy, *Treasurer*
EMP: 7 **EST:** 1952
SQ FT: 9,900
SALES (est): 800K **Privately Held**
SIC: 3469 Metal stampings

Prospect - New Haven County (G-6994)   GEOGRAPHIC SECTION

(G-6994)
BIG DIPPER ICE CREAM FCTRY INC
91 Waterbury Rd (06712-1223)
P.O. Box 7305 (06712-0305)
PHONE..................203 758-3200
Barbara Rowe, *President*
Harry W Rowe III, *Vice Pres*
EMP: 20
SQ FT: 2,880
SALES (est): 756.7K **Privately Held**
SIC: 5812 2024 Ice cream stands or dairy bars; ice cream & frozen desserts

(G-6995)
BIOGRAPHICAL PUBLISHING CO
95 Sycamore Dr (06712-1493)
PHONE..................203 758-3661
John Guevin, *Owner*
EMP: 1 EST: 1991
SALES (est): 19.4K **Privately Held**
SIC: 2741 Miscellaneous publishing

(G-6996)
C F D ENGINEERING COMPANY (PA)
194 Cook Rd (06712-1899)
PHONE..................203 758-4148
William Flaherty, *President*
William A Finn III, *Vice Pres*
EMP: 20
SQ FT: 2,400
SALES (est): 1.5MM **Privately Held**
WEB: www.naugatuckmfg.com
SIC: 3469 Stamping metal for the trade

(G-6997)
COMMSCOPE TECHNOLOGIES LLC
33 Union City Rd Ste 2 (06712-1550)
PHONE..................203 699-4100
Peter Sandore, *Branch Mgr*
EMP: 10 **Publicly Held**
WEB: www.andrew.com
SIC: 3663 Radio & TV communications equipment
HQ: Commscope Technologies Llc
  4 Westbrook Corporate Ctr
  Westchester IL 60154
  708 236-6600

(G-6998)
CURTISS WOODWORKING INC
123 Union City Rd (06712-1030)
PHONE..................203 527-9305
Dale R Curtiss, *President*
Lisa Curtiss, *Vice Pres*
Isabelle Curtiss, *Admin Sec*
EMP: 12
SQ FT: 10,000
SALES (est): 2.3MM **Privately Held**
WEB: www.curtisswoodworking.com
SIC: 2599 2431 Cabinets, factory; millwork

(G-6999)
CUTTING EDGE SGNS GRAPHICS LLC
Also Called: Signs & Shirts
21a Gramar Ave (06712-1091)
PHONE..................203 758-7776
Paul Ricchezza,
EMP: 1
SQ FT: 2,000
SALES (est): 141.4K **Privately Held**
SIC: 2759 3993 Screen printing; signs & advertising specialties

(G-7000)
DAVES PAVING AND CONSTRUCTION
105 Waterbury Rd Ste 5 (06712-1233)
PHONE..................203 753-4992
David Coretto, *Owner*
EMP: 3
SQ FT: 2,000
SALES (est): 200K **Privately Held**
SIC: 3531 Pavers

(G-7001)
EAST MOUNTAIN OIL CO LLC
21 Gramar Ave (06712-1017)
PHONE..................203 757-7774
Melanie Ramph, *Manager*
EMP: 2
SALES (est): 132.6K **Privately Held**
SIC: 1389 Oil field services

(G-7002)
EDWARDS & SCHMIDT LLC
16 Waterbury Rd (06712-1255)
PHONE..................203 393-5666
Benjamin F Edwards, *Manager*
EMP: 2
SALES (est): 158.3K **Privately Held**
SIC: 3011 Tires & inner tubes

(G-7003)
ERRICHETTI WOODWORKS LLC
15 Bronson Rd (06712-1002)
PHONE..................203 528-3977
Daniel Errichetti, *Principal*
EMP: 2
SALES (est): 87.1K **Privately Held**
SIC: 2431 Millwork

(G-7004)
HIGHLAND WOODWORKS
21 Gramar Ave (06712-1017)
PHONE..................203 758-6625
Arthur Tyrrell, *Principal*
EMP: 2 EST: 2008
SALES (est): 204.1K **Privately Held**
SIC: 2431 Millwork

(G-7005)
KELBY STUCCO LLC
5 Barry Ln (06712-1202)
PHONE..................203 527-9501
Donald F Kelliher, *Principal*
EMP: 1 EST: 2008
SALES (est): 83.1K **Privately Held**
SIC: 3299 Stucco

(G-7006)
KMS CANDLE COMPANY LLC
10 Birchwood Ter (06712-1301)
PHONE..................203 758-3821
Kristina Semrow, *Principal*
EMP: 1
SALES (est): 107.4K **Privately Held**
SIC: 3999 Candles

(G-7007)
LEADING EDGE PRINTERS LLC
27 Cornwall Ave (06712-1715)
PHONE..................203 592-4477
Robert S Molnar, *Principal*
EMP: 2
SALES (est): 92.3K **Privately Held**
SIC: 2752 Commercial printing, lithographic

(G-7008)
MARC TOOL & DIE INC
23 Oak Ln (06712-1315)
PHONE..................203 758-5933
Gaetan Marcoux, *President*
Marie Marcoux, *Principal*
Bart Marcoux, *Vice Pres*
EMP: 3
SALES (est): 150K **Privately Held**
SIC: 3544 Special dies & tools; jigs & fixtures; industrial molds

(G-7009)
MARIO PRECISION PRODUCTS
19 Wihbey Dr (06712-1466)
PHONE..................203 758-3101
Mario Dias, *Owner*
EMP: 3
SALES: 50K **Privately Held**
SIC: 3451 Screw machine products

(G-7010)
MDN ASSOC INC
18 Robindale Dr (06712-1439)
PHONE..................203 758-6721
Michael J Rasmussen, *President*
EMP: 2
SALES (est): 220.7K **Privately Held**
SIC: 3545 Machine tool accessories

(G-7011)
MONTAMBAULT RIVA
Also Called: Address For Success
25 Luke St (06712-1428)
PHONE..................203 758-4981
EMP: 2
SALES (est): 100K **Privately Held**
SIC: 2621 2754 Paper Mill Gravure Commercial Printing

(G-7012)
OPTIMUM WELDING SOLUTIONS LLC
25 Gramar Ave Unit B (06712-1017)
PHONE..................203 598-8489
Liane Toupin,
EMP: 1 EST: 2017
SALES (est): 37.6K **Privately Held**
SIC: 7692 Welding repair

(G-7013)
OXFORD GENERAL INDUSTRIES INC
3 Gramar Ave (06712-1017)
P.O. Box 7033 (06712-0033)
PHONE..................203 758-4467
D L Carnaroli, *Vice Pres*
Brian Barrett, *Vice Pres*
Donna L Carnaroli, *Vice Pres*
Gordon Eckman, *Vice Pres*
EMP: 11
SQ FT: 25,000
SALES (est): 1.8MM **Privately Held**
SIC: 3499 3544 3542 Machine bases, metal; special dies, tools, jigs & fixtures; machine tools, metal forming type

(G-7014)
PACKARD INC
Also Called: Packard Specialties
6 Industrial Rd (06712-1018)
P.O. Box 7238 (06712-0238)
PHONE..................203 758-6219
John F Jones, *President*
Carol Jones, *Vice Pres*
Paul Bird, *Engineer*
EMP: 20 EST: 1980
SQ FT: 15,000
SALES (est): 4.4MM **Privately Held**
WEB: www.packardinc.com
SIC: 3565 3569 Packaging machinery; assembly machines, non-metalworking

(G-7015)
PALLASIAN SOFTWARE LLC
6 Rolling Ridge Ct (06712-1737)
PHONE..................203 758-5868
Michael Arisian, *Principal*
EMP: 2
SALES (est): 78.4K **Privately Held**
SIC: 7372 Prepackaged software

(G-7016)
POLAR INDUSTRIES INC (PA)
32 Gramar Ave (06712-1016)
P.O. Box 7075 (06712-0075)
PHONE..................203 758-6651
Eugene R Lewis, *Ch of Bd*
David L Lewis, *President*
Mike Accuosti, *Controller*
▲ EMP: 35
SALES (est): 6.4MM **Privately Held**
WEB: www.polarcentral.com
SIC: 2821 Polystyrene resins

(G-7017)
PROSPECT FLOORING
19a Scott Rd (06712-1331)
PHONE..................203 758-4207
Paul Bresnahan, *President*
Anita Bresnahan, *Vice Pres*
Eric Bresnahan,
EMP: 3 EST: 1973
SALES: 175K **Privately Held**
SIC: 5713 2591 7359 Floor covering stores; blinds vertical; home cleaning & maintenance equipment rental services

(G-7018)
PROSPECT INDUSTRIES LLC
Also Called: CMS Automation
4 Catherine Dr (06712-1302)
PHONE..................203 758-3736
Tammy Canfield, *CFO*
Tammy Liscomb, *Mng Member*
EMP: 2 EST: 2011
SQ FT: 2,500
SALES (est): 530.1K **Privately Held**
SIC: 3569 Liquid automation machinery & equipment

(G-7019)
PROSPECT MACHINE PRODUCTS INC
139 Union City Rd (06712-1031)
P.O. Box 7016 (06712-0016)
PHONE..................203 758-4448
Richard Laurenzi, *President*
David Boiano, *Engineer*
Karen McWhirt, *Controller*
Anthony Romero, *Sales Staff*
EMP: 23
SQ FT: 20,000
SALES (est): 6.8MM **Privately Held**
SIC: 3469 8711 Stamping metal for the trade; machine tool design

(G-7020)
PROSPECT PAGES LLC
50 Waterbury Rd Ste C (06712-1259)
P.O. Box 7100 (06712-0100)
PHONE..................203 758-6934
Gwenn Fischer, *Mng Member*
EMP: 2
SALES (est): 180.3K **Privately Held**
SIC: 2711 Newspapers, publishing & printing

(G-7021)
PROSPECT PRINTING LLC
16 Waterbury Rd (06712-1255)
P.O. Box 7242 (06712-0242)
PHONE..................203 758-6007
Angela Halloran, *Cust Mgr*
Paul Dipietro, *Accounts Exec*
Mark Deloia,
Mike Ambrose,
Anthony Bracco,
EMP: 10
SQ FT: 5,500
SALES (est): 1.8MM **Privately Held**
SIC: 2752 Commercial printing, offset

(G-7022)
PRS MOBILE LLC
2 New Haven Rd (06712-1623)
PHONE..................203 909-5249
EMP: 1 EST: 2018
SALES (est): 37.5K **Privately Held**
SIC: 2741 Miscellaneous publishing

(G-7023)
RED BARN INNOVATIONS
Also Called: Friction Force
8 Tress Rd (06712-1727)
PHONE..................203 393-0778
Thomas Allen, *Owner*
EMP: 5
SALES (est): 0 **Privately Held**
SIC: 3569 General industrial machinery

(G-7024)
SGA COMPONENTS GROUP LLC
13 Gramar Ave (06712-1017)
PHONE..................203 758-3702
Robert N Morin,
EMP: 8
SQ FT: 5,000
SALES (est): 600K **Privately Held**
WEB: www.sgalt.com
SIC: 3451 Screw machine products

(G-7025)
SHELDON PRECISION LLC
10 Industrial Rd (06712-1018)
PHONE..................203 758-4441
John Hoskins Jr, *CEO*
EMP: 50
SQ FT: 17,500
SALES: 12MM **Privately Held**
SIC: 3451 Screw machine products

(G-7026)
THERMO CONDUCTOR SERVICES INC
3 Industrial Rd (06712-1039)
P.O. Box 7191 (06712-0191)
PHONE..................203 758-6611
Mark Baker, *President*
▲ EMP: 5
SALES (est): 1MM **Privately Held**
SIC: 3312 Blast furnaces & steel mills

Putnam — Windham County

(G-7027) TSS & A INC
Also Called: Triple Stitch Sportswear
115 Waterbury Rd (06712-1254)
P.O. Box 7036 (06712-0036)
PHONE..................800 633-3536
Joseph Commendatore, *President*
Nicholas D'Eramo, *Vice Pres*
EMP: 13
SQ FT: 3,000
SALES (est): 1.5MM **Privately Held**
WEB: www.triplestitch.com
SIC: 2395 7336 Embroidery products, except schiffli machine; silk screen design; creative services to advertisers, except writers

Putnam
Windham County

(G-7028) AEROTECH FASTENERS INC
1 Ridge Rd (06260-3034)
PHONE..................860 928-6300
Erik Sandberg-Diment, *President*
Frank Di Rienzo, *Vice Pres*
EMP: 13
SQ FT: 18,000
SALES (est): 2MM **Privately Held**
WEB: www.aerotechfasteners.com
SIC: 3452 Screws, metal; rivets, metal

(G-7029) AMR MACHINES LLC
77 Industrial Park Rd # 6 (06260-3005)
PHONE..................860 336-6208
Austin Riley,
EMP: 1
SALES (est): 201.1K **Privately Held**
SIC: 3541 Machine tools, metal cutting type

(G-7030) APOGEE CORPORATION (PA)
Also Called: Impact Plastics
5 Highland Dr (06260-3010)
PHONE..................860 963-1976
Christopher L Ryan, *Principal*
David Kingeter, *Chairman*
Steven M Ryan, *Treasurer*
Christopher Ryan, *Admin Sec*
▲ **EMP:** 60 **EST:** 1970
SALES (est): 10MM **Privately Held**
WEB: www.impactplastics-ct.com
SIC: 3081 Unsupported plastics film & sheet

(G-7031) BARNES CONCRETE CO INC
873 Providence Pike (06260-2606)
PHONE..................860 928-7242
David Barnes, *President*
Bruce Barnes, *Vice Pres*
EMP: 20
SQ FT: 2,500
SALES: 4MM **Privately Held**
SIC: 3273 Ready-mixed concrete

(G-7032) CASTROL INDUSTRIAL N AMER INC
251 Kennedy Dr (06260-1628)
PHONE..................860 928-5100
Dan Caissie, *Branch Mgr*
EMP: 5
SALES (corp-wide): 298.7B **Privately Held**
SIC: 2992 Lubricating oils & greases
HQ: Castrol Industrial North America Inc.
150 W Warrenville Rd
Naperville IL 60563
877 641-1600

(G-7033) CENTRAL CONSTRUCTION INDS LLC
Also Called: CCI
30 Harris St (06260-1907)
P.O. Box 229 (06260-0229)
PHONE..................860 963-8902
Lloyd Frink,
Bruce A Richards,
EMP: 20 **EST:** 1996

SALES (est): 5.6MM **Privately Held**
WEB: www.ccict.com
SIC: 3441 1542 1521 Fabricated structural metal; nonresidential construction; single-family housing construction

(G-7034) CHASE GRAPHICS INC
124 School St (06260-1613)
PHONE..................860 315-9006
James St Jean, *President*
Debra St Jean, *Vice Pres*
Jennifer Beckett, *Executive*
Nadeau Carolyn, *Graphic Designe*
Kathleen Guertin, *Graphic Designe*
EMP: 11
SQ FT: 4,500
SALES (est): 1.8MM **Privately Held**
WEB: www.chasegraphics.com
SIC: 2752 Commercial printing, offset

(G-7035) CONNECTICUT TOOL CO INC
6 Highland Dr (06260-3007)
PHONE..................860 928-0565
Philip Durand, *Chairman*
Stephen Durand, *Vice Pres*
Claire Durand, *Admin Sec*
EMP: 24
SQ FT: 13,500
SALES (est): 4.4MM **Privately Held**
WEB: www.conntool.com
SIC: 3089 3544 Injection molding of plastics; special dies, tools, jigs & fixtures

(G-7036) CONNTROL INTERNATIONAL INC
135 Park Rd (06260-3032)
P.O. Box 645 (06260-0645)
PHONE..................860 928-0567
Ronald Braaten, *President*
Willie O Pritchard, *Admin Sec*
EMP: 12
SQ FT: 13,000
SALES (est): 1.4MM **Privately Held**
WEB: www.conntrol.com
SIC: 3625 Relays & industrial controls

(G-7037) CONTROL CONCEPTS INC (PA)
Also Called: Merlyn
100 Park St (06260-2332)
PHONE..................860 928-6551
Henry D Tiffany III, *President*
Serena Rutherford, *Bookkeeper*
Jonathan Larrabee, *Admin Sec*
◆ **EMP:** 12
SQ FT: 8,200
SALES: 3.5MM **Privately Held**
WEB: www.speedswitch.com
SIC: 3625 3613 3566 Switches, electronic applications; switches, electric power except snap, push button, etc.; speed changers, drives & gears

(G-7038) CREATIVE ENVELOPE INC
26 Highland Dr (06260-3007)
P.O. Box 588 (06260-0588)
PHONE..................860 963-1231
Richard A Sherman, *President*
▲ **EMP:** 4
SQ FT: 5,000
SALES (est): 843K **Privately Held**
WEB: www.creativeenvelope.com
SIC: 2759 Commercial printing

(G-7039) DIMENSION-POLYANT INC
78 Highland Dr (06260-3037)
PHONE..................860 928-8300
John E Gluek Jr, *President*
Kenneth Madsen, *Vice Pres*
Karin Ruckwardt, *Treasurer*
Don Swanson, *Controller*
Becky Tellier, *Info Tech Mgr*
◆ **EMP:** 35
SQ FT: 50,000
SALES (est): 7MM **Privately Held**
WEB: www.dimension-polyant.com
SIC: 2211 2221 2394 Sail cloth; broadwoven fabric mills, manmade; canvas & related products

(G-7040) ENSINGER PRCSION CMPONENTS INC
Also Called: Plastock
11 Danco Rd (06260-3001)
PHONE..................860 928-7911
Matt McKenney, *General Mgr*
Roland Comtois, *Engineer*
▲ **EMP:** 65
SQ FT: 66,000
SALES (est): 7MM
SALES (corp-wide): 533.1MM **Privately Held**
WEB: www.putnamprecisionmolding.com
SIC: 3089 Injection molding of plastics
HQ: Ensinger Industries, Inc.
365 Meadowlands Blvd
Washington PA 15301
724 746-6050

(G-7041) FLUID COATING TECHNOLOGY INC
48 Industrial Park Rd (06260-3003)
PHONE..................860 963-2505
Nathan Rosebrooks, *President*
Roger De Bruyn, *Vice Pres*
Janet Hill, *Technology*
EMP: 5
SQ FT: 5,500
SALES (est): 806.3K **Privately Held**
WEB: www.fct-inc.com
SIC: 3229 Fiber optics strands

(G-7042) FOSTER CORPORATION (HQ)
Also Called: Foster Delivery Science
45 Ridge Rd (06260-3034)
PHONE..................860 928-4102
Larry Acquarulo, *CEO*
Hank Hague, *COO*
Carmella Robles, *Prdtn Mgr*
Art Beshaw, *Production*
Carol-Lynn Maynard, *Buyer*
▲ **EMP:** 65
SQ FT: 43,000
SALES (est): 14.3MM **Privately Held**
SIC: 3087 Custom compound purchased resins

(G-7043) FOSTER DELIVERY SCIENCE INC (DH)
36 Ridge Rd (06260-3035)
PHONE..................860 928-4102
Hank Hague, *CFO*
EMP: 12
SALES (est): 1.6MM **Privately Held**
SIC: 2834 Pharmaceutical preparations
HQ: Foster Corporation
45 Ridge Rd
Putnam CT 06260
860 928-4102

(G-7044) FOSTER DELIVERY SCIENCE INC
45 Ridge Rd (06260-3034)
PHONE..................860 630-4515
Lawrence Acquarulo, *CEO*
EMP: 12 **Privately Held**
SIC: 2834 Tablets, pharmaceutical
HQ: Foster Delivery Science, Inc.
36 Ridge Rd
Putnam CT 06260
860 928-4102

(G-7045) GRAPHICS UNLIMITED
445 School St (06260-1349)
P.O. Box 262, Pomfret (06258-0262)
PHONE..................860 928-1407
Joel Perry, *Owner*
Aaron Perry, *Manager*
EMP: 5
SALES: 560K **Privately Held**
SIC: 7389 3993 Lettering & sign painting services; signs & advertising specialties

(G-7046) IMMERSIVE CUSTOM COATINGS
30 Chassey St (06260-1747)
PHONE..................401 636-1196
Chris Morris, *Principal*
EMP: 2

SALES (est): 81.5K **Privately Held**
SIC: 3479 Metal coating & allied service

(G-7047) INTERNATIONAL PAPER COMPANY
175 Park Rd (06260-3040)
PHONE..................860 928-7901
Anita Santerre, *Human Res Mgr*
Don Davis, *Manager*
Kevin Shead, *Manager*
EMP: 130
SALES (corp-wide): 23.3B **Publicly Held**
WEB: www.internationalpaper.com
SIC: 2621 Paper mills
PA: International Paper Company
6400 Poplar Ave
Memphis TN 38197
901 419-9000

(G-7048) J B CONCRETE PRODUCTS INC
1 Arch St (06260)
P.O. Box 387 (06260-0387)
PHONE..................860 928-9365
John W Barnes Sr, *President*
Heather Barnes, *Admin Sec*
EMP: 5 **EST:** 1969
SQ FT: 9,000
SALES (est): 883.4K **Privately Held**
SIC: 3272 Tanks, concrete; septic tanks, concrete; steps, prefabricated concrete

(G-7049) JAMES WRIGHT PRECISION PDTS
20 Mechanics St (06260-1315)
P.O. Box 924 (06260-0924)
PHONE..................860 928-7756
Robert A Main Jr, *President*
Susan Main, *Corp Secy*
William Main, *Vice Pres*
EMP: 12 **EST:** 1975
SQ FT: 7,500
SALES (est): 1.9MM
SALES (corp-wide): 35.5MM **Privately Held**
WEB: www.jwpp.com
SIC: 3451 Screw machine products
PA: Main, Robert A & Sons Holding Company Inc
555 Goffle Rd
Wyckoff NJ 07481
201 447-3700

(G-7050) JIMS MACHINE SHOP INC
475 School St (06260-2430)
PHONE..................860 928-5151
James Fitzsimmons, *President*
EMP: 1
SALES (est): 179.9K **Privately Held**
SIC: 3545 Precision tools, machinists'

(G-7051) KAPSTONE PAPER AND PACKG CORP
25 Intervale St (06260-1312)
PHONE..................860 928-2211
EMP: 3
SALES (corp-wide): 16.2B **Publicly Held**
SIC: 2653 Corrugated & solid fiber boxes
HQ: Kapstone Paper And Packaging Corporation
1000 Abernathy Rd
Atlanta GA 30328
770 448-2193

(G-7052) NATIONAL CHROMIUM COMPANY INC
10 Senexet Rd (06260-1039)
PHONE..................860 928-7965
John Miller, *President*
Whitby K Ellsworth, *Admin Sec*
EMP: 11 **EST:** 1941
SQ FT: 9,000
SALES (est): 1.4MM **Privately Held**
WEB: www.nationalchromium.com
SIC: 3471 Chromium plating of metals or formed products; electroplating & plating; electroplating of metals or formed products

Putnam - Windham County (G-7053)

(G-7053)
NEW ENGLAND PLASMA DEV CORP
14 Highland Dr (06260-3007)
P.O. Box 369 (06260-0369)
PHONE....................860 928-6561
Peter J Olshewski, *President*
Maureen Olshewski, *Vice Pres*
EMP: 10
SQ FT: 3,800
SALES (est): 1.9MM **Privately Held**
WEB: www.neplasma.com
SIC: 3541 Machine tools, metal cutting type

(G-7054)
NUTMEG CONTAINER CORPORATION (HQ)
100 Canal St (06260-1912)
PHONE....................860 963-6727
Harry A Perkins, *CEO*
Charles Pious, *President*
James Pious, *Exec VP*
EMP: 100
SQ FT: 25,000
SALES (est): 15.9MM
SALES (corp-wide): 121.1MM **Privately Held**
SIC: 2653 Boxes, corrugated: made from purchased materials
PA: Connecticut Container Corp.
455 Sackett Point Rd
North Haven CT 06473
203 248-2161

(G-7055)
OMNICRON ELECTRONICS
554 Liberty Hwy Ste 2 (06260-2728)
P.O. Box 623 (06260-0623)
PHONE....................860 928-0377
William Jones, *Owner*
EMP: 6 **EST:** 1976
SQ FT: 4,000
SALES (est): 200K **Privately Held**
SIC: 3651 3677 Recording machines, except dictation & telephone answering; coupling transformers

(G-7056)
OPTICONX INC
45 Danco Rd (06260-3001)
PHONE....................888 748-6855
Patricia Doherty, *President*
Paul Doherty, *Vice Pres*
Paul Langlois, *VP Mfg*
Mark Lavallee, *Regl Sales Mgr*
EMP: 25
SQ FT: 16,000
SALES (est): 5.8MM **Privately Held**
WEB: www.opticonx.com
SIC: 3661 Fiber optics communications equipment

(G-7057)
PALLFLEX PRODUCTS COMPANY
125 Kennedy Dr (06260-1945)
PHONE....................860 928-7761
Lawrence D Kingsley, *President*
Ronald Hoffman, *Chairman*
Joseph Doherty, *Vice Pres*
Lisa McDermott, *CFO*
▲ **EMP:** 50 **EST:** 1990
SALES (est): 11.4MM
SALES (corp-wide): 19.8B **Publicly Held**
WEB: www.pall.com
SIC: 3569 Filters, general line: industrial
HQ: Pall Corporation
25 Harbor Park Dr
Port Washington NY 11050
516 484-5400

(G-7058)
PHILLIPS-MOLDEX COMPANY
161 Park Rd (06260-3032)
PHONE....................860 928-0401
Lawrence C Moon Jr, *President*
Robert Gaura, *Vice Pres*
Gregory Mickelson, *Vice Pres*
Keld Rasmussen, *Vice Pres*
Jennifer Lyons, *Admin Sec*
EMP: 25
SALES (est): 5.7MM
SALES (corp-wide): 43.3MM **Privately Held**
SIC: 3089 Injection molding of plastics
PA: C. Cowles & Company
126 Bailey Rd
North Haven CT 06473
203 865-3117

(G-7059)
POLYMEDEX DISCOVERY GROUP INC (PA)
45 Ridge Rd (06260-3034)
PHONE....................860 928-4102
Lawrence A Acquarulo Jr, *President*
Hank Hague, *COO*
EMP: 15
SALES (est): 17.7MM **Privately Held**
SIC: 3082 3083 6719 Tubes, unsupported plastic; laminated plastics plate & sheet; investment holding companies, except banks

(G-7060)
PRISON PUBLICATIONS INC
107 Providence St (06260-1542)
PHONE....................860 928-4055
EMP: 6
SALES (est): 411.8K **Privately Held**
SIC: 2741 Miscellaneous publishing

(G-7061)
R W E INC
91 Highland Dr (06260-3010)
P.O. Box 431 (06260-0431)
PHONE....................860 974-1101
Eric Whittenburg, *President*
Robin Whittenburg, *Vice Pres*
Steve Labonte, *Engineer*
Bob Laroche, *Engineer*
EMP: 34
SQ FT: 15,000
SALES: 5MM **Privately Held**
WEB: www.erwinc.com
SIC: 3444 Sheet metal specialties, not stamped

(G-7062)
RAWSON MANUFACTURING INC (PA)
99 Canal St (06260-1909)
PHONE....................860 928-4458
James Rawson, *President*
Ben Rawson, *Vice Pres*
Jim Rawson, *Branch Mgr*
Donna Rawson, *Admin Sec*
EMP: 17
SQ FT: 24,299
SALES (est): 3MM **Privately Held**
WEB: www.rawsonscreens.com
SIC: 3531 Construction machinery

(G-7063)
RENCHEL TOOL INC
51 Ridge Rd (06260-3034)
PHONE....................860 315-9017
Ronald Williams, *President*
Brenda Williams, *Corp Secy*
Robert McCurry, *Vice Pres*
Shane Szall, *Vice Pres*
Renee Williams, *Admin Asst*
EMP: 12
SQ FT: 3,000
SALES (est): 2.6MM **Privately Held**
WEB: www.rencheltoolinc.com
SIC: 3599 Machine shop, jobbing & repair

(G-7064)
SHIPPEE SOLAR AND CNSTR LLC
111 Sabin St (06260-1844)
PHONE....................860 630-0322
Denise Shippee,
EMP: 2
SALES (est): 154.8K **Privately Held**
SIC: 3433 Heating equipment, except electric

(G-7065)
SHOPPERS-TURNPIKE CORPORATION
Also Called: Shoppers Guide
70 Main St (06260-1918)
P.O. Box 529 (06260-0529)
PHONE....................860 928-3040
Dennis E Neumann, *President*
Wilbur D Neumann, *President*
EMP: 18
SQ FT: 2,000
SALES (est): 1.5MM **Privately Held**
WEB: www.shopperturnpike.com
SIC: 2741 Guides: publishing only, not printed on site

(G-7066)
SLATER HILL TOOL LLC
77 Industrial Park Rd (06260-3005)
PHONE....................860 963-0415
Josh W Nason, *Principal*
EMP: 3
SALES (est): 220K **Privately Held**
SIC: 3599 3546 Machine shop, jobbing & repair; power-driven handtools

(G-7067)
SONOCO
29 Park Rd (06260-3044)
PHONE....................860 928-7795
EMP: 6
SALES (est): 1MM **Privately Held**
SIC: 2631 Paperboard mills

(G-7068)
SONOCO PRTECTIVE SOLUTIONS INC
29 Park Rd (06260-3044)
PHONE....................860 928-7795
Emil Castagna, *Prdtn Mgr*
Ken Blandina, *Foreman/Supr*
EMP: 48
SQ FT: 80,000
SALES (corp-wide): 5.3B **Publicly Held**
WEB: www.tuscarora.com
SIC: 3086 2821 2671 Packaging & shipping materials, foamed plastic; plastics materials & resins; packaging paper & plastics film, coated & laminated
HQ: Sonoco Protective Solutions, Inc.
1 N 2nd St
Hartsville SC 29550
843 383-7000

(G-7069)
SPECTRAL LLC (PA)
Also Called: Spectral Products
111 Highland Dr (06260-3010)
PHONE....................860 928-7726
Sheila Dupre, *Manager*
Yu H Hahn,
▲ **EMP:** 5
SALES: 1.5MM **Privately Held**
SIC: 3826 Analytical instruments

(G-7070)
SPECTRAL OPTICS INC
111 Highland Dr (06260-3010)
PHONE....................978 682-1302
Joung Hwa Namgung, *Partner*
Jin Im Kim, *Principal*
Daze Lee, *Principal*
EMP: 1 **EST:** 2015
SALES (est): 85.6K **Privately Held**
SIC: 3827 Optical instruments & lenses

(G-7071)
SUPERIOR PLAS EXTRUSION CO INC (PA)
Also Called: Town of Putnam
5 Highland Dr (06260-3010)
PHONE....................860 963-1976
David P Kingeter, *President*
Steven M Ryan, *Treasurer*
Stephen Stedioso, *Controller*
Denis A Chaves, *Admin Sec*
▲ **EMP:** 44
SQ FT: 50,000
SALES (est): 12.6MM **Privately Held**
WEB: www.impactputnam.com
SIC: 3081 Plastic film & sheet

(G-7072)
TEN 22 INC
Also Called: Putnam Town Crier & N E Ledger
158 Main St Ste 9 (06260-1965)
PHONE....................860 963-1050
Linda Lemmon, *President*
EMP: 1
SALES (est): 88.8K **Privately Held**
SIC: 2711 Newspapers, publishing & printing

(G-7073)
TERRIS AFFORDABLE EMBROIDERY
144 Providence St (06260-1532)
PHONE....................860 928-0552
Terri Larochelle, *Owner*
EMP: 1
SALES (est): 77.1K **Privately Held**
SIC: 2284 Embroidery thread

(G-7074)
TERRIS EMBROIDERY
96 Front St (06260-1643)
PHONE....................860 928-0552
Terri Larochelle, *Principal*
EMP: 1 **EST:** 2014
SALES (est): 69.2K **Privately Held**
SIC: 2395 Embroidery products, except schiffli machine

(G-7075)
UNIBOARD CORP
Also Called: Teleboardusa.com
570 River Rd (06260-2929)
P.O. Box 2 (06260-0002)
PHONE....................860 428-5979
Martin Fey, *President*
Bill Butler, *Vice Pres*
Erik Fey, *Director*
EMP: 6
SALES (est): 380K **Privately Held**
SIC: 3949 Water sports equipment

(G-7076)
US BUTTON CORPORATION
328 Kennedy Dr (06260-1629)
PHONE....................860 928-2707
Larry Jacobs, *President*
◆ **EMP:** 140
SQ FT: 100,000
SALES (est): 21.1MM **Privately Held**
WEB: www.usbutton.com
SIC: 3965 Buttons & parts

(G-7077)
VILLAGER NEWSPAPERS
107 Providence St (06260-1542)
PHONE....................860 928-1818
Ron Tremblay, *Principal*
EMP: 5
SALES (est): 157.9K **Privately Held**
SIC: 2711 Commercial printing & newspaper publishing combined; newspapers, publishing & printing

(G-7078)
WILLIAMS MOLD & MACHINE
407 Chase Rd (06260-2812)
PHONE....................860 928-3522
Kenneth Williams, *Owner*
EMP: 1 **EST:** 1996
SALES (est): 87.5K **Privately Held**
SIC: 3599 Machine shop, jobbing & repair

(G-7079)
WINDHAM CONTAINER CORPORATION
30 Park Rd (06260-3030)
P.O. Box 944 (06260-0944)
PHONE....................860 928-7934
Gordie Mauer, *President*
Jeanine Mauer, *Treasurer*
EMP: 20 **EST:** 1958
SQ FT: 45,000
SALES (est): 4MM **Privately Held**
WEB: www.windhamcontainer.com
SIC: 2653 2671 Boxes, corrugated: made from purchased materials; packaging paper & plastics film, coated & laminated

(G-7080)
WOODSTOCK LINE CO
91 Canal St (06260-1947)
PHONE....................860 928-6557
Bernard Phaneuf, *President*
Dale Johnson, *Manager*
▲ **EMP:** 15 **EST:** 1946
SQ FT: 22,000
SALES (est): 2.1MM **Privately Held**
WEB: www.woodstockline.com
SIC: 2298 Cord, braided; fishing lines, nets, seines: made in cordage or twine mills

▲ = Import ▼ = Export
◆ = Import/Export

(G-7081)
WOOLWORKS LTD
154 Main St B (06260-1932)
PHONE..................................860 963-1228
Jennifer Ruggirello, *Principal*
EMP: 3
SALES (est): 160K **Privately Held**
SIC: 3229 Yarn, fiberglass

Quaker Hill
New London County

(G-7082)
HANNA RES & CONSULTING LLC
72 Old Colchester Rd (06375-1008)
PHONE..................................860 443-0443
John Hanna,
Bonnie Hanna,
EMP: 1
SALES (est): 56K **Privately Held**
SIC: 7372 Educational computer software

(G-7083)
MISFIT PUBLISHING CO LLC
11 Totoket Rd (06375-1328)
PHONE..................................860 444-6796
Joseph Podurgiel, *Principal*
EMP: 1
SALES (est): 56.1K **Privately Held**
SIC: 2741 Miscellaneous publishing

(G-7084)
RHODE ISLAND RACEWAY LLC
846 Vauxhall Street Ext (06375-1031)
PHONE..................................860 701-0192
Jonathan Avery, *Principal*
EMP: 3
SALES (est): 160.7K **Privately Held**
SIC: 3644 Raceways

(G-7085)
T&K TECHNICAL SERVICES LLC
Also Called: Pjtrepanier Tktechserv.com
26 Upper Bartlett Rd (06375-1031)
PHONE..................................860 235-5882
Paul Trepanier, *CEO*
Michael B Keith, *CFO*
Michael Keith, *CFO*
EMP: 5
SALES (est): 279.7K **Privately Held**
SIC: 8711 3674 5999 3679 Electrical or electronic engineering; solid state electronic devices; training materials, electronic; harness assemblies for electronic use: wire or cable

(G-7086)
USES MFG INC
152 Old Colchester Rd (06375-1025)
P.O. Box 156 (06375-0156)
PHONE..................................860 443-8737
Brian Wohlforth, *President*
Edmund Wohlforth, *Vice Pres*
Doris Wohlforth, *Treasurer*
EMP: 4
SQ FT: 2,500
SALES (est): 450.6K **Privately Held**
WEB: www.usesmfg.com
SIC: 3825 Energy measuring equipment, electrical

Redding
Fairfield County

(G-7087)
A FAMILY FARM
Also Called: Pegasus Productions
145 Mountain Rd (06896-2715)
PHONE..................................203 438-5497
Mike Ammirata, *Owner*
Margaret Ammirata, *Owner*
EMP: 2 **EST:** 2000
SALES (est): 180.5K **Privately Held**
SIC: 3523 Potato diggers, harvesters & planters

(G-7088)
ALTERNATE INC
30 Orchard Dr (06896-2911)
P.O. Box 811, Georgetown (06829-0811)
PHONE..................................203 938-4125
Don Smiffen, *Owner*
Sharon Smiffen, *Principal*
EMP: 1
SALES (est): 78.8K **Privately Held**
SIC: 5251 3812 Tools; compasses & accessories

(G-7089)
AMERICAN ACTUATOR CORPORATION
292 Newtown Tpke (06896-2418)
P.O. Box 113096, Stamford (06911-3096)
PHONE..................................203 324-6334
Joseph Fowler, *President*
Evelyn Fowler, *Corp Secy*
EMP: 14
SQ FT: 1,800
SALES (est): 1.5MM **Privately Held**
SIC: 3542 Machine tools, metal forming type

(G-7090)
ARMORED SHIELD TECHNOLOGIES
Also Called: Cable Manufacturing Business
3655 W Mcfadden Ave (06896)
PHONE..................................714 848-5796
Christopher Badinelli, *President*
▲ **EMP:** 15
SQ FT: 10,000
SALES (est): 2.3MM **Privately Held**
WEB: www.cablemanufacturing.com
SIC: 3496 Cable, uninsulated wire: made from purchased wire

(G-7091)
CROSSFIELD CONCEPTS INC
105 Cross Hwy (06896-2406)
PHONE..................................203 938-5667
Laurie Heiss, *President*
EMP: 1
SALES (est): 54K **Privately Held**
SIC: 2741 Business service newsletters: publishing & printing

(G-7092)
GE OIL & GAS ESP INC
78 Black Rock Tpke (06896-3010)
PHONE..................................405 670-1431
EMP: 30
SALES (corp-wide): 121.6B **Publicly Held**
WEB: www.woodgroup-esp.com
SIC: 1389 Testing, measuring, surveying & analysis services
HQ: Ge Oil & Gas Esp, Inc.
5500 Se 59th St
Oklahoma City OK 73135
405 670-1431

(G-7093)
GOLD LINE CONNECTOR INC (PA)
40 Great Pasture Rd (06896-2303)
P.O. Box 500 (06896-0500)
PHONE..................................203 938-2588
Martin Miller, *President*
Marjorie Miller, *Vice Pres*
EMP: 30 **EST:** 1961
SALES (est): 2.2MM **Privately Held**
WEB: www.gold-line.com
SIC: 3825 3663 3643 3829 Radio apparatus analyzers; citizens' band (CB) radio; marine radio communications equipment; connectors, electric cord; measuring & controlling devices

(G-7094)
HEIDI M GREENE INC
18 Lonetown Rd (06896)
P.O. Box 148 (06896-0148)
PHONE..................................203 938-4132
Heidi M Greene, *President*
EMP: 2 **EST:** 1999
SALES (est): 164.3K **Privately Held**
WEB: www.heidiaishman.com
SIC: 2299 Yarns, specialty & novelty

(G-7095)
INTELLIGRATED SYSTEMS OHIO LLC
3 Costa Ln (06896-1401)
PHONE..................................203 938-8404
Jeff Dooley, *Principal*
EMP: 1
SALES (corp-wide): 41.8B **Publicly Held**
WEB: www.fkilogistex.com
SIC: 3535 Conveyors & conveying equipment
HQ: Intelligrated Systems Of Ohio, Llc
7901 Innovation Way
Mason OH 45040
513 701-7300

(G-7096)
LITTLEFINGERS SOFTWARE
5 Chapman Pl (06896-1224)
PHONE..................................203 938-2684
Amy S Gallen, *Owner*
EMP: 1
SALES: 50K **Privately Held**
WEB: www.littlefingers.com
SIC: 7372 5734 Prepackaged software; computer & software stores

(G-7097)
LOCAL TRAFFIC FUSION LLC
431 Newtown Tpke (06896-2014)
PHONE..................................203 938-8862
Anthony Wahl, *President*
EMP: 1
SALES (est): 42.1K **Privately Held**
SIC: 2099 Coconut, desiccated & shredded

(G-7098)
LOLLIPOP KIDS LLC
13 Woodland Drive Ext (06896-3407)
PHONE..................................203 664-1799
EMP: 3
SALES (est): 111.3K **Privately Held**
SIC: 2064 Lollipops & other hard candy

(G-7099)
M P ROBINSON PRODUCTION
77 Topstone Rd (06896-1816)
PHONE..................................203 938-1336
Martin Robinson, *Owner*
Lore K Wright, *Nurse*
EMP: 20 **EST:** 1994
SALES (est): 613.3K **Privately Held**
SIC: 3999 3569 Puppets & marionettes; general industrial machinery

(G-7100)
MC MAHON PUBLISHING CO
83 Peaceable St (06896-3198)
PHONE..................................203 544-8389
Raymond Mc Mahon, *Principal*
Kate Carmody, *Sales Staff*
EMP: 2
SALES (est): 135.9K **Privately Held**
SIC: 2741 Miscellaneous publishing

(G-7101)
MICHAEL DUPONT
1 Beeholm Rd (06896-3302)
PHONE..................................203 434-0650
Michael Dupont, *Principal*
EMP: 2
SALES (est): 81.8K **Privately Held**
SIC: 2879 Agricultural chemicals

(G-7102)
MICHAEL JAMES DISTLER
34 Wagon Wheel Rd (06896-1619)
PHONE..................................203 241-4574
Michael Distler, *Principal*
EMP: 2
SALES (est): 62.3K **Privately Held**
SIC: 2085 Distilled & blended liquors

(G-7103)
MILLER TINA-ATTORNEY
81 Seventy Acre Rd (06896-2723)
PHONE..................................203 938-8507
Tina Miller, *Owner*
EMP: 1
SALES (est): 49.7K **Privately Held**
SIC: 2711 Newspapers, publishing & printing

(G-7104)
NEC A NEC WOODS INC
57 Seventy Acre Rd (06896-2705)
PHONE..................................203 431-0621
Susan McNeill, *President*
EMP: 2
SALES (est): 184.7K **Privately Held**
SIC: 2511 5712 Children's wood furniture; custom made furniture, except cabinets

(G-7105)
OPENIAM SOFTWARE LLC
49 Whortleberry Rd (06896-1323)
PHONE..................................203 202-7186
EMP: 2
SALES (est): 91.3K **Privately Held**
SIC: 7372 Prepackaged Software Services

(G-7106)
REDDING CREAMERY LLC
2 Marli Ln (06896-1919)
P.O. Box 4137, Stamford (06907-0137)
PHONE..................................203 938-2766
Maya Curto, *Principal*
EMP: 2
SALES (est): 111.3K **Privately Held**
SIC: 2021 Creamery butter

(G-7107)
SCHWANK ARCHTCTURAL WOODWORKER
111 Redding Rd (06896-3213)
PHONE..................................203 912-0109
Stephen Schwank, *Owner*
EMP: 1
SALES (est): 50.1K **Privately Held**
SIC: 2434 2431 Wood kitchen cabinets; millwork

(G-7108)
SHARPS & FLATS
16 Sullivan Dr (06896-2509)
PHONE..................................203 438-3300
Joanne Galli, *Principal*
EMP: 2
SALES (est): 135.8K **Privately Held**
SIC: 3931 Musical instruments

(G-7109)
SHAWNEE CHEMICAL
429 Rock House Rd (06896-3401)
PHONE..................................203 938-3003
Richard Bradley, *Principal*
EMP: 4
SALES (est): 149.8K **Privately Held**
SIC: 3795 Tanks & tank components

(G-7110)
STEPHANIE LAUREN LLC
32 High Ridge Rd (06896-2019)
PHONE..................................203 938-0364
Susan Fow, *Principal*
EMP: 1 **EST:** 2010
SALES (est): 79.1K **Privately Held**
SIC: 3999 Pet supplies

(G-7111)
TWISKO PRESS LLC
331 Redding Rd (06896-2925)
PHONE..................................203 938-3466
Brian Meehl, *Principal*
EMP: 1
SALES (est): 41.3K **Privately Held**
SIC: 2741 Miscellaneous publishing

(G-7112)
UNICORN PRESS LLC
17 Church Hill Rd (06896-2106)
PHONE..................................203 938-7405
Jan L Kardys, *Principal*
EMP: 2
SALES (est): 123.2K **Privately Held**
SIC: 2741 Miscellaneous publishing

Ridgefield
Fairfield County

(G-7113)
283 INDUSTRIES INC
3 Mallory Hill Rd (06877-6302)
PHONE..................................203 276-8956
Marjory Savino, *Principal*

Ridgefield - Fairfield County (G-7114)

EMP: 3 EST: 2012
SALES (est): 191.8K **Privately Held**
SIC: 3999 Manufacturing industries

(G-7114)
AC TEK INSTRUMENTS
34 Loren Ln (06877-2401)
PHONE..................203 431-0825
Amy Zhang, *Owner*
EMP: 1
SALES (est): 80.2K **Privately Held**
WEB: www.actekinstruments.com
SIC: 3829 Measuring & controlling devices

(G-7115)
ACE TIRE & AUTO CENTER INC
861 Ethan Allen Hwy (06877-2801)
PHONE..................203 438-4042
Richard Desrochers, *Administration*
EMP: 11
SALES (est): 1MM **Privately Held**
SIC: 3011 Automobile tires, pneumatic

(G-7116)
AMSYS INC
Also Called: Amsys Computer
900 Ethan Allen Hwy Ste 1 (06877-2832)
P.O. Box 797, Brookfield (06804-0797)
PHONE..................203 431-8814
Edward Heere, *President*
John M Dougall, *Vice Pres*
Geoffrey Langdon, *Vice Pres*
John Mc Dougall, *Vice Pres*
Donna Heere, *Treasurer*
EMP: 22
SQ FT: 5,000
SALES (est): 2.5MM **Privately Held**
WEB: www.amsys.net
SIC: 7373 7379 7378 3571 Systems integration services; computer related consulting services; computer maintenance & repair; electronic computers; computer software systems analysis & design, custom;

(G-7117)
API WIZARD LLC
10 Hamilton Rd (06877-4320)
PHONE..................914 764-5726
Richard Volpitta, *Mng Member*
EMP: 9 EST: 2016
SALES (est): 204.2K **Privately Held**
SIC: 7372 7389 Utility computer software;

(G-7118)
BAILEY AVENUE KITCHENS
904 Ethan Allen Hwy (06877-2826)
PHONE..................203 438-4868
David Adams, *Owner*
EMP: 6
SALES (est): 367.5K **Privately Held**
WEB: www.baileyavenuekitchens.com
SIC: 2434 Wood kitchen cabinets

(G-7119)
BOARD SILLY CUSTOM SAWMILL LLC
318 Ethan Allen Hwy (06877-4722)
PHONE..................203 438-3631
Robert Dermer, *Mng Member*
EMP: 3
SALES (est): 270K **Privately Held**
SIC: 5211 2421 Lumber products; sawmills & planing mills, general

(G-7120)
BOEHRINGER INGELHEIM CORP (DH)
900 Ridgebury Rd (06877-1058)
P.O. Box 368 (06877-0368)
PHONE..................203 798-9988
Hans-Peter Grau, *President*
Paul Fonteyne, *Principal*
Philip I Datlow, *Counsel*
Albert Ros, *Exec VP*
Kathleen Hirst, *Vice Pres*
◆ EMP: 1500
SQ FT: 266,000
SALES (est): 1.2B
SALES (corp-wide): 20B **Privately Held**
WEB: www.us.boehringer-ingelheim.com
SIC: 2834 6221 Medicines, capsuled or ampuled; veterinary pharmaceutical preparations; commodity traders, contracts

(G-7121)
BOEHRINGER INGELHEIM PHARMA (DH)
900 Ridgebury Rd (06877-1058)
P.O. Box 368 (06877-0368)
PHONE..................203 798-9988
Paul Fonteyne, *CEO*
Andreas Barner, *President*
Jay Fine, *Vice Pres*
Graham Goodrich, *Vice Pres*
Stefan Rinn Sr, *Vice Pres*
▲ EMP: 1300
SQ FT: 1,326,000
SALES (est): 293.6MM
SALES (corp-wide): 20B **Privately Held**
SIC: 2834 Drugs acting on the cardiovascular system, except diagnostic; drugs acting on the respiratory system
HQ: Boehringer Ingelheim Corporation
900 Ridgebury Rd
Ridgefield CT 06877
203 798-9988

(G-7122)
BOEHRINGER INGELHEIM USA CORP (DH)
900 Ridgebury Rd (06877-1058)
P.O. Box 368 (06877-0368)
PHONE..................203 798-9988
Andreas Barner, *Ch of Bd*
Marla S Persky, *Senior VP*
Genevieve Faith, *Project Mgr*
Scott Pennino, *Research*
Stefan Rinn, *CFO*
▲ EMP: 102
SALES (est): 1.1B
SALES (corp-wide): 20B **Privately Held**
SIC: 2834 Medicines, capsuled or ampuled
HQ: Boehringer Ingelheim Auslandsbeteiligungs Gmbh
Binger Str. 173
Ingelheim Am Rhein
613 277-0

(G-7123)
BOEHRNGER INGELHEIM ROXANE INC
175 Briar Ridge Rd (06877)
PHONE..................203 798-5555
EMP: 32
SALES (corp-wide): 16.5B **Privately Held**
SIC: 2834 Manufactures Pharmaceutical Preparations
HQ: Boehringer Ingelheim Roxane, Inc.
1809 Wilson Rd
Columbus OH 43228
614 276-4000

(G-7124)
BOTTOMLINE TECHNOLOGIES DE INC
17 Weir Farm Ln (06877-6000)
PHONE..................203 431-9787
Larry George, *Vice Pres*
EMP: 1
SALES (corp-wide): 421.9MM **Publicly Held**
WEB: www.bottomline.com
SIC: 7372 Application computer software
PA: Bottomline Technologies (De), Inc.
325 Corporate Dr Ste 300
Portsmouth NH 03801
603 436-0700

(G-7125)
BRANDMARK STUDIOS LLC
16 Whitewood Hollow Ct (06877-3405)
PHONE..................203 438-9400
Betsy Brand, *Principal*
EMP: 2
SALES (est): 192.9K **Privately Held**
SIC: 3949 Bowling balls

(G-7126)
BRANDSTROM INSTRUMENTS INC
85 Ethan Allen Hwy (06877-6226)
PHONE..................203 544-9341
Arvid A Brandstrom, *CEO*
Thomas Allard, *Vice Pres*
▼ EMP: 25
SQ FT: 5,000
SALES (est): 4.8MM **Privately Held**
WEB: www.brandstrominstruments.com
SIC: 3728 3812 Aircraft parts & equipment; infrared object detection equipment

(G-7127)
CHERNER CHAIR COMPANY LLC
218 North St (06877-2538)
P.O. Box 509 (06877-0509)
PHONE..................203 894-4702
Thomas Cherner,
Ben Cherner,
▲ EMP: 5
SQ FT: 5,000
SALES (est): 557.5K **Privately Held**
WEB: www.chernerchair.com
SIC: 2511 Wood household furniture

(G-7128)
CITRA SOLV LLC
188 Shadow Lake Rd (06877-1032)
P.O. Box 2597, Danbury (06813-2597)
PHONE..................203 778-0881
Sherrill Tedino, *Accounting Mgr*
Eric Zeitler, *Regl Sales Mgr*
Cindy Howley, *Sales Staff*
Steven Zeitler,
Melissa Zeitler,
EMP: 7
SALES (est): 1.5MM **Privately Held**
WEB: www.citrasolv.com
SIC: 2842 Specialty cleaning, polishes & sanitation goods

(G-7129)
CONANT VALLEY JAMS
11 Wilton Rd W (06877-5606)
PHONE..................203 403-3811
EMP: 2
SALES (est): 62.3K **Privately Held**
SIC: 2033 Jams, jellies & preserves: packaged in cans, jars, etc.

(G-7130)
CONTROLLED INTERFACES LLC
34 Farm Hill Rd (06877-3729)
P.O. Box 933 (06877-8933)
PHONE..................917 328-4471
Jeffrey Menoher, *Principal*
EMP: 1
SALES (est): 55.1K **Privately Held**
SIC: 3999 Manufacturing industries

(G-7131)
CROSSROADS SIGNS
679 Danbury Rd Ste 2 (06877-2757)
PHONE..................203 894-5938
Paul Fitzpatrick, *Owner*
EMP: 2
SALES (est): 162K **Privately Held**
SIC: 3993 Electric signs

(G-7132)
CURBSIDE COMPOST LLC
65 Spring Valley Rd (06877-1218)
P.O. Box 188 (06877-0188)
PHONE..................914 646-6890
Nicholas Skeadas, *Principal*
EMP: 4
SALES (est): 159.5K **Privately Held**
SIC: 2875 Compost

(G-7133)
CUSTOM TS N MORE LLC
135 Ethan Allen Hwy (06877-6207)
PHONE..................203 438-1592
Arthur F Crabtree, *Owner*
EMP: 3
SALES (est): 333K **Privately Held**
SIC: 2759 Screen printing

(G-7134)
D T TECHNOLOGIES INC
139 Sleepy Hollow Rd (06877-2326)
PHONE..................203 312-3527
Frank Dentrone, *Principal*
EMP: 1
SALES (est): 104.2K **Privately Held**
SIC: 3541 Machine tools, metal cutting type

(G-7135)
DEBORAH ANNS HMMADE CHOCOLATES
453 Main St (06877-4513)
PHONE..................203 438-0065
Michael Grissman, *Partner*
Deborah Backes, *Partner*
EMP: 2
SALES (est): 204.1K **Privately Held**
SIC: 2064 5145 Chocolate candy, except solid chocolate; candy

(G-7136)
DJ SPORTSWARE
17 Woodstone Rd (06877-3205)
PHONE..................203 438-0078
Joseph Chelednik, *President*
EMP: 1
SALES (est): 10.1K **Privately Held**
SIC: 2386 Garments, leather

(G-7137)
ECONOMY PRINTING & COPY CENTER
Also Called: Village Printer
971 Ethan Allen Hwy (06877-2802)
PHONE..................203 438-7401
Lisa D Witt, *Manager*
EMP: 4
SALES (corp-wide): 989.6K **Privately Held**
SIC: 2752 7334 Commercial printing, offset; photocopying & duplicating services
PA: Economy Printing & Copy Center
128 E Liberty St Ste 4
Danbury CT 06810
203 792-5610

(G-7138)
EDUCATIONAL RESOURCES NETWORK
4 Sarah Bishop Rd (06877-1215)
PHONE..................203 866-9973
R D Lenoue, *President*
EMP: 2
SALES (est): 6MM **Privately Held**
WEB: www.ern4schools.com
SIC: 8743 2731 7313 Sales promotion; textbooks: publishing only, not printed on site; printed media advertising representatives

(G-7139)
ELEMENTALS LLC
158 Main St (06877-4931)
PHONE..................203 438-1848
Pamela A Leahy, *Principal*
EMP: 1 EST: 2009
SALES (est): 101.6K **Privately Held**
SIC: 2833 Botanical products, medicinal: ground, graded or milled

(G-7140)
FACTOR INDUSTRIES LLC
68 Topstone Rd (06877-3411)
PHONE..................203 244-5429
Ryan Eckhoff, *Owner*
EMP: 1
SALES (est): 55.5K **Privately Held**
SIC: 3999 Manufacturing industries

(G-7141)
FORGETFUL GENTLEMAN LLC
54 Hobby Dr (06877-1930)
PHONE..................203 431-2486
Nate Pan,
EMP: 2
SALES (est): 120K **Privately Held**
SIC: 3499 2678 Novelties & giftware, including trophies; stationery products

(G-7142)
FREMCO LLC
8 Redwood Ln (06877-3344)
P.O. Box 791 (06877-0791)
PHONE..................203 857-0522
Lloyd Fremed,
Camille Fremed,
Lloyd J Fremed,
EMP: 10
SQ FT: 1,600
SALES (est): 1.7MM **Privately Held**
WEB: www.scanandprint.com
SIC: 3577 Printers, computer

GEOGRAPHIC SECTION
Ridgefield - Fairfield County (G-7177)

(G-7143)
FUR SIDE LLC
622 Main St (06877-3825)
PHONE..................................203 403-3369
Sheryl Oliveira, *Principal*
EMP: 2 **EST:** 2010
SALES (est): 124.9K **Privately Held**
SIC: 3999 Furs

(G-7144)
GREYCOURT PUBLISHING LLC
11 Conant Rd (06877-4317)
PHONE..................................203 894-1535
Mark Winkler, *Owner*
EMP: 1 **EST:** 2011
SALES (est): 60.7K **Privately Held**
SIC: 2741 Miscellaneous publishing

(G-7145)
HAMLETHUB LLC
37 Danbury Rd Ste 202 (06877-4079)
PHONE..................................203 431-6400
Steven Blackburn, *Editor*
Peter Flier, *Editor*
Rachel Lampen, *Editor*
Lauterborn Mike, *Editor*
Sandy Vas, *Editor*
EMP: 5 **EST:** 2011
SALES (est): 450K **Privately Held**
SIC: 2711 Newspapers: publishing only, not printed on site

(G-7146)
HERSAM ACORN CMNTY PUBG LLC (HQ)
16 Bailey Ave (06877-4512)
PHONE..................................203 438-6544
Martin Hersam,
EMP: 16
SALES (est): 3.7MM
SALES (corp-wide): 5.3MM **Privately Held**
SIC: 2711 Newspapers, publishing & printing
PA: Hersam Acorn Newspapers, Llc
16 Bailey Ave
Ridgefield CT
203 438-6000

(G-7147)
INSIDE TRACK
18 Lost Mine Pl (06877-3435)
PHONE..................................203 431-4540
Gisela Schoell, *Manager*
EMP: 1
SALES (est): 57.9K **Privately Held**
WEB: www.inside-track-online.com
SIC: 2731 Book publishing

(G-7148)
J S DENTAL MANUFACTURING INC
Also Called: J S Dental
196 N Salem Rd (06877-3127)
P.O. Box 904 (06877-8904)
PHONE..................................203 438-8832
Inga Engstrom, *CEO*
Mats Engstrom, *President*
Gerhard Kiklas, *Sales Mgr*
Sue St Hilaire, *Manager*
EMP: 7
SQ FT: 6,000
SALES (est): 1.4MM **Privately Held**
WEB: www.jsdental.com
SIC: 3843 Dental equipment

(G-7149)
JAMES CALLAHAN
55 Buck Hill Rd (06877-2702)
PHONE..................................914 641-2852
James Callahan, *Principal*
EMP: 3
SALES (est): 195.5K **Privately Held**
SIC: 2411 Logging

(G-7150)
JM SHEA LLC
Also Called: J M Shea Assc
25 Hessian Dr (06877-2417)
P.O. Box 108 (06877-0108)
PHONE..................................203 431-4435
Joseph Shea, *Mng Member*
EMP: 1
SALES (est): 141.7K **Privately Held**
SIC: 2621 Wallpaper (hanging paper)

(G-7151)
JOSEPH MANUFACTURING CO
18 Thunder Hill Ln (06877-3107)
PHONE..................................203 431-6400
EMP: 1 **EST:** 2011
SALES (est): 50K **Privately Held**
SIC: 3999 Mfg Misc Products

(G-7152)
JRC PUBLISHING LLC
20 Mckeon Pl (06877-1043)
PHONE..................................203 942-2726
John Malley, *Principal*
EMP: 1
SALES (est): 63.1K **Privately Held**
SIC: 2741 Miscellaneous publishing

(G-7153)
KIELO AMERICA INC
163 Branchville Rd (06877-5127)
PHONE..................................203 431-3999
EMP: 3 **EST:** 1984
SALES (est): 270K **Privately Held**
SIC: 2253 5632 Mfgs & Ret Hand Knit Women's Clothing

(G-7154)
LITIGATION ANALYTICS INC (PA)
127 Main St Bldg Ii (06877-4932)
P.O. Box 1105 (06877-9105)
PHONE..................................203 431-0300
John Scarbrough, *President*
John Morsen, *Admin Sec*
EMP: 15
SQ FT: 3,000
SALES (est): 2MM **Privately Held**
WEB: www.litigationanalytics.com
SIC: 8732 7372 Business analysis; prepackaged software

(G-7155)
MODERN NUTRITION & BIOTECH
61 Overlook Dr (06877-3711)
PHONE..................................203 244-5830
Jan Dong, *Vice Pres*
EMP: 4
SALES (est): 250K **Privately Held**
SIC: 2833 Medicinals & botanicals

(G-7156)
MORAN WOODWORKING LLC
636 Ethan Allen Hwy (06877-3431)
PHONE..................................203 438-0477
Cliff Moran, *Principal*
EMP: 1
SQ FT: 2,500
SALES (est): 141.7K **Privately Held**
SIC: 2511 Wood household furniture

(G-7157)
NORILSK NICKEL USA INC
3 Turtle Ridge Ct (06877-1060)
PHONE..................................203 730-0676
EMP: 3 **EST:** 2011
SALES (est): 171.6K **Privately Held**
SIC: 3356 Nickel

(G-7158)
NORTHEAST CABINET DESIGN
18 Bailey Ave (06877-4512)
PHONE..................................203 438-1709
Simon Johnson, *Principal*
Kimberly Jonson, *Principal*
EMP: 4
SALES (est): 543.9K **Privately Held**
WEB: www.northeastcabinetdesign.com
SIC: 2434 Wood kitchen cabinets

(G-7159)
OLD ROAD SOFTWARE INC
87 Grandview Dr (06877-3013)
PHONE..................................914 755-1329
EMP: 2 **EST:** 2009
SALES (est): 131.8K **Privately Held**
SIC: 7372 Prepackaged software

(G-7160)
PICKADENT INC
196 N Salem Rd Ste 2 (06877-3127)
P.O. Box 4185, Danbury (06813-4185)
PHONE..................................203 431-8716
Mats Engstrom, *President*
Inga Engstrom, *Vice Pres*
▼ **EMP:** 3

SQ FT: 3,000
SALES: 301.1K **Privately Held**
SIC: 3843 Dental equipment & supplies

(G-7161)
PILLA INC
908 Ethan Allen Hwy (06877-2826)
PHONE..................................203 894-3265
Phillip Pilla, *President*
Carlo Pilla, *Adv Board Mem*
Ryan Carey, *Sales Staff*
Dan Fireman, *Director*
EMP: 4
SALES (est): 509.6K **Privately Held**
SIC: 3851 5941 Eyeglasses, lenses & frames; specialty sport supplies

(G-7162)
PINNACLE POLYMERS LLC
31 Bailey Ave Ste 4 (06877-4533)
PHONE..................................203 313-4116
EMP: 3
SALES (corp-wide): 44.9MM **Privately Held**
SIC: 2821 Mfg Plastic Materials/Resins
PA: Pinnacle Polymers, Llc
1 Pinnacle Ave
Garyville LA 70051
985 535-2000

(G-7163)
PLANET TECHNOLOGIES INC
96 Danbury Rd (06877-4069)
PHONE..................................800 255-3749
Scott L Glenn, *Ch of Bd*
Edward J Steube, *President*
Bret Megargel, *Vice Pres*
Francesca Dinota, *CFO*
EMP: 11
SQ FT: 13,317
SALES: 8MM **Privately Held**
SIC: 3564 Air cleaning systems; air purification equipment; filters, air: furnaces, air conditioning equipment, etc.

(G-7164)
POINTPHARMA LLC
127 Rising Ridge Rd (06877-5820)
PHONE..................................203 668-8543
Nancy Lizzul Sumberaz, *Principal*
EMP: 2
SALES (est): 125.7K **Privately Held**
SIC: 2834 Pharmaceutical preparations

(G-7165)
QUARTER MILE
91 Peaceable St (06877-4811)
PHONE..................................203 438-9718
P Kevin McNamara, *Principal*
EMP: 1
SALES (est): 65.2K **Privately Held**
SIC: 3131 Quarters

(G-7166)
RETAIL PRINT SOLUTIONS
300 West Ln (06877-5323)
PHONE..................................203 438-5457
Marshall Odeen, *Principal*
EMP: 2
SALES (est): 169.5K **Privately Held**
SIC: 2752 Commercial printing, lithographic

(G-7167)
RIDGEFELD SCRNPRINTING EMB LLC
71 Hussars Camp Pl (06877-1430)
PHONE..................................203 438-1203
Robert Dinucci, *Principal*
EMP: 2
SALES (est): 145.2K **Privately Held**
SIC: 2395 Embroidery & art needlework

(G-7168)
RIDGEFIELD OVERHEAD DOOR LLC
703 Danbury Rd Ste 4 (06877-2737)
P.O. Box 928 (06877-8928)
PHONE..................................203 431-3667
Paul Peloquin,
Nancy Peloquin,
EMP: 7
SALES: 1.1MM **Privately Held**
SIC: 2431 Garage doors, overhead: wood

(G-7169)
RUSSELL AMY KAHN (PA)
225 S Salem Rd (06877-4832)
PHONE..................................203 438-2133
Amy Kahn Russell, *Owner*
EMP: 10
SALES (est): 1.5MM **Privately Held**
WEB: www.supplementsny.net
SIC: 3911 Jewelry, precious metal

(G-7170)
RX ANALYTIC INC
6 Bob Hill Rd (06877-2006)
PHONE..................................203 733-0837
Michael Goldstein, *Ch of Bd*
Joan Goldstein, *Vice Pres*
EMP: 6
SALES (est): 397.2K **Privately Held**
SIC: 2834 Pharmaceutical preparations

(G-7171)
SAFETY DISPATCH INC
57 Jefferson Dr (06877-5919)
PHONE..................................203 885-5722
Carrie Shields, *President*
John Shields, *Sales Staff*
EMP: 3
SALES (est): 120K **Privately Held**
SIC: 3842 Personal safety equipment

(G-7172)
SEWN IN AMERICA INC (PA)
Also Called: Sia
54 Danbury Rd Ste 240 (06877-4019)
PHONE..................................203 438-9149
John Mc Loughlin, *President*
▲ **EMP:** 80
SALES (est): 6MM **Privately Held**
WEB: www.sewninamerica.com
SIC: 2326 Men's & boys' work clothing

(G-7173)
SILICON CATALYST LLC
258 W Mountain Rd (06877-2917)
PHONE..................................203 240-0499
Daniel J Armbrust,
Daniel Armbrust,
Rick Lazansky,
Mike Nooney,
EMP: 3
SALES (est): 167.3K **Privately Held**
SIC: 3674 Semiconductors & related devices

(G-7174)
SONIAS CHOCOLATERIE INC
6 Ascot Way (06877-5503)
PHONE..................................203 438-5965
EMP: 10
SALES (est): 400K **Privately Held**
SIC: 2064 Mfg Candy/Confectionery

(G-7175)
SOUND CUSTOM WOODWORKING & DES
260 North St (06877-2529)
PHONE..................................203 948-5594
Leo A Castagna, *Manager*
EMP: 2
SALES (est): 154.1K **Privately Held**
SIC: 2431 Millwork

(G-7176)
TRITON EXCIMER GROUP LLC
241 Ethan Allen Hwy (06877-6208)
PHONE..................................203 733-1063
Dominick A Pagano, *Principal*
EMP: 1
SALES: 500K **Privately Held**
SIC: 3999 Manufacturing industries

(G-7177)
TRITON THALASSIC TECH INC (PA)
241 Ethan Allen Hwy (06877-6208)
PHONE..................................203 438-0633
Barry Ressler, *President*
Stephenson Ward, *CFO*
EMP: 5
SQ FT: 40,000
SALES (est): 474.2K **Privately Held**
WEB: www.t3i-uv.com
SIC: 3641 Ultraviolet lamps

Ridgefield - Fairfield County (G-7178)

(G-7178)
ULLMAN DEVICES CORPORATION
664 Danbury Rd (06877-2720)
P.O. Box 398 (06877-0398)
PHONE.................203 438-6577
Steve Gorden, *CEO*
Edward Coleman, *President*
Benjamin Ungar, *Vice Pres*
Bernard Jaffe, *Treasurer*
Janet Lemma, *Admin Sec*
▲ **EMP:** 70 **EST:** 1935
SQ FT: 15,000
SALES (est): 12.1MM **Privately Held**
SIC: 3423 Mechanics' hand tools

(G-7179)
UNIMELON INC
5 Taylor Ct (06877-1047)
PHONE.................201 774-2786
Arun T Chinnaraju, *President*
EMP: 1
SALES (est): 55.4K **Privately Held**
SIC: 7371 7372 Computer software systems analysis & design, custom; computer software writers, freelance; computer software development; application computer software; business oriented computer software

(G-7180)
VITAL HEALTH PUBLISHING INC
149 Old Branchville Rd (06877-6013)
PHONE.................203 438-3229
David Richard, *President*
EMP: 3 **EST:** 1998
SALES (est): 220.9K **Privately Held**
SIC: 2731 Books: publishing only

(G-7181)
WALPOLE WOODWORKERS INC
Also Called: Walpole Fence Company
346 Ethan Allen Hwy (06877-4722)
PHONE.................508 668-2800
Robert Booth, *Branch Mgr*
EMP: 30
SQ FT: 1,000
SALES (corp-wide): 83.9MM **Privately Held**
WEB: www.walpolewoodworkers.com
SIC: 2499 5211 5712 2452 Fencing, wood; fencing; outdoor & garden furniture; prefabricated wood buildings; prefabricated metal buildings; wood household furniture
PA: Walpole Outdoors Llc
100 Rver Ridge Dr Ste 302
Norwood MA 02062
508 668-2800

(G-7182)
WARREN PRESS INC
Also Called: Village Printers
470 Main St Ste 1 (06877-4516)
PHONE.................203 431-0011
Fax: 203 431-9985
EMP: 1
SALES (corp-wide): 1.4MM **Privately Held**
SIC: 2759 2752 7338 2789 Commercial Printing Lithographic Coml Print Secy/Court Reporting Svc Bookbinding/Related Work
PA: The Warren Press Inc
128 E Liberty St Ste 4
Danbury CT
203 792-7762

(G-7183)
WEEKLY RETAIL SERVICE LLC
94 Cooper Rd (06877-6106)
PHONE.................203 244-5150
Thomas Smith, *Principal*
EMP: 2
SALES (est): 90.5K **Privately Held**
SIC: 2711 Newspapers

(G-7184)
WHIPSTICK CREAMERY LLC
43 Whipstick Rd (06877-5009)
PHONE.................203 438-2203
Richard Sica, *Principal*
EMP: 2
SALES (est): 107.3K **Privately Held**
SIC: 2021 Creamery butter

(G-7185)
WORD FOR WORDS LLC
12 Abbott Ave (06877-4407)
PHONE.................203 894-1908
Adele M Annesi, *Principal*
EMP: 2
SALES (est): 129.4K **Privately Held**
SIC: 2741 Miscellaneous publishing

(G-7186)
WRENFIELD GROUP INC
Also Called: Rally For A Cure
27 Governor St (06877-4657)
P.O. Box 855, Wilton (06897-0855)
PHONE.................203 438-0090
EMP: 20
SALES (est): 1.6MM **Privately Held**
SIC: 8742 8743 2385 Management Consulting Services Public Relations Services Mfg Waterproof Outerwear

(G-7187)
ZACTECH ULTRASONICS LLC
199 Ethan Allen Hwy (06877-6212)
PHONE.................203 438-0004
Joseph Zaccone, *Principal*
EMP: 1
SQ FT: 2,000
SALES (est): 131.5K **Privately Held**
SIC: 3829 Gauging instruments, thickness ultrasonic

(G-7188)
ZANDER WOOD WORKS LLC
137 Ethan Allen Hwy (06877-6238)
PHONE.................203 493-5066
David Zander, *Principal*
EMP: 1
SALES (est): 65.4K **Privately Held**
SIC: 2431 Millwork

Riverside
Fairfield County

(G-7189)
ALEXANDER TULCHINSKY VIOLINS
35 Marks Rd (06878-2324)
PHONE.................203 698-7844
EMP: 2 **EST:** 2016
SALES (est): 85.9K **Privately Held**
SIC: 3931 Violins & parts

(G-7190)
CHIAPPETTAS WELDING
21 Sheephill Rd (06878-1403)
PHONE.................203 637-1522
Paul W Chiappetta, *Owner*
EMP: 1
SALES: 200K **Privately Held**
SIC: 7692 Welding repair

(G-7191)
CURRIE & KINGSTON LLC
1111 E Putnam Ave (06878-1335)
PHONE.................203 698-9428
Louis Van Leeuwen, *CEO*
EMP: 1 **EST:** 2014
SALES (est): 42K **Privately Held**
SIC: 2434 Wood kitchen cabinets

(G-7192)
DP MARINE LLC
34 Lockwood Ln (06878-1708)
PHONE.................917 705-7435
Jacques Guillet,
Pierre Guillet,
EMP: 5 **EST:** 2017
SALES (est): 253.7K **Privately Held**
SIC: 3531 Marine related equipment

(G-7193)
DRUNK ALPACA LLC
23 Hoover Rd (06878-1421)
PHONE.................646 415-4995
Stephania Halverson, *President*
EMP: 1
SALES (est): 124.9K **Privately Held**
SIC: 2231 Alpacas, mohair: woven

(G-7194)
DULCIFY LLC
175 Riverside Ave (06878-2212)
PHONE.................203 344-1671
Christophe Armero,
EMP: 1
SALES (est): 57.4K **Privately Held**
SIC: 2099 Sugar

(G-7195)
EXPERIENCE PUBLISHING INC
4 William St (06878-2118)
PHONE.................203 637-2324
Andrew Bein, *President*
EMP: 2
SALES (est): 178.5K **Privately Held**
SIC: 2741 Miscellaneous publishing

(G-7196)
MATTITUCK VINEYARDS LLC
33 Gilliam Ln (06878-2200)
PHONE.................203 637-4457
Alexander Jackson, *Principal*
EMP: 2
SALES (est): 97.3K **Privately Held**
SIC: 2084 Wines, brandy & brandy spirits

(G-7197)
MONOGRAM MARY LLC
8 Somerset Ln (06878-1608)
PHONE.................203 536-9526
Brooke Labriola Shepard, *Principal*
EMP: 1 **EST:** 2017
SALES (est): 57.6K **Privately Held**
SIC: 2395 Embroidery & art needlework

(G-7198)
NATIONAL INSTRUMENTS CORP
1117 E Putnam Ave Ste 240 (06878-1333)
PHONE.................203 661-6795
James Truchard, *President*
EMP: 1
SALES (corp-wide): 1.3B **Publicly Held**
WEB: www.ni.com
SIC: 7372 Prepackaged software
PA: National Instruments Corporation
11500 N Mopac Expy
Austin TX 78759
512 683-0100

(G-7199)
PORCELANOSA NEW YORK INC
1063 E Putnam Ave (06878-1305)
PHONE.................203 698-7618
Reana Coursey, *Branch Mgr*
EMP: 13
SALES (corp-wide): 16.3MM **Privately Held**
SIC: 5032 3253 Ceramic wall & floor tile; ceramic wall & floor tile
HQ: Porcelanosa New York, Inc.
600 State Rt 17
Ramsey NJ 07446
408 467-9400

(G-7200)
PRINTING SOLUTIONS LLC
1117 E Putnam Ave Ste 249 (06878-1333)
PHONE.................203 965-0090
Scott Muller, *Principal*
EMP: 2 **EST:** 2001
SALES (est): 297.3K **Privately Held**
SIC: 2752 Commercial printing, offset

(G-7201)
RIVERSIDE EXPRESS
1117 E Putnam Ave Ste 264 (06878-1333)
PHONE.................203 326-1245
Pedro Martinez, *Partner*
Naelida Martinez, *Partner*
EMP: 2
SQ FT: 300
SALES (est): 50K **Privately Held**
SIC: 2037 Fruit juices

(G-7202)
TRIBAL WEAR
27 Summit Rd (06878-2104)
PHONE.................203 637-7884
David Fescier, *Owner*
EMP: 3
SALES (est): 50K **Privately Held**
SIC: 2329 2339 Jackets (suede, leatherette, etc.), sport: men's & boys'; jackets, untailored: women's, misses' & juniors'

(G-7203)
TURQ LLC
123 Lockwood Rd (06878-1827)
PHONE.................203 344-1257
Susan White, *CEO*
▲ **EMP:** 5
SALES (est): 299.2K **Privately Held**
SIC: 2329 Men's & boys' sportswear & athletic clothing

(G-7204)
VINEYARD BROTHERS LLC
29 Normandy Ln (06878-2410)
PHONE.................203 637-0381
Shepherd P Murray, *Manager*
EMP: 2
SALES (est): 66K **Privately Held**
SIC: 2084 Wines

(G-7205)
WEIGH & TEST SYSTEMS INC
Also Called: Wagner Instruments
17 Wilmot Ln Ste 2 (06878-1633)
P.O. Box 1217, Greenwich (06836-1217)
PHONE.................203 698-9681
William B Wagner, *President*
Pierrette Wagner, *Vice Pres*
▲ **EMP:** 10
SQ FT: 2,000
SALES: 1MM **Privately Held**
WEB: www.wagnerforce.com
SIC: 3829 Measuring & controlling devices

Riverton
Litchfield County

(G-7206)
DURALITE INCORPORATED
15 School St (06065-1013)
PHONE.................860 379-3113
Elliott E Jessen, *Ch of Bd*
Mark Jessen, *President*
Dale L Smith, *Vice Pres*
Jeanette Smith, *Treasurer*
Vickie Clarke, *Sales Staff*
▲ **EMP:** 10 **EST:** 1946
SQ FT: 5,500
SALES (est): 2MM **Privately Held**
WEB: www.duralite.com
SIC: 3567 Heating units & devices, industrial: electric

(G-7207)
GREENWOOD GLASS
3 Robertsville Rd 242 (06065)
PHONE.................860 738-9464
Peter Greenwood, *Owner*
EMP: 1
SQ FT: 550
SALES: 70K **Privately Held**
WEB: www.petergreenwood.com
SIC: 3229 5719 Pressed & blown glass; glassware

(G-7208)
HITCHCOCK CHAIR COMPANY LTD (DH)
13 Riverton Rd (06065-1205)
P.O. Box 409, New Hartford (06057-0409)
PHONE.................860 738-0141
Ron Coleman, *President*
Richard Swenson, *Managing Prtnr*
Robin Faccenda, *Chairman*
Nancy Swenson, *Administration*
EMP: 2
SQ FT: 110,000
SALES (est): 6.4MM
SALES (corp-wide): 182.4MM **Privately Held**
SIC: 2511 Wood household furniture
HQ: Hitchcock Holding Company, Inc.
31 Industrial Park Rd
New Hartford CT 06057
860 738-0141

(G-7209)
LEE BROWN CO LLC
91 Old Forge Rd (06065-1213)
P.O. Box 263 (06065-0263)
PHONE.................860 379-4706
Peter Lee Brown, *Owner*
EMP: 10

Rockfall
Middlesex County

(G-7210)
AIRCRAFT FORGED TOOL COMPANY
98 Cedar St (06481-2038)
PHONE..................................860 347-3778
William Piantek, *President*
EMP: 3 **EST:** 1957
SQ FT: 1,200
SALES (est): 340.1K **Privately Held**
SIC: 3545 Machine tool accessories

(G-7211)
CONNECTICUT FOREST & PARK ASSN
Also Called: CFPA
16 Meriden Rd (06481-2945)
PHONE..................................860 346-2372
Cva Liz Hughes, *Manager*
E Hammerling, *Exec Dir*
Eric Hammerling, *Exec Dir*
Beth Bernard, *Program Dir*
Amelia Graham, *Assistant*
EMP: 10
SALES (est): 1.2MM **Privately Held**
WEB: www.ctwoodlands.org
SIC: 8999 2721 Natural resource preservation service; periodicals

(G-7212)
FRESH PRINTS OF CT LLC
21 Cedar St (06481-2035)
PHONE..................................860 398-4893
Kathryn Ziegler, *Principal*
EMP: 2 **EST:** 2016
SALES (est): 101.5K **Privately Held**
SIC: 2752 Commercial printing, lithographic

(G-7213)
J F TOOL INC
205 Main St Ste C (06481-2081)
P.O. Box 158 (06481-0158)
PHONE..................................860 349-3063
Rebeca Meadows, *President*
John Meadows Jr, *President*
EMP: 9
SQ FT: 12,000
SALES (est): 760K **Privately Held**
WEB: www.jftool.com
SIC: 3544 3545 Dies & die holders for metal cutting, forming, die casting; tools & accessories for machine tools

(G-7214)
LOYAL FENCE COMPANY LLC
1 Lorraine Ter (06481-2067)
PHONE..................................203 530-7046
Frank Garcia,
EMP: 7 **EST:** 2013
SALES (est): 386.1K **Privately Held**
SIC: 3446 Fences, gates, posts & flagpoles

(G-7215)
ROGERS MANUFACTURING COMPANY
Also Called: Mery Manufacturing
72 Main St (06481-2001)
P.O. Box 155 (06481-0155)
PHONE..................................860 346-8648
Vincent J Bitel Jr, *President*
Elaine B Cunningham, *Vice Pres*
▲ **EMP:** 100 **EST:** 1891
SQ FT: 65,000
SALES (est): 21.4MM **Privately Held**
SIC: 3089 Injection molded finished plastic products

(G-7216)
WADSWORTH FALLS MFG CO
72 Main St (06481-2001)
P.O. Box 155 (06481-0155)
PHONE..................................860 346-3644
Vincent J Bitel, *President*
Emma J Bitel, *Director*
EMP: 10
SALES (est): 1.1MM **Privately Held**
SIC: 3442 Window & door frames

Rocky Hill
Hartford County

(G-7217)
A-1 ASPHALT PAVING
925 New Britain Ave (06067-1707)
P.O. Box 274 (06067-0274)
PHONE..................................860 436-6085
Gabby Thompson, *Owner*
EMP: 5 **EST:** 2011
SALES (est): 393.8K **Privately Held**
SIC: 2951 Asphalt paving mixtures & blocks

(G-7218)
ADEMCO INC
Also Called: ADI Global Distribution
712 Brook St (06067-3447)
PHONE..................................860 257-3266
EMP: 3
SALES (corp-wide): 4.8B **Publicly Held**
SIC: 5063 3669 3822 Electrical apparatus & equipment; emergency alarms; auto controls regulating residntl & coml environmt & applncs
HQ: Ademco Inc.
1985 Douglas Dr N
Golden Valley MN 55422
800 468-1502

(G-7219)
ADVANCED DRAINAGE SYSTEMS INC
520 Cromwell Ave (06067-1864)
PHONE..................................860 529-8188
Ron Vitarelli, *Branch Mgr*
EMP: 32
SALES (corp-wide): 1.3B **Publicly Held**
SIC: 3272 3084 Pipe, concrete or lined with concrete; plastics pipe
PA: Advanced Drainage Systems, Inc.
4640 Trueman Blvd
Hilliard OH 43026
614 658-0050

(G-7220)
AEROSPACE COMPONENTS MFRS INC
1090 Elm St Ste 202 (06067-1849)
P.O. Box 736 (06067-0736)
PHONE..................................860 513-3205
Randy Plis, *Principal*
EMP: 2
SALES (est): 338.8K **Privately Held**
SIC: 3728 Aircraft parts & equipment

(G-7221)
ARC DYNAMICS INC
28 Belamose Ave Ste C (06067-3795)
P.O. Box 656 (06067-0656)
PHONE..................................860 563-1006
Dave Pracon, *President*
Virginia Pracon, *Vice Pres*
EMP: 5
SQ FT: 4,000
SALES (est): 920.7K **Privately Held**
WEB: www.arcdynamics.com
SIC: 3441 Fabricated structural metal

(G-7222)
BELLA NAIL & SPA LLC
945 Cromwell Ave Ste 19 (06067-3008)
PHONE..................................860 436-3119
Kim Bora, *Principal*
EMP: 1
SALES (est): 77.7K **Privately Held**
SIC: 3421 7991 Clippers, fingernail & toenail; spas

(G-7223)
BINGHAM & TAYLOR CORP (HQ)
1022 Elm St (06067-1809)
P.O. Box 939, Culpeper VA (22701-0939)
PHONE..................................540 825-8334
Laura T Grondin, *CEO*
Lincoln Thompson, *Vice Pres*
Phil Ferrari, *CFO*
John Gould, *Controller*
Jay Corazza, *Sales Staff*
▲ **EMP:** 3
SALES (est): 20.8MM
SALES (corp-wide): 51.9MM **Privately Held**
WEB: www.binghamandtaylor.com
SIC: 3321 Cast iron pipe & fittings
PA: Virginia Industries, Inc.
1022 Elm St
Rocky Hill CT 06067
860 571-3600

(G-7224)
BIZ WIZ PRINT & COPY CTR LLC (PA)
781 Cromwell Ave Ste E (06067-3000)
PHONE..................................860 721-0040
Kelly Dotson,
Chris Dotson,
EMP: 5
SALES (est): 638.5K **Privately Held**
SIC: 2759 Commercial printing

(G-7225)
CARRIER CORP
175 Capital Blvd Ste 400 (06067-3914)
PHONE..................................860 728-7000
Bob Cardin, *Principal*
EMP: 2
SALES (est): 85.1K **Privately Held**
SIC: 3812 Search & navigation equipment

(G-7226)
CCO LLC
Also Called: Sams Food Stores
2138 Silas Deane Hwy # 101 (06067-2317)
PHONE..................................860 757-3434
Nasim Khalid, *Mng Member*
EMP: 3
SALES (est): 124.5K **Privately Held**
SIC: 5411 3496 Grocery stores; grocery carts, made from purchased wire

(G-7227)
CONNECTICUT CANDLE GROUP
19a Carillon Dr (06067-2501)
PHONE..................................860 924-1766
EMP: 1
SALES (est): 39.6K **Privately Held**
SIC: 3999 Candles

(G-7228)
CONNECTICUT RADIO INC
1208 Cromwell Ave Ste C (06067-3436)
P.O. Box 487 (06067-0487)
PHONE..................................860 563-4867
Don Bighinatti, *President*
Bill Charamut, *Vice Pres*
EMP: 8
SQ FT: 1,000
SALES (est): 1.5MM **Privately Held**
WEB: www.connradio.com
SIC: 5065 3663 Communication equipment; radio broadcasting & communications equipment

(G-7229)
CROMWELL CHRONICLE
222 Dividend Rd (06067-3740)
P.O. Box 289 (06067-0289)
PHONE..................................860 257-8715
Ralph Rarey, *Principal*
EMP: 4
SALES (est): 138.4K **Privately Held**
SIC: 2711 Job printing & newspaper publishing combined

(G-7230)
CUMMINS INC
Also Called: Metropower
914 Cromwell Ave (06067-3004)
PHONE..................................860 529-7474
Robert Gayle, *Site Mgr*
Rusty Graham, *Branch Mgr*
EMP: 38
SALES (corp-wide): 23.7B **Publicly Held**
SIC: 5084 3519 Engines, gasoline; internal combustion engines
PA: Cummins Inc.
500 Jackson St
Columbus IN 47201
812 377-5000

(G-7231)
CUSTOM PUBLISHING DESIGN GROUP
35 Cold Spring Rd Ste 321 (06067-3163)
PHONE..................................860 513-1213
Douglas Hatch, *President*
EMP: 18
SALES (est): 1.6MM **Privately Held**
WEB: www.mycompanymagazine.com
SIC: 2741 Business service newsletters: publishing & printing

(G-7232)
D&R MARINE UPHOLSTERY & CANVAS
369 Old Main St (06067-1507)
PHONE..................................860 989-9646
Raymond Accardo, *Owner*
EMP: 2
SALES (est): 162K **Privately Held**
SIC: 2211 Canvas

(G-7233)
DAILY MART
2204 Silas Deane Hwy (06067-2315)
PHONE..................................860 529-5210
EMP: 6
SALES (est): 210K **Privately Held**
SIC: 2711 Newspapers-Publishing/Printing

(G-7234)
DESAI MUKESH
Also Called: PBM Printers & Copy Center
632 Cromwell Ave (06067-1843)
PHONE..................................860 529-4141
Mukesh Desai, *Owner*
EMP: 2
SQ FT: 1,200
SALES (est): 199.3K **Privately Held**
SIC: 2759 2791 2789 Commercial printing; typesetting; bookbinding & related work

(G-7235)
DRAGONLAB LLC
1275 Cromwell Ave Ste C6 (06067-3430)
PHONE..................................860 436-9221
Michael Williams, *President*
▲ **EMP:** 3 **EST:** 2008
SALES (est): 360.6K **Privately Held**
SIC: 2869 3821 Laboratory chemicals, organic; centrifuges, laboratory; hotplates, laboratory

(G-7236)
DYNAMIC BLDG ENRGY SLTIONS LLC
70 Inwood Rd (06067-3441)
PHONE..................................860 571-8590
Robert Musselman, *Branch Mgr*
EMP: 2 **Privately Held**
SIC: 3569 Filters
PA: Dynamic Building & Energy Solutions Llc
183 Provdnc New London
North Stonington CT 06359

(G-7237)
EDISON ATLAS LLC
1275 Cromwell Ave Ste F1 (06067-3432)
PHONE..................................860 335-6455
EMP: 2
SALES (est): 73.4K **Privately Held**
SIC: 3465 Moldings or trim, automobile: stamped metal

(G-7238)
FRONTIER VISION TECH INC
Also Called: Evogence
2080 Silas Deane Hwy # 203 (06067-2334)
PHONE..................................860 953-0240
Timur Y Ruban, *President*
Thomas Jacob, *Vice Pres*
Susan Azano, *Administration*
EMP: 43
SQ FT: 5,000
SALES (est): 2.9MM **Privately Held**
SIC: 3571 3577 7378 5045 Computers, digital, analog or hybrid; graphic displays, except graphic terminals; input/output equipment, computer; computer maintenance & repair; computers, peripherals & software; systems integration services; radio & TV communications equipment

Rocky Hill - Hartford County (G-7239)   GEOGRAPHIC SECTION

(G-7239)
GULF MANUFACTURING INC
645 Cromwell Ave (06067)
P.O. Box 430 (06067-0430)
PHONE..................860 529-8601
James Murphy, *President*
Julie Murphy, *Admin Sec*
EMP: 23
SQ FT: 8,000
SALES (est): 2.4MM **Privately Held**
SIC: 3441 3599 Fabricated structural metal; machine shop, jobbing & repair

(G-7240)
HARTFORD ELECTRIC SUP CO INC
ASG
70 Inwood Rd (06067-3441)
PHONE..................860 760-4887
Bill Thompson, *Division Mgr*
EMP: 11
SALES (corp-wide): 38.5MM **Privately Held**
SIC: 3679 Electronic loads & power supplies
PA: The Hartford Electric Supply Company Inc
  30 Inwood Rd Ste 1
  Rocky Hill CT 06067
  860 236-6363

(G-7241)
HARTFORD TECHNOLOGIES INC
1022 Elm St (06067-1809)
PHONE..................860 571-3602
Laura T Grondin, *President*
Lincoln Thomson, *Vice Pres*
Christopher Cowles, *CFO*
Lori Landry, *Human Res Mgr*
Vickie Brown, *Sales Staff*
▲ **EMP:** 27
SALES (est): 7.9MM
SALES (corp-wide): 51.9MM **Privately Held**
WEB: www.hartfordtechnologies.com
SIC: 3562 3399 Ball & roller bearings; steel balls
PA: Virginia Industries, Inc.
  1022 Elm St
  Rocky Hill CT 06067
  860 571-3600

(G-7242)
HBL AMERICA INC (HQ)
Also Called: Hbl Batteries
712 Brook St Ste 107 (06067-3447)
PHONE..................860 257-9800
James McAuliffe, *President*
Robert Herritty, *Director*
◆ **EMP:** 8
SQ FT: 10,000
SALES (est): 1.3MM **Privately Held**
SIC: 3691 Storage batteries

(G-7243)
HBL AMERICA INC
Also Called: Hbl Power Systems Limited
712 Brook St Ste 107 (06067-3447)
PHONE..................860 257-9800
EMP: 2
SALES (est): 88.3K **Privately Held**
SIC: 3691 Storage batteries
HQ: Hbl America Inc.
  712 Brook St Ste 107
  Rocky Hill CT 06067
  860 257-9800

(G-7244)
HENKEL CORPORATION (DH)
1 Henkel Way (06067-3581)
PHONE..................860 571-5100
Hans Van Bylen, *CEO*
Steve Ritchie, *Regional Mgr*
Amy Wergeles, *Counsel*
Jan-Dirk Auris, *Exec VP*
Kathrin Menges, *Exec VP*
EMP: 1
SQ FT: 60,000
SALES (est): 558.3K
SALES (corp-wide): 22.7B **Privately Held**
SIC: 2841 2891 Soap & other detergents; adhesives & sealants

HQ: Henkel Of America, Inc.
  1 Henkel Way
  Rocky Hill CT 06067
  860 571-5100

(G-7245)
HENKEL LOCTITE CORPORATION (DH)
1 Henkel Way (06067-3581)
PHONE..................860 571-5100
Jeffrey C Piccolomini, *CEO*
Peter Dowling, *President*
Heinrich Grun, *President*
Steven T Merkel, *President*
Donna Garrigues, *General Mgr*
◆ **EMP:** 40
SQ FT: 500,000
SALES (est): 50.7MM
SALES (corp-wide): 22.7B **Privately Held**
SIC: 2891 3677 8731 8711 Adhesives; sealants; inductors, electronic; commercial physical research; engineering services
HQ: Henkel Us Operations Corporation
  1 Henkel Way
  Rocky Hill CT 06067
  860 571-5100

(G-7246)
HENKEL OF AMERICA INC (HQ)
1 Henkel Way (06067-3581)
PHONE..................860 571-5100
Dr Lothar Steinebach, *Ch of Bd*
Nicole Bernabo, *Counsel*
William B Read III, *Senior VP*
Frederic Chupin, *Vice Pres*
Patrick Courtney, *Vice Pres*
▲ **EMP:** 421 **EST:** 1979
SQ FT: 60,000
SALES (est): 1.7B
SALES (corp-wide): 22.7B **Privately Held**
SIC: 2843 2821 2833 2899 Surface active agents; plastics materials & resins; thermoplastic materials; medicinals & botanicals; vitamins, natural or synthetic: bulk, uncompounded; chemical preparations; adhesives; fatty acid esters, aminos, etc.
PA: Henkel Ag & Co. Kgaa
  Henkelstr. 67
  Dusseldorf 40589
  211 797-0

(G-7247)
HENKEL US OPERATIONS CORP (DH)
1 Henkel Way (06067-3581)
PHONE..................860 571-5100
Hans Van Bylen, *CEO*
Dr Jochen Krautter, *Ch of Bd*
Stephan Fuesti-Molnar, *President*
Chris Hallsey, *President*
Jeffrey C Piccolomini, *President*
◆ **EMP:** 400
SQ FT: 60,000
SALES (est): 1.7B
SALES (corp-wide): 22.7B **Privately Held**
WEB: www.handheld.com
SIC: 2843 2821 2833 2899 Surface active agents; plastics materials & resins; thermoplastic materials; medicinals & botanicals; vitamins, natural or synthetic: bulk, uncompounded; chemical preparations; adhesives
HQ: Henkel Of America, Inc.
  1 Henkel Way
  Rocky Hill CT 06067
  860 571-5100

(G-7248)
HEXPLORA LLC
10 Waterchase Dr Iii Fl (06067)
PHONE..................860 760-7601
Srinivas Pendyala, *CEO*
SAI Alahari, *Principal*
Ravi Obbu, *COO*
EMP: 2
SQ FT: 2,700
SALES (est): 108.5K **Privately Held**
SIC: 7372 7374 Application computer software; data processing service

(G-7249)
IDEMIA IDENTITY & SEC USA LLC
101 Hammer Mill Rd (06067-3771)
PHONE..................860 529-2559
Jim Lyons, *Branch Mgr*
EMP: 6
SALES (corp-wide): 4.6B **Privately Held**
SIC: 3089 Identification cards, plastic
HQ: Idemia Identity & Security Usa Llc
  11951 Freedom Dr Fl 18
  Reston VA 20190

(G-7250)
INGERSOLL-RAND COMPANY
716 Brook St Ste 130 (06067-3433)
PHONE..................860 616-6600
Mike Carey, *Manager*
EMP: 75 **Privately Held**
SIC: 1711 3561 Plumbing, heating, air-conditioning contractors; pumps & pumping equipment
HQ: Ingersoll-Rand Company
  800 Beaty St Ste B
  Davidson NC 28036
  704 655-4000

(G-7251)
INTERSEC LLC
1275 Cromwell Ave Ste B3 (06067-3421)
PHONE..................860 985-3158
Peter Sywenkyj, *Mng Member*
EMP: 5 **EST:** 2015
SALES (est): 423.2K **Privately Held**
SIC: 3949 8742 Sporting & athletic goods; marketing consulting services

(G-7252)
JAMES J SCOTT LLC
38 New Britain Ave Ste 3 (06067-1197)
PHONE..................860 571-9200
Scott Mokoski, *CFO*
James J Mokoski,
James F Mokoski,
James Mokoski,
Scott P Mokoski,
◆ **EMP:** 6
SQ FT: 6,800
SALES (est): 1.1MM **Privately Held**
SIC: 3592 5088 3545 Valves; aircraft & parts; tools & accessories for machine tools

(G-7253)
JOHNSON CONTROLS INC
27 Inwood Rd (06067-3412)
PHONE..................860 571-3300
Dave Clark, *Vice Pres*
EMP: 8 **Privately Held**
SIC: 2531 Seats, automobile
HQ: Johnson Controls, Inc.
  5757 N Green Bay Ave
  Milwaukee WI 53209
  414 524-1200

(G-7254)
LINVAR LLC
2189 Silas Deane Hwy # 15 (06067-2324)
PHONE..................860 951-3818
Joseph Ramondetta, *President*
EMP: 5
SALES (est): 486.8K **Privately Held**
SIC: 3443 5084 Bins, prefabricated metal plate; materials handling machinery

(G-7255)
LUXPOINT INC
101 Hammer Mill Rd Ste K (06067-3771)
PHONE..................860 982-9588
Paul Sanders, *Director*
EMP: 2
SQ FT: 10,000
SALES (est): 319.8K **Privately Held**
SIC: 3829 Measuring & controlling devices

(G-7256)
MAXON CORPORATION
712 Brook St Ste 106 (06067-3447)
PHONE..................860 571-6411
EMP: 2
SALES (corp-wide): 41.8B **Publicly Held**
SIC: 3433 Heating equipment, except electric

HQ: Maxon Corporation
  201 E 18th St
  Muncie IN 47302
  765 284-3304

(G-7257)
MERRIFIELD PAINT COMPANY INC
47 Inwood Rd (06067-3412)
PHONE..................860 529-1583
John Merrifield Jr, *President*
Douglas A Merrifield, *Vice Pres*
Paige M Merrifield, *Admin Sec*
EMP: 3 **EST:** 1946
SQ FT: 3,000
SALES (est): 615.5K **Privately Held**
WEB: www.merrifieldpaint.com
SIC: 2851 5231 Paints & paint additives; paint

(G-7258)
MTU AERO ENGINES N AMER INC
795 Brook St 5 (06067-3403)
PHONE..................860 258-9700
Alarm Eerube, *President*
EMP: 3
SALES (corp-wide): 5.2B **Privately Held**
SIC: 3812 Airspeed instrumentation (aeronautical instruments)
HQ: Mtu Aero Engines North America Inc.
  795 Brook St Bldg 5
  Rocky Hill CT 06067
  860 258-9700

(G-7259)
NQ INDUSTRIES INC
1275 Cromwell Ave Ste A9 (06067-3428)
PHONE..................860 258-3466
William Carey, *CEO*
▲ **EMP:** 7
SQ FT: 3,000
SALES (est): 700K **Privately Held**
SIC: 3564 Air cleaning systems

(G-7260)
OLIVE OILS AND BALSAMICS LLC
35 New Rd (06067-1703)
PHONE..................860 563-0105
Anna Flynn, *Principal*
EMP: 3
SALES (est): 110.5K **Privately Held**
SIC: 2079 Olive oil

(G-7261)
OXY COUTURE LLC
228 Raymond Rd (06067-1225)
PHONE..................860 257-8750
Tracy Lanciotto, *Principal*
EMP: 2
SALES (est): 157.7K **Privately Held**
SIC: 3829 Breathalyzers

(G-7262)
PDQ INC (PA)
24 Evans Rd (06067-3734)
PHONE..................860 529-9051
Ronald Gronback Sr, *President*
Ronald G Gronback Jr, *President*
Barbara Downey, *Office Mgr*
EMP: 25
SQ FT: 6,000
SALES (est): 4.7MM **Privately Held**
WEB: www.pdqcorp.com
SIC: 3724 Aircraft engines & engine parts

(G-7263)
PETERS MACHINE COMPANY
1275 Cromwell Ave Ste B8 (06067-3429)
PHONE..................860 529-3672
Peter Vago, *Owner*
EMP: 1
SQ FT: 850
SALES (est): 88K **Privately Held**
SIC: 3599 Machine shop, jobbing & repair

(G-7264)
RARE REMINDER INCORPORATED
222 Dividend Rd (06067-3740)
P.O. Box 289 (06067-0289)
PHONE..................860 563-9386
Kevin Rarey, *President*
Greg Barden, *General Mgr*

▲ = Import ▼=Export
◆ =Import/Export

James Klatt, *Vice Pres*
Rob Zappulla, *Accounts Exec*
Libby Lord, *Consultant*
EMP: 50 **EST:** 1953
SQ FT: 14,300
SALES (est): 5.4MM **Privately Held**
WEB: www.rarereminder.com
SIC: 2741 2752 Shopping news: publishing & printing; commercial printing, offset

(G-7265)
SOS SECURITY INCORPORATED
2264 Silas Deane Hwy (06067-2333)
PHONE.................860 563-2121
Mike Macdoanald, *Branch Mgr*
Joseph Flaherty, *Supervisor*
EMP: 1
SALES (corp-wide): 103.4MM **Privately Held**
SIC: 3699 Security control equipment & systems
PA: Sos Security Incorporated
  1915 Us Highway 46 Ste 1
  Parsippany NJ 07054
  973 402-6600

(G-7266)
SOUND MARKETING CONCEPTS
1800 Silas Deane Hwy # 7 (06067-1331)
P.O. Box 890271, Charlotte NC (28289-0271)
PHONE.................860 257-9367
Steve Avroch,
EMP: 3
SQ FT: 1,500
SALES (est): 229.4K **Privately Held**
WEB: www.soundmarketingconcepts.com
SIC: 7389 3993 Telephone services; signs & advertising specialties

(G-7267)
SYSTEMATICS INC
1275 Cromwell Ave Ste B1 (06067-3429)
PHONE.................860 721-0706
EMP: 11
SALES (corp-wide): 11.6MM **Privately Held**
SIC: 3572 Mfg Computer Storage Devices
PA: Systematics, Inc.
  238 Cherry St Ste C
  Shrewsbury MA 01545
  508 366-1306

(G-7268)
TARGET MARKETING ASSOC INC
35 Cold Spring Rd Ste 224 (06067-3162)
P.O. Box 566 (06067-0566)
PHONE.................860 571-7294
Gregory Reynolds, *President*
EMP: 3
SALES (est): 303.8K **Privately Held**
WEB: www.targetmarketingreps.com
SIC: 3721 Aircraft

(G-7269)
TORNIK INC
16 Old Forge Rd B (06067-3729)
PHONE.................860 282-6081
Edward S Stephens, *President*
Josue Negron, *Senior Buyer*
Jill Tyldsley, *Buyer*
Stephen Gormley, *Engineer*
David Cobbol, *Manager*
▲ **EMP:** 110
SQ FT: 21,000
SALES (est): 29.1MM **Privately Held**
WEB: www.tornik.com
SIC: 3679 8711 Harness assemblies for electronic use: wire or cable; electrical or electronic engineering

(G-7270)
UNITED SEATING & MOBILITY LLC (PA)
Also Called: Numotion
1111 Cromwell Ave (06067-3449)
PHONE.................860 761-0700
Mike Swinford, *CEO*
Mary Gorny, *Opers Mgr*
Julie Abrams, *Benefits Mgr*
Joe McKnight, *Sales Staff*
Rich Salm, *Manager*
EMP: 8
SALES (est): 947.7K **Privately Held**
SIC: 3842 Wheelchairs

(G-7271)
VIRGINIA INDUSTRIES INC (PA)
1022 Elm St (06067-1809)
PHONE.................860 571-3600
Laura T Grondin, *President*
Douglas Ericson, *Project Engr*
Carrie Sweeney, *Accountant*
Lincoln L Thompson Jr, *Shareholder*
▲ **EMP:** 5
SQ FT: 128,000
SALES (est): 51.9MM **Privately Held**
WEB: www.virginiaindustries.com
SIC: 3562 3084 3321 3568 Ball & roller bearings; plastics pipe; cast iron pipe & fittings; bearings, plain

(G-7272)
VITAL SIGNS MEDICAL LLC
318 Old Main St (06067-1508)
PHONE.................860 563-4969
Marc A Gorski, *Principal*
EMP: 2
SALES (est): 144.9K **Privately Held**
SIC: 3993 Signs & advertising specialties

(G-7273)
WETHERSFIELD OFFSET INC
1795 Silas Deane Hwy (06067-1305)
PHONE.................860 721-8236
Joseph P Amaio, *President*
Michelle Morro, *Accounts Mgr*
EMP: 5
SALES (est): 531.2K **Privately Held**
SIC: 2752 Commercial printing, offset

(G-7274)
WETHERSFIELD PRINTING CO INC
1795 Silas Deane Hwy (06067-1305)
PHONE.................860 721-8236
Joseph Amaio, *President*
Barbara Amaio, *Corp Secy*
EMP: 12
SQ FT: 7,500
SALES (est): 1.4MM **Privately Held**
WEB: www.wethersfieldoffset.com
SIC: 2752 Commercial printing, offset

Roxbury
Litchfield County

(G-7275)
CHIP - MAR INC
2 Moosehorn Rd (06783-1107)
P.O. Box 245 (06783-0245)
PHONE.................860 355-4854
Mary Folwell, *President*
Robert Ognan, *Vice Pres*
EMP: 2
SALES (est): 183.1K **Privately Held**
SIC: 3599 Machine shop, jobbing & repair

(G-7276)
CLASSIC SHOTGUNS
58 Garnet Rd (06783-2033)
P.O. Box 134 (06783-0134)
PHONE.................860 354-4648
Carolee Fairchild, *Partner*
Richard Fairchild, *Partner*
EMP: 2
SALES: 90K **Privately Held**
SIC: 3482 Shotgun ammunition: empty, blank or loaded

(G-7277)
GEORGE BULLOCK & SONS INC
28 Minor Bridge Rd (06783-2017)
PHONE.................860 355-1243
Kenneth Bullock, *President*
EMP: 1
SQ FT: 2,000
SALES (est): 342.5K **Privately Held**
SIC: 5084 2752 Industrial machinery & equipment; commercial printing, offset

(G-7278)
LAUFER TEKNIK
360 Southbury Rd (06783-2102)
PHONE.................860 355-4484
Sam Laufer, *Owner*
▲ **EMP:** 1
SALES: 500K **Privately Held**
SIC: 3651 Audio electronic systems

(G-7279)
MINE HILL DISTILLERY
5 Mine Hill Rd (06783-1323)
PHONE.................860 210-1872
Elliott B Davis, *President*
EMP: 4
SALES (est): 265.2K **Privately Held**
SIC: 2085 Distilled & blended liquors

(G-7280)
OLD LEATHER WALLET COMPANY LLC
8 Wellers Bridge Rd (06783-1616)
PHONE.................860 350-9868
Theresa Gallagher-Krebs, *Principal*
EMP: 1
SALES (est): 72.3K **Privately Held**
SIC: 3172 Wallets

(G-7281)
RONACO INDUSTRIES INC
141 Bacon Rd (06783-1918)
PHONE.................203 979-7712
Richard Pober, *Principal*
EMP: 2
SALES (est): 74.6K **Privately Held**
SIC: 3999 Manufacturing industries

(G-7282)
ROXBURY CABINET CO LLC
16 Evergreen Ln (06783-1331)
PHONE.................203 994-9855
Brent Benner, *Principal*
EMP: 1
SALES (est): 205.3K **Privately Held**
SIC: 2434 Wood kitchen cabinets

(G-7283)
SCOTT C PARKER
80 Transylvania Rd (06783-2107)
PHONE.................860 355-9738
Scott C Parker, *Owner*
Patricia Parker, *Co-Owner*
EMP: 2
SALES (est): 171.1K **Privately Held**
SIC: 2391 Curtains & draperies

(G-7284)
SHIPSTIK LLC
30 Sentry Hill Rd (06783-1303)
PHONE.................203 417-8022
Sara Howard, *Principal*
EMP: 1
SALES (est): 120.8K **Privately Held**
SIC: 3732 Boat building & repairing

(G-7285)
SOFTWARE MATTERS
38 River Rd (06783-1614)
P.O. Box 25 (06783-0025)
PHONE.................860 354-8804
William Chin, *Owner*
EMP: 1
SALES (est): 93.6K **Privately Held**
SIC: 7372 Prepackaged software

(G-7286)
WORLDWIDE PRODUCTS INC
58 Mallory Rd (06783-2038)
PHONE.................855 972-2867
Stephen J Parzuchowski, *President*
EMP: 1
SALES (est): 127.2K **Privately Held**
SIC: 3578 Point-of-sale devices; automatic teller machines (ATM)

Salem
New London County

(G-7287)
CARLI FARM & EQUIPMENT LLC
40 Mill Ln (06420-3519)
PHONE.................860 908-3227
Victor Carli,
Rance V Carli,
EMP: 5 **EST:** 2009
SQ FT: 5,500
SALES (est): 34.3K **Privately Held**
SIC: 3498 Fabricated pipe & fittings

(G-7288)
DUNDORF DESIGNS USA INC
Also Called: Distinctive Designs USA
426 Forsyth Rd (06420-4018)
PHONE.................860 859-2955
David Dundorf, *President*
EMP: 4
SALES (est): 320K **Privately Held**
SIC: 3993 2499 Signs & advertising specialties; carved & turned wood

(G-7289)
GS RUFF STUFF
49 Rattlesnake Ledge Rd (06420-3626)
PHONE.................860 859-9355
Gary Getty, *Owner*
Linda M Getty, *Co-Owner*
EMP: 2 **EST:** 1997
SALES: 400K **Privately Held**
SIC: 1411 4213 Granite, dimension-quarrying; heavy hauling

(G-7290)
MARY JEANS MUSICAL INSTRS LLC
204 West Rd (06420-3506)
PHONE.................860 887-0633
Mary Simpson, *Principal*
EMP: 1 **EST:** 2017
SALES (est): 41K **Privately Held**
SIC: 3931 Musical instruments

(G-7291)
SALEM VLY FARMS ICE CREAM INC
20 Darling Rd (06420-3906)
PHONE.................860 859-2980
David Bingham, *President*
Tiffany B Cunningham, *Vice Pres*
Anne W Bingham, *Admin Sec*
EMP: 8
SALES (est): 695.4K **Privately Held**
SIC: 2024 Ice cream, bulk

(G-7292)
STEED READ HORSEMANS CLASSIFIE
16b Mill Ln (06420-3539)
PHONE.................860 859-0770
Dana Stillwell,
EMP: 3
SALES: 350K **Privately Held**
WEB: www.steedread.com
SIC: 2721 0752 Periodicals: publishing only; animal specialty services

(G-7293)
WINGS N THINGS
26 New London Rd Ste 1 (06420-4052)
PHONE.................860 859-9514
Marion Brick, *Owner*
EMP: 1 **EST:** 2009
SALES (est): 61K **Privately Held**
SIC: 3999 Pet supplies

Salisbury
Litchfield County

(G-7294)
CARLO HUBER SELECTIONS INC
210 Between The Lakes Rd (06068-1612)
PHONE.................917 742-0601
Carlo Huber, *President*
EMP: 2
SALES (est): 84.7K **Privately Held**
SIC: 2084 Wines

(G-7295)
CEDAR RIDGE OIL CO
349 Taconic Rd (06068-1208)
PHONE.................860 435-9398
Ann Grumpelt, *Director*
EMP: 1
SALES (est): 78.4K **Privately Held**
SIC: 1389 Oil field services

(G-7296)
PRESENT TIME VISIONS
12 Slater Rd (06068-1211)
PHONE.................860 435-4997
Lynne Stanton, *Principal*

EMP: 1
SALES (est): 81K **Privately Held**
SIC: 3423 Jewelers' hand tools

(G-7297)
SALISBURY ARTISANS
80 Factory St (06068)
PHONE..................860 435-0344
David Bowen, *Owner*
EMP: 1
SQ FT: 3,000
SALES (est): 116.1K **Privately Held**
WEB: www.salisburyartisans.com
SIC: 2431 5712 Doors, combination screen-storm, wood; window frames, wood; window sashes, wood; custom made furniture, except cabinets

(G-7298)
SERENA GRANBERY WELDING
82 Indian Cave Rd (06068-1812)
PHONE..................860 435-2322
Serena Granbery, *Owner*
EMP: 1
SALES (est): 38.4K **Privately Held**
SIC: 7692 Welding repair

Sandy Hook
Fairfield County

(G-7299)
AL HUPPENTHAL
2 Hearthstone Ln (06482-1098)
P.O. Box 698, Newtown (06470-0698)
PHONE..................203 364-1028
Al Huppenthal, *Owner*
EMP: 2
SALES (est): 131.7K **Privately Held**
SIC: 7372 Prepackaged software

(G-7300)
BOMBA INDUSTRIES LLC
6 Crown Hill Dr (06482-1506)
PHONE..................203 304-9051
Gregory L Bomba, *Principal*
EMP: 2
SALES (est): 143.2K **Privately Held**
SIC: 3999 Manufacturing industries

(G-7301)
BRW ASSOCIATES INC
44 Great Ring Rd (06482-1652)
PHONE..................203 426-3318
Neal Berko, *President*
Joanne Berko, *Vice Pres*
EMP: 2
SALES (est): 2MM **Privately Held**
SIC: 3448 Prefabricated metal components

(G-7302)
CABINETMAKERS CHOICE LLC
32 Gelding Hill Rd (06482-1434)
P.O. Box 729, Newtown (06470-0729)
PHONE..................203 426-3247
Neil Ratner,
EMP: 1
SALES (est): 119.1K **Privately Held**
SIC: 2434 Wood kitchen cabinets

(G-7303)
COASTAL CANVAS
24 Poplar Dr (06482-1276)
P.O. Box 254, Newtown (06470-0254)
PHONE..................203 270-7408
Michael Agius, *Owner*
EMP: 1
SALES (est): 51.2K **Privately Held**
SIC: 2211 Canvas

(G-7304)
COMPUTER WAREHOUSE
42 Valley Field Rd S (06482-1094)
PHONE..................203 426-1034
Thomas Depall, *Owner*
EMP: 1
SALES (est): 77K **Privately Held**
SIC: 3575 Computer terminals, monitors & components

(G-7305)
CONN ENGINEERING ASSOC CORP
Also Called: Ceac
27 Philo Curtis Rd (06482-1245)
P.O. Box 656 (06482-0656)
PHONE..................203 426-4733
Gregory Jossick, *President*
Sandra Jossick, *Corp Secy*
Ziad Fakhoury, *Exec VP*
Jeffrey Jossick, *Vice Pres*
Nick Sopchak, *Manager*
▲ EMP: 14 EST: 1967
SQ FT: 6,000
SALES (est): 2.5MM **Privately Held**
WEB: www.ceacpowder.com
SIC: 3399 Powder, metal

(G-7306)
CT PYRO MFG LLC
15 Glen Rd (06482-1161)
PHONE..................203 856-8313
Jim Widmann, *President*
EMP: 2
SALES (est): 174.2K **Privately Held**
SIC: 3999 Manufacturing industries

(G-7307)
CURTIS CORPORATION A DEL CORP
44 Berkshire Rd (06482-1499)
PHONE..................203 426-5861
Donald Droppo, *President*
William Peck, *Corp Secy*
EMP: 155
SQ FT: 112,000
SALES (est): 24.8MM **Privately Held**
SIC: 2657 Folding paperboard boxes

(G-7308)
CURTIS PACKAGING CORPORATION
44 Berkshire Rd (06482-1428)
PHONE..................203 426-5861
Donald R Droppo Jr, *Ch of Bd*
Donald Droppo Jr, *President*
William F Peck, *Senior VP*
Kerry Brown, *Safety Mgr*
Jared Unterborn, *QC Mgr*
▲ EMP: 130
SQ FT: 150,000
SALES: 13.8K **Privately Held**
WEB: www.curtispackaging.com
SIC: 2657 Folding paperboard boxes

(G-7309)
DESIGN LTD
62 Underhill Rd (06482-1207)
PHONE..................203 426-5539
Jane Sharpe, *Owner*
EMP: 2
SALES (est): 152.8K **Privately Held**
WEB: www.design-ltd.com
SIC: 2452 Log cabins, prefabricated, wood

(G-7310)
DOORS TO EXPLORE INC
16 Chestnut Hill Rd (06482-1519)
PHONE..................978 761-7210
Kelley T Johnson, *President*
Kelley Johnson, *President*
EMP: 1 EST: 2016
SALES (est): 45.4K **Privately Held**
SIC: 2741

(G-7311)
FRANCE VOILES CO INC
75 Glen Rd Ste 300 (06482-1191)
PHONE..................203 364-9454
Steve Morris, *President*
▲ EMP: 1
SALES (est): 208.5K **Privately Held**
SIC: 3552 Textile machinery

(G-7312)
FRATES CUSTOM CABINETRY
6a Russett Rd (06482-1455)
PHONE..................203 994-1108
Robert Frate, *Owner*
EMP: 1
SALES (est): 75.7K **Privately Held**
SIC: 1751 3999 Cabinet & finish carpentry; barber & beauty shop equipment

(G-7313)
G H TOOL INC
26 Berkshire Rd (06482-1321)
PHONE..................203 270-0566
Gabor Hajzer, *President*
EMP: 2
SALES (est): 241.9K **Privately Held**
SIC: 3599 Machine shop, jobbing & repair

(G-7314)
GINTYS WELDING SERVICE INC
Also Called: Ginty's
29 Philo Curtis Rd (06482-1245)
PHONE..................203 270-3399
EMP: 2
SALES (est): 150K **Privately Held**
SIC: 7692 3444 Welding Repair Mfg Sheet Metalwork

(G-7315)
HENDRICKSON GROUP
11 Washington Ave (06482-1339)
PHONE..................203 426-9266
Frances Hendrickson, *Owner*
EMP: 1 EST: 1988
SALES (est): 43.9K **Privately Held**
SIC: 2741 Music book & sheet music publishing

(G-7316)
HURLEY WOODWORKING LLC
68 Jeremiah Rd (06482-1407)
PHONE..................818 643-5809
Stephanie Hurley,
EMP: 1
SALES (est): 54.1K **Privately Held**
SIC: 2431 Millwork

(G-7317)
JAMES WOZNICK
Also Called: Amazing Signs
2 Rocky Wood Dr (06482-1479)
PHONE..................203 426-5585
James Woznick, *Owner*
William Braswell, *Executive*
EMP: 1
SALES (est): 85.4K **Privately Held**
SIC: 3993 Signs & advertising specialties

(G-7318)
KARIBA WOODWORKS
25 Riverside Rd (06482-1214)
PHONE..................203 246-8917
Nicole Capener, *Principal*
EMP: 2 EST: 2016
SALES (est): 113.4K **Privately Held**
SIC: 2431 Millwork

(G-7319)
LISERN ENTERPRISES INC
57 Lakeview Ter (06482-1410)
PHONE..................203 426-9079
E Willvonseder, *President*
EMP: 2
SALES (corp-wide): 205.7K **Privately Held**
SIC: 3089 Coloring & finishing of plastic products
PA: Lisern Enterprises Inc
550 Shore Acres Dr
Mamaroneck NY

(G-7320)
LOMBARDO INDUSTRIES LLC
42 Berkshire Rd (06482-1335)
PHONE..................203 948-8562
Phillip Lombardo, *Owner*
EMP: 1
SALES (est): 39.6K **Privately Held**
SIC: 3999 Manufacturing industries

(G-7321)
MAPLE CRAFT FOODS LLC
6 Cider Mill Rd (06482-1587)
PHONE..................203 913-7066
EMP: 4
SALES (est): 99.1K **Privately Held**
SIC: 2099 Food preparations

(G-7322)
MURPHY INDUSTRIES LLC
37 Great Ring Rd (06482-1638)
PHONE..................203 426-1772
Michael W Murphy, *Manager*
EMP: 1 EST: 2001

SALES (est): 51.2K **Privately Held**
SIC: 3999 Manufacturing industries

(G-7323)
NCC
14 Osborne Hill Rd (06482-1533)
PHONE..................203 966-8307
Douglas Dean, *President*
EMP: 1
SALES (est): 41K **Privately Held**
SIC: 3915 Jewelers' materials & lapidary work

(G-7324)
OFF THE HOOKHANDMADECROCHETLLC
96 High Rock Rd (06482-1671)
PHONE..................203 912-1638
Wendy Decarlo,
EMP: 2 EST: 2017
SALES (est): 100.8K **Privately Held**
SIC: 2399 Hand woven & crocheted products

(G-7325)
PETER ORTALI & ASSOCIATES LLC
45 New Lebbon Rd (06482-1626)
PHONE..................203 571-8023
Peter Ortali, *Principal*
EMP: 2
SALES (est): 103.7K **Privately Held**
SIC: 8742 3993 7311 Management consulting services; advertising artwork; advertising agencies

(G-7326)
PHOENIX MEMORIAL PRINTING LLC
18 Evergreen Rd (06482-1003)
PHONE..................203 364-9617
Stephen Agnew, *Principal*
EMP: 2
SALES (est): 118.8K **Privately Held**
SIC: 2752 Commercial printing, lithographic

(G-7327)
Q-LANE TURNSTILES LLC
52 Riverside Rd (06482-1213)
PHONE..................860 410-1801
Ed Jacobsen, *Manager*
EMP: 11 EST: 2016
SALES (est): 619.9K **Privately Held**
SIC: 3829 7382 1731 3669 Automatic turnstiles & related apparatus; protective devices, security; safety & security specialization; pedestrian traffic control equipment

(G-7328)
ROOST CANDLE CO LLC
16 Gelding Hill Rd (06482-1453)
PHONE..................203 270-6577
Glenn R Schicker, *Principal*
EMP: 2
SALES (est): 62.5K **Privately Held**
SIC: 3999 Candles

(G-7329)
SANDY HOOK WELDING & FABG
4 Forest Dr (06482-1228)
PHONE..................203 731-9844
Joseph McCarthy, *Principal*
EMP: 1
SALES (est): 80.4K **Privately Held**
SIC: 7692 Welding repair

(G-7330)
SMOKEY MOUNTAIN CHEW INC
107 Church Hill Rd (06482-1194)
P.O. Box 3608, Newtown (06470-3608)
PHONE..................203 304-9200
Daniel R Calandro, *Principal*
EMP: 4
SALES (est): 730K **Privately Held**
SIC: 5194 2111 Smoking tobacco; cigarettes

(G-7331)
USA CIRCUITS LLC
114 Lakeview Ter (06482-1482)
PHONE..................203 364-1378
Thomas Cheung, *Principal*
EMP: 3 EST: 2010

Scotland
Windham County

(G-7332)
HARDWOOD LUMBER MANUFACTURING
Also Called: Scotland Hardwoods
111 Ziegler Rd (06264)
P.O. Box 328 (06264-0328)
PHONE..................860 423-2447
Brian Park, *Manager*
EMP: 20
SALES (corp-wide): 57.5MM **Privately Held**
SIC: 5031 2421 Lumber: rough, dressed & finished; sawmills & planing mills, general
PA: Hardwood Lumber Manufacturing, Inc
567 N Charlotte Ave
Waynesboro VA 22980
540 946-9150

(G-7333)
SCOTLAND HARDWOODS LLC
117 Ziegler Rd (06264)
P.O. Box 328 (06264-0328)
PHONE..................860 423-1233
Peter J Rossi, *Mng Member*
Andrew Becker,
▼ **EMP:** 34
SQ FT: 45,000
SALES (est): 5.6MM **Privately Held**
SIC: 2421 Lumber: rough, sawed or planed
PA: New England Timber Resources Inc
162 West St Ste A
Cromwell CT
860 632-3505

Seymour
New Haven County

(G-7334)
12 PAWS PUBLISHING LLC
78 Birchwood Rd (06483-3806)
PHONE..................203 232-4534
Katie Melko, *Manager*
EMP: 1
SALES (est): 37.5K **Privately Held**
SIC: 2741 Miscellaneous publishing

(G-7335)
AIR-VAC ENGINEERING CO INC (PA)
30 Progress Ave Ste 2 (06483-3935)
P.O. Box 216 (06483-0216)
PHONE..................203 888-9900
Clifford S Lasto, *President*
Jeffrey S Duhaime, *Vice Pres*
Howard C Lasto, *Treasurer*
Brett Lasto, *Director*
Gary R Duhaime, *Admin Sec*
EMP: 22 **EST:** 1959
SQ FT: 25,000
SALES (est): 4.8MM **Privately Held**
SIC: 3548 Soldering equipment, except hand soldering irons

(G-7336)
BRIAN CHENEY (PA)
Also Called: Magivac Sales
869 S Main St (06483-3233)
PHONE..................203 734-4793
Bryan Cheney, *Owner*
EMP: 1 **EST:** 1995
SQ FT: 2,000
SALES (est): 159.1K **Privately Held**
SIC: 5722 5211 1731 3699 Vacuum cleaners; lumber & other building materials; computer installation; door opening & closing devices, electrical

(G-7337)
CANOGA PERKINS CORPORATION
100 Bank St (06483-2806)
PHONE..................203 888-7914
Steve Hannay, *Branch Mgr*
EMP: 3
SALES (corp-wide): 1B **Privately Held**
WEB: www.canoga.com
SIC: 3661 Modems
HQ: Canoga Perkins Corporation
20600 Prairie St
Chatsworth CA 91311
818 718-6300

(G-7338)
CASPARI INC (PA)
99 Cogwheel Ln (06483-3900)
PHONE..................203 888-1100
Douglas H Stevens, *Ch of Bd*
Lisa Fingeret, *Vice Pres*
Caralyn Stevens, *Vice Pres*
Gloria Finkenauer, *CFO*
Tracy Peters, *Credit Mgr*
◆ **EMP:** 16
SQ FT: 35,000
SALES (est): 36.3MM **Privately Held**
SIC: 2771 Greeting cards

(G-7339)
CENTURY SOFTWARE SYSTEMS
26 Sagamore Dr (06483-2058)
PHONE..................203 888-5233
Stewart Harris, *Owner*
EMP: 2 **EST:** 1982
SALES (est): 114K **Privately Held**
SIC: 7372 Prepackaged software

(G-7340)
CIRCUIT BREAKER SALES NE INC
Also Called: CBS Ne
79 Main St (06483-3122)
PHONE..................203 888-7500
Finley Ledbetter, *President*
Ray Kinney, *Vice Pres*
Stephen Raccio, *Project Mgr*
EMP: 35
SALES (est): 2MM **Privately Held**
SIC: 5063 3699 Electrical supplies; electrical equipment & supplies
PA: Group Cbs, Inc.
1315 Columbine Dr
Gainesville TX 76240

(G-7341)
CONNECTCUT DGITAL GRAPHICS LLC
100 S Main St (06483-3329)
PHONE..................203 888-6509
James L Petzold,
EMP: 1
SALES (est): 92.9K **Privately Held**
SIC: 3993 Signs & advertising specialties

(G-7342)
CONNECTICUT CUSTOM WDWRK LLC
57 Botsford Rd (06483-2303)
PHONE..................203 888-3948
EMP: 2
SALES (est): 133.1K **Privately Held**
SIC: 2431 Mfg Millwork

(G-7343)
CT FILMS LLC
38 N Benham Rd (06483-2247)
PHONE..................203 734-8307
Rosalie Averill, *Principal*
EMP: 1
SALES (est): 74.8K **Privately Held**
SIC: 3861 Motion picture film

(G-7344)
E S WILLIAMS CO
61 Washington Ave (06483-3126)
PHONE..................203 888-0093
EMP: 2
SALES (est): 131.4K **Privately Held**
SIC: 3559 Sewing machines & attachments, industrial

(G-7345)
EDKO CABINETS LLC
101 Derby Ave Apt 1 (06483-3156)
PHONE..................203 463-8346
Edward Konopka,
EMP: 2
SQ FT: 3,600
SALES (est): 229K **Privately Held**
SIC: 2511 2541 Wood household furniture; wood partitions & fixtures

(G-7346)
FRANK DEMARTINO AND SONS
Also Called: Demartino Packing
66 Old Ansonia Rd (06483-3515)
PHONE..................203 734-1074
Frank Demartino, *Owner*
EMP: 3
SQ FT: 2,500
SALES (est): 218.5K **Privately Held**
WEB: www.frankdemartino.com
SIC: 5154 2011 Auctioning livestock; beef products from beef slaughtered on site

(G-7347)
G & M TOOL COMPANY
45 Highland Rd (06478-1694)
PHONE..................203 888-9354
George Maciulewski, *Owner*
EMP: 3
SQ FT: 1,200
SALES (est): 308.2K **Privately Held**
SIC: 3599 Machine shop, jobbing & repair; custom machinery

(G-7348)
GREENWICH WORKSHOP INC (PA)
Also Called: Gws Marketing Associates
151 Main St (06483-3137)
P.O. Box 231 (06483-0231)
PHONE..................203 881-3336
Vincent Grabowski, *President*
Michael Meskill, *Chairman*
Jane Capua, *Sales Mgr*
Jim Oberempt, *Manager*
▲ **EMP:** 35
SQ FT: 28,000
SALES (est): 8.3MM **Privately Held**
WEB: www.greenwichworkshop.com
SIC: 5199 5999 8412 2731 Art goods; art dealers; art gallery; book publishing

(G-7349)
HAYNES AGGREGATES - DEEP RIVER
30d Progress Ave (06483)
PHONE..................203 888-8100
Thomas Haynes, *Principal*
EMP: 2
SALES (est): 170.7K **Privately Held**
SIC: 1481 Nonmetallic mineral services

(G-7350)
HOUSATONIC WIRE CO
109 River St (06483-2639)
PHONE..................203 888-9670
EMP: 12 **EST:** 1972
SQ FT: 65,000
SALES (est): 132.2K **Privately Held**
SIC: 3315 Mfg Steel Wire/Related Products

(G-7351)
INFORMATION SECURITY ASSOC LLC
Also Called: ISA
6 Spruce Brook Rd (06483-2220)
PHONE..................203 736-9587
Horace Edgerton,
Sabrina Edgerton,
EMP: 2
SALES (est): 248.1K **Privately Held**
SIC: 3825 Instruments to measure electricity

(G-7352)
JV PRECISION MACHINE CO
71 Cogwheel Ln (06483-3919)
PHONE..................203 888-0748
Josef Visinski Jr, *President*
Andrew Visinski, *Treasurer*
EMP: 30
SQ FT: 42,000
SALES (est): 5.3MM **Privately Held**
WEB: www.jvprecision.net
SIC: 3599 Machine shop, jobbing & repair

(G-7353)
KINETIC DEVELOPMENT GROUP LLC
Also Called: Kdg
71 Cogwheel Ln (06483-3919)
PHONE..................203 888-4321
Darren Mellors, *Mng Member*
Charles Lafferty, *Mng Member*
Josef Visinski, *Administration*
EMP: 5
SQ FT: 72,000
SALES (est): 527.1K **Privately Held**
SIC: 3484 Guns (firearms) or gun parts, 30 mm. & below

(G-7354)
MARMON UTILITY LLC
Also Called: Kerite
49 Day St (06483-3401)
PHONE..................203 881-5358
Edmund Sleight, *President*
Wayne Yakich, *Mng Member*
Michael Garratt, *Mng Member*
Craig Phelon, *Mng Member*
Robert W Webb, *Mng Member*
◆ **EMP:** 31 **EST:** 1996
SALES (est): 10.6MM
SALES (corp-wide): 225.3B **Publicly Held**
SIC: 3315 3357 Wire, steel: insulated or armored; cable, steel: insulated or armored; nonferrous wiredrawing & insulating
HQ: The Marmon Group Llc
181 W Madison St Ste 2600
Chicago IL 60602

(G-7355)
MATTHEW WARREN INC
Also Called: Raf Electronic Hardware
95 Silvermine Rd Ste 1 (06483-3915)
PHONE..................203 888-2133
Nick Russo, *Vice Pres*
Brian Stach, *Plant Mgr*
Kathy Mullen, *Accounts Mgr*
David Granger, *Sales Staff*
Mike Heywosz, *Sales Staff*
EMP: 8
SALES (corp-wide): 185.9MM **Privately Held**
SIC: 3451 3452 Screw machine products; bolts, nuts, rivets & washers
HQ: Matthew Warren, Inc.
9501 Tech Blvd Ste 401
Rosemont IL 60018
847 349-5760

(G-7356)
MB SYSTEMS LLC
9 Old Town Rd (06483-2416)
PHONE..................203 881-1583
Martin Opitz, *CEO*
Robert Splaine, *Mng Member*
EMP: 2
SALES: 100K **Privately Held**
SIC: 3825 Engine electrical test equipment

(G-7357)
MICROBOARD PROCESSING INC
Also Called: M P I
36 Cogwheel Ln (06483-3922)
PHONE..................203 881-4300
Craig Hoekenga, *Ch of Bd*
Nicole Russo, *President*
Bryan Brady, *Vice Pres*
Ted Labowski, *Vice Pres*
Tyler Allen, *Production*
▲ **EMP:** 105
SQ FT: 60,000
SALES (est): 35.5MM **Privately Held**
WEB: www.microboard.com
SIC: 3672 7629 Circuit boards, television & radio printed; circuit board repair

(G-7358)
NEW ENGLAND CAP COMPANY
Also Called: Om Cass Swiss
756 Derby Ave (06483-2412)
PHONE..................203 736-6184
Mike Murjani, *Mng Member*
EMP: 16
SQ FT: 16,000
SALES: 600K **Privately Held**
WEB: www.newenglandcap.com
SIC: 2353 Hats, caps & millinery

(G-7359)
NEW ENGLAND CUSTOM BUILT LLC
133 West St Apt 29g (06483-2634)
PHONE..................203 828-6480
Christopher Cowell, *Principal*
EMP: 1

Seymour - New Haven County (G-7360)

SALES (est): 38.7K **Privately Held**
SIC: 2395 Embroidery & art needlework

(G-7360)
PHOENIX MACHINE INC
279 Pearl St (06483-3719)
PHONE..................................203 888-1135
Al Pokrywka, *President*
EMP: 5
SQ FT: 3,500
SALES: 390K **Privately Held**
SIC: 3599 7692 Machine shop, jobbing & repair; welding repair

(G-7361)
PLASTIC MOLDING TECHNOLOGY
92 Cogwheel Ln (06483-3923)
PHONE..................................203 881-1811
Charles Sholtis, *Principal*
EMP: 4
SALES (est): 310.9K **Privately Held**
SIC: 3089 Injection molding of plastics

(G-7362)
PORTA DOOR CO
65 Cogwheel Ln (06483-3919)
PHONE..................................203 888-6191
Peter Romanos, *President*
Chris Malizia, *Vice Pres*
EMP: 31
SQ FT: 20,000
SALES (est): 3.8MM **Privately Held**
WEB: www.portadoor.com
SIC: 2434 5712 2431 Wood kitchen cabinets; furniture stores; millwork

(G-7363)
PRECISION AEROSPACE INC
88 Cogwheel Ln (06483-3923)
PHONE..................................203 888-3022
Jack E Hillman Sr, *CEO*
Jack E Hillman Jr, *President*
Jeffrey W Hillman, *Vice Pres*
Janice Hillman Frost, *Admin Sec*
Dorothy Hillman, *Admin Sec*
EMP: 40
SQ FT: 16,000
SALES (est): 8.1MM **Privately Held**
SIC: 3728 Aircraft parts & equipment

(G-7364)
PROTECTIVE HOME COATINGS LLC
18 Buckingham Rd (06483-2208)
PHONE..................................203 410-5826
James Verrinder, *Principal*
EMP: 2
SALES (est): 81.5K **Privately Held**
SIC: 3479 Metal coating & allied service

(G-7365)
RETINA SYSTEMS INC
146 Day St (06483-3403)
PHONE..................................203 881-1311
Floyd Moir, *President*
George Wixon, *Engineer*
Billie Guliuzza, *Accountant*
Melanie Anderson, *Sales Staff*
Karl Cressotti, *Director*
▲ EMP: 25
SQ FT: 14,000
SALES (est): 5.5MM **Privately Held**
WEB: www.retinasystems.com
SIC: 3827 Lenses, optical: all types except ophthalmic

(G-7366)
SAFE WATER
371 Roosevelt Dr (06483-2120)
PHONE..................................203 732-4806
Vincent Veccharelli, *Owner*
EMP: 3 EST: 1999
SALES (est): 142.9K **Privately Held**
WEB: www.safewater.com
SIC: 3589 Water filters & softeners, household type

(G-7367)
STATE CUTTER GRINDING SVC INC
481 N Main St (06483-2945)
P.O. Box 245 (06483-0245)
PHONE..................................203 888-8821
Jack Saldamarco, *President*
James Saldamarco, *Vice Pres*
Donna Duclos, *Manager*
EMP: 6 EST: 1967
SQ FT: 17,000
SALES: 857.9K **Privately Held**
WEB: www.statecutter.com
SIC: 7389 3599 Grinding, precision: commercial or industrial; machine shop, jobbing & repair

(G-7368)
THULE INC (DH)
42 Silvermine Rd (06483-3928)
PHONE..................................203 881-9600
Fred Clark, *President*
Maureen Murphy-Parente, *Vice Pres*
Gary Vehrenkamp, *Vice Pres*
Fred Wyckoff, *Vice Pres*
Elizabeth Santana, *Project Mgr*
◆ EMP: 157
SALES (est): 120.4MM **Privately Held**
WEB: www.karriteus.com
SIC: 3714 5021 Tops, motor vehicle; racks

(G-7369)
THULE CANADA HOLDING LLC
42 Silvermine Rd (06483-3928)
PHONE..................................203 881-4919
Edmund Farmer, *Vice Pres*
Mark Cohen, *CFO*
▲ EMP: 2
SALES (est): 291.2K **Privately Held**
WEB: www.thuleus.com
SIC: 3429 Bicycle racks, automotive
HQ: Thule, Inc.
42 Silvermine Rd
Seymour CT 06483
203 881-9600

(G-7370)
THULE HOLDING INC (DH)
42 Silvermine Rd (06483-3928)
PHONE..................................203 881-9600
Fred Clark, *President*
Moreen Parente, *Vice Pres*
Patrick Monahan, *VP Opers*
Tom Chimenti, *Director*
Stewart Semeraro, *Maintence Staff*
EMP: 13
SALES (est): 120.4MM **Privately Held**
SIC: 3792 3714 Travel trailers & campers; tops, motor vehicle
HQ: Thule Holding Ab
Fosievagen 13
Malmo
406 359-000

(G-7371)
ULTRA MFG LLC
43 Patton Ave (06483-3531)
PHONE..................................203 888-1180
Ben Wrogg, *Owner*
EMP: 1
SALES (est): 88.6K **Privately Held**
SIC: 3312 3999 Tool & die steel; manufacturing industries

(G-7372)
VERNIER METAL FABRICATING INC
Also Called: V M F
26 Progress Ave (06483-3921)
PHONE..................................203 881-3133
Edward Zerjav, *President*
John J Zerjav, *Vice Pres*
Robert Zerjav, *Treasurer*
Barbara Zerjav, *Admin Sec*
EMP: 70
SQ FT: 54,000
SALES (est): 15.7MM **Privately Held**
WEB: www.vmf.com
SIC: 3441 3444 Fabricated structural metal; sheet metalwork

(G-7373)
WILDFLOUR CUPCAKES SWEETS LLC
18 Bank St (06483-2802)
PHONE..................................203 828-6576
Alyssa Dematteo, *Principal*
EMP: 2
SALES (est): 193.6K **Privately Held**
SIC: 2051 Bread, cake & related products

(G-7374)
WORMS EYE
66 Briarwood Dr (06483-3045)
PHONE..................................203 888-0895
Regene Chernaunkan, *Owner*
EMP: 1
SALES (est): 99K **Privately Held**
SIC: 3944 Craft & hobby kits & sets

(G-7375)
XAMAX INDUSTRIES INC
63 Silvermine Rd (06483-3915)
PHONE..................................203 888-7200
Martin J Weinberg, *President*
Carol Evancovitch, *Marketing Mgr*
Bill Pisani, *Marketing Staff*
Margaret Pederson, *Admin Sec*
▲ EMP: 50
SQ FT: 36,000
SALES (est): 21.8MM **Privately Held**
WEB: www.xamax.com
SIC: 2621 2297 Insulation siding, paper; nonwoven fabrics

Sharon
Litchfield County

(G-7376)
BRISTOW STUDIO GLASS
139 Sharon Valley Rd (06069-2093)
PHONE..................................860 364-1670
Tim Bristow, *Owner*
Karen Bristow, *Owner*
EMP: 2
SALES (est): 68.1K **Privately Held**
SIC: 3229 Pressed & blown glass

(G-7377)
DBO HOME LLC
25 Millerton Rd (06069-2068)
PHONE..................................860 364-6008
Dana M Brandwein, *Principal*
EMP: 2
SALES (est): 107.4K **Privately Held**
SIC: 3229 7389 2519 Tableware, glass or glass ceramic; ; rattan furniture: padded or plain

(G-7378)
DOMUS VI LLC
85 Herb Rd (06069-2332)
P.O. Box 139, Washington Depot (06794-0139)
PHONE..................................860 619-0707
Robert W Ensign,
EMP: 1
SALES (est): 51.4K **Privately Held**
SIC: 0782 3523 0711 7699 Lawn care services; tractors, farm; plowing services; cleaning services

(G-7379)
GREEN EDITORIAL
Also Called: Design Books
139 Calkinstown Rd (06069-2126)
PHONE..................................860 364-5100
Nancy Green, *Partner*
Walton Green, *Partner*
EMP: 2
SALES (est): 120K **Privately Held**
SIC: 2731 Books: publishing only

(G-7380)
GREY HOUSE PUBLISHING INC
23 N Main St (06069-2075)
PHONE..................................860 364-1444
Richard Gottlieb, *Branch Mgr*
EMP: 2
SALES (corp-wide): 5.3MM **Privately Held**
SIC: 2741 Miscellaneous publishing
PA: Grey House Publishing, Inc.
4919 Route 22
Amenia NY 12501
518 789-8700

(G-7381)
ONE PAIR OF HANDS
79 Gay St (06069-2001)
P.O. Box 484 (06069-0484)
PHONE..................................860 364-0027
Samuel Fitzgerald, *Owner*
EMP: 1
SALES (est): 56.7K **Privately Held**
WEB: www.bainrealestate.com
SIC: 3269 Stoneware pottery products

(G-7382)
PRS WOODS LLC
94 Lambert Rd (06069-2217)
PHONE..................................860 364-5173
Patricia Purdy, *Principal*
EMP: 1
SALES (est): 43.6K **Privately Held**
SIC: 2741 Miscellaneous publishing

(G-7383)
SANDPIPER ELECTRONICS INC
95 Westwoods Road 1 (06069-2234)
PHONE..................................860 364-5558
Joe Lomask, *President*
EMP: 2
SALES (corp-wide): 3.7MM **Privately Held**
WEB: www.buxco.com
SIC: 3571 Electronic computers
PA: Sandpiper Electronics, Inc.
2033 Corporate Dr Ste 1
Wilmington NC 28405
910 794-6980

(G-7384)
TCG GREEN TECHNOLOGIES INC
Also Called: Turtle Clan Global
1 Skiff Mountain Rd (06069-2224)
P.O. Box 861 (06069-0861)
PHONE..................................860 364-4694
Albert Snow, *President*
Lesley Burton-Dallas, *Chairman*
▲ EMP: 10 EST: 2013
SALES (est): 601.5K **Privately Held**
SIC: 3291 2851 Abrasive products; coating, air curing

Shelton
Fairfield County

(G-7385)
A & I CONCENTRATE LLC
2 Corporate Dr Ste 136 (06484-6274)
PHONE..................................203 447-1938
David Rothacker, *Vice Pres*
Don Vultaggio, *Mng Member*
Joseph Misinonile, *Manager*
Thomas O'Hara,
EMP: 10
SALES: 9.9MM **Privately Held**
SIC: 3556 5181 Food products machinery; beer & ale

(G-7386)
A&A HOME SOLUTIONS
440 Nichols Ave (06484-5704)
PHONE..................................203 993-1735
EMP: 1
SALES (est): 84K **Privately Held**
SIC: 1521 3646 Single-Family House Construction Mfg Commercial Lighting Fixtures

(G-7387)
ABC SIGN CORPORATION
30 Controls Dr Ste 1 (06484-6157)
PHONE..................................203 513-8110
Gus De Santy, *CEO*
Greg De Santy, *President*
EMP: 25 EST: 1955
SQ FT: 20,000
SALES (est): 4.6MM **Privately Held**
WEB: www.abcsigncorp.com
SIC: 3993 Signs, not made in custom sign painting shops

(G-7388)
ACTION PRINTING
415 Howe Ave Ste 328 (06484-3169)
PHONE..................................203 366-4413
Glenn Niestemski, *Owner*
EMP: 2
SQ FT: 520

GEOGRAPHIC SECTION

SALES (est): 140K **Privately Held**
SIC: **2759** 2791 2752 Visiting cards (including business): printing; promotional printing; menus: printing; envelopes: printing; typesetting; commercial printing, lithographic

(G-7389)
AFRICAN LINK
788 Long Hill Ave (06484-5409)
P.O. Box 5132, New York NY (10185-5132)
PHONE..................................203 925-1632
Frank Adae, *Owner*
EMP: 1
SALES (est): 50K **Privately Held**
WEB: www.africanlinkmagazine.com
SIC: **2731** Book publishing

(G-7390)
AL-LYNN SALES LLC
25 Brook St Ste 102 (06484-2332)
PHONE..................................203 922-7840
Marilyn Ragozzine, *Opers Mgr*
Nicole Kowalewski, *Natl Sales Mgr*
Gail Cheney, *Sales Staff*
Kara Iarossi, *Sales Staff*
Mike Ragozzine, *Mng Member*
EMP: 9
SQ FT: 2,000
SALES (est): 1MM **Privately Held**
WEB: www.al-lynn.com
SIC: **5699** 2395 Uniforms; embroidery products, except schiffli machine

(G-7391)
ALBERT GRAMESTY AND DAWN GRAME
19 Wakeley St (06484-4511)
PHONE..................................203 924-7947
Albert Gramesty, *Partner*
EMP: 2
SALES (est): 106.6K **Privately Held**
SIC: **3993** Signs & advertising specialties

(G-7392)
ALPHA-CORE INC
6 Waterview Dr (06484-4300)
PHONE..................................203 954-0050
Peder Ulrik Poulsen, *President*
Sandu Pescaru, *Vice Pres*
◆ EMP: 20
SQ FT: 25,000
SALES (est): 2.8MM **Privately Held**
SIC: **3679** 5731 3612 3549 Cores, magnetic; radio, television & electronic stores; transformers, except electric; metalworking machinery; nonferrous wiredrawing & insulating; aluminum rolling & drawing

(G-7393)
AMERICAN SPECIALTY CO INC
762 River Rd (06484-5465)
P.O. Box 670, Northford (06472-0670)
PHONE..................................203 929-5324
James W Monde, *President*
Emil J Monde, *Vice Pres*
Gina Kenyon, *Accounting Mgr*
EMP: 10 EST: 1957
SQ FT: 12,000
SALES (est): 956.1K **Privately Held**
SIC: **3493** Steel springs, except wire

(G-7394)
AMERICAN ULTRAVIOLET
22 Ivy Grove Ct (06484-3824)
PHONE..................................203 926-0140
John Andros, *Principal*
EMP: 2
SALES (est): 161.4K **Privately Held**
SIC: **3826** Ultraviolet analytical instruments

(G-7395)
ANCO ENGINEERING INC
217 Long Hill Cross Rd (06484-6145)
PHONE..................................203 925-9235
Lucian S Leszczynski, *President*
Daniel Leszczynski, *Vice Pres*
Lucian Leszczynski Jr, *Vice Pres*
Ann Leszczynski, *Treasurer*
Vicky Deleon, *Accounts Mgr*
EMP: 85 EST: 1981
SQ FT: 100,000
SALES (est): 22MM **Privately Held**
WEB: www.ancoeng.com
SIC: **3441** 3444 Fabricated structural metal; sheet metal specialties, not stamped

(G-7396)
ANTHONY S FUEL
56 Great Oak Rd (06484-5208)
PHONE..................................203 513-7400
Anthony Frank Mobilio, *Principal*
EMP: 3
SALES (est): 433K **Privately Held**
SIC: **2869** Fuels

(G-7397)
ARP WELDING & REPAIR LLC
38 Button Rd (06484-2746)
PHONE..................................203 924-6811
Adam Patrick, *Principal*
EMP: 1 EST: 2015
SALES (est): 36.7K **Privately Held**
SIC: **7692** Welding repair

(G-7398)
BAGELA USA LLC
70 Platt Rd (06484-5339)
PHONE..................................203 944-0525
Greg Harla, *General Mgr*
Gregory Harla,
▲ EMP: 5
SALES (est): 959K **Privately Held**
SIC: **3531** Construction machinery

(G-7399)
BAINGAN LLC
94 River Rd (06484-5618)
PHONE..................................203 924-2626
Shrijana Kandel, *Principal*
EMP: 4
SALES (est): 384.2K **Privately Held**
SIC: **3421** Table & food cutlery, including butchers'

(G-7400)
BAKERY ENGINEERING/WINKLER INC
Also Called: Winkler USA
2 Trap Falls Rd Ste 105 (06484-4670)
PHONE..................................203 929-8630
Dan Wilzinski, *President*
Carl Petterson, *Vice Pres*
Kim Rodriguez, *Administration*
EMP: 19
SQ FT: 15,000
SALES (est): 3.4MM **Privately Held**
WEB: www.krausectp.com
SIC: **3556** Ovens, bakery; bakery machinery

(G-7401)
BALDWIN GRAPHIC SYSTEMS INC
12 Commerce Dr (06484-6202)
PHONE..................................203 925-1100
Fax: 203 929-7856
EMP: 2
SALES (est): 216K **Privately Held**
SIC: **3555** Mfg Printing Trades Machinery

(G-7402)
BAM CUSTOM PRINTING
51a Armstrong Rd (06484-6104)
PHONE..................................888 583-6690
EMP: 2
SALES (est): 83.9K **Privately Held**
SIC: **2752** Commercial printing, lithographic

(G-7403)
BETA PHARMA INC
1 Enterprise Dr Ste 408 (06484-7624)
PHONE..................................203 315-5062
Don Zhang, *President*
Mehrnaz Kamal, *Exec VP*
Michael Costanzo, *Director*
Jidong Liu, *Director*
◆ EMP: 12
SQ FT: 4,800
SALES (est): 2.6MM **Privately Held**
WEB: www.betapharma.com
SIC: **2834** 8731 Pharmaceutical preparations; commercial physical research

(G-7404)
BETA SHIM CO
11 Progress Dr (06484-6218)
PHONE..................................203 926-1150
John P McCue, *President*
Mark Lovallo, *Vice Pres*
Scott McCue, *Vice Pres*
Zach Pratt, *Vice Pres*
Kevin McCue, *Sales Staff*
EMP: 47
SQ FT: 21,000
SALES (est): 12.5MM **Privately Held**
WEB: www.betashim.com
SIC: **3499** 3469 Shims, metal; metal stampings

(G-7405)
BEYOND INVITE
46 Brownson Dr (06484-2713)
PHONE..................................203 219-9434
EMP: 2
SALES (est): 104.7K **Privately Held**
SIC: **2759** Invitations: printing

(G-7406)
BIC CONSUMER PDTS MFG CO INC
1 Bic Way Ste 1 # 1 (06484-6223)
PHONE..................................203 783-2000
Bruno Bich, *Ch of Bd*
Patrick Cordle, *Vice Pres*
Eileen Barcello, *Opers Staff*
Carlos Avila, *Marketing Staff*
Keith Anderson, *Admin Mgr*
▲ EMP: 1
SALES (est): 382.3K
SALES (corp-wide): 791.2MM **Privately Held**
WEB: www.biceveryday.com
SIC: **3951** Ball point pens & parts
HQ: Bic Usa Inc.
1 Bic Way Ste 1 # 1
Shelton CT 06484
203 783-2000

(G-7407)
BIC CORPORATION (HQ)
Also Called: Bic Graphic USA
1 Bic Way Ste 1 # 1 (06484-6223)
PHONE..................................203 783-2000
Mario Guevara, *CEO*
Bruno Bich, *Ch of Bd*
Pauline Dantas, *President*
David Houston, *Business Mgr*
Nikita Minchenko, *Business Mgr*
▲ EMP: 900 EST: 1958
SQ FT: 800,000
SALES (est): 1.4B
SALES (corp-wide): 791.2MM **Privately Held**
WEB: www.biclink.com
SIC: **3951** 2899 3999 3421 Ball point pens & parts; correction fluid; cigarette lighters, except precious metal; razor blades & razors; watersports equipment & supplies; lead pencils & art goods
PA: Societe Bic
14 Rue Jeanne D Asnieres
Clichy 92110
800 101-214

(G-7408)
BIC USA INC (DH)
1 Bic Way Ste 1 # 1 (06484-6223)
PHONE..................................203 783-2000
Kazufumi Ikeda, *Ch of Bd*
Don Cummins, *President*
Steven A Burkhart, *Vice Pres*
Barry Johnson, *Vice Pres*
David T Kimball, *Vice Pres*
▲ EMP: 200
SQ FT: 15,000
SALES (est): 133.1MM
SALES (corp-wide): 791.2MM **Privately Held**
WEB: www.biceveryday.com
SIC: **3951** 2899 3999 3421 Ball point pens & parts; correction fluid; cigarette lighters, except precious metal; razor blades & razors
HQ: Bic Corporation
1 Bic Way Ste 1 # 1
Shelton CT 06484
203 783-2000

(G-7409)
BRENNAN REALTY LLC (PA)
Also Called: Aggregate Products
70 Platt Rd (06484-5339)
P.O. Box 788 (06484-0788)
PHONE..................................203 929-6314
Nicholas Teodosio, *General Mgr*
Kevin Hogan, *Vice Pres*
Erik Guerra, *Project Mgr*
Matthew Brennan, *Opers Staff*
Greg Harla, *Manager*
EMP: 125
SQ FT: 25,000
SALES (est): 14.3MM **Privately Held**
SIC: **1623** 1542 1442 8741 Water, sewer & utility lines; commercial & office building, new construction; sand mining; gravel mining; management services

(G-7410)
BRIDGEPORT MAGNETICS GROUP INC
6 Waterview Dr (06484-4300)
PHONE..................................203 954-0050
Ulrik Poulsen, *President*
Sandu Pescaru, *Vice Pres*
Charlotte Poulsen, *Admin Sec*
▲ EMP: 27
SALES (est): 6.3MM **Privately Held**
SIC: **3357** 3679 3612 Magnet wire, non-ferrous; cores, magnetic; power transformers, electric

(G-7411)
CANVAS PRODUCTS
383 Isinglass Rd (06484-5708)
PHONE..................................203 225-0507
Paul Yacovelli, *Owner*
EMP: 1
SALES: 100K **Privately Held**
SIC: **2394** Awnings, fabric: made from purchased materials

(G-7412)
CCL INDUSTRIES CORPORATION (DH)
Also Called: CCL Label
15 Controls Dr (06484-6111)
PHONE..................................203 926-1253
Geoffrey T Martin, *CEO*
Wayne M E McLeod, *President*
Peter Fleissner, *Vice Pres*
Gina Bockiaro, *Production*
Pam Vath, *Purch Mgr*
▲ EMP: 85
SQ FT: 38,000
SALES (est): 1B
SALES (corp-wide): 3.9B **Privately Held**
SIC: **2759** 2992 3411 2819 Flexographic printing; lubricating oils & greases; aluminum cans; industrial inorganic chemicals; cosmetic preparations
HQ: Ccl International Inc
105 Gordon Baker Rd Suite 800
North York ON
416 756-8500

(G-7413)
CCL LABEL INC
15 Controls Dr (06484-6111)
PHONE..................................203 926-1253
EMP: 190
SALES (corp-wide): 3.9B **Privately Held**
SIC: **2759** 3411 2671 Flexographic printing; letterpress printing; aluminum cans; packaging paper & plastics film, coated & laminated
HQ: Ccl Label, Inc.
161 Worcester Rd Ste 603
Framingham MA 01701
508 872-4511

(G-7414)
CCL LABEL (DELAWARE) INC (DH)
15 Controls Dr (06484-6111)
PHONE..................................203 926-1253
Serge De Paoli, *President*
Art Hunsinger, *President*
Ronald Perin, *Vice Pres*
Victor Theriault, *Vice Pres*
David Blackwell, *Production*
▲ EMP: 4
SQ FT: 30,000

Shelton - Fairfield County (G-7415)

SALES (est): 197.1MM
SALES (corp-wide): 3.9B **Privately Held**
SIC: **2759** Labels & seals: printing
HQ: Ccl Label, Inc.
161 Worcester Rd Ste 603
Framingham MA 01701
508 872-4511

(G-7415)
CENTRIX INC
770 River Rd (06484-5430)
PHONE.................................203 929-5582
William B Dragan, *President*
John J Discko Jr, *Vice Pres*
John Discko, *Vice Pres*
Hank Buddrus, *Manager*
Paul Fattibene, *Admin Sec*
▲ EMP: 103
SQ FT: 50,000
SALES (est): 21.5MM **Privately Held**
SIC: **3843** Dental equipment; dental materials

(G-7416)
CHANDLER FURNITURE & WDWRK LLC
17 Bonnie Brook Dr (06484-5700)
PHONE.................................203 895-6289
Alcides Barros, *Principal*
EMP: 1
SALES (est): 67.5K **Privately Held**
SIC: **2431** Millwork

(G-7417)
CHRIS KRAWCZYK WOODWORK LLC
105 Toas St (06484-5528)
PHONE.................................203 895-5785
EMP: 1
SALES (est): 54.1K **Privately Held**
SIC: **2431** Millwork

(G-7418)
CHROMALLOY COMPONENT SVCS INC
415 Howe Ave (06484-3166)
PHONE.................................203 924-1666
Dan Martin, *Branch Mgr*
EMP: 8
SALES (corp-wide): 2.4B **Publicly Held**
HQ: Chromalloy Component Services, Inc.
303 Industrial Park Rd
San Antonio TX 78226
210 331-2300

(G-7419)
CHROMATIONS LLC
20 Elderberry Ln (06484-3757)
PHONE.................................203 929-8007
EMP: 1
SALES (est): 67.2K **Privately Held**
SIC: **3949** Mfg Sporting/Athletic Goods

(G-7420)
CISSE PUBLICATIONS LLC
18 Kimberly Dr (06484-5773)
PHONE.................................203 685-4189
Tarek Sobh, *Principal*
Tarek M Sobh, *Principal*
EMP: 1 EST: 2012
SALES (est): 94.6K **Privately Held**
SIC: **2741** Miscellaneous publishing

(G-7421)
COMET TECHNOLOGIES USA INC (DH)
Also Called: Yxlon International
100 Trap Falls Road Ext (06484-4646)
PHONE.................................203 447-3200
Robert Jardim, *President*
Stephan Haferl, *General Mgr*
Dirk Steiner, *Business Mgr*
Jeremy Simon, *Vice Pres*
Paul Wade, *Engineer*
◆ EMP: 30
SQ FT: 16,421
SALES (est): 139.5MM
SALES (corp-wide): 439MM **Privately Held**
WEB: www.yxlon.com
SIC: **3844** 3829 X-ray apparatus & tubes; measuring & controlling devices

HQ: Comet Ag
Herrengasse 10
Flamatt FR 3175
317 449-000

(G-7422)
CONNECTICUT FINE BLANKING
25 Forest Pkwy (06484-6122)
PHONE.................................203 925-0012
Jim Flynn, *Manager*
EMP: 2 EST: 2001
SALES (est): 158.1K **Privately Held**
SIC: **3469** Metal stampings

(G-7423)
CONNER PRINTING
Also Called: Conner, James A Printer
226 Leavenworth Rd (06484-1881)
PHONE.................................203 929-2070
James Conner, *Owner*
EMP: 2
SQ FT: 2,200
SALES: 400K **Privately Held**
SIC: **2752** 2791 2789 Commercial printing, offset; typesetting; bookbinding & related work

(G-7424)
CTS SERVICES LLC
15 Rayo Dr (06484-2450)
PHONE.................................203 268-5865
Daryl D Bouchard, *Mng Member*
EMP: 4 EST: 2012
SALES (est): 216.6K **Privately Held**
SIC: **2869** Fuels

(G-7425)
CYA TECHNOLOGIES INC
3 Enterprise Dr Ste 408 (06484-4696)
PHONE.................................203 513-3111
Wayne Crandall, *President*
Uma Annareddy, *Consultant*
Clint Karlin, *Info Tech Dir*
Scott Young, *Software Engr*
Ken Schietinger, *Analyst*
EMP: 50
SALES (est): 3.8MM **Privately Held**
WEB: www.cya.com
SIC: **7372** Application computer software

(G-7426)
DAC SYSTEMS INC
4 Armstrong Rd Ste 12 (06484-4721)
PHONE.................................203 924-7000
Mark G Nickson, *President*
EMP: 10
SQ FT: 4,000
SALES (est): 1.6MM **Privately Held**
WEB: www.dacsystems.com
SIC: **3661** Telephones & telephone apparatus

(G-7427)
DAN BEARD INC
Also Called: Island Sand & Gravel Pit
64 Hawthorne Ave (06484-4437)
P.O. Box 71 (06484-0071)
PHONE.................................203 924-4346
Jeff Rhodes, *Manager*
EMP: 15
SALES (corp-wide): 3.2MM **Privately Held**
WEB: www.danbeard.com
SIC: **3281** 5032 1442 Cut stone & stone products; brick, stone & related material; construction sand & gravel
PA: Dan Beard Inc
Mary St
Shelton CT 06484
203 924-1575

(G-7428)
DARK FIELD TECHNOLOGIES INC
5 Research Dr (06484-6232)
PHONE.................................203 298-0731
Timothy A Potts, *President*
Jamila E Potts, *Vice Pres*
Jamila Potts, *Manager*
EMP: 15
SQ FT: 10,000
SALES: 1.1MM **Privately Held**
WEB: www.darkfield.com
SIC: **8711** 3577 Electrical or electronic engineering; optical scanning devices

(G-7429)
DDK INDUSTRIES LLC
70 Center St (06484-3242)
PHONE.................................203 641-4218
Kevin Zdanowicz, *Principal*
EMP: 2 EST: 2014
SALES (est): 183.2K **Privately Held**
SIC: **3999** Manufacturing industries

(G-7430)
DERBY CELLULAR PRODUCTS INC
680 Bridgeport Ave Ste 3 (06484-4705)
PHONE.................................203 735-4661
Frank Osak Jr, *President*
Allan Cribbines, *President*
Charles Drabek, *Vice Pres*
Michael Osak, *Vice Pres*
EMP: 145
SQ FT: 161,000
SALES (est): 20.3MM **Privately Held**
WEB: www.derbycellularproducts.com
SIC: **3053** Gaskets & sealing devices

(G-7431)
DERMAPAC INC
33 Hull St Ste 4 (06484-3329)
P.O. Box 852 (06484-0852)
PHONE.................................203 924-7148
Arlene H Tuchband, *President*
Ida Reichlin, *Corp Secy*
Steven Tuchband, *Vice Pres*
EMP: 5
SQ FT: 4,000
SALES (est): 734.1K **Privately Held**
SIC: **5047** 3842 Hospital equipment & furniture; dressings, surgical

(G-7432)
DIGATRON POWER ELECTRONICS INC
50 Waterview Dr (06484-4376)
PHONE.................................203 446-8000
Rolf Beckers, *Ch of Bd*
Mark Clark, *Engineer*
Paula Fernandes, *Finance*
Kyra Materasso, *Admin Asst*
▲ EMP: 35
SQ FT: 16,000
SALES (est): 9.1MM
SALES (corp-wide): 177.9K **Privately Held**
SIC: **3629** 3625 3825 Battery chargers, rectifying or nonrotating; motor controls, electric; battery testers, electrical
HQ: Digatron Power Electronics Gmbh
Tempelhofer Str. 12-14
Aachen 52068
241 168-090

(G-7433)
DONUT STOP
368 Howe Ave (06484-3127)
PHONE.................................203 924-7133
Maria Bobotsis, *Owner*
EMP: 5
SALES (est): 160K **Privately Held**
SIC: **2051** 5461 Doughnuts, except frozen; doughnuts

(G-7434)
EBEAM FILM LLC
240 Long Hill Cross Rd (06484-6161)
PHONE.................................203 926-0100
EMP: 12
SALES (est): 820.5K **Privately Held**
SIC: **3861** 3577 7374 8731 Mfg Photo Equip/Supplies Mfg Computer Peripherals Data Processing/Prep Coml Physical Research Commercial Photography

(G-7435)
EDGEWELL PER CARE BRANDS LLC (HQ)
Also Called: Energizer
6 Research Dr (06484-6228)
PHONE.................................203 944-5500
David Hatfield, *CEO*
Ward Klein, *Ch of Bd*
Daniel J Sescleifer, *Exec VP*
Corey Barrette, *Vice Pres*
Stephanie Lynn, *Vice Pres*
◆ EMP: 370

SALES (est): 3.7B
SALES (corp-wide): 2.2B **Publicly Held**
WEB: www.evereadly.com
SIC: **3421** 2844 2676 Razor blades & razors; lotions, shaving; tampons, sanitary: made from purchased paper
PA: Edgewell Personal Care Company
1350 Tmberlake Manor Pkwy
Chesterfield MO 63017
314 594-1900

(G-7436)
EDWARD D SEGEN CO
100 Trap Falls Road Ext (06484-4646)
PHONE.................................203 929-8700
Alain R Samson, *Principal*
EMP: 2
SALES (est): 135.4K **Privately Held**
SIC: **3544** Special dies, tools, jigs & fixtures

(G-7437)
ELECTRI-CABLE ASSEMBLIES INC
70 Shelton Technology Ctr (06484-6406)
PHONE.................................203 924-6617
EMP: 2
SALES (est): 88.3K **Privately Held**
SIC: **3645** Residential lighting fixtures

(G-7438)
ELVEX CORPORATION
2 Mountain View Dr (06484-6419)
PHONE.................................203 743-2488
Jeffrey Begoon, *President*
Walter Fred Ravetto, *Vice Pres*
Richard Sustello, *Vice Pres*
▲ EMP: 15
SQ FT: 12,000
SALES (est): 3.3MM **Privately Held**
WEB: www.elvex.com
SIC: **3842** 5099 Personal safety equipment; safety equipment & supplies

(G-7439)
ENFIELD TECHNOLOGIES LLC
50 Waterview Dr Ste 120 (06484-4377)
PHONE.................................203 375-3100
Ken Barbee, *Engineer*
Alady Cubas, *Info Tech Mgr*
R Edwin Howe,
Rosa Trombetta, *Admin Asst*
Vince McCarroll,
▼ EMP: 10
SQ FT: 6,000
SALES (est): 2.2MM **Privately Held**
WEB: www.enfieldtech.com
SIC: **3492** 3494 Fluid power valves & hose fittings; valves & pipe fittings

(G-7440)
ENGINEERED FIBERS TECH LLC
88 Long Hill Cross Rd # 4 (06484-4783)
PHONE.................................203 922-1810
Robert E Evans, *Mng Member*
Andy Honkamp, *Manager*
David Merrill,
▲ EMP: 12
SQ FT: 18,000
SALES: 4.5MM **Privately Held**
WEB: www.eftfibers.com
SIC: **8711** 5169 2299 Engineering services; manmade fibers; flock (recovered textile fibers)

(G-7441)
EPDM COATINGS
15 Rushbrooke Ln (06484-6154)
PHONE.................................203 225-0104
Kellie Allister, *Principal*
Asif Hyded, *Info Tech Dir*
EMP: 2 EST: 2009
SALES (est): 284.3K **Privately Held**
SIC: **5033** 2952 2429 Roofing, asphalt & sheet metal; roofing materials; shingle & shingle mills

(G-7442)
FAIRFIELD COUNTY GAZETTE
11 Woodlawn Ter (06484-5721)
PHONE.................................203 929-1405
Evelyn Pellino, *Manager*
EMP: 1
SALES (est): 60.4K **Privately Held**
SIC: **2711** Newspapers, publishing & printing

▲ = Import ▼ = Export
◆ = Import/Export

GEOGRAPHIC SECTION
Shelton - Fairfield County (G-7471)

(G-7443)
FAIRWAY AND GREENE INC
2 Enterprise Dr Ste 505 (06484-4657)
PHONE.....................203 926-1881
Todd Martin, *Principal*
Todd Fontaine, *Manager*
▲ **EMP:** 2
SALES (est): 122.8K **Privately Held**
SIC: 2389 Apparel & accessories

(G-7444)
FIVE STAR PRODUCTS INC
60 Parrott Dr (06484-4733)
PHONE.....................203 336-7900
Wilfred A Martinez, *CEO*
David Babcock, *President*
David S Babcock, *Chairman*
Brian R Feidt, *Vice Pres*
Terry Stysly, *Vice Pres*
▲ **EMP:** 30
SALES (est): 11.3MM **Privately Held**
SIC: 3273 2891 2899 2851 Ready-mixed concrete; adhesives & sealants; chemical preparations; paints & allied products

(G-7445)
FLEXIINTERNATIONAL SFTWR INC (PA)
2 Trap Falls Rd Ste 501 (06484-7623)
PHONE.....................203 925-3040
Stefan R Bothe, *Ch of Bd*
Maureen M Okerstrom, *President*
Dmitry G Trudov, *President*
Mary Brandon, *Vice Pres*
EMP: 34
SQ FT: 25,000
SALES (est): 9.9MM **Publicly Held**
SIC: 7372 Application computer software

(G-7446)
FOOTNOTE JOURNAL LLC
87 Ten Coat Ln (06484-2287)
PHONE.....................203 924-0391
Thomas Kilfoyle, *Manager*
EMP: 2
SALES (est): 104.1K **Privately Held**
SIC: 2711 Newspapers, publishing & printing

(G-7447)
FROG PRINTS PUBLISHING LLC
22 Cold Spring Cir (06484-4805)
PHONE.....................610 425-0090
Christine O'Neil-Bell, *Principal*
EMP: 2
SALES (est): 55K **Privately Held**
SIC: 2741 Miscellaneous publishing

(G-7448)
GAIDA WELDING CO & MAR REPR
57 West St (06484-2217)
P.O. Box 46, Stratford (06615-0046)
PHONE.....................203 924-4868
John Gaida, *Partner*
Josephine Gaida, *Partner*
EMP: 2
SALES (est): 231.2K **Privately Held**
SIC: 1799 7692 7699 Welding on site; welding repair; boat repair

(G-7449)
GLASS SOURCE LLC
410 Howe Ave (06484-3127)
PHONE.....................203 924-4368
Michael Skertic, *Mng Member*
EMP: 5
SALES (est): 317.9K **Privately Held**
WEB: www.theglasssource.com
SIC: 3231 5231 1799 Stained glass: made from purchased glass; glass, leaded or stained; sandblasting of building exteriors

(G-7450)
GLITZY LADY
255 Kneen St Unit 20 (06484-3958)
PHONE.....................203 924-5663
Sharon Brown, *Owner*
EMP: 1
SALES: 75K **Privately Held**
SIC: 3961 Costume jewelry

(G-7451)
GOLDEN OYSTER COMPANY
9 Pueblo Trl (06484-4930)
PHONE.....................203 929-3389
Zbigniew Zadrozny, *Owner*
EMP: 1
SALES (est): 93.5K **Privately Held**
SIC: 2091 Oysters, preserved & cured

(G-7452)
GRAHAM WHITEHEAD & MANGER CO
431 Howe Ave (06484-3144)
PHONE.....................978 887-0430
Robert C Manger, *Vice Pres*
Lyle Graham, *Branch Mgr*
EMP: 1
SALES (corp-wide): 450.1K **Privately Held**
SIC: 3315 Fencing made in wiredrawing plants
PA: Graham, Whitehead & Manger Co., Inc
   462 Boston St Ste 2-1
   Topsfield MA 01983
   203 922-9225

(G-7453)
GRAYWOLF SENSING SOLUTIONS LLC (PA)
6 Research Dr Ste 110 (06484-6228)
PHONE.....................203 402-0477
Richard T Stonier, *President*
Juan Irizarry-Hernan, *Engineer*
Randy Nunley, *Regl Sales Mgr*
Erik Anderson, *Sales Staff*
Rick Stonier, *Sales Staff*
EMP: 9
SALES (est): 2.3MM **Privately Held**
WEB: www.wolfsense.com
SIC: 3822 Auto controls regulating residntl & coml environmt & applncs

(G-7454)
GREAT LAKES CHEMICAL CORP (DH)
2 Armstrong Rd Ste 101 (06484-4735)
PHONE.....................203 573-2000
Craig Rogerson, *CEO*
Anne Noonan, *President*
◆ **EMP:** 50 **EST:** 1932
SALES (est): 668.9MM
SALES (corp-wide): 8.2B **Publicly Held**
WEB: www.glcc.com
SIC: 2899 2842 Fire retardant chemicals; sanitation preparations, disinfectants & deodorants
HQ: Lanxess Solutions Us Inc.
   2 Armstrong Rd Ste 101
   Shelton CT 06484
   203 573-2000

(G-7455)
H J BAKER & BROTHER INC
2 Corporate Dr Ste 545 (06484-6279)
PHONE.....................501 664-4870
Mark Hohnbaum, *President*
Ercole John, *Treasurer*
Diane Lewan, *Office Mgr*
Alessandra Gaun, *Executive Asst*
EMP: 2
SALES (est): 62.3K **Privately Held**
SIC: 2048 Prepared feeds

(G-7456)
HAMDEN BREWING COMPANY LLC
819 Bridgeport Ave (06484-4714)
PHONE.....................203 247-4677
EMP: 3 **EST:** 2008
SALES (est): 134.2K **Privately Held**
SIC: 2082 Mfg Malt Beverages

(G-7457)
HAMWORTHY PEABODY COMBUSTN INC (DH)
Also Called: John Zink Company
6 Armstrong Rd Ste 2 (06484-4722)
PHONE.....................203 922-1199
Lawrence Berry, *President*
Anthony R Baker, *Vice Pres*
▲ **EMP:** 23 **EST:** 1920
SALES (est): 5.9MM
SALES (corp-wide): 40.6B **Privately Held**
WEB: www.hamworthy-peabody.com
SIC: 3433 3567 3561 Gas burners, industrial; oil burners, domestic or industrial; industrial furnaces & ovens; pumps & pumping equipment
HQ: John Zink Company, Llc
   11920 E Apache St
   Tulsa OK 74116
   918 234-1800

(G-7458)
HANDHOLD ADAPTIVE LLC
2 Arden Ln (06484-1907)
PHONE.....................203 526-6313
Daniel Tedesco,
EMP: 2
SALES: 30K **Privately Held**
SIC: 7372 Business oriented computer software

(G-7459)
HARD-CORE SELF DEFENSE
500 River Rd (06484-4540)
PHONE.....................203 231-2344
EMP: 3
SALES (est): 206.5K **Privately Held**
SIC: 3812 Defense systems & equipment

(G-7460)
HARRY TUTUNJIAN
Also Called: Speedy Sign Design
44 Ridgewood Ct (06484-3825)
PHONE.....................203 944-9444
Harry Tutunjian, *Owner*
EMP: 1
SALES (est): 57.7K **Privately Held**
SIC: 3993 Signs & advertising specialties

(G-7461)
HASLER INC
19 Forest Pkwy (06484-6135)
P.O. Box 858 (06484-0903)
PHONE.....................203 301-3400
John Vavra, *Principal*
EMP: 3
SALES (est): 322.9K **Privately Held**
SIC: 3579 Mailing machines

(G-7462)
HC INNOVATIONS INC
10 Progress Dr 200 (06484-6216)
PHONE.....................203 925-9600
Salvatore V Bastardi, *Division Pres*
R Scott Walker, *Officer*
EMP: 2
SALES: 27.8MM **Privately Held**
SIC: 3714 Motor vehicle parts & accessories

(G-7463)
HEARST CORPORATION
Also Called: Milford Mirror, The
1000 Bridgeport Ave (06484-4660)
PHONE.....................203 926-2080
Jill Dion, *Principal*
EMP: 3
SALES (corp-wide): 8.3B **Privately Held**
SIC: 2711 Newspapers
PA: The Hearst Corporation
   300 W 57th St Fl 42
   New York NY 10019
   212 649-2000

(G-7464)
HIGH FIRE SERVICING LLC
63 Cranston Ave (06484-5543)
PHONE.....................203 924-6562
Jeffrey Quickel Jr, *Owner*
EMP: 2
SALES (est): 91.6K **Privately Held**
SIC: 1389 Roustabout service

(G-7465)
HJ BAKER & BRO LLC (PA)
2 Corporate Dr Ste 545 (06484-6279)
PHONE.....................203 682-9200
Christopher Smith, *CEO*
David Smith, *President*
Andy Lee, *Business Mgr*
Steve Azzarello, *Exec VP*
Jack L Williams, *Exec VP*
◆ **EMP:** 40 **EST:** 1850
SQ FT: 12,500
SALES (est): 135.8MM **Privately Held**
SIC: 2048 5191 5052 Poultry feeds; feed; fertilizer & fertilizer materials; sulfur

(G-7466)
HOT TOPS LLC
240 Long Hill Cross Rd # 4 (06484-6161)
PHONE.....................203 926-2067
Michael Conroy, *Vice Pres*
Kathleen Conroy, *MIS Mgr*
Kathy Conroy,
EMP: 10
SQ FT: 9,000
SALES: 1.5MM **Privately Held**
WEB: www.hottops.com
SIC: 7336 3993 2396 2395 Silk screen design; signs & advertising specialties; automotive & apparel trimmings; pleating & stitching

(G-7467)
HOUSATONIC MCH & PROTOTYPE LLC
14 Audubon Ln (06484-4366)
PHONE.....................203 922-2714
Alfred Languerand, *Partner*
EMP: 2
SALES: 20K **Privately Held**
SIC: 3699 Electrical equipment & supplies

(G-7468)
HUBBELL INCORPORATED (PA)
40 Waterview Dr (06484-4300)
PHONE.....................475 882-4000
David G Nord, *Ch of Bd*
Gerben W Bakker, *President*
David Bruce, *Regional Mgr*
Gary Robinson, *District Mgr*
An-Ping Hsieh, *Senior VP*
EMP: 65 **EST:** 1888
SALES: 4.4B **Publicly Held**
WEB: www.hubbell.com
SIC: 3699 3678 Electrical equipment & supplies; electronic connectors

(G-7469)
HUBBELL INCORPORATED DELAWARE
Hubbell Wiring Device-Kellems
40 Waterview Dr (06484-4300)
P.O. Box 1000 (06484-1000)
PHONE.....................475 882-4800
Gary Amato, *Vice Pres*
James Landolina, *Vice Pres*
John Van Cleve, *Sales Staff*
Carolyn Niper, *Administration*
EMP: 200
SQ FT: 21,600
SALES (corp-wide): 4.4B **Publicly Held**
SIC: 3643 Current-carrying wiring devices
HQ: Hubbell Incorporated (Delaware)
   40 Waterview Dr
   Shelton CT 06484
   475 882-4000

(G-7470)
HUBBELL INCORPORATED DELAWARE (HQ)
40 Waterview Dr (06484-4300)
PHONE.....................475 882-4000
Gary Amato, *CEO*
Mark Mozdzer, *Engineer*
Eunice Frank, *Finance Dir*
Chris Kyle, *Director*
Javier Piraneque, *Director*
EMP: 80
SALES (est): 53.6MM
SALES (corp-wide): 4.4B **Publicly Held**
WEB: www.hubbell.com
SIC: 3643 Current-carrying wiring devices
PA: Hubbell Incorporated
   40 Waterview Dr
   Shelton CT 06484
   475 882-4000

(G-7471)
HUNTINGTON CAPITAL MGT LLC
41 Patricia Dr (06484-3558)
PHONE.....................203 339-2126
Rafael Carmelo, *Mng Member*
EMP: 1
SALES (est): 405K **Privately Held**
SIC: 2099 5149 Sugar; wine makers' equipment & supplies

Shelton - Fairfield County (G-7472)

(G-7472)
I LEVEL SIGN AND GRAPHICS
Also Called: I Level Sign Company
42 New Castle Dr (06484-5011)
PHONE..................................203 256-9486
Meredith Mortimer, *Principal*
EMP: 1
SALES (est): 119K **Privately Held**
SIC: 3993 Signs & advertising specialties

(G-7473)
IKIGAI FOODS LLC
19 Beverly Hill Dr (06484-5105)
PHONE..................................203 954-8083
Richard B Harvey, *Principal*
EMP: 3
SALES (est): 145.9K **Privately Held**
SIC: 2099 Food preparations

(G-7474)
IMAGE GRAPHICS INC
240 Long Hill Croct Rd (06484)
PHONE..................................203 926-0100
EMP: 20 EST: 1974
SALES: 1.5MM **Privately Held**
SIC: 7374 3577 3825 3572 Scanning And Converting Paper Documents Mfg High Resolution Film Recorders

(G-7475)
INDUSTRIAL WOOD PRODUCT CO
84 Platt Rd (06484-5340)
PHONE..................................203 735-2374
H William Karcher, *President*
William H Karcher, *Trustee*
Susanne Karcher, *Vice Pres*
William Karcher, *VP Mfg*
EMP: 5
SALES: 500K **Privately Held**
SIC: 2431 2511 2434 1751 Ornamental woodwork: cornices, mantels, etc.; wood household furniture; wood kitchen cabinets; cabinet & finish carpentry

(G-7476)
INFINITE AUDIO LLC
61 Montgomery St (06484-4358)
PHONE..................................203 924-2558
EMP: 2 EST: 2005
SALES (est): 110K **Privately Held**
SIC: 3651 Mfg Home Audio/Video Equipment

(G-7477)
INFORM INC
Also Called: Visible Record Systems
25 Brook St Ste 200 (06484-2332)
P.O. Box 785 (06484-0785)
PHONE..................................203 924-9929
Bill Carlson, *President*
David Carlson, *Corp Secy*
Greg Mattei, *Accounts Exec*
EMP: 8
SQ FT: 10,000
SALES (est): 1.4MM **Privately Held**
WEB: www.informprinting.com
SIC: 2752 Business forms, lithographed

(G-7478)
INKBYTE LLC
35 Nutmeg Ln (06484-1717)
PHONE..................................203 939-1140
Duke Parnter, *Principal*
EMP: 2
SALES (est): 83.9K **Privately Held**
SIC: 2752 Commercial printing, lithographic

(G-7479)
INLINE PLASTICS CORP (PA)
Also Called: Surelock Division
42 Canal St (06484-3265)
PHONE..................................203 924-5933
Thomas Orkisz, *President*
Paul Bertuglia, *Vice Pres*
Augie Lanzetta, *Vice Pres*
Sam Maida, *Plant Mgr*
Shane Woodall, *Prdtn Mgr*
◆ EMP: 190
SQ FT: 312,000
SALES (est): 68.5MM **Privately Held**
WEB: www.inlineplastics.com
SIC: 3089 Injection molding of plastics; trays, plastic

(G-7480)
ITT WATER & WASTEWATER USA INC (HQ)
1 Greenwich Pl Ste 2 (06484-7603)
PHONE..................................262 548-8181
Ron Port, *President*
Frank Oliveira, *Vice Pres*
Jonny Sandstedt, *Vice Pres*
◆ EMP: 70 EST: 1957
SQ FT: 35,000
SALES (est): 52.8MM **Publicly Held**
WEB: www.flygtus.com
SIC: 3561 Pumps & pumping equipment

(G-7481)
JOHN ZINK COMPANY LLC
Also Called: John Zink -Todd Combustn Group
2 Armstrong Rd Fl 3 (06484-4735)
PHONE..................................203 925-0380
Andrew Darrieau, *Principal*
Timothy Webster, *Plant Mgr*
EMP: 100
SQ FT: 45,000
SALES (est): 6.1MM **Privately Held**
SIC: 3433 8711 5074 Oil burners, domestic or industrial; gas burners, industrial; engineering services; oil burners

(G-7482)
K C K PUBLISHING
127 Toas St (06484-5530)
PHONE..................................203 924-1147
EMP: 1 EST: 2000
SALES (est): 47K **Privately Held**
SIC: 2731 Books-Publishing/Printing

(G-7483)
KENO GRAPHIC SERVICES INC
1 Parrott Dr Ste 100 (06484-4853)
PHONE..................................203 925-7722
Daniel Kennedy, *President*
Bill Kennedy Jr, *Vice Pres*
Lisa Schmidt, *Production*
Kim Yerrington, *Production*
William Kennedy Jr, *Treasurer*
EMP: 27
SALES (est): 3.9MM **Privately Held**
SIC: 2759 Screen printing

(G-7484)
KENZINC LLC
7 Acadia Ln Unit 5303 (06484-4472)
PHONE..................................203 307-5369
Drew Pickering Jr, *President*
EMP: 5
SQ FT: 1,200
SALES (est): 154.7K **Privately Held**
SIC: 8711 3841 3724 Aviation &/or aeronautical engineering; surgical & medical instruments; aircraft engines & engine parts

(G-7485)
LAMOR USA CORPORATION
2 Enterprise Dr Ste 404 (06484-4657)
PHONE..................................203 888-7700
Daniel Beyer, *General Mgr*
Stephen J Reilly, *Vice Pres*
Juri Tubashov, *Export Mgr*
Annika Blomqvist, *Controller*
Jim Gianacopolos, *Sales Staff*
◆ EMP: 4 EST: 1960
SQ FT: 30,000
SALES (est): 4.8MM **Privately Held**
SIC: 3559 Chemical machinery & equipment

(G-7486)
LANXESS SOLUTIONS US INC (DH)
Also Called: Chemtura USA
2 Armstrong Rd Ste 101 (06484-4735)
PHONE..................................203 573-2000
Antonis Papadourakis, *President*
Alfred F Ingulli, *Exec VP*
Darlene Stott, *Safety Mgr*
Elizabeth Goodwin, *Production*
Frederic Schott, *CFO*
EMP: 22

SALES (est): 1.1B
SALES (corp-wide): 8.2B **Privately Held**
WEB: www.cromptoncorp.com
SIC: 2869 2843 2821 2911 Industrial organic chemicals; surface active agents; plastics materials & resins; polystyrene resins; residues; petrolatums, nonmedicinal; fire retardant chemicals; oxidizers, inorganic; water treating compounds; sanitation preparations, disinfectants & deodorants; degreasing solvent
HQ: Lanxess Deutschland Gmbh
Kennedyplatz 1
Koln 50679
221 888-50

(G-7487)
LATEX FOAM INTERNATIONAL LLC (HQ)
Also Called: Latex Foam Products
510 River Rd (06484-4517)
PHONE..................................203 924-0700
Joanne Osmolik, *VP Human Res*
Robert L Jenkins, *Mng Member*
Christy Kriz, *Manager*
Dave Fisher,
Steven Russo,
◆ EMP: 87
SALES (est): 39.1MM **Privately Held**
SIC: 2392 3069 Household furnishings; foam rubber
PA: Latex Foam International Holdings, Inc.
510 River Rd
Shelton CT 06484
203 924-0700

(G-7488)
LATEX FOAM INTL HOLDINGS INC (PA)
Also Called: Talalay Global
510 River Rd (06484-4517)
PHONE..................................203 924-0700
Marc Navarre, *CEO*
David T Fisher, *President*
Steve Turner, *Vice Pres*
Steve Tolmich, *Purch Mgr*
Steven Watson, *Treasurer*
◆ EMP: 200 EST: 1975
SQ FT: 284,000
SALES (est): 39.1MM **Privately Held**
SIC: 3069 Latex, foamed

(G-7489)
LECLAIRE FUEL OIL LLC
97 Unit 3 Bridgeport Ave (06484)
PHONE..................................203 922-1512
Richard Leclaire, *Principal*
EMP: 3
SALES (est): 310K **Privately Held**
SIC: 2911 Oils, fuel

(G-7490)
LEX PRODUCTS LLC (PA)
15 Progress Dr (06484-6218)
PHONE..................................203 363-3738
Robert R Luther, *CEO*
Joseph Birchak, *Vice Pres*
Dawn Tuthill, *Vice Pres*
Brayner Recinos, *Production*
Doreen Cordeiro, *Senior Buyer*
▲ EMP: 150
SQ FT: 18,000
SALES (est): 54MM **Privately Held**
WEB: www.lex-mps.com
SIC: 3829 3315 3643 3613 Measuring & controlling devices; cable, steel: insulated or armored; current-carrying wiring devices; switchboards & parts, power

(G-7491)
LOANWORKS SERVICING LLC
3 Corporate Dr Ste 208 (06484-6278)
PHONE..................................203 402-7304
Joe Caravetta, *Director*
EMP: 6 EST: 2009
SALES (est): 431.7K **Privately Held**
SIC: 1389 Roustabout service

(G-7492)
LOOKINGFORSOLUTIONSCOM LLC
4 Research Dr Ste 402 (06484-6242)
PHONE..................................475 239-5773
Shahin Baghai,
EMP: 1

SALES (est): 41.6K **Privately Held**
SIC: 3999 Manufacturing industries

(G-7493)
MACHINE BUILDERS NENG LLC
33 Hull St Ste 6a (06484-3329)
PHONE..................................203 922-9446
Leon Tyrrell,
EMP: 12
SQ FT: 8,000
SALES (est): 1.8MM **Privately Held**
SIC: 7699 3541 Industrial equipment services; milling machines

(G-7494)
MACRO SYSTEMS INC
20 Hubbell Ln (06484-2166)
PHONE..................................203 225-6266
John Tokarczyk, *President*
Sandra Tokarczyk, *Vice Pres*
Johnathan Tokarczyk, *Finance*
EMP: 3
SQ FT: 1,600
SALES: 230K **Privately Held**
WEB: www.macrosystemsinc.com
SIC: 3827 Optical comparators

(G-7495)
MANDREL
65 Philip Dr (06484-5132)
PHONE..................................410 507-7767
Tara Gallant, *Principal*
EMP: 2
SALES (est): 82.7K **Privately Held**
SIC: 3545 Mandrels

(G-7496)
MARSARS WATER RESCUE SYSTEMS
8 Algonkin Rd (06484-4903)
PHONE..................................203 924-7315
Robert E Davis, *President*
Michelle Davis, *Vice Pres*
EMP: 8
SQ FT: 2,000
SALES (est): 717K **Privately Held**
WEB: www.marsars.com
SIC: 3561 Pumps, domestic: water or sump

(G-7497)
MERCANTILE DEVELOPMENT INC
10 Waterview Dr (06484-4300)
P.O. Box 825 (06484-0825)
PHONE..................................203 922-8880
F Alan Fankhanel, *President*
Tim Miller, *General Mgr*
Frank Digiovanni, *COO*
Lucia Furman, *Vice Pres*
Alan Sankhanel, *Purch Agent*
◆ EMP: 38 EST: 1947
SQ FT: 138,960
SALES (est): 12.7MM **Privately Held**
WEB: www.mdiwipers.com
SIC: 2679 Paper products, converted

(G-7498)
METALS EDGE WELDING LLC
135 Big Horn Rd (06484-1873)
PHONE..................................203 500-5644
Matthew Shafransky, *Principal*
EMP: 1
SALES (est): 45.9K **Privately Held**
SIC: 7692 Welding repair

(G-7499)
MICHAEL J MACISCO
Also Called: Keys-Plus
318 Meadowridge Rd (06484-2157)
PHONE..................................203 924-0013
Michael J Macisco, *Owner*
EMP: 1 EST: 1982
SALES (est): 133.8K **Privately Held**
SIC: 5072 3429 Hardware; manufactured hardware (general)

(G-7500)
MICROPHASE CORPORATION
100 Trap Falls Road Ext # 400 (06484-4646)
PHONE..................................203 866-8000
Amos Kohn, *CEO*
Necdet F Ergul, *President*
Jeffrey R F Peterson, *Corp Secy*

Jorge Lopez, *Production*
Bob Pasciucco, *QA Dir*
EMP: 26
SQ FT: 23,898
SALES: 9.1MM
SALES (corp-wide): 27.1MM **Publicly Held**
WEB: www.microphase.com
SIC: 3663 3677 3674 3661 Microwave communication equipment; electronic coils, transformers & other inductors; semiconductors & related devices; telephone & telegraph apparatus; household audio & video equipment
HQ: Digital Power Corporation
48430 Lakeview Blvd
Fremont CA 94538
510 657-2635

(G-7501)
MILITARYLIFE PUBLISHING LLC
4 Research Dr (06484-6280)
PHONE..................................203 402-7234
Vincent Santoro,
EMP: 2
SALES: 700K **Privately Held**
SIC: 2741 Miscellaneous publishing

(G-7502)
MINUTEMAN PRESS
42 Bridgeport Ave (06484-3212)
PHONE..................................203 445-6971
EMP: 2
SALES (est): 83.9K **Privately Held**
SIC: 2752 Commercial printing, lithographic

(G-7503)
MINUTEMAN PRESS LLC
427b Howe Ave (06484-3111)
PHONE..................................203 922-9228
Harry Burlakoff,
EMP: 2
SALES (est): 303.9K **Privately Held**
SIC: 2752 Commercial printing, lithographic

(G-7504)
MITCHELL WODS PHRMCUTICALS LLC
4 Corporate Dr Ste 287 (06484-6240)
PHONE..................................203 258-1305
Mark Farber,
Anthony Lancia,
Irving Wainer,
EMP: 1
SQ FT: 50,000
SALES (est): 86.6K **Privately Held**
SIC: 2834 Druggists' preparations (pharmaceuticals)

(G-7505)
MOTORCYCLISTS POST
11 Haven Ln (06484-2017)
PHONE..................................203 929-9409
Leo Castell, *Owner*
EMP: 4
SALES (est): 180.7K **Privately Held**
SIC: 2721 Periodicals

(G-7506)
NAIAD DYNAMICS US INC (HQ)
Also Called: Naiad Marine Systems
50 Parrott Dr (06484-4733)
PHONE..................................203 929-6355
John D Venables, *President*
Dave Archambault, *General Mgr*
Steve Colliss, *General Mgr*
Charlotte Gore, *Vice Pres*
Eric Paulson, *Engineer*
▲ **EMP:** 50
SQ FT: 26,500
SALES (est): 16.9MM **Privately Held**
WEB: www.naiad.com
SIC: 3531 3625 3569 3599 Marine related equipment; marine & navy auxiliary controls; assembly machines, non-metalworking; machine & other job shop work; aircraft parts & equipment; military ships, building & repairing

(G-7507)
NAIAD MARITIME GROUP INC (PA)
Also Called: Naiad Dynamics
50 Parrott Dr (06484-4733)
PHONE..................................203 944-1932
John Venables, *President*
EMP: 50
SALES (est): 21.7MM **Privately Held**
SIC: 6719 3731 3531 Personal holding companies, except banks; shipbuilding & repairing; marine related equipment

(G-7508)
NEVAMAR COMPANY LLC (HQ)
Also Called: Nevamar Distributors
1 Corporate Dr Ste 725 (06484-6230)
PHONE..................................203 925-1556
Jeffrey Muller, *Mng Member*
Jim Tees,
▲ **EMP:** 300
SALES (est): 82.1MM **Privately Held**
SIC: 3089 5162 Panels, building: plastic; plastics materials & basic shapes

(G-7509)
NEW ENGLAND STAIR COMPANY INC
1 White St (06484-3117)
P.O. Box 763 (06484-0763)
PHONE..................................203 924-0606
William J Sylvia, *President*
Matthew Sylvia, *Admin Sec*
EMP: 21
SQ FT: 25,000
SALES (est): 4.3MM **Privately Held**
WEB: www.newenglandstair.com
SIC: 2431 Staircases & stairs, wood

(G-7510)
NEWCO CONDENSER INC
40 Waterview Dr (06484-4300)
PHONE..................................475 882-4000
EMP: 4 **EST:** 2007
SALES (est): 187.4K
SALES (corp-wide): 4.4B **Publicly Held**
SIC: 3264 3699 3675 3674 Insulators, electrical: porcelain; electrical equipment & supplies; electronic capacitors; semiconductors & related devices; switchgear & switchboard apparatus
PA: Hubbell Incorporated
40 Waterview Dr
Shelton CT 06484
475 882-4000

(G-7511)
NEWCO LIGHTING INC (HQ)
40 Waterview Dr (06484-4300)
PHONE..................................475 882-4000
David G Nord, *President*
EMP: 5
SALES (est): 46MM
SALES (corp-wide): 4.4B **Publicly Held**
SIC: 3646 Fluorescent lighting fixtures, commercial; ceiling systems, luminous
PA: Hubbell Incorporated
40 Waterview Dr
Shelton CT 06484
475 882-4000

(G-7512)
NINETY-NINE CENT PUBG LLC
132 New St (06484-2324)
PHONE..................................203 922-9917
John S Stroud, *Principal*
EMP: 1
SALES (est): 79.3K **Privately Held**
SIC: 2741 Miscellaneous publishing

(G-7513)
NORCELL INC (DH)
2 Corporate Dr Fl 5 (06484-6238)
PHONE..................................203 254-5292
Mark Cassidy, *President*
Leslie Santore, *CFO*
Sperre Lars, *Human Res Mgr*
Michael Cross, *Manager*
Stig Stene, *Representative*
▲ **EMP:** 15
SQ FT: 3,600
SALES (est): 3.1MM
SALES (corp-wide): 3.1B **Privately Held**
WEB: www.norske-skog-utmark.com
SIC: 2621 Printing paper
HQ: Cellmark Ab
Lilla Bommen 3c
Goteborg 411 0
311 900-07

(G-7514)
NOVAMONT NORTH AMERICA INC
1000 Bridgeport Ave # 304 (06484-4676)
PHONE..................................203 744-8801
Alessandro Ferlito, *President*
Gaetano Lo Monaco, *Principal*
Paul Darby, *Manager*
EMP: 13 **EST:** 2010
SALES (est): 2.5MM **Privately Held**
SIC: 3821 Chemical laboratory apparatus
HQ: Novamont Spa
Via Giacomo Fauser 8
Novara NO 28100
032 169-9611

(G-7515)
NUTMEG BREWING REST GROUP LLC
Also Called: Southport Brewing Company
819 Bridgeport Ave (06484-4714)
PHONE..................................203 256-2337
William Dasilva,
David Rutigliano,
EMP: 50
SQ FT: 3,200
SALES (est): 4.2MM **Privately Held**
SIC: 2082 Beer (alcoholic beverage)

(G-7516)
O C TANNER COMPANY
2 Corporate Dr Ste 935 (06484-6250)
PHONE..................................203 944-5430
Christopher Osinski, *Manager*
EMP: 3
SALES (corp-wide): 378.7MM **Privately Held**
WEB: www.octanner.com
SIC: 3911 Jewelry, precious metal
PA: O. C. Tanner Company
1930 S State St
Salt Lake City UT 84115
801 486-2430

(G-7517)
O E M CONTROLS INC (PA)
10 Controls Dr (06484-6100)
P.O. Box 894 (06484-0894)
PHONE..................................203 929-8431
S Brian Simons, *President*
Keith T Simons, *Vice Pres*
Robert D Rose, *Plant Mgr*
Harold Meeker, *Design Engr*
Ken Pontbriant, *Electrical Engi*
EMP: 200 **EST:** 1966
SQ FT: 56,000
SALES (est): 34.2MM **Privately Held**
WEB: www.oemcontrols.com
SIC: 3625 3229 3577 Electric controls & control accessories, industrial; switches, electric power; fiber optics strands; computer peripheral equipment

(G-7518)
OERLIKON AM MEDICAL INC
Also Called: (PARENT IS OERLIKON USA HOLDING INC, TRAFFORD, PA.)
10 Constitution Blvd S (06484-4302)
PHONE..................................203 712-1030
Ottavio Disanto, *CEO*
Thomas Barret, *President*
Nancy Theodorides, *Treasurer*
Mark Zembrzuski, *Admin Sec*
Adreana Di Santo, *Assistant*
EMP: 75
SQ FT: 30,000
SALES (est): 14.3MM
SALES (corp-wide): 2.6B **Privately Held**
WEB: www.disanto.com
SIC: 3841 Surgical instruments & apparatus
PA: Oc Oerlikon Corporation Ag, Pfaffikon
Churerstrasse 120
PfAffikon SZ 8808
583 609-696

(G-7519)
OPEL CONNECTICUT SOLAR LLC
3 Corporate Dr Ste 204 (06484-6210)
P.O. Box 555, Storrs Mansfield (06268-0555)
PHONE..................................203 612-2366
Robert G Pico, *President*
France Pagnot, *General Mgr*
Susanne Schaefer, *General Mgr*
Johan Brusing, *District Mgr*
Andrew Carlson, *Engineer*
▲ **EMP:** 27
SQ FT: 5,500
SALES (est): 3.4MM **Privately Held**
SIC: 3674 Photovoltaic devices, solid state

(G-7520)
OPTIMA SPECIALTY CHEMICAL
8 Huntington St 332 (06484-5212)
PHONE..................................203 929-2031
Liane Puleo, *Partner*
Steve Puleo, *Partner*
EMP: 3 **EST:** 1998
SALES (est): 594.8K **Privately Held**
WEB: www.optimaspecialty.com
SIC: 5122 2833 5169 Cosmetics; vitamins, natural or synthetic: bulk, uncompounded; organic chemicals, synthetic

(G-7521)
ORCHID ORTHPD SOLUTIONS LLC
Also Called: Orchid Design
80 Shelton Technology Ctr (06484-6406)
PHONE..................................203 922-0105
Steve McGuire, *General Mgr*
Tim Greenwood, *Engineer*
Paul Strahm, *Engineer*
Stephen Maguire, *Executive*
EMP: 1
SALES (corp-wide): 319MM **Privately Held**
SIC: 3842 Orthopedic appliances
HQ: Orchid Orthopedic Solutions Llc
1489 Cedar St
Holt MI 48842
517 694-2300

(G-7522)
PANOLAM INDUSTRIES INC (HQ)
Also Called: Panolam Surface System
1 Corporate Dr Ste 725 (06484-6230)
PHONE..................................203 925-1556
Robert Muller, *President*
Alan S Kabus, *President*
Lawrence Grossman, *Exec VP*
Vincent Miceli, *CFO*
Jeffery Muller, *Admin Sec*
▲ **EMP:** 40
SALES (est): 265.6MM **Privately Held**
WEB: www.panolam.com
SIC: 3089 3083 Panels, building: plastic; laminated plastics plate & sheet

(G-7523)
PANOLAM INDUSTRIES INTL INC (PA)
Also Called: Panolam Surface Systems
1 Corporate Dr Ste 725 (06484-6230)
PHONE..................................203 925-1556
Peter Jones, *President*
Nevin Caldwell, *COO*
Mike Conti, *Vice Pres*
Beth Cocca, *Purchasing*
Robert Vail, *Research*
▲ **EMP:** 40
SALES (est): 546.2MM **Privately Held**
SIC: 2493 3089 Particleboard products; particleboard, plastic laminated; panels, building: plastic

(G-7524)
PERIODIC TABLEWARE LLC
415 Howe Ave Ste 110 (06484-3182)
PHONE..................................310 428-4250
Marshall Jamshidi, *Principal*
EMP: 10 **EST:** 2013
SALES (est): 1MM **Privately Held**
SIC: 3229 3231 Tableware, glass or glass ceramic; laboratory glassware

Shelton - Fairfield County (G-7525)

(G-7525)
PERKINELMER INC
Perkinelmer Life and Analytic
710 Bridgeport Ave (06484-4794)
PHONE.................................203 925-4600
Gary Grecsek, *Vice Pres*
Vinod Aliminate, *Project Mgr*
Erika Garrison, *Project Mgr*
James Haydu, *Mfg Mgr*
Richard Franklin, *Purch Mgr*
EMP: 8
SALES (corp-wide): 2.7B **Publicly Held**
WEB: www.perkinelmer.com
SIC: 3826 Analytical instruments
PA: Perkinelmer, Inc.
    940 Winter St
    Waltham MA 02451
    781 663-6900

(G-7526)
PERKINELMER HLTH SCIENCES INC
710 Bridgeport Ave (06484-4794)
PHONE.................................203 925-4600
EMP: 135
SALES (corp-wide): 2.7B **Publicly Held**
SIC: 3826 Analytical instruments
HQ: Perkinelmer Health Sciences, Inc.
    940 Winter St
    Waltham MA 02451
    781 663-6900

(G-7527)
PIONEER PLASTICS CORPORATION (HQ)
Also Called: Pionite Decorative Surfaces
1 Corporate Dr Ste 725 (06484-6230)
PHONE.................................203 925-1556
Alan S Kabus, *President*
Robert Muller, *President*
Jeffrey Muller, *COO*
Larry Grossman, *CFO*
Vincent Miceli, *CFO*
◆ **EMP:** 89
SQ FT: 560,000
SALES (est): 204MM **Privately Held**
SIC: 3083 3087 Laminated plastics plate & sheet; custom compound purchased resins

(G-7528)
PITNEY BOWES INC
27 Waterview Dr (06484-4301)
PHONE.................................203 792-1600
David Cavanaugh, *Opers Staff*
Brian Baxendale, *Branch Mgr*
Thomas McGrath, *Manager*
EMP: 35
SALES (corp-wide): 3.5B **Publicly Held**
SIC: 3579 Mailing machines
PA: Pitney Bowes Inc.
    3001 Summer St Ste 3
    Stamford CT 06905
    203 356-5000

(G-7529)
PITNEY BOWES INC
27 Waterview Dr (06484-4301)
PHONE.................................203 922-4000
Barret S Johnson, *President*
EMP: 35
SALES (corp-wide): 3.5B **Publicly Held**
SIC: 3579 7359 Postage meters; business machine & electronic equipment rental services
PA: Pitney Bowes Inc.
    3001 Summer St Ste 3
    Stamford CT 06905
    203 356-5000

(G-7530)
PITNEY BOWES INC
27 Waterview Dr (06484-4301)
PHONE.................................203 356-5000
EMP: 35
SALES (corp-wide): 3.5B **Publicly Held**
SIC: 3579 7359 3661 8744 Mailing machines; postage meters; forms handling equipment; business machine & electronic equipment rental services; facsimile equipment; facilities support services
PA: Pitney Bowes Inc.
    3001 Summer St Ste 3
    Stamford CT 06905
    203 356-5000

(G-7531)
PLAYTEX PRODUCTS LLC (HQ)
6 Research Dr Ste 400 (06484-6228)
P.O. Box 889 (06484-0889)
PHONE.................................203 944-5500
Thomas Schultz, *Development*
Neil P Defeo, *Mng Member*
Perry R Beadon,
James S Cook,
Kris Kelley,
▼ **EMP:** 100
SQ FT: 59,100
SALES (est): 473.3MM
SALES (corp-wide): 2.2B **Publicly Held**
WEB: www.playtexproductsinc.com
SIC: 2676 3069 2844 3842 Tampons, sanitary: made from purchased paper; diapers, paper (disposable): made from purchased paper; nipples, rubber; baby pacifiers, rubber; bibs, vulcanized rubber or rubberized fabric; water bottles, rubber; suntan lotions & oils; hair preparations, including shampoos; towelettes, premoistened; gloves, safety
PA: Edgewell Personal Care Company
    1350 Tmberlake Manor Pkwy
    Chesterfield MO 63017
    314 594-1900

(G-7532)
PR-MX HOLDINGS COMPANY LLC (HQ)
Also Called: Precision Resource Mexico
25 Forest Pkwy (06484-6122)
PHONE.................................203 925-0012
Peter Wolcott,
Scott Fabricant,
Charles Polatsek,
John Weiland,
EMP: 15
SQ FT: 70,000
SALES (est): 1.7MM
SALES (corp-wide): 260.1MM **Privately Held**
WEB: www.precisionresource.com
SIC: 3469 Metal stampings
PA: Precision Resource, Inc.
    25 Forest Pkwy
    Shelton CT 06484
    203 925-0012

(G-7533)
PRECISE CIRCUIT COMPANY INC
155 Myrtle St (06484-4062)
PHONE.................................203 924-2512
Thomas Misencik, *President*
Roseann Misencik, *Admin Sec*
EMP: 25
SQ FT: 15,000
SALES (est): 3.4MM **Privately Held**
WEB: www.precisecircuit.com
SIC: 3672 Circuit boards, television & radio printed

(G-7534)
PRECISION RESOURCE INC (PA)
25 Forest Pkwy (06484-6122)
PHONE.................................203 925-0012
Peter Wolcott, *CEO*
Charles Polatsek, *Vice Pres*
Mony Singh, *Engineer*
Gregory Chvirko, *Design Engr*
Dan Bazar, *Manager*
▲ **EMP:** 176 **EST:** 1953
SQ FT: 100,000
SALES (est): 260.1MM **Privately Held**
WEB: www.precisionresource.com
SIC: 3469 Stamping metal for the trade

(G-7535)
PRECISION RSURCE INTL SLS CORP
25 Forest Pkwy (06484-6122)
PHONE.................................203 925-0012
EMP: 2
SALES (est): 110K **Privately Held**
SIC: 3469 Stamping metal for the trade

(G-7536)
PREFERRED PDT & MKTG GROUP LLC
415 Howe Ave Ste 103 (06484-3174)
PHONE.................................203 567-0221
Celeste S McGorty,
EMP: 3
SALES: 80K **Privately Held**
WEB: www.ppmgllc.com
SIC: 3679 Electronic components

(G-7537)
PREFERRED TOOL & DIE INC (PA)
Also Called: Preferred Precision
30 Forest Pkwy (06484-6122)
PHONE.................................203 925-8525
Michael Fortin, *President*
Virginia Fortin, *President*
Wayne Fortin, *Vice Pres*
Kim Oconnor, *Office Mgr*
EMP: 82
SQ FT: 26,000
SALES (est): 17.2MM **Privately Held**
SIC: 3469 3544 Stamping metal for the trade; special dies & tools

(G-7538)
PREFERRED TOOL & DIE INC
Preferred Precision
19 Forest Pkwy (06484-6135)
PHONE.................................203 925-8525
Mark Testani, *Branch Mgr*
EMP: 40
SALES (est): 5.2MM
SALES (corp-wide): 17.2MM **Privately Held**
SIC: 3545 Precision tools, machinists'
PA: Preferred Tool & Die, Inc.
    30 Forest Pkwy
    Shelton CT 06484
    203 925-8525

(G-7539)
PREMIER MFG GROUP INC
Also Called: Electri-Cable Assemblies
10 Mountain View Dr (06484-6403)
PHONE.................................203 924-6617
Russell Hayden, *President*
David Black, *Treasurer*
EMP: 60
SALES (est): 15.5MM
SALES (corp-wide): 2.7B **Publicly Held**
SIC: 3645 2541 Residential lighting fixtures; office fixtures, wood
HQ: Group Dekko, Inc.
    2505 Dekko Dr
    Garrett IN 46738

(G-7540)
PUCKS PUTTERS & FUEL LLC (PA)
784 River Rd (06484-5430)
PHONE.................................203 494-3952
Steven Genova, *Principal*
EMP: 3 **EST:** 2012
SALES (est): 871.9K **Privately Held**
SIC: 2869 Fuels

(G-7541)
QDS LLC
120 Long Hill Cross Rd (06484-6180)
PHONE.................................203 338-9668
Paul Christian, *Principal*
Frank Harrington, *Manager*
Dave Christian, *Technical Staff*
EMP: 3
SALES (est): 278.6K **Privately Held**
SIC: 3999 Manufacturing industries

(G-7542)
QUALEDI INC
1 Trap Falls Rd Ste 206 (06484-4672)
P.O. Box 623, Stratford (06615-0623)
PHONE.................................203 538-5320
Stephen A Morocco, *Branch Mgr*
EMP: 9
SALES (corp-wide): 1.2MM **Privately Held**
SIC: 7372 Prepackaged software
PA: Qualedi Inc
    121 W Main St Ste 4
    Milford CT 06460
    203 874-4334

(G-7543)
RAPID SLICER LLC
16 Crystal Ln (06484-5776)
PHONE.................................203 610-3673
Cynthia Fox, *CEO*
Robert Fox, *Principal*
EMP: 2
SALES (est): 88.9K **Privately Held**
SIC: 3089 Kitchenware, plastic

(G-7544)
RCD LLC
230 Long Hill Cross Rd (06484-6160)
PHONE.................................203 712-1900
Harry Holiday III, *Branch Mgr*
Kelly Hicks, *Info Tech Mgr*
EMP: 1 **Privately Held**
SIC: 3312 Tool & die steel & alloys
PA: Rcd Llc
    1107 Springfield Rd
    Lebanon MO 65536

(G-7545)
RED APPLE CREATIVE US INC
38 Ann Ave (06484-4402)
PHONE.................................212 453-2540
EMP: 2
SALES (est): 85.9K **Privately Held**
SIC: 3571 Mfg Electronic Computers

(G-7546)
REIS FLOOR FINISHING
46 Cathy Dr (06484-5207)
PHONE.................................203 367-1273
Paul M Reis, *Owner*
EMP: 1
SALES (est): 150K **Privately Held**
SIC: 2435 Hardwood plywood, prefinished

(G-7547)
RUSSELL SPEEDERS CAR WASH LLC
811 River Rd (06484-5432)
PHONE.................................203 925-0083
EMP: 2
SALES (corp-wide): 2.6MM **Privately Held**
SIC: 7542 3714 Washing & polishing, automotive; filters: oil, fuel & air, motor vehicle
PA: Russell Speeder's Car Wash, Llc
    270 Main Ave
    Norwalk CT 06851
    203 847-8669

(G-7548)
RUSTIC RSTRTIONS RACE CARS LLC
3 Spoke Dr (06484-4832)
PHONE.................................203 929-4813
Bruce Belco, *Principal*
EMP: 2
SALES (est): 102.8K **Privately Held**
SIC: 3711 Automobile assembly, including specialty automobiles

(G-7549)
SAFETY BAGS INC
2 Corporate Dr Ste 250 (06484-6239)
P.O. Box 553 (06484-0553)
PHONE.................................203 242-0727
Dori Decarlo, *CEO*
EMP: 3
SALES: 500K **Privately Held**
SIC: 2673 Plastic bags: made from purchased materials

(G-7550)
SANDRA MERCIER PROCACCIN
234 Deer Run (06484-2874)
PHONE.................................203 929-6968
Sandra Mercier, *Owner*
EMP: 2
SALES (est): 100K **Privately Held**
SIC: 3999 Hair, dressing of, for the trade

(G-7551)
SATIN AMERICAN CORPORATION
40 Oliver Ter (06484-5384)
P.O. Box 619 (06484-0619)
PHONE.................................203 929-6363
Joseph Satin, *President*
Leo Disorbo, *Vice Pres*
Anthony Ciccaglione, *VP Sales*
EMP: 35
SQ FT: 55,000
SALES (est): 7.6MM **Privately Held**
WEB: www.satinamerican.com
SIC: 3613 Switchgear & switchboard apparatus

▲ = Import ▼ = Export
◆ = Import/Export

GEOGRAPHIC SECTION
Shelton - Fairfield County (G-7581)

(G-7552)
SEAWOLFS PRODUCTS CO
18 Longview Rd (06484-4814)
PHONE.................................203 225-0110
Michael Zilinek, *CEO*
EMP: 2
SALES (est): 124.6K **Privately Held**
SIC: 3999 Manufacturing industries

(G-7553)
SHEAFFER PEN CORP
1 Bic Way Ste 1 (06484-6223)
PHONE.................................203 783-2894
EMP: 300 **EST:** 1960
SALES (est): 18.8MM **Privately Held**
SIC: 2621 Paper Mill

(G-7554)
SHORELINE BREWING COMPANY LLC
819 Bridgeport Ave (06484-4714)
PHONE.................................203 225-7734
William Da Silva, *CEO*
EMP: 2
SALES (est): 150K **Privately Held**
SIC: 2082 Beer (alcoholic beverage)

(G-7555)
SIGN IN SOFT INC
1 Waterview Dr (06484-4368)
PHONE.................................203 216-3046
Peter Pynadath, *President*
Sridhar Rapelli, *Principal*
EMP: 4
SALES (est): 98.6K **Privately Held**
SIC: 3993 5045 5049 Signs & advertising specialties; computer software; optical goods

(G-7556)
SIKORSKY AIRCRAFT CORPORATION
1 Far Mill Xing (06484-6121)
PHONE.................................203 386-7861
Filmson Alexander, *Branch Mgr*
EMP: 715 **Publicly Held**
SIC: 3721 Helicopters
HQ: Sikorsky Aircraft Corporation
    6900 Main St
    Stratford CT 06614

(G-7557)
SORGE INDUSTRIES INC
289 Coram Rd (06484-4529)
PHONE.................................203 924-8900
Thomas Sorge, *President*
Susan K Sorge, *Corp Secy*
EMP: 6
SQ FT: 3,000
SALES (est): 973.8K **Privately Held**
SIC: 7692 3446 Welding repair; stairs, staircases, stair treads: prefabricated metal

(G-7558)
SPINE WAVE INC
3 Enterprise Dr Ste 210 (06484-4696)
PHONE.................................203 944-9494
Mark Loguidice, *President*
Hal Jungerheld, *Exec VP*
Ronnie Smith, *Vice Pres*
Tom Wilson, *Vice Pres*
Beth Stuart, *Research*
EMP: 100
SALES (est): 21MM **Privately Held**
SIC: 3841 Surgical & medical instruments

(G-7559)
STONEAGE LLC
36 Narragansett Trl (06484-4911)
PHONE.................................203 926-1133
EMP: 3
SALES: 180K **Privately Held**
SIC: 3281 Mfg Cut Stone/Products

(G-7560)
SWPCI
Also Called: Track Fresh
18 Longview Rd (06484-4814)
PHONE.................................203 278-6400
EMP: 2 **EST:** 2011
SALES (est): 134.8K **Privately Held**
SIC: 3714 Motor vehicle parts & accessories

(G-7561)
SYFERLOCK TECHNOLOGY CORP
917 Bridgeport Ave Ste 5 (06484-4679)
PHONE.................................203 292-5441
Robert D Russo, *President*
Francis Laplante, *Technology*
Abu Marcose, *Technology*
EMP: 7 **EST:** 2008
SALES (est): 876.4K **Privately Held**
SIC: 3577 5045 Computer peripheral equipment; computer software

(G-7562)
SYSTEM INTGRTION CNSULTING LLC
Also Called: Allegra Print & Imaging
1000 Bridgeport Ave 1-3 (06484-4660)
PHONE.................................203 926-9599
Gary Bean, *CEO*
EMP: 5
SQ FT: 300
SALES: 900K **Privately Held**
SIC: 2752 Commercial printing, offset

(G-7563)
TANGOE US INC
1 Waterview Dr Ste 200 (06484-4368)
PHONE.................................203 859-9300
Robert Irwin, *CEO*
Ajesh Appukuttan, *Chief*
Chris Newman, *Vice Pres*
Michael Niziolek, *Vice Pres*
Neal Poretsky, *Vice Pres*
EMP: 300
SALES (corp-wide): 491.5MM **Privately Held**
SIC: 7372 Prepackaged software
HQ: Tangoe Us, Inc.
    1 Waterview Dr Ste 200
    Shelton CT 06484
    973 257-0300

(G-7564)
TANGOE US INC (HQ)
1 Waterview Dr Ste 200 (06484-4368)
PHONE.................................973 257-0300
Robert Irwin, *CEO*
Marc Culver, *Vice Pres*
Chris Taylor, *CFO*
Rick Young, *CFO*
Sidra Berman, *Chief Mktg Ofcr*
EMP: 120
SQ FT: 66,000
SALES (est): 491.5MM **Privately Held**
WEB: www.tangoe.com
SIC: 7372 Application computer software
PA: Tangoe, Llc
    6410 Poplar Ave Ste 200
    Memphis TN 38119
    901 752-6200

(G-7565)
THOMAS MEADE
Also Called: Meade Computer Services
40 Beacon Hill Ter (06484-5904)
PHONE.................................203 209-7591
Thomas Meade, *Owner*
EMP: 3
SALES: 80K **Privately Held**
SIC: 7379 3699 Computer related consulting services; security control equipment & systems

(G-7566)
THREADS OF EVIDENCE LLC
52 Oronoque Trl (06484-4949)
PHONE.................................203 929-5209
Mary McQuillan, *Mng Member*
EMP: 4
SALES (est): 220K **Privately Held**
SIC: 2391 Curtains & draperies

(G-7567)
THURSDAYS CHILD PUBLISHING LLC
7 Tulip Ln (06484-2632)
PHONE.................................203 929-5080
M Hernon Macdonald, *Principal*
EMP: 2
SALES (est): 87.8K **Privately Held**
SIC: 2741 Miscellaneous publishing

(G-7568)
TIGER-SUL PRODUCTS LLC
4 Armstrong Rd Ste 220 (06484-4721)
P.O. Box 5, Atmore AL (36504-0005)
PHONE.................................251 202-3850
Don Cherry, *President*
▼ **EMP:** 50
SALES (est): 12.6MM
SALES (corp-wide): 74.2MM **Privately Held**
SIC: 2819 Sulfur, recovered or refined, incl. from sour natural gas
PA: Platte River Equity Iii, L.P.
    200 Fillmore St Ste 200 # 200
    Denver CO 80206
    303 292-7300

(G-7569)
TREIF USA INC
50 Waterview Dr Ste 130 (06484-4377)
PHONE.................................203 929-9930
Guenter Becker, *President*
Cornelia Bischoff, *Sales Staff*
Roger Costello, *Sales Staff*
Andres Sigcha, *Sales Staff*
Alicia Clayton, *Office Mgr*
◆ **EMP:** 15
SQ FT: 12,000
SALES (est): 3.4MM
SALES (corp-wide): 62.6MM **Privately Held**
SIC: 3556 5046 Food products machinery; commercial equipment
PA: T R E I F - Maschinenbau Gesellschaft Mit Beschrankter Haftung
    Toni-Reifenhauser-Str. 1
    Oberlahr 57641
    268 594-40

(G-7570)
TRI SOURCE INC
84 Platt Rd (06484-5340)
PHONE.................................203 924-7030
Edward Hyland, *President*
Anita Hampel, *Corp Secy*
EMP: 12
SQ FT: 17,000
SALES: 1.5MM **Privately Held**
WEB: www.trisourceinc.com
SIC: 3679 8732 Power supplies, all types: static; market analysis or research

(G-7571)
TRUMBULL TRANSFER LLC
12 Commerce Dr (06484-6202)
PHONE.................................203 377-2487
Rosario Bacarella, *Principal*
EMP: 1
SALES (est): 110.2K **Privately Held**
SIC: 2711 Newspapers, publishing & printing

(G-7572)
TRYON MANUFACTURING COMPANY
30 Oliver Ter (06484-5336)
P.O. Box 242 (06484-0242)
PHONE.................................203 929-0464
George Fairbanks Jr, *Owner*
EMP: 6 **EST:** 1917
SQ FT: 4,000
SALES (est): 686.4K **Privately Held**
SIC: 3451 Screw machine products

(G-7573)
ULTIMATE WOODWORKING LLC
16 Fair Oaks Dr (06484-3407)
PHONE.................................203 243-3367
Jacek Supronowicz, *Principal*
EMP: 2
SALES (est): 93.5K **Privately Held**
SIC: 2431 Millwork

(G-7574)
UNEEDA WELDER
25 Oak Hill Ln (06484-5927)
PHONE.................................203 929-4507
William Kettles, *Owner*
EMP: 1
SALES (est): 57K **Privately Held**
SIC: 7692 Welding repair

(G-7575)
UNILEVER ASCC AG
3 Corporate Dr (06484-6222)
PHONE.................................203 381-2482
EMP: 300
SALES (corp-wide): 58.3B **Privately Held**
SIC: 2841 2099 Soap & other detergents; syrups
HQ: Unilever Ascc Ag
    Spitalstrasse 5
    Schaffhausen SH
    526 315-000

(G-7576)
UNITEC PARTS CO
1 Enterprise Dr Ste 205 (06484-4631)
PHONE.................................919 627-0192
EMP: 2
SALES (est): 95.5K **Privately Held**
SIC: 3534 Elevators & moving stairways

(G-7577)
UNITED AERO GROUP LLC
12 Commerce Dr (06484-6202)
PHONE.................................203 283-9524
Joshua Gelder,
James Gelder,
EMP: 8
SQ FT: 81,000
SALES (est): 3.9MM **Privately Held**
SIC: 3728 Aircraft parts & equipment

(G-7578)
VERTICAL EDGE LLC
283 Eagles Lndg (06484-2879)
PHONE.................................203 513-2806
Matthew P Kranz, *Principal*
EMP: 1 **EST:** 2010
SALES (est): 74K **Privately Held**
SIC: 2591 Blinds vertical

(G-7579)
VIKING TOOL COMPANY
435 Access Rd (06484)
P.O. Box 808 (06484-0808)
PHONE.................................203 929-1457
Ole C Severson Jr, *President*
Ole C Severson III, *Treasurer*
James J Severson, *Admin Sec*
EMP: 35 **EST:** 1946
SQ FT: 10,000
SALES (est): 5MM **Privately Held**
WEB: www.vikingtool.com
SIC: 3541 5084 3545 Machine tools, metal cutting type; industrial machinery & equipment; machine tool accessories

(G-7580)
VISHAY AMERICAS INC (HQ)
1 Greenwich Pl (06484-7603)
PHONE.................................203 452-5648
Gerald Paul, *CEO*
Marc Zandman, *Ch of Bd*
EMP: 500
SALES (est): 363.2MM
SALES (corp-wide): 3B **Publicly Held**
SIC: 3676 3674 Electronic resistors; semiconductors & related devices
PA: Vishay Intertechnology, Inc.
    63 Lancaster Ave
    Malvern PA 19355
    610 644-1300

(G-7581)
VITEC PRODUCTION SOLUTIONS INC (HQ)
14 Progress Dr (06484-6216)
PHONE.................................203 929-1100
Dan Fitzpatrick, *President*
Michael Accardi, *Vice Pres*
Curt Dann, *Treasurer*
Penny Lock, *Sales Staff*
Matthew Danilowicz, *Director*
▲ **EMP:** 100 **EST:** 1970
SALES (est): 31.1MM
SALES (corp-wide): 495MM **Privately Held**
WEB: www.antonbauer.com
SIC: 3861 3692 Cameras & related equipment; primary batteries, dry & wet
PA: The Vitec Group Plc.
    Bridge House
    Richmond TW9 1
    208 332-4600

Shelton - Fairfield County (G-7582)

(G-7582)
VOGEL OPTICS LLC
12 Old Coram Rd (06484-4257)
PHONE.....................203 925-9619
Steven Vogel, *Principal*
EMP: 1 EST: 2011
SALES (est): 47.8K Privately Held
SIC: 3229 Optical glass

(G-7583)
WARREN COMPUTER SERVICES
79 Fairlane Dr (06484-1983)
PHONE.....................203 929-5725
Warren McGuire, *Owner*
EMP: 6
SALES (est): 88.2K Privately Held
SIC: 7374 7372 Data processing & preparation; prepackaged software

(G-7584)
WEST-CONN TOOL AND DIE INC
128 Long Hill Cross Rd (06484-6169)
PHONE.....................203 538-5081
David Marasco, *President*
Laura Pinciaro, *Vice Pres*
Dave Zell, *Opers Staff*
Shelley Schneider, *Administration*
EMP: 11 EST: 1983
SQ FT: 15,900
SALES (est): 2.2MM Privately Held
SIC: 3544 Special dies & tools

(G-7585)
WHEELS OF HOPE INC
44 Brownson Dr (06484-2713)
PHONE.....................203 305-5762
Kris Heaton, *Principal*
EMP: 2
SALES (est): 185.2K Privately Held
SIC: 3312 Blast furnaces & steel mills

(G-7586)
WICKS BUSINESS INFORMATION LLC (PA)
Also Called: Treasury & Risk Management
4 Research Dr Ste 402 (06484-6242)
PHONE.....................203 334-2002
Douglas J Manoni,
EMP: 10 EST: 1999
SALES: 20MM Privately Held
WEB: www.assetnews.com
SIC: 2721 2711 Magazines: publishing only, not printed on site; newspapers: publishing only, not printed on site

(G-7587)
WIFFLE BALL INCORPORATED
275 Bridgeport Ave (06484-3827)
P.O. Box 193 (06484-0193)
PHONE.....................203 924-4643
David J Mullany, *President*
Stephen A Mullany, *Vice Pres*
EMP: 15 EST: 1953
SQ FT: 20,000
SALES (est): 2.5MM Privately Held
WEB: www.wiffle.com
SIC: 3949 Sporting & athletic goods

(G-7588)
WOODS LIGHTNING PROTECTION
31 School St (06484-1825)
P.O. Box 348 (06484-0348)
PHONE.....................203 929-1868
Drew M Curtiss,
Nancy Curtiss,
EMP: 9 EST: 1868
SALES (est): 1MM Privately Held
SIC: 1799 3643 Lightning conductor erection; lightning protection equipment

(G-7589)
XYLEM WATER SOLUTIONS USA INC
1000 Bridgeport Ave # 402 (06484-4660)
PHONE.....................203 450-3715
Mong Liu, *Analyst*
EMP: 25 Publicly Held
SIC: 3561 Pumps & pumping equipment
HQ: Xylem Water Solutions U.S.A., Inc.
4828 Prkwy Plz Blvd 200
Charlotte NC 28217

Sherman
Fairfield County

(G-7590)
ALPHA 1C LLC
3 Leach Hollow Rd (06784-2302)
PHONE.....................860 354-7979
Barbara Dankenbring, *Vice Pres*
Al Kenney, *Mng Member*
EMP: 6
SALES (est): 464.4K Privately Held
SIC: 3826 Analytical instruments

(G-7591)
CANDLE WOODWORKS
50 Route 37 E (06784-1427)
PHONE.....................860 350-4390
Joseph Keneally, *Owner*
EMP: 2
SALES (est): 120K Privately Held
SIC: 2431 Millwork

(G-7592)
CLANCY WOODWORKING LLC
12 Anderson Rd E (06784-1014)
PHONE.....................860 355-3655
Brian Clancy, *Principal*
EMP: 4
SALES (est): 357.6K Privately Held
SIC: 2431 Millwork

(G-7593)
COMPOSITE TRUCK BODY LLC
3 Nutmeg Ln (06784-2219)
PHONE.....................800 735-1668
Patti Tagani, *Office Mgr*
Renee Harris, *Manager*
Daniel O'Connell,
Francois Boisvert,
EMP: 4
SALES: 550K Privately Held
SIC: 5012 3713 7389 Truck bodies; utility truck bodies;

(G-7594)
DUBE AIR LLC
8 Brookside Ln (06784-1650)
PHONE.....................860 355-1705
Arthur J Dube, *Manager*
EMP: 2
SALES (est): 186.9K Privately Held
WEB: www.dubeair.com
SIC: 3721 Aircraft

(G-7595)
GODFREY CEMETARY MAINT LLC
4 Briarwood Dr (06784-1326)
PHONE.....................203 858-4035
Kevin Godfrey, *President*
EMP: 2
SALES (est): 194.2K Privately Held
SIC: 3281 Burial vaults, stone

(G-7596)
JAMES M MUNCH
Also Called: JM Logging Forestry
48 Route 37 S (06784-1529)
PHONE.....................802 353-3114
James Munch, *Principal*
EMP: 3
SALES (est): 212.2K Privately Held
SIC: 2411 Logging

(G-7597)
LINDSAY GRAPHICS
9 Partridge Trl (06784-1744)
PHONE.....................860 355-8744
Lindsay Ward, *Owner*
EMP: 1
SALES (est): 32.6K Privately Held
SIC: 2731 Book publishing

(G-7598)
MID-ISLAND AGGREGATES/DISTRIBU
5 Highview Ln (06784-1237)
PHONE.....................860 605-6753
Brian Heidel, *Mng Member*
Brian J Heidel,
Peggie Heidel,
EMP: 2
SALES: 100K Privately Held
SIC: 1423 5032 Crushed & broken granite; brick, stone & related material

(G-7599)
P L WOODWORKING
4 Deer Hill Rd (06784-2321)
PHONE.....................860 354-6855
Paul Levine, *President*
EMP: 6
SALES: 100K Privately Held
SIC: 2434 Wood kitchen cabinets

(G-7600)
PALUMBO SAND & GRAVEL
4 Old Greenwoods Rd (06784-1522)
PHONE.....................860 350-5322
Anthony Palumbo, *Principal*
EMP: 2
SALES (est): 118.7K Privately Held
SIC: 1442 Construction sand & gravel

(G-7601)
PHOCUSWRIGHT INC (PA)
1 Route 37 E Ste 200 (06784-1406)
P.O. Box 760 (06784-0760)
PHONE.....................860 350-4084
Phillip Wolf, *CEO*
Thomas L Kemp, *President*
Phillip Ferri, *Corp Secy*
Carol Hutzelman, *Senior VP*
Peter Comeau, *Vice Pres*
EMP: 22
SALES (est): 3.1MM Privately Held
WEB: www.phocuswright.com
SIC: 8742 2759 Marketing consulting services; publication printing

(G-7602)
PRIVATE COMMUNICATIONS CORP
Also Called: Private Wifi
39 Holiday Point Rd (06784-1628)
P.O. Box 159 (06784-0159)
PHONE.....................860 355-2718
Kent Lawson, *President*
EMP: 12
SQ FT: 4,000
SALES (est): 1.2MM Privately Held
WEB: www.privatewifi.com
SIC: 7372 Prepackaged software

(G-7603)
ROSSOMANO PICTURES
35 Route 37 S (06784-1500)
PHONE.....................203 241-5087
Brian McAward, *Owner*
EMP: 1
SALES: 82K Privately Held
SIC: 7336 3651 Film strip, slide & still film production; video cassette recorders/players & accessories

(G-7604)
SACRED GRUNDS COF ROASTERS LLC
1 Route 37 E Ste 1 # 1 (06784-1407)
PHONE.....................860 717-2871
John Rich,
EMP: 1
SALES (est): 54K Privately Held
SIC: 2095 5499 Coffee roasting (except by wholesale grocers); coffee

(G-7605)
TEKCAST INDUSTRIES
6 Oak Dr (06784-1634)
PHONE.....................860 799-6464
EMP: 2
SALES (est): 106.6K Privately Held
SIC: 3544 Special dies, tools, jigs & fixtures

(G-7606)
WHITE SILO FARM
32 Route 37 E (06784-1427)
PHONE.....................860 355-0271
Ralph Gorman, *Owner*
EMP: 1
SALES (est): 75K Privately Held
SIC: 2084 Wines

(G-7607)
WINE CAPP INC
35 Mauweehoo Hl (06784-2312)
PHONE.....................860 355-0521
Steven Roffwarg, *President*
EMP: 2 EST: 1989
SALES (est): 180K Privately Held
SIC: 2741 Miscellaneous publishing

Simsbury
Hartford County

(G-7608)
A & D DENTAL INNOVATIONS LLC
40 Fawnbrook Ln (06070-2610)
PHONE.....................888 374-5134
EMP: 2
SALES (est): 236.2K Privately Held
SIC: 3843 Mfg Dental Equipment/Supplies

(G-7609)
ADVANCED VACUUM TECHNOLOGY INC
Also Called: Avt
7 Herman Dr Ste E (06070-3501)
P.O. Box 386, East Granby (06026-0386)
PHONE.....................860 653-4176
James Capazzi, *President*
Cheryl Capazzi, *CFO*
▲ EMP: 2
SQ FT: 5,000
SALES (est): 424K Privately Held
WEB: www.advactec.com
SIC: 7699 3548 3545 8331 Welding equipment repair; welding & cutting apparatus & accessories; machine tool attachments & accessories; job training services

(G-7610)
ALLIANCES BY ALISA LLC
14 Northgate (06070-1021)
PHONE.....................860 869-1509
Alisa Gaudiosi, *Principal*
EMP: 2
SALES (est): 127.3K Privately Held
SIC: 2836 Culture media

(G-7611)
ANTRIM HOUSE
21 Goodrich Rd (06070-1804)
PHONE.....................860 217-0023
Robert McQuilkin, *Principal*
EMP: 1
SALES (est): 72.8K Privately Held
SIC: 2741 Miscellaneous publishing

(G-7612)
AUTOMATION & SERVO TECH
15 Hunting Ridge Dr (06070-1806)
PHONE.....................860 658-5172
Edward Crofton, *President*
EMP: 2 EST: 2001
SALES (est): 138.8K Privately Held
SIC: 3625 Motor controls, electric

(G-7613)
BMI CAD SERVICES INC
8a Herman Dr (06070-1404)
P.O. Box 522 (06070-0522)
PHONE.....................860 658-0808
Bradford T Martin, *President*
Karen A Martin, *Vice Pres*
Karen Martin, *Vice Pres*
EMP: 10
SALES (est): 1.6MM Privately Held
SIC: 3599 Machine shop, jobbing & repair

(G-7614)
CONTAINMENT SOLUTIONS INC
35 Ichabod Rd (06070-2812)
PHONE.....................860 651-4371
Scott Knake, *Branch Mgr*
EMP: 128 Privately Held
WEB: www.containmentsolutions.com
SIC: 3443 Fabricated plate work (boiler shop)
HQ: Containment Solutions, Inc.
333 N Rivershire Dr # 190
Conroe TX 77304

GEOGRAPHIC SECTION — Simsbury - Hartford County

(G-7615)
DESIGNS & PROTOTYPES LTD
Also Called: D & P Instruments
1280 Hopmeadow St Ste E (06070-1425)
PHONE..................860 658-0458
Winthrop Wadsworth, *Branch Mgr*
EMP: 3
SALES (est): 416.9K **Privately Held**
WEB: www.dpinstruments.com
SIC: 3826 Analytical instruments
PA: Designs & Prototypes, Ltd.
  10 White Oak Dr Apt 113
  Exeter NH 03833

(G-7616)
DIAGNOSTIC DEVICES INC
Also Called: D D I
11 Windham Dr (06070-1227)
PHONE..................860 651-6583
Hemchandra Shertukde, *President*
EMP: 2 **Privately Held**
WEB: www.diagnostic-devices.com
SIC: 3612 Transformers, except electric
PA: Diagnostic Devices Inc.
  50 Wolcott Rd
  Simsbury CT 06070

(G-7617)
DIAGNOSTIC DEVICES INC (PA)
Also Called: D D I
50 Wolcott Rd (06070-1416)
P.O. Box 362 (06070-0362)
PHONE..................860 651-6583
Hemchandra Shertukde, *President*
Rekha Shertukde,
Brenda Kreuzer, *Executive Asst*
EMP: 2
SQ FT: 200
SALES: 50K **Privately Held**
SIC: 3612 Transformers, except electric

(G-7618)
DYNO NOBEL INC
660 Hopmeadow St (06070-2420)
P.O. Box 2006 (06070-7603)
PHONE..................860 843-2000
Dave Mains, *Engineer*
Jock Muir, *Branch Mgr*
Rudy Maurer, *Manager*
Robert Cooper, *Technology*
Nathan Burnette, *IT/INT Sup*
EMP: 150 **Privately Held**
SIC: 2892 Detonators & detonating caps
HQ: Dyno Nobel Inc.
  2795 E Cottonwood Pkwy # 500
  Salt Lake City UT 84121
  801 364-4800

(G-7619)
ENSIGN BICKFORD INDUSTRIES
100 Grist Mill Ln (06070-2484)
P.O. Box 7 (06070-0007)
PHONE..................203 843-2126
EMP: 13
SALES (est): 301K **Privately Held**
SIC: 3999 Manufacturing industries

(G-7620)
ENSIGN-BICKFORD AROSPC DEF CO (HQ)
Also Called: EBA&d
640 Hopmeadow St (06070-2420)
P.O. Box 429 (06070-0429)
PHONE..................860 843-2289
Brendan Walsh, *President*
Brendan M Walsh, *President*
Jeremy Stewart, *General Mgr*
Jonathan Lutz, *Business Mgr*
P Franklin, *Opers Staff*
▲ EMP: 277
SQ FT: 150,000
SALES (est): 144.2MM
SALES (corp-wide): 196.2MM **Privately Held**
WEB: www.eba-d.com
SIC: 2892 Detonators & detonating caps
PA: Ensign-Bickford Industries, Inc.
  999 17th St Ste 900
  Denver CO 80202
  860 843-2000

(G-7621)
ENSIGN-BICKFORD COMPANY (HQ)
125 Powder Forest Dr (06070)
P.O. Box 711 (06070-0711)
PHONE..................860 843-2001
Scott M Deakin, *President*
Charles Difatta, *President*
Anna Fusari, *Accountant*
Rich Stewart, *Technical Staff*
Dorothy T Hammett, *General Counsel*
▲ EMP: 7
SQ FT: 11,000
SALES (est): 11.1MM
SALES (corp-wide): 196.2MM **Privately Held**
SIC: 2892 Detonators & detonating caps
PA: Ensign-Bickford Industries, Inc.
  999 17th St Ste 900
  Denver CO 80202
  860 843-2000

(G-7622)
ENSIGN-BICKFORD INDUSTRIES INC
630 Hopmeadow St Rm 20 (06070-2420)
PHONE..................860 658-4411
Michael Long, *Vice Pres*
EMP: 35
SALES (corp-wide): 196.2MM **Privately Held**
WEB: www.e-bind.com
SIC: 3089 8742 3613 3489 Plastic processing; management consulting services; switchgear & switchboard apparatus; ordnance & accessories; ammunition, except for small arms; explosives
PA: Ensign-Bickford Industries, Inc.
  999 17th St Ste 900
  Denver CO 80202
  860 843-2000

(G-7623)
ENSIGN-BICKFORD RENEWABLE ENER
125 Powder Forest Dr (06070)
PHONE..................860 843-2000
Caleb E White, *President*
Scott M Deakin, *Treasurer*
Will Silton, *Director*
Dorothy Hammett, *Admin Sec*
EMP: 20
SALES (est): 2MM
SALES (corp-wide): 196.2MM **Privately Held**
SIC: 2421 Wood chips, produced at mill
PA: Ensign-Bickford Industries, Inc.
  999 17th St Ste 900
  Simsbury CT 80202
  860 843-2000

(G-7624)
EQUIPMENT DESIGNS ASSOCIATE
11 Long View Dr (06070-2611)
PHONE..................860 217-1573
William Abramczyk,
EMP: 2
SALES (est): 236.6K **Privately Held**
SIC: 3543 Industrial patterns

(G-7625)
ETHICON INC
31 Pine Glen Rd (06070-2743)
PHONE..................860 658-7653
Tom Glass, *Manager*
EMP: 1
SALES (corp-wide): 81.5B **Publicly Held**
WEB: www.ethiconinc.com
SIC: 3842 Ligatures, medical
HQ: Ethicon Inc.
  Us Route 22
  Somerville NJ 08876
  732 524-0400

(G-7626)
FIRST LIGHT SOFTWARE INC
6 Deepwood Rd (06070-1608)
PHONE..................860 217-0673
Maryann Light, *Owner*
EMP: 2
SALES (est): 95K **Privately Held**
SIC: 7372 Prepackaged software

(G-7627)
GLASS DESIGN STUDIO
2 Mathers Xing (06070-2477)
PHONE..................860 651-4233
Carol Ellen, *Owner*
EMP: 1
SALES (est): 41.6K **Privately Held**
SIC: 3211 Flat glass

(G-7628)
GLASS MASTER LLC
24 Deepwood Rd (06070-1652)
PHONE..................860 658-0040
EMP: 2 EST: 2005
SALES (est): 150K **Privately Held**
SIC: 3231 Mfg Products-Purchased Glass

(G-7629)
INTEGRITY GRAPHICS INC
42 Carver Cir (06070-2020)
PHONE..................800 343-1248
Joseph E La Valla, *President*
Michael Hart, *Exec VP*
Josh Bainton, *Vice Pres*
Tom Shaw, *Vice Pres*
Walter August, *VP Opers*
EMP: 62
SALES: 17MM **Privately Held**
WEB: www.integrity-usa.com
SIC: 2752 Commercial printing, offset

(G-7630)
INTERCTIVE PRINT SOLUTIONS LLC
411 Bushy Hill Rd (06070-2826)
PHONE..................860 217-0412
Charles Eugene Dipace, *Principal*
EMP: 2
SALES (est): 129.7K **Privately Held**
SIC: 2752 Commercial printing, lithographic

(G-7631)
J FOSTER ICE CREAM
894 Hopmeadow St (06070-1825)
PHONE..................860 651-1499
John Darcangelo, *Branch Mgr*
EMP: 5
SALES (est): 268.1K **Privately Held**
SIC: 2024 5812 Ice cream & frozen desserts; ice cream stands or dairy bars
PA: J Foster Ice Cream
  4 Bailey Rd
  Avon CT 06001

(G-7632)
LW GLOBAL LLC
36 Metacom Dr (06070-1850)
PHONE..................860 519-7134
William Shipman, *Mng Member*
EMP: 1
SALES: 200K **Privately Held**
SIC: 2079 Cooking oils, except corn: vegetable refined

(G-7633)
MANDEL VILAR PRESS
19 Oxford Ct (06070-2174)
PHONE..................806 790-4731
EMP: 1
SALES (est): 37.5K **Privately Held**
SIC: 2741 Miscellaneous publishing

(G-7634)
MICHAUD INDUSTRIES LLC
72 Riverside Rd (06070-2517)
PHONE..................860 408-0907
Robertson J Michaud, *Principal*
EMP: 2
SALES (est): 136.4K **Privately Held**
SIC: 3999 Barber & beauty shop equipment

(G-7635)
MICROTOOLS INC
714 Hopmeadow St Ste 14 (06070-2234)
P.O. Box 624 (06070-0624)
PHONE..................860 651-6170
Bob Japenga, *President*
Barbara Japenga, *Shareholder*
Nancy Lehman, *Shareholder*
Joseph Lehman, *Admin Sec*
EMP: 8
SQ FT: 900
SALES: 347K **Privately Held**
WEB: www.mtiemail.com
SIC: 7371 3825 Computer software development; computer software development & applications; test equipment for electronic & electrical circuits

(G-7636)
MJ TOOL & MANUFACTURING INC
11 Herman Dr Ste B (06070-1463)
P.O. Box 13 (06070-0013)
PHONE..................860 352-2688
Gustav Jaeggi, *President*
Marie Jaeggi, *Admin Sec*
EMP: 3 EST: 1981
SALES: 250K **Privately Held**
SIC: 3599 Machine & other job shop work

(G-7637)
NEW ENGLAND TOY LLC
4 Mclean St (06070-2121)
PHONE..................860 655-6089
Joshua Livingston,
▲ EMP: 1
SALES (est): 97.5K **Privately Held**
SIC: 3942 7389 Dolls & stuffed toys;

(G-7638)
PAINTED TILES CO
58 Laurel Ln (06070-1518)
PHONE..................860 658-7218
Jane Kozlak, *Owner*
EMP: 1
SALES (est): 71.4K **Privately Held**
WEB: www.painted-tiles.com
SIC: 3261 7389 3253 Sinks, vitreous china; hand painting, textile; ceramic wall & floor tile

(G-7639)
PHARMAVITE CORP
10 Station St (06070-2258)
PHONE..................860 651-1885
Thomas Leloup, *Principal*
Jim Maresca, *Purch Agent*
Federico Troiani, *Mktg Dir*
Erez Levy, *Manager*
John Newcomb, *Manager*
EMP: 6 EST: 1997
SALES: 533K **Privately Held**
SIC: 2834 Vitamin preparations

(G-7640)
PLASCO LLC
3 Pennington Dr (06070-2648)
PHONE..................860 217-1187
Gerald W Marcum, *Principal*
EMP: 2
SALES (est): 160.4K **Privately Held**
SIC: 3089 Injection molding of plastics

(G-7641)
PRECISION METAL MANUFACTURING
34 Northgate (06070-1033)
PHONE..................973 253-0500
EMP: 2
SALES (est): 62.5K **Privately Held**
SIC: 3999 Manufacturing industries

(G-7642)
RE-STYLE YOUR CLOSETS LLC
86 E Weatogue St (06070-2525)
PHONE..................860 658-9450
Heather Feinsinger, *Principal*
EMP: 4
SALES (est): 287.4K **Privately Held**
SIC: 2673 Wardrobe bags (closet accessories): from purchased materials

(G-7643)
RUNWAY LIQUIDATION LLC
Also Called: Bcbg
2320 Gala St (06070)
PHONE..................561 279-4444
EMP: 2
SALES (corp-wide): 570.1MM **Privately Held**
SIC: 2335 Women's, juniors' & misses' dresses
HQ: Runway Liquidation, Llc
  2761 Fruitland Ave
  Vernon CA 90058
  323 589-2224

Simsbury - Hartford County (G-7644)

(G-7644)
SHELBRACK WOODWORKING
15 Nod Brook Dr (06070-3015)
PHONE..................................860 431-5028
Wayne S Shelbrack, *Principal*
EMP: 2
SALES (est): 24.6K **Privately Held**
SIC: 2431 Millwork

(G-7645)
SIEMENS AG
24 Old Barge Rd (06070-1741)
PHONE..................................860 651-1399
EMP: 2
SALES (est): 88.3K **Privately Held**
SIC: 3661 Telephones & telephone apparatus

(G-7646)
SIGNS DIRECT INC
4 Woods Ln (06070-2441)
PHONE..................................860 658-9589
Shannon M Conover, *President*
EMP: 1
SALES (est): 107K **Privately Held**
SIC: 3993 Signs & advertising specialties

(G-7647)
SIMSBURY PRECISION PRODUCTS
11 Herman Dr Ste C (06070-1463)
PHONE..................................860 658-6909
Bruce Staubley, *President*
EMP: 8 **EST:** 1966
SQ FT: 4,800
SALES (est): 1.2MM **Privately Held**
SIC: 3599 Machine shop, jobbing & repair

(G-7648)
SPECIALTY SAW INC
30 Wolcott Rd (06070-1445)
PHONE..................................860 658-4419
David Bryan Nagy, *President*
Beverly Stillbach Nagy, *Admin Sec*
▲ **EMP:** 25
SQ FT: 11,000
SALES (est): 6.5MM **Privately Held**
WEB: www.specialtysaw.com
SIC: 3425 Saw blades for hand or power saws

(G-7649)
TALCOTT MOUNTAIN ENGINEERING
22 Talcott Mountain Rd (06070-2515)
PHONE..................................860 651-3141
James Miller, *President*
▲ **EMP:** 12 **EST:** 1997
SALES (est): 1.7MM **Privately Held**
SIC: 3561 Pumps & pumping equipment

(G-7650)
VALLEY PRESS INC
540 1/2 Hopmeadow St (06070)
PHONE..................................860 651-4700
Keith Turley, *Mng Member*
EMP: 25 **EST:** 2009
SALES (est): 241K **Privately Held**
SIC: 2741 Miscellaneous publishing

(G-7651)
XIN YONG CHEN
773 Hopmeadow St (06070-2206)
PHONE..................................860 651-4937
Chun Fong LI, *Principal*
EMP: 1
SALES (est): 71.6K **Privately Held**
SIC: 3421 Table & food cutlery, including butchers

(G-7652)
XOLVI LLC
207 Great Pond Rd (06070-1527)
PHONE..................................339 222-3616
EMP: 2
SALES (est): 92.3K **Privately Held**
SIC: 7372 7389 Prepackaged Software Services

Somers
Tolland County

(G-7653)
CONNECTICUT CUSTOM WOODWORKING
31 Pine Knob Rd (06071-1603)
PHONE..................................860 741-8946
Christopher Such, *Principal*
EMP: 2
SALES (est): 23.2K **Privately Held**
SIC: 2431 Millwork

(G-7654)
CT FIBEROPTICS INC
64 Field Rd Ste 11 (06071-2043)
PHONE..................................860 763-4341
John Plocharczyk, *President*
EMP: 10
SQ FT: 4,500
SALES (est): 1.1MM **Privately Held**
WEB: www.ctfiberoptics.com
SIC: 3827 Optical instruments & lenses

(G-7655)
DAIGLES DIVERSFD WLDG SVC LLC
19 Haystack Ln (06071-2244)
PHONE..................................860 265-3024
Dawn Daigle, *Principal*
Scott Daigle, *Agent*
EMP: 6 **EST:** 2010
SALES (est): 328.5K **Privately Held**
SIC: 7692 Welding repair

(G-7656)
DYMOTEK CORPORATION
24 Scitico Rd (06071)
PHONE..................................800 788-1984
EMP: 6
SALES (est): 427.3K **Privately Held**
SIC: 3089 Injection molding of plastics

(G-7657)
EQUESTRIAN COLLECTION
62 South Rd (06071-2157)
P.O. Box 232 (06071-0232)
PHONE..................................860 749-2964
Judy H Cox, *Owner*
EMP: 1 **EST:** 1997
SALES (est): 57.6K **Privately Held**
SIC: 5699 3199 Miscellaneous apparel & accessories; equestrian related leather articles

(G-7658)
FILTER FAB INC
Also Called: Filter Fabrication
23b Eleanor Rd (06071-1632)
PHONE..................................860 749-6381
David Marini, *President*
Catherine Marini, *Vice Pres*
EMP: 5 **EST:** 1992
SALES (est): 275K **Privately Held**
SIC: 3599 Air intake filters, internal combustion engine, except auto

(G-7659)
FOREST REMODELING
122 Hampden Rd (06071-1270)
PHONE..................................413 222-7953
Edward J Forest, *Owner*
EMP: 5
SALES (est): 500K **Privately Held**
SIC: 2434 Wood kitchen cabinets

(G-7660)
FRONTLINE SCREEN PRINTING & EM
19 Bradfield Dr (06071-1623)
PHONE..................................860 749-0232
Brian Carra, *Partner*
EMP: 2
SALES (est): 200.8K **Privately Held**
SIC: 2759 Screen printing

(G-7661)
HORSE RIDGE CELLARS LLC (PA)
11 South Rd (06071-2109)
P.O. Box 52 (06071-0052)
PHONE..................................860 763-5380
Jed Benedict,
▲ **EMP:** 2 **EST:** 1999
SALES (est): 543K **Privately Held**
WEB: www.horseridgecellars.com
SIC: 2084 Wine cellars, bonded: engaged in blending wines

(G-7662)
JENNINGS ASSOCIATES INC
541 Main St (06071-2009)
PHONE..................................860 749-4281
William F Blythe Jr, *President*
Philip W Shuman, *Director*
EMP: 2 **EST:** 1937
SQ FT: 1,600
SALES (est): 100K **Privately Held**
SIC: 3469 Metal stampings

(G-7663)
JOHN CUTTER
14 Olmsted Manor Dr (06071-2116)
PHONE..................................860 749-0015
John Cutter, *Principal*
EMP: 1
SALES (est): 90.7K **Privately Held**
SIC: 1389 Construction, repair & dismantling services

(G-7664)
KULAS SYSTEMS INC
64 Field Rd Ste 2d (06071-2043)
PHONE..................................860 749-6645
William Kulas, *President*
Kerry Victoria Kulas, *Director*
EMP: 2
SQ FT: 1,600
SALES (est): 323.5K **Privately Held**
SIC: 3823 Thermocouples, industrial process type

(G-7665)
NARRAGANSETT YACHT SERVIC
200 Battle St (06071-1645)
PHONE..................................860 763-1980
Bud Wagner, *Owner*
EMP: 2
SALES (est): 157.9K **Privately Held**
SIC: 3732 Boat building & repairing

(G-7666)
OLIVE SABOR OIL CO
22 Brookford Rd (06071-1253)
PHONE..................................860 922-7483
Luis Valentin, *Principal*
EMP: 3
SALES (est): 91.3K **Privately Held**
SIC: 2079 Olive oil

(G-7667)
PARKER SEPTIC SERVICE
Also Called: Parker Saw Mill
77 South Rd (06071-2109)
PHONE..................................860 749-8220
Perlin A Parker Jr, *Partner*
Susan Parker, *Partner*
EMP: 17
SALES (est): 805.3K **Privately Held**
SIC: 7699 2421 Septic tank cleaning service; sawmills & planing mills, general

(G-7668)
POP MOODY WELDING SERVICES
712 Stafford Rd (06071-1314)
PHONE..................................860 749-9537
David E Moody, *Owner*
EMP: 1
SALES (est): 76.5K **Privately Held**
SIC: 1799 7692 Welding on site; welding repair

(G-7669)
SOAPSTONE MEDIA INC
Also Called: Mvp Visuals
27 Quality Ave Ste B (06071-1840)
PHONE..................................860 749-0455
Benjamin Camerota, *President*
Theresa Camerota, *Principal*
EMP: 3 **EST:** 2012
SALES (est): 317.1K **Privately Held**
SIC: 5131 2399 5999 2394 Flags & banners; banners, pennants & flags; banners, flags, decals & posters; canopies, fabric: made from purchased materials

(G-7670)
SOMERS MUSIC PUBLICATIONS
45 Kibbe Dr (06071-2111)
PHONE..................................860 763-0366
EMP: 1
SALES (est): 52K **Privately Held**
SIC: 2741 Misc Publishing

(G-7671)
STAFFORD PAPER COMPANY
34 Egypt Rd Ste D (06071-2023)
P.O. Box 174 (06071-0174)
PHONE..................................860 749-0787
Frank Caponera, *Partner*
Mary Ann Caponera, *Partner*
EMP: 2
SQ FT: 5,000
SALES (est): 300K **Privately Held**
SIC: 2679 Paper products, converted

(G-7672)
STAR STEEL STRUCTURES INC
392 Four Bridges Rd (06071-1107)
P.O. Box 535 (06071-0535)
PHONE..................................860 763-5681
Kurt Knoefel, *President*
Karl Milikowski, *Chairman*
Mark Milikowski, *Corp Secy*
Neal Farnham, *Vice Pres*
EMP: 9
SQ FT: 9,000
SALES (est): 1.2MM **Privately Held**
SIC: 3448 Greenhouses: prefabricated metal

(G-7673)
STS MOTORSPORTS GRAPHICS
16 Egypt Rd (06071-2023)
PHONE..................................860 698-6697
EMP: 2
SALES (est): 73.2K **Privately Held**
SIC: 2759 Commercial printing

(G-7674)
TOMMYS SUPPLIES LLC
34 Egypt Rd Unit A (06071-2023)
PHONE..................................860 265-2199
Tommy Ringwalt,
▲ **EMP:** 3
SALES (est): 354.2K **Privately Held**
SIC: 5999 5094 2389 Toiletries, cosmetics & perfumes; jewelry; apparel for handicapped

(G-7675)
VORTEX MANUFACTURING
60 Sunshine Farms Dr (06071-2028)
PHONE..................................860 749-9769
George Gergely, *Owner*
EMP: 3
SQ FT: 4,000
SALES (est): 250K **Privately Held**
SIC: 3599 Custom machinery

(G-7676)
WAKEEN GALLERY
128 Parker Rd (06071-2221)
PHONE..................................860 763-4565
Sandra Wakeen, *Owner*
EMP: 1
SALES (est): 58.3K **Privately Held**
SIC: 2741 Business service newsletters: publishing & printing

(G-7677)
WINK INK LLC
Also Called: Sue's Shirt Creations
154 Main St (06071)
PHONE..................................860 202-8709
Michelle Wink, *Manager*
Chad Wink,
Susan Janssen,
EMP: 4 **EST:** 2016
SQ FT: 1,700
SALES (est): 343K **Privately Held**
SIC: 2759 Commercial printing; promotional printing; imprinting; screen printing

Somersville
Tolland County

(G-7678)
CARBON PRODUCTS INC
40 Scitico Rd (06072)
P.O. Box N (06072-0914)
PHONE................................860 749-0614
Peter Ouellet, *President*
◆ **EMP:** 9
SQ FT: 18,000
SALES (est): 1.2MM **Privately Held**
SIC: 3624 Carbon & graphite products

South Glastonbury
Hartford County

(G-7679)
AUTOMATED GRAPHIC SYSTEMS INC
287 Great Pond Rd (06073-3106)
PHONE................................860 659-1076
EMP: 2 **EST:** 1975
SALES (est): 97K **Privately Held**
SIC: 2759 Commercial Printing

(G-7680)
FUNDRSING WITH CNDLE FNDRISERS
97 Overshot Dr (06073-2231)
PHONE................................860 384-3691
EMP: 1 **EST:** 2017
SALES (est): 39.6K **Privately Held**
SIC: 3999 Candles

(G-7681)
O W HEAT TREAT INC
77 Great Pond Rd (06073-3104)
PHONE................................860 430-6709
EMP: 4 **EST:** 2016
SALES (est): 347.5K **Privately Held**
SIC: 3398 Metal heat treating

(G-7682)
RIVER VALLEY PHOTOGRAPHIC LLC
Also Called: Eric Lindquist Photography
908 Main St 2ff (06073-2229)
PHONE................................860 368-0882
Eric Lindquist, *Owner*
EMP: 1
SALES (est): 73.1K **Privately Held**
SIC: 7335 3861 7221 Commercial photography; photographic studio, commercial; photographic equipment & supplies; home photographer

South Kent
Litchfield County

(G-7683)
BOOMERANG CONSIGNMENT
90 S Kent Rd (06785-1112)
PHONE................................203 788-9002
Kathleen Lee, *Manager*
EMP: 1
SALES (est): 47K **Privately Held**
SIC: 3949 Boomerangs

(G-7684)
PAUL RAMEE LLC
71 Bulls Bridge Rd (06785-1120)
PHONE................................860 927-7135
Paul Ramee, *Mng Member*
EMP: 1
SALES (est): 326.7K **Privately Held**
SIC: 3949 Shafts, golf club

South Lyme
New London County

(G-7685)
R L PRITCHARD & CO INC
1 North Rd (06376)
PHONE................................203 393-0260
Susan Paisley, *President*
EMP: 1
SALES (est): 47.2K **Privately Held**
SIC: 2824 Organic fibers, noncellulosic

(G-7686)
TS WHITMAN CUSTOM WDWKG LLC
389 Shore Rd (06376-9992)
PHONE................................860 575-1923
Thomas S Whitman III, *Administration*
EMP: 1 **EST:** 2017
SALES (est): 58.5K **Privately Held**
SIC: 2431 Millwork

South Windham
Windham County

(G-7687)
HARWEST HOLDINGS ONE INC
1102 Windham Rd (06266)
P.O. Box 96 (06266-0096)
PHONE................................860 423-8334
Robert Mongell, *President*
Anthony Williams, *Chairman*
Joseph Loffredo, *Vice Pres*
Catherine Salemma, *Sales Mgr*
Stuart Alexander, *CTO*
EMP: 35
SALES (est): 3.8MM **Privately Held**
SIC: 3599 Machine shop, jobbing & repair

(G-7688)
IVES WELDING SERVICE
299 Old S Windham Rd (06266)
P.O. Box 14 (06266-0014)
PHONE................................860 423-6139
Richard Ives, *Owner*
EMP: 1
SALES (est): 59K **Privately Held**
SIC: 7692 7699 Welding repair; welding equipment repair

(G-7689)
JANES NORMAN & JACQUELINE MACH
74 Machine Shop Hill Rd (06266-1118)
PHONE................................860 423-1932
Norman Janes, *Principal*
Jacqueline Janes, *Bd of Directors*
EMP: 2
SALES (est): 154.8K **Privately Held**
SIC: 3599 Machine shop, jobbing & repair

(G-7690)
MICRO PRECISION LLC
1102 Windham Rd (06266)
P.O. Box 96 (06266-0096)
PHONE................................860 423-4575
Robert Mongell,
John Desrosier,
Hadley Mongell,
EMP: 29
SALES (est): 6.2MM **Privately Held**
SIC: 3599 Machine shop, jobbing & repair

(G-7691)
MITERED EDGE WOODWORKING
186 Babcock Hill Rd (06266-1104)
PHONE................................860 576-6657
Stephen Gallen, *Principal*
EMP: 1
SALES (est): 58.2K **Privately Held**
SIC: 2431 Millwork

(G-7692)
NATHAN AIRCHIME INC
1102 Windham Rd (06266)
P.O. Box 96 (06266-0096)
PHONE................................860 423-4575
▲ **EMP:** 8
SALES (est): 1.3MM **Privately Held**
SIC: 3714 Horns, motor vehicle

(G-7693)
WATER & AIR INC (PA)
Also Called: All You Need For Sleep
885 Windham Rd (06266-1132)
P.O. Box 196 (06266-0196)
PHONE................................860 423-0234
Mark Gadarowski, *President*
EMP: 5
SQ FT: 4,500
SALES (est): 959.1K **Privately Held**
WEB: www.allyouneedforsleep.com
SIC: 5712 2515 Mattresses; bedding & bedsprings; waterbeds & accessories; mattresses & foundations

(G-7694)
WENTWORTH MANUFACTURING LLC (PA)
1102 Windham Rd (06266-1131)
P.O. Box 96 (06266-0096)
PHONE................................860 423-4575
Joseph Loffredo,
EMP: 35 **EST:** 1981
SQ FT: 7,000
SALES (est): 19.7MM **Privately Held**
WEB: www.microprecisiongroup.com
SIC: 3599 Machine shop, jobbing & repair

(G-7695)
WINDHAM AUTOMATED MACHINES INC
Also Called: W A M
1102 Windham Rd (06266)
PHONE................................860 208-5297
Christopher H Ramm, *President*
EMP: 19
SALES (est): 2.5MM **Privately Held**
WEB: www.windhamautomated.com
SIC: 3559 Automotive related machinery

South Windsor
Hartford County

(G-7696)
A C T MANUFACTURING LLC
Also Called: Act Manufacturing
55 Glendale Rd (06074-2415)
PHONE................................860 289-8837
Richard Rondinone, *Owner*
EMP: 3
SQ FT: 2,600
SALES (est): 200K **Privately Held**
SIC: 3599 Machine shop, jobbing & repair

(G-7697)
AA INDUSTRIES LLC
223 Nutmeg Rd S (06074-3461)
PHONE................................860 291-8929
Aneudy Alvarez, *President*
John Tracey, *Maintence Staff*
James Ferranti, *Contractor*
Paige Sarazin, *Contractor*
EMP: 2
SALES (est): 248.5K **Privately Held**
SIC: 3999 Manufacturing industries

(G-7698)
ABLE MANUFACTURING CO LLC
381 Governors Hwy Ste A (06074-2517)
PHONE................................860 282-6108
Dyalal Bhut,
EMP: 2
SALES (est): 339.1K **Privately Held**
SIC: 3599 Machine shop, jobbing & repair

(G-7699)
ACCUTURN MFG CO LLC
100 Commerce Way (06074-1151)
PHONE................................860 289-6355
Hasu Viroja,
Sunny Viroja,
EMP: 10
SQ FT: 2,000
SALES (est): 781.8K **Privately Held**
SIC: 3812 Acceleration indicators & systems components, aerospace

(G-7700)
ACIER FAB LLC
105 Edwin Rd (06074-2436)
PHONE................................860 282-1211
Robert Mathiau, *Principal*
EMP: 2
SALES (est): 156.1K **Privately Held**
SIC: 3444 Sheet metalwork

(G-7701)
AERO TUBE TECHNOLOGIES LLC
425 Sullivan Ave Ste 8 (06074-1947)
PHONE................................860 289-2520
Charlie Agreda, *Vice Pres*
Dean Tulamaris,
EMP: 25
SALES (est): 6.2MM **Privately Held**
SIC: 3728 Aircraft parts & equipment

(G-7702)
AERO-MED LTD
571 Nutmeg Rd N (06074-2461)
PHONE................................860 659-2270
Daniel Del Mastro, *Branch Mgr*
EMP: 8
SALES (corp-wide): 145.5B **Publicly Held**
SIC: 3843 Dental equipment & supplies
HQ: Aero-Med, Ltd.
85 Commerce St
Glastonbury CT 06033
860 659-0602

(G-7703)
AIR CRUISERS CO
45 S Satellite Rd Ste 2 (06074-5407)
PHONE................................732 681-3527
E Dehaas, *Finance*
EMP: 2
SALES (est): 93.3K **Privately Held**
SIC: 2531 Public building & related furniture

(G-7704)
ALLIED METAL FINISHING L L C
379 Chapel Rd (06074-4104)
P.O. Box 26 (06074-0026)
PHONE................................860 290-8865
Joseph A Toce, *Mng Member*
EMP: 8
SALES (est): 1MM **Privately Held**
WEB: www.alliedmetalfinishing.com
SIC: 3471 Finishing, metals or formed products

(G-7705)
AMERICAN DESIGN & MFG INC
145 Commerce Way (06074-1152)
PHONE................................860 282-2719
Adam Vyskocil, *Principal*
Daniel Lessard, *Vice Pres*
Daniel W Jordan, *Vice Pres*
EMP: 35
SQ FT: 33,000
SALES (est): 13.1MM **Privately Held**
WEB: www.americandes-mfg.com
SIC: 3829 3724 Testers for checking hydraulic controls on aircraft; aircraft engines & engine parts; lubricating systems, aircraft

(G-7706)
AMERICAN METALLIZING
401 Governors Hwy (06074-2510)
PHONE................................860 289-1677
Paul Oliva, *CEO*
EMP: 3
SALES (est): 341.7K **Privately Held**
WEB: www.americanmetallizing.com
SIC: 3479 3599 Coating of metals & formed products; industrial machinery

(G-7707)
AMK WELDING INC (HQ)
Also Called: Amk Technical Services
283 Sullivan Ave (06074-1914)
PHONE................................860 289-5634
Daniel R Godin, *President*
Joan Silvestri, *Info Tech Mgr*
EMP: 29 **EST:** 2009

South Windsor - Hartford County (G-7708)   GEOGRAPHIC SECTION

SALES (est): 3.8MM
SALES (corp-wide): 368.4MM **Privately Held**
SIC: **7692** 3398 7699 Welding repair; metal heat treating; aviation propeller & blade repair
PA: Meyer Tool, Inc.
3055 Colerain Ave
Cincinnati OH 45225
513 681-7362

(G-7708)
AMOUN PITA & DISTRIBUTION LLC
Also Called: Amoun Bakery & Distribution
361 Pleasant Valley Rd (06074-3427)
PHONE..................................866 239-9990
Mohsen Youssef, *President*
EMP: 39
SQ FT: 9,000
SALES (est): 1.6MM **Privately Held**
SIC: **5461** 2051 Bread; bread, cake & related products

(G-7709)
ANDRE FURNITURE INDUSTRIES
55 Sandra Dr Ste 1 (06074-1039)
PHONE..................................860 528-8826
Andre K Charbonneau, *Owner*
EMP: 8
SQ FT: 12,000
SALES: 800K **Privately Held**
SIC: **2511** Wood household furniture

(G-7710)
APPLIED SOFTWARE
905 Main St (06074-3322)
PHONE..................................860 289-9153
David Singer, *Owner*
Charisse Smith, *Vice Pres*
David Nater, *Accountant*
Mark Martinez, *Technical Staff*
EMP: 2
SALES (est): 120K **Privately Held**
WEB: www.keystoneauctions.com
SIC: **7372** Prepackaged software

(G-7711)
ATI LADISH MACHINING INC
Also Called: Aerex Manufacturing
34 S Satellite Rd (06074-3445)
PHONE..................................860 688-3688
Richard Cleary, *Branch Mgr*
EMP: 95 **Publicly Held**
SIC: **3724** Aircraft engines & engine parts
HQ: Ati Ladish Machining, Inc.
311 Prestige Park Rd
East Hartford CT 06108
860 688-3688

(G-7712)
ATLANTIC FABRICATING CO INC
71 Edwin Rd (06074-2476)
P.O. Box 433 (06074-0433)
PHONE..................................860 291-9882
William S Johnson, *President*
Susan Johnson, *Admin Sec*
EMP: 10
SQ FT: 7,500
SALES (est): 1.5MM **Privately Held**
WEB: www.atlfab.com
SIC: **3441** Fabricated structural metal

(G-7713)
ATLAS METAL WORKS LLC
48 Commerce Way (06074-1151)
PHONE..................................860 282-1030
Peter Saxon, *Opers Mgr*
Shaun Miller, *Prdtn Mgr*
Gary Allard, *Mng Member*
Dennis Larose,
EMP: 12
SALES: 1.9MM **Privately Held**
WEB: www.atlasmetalworksllc.com
SIC: **3441** Fabricated structural metal

(G-7714)
ATLAS PRECISION MFG LLC
508 Burnham St (06074-4102)
PHONE..................................860 290-9114
Waclaw Dybinski, *Mng Member*
EMP: 25
SQ FT: 20,000
SALES (est): 3MM **Privately Held**
SIC: **3599** Machine shop, jobbing & repair

(G-7715)
AXOL MEDIA INC
1502 Mill Pond Dr (06074-3552)
PHONE..................................650 315-1743
Christian Baer, *President*
EMP: 1
SALES (est): 37.5K **Privately Held**
SIC: **2741**

(G-7716)
BACKYARD CANDLES LLC
116 Debbie Dr (06074-1817)
PHONE..................................860 644-9561
Justin Healy, *Owner*
EMP: 2
SALES (est): 62.5K **Privately Held**
SIC: **3999** Candles

(G-7717)
BARKER STEEL LLC
30 Talbot Ln (06074-5401)
PHONE..................................860 282-1860
Raymond Kandolin, *Branch Mgr*
EMP: 30
SALES (corp-wide): 25B **Publicly Held**
WEB: www.barker.com
SIC: **3449** 5085 Bars, concrete reinforcing; fabricated steel; industrial supplies
HQ: Barker Steel Llc
55 Sumner St Ste 1
Milford MA 01757
800 363-3953

(G-7718)
BLASTING TECHNIQUES INC
350 Chapel Rd Ste A2 (06074-4181)
PHONE..................................860 528-4717
Adella Fiori, *President*
Martin Fiori, *Admin Sec*
EMP: 5
SQ FT: 4,400
SALES (est): 639.3K **Privately Held**
WEB: www.blastingtechniques.com
SIC: **1799** 3398 3471 Sandblasting of building exteriors; shot peening (treating steel to reduce fatigue); cleaning, polishing & finishing

(G-7719)
BODYCOTE THERMAL PROC INC
45 Connecticut Ave (06074-3475)
PHONE..................................860 282-1371
Mike Sakelakos, *Branch Mgr*
EMP: 40
SALES (corp-wide): 935.8MM **Privately Held**
SIC: **3398** Brazing (hardening) of metal
HQ: Bodycote Thermal Processing, Inc.
12700 Park Central Dr # 700
Dallas TX 75251
214 904-2420

(G-7720)
C & T PRINT FINISHING INC
67 Commerce Way (06074-1152)
PHONE..................................860 282-0616
Jeffrey Cole, *President*
Mary Ann Cole, *Treasurer*
EMP: 10
SQ FT: 9,500
SALES (est): 4.9MM **Privately Held**
WEB: www.ctpf.com
SIC: **2675** Paper die-cutting

(G-7721)
C MATHER COMPANY INC
Also Called: Mathertops
339 Chapel Rd (06074-4104)
PHONE..................................860 528-5667
Thomas Mather, *President*
James Fromerth, *Vice Pres*
Clayton D Mather, *Shareholder*
Richard Mather, *Admin Sec*
EMP: 9
SQ FT: 10,000
SALES (est): 1.3MM **Privately Held**
WEB: www.mathertops.com
SIC: **2542** 2821 2541 Counters or counter display cases: except wood; plastics materials & resins; wood partitions & fixtures

(G-7722)
CAPEWELL AERIAL SYSTEMS LLC (PA)
105 Nutmeg Rd S (06074-5400)
PHONE..................................860 610-0700
Marie McCoy, *Human Res Mgr*
Richard Wheeler, *Mng Member*
▲ EMP: 100
SALES (est): 45.4MM **Privately Held**
SIC: **3531** Aerial work platforms: hydraulic/elec. truck/carrier mounted

(G-7723)
CAPSTONE MANUFACTURING INC
1257 John Fitch Blvd 2 (06074-2431)
PHONE..................................413 636-6170
Rebecca L Work, *CEO*
Mark Work, *President*
EMP: 2
SALES (est): 140K **Privately Held**
SIC: **3489** 3482 3761 3724 Ordnance & accessories; small arms ammunition; guided missiles & space vehicles; turbines, aircraft type; casings, sheet metal

(G-7724)
CARL ASSOCIATES INC
1257 John Fitch Blvd 3 (06074-2431)
PHONE..................................860 749-7620
Susan Carl, *President*
EMP: 4
SALES (est): 516K **Privately Held**
WEB: www.carl-associates.com
SIC: **3599** Machine shop, jobbing & repair

(G-7725)
CARL RIZZO & ASSOCIATES
68 Mark Dr (06074-1435)
PHONE..................................860 644-5849
Mark Rizzo, *Owner*
EMP: 1
SALES (est): 55K **Privately Held**
SIC: **3999** Manufacturing industries

(G-7726)
CARLAS PASTA INC
50 Talbot Ln (06074-5401)
PHONE..................................860 436-4042
Carla Squatrito, *President*
Keith Branham, *Regional Mgr*
John Koch, *Regional Mgr*
Dawn Iannacone, *Business Mgr*
Sandro Squatrito, *Vice Pres*
▲ EMP: 145
SQ FT: 13,000
SALES: 72MM **Privately Held**
WEB: www.carlaspasta.com
SIC: **2098** Macaroni & spaghetti

(G-7727)
CENTRAL CONN COOPERATIVE FARME
1050 Sullivan Ave Ste A3 (06074-2000)
P.O. Box 8500 (06074)
PHONE..................................860 649-4523
Daniel Logue, *President*
Arthur Guzman, *President*
Donald Domina, *General Mgr*
Walter Bradway, *Vice Pres*
Morris Stollman, *Vice Pres*
EMP: 40
SQ FT: 35,000
SALES (est): 19.1MM **Privately Held**
WEB: www.cccfeeds.com
SIC: **5191** 5153 2041 Feed; grains; flour & other grain mill products

(G-7728)
CHALLENGE SAILCLOTH
560 Nutmeg Rd N (06074-2458)
PHONE..................................860 871-8030
Bob Bainbridge, *President*
EMP: 2
SALES (est): 131.7K **Privately Held**
SIC: **5131** 2221 Piece goods & other fabrics; broadwoven fabric mills, manmade

(G-7729)
CLEARLY CLEAN PRODUCTS LLC (PA)
225 Oakland Rd Ste 401 (06074-2896)
PHONE..................................860 646-1040
Gary D Colby, *General Counsel*
Jeffrey Maguire,
EMP: 17
SALES (est): 8.7MM **Privately Held**
WEB: www.peelatray.com
SIC: **3089** Plastic containers, except foam

(G-7730)
COBURN TECHNOLOGIES
83 Gerber Rd W (06074-3230)
PHONE..................................800 262-8761
EMP: 2
SALES (est): 104.2K **Privately Held**
SIC: **3827** Optical instruments & lenses

(G-7731)
COBURN TECHNOLOGIES INC (PA)
83 Gerber Rd W (06074-3230)
PHONE..................................860 648-6600
Edward G Jepsen, *CEO*
Michael Dolen, *Vice Pres*
Mike Dolen, *Vice Pres*
Wayne Labrecque, *Vice Pres*
Jared Selley, *Mfg Spvr*
◆ EMP: 141
SALES (est): 48MM **Privately Held**
SIC: **3851** 3827 Ophthalmic goods; optical instruments & lenses

(G-7732)
COBURN TECHNOLOGIES INTL INC (HQ)
55 Gerber Rd E (06074-3244)
PHONE..................................860 648-6600
Edward G Jepsen, *CEO*
Alex Incera, *President*
Mike Dolen, *Vice Pres*
Wayne Labrecque, *Vice Pres*
EMP: 4
SQ FT: 65,000
SALES: 37MM **Privately Held**
SIC: **5049** 3827 7699 Optical goods; optical instruments & lenses; optical instrument repair

(G-7733)
COBURN TECNOLOGIES CANADA
55 Gerber Rd E (06074-3244)
PHONE..................................860 648-6710
EMP: 96
SALES (est): 324.8K **Privately Held**
SIC: **5049** 7699 3827 Whol Professional Equipment Repair Services Mfg Optical Instruments/Lenses
HQ: Coburn Technologies International, Inc.
55 Gerber Rd E
South Windsor CT 06074

(G-7734)
COMPETITIVE EDGE COATINGS LLC
185 Nutmeg Rd S (06074-3461)
PHONE..................................860 882-0762
Damon Schuster,
Christopher Scutnik,
EMP: 3
SQ FT: 5,000
SALES (est): 263.9K **Privately Held**
SIC: **3479** Coating of metals & formed products

(G-7735)
CONNECTICUT PLASMA TECH LLC
273 Chapel Rd (06074-4104)
P.O. Box 58 (06074-0058)
PHONE..................................860 289-5500
James J Jasmin, *Mng Member*
Robert Lempicki, *Mng Member*
EMP: 13
SALES (est): 1.2MM **Privately Held**
SIC: **3479** Coating of metals & formed products

(G-7736)
CR FABRICATION LLC
10 Thomas St (06074-1514)
PHONE..................................860 377-1629
Christopher Radkovitch, *Principal*
EMP: 2 EST: 2012
SALES (est): 149.4K **Privately Held**
SIC: **3499** Novelties & giftware, including trophies

GEOGRAPHIC SECTION

South Windsor - Hartford County (G-7764)

(G-7737)
CRAMER COMPANY
105 Nutmeg Rd S (06074-5400)
PHONE..................860 291-8402
Kenneth Mac Cormac, *President*
EMP: 5
SALES (est): 374.6K **Privately Held**
SIC: 3621 Motors & generators

(G-7738)
CT COMPOSITES & MARINE SVC LLC
620 Sullivan Ave (06074-1919)
PHONE..................860 282-0100
Tom Krivickas,
EMP: 8
SALES (est): 473.4K **Privately Held**
SIC: 3083 Laminated plastics plate & sheet

(G-7739)
DOOSAN FUEL CELL AMERICA INC (HQ)
195 Governors Hwy (06074-2419)
PHONE..................860 727-2200
Jeff Hyungrak Chung, *President*
Chankyo Chung, *General Mgr*
Michael Coskun, *General Mgr*
Minchul Kim, *Corp Secy*
Tiffany Eisenbise, *Counsel*
◆ EMP: 150
SQ FT: 238,711
SALES (est): 57.1MM **Privately Held**
SIC: 3674 7629 Fuel cells, solid state; electronic equipment repair

(G-7740)
DST OUTPUT EAST LLC (DH)
125 Ellington Rd (06074-4112)
PHONE..................816 221-1234
Steven J Towle, *CEO*
Tebbetts Al, *Opers Staff*
Jasmin Hrnjic, *Production*
Michael Ponting, *Financial Analy*
Dave Knybel, *Manager*
EMP: 20
SQ FT: 30,000
SALES (est): 8.1MM
SALES (corp-wide): 4.3B **Publicly Held**
WEB: www.output.net
SIC: 2759 Laser printing

(G-7741)
DYCO INDUSTRIES INC
229 S Satellite Rd (06074-3474)
PHONE..................860 289-4957
David Dyke, *President*
Barbara Dyke, *Senior VP*
Chris Van Dyke, *Vice Pres*
Paul Socolosky, *Opers Mgr*
Kaylin S Dyke, *Admin Sec*
EMP: 30
SQ FT: 24,000
SALES (est): 6.7MM **Privately Held**
SIC: 3446 7692 3444 Architectural metalwork; welding repair; sheet metalwork

(G-7742)
EAGLE TISSUE LLC
70 Bidwell Rd (06074-2412)
PHONE..................860 282-2535
Robert E Costa, *President*
Dan Sforza, *Vice Pres*
Richard Costa,
Teresa Costa,
▲ EMP: 14
SQ FT: 21,000
SALES (est): 3.5MM **Privately Held**
WEB: www.eagletissue.com
SIC: 2679 Wrappers, paper (unprinted): made from purchased material

(G-7743)
EAST COAST PRECISION GRINDING
259 Sullivan Ave Ste D (06074-1921)
PHONE..................860 289-1010
EMP: 2 EST: 2011
SALES (est): 110K **Privately Held**
SIC: 3599 Mfg Industrial Machinery

(G-7744)
EAST COAST STAIRS CO INC
125 Bidwell Rd (06074-2443)
PHONE..................860 528-7096
Richard Hall, *President*
EMP: 6
SALES (est): 1.8MM **Privately Held**
SIC: 2431 Staircases & stairs, wood

(G-7745)
EAST WINDSOR METAL FABG INC
91 Glendale Rd (06074-2415)
P.O. Box 357, East Windsor Hill (06028-0357)
PHONE..................860 528-7107
Peter Hughes, *President*
Mary Ellen Brennan, *Vice Pres*
James Hughes, *Vice Pres*
Josephine Hughes, *Admin Sec*
EMP: 11
SQ FT: 20,000
SALES (est): 1MM **Privately Held**
WEB: www.eastwindsor-ct.gov
SIC: 3444 7692 3446 3441 Metal housings, enclosures, casings & other containers; welding repair; architectural metalwork; fabricated structural metal

(G-7746)
EASTERN TRUCK & MACHINE LLC
23 Barbara Rd (06074-3403)
PHONE..................860 528-0258
Adam Randazzo, *Principal*
EMP: 2
SALES (est): 98.6K **Privately Held**
SIC: 3599 Industrial machinery

(G-7747)
ELECTRO-METHODS INC (PA)
330 Governors Hwy (06074-2422)
P.O. Box 54 (06074-0054)
PHONE..................860 289-8661
Randall Fries, *President*
William W Soucy, *Vice Pres*
Dani Stephens, *Vice Pres*
William Soucy, *VP Mfg*
Jeff Paradis, *Foreman/Supr*
EMP: 121 EST: 1965
SQ FT: 101,000
SALES (est): 40.6MM **Privately Held**
WEB: www.electro-methods.com
SIC: 3724 7629 3728 3829 Aircraft engines & engine parts; aircraft electrical equipment repair; panel assembly (hydromatic propeller test stands), aircraft; testing equipment: abrasion, shearing strength, etc.; search & navigation equipment

(G-7748)
ELECTRO-METHODS INC
525 Nutmeg Rd N (06074-2461)
P.O. Box 54 (06074-0054)
PHONE..................860 289-8661
Randall Fries, *Branch Mgr*
EMP: 79
SALES (corp-wide): 40.6MM **Privately Held**
WEB: www.electro-methods.com
SIC: 3724 Aircraft engines & engine parts
PA: Electro-Methods, Inc.
330 Governors Hwy
South Windsor CT 06074
860 289-8661

(G-7749)
ENCORE OPTICS
140 Commerce Way (06074-1151)
PHONE..................860 282-0082
Paul Zito, *Owner*
▲ EMP: 15
SALES (est): 2.2MM **Privately Held**
SIC: 3851 Eyeglasses, lenses & frames

(G-7750)
ENGINEERING SERVICES & PDTS CO (PA)
Also Called: Clearspan
1395 John Fitch Blvd (06074-1029)
PHONE..................860 528-1119
Barry Goldsher, *President*
Charles R Clark Jr, *Corp Secy*
Matthew K Niaura, *Vice Pres*
Matthew Niaura, *Vice Pres*
Tania Tomoroga, *Creative Dir*
◆ EMP: 88
SQ FT: 51,281
SALES (est): 73.6MM **Privately Held**
WEB: www.esapco.com
SIC: 3523 5083 3081 Dairy equipment (farm); hog feeding, handling & watering equipment; poultry brooders, feeders & waterers; poultry equipment; agricultural machinery; polyethylene film

(G-7751)
ESTEEM MANUFACTURING CORP
175 S Satellite Rd (06074-3474)
PHONE..................860 282-9964
David Kostyk, *President*
Shawn Dietz, *Vice Pres*
Keith Maciolek, *QA Dir*
Joel Newcomb, *Director*
Suzanne Kostyk, *Admin Sec*
EMP: 35
SQ FT: 10,000
SALES (est): 6.5MM **Privately Held**
WEB: www.esteemmfg.com
SIC: 3599 Machine shop, jobbing & repair

(G-7752)
ETHICAL SOLUTIONS LLC
Also Called: Ethicalchem
177 Governors Hwy (06074-2419)
PHONE..................860 490-8124
Charles B Shephard,
Jean Edward Shephard III,
EMP: 2
SALES (est): 160.4K **Privately Held**
SIC: 2865 2869 5169 Chemical indicators; industrial organic chemicals; adhesives, chemical

(G-7753)
EVOAERO INC
425 Sullivan Ave Ste 5 (06074-1947)
PHONE..................860 289-2520
Pedro J Agreda, *President*
Victoria Salas, *Info Tech Mgr*
Juan C Agreda, *Admin Sec*
EMP: 65
SALES (est): 19MM **Privately Held**
WEB: www.candpmachine.com
SIC: 3728 Aircraft parts & equipment

(G-7754)
EVOQUA WATER TECHNOLOGIES LLC
88 Nutmeg Rd S (06074-3469)
PHONE..................860 528-6512
Robert Rohan, *Manager*
EMP: 26
SALES (corp-wide): 1.3B **Publicly Held**
SIC: 3589 Water filters & softeners, household type
HQ: Evoqua Water Technologies Llc
210 6th Ave Ste 3300
Pittsburgh PA 15222
724 772-0044

(G-7755)
EXPERIMENTAL PROTOTYPE PDTS CO
248 Chapel Rd (06074-4103)
PHONE..................860 289-4948
Robert H Ainsworth Jr, *President*
William Ainsworth Sr, *Vice Pres*
Robert Ainsworth Sr, *Admin Sec*
EMP: 10
SQ FT: 2,500
SALES (est): 1.7MM **Privately Held**
SIC: 3599 Machine shop, jobbing & repair

(G-7756)
FIBRE OPTIC PLUS INC
585 Nutmeg Rd N (06074-2461)
PHONE..................860 646-3581
Donald E Ballsieper, *President*
Sylvia Ballsieper, *Vice Pres*
Greg Brown, *Manager*
EMP: 13
SQ FT: 2,400
SALES (est): 3.2MM **Privately Held**
WEB: www.fibreopticplus.com
SIC: 3661 Fiber optics communications equipment

(G-7757)
GENERAL SEATING SOLUTIONS LLC
45 S Satellite Rd Ste 5 (06074-5407)
PHONE..................860 242-3307
Anthony Nash,
Antonio Medina,
EMP: 10
SALES (est): 1.1MM **Privately Held**
WEB: www.generalseatingsolutions.com
SIC: 2599 7641 Restaurant furniture, wood or metal; bar furniture; hotel furniture; reupholstery

(G-7758)
GERBER COBURN OPTICAL INC (HQ)
55 Gerber Rd E (06074-3244)
PHONE..................800 843-1479
Alex Incera, *President*
Wayne Labrecque, *Vice Pres*
Mitzi Blayton, *Finance Mgr*
◆ EMP: 120
SQ FT: 60,000
SALES (est): 11MM **Privately Held**
SIC: 3851 3827 Ophthalmic goods; optical instruments & lenses

(G-7759)
GHEZZI ENTERPRISES INC
Also Called: G-Force Signs & Graphics
52 Connecticut Ave Ste B (06074-3429)
PHONE..................860 787-5338
Gregory Ghezzi, *CEO*
EMP: 2
SALES (est): 79.8K **Privately Held**
SIC: 3993 Signs & advertising specialties

(G-7760)
GLOBAL TRBINE CMPNENT TECH LLC
125 S Satellite Rd (06074-3474)
PHONE..................860 528-4722
William W Baker, *Opers Staff*
Brian Fielding, *QC Mgr*
Edmund Autuori, *Executive*
Carla Diniz, *Executive*
EMP: 35
SQ FT: 20,000
SALES (est): 6.6MM **Privately Held**
WEB: www.globalturbine.com
SIC: 3728 3724 Aircraft parts & equipment; aircraft engines & engine parts

(G-7761)
GNB WOODWORKING LLC
381 Governors Hwy (06074-2517)
PHONE..................860 282-0595
EMP: 1
SALES (est): 80K **Privately Held**
SIC: 2431 Mfg Millwork

(G-7762)
GOLDPOINT PUBLISHING LLC
258 Lefoll Blvd (06074-4262)
PHONE..................860 432-8934
Stephen Raiken, *Principal*
EMP: 2
SALES (est): 60.1K **Privately Held**
SIC: 2741 Miscellaneous publishing

(G-7763)
GOLIK MACHINE CO
154 Commerce Way (06074-1151)
PHONE..................860 610-0095
Chris Golik, *Owner*
EMP: 4
SQ FT: 2,000
SALES (est): 750K **Privately Held**
SIC: 3599 Machine shop, jobbing & repair

(G-7764)
GRANITE & KITCHEN STUDIO LLC
313 Pleasant Valley Rd (06074-5411)
PHONE..................860 290-4444
Ahmed Eldirany, *Mng Member*
▲ EMP: 5 EST: 2012
SQ FT: 8,000
SALES (est): 542.7K **Privately Held**
SIC: 3281 Curbing, granite or stone

South Windsor - Hartford County (G-7765) — GEOGRAPHIC SECTION

(G-7765)
GREEN TOMATILLO LLC
935 Sullivan Pl Ctr (06074)
PHONE 860 749-0172
Ruben Huerta,
EMP: 2
SALES (est): 82.1K **Privately Held**
SIC: 2066 Chocolate liquor

(G-7766)
H & B TOOL & ENGINEERING CO
481 Sullivan Ave (06074-1942)
P.O. Box 717 (06074-0717)
PHONE 860 528-9341
Michael Gennelli, *Ch of Bd*
Janice Proll, *President*
Bob Dionizio, *Managing Dir*
Michael Giannelli, *Vice Pres*
Darlene Parker, *Purch Mgr*
EMP: 50 EST: 1960
SQ FT: 33,000
SALES (est): 8.6MM **Privately Held**
SIC: 3599 3823 3728 3545 Machine shop, jobbing & repair; industrial instrmnts msrmnt display/control process variable; aircraft parts & equipment; machine tool accessories

(G-7767)
HANCOCK LOGGING & FORESTRY MGT
Also Called: Stovewood Acres
147 Foster Rd (06074-2530)
PHONE 860 289-5647
Philip Hancock, *Owner*
EMP: 2
SALES (est): 250K **Privately Held**
SIC: 2411 4212 5989 Logging camps & contractors; lumber (log) trucking, local; wood (fuel)

(G-7768)
HERMAN SCHMIDT PRECISION WORKH
26 Sea Pave Rd (06074-4155)
PHONE 860 289-3347
Thomas Duff III, *President*
EMP: 8
SALES (est): 351.8K **Privately Held**
SIC: 3544 Special dies, tools, jigs & fixtures

(G-7769)
HERMANN SCHMIDT COMPANY INC
26 Sea Pave Rd (06074-4155)
PHONE 860 289-3347
Peter Schmidt, *President*
EMP: 10
SALES (est): 1.5MM **Privately Held**
SIC: 3545 Precision measuring tools

(G-7770)
HEXCEL CORPORATION
250 Nutmeg Rd S (06074-3498)
PHONE 925 520-3232
Jason Eddy, *President*
Nick Stanage, *President*
EMP: 99
SALES (est): 9.6MM
SALES (corp-wide): 2.1B **Publicly Held**
SIC: 3324 Aerospace investment castings, ferrous
PA: Hexcel Corporation
281 Tresser Blvd Ste 1503
Stamford CT 06901
203 969-0666

(G-7771)
HGH INDUSTRIES LLC
43 Sally Dr (06074-3500)
PHONE 860 644-1150
Herbert Hoyne, *Mng Member*
John Hoyne,
EMP: 3
SALES (est): 240K **Privately Held**
SIC: 3545 Machine tool accessories

(G-7772)
HI HEAT COMPANY INC
32 Glendale Rd (06074-2416)
PHONE 860 528-9315
Leonard Werner, *President*
Prairie Brown, *Vice Pres*
EMP: 3
SQ FT: 22,000
SALES: 1MM **Privately Held**
WEB: www.hi-heat.com
SIC: 3567 Industrial furnaces & ovens

(G-7773)
HOYA CORPORATION
Also Called: Hoya Optcal Labs Amrc-Hartford
580 Nutmeg Rd N (06074-2458)
PHONE 860 289-5379
Joe Bassler, *Branch Mgr*
EMP: 252 **Privately Held**
SIC: 3851 5049 Ophthalmic goods; optical goods
HQ: Hoya Corporation
651 E Corporate Dr
Lewisville TX 75057
972 221-4141

(G-7774)
INTERIOR PLANTWORKS INC
369 Main St (06074-3910)
PHONE 860 289-9499
David Fromson, *Branch Mgr*
EMP: 1
SALES (corp-wide): 208.3K **Privately Held**
WEB: www.interiorplantworks.com
SIC: 0782 3699 Landscape contractors; Christmas tree ornaments, electric
PA: Interior Plantworks Inc
52 Oakwood Dr
South Windsor CT 06074
860 289-9499

(G-7775)
INTERIOR PLANTWORKS INC (PA)
52 Oakwood Dr (06074-2815)
PHONE 860 289-9499
David Fromson, *President*
EMP: 1
SQ FT: 2,400
SALES (est): 333K **Privately Held**
WEB: www.interiorplantworks.com
SIC: 0782 3699 3999 5992 Landscape contractors; Christmas tree ornaments, electric; Christmas tree ornaments, except electrical & glass; florists

(G-7776)
JAD LLC
Also Called: Industronics Service
489 Sullivan Ave (06074-1942)
P.O. Box 649 (06074-0649)
PHONE 860 289-1551
James L Wyse, *President*
Dean P Hills, *Mng Member*
EMP: 25
SQ FT: 14,000
SALES (est): 6.2MM **Privately Held**
WEB: www.industronics.com
SIC: 3823 3567 5084 3433 Temperature instruments: industrial process type; thermocouples, industrial process type; industrial furnaces & ovens, controlling instruments & accessories; heating equipment, except electric

(G-7777)
JHS RESTORATION INC
170 Strong Rd (06074-1013)
PHONE 860 757-3870
Bonnie M Snyder, *President*
John Snyder, *Vice Pres*
EMP: 10
SALES: 600K **Privately Held**
SIC: 3444 1761 Roof deck, sheet metal; roofing, siding & sheet metal work

(G-7778)
JL AEROTECH INC
475 Buckland Rd Ste 103 (06074-3738)
PHONE 860 248-8628
Brian Sohn, *President*
Kangho Son, *Director*
EMP: 3 EST: 2016
SALES (est): 1.5MM **Privately Held**
SIC: 3324 Aerospace investment castings, ferrous

(G-7779)
JONES METAL PRODUCTS CO INC
22 Schwier Rd Ste 1 (06074-1940)
PHONE 860 289-8023
Kevin R Jones, *President*
EMP: 5 EST: 1964
SQ FT: 11,000
SALES: 750K **Privately Held**
SIC: 3444 Sheet metal specialties, not stamped

(G-7780)
JUDITH E GOLDSTEIN COMPANY
66 Windshire Dr (06074-2133)
PHONE 860 644-4646
Judith E Goldstein, *Owner*
EMP: 1
SALES (est): 77.2K **Privately Held**
SIC: 3339 Precious metals

(G-7781)
K2 MANUFACTURING INC
1257 John Fitch Blvd (06074-2431)
PHONE 413 636-6170
Mark Work, *President*
EMP: 2
SALES (est): 62.5K **Privately Held**
SIC: 3999 Manufacturing industries

(G-7782)
KASHETA POWER EQUIPMENT
1275 John Fitch Blvd (06074-2431)
PHONE 860 528-8421
Edward Kasheta Jr, *President*
Susan Kasheta, *Admin Sec*
EMP: 5
SQ FT: 2,400
SALES (est): 977.3K **Privately Held**
SIC: 3568 Power transmission equipment

(G-7783)
KEYSTONE PAPER & BOX CO INC
31 Edwin Rd (06074-2413)
P.O. Box 355, East Windsor Hill (06028-0355)
PHONE 860 291-0027
James Rutt, *President*
John Goodenow, *Admin Sec*
EMP: 52
SQ FT: 61,000
SALES (est): 17.7MM **Privately Held**
WEB: www.keystonepaperbox.com
SIC: 2657 2631 Folding paperboard boxes; container, packaging & boxboard

(G-7784)
KK MANUFACTURING LLC
Also Called: Koffee Karousel
27 Stonehenge Rd (06074-2524)
PHONE 860 644-5330
EMP: 1
SQ FT: 3,200
SALES: 400K **Privately Held**
SIC: 3581 Mfg Vending Machines

(G-7785)
L T A GROUP INC
Also Called: Argix Direct
694 Nutmeg Rd N (06074-2433)
PHONE 860 291-9911
EMP: 25
SALES (est): 2.5MM **Privately Held**
SIC: 3743 Mfg Railroad Equipment

(G-7786)
LANDMARK SIGN SERVICE
123 Pine Knob Dr (06074-2330)
P.O. Box 260101, Hartford (06126-0101)
PHONE 860 474-5305
EMP: 2
SALES (est): 64.9K **Privately Held**
SIC: 3993 Signs & advertising specialties

(G-7787)
LEAPS & BONES LLC
81 Evergreen Way (06074-6975)
PHONE 860 648-9708
Amy Kenkel, *President*
EMP: 2
SALES (est): 171.1K **Privately Held**
SIC: 3999 Pet supplies

(G-7788)
LIGHTHOUSE INTERNATIONAL LLC
125 S Satellite Rd (06074-3474)
PHONE 860 528-4722
Edmond Autuori,
EMP: 20
SALES (est): 1.5MM **Privately Held**
SIC: 3724 Aircraft engines & engine parts

(G-7789)
MARKANY NA LLC
152 Deming St (06074-3740)
PHONE 914 656-7073
Gary Raytar, *Managing Dir*
EMP: 2
SALES (est): 140K **Privately Held**
SIC: 3577 Computer peripheral equipment

(G-7790)
MARKOW RACE CARS
701 Nutmeg Rd N Ste 1 (06074-2437)
PHONE 860 610-0776
Ronald Siemienski, *Principal*
EMP: 3
SALES (est): 380.5K **Privately Held**
SIC: 3711 Automobile assembly, including specialty automobiles

(G-7791)
MASSCONN DISTRIBUTE CPL
12 Commerce Way (06074-1151)
PHONE 860 882-0717
Brian Hastings, *Principal*
EMP: 85
SALES (est): 11.7MM **Privately Held**
SIC: 2051 Doughnuts, except frozen

(G-7792)
MEYER GAGE CO INC
230 Burnham St (06074-4193)
PHONE 860 528-6526
John Meyer, *CEO*
James Meyer, *Vice Pres*
Stephanie Antrum, *Sales Mgr*
▲ EMP: 18
SQ FT: 28,000
SALES: 3.6MM **Privately Held**
WEB: www.meyergage.com
SIC: 3545 Gauges (machine tool accessories)

(G-7793)
MH RHODES CRAMER LLC
105 Nutmeg Rd S (06074-5400)
PHONE 860 291-8402
Robert G McCreary III,
▲ EMP: 3
SALES (est): 260K **Privately Held**
SIC: 3613 5012 Time switches, electrical switchgear apparatus; motorized cycles

(G-7794)
MICHAEL ZOPPA
Also Called: Zoppa Studio
23 Sea Pave Rd (06074-4156)
PHONE 860 289-5881
Michael Zoppa, *Owner*
Stephen Zoppa, *Opers Mgr*
June Zoppa, *Office Mgr*
EMP: 9
SQ FT: 3,800
SALES (est): 1MM **Privately Held**
SIC: 7336 3993 2396 Silk screen design; signs & advertising specialties; automotive & apparel trimmings

(G-7795)
NETSOURCE INC
350 Pleasant Valley Rd (06074-3428)
PHONE 860 282-8994
EMP: 1 **Privately Held**
SIC: 3496 Miscellaneous fabricated wire products
PA: Netsource, Inc.
260 Progress Dr
Manchester CT 06042

(G-7796)
NEYRA INDUSTRIES INC
239 Sullivan Ave (06074-1914)
P.O. Box 588 (06074-0588)
PHONE 860 289-4359
Randy Lee, *Regional Mgr*
EMP: 6
SQ FT: 4,000
SALES (corp-wide): 15.2MM **Privately Held**
WEB: www.neyra.com
SIC: 2952 Coating compounds, tar; roofing felts, cements or coatings

GEOGRAPHIC SECTION
South Windsor - Hartford County (G-7827)

PA: Neyra Industries, Inc.
10700 Evendale Dr
Cincinnati OH 45241
513 733-1000

(G-7797)
NUTMEG FOOD BROKERS LLC
130 Mcgrath Rd (06074-1124)
PHONE..............................860 289-9566
Michael Flaherty, *Owner*
EMP: 2
SALES (est): 109.4K **Privately Held**
SIC: 2099 Food preparations

(G-7798)
NUWAY TOBACCO COMPANY
200 Sullivan Ave Ste 2 (06074-1953)
P.O. Box 415, East Windsor Hill (06028-0415)
PHONE..............................860 289-6414
Raymond A Voorhies, *CEO*
Anne S King, *Vice Pres*
Thomas Kirby, *CFO*
Jean E Shepard III, *Asst Treas*
James T Farrell, *Admin Sec*
◆ **EMP:** 85 **EST:** 1951
SQ FT: 65,000
SALES (est): 28.4MM **Privately Held**
SIC: 2131 5159 Chewing & smoking tobacco; tobacco, leaf

(G-7799)
O & W HEAT TREAT INC
Also Called: Ohlheiser, H R Jr Pe
1 Bidwell Rd (06074-2411)
PHONE..............................860 528-9239
Harold R Ohlheiser Jr, *President*
Patrick Ohlheiser, *Vice Pres*
Robert Simmons, *QC Mgr*
Vicki S Sanborn, *Manager*
Vicky Sanborn, *Manager*
EMP: 13 **EST:** 1963
SQ FT: 10,500
SALES (est): 1.8MM **Privately Held**
WEB: www.owheattreat.com
SIC: 8742 3398 Management consulting services; brazing (hardening) of metal

(G-7800)
OLD THYME COUNTRY CANDLES
807 Twin Circle Dr (06074-2618)
PHONE..............................860 655-2583
Heath Johnstone, *Principal*
EMP: 1 **EST:** 2016
SALES (est): 39.6K **Privately Held**
SIC: 3999 Candles

(G-7801)
OXFORD PERFORMANCE MTLS INC
30 S Satellite Rd (06074-3445)
PHONE..............................860 698-9300
Scott Defelice, *President*
Paul Martin, *President*
Severine Valdant Zygmont, *President*
Severine Zygmont, *President*
Larry Varholak, *Vice Pres*
◆ **EMP:** 35
SQ FT: 16,000
SALES (est): 253K **Privately Held**
SIC: 2821 Plastics materials & resins

(G-7802)
OXPEKK PERFORMANCE MTLS INC
30 S Satellite Rd (06074-3445)
PHONE..............................860 698-9300
Scott Defelice, *President*
Bernard Plishtin, *Officer*
EMP: 15
SALES (est): 1.8MM **Privately Held**
SIC: 2821 Thermoplastic materials

(G-7803)
P & M WELDING CO LLC
Also Called: P&M Welding
38 Edwin Rd (06074-2414)
PHONE..............................860 528-2077
John Chesanek, *Mng Member*
Cynthia Chesanek,
EMP: 3
SQ FT: 10,000
SALES (est): 350K **Privately Held**
SIC: 7692 Welding repair

(G-7804)
PAVERS OF NEW ENGLAND INC
1370 John Fitch Blvd (06074-1017)
PHONE..............................860 289-7778
Robert Bellody, *Principal*
EMP: 1
SALES (est): 89.1K **Privately Held**
SIC: 3531 Pavers

(G-7805)
PIONEER ARSPC DEF SYSTEMS CORP
45 S Satellite Rd (06074-5407)
PHONE..............................860 528-0092
John Smith, *President*
EMP: 1
SQ FT: 500
SALES (est): 83K **Privately Held**
SIC: 8711 2399 Engineering services; parachutes

(G-7806)
PLAS-TEC COATINGS INC
68 Mascolo Rd (06074-3312)
PHONE..............................860 289-6029
Richard Cyr, *President*
Brian Cyr, *Vice Pres*
Sandra Cyr, *Treasurer*
EMP: 10
SQ FT: 10,000
SALES (est): 1.5MM **Privately Held**
WEB: www.plas-teccoatings.com
SIC: 3479 Coating of metals & formed products

(G-7807)
PLASMA TECHNOLOGY INCORPORATED
70 Rye St (06074-1218)
PHONE..............................860 282-0659
Richard Petersen, *Branch Mgr*
Rich Petersen, *Manager*
EMP: 35
SQ FT: 12,000
SALES (corp-wide): 17.4MM **Privately Held**
SIC: 2836 3471 Plasmas; plating & polishing
PA: Plasma Technology Incorporated
1754 Crenshaw Blvd
Torrance CA 90501
310 320-3373

(G-7808)
PODUNK POPCORN
245 Barber Hill Rd (06074-1659)
PHONE..............................860 648-9565
EMP: 3
SALES (est): 131.9K **Privately Held**
SIC: 2099 Food preparations

(G-7809)
POWER TURBINE COMPONENTS LLC
125 S Satellite Rd (06074-3474)
PHONE..............................860 291-8885
Carla Rodrigues, *Info Tech Mgr*
Edmund Autuori,
EMP: 1
SALES (est): 110K **Privately Held**
SIC: 3728 Aircraft parts & equipment

(G-7810)
POWERSCREEN CONNECTICUT INC
Also Called: Powerscreen England
140 Nutmeg Rd S (06074-3468)
PHONE..............................860 627-6596
Michael Sheelan, *President*
Bernadette Sheelan, *CFO*
Sean Clifford, *Sales Staff*
Jeff Morrow, *Sales Staff*
▲ **EMP:** 10
SQ FT: 11,000
SALES (est): 2.8MM **Privately Held**
SIC: 3532 Crushing, pulverizing & screening equipment

(G-7811)
PRESSURE BLAST MFG CO INC
205 Nutmeg Rd S Ste E (06074-5406)
PHONE..............................800 722-5278
Lowell W Mc Mullen III, *Ch of Bd*
Ted Clifford, *Treasurer*
Stephen Zavarella, *Admin Sec*
EMP: 15 **EST:** 1958
SQ FT: 25,000
SALES: 2MM **Privately Held**
SIC: 3629 3469 3291 Blasting machines, electrical; machine parts, stamped or pressed metal; abrasive products

(G-7812)
PRINTED COMMUNICATIONS
400 Chapel Rd Ste L1 (06074-4159)
PHONE..............................860 436-9619
Wayne Egienbaum, *Manager*
EMP: 7
SALES (est): 201.6K **Privately Held**
SIC: 2711 Commercial printing & newspaper publishing combined

(G-7813)
PROGRAM DYNAMIX INC
1155 Main St (06074-2453)
PHONE..............................860 282-0695
Jonathon Singer, *CEO*
Jonathan Singer, *CEO*
▲ **EMP:** 1
SALES (est): 140.1K **Privately Held**
SIC: 3312 Blast furnaces & steel mills

(G-7814)
PROGRESSIVE SHEETMETAL LLC
36 Mascolo Rd (06074-3312)
PHONE..............................860 436-9884
Keith Beaulieu, *Mng Member*
Andrea Beaulieu,
EMP: 36
SQ FT: 13,600
SALES: 5MM **Privately Held**
SIC: 3444 Sheet metalwork

(G-7815)
PROQUEST INC
171 Trumbull Ln (06074-2370)
PHONE..............................860 644-2392
EMP: 1
SALES (est): 37.5K **Privately Held**
SIC: 2741 Miscellaneous publishing

(G-7816)
PULSE INTERNATIONAL INC
2 Jeffrey Rd (06074-5410)
P.O. Box 416 (06074-0416)
PHONE..............................860 290-7878
Brett Bryan, *President*
▲ **EMP:** 2
SALES (est): 164.6K **Privately Held**
SIC: 2899 Ink or writing fluids

(G-7817)
REAL MANUFACTURING LLC
524 Sullivan Ave Ste 8 (06074-1920)
PHONE..............................860 757-3975
Suresh Bhut,
EMP: 1
SALES (est): 120K **Privately Held**
SIC: 3812 Acceleration indicators & systems components, aerospace

(G-7818)
REDLAND BRICK INC
Also Called: K F Brick Plant
1440 John Fitch Blvd (06074-1036)
PHONE..............................860 528-1311
Simon Whalley, *Director*
EMP: 130
SALES (corp-wide): 8.1MM **Privately Held**
WEB: www.redlandbrick.com
SIC: 3255 3251 Brick, clay refractory; brick & structural clay tile
HQ: Redland Brick Inc.
15718 Clear Spring Rd
Williamsport MD 21795
301 223-7700

(G-7819)
RICHMOND PRESS
676 Main St (06074-3902)
PHONE..............................860 649-0552
EMP: 1 **EST:** 2012
SALES (est): 37.5K **Privately Held**
SIC: 2741 Miscellaneous publishing

(G-7820)
SATELLITE TOOL & MCH CO INC
185 Commerce Way Ste 1 (06074-1154)
PHONE..............................860 290-8558
J Mark Lukasik, *CEO*
Jack Lukasik, *President*
Jan Lukasik, *President*
Monica Marselli, *Vice Pres*
EMP: 50 **EST:** 1975
SQ FT: 10,000
SALES (est): 15.7MM **Privately Held**
SIC: 3728 Aircraft parts & equipment

(G-7821)
SIFTEX EQUIPMENT COMPANY
Also Called: American Pulley Cover
52 Connecticut Ave Ste D (06074-3484)
PHONE..............................860 289-8779
Steven Weil, *President*
◆ **EMP:** 25
SQ FT: 12,000
SALES (est): 4.5MM **Privately Held**
WEB: www.siftex.com
SIC: 3089 Ducting, plastic

(G-7822)
SKILLCRAFT MACHINE TOOL CO
255 Nutmeg Rd S (06074-5403)
PHONE..............................860 953-1246
Thomas Litke, *President*
Gail Clark, *Project Mgr*
Todd Koplin, *Engineer*
Jacob Litke, *Engineer*
Jim Bailey, *Info Tech Mgr*
EMP: 15 **EST:** 1946
SALES (est): 4.2MM **Privately Held**
SIC: 3423 3544 Wrenches, hand tools; special dies & tools

(G-7823)
SMR METAL TECHNOLOGY
524 Sullivan Ave Ste 15 (06074-1946)
PHONE..............................860 291-8259
Sharon M Riley, *Owner*
EMP: 7
SALES (est): 972.6K **Privately Held**
SIC: 3443 Metal parts

(G-7824)
SOURCE LOUDSPEAKERS
Also Called: Source Technologies
701 Nutmeg Rd N Ste 2 (06074-2437)
PHONE..............................860 918-3088
John Sollecito, *Owner*
◆ **EMP:** 3
SQ FT: 3,000
SALES: 300K **Privately Held**
SIC: 3651 Loudspeakers, electrodynamic or magnetic

(G-7825)
SOUTH WIND MUSIC PUBG LLC
40 Steep Rd (06074-1340)
PHONE..............................860 644-2357
Alexander Bordonaro, *Principal*
EMP: 1
SALES (est): 41.3K **Privately Held**
SIC: 2741 Miscellaneous publishing

(G-7826)
SOUTH WINDSOR GOLF COURSE LLC
Also Called: Topstone Golf Course
516 Griffin Rd (06074-1324)
PHONE..............................860 648-4653
John J Kelly Sr, *Mng Member*
EMP: 60
SALES (est): 2.4MM **Privately Held**
WEB: www.topstonegc.com
SIC: 7997 3631 Golf club, membership; barbecues, grills & braziers (outdoor cooking)

(G-7827)
SOUTH WINDSOR QUALITY BLACK MO
287 Oakland Rd (06074-3824)
PHONE..............................860 385-2740
EMP: 2 **EST:** 2010
SALES (est): 110K **Privately Held**
SIC: 3544 Mfg Dies/Tools/Jigs/Fixtures

South Windsor - Hartford County

(G-7828)
SPACE TOOL & MACHINE CO INC
130 Commerce Way Ste 1 (06074-1151)
PHONE.................................860 290-8599
Thomas Luaasik, *President*
EMP: 5 **EST:** 1975
SALES (est): 440K **Privately Held**
SIC: 3599 Machine shop, jobbing & repair

(G-7829)
STEELTECH BUILDING PDTS INC
636 Nutmeg Rd N (06074-2433)
PHONE.................................860 290-8930
J Robert Denton, *Chairman*
Steve Iacino, *Vice Pres*
Steve Rich, *Vice Pres*
EMP: 51 **EST:** 1965
SQ FT: 38,000
SALES (est): 19.1MM **Privately Held**
WEB: www.econstructionspecialties.com
SIC: 3441 1791 5072 5031 Fabricated structural metal; structural steel erection; hardware; doors; door frames, all materials; partitions

(G-7830)
STM INDUSTRIES LLC
185 Commerce Way (06074-1152)
PHONE.................................860 785-8419
Jack Lukasik, *Principal*
EMP: 2
SALES (est): 94.3K **Privately Held**
SIC: 3999 Manufacturing industries

(G-7831)
STONEWALL KITCHEN LLC
400 Evergreen Way # 408 (06074-6967)
PHONE.................................860 648-9215
Silvester Linda, *Branch Mgr*
EMP: 120 **Privately Held**
SIC: 2514 Metal kitchen & dining room furniture
PA: Stonewall Kitchen, Llc
2 Stonewall Ln
York ME 03909

(G-7832)
TELEFUNKEN USA LLC
Also Called: Telefunken Elektro Acoustic
300 Pleasant Valley Rd E (06074-5408)
PHONE.................................860 882-5919
Alan Veniscofsky, *Sales Executive*
Toni Fishman,
▲ **EMP:** 15
SQ FT: 10,000
SALES: 2MM **Privately Held**
WEB: www.telefunkenusa.com
SIC: 3651 Microphones

(G-7833)
TICKET SOFTWARE LLC
83 Gerber Rd W (06074-3230)
PHONE.................................860 644-0422
Donald J Vaccaro, *Branch Mgr*
EMP: 3
SALES (corp-wide): 12.4MM **Privately Held**
SIC: 7372 Business oriented computer software
HQ: Ticket Software, Llc
75 Gerber Rd E
South Windsor CT 06074
860 644-4000

(G-7834)
TOMKIEL FURNITURE
84 Jessica Dr (06074-1822)
PHONE.................................860 871-7632
Mark Tomkiel, *Owner*
EMP: 2
SALES (est): 194.6K **Privately Held**
WEB: www.tomkielcc.com
SIC: 2434 Wood kitchen cabinets

(G-7835)
TRUE POSITION MFG LLC
40 Sandra Dr Ste 3 (06074-1043)
PHONE.................................860 291-2987
Richard Stathers,
Jeffrey Stathers,
EMP: 8
SQ FT: 2,000

SALES (est): 1MM **Privately Held**
SIC: 3549 Metalworking machinery

(G-7836)
UNITED TECHNOLOGIES CORP
Also Called: Power Systems Division
Governors Hwy (06074)
PHONE.................................860 727-2200
Jan Vandokkum, *Branch Mgr*
EMP: 255
SALES (corp-wide): 66.5B **Publicly Held**
WEB: www.utc.com
SIC: 3724 Aircraft engines & engine parts
PA: United Technologies Corporation
10 Farm Springs Rd
Farmington CT 06032
860 728-7000

(G-7837)
US AVIONICS INC / SUPERABR
Also Called: US Avionics
1265 John Fitch Blvd # 3 (06074-2456)
P.O. Box 599 (06074-0599)
PHONE.................................860 528-1114
Sari Alt, *Principal*
EMP: 5
SALES (est): 480.9K **Privately Held**
SIC: 3541 Grinding machines, metalworking

(G-7838)
VIOLIN PERFORMANCE CO
677 Rye St (06074-1229)
PHONE.................................860 836-8647
Jonathan Bonds, *Principal*
EMP: 2
SALES (est): 121.1K **Privately Held**
SIC: 3931 Violins & parts

(G-7839)
WAYBEST FOODS INC
1510 John Fitch Blvd (06074-1019)
PHONE.................................860 289-7948
Stanley Karasinski, *President*
S Karasinski, *Office Mgr*
EMP: 9
SALES (est): 859.3K **Privately Held**
SIC: 2015 Poultry sausage, luncheon meats & other poultry products

Southbury
New Haven County

(G-7840)
ABSOLUTE PRECISION CO
234 Bates Rock Rd (06488-3216)
PHONE.................................203 767-9066
James Muller, *Owner*
EMP: 4
SALES (est): 220.1K **Privately Held**
SIC: 3724 Aircraft engines & engine parts

(G-7841)
ADIRONDACK LKFRONT RETREAT LLC
77 Main St N (06488-2200)
PHONE.................................203 267-5882
EMP: 2 **EST:** 2008
SALES (est): 186.2K **Privately Held**
SIC: 2879 Mfg Agricultural Chemicals

(G-7842)
ADVANCED PROTOTYPE DEVELOPMENT
7 Stiles Rd (06488-1241)
PHONE.................................203 267-1262
Robert Bedard, *Owner*
EMP: 3
SALES: 190K **Privately Held**
SIC: 2514 Medicine cabinets & vanities: metal

(G-7843)
ALFRO CUSTOM MANUFACTURING CO
99 Old Woodbury Rd (06488-1933)
PHONE.................................203 264-6246
EMP: 2
SQ FT: 5,000
SALES (est): 280K **Privately Held**
SIC: 3469 Mfg Machine Parts

(G-7844)
ARC SERVICES
190 High Meadow Dr (06488-2620)
PHONE.................................203 264-0866
Tom Hudak, *Principal*
EMP: 1
SALES (est): 71.8K **Privately Held**
SIC: 2395 Embroidery products, except schiffli machine

(G-7845)
BLACK DOG BOAT WORKS LLC
155 Lakemere Dr (06488-2566)
PHONE.................................203 264-5823
Lee Heinzman, *Manager*
EMP: 1
SALES (est): 140K **Privately Held**
SIC: 3732 Boat building & repairing

(G-7846)
BTAC PUBLICATIONS
391 Berkshire Rd (06488-2043)
PHONE.................................203 560-7742
Richard Schnitzel, *Principal*
EMP: 1 **EST:** 2017
SALES (est): 37.5K **Privately Held**
SIC: 2741 Miscellaneous publishing

(G-7847)
CAREY AUTOMATIC DOOR LLC
35 Forest Rd (06488-2405)
PHONE.................................203 267-4278
Lisa M Carey,
EMP: 3
SALES (est): 500K **Privately Held**
SIC: 3442 Metal doors, sash & trim

(G-7848)
COMSAT INC
2120 River Rd (06488-1147)
PHONE.................................203 264-4091
Guy White, *Branch Mgr*
EMP: 14
SALES (corp-wide): 20.8MM **Privately Held**
SIC: 3663 Radio & TV communications equipment
HQ: Comsat, Inc.
2550 Wasser Ter Ste 600
Herndon VA 20171
571 599-3600

(G-7849)
CT SPRAYFOAM INDUSTRIES LLC
571 Main St N (06488-1806)
PHONE.................................203 232-0961
Stephen Ouellet, *Manager*
EMP: 2 **EST:** 2008
SALES (est): 90.2K **Privately Held**
SIC: 3999 Manufacturing industries

(G-7850)
CUSTOM COMPUTER SYSTEMS
250 Main St S (06488-2263)
PHONE.................................203 264-7808
EMP: 3
SALES (est): 51.5K **Privately Held**
SIC: 7374 7372 Data Processing/Preparation Prepackaged Software Services

(G-7851)
DAVID O WELLS CUSTOM CABINETRY
172 Jacob Rd (06488-2718)
PHONE.................................203 231-0280
David Wells, *Principal*
EMP: 2
SALES (est): 186.7K **Privately Held**
SIC: 2434 Wood kitchen cabinets

(G-7852)
EXPONENT PUBLISHING CO
949a Heritage Vlg (06488-1353)
PHONE.................................203 264-1130
EMP: 1 **EST:** 2015
SALES (est): 37.5K **Privately Held**
SIC: 2741 Miscellaneous publishing

(G-7853)
FURNACE CONCEPTS
Also Called: Freezer Concepts
186 Beecher Dr (06488-1942)
P.O. Box 863 (06488-0863)
PHONE.................................203 264-7856

Angelo Makris, *President*
EMP: 2
SALES: 565K **Privately Held**
WEB: www.freezer-concepts.com
SIC: 3567 1711 Industrial furnaces & ovens; plumbing, heating, air-conditioning contractors

(G-7854)
GALATA CHEMICALS LLC (HQ)
464 Heritage Rd Ste A1 (06488-3863)
PHONE.................................203 236-9000
Luc De Temmerman, *CEO*
Steven McKeown, *President*
Brian Johnson, *Vice Pres.*
Joseph Falsbury, *CFO*
▲ **EMP:** 10
SQ FT: 4,000
SALES (est): 150.3MM **Privately Held**
SIC: 5169 3999 2821 Organic chemicals, synthetic; atomizers, toiletry; polyvinyl chloride resins (PVC)

(G-7855)
GLAXOSMITHKLINE LLC
186 Beecher Dr (06488-1942)
PHONE.................................203 232-5145
EMP: 26
SALES (corp-wide): 39.5B **Privately Held**
SIC: 2834 Pharmaceutical preparations
HQ: Glaxosmithkline Llc
5 Crescent Dr
Philadelphia PA 19112
215 751-4000

(G-7856)
HIDDEN MEADOW ALPACA
901 Kettletown Rd (06488-2641)
PHONE.................................203 262-1669
EMP: 2
SALES (est): 123.3K **Privately Held**
SIC: 2231 Alpacas, mohair: woven

(G-7857)
HILL HOUSE PRESS LLC
327 Turrill Brook Dr (06488-1045)
PHONE.................................203 405-1158
Sara Beth Videtto, *Owner*
EMP: 1
SALES (est): 37.5K **Privately Held**
SIC: 2741 Miscellaneous publishing

(G-7858)
HISTORICAL ART PRINTS
464 Burr Rd (06488-2788)
P.O. Box 660 (06488-0660)
PHONE.................................203 262-6680
Don Troiani, *Owner*
Donna O'Brien, *Office Mgr*
EMP: 3
SALES: 1MM **Privately Held**
WEB: www.historicalartprints.com
SIC: 2741 Art copy: publishing only, not printed on site

(G-7859)
ILLICIT INDUSTRIES
325 Berkshire Rd (06488-2041)
PHONE.................................203 264-6293
EMP: 1
SALES (est): 39.6K **Privately Held**
SIC: 3999 Manufacturing industries

(G-7860)
IMAGE IN MOTION
679 Jacob Rd (06488-2724)
PHONE.................................203 264-6784
Laurie Ryer, *Owner*
EMP: 1
SALES (est): 94.6K **Privately Held**
SIC: 3861 Lantern slide plates, sensitized

(G-7861)
INNOVATIVE SOFTWARE
134 Lower Fish Rock Rd (06488-2139)
PHONE.................................203 264-1564
Lisa Cooper Munson, *Owner*
EMP: 1
SALES (est): 80.9K **Privately Held**
SIC: 7372 Prepackaged software

▲ = Import ▼=Export
◆ =Import/Export

GEOGRAPHIC SECTION

Southington - Hartford County (G-7893)

(G-7862)
INTERNATIONAL CONTACT TECH
Also Called: I C T
1432 Old Waterbury Rd # 6 (06488-3905)
PHONE.................................203 264-5757
Joseph Baker, *President*
Paul J Geary, *Vice Pres*
▲ **EMP:** 20 **EST:** 1993
SALES (est): 3.2MM **Privately Held**
SIC: 3825 Test equipment for electronic & electric measurement

(G-7863)
INTERNATIONAL MINES OUTLET
351 Peter Rd (06488)
P.O. Box 128 (06488-0128)
PHONE.................................203 264-9207
Anita Barney, *Principal*
EMP: 1
SALES (est): 113.3K **Privately Held**
SIC: 3915 Lapidary work, contract or other

(G-7864)
KAN PAK LLC
425 Main St N (06488-3804)
PHONE.................................203 933-6631
Art Mc Farrin, *Manager*
EMP: 5
SALES (corp-wide): 1.3B **Privately Held**
WEB: www.mixology.com
SIC: 2024 Ice cream & frozen desserts
HQ: Kan. Pak, Llc
   151 S Whittier Rd
   Wichita KS 67207
   620 442-6820

(G-7865)
KAYA SOFTWARE LLC
19 Greenwood Dr (06488-1887)
PHONE.................................203 267-7817
Michael Pellegrini,
EMP: 2
SALES (est): 132.1K **Privately Held**
SIC: 7372 Prepackaged software

(G-7866)
MBSIINET INC
194 Main St N (06488-3806)
P.O. Box 425 (06488-0425)
PHONE.................................888 466-2744
Tim Thomas, *President*
Carolyn Thomas, *CFO*
EMP: 12 **EST:** 1992
SALES (est): 1MM **Privately Held**
WEB: www.profic.com
SIC: 7372 Business oriented computer software

(G-7867)
METAL COMPONENTS MFG
43 Bagley Rd (06488-2418)
PHONE.................................203 267-5510
William D Dwyer, *Principal*
EMP: 2
SALES (est): 113.3K **Privately Held**
SIC: 3999 Manufacturing industries

(G-7868)
MICHAELS WOODWORKING LLC
474 S Flat Hill Rd (06488-2003)
PHONE.................................203 470-0867
Michael Liotta, *Principal*
EMP: 2
SALES (est): 198.2K **Privately Held**
SIC: 2431 Millwork

(G-7869)
MICRO-PROBE INCORPORATED
Also Called: Form Factor
2 Pomperaug Office Park # 103 (06488-2288)
PHONE.................................203 267-6446
Todd Martin, *Branch Mgr*
EMP: 3 **Publicly Held**
SIC: 3674 Semiconductors & related devices
HQ: Micro-Probe Incorporated
   617 River Oaks Pkwy
   San Jose CA 95134
   408 457-3900

(G-7870)
O & G INDUSTRIES INC
236 Roxbury Rd (06488-1234)
PHONE.................................203 263-2195
John Jenkins, *Chief Mktg Ofcr*
Johnathan Jacobs, *MIS Mgr*
EMP: 52
SALES (corp-wide): 538MM **Privately Held**
WEB: www.ogind.com
SIC: 5032 2951 1542 Sand, construction; gravel; asphalt paving mixtures & blocks; commercial & office building, new construction
PA: O & G Industries, Inc.
   112 Wall St
   Torrington CT 06790
   860 489-9261

(G-7871)
PAUL MAXX INDUSTRIES LLC
6 Freedom Cir (06488-3004)
P.O. Box 301 (06488-0301)
PHONE.................................203 417-2446
M Karam, *Bd of Directors*
EMP: 2 **EST:** 2018
SALES (est): 102.2K **Privately Held**
SIC: 3999 Manufacturing industries

(G-7872)
PERRELLA SPECIALTIES
Also Called: Perrella Guide Service
278 W Purchase Rd (06488-1004)
PHONE.................................203 264-1758
Robert Perrella, *Owner*
EMP: 1
SALES (est): 25K **Privately Held**
SIC: 3829 Thermometers & temperature sensors

(G-7873)
RAF INDUSTRIES LLC
257 Strongtown Rd (06488-2445)
PHONE.................................203 228-4290
Ronald Farina, *Principal*
▲ **EMP:** 2 **EST:** 2010
SALES (est): 145.4K **Privately Held**
SIC: 3999 Pet supplies

(G-7874)
REAL WOMEN INTERNATIONAL LLC
Also Called: Jolie Montre
385 Main St S Ste 404 (06488-4247)
PHONE.................................212 719-3130
Mark Levine, *President*
Rundah Arafat, *Manager*
EMP: 3
SALES (est): 500K **Privately Held**
SIC: 3873 Watches, clocks, watchcases & parts

(G-7875)
ROCKEFELLER TREASURY SERVICES
905 Georges Hill Rd (06488-2668)
PHONE.................................203 264-8404
Barbara Rockefeller, *President*
Lawrence Johnson, *Corp Secy*
EMP: 2
SALES (est): 250K **Privately Held**
WEB: www.rts-forex.com
SIC: 2741 Newsletter publishing

(G-7876)
RODGER CRAIG
380 Old Waterbury Rd # 12 (06488-1843)
PHONE.................................203 264-8843
Rodger Craig, *Principal*
EMP: 2
SALES (est): 188.2K **Privately Held**
SIC: 1381 Service well drilling

(G-7877)
ROMANO CONSTRUCTION LLC
315 Old Waterbury Rd (06488-1865)
PHONE.................................203 223-3136
Christopher Romano, *Principal*
EMP: 2
SALES (est): 138.7K **Privately Held**
SIC: 3089 Injection molded finished plastic products

(G-7878)
SOUTHBURY PRINTING CENTRE INC
385 Main St S Ste 107 (06488-4292)
PHONE.................................203 264-0102
Fredrick Plescia Jr, *President*
EMP: 9
SQ FT: 1,500
SALES (est): 1.6MM **Privately Held**
SIC: 2752 Commercial printing, offset

(G-7879)
SOUTHFORD KINDLING COMPANY LLC
94 Bridle Path Rd (06488-4406)
PHONE.................................203 394-2148
Brett John Sandor, *Principal*
EMP: 2 **EST:** 2017
SALES (est): 130.7K **Privately Held**
SIC: 2899 Chemical preparations

(G-7880)
TMF INCORPORATED
1266 Main St S Ste 3 (06488-2136)
PHONE.................................203 267-7364
Todd Decater, *President*
EMP: 4
SQ FT: 4,000
SALES (est): 1MM **Privately Held**
WEB: www.tmslitho.com
SIC: 3549 3544 Metalworking machinery; special dies, tools, jigs & fixtures

(G-7881)
TRAP ROCK QUARRY
236 Roxbury Rd (06488-1234)
PHONE.................................203 263-2195
John Jenkins, *Principal*
EMP: 3 **EST:** 1994
SALES (est): 136.1K **Privately Held**
SIC: 1422 Crushed & broken limestone

(G-7882)
VICTORS HOT HOUSE LLC
101 Pomperaug Trl (06488-2082)
PHONE.................................203 264-0939
Victor Swyrydenko,
EMP: 2
SALES (est): 120K **Privately Held**
SIC: 2099 Ready-to-eat meals, salads & sandwiches

(G-7883)
W G WOODWORKING
1370 Kettletown Rd (06488-4629)
PHONE.................................203 262-8308
EMP: 2
SALES (est): 130K **Privately Held**
SIC: 2431 Millwork, Nsk

(G-7884)
WALLY-B WELDING
556 Berkshire Rd (06488-2073)
PHONE.................................203 264-3853
Walter Bates, *Owner*
Cynthia Bates, *Co-Owner*
EMP: 1
SALES (est): 20K **Privately Held**
SIC: 7692 Welding repair

(G-7885)
WESTFAIR ELECTRIC CONTRACTORS
1181 Main St S (06488-2157)
PHONE.................................203 586-1760
EMP: 2
SALES (est): 93.7K **Privately Held**
SIC: 5082 3699 General construction machinery & equipment; electrical equipment & supplies

(G-7886)
WILLOUGHBY & CO LLC
Also Called: Sb USA
427 Old Poverty Rd (06488-1760)
P.O. Box 938, Middlebury (06762-0938)
PHONE.................................203 709-1464
Kate Willoughby,
▲ **EMP:** 1
SALES (est): 810K **Privately Held**
SIC: 3821 Laboratory equipment: fume hoods, distillation racks, etc.; laboratory furniture

Southington
Hartford County

(G-7887)
ACUCUT INC
200 Town Line Rd (06489-1145)
PHONE.................................860 793-7012
Scott Barmore, *CEO*
Judith Barmore, *Ch of Bd*
Michael Barmore, *President*
Larry Mc Nellis, *President*
Ray Lemay, *Vice Pres*
EMP: 48 **EST:** 1978
SQ FT: 30,000
SALES (est): 9.2MM **Privately Held**
WEB: www.acucut.com
SIC: 3599 Machine shop, jobbing & repair; electrical discharge machining (EDM)

(G-7888)
AGA MILL WORK LLC
178 Newell St (06489-1123)
PHONE.................................860 426-9901
Walenty Kolodziejczyk, *Principal*
EMP: 2
SALES (est): 255.2K **Privately Held**
SIC: 2431 Millwork

(G-7889)
AMERICAN STANDARD COMPANY
Also Called: Florian Tools
157 Water St (06489-3018)
PHONE.................................860 628-9643
▲ **EMP:** 25 **EST:** 1937
SQ FT: 20,000
SALES (est): 4.2MM **Privately Held**
SIC: 3469 3312 5261 Mfg Metal Stampings Blast Furnace-Steel Works Ret Nursery/Garden Supplies

(G-7890)
ANDERSON PUBLISHING LLC
24 Mooreland Dr (06489-2900)
P.O. Box 786 (06489-0786)
PHONE.................................860 621-2192
Joan Anderson, *Mng Member*
Anderson Publishing, *E-Business*
EMP: 3
SALES (est): 308.5K **Privately Held**
WEB: www.andersonpublish.com
SIC: 2752 Commercial printing, lithographic

(G-7891)
APAROS ELECTRIC MOTOR SERVICE
Also Called: Aparo's Electric Motor Repair
134 Industrial Dr (06489-1182)
PHONE.................................860 276-2044
Steven Aparo, *President*
Stephen Aparo, *President*
Daniel Aparo, *Treasurer*
Marie Aparo, *Admin Sec*
EMP: 5
SQ FT: 2,400
SALES (est): 500K **Privately Held**
SIC: 7694 5063 5999 Electric motor repair; motors, electric; motors, electric

(G-7892)
ARTWORK EMBROIDERY
36 Long Bottom Rd (06489-1311)
PHONE.................................860 620-0456
Rich Kelly, *Principal*
EMP: 1
SALES (est): 46.7K **Privately Held**
SIC: 2395 Embroidery & art needlework

(G-7893)
AZ COPY CENTER INC
Also Called: A Z Copy Center
298 Captain Lewis Dr (06489-1153)
PHONE.................................860 621-7325
Steven J Adduci, *President*
EMP: 4
SQ FT: 1,200
SALES (est): 61.3K **Privately Held**
SIC: 2759 Commercial printing

Southington - Hartford County (G-7894)

(G-7894)
BAUMER LTD (DH)
Also Called: Baumer Electric
122 Spring St Ste C6 (06489-1534)
PHONE..................................860 621-2121
Milan Ralbovsky, *President*
Rudi Rincker, *Vice Pres*
Ernst Attinger, *Project Mgr*
Lynn Laroche, *Purch Agent*
Correia Manuel, *QC Mgr*
▲ **EMP:** 10
SQ FT: 4,500
SALES (est): 6.7MM
SALES (corp-wide): 392.5K **Privately Held**
WEB: www.baumerelectric.com
SIC: 5084 3625 Measuring & testing equipment, electrical; switches, electric power
HQ: Baumer Holding Ag
    Hummelstrasse 17
    Frauenfeld TG 8500
    527 281-122

(G-7895)
BELLA HISPANIOLA ENTPS LLC
384 Lazy Ln (06489-1733)
PHONE..................................860 628-0105
Beatrice Ferry, *Principal*
EMP: 2
SALES (est): 88.9K **Privately Held**
SIC: 2311 Men's & boys' suits & coats

(G-7896)
BOBS VENDING
42 Vermont Ave (06489-3206)
PHONE..................................860 426-1232
Robert Kowalczyk, *Owner*
EMP: 1
SALES (est): 93K **Privately Held**
SIC: 3581 Automatic vending machines

(G-7897)
BRACONE METAL SPINNING INC
39 Depaolo Dr (06489-1021)
PHONE..................................860 628-5927
Christina Bracone, *President*
EMP: 20
SQ FT: 15,000
SALES (est): 3.3MM **Privately Held**
SIC: 3599 3469 Machine & other job shop work; spinning metal for the trade

(G-7898)
BROPHY METAL PRODUCTS INC
364 Old Turnpike Rd (06489)
P.O. Box 650 (06489-0650)
PHONE..................................860 621-3636
George E Brophy, *President*
Michael Brophy, *Vice Pres*
EMP: 2 **EST:** 1962
SQ FT: 8,000
SALES: 200K **Privately Held**
SIC: 3451 Screw machine products

(G-7899)
BUTTERFLY PRESS LLC
229 Loper St (06489-1852)
PHONE..................................860 621-2883
Angela Salonia, *Owner*
EMP: 1 **EST:** 2011
SALES (est): 61.1K **Privately Held**
SIC: 2741 Miscellaneous publishing

(G-7900)
C C PRECISION PRODUCTS CO INC
607 Old Turnpike Rd (06489)
P.O. Box 488 (06489-0488)
PHONE..................................860 628-4403
Charles Labbe, *President*
Carol Labbe, *Vice Pres*
EMP: 2
SQ FT: 3,600
SALES (est): 268K **Privately Held**
SIC: 3451 Screw machine products

(G-7901)
C V TOOL COMPANY INC (PA)
44 Robert Porter Rd (06489-1159)
PHONE..................................978 353-7901
Carmine Votino, *President*
Assunta Votino, *Corp Secy*
Kenneth Mattson, *Plant Mgr*
Filomena Maria Hurley, *Manager*
John Votino, *Manager*
EMP: 32 **EST:** 1980
SQ FT: 35,000
SALES (est): 10MM **Privately Held**
WEB: www.cvtool.com
SIC: 3599 3728 7692 3544 Machine shop, jobbing & repair; aircraft parts & equipment; welding repair; special dies, tools, jigs & fixtures; machine tools, metal cutting type

(G-7902)
CAMLOCK SYSTEMS INC
109 Industrial Dr (06489-1182)
PHONE..................................860 378-0302
Thomas J Divito, *President*
Bin Carroll, *Treasurer*
Melissa Jarrell, *Sales Staff*
▲ **EMP:** 2
SALES (est): 295.2K **Privately Held**
SIC: 3429 Locks or lock sets

(G-7903)
CAPTIVE GLOBAL LLC
22 Summit Farms Rd (06489-1524)
PHONE..................................860 302-6706
Christina Mancini,
EMP: 2
SALES (est): 100K **Privately Held**
SIC: 2741 Miscellaneous publishing

(G-7904)
CARBIDE TECHNOLOGY INC
55 Captain Lewis Dr (06489-1148)
PHONE..................................860 621-8981
Robert Burz, *President*
Judith Burz, *Shareholder*
EMP: 5
SQ FT: 6,000
SALES: 500K **Privately Held**
WEB: www.carbidetechnology.net
SIC: 2819 Carbides; inorganic acids, except nitric & phosphoric

(G-7905)
CKG WELDING FABRICATION LLC
217 Flanders Rd (06489-2843)
PHONE..................................860 628-7129
Clifford R Stakey, *Principal*
EMP: 2
SALES (est): 82.8K **Privately Held**
SIC: 7692 Welding repair

(G-7906)
CLEAR AUTOMATION LLC
85 Robert Porter Rd (06489-1152)
PHONE..................................860 621-2955
Ronald McCleary, *President*
Bruce Barnes, *Engineer*
Brett Bechtel, *Engineer*
Michael Powers, *Engineer*
Steve Serina, *Engineer*
▲ **EMP:** 27
SQ FT: 31,000
SALES: 5.7MM **Privately Held**
WEB: www.clearautomation.com
SIC: 3549 Assembly machines, including robotic

(G-7907)
COMPANION INDUSTRIES INC
891 W Queen St (06489-1094)
PHONE..................................860 628-0504
Ken Paul, *President*
Vincent Roy, *Vice Pres*
Vinny Roy, *Opers Mgr*
Steve Tosta, *Admin Sec*
EMP: 70
SQ FT: 34,000
SALES (est): 12.9MM **Privately Held**
WEB: www.companionind.com
SIC: 3469 Stamping metal for the trade

(G-7908)
CONNECTICUT SIGN FACTORY
11 Hart St (06489-2440)
PHONE..................................860 833-5689
EMP: 2
SALES (est): 66K **Privately Held**
SIC: 3993 Signs & advertising specialties

(G-7909)
CRS I GROUP INC
130 Ciccolella Ct (06489-1354)
PHONE..................................860 593-4886
Timothy Richardson, *Principal*
EMP: 1
SALES (est): 69.7K **Privately Held**
SIC: 3993 Signs & advertising specialties

(G-7910)
D F ARSZYLA WELL DRILLING INC
1255 East St (06489-4405)
PHONE..................................860 628-6156
Ann Arszyla, *President*
Martha Boga, *Corp Secy*
Jeffrey Boga, *Shareholder*
EMP: 2 **EST:** 1950
SALES (est): 237.6K **Privately Held**
SIC: 1381 1781 Service well drilling; water well drilling

(G-7911)
DAVID SMITH
66 N Summit St (06489-3045)
PHONE..................................860 877-3232
David Smith, *Owner*
EMP: 1
SALES (est): 44.1K **Privately Held**
SIC: 7379 7372 Computer related consulting services; application computer software;

(G-7912)
DEE ZEE ICE LLC
93 Industrial Dr (06489-1181)
PHONE..................................860 276-3500
Robert L Rogers, *Mng Member*
Carl Verderame III, *Info Tech Mgr*
EMP: 15
SQ FT: 2,000
SALES (est): 2.2MM **Privately Held**
SIC: 2097 Ice cubes

(G-7913)
DEMO AGENT SALES LLC
312 Mill St (06489-4717)
PHONE..................................860 621-3303
William F McGloin, *Manager*
EMP: 2
SALES (est): 87K **Privately Held**
SIC: 2819 Industrial inorganic chemicals

(G-7914)
DENCO COUNTER-BORE LLC
30 Peters Cir (06489-3713)
P.O. Box 875 (06489-0875)
PHONE..................................860 276-0782
Dennis Glatz,
Chris Glatz,
Patricia Glatz,
EMP: 3
SALES: 100K **Privately Held**
SIC: 3541 Machine tools, metal cutting type

(G-7915)
DIGIT-X INC
173 Hart St (06489-2442)
PHONE..................................860 620-1221
Alex Churilov, *Principal*
▲ **EMP:** 1
SALES (est): 70.5K **Privately Held**
SIC: 3993 Signs & advertising specialties

(G-7916)
DONNAS CANVAS CREATIONS
100 Forest Ln (06489-3915)
PHONE..................................860 276-0327
Donna R Perkins, *Owner*
EMP: 2 **EST:** 2015
SALES (est): 74.4K **Privately Held**
SIC: 2211 Canvas

(G-7917)
ECR ENTERPRISES LLC
Also Called: Yuya Paperie
77 Knollwood Rd (06489-1729)
PHONE..................................860 426-3098
Julio N Pazos, *Mng Member*
Erika Pazos,
EMP: 1
SALES: 72K **Privately Held**
SIC: 2754 7389 Stationery & invitation printing, gravure; design services

(G-7918)
ETHICON INC
Also Called: Ethicon Endo - Surgery
201 W Queen St (06489-1138)
PHONE..................................860 621-9111
John Callen, *Manager*
EMP: 300
SALES (corp-wide): 81.5B **Publicly Held**
WEB: www.ethiconinc.com
SIC: 3842 Ligatures, medical
HQ: Ethicon Inc.
    Us Route 22
    Somerville NJ 08876
    732 524-0400

(G-7919)
EX MODEL ENGINES
39 Amato Cir (06489-2456)
PHONE..................................860 681-2451
EMP: 2 **EST:** 2014
SALES (est): 163.2K **Privately Held**
SIC: 3519 Internal combustion engines

(G-7920)
EXPLICIT AIRBRUSH
45 Railroad Ave (06489-3561)
PHONE..................................860 582-6038
Jamie Chasse, *Owner*
EMP: 1
SALES: 62K **Privately Held**
SIC: 3952 Brushes, air, artists'

(G-7921)
F F SCREW PRODUCTS INC
Also Called: Ff Screw Products
888 W Queen St (06489-1033)
PHONE..................................860 621-4567
Frank Fragola, *President*
Mary Fragola, *Vice Pres*
▲ **EMP:** 25
SQ FT: 15,000
SALES (est): 6MM **Privately Held**
SIC: 3089 3451 Fittings for pipe, plastic; screw machine products

(G-7922)
F K BEARINGS INC
865 W Queen St (06489-1032)
PHONE..................................860 621-4567
Frank Fragola, *CEO*
Alfonso Fragola, *Vice Pres*
▲ **EMP:** 15
SQ FT: 15,000
SALES (est): 7MM **Privately Held**
WEB: www.fkrodends.com
SIC: 5085 3568 Bearings; power transmission equipment

(G-7923)
FIBERGLASS REPAIRS &
209 Meriden Ave (06489-3673)
PHONE..................................860 628-4962
Marcel J Duprey, *Mng Member*
EMP: 3
SALES (est): 213.8K **Privately Held**
SIC: 1799 3229 Kitchen & bathroom remodeling; glass fiber products

(G-7924)
FIRE TECHNOLOGY INC
122 Spring St (06489-1534)
PHONE..................................860 276-2181
Benjamin S Wysocki Jr, *Principal*
EMP: 4
SALES (est): 689.8K **Privately Held**
SIC: 3569 Sprinkler systems, fire; automatic

(G-7925)
FIVES N AMERCN COMBUSTN INC
999 Andrews St (06489-2911)
PHONE..................................216 271-6000
EMP: 43
SALES (corp-wide): 871.2K **Privately Held**
SIC: 3433 Heating equipment, except electric
HQ: Fives North American Combustion, Inc.
    4455 E 71st St
    Cleveland OH 44105
    216 271-6000

Southington - Hartford County

(G-7926)
GEMCO MANUFACTURING CO INC
555 W Queen St (06489-1178)
PHONE..............860 628-5529
Mark Divenere, *President*
Annmarie Johnson, *Business Mgr*
Andrew White, *VP Mfg*
EMP: 21 **EST:** 1943
SQ FT: 40,000
SALES (est): 4.7MM **Privately Held**
WEB: www.gemcomfg.com
SIC: 3469 3495 3496 Stamping metal for the trade; wire springs; woven wire products

(G-7927)
GENERAL MACHINE COMPANY INC
1223 Mount Vernon Rd (06489-2116)
PHONE..............860 426-9295
Mary Grzegorzk, *President*
Walentyn Grzegorzk, *Vice Pres*
EMP: 10
SQ FT: 2,500
SALES (est): 930K **Privately Held**
SIC: 3599 Machine shop, jobbing & repair

(G-7928)
GLACIER PUBLISHING
40 Oak St (06489-3217)
PHONE..............860 621-7644
Jack Lautier, *Owner*
EMP: 1
SALES (est): 34.7K **Privately Held**
SIC: 2731 Book publishing

(G-7929)
GLOBE TOOL & MET STAMPG CO INC
95 Robert Porter Rd (06489-1161)
PHONE..............860 621-6807
Reginald J Cote, *CEO*
Michelle Cote Knuth, *President*
Paul Cote, *Vice Pres*
Phyllis B Cote, *Admin Sec*
EMP: 35 **EST:** 1945
SQ FT: 31,000
SALES (est): 7.2MM **Privately Held**
WEB: www.globe-tool.com
SIC: 3469 3544 Stamping metal for the trade; die sets for metal stamping (presses)

(G-7930)
GOODY CANDLES LLC
434 Pleasant St (06489-2710)
PHONE..............860 426-9436
Michael Goodrich, *Manager*
EMP: 2
SALES (est): 130.5K **Privately Held**
SIC: 3999 Candles

(G-7931)
GORDON CORPORATION
170 Spring St Unit 3 (06489-1532)
PHONE..............860 628-4775
Anthony Prepiatti, *President*
David Gross, *Vice Pres*
Sue Devine, *Administration*
EMP: 79
SQ FT: 50,000
SALES (est): 15.5MM **Privately Held**
WEB: www.gordoncelladoor.com
SIC: 3317 3442 Steel pipe & tubes; metal doors

(G-7932)
HANDYSCAPE LLC
43 Sandy Pine Dr (06489-6016)
PHONE..............860 318-1067
Alan Seibert, *Principal*
EMP: 3
SALES (est): 261.8K **Privately Held**
SIC: 2851 Removers & cleaners

(G-7933)
HELIX MOORING SYSTEMS
170 Spring St (06489-1514)
PHONE..............860 628-0933
George Brown, *Owner*
EMP: 1
SALES (est): 77K **Privately Held**
SIC: 3449 Miscellaneous metalwork

(G-7934)
HIGH TECH PRECISION MFG L L C
43 Aircraft Rd (06489-1402)
P.O. Box 709 (06489-0709)
PHONE..............860 621-7242
Stanley Maciorowski,
EMP: 3 **EST:** 2000
SQ FT: 5,000
SALES: 325K **Privately Held**
SIC: 3599 Machine shop, jobbing & repair

(G-7935)
HOLM CORRUGATED CONTAINER INC
Metals Dr (06489)
P.O. Box 477 (06489-0477)
PHONE..............860 628-5559
Robert E Holm, *President*
Francine Holm, *Admin Sec*
EMP: 26
SQ FT: 25,000
SALES (est): 6MM **Privately Held**
SIC: 2653 Boxes, corrugated: made from purchased materials

(G-7936)
HOYT MANUFACTURING CO INC
37 W Center St Ste LI1 (06489-3501)
PHONE..............860 628-2050
Carl H Schmidt, *Vice Pres*
Jason David Hoyt, *Vice Pres*
EMP: 6
SALES (est): 625.6K **Privately Held**
SIC: 3469 Machine parts, stamped or pressed metal

(G-7937)
ICI DULUX PAINTS
320 Queen St (06489-1871)
PHONE..............860 621-8661
Larry Houtryve, *Manager*
EMP: 2 **EST:** 2008
SALES (est): 68.7K **Privately Held**
SIC: 5231 5198 2851 Paint; paints; paints & allied products

(G-7938)
INSPIRED MACHINE SHOP
122 Spring St Ste D3 (06489-1534)
PHONE..............860 628-7822
William Bishop, *Owner*
EMP: 1
SQ FT: 1,500
SALES: 40K **Privately Held**
SIC: 3599 Machine shop, jobbing & repair

(G-7939)
INTEGRITY CUSTOM WDWKG LLC
137 Walnut St (06489-2335)
PHONE..............860 302-3726
EMP: 1
SALES (est): 54.1K **Privately Held**
SIC: 2431 Millwork

(G-7940)
INTERNATIONAL PLATING TECH LLC
75 Aircraft Rd Ste 3 (06489-1443)
PHONE..............860 589-2212
Lucien Dallaire, *President*
EMP: 2
SALES (est): 116.6K **Privately Held**
SIC: 3559 Special industry machinery

(G-7941)
J J INDUSTRIES CONN INC
125 W Queen St (06489-1126)
PHONE..............860 628-4655
Todd Sanzone, *President*
Kathleen Sanzone, *Vice Pres*
Jon Salvitti, *Sales Mgr*
Pete Wallace, *Sales Staff*
Wendy Perkins, *Office Mgr*
EMP: 14
SQ FT: 2,000
SALES (est): 2.8MM **Privately Held**
WEB: www.jjindustries.com
SIC: 3545 Machine tool accessories

(G-7942)
JEM SPECIAL TOOL CO LLC
116 N Star Dr (06489-3858)
PHONE..............860 276-9767
Robert Ginsyski,
Robert Grzywinski,
EMP: 2
SALES: 70K **Privately Held**
SIC: 3599 Machine & other job shop work

(G-7943)
JET TOOL & CUTTER MFG INC
125 W Queen St (06489-1126)
PHONE..............860 621-5381
Ronald Sanzone, *CEO*
Todd Sanzone, *President*
James J Devito, *Director*
Thomas Albert, *Shareholder*
Christy Sanzone, *Admin Sec*
EMP: 24
SQ FT: 3,400
SALES (est): 4.6MM **Privately Held**
WEB: www.jettool.com
SIC: 3545 Machine tool accessories

(G-7944)
JFN MANUFACTURING LLC
76 Berlin St (06489-3759)
PHONE..............860 621-0069
John F Nelson, *Principal*
EMP: 2 **EST:** 2010
SALES (est): 127.2K **Privately Held**
SIC: 3999 Manufacturing industries

(G-7945)
JOHNSON & JOHNSON
201 W Queen St (06489-1138)
PHONE..............860 621-9111
James Goodrich, *Principal*
Henry Staszak, *Info Tech Mgr*
EMP: 2 **EST:** 2016
SALES (est): 95.3K **Privately Held**
SIC: 3841 Surgical & medical instruments

(G-7946)
KORDYS WELDING INC
162 Pratt St (06489-4254)
PHONE..............860 621-2271
Edward P Kordys, *President*
Cynthia K Dripchak, *Vice Pres*
Mildred Kordys, *Treasurer*
EMP: 1
SQ FT: 900
SALES (est): 54.6K **Privately Held**
SIC: 7692 Welding repair

(G-7947)
LIGHT METALS COLORING CO INC
Also Called: L M C
270 Spring St (06489-1589)
PHONE..............860 621-0145
Richard William Fleet, *President*
Mark Thomas, *Admin Sec*
EMP: 100 **EST:** 1945
SQ FT: 27,000
SALES (est): 14.8MM **Privately Held**
WEB: www.lightmetalscoloring.com
SIC: 3471 Anodizing (plating) of metals or formed products; coloring & finishing of aluminum or formed products

(G-7948)
M & M CARBIDE INC
290 Center St (06489-3112)
PHONE..............860 628-2002
Marcial Mendez, *President*
Carmen Mendez, *Vice Pres*
EMP: 5
SQ FT: 1,500
SALES: 400K **Privately Held**
SIC: 3545 7699 Cutting tools for machine tools; industrial tool grinding

(G-7949)
M & W INDUSTRIES INC
29 Depaolo Dr (06489-1021)
PHONE..............860 621-7358
Dan Sebastian, *CEO*
John R Bagnuolo, *COO*
Scottie Pennington, *Opers Mgr*
EMP: 2 **EST:** 1979
SALES (est): 428.1K **Privately Held**
SIC: 3999 Barber & beauty shop equipment

(G-7950)
MASTERCRAFT TOOL AND MCH CO
100 Newell St (06489-1123)
PHONE..............860 628-5551
Stephen Lassy, *President*
Brian J Lassy, *Vice Pres*
Brian Lassy, *Vice Pres*
Michael Lassy, *Vice Pres*
Alec Konovalov, *QC Mgr*
EMP: 19
SALES (est): 3.5MM **Privately Held**
WEB: www.mastercrafttool-mach.com
SIC: 3469 3443 3544 Stamping metal for the trade; air coolers, metal plate; special dies & tools

(G-7951)
MATSUTEK ENTERPRISES LLC
213 Wedgewood Rd (06489-2845)
PHONE..............860 276-2464
David Alexander, *Mng Member*
EMP: 1
SALES: 8MM **Privately Held**
SIC: 3635 Household vacuum cleaners
PA: Matsutek Enterprises Co., Ltd.
2f, No. 2, Lane 15, Ziqiang St.
New Taipei City TAP 23678

(G-7952)
MATTHEW WARREN INC
Also Called: Economy Spring
29 Depaolo Dr (06489-1021)
PHONE..............860 621-7358
Leonide Charette, *Branch Mgr*
EMP: 89
SALES (corp-wide): 185.9MM **Privately Held**
SIC: 3495 3493 Precision springs; steel springs, except wire; coiled flat springs; torsion bar springs
HQ: Matthew Warren, Inc.
9501 Tech Blvd Ste 401
Rosemont IL 60018
847 349-5760

(G-7953)
METTLER PACKAGING LLC ✪
100 Queen St Ste 5 (06489-2052)
PHONE..............860 628-6193
EMP: 2 **EST:** 2019
SALES (est): 90.7K **Privately Held**
SIC: 2674 Bags: uncoated paper & multi-wall

(G-7954)
MIDSUN GROUP INC (PA)
135 Redstone St (06489-1129)
P.O. Box 864 (06489-0864)
PHONE..............860 378-0100
Robert Vojtila, *President*
Brad Macculloch, *General Mgr*
Herebert Kleinegger, *Engineer*
Mark C Hatje, *Treasurer*
Peggy Cameron, *Bookkeeper*
EMP: 9
SQ FT: 20,000
SALES (est): 13.8MM **Privately Held**
WEB: www.midsungroup.com
SIC: 5169 2869 Chemicals & allied products; silicones

(G-7955)
MILL MACHINE TOOL & DIE CO
280 Mill St (06489-4715)
PHONE..............860 628-6700
John D'Angelo, *Owner*
EMP: 3
SQ FT: 6,000
SALES (est): 228.3K **Privately Held**
SIC: 3599 Machine shop, jobbing & repair

(G-7956)
NEW ENGLAND PLC SYSTEMS LLC
453 N Main St Pmb 364 (06489-2521)
PHONE..............860 793-2975
Mike Dalena, *Owner*
EMP: 1
SALES (est): 110K **Privately Held**
SIC: 3542 Robots for metal forming: pressing, extruding, etc.; computer integrated systems design

(G-7957)
NEWCOMB SPRING CORP
235 Spring St (06489-1542)
PHONE..................860 621-0111
George D Jacobson, *Manager*
EMP: 27
SALES (corp-wide): 71.2MM **Privately Held**
WEB: www.newcombspring.com
SIC: 3495 3493 Wire springs; steel springs, except wire
PA: Spring Newcomb Corp
  5408 Panola Indus Blvd
  Decatur GA 30035
  770 981-2803

(G-7958)
NEWCOMB SPRINGS CONNECTICUT
235 Spring St (06489-1542)
PHONE..................860 621-0111
Robert Jacobson, *President*
Kurt Tonhaeuser, *General Mgr*
Donald Jacobson, *Chairman*
Charly Vaichus, *Engineer*
Keith Porter, *Director*
EMP: 50
SQ FT: 80,000
SALES (est): 8.2MM **Privately Held**
SIC: 3495 Wire springs

(G-7959)
NORTHEAST CARBIDE INC
Also Called: Springs Manufacturer Supply Co
525 W Queen St (06489-1192)
PHONE..................860 628-2515
William Lyons III, *President*
Ralph Parlado, *Vice Pres*
Marianne Caiaze, *Office Mgr*
EMP: 15
SQ FT: 10,000
SALES (est): 2.1MM **Privately Held**
WEB: www.springmfrssupply.com
SIC: 3544 Special dies & tools; jigs & fixtures

(G-7960)
NORTHEAST PIPELINE SERVICE LLC
156 Old Turnpike Rd (06489-3632)
PHONE..................860 621-6921
Dana Seitz, *Mng Member*
EMP: 2
SALES (est): 233.2K **Privately Held**
SIC: 3491 Water works valves

(G-7961)
OWEN TOOL AND MFG CO INC
149 Aircraft Rd (06489-1404)
P.O. Box 8, Plainville (06062-0008)
PHONE..................860 628-6540
Thomas Owen, *President*
EMP: 8 EST: 1941
SQ FT: 10,000
SALES (est): 1.1MM **Privately Held**
WEB: www.owen-tool.com
SIC: 3469 Stamping metal for the trade

(G-7962)
PROTEK SKI RACING INC
85 Ladyslipper Ln (06489-1082)
PHONE..................860 628-9643
Sean Florian, *President*
Beth Florian, *Principal*
EMP: 1
SALES (est): 74.3K **Privately Held**
SIC: 3949 5085 Ice skates, parts & accessories; gears

(G-7963)
QUANTUM BPOWER SOUTHINGTON LLC
49 Depaolo Dr (06489-1021)
PHONE..................860 201-0621
Mike Curtis, *Director*
Kevin J Boucher,
EMP: 4 EST: 2016
SALES (est): 104K **Privately Held**
SIC: 3572 Computer storage devices

(G-7964)
R & D SERVICES LLC
45 Old Turnpike Rd (06489-3633)
PHONE..................860 628-5205
Kevin Johnston, *CEO*
Dan Mac Kenzie, *Manager*
Stan Mac Kenzie, *Manager*
Linda Johnston,
Donald Mac Kenzie,
EMP: 5
SQ FT: 1,400
SALES (est): 680.3K **Privately Held**
SIC: 2026 Yogurt

(G-7965)
RECOR WELDING CENTER INC
86 Gannet Dr (06489-1758)
PHONE..................860 573-1942
Sonia Bourget, *Admin Sec*
EMP: 3
SALES: 394K **Privately Held**
SIC: 7692 Welding repair

(G-7966)
REGISTER FOR PUBLICATIONS
22 Summit Farms Rd (06489-1524)
P.O. Box 798 (06489-0798)
PHONE..................860 302-6706
EMP: 1
SALES (est): 52.2K **Privately Held**
SIC: 2741 Miscellaneous publishing

(G-7967)
REM CHEMICALS INC (PA)
Also Called: R E M
325 W Queen St (06489-1177)
PHONE..................860 621-6755
Mark D Michaud, *President*
Lori Bailey, *Facilities Mgr*
Justin Michaud, *Opers Staff*
Vincent Cline, *Project Engr*
Louise B Michaud, *Treasurer*
▲ EMP: 17 EST: 1965
SQ FT: 14,500
SALES (est): 8MM **Privately Held**
WEB: www.remchem.com
SIC: 2899 Chemical preparations

(G-7968)
ROSE TO OCCASSION LLC
Also Called: Rose To The Occasion Florist
92 Monarch Dr (06489-4367)
PHONE..................860 628-6880
Laure Jo Powell, *Mng Member*
EMP: 3 EST: 1997
SALES (est): 125K **Privately Held**
SIC: 5992 3944 5947 Flowers, fresh; craft & hobby kits & sets; gift baskets

(G-7969)
ROYCE INDUSTRIES INC (PA)
357 Captain Lewis Dr (06489-1170)
P.O. Box 545, Farmington (06034-0545)
PHONE..................860 674-2700
Tracey Mencio, *CEO*
Peter Fazzone Jr, *Ch of Bd*
◆ EMP: 17
SQ FT: 5,000
SALES: 3MM **Privately Held**
WEB: www.integrated-mfg.com
SIC: 5085 3679 Valves & fittings; electronic switches

(G-7970)
SAUCIER WELDING SERVICES
252 Washington Dr (06489-4361)
P.O. Box 1040 (06489-5040)
PHONE..................860 747-4577
Clayton Saucier, *Owner*
EMP: 2 EST: 1982
SALES (est): 85K **Privately Held**
SIC: 7692 Welding repair

(G-7971)
SAUCIERS MISC METAL WORKS LLC
89 Birch St (06489-1120)
P.O. Box 1040 (06489-5040)
PHONE..................860 747-4577
Clayton Saucier,
Clayton R Saucier,
EMP: 4
SQ FT: 2,400
SALES (est): 362K **Privately Held**
SIC: 7692 Welding repair

(G-7972)
SCRIPTURAL RES & PUBG CO INC
550 N Main St (06489-2025)
PHONE..................860 609-5138
Robert Ramos, *Principal*
EMP: 1
SALES (est): 37.5K **Privately Held**
SIC: 2741 Miscellaneous publishing

(G-7973)
SENS ALL INC
85 Water St (06489-3017)
P.O. Box 626 (06489-0626)
PHONE..................860 628-8379
Walter E Jacobson Sr, *President*
Walter E Jacobson Jr, *Vice Pres*
EMP: 4 EST: 1982
SALES (est): 516.6K **Privately Held**
SIC: 3829 Pressure transducers

(G-7974)
SMARTPAY SOLUTIONS
200 Executive Blvd Ste 3a (06489-1042)
PHONE..................860 986-7659
Gavin Forrester, *Principal*
EMP: 3
SALES (est): 235.5K **Privately Held**
SIC: 7372 Prepackaged software

(G-7975)
SMITHS MEDICAL ASD INC
Also Called: Medex Southington
201 W Queen St (06489-1194)
PHONE..................860 621-9111
Darren Hodkinson, *Opers Staff*
Massimo Castaldi, *Engineer*
John Hemsted, *Branch Mgr*
Richard Flynn, *Director*
EMP: 341
SALES (corp-wide): 4.1B **Privately Held**
SIC: 3841 IV transfusion apparatus
HQ: Smiths Medical Asd, Inc.
  6000 Nathan Ln N Ste 100
  Plymouth MN 55442
  763 383-3000

(G-7976)
SOFTWARE ESTABLISHMENT LLC
42 Clearview Ct (06489-3461)
PHONE..................860 426-2700
Arthur L Wilkes, *Principal*
EMP: 2
SALES (est): 109K **Privately Held**
SIC: 7372 Prepackaged software

(G-7977)
SOUTHINGTON METAL FABG CO
95 Corporate Dr (06489-1085)
P.O. Box 456 (06489-0456)
PHONE..................860 621-0149
John Brunalli, *President*
Tom Beland, *General Mgr*
James Needham, *Corp Secy*
EMP: 10 EST: 1967
SQ FT: 17,500
SALES (est): 1.9MM **Privately Held**
SIC: 3446 Stairs, fire escapes, balconies, railings & ladders; fences, gates, posts & flagpoles

(G-7978)
SOUTHINGTON TRANSM AUTO REPR
1900 West St (06489-1030)
PHONE..................860 329-0381
Richard Singer, *Principal*
EMP: 4
SALES (est): 463.5K **Privately Held**
SIC: 3714 Power transmission equipment, motor vehicle

(G-7979)
SPECIALTY PRODUCTS MFG LLC
251 Captain Lewis Dr (06489-1155)
PHONE..................860 621-6969
David Randall, *Mng Member*
EMP: 6
SQ FT: 6,000
SALES (est): 929.7K **Privately Held**
SIC: 3429 3451 Locks or lock sets; screw machine products

(G-7980)
STAMPTECH INCORPORATED
445 W Queen St Ste 100 (06489-1171)
PHONE..................860 628-9090
Anthony Amato, *President*
Pat Clavet, *Admin Sec*
▲ EMP: 18
SALES (est): 10.3MM **Privately Held**
SIC: 5051 3542 Metals service centers & offices; machine tools, metal forming type

(G-7981)
STANLEY BLACK & DECKER INC
400 Executive Blvd (06489-6027)
PHONE..................860 460-9122
EMP: 2
SALES (est): 72K **Privately Held**
SIC: 3546 Power-driven handtools

(G-7982)
STEP SAVER INC
Also Called: Observer, The
213 Spring St (06489-1530)
PHONE..................860 621-6751
William B Pape, *President*
Douglas Guersney, *Exec VP*
Kevin Smalley, *Prdtn Mgr*
Andrew Laforge, *Sales Staff*
Mike Chaiken, *Manager*
EMP: 45
SQ FT: 17,000
SALES (est): 3MM **Privately Held**
SALES (corp-wide): 24MM **Privately Held**
WEB: www.stepsaver.com
SIC: 2741 2752 2791 2789 Shopping news; publishing & printing; commercial printing, lithographic; typesetting; bookbinding & related work
PA: American-Republican, Incorporated
  389 Meadow St
  Waterbury CT 06702
  203 574-3636

(G-7983)
SUPREME STORM SERVICES LLC
49 Depaolo Dr (06489-1021)
PHONE..................860 201-0642
Ronald Wuennemann,
Kevin Boucher,
Joseph Calvanese,
EMP: 3 EST: 2016
SALES (est): 91.3K **Privately Held**
SIC: 2099 4222 5149 8744 Food preparations; warehousing, cold storage or refrigerated; groceries & related products;

(G-7984)
TECHNOLOGY INF PARTERS
302 Stonegate Rd (06489-3831)
PHONE..................860 985-8760
Technology Parters, *Principal*
EMP: 2
SALES (est): 85.9K **Privately Held**
SIC: 3577 Computer peripheral equipment

(G-7985)
THADIEO LLC
405 Queen St Ste M (06489-1823)
PHONE..................860 621-4500
Michael Thadieo, *Principal*
EMP: 4 EST: 2008
SALES (est): 154K **Privately Held**
SIC: 2051 Bread, cake & related products

(G-7986)
THOMAS CONCRETE
111 Ciccio Rd (06489-2104)
PHONE..................860 628-4957
Thomas Alfieri, *Owner*
EMP: 1
SALES (est): 70.5K **Privately Held**
SIC: 3273 Ready-mixed concrete

(G-7987)
THOMAS PRODUCTS LTD
987 West St (06489-1023)
PHONE..................860 621-9101
Thomas Duksa, *President*
Paul Cameron, *Controller*
EMP: 20
SQ FT: 20,000

GEOGRAPHIC SECTION

Stafford Springs - Tolland County (G-8015)

SALES (est): 3.8MM **Privately Held**
WEB: www.thomasprod.com
SIC: **3625** 3643 Flow actuated electrical switches; current-carrying wiring devices

(G-7988)
THORNTON AND COMPANY INC
132 Main St Ste 2a 3 (06489-2561)
PHONE.................................860 628-6771
Paul P Thornton, *President*
Nate Deangelis, *Vice Pres*
Jake Thornton, *Vice Pres*
Lisa Vaccaro, *Admin Sec*
◆ EMP: 10
SQ FT: 3,000
SALES (est): 4.3MM **Privately Held**
SIC: **2821** 5162 Polyethylene resins; plastics products

(G-7989)
TOOL 2000
327 Captain Lewis Dr (06489-1170)
PHONE.................................860 620-0020
Andrzej Siwek, *Owner*
EMP: 4
SALES (est): 328.1K **Privately Held**
SIC: **3423** 7389 Hand & edge tools; hand tool designers

(G-7990)
TRI MAR MANUFACTURING COMPAN
191 Captain Lewis Dr (06489-1144)
PHONE.................................860 628-4791
Keith Martinelli, *President*
Martin Martinelli, *Corp Secy*
Kevin Martinelli, *Vice Pres*
David Martinelli, *Asst Treas*
EMP: 13
SQ FT: 6,000
SALES (est): 2.1MM **Privately Held**
WEB: www.marathonrecruiters.com
SIC: **3599** Machine shop, jobbing & repair

(G-7991)
UTICA SPRING COMPANY INC
474 Churchill St (06489-1001)
PHONE.................................860 628-6165
David Drozd, *President*
Elizabeth Drozd, *Admin Sec*
EMP: 2
SALES (est): 2.3MM **Privately Held**
SIC: **3495** 7389 Wire springs;

(G-7992)
VANGUARD PLASTICS CORPORATION
100 Robert Porter Rd (06489-1160)
PHONE.................................860 628-4736
Lawrence J Budnick Jr, *CEO*
Christopher Budnick, *President*
Marsha A Budnick, *Vice Pres*
Daren Fippinger, *Vice Pres*
Kimberly Lagace, *Vice Pres*
▲ EMP: 45
SQ FT: 22,500
SALES (est): 9.3MM **Privately Held**
WEB: www.vanguardplastics.com
SIC: **3089** Injection molding of plastics

(G-7993)
VERZATEC INC
119 Sabina Dr (06489-2449)
PHONE.................................860 628-0511
Darryl Upson, *Director*
EMP: 3
SALES (est): 335.2K **Privately Held**
SIC: **3599** Machine shop, jobbing & repair

(G-7994)
VISUAL IMPACT SIGNS
115 Meeker Rd (06489-2222)
PHONE.................................860 621-7446
Christopher Dziob, *Principal*
EMP: 1
SALES (est): 103.8K **Privately Held**
SIC: **3993** Signs & advertising specialties

(G-7995)
WELD-ALL INC
987 West St (06489-1023)
PHONE.................................860 621-3156
Thomas R Duksa, *President*
Clara Duksa, *Admin Sec*
EMP: 15

SQ FT: 10,000
SALES (est): 1.7MM **Privately Held**
SIC: **3599** 7692 Machine shop, jobbing & repair; welding repair

(G-7996)
WTP MACHINE ROBOTICS
41 Water St (06489-3017)
PHONE.................................860 716-7281
EMP: 2
SALES (est): 115.1K **Privately Held**
SIC: **3549** Assembly machines, including robotic

(G-7997)
YARDE METALS INC (HQ)
45 Newell St (06489-1424)
PHONE.................................860 406-6061
William K Sales Jr, *CEO*
Matthew L Smith, *President*
Carla Lewis, *Vice Pres*
Doug Jones, *Facilities Mgr*
Douglas Candreva, *Opers Staff*
◆ EMP: 425
SQ FT: 500,000
SALES (est): 240.1MM
SALES (corp-wide): 11.5B **Publicly Held**
WEB: www.yarde.com
SIC: **3499** 5051 Safe deposit boxes or chests, metal; aluminum bars, rods, ingots, sheets, pipes, plates, etc.
PA: Reliance Steel & Aluminum Co.
350 S Grand Ave Ste 5100
Los Angeles CA 90071
213 687-7700

Southport
Fairfield County

(G-7998)
AIRIGAN SOLUTIONS LLC
Also Called: Negg Maker, The
107 John St Ste 1c (06890-1466)
PHONE.................................203 594-7781
Sheila M Torgan, *Mng Member*
Margaret B Tyler,
EMP: 2
SALES (est): 88.3K **Privately Held**
SIC: **3631** 5023 Household cooking equipment; kitchen tools & utensils

(G-7999)
ASYLUM DISTILLERY
105 Waterville Rd (06890-1056)
PHONE.................................203 209-0146
Robert Schulten, *Principal*
EMP: 3
SALES (est): 111.3K **Privately Held**
SIC: **2085** Distilled & blended liquors

(G-8000)
BRAND FACTORY AGENCY
450 Center St Apt 9 (06890-1447)
PHONE.................................203 984-6178
Jay Goldman, *Owner*
▲ EMP: 1
SALES (est): 81.9K **Privately Held**
SIC: **2599** Factory furniture & fixtures

(G-8001)
C O JELLIFF CORPORATION (PA)
354 Pequot Ave Ste 300 (06890-1485)
PHONE.................................203 259-1615
Wilmot F Wheeler Jr, *Ch of Bd*
Geoffrey Wheeler, *President*
Rand Glucroft, *Vice Pres*
Halsted W Wheeler, *Treasurer*
▲ EMP: 62
SQ FT: 40,000
SALES (est): 12.8MM **Privately Held**
WEB: www.jelliff.com
SIC: **3496** Woven wire products; mesh, made from purchased wire

(G-8002)
CENTER FOR DISCOVERY
1320 Mill Hill Rd (06890-3017)
PHONE.................................203 955-1381
Alyse Peekman, *Principal*
EMP: 50 EST: 2012

SALES (est): 3.7MM **Privately Held**
SIC: **3822** Liquid level controls, residential or commercial heating

(G-8003)
DELL SOFTWARE INC
Also Called: Quest Software
49 John St (06890-1484)
PHONE.................................203 259-0326
EMP: 1
SALES (corp-wide): 23.2B **Publicly Held**
SIC: **7372** Prepackaged Software Services
HQ: Dell Software, Inc.
5 Polaris Way
Aliso Viejo CA 92656
949 754-8000

(G-8004)
INTERNATIONAL SOCCER & RUGBY
3683 Post Rd (06890-1113)
PHONE.................................203 254-1979
Gus Avalos, *Branch Mgr*
EMP: 5 **Privately Held**
SIC: **3949** Fencing equipment (sporting goods)
PA: International Soccer & Rugby Imports, Llc
3683 Post Rd Unit 1
Fairfield CT 06430

(G-8005)
KASSON JEWELERS OF SOUTHPORT
393 Pequot Ave (06890-1346)
PHONE.................................203 319-0021
Alan Kasson, *President*
Adam Kasson, *Marketing Staff*
Susan Kasson, *Admin Sec*
EMP: 6
SALES (est): 843.8K **Privately Held**
WEB: www.kassonjewelers.com
SIC: **5944** 3911 Jewelry, precious stones & precious metals; jewelry, precious metal

(G-8006)
MACWEAR LLC (PA)
Also Called: Macwear Athletic Apparel & Eqp
3300 Post Rd (06890-1383)
PHONE.................................203 579-4277
Jim Mc Aleavey,
EMP: 3
SALES (est): 776.7K **Privately Held**
SIC: **7389** 5941 5699 2759 Embroidering of advertising on shirts, etc.; sporting goods & bicycle shops; customized clothing & apparel; screen printing

(G-8007)
REAL DATA INC
657 Mill Hill Rd (06890-3011)
P.O. Box 691 (06890-0691)
PHONE.................................203 255-2732
Frank Gallinelli, *President*
A J Gallinelli, *Vice Pres*
EMP: 2
SQ FT: 1,000
SALES: 200K **Privately Held**
WEB: www.realdataexchange.com
SIC: **7371** 2741 Computer software development; technical manuals: publishing only, not printed on site

(G-8008)
RESOLUTE FP US INC
97 Village Ln (06890-1149)
PHONE.................................203 292-6560
Breen Blaine, *Branch Mgr*
EMP: 438
SALES (corp-wide): 3.7B **Privately Held**
SIC: **2621** Newsprint paper
HQ: Resolute Fp Us Inc.
5300 Cureton Ferry Rd
Catawba SC 29704
803 981-8000

(G-8009)
SIGN CREATIONS
89 Arbor Dr (06890-1190)
PHONE.................................203 259-8330
Mark Milosky, *Owner*
EMP: 3
SALES (est): 180.8K **Privately Held**
WEB: www.signcreations.com
SIC: **3993** Signs, not made in custom sign painting shops

(G-8010)
STURM RUGER & COMPANY INC (PA)
1 Lacey Pl (06890-1207)
PHONE.................................203 259-7843
C Michael Jacobi, *Ch of Bd*
Michael O Fifer, *Vice Ch Bd*
Christopher J Killoy, *President*
Michael Fifer, *Vice Chairman*
Thomas P Sullivan, *Senior VP*
▲ EMP: 277 EST: 1949
SQ FT: 25,000
SALES: 495.6MM **Publicly Held**
WEB: www.ruger-firearms.com
SIC: **3484** 3324 Pistols or pistol parts, 30 mm. & below; revolvers or revolver parts, 30 mm. & below; rifles or rifle parts, 30 mm. & below; shotguns or shotgun parts, 30 mm. & below; commercial investment castings, ferrous

(G-8011)
SUPERIOR PLATING COMPANY
2 Lacey Pl (06890-1241)
PHONE.................................203 255-1501
John L Raymond, *President*
EMP: 75
SQ FT: 20,000
SALES (est): 9.2MM
SALES (corp-wide): 6.7MM **Privately Held**
WEB: www.superiorplatingco.com
SIC: **3471** Electroplating of metals or formed products; finishing, metals or formed products
PA: Superior Technology Corp.
Lacey Pl
Southport CT 06890
203 255-1501

(G-8012)
SUPERIOR TECHNOLOGY CORP (PA)
Lacey Pl (06890)
PHONE.................................203 255-1501
John L Raymond, *President*
EMP: 120 EST: 1974
SQ FT: 30,000
SALES (est): 6.7MM **Privately Held**
SIC: **3471** Electroplating of metals or formed products; chromium plating of metals or formed products

(G-8013)
THOMAS BERNHARD BUILDING SYS
Also Called: B T Building Systems
281 Pequot Ave (06890-1360)
PHONE.................................203 925-0414
Harold C Thomas, *Principal*
Bryan Maloney, *CFO*
Van H Bernhard,
EMP: 35
SQ FT: 110,000
SALES (est): 3.3MM **Privately Held**
WEB: www.btbuildingsystems.com
SIC: **2439** 5211 2435 Trusses, wooden roof; home centers; hardwood veneer & plywood

(G-8014)
YES FINE WOODWORKING LLC
183 Barberry Rd (06890-1057)
PHONE.................................203 255-6366
Stephen G Yale, *Manager*
EMP: 2
SALES (est): 117.1K **Privately Held**
SIC: **2431** Millwork

Stafford Springs
Tolland County

(G-8015)
3M PURIFICATION INC
32 River Rd (06076-1500)
PHONE.................................860 684-8628
Michael Bristol, *Opers-Prdtn-Mfg*
EMP: 150
SALES (corp-wide): 32.7B **Publicly Held**
WEB: www.cuno.com
SIC: **3677** Filtration devices, electronic

Stafford Springs - Tolland County (G-8016)   GEOGRAPHIC SECTION

HQ: 3m Purification Inc.
400 Research Pkwy
Meriden CT 06450
203 237-5541

(G-8016)
AMERICAN SLEEVE BEARING LLC
1 Spring St (06076-1504)
PHONE..................860 684-8060
Ozzie Avery, Office Mgr
Howard Buckland,
▲ EMP: 35 EST: 1982
SQ FT: 60,000
SALES (est): 9.4MM Privately Held
WEB: www.asbbearings.com
SIC: 3568 3366 Bearings, plain; copper foundries

(G-8017)
AMERICAN WOOLEN COMPANY INC
8 Furnace Ave (06076-1223)
PHONE..................860 684-2766
Jacob Harrison Long, CEO
Katherine J Knight, President
Michael Fournier, Opers Staff
Giuseppe Monteleone, Opers Staff
Lisa Cornish, Treasurer
EMP: 3
SALES (est): 701.1K Privately Held
SIC: 2211 7389 Stretch fabrics, cotton; textile designers

(G-8018)
BALSAM WOODS FARM
Also Called: Realmaplesyrup.com
4 Clinton St (06076-1106)
PHONE..................860 265-1800
David Broer, Owner
EMP: 3
SALES (est): 78K Privately Held
SIC: 2099 Sugar, industrial maple

(G-8019)
BENOIT SIGNS & GRAPHICS
7 Hicks Ave (06076-1415)
PHONE..................860 870-8300
EMP: 1 EST: 2002
SALES (est): 56K Privately Held
SIC: 3993 Mfg Signs/Advertising Specialties

(G-8020)
CATHYS COUNTRY SCENTS CANDLES
100 Monson Rd (06076-3622)
PHONE..................860 458-8219
Cathy Pastula, Principal
EMP: 2
SALES (est): 62.5K Privately Held
SIC: 3999 Candles

(G-8021)
CORKTEC INC
17 Middle River Dr (06076-1034)
PHONE..................860 851-9417
Allen Gmanan, President
Nathan Lee, Opers Mgr
▲ EMP: 2
SALES (est): 208.5K Privately Held
WEB: www.corktec.com
SIC: 2499 Cork & cork products

(G-8022)
CROTEAU DEVELOPMENT GROUP INC
25 West St (06076-1325)
P.O. Box 150 (06076-0150)
PHONE..................860 684-3605
Jim Croteau, President
EMP: 3
SQ FT: 11,000
SALES (est): 600K Privately Held
SIC: 3444 3585 Sheet metalwork; ice making machinery

(G-8023)
D&D PRINTING ENTERPRISES (PA)
30 Conklin Rd (06076-4202)
PHONE..................860 684-2023
David Tyrell, Partner
Donna Tyrell, Partner
EMP: 2

SALES: 150K Privately Held
SIC: 2752 5199 Commercial printing, offset; advertising specialties

(G-8024)
DALLA CORTE LUMBER
12 Minor Rd (06076-4215)
PHONE..................860 875-9480
Keven Dallacorte, President
EMP: 3
SALES (est): 296.5K Privately Held
SIC: 2421 Sawmills & planing mills, general

(G-8025)
DAVES LOGGING
252 Hydeville Rd (06076-3802)
PHONE..................860 684-6533
Dave Worthington, Owner
EMP: 1
SALES (est): 112.2K Privately Held
SIC: 2411 Logging camps & contractors

(G-8026)
DIANNA BLANCHARD
Also Called: Candle D' Lites
4 Spellman Rd (06076-3610)
PHONE..................860 684-4874
Dianna Blanchard, Owner
EMP: 2
SQ FT: 1,200
SALES (est): 37.2K Privately Held
SIC: 3999 Candles

(G-8027)
DIVISION 5 LLC
99 Cooper Ln (06076-1312)
PHONE..................860 752-4127
Conrad Barker, Business Mgr
Alex Pumiglia, Project Mgr
EMP: 7
SALES (est): 2.2MM Privately Held
SIC: 3441 Fabricated structural metal

(G-8028)
EDGEWATER INTERNATIONAL LLC
Also Called: Rec Components
17 Middle River Dr (06076-1034)
PHONE..................860 851-9014
Bill Purtill, Controller
Alan Gnann,
Linda L Gnann,
▲ EMP: 15
SQ FT: 15,000
SALES (est): 2MM Privately Held
WEB: www.recoilguides.com
SIC: 3949 Fishing equipment

(G-8029)
FDM LLC
16 Woodland Dr (06076-1636)
P.O. Box 69 (06076-0069)
PHONE..................860 684-7466
Francis J Moriarty,
EMP: 2
SALES (est): 128.7K Privately Held
SIC: 3545 Precision tools, machinists'

(G-8030)
FLEETPRINTERS LLC
163 Diamond Ledge Rd (06076-3112)
PHONE..................860 684-2352
Galen Cromwell, Manager
EMP: 2
SALES (est): 90.5K Privately Held
SIC: 2752 Commercial printing, lithographic

(G-8031)
HOBBS MEDICAL INC
8 Spring St (06076-1505)
PHONE..................860 684-5875
Joanna Warner, President
Wayne Singer, Purchasing
Edward Page, Engineer
EMP: 22
SQ FT: 10,000
SALES (est): 4.6MM Privately Held
WEB: www.hobbsmedical.com
SIC: 3841 3845 Surgical & medical instruments; electromedical equipment

(G-8032)
LUCHON CABINET WOODWORK
140 Buckley Hwy (06076-4407)
PHONE..................860 684-5037
Jeff Luchon, Owner
EMP: 3
SALES (est): 411.4K Privately Held
WEB: www.luchoncabinet.com
SIC: 2434 Wood kitchen cabinets

(G-8033)
MSJ INVESTMENTS INC
Also Called: Rmi
72 W Stafford Rd Ste 3 (06076-1000)
PHONE..................860 684-9956
Mark S Jewson, President
EMP: 10
SQ FT: 4,000
SALES: 5MM Privately Held
WEB: www.msjinvestments.com
SIC: 3724 3812 Aircraft engines & engine parts; aircraft/aerospace flight instruments & guidance systems

(G-8034)
PRESTIGE CABINETRY
2 Rice Rd (06076-1679)
PHONE..................860 558-2784
EMP: 2
SALES (est): 119.9K Privately Held
SIC: 2434 Wood kitchen cabinets

(G-8035)
ROSSI PTER SIGNS LETTERING LLC
34 West St (06076-1338)
PHONE..................860 684-9229
Peter Rossi, President
EMP: 2
SQ FT: 1,040
SALES (est): 252.4K Privately Held
SIC: 3993 Signs & advertising specialties

(G-8036)
S P JOHNSON INC
20 Bowles Rd (06076-4100)
PHONE..................860 871-8664
Stephen P Johnson, President
Steve Johnson, President
Joan Johnson, Vice Pres
EMP: 2
SALES: 40K Privately Held
SIC: 3599 Machine & other job shop work

(G-8037)
SERAFIN SULKY CO
65 Buckley Hwy (06076-4426)
PHONE..................860 684-2986
Elmo Serafin, President
Michael Serafin, Treasurer
Marjorie Serafin, Admin Sec
EMP: 5
SQ FT: 5,000
SALES (est): 694.8K Privately Held
SIC: 3799 7699 Carriages, horse drawn; horse drawn vehicle repair

(G-8038)
SKYLINE QUARRY
110 Conklin Rd (06076-4204)
PHONE..................860 875-3580
Wayne C Williams, Partner
Carolyn Williams, Partner
EMP: 25
SQ FT: 1,500
SALES (est): 2.9MM Privately Held
SIC: 3281 1442 1423 5032 Stone, quarrying & processing of own stone products; construction sand & gravel; crushed & broken granite; building stone

(G-8039)
SOAPSTONE LANDING LLC
32 Gulf Rd (06076-4019)
PHONE..................860 875-6200
Anthony Jetmore, Principal
EMP: 1 EST: 2010
SALES (est): 91.2K Privately Held
SIC: 1499 Soapstone mining

(G-8040)
STAFFORD PRECISION TOOL LLC
25 West St (06076-1325)
P.O. Box 69 (06076-0069)
PHONE..................860 684-0471
Faran Moriarty,
Donna Moriarty,
EMP: 1 EST: 1997
SALES (est): 113K Privately Held
SIC: 3544 Special dies, tools, jigs & fixtures

(G-8041)
TE CONNECTIVITY CORPORATION
Tyco Elec Stafford Sprng Div
15 Tyco Dr (06076)
PHONE..................860 684-8000
Robert Peirce, General Mgr
EMP: 110
SALES (corp-wide): 13.9B Privately Held
WEB: www.raychem.com
SIC: 3549 3672 Assembly machines, including robotic; printed circuit boards
HQ: Te Connectivity Corporation
1050 Westlakes Dr
Berwyn PA 19312
610 893-9800

(G-8042)
TETRAULT & SONS INC
Also Called: Awnair
75 Tetrault Rd (06076-3134)
PHONE..................860 872-9187
Alan Tetrault, President
Jayne Tetrault, Treasurer
Joan Beaudet, Admin Sec
EMP: 6
SALES (est): 925.1K Privately Held
SIC: 3444 2394 1799 1751 Awnings, sheet metal; awnings, fabric: made from purchased materials; awning installation; window & door installation & erection; curtains & draperies; patio & deck construction & repair

(G-8043)
TTM PRINTED CIRCUIT GROUP INC
15 Industrial Park Dr (06076-3612)
PHONE..................860 684-8000
Bob Pierce, General Mgr
EMP: 165
SALES (corp-wide): 2.8B Publicly Held
WEB: www.printedcircuits.tycoelectronics.com
SIC: 3672 Printed circuit boards
HQ: Ttm Printed Circuit Group, Inc.
2630 S Harbor Blvd
Santa Ana CA 92704

(G-8044)
TTM TECHNOLOGIES INC
4 Old Monson Rd (06076-3319)
PHONE..................860 684-5881
Phil Titterton, General Mgr
EMP: 400
SALES (corp-wide): 2.8B Publicly Held
WEB: www.ttmtechnologies.com
SIC: 3672 Printed circuit boards
PA: Ttm Technologies, Inc.
200 Sandpointe Ave # 400
Santa Ana CA 92707
714 327-3000

(G-8045)
TTM TECHNOLOGIES INC
20 Industrial Park Dr (06076-3613)
PHONE..................860 684-8000
Keith Wood, Branch Mgr
EMP: 100
SALES (corp-wide): 2.8B Publicly Held
WEB: www.ttmtechnologies.com
SIC: 3672 Printed circuit boards
PA: Ttm Technologies, Inc.
200 Sandpointe Ave # 400
Santa Ana CA 92707
714 327-3000

(G-8046)
URG GRAPHICS INC (PA)
12 Fox Hill Dr (06076-3742)
PHONE..................860 928-0835
Arthur Etchells, CEO

▲ = Import ▼=Export
◆ =Import/Export

Rennie Cercone, *President*
Helen R Etchells, *Vice Pres*
J Paul Etchells, *Admin Sec*
EMP: 24
SQ FT: 19,000
SALES (est): 1.6MM **Privately Held**
SIC: 2796 Engraving platemaking services

(G-8047)
WORTHINGTON LOGGING
6 Crow Hill Rd (06076-3124)
PHONE..................................860 684-9605
Brian Worthington, *Owner*
Jennifer Worthington, *Co-Owner*
EMP: 2
SALES: 90K **Privately Held**
SIC: 2411 Timber, cut at logging camp

Stamford
Fairfield County

(G-8048)
170 MOUNTAINWOOD ROAD LLC
134 Forest St (06901-2133)
PHONE..................................203 252-4284
Brian Bello, *Principal*
EMP: 2
SALES (est): 50.2K **Privately Held**
SIC: 2499 Wood products

(G-8049)
20/20 SOFTWARE INC
2001 W Main St Ste 270 (06902-4540)
PHONE..................................203 316-5500
Donald Resnick, *President*
Sheron Resnick, *Vice Pres*
EMP: 8
SQ FT: 1,200
SALES (est): 994.2K **Privately Held**
WEB: www.2020soft.net
SIC: 3695 7389 4813 Computer software tape & disks: blank, rigid & floppy; design services;

(G-8050)
5 STAR PRINTING
9 Old North Stamford Rd 35a (06905-3929)
PHONE..................................203 975-1000
Janice Lederman, *Owner*
EMP: 2
SALES (est): 110K **Privately Held**
WEB: www.5starprinting.com
SIC: 2759 2752 Commercial printing; commercial printing, lithographic

(G-8051)
A GERBER CORP
110 Idlewood Dr (06905-2406)
PHONE..................................203 918-1913
Akemi Gerber Stuart, *President*
EMP: 3
SALES: 200K **Privately Held**
SIC: 2326 Industrial garments, men's & boys'

(G-8052)
A S FINE FOODS
Also Called: A-S Catering
856 High Ridge Rd (06905-1911)
PHONE..................................203 322-3899
Jack Marnaia, *President*
EMP: 65
SALES (est): 5.2MM **Privately Held**
SIC: 2032 Italian foods: packaged in cans, jars, etc.

(G-8053)
A TO A STUDIO SOLUTIONS LTD
47 Euclid Ave (06902-6230)
PHONE..................................203 388-9050
Wahler Allan, *President*
Carol Wahler, *CFO*
EMP: 10
SALES: 1.5MM **Privately Held**
SIC: 7374 2759 2791 7336 Computer graphics service; laser printing; poster & decal printing & engraving; screen printing; typographic composition, for the printing trade; graphic arts & related design

(G-8054)
A1 COMMERCIAL PRINTING CO LLC
9 Old North Stamford Rd 35a (06905-3929)
PHONE..................................203 975-1000
Janice Lederman, *Principal*
EMP: 2 **EST:** 2010
SALES (est): 122.7K **Privately Held**
SIC: 2752 Commercial printing, offset

(G-8055)
ABB ENTERPRISE SOFTWARE INC
900 Long Ridge Rd (06902-1139)
PHONE..................................203 329-8771
Nils Leffler, *Vice Pres*
Gregory E Sages, *CFO*
R Norton, *Treasurer*
John W Cutler Jr, *Branch Mgr*
Eugene E Madara, *Director*
EMP: 10
SALES (corp-wide): 36.4B **Privately Held**
WEB: www.elsterelectricity.com
SIC: 3612 Transformers, except electric
HQ: Abb Inc.
  305 Gregson Dr
  Cary NC 27511

(G-8056)
ACCENT SIGNS LLC
130 Lenox Ave Ste 21 (06906-2337)
PHONE..................................203 975-8688
John Massari,
Jill Massari,
EMP: 4
SQ FT: 2,000
SALES: 500K **Privately Held**
WEB: www.accent-signs.com
SIC: 3993 Signs, not made in custom sign painting shops

(G-8057)
ACCURATE TOOL & DIE INC
16 Leon Pl (06902-5508)
PHONE..................................203 967-1200
Jeffrey Salvatore, *President*
▲ **EMP:** 22 **EST:** 1956
SQ FT: 14,500
SALES (est): 3.6MM **Privately Held**
SIC: 3599 3544 Machine shop, jobbing & repair; special dies & tools

(G-8058)
ACI INDUSTRIES CONVERTING LTD
1266 E Main St Ste 700r (06902-3507)
PHONE..................................740 368-4166
EMP: 2
SALES (corp-wide): 3.8MM **Privately Held**
SIC: 2676 Towels, napkins & tissue paper products
HQ: Aci Industries Converting, Ltd.
  970 Pittsburgh Dr
  Delaware OH 43015
  740 368-4160

(G-8059)
ACME SIGN CO (PA)
12 Research Dr (06906-1419)
P.O. Box 2345 (06906-0345)
PHONE..................................203 324-2263
Stephen Trell, *President*
Jeff Trell, *Vice Pres*
EMP: 18
SQ FT: 7,000
SALES (est): 2.3MM **Privately Held**
WEB: www.acmesignco.com
SIC: 3993 3953 5099 5719 Signs & advertising specialties; textile marking stamps, hand: rubber or metal; signs, except electric; rubber stamps; lighting fixtures; rubber stamps

(G-8060)
ACQUISITIONS CONTROLLED SVCS
55 Woodland Pl Apt 4 (06902-6962)
P.O. Box 106, Riverside (06878-0106)
PHONE..................................203 327-6364
Kenneth Thron, *President*
Deborah Thron, *Admin Sec*
EMP: 3
SQ FT: 6,000
SALES: 1.5MM **Privately Held**
SIC: 3441 Fabricated structural metal

(G-8061)
ACTION LETTER INC (PA)
11 Elm Ct (06902-5117)
PHONE..................................203 323-2466
Ellen Connery, *President*
Carlos Lopez, *Prdtn Mgr*
Fanny Chafloque, *Production*
David Chilenskas, *Info Tech Mgr*
Meg Orner, *Business Dir*
EMP: 20
SALES (est): 4.5MM **Privately Held**
SIC: 7331 7334 2791 2752 Mailing list compilers; photocopying & duplicating services; typesetting; commercial printing, lithographic

(G-8062)
ADIRONDACK WOOD PRODUCTS LLC
174 Larkspur Rd (06903-3409)
PHONE..................................203 322-4518
Joseph Dastoli III, *Partner*
EMP: 2
SALES: 120K **Privately Held**
SIC: 2511 5712 Lawn furniture: wood; furniture stores

(G-8063)
AFROASIA PUBLICATION LLC
132 Hope St Unit B (06906-2544)
PHONE..................................917 692-3937
Zarri Gul, *Administration*
EMP: 1
SALES (est): 62.8K **Privately Held**
SIC: 2741 Miscellaneous publishing

(G-8064)
AFTEL CORP
137 Big Oak Rd (06903-4635)
PHONE..................................203 329-2273
Arthur Feldman, *President*
EMP: 2
SALES (est): 170.5K **Privately Held**
SIC: 3829 Measuring & controlling devices

(G-8065)
AG JEWELRY DESIGNS LLC (PA)
1 Stamford Plz (06901-3271)
PHONE..................................800 643-0978
Michael Soutar,
Mary K Soutar,
EMP: 4
SQ FT: 3,600
SALES: 1MM **Privately Held**
SIC: 3911 5094 Jewelry, precious metal; jewelry & precious stones

(G-8066)
AG SEMICONDUCTOR SERVICES LLC
1111 Summer St Fl 4 (06905-5511)
PHONE..................................203 322-5300
Albert P Vasquez,
Joshua Brain,
Julian Gates,
▼ **EMP:** 30
SQ FT: 10,000
SALES: 15MM **Privately Held**
SIC: 3674 Semiconductors & related devices

(G-8067)
AGI-SHOREWOOD GROUP US LLC
300 Atlantic St Ste 206 (06901-3514)
PHONE..................................203 324-4839
Timothy J Facio, *Vice Pres*
Jacob D Hudson, *Vice Pres*
Donald K Eldert, *CFO*
Philip E Schuch, *Treasurer*
◆ **EMP:** 1005 **EST:** 1966
SALES (est): 70.1K
SALES (corp-wide): 2.9B **Privately Held**
WEB: www.shorepak.com
SIC: 2671 2652 2657 Packaging paper & plastics film, coated & laminated; setup paperboard boxes; folding paperboard boxes
PA: Atlas Holdings, Llc
  100 Northfield St
  Greenwich CT 06830
  203 622-9138

(G-8068)
AICAS INC
6 Landmark Sq Ste 400 (06901-2711)
PHONE..................................203 359-5705
James J Hunt, *CEO*
EMP: 2
SALES (est): 150.1K **Privately Held**
SIC: 7372 7371 7373 Prepackaged software; computer software development & applications; systems software development services

(G-8069)
AIRCASTLE ADVISOR LLC
201 Tresser Blvd Ste 400 (06901-3435)
PHONE..................................203 504-1020
Roy Chandran, *Exec VP*
Michael Kriedberg, *Ch Credit Ofcr*
Ron Wainshal, *Mng Member*
Marie Gannon, *Manager*
J Robert Peart, *CIO*
EMP: 78
SALES (est): 11.3MM **Publicly Held**
WEB: www.aircastle.com
SIC: 7359 3721 Aircraft rental; aircraft
PA: Aircastle Limited
  201 Tresser Blvd Ste 400
  Stamford CT 06901

(G-8070)
AIRTECH OF STAMFORD INC
21 Anthony St (06902-4791)
PHONE..................................203 323-3959
John Delelle, *President*
Lucio Bortot, *Vice Pres*
Tim Walkley, *Opers Staff*
Rose Bernadel, *Office Mgr*
Christopher Hanulik, *Shareholder*
EMP: 30
SQ FT: 8,400
SALES: 5.5MM **Privately Held**
WEB: www.airtech-hvac.com
SIC: 1711 1761 3444 Heating & air conditioning contractors; ventilation & duct work contractor; sheet metalwork; sheet metalwork

(G-8071)
ALLIANCE WATER TREATMENT CO
28 Coachlamp Ln (06902-2005)
P.O. Box 3036 (06905-0036)
PHONE..................................203 323-9968
John F Piatek, *President*
Laure Kovacs, *Office Mgr*
EMP: 6
SALES (est): 550K **Privately Held**
WEB: www.allianceh2o.com
SIC: 3589 Water treatment equipment, industrial

(G-8072)
ALLIED CONTROLS INC
25 Forest St Apt 14a (06901-1860)
PHONE..................................860 628-8443
Mohd Aslami, *President*
Charles De Luca, *Vice Pres*
EMP: 11
SQ FT: 25,000
SALES: 596.6K **Privately Held**
WEB: www.alliedcontrols.com
SIC: 3643 3613 3625 Current-carrying wiring devices;*switchgear & switchboard apparatus; relays, for electronic use

(G-8073)
AMERICAN ART HERITAGE PUBG
66 Broad St Ste 4 (06901-2314)
PHONE..................................203 973-0564
Natalie Alexander, *Owner*
EMP: 2 **EST:** 2007
SALES (est): 82.9K **Privately Held**
SIC: 2741 Art copy & poster publishing

(G-8074)
AMERICAN BANKNOTE CORPORATION (PA)
Also Called: Abcorp
1055 Washington Blvd Fl 6 (06901-2216)
PHONE..................................203 941-4090
Steven G Singer, *CEO*
Jack Barnett, *Vice Pres*
David Kober, *Vice Pres*
Steve Andrews, *CFO*

Hilgren Randy, *Sales Staff*
◆ **EMP:** 6
SQ FT: 8,020
SALES (est): 292.8MM **Privately Held**
WEB: www.americanbanknote.com
SIC: 2759 2752 2621 Commercial printing; cards, lithographed; card paper

(G-8075)
AMERICAN INDUS ACQISITION CORP (PA)
Also Called: Aiac
1 Harbor Point Rd # 1700 (06902-7317)
PHONE 203 952-9212
Leonard Levie, *President*
John Isella, *Exec VP*
Siobhan Sweeney-Cordova, *Exec VP*
Ian Fichtenbaum, *Senior VP*
Brandon Stewar, *Senior VP*
EMP: 1
SQ FT: 2,000
SALES: 1B **Privately Held**
SIC: 3443 Heat exchangers: coolers (after, inter), condensers, etc.

(G-8076)
AMERICAN KRAFT PAPER INDS LLC
1 Harbor Point Rd # 1700 (06902-7317)
PHONE 203 323-1916
EMP: 1
SALES (est): 57.5K **Privately Held**
SIC: 2621 Kraft paper

(G-8077)
AMERICAN PROTOTYPE HOB
203 Sylvan Knoll Rd (06902-5341)
P.O. Box 2305 (06906-0305)
PHONE 203 323-6832
EMP: 2
SALES (est): 117.1K **Privately Held**
SIC: 3999 Manufacturing industries

(G-8078)
AMERICAN SOLAR & ALTERMATIVE
Also Called: ASAP
2777 Summer St Ste 204 (06905-4383)
PHONE 203 324-7186
EMP: 2
SALES (est): 334.7K **Privately Held**
SIC: 3648 5074 Mfg Lighting Equipment Whol Plumbing Equipment/Supplies

(G-8079)
AMERICAN UNMANNED SYSTEMS LLC
460 Summer St (06901-1301)
PHONE 203 406-7611
Dorothea Smith, *Vice Pres*
Peter Muhlrad, *Marketing Staff*
EMP: 5
SALES (est): 370.8K **Privately Held**
SIC: 3519 3724 5088 Controls, remote, for boats; aircraft engines & engine parts; helicopter parts

(G-8080)
AMPCO PUBLISHING & PRTG CORP
130 Lenox Ave Ste 32 (06906-2337)
P.O. Box 8239 (06905-8239)
PHONE 203 325-1509
Daniel Sposi Sr, *President*
Maryann Sposi, *Vice Pres*
EMP: 4
SQ FT: 3,000
SALES (est): 526.1K **Privately Held**
SIC: 2752 Commercial printing, offset

(G-8081)
AMPHENOL CORPORATION
Amphenol Nexus Technologies
50 Sunnyside Ave (06902-7641)
PHONE 203 327-7300
Fereidoun A Farahani, *Manager*
EMP: 60
SALES (corp-wide): 8.2B **Publicly Held**
SIC: 3643 Electric switches; connectors & terminals for electrical devices
PA: Amphenol Corporation
358 Hall Ave
Wallingford CT 06492
203 265-8900

(G-8082)
AMPHENOL NEXUS TECHNOLOGIES
50 Sunnyside Ave (06902-7641)
PHONE 203 327-7300
Fereidoun A Farahani, *General Mgr*
EMP: 60 **EST:** 1961
SQ FT: 16,000
SALES (est): 11.6MM
SALES (corp-wide): 8.2B **Publicly Held**
WEB: www.nexus.com
SIC: 3643 Electric connectors; electric switches
PA: Amphenol Corporation
358 Hall Ave
Wallingford CT 06492
203 265-8900

(G-8083)
AMS STRATEGIC MANAGEMENT INC
Also Called: AMS Supply Management
201 Commons Park S # 702 (06902-7066)
P.O. Box 674, Harriman NY (10926-0674)
PHONE 845 500-5635
Michelle Sanchez, *Business Mgr*
EMP: 2 **EST:** 2014
SALES (est): 232.8K **Privately Held**
SIC: 8741 5088 3585 3711 Business management; transportation equipment & supplies; aircraft & space vehicle supplies & parts; aeronautical equipment & supplies; aircraft equipment & supplies; refrigeration & heating equipment; military motor vehicle assembly; intercommunication systems, electric; radio frequency measuring equipment

(G-8084)
ANDREW LAMBERT
175 Atlantic St (06901-3500)
PHONE 203 249-6310
Andrew Lambert, *Owner*
EMP: 1
SALES (est): 53.4K **Privately Held**
SIC: 3679 Electronic circuits

(G-8085)
ANGELA COSMAI INC
383 Janes Ln (06903-4820)
PHONE 203 329-7403
Angela Cosmai, *President*
Daniel Nault, *Vice Pres*
EMP: 2
SQ FT: 2,000
SALES: 250K **Privately Held**
SIC: 2844 Hair preparations, including shampoos

(G-8086)
ANJAR CO
42 Russet Rd (06903-1822)
PHONE 203 321-1023
James Becker, *Partner*
Jonathan Becker, *Partner*
David Schlatter, *Manager*
EMP: 5
SQ FT: 1,000
SALES (est): 340K **Privately Held**
WEB: www.anjar.com
SIC: 3944 3942 Games, toys & children's vehicles; dolls & stuffed toys

(G-8087)
ANOTHERCREATIONBYMICHELE
1351 Riverbank Rd (06903-2026)
PHONE 203 322-4277
Michele Pulver, *Mng Member*
EMP: 2
SALES (est): 2.5MM **Privately Held**
WEB: www.anothercreation.com
SIC: 2771 Greeting cards

(G-8088)
APIJECT SYSTEMS CORP (PA)
2 High Ridge Park (06905-1350)
PHONE 203 461-7121
Jay Walker, *CEO*
EMP: 2
SALES: 500K **Privately Held**
SIC: 3999 Manufacturing industries

(G-8089)
AR ROBINSON PRINTING
215 Lawn Ave (06902-3115)
PHONE 203 961-1787
Alvin Robinson, *Principal*
EMP: 2
SALES (est): 212.9K **Privately Held**
SIC: 2752 Commercial printing, lithographic

(G-8090)
ARCADIA ARCHITECTURAL PDTS INC
110 Viaduct Rd (06907-2707)
PHONE 203 316-8000
Robert Sayour, *President*
◆ **EMP:** 25
SALES (est): 5.9MM **Privately Held**
WEB: www.arcadiaproducts.com
SIC: 3442 Metal doors, sash & trim

(G-8091)
ARCCOS GOLF LLC
700 Canal St Ste 19 (06902-5921)
PHONE 844 692-7226
Sal Syed, *Owner*
Ammad Faisal, *COO*
Stephanie Boms, *Vice Pres*
Ryan Smith, *Opers Staff*
Jared Rapoport, *Sales Mgr*
EMP: 28
SQ FT: 4,500
SALES (est): 2.5MM **Privately Held**
SIC: 3679 Electronic circuits

(G-8092)
ARISTO DATA SYSTEMS
1010 Summer St Ste 102a (06905-5533)
PHONE 203 322-1113
Jo Friedlander,
Steven J Monk,
EMP: 2
SALES (est): 235K **Privately Held**
SIC: 7372 Business oriented computer software

(G-8093)
ARNOW SILK SCREENING LLC
31 Viaduct Rd Ste 2 (06907-2719)
PHONE 203 964-1963
Marylee Arnow, *Manager*
EMP: 2
SALES (est): 191.1K **Privately Held**
SIC: 2759 Screen printing

(G-8094)
ARRAYENT HEALTH LLC
1266 E Main St Ste 700r (06902-3507)
PHONE 973 568-0323
Kevin Jones, *CEO*
Stephen Maccaux, *Sales Staff*
EMP: 2
SALES (est): 149.4K **Privately Held**
SIC: 3577 Computer peripheral equipment

(G-8095)
ART OF WELLBEING LLC
230 Saddle Hill Rd (06903-2301)
PHONE 917 453-3009
Michiel Nolet, *CEO*
Igor Shindel, *COO*
EMP: 5
SALES: 80K **Privately Held**
SIC: 7372 7389 Prepackaged software;

(G-8096)
ARTHUR G BYRNE CO INC
88 Erskine Rd (06903-1023)
PHONE 203 461-8805
Arthur Byrne, *President*
EMP: 2
SALES (est): 240K **Privately Held**
SIC: 3465 Body parts, automobile: stamped metal

(G-8097)
ASSET VANTAGE INC
1 Dock St Ste 201 (06902-5836)
PHONE 475 218-2639
EMP: 1
SALES (est): 30.7K **Privately Held**
SIC: 7372 Prepackaged software

(G-8098)
ATLANTIC STREET CAPITL MGT LLC (PA)
281 Tresser Blvd Fl 6 (06901-3246)
PHONE 203 428-3150
Peter Shabecoff, *Managing Prtnr*
Andy Wilkins, *Managing Prtnr*
Brian Cooper, *Vice Pres*
Iris Rosken, *CFO*
Christina Garceau, *Executive Asst*
EMP: 50
SALES (est): 482.8MM **Privately Held**
WEB: www.atlanticstreetcapital.com
SIC: 6799 2099 Venture capital companies; food preparations

(G-8099)
AVALON IT SYSTEMS
35 6th St (06905-4603)
PHONE 203 323-7000
Fernando Alvarenga, *Principal*
EMP: 2
SALES (est): 113.8K **Privately Held**
SIC: 7372 Business oriented computer software

(G-8100)
AVOLON AEROSPACE NEW YORK INC
700 Canal St 2nd (06902-5921)
PHONE 203 663-5490
Karla Micklo, *Assistant VP*
Dorothea Peterson, *Assistant VP*
Lisa Janiga, *Vice Pres*
Debbie McAdam, *Vice Pres*
Kathleen Murphy, *Vice Pres*
EMP: 7
SALES (est): 246.3K **Privately Held**
SIC: 3721 Aircraft
PA: Avolon Aerospace Leasing Limited
Building 1
Dublin

(G-8101)
AVRIO HEALTH LP
201 Tresser Blvd (06901-3435)
PHONE 888 827-0624
John Stewart, *Managing Prtnr*
Edward Mahony, *Partner*
EMP: 1500
SALES (est): 88.5MM **Privately Held**
SIC: 2834 Pharmaceutical preparations
PA: Purdue Pharma L.P.
201 Tresser Blvd Fl 1
Stamford CT 06901

(G-8102)
AZ WOODWORKING LLC
14 Dora St Apt 2 (06902-9407)
PHONE 203 595-9063
Adam Zagaja, *Principal*
EMP: 2
SALES (est): 92.8K **Privately Held**
SIC: 2431 Millwork

(G-8103)
B & F ELECTRIC MOTORS LLC
156 Magee Ave (06902-5908)
PHONE 203 359-2626
Charles Solon,
Michael Solon,
EMP: 2
SALES (est): 322.8K **Privately Held**
SIC: 5063 7694 Motors, electric; electric motor repair

(G-8104)
B-E INDUSTRIES
225 Pinewood Rd (06903-2521)
PHONE 203 357-8055
EMP: 2
SALES (est): 84K **Privately Held**
SIC: 3999 Mfg Misc Products

(G-8105)
BAE SYSTEMS APPLIED INTEL INC
21 Harbor View Ave (06902-5913)
PHONE 203 323-0066
EMP: 2 **EST:** 2016
SALES (est): 77.4K **Privately Held**
SIC: 3812 3721 Aircraft/aerospace flight instruments & guidance systems; non-motorized & lighter-than-air aircraft

GEOGRAPHIC SECTION
Stamford - Fairfield County (G-8138)

(G-8106)
BAL INTERNATIONAL INC
281 Tresser Blvd Fl 12 (06901-3238)
PHONE.................................203 359-6775
Emilio Galetzki, *President*
Elliott Levy, *Vice Pres*
Edward Thomas Jr, *Treasurer*
Richard Southey, *Director*
EMP: 25
SALES (est): 2.1MM **Privately Held**
SIC: 3339 Precious metals

(G-8107)
BAM ELECTRIC LLC
12 Sandy Ln (06905-2133)
PHONE.................................203 595-0008
EMP: 2
SALES (est): 210K **Privately Held**
SIC: 3699 Mfg Electrical Equipment/Supplies

(G-8108)
BEAUTIFUL TABLES LLC
53 W Bank Ln (06902-1309)
PHONE.................................203 602-9969
Savka Wisecup,
EMP: 1
SALES (est): 73.3K **Privately Held**
SIC: 2392 Tablecloths: made from purchased materials

(G-8109)
BELDOTTI BAKERIES
Also Called: Cerbone Bakery
605 Newfield Ave (06905-3302)
PHONE.................................203 348-9029
James Beldotti Jr, *Partner*
Michael Beldotti, *Partner*
EMP: 15
SQ FT: 3,000
SALES (est): 903.5K **Privately Held**
SIC: 2051 2052 Bakery: wholesale or wholesale/retail combined; cookies & crackers

(G-8110)
BEP FLAVOR HOLDINGS LLC (PA)
201 Tresser Blvd Ste 320 (06901-3435)
PHONE.................................203 595-4520
Donald L Hawks III,
EMP: 2
SALES (est): 19.2MM **Privately Held**
SIC: 2087 Flavoring extracts & syrups

(G-8111)
BEST GASKETS
41 Orange St (06902-4276)
PHONE.................................914 347-1971
Nare Pesso, *Owner*
EMP: 2
SALES (est): 74.7K **Privately Held**
SIC: 3053 Gaskets, packing & sealing devices

(G-8112)
BIROTECH INC
29 Sunnyside Ave Ste 4 (06902-7607)
PHONE.................................203 968-5080
Maria Szebeni, *President*
Larry Szebeni, *Exec VP*
EMP: 4
SQ FT: 1,750
SALES: 425K **Privately Held**
SIC: 3469 3724 Metal stampings; aircraft engines & engine parts

(G-8113)
BLU & GRAE MUSIC
1901 Long Ridge Rd (06903-3201)
PHONE.................................857 204-3095
Geoffrey Gamere, *Principal*
EMP: 1
SALES (est): 53.8K **Privately Held**
SIC: 3931 Recorders (musical instruments)

(G-8114)
BOTTARGA BROTHERS LLC
263 Brookdale Rd (06903-4118)
PHONE.................................203 355-1134
Jean Madar, *Software Dev*
Herbert Madar,
EMP: 2
SALES (est): 159.4K **Privately Held**
SIC: 2091 Fish, cured

(G-8115)
BOTTOM LINE INC (PA)
Also Called: Bottom Line Publications
3 Landmark Sq Ste 230 (06901-2501)
PHONE.................................203 973-5900
Margie Abramas, *President*
Martin Edelston, *Chairman*
Rita Edelston, *Vice Pres*
Sam Edelston, *Vice Pres*
Marilyn Knowlton, *Research*
EMP: 80
SQ FT: 22,000
SALES (est): 21.4MM **Privately Held**
WEB: www.bottomlinepublications.com
SIC: 2721 Magazines: publishing only, not printed on site

(G-8116)
BRADT ENTERPRISES LLC
200 W Hill Rd (06902-1712)
PHONE.................................203 323-8501
George Bradt, *Owner*
EMP: 1
SALES (est): 41.4K **Privately Held**
SIC: 2731 Books: publishing & printing

(G-8117)
BRAIN PARADE LLC
1177 High Ridge Rd (06905-1221)
PHONE.................................203 329-8136
James McClafferty, *Principal*
EMP: 5
SALES (est): 500K **Privately Held**
SIC: 3695 Computer software tape & disks: blank, rigid & floppy

(G-8118)
BRAINBEAT INC
6 Landmark Sq Fl 4 (06901-2704)
PHONE.................................917 291-9747
Suguna Sanakkayala, *President*
EMP: 1
SALES (est): 64.9K **Privately Held**
SIC: 3944 Board games, children's & adults'

(G-8119)
BRANBROKS DNTL STFFING SLTIONS
61 Quintard Ter (06902-3902)
PHONE.................................704 784-1056
EMP: 2
SALES (est): 90K **Privately Held**
SIC: 3674 Semiconductors & related devices

(G-8120)
BROOKSIDE FLVORS INGRDENTS LLC (HQ)
201 Tresser Blvd Ste 320 (06901-3435)
PHONE.................................203 595-4520
Donald L Hawks III, *President*
Richard Nikola, *COO*
William Gambrell, *Vice Pres*
Gaetan Sourceau, *CFO*
EMP: 88
SALES (est): 19.2MM **Privately Held**
SIC: 2087 Flavoring extracts & syrups
PA: Bep Flavor Holdings Llc
    201 Tresser Blvd Ste 320
    Stamford CT 06901
    203 595-4520

(G-8121)
BRUCE KAHN
225 Pinewood Rd (06903-2521)
PHONE.................................203 329-7441
Bruce Kahn, *Owner*
EMP: 1 EST: 2010
SALES (est): 58.6K **Privately Held**
SIC: 2514 Novelty furniture, household: metal

(G-8122)
BTX INDUSTRIES
84 W Park Pl (06901-2211)
PHONE.................................203 359-4870
Bill Avery, *CEO*
EMP: 1
SALES (est): 51.1K **Privately Held**
SIC: 3999 Manufacturing industries

(G-8123)
C C D CENTER
24 Roxbury Rd (06902-1220)
PHONE.................................203 348-0052
Eileen Towne, *Manager*
EMP: 1
SALES (est): 54.5K **Privately Held**
SIC: 3229 Pressed & blown glass

(G-8124)
C J S MILLWORK INC
425 Fairfield Ave Ste 12 (06902-7588)
PHONE.................................203 708-0080
Chris Sculti, *President*
Steve Scenna, *Manager*
EMP: 10 EST: 1996
SALES (est): 1.2MM **Privately Held**
WEB: www.cjsmillwork.com
SIC: 2431 Millwork

(G-8125)
CABALLROS HRDWOOD FLORS PNTINC
2 Myano Ct (06902-2108)
PHONE.................................914 312-0695
Olvin Caballeros, *Principal*
EMP: 1 EST: 2016
SALES (est): 55K **Privately Held**
SIC: 2426 Hardwood dimension & flooring mills

(G-8126)
CADMUS
200 1st Stamford Pl Fl 2 (06902-6753)
PHONE.................................203 595-3000
Scott J Goodwin, *CFO*
Scott Grant, *Manager*
John Lindquist, *Technology*
EMP: 6
SALES (est): 461K **Privately Held**
SIC: 2752 Commercial printing, lithographic

(G-8127)
CARA THERAPEUTICS INC
107 Elm St Fl 9 (06902-3834)
PHONE.................................203 406-3700
Derek Chalmers, *President*
Frederique Menzaghi, *Senior VP*
Mani Mohindru, *CFO*
Richard Makara, *Controller*
Scott M Terrillion, *Ch Credit Ofcr*
EMP: 37
SQ FT: 24,000
SALES (est): 13.4MM **Privately Held**
WEB: www.caratherapeutics.com
SIC: 2834 8731 Pharmaceutical preparations; commercial physical research; biotechnical research, commercial

(G-8128)
CARLA WAY
65 High Ridge Rd 287 (06905-3800)
PHONE.................................203 351-7815
EMP: 1
SALES (est): 52K **Privately Held**
SIC: 3951 Mfg Pens/Mechanical Pencils

(G-8129)
CASARO LABS LTD
1100 Summer St Ste 203 (06905-5520)
PHONE.................................203 353-8500
Ron Viccari, *President*
Sam Lubliner, *Vice Pres*
▲ EMP: 7
SQ FT: 2,200
SALES (est): 1MM **Privately Held**
SIC: 2844 Cosmetic preparations

(G-8130)
CASE CONCEPTS INTL LLC (PA)
112 Prospect St Unit A (06901-1207)
PHONE.................................203 883-8602
Ed Bell, *Vice Pres*
Tony Lee, *Manager*
Raul Riveros,
Edward Bell,
▲ EMP: 16
SQ FT: 7,500
SALES: 2.2MM **Privately Held**
WEB: www.caseconcepts.com
SIC: 3161 Attache cases

(G-8131)
CASTLETON COMMODITIES (HQ)
2200 Atlantic St Ste 800 (06902-6834)
PHONE.................................203 564-8100
EMP: 5 EST: 2016
SALES (est): 474.8K **Privately Held**
SIC: 4923 1382 6799 Gas transmission & distribution; oil & gas exploration services; commodity investors

(G-8132)
CAVEGRL LLC
34 Clifford Ave (06905-3607)
PHONE.................................914 261-5801
Erica Pesso,
EMP: 1
SALES (est): 42.9K **Privately Held**
SIC: 2064 Granola & muesli, bars & clusters

(G-8133)
CCI CORPUS CHRISTI LLC
2200 Atlantic St Ste 800 (06902-6834)
PHONE.................................203 564-8100
Michale Dowling, *President*
EMP: 4
SALES (est): 260.3K **Privately Held**
SIC: 2911 Petroleum refining
PA: Castleton Commodities International Llc
    2200 Atlantic St Ste 800
    Stamford CT 06902

(G-8134)
CCI CYRUS RIVER TERMINAL LLC
2200 Atlantic St Ste 800 (06902-6834)
PHONE.................................203 761-8000
William C Reed II, *President*
EMP: 9 EST: 2008
SALES (est): 800.4K **Privately Held**
SIC: 3999 Dock equipment & supplies, industrial
HQ: Cci Us Asset Holdings Llc
    2200 Atlantic St Ste 800
    Stamford CT 06902
    203 564-8100

(G-8135)
CCI EAST TEXAS UPSTREAM LLC
2200 Atlantic St Ste 800 (06902-6834)
PHONE.................................203 564-8100
Joseph Rothbauer, *Principal*
EMP: 7 EST: 2017
SALES (est): 110.6K **Privately Held**
SIC: 4923 1382 6799 Gas transmission & distribution; oil & gas exploration services; commodity investors
HQ: Castleton Commodities Upstream Ii Llc
    2200 Atlantic St Ste 800
    Stamford CT 06902
    203 564-8100

(G-8136)
CCI ROBINSONS BEND LLC
2200 Atlantic St Ste 800 (06902-6834)
PHONE.................................203 564-8571
Craig Jarchow, *President*
EMP: 4
SALES (est): 172.6K **Privately Held**
SIC: 1311 Crude petroleum & natural gas
PA: Castleton Commodities International Llc
    2200 Atlantic St Ste 800
    Stamford CT 06902

(G-8137)
CEMA PUBLISHING LLC
56 Maitland Rd (06906-2103)
PHONE.................................585 317-3724
Charleen E Merced Agosto, *Principal*
EMP: 1
SALES (est): 41.3K **Privately Held**
SIC: 2741 Miscellaneous publishing

(G-8138)
CENVEO INC
200 1st Stamford Pl (06902-6753)
PHONE.................................203 595-3000
EMP: 80

Stamford - Fairfield County (G-8139)

SALES: 1.6B **Privately Held**
WEB: www.mail-well.com
SIC: **2677** 2679 Envelopes; tags & labels, paper

(G-8139)
CENVEO CORPORATION
200 Frst Stamford Pl Fl 2 (06902)
PHONE...................................303 790-8023
EMP: 40 EST: 1993
SALES (est): 1.3B **Privately Held**
WEB: www.mail-wellenvelope.com
SIC: **2677** 2752 2759 Envelopes; commercial printing, lithographic; color lithography; promotional printing, lithographic; catalogs, lithographed; labels & seals: printing

(G-8140)
CENVEO ENTERPRISES INC (PA)
200 First Stamford Pl # 2 (06902-6753)
PHONE...................................203 595-3000
Robert G Burton Jr, *Ch of Bd*
Greg Suek, *Client Mgr*
Tony Fleshman, *Sales Staff*
Tom Krubl, *Sales Staff*
Scott Reid, *Sales Staff*
EMP: 4
SALES (est): 2.6B **Privately Held**
SIC: **2677** 2679 Envelopes; tags & labels, paper

(G-8141)
CENVEO WORLDWIDE LIMITED (DH)
Also Called: Lightninglabel.com
200 First Stamford Pl # 2 (06902-6753)
PHONE...................................203 595-3000
Robert G Burton, *CEO*
Michael G Burton, *President*
Marivel Medina, *Publisher*
Glenn Eddleman, *General Mgr*
Marcia Berry, *Counsel*
EMP: 11
SALES (est): 2.8B
SALES (corp-wide): 2.6B **Privately Held**
SIC: **2677** 2679 Envelopes; tags & labels, paper
HQ: Cwl Enterprises, Inc.
200 First Stamford Pl # 2
Stamford CT 06902
303 790-8023

(G-8142)
CHEF GRETCHEN LLC
1184 Newfield Ave (06905-1409)
PHONE...................................203 252-8892
Gretchen Raymond,
EMP: 2
SALES: 65K **Privately Held**
SIC: **3999** 5963 5199 Manufacturing industries; food services, direct sales; non-durable goods

(G-8143)
CHIEF EXECUTIVE GROUP LLC (PA)
9 W Broad St Ste 430 (06902-3764)
PHONE...................................785 832-0303
Marshall Cooper, *CEO*
Lynn Whylly, *Editor*
Wayne Cooper, *Chairman*
Melanie Haniph, *Vice Pres*
Gabriella Kallay, *Vice Pres*
EMP: 14
SQ FT: 4,200
SALES: 6MM **Privately Held**
SIC: **2721** 2741 7319 8611 Magazines: publishing only, not printed on site; business service newsletters: publishing & printing; media buying service; business associations; management consulting services

(G-8144)
CHIEF EXECUTIVE GROUP LP (PA)
Also Called: Chief Executive Magazine
9 W Broad St Ste 430 (06902-3764)
PHONE...................................203 930-2700
Edward Kopko, *CEO*
Bobbiann Victory, *Research Analys*
EMP: 23
SQ FT: 6,600

SALES (est): 2.5MM **Privately Held**
SIC: **2721** 8742 Magazines: publishing only, not printed on site; management consulting services

(G-8145)
CHUNGHUA CABINET CT INC
120 Viaduct Rd (06907-2707)
PHONE...................................718 886-4588
EMP: 1
SALES (est): 53.7K **Privately Held**
SIC: **2434** Wood kitchen cabinets

(G-8146)
CIETRADE SYSTEMS INC
263 Tresser Blvd Ste 1030 (06901-3236)
PHONE...................................203 323-0074
David Haber, *President*
Richard Hamilton, *Managing Prtnr*
Marc Covey, *Software Dev*
Suzanne Haber, *Director*
EMP: 2 EST: 1999
SALES (est): 227.2K **Privately Held**
WEB: www.socialsoftwarecompany.com
SIC: **7372** Business oriented computer software

(G-8147)
CINE MAGNETICS INC (PA)
Also Called: CMI Media Management
9 W Broad St Ste 250 (06902-3758)
P.O. Box 862, Armonk NY (10504-0862)
PHONE...................................914 273-7600
Robert Pastore, *President*
Joseph J Barber Jr, *Chairman*
Stephen Kushel, *Admin Sec*
▲ EMP: 105
SQ FT: 62,282
SALES (est): 18.9MM **Privately Held**
WEB: www.cmvdl.com
SIC: **7819** 7221 3861 7384 Video tape or disk reproduction; photographer, still or video; photographic processing chemicals; photofinish laboratories

(G-8148)
CITA LLC
25 Forest St Apt 6k (06901-1855)
PHONE...................................203 545-7035
Gergana Genova,
EMP: 1
SALES (est): 39.7K **Privately Held**
SIC: **7372** Application computer software

(G-8149)
CITY DATA CABLE CO
34 Parker Ave (06906-1712)
PHONE...................................203 327-7917
Greg Burns, *President*
EMP: 3
SALES (est): 197.3K **Privately Held**
SIC: **3315** Steel wire & related products

(G-8150)
CLEMONS PRODUCTIONS INC
Also Called: Thought For The Week
875 Westover Rd (06902-1319)
PHONE...................................203 316-9394
Mark Connolly, *President*
EMP: 6
SALES: 323.1K **Privately Held**
SIC: **4832** 2721 Radio broadcasting stations; magazines: publishing & printing

(G-8151)
COFCO AMERICAS RESOURCES CORP (PA)
Also Called: Cofco-Agri Coffee Cotton Grain
4 Stamford Plz (06902-3834)
PHONE...................................203 252-5200
William J Cronin, *President*
David E Behrends, *Exec VP*
Eric Twombly, *Treasurer*
Joseph P Limone, *Admin Sec*
EMP: 280
SQ FT: 48,060
SALES (est): 335.4MM **Privately Held**
SIC: **6221** 5153 5149 2099 Commodity dealers, contracts; grain & field beans; cocoa; sugar

(G-8152)
COMANCHE CLEAN ENERGY CORP
1 Dock St Ste 101 (06902-5872)
PHONE...................................203 326-4570
EMP: 3 EST: 2007
SALES (est): 170K **Privately Held**
SIC: **2842** Mfg Polish/Sanitation Goods

(G-8153)
COMICANA INC
61 Studio Rd (06903-4724)
PHONE...................................203 968-0748
Mort Walker, *President*
Greg Walker, *Vice Pres*
Brian Walker, *Admin Sec*
EMP: 9
SALES: 1.2MM **Privately Held**
SIC: **2721** 2731 Comic books: publishing only, not printed on site; books: publishing & printing

(G-8154)
COMPANY OF COCA-COLA BOTTLING
333 Ludlow St Ste 8 (06902-6991)
PHONE...................................203 905-3900
Ann Ellam, *Manager*
EMP: 80 **Privately Held**
WEB: www.coke.com
SIC: **2086** Bottled & canned soft drinks
HQ: Coca-Cola Bottling Company Of Southeastern New England, Inc.
150 Waterford Parkway S
Waterford CT 06385
860 443-2816

(G-8155)
COMPUTER PRGRM & SYSTEMS INC (PA)
Also Called: Actuaries Division
1011 High Ridge Rd # 208 (06905-1604)
PHONE...................................203 324-9203
Samuel Urda, *President*
Allan Aferrone, *Vice Pres*
Peter O'Karma, *Vice Pres*
Peter Okarma, *Vice Pres*
Gabriela Solis, *Office Mgr*
EMP: 7
SQ FT: 3,000
SALES (est): 2.2MM **Privately Held**
WEB: www.cccdinc.org
SIC: **7372** 8742 8999 Prepackaged software; management consulting services; actuarial consultant

(G-8156)
CONAIR CORPORATION (PA)
Also Called: Personal Care Appliances Div
1 Cummings Point Rd (06902-7901)
PHONE...................................203 351-9000
James M Dubin, *Ch of Bd*
Ronald T Diamond, *President*
Andrea Hoffman, *Regional Mgr*
Lawrence Cruz, *Counsel*
Michael Baldino, *Vice Pres*
◆ EMP: 366 EST: 1959
SALES: 2B **Privately Held**
WEB: www.conair.com
SIC: **3634** 3631 3639 3999 Electric housewares & fans; hair dryers, electric; curling irons, electric; hair curlers, electric; household cooking equipment; major kitchen appliances, except refrigerators & stoves; barber & beauty shop equipment

(G-8157)
CONNECTICUT NEWSPAPERS INC
75 Tresser Blvd (06901-3329)
PHONE...................................203 964-2200
Durham Monsma, *Principal*
EMP: 6
SALES (est): 279.2K **Privately Held**
SIC: **2711** Newspapers, publishing & printing

(G-8158)
CONSTITUTION SPARKLER SALES
505 W Hill Rd (06902-1506)
PHONE...................................203 324-5159
Gerald Kijek, *Principal*
EMP: 2

SALES (est): 175.4K **Privately Held**
SIC: **2899** Fireworks

(G-8159)
CONTEMPRARY LIGHTS STAGING LLC
425 Fairfield Ave Ste 4 (06902-7529)
PHONE...................................203 359-8200
Patrick J Eagleton,
EMP: 1
SALES: 1.1MM **Privately Held**
WEB: www.lightsandstaging.com
SIC: **3648** Stage lighting equipment

(G-8160)
CORELLI INDUSTRIES LLC
94 Elaine Dr (06902-8332)
PHONE...................................203 356-9058
Lucy Corelli, *Manager*
EMP: 1
SALES (est): 60.7K **Privately Held**
SIC: **3999** Manufacturing industries

(G-8161)
CORINTH ACQUISITION CORP (PA)
Also Called: United Pioneer Company
2777 Summer St Ste 206 (06905-4383)
PHONE...................................203 504-6260
Bernard Braverman, *President*
Michael Braverman, *Vice Pres*
▲ EMP: 5
SQ FT: 3,000
SALES: 22.4MM **Privately Held**
SIC: **2311** Coats, overcoats & vests

(G-8162)
CPC SOFTWARE LLC
197 Lawn Ave (06902-3114)
PHONE...................................203 348-9684
Debra T Cuozzo, *Principal*
EMP: 2
SALES (est): 117.3K **Privately Held**
SIC: **7372** Prepackaged software

(G-8163)
CRAFTSMEN PRINTING GROUP INC
104 Lincoln Ave (06902-3121)
PHONE...................................203 327-2817
James Zygmont, *President*
Marcia Gogliettino, *Treasurer*
EMP: 7
SQ FT: 1,600
SALES (est): 759.9K **Privately Held**
SIC: **2752** Commercial printing, offset

(G-8164)
CRAFTY BABY TM LLC
193 Minivale Rd (06907-1210)
PHONE...................................203 921-1179
Jill Chuckas, *Mng Member*
EMP: 1
SALES (est): 78.9K **Privately Held**
SIC: **2361** Dresses: girls', children's & infants'

(G-8165)
CRANE AEROSPACE INC (DH)
100 Stamford Pl (06902-6740)
PHONE...................................203 363-7300
Max H Mitchell, *CEO*
Curtis A Baron Jr, *Vice Pres*
EMP: 152
SALES (est): 475.3MM
SALES (corp-wide): 3.3B **Publicly Held**
SIC: **3492** Control valves, fluid power: hydraulic & pneumatic

(G-8166)
CRANE CO (PA)
100 1st Stamford Pl # 300 (06902-6740)
PHONE...................................203 363-7300
Robert S Evans, *Ch of Bd*
Max H Mitchell, *President*
Lee-Ann Etter, *President*
Fidias Silva, *District Mgr*
Ken Jacobs, *Counsel*
▲ EMP: 56 EST: 1855

SALES: 3.3B **Publicly Held**
WEB: www.craneco.com
SIC: 3492 3494 3594 3589 Control valves, fluid power: hydraulic & pneumatic; pipe fittings; pumps, hydraulic power transfer; pumps, hydraulic, aircraft; water treatment equipment, industrial; aircraft parts & equipment; brakes, aircraft; aircraft assemblies, subassemblies & parts; military aircraft equipment & armament; lumber, plywood & millwork; doors & windows; building materials, exterior; building materials, interior

(G-8167)
CRANE CONTROLS INC (DH)
100 Stamford Pl (06902-6740)
PHONE....................................203 363-7300
Andrew Krawitt, *Principal*
EMP: 5
SALES (est): 29.3MM
SALES (corp-wide): 3.3B **Publicly Held**
SIC: 3492 Control valves, fluid power: hydraulic & pneumatic

(G-8168)
CRANE INTL HOLDINGS INC (HQ)
100 Stamford Pl (06902-6740)
PHONE....................................203 363-7300
Max H Mitchell, *CEO*
Curtis Robb, *President*
EMP: 9
SALES (est): 1.2B
SALES (corp-wide): 3.3B **Publicly Held**
SIC: 3492 Control valves, fluid power: hydraulic & pneumatic
PA: Crane Co.
    100 1st Stamford Pl # 300
    Stamford CT 06902
    203 363-7300

(G-8169)
CREATIVE STONE GROUP INC
444 Bedford St Apt 4e (06901-1507)
PHONE....................................203 554-7773
Sheila Breland, *Vice Pres*
EMP: 3
SALES (est): 119K **Privately Held**
SIC: 7299 7336 8611 7374 Personal document & information services; commercial art & graphic design; growers' marketing advisory service; data processing service; periodicals: publishing & printing;

(G-8170)
CRYSTAL NAILS AND SPA OF SH
20 Magee Ave (06902-5907)
PHONE....................................203 323-0551
Aeran Kang, *Owner*
EMP: 2
SALES (est): 54K **Privately Held**
SIC: 2844 Manicure preparations

(G-8171)
CUNNINGHAM INDUSTRIES INC
102 Lincoln Ave Ste 3 (06902-3103)
PHONE....................................203 324-2942
Frederick E Cunningham, *President*
EMP: 3 EST: 1953
SQ FT: 2,000
SALES (est): 250K **Privately Held**
WEB: www.cunningham-ind.com
SIC: 3566 5734 3462 Gears, power transmission, except automotive; software, business & non-game; computer peripheral equipment; iron & steel forgings

(G-8172)
CUSTOM SIGN SOLUTIONS LLC
93 Prospect St (06901-1615)
PHONE....................................203 975-8344
Virgil Williams,
EMP: 2
SALES (est): 206.7K **Privately Held**
SIC: 3993 Signs, not made in custom sign painting shops

(G-8173)
CUSTOM TEE
400 Main St Ste 510 (06901-3004)
PHONE....................................718 450-1210
Jose Rios, *Principal*
EMP: 2

SALES (est): 83.9K **Privately Held**
SIC: 2752 Commercial printing, lithographic

(G-8174)
CWL ENTERPRISES INC (HQ)
200 First Stamford Pl # 2 (06902-6753)
PHONE....................................303 790-8023
Robert G Burton Jr, *Ch of Bd*
EMP: 4
SALES (est): 1.9B
SALES (corp-wide): 2.6B **Privately Held**
SIC: 2677 2679 Envelopes; tags & labels, paper
PA: Cenveo Enterprises, Inc.
    200 First Stamford Pl # 2
    Stamford CT 06902
    203 595-3000

(G-8175)
CYLINDER VODKA INC
101 Washington Blvd # 1223 (06902-7061)
PHONE....................................203 979-0792
Stylianos D Stavrianos, *President*
Alexis M Navarro, *Admin Sec*
EMP: 3
SALES (est): 122K **Privately Held**
SIC: 2085 Vodka (alcoholic beverage)

(G-8176)
CYTEC INDUSTRIES INC
1937 W Main St Ste 1 (06902-4578)
P.O. Box 60 (06904-0060)
PHONE....................................203 321-2200
Qi Dai, *Research*
William Haseltine, *Research*
Philip D Kutzenco, *Research*
Min Wang, *Research*
Bill Moore, *Manager*
EMP: 78
SALES (corp-wide): 12.8MM **Privately Held**
SIC: 2899 8731 Chemical preparations; commercial physical research
HQ: Cytec Industries Inc.
    4500 Mcginnis Ferry Rd
    Alpharetta GA 30005

(G-8177)
D & J TEXTILE LLC
31 Congress St Ste 2 (06902-7609)
PHONE....................................203 569-7754
Daniel Medina,
EMP: 1
SALES (est): 78.6K **Privately Held**
SIC: 2299 Fabrics: linen, jute, hemp, ramie

(G-8178)
DAN CHICHESTER
104 Soundview Ave (06902-6138)
PHONE....................................203 722-4619
Dan Chichester, *Executive*
EMP: 1
SALES (est): 49.1K **Privately Held**
SIC: 3861 Photographic equipment & supplies

(G-8179)
DANONE HOLDINGS INC
208 Harbor Dr Fl 3 (06902-7467)
PHONE....................................203 229-7000
Jim Stevens, *CEO*
EMP: 1300
SALES (est): 21.7K
SALES (corp-wide): 762.4MM **Privately Held**
SIC: 2086 Pasteurized & mineral waters, bottled & canned
HQ: Danone Us, Llc
    1 Maple Ave
    White Plains NY 10605
    914 872-8400

(G-8180)
DASCO SUPPLY LLC
Also Called: Dunphey Associates Supply Co
43 Homestead Ave (06902-7262)
PHONE....................................203 388-0095
Gene Brown, *Manager*
EMP: 4
SALES (corp-wide): 4.5B **Publicly Held**
SIC: 3585 Air conditioning units, complete: domestic or industrial

HQ: Dasco Supply, Llc
    9 Whippany Rd Bldngd
    Whippany NJ 07981
    973 884-1390

(G-8181)
DATAQUEST KOREA INC
56 Top Gallant Rd (06902-7747)
PHONE....................................239 561-4862
Christopher J Lafond, *Principal*
EMP: 3 EST: 2001
SALES (est): 207K **Privately Held**
SIC: 3695 Computer software tape & disks: blank, rigid & floppy

(G-8182)
DAVID WEISMAN LLC
30 Mill Valley Ln (06903-1642)
PHONE....................................203 322-9978
David W Weisman,
EMP: 6
SALES (est): 779.1K **Privately Held**
SIC: 3567 Industrial furnaces & ovens

(G-8183)
DEER CREEK FABRICS INC
509 Glenbrook Rd (06906-1825)
PHONE....................................203 964-0922
Steven Lucier, *President*
Jill Cooper, *Vice Pres*
Mary Ann Lucier, *Vice Pres*
EMP: 7
SQ FT: 3,000
SALES (est): 2.2MM **Privately Held**
WEB: www.deercreekfabrics.com
SIC: 2221 Broadwoven fabric mills, man-made

(G-8184)
DEVIN DAVID
Also Called: Olive Oil Mediterranean
12 Long Ridge Rd (06905-3802)
PHONE....................................203 322-4000
David Devin, *Owner*
EMP: 1
SQ FT: 900
SALES (est): 55.4K **Privately Held**
SIC: 2079 Olive oil

(G-8185)
DIGITAL BOB
51 Northwood Ln (06903-4335)
PHONE....................................203 322-5732
Robert Kolb, *Manager*
EMP: 2 EST: 2016
SALES (est): 88.3K **Privately Held**
SIC: 3669 Communications equipment

(G-8186)
DIRECT ENERGY INC (HQ)
263 Tresser Blvd Fl 8 (06901-3236)
PHONE....................................800 260-0300
Deryk King, *CEO*
Badar Khan, *Senior VP*
Keith Mac Arthur, *Director*
▲ EMP: 17
SALES (est): 284.8MM **Privately Held**
SIC: 4911 1311 Electric services; natural gas production

(G-8187)
DIY AWARDS LLC (PA)
1 Atlantic St Ste 705 (06901-2402)
PHONE....................................800 810-1216
Daniel WEI Xu,
EMP: 5
SALES: 700K **Privately Held**
SIC: 2499 Trophy bases, wood

(G-8188)
DOUBLE DIAMOND CONSTRUCTION
11 Deleo Dr (06906-1006)
PHONE....................................203 357-7757
Joseph G Pierni Jr, *Partner*
Lena Pierni, *Partner*
EMP: 2
SALES: 500K **Privately Held**
SIC: 3531 1711 Excavators: cable, clamshell, crane, derrick, dragline, etc.; plumbing contractors

(G-8189)
DSAR COMPANY
3 Nash Pl Ste 7 (06906-2524)
PHONE....................................203 324-6456
Hillel Disraelly, *Owner*
Barbi Strair Disraelly, *Partner*
EMP: 3
SALES (est): 200.9K **Privately Held**
SIC: 7379 7372 Data processing consultant; operating systems computer software

(G-8190)
EARTH ANIMAL VENTURES INC
49 John St (06902-5845)
PHONE....................................717 271-6393
EMP: 8 EST: 2011
SALES (est): 673.1K **Privately Held**
SIC: 2048 Feed supplements

(G-8191)
EAST COAST HOCKEY DEPOT LLC
3 Old Long Ridge Rd (06903-1620)
PHONE....................................203 247-3476
Sergey Barinov,
EMP: 1
SALES (est): 47K **Privately Held**
SIC: 3949 Hockey equipment & supplies, general

(G-8192)
ECOLOGIC ENERGY SOLUTIONS LLC
48 Union St Ste 14 (06906-1342)
PHONE....................................203 889-0505
Jeremy Klein, *Office Mgr*
Justin Breiner,
Brian Bodell,
EMP: 25
SALES (est): 2.9MM
SALES (corp-wide): 1.3B **Publicly Held**
SIC: 3296 1742 Fiberglass insulation; insulation, buildings
PA: Installed Building Products, Inc.
    495 S High St Ste 50
    Columbus OH 43215
    614 221-3399

(G-8193)
EFFIHEALTH LLC
259 Main St Apt 3 (06901-2933)
PHONE....................................888 435-3108
Jack Nail,
EMP: 5
SALES (est): 278K **Privately Held**
SIC: 2833 Vitamins, natural or synthetic: bulk, uncompounded

(G-8194)
ELIZABETH ARDEN INC
300 Main St Ste 800 (06901-3033)
PHONE....................................203 905-1700
Todd Walter, *CEO*
Curt Lee, *Asst Controller*
Kimberly Pisco, *Human Res Dir*
Blake Shapiro, *Manager*
EMP: 2 **Publicly Held**
SIC: 2844 Toilet preparations
HQ: Elizabeth Arden, Inc.
    880 Sw 145th Ave Ste 200
    Pembroke Pines FL 33027

(G-8195)
EMSC LLC
2009 Summer St Ste 201 (06905-5023)
PHONE....................................203 268-5101
Andrew Krzywosz, *President*
Cathie Krzywosz, *General Mgr*
EMP: 6 EST: 1987
SALES (est): 299.4K **Privately Held**
WEB: www.emsc-llc.com
SIC: 3612 Transformers, except electric

(G-8196)
EOWS MIDLAND INC
1 Landmark Sq Fl 11 (06901-2603)
PHONE....................................203 358-5705
Charles Drimal, *President*
EMP: 32
SALES: 1.8MM **Privately Held**
SIC: 1381 Drilling oil & gas wells

Stamford - Fairfield County (G-8197)

(G-8197)
EQUINOR SHIPPING INC
120 Long Ridge Rd 3eo1 (06902-1839)
PHONE..................203 978-6900
Alexander Murray, *President*
Gary A Turiano, *CFO*
Charles O Brien, *Admin Sec*
EMP: 4
SALES: 3.8MM **Privately Held**
SIC: 5172 1382 5113 Crude oil; oil & gas exploration services; shipping supplies

(G-8198)
EQUINOR US HOLDINGS INC (DH)
120 Long Ridge Rd 3eo1 (06902-1839)
PHONE..................203 978-6900
Bent Rune Solheim, *CEO*
Helge Haugane, *President*
Eyvind Aven, *Vice Pres*
Martin Pastore, *Vice Pres*
Fredrik Rydin, *Vice Pres*
▲ **EMP:** 119
SQ FT: 56,000
SALES: 7.7B
SALES (corp-wide): 76.3B **Privately Held**
SIC: 5172 1382 Crude oil; oil & gas exploration services

(G-8199)
EVERCEL INC (PA)
1055 Washington Blvd Fl 8 (06901-2251)
PHONE..................781 741-8800
James D Gerson, *Ch of Bd*
Garry A Prime, *President*
Daniel J McCarthy, *COO*
Anthony P Kiernan, *CFO*
EMP: 94
SALES (est): 5.4MM **Publicly Held**
SIC: 3691 Alkaline cell storage batteries

(G-8200)
EVERGREEN ALUMINUM LLC
Also Called: Glencore, Eaar, Switzerland
301 Tresser Blvd Ste 1500 (06901-3280)
PHONE..................203 328-4900
Cheryl Driscoll, *Director*
Charles Reali,
James Croker,
EMP: 12
SALES (est): 1MM **Privately Held**
WEB: www.evergrnal.com
SIC: 3334 Primary aluminum

(G-8201)
EVERGREEN PRINTING
61 Seaview Ave (06902-6021)
PHONE..................203 323-4717
EMP: 2 **EST:** 2013
SALES (est): 83.9K **Privately Held**
SIC: 2752 Commercial printing, lithographic

(G-8202)
FAST SIGN
95 Atlantic St (06901-2403)
PHONE..................203 348-0222
EMP: 2
SALES (est): 170.9K **Privately Held**
SIC: 3993 Signs & advertising specialties

(G-8203)
FENRIR INDUSTRIES INC
652 Glenbrook Rd 6-202 (06906-1410)
P.O. Box 2027 (06906-0027)
PHONE..................203 977-0671
Bob Muller, *President*
Elizabeth Muller, *Vice Pres*
Elizabeth B Muller, *Admin Sec*
EMP: 15
SQ FT: 8,000
SALES (est): 1.4MM **Privately Held**
WEB: www.fenrir.com
SIC: 5999 3482 3483 3489 Police supply stores; small arms ammunition; ammunition, except for small arms; ordnance & accessories

(G-8204)
FINANCIAL NAVIGATOR INC
1 Dock St Ste 200 (06902-5837)
PHONE..................800 468-3636
Edward Van Deman, *CEO*
Kevin Whalen, *CFO*
Luke Van Deman, *Marketing Staff*
David Campbell, *CTO*
John Van Deman, *Director*
EMP: 3
SALES (est): 708.2K **Privately Held**
WEB: www.finnav.com
SIC: 7371 7372 Computer software development; application computer software
PA: Asset Vantage, Inc.
 1 Dock St Ste 200
 Stamford CT 06902
 800 468-3636

(G-8205)
FIRST RESERVE FUND VIII LP
290 Harbor Dr (06902-8700)
PHONE..................203 661-6601
William Macaulay, *CEO*
William Honeybourne, *Managing Dir*
EMP: 2
SALES (est): 193.9K **Privately Held**
SIC: 3533 3491 7699 Oil & gas field machinery; pressure valves & regulators, industrial; industrial equipment services

(G-8206)
FPR PINEDALE LLC
58 Commerce Rd (06902-4506)
PHONE..................203 542-6000
Centaurus Capital LP,
Freepoint Resources LLC,
EMP: 5
SALES (est): 14.9MM **Privately Held**
SIC: 1311 Natural gas production

(G-8207)
FRANK ALEXANDER WEEMS PUBG LLC
261 Montauk Dr Apt 212 (06902-6429)
PHONE..................203 898-4654
Nadira Pankey, *Principal*
EMP: 1
SALES (est): 41.8K **Privately Held**
SIC: 2741 Miscellaneous publishing

(G-8208)
FRANKLIN LIQUOR STORE
99 North St (06902-2420)
PHONE..................203 323-1356
Robert Daly, *Owner*
EMP: 1
SALES (est): 161.4K **Privately Held**
SIC: 5921 2086 Beer (packaged); bottled & canned soft drinks

(G-8209)
FRC FOUNDERS CORPORATION (PA)
Also Called: F R C
290 Harbor Dr (06902-8700)
PHONE..................203 661-6601
Christopher Tracey, *Asst Controller*
Terry Longman, *Info Tech Mgr*
John A Hill,
William Honeybourne,
William Macaulay,
EMP: 30
SALES (est): 574.6MM **Privately Held**
SIC: 8741 1311 1389 8731 Financial management for business; crude petroleum & natural gas; oil field services; gas field services; energy research; petroleum industry machinery

(G-8210)
FREDERICK PURDUE COMPANY INC (PA)
Also Called: Purdue Pharma
201 Tresser Blvd (06901-3435)
PHONE..................203 588-8000
John H Stewart, *President*
Andy Ritter, *Business Mgr*
Richard Inz, *Counsel*
Alan Koller, *Counsel*
Stuart D Baker, *Exec VP*
▲ **EMP:** 310
SQ FT: 90,000
SALES (est): 88.5MM **Privately Held**
SIC: 2834 5122 Pharmaceutical preparations; pharmaceuticals

(G-8211)
FUJIFILM ELCTRNIC MTLS USA INC
Also Called: Fujifilm NDT Systems
419 West Ave (06902-6343)
PHONE..................203 363-3360
Jim Bonne, *Project Mgr*
Jeffery Buchanan, *Project Mgr*
Brian Higgins, *Controller*
Keith Roth, *Controller*
Helen Block, *Human Res Dir*
EMP: 9 **Privately Held**
SIC: 5043 3861 Photographic equipment & supplies; photographic equipment & supplies
HQ: Fujifilm Electronic Materials U.S.A., Inc.
 80 Circuit Dr
 North Kingstown RI 02852
 401 522-9499

(G-8212)
GCOOPER LEGACY PUBLISHING LLC
65 Judy Ln (06906-2102)
PHONE..................203 357-1483
Starr Merritt, *Principal*
EMP: 1
SALES (est): 37.5K **Privately Held**
SIC: 2741 Miscellaneous publishing

(G-8213)
GENERAL NETWORK SERVICE INC
6 Landmark Sq Ste 400 (06901-2711)
PHONE..................203 359-5735
Jason Liu, *President*
EMP: 1
SALES (est): 59.1K **Privately Held**
SIC: 7371 3663 Computer software development & applications; mobile communication equipment

(G-8214)
GENESIS ALKALI LLC
1 Stamford Plz 263 (06901-3271)
PHONE..................215 299-6773
Kathy Harper, *Manager*
EMP: 60 **Publicly Held**
SIC: 2812 Sodium bicarbonate
HQ: Genesis Alkali, Llc
 919 Milam St Ste 2100
 Houston TX 77002
 713 860-2500

(G-8215)
GENEVE CORPORATION (HQ)
96 Cummings Point Rd (06902-7975)
PHONE..................203 358-8000
Edward Netter, *Ch of Bd*
F Peter Zoch III, *President*
Robert T Keiser, *Senior VP*
Steven P Lapin, *Senior VP*
Ronald G Strackbein, *Vice Pres*
EMP: 20
SQ FT: 12,000
SALES (est): 297.6MM
SALES (corp-wide): 269.1MM **Privately Held**
SIC: 5961 3483 6282 Educational supplies & equipment, mail order; mail order house; ammunition components; investment counselors
PA: Geneve Holdings, Inc.
 96 Cummings Point Rd
 Stamford CT 06902
 203 358-8000

(G-8216)
GENEVE HOLDINGS INC (PA)
96 Cummings Point Rd (06902-7919)
PHONE..................203 358-8000
Edward Netter, *Ch of Bd*
F Peter Zoch II, *President*
Robert Keiser, *Vice Pres*
◆ **EMP:** 5
SQ FT: 15,000
SALES (est): 269.1MM **Privately Held**
WEB: www.ihc-geneve.com
SIC: 3462 6331 Ordnance forgings, ferrous; fire, marine & casualty insurance & carriers

(G-8217)
GOLDEN SUN INC
Also Called: Newhall Labs
5 High Ridge Park Ste 200 (06905-1326)
PHONE..................800 575-7960
Jon Achenbaum, *CEO*
Dario Margve, *Chairman*
Ian Mactaggart, *Vice Pres*
Chris Conley, *CFO*
▲ **EMP:** 19
SQ FT: 20,000
SALES (est): 2.8MM **Privately Held**
WEB: www.goldensun.com
SIC: 2844 Hair preparations, including shampoos; cosmetic preparations; lipsticks
HQ: Golden Sun Holdings, Inc.
 5 High Ridge Park Ste 100
 Stamford CT 06905
 203 595-5228

(G-8218)
GOLF RESEARCH ASSOCIATES
Also Called: Shotbyshop.com
2810 High Ridge Rd (06903-1808)
PHONE..................203 968-1608
Peter Sanders, *Managing Prtnr*
Molly Sanders, *Partner*
EMP: 3
SALES (est): 125K **Privately Held**
WEB: www.shotbyshot.com
SIC: 7372 Application computer software

(G-8219)
GRANATA SIGNS LLC
Also Called: Granata Sign Co
80 Lincoln Ave 90 (06902-3102)
PHONE..................203 358-0780
John Granata, *Owner*
Daniel Petrone, *Manager*
EMP: 6
SQ FT: 6,000
SALES (est): 626K **Privately Held**
WEB: www.granatasigns.com
SIC: 3993 Signs & advertising specialties

(G-8220)
GREEN SHUTTER INC
439 Courtland Ave (06906-1813)
PHONE..................203 359-3863
Gregg Rosinsky, *Principal*
EMP: 2
SALES (est): 168.8K **Privately Held**
SIC: 3442 Shutters, door or window: metal

(G-8221)
GREENWICH TIME
44 Columbus Pl Apt 9 (06907-1614)
PHONE..................203 253-2922
Katelyn L Imbornoni, *Principal*
EMP: 4
SALES (est): 117K **Privately Held**
SIC: 2711 Newspapers, publishing & printing

(G-8222)
HALLS EDGE INC
420 Fairfield Ave Ste 3 (06902-7550)
PHONE..................203 653-2281
David Hall, *President*
EMP: 3
SQ FT: 2,500
SALES: 500K **Privately Held**
WEB: www.hallsedge.com
SIC: 3429 Cabinet hardware

(G-8223)
HAMPTON ASSOCIATES LLC
287 Hamilton Ave Apt 4c (06902-3539)
PHONE..................203 817-0161
Victoria Hampton,
EMP: 1 **EST:** 2010
SALES (est): 49.5K **Privately Held**
SIC: 7291 2759 Tax return preparation services; financial note & certificate printing & engraving

(G-8224)
HARMAN BECKER AUTOMOTIVE SYSTE
400 Atlantic St Ste 15 (06901-3533)
PHONE..................203 328-3501
EMP: 3

SALES (est): 125.2K **Privately Held**
SIC: 3651 Household audio & video equipment
HQ: Harman International Industries Incorporated
400 Atlantic St Ste 15
Stamford CT 06901
203 328-3500

(G-8225)
HARMAN CONSUMER INC
Also Called: Jbl
400 Atlantic St Ste 1500 (06901-3512)
PHONE..................................203 328-3500
Dinesh Paliwal, *CEO*
Joe Hacker, *Vice Pres*
Chet Simon, *Vice Pres*
Chad Beck, *Engineer*
Raul Gonzalez, *Engineer*
EMP: 5 **EST:** 1979
SALES (est): 555.4K **Privately Held**
SIC: 3651 Audio electronic systems

(G-8226)
HARMAN INTERNATIONAL INDS INC (DH)
400 Atlantic St Ste 15 (06901-3533)
PHONE..................................203 328-3500
Dinesh C Paliwal, *President*
Michael Mauser, *President*
Mike Peters, *President*
Valerie Freeman, *Business Mgr*
Sanjay Dhawan, *Exec VP*
▲ **EMP:** 277
SALES (est): 5B **Privately Held**
WEB: www.harman.com
SIC: 3651 Household audio equipment
HQ: Samsung Electronics America, Inc.
85 Challenger Rd Fl 7
Ridgefield Park NJ 07660
201 229-4000

(G-8227)
HARMAN INTERNATIONAL INDS INC
Also Called: Harman Consumer Group Division
400 Atlantic St Ste 15 (06901-3533)
PHONE..................................203 328-3500
EMP: 3 **Privately Held**
SIC: 3651 Household audio equipment
HQ: Harman International Industries Incorporated
400 Atlantic St Ste 15
Stamford CT 06901
203 328-3500

(G-8228)
HARMAN INTERNATIONAL INDS INC
400 Atlantic St Fl 5 (06901-3519)
PHONE..................................203 328-3500
EMP: 130
SALES (corp-wide): 6.1B **Publicly Held**
SIC: 3651 Household Audio And Video Equipment
PA: Harman International Industries Incorporated
400 Atlantic St Ste 15
Stamford CT 06901
203 328-3500

(G-8229)
HARMAN KG HOLDING LLC (DH)
400 Atlantic St Ste 1500 (06901-3512)
PHONE..................................203 328-3500
Dinesh C Paliwal, *Ch of Bd*
EMP: 13
SALES (est): 504.9MM **Privately Held**
SIC: 3651 Household audio equipment
HQ: Harman International Industries Incorporated
400 Atlantic St Ste 15
Stamford CT 06901
203 328-3500

(G-8230)
HARVEST HILL HOLDINGS LLC (PA)
1 High Ridge Park Fl 2 (06905-1322)
PHONE..................................203 914-1620
Tim Voelkerding, *President*
Michael McNiff, *Vice Pres*
Thomas Diana, *Director*

Eduardo Gonzalez, *Director*
EMP: 13
SALES (est): 1.3B
SALES (corp-wide): 1.2B **Privately Held**
SIC: 2086 5499 Fruit drinks (less than 100% juice): packaged in cans, etc.; soft drinks

(G-8231)
HEARST COMMUNICATIONS INC
9a Riverbend Dr S (06907-2524)
PHONE..................................203 964-2200
EMP: 2
SALES (est): 62.9K **Privately Held**
SIC: 2711 Newspapers

(G-8232)
HENKEL CONSUMER GOODS INC (DH)
200 Elm St (06902-3800)
PHONE..................................475 210-0230
Norbert Koll, *President*
Rebecca Woodcock, *Business Mgr*
Valerie Pochron, *Counsel*
Adil Choudhry, *Vice Pres*
Steven Essick, *Vice Pres*
◆ **EMP:** 600
SALES (est): 1.3B
SALES (corp-wide): 22.7B **Privately Held**
SIC: 2841 Soap & other detergents
HQ: Henkel Us Operations Corporation
1 Henkel Way
Rocky Hill CT 06067
860 571-5100

(G-8233)
HEXCEL CORPORATION (PA)
281 Tresser Blvd Ste 1503 (06901-3261)
PHONE..................................203 969-0666
Nick L Stanage, *Ch of Bd*
Thierry Merlot, *President*
Colleen Pritchett, *President*
Brett Schneider, *President*
Timothy Swords, *President*
EMP: 26
SALES: 2.1B **Publicly Held**
WEB: www.hexcel.com
SIC: 3728 3089 3624 2891 Aircraft parts & equipment; fiberglass doors; fibers, carbon & graphite; adhesives; epoxy adhesives; sealants; honeycombed metal; epoxy resins

(G-8234)
HEXCEL CORPORATION
281 Tresser Blvd Ste 1503 (06901-3261)
PHONE..................................203 969-0666
EMP: 2
SALES (corp-wide): 2.1B **Publicly Held**
SIC: 2821 Plastics materials & resins
PA: Hexcel Corporation
281 Tresser Blvd Ste 1503
Stamford CT 06901
203 969-0666

(G-8235)
HEXCEL POTTSVILLE CORPORATION
2 Stamford Plz 16thf (06901-3263)
PHONE..................................203 969-0666
Wayne C Pensky, *President*
Jack Parker, *Manager*
EMP: 4 **EST:** 1998
SALES (est): 82.4K
SALES (corp-wide): 2.1B **Publicly Held**
SIC: 3728 Aircraft parts & equipment
PA: Hexcel Corporation
281 Tresser Blvd Ste 1503
Stamford CT 06901
203 969-0666

(G-8236)
HIGH RIDGE BRANDS CO (PA)
333 Ludlow St Ste 2 (06902-6991)
PHONE..................................203 674-8080
Patricia Lopez, *CEO*
Amanda D H Allen, *CFO*
EMP: 65
SALES (est): 80.4MM **Privately Held**
WEB: www.highridgebrands.com
SIC: 2844 Toilet preparations

(G-8237)
HIGH RIDGE COPY INC
Also Called: High Ridge Printing & Copy Ctr
1009 High Ridge Rd (06905-1602)
PHONE..................................203 329-1889
Jon De Crescenzo, *President*
Christine De Crescenzo, *Corp Secy*
EMP: 10
SQ FT: 25,000
SALES (est): 1.4MM **Privately Held**
WEB: www.highridgecapital.com
SIC: 2752 Commercial printing, offset

(G-8238)
HILLSIDE CAPITAL INC DE CORP (HQ)
201 Tresser Blvd Ste 200 (06901-3435)
PHONE..................................203 618-0202
John N Irwin III, *President*
EMP: 12
SQ FT: 7,000
SALES (est): 1.7MM
SALES (corp-wide): 7.3MM **Privately Held**
WEB: www.hillsidecapital.com
SIC: 2711 Commercial printing & newspaper publishing combined
PA: Brookside International Inc
201 Tresser Blvd Ste 200
Stamford CT 06901
203 595-4500

(G-8239)
HISPANIC COMMUNICATIONS LLC
400 Main St (06901-3004)
PHONE..................................203 674-6793
Norma Rodriguez, *President*
EMP: 4
SALES (est): 149.6K **Privately Held**
SIC: 2711 Newspapers, publishing & printing

(G-8240)
HOFFMAN ENGINEERING LLC (DH)
8 Riverbend Dr (06907-2629)
P.O. Box 4430 (06907-0430)
PHONE..................................203 425-8900
Andrew Sadlon, *President*
Mark Bohacs, *Business Mgr*
Carla Hill, *Vice Pres*
Ken Wagner, *Vice Pres*
Chris Moher, *VP Opers*
EMP: 63 **EST:** 1987
SQ FT: 30,000
SALES (est): 20.7MM
SALES (corp-wide): 57.7MM **Privately Held**
WEB: www.hoffmanengineering.com
SIC: 8734 3647 3826 3825 Testing laboratories; aircraft lighting fixtures; photometers; instruments to measure electricity; semiconductors & related devices; electronic computers
HQ: Aeronautical & Gi Holdings Limited
Fleets Point House Willis Way
Poole
120 268-5661

(G-8241)
HOPE KIT CBINETS STONE SUP LLC
308 Hope St (06906-1704)
PHONE..................................203 504-3164
Ren Chanz, *Branch Mgr*
EMP: 1
SALES (corp-wide): 800.6K **Privately Held**
SIC: 2434 Wood kitchen cabinets
PA: Hope Kitchen Cabinets & Stone Supply, Llc
1901 Commerce Dr
Bridgeport CT 06605
203 610-6147

(G-8242)
HXB INDUSTRIES LLC
7 Bend Of River Ln (06902-1301)
PHONE..................................203 348-5922
Harvey Cohen, *Principal*
EMP: 1 **EST:** 2008
SALES (est): 62.2K **Privately Held**
SIC: 3999 Manufacturing industries

(G-8243)
ICT BUSINESS
17 Bridge St (06905-4501)
PHONE..................................203 595-9452
EMP: 3
SALES (est): 140K **Privately Held**
SIC: 3842 Mfg Surgical Appliances/Supplies

(G-8244)
IM YOUR TYPE LLC
10 Reynolds Ave (06905-4120)
PHONE..................................203 967-4063
Diana Dellapietro, *Principal*
EMP: 1
SALES (est): 57.6K **Privately Held**
SIC: 2791 Typesetting

(G-8245)
IMPERIAL METALWORKS LLC
92 Coolidge Ave (06906-2406)
P.O. Box 2761 (06906-0761)
PHONE..................................203 791-8567
Harry Van Dyke, *Principal*
EMP: 3
SALES (est): 290.9K **Privately Held**
SIC: 3446 Stairs, staircases, stair treads: prefabricated metal

(G-8246)
IMPRESSION POINT INC
500 West Ave Ste 4 (06902-6360)
PHONE..................................203 353-8800
Robert Labanca, *CEO*
Mary Labanca, *Treasurer*
EMP: 15
SQ FT: 5,000
SALES (est): 1.6MM **Privately Held**
WEB: www.impressionpt.com
SIC: 2752 Commercial printing, offset

(G-8247)
INDUSTRIAL SHIPG ENTPS MGT LLC
2187 Atlantic St (06902-6880)
PHONE..................................203 504-5800
EMP: 5
SALES (est): 393.2K **Privately Held**
SIC: 3429 Mfg Hardware

(G-8248)
INFORMA BUSINESS MEDIA INC
Also Called: Electronic Magazine
11 Riverbend Dr S (06907-2524)
P.O. Box 4232 (06907-0232)
PHONE..................................203 358-9900
Florence Torres, *Managing Dir*
Frank L Hajdu, *Pub Rel Mgr*
Charles Usher, *Branch Mgr*
EMP: 100
SALES (corp-wide): 3B **Privately Held**
SIC: 2721 Magazines: publishing & printing
HQ: Informa Business Media, Inc.
605 3rd Ave
New York NY 10158
212 204-4200

(G-8249)
INFORMA BUSINESS MEDIA INC
National Ctr For Database Mktg
11 River Band Dry S (06906)
P.O. Box 4949 (06907-0949)
PHONE..................................203 358-9900
Ryan Heart, *Director*
EMP: 110
SALES (corp-wide): 3B **Privately Held**
SIC: 2721 Marketing Logistics And Conference Coordination
HQ: Informa Business Media, Inc.
605 3rd Ave
New York NY 10158
212 204-4200

(G-8250)
INK TANK INDUSTRIES LLC
1069 E Main St (06902-4311)
PHONE..................................203 274-2717
Virginia T Peters, *Principal*
EMP: 1
SALES (est): 65.1K **Privately Held**
SIC: 3999 Manufacturing industries

Stamford - Fairfield County (G-8251)

(G-8251)
INSTALLED BUILDING PDTS INC
43 Crescent St Apt 19 (06906-1853)
PHONE..................203 889-0505
Justin Breiner, *Branch Mgr*
EMP: 5
SALES (corp-wide): 1.3B **Publicly Held**
SIC: 3296 Fiberglass insulation
PA: Installed Building Products, Inc.
495 S High St Ste 50
Columbus OH 43215
614 221-3399

(G-8252)
INTANGIBLE MATTER LLC
151 Courtland Ave (06902-3494)
PHONE..................203 219-9619
Diego Medina-Bernal,
Flavio Lici,
Andres Peguero,
Kevin Phun,
EMP: 4
SALES (est): 89.7K **Privately Held**
SIC: 7371 2741 Custom computer programming services; miscellaneous publishing

(G-8253)
INTERNATIONAL MKTG STRATEGIES
Also Called: Marine Money
1 Stamford Lndg (06902-7229)
PHONE..................203 406-0106
James Lawrence, *Chairman*
Jill Lawrence, *Vice Pres*
Gail Karlshoej, *Marketing Staff*
EMP: 11
SQ FT: 4,000
SALES: 1MM **Privately Held**
WEB: www.intmarketingstrategies.com
SIC: 2721 Trade journals: publishing only, not printed on site

(G-8254)
INTERNATIONAL PAPER - 16 INC (HQ)
281 Tresser Blvd (06901-3284)
PHONE..................203 329-8544
Robert Amen, *President*
Charles Greenberg, *Vice Pres*
Syvert Nerheim, *Vice Pres*
Donald Folley, *Treasurer*
EMP: 4
SQ FT: 50,000
SALES: 5.9MM
SALES (corp-wide): 23.3B **Publicly Held**
SIC: 2621 2611 Paper mills; pulp mills
PA: International Paper Company
6400 Poplar Ave
Memphis TN 38197
901 419-9000

(G-8255)
INTERNATIONAL ROBOTICS INC
1074 Hope St Ste 206 (06907-2113)
PHONE..................914 325-7773
EMP: 2
SALES (est): 95.5K **Privately Held**
SIC: 3535 Robotic conveyors

(G-8256)
INTERNATIONAL ROBOTICS INC
761 Stillwater Rd (06902-1726)
P.O. Box 11474, Naples FL (34101-1474)
PHONE..................914 630-1060
Robert Doornic, *CEO*
EMP: 10
SALES (est): 1MM **Privately Held**
SIC: 3535 Robotic conveyors

(G-8257)
IORFINO WOODWORKING
97 Blue Ridge Dr (06903-4924)
PHONE..................203 329-1075
Enzo F Iorfino, *Principal*
EMP: 1
SALES (est): 167.6K **Privately Held**
WEB: www.iorfinowoodworking.com
SIC: 2431 Millwork

(G-8258)
IPSOGEN
700 Canal St Ste 5 (06902-5921)
PHONE..................203 504-8583
Susan Hertzberg, *Principal*
EMP: 4
SALES (est): 321.8K **Privately Held**
SIC: 3841 Surgical instruments & apparatus

(G-8259)
IRONMAN WELDING L L C
420 Courtland Ave (06906-1834)
PHONE..................203 979-4063
Anthony Canzoneri, *President*
EMP: 1
SALES (est): 194.8K **Privately Held**
SIC: 7692 Welding repair

(G-8260)
ISUPPORTWS INC
Also Called: JI Services
65 High Ridge Rd (06905-3800)
PHONE..................203 569-7600
Joseph Liscek, *President*
EMP: 15
SQ FT: 5,000
SALES (est): 750K **Privately Held**
SIC: 7379 7371 3699 6211 Computer related consulting services; computer related maintenance services; ; computer software development & applications; computer software development; computer software systems analysis & design, custom; security devices; security control equipment & systems; distributors, security; security systems services

(G-8261)
J SQUARED SOFTWARE
1127 High Ridge Rd (06905-1203)
PHONE..................203 325-0275
Judd Love, *Owner*
Les Kerper, *Manager*
EMP: 2
SALES (est): 130.8K **Privately Held**
SIC: 7372 Prepackaged software

(G-8262)
JDM-GREENWOOD LLC
50 Glenbrook Rd Apt 5a (06902-2950)
PHONE..................203 358-4816
Joanne Rubin, *Principal*
EMP: 1
SALES (est): 47.8K **Privately Held**
SIC: 2499 Wood products

(G-8263)
JKL SPECIALTY FOODS INC
417 Shippan Ave Ste 2 (06902-6189)
P.O. Box 4607 (06907-0607)
PHONE..................203 541-3990
Ken Liu, *President*
Judy Chan, *Vice Pres*
▼ **EMP:** 10
SALES (est): 1.4MM **Privately Held**
WEB: www.asianmenusauces.com
SIC: 2035 Pickles, sauces & salad dressings

(G-8264)
JN CONSTRUCTION LLC
341 Shippan Ave Apt 2 (06902-6087)
PHONE..................914 483-2998
John J Aguirre,
EMP: 1
SALES (est): 50.9K **Privately Held**
SIC: 1442 Construction sand & gravel

(G-8265)
JOE VALENTINE MACHINE COMPANY
77 Southfield Ave Ste 2 (06902-7690)
PHONE..................203 356-9776
Joseph Valentine, *President*
Patricia Valentine, *Vice Pres*
EMP: 5
SALES (est): 600.8K **Privately Held**
SIC: 3599 Machine shop, jobbing & repair

(G-8266)
JOESJUICECOM LLC
25 Elmbrook Dr (06906-1110)
PHONE..................203 824-1854
Joseph Gatto,
EMP: 1
SALES (est): 84.1K **Privately Held**
SIC: 2899 Water treating compounds

(G-8267)
JOHANNES SULEK JEWELRY
Also Called: J S Jewelry
13 Opper Rd (06903-4705)
PHONE..................203 968-1729
Johannes Sulek, *Owner*
EMP: 1
SALES: 140K **Privately Held**
SIC: 3911 5094 7631 Jewelry, precious metal; jewelry; jewelry repair services

(G-8268)
JORNIK MAN CORP
652 Glenbrook Rd Ste 2 (06906-1410)
PHONE..................203 969-0500
Jacqueline Herz, *President*
Jordie Freedman, *VP Sls/Mktg*
Elyse Strauss, *Sales Executive*
Peter Herz, *Admin Sec*
▲ **EMP:** 19
SQ FT: 7,500
SALES (est): 3.1MM **Privately Held**
WEB: www.jornik.com
SIC: 3993 2396 Signs & advertising specialties; automotive & apparel trimmings

(G-8269)
JORNIK SCREEN PRINTING
652 Glenbrook Rd 8-201 (06906-1424)
PHONE..................203 969-0500
Jacqueline Herz, *Principal*
EMP: 2
SALES (est): 145.7K **Privately Held**
SIC: 2752 Commercial printing, lithographic

(G-8270)
JS MCCARTHY CO INC
Also Called: Printech
652 Glenbrook Rd 4-101 (06906-1410)
PHONE..................203 355-7600
Aslam Devale, *Managing Dir*
Jennifer Ponzini, *Production*
Arthur Zale, *Production*
Joseph Testa, *Sales Staff*
Raghav Gowda, *Marketing Staff*
EMP: 50
SALES (corp-wide): 35MM **Privately Held**
SIC: 2752 Commercial printing, offset
PA: J.S. Mccarthy Co., Inc.
15 Darin Dr
Augusta ME 04330
207 622-6241

(G-8271)
JV SHEET METAL
58 East Ave (06902-6117)
PHONE..................203 540-0383
Elizabeth Tineo, *Owner*
EMP: 2 **EST:** 2014
SALES (est): 190.8K **Privately Held**
SIC: 3444 Sheet metalwork

(G-8272)
K A F MANUFACTURING CO INC
14 Fahey St (06907-2216)
PHONE..................203 324-3012
John Feighery, *President*
Sharon Feighery, *Admin Sec*
EMP: 22 **EST:** 1971
SQ FT: 11,500
SALES: 5MM **Privately Held**
WEB: www.kaf.com
SIC: 3826 3562 Analytical instruments; ball & roller bearings

(G-8273)
K&M WOODWORKING LLC
25 E Walnut St (06902-6905)
PHONE..................203 406-0694
Karol Tyszka, *Principal*
EMP: 2
SALES (est): 123.7K **Privately Held**
SIC: 2431 Millwork

(G-8274)
K29
149 Emery Dr E (06902-2035)
PHONE..................203 961-9662
Len G Kunin, *Principal*
EMP: 1

SALES (est): 77.4K **Privately Held**
SIC: 2844 Toilet preparations

(G-8275)
KIEFFER ASSOCIATES INC
Also Called: Betoel Publishers
86 Wallacks Dr (06902-7125)
PHONE..................203 323-3437
EMP: 3
SALES: 35K **Privately Held**
SIC: 2731 Books-Publishing/Printing

(G-8276)
KITCHENS BY DEANE INC
1267 E Main St (06902-3538)
PHONE..................203 327-7008
Carrie Ann Deane, *Principal*
Lawrence Ciambriello, *Project Mgr*
Michael Pellas, *Opers Staff*
Peter M Dean, *Manager*
EMP: 22
SQ FT: 2,500
SALES: 8MM **Privately Held**
WEB: www.kitchensbydeane.com
SIC: 5712 2431 Cabinet work, custom; millwork

(G-8277)
KOHINOOR USA
46 Southfield Ave (06902-7236)
PHONE..................203 388-1850
Scott Gress, *Principal*
EMP: 1
SALES (est): 51K **Privately Held**
SIC: 2399 Fabricated textile products

(G-8278)
KOSTAS CSTM IR FBRICATIONS LLC
21 Judy Ln (06906-2102)
PHONE..................203 667-0881
Atheena Kouskousoglou, *Principal*
EMP: 1
SALES (est): 27.6K **Privately Held**
SIC: 7692 Welding repair

(G-8279)
KOSTAS CUSTOM IR FABRICATIONS
42 Lockwood Ave (06902-4218)
PHONE..................203 328-1308
Atheena Kouskousoglou, *Principal*
EMP: 4
SALES (est): 418.1K **Privately Held**
SIC: 5064 3441 Irons; fabricated structural metal

(G-8280)
LAYLAS FALAFEL
936 High Ridge Rd (06905-1601)
PHONE..................203 685-2830
Imad Sakakini, *Principal*
EMP: 4
SALES (est): 268.1K **Privately Held**
SIC: 3421 Table & food cutlery, including butchers'

(G-8281)
LEISURE LEARNING PRODUCTS INC
Also Called: Leisure Group
652 Glenbrook Rd Bldg 8 (06906-1410)
P.O. Box 2697 (06906-0697)
PHONE..................203 325-2800
Richard Bendett, *President*
Christine Binsteiner, *Vice Pres*
▲ **EMP:** 18
SQ FT: 15,000
SALES: 5MM **Privately Held**
WEB: www.mightymind.com
SIC: 3999 5092 Education aids, devices & supplies; toys & games; educational toys

(G-8282)
LESCO
52b Poplar St (06907-2718)
PHONE..................203 353-0061
Rick Linsaoey, *Admin Sec*
EMP: 2
SALES (est): 75.6K **Privately Held**
SIC: 3999 Manufacturing industries

GEOGRAPHIC SECTION
Stamford - Fairfield County (G-8309)

(G-8283)
LETTERING INC OF NEW YORK (PA)
255 Mill Rd (06903-1625)
PHONE..................203 329-7759
Karin Krumpelbeck, *President*
John Krumpelbeck, *Vice Pres*
EMP: 22
SALES (est): 2MM **Privately Held**
SIC: 7336 2791 Commercial art & graphic design; typesetting

(G-8284)
LEXA INTERNATIONAL CORPORATION (PA)
1 Landmark Sq Ste 407 (06901-2601)
PHONE..................203 326-5200
Antonia Axson Johnson, *Ch of Bd*
P Goeran Ennerfelt, *Vice Ch Bd*
John Pascale, *Vice Pres*
Charles W Seitz, *Vice Pres*
▲ EMP: 14 EST: 1920
SQ FT: 12,000
SALES (est): 546.7MM **Privately Held**
WEB: www.axeljohnson.com
SIC: 5171 3822 Petroleum bulk stations; auto controls regulating residntl & coml environmt & applncs

(G-8285)
LINK SYSTEMS INC
Also Called: Prolease
1 Dock St Ste 200 (06902-5837)
PHONE..................203 274-9702
Alan Bushell, *CEO*
Susan Wall, *CFO*
EMP: 15
SALES (est): 1.6MM
SALES (corp-wide): 121.8MM **Privately Held**
SIC: 7371 7372 7379 7389 Computer software development; business oriented computer software; computer related consulting services.
PA: Mri Software Llc
   28925 Fountain Pkwy
   Solon OH 44139
   800 321-8770

(G-8286)
LITTLE JOES UPHOLSTERY
Also Called: Little Joe Upholstery
94 Franklin St (06901-1310)
PHONE..................203 975-2871
Joe Delmore, *Owner*
Marie Antoline, *Admin Sec*
EMP: 1
SALES (est): 79.2K **Privately Held**
SIC: 2512 7641 Upholstered household furniture; furniture upholstery repair

(G-8287)
LOCALLIVE NETWORKS INC
175 Atlantic St Ste 2 (06901-3530)
PHONE..................877 355-6225
Nelson Santos, *CEO*
EMP: 5
SALES (est): 339.6K **Privately Held**
SIC: 7372 Application computer software

(G-8288)
LONGFORDS ICE CREAM LTD
Also Called: Longford's Own
425 Fairfield Ave Ste 25 (06902-7547)
PHONE..................914 935-9469
Nolan West, *President*
Patricia Sudbay West, *Vice Pres*
EMP: 12
SQ FT: 3,000
SALES (est): 1.2MM **Privately Held**
WEB: www.longfordsicecream.com
SIC: 2024 5143 Ice cream & frozen desserts; dairy products, except dried or canned

(G-8289)
LOS ANGLES TMES CMMNCTIONS LLC
Also Called: Outdoor Life Channel
250 Harbor Dr (06902-7444)
PHONE..................203 965-6434
Peter Englehart, *Vice Pres*
EMP: 149
SALES (corp-wide): 846.2MM **Privately Held**
SIC: 2711 Newspapers
PA: Los Angeles Times Communications, Llc
   2300 E Imperial Hwy
   El Segundo CA 90245
   213 237-5000

(G-8290)
LOVESAC COMPANY (PA)
2 Landmark Sq Ste 300 (06901-2410)
PHONE..................888 636-1223
Shawn Nelson, *CEO*
Andrew Heyer, *Ch of Bd*
Jack Krause, *President*
Donna Dellomo, *CFO*
Annette Cetta, *Manager*
EMP: 6
SQ FT: 15,730
SALES: 165.8MM **Publicly Held**
SIC: 5712 2519 Furniture stores;

(G-8291)
LOXO ONCOLOGY INC (HQ)
281 Tresser Blvd Fl 9 (06901-3238)
PHONE..................203 653-3880
Joshua H Bilenker MD, *President*
Jacob S Van Naarden, *COO*
James Pierson, *Vice Pres*
Michael Rothenberg MD, *Vice Pres*
Sara Slifka, *Vice Pres*
EMP: 50
SQ FT: 36,400
SALES: 21.3MM
SALES (corp-wide): 24.5B **Publicly Held**
SIC: 2834 Pharmaceutical preparations
PA: Eli Lilly And Company
   Lilly Corporate Ctr
   Indianapolis IN 46285
   317 276-2000

(G-8292)
M & B AUTOMOTIVE MACHINE SHOP
443 Elm St (06902-5112)
P.O. Box 2336 (06906-0336)
PHONE..................203 348-6134
Michael Lessard, *President*
EMP: 4
SQ FT: 800
SALES (est): 481.4K **Privately Held**
SIC: 3599 5531 7539 Machine shop, jobbing & repair; automotive & home supply stores; machine shop, automotive

(G-8293)
M H PIERCE & CO
11 Ledge Ter (06905-3323)
PHONE..................203 327-2970
Morton Hollinger, *Owner*
EMP: 2 EST: 1957
SQ FT: 1,700
SALES (est): 109.8K **Privately Held**
SIC: 2389 5094 Clergymen's vestments; jewelry

(G-8294)
MALABAR BAY LLC
Also Called: Jaye's Studio
1127 High Ridge Rd # 159 (06905-1203)
PHONE..................203 359-9714
Lalan K Shrikam, *Mng Member*
EMP: 7
SQ FT: 4,000
SALES (est): 1.8MM **Privately Held**
SIC: 2389 5632 Men's miscellaneous accessories; women's accessory & specialty stores; apparel accessories; lingerie (outerwear)

(G-8295)
MANDALAY INDUSTRIES LLC
82 Akbar Rd (06902-1402)
PHONE..................203 324-4033
Howard G Kraus, *Principal*
EMP: 1
SALES (est): 63.1K **Privately Held**
SIC: 3999 Barber & beauty shop equipment

(G-8296)
MARILYN GEHRING
Also Called: Stained Glass Apple, The
496 Glenbrook Rd (06906-1821)
PHONE..................203 358-8700
Marilyn Gehring, *Owner*
EMP: 1
SALES (est): 52K **Privately Held**
SIC: 3211 5231 3231 3229 Flat glass; glass, leaded or stained; products of purchased glass; pressed & blown glass

(G-8297)
MARINERO EXPRESS 809 EAST
809 E Main St (06902-3807)
PHONE..................203 487-0636
Jose L Marinero, *Principal*
EMP: 7 EST: 2009
SALES (est): 887.5K **Privately Held**
SIC: 3578 Automatic teller machines (ATM)

(G-8298)
MAYBORN USA INC
Also Called: Mayborn Group
1010 Washington Blvd # 11 (06901-2202)
P.O. Box 5003, Westport (06881-5003)
PHONE..................781 269-7490
Steve Parkin, *CEO*
Brenda O'Grady Liistro, *President*
Chris Parsons, *General Mgr*
George Idicula, *Corp Secy*
Sean Neasham, *QC Mgr*
▲ EMP: 13
SQ FT: 3,000
SALES (est): 32.5MM
SALES (corp-wide): 237.9MM **Privately Held**
WEB: www.maws-usa.com
SIC: 3069 3085 3634 3821 Baby pacifiers, rubber; nipples, rubber; teething rings, rubber; plastics bottles; bottle warmers, electric; household; sterilizers
HQ: Mayborn Group Limited
   Mayborn House, Balliol Business Park
   Newcastle-Upon-Tyne NE23
   191 250-1864

(G-8299)
MCINNIS USA INC
850 Canal St (06902-6943)
PHONE..................203 890-9950
Herve Mallet, *CEO*
James Braselton, *Senior VP*
Claude Ferland, *CFO*
EMP: 40 EST: 2013
SALES (est): 5.6MM
SALES (corp-wide): 28.4MM **Privately Held**
SIC: 3241 Cement, hydraulic
PA: Ciment Mcinnis Inc
   1350 Boul Rene-Levesque O Bureau 205
   Montreal QC H3G 2
   438 382-3331

(G-8300)
MD SOLARSCIENCES CORPORATION
9 W Broad St Ste 320 (06902-3758)
PHONE..................203 857-0095
Robert Friedman, *CEO*
Paul Ainsworth, *President*
Scott Friedman, *Vice Pres*
Beth Hale, *Opers Mgr*
▲ EMP: 12
SQ FT: 2,500
SALES (est): 713.1K **Privately Held**
SIC: 2834 Pharmaceutical preparations

(G-8301)
MEADWESTVACO PACKG SYSTEMS LLC
Also Called: Meadwestvaco Texas
1 High Ridge Park (06905-1323)
PHONE..................409 276-3137
John Luke, *Principal*
EMP: 5
SALES (est): 380K **Privately Held**
SIC: 4215 2679 Package delivery, vehicular; paperboard products, converted

(G-8302)
MEDHUMOR MED PUBLICATIONS LLC
1127 High Ridge Rd # 332 (06905-1203)
PHONE..................203 550-9041
Stuart C Silverstein, *Manager*
EMP: 1
SALES (est): 23.1K **Privately Held**
WEB: www.passtheboards.com
SIC: 2741 Miscellaneous publishing

(G-8303)
MEDI PRODUCTS
30 Nurney St (06902-4617)
PHONE..................203 324-3711
Kevin Lyons, *Principal*
EMP: 2 EST: 2018
SALES (est): 86.6K **Privately Held**
SIC: 3841 Surgical & medical instruments

(G-8304)
MEDICAL IMAGING GROUP INC (PA)
216 Cascade Rd (06903-4210)
PHONE..................203 588-1921
Thomas Leiper, *President*
EMP: 2
SALES (est): 342.7K **Privately Held**
SIC: 3861 X-ray film

(G-8305)
MEDITERRANEAN SNACK FD CO LLC
1111 Summer St Ste 5a (06905-5511)
PHONE..................973 402-2644
Vincent James,
◆ EMP: 12
SQ FT: 2,500
SALES (est): 3.8MM
SALES (corp-wide): 10.4MM **Privately Held**
WEB: www.mediterraneansnackfoods.com
SIC: 2096 Potato chips & similar snacks
PA: American Halal Company, Inc
   1111 Summer St Fl 5
   Stamford CT 06905
   203 961-1954

(G-8306)
MELEGA INC
Also Called: AlphaGraphics
47 W Main St (06902-5030)
PHONE..................203 961-8703
Fax: 203 961-8715
EMP: 6
SQ FT: 2,000
SALES (est): 1.2MM **Privately Held**
SIC: 2752 Comm Prtg Litho

(G-8307)
METABEV INC (PA)
50 Soundview Dr (06902-7113)
PHONE..................203 967-8502
John Sbordone, *President*
Carlos Mendez, *Vice Pres*
Christopher Scinto, *Vice Pres*
Pamela Stewart, *Vice Pres*
Jon Mendez, *Warehouse Mgr*
EMP: 10
SALES: 2.8MM **Privately Held**
WEB: www.sukkaronline.com
SIC: 8742 2087 Food & beverage consultant; flavoring extracts & syrups; concentrates, flavoring (except drink); extracts, flavoring; powders, flavoring (except drink)

(G-8308)
MICROSHIELD LLC
200 Henry St (06902-5875)
P.O. Box 9, North Grosvenordale (06255-0009)
PHONE..................800 553-1290
Stephen Stacy, *Engineer*
Stephen M Stacy,
EMP: 1
SALES (est): 193.1K **Privately Held**
SIC: 3564 Filters, air: furnaces, air conditioning equipment, etc.

(G-8309)
MIDSTATE PRINTING GROUP LLC
1 Bank St Ste 401 (06901-3074)
PHONE..................203 998-7575
Richard Fedeli Jr, *Mng Member*
EMP: 3
SQ FT: 1,000
SALES (est): 300K **Privately Held**
SIC: 7389 2752 Packaging & labeling services; commercial printing, lithographic

---

(PA)=Parent Co (HQ)=Headquarters (DH)=Div Headquarters
✪ = New Business established in last 2 years

Stamford - Fairfield County (G-8310)

(G-8310)
MILLENNIUM SHADE & SIGN LLC
29 Sunnyside Ave Ste 2 (06902-7607)
PHONE 203 968-5080
Larry L Szebeni, *Principal*
EMP: 1 **EST:** 2015
SALES (est): 52.7K **Privately Held**
SIC: 3993 Signs & advertising specialties

(G-8311)
MIND2MIND EXCHANGE LLC
32 Mill Brook Rd (06902-1018)
PHONE 203 856-0981
Faisal Hoque, *Principal*
Edward Burke,
EMP: 4
SALES (est): 276K **Privately Held**
SIC: 7372 Application computer software

(G-8312)
MINDTRAINR LLC
107 Revonah Cir (06905-4026)
PHONE 914 799-1515
Marvin Schildkraut, *Mng Member*
EMP: 5 **EST:** 2015
SALES (est): 58K **Privately Held**
SIC: 7372 7389 Application computer software;

(G-8313)
MONDO SAUCE LLC
151 Courtland Ave Apt 5e (06902-9101)
PHONE 206 714-0390
Mitchell Kling,
EMP: 1
SALES (est): 39.6K **Privately Held**
SIC: 3999 Manufacturing industries

(G-8314)
MOSAIC RECORDS INC
425 Fairfield Ave Ste 1 (06902-7533)
PHONE 203 327-7111
Michael Cuscuna, *President*
Frances Lourie, *Treasurer*
EMP: 7
SQ FT: 4,000
SALES (est): 1.2MM **Privately Held**
WEB: www.truebluemusic.com
SIC: 3652 7922 Phonograph records, prerecorded; compact laser discs, prerecorded; theatrical producers & services

(G-8315)
MOWMEDIA LLC
85 Camp Ave Apt 10l (06907-1839)
PHONE 203 240-6416
Mike Wiston,
EMP: 2
SALES (est): 59.2K **Privately Held**
SIC: 2741

(G-8316)
MURPHY & SONS WELDING & REPAIR
Also Called: T Murphy Auto Repair
117 North St (06901-1016)
PHONE 203 635-3372
Terrance W Murphy, *Owner*
EMP: 2
SALES (est): 95.1K **Privately Held**
SIC: 7692 Welding repair

(G-8317)
N A B FINE WOODWORKING LLC
50 Euclid Ave Apt 2 (06902-6289)
PHONE 203 667-3922
Nelson Berganza, *Principal*
EMP: 2 **EST:** 2016
SALES (est): 65.4K **Privately Held**
SIC: 2499 Wood products

(G-8318)
NEAR OAK LLC
Also Called: Amber Synthetics
1011 High Ridge Rd (06905-1610)
PHONE 203 329-6500
Thomas J Castrovinci, *President*
Susan Orr, *Vice Pres*
Stacy Dumas, *Marketing Staff*
Gwen Langer, *Office Mgr*
Diane M Castrovinci, *Admin Sec*
◆ **EMP:** 7

SALES (est): 2.5MM **Privately Held**
WEB: www.amsyn.com
SIC: 5169 2899 Chemicals, industrial & heavy; chemical preparations

(G-8319)
NELSON & MILLER ASSOCIATES
5 Hillandale Ave Ste F (06902-2843)
PHONE 203 356-9694
Denis O'Malley, *Owner*
EMP: 3
SALES (est): 227.8K **Privately Held**
SIC: 2741 Miscellaneous publishing

(G-8320)
NERJAN DEVELOPMENT COMPANY
101 West Ave (06902-4696)
PHONE 203 325-3228
Blake Zizzi, *President*
Robert Zizzi, *Vice Pres*
Cynthia Zizzi, *Admin Sec*
EMP: 6
SQ FT: 3,300
SALES (est): 956.6K **Privately Held**
WEB: www.nerjan.com
SIC: 3599 Machine shop, jobbing & repair

(G-8321)
NEW BEGINNINGS SEA GLASS LLC
40 Club Cir (06905-2115)
PHONE 203 329-7623
Betsy Oreilly, *Owner*
EMP: 1
SALES (est): 56.7K **Privately Held**
SIC: 3944 7389 Craft & hobby kits & sets;

(G-8322)
NEW CANAAN OLIVE OIL LLC
47 Blachley Rd (06902-4318)
PHONE 845 240-3294
Heidi Lindblad Burrows, *Principal*
EMP: 3 **EST:** 2013
SALES (est): 202.5K **Privately Held**
SIC: 2079 Olive oil

(G-8323)
NEW ENGLAND TILE & STONE INC
85 Old Long Ridge Rd # 2 (06903-1641)
PHONE 914 481-4488
Robert Nardozzi, *President*
EMP: 10
SALES (est): 1.3MM **Privately Held**
SIC: 2499 Tiles, cork

(G-8324)
NEW HOPE WLDG FABRICATION LLC
914 E Main St Ste 9 (06902-4055)
PHONE 203 357-0080
Christian Browning,
EMP: 1
SQ FT: 44,000
SALES (est): 222.3K **Privately Held**
SIC: 3548 Welding & cutting apparatus & accessories

(G-8325)
NEW HORIZON MACHINE CO INC
36 Ludlow St (06902-6914)
PHONE 203 316-9355
Antoinette Balbi, *President*
Carmello Balbi, *Vice Pres*
EMP: 8 **EST:** 1978
SQ FT: 5,500
SALES (est): 1.2MM **Privately Held**
WEB: www.newhorizonmachine.com
SIC: 3599 Machine shop, jobbing & repair

(G-8326)
NEW YORK TRANSIT SHOES
2828 High Ridge Rd (06903-1808)
PHONE 203 968-6642
Bruce Victor, *Principal*
EMP: 1 **EST:** 2001
SALES (est): 56.9K **Privately Held**
SIC: 3999 Manufacturing industries

(G-8327)
NEWTEC AMERICA INC
1055 Washington Blvd Fl 6 (06901-2216)
PHONE 203 323-0042
Emmanuel Schellekens, *CEO*

Serge Van Herck, *CEO*
Raymond Pieck, *President*
Timy Abraham, *Engineer*
Geert Tackaert, *CFO*
EMP: 11 **EST:** 1997
SQ FT: 3,700
SALES (est): 2.7MM **Privately Held**
WEB: www.newtecamerica.com
SIC: 3663 Satellites, communications
HQ: St Engineering Idirect (Europe) Cy
Laarstraat 5
Sint-Niklaas 9100
378 065-00

(G-8328)
NEXVUE INFORMATION SYSTEMS INC
65 Broad St (06901-2374)
PHONE 203 327-0800
Dan Schwartz, *President*
Gary Frey, *Vice Pres*
EMP: 15
SALES (est): 1.8MM **Privately Held**
WEB: www.nexvue.com
SIC: 7372 Business oriented computer software

(G-8329)
NON-INVASIVE MED SYSTEMS LLC
1 Harbor Point Rd # 2050 (06902-7352)
PHONE 914 462-0701
Arthur Rappaport, *President*
EMP: 3
SALES (est): 207K **Privately Held**
SIC: 3845 Ultrasonic scanning devices, medical

(G-8330)
NORTHEASTERN METALS CORP
130 Lenox Ave Ste 23 (06906-2337)
PHONE 203 348-8088
Charles Schemera, *President*
Fred Lorenzen, *Treasurer*
EMP: 7
SQ FT: 2,500
SALES: 9MM **Privately Held**
SIC: 3339 5094 5084 Precious metals; precious metals; cleaning equipment, high pressure, sand or steam

(G-8331)
NOVAERUS US INC (PA)
35 Melrose Pl (06902-7516)
PHONE 813 304-2468
Kevin Maughan, *President*
Timothy Powell, *Vice Pres*
Eric Murphy, *Treasurer*
EMP: 10
SALES (est): 2.3MM **Privately Held**
SIC: 3564 Air cleaning systems

(G-8332)
NOVATEK MEDICAL INC
Also Called: Cloodloc
1 Strawberry Hill Ave (06902-2609)
P.O. Box 4963, Greenwich (06831-0419)
PHONE 203 356-0156
Gail Kirhoffer, *President*
EMP: 3
SALES (est): 206K **Privately Held**
SIC: 3841 3845 Blood transfusion equipment; electromedical apparatus

(G-8333)
NUTMEG ARCHITECTURAL WDWRK INC
48 Union St Ste 14 (06906-1342)
PHONE 203 325-4434
Tito Cerretani, *President*
Glenn Silkman, *Vice Pres*
EMP: 20
SQ FT: 22,300
SALES (est): 2.7MM **Privately Held**
SIC: 2522 Cabinets, office: except wood

(G-8334)
NYC GRIND SPORTS MARKETING LLC
1127 High Ridge Rd (06905-1203)
PHONE 917 513-0590
Jerry Tarantola, *Principal*
EMP: 2
SALES (est): 108.8K **Privately Held**
SIC: 3599 Grinding castings for the trade

(G-8335)
O & G INDUSTRIES INC
686 Canal St (06902-5904)
PHONE 203 977-1618
Ray Oneglia, *Branch Mgr*
EMP: 28
SALES (corp-wide): 538MM **Privately Held**
WEB: www.ogind.com
SIC: 2951 Asphalt paving mixtures & blocks
PA: O & G Industries, Inc.
112 Wall St
Torrington CT 06790
860 489-9261

(G-8336)
O & G INDUSTRIES INC
40 Meadow St (06902-5919)
PHONE 203 323-1111
Jack Harding, *Branch Mgr*
EMP: 50
SQ FT: 10,000
SALES (corp-wide): 538MM **Privately Held**
WEB: www.ogind.com
SIC: 5211 3273 1542 3281 Brick; ready-mixed concrete; commercial & office building, new construction; cut stone & stone products; concrete products; construction sand & gravel
PA: O & G Industries, Inc.
112 Wall St
Torrington CT 06790
860 489-9261

(G-8337)
ODOROX IAQ INC
1266 E Main St Ste 700r (06902-3507)
PHONE 203 541-5577
Harry Hirschfeld, *Principal*
EMP: 3
SALES (est): 209.1K **Privately Held**
SIC: 3442 Molding, trim & stripping

(G-8338)
OLD NI INCORPORATED
50 Sunnyside Ave (06902-7641)
PHONE 203 327-7300
William H Flanagan, *Principal*
EMP: 3
SALES (est): 160.5K **Privately Held**
SIC: 3643 Current-carrying wiring devices

(G-8339)
OLIVE CHIAPPETTA OIL LLC
50 Mathews St (06902-4434)
PHONE 203 223-3655
Pat Chiappetta, *Principal*
EMP: 3
SALES (est): 186.9K **Privately Held**
SIC: 2079 Olive oil

(G-8340)
OMEGA ENGINEERING INC
1 Omega Dr (06907-2336)
P.O. Box 2699 (06906-0699)
PHONE 203 359-7922
Dewana Harris, *Materials Mgr*
Weidong Tao, *Purch Agent*
Jennifer Obrien, *Purchasing*
John Ricciuti, *Purchasing*
James Bizak, *Engineer*
EMP: 5
SALES (corp-wide): 2B **Privately Held**
WEB: www.omega.com
SIC: 3823 Industrial instrmnts msrmnt display/control process variable
HQ: Omega Engineering, Inc.
800 Connecticut Ave 5n01
Norwalk CT 06854
203 359-1660

(G-8341)
OMEGA INTERNATIONAL CORP
1 Omega Dr (06907-2336)
P.O. Box 4047 (06907-0047)
PHONE 203 359-1660
Betty Hollander, *President*
Cyrus Grimes, *Engineer*
Richard Kremheller, *Treasurer*
John Bach, *Sales Engr*
EMP: 2
SALES (est): 459.7K **Privately Held**
SIC: 3823 Industrial instrmnts msrmnt display/control process variable

GEOGRAPHIC SECTION

Stamford - Fairfield County (G-8370)

(G-8342)
OPTAMARK CT LLC
15 Bank St Ste 1 (06901-3037)
PHONE 203 325-1180
Tarang Gosalia,
EMP: 3 **EST:** 2017
SALES (est): 58.5K
SALES (corp-wide): 320.5K **Privately Held**
SIC: 2752 Commercial printing, lithographic
PA: Optamark Llc
  865 E Washington St
  North Attleboro MA 02760
  508 643-1017

(G-8343)
OPTICAL DESIGN ASSOCIATES
600 Summer St (06901-4404)
PHONE 203 249-6408
Lev Sakim, Owner
EMP: 3
SALES (est): 245.8K **Privately Held**
SIC: 3827 Optical instruments & lenses

(G-8344)
OPTICAL ENERGY TECHNOLOGIES
472 Westover Rd (06902-1930)
PHONE 203 357-0626
Gerald Falbel, President
Gerald Falbel, President
Judith Falbel, Admin Sec
EMP: 5
SALES: 200K **Privately Held**
WEB: www.opticalenergy.com
SIC: 3433 8742 Solar heaters & collectors; industry specialist consultants

(G-8345)
ORACLE AMERICA INC
900 Long Ridge Rd Bldg 1 (06902-1139)
PHONE 203 703-3000
Lou Cusano, Sales Staff
Steven McLaughlin, Branch Mgr
Diane Reichert, Manager
Kim Laregina, Technical Staff
Kazim Isfahani, Director
EMP: 51
SALES (corp-wide): 39.5B **Publicly Held**
SIC: 3571 7379 7373 7372 Minicomputers; computer related consulting services; systems integration services; operating systems computer software; microprocessors
HQ: Oracle America, Inc.
  500 Oracle Pkwy
  Redwood City CA 94065
  650 506-7000

(G-8346)
ORTHOZON TECHNOLOGIES LLC
175 Atlantic St Ste 206 (06901-3500)
PHONE 203 989-4937
Joshua Aferzon,
EMP: 5
SQ FT: 1,000
SALES (est): 420K **Privately Held**
SIC: 3841 Surgical & medical instruments

(G-8347)
OUTER OFFICE
218 Quarry Rd (06903-5004)
P.O. Box 16815 (06905-8815)
PHONE 203 329-8600
Sandy Golove, Partner
Fred Golove, Partner
EMP: 2
SALES (est): 142.5K **Privately Held**
WEB: www.the-outer-office.com
SIC: 2741 7338 Miscellaneous publishing; secretarial & typing service

(G-8348)
P & S PRINTING LLC
Also Called: Minuteman Press
513 Summer St (06901-1314)
PHONE 203 327-9818
Peter Sandler,
EMP: 5
SQ FT: 2,000
SALES (est): 839.4K **Privately Held**
SIC: 2752 Commercial printing, lithographic

(G-8349)
P C I GROUP
652 Glenbrook Rd 3-201 (06906-1443)
PHONE 203 327-0410
Mary Ferrara, President
Anne Chiapetta, Vice Pres
EMP: 10
SQ FT: 4,500
SALES (est): 1.7MM **Privately Held**
WEB: www.pcigroup.net
SIC: 2752 7336 Commercial printing, offset; graphic arts & related design

(G-8350)
PARFUMS DE COEUR LTD (PA)
Also Called: PDC Brands
750 E Main St (06902-3831)
PHONE 203 655-8807
James Stammer, President
Mark A Laracy, Chairman
James E Rogers, COO
John F Owen, CFO
Edward Kaminski, Treasurer
◆ **EMP:** 30
SQ FT: 13,000
SALES (est): 30.6MM **Privately Held**
WEB: www.pdcpm.com
SIC: 2844 Perfumes, natural or synthetic

(G-8351)
PASSUR AEROSPACE INC (PA)
1 Landmark Sq Ste 1900 (06901-2671)
PHONE 203 622-4086
James T Barry, President
Keith D Wichman, General Mgr
G S Beckwith Gilbert, Chairman
Timothy Campbell, Exec VP
Tim Cinello, Vice Pres
EMP: 44
SQ FT: 5,300
SALES: 14.8MM **Publicly Held**
WEB: www.passur.com
SIC: 3812 Search & navigation equipment

(G-8352)
PAULS MARBLE DEPOT LLC
Also Called: Extile.com
40 Warshaw Pl Ste 1 (06902-6354)
PHONE 203 978-0669
Parag Adalja, Mng Member
▲ **EMP:** 13
SQ FT: 28,000
SALES (est): 2.8MM **Privately Held**
SIC: 3272 5032 Tile, precast terrazzo or concrete; marble building stone

(G-8353)
PAWTRAIT INC
38 Pine Hill Ter (06903-4929)
PHONE 848 992-4599
Andrew Wind, Principal
EMP: 1
SALES (est): 36K **Privately Held**
SIC: 7372 Application computer software

(G-8354)
PEANUT BUTTER AND JELLY
500 Bedford St Apt 227 (06901-1513)
PHONE 203 504-2280
EMP: 3
SALES (est): 83K **Privately Held**
SIC: 2099 Mfg Food Preparations

(G-8355)
PEERLESS SYSTEMS CORPORATION (DH)
1055 Washington Blvd Fl 8 (06901-2251)
PHONE 203 350-0040
Anthony Bonid, CEO
Lodovico De Visconti, President
EMP: 11
SQ FT: 1,200
SALES: 3.6MM
SALES (corp-wide): 4.6MM **Privately Held**
SIC: 7372 7371 Prepackaged software; custom computer programming services
HQ: Mobius Acquisition, Llc
  1000 Mcknight Park Dr
  Pittsburgh PA 15237
  412 281-7000

(G-8356)
PEGASUS CAPITAL ADVISORS LP (PA)
750 E Main St (06902-3831)
PHONE 203 869-4400
Craig Cogut, Managing Prtnr
Greg Gish, Managing Prtnr
Daniel Stencel, Managing Prtnr
Brian Friedman, Vice Pres
Anne Frank-Shapiro, Officer
EMP: 25
SALES (est): 54.6MM **Publicly Held**
SIC: 3646 3648 Commercial indusl & institutional electric lighting fixtures; street lighting fixtures

(G-8357)
PELICAN ISLAND PUBLISHING
41 Foxwood Rd (06903-2209)
PHONE 908 227-0991
EMP: 2
SALES (est): 85K **Privately Held**
SIC: 2741 Miscellaneous publishing

(G-8358)
PERSONALLY YOURS
45 Idlewood Pl (06905-2410)
PHONE 203 329-6645
Moreen Pape, Owner
EMP: 1
SALES (est): 79.8K **Privately Held**
SIC: 2282 Embroidery yarn: twisting, winding or spooling

(G-8359)
PF LABORATORIES INC (HQ)
201 Tresser Blvd Ste 324 (06901-3435)
PHONE 973 256-3100
John Stewart, President
David Long, Senior VP
Russ Gasdia, Vice Pres
Bert Weinstein, Vice Pres
Yuning Chang, Research
EMP: 150
SQ FT: 300,000
SALES (est): 16.9MM **Privately Held**
SIC: 2834 Pharmaceutical preparations

(G-8360)
PHARMACEUTICAL RES ASSOC INC (HQ)
201 Tresser Blvd (06901-3435)
PHONE 203 588-8000
Stuart Baker, Vice Pres
Howard Udell, Vice Pres
EMP: 3
SQ FT: 90,000
SALES (est): 60.6MM **Privately Held**
SIC: 2834 5122 Pharmaceutical preparations; pharmaceuticals; proprietary (patent) medicines

(G-8361)
PILOT SOFTWARE INC
144 Morgan St Ste 1 (06905-5433)
PHONE 203 252-2463
Boris Mayzler, Principal
EMP: 2
SALES (est): 164.3K **Privately Held**
SIC: 7372 Prepackaged software

(G-8362)
PITNEY BOWES INC (PA)
3001 Summer St Ste 3 (06905-4321)
PHONE 203 356-5000
Michael I Roth, Ch of Bd
Marc B Lautenbach, President
Jason C Dies, President
Robert Guidotti, President
Denise Wray, Partner
◆ **EMP:** 3500 **EST:** 1920
SALES: 3.5B **Publicly Held**
WEB: www.pb.com
SIC: 3579 7359 3661 8744 Mailing machines; postage meters; forms handling equipment; business machine & electronic equipment rental services; facsimile equipment; facilities support services; prepackaged software

(G-8363)
PITNEY BOWES INC
300 Stamford Pl Ste 200 (06902-6735)
PHONE 203 356-5000
Mark Flynn, Branch Mgr
EMP: 35
SALES (corp-wide): 3.5B **Publicly Held**
SIC: 3579 7359 Postage meters; business machine & electronic equipment rental services
PA: Pitney Bowes Inc.
  3001 Summer St Ste 3
  Stamford CT 06905
  203 356-5000

(G-8364)
PITNEY BOWES SOFTWARE INC
3001 Summer St Ste 3 (06905-4321)
PHONE 603 595-2060
Andrea Goldberg, Vice Pres
Bob Guidltti, Branch Mgr
EMP: 2
SALES (corp-wide): 3.5B **Publicly Held**
SIC: 7372 Prepackaged software
HQ: Pitney Bowes Software Inc.
  27 Waterview Dr
  Shelton CT 06484
  855 839-5119

(G-8365)
PMOYS LLC
Soundview Plz (06902)
PHONE 203 541-0995
Emmett Woodward,
EMP: 1
SALES (est): 32.7K **Privately Held**
SIC: 7372 7389 Application computer software;

(G-8366)
POINTER PRESS
41 Minivale Rd (06907-1204)
PHONE 203 355-0677
EMP: 1 **EST:** 2017
SALES (est): 37.5K **Privately Held**
SIC: 2741 Miscellaneous publishing

(G-8367)
POLYMER ENGINEERED PDTS INC (PA)
595 Summer St Ste 2 (06901-1407)
PHONE 203 324-3737
Leslie Klein, CEO
Sheila Klein, Director
▲ **EMP:** 100 **EST:** 1970
SQ FT: 8,500
SALES (est): 13.9MM **Privately Held**
SIC: 3089 Injection molding of plastics

(G-8368)
POLYONE CORPORATION
70 Carlisle Pl (06902-7630)
PHONE 203 327-6010
Julie A McAlindon, Manager
EMP: 9 **Publicly Held**
SIC: 2821 Plastics materials & resins
PA: Polyone Corporation
  33587 Walker Rd
  Avon Lake OH 44012

(G-8369)
POZZI FMLY WINE & SPIRITS LLC
37 Old Well Rd (06907-1128)
PHONE 646 422-9134
Daniele Pozzi,
Barbara Pozzi,
EMP: 3
SALES: 3MM **Privately Held**
SIC: 2084 Wines

(G-8370)
PRA HOLDINGS INC
1 Stamford Forum (06901-3516)
PHONE 203 853-0123
Stuart Baker, President
Howard Udell, Vice Pres
EMP: 3
SQ FT: 90,000
SALES (est): 61.2MM
SALES (corp-wide): 2.8B **Publicly Held**
SIC: 2834 5122 8742 Pharmaceutical preparations; pharmaceuticals; industry specialist consultants
PA: Pra Health Sciences, Inc.
  4130 Parklake Ave Ste 400
  Raleigh NC 27612
  919 786-8200

Stamford - Fairfield County (G-8371)

(G-8371)
PRECISION PRESS LLC
149 Skyview Dr (06902-1512)
PHONE..................203 359-0211
Joshua Greene, *Principal*
EMP: 2
SALES (est): 129.5K **Privately Held**
SIC: 2752 Commercial printing, offset

(G-8372)
PRESIDIUM USA INC
100 Stamford Pl (06902-6740)
PHONE..................203 674-9374
EMP: 3
SALES (est): 306.9K **Privately Held**
SIC: 2821 Plastics materials & resins

(G-8373)
PRINERTECHS
255 Strawberry Hill Ave (06902-2547)
PHONE..................203 249-6646
Nick Santagata, *Principal*
EMP: 2
SALES (est): 83.9K **Privately Held**
SIC: 2752 Commercial printing, lithographic

(G-8374)
PRINTER TECHS LLC
44 Commerce Rd (06902-4561)
PHONE..................203 322-1160
Nicholas J Santagata Jr, *Manager*
EMP: 2
SALES (est): 127.7K **Privately Held**
SIC: 2752 Commercial printing, lithographic

(G-8375)
PRINTING SOLUTIONS & RESOURCES
16 Dyke Ln (06902-7313)
PHONE..................203 965-0090
Scott Muller, *President*
EMP: 1
SQ FT: 15,000
SALES (est): 101K **Privately Held**
WEB: www.printscott.com
SIC: 2752 Commercial printing, lithographic

(G-8376)
PROTEGRITY USA INC (PA)
333 Ludlow St Ste 8 (06902-6991)
PHONE..................203 326-7200
Rick Farnell, *CEO*
Jay Wolf, *Controller*
Jeffra Ruesink, *VP Sales*
Eileen Garry, *Chief Mktg Ofcr*
EMP: 22
SQ FT: 8,000
SALES (est): 18.3MM **Privately Held**
WEB: www.protegrity.com
SIC: 7372 Prepackaged software

(G-8377)
PURDUE PHARMA INC
201 Tresser Blvd Fl 1 (06901-3432)
PHONE..................203 588-8000
Mark Timney, *CEO*
Stuart D Baker, *Exec VP*
Edward B Mahony, *CFO*
Laykea Tafesse, *Associate Dir*
EMP: 2 EST: 1991
SQ FT: 90,000
SALES (est): 406.4K **Privately Held**
WEB: www.purduepharma.com
SIC: 2834 5122 Pills, pharmaceutical; pharmaceuticals
PA: Purdue Pharma L.P.
201 Tresser Blvd Fl 1
Stamford CT 06901

(G-8378)
PURDUE PHARMA LP (PA)
201 Tresser Blvd Fl 1 (06901-3432)
PHONE..................203 588-8000
Steve Miller, *Partner*
Stuart D Baker, *Exec VP*
Alan W Dunton, *Senior VP*
Jean-Jacques Charhon, *CFO*
Edward B Mahony, *CFO*
▲ EMP: 256
SQ FT: 500,000
SALES (est): 484.4MM **Privately Held**
SIC: 2834 5122 Pharmaceutical preparations; pharmaceuticals

(G-8379)
PURDUE PHARMA MANUFACTURING LP
1 Stamford Forum 201 (06901-3516)
PHONE..................252 265-1924
David Lundie, *Senior VP*
Stuart D Baker, *Vice Pres*
Edward Mahony, *Vice Pres*
Phillip Strassburger, *Vice Pres*
▲ EMP: 32 EST: 2013
SALES (est): 2.4MM **Privately Held**
SIC: 2834 Chlorination tablets & kits (water purification)
PA: Purdue Pharma L.P.
201 Tresser Blvd Fl 1
Stamford CT 06901

(G-8380)
PURDUE PHARMACEUTICAL PDTS LP
1 Stamford Forum (06901-3516)
PHONE..................203 588-5000
John Stewart, *Partner*
Purdue Pharmeceutical Products, *General Ptnr*
Edward Mahoney, *CFO*
EMP: 2
SALES (est): 338.5K **Privately Held**
SIC: 2834 Pharmaceutical preparations
PA: Purdue Pharma L.P.
201 Tresser Blvd Fl 1
Stamford CT 06901

(G-8381)
PURDUE PHARMACEUTICALS LP
1 Stamford Forum (06901-3516)
PHONE..................252 265-1900
Edward Mahony, *Exec VP*
Stuart D Baker, *Exec VP*
David Long, *Senior VP*
Saeed Motahari, *Senior VP*
EMP: 11
SALES (est): 7.3MM **Privately Held**
SIC: 5122 2834 Pharmaceuticals; pharmaceutical preparations
PA: Purdue Pharma L.P.
201 Tresser Blvd Fl 1
Stamford CT 06901

(G-8382)
PURITAN LANE LLC
59 Puritan Ln (06906-1616)
PHONE..................203 602-5555
Ferdinando Delpeschio,
EMP: 2
SALES (est): 87.2K **Privately Held**
SIC: 3711 Motor vehicles & car bodies

(G-8383)
PUZZLE RINGS CREATIONS LLC
6 Donata Ln (06905-1908)
PHONE..................203 550-1591
Ambroz Pergjoni, *Principal*
EMP: 1
SALES (est): 67.6K **Privately Held**
SIC: 3944 Puzzles

(G-8384)
RAIN CARBON INC
10 Signal Rd (06902-7909)
PHONE..................203 406-0535
Jagan Nellore, *CEO*
Gerard Sweeney, *President*
Gunther Weymans, *COO*
Paul Francese, *CFO*
Matthew Scott Hansen,
EMP: 6 EST: 2010
SALES (est): 175.2K **Privately Held**
SIC: 3624 Carbon & graphite products
PA: Rain Industries Limited
Rain Center, No. 34
Hyderabad TS 50007

(G-8385)
RAIN CII CARBON LLC
10 Signal Rd (06902-7909)
PHONE..................203 406-0535
Gerard Sweeney, *Branch Mgr*
EMP: 15 **Privately Held**
SIC: 2999 8741 8748 Coke, calcined petroleum: made from purchased materials; financial management for business; environmental consultant
HQ: Rain Cii Carbon Llc
2627 Chestnut Ridge Dr # 200
Kingwood TX 77339
281 318-2400

(G-8386)
RELATIVE GOURMET II
30 Spring St (06901-1701)
PHONE..................203 358-4602
EMP: 1 EST: 2011
SALES (est): 93.1K **Privately Held**
SIC: 3421 Table & food cutlery, including butchers'

(G-8387)
RESINALL CORP (DH)
3065 High Ridge Rd (06903-1301)
P.O. Box 195, Severn NC (27877-0195)
PHONE..................203 329-7100
Elaine Godina, *President*
Harry Anderson, *Project Mgr*
Joyce Sullivan, *Buyer*
Lee T Godina, *Treasurer*
▼ EMP: 10 EST: 1979
SQ FT: 4,000
SALES (est): 65.3MM
SALES (corp-wide): 997.6MM **Privately Held**
WEB: www.resinall.com
SIC: 2821 Thermosetting materials; thermoplastic materials
HQ: Ergon Chemicals, Llc
2829 Lakeland Dr Ste 2000
Flowood MS 39232
601 933-3000

(G-8388)
REVOLUTION LIGHTING (HQ)
177 Broad St Fl 12 (06901-5002)
PHONE..................203 504-1111
Robert V Lapenta, *President*
EMP: 3 EST: 2016
SQ FT: 6,625
SALES (est): 1.3MM
SALES (corp-wide): 99.9MM **Publicly Held**
SIC: 3674 3641 3993 Light emitting diodes; electric light bulbs, complete; signs & advertising specialties
PA: Revolution Lighting Technologies, Inc.
177 Broad St Fl 12
Stamford CT 06901
203 504-1111

(G-8389)
REVOLUTION LIGHTING TECH INC (PA)
177 Broad St Fl 12 (06901-5002)
PHONE..................203 504-1111
Robert V Lapenta, *Ch of Bd*
Richard Hanlon, *COO*
Jon Barker, *Vice Pres*
Doug Cotter, *Vice Pres*
John Poerstel, *Vice Pres*
EMP: 111
SQ FT: 16,626
SALES (est): 99.9MM **Publicly Held**
WEB: www.nexxuslighting.com
SIC: 3674 3641 3993 Light emitting diodes; electric light bulbs, complete; signs & advertising specialties

(G-8390)
REVOLUTION LIGHTING TECH INC
177 Broad St Fl 12 (06901-5002)
PHONE..................203 504-1111
Susan Knox, *Branch Mgr*
EMP: 14
SALES (corp-wide): 99.9MM **Publicly Held**
WEB: www.nexxuslighting.com
SIC: 3993 Signs & advertising specialties
PA: Revolution Lighting Technologies, Inc.
177 Broad St Fl 12
Stamford CT 06901
203 504-1111

(G-8391)
REXEL
390 Fairfield Ave (06902-7202)
PHONE..................203 969-6601
EMP: 4
SALES (est): 395.1K **Privately Held**
SIC: 5063 3699 Whol Electrical Equipment Mfg Electrical Equipment/Supplies

(G-8392)
REYNOLDS AND REYNOLDS COMPANY
102 Fieldstone Ter (06902-2573)
PHONE..................203 323-3748
Noel Cerniglia, *Manager*
EMP: 1
SALES (corp-wide): 1.5B **Privately Held**
WEB: www.reyrey.com
SIC: 7372 Application computer software
HQ: The Reynolds And Reynolds Company
1 Reynolds Way
Kettering OH 45430
937 485-2000

(G-8393)
RISEANDSHINE CORPORATION (PA)
Also Called: Rise Brewing Co
425 Fairfield Ave 1a11 (06902-7538)
PHONE..................917 599-7541
Grant Gyesky, *CEO*
EMP: 18
SALES (est): 2.8MM **Privately Held**
SIC: 2095 Instant coffee

(G-8394)
RLP INC
Also Called: Amusements Unlimited
12 Magee Ave (06902-5907)
PHONE..................203 359-2504
Richard Preli, *President*
▲ EMP: 3
SQ FT: 3,000
SALES: 500K **Privately Held**
SIC: 3999 Coin-operated amusement machines

(G-8395)
ROBERT CHANG
1500 Bedford St Apt 203 (06905-4725)
PHONE..................203 737-2264
Robert Chang, *CEO*
EMP: 1
SALES (est): 47.2K **Privately Held**
SIC: 2841 Soap & other detergents

(G-8396)
ROBERT L LOVALLO
Also Called: Roblo Woodworks
127 Myrtle Ave (06902-3906)
PHONE..................203 324-6655
Robert L Lovallo, *Owner*
EMP: 7 EST: 1956
SQ FT: 2,500
SALES (est): 551K **Privately Held**
WEB: www.sallylamb.com
SIC: 2434 2541 2431 Wood kitchen cabinets; wood partitions & fixtures; staircases & stairs, wood

(G-8397)
ROLLEASE ACMEDA INC (PA)
750 E Main St 7 (06902-3831)
PHONE..................203 964-1573
Derick Marsch, *President*
Greg Farr, *Senior VP*
Thomas Gilboy, *Vice Pres*
Tom Gilboy, *CFO*
Kevin Leon, *Human Res Mgr*
◆ EMP: 97 EST: 1980
SQ FT: 54,000
SALES (est): 26.7MM **Privately Held**
WEB: www.rollease.com
SIC: 3568 2591 Clutches, except vehicular; drapery hardware & blinds & shades; window shade rollers & fittings; window blinds

(G-8398)
ROSCO HOLDINGS INC (PA)
52 Harbor View Ave (06902-5914)
PHONE..................203 708-8900
Stanford Miller, *President*
Ron Knell, *Business Mgr*
Mark Engel, *COO*
Stan Schwartz, *Exec VP*
Cindi Carriero, *Inv Control Mgr*
▲ EMP: 60
SQ FT: 20,000

SALES (est): 7.7MM **Privately Held**
SIC: 3861 Motion picture apparatus & equipment

(G-8399)
ROSCO LABORATORIES INC (HQ)
52 Harbor View Ave (06902-5947)
PHONE..................203 708-8900
Stanford Miller, *Ch of Bd*
Mark Engel, *President*
Diane Ricci, *General Mgr*
Stan Schwartz, *Exec VP*
Cristian Arroyo, *Vice Pres*
▲ **EMP:** 25 **EST:** 1921
SQ FT: 40,000
SALES (est): 7.6MM **Privately Held**
WEB: www.rosco.com
SIC: 3861 Motion picture apparatus & equipment

(G-8400)
SAFE LASER THERAPY LLC
1747 Summer St Ste 4 (06905-5144)
PHONE..................203 261-4400
Malti G Gupta, *President*
EMP: 4 **EST:** 2008
SALES (est): 274K **Privately Held**
SIC: 3845 8093 7999 Laser systems & equipment, medical; weight loss clinic, with medical staff; physical fitness instruction

(G-8401)
SAINTE-ANNE CUSTOM WOODWORK
50 Euclid Ave (06902-6289)
PHONE..................203 961-9403
Ange Rossel-Y-Ferrer, *Principal*
EMP: 1
SALES (est): 57.6K **Privately Held**
SIC: 2431 Millwork

(G-8402)
SANFORD REDMOND INC
746 Riverbank Rd (06903-3514)
PHONE..................203 351-9800
Jonathan Sanford, *CEO*
EMP: 8 **EST:** 1953
SALES (est): 1.5MM **Privately Held**
WEB: www.sanfordredmond.com
SIC: 3565 Packaging machinery

(G-8403)
SCINETX LLC
Also Called: Capital Venture
1836 Long Ridge Rd (06903-3234)
PHONE..................203 355-3676
Louis G Cornacchia, *Mng Member*
EMP: 4 **EST:** 2009
SALES (est): 100K **Privately Held**
SIC: 3663 Microwave communication equipment

(G-8404)
SCITECH INTERNATIONAL LLC
Also Called: Scitech Ingredients
50 Soundview Dr (06902-7113)
PHONE..................203 967-8502
John Sbordone,
Steve Carlin,
William Gambrell,
Jack Manno,
Carlos Mendez,
EMP: 7
SQ FT: 1,800
SALES (est): 279.1K **Privately Held**
WEB: www.scitech1.com
SIC: 2087 Flavoring extracts & syrups

(G-8405)
SCRIBBLING SCRIBE
79 Hickory Rd (06903-2932)
PHONE..................203 329-7140
Sue Ellen Bache, *Owner*
EMP: 1
SALES (est): 58K **Privately Held**
SIC: 2759 Invitation & stationery printing & engraving

(G-8406)
SECLINGUA INC
52 Mill Valley Ln (06903-1642)
PHONE..................203 922-4560
Matthew Smith, *CEO*

EMP: 2
SQ FT: 10,000
SALES (est): 147K **Privately Held**
SIC: 3571 3845 3841 Electronic computers; electromedical equipment; medical instruments & equipment, blood & bone work

(G-8407)
SEESMART INC
Also Called: Revolution Lighting
177 Broad St Fl 12 (06901-5002)
PHONE..................203 504-1111
James Depalma, *President*
Ken Ames, *Vice Pres*
Marvin Tsai, *Purchasing*
Olivia Wu, *Purchasing*
Jonathan Miller, *CFO*
▲ **EMP:** 27
SALES (est): 6.1MM
SALES (corp-wide): 99.9MM **Publicly Held**
SIC: 3645 3646 Residential lighting fixtures; commercial indusl & institutional electric lighting fixtures
PA: Revolution Lighting Technologies, Inc.
177 Broad St Fl 12
Stamford CT 06901
203 504-1111

(G-8408)
SEKISUI DIAGNOSTICS LLC
500 West Ave (06902-6360)
PHONE..................203 602-7777
Adele Ozanne, *Branch Mgr*
Les Deluca, *Director*
EMP: 7 **Privately Held**
SIC: 3841 Diagnostic apparatus, medical
HQ: Sekisui Diagnostics, Llc
1 Wall St Ste 301
Burlington MA 01803

(G-8409)
SENIOR NETWORK INC
777 Summer St Ste 103 (06901-1085)
PHONE..................203 969-2700
Frederick Adler, *President*
Larry Brown, *Exec VP*
EMP: 34
SALES (est): 3.3MM **Privately Held**
WEB: www.seniornetwork.com
SIC: 2741 Miscellaneous publishing

(G-8410)
SENIOR RESOURCE PUBLISHING LLC
27 5th St (06905-5013)
PHONE..................203 295-3477
Gary Ferone, *Principal*
EMP: 1 **EST:** 2014
SALES (est): 52K **Privately Held**
SIC: 2741 Miscellaneous publishing

(G-8411)
SHENONDAH VLY SPECIALTY FOODS
Also Called: Valley of Mexico
28 Intervale Rd (06905-1308)
PHONE..................203 348-0402
Stephen Bowling, *President*
EMP: 3
SALES (est): 190K **Privately Held**
WEB: www.valleyofmexico.com
SIC: 2032 Canned specialties

(G-8412)
SHIPPAN LIQUORS
316 Shippan Ave (06902-6014)
PHONE..................203 348-0925
Kamlesh Rana, *Owner*
EMP: 2
SALES (est): 73.9K **Privately Held**
SIC: 2086 5921 Bottled & canned soft drinks; liquor stores

(G-8413)
SHORE THERAPEUTICS INC
177 Broad St Ste 1101 (06901-2048)
PHONE..................646 562-1243
EMP: 4
SALES (est): 140K **Privately Held**
SIC: 2834 Mfg Pharmaceutical Preparations

(G-8414)
SIGG SWITZERLAND (USA) INC
1177 High Ridge Rd (06905-1221)
PHONE..................203 321-1232
Daniel McNamara, *Vice Pres*
▲ **EMP:** 9
SALES (est): 1.1MM **Privately Held**
SIC: 2086 Bottled & canned soft drinks

(G-8415)
SIGN A RAMA INC
Also Called: Sign-A-Rama
854 High Ridge Rd (06905-1911)
PHONE..................203 674-8900
Adam Cohen, *Principal*
EMP: 2
SALES (est): 190.4K **Privately Held**
SIC: 3993 Signs & advertising specialties

(G-8416)
SIGNCRAFTERS INC
874 E Main St (06902-3926)
PHONE..................203 353-9535
Paul D Muenzen, *President*
EMP: 5
SALES (est): 374.4K **Privately Held**
SIC: 3993 Signs, not made in custom sign painting shops

(G-8417)
SIGNS OF SUCCESS INC
1084 Hope St (06907-1823)
PHONE..................203 329-3374
Richard Farber, *President*
EMP: 3
SALES (est): 395.2K **Privately Held**
SIC: 3993 Signs & advertising specialties

(G-8418)
SIGNS PRO LLC
100 Research Dr (06906-1400)
PHONE..................203 323-9994
Jose Palacios,
EMP: 2
SALES (est): 256.1K **Privately Held**
WEB: www.signspro.net
SIC: 3993 Signs, not made in custom sign painting shops

(G-8419)
SILGAN CLOSURES INTL HOLDG CO
4 Landmark Sq (06901-2502)
PHONE..................203 975-7110
EMP: 2
SALES (est): 73.4K **Privately Held**
SIC: 3411 Metal cans

(G-8420)
SILGAN CONTAINERS CORPORATION
4 Landmark Sq (06901-2502)
PHONE..................203 975-7110
EMP: 12
SALES (corp-wide): 4.4B **Publicly Held**
SIC: 3411 Metal cans
HQ: Silgan Containers Corporation
21600 Oxnard St Ste 1600
Woodland Hills CA 91367
818 348-3700

(G-8421)
SILGAN HOLDINGS INC (PA)
4 Landmark Sq Ste 400 (06901-2502)
PHONE..................203 975-7110
Anthony J Allott, *Ch of Bd*
Adam J Greenlee, *President*
Thomas J Snyder, *President*
Frank W Hogan III, *Senior VP*
B Frederik Prinzen, *Senior VP*
EMP: 107
SALES: 4.4B **Publicly Held**
WEB: www.silgan.com
SIC: 3411 3085 3089 Food & beverage containers; aluminum cans; plastics bottles; plastic containers, except foam; plastic kitchenware, tableware & houseware

(G-8422)
SIMCHA DESIGNS
53 Boxwood Dr (06906-1506)
PHONE..................203 273-1593
Judith Cahn, *Owner*
EMP: 1

SALES (est): 93.4K **Privately Held**
SIC: 2754 Invitations: gravure printing

(G-8423)
SIMPLY SIGNS
48 Putter Dr (06907-1238)
PHONE..................203 595-0123
Jami Sherwood, *Owner*
EMP: 2
SALES (est): 100K **Privately Held**
SIC: 3993 Signs & advertising specialties

(G-8424)
SKYTHINK INC
1 Rock Spring Rd Apt 4 (06906-1945)
PHONE..................203 324-1108
EMP: 2 **EST:** 2016
SALES (est): 56.5K **Privately Held**
SIC: 7372 Prepackaged Software Services

(G-8425)
SMART ALEX FOODS LLC
41 Shelter Rock Rd (06903-3530)
PHONE..................203 322-3368
Bruce Miller,
Maria Miller,
EMP: 2
SALES (est): 90.4K **Privately Held**
SIC: 2096 Potato chips & similar snacks

(G-8426)
SMART POLISHING
24 Betts Ave (06902-6465)
PHONE..................203 559-1541
Edgar Cavero, *Principal*
EMP: 3 **EST:** 2010
SALES (est): 134K **Privately Held**
SIC: 3471 Polishing, metals or formed products

(G-8427)
SOLAIS LIGHTING INC
650 West Ave (06902-6325)
PHONE..................203 683-6222
James Leahy, *President*
Ken Hurd, *Senior VP*
Glenn Bordfeld, *Vice Pres*
Rob Limroth, *Vice Pres*
Colleen Kelly Kishore, *Controller*
EMP: 10
SALES (est): 161.3K
SALES (corp-wide): 23.5B **Publicly Held**
SIC: 3648 Lighting equipment
HQ: Powersecure, Inc.
1609 Heritage Commerce Ct
Wake Forest NC 27587
919 556-3056

(G-8428)
SOLDIER SOCKS
90 Fairfield Ave (06902-5021)
PHONE..................203 832-2005
EMP: 4 **EST:** 2011
SALES (est): 324.9K **Privately Held**
SIC: 2252 Socks

(G-8429)
SONIC WELDING CO
18 West Ave (06902-4644)
PHONE..................203 348-8021
Gino Lupinachi, *Owner*
Robert Kelley, *Owner*
EMP: 1
SQ FT: 2,000
SALES (est): 56.2K **Privately Held**
SIC: 7692 3599 Welding repair; machine shop, jobbing & repair

(G-8430)
SOUTH BEND ETHANOL LLC
107 Elm St (06902-3834)
PHONE..................203 326-8132
Bill Bronin,
EMP: 50
SALES (est): 56.8MM
SALES (corp-wide): 1.5B **Privately Held**
SIC: 1311 Natural gas production
HQ: Vitol Americas Corp.
2925 Richmond Ave Ste 11
Houston TX 77098

(G-8431)
SOUTHWIRE COMPANY LLC
Also Called: Seatek Wireless
392 Pacific St (06902-5816)
PHONE..................203 324-0067

Stamford - Fairfield County (G-8432) — GEOGRAPHIC SECTION

EMP: 19
SALES (corp-wide): 2.2B Privately Held
SIC: 3423 Hand & edge tools
PA: Southwire Company, Llc
1 Southwire Dr
Carrollton GA 30119
770 832-4242

(G-8432)
SPARTECH LLC
Also Called: Polycast
69 Southfield Ave (06902-7614)
PHONE 203 327-6010
Julie A McAlindon, *Manager*
EMP: 185
SALES (corp-wide): 961.3MM Privately Held
WEB: www.spartech.com
SIC: 3089 3081 2821 Plastic processing; unsupported plastics film & sheet; plastics materials & resins
PA: Spartech Llc
11650 Lkeside Crossing Ct
Saint Louis MO 63146
314 569-7400

(G-8433)
SPEED PRINTING & GRAPHICS INC
Also Called: S P & G
330 Fairfield Ave Ste 3 (06902-7248)
PHONE 203 324-4000
Steven Seifert, *President*
John Schnefke, *Sales Staff*
EMP: 6
SQ FT: 2,800
SALES (est): 927K Privately Held
WEB: www.sp-g.com
SIC: 2752 2759 Commercial printing, offset; commercial printing

(G-8434)
SPIERS WELDING SERVICE
1277 Long Ridge Rd (06903-4431)
PHONE 203 322-1004
Malcolm Spiers, *Owner*
EMP: 1
SALES (est): 85.1K Privately Held
SIC: 7692 1799 Welding repair; ornamental metal work

(G-8435)
SPX CORPORATION
2001 W Main St Ste 222 (06902-4542)
PHONE 203 356-9308
Richard Inzitari, *Branch Mgr*
EMP: 2
SALES (corp-wide): 1.5B Publicly Held
WEB: www.spx.com
SIC: 3443 Cooling towers, metal plate
PA: Spx Corporation
13320a Balntyn Corp Pl
Charlotte NC 28277
980 474-3700

(G-8436)
STAMFORD CAPITAL GROUP INC (PA)
1266 E Main St (06902-3546)
PHONE 800 977-7837
Patton Corrigan, *President*
Evan Tessler, *Vice Pres*
EMP: 1675
SALES (est): 52.8MM Privately Held
SIC: 2741 6211 Guides: publishing only, not printed on site; investment bankers

(G-8437)
STAMFORD FORGE & METAL CFT INC
63 Victory St (06902-5614)
PHONE 203 348-8290
Chris Salvator, *President*
EMP: 3 EST: 1970
SQ FT: 3,500
SALES: 500K Privately Held
SIC: 3446 Architectural metalwork

(G-8438)
STAMFORD IRON & STL WORKS INC
347 Courtland Ave (06906-2201)
P.O. Box 2190 (06906-0190)
PHONE 203 324-6751
Joseph Fuss Jr, *President*

Thomas Pettit Jr, *Vice Pres*
EMP: 15 EST: 1957
SQ FT: 4,500
SALES (est): 4MM Privately Held
WEB: www.clcstamford.org
SIC: 3441 Fabricated structural metal

(G-8439)
STAMFORD RISK ANALYTICS LLC
263 Tresser Blvd Fl 9 (06901-3236)
PHONE 203 559-0883
Ali Samad-Khan, *President*
EMP: 11
SALES (est): 669.2K Privately Held
WEB: www.opriskadvisory.com
SIC: 7372 Business oriented computer software

(G-8440)
STAMFORD RPM RACEWAY LLC
600 West Ave (06902-6325)
PHONE 203 323-7223
Eyal Farage, *Principal*
EMP: 3
SALES (est): 106.9K Privately Held
SIC: 3644 Raceways

(G-8441)
STEPHANIE MARK
Also Called: Pyridiam Block
181 Turn Of River Rd (06905-1338)
PHONE 203 329-7562
Stephanie Mark, *Principal*
EMP: 1
SALES (est): 56.7K Privately Held
SIC: 3272 3449 0181 Well curbing, concrete; curtain walls for buildings, steel; mats, preseeded: soil erosion, growing of

(G-8442)
STERLING GAS DRLG FUND 1982 LP
1 Landmark Sq (06901-2603)
PHONE 203 358-5700
Charles E Drimal Jr, *CEO*
EMP: 2
SALES (est): 92.9K Privately Held
SIC: 1381 Drilling oil & gas wells

(G-8443)
STEVEN ROSENBURG
Also Called: Hammersmith
148 Old Long Ridge Rd (06903-1616)
PHONE 203 329-8798
Steven Rosenburg, *Owner*
EMP: 2
SALES: 90K Privately Held
SIC: 3446 5945 3441 3272 Architectural metalwork; hobby, toy & game shops; fabricated structural metal; concrete products

(G-8444)
STORA ENSO N AMERCN SLS INC (HQ)
201 Broad St (06901-2004)
PHONE 203 541-5178
Peter Mersmann, *President*
Brent Saunders, *Vice Pres*
Reto Leuenberger, *Admin Sec*
Robert Zitnay, *Admin Sec*
▲ EMP: 5
SQ FT: 5,000
SALES (est): 2MM
SALES (corp-wide): 12B Privately Held
SIC: 2671 Packaging paper & plastics film, coated & laminated
PA: Stora Enso Oyj
Kanavaranta 1
Helsinki 00160
204 613-1

(G-8445)
STORMWATERWORKSCOM LLC
48 Union St Ste M (06906-1343)
PHONE 203 324-0045
Nanda T Zimmerman,
EMP: 2
SALES (est): 254.9K Privately Held
WEB: www.stormwaterworks.com
SIC: 3569 5999 Filters, general line: industrial; safety supplies & equipment

(G-8446)
STRATEGIC INSIGHTS INC
Also Called: Plan & Sponsor
1055 Washington Blvd # 400 (06901-2216)
PHONE 203 595-3200
Joel Mandelbaum, *CEO*
Michael Garity, *Vice Pres*
Lynn Connelly, *Production*
Lisa Reilly, *Sales Staff*
Steve Soccorso, *Sales Staff*
EMP: 2 Privately Held
SIC: 2721 Magazines: publishing only, not printed on site
PA: Strategic Insights, Inc.
805 3rd Ave
New York NY 10022

(G-8447)
SUBTLE-T LLC
225 Greenwich Ave (06901-6704)
PHONE 203 273-6061
Joseph Gundeck, *Manager*
EMP: 1 EST: 2011
SQ FT: 370
SALES (est): 52K Privately Held
SIC: 2086 Iced tea & fruit drinks, bottled & canned

(G-8448)
SUBURBAN INDUSTRIES INC
1 Shore Rd Unit 14 (06902-7546)
PHONE 203 716-8085
Joseph R Neal, *Principal*
EMP: 1
SALES (est): 99.4K Privately Held
SIC: 3999 Manufacturing industries

(G-8449)
SUMMER CAMP STORIES LLC
35 Toilsome Brook Rd (06905-3952)
PHONE 203 705-1600
Elliot Sloyer,
EMP: 1 EST: 2014
SALES (est): 36.6K Privately Held
SIC: 2731 Book publishing

(G-8450)
SUMMER STREET PRESS LLC
460 Summer St (06901-1301)
PHONE 203 978-0098
Judy Glickman, *Co-Founder*
Nicolas Mandelkern,
EMP: 12
SQ FT: 3,500
SALES (est): 1MM Privately Held
WEB: www.summerstreetpress.com
SIC: 2731 Book publishing

(G-8451)
SUNNYSIDE FAB & WELDING INC
55 Sunnyside Ave (06902-7603)
PHONE 203 348-5040
Thomas Krasniewicz, *President*
EMP: 1
SALES (est): 184.4K Privately Held
SIC: 3499 Welding tips, heat resistant: metal

(G-8452)
SURFACE MOUNT DEVICES LLC
Also Called: S M D
16 Acre View Dr (06903-2507)
PHONE 203 322-8290
Douglas Muller, *President*
EMP: 3
SQ FT: 4,000
SALES: 100K Privately Held
SIC: 3679 3678 Sockets, electronic tube; electronic connectors

(G-8453)
SWAROVSKI NORTH AMERICA LTD
100 Greyrock Pl (06901-3118)
PHONE 203 462-3357
Jose Melendez, *Branch Mgr*
EMP: 7
SALES (corp-wide): 4.7B Privately Held
SIC: 3961 Costume jewelry
HQ: Swarovski North America Limited
1 Kenney Dr
Cranston RI 02920
401 463-6400

(G-8454)
SWEET LEAF TEA COMPANY (DH)
900 Long Ridge Rd Bldg 2 (06902-1140)
PHONE 203 863-0263
Dan Costello, *CEO*
Clayton Christopher, *President*
David Smith, *Vice Pres*
Brian Goldberg, *CFO*
▲ EMP: 12
SQ FT: 2,000
SALES (est): 10.1MM
SALES (corp-wide): 92B Privately Held
WEB: www.sweetleaftea.com
SIC: 2086 Iced tea & fruit drinks, bottled & canned

(G-8455)
SYSDYNE TECHNOLOGIES LLC
9 Riverbend Dr S (06907-2524)
PHONE 203 327-3649
Hongbo Liu, *Engineer*
Derek Dukes, *Office Mgr*
Matt Hughes, *Manager*
Jill Zhang,
▲ EMP: 10
SQ FT: 3,500
SALES (est): 2.2MM Privately Held
WEB: www.sysdyne.com
SIC: 3679 Commutators, electronic

(G-8456)
T-S DISPLAY SYSTEMS INC
Also Called: Tele-Spot Systems
76 Progress Dr (06902-3600)
PHONE 203 964-0575
John J Mauro, *President*
Darrell Schneider, *Vice Pres*
▼ EMP: 6
SQ FT: 3,700
SALES: 7MM Privately Held
SIC: 3669 7629 Highway signals, electric; traffic signals, electric; electronic equipment repair

(G-8457)
TAGETIK NORTH AMERICA LLC
Also Called: Cch Tagetik
9 W Broad St Ste 400 (06902-3764)
PHONE 203 391-7520
Pierluigi Pierallini, *President*
Marco Pierallini, *Exec VP*
Nicola Pierallini, *CFO*
EMP: 5
SALES (est): 1.2MM
SALES (corp-wide): 4.8B Privately Held
SIC: 7372 Business oriented computer software
HQ: Tagetik Software Srl
Via Franklyn Delano Roosevelt 103
Lucca LU 55100
058 396-811

(G-8458)
TAVISCA LLC
6 High Ridge Park (06905-1327)
PHONE 203 956-1000
Priyanka Ratnacarkhi, *Managing Prtnr*
EMP: 5
SALES (est): 180.8K
SALES (corp-wide): 699.8MM Privately Held
SIC: 7372 Prepackaged software
PA: Cxloyalty
6 High Ridge Park
Stamford CT 06905
203 956-1000

(G-8459)
TBS ADJUSTING INC
35 Lawton Ave (06907-1918)
PHONE 203 274-5525
EMP: 1
SALES (est): 60K Privately Held
SIC: 3531 Construction machinery

(G-8460)
TECH-REPRO INC
Also Called: Rapid Press
555 Summer St Ste 1 (06901-1413)
PHONE 203 348-8884
William Fishman, *President*
Hillary Huaman, *Vice Pres*
Curt Lepper, *Project Mgr*
Bill Fishman, *Sales Staff*
EMP: 10 EST: 1979

SALES (est): 1.5MM **Privately Held**
SIC: 7334 2752 2791 2789 Photocopying & duplicating services; commercial printing, offset; typesetting; bookbinding & related work

(G-8461)
TECLENS LLC
9 Riverbend Dr S Ste C (06907-2524)
PHONE.................................919 824-5224
David Acker, *CEO*
Patrick Lopath, *COO*
EMP: 3
SALES (est): 160.7K **Privately Held**
SIC: 3845 Electromedical apparatus

(G-8462)
TEDDY S CUSTOM METALWORKS INC
100 Research Dr Ste 1 (06906-1400)
PHONE.................................203 359-6927
Sam Boccuzzi, *President*
Teddy Boccuzzi, *Vice Pres*
EMP: 4
SQ FT: 1,500
SALES (est): 342.7K **Privately Held**
SIC: 1799 3446 Ornamental metal work; stairs, staircases, stair treads: prefabricated metal

(G-8463)
TEKTRONIX GRAPHICS PRINTING
456 Glenbrook Rd Ste 2 (06906-1800)
PHONE.................................203 359-8003
EMP: 2 **EST:** 2007
SALES (est): 122.8K **Privately Held**
SIC: 2752 Commercial printing, offset

(G-8464)
THE DID COLLECTION
42 Van Buskirk Ave (06902-6120)
PHONE.................................203 807-4305
Denise Campos, *Owner*
Andres Campos, *Owner*
EMP: 2
SALES (est): 148.9K **Privately Held**
SIC: 3961 5632 Jewelry apparel, non-precious metals; handbags

(G-8465)
THIS OLD HOUSE VENTURES LLC
2 Harbor Dr (06902)
PHONE.................................475 209-8665
Eric Thorkilsen, *CEO*
EMP: 50
SALES (est): 1.5MM **Privately Held**
SIC: 2721 7299 Magazines: publishing only, not printed on site; home improvement & renovation contractor agency

(G-8466)
THOMAS DESIGN GROUP LLC
Also Called: Peekaboopumpkin.com
360 Fairfield Ave (06902-7249)
PHONE.................................203 588-1910
Alexander M Thomas,
Alex Thomas,
Kimberly Thomas,
EMP: 6
SQ FT: 3,000
SALES (est): 914.7K **Privately Held**
SIC: 2621 Stationery, envelope & tablet papers

(G-8467)
THOMSON REUTERS RISK MGT INC
1 Station Pl (06902-6800)
PHONE.................................203 539-8000
Jamie A Kagan, *President*
Sean Cannizzaro, *Admin Sec*
EMP: 2
SALES (est): 62.9K **Privately Held**
SIC: 2711 Newspapers, publishing & printing

(G-8468)
THOMSON REUTERS US LLC (DH)
1 Station Pl Ste 6 (06902-6893)
PHONE.................................203 539-8000
Dick Harington, *CEO*
Patrick Naughton, *Business Mgr*

Edward Friedland, *Vice Pres*
Michael Moore, *Vice Pres*
Wendy Spiesman, *Human Res Dir*
EMP: 46
SALES (est): 405.3MM
SALES (corp-wide): 10.6B **Publicly Held**
SIC: 2711 Newspapers, publishing & printing
HQ: Thomson Reuters Corporation
3 Times Sq
New York NY 10036
646 223-4000

(G-8469)
TIFFANY PRESS INC
68 Saddle Hill Rd (06903-2304)
PHONE.................................914 806-2245
EMP: 1 **EST:** 2016
SALES (est): 37.5K **Privately Held**
SIC: 2741 Miscellaneous publishing

(G-8470)
TOP OF LINE DRAPERY & UPHL
90 Lincoln Ave (06902-3120)
PHONE.................................203 348-0000
Jehad S Badr, *Manager*
EMP: 2
SALES (est): 200.6K **Privately Held**
SIC: 2391 2221 Curtains & draperies; upholstery, tapestry & wall covering fabrics

(G-8471)
TORQMASTER INC
Also Called: Torqmaster International
200 Harvard Ave (06902-6351)
PHONE.................................203 326-5945
Garrett Bebell, *President*
Dr Martin Waine, *Vice Pres*
Victor A Ceci, *Engineer*
Rob Mozdzer, *Project Engr*
Andy Macdowell, *CFO*
◆ **EMP:** 45
SQ FT: 20,000
SALES (est): 7.5MM **Privately Held**
WEB: www.torqmaster.com
SIC: 3499 Friction material, made from powdered metal

(G-8472)
TRADEWINDS
1010 Washington Blvd # 3 (06901-2202)
PHONE.................................203 324-2994
Aase Jakobsen, *Manager*
V Tricolo, *Manager*
EMP: 4
SALES (corp-wide): 800.4MM **Privately Held**
SIC: 2711 Newspapers
HQ: Nhst Global Publications As
Christian Krohgs Gate 16
Oslo 0186
755 449-00

(G-8473)
TRANE US INC
47 Harbor View Ave (06902-5913)
PHONE.................................203 295-2170
EMP: 2 **Privately Held**
SIC: 3585 Refrigeration & heating equipment
HQ: Trane U.S. Inc.
3600 Pammel Creek Rd
La Crosse WI 54601
608 787-2000

(G-8474)
TRANE US INC
390 Fairfield Ave (06902-7202)
PHONE.................................800 544-1642
James Shultz, *Manager*
EMP: 2 **Privately Held**
SIC: 3585 Refrigeration & heating equipment
HQ: Trane U.S. Inc.
3600 Pammel Creek Rd
La Crosse WI 54601
608 787-2000

(G-8475)
TRI LLC
34 Crescent St Apt 1i (06906-1840)
PHONE.................................203 353-8418
Glenn Wecker, *Principal*
EMP: 3 **EST:** 2008
SALES (est): 183.6K **Privately Held**
SIC: 3281 Cut stone & stone products

(G-8476)
TRONOX INCORPORATED (DH)
1 Stamford Plz (06901-3271)
PHONE.................................203 705-3800
Thomas Casey, *Ch of Bd*
John D Romano, *Exec VP*
Michael J Foster, *Vice Pres*
Daniel Greenwell, *CFO*
Edward G Ritter,
◆ **EMP:** 200
SALES (est): 378.5MM **Privately Held**
WEB: www.tieandtimber.com
SIC: 2421 2819 Railroad ties, sawed; sodium compounds or salts, inorg., ex. refined sod. chloride
HQ: Tronox Us Holdings Inc.
3301 Nw 150th St
Oklahoma City OK 73134
405 775-5000

(G-8477)
TRONOX LIMITED
1 Stamford Plz (06901-3271)
PHONE.................................203 705-3800
EMP: 4 **Privately Held**
SIC: 1099 Titanium ore mining
PA: Tronox Limited
Lot 22 Mason Rd
Kwinana WA 6167

(G-8478)
TRONOX LLC (PA)
263 Tresser Blvd Ste 1100 (06901-3227)
PHONE.................................203 705-3800
Tom Casey, *CEO*
Jean-Francois Turgeon, *Exec VP*
Timothy Carlson, *Vice Pres*
John Romano, *Vice Pres*
Daniel Blue, *Bd of Directors*
EMP: 24 **EST:** 2012
SALES (est): 29.4MM **Privately Held**
SIC: 1241 1442 Coal mining services; sand mining

(G-8479)
TSTY BRANDS INC
155 Frederick St Apt 2l (06902-5282)
PHONE.................................203 609-4391
Andrzej Witek, *President*
Krzysztof Witek, *Vice Pres*
EMP: 2
SALES (est): 84.5K **Privately Held**
SIC: 2035 Vegetables, brined; vegetables, pickled

(G-8480)
UNGER PUBLISHING LLC
700 Canal St Ste 4 (06902-5921)
PHONE.................................203 588-1363
Suni E Unger,
EMP: 1
SALES (est): 77K **Privately Held**
SIC: 2711 Newspapers, publishing & printing

(G-8481)
US GAMES SYSTEMS INC
Also Called: Cove Press
179 Ludlow St (06902-6900)
PHONE.................................203 353-8400
Stuart R Kaplan, *Ch of Bd*
Ricardo Cruz, *Treasurer*
Michael Kaplan, *Accounts Mgr*
Luis Cardez, *Manager*
Paula Palmer, *Creative Dir*
◆ **EMP:** 20
SQ FT: 22,000
SALES (est): 2.5MM **Privately Held**
WEB: www.usgamesinc.com
SIC: 2741 5092 3944 2752 Miscellaneous publishing; playing cards; games, toys & children's vehicles; commercial printing, lithographic

(G-8482)
US SMOKELESS TOBACCO CO LLC
6 High Ridge Park Bldg A (06905-1327)
P.O. Box 85107, Richmond VA (23285-5107)
PHONE.................................203 661-1100
EMP: 61
SALES (est): 15.4MM
SALES (corp-wide): 25.4B **Publicly Held**
SIC: 2131 Chewing And Smoking Tobacco

HQ: Ust Llc
6 High Ridge Park Bldg A
Stamford CT 06905
203 817-3000

(G-8483)
UST LLC (HQ)
6 High Ridge Park Bldg A (06905-1327)
P.O. Box 85107, Richmond VA (23285-5107)
PHONE.................................203 817-3000
Rich A Kohlberger, *Exec VP*
Richard A Kohlberger, *Exec VP*
Richard Kohlberger, *Exec VP*
Raymond Silcock, *Senior VP*
Gary B Glass, *Vice Pres*
◆ **EMP:** 9
SALES (est): 43.6MM
SALES (corp-wide): 25.3B **Publicly Held**
WEB: www.ustshareholder.com
SIC: 2131 2084 2621 3999 Chewing & smoking tobacco; chewing tobacco; wines, brandy & brandy spirits; cigarette paper; pipe cleaners
PA: Altria Group, Inc.
6601 W Broad St
Richmond VA 23230
804 274-2200

(G-8484)
VINO ET AL LLC
53 Wire Mill Rd (06903-4414)
PHONE.................................203 405-3931
Hemant Sujan, *Principal*
EMP: 2
SALES (est): 112.9K **Privately Held**
SIC: 2084 Wines, brandy & brandy spirits

(G-8485)
VIRIDIAN ENERGY LLC
1055 Washington Blvd Fl 7 (06901-2252)
PHONE.................................203 663-5089
EMP: 99 **EST:** 2009
SALES (est): 11.6MM
SALES (corp-wide): 25.3MM **Privately Held**
SIC: 5211 1311 Ret Lumber/Building Materials Crude Petroleum/Natural Gas Production
PA: Crius Energy, Llc
1055 Washington Blvd
Stamford CT 06854
203 663-5089

(G-8486)
VISTAR FOUNDATION INC
75 Ridge Brook Dr (06903-1226)
PHONE.................................203 968-1995
Ron Friedman, *Principal*
EMP: 2
SALES (est): 205K **Privately Held**
SIC: 3721 Research & development on aircraft by the manufacturer

(G-8487)
WAGZ INC
Also Called: Link AKC
1 Landmark Sq Ste 505 (06901-2632)
PHONE.................................203 553-9336
Herbie Calves, *Branch Mgr*
EMP: 6
SALES (corp-wide): 1.5MM **Privately Held**
SIC: 3663
PA: Wagz, Inc.
230 Commerce Way Ste 325
Portsmouth NH 03801
603 570-6015

(G-8488)
WALPOLE WOODWORKERS INC
129 Interlaken Rd (06903-5026)
PHONE.................................203 595-9930
EMP: 1
SALES (corp-wide): 83.9MM **Privately Held**
SIC: 2431 Millwork
PA: Walpole Outdoors Llc
100 Rver Ridge Dr Ste 302
Norwood MA 02062
508 668-2800

Stamford - Fairfield County (G-8489)

(G-8489)
WEDDLES LLC
2052 Shippan Ave (06902-8208)
PHONE 203 964-1888
Peter D Weddle, *Mng Member*
EMP: 1
SALES (est): 92.5K Privately Held
SIC: 2731 Book publishing

(G-8490)
WENDON COMPANY INC
17 Irving Ave (06902-6622)
PHONE 203 348-6272
Michael Montanaro, *President*
Donald Bosak, *Vice Pres*
Gerry Sarfaty, *Foreman/Supr*
EMP: 18 EST: 1961
SQ FT: 13,000
SALES (est): 7.2MM Privately Held
WEB: www.wendon.net
SIC: 3599 Machine shop, jobbing & repair

(G-8491)
WENDON TECHNOLOGIES INC
Also Called: Stamford Fabricating
17 Irving Ave (06902-6622)
P.O. Box 112875 (06911-2875)
PHONE 203 348-6271
Julius Bogdan, *President*
EMP: 60
SQ FT: 20,000
SALES (est): 8.7MM Privately Held
SIC: 3444 Sheet metalwork

(G-8492)
WESTROCK COMMERCIAL LLC
1635 Coining Dr (06902)
PHONE 203 595-3130
EMP: 4 EST: 2013
SALES (est): 381.7K Privately Held
SIC: 2752 Commercial printing, lithographic

(G-8493)
WILLIAM A WEINERT CANVAS
98 Pinewood Rd (06903-2520)
PHONE 203 595-0580
William Weinert, *Owner*
EMP: 1
SALES (est): 48K Privately Held
SIC: 2394 Canvas & related products

(G-8494)
WILSON PARTITIONS
110 Viaduct Rd (06907-2707)
PHONE 203 316-8033
EMP: 1
SALES (est): 57.6K Privately Held
SIC: 3334 Primary aluminum

(G-8495)
WILSON PARTITIONS INC
Also Called: Arcadia
120 Viaduct Rd (06907-2707)
PHONE 203 316-8033
Jim Schladen, *Owner*
Sean Boylan, *General Mgr*
▼ EMP: 13
SALES (est): 1.1MM Privately Held
SIC: 3334 Primary aluminum

(G-8496)
WINESPEAK PRESS LLC
38 Janice Rd (06905-2315)
PHONE 203 968-8882
EMP: 2 EST: 2008
SALES (est): 86K Privately Held
SIC: 2741 Misc Publishing

(G-8497)
WINSOL CLEAN ENERGY LLC
112 Prospect St Fl 3 (06901-1207)
PHONE 203 216-1972
David Bennett, *Branch Mgr*
EMP: 1
SALES (corp-wide): 160.6K Privately Held
SIC: 3511 Turbines & turbine generator sets & parts
PA: Winsol Economic Development Corporation
112 Prospect St Fl 3
Stamford CT 06901
203 216-1972

(G-8498)
WINSOL ECONOMIC DEV CORP (PA)
112 Prospect St Fl 3 (06901-1207)
PHONE 203 216-1972
David Bennett, *CFO*
EMP: 2 EST: 2014
SQ FT: 200
SALES (est): 160.6K Privately Held
SIC: 3511 Turbines & turbine generator sets & parts

(G-8499)
WOOD WORKS BY ARANDA LLC
652 Glenbrook Rd 3-301 (06906-1410)
PHONE 203 908-3010
Manuel Aranda, *Principal*
EMP: 2
SALES (est): 131.8K Privately Held
SIC: 2431 Millwork

(G-8500)
WOODWAY PRINT INC
48 Union St Ste 21 (06906-1342)
PHONE 203 323-6423
Arnold Feintuck, *President*
EMP: 3 EST: 1961
SALES (est): 355.2K Privately Held
SIC: 2752 Commercial printing, offset

(G-8501)
WOOLWORKS INTERNATIONAL LTD (PA)
379 Old Long Ridge Rd (06903-1133)
PHONE 203 661-7076
Pascale Henault-Bertrand, *President*
EMP: 1
SALES (est): 129.4K Privately Held
SIC: 2721 Periodicals

(G-8502)
WORLD WRESTLING ENTRMT INC (PA)
1241 E Main St (06902-3520)
PHONE 203 352-8600
Michael J Luisi, *President*
Paul Levesque, *Exec VP*
James Rosenstock, *Exec VP*
Blake T Bilstad, *Senior VP*
Sarah Cummins, *Senior VP*
▲ EMP: 164
SQ FT: 94,200
SALES: 930.1MM Publicly Held
WEB: www.wwe.com
SIC: 7812 7929 2721 Television film production; video tape production; entertainment group; magazines: publishing only, not printed on site

(G-8503)
XINTEKIDEL INC
Also Called: Intelvideo
56 W Broad St (06902-3715)
PHONE 203 348-9229
John Rossi, *President*
Marie Rossi, *Admin Sec*
EMP: 5
SQ FT: 2,000
SALES: 1MM Privately Held
WEB: www.xintekvideo.com
SIC: 3663 3651 Television broadcasting & communications equipment; household audio & video equipment

(G-8504)
YUMMYEARTH LLC (PA)
Also Called: Yumearth
9 W Broad St Ste 440 (06902-3764)
PHONE 203 276-1259
Sergio Bicas, *CEO*
Rob Wunder, *CFO*
▲ EMP: 4
SQ FT: 4
SALES (est): 7.2MM Privately Held
WEB: www.yummyearth.com
SIC: 2064 Lollipops & other hard candy

(G-8505)
Z-LODA SYSTEMS INC
111 Prospect St (06901-1221)
PHONE 203 359-2991
Clifford Mollo, *President*
EMP: 4
SALES (est): 471.9K Privately Held
WEB: www.z-loda.com
SIC: 3535 Conveyors & conveying equipment

(G-8506)
ZHAO LLC
28 Glenbrook Rd Unit 28 # 28 (06902)
PHONE 401 864-7186
Lili Zhao, *Mng Member*
EMP: 2
SALES (est): 102.4K Privately Held
SIC: 2393 Textile bags

Sterling
Windham County

(G-8507)
AUSTIN POWDER COMPANY
332 Ekonk Hill Rd (06377)
PHONE 860 564-5466
William Schappert, *Manager*
EMP: 26
SALES (corp-wide): 567.4MM Privately Held
SIC: 2892 Explosives
HQ: Austin Powder Company
25800 Science Park Dr # 300
Cleveland OH 44122
216 464-2400

(G-8508)
BRIAN ARNIO
Also Called: Brian Arnio Welding and Fabg
556 Margaret Henry Rd (06377-1510)
PHONE 860 779-2983
Brian Arnio, *Owner*
EMP: 4
SQ FT: 2,400
SALES (est): 206.9K Privately Held
SIC: 7699 3443 Industrial equipment services; fabricated plate work (boiler shop)

(G-8509)
DETOTEC NORTH AMERICA INC
401 Snake Meadow Hill Rd (06377-1713)
P.O. Box 276 (06377-0276)
PHONE 860 564-1012
Tim Obrien, *President*
Martha Obrien, *Admin Sec*
▲ EMP: 9
SQ FT: 100
SALES (est): 1.6MM Privately Held
WEB: www.detotec.com
SIC: 2298 Cordage & twine

(G-8510)
JORDAN SAW MILL L L C
Also Called: Jordan Sawmill
201 Saw Mill Hill Rd (06377-1405)
PHONE 860 774-0247
Kevin Jordan, *Mng Member*
EMP: 10
SQ FT: 20,000
SALES (est): 1.3MM Privately Held
SIC: 2421 Sawmills & planing mills, general

(G-8511)
KAMELOT KREATIONS LLC
50 Hungry Hill Rd (06377-1818)
PHONE 860 564-7399
James Evans, *Mng Member*
James G Evans,
Loreen Evans,
EMP: 2
SALES (est): 77.5K Privately Held
SIC: 2395 7389 Embroidery & art needlework;

(G-8512)
MAXAM INITIATION SYSTEMS LLC
74 Dixon Rd (06377-1503)
PHONE 860 774-3507
Pierre Labelle, *General Mgr*
◆ EMP: 12
SALES (est): 2.3MM Privately Held
SIC: 2892 Explosives

(G-8513)
MAXAM NORTH AMERICA INC
74 Dixon Rd (06377-1503)
PHONE 860 774-2333
EMP: 3
SALES (corp-wide): 48.6MM Privately Held
SIC: 2892 Explosives
HQ: Maxam North America, Inc.
433 Las Colinas Blvd E # 900
Irving TX 75039
801 233-6000

(G-8514)
NU-STONE MFG & DISTRG LLC
160 Sterling Rd (06377-2006)
PHONE 860 564-6555
Charlie Corson, *Owner*
EMP: 7
SALES (est): 397.5K Privately Held
SIC: 1429 Igneous rock, crushed & broken-quarrying

(G-8515)
OLD COACH HOME SALES
242 Harris Rd (06377-1508)
PHONE 860 774-1379
Michael Angelo, *Owner*
Gerry Scott, *Owner*
EMP: 22
SQ FT: 3,600
SALES (est): 22MM Privately Held
SIC: 2451 Mobile homes

(G-8516)
SAW MILL SHEET METAL LLC
143 Saw Mill Hill Rd (06377-1421)
PHONE 860 779-3194
James McGarry, *President*
EMP: 2
SALES (est): 309.5K Privately Held
SIC: 3444 Sheet metalwork

(G-8517)
STERLING PRECISION MACHINING
112 Industrial Park Rd (06377)
P.O. Box 236 (06377-0236)
PHONE 860 564-4043
Carmine Demarco, *President*
Ellen W De Marco, *Vice Pres*
Rick Demarco, *Treasurer*
Dave Demarco, *Admin Sec*
EMP: 13
SQ FT: 12,000
SALES (est): 1.8MM Privately Held
WEB: www.spmachining.com
SIC: 3599 Machine shop, jobbing & repair

(G-8518)
STERLING SAND AND GRAVEL LLC
485 Saw Mill Hill Rd (06377-1407)
PHONE 860 774-3985
Erick E Smith, *Manager*
EMP: 6
SALES (est): 303K Privately Held
SIC: 1442 Construction sand & gravel

(G-8519)
WESTMINSTER TOOL INC
51 Industrial Park Rd (06377-1804)
PHONE 860 317-1039
EMP: 2
SALES (est): 124.1K Privately Held
SIC: 3599 Machine shop, jobbing & repair

Stevenson
Fairfield County

(G-8520)
ANODIC INCORPORATED
1480 Monroe Tpke (06491)
P.O. Box 52 (06491-0052)
PHONE 203 268-9966
Ronald Buttner, *President*
EMP: 19 EST: 1951
SQ FT: 16,000
SALES (est): 2.4MM Privately Held
WEB: www.anodic.com
SIC: 3471 Finishing, metals or formed products

▲ = Import ▼ = Export
◆ = Import/Export

Stonington
New London County

(G-8521)
ALTERIS RENEWABLES INC
32 Taugwonk Spur Rd 12n (06378-2036)
PHONE..........................860 535-3370
Mike Kocsmiersky, *Principal*
EMP: 2 **EST:** 2010
SALES (est): 143.3K **Privately Held**
SIC: 3585 Heating equipment, complete

(G-8522)
AQUATIC MAMMALS JOURNAL NFP
222 Wolf Neck Rd (06378-1532)
PHONE..........................860 514-4704
Justin Gregg, *Vice Pres*
Kelly Melillo, *Research*
Kathleen Dudzinski, *Manager*
EMP: 2
SALES (est): 73.1K **Privately Held**
SIC: 2721 Periodicals

(G-8523)
BARNARD-MAINE LTD
1 Cross St (06378-1303)
PHONE..........................860 535-9485
Brian Barnard, *Owner*
Carol Barnard, *Office Mgr*
EMP: 1
SALES (est): 63K **Privately Held**
WEB: www.barnard-maine.com
SIC: 2323 Bow ties, men's & boys': made from purchased materials

(G-8524)
BEERD BREWING CO LLC
22 Bayview Ave (06378-1142)
PHONE..........................585 771-7428
Aaron Simon Cini, *Mng Member*
EMP: 15
SALES (est): 1.7MM **Privately Held**
SIC: 2082 Beer (alcoholic beverage)

(G-8525)
CLASSIC FRAMERS
211 Cove Rd (06378-2306)
PHONE..........................401 596-6820
EMP: 2
SALES (est): 162.4K **Privately Held**
SIC: 7699 2499 Repair Services Mfg Wood Products

(G-8526)
COASTAL INDUSTRIES LLC
3 Walnut St (06378-2758)
PHONE..........................860 535-9043
Robert Lewandowski, *President*
EMP: 1
SALES (est): 86.8K **Privately Held**
SIC: 3999 Manufacturing industries

(G-8527)
EMULSION LLC
34 Taugwonk Spur Rd # 3 (06378-2037)
PHONE..........................860 440-8685
EMP: 2
SALES (est): 222.5K **Privately Held**
SIC: 2752 Commercial printing, lithographic

(G-8528)
FRANK OBUCHOWSKI
Also Called: White Eagle Printing Co
50 Ashworth Ave (06378-3003)
PHONE..........................860 535-4739
Frank Obuchowski, *Owner*
EMP: 2
SQ FT: 3,200
SALES (est): 153.8K **Privately Held**
WEB: www.brasscitytrophy-gifts.com
SIC: 2752 2789 Commercial printing, lithographic; bookbinding & related work

(G-8529)
GREENHAVEN CABINETRY & MILLWOR
338 Elm St (06378-2926)
PHONE..........................860 535-1106
Robert D Wood, *Principal*
EMP: 3
SALES (est): 391.4K **Privately Held**
SIC: 2434 Wood kitchen cabinets

(G-8530)
JAK INDUSTRIES LLC
493 Pequot Trl (06378-2224)
PHONE..........................877 964-2725
Ryan Kennedy, *President*
EMP: 1 **EST:** 2017
SALES (est): 48.3K **Privately Held**
SIC: 3999 Manufacturing industries

(G-8531)
JAMES J CHASSE
Also Called: J.C. Engineering & Project MGT
578 New London Tpke (06378-1614)
P.O. Box 633, Old Mystic (06372-0633)
PHONE..........................860 572-0838
James J Chasse, *Owner*
EMP: 1
SALES (est): 109.1K **Privately Held**
SIC: 3565 Labeling machines, industrial

(G-8532)
JAW PRECISION MACHINING LLC
44 Taugwonk Spur Rd # 1 (06378-2035)
PHONE..........................860 535-0615
Jeff Washburn, *Owner*
EMP: 3
SALES (est): 290.2K **Privately Held**
SIC: 3599 Machine shop, jobbing & repair

(G-8533)
JCASCIO SOFTWARE INC
10 Juniper Ln (06378-2332)
PHONE..........................860 535-2864
EMP: 2 **EST:** 2005
SALES (est): 130K **Privately Held**
SIC: 7372 Prepackaged Software Services

(G-8534)
LARKIN LITHO
131 Elm St (06378-1163)
PHONE..........................860 535-0116
M Larkin, *Principal*
EMP: 2
SALES (est): 116.8K **Privately Held**
SIC: 2759 Commercial printing

(G-8535)
PERRY S SAWYER
1307 Pequot Trl (06378-1928)
PHONE..........................860 572-9473
Perry S Sawyer, *Principal*
EMP: 1
SALES (est): 79.8K **Privately Held**
SIC: 2411 Logging camps & contractors

(G-8536)
PMW MARINE REPAIR
228 N Water St (06378-1023)
PHONE..........................860 535-3064
John Pereira, *Owner*
EMP: 1
SALES: 100K **Privately Held**
SIC: 3732 Boat building & repairing

(G-8537)
REFINED DESIGNS
779 Stonington Rd (06378-2529)
PHONE..........................860 535-7273
Michael Hanos, *Owner*
EMP: 2
SALES (est): 98.9K **Privately Held**
SIC: 2499 Decorative wood & woodwork

(G-8538)
STONINGTON BOAT WORKS LLC
228 N Water St (06378-1023)
PHONE..........................860 535-0332
William Mills, *Mng Member*
EMP: 1
SALES (est): 143.2K **Privately Held**
SIC: 3732 Boats, fiberglass: building & repairing

(G-8539)
STONINGTON CUSTOM CANVAS LLC
501 Stonington Rd (06378-2823)
P.O. Box 29 (06378-0029)
PHONE..........................860 213-1240
Paul D Stiephaudt, *Principal*
EMP: 1
SALES (est): 100.9K **Privately Held**
SIC: 2394 Awnings, fabric: made from purchased materials

(G-8540)
STONINGTON VINEYARDS INC
523 Taugwonk Rd (06378-1805)
P.O. Box 463 (06378-0463)
PHONE..........................860 535-1222
Cornelius H Smith, *President*
EMP: 9
SQ FT: 11,000
SALES (est): 825K **Privately Held**
WEB: www.stoningtonvineyards.com
SIC: 2084 Wines

(G-8541)
TOMS NEWS
133 Water St (06378-1324)
PHONE..........................860 535-1276
Tom Rezenes, *Owner*
EMP: 1
SALES (est): 59.8K **Privately Held**
SIC: 2711 Newspapers

(G-8542)
ZUCKERMAN HRPSICHORDS INTL LLC
65 Cutler St (06378-1004)
P.O. Box 151 (06378-0151)
PHONE..........................860 535-1715
Richard Auber,
David Jacques Way,
EMP: 6
SQ FT: 10,000
SALES (est): 814.8K **Privately Held**
WEB: www.zhi.net
SIC: 3931 Harpsichords; pianos, all types: vertical, grand, spinet, player, etc.; pipes, organ

Storrs
Tolland County

(G-8543)
BIORASIS INC
23 Fellen Rd (06268-2520)
PHONE..........................860 429-3592
Malti Jain, *President*
Michail Kastellorizios, *Research*
EMP: 4
SALES (est): 292.6K **Privately Held**
SIC: 3841 Diagnostic apparatus, medical

(G-8544)
CABINET WORKS LLC
895 Mansfield City Rd (06268-2759)
PHONE..........................860 450-0803
EMP: 1 **EST:** 1999
SQ FT: 1,875
SALES (est): 96K **Privately Held**
SIC: 2434 Mfg Custom Cabinets

(G-8545)
CHAMPION ENTERPRISES INC
19 Greenfield Ln (06268-1250)
PHONE..........................860 429-3537
Nayna Chheda, *Principal*
EMP: 2
SALES (est): 199K **Privately Held**
SIC: 2451 Mobile homes

(G-8546)
CHARLES RIVER LABORATORIES INC
67 Baxter Rd (06268-1109)
PHONE..........................860 429-7261
Candace Brewer, *Auditor*
Seador Girshick, *Manager*
EMP: 25
SALES (corp-wide): 2.2B **Publicly Held**
WEB: www.criver.com
SIC: 2836 8731 2835 Vaccines; commercial physical research; in vitro & in vivo diagnostic substances
HQ: Charles River Laboratories, Inc.
251 Ballardvale St
Wilmington MA 01887
781 222-6000

(G-8547)
COMA SKATEBOARDS
10 Fern Rd (06268-2706)
PHONE..........................860 933-4830
EMP: 2
SALES (est): 79.5K **Privately Held**
SIC: 3949 Skateboards

(G-8548)
ESSENTALIA LLC
69 Summit Rd (06268-1421)
PHONE..........................860 617-5106
George Hoag, *Principal*
EMP: 2
SALES (est): 140.1K **Privately Held**
SIC: 2844 Toilet preparations

(G-8549)
GEORGE BAILEY
75 Crane Hill Rd (06268-2811)
PHONE..........................860 423-2136
George Bailey, *Owner*
EMP: 1
SALES (est): 79.2K **Privately Held**
WEB: www.ctbaileys.org
SIC: 2099 Food preparations

(G-8550)
ORTEOPONIX LLC
22 Scottron Dr (06268)
PHONE..........................203 804-9775
Michael Zilm, *CEO*
EMP: 3
SALES (est): 155.3K **Privately Held**
SIC: 3842 Grafts, artificial: for surgery

(G-8551)
SOBRIO LLC
Longley 270 Mid Trnpk 203 (06269-0001)
PHONE..........................860 880-1990
Nadav Ullman,
Thomas Bachant,
EMP: 2
SALES (est): 130K **Privately Held**
SIC: 7372 Application computer software

Storrs Mansfield
Tolland County

(G-8552)
AQUATIC SENSOR NETWRK TECH LLC
Also Called: Aquasent
30 Beacon Hill Dr (06268-2756)
PHONE..........................860 429-4303
Yong MA, *General Mgr*
Jun Hong Cui, *Principal*
Janny Liao, *Manager*
▲ **EMP:** 10 **EST:** 2012
SALES (est): 1.2MM **Privately Held**
SIC: 3669 Sirens, electric: vehicle, marine, industrial & air raid

(G-8553)
CONN DAILY CAMPUS
Also Called: Daily Campus, The
11 Dog Ln (06268-2206)
PHONE..........................860 486-3407
Jim Acton, *Principal*
EMP: 4
SALES (est): 269.6K **Privately Held**
SIC: 2711 Newspapers, publishing & printing

(G-8554)
D AND L WELDING LLC
309 S Eagleville Rd (06268-2005)
PHONE..........................860 429-8259
David Roy, *Principal*
EMP: 1 **EST:** 1996
SALES (est): 175K **Privately Held**
SIC: 7692 Welding repair

(G-8555)
DESIATO SAND & GRAVEL CORP
999 Stafford Rd (06268-1803)
PHONE..........................860 429-6479
Phillip Desiato, *President*
Sam Schrager, *Admin Sec*
EMP: 23
SQ FT: 8,600

Storrs Mansfield - Tolland County (G-8556)

SALES (est): 3.4MM **Privately Held**
SIC: **1794** 5211 5032 1442 Excavation work; sand & gravel; brick, stone & related material; construction sand & gravel

(G-8556)
GRINDING SYSTEM SERVICES LLC
673 Chaffeeville Rd (06268-2337)
PHONE.................................860 208-5196
EMP: 1
SALES (est): 57.2K **Privately Held**
SIC: **3999** Custom pulverizing & grinding of plastic materials

(G-8557)
ODIS INC
22 Quail Run Rd (06268-2768)
P.O. Box 555 (06268-0555)
PHONE.................................860 450-8407
Lee Pierhal, *President*
◆ EMP: 4
SALES: 1MM **Privately Held**
SIC: **3827** Optical instruments & lenses

(G-8558)
R AND R PUBLISHING LLC
42 Fern Rd (06268-2706)
PHONE.................................860 944-2085
Rebekah Salamack, *Principal*
EMP: 1
SALES (est): 38.8K **Privately Held**
SIC: **2741** Miscellaneous publishing

(G-8559)
SAIL SPARS DESIGN LLC
455 Gurleyville Rd (06268-1415)
PHONE.................................860 429-9866
James Gretzky,
Sarah L Gretzky,
EMP: 2
SALES: 200K **Privately Held**
SIC: **2394** 8742 Sails: made from purchased materials; business consultant

(G-8560)
SANDBALLZ INTERNATIONAL LLC
832 Stafford Rd (06268-2023)
PHONE.................................860 465-9628
George Kronen, *Principal*
EMP: 3
SALES (est): 154K **Privately Held**
SIC: **1455** Kaolin & ball clay

(G-8561)
WILLARD J STEARNS & SONS INC
Also Called: Mountain Dairy
50 Stearns Rd (06268-2701)
PHONE.................................860 423-9289
Willard C Stearns, *CEO*
David Stearns, *Vice Pres*
Arthur B Stearns, *Treasurer*
Sarah Vooys, *Cust Mgr*
Leslie H Stearns, *Director*
EMP: 35
SALES: 4MM **Privately Held**
WEB: www.mountaindairy.com
SIC: **2026** 0241 Fluid milk; dairy farms

Stratford
Fairfield County

(G-8562)
(FAST) INTERNATIONAL INC (PA)
Also Called: Kitchen Brains
905 Honeyspot Rd (06615-7140)
PHONE.................................203 380-3489
Bernard Koether, *CEO*
Christian Koether, *President*
Rosamond Koether, *Vice Pres*
Sany Langdon, *Controller*
EMP: 2
SALES (est): 236.2K **Privately Held**
SIC: **3625** Timing devices, electronic

(G-8563)
A&D SCHNEIDER LLC
111 Morningside Ter (06614-2853)
PHONE.................................203 870-9474
Aileen Schneider,
Aileen Chua-Schneider,
Darryl Schneider,
EMP: 2
SALES (est): 116K **Privately Held**
SIC: **5944** 3911 7389 Jewelry, precious stones & precious metals; jewelry, precious metal; jewelry apparel;

(G-8564)
ADVANCED GRAPHICS INC
55 Old South Ave (06615-7368)
P.O. Box 656 (06615-0656)
PHONE.................................203 378-0471
John Alesevich, *President*
Jim Auten, *Opers Mgr*
Kim Auten, *Office Mgr*
Bonnie Alesevich, *Admin Sec*
EMP: 24 EST: 1976
SQ FT: 11,000
SALES (est): 3.4MM **Privately Held**
WEB: www.advanced-graphics.com
SIC: **3479** 2759 2396 Painting of metal products; etching on metals; screen printing; automotive & apparel trimmings

(G-8565)
AGISSAR CORPORATION
526 Benton St (06615-7351)
PHONE.................................203 375-8662
James Foley, *President*
Suzanne Rassiga, *Vice Pres*
EMP: 64
SQ FT: 15,500
SALES (est): 13.5MM **Privately Held**
WEB: www.agissar.com
SIC: **3579** 7629 5044 Mailing machines; business machine repair, electric; office equipment; mailing machines

(G-8566)
ALBERT E ERICKSON CO
1111 Honeyspot Rd Ste 1 (06615-7144)
PHONE.................................203 386-8931
Bernice Erickson, *Corp Secy*
Donald Erickson, *Vice Pres*
Mary Erickson, *Treasurer*
EMP: 15 EST: 1952
SQ FT: 15,000
SALES (est): 2.1MM **Privately Held**
SIC: **3599** Machine shop, jobbing & repair; machine & other job shop work

(G-8567)
ALL LEAGUE EMBROIDERY
171 Bruce Ave (06615-6102)
PHONE.................................203 377-7215
Charles Caruso, *Owner*
EMP: 1
SALES (est): 62.6K **Privately Held**
WEB: www.allleague.net
SIC: **2395** Embroidery & art needlework

(G-8568)
AMERICAN RECREATIONAL INDS
630 Surf Ave (06615-6728)
PHONE.................................203 375-5900
Basil D Rissolo, *President*
EMP: 1
SALES (est): 53.4K **Privately Held**
SIC: **3999** Manufacturing industries

(G-8569)
APTARGROUP INC
Aptar Stratford
125 Access Rd (06615-7414)
PHONE.................................203 377-8100
Phil Miller, *Vice Pres*
John Sullo, *Opers Staff*
Anthony Mancini, *Mfg Staff*
Colin Francis, *Purchasing*
Amy Flood, *Human Res Mgr*
EMP: 350 **Publicly Held**
SIC: **3089** 3499 Closures, plastic; aerosol valves, metal
PA: Aptargroup, Inc.
    265 Exchange Dr Ste 100
    Crystal Lake IL 60014

(G-8570)
ARROW MARKETING INC
7365 Main St Ste 8 (06614-1300)
PHONE.................................203 375-7541
Judith Seid, *President*
▲ EMP: 2
SALES (est): 212.4K **Privately Held**
SIC: **2621** Packaging paper

(G-8571)
ASHCRFT-NGANO KIKI HLDINGS INC (HQ)
250 E Main St (06614-5145)
PHONE.................................203 378-8281
Steven A Culmone, *CEO*
EMP: 1
SALES (est): 222.1MM **Privately Held**
SIC: **3823** 3679 3663 3625 Pressure gauges, dial & digital; transducers, electrical; transmitter-receivers, radio; switches, electric power

(G-8572)
ASHCROFT INC (DH)
250 E Main St (06614-5145)
PHONE.................................203 378-8281
Steven Culmone, *CEO*
◆ EMP: 450
SQ FT: 325,000
SALES (est): 195.7MM **Privately Held**
SIC: **3823** 3679 3663 3625 Pressure gauges, dial & digital; transducers, electrical; transmitter-receivers, radio; switches, electric power
HQ: Ashcroft Nagano Keiki Holdings, Inc.
    250 E Main St
    Stratford CT 06614
    203 378-8281

(G-8573)
ASHCROFT INC
Heise
250 E Main St (06614-5145)
PHONE.................................203 378-8281
Gene Urbinati, *Branch Mgr*
EMP: 35 **Privately Held**
SIC: **3825** Instruments to measure electricity
HQ: Ashcroft Inc.
    250 E Main St
    Stratford CT 06614
    203 378-8281

(G-8574)
ATLANTIC SAIL & CANVAS CO
1962 Elm St (06615-6331)
PHONE.................................203 254-1315
Chris Johannessen, *Principal*
EMP: 1
SALES (est): 76.4K **Privately Held**
SIC: **2211** Canvas

(G-8575)
B & C INDUSTRIES
3125 Broadbridge Ave (06614-2502)
PHONE.................................203 572-0265
EMP: 1 EST: 2010
SALES: 80K **Privately Held**
SIC: **3443** Mfg Fabricated Plate Work

(G-8576)
B/E AEROSPACE INC
Also Called: Klx Aerospace Solutions
650 Long Beach Blvd (06615-7168)
PHONE.................................203 380-5000
Jason Lewis, *Branch Mgr*
EMP: 4
SALES (corp-wide): 66.5B **Publicly Held**
WEB: www.beaerospace.com
SIC: **3728** Aircraft parts & equipment
HQ: B/E Aerospace, Inc.
    1400 Corporate Center Way
    Wellington FL 33414
    561 791-5000

(G-8577)
BARA ESSENTIALS LLC
3164 Broadbridge Ave (06614-2503)
PHONE.................................203 428-1786
Tracey Williams, *CEO*
EMP: 1
SALES (est): 72.6K **Privately Held**
SIC: **2841** 2844 7389 Textile soap; face creams or lotions;

(G-8578)
BARGAIN NEWS FREE CLASSIFIED A
720 Barnum Avenue Cutoff (06614-5037)
PHONE.................................203 377-3000
Carol Leach, *Manager*
EMP: 80
SALES (est): 2.1MM **Privately Held**
SIC: **2711** 2721 Newspapers; periodicals

(G-8579)
BARNEYS SIGN SERVICE INC
Also Called: A Barney's Sign
45 Seymour St Ste 3 (06615-6170)
PHONE.................................203 878-3763
Charles Barnes Jr, *President*
Amelia Barnes, *Admin Sec*
EMP: 5
SALES (est): 396.1K **Privately Held**
SIC: **3993** Signs & advertising specialties

(G-8580)
BARNUM WASH & DRY
2370 Barnum Ave (06615-5520)
PHONE.................................203 870-6099
Patrick Lorent, *Principal*
EMP: 2
SALES (est): 130K **Privately Held**
SIC: **3578** Automatic teller machines (ATM)

(G-8581)
BEAUTIFUL PUBLICATIONS
1345 Barnum Ave Ste 115 (06614-5422)
PHONE.................................347 508-2798
Tracy Wilson, *Principal*
EMP: 2
SALES (est): 50K **Privately Held**
SIC: **2741** Miscellaneous publishing

(G-8582)
BECK INDUSTRIES LLC
103 Jamestown Rd (06614-1606)
PHONE.................................203 260-8864
Bruce Beckmann Sol, *Principal*
EMP: 2 EST: 2016
SALES (est): 108.4K **Privately Held**
SIC: **3599** Industrial machinery

(G-8583)
BELAIR AVIATION
20 Wigwam Ln (06614)
PHONE.................................203 380-8993
Steve Kacenski, *Principal*
EMP: 2
SALES (est): 202.7K **Privately Held**
SIC: **3721** Aircraft

(G-8584)
BLASE MANUFACTURING COMPANY (PA)
Also Called: Blase Tool & Manufacturing Co
60 Watson Blvd Ste 3 (06615-7165)
PHONE.................................203 375-5646
John Blase, *President*
EMP: 55
SQ FT: 60,000
SALES (est): 9.4MM **Privately Held**
WEB: www.blasemfg.com
SIC: **3469** Stamping metal for the trade

(G-8585)
BREMSER TECHNOLOGIES INC
305 Sniffens Ln (06615-7558)
PHONE.................................203 378-8486
Helma Chartier, *President*
Eric Chartier, *Vice Pres*
Eric Helma, *Vice Pres*
EMP: 10 EST: 1949
SQ FT: 5,000
SALES: 500K **Privately Held**
WEB: www.bremsertech.com
SIC: **3544** 5084 Special dies & tools; industrial machinery & equipment

(G-8586)
BRIAN CODY
211 Plymouth St (06614-4126)
PHONE.................................203 331-7382
Brian Cody, *Owner*
EMP: 1 EST: 2015
SALES (est): 60.1K **Privately Held**
SIC: **3641** Electric lamps

(G-8587)
BRIDGEPORT BURIAL VAULT CO
544 Surf Ave (06615-6725)
PHONE.................................203 375-7375
Dennis McNamara, *President*
Carla Mc Namara, *Corp Secy*
EMP: 3 EST: 1946

GEOGRAPHIC SECTION — Stratford - Fairfield County (G-8616)

SQ FT: 12,000
SALES: 500K **Privately Held**
SIC: **3272** Burial vaults, concrete or precast terrazzo; monuments, concrete

(G-8588)
BRIDGEPORT FITTINGS LLC
705 Lordship Blvd (06615-7313)
P.O. Box 619, Bridgeport (06601-0619)
PHONE 203 377-5944
Paul Suzio, *President*
Tom Auray, *Controller*
Robin Hull, *Admin Asst*
▲ EMP: 200
SQ FT: 135,000
SALES (est): 46.3MM **Privately Held**
WEB: www.bptfittings.com
SIC: **3644** Electric conduits & fittings
PA: Nsi Industries, Llc
 9730 Northcross Center Ct
 Huntersville NC 28078

(G-8589)
BRIDGEPORT INSULATED WIRE CO
514 Surf Ave (06615-6725)
PHONE 203 375-9579
Wayne Gombar, *Opers-Prdtn-Mfg*
EMP: 25
SQ FT: 2,200
SALES (corp-wide): 5.6MM **Privately Held**
SIC: **3357** 3496 Nonferrous wiredrawing & insulating; miscellaneous fabricated wire products
PA: The Bridgeport Insulated Wire Company
 51 Brookfield Ave
 Bridgeport CT 06610
 203 333-3191

(G-8590)
BUCKLEY ASSOCIATES INC
350 Long Beach Blvd (06615-7167)
PHONE 203 380-2405
Mike Gagnon, *Sales Staff*
Mike Gajnon, *Branch Mgr*
EMP: 9
SALES (corp-wide): 59MM **Privately Held**
SIC: **5075** 3444 Warm air heating equipment & supplies; air conditioning equipment, except room units; ducts, sheet metal
PA: Buckley Associates, Inc.
 385 King St
 Hanover MA 02339
 781 878-5000

(G-8591)
C LIBBY LEONARD
Also Called: Pro Line Sports Design
171 Bruce Ave (06615-6102)
PHONE 203 375-6205
Leonard C Libby, *Owner*
EMP: 2
SALES (est): 120K **Privately Held**
SIC: **2759** 2396 Screen printing; automotive & apparel trimmings

(G-8592)
CARALA VENTURES LTD
Also Called: Classics of Golf
120 Research Dr (06615-7126)
PHONE 800 483-6449
Michael P Beckerich, *President*
EMP: 28
SQ FT: 10,000
SALES (est): 2.3MM **Privately Held**
WEB: www.classicsofgolf.com
SIC: **2731** Book publishing

(G-8593)
CARBTROL CORPORATION
200 Benton St (06615-7330)
PHONE 203 337-4340
Chris Rotondo, *President*
Kenneth Lanouette, *President*
Heather Mroz, *Vice Pres*
Austin Shepherd, *Vice Pres*
Mary Nelson, *Purch Agent*
EMP: 20
SALES (est): 5.3MM **Privately Held**
WEB: www.carbtrol.com
SIC: **2819** Charcoal (carbon), activated

(G-8594)
CAREER CONCEPTS
3841 Main St (06614-3546)
PHONE 203 378-9943
Terence Blake, *Principal*
EMP: 1
SALES (est): 42.5K **Privately Held**
SIC: **2731** Book publishing

(G-8595)
CHRIS CROSS LLC
Also Called: Prestige Remodeling
294 Benton St (06615-7330)
P.O. Box 321135, Fairfield (06825-6135)
PHONE 203 386-8426
John Cross, *Manager*
EMP: 4
SALES (est): 403.6K **Privately Held**
SIC: **2434** Wood kitchen cabinets

(G-8596)
COATING DESIGN GROUP INC
430 Sniffens Ln (06615-7559)
PHONE 203 878-3663
William L Roy, *President*
Kathryn G Cunningham, *Corp Secy*
Katherine Cunningham, *Human Res Mgr*
Kevin Joseph, *Exec Dir*
Miguel Segui, *Technician*
EMP: 20
SQ FT: 11,500
SALES (est): 4.2MM **Privately Held**
WEB: www.coatingdesigngroup.com
SIC: **3827** 3089 Optical instruments & lenses; coloring & finishing of plastic products

(G-8597)
CONNECTICUT BREAKER CO INC
680 Surf Ave (06615-6733)
PHONE 203 378-2240
John Nedavaska, *President*
Paul Zezima, *Admin Sec*
EMP: 2
SQ FT: 3,000
SALES (est): 89K **Privately Held**
SIC: **3613** 8734 Circuit breakers, air; product testing laboratory, safety or performance

(G-8598)
CONNECTICUT MACHINE & WELDING
Also Called: Rollins Transmission Service
425 Harding Ave (06615-7248)
P.O. Box 249 (06615-0249)
PHONE 203 502-2605
Wayne J Rollins, *President*
Gary Rollins, *Treasurer*
Glenn A Rollins, *Admin Sec*
EMP: 20
SQ FT: 7,000
SALES (est): 965K **Privately Held**
WEB: www.rollinstransmission.com
SIC: **3599** Machine shop, jobbing & repair

(G-8599)
CORPORATE EXPRESS CT
400 Long Beach Blvd Ste 1 (06615-7180)
PHONE 203 455-2500
Peter Guala, *President*
EMP: 3
SALES (est): 189.9K **Privately Held**
SIC: **7363** 2741 Office help supply service; miscellaneous publishing

(G-8600)
COTE DIVOIRE IMPORTS
260 Prayer Spring Rd (06614-1322)
PHONE 203 243-4841
Vera Maximin, *President*
EMP: 1 EST: 2014
SALES (est): 72.1K **Privately Held**
SIC: **2095** 2066 Roasted coffee; freeze-dried coffee; instant cocoa

(G-8601)
CSS INDUSTRIES LLC
220 Whippoorwill Ln (06614-2487)
PHONE 203 521-5246
EMP: 2 EST: 2010
SALES (est): 115K **Privately Held**
SIC: **3999** Manufacturing industries

(G-8602)
CUESCRIPT INC
555 Lordship Blvd Unit F (06615-7156)
PHONE 203 763-4030
Michael Accardi, *President*
EMP: 7 EST: 2014
SALES (est): 658.4K **Privately Held**
SIC: **3663** Radio & TV communications equipment

(G-8603)
D & L ENGINEERING COMPANY
564 Surf Ave (06615-6725)
PHONE 203 375-5856
Judith Di Libro, *President*
Judith M Delibro, *Director*
EMP: 5
SQ FT: 3,000
SALES: 200K **Privately Held**
SIC: **3599** Machine shop, jobbing & repair

(G-8604)
DEFINED DESIGN CREATIVE ART
2505 Main St Ste 226b (06615-5839)
PHONE 203 378-2571
Edward Sanetti, *Mng Member*
EMP: 1 EST: 2013
SALES (est): 85.4K **Privately Held**
SIC: **7336** 3993 Package design; signs & advertising specialties

(G-8605)
DELTA LEVEL LLC
Also Called: Delta Level Defense
40 Embree St (06615-6710)
PHONE 203 919-1514
Ryan Gisolfi, *Mng Member*
EMP: 2
SALES (est): 153.1K **Privately Held**
SIC: **3812** Defense systems & equipment

(G-8606)
DICTAPHONE CORPORATION (HQ)
3191 Broadbridge Ave (06614-2559)
PHONE 203 381-7000
Robert Schwager, *Ch of Bd*
Daniel P Hart, *Senior VP*
Joseph Delaney, *Senior VP*
Thomas C Hodge, *Senior VP*
Ed Rucinski, *Senior VP*
▲ EMP: 200 EST: 1881
SQ FT: 100,000
SALES (est): 222.2MM **Publicly Held**
WEB: www.dictaphone.com
SIC: **3579** 3825 3695 3577 Dictating machines; instruments to measure electricity; magnetic & optical recording media; computer peripheral equipment

(G-8607)
ELECTRIC ENTERPRISE INC
1410 Stratford Ave (06615-6417)
PHONE 203 378-7311
Raymond S Sierakowski, *President*
Mary Jo Sierakowski, *Admin Sec*
EMP: 11
SQ FT: 3,200
SALES (est): 2MM **Privately Held**
WEB: www.electricenterprise.com
SIC: **7694** 5063 Electric motor repair; motors, electric

(G-8608)
ELIUS DELIGHT SNACKS LLC
1915 Stratford Ave (06615-6426)
PHONE 646 302-4948
Eliu Garcia, *Mng Member*
EMP: 1
SQ FT: 3,800
SALES: 40K **Privately Held**
SIC: **5441** 2052 2051 Confectionery; cookies & crackers; cakes, pies & pastries

(G-8609)
FAIRFIELD WOODWORKS LLC
Also Called: Fairfield Wood Works
365 Sniffens Ln (06615-7558)
PHONE 203 380-9842
David Evans,
Mark Bento,
EMP: 18
SQ FT: 10,500
SALES (est): 2.4MM **Privately Held**
SIC: **2431** Millwork

(G-8610)
FOOD ATMTN - SVC TCHNIQUES INC (PA)
Also Called: Fast
905 Honeyspot Rd (06615-7140)
PHONE 203 377-4414
Timothy Lane, *CEO*
Bernard G Koether II, *Ch of Bd*
Bernard Johnson, *President*
George F Koether, *President*
Reza Khani, *COO*
◆ EMP: 130
SQ FT: 100,000
SALES (est): 31.3MM **Privately Held**
WEB: www.fastinc.com
SIC: **3823** 3822 Time cycle & program controllers, industrial process type; temperature controls, automatic

(G-8611)
FRANK ROTH CO INC
1795 Stratford Ave (06615-6442)
PHONE 203 377-2155
Walker Woodworth, *President*
Cornelia Toffolo, *Corp Secy*
Marissa Woodworth, *Treasurer*
EMP: 60 EST: 1934
SQ FT: 14,000
SALES (est): 9MM **Privately Held**
WEB: www.frankroth.com
SIC: **3599** 3325 3841 3751 Machine shop, jobbing & repair; machine & other job shop work; alloy steel castings, except investment; surgical & medical instruments; motorcycles, bicycles & parts

(G-8612)
FREDDIE NELSON WOODWORKS
493 Sedgewick Ave (06615-6969)
PHONE 203 378-2330
Freddie Nelson, *Principal*
EMP: 1 EST: 2017
SALES (est): 54.1K **Privately Held**
SIC: **2431** Millwork

(G-8613)
FS SIGNS LLC
1895 Stratford Ave (06615-6426)
PHONE 203 612-4447
Geovanna Granda, *Principal*
EMP: 1
SALES (est): 55.7K **Privately Held**
SIC: **3993** Signs & advertising specialties

(G-8614)
FUNCTIONAL CONCEPTS LLC
166 Holmes St (06615-6515)
P.O. Box 29 (06615-0029)
PHONE 203 813-0157
Edward C Kaine,
EMP: 3 EST: 2009
SALES (est): 150K **Privately Held**
SIC: **8093** 7371 8742 2741 Rehabilitation center, outpatient treatment; custom computer programming services; hospital & health services consultant;

(G-8615)
GARCIA PRINTING INC
860 Honeyspot Rd (06615-7159)
PHONE 203 378-6200
Cesar A Garcia, *President*
EMP: 6
SQ FT: 5,000
SALES (est): 810K **Privately Held**
SIC: **2752** Commercial printing, offset

(G-8616)
GARY TOOL COMPANY
26 Grant St (06615-6188)
PHONE 203 377-3077
Raymond Anderson Jr, *President*
Cristine Ansder, *President*
EMP: 7
SQ FT: 10,000
SALES (est): 1.2MM **Privately Held**
SIC: **3541** 3544 Machine tools, metal cutting: exotic (explosive, etc.); jigs & fixtures

Stratford - Fairfield County (G-8617)

(G-8617)
GEORGE H OLSON STEEL CO INC
Also Called: Olson, G H Steel
245 Access Rd (06615-7414)
PHONE.................................203 375-5656
George H Olson, *President*
Mary Ann Gentile, *Admin Sec*
EMP: 25 **EST:** 1944
SQ FT: 2,800
SALES (est): 2.1MM **Privately Held**
SIC: 1791 3441 Structural steel erection; fabricated structural metal

(G-8618)
GLYNE MANUFACTURING CO INC
380 E Main St (06614-5145)
PHONE.................................203 375-4495
Bruce McGalliard, *President*
Thomas Frei, *Vice Pres*
Tom Frei, *Vice Pres*
Ben McGalliard, *Vice Pres*
Marge Barrett, *Office Mgr*
EMP: 16
SQ FT: 9,600
SALES (est): 3.7MM **Privately Held**
WEB: www.glyne.com
SIC: 3728 Aircraft parts & equipment

(G-8619)
GOOD EARTH TREE CARE INC
540 Longbrook Ave (06614-5115)
P.O. Box 565, Botsford (06404-0565)
PHONE.................................203 375-7962
Jennifer Damon, *Principal*
▲ **EMP:** 5
SQ FT: 1,500
SALES (est): 831K **Privately Held**
SIC: 0783 2873 4953 5199 Removal services, bush & tree; fertilizers: natural (organic), except compost; recycling, waste materials; baling of wood shavings for mulch

(G-8620)
GRAFTED COATINGS INC
Also Called: We Make Paint
400 Surf Ave (06615-6723)
PHONE.................................203 377-9979
James A Bolton, *President*
Joanne M Young, *Treasurer*
Alice Irene Bolton, *Admin Sec*
EMP: 15
SQ FT: 12,000
SALES (est): 2.4MM **Privately Held**
WEB: www.graftedcoatings.com
SIC: 2891 5198 Sealants; paints

(G-8621)
HAMPFORD RESEARCH INC
1255 W Broad St (06615-5746)
P.O. Box 1073 (06615-8573)
PHONE.................................203 380-2852
EMP: 1
SALES (corp-wide): 3.8MM **Privately Held**
SIC: 2869 Industrial organic chemicals
PA: Hampford Research, Inc.
54 Veterans Blvd
Stratford CT 06615
203 375-1137

(G-8622)
HAMPFORD RESEARCH INC (PA)
54 Veterans Blvd (06615-5111)
PHONE.................................203 375-1137
Clare C Hampford Donahue, *President*
Randy Dieckman, *Plant Mgr*
John Teator, *Engineer*
Jennifer Ricciardi, *Manager*
Timothy Hampford, *Executive*
▲ **EMP:** 34
SQ FT: 100,000
SALES (est): 3.8MM **Privately Held**
WEB: www.hampfordresearch.com
SIC: 2869 8731 Industrial organic chemicals; commercial physical research

(G-8623)
HANGER PRSTHETCS & ORTHO INC
1985 Barnum Ave (06615-5512)
PHONE.................................203 377-8820
Nathan Seversky, *Manager*
EMP: 7
SALES (corp-wide): 1B **Publicly Held**
SIC: 3842 Prosthetic appliances
HQ: Hanger Prosthetics & Orthotics, Inc.
10910 Domain Dr Ste 300
Austin TX 78758
512 777-3800

(G-8624)
HERFF JONES LLC
71 Vought Pl (06614-2949)
PHONE.................................203 368-9344
Herff Jones, *Branch Mgr*
EMP: 10
SALES (corp-wide): 1.1B **Privately Held**
SIC: 3911 Jewelry, precious metal
HQ: Herff Jones, Llc
4501 W 62nd St
Indianapolis IN 46268
800 419-5462

(G-8625)
HI TEK RACING LLC
7365 Main St Ste 8 (06614-1300)
P.O. Box 183 (06615-0183)
PHONE.................................203 378-5210
Tom Kolhawik,
Julie Kolhawik,
EMP: 2
SALES (est): 198.7K **Privately Held**
WEB: www.hitekracing.com
SIC: 3625 Timing devices, electronic

(G-8626)
HI-TECH PACKAGING INC
1 Bruce Ave (06615-6102)
PHONE.................................203 378-2700
Michael Rappa, *President*
Alfred Thibault, *Senior VP*
EMP: 28
SQ FT: 40,000
SALES (est): 5.4MM **Privately Held**
SIC: 2448 2653 3086 Pallets, wood; boxes, corrugated: made from purchased materials; carpet & rug cushions, foamed plastic

(G-8627)
HOUSATONIC BOAT WORKS LLC
485 Chapel St (06614-1642)
PHONE.................................203 375-3161
Terry Cappellieri, *Principal*
EMP: 2 **EST:** 2007
SALES (est): 122.9K **Privately Held**
SIC: 3732 Boat building & repairing

(G-8628)
HUDSON PAPER COMPANY (PA)
Also Called: Hupaco
1341 W Broad St Ste 4 (06615-5761)
PHONE.................................203 378-8759
Richard Wilk, *President*
Bonnie S Wilk, *Vice Pres*
Brian Wilk, *Treasurer*
Richard M Wilk, *Treasurer*
▲ **EMP:** 35
SQ FT: 80,000
SALES (est): 16.4MM **Privately Held**
WEB: www.hudsonpaper.com
SIC: 5113 5199 5947 2674 Bags, paper & disposable plastic; boxes & containers; paper & products, wrapping or coarse; packaging materials; party favors; bags: uncoated paper & multiwall; boxes, newsboard, metal edged: made from purchased materials

(G-8629)
HYDRO-FLEX INC
Also Called: Necs
534 Surf Ave (06615-6725)
PHONE.................................203 269-5599
James William, *President*
Chester Cornacchia, *Principal*
Eileen Kelly, *Principal*
EMP: 4
SQ FT: 20,000
SALES (est): 250K **Privately Held**
SIC: 3999 Pipe cleaners

(G-8630)
I95 SIGNS LLC
300 Honeyspot Rd (06615-6815)
PHONE.................................203 296-2141
EMP: 1
SALES (est): 46K **Privately Held**
SIC: 3993 Signs & advertising specialties

(G-8631)
IMPERIAL METAL FINISHING INC
920 Honeyspot Rd (06615-7112)
PHONE.................................203 377-1229
Vincent Bevacqua, *President*
Frank Bevacqua, *Vice Pres*
John Bevacqua Jr, *Vice Pres*
EMP: 9
SQ FT: 13,000
SALES: 850K **Privately Held**
SIC: 3479 Painting of metal products; coating of metals & formed products

(G-8632)
INNARAH INC
838 Woodend Rd (06615-7324)
P.O. Box 335 (06615-0335)
PHONE.................................203 873-0015
Manozoor Jaffery, *President*
▲ **EMP:** 5
SALES (est): 473.3K **Privately Held**
SIC: 2844 Cosmetic preparations

(G-8633)
INNOTEQ INC (PA)
555 Lordship Blvd (06615-7156)
P.O. Box 1640, Pleasantville NJ (08232-6640)
PHONE.................................203 659-4444
Craig J Berry, *President*
Laurie Koppe, *General Mgr*
John Ledonne, *Director*
▼ **EMP:** 40
SQ FT: 25,000
SALES (est): 8.9MM **Privately Held**
SIC: 2834 Pharmaceutical preparations

(G-8634)
J & B WOODWORKING
55 Anson St (06614-2802)
PHONE.................................203 377-4682
Jordan Liscinsky, *Owner*
Kelley Liscinsky, *Co-Owner*
EMP: 2
SALES (est): 121.6K **Privately Held**
SIC: 2499 Decorative wood & woodwork

(G-8635)
JA CUSTOM WOODWORK
35 Soundview Ave (06615-6242)
PHONE.................................203 540-5747
Jacek Andrychowski, *Owner*
EMP: 1
SALES (est): 91.4K **Privately Held**
SIC: 2431 Millwork

(G-8636)
JGS PROPERTIES LLC
Also Called: R A Lalli
1805 Stratford Ave (06615-6426)
PHONE.................................203 378-7508
Geza Scap, *Owner*
Julie Scap, *Vice Pres*
Peter Kirby, *Manager*
EMP: 30 **EST:** 1953
SQ FT: 25,000
SALES (est): 5.6MM **Privately Held**
SIC: 3444 Sheet metal specialties, not stamped

(G-8637)
JOE & SON WLDG FABRICATION LLC
7 Raven Ter (06614-3330)
PHONE.................................203 380-2072
Joseph Pacific, *Principal*
EMP: 1
SALES (est): 61.4K **Privately Held**
SIC: 7692 Welding repair

(G-8638)
JUDGE TOOL & GAGE INC
Also Called: Judge Tool Sales Company
555 Lordship Blvd Unit A (06615-7156)
PHONE.................................800 214-5990
Joseph Palmer, *CEO*
Bob Ratzenberger, *Sales Staff*
Gwen Palmer, *Admin Sec*
EMP: 4 **EST:** 1958
SQ FT: 1,800
SALES (est): 765.3K **Privately Held**
WEB: www.judgetool.com
SIC: 3829 Nuclear instrument modules

(G-8639)
KIMBERLY-CLARK CORPORATION
137 Ryegate Ter (06615-7659)
PHONE.................................973 986-8454
Ryan Wagner, *Branch Mgr*
EMP: 202
SALES (corp-wide): 18.4B **Publicly Held**
SIC: 2621 2676 Paper mills; infant & baby paper products
PA: Kimberly-Clark Corporation
351 Phelps Dr
Irving TX 75038
972 281-1200

(G-8640)
KIMS NAIL CORPORATION
Also Called: Kim's Nail Salon
7365 Main St Ste 11 (06614-1300)
PHONE.................................203 380-8608
Euneui Jo, *Principal*
EMP: 3
SALES (est): 30K **Privately Held**
SIC: 2844 Manicure preparations

(G-8641)
KINGSLEY PRINTING ASSOC LLC
4883 Main St (06614-3646)
PHONE.................................203 345-6046
David Kingsley Adnett, *Principal*
EMP: 2
SALES (est): 140K **Privately Held**
SIC: 2752 Commercial printing, lithographic

(G-8642)
KIT ARCHITECTURAL DESIGNS LLC
825 Barnum Avenue Cutoff (06614-5027)
PHONE.................................203 378-6911
John Rehm, *Partner*
EMP: 2
SQ FT: 8,000
SALES (est): 247.7K **Privately Held**
SIC: 2434 Wood kitchen cabinets

(G-8643)
KUB TECHNOLOGIES INC
Also Called: Kubtec
111 Research Dr (06615-7126)
PHONE.................................203 364-8544
Vikram Butani, *President*
Preeti Butani, *Vice Pres*
▼ **EMP:** 28
SQ FT: 10,000
SALES (est): 4.3MM **Privately Held**
WEB: www.kubtec.com
SIC: 3844 X-ray apparatus & tubes

(G-8644)
M & D COATINGS LLC
167 Avon St (06615-6744)
PHONE.................................203 380-9466
Jeffrey Dumas, *Manager*
▲ **EMP:** 8
SALES (est): 948.5K **Privately Held**
SIC: 2851 Paints, waterproof

(G-8645)
MAJOR TIRE CO LLC
80 Century Dr Ste 2 (06615-7365)
PHONE.................................203 543-0334
David Mihalov,
Charles Willinger,
EMP: 1
SALES (est): 135.3K **Privately Held**
SIC: 3011 5531 Retreading materials, tire; automotive & home supply stores

(G-8646)
MALUX MACHINE LLC
360 Sniffens Ln (06615-7592)
PHONE.................................203 526-1834
Marek Malyszko, *Principal*
EMP: 1 **EST:** 2014
SQ FT: 800
SALES (est): 79.2K **Privately Held**
SIC: 3599 Machine shop, jobbing & repair

▲ = Import ▼ = Export
◆ = Import/Export

GEOGRAPHIC SECTION
Stratford - Fairfield County (G-8674)

(G-8647)
MANAGEMENT HLTH SOLUTIONS INC (PA)
Also Called: Syft
99 Hawley Ln Ste 1201 (06614-1202)
P.O. Box 320548, Fairfield (06825-0548)
PHONE..................................888 647-4621
Todd J Plesko, *CEO*
Brian Campbell, *President*
Edward Murphy, *Chairman*
Miriam Achour, *Vice Pres*
Steven Herz, *Vice Pres*
EMP: 31
SQ FT: 1,200
SALES (est): 22.7MM **Privately Held**
SIC: 7372 8742 Business oriented computer software; materials mgmt. (purchasing, handling, inventory) consultant

(G-8648)
MCMELLON BROS INCORPORATED
915 Honeyspot Rd (06615-7192)
PHONE..................................203 375-5685
Thomas Miller, *President*
Hans Hanshaffner, *Vice Pres*
Reberta Miller, *Vice Pres*
Elizabeth Austin, *Engineer*
Alan Brown, *Marketing Staff*
EMP: 27 **EST:** 1951
SQ FT: 20,000
SALES (est): 6.3MM **Privately Held**
WEB: www.mcmellonbros.com
SIC: 3728 3452 Aircraft parts & equipment; bolts, nuts, rivets & washers

(G-8649)
MEDIA METRIX LLC
999 Oronoque Ln Ste 3b (06614-1379)
PHONE..................................203 386-0228
Mark A O'Halloran,
EMP: 2
SQ FT: 2,000
SALES: 1.2MM **Privately Held**
SIC: 2741 7311 Directories, telephone: publishing & printing; advertising agencies

(G-8650)
MEREDITH GRAPHICS & DESIGN
375 N Abram St (06614-2966)
PHONE..................................203 375-1039
Hazel Meredith, *Owner*
EMP: 2
SALES: 50K **Privately Held**
SIC: 2791 7336 Typesetting; graphic arts & related design

(G-8651)
MORTHANOSCOM LLC
4 Ocean Ave (06615-7748)
PHONE..................................203 378-2414
John Morthanos,
EMP: 2
SALES (est): 128.2K **Privately Held**
SIC: 8742 2721 7313 Business planning & organizing services; corporate objectives & policies consultant; materials mgmt. (purchasing, handling, inventory) consultant; magazines: publishing only, not printed on site; statistical reports (periodicals): publishing only; radio, television, publisher representatives

(G-8652)
MURRAY SIGNS & DESIGNS BOB
118 Winter St (06614-4740)
PHONE..................................203 375-7351
Robert Murray, *Owner*
EMP: 1
SALES (est): 67K **Privately Held**
SIC: 3993 Signs & advertising specialties

(G-8653)
NATURE PLUS INC
55 Rachel Dr (06615-6411)
PHONE..................................203 380-0316
Jon Sedgwick, *President*
EMP: 7
SQ FT: 5,100
SALES (est): 834K **Privately Held**
SIC: 2842 Cleaning or polishing preparations; industrial plant disinfectants or deodorants; disinfectants, household or industrial plant; sanitation preparations, disinfectants & deodorants

(G-8654)
NORTHASTERN COMMUNICATIONS INC
255 Hathaway Dr Ste 3 (06615-7370)
PHONE..................................203 381-9008
Julie Reibold, *Branch Mgr*
EMP: 10
SALES (est): 403.7K
SALES (corp-wide): 9MM **Privately Held**
WEB: www.norcomct.com
SIC: 5999 3663 Telephone & communication equipment; radio broadcasting & communications equipment
PA: Northeastern Communications, Inc.
  7 Great Hill Rd
  Naugatuck CT 06770
  203 575-9008

(G-8655)
NORWALK COMPRESEER COMPANY
1650 Stratford Ave (06615-6419)
PHONE..................................203 386-1234
Arthur McCauley, *Ch of Bd*
Jeff Barker, *Sales Staff*
Brian Benway, *Maintence Staff*
▼ **EMP:** 45
SQ FT: 33,000
SALES (est): 9MM **Privately Held**
SIC: 3563 Air & gas compressors

(G-8656)
NORWALK COMPRESSOR INC
1650 Stratford Ave (06615-6419)
PHONE..................................203 386-1234
Arthur Cauley, *Principal*
Mario Perrotta, *Webmaster*
Chris McCauley, *Executive*
▲ **EMP:** 6
SALES (est): 1.9MM **Privately Held**
SIC: 3563 Air & gas compressors

(G-8657)
NORWALK POWDERED METALS INC
Also Called: Npm
30 Moffitt St (06615-6718)
PHONE..................................203 338-8000
Thomas A Blumenthal, *President*
Ann Blumenthal, *Vice Pres*
Richard Webb, *Vice Pres*
Henry Adams, *VP Sales*
EMP: 70 **EST:** 1957
SQ FT: 34,000
SALES (est): 14.4MM **Privately Held**
SIC: 3399 Powder, metal

(G-8658)
NUANCE COMMUNICATIONS INC
3191 Broadbridge Ave Fl 2 (06614-2566)
PHONE..................................781 565-5000
Ed Rucinski, *Exec VP*
Simon Howes, *Vice Pres*
Betsy Hipp, *Senior Mgr*
EMP: 4 **Publicly Held**
SIC: 7372 Prepackaged software
PA: Nuance Communications, Inc.
  1 Wayside Rd
  Burlington MA 01803

(G-8659)
NUOVO PASTA PRODUCTIONS LTD
1330 Honeyspot Road Ext (06615-7115)
PHONE..................................203 380-4090
Carl L Zuanelli, *President*
Tom Quinn, *Exec VP*
Kevin Sterner, *Regl Sales Mgr*
Michael Voelker, *Manager*
◆ **EMP:** 150
SQ FT: 40,000
SALES: 36MM **Privately Held**
SIC: 2099 Packaged combination products: pasta, rice & potato

(G-8660)
PALMERO HEALTHCARE LLC
120 Goodwin Pl (06615-6790)
PHONE..................................203 377-6424
Karen Neiner, *President*
Bernie Dutton, *COO*
Beth Wade, *Sales Staff*
EMP: 13
SALES (est): 3.6MM **Privately Held**
SIC: 3843 Dental equipment & supplies

(G-8661)
PANEL SHOP INC
100 Lupes Dr (06615-6436)
PHONE..................................203 377-6208
Steve Hall, *President*
Mark Barton, *Vice Pres*
EMP: 2
SQ FT: 2,000
SALES (est): 200K **Privately Held**
SIC: 3444 Sheet metalwork

(G-8662)
PARK CITY PACKAGING INC (PA)
Also Called: Pack Center , The
480 Sniffens Ln (06615-7559)
PHONE..................................203 378-7384
C Richard Polzello, *CEO*
Lisa Morgan, *Human Resources*
Steve Ciukenda, *Manager*
Troy Manson, *Manager*
EMP: 35 **EST:** 1954
SQ FT: 25,000
SALES (est): 9MM **Privately Held**
WEB: www.thepackcenter.com
SIC: 4783 5199 2679 Packing goods for shipping; packaging materials; corrugated paper: made from purchased material

(G-8663)
PENMAR INDUSTRIES INC
Also Called: Spec Label Systems
35 Ontario St (06615-7135)
PHONE..................................203 853-4868
Elizabeth Soegaard, *President*
Eddy W Rodriguez, *President*
Jeffrey Dais, *Principal*
Sandi Gould, *Purch Mgr*
Jose A Soegaard III, *Treasurer*
EMP: 14
SQ FT: 11,500
SALES (est): 4.7MM **Privately Held**
WEB: www.penmar-industries.com
SIC: 5199 5113 2671 Packaging materials; shipping supplies; packaging paper & plastics film, coated & laminated

(G-8664)
PEPSI-COLA METRO BTLG CO INC
Also Called: Pepsico
355 Benton St (06615-7329)
PHONE..................................203 375-2484
Carlos Salgado, *Plant Mgr*
Spencer Bresette, *Sales Staff*
Todd Bixby, *Manager*
EMP: 400
SALES (corp-wide): 64.6B **Publicly Held**
WEB: www.pbg.com
SIC: 2086 Carbonated soft drinks, bottled & canned
HQ: Pepsi-Cola Metropolitan Bottling Company, Inc.
  1111 Westchester Ave
  White Plains NY 10604
  914 767-6000

(G-8665)
PICTURE PERFECT PRINTING INC
335 Sniffens Ln (06615-7558)
PHONE..................................203 386-9696
Peter Bartush, *Owner*
EMP: 2
SALES (est): 184.6K **Privately Held**
SIC: 2759 Screen printing

(G-8666)
POLEP DISTRIBUTION SERVICES J
1075 Honeyspot Rd (06615-7113)
PHONE..................................203 378-2193
Ryan Payeur, *Principal*
EMP: 2
SALES (est): 122.2K **Privately Held**
SIC: 5194 5099 2111 Tobacco & tobacco products; durable goods; cigarettes

(G-8667)
PREFERRED PRODUCTS CO INC
55 Browning St Ste 1 (06615-7154)
PHONE..................................203 375-9139
Neil W Muirhead, *President*
EMP: 1
SQ FT: 2,000
SALES (est): 127.5K **Privately Held**
SIC: 3599 Machine shop, jobbing & repair

(G-8668)
PREMIER GRAPHICS LLC
Also Called: Premier Prtg Mailing Solutions
860 Honeyspot Rd Ste 1 (06615-7159)
PHONE..................................800 414-1624
Tim Chiccese, *President*
EMP: 55
SQ FT: 33,000
SALES (est): 13.3MM **Privately Held**
SIC: 2721 Periodicals: publishing & printing

(G-8669)
PROFESSIONAL MKTG SVCS INC
Also Called: Pmsi
300 Long Beach Blvd Ste 6 (06615-7153)
PHONE..................................203 610-6222
Marty Bear, *President*
EMP: 10
SQ FT: 3,500
SALES: 7MM **Privately Held**
SIC: 5199 2678 Advertising specialties; stationery products

(G-8670)
PROGRESSIVE HYDRAULICS INC
590 Lordship Blvd Unit 1 (06615-7123)
PHONE..................................203 386-0885
Dave Schatteman, *Branch Mgr*
EMP: 1
SALES (corp-wide): 25.4MM **Privately Held**
SIC: 3492 Hose & tube couplings, hydraulic/pneumatic
PA: Progressive Hydraulics, Inc.
  350 N Midland Ave
  Saddle Brook NJ 07663
  201 791-3400

(G-8671)
PROTECTION INDUSTRIES CORP (PA)
2897 Main St (06614-4938)
P.O. Box 1832, New York NY (10156-1832)
PHONE..................................203 375-9393
William J Hill, *Ch of Bd*
Donna Z Hill, *President*
William Hill, *Principal*
EMP: 9
SALES (est): 2.6MM **Privately Held**
SIC: 5063 3669 Control & signal wire & cable, including coaxial; fire detection systems, electric

(G-8672)
RAGS A MUFFIN
120 Kings Row (06614-1652)
PHONE..................................203 377-7063
Charlene Kendrick, *Owner*
EMP: 1
SALES (est): 67K **Privately Held**
SIC: 3942 Dolls, except stuffed toy animals

(G-8673)
RAVEN AD SPECIALTIES
52 Raven Ter (06614-3329)
PHONE..................................203 521-8687
Nancy M RE, *Owner*
EMP: 1
SALES (est): 34.4K **Privately Held**
SIC: 5699 2771 5112 Customized clothing & apparel; greeting cards; greeting cards

(G-8674)
REDCO AUDIO INC
1701 Stratford Ave (06615-6421)
PHONE..................................203 502-7600
David Berliner, *President*

Stratford - Fairfield County (G-8675)

Peter Greenwood, *Engineer*
Marc Lelyveld, *Sales Staff*
▲ **EMP:** 14
SQ FT: 6,000
SALES (est): 2.9MM **Privately Held**
WEB: www.redco.com
SIC: 3496 3651 1761 Cable, uninsulated wire; made from purchased wire; household audio equipment; sheet metalwork

(G-8675)
SAUGATUCK KITCHENS LLC
125 Bruce Ave (06615-6102)
PHONE 203 334-1099
Sonia Fernandez-Wells,
David Wells,
Nicolas Wells,
Oliver Wells,
EMP: 5
SQ FT: 20,000
SALES (est): 118.7K **Privately Held**
SIC: 2092 Crabcakes, frozen

(G-8676)
SEABOARD INDUSTRIES INC
100 Benton St Unit A (06615-7310)
PHONE 973 427-8500
EMP: 2 **EST:** 2014
SALES (est): 59.4K **Privately Held**
SIC: 3999 Manufacturing industries

(G-8677)
SIKORSKY AIRCRAFT CORPORATION
1825 Main St (06615-6528)
P.O. Box 9729 (06615-9129)
PHONE 203 386-4000
Steven Finger, *President*
EMP: 600 **Publicly Held**
WEB: www.sikorsky.com
SIC: 3724 Aircraft engines & engine parts
HQ: Sikorsky Aircraft Corporation
6900 Main St
Stratford CT 06614

(G-8678)
SIKORSKY AIRCRAFT CORPORATION (HQ)
6900 Main St (06614-1385)
P.O. Box 9729 (06615-9129)
PHONE 203 386-4000
Daniel Schultz, *President*
John Palumbo, *Senior VP*
Judith E Bankowski, *Vice Pres*
Chris Buiten, *Vice Pres*
Stephen B Estill, *Vice Pres*
◆ **EMP:** 2093
SALES (est): 2.9B **Publicly Held**
WEB: www.sikorsky.com
SIC: 3721 4581 5599 Helicopters; aircraft maintenance & repair services; aircraft dealers

(G-8679)
SIKORSKY EXPORT CORPORATION
6900 Main St (06614-1378)
PHONE 203 386-4000
Mick Maurer, *President*
▼ **EMP:** 300
SALES (est): 19MM **Publicly Held**
WEB: www.sikorskyarchives.com
SIC: 3721 Helicopters
HQ: Sikorsky Aircraft Corporation
6900 Main St
Stratford CT 06614

(G-8680)
SIKORSKY INTERNATIONAL PRODUCT
6900 Main St (06614-1378)
PHONE 203 375-0095
Jeffrey Pino, *President*
▼ **EMP:** 2
SALES (est): 250.2K **Privately Held**
SIC: 3721 4581 Helicopters; aircraft servicing & repairing

(G-8681)
SKYTECH MACHINING INC
765 Woodend Rd (06615-7323)
PHONE 203 378-9994
Carlos Lobo, *President*
Antonio Da Silva, *Vice Pres*
EMP: 5
SQ FT: 3,200
SALES: 650K **Privately Held**
WEB: www.skytechmachining.com
SIC: 3599 Machine shop, jobbing & repair

(G-8682)
SNEHAM MANUFACTURING INC
727 Honeyspot Rd Ste 99 (06615-7172)
PHONE 203 610-6669
Suja Thomas, *President*
Saji Thomas, *Principal*
EMP: 4
SQ FT: 4,000
SALES (est): 370K **Privately Held**
SIC: 3599 Machine shop, jobbing & repair

(G-8683)
SONIC CORP
1 Research Dr (06615-7184)
PHONE 203 375-0063
Robert Brakeman III, *President*
Richard Cizik, *Purch Mgr*
Bill Brakeman, *Engineer*
Petra Ortiz, *Manager*
Claire C Skidd, *Admin Sec*
EMP: 12
SQ FT: 10,000
SALES (est): 3MM **Privately Held**
WEB: www.sonicmixing.com
SIC: 3556 3561 3552 3554 Mixers, feed, except agricultural; pumps & pumping equipment; textile machinery; paper industries machinery

(G-8684)
SPOT WELDERS INC
1021 Honeyspot Rd (06615-7113)
PHONE 203 386-8938
Alphonse L Silvestri, *President*
Florence Silvestri, *Vice Pres*
James V Silvestri, *Treasurer*
Deborah Silvestri, *Admin Sec*
EMP: 2
SQ FT: 3,400
SALES (est): 150K **Privately Held**
SIC: 7692 Welding repair

(G-8685)
STERLING TOOL DIE & MFG CO
1135 James Farm Rd (06614-1047)
PHONE 203 378-0893
Marty Kosh, *Vice Pres*
EMP: 2
SALES (est): 83.2K **Privately Held**
SIC: 3544 Special dies, tools, jigs & fixtures

(G-8686)
STRATFORD STEEL LLC
185 Masarik Ave (06615)
PHONE 203 612-7350
Michael Matkovic, *Mng Member*
EMP: 40
SQ FT: 13,000
SALES: 5MM **Privately Held**
SIC: 3441 Fabricated structural metal

(G-8687)
STRATON INDUSTRIES INC
180 Surf Ave (06615-7137)
PHONE 203 375-4488
Edward J Cremin, *CEO*
David E Cremin, *President*
James Jarusinsky, *Engineer*
Kathleen McCann, *VP Sls/Mktg*
Marie Brackett, *Accounting Mgr*
EMP: 52 **EST:** 1961
SQ FT: 12,000
SALES (est): 14MM **Privately Held**
WEB: www.straton.com
SIC: 3544 3599 3721 3728 Special dies & tools; jigs & fixtures; machine & other job shop work; research & development on aircraft by the manufacturer; alighting (landing gear) assemblies, aircraft

(G-8688)
STRINGS BY AURORA LLC
514 Surf Ave (06615-6725)
PHONE 203 583-9929
Christopher L Pelletier,
EMP: 1
SALES (est): 49.9K **Privately Held**
SIC: 3931 Guitars & parts, electric & non-electric

(G-8689)
SUCCESS APP
54 Melville St (06615-5722)
PHONE 203 218-6264
Paul Brault, *Principal*
EMP: 2
SALES (est): 62.1K **Privately Held**
SIC: 7372 Prepackaged software

(G-8690)
SUPER SEAL CORP
45 Seymour St (06615-6170)
P.O. Box 394 (06615-0394)
PHONE 203 378-5015
William Newbauer Jr, *President*
Einer Dineson, *Admin Sec*
▲ **EMP:** 10
SQ FT: 12,000
SALES (est): 1.2MM **Privately Held**
SIC: 3089 Molding primary plastic

(G-8691)
SUPPLEMENT TECH LLC
Also Called: Supplements Unlimited
1625 Main St (06615-6526)
PHONE 203 377-5551
James Shaham, *Mng Member*
Kamal Shaham, *Mng Member*
EMP: 2
SQ FT: 5,000
SALES (est): 232K **Privately Held**
SIC: 2023 Dietary supplements, dairy & non-dairy based

(G-8692)
SURF METAL CO INC
460 Lordship Blvd (06615-7123)
PHONE 203 375-2211
James Chacho Jr, *President*
Dorie Chacho, *Admin Sec*
EMP: 5
SQ FT: 4,000
SALES (est): 450K **Privately Held**
SIC: 3341 5093 Lead smelting & refining (secondary); ferrous metal scrap & waste

(G-8693)
T C KITCHENS INC
416 Jackson Ave (06615-6118)
PHONE 203 375-4469
Anthony Cacavollia, *President*
EMP: 2
SALES (est): 197.4K **Privately Held**
SIC: 2434 2541 5722 Wood kitchen cabinets; counters or counter display cases, wood; household appliance stores

(G-8694)
THE MERRILL ANDERSON CO INC
1166 Barnum Ave (06614-5427)
PHONE 203 377-4996
Samuel H Heitzman, *Ch of Bd*
Thomas Gerrity, *President*
Samuel Simpson, *Treasurer*
Paula Tkacs, *Art Dir*
Jim Gust, *Senior Editor*
EMP: 12
SQ FT: 7,500
SALES (est): 1.4MM **Privately Held**
WEB: www.merrillanderson.com
SIC: 2741 8742 Business service newsletters: publishing & printing; marketing consulting services

(G-8695)
THOMAS MANUFACTURING LLC
378 Highland Ave (06614-3223)
PHONE 203 209-4568
Keren L Thomas, *Principal*
EMP: 1 **EST:** 2009
SALES (est): 59.5K **Privately Held**
SIC: 3999 Manufacturing industries

(G-8696)
TINAS HEAVENLY TREATS
35 Meadowview Ave (06615-7420)
PHONE 203 543-3560
Tina Sadler,
EMP: 2
SALES (est): 62.3K **Privately Held**
SIC: 2051 Bread, cake & related products

(G-8697)
TOPCAT LLC
120 Goodwin Pl (06615-6713)
PHONE 203 610-6544
Bernie Dutton, *President*
EMP: 3 **EST:** 2015
SALES (est): 78.5K **Privately Held**
SIC: 4813 2842 ; sanitation preparations, disinfectants & deodorants

(G-8698)
TOTAL PTRCHEMICALS REF USA INC
125 Ontario St (06615-7135)
PHONE 203 375-0668
Donna Kovac, *Branch Mgr*
EMP: 30
SALES (corp-wide): 8.4B **Publicly Held**
SIC: 2821 Plastics materials & resins
HQ: Total Petrochemicals & Refining Usa, Inc.
1201 La St Ste 1800
Houston TX 77002
713 483-5000

(G-8699)
TYGER TOOL INC
45 Sperry Ave (06615-7317)
PHONE 203 375-4344
Mark Bracchi, *President*
Darrell Ingram, *Corp Secy*
Paul Ferencz, *Vice Pres*
Kimberly Smircich, *Office Mgr*
Jackie Mata, *Manager*
EMP: 10
SQ FT: 4,800
SALES: 1MM **Privately Held**
WEB: www.tygertool.com
SIC: 3469 3549 Machine parts, stamped or pressed metal; metalworking machinery

(G-8700)
UNLIMITED WOODWORKING
205 York St (06615-7953)
PHONE 203 380-2340
Frank Lipinsky, *Principal*
EMP: 2
SALES (est): 154.6K **Privately Held**
SIC: 2431 Millwork

(G-8701)
USC TECHNOLOGIES LLC
175 Garfield Ave (06615-7103)
PHONE 203 378-9622
Robert Reath, *Manager*
EMP: 4
SALES (est): 133.8K **Privately Held**
SIC: 3471 Electroplating & plating

(G-8702)
VIDEO MESSENGERCOM CORP
Also Called: Video Messenger Co
862 Judson Pl (06615-5933)
PHONE 203 358-8842
Joe Romano, *President*
Charles Corsello, *Vice Pres*
Peter Murphyprincipal, *Natl Sales Mgr*
George Hayman, *Technical Dir*
Brad Jeske, *Associate*
EMP: 8
SQ FT: 5,000
SALES: 2MM **Privately Held**
WEB: www.videomessenger.com
SIC: 7941 6719 3663 Sports promotion; investment holding companies, except banks; encryption devices

(G-8703)
VO LEATHER INC
489a Commanche Ln (06614-8283)
PHONE 203 345-8442
Thomas Weinstein, *Ch of Bd*
EMP: 2
SALES (est): 199.4K **Privately Held**
SIC: 3199 Leather goods

(G-8704)
WARRIOR PRECISION
264 Seymour St (06615-6232)
PHONE 203 375-8154
Craig Ferrero, *Owner*
EMP: 1
SQ FT: 1,200

SALES (est): 110K **Privately Held**
SIC: 3599 Machine shop, jobbing & repair

(G-8705)
WATERFALLS
296 1st Ave (06615-7501)
PHONE.....................203 377-1540
Katharina Eoshea, *Principal*
EMP: 1
SALES (est): 63K **Privately Held**
SIC: 3999 Manufacturing industries

(G-8706)
WELDING ON WHEELS SERVICES LLC
163 Jackson Ave (06615-6215)
PHONE.....................203 449-6273
Josue Gotay, *Principal*
EMP: 1
SALES (est): 103.7K **Privately Held**
SIC: 7692 Welding repair

(G-8707)
WESTPORT PRECISION LLC
280 Hathaway Dr (06615-7344)
PHONE.....................203 378-2175
Carlos Mora, *Purch Mgr*
Tom Fischetti, *Sales Engr*
Judd Mellott,
Robert Zawadski,
EMP: 53
SQ FT: 25,000
SALES (est): 12.2MM **Privately Held**
WEB: www.westportprecision.com
SIC: 3599 Machine shop, jobbing & repair

(G-8708)
WHATS YOUR SIGN LLC
1097 Hillside Ave (06614-4803)
PHONE.....................814 823-7807
Hillary Stickney, *Mng Member*
EMP: 1
SALES (est): 46K **Privately Held**
SIC: 3993 Signs & advertising specialties

(G-8709)
WIRED INC
3010 Huntington Rd (06614-1142)
PHONE.....................601 992-0490
EMP: 2
SALES (est): 69.9K **Privately Held**
SIC: 3479 Metal coating & allied service

(G-8710)
WJ KETTLEWORKS LLC
55 Sperry Ave (06615-7317)
PHONE.....................203 377-5000
William J Kettles,
EMP: 3
SALES (est): 220K **Privately Held**
SIC: 3272 Concrete stuctural support & building material

(G-8711)
XAVIER MARCUS
Also Called: L 'espoir
25 Washburn Dr (06614-1735)
PHONE.....................203 543-2032
Xavier Marcus, *Owner*
EMP: 1
SALES (est): 57.9K **Privately Held**
SIC: 3559 3484 1799 1542 Semiconductor manufacturing machinery; machine guns or machine gun parts, 30 mm. & below; cleaning new buildings after construction; commercial & office building, new construction

(G-8712)
XG INDUSTRIES LLC
53 Hancock St (06615-6204)
PHONE.....................475 282-4643
Marx Bowens,
EMP: 11 **EST:** 2016
SALES (est): 2.6MM **Privately Held**
SIC: 2891 Adhesives & sealants

(G-8713)
YALE COMFORT SHOE CENTER INC
305 Boston Ave Fl 1 (06614-5246)
PHONE.....................203 338-8345
Marie Kaufman, *Principal*
EMP: 1
SALES (corp-wide): 591.3K **Privately Held**
SIC: 3842 Prosthetic appliances
PA: Yale Comfort Shoe Center Inc
627 Chapel St 629
New Haven CT 06511
203 777-2396

Suffield
Hartford County

(G-8714)
ARCOR SYSTEMS LLC
4 Kenny Roberts Mem Dr (06078-2529)
PHONE.....................860 370-9780
Gary Francoeur,
EMP: 2
SALES (est): 136.5K **Privately Held**
SIC: 3599 Machine shop, jobbing & repair

(G-8715)
BLESSED CREEK
908 Overhill Dr (06078-1944)
PHONE.....................860 416-3692
Jean Wild, *President*
EMP: 4
SALES (est): 308.8K **Privately Held**
SIC: 2844 Toilet preparations

(G-8716)
CADENCE CT INC
4 Kenny Roberts Mem Dr (06078-2529)
PHONE.....................860 370-9780
Alan Connor, *President*
EMP: 75
SQ FT: 30,000
SALES: 10MM
SALES (corp-wide): 55.1MM **Privately Held**
SIC: 3699 Laser welding, drilling & cutting equipment
PA: Cadence, Inc.
9 Technology Dr
Staunton VA 24401
540 248-2200

(G-8717)
DOUGHERTY SONS FUR STRETCHERS
878 North St (06078-1626)
PHONE.....................860 839-0096
Blake Dougherty, *Principal*
EMP: 2
SALES (est): 86.6K **Privately Held**
SIC: 3842 Stretchers

(G-8718)
EVANS COOLING SYSTEMS INC (PA)
1 Mountain Rd Ste 1 # 1 (06078-2163)
PHONE.....................860 668-1114
John W Evans, *President*
Catherine Wright, *General Mgr*
Jeffrey Bye, *COO*
Jeff Bye, *Vice Pres*
Andy Barbieri, *Sales Staff*
▼ **EMP:** 7
SALES (est): 1.5MM **Privately Held**
SIC: 3559 3724 Automotive related machinery; cooling systems, aircraft engine

(G-8719)
GAS TURBINE SUPPLY AND SVC LLC
120 Barndoor Hills Rd (06078-1350)
PHONE.....................860 254-5651
David A Leason,
▲ **EMP:** 1
SQ FT: 1,800
SALES (est): 272.5K **Privately Held**
SIC: 3511 Turbines & turbine generator set units, complete

(G-8720)
GAY TOOL & MACHINE
129 Kent Ave (06078-2229)
PHONE.....................860 668-5054
Stephen Bycenski, *Owner*
EMP: 1 **EST:** 1965
SQ FT: 1,500
SALES (est): 113.2K **Privately Held**
SIC: 3724 Aircraft engines & engine parts

(G-8721)
HP HOOD LLC
Ice Cream Division
1250 East St S (06078-2498)
PHONE.....................860 623-4435
Rick Kovarik, *Opers Mgr*
Scott Whitman, *Engineer*
Dana Johnson, *Sales Staff*
Joseph McFadden, *Sales Staff*
Derek Frost, *Analyst*
EMP: 225
SQ FT: 147,000
SALES (corp-wide): 2.2B **Privately Held**
WEB: www.hphood.com
SIC: 2024 Ice cream & frozen desserts
PA: Hp Hood Llc
6 Kimball Ln Ste 400
Lynnfield MA 01940
617 887-8441

(G-8722)
J J LANE DESIGNS
45 Shad Row (06078-1922)
PHONE.....................860 849-0815
Alison Gill, *Owner*
EMP: 1
SALES (est): 30.3K **Privately Held**
SIC: 5961 5944 3911 ; jewelry stores; jewelry apparel

(G-8723)
KONGSBERG ACTUATION (HQ)
Also Called: Kongsberg Automotive
1 Firestone Dr (06078-2611)
PHONE.....................860 668-1285
Hennings Jensen, *CEO*
Jonathan Day, *President*
James Fuda, *Treasurer*
Rachel Baxter, *Admin Sec*
▲ **EMP:** 6
SALES (est): 20.7MM **Privately Held**
SIC: 3052 Rubber & plastics hose & beltings

(G-8724)
M & J BUS INC
1353 South St (06078-2528)
PHONE.....................860 668-6526
EMP: 2
SALES (est): 115.3K **Privately Held**
SIC: 7519 5012 3711 Recreational vehicle rental; buses; buses, all types, assembly of

(G-8725)
MARKOWSKI FARM
101 3rd St (06078-1824)
PHONE.....................860 668-5033
Peter Markowski, *Owner*
EMP: 2
SALES (est): 190K **Privately Held**
SIC: 2141 Tobacco stemming & redrying

(G-8726)
METAL FINISH EQP & SUP CO INC
Also Called: Metfin Shot Blast Systems
19 Kenny Roberts Mem Dr (06078-2500)
PHONE.....................860 668-1050
Richard Rush, *CEO*
Nancy Austermann, *Business Mgr*
Robert Rush, *Vice Pres*
Corinne Smith, *Design Engr*
George Giles, *VP Sales*
▲ **EMP:** 27
SQ FT: 10,000
SALES (est): 14.9MM **Privately Held**
WEB: www.metfin.com
SIC: 5084 2892 Materials handling machinery; machine tools & accessories; explosives

(G-8727)
MOBILE MINI INC
911 S St Mach 1 Indus Par 1 Mach (06078)
PHONE.....................860 668-1888
Brian Lowder, *Manager*
EMP: 20
SALES (corp-wide): 593.2MM **Publicly Held**
SIC: 3448 3441 3412 7359 Buildings, portable: prefabricated metal; fabricated structural metal; drums, shipping: metal; shipping container leasing
PA: Mobile Mini, Inc.
4646 E Van Buren St # 400
Phoenix AZ 85008
480 894-6311

(G-8728)
PATRIOTIC SPIRIT
251 Hill St (06078-1507)
PHONE.....................704 239-4289
Chris Seman, *Owner*
EMP: 1
SALES (est): 72.4K **Privately Held**
SIC: 3553 Woodworking machinery

(G-8729)
PRAXAIR INC
1 U Car St (06078-2454)
PHONE.....................860 292-5400
Jim Bozzone, *Opers-Prdtn-Mfg*
EMP: 64
SQ FT: 4,832 **Privately Held**
SIC: 2813 Industrial gases
HQ: Praxair, Inc.
10 Riverview Dr
Danbury CT 06810
203 837-2000

(G-8730)
PRICING EXCELLENCE LLC
Also Called: Data Ladder
68 Bridge St Unit 304 (06078-3108)
PHONE.....................866 557-8102
Nathan Krol, *Mng Member*
EMP: 1
SALES (est): 113.1K **Privately Held**
SIC: 8742 7371 7372 Financial consultant; computer software development; business oriented computer software

(G-8731)
PRO GRAPHICS INC
378 Thompsonville Rd (06078-1312)
PHONE.....................860 668-9067
EMP: 15
SQ FT: 4,000
SALES (est): 1.2MM **Privately Held**
SIC: 7336 2752 Graphic Art Service

(G-8732)
RALPH B FLETCHER LOGGING & LAN
834 East St S (06078-2402)
PHONE.....................860 668-5404
Ralph B Fletcher, *Owner*
EMP: 3
SALES (est): 187.5K **Privately Held**
SIC: 2411 Logging camps & contractors

(G-8733)
ROAMING RACEWAY AND RR LLC
755 Sheldon St (06078-2052)
PHONE.....................413 531-3390
Danny Decosmo, *Principal*
EMP: 4
SALES (est): 266.6K **Privately Held**
SIC: 3644 Raceways

(G-8734)
ROARING ACRES ALPACAS LLC
685 Hale St (06078-2505)
PHONE.....................860 668-7075
Alison Mnich, *Principal*
EMP: 2
SALES (est): 85.5K **Privately Held**
SIC: 2231 Alpacas, mohair: woven

(G-8735)
SAVAGE ARMS INC
118 Mountain Rd (06078-2068)
PHONE.....................860 668-7049
Brian Herrick, *Principal*
EMP: 2 **EST:** 2011
SALES (est): 160K **Privately Held**
SIC: 3484 Small arms

(G-8736)
STONE IMAGE CUSTOM CONCRETE
1186 Old Coach Xing (06078-1538)
PHONE.....................860 668-2434
Robert Heim, *Principal*
EMP: 3

Suffield - Hartford County (G-8737)

SALES (est): 228.8K **Privately Held**
SIC: 3272 Cast stone, concrete

(G-8737)
UNITED GEAR & MACHINE CO INC
1087 East St S (06078-2405)
PHONE................860 623-6618
William J Malec, *President*
Genevieve Malec, *Corp Secy*
EMP: 10 EST: 1955
SALES (est): 1.5MM **Privately Held**
SIC: 3599 3462 Machine shop, jobbing & repair; gears, forged steel

(G-8738)
WELDINGRODSCOM LLC
1242 South St (06078-2522)
P.O. Box 3263, Windsor Locks (06096-3263)
PHONE................888 935-3703
David Miller, *Mng Member*
EMP: 2
SALES (est): 149.8K **Privately Held**
SIC: 3356 Welding rods

(G-8739)
WOODWORKERS RESOURCE
10 Wren Dr (06078)
PHONE................860 668-4100
Frank Tomeo, *Owner*
EMP: 2
SALES (est): 179.8K **Privately Held**
SIC: 2499 Decorative wood & woodwork

Taftville
New London County

(G-8740)
C B FABRICATION
342 Norwich Ave (06380-1224)
PHONE................860 889-8030
David Morgenstein, *Owner*
EMP: 1
SQ FT: 2,500
SALES (est): 113K **Privately Held**
SIC: 5531 3711 Automotive parts; speed shops, including race car supplies; automobile assembly, including specialty automobiles

(G-8741)
GP INDUSTRIES
500 Norwich Ave Ste 7 (06380-1335)
PHONE................860 859-9938
Vesselin Zaprianov, *President*
EMP: 7
SALES (est): 552.6K **Privately Held**
SIC: 3089 Battery cases, plastic or plastic combination

(G-8742)
PROKOP SIGN CO
Also Called: Prokop Signs & Graphics
338 Norwich Ave (06380-1254)
PHONE................860 889-6265
Francis Houle, *Owner*
Karen Houle, *Co-Owner*
EMP: 3
SALES (est): 283K **Privately Held**
WEB: www.prokopsigns.com
SIC: 3993 Signs & advertising specialties

Tariffville
Hartford County

(G-8743)
ANCHOR OVERHEAD DOOR SALES
24 Wooster Rd (06081-9656)
P.O. Box 552 (06081-0552)
PHONE................860 651-6560
Eugene D Holt, *Principal*
EMP: 1
SALES (est): 146.7K **Privately Held**
SIC: 2431 Garage doors, overhead: wood

(G-8744)
APPLIED POROUS TECH INC
2 Tunxis Rd Ste 103 (06081-9687)
P.O. Box 569 (06081-0569)
PHONE................860 408-9793
Edward Swiniarski, *President*
Heidi Eisenhaure, *Vice Pres*
▲ EMP: 12
SQ FT: 7,500
SALES (est): 1.8MM **Privately Held**
WEB: www.appliedporous.com
SIC: 3569 Filters, general line: industrial; filters

(G-8745)
VERTICAL REALMS LLC
38 White Water Turn (06081-9649)
PHONE................860 508-5273
Linda S Boyd, *Principal*
EMP: 1
SALES (est): 69.4K **Privately Held**
SIC: 2591 Blinds vertical

Terryville
Litchfield County

(G-8746)
ADVANCED MICRO CONTROLS INC
Also Called: Amci
20 Gear Dr (06786-7314)
PHONE................860 585-1254
William Erb, *President*
Richard Eykelhoff, *General Mgr*
Stancho Djiev, *Engineer*
Stanko Mantchev, *Design Engr*
Bob Alesio, *Sales Dir*
◆ EMP: 38
SQ FT: 16,000
SALES: 10.3MM **Privately Held**
WEB: www.amciworld.com
SIC: 3625 Controls for adjustable speed drives

(G-8747)
ALLREAD PRODUCTS CO LLC
22 S Main St (06786-6212)
PHONE................860 589-3566
William Allread,
EMP: 19
SQ FT: 8,000
SALES: 1MM **Privately Held**
WEB: www.allreadproducts.com
SIC: 3399 2821 Powder, metal; plastics materials & resins

(G-8748)
C-B MANUFACTURING & TOOL CO
118 Napco Dr (06786-7309)
P.O. Box 61 (06786-0061)
PHONE................860 583-5402
Bruce Czaplicki, *President*
Sally Czaplicki, *Vice Pres*
EMP: 4 EST: 1963
SQ FT: 4,000
SALES: 240K **Privately Held**
WEB: www.rimfg.com
SIC: 3599 Machine shop, jobbing & repair

(G-8749)
CASTLE TECHNOLOGIES INC
5 Cross Rd (06786-5800)
PHONE................860 582-7299
George Castle, *President*
EMP: 1
SALES: 200K **Privately Held**
SIC: 3544 Special dies, tools, jigs & fixtures

(G-8750)
CPS MILLWORKS LLC
5 Katy Ct (06786-5703)
PHONE................860 283-4276
Claudia Senetcen,
EMP: 1
SALES (est): 39.6K **Privately Held**
SIC: 3999 Manufacturing industries

(G-8751)
DRILL RITE CARBIDE TOOL CO
6 Orchard St (06786-6017)
PHONE................860 583-3200
Donald Tanguay, *President*
EMP: 5
SALES (est): 403.8K **Privately Held**
SIC: 3545 Cutting tools for machine tools

(G-8752)
ELM PRESS INCORPORATED
16 Tremco Dr (06786-7312)
PHONE................860 583-3600
Victor L Losure, *President*
Dennis Martel, *Mfg Staff*
Julie McNellis, *Manager*
Joel A Zinn, *Admin Sec*
EMP: 40 EST: 1961
SQ FT: 13,200
SALES (est): 7.6MM **Privately Held**
WEB: www.elmpress.com
SIC: 2752 2791 2789 2759 Commercial printing, offset; typesetting; bookbinding & related work; commercial printing

(G-8753)
ES METAL FABRICATIONS INC
11 Allread Dr (06786-7300)
PHONE................860 585-6067
Eric Schleich, *President*
Russell Schleich, *Vice Pres*
Arianna Devre, *Office Mgr*
▲ EMP: 17
SQ FT: 6,000
SALES (est): 3.6MM **Privately Held**
WEB: www.esmetal.com
SIC: 3441 Fabricated structural metal

(G-8754)
EXTERIOR TRIM SPECIALITIES LLC
84 Napco Dr (06786-7315)
PHONE................860 261-5194
EMP: 2
SALES (est): 197.4K **Privately Held**
SIC: 2431 Millwork

(G-8755)
FURNACE SOURCE LLC
99 Agney Ave (06786-6224)
PHONE................860 582-4201
Marshall Klimasewiski,
EMP: 18
SALES (est): 4.2MM **Privately Held**
WEB: www.thefurnacesource.com
SIC: 3567 3841 Industrial furnaces & ovens; medical instruments & equipment, blood & bone work

(G-8756)
FX MODELS LLC
111 Seymour Rd (06786-4512)
PHONE................860 589-5279
Marc L Dantonio, *Principal*
Jodi D Antonio,
Ed Miarecki,
EMP: 4
SALES: 80K **Privately Held**
WEB: www.fxmodels.com
SIC: 3999 7812 Models, except toy; industrial motion picture production

(G-8757)
GENOVESE MANUFACTURING CO
8 Bombard Ct (06786-4403)
P.O. Box 2112, Bristol (06011-2112)
PHONE................860 582-9944
Mike Genovese, *Vice Pres*
Vincent Genovese Jr, *Shareholder*
EMP: 10
SQ FT: 15,000
SALES (est): 1.7MM **Privately Held**
SIC: 3599 Machine shop, jobbing & repair

(G-8758)
GLEN MANUFACTURING CO INC
19 Church St (06786-5112)
P.O. Box 101 (06786-0101)
PHONE................860 589-0881
Christopher M Davey, *President*
EMP: 2 EST: 1963
SALES: 500K **Privately Held**
SIC: 3469 Stamping metal for the trade

(G-8759)
GRAHAM TOOL AND MACHINE LLC
9 Container Dr (06786-7302)
PHONE................860 585-1261
Michael Graham, *Mng Member*
EMP: 6
SQ FT: 3,300
SALES (est): 869.6K **Privately Held**
SIC: 3599 Machine shop, jobbing & repair

(G-8760)
GRASSCHOPPERS LLC
29 Hillside Ave (06786-5401)
PHONE................860 294-1620
Jamie Clark, *Principal*
EMP: 1
SALES (est): 54.6K **Privately Held**
SIC: 3751 Motorcycles & related parts

(G-8761)
KEMBY MANUFACTURING
56 E Orchard St (06786-6113)
P.O. Box 116 (06786-0116)
PHONE................860 582-2850
Brad York, *Owner*
EMP: 3
SQ FT: 2,400
SALES (est): 100K **Privately Held**
SIC: 3451 Screw machine products

(G-8762)
LAURETANO SIGN GROUP INC
1 Tremco Dr (06786-7311)
PHONE................860 582-0233
Michael Lauretano, *President*
Patrick Byrne, *President*
Joanne West, *Corp Secy*
EMP: 50
SQ FT: 28,000
SALES (est): 9.3MM **Privately Held**
WEB: www.lauretano.com
SIC: 3993 Electric signs

(G-8763)
LORANCTIS ORGNAL WOODWORKS LLC
78 Allen St (06786-6402)
PHONE................860 924-8810
Thomas J R Lorancaitis, *Principal*
EMP: 1
SALES (est): 54.1K **Privately Held**
SIC: 2431 Millwork

(G-8764)
MALCO INC
Also Called: Brass Traditions
38 Napco Dr (06786-7307)
P.O. Box 326 (06786-0326)
PHONE................860 584-0446
Michael L Theriault, *President*
Allen J Theriault, *Vice Pres*
Allen Theriault, *Vice Pres*
EMP: 11 EST: 1972
SQ FT: 8,000
SALES (est): 1.8MM **Privately Held**
WEB: www.malco.com
SIC: 3648 Lighting equipment

(G-8765)
MICHAUD TOOL CO INC
122 Napco Dr (06786-7309)
P.O. Box 430 (06786-0430)
PHONE................860 582-6785
Roy Michaud, *President*
Darlene Michaud, *Corp Secy*
James Michaud, *Vice Pres*
EMP: 5
SQ FT: 4,500
SALES (est): 623.9K **Privately Held**
SIC: 3599 3544 Electrical discharge machining (EDM); special dies & tools

(G-8766)
NEW ENGLAND FUELS & ENERGY LLC
86 Allen St (06786-6403)
PHONE................860 585-5917
James Schultz, *Principal*
EMP: 3 EST: 2010
SALES (est): 168.9K **Privately Held**
SIC: 2869 Fuels

GEOGRAPHIC SECTION
Thomaston - Litchfield County (G-8795)

(G-8767)
NORTH EAST FASTENERS CORP
8 Tremco Dr (06786-7312)
P.O. Box 322 (06786-0322)
PHONE..................................860 589-3242
Eric Webster, *President*
Diane Webster, *Vice Pres*
Joseph Longo, *QC Mgr*
Mike Dichello, *Info Tech Dir*
▲ **EMP:** 22 **EST:** 1963
SQ FT: 9,000
SALES (est): 3.7MM **Privately Held**
WEB: www.nef1.com
SIC: 3452 3316 Screws, metal; cold finishing of steel shapes

(G-8768)
R & I MANUFACTURING CO
118 Napco Dr (06786-7309)
PHONE..................................860 589-6364
Bruce Czatlicki, *Owner*
EMP: 10 **EST:** 1968
SQ FT: 2,400
SALES (est): 1.1MM **Privately Held**
SIC: 3535 Robotic conveyors

(G-8769)
RAY MACHINE CORPORATION
84 Town Hill Rd (06786-5802)
P.O. Box 47 (06786-0047)
PHONE..................................860 582-8202
Raymond Lassy, *President*
Brian Lassy, *Vice Pres*
EMP: 20 **EST:** 1955
SQ FT: 15,000
SALES: 700K **Privately Held**
WEB: www.raymachinecorp.com
SIC: 3545 3544 Precision tools, machinists'; special dies & tools; jigs: inspection, gauging & checking

(G-8770)
SNOWATHOME LLC
84 Napco Dr Ste 6 (06786-7315)
PHONE..................................860 584-2991
Matt Pittman, *Principal*
Alissa Pittman, *COO*
▲ **EMP:** 3
SALES (est): 401.8K **Privately Held**
SIC: 3585 Snowmaking machinery

(G-8771)
SPARGO MACHINE PRODUCTS INC
6 Gear Dr (06786-7314)
PHONE..................................860 583-3925
Randy Spargo, *President*
Carole Spargo, *Admin Sec*
EMP: 11
SALES (est): 1.9MM **Privately Held**
SIC: 3599 Machine shop, jobbing & repair

(G-8772)
STITCHES & SEAMS USA LLC
412 Main St Apt 16 (06786-5609)
PHONE..................................708 872-7326
Frank Ippolito, *Principal*
EMP: 1
SALES (est): 40.7K **Privately Held**
SIC: 2395 Embroidery & art needlework

(G-8773)
SUPERIOR WELDING
15 Ridge Rd (06786-4515)
PHONE..................................860 584-2632
James Bourgoin, *Principal*
EMP: 1
SALES (est): 36.9K **Privately Held**
SIC: 7692 Welding repair

(G-8774)
TECHNOLOGY PLASTICS LLC
75 Napco Dr (06786-7305)
PHONE..................................806 583-1590
Tom Fernandes, *CEO*
Edward Butkevich,
▲ **EMP:** 15
SQ FT: 46,000
SALES (est): 2.2MM **Privately Held**
SIC: 3089 Injection molding of plastics

(G-8775)
TRIEM INDUSTRIES LLC
105 Napco Dr (06786-7310)
PHONE..................................203 888-1212
Lea Mola, *General Mgr*
Douglas A Mola, *Mng Member*
Robert D Mola,
▲ **EMP:** 28
SQ FT: 23,000
SALES (est): 5.8MM **Privately Held**
WEB: www.triemindustries.com
SIC: 3452 Screws, metal

(G-8776)
UNIPRISE INTERNATIONAL INC
Also Called: Uniprise Sales
50 Napco Dr (06786-7307)
P.O. Box 369 (06786-0369)
PHONE..................................860 589-7262
Philip Porter, *President*
Douglas Porter, *Vice Pres*
EMP: 24
SQ FT: 10,000
SALES (est): 4.7MM **Privately Held**
SIC: 3599 3423 Tubing, flexible metallic; soldering tools

(G-8777)
VICTORY FUEL LLC
248 Main St (06786-5901)
PHONE..................................860 585-0532
Samuel J Gizzie Jr, *Owner*
EMP: 8
SALES (est): 903.6K **Privately Held**
SIC: 2869 Fuels

Thomaston
Litchfield County

(G-8778)
ALBEA THOMASTON INC
60 Electric Ave (06787-1617)
PHONE..................................860 283-2000
Francois Luscan, *CEO*
Axel Moreau, *Exec VP*
Carlos Amaro, *Opers Mgr*
Joseph Eharth, *Engineer*
Roger Pappineau, *Engineer*
▲ **EMP:** 370
SQ FT: 150,000
SALES (est): 121.4MM **Privately Held**
SIC: 2844 Cosmetic preparations
HQ: Albea Americas, Inc.
191 State Route 31 N
Washington NJ 07882

(G-8779)
BALDWIN THREAD ROLLING
40 Hillside Ave (06787-1442)
PHONE..................................860 283-4948
Raymond Baldwin, *Owner*
EMP: 1
SALES (est): 74.6K **Privately Held**
SIC: 3541 Screw & thread machines

(G-8780)
BEARDSWORTH GROUP INC
1085 Waterbury Rd (06787-2028)
P.O. Box 358, Woodbury (06798-0358)
PHONE..................................860 283-4014
Douglas Beardsworth, *President*
Carrie Beardsworth, *Admin Sec*
▲ **EMP:** 5
SALES (est): 885.2K **Privately Held**
WEB: www.beardsworthgroup.com
SIC: 3565 5084 Packaging machinery; industrial machinery & equipment

(G-8781)
BIEDERMANN MFG INDS INC
Also Called: B M I South
135 S Main St (06787-1754)
PHONE..................................860 283-8268
Fax: 860 283-5222
EMP: 50
SALES (corp-wide): 5.7MM **Privately Held**
SIC: 3451 Mfr Screw Machine Products
PA: Biedermann Manufacturing Industries Incorporated
4500 Preslyn Dr
Raleigh NC
919 878-7776

(G-8782)
BROOKFIELD INDUSTRIES INC
99 W Hillside Ave (06787-1433)
PHONE..................................860 283-6211
Karl P Kinzer, *President*
Chris S Kinzer, *Vice Pres*
EMP: 25
SQ FT: 10,000
SALES: 4.7MM **Privately Held**
WEB: www.brookfieldindustries.com
SIC: 3699 3429 Electrical equipment & supplies; manufactured hardware (general)

(G-8783)
CARTER INV HOLDINGS CORP (HQ)
401 Watertown Rd (06787-1990)
PHONE..................................860 283-5801
Jon Carter, *CEO*
EMP: 3 **EST:** 2012
SALES (est): 49.5MM **Privately Held**
SIC: 1731 3621 7694 Electrical work; motors & generators; armature rewinding shops
PA: Ward Leonard Holdings Llc
401 Watertown Rd
Thomaston CT 06787
860 283-5801

(G-8784)
CHANDLER INDUSTRIES LLC
117 E Main St (06787-1611)
PHONE..................................860 283-8147
Holly Chandler, *Principal*
EMP: 2
SALES (est): 83.7K **Privately Held**
SIC: 3999 Candles

(G-8785)
CHAPMAN LUMBER INC
Also Called: Benjamin Moore Authorized Ret
224 Watertown Rd (06787-1920)
PHONE..................................860 283-6213
David Chapman, *President*
Stewart Chapman, *Vice Pres*
Stuart Chapman, *Vice Pres*
Denise Hayes, *Department Mgr*
EMP: 30 **EST:** 1952
SQ FT: 50,000
SALES (est): 7MM **Privately Held**
WEB: www.chapmanlumberinc.com
SIC: 5211 2431 5231 Millwork & lumber; millwork; paint, glass & wallpaper

(G-8786)
CORESLAB STRUCTURES CONN INC
1023 Waterbury Rd (06787-2028)
P.O. Box 279 (06787-0279)
PHONE..................................860 283-8281
Mario Franciosa, *President*
Frank Franciosa, *Corp Secy*
Leon Grant, *Vice Pres*
Herman Pelletier, *Plant Mgr*
Angela Kackowski, *Human Res Dir*
EMP: 80
SQ FT: 45,000
SALES (est): 14MM
SALES (corp-wide): 27.3MM **Privately Held**
SIC: 8712 1771 3272 Architectural services; concrete work; precast terrazo or concrete products
HQ: Coreslab Structures (Ont) Inc
205 Coreslab Dr
Dundas ON L9H 0
905 689-3993

(G-8787)
DON S SCREW MACHINE PDTS LLC
247 Old Northfield Rd (06787-1140)
PHONE..................................860 283-6448
Donald Carl Schlicher,
EMP: 3
SALES (est): 114.3K **Privately Held**
SIC: 3451 Screw machine products

(G-8788)
EDWARD SEGAL INC
360 Reynolds Bridge Rd (06787-1914)
P.O. Box 429 (06787-0429)
PHONE..................................860 283-5821
David Segal, *President*

Mike Gerback, *COO*
Margaret Bartone, *Purchasing*
Tommy Trufan, *Engineer*
Richard Segal, *Shareholder*
▲ **EMP:** 20 **EST:** 1942
SQ FT: 20,000
SALES (est): 4.5MM **Privately Held**
SIC: 3559 Buttonhole & eyelet machines & attachments, industrial

(G-8789)
ELEMENT 119 LLC
296 Reynolds Bridge Rd (06787-1996)
PHONE..................................860 358-0119
Andrew Zeppa, *President*
EMP: 10
SQ FT: 4,000
SALES (est): 4MM **Privately Held**
SIC: 2851 Undercoatings, paint; lacquers, varnishes, enamels & other coatings

(G-8790)
FUTURE SWISS
41 Electric Ave (06787-1651)
PHONE..................................860 283-4358
Alfred R Smith, *Principal*
EMP: 2
SALES (est): 144K **Privately Held**
SIC: 3446 Ornamental metalwork

(G-8791)
HALLDEN SHEAR SERVICE OF AMER
Also Called: Hallden America
290 Reynolds Bridge Rd (06787-1975)
P.O. Box 217 (06787-0217)
PHONE..................................860 283-4386
Mary Lou Osterman, *President*
John Osterman Sr, *Vice Pres*
EMP: 3
SQ FT: 2,400
SALES (est): 359.7K **Privately Held**
WEB: www.hallden.com
SIC: 7699 3541 Tool repair services; sawing & cutoff machines (metalworking machinery)

(G-8792)
INTRASONICS INC
1401 Waterbury Rd (06787-2030)
P.O. Box 186 (06787-0186)
PHONE..................................860 283-8040
Keith Rogozinski, *President*
Peter Rogozinski, *Vice Pres*
Donald Charette, *Admin Sec*
EMP: 5
SALES (est): 726.2K **Privately Held**
WEB: www.intrasonics.com
SIC: 3599 Machine shop, jobbing & repair

(G-8793)
J & J PRECISION EYELET INC
116 Waterbury Rd (06787-1829)
PHONE..................................860 283-8243
John Stephen Maxwell, *President*
EMP: 70
SQ FT: 3,000
SALES: 13.7MM **Privately Held**
WEB: www.jjprecision.com
SIC: 3965 2834 3469 Eyelets, metal: clothing, fabrics, boots or shoes; pharmaceutical preparations; stamping metal for the trade

(G-8794)
JFS INDUSTRIES
90 Walnut St Apt B (06787-1553)
PHONE..................................203 592-0754
EMP: 3
SALES (est): 146.3K **Privately Held**
SIC: 3999 Manufacturing industries

(G-8795)
K-TEC LLC
33 River St Ste 2 (06787-1714)
PHONE..................................860 283-8875
Christine Misluk, *Manager*
Milan Keklak,
EMP: 4
SALES: 175K **Privately Held**
WEB: www.ktecmolding.com
SIC: 3089 Injection molding of plastics

Thomaston - Litchfield County (G-8796)

(G-8796)
LASER TOOL COMPANY INC
98 N Main St (06787-1654)
P.O. Box 278 (06787-0278)
PHONE 860 283-8284
Faye Duquette, *President*
EMP: 15
SQ FT: 4,840
SALES (est): 2MM **Privately Held**
SIC: **3541** Machine tools, metal cutting type

(G-8797)
METALLON INC
1415 Waterbury Rd (06787-2030)
PHONE 860 283-8265
Paul P Ayoub, *Principal*
Dennis Hayes, *Project Mgr*
Suzann Ackers, *Office Mgr*
Elfriede Fieldman, *Branch Mgr*
Roger Porter, *Manager*
EMP: 50
SQ FT: 30,000
SALES (est): 11.6MM **Privately Held**
WEB: www.metallon.com
SIC: **3469** **3728** Stamping metal for the trade; aircraft assemblies, subassemblies & parts

(G-8798)
NATIONAL SPRING & STAMPING INC
135 S Main St Ste 8 (06787-1754)
P.O. Box 369 (06787-0369)
PHONE 860 283-0203
Walter Janczyk, *President*
William Yeske III, *Corp Secy*
Raymond Kowalec, *Vice Pres*
EMP: 22
SQ FT: 8,000
SALES (est): 4.3MM **Privately Held**
WEB: www.nationalsprings.com
SIC: **3495** **3469** Wire springs; stamping metal for the trade

(G-8799)
NOLAN WOODWORKING LLC
135 S Main St Ste 14 (06787-1754)
PHONE 860 283-6000
EMP: 2
SALES (est): 59.5K **Privately Held**
SIC: **2431** Millwork

(G-8800)
PALMER DEEP DRAW STAMPING LLC
135 S Main St (06787-1754)
P.O. Box 120 (06787-0120)
PHONE 860 880-8022
Martin J Palmer,
EMP: 1
SQ FT: 5,000
SALES: 500K **Privately Held**
SIC: **3221** Cosmetic jars, glass

(G-8801)
QUALITY ROLLING DEBURRING INC
135 S Main St Ste 3 (06787-1754)
P.O. Box 128 (06787-0128)
PHONE 860 283-0271
George Lacapra, *Ch of Bd*
George Lacapra Jr, *President*
Ronald Stango, *Director*
EMP: 90 EST: 1949
SQ FT: 110,000
SALES (est): 8.6MM **Privately Held**
WEB: www.qualityrolling.com
SIC: **3471** Finishing, metals or formed products

(G-8802)
REYNOLDS CARBIDE DIE CO INC
27 Reynolds Bridge Rd (06787-1910)
P.O. Box 326 (06787-0326)
PHONE 860 283-8246
James Zaccaria, *President*
Michael Masi Jr, *Vice Pres*
EMP: 35 EST: 1971
SQ FT: 12,000
SALES (est): 5.9MM **Privately Held**
WEB: www.rcdinc.com
SIC: **3552** **3544** Textile machinery; special dies & tools

(G-8803)
RISDON MANUFACTURING CO
60 Electric Ave (06787-1617)
PHONE 860 283-2000
Robert Brands, *Principal*
EMP: 2
SALES (est): 149.2K **Privately Held**
SIC: **3999** Manufacturing industries

(G-8804)
S & M SWISS PRODUCTS INC
135 S Main St Ste 7 (06787-1754)
PHONE 860 283-4020
Gerald Maccione, *President*
EMP: 4 EST: 1978
SQ FT: 5,400
SALES (est): 552.4K **Privately Held**
SIC: **3451** Screw machine products

(G-8805)
SELECTIVES LLC
166 Litchfield St (06787-1427)
P.O. Box 336 (06787-0336)
PHONE 860 585-1956
EMP: 5
SALES (est): 475.2K **Privately Held**
SIC: **3089** Mfg Plastic Products

(G-8806)
STEVENS COMPANY INCORPORATED
1085 Waterbury Rd 1 (06787-2028)
P.O. Box 428 (06787-0428)
PHONE 860 283-8201
Doug Stevens, *President*
Jannette Stevens, *President*
Adelina Otano, *Buyer*
Michele Caulfield, *Admin Sec*
▲ EMP: 65
SQ FT: 40,000
SALES: 5.1MM **Privately Held**
WEB: www.stevenscompanyinc.com
SIC: **3469** **3965** Metal stampings; eyelets, metal: clothing, fabrics, boots or shoes

(G-8807)
STEWART EFI LLC (PA)
45 Old Waterbury Rd (06787-1903)
PHONE 860 283-8213
Mike Morrissey, *President*
Angel Sanchez, *Plant Mgr*
Debbie Eckert, *Buyer*
Chris Carey, *Engineer*
Marty Dionne, *Engineer*
EMP: 105
SQ FT: 98,000
SALES (est): 64.6MM **Privately Held**
WEB: www.stewartefi.com
SIC: **3469** Stamping metal for the trade

(G-8808)
STEWART EFI LLC
332 Reynolds Bridge Rd (06787-1914)
PHONE 860 283-2523
Daniel Stokes, *Manager*
EMP: 25
SALES (corp-wide): 64.6MM **Privately Held**
WEB: www.stewartefi.com
SIC: **3469** Metal stampings
PA: Stewart Efi, Llc
   45 Old Waterbury Rd
   Thomaston CT 06787
   860 283-8213

(G-8809)
STEWART EFI CONNECTICUT LLC
45 Old Waterbury Rd (06787-1903)
PHONE 860 283-8213
Daniel Stokes, *Mng Member*
Phillip Rejeski,
Bernie Rosselli,
EMP: 110
SQ FT: 98,000
SALES (est): 18.7MM
SALES (corp-wide): 64.6MM **Privately Held**
WEB: www.stewartefi.com
SIC: **3469** Metal stampings
PA: Stewart Efi, Llc
   45 Old Waterbury Rd
   Thomaston CT 06787
   860 283-8213

(G-8810)
STEWART EFI TEXAS LLC
45 Old Waterbury Rd (06787-1903)
PHONE 860 283-8213
Dan Stokes, *Mng Member*
EMP: 2
SALES (est): 97.7K **Privately Held**
SIC: **3469** Stamping metal for the trade

(G-8811)
SUMMIT CORPORATION OF AMERICA
Also Called: Summit Finishing Division
1430 Waterbury Rd (06787-2098)
PHONE 860 283-4391
Harry M Scoble, *Principal*
Larry Buhl, *Director*
Daniel Stokes, *Director*
Linda L Scapellati, *Admin Sec*
▲ EMP: 83
SQ FT: 140,000
SALES (est): 23.7MM **Privately Held**
WEB: www.scact.com
SIC: **3471** **3479** Electroplating of metals or formed products; etching on metals

(G-8812)
THOMASTN-MDTOWN SCREW MCH PDTS
550 N Main St (06787-1315)
P.O. Box 249 (06787-0249)
PHONE 860 283-9796
Robert P Lyman, *President*
Celeste Parsons, *Vice Pres*
EMP: 15 EST: 1963
SQ FT: 7,500
SALES (est): 2.2MM **Privately Held**
WEB: www.mypww.com
SIC: **3451** Screw machine products

(G-8813)
THOMASTON INDUSTRIES INC
41 Electric Ave (06787-1651)
P.O. Box 308 (06787-0308)
PHONE 860 283-4358
Dennis Diemand, *President*
EMP: 10
SALES (est): 1.7MM **Privately Held**
SIC: **3451** Screw machine products; barber & beauty shop equipment

(G-8814)
TREADWELL CORPORATION
341 Railroad St (06787-1667)
P.O. Box 458 (06787-0458)
PHONE 860 283-7600
John A Johnson, *CEO*
Robert Johnson, *COO*
Steven Malaspina, *Exec VP*
Michael Patruski, *Vice Pres*
EMP: 33
SQ FT: 30,000
SALES (est): 16.3MM **Privately Held**
WEB: www.treadwellcorp.com
SIC: **3564** Air purification equipment

(G-8815)
TYLER AUTOMATICS INCORPORATED
Also Called: Thomaston Swiss
437 S Main St (06787-1816)
P.O. Box 247 (06787-0247)
PHONE 860 283-5878
George Kowaleski, *President*
EMP: 20 EST: 1947
SQ FT: 20,000
SALES (est): 5.9MM **Privately Held**
SIC: **3451** Screw machine products

(G-8816)
UNIMETAL SURFACE FINISHING LLC (PA)
135 S Main St (06787-1754)
P.O. Box 902 (06787-0902)
PHONE 860 283-0271
Armand Deangelis, *Plant Mgr*
Ron Stango, *Facilities Mgr*
Marco Quintana, *Engineer*
Michele Sovia, *Sales Staff*
George Lacapra Jr, *Mng Member*
EMP: 50 EST: 2011
SALES (est): 22.7MM **Privately Held**
SIC: **2843** Finishing agents

(G-8817)
VALLEY WELDING CO INC
164 S Main St (06787-1741)
PHONE 860 283-5768
Paul Yoos, *President*
Christine Yoos, *Admin Sec*
EMP: 1
SALES (est): 189.1K **Privately Held**
SIC: **7692** **3441** Welding repair; fabricated structural metal

(G-8818)
WARD LEONARD CT LLC (DH)
401 Watertown Rd (06787-1990)
PHONE 860 283-5801
Jon Carter, *CEO*
Mike Clute, *President*
Margaret Pellegren, *Editor*
Bill Berger, *Business Mgr*
April Brodeur, *Materials Mgr*
◆ EMP: 199
SQ FT: 135,000
SALES (est): 49.5MM
SALES (corp-wide): 49.5MM **Privately Held**
SIC: **3621** **3625** Motors, electric; motor controls, electric
HQ: Ward Leonard Operating Llc
   401 Watertown Rd
   Thomaston CT 06787
   860 283-5801

(G-8819)
WARD LEONARD CT LLC
401 Watertown Rd (06787-1990)
PHONE 860 283-2294
Jon Carter, *President*
EMP: 56
SQ FT: 150,000
SALES (corp-wide): 49.5MM **Privately Held**
SIC: **3621** Generators & sets, electric
HQ: Ward Leonard Ct Llc
   401 Watertown Rd
   Thomaston CT 06787
   860 283-5801

(G-8820)
WARD LEONARD HOLDINGS LLC (PA)
401 Watertown Rd (06787-1990)
PHONE 860 283-5801
Jon Carter, *CEO*
Philip Cordeiro, *Electrical Engi*
EMP: 4
SALES (est): 49.5MM **Privately Held**
SIC: **1731** **3621** **7694** Electrical work; motors & generators; armature rewinding shops

(G-8821)
WARD LEONARD INV HOLDINGS LLC (DH)
401 Watertown Rd (06787-1990)
PHONE 860 283-5801
Mike Clute, *President*
EMP: 3
SALES (est): 49.5MM **Privately Held**
SIC: **1731** **3621** **7694** Electrical work; motors & generators; armature rewinding shops
HQ: Carter Investment Holdings Corp.
   401 Watertown Rd
   Thomaston CT 06787
   860 283-5801

(G-8822)
WARD LEONARD OPERATING LLC (DH)
401 Watertown Rd (06787-1990)
PHONE 860 283-5801
Mike Clute, *President*
EMP: 3 EST: 1994
SALES (est): 49.5MM
SALES (corp-wide): 49.5MM **Privately Held**
SIC: **1731** **3621** **7694** Electrical work; motors & generators; armature rewinding shops
HQ: WI Intermediate Holdings, Llc
   401 Watertown Rd
   Thomaston CT 06787
   860 283-5801

▲ = Import ▼ = Export
◆ = Import/Export

GEOGRAPHIC SECTION

Tolland - Tolland County (G-8854)

(G-8823)
WARD LONARD HOUMA HOLDINGS LLC
401 Watertown Rd (06787-1990)
PHONE..................................860 283-5801
Mike Clute, *President*
EMP: 1
SALES (est): 71.7K
SALES (corp-wide): 49.5MM **Privately Held**
SIC: 1731 3621 7694 Electrical work; motors & generators; armature rewinding shops
HQ: Wl Intermediate Holdings, Llc
401 Watertown Rd
Thomaston CT 06787
860 283-5801

(G-8824)
WHYCO FINISHING TECH LLC
670 Waterbury Rd (06787-2099)
PHONE..................................860 283-5826
William Nicholas Post, *President*
Mike Patrick, *Engineer*
EMP: 47
SQ FT: 100,000
SALES: 6MM **Privately Held**
SIC: 3471 Plating of metals or formed products; chromium plating of metals or formed products

(G-8825)
WL INTERMEDIATE HOLDINGS LLC (DH)
401 Watertown Rd (06787-1990)
PHONE..................................860 283-5801
Mike Clute, *President*
EMP: 3
SALES (est): 49.5MM **Privately Held**
SIC: 1731 3621 7694 Electrical work; motors & generators; armature rewinding shops
HQ: Ward Leonard Investment Holdings Llc
401 Watertown Rd
Thomaston CT 06787
860 283-5801

(G-8826)
WTM COMPANY
135 S Main St Ste 12 (06787-1754)
P.O. Box 226 (06787-0226)
PHONE..................................860 283-5871
Stanley E Mossey, *President*
John R Laone, *President*
EMP: 5
SQ FT: 7,500
SALES (est): 880K **Privately Held**
SIC: 3429 Metal fasteners

(G-8827)
ZERO CHECK LLC
297 Reynolds Bridge Rd (06787-1974)
P.O. Box 903 (06787-0903)
PHONE..................................860 283-5629
James Upton,
EMP: 8 **EST:** 1983
SQ FT: 8,600
SALES (est): 1.3MM **Privately Held**
WEB: www.zerocheck.com
SIC: 3545 Gauges (machine tool accessories)

Thompson
Windham County

(G-8828)
AJ MFG
999 Quaddick Town Farm Rd (06277-2918)
P.O. Box 435 (06277-0435)
PHONE..................................860 963-7622
Pamela Bellavance, *Owner*
EMP: 5
SALES (est): 547.1K **Privately Held**
SIC: 2273 Floor coverings: paper, grass, reed, coir, sisal, jute, etc.

(G-8829)
B H DAVIS CO
227 Riverside Dr (06277-2713)
P.O. Box 70, Grosvenor Dale (06246-0070)
PHONE..................................860 923-2771
Bernard Davis, *Owner*
EMP: 3
SQ FT: 3,000
SALES: 100K **Privately Held**
SIC: 2431 5712 Millwork; cabinet work, custom

(G-8830)
BEN BARRETTS LLC
129 Robbins Rd (06277-2846)
PHONE..................................860 928-9373
Bernard Barrett, *President*
EMP: 5
SALES (est): 371.8K **Privately Held**
SIC: 2426 5031 5023 5211 Hardwood dimension & flooring mills; lumber, plywood & millwork; wood flooring; flooring, wood

(G-8831)
BRANDY HILL LOGGING
334 Brandy Hill Rd (06277-2425)
PHONE..................................860 923-3175
Robert W Kneeland, *Owner*
EMP: 1
SALES (est): 91.3K **Privately Held**
SIC: 2411 Logging

(G-8832)
CENTURY TOOL CO INC
753 Thompson Rd (06277-1939)
P.O. Box 314 (06277-0314)
PHONE..................................860 923-9523
Joseph Simonelli, *President*
EMP: 18
SQ FT: 8,000
SALES: 1.5MM **Privately Held**
WEB: www.centurytoolco.com
SIC: 3544 Special dies, tools, jigs & fixtures

(G-8833)
COURNOYER FLR SANDING FINSHG
424 Quaddick Rd (06277-2909)
PHONE..................................860 963-7088
William Cournoyer, *Owner*
EMP: 2
SALES: 50K **Privately Held**
SIC: 3553 Sanding machines, except portable floor sanders: woodworking

(G-8834)
HECK D TOOL LLC
Also Called: D Heck Tool
1250 Thompson Rd (06277-1321)
PHONE..................................860 935-9274
Dana Heckendorf, *President*
EMP: 2
SQ FT: 750
SALES: 200K **Privately Held**
SIC: 3089 3544 Injection molding of plastics; special dies, tools, jigs & fixtures

(G-8835)
JS INDUSTRIES
526 Quaddick Rd (06277-2911)
PHONE..................................860 928-0786
Joe Suich, *Principal*
EMP: 3 **EST:** 2017
SALES (est): 174.5K **Privately Held**
SIC: 3999 Manufacturing industries

(G-8836)
KEDO KONCEPTS LLC
310 W Thompson Rd (06277-2605)
PHONE..................................860 315-7392
Jeffrey S Thebado,
EMP: 1
SALES (est): 91.8K **Privately Held**
SIC: 3993 Electric signs

(G-8837)
LINCOLN PRECISION MACHINE INC
923 Thompson Rd (06277-1909)
PHONE..................................860 923-9358
Ronald Lincoln, *President*
Todd Lincoln, *Vice Pres*
EMP: 5 **EST:** 1997
SALES: 400K **Privately Held**
SIC: 3599 Machine shop, jobbing & repair

(G-8838)
LISA BARRETTE
38 Ballard Rd (06277-2801)
PHONE..................................860 928-0599
Lisa Barrette, *Principal*
EMP: 1
SALES (est): 39.6K **Privately Held**
SIC: 3999 Barrettes

(G-8839)
LITTLE T QARTER MIDGET CLB INC
205 E Thompson Rd (06277-1929)
PHONE..................................860 823-7258
Joseph Ferreira, *Principal*
EMP: 2 **EST:** 2014
SALES: 69.5K **Privately Held**
SIC: 3131 Quarters

(G-8840)
MOLDVISION LLC
316 County Home Rd (06277-2845)
PHONE..................................860 315-1025
John Carpenter, *President*
EMP: 3
SALES (est): 175.5K **Privately Held**
SIC: 3544 Industrial molds

(G-8841)
NUMA TOOL COMPANY (PA)
646 Thompson Rd (06277-2214)
P.O. Box 348 (06277-0348)
PHONE..................................860 923-9551
Ralph H Leonard, *President*
Laurene Darling, *Purch Mgr*
Mark Stickney, *CFO*
Dena Dugas, *Info Tech Mgr*
Wendy Bouchey, *Administration*
▼ **EMP:** 80
SQ FT: 52,000
SALES: 16MM **Privately Held**
WEB: www.numadth.com
SIC: 3532 3531 3533 5082 Drills & drilling equipment, mining (except oil & gas); hammer mills (rock & ore crushing machines), portable; oil & gas field machinery; general construction machinery & equipment; quarrying machinery & equipment

(G-8842)
R&R WOODWORKING
11 Lakeside Dr (06277-2907)
PHONE..................................508 202-3543
Robert Stlaurent, *Principal*
EMP: 1
SALES (est): 54.1K **Privately Held**
SIC: 2431 Millwork

(G-8843)
RENEWABLE ENERGY NATURAL RES
144 New Rd (06277-1913)
PHONE..................................860 923-1091
Robert Neundorf, *Mng Member*
EMP: 5
SALES (est): 216.6K **Privately Held**
SIC: 1796 3559 3589 8999 Power generating equipment installation; refinery, chemical processing & similar machinery; water purification equipment, household type; natural resource preservation service

(G-8844)
TOTAL DRILLING SUPPLY LLC
144 New Rd (06277-1913)
PHONE..................................860 923-1091
Robert Neundorf, *President*
Debra Neundorf, *CFO*
EMP: 2 **EST:** 2012
SALES (est): 124.5K **Privately Held**
SIC: 1381 Drilling oil & gas wells

Tolland
Tolland County

(G-8845)
3D SOLUTIONS LLC
60 Industrial Park Rd W (06084-2867)
PHONE..................................860 454-7302
Shawn Yates, *General Mgr*
EMP: 2
SALES (est): 394.1K **Privately Held**
SIC: 3599 Chemical milling job shop

(G-8846)
A Z WELDING
38 Goose Ln (06084-3411)
PHONE..................................860 872-1301
Daniel Martin, *Owner*
EMP: 1
SALES (est): 76.3K **Privately Held**
SIC: 7692 Welding repair

(G-8847)
ACCU-RITE TOOL & MFG CO
23 Industrial Park Rd W B (06084-2861)
PHONE..................................860 688-4844
Steve Gessay, *President*
Christophe Gessay, *Vice Pres*
EMP: 11 **EST:** 1956
SQ FT: 6,500
SALES: 1.1MM **Privately Held**
SIC: 3545 Machine tool attachments & accessories

(G-8848)
AMERICAN CUSTOM FINE WOODWRKNG
714 Crystal Lake Rd 2b (06084-2179)
PHONE..................................860 871-8783
Jennifer Norman, *Principal*
EMP: 2
SALES (est): 126.6K **Privately Held**
SIC: 2431 Millwork

(G-8849)
APPLE PUBLICATIONS ✪
105 Williams Way (06084-2533)
PHONE..................................860 392-8348
EMP: 1 **EST:** 2019
SALES (est): 37.5K **Privately Held**
SIC: 2741 Miscellaneous publishing

(G-8850)
B & D MACHINE INC
30 Industrial Park Rd E (06084-2805)
P.O. Box 791 (06084-0791)
PHONE..................................860 871-9226
Robert Stutz, *President*
Donald Gagnon, *Vice Pres*
Kenneth Gibbons, *Treasurer*
EMP: 12
SQ FT: 9,000
SALES: 1.5MM **Privately Held**
WEB: www.bdmachine.net
SIC: 3544 Industrial molds

(G-8851)
BAYTEK SIGN CO
169 Goose Ln (06084-3822)
PHONE..................................860 872-9279
Lynn Mullen, *President*
EMP: 1 **EST:** 1995
SALES (est): 130.8K **Privately Held**
SIC: 3993 Signs & advertising specialties

(G-8852)
BLUE CHIP TOOL
40 Tolland Stage Rd D4 (06084-2341)
PHONE..................................860 875-7999
Fred Bulach, *Owner*
EMP: 3
SALES: 250K **Privately Held**
SIC: 3545 Precision tools, machinists'

(G-8853)
C&S COLLECTIBLES
129 Torry Rd (06084-3037)
PHONE..................................860 872-6825
Scott Dean, *Owner*
Charlene Dean, *Owner*
EMP: 2 **EST:** 1992
SALES (est): 70.9K **Privately Held**
SIC: 3999 5947 2771 Manufacturing industries; gift, novelty & souvenir shop; greeting cards

(G-8854)
CLASSIC JIG GRINDING
38 Gerber Dr (06084-2851)
PHONE..................................860 870-4900
Ann T Morrin, *Principal*
EMP: 2
SALES (est): 251K **Privately Held**
SIC: 3599 Grinding castings for the trade; machine shop, jobbing & repair

Tolland - Tolland County (G-8855)   GEOGRAPHIC SECTION

(G-8855)
CONNECTICUT COMPONENTS INC
Also Called: Cciyes
60 Industrial Park Rd W # 2 (06084-2838)
PHONE..................................860 633-0277
Kimberly Jean Giansanti, *President*
Toni Cardone, *Opers Mgr*
Mike Pylkowski, *Sales Staff*
John Neligon, *Sales Executive*
▲ **EMP:** 6 **EST:** 1973
SALES: 3MM **Privately Held**
WEB: www.cciyes.com
SIC: 3999 Advertising display products

(G-8856)
CRISTA GRASSO LLC
Also Called: Criscara
55 Kendall Mountain Rd (06084-2121)
P.O. Box 868 (06084-0868)
PHONE..................................347 946-2533
Crista Grasso,
Jeremy Pollack,
EMP: 2
SALES (est): 151K **Privately Held**
SIC: 3961 5139 5632 7389 Costume jewelry; shoe accessories; women's dancewear, hosiery & lingerie; costume jewelry;

(G-8857)
D D M METAL FINISHING CO INC
25 Industrial Park Rd W (06084-2806)
P.O. Box 687 (06084-0687)
PHONE..................................860 872-4683
Daniel R Castonguay, *President*
EMP: 8
SQ FT: 2,500
SALES (est): 1MM **Privately Held**
SIC: 3471 Buffing for the trade; finishing, metals or formed products; polishing, metals or formed products

(G-8858)
DALBERGIA LLC (PA)
58 Gerber Dr (06084-2851)
PHONE..................................860 870-2500
Charles E Wilson, *Manager*
EMP: 3
SALES (est): 343.2K **Privately Held**
SIC: 2431 Millwork

(G-8859)
DARI-FARMS ICE CREAM CO INC
55 Gerber Dr (06084-2851)
PHONE..................................860 872-8313
EMP: 13
SALES (est): 1.9MM **Privately Held**
SIC: 2024 Mfg Ice Cream/Frozen Desert

(G-8860)
DATA TECHNOLOGY INC
24 Industrial Park Rd W (06084-2806)
PHONE..................................860 871-8082
David Buckley, *CEO*
Peter Morrissey, *Senior VP*
Terry Grainger, *Engineer*
Carlos Cifuentes, *Sales Staff*
Michael Cooksey, *Manager*
EMP: 25 **EST:** 1960
SQ FT: 29,000
SALES (est): 2.8MM
SALES (corp-wide): 258.7MM **Privately Held**
WEB: www.data-technology.com
SIC: 3577 3829 3827 Computer peripheral equipment; surveying instruments & accessories; map plotting instruments; optical instruments & lenses
PA: Gerber Scientific Llc
24 Indl Pk Rd W
Tolland CT 06084
860 871-8082

(G-8861)
DIVERSIS CAPITAL LLC
Also Called: Dari-Farms Ice Cream
1 Dari Farms Way (06084-2850)
PHONE..................................860 872-8313
EMP: 1
SALES (corp-wide): 33.3MM **Privately Held**
SIC: 2024 Ice cream & frozen desserts

PA: Diversis Capital, Llc
1100 Glendon Ave Ste 920
Los Angeles CA 90024
310 396-4200

(G-8862)
E AND S GAGE INC
Also Called: E & S Gauge Company
38 Gerber Dr (06084-2851)
PHONE..................................860 872-5917
Kevin S Hilinski, *President*
EMP: 12 **EST:** 1953
SQ FT: 2,500
SALES: 1.6MM **Privately Held**
SIC: 3545 3544 Gauges (machine tool accessories); special dies, tools, jigs & fixtures

(G-8863)
ENVIRONICS INC
69 Industrial Park Rd E (06084-2873)
PHONE..................................860 872-1111
Catherine S Dunn, *CEO*
Terrence P Dunn, *President*
Cathy Dunnn, *Vice Pres*
Rachel M Stansel, *Vice Pres*
David Freitag, *Engineer*
EMP: 20
SQ FT: 15,000
SALES: 4.1MM **Privately Held**
WEB: www.environics.com
SIC: 3823 3821 Gas flow computers, industrial process type; calibration tapes for physical testing machines

(G-8864)
GERBER SCIENTIFIC LLC (PA)
24 Indl Pk Rd W (06084)
PHONE..................................860 871-8082
Michael Elia, *President*
Ngo Duong, *General Mgr*
Patti Burmahl, *Vice Pres*
Steven Gore, *Vice Pres*
John Henderson, *Vice Pres*
◆ **EMP:** 200 **EST:** 1948
SQ FT: 250,000
SALES: 258.7MM **Privately Held**
WEB: www.gerberscientific.com
SIC: 3993 7336 3851 7372 Signs & advertising specialties; commercial art & graphic design; lenses, ophthalmic; prepackaged software; magnetic ink & optical scanning devices

(G-8865)
GERBER TECHNOLOGY LLC (HQ)
24 Industrial Park Rd W (06084-2806)
PHONE..................................860 871-8082
Mohit Uberoi, *CEO*
Scott Schinlever, *President*
Patricia L Burmahl, *Senior VP*
Steven Gore, *Senior VP*
Peter Morrissey, *Senior VP*
◆ **EMP:** 344
SQ FT: 260,000
SALES (est): 242.6MM
SALES (corp-wide): 255.3MM **Privately Held**
SIC: 3559 7371 Foundry machinery & equipment; custom computer programming services
PA: American Industrial Partners, L.P.
1 Maritime Plz Ste 1925
San Francisco CA 94111
415 788-7354

(G-8866)
INOCRAFT PRODUCTS INC
Also Called: Keola Sandals
77 Bucks Xing (06084-2281)
P.O. Box 551, Brooklyn (06234-0551)
PHONE..................................860 933-0485
Charles McLeish, *CEO*
Andrew McLeish, *President*
▲ **EMP:** 26
SQ FT: 3,500
SALES (est): 6MM **Privately Held**
SIC: 5191 3021 Garden supplies; rubber & plastics footwear

(G-8867)
KH INDUSTRIES LLC
30 White Birch Dr (06084-3723)
PHONE..................................860 875-4779
Kevin Houle, *Principal*

EMP: 1 **EST:** 2014
SALES (est): 46.7K **Privately Held**
SIC: 3999 Manufacturing industries

(G-8868)
LOON MEDICAL INC
1 Technology Dr (06084-3902)
PHONE..................................860 373-0217
Kevin Miller, *President*
EMP: 5
SALES (est): 373.7K **Privately Held**
SIC: 3845 Electrotherapeutic apparatus

(G-8869)
MACROSCOPIC SOLUTIONS LLC
1 Technology Dr (06084-3902)
PHONE..................................410 870-5566
Mark Smith,
EMP: 2
SALES (est): 205K **Privately Held**
SIC: 3861 3826 3827 8099 Photographic instruments, electronic; microscopes, electron & proton; microscopes, except electron, proton & corneal; medical photography & art; soil analysis

(G-8870)
MH WOODWORKING INC
327 Sugar Hill Rd (06084-2136)
PHONE..................................860 871-7321
Michael P Hagen, *Principal*
EMP: 2
SALES (est): 153.9K **Privately Held**
SIC: 2431 Millwork

(G-8871)
MOTHERSTAR ONLINE LLC
103 Mountain Spring Rd (06084-2930)
PHONE..................................860 896-1869
EMP: 2
SALES (est): 81.4K **Privately Held**
SIC: 3599 Industrial machinery

(G-8872)
NORTHEAST STAIR COMPANY LLC
185 Buff Cap Rd (06084-2613)
PHONE..................................860 875-3358
William Drzyzga,
Pat Drzyzga,
EMP: 6
SALES (est): 650K **Privately Held**
WEB: www.northeasttimes.com
SIC: 2431 Millwork

(G-8873)
NORTHEAST VINEYARD SVCS LLC
66 Shanda Ln (06084-3951)
PHONE..................................860 872-8239
Geoffrey Desmarais, *Principal*
EMP: 2
SALES (est): 62.3K **Privately Held**
SIC: 2084 Wines

(G-8874)
NOVATECH
184 Goose Ln (06084-3821)
P.O. Box 1063 (06084-1063)
PHONE..................................860 871-4180
Eugene Hunt, *Owner*
EMP: 2
SALES: 300K **Privately Held**
SIC: 3821 Laboratory apparatus & furniture

(G-8875)
PENNEY SOFTWARE SERVICES
84 Angela Dr (06084-3128)
PHONE..................................860 870-3443
Beth Penny, *Owner*
EMP: 1 **EST:** 2001
SALES (est): 78.9K **Privately Held**
SIC: 7372 Prepackaged software

(G-8876)
QUICK & DIRTY PRESS
16 Wonderview Dr (06084-2826)
PHONE..................................860 817-0912
EMP: 1 **EST:** 2016
SALES (est): 37.5K **Privately Held**
SIC: 2741 Miscellaneous publishing

(G-8877)
SHIMMER LLC
443 Buff Cap Rd (06084-2225)
PHONE..................................860 875-4701
Sharon Cormier, *Partner*
Simone Dion, *Partner*
EMP: 2
SALES (est): 127.8K **Privately Held**
SIC: 3999 Candles

(G-8878)
SOLDREAM SPCIAL PROCESS - WLDG
203 Hartford Tpke (06084-2821)
PHONE..................................860 858-5247
Vlad Dzhatiev, *Opers Staff*
Maggie Pytel, *Purch Mgr*
EMP: 3
SALES (est): 165.2K **Privately Held**
SIC: 3599 Machine shop, jobbing & repair

(G-8879)
SWAHILI AVIATION AEROSPACE LLC
3 Charlotte Dr (06084-2153)
PHONE..................................860 268-3639
Oluwole Oyelola, *President*
▼ **EMP:** 5
SQ FT: 2,400
SALES (est): 250K **Privately Held**
SIC: 4581 3812 2899 Aircraft maintenance & repair services; aircraft control systems, electronic; chemical supplies for foundries

(G-8880)
SYSTEMS AND TECH INTL INC
24 Goose Ln Ste 5 (06084-3417)
PHONE..................................860 871-0401
Joseph J Mahar, *President*
EMP: 5
SQ FT: 1,500
SALES (est): 690.5K **Privately Held**
SIC: 3548 5065 Soldering equipment, except hand soldering irons; electronic parts & equipment; semiconductor devices

(G-8881)
TITANIUM INDUSTRIES INC
362 Mile Hill Rd (06084-3605)
PHONE..................................860 870-3939
Brett Paddock, *CEO*
Mike Melanio, *Broker*
James Bundschuh, *Sales Staff*
Jamie Moccia, *Marketing Staff*
Kristen Ferment, *Manager*
EMP: 3 **Privately Held**
SIC: 3356 Titanium
PA: Titanium Industries, Inc.
18 Green Pond Rd Ste 1
Rockaway NJ 07866

(G-8882)
TOLLAND ARCHITECTURAL WDWKG LLC
Also Called: Tolland Architectural Wdwkg
526 Tolland Stage Rd (06084-2924)
P.O. Box 1129 (06084-1129)
PHONE..................................860 875-9841
Richard Rizzy, *Mng Member*
Linda Rizy,
Richard Rizy,
EMP: 2
SALES (est): 359K **Privately Held**
SIC: 2541 2431 Cabinets, lockers & shelving; millwork

(G-8883)
TOOLMAX DESIGNING TOOLING INC
69 Industrial Park Rd E A (06084-2873)
P.O. Box 103 (06084-0103)
PHONE..................................860 871-7265
Michael A Tyler, *President*
Sally A Tyler, *Corp Secy*
EMP: 4
SALES (est): 501.8K **Privately Held**
SIC: 3423 Hand & edge tools

▲ = Import ▼=Export
◆ =Import/Export

Torrington
Litchfield County

(G-8884)
588 SMAINST LLC
588 S Main St Rear (06790-6944)
PHONE..................860 482-1625
Jane S St Pierre, *Principal*
EMP: 2
SALES (est): 123.2K **Privately Held**
SIC: 3965 Needles, hand or machine

(G-8885)
A V I INTERNATIONAL INC
3240 Winsted Rd (06790-2233)
PHONE..................860 482-8345
Clifford W Burell, *President*
Adon Burrell, *Treasurer*
Deborah A Burrell, *Admin Sec*
◆ **EMP:** 8
SQ FT: 4,600
SALES (est): 1.9MM **Privately Held**
WEB: www.avipumps.com
SIC: 7699 3561 Pumps & pumping equipment repair; pumps & pumping equipment

(G-8886)
ACE MARINE SERVICE INC
511 Migeon Ave (06790-4643)
PHONE..................860 489-5960
Greg Mantz, *President*
EMP: 6
SQ FT: 5,000
SALES (est): 1.1MM **Privately Held**
SIC: 5551 3732 4491 Outboard motors; motorboats, inboard or outboard: building & repairing; docks, piers & terminals

(G-8887)
ACTION SIGNS
610 Migeon Ave (06790-4644)
PHONE..................860 496-1232
Gus Dellaghelfa, *Owner*
EMP: 1
SQ FT: 1,000
SALES (est): 145.8K **Privately Held**
SIC: 7389 3993 Lettering service; sign painting & lettering shop; signs & advertising specialties

(G-8888)
ALC MANUFACTURING LLC
323 Technology Park Dr (06790-2594)
PHONE..................860 496-0883
John Birden, *Principal*
EMP: 1
SALES (est): 50.3K **Privately Held**
SIC: 3999 Manufacturing industries

(G-8889)
ALLIANCE CARPET CUSHION CO (HQ)
180 Church St (06790-5225)
P.O. Box 1174 (06790-1174)
PHONE..................860 489-4273
Jack Lens, *Principal*
▲ **EMP:** 60
SALES (est): 28.4MM
SALES (corp-wide): 9.9B **Publicly Held**
SIC: 1771 2273 Flooring contractor; carpets & rugs
PA: Mohawk Industries, Inc.
160 S Industrial Blvd
Calhoun GA 30701
706 629-7721

(G-8890)
ALPHA MAGNETICS & COILS INC
527 Westledge Dr (06790-4490)
PHONE..................860 496-0122
Shiban Qasba, *President*
▲ **EMP:** 4
SALES (est): 250K **Privately Held**
SIC: 3677 5731 Electronic transformers; inductors, electronic; coil windings, electronic; radio, television & electronic stores

(G-8891)
ALTEK COMPANY
89 Commercial Blvd Ste 1 (06790-7215)
P.O. Box 1128 (06790-1128)
PHONE..................860 482-7626
Stephen Altschuler, *President*
Joan Altschuler, *Admin Sec*
EMP: 180
SALES (est): 909.6K **Privately Held**
WEB: www.altekcompany.com
SIC: 3625 Relays & industrial controls

(G-8892)
ALTEK ELECTRONICS INC
89 Commercial Blvd (06790-7215)
P.O. Box 1128 (06790-1128)
PHONE..................860 482-7626
David Altschuler, *CEO*
Stephen Altschuler, *Ch of Bd*
Sabrina Beck, *Vice Pres*
▲ **EMP:** 170
SQ FT: 65,000
SALES (est): 27.8MM **Privately Held**
WEB: www.electronics.altekcompany.com
SIC: 3825 3599 3625 3672 Measuring instruments & meters, electric; machine & other job shop work; control equipment, electric; printed circuit boards; nonferrous wiredrawing & insulating

(G-8893)
AMELIA CABINET CO LLC
89 Colt Ave (06790-6521)
PHONE..................860 638-9047
EMP: 1
SALES (est): 64.2K **Privately Held**
SIC: 2434 Wood kitchen cabinets

(G-8894)
AMERICAN-REPUBLICAN INC
122 Franklin St (06790-5508)
PHONE..................860 496-9301
EMP: 107
SALES (corp-wide): 24MM **Privately Held**
SIC: 2711 Newspapers, publishing & printing
PA: American-Republican, Incorporated
389 Meadow St
Waterbury CT 06702
203 574-3636

(G-8895)
AN DESIGNS INC
111 Putter Ln (06790-2360)
PHONE..................860 618-0183
Robert Nilsson, *President*
EMP: 5
SALES (est): 570K **Privately Held**
SIC: 3423 Mechanics' hand tools

(G-8896)
ANDRITZ SHW INC
90 Commercial Blvd (06790-3097)
P.O. Box 238 (06790-0238)
PHONE..................860 496-8888
George Shank, *CEO*
George L Shank, *CEO*
Ulrich Severing, *President*
▲ **EMP:** 30
SQ FT: 50,000
SALES: 8.1MM
SALES (corp-wide): 416.3MM **Privately Held**
WEB: www.shwinc.com
SIC: 3554 Paper industries machinery
HQ: Shw Casting Technologies Gmbh
Stiewingstr. 101
Aalen 73433
736 137-0239

(G-8897)
APTAR INC
301 Ella Grasso Ave (06790-2346)
PHONE..................860 489-6249
Wayne Maw, *Principal*
Mike Smegielski, *Materials Mgr*
Lise Fitzpatrick, *Office Mgr*
Glenys Teixeira, *Manager*
Sue Christian, *Supervisor*
EMP: 3
SALES (est): 717.7K **Privately Held**
SIC: 3083 Plastic finished products, laminated

(G-8898)
ASTI COMPANY INC
953 S Main St (06790-6941)
PHONE..................860 482-2675
Americo Marola, *President*
Edna Marola, *Vice Pres*
EMP: 3 **EST:** 1977
SQ FT: 2,400
SALES: 85K **Privately Held**
SIC: 3089 Bearings, plastic; molding primary plastic

(G-8899)
AWNINGS PLUS LLC
148 Sherwood Dr (06790-4231)
PHONE..................860 496-7996
Steve Howe,
Colleen Howe,
EMP: 2
SALES (est): 236.4K **Privately Held**
SIC: 2394 5999 Awnings, fabric: made from purchased materials; awnings

(G-8900)
BAGOGAMES LLC
79 Lewis St (06790-6705)
PHONE..................860 801-7462
Trevor Kincaid,
Christopher Newton,
EMP: 2
SALES (est): 105.1K **Privately Held**
SIC: 2741

(G-8901)
BEEN PRINTED LLC
Also Called: Been Printing
66 Torrington Heights Rd (06790-5637)
PHONE..................860 618-3600
Ben Veilleux, *Mng Member*
EMP: 2 **EST:** 2010
SALES (est): 188.9K **Privately Held**
SIC: 2759 Screen printing

(G-8902)
BENDER SHOWROOM
29 Main St (06790-5304)
PHONE..................860 618-2944
David Bender, *Owner*
EMP: 1
SALES (est): 105K **Privately Held**
SIC: 3553 Cabinet makers' machinery

(G-8903)
BETTER BAKING BY BETH
270 W Hill Rd (06790-2337)
PHONE..................860 482-4706
Beth Zukowski, *Principal*
EMP: 8
SALES (est): 721.6K **Privately Held**
SIC: 2051 Bread, cake & related products

(G-8904)
BEY-LOW MOLDS
80 Sunrise Dr (06790-5848)
PHONE..................860 482-6561
Alan Beyer, *Owner*
EMP: 3
SALES (est): 159.7K **Privately Held**
SIC: 3089 Molding primary plastic

(G-8905)
BICRON ELECTRONICS COMPANY (PA)
427 Goshen Rd (06790-2601)
PHONE..................860 482-2524
Chris Skomorowski, *President*
Philip Rueger, *Opers Staff*
William J Zeronsa, *Treasurer*
Lisa Skomorowski, *Admin Sec*
◆ **EMP:** 79 **EST:** 1964
SQ FT: 30,000
SALES (est): 13.3MM **Privately Held**
WEB: www.bicronusa.com
SIC: 3612 3679 3677 Power transformers, electric; solenoids for electronic applications; electronic coils, transformers & other inductors

(G-8906)
BRISTOL PRESS
Also Called: Thomaston Express, The Div
188 Main St (06790)
P.O. Box 2158, Bristol (06011-2158)
PHONE..................860 584-0501
Robert Jelenic, *President*
Jazzya Coakley, *Opers Staff*
Bradford Carroll, *Manager*
EMP: 100 **EST:** 1871
SQ FT: 24,000
SALES (est): 4.1MM
SALES (corp-wide): 697.5MM **Privately Held**
WEB: www.journalregister.com
SIC: 2711 Commercial printing & newspaper publishing combined
PA: Journal Register Company
5 Hanover Sq Fl 25
New York NY 10004

(G-8907)
BROTHERS & SONS SUGAR HOUSE
998 Saw Mill Hill Rd (06790-2121)
PHONE..................860 489-2719
Frances Schoonmaker, *Owner*
EMP: 4 **EST:** 1992
SALES (est): 241K **Privately Held**
SIC: 2099 Maple syrup

(G-8908)
C WEST WOODWORKS
143 Hoerle Blvd (06790-3244)
PHONE..................860 309-7362
Charles West, *Principal*
EMP: 1
SALES (est): 58.8K **Privately Held**
SIC: 2431 Millwork

(G-8909)
CARIN INDUSTRIES INC
78 N Elm St (06790-4603)
PHONE..................860 489-1122
EMP: 2 **EST:** 2015
SALES (est): 91.7K **Privately Held**
SIC: 3999 Manufacturing industries

(G-8910)
CHANNYS CANDLES LLC
62 Charles St (06790-3818)
PHONE..................860 313-9139
Chantelle Spellman,
EMP: 1
SALES (est): 39.6K **Privately Held**
SIC: 3999 Candles

(G-8911)
CLS DESIGN GROUP
131 Lawrence Ln (06790-4445)
PHONE..................860 307-2810
Theodore S Langston, *Owner*
EMP: 1 **EST:** 1997
SALES: 21.6K **Privately Held**
SIC: 3571 7384 7311 Personal computers (microcomputers); photograph developing & retouching; advertising agencies

(G-8912)
COLONIAL BRONZE COMPANY
511 Winsted Rd (06790-2932)
P.O. Box 207 (06790-0207)
PHONE..................860 489-9233
Jamie V Gregg, *CEO*
▲ **EMP:** 55
SQ FT: 50,000
SALES (est): 10.7MM **Privately Held**
WEB: www.colonialbronze.com
SIC: 3429 3432 Builders' hardware; plumbing fixture fittings & trim

(G-8913)
COMMERCIAL SEWING INC
65 Grant St (06790-6899)
P.O. Box 1173 (06790-1173)
PHONE..................860 482-5509
Samuel G Mazzarelli, *CEO*
Greg Perosino, *President*
David Mazzarelli, *Vice Pres*
Stephen Mazzarelli, *Vice Pres*
▲ **EMP:** 140 **EST:** 1967
SQ FT: 30,000
SALES (est): 26.7MM **Privately Held**
WEB: www.commercialsewing.com
SIC: 3161 2394 Luggage; liners & covers, fabric: made from purchased materials

(G-8914)
CONAIR CORPORATION
Also Called: Waring Products Division
314 Ella Grasso Ave (06790-2345)
P.O. Box 3201 (06790-8181)
PHONE..................800 492-7464

Torrington - Litchfield County (G-8915)

Jane Deblasi, *Traffic Mgr*
Donald Apperson, *Project Engr*
Fran Ney, *Marketing Staff*
Richard Dombroski, *Manager*
Brian Lahti, *Manager*
EMP: 66
SALES (corp-wide): 2B **Privately Held**
WEB: www.conair.com
SIC: 3634 5064 8741 7629 Electric housewares & fans; electrical appliances, television & radio; management services; electrical repair shops; food products machinery; construction machinery
PA: Conair Corporation
    1 Cummings Point Rd
    Stamford CT 06902
    203 351-9000

(G-8915)
CONNECTCUT PRCSION CMPNNTS LLC
Also Called: CP
588 S Main St Rear (06790-6944)
PHONE..........................860 489-8621
Deb Guilmart,
Mike St Pierre,
EMP: 6
SQ FT: 4,200
SALES (est): 588.3K **Privately Held**
SIC: 3965 Needles, hand or machine

(G-8916)
CREATIVE EDGE SOLUTIONS L
960 Migeon Ave (06790-4525)
PHONE..........................860 626-0007
Matthew L Newton Sr, *Principal*
EMP: 1
SALES (est): 64.2K **Privately Held**
SIC: 3993 Signs & advertising specialties

(G-8917)
DAWN HILL ENTERPRISES LLC
Also Called: Dawn Hill Designs
66 Elmwood Ter (06790-3236)
PHONE..........................860 496-9188
Dawn Hill, *Owner*
EMP: 1
SQ FT: 168
SALES (est): 70.4K **Privately Held**
SIC: 7389 8999 5094 3911 Design services; artist; jewelry; pearl jewelry, natural or cultured; costume jewelry, ex. precious metal & semiprecious stones

(G-8918)
DUCDUC LLC
100 Lawton St (06790-6715)
PHONE..........................860 482-1322
EMP: 2
SALES (est): 269.3K **Privately Held**
SIC: 5712 2519 Furniture stores; household furniture, except wood or metal: upholstered

(G-8919)
DYMAX CORPORATION
Also Called: Dymax Oligomers & Coatings
51 Greenwoods Rd (06790-2349)
PHONE..........................860 626-7006
EMP: 9
SALES (corp-wide): 103.6MM **Privately Held**
SIC: 2869 Industrial organic chemicals
PA: Dymax Corporation
    318 Industrial Ln Ste 1
    Torrington CT 06790
    860 482-1010

(G-8920)
DYMAX MATERIALS INC (HQ)
51 Greenwoods Rd (06790-2349)
PHONE..........................860 482-1010
Andrew Bachman, *President*
Jane Bachman, *Vice Pres*
EMP: 3
SQ FT: 20,000
SALES (est): 2.5MM
SALES (corp-wide): 103.6MM **Privately Held**
SIC: 2869 Industrial organic chemicals
PA: Dymax Corporation
    318 Industrial Ln Ste 1
    Torrington CT 06790
    860 482-1010

(G-8921)
DYMAX OLIGOMERS & COATINGS
318 Industrial Ln (06790-7709)
PHONE..........................860 626-7006
Roberta E Hagstrom, *President*
Greg Bachmann, *Chairman*
▲ **EMP:** 10
SQ FT: 15,000
SALES (est): 2.5MM
SALES (corp-wide): 103.6MM **Privately Held**
WEB: www.bomarspecialties.com
SIC: 2869 Industrial organic chemicals
HQ: Dymax Materials, Inc.
    51 Greenwoods Rd
    Torrington CT 06790

(G-8922)
EMSON INC
301 Ella Grasso Ave (06790-2346)
PHONE..........................860 489-6249
Tom Griffin, *Manager*
EMP: 2
SALES (est): 111.3K **Privately Held**
SIC: 2295 Resin or plastic coated fabrics

(G-8923)
FCT ELECTRONICS LP
187 Commercial Blvd (06790-3098)
PHONE..........................860 482-2800
Toni Kling, *Managing Prtnr*
Anton Kling, *Partner*
Siegfried Ratzel, *Partner*
Daniel J Schreck, *General Ptnr*
Samantha Scanlon, *Project Mgr*
▲ **EMP:** 55
SQ FT: 26,500
SALES (est): 41.1MM **Privately Held**
WEB: www.fctelectronics.com
SIC: 5065 3678 Connectors, electronic; electronic connectors

(G-8924)
FEDERAL BUSINESS PRODUCTS INC
368 Ella Grasso Ave (06790-2345)
PHONE..........................860 482-6231
Bob Beltrandi, *Branch Mgr*
EMP: 70
SQ FT: 32,500
SALES (corp-wide): 20MM **Privately Held**
WEB: www.feddirect.com
SIC: 7389 2761 Personal service agents, brokers & bureaus; manifold business forms
PA: Federal Business Products Inc
    150 Clove Rd Ste 5
    Little Falls NJ 07424
    973 667-9800

(G-8925)
FOOTHILLS TRADER CLASSIFIED
59 Field St (06790-4955)
PHONE..........................860 489-3121
Wesley Rowe, *Publisher*
EMP: 2
SALES (est): 111.1K **Privately Held**
SIC: 2711 Newspapers

(G-8926)
FRANKLIN PRINT SHOPPE INC
48 Main St (06790-5303)
PHONE..........................860 496-9516
Jean Murphy, *President*
EMP: 4
SQ FT: 1,000
SALES (est): 314.6K **Privately Held**
WEB: www.franklinprintshoppe.com
SIC: 2752 2791 Commercial printing, lithographic; typesetting

(G-8927)
FUELCELL ENERGY INC
Also Called: Fuel Cell Manufacturing
539 Technology Park Dr (06790-2594)
PHONE..........................860 496-1111
Christopher R Bentley, *President*
Lori Deane, *Purch Agent*
Tom Lucas, *Engineer*
Jill Crossman, *Executive*
Rebecca Budny, *Technician*
EMP: 35
SALES (corp-wide): 89.4MM **Publicly Held**
WEB: www.fuelcellenergy.com
SIC: 3674 3621 3699 Fuel cells, solid state; motors & generators; electrical equipment & supplies
PA: Fuelcell Energy, Inc.
    3 Great Pasture Rd
    Danbury CT 06810
    203 825-6000

(G-8928)
G L YAROCKI & COMPANY
679 Riverside Ave (06790-4535)
PHONE..........................860 482-9215
George L Yarocki, *Owner*
George Yarocki, *Owner*
EMP: 2
SQ FT: 14,000
SALES: 500K **Privately Held**
WEB: www.oldmc-lit.com
SIC: 3531 Construction machinery attachments; backhoe mounted, hydraulically powered attachments

(G-8929)
GARY MORRIS CLUBMAKER
475 Harwinton Ave (06790-6543)
PHONE..........................860 482-5929
Gary Morris, *Owner*
EMP: 1
SALES (est): 51.2K **Privately Held**
SIC: 3949 Shafts, golf club

(G-8930)
GREGOR TECHNOLOGIES LLC
529 Technology Park Dr (06790-2594)
PHONE..........................860 482-2569
David H Hannah,
Janice Gregorich,
John Gregorich,
EMP: 49
SQ FT: 40,000
SALES (est): 11.7MM
SALES (corp-wide): 11.5B **Publicly Held**
WEB: www.gregortech.com
SIC: 3599 Machine shop, jobbing & repair
HQ: Metals Usa Holdings Corp.
    4901 Nw 17th Way Ste 405
    Fort Lauderdale FL 33309
    954 202-4000

(G-8931)
HANGER PRSTHETCS & ORTHO INC
811 E Main St Ste B (06790-3930)
PHONE..........................860 482-5611
Scott Greenstein, *Branch Mgr*
EMP: 7
SALES (corp-wide): 1B **Publicly Held**
SIC: 3842 Surgical appliances & supplies
HQ: Hanger Prosthetics & Orthotics, Inc.
    10910 Domain Dr Ste 300
    Austin TX 78758
    512 777-3800

(G-8932)
HART TECHNOLOGY LLC
70 Suncrest Ct (06790-3086)
PHONE..........................860 482-6160
James J Hlavacek, *Principal*
EMP: 1
SALES (est): 93.4K **Privately Held**
WEB: www.hart-technology.com
SIC: 2911 Oils, fuel

(G-8933)
HUTCH WELDING COMPANY
153 Durand St (06790-3130)
PHONE..........................860 496-9082
David Hutchinson, *Owner*
EMP: 1
SALES (est): 53K **Privately Held**
SIC: 7692 Welding repair

(G-8934)
IDA DEAN
Also Called: Ida's Bridal Suite
98 Main St (06790-5337)
PHONE..........................860 482-3589
Ida Dean, *Owner*
EMP: 1
SALES (est): 79.3K **Privately Held**
SIC: 5621 2253 5699 Bridal shops; dresses & skirts; custom tailor

(G-8935)
IFFLAND LUMBER COMPANY INC
747 S Main St (06790-6926)
P.O. Box 477 (06790-0477)
PHONE..........................860 489-9218
Earl Iffland, *President*
Thomas Iffland, *Treasurer*
Jim Frink, *Sales Staff*
Lee Parente, *Sales Staff*
Fred Stiles, *Sales Associate*
EMP: 35 **EST:** 1972
SQ FT: 100,000
SALES (est): 8.1MM **Privately Held**
WEB: www.ifflandlumber.com
SIC: 5211 3273 Planing mill products & lumber; ready-mixed concrete

(G-8936)
INDUSTRIAL SAWS INC
105 Summer St (06790-6333)
PHONE..........................860 496-7000
James Campbell, *President*
EMP: 5
SQ FT: 5,000
SALES (est): 773.8K **Privately Held**
SIC: 7699 3559 5084 Sewing machine repair shop; sewing machines & attachments, industrial; sewing machines, industrial

(G-8937)
JEFF MANUFACTURING CO INC
679 Riverside Ave (06790-4535)
PHONE..........................860 482-8845
Jeff Roesing, *President*
Jeff Currier, *Vice Pres*
EMP: 10
SQ FT: 2,000
SALES: 1.4MM **Privately Held**
SIC: 7692 3599 Welding repair; machine & other job shop work

(G-8938)
JENNIFERS TAILOR SHOP
539 Main St (06790-3702)
PHONE..........................860 489-8968
Jennifer Sung, *Owner*
EMP: 1
SALES (est): 40.7K **Privately Held**
SIC: 2395 5699 7219 Embroidery products, except schiffli machine; dressmakers, custom; garment alteration & repair shop

(G-8939)
JOHN SAMUEL GROUP
25 Fairview St (06790-6056)
PHONE..........................860 806-5734
John Samuel, *CEO*
EMP: 6
SALES (est): 302.2K **Privately Held**
SIC: 5999 3651 Audio-visual equipment & supplies; audio electronic systems

(G-8940)
JONMANDY CORPORATION
151 Ella Grasso Ave Ste 3 (06790-2351)
P.O. Box 324, Goshen (06756-0324)
PHONE..........................860 482-2354
Donald Nardozzi, *President*
Marilyn Nardozzi, *Vice Pres*
Tom Nardozzi, *Admin Sec*
EMP: 3
SQ FT: 4,000
SALES: 300K **Privately Held**
WEB: www.jonmandy.com
SIC: 3479 Painting of metal products

(G-8941)
K-TECH INTERNATIONAL
56 Ella Grasso Ave (06790-2341)
PHONE..........................860 489-9399
Samuel J Massameno, *President*
Samuel Massameno, *President*
Kay E Massameno, *Vice Pres*
Michelle Allen, *Purch Mgr*
Samuel Fiorello, *QC Mgr*
EMP: 25
SQ FT: 10,800
SALES (est): 6.8MM **Privately Held**
WEB: www.ktechonline.com
SIC: 3534 3661 3499 Elevators & equipment; telephone & telegraph apparatus; barricades, metal

GEOGRAPHIC SECTION — Torrington - Litchfield County

(G-8942) KENT SCIENTIFIC CORPORATION
1116 Litchfield St (06790-6029)
PHONE 860 626-1172
Andrew H Ide, *President*
Deborah Ide, *Vice Pres*
Judi Stella, *Cust Mgr*
Michelle Durham, *Sales Staff*
Eugene Marino, *Marketing Mgr*
▲ EMP: 10
SQ FT: 4,500
SALES: 3.5MM Privately Held
WEB: www.kentscientific.com
SIC: 3845 Patient monitoring apparatus; respiratory analysis equipment, electromedical

(G-8943) LITTLE INDIA PUBLICATIONS INC
Also Called: Noble Publishing
408 Windtree St (06790-3033)
P.O. Box 249, Walpole MA (02081-0249)
PHONE 212 560-0608
Achal Mehra, *President*
Megha Parikh, *Manager*
▲ EMP: 12
SALES: 1.4MM Privately Held
WEB: www.littleindia.com
SIC: 2721 Magazines: publishing & printing

(G-8944) LUNDGREN CENTERLESS GRINDING
3263 Torringford St (06790-8505)
PHONE 860 482-4927
John Lundgren, *Owner*
EMP: 2 EST: 1966
SALES (est): 187.5K Privately Held
SIC: 3599 Grinding castings for the trade

(G-8945) M & Z ENGINEERING INC
643 Riverside Ave (06790-4535)
PHONE 860 496-0282
Michael Dedkiewicz, *President*
Zbiginew Dedkiewicz, *Corp Secy*
EMP: 6
SQ FT: 10,000
SALES (est): 730K Privately Held
SIC: 3599 3471 Custom machinery; electroplating & plating

(G-8946) M-FAB LLC
52 Norwood St (06790-4632)
PHONE 860 496-0055
Andre Cloutier, *President*
James Dion, *CFO*
EMP: 8
SQ FT: 35,000
SALES: 961.1K Privately Held
SIC: 3599 Ties, form: metal

(G-8947) MC KEON COMPUTER SERVICES
142 Cedar Ln (06790-2301)
PHONE 860 496-7171
EMP: 1 EST: 1994
SALES (est): 71K Privately Held
SIC: 7372 7371 7379 7389 Prepackaged Software Svcs Custom Computer Programing Computer Related Svcs Bus Svcs Data Processing/Prep Bus Cnsltng Svcs

(G-8948) MILLWORK SHOP LLC
39 Putter Ln (06790-2360)
PHONE 860 489-8848
Jonathan Dowd, *Mng Member*
James Dowd,
EMP: 3
SQ FT: 3,000
SALES: 300K Privately Held
WEB: www.millworkshop.com
SIC: 2431 Millwork

(G-8949) MINUTEMAN PRESS
257 Main St Bsmt A (06790-5206)
PHONE 860 496-7525
Richard J Arcelaschi, *Owner*
EMP: 2
SALES (est): 190.1K Privately Held
SIC: 2752 Commercial printing, lithographic

(G-8950) MOHAWK INDUSTRIES INC
180 Church St (06790-5225)
PHONE 706 629-7721
Tina Dileo, *Principal*
Tommy Woods, *Manager*
EMP: 3
SALES (est): 80.7K Privately Held
SIC: 2273 Finishers of tufted carpets & rugs

(G-8951) MOLEX LLC
187 Commercial Blvd (06790-3098)
PHONE 860 482-2800
EMP: 2
SALES (est): 90K Privately Held
SIC: 3678 Electronic connectors

(G-8952) NORSE INC
100 South Rd (06790-2441)
PHONE 860 482-1532
Alfred C Langer, *President*
Christopher Langer, *Treasurer*
Karen Langer, *Sales Staff*
EMP: 6
SQ FT: 8,800
SALES: 1.5MM Privately Held
WEB: www.norse.net
SIC: 3429 Metal fasteners

(G-8953) ODDO PRINT SHOP INC
Also Called: Oddo Print Shop & Copy Center
142 E Main St (06790-5429)
PHONE 860 489-6585
Patricia Meneguzzo, *President*
Lisa Meneguzzo, *Admin Sec*
Lisa J Meneguzzo, *Admin Sec*
EMP: 8 EST: 1946
SALES (est): 1.1MM Privately Held
WEB: www.oddoprint.com
SIC: 2752 7334 2791 7331 Commercial printing, offset; photocopying & duplicating services; typesetting; mailing service

(G-8954) ORBAN DESIGNS LLC
339 Allison Dr (06790-3153)
PHONE 860 605-7975
John Orban, *CEO*
EMP: 1 EST: 2011
SALES: 75K Privately Held
SIC: 3089 Holders: paper towel, grocery bag, etc.: plastic

(G-8955) PACKAGING CONCEPTS ASSOC LLC
Also Called: PCA
230 Ella Grasso Ave (06790-8513)
PHONE 860 489-0480
Guy Ferrelli, *Opers Mgr*
Emil Meshberg, *Mng Member*
David Meshberg,
▲ EMP: 5
SQ FT: 1,500
SALES (est): 1MM Privately Held
SIC: 3085 Plastics bottles

(G-8956) PANACOL-USA INC
142 Industrial Ln (06790-2325)
PHONE 860 738-7449
Gary Grosclaude, *President*
Richard Wick, *Vice Pres*
David Devaux, *Engineer*
Richard Golebiewski, *Marketing Staff*
Susan Beckwith, *Office Mgr*
EMP: 15
SQ FT: 34,000
SALES (est): 2.2MM Privately Held
WEB: www.tangentindinc.com
SIC: 2891 Adhesives & sealants

(G-8957) PHOTO ARTS LIMITED
44 Putter Ln (06790-2359)
PHONE 860 489-1170
Mark Langenheim, *Owner*
EMP: 3
SQ FT: 7,500
SALES (est): 342.6K Privately Held
WEB: www.photoartslimited.com
SIC: 7336 2752 Graphic arts & related design; commercial printing, offset

(G-8958) PINKHAM WOODWORKING
239 Dorothy Dr (06790-4272)
PHONE 860 733-3903
Jeremy Pinkham, *Principal*
EMP: 1 EST: 2015
SALES (est): 54.1K Privately Held
SIC: 2431 Millwork

(G-8959) PRECISION MOLD AND POLSG LLC
301 Ella Grasso Ave (06790-2346)
PHONE 860 489-6249
Mark R Gower, *Principal*
EMP: 2
SALES (est): 142.9K Privately Held
SIC: 3544 Industrial molds

(G-8960) PRINT MASTER LLC
1219 E Main St (06790-3963)
PHONE 860 482-8152
Judy McKay, *Partner*
Tom McKay,
EMP: 4 EST: 1974
SQ FT: 3,600
SALES: 500K Privately Held
SIC: 2752 Commercial printing, offset

(G-8961) PULP PAPER PRODUCTS INC
30 Norwood St (06790-4632)
PHONE 860 806-0143
Eric Haggard, *President*
▲ EMP: 4
SALES (est): 587.4K Privately Held
WEB: www.pulpproducts.com
SIC: 2678 Stationery products

(G-8962) QUEST PLASTICS INC
89 Commercial Blvd Ste 3 (06790-7215)
PHONE 860 489-1404
James A Bean, *President*
Jim Bean, *President*
Alan Bean, *Admin Sec*
EMP: 17
SQ FT: 26,000
SALES (est): 3.5MM Privately Held
SIC: 3089 3559 Injection molding of plastics; glass making machinery: blowing, molding, forming, etc.

(G-8963) RAPID TRUCK SERVICE INC
1745 Torringford West St (06790-3047)
P.O. Box 1904 (06790-1904)
PHONE 860 482-5500
EMP: 1
SQ FT: 2,000
SALES (est): 93K Privately Held
SIC: 7538 7692 Truck Repair & Welding

(G-8964) REIDVILLE HYDRAULICS & MFG INC
175 Industrial Ln (06790-2326)
PHONE 860 496-1133
Larry J Becker, *Principal*
Jeanette Becker, *Admin Sec*
▲ EMP: 25 EST: 1955
SQ FT: 23,000
SALES (est): 5.6MM Privately Held
WEB: www.reidvillehydraulics.com
SIC: 3594 3599 Motors: hydraulic, fluid power or air; machine shop, jobbing & repair

(G-8965) RUBCO PRODUCTS COMPANY
1697 E Main St (06790-3520)
PHONE 860 496-1178
Glenn Rubenoff, *Owner*
EMP: 4 EST: 1939
SQ FT: 11,000
SALES (est): 343.9K Privately Held
SIC: 3052 Rubber hose

(G-8966) SAPPHIRE MLTNATIONAL GROUP INC
21 Prospect St Ste B (06790-6359)
PHONE 860 693-1233
John P Law, *President*
Amanda Mainville, *Business Mgr*
Tom Yang, *Corp Secy*
Carsten Bo Skoett, *Vice Pres*
EMP: 9 EST: 2015
SQ FT: 7,700
SALES: 3.5MM Privately Held
SIC: 5063 3648 Flashlights; spotlights

(G-8967) SCOTT OLSON ENTERPRISES LLC
Also Called: CT Pellet
1707 E Main St (06790-3520)
PHONE 860 482-4391
Scott Olson, *Mng Member*
EMP: 4
SQ FT: 65,000
SALES (est): 550.1K Privately Held
SIC: 3484 Pellet & BB guns

(G-8968) SCREEN-TECH INC
230 Ella Grasso Ave (06790-2343)
PHONE 860 496-8016
David Butkevich, *President*
EMP: 6
SQ FT: 5,700
SALES (est): 490K Privately Held
WEB: www.screen-tech.com
SIC: 3552 Silk screens for textile industry

(G-8969) SEITZ LLC
212 Industrial Ln (06790-2325)
PHONE 860 489-0476
Mike Sullivan, *CEO*
Ed Butler, *President*
Lorie Nicholson, *Business Mgr*
Chuck Ducey, *Exec VP*
Mike Beaman, *Vice Pres*
▲ EMP: 50 EST: 1951
SQ FT: 80,000
SALES (est): 71.4MM Privately Held
WEB: www.seitzcorp.com
SIC: 5084 3089 Industrial machine parts; injection molded finished plastic products

(G-8970) SHARON MASONRY
55 Norton St (06790-5830)
PHONE 860 307-7427
EMP: 2
SALES (est): 63.8K Privately Held
SIC: 2024 Yogurt desserts, frozen

(G-8971) SOLTIS SPEED EQUIPMENT
186 N Elm St (06790-4605)
PHONE 860 489-0119
Christopher Soltis, *Owner*
EMP: 2
SQ FT: 4,000
SALES (est): 180K Privately Held
SIC: 5531 3599 Automotive parts; catapults

(G-8972) STEPHEN MAZZARELLI
1880 Mountain Rd (06790-2107)
PHONE 860 482-8200
Stephen Mazzarelli, *Owner*
EMP: 1
SALES (est): 52.7K Privately Held
SIC: 3999 Manufacturing industries

(G-8973) STITCH IN TIME EMB SVCS LLC
80 Culvert St (06790-5144)
PHONE 860 496-0226
Ian Jones, *Principal*
EMP: 1
SALES (est): 50.4K Privately Held
SIC: 2395 Embroidery & art needlework

(G-8974) STONE INNOVATIONS
47 Hitchcock Way (06790)
PHONE 203 347-8536
Ron Stone, *Owner*

Torrington - Litchfield County

EMP: 1
SALES (est): 84K **Privately Held**
SIC: 3949 Sporting & athletic goods

(G-8975)
T AND A INDUSTRIES LLC
134 New Harwinton Rd (06790-5645)
PHONE..................860 309-9211
Timothy D Riccucci, *Administration*
EMP: 2
SALES (est): 158.1K **Privately Held**
SIC: 3999 Manufacturing industries

(G-8976)
TECHNICAL INDUSTRIES INC (PA)
336 Pinewoods Rd (06790-2350)
PHONE..................860 489-2160
Susan O Parent, *President*
R Dale Smith, *Vice Pres*
EMP: 52
SQ FT: 25,000
SALES (est): 19.7MM **Privately Held**
WEB: www.technicalindustriesinc.com
SIC: 3089 Injection molding of plastics

(G-8977)
THOMAS LA GANGA
Also Called: Colonial Welding Service
612 S Main St (06790-6920)
PHONE..................860 489-0920
Thomas La Ganga, *Owner*
EMP: 5
SQ FT: 8,000
SALES (est): 294.1K **Privately Held**
SIC: 7692 7699 3444 3441 Welding repair; industrial machinery & equipment repair; sheet metalwork; fabricated structural metal

(G-8978)
TOCE BROTHERS INCORPORATED (PA)
145 E Main St (06790)
PHONE..................860 496-2080
Russell Barrett, *President*
Dominic Toce, *President*
Debra Lopardo, *Sales Staff*
Russel Barrett, *Information Mgr*
Debra A Lopardo, *Admin Sec*
▲ EMP: 30
SQ FT: 13,800
SALES (est): 16.8MM **Privately Held**
SIC: 5531 5014 3011 Automotive tires; tires & tubes; tires & inner tubes

(G-8979)
TORRINGTON BRUSH WORKS INC
63 Avenue A (06790-6519)
P.O. Box 56 (06790-0056)
PHONE..................860 482-3517
Sidney Fitzgerald, *Principal*
Richard McKenna, *Materials Mgr*
EMP: 3
SQ FT: 12,750
SALES (corp-wide): 1.4MM **Privately Held**
WEB: www.brusheswholesale.com
SIC: 3991 Brooms & brushes
PA: Torrington Brush Works Inc
   4377 Independence Ct
   Sarasota FL 34234
   941 355-1499

(G-8980)
TORRINGTON DIESEL CORPORATION
287 Old Winsted Rd (06790-2420)
PHONE..................860 496-9948
Pierre Bauchiero, *President*
EMP: 5
SQ FT: 2,400
SALES (est): 821.6K **Privately Held**
SIC: 7692 7538 Welding repair; general truck repair

(G-8981)
TORRINGTON DISTRIBUTORS INC (PA)
Also Called: Tdi
43 Norfolk St (06790-4825)
PHONE..................860 482-4464
James Allen Mazzarelli, *President*
Teresa L Asklar, *Vice Pres*
▲ EMP: 25 EST: 1974
SQ FT: 17,000
SALES (est): 6.1MM **Privately Held**
WEB: www.torringtondistributors.com
SIC: 2531 Seats, aircraft

(G-8982)
TORRINGTON IG PARTNERS LLC
59 Field St (06790-4942)
PHONE..................860 482-7868
EMP: 2
SALES (est): 160K **Privately Held**
SIC: 7372 Prepackaged Software Services

(G-8983)
TORRINGTON INDUSTRIES INC (PA)
Also Called: Torrington Ready-Mix
112 Wall St (06790-5416)
P.O. Box 1031, Litchfield (06759-1031)
PHONE..................860 489-9261
Theodore Zoli Jr, *President*
Joseph Dubay, *Vice Pres*
Pierce Campbell, *Treasurer*
Jeanne Danaher, *Admin Sec*
EMP: 2 EST: 1942
SQ FT: 1,200
SALES (est): 1.9MM **Privately Held**
SIC: 3273 3272 Ready-mixed concrete; building stone, artificial: concrete; stone, cast concrete

(G-8984)
TORRINGTON LUMBER COMPANY
281 Church St (06790-5208)
PHONE..................860 482-3529
Donna Fabro, *President*
Eugene Farely, *Vice Pres*
Daniel Farley, *CPA*
Daniel T Farley, *Admin Sec*
EMP: 6
SQ FT: 49,800
SALES (est): 804.9K **Privately Held**
WEB: www.tlcdoor.com
SIC: 2431 Doors & door parts & trim, wood; windows & window parts & trim, wood

(G-8985)
TSMC INC
100 Lawton St (06790-6715)
PHONE..................860 283-8265
Allen M Sperry Sr, *Ch of Bd*
Paul Ayoub, *President*
▲ EMP: 2 EST: 1848
SQ FT: 345,000
SALES (est): 548.7K **Privately Held**
WEB: www.turnerseymour.com
SIC: 3315 5051 Nails, steel: wire or cut; cable, wire

(G-8986)
UPPER VALLEY MOLD LLC
481 Guerdat Rd (06790-2846)
PHONE..................860 489-8282
Teofilo M Pleil, *Principal*
EMP: 3
SALES (est): 197.8K **Privately Held**
SIC: 3544 Industrial molds

(G-8987)
VR INDUSTRIES LLC
27 Elton St (06790-6702)
P.O. Box 1147 (06790-1147)
PHONE..................860 618-2772
Mark Bastiaanse, *Owner*
EMP: 1
SALES (est): 61K **Privately Held**
SIC: 3999 Manufacturing industries

(G-8988)
WHITE DOG WOODWORKING LLC
199 W Pearl Rd (06790-3026)
PHONE..................860 482-3776
Thomas C Officer, *Manager*
EMP: 4
SALES (est): 417.7K **Privately Held**
SIC: 2431 Millwork

(G-8989)
WHITING LIGHTING LLC
839 Main St Apt 79 (06790-3362)
PHONE..................860 626-0734
Woodrow Dick, *Principal*
EMP: 2
SALES (est): 98.3K **Privately Held**
SIC: 3648 Lighting equipment

(G-8990)
WIRE CUTTING PRECISION
30 Norwood St (06790-4632)
PHONE..................860 496-9302
Steve Dougal, *Principal*
EMP: 2 EST: 2010
SALES (est): 116.6K **Privately Held**
SIC: 3599 Industrial machinery

(G-8991)
WITTMANN BATTENFELD INC (DH)
1 Technology Park Dr (06790-2594)
PHONE..................860 496-9603
Michael Wittmann, *CEO*
Dave Cantey, *Safety Mgr*
Nancy Sabia, *Production*
Greg Peck, *Senior Buyer*
Lynn Farley, *Buyer*
▲ EMP: 80
SQ FT: 40,000
SALES (est): 100.2MM
SALES (corp-wide): 2.6MM **Privately Held**
WEB: www.wittmann-ct.com
SIC: 3559 5084 Robots, molding & forming plastics; industrial machinery & equipment
HQ: Wittmann Kunststoffgerate
    Gesellschaft M.B.H.
    LichtblaustraBe 10
    Wien 1220
    125 039-0

(G-8992)
WRITE WAY SIGNS & DESIGN INC
73 Migeon Ave (06790-4813)
PHONE..................860 482-8893
Jared Servin, *Manager*
Kelly Lund, *Graphic Designe*
EMP: 6
SQ FT: 3,800
SALES (est): 919.6K **Privately Held**
WEB: www.writewaysigns.com
SIC: 3993 Signs & advertising specialties

(G-8993)
X44 LLC
Also Called: X44 Project, The
23 Pershing St (06790-5716)
PHONE..................860 480-5560
Jeff Schroeder, *General Mgr*
Jeffrey Schroeder,
EMP: 1
SALES (est): 69.8K **Privately Held**
SIC: 5941 3949 3944 5945 Team sports equipment; winter sports equipment; water sports equipment; games, toys & children's vehicles; children's toys & games, except dolls;

Trumbull
Fairfield County

(G-8994)
5N PLUS CORP
120 Corporate Dr (06611-1387)
PHONE..................608 846-1357
Jacques L'Ecuyer, *CEO*
Nicholas Audet, *Vice Pres*
Jean Bernier, *Vice Pres*
Christophe Gauder, *Vice Pres*
Sebastian Voigt, *Vice Pres*
▲ EMP: 18
SALES (est): 7.4MM **Privately Held**
SIC: 5074 2899 Heating equipment & panels, solar; chemical preparations

(G-8995)
5N PLUS WISCONSIN INC
120 Corporate Dr (06611-1387)
PHONE..................203 384-0331
Teri Beckoff, *Principal*

Paul Tancell, *Vice Pres*
Jason Merrell, *Research*
Richard Perron, *CFO*
▲ EMP: 16 EST: 1969
SQ FT: 40,000
SALES (est): 7.5MM
SALES (corp-wide): 218MM **Privately Held**
SIC: 3341 Secondary nonferrous metals
PA: 5n Plus Inc
    4385 Rue Garand
    Saint-Laurent QC H4R 2
    514 856-0644

(G-8996)
83 ERNA AVENUE LLC
21 Blue Ridge Dr (06611-4001)
PHONE..................203 243-7426
Dianne Stempien, *Principal*
EMP: 1
SALES (est): 54.1K **Privately Held**
SIC: 3541 Machine tools, metal cutting type

(G-8997)
AMERICAN GRIPPERS INC
Also Called: A G I Automation
171 Spring Hill Rd (06611-1327)
PHONE..................203 459-8345
Peter Farkas, *President*
John Barnes, *Vice Pres*
EMP: 23
SALES (est): 3MM **Privately Held**
WEB: www.agi-automation.com
SIC: 3545 Machine tool accessories

(G-8998)
AMERICAN PRONT AND SIGN
6 Gwendolyn Dr (06611-2428)
PHONE..................203 400-2155
Leonard Provenzano, *Principal*
EMP: 1
SALES (est): 46.9K **Privately Held**
SIC: 3993 Signs & advertising specialties

(G-8999)
ANSEL LABEL AND PACKAGING CORP
204 Spring Hill Rd Ste 3 (06611-1356)
PHONE..................203 452-0311
William San Fan Andre, *Ch of Bd*
Jeff San Fan Andre, *President*
Harold Smyth, *Treasurer*
Clifford Albers, *VP Sales*
EMP: 22
SQ FT: 13,364
SALES (est): 3MM **Privately Held**
SIC: 2759 2671 Labels & seals: printing; packaging paper & plastics film, coated & laminated

(G-9000)
ATK GOLF SERVICES
25 Hills Point Rd (06611-1713)
PHONE..................203 615-2099
EMP: 2
SALES (est): 86K **Privately Held**
SIC: 3764 Propulsion units for guided missiles & space vehicles

(G-9001)
AVERY ABRASIVES INC
2225 Reservoir Ave Ste 1 (06611-4795)
PHONE..................203 372-3513
Craig F Avery, *President*
Ray Soto, *Opers Mgr*
Robert J Berta, *Admin Sec*
▲ EMP: 35 EST: 1960
SQ FT: 42,000
SALES (est): 6.2MM **Privately Held**
SIC: 3291 Wheels, abrasive

(G-9002)
BAGHAI SHAHIN
95 Cranbury Dr (06611-1466)
PHONE..................203 268-6287
Shahin Baghai, *CEO*
EMP: 2 EST: 2017
SALES (est): 86K **Privately Held**
SIC: 3721 Aircraft

(G-9003)
BARON TECHNOLOGY INC
62 Spring Hill Rd (06611-1328)
PHONE..................203 452-0515
David Baron, *President*

Frank Baron, *Chairman*
Ruth Baron, *Corp Secy*
Karlo Glad, *Vice Pres*
Karla Glad, *Office Mgr*
EMP: 45
SQ FT: 5,300
SALES (est): 9.9MM **Privately Held**
WEB: www.baronengraving.com
SIC: 2759 3231 2796 Engraving; products of purchased glass; platemaking services

(G-9004)
BIOMETRICS INC (PA)
115 Technology Dr Cp102 (06611-6342)
PHONE.....................203 261-1162
David Rooney, *President*
Robert Dzurenda, *President*
Ian Engelman, *Shareholder*
EMP: 8
SALES (est): 862.9K **Privately Held**
WEB: www.biometricsct.com
SIC: 3842 Limbs, artificial; braces, orthopedic

(G-9005)
BLAIRDEN PRECISION INSTRS INC
Also Called: Cooper Surgical
95 Corporate Dr (06611-1350)
PHONE.....................203 799-2000
Kerry L Blair, *President*
Dan Polly, *Regl Sales Mgr*
▲ **EMP:** 9
SQ FT: 13,000
SALES (est): 2MM **Privately Held**
WEB: www.coopersurgical.com
SIC: 3841 Surgical instruments & apparatus

(G-9006)
BLUE CRYSTAL ENTERPRISES LLC
43 Wedgewood Rd (06611-1638)
PHONE.....................203 856-5397
Cindy Bartlett-Niebuhr,
EMP: 1
SALES (est): 25K **Privately Held**
SIC: 7372 7389 Application computer software;

(G-9007)
BRIDGE INNVATIONS VENTURES LLC
286 Strobel Rd (06611-3330)
PHONE.....................203 520-8241
Oleg Shikhman, *President*
EMP: 1
SALES (est): 55K **Privately Held**
SIC: 3841 7389 Surgical & medical instruments;

(G-9008)
CADESK COMPANY LLC (PA)
88 Cottage St (06611-2830)
PHONE.....................203 268-8083
Michael G Pagett, *Principal*
Robert Hutcheon, *Director*
EMP: 3
SALES (est): 302.2K **Privately Held**
SIC: 3577 Computer peripheral equipment

(G-9009)
CANINE CORE INDUSTRIES LLC
232 Teller Rd (06611-1451)
PHONE.....................203 459-1584
Elizabeth Vinas, *Principal*
EMP: 1
SALES (est): 51.4K **Privately Held**
SIC: 3999 Manufacturing industries

(G-9010)
CAR BUYERS MARKET
30 Nutmeg Dr Ste B (06611-5453)
P.O. Box 110317 (06611-0317)
PHONE.....................516 482-0292
John Roy, *President*
Robert Fitting, *Treasurer*
EMP: 30 **EST:** 1958
SQ FT: 1,800
SALES (est): 1.6MM **Privately Held**
SIC: 2711 5521 Newspapers: publishing only, not printed on site; used car dealers

(G-9011)
CHRIS DEDURA
33 Hillside Ave (06611-4525)
PHONE.....................203 257-7304
Chris Dedura, *Principal*
EMP: 1
SALES (est): 71.7K **Privately Held**
SIC: 2431 Millwork

(G-9012)
COACH INC
5065 Main St Ste P2114 (06611-4223)
PHONE.....................203 372-0208
EMP: 15
SALES (corp-wide): 4.4B **Publicly Held**
SIC: 3171 Mfg Women's Handbags/Purses
PA: Coach, Inc.
10 Hudson Yards
New York NY 10001
212 594-1850

(G-9013)
COLMEC USA INC
35 Nutmeg Dr (06611-5431)
PHONE.....................203 502-8822
Martin Yonnone, *President*
Frank Ferrante, *Admin Sec*
EMP: 2
SALES (est): 398K **Privately Held**
SIC: 3559 Rubber working machinery, including tires

(G-9014)
CONOPCO INC
Also Called: Thomas J Lipton
75 Merritt Blvd (06611-5435)
PHONE.....................708 606-0540
Andrea Misek, *Administration*
EMP: 50
SALES (corp-wide): 58.3B **Privately Held**
SIC: 2099 2034 2033 2098 Tea blending; seasonings: dry mixes; seasonings & spices; soup mixes; spaghetti & other pasta sauce: packaged in cans, jars, etc.; noodles (e.g. egg, plain & water); dry; ice cream, packaged: molded, on sticks, etc.
HQ: Conopco, Inc.
700 Sylvan Ave
Englewood Cliffs NJ 07632
201 894-7760

(G-9015)
CONOPCO INC
Also Called: Slim-Fast Foods Company
75 Merritt Blvd (06611-5435)
PHONE.....................203 381-3557
Eric Walsh, *President*
EMP: 99
SALES (corp-wide): 58.3B **Privately Held**
SIC: 2037 Frozen fruits & vegetables
HQ: Conopco, Inc.
700 Sylvan Ave
Englewood Cliffs NJ 07632
201 894-7760

(G-9016)
COOPERSURGICAL INC
Also Called: Wallach Surgical
120 Corporate Dr (06611-1387)
PHONE.....................203 601-5200
EMP: 6
SALES (corp-wide): 2.5B **Publicly Held**
SIC: 5047 3842 Medical equipment & supplies; gynecological supplies & appliances
HQ: Coopersurgical, Inc.
95 Corporate Dr
Trumbull CT 06611

(G-9017)
COOPERSURGICAL INC (HQ)
95 Corporate Dr (06611-1350)
PHONE.....................203 601-5200
Paul Remmell, *President*
Pam Holler, *General Mgr*
Bryan Hickman, *Regional Mgr*
Amy Strack, *Regional Mgr*
Robert D Auerbach, *Exec VP*
◆ **EMP:** 180
SQ FT: 92,000
SALES (est): 185.5MM
SALES (corp-wide): 2.5B **Publicly Held**
SIC: 5047 3842 3841 3845 Medical equipment & supplies; gynecological supplies & appliances; surgical & medical instruments; electromedical equipment
PA: The Cooper Companies Inc
6140 Stoneridge Mall Rd # 590
Pleasanton CA 94588
925 460-3600

(G-9018)
CREATIVE CUPOLAS
10 Sutton Pl (06611-3732)
PHONE.....................203 261-2178
Robert Langer, *President*
EMP: 1
SALES (est): 57.6K **Privately Held**
SIC: 3999 Manufacturing industries

(G-9019)
DEFELICE WOODWORKING INC
50 Oakland Dr (06611-1912)
PHONE.....................203 445-0199
Thomas P Defelice, *President*
EMP: 1 **EST:** 2001
SALES (est): 120.7K **Privately Held**
WEB: www.defelicewoodworking.com
SIC: 2431 Millwork

(G-9020)
DELCON INDUSTRIES
31 Frenchtown Rd (06611-4729)
PHONE.....................203 371-5711
EMP: 3
SALES (est): 190.1K **Privately Held**
SIC: 3999 Manufacturing industries

(G-9021)
DIRECTV
6058 Main St (06611-2436)
PHONE.....................203 445-2876
EMP: 2 **EST:** 2012
SALES (est): 120K **Privately Held**
SIC: 3663 Mfg Radio/Tv Communication Equipment

(G-9022)
E-LITE TECHNOLOGIES INC
2285 Reservoir Ave (06611-4752)
PHONE.....................203 371-2070
Mark Appelberg, *President*
Gustaf T Appelberg, *Chairman*
EMP: 11
SQ FT: 10,600
SALES (est): 1.9MM **Privately Held**
WEB: www.e-lite.com
SIC: 3645 Residential lighting fixtures

(G-9023)
EAGLE CONSULTING LLC
Also Called: Rh Rosen Group
180 Merrimac Dr (06611-1742)
PHONE.....................203 445-1740
Richard Rosen,
EMP: 1
SALES (est): 88.8K **Privately Held**
SIC: 8748 7372 Business consulting; prepackaged software

(G-9024)
ELENE A MOORE
Also Called: Moore Precisionworks
400 Booth Hill Rd (06611-4004)
PHONE.....................203 377-0248
Elene A Moore, *Owner*
EMP: 2 **EST:** 1998
SALES (est): 182.1K **Privately Held**
SIC: 3599 Machine shop, jobbing & repair

(G-9025)
ELMO NASH INDUSTRIES
9 Trefoil Dr (06611-1330)
PHONE.....................203 459-3648
EMP: 1 **EST:** 2011
SALES (est): 64K **Privately Held**
SIC: 3999 Mfg Misc Products

(G-9026)
FAIRFIELD CNTY STUMP GRINDING
35 Corporate Dr Ste 1045 (06611-1355)
PHONE.....................203 261-7867
Mike Shea, *Owner*
EMP: 2
SALES (est): 192.2K **Privately Held**
SIC: 3599 0783 Grinding castings for the trade; removal services, bush & tree

(G-9027)
FRED RADFORD
Also Called: Radford, F Castings Plastic ML
135 Pinewood Trl (06611-3312)
PHONE.....................203 377-6189
Fred Radford, *Owner*
Margaret Radford, *Co-Owner*
EMP: 4
SALES (est): 1MM **Privately Held**
WEB: www.fredradford.com
SIC: 3369 3366 3089 Castings, except die-castings, precision; castings (except die); molding primary plastic

(G-9028)
GARDNER DENVER NASH LLC (DH)
2 Trefoil Dr (06611-1330)
P.O. Box 130, Bentleyville PA (15314-0130)
PHONE.....................203 459-3923
Barry Pennypacker, *CEO*
Armando Castorena, *Vice Pres*
T Duane Morgan, *Vice Pres*
Brent A Walters, *Vice Pres*
Helen Cornell, *CFO*
▲ **EMP:** 75
SQ FT: 42,000
SALES (est): 331.1MM
SALES (corp-wide): 2.6B **Publicly Held**
WEB: www.nasheng.com
SIC: 5084 3563 8711 3561 Compressors, except air conditioning; air & gas compressors including vacuum pumps; engineering services; pumps & pumping equipment

(G-9029)
GETTYSBURG PUBLISHING LLC
192 Edison Rd (06611-4139)
P.O. Box 110271 (06611-0271)
PHONE.....................203 268-7111
Kevin Drake, *Owner*
EMP: 2
SALES (est): 117.5K **Privately Held**
SIC: 2741 Miscellaneous publishing

(G-9030)
GRASSY MEADOWS LAWN CARE
849 Plattsville Rd (06611-3525)
PHONE.....................203 856-3823
Robert A Cerulli, *Owner*
EMP: 2 **EST:** 2007
SALES (est): 102.3K **Privately Held**
SIC: 0782 3523 Lawn care services; spraying services, lawn; fertilizing machinery, farm

(G-9031)
GRDN WOODWORKS
3 Raynor Ave (06611-4331)
PHONE.....................203 814-6446
EMP: 2 **EST:** 2010
SALES (est): 176.4K **Privately Held**
SIC: 2431 Millwork

(G-9032)
GYNION LLC
286 Strobel Rd (06611-3330)
PHONE.....................203 520-8241
Oleg Shikhman, *CEO*
EMP: 1
SALES (est): 68.6K **Privately Held**
SIC: 3841 Surgical & medical instruments

(G-9033)
HELICOPTER SUPPORT INC (DH)
Also Called: Sikorsky Commercial
124 Quarry Rd (06611-4816)
P.O. Box 111068 (06611-0868)
PHONE.....................203 416-4000
David Adler, *President*
John Chimini, *Exec VP*
Christopher Bogan, *Vice Pres*
Rajeev Bhalla, *Treasurer*
Richard S Caswell, *Treasurer*
◆ **EMP:** 265
SQ FT: 183,000

Trumbull - Fairfield County (G-9034)   **GEOGRAPHIC SECTION**

SALES (est): 163.3MM **Publicly Held**
WEB: www.hsius.com
SIC: **5088** 4581 3728 Helicopter parts; aircraft maintenance & repair services; aircraft parts & equipment; aircraft body & wing assemblies & parts

(G-9034)
HERSAM ACORN CMNTY PUBG LLC
Also Called: Trumbull Printing
205 Spring Hill Rd (06611-1327)
PHONE..................203 261-2548
Gus Semon, *Manager*
EMP: 15
SALES (corp-wide): 5.3MM **Privately Held**
SIC: **2711** Newspapers, publishing & printing
HQ: Hersam Acorn Community Publishing, Llc
   16 Bailey Ave
   Ridgefield CT 06877

(G-9035)
HOME DIAGNOSTICS CORP
1 Trefoil Dr (06611-6352)
PHONE..................203 445-1170
George Holley, *President*
Donald Parson, *Admin Sec*
EMP: 200
SQ FT: 20,000
SALES (est): 11.1MM **Privately Held**
SIC: **3845** 8731 3841 Electromedical apparatus; medical research, commercial; electronic research; surgical & medical instruments

(G-9036)
INTERNATIONAL SYSTEMS CONS
58 Firehouse Rd (06611-2675)
PHONE..................203 268-1045
David Anand, *Owner*
EMP: 1
SALES (est): 140K **Privately Held**
SIC: **7377** 7372 Computer rental & leasing; prepackaged software

(G-9037)
JOHN OLSEN
Also Called: P D M Company
19 Meadow Rd (06611-2020)
P.O. Box 682 (06611-0682)
PHONE..................203 624-5544
John Olsen, *Owner*
Ron Johnson, *CTO*
Hannon Russell, *CTO*
EMP: 2
SALES (est): 210K **Privately Held**
SIC: **3625** 3613 Relays & industrial controls; switchgear & switchboard apparatus

(G-9038)
JPO SOLUTIONS INC
Also Called: Jpo Absorbents
30 Nutmeg Dr Ste F (06611-5453)
P.O. Box 5208, Topeka KS (66605-0208)
PHONE..................203 502-8609
EMP: 2
SALES (est): 219.5K **Privately Held**
SIC: **3569** Industrial shock absorbers

(G-9039)
KIMBERLY BON PUBLISHING LLC
655 Booth Hill Rd (06611-4007)
PHONE..................203 258-9829
Kimberly Vecchione-Bon, *Principal*
EMP: 1
SALES (est): 90K **Privately Held**
SIC: **2741** 7389 Miscellaneous publishing;

(G-9040)
KIMLAR INDUSTRIES LLC
53 Flint St (06611-3059)
PHONE..................203 220-2200
Larry F Ciambriello, *Principal*
Desmond Hussey, *Vice Pres*
John Ciccone, *Human Res Mgr*
Stephanie Green, *Marketing Staff*
Peter Miller, *Info Tech Mgr*
EMP: 2
SALES (est): 103.3K **Privately Held**
SIC: **3999** Manufacturing industries

(G-9041)
LADY ANNE COSMETICS INC
Also Called: Ecogenics
78 Russ Rd (06611-3434)
PHONE..................203 372-6972
Ann McDonnell, *President*
▲ EMP: 5
SQ FT: 1,500
SALES (est): 865.1K **Privately Held**
WEB: www.ecogenics.com
SIC: **2844** 5122 5999 Face creams or lotions; drugs, proprietaries & sundries; toiletries, cosmetics & perfumes

(G-9042)
LATERAL THINKING SOFTWARE SYS
835 Daniels Farm Rd (06611-2601)
PHONE..................203 452-9713
Enzo Maini, *Principal*
EMP: 2
SALES (est): 101K **Privately Held**
SIC: **7372** Prepackaged software

(G-9043)
LEICHSENRING STUDIOS LLC
9 Oxen Hill Rd (06611-2540)
P.O. Box 532 (06611-0532)
PHONE..................203 452-7710
Sharon Leichsenring,
EMP: 1
SALES (est): 84.1K **Privately Held**
SIC: **3993** Displays, paint process

(G-9044)
LRP CONFERENCES LLC
Also Called: Professional Media Group
35 Nutmeg Dr (06611-5431)
PHONE..................203 663-0100
Joseph Hanson, *Mng Member*
EMP: 42
SALES (corp-wide): 111.8MM **Privately Held**
SIC: **2759** Magazines: printing
HQ: Lrp Conferences, Llc
   360 Hiatt Dr
   Palm Beach Gardens FL 33418
   215 784-0860

(G-9045)
M T D CORPORATION
171 Spring Hill Rd (06611-1327)
PHONE..................203 261-3721
Dorothy Bertini, *President*
Milo Bertini, *Vice Pres*
Steve Seifert, *Marketing Staff*
EMP: 15
SQ FT: 9,000
SALES (est): 1MM **Privately Held**
SIC: **3599** Machine shop, jobbing & repair

(G-9046)
MATTHEW RYAN WOODWORKING LLC
5778 Main St (06611-3136)
PHONE..................203 268-8469
Matthew R O Cheskey, *Principal*
EMP: 2
SALES (est): 106.4K **Privately Held**
SIC: **2431** Millwork

(G-9047)
MCGURK INDUSTRIES
49 Meadow Rd (06611-2049)
PHONE..................917 524-5132
Joe McGurk, *Principal*
EMP: 2
SALES (est): 115.3K **Privately Held**
SIC: **3999** Manufacturing industries

(G-9048)
MINUTEMAN ARMS LLC
35 Washington St (06611-4668)
PHONE..................203 268-4853
Joseph Seminoro, *Principal*
EMP: 2
SALES (est): 105.1K **Privately Held**
SIC: **2752** Commercial printing, offset

(G-9049)
MINUTEMAN PRESS
14 Kitcher Ct (06611-1015)
PHONE..................203 261-8318
EMP: 2

SALES (est): 83.9K **Privately Held**
SIC: **2752** 2741 Commercial printing, lithographic; miscellaneous publishing

(G-9050)
MORNING SUN OF TRUMBULL LLC
98 Cottage St (06611-2829)
PHONE..................203 220-8509
Kevin Tran, *Principal*
EMP: 2
SALES (est): 66K **Privately Held**
SIC: **1221** Bituminous coal & lignite-surface mining

(G-9051)
NORTHEAST DRONE SERVICES LLC
115 Technology Dr A201 (06611-6337)
PHONE..................203 220-6478
Richard Zini, *Principal*
EMP: 2
SALES (est): 105.6K **Privately Held**
SIC: **3721** Motorized aircraft

(G-9052)
OPTICARE EYE HEALTH & VISION
925 White Plains Rd Ste 5 (06611-4583)
PHONE..................203 261-2619
Sharon Marrone, *Manager*
Crystal Seaforth, *Manager*
EMP: 3
SALES (est): 178.3K **Privately Held**
SIC: **5995** 3851 Contact lenses, prescription; contact lenses; eyeglasses, lenses & frames

(G-9053)
ORIGIO MIDATLANTIC DEVICES INC
75 Corporate Dr (06611-1350)
PHONE..................856 762-2000
Paul Rennell, *CEO*
Terrance J Fortino, *CEO*
◆ EMP: 22
SQ FT: 11,000
SALES (est): 3.8MM **Privately Held**
WEB: www.midatlanticdiagnostics.com
SIC: **3821** 5047 Laboratory equipment: fume hoods, distillation racks, etc.; medical laboratory equipment
HQ: Origio Inc.
   2400 Hunters Way
   Charlottesville VA 22911

(G-9054)
PANCOAST ASSOCIATES INC
Also Called: Exact Printing & Graphics
25 Mariner Cir (06611-1721)
PHONE..................203 377-6571
Charles Pancoast, *President*
Bruce Pancoast, *Corp Secy*
Richard Pancoast, *Vice Pres*
EMP: 3
SQ FT: 3,300
SALES: 350K **Privately Held**
SIC: **7334** 2752 2791 2789 Photocopying & duplicating services; commercial printing, lithographic; typesetting; bookbinding & related work

(G-9055)
PFIZER INC
9 Pinehurst St (06611-2414)
PHONE..................860 441-4568
EMP: 2
SALES (corp-wide): 53.6B **Publicly Held**
SIC: **2834** Pharmaceutical preparations
PA: Pfizer Inc.
   235 E 42nd St
   New York NY 10017
   212 733-2323

(G-9056)
PREUSSER RESEARCH GROUP INC (PA)
7100 Main St (06611-1314)
PHONE..................203 459-8700
David Preusser, *President*
Robert Chaffe, *Research*
Julie Tison, *Research*
Robert G Ulmer, *Treasurer*
Katie Raboin, *Sales Staff*
EMP: 15

SALES (est): 1.1MM **Privately Held**
WEB: www.preussergroup.com
SIC: **8748** 3669 Traffic consultant; pedestrian traffic control equipment

(G-9057)
PRINTER SOURCE INC
101 Merritt Blvd Ste 21 (06611-5450)
PHONE..................800 788-5101
EMP: 2
SALES (est): 83.9K **Privately Held**
SIC: **2752** Commercial printing, lithographic

(G-9058)
QUANTUM HEALTH PRESS
5520 Park Ave Ste 301 (06611-3465)
PHONE..................203 396-0222
EMP: 2 EST: 2008
SALES (est): 89K **Privately Held**
SIC: **2741** Misc Publishing

(G-9059)
R & A PRECIOUS METALS LLC
3 Plumb Creek Rd (06611-1492)
PHONE..................203 220-8265
Amir Akhundzadeh, *Owner*
EMP: 1
SALES (est): 70.1K **Privately Held**
SIC: **3339** Precious metals

(G-9060)
R S INDUSTRIES LLC
51 Bassick Rd (06611-2909)
PHONE..................203 261-1146
Ryan Bogen, *Principal*
EMP: 2
SALES (est): 93.3K **Privately Held**
SIC: **3999** Manufacturing industries

(G-9061)
RAMPAGE LLC
38 Palisade Ave (06611-3040)
PHONE..................203 930-1022
Rich Peterson,
EMP: 12
SALES (est): 745K **Privately Held**
WEB: www.rampag.
SIC: **3949** Skateboards

(G-9062)
REAL SLTONS EDCTL CNSLTING INC
Also Called: Rs Tutoring
67 Driftwood Ln (06611-1803)
PHONE..................203 220-2279
Ronald C Sabad, *President*
EMP: 2
SALES (est): 400K **Privately Held**
SIC: **8299** 2731 Tutoring school; textbooks: publishing only, not printed on site

(G-9063)
REBLEE INC (PA)
Also Called: Bridgeport Plastics Co
27 Bonazzo Dr (06611-5226)
PHONE..................203 372-3338
Lee Bonazzo, *President*
EMP: 2
SQ FT: 5,000
SALES (est): 1.1MM **Privately Held**
SIC: **3089** Injection molding of plastics

(G-9064)
RELIABLE PRINTING LLC
4 Daniels Farm Rd Ste 268 (06611-3900)
PHONE..................203 261-8867
Gerald Dooda, *Manager*
EMP: 1
SALES (est): 87.6K **Privately Held**
SIC: **2752** Commercial printing, lithographic

(G-9065)
RTS CORPORATION
115 Technology Dr A201 (06611-6339)
PHONE..................203 459-9835
Dennis C Rotunno, *President*
EMP: 2
SALES (est): 277.9K **Privately Held**
SIC: **1382** Oil & gas exploration services

▲ = Import ▼ = Export
◆ = Import/Export

GEOGRAPHIC SECTION

Uncasville - New London County (G-9096)

(G-9066)
RUCH INDUSTRIES LLC
686 Fairchild Rd (06611-3669)
PHONE..................................203 268-6514
Joseph J Ruchalski, *Principal*
EMP: 1
SALES (est): 50.4K **Privately Held**
SIC: 3999 Manufacturing industries

(G-9067)
RUNWAY LIQUIDATION LLC
Also Called: Bcbg
15 Corporate Dr (06611-1351)
PHONE..................................239 337-2020
EMP: 2
SALES (corp-wide): 570.1MM **Privately Held**
SIC: 2335 Women's, juniors' & misses' dresses
HQ: Runway Liquidation, Llc
2761 Fruitland Ave
Vernon CA 90058
323 589-2224

(G-9068)
S G R WOODWORKS
2 Woodfield Dr (06611-1228)
PHONE..................................203 216-3327
EMP: 1 **EST:** 2017
SALES (est): 59.5K **Privately Held**
SIC: 2431 Millwork

(G-9069)
SAIGEWORKS LLC
138 Chestnut Hill Rd (06611-4114)
PHONE..................................203 767-1035
Timothy Dolan,
EMP: 2
SALES (est): 94.5K **Privately Held**
SIC: 4961 8711 3433 Steam heating systems (suppliers of heat); energy conservation engineering; boilers, low-pressure heating: steam or hot water

(G-9070)
SCAN TOOL & MOLD INC
2 Trefoil Dr (06611-1330)
PHONE..................................203 459-4950
John F Gotch Jr, *President*
Joe Heeran, *QC Mgr*
Jan Gallagher, *Bookkeeper*
Nancy Ares, *Supervisor*
Lynn Tomas, *Admin Asst*
▲ **EMP:** 26
SQ FT: 32,500
SALES (est): 6.1MM **Privately Held**
WEB: www.scantoolinc.com
SIC: 3089 3544 Injection molding of plastics; industrial molds

(G-9071)
SCOTT AMERICAN LLC
6 Regency Cir (06611-1391)
PHONE..................................203 733-5512
Frank Scott, *Principal*
EMP: 1
SALES (est): 55.5K **Privately Held**
SIC: 2741 Miscellaneous publishing

(G-9072)
SECUREMARK DECAL CORP
20 Nutmeg Dr (06611-5414)
PHONE..................................773 622-6815
Norman Hoffderg, *President*
Jim Chmura, *General Mgr*
Paul Choiniere, *Opers Mgr*
James Leach, *Opers Mgr*
George Houston, *QC Dir*
EMP: 15
SALES (est): 2.1MM **Privately Held**
SIC: 2672 Labels (unprinted), gummed: made from purchased materials

(G-9073)
SHADOW GRAPHICS
21 Cottage St (06611-2827)
PHONE..................................203 590-3533
EMP: 1
SALES (est): 53.7K **Privately Held**
SIC: 7336 2759 Graphic arts & related design; commercial printing

(G-9074)
SIGN-IT LLC
672 White Plains Rd (06611-4513)
PHONE..................................203 377-8831
Jonathan Spodnick, *Principal*
EMP: 1
SALES (est): 46K **Privately Held**
SIC: 3993 Signs & advertising specialties

(G-9075)
SOLANA PUBLISHING LLC
2361 Huntington Rd (06611-5440)
PHONE..................................203 380-2851
Edwin Rosado, *Principal*
EMP: 1
SALES (est): 37.5K **Privately Held**
SIC: 2741 Miscellaneous publishing

(G-9076)
SPOTS AND LADYBUGS LLC
45 Hilltop Dr (06611-5106)
PHONE..................................203 378-8232
Alison Zajac, *Mng Member*
Ailis Martin,
EMP: 2
SALES: 60K **Privately Held**
SIC: 3944 7389 Craft & hobby kits & sets;

(G-9077)
STEPHEN WENNING
43 Clemens Ave (06611-1958)
PHONE..................................203 906-9273
Stephen Wenning, *Principal*
EMP: 2
SALES (est): 140.2K **Privately Held**
SIC: 2431 Millwork

(G-9078)
SURYS INC
20 Nutmeg Dr (06611-5414)
PHONE..................................203 333-5503
Richard Salomone, *CEO*
▲ **EMP:** 202
SALES (est): 17.3MM
SALES (corp-wide): 177.9M **Privately Held**
SIC: 2679 2759 Tags & labels, paper; labels & seals: printing
HQ: Surys
Parc D Activite G Eiffel
Bussy-Saint-Georges 77600
164 763-100

(G-9079)
SWAN CABINETRY
844 Daniels Farm Rd (06611-2602)
PHONE..................................203 667-7026
Charles Anello, *Partner*
EMP: 1
SALES (est): 62.1K **Privately Held**
SIC: 2434 Wood kitchen cabinets

(G-9080)
SWAROVSKI NORTH AMERICA LTD
5065 Main St (06611-4204)
PHONE..................................203 372-0336
White Thayer, *Branch Mgr*
EMP: 4
SALES (corp-wide): 4.7B **Privately Held**
SIC: 3961 Costume jewelry
HQ: Swarovski North America Limited
1 Kenney Dr
Cranston RI 02920
401 463-6400

(G-9081)
THOMAS J LIPTON INC
Also Called: Unilever Foods Chill
75 Merritt Blvd (06611-5435)
PHONE..................................206 381-3500
◆ **EMP:** 2200 **EST:** 2006
SALES (est): 18.5MM **Privately Held**
SIC: 2099 2034 2035 2033 Mfg Food Preparations Mfg Dhydrtd Fruit/Vegtbl

(G-9082)
TRUMBULL PRINTING INC
205 Spring Hill Rd (06611-1327)
PHONE..................................203 261-2548
Steve Huhta, *President*
Tiberio Moniz, *President*
William McCann, *CFO*
Walter Cooper, *Manager*
Sharon Esares,
EMP: 150
SQ FT: 80,000
SALES (est): 32.6MM **Privately Held**
SIC: 2752 Commercial printing, offset

(G-9083)
TWICE BAKED TWINS LLC
6486 Main St (06611-1311)
PHONE..................................203 368-8841
Judith Vig, *Manager*
EMP: 1
SALES (est): 51.5K **Privately Held**
SIC: 2711 Newspapers, publishing & printing

(G-9084)
UCHISEARCH LLC
15 Wedgewood Rd (06611-1638)
PHONE..................................203 268-9096
Steve Wilson, *President*
EMP: 1
SALES (est): 86.3K **Privately Held**
SIC: 3572 Computer storage devices

(G-9085)
UNILEVER HOME AND PER CARE NA
Also Called: Unilever Hpc NA
75 Merritt Blvd (06611-5435)
PHONE..................................203 502-0086
Frederick Baumer, *Principal*
◆ **EMP:** 78
SALES (est): 37.5MM **Privately Held**
SIC: 2841 2844 Soap & other detergents; shampoos, rinses, conditioners: hair

(G-9086)
UNILEVER HPC USA
45 Commerce Dr (06611-5403)
PHONE..................................203 381-3311
Richard McNabb, *Director*
EMP: 4 **EST:** 2010
SALES (est): 342.6K **Privately Held**
SIC: 2844 Deodorants, personal

(G-9087)
UNILEVER TRUMBULL RES SVCS INC (HQ)
Also Called: Unilever Hpc USA
40 Merritt Blvd (06611-5413)
PHONE..................................203 502-0086
Peter Gallagher, *President*
Jason Harcup, *Vice Pres*
John Weir, *Vice Pres*
◆ **EMP:** 3
SALES (est): 1.7MM
SALES (corp-wide): 58.3B **Privately Held**
SIC: 2844 Toilet preparations
PA: Unilever N.V.
Weena 455
Rotterdam
102 174-000

(G-9088)
UNITED STTS SGN & FBRCTION
Also Called: US Sign
1 Trefoil Dr Ste 2 (06611-6352)
PHONE..................................203 601-1000
George Holley, *Ch of Bd*
Ron Eppert, *Vice Pres*
David Helmers, *Engineer*
Alan Posner, *CFO*
Eppert Diane, *Office Mgr*
EMP: 40
SQ FT: 40,000
SALES (est): 7.1MM **Privately Held**
WEB: www.ussign.com
SIC: 3953 3993 3444 3356 Marking devices; signs & advertising specialties; sheet metalwork; nonferrous rolling & drawing

(G-9089)
UNIVERSAL PRECISION MFG
21 Leffert Rd (06611-4949)
PHONE..................................203 374-9809
Ron Bouffard, *Owner*
EMP: 3
SQ FT: 600
SALES (est): 254.7K **Privately Held**
SIC: 3545 3546 Cutting tools for machine tools; power-driven handtools

(G-9090)
URBAN EXPOSITION LLC (DH)
Also Called: Clarion Ux
35 Nutmeg Dr Ste 125 (06611-5456)
PHONE..................................203 242-8717
Christina Bell, *Vice Pres*
Mike Carlucci, *Vice Pres*
Donna Guess, *Vice Pres*
Wendy Booth, *Opers Mgr*
Karen Gillis, *Buyer*
▲ **EMP:** 25
SQ FT: 3,800
SALES (est): 9.5MM **Privately Held**
WEB: www.urban-expo.com
SIC: 7389 8741 2721 7299 Convention & show services; management services; magazines: publishing & printing; party planning service
HQ: Clarion Events Limited
Bedford House
London SW6 3
207 384-7700

(G-9091)
VAZZANOS CATERING LLC
2456 Huntington Tpke (06611-4019)
PHONE..................................203 378-3331
Christopher Vazzano,
EMP: 10
SALES (est): 304K **Privately Held**
SIC: 5812 2599 Family restaurants; caterers; bar, restaurant & cafeteria furniture

(G-9092)
VIGIRODA ENTERPRISES INC
104 Garwood Rd (06611-2231)
PHONE..................................203 268-6117
Frank Ferraro, *President*
Edward J Cremin, *Mfg Mgr*
EMP: 5
SQ FT: 6,000
SALES (est): 427.3K **Privately Held**
SIC: 3631 Barbecues, grills & braziers (outdoor cooking)

(G-9093)
W S POLYMERS
93 Calhoun Ave (06611-2455)
PHONE..................................203 268-1557
Wayne D Stokes, *Owner*
EMP: 6
SALES (est): 428K **Privately Held**
SIC: 2821 Thermoplastic materials

(G-9094)
WALLACH SURGICAL DEVICES INC (PA)
75 Corporate Dr (06611-1350)
PHONE..................................203 799-2000
Nicholas J Pichotta, *CEO*
Paul L Remmell, *President*
Tina Allan, *Business Mgr*
Carol R Kaufman, *Vice Pres*
Dan Wallach, *Admin Sec*
▲ **EMP:** 31
SQ FT: 40,000
SALES (est): 2.5MM **Privately Held**
SIC: 3841 Surgical & medical instruments

(G-9095)
WALLACH SURGICAL DEVICES INC
95 Corporate Dr (06611-1350)
PHONE..................................800 243-2463
Nicholas J Pichotta, *Branch Mgr*
EMP: 14
SALES (corp-wide): 2.5MM **Privately Held**
SIC: 3841 Surgical & medical instruments
PA: Wallach Surgical Devices, Inc.
75 Corporate Dr
Trumbull CT 06611
203 799-2000

Uncasville
New London County

(G-9096)
BOCCELLI
1 Mohegan Sun Blvd 621c (06382-1355)
PHONE..................................860 862-9300
Linda Nelson, *Manager*
EMP: 5
SALES (est): 290.5K **Privately Held**
SIC: 3172 Handbags, regardless of material: men's

Uncasville - New London County (G-9097)

(G-9097)
COUNTRY CREATIONS BY CAROL
Also Called: Ducky O Soat Company
103 Moxley Rd (06382-2301)
PHONE..................860 848-0276
Carol Kernozek, Owner
EMP: 1
SALES (est): 50K Privately Held
SIC: 3471 Decorative plating & finishing of formed products

(G-9098)
KRA-ZE LLC
32 Cedar Ln (06382-1202)
PHONE..................860 892-8025
Carl Brown, Principal
EMP: 1
SALES (est): 131.7K Privately Held
SIC: 2085 Bourbon whiskey

(G-9099)
MOHEGAN WOOD PELLETS LLC
13 Crow Hill Rd (06382-1118)
PHONE..................860 862-6100
Kevin Brown,
EMP: 1
SALES (est): 67.2K Privately Held
SIC: 2493 Reconstituted wood products

(G-9100)
NORTHEAST WOOD PRODUCTS LLC
Also Called: Thermaglo
13 Crow Hill Rd (06382-1118)
PHONE..................860 862-6350
Guy J Mozzicato, President
Michael D Reid, Senior VP
Kenneth N Wycherley, Senior VP
EMP: 25
SQ FT: 20,000
SALES (est): 2.3MM Privately Held
SIC: 3999 Burnt wood articles

(G-9101)
OLD FARMERS ALMANAC
1 Mohegan Sun Blvd (06382-1355)
PHONE..................860 862-9100
Howard Catcher, Owner
EMP: 2
SALES (est): 103.2K Privately Held
SIC: 2711 Newspapers

(G-9102)
PEPSI-COLA METRO BTLG CO INC
260 Gallivan Ln (06382-1121)
PHONE..................860 848-1231
Paul Andreotta, Manager
EMP: 40
SALES (corp-wide): 64.6B Publicly Held
WEB: www.joy-of-cola.com
SIC: 2086 Carbonated soft drinks, bottled & canned
HQ: Pepsi-Cola Metropolitan Bottling Company, Inc.
1111 Westchester Ave
White Plains NY 10604
914 767-6000

(G-9103)
QUICKSAND BLASTING
107 Jerome Rd (06382-2525)
PHONE..................860 848-4482
George Taylor, Owner
EMP: 1
SALES (est): 92K Privately Held
SIC: 3471 1799 Sand blasting of metal parts; athletic & recreation facilities construction

(G-9104)
TECH-AIR INCORPORATED
152 Route 163 (06382-2118)
P.O. Box 363 (06382-0363)
PHONE..................860 848-1287
Richard Hubbert, President
Donald L Hubbert, Vice Pres
Michael F Hubbert, Vice Pres
Jeanette B Hubbert, Admin Sec
EMP: 34 EST: 1978
SQ FT: 13,000
SALES (est): 6.3MM Privately Held
SIC: 3444 1761 Sheet metalwork; sheet metalwork

(G-9105)
THAMES RIVER FURNITURE LLC
5 Red Cedar Ave (06382-2517)
PHONE..................201 312-2050
David Collins,
EMP: 2
SALES (est): 90.4K Privately Held
SIC: 2599 Furniture & fixtures

(G-9106)
TONI LELAND
Also Called: Equine Graphics
58 Indian Hill Rd (06382-2071)
PHONE..................860 892-8890
Toni Leland, Owner
EMP: 2 EST: 1985
SALES (est): 100K Privately Held
WEB: www.smallhorse.com
SIC: 8748 2731 Publishing consultant; book publishing

(G-9107)
TOWN OF MONTVILLE
Also Called: Montville Sewer Plant
83 Pink Row (06382-2427)
PHONE..................860 848-3830
Mike Didato, Manager
EMP: 13 Privately Held
SIC: 3589 Water treatment equipment, industrial
PA: Town Of Montville
310 Nrwich New Lndon Tpke
Uncasville CT 06382
860 848-3030

(G-9108)
WESTROCK CP LLC
125 Depot Rd (06382-2441)
PHONE..................860 848-1500
Paul Hayes, Branch Mgr
EMP: 115
SALES (corp-wide): 16.2B Publicly Held
WEB: www.sto.com
SIC: 2631 Corrugating medium
HQ: Westrock Cp, Llc
1000 Abernathy Rd
Atlanta GA 30328

Union
Tolland County

(G-9109)
CAVAR INDUSTRIES LLC
38 Mashapaug Rd (06076-4718)
PHONE..................860 684-0706
EMP: 1
SALES (est): 67.1K Privately Held
SIC: 3999 Mfg Misc Products

Unionville
Hartford County

(G-9110)
AIR TOOL SALES & SERVICE CO (PA)
1 Burnham Ave (06085-1225)
P.O. Box 218 (06085-0218)
PHONE..................860 673-2714
Niles O Lindstedt, President
EMP: 9
SQ FT: 15,000
SALES (est): 1.5MM Privately Held
SIC: 3546 5084 5072 7699 Power-driven handtools; pneumatic tools & equipment; power tools & accessories; power handtools; power tool repair; work clothing; tool repair, electric

(G-9111)
AUTOMATECH INC
21 Westview Ter (06085-1459)
PHONE..................860 673-5940
John Murry, Manager
EMP: 10 Privately Held
SIC: 7372 Prepackaged software
PA: Automatech, Inc.
138 Industrial Park Rd
Plymouth MA 02360

(G-9112)
CHAS W HOUSE & SONS INC
19 Perry St (06085-1021)
PHONE..................860 673-2518
Matthew Bristiw, President
Patricia Burwood, Vice Pres
EMP: 65
SQ FT: 140,000
SALES (est): 4.7MM Privately Held
SIC: 2231 3053 Felts, woven: wool, mohair or similar fibers; blankets & blanketings: wool or similar fibers; billiard cloths; gaskets, all materials

(G-9113)
DATA MANAGEMENT INCORPORATED
Also Called: Threshold
557 New Britain Ave (06085)
P.O. Box 789, Farmington (06034-0789)
PHONE..................860 677-8586
Daniel A Hincks, CEO
Brian Gallagher, President
Josette Lumbruno, Marketing Staff
Ronald Coleman, Manager
Katrina Welch, Executive
EMP: 45 EST: 1961
SQ FT: 6,000
SALES: 7.2MM Privately Held
WEB: www.checksforms.com
SIC: 2752 2782 Commercial printing, offset; account books

(G-9114)
EDGEWOOD PROSPECT LLC
15 Edgewood St (06085-1111)
PHONE..................860 255-7799
Kerry Laberge, Principal
EMP: 1
SALES (est): 50.2K Privately Held
SIC: 2499 Wood products

(G-9115)
FIREHOUSE DISCOUNT OIL LLC (PA)
17 Depot Pl Ste C (06085-6202)
PHONE..................860 404-1827
Brian C Damato,
Robert E Lavoie,
EMP: 3 EST: 2008
SALES (est): 374.2K Privately Held
SIC: 2869 Fuels

(G-9116)
KARGER S PUBLISHERS INC
26 W Avon Rd (06085-1162)
PHONE..................860 675-7834
EMP: 5
SALES (est): 528.7K Privately Held
SIC: 2721 Periodicals Publishing/Printing
PA: S. Karger Ag
Allschwilerstrasse 10
Basel BS 4055
613 061-111

(G-9117)
KEITH REED INDUSTRIES LLC
22 Stonegate (06085-1468)
PHONE..................860 677-7739
Keith Reed, Principal
EMP: 1
SALES (est): 44.7K Privately Held
SIC: 3999 Manufacturing industries

(G-9118)
M SQUARED WOODWORKING LLC
66 Litchfield Rd (06085-1318)
PHONE..................860 673-6079
Michael Montelius, Principal
EMP: 2
SALES (est): 162.9K Privately Held
SIC: 2431 Millwork

(G-9119)
MADIGAN MILLWORK INC
150 New Britain Ave (06085-1221)
PHONE..................860 673-7601
James Madigan, President
Regina Madigan, Admin Sec
EMP: 9
SQ FT: 20,000
SALES (est): 1.5MM Privately Held
SIC: 2431 2511 Woodwork, interior & ornamental; wood household furniture

(G-9120)
MAJESTIC PRESS
55 Railroad Ave (06085-1047)
PHONE..................860 673-2064
William Nawrocki, Owner
EMP: 1 EST: 1953
SQ FT: 3,200
SALES: 314.2K Privately Held
WEB: www.majesticpress.com
SIC: 2752 2759 Commercial printing, offset; letterpress printing

(G-9121)
MOMMY & ME
9 School St (06085-1018)
PHONE..................860 269-6226
Seong Yun Choi, Owner
EMP: 2
SALES (est): 126.1K Privately Held
SIC: 5712 2389 Furniture stores; apparel & accessories

(G-9122)
MVP SYSTEMS SOFTWARE INC
29 Mill St Ste 8 (06085-1484)
PHONE..................860 269-3112
EMP: 11
SQ FT: 2,200
SALES (est): 900.3K Privately Held
SIC: 7372 Prepackaged Software Services

(G-9123)
NOVA MACHINING LLC
16 E Shore Blvd (06085-1510)
PHONE..................860 675-8131
Mariusz Wroblewski, Manager
EMP: 3
SALES (est): 180K Privately Held
SIC: 3599 Machine shop, jobbing & repair

(G-9124)
OLDE TYME COUNTRY CANDLES
8 Mohawk Dr (06085-1410)
PHONE..................860 673-5086
Beverly La Plume, Owner
EMP: 1
SALES (est): 52K Privately Held
SIC: 3999 5947 Candles; gift, novelty & souvenir shop

(G-9125)
RANSOM SKATEBOARDS AND APP
178 Plainville Ave (06085-1206)
PHONE..................860 538-5577
Randy Long, Owner
EMP: 2
SALES (est): 147.2K Privately Held
SIC: 3949 Skateboards

(G-9126)
S KARGER PUBLISHERS INC
26 W Avon Rd (06085-1162)
P.O. Box 529 (06085-0529)
PHONE..................860 675-7834
Petra Schlegel, Managing Dir
Iola Gulijew, Business Mgr
Kyle Hurley, Sales Staff
Thomas Nold, Marketing Mgr
Rachele Loetscher, Marketing Staff
EMP: 5
SALES (est): 448.8K
SALES (corp-wide): 51.6MM Privately Held
SIC: 2731 2721 Book publishing; periodicals
PA: S. Karger Ag
Allschwilerstrasse 10
Basel BS 4055
613 061-111

(G-9127)
SARAH MAY BLOCK21PRINTS
39 Forest St (06085-1201)
PHONE..................860 604-4004
Sarah C May, Owner
EMP: 2
SALES (est): 83.9K Privately Held
SIC: 2752 Commercial printing, lithographic

GEOGRAPHIC SECTION

Vernon Rockville - Tolland County (G-9158)

(G-9128)
SHERRIC GROUP LLC
Also Called: Innova Motors
77 Lido Rd (06085-1563)
PHONE..................860 673-3924
Eric M Solliday,
EMP: 2
SALES: 462.2K **Privately Held**
SIC: 3699 Electrical equipment & supplies

Vernon
Tolland County

(G-9129)
ADOLF GORDON CORPORATION
142 Echo Dr (06066-5939)
PHONE..................860 872-9037
Eileen Lieberman, *President*
Joshua Lieberman, *Vice Pres*
EMP: 2
SALES (est): 900K **Privately Held**
WEB: www.adolfgordoncorporation.com
SIC: 3842 5047 Orthopedic appliances; medical equipment & supplies

(G-9130)
AMERICAN SPECIALTY PDTS LLC
101 Industrial Park Rd (06066-5538)
PHONE..................860 871-2279
Andrew Robinson,
Robert Morton,
EMP: 6
SQ FT: 4,000
SALES (est): 1MM **Privately Held**
WEB: www.aspusaonline.com
SIC: 3599 8711 3643 Machine shop, jobbing & repair; engineering services; current-carrying wiring devices

(G-9131)
AROMALITE CANDLE CO LLC
242 Tlcttvlle Rd Unit 207 (06066)
PHONE..................860 872-1029
Jennifer A Kaufmann, *Manager*
EMP: 2
SALES (est): 141K **Privately Held**
SIC: 3999 Candles

(G-9132)
BK INDUSTRIES LLC
75 Hockanum Blvd (06066-4056)
PHONE..................832 744-3067
Benjamin Kantor, *Principal*
EMP: 1
SALES (est): 47.3K **Privately Held**
SIC: 3999 Manufacturing industries

(G-9133)
BNL INDUSTRIES INC
30 Industrial Park Rd (06066-5523)
PHONE..................860 870-6222
Leonard Bosh Jr, *President*
Dennis Grogan, *General Mgr*
Rick Rasimas, *Plant Mgr*
Ryan Wheeler, *Plant Mgr*
Rasimas Rick, *Prdtn Mgr*
EMP: 40
SQ FT: 27,000
SALES (est): 10.6MM **Privately Held**
WEB: www.valves.net
SIC: 3491 Industrial valves

(G-9134)
BRAVO LLC
Also Called: Manchester Packing
1084 Hartford Tpke (06066-4413)
PHONE..................860 896-1899
David Bogner, *Manager*
EMP: 20
SALES (est): 2.4MM
SALES (corp-wide): 5.6MM **Privately Held**
SIC: 2047 Dog food
PA: Bravo , Llc
  349 Wetherell St
  Manchester CT 06040
  866 922-9222

(G-9135)
CONNECTICUT MILLWORK INC
80 Spring St (06066-3452)
P.O. Box 71 (06066-0071)
PHONE..................860 875-2860
Gregory A Stewart, *President*
EMP: 9
SQ FT: 6,000
SALES (est): 1.4MM **Privately Held**
SIC: 2431 Millwork

(G-9136)
CRYSTAL TOOL AND MACHINE CO
Also Called: Ridgeway Racing
114 Brooklyn St (06066-6708)
P.O. Box 504 (06066-0504)
PHONE..................860 870-7431
John D Yedziniak Jr, *Owner*
EMP: 6
SQ FT: 4,000
SALES (est): 450K **Privately Held**
SIC: 3599 Machine shop, jobbing & repair

(G-9137)
DIVISION X SPECIALTIES LLC
75 Diane Dr (06066-6205)
PHONE..................860 402-7736
Scott Wyllie, *Mng Member*
EMP: 2 EST: 2015
SALES (est): 140.6K **Privately Held**
SIC: 3089 8711 1541 Plastic hardware & building products; construction & civil engineering; industrial buildings, new construction

(G-9138)
FAMILY RACEWAY LLC
11 Earl St (06066-3734)
PHONE..................860 896-0171
Kimberly Cavaliere, *Principal*
EMP: 3
SALES (est): 157.7K **Privately Held**
SIC: 3644 Raceways

(G-9139)
HANGER PRSTHETCS & ORTHO INC
428 Hartford Tpke Ste 103 (06066-4841)
PHONE..................860 871-0905
Paul Armstrong, *Manager*
EMP: 4
SALES (corp-wide): 1B **Publicly Held**
SIC: 3842 Surgical appliances & supplies
HQ: Hanger Prosthetics & Orthotics, Inc.
  10910 Domain Dr Ste 300
  Austin TX 78758
  512 777-3800

(G-9140)
INNOVATIVE SIGNS LLC
536 Talcottville Rd (06066-2310)
PHONE..................860 870-7446
John Kurowski, *Manager*
EMP: 2
SALES (est): 207K **Privately Held**
SIC: 3993 Signs & advertising specialties

(G-9141)
INSIGHT ENTERPRISES INC
32 Lily Ln (06066-5269)
PHONE..................860 647-0848
Paul Rouleau Jr, *Branch Mgr*
EMP: 1 **Publicly Held**
SIC: 7372 Prepackaged software
PA: Insight Enterprises, Inc.
  6820 S Harl Ave
  Tempe AZ 85283

(G-9142)
JUST NEON COMPANY
37 Oxbow Dr (06066-4324)
PHONE..................860 881-7446
EMP: 2
SALES (est): 143.9K **Privately Held**
SIC: 2813 Neon

(G-9143)
MIKRO INDUSTRIAL FINISHING CO
170 W Main St (06066-3560)
PHONE..................860 875-6357
Steven Wakefield, *President*
Carla Wakefield, *Vice Pres*
Mikro Kressner, *Sales Engr*
Mike Wakefield, *Sales Staff*
Karen Claing, *Office Mgr*
EMP: 9
SQ FT: 10,500
SALES (est): 1.6MM **Privately Held**
WEB: www.mikro1.com
SIC: 5084 3559 Machine tools & metal-working machinery; metal finishing equipment for plating, etc.

(G-9144)
MILLER PROFESSIONAL TRANS SVC
8 Bancroft Rd (06066-3506)
PHONE..................860 871-6818
Samuel Miller, *Principal*
EMP: 4
SALES (est): 230K **Privately Held**
SIC: 3715 Truck trailers

(G-9145)
MORE THAN ASLEEP PUBG LLC
38 Zoey Dr (06066-5723)
PHONE..................860 872-5757
Maureen E Czick, *Principal*
EMP: 1
SALES (est): 49.9K **Privately Held**
SIC: 2741 Miscellaneous publishing

(G-9146)
MT HOPE CEMETERY ASSOCIATION
41 Elm Hill Rd (06066-5209)
PHONE..................860 643-4264
Linda Welles, *Principal*
EMP: 1 EST: 2014
SALES (est): 101.4K **Privately Held**
SIC: 3272 Grave markers, concrete

(G-9147)
MYCO TOOL & MANUFACTURING INC
176 Bolton Rd Ste 6 (06066-5527)
PHONE..................860 875-7340
Michael Simard, *President*
Linda Simard, *Corp Secy*
EMP: 3
SQ FT: 4,000
SALES (est): 400K **Privately Held**
WEB: www.manufacturingworkers.com
SIC: 3599 Machine shop, jobbing & repair

(G-9148)
NEISS CORP
29 Naek Rd (06066-3942)
PHONE..................860 872-8528
John Cratty, *President*
Bonnie Cratty, *Admin Sec*
EMP: 10
SQ FT: 8,000
SALES (est): 916.8K **Privately Held**
SIC: 2521 Panel systems & partitions (free-standing), office: wood

(G-9149)
PARAGON PUBLICATIONS
124 Rollingview Dr (06066-5837)
PHONE..................860 875-4366
Robert Shoemaker, *Principal*
EMP: 2
SALES (est): 150.4K **Privately Held**
SIC: 2759 Publication printing

(G-9150)
PRECISION PLATING CORP
1050 Hartford Tpke (06066-4487)
P.O. Box 506, Vernon Rockville (06066-0506)
PHONE..................860 875-9267
Richard Goulet, *President*
EMP: 2
SQ FT: 3,000
SALES (est): 241.7K **Privately Held**
WEB: www.ppc1904.com
SIC: 3471 Buffing for the trade; chromium plating of metals or formed products; polishing, metals or formed products

(G-9151)
REMINDER BROADCASTER
Also Called: Reminder Media
130 Old Town Rd (06066-2322)
P.O. Box 27 (06066-0027)
PHONE..................860 875-3366
Ken Hovland, *President*
EMP: 99
SALES (est): 2.8MM **Privately Held**
SIC: 2711 Newspapers

(G-9152)
SILVER LINING TECHNOLOGIES LLC
48 Rainbow Trl (06066-5919)
PHONE..................860 539-4182
Stephen D Deltatto, *Principal*
EMP: 2
SALES (est): 162.1K **Privately Held**
SIC: 3479 Metal coating & allied service

(G-9153)
SUNNY PUBLISHING COMPANY LLC
1134 Hartford Tpke (06066-4598)
PHONE..................203 619-3831
EMP: 2 EST: 2012
SALES (est): 82K **Privately Held**
SIC: 2741 Misc Publishing

(G-9154)
TEK INDUSTRIES INC
48 Hockanum Blvd Unit 1 (06066-7048)
PHONE..................860 870-0001
Mark Matheny, *President*
Deborah Gordon, *Vice Pres*
EMP: 32
SALES (est): 7.1MM **Privately Held**
WEB: www.tekind.com
SIC: 3672 7373 8711 Printed circuit boards; turnkey vendors, computer systems; designing: ship, boat, machine & product

(G-9155)
TOLLAND MACHINE CO
1050 Hartford Tpke (06066-4487)
P.O. Box 82 (06066-0082)
PHONE..................860 872-4863
Lance Shackway, *Owner*
EMP: 6
SQ FT: 7,500
SALES (est): 1MM **Privately Held**
WEB: www.tollandmachine.com
SIC: 3599 Machine shop, jobbing & repair

(G-9156)
TOWN OF VERNON
Also Called: Water Treatment Plant
100 Windsorville Rd (06066-2315)
PHONE..................860 870-3545
Robert Grasis, *General Mgr*
EMP: 17 **Privately Held**
WEB: www.vernonctpolice.com
SIC: 3589 Water treatment equipment, industrial
PA: Town Of Vernon
  14 Park Pl
  Vernon CT 06066
  860 870-3690

(G-9157)
VENTURES LLC DOT COM LLC
35-31 Tlcottville Rd 23 (06066)
PHONE..................203 930-8972
Leonard Wells,
EMP: 5
SALES (est): 535.4K **Privately Held**
SIC: 3556 Roasting machinery: coffee, peanut, etc.

Vernon Rockville
Tolland County

(G-9158)
ABA-PGT INC
140 Bolton Rd (06066-5512)
PHONE..................860 872-2058
Sam Pierson, *Branch Mgr*
EMP: 4
SALES (est): 250.5K
SALES (corp-wide): 30.5MM **Privately Held**
WEB: www.abapgt.com
SIC: 3089 Injection molding of plastics
PA: Aba-Pgt Inc.
  10 Gear Dr
  Manchester CT 06042
  860 649-4591

Vernon Rockville - Tolland County (G-9159)

(G-9159)
ALTERNATIVE CHOICE LLC
5 Lawrence St (06066-3308)
PHONE...................................860 875-7529
Jerry Kish, *Owner*
EMP: 1
SALES (est): 64.4K **Privately Held**
SIC: 2843 Processing assistants

(G-9160)
ATLAS HOBBING AND TOOL CO INC
Also Called: American Molding Product
20 Mountain St (06066-3310)
PHONE...................................860 870-9226
Mehmed Ramic, *President*
Supie Polo, *Corp Secy*
Raum Bombard, *Vice Pres*
Ron Bombard, *Manager*
EMP: 17
SQ FT: 2,400
SALES (est): 2.3MM **Privately Held**
SIC: 3089 Molding primary plastic

(G-9161)
B & A DESIGN INC
255 Bamforth Rd (06066-5629)
P.O. Box 3153 (06066-2053)
PHONE...................................860 871-0134
Robert E Triggs Jr, *President*
Ann Triggs, *Vice Pres*
EMP: 3
SALES (est): 40K **Privately Held**
SIC: 3559 3613 Electronic component making machinery; control panels, electric

(G-9162)
BLIND CRAFTERS
615 Talcottville Rd (06066-2319)
PHONE...................................860 896-0366
EMP: 2
SALES (est): 126.1K **Privately Held**
SIC: 2431 Blinds (shutters), wood

(G-9163)
BOSS INDUSTRIES
133 West St (06066-2901)
PHONE...................................860 819-1637
Abigael Sutherland, *Principal*
EMP: 2 EST: 2017
SALES (est): 80.6K **Privately Held**
SIC: 3999 Manufacturing industries

(G-9164)
CLEMSON SHEET METAL LLC
344 Somers Rd Unit 1 (06066)
PHONE...................................860 871-9369
Alan Clemson, *Owner*
EMP: 3 EST: 2007
SALES (est): 318.4K **Privately Held**
SIC: 3444 Sheet metalwork

(G-9165)
CONNECTICUT AEROSPACE INC
101 Industrial Park Rd (06066-5538)
PHONE...................................860 872-0036
Chris Clark, *Principal*
EMP: 2
SALES (est): 94.5K **Privately Held**
SIC: 3812 Aircraft/aerospace flight instruments & guidance systems

(G-9166)
D & D PRINTING & ADVERTISING
1264 Hartford Tpke (06066-4528)
PHONE...................................860 871-7774
Don Tyrell, *Principal*
EMP: 2
SALES (est): 138.4K **Privately Held**
SIC: 2752 Commercial printing, lithographic

(G-9167)
DANCO MANUFACTURING LLC
77 Industrial Park Rd # 13 (06066-5500)
PHONE...................................860 870-1706
Angelo Daniele,
Mario Daniele,
EMP: 2
SQ FT: 400
SALES (est): 400K **Privately Held**
SIC: 3469 3545 Machine parts, stamped or pressed metal; machine tool accessories

(G-9168)
FISHER ELECTRONICS
6 Brighton Ln (06066-5805)
PHONE...................................860 646-7779
Jack Fisher, *Owner*
EMP: 2
SALES (est): 106.2K **Privately Held**
SIC: 3663 7622 Radio broadcasting & communications equipment; radio repair & installation

(G-9169)
I-LOGIC SOFTWARE
655 Talcottville Rd (06066-2354)
PHONE...................................860 875-7760
Douglas Rudd, *Owner*
EMP: 2
SALES (est): 114.7K **Privately Held**
WEB: www.i-logic.com
SIC: 7372 Prepackaged software

(G-9170)
IREX MACHINE INC
77 Industrial Park Rd (06066-5500)
PHONE...................................860 870-1677
Ireneusz Kotlewski, *President*
EMP: 2
SALES (est): 153.9K **Privately Held**
SIC: 3599 Industrial machinery

(G-9171)
NEW TECHNOLOGIES MFG INC
63 Duncaster Ln (06066-4805)
PHONE...................................860 872-7605
Thomas Richard Kroegel, *Principal*
EMP: 1
SALES (est): 66.2K **Privately Held**
SIC: 3949 5941 Archery equipment, general; archery supplies

(G-9172)
NURSES ALARM SYSTEMS INC
27 Naek Rd Ste 6 (06066-3965)
PHONE...................................860 872-0025
Lynne Swalec, *Principal*
Connie Miessau, *Production*
EMP: 2
SALES (est): 286.2K **Privately Held**
SIC: 3822 Building services monitoring controls, automatic

(G-9173)
PAMELAS PATTERNS
613 Talcottville Rd (06066-2319)
PHONE...................................610 534-4182
Pamela Leggett, *Principal*
EMP: 2
SALES (est): 188.5K **Privately Held**
SIC: 3543 Industrial patterns

(G-9174)
PIO TEE GIO LLC
482 Talcottville Rd (06066-4019)
PHONE...................................860 280-7073
Harbhajan Singh, *Owner*
EMP: 2 EST: 2016
SALES (est): 101.9K **Privately Held**
SIC: 2759 Screen printing

(G-9175)
POSH PUPS LLC
56 Hyde Ave (06066-4503)
PHONE...................................860 454-4055
Bill Soucy, *Principal*
EMP: 2 EST: 2011
SALES (est): 141.7K **Privately Held**
SIC: 3999 Pet supplies

(G-9176)
POTTERS INK INC
84 Grove St C (06066-3742)
PHONE...................................860 896-5909
EMP: 1 EST: 2011
SALES (est): 63.2K **Privately Held**
SIC: 3961 Mfg Costume Jewelry

(G-9177)
RMI INC
Also Called: Stafford Reminder
130 Old Town Rd (06066-2322)
P.O. Box 27 (06066-0027)
PHONE...................................860 875-3366
Kenneth A Hovland Jr, *President*
George Cunningham, *Corp Secy*
Keith A Hovland, *Vice Pres*
EMP: 200
SQ FT: 30,000
SALES (est): 10.3MM **Privately Held**
SIC: 2711 2752 Newspapers, publishing & printing; commercial printing, offset

(G-9178)
SIGN A RAMA
Also Called: Sign-A-Rama
536 Talcottville Rd (06066-2310)
PHONE...................................860 870-7446
John Kurowski, *Owner*
EMP: 2
SALES (est): 144.5K **Privately Held**
SIC: 3993 Signs & advertising specialties

(G-9179)
SIGN CONNECTION INC
101 West St (06066-2954)
PHONE...................................860 870-8855
Bodin Muschinsky, *President*
Evon Muschinsky, *Vice Pres*
EMP: 6
SQ FT: 2,900
SALES: 200K **Privately Held**
SIC: 3993 Signs & advertising specialties

(G-9180)
SOLDREAM INC
129 Reservoir Rd (06066-5705)
PHONE...................................860 871-6883
Jarek Kalecinski, *President*
Jadwiga Kalecinski, *President*
Anthony Steullet, *Vice Pres*
Richard Letellier, *QC Mgr*
Rob Renaud, *QC Mgr*
▼ EMP: 49
SQ FT: 20,000
SALES (est): 15.3MM **Privately Held**
WEB: www.soldream.com
SIC: 3829 Measuring & controlling devices

(G-9181)
THERMA-SCAN INC
43 Claire Rd (06066-4821)
P.O. Box 121, Ellington (06029-0121)
PHONE...................................860 872-9770
Gayle Carroll, *CEO*
George Carroll, *President*
EMP: 3
SALES (est): 253.7K **Privately Held**
SIC: 2759 Thermography

(G-9182)
TIM POLOSKI
38 Risley Rd (06066-5923)
PHONE...................................860 508-6566
Timothy Poloski, *Owner*
EMP: 4
SALES (est): 182.7K **Privately Held**
SIC: 3479 Metal coating & allied service

(G-9183)
TOWN OF VERNON
Also Called: Water Pollution Control Dept
5 Park St Fl 2 (06066-3211)
P.O. Box 147 (06066-0147)
PHONE...................................860 870-3699
David Ignatowicz, *Director*
EMP: 4 **Privately Held**
WEB: www.vernonctpolice.com
SIC: 3589 Sewage & water treatment equipment
PA: Town Of Vernon
14 Park Pl
Vernon CT 06066
860 870-3690

(G-9184)
TROPHY SHOP
214 Hartford Tpke (06066-4701)
P.O. Box 2353 (06066-1753)
PHONE...................................860 871-0867
Edward Dymon, *Owner*
EMP: 1
SALES (est): 54.4K **Privately Held**
SIC: 5999 5099 3993 Trophies & plaques; signs, except electric; signs & advertising specialties

(G-9185)
UNITED PHOTONICS LLC
42 Diane Dr (06066-6237)
PHONE...................................617 752-2073
Scott Nelson, *Principal*
EMP: 4 EST: 2016
SALES (est): 285.6K **Privately Held**
SIC: 3661 Fiber optics communications equipment

(G-9186)
VERNON PRINTING CO INC
Also Called: Minuteman Press
352 Hartford Tpke Ste 9 (06066-4733)
PHONE...................................860 872-1826
Amy Steiman, *President*
Joel Steinman, *Exec VP*
Joel Steiman, *Vice Pres*
EMP: 8
SALES (est): 176.3K **Privately Held**
SIC: 2752 2791 2789 Commercial printing, lithographic; typesetting; bookbinding & related work

Voluntown
New London County

(G-9187)
CHARLES RIVER LABORATORIES INC
425 Pendleton Hill Rd (06384-2107)
PHONE...................................860 376-1240
Lydia Cary, *Administration*
EMP: 30
SALES (corp-wide): 2.2B **Publicly Held**
WEB: www.criver.com
SIC: 2836 Biological products, except diagnostic
HQ: Charles River Laboratories, Inc.
251 Ballardvale St
Wilmington MA 01887
781 222-6000

(G-9188)
COLEMAN DRILLING & BLASTING
1458 Hopeville Rd (06384)
PHONE...................................860 376-3813
Robert Coleman, *President*
EMP: 5
SALES (est): 2MM **Privately Held**
WEB: www.colemandrillingandblasting.com
SIC: 1381 1629 Drilling oil & gas wells; blasting contractor, except building demolition

(G-9189)
JEWETT CITY TOOL AND DIE CO
576 Beach Pond Rd (06384-1912)
PHONE...................................860 376-0455
Michael J Magario, *Partner*
Joseph F Magario, *Partner*
EMP: 2
SQ FT: 900
SALES (est): 110K **Privately Held**
SIC: 3544 3599 Special dies & tools; machine shop, jobbing & repair

(G-9190)
LOVING LIFE LLC
363 Rockville Rd (06384-2018)
PHONE...................................860 326-1459
Lauren Richmond,
EMP: 1
SALES: 180K **Privately Held**
SIC: 5961 7372 7389 ; application computer software;

(G-9191)
SUGAR RUN K9 LLC
Also Called: Srk9
43 Valley Dr (06384-1731)
PHONE...................................860 591-4193
Pamela Deveau-Delaney, *CEO*
EMP: 1
SALES: 950K **Privately Held**
SIC: 8748 8331 5999 3577 Safety training service; manpower training; educational aids & electronic training materials; data conversion equipment, media-to-media: computer; animal training services

Wallingford
New Haven County

(G-9192)
111 BRENTWOOD LLC
15 Taylor Ln (06492-6019)
PHONE................................203 284-5065
Mark Wollen, *Principal*
EMP: 2
SALES (est): 65.4K **Privately Held**
SIC: 2499 Wood products

(G-9193)
A LINE DESIGN INC
18 Martin Trl (06492-2622)
PHONE................................203 294-0080
John Arrigoni, *President*
EMP: 5
SALES (est): 525.1K **Privately Held**
WEB: www.alinedesign.com
SIC: 3423 Hand & edge tools

(G-9194)
A S J SPECIALTIES LLC
2 Toms Dr (06492-2558)
PHONE................................203 284-8650
Anthony Savo Jr,
Sheila Savo,
EMP: 3
SALES (est): 80K **Privately Held**
SIC: 2541 2434 Table or counter tops, plastic laminated; wood kitchen cabinets

(G-9195)
ACCENT SCREENPRINTING
186 Center St (06492-4142)
PHONE................................203 284-8601
EMP: 3 **EST:** 2010
SALES (est): 255.1K **Privately Held**
SIC: 2759 Commercial Printing

(G-9196)
ACCOLADE FURNITURE LLC
340 Quinnipiac St (06492-4050)
PHONE................................203 265-0524
Timothy H Fagan,
EMP: 1
SALES (est): 129.4K **Privately Held**
WEB: www.accoladefurniture.com
SIC: 2519 Household furniture

(G-9197)
ACCURATE AUTOMATION LLC
29 Pequot Rd (06492-2813)
PHONE................................203 988-9426
Clement Hall,
EMP: 2
SQ FT: 2,000
SALES: 250K **Privately Held**
SIC: 3559 Electronic component making machinery

(G-9198)
AERO PRECISION MFG LLC
71 S Turnpike Rd (06492-3421)
PHONE................................203 675-7625
Frank Jukic, *Principal*
EMP: 8 **EST:** 2007
SALES (est): 853.8K **Privately Held**
SIC: 3999 Manufacturing industries

(G-9199)
ALLNEX USA INC
Also Called: Evonic Cyro
528 S Cherry St (06492-4458)
PHONE................................203 269-4481
Linda Harroch, *CEO*
Benoit Debecker, *Vice Pres*
Robert Wood, *Engineer*
Duncan Taylor, *CFO*
Kevin Gildea, *Manager*
EMP: 99
SALES (corp-wide): 177.9K **Privately Held**
SIC: 2821 Plastics materials & resins
HQ: Allnex Usa Inc.
9005 Westside Pkwy
Alpharetta GA
800 433-2873

(G-9200)
ALLOY METALS INC (PA)
34b Barnes Indus Rd S (06492-2438)
P.O. Box 336, Roseville MI (48066-0336)
PHONE................................203 774-3270
John Melanson, *President*
Erin St Thomas, *Manager*
▲ **EMP:** 13
SALES (est): 1.3MM **Privately Held**
SIC: 3351 Copper & copper alloy sheet, strip, plate & products

(G-9201)
AMERICAN PERFORMANCE PDTS LLC
7 Atwater Pl (06492-1774)
PHONE................................203 269-4468
Ronald P Normandin, *Mng Member*
Andrew Debaise,
EMP: 6
SQ FT: 13,000
SALES: 350K **Privately Held**
SIC: 3444 Sheet metalwork

(G-9202)
AMERICAN STONECRAFTERS INC
Also Called: A American Stone & Countertop
224 S Whittlesey Ave (06492-4511)
PHONE................................203 514-9725
Fax: 203 269-7471
EMP: 5
SALES (est): 510K **Privately Held**
SIC: 2542 3281 5999 5032 Mfg Nonwd Partition/Fixt Mfg Cut Stone/Products Ret Misc Merchandise Whol Brick/Stone Matrls

(G-9203)
AMETEK INC
Also Called: Ametek Specialty Metal Pdts
21 Toelles Rd (06492-4456)
P.O. Box 5807 (06492-7607)
PHONE................................203 265-6731
David Jenkins, *President*
Brian McConnell, *Project Mgr*
Andrew Vidmar, *Project Mgr*
Robert Kowalczyk, *Opers Staff*
John Lalena, *Buyer*
EMP: 105
SALES (corp-wide): 4.8B **Publicly Held**
SIC: 3452 3823 3399 3331 Bolts, metal; industrial instrmnts msrmnt display/control process variable; iron, powdered; primary copper; steel wire & related products; gaskets, packing & sealing devices
PA: Ametek, Inc.
1100 Cassatt Rd
Berwyn PA 19312
610 647-2121

(G-9204)
AMPHENOL CORPORATION (PA)
358 Hall Ave (06492-3574)
P.O. Box 5030 (06492-7530)
PHONE................................203 265-8900
R Adam Norwitt, *President*
Lance E D'Amico, *Senior VP*
William J Doherty, *Senior VP*
Zachary W Raley, *Senior VP*
David Silverman, *Senior VP*
▼ **EMP:** 85
SALES: 8.2B **Publicly Held**
SIC: 3678 3643 3661 Electronic connectors; connectors & terminals for electrical devices; fiber optics communications equipment

(G-9205)
AMPHENOL FUNDING CORP
358 Hall Ave (06492-3574)
PHONE................................203 265-8900
Adam R Norwitt, *CEO*
Edward G Jepsen, *CFO*
EMP: 2
SALES (est): 147.9K **Privately Held**
SIC: 3678 Electronic connectors

(G-9206)
AMPHENOL INTERNATIONAL LTD (HQ)
358 Hall Ave (06492-3574)
PHONE................................203 265-8900
EMP: 3

SALES (est): 1.8MM
SALES (corp-wide): 8.2B **Publicly Held**
SIC: 3678 Electronic connectors
PA: Amphenol Corporation
358 Hall Ave
Wallingford CT 06492
203 265-8900

(G-9207)
APCT-CT INC
Also Called: Apct Global
340 Quinnipiac St Unit 25 (06492-4050)
P.O. Box 309 (06492-0309)
PHONE................................203 284-1215
Steve Robinson, *President*
Tracy Conway, *Controller*
▲ **EMP:** 5
SQ FT: 2,500
SALES (est): 2.8MM
SALES (corp-wide): 26.7MM **Privately Held**
SIC: 3672 Printed circuit boards
PA: Apct, Inc.
3495 De La Cruz Blvd
Santa Clara CA 95054
408 727-6442

(G-9208)
APCT-WALLINGFORD INC
Also Called: Tech Circuits
340 Quinnipiac St Unit 25 (06492-4050)
P.O. Box 309 (06492-0309)
PHONE................................203 269-3311
Steve Robinson, *President*
Greg Elder, *CFO*
Kimberly Johnson, *Sales Staff*
Pat Fusco, *Department Mgr*
Deke Lein, *Manager*
EMP: 45
SQ FT: 46,000
SALES (est): 8.4MM
SALES (corp-wide): 26.7MM **Privately Held**
WEB: www.techcircuits.com
SIC: 3672 Circuit boards, television & radio printed
PA: Apct, Inc.
3495 De La Cruz Blvd
Santa Clara CA 95054
408 727-6442

(G-9209)
AQUA COMFORT TECHNOLOGIES LLC (PA)
8 Fairfield Blvd Ste 1 (06492-1890)
PHONE................................203 265-0100
Dan Tighe, *Mktg Coord*
Ramona Sukhraj, *Marketing Staff*
David Rybacki, *Mng Member*
Mark Coleman, *Mng Member*
Timothy Hart, *Mng Member*
EMP: 2
SALES (est): 673K **Privately Held**
SIC: 3648 Swimming pool lighting fixtures

(G-9210)
AQUACOMFORT SOLUTIONS LLC
8 Fairfield Blvd Ste 5 (06492-1890)
PHONE................................203 265-0100
Carol Yeager, *CFO*
EMP: 2
SALES (est): 150.4K **Privately Held**
SIC: 3433 Heaters, swimming pool: oil or gas

(G-9211)
ARNCO SIGN COMPANY
1133 S Broad St (06492-1713)
PHONE................................203 238-1224
Paul Cohen, *President*
Marc Cohen, *Vice Pres*
EMP: 25
SQ FT: 15,000
SALES (est): 2.8MM **Privately Held**
SIC: 7389 3993 Crane & aerial lift service; electric signs

(G-9212)
ARRIS TECHNOLOGY INC
15 Sterling Dr (06492-1843)
PHONE................................678 473-8493
EMP: 10
SALES (est): 1.1MM **Privately Held**
SIC: 3661 Telephone & telegraph apparatus

(G-9213)
ATLANTIC EQP INSTALLERS INC
55 N Plains Industrial Rd (06492-5841)
P.O. Box 547 (06492-0547)
PHONE................................203 284-0402
Robert J Huelsman, *President*
Donald J Huelsman, *Vice Pres*
Bill Bohne, *CFO*
William E Bohne, *CFO*
Robert K Huelsman, *Shareholder*
EMP: 22 **EST:** 1981
SQ FT: 12,000
SALES (est): 6.8MM **Privately Held**
SIC: 3441 1796 Fabricated structural metal; installing building equipment

(G-9214)
ATLAS FILTRI NORTH AMERICA LLC
1068 N Farms Rd Ste 3 (06492-5939)
PHONE................................203 284-0080
Gary Fappino, *CEO*
Daniele Costantini, *Vice Pres*
EMP: 12
SQ FT: 24,000
SALES: 1.5MM **Privately Held**
SIC: 3589 Water treatment equipment, industrial

(G-9215)
AUTOMAR NE LLC
329 Main St Ste 108 (06492-2291)
PHONE................................203 793-7630
Theresa L Defilio, *Principal*
EMP: 2
SALES (est): 197K **Privately Held**
SIC: 3537 Bomb lifts & trucks

(G-9216)
AXIS LASER
7 Atwater Pl (06492-1774)
PHONE................................203 284-9455
Paul Best, *Owner*
EMP: 4 **EST:** 2007
SALES (est): 349.1K **Privately Held**
SIC: 3444 Sheet metal specialties, not stamped

(G-9217)
B 9 AIR QUALITY SERVICES LLC
121 N Plains Industrial R (06492-2352)
PHONE................................203 387-1709
Brent Borgnine, *Mng Member*
EMP: 7
SALES: 400K **Privately Held**
SIC: 7699 2679 Cleaning services; building, insulating & packaging paper

(G-9218)
B H S INDUSTRIES LTD
23 N Plains Industrial Rd # 3 (06492-2345)
PHONE................................203 284-9764
Fax: 203 265-5999
EMP: 8
SQ FT: 3,600
SALES (est): 490K **Privately Held**
SIC: 3369 Manufactures Industrial And Giftware Castings

(G-9219)
BEI HOLDINGS INC
6 Capital Dr (06492-2318)
PHONE................................203 741-9300
Michael Salamone, *President*
EMP: 15
SALES (est): 587.6K **Privately Held**
SIC: 3695 Magnetic & optical recording media

(G-9220)
BOARDMAN SILVERSMITHS INC
22 N Plains Industrial Rd 6c (06492-2341)
PHONE................................203 265-9978
Burton Boardman, *President*
EMP: 15
SALES (est): 2.3MM **Privately Held**
WEB: www.boardmansilversmiths.com
SIC: 3914 Silverware; pewter ware

(G-9221)
BOND-BILT GARAGES INC
30 N Plains Industrial Rd # 16 (06492-2357)
PHONE................................203 269-3375
Kenneth Kaye, *President*

Wallingford - New Haven County (G-9222)

Arlene Kaye, *Admin Sec*
EMP: 6 **EST:** 1961
SQ FT: 2,400
SALES: 1.9MM **Privately Held**
SIC: 2452 Prefabricated buildings, wood

(G-9222)
BRITTANY COMPANY INC
193 S Cherry St (06492-4017)
P.O. Box 221 (06492-0221)
PHONE 203 269-7859
Thaddeus Swierczynski, *President*
Thaddeau Sivernyznski, *President*
EMP: 5
SQ FT: 7,500
SALES: 1MM **Privately Held**
WEB: www.brittanycompany.com
SIC: 3444 1761 Sheet metal specialties, not stamped; roofing, siding & sheet metal work

(G-9223)
BROAD PEAK MANUFACTURING LLC
10 Beaumont Rd Ste 1 (06492-2455)
PHONE 203 678-4664
Levi Citarella,
EMP: 20 **EST:** 2015
SALES: 1.7MM **Privately Held**
SIC: 3471 Cleaning, polishing & finishing

(G-9224)
BROWNE HANSEN LLC
44 School House Rd (06492-3434)
PHONE 203 269-0557
Ronald Hansen Jr, *Mng Member*
Frederick Browne, *Mng Member*
Steven Browne,
Kelly O Neil,
EMP: 6
SQ FT: 50,000
SALES (est): 521.2K **Privately Held**
SIC: 2844 Suntan lotions & oils

(G-9225)
CARDIOXYL PHARMACEUTICALS INC
5 Research Pkwy (06492-1951)
PHONE 919 869-8586
Christopher A Kroeger, *President*
Doug Cowart, *Exec VP*
EMP: 7
SALES (est): 785.2K
SALES (corp-wide): 22.5B **Publicly Held**
WEB: www.cardioxyl.com
SIC: 2834 Druggists' preparations (pharmaceuticals)
PA: Bristol-Myers Squibb Company
430 E 29th St Fl 14
New York NY 10016
212 546-4000

(G-9226)
CHARTER OAK AUTOMATION LLC
340 Quinnipiac St Ste 19 (06492-4050)
PHONE 203 562-0699
Randall Betta,
Mark Herman,
Loudon Page,
▲ **EMP:** 4
SALES (est): 563.2K **Privately Held**
SIC: 3541 3549 Vertical turning & boring machines (metalworking); metalworking machinery

(G-9227)
CIDRA CHEMICAL MANAGEMENT INC (HQ)
50 Barnes Park Rd N # 103 (06492-5920)
PHONE 203 265-0035
F Kevin Didden, *President*
Michael Grillo, *Vice Pres*
John Viega, *Opers Mgr*
Gary Hokunson, *CFO*
EMP: 70
SALES (est): 8.7MM **Privately Held**
WEB: www.cidra.com
SIC: 3823 Flow instruments, industrial process type

(G-9228)
CIDRA CORPORATE SERVICES INC
50 Barnes Park Rd N (06492-5920)
PHONE 203 265-0035
Kevin Didden, *President*
F Kevin Didden, *President*
John Viega, *COO*
Michael Grillo, *Vice Pres*
Gary Hokunson, *Treasurer*
EMP: 70
SALES (est): 15.6MM **Privately Held**
WEB: www.cidra.com
SIC: 3823 Industrial flow & liquid measuring instruments
PA: Cidra Holdings Llc
50 Barnes Park Rd N # 103
Wallingford CT 06492

(G-9229)
CIDRA CORPORATION
50 Barnes Park Rd N # 103 (06492-5920)
PHONE 203 265-0035
F Kevin Didden, *CEO*
Patrick Curry, *President*
Martin Putnam, *President*
Marc Grammatico, *Vice Pres*
John Viega, *Vice Pres*
▼ **EMP:** 95
SALES (est): 22MM **Privately Held**
SIC: 3823 Industrial flow & liquid measuring instruments

(G-9230)
CIDRA MINERAL PROCESSING INC
50 Barnes Park Rd N (06492-5920)
PHONE 203 265-0035
F Kevin Didden, *President*
Michael Grillo, *Vice Pres*
John Viega, *Opers Mgr*
Gary Hokunson, *CFO*
EMP: 70
SALES (est): 527.4K **Privately Held**
WEB: www.cidra.com
SIC: 3823 Flow instruments, industrial process type; industrial flow & liquid measuring instruments
PA: Cidra Holdings Llc
50 Barnes Park Rd N # 103
Wallingford CT 06492

(G-9231)
CIDRA OILSANDS INC (HQ)
50 Barnes Park Rd N (06492-5920)
PHONE 203 265-0035
F Kevin Didden, *President*
Michael Grillo, *Vice Pres*
Gary Hokunson, *CFO*
EMP: 6
SALES (est): 4.9MM **Privately Held**
WEB: www.cidra.com
SIC: 3823 Gas flow computers, industrial process type; flow instruments, industrial process type

(G-9232)
CLG ENTERPRISES INC
Also Called: BEI
6 Capital Dr (06492-2318)
PHONE 203 741-9300
Michael Salamone, *Branch Mgr*
EMP: 11
SQ FT: 14,000
SALES (corp-wide): 7.2MM **Privately Held**
SIC: 7382 3572 5999 Protective devices, security; tape recorders for computers; alarm & safety equipment stores
PA: Clg Enterprises, Inc.
47 Masters Ln
Milford CT 06461
203 887-1093

(G-9233)
COLORS INK
40 Capital Dr (06492-2318)
PHONE 203 269-4000
Sema Sargin, *President*
Oguc Sargin, *Vice Pres*
EMP: 4
SQ FT: 4,000
SALES (est): 800K **Privately Held**
SIC: 3952 5084 Ink, drawing: black & colored; printing trades machinery, equipment & supplies

(G-9234)
COMMAND TOOLING SYSTEMS
16 Cliffside Dr (06492-1924)
PHONE 203 284-9615
Bob R Russo, *Principal*
EMP: 1
SALES (est): 54.1K **Privately Held**
SIC: 3545 Machine tool accessories

(G-9235)
COMPONENT ENGINEERS INC
Also Called: C E I
108 N Plains Indus Rd (06492-2334)
PHONE 203 269-0557
Ronald Hansen Jr, *CEO*
Rick Griffin, *COO*
Anthony Bracale, *Vice Pres*
Clayton Oliver, *CFO*
Brittany Ryan, *Human Resources*
◆ **EMP:** 95
SQ FT: 52,000
SALES (est): 27.6MM **Privately Held**
WEB: www.componenteng.com
SIC: 3469 Stamping metal for the trade

(G-9236)
CONCEPT TEAM ASSOCIATES LLC
41 Hill Ave (06492-2257)
PHONE 203 269-5152
Peter Doyle,
Carol Ryan,
EMP: 2
SALES (est): 220K **Privately Held**
SIC: 3471 Plating of metals or formed products

(G-9237)
CONFORMIS INC
10 Beaumont Rd Ste 4 (06492-2455)
PHONE 203 793-7178
Mark Augusti, *CEO*
EMP: 202 **Publicly Held**
SIC: 3996 Hard surface floor coverings
PA: Conformis, Inc.
600 Technology Park Dr # 3
Billerica MA 01821

(G-9238)
CONNECTICUT HYPODERMICS INC
519 Main St (06492-1723)
PHONE 203 265-4881
Leonard Tutolo, *Ch of Bd*
Steven Tutolo, *President*
Robert Kwasniewski, *Project Mgr*
Donna Wilson, *QC Mgr*
Mark Tutolo, *Treasurer*
◆ **EMP:** 90
SQ FT: 30,000
SALES (est): 21MM **Privately Held**
WEB: www.connhypo.com
SIC: 3841 Hypodermic needles & syringes

(G-9239)
COOL-IT LLC
340 Quinnipiac St (06492-4050)
P.O. Box 309 (06492-0309)
PHONE 203 284-4848
Gregory Peterson,
Ashley Dean, *Admin Sec*
Randy Peterson,
EMP: 4 **EST:** 2012
SALES (est): 190K **Privately Held**
SIC: 3089 Plastic containers, except foam

(G-9240)
CORCO MFG
550 Woodhouse Ave (06492-5418)
PHONE 203 284-1831
EMP: 1
SALES (est): 49.9K **Privately Held**
SIC: 3999 Manufacturing industries

(G-9241)
CORRU SEALS INC
Also Called: Nicholsons
24 Capital Dr (06492-2318)
PHONE 203 284-0319
T P Nicholson, *CEO*
William Warner, *President*
EMP: 19
SQ FT: 8,000
SALES (est): 3.6MM **Privately Held**
WEB: www.corru-seals.com
SIC: 3053 Gaskets, all materials

(G-9242)
CRUSH CLUB LLC
65 S Colony St (06492-4150)
P.O. Box 1827 (06492-7127)
PHONE 203 626-9545
Frank Martone, *President*
EMP: 3
SALES (est): 268.1K **Privately Held**
SIC: 2084 Wines

(G-9243)
CT ACQUISITIONS LLC
Also Called: Danver
1 Grand St (06492-3509)
PHONE 888 441-0537
Alex Drozd, *Plant Mgr*
Johnson Clark, *Sales Staff*
Denise Litchfield, *Sales Associate*
Philip Zaleon, *Mktg Dir*
Mitchell Slater, *Mng Member*
EMP: 50 **EST:** 1998
SQ FT: 52,000
SALES: 8.5MM **Privately Held**
WEB: www.danver.com
SIC: 2514 Kitchen cabinets: metal

(G-9244)
CUSTOM CHROME PLATING
400 S Orchard St (06492-4500)
PHONE 203 265-5667
Jerry Sofocli, *Manager*
EMP: 3
SALES (est): 115.8K **Privately Held**
SIC: 3471 Chromium plating of metals or formed products

(G-9245)
CYTEC INDUSTRIES INC
Cyro Industries
5 S Cherry St (06492)
P.O. Box 425 (06492-7050)
PHONE 203 284-4334
Robert A Leitzman, *Principal*
Patricia Harrison, *Mktg Dir*
EMP: 120
SALES (corp-wide): 12.8MM **Privately Held**
SIC: 3083 2821 2899 Laminated plastics plate & sheet; plastics materials & resins; hydrofluoric acid compound, for etching or polishing glass
HQ: Cytec Industries Inc.
4500 Mcginnis Ferry Rd
Alpharetta GA 30005

(G-9246)
DANAHER TOOL GROUP
61 Barnes Industrial Park (06492-1845)
PHONE 203 284-7000
Lawrence Culp Jr, *CEO*
EMP: 15
SALES (est): 2.2MM **Privately Held**
SIC: 3823 Water quality monitoring & control systems

(G-9247)
DAVID J WEBER
Also Called: Weber Audio Systems
131 N Colony St (06492-3631)
PHONE 203 949-9198
David J Weber, *Owner*
EMP: 1
SQ FT: 800
SALES: 150K **Privately Held**
SIC: 3651 5731 Audio electronic systems; radio, television & electronic stores

(G-9248)
DEMARTINO FIXTURE CO INC
Also Called: Chefs Equipment Emporium
920 S Colony Rd (06492-5263)
PHONE 203 269-3971
Dominick Demartino, *President*
Michele Salvatore, *Corp Secy*
Pasquale Salvatore, *Vice Pres*
EMP: 40
SQ FT: 150,000

SALES (est): 9.4MM **Privately Held**
WEB: www.chefsequip.com
SIC: **3585** Refrigeration equipment, complete; cabinets, show & display, refrigerated; counters & counter display cases, refrigerated

(G-9249)
DEXMET CORPORATION
22 Barnes Industrial Rd S (06492-2462)
PHONE....................203 294-4440
Tim Poor, *CEO*
▲ EMP: 65
SALES (est): 12.5MM **Privately Held**
SIC: **3497** Metal foil & leaf

(G-9250)
DIRECTIONAL TECHNOLOGIES INC
89 N Main St (06492-3709)
PHONE....................203 294-9200
Katherine M Sequino, *Principal*
Mike Sequino, *Vice Pres*
Katherine Sequino, *Engineer*
EMP: 2
SALES (est): 110K **Privately Held**
SIC: **1381** Directional drilling oil & gas wells

(G-9251)
DNE SYSTEMS INC (DH)
50 Barnes Industrial Park (06492)
P.O. Box 30 (06492-0030)
PHONE....................203 265-7151
William Gill, *President*
Wayne Addy, *Engineer*
Ron Hanley, *Human Res Dir*
Meredith Ieraci, *Human Res Dir*
Karl Forsander, *Director*
EMP: 2
SALES (est): 7.5MM
SALES (corp-wide): 984.8MM **Privately Held**
SIC: **3357** Communication wire
HQ: Ultra Electronics Defense Inc.
4101 Smith School Rd
Austin TX 78744
512 327-6795

(G-9252)
DOCTOR STUFF LLC
20 N Plains Industrial Rd # 1 (06492-2300)
PHONE....................203 785-8475
Kathleen Bouvier, *Principal*
Nora Laverty,
EMP: 6
SALES (est): 643.8K **Privately Held**
SIC: **2759** 8711 Commercial printing; consulting engineer

(G-9253)
DRINKIN HATS LLC
10 Huntington Ridge Rd (06492-5331)
PHONE....................203 265-3489
Timothy Keogh Jr, *Principal*
EMP: 1 EST: 2010
SALES (est): 55.4K **Privately Held**
SIC: **2353** Hats, caps & millinery

(G-9254)
DUPONT GUY OFFICE
21 Cassella Dr (06492-1615)
PHONE....................203 679-0358
Guy Dupont, *Principal*
EMP: 1
SALES (est): 74.9K **Privately Held**
SIC: **2879** Agricultural chemicals

(G-9255)
E & A ENTERPRISES INC
Also Called: Northeast Thermography
10 Capital Dr A (06492-2318)
PHONE....................203 250-8050
Elliott L Greenspan, *President*
Anita Greenspan, *Corp Secy*
EMP: 20
SQ FT: 10,000
SALES (est): 2MM **Privately Held**
SIC: **2759** Thermography; visiting cards (including business): printing; invitation & stationery printing & engraving; envelopes: printing

(G-9256)
E-J ELECTRIC T & D LLC
53 N Plains Industrial Rd (06492-5808)
PHONE....................203 626-9625
Joe Rubino, *General Mgr*
Anthony Edward Mann,
EMP: 80 EST: 2009
SALES (est): 25MM **Privately Held**
SIC: **3699** 1731 Electrical equipment & supplies; electrical work

(G-9257)
ENAQUA
57 Grieb Trl (06492-2655)
PHONE....................203 269-9890
Manoj Ghawaj, *CEO*
EMP: 1
SALES (est): 68.2K **Privately Held**
SIC: **3999** Manufacturing industries

(G-9258)
ETHOSENERGY COMPONENT REPR LLC
Also Called: Wood Group Component Repair
34 Capital Dr (06492-2318)
PHONE....................203 949-8144
Bert Voisine, *President*
EMP: 35
SQ FT: 15,000
SALES (est): 388.8K
SALES (corp-wide): 10B **Privately Held**
WEB: www.woodgroupgts.com
SIC: **3724** Turbines, aircraft type
HQ: Ethosenergy Gts Holdings (Us), Llc
2800 North Loop W # 1100
Houston TX 77092

(G-9259)
EVEREST ISLES LLC
616 N Elm St (06492-3270)
PHONE....................203 561-5128
Jeffrey Hladky, *President*
Ross Fenton, *Comms Dir*
EMP: 5
SALES (est): 608.3K **Privately Held**
SIC: **2329** Bathing suits & swimwear: men's & boys'

(G-9260)
EVOLUTION STUCCO LLC
35 Old Colony Rd (06492-2425)
PHONE....................203 507-3639
Julio C Obando, *Principal*
EMP: 1
SALES (est): 48.5K **Privately Held**
SIC: **3299** Stucco

(G-9261)
EXECUTIVE GRAPHIC SYSTEMS LLC
61 N Plains Industrial Rd # 184 (06492-5841)
PHONE....................203 678-6432
Robert T Desalle Jr, *Mng Member*
EMP: 1
SALES (est): 155.8K **Privately Held**
SIC: **3993** 2759 Name plates: except engraved, etched, etc.: metal; engraving

(G-9262)
EXOCETUS ATONOMOUS SYSTEMS LLC
7 Laser Ln (06492-1928)
PHONE....................860 512-7260
Joseph Turner, *COO*
EMP: 1
SALES (est): 60K **Privately Held**
SIC: **3731** Submersible marine robots, manned or unmanned

(G-9263)
EXOCETUS AUTONOMOUS SYSTEMS
7 Laser Ln (06492-1928)
PHONE....................860 512-7260
William Turner, *CEO*
Joseph Turner, *COO*
EMP: 5 EST: 2017
SALES (est): 348.3K **Privately Held**
SIC: **3731** 3812 Submersible marine robots, manned or unmanned; search & detection systems & instruments

(G-9264)
EXPERT EMBROIDERY
121 N Plains Indus Ste G (06492-5883)
PHONE....................203 269-9675
Chris Fjuer, *President*
EMP: 15
SALES (est): 870.3K **Privately Held**
SIC: **2395** Embroidery products, except schiffli machine

(G-9265)
EYLWARD TIMBER CO
13 Quince St (06492-2964)
PHONE....................203 265-4276
Mike Eylward, *Owner*
EMP: 9
SALES (est): 806.7K **Privately Held**
SIC: **2421** 5099 Sawmills & planing mills, general; firewood

(G-9266)
FIBERGLASS ENGR & DESIGN CO
Also Called: Fedco
25 N Plains Industrial Hw (06492-6804)
PHONE....................203 265-1644
Dave Papoosha, *President*
EMP: 4
SQ FT: 13,000
SALES (est): 500K **Privately Held**
SIC: **3089** 3792 Plastic processing; travel trailers & campers

(G-9267)
FISHER MFG SYSTEMS INC
20 N Plains Industrial Rd # 12 (06492-6811)
PHONE....................203 250-8033
EMP: 1 **Privately Held**
SIC: **3599** Machine shop, jobbing & repair
PA: Fisher Manufacturing Systems, Inc.
20 N Plains Industrial Rd # 12
Wallingford CT 06492

(G-9268)
FISHER MFG SYSTEMS INC (PA)
Also Called: Fisher Products
20 N Plains Industrial Rd # 12 (06492-6811)
PHONE....................203 269-3846
Curtis Fisher, *President*
Sharon Fisher, *Admin Sec*
EMP: 10
SQ FT: 10,000
SALES (est): 1MM **Privately Held**
WEB: www.fishermfgsystems.com
SIC: **3599** Machine shop, jobbing & repair

(G-9269)
FOUGERA PHARMACEUTICALS INC
Byk-Chemie USA
524 S Cherry St (06492-4453)
P.O. Box 5670 (06492-7651)
PHONE....................203 265-2086
Darryl Jackson, *Publisher*
Wolfgang Zinnert, *Manager*
EMP: 69
SALES (corp-wide): 51.9B **Privately Held**
SIC: **2851** Paints & allied products
HQ: Fougera Pharmaceuticals Inc.
60 Baylis Rd
Melville NY 11747
631 454-7677

(G-9270)
FRANK PRINTING CO R
184 Center St (06492-4142)
PHONE....................203 265-6152
Richard Frank, *Owner*
EMP: 3
SQ FT: 1,300
SALES (est): 265.5K **Privately Held**
SIC: **2759** Letterpress printing

(G-9271)
FRIES SPINNING & STAMPINGS
65 Washington St (06492-3565)
P.O. Box 368 (06492-0368)
PHONE....................203 265-1678
William E Cook Jr, *President*
Peter Cook, *Vice Pres*
Mark Soderstrom, *Admin Sec*
EMP: 1
SQ FT: 14,000
SALES (est): 900K **Privately Held**
SIC: **3469** Spinning metal for the trade

(G-9272)
FRONT PORCH BREWING
226 N Plns Ind Rd Unit 4 (06492-2397)
PHONE....................203 679-1096
James Flynn, *Owner*
EMP: 5
SALES (est): 139.9K **Privately Held**
SIC: **2082** Beer (alcoholic beverage)

(G-9273)
G & G BEVERAGE DISTRIBUTORS
Also Called: G & G Recycling Center
207 Church St (06492-6202)
P.O. Box 4488 (06492-7565)
PHONE....................203 949-6220
Mark Gingras, *President*
Tom Larosa, *General Mgr*
Chris Gingras, *Corp Secy*
Mary Brockett, *Production*
Christine Gingras, *Treasurer*
▲ EMP: 62
SQ FT: 54,000
SALES (est): 21MM **Privately Held**
WEB: www.ggbeverage.com
SIC: **5181** 5149 4953 2086 Beer & other fermented malt liquors; soft drinks; water, distilled; recycling, waste materials; bottled & canned soft drinks

(G-9274)
GARDNER WELDING LLC
850 S Colony Rd (06492-5260)
PHONE....................203 265-1036
Lee Biega, *Owner*
EMP: 1
SQ FT: 2,800
SALES (est): 100K **Privately Held**
SIC: **7692** 1799 Welding repair; welding on site

(G-9275)
GEORGE S PREISNER JEWELERS
Also Called: Preisner, George S Pewter Co
150 Center St (06492-4114)
P.O. Box 460 (06492-0460)
PHONE....................203 265-0057
George S Preisner, *President*
Erna Damm, *Vice Pres*
EMP: 5
SQ FT: 5,280
SALES (est): 280K **Privately Held**
SIC: **3914** 3911 Pewter ware; jewelry, precious metal

(G-9276)
GLASS INDUSTRIES AMERICA LLC
340 Quinnipiac St Unit 9 (06492-4050)
PHONE....................203 269-6700
Livia Liburdi, *Manager*
George Sutherland,
EMP: 15
SALES (est): 1.7MM **Privately Held**
SIC: **3231** 5023 Decorated glassware: chipped, engraved, etched, etc.; kitchenware

(G-9277)
GOUVEIA VINEYARDS LLC
1339 Whirlwind Hill Rd (06492-2727)
PHONE....................203 265-5526
Mary L Gouveia, *Principal*
EMP: 2
SALES (est): 227.4K **Privately Held**
SIC: **2084** Wines

(G-9278)
HARBY POWER SOLUTIONS LLC
105 S Elm St (06492-4705)
PHONE....................203 265-0012
Byron Brewer Jr, *Principal*
EMP: 2
SALES (est): 156.9K **Privately Held**
SIC: **3629** Electrical industrial apparatus

(G-9279)
HATCAMS LLC
168 N Plains Industrial (06492-2377)
PHONE....................203 303-7250

EMP: 1
SALES (est): 56K **Privately Held**
SIC: 3651 Mfg Home Audio/Video Equipment

(G-9280)
HERBASWAY LABORATORIES LLC
101 N Plains Indstrl Rd (06492-2360)
PHONE.................................203 269-6991
Lorraine St John, *Exec VP*
Franklin M Saintjohn,
▲ EMP: 49
SALES (est): 6.1MM **Privately Held**
WEB: www.herbasway.com
SIC: 2099 8731 2087 5149 Tea blending; commercial physical research; flavoring extracts & syrups; organic & diet foods

(G-9281)
HIGH ENERGY X-RAYS INTL CORP
Also Called: Hexi
57 N Plains Industrial Rd B (06492-5841)
P.O. Box 457 (06492-0457)
PHONE.................................203 909-9777
Sereymeth Kong, *Vice Pres*
EMP: 3
SALES (est): 175.3K **Privately Held**
SIC: 3844 Radiographic X-ray apparatus & tubes

(G-9282)
HITACHI ALOKA MEDICAL LTD
10 Fairfield Blvd (06492-5903)
PHONE.................................203 269-5088
Minoru Yoshizumi, *President*
EMP: 99
SALES (est): 8.5MM **Privately Held**
SIC: 3841 5047 3829 Surgical & medical instruments; hospital equipment & furniture; measuring & controlling devices

(G-9283)
HITACHI ALOKA MEDICAL AMER INC
10 Fairfield Blvd (06492-5903)
PHONE.................................203 269-5088
David R Famiglietti, *President*
Randy R Baraso, *Business Mgr*
Angela Van Arsdale, *QC Mgr*
Ray Koba, *Treasurer*
EMP: 99
SALES (est): 19.7MM **Privately Held**
WEB: www.aloka.com
SIC: 3841 5047 3829 Surgical & medical instruments; hospital equipment & furniture; measuring & controlling devices
PA: Hitachi, Ltd.
1-6-6, Marunouchi
Chiyoda-Ku TKY 100-0

(G-9284)
HOLO-KROME USA
61 Barnes Industrial Park (06492-1845)
PHONE.................................800 879-6205
Bart Letniowski, *Engineer*
Orlando Castaneda, *Manager*
EMP: 30 EST: 2018
SALES (est): 2.2MM **Privately Held**
SIC: 3452 Bolts, nuts, rivets & washers

(G-9285)
HYDEVILLE MANFACTURING INC
340 Quinnipiac St (06492-4050)
PHONE.................................203 265-0524
Timothy Fagan, *President*
EMP: 2
SALES (est): 250K **Privately Held**
SIC: 8712 2499 Architectural services; decorative wood & woodwork

(G-9286)
IDEX HEALTH & SCIENCE LLC
50 Barnes Park Rd N (06492-5920)
PHONE.................................203 774-4422
EMP: 2
SALES (corp-wide): 2.4B **Publicly Held**
SIC: 3561 Industrial pumps & parts
HQ: Idex Health & Science Llc
600 Park Ct
Rohnert Park CA 94928
707 588-2000

(G-9287)
IMAGE360
Also Called: Signs By Tomorrow
163 N Plains Indus Rd (06492-2332)
PHONE.................................203 949-0726
Tim Keogh, *President*
EMP: 14
SQ FT: 5,600
SALES: 700K **Privately Held**
SIC: 3993 Signs & advertising specialties

(G-9288)
INNOVATIVE MFG SYSTEMS LLC
53 High Hill Rd (06492-1903)
PHONE.................................203 284-2605
Thomas E Massaro, *Principal*
EMP: 1
SALES (est): 60.7K **Privately Held**
SIC: 3999 Manufacturing industries

(G-9289)
INTERACTER INC
10 Beaumont Rd Ste 1 (06492-2455)
PHONE.................................203 949-0199
Bob Besch, *President*
EMP: 2 EST: 2013
SALES (est): 232.1K **Privately Held**
SIC: 5063 3691 Batteries; storage batteries

(G-9290)
ITS NEW ENGLAND INC
8 Capital Dr (06492-2318)
PHONE.................................203 265-8100
Brian Russell, *President*
EMP: 4 EST: 2010
SALES (est): 467.9K **Privately Held**
SIC: 3579 Office machines

(G-9291)
J & L TOOL COMPANY INC
368 N Cherry Street Ext (06492-2309)
PHONE.................................203 265-6237
Leonard Rossicone Sr, *President*
Jason Rossicone, *Vice Pres*
Leonard Rossicone Jr, *Vice Pres*
Nancy Rossicone, *Vice Pres*
EMP: 25
SQ FT: 12,000
SALES (est): 3.4MM **Privately Held**
SIC: 3544 Industrial molds; forms (molds), for foundry & plastics working machinery

(G-9292)
J&L PLASTIC MOLDING LLC
368 N Cherry Street Ext (06492-2309)
PHONE.................................203 265-6237
Al Kunst, *Production*
Michael Griglun, *QC Mgr*
Marty Kellaher, *VP Sales*
Leonard Rossicone,
Leonard Rossicone Jr,
▲ EMP: 7
SQ FT: 12,000
SALES (est): 1.4MM **Privately Held**
WEB: www.jlmolding.com
SIC: 3089 Molding primary plastic; injection molding of plastics

(G-9293)
JAMES H QUINN
Also Called: Quinn Capentry & Painting
60 Lee Ave (06492-3610)
PHONE.................................203 809-6046
James Quinn, *Owner*
EMP: 1
SALES (est): 82K **Privately Held**
SIC: 2431 Woodwork, interior & ornamental

(G-9294)
JEM MANUFACTURING INC
Also Called: American Industrial Rbr Pdts
20 N Plains Industrial Rd # 12 (06492-6811)
PHONE.................................203 250-9404
Ian Robinson, *President*
EMP: 6
SALES (est): 652.2K **Privately Held**
SIC: 3061 Mechanical rubber goods

(G-9295)
JIMMYS CLEANERS & ALTERATIONS
200 Church St Ste 9 (06492-2274)
PHONE.................................203 294-1006
Hak Roh, *Owner*
EMP: 1
SALES (est): 67.2K **Privately Held**
SIC: 2842 Drycleaning preparations

(G-9296)
KERRY D HOGAN
7 Morgan Dr (06492-2640)
PHONE.................................203 213-4624
Kerry Hogan, *Owner*
EMP: 2
SALES (est): 175K **Privately Held**
SIC: 2431 Millwork

(G-9297)
KINAMOR INCORPORATED
Also Called: Kinamor Plastics
63 N Plains Industrial Rd (06492-5841)
PHONE.................................203 269-0380
John Romanik Sr, *CEO*
John Romanik Jr, *Vice Pres*
Mary Romanik, *Vice Pres*
▲ EMP: 29
SQ FT: 15,000
SALES (est): 5.2MM **Privately Held**
WEB: www.kinamorinc.com
SIC: 3089 3441 2396 Injection molding of plastics; fabricated structural metal; automotive & apparel trimmings

(G-9298)
KOVACS MACHINE AND TOOL CO
50 N Plains Industrial Rd (06492-2372)
PHONE.................................203 269-4949
Allen Cuccaro, *President*
Peter Albrycht, *Vice Pres*
Michael Frank, *Vice Pres*
EMP: 37 EST: 1967
SQ FT: 8,000
SALES (est): 5.4MM **Privately Held**
SIC: 3599 3544 Machine shop, jobbing & repair; special dies, tools, jigs & fixtures

(G-9299)
KRAFTY KAKES INC
39 N Plains Industrial Rd E (06492-2346)
PHONE.................................203 284-0299
Tom Conlon, *President*
EMP: 4
SALES (est): 355.7K **Privately Held**
SIC: 2051 Bread, all types (white, wheat, rye, etc): fresh or frozen

(G-9300)
L R BROWN MANUFACTURING CO
53 Prince St (06492-4119)
P.O. Box 282 (06492-0282)
PHONE.................................203 265-5639
Charles Liedke Sr, *President*
Charles Liedke Jr, *Vice Pres*
Robert Liedke, *Vice Pres*
Fran Liedke, *Admin Sec*
Frances Liedke, *Admin Sec*
EMP: 8 EST: 1949
SQ FT: 5,000
SALES (est): 300K **Privately Held**
SIC: 3599 3542 Custom machinery; rebuilt machine tools, metal forming types

(G-9301)
LAWRENCE HOLDINGS INC (PA)
34b Barnes Indus Rd S (06492-2438)
P.O. Box 336, Roseville MI (48066-0336)
PHONE.................................203 949-1600
Lawrence Buhl III, *CEO*
K C Jones, *CFO*
EMP: 17
SALES (est): 37.7MM **Privately Held**
SIC: 3469 3089 3544 Stamping metal for the trade; automotive parts, plastic; special dies, tools, jigs & fixtures

(G-9302)
LEE MANUFACTURING INC
46 Barnes Industrial Rd S (06492-2438)
P.O. Box 758 (06492-0758)
PHONE.................................203 284-0466
George M Eames IV, *President*
George M Eames III, *Director*
EMP: 60
SQ FT: 40,000
SALES (est): 10.9MM **Privately Held**
WEB: www.leemanufacturing.com
SIC: 3444 Metal housings, enclosures, casings & other containers

(G-9303)
LINGOL CORPORATION
415 S Cherry St (06492-4428)
P.O. Box 791 (06492-0791)
PHONE.................................203 265-3608
Peter W Lindenfelser, *Vice Pres*
Ruth B Lindenfelser, *Admin Sec*
EMP: 10
SALES (est): 1.4MM **Privately Held**
SIC: 3089 Plastic processing

(G-9304)
LODEN SOFTWARE
37 Jamestown Cir (06492-2138)
PHONE.................................203 949-9416
Jeffrey Loden, *Owner*
Julie Phelps, *Research*
EMP: 1 EST: 2009
SALES (est): 62K **Privately Held**
SIC: 7372 Home entertainment computer software

(G-9305)
LOGANS RUN TRNSP SVC LLC
Also Called: Tyler's Total Truck Service
226 N Plains Industrl 8 (06492-2397)
PHONE.................................203 679-0870
Bobby Bruneau, *Vice Pres*
EMP: 1
SALES (corp-wide): 937.5K **Privately Held**
SIC: 3531 Trucks, off-highway
PA: Logan's Run Transportation Service "llc"
226 N Plns Indstrl 8
Wallingford CT 06492
203 679-0870

(G-9306)
LOGO SPORTSWEAR INC
12 Beaumont Rd (06492-2402)
PHONE.................................203 678-4700
Patrick Cerreta, *CEO*
Tom Kordik, *Opers Staff*
Josh Ferguson, *Sales Mgr*
Terry Halloran, *Sales Staff*
Frederick Swan, *Sales Staff*
EMP: 6 EST: 2015
SQ FT: 15,000
SALES (est): 617.7K
SALES (corp-wide): 851.2K **Privately Held**
SIC: 2759 5699 Screen printing; customized clothing & apparel; sports apparel
PA: Digital Room Llc
8000 Haskell Ave
Van Nuys CA 91406
310 575-4440

(G-9307)
LOST CODE SOFTWARE LLC
49 Hanover St (06492-1641)
PHONE.................................203 626-9133
EMP: 2 EST: 2010
SALES (est): 120K **Privately Held**
SIC: 7372 Prepackaged Software Services

(G-9308)
LYONS UPHOLSTERY SHOP INC
Also Called: Lyons Upholstery & Carpet Shop
864 N Colony Rd (06492-2410)
PHONE.................................203 269-3782
James Mercuri, *President*
Patricia Koniuta, *Vice Pres*
EMP: 4
SQ FT: 6,000
SALES: 100K **Privately Held**
SIC: 7641 5713 2391 Reupholstery; carpets; curtains & draperies

(G-9309)
MAGNA-WIND INC
Also Called: Magna-Wind Electric Motor Repr
130 S Turnpike Rd (06492-4398)
PHONE.................................203 269-4749
Peter Kulak, *President*
Cecilia O'Rourke, *President*

GEOGRAPHIC SECTION
Wallingford - New Haven County (G-9337)

EMP: 5
SQ FT: 7,200
SALES (est): 1.4MM **Privately Held**
WEB: www.magna-wind.com
SIC: 5063 7694 Motors, electric; electric motor repair

(G-9310)
MAGNETEC CORPORATION
Also Called: Ithaca Peripherals Div
7 Laser Ln (06492-1928)
PHONE.................................203 949-9933
Bart C Shuldman, *President*
David Ritchie, *President*
John Cygielnik, *Senior VP*
Michael Kumpf, *Senior VP*
Lucy H Staley, *Senior VP*
EMP: 100 **EST:** 1973
SQ FT: 44,000
SALES (est): 47MM **Publicly Held**
WEB: www.magnetec.com
SIC: 3577 Printers, computer
PA: Transact Technologies Incorporated
2319 Whitney Ave Ste 3b
Hamden CT 06518

(G-9311)
MAK METAL FAB
89 N Plains Industrial Rd (06492-5847)
PHONE.................................203 213-0269
EMP: 1
SALES (est): 54.3K **Privately Held**
SIC: 3499 Fabricated metal products

(G-9312)
MARLIN COMPANY (PA)
10 Research Pkwy Ste 4 (06492-1963)
PHONE.................................203 294-9800
Frank Kenna III, *CEO*
Eric Auxt, *Regional Mgr*
David Cook, *Regional Mgr*
Paul Faits, *Regional Mgr*
Mike Healy, *Regional Mgr*
EMP: 60
SQ FT: 20,000
SALES (est): 27.8MM **Privately Held**
WEB: www.themarlincompany.com
SIC: 8748 8732 2731 Communications consulting; business research service; pamphlets: publishing & printing

(G-9313)
MATERIALS PROC DEV GROUP LLC
7 Swan Ave (06492-1624)
PHONE.................................203 269-6617
Robert Hancock, *Owner*
EMP: 3
SALES (est): 241.5K **Privately Held**
SIC: 2851 Shellac (protective coating)

(G-9314)
MATTHEWS PRINTING CO
10 Marshall St (06492-4097)
P.O. Box 456 (06492-0456)
PHONE.................................203 265-0363
Dean De Negris, *President*
Gail De Negris, *Admin Sec*
EMP: 10
SQ FT: 4,000
SALES (est): 1.5MM **Privately Held**
SIC: 2752 2759 Commercial printing, offset; letterpress printing

(G-9315)
MAX-TEK LLC
Also Called: Max-Tek Ue Superabrasive Mch
48 N Plains Industrial Rd # 1 (06492-2351)
PHONE.................................860 372-4900
Edward Elie, *President*
▲ **EMP:** 10
SALES (est): 2MM **Privately Held**
SIC: 3541 Machine tools, metal cutting type

(G-9316)
MEALS BY MICHAEL
Also Called: Personal Service
8 Mulligan Dr (06492-5457)
PHONE.................................203 294-1770
Michael G Kisiel, *Owner*
EMP: 1
SALES (est): 44.2K **Privately Held**
SIC: 2099 Ready-to-eat meals, salads & sandwiches

(G-9317)
MEASUREMENT SYSTEMS INC
Also Called: Ultra Elec Measurement Systems
50 Barnes Park Rd N # 102 (06492-5940)
PHONE.................................203 949-3500
Peter Crawford, *President*
Ken L Tasch, *President*
Larry Falco, *Vice Pres*
EMP: 42
SQ FT: 19,500
SALES (est): 13.5MM
SALES (corp-wide): 984.8MM **Privately Held**
WEB: www.ultra-msi.com
SIC: 3625 3577 Electric controls & control accessories, industrial; computer peripheral equipment
PA: Ultra Electronics Holdings Plc
417 Bridport Road
Greenford MIDDX UB6 8
208 813-4567

(G-9318)
MICHELE SCHIANO DI COLA INC
11 S Colony St (06492-4150)
PHONE.................................203 265-5301
Cindy Fiorentino, *President*
EMP: 2
SALES (est): 273.1K **Privately Held**
SIC: 2041 3531 Pizza dough, prepared; crushers, grinders & similar equipment

(G-9319)
MICRO PRINTING LLC
216 Center St (06492-4142)
PHONE.................................203 265-5578
Anthony Diep, *Mng Member*
Justin Brangiero,
EMP: 2
SALES (est): 111.1K **Privately Held**
SIC: 2759 Business forms: printing

(G-9320)
MICROMOD AUTOMATION & CONTROLS
10 Capital Dr (06492-2318)
PHONE.................................585 321-9209
Eric Vangellow, *President*
Jeffrey Galvin, *Sales Engr*
Kirk Jaynes, *Technical Staff*
EMP: 16
SALES (est): 3MM **Privately Held**
SIC: 3823 Industrial process control instruments

(G-9321)
MICROMOD AUTOMTN & CONTRLS LLC
10 Capital Dr (06492-2318)
PHONE.................................585 321-9200
Sohil Patel, *President*
Pat Carpenter, *Purch Mgr*
Rick Warner, *Manager*
Bill White, *Technical Staff*
EMP: 20
SALES (est): 4MM **Privately Held**
WEB: www.micmod.com
SIC: 3625 Industrial controls: push button, selector switches, pilot

(G-9322)
MIDSTATE ELECTRONICS CO
71 S Turnpike Rd Ste 2 (06492-3421)
PHONE.................................203 265-9900
Josh Reed, *President*
Denice Handwerk, *Vice Pres*
Gerri Duplease, *Purchasing*
Andrew Cordes, *Accounting Mgr*
Osullivan Patty, *Accounting Mgr*
▲ **EMP:** 18 **EST:** 1977
SQ FT: 7,774
SALES (est): 9.8MM **Privately Held**
WEB: www.midstateelectronics.com
SIC: 5065 3672 Electronic parts; printed circuit boards

(G-9323)
MIKCO MANUFACTURING INC
14 Village Ln (06492-2427)
P.O. Box 764 (06492-0764)
PHONE.................................203 269-2250
Michael J Boissy, *President*
Michael S Boissy, *Vice Pres*
Betty Boissy, *Executive*
Betty J Boissy, *Shareholder*
EMP: 14
SQ FT: 9,000
SALES (est): 2.5MM **Privately Held**
SIC: 3599 Machine shop, jobbing & repair

(G-9324)
MORRIS PRECISION TOOL INC
50 N Plains Industrial Rd (06492-2333)
PHONE.................................203 284-8488
David Harkness, *Owner*
EMP: 2
SALES (est): 125.4K **Privately Held**
SIC: 3599 Machine shop, jobbing & repair

(G-9325)
NATIONAL FILTER MEDIA CORP
9 Fairfield Blvd (06492-1828)
PHONE.................................203 741-2225
Denis Charest, *Branch Mgr*
EMP: 40
SQ FT: 32,745
SALES (corp-wide): 922.9MM **Privately Held**
WEB: www.nfm-filter.com
SIC: 3569 Jack screws; filters, general line: industrial
HQ: The National Filter Media Corporation
691 N 400 W
Salt Lake City UT 84103
801 363-6736

(G-9326)
NN INC
6 Northrop Indus Pk Rd W (06492-1962)
PHONE.................................203 793-7132
EMP: 3
SALES (corp-wide): 770.6MM **Publicly Held**
SIC: 3562 Ball bearings & parts
PA: Nn, Inc.
6210 Ardrey Kell Rd
Charlotte NC 28277
980 264-4300

(G-9327)
NOMIS ENTERPRISES
90 Northford Rd (06492-5519)
PHONE.................................631 821-3120
Susan Simon, *Owner*
EMP: 3
SALES (est): 40K **Privately Held**
SIC: 2329 3993 5999 2399 Men's & boys' athletic uniforms; signs & advertising specialties; banners, flags, decals & posters; emblems, badges & insignia: from purchased materials; embroidering of advertising on shirts, etc.

(G-9328)
NORTH HAVEN MANUFACTURING CO
25 George St (06492-4008)
PHONE.................................203 284-8578
Robert Rinaldi, *President*
EMP: 2
SQ FT: 8,500
SALES: 170K **Privately Held**
SIC: 3545 3541 Gauges (machine tool accessories); robots for drilling, cutting, grinding, polishing, etc.

(G-9329)
NU LINE DESIGN LLC
Also Called: Nu Line Signs
21 N Plains Industrial Rd (06492-2382)
PHONE.................................203 949-0726
Susan Keogh,
Tim Keogh,
EMP: 4
SQ FT: 2,600
SALES: 190K **Privately Held**
SIC: 3993 7389 4493 Signs & advertising specialties; sign painting & lettering shop; boat yards, storage & incidental repair

(G-9330)
NUCOR STEEL CONNECTICUT INC
Also Called: Nucor Bar Mill Group
35 Toelles Rd (06492-4419)
P.O. Box 928 (06492-0928)
PHONE.................................203 265-0615
Mark Brando, *Principal*
Selma Notaro, *Purch Agent*
Rolf Kuhn, *Controller*
Lisa Greenier, *Senior Mgr*
Maria Dias, *Supervisor*
▲ **EMP:** 157
SQ FT: 227,120
SALES (est): 71.8MM
SALES (corp-wide): 25B **Publicly Held**
WEB: www.nucor.com
SIC: 3312 3449 3496 Rods, iron & steel: made in steel mills; bars, concrete reinforcing: fabricated steel; mesh, made from purchased wire
PA: Nucor Corporation
1915 Rexford Rd Ste 400
Charlotte NC 28211
704 366-7000

(G-9331)
ON TRACK KARTING INC (PA)
984 N Colony Rd (06492-1860)
PHONE.................................203 626-0464
Martin Tyrrel, *Principal*
▲ **EMP:** 15
SALES (est): 2.2MM **Privately Held**
SIC: 3799 Go-carts, except children's

(G-9332)
PARADISE HLLS VNYRD WINERY LLC
15 Windswept Hill Rd (06492-2755)
PHONE.................................203 284-0123
Albert Ruggiero,
EMP: 6
SALES (est): 532.4K **Privately Held**
SIC: 2084 Wines

(G-9333)
PAUWAY CORP
63 N Cherry St Ste 2 (06492-2363)
PHONE.................................203 265-3939
Wayne Rydzy, *President*
Paulette Rydzy, *Admin Sec*
EMP: 15
SALES (est): 1.9MM **Privately Held**
WEB: www.pauwaycorp.com
SIC: 3479 Painting of metal products

(G-9334)
PEACH PRINTING SOLUTIONS
18 Chimney Sweep Rd (06492-1656)
PHONE.................................203 793-7381
Lynne Bahr, *President*
EMP: 2
SALES (est): 102.1K **Privately Held**
SIC: 2752 Commercial printing, lithographic

(G-9335)
PERRIN MANUFACTURING
102 Liney Hall Ln (06492-2710)
PHONE.................................203 265-1325
Ron Perrin, *Owner*
EMP: 1
SALES (est): 94K **Privately Held**
WEB: www.jean-perrin.com
SIC: 3465 Body parts, automobile: stamped metal

(G-9336)
POWER CONTROLS INC
801 N Main Street Ext (06492-2463)
PHONE.................................203 284-0235
Ronald Nash, *President*
Karen Nash, *Admin Sec*
EMP: 14
SQ FT: 7,500
SALES (est): 2.4MM **Privately Held**
WEB: www.powercontrols.com
SIC: 3679 Power supplies, all types: static

(G-9337)
PPG INDUSTRIES INC
22 Barnes Industrial Rd S (06492-2462)
PHONE.................................203 294-4440
Michael McGarry, *Branch Mgr*
EMP: 65
SALES (corp-wide): 15.3B **Publicly Held**
SIC: 3497 Metal foil & leaf
PA: Ppg Industries, Inc.
1 Ppg Pl
Pittsburgh PA 15272
412 434-3131

Wallingford - New Haven County (G-9338)

(G-9338)
PRALINES INC
Also Called: Pralines Central
30 N Plains Industrial Rd # 12
(06492-2357)
PHONE...................203 284-8847
Dana Torre, *President*
EMP: 11
SQ FT: 1,900
SALES (est): 1.3MM **Privately Held**
WEB: www.pralines.com
SIC: 2024 Ice cream, bulk

(G-9339)
PRAXAIR INC
10 Research Pkwy (06492-1963)
PHONE...................203 793-1200
Lori M Lieser, *Vice Pres*
Steven Christie, *Treasurer*
Maria Scarpa, *Director*
Robert S Zuccaro, *Director*
Stephen Sonnone, *Admin Sec*
EMP: 20 **Privately Held**
SIC: 2813 Industrial gases
HQ: Praxair, Inc.
10 Riverview Dr
Danbury CT 06810
203 837-2000

(G-9340)
PRECISION DEVICES INC (PA)
55 N Plains Industrial Rd (06492-5841)
PHONE...................203 265-9308
William P Bacha Jr, *President*
Mark Hoover, *Vice Pres*
Christine Bacha, *Admin Sec*
EMP: 17 **EST:** 1981
SQ FT: 8,000
SALES (est): 4MM **Privately Held**
SIC: 7694 5063 Electric motor repair; electrical apparatus & equipment

(G-9341)
PRECISION ENGINEERED PDTS LLC
Also Called: Pep Connecticut Plastics
6 Northrop Indus Pk Rd W (06492-1962)
PHONE...................203 265-3299
Claire Webb, *Manager*
EMP: 40
SALES (corp-wide): 770.6MM **Publicly Held**
SIC: 3089 Plastic processing
HQ: Precision Engineered Products Llc
110 Frank Mossberg Dr
Attleboro MA 02703
508 226-5600

(G-9342)
PRECISION PRODUCTS
8 Enterprise Rd (06492-1894)
PHONE...................203 265-2061
Fax: 203 269-0367
EMP: 2 **EST:** 2010
SALES (est): 127.7K **Privately Held**
SIC: 3599 Mfg Industrial Machinery

(G-9343)
PROTON ENERGY SYSTEMS INC
Also Called: Proton Onsite
10 Technology Dr (06492-1955)
PHONE...................203 678-2000
Anders Soreng, *CEO*
David T Bow, *Senior VP*
John A Zagaja III, *Senior VP*
Everett Anderson, *Vice Pres*
Albert Cortina, *Electrical Engi*
▲ **EMP:** 90
SQ FT: 98,703
SALES (est): 33.6MM **Privately Held**
WEB: www.protonenergy.com
SIC: 3569 Gas producers, generators & other gas related equipment; gas generators; generators: steam, liquid oxygen or nitrogen
PA: Nel Asa
Karenslyst Alle 20
Oslo 0278

(G-9344)
PROTRONIX INC
28 Parker St (06492-2320)
PHONE...................203 269-5858
Don Rosadini Jr, *President*
Janis Rosadini, *Admin Sec*
EMP: 10
SQ FT: 3,500
SALES (est): 1.6MM **Privately Held**
SIC: 3679 Electronic circuits

(G-9345)
QUALITY ENGINEERING SVCS INC
122 N Plains Indus Rd (06492-2386)
PHONE...................203 269-5054
Richard Addy, *President*
Tom Addy, *General Mgr*
Gregory Whitehouse, *Vice Pres*
Pam Smith, *Office Mgr*
James Gibson, *Executive*
EMP: 30
SQ FT: 10,000
SALES (est): 6.8MM **Privately Held**
SIC: 8711 3449 3544 Mechanical engineering; miscellaneous metalwork; special dies, tools, jigs & fixtures

(G-9346)
R & D PRECISION INC
63 N Cherry St Ste 1 (06492-2363)
PHONE...................203 284-3396
William D Harkness, *President*
Robin Harkness, *Admin Sec*
EMP: 19
SQ FT: 14,000
SALES (est): 3.5MM **Privately Held**
SIC: 3444 Sheet metal specialties, not stamped

(G-9347)
RACING TIMES
428 Main St (06492-2275)
PHONE...................203 298-2899
Alan Joseph Piquette, *Partner*
EMP: 25
SQ FT: 2,300
SALES: 98K **Privately Held**
SIC: 2721 Magazines: publishing & printing

(G-9348)
RAMAN POWER TECHNOLOGIES LLC
Also Called: Allard Electronics
46 Capital Dr (06492-2318)
PHONE...................203 695-4885
Tom Watson, *General Mgr*
Surendra Patel, *Mng Member*
EMP: 5
SQ FT: 2,200
SALES (est): 801.6K **Privately Held**
SIC: 5084 3679 Controlling instruments & accessories; measuring & testing equipment, electrical; static power supply converters for electronic applications

(G-9349)
REALTRAPS LLC
Also Called: Realtraps Manufacturing
47 N Plains Industrial Rd F (06492-5831)
PHONE...................203 294-4285
Douglas Ferrara,
Ethan Winer,
EMP: 2
SQ FT: 2,300
SALES: 100K **Privately Held**
WEB: www.ethanwiner.com
SIC: 3296 Acoustical board & tile, mineral wool

(G-9350)
RESPIRONICS INC
5 Technology Dr (06492-1942)
PHONE...................203 697-6490
Dorita A Pishko, *Branch Mgr*
EMP: 164
SALES (corp-wide): 20.8B **Privately Held**
SIC: 3842 Surgical appliances & supplies
HQ: Respironics, Inc.
1001 Murry Ridge Ln
Murrysville PA 15668
724 387-5200

(G-9351)
RESPIRONICS NOVAMETRIX LLC
5 Technology Dr (06492-1942)
PHONE...................203 697-6475
Philip F Nuzzo, *Plant Mgr*
▲ **EMP:** 150 **EST:** 1978
SQ FT: 53,000
SALES (est): 15.4MM
SALES (corp-wide): 20.8B **Privately Held**
SIC: 3841 3845 Surgical & medical instruments; electromedical equipment
HQ: Respironics, Inc.
1001 Murry Ridge Ln
Murrysville PA 15668
724 387-5200

(G-9352)
RF PRINTING LLC
Also Called: AlphaGraphics
200 Church St Ste 5 (06492-2274)
P.O. Box 302, Guilford (06437-0302)
PHONE...................203 265-9939
Richard W Fuhrman, *Mng Member*
EMP: 6
SALES: 500K **Privately Held**
SIC: 2752 Commercial printing, lithographic

(G-9353)
RICCI CABINET &STAIR CO
110 Constitution St (06492-3825)
PHONE...................203 889-6511
EMP: 2
SALES (est): 143.3K **Privately Held**
SIC: 2434 Wood kitchen cabinets

(G-9354)
RICHARD WOODWORKING
7 Sunny Ct (06492-5235)
PHONE...................203 265-0887
EMP: 1
SALES (est): 54.1K **Privately Held**
SIC: 2431 Millwork

(G-9355)
RICHARDS CREATIVE INTERIORS
1060 S Colony Rd (06492-5231)
PHONE...................203 484-0361
Antoinette Gallo, *Principal*
EMP: 2
SALES (est): 130.6K **Privately Held**
SIC: 2842 5169 5712 7641 Window cleaning preparations; specialty cleaning & sanitation preparations; customized furniture & cabinets; upholstery work

(G-9356)
ROBISON MUSIC MEDIA & PUBG LLC
15 Sullivan Rd (06492-1637)
PHONE...................203 858-8106
Tiger Robison,
EMP: 1
SALES (est): 52.4K **Privately Held**
SIC: 2731 7371 7389 Book music: publishing & printing; computer software writers, freelance;

(G-9357)
ROCK HARD OFFROAD LLC
168 N Plains Indus Rd (06492-2377)
PHONE...................860 919-3118
EMP: 2
SALES: 100K **Privately Held**
WEB: www.rockhardoffroad.com
SIC: 3711 Motor vehicles & car bodies

(G-9358)
ROEHM AMERICA LLC
528 S Cherry St (06492-4458)
PHONE...................203 269-4481
Peter Stein, *Manager*
Jeffrey Zgorski, *Manager*
EMP: 50
SALES (corp-wide): 208.6MM **Privately Held**
SIC: 2821 Plastics materials & resins
PA: Roehm America Llc
299 Jefferson Rd
Parsippany NJ 07054
973 929-8000

(G-9359)
ROKAP INC
Also Called: Sign Stop
1002 Yale Ave (06492-5923)
PHONE...................203 265-6895
Rosalind Kaplan, *President*
Seth Kaplan, *Vice Pres*
Russ Kaplan, *Admin Sec*
EMP: 7
SQ FT: 4,200
SALES (est): 1MM **Privately Held**
WEB: www.signstopsigns.com
SIC: 3993 7699 7532 7389 Signs, not made in custom sign painting shops; boat repair; truck painting & lettering; engraving service

(G-9360)
ROODLE RICE & NOODLE BAR
1263 S Broad St (06492-1737)
PHONE...................203 269-9899
EMP: 4 **EST:** 2016
SALES (est): 218.6K **Privately Held**
SIC: 2098 Noodles (e.g. egg, plain & water), dry

(G-9361)
ROWLAND TECHNOLOGIES INC
320 Barnes Rd (06492-1804)
PHONE...................203 269-9500
Stephen J Dimugno, *President*
Peter J Connerton Jr, *Exec VP*
Michael A Iovene, *Admin Sec*
◆ **EMP:** 75
SQ FT: 40,000
SALES (est): 27.4MM **Privately Held**
WEB: www.rowlandtechnologies.com
SIC: 3081 Plastic film & sheet

(G-9362)
RUCKUS WIRELESS INC
Also Called: Broadband Communication Div
15 Sterling Dr (06492-1843)
PHONE...................203 303-6400
John Caezza, *Division Pres*
EMP: 20
SALES (corp-wide): 6.7B **Privately Held**
WEB: www.c-cor.net
SIC: 3661 Fiber optics communications equipment
HQ: Ruckus Wireless, Inc.
350 W Java Dr
Sunnyvale CA 94089
650 265-4200

(G-9363)
RUSSELL ORGANICS LLC
329 Main St Ste 208 (06492-2273)
PHONE...................203 285-6633
Richard Russell, *CEO*
◆ **EMP:** 7
SALES: 3MM **Privately Held**
SIC: 2844 Cosmetic preparations

(G-9364)
S & S SEALCOATING LLC
5 Barker Dr (06492-1773)
PHONE...................203 284-0054
Gary Stanley, *Principal*
EMP: 4
SALES (est): 421.6K **Privately Held**
SIC: 2891 Adhesives & sealants

(G-9365)
SHIRT GRAPHIX
198 Center St (06492-4142)
PHONE...................203 294-1656
Ed Zielinski, *Owner*
EMP: 3
SALES (est): 334.5K **Privately Held**
SIC: 2759 2395 Screen printing; embroidery products, except schiffli machine

(G-9366)
SIAM VALEE
20 Ives Rd (06492-2484)
PHONE...................203 269-6888
EMP: 3 **EST:** 2007
SALES (est): 224.3K **Privately Held**
SIC: 3993 Signs & advertising specialties

(G-9367)
SILVER ARROW PUBLISHER LLC
71 Curtis Ave Apt 3 (06492-3707)
PHONE...................203 265-4653
Patrick Fenton, *Principal*
EMP: 2
SALES (est): 69.2K **Privately Held**
SIC: 2711 Newspapers

▲ = Import ▼=Export
◆ =Import/Export

GEOGRAPHIC SECTION
Wallingford - New Haven County (G-9393)

(G-9368)
SIMPLY CANVAS LLC
39 Reynolds Dr (06492-3933)
PHONE 203 265-0659
Lillian M Haines, *Principal*
EMP: 1 **EST:** 2008
SALES (est): 71.6K **Privately Held**
SIC: 2211 Canvas

(G-9369)
SIMSON PRODUCTS CO INC
50 N Plains Industrial Rd (06492-2333)
PHONE 203 265-9882
Allen Cuccaro, *President*
Michael Frank, *Admin Sec*
EMP: 12
SALES (est): 1.3MM **Privately Held**
SIC: 3599 Machine shop, jobbing & repair

(G-9370)
SNOWDOG SOFTWARE LLC
32 Southview Dr (06492-4935)
PHONE 203 265-7116
Tracey Brown, *Mng Member*
EMP: 1
SALES (est): 61.4K **Privately Held**
WEB: www.katieb.com
SIC: 7372 Prepackaged software

(G-9371)
SOUTHERN CONN PALLET CO INC
346 Quinnipiac St (06492-4053)
P.O. Box 4566 (06492-7566)
PHONE 203 265-1313
James Waldeck, *President*
EMP: 7
SQ FT: 10,000
SALES (est): 1.3MM **Privately Held**
SIC: 2448 Pallets, wood

(G-9372)
SPECIALTY CABLE CORP
2 Tower Dr (06492-1877)
P.O. Box 50 (06492-0050)
PHONE 203 265-7126
Kim Bowen, *CEO*
Carl Shanahan, *President*
Christopher Lambert, *Purch Mgr*
David Severino, *Accountant*
James Streifel, *Marketing Mgr*
EMP: 70
SQ FT: 65,000
SALES (est): 30.1MM **Privately Held**
SIC: 3357 3315 5063 Nonferrous wire-drawing & insulating; cable, steel: insulated or armored; wire & cable

(G-9373)
SPECIALTY COMPONENTS INC (PA)
14 Village Ln Ste 1 (06492-2459)
PHONE 203 284-9112
Marc Hadarik, *President*
Amy Hadarik, *Admin Sec*
EMP: 5 **EST:** 1975
SQ FT: 17,000
SALES (est): 1.3MM **Privately Held**
WEB: www.specialtycomponents.com
SIC: 3599 Machine shop, jobbing & repair

(G-9374)
SPECIALTY COMPONENTS INC
14 Village Ln (06492-2459)
PHONE 203 284-9112
Jam Hadararick, *Owner*
EMP: 4
SALES (corp-wide): 1.3MM **Privately Held**
WEB: www.specialtycomponents.com
SIC: 3829 Measuring & controlling devices
PA: Specialty Components, Inc.
    14 Village Ln Ste 1
    Wallingford CT 06492
    203 284-9112

(G-9375)
STABAN ENGINEERING CORP
65 N Plains Industrial Rd (06492-5832)
P.O. Box 8 (06492-0008)
PHONE 203 294-1997
Dennis Bandecchi, *President*
Todd Widener, *Vice Pres*
EMP: 14
SQ FT: 16,500
SALES (est): 4.2MM **Privately Held**
SIC: 3565 Packing & wrapping machinery

(G-9376)
STATE WELDING & FABG INC
107 N Cherry St (06492-2305)
PHONE 203 294-4071
Charles Mascola, *President*
EMP: 7
SQ FT: 18,000
SALES (est): 1.5MM **Privately Held**
SIC: 3441 7692 Building components, structural steel; welding repair

(G-9377)
STRAIN MEASUREMENT DEVICES INC
55 Barnes Park Rd N (06492-1883)
PHONE 203 294-5800
Frederick E Jackson, *President*
Daniel Shapiro, *Vice Pres*
Linda Anderson, *Production*
Eduard Krutyanskiy, *Engineer*
Jason Michaud, *Controller*
EMP: 25
SQ FT: 14,000
SALES (est): 6.3MM **Privately Held**
WEB: www.smdsensors.com
SIC: 3829 3674 Measuring & controlling devices; strain gages, solid state

(G-9378)
STUCCO DEPOT LLC
150 N Plains Indus Rd (06492-2353)
PHONE 203 430-9186
David Bowlby, *President*
EMP: 2
SQ FT: 6,000
SALES: 800K **Privately Held**
SIC: 3299 Stucco

(G-9379)
TECHNICAL METAL FINISHING INC
Also Called: T M F
29 Capital Dr (06492-5818)
PHONE 203 284-7825
Levi Citarella, *President*
Alfred Matarese, *Principal*
Phillip Milidaneri, *Vice Pres*
Phillip Milidantri, *Vice Pres*
EMP: 23
SALES (est): 2.8MM **Privately Held**
SIC: 3471 Finishing, metals or formed products

(G-9380)
TENOVA INC
1070 N Farms Rd Ste 3b (06492-5931)
PHONE 203 265-5684
Frank Byus, *Principal*
Mark Olean, *Engineer*
Bonnie Daigle, *Accounting Mgr*
EMP: 20
SALES (corp-wide): 355.8K **Privately Held**
SIC: 8711 5084 3325 Industrial engineers; industrial machinery & equipment; rolling mill rolls, cast steel
HQ: Tenova Inc.
    100 Corporate Center Dr # 100
    Coraopolis PA 15108
    412 262-2240

(G-9381)
THERMOSPAS HOT TUB PRODUCTS
10 Research Pkwy Ste 300 (06492-1963)
PHONE 203 303-0005
Andrew Tournas, *President*
Paul Anderson, *Sales Staff*
EMP: 35
SALES (est): 5.2MM **Privately Held**
SIC: 3999 Hot tubs
HQ: Sundance Spas, Inc.
    13925 City Center Dr # 200
    Chino Hills CA 91709
    909 606-7733

(G-9382)
THYSSENKRUPP MATERIALS NA INC
Also Called: Copper and Brass Sales Div
5 Sterling Dr (06492-1843)
PHONE 203 265-1567
Gene Dixon, *Credit Mgr*
EMP: 28
SALES (corp-wide): 39.8B **Privately Held**
SIC: 5162 3444 Plastics sheets & rods; sheet metalwork
HQ: Thyssenkrupp Materials Na, Inc.
    22355 W 11 Mile Rd
    Southfield MI 48033
    248 233-5600

(G-9383)
THYSSENKRUPP MATERIALS NA INC
Copper and Brass Sales Div
5 Sterling Dr (06492-1843)
PHONE 610 586-1800
Frank Kavani, *Branch Mgr*
EMP: 40
SALES (corp-wide): 39.8B **Privately Held**
SIC: 5052 3341 Coal & other minerals & ores; secondary nonferrous metals
HQ: Thyssenkrupp Materials Na, Inc.
    22355 W 11 Mile Rd
    Southfield MI 48033
    248 233-5600

(G-9384)
TICO TITANIUM INC (PA)
Also Called: Lhi Metals
34b Barnes Indus Rd S (06492-2438)
P.O. Box 336, Roseville MI (48066-0336)
PHONE 248 446-0400
Lawrence Buhl III, *CEO*
Gary C Johnson, *President*
Jeffrey A White, *Vice Pres*
James D Morell, *CFO*
Lawrence Coassin, *Admin Sec*
▲ **EMP:** 31
SQ FT: 60,500
SALES (est): 17.8MM **Privately Held**
WEB: www.ticotitanium.com
SIC: 5051 3452 3441 3356 Nonferrous metal sheets, bars, rods, etc.; copper; zinc; aluminum bars, rods, ingots, sheets, pipes, plates, etc.; bolts, nuts, rivets & washers; fabricated structural metal; nonferrous rolling & drawing

(G-9385)
TIMES FIBER COMMUNICATIONS INC (HQ)
358 Hall Ave (06492-3574)
P.O. Box 384 (06492-7006)
PHONE 203 265-8500
Adam R Norwitt, *President*
Greg Lamto, *CFO*
◆ **EMP:** 54
SQ FT: 15,000
SALES (est): 166.5MM
SALES (corp-wide): 8.2B **Publicly Held**
WEB: www.timesfiber.com
SIC: 3357 Coaxial cable, nonferrous
PA: Amphenol Corporation
    358 Hall Ave
    Wallingford CT 06492
    203 265-8900

(G-9386)
TIMES MICROWAVE SYSTEMS INC (HQ)
358 Hall Ave (06492-3574)
P.O. Box 5039 (06492-7539)
PHONE 203 949-8400
Bill Callahan, *General Mgr*
Bill McLaughlin, *Engineer*
Miriam Gatter, *Administration*
▲ **EMP:** 300
SQ FT: 154,000
SALES (est): 62.9MM
SALES (corp-wide): 8.2B **Publicly Held**
WEB: www.timesmicrowave.com
SIC: 3679 3357 3678 Microwave components; nonferrous wiredrawing & insulating; electronic connectors
PA: Amphenol Corporation
    358 Hall Ave
    Wallingford CT 06492
    203 265-8900

(G-9387)
TIMES WIRE AND CABLE COMPANY (HQ)
Also Called: Amphenol
358 Hall Ave (06492-3574)
PHONE 203 949-8400
Mark St Hilaire, *General Mgr*
EMP: 7
SALES (est): 1.9MM
SALES (corp-wide): 8.2B **Publicly Held**
SIC: 3643 5063 Current-carrying wiring devices; electronic wire & cable
PA: Amphenol Corporation
    358 Hall Ave
    Wallingford CT 06492
    203 265-8900

(G-9388)
TIMNA MANUFACTURING INC
204 N Plains Indus Rd (06492-2358)
PHONE 203 265-4656
Sharon A Nagy, *President*
Frank A Nagy, *Treasurer*
EMP: 9
SQ FT: 5,000
SALES (est): 1.2MM **Privately Held**
SIC: 3599 Machine shop, jobbing & repair

(G-9389)
TOMS SEAMLESS GUTTERS INC
54 Ridgewood Rd (06492-2119)
PHONE 203 269-2296
Thomas Hulett II, *President*
Marjorie Hulett, *Corp Secy*
EMP: 2
SALES (est): 195.6K **Privately Held**
SIC: 1761 3444 Gutter & downspout contractor; gutters, sheet metal

(G-9390)
TOTAL CONTROL INC
130 S Turnpike Rd (06492-4320)
PHONE 203 269-4749
Peter Kulak, *President*
EMP: 8
SALES (est): 2.2MM **Privately Held**
WEB: www.totalcontrol-online.com
SIC: 7694 Electric motor repair

(G-9391)
TROD NOSSEL PRDCTNS & RCRDNG S
Also Called: Tna Records & Studios
10 George St (06492-4008)
P.O. Box 57 (06492-0057)
PHONE 203 269-4465
Thomas J Cavalier, *President*
Richard Robinson, *Admin Sec*
EMP: 4
SQ FT: 5,000
SALES (est): 330K **Privately Held**
WEB: www.cdduping.com
SIC: 7389 7812 3695 3652 Recording studio, noncommercial records; artists' agents & brokers; motion picture & video production; magnetic & optical recording media; pre-recorded records & tapes

(G-9392)
TRUE PUBLISHING COMPANY
Also Called: Cheshire Herald
125 Grandview Ave (06492-5157)
P.O. Box 247, Cheshire (06410-0247)
PHONE 203 272-5316
Joseph Jakubisyn, *President*
Maureen Jakubisyn, *Treasurer*
Debbie Eckert, *Representative*
EMP: 13 **EST:** 1953
SALES: 1MM **Privately Held**
WEB: www.cheshireherald.com
SIC: 2711 Newspapers: publishing only, not printed on site

(G-9393)
ULBRICH STAINLESS STEELS
Also Called: Ulbrich Steel
1 Dudley Ave (06492-4457)
P.O. Box 610 (06492-0610)
PHONE 203 269-2507
Mike Marzik, *Opers Mgr*
Lisa Aurora, *Purch Mgr*
Bob Ferguson, *Inv Control Mgr*
Rob Giapponi, *Sales/Mktg Mgr*
Allie Clark, *Associate*
EMP: 180

(PA)=Parent Co (HQ)=Headquarters (DH)=Div Headquarters
○ = New Business established in last 2 years

Wallingford - New Haven County (G-9394)

SALES (corp-wide): 224.5MM **Privately Held**
WEB: www.ulbrich.com
SIC: 3316 3547 3356 3339 Cold finishing of steel shapes; rolling mill machinery; nonferrous rolling & drawing; primary nonferrous metals; blast furnaces & steel mills
PA: Ulbrich Stainless Steels & Special Metals, Inc.
153 Washington Ave
North Haven CT 06473
203 239-4481

(G-9394)
ULTIMATE GROWERS LLC
30 Mapleview Rd (06492-2534)
PHONE.................203 269-9027
Mary Cone, *President*
EMP: 1 EST: 2000
SALES (est): 112.2K **Privately Held**
SIC: 3295 Minerals, ground or treated

(G-9395)
UNHOLTZ-DICKIE CORPORATION (PA)
6 Brookside Dr (06492-1893)
PHONE.................203 265-9875
Michael K Reen, *President*
Gerald K Reen, *Corp Secy*
▲ EMP: 44 EST: 1958
SQ FT: 40,000
SALES (est): 12.4MM **Privately Held**
WEB: www.udco.com
SIC: 3829 Vibration meters, analyzers & calibrators

(G-9396)
UPSCALE WELDING & FABRICA
418 S Cherry St (06492-4431)
PHONE.................203 265-0800
Robert Giza, *Principal*
EMP: 1
SALES (est): 64.1K **Privately Held**
SIC: 7692 Welding repair

(G-9397)
US FILTER SURFACE PREPARATIO
29 Capital Dr (06492-5818)
PHONE.................203 284-7825
EMP: 2 EST: 2011
SALES (est): 130K **Privately Held**
SIC: 3569 Mfg General Industrial Machinery

(G-9398)
UTE BRINKMANN GEIGENBAUMEISTER
84 S Orchard St (06492-4131)
PHONE.................203 265-7456
Ute Brinkmann, *Principal*
EMP: 1
SALES (est): 67.1K **Privately Held**
SIC: 3931 Musical instruments

(G-9399)
VALUE PRINT INCORPORATED
34 Mellor Dr (06492-4953)
PHONE.................203 265-1371
John L Kastukevich, *President*
Mary R Kastukevich, *Admin Sec*
EMP: 11
SQ FT: 5,000
SALES (est): 1MM **Privately Held**
SIC: 2752 Commercial printing, offset

(G-9400)
VENTUREOUT PUBLICATIONS LLC
19 Country Way (06492-5358)
PHONE.................203 668-9162
Margaret Griffin, *Principal*
EMP: 2
SALES (est): 142.8K **Privately Held**
SIC: 2741 Miscellaneous publishing

(G-9401)
VERTIV CORPORATION
8 Fairfield Blvd Ste 4 (06492-1890)
PHONE.................203 294-6020
Bob Paradiso, *Manager*
EMP: 10

SALES (corp-wide): 2.9B **Privately Held**
WEB: www.liebert.com
SIC: 3823 Industrial instrmnts msrmnt display/control process variable
HQ: Vertiv Corporation
1050 Dearborn Dr
Columbus OH 43085
614 888-0246

(G-9402)
WEATHERFORD INTERNATIONAL LLC
8 Enterprise Rd (06492-1835)
PHONE.................203 294-0190
Lorraine Matuskiewicz, *Senior Buyer*
Christopher McDowell, *Engineer*
Kevin Didden, *Branch Mgr*
EMP: 25 **Privately Held**
WEB: www.weatherford.com
SIC: 1389 Oil field services
HQ: Weatherford International, Llc
2000 Saint James Pl
Houston TX 77056
713 693-4000

(G-9403)
WINSLOW MANUFACTURING INC
68 N Plains Indus Hwy (06492-2331)
P.O. Box 772 (06492-0772)
PHONE.................203 269-1977
George Ehinger, *President*
Susie Stern, *Shareholder*
EMP: 15
SQ FT: 13,000
SALES (est): 2.1MM **Privately Held**
SIC: 3451 Screw machine products

(G-9404)
WOOD-N-TAP
970 N Colony Rd Ste 2 (06492-5900)
PHONE.................203 265-9663
Joe Derricho, *Branch Mgr*
EMP: 1
SALES (corp-wide): 1.7MM **Privately Held**
PA: Wood-N-Tap
99 Sisson Ave
Hartford CT 06106
860 206-6284

(G-9405)
Z-MEDICA LLC
4 Fairfield Blvd Ste 1 (06492-1857)
PHONE.................203 294-0000
Eric Compton, *CEO*
Edward Hallaran, *President*
David Clarke, *Vice Pres*
Scott Garrett, *Vice Pres*
Denny Lo, *Vice Pres*
▲ EMP: 68
SQ FT: 20,000
SALES (est): 20.5MM **Privately Held**
SIC: 5047 2211 Medical equipment & supplies; bandages, gauzes & surgical fabrics, cotton

Warren
Litchfield County

(G-9406)
ALFRED BROWN CABINETRY LLC (PA)
24 Kent Rd (06754-1600)
PHONE.................860 868-7261
Alfred H Brown, *Manager*
EMP: 2 EST: 2001
SALES (est): 242.3K **Privately Held**
SIC: 2434 Wood kitchen cabinets

(G-9407)
CORNWALL BRIDGE POTTERY INC
69 Kent Rd (06754-1601)
P.O. Box 134, Cornwall Bridge (06754-0134)
PHONE.................860 672-6545
Todd Piker, *President*
EMP: 2
SQ FT: 5,000

SALES (est): 225.2K **Privately Held**
WEB: www.cbpots.com
SIC: 5719 3269 3263 Pottery; pottery cooking & kitchen articles; semivitreous table & kitchenware

(G-9408)
FLOATING WORLD EDITIONS
26 Jack Corner Rd (06777-1212)
PHONE.................860 868-0890
Ray Furse, *President*
Maryellen Sesdelli, *Vice Pres*
EMP: 2
SALES: 125K **Privately Held**
SIC: 2741 Maps: publishing only, not printed on site

(G-9409)
WARREN TRADING COMPANY
14 Brick School Rd (06754-1421)
PHONE.................860 868-7848
Theodore A Seavey, *Owner*
EMP: 1
SALES (est): 81.2K **Privately Held**
SIC: 5941 3949 Firearms; sporting & athletic goods

(G-9410)
WYNDEMERE PUBLISHING LLC
22 Partridge Rd (06754-1726)
PHONE.................860 868-1490
Kerri Byrnes, *Principal*
EMP: 1 EST: 2018
SALES (est): 37.5K **Privately Held**
SIC: 2741 Miscellaneous publishing

Washington
Litchfield County

(G-9411)
AMERICAN CT RNG BNDER INDEX &
42 Sabbaday Ln (06793-1305)
PHONE.................860 868-7900
Peter Tagley, *President*
Diana Tagley, *Corp Secy*
EMP: 17
SQ FT: 14,000
SALES: 1MM **Privately Held**
WEB: www.ringbinders.com
SIC: 2782 2678 2675 Looseleaf binders & devices; stationery products; die-cut paper & board

(G-9412)
CHARLES A BOUCHER CO INC
30 Dark Entry Rd (06793-1103)
PHONE.................860 868-2881
Charles A Boucher, *President*
Barbara Boucher, *Corp Secy*
Charles Boucher Jr, *Vice Pres*
EMP: 5
SALES: 800K **Privately Held**
SIC: 1522 1542 2431 Residential construction; commercial & office building, new construction; millwork

(G-9413)
EDIBLE NUTMEG
90 Old Litchfield Rd (06793-1111)
P.O. Box 222, Washington Depot (06794-0222)
PHONE.................818 383-4603
Dana Jackson, *Principal*
EMP: 2 EST: 2015
SALES (est): 126.6K **Privately Held**
SIC: 2721 Magazines: publishing & printing

(G-9414)
TURKEY TAIL PUBLISHING LLC
68 Carmel Hill Rd (06793-1605)
PHONE.................860 671-0800
Joseph Gervasio, *Manager*
EMP: 1
SALES (est): 37.5K **Privately Held**
SIC: 2741 Miscellaneous publishing

(G-9415)
WASHINGTON COPPER WORKS INC
49 South St (06793-1516)
PHONE.................860 868-7637
Serge L Miller, *President*

EMP: 3
SALES (est): 288.5K **Privately Held**
WEB: www.washingtoncopperworks.com
SIC: 3645 5719 5063 Residential lighting fixtures; lighting fixtures; lighting fixtures

Washington Depot
Litchfield County

(G-9416)
BERKSHIRE PHOTONICS LLC
88 Bee Brook Rd (06794-1202)
P.O. Box 595 (06794-0595)
PHONE.................860 868-0412
Denise Roka, *Purch Mgr*
Brad Jones, *Executive*
Jeffrey Miller, *Admin Asst*
EMP: 8
SQ FT: 2,200
SALES: 1.2MM **Privately Held**
WEB: www.berkshirephotonics.com
SIC: 3559 Optical lens machinery

(G-9417)
CUSTOM WOODWORKING
3 Church Hill Rd (06794-1402)
PHONE.................860 868-0257
Bruce Bronson, *Owner*
EMP: 1
SALES (est): 91.2K **Privately Held**
SIC: 2431 Millwork

(G-9418)
MIKES PLOWING & MAINTENANCE
41 W Morris Rd (06794-1302)
P.O. Box 372 (06794-0372)
PHONE.................860 868-1413
Mike Parent, *Owner*
EMP: 1
SALES (est): 51.5K **Privately Held**
SIC: 0781 3524 Landscape services; snowblowers & throwers, residential

(G-9419)
NICHOLS WOODWORKING LLC (PA)
136 Walker Brook Rd S (06794)
PHONE.................860 350-4223
Franklin Nichols, *Principal*
EMP: 3
SALES (est): 782.3K **Privately Held**
SIC: 2431 Millwork

Waterbury
New Haven County

(G-9420)
77 MATTATUCK HEIGHTS LLC
77 Mattatuck Heights Rd (06705-3832)
PHONE.................203 597-9338
Jim Xhema,
▲ EMP: 20
SALES (est): 2.3MM **Privately Held**
SIC: 2431 Woodwork, interior & ornamental

(G-9421)
911 MOTORSPORTS LLC
520 Watertown Ave (06708-2205)
PHONE.................203 755-8405
William Strakosch, *Owner*
EMP: 4 EST: 2008
SALES (est): 384.2K **Privately Held**
SIC: 7532 3713 3711 Lettering & painting services; truck & bus bodies; automobile bodies, passenger car, not including engine, etc.

(G-9422)
ABAIR MANUFACTURING COMPANY
Also Called: Abair Assemblies
250 Mill St Ste 2 (06706-1209)
PHONE.................203 757-0112
EMP: 19
SQ FT: 10,000
SALES: 720K **Privately Held**
SIC: 3711 Automobile Component Assembly

Waterbury - New Haven County

(G-9423)
ADVANCED MACHINE SERVICES LLC (PA)
2056 Thomaston Ave (06704-1038)
PHONE...............................203 888-6600
Christopher G Mackenzie,
Chris Mackenzie,
EMP: 4
SQ FT: 3,100
SALES (est): 711.2K Privately Held
WEB: www.precisionspindle.com
SIC: 3552 3542 7389 Spindles, textile; spinning, spline rolling & winding machines; grinding, precision: commercial or industrial

(G-9424)
AI DIVESTITURES INC
245 Freight St (06702-1818)
PHONE...............................203 575-5727
Stuart L Daniels, Director
EMP: 4
SALES (est): 228.4K
SALES (corp-wide): 1.9B Publicly Held
SIC: 2869 Hydraulic fluids, synthetic base
PA: Element Solutions Inc
    1450 Centrepark Blvd # 210
    West Palm Beach FL 33401
    561 207-9600

(G-9425)
ALENT INC
245 Freight St (06702-1818)
PHONE...............................203 575-5727
Allan Macdonald, Principal
EMP: 70
SALES (est): 1.1MM
SALES (corp-wide): 1.9B Publicly Held
SIC: 3699 Electrical equipment & supplies
HQ: Macdermid, Incorporated
    245 Freight St
    Waterbury CT 06702
    203 575-5700

(G-9426)
ALENT USA HOLDING INC
245 Freight St (06702-1818)
PHONE...............................203 575-5727
Steven Corbett, President
William Gorgone, Vice Pres
Robert Landry, Vice Pres
Allan Macdonald, Vice Pres
Joseph M Creighton, Treasurer
EMP: 279
SALES (est): 230.9M
SALES (corp-wide): 1.9B Publicly Held
SIC: 3699 3356 3341 3313 Electrical equipment & supplies; solder: wire, bar, acid core, & rosin core; lead smelting & refining (secondary); tin smelting & refining (secondary); alloys, additive, except copper: not made in blast furnaces; lead smelting & refining (primary); tin refining (primary); fluxes: brazing, soldering, galvanizing & welding
PA: Element Solutions Inc
    1450 Centrepark Blvd # 210
    West Palm Beach FL 33401
    561 207-9600

(G-9427)
AMERICAN ELECTRO PRODUCTS INC
1358 Thomaston Ave (06704-1791)
P.O. Box 4129 (06704-0129)
PHONE...............................203 756-7051
Dennis Burke, President
James Moore, Plant Mgr
John Krin, CFO
EMP: 135 EST: 1950
SALES (est): 19.1MM
SALES (corp-wide): 15MM Privately Held
SIC: 3471 Electroplating of metals or formed products
PA: National Integrated Industries, Inc.
    322 Main St
    Farmington CT 06032
    860 677-7995

(G-9428)
AMERICAN PLASTIC PRODUCTS INC
2114 Thomaston Ave (06704-1013)
P.O. Box 4429 (06704-0429)
PHONE...............................203 596-2410
Dennis M Burke, President
EMP: 135
SQ FT: 5,000
SALES (est): 35.9MM
SALES (corp-wide): 15MM Privately Held
WEB: www.amerplastic.com
SIC: 3089 Injection molding of plastics
PA: National Integrated Industries, Inc.
    322 Main St
    Farmington CT 06032
    860 677-7995

(G-9429)
AMERICAN-REPUBLICAN INC (PA)
Also Called: Republican-American
389 Meadow St (06702-1808)
P.O. Box 2090 (06722-2090)
PHONE...............................203 574-3636
William B Pape, President
Jennine Goldenberg, Human Res Mgr
Jeff Guerrette, Accounts Exec
Michael Degirolamo, Librarian
Ed Winters, Director
EMP: 79
SQ FT: 110
SALES (est): 24MM Privately Held
WEB: www.rep-am.com
SIC: 2711 2752 Newspapers, publishing & printing; commercial printing, lithographic

(G-9430)
AMODIOS INC (PA)
Also Called: Pilot Seasonings
40 Falls Ave Ste 4 (06708-1054)
PHONE...............................203 573-1229
Joseph R Summa, President
Fred Schnaars Jr, Corp Secy
Richard Rogers, Vice Pres
EMP: 12 EST: 1981
SQ FT: 12,000
SALES (est): 1.3MM Privately Held
WEB: www.pilotseasoning.com
SIC: 2099 2051 Spices, including grinding; bread, cake & related products

(G-9431)
ANGEL FUEL LLC
56 Knoll St (06705-1813)
PHONE...............................203 597-8759
Angel L Morales, Manager
EMP: 7
SALES (est): 656.1K Privately Held
SIC: 3443 Fuel tanks (oil, gas, etc.): metal plate

(G-9432)
APPS SCREEN PRINTING LLC
150 E Aurora St Ste D (06708-2039)
PHONE...............................860 938-7596
Andrea Persechino, Principal
EMP: 2
SALES (est): 83.9K Privately Held
SIC: 2752 Commercial printing, lithographic

(G-9433)
ARCHITECTURAL SUPPLEMENTS LLC
567 S Leonard St Bldg 1b (06708-4300)
PHONE...............................203 591-5505
Phil Feinman, Ch of Bd
Steven C Decker, Partner
▲ EMP: 18
SQ FT: 50,000
SALES (est): 4.2MM Privately Held
SIC: 3089 3412 Plastic containers, except foam; metal barrels, drums & pails

(G-9434)
ARMED & READY ALARM SYSTEM
112 Fieldwood Rd (06704-1107)
P.O. Box 591, Oxford (06478-0591)
PHONE...............................203 596-0327
Shawn Burch, Owner
EMP: 15
SALES (est): 1.2MM Privately Held
SIC: 3273 Ready-mixed concrete

(G-9435)
ATI FLAT RLLED PDTS HLDNGS LLC
271 Railroad Hill St (06708-4306)
PHONE...............................203 756-7414
Jose Reyes, Manager
Richard Deming, Technician
EMP: 10 Publicly Held
WEB: www.alleghenyludlum.com
SIC: 3312 5051 Stainless steel; steel
HQ: Ati Flat Rolled Products Holdings, Llc
    1000 Six Ppg Pl
    Pittsburgh PA 15222
    412 394-3047

(G-9436)
BAR WORK MANUFACTURING CO INC
1198 Highland Ave (06708-4911)
PHONE...............................203 753-4103
William Steinen Jr, President
John J Scopelliti, Vice Pres
Jr C Jung, Executive
John B Dangler, Admin Sec
EMP: 14 EST: 1951
SQ FT: 24,000
SALES (est): 2.4MM
SALES (corp-wide): 15.3MM Privately Held
WEB: www.bar-work.com
SIC: 3451 Screw machine products
PA: Wm. Steinen Mfg. Co.
    29 E Halsey Rd
    Parsippany NJ 07054
    973 887-6400

(G-9437)
BARBARA JONES
31 Granger St (06705-2216)
P.O. Box 4712 (06704-0712)
PHONE...............................203 596-9219
EMP: 2
SALES (est): 65.5K Privately Held
SIC: 2711 Newspapers

(G-9438)
BERNELL TOOL & MFG CO
181 Mulloy Rd (06705-3439)
PHONE...............................203 756-4405
Charles Famiglietti, President
Margaret Famiglietti, Corp Secy
EMP: 5
SQ FT: 3,400
SALES (est): 200K Privately Held
SIC: 3541 5084 Machine tools, metal cutting type; industrial machinery & equipment

(G-9439)
BOBKEN AUTOMATICS INC
1495 Thomaston Ave Ste 2 (06704-1744)
P.O. Box 131, Oakville (06779-0131)
PHONE...............................203 757-5525
Bob Piazzaroli, President
Ursula Piazzaroli, Admin Sec
EMP: 6
SALES (est): 821.5K Privately Held
SIC: 3451 Screw machine products

(G-9440)
BPREX HALTHCARE BROOKVILLE INC
574 E Main St (06702-1706)
P.O. Box 808 (06720-0808)
PHONE...............................203 754-4141
Kevin Edwards, Opers-Prdtn-Mfg
EMP: 195
SQ FT: 100,000 Publicly Held
SIC: 3089 Caps, plastic; closures, plastic
HQ: Bprex Healthcare Brookville Inc.
    1899 N Wilkinson Way
    Perrysburg OH 43551

(G-9441)
BRASS CITY CUSTOM
98 Glenstone Rd (06705-3731)
PHONE...............................860 995-9321
Jonathan Kane, Principal
EMP: 2
SALES (est): 83.9K Privately Held
SIC: 2752 Commercial printing, lithographic

(G-9442)
BRASS CITY GAMERS TOURNAMENT
300 Schraffts Dr (06705-3248)
PHONE...............................203 584-3359
Jeriel Navarro, CEO
Hector Navarro-Ramos, President
EMP: 1
SALES (est): 32.7K Privately Held
SIC: 7372 7389 Prepackaged software;

(G-9443)
BRASS CITY TILE DESIGNS LLC
29 S Commons Rd Ste 3 (06704-1060)
PHONE...............................203 597-8764
Martin Niatopsky, Owner
EMP: 2
SALES (est): 115.4K Privately Held
SIC: 2499 3253 5032 Tiles, cork; ceramic wall & floor tile; ceramic wall & floor tile

(G-9444)
BYRNE GROUP INC
Also Called: Minuteman Tress
170 Grand St (06702-1909)
PHONE...............................203 573-0100
Matt Byrne, President
Tiffany Byrne, Vice Pres
EMP: 3
SALES (est): 114.2K Privately Held
SIC: 2752 Commercial printing, lithographic

(G-9445)
C F D ENGINEERING COMPANY
Naugatuck Manufacturing Div
105 Avenue Of Industry (06705-3902)
P.O. Box 3175 (06705-0175)
PHONE...............................203 754-2807
Chuck Adminson, Manager
EMP: 17
SALES (corp-wide): 1.5MM Privately Held
WEB: www.naugatuckmfg.com
SIC: 3823 Industrial flow & liquid measuring instruments
PA: The C F D Engineering Company
    194 Cook Rd
    Prospect CT 06712
    203 758-4148

(G-9446)
CARPIN MANUFACTURING INC
411 Austin Rd (06705-3763)
P.O. Box 471 (06720-0471)
PHONE...............................203 574-2556
Ralph H Carpinella, Ch of Bd
Ralph Carpinella, Chairman
Rachel Albanese, Controller
James Bachis, Sales Staff
David Ferraro, Officer
▲ EMP: 90
SQ FT: 60,000
SALES (est): 24.8MM Privately Held
WEB: www.carpin.com
SIC: 3469 3089 3441 Metal stampings; injection molding of plastics; fabricated structural metal

(G-9447)
CAVALLO MANUFACTURING LLC
289 Fairfield Ave (06708-4061)
PHONE...............................203 596-8007
Vito Cavallo, Principal
EMP: 1
SALES (est): 61.1K Privately Held
SIC: 3999 Manufacturing industries

(G-9448)
CAVTECH INDUSTRIES
217 Interstate Ln (06705-2642)
PHONE...............................203 437-8764
Sam Cavallo, Owner
EMP: 4
SQ FT: 6,500
SALES: 500K Privately Held
SIC: 3599 Machine shop, jobbing & repair

(G-9449)
CHEMTURA RECEIVABLES LLC
199 Benson Rd (06749-0001)
PHONE...............................203 573-3327
EMP: 5 EST: 2008

Waterbury - New Haven County (G-9450)

SALES (est): 20.6K **Privately Held**
SIC: 2879 Insecticides, agricultural or household

(G-9450)
CLASSIC TOOL & MFG INC
112 Porter St (06708-3819)
PHONE..................................203 755-6313
Robert Druan, *President*
EMP: 4
SALES (est): 329.8K **Privately Held**
SIC: 3544 Special dies, tools, jigs & fixtures

(G-9451)
CLASSIC TOOL & MFG LLC
112 Porter St (06708-3819)
PHONE..................................203 755-6313
Robert J Druan, *Manager*
EMP: 3
SALES (est): 264.4K **Privately Held**
SIC: 3999 Manufacturing industries

(G-9452)
CLY-DEL MANUFACTURING COMPANY
151 Sharon Rd (06705-4041)
P.O. Box 1367 (06721-1367)
PHONE..................................203 574-2100
Robert W Garthwait Jr, *President*
Robert W Garthwait, *Chairman*
Bruce Weingart, *Plant Mgr*
Charles W Henry, *Admin Sec*
▲ **EMP:** 210
SQ FT: 185,000
SALES (est): 56.4MM **Privately Held**
WEB: www.cly-del.com
SIC: 3469 Metal stampings

(G-9453)
COLONIAL CORRUGATED PDTS INC
118 Railroad Hill St (06708-4320)
P.O. Box 2753 (06723-2753)
PHONE..................................203 597-1707
Jack Bair, *President*
Angela Derkins, *Admin Sec*
EMP: 40
SALES (est): 6.1MM **Privately Held**
WEB: www.colonialcorrugated.com
SIC: 2653 Boxes, corrugated: made from purchased materials

(G-9454)
COMMERCIAL SERVICE
45 Freight St Rm 1 (06702-1814)
PHONE..................................203 755-0166
Janis McConnell, *Owner*
EMP: 1 **EST:** 1945
SQ FT: 1,100
SALES (est): 145.1K **Privately Held**
SIC: 2752 7338 7334 Commercial printing, offset; word processing service; photocopying & duplicating services

(G-9455)
CREATIVE RACK SOLUTIONS INC
365 Thomaston Ave (06702-1024)
P.O. Box 750, Southington (06489-0750)
PHONE..................................203 755-2102
Bill Camp, *President*
William Camp, *President*
EMP: 4
SQ FT: 1,000
SALES (est): 582.7K **Privately Held**
WEB: www.crea-sol.com
SIC: 3498 Tube fabricating (contract bending & shaping)

(G-9456)
CREATIVE WOODWORKING LLC
515 Pierpont Rd (06705-3909)
PHONE..................................203 518-0336
Sobers Luton, *Principal*
EMP: 1
SALES (est): 41.5K **Privately Held**
SIC: 2499 Wood products

(G-9457)
CUSTOMIZED FOODS MFG LLC
8 S Commons Rd (06704-1035)
PHONE..................................203 759-1645
Al Poe, *Principal*
EMP: 8

SALES (est): 518.8K **Privately Held**
SIC: 3999 Manufacturing industries

(G-9458)
D & M PACKING LLC
407 Brookside Rd Ste 1 (06708-1453)
PHONE..................................203 591-8986
David Miller, *President*
Aziz Debbagh,
▲ **EMP:** 28 **EST:** 2013
SALES (est): 722.9K **Privately Held**
SIC: 5149 2032 Organic & diet foods; natural & organic foods; ethnic foods: canned, jarred, etc.; Italian foods: packaged in cans, jars, etc.

(G-9459)
DA SILVA KLANKO LTD
Also Called: Love 'n Herbs
70 Deerwood Ln Unit 8 (06704-1665)
PHONE..................................203 756-4932
Maria B Klanko, *President*
Donald Klanko, *Corp Secy*
Peter J Klanko, *Vice Pres*
EMP: 3
SALES (est): 850K **Privately Held**
SIC: 2035 Dressings, salad: raw & cooked (except dry mixes)

(G-9460)
DANGELO FAMILY LLC
460 Fairfield Ave (06708-4042)
PHONE..................................203 235-1238
EMP: 1
SALES (est): 54.3K **Privately Held**
SIC: 3499 Fabricated metal products

(G-9461)
DANGEROUS INDUSTRIES QUALITY
13 Harriet Ave Fl 3 (06708-3703)
PHONE..................................860 986-0879
Wilfredo Vargas, *Principal*
EMP: 1 **EST:** 2013
SALES (est): 39.6K **Privately Held**
SIC: 3999 Manufacturing industries

(G-9462)
DARLING INTERNATIONAL INC
172 E Aurora St (06708-2047)
PHONE..................................203 597-0773
EMP: 2
SALES (est): 83K **Privately Held**
SIC: 2077 Animal fats, oils & meals

(G-9463)
DASCO WELDED PRODUCTS INC
2038 Thomaston Ave (06704-1036)
PHONE..................................203 754-9353
Daren Edward Thornberg, *President*
Patrick Hale, *Vice Pres*
EMP: 11
SQ FT: 3,000
SALES (est): 1.2MM **Privately Held**
SIC: 3444 Sheet metalwork

(G-9464)
DAVID R WTTRWRTH SON SIGNS LLC
71 Mountain View Dr (06706-2825)
PHONE..................................203 753-3666
David R Watterworth, *Principal*
EMP: 1
SALES (est): 82.7K **Privately Held**
SIC: 3993 Signs & advertising specialties

(G-9465)
DIANAS CANDLES AND SOAP LLC
206 Long Hill Rd (06704-3716)
PHONE..................................203 527-4028
Sudesh Sookram, *Principal*
EMP: 1
SALES (est): 39.6K **Privately Held**
SIC: 3999 Candles

(G-9466)
DONALD E BASIL INC
76 Sabal Dr (06708-2150)
PHONE..................................203 574-0149
Donald E Basil, *President*
EMP: 2

SALES (est): 210K **Privately Held**
SIC: 3699 Automotive driving simulators (training aids), electronic

(G-9467)
DURCO MANUFACTURING CO INC
493 S Leonard St (06708-4315)
PHONE..................................203 575-0446
F Donald Ek, *CEO*
Sabastian Corona, *President*
Barbara Williams, *Treasurer*
EMP: 8
SQ FT: 5,000
SALES (est): 1.4MM **Privately Held**
WEB: www.durcomfg.com
SIC: 3451 Screw machine products

(G-9468)
DUROS WELDING SERVICES
353 Highland Dr (06708-3663)
PHONE..................................203 982-6978
EMP: 1 **EST:** 2015
SALES (est): 39.9K **Privately Held**
SIC: 7692 Welding repair

(G-9469)
E & J PARTS CLEANING INC
1669 Thomaston Ave (06704-1026)
P.O. Box 4250 (06704-0250)
PHONE..................................203 757-1716
Everett Hardick, *President*
EMP: 11
SALES (est): 1.1MM **Privately Held**
WEB: www.ejpartscleaning.com
SIC: 7349 Cleaning & descaling metal products; cleaning service, industrial or commercial

(G-9470)
EDS JEWELRY LLC
625 Wolcott St Ste 14 (06705-1342)
PHONE..................................203 757-0018
Eduardo Perez, *Principal*
EMP: 2 **EST:** 2008
SALES (est): 96.3K **Privately Held**
SIC: 3423 Jewelers' hand tools

(G-9471)
EDWIN PUBLISHING COMPANY
70 Edwin Ave (06708-2238)
PHONE..................................203 228-9396
David R Zackin, *Principal*
EMP: 1 **EST:** 2010
SALES (est): 59.1K **Privately Held**
SIC: 2741 Miscellaneous publishing

(G-9472)
EEMAX INC (DH)
400 Captain Neville Dr (06705-3811)
PHONE..................................203 267-7890
Kevin M Ruppelt, *President*
Jens Bolleyer, *Vice Pres*
Mike Burns, *Plant Mgr*
Mark Smola, *QC Mgr*
Chris Hayden, *Engineer*
▲ **EMP:** 80
SQ FT: 16,000
SALES (est): 14.2MM **Privately Held**
WEB: www.eemax.com
SIC: 3639 Hot water heaters, household
HQ: Rheem Manufacturing Company Inc
1100 Abernathy Rd # 1700
Atlanta GA 30328
770 351-3000

(G-9473)
ELECTRONIC CONNECTION CORP
112 Porter St (06708-3819)
PHONE..................................860 243-3356
Ray Gorski Jr, *President*
Ronald Gorski, *Vice Pres*
Melinda Farley, *Manager*
EMP: 20
SQ FT: 8,000
SALES (est): 3.3MM **Publicly Held**
WEB: www.eccwire.com
SIC: 3679 Harness assemblies for electronic use: wire or cable
PA: Air Industries Group
1460 5th Ave
Bay Shore NY 11706

(G-9474)
ELECTRONIC FILM CAPACITORS
Also Called: EFC
41 Interstate Ln (06705-2639)
PHONE..................................203 755-5629
Jay Weiner, *President*
Leonard Gelonese, *Engineer*
Bob Fountain, *Sales Executive*
Jessica Gadzik, *Marketing Staff*
Anglea Sousa, *Admin Sec*
EMP: 47
SQ FT: 15,000
SALES (est): 7MM **Privately Held**
WEB: www.filmcapacitors.com
SIC: 3675 Electronic capacitors

(G-9475)
ELEMENT SOLUTIONS INC
245 Freight St (06702-1818)
PHONE..................................203 575-5850
EMP: 25
SALES (corp-wide): 1.9B **Publicly Held**
SIC: 2899 2869 Chemical preparations; hydraulic fluids, synthetic base
PA: Element Solutions Inc
1450 Centrepark Blvd # 210
West Palm Beach FL 33401
561 207-9600

(G-9476)
EYELET CRAFTERS INC
2712 S Main St (06706-2647)
P.O. Box 2542 (06723-2542)
PHONE..................................203 757-9221
Robert A Finkenzeller, *President*
William E Finkenzeller, *Vice Pres*
Harriet Finkenzeller, *Admin Sec*
Frank T Healey, *Asst Sec*
EMP: 65
SQ FT: 30,000
SALES (est): 16.6MM **Privately Held**
WEB: www.eyeletcrafters.com
SIC: 3469 3471 Stamping metal for the trade; finishing, metals or formed products

(G-9477)
EYELET DESIGN INC
574 E Main St (06702-1706)
P.O. Box 808 (06720-0808)
PHONE..................................203 754-4141
Robert L Hughes, *President*
Card Chris, *Safety Mgr*
Ken Schoppmann, *QC Mgr*
Craig Parker, *Engineer*
Claudia M Hughes, *Treasurer*
EMP: 100
SQ FT: 130,000
SALES (est): 15.5MM **Privately Held**
WEB: www.eyeletdesign.com
SIC: 3469 3466 Stamping metal for the trade; crowns & closures

(G-9478)
EYELETS FOR INDUSTRY INC
47 Stevens St (06704-1020)
PHONE..................................203 754-6502
Jim Troland, *Principal*
EMP: 1
SALES (est): 72K **Privately Held**
SIC: 2395 Eyelet making, for the trade

(G-9479)
FABOR FOURSLIDE INC
44 Railroad Hill St (06708-4320)
P.O. Box 2420 (06722-2420)
PHONE..................................203 753-4380
EMP: 5
SQ FT: 6,000
SALES (est): 400K **Privately Held**
SIC: 3469 Manufacturer Of Metal Stampings

(G-9480)
FASCIAS CHOCOLATES INC
44 Chase River Rd (06704-1408)
PHONE..................................203 753-0515
Carmen Romeo, *President*
Lynne Fascia Moanes, *Vice Pres*
Louise Fascia Romeo, *Admin Sec*
EMP: 15
SQ FT: 18,000

SALES (est): 590K **Privately Held**
SIC: **5441** 2064 Confectionery produced for direct sale on the premises; candy & other confectionery products

(G-9481)
FOAM PLASTICS NEW ENGLAND INC
32 Gramar Ave (06712-1016)
P.O. Box 7075, Prospect (06712-0075)
PHONE..................203 758-6651
David L Lewis, *President*
Eugene R Lewis, *Admin Sec*
EMP: 4
SQ FT: 96,000
SALES (est): 570K **Privately Held**
SIC: **3086** Insulation or cushioning material, foamed plastic

(G-9482)
FORUM PLASTICS LLC
105 Progress Ln (06705-3830)
PHONE..................203 754-0777
Joseph Pasqualucci, *Principal*
Mark Polinsky, *Engineer*
Brian Labrec, *Sales Staff*
EMP: 44
SALES (est): 15.8MM **Privately Held**
SIC: **2821** Thermoplastic materials

(G-9483)
G F GRINDING TOOL MFG CO INC
649 Captain Neville Dr (06705-3826)
PHONE..................203 757-6244
John Fratamico, *President*
EMP: 3 EST: 1968
SALES: 175K **Privately Held**
SIC: **3599** Machine shop, jobbing & repair

(G-9484)
G S S INDUSTRIES
44 Railroad Hill St (06708-4320)
P.O. Box 2420 (06722-2420)
PHONE..................203 755-6644
George Strobel Jr, *Owner*
George Stobel, *Accounting Dir*
EMP: 2
SQ FT: 1,500
SALES (est): 192.3K **Privately Held**
WEB: www.lexusofakron-canton.com
SIC: **3999** Barber & beauty shop equipment

(G-9485)
GEM MANUFACTURING CO INC (PA)
78 Brookside Rd (06708-1402)
P.O. Box 4550 (06704-0550)
PHONE..................203 574-1466
Robert C Caulfield Jr, *President*
Gerard Berthiaume, *Vice Pres*
Mark G Caulfield, *Vice Pres*
Kaitlin Dwyer, *Manager*
Christopher C Gemino, *Admin Sec*
◆ EMP: 90 EST: 1943
SQ FT: 84,000
SALES (est): 19.5MM **Privately Held**
WEB: www.gemmfg.com
SIC: **3469** Stamping metal for the trade

(G-9486)
GENERAL HEAT TREATING CO
80 Fulkerson Dr (06708-1409)
PHONE..................203 755-5441
Larry Maknis, *President*
Tracy Maknis, *Treasurer*
Tracey Maknis, *Admin Sec*
EMP: 6
SQ FT: 7,000
SALES (est): 911.5K **Privately Held**
SIC: **3398** Metal heat treating

(G-9487)
GENERAL WELDING COMPANY INC
28 Broadway St (06705-3849)
PHONE..................203 753-6988
Larry Berluti, *President*
EMP: 2
SQ FT: 1,000
SALES (est): 204.7K **Privately Held**
SIC: **7692** Welding repair

(G-9488)
GLOBAL BRASS & COPPER LLC (PA)
Also Called: Somers Thin Strip
215 Piedmont St (06706-2152)
PHONE..................203 597-5000
Tom Werner, *Vice Pres*
William M Fautch, *Vice Pres*
Mike Houston, *Vice Pres*
Dale R Taylor, *Vice Pres*
Brian Weyel, *Supervisor*
▲ EMP: 5 EST: 2010
SQ FT: 150,000
SALES (est): 2.3MM **Privately Held**
SIC: **3351** Copper rolling & drawing

(G-9489)
GLOBAL BRASS & COPPER LLC
Also Called: Somers Thin Strip
94 Baldwin Ave (06706-1853)
PHONE..................203 597-5000
EMP: 1
SALES (est): 170.9K
SALES (corp-wide): 2.3MM **Privately Held**
SIC: **3351** Copper rolling & drawing
PA: Global Brass & Copper, Llc
215 Piedmont St
Waterbury CT 06706
203 597-5000

(G-9490)
GM HOME SOLUTIONS
59 Fairview St (06710-1829)
PHONE..................305 608-9721
EMP: 2
SALES (est): 95.9K **Privately Held**
SIC: **3716** Motor homes

(G-9491)
GROTTO ALWAYS INC
Also Called: Tasteful Gift Baskets By Mrs G
634 Watertown Ave (06708-2207)
PHONE..................203 754-0295
Joseph Graziosa, *President*
Bernadette Graziosa, *Vice Pres*
James Westwood, *CFO*
EMP: 10
SQ FT: 3,000
SALES (est): 450K **Privately Held**
SIC: **5812** 5499 2098 2097 Italian restaurant; food gift baskets; macaroni & spaghetti; manufactured ice

(G-9492)
GUISEPPE MAZZETTINI
Also Called: MJM Islet
270 Bradley Ave (06708-4438)
PHONE..................203 597-9035
Guiseppe Mazzettini, *Partner*
Mario Mazzettini, *Partner*
EMP: 1
SALES (est): 100K **Privately Held**
SIC: **3541** Machine tool replacement & repair parts, metal cutting types

(G-9493)
H&H TOOL LLC
59 Nichols Rd (06716-2716)
PHONE..................203 879-4519
C Heller, *Principal*
EMP: 2
SALES (est): 138.6K **Privately Held**
SIC: **3423** Wrenches, hand tools

(G-9494)
H&T WATERBURY INC
Also Called: Bouffard Metal Goods
984 Waterville St (06710-1015)
P.O. Box 4700 (06704-0700)
PHONE..................203 574-2240
Reinhard S Scholle, *General Mgr*
Christian Diemer, *Principal*
Daniel D Moffa, *Vice Pres*
Ronald T Turmel, *Vice Pres*
David Sorensen, *QC Mgr*
▲ EMP: 150
SQ FT: 128,000
SALES (est): 39.3MM
SALES (corp-wide): 125.1K **Privately Held**
SIC: **3469** Stamping metal for the trade

PA: Sdruzeni Firem Heitkamp&Thumann Group
Havlickova 540/28
Hustopece

(G-9495)
HALCO INC
Also Called: Waterbury Plating
114 Porter St (06708-3819)
P.O. Box 2545 (06723-2545)
PHONE..................203 575-9450
Glen Harper, *President*
Bob Lanz, *Vice Pres*
EMP: 75 EST: 1941
SQ FT: 55,000
SALES (est): 10.1MM **Privately Held**
WEB: www.waterburyplating.com
SIC: **3471** 3479 Electroplating of metals or formed products; painting of metal products

(G-9496)
HARDCORE SWEET CUPCAKES LLC
784 Cooke St (06710-1112)
PHONE..................203 808-5547
Danette McEvoy, *Principal*
EMP: 4
SALES (est): 166.6K **Privately Held**
SIC: **2051** Bread, cake & related products

(G-9497)
HAYDON KERK MTION SLUTIONS INC
1500 Meriden Rd (06705-3982)
P.O. Box 3329 (06705-0329)
PHONE..................203 756-7441
John P Norris, *President*
Frank Morton, *General Mgr*
Robert S Feit, *Vice Pres*
James Bostwick, *Engineer*
William J Burke, *Treasurer*
▲ EMP: 140 EST: 1963
SQ FT: 42,000
SALES (est): 39.3MM
SALES (est): 4.8B **Publicly Held**
WEB: www.hsi-inc.com
SIC: **3823** Industrial instrmnts msrmnt display/control process variable
PA: Ametek, Inc.
1100 Cassatt Rd
Berwyn PA 19312
610 647-2121

(G-9498)
HOMAR MOLDS & MODELS CO
64 Diane Ter (06705-3523)
PHONE..................203 753-9017
Robert Scarpa, *Owner*
EMP: 2
SQ FT: 1,500
SALES: 50K **Privately Held**
SIC: **3089** Molding primary plastic

(G-9499)
HOTSEAT CHASSIS INC
Also Called: Semipilot
20 S Commons Rd (06704-1035)
PHONE..................860 582-5031
Jay Leboff, *President*
EMP: 6
SALES: 750K **Privately Held**
WEB: www.hotseatinc.com
SIC: **7372** 5999 Educational computer software; educational aids & electronic training materials; education aids, devices & supplies

(G-9500)
HOUSTON MACDERMID INC
245 Freight St (06702-1818)
PHONE..................203 575-5700
EMP: 3
SALES (est): 123.2K
SALES (corp-wide): 1.9B **Publicly Held**
SIC: **2869** Hydraulic fluids, synthetic base
PA: Element Solutions Inc
1450 Centrepark Blvd # 210
West Palm Beach FL 33401
561 207-9600

(G-9501)
HUBBARD-HALL INC (PA)
563 S Leonard St (06708-4316)
P.O. Box 790 (06720-0790)
PHONE..................203 756-5521

Molly Kellogg, *President*
Gerard Mastropietro, *COO*
Jeff Davis, *Senior VP*
Robert Farrell, *Senior VP*
Charles T Kellogg, *CFO*
◆ EMP: 111 EST: 1971
SQ FT: 90,000
SALES (est): 55.3MM **Privately Held**
WEB: www.hubbardhall.com
SIC: **5169** 3471 2899 2842 Chemicals, industrial & heavy; finishing, metals or formed products; chemical preparations; specialty cleaning, polishes & sanitation goods

(G-9502)
I AND U LLC
Also Called: Pan Del Cielo
66 Mattatuck Heights Rd (06705-3831)
PHONE..................860 803-1491
Tony Tasilva, *President*
Ivania Lorenzo, *Vice Pres*
EMP: 6
SQ FT: 2,500
SALES: 600K **Privately Held**
SIC: **2051** Bread, cake & related products

(G-9503)
ILLINOIS TOOL WORKS INC
ITW Drawform Waterbury
1240 Wolcott St (06705-1320)
PHONE..................203 574-2119
Rob Webber, *Branch Mgr*
EMP: 140
SALES (corp-wide): 14.7B **Publicly Held**
SIC: **3482** 3469 3448 Small arms ammunition; metal stampings; prefabricated metal buildings
PA: Illinois Tool Works Inc.
155 Harlem Ave
Glenview IL 60025
847 724-7500

(G-9504)
INDUSTRIAL DRIVES CONTRLS INC (PA)
165 Homer St (06704-1729)
PHONE..................203 753-5103
Jack Traver Jr, *President*
Jack Traver Sr, *Treasurer*
Brian Aurell, *Manager*
Elaine Traver, *Admin Sec*
EMP: 11
SQ FT: 5,000
SALES (est): 16MM **Privately Held**
SIC: **5063** 7694 Motors, electric; electric motor repair

(G-9505)
INFINITY STONE INC
1261 Meriden Rd (06705-3637)
PHONE..................203 575-9484
Michael Amendola, *President*
Ellen Labriola, *Sales Staff*
EMP: 10 EST: 2014
SALES (est): 290.3K **Privately Held**
SIC: **1411** 3944 Marble, dimension-quarrying; marbles (toys)

(G-9506)
ITW DRAWFORM INC
1240 Wolcott St (06705-1320)
PHONE..................203 574-3200
Gills Boehm, *Principal*
Burt Hanson, *Foreman/Supr*
EMP: 29
SALES (est): 5.9MM **Privately Held**
SIC: **3469** Metal stampings

(G-9507)
J & R PROJECTS
1509 Wolcott Rd (06716-1321)
PHONE..................203 879-2347
James F Rideout Sr, *Partner*
James Rideout Jr, *Partner*
EMP: 3
SQ FT: 1,600
SALES (est): 323K **Privately Held**
SIC: **3451** Screw machine products

(G-9508)
JA ELECTRONICS LLC
121 Bennett Ave (06708-4046)
PHONE..................860 921-7549
Philip Petkin, *Principal*
EMP: 1

Waterbury - New Haven County (G-9509)

SALES (est): 88K Privately Held
SIC: 3679 8711 Electronic components; engineering services

(G-9509)
JIMBPA ENTERPRISES LLC
36 Wheeler St (06704-1720)
PHONE..................203 755-9237
James L Baranoski, Principal
EMP: 2
SALES (est): 64.5K Privately Held
SIC: 7378 5734 5084 3999 Computer maintenance & repair; computer & software stores; industrial machinery & equipment; manufacturing industries

(G-9510)
JL LUCAS MACHINERY CO INC
429 Brookside Rd (06708-1418)
P.O. Box 4220 (06704-0220)
PHONE..................203 597-1300
John Pelletier, President
Judy Pelletier, Admin Sec
▲ EMP: 18
SQ FT: 20,000
SALES (est): 3.3MM Privately Held
WEB: www.jllucas.com
SIC: 3541 5084 Machine tools, metal cutting type; machine tools & accessories

(G-9511)
JO VEK TOOL AND DIE MFG CO
2121 Thomaston Ave (06704)
PHONE..................203 755-1884
Frank Longo, President
Chris Longo, Corp Secy
EMP: 6 EST: 1953
SQ FT: 10,200
SALES (est): 1MM Privately Held
SIC: 3469 3965 3312 Stamping metal for the trade; eyelets, metal: clothing, fabrics, boots or shoes; tool & die steel

(G-9512)
JOHN HYCHKO
Also Called: Valley Truckstop
299 Sheffield St (06704-1010)
PHONE..................203 757-3458
John Hychko, Owner
EMP: 4
SQ FT: 14,400
SALES (est): 526.9K Privately Held
SIC: 1442 1794 Construction sand & gravel; excavation & grading, building construction

(G-9513)
JOMA INCORPORATED
185 Interstate Ln (06705-2640)
PHONE..................203 759-0848
Francis X Macary, President
▲ EMP: 20 EST: 1953
SQ FT: 20,000
SALES (est): 4MM Privately Held
SIC: 3469 Stamping metal for the trade

(G-9514)
K CHEF INC
108 Edwin Ave (06708-2238)
PHONE..................646 778-8396
Karen Williams, President
EMP: 1
SALES: 94K Privately Held
SIC: 2087 Beverage bases

(G-9515)
KNIGHT INC
Also Called: Knight Manufacturing
47 Stevens St (06704-1020)
P.O. Box 4343 (06704-0343)
PHONE..................203 754-6502
Jim Troland, President
EMP: 5
SQ FT: 12,000
SALES (est): 750.7K Privately Held
SIC: 3965 Eyelets, metal: clothing, fabrics, boots or shoes

(G-9516)
L C M TOOL CO
68 Diane Ter (06705-3523)
P.O. Box 3245 (06705-0245)
PHONE..................203 757-1575
Dante Carrafa, President
Michele Longo, Vice Pres
Sebastian Longo, Treasurer
Mario Longo, Admin Sec
EMP: 9 EST: 1966
SALES: 1.1MM Privately Held
WEB: www.lcmtool.com
SIC: 3541 Screw & thread machines

(G-9517)
LEELYND CORP
546 S Main St (06706-1015)
PHONE..................203 753-9137
Thomas Deleon, President
EMP: 3
SQ FT: 3,500
SALES (est): 448.9K Privately Held
SIC: 3469 Machine parts, stamped or pressed metal

(G-9518)
LUIS PRESSURE WASHER
47 Esther Ave (06708-4818)
PHONE..................203 706-7399
Luis Rodriguez, Principal
EMP: 3 EST: 2011
SALES (est): 188.8K Privately Held
SIC: 3452 Washers

(G-9519)
LUVATA WATERBURY INC
2121 Thomaston Ave Ste 1 (06704)
PHONE..................203 753-5215
James C Lajewski, President
Jukka Somerkoski, Info Tech Mgr
Gwen Gilbert, Director
Pekka Kleemola, Admin Sec
▲ EMP: 66
SQ FT: 210,000
SALES (est): 27.7MM Privately Held
SIC: 3357 Magnet wire, nonferrous
HQ: Luvata Pori Oy
   Kuparitie 5
   Pori 28330
   262 661-11

(G-9520)
LYONS SLITTING INC
46 Mattatuck Heights Rd (06705-3831)
PHONE..................203 755-4564
Brad Lyons, President
EMP: 10
SQ FT: 12,000
SALES (est): 936.8K Privately Held
WEB: www.lyonsslitting.com
SIC: 7389 3444 Metal slitting & shearing; sheet metalwork

(G-9521)
M & M PALLET INC
360 Baldwin St (06706-1304)
PHONE..................203 754-2606
Donna Gilbert, President
Marsel Frappier, Principal
Tina Santos, Vice Pres
Jacques Frappier, Admin Sec
EMP: 2
SALES (est): 239.1K Privately Held
SIC: 2448 Pallets, wood

(G-9522)
MACDERMID INCORPORATED (HQ)
Also Called: Macdermid Prfmce Solutions
245 Freight St (06702-1818)
P.O. Box 671 (06720-0671)
PHONE..................203 575-5700
Scot Benson, President
Ken Southwell, General Mgr
Frank J Monteiro, COO
Aaron Bowman, Counsel
Patricia Gaglione, Vice Pres
◆ EMP: 200 EST: 1922
SQ FT: 51,700
SALES: 430.2MM
SALES (corp-wide): 1.9B Publicly Held
WEB: www.macdermid.com
SIC: 2842 2992 2752 3577 Cleaning or polishing preparations; lubricating oils; offset & photolithographic printing; printers & plotters; plating compounds
PA: Element Solutions Inc
   1450 Centrepark Blvd # 210
   West Palm Beach FL 33401
   561 207-9600

(G-9523)
MACDERMID INCORPORATED
245 Freight St (06702-1818)
PHONE..................262 242-2892
EMP: 2
SALES (corp-wide): 1.9B Publicly Held
SIC: 2899 Chemical preparations
HQ: Macdermid, Incorporated
   245 Freight St
   Waterbury CT 06702
   203 575-5700

(G-9524)
MACDERMID INCORPORATED
Also Called: Mac Dermid Elec Solution
245 Freight St (06702-1818)
PHONE..................203 575-5700
Richard A Nave, Branch Mgr
EMP: 38
SALES (est): 1.9B Publicly Held
WEB: www.macdermid.com
SIC: 2899 Plating compounds
HQ: Macdermid, Incorporated
   245 Freight St
   Waterbury CT 06702
   203 575-5700

(G-9525)
MACDERMID ACUMEN INC
245 Freight St (06702-1818)
PHONE..................203 575-5700
EMP: 4 EST: 1997
SALES (est): 232.8K
SALES (corp-wide): 1.9B Publicly Held
SIC: 2899 Chemical preparations
PA: Element Solutions Inc
   1450 Centrepark Blvd # 210
   West Palm Beach FL 33401
   561 207-9600

(G-9526)
MACDERMID AG SOLUTIONS INC
Also Called: Agriphar Crop Solutions
245 Freight St (06702-1818)
PHONE..................203 575-5727
Frank Monteiro, President
Michael Kennedy, Treasurer
John Cordani, Admin Sec
EMP: 15 EST: 2014
SQ FT: 50,000
SALES (est): 35.6MM
SALES (corp-wide): 1.9B Publicly Held
SIC: 2879 Agricultural chemicals
HQ: Macdermid, Incorporated
   245 Freight St
   Waterbury CT 06702
   203 575-5700

(G-9527)
MACDERMID ANION INC
245 Freight St (06702-1818)
PHONE..................203 575-5700
EMP: 3 EST: 2002
SALES (est): 123.2K
SALES (corp-wide): 1.9B Publicly Held
SIC: 2869 Hydraulic fluids, synthetic base
PA: Element Solutions Inc
   1450 Centrepark Blvd # 210
   West Palm Beach FL 33401
   561 207-9600

(G-9528)
MACDERMID BRAZIL INC
245 Freight St (06702-1818)
PHONE..................203 575-5700
EMP: 3
SALES (est): 123.2K
SALES (corp-wide): 1.9B Publicly Held
SIC: 2869 Hydraulic fluids, synthetic base
PA: Element Solutions Inc
   1450 Centrepark Blvd # 210
   West Palm Beach FL 33401
   561 207-9600

(G-9529)
MACDERMID OVERSEAS ASIA LTD (HQ)
245 Freight St (06702-1818)
PHONE..................203 575-5799
EMP: 5 EST: 1983
SALES (est): 8MM
SALES (corp-wide): 1.9B Publicly Held
SIC: 2899 Chemical preparations
PA: Element Solutions Inc
   1450 Centrepark Blvd # 210
   West Palm Beach FL 33401
   561 207-9600

(G-9530)
MACDERMID PRINTING SOLUTIONS
245 Freight St (06702-1818)
PHONE..................203 575-5727
Ted Antonellis, Research
Jun Nable, Research
Eric Wetmore, Engineer
Deborah Gorzelany, Credit Staff
Holly Delaurentis, Financial Analy
EMP: 6
SALES (est): 488K
SALES (corp-wide): 1.9B Publicly Held
SIC: 2899 Chemical preparations
PA: Element Solutions Inc
   1450 Centrepark Blvd # 210
   West Palm Beach FL 33401
   561 207-9600

(G-9531)
MACDERMID SOUTH AMERICA INC
245 Freight St (06702-1818)
PHONE..................203 575-5700
EMP: 3
SALES (est): 123.2K
SALES (corp-wide): 1.9B Publicly Held
SIC: 2869 Hydraulic fluids, synthetic base
PA: Element Solutions Inc
   1450 Centrepark Blvd # 210
   West Palm Beach FL 33401
   561 207-9600

(G-9532)
MACDERMID SOUTH ATLANTIC INC
245 Freight St (06702-1818)
PHONE..................203 575-5700
EMP: 3
SALES (est): 150.1K
SALES (corp-wide): 1.9B Publicly Held
SIC: 2869 Hydraulic fluids, synthetic base
PA: Element Solutions Inc
   1450 Centrepark Blvd # 210
   West Palm Beach FL 33401
   561 207-9600

(G-9533)
MANUFCTRING ALNCE SVC CORP INC
173 Interstate Ln (06705-2661)
PHONE..................203 596-1900
Pastsy A Guarino, Principal
EMP: 1
SALES (est): 162.9K Privately Held
SIC: 3999 Manufacturing industries

(G-9534)
MARJAN INC
44 Railroad Hill St (06708-4320)
P.O. Box 2420 (06722-2420)
PHONE..................203 573-1742
George Strobel Sr, President
William C Strobel, Vice Pres
George Strobel Jr, Treasurer
Richard Strobel, Admin Sec
▲ EMP: 19
SQ FT: 17,000
SALES (est): 2MM Privately Held
WEB: www.marjaninc.com
SIC: 3479 Hot dip coating of metals or formed products; coating of metals & formed products

(G-9535)
MASTER ENGRV & PRINTERY INC (PA)
Also Called: Waterbury Printing
45 Westridge Dr (06708-3336)
PHONE..................203 723-2779
Rocco Corso, President
Roselyn Goldman, Bookkeeper
EMP: 8
SQ FT: 4,800
SALES (est): 844.3K Privately Held
SIC: 2759 2791 2789 2752 Invitation & stationery printing & engraving; typesetting; bookbinding & related work; commercial printing, lithographic

▲ = Import ▼ = Export
◆ = Import/Export

Waterbury - New Haven County

(G-9536)
MATERIAL PROMOTIONS INC
145 Railroad Hill St (06708-4306)
PHONE..................203 757-8900
Peter Bove, *President*
EMP: 4 **EST:** 2007
SALES (est): 550.6K **Privately Held**
SIC: 2752 Commercial printing, lithographic

(G-9537)
MATTATUCK ALARM CO INC
161 Fairfield Ave (06708-4060)
PHONE..................203 754-0541
Mike Monteiro, *Principal*
EMP: 1
SALES (est): 99.2K **Privately Held**
SIC: 3669 Burglar alarm apparatus, electric

(G-9538)
MCLEOD OPTICAL COMPANY INC
451 Meriden Rd Ste 3 (06705-2248)
PHONE..................203 754-2187
Daniel Mattaboni, *Manager*
EMP: 7
SALES (corp-wide): 5.8MM **Privately Held**
SIC: 3851 Ophthalmic goods
PA: Mcleod Optical Company, Inc.
50 Jefferson Park Rd
Warwick RI 02888
401 467-3000

(G-9539)
MERCURY FUEL SERVICE INC (PA)
43 Lafayette St (06708-3897)
PHONE..................203 756-7284
Michael Devino Jr, *President*
Tebbets Kelley, *District Mgr*
David F Devino, *Vice Pres*
Jim Scully, *Project Mgr*
Martin F Devino, *Treasurer*
EMP: 100
SQ FT: 12,000
SALES (est): 105.1MM **Privately Held**
SIC: 5172 5541 5411 5983 Gasoline; fuel oil; filling stations, gasoline; convenience stores, chain; fuel oil dealers; warm air heating & air conditioning contractor; petroleum refining

(G-9540)
METALLON INC
2120 Thomaston Ave (06704-1013)
PHONE..................203 437-8540
Suzann Ackers, *Office Mgr*
EMP: 1 **EST:** 2015
SALES (est): 65.7K **Privately Held**
SIC: 3499 Fabricated metal products

(G-9541)
MEXI-GRILL LLC
495 Union St (06706-1292)
PHONE..................203 574-2127
EMP: 4 **EST:** 2011
SALES (est): 180K **Privately Held**
SIC: 3421 Mfg Cutlery

(G-9542)
MICROBEST INC
670 Captain Neville Dr # 1 (06705-3855)
PHONE..................203 597-0355
Steven Griffin, *President*
Edward McNerney, *Vice Pres*
Michael Altberg, *Vice Pres*
Paul Lemay, *Vice Pres*
Elaine M Studwell, *Vice Pres*
EMP: 135
SQ FT: 43,000
SALES (est): 41.7MM **Privately Held**
WEB: www.microbest.com
SIC: 3451 3541 Screw machine products; machine tools, metal cutting type

(G-9543)
MILITE BAKERY
Also Called: Arturo Milite and Spinella Bky
53 Interstate Ln (06705-2658)
PHONE..................203 753-9451
Ralph Spinella, *Owner*
EMP: 8 **EST:** 1932
SALES (est): 468.2K **Privately Held**
SIC: 2051 5461 Bread, all types (white, wheat, rye, etc): fresh or frozen; rolls, bread type: fresh or frozen; bakeries

(G-9544)
MIRROR POLISHING & PLTG CO INC
346 Huntingdon Ave (06708-1430)
PHONE..................203 574-5400
Gary Nalband, *President*
Glenn Geddis, *Engineer*
Penny Nalband, *Human Res Mgr*
◆ **EMP:** 40
SQ FT: 85,000
SALES (est): 6.3MM **Privately Held**
WEB: www.mpp.net
SIC: 3471 5719 Chromium plating of metals or formed products; finishing, metals or formed products; mirrors

(G-9545)
MITCHELL-BATE COMPANY
365 Thomaston Ave (06702-1024)
P.O. Box 1707 (06721-1707)
PHONE..................203 233-0862
Donald C Lang Jr, *President*
Scott Lang, *Vice Pres*
Peter Dimaria, *Representative*
EMP: 30 **EST:** 1955
SQ FT: 15,000
SALES (est): 5.8MM **Privately Held**
SIC: 2542 3479 3443 Racks, merchandise display or storage: except wood; coating of metals with plastic or resins; fabricated plate work (boiler shop)

(G-9546)
MIX BOX
495 Union St Ste 1024 (06706-1293)
PHONE..................203 591-8887
Hang Gao, *Owner*
EMP: 2
SALES (est): 73.7K **Privately Held**
SIC: 3961 Costume jewelry

(G-9547)
MJM MARGA LLC
561 Sylvan Ave (06706-1945)
PHONE..................203 597-9035
Joe Mazzettini, *Owner*
EMP: 1
SALES (est): 39.6K **Privately Held**
SIC: 3999 Manufacturing industries

(G-9548)
MUNICIPAL STADIUM
1200 Watertown Ave (06708-1760)
PHONE..................203 755-4019
Tom Gorman, *Manager*
EMP: 2
SALES (est): 105.4K **Privately Held**
SIC: 2741 Miscellaneous publishing

(G-9549)
MVC AQUATIC MACHINE SHOP
17 Highview St (06708-4917)
PHONE..................203 598-5747
Michael Cappelietti, *Principal*
EMP: 2
SALES (est): 120K **Privately Held**
SIC: 3599 Machine shop, jobbing & repair

(G-9550)
MY CITIZENS NEWS
389 Meadow St (06702-1808)
PHONE..................203 729-2228
Paul Roth, *Publisher*
EMP: 5
SALES (est): 194.2K **Privately Held**
SIC: 2711 Newspapers, publishing & printing

(G-9551)
MY TOOL COMPANY INC
1212 S Main St (06706-1747)
PHONE..................203 755-2333
Fax: 203 755-4744
EMP: 4
SQ FT: 5,000
SALES (est): 500K **Privately Held**
SIC: 3599 3544 Mfg Industrial Machinery Mfg Dies/Tools/Jigs/Fixtures

(G-9552)
NAPP PRINTING PLATE DIST INC
245 Freight St (06702-1818)
PHONE..................203 575-5727
Frank Monteiro, *Principal*
EMP: 7
SALES (est): 913.6K
SALES (corp-wide): 1.9B **Publicly Held**
SIC: 2752 Commercial printing, offset
PA: Element Solutions Inc
1450 Centrepark Blvd # 210
West Palm Beach FL 33401
561 207-9600

(G-9553)
NATIONAL INTEGRATED INDS INC
Also Called: American Electro Products Div
1358 Thomaston Ave (06704-1791)
P.O. Box 4129 (06704-0129)
PHONE..................203 756-7051
Dennis Burke, *President*
James Moore, *Plant Mgr*
Joseph Gannon, *Purchasing*
John Krin, *Controller*
Angela Ciccone, *Human Res Dir*
EMP: 100
SALES (est): 9.2MM
SALES (corp-wide): 15MM **Privately Held**
SIC: 3471 Electroplating of metals or formed products
PA: National Integrated Industries, Inc.
322 Main St
Farmington CT 06032
860 677-7995

(G-9554)
NAUGATUCK VLY PHOTO ENGRV INC
2148 S Main St (06706-2639)
PHONE..................203 756-7345
Daniel Semeraro, *President*
Frank Semeraro, *Vice Pres*
Nancy Semeraro, *Admin Sec*
EMP: 4
SALES (est): 544.3K **Privately Held**
SIC: 2754 2752 Commercial printing, gravure; commercial printing, lithographic

(G-9555)
NELCOTE INC
172 E Aurora St Ste A (06708-2048)
PHONE..................203 509-5247
Patrick Haywood, *Principal*
EMP: 2
SALES (est): 114.6K **Privately Held**
SIC: 3089 Plastics products

(G-9556)
NELSON HEAT TREATING CO INC
2046 N Main St (06704-2365)
PHONE..................203 754-0670
James La France, *President*
James Lafrance, *President*
EMP: 11
SQ FT: 6,000
SALES (est): 1.5MM **Privately Held**
SIC: 3398 Metal heat treating

(G-9557)
NEOPERL INC
171 Mattatuck Heights Rd (06705-3832)
PHONE..................203 756-8891
Frederic Fraisse, *Managing Dir*
Michael Moraniec, *Senior VP*
Marie Helene Pernin, *Vice Pres*
Mike Moraniec, *VP Opers*
Chris Manning, *QC Mgr*
▲ **EMP:** 60 **EST:** 1927
SQ FT: 60,000
SALES (est): 11.1MM
SALES (corp-wide): 355.8K **Privately Held**
WEB: www.neoperl.com
SIC: 3432 5074 3088 Plumbers' brass goods: drain cocks, faucets, spigots, etc.; plumbers' brass goods & fittings; plastics plumbing fixtures
PA: Neoperl Holding Ag
Pfeffingerstrasse 21
Reinach BL
617 167-411

(G-9558)
NEW ENGLAND DIE CO INC
48 Ford Ave (06708-1408)
PHONE..................203 574-5140
Joseph Almeida, *President*
Joseph Almeida Jr, *President*
Shelly Almeida, *Admin Sec*
EMP: 12 **EST:** 1941
SQ FT: 10,000
SALES (est): 1.8MM **Privately Held**
WEB: www.newenglanddie.com
SIC: 3541 Electrical discharge erosion machines; drilling & boring machines

(G-9559)
NEW ENGLAND POST A SIGN
215 Oakville Ave (06708-1617)
PHONE..................203 635-3171
Meghan Edwards, *Principal*
EMP: 1 **EST:** 2017
SALES (est): 46K **Privately Held**
SIC: 3993 Signs & advertising specialties

(G-9560)
NEWMARK MEDICAL COMPONENTS INC
2670 S Main St (06706-2616)
P.O. Box 1030 (06721-1030)
PHONE..................203 753-1158
James Behuniak, *Ch of Bd*
David W Mieczkowski, *President*
Thomas Tassis, *Corp Secy*
EMP: 14 **EST:** 2010
SQ FT: 15,000
SALES (est): 1.9MM
SALES (corp-wide): 20.2MM **Privately Held**
SIC: 3841 Medical instruments & equipment, blood & bone work
PA: The Platt Brothers & Company
2670 S Main St
Waterbury CT 06706
203 753-4194

(G-9561)
NORTH EAST POWDER COATING
112 Porter St (06708-3819)
PHONE..................203 573-1543
David D Daigle, *Principal*
EMP: 2 **EST:** 2009
SALES (est): 94.9K **Privately Held**
SIC: 3479 Coating of metals & formed products

(G-9562)
NOUJAIM TOOL CO INC
412 Chase River Rd (06704-1401)
PHONE..................203 753-4441
Joseph Noujaim, *President*
Selim G Noujaim, *President*
Jospoh Noujaim, *Owner*
Kenneth Colson, *General Mgr*
Naim Noujaim, *Vice Pres*
EMP: 23
SQ FT: 5,500
SALES (est): 4.4MM **Privately Held**
WEB: www.noujaimtools.com
SIC: 3599 3544 Machine shop, jobbing & repair; special dies, tools, jigs & fixtures

(G-9563)
NT LAWN SERVICE
142 Fillmore St (06705-2439)
PHONE..................203 573-0285
Nuro Tairovski, *Principal*
EMP: 1
SALES (est): 91.4K **Privately Held**
SIC: 3444 Metal roofing & roof drainage equipment

(G-9564)
NUTMEG WELDING COMPANY INC
92 Rockaway Ave (06705-2937)
PHONE..................203 756-7458
Philip Forino, *President*
Cheryl Forino, *Admin Sec*
EMP: 2 **EST:** 1952
SALES: 390K **Privately Held**
SIC: 7692 3441 Welding repair; fabricated structural metal

Waterbury - New Haven County (G-9565) — GEOGRAPHIC SECTION

(G-9565)
NYLO METAL FINISHING LLC
730 N Main St Ste 1 (06704-3510)
P.O. Box 4960 (06704-0960)
PHONE...........................203 574-5477
Olyn Jaboin,
▲ EMP: 6 EST: 2000
SALES (est): 689.3K Privately Held
WEB: www.nylometalfinishing.com
SIC: 3471 Electroplating of metals or formed products

(G-9566)
OAK HILL INDUSTRIES INC
2457 E Main St Ste 1j (06705-2684)
PHONE...........................203 755-4400
Martha Guarino, *Principal*
EMP: 1
SALES (est): 56.1K Privately Held
SIC: 3999 Manufacturing industries

(G-9567)
OAKVILLE QUALITY PRODUCTS LLC
Also Called: Bobken Automatics
1495 Thomaston Ave Ste 2 (06704-1744)
PHONE...........................203 757-5525
Mark Newton,
EMP: 10
SALES (est): 1.4MM Privately Held
SIC: 3599 Machine shop, jobbing & repair

(G-9568)
ODYSSEY JEWELRY
495 Union St Ofc (06706-1295)
PHONE...........................203 574-4956
Ronnie Hypes, *Principal*
EMP: 1
SALES (est): 56.6K Privately Held
SIC: 3911 Jewelry, precious metal

(G-9569)
OIL PURIFICATION SYSTEMS INC
2176 Thomaston Ave (06704-1013)
PHONE...........................203 346-1800
Greg Slawson, *CEO*
William F Esposito, *President*
Mark Smith, *CFO*
Beth Muller, *Software Dev*
▲ EMP: 15
SQ FT: 1,200
SALES (est): 3.4MM Privately Held
WEB: www.oilpursys.com
SIC: 3533 Oil field machinery & equipment

(G-9570)
OLIVE OIL FACTORY LLC
197 Huntingdon Ave (06708-1413)
PHONE...........................203 591-8986
Laura Miller, *CFO*
David B Miller Jr,
EMP: 12
SQ FT: 2,000
SALES (est): 1.4MM Privately Held
WEB: www.theoliveoilfactory.com
SIC: 7389 5812 2079 Packaging & labeling services; eating places; olive oil

(G-9571)
OPTICARE HEALTH SYSTEMS INC (HQ)
87 Grandview Ave Ste A (06708-2523)
PHONE...........................203 574-2020
Nancy Noll, *President*
Pam Skeens, *Regional Mgr*
Tom Carr, *Vice Pres*
Brian M Wood, *Treasurer*
Mary Graveline, *Admin Sec*
EMP: 150
SALES (est): 21MM Privately Held
SALES (corp-wide): 584.2MM Privately Held
WEB: www.opticare.com
SIC: 8042 5995 3841 Offices & clinics of optometrists; optical goods stores; eyeglasses, prescription; contact lenses, prescription; eye examining instruments & apparatus
PA: Refac Optical Group
    1 Harmon Dr
    Blackwood NJ 08012
    856 228-1000

(G-9572)
PACKAGING AND CRATING TECH LLC
150 Mattatuck Heights Rd (06705-3893)
PHONE...........................203 759-1799
David Goodrich,
Claude Michael Jackson,
EMP: 6
SALES (est): 903.9K Privately Held
SIC: 2671 3089 Packaging paper & plastics film, coated & laminated; blister or bubble formed packaging, plastic

(G-9573)
PACT INC
150 Mattatuck Heights Rd (06705-3893)
PHONE...........................203 759-1799
Rodger Mort, *President*
David Goodrich, *President*
EMP: 17
SALES (est): 2.8MM Privately Held
SIC: 2631 Packaging board

(G-9574)
PALLADIN PRECISION PDTS INC
57 Bristol St (06708-4901)
PHONE...........................203 574-0246
Anthony Palladino, *President*
Dean Palladino, *Vice Pres*
Gary Wininger, *QC Dir*
Lynne R Palladino, *Treasurer*
Sandy Palladino, *Office Mgr*
EMP: 25
SQ FT: 20,000
SALES (est): 5.9MM Privately Held
WEB: www.palladin.com
SIC: 3451 Screw machine products

(G-9575)
PHARMACAL RESEARCH LABS INC
562 Captain Neville Dr # 1 (06705-3875)
P.O. Box 369, Naugatuck (06770-0369)
PHONE...........................203 755-4908
Kenneth Shapiro, *President*
Bill Fleischer, *Vice Pres*
Jerry Shapiro, *CFO*
Warren Ball, *Sales Staff*
Danielle Boulais, *Sales Staff*
◆ EMP: 34
SQ FT: 14,500
SALES (est): 8.5MM Privately Held
WEB: www.pharmacal.com
SIC: 2841 Soap & other detergents

(G-9576)
PHILIPS ULTRASOUND INC
Igc Advanced Superconductors
1875 Thomaston Ave Ste 5 (06704-1034)
PHONE...........................203 753-5215
Richard Lienhardt, *Manager*
EMP: 95
SALES (corp-wide): 20.8B Privately Held
SIC: 3845 Electromedical equipment
HQ: Philips Ultrasound, Inc.
    22100 Bothell Everett Hwy
    Bothell WA 98021
    800 982-2011

(G-9577)
PIECES OF TIME SCRAPBOOK
32 Devonshire Rd (06716-2648)
PHONE...........................203 879-2678
Jennifer Cummings, *Owner*
EMP: 1
SALES (est): 47K Privately Held
SIC: 2782 Scrapbooks

(G-9578)
PLASMA COATINGS INC
758 E Main St (06702-1712)
P.O. Box 10006 (06725-0006)
PHONE...........................203 598-3100
Gary Carlo, *President*
Jody Leblanc, *Sales Staff*
EMP: 3
SALES (est): 405.5K Privately Held
SIC: 2836 Plasmas

(G-9579)
PLASTI-COAT
137 Brookside Rd (06708-1427)
PHONE...........................203 755-3741
EMP: 2
SALES (est): 69.9K Privately Held
SIC: 3479 Coating/Engraving Service

(G-9580)
PLATT BROTHERS & COMPANY (PA)
2670 S Main St (06706-2616)
PHONE...........................203 753-4194
Milton Grile, *Ch of Bd*
James P Behuniak, *President*
David W Mieczkowski, *President*
James J Goggins, *Corp Secy*
John Greaney, *Vice Pres*
EMP: 98 EST: 1830
SQ FT: 120,000
SALES (est): 20.2MM Privately Held
WEB: www.plattbros.com
SIC: 3356 3357 3965 3272 Zinc & zinc alloy: rolling, drawing or extruding; nonferrous wiredrawing & insulating; eyelets, metal; clothing, fabrics, boots or shoes; terrazzo products, precast; metal stampings

(G-9581)
PONY EXPRESS PRINT CO
51 Newport Dr (06705-2511)
PHONE...........................203 592-7095
EMP: 2
SALES (est): 83.9K Privately Held
SIC: 2752 Commercial printing, lithographic

(G-9582)
PORTER PRESTON INC
61 Mattatuck Heights Rd # 2 (06705-3854)
PHONE...........................203 753-1113
John P Birtwell, *President*
Steven P Gilmore, *Vice Pres*
Tom Russell, *Plant Mgr*
Michelle Clark, *Accountant*
Kathy Moran, *Sales Staff*
EMP: 29
SALES: 6MM Privately Held
WEB: www.porterpreston.com
SIC: 2591 Window blinds

(G-9583)
POWER COVER USA LLC
37 Commons Ct Ste 3 (06704-1400)
PHONE...........................203 755-2687
Erik Noeding,
Jill Noeding,
EMP: 4
SALES (est): 1MM Privately Held
SIC: 2399 3537 Automotive covers, except seat & tire covers; loading docks; portable, adjustable & hydraulic

(G-9584)
PRECISION DIP COATING LLC
176 Chase River Rd (06704-1441)
PHONE...........................203 805-4564
Gary Santoro,
Charlene Santoro,
EMP: 5
SALES (est): 630K Privately Held
WEB: www.precisiondipcoating.com
SIC: 3291 2821 Coated abrasive products; molding compounds, plastics

(G-9585)
PREMIERE
1159 Highland Ave (06704-4943)
PHONE...........................203 756-0178
EMP: 2
SALES (est): 59.2K Privately Held
SIC: 2741 Miscellaneous publishing

(G-9586)
PREMIERE PACKG PARTNERS LLC
197 Huntingdon Ave (06708-1413)
PHONE...........................203 694-0003
Michael O'Gorman,
EMP: 25
SALES (est): 809.2K Privately Held
SIC: 2099 Food preparations

(G-9587)
PREYCO MFG CO INC
1184 N Main St (06704-3114)
P.O. Box 4057 (06704-0057)
PHONE...........................203 574-4545
Dennis Laperrierre, *President*
Susan Laperriere, *Director*
EMP: 3 EST: 1960
SQ FT: 8,000
SALES (est): 450K Privately Held
WEB: www.preyco.com
SIC: 3469 Stamping metal for the trade

(G-9588)
PRIMO PRESS LLC
67 Meriden Rd (06705-1933)
PHONE...........................203 527-7904
Andrew Rosado, *Principal*
EMP: 2 EST: 2017
SALES (est): 59.2K Privately Held
SIC: 2741 Miscellaneous publishing

(G-9589)
PRODUCTION DECORATING CO INC
184 Railroad Hill St (06708-4307)
PHONE...........................203 574-2975
Frank Hartnett, *President*
Brendan Hartnett, *Vice Pres*
EMP: 20
SQ FT: 11,000
SALES (est): 2.5MM Privately Held
SIC: 2759 Screen printing

(G-9590)
PROXTALKERCOM LLC (PA)
Also Called: Logantech
327 Huntingdon Ave (06708-1413)
PHONE...........................203 721-6074
Mary Wyatt, *General Mgr*
Glen Dobbs,
Kevin Miller,
EMP: 7
SALES (est): 570.3K Privately Held
SIC: 3651 Audio electronic systems

(G-9591)
QSCEND TECHNOLOGIES INC
231 Bank St (06702-2213)
PHONE...........................203 757-6000
Keith Lebeau, *President*
Irene Lebeau, *Comptroller*
Jessica Chase, *VP Sales*
Kristee Trelli, *Mktg Coord*
Paul Bentley, *Manager*
EMP: 21
SALES (est): 2.9MM Privately Held
WEB: www.qscend.com
SIC: 7372 Application computer software

(G-9592)
RAYPAX MANUFACTURING CO INC
21 Tremont St (06708-2217)
PHONE...........................203 758-7416
EMP: 8 EST: 1960
SQ FT: 17,370
SALES (est): 65.1K Privately Held
SIC: 3451 Mfg Screw Machine Products

(G-9593)
RICHARD DUDGEON INC
24 Swift Pl (06710-2026)
PHONE...........................203 336-4459
Allen D Haight, *Ch of Bd*
Allen Haight, *Ch of Bd*
EMP: 6 EST: 1849
SQ FT: 19,000
SALES (est): 2MM Privately Held
WEB: www.dudgeonjacks.com
SIC: 3569 7353 Jacks, hydraulic; heavy construction equipment rental

(G-9594)
ROBRAN INDUSTRIES INC
15 Palma Cir (06704-1639)
PHONE...........................203 510-6292
Matthew D Brandimarte, *CEO*
EMP: 1
SALES (est): 110.1K Privately Held
SIC: 2493 3531 4911 Particleboard products; pavers; generation, electric power

(G-9595)
RV PARTS & ELECTRIC INC
Also Called: Mople Home Xixit
385 S Leonard St (06704-4309)
PHONE...........................203 754-5962
Thomas Hedman, *President*
Pat Hedman, *Vice Pres*
EMP: 2

▲ = Import ▼ = Export
◆ = Import/Export

Waterbury - New Haven County (G-9626)

SALES (est): 170K **Privately Held**
SIC: 7538 5561 2451 Recreational vehicle repairs; recreational vehicle parts & accessories; mobile homes, industrial or commercial use

(G-9596)
S & L SYSTEMS
60 Fiske St (06710-1311)
PHONE.....................203 757-6159
Wayne Adams, *Owner*
EMP: 3
SALES (est): 260K **Privately Held**
SIC: 5734 2741 Computer & software stores; music, sheet: publishing only, not printed on site

(G-9597)
SALESCHAIN LLC
61 Mattatuck Heights Rd # 201 (06705-3839)
PHONE.....................203 262-1611
Tim Szczygiel, *President*
Robert Schuldt, *Project Mgr*
Jennifer Boucher, *Sr Project Mgr*
Douglas Uhl, *Director*
EMP: 10
SALES (est): 1.6MM **Privately Held**
WEB: www.saleschain.com
SIC: 7372 Prepackaged software

(G-9598)
SANDUR TOOL CO
853 Hamilton Ave (06706-1998)
PHONE.....................203 753-0004
Anthony Durso Jr, *President*
Jean Gaudiosi, *Finance Mgr*
EMP: 7 EST: 1955
SQ FT: 5,000
SALES: 1.5MM **Privately Held**
SIC: 3544 Special dies & tools

(G-9599)
SEGA READY MIX INCORPORATED
310 Chase River Rd (06704-1401)
PHONE.....................203 465-1052
Mark Whitlock, *Manager*
EMP: 8
SALES (corp-wide): 2MM **Privately Held**
SIC: 3273 Ready-mixed concrete
PA: Sega Ready Mix, Incorporated
519 Danbury Rd
New Milford CT 06776
860 354-3969

(G-9600)
SEIDEL INC
Also Called: Anodizing
1883 Thomaston Ave (06704-1039)
P.O. Box 4727 (06704-0727)
PHONE.....................203 757-7349
Michael Ritzenhoff, *Vice Pres*
Donna Van Nostrand, *Purchasing*
EMP: 95
SALES (corp-wide): 86.4MM **Privately Held**
SIC: 3471 Polishing, metals or formed products
PA: Seidel Gmbh & Co. Kg
Rosenstr. 8
Marburg 35037
642 160-40

(G-9601)
SEIDEL INC
2223 Thomaston Ave (06704-1000)
PHONE.....................203 757-7349
Michael Ritzenhoff, *President*
Stephen Maclean, *Manager*
▲ EMP: 70
SQ FT: 75,000
SALES (est): 12.1MM **Privately Held**
WEB: www.seidel.com
SIC: 3471 Electroplating of metals or formed products

(G-9602)
SHEILA P PATRICK
Also Called: Printing Plus
179 Dwight St (06704-1816)
PHONE.....................203 575-1716
Sheila P Patrick, *Owner*
EMP: 5
SALES (est): 306.6K **Privately Held**
SIC: 2759 Commercial printing

(G-9603)
SHELDON PRECISION LLC
10 Industrial Rd (06712-1018)
PHONE.....................203 758-4441
EMP: 3
SALES (est): 430.7K **Privately Held**
SIC: 3451 Mfg Screw Machine Products

(G-9604)
SON OF A STITCH
28 E Main St (06702-2325)
PHONE.....................203 527-3432
EMP: 1
SALES (est): 61.3K **Privately Held**
SIC: 2395 Embroidery products, except schiffli machine

(G-9605)
SPECIALTY POLYMERS INC
245 Freight St (06702-1818)
PHONE.....................203 575-5727
John Cordani, *President*
EMP: 4 EST: 2017
SALES (est): 232.2K
SALES (corp-wide): 1.9B **Publicly Held**
SIC: 2822 Ethylene-propylene rubbers, EPDM polymers
PA: Element Solutions Inc
1450 Centrepark Blvd # 210
West Palm Beach FL 33401
561 207-9600

(G-9606)
SPINELLA BAKERY
53 Interstate Ln (06705-2658)
PHONE.....................203 753-9451
Ralph Spinella Jr, *Owner*
EMP: 12 EST: 1934
SQ FT: 4,000
SALES (est): 964.5K **Privately Held**
SIC: 2051 Bread, cake & related products

(G-9607)
STATELY STAIR CO INC
3810 E Main St (06705-3853)
PHONE.....................203 575-1966
Nick Pennacchio, *President*
Elizabeth Adams, *General Mgr*
EMP: 23
SQ FT: 12,000
SALES (est): 3.3MM **Privately Held**
WEB: www.touristnetuk.com
SIC: 2431 3446 Staircases & stairs, wood; stair railings, wood; stairs, staircases, stair treads: prefabricated metal

(G-9608)
STRAPLESS SUSPENDERS
16 Pleasant St (06706-1322)
PHONE.....................203 709-0992
EMP: 1
SALES (est): 42.5K **Privately Held**
SIC: 2389 Suspenders

(G-9609)
TATER BATS LLC
82 Woodhaven St (06708-2306)
PHONE.....................203 510-4054
Sigfredo Vargas Jr, *Principal*
EMP: 2
SALES (est): 154K **Privately Held**
SIC: 3949 Sporting & athletic goods

(G-9610)
TECHNO MTAL POST WATERTOWN LLC
88 Meadowbrook Dr (06706-2722)
PHONE.....................203 755-6403
Sylvain Halle,
EMP: 3 EST: 2007
SALES (est): 391.3K **Privately Held**
SIC: 3272 2491 Poles & posts, concrete; piles, foundation & marine construction: treated wood

(G-9611)
TESCO RESOURCES INC
170 Freight St (06702-1804)
PHONE.....................203 754-3900
Hank Berberat, *President*
Delores Marino, *Corp Secy*
Tammy Berberat, *Vice Pres*
EMP: 4
SQ FT: 4,000
SALES: 1.8MM **Privately Held**
WEB: www.tescotank.com
SIC: 3443 Tanks, standard or custom fabricated: metal plate

(G-9612)
TODD LUCIEN MENDES LLC
63 Tracy Ave (06706-2142)
PHONE.....................203 228-3134
Todd L Mendes, *Principal*
EMP: 2
SALES (est): 183.1K **Privately Held**
SIC: 2431 Millwork

(G-9613)
TOOL THE SOMMA COMPANY
109 Scott Rd (06705-3202)
P.O. Box 2559 (06723-2559)
PHONE.....................203 753-2114
Eric A Somma, *President*
Thomas R Minuto, *Vice Pres*
Gerard H Somma, *Vice Pres*
Jerry Somma, *Vice Pres*
Dick Noti, *Purch Agent*
EMP: 25 EST: 1939
SQ FT: 27,000
SALES (est): 5.7MM **Privately Held**
WEB: www.somma.com
SIC: 3545 Cutting tools for machine tools; tool holders; collets (machine tool accessories)

(G-9614)
TOP SOURCE INC
490 S Main St (06706-1018)
PHONE.....................203 753-6490
Danna M Gizzie, *President*
EMP: 3
SALES (est): 800K **Privately Held**
SIC: 3131 Counters

(G-9615)
TOWER PRINTING INC
1713 Thomaston Ave (06704-1042)
P.O. Box 911 (06720-0911)
PHONE.....................203 757-1030
Kathy A Galullo, *Vice Pres*
Peter Galullo, *Treasurer*
Doug F Galullo, *Treasurer*
Douglas F Galullo, *Treasurer*
Peter H Galullo, *Admin Sec*
EMP: 3 EST: 1960
SQ FT: 6,000
SALES (est): 1.3MM **Privately Held**
SIC: 2752 7336 Business forms, lithographed; graphic arts & related design

(G-9616)
TPS ACQUISITION LLC (PA)
151 Sharon Rd (06705-4044)
PHONE.....................860 589-5511
Robert W Garthwait Jr,
David Elliot,
Peter K Gersky,
Thaddeus M Sendzimir,
EMP: 5 EST: 2013
SALES (est): 62.8MM **Privately Held**
SIC: 3324 Steel investment foundries

(G-9617)
TRAVER ELECTRIC MOTOR CO INC
151 Homer St (06704-1729)
PHONE.....................203 753-5103
Jack E Traver, *President*
Julia Blake, *Sales Staff*
Elaine Traver, *Admin Sec*
EMP: 25
SQ FT: 14,000
SALES (est): 5.3MM **Privately Held**
WEB: www.traveridc.com
SIC: 7694 5063 Electric motor repair; electrical supplies

(G-9618)
TRITEX CORPORATION
Also Called: Haydon Motion Europe
1500 Meriden Rd (06705-3982)
P.O. Box 3329 (06705-0329)
PHONE.....................203 756-7441
John Norris, *President*
▲ EMP: 250
SQ FT: 42,000
SALES (est): 31.2MM **Privately Held**
SIC: 3679 3621 Switches, stepping; motors, electric

(G-9619)
TRUELOVE MACLEAN INC
984 Waterville St (06710-1015)
P.O. Box 4700 (06704-0700)
PHONE.....................203 574-2240
John Benaglio, *Principal*
Ron Turmel, *Vice Pres*
Harald Langerbeins, *CFO*
Daniel Moffa, *VP Finance*
Lori Dangelo, *Human Res Mgr*
EMP: 2
SALES (est): 179.8K **Privately Held**
SIC: 3469 Stamping metal for the trade

(G-9620)
UNIROYAL CHEMICAL CORPORATION
Benson Road (06749-0001)
PHONE.....................203 573-2000
Walter Ruc, *Principal*
EMP: 1
SALES (est): 123.3K **Privately Held**
SIC: 2869 Industrial organic chemicals

(G-9621)
VIKING PLATINUM LLC
46 Municipal Rd (06708-4305)
PHONE.....................203 574-7979
EMP: 14
SQ FT: 21,500
SALES (est): 1.1MM **Privately Held**
SIC: 3341 Secondary Nonferrous Metal Producer

(G-9622)
VILLE SWISS AUTOMATICS INC
205 Cherry St (06702-1610)
P.O. Box 4068 (06704-0068)
PHONE.....................203 756-2825
John Petro, *President*
Miriam Hernandez, *Corp Secy*
EMP: 14
SQ FT: 7,800
SALES (est): 2.5MM **Privately Held**
WEB: www.villeswiss.com
SIC: 3451 Screw machine products

(G-9623)
VOCALIS LIMITED
100 Avalon Cir (06710-1100)
PHONE.....................203 753-5244
Mary Gretchen Iorio, *President*
Charles Beyer, *Vice Pres*
EMP: 2 EST: 1998
SALES: 10K **Privately Held**
WEB: www.vocalisesl.com
SIC: 2741 2731 Miscellaneous publishing; books: publishing only

(G-9624)
VOLTARC TECHNOLOGIES INC
400 Captain Neville Dr (06705-3811)
PHONE.....................203 753-6366
Louise Kessler, *Principal*
EMP: 1 EST: 2016
SALES (est): 61.6K **Privately Held**
SIC: 3641 Electric lamps

(G-9625)
W CANNING INC
245 Freight St (06702-1818)
PHONE.....................203 575-5727
EMP: 4
SALES (est): 217.9K
SALES (corp-wide): 1.9B **Publicly Held**
SIC: 2899 Chemical preparations
PA: Element Solutions Inc
1450 Centrepark Blvd # 210
West Palm Beach FL 33401
561 207-9600

(G-9626)
WATERBURY CPL LLC
535 Watertown Ave (06708-2200)
PHONE.....................203 592-4069
Antonio Batista, *Principal*
EMP: 1
SALES (est): 101.5K **Privately Held**
SIC: 3421 Table & food cutlery, including butchers'

Waterbury - New Haven County (G-9627)

(G-9627)
WATERBURY LEATHERWORKS CO
1691 Thomaston Ave Ste 3 (06704-1044)
PHONE....................203 755-7789
Ernest Bentley, *President*
Russ Kaye, *Vice Pres*
EMP: 12
SQ FT: 14,000
SALES (est): 1.1MM **Privately Held**
SIC: 3172 Personal leather goods

(G-9628)
WATERBURY ROLLING MILLS INC
215 Piedmont St (06706-2152)
PHONE....................203 597-5000
Pat Kelly, *General Mgr*
EMP: 95 **EST:** 1906
SQ FT: 100,000
SALES: 18.5MM
SALES (corp-wide): 6.9B **Publicly Held**
WEB: www.olin.com
SIC: 3351 3312 3356 Bronze rolling & drawing; rolled or drawn shapes: copper & copper alloy; blast furnaces & steel mills; nickel & nickel alloy: rolling, drawing or extruding
PA: Olin Corporation
 190 Carondelet Plz # 1530
 Saint Louis MO 63105
 314 480-1400

(G-9629)
WATERBURY SCREW MACHINE
319 Thomaston Ave (06702-1024)
PHONE....................203 756-8084
Matt Corcoran, *Principal*
Matthew Corcoran, *Principal*
EMP: 6
SALES (est): 637.7K **Privately Held**
SIC: 3451 Screw machine products

(G-9630)
WATERBURY SCREW MCH PDTS CO
311 Thomaston Ave Ste 319 (06702-1024)
P.O. Box 2576 (06723-2576)
PHONE....................203 756-8084
Matthew Corcoran, *President*
EMP: 30 **EST:** 1938
SQ FT: 13,500
SALES (est): 5.2MM **Privately Held**
SIC: 3451 Screw machine products

(G-9631)
WATERBURY SWISS AUTOMATICS
43 Mattatuck Heights Rd (06705-3832)
P.O. Box 3128 (06705-0128)
PHONE....................203 573-8584
Neil Tremaglio Jr, *President*
Jerry Beaudoin, *General Mgr*
Alba Tremaglio, *Vice Pres*
Tom Hotham, *Purchasing*
EMP: 27 **EST:** 1950
SQ FT: 11,500
SALES (est): 5.5MM **Privately Held**
SIC: 3451 Screw machine products

(G-9632)
WCES INC
Also Called: Inc, Waterbury
225 S Leonard St (06708-4247)
P.O. Box 33 (06720-0033)
PHONE....................203 573-1325
Lisa Meyer, *President*
Donald Martelli, *General Mgr*
EMP: 14
SQ FT: 18,000
SALES (est): 1.6MM **Privately Held**
WEB: www.wces.com
SIC: 3469 Metal stampings

(G-9633)
WHITE WELDING COMPANY INC
44 N Elm St (06702-1512)
PHONE....................203 753-1197
Leo Tomaiolo, *Corp Secy*
Robert Tomaiolo, *Vice Pres*
Mark Krause, *Treasurer*
EMP: 8
SQ FT: 10,000
SALES: 1MM **Privately Held**
WEB: www.whitewelding.com
SIC: 3444 7692 Metal housings, enclosures, casings & other containers; welding repair

(G-9634)
WIRE BURN INDUSTRIES LLC
546 S Main St (06706-1015)
PHONE....................203 597-9424
Thomas Deleon, *Principal*
EMP: 2 **EST:** 2008
SALES (est): 137K **Privately Held**
SIC: 3999 Manufacturing industries

(G-9635)
WOLCOTT COMMUNITY NEWS LL
18 Hilltop Dr (06716-1508)
PHONE....................203 879-3900
Julie Moore, *Owner*
EMP: 2
SALES (est): 148.8K **Privately Held**
SIC: 2711 Commercial printing & newspaper publishing combined

(G-9636)
WOODFREE CRATING SYSTEMS INC
150 Mattatuck Heights Rd (06705-3893)
PHONE....................203 759-1799
David Goodrich, *President*
Michael Jackson, *Admin Sec*
EMP: 12
SQ FT: 17,900
SALES: 2.8MM **Privately Held**
WEB: www.woodfreecrating.com
SIC: 2449 Rectangular boxes & crates, wood

(G-9637)
XTREME DETAIL
600 Meriden Rd (06705-2320)
PHONE....................203 753-6608
EMP: 2 **EST:** 2009
SALES (est): 69K **Privately Held**
SIC: 2842 Mfg Polish/Sanitation Goods

Waterford
New London County

(G-9638)
210 INNOVATION LLC
4 Donna St (06385-2512)
PHONE....................860 444-1986
James Ritchie, *Partner*
James Marquis, *Partner*
EMP: 2 **EST:** 1997
SALES (est): 149.5K **Privately Held**
SIC: 3842 Wheelchairs

(G-9639)
ADVANCED REASONING
82 Boston Post Rd Ste 3 (06385-2425)
P.O. Box 41 (06385-0041)
PHONE....................860 437-0508
John Lehet, *President*
EMP: 5
SALES: 480K **Privately Held**
WEB: www.advreason.com
SIC: 7372 Prepackaged software

(G-9640)
AIRGAS USA LLC
130 Cross Rd (06385-1204)
PHONE....................860 442-0363
Dwayne Gawronski, *Branch Mgr*
EMP: 2
SALES (corp-wide): 125.9MM **Privately Held**
WEB: www.abcodelivers.com
SIC: 5047 3548 Medical equipment & supplies; welding apparatus
HQ: Airgas Usa, Llc
 259 N Radnor Chester Rd
 Radnor PA 19087
 610 687-5253

(G-9641)
AIRGAS USA LLC
130 Cross Rd (06385-1204)
PHONE....................860 442-0363
Andy Way, *Principal*
EMP: 35
SALES (corp-wide): 125.9MM **Privately Held**
SIC: 5084 2813 Welding machinery & equipment; industrial gases
HQ: Airgas Usa, Llc
 259 N Radnor Chester Rd
 Radnor PA 19087
 610 687-5253

(G-9642)
BATROLLING4U LLC
40b Cross Rd (06385-1627)
PHONE....................860 439-1994
Jeffrey S Burdsall, *Principal*
EMP: 2
SALES (est): 180.4K **Privately Held**
SIC: 3949 Sporting & athletic goods

(G-9643)
BESTWAY FOOD AND FUEL
6 Boston Post Rd (06385-2402)
PHONE....................860 447-0729
Chirag Patel, *Owner*
EMP: 5
SALES (est): 235.5K **Privately Held**
SIC: 2869 Fuels

(G-9644)
CARDOROS INC
Also Called: Orsini's Sausages
5 Giovanni Dr (06385-1724)
P.O. Box 214 (06385-0214)
PHONE....................860 442-2907
Carl Orsini, *President*
EMP: 2
SALES: 25K **Privately Held**
SIC: 2013 Sausages & other prepared meats

(G-9645)
CJBOWS
35 Yorkshire Dr (06385-1718)
PHONE....................860 287-5053
Christine Caldrello, *Owner*
EMP: 1
SALES (est): 76.3K **Privately Held**
SIC: 2339 Women's & misses' accessories

(G-9646)
COASTAL STEEL CORPORATION
10 Mallard Ln (06385-1110)
PHONE....................860 443-4073
Glenn Ahnert, *President*
Susan Ahnert, *Treasurer*
EMP: 20
SQ FT: 22,000
SALES (est): 2.3MM **Privately Held**
SIC: 3441 Fabricated structural metal

(G-9647)
COCA-COLA COMPANY
150 Parkway S (06385)
PHONE....................860 443-2816
Steven K Perrelli, *Treasurer*
EMP: 3
SALES (corp-wide): 31.8B **Publicly Held**
WEB: www.cocacola.com
SIC: 2086 Bottled & canned soft drinks
PA: The Coca-Cola Company
 1 Coca Cola Plz Nw
 Atlanta GA 30313
 404 676-2121

(G-9648)
CONNECTICUT WOODWORKS LLC
39 Braman Rd (06385-3502)
PHONE....................860 367-7449
Aaron Robert Robarge, *Principal*
EMP: 1
SALES (est): 54.1K **Privately Held**
SIC: 2431 Millwork

(G-9649)
CRITICAL SCRN PRINTG & EMB
82 Boston Post Rd (06385-2425)
PHONE....................860 443-4327
James Monahan, *President*
EMP: 2
SALES (est): 214.8K **Privately Held**
SIC: 2752 Commercial printing, lithographic

(G-9650)
CRITICAL SIGNS GRAPHICS &
1068 Hartford Tpke Ste 4 (06385-4039)
PHONE....................860 443-7446
Shawn Monahan,
EMP: 1
SALES (est): 147.7K **Privately Held**
SIC: 3993 Signs & advertising specialties

(G-9651)
CRITICAL SIGNS & GRAPHICS
106 Boston Post Rd (06385-2426)
P.O. Box 525 (06385-0525)
PHONE....................860 443-7446
Shawn Monahan, *Owner*
Deigo Monhann, *Manager*
EMP: 1
SALES (est): 83.2K **Privately Held**
SIC: 3993 Signs & advertising specialties

(G-9652)
DEFENDER INDUSTRIES INC
Also Called: Defender Warehouse Outlet Str
42 Great Neck Rd (06385-3334)
PHONE....................860 701-3400
Stephan Lance, *President*
Sheldon Lance, *Principal*
Paul Gasperini, *Editor*
Chris Synott, *Editor*
Andrew Lance, *Exec VP*
◆ **EMP:** 120 **EST:** 1938
SQ FT: 109,000
SALES (est): 60.1MM **Privately Held**
WEB: www.defender.com
SIC: 5551 5961 5088 2394 Marine supplies; mail order house; marine supplies; canvas & related products; canvas covers & drop cloths; resin or plastic coated fabrics

(G-9653)
FASTSIGNS
40 Boston Post Rd (06385-2424)
PHONE....................860 437-7446
Anthony Sabilia, *President*
Vincent Accurso, *Sales Staff*
EMP: 2
SALES (est): 141.8K **Privately Held**
SIC: 3993 Signs & advertising specialties

(G-9654)
HARJANI HITESH
Also Called: In Style Fragrances
850 Hartford Tpke H109 (06385-4238)
PHONE....................860 913-6032
Hitesh Harjani, *Owner*
EMP: 3
SALES: 84K **Privately Held**
WEB: www.instylefragrances.com
SIC: 2844 Toilet preparations

(G-9655)
HARSHA INC
850 Hartford Tpke (06385-4238)
PHONE....................860 439-1466
Dinesh Vachhani, *Vice Pres*
EMP: 4
SALES (est): 264.3K **Privately Held**
SIC: 2052 Bakery products, dry

(G-9656)
JAYPRO SPORTS LLC
Also Called: US Athletic Equipment
976 Hartford Tpke Ste B (06385-4044)
PHONE....................860 447-3001
Michael J Ferrara,
Mark Ferrara,
▲ **EMP:** 50 **EST:** 1953
SALES (est): 3.7MM **Privately Held**
WEB: www.jaypro.com
SIC: 3949 5091 Sporting & athletic goods; sporting & recreation goods

(G-9657)
KOBYLUCK READY-MIX INC
24 Industrial Dr (06385-4026)
PHONE....................860 444-9604
Matthew T Kobyluck, *President*
Daniel W Kobyluck, *Vice Pres*
Joshua E Kobyluck, *Vice Pres*
Mark N Kobyluck, *Vice Pres*
Maureen A Kobyluck, *Vice Pres*
EMP: 10 **EST:** 1995
SALES (est): 2.5MM **Privately Held**
SIC: 3271 Blocks, concrete or cinder: standard

(G-9658)
KOBYLUCK SAND AND GRAVEL INC
24 Industrial Dr (06385-4026)
PHONE..................860 444-9600
Daniel W Kobyluck, *President*
Maureen Kobyluck, *Admin Sec*
EMP: 15
SALES (est): 3.8MM **Privately Held**
SIC: **1442** Common sand mining; gravel mining

(G-9659)
LLOYD P MCDONALD
112 Cross Rd (06385-1204)
PHONE..................860 447-1787
Lloyd P McDonald, *Principal*
EMP: 2
SALES (est): 171.1K **Privately Held**
SIC: **3843** Enamels, dentists'

(G-9660)
M & J BUS CO INC
30 Fargo Rd (06385-4012)
PHONE..................860 437-3721
Mike Bebe, *Owner*
EMP: 2
SALES (est): 80.7K **Privately Held**
SIC: **7519** 5012 3711 Recreational vehicle rental; buses; buses, all types, assembly of

(G-9661)
MAGO POINT CANVAS
362 Mago Point Way (06385-3145)
PHONE..................860 442-2111
EMP: 1
SALES (est): 55.3K **Privately Held**
SIC: **2211** Canvas

(G-9662)
MASON PRESS INC
139 Oswegatchie Rd (06385-1428)
PHONE..................860 625-3707
Tony Northrup, *President*
EMP: 2
SALES (est): 127.4K **Privately Held**
SIC: **2741** Miscellaneous publishing

(G-9663)
MISTRAS GROUP INC
6 Mill Ln (06385-2616)
PHONE..................860 447-2474
Alfonso Gianfanti, *General Mgr*
EMP: 40 **Publicly Held**
SIC: **3829** Measuring & controlling devices
PA: Mistras Group, Inc.
 195 Clarksville Rd Ste 2
 Princeton Junction NJ 08550

(G-9664)
NOVELTY TEXTILE MILLS LLC
24 Spithead Rd (06385-1917)
PHONE..................860 774-5000
Allan Taylor, *President*
EMP: 4
SALES (est): 310K **Privately Held**
SIC: **2258** Lace & warp knit fabric mills

(G-9665)
OFFSHORE CANVAS & CUSHIONS LLC
249 Shore Rd (06385-3430)
PHONE..................860 442-7803
Kevin Connors, *Principal*
EMP: 1 EST: 2010
SALES (est): 51.5K **Privately Held**
SIC: **2211** Canvas

(G-9666)
PRICE-DRISCOLL CORPORATION
17 Industrial Dr (06385-4010)
PHONE..................860 442-3575
Philip C Barth, *President*
Linda Paquette, *Opers Mgr*
Nancy Arzamarski, *Accounts Exec*
Robert Walter, *Manager*
Jessica Kelliher, *Administration*
EMP: 8 EST: 1947
SQ FT: 12,000
SALES (est): 2MM **Privately Held**
WEB: www.price-driscoll.com
SIC: **2992** Re-refining lubricating oils & greases

(G-9667)
RODNEY TULBA WELDING & FABG
Also Called: R Tulba Welding
1 Myrock Ave (06385-3007)
PHONE..................860 442-9840
Rodney Tulba, *Owner*
EMP: 1
SALES (est): 55.4K **Privately Held**
SIC: **7692** Welding repair

(G-9668)
SALEM STONE DESIGN INC
18a Industrial Dr (06385-4026)
PHONE..................860 439-1234
John Kim, *President*
Arthur Singer, *President*
William Singer, *Vice Pres*
Debra Deutermann, *Sales Mgr*
Stacey Singer, *Admin Sec*
EMP: 10
SQ FT: 5,000
SALES (est): 989.2K **Privately Held**
SIC: **1799** 3281 3269 Counter top installation; granite, cut & shaped; cookware: stoneware, coarse earthenware & pottery

(G-9669)
SECONN AUTOMATION SOLUTIONS
147 Cross Rd (06385-1216)
P.O. Box 294 (06385-0294)
PHONE..................860 442-4325
Robert Mareli, *CEO*
EMP: 16 EST: 1956
SQ FT: 2,600
SALES (est): 10.3MM **Privately Held**
SIC: **3444** Sheet metalwork

(G-9670)
SECONN FABRICATION LLC
180 Cross Rd (06385-1215)
PHONE..................860 443-0000
Lisa Robison, *Mfg Staff*
Robert J Marelli Jr,
EMP: 65
SQ FT: 60,000
SALES (est): 15.3MM **Privately Held**
WEB: www.seconn.com
SIC: **3444** Sheet metal specialties, not stamped

(G-9671)
SMOOTHIE KING
Also Called: Smoothie King
106 Boston Post Rd Ste A (06385-2426)
PHONE..................860 574-9382
EMP: 2 EST: 2017
SALES (est): 31.7K **Privately Held**
SIC: **5812** 2024 Ice cream, soft drink & soda fountain stands; ice cream & frozen desserts

(G-9672)
SONALYSTS INC (PA)
215 Parkway N (06385)
P.O. Box 280 (06385-0280)
PHONE..................860 442-4355
Lawrence F Clark, *Ch of Bd*
Milton L Stretton, *President*
Andrew N Toriello, *President*
Glenn Abbott, *Editor*
David Coleman, *Exec VP*
EMP: 275
SQ FT: 38,000
SALES (est): 91.7MM **Privately Held**
WEB: www.sonalysts.com
SIC: **8711** 7373 8748 8732 Consulting engineer; systems engineering, computer related; systems engineering consultant, ex. computer or professional; business research service; displays & cutouts, window & lobby

(G-9673)
SPORTEES LLC
262 Boston Post Rd Unit 8 (06385-2053)
PHONE..................860 440-3922
Thomas J Harrington,
EMP: 3
SQ FT: 1,000
SALES (est): 205.7K **Privately Held**
SIC: **2759** Screen printing

(G-9674)
TACDAB LLC
611 Vauxhall Street Ext (06385-4303)
PHONE..................860 447-9023
Barbara Schubler,
EMP: 1
SALES (est): 12K **Privately Held**
SIC: **3944** Railroad models: toy & hobby

(G-9675)
VIKING ENTERPRISES INC
41 Millstone Rd (06385-3116)
PHONE..................860 440-0728
David Engdall, *President*
William Engdall, *Director*
EMP: 4
SALES (est): 175K **Privately Held**
SIC: **3441** Fabricated structural metal

(G-9676)
WATER TRANSIT SERVICES LLC
22 Prindiville Ave (06385-3514)
PHONE..................860 625-3625
Matthew Lynch, *Owner*
EMP: 1 EST: 2006
SALES (est): 170.3K **Privately Held**
SIC: **7699** 3647 Boat repair; boat & ship lighting fixtures

(G-9677)
YOST MANUFACTURING & SUPPLY
1018 Hartford Tpke (06385-4032)
P.O. Box 263 (06385-0263)
PHONE..................860 447-9678
George P Yost, *President*
Andrew Saad, *General Mgr*
Albert G Yost Jr, *Vice Pres*
EMP: 10
SQ FT: 5,000
SALES (est): 710K **Privately Held**
SIC: **3444** Gutters, sheet metal

Watertown
Litchfield County

(G-9678)
6 BROOKWOOD DRIVE LLC
329 Lovley Dr (06795-3162)
PHONE..................860 945-3456
William Peck, *Principal*
EMP: 1 EST: 2016
SALES (est): 41.5K **Privately Held**
SIC: **2499** Wood products

(G-9679)
ADVANCED SPECIALIST LLC
162 Commercial St (06795-3309)
PHONE..................860 945-9125
Gardner W Gage, *Principal*
Steve Gage, *VP Mfg*
▲ EMP: 8
SALES (est): 796.2K **Privately Held**
SIC: **3999** Manufacturing industries

(G-9680)
AMERICAN PRECISION PRODUCT LLC
81 Winding Brook Farm Rd (06795-1743)
PHONE..................860 274-7301
Mj Bouffard, *Mng Member*
▲ EMP: 2
SALES (est): 416K **Privately Held**
SIC: **5084** 3469 Industrial machine parts; metal stampings

(G-9681)
AMRO TOOL CO
127 Echo Lake Rd Ste 26 (06795-2657)
PHONE..................860 274-9766
Robert Valunas, *Owner*
EMP: 3
SALES (est): 386.6K **Privately Held**
SIC: **3546** Cartridge-activated hand power tools

(G-9682)
APPLE HILL WOODWORKING LLC
155 Apple Hill Dr (06795-1147)
PHONE..................860 945-6102
Scott David Jack, *Owner*
EMP: 2
SALES (est): 126.1K **Privately Held**
SIC: **2431** Millwork

(G-9683)
BEANS INC
2213 Litchfield Rd (06795-1006)
PHONE..................860 945-9234
Danielle Brennan, *President*
EMP: 4
SALES (est): 189K **Privately Held**
SIC: **2051** Bakery: wholesale or wholesale/retail combined

(G-9684)
BLAIS WOODWORKS LLC
1216 Guernseytown Rd (06795-1251)
PHONE..................860 274-2906
Laura Blais, *Owner*
EMP: 2
SALES (est): 184.2K **Privately Held**
SIC: **2431** Millwork

(G-9685)
BRAXTON MANUFACTURING CO INC
858 Echo Lake Rd (06795-1636)
P.O. Box 429 (06795-0429)
PHONE..................860 274-6781
Thomas Ordway, *President*
Shirley Bridge, *Production*
Robert G Dionne, *Treasurer*
Joseph E Triano, *Admin Sec*
EMP: 170
SQ FT: 60,000
SALES (est): 30.7MM **Privately Held**
WEB: www.braxtonmfg.com
SIC: **3965** 3769 3577 Eyelets, metal; clothing, fabrics, boots or shoes; guided missile & space vehicle parts & auxiliary equipment; computer peripheral equipment

(G-9686)
BRISTOL INC (HQ)
Also Called: Emerson Rmote Automtn Solution
1100 Buckingham St (06795-6602)
P.O. Box 36911, Saint Louis MO (63136-9011)
PHONE..................860 945-2200
Craig T Llewlyn, *President*
Craig Llewlyn, *President*
Warren Howard, *Vice Pres*
Richard Denomme, *Engineer*
Fred Dinicola, *Engineer*
▲ EMP: 300 EST: 1980
SQ FT: 190,000
SALES (est): 110.6MM
SALES (corp-wide): 17.4B **Publicly Held**
WEB: www.bristolbabcock.com
SIC: **3823** Industrial process control instruments; industrial process measurement equipment; digital displays of process variables
PA: Emerson Electric Co.
 8000 West Florissant Ave
 Saint Louis MO 63136
 314 553-2000

(G-9687)
BRISTOL BABCOCK EMPLOYEES FEDE
1100 Buckingham St (06795-6602)
PHONE..................860 945-2200
Doris Lapagalia, *President*
Neil Mascola, *Vice Pres*
Mary E Sportino, *Treasurer*
EMP: 1
SQ FT: 190,000
SALES (est): 282.3K **Privately Held**
WEB: www.bristolbabcock.ca
SIC: **6061** 3825 3823 3625 Federal credit unions; instruments to measure electricity; industrial instrmnts msrmnt display/control process variable; relays & industrial controls; computer peripheral equipment; electronic computers

(G-9688)
C&G MFG
126 Skilton Rd (06795-1213)
PHONE..................860 274-9785
Thomas Ciarlo, *Owner*
EMP: 2

Watertown - Litchfield County (G-9689)

SALES (est): 302.6K **Privately Held**
SIC: 3559 3999 Semiconductor manufacturing machinery; manufacturing industries

(G-9689)
C-TECH MANUFACTURING CO LLC
27 Siemon Company Dr (06795-2654)
PHONE.................860 274-6879
Thomas Ciarlo, *Mng Member*
EMP: 1
SALES (est): 224.4K **Privately Held**
SIC: 3451 5085 Screw machine products; fasteners, industrial: nuts, bolts, screws, etc.

(G-9690)
CARE CONNECTION LLC
38 Breezy Knoll Dr (06795-1323)
PHONE.................860 274-1251
Debra Gianetto, *Mng Member*
EMP: 1
SALES (est): 94K **Privately Held**
SIC: 3669 Emergency alarms

(G-9691)
CGL INC
Also Called: Anco Tool & Manufacturing
1094 Echo Lake Rd (06795-1635)
P.O. Box 698 (06795-0698)
PHONE.................860 945-6166
Charles G Lacombe, *President*
Charles J Lacombe, *Vice Pres*
Donald Melason, *Vice Pres*
Nicholas Meglio, *QC Mgr*
EMP: 12 EST: 1956
SALES (est): 3.1MM **Privately Held**
WEB: www.ancotool.com
SIC: 3544 3599 3469 Special dies & tools; electrical discharge machining (EDM); metal stampings

(G-9692)
CICCHETTI & CO LLC
124 Winding Brook Farm Rd (06795-1742)
PHONE.................860 945-0424
Richard Cichetti,
EMP: 1
SALES (est): 59.4K **Privately Held**
SIC: 3999 Manufacturing industries

(G-9693)
CLEARCLAD COATINGS LLC
11 Pepperidge Tree Rd (06795-1804)
PHONE.................860 945-9200
Phillip Dunleavy, *Branch Mgr*
EMP: 1 **Privately Held**
WEB: www.clearclad.net
SIC: 2869 Industrial organic chemicals
PA: Clearclad Coatings Llc
    16910 Lathrop Ave
    Harvey IL

(G-9694)
CLICK BOND INC
18 Park Rd (06795-1618)
PHONE.................860 274-5435
Charles G Hutter III, *CEO*
EMP: 50
SALES (corp-wide): 59.8MM **Privately Held**
SIC: 3452 Bolts, metal; rivets, metal; screws, metal
HQ: Click Bond, Inc.
    2151 Lockheed Way
    Carson City NV 89706
    775 885-8000

(G-9695)
CONNECTICUT CARVED SIGN CO LLC
140 Circuit Ave (06795-1702)
PHONE.................860 274-2039
William Lutkus, *Principal*
EMP: 1
SALES (est): 75.4K **Privately Held**
SIC: 3993 Signs & advertising specialties

(G-9696)
COVIT AMERICA INC
Also Called: Albea Metal Americas
1 Seemar Rd (06795-1638)
PHONE.................860 274-6791
Henry F Seebach Jr, *President*
John Spino, *General Mgr*
Douglas Jerman, *Plant Mgr*
Lisa Mudry, *Human Res Mgr*
▲ EMP: 375
SALES (est): 84.9MM **Privately Held**
SIC: 3086 Packaging & shipping materials, foamed plastic
HQ: Albea Services
    Zac Des Barbanniers Le Signac
    Gennevilliers 92230
    181 932-000

(G-9697)
CRYSTAL ROCK HOLDINGS INC (HQ)
1050 Buckingham St (06795-6602)
PHONE.................860 945-0661
Peter K Baker, *President*
Jack Baker, *Exec VP*
John B Baker, *Exec VP*
David Jurasek, *CFO*
Brandon Sereni, *Sales Staff*
▲ EMP: 41
SQ FT: 67,000
SALES: 59MM
SALES (corp-wide): 2.2B **Privately Held**
SIC: 2086 3589 Mineral water, carbonated: packaged in cans, bottles, etc.; water, pasteurized: packaged in cans, bottles, etc.; coffee brewing equipment
PA: Cott Corporation
    6525 Viscount Rd
    Mississauga ON L4V 1
    905 672-1900

(G-9698)
CRYSTAL ROCK SPRING WATER CO
Also Called: Crystal Rock Water & Coffee Co
1050 Buckingham St (06795-6602)
PHONE.................860 945-0661
Peter Baker, *President*
Jack Baker, *Exec VP*
John B Baker, *Exec VP*
Dale Dame, *Production*
Bruce Macdonald, *CFO*
▲ EMP: 315 EST: 1914
SQ FT: 67,000
SALES (est): 63.2MM
SALES (corp-wide): 2.2B **Privately Held**
WEB: www.crystalrock.com
SIC: 5149 5499 2086 2899 Mineral or spring water bottling; coffee & tea; soft drinks; water: distilled mineral or spring; coffee; soft drinks; bottled & canned soft drinks; chemical preparations
HQ: Crystal Rock Holdings, Inc.
    1050 Buckingham St
    Watertown CT 06795

(G-9699)
CUSTOMIZED WOODWORKING LLC
109 Skilton Rd (06795-1214)
PHONE.................860 274-4025
Joseph Sklanka Jr, *Principal*
EMP: 1
SALES (est): 85.2K **Privately Held**
SIC: 2431 Millwork

(G-9700)
DAADS LLC
Also Called: Daad Motorcyle Emporuim
1376 Main St (06795-3110)
PHONE.................860 274-1589
Diane Delaurentis, *Owner*
EMP: 1
SALES (est): 192.6K **Privately Held**
SIC: 3751 Motorcycles & related parts

(G-9701)
DEMSEY MANUFACTURING CO INC
78 New Wood Rd (06795-3339)
PHONE.................860 274-6209
Richard A Demsey, *President*
Scott Demsey, *General Mgr*
Laura Harrington, *Office Mgr*
EMP: 35 EST: 1954
SQ FT: 35,000
SALES (est): 8.7MM **Privately Held**
WEB: www.demseyelets.com
SIC: 3469 Metal stampings

(G-9702)
DISTINCTIVE STEERING WHEELS
189 Chimney Rd (06795-1682)
PHONE.................860 274-9087
John M Augelli, *Principal*
EMP: 3
SALES (est): 165.2K **Privately Held**
SIC: 3465 Hub caps, automobile: stamped metal

(G-9703)
ECI SCREEN PRINT INC
15 Mountain View Rd (06795-1648)
P.O. Box 116, Thomaston (06787-0116)
PHONE.................860 283-9849
Edward Cook, *President*
Eleanor Maynard, *COO*
Irma Diaz, *Vice Pres*
Girolimon Mark, *Opers Mgr*
Brett Owen, *Sales Staff*
EMP: 12
SQ FT: 13,000
SALES (est): 2.5MM **Privately Held**
WEB: www.eciscreenprint.com
SIC: 2759 Screen printing

(G-9704)
EXPANSION SOFTWARE LLC
1064 Middlebury Rd (06795-3200)
PHONE.................860 274-0338
George T Porto Jr, *Principal*
EMP: 2
SALES (est): 151.7K **Privately Held**
SIC: 7372 Prepackaged software

(G-9705)
EYELET TOOLMAKERS INC
40 Callender Rd (06795-1628)
P.O. Box 402 (06795-0402)
PHONE.................860 274-5423
Albinas Rickevicius, *President*
Linda Rickevicius, *Vice Pres*
Anna Rickevicius, *Admin Sec*
EMP: 40
SQ FT: 30,000
SALES (est): 5.2MM **Privately Held**
WEB: www.eyelettoolmakers.com
SIC: 3469 Stamping metal for the trade

(G-9706)
FASHION HOME PRODUCTS
604 Guernseytown Rd (06795-1836)
P.O. Box 285 (06795-0285)
PHONE.................860 274-0824
Viviana Osborne, *Owner*
EMP: 2
SALES: 1K **Privately Held**
SIC: 2259 Curtains & bedding, knit

(G-9707)
FRANK PORTO
Also Called: Precision Welding
27 Walnut St (06795-1920)
PHONE.................203 596-0811
Frank Porto, *Owner*
EMP: 1
SALES (est): 98.9K **Privately Held**
SIC: 3441 7692 3498 Fabricated structural metal; welding repair; fabricated pipe & fittings

(G-9708)
GENERAL WLDG & FABRICATION INC
977 Echo Lake Rd (06795-1639)
PHONE.................860 274-9668
Holly A Herbert, *President*
Jay N Herbert, *Corp Secy*
EMP: 13
SQ FT: 12,400
SALES (est): 3.7MM **Privately Held**
SIC: 7692 Welding repair

(G-9709)
GLOBAL MACHINE MOVERS LLC
Also Called: Gmb
58 Commercial St (06795-3368)
PHONE.................860 484-4449
Joe Wihbey, *Owner*
Luis Santiago, *Sales Staff*
◆ EMP: 16
SQ FT: 24,000
SALES (est): 6.3MM **Privately Held**
SIC: 5084 3599 Materials handling machinery; flexible metal hose, tubing & bellows

(G-9710)
GLOBAL STEERING SYSTEMS LLC (PA)
Also Called: G S S
156 Park Rd (06795-1616)
P.O. Box 210 (06795-0210)
PHONE.................860 945-5400
Larry Finnell, *CEO*
Julio Costa, *Vice Pres*
Scott Filion, *Vice Pres*
Gabe Rosa, *Vice Pres*
Eileen Meade, *Purch Mgr*
◆ EMP: 131
SQ FT: 180,000
SALES (est): 54.6MM **Privately Held**
SIC: 3714 Motor vehicle steering systems & parts

(G-9711)
HAWK RIDGE WINERY LLC
28 Plungis Rd (06795-1321)
P.O. Box 410 (06795-0410)
PHONE.................860 274-7440
John M McHugh, *Principal*
EMP: 2
SALES (est): 123.7K **Privately Held**
SIC: 2084 Wines

(G-9712)
IRONHORSE INDUSTRIES LLC
11 Vista Dr (06795-1653)
PHONE.................203 598-8720
EMP: 2
SALES (est): 127.8K **Privately Held**
SIC: 3999 Manufacturing industries

(G-9713)
JAMES A BLAZYS
Also Called: Old Harbor Fine Handcrafted
280 Lake Winnemaug Rd (06795-3048)
PHONE.................860 274-3857
James A Blazys, *Owner*
EMP: 1 EST: 2002
SALES (est): 138.6K **Privately Held**
SIC: 7692 Welding repair

(G-9714)
KOSTER KEUNEN INC
1021 Echo Lake Rd (06795-1639)
PHONE.................860 945-3333
John Koster, *Ch of Bd*
Henry Muschio, *Vice Pres*
Michael Samson, *Sales Mgr*
Eva Lippai, *Manager*
EMP: 3
SALES (est): 209.9K **Privately Held**
SIC: 2911 Mineral waxes, natural

(G-9715)
KOSTER KEUNEN LLC (PA)
1021 Echo Lake Rd (06795-1639)
PHONE.................860 945-3333
Joe Iorfino, *Opers Staff*
John Koster,
Joanna Koster,
◆ EMP: 14
SALES (est): 9.3MM **Privately Held**
SIC: 2999 2834 2671 2842 Waxes, petroleum: not produced in petroleum refineries; pharmaceutical preparations; bread wrappers, waxed or laminated: purchased material; floor waxes; furniture polish or wax; waxes for wood, leather & other materials

(G-9716)
KOSTER KEUNEN MFG INC
1021 Echo Lake Rd (06795-1639)
P.O. Box 69 (06795-0069)
PHONE.................860 945-3333
John F Koster, *President*
Robert Behrer, *Vice Pres*
Henry Muschio, *VP Opers*
Jessica Dynda, *Sales Staff*
◆ EMP: 60
SQ FT: 100,000
SALES (est): 13.1MM **Privately Held**
WEB: www.kosterkeunen.com
SIC: 2911 Mineral waxes, natural

Watertown - Litchfield County

(G-9717)
OIL GUY LLC
70 Farmdale Rd (06795-2319)
PHONE...................203 910-2752
Patrick Crimmins, *Principal*
EMP: 2
SALES (est): 88.8K Privately Held
SIC: 1311 Crude petroleum & natural gas

(G-9718)
ORDINARY JOES
253 Buckingham St (06779-1730)
PHONE...................860 945-1500
Joseph Romano, *Principal*
EMP: 2
SALES (est): 184.3K Privately Held
SIC: 2599 Bar, restaurant & cafeteria furniture

(G-9719)
PAMELA D SIEMON LCSW LLC
51 Depot St Ste 207 (06795-2667)
PHONE...................203 232-8009
Pamela D Siemon, *Principal*
EMP: 2 EST: 2018
SALES (est): 88.3K Privately Held
SIC: 3661 Telephones & telephone apparatus

(G-9720)
PEACHWAVE OF WATERTOWN
1156 Main St (06795-2918)
PHONE...................203 942-4949
Kelly Dun, *Managing Prtnr*
EMP: 4 EST: 2012
SALES (est): 218.3K Privately Held
SIC: 2026 Yogurt

(G-9721)
PERGENEX SOFTWARE LLC
410 Winding Brook Farm Rd (06795-1746)
PHONE...................860 274-7318
Frank Perugini, *Principal*
EMP: 2
SALES (est): 160.5K Privately Held
SIC: 7372 Application computer software

(G-9722)
PETRON AUTOMATION INC
65 Mountain View Rd (06795-1648)
P.O. Box 399 (06795-0399)
PHONE...................860 274-9091
Michael Petro Jr, *President*
Mary Felcher, *CFO*
EMP: 24
SQ FT: 7,500
SALES (est): 5.1MM Privately Held
WEB: www.petronautomation.com
SIC: 3451 Screw machine products

(G-9723)
PRIME ENGNEERED COMPONENTS INC
1012 Buckingham St (06795-6602)
PHONE...................860 274-6773
Dennis J Izzo, *President*
Mark Izzo, *Vice Pres*
EMP: 3
SALES (est): 295.4K Privately Held
SIC: 3451 Screw machine products

(G-9724)
PRIME PUBLISHERS INC
Also Called: Town Times
449 Main St (06795-2628)
P.O. Box 1 (06795-0001)
PHONE...................860 274-6721
Annette Linster, *CFO*
Walter Mazurosky, *Adv Mgr*
Terry Pfeifer, *Manager*
EMP: 6
SALES (corp-wide): 5MM Privately Held
SIC: 2711 Newspapers: publishing only, not printed on site
PA: Prime Publishers Inc
    90 Middle Quarter Rd
    Woodbury CT
    203 263-2116

(G-9725)
PRIME SCREW MACHINE PDTS INC (PA)
Also Called: Prime Engineered Components
1012 Buckingham St (06795-1667)
P.O. Box 359 (06795-0359)
PHONE...................860 274-6773
Dennis Izzo, *President*
Mark Izzo, *Vice Pres*
Prima Izzo, *Admin Sec*
EMP: 61
SQ FT: 32,000
SALES (est): 12.5MM Privately Held
WEB: www.primesmp.com
SIC: 3451 Screw machine products

(G-9726)
PROFESSIONAL TRADES NETWRK LLC
1100 Buckingham St (06795-6602)
P.O. Box 327 (06795-0327)
PHONE...................860 567-0173
Matthew Fenn,
EMP: 2
SALES (est): 244.9K Privately Held
SIC: 2521 5031 Wood office furniture; kitchen cabinets

(G-9727)
PROTOPAC INC
Also Called: Protopac Printing Services
120 Echo Lake Rd (06795-2664)
PHONE...................860 274-6796
Hugh J Langin, *President*
Stephen Langin, *Treasurer*
Hugh F Langin, *Controller*
Susan Langin, *Admin Sec*
EMP: 9 EST: 1979
SQ FT: 3,000
SALES: 900K Privately Held
WEB: www.protopac.com
SIC: 3496 2752 Wire winding; commercial printing, offset

(G-9728)
QUALITY SIGNS OF WATERTOWN
140 Circuit Ave (06795-1702)
P.O. Box 553 (06795-0553)
PHONE...................860 274-4828
William Letkus, *Owner*
EMP: 1
SALES: 40K Privately Held
SIC: 3993 Signs & advertising specialties

(G-9729)
RAM ARTS SIGNS
24 Ledgewood Rd (06795-1304)
PHONE...................860 274-6833
Richard Mikush, *Owner*
EMP: 2
SALES: 90K Privately Held
SIC: 3993 Signs & advertising specialties

(G-9730)
RED APPLE CHEESE LLC (PA)
27 Siemon Co Dr Ste 231w (06795-2654)
PHONE...................203 755-5579
Paul Brzezienski,
Salvatore Distasio,
▲ EMP: 9
SQ FT: 700
SALES (est): 2.5MM Privately Held
WEB: www.redapplecheese.com
SIC: 2022 Cheese, natural & processed

(G-9731)
RTC MFG CO INC
1094 Echo Lake Rd (06795-1635)
P.O. Box 698 (06795-0698)
PHONE...................800 888-3701
Carolyn A Locombe, *President*
Charles J Lacombe, *Vice Pres*
Charles G Lacombe, *Treasurer*
Gene Mc Redmond, *Accountant*
Carolyn A Lacombe, *Director*
EMP: 5
SQ FT: 3,000
SALES: 160K Privately Held
SIC: 3469 Stamping metal for the trade

(G-9732)
S HASSEL GOLF WORKS
55 Morehouse Rd (06795-2315)
PHONE...................860 274-4011
Scott Hassel, *Owner*
EMP: 1
SALES (est): 33.9K Privately Held
SIC: 7999 3949 Golf professionals; golf club & equipment repair; shafts, golf club

(G-9733)
SHELTERLOGIC CORP (HQ)
150 Callender Rd (06795-1628)
PHONE...................860 945-6442
James Raymond, *CEO*
Rob Silinski, *President*
Jon Slaughter, *Vice Pres*
Ken Smith, *Vice Pres*
Joann Trezza, *Vice Pres*
◆ EMP: 151
SALES (est): 121.5MM Privately Held
SIC: 2394 5091 Tents: made from purchased materials; camping equipment & supplies
PA: Slogic Holding Corp.
    36 Grove St
    New Canaan CT 06840
    203 966-2800

(G-9734)
SIEMON COMPANY (PA)
Also Called: Siemon Global Project Services
101 Siemon Company Dr (06795-2651)
PHONE...................860 945-4200
Carl N Siemon, *President*
CK Siemon, *President*
John Siemon, *Vice Pres*
Brian Wheelock, *Plant Mgr*
Lance Lorusso, *Senior Buyer*
◆ EMP: 537
SQ FT: 200,000
SALES (est): 156.3MM Privately Held
SIC: 3643 3089 3679 3469 Electric connectors; thermoformed finished plastic products; harness assemblies for electronic use: wire or cable; metal stampings; switchgear & switchboard apparatus; nonferrous wiredrawing & insulating

(G-9735)
SIEMON COMPANY
Siemon Electronics Co
101 Siemon Company Dr (06795-2651)
PHONE...................860 945-4218
Carl Siemon, *President*
Carly Achenbach, *Sales Staff*
John Sturges Jr, *Payroll Mgr*
EMP: 22
SALES (corp-wide): 156.3MM Privately Held
SIC: 3643 Current-carrying wiring devices
PA: The Siemon Company
    101 Siemon Company Dr
    Watertown CT 06795
    860 945-4200

(G-9736)
SIGN AND WONDERS LLC
98 Birch St (06795-2757)
PHONE...................860 274-8526
Dan E Rubelman,
EMP: 2
SALES: 140K Privately Held
SIC: 3993 Signs & advertising specialties

(G-9737)
SOLLA EYELET PRODUCTS INC
50 Seemar Rd (06795-1638)
PHONE...................860 274-5729
Louis Solla, *CEO*
Salvatore L Solla, *Vice Pres*
EMP: 20
SQ FT: 9,000
SALES (est): 3.2MM Privately Held
SIC: 3469 Metal stampings

(G-9738)
STANLEY STEEMER INTL INC
46 Meadow Ln (06795-2416)
PHONE...................860 274-5540
EMP: 34
SALES (corp-wide): 227.2MM Privately Held
SIC: 7217 3635 6794 5713 Carpet & furniture cleaning on location; household vacuum cleaners; franchises, selling or licensing; carpets
PA: Stanley Steemer International, Inc.
    5800 Innovation Dr
    Dublin OH 43016
    614 764-2007

(G-9739)
SUMAL ENTERPRISES LLC
Also Called: Town & Country Cleaners & Tlrs
620 Main St (06795-2614)
PHONE...................860 945-3337
Malini S Jadav,
EMP: 5
SALES (est): 488K Privately Held
SIC: 3582 Commercial laundry equipment

(G-9740)
THREE KINGS PRODUCTS LLC
1021 Echo Lake Rd (06795-1639)
P.O. Box 69 (06795-0069)
PHONE...................860 945-5294
John Coster, *Owner*
▲ EMP: 3
SALES (est): 317.9K Privately Held
WEB: www.threekingsproducts.com
SIC: 2899 3999 Incense; manufacturing industries

(G-9741)
TIMBER-TOP INC
210 Hopkins Rd (06795-1549)
P.O. Box 517 (06795-0517)
PHONE...................860 274-6706
Jay P Fischer, *President*
Justin T Fischer, *General Mgr*
Nancy Fischer, *Info Tech Mgr*
EMP: 3 EST: 1957
SALES: 500K Privately Held
SIC: 3965 3399 5072 Fasteners; metal fasteners; miscellaneous fasteners

(G-9742)
TRIPLE PLAY SPORTS
16 Straits Tpke (06795-3119)
PHONE...................860 417-2877
Tom Daddona, *Partner*
EMP: 10
SALES (est): 926K Privately Held
SIC: 2599 Bar, restaurant & cafeteria furniture

(G-9743)
TRUELOVE & MACLEAN INC
57 Callender Rd (06795-1627)
P.O. Box 268 (06795-0268)
PHONE...................860 274-9600
Richard L Bouffard, *President*
Grant Demerchant, *Vice Pres*
Mario Lambiase, *Vice Pres*
Terry Colby, *Design Engr*
Dan Moffa, *Finance Dir*
▲ EMP: 124 EST: 1998
SQ FT: 105,000
SALES (est): 28.3MM Privately Held
WEB: www.trueloveandmaclean.com
SIC: 3469 Stamping metal for the trade

(G-9744)
UTITEC INC (HQ)
169 Callender Rd (06795-1627)
P.O. Box 370 (06795-0370)
PHONE...................860 945-0605
Carl Contadini, *President*
Kara Harlow, *Human Res Dir*
EMP: 65
SALES (est): 13.6MM
SALES (corp-wide): 13.9MM Privately Held
SIC: 3841 3341 3469 Surgical & medical instruments; platinum group metals, smelting & refining (secondary); pressure cookers, stamped or drawn metal
PA: Utitec Holdings, Inc.
    169 Callender Rd
    Watertown CT 06795
    860 945-0601

(G-9745)
UTITEC HOLDINGS INC (PA)
169 Callender Rd (06795-1627)
P.O. Box 370 (06795-0370)
PHONE...................860 945-0601
Bob Oppici, *Principal*
Ronald Lipeika, *COO*
EMP: 8

Watertown - Litchfield County (G-9746)

SALES (est): 13.9MM **Privately Held**
SIC: 3841 3469 Surgical & medical instruments; pressure cookers, stamped or drawn metal; electronic enclosures, stamped or pressed metal

(G-9746)
VICTORIA ART & FRAME LLC
81 Winding Brook Farm Rd (06795-1743)
PHONE..................860 274-8222
EMP: 2 EST: 2013
SALES (est): 178.8K **Privately Held**
SIC: 3499 Picture frames, metal

(G-9747)
VITIS PRESS
1083 Bunker Hill Rd (06795-3240)
PHONE..................860 921-8570
EMP: 2 EST: 2014
SALES (est): 74.8K **Privately Held**
SIC: 2741 Miscellaneous publishing

(G-9748)
WATERTOWN JIG BORE SERVICE INC
29 New Wood Rd (06795-3314)
PHONE..................860 274-5898
Fax: 860 274-7830
EMP: 16
SQ FT: 7,000
SALES (est): 1.4MM **Privately Held**
SIC: 3544 3541 Mfg Dies/Tools/Jigs/Fixtures Mfg Machine Tools-Cutting

(G-9749)
WATERTOWN PLASTICS INC
830 Echo Lake Rd (06795-1636)
P.O. Box 309 (06795-0309)
PHONE..................860 274-7535
Jonathan Andrew, *President*
Diane Andrew, *Corp Secy*
Mike Andrew, *Vice Pres*
Edward Nickles, *Vice Pres*
Laurie Smith, *Office Mgr*
EMP: 36
SQ FT: 15,000
SALES (est): 9.3MM **Privately Held**
WEB: www.watertownplastics.com
SIC: 3089 3544 Injection molding of plastics; industrial molds

(G-9750)
WIRE TECH LLC
1094 Echo Lake Rd (06795-1635)
PHONE..................860 945-9473
Charles G Lacompe,
Charles J Lacompe,
EMP: 6
SQ FT: 3,000
SALES (est): 558.7K **Privately Held**
SIC: 3599 Electrical discharge machining (EDM)

(G-9751)
WORLDSCREEN INC
843 Echo Lake Rd (06795-1637)
PHONE..................860 274-9218
Stephen P Lukos, *President*
Carol Anne Lukos, *Manager*
EMP: 3
SALES (est): 258.7K **Privately Held**
SIC: 3851 Glasses, sun or glare

Wauregan
Windham County

(G-9752)
BROOKWOOD LAMINATING INC
Also Called: Brookwood Roll Goods Group
275 Putnam Rd (06387)
PHONE..................860 774-5001
Amber M Brookman, *President*
Martin Handley, *General Mgr*
Robert Vander Meulen, *Vice Pres*
Joseph Trumpetto, *Treasurer*
▲ EMP: 53
SQ FT: 50,000
SALES (est): 12.8MM **Privately Held**
SIC: 2295 2269 Laminating of fabrics; finishing plants

HQ: Brookwood Companies Incorporated
485 Madison Ave Ste 500
New York NY 10022
212 551-0100

(G-9753)
FORTERRA PIPE & PRECAST LLC
174 All Hallows Rd (06387)
PHONE..................860 564-9000
George Stevens, *General Mgr*
EMP: 19
SALES (corp-wide): 1.4B **Publicly Held**
SIC: 3272 Concrete products, precast
HQ: Forterra Pipe & Precast, Llc
511 E John Carpenter Fwy
Irving TX 75062
469 458-7973

(G-9754)
WAUREGAN MACHINE SHOP
51 S Walnut St (06387-8700)
P.O. Box 212 (06387-0212)
PHONE..................860 774-0686
Daniel Maheu, *Owner*
EMP: 3
SQ FT: 4,800
SALES: 120K **Privately Held**
SIC: 3599 Machine shop, jobbing & repair

Weatogue
Hartford County

(G-9755)
BIOMASS ENERGY LLC
125 Powder Forest Dr (06089-7943)
PHONE..................540 872-3300
Mark Boivin, *Principal*
EMP: 20
SALES (est): 2.2MM **Privately Held**
SIC: 2421 Wood chips, produced at mill

(G-9756)
JONATHAN DAVID HUMPHERYS
Also Called: Simple Card Sort
78 Simsbury Manor Dr (06089-9749)
PHONE..................415 847-3032
Jonathan Humpherys, *Owner*
EMP: 1
SALES (est): 36K **Privately Held**
SIC: 7372 Prepackaged software

(G-9757)
LEATHERBY
19 Deer Park Rd (06089-9703)
PHONE..................860 658-6166
Richard Goldberg, *Owner*
EMP: 3
SALES: 75K **Privately Held**
SIC: 3171 3161 5948 3172 Women's handbags & purses; satchels; luggage & leather goods stores; leather goods, except luggage & shoes; wallets

(G-9758)
LEATHERWORKS
18 Butternut Ln (06089-9739)
PHONE..................860 658-6178
Arthur N Levin, *Principal*
EMP: 1
SALES (est): 84.9K **Privately Held**
SIC: 3199 Leather goods

(G-9759)
RC CONNECTORS LLC
146 Hopmeadow St (06089-7908)
PHONE..................860 413-2196
John D Ritson, *Principal*
EMP: 3
SALES (est): 289K **Privately Held**
SIC: 3678 Electronic connectors

(G-9760)
VEEDER-ROOT COMPANY (HQ)
125 Powder Forest Dr Fl 1 (06089-7943)
P.O. Box 2003, Simsbury (06070-7684)
PHONE..................860 651-2700
Brian Burnett, *President*
Martin Gafinowitz, *Vice Pres*
Jamey Greene, *Vice Pres*
Don Murashima, *Vice Pres*
Bradley Davis, *Project Mgr*
◆ EMP: 80

SQ FT: 25,000
SALES (est): 98.5MM
SALES (corp-wide): 6.4B **Publicly Held**
SIC: 3823 3824 Industrial instrmnts msrmnt display/control process variable; mechanical measuring meters; gas meters, domestic & large capacity: industrial
PA: Fortive Corporation
6920 Seaway Blvd
Everett WA 98203
425 446-5000

West Cornwall
Litchfield County

(G-9761)
CHESTNUT WDWKG & ANTIQ FLRG CO
14 Great Hollow Rd (06796-1806)
PHONE..................860 672-4300
Bob Friedman, *President*
Karen Friedman, *Treasurer*
EMP: 2
SALES: 200K **Privately Held**
WEB: www.chestnutwoodworking.com
SIC: 2431 Millwork

(G-9762)
CLOVERDALE INC
Also Called: Cloverdale Cleaner
5 Smith Pl (06796-1116)
P.O. Box 268 (06796-0268)
PHONE..................860 672-0216
Harry L Colley II, *President*
EMP: 5
SALES (est): 390K **Privately Held**
WEB: www.cloverdale.com
SIC: 2842 5169 4959 Specialty cleaning preparations; cleaning or polishing preparations; degreasing solvent; chemicals & allied products; environmental cleanup services

(G-9763)
HEDDEN FOREST PRODUCTS
87 Cream Hill Rd (06796-1203)
PHONE..................860 672-6023
Steve Hedden, *Owner*
EMP: 2
SQ FT: 1,500
SALES (est): 205.7K **Privately Held**
SIC: 2421 Sawmills & planing mills, general

(G-9764)
IAN INGERSOLL CABINETMAKER
422 Sharon Goshen Tpke (06796-1122)
PHONE..................860 672-6334
Ian Ingersoll, *Owner*
EMP: 10
SQ FT: 2,000
SALES: 1.2MM **Privately Held**
WEB: www.ianingersoll.com
SIC: 5712 2511 Cabinet work, custom; chairs, household, except upholstered: wood

(G-9765)
TIM PRENTICE
129 Lake Rd (06796-1402)
PHONE..................860 672-6728
Tim Prentice, *Owner*
EMP: 3 EST: 1989
SQ FT: 576
SALES (est): 140K **Privately Held**
WEB: www.timprentice.com
SIC: 3299 Architectural sculptures: gypsum, clay, papier mache, etc.

West Granby
Hartford County

(G-9766)
BELMEADE GROUP LLC
Also Called: Belmeade Signs
46 Simsbury Rd (06090-1401)
PHONE..................860 413-3569
Jean-Luc Godard,
EMP: 3

SALES (est): 121K **Privately Held**
SIC: 3993 Signs & advertising specialties

(G-9767)
JEROME RIDEL
Also Called: R S Enterprise
15 Hampsted Rd (06090)
PHONE..................860 379-1774
Jerome Ridel, *Owner*
EMP: 4
SALES (est): 189.7K **Privately Held**
SIC: 3599 Machine shop, jobbing & repair

West Hartford
Hartford County

(G-9768)
32 DEGREES LLC
216 South St (06110-1931)
PHONE..................978 602-2007
◆ EMP: 1
SALES (est): 98K **Privately Held**
SIC: 5611 5136 5137 2353 Ret Men's/Boy's Clothing Whol Mens/Boys Clothing Whol Women/Child Clothng Mfg Hats/Caps/Millinery Bus Servs Non-Comcl Site

(G-9769)
A PIECE OF PZZLE BHVRAL INTRVE
1100 New Britain Ave # 105 (06110-2427)
PHONE..................860 250-8054
Amy Lavoie, *Principal*
EMP: 1
SALES (est): 41K **Privately Held**
SIC: 3944 Puzzles

(G-9770)
ABBOTT BALL COMPANY
19 Railroad Pl (06110-2384)
P.O. Box 330100 (06133-0100)
PHONE..................860 236-5901
Craig W Bond, *President*
Patricia Dacunha, *Human Res Mgr*
▲ EMP: 75
SALES (est): 21.5MM **Privately Held**
WEB: www.abbottball.com
SIC: 3399 Steel balls

(G-9771)
ABBYDABBY
2523 Albany Ave (06117-2308)
PHONE..................860 586-8832
Andrea Matteson, *Manager*
EMP: 6 EST: 2010
SALES (est): 280.7K **Privately Held**
SIC: 2024 Ice cream, bulk

(G-9772)
ACME TYPESETTING SERVICE CO
47 Cody St (06110-1901)
PHONE..................860 953-1470
Jeffrey F Lewis, *Owner*
EMP: 5
SALES: 220K **Privately Held**
SIC: 2791 2759 Typesetting; commercial printing

(G-9773)
ALMOND SAND ELEPHANTS
11 Craigmoor Rd (06107-1210)
PHONE..................860 232-4888
Sally Lynch, *Owner*
EMP: 2
SALES (est): 66K **Privately Held**
SIC: 1442 Construction sand & gravel

(G-9774)
ANDERSON SPECIALTY COMPANY
81 Custer St (06110-1908)
PHONE..................860 953-6630
Kenneth Swanson, *President*
EMP: 6 EST: 1940
SQ FT: 5,600
SALES (est): 935.1K **Privately Held**
SIC: 3398 Metal heat treating

GEOGRAPHIC SECTION

West Hartford - Hartford County (G-9804)

(G-9775)
ARBOT SOFTWARE
1245 Farmington Ave Fl 2 (06107-2667)
PHONE..................860 209-8460
Seth Baker, *Principal*
EMP: 2
SALES (est): 186.5K Privately Held
SIC: 7372 Prepackaged software

(G-9776)
ATLAS METAL AND WOOD WORKS LLC
2 Auburn Rd (06119-1301)
PHONE..................805 450-7031
Christoph Glueck, *Principal*
EMP: 1
SALES (est): 54.1K Privately Held
SIC: 2431 Millwork

(G-9777)
AUTOMATION INC
707 Oakwood Ave (06110-1508)
P.O. Box 330346 (06133-0346)
PHONE..................860 236-5991
Ronald D Hall, *President*
Robert C Dodge, *Vice Pres*
Stephanie Dodge, *Vice Pres*
Alice L Hall, *Admin Sec*
EMP: 11 EST: 1963
SQ FT: 5,000
SALES: 2.3MM Privately Held
WEB: www.automationincct.com
SIC: 3569 5085 Lubrication equipment, industrial; industrial supplies

(G-9778)
BELLABLE LLC
1245 Farmington Ave Ste 1 (06107-2667)
PHONE..................800 212-2603
Engel Sanchez,
EMP: 1
SALES: 100K Privately Held
SIC: 5961 2741 7389 ; ; business services

(G-9779)
BERTRAM SIRKIN
Also Called: Photobert Cheatsheets
200 Mohegan Dr (06117-1426)
PHONE..................860 656-7446
Bertram Sirkin, *Owner*
EMP: 3
SALES: 140K Privately Held
SIC: 2741 Guides: publishing & printing

(G-9780)
BUSINESS & PROF MICROCOMPTER
Also Called: B P Mug
15 Cassandra Blvd Apt 203 (06107-3147)
PHONE..................860 231-7302
Paul Silversmith, *Treasurer*
EMP: 1
SALES (est): 110K Privately Held
WEB: www.bpmug.org
SIC: 7372 Educational computer software

(G-9781)
C & L AUTOMOTIVE MACHINE SHOP
67 Grassmere Ave (06110-1216)
PHONE..................860 523-5268
William Leonarde, *Owner*
EMP: 1 EST: 1976
SQ FT: 1,000
SALES (est): 202K Privately Held
SIC: 3599 Machine shop, jobbing & repair

(G-9782)
CABINET HARWARD SPECIALTI
50 Chelton Ave (06110-1205)
PHONE..................860 231-1192
Art Roth, *Owner*
EMP: 7
SALES (est): 555.5K Privately Held
SIC: 2434 Wood kitchen cabinets

(G-9783)
CAMPUS YELLOW PAGES LLC
Also Called: High School Counselor Connect
79 High Wood Rd (06117-1117)
P.O. Box 270071 (06127-0071)
PHONE..................860 523-9909
Gary Dinowitz,
Heather Dinowitz,
Glen Hauser,
EMP: 5
SALES: 1MM Privately Held
WEB: www.campusyellowpages.com
SIC: 2741 7374 Directories: publishing only, not printed on site; data processing service

(G-9784)
CANVAS LLC
608 Park Rd (06107-3441)
PHONE..................860 986-8553
Tara Cantor, *Principal*
EMP: 1
SALES (est): 55.8K Privately Held
SIC: 2394 Canvas & related products

(G-9785)
CAPITOL CITY BURIAL VAULTS
111 South St (06110-1928)
PHONE..................860 953-1060
EMP: 2
SALES (est): 95.8K Privately Held
SIC: 3272 Burial vaults, concrete or pre-cast terrazzo

(G-9786)
CCR PRODUCTS LLC
167 South St (06110-1928)
P.O. Box 330186 (06133-0186)
PHONE..................860 953-0499
Craig Bond,
▲ EMP: 20
SQ FT: 14,000
SALES (est): 4.4MM Privately Held
WEB: www.ccrproducts.com
SIC: 3312 3399 Hot-rolled iron & steel products; tacks, nonferrous metal or wire

(G-9787)
CENTRAL OPTICAL
33 Lasalle Rd (06107-2304)
PHONE..................860 236-2329
Carl Zyskowski, *Principal*
EMP: 2
SALES (est): 306.4K Privately Held
WEB: www.centralopticaeyes.com
SIC: 5995 3851 Opticians; ophthalmic goods

(G-9788)
CHROMATIC PRESS US INC
84 Woodrow St (06107-2729)
P.O. Box 270138 (06127-0138)
PHONE..................860 796-7667
Magda Erik-Soussi, *Director*
Lianne Sentar, *Director*
EMP: 5
SALES (est): 101.4K Privately Held
SIC: 2711 Newspapers

(G-9789)
COLT DEFENSE EMPLYE PLN (HQ)
547 New Park Ave (06110-1336)
PHONE..................860 232-4489
William Keys, *President*
James Battaglini, *Exec VP*
Carlton Chen, *Vice Pres*
Richard Nadeau, *CFO*
EMP: 2
SQ FT: 250,000
SALES (est): 10MM
SALES (corp-wide): 287.9MM Privately Held
SIC: 3484 Small arms; machine guns or machine gun parts, 30 mm. & below; carbines, 30 mm. & below
PA: Colt Defense Holding Llc
547 New Park Ave
West Hartford CT 06110
860 232-4489

(G-9790)
COLT DEFENSE LLC (HQ)
Also Called: Colt Defense Holding
547 New Park Ave (06110-1336)
PHONE..................860 232-4489
Dennis Veilleux, *CEO*
Alejandro Fuster, *Mktg Dir*
James R Battaglini,
EMP: 380
SQ FT: 250,000
SALES: 277.9MM
SALES (corp-wide): 110.2MM Privately Held
WEB: www.colt.com
SIC: 3484 Machine guns or machine gun parts, 30 mm. & below; carbines, 30 mm. & below
PA: Colt Defense Holding Llc
547 New Park Ave
West Hartford CT 06110
860 232-4489

(G-9791)
COLTS MANUFACTURING CO LLC (DH)
547 New Park Ave (06110-1336)
P.O. Box 1868, Hartford (06144-1868)
PHONE..................860 236-6311
Dennis Veilleux, *CEO*
Donald E Zilkha, *Ch of Bd*
William M Keys, *President*
Michael Buchner, *Vice Pres*
Nico Colaiocco, *Opers Staff*
EMP: 160
SQ FT: 300,000
SALES: 53.1MM
SALES (corp-wide): 110.2MM Privately Held
SIC: 3484 Guns (firearms) or gun parts, 30 mm. & below

(G-9792)
COMPONENT CONCEPTS INC
Also Called: Celtic Co
26 Hammick Rd (06107-1221)
PHONE..................860 523-4066
Michael Clifford, *President*
Michael David Clifford, *Director*
EMP: 5
SALES: 3.2MM Privately Held
WEB: www.comcpt.com
SIC: 3678 3679 3625 5065 Electronic connectors; electronic switches; relays, for electronic use; electronic parts

(G-9793)
CONNECTCUT BOILER REPR MFG INC
Also Called: Cbr
694 Oakwood Ave (06110-1507)
PHONE..................860 953-9117
Peter J Royer, *President*
Tony Pentlicki, *Foreman/Supr*
Irene L Royer, *Treasurer*
Sharon E Royer, *Admin Sec*
EMP: 20
SQ FT: 12,000
SALES (est): 4.5MM Privately Held
SIC: 7699 1711 3443 Boiler repair shop; boiler & furnace contractors; smokestacks, boiler plate

(G-9794)
CONNECTICUT VINEYARD & WINERY
433 S Main St Ste 309 (06110-2815)
PHONE..................860 307-3550
Keith Bishop, *Principal*
EMP: 2 EST: 2013
SALES: 71.6K Privately Held
SIC: 2084 Wines

(G-9795)
CREATIVE ENHANCEMENT INC
1028 Boulevard Ste 243 (06119-1801)
PHONE..................860 833-8493
Saundra Magana, *President*
EMP: 27
SQ FT: 2,000
SALES: 250K Privately Held
SIC: 7389 2339 Interior design services; women's & misses' outerwear

(G-9796)
CRICKET PRESS INC
236 Park Rd (06119-2018)
PHONE..................860 521-9279
Michelle Confessore, *President*
Greg Confessore, *Vice Pres*
Michelle T Confessore, *Treasurer*
Carol Teasdale, *Treasurer*
EMP: 6
SQ FT: 2,000
SALES (est): 525.1K Privately Held
WEB: www.cricketpress.net
SIC: 2752 Commercial printing, offset

(G-9797)
D & M TOOL COMPANY INC
17 Grassmere Ave (06110-1216)
P.O. Box 330631 (06133-0631)
PHONE..................860 236-6037
Fax: 860 236-6037
EMP: 5 EST: 1966
SQ FT: 4,000
SALES: 300K Privately Held
SIC: 3544 3724 3545 Mfg Dies Tools Jigs Aircraft Parts & Gauges

(G-9798)
DAVID H JOHNSON INC
137 Woodpond Rd (06107-3540)
PHONE..................860 677-5595
David H Johnson, *President*
EMP: 3
SQ FT: 2,000
SALES: 3MM Privately Held
SIC: 5172 5075 3563 5078 Lubricating oils & greases; compressors, air conditioning; air & gas compressors; refrigeration equipment & supplies; compressors, except air conditioning

(G-9799)
DELTA-SOURCE LLC
138 Beacon Hill Dr (06117-1006)
PHONE..................860 461-1600
Daniel Barash, *Principal*
EMP: 10 EST: 2010
SALES (est): 408.9K Privately Held
SIC: 3999 Manufacturing industries

(G-9800)
DIGYSOL LLC
34 Miamis Rd (06117-2223)
PHONE..................860 232-1614
Thomas Freund, *Principal*
EMP: 1 EST: 2014
SALES (est): 85.9K Privately Held
SIC: 3829 Measuring & controlling devices

(G-9801)
DOOR STEP PREP LLC
51 Thomson Rd (06107-2535)
PHONE..................860 550-0460
Linda Houde,
EMP: 3
SALES (est): 266.4K Privately Held
SIC: 3845 Colonascopes, electromedical

(G-9802)
DWELLING LLC
149 Raymond Rd (06107-2537)
PHONE..................860 521-1935
Gloria R Delaney, *Mng Member*
EMP: 1
SQ FT: 3,000
SALES (est): 98.8K Privately Held
SIC: 2282 Needle & handicraft yarns: twisting, winding or spooling

(G-9803)
EAGLE INVESTMENT SYSTEMS LLC
65 Lasalle Rd Ste 305 (06107-2325)
PHONE..................860 561-4602
Greg Gruber, *Vice Pres*
Jeremy Shaw, *Opers Staff*
Akhar Mathews, *Engineer*
Linda Mongillo, *Accountant*
Catherine Anderson, *Technical Staff*
EMP: 11
SALES (corp-wide): 16.3B Publicly Held
SIC: 6722 6282 8721 7372 Management investment, open-end; investment advisory service; accounting services, except auditing; business oriented computer software
HQ: Eagle Investment Systems Llc
45 William St
Wellesley MA 02481

(G-9804)
EAGLE PRINTING CO
7a Andover Dr (06110-1502)
PHONE..................860 953-2152
EMP: 2

(PA)=Parent Co (HQ)=Headquarters (DH)=Div Headquarters
✪ = New Business established in last 2 years

SALES (est): 15.7K **Privately Held**
SIC: 2752 Lithographic Commercial Printing

(G-9805)
EFITZGERALD PUBLISHING LLC
319 Ridgewood Rd (06107-3515)
PHONE.................................860 904-7250
Patrice Fitzgerald, *Principal*
EMP: 3
SALES (est): 87.9K **Privately Held**
SIC: 2711 Newspapers

(G-9806)
EL MAR INC
Also Called: Uncle Bill's Tweezers
38 Cody St 2 (06110-1904)
P.O. Box 925, Avon (06001-0925)
PHONE.................................860 729-7232
Glen Baron, *President*
EMP: 9
SQ FT: 5,000
SALES (est): 700K **Privately Held**
SIC: 3599 Machine & other job shop work

(G-9807)
ELEMENTS LLC
945 Farmington Ave (06107-2203)
PHONE.................................860 231-8011
Sarah Howes, *Principal*
EMP: 3
SALES (est): 193K **Privately Held**
SIC: 2819 Industrial inorganic chemicals

(G-9808)
ELM-CAP INDUSTRIES INC
111 South St (06110-1928)
P.O. Box 330099 (06133-0099)
PHONE.................................860 953-1060
R Thomas Abbate, *President*
EMP: 45 EST: 1914
SALES (est): 6.1MM **Privately Held**
SIC: 3272 Burial vaults, concrete or precast terrazzo; concrete products, precast

(G-9809)
EYELASH EXTENSIONS AND MORE
998 Farmington Ave (06107-2162)
PHONE.................................860 951-9355
Esther Nicholls, *Owner*
EMP: 12
SQ FT: 900
SALES (est): 330.1K **Privately Held**
SIC: 3999 Eyelashes, artificial

(G-9810)
FIELD ENERGY LLC
17 Fawn Brk (06117-1032)
PHONE.................................860 817-2654
Hiro Hara, *Mng Member*
EMP: 2
SALES (est): 173.8K **Privately Held**
SIC: 5169 2099 0182 Essential oils; food preparations; food crops grown under cover

(G-9811)
FREEDOM PROPERTIES
1865 Boulevard (06107-2823)
PHONE.................................860 508-3349
Michael Krupa, *President*
Melody Nichols, *Bookkeeper*
EMP: 2
SALES (est): 150K **Privately Held**
SIC: 1442 Construction sand & gravel

(G-9812)
FRESH INK LLC
216 Park Rd (06119-2015)
PHONE.................................860 656-7013
David Austin, *Principal*
EMP: 2
SALES (est): 170K **Privately Held**
SIC: 2759 Screen printing

(G-9813)
GRADUATE GROUP
Also Called: Graduate Group Booksellers
25 Norwood Rd (06117-2234)
PHONE.................................860 233-2330
Mara Whitman, *Owner*
EMP: 1 EST: 1964

SALES (est): 46.8K **Privately Held**
WEB: www.graduategroup.com
SIC: 2731 7338 Book publishing; secretarial & court reporting

(G-9814)
GREENMAKER INDUSTRIES CONN LLC
697 Oakwood Ave (06110-1506)
PHONE.................................860 761-2830
John Di Stefano, *Mfg Staff*
Mike Jalbert, *Sales Staff*
Sarah Beaty, *Mng Member*
Cheryl Buller,
John Distefano,
EMP: 16
SALES (est): 2.2MM **Privately Held**
SIC: 2851 Paints & allied products

(G-9815)
HAR-CONN CHROME COMPANY (PA)
603 New Park Ave (06110-1380)
P.O. Box 330189 (06133-0189)
PHONE.................................860 236-6801
Kent N Backus, *CEO*
Tim Backus, *President*
Fred Gariepy, *General Mgr*
Daniel Backus, *Vice Pres*
Scherry Rowland, *Purchasing*
EMP: 70 EST: 1948
SQ FT: 40,000
SALES (est): 17.2MM **Privately Held**
WEB: www.har-conn.com
SIC: 3471 Plating of metals or formed products; finishing, metals or formed products

(G-9816)
HARTFORD COURANT COMPANY
141 South St Ste E (06110-1963)
PHONE.................................860 560-3747
George Madera, *Branch Mgr*
EMP: 15
SALES (corp-wide): 1B **Publicly Held**
WEB: www.courantnie.com
SIC: 2711 Newspapers, publishing & printing
HQ: The Hartford Courant Company Llc
285 Broad St
Hartford CT 06115
860 241-6200

(G-9817)
HARTFORD GAUGE CO
23 Brook St (06110-2350)
P.O. Box 1975, Boerne TX (78006-6975)
PHONE.................................860 233-9619
EMP: 4 EST: 1941
SQ FT: 6,000
SALES: 500K **Privately Held**
SIC: 3545 3544 Mfg Gages Jigs & Tools

(G-9818)
HARTFORD MONTHLY MEETING
144 Quaker Ln S (06119-1636)
PHONE.................................860 232-3631
EMP: 4 EST: 2015
SALES (est): 141.3K **Privately Held**
SIC: 2711 Newspapers

(G-9819)
HARTFORD SEAMLESS GUTTERS
41 Crossroads Plz (06117-2402)
PHONE.................................860 266-2516
EMP: 4 EST: 2016
SALES (est): 279.8K **Privately Held**
SIC: 3089 3444 Gutters (glass fiber reinforced, fiberglass or plastic; gutters, sheet metal

(G-9820)
IMPACT SALES & MARKETING LLC
48 Carlyle Rd (06117-1325)
PHONE.................................860 523-5366
Ira Gold, *Owner*
EMP: 4
SALES (est): 327K **Privately Held**
SIC: 3651 Household audio & video equipment

(G-9821)
INITIAL STEP MONOGRAMMING
635 New Park Ave Ste 2a (06110-1338)
PHONE.................................860 665-0542
Michael Reddy, *Partner*
Joan Maradie, *Partner*
Gloria Reddy, *Partner*
EMP: 3
SQ FT: 1,000
SALES (est): 301.7K **Privately Held**
SIC: 2395 Embroidery & art needlework

(G-9822)
IONA PRESS
1245 Farmington Ave (06107-2667)
P.O. Box 270811 (06127-0811)
PHONE.................................860 841-5006
EMP: 1
SALES (est): 37.5K **Privately Held**
SIC: 2741 Miscellaneous publishing

(G-9823)
IRON AND GRAIN CO LLC
183 Webster Hill Blvd (06107-3748)
PHONE.................................860 840-2179
Tate Norden, *Principal*
EMP: 2
SALES (est): 62K **Privately Held**
SIC: 3462 Iron & steel forgings

(G-9824)
JOBIN MACHINE INC
37 Custer St (06110-1907)
PHONE.................................860 953-1631
George Kiss, *President*
Barry Kalin, *General Mgr*
David Chapdelaine, *Mfg Mgr*
Erica Kiss Ames, *Treasurer*
EMP: 28
SQ FT: 9,500
SALES (est): 7MM **Privately Held**
SIC: 3728 3714 Aircraft parts & equipment; motor vehicle parts & accessories

(G-9825)
LA CARE INDUSTRIES LLC
54 W Ridge Dr (06117-2046)
P.O. Box 370454 (06137-0454)
PHONE.................................860 231-7772
Arthur Green, *President*
Leonard Berlind, *Principal*
▲ EMP: 2
SALES (est): 153.1K **Privately Held**
SIC: 3999 Manufacturing industries

(G-9826)
LED LIGHTING HUB
193 Simsbury Rd (06117-1450)
PHONE.................................860 232-7141
Peter Goldsmith, *Owner*
EMP: 2
SALES (est): 124.2K **Privately Held**
SIC: 3648 Lighting equipment

(G-9827)
LEGACY CORP
555 New Park Ave (06110-1348)
PHONE.................................860 236-6500
Dee Koch, *Finance Mgr*
EMP: 1
SALES (est): 39.7K **Privately Held**
SIC: 3231 Products of purchased glass

(G-9828)
LEGRAND HOLDING INC (DH)
60 Woodlawn St (06110-2326)
PHONE.................................860 233-6251
John P Selldorff, *CEO*
Giles Schnep, *President*
Jim Waddell, *President*
Kenneth Ruh, *General Mgr*
Lori Kelly, *District Mgr*
▲ EMP: 30
SALES (est): 1.8B
SALES (corp-wide): 21.2MM **Privately Held**
SIC: 3643 6719 Current-carrying wiring devices; investment holding companies, except banks
HQ: Legrand France
128 Av Du Mal De Lattre De Tassigny
Limoges 87000
555 067-272

(G-9829)
LEMAC IRON WORKS INC
18 Brainard Rd (06117-2201)
PHONE.................................860 232-7380
Michael Levy, *President*
Max Levy, *Vice Pres*
EMP: 3 EST: 1963
SQ FT: 10,000
SALES (est): 242.3K **Privately Held**
SIC: 7692 3441 5032 Welding repair; fabricated structural metal; concrete building products

(G-9830)
LEWTAN INDUSTRIES CORPORATION
Also Called: Abbott Manufacturing
57 Loomis Dr Apt A1 (06107-2035)
P.O. Box 2049, Hartford (06145-2049)
PHONE.................................860 278-9800
Marvin Lewtan, *Ch of Bd*
Douglas Lewtan, *President*
▲ EMP: 75 EST: 1947
SQ FT: 35,000
SALES (est): 8.7MM **Privately Held**
WEB: www.lewtan8.com
SIC: 3993 Signs & advertising specialties

(G-9831)
LIFE PUBLICATIONS
Also Called: White Publishing
106 South St Ste 5 (06110-1965)
PHONE.................................860 953-0444
Christopher White, *Owner*
Chris White, *Opers Dir*
EMP: 30
SALES (est): 1.6MM **Privately Held**
SIC: 2711 Newspapers: publishing only, not printed on site

(G-9832)
MANUFACTURERS COML FIN LLC
Also Called: Electro-Flex Heat
1022 Boulevard (06119-1801)
P.O. Box 88, Bloomfield (06002-0088)
PHONE.................................860 242-6287
Delly Lugo, *Finance Mgr*
Sandy Tetreault, *Sales Executive*
EMP: 31
SALES (est): 8.6MM **Privately Held**
SIC: 3567 Heating units & devices, industrial: electric

(G-9833)
MARATHON ENTERPRISES LLC
9 Rushleigh Rd (06117-2922)
PHONE.................................860 888-6294
EMP: 2
SALES (est): 95.5K **Privately Held**
SIC: 3537 Trucks, tractors, loaders, carriers & similar equipment

(G-9834)
MARKETING SLTONS UNLIMITED LLC
109 Talcott Rd (06110-1228)
PHONE.................................860 523-0670
Heidi Anderson Buckley, *President*
EMP: 22
SALES (est): 4.9MM **Privately Held**
SIC: 2752 Commercial printing, offset

(G-9835)
MBSW INC
41 Plainfield Rd (06117-1936)
PHONE.................................860 243-0303
Theodore L Zachs, *President*
Jed Zachs, *Vice Pres*
Ross Zachs, *Treasurer*
▲ EMP: 75 EST: 1939
SQ FT: 45,000
SALES (est): 9MM **Privately Held**
WEB: www.cthruruler.com
SIC: 3089 3953 2782 Injection molded finished plastic products; stencils, painting & marking; letters (marking devices), metal; scrapbooks, albums & diaries

(G-9836)
METALPUCK CO LLC
25 Common Dr (06107-3200)
PHONE.................................860 561-5936
Teresa M Stanton, *Principal*
EMP: 2 EST: 2007

SALES (est): 128.7K **Privately Held**
SIC: 3441 Fabricated structural metal

(G-9837)
NEW ENGLAND GRAN CABINETS LLC
8 Cody St (06110-1903)
PHONE..................................860 310-2981
Wenbo MA, *Mng Member*
EMP: 6
SALES (est): 546K **Privately Held**
SIC: 3281 Curbing, granite or stone

(G-9838)
NORTH SHORE PUBLISHING LLC
111 Stoner Dr (06107-1307)
PHONE..................................860 561-8768
Robert D Lachange, *Principal*
EMP: 1
SALES (est): 49K **Privately Held**
SIC: 2741 Miscellaneous publishing

(G-9839)
NORTHEAST SEALCOAT INC
38 Jansen Ct (06110-1913)
PHONE..................................860 953-4400
Gary Sharkevich Jr, *President*
EMP: 2
SALES (est): 210K **Privately Held**
SIC: 2851 1799 Lacquers, varnishes, enamels & other coatings; coating, caulking & weather, water & fireproofing

(G-9840)
NUTTY COW INC
126 Brewster Rd (06117-2101)
PHONE..................................626 888-9269
Cara Paiuk, *Principal*
Alejandro Paiuk, *Principal*
EMP: 2
SALES (est): 130K **Privately Held**
SIC: 2022 Imitation cheese

(G-9841)
ORTRONICS INC
Also Called: Legrand
60 Woodlawn St (06110-2326)
PHONE..................................877 295-3472
Kirsten Mathis, *Regional Mgr*
Jeff Thompson, *District Mgr*
Ken Freeman, *Vice Pres*
Harold Jepsen, *Vice Pres*
Steve Killius, *Vice Pres*
EMP: 7
SALES (corp-wide): 21.2MM **Privately Held**
SIC: 3577 3357 Computer peripheral equipment; communication wire
HQ: Ortronics, Inc.
    125 Eugene Oneill Dr # 140
    New London CT 06320
    860 445-3900

(G-9842)
PAL TECHNOLOGIES LLC
9 Tolles St (06110-1504)
PHONE..................................860 953-1984
EMP: 3
SQ FT: 6,000
SALES: 600K **Privately Held**
SIC: 3599 Mfg Industrial Machinery

(G-9843)
PETER KELSEY PUBLISHING INC
Also Called: Atlantic Law Book Company, The
22 Grassmere Ave (06110-1215)
PHONE..................................860 231-9300
Richard Epstein, *President*
Barbara Marriot, *Vice Pres*
EMP: 2
SQ FT: 600
SALES (est): 178.6K **Privately Held**
WEB: www.atlntc.com
SIC: 2731 8111 5192 Textbooks: publishing & printing; legal services; books

(G-9844)
PETRUNTI DESIGN & WDWKG LLC
23c Andover Dr (06110-1502)
PHONE..................................860 953-5332
William Petrunti, *Owner*
Bill Petrunti,

EMP: 4
SALES (est): 476.6K **Privately Held**
SIC: 2431 Millwork

(G-9845)
PICK & MIX CORP
1234 Farmington Ave Ste 3 (06107-2670)
PHONE..................................860 521-1521
Ho Y Joo, *Principal*
EMP: 4
SALES (est): 233.4K **Privately Held**
SIC: 3273 Ready-mixed concrete

(G-9846)
PPG INDUSTRIES INC
141 South St (06110-1963)
PHONE..................................860 953-1153
Milian Totolici, *Branch Mgr*
EMP: 2
SALES (corp-wide): 15.3B **Publicly Held**
SIC: 2851 Paints & allied products
PA: Ppg Industries, Inc.
    1 Ppg Pl
    Pittsburgh PA 15272
    412 434-3131

(G-9847)
PRINT MGT & CONSULTING LLC
26 Westland Ave (06107-2732)
PHONE..................................860 521-7444
Steven Mayville, *Principal*
EMP: 2
SALES (est): 210K **Privately Held**
SIC: 2752 Commercial printing, lithographic

(G-9848)
RBF FROZEN DESSERTS LLC
240 Park Rd Ste 3 (06119-2040)
PHONE..................................516 474-6488
Thomas Marshall, *Mng Member*
EMP: 12
SQ FT: 20,000
SALES (est): 605K **Privately Held**
SIC: 2024 Ice cream & frozen desserts

(G-9849)
READY TOOL COMPANY (HQ)
1 Carney Rd (06110-1937)
PHONE..................................860 524-7811
Joseph Wagner, *President*
Daniel Piendak, *Engineer*
Dave Brunette, *Mktg Dir*
EMP: 20 EST: 1908
SQ FT: 40,000
SALES (est): 1.6MM
SALES (corp-wide): 43.9MM **Privately Held**
WEB: www.readytool.com
SIC: 3541 Machine tools, metal cutting type
PA: The United Tool And Die Company
    1 Carney Rd
    West Hartford CT 06110
    860 246-6531

(G-9850)
RECREATIONAL EQUIPMENT INC
1417 New Britain Ave (06110)
PHONE..................................860 313-0128
EMP: 1
SALES (est): 47K **Privately Held**
SIC: 3949 Sporting & athletic goods

(G-9851)
RELATIONAL DATA SOLUTIONS LLC
123 Thomas St (06119-2340)
PHONE..................................860 231-7682
Denise Rogers, *Principal*
EMP: 2
SALES (est): 113K **Privately Held**
SIC: 7372 Prepackaged software

(G-9852)
ROBUST SOFTWARE LLC
64 Whitehill Dr (06117-2052)
PHONE..................................860 231-9880
EMP: 2
SALES (est): 79.6K **Privately Held**
SIC: 7372 Prepackaged Software Services

(G-9853)
RUGSALECOM LLC
17 S Main St (06107-2407)
PHONE..................................860 756-0959
Charles Kaoud,
EMP: 5
SALES (est): 598.9K **Privately Held**
SIC: 2273 5713 Floor coverings, textile fiber; rugs

(G-9854)
SEAN CHRISTIAN LEATHER LLC
134 Abbotsford Ave (06110-2204)
PHONE..................................787 690-7039
Anibal Carrero, *Principal*
EMP: 1
SALES (est): 83K **Privately Held**
SIC: 3111 7389 Leather processing;

(G-9855)
SIGN OF FLYING TURTLE LLC
68 Kingswood Rd (06119-1539)
PHONE..................................860 830-3132
Steven Karas, *Principal*
EMP: 1 EST: 2010
SALES (est): 68.7K **Privately Held**
SIC: 3993 Signs & advertising specialties

(G-9856)
SMARTCAP INNOVATIONS LLC
121 Walbridge Rd (06119-1052)
PHONE..................................860 878-4688
Rodney Powell,
Claudio Borea, *Admin Sec*
EMP: 2
SALES (est): 88.3K **Privately Held**
SIC: 3648 Street lighting fixtures; outdoor lighting equipment

(G-9857)
SOFTSTORMS LLC
35 Hollywood Ave (06110-2216)
PHONE..................................860 578-8515
EMP: 2
SALES (est): 84.7K **Privately Held**
SIC: 7372 Prepackaged Software Services

(G-9858)
SORENSON LIGHTED CONTROLS INC (PA)
Also Called: Solico
100 Shield St (06110-1920)
PHONE..................................860 527-3092
Robert C Sorenson Jr, *President*
John D Gallery, *Exec VP*
Fred Kundahl, *Exec VP*
Wesley T Sorenson II, *Vice Pres*
Suzanne Ferguson, *Sales Staff*
▲ EMP: 62 EST: 1960
SQ FT: 25,000
SALES (est): 18.7MM **Privately Held**
WEB: www.solico.com
SIC: 3648 Lighting equipment

(G-9859)
SOUTH BEACH INC
Also Called: South Beach Swimsuits
12 Cody St (06110-1903)
PHONE..................................860 953-0038
Donna Grossman, *President*
Bennett Grossman, *Vice Pres*
Ashley Backman, *Treasurer*
EMP: 2
SALES (est): 236.8K **Privately Held**
SIC: 5632 2339 Lingerie (outerwear); bathing suits: women's, misses' & juniors'

(G-9860)
SPORTS CENTER
200 Bloomfield Ave (06117-1545)
PHONE..................................860 768-4650
Ted Stavropoulos, *Director*
EMP: 2 EST: 2013
SALES (est): 112.1K **Privately Held**
SIC: 3949 Gymnasium equipment

(G-9861)
SPV INDUSTRIES LLC
9 Tolles St (06110-1504)
PHONE..................................860 953-5928
Wendy Palacios,
EMP: 3
SALES (est): 261.9K **Privately Held**
SIC: 3999 Manufacturing industries

(G-9862)
STOCK BAR CANDLES LLC
105 Beechwood Rd (06107-3600)
PHONE..................................860 805-1986
Amelia E Yungk, *Principal*
EMP: 1
SALES (est): 57.1K **Privately Held**
SIC: 3999 Candles

(G-9863)
SWANSON TOOL MANUFACTURING INC
71 Custer St (06110-1908)
P.O. Box 330318 (06133-0318)
PHONE..................................860 953-1641
Kenneth Swanson Jr, *CEO*
Kenneth W Swanson Sr, *CEO*
Annlouise Swanson, *Treasurer*
Merle Nicoletta, *Technology*
EMP: 25
SQ FT: 19,000
SALES (est): 6.5MM **Privately Held**
WEB: www.swansongage.com
SIC: 3545 5084 5251 Threading tools (machine tool accessories); gauges (machine tool accessories); threading tools; tools

(G-9864)
TALL TREES PRESS
54 Henley Way (06117-1451)
PHONE..................................860 233-7024
June Sidran Mandelk, *Owner*
EMP: 1
SALES (est): 49.1K **Privately Held**
SIC: 2741 Miscellaneous publishing

(G-9865)
THINK AHEAD SOFTWARE LLC (PA)
30 Wardwell Rd (06107-2734)
PHONE..................................860 463-9786
Richard M Spear, *Principal*
EMP: 3
SALES (est): 1.1MM **Privately Held**
SIC: 7372 Prepackaged software

(G-9866)
THIRDSHIFT PUBLISHING
215 Raymond Rd (06107-2539)
PHONE..................................860 521-6613
Jim Rigby, *Owner*
EMP: 1
SALES (est): 81.3K **Privately Held**
SIC: 2741 Miscellaneous publishing

(G-9867)
TINY B CODE LLC
38 N Main St Apt 30 (06107-1907)
PHONE..................................617 308-9635
Darren Lafreniere,
EMP: 1
SALES: 50K **Privately Held**
SIC: 7372 Prepackaged software

(G-9868)
TRIATIC INCORPORATED
22 Grassmere Ave (06110-1215)
PHONE..................................860 236-2298
William Plourd, *President*
Bill Kauffman, *Admin Sec*
EMP: 11
SQ FT: 10,000
SALES (est): 1.3MM **Privately Held**
WEB: www.triaticinc.com
SIC: 3291 Artificial abrasives

(G-9869)
TRIUMPH ENG CTRL SYSTEMS LLC
Also Called: Goodrich
1 Charter Oak Blvd (06110-1328)
PHONE..................................860 236-0651
Alec Searle, *Vice Pres*
Scott Maze, *Business Anlyst*
Don Fortier, *Business Dir*
EMP: 560 EST: 2013
SALES (est): 200.8MM **Publicly Held**
SIC: 3728 3724 3812 Aircraft body & wing assemblies & parts; aircraft engines & engine parts; aircraft control instruments
PA: Triumph Group, Inc.
    899 Cassatt Rd Ste 210
    Berwyn PA 19312

West Hartford - Hartford County (G-9870) — GEOGRAPHIC SECTION

(G-9870)
TRIUMPH ENG CTRL SYSTEMS LLC
1 Talcott Rd (06110)
PHONE..................................860 236-0651
EMP: 14
SALES (est): 2.4MM **Privately Held**
SIC: 3812 Mfg Search/Navigation Equipment

(G-9871)
UNITED TOOL AND DIE COMPANY (PA)
1 Carney Rd (06110-1982)
PHONE..................................860 246-6531
Julie Susan Wagner, *CEO*
Joseph Wagner, *President*
Charles Zien, *Vice Pres*
Sheila Suchecki, *Purch Mgr*
David Hussey, *Treasurer*
EMP: 115 **EST:** 1925
SQ FT: 150,000
SALES (est): 43.9MM **Privately Held**
WEB: www.utdco.com
SIC: 3724 3541 3769 Aircraft engines & engine parts; machine tools, metal cutting type; guided missile & space vehicle parts & auxiliary equipment

(G-9872)
WEST HARTFORD STONE MULCH LLC
154 Reed Ave (06110-1510)
PHONE..................................860 461-7616
Robert Dignoti, *Mng Member*
EMP: 3
SALES (est): 144.7K **Privately Held**
SIC: 1411 3272 1442 0782 Dimension stone; building stone, artificial; concrete; construction sand & gravel; mulching services, lawn

(G-9873)
WIPL-D (USA) LLC
103 High Ridge Rd (06117-1815)
PHONE..................................860 570-0678
Zoran Maricevic, *Principal*
Marija Bozic, *Sales Staff*
Sladjana Vukajlovic, *Sales Staff*
EMP: 2 **EST:** 2013
SALES (est): 92.1K **Privately Held**
SIC: 7372 Prepackaged software

(G-9874)
WIREMOLD COMPANY (DH)
60 Woodlawn St (06110-2383)
PHONE..................................860 233-6251
John P Selldorff, *CEO*
Brian Dibella, *President*
Adam Hayes, *District Mgr*
Thomas Feiden, *Vice Pres*
Steve Knudsen, *Project Mgr*
◆ **EMP:** 750 **EST:** 1919
SQ FT: 226,000
SALES (est): 387.7MM
SALES (corp-wide): 21.2MM **Privately Held**
SIC: 3643 3496 3315 3644 Current-carrying wiring devices; miscellaneous fabricated wire products; steel wire & related products; raceways
HQ: Legrand Holding, Inc.
60 Woodlawn St
West Hartford CT 06110
860 233-6251

(G-9875)
WIREMOLD COMPANY
21 Railroad Pl (06110-2344)
PHONE..................................860 263-3115
John P Selldorff, *CEO*
EMP: 15
SALES (corp-wide): 21.2MM **Privately Held**
SIC: 3644 Noncurrent-carrying wiring services
HQ: Wiremold Company
60 Woodlawn St
West Hartford CT 06110
860 233-6251

(G-9876)
WIREMOLD LEGRAND CO CENTEREX
60 Woodlawn St (06110-2326)
PHONE..................................877 295-3472
Amy Gerakos, *Principal*
Joe Milheiro, *Engineer*
EMP: 37
SALES (est): 6.5MM **Privately Held**
SIC: 3644 Noncurrent-carrying wiring services

(G-9877)
WOOD POND PRESS
365 Ridgewood Rd (06107-3517)
PHONE..................................860 521-0389
Richard Woodworth, *Owner*
EMP: 2
SALES (est): 80.3K **Privately Held**
WEB: www.getawayguides.com
SIC: 2731 Books: publishing only

West Haven
New Haven County

(G-9878)
A LITTLE SOY CANDLE CO LLC
30 Pauline Ave (06516-6927)
PHONE..................................860 877-6001
Jordan Crooms, *Administration*
EMP: 1
SALES (est): 39.6K **Privately Held**
SIC: 3999 Candles

(G-9879)
AA & B CO
284 2nd Ave (06516-5126)
PHONE..................................203 933-9110
Alex Borodkin, *Owner*
Eugene Borodkin, *Corp Secy*
Mark Borodkin, *Vice Pres*
EMP: 6
SALES (est): 250.6K **Privately Held**
SIC: 3089 Plastic hardware & building products

(G-9880)
AAM WELDING + FABRICATION LLC
67 Phillips Ter (06516-4109)
PHONE..................................203 479-4339
Angelo Messina, *Manager*
EMP: 1
SALES (est): 160.6K **Privately Held**
SIC: 3714 Motor vehicle parts & accessories

(G-9881)
ADDISON INDUSTRIES LLC
23 Sarah Ct (06516-6515)
PHONE..................................203 809-0254
Lawrence R Jennes, *Manager*
EMP: 1
SALES (est): 39.6K **Privately Held**
SIC: 3999 Manufacturing industries

(G-9882)
ALLEXCEL INC
135 Wood St Ste 200 (06516-3700)
PHONE..................................203 764-2036
Anil R Diwan, *President*
Jayant Tatake, *Vice Pres*
EMP: 2 **EST:** 2001
SALES (est): 386.6K **Privately Held**
SIC: 7372 Application computer software

(G-9883)
AMERIFIX LLC
278 Washington Ave (06516-5327)
PHONE..................................203 931-7290
Richard L Moore,
Ellen L Manning-Moore,
EMP: 9
SQ FT: 22,000
SALES (est): 960K **Privately Held**
SIC: 2491 Millwork, treated wood

(G-9884)
AMPOL TOOL INC
44 Hamilton St (06516-2321)
PHONE..................................203 932-3161
Jerzy Kozlowski, *President*
EMP: 5
SQ FT: 4,500
SALES: 500K **Privately Held**
SIC: 3423 Hand & edge tools

(G-9885)
AUTOPART INTERNATIONAL INC
732 Washington Ave (06516-3754)
PHONE..................................203 931-9189
Roger Patkin, *Principal*
EMP: 11
SALES (corp-wide): 9.5B **Publicly Held**
WEB: www.autopartintl.com
SIC: 5531 5013 3714 Automobile & truck equipment & parts; exhaust systems (mufflers, tail pipes, etc.); exhaust systems & parts, motor vehicle
HQ: Autopart International, Inc.
192 Mansfield Ave
Norton MA 02766
781 784-1111

(G-9886)
CANNELLI PRINTING CO INC
39 Wood St (06516-3843)
PHONE..................................203 932-1719
Victor Cannelli, *President*
Rose Cannelli, *Vice Pres*
EMP: 9
SALES (est): 1.5MM **Privately Held**
WEB: www.cannelli.com
SIC: 2752 2759 Commercial printing, offset; lithographing on metal; card printing & engraving, except greeting; embossing on paper

(G-9887)
CLG SOLUTIONS LLC
123 Dogburn Rd (06516-2101)
PHONE..................................203 507-1105
Thomas Goldenberg,
EMP: 1
SALES (est): 35.4K **Privately Held**
SIC: 7372 Application computer software

(G-9888)
CODEBRIDGE SOFTWARE INC
91 Honor Rd (06516-6837)
PHONE..................................203 535-0517
Pedro Rodriguez Jr, *Principal*
EMP: 3
SALES (est): 165.3K **Privately Held**
SIC: 7372 Prepackaged software

(G-9889)
COLONIAL WOOD PRODUCTS INC
250 Callegari Dr (06516-6234)
PHONE..................................203 932-9003
Kevin Donovan, *President*
William Donovan Jr, *Vice Pres*
EMP: 15 **EST:** 1938
SQ FT: 10,000
SALES: 2MM **Privately Held**
SIC: 2431 2441 Millwork; boxes, wood

(G-9890)
CONCO WOOD WORKING INC
755 1st Ave (06516-2712)
P.O. Box 17176, Stamford (06907-7176)
PHONE..................................203 934-9665
Louis M Cutaneo, *President*
EMP: 9
SQ FT: 27,000
SALES (est): 1MM **Privately Held**
WEB: www.concowoodworking.com
SIC: 2521 2522 Wood office furniture; office furniture, except wood

(G-9891)
CONNECTCUT CSWORK SPCLISTS LLC
755 1st Ave Ste B (06516-2712)
PHONE..................................203 934-9665
Lou Cunaeo Jr, *Principal*
EMP: 2 **EST:** 2014
SALES (est): 220.1K **Privately Held**
SIC: 3523 Farm machinery & equipment

(G-9892)
CONNECTICUT CANDLE LLC
25 Ranchwood Dr (06516-3917)
PHONE..................................203 937-7330
Kristen M Teshoney, *Principal*
EMP: 1
SALES (est): 65.6K **Privately Held**
SIC: 3999 Candles

(G-9893)
COSMOS FOOD PRODUCTS INC
200 Callegari Dr (06516-6234)
PHONE..................................800 942-6766
Cosmo N Laudano, *President*
Lisa L Laudano, *Vice Pres*
Mario Laudano, *Treasurer*
Mark C Laudano, *Treasurer*
Lauren N Laudano, *Admin Sec*
▲ **EMP:** 40
SQ FT: 25,000
SALES (est): 9.1MM **Privately Held**
WEB: www.cosmosfoods.com
SIC: 2033 Canned fruits & specialties

(G-9894)
COVERIS ADVANCED COATINGS
351 Morgan Ln (06516-4135)
PHONE..................................413 244-9685
Gordon Thompson, *Manager*
EMP: 1 **EST:** 2014
SALES (est): 158.9K **Privately Held**
SIC: 2621 Paper mills

(G-9895)
DANDREA CORPORATION
Also Called: Dunkin' Donuts
985 Boston Post Rd (06516-1727)
PHONE..................................203 932-6000
Frank D'Andrea, *President*
EMP: 16
SALES (est): 745.3K **Privately Held**
SIC: 5461 2051 Doughnuts; doughnuts, except frozen

(G-9896)
DEITSCH PLASTIC COMPANY INC
14 Farwell St (06516-1717)
P.O. Box 26005 (06516-8005)
PHONE..................................203 934-6601
Mordecoi Deitsch, *President*
Joseph Deitsch, *Vice Pres*
Bob Frank, *Purchasing*
Moti Sandman, *Asst Controller*
Mendel Deitsch, *Manager*
◆ **EMP:** 68 **EST:** 1954
SQ FT: 200,000
SALES (est): 13.8MM **Privately Held**
WEB: www.deitschplastic.com
SIC: 2221 2295 Broadwoven fabric mills, manmade; plastic coated yarns or fabrics

(G-9897)
DESIGN SHOP LLC
170 Wood St (06516-3759)
PHONE..................................203 937-1651
David Hallock, *Mng Member*
EMP: 2
SQ FT: 4,000
SALES: 500K **Privately Held**
WEB: www.designshop.com
SIC: 2434 5712 Wood kitchen cabinets; cabinet work, custom; cabinets, except custom made: kitchen

(G-9898)
DEVICE42 INC
600 Saw Mill Rd (06516-4007)
PHONE..................................203 409-7242
Raj Jalen, *CEO*
Maggie Berkovich, *Business Mgr*
Greg Osborne, *Senior Engr*
Stephen Timms, *Risk Mgmt Dir*
EMP: 14
SALES (est): 564.9K **Privately Held**
SIC: 7372 Prepackaged software

(G-9899)
DIETZGEN CORPORATION
351 Morgan Ln (06516)
PHONE..................................813 849-4334
EMP: 2 **EST:** 2017
SALES (est): 225.7K **Privately Held**
SIC: 2679 Paper products, converted

(G-9900)
DJ CABINETS
627 Main St (06516-4820)
PHONE..................................203 243-0032
David Jennings, *Principal*
EMP: 1

▲ = Import ▼ = Export
◆ = Import/Export

GEOGRAPHIC SECTION — West Haven - New Haven County

SALES (est): 93.2K **Privately Held**
SIC: 2434 Wood kitchen cabinets

(G-9901)
DL DISTRIBUTORS LLC
343 Beach St (06516-6176)
PHONE.................................203 931-1724
EMP: 4
SALES (est): 254.6K **Privately Held**
SIC: 2051 Mfg Bread/Related Products

(G-9902)
DURANTES PASTA INC
78 Fenwick St (06516-1120)
PHONE.................................203 387-5560
Amedeo Durante, *President*
EMP: 3
SALES (est): 275.2K **Privately Held**
SIC: 2099 5149 Pasta, uncooked: packaged with other ingredients; groceries & related products

(G-9903)
DUROL LABORATORIES LLC
Also Called: Durol Cosmetic Laboratories
5 Knight Ln (06516-2940)
PHONE.................................866 611-9694
Ade Aminu, *CEO*
EMP: 10 EST: 2010
SQ FT: 11,000
SALES (est): 720K **Privately Held**
SIC: 2844 Face creams or lotions

(G-9904)
E O MANUFACTURING COMPANY INC
474 Frontage Rd (06516-4154)
PHONE.................................203 932-5981
Peter Lemere Jr, *President*
EMP: 23 EST: 1945
SQ FT: 8,748
SALES: 1MM **Privately Held**
SIC: 3599 Machine shop, jobbing & repair

(G-9905)
E&D LANDSCAPING
91 Cynthia Dr (06516-2907)
PHONE.................................203 934-4088
Don Hurley, *Partner*
EMP: 3
SALES (est): 195.2K **Privately Held**
SIC: 0781 0782 3444 1799 Landscape services; landscape contractors; mail chutes, sheet metal; fence construction

(G-9906)
ERA WIRE INC
19 Locust St (06516-2022)
PHONE.................................203 933-0480
Richard T Rae, *President*
Katherine Rae, *Vice Pres*
EMP: 11
SQ FT: 5,000
SALES (est): 2MM **Privately Held**
WEB: www.erawire.com
SIC: 3496 Miscellaneous fabricated wire products

(G-9907)
FAGAN DESIGN & FABRICATION
44 Railroad Ave (06516-4132)
PHONE.................................203 937-1874
Jay Fagan, *President*
Lisa Spetrini, *Office Mgr*
EMP: 4
SQ FT: 20,000
SALES (est): 600K **Privately Held**
SIC: 2431 2499 Ornamental woodwork: cornices, mantels, etc.; porch columns, wood; carved & turned wood

(G-9908)
FED RUSSELL LLC
Also Called: Rockhouse
52 Collis St (06516-3505)
PHONE.................................203 934-2501
John McCarthy, *Software Dev*
Curtis Moye, *Director*
Joe Palombo,
EMP: 3
SALES: 1.5MM **Privately Held**
SIC: 7812 2721 Video production; magazines: publishing only, not printed on site

(G-9909)
FIRE & IRON
298 Platt Ave (06516-4837)
PHONE.................................203 934-3756
EMP: 3
SALES (est): 130K **Privately Held**
SIC: 3842 Mfg Surgical Appliances/Supplies

(G-9910)
FUSION MEDICAL CORPORATION
44 Church St (06516-4927)
PHONE.................................860 906-7856
Wayne Conwin, *CEO*
EMP: 2 EST: 2007
SQ FT: 1,000
SALES (est): 150.7K **Privately Held**
SIC: 3841 Bone plates & screws

(G-9911)
GENALCO INC
44 W Clark St (06516-3541)
PHONE.................................203 932-5991
EMP: 2
SALES (est): 85.6K **Privately Held**
SIC: 3494 Valves & pipe fittings

(G-9912)
GHP MEDIA INC (PA)
475 Heffernan Dr (06516-4151)
PHONE.................................203 479-7500
John Robinson, *CEO*
Fred Hoxsie, *Managing Prtnr*
Scott Carter, *Exec VP*
Marc Server, *Vice Pres*
Dave Sweet, *Vice Pres*
EMP: 109
SQ FT: 11,000
SALES (est): 21.2MM **Privately Held**
WEB: www.gist-image.com
SIC: 2752 2796 Commercial printing, offset; color separations for printing

(G-9913)
GNGWOODWORKING
39 Carlson Rd (06516-2902)
PHONE.................................203 996-5255
Diane E Gray, *Principal*
EMP: 2
SALES (est): 137.3K **Privately Held**
SIC: 2431 Millwork

(G-9914)
HARBISONWALKER INTL INC
163 Boston Post Rd (06516-2038)
PHONE.................................203 934-7960
Robert Murray, *Branch Mgr*
EMP: 4
SALES (corp-wide): 703.8MM **Privately Held**
WEB: www.hwr.com
SIC: 3255 Clay refractories
HQ: Harbisonwalker International, Inc.
    1305 Cherrington Pkwy # 100
    Moon Township PA 15108

(G-9915)
HOLLUMS SHEET METAL LLC
47 Dana St (06516-2710)
PHONE.................................203 640-4970
Tony Hollums, *Principal*
EMP: 1
SALES (est): 82.7K **Privately Held**
SIC: 3444 Sheet metalwork

(G-9916)
IMANI MAGAZINE/FMI
15 Boylston St (06516-3383)
PHONE.................................203 809-2565
Corrine Thomas, *Principal*
EMP: 3
SALES (est): 161.7K **Privately Held**
SIC: 2721 Periodicals

(G-9917)
J G M WOODWORKS
190 Jaffrey St (06516-2218)
PHONE.................................203 934-3726
EMP: 1
SALES (est): 54.1K **Privately Held**
SIC: 2431 Millwork

(G-9918)
JLC INDUSTRIES
362 2nd Ave (06516-5134)
PHONE.................................315 761-8051
John Mitchell, *Principal*
EMP: 1 EST: 2018
SALES (est): 39.6K **Privately Held**
SIC: 3999 Manufacturing industries

(G-9919)
JMK TOOL CO
184 Forest Rd (06516-1301)
P.O. Box 26496 (06516-0959)
PHONE.................................203 937-1229
Joseph Kalocsai, *Owner*
Maria Kalocsai, *Co-Owner*
EMP: 2
SALES (est): 155.6K **Privately Held**
SIC: 3728 Aircraft parts & equipment

(G-9920)
JUPITER COMMUNICATIONS LLC
755 1st Ave (06516-2712)
PHONE.................................475 238-7082
Ethan Odin, *Mng Member*
Rose Mannon, *Admin Sec*
EMP: 12
SQ FT: 16,000
SALES (est): 3.9MM **Privately Held**
WEB: www.jupitercommunications.net
SIC: 2752 2791 Commercial printing, offset; typesetting, computer controlled

(G-9921)
JUST CALL JASON LLC
44 Tyler St (06516-6822)
PHONE.................................203 934-3127
Jason Valdivieso,
EMP: 1
SALES (est): 65K **Privately Held**
WEB: www.justcalljason.net
SIC: 7694 Electric motor repair

(G-9922)
K & D PRECISION MANUFACTURING
25 High St (06516-2020)
PHONE.................................203 931-9550
David Crowley, *Partner*
Kenneth Rasmussen, *Partner*
EMP: 2
SQ FT: 2,400
SALES: 500K **Privately Held**
SIC: 3612 Specialty transformers

(G-9923)
KEMPER MANUFACTURING CORP
5 Clinton Pl (06516-2808)
PHONE.................................203 934-1600
Cathy Harter, *President*
▲ EMP: 20
SQ FT: 10,000
SALES (est): 2.4MM **Privately Held**
WEB: www.straplady.com
SIC: 2399 Belting & belt products

(G-9924)
KRAMER PRINTING COMPANY INC
270 Front Ave (06516-2800)
PHONE.................................203 933-5416
Richard Kramer, *President*
Don Schmitz, *Manager*
Ilene J Kramer, *Director*
Marcy Kramer-Ide, *Admin Sec*
EMP: 13
SQ FT: 7,800
SALES: 700K **Privately Held**
SIC: 2752 2759 Commercial printing, offset; promotional printing

(G-9925)
KX TECHNOLOGIES LLC (DH)
55 Railroad Ave (06516-4143)
PHONE.................................203 799-9000
John J Goody, *Mng Member*
Bruce R Belcher,
Frank A Brigano PHD,
Leon R Drake II,
▲ EMP: 12
SQ FT: 67,000
SALES (est): 27.8MM
SALES (corp-wide): 225.3B **Publicly Held**
SIC: 3589 Water purification equipment, household type; water filters & softeners, household type

(G-9926)
LIGHT FANTASTIC REALTY INC
Also Called: Fraqtir
114 Boston Post Rd (06516-2043)
PHONE.................................203 934-3441
Allison K Schieffelin, *CEO*
David R Pfund, *President*
Suzanne Carroll, *Exec VP*
Joseph R Zaharewicz, *Vice Pres*
Cynthia Hoboken, *CFO*
▲ EMP: 125
SQ FT: 100,000
SALES (est): 16.3MM **Privately Held**
WEB: www.elliptipar.com
SIC: 3647 3645 Dome lights, automotive; residential lighting fixtures

(G-9927)
M & S MACHINE TOOL COMPANY
744 Washington Ave Ste 8 (06516-3797)
PHONE.................................203 933-8920
Michael Bramwell, *President*
Frank Bramwell, *Admin Sec*
EMP: 2
SQ FT: 5,000
SALES (est): 372.4K **Privately Held**
SIC: 3728 Aircraft parts & equipment

(G-9928)
MACDERMID ENTHONE INC (HQ)
350 Frontage Rd (06516-4130)
PHONE.................................203 934-8611
Scott Benson, *President*
Emmanuel Colchen, *President*
Hector Grimes, *General Mgr*
Bob Haskins, *Vice Pres*
Pingping Ye, *Research*
◆ EMP: 158
SALES (est): 152MM
SALES (corp-wide): 1.9B **Publicly Held**
WEB: www.enthone.com
SIC: 2899 Chemical preparations
PA: Element Solutions Inc
    1450 Centrepark Blvd # 210
    West Palm Beach FL 33401
    561 207-9600

(G-9929)
MAD SPORTSWEAR LLC
100 Putney Dr (06516-2931)
PHONE.................................203 932-4868
David Ruotolo,
Anthony Mantone,
Michael Volpe,
EMP: 3
SQ FT: 3,000
SALES (est): 154.9K **Privately Held**
WEB: www.madsportswear.com
SIC: 2395 2759 Embroidery & art needlework; screen printing

(G-9930)
MANUFACTURERS ASSOCIATES INC
45 Railroad Ave (06516-4143)
P.O. Box 4419, Hamden (06514-0419)
PHONE.................................203 931-4344
Lonnie Parillo, *President*
EMP: 20
SQ FT: 25,000
SALES: 1.8MM **Privately Held**
SIC: 3451 Screw machine products

(G-9931)
MANUFACTURING ASSISTS
36 Hillside Ave (06516-6706)
PHONE.................................203 934-6574
Joseph Cullen, *Principal*
EMP: 1 EST: 2010
SALES (est): 61.7K **Privately Held**
SIC: 3999 Manufacturing industries

(G-9932)
MAREL CORPORATION
5 Saw Mill Rd (06516-4111)
PHONE.................................203 934-8187
John Rice, *President*
Tim McNeil, *Vice Pres*

West Haven - New Haven County (G-9933)

Elizabeth Rice, *Admin Sec*
EMP: 11
SALES (est): 1.4MM **Privately Held**
SIC: 3841 5047 Surgical & medical instruments; hospital equipment & furniture

(G-9933)
MAX PADRO
Also Called: Sector 1 Defense
13 Cullen Ave (06516-1235)
PHONE..................203 530-0616
Max Padro, *Principal*
EMP: 1 **EST:** 2017
SALES (est): 69.9K **Privately Held**
SIC: 3812 Defense systems & equipment

(G-9934)
MB SOFTWARE DEVELOPMENT
109 Coleman St (06516-3241)
PHONE..................203 928-0436
EMP: 2 **EST:** 2011
SALES (est): 110K **Privately Held**
SIC: 7372 Prepackaged Software Services

(G-9935)
MCNEIL HEALTHCARE INC
5 Saw Mill Rd (06516-4111)
PHONE..................203 934-8187
Tim McNeil, *President*
EMP: 3
SALES (est): 14.2K **Privately Held**
SIC: 3842 Surgical appliances & supplies

(G-9936)
METRO SIGNS LLC
912 Boston Post Rd (06516-1838)
PHONE..................203 933-0333
Bashir Hussain, *Principal*
EMP: 1
SALES (est): 109K **Privately Held**
SIC: 3993 Signs & advertising specialties

(G-9937)
MICHAEL VIOLANO
Also Called: Vio's Sport Shack West Haven
487 Campbell Ave (06516-5018)
PHONE..................203 934-3368
Michael Violano, *Owner*
EMP: 5
SQ FT: 2,800
SALES (est): 343.4K **Privately Held**
SIC: 5699 5136 5137 2396 Sports apparel; uniforms & work clothing; sportswear, men's & boys'; sportswear, women's & children's; screen printing on fabric articles; embroidery products, except schiffli machine

(G-9938)
MORTON WOOD WORKS
362 2nd Ave (06516-5134)
PHONE..................203 594-6678
EMP: 2 **EST:** 2017
SALES (est): 84.3K **Privately Held**
SIC: 2431 Millwork

(G-9939)
NEW ENGLAND NONWOVENS LLC
283 Dogburn Rd (06516)
PHONE..................203 891-0851
John Guchmanowicz, *Mng Member*
Alan Lapoint,
EMP: 19 **EST:** 2008
SALES (est): 4MM **Privately Held**
SIC: 2297 Nonwoven fabrics

(G-9940)
O BERK COMPANY NENG LLC
300 Callegari Dr (06516-6255)
PHONE..................203 932-8000
Marc Gaelen, *President*
Brenda Evans, *Vice Pres*
Brenda Kursawe,
▲ **EMP:** 10 **EST:** 1933
SALES (est): 4.1MM
SALES (corp-wide): 57.8MM **Privately Held**
SIC: 5085 2759 3999 5047 Bottler supplies; crowns & closures, metal; plastic bottles; screen printing; gold stamping, except books; hospital equipment & supplies
PA: The O Berk Company L L C
3 Milltown Ct
Union NJ 07083
800 631-7392

(G-9941)
OMI INTERNATIONAL CORPORATION
350 Frontage Rd (06516-4130)
PHONE..................203 575-5727
EMP: 4
SALES (est): 209.5K
SALES (corp-wide): 1.9B **Publicly Held**
SIC: 2899 Chemical preparations
PA: Element Solutions Inc
1450 Centrepark Blvd # 210
West Palm Beach FL 33401
561 207-9600

(G-9942)
PANAGRAFIX INC
Also Called: USA Notepads
50 Fresh Meadow Rd (06516-1445)
PHONE..................203 691-5529
EMP: 28
SALES (corp-wide): 3.8MM **Privately Held**
SIC: 2678 Tablets & pads, book & writing: from purchased materials
PA: Panagrafix, Inc.
75 Cascade Blvd
Milford CT

(G-9943)
PANZA WOODWORK & SUPPLY LLC
4 Hugo St (06516-1308)
PHONE..................203 934-3430
John Panza, *Principal*
Ed Panza,
EMP: 5 **EST:** 1994
SQ FT: 2,700
SALES (est): 550K **Privately Held**
SIC: 3429 Furniture builders' & other household hardware

(G-9944)
PINPOINT PROMOTIONS & PRTG LLC
45 Railroad Ave (06516-4143)
PHONE..................203 301-4273
Steve Gentile, *Managing Prtnr*
Jillian Putterman, *Project Mgr*
Stan Martinez, *Production*
EMP: 17
SALES (est): 3MM **Privately Held**
SIC: 2752 Commercial printing, lithographic

(G-9945)
POCKET PARKS PUBLISHING LLC
116 Cherry Ln (06516-5600)
PHONE..................203 499-7416
Rosemary O'Brien,
EMP: 1 **EST:** 2013
SALES (est): 48.9K **Privately Held**
SIC: 2741 2731 Miscellaneous publishing; books: publishing & printing

(G-9946)
POLYMER FILMS INC
301 Heffernan Dr (06516-4151)
PHONE..................203 932-3000
John Watson, *President*
Mary Watson, *Corp Secy*
Tom Tchang, *Vice Pres*
Robert Watson, *Vice Pres*
James Watson, *CFO*
EMP: 25 **EST:** 1963
SQ FT: 88,000
SALES (est): 271.1K **Privately Held**
WEB: www.watsonfoods.com
SIC: 3081 2671 Plastic film & sheet; packaging paper & plastics film, coated & laminated

(G-9947)
PRO-TECH ENTERPRISES LLC
375 Morgan Ln Ste 102 (06516-4158)
P.O. Box 26172 (06516-0961)
PHONE..................203 931-9668
Jenny Tsao, *Principal*
▲ **EMP:** 2 **EST:** 1995
SALES (est): 300.2K **Privately Held**
SIC: 3562 Ball & roller bearings

(G-9948)
PROIRON LLC
1 Calgery Dr (06516)
PHONE..................203 934-7967
James Charbonneau, *General Mgr*
Stephanie Siclari, *Vice Pres*
Mary F Charbonneau,
EMP: 4
SALES (est): 698.7K **Privately Held**
SIC: 3542 Metal deposit forming machines

(G-9949)
ROBERT KENNETH ANDRADE LLC
975 Campbell Ave (06516-2707)
PHONE..................203 937-8697
Robert B Andrade, *Manager*
Robert Andrade, *Manager*
EMP: 2
SALES (est): 125K **Privately Held**
SIC: 3713 Automobile wrecker truck bodies

(G-9950)
ROSS COPY & PRINT LLC
611 Campbell Ave (06516-4481)
PHONE..................203 933-8732
Raymond Ross,
EMP: 2
SQ FT: 1,200
SALES (est): 274.1K **Privately Held**
SIC: 2752 5943 Commercial printing, offset; office forms & supplies

(G-9951)
SABATINO NORTH AMERICA LLC (PA)
Also Called: Speedy Food Group USA
135 Front Ave (06516-2811)
PHONE..................718 328-4120
Vincent Jeanseaume, *Vice Pres*
Vincent Gentile, *Regl Sales Mgr*
Federico Balestra,
▲ **EMP:** 25
SQ FT: 42,000
SALES (est): 13.6MM **Privately Held**
SIC: 2033 Mushrooms: packaged in cans, jars, etc.

(G-9952)
SAVIN ROCK PRINTING
145 Boston Post Rd (06516-2026)
PHONE..................203 500-1577
EMP: 2
SALES (est): 92.3K **Privately Held**
SIC: 2752 Commercial printing, lithographic

(G-9953)
SCHRAFEL PAPERBOARD CONVERTING
82 W Clark St Ste 1 (06516-3559)
PHONE..................203 931-1700
Richard B Schrafel, *President*
Robert A Schrafel, *Corp Secy*
Robert Schrafel, *Treasurer*
Joseph Vece, *Sales Executive*
Diane Wilson, *Manager*
EMP: 25
SQ FT: 101,000
SALES (est): 4.8MM **Privately Held**
SIC: 2679 2631 Paperboard products, converted; paperboard mills

(G-9954)
SHAGMEISTERS ENTERPRISES
94 4th Ave (06516-3742)
PHONE..................203 937-5584
EMP: 2
SALES (est): 56.5K **Privately Held**
SIC: 7372 Prepackaged software

(G-9955)
SKIN & CO NORTH AMERICA LLC
135 Front Ave (06516-2811)
PHONE..................888 444-9771
Federico Balestra,
Guido Balestra,
Marina Balestra,
EMP: 2
SALES (est): 107.7K **Privately Held**
SIC: 2844 2836 7389 Face creams or lotions; suntan lotions & oils; serums; cosmetic kits, assembling & packaging

(G-9956)
SUBURBAN VOICES PUBLISHING LLC
Also Called: West Haven Voice
840 Boston Post Rd Ste 2 (06516-1848)
PHONE..................203 934-6397
William Riccio, *President*
Maurizio Girotto, *Prdtn Mgr*
EMP: 4
SALES (est): 100K **Privately Held**
WEB: www.whvoice.com
SIC: 2711 Newspapers, publishing & printing

(G-9957)
SYLVAN R SHEMITZ DESIGNS LLC
Also Called: Lighting Quotient, The
114 Boston Post Rd (06516-2043)
PHONE..................203 934-3441
Allison K Schieffelin, *President*
Emily Tkach, *Materials Mgr*
Eric Henault, *Engineer*
Ken Pask, *Design Engr*
Cindy Hoboken, *CFO*
▲ **EMP:** 102 **EST:** 2014
SALES (est): 22MM **Privately Held**
SIC: 3646 Commercial indusl & institutional electric lighting fixtures

(G-9958)
THERACOUR PHARMA INC
135 Wood St Ste 8 (06516-3700)
PHONE..................203 937-6137
Anil Diwan, *President*
EMP: 2
SALES (est): 88.3K **Privately Held**
SIC: 2834 Pharmaceutical preparations

(G-9959)
THERMAXX LLC (PA)
14 Farwell St (06516-1717)
PHONE..................203 672-1021
Mike Bannon, *Mng Member*
EMP: 7
SALES (est): 60.5K **Privately Held**
SIC: 3443 Jackets, industrial: metal plate

(G-9960)
WATSON LLC (DH)
301 Heffernan Dr (06516-4151)
PHONE..................203 932-3000
James Watson, *President*
Gavin Watson, *COO*
Moira Watson, *Vice Pres*
Gary Wada, *Prdtn Mgr*
Delyan Ivanov, *Purch Mgr*
◆ **EMP:** 277
SQ FT: 220,000
SALES (est): 76.1MM **Privately Held**
SIC: 2045 2833 2087 2051 Prepared flour mixes & doughs; vitamins, natural or synthetic: bulk, uncompounded; flavoring extracts & syrups; bread, cake & related products

(G-9961)
WELCH MATERIALS INC
334 Main St (06516-4423)
PHONE..................203 691-1721
Gloria Shao, *President*
EMP: 1
SALES (est): 64.3K **Privately Held**
SIC: 3826 Chromatographic equipment, laboratory type

(G-9962)
WEST HAVEN TOOL & MFG LLC
Also Called: West Haven Tool & Mfg
1 Hart St (06516-3847)
PHONE..................203 932-1735
Darren Smith,
Robert Smith,
EMP: 2
SQ FT: 2,500
SALES (est): 301K **Privately Held**
SIC: 3544 Special dies, tools, jigs & fixtures

GEOGRAPHIC SECTION

Westbrook - Middlesex County (G-9994)

(G-9963)
WEST MONT GROUP
14 Gilbert St Ste 202 (06516-1639)
PHONE..................................203 931-1033
Jeff Carter, *Owner*
EMP: 6
SALES (est): 408.2K **Privately Held**
SIC: 2434 7389 Wood kitchen cabinets; design services

(G-9964)
WESTMOUNT GROUP LLC
14b Gilbert St M202 (06516)
PHONE..................................203 931-1033
Jeffrey H Carter, *Principal*
EMP: 5
SALES (est): 539.1K **Privately Held**
SIC: 2599 Cabinets, factory

(G-9965)
WHHS B WING ELEVATOR ✪
1 Circle St (06516-5256)
PHONE..................................203 288-5949
EMP: 2 EST: 2019
SALES (est): 83.9K **Privately Held**
SIC: 2752 Commercial printing, lithographic

(G-9966)
WOODLAND POWER PRODUCTS INC
72 Acton St (06516-1704)
PHONE..................................888 531-7253
James C Whitney PHD, *President*
Matthew Coz, *General Mgr*
Ethan Hershman, *Vice Pres*
Dave Troop, *Mfg Mgr*
Kenneth Rowe, *Accounts Mgr*
▲ EMP: 25
SQ FT: 15,000
SALES (est): 9.4MM **Privately Held**
WEB: www.cyclonerake.com
SIC: 3524 Lawn & garden equipment

(G-9967)
YOLANDA DUBOSE RECORDS AND
105 W Prospect St (06516-3540)
P.O. Box 5034, Milford (06460-1434)
PHONE..................................203 823-6699
Yolanda Dubose, *Mng Member*
EMP: 10
SALES (est): 275K **Privately Held**
SIC: 2782 7929 7389 Record albums; entertainment service;

(G-9968)
YOURLIGHTINGSOURCE CO LLC
17 Ivy St (06516-5741)
PHONE..................................917 439-6501
Joseph Trerotola, *Principal*
EMP: 1 EST: 2008
SALES (est): 91.5K **Privately Held**
SIC: 3648 Lighting equipment

West Redding
Fairfield County

(G-9969)
ESTEN MCGEE INC
4 Old Mill Rd (06896-3204)
PHONE..................................203 544-2000
Timothy Bogelman, *Principal*
EMP: 1
SALES (est): 9K **Privately Held**
SIC: 2679 Paper products, converted

(G-9970)
PARKHILL PUBLISHING LLC
32 Drummer Ln (06896-1414)
PHONE..................................203 938-9199
EMP: 2
SALES (est): 86K **Privately Held**
SIC: 2741 Misc Publishing

West Simsbury
Hartford County

(G-9971)
AD EMBROIDERY LLC
350 W Mountain Rd (06092-2913)
PHONE..................................860 651-4410
EMP: 1
SALES (est): 56.5K **Privately Held**
SIC: 2395 Embroidery & art needlework

(G-9972)
BELO WOODWORKING LLC
53 W Mountain Rd (06092-2306)
PHONE..................................727 249-8514
Frank Belo, *Owner*
EMP: 1
SALES (est): 54.1K **Privately Held**
SIC: 2431 Millwork

(G-9973)
BWD PUBLISHING LLC
11 Roswell Rd (06092-2816)
PHONE..................................860 651-1966
Bruce Deckert, *Principal*
EMP: 1
SALES (est): 37.5K **Privately Held**
SIC: 2741 Miscellaneous publishing

(G-9974)
CLEAR & SIMPLE INC
5 Notch Rd (06092-2710)
PHONE..................................860 658-1204
Tony Pereira, *President*
Anthony Pereira III, *Vice Pres*
EMP: 3
SALES (est): 209K **Privately Held**
WEB: www.clear-simple.com
SIC: 7371 7379 2731 Computer software development; computer related consulting services; books: publishing only

(G-9975)
CRAIG DASCANIO
Also Called: Windfall Woodworking
250 Farms Village Rd Rear (06092-2407)
P.O. Box 344 (06092-0344)
PHONE..................................860 651-0466
Craig Dascanio, *Owner*
EMP: 1
SQ FT: 3,000
SALES (est): 109.8K **Privately Held**
SIC: 2511 2512 5712 Wood household furniture; upholstered household furniture; custom made furniture, except cabinets

(G-9976)
CTL CORPORATION
10 Rocklyn Ct (06092-2623)
PHONE..................................860 651-9173
Carl Fink, *President*
Lynn Fink, *Chairman*
EMP: 4
SALES (est): 363.2K **Privately Held**
WEB: www.glovebags.com
SIC: 3842 Clothing, fire resistant & protective

(G-9977)
D E SIRMAN SPECIALTY COMPANY
111 Westledge Rd (06092-2011)
PHONE..................................860 658-6336
Dave E Sirman, *Owner*
EMP: 1
SALES (est): 63.1K **Privately Held**
SIC: 3999 Identification badges & insignia

(G-9978)
DAVENPORT KITCHEN & BATH LLC
20 Mountain View Rd (06092)
P.O. Box 601 (06092-0601)
PHONE..................................860 323-0630
Andrew Davenport,
EMP: 1
SALES (est): 105.6K **Privately Held**
SIC: 2499 Kitchen, bathroom & household ware: wood

(G-9979)
EDMUND PRICE
78 Woodchuck Hill Rd (06092-2321)
PHONE..................................860 658-1441
Edmund Price, *Owner*
EMP: 1
SALES (est): 124.4K **Privately Held**
SIC: 2421 Cut stock, softwood

(G-9980)
MCCANN SALES INC
9 Case Cir (06092-2201)
P.O. Box 280 (06092-0280)
PHONE..................................860 614-0992
Michael J Cellerino, *President*
EMP: 1
SALES (est): 153.6K **Privately Held**
SIC: 3312 3363 Structural shapes & pilings, steel; aluminum die-castings

(G-9981)
MEDPIPES
19 Drumlin Rd (06092-2909)
PHONE..................................860 658-7300
Peter Gensheimer, *Principal*
EMP: 2
SALES (est): 122.8K **Privately Held**
WEB: www.medpipes.com
SIC: 7372 Prepackaged software

(G-9982)
SEASONS MEDIA LLC
6 Sharlin Dr (06092-2712)
P.O. Box 92 (06092-0092)
PHONE..................................860 413-2022
James P Tully,
EMP: 1
SALES: 400K **Privately Held**
SIC: 2721 7389 Magazines: publishing only, not printed on site;

(G-9983)
SUMMIT ATELIER
2 Old Stone Xing (06092-2821)
PHONE..................................646 284-0304
Brewse Monier-Williams, *Principal*
EMP: 2
SALES (est): 135.6K **Privately Held**
SIC: 2431 Millwork

(G-9984)
WARREN WOODWORKING LLC
31 Canton Rd (06092-2806)
PHONE..................................860 408-0030
Christopher Warren, *Principal*
EMP: 2
SALES (est): 143.9K **Privately Held**
SIC: 2431 Millwork

West Suffield
Hartford County

(G-9985)
CASE ASSOCIATION
2750 Mountain Rd (06093-3110)
PHONE..................................860 989-6533
Rebecca Morris, *President*
EMP: 2 EST: 2017
SALES (est): 85.9K **Privately Held**
SIC: 3523 Farm machinery & equipment

(G-9986)
DEBBIE PILEIKA INTERIORS
30 Chestnut Cir (06093-2102)
PHONE..................................860 668-6324
Debbie Pileika, *Owner*
EMP: 1
SALES (est): 87.9K **Privately Held**
SIC: 2591 Window shades

(G-9987)
LADY AND THE LEOPARD
935 N Grand St (06093-2503)
PHONE..................................413 531-4811
Solveig Pflueger MD, *Owner*
EMP: 1
SALES (est): 64.3K **Privately Held**
SIC: 2335 5699 Dresses, paper: cut & sewn; costumes, masquerade or theatrical

(G-9988)
ONSITE MAMMOGRAPHY
70 Sunset Dr (06093-2135)
PHONE..................................860 254-5097
Carl Schmidt, *CEO*
EMP: 2
SALES (est): 174K **Privately Held**
SIC: 3829 Medical diagnostic systems, nuclear

Westbrook
Middlesex County

(G-9989)
AGW CLSSIC HARDWOOD FLOORS LLC
1871 Boston Post Rd (06498-2183)
PHONE..................................203 640-3106
Jeannine Veinot Amendola,
Armand Amendola,
EMP: 21
SALES (est): 1.2MM **Privately Held**
SIC: 1751 1752 2499 5713 Carpentry work; wood floor installation & refinishing; decorative wood & woodwork; floor covering stores

(G-9990)
AIUDI CONCRETE INC
129 Norris Ave (06498)
PHONE..................................860 399-9289
Elmo Aiudi, *President*
EMP: 8
SQ FT: 1,939
SALES (est): 1.4MM **Privately Held**
WEB: www.aiudiconcrete.com
SIC: 3273 Ready-mixed concrete

(G-9991)
ATLANTIC OUTBOARD INC
475 Boston Post Rd (06498-1783)
P.O. Box 55 (06498-0055)
PHONE..................................860 399-6773
Paul Cusson, *President*
Brittany Friel, *Sales Associate*
Dave Steele, *Manager*
Gina Trasacco, *Office Admin*
Bob Charrette, *Master*
EMP: 5
SQ FT: 5,000
SALES (est): 1.1MM **Privately Held**
WEB: www.atlanticoutboard.com
SIC: 7699 5551 3519 Boat repair; outboard boats; marine engines

(G-9992)
B&D INDUSTRIES LLC
157 Lttle Stannard Bch Rd (06498-2003)
PHONE..................................860 604-2404
Francene Barrett, *Principal*
EMP: 1
SALES (est): 55.1K **Privately Held**
SIC: 3999 Atomizers, toiletry

(G-9993)
CHERYL AIUDI & SON LLC
58 Sagamore Terrace Rd (06498-2124)
PHONE..................................860 575-8462
Cheryl Aiudi Cook, *Mng Member*
EMP: 2
SALES (est): 132.6K **Privately Held**
SIC: 3433 Heaters, swimming pool: oil or gas

(G-9994)
CLINTON NURSERY PRODUCTS INC (PA)
517 Pond Meadow Rd (06498-1493)
P.O. Box 679 (06498-0679)
PHONE..................................860 399-3000
David Richards, *President*
Warren Richards Jr, *Chairman*
Peter Richards, *Vice Pres*
Jim Galvin, *CFO*
EMP: 250
SQ FT: 50,000
SALES: 45MM **Privately Held**
SIC: 5191 2879 5193 2875 Fertilizer & fertilizer materials; soil, potting & planting; agricultural chemicals; nursery stock; potting soil, mixed

Westbrook - Middlesex County (G-9995)

(G-9995)
EASTERN UTILITY PRODUCTS LLC
246 Toby Hill Rd (06498-3521)
PHONE..................................860 399-1724
Mike Hugrue, *Principal*
Mike Shugrue,
EMP: 1
SALES (est): 97.7K **Privately Held**
SIC: 5074 3824 Boilers, power (industrial); fluid meters & counting devices

(G-9996)
ENTEREX AMERICA LLC
2046 Boston Post Rd Ste 2 (06498-2188)
PHONE..................................860 661-4635
John Kolb,
▲ EMP: 2
SQ FT: 20,000
SALES (est): 227.3K
SALES (corp-wide): 41.9MM **Privately Held**
SIC: 3433 3585 Radiators, except electric; air conditioning equipment, complete; air conditioning units, complete: domestic or industrial; air conditioning, motor vehicle
PA: Yangzhou Enterex Industrial Co., Ltd.
No.5,Jinyuan Rd,Guangling Dist.,
Yangzhou 22500
514 877-8218

(G-9997)
GARDEN IRON LLC
47 Westbrook Indust Pk Rd (06498-1524)
PHONE..................................860 767-9917
Christopher R Anderson,
EMP: 7
SALES (est): 848K **Privately Held**
WEB: www.gardeniron.com
SIC: 1799 3446 Ornamental metal work; ornamental metalwork

(G-9998)
INNOPHASE CORP
18 Sea Scape Dr (06498-1969)
P.O. Box 755 (06498-0755)
PHONE..................................860 399-2269
Allen Brownstein, *President*
Amy N Amenta, *Manager*
EMP: 3
SALES: 100K **Privately Held**
SIC: 2819 8732 8999 Industrial inorganic chemicals; research services, except laboratory; chemical consultant

(G-9999)
KEELINGS
1566 Boston Post Rd (06498-2045)
PHONE..................................860 399-4527
EMP: 1
SALES (est): 56K **Privately Held**
SIC: 3645 Residential Lighting Fixtures

(G-10000)
LEE COMPANY (PA)
2 Pettipaug Rd (06498-1500)
P.O. Box 424 (06498-0424)
PHONE..................................860 399-6281
William W Lee, *President*
Leighton Lee III, *Chairman*
Jeff Svadlenak, *District Mgr*
Robert M Lee, *Exec VP*
Thomas Lee, *Exec VP*
▲ EMP: 775 EST: 1949
SQ FT: 365,000
SALES: 207.5MM **Privately Held**
WEB: www.eeco.com
SIC: 3823 3841 3812 3728 Fluidic devices, circuits & systems for process control; surgical & medical instruments; search & navigation equipment; aircraft parts & equipment; motor vehicle parts & accessories

(G-10001)
LEE COMPANY
22 Pequot Park Rd (06498-1466)
PHONE..................................860 399-6281
Mark Raasch, *Mfg Spvr*
Steve Hanssen, *Senior Buyer*
Robert Merrick, *Chief Engr*
Ed Jones, *Branch Mgr*
EMP: 20
SALES (corp-wide): 207.5MM **Privately Held**
SIC: 3823 Industrial instrmnts msrmnt display/control process variable
PA: The Lee Company
2 Pettipaug Rd
Westbrook CT 06498
860 399-6281

(G-10002)
LIBERTY SERVICES LLC
Also Called: Canvas and Sail Repair Company
790 Boston Post Rd (06498-2189)
PHONE..................................860 399-0077
Billy Liberty, *Manager*
Debbie Liberty,
EMP: 4
SALES (est): 379.8K **Privately Held**
SIC: 2394 Sails: made from purchased materials

(G-10003)
MARGARET WITHAM
Also Called: Lighthouse Signs
662 Boston Post Rd (06498-1877)
PHONE..................................860 399-6403
Margaret Witham, *Owner*
Tucker Reynolds, *Co-Owner*
EMP: 2
SQ FT: 4,000
SALES: 200K **Privately Held**
SIC: 3993 Signs & advertising specialties

(G-10004)
MEADE DAILY GROUP LLC
103 Cold Spring Dr (06498-3511)
PHONE..................................860 399-7342
Eileen M Daily, *Manager*
EMP: 3
SALES (est): 116.8K **Privately Held**
SIC: 2711 Newspapers, publishing & printing

(G-10005)
PURFX INC
51 Brookwood Dr (06498-1576)
P.O. Box 227 (06498-0227)
PHONE..................................860 399-4045
Arno Utegg, *President*
EMP: 3
SALES: 2.4MM **Privately Held**
SIC: 3677 Filtration devices, electronic

(G-10006)
RA SENFT INC
159 Wesley Ave (06498-1842)
PHONE..................................860 399-5967
Vivian Senft, *President*
Richard A Senft, *President*
EMP: 2
SQ FT: 4,000
SALES: 40K **Privately Held**
SIC: 3599 7538 7539 Machine shop, jobbing & repair; engine rebuilding: automotive; machine shop, automotive

(G-10007)
SCRAPBOOK CLUBHOUSE
20 Westbrook Pl (06498-3902)
PHONE..................................860 399-4443
Sharon Cooke, *Owner*
EMP: 10
SALES (est): 659.5K **Privately Held**
SIC: 2782 Scrapbooks

(G-10008)
SHORELINE BOILER & WELDING LLC
43 Pepperidge Ave (06498-1941)
PHONE..................................860 575-0944
William Delorenze, *Principal*
EMP: 4
SALES (est): 104.2K **Privately Held**
SIC: 7699 7692 Boiler repair shop; welding repair

(G-10009)
SOUND YACHTS LLC
333 Boston Post Rd Fl 2 (06498-1748)
PHONE..................................860 399-8800
EMP: 1
SALES (est): 54.6K **Privately Held**
SIC: 3732 Yachts, building & repairing

(G-10010)
SSHC INC
Also Called: Solid State Heating
1244 Old Clinton Rd (06498-1871)
P.O. Box 769, Old Saybrook (06475-0769)
PHONE..................................860 399-5434
Richard Watson, *President*
Susan Watson, *Vice Pres*
William C Bieluch Jr, *Admin Sec*
EMP: 15
SALES (est): 3MM **Privately Held**
WEB: www.heatnow.net
SIC: 3567 1711 Heating units & devices, industrial: electric; plumbing, heating, air-conditioning contractors

(G-10011)
TOPSIDE CANVAS UPHOLSTERY
768 Boston Post Rd (06498-1846)
PHONE..................................860 399-4845
Robert Ramsdell, *President*
Maureen Ramsdell, *President*
EMP: 7
SQ FT: 2,400
SALES: 150K **Privately Held**
SIC: 2394 Canvas & related products

(G-10012)
TRIAD CONCEPTS INC
51 Brookwood Dr (06498-1576)
PHONE..................................860 399-4045
Arno E Utegg Sr, *President*
Linda Willard, *Opers Staff*
EMP: 2
SALES (est): 160.3K **Privately Held**
SIC: 3569 Filters & strainers, pipeline

(G-10013)
VERONICA MATTHEWS MINERALS
287 Hammock Rd N (06498-1744)
P.O. Box 588 (06498-0588)
PHONE..................................860 399-0063
Veronica Matthews, *Owner*
EMP: 2 EST: 1992
SALES (est): 143.6K **Privately Held**
SIC: 1481 Mine & quarry services, non-metallic minerals

(G-10014)
WATERSIDE VENDING LLC
643 Old Clinton Rd (06498-1760)
PHONE..................................860 399-6039
Jill Newberg, *Mng Member*
Richard Newberg Jr,
EMP: 3
SALES: 180K **Privately Held**
SIC: 3581 Automatic vending machines

(G-10015)
WESTBROOK CON BLOCK CO INC
Cold Spring Brook Ind Par (06498)
PHONE..................................860 399-6201
Rose Maksin, *Manager*
EMP: 25
SALES (corp-wide): 3.6MM **Privately Held**
WEB: www.westbrookblock.com
SIC: 3271 Blocks, concrete or cinder: standard
PA: Westbrook Concrete Block Company, Inc.
439 Spencer Plains Rd
Westbrook CT
860 399-6201

Weston
Fairfield County

(G-10016)
360ALUMNI INC
1 Norfield Rd (06883-2111)
PHONE..................................203 253-5860
Christina Balotescu, *CEO*
EMP: 7
SQ FT: 1,200
SALES (est): 328.6K **Privately Held**
SIC: 7372 Prepackaged software

(G-10017)
AMT MICROPURE INC
14 Mountain View Dr (06883-1306)
P.O. Box 904, Georgetown (06829-0904)
PHONE..................................203 226-7938
B Anthony McNulty, *President*
EMP: 3
SALES (est): 28.6K **Privately Held**
SIC: 3556 Food products machinery

(G-10018)
AUTOMOTIVE COOP COUPONING INC
Also Called: Auto Merchandising Depot
27 Cardinal Rd (06883-2448)
PHONE..................................203 227-2722
Peter D Shafer, *President*
Janica Shafer, *Admin Sec*
EMP: 5 EST: 1992
SALES: 1MM **Privately Held**
SIC: 3993 7331 7311 8742 Signs & advertising specialties; direct mail advertising services; advertising agencies; business consultant

(G-10019)
BENENSON FAMILY REALTY LLC
102 Ladder Hill Rd N (06883-1127)
PHONE..................................919 544-7839
EMP: 2
SALES (est): 83.9K **Privately Held**
SIC: 2752 Commercial printing, lithographic

(G-10020)
BLANK CANVAS INTERIORS LLC
73 Norfield Rd (06883-2245)
PHONE..................................203 226-5602
Nancy E Cannon, *Principal*
EMP: 1
SALES (est): 84K **Privately Held**
SIC: 2211 Canvas

(G-10021)
CAPSTAN INC
263 Georgetown Rd (06883-1226)
PHONE..................................508 384-3100
W Macleod Snaith, *President*
EMP: 2
SALES (est): 120.4K **Privately Held**
SIC: 3441 Fabricated structural metal

(G-10022)
CELL NIQUE
12 Old Stage Coach Rd (06883-1908)
P.O. Box 1131 (06883-0131)
PHONE..................................888 417-9343
EMP: 3
SALES (est): 146.7K **Privately Held**
SIC: 2086 Bottled & canned soft drinks

(G-10023)
CREATIVE MEDIA APPLICATIONS
22 Old Orchard Dr (06883-1309)
PHONE..................................203 226-0544
Barbara Stewart, *President*
Daniel Oelsen, *Vice Pres*
Lary Rosenblatt, *Vice Pres*
EMP: 15
SQ FT: 1,500
SALES: 800K **Privately Held**
WEB: www.cmacontent.com
SIC: 2731 Book publishing

(G-10024)
CROCHET AWAY 203
159 Georgetown Rd (06883-1042)
PHONE..................................203 690-7904
Jessica Gecinceis, *Principal*
EMP: 1
SALES (est): 40.9K **Privately Held**
SIC: 2399 Hand woven & crocheted products

(G-10025)
ERNEST FERRARO
2 High Noon Rd (06883-2523)
PHONE..................................914 921-4376
Ernest-Wn-Bced Ferraro, *Administration*
EMP: 1

GEOGRAPHIC SECTION

Westport - Fairfield County (G-10061)

SALES (est): 47K **Privately Held**
SIC: 3949 Sporting & athletic goods

(G-10026)
FEZZA INC
14 Riverfield Dr (06883-2909)
PHONE.................203 222-9721
Andrew Fezza, *President*
Marilyn Fezza, *Vice Pres*
EMP: 2
SALES (est): 120.4K **Privately Held**
SIC: 2321 Men's & boys' furnishings

(G-10027)
HOPEWELL HARMONY LLC
11 Lilac Ln (06883-3032)
PHONE.................203 222-2268
▲ EMP: 2
SALES (est): 100.1K **Privately Held**
SIC: 3999 Beekeepers' supplies

(G-10028)
INSPIRED BRANDS INTL LLC
25 Lords Hwy (06883-1607)
PHONE.................203 722-5629
Robert Micahel Levi, *Mng Member*
EMP: 1
SALES (est): 81.3K **Privately Held**
SIC: 3411 Food & beverage containers

(G-10029)
INSTANT STYLE HOME STAGING
1 Meadowbrook Ln (06883-1008)
PHONE.................203 417-0131
Britt Bast, *Partner*
EMP: 2
SALES (est): 100.1K **Privately Held**
SIC: 2752 Commercial printing, lithographic

(G-10030)
JACOBY
11 Blueberry Hill Rd (06883-2402)
PHONE.................203 227-2220
Douglas Jacoby, *President*
EMP: 1
SALES (est): 37.5K **Privately Held**
SIC: 2741 Miscellaneous publishing

(G-10031)
KISS-U CORPS LLC
Also Called: Kiss-U Tissue
14 Lilac Ln (06883-3008)
PHONE.................203 226-7730
▲ EMP: 1
SALES (est): 130K **Privately Held**
SIC: 2621 2675 Paper Mill Mfg Die-Cut Paper/Paperboard

(G-10032)
LANGNER PRESS LLC
31 Langner Ln (06883-1218)
PHONE.................203 226-7752
Michele Perkins,
EMP: 1
SALES (est): 43.7K **Privately Held**
SIC: 2741 Miscellaneous publishing

(G-10033)
NANCY TENENBAUM FILMS
41 Lyons Plain Rd (06883-2905)
PHONE.................203 221-6830
Nancy Tenenbaum, *Principal*
EMP: 1
SALES (est): 76.9K **Privately Held**
SIC: 3861 Reproduction machines & equipment

(G-10034)
NORTHAST TNNIS PBLICATIONS LLC
17 Walnut Ln (06883-1417)
PHONE.................203 984-1088
Joseph F Watson, *Principal*
EMP: 1
SALES (est): 46.6K **Privately Held**
SIC: 2741 Miscellaneous publishing

(G-10035)
PAUL GAFFNEY
8 Brookwood Ln (06883-1232)
PHONE.................203 221-1249
Paul Gaffney, *Founder*
EMP: 1

SALES (est): 90K **Privately Held**
SIC: 3674 Semiconductors & related devices

(G-10036)
PMC TECHNOLOGIES LLC
31 Glenwood Rd (06883-2310)
PHONE.................203 222-0000
Patrick Chila,
EMP: 7
SALES: 500K **Privately Held**
SIC: 3651 Household audio & video equipment

(G-10037)
PUBLISHING DIMENSIONS LLC
15 Treadwell Ln (06883-1949)
PHONE.................203 856-7716
Ken Brooks,
EMP: 4
SALES (est): 134.2K **Privately Held**
SIC: 2741 Miscellaneous publishing

(G-10038)
PUDDINGSTONE PUBLISHING LLC
163 Weston Rd (06883-2718)
PHONE.................203 454-3939
Rush L Workman, *Principal*
EMP: 1
SALES (est): 53.5K **Privately Held**
SIC: 2741 Miscellaneous publishing

(G-10039)
SAFESTART SYSTEMS LLC
80 Wells Hill Rd (06883-2625)
PHONE.................203 221-0652
Kathleen Lombard, *Vice Pres*
EMP: 2
SALES (est): 267.8K **Privately Held**
WEB: www.safestartsystems.com
SIC: 3625 Relays & industrial controls

(G-10040)
SOUNDVIEW HORIZONS DGTL LDRSHP
26 Soundview Farm (06883-2628)
PHONE.................203 292-0880
Lisa Mainiero Mangini,
EMP: 1
SALES (est): 57.6K **Privately Held**
SIC: 7372 7389 Educational computer software;

(G-10041)
US-MALABAR COMPANY INC
25 Timber Mill Ln (06883-2727)
PHONE.................203 226-1773
Matthew Mathai, *President*
Claudia Young, *Director*
▲ EMP: 6
SALES (est): 484.8K **Privately Held**
SIC: 3365 7389 Aluminum & aluminum-based alloy castings;

(G-10042)
VAN DEUSEN & LEVITT ASSOC INC
14 Wood Hill Rd (06883-1603)
PHONE.................203 445-6244
Glenn C Van Deusen, *President*
EMP: 40
SALES (est): 2.1MM **Privately Held**
SIC: 3953 Irons, marking or branding

(G-10043)
VANILLA POLITICS LLC
203 Godfrey Rd E (06883-1404)
PHONE.................203 221-0895
Paula Zipkis, *Principal*
EMP: 1
SALES (est): 57K **Privately Held**
SIC: 1721 2621 7999 8999 Residential painting; writing paper; yoga instruction; artist

(G-10044)
VERTICAL VENTURES INTL LLC
40 Hackberry Hill Rd (06883-1825)
PHONE.................203 227-1364
J Hough, *Principal*
EMP: 2
SALES (est): 161K **Privately Held**
SIC: 2591 Drapery hardware & blinds & shades

(G-10045)
WEBWRITE PUBLISHING LLC
134 Georgetown Rd (06883-1004)
PHONE.................203 544-9728
Lee Miller, *Principal*
EMP: 1
SALES (est): 75.9K **Privately Held**
SIC: 2741 Miscellaneous publishing

(G-10046)
WMW LLC
13 Scatacook Trl (06883-1312)
P.O. Box 997, Georgetown (06829-0997)
PHONE.................203 227-4992
William McDonough,
EMP: 2
SALES: 30K **Privately Held**
SIC: 3823 Humidity instruments, industrial process type

(G-10047)
WOODS END INC
Also Called: Bee-Commerce.com
11 Lilac Ln (06883-3032)
PHONE.................203 226-6303
Howland Blackiston, *President*
Ed Weiss, *Vice Pres*
EMP: 8
SALES (est): 749.9K **Privately Held**
SIC: 2842 7379 Beeswax, processing of; computer related consulting services

Westport
Fairfield County

(G-10048)
8 TIMES LLC
12 Juniper Rd (06880-2535)
PHONE.................203 227-7575
Keith Lombardo, *Principal*
EMP: 4
SALES (est): 164.3K **Privately Held**
SIC: 2711 Newspapers, publishing & printing

(G-10049)
A-1 GARAGE DOOR CO
Also Called: A-1 Garage Door Specialties
8 Surf Rd (06880-6731)
PHONE.................203 866-6620
EMP: 1 EST: 1972
SALES: 100K **Privately Held**
SIC: 5211 3699 Ret Lumber/Building Materials Mfg Electrical Equipment/Supplies

(G-10050)
AFFICIENCY INC
606 Post Rd E (06880-4540)
PHONE.................718 496-9071
Mark Scafaro, *CEO*
EMP: 2
SALES: 500K **Privately Held**
SIC: 7372 Application computer software

(G-10051)
AIRTIME PUBLISHING INC
191 Post Rd W (06880-4625)
PHONE.................203 454-4773
▲ EMP: 30
SALES (est): 1.9MM **Privately Held**
SIC: 2721 Periodicals-Publishing/Printing

(G-10052)
ALPINE MANAGEMENT GROUP LLC
Also Called: Alpine Art & Mirror
25 Sylvan Rd S Ste B (06880-4637)
PHONE.................954 531-1692
Jeffrey Spitzer, *Mng Member*
EMP: 5 EST: 2011
SALES (est): 294.4K **Privately Held**
SIC: 3999 2499 Framed artwork; picture & mirror frames, wood

(G-10053)
ALSIP ACQUISITION LLC
315 Post Rd W (06880-4739)
PHONE.................203 202-7777
EMP: 2
SALES (est): 98.1K **Privately Held**
SIC: 2672 Mfg Coated/Laminated Paper

(G-10054)
AMERICAN NATURAL SODA ASH CORP (PA)
Also Called: Ansac
15 Riverside Ave Ste 2 (06880-4245)
PHONE.................203 226-9056
John M Andrews, *President*
Janice Osullivan, *President*
Samuel R Blood, *Vice Pres*
Ravi Kuruppu, *Vice Pres*
Daniel Martinez, *Vice Pres*
◆ EMP: 20
SQ FT: 9,000
SALES (est): 49.5MM **Privately Held**
WEB: www.ansac.com
SIC: 1474 Soda ash (natural) mining

(G-10055)
AMERICAN TRADE FAIRS ORG
Also Called: Atfo
250 Main St Ste 101 (06880-2431)
P.O. Box 489 (06881-0489)
PHONE.................203 221-0114
Michael Montanaro, *Partner*
EMP: 3
SALES (est): 137.8K **Privately Held**
SIC: 2741 Miscellaneous publishing

(G-10056)
AMG DEVELOPMENT LLC
1698 Post Rd E (06880-5652)
PHONE.................203 292-8444
Dom L Gatto, *Mng Member*
EMP: 2
SQ FT: 1,200
SALES: 200K **Privately Held**
SIC: 3841 5943 5112 Surgical & medical instruments; stationery stores; office supplies

(G-10057)
ANDREE BROOKS
15 Hitchcock Rd (06880-2630)
PHONE.................203 226-9834
Andree Brooks, *Principal*
EMP: 2
SALES (est): 94K **Privately Held**
SIC: 2731 Book publishing

(G-10058)
ASTRALIS ROCKETRY CORP
4 Davis Ln (06880-4115)
PHONE.................203 254-0427
EMP: 1 EST: 2006
SALES (est): 110K **Privately Held**
SIC: 3724 Mfg Aircraft Engines/Parts

(G-10059)
BAKER GRAPHICS CORPORATION
Also Called: Baker Grphics Reproduction Ctr
1753 Post Rd E (06880-5606)
PHONE.................203 226-6928
Richard Baker, *President*
Marita Baker, *Vice Pres*
EMP: 25
SQ FT: 6,500
SALES (est): 2.5MM **Privately Held**
WEB: www.bakergraphics.net
SIC: 7334 2752 Photocopying & duplicating services; commercial printing, offset

(G-10060)
BB SHADES
Also Called: Beebe Company
62 Hills Ln (06880-2907)
PHONE.................203 849-9345
Cynthia Beebe, *Owner*
EMP: 2
SALES (est): 145.2K **Privately Held**
SIC: 3645 Lamp shades, metal

(G-10061)
BONENFANTS DRV YOUR AUTO SVC
23 Reichert Cir (06880-2642)
PHONE.................203 222-2239
Patricia Bonenfant, *President*
Ron Bonenfant, *Principal*
EMP: 1
SALES (est): 91.3K **Privately Held**
SIC: 3949 7538 Driving ranges, golf, electronic; general automotive repair shops

---

(PA)=Parent Co (HQ)=Headquarters (DH)=Div Headquarters
✪ = New Business established in last 2 years

Westport - Fairfield County (G-10062)

(G-10062)
C C AND P
2 Fairview Dr (06880-1702)
PHONE 203 222-8260
Bob Duffy, *Manager*
EMP: 2
SALES (est): 80.6K **Privately Held**
SIC: 2759 Commercial printing

(G-10063)
CHARLES ALAIN PUBLISHING LTD
27 Cross Hwy (06880-2139)
PHONE 203 226-2882
Mike Toma, *Owner*
EMP: 1
SALES (est): 55.2K **Privately Held**
SIC: 2731 5942 Book publishing; book stores

(G-10064)
CHESSCO INDUSTRIES INC (PA)
1330 Post Rd E Ste 2 (06880-5539)
PHONE 203 255-2804
Jeffrey Radler, *President*
Louis Radler, *Vice Pres*
Shaun Daly, *Plant Mgr*
Michael J Daly, *Treasurer*
Albert J Kleban, *Admin Sec*
▲ EMP: 41
SQ FT: 2,000
SALES (est): 8.5MM **Privately Held**
WEB: www.processresearch.com
SIC: 3291 2911 2992 2899 Abrasive products; oils, lubricating; cutting oils, blending: made from purchased materials; chemical preparations; adhesives & sealants; plastics materials & resins

(G-10065)
COASTALOGIX LLC
1771 Post Rd E 205 (06880-5606)
PHONE 203 521-4770
Ryan Moran, *Mng Member*
EMP: 2 EST: 2015
SQ FT: 2,000
SALES (est): 62.1K **Privately Held**
SIC: 7372 Business oriented computer software

(G-10066)
COMMERCE CONNECT MEDIA INC
Also Called: Cygnus Business Media
830 Post Rd E Fl 2 (06880-5222)
PHONE 800 547-7377
Paul Mackler, *CEO*
EMP: 2188
SALES (est): 66.9MM **Privately Held**
WEB: www.abry.com
SIC: 2721 Magazines: publishing & printing
PA: Abry Partners, Inc.
   888 Boylston St Ste 1600
   Boston MA 02199

(G-10067)
COMMUNITY BRANDS HOLDINGS LLC
Also Called: Tripbuilder Media
180 Post Rd E Ste 200 (06880-3414)
PHONE 203 227-1255
EMP: 15
SALES (corp-wide): 13.5MM **Privately Held**
SIC: 7372 Prepackaged software
PA: Community Brands Holdings, Llc
   9620 Executive Center Dr
   Saint Petersburg FL 33702
   727 827-0046

(G-10068)
COMPASS GROUP MANAGEMENT LLC (PA)
301 Riverside Ave (06880-4806)
PHONE 203 221-1703
Pat Maciariello, *COO*
Timothy Chiodo, *Vice Pres*
Joe Massoud,
Alan Offenberg,
EMP: 16
SALES (est): 4.7MM **Privately Held**
WEB: www.compassequity.com
SIC: 6282 3547 Investment advisory service; rolling mill machinery

(G-10069)
CONVERGENT SOLUTIONS LLC
3 Baywood Ln (06880-4036)
PHONE 203 293-3534
Nancy Mahmoud, *Principal*
EMP: 3
SALES (est): 108.9K **Privately Held**
SIC: 3674 Semiconductors & related devices

(G-10070)
COYOTE SOFTWARE
53 Cross Hwy (06880-2144)
PHONE 203 227-6510
Vincent Macilvain, *Principal*
EMP: 2
SALES (est): 87.8K **Privately Held**
SIC: 7372 Prepackaged software

(G-10071)
CRAVE FOODS LLC
33 Danbury Ave (06880-6822)
PHONE 203 227-6868
Amy Mandelbaum, *Principal*
EMP: 2 EST: 2012
SALES (est): 96.2K **Privately Held**
SIC: 2099 Food preparations

(G-10072)
CT ORGANIZER LLC
8 Washington Ave (06880-2546)
PHONE 203 858-5824
Maria A Hildebrandt, *Owner*
EMP: 1 EST: 2015
SALES: 20K **Privately Held**
SIC: 3089 Organizers for closets, drawers, etc.: plastic

(G-10073)
CUERO OPERATING
Also Called: Quero Shoes
34 Meeker Rd (06880-1708)
PHONE 203 253-8651
Randy Shuken,
EMP: 4
SALES: 1.5MM **Privately Held**
SIC: 3111 5661 Shoe leather; shoe stores

(G-10074)
DOMINO MEDIA GROUP INC
Also Called: Domino.com
16 Taylor Pl (06880-4313)
PHONE 877 223-7844
Cliff Sirlin, *CEO*
Andy Appelbaum, *Principal*
Aaron Wallace, *Treasurer*
Phuong Nguyen, *Graphic Designe*
EMP: 30 EST: 2012
SQ FT: 1,500
SALES (est): 3MM **Privately Held**
SIC: 2721 5712 Magazines: publishing only, not printed on site; furniture stores

(G-10075)
E11EVEN LLC
35 Post Rd W (06880-4205)
P.O. Box 370055, West Hartford (06137-0055)
PHONE 855 246-6233
Bernard Moran,
EMP: 2
SALES (est): 175.7K **Privately Held**
SIC: 3944 Board games, puzzles & models, except electronic

(G-10076)
EARNIX INC
191 Post Rd W (06880-4625)
PHONE 203 557-8077
Meryl Golden, *Branch Mgr*
EMP: 10 **Privately Held**
SIC: 7372 Business oriented computer software
PA: Earnix Ltd
   4 Ariel Sharon
   Givataim
   375 382-92

(G-10077)
EK PUBLISHING LLC
88 Compo Rd S (06880-5054)
PHONE 203 246-9683
Thomas J Kalb, *Principal*
EMP: 1
SALES (est): 63K **Privately Held**
SIC: 2741 Miscellaneous publishing

(G-10078)
ELLIPSON DATA LLC
21 Bridge Sq (06880-5900)
PHONE 203 227-5520
Bernhard Keppler,
EMP: 3
SALES: 500K **Privately Held**
SIC: 3577 Computer peripheral equipment

(G-10079)
FENTON CORP
191 Post Rd W (06880-4625)
PHONE 203 221-2788
Harrison Kwan, *President*
Florence Lee, *Bookkeeper*
Michael Brown, *Senior Mgr*
EMP: 10 EST: 1993
SALES (est): 910.2K **Privately Held**
SIC: 3663 5065 Radio & TV communications equipment; communication equipment

(G-10080)
FIDDLE HORSE FARM LLC
95 Bayberry Ln (06880-4000)
PHONE 203 557-3285
Ronald Friedson, *General Mgr*
Ronald S Friedson,
EMP: 1
SALES: 750K **Privately Held**
SIC: 2329 2339 3199 5699 Riding clothes:, men's, youths' & boys'; riding habits: women's, misses' & juniors'; equestrian related leather articles; riding apparel; saddlery & equestrian equipment

(G-10081)
FIRST AVIATION SERVICES INC (PA)
15 Riverside Ave (06880-4245)
PHONE 203 291-3300
Aaron P Hollander, *President*
Joshua Krotec, *Senior VP*
Janelle Miller, *CFO*
Joy Karageorge, *Executive Asst*
Joy Sideleau, *Executive Asst*
EMP: 4
SQ FT: 3,000
SALES (est): 31.7MM **Privately Held**
SIC: 3728 3724 Aircraft parts & equipment; aircraft engines & engine parts

(G-10082)
FIRST EQUITY GROUP INC (PA)
15 Riverside Ave Ste 1 (06880-4245)
PHONE 203 291-7700
Aaron Hollander, *CEO*
Larissa Strautman, *Admin Sec*
EMP: 15
SQ FT: 3,000
SALES (est): 17.9MM **Privately Held**
SIC: 3724 7389 Aircraft engines & engine parts; brokers, business: buying & selling business enterprises

(G-10083)
FJB AMERICA LLC
8 Wright St Ste 107 (06880-3114)
PHONE 203 682-2424
Francisco Barreto, *Mng Member*
Jacqueline Barreto,
▲ EMP: 3
SALES (est): 3MM **Privately Held**
SIC: 2095 Roasted coffee

(G-10084)
FLOTTEC INTERNATIONAL SLS CORP
Also Called: Fife
3 Meeker Rd (06880-1704)
PHONE 973 588-4717
John E Tober, *President*
Frank R Cappuccitti, *Director*
EMP: 4 EST: 2014
SQ FT: 800
SALES: 4MM
SALES (corp-wide): 1MM **Privately Held**
SIC: 2899 Chemical preparations
PA: Flottec Llc
   5 Hillcrest Rd
   Boonton NJ 07005
   973 588-4717

(G-10085)
FOUR SIX JULIET LLC
11 Bermuda Rd (06880-6702)
PHONE 203 227-1557
Todd M Freeman,
Nikola Freeman,
EMP: 2
SALES (est): 130.9K **Privately Held**
SIC: 3721 Aircraft

(G-10086)
FUEL FOR HUMANITY INC
11 Hedley Farms Rd (06880-6335)
PHONE 203 255-5913
Jerid O'Connell, *Principal*
EMP: 3
SALES (est): 174.5K **Privately Held**
SIC: 2869 Fuels

(G-10087)
GALLAGHER KATIE PUBLISHERS REP
3 Ridgewood Ln (06880-3107)
PHONE 203 221-7140
EMP: 1
SALES (est): 62K **Privately Held**
SIC: 2741 Misc Publishing

(G-10088)
GEMMA ORO INC
2 Coach Ln (06880-2107)
PHONE 203 227-0774
Perry Gandelman, *President*
Nanette Gandelman, *Vice Pres*
EMP: 5
SQ FT: 850
SALES (est): 486.8K **Privately Held**
SIC: 3911 Jewelry, precious metal

(G-10089)
GINTER HILL CORPORATION
1 Flower Farm Ln (06880-5536)
PHONE 203 293-4301
Zhiyong Fan, *Director*
EMP: 2
SALES (est): 110.9K **Privately Held**
SIC: 3089 Injection molding of plastics

(G-10090)
GLOBAL PALATE FOODS LLC
161 Cross Hwy (06880-2245)
PHONE 203 543-3028
Craig Kyzar, *Principal*
EMP: 3 EST: 2011
SALES (est): 187.9K **Privately Held**
SIC: 2099 Food preparations

(G-10091)
GLOSYSTEMS INC
3 Tarone Dr (06880-4725)
PHONE 203 227-2464
Allan Curtis, *President*
EMP: 2
SALES: 10MM **Privately Held**
WEB: www.goatomic.net
SIC: 3675 Condensers, electronic

(G-10092)
GOOD EARTH MILLWORK LLC
292 Post Rd E (06880-3628)
PHONE 203 226-7958
Michael Greenberg, *Manager*
EMP: 2
SALES (est): 153.3K **Privately Held**
SIC: 2431 Millwork

(G-10093)
GREENPORT FOODS LLC
191 Post Rd W (06880-4625)
PHONE 203 221-2673
Eduardo Bembibre, *General Mgr*
Carlos Grego, *Principal*
Scott Goodyear, *Natl Sales Mgr*
Corina Hoffman, *Consultant*
◆ EMP: 11
SALES (est): 3.1MM **Privately Held**
SIC: 2091 Seafood products: packaged in cans, jars, etc.

(G-10094)
GSV INC
191 Post Rd W (06880-4625)
PHONE 203 221-2690
Sagi Matza, *Ch of Bd*
Gilad Gat, *President*

▲ = Import ▼=Export
◆ =Import/Export

GEOGRAPHIC SECTION
Westport - Fairfield County (G-10124)

Yoav Bitter, *Principal*
EMP: 2
SQ FT: 150
SALES (est): 267.9K **Privately Held**
WEB: www.gsv.com
SIC: 1311 Crude petroleum & natural gas

(G-10095)
HILLS POINT INDUSTRIES LLC (PA)
191 Post Rd W (06880-4625)
PHONE..................917 515-8650
Marissa Saporta,
Jennifer Richter,
▼ **EMP:** 3
SALES (est): 2MM **Privately Held**
SIC: 2392 Household furnishings

(G-10096)
ILLUME HEALTH LLC
20 Ketchum St (06880-5939)
PHONE..................203 242-7801
Kristyn Miller, *Director*
Howard Steinberg,
EMP: 1
SQ FT: 800
SALES (est): 36K **Privately Held**
SIC: 7372 Prepackaged software

(G-10097)
IN STORE EXPERIENCE INC
49 Richmondville Ave # 102 (06880-2050)
PHONE..................203 221-4777
Christopher S Anderson, *CEO*
Deborah Anderson, *Vice Pres*
Greg Cuccinello, *Vice Pres*
George Martocchio, *Vice Pres*
Adam Silverstein, *Vice Pres*
▲ **EMP:** 26
SALES (est): 4.7MM **Privately Held**
SIC: 2542 Fixtures, store: except wood

(G-10098)
INDULGE BY MERSENE LLC
20 Railroad Pl (06880-5912)
PHONE..................203 644-6172
Mersene Norbom, *Mng Member*
EMP: 2
SALES (est): 260.7K **Privately Held**
SIC: 2449 Baskets: fruit & vegetable, round stave, till, etc.

(G-10099)
INDUSTRIAL SALES CORP (PA)
Also Called: Industrial Sales Supply
727 Post Rd E (06880-5219)
PHONE..................203 227-5988
James Hornung, *President*
Robert Hornung, *Vice Pres*
▲ **EMP:** 11
SALES (est): 2.1MM **Privately Held**
SIC: 2431 Windows & window parts & trim, wood

(G-10100)
INFIRST HEALTHCARE INC
8 Church Ln (06880-3508)
PHONE..................203 222-1300
Manfred Scheske, *CEO*
James Barickman, *President*
Philip Lindsell, *CFO*
John Linderman, *Director*
EMP: 7
SQ FT: 5,000
SALES: 22.8MM
SALES (corp-wide): 17MM **Privately Held**
SIC: 2834 Drugs acting on the respiratory system
PA: Infirst Healthcare Limited
Central Point
London EC2Y
207 153-6600

(G-10101)
INSTINCTIVE WORKS LLC
5 Spicer Ct (06880-4527)
PHONE..................203 434-8094
Stuart David Farnworth,
Tony Yao,
EMP: 5 **EST:** 2013
SQ FT: 1,000
SALES: 250K **Privately Held**
SIC: 3633 Household laundry equipment

(G-10102)
INTEGER-COMFAB ENTERPRISES LLC
Also Called: Integer Confab
1771 Post Rd E 21 (06880-5606)
PHONE..................646 620-9112
Kenneth Bird,
EMP: 1 **EST:** 2008
SALES: 0 **Privately Held**
SIC: 2741 7389 ;

(G-10103)
INTENSITY THERAPEUTICS INC
61 Wilton Rd Ste 3 (06880-3121)
PHONE..................203 682-2434
Lewis Bender, *CEO*
Ian B Walters, *Chief Mktg Ofcr*
EMP: 2 **EST:** 2012
SALES (est): 254.9K **Privately Held**
SIC: 2834 Solutions, pharmaceutical

(G-10104)
INVERSE MEDIA LLC
2 Evergreen Ave (06880-2560)
PHONE..................203 255-9620
Chris Thomas, *President*
EMP: 4
SALES (est): 260K **Privately Held**
WEB: www.inversemedia.com
SIC: 7374 7372 Computer graphics service; prepackaged software

(G-10105)
IWCO DIRECT
1276 Post Rd E (06880-5505)
PHONE..................203 557-4303
EMP: 2 **EST:** 2010
SALES (est): 123K **Privately Held**
SIC: 3577 Optical scanning devices

(G-10106)
JUICE PUBLISHING LLC
80 Compo Rd N (06880-2508)
PHONE..................203 226-5715
Charles J Durkin III, *Principal*
EMP: 1 **EST:** 2013
SALES (est): 68.2K **Privately Held**
SIC: 2741 Miscellaneous publishing

(G-10107)
KERRY R WOOD
2 Hideaway Ln (06880-6115)
PHONE..................203 221-7780
Kerry Wood, *Owner*
EMP: 7
SALES (est): 419.8K **Privately Held**
SIC: 2035 2099 Dressings, salad: raw & cooked (except dry mixes); salads, fresh or refrigerated

(G-10108)
KNOX ENTERPRISES INC (PA)
830 Post Rd E Ste 205 (06880-5222)
PHONE..................203 226-6408
Paul K Kelly, *CEO*
Frederick A Rossetti, *COO*
Jeffrey B Gaynor, *Exec VP*
◆ **EMP:** 3
SQ FT: 2,500
SALES (est): 10.6MM **Privately Held**
SIC: 2671 3496 Packaging paper & plastics film, coated & laminated; miscellaneous fabricated wire products

(G-10109)
KNOX INDUSTRIES INC
830 Post Rd E Ste 205 (06880-5222)
PHONE..................203 226-6408
Frederick Rossetti, *President*
Jeffrey B Gaynor, *Admin Sec*
◆ **EMP:** 142
SQ FT: 860
SALES: 8.1MM
SALES (corp-wide): 10.6MM **Privately Held**
SIC: 2679 Paper products, converted
PA: Knox Enterprises Inc
830 Post Rd E Ste 205
Westport CT 06880
203 226-6408

(G-10110)
KTCR HOLDING
4 Pheasant Ln (06880-1709)
PHONE..................203 227-4115
Joshua Rizack, *Owner*
EMP: 8
SALES (est): 327.1K **Privately Held**
SIC: 3621 Motors & generators

(G-10111)
LDA PUBLISHERS
12 Little Fox Ln (06880-1403)
PHONE..................203 438-1484
EMP: 1
SALES (est): 49K **Privately Held**
SIC: 2741 Miscellaneous Publishing, Nsk

(G-10112)
LH GAULT & SON INCORPORATED
11 Ferry Ln W (06880-5808)
P.O. Box 2030 (06880-0030)
PHONE..................203 227-5181
Samuel M Gault, *President*
Jim Hickey, *General Mgr*
William L Gault, *Chairman*
Debbie Finan, *Controller*
Tina Bahr, *Accounts Mgr*
▲ **EMP:** 65
SQ FT: 40,000
SALES (est): 41.5MM **Privately Held**
SIC: 1411 5032 3441 5211 Granite dimension stone; building stone; granite building stone; marble building stone; gravel; fabricated structural metal; sand & gravel; drainage system construction; pavers

(G-10113)
LIME ROCK RESOURCES GP III LP
274 Riverside Ave (06880-4808)
PHONE..................203 293-2750
Blair Barlow, *Director*
EMP: 1 **EST:** 2014
SALES (est): 65.6K
SALES (corp-wide): 4.1MM **Privately Held**
SIC: 1422 Lime rock, ground
PA: Lime Rock Management Lp
274 Riverside Ave Ste 3b
Westport CT 06880
203 293-2750

(G-10114)
LUMENDI LLC
253 Post Rd W (06880-4737)
PHONE..................203 528-0316
Michael Parrilla, *COO*
Eric Coolidge, *Vice Pres*
EMP: 7
SQ FT: 4,000
SALES (est): 1.2MM **Privately Held**
SIC: 3841 Surgical & medical instruments

(G-10115)
MAGNESIUM INTERACTIVE LLC
171 Roseville Rd (06880-2618)
PHONE..................917 609-1306
John C Dodd, *Principal*
EMP: 4
SALES (est): 120.9K **Privately Held**
SIC: 3356 Magnesium

(G-10116)
MAGNUSS SERVICES INC
580 Riverside Ave Apt 104 (06880-5957)
PHONE..................347 703-0750
James Rhodes, *CEO*
Edward Shergalis, *COO*
EMP: 1 **EST:** 2013
SALES (est): 71.4K **Privately Held**
SIC: 3731 Commercial cargo ships, building & repairing

(G-10117)
MANTROSE-HAEUSER CO INC (HQ)
100 Nyala Farms Rd (06880-6266)
PHONE..................203 454-1800
William J Barrie, *President*
Stephen A Santos, *Senior VP*
Susan Wahler, *Export Mgr*
Katie Fontaine, *Research*
Xiangdong Gan, *Research*
▲ **EMP:** 29
SALES (est): 22MM
SALES (corp-wide): 5.5B **Publicly Held**
WEB: www.mantrose.com
SIC: 2064 2066 2851 0723 Candy & other confectionery products; chocolate & cocoa products; paints & allied products; crop preparation services for market; medicinals & botanicals; drugs, proprietaries & sundries
PA: Rpm International Inc.
2628 Pearl Rd
Medina OH 44256
330 273-5090

(G-10118)
MASON MEDICAL COMMUNICATIONS
10 Covlee Dr (06880-6405)
P.O. Box 216, Greens Farms (06838-0216)
PHONE..................203 227-9252
Howard Mason, *President*
Jacqueline Mason, *Corp Secy*
EMP: 5
SQ FT: 1,000
SALES (est): 405.3K **Privately Held**
SIC: 2721 Magazines: publishing only, not printed on site

(G-10119)
MERCURY FUEL SERVICE INC
322 Post Rd E (06880-3619)
PHONE..................203 291-0833
Imtiaz Siddiquee, *Manager*
EMP: 1
SALES (corp-wide): 105.1MM **Privately Held**
SIC: 2869 Fuels
PA: Mercury Fuel Service Inc
43 Lafayette St
Waterbury CT 06708
203 756-7284

(G-10120)
MEV TECHNOLOGIES LLC
Also Called: Mev Photonics
9 Janson Dr (06880-2515)
PHONE..................203 227-4723
Milan Milosevic, *General Mgr*
Violet Milosevic,
EMP: 2
SALES (est): 300.2K **Privately Held**
SIC: 3827 Optical instruments & lenses

(G-10121)
MINUTEMAN NEWSPAPER (PA)
1175 Post Rd E Ste 3e (06880-5400)
PHONE..................203 226-8877
Paula Walsh, *Manager*
EMP: 24 **Privately Held**
SIC: 2711 Newspapers: publishing only, not printed on site

(G-10122)
MIX N MATCH LLC
19 Pequot Trl (06880-2929)
PHONE..................203 227-9588
Cheryl Herman, *Manager*
EMP: 1
SALES (est): 99.6K **Privately Held**
WEB: www.mistral.org
SIC: 3273 Ready-mixed concrete

(G-10123)
MOFFLY PUBLICATIONS INC
Also Called: Westport Magazine
205 Main St Ste 1 (06880-3206)
PHONE..................203 222-0600
John W Moffly, *Branch Mgr*
EMP: 11
SALES (corp-wide): 4.4MM **Privately Held**
WEB: www.mofflypub.com
SIC: 2721 Magazines: publishing only, not printed on site
PA: Moffly Publications Inc
205 Main St Ste 1
Westport CT 06880
203 222-0600

(G-10124)
MOFFLY PUBLICATIONS INC (PA)
Also Called: Greenwich Magazine
205 Main St Ste 1 (06880-3206)
PHONE..................203 222-0600
Jonathan Moffly, *CEO*

Westport - Fairfield County (G-10125)

John W Moffly IV, *Chairman*
Donna C Moffly, *Vice Pres*
Elena Moffly, *Treasurer*
EMP: 23
SQ FT: 4,500
SALES (est): 4.4MM **Privately Held**
WEB: www.mofflypub.com
SIC: 2721 Magazines: publishing only, not printed on site

(G-10125)
MR BOLTONS MUSIC INC
31 Kings Hwy N (06880-3002)
PHONE..................................646 578-8081
Micheal Bolotin, *President*
EMP: 3
SALES (est): 229.1K **Privately Held**
SIC: 2741 Music, sheet: publishing & printing

(G-10126)
MURDOCH AND CO
3 Sniffen Rd (06880-1222)
PHONE..................................203 226-2800
Dan Murdoch, *Partner*
Jean Murdoch, *Partner*
EMP: 2
SALES (est): 132.9K **Privately Held**
SIC: 7389 3993 7319 Appraisers, except real estate; trade show arrangement; signs & advertising specialties; display advertising service

(G-10127)
NATURESEAL INC
1175 Post Rd E Ste 3b (06880-5400)
PHONE..................................203 454-1800
William J Barrie, *President*
Sue O'Rourke, *Vice Pres*
Edward W Moore, *Admin Sec*
EMP: 31 **EST:** 2008
SALES (est): 1.5MM
SALES (corp-wide): 5.5B **Publicly Held**
SIC: 0723 2037 Crop preparation services for market; frozen fruits & vegetables
HQ: Mantrose-Haeuser Co., Inc.
100 Nyala Farms Rd
Westport CT 06880

(G-10128)
NEWMANS OWN INC (PA)
Also Called: Newman's Own Organics
1 Morningside Dr N Ste 1 # 1 (06880-3847)
PHONE..................................203 222-0136
Thomas Indoe, *President*
Tom Indoe, *COO*
Lori Dibiase, *Vice Pres*
William Lee, *Vice Pres*
Jeffrey Smith, *VP Opers*
▼ **EMP:** 28
SQ FT: 4,200
SALES (est): 19MM **Privately Held**
WEB: www.newmansown.com
SIC: 2035 2086 Dressings, salad: raw & cooked (except dry mixes); lemonade: packaged in cans, bottles, etc.

(G-10129)
NSF GOURMET PRODUCTS
940 Post Rd E (06880-5342)
PHONE..................................203 856-4995
Fred Ketcher, *Owner*
EMP: 1
SALES (est): 5K **Privately Held**
SIC: 2079 Olive oil

(G-10130)
NVIZIX CORP
381 Main St (06880-2005)
PHONE..................................203 222-8723
Elie Track, *CEO*
Christopher Sanzeni, *VP Opers*
David Winn, *CTO*
EMP: 3
SALES (est): 210K **Privately Held**
WEB: www.nvizix.com
SIC: 3827 Optical elements & assemblies, except ophthalmic

(G-10131)
NYTEX PETROLEUM INC
1771 Post Rd E Ste 133 (06880-5606)
PHONE..................................203 261-6329
Robert January, *President*
EMP: 2
SALES (est): 77.1K **Privately Held**
SIC: 1389 Oil consultants

(G-10132)
ONE KID LLC (PA)
188 Compo Rd S (06880-5019)
PHONE..................................203 254-9978
Eric Autard,
▲ **EMP:** 3 **EST:** 1998
SALES (est): 342.8K **Privately Held**
WEB: www.onekid.com
SIC: 2369 Girls' & children's outerwear

(G-10133)
ONION HILL PRESS LLC
17 Buena Vista Dr (06880-6602)
PHONE..................................203 227-4895
Totney Benson,
Kassie Foss,
EMP: 2
SALES (est): 110K **Privately Held**
WEB: www.onionhilldesigns.com
SIC: 2771 Greeting cards

(G-10134)
ONLINE RIVER LLC
606 Post Rd E Ste 723 (06880-4540)
PHONE..................................203 801-5900
Todd Landen, *Mng Member*
EMP: 14
SALES (est): 2.2MM **Privately Held**
SIC: 5099 3829 5045 3577 Novelties, durable; turnstiles, equipped with counting mechanisms; computer software; computer peripheral equipment; tags: printing; hand & edge tools

(G-10135)
OUR TOWN CRIER
36 Lyons Plains Rd (06880-1305)
PHONE..................................203 400-5000
EMP: 3
SALES (est): 126.9K **Privately Held**
SIC: 2711 Newspapers, publishing & printing

(G-10136)
OWLSTONE INC (PA)
19 Ludlow Rd Ste 202 (06880-3040)
PHONE..................................203 908-4848
Bret Bader, *CEO*
Ashley Wilks, *Business Mgr*
Thomas Finn, *CFO*
EMP: 6
SQ FT: 2,771
SALES (est): 4.6MM **Privately Held**
SIC: 3826 3829 Analytical instruments; measuring & controlling devices

(G-10137)
PALLET INC LLC
41 Charcoal Hill Rd (06880-1635)
PHONE..................................203 227-8148
Mark Ancona, *Principal*
EMP: 3
SALES (est): 156.7K **Privately Held**
SIC: 2448 Pallets, wood & wood with metal

(G-10138)
PENINSULA PUBLISHING
1630 Post Rd E Unit 312 (06880-5647)
PHONE..................................203 292-5621
Charles Wiseman, *Owner*
EMP: 3
SALES (est): 50K **Privately Held**
SIC: 2731 Books: publishing only

(G-10139)
PENOTTI USA INC
4 Maple Grove Ave (06880-4917)
P.O. Box 2864 (06880-0864)
PHONE..................................203 341-9494
Marcel Peteers, *President*
Stanley Rottell, *Director*
EMP: 2
SALES (est): 133.9K **Privately Held**
SIC: 2064 Chocolate candy, except solid chocolate

(G-10140)
PETER HANNAN
Also Called: Arbor Computer Systems
117 Weston Rd (06880-1311)
P.O. Box 548 (06881-0548)
PHONE..................................203 226-4335
Peter Hannan, *Owner*
EMP: 2
SALES (est): 140.1K **Privately Held**
SIC: 7372 Prepackaged software

(G-10141)
POLAR BEAR INDUSTRIES LLC
2 Plunkett Pl (06880-2732)
P.O. Box 1116, Greens Farms (06838-1116)
PHONE..................................203 858-4396
John J Mori,
EMP: 2 **EST:** 2012
SALES (est): 91.1K **Privately Held**
SIC: 3999 Manufacturing industries

(G-10142)
PPC BOOKS LTD
Also Called: Publishing Packagers
335 Post Rd W (06880)
PHONE..................................203 226-6644
Christopher Watson, *President*
EMP: 4
SQ FT: 1,200
SALES (est): 200K **Privately Held**
SIC: 2732 2731 2721 Books: printing & binding; book publishing; periodicals

(G-10143)
PREMIER FOODS INC
Also Called: Sharwood's
31 Imperial Ave (06880-4303)
P.O. Box 5013 (06881-5013)
PHONE..................................203 226-6577
Neil Turpin, *CEO*
EMP: 2 **EST:** 2012
SALES (est): 211.9K **Privately Held**
SIC: 2033 Canned fruits & specialties
HQ: Premier Foods Group Limited
Premier House, Centrium Business Park
St Albans HERTS AL1 2

(G-10144)
PUZZLESOCIAL LLC
29 W Parish Rd (06880-5332)
PHONE..................................917 515-1030
James E Balise III, *Mng Member*
EMP: 1
SALES (est): 70K **Privately Held**
SIC: 3944 Electronic games & toys

(G-10145)
RAND MEDIA CO LLC
265 Post Rd W (06880-4746)
PHONE..................................203 226-8727
EMP: 4
SALES (est): 100K **Privately Held**
SIC: 2741 Misc Publishing

(G-10146)
REALIZERS GROUP LLC
15 Danbury Ave (06880-6820)
PHONE..................................203 253-9510
John Lamie,
EMP: 2
SALES (est): 62.5K **Privately Held**
SIC: 3999 Manufacturing industries

(G-10147)
RECYCLE 4 VETS LLC
Also Called: R4v
518 Riverside Ave Ste 1 (06880-5741)
PHONE..................................203 222-7300
Tracy Troy,
John Mangan,
Brendan Reilly,
EMP: 7
SALES (est): 565.9K **Privately Held**
SIC: 5112 3861 3577 Stationery & office supplies; photographic processing chemicals; readers, sorters or inscribers, magnetic ink

(G-10148)
RENAISSANCE STUDIO INC
188 Imperial Ave (06880-4913)
PHONE..................................203 226-9674
Peter M Green, *President*
Tina Green, *Vice Pres*
EMP: 2 **EST:** 1973
SALES (est): 246.1K **Privately Held**
WEB: www.renaissancestudios.com
SIC: 3231 7336 Stained glass: made from purchased glass; commercial art & graphic design

(G-10149)
RJ CABINETRY LLC
943 Post Rd E (06880-5362)
PHONE..................................203 515-8401
Ruben Reinoso, *Principal*
EMP: 3
SALES (est): 187.7K **Privately Held**
SIC: 2434 Wood kitchen cabinets

(G-10150)
ROBERT WARREN LLC (PA)
Also Called: Lance International
1 Sprucewood Ln (06880-4022)
PHONE..................................203 247-3347
Murray Doscher,
Ed Diamond,
EMP: 50 **EST:** 1974
SQ FT: 18,000
SALES (est): 9.8MM **Privately Held**
WEB: www.lanceintl.com
SIC: 3679 Harness assemblies for electronic use: wire or cable

(G-10151)
ROGERS SEPTIC TANKS INC
1480 Post Rd E (06880-5509)
PHONE..................................203 259-9947
Roger Thoele, *President*
EMP: 15 **EST:** 1947
SQ FT: 2,000
SALES (est): 1.5MM **Privately Held**
SIC: 3272 Septic tanks, concrete

(G-10152)
ROSS TYPE
7 Lincoln St (06880-4202)
PHONE..................................203 227-2007
Randi Ross, *Owner*
EMP: 2
SALES (est): 201.8K **Privately Held**
SIC: 2752 Commercial printing, lithographic

(G-10153)
SAATVA INC
8 Wright St Ste 108 (06880-3114)
PHONE..................................877 672-2882
Ron Rudzin, *CEO*
Edward Seidner, *Vice Pres*
Robin Belliveau, *Human Res Dir*
Krista Deshayes, *Mktg Dir*
Robert Kramer, *Business Anlyst*
EMP: 31
SALES (est): 3.7MM **Privately Held**
SIC: 2515 Mattresses & bedsprings

(G-10154)
SATORI AUDIO LLC
Also Called: Satori Nyc
180 Post Rd E Ste 201 (06880-3414)
PHONE..................................203 571-6050
Jeffrey Warshaw, *Mng Member*
EMP: 4
SALES (est): 146.9K **Privately Held**
SIC: 7372 Application computer software

(G-10155)
SHELL SHOCK TECHNOLOGIES LLC
38 Owenoke Park (06880-6833)
PHONE..................................203 557-3256
Andrew Vallance, *Vice Pres*
Craig F Knight, *Mng Member*
EMP: 6 **EST:** 2015
SALES: 1MM **Privately Held**
SIC: 3482 Cartridge cases for ammunition, 30 mm. & below

(G-10156)
SHERWOOD GROUP INC (PA)
Also Called: Albe Furs
286 Post Rd E (06880-3614)
PHONE..................................203 227-5288
Ben Berman, *President*
Leon Skolnik, *Vice Pres*
George Lotkin, *Treasurer*
EMP: 12
SQ FT: 3,400
SALES (est): 1.3MM **Privately Held**
WEB: www.albefurs.com
SIC: 5632 2371 Furriers; fur apparel, made to custom order; fur coats & other fur apparel; coats, fur

GEOGRAPHIC SECTION

Wethersfield - Hartford County (G-10187)

(G-10157)
SHIRE RGENERATIVE MEDICINE INC (DH)
36 Church Ln (06880-3505)
PHONE.................................877 422-4363
Kevin Rakin, *President*
Kathy McGee, *Senior VP*
Charles E Hart PHD, *Vice Pres*
Mark McElligott, *Engineer*
Kevin C O'Boyle, *CFO*
EMP: 4
SALES (est): 15.4MM
SALES (corp-wide): 15.1B **Privately Held**
WEB: www.advancedtissue.com
SIC: 2834 Pharmaceutical preparations
HQ: Shire Us Holdings Llc
9200 Brookfield Ct # 108
Florence KY 41042
859 669-8000

(G-10158)
SIDNEY DOBSON
Also Called: D & D Refuse
7 Palmieri Rd (06880-4157)
PHONE.................................203 255-5545
Sidney Dobson, *Owner*
EMP: 2
SALES (est): 177.7K **Privately Held**
SIC: 3713 Garbage, refuse truck bodies

(G-10159)
SIGMAVOIP LLC
980 Post Rd E Ste 3 (06880-5359)
P.O. Box 309, Middlefield (06455-0309)
PHONE.................................203 541-5450
Charles Ambrosecchia,
EMP: 7
SALES (est): 493.7K **Privately Held**
SIC: 4813 3661 Voice telephone communications; telephones & telephone apparatus

(G-10160)
STEPPING STONES MARBLE
420 Post Rd W (06880-4744)
PHONE.................................203 293-4796
Anthony Corelli, *Manager*
EMP: 2 **EST:** 2008
SALES (est): 160.7K **Privately Held**
SIC: 2426 Flooring, hardwood

(G-10161)
STYLE AND GRACE LLC
101 Franklin St Ste 3 (06880-5966)
PHONE.................................917 751-2043
Paris Gordon, *CEO*
EMP: 3
SQ FT: 1,000
SALES (est): 900K **Privately Held**
SIC: 2389 Men's miscellaneous accessories

(G-10162)
SUMMER STREET CONTENT LLC
1771 Post Rd E (06880-5606)
PHONE.................................203 536-9845
Nicolas D Mandelkern, *President*
EMP: 1
SALES (est): 56.9K **Privately Held**
SIC: 2741 Miscellaneous publishing

(G-10163)
TEREX CORPORATION (PA)
200 Nyala Farms Rd Ste 2 (06880-6261)
PHONE.................................203 222-7170
John L Garrison Jr, *Ch of Bd*
James Barr, *General Mgr*
Terri Paynter, *Editor*
Robert Brown, *Vice Pres*
Damian Kitson, *Vice Pres*
◆ **EMP:** 15
SALES: 5.1B **Publicly Held**
WEB: www.terex.com
SIC: 3537 3531 Industrial trucks & tractors; lift trucks, industrial: fork, platform, straddle, etc.; stackers, power (industrial truck stackers); straddle carriers, mobile; cranes

(G-10164)
TEREX USA LLC (HQ)
Also Called: Cedarapids
200 Nyala Farms Rd (06880-6265)
PHONE.................................203 222-7170
Gary Pils, *Credit Staff*
Ethan Waller, *Regl Sales Mgr*
Jodi Robledo, *Sales Staff*
Gerald Corder, *Marketing Mgr*
Ronald M Defeo, *Mng Member*
◆ **EMP:** 335 **EST:** 1923
SQ FT: 61,700
SALES (est): 232.9MM
SALES (corp-wide): 5.1B **Publicly Held**
SIC: 3532 Crushing, pulverizing & screening equipment
PA: Terex Corporation
200 Nyala Farms Rd Ste 2
Westport CT 06880
203 222-7170

(G-10165)
TEXTSPEAK CORPORATION
Also Called: Textspeak Design
55 Greens Farms Rd (06880-6149)
PHONE.................................203 803-1069
Nancy Stogel, *President*
Scott Stogel, *Vice Pres*
EMP: 11 **EST:** 2000
SALES (est): 363.7K **Privately Held**
SIC: 4899 3845 Communication signal enhancement network system; audiological equipment, electromedical

(G-10166)
TEYS (USA) INC
191 Post Rd W (06880-4625)
PHONE.................................203 227-0481
Dorith Marol, *Manager*
EMP: 3
SALES (est): 285.6K **Privately Held**
SIC: 2011 Meat packing plants

(G-10167)
THT INC
33 Riverside Ave Ste 506 (06880-4223)
PHONE.................................203 226-6408
Paul K Kelly, *CEO*
EMP: 3
SALES (est): 196.7K **Privately Held**
SIC: 2671 Packaging paper & plastics film, coated & laminated

(G-10168)
TOTS411 LLP
8 Carolyn Pl (06880-3101)
PHONE.................................203 558-5369
Claudia Sawyer, *Managing Prtnr*
Tracy Levites, *Partner*
EMP: 2
SALES (est): 93.2K **Privately Held**
SIC: 2741 Directories: publishing & printing

(G-10169)
ULTRA GOLDEN SOFTWARE LLC
35 Narrow Rocks Rd (06880-6017)
PHONE.................................203 227-4009
Deanna B Davis, *Principal*
EMP: 2 **EST:** 2009
SALES (est): 143.8K **Privately Held**
SIC: 7372 Application computer software

(G-10170)
UPON A ONCE PILLOW LLC
4 Sunnyside Ln (06880-1710)
P.O. Box 172 (06881-0172)
PHONE.................................203 222-1717
Ellen Gang,
EMP: 1
SALES (est): 68.4K **Privately Held**
SIC: 2392 Cushions & pillows

(G-10171)
VARPRO INC
4 Shadbush Ln Pmb 2224 (06880-1838)
P.O. Box 2224 (06880-0224)
PHONE.................................203 227-6876
Peter Brink, *President*
Sandra Brink, *Treasurer*
EMP: 20
SQ FT: 2,000
SALES (est): 1.2MM **Privately Held**
SIC: 2371 8742 Apparel, fur; management consulting services

(G-10172)
VIDEO TECHNOLOGIES GROUP LLC
21 Charles St Ste 116 (06880-5803)
PHONE.................................203 341-0474
Clifford R Allen,
Robert B Spencer,
EMP: 2
SALES (est): 404.1K **Privately Held**
SIC: 3663 Television broadcasting & communications equipment

(G-10173)
WALPOLE WOODWORKERS INC
Also Called: Walpole Outdoors
1835 Post Rd E Ste 6 (06880-5678)
PHONE.................................203 255-9010
Linda Bartlle, *Manager*
EMP: 4
SALES (corp-wide): 83.9MM **Privately Held**
WEB: www.walpolewoodworkers.com
SIC: 2499 5211 5712 2452 Fencing, wood; fencing; outdoor & garden furniture; prefabricated wood buildings; wood household furniture
PA: Walpole Outdoors Llc
100 Rver Ridge Dr Ste 302
Norwood MA 02062
508 668-2800

(G-10174)
WESPORT SIGNS
1761 Post Rd E (06880-5606)
PHONE.................................203 557-3668
EMP: 1 **EST:** 2017
SALES (est): 46K **Privately Held**
SIC: 3993 Signs & advertising specialties

(G-10175)
WESTPORT MODEL WORKS
24 Cob Dr (06880-2113)
PHONE.................................203 226-2798
EMP: 2
SALES (est): 110.4K **Privately Held**
SIC: 3944 Games, toys & children's vehicles

(G-10176)
WINNER PRODUCING CO
31 Bulkley Ave N (06880-4113)
PHONE.................................203 259-7576
Mark Naftalin, *Principal*
EMP: 2
SALES (est): 120.1K **Privately Held**
WEB: www.bluespower.com
SIC: 1311 Crude petroleum & natural gas

(G-10177)
WIZARD TOO LLC
34 Little Fox Ln (06880-1403)
PHONE.................................203 984-7180
Ronald Leong,
EMP: 3
SALES (est): 129.4K **Privately Held**
SIC: 2741 Miscellaneous publishing

(G-10178)
YUMI ECOSOLUTIONS INC
4 Bruce Ln (06880-1701)
PHONE.................................203 803-1880
Virginia P'An, *CEO*
Albert P'An, *Senior VP*
Sandra Welwood, *Controller*
▲ **EMP:** 2
SALES (est): 513.3K **Privately Held**
SIC: 5113 2679 Disposable plates, cups, napkins & eating utensils; pressed fiber products from wood pulp: from purchased goods

Wethersfield
Hartford County

(G-10179)
A HELIUM PLUS BALLOONS LLC
94 Albert Ave (06109-1057)
PHONE.................................860 833-1761
Diaram T Gopaul, *Principal*
EMP: 3 **EST:** 2018
SALES (est): 123.2K **Privately Held**
SIC: 2813 Helium

(G-10180)
ARROW WINDOW SHADE MFG CO
1252 Berlin Tpke (06109-1004)
PHONE.................................860 956-3570
Kris T Hoskins, *Principal*
Madelyn A Hoskins, *Vice Pres*
Donald B Hoskins, *Treasurer*
EMP: 3
SQ FT: 2,200
SALES (est): 350K **Privately Held**
SIC: 2591 5719 7699 Window shades; blinds vertical; venetian blinds; window shades; vertical blinds; venetian blinds; window blind repair services

(G-10181)
ARROW WINDOW SHADE MFG CO MRDN
47 Oxford St (06109-1724)
PHONE.................................860 563-4035
Oscar Laraia, *President*
EMP: 12
SALES (est): 930K **Privately Held**
SIC: 2591 5719 Venetian blinds; venetian blinds

(G-10182)
B & G INDUSTRIES LLC
25 Knight St (06109-2834)
PHONE.................................860 571-8873
David E Breiner, *Principal*
Grant R Golub,
EMP: 2 **EST:** 2010
SALES (est): 183.4K **Privately Held**
SIC: 3699 Electrical equipment & supplies

(G-10183)
BARRY E LEONARD
390 Nott St (06109-1626)
PHONE.................................860 951-5105
Barry E Leonard, *Owner*
▲ **EMP:** 2
SALES (est): 214.6K **Privately Held**
SIC: 3599 Machine shop, jobbing & repair

(G-10184)
BLACK & DECKER (US) INC
Also Called: Dewalt Service Center 050
662 Silas Deane Hwy (06109-3053)
PHONE.................................860 563-5800
John Walls, *Manager*
EMP: 6
SQ FT: 4,000
SALES (corp-wide): 13.9B **Publicly Held**
WEB: www.dewalt.com
SIC: 3546 Power-driven handtools
HQ: Black & Decker (U.S.) Inc.
1000 Stanley Dr
New Britain CT 06053
860 225-5111

(G-10185)
CAP-TECH PRODUCTS INC
61 Arrow Rd Ste 11 (06109-1301)
P.O. Box 290123 (06129-0123)
PHONE.................................860 490-5078
Lucia Capobianco, *President*
Sergio Capobianco, *Admin Sec*
EMP: 10
SQ FT: 4,500
SALES (est): 954K **Privately Held**
WEB: www.captechproducts.com
SIC: 2399 2221 Parachutes; manmade & synthetic broadwoven fabrics

(G-10186)
CARTE MEDICAL CORP
850 Silas Deane Hwy (06109-3443)
PHONE.................................860 258-1970
EMP: 2
SALES (est): 104.2K **Privately Held**
SIC: 3825 Network analyzers

(G-10187)
CKH INDUSTRIES INC
365 Silas Deane Hwy Ste 1 (06109-2121)
PHONE.................................860 563-2999
Kenneth Cline, *Branch Mgr*
EMP: 71

Wethersfield - Hartford County (G-10188)

SALES (corp-wide): 14.6MM **Privately Held**
SIC: 3442 Window & door frames
PA: Ckh Industries Inc
520 Temple Hill Rd
New Windsor NY 12553
845 561-9000

(G-10188)
CLEAR WATER MANUFACTURING CORP (PA)
900 Wells Rd (06109-2417)
PHONE..................................860 372-4907
Patrick Sullivan, *President*
Mike Cackowski, *VP Mfg*
Kelly Thompson, *CFO*
Bob Solar, *Accounts Mgr*
Penny Harris, *Sales Staff*
EMP: 8
SALES (est): 1.9MM **Privately Held**
SIC: 3498 Fabricated pipe & fittings

(G-10189)
CORPORATE CONNECTICUT MAG LLC
912 Silas Deane Hwy (06109-3434)
PHONE..................................860 257-0500
Anders G Helm, *Principal*
EMP: 3
SALES (est): 197.6K **Privately Held**
SIC: 2721 Magazines: publishing only, not printed on site

(G-10190)
DIRECTORY ASSISTANTS INC
1321 Silas Deane Hwy 2f (06109-4302)
PHONE..................................860 633-0122
David Ford, *President*
Michael Cody, *Exec VP*
Nancy Claffey, *Accounts Mgr*
Nancy Arruda, *Manager*
EMP: 25
SALES (est): 3.9MM **Privately Held**
WEB: www.yellowpagehelp.com
SIC: 7311 2741 Advertising consultant; miscellaneous publishing

(G-10191)
DOSS CORPORATION
102 Orchard Hill Dr (06109-2420)
PHONE..................................860 721-7384
Vijaya L Murthy, *President*
Mal V Murthy, *Vice Pres*
EMP: 3
SQ FT: 2,000
SALES: 300K **Privately Held**
SIC: 3089 Injection molded finished plastic products; injection molding of plastics

(G-10192)
EASTWOOD PRINTING INC
501 Middletown Ave (06109-3809)
P.O. Box 290271 (06129-0271)
PHONE..................................860 529-6673
Lewis Eastwood, *President*
Ellen Eastwood, *Admin Sec*
EMP: 10
SQ FT: 2,500
SALES (est): 1MM **Privately Held**
WEB: www.eastwoodprinting.com
SIC: 2759 Commercial printing

(G-10193)
GIRL COP PUBLISHING LLC
45 Prospect St (06109-3756)
PHONE..................................860 529-3424
Mark Franco, *Principal*
EMP: 2
SALES (est): 104.3K **Privately Held**
SIC: 2741 Miscellaneous publishing

(G-10194)
GOTHERS & MARTIN WDWKG LLC
16 State St (06109-1846)
PHONE..................................860 982-4193
Timothy Gothers, *Principal*
EMP: 1
SALES (est): 146.2K **Privately Held**
SIC: 2431 Woodwork, interior & ornamental

(G-10195)
HALURGITE PUBLISHING LLC
108 Round Hill Rd (06109-2521)
PHONE..................................860 563-0372
John M Halstead, *Principal*
EMP: 1
SALES (est): 51.5K **Privately Held**
SIC: 2741 Miscellaneous publishing

(G-10196)
HEDGES & HEDGES LTD
Also Called: Copies Now
1155 Silas Deane Hwy # 3 (06109-4331)
PHONE..................................860 257-3170
Robert Hedges, *President*
EMP: 8
SQ FT: 1,800
SALES (est): 865.9K **Privately Held**
SIC: 7334 2791 Photocopying & duplicating services; typesetting

(G-10197)
INDUSTRIAL PRSSURE WASHERS LLC
500 Ridge Rd (06109-1925)
PHONE..................................860 608-6153
Richard Senokosoff,
Patti Senokosoff,
EMP: 3 EST: 2011
SALES (est): 335.4K **Privately Held**
SIC: 3452 3548 Bolts, metal; rivets, metal; screws, metal; welding apparatus

(G-10198)
INFOCUS DRONEWORX LLC
1077 Silas Deane Hwy (06109-4229)
PHONE..................................860 499-0789
Michael C Millrod,
EMP: 2
SALES (est): 86K **Privately Held**
SIC: 3721 Motorized aircraft

(G-10199)
INTEGRATED WOODWORKS LLC
140 Carriage Hill Dr (06109-4104)
PHONE..................................860 563-4537
Steven Pace, *Principal*
EMP: 1
SALES (est): 70.4K **Privately Held**
SIC: 2431 Millwork

(G-10200)
INTERFLON OF NEW ENGLAND
310 Forest Dr (06109-1434)
PHONE..................................860 305-8976
Robert Shampain, *Principal*
EMP: 1
SALES (est): 141.4K **Privately Held**
SIC: 2992 Lubricating oils & greases

(G-10201)
J & T PRINTING LLC
46 2 Silas Deane Hwy (06109)
PHONE..................................860 529-4628
Jeffrey W Foley, *Principal*
EMP: 3
SALES (est): 262.5K **Privately Held**
SIC: 2752 Commercial printing, lithographic

(G-10202)
JOHN OLDHAM STUDIOS INC
888 Wells Rd (06109-2417)
PHONE..................................860 529-3331
John W Oldham Jr, *President*
Mark Oldham, *Vice Pres*
Jennifer Jenkins, *Office Mgr*
Patrica Oldham, *Admin Sec*
▲ EMP: 24 EST: 1931
SQ FT: 86,000
SALES (est): 3.3MM **Privately Held**
WEB: www.oldhamstudios.com
SIC: 3993 7389 Displays & cutouts, window & lobby; displays, paint process; design services

(G-10203)
KAHN AND COMPANY INCORPORATED
885 Wells Rd (06109-2499)
PHONE..................................860 529-8643
Jeffrey S Kahn, *President*
David A Kahn, *Vice Pres*
Gerhard Merkle, *Vice Pres*
Bob Gittleman, *Controller*
Robert Bailey, *Manager*
EMP: 2
SQ FT: 50,000
SALES (est): 412.8K **Privately Held**
WEB: www.kahn.com
SIC: 3826 3823 3825 3822 Gas testing apparatus; absorption analyzers: infrared, X-ray, etc.: industrial; test equipment for electronic & electric measurement; auto controls regulating residntl & coml environmt & applncs; measuring & controlling devices; dynamometer instruments

(G-10204)
KAHN INDUSTRIES INC
885 Wells Rd (06109-2499)
PHONE..................................860 529-8643
Jeffrey S Kahn, *President*
Gerhard Merkle, *Vice Pres*
David Kahn, *Admin Sec*
▼ EMP: 20
SQ FT: 50,000
SALES: 7MM **Privately Held**
SIC: 3829 Dynamometer instruments

(G-10205)
KAHN INSTRUMENTS INCORPORATED
885 Wells Rd (06109-2416)
PHONE..................................860 529-8643
Jeffrey Kahn, *President*
EMP: 7
SQ FT: 50,000
SALES: 5.3MM **Privately Held**
SIC: 5084 3823 Instruments & control equipment; moisture meters, industrial process type

(G-10206)
KELL-STROM TOOL CO INC (PA)
214 Church St (06109-2397)
PHONE..................................860 529-6851
Francis P Kelly, *President*
Robert Kelly, *Vice Pres*
Jerry Edison, *Production*
Gary Viola, *Purch Mgr*
Thomas J Kelly, *Treasurer*
EMP: 39
SALES (est): 9.1MM **Privately Held**
SIC: 3429 3599 3423 Aircraft hardware; machine shop, jobbing & repair; hand & edge tools

(G-10207)
KELL-STROM TOOL INTL INC
214 Church St (06109-2316)
PHONE..................................860 529-6851
Francis P Kelly, *President*
Robert M Kelly, *Vice Pres*
Thomas J Kelly, *Treasurer*
Peter J Kelly, *Admin Sec*
EMP: 39 EST: 1942
SQ FT: 30,000
SALES (est): 7.1MM **Privately Held**
SIC: 3429 3599 5072 5085 Aircraft hardware; machine shop, jobbing & repair; hand tools; industrial supplies; welding repair; hand & edge tools
PA: The Kell-Strom Tool Co Incorporated
214 Church St
Wethersfield CT 06109

(G-10208)
KEYWAY INC
3 Wells Rd (06109-3041)
PHONE..................................860 571-9181
Richard Casciano, *President*
Nancy Casciano, *Admin Sec*
EMP: 3
SQ FT: 2,400
SALES: 300K **Privately Held**
WEB: www.keyway.com
SIC: 3599 Machine shop, jobbing & repair

(G-10209)
LEONA CORP
Also Called: Altman Orthotics & Prosthetics
638 Silas Deane Hwy (06109-3053)
PHONE..................................860 257-3840
John Miller, *President*
Kim Miller, *Vice Pres*
EMP: 3
SALES (est): 230K **Privately Held**
SIC: 3842 Prosthetic appliances

(G-10210)
LINDA CASE WRITING GRAPHIC
103 Park Ave (06109-1633)
PHONE..................................860 563-5713
L Case, *Principal*
EMP: 2 EST: 2015
SALES (est): 88.6K **Privately Held**
SIC: 2759 Commercial printing

(G-10211)
MERRITT MACHINE COMPANY
Also Called: Arrow Tool Division
61 Arrow Rd Ste 5 (06109-1358)
PHONE..................................860 257-4484
Fax: 860 529-2509
EMP: 3
SQ FT: 40,000
SALES: 400K **Privately Held**
SIC: 3599 Machine Shop

(G-10212)
MINUTEMAN PRESS
462 Silas Deane Hwy (06109-2104)
PHONE..................................860 529-4628
Taunya Foley, *Owner*
EMP: 4
SALES (est): 351.4K **Privately Held**
SIC: 2752 Commercial printing, lithographic

(G-10213)
MOZZICATO FMLY INVESTMENTS LLC
Also Called: Sam Maulucci & Sons
631 Ridge Rd (06109-2617)
PHONE..................................860 296-0426
Rino Mozzicato, *Mng Member*
EMP: 7
SQ FT: 1,200
SALES (est): 656.2K **Privately Held**
SIC: 2022 5143 Cheese, natural & processed; cheese

(G-10214)
PATRIOT ENVELOPE LLC
501 Middletown Ave (06109-3809)
PHONE..................................860 529-1553
Lewis Eastwood,
EMP: 3
SALES (est): 210K **Privately Held**
SIC: 2759 Envelopes: printing

(G-10215)
PROGRESS MANUFACTURING LLC
334 Back Ln (06109-3902)
PHONE..................................860 563-6254
Frederick S Krol, *President*
EMP: 1
SALES (est): 52.1K **Privately Held**
SIC: 3999 Manufacturing industries

(G-10216)
RAFFAELE RUBERTO LLC
214 Amherst St (06109-1906)
PHONE..................................860 573-4094
Raffaele Ruberto,
EMP: 1
SALES (est): 77.8K **Privately Held**
SIC: 2844 Face creams or lotions

(G-10217)
READY TOOL LLC
6 Palomina Way (06109-3900)
PHONE..................................860 436-2128
Santo Pirrotta, *President*
EMP: 2 EST: 2017
SALES (est): 168.6K **Privately Held**
SIC: 3599 Machine shop, jobbing & repair

(G-10218)
REFLEX LTG GROUP OF CT LLC
1290 Silas Deane Hwy 1a (06109-4337)
PHONE..................................860 666-1548
Paul Mustone,
EMP: 2
SALES (est): 133.1K **Privately Held**
SIC: 3648 Lighting equipment

Willimantic
Windham County

(G-10219)
49 HIGH ST LLC
49 High St (06226-2223)
PHONE.................................860 423-9496
Justin Smith, *Manager*
EMP: 1
SALES (est): 90.3K **Privately Held**
SIC: 3421 Table & food cutlery, including butchers'

(G-10220)
ALL SMILES DENTAL
1003 Main St (06226-2111)
PHONE.................................860 450-9237
Patricia Sartori, *Principal*
EMP: 2
SALES (est): 204.5K **Privately Held**
SIC: 3843 Enamels, dentists'

(G-10221)
ARCH PARENT INC
82 Storrs Rd (06226-4001)
PHONE.................................860 336-4856
EMP: 3 **Privately Held**
SIC: 2752 Commercial printing, lithographic
HQ: Arch Parent Inc.
9 W 57th St Fl 31
New York NY 10019
212 796-8500

(G-10222)
CHRONICLE PRINTING COMPANY
Also Called: Chronicle, The
1 Chronicle Rd (06226-1932)
P.O. Box 229 (06226-0229)
PHONE.................................860 423-8466
Lucy B Crosbie, *President*
Jean Beckley, *Director*
EMP: 86 EST: 1877
SQ FT: 22,000
SALES (est): 6MM **Privately Held**
WEB: www.thechronicle.com
SIC: 2711 Commercial printing & newspaper publishing combined

(G-10223)
CRISTINA ILIES
1671 Main St (06226-1127)
PHONE.................................860 456-3153
Cristina Ilies, *Principal*
EMP: 2 EST: 2011
SALES (est): 102K **Privately Held**
SIC: 3843 Enamels, dentists'

(G-10224)
DIMENSION ZERO LTD
52 Prospect St (06226)
PHONE.................................860 325-7073
Nuemarcus Brooks, *Ch of Bd*
Marcus Brooks, *Principal*
EMP: 1
SALES (est): 30K **Privately Held**
SIC: 8732 3826 8399 Commercial non-physical research; analytical instruments; spectroscopic & other optical properties measuring equipment; community development groups; social change association

(G-10225)
EASTERN CANVAS WORKS
88 Windham Rd (06226-3524)
PHONE.................................860 245-9174
EMP: 1 EST: 2012
SALES (est): 46.5K **Privately Held**
SIC: 2211 Canvas

(G-10226)
EASTERN CONNECTICUT
42 Boston Post Rd (06226-2920)
PHONE.................................860 423-1972
William Soucy, *Branch Mgr*
Paula Goyette, *Education*
EMP: 10
SALES (est): 480K **Privately Held**
SIC: 1389 7389 Testing, measuring, surveying & analysis services; inspection & testing services

(G-10227)
GENERAL CABLE INDUSTRIES INC
Also Called: Willimantic, CT Plant
1600 Main St (06226-1128)
PHONE.................................860 456-8000
Jim Barney, *President*
Solomon Mulugeta, *Engrg Mgr*
Stew Later, *VP Sales*
Deb Boisvert, *Manager*
Joe Kidder, *Manager*
EMP: 148 **Privately Held**
WEB: www.generalcable.com
SIC: 3496 3357 Miscellaneous fabricated wire products; communication wire
HQ: General Cable Industries, Inc.
4 Tesseneer Dr
Highland Heights KY 41076

(G-10228)
GUARANTEED QUALITY PARTS L L C
Also Called: Gqp
120 Union St (06226-3004)
PHONE.................................860 450-0419
Damien Hazley, *Vice Pres*
John Hazley,
EMP: 3
SQ FT: 7,200
SALES (est): 90K **Privately Held**
WEB: www.parts.com
SIC: 5051 3469 Cable, wire; machine parts, stamped or pressed metal

(G-10229)
GULEMO INC
Also Called: Willimantic Instant Print
2 Birch St (06226-2103)
P.O. Box 467 (06226-0467)
PHONE.................................860 456-1151
Gunnel Stenberg, *President*
Lena Fontaine, *Admin Sec*
EMP: 8
SALES (est): 1.2MM **Privately Held**
WEB: www.gulemo.com
SIC: 2752 Commercial printing, offset

(G-10230)
HORIZONS UNLIMITED INC
Also Called: Quality Sign Crafters
90 S Park St Ste 1 (06226-3336)
P.O. Box 35 (06226-0035)
PHONE.................................860 423-1931
Richard Napolitano, *President*
Lisa Napolitano, *Admin Sec*
EMP: 12 EST: 1995
SQ FT: 15,000
SALES: 1MM **Privately Held**
WEB: www.qscct.com
SIC: 3993 Signs & advertising specialties

(G-10231)
JACOB SPORTZ LLC
28 Ash Ave (06226-1602)
PHONE.................................860 450-1073
Elizabeth Dunnack, *Principal*
Christopher Rallo, *Vice Pres*
Tania Eaton, *Branch Mgr*
EMP: 2
SALES (est): 102.3K **Privately Held**
SIC: 3949 5091 Sporting & athletic goods; sporting & recreation goods

(G-10232)
JOHN DEMARCHI
23 Potter St (06226-3517)
PHONE.................................860 649-9685
John Demarchi, *Principal*
EMP: 1
SALES (est): 40.9K **Privately Held**
SIC: 2399 Fabricated textile products

(G-10233)
MARC BOULEY
Also Called: M B Machine
28 Young St (06226-3333)
PHONE.................................860 450-1713
Marc Bouley, *Owner*
EMP: 6
SQ FT: 1,500
SALES (est): 29.3K **Privately Held**
SIC: 3599 7692 Machine shop, jobbing & repair; welding repair

(G-10234)
POLYMATH SOFTWARE
42 Carey St (06226-2622)
P.O. Box 523 (06226-0523)
PHONE.................................860 423-5823
Michael Cutlip, *Owner*
EMP: 4
SALES (est): 304.9K **Privately Held**
WEB: www.polymath-software.com
SIC: 7372 Business oriented computer software

(G-10235)
QMDI PRESS SERVICES LLC (PA)
322 Main St Ste 1 (06226-3152)
PHONE.................................860 942-8822
Anthony Tatulli, *Mng Member*
EMP: 2
SALES (est): 210.7K **Privately Held**
SIC: 2752 Commercial printing, lithographic

(G-10236)
SIGNS PLUS LLC
700 Main St (06226-2651)
PHONE.................................860 423-3048
Deborah Patten, *General Mgr*
Joseph Duvall,
EMP: 3
SALES (est): 273.2K **Privately Held**
SIC: 3993 5999 Signs, not made in custom sign painting shops; banners, flags, decals & posters

(G-10237)
VEEDER-ROOT CO
407 Jackson St (06226-1738)
PHONE.................................860 450-0895
EMP: 2 EST: 2011
SALES (est): 100K **Privately Held**
SIC: 3599 Mfg Industrial Machinery

(G-10238)
WILLIAM MAGENAU & COMPANY INC
42 Walnut St (06226-2360)
P.O. Box 347 (06226-0347)
PHONE.................................860 423-7713
Harry M Crowther, *President*
Hazel G Crowther, *Admin Sec*
EMP: 4
SQ FT: 5,000
SALES (est): 616.7K **Privately Held**
SIC: 5085 3452 Tools; bolts, nuts, rivets & washers

(G-10239)
WILLIMANTIC BREWING CO LLC
967 Main St (06226-2330)
PHONE.................................860 423-6777
Andrew Matika, *General Mgr*
Karen Gilbransen, *Mktg Coord*
David Scott Wollner, *Manager*
EMP: 1
SALES (est): 168.6K **Privately Held**
SIC: 2082 Beer (alcoholic beverage)

(G-10240)
WILLIMANTIC WASTE PAPER CO INC (PA)
185 Recycling Way (06226-1944)
P.O. Box 239 (06226-0239)
PHONE.................................860 423-4527
Mary Lou De Vivo, *President*
Bridget De Vivo, *Vice Pres*
Thomas E Devivo, *Vice Pres*
Timothy Devivo, *Treasurer*
Peace Omo-Edo, *Controller*
▲ EMP: 120
SQ FT: 70,000
SALES (est): 52.7MM **Privately Held**
SIC: 5093 3341 2611 Waste paper; secondary nonferrous metals; pulp mills

(G-10241)
WINDHAM MATERIALS LLC (PA)
79 Boston Post Rd (06226)
P.O. Box 346 (06226-0346)
PHONE.................................860 456-4111
Steve Aiudi, *President*
Dave Doremus, *Vice Pres*
EMP: 100
SQ FT: 12,000
SALES (est): 6.9MM **Privately Held**
SIC: 5032 5211 1542 3273 Sand, construction; gravel; sand & gravel; institutional building construction; commercial & office building, new construction; commercial & office buildings, renovation & repair; shopping center construction; ready-mixed concrete

(G-10242)
ZOKS HOMEBREWING & WINEMAKING
18 North St (06226-2509)
PHONE.................................860 456-7704
Paul Zocco, *Owner*
EMP: 1 EST: 2000
SALES (est): 108.3K **Privately Held**
WEB: www.homemadebrew.net
SIC: 2084 Wines

Willington
Tolland County

(G-10243)
1ST VERTICAL LLC
65 Balazs Rd (06279-2402)
PHONE.................................860 458-0120
George Marco, *Owner*
EMP: 1 EST: 2011
SALES (est): 74.1K **Privately Held**
SIC: 2591 Blinds vertical

(G-10244)
ADVANCE SOFTWARE LLC
65 Jared Sparks Rd (06279-1503)
PHONE.................................860 429-3721
Rick Baker, *VP Sales*
Iain Baker, *Manager*
EMP: 2
SALES (est): 164.7K **Privately Held**
WEB: www.advance-soft.com
SIC: 7372 Business oriented computer software

(G-10245)
ANYTHING PRINTED LLC
Also Called: Anything Printed Copy Center
331 River Rd (06279-1633)
P.O. Box 376 (06279-0376)
PHONE.................................860 429-1244
Joseph S Varholy, *President*
Joe Barholy, *President*
Pam Barholy, *President*
EMP: 2
SQ FT: 6,000
SALES: 400K **Privately Held**
SIC: 2759 Commercial printing

(G-10246)
CABLE TECHNOLOGY INC
73 River Rd (06279-1830)
PHONE.................................860 429-7889
Michael Cariglia, *President*
Brian Beyor, *General Mgr*
Carl Beyor, *Vice Pres*
EMP: 25 EST: 1982
SQ FT: 35,000
SALES (est): 4.5MM **Privately Held**
SIC: 3677 3357 Electronic coils, transformers & other inductors; nonferrous wiredrawing & insulating

(G-10247)
CHANGESURFER CONSULTING
56 Daleville School Rd (06279-2106)
PHONE.................................312 702-3742
James Hughes, *Owner*
EMP: 1
SALES (est): 46.6K **Privately Held**
SIC: 3423 Hand & edge tools

(G-10248)
GROVER D & SONS LLC
156 Old Farms Rd (06279-1721)
PHONE.................................860 429-9420
Dennis Grover, *Mng Member*
Debra Grover,
EMP: 2
SALES (est): 125.4K **Privately Held**
SIC: 3441 Fabricated structural metal

Willington - Tolland County (G-10249)

(G-10249)
HARTFORD STONE WORKS INC
3 Lisa Ln (06279-2241)
PHONE..................860 684-7995
Christine Reilly, *President*
Joseph M Reilly, *Vice Pres*
EMP: 2
SALES (est): 142.6K **Privately Held**
SIC: 3281 5032 Marble, building: cut & shaped; building stone

(G-10250)
HOUSE OF BUBBA LLC
106 Clint Eldredge Rd (06279-1734)
PHONE..................860 429-4250
Tammy L E Gifford,
Tammy Gifford,
EMP: 2
SALES (est): 170K **Privately Held**
SIC: 3911 7389 7373 3369 Jewelry, precious metal; apparel designers, commercial; computer-aided design (CAD) systems service; castings, except die-castings, precision; silversmithing

(G-10251)
KUCKO CHAIN SAW SUPPLIES
65 Kucko Rd (06279-2310)
PHONE..................860 684-3887
Henry Kucko, *Owner*
EMP: 1
SALES (est): 118.6K **Privately Held**
SIC: 3546 Saws & sawing equipment

(G-10252)
NELSON ARCHTCTURAL RESTORATION
40 Fisher Hill Rd (06279-1605)
PHONE..................860 429-3830
Randall Nelson, *Owner*
EMP: 1
SALES (est): 98K **Privately Held**
WEB: www.nae-us.com
SIC: 8712 3299 Architectural services; architectural sculptures: gypsum, clay, papier mache, etc.

(G-10253)
PETRO-TECH INDUSTRIES LLC
16 Laurel Dr (06279-2247)
PHONE..................860 881-5890
EMP: 1
SALES (est): 49.1K **Privately Held**
SIC: 3999 Manufacturing industries

(G-10254)
PJ SPECIALTIES
7 Luchon Rd (06279-1616)
P.O. Box 41 (06279-0041)
PHONE..................860 429-7626
William Hodge, *Owner*
EMP: 10
SALES: 300K **Privately Held**
WEB: www.pjspecialties.com
SIC: 7336 2395 Silk screen design; embroidery & art needlework

(G-10255)
R & M LOGGING
268 River Rd (06279-1631)
PHONE..................860 429-6209
EMP: 2
SALES (est): 81.7K **Privately Held**
SIC: 2411 Logging

(G-10256)
RICH SIGNS & DESIGNS
55 Timber Ln (06279-1837)
PHONE..................860 429-2165
John Peterson, *Principal*
EMP: 2
SALES (est): 94.9K **Privately Held**
SIC: 3993 Signs & advertising specialties

(G-10257)
SAVOIR CONSULTING & MFG CO LLC
102 Latham Rd (06279-1916)
PHONE..................860 933-7614
Roland D Savior Jr,
EMP: 1
SALES (est): 100.8K **Privately Held**
SIC: 3544 Industrial molds

(G-10258)
SHERRI MASINDA
216 Luchon Rd (06279-1644)
PHONE..................860 429-4988
Mark Masinda, *Owner*
EMP: 1
SALES (est): 114.9K **Privately Held**
SIC: 2834 Vitamin, nutrient & hematinic preparations for human use

(G-10259)
TOMS TAZ LURES
245 River Rd (06279-1630)
PHONE..................860 429-0307
EMP: 2
SALES (est): 149.4K **Privately Held**
SIC: 3949 Snowshoes

(G-10260)
TRUMBULL RECREATION SUPPLY CO
148 River Rd (06279-1629)
P.O. Box 109 (06279-0109)
PHONE..................860 429-6604
Francis Kosowicz Sr, *President*
EMP: 7
SALES (est): 1MM **Privately Held**
SIC: 3088 Shower stalls, fiberglass & plastic

(G-10261)
WHITNEY PRATT
64 Cemetery Rd (06279-2300)
PHONE..................860 565-6431
Peter Kelly, *Principal*
Bret Lynch, *Manager*
Lloyd Torrey, *Administration*
EMP: 2 EST: 2018
SALES (est): 86K **Privately Held**
SIC: 3724 Aircraft engines & engine parts

Wilton
Fairfield County

(G-10262)
2 GIRL A TRUNK
35 Dudley Rd (06897-3508)
PHONE..................203 762-0360
Carol Schuler, *Principal*
EMP: 3
SALES (est): 231.4K **Privately Held**
SIC: 3161 Trunks

(G-10263)
21ST CENTURY FOX AMERICA INC
20 Westport Rd (06897-4549)
PHONE..................203 563-6600
Ralph Masiello, *President*
Carey Chase, *Chairman*
Linda Campbell, *Area Mgr*
Paul Schmidt, *Vice Pres*
Joe Poulos, *Engineer*
EMP: 8
SALES (corp-wide): 90.2B **Publicly Held**
SIC: 2711 Newspapers: publishing only, not printed on site
HQ: 21st Century Fox America, Inc.
1211 Ave Of The Americas
New York NY 10036
212 852-7000

(G-10264)
22 CANDLES
188 Chestnut Hill Rd (06897-4109)
PHONE..................203 577-5540
Natasha Babchak, *Principal*
EMP: 1
SALES (est): 39.6K **Privately Held**
SIC: 3999 Candles

(G-10265)
A FLOOD OF PAPER
94 Old Ridgefield Rd (06897-3017)
PHONE..................203 529-3030
David Gillaugh, *President*
EMP: 2
SALES (est): 152.8K **Privately Held**
SIC: 2754 Stationery & invitation printing, gravure

(G-10266)
AARONS ENTERPRISES
24 Old Hwy (06897-3111)
PHONE..................203 762-9764
Aaron Nachbar, *Owner*
EMP: 1
SALES (est): 159.6K **Privately Held**
SIC: 5032 1381 Brick, stone & related material; service well drilling

(G-10267)
AIR AGE INC
88 Danbury Rd Ste 2b (06897-4423)
PHONE..................203 431-9000
Louis Defrancesco Jr, *President*
Louis De Francesco Jr, *President*
Yvonne De Francesco, *Exec VP*
Carol Shepherd, *CFO*
Yelena Trakht, *Accounting Mgr*
EMP: 27 EST: 1929
SQ FT: 9,675
SALES (est): 5MM **Privately Held**
WEB: www.airage.com
SIC: 2721 2731 Magazines: publishing only, not printed on site; books: publishing & printing

(G-10268)
ALBERTO CASTILLO
Also Called: Zara Tool & Die Co
7 Mather St (06897-5012)
PHONE..................203 834-1486
Alberto Castillo, *Owner*
EMP: 2
SALES (est): 96.9K **Privately Held**
SIC: 3544 Special dies & tools

(G-10269)
AMANDAS DAILY IDEAS LLC
24 Glen Hill Rd (06897-2420)
PHONE..................203 761-8599
Amanda Lord, *Principal*
EMP: 2
SALES (est): 105K **Privately Held**
SIC: 2711 Newspapers, publishing & printing

(G-10270)
ASML US LLC
77 Danbury Rd (06897-4407)
PHONE..................203 761-4000
Michael Brennan, *Superintendent*
Noreen Harned, *Vice Pres*
Gary Zhang, *Vice Pres*
Terry Blakeslee, *Engineer*
David Calabro, *Engineer*
EMP: 800
SALES (corp-wide): 12.5B **Privately Held**
SIC: 3555 Lithographic stones
HQ: Asml Us, Llc
2650 W Geronimo Pl
Chandler AZ 85224
480 696-2888

(G-10271)
BEIERSDORF INC (DH)
45 Danbury Rd (06897-4405)
PHONE..................203 563-5800
Amy Nenner, *Vice Pres*
Kathy Shea, *Vice Pres*
Mauricio Valdes, *Vice Pres*
Joerg Disseld, *CFO*
Alex Lund, *Marketing Staff*
▲ EMP: 9
SQ FT: 300,000
SALES (est): 223.4MM
SALES (corp-wide): 11.8B **Privately Held**
WEB: www.bdfusa.com
SIC: 2844 Face creams or lotions
HQ: Beiersdorf North America Inc.
45 Danbury Rd
Wilton CT 06897
203 563-5800

(G-10272)
BEIERSDORF NORTH AMERICA INC (DH)
45 Danbury Rd (06897-4405)
PHONE..................203 563-5800
James A Kenton, *CEO*
Bill Graham, *President*
Stefan Heidenreich, *Chairman*
Sarah Simpson, *Business Mgr*
Jorg Diesfeld, *Vice Pres*
▲ EMP: 10
SALES (est): 223.4MM
SALES (corp-wide): 11.8B **Privately Held**
SIC: 2844 5122 3842 2841 Face creams or lotions; antiseptics; bandages & dressings; stockinette, surgical; soap: granulated, liquid, cake, flaked or chip; tape, pressure sensitive: made from purchased materials
HQ: Beiersdorf Ag
Unnastr. 48
Hamburg 20253
404 909-0

(G-10273)
BIOWAVE INNOVATIONS LLC
274 Ridgefield Rd (06897-2335)
PHONE..................203 982-8157
Donald Rabinovitch, *President*
EMP: 191
SALES (est): 8.5MM **Privately Held**
SIC: 3844 X-ray apparatus & tubes

(G-10274)
BLUE BUFFALO COMPANY LTD (DH)
11 River Rd Ste 200 (06897-6011)
PHONE..................203 762-9751
Kurt Schmidt, *CEO*
William Bishop, *Principal*
Bill Bishop, *Chairman*
Brenda Gonzalez, *Regional Mgr*
Debbie Skibo, *Regional Mgr*
EMP: 277
SALES (est): 441.6MM
SALES (corp-wide): 16.8B **Publicly Held**
SIC: 2047 5149 Dog & cat food; pet foods
HQ: Blue Buffalo Pet Products, Inc.
11 River Rd Ste 103
Wilton CT 06897
203 762-9751

(G-10275)
BLUE BUFFALO PET PRODUCTS INC (HQ)
11 River Rd Ste 103 (06897-6011)
P.O. Box 770 (06897-0770)
PHONE..................203 762-9751
William Bishop Jr, *President*
Kathryn K Garrison, *Vice Pres*
Gerald J Morris, *Vice Pres*
Mike Nathenson, *Treasurer*
Christian Setterlund, *Marketing Staff*
EMP: 47
SQ FT: 41,000
SALES: 1.2B
SALES (corp-wide): 16.8B **Publicly Held**
SIC: 2048 Canned pet food (except dog & cat)
PA: General Mills, Inc.
1 General Mills Blvd
Minneapolis MN 55426
763 764-7600

(G-10276)
BOTTOMLINE TECHNOLOGIES DE INC
187 Danbury Rd Ste 204 (06897-4079)
PHONE..................203 761-1289
Robert A Eberle, *President*
Beate Dayton, *Auditor*
Benjamin Nutting, *Technology*
Bob Mullen, *Director*
EMP: 1
SALES (corp-wide): 421.9MM **Publicly Held**
SIC: 7372 Business oriented computer software
PA: Bottomline Technologies (De), Inc.
325 Corporate Dr Ste 300
Portsmouth NH 03801
603 436-0700

(G-10277)
BUCHANAN MINERALS LLC (DH)
57 Danbury Rd Ste 201 (06897-4439)
PHONE..................304 392-1000
Arold R Spindler, *CEO*
Garold Spindler, *CEO*
James Campbell, *COO*
Robert Cline, *Vice Pres*
EMP: 53
SALES (est): 5.3MM
SALES (corp-wide): 1.9B **Privately Held**
SIC: 1241 Mining services: bituminous

▲ = Import ▼ = Export
◆ = Import/Export

GEOGRAPHIC SECTION
Wilton - Fairfield County (G-10309)

HQ: Coronado Coal Llc
  57 Danbury Rd Ste 201
  Wilton CT 06897
  203 761-1291

(G-10278)
BUFFALO INDUSTRIAL FABRICS INC
372 Danbury Rd Ste 199 (06897-2523)
P.O. Box 607 (06897-0607)
PHONE.................................203 553-9400
Stewart Ehrenhaus, *President*
EMP: 5
SQ FT: 1,500
SALES (est): 702.8K **Privately Held**
SIC: 2281 Weaving yarn, spun

(G-10279)
BUSINESS MARKETING & PUBG INC
13 Silvermine Woods (06897-4235)
P.O. Box 7457 (06897-7457)
PHONE.................................203 834-9959
Donna L Young, *Principal*
EMP: 1
SALES (est): 55.2K **Privately Held**
SIC: 2741 Miscellaneous publishing

(G-10280)
CHILDRENS HEALTH MARKET INC
27 Cannon Rd Ste 1b (06897-2627)
P.O. Box 7294 (06897-7294)
PHONE.................................203 762-2938
Nancy M Grace, *President*
Timothy C Grace, *Principal*
James C Grace, *Admin Sec*
EMP: 7
SQ FT: 1,400
SALES (est): 782.3K **Privately Held**
WEB: www.thegreatbodyshop.net
SIC: 2741 8748 Miscellaneous publishing; business consulting

(G-10281)
CLASSIC SIGN & GRAPHICS
Also Called: Classic Sign Company
23 Gaylord Dr N (06897-3932)
PHONE.................................203 834-1145
Mark Lussier, *Owner*
EMP: 1
SALES (est): 92.7K **Privately Held**
SIC: 3993 Signs & advertising specialties

(G-10282)
CORONADO GROUP LLC (PA)
57 Danbury Rd Ste 201 (06897-4439)
PHONE.................................203 761-1291
Jeff Bitzer, *Vice Pres*
Garold R Spindler, *Mng Member*
EMP: 6 EST: 2015
SALES (est): 1.9B **Privately Held**
SIC: 1241 Coal mining services

(G-10283)
CORTINA LEARNING INTL INC (PA)
Also Called: Cortina Famous Schools
33 Catalpa Rd (06897-2002)
PHONE.................................800 245-2145
Robert E Livesey, *President*
Robert Ellis, *Vice Pres*
Magdalen B Livesey, *Admin Sec*
EMP: 12 EST: 1882
SALES (est): 1.6MM **Privately Held**
WEB: www.cortina-french.com
SIC: 2731 8249 Books: publishing only; correspondence school

(G-10284)
COTTON PRESS LLC
596 Nod Hill Rd (06897-1303)
PHONE.................................203 257-7958
Dylan Cotton, *Principal*
EMP: 2
SALES (est): 119.2K **Privately Held**
SIC: 2741 Miscellaneous publishing

(G-10285)
CROTON INDUSTRIES EAST AFRICA
18 Banks Dr (06897-3202)
PHONE.................................407 947-4381
Larisa Warhol, *Principal*
Myles Lutheran, *Principal*
EMP: 2
SALES (est): 82.9K **Privately Held**
SIC: 3999 Manufacturing industries

(G-10286)
CULTURE MEDIA LLC
944 Danbury Rd (06897-4909)
PHONE.................................203 470-5918
EMP: 2
SALES (est): 74.4K **Privately Held**
SIC: 2836 Culture media

(G-10287)
CYCLING SPORTS GROUP INC (HQ)
Also Called: Cannondale Sports Group
1 Cannondale Way (06897-4319)
PHONE.................................608 268-8916
Peter Woods, *President*
Matt Takovich, *Credit Staff*
Kevin Bennett, *Sales Dir*
Brian Immel, *Marketing Staff*
Burton Avery, *Manager*
◆ EMP: 70
SQ FT: 32,500
SALES (est): 112.7MM
SALES (corp-wide): 2.6B **Privately Held**
SIC: 3751 2329 Bicycles & related parts; men's & boys' sportswear & athletic clothing; athletic (warmup, sweat & jogging) suits: men's & boys'
PA: Industries Dorel Inc, Les
  1255 Av Greene Bureau 300
  Westmount QC H3Z 2
  514 934-3034

(G-10288)
DAMPITS LLC
98 Ridgefield Rd (06897-2427)
PHONE.................................203 210-7946
David Hollander, *Principal*
EMP: 3
SALES (est): 296.3K **Privately Held**
SIC: 3634 Electric housewares & fans

(G-10289)
DIETZE & ASSOCIATES LLC
Also Called: Dietze Associates
88 Danbury Rd Ste 1a (06897-4423)
PHONE.................................203 762-3500
Herlof Sorensen, *Branch Mgr*
EMP: 14
SALES (est): 621K
SALES (corp-wide): 2.4MM **Privately Held**
SIC: 1311 Crude petroleum & natural gas
PA: Dietze & Associates Llc
  88 Danbury Rd Ste 1a
  Wilton CT 06897
  203 762-3500

(G-10290)
EHRICHED STITCH LLC
196 Danbury Rd (06897-4029)
PHONE.................................203 210-5107
Suzanne E Vallerie, *Principal*
EMP: 2 EST: 2012
SALES (est): 250.5K **Privately Held**
SIC: 3552 Embroidery machines

(G-10291)
END GRAIN WOODWORKS LLC
73 Old Driftway (06897-2316)
PHONE.................................203 817-7154
Kieran McCauley, *Principal*
EMP: 1
SALES (est): 93.4K **Privately Held**
SIC: 2431 Millwork

(G-10292)
ERIC NORDLUND WELDING
140 Old Mill Rd (06897-5020)
PHONE.................................203 544-8293
Eric Nordlund, *Principal*
EMP: 1 EST: 2009
SALES (est): 53K **Privately Held**
SIC: 7692 Welding repair

(G-10293)
ERIELLE MEDIA LLC
341 Newtown Tpke (06897-3605)
PHONE.................................203 563-9159
Eric Feidner,
Marcelle Soviero,
EMP: 2

SALES (est): 96.2K **Privately Held**
SIC: 2741 Miscellaneous publishing

(G-10294)
FACET SKIS
46 Mollbrook Dr (06897-4709)
PHONE.................................203 529-3681
EMP: 2 EST: 2013
SALES (est): 112K **Privately Held**
SIC: 3949 Sporting & athletic goods

(G-10295)
FEDERICI BRANDS LLC
195 Danbury Rd (06897-4075)
PHONE.................................203 762-7667
Jeff Livingston, *President*
James Federici, *Principal*
Lynn Federici, *VP Opers*
Joseph Cincotta, *Research*
John Roth, *CFO*
▲ EMP: 19
SALES (est): 3.3MM **Privately Held**
SIC: 3273 Ready-mixed concrete

(G-10296)
FINE WOODWORKING
143 Cheesespring Rd (06897-2306)
PHONE.................................203 762-8197
EMP: 2 EST: 2017
SALES (est): 85.2K **Privately Held**
SIC: 2431 Millwork

(G-10297)
FROSTBITE LLC
46 Mollbrook Dr (06897-4709)
PHONE.................................203 240-3449
Mike Migoiorino, *Mng Member*
EMP: 1
SALES (est): 82.7K **Privately Held**
SIC: 3949 5941 7389 Snow skis; skiing equipment;

(G-10298)
GREGORYS SAWMILL LLC
3 Pimpewaug Rd (06897-2713)
PHONE.................................203 762-8298
Taber Gregory,
EMP: 2
SALES (est): 40K **Privately Held**
SIC: 2421 Sawmills & planing mills, general

(G-10299)
GROUP WORKS
50 Powder Horn Hill Rd (06897-3123)
P.O. Box 7269 (06897-7269)
PHONE.................................203 834-7905
Shane Scott, *Owner*
EMP: 4
SALES (est): 266.9K **Privately Held**
WEB: www.groupworksllc.com
SIC: 3949 1799 Swimming pools, except plastic; swimming pool construction

(G-10300)
IMAGIN MINERALS
Also Called: Saint Cloud Mining
32 Bryant (06897)
PHONE.................................203 762-1249
Pat Freeman, *Chairman*
EMP: 2
SALES (est): 117.5K **Privately Held**
WEB: www.imaginminerals.com
SIC: 1081 Metal mining services

(G-10301)
IMPERIAL SUGAR COMPANY
40 Danbury Rd (06897-4441)
P.O. Box 810 (06897-0810)
PHONE.................................203 761-8474
Peggy Jenkins, *Buyer*
Jeana Hines, *VP Sales*
John Sheptor, *Branch Mgr*
EMP: 205
SALES (corp-wide): 37.6B **Privately Held**
SIC: 5149 2062 Sugar, refined; granulated cane sugar from purchased raw sugar or syrup
HQ: Imperial Sugar Company
  3 Sugar Creek Center Blvd # 500
  Sugar Land TX 77478
  281 491-9181

(G-10302)
INFORMATION TODAY INC
Online
88 Danbury Rd Ste 2c (06897-4423)
PHONE.................................203 761-1466
John Sculley, *Partner*
Adam Pemberton, *Manager*
EMP: 14
SALES (corp-wide): 20.3MM **Privately Held**
WEB: www.infotoday.com
SIC: 2721 2731 7389 Magazines: publishing only, not printed on site; book publishing; convention & show services
PA: Information Today, Inc.
  143 Old Marlton Pike
  Medford NJ 08055
  609 654-6266

(G-10303)
INTERNATIONAL GARRETT-HEWITT
228 Danbury Rd (06897-4008)
PHONE.................................203 761-1542
Jason Clerke, *Principal*
Deirdre Larosa, *Accounts Mgr*
EMP: 1
SALES (est): 45.1K **Privately Held**
SIC: 3991 Brooms

(G-10304)
JAMES P KING
Also Called: Brown House Communications
108 Pond Rd (06897-3220)
PHONE.................................203 834-0050
James P King, *Owner*
EMP: 1
SALES (est): 78K **Privately Held**
SIC: 2741 Newsletter publishing; technical manuals: publishing only, not printed on site

(G-10305)
JPG CONSULTING INC
65 Heather Ln (06897-4130)
PHONE.................................203 247-2730
Johnathan P Griep, *President*
Jonathan P Griep, *President*
Joseph Griep, *Vice Pres*
Mark Griep, *Treasurer*
Martha E Griep, *Admin Sec*
EMP: 3
SALES (est): 199K **Privately Held**
SIC: 7372 Business oriented computer software

(G-10306)
JSAN PUBLISHING LLC
14 Woodway Ln (06897-4730)
PHONE.................................203 210-5495
James Beecher, *Principal*
EMP: 2 EST: 2008
SALES (est): 165.2K **Privately Held**
SIC: 2741 Miscellaneous publishing

(G-10307)
L & L CAPITAL PARTNERS LLC
57 Danbury Rd Ste 3 (06897-4439)
PHONE.................................203 834-6222
Bulkeley Griswold, *Partner*
Steve Rossetter,
EMP: 17
SQ FT: 2,500
SALES (est): 2MM **Privately Held**
WEB: www.llcapitalpartners.net
SIC: 6726 2511 Investment offices; wood household furniture

(G-10308)
LAB SOFTWARE ASSOCIATES
48 Old Driftway (06897-2315)
PHONE.................................203 762-1342
James Cooper, *Owner*
EMP: 2
SALES (est): 132.2K **Privately Held**
SIC: 7372 Prepackaged software

(G-10309)
LEASEFISH LLC
11 Bayberry Ln (06897-3302)
PHONE.................................203 293-3603
Rafael Ceron,
Jeffrey Jacobson,
Luciano Sampaio,
EMP: 3

(PA)=Parent Co (HQ)=Headquarters (DH)=Div Headquarters
✪ = New Business established in last 2 years

2020 Harris Connecticut Manufacturers Directory

Wilton - Fairfield County (G-10310)

SALES (est): 86.5K **Privately Held**
SIC: 2741

(G-10310)
LOUIS DREYFUS HOLDING COMPANY (HQ)
40 Danbury Rd (06897-4441)
PHONE.................................203 761-2000
Hal Wolkin, *President*
Ernest F Steiner, *Director*
Carol Aronoff, *Admin Sec*
◆ EMP: 350
SQ FT: 70,000
SALES (est): 168.7MM
SALES (corp-wide): 2.9MM **Privately Held**
SIC: 6221 5153 6512 6531 Commodity traders, contracts; grains; commercial & industrial building operation; real estate managers; natural gas production
PA: Impala Sas
    4 Rue Euler
    Paris 8e Arrondissement 75008
    145 623-786

(G-10311)
M&G BERMAN INC
67 Pond Rd (06897-3226)
PHONE.................................203 834-8754
Murray Berman, *Owner*
EMP: 4
SALES (est): 210.8K **Privately Held**
SIC: 2711 Newspapers

(G-10312)
MKRS CORPORATION
32 Blueberry Hill Pl (06897-1406)
PHONE.................................203 762-2662
Rohit Sharma, *Principal*
EMP: 6
SALES (est): 101.4K **Privately Held**
SIC: 2711 Newspapers

(G-10313)
MONTAGE SOFTWARE SYSTEMS INC
76 Hillbrook Rd (06897-1708)
P.O. Box 7574 (06897-7574)
PHONE.................................203 834-1144
Jim Alonso, *President*
Kathryn Alonso, *Vice Pres*
EMP: 3
SALES (est): 171.1K **Privately Held**
WEB: www.montagesoftware.com
SIC: 7371 7372 Computer software development; prepackaged software

(G-10314)
MPI SYSTEMS INC
28 Powder Horn Hill Rd (06897-3121)
PHONE.................................203 762-2260
Richard Kaye, *President*
Annette G Kaye, *Vice Pres*
EMP: 5
SALES (est): 487.5K **Privately Held**
WEB: www.mpisystems.com
SIC: 7372 Prepackaged software

(G-10315)
NANTUCKET SPIDER LLC
49 Liberty St (06897-3218)
P.O. Box 536 (06897-0536)
PHONE.................................203 423-3031
Jeffrey Busch,
Nancy Jack,
EMP: 2
SALES: 100K **Privately Held**
SIC: 5191 2879 Insecticides; insecticides & pesticides

(G-10316)
OPTICAL RESEARCH TECHNOLOGIES
310 Hurlbutt St (06897-2605)
P.O. Box 398 (06897-0398)
PHONE.................................203 762-9063
John Wilson, *Owner*
EMP: 3
SALES: 1.5MM **Privately Held**
WEB: www.wiltonsingers.com
SIC: 3827 Lenses, optical: all types except ophthalmic

(G-10317)
OUTPOST EXPLORATION LLC
7 Broad Axe Ln (06897-3904)
PHONE.................................203 762-7206
Paul Mazzarulli, *Principal*
EMP: 3 EST: 2015
SALES (est): 127K **Privately Held**
SIC: 1311 Crude petroleum & natural gas

(G-10318)
PEMBERTON PRESS INC
462 Danbury Rd (06897-2132)
PHONE.................................203 761-1466
EMP: 1
SALES (est): 37.5K **Privately Held**
SIC: 2741 Miscellaneous publishing

(G-10319)
PERRY HEIGHTS PRESS LLC
Also Called: Readily Apparent
610 Nod Hill Rd (06897-1305)
P.O. Box 102, Georgetown (06829-0102)
PHONE.................................203 767-6509
Brendan Hanrahan,
Nancy Hanrahan,
EMP: 2
SALES (est): 25K **Privately Held**
SIC: 2741 7373 Miscellaneous publishing; computer integrated systems design; computer systems analysis & design

(G-10320)
POLSTAL CORPORATION
10 Admiral Ln (06897-4710)
PHONE.................................203 849-7788
Peter Wycislo, *President*
Danuta Wycislo, *Vice Pres*
▲ EMP: 4
SALES (est): 302K **Privately Held**
SIC: 3325 3295 3315 Steel foundries; graphite, natural: ground, pulverized, refined or blended; steel wire & related products

(G-10321)
PRINT PRODUCERS LLC
1042 Ridgefield Rd (06897-1006)
PHONE.................................203 761-9877
Joanne Cerrone, *Manager*
Rick Smith, *Manager*
EMP: 2
SALES (est): 250K **Privately Held**
SIC: 2759 Commercial printing

(G-10322)
PROSPEROUS PRINTING LLC
Also Called: Paul's Prosperous Printing
35 Danbury Rd Ste 4 (06897-4428)
PHONE.................................203 834-1962
Paul Hafter, *Mng Member*
EMP: 3
SQ FT: 1,700
SALES (est): 352.4K **Privately Held**
SIC: 2752 2791 2789 Commercial printing, offset; typesetting; bookbinding & related work

(G-10323)
RACEMYFACE LLC
82 Village Ct (06897-4547)
PHONE.................................203 285-8090
Levente Hatvani,
EMP: 2
SALES (est): 101.2K **Privately Held**
SIC: 7372 Application computer software

(G-10324)
RAVAGO AMERICAS LLC
Muehlstein
10 Westport Rd (06897-4543)
PHONE.................................203 855-6000
David Roesner, *Plant Mgr*
Margarita Salazar, *Export Mgr*
Judson Roszman, *Manager*
Wyatt Stine, *Manager*
EMP: 50
SALES (corp-wide): 1.9MM **Privately Held**
SIC: 2821 Plastics materials & resins
HQ: Ravago Americas Llc
    1900 Summit Tower Blvd
    Orlando FL 32810
    407 875-9595

(G-10325)
ROCKWELL ART & FRAMING LLC (PA)
Also Called: Wilton Art Framing
151 Old Ridgefield Rd # 101 (06897-3058)
PHONE.................................203 762-8311
Hector Rosario, *Owner*
EMP: 6
SQ FT: 1,500
SALES (est): 700.9K **Privately Held**
SIC: 2499 Picture & mirror frames, wood

(G-10326)
SABOL ASSOCIATES
50 Village Walk (06897-4042)
PHONE.................................203 762-2183
Denise Sabol, *Owner*
EMP: 1
SALES (est): 49K **Privately Held**
WEB: www.sabolassoc.com
SIC: 8742 3843 Marketing consulting services; dental equipment & supplies

(G-10327)
SALTBOX PRESS LLC
522 Ridgefield Rd (06897-1926)
PHONE.................................203 762-9731
Lynda Campbell, *Principal*
EMP: 1
SALES (est): 59.3K **Privately Held**
SIC: 2741 Miscellaneous publishing

(G-10328)
SERVCO OIL INC
387 Danbury Rd (06897-2529)
PHONE.................................203 762-7994
Mike Buono, *General Mgr*
Philip Olkoski, *Controller*
EMP: 2
SALES (est): 81.9K **Privately Held**
SIC: 1321 7372 Propane (natural) production; application computer software

(G-10329)
SHIELD GROUP
64 Danbury Rd Ste 700 (06897-4470)
PHONE.................................203 981-6169
EMP: 2 EST: 2016
SALES (est): 67K **Privately Held**
SIC: 2329 Men's & boys' clothing

(G-10330)
SHILLER AND COMPANY INC
Also Called: Shillermath
258 Thunder Lake Rd (06897-1339)
PHONE.................................203 210-5208
Larry Shiller, *President*
EMP: 90
SALES (est): 1,000K **Privately Held**
SIC: 2741 Miscellaneous publishing

(G-10331)
SIDEL & MCELWREATH LLC
142 Old Kings Hwy (06897-3726)
PHONE.................................203 834-2946
Evan Pepper, *Principal*
EMP: 1
SALES (est): 44.7K **Privately Held**
SIC: 3999 Wreaths, artificial

(G-10332)
SLV CONSULTING INC
6 Forest Ln (06897-1913)
PHONE.................................917 892-4034
Dharmesh Vazarkar, *Principal*
EMP: 2
SALES (est): 111.8K **Privately Held**
SIC: 7372 Prepackaged software

(G-10333)
SPRAYFOAMPOLYMERSCOM LLC
134 Old Ridgefield Rd # 3 (06897-3048)
P.O. Box 1182, New Canaan (06840-1182)
PHONE.................................800 853-1577
Richard Ettinger, *President*
EMP: 3
SALES (est): 870.6K **Privately Held**
SIC: 3086 5199 Insulation or cushioning material, foamed plastic; plastics foam

(G-10334)
STARTECH ENVIRONMENTAL CORP (PA)
88 Danbury Rd Ste 2b (06897-4423)
PHONE.................................203 762-2499
Joseph F Longo, *Ch of Bd*
Ralph N Dechiaro, *Vice Pres*
Peter J Scanlon, *CFO*
EMP: 14
SQ FT: 5,612
SALES (est): 157.4K **Privately Held**
WEB: www.startech.net
SIC: 3559 Recycling machinery

(G-10335)
SYNERGY SOLUTIONS LLC
276 Newtown Tpke (06897-4715)
PHONE.................................203 762-1153
Barney Stevenson,
EMP: 5
SALES (est): 400K **Privately Held**
WEB: www.solves-it.com
SIC: 7372 Prepackaged software

(G-10336)
SYZYGY HALTHCARE SOLUTIONS LLC
33 Cannon Rd (06897-2619)
P.O. Box 588, Westport (06881-0588)
PHONE.................................203 226-4449
John Linderman, *Mng Member*
EMP: 4
SQ FT: 5,000
SALES (est): 300K **Privately Held**
SIC: 2834 Pharmaceutical preparations

(G-10337)
TESTING TECHNOLOGIES INC
30 Spoonwood Rd (06897-4114)
PHONE.................................212 835-3617
Sean Selinger, *Director*
EMP: 2
SALES (est): 144.9K **Privately Held**
SIC: 2752 Commercial printing, lithographic

(G-10338)
TOWN OF WILTON
Also Called: Public Works Dept
238 Danbury Rd (06897-4058)
PHONE.................................203 563-0152
Thomas Therkepple, *Director*
EMP: 4 **Privately Held**
SIC: 3531 Drags, road (construction & road maintenance equipment)
PA: Town Of Wilton
    238 Danbury Rd
    Wilton CT 06897
    203 563-0100

(G-10339)
ULTIMATE INK LLC
681 Danbury Rd Ste 1 (06897-5024)
PHONE.................................203 762-0602
James Gerwect,
EMP: 5
SQ FT: 500
SALES (est): 100K **Privately Held**
SIC: 2261 Screen printing of cotton broadwoven fabrics

(G-10340)
WFV CABINETMAKER
760 Ridgefield Rd (06897-1415)
PHONE.................................203 761-9109
William Verill, *Owner*
EMP: 1
SALES (est): 67.8K **Privately Held**
SIC: 2434 Wood kitchen cabinets

(G-10341)
WHEELS 45
386 Danbury Rd (06897-2510)
PHONE.................................203 762-8684
John Sanini, *Principal*
EMP: 2
SALES (est): 156.4K **Privately Held**
SIC: 3312 Wheels

(G-10342)
YOURCOVER LLC
11 Grumman Hill Rd Ste 2 (06897-4500)
PHONE.................................203 563-9233
Michele Kolier, *Marketing Staff*
Mark Kolier,

GEOGRAPHIC SECTION

Windsor - Hartford County (G-10369)

Michelle Kolier,
EMP: 2
SALES (est): 264.3K **Privately Held**
WEB: www.yourcover.com
SIC: 2621 Cover paper

Winchester Center
Litchfield County

(G-10343)
BEAR MARKET
397 Colebrook River Rd (06098)
PHONE................................860 379-8943
Molly Silver, *Owner*
EMP: 3
SALES (est): 172.1K **Privately Held**
SIC: 3944 Craft & hobby kits & sets

(G-10344)
CUSTOM INTERIORS
152 Colebrook River Rd (06098-2205)
PHONE................................860 738-8754
Glen Lauzier, *Principal*
EMP: 4
SALES (est): 658K **Privately Held**
SIC: 2434 Wood kitchen cabinets

Windham
Windham County

(G-10345)
E & J ANDRYCHOWSKI FARMS
257 Brick Top Rd (06280-1006)
PHONE................................860 423-4124
Robert Andrychowski, *Owner*
EMP: 3
SALES: 75K **Privately Held**
SIC: 2011 Meat packing plants

(G-10346)
GEBHARDTS SAWMILL
101 Ballamahack Rd (06280-1102)
PHONE................................860 423-0123
David Gebhardt, *Owner*
EMP: 1
SALES (est): 88.3K **Privately Held**
SIC: 2421 Sawmills & planing mills, general

(G-10347)
J P FABRICATION AND RPS LLC
622 Jerusalem Rd (06280-1512)
PHONE................................860 423-8993
James L Palmer, *Owner*
EMP: 1
SALES (est): 113.8K **Privately Held**
SIC: 3599 Machine shop, jobbing & repair

(G-10348)
JOHNS FLOOR SANDING
75 Mullen Hill Rd (06280-1416)
P.O. Box 28 (06280-0028)
PHONE................................860 423-3852
John Rood, *Owner*
EMP: 2
SALES (est): 166.4K **Privately Held**
SIC: 3553 Sanding machines, except portable floor sanders: woodworking

(G-10349)
L & M LOGGING LLC
5 George St (06280-1115)
PHONE................................860 208-9884
Earl Messier, *Principal*
EMP: 2 **EST:** 2017
SALES (est): 81.7K **Privately Held**
SIC: 2411 Logging

Windsor
Hartford County

(G-10350)
A & A PRODUCTS AND SERVICES
610 Hayden Station Rd (06095-1338)
PHONE................................860 683-0879
Fred Saleh, *Owner*
EMP: 3
SALES (est): 201.7K **Privately Held**
SIC: 3471 Plating & polishing

(G-10351)
A&S INNERSPRINGS USA LLC
4 Market Cir (06095-1422)
PHONE................................860 298-0401
Brian Akchin, *VP Sales*
Deborah Covey, *Mng Member*
EMP: 4 **EST:** 2016
SALES (est): 237.5K
SALES (corp-wide): 162.3MM **Privately Held**
SIC: 2515 Mattresses & bedsprings
PA: Agro Holding Gmbh
Senfdamm 21
Bad Essen 49152
547 294-200

(G-10352)
AAR CORP
754 Rainbow Rd (06095-1004)
PHONE................................619 545-6129
EMP: 2
SALES (corp-wide): 2B **Publicly Held**
SIC: 3724 Aircraft engines & engine parts
PA: Aar Corp.
1100 N Wood Dale Rd
Wood Dale IL 60191
630 227-2000

(G-10353)
ABB ENTERPRISE SOFTWARE INC
Also Called: Corporate
5 Waterside Xing Fl 3-2 (06095-1595)
PHONE................................860 285-0183
Steve Alger, *Branch Mgr*
EMP: 76
SALES (corp-wide): 36.4B **Privately Held**
WEB: www.elsterelectricity.com
SIC: 3612 Transformers, except electric
HQ: Abb Inc.
305 Gregson Dr
Cary NC 27511

(G-10354)
ACCUTRON INC
149 Addison Rd (06095-2102)
PHONE................................860 683-8300
Vijay R Faldu, *President*
Bhagwati Faldu, *COO*
Bharat R Faldu, *Vice Pres*
Bhagwati R Faldu, *Treasurer*
Parin Patel, *CTO*
▲ **EMP:** 110
SQ FT: 55,000
SALES: 25MM **Privately Held**
WEB: www.accutroninc.com
SIC: 3672 3613 3441 Printed circuit boards; control panels, electric; fabricated structural metal

(G-10355)
AERO GEAR INCORPORATED
1050 Day Hill Rd (06095-4728)
PHONE................................860 688-0888
Douglas B Rose, *President*
Roger Burdick, *COO*
Craig W Scott, *CFO*
Steve Hill, *Manager*
Shane Allen, *Maintence Staff*
◆ **EMP:** 140
SQ FT: 78,000
SALES (est): 40.5MM **Privately Held**
WEB: www.aerogear.com
SIC: 3728 Gears, aircraft power transmission

(G-10356)
AIM VINYL SIGNS
105 Longview Dr (06095-3806)
PHONE................................203 868-1413
EMP: 1
SALES (est): 46K **Privately Held**
SIC: 3993 Signs & advertising specialties

(G-10357)
AKO INC
Also Called: Torque Specialties
50 Baker Hollow Rd (06095-2133)
P.O. Box 1283, Enfield (06083-1283)
PHONE................................860 298-9765
Patrick Pierce, *CEO*
Doris Leclerc, *President*
Rachel Leclerc, *Admin Sec*
EMP: 20
SQ FT: 17,800
SALES (est): 4.6MM **Privately Held**
WEB: www.akotorque.com
SIC: 3825 3545 3621 3823 Test equipment for electronic & electric measurement; machine tool accessories; torque motors, electric; industrial instrmnts msrmnt display/control process variable; product testing laboratories

(G-10358)
ALSTOM POWER CO
175 Addison Rd (06095-2178)
PHONE................................860 688-1911
EMP: 10
SALES (est): 650K
SALES (corp-wide): 121.6B **Publicly Held**
SIC: 3569 8711 Liquid automation machinery & equipment; professional engineer
PA: General Electric Company
41 Farnsworth St
Boston MA 02210
617 443-3000

(G-10359)
ALSTOM RENEWABLE US LLC
Also Called: GE Renewable Energy USA
200 Great Pond Dr (06095-1564)
PHONE................................860 688-1911
Teresa Rivera, *Technology*
Kevin Hulse, *Director*
EMP: 3
SALES (corp-wide): 121.6B **Publicly Held**
SIC: 3621 Power generators
HQ: Alstom Renewable Us Llc
8000 E Maplewood Ave # 105
Greenwood Village CO 80111
303 730-4000

(G-10360)
ALVEST (USA) INC (HQ)
812 Bloomfield Ave (06095-2340)
PHONE................................860 602-3400
Mark Garlasco, *CEO*
Shaun Doyle, *Technician*
EMP: 29
SALES (est): 331MM
SALES (corp-wide): 28.3MM **Privately Held**
WEB: www.tldusa.com
SIC: 3585 3535 Air conditioning equipment, complete; unit handling conveying systems
PA: Lbo France Gestion
148 Rue De L Universite
Paris 7e Arrondissement 75007
140 627-767

(G-10361)
AMBROSONICS
229 Rollingbrook (06095-1363)
PHONE................................860 752-9022
Eric Ambrosinos, *Owner*
Elanie Ambrosinos, *Owner*
EMP: 1 **EST:** 1984
SALES (est): 102.9K **Privately Held**
WEB: www.ambrosonics.com
SIC: 3679 Electronic circuits

(G-10362)
APCOMPOWER INC (DH)
200 Great Pond Dr (06095-1556)
P.O. Box 500 (06095-0711)
PHONE................................860 688-1911
Eric A Heruser, *President*
Jeff Skipton, *President*
James M Carroll, *Vice Pres*
Thomas Kehoe, *Vice Pres*
Theordore P Sharp, *Vice Pres*
EMP: 47
SQ FT: 58,000
SALES (est): 62.2MM
SALES (corp-wide): 121.6B **Publicly Held**
WEB: www.apcompower.net
SIC: 8711 3443 1629 Engineering services; fabricated plate work (boiler shop); power plant construction
HQ: Ge Steam Power, Inc.
175 Addison Rd
Windsor CT 06095
866 257-8664

(G-10363)
APPLIED RUBBER & PLASTICS INC
100 Skitchewaug St (06095-4605)
PHONE................................860 987-9018
Brendan Ward Farrell, *President*
Patricia C Farrell, *Admin Sec*
Crystal Vono, *Admin Asst*
▲ **EMP:** 15
SQ FT: 20,000
SALES (est): 2.6MM **Privately Held**
WEB: www.appliedrubber-plastics.com
SIC: 3061 5085 Mechanical rubber goods; rubber goods, mechanical

(G-10364)
ARROW SPACE DEBURRING
610 Hayden Station Rd B (06095-1338)
PHONE................................860 683-0879
Fred Solah, *Owner*
EMP: 2
SALES (est): 87.7K **Privately Held**
SIC: 3471 Cleaning, polishing & finishing

(G-10365)
ARROWHEAD GROUP LLC
159 Ethan Dr (06095-1672)
PHONE................................954 771-5115
Luis Marcelino, *Manager*
EMP: 2
SALES (est): 104.4K **Privately Held**
SIC: 2752 Commercial printing, lithographic

(G-10366)
ASTRO AIRCOM LLC
610 Hayden Station Rd (06095-1338)
PHONE................................860 688-3320
John Muth, *General Mgr*
Dariusz Demusz,
EMP: 7
SQ FT: 5,000
SALES: 1MM **Privately Held**
SIC: 3599 Machine shop, jobbing & repair

(G-10367)
BARNES GROUP INC
Also Called: Barnes Aerospace
169 Kennedy Rd (06095-2043)
PHONE................................860 298-7740
Dawn Johnson, *Division Mgr*
Ted McCrow, *Division Mgr*
David Brunner, *Business Mgr*
Williams Brent, *Facilities Mgr*
Steve Donoviel, *Production*
EMP: 1434
SQ FT: 160,000
SALES (corp-wide): 1.5B **Publicly Held**
WEB: www.barnesgroupinc.com
SIC: 3724 Aircraft engines & engine parts
PA: Barnes Group Inc.
123 Main St
Bristol CT 06010
860 583-7070

(G-10368)
BLOOMY CONTROLS INC (PA)
Also Called: Bloomy Energy Systems
839 Marshall Phelps Rd (06095-2170)
PHONE................................860 298-9925
Peter Blume, *President*
George Stein, *Principal*
Robert Cornwell, *Vice Pres*
Jonathan Rarey, *Engineer*
Jean Grant, *Finance Mgr*
EMP: 41
SQ FT: 6,000
SALES (est): 6.4MM **Privately Held**
WEB: www.bloomy.com
SIC: 5084 3825 3679 Industrial machinery & equipment; instruments to measure electricity; electronic switches

(G-10369)
BURTECK LLC
863 Marshall Phelps Rd (06095-2108)
PHONE................................860 206-8872
Chris Dobosz, *Engineer*
Joseph Corraccio, *Design Engr*
Pete Burgess, *Mng Member*
John Eastham, *Program Mgr*
Cienciwa Michael, *Program Mgr*
EMP: 11
SALES (est): 2.2MM **Privately Held**
SIC: 3089 Injection molding of plastics

Windsor - Hartford County (G-10370) — GEOGRAPHIC SECTION

(G-10370)
C & C LOGGING
416 Pigeon Hill Rd (06095-2157)
PHONE..................860 683-0071
Grace Cranouski, *Principal*
EMP: 8
SALES (est): 723.1K **Privately Held**
SIC: 2411 Logging camps & contractors

(G-10371)
CARBIDE SOLUTIONS LLC
800 Marshall Phelps Rd (06095-2143)
PHONE..................860 515-8665
Alan M Stanek, *Principal*
EMP: 4 EST: 2015
SALES (est): 213K **Privately Held**
SIC: 2819 Carbides

(G-10372)
CHANTYS CLOSET
1210 Matianuck Ave (06095-3295)
PHONE..................860 752-4512
Robin Allen, *Principal*
EMP: 1
SALES (est): 33K **Privately Held**
SIC: 3942 Dolls & doll clothing

(G-10373)
CHROMALLOY COMPONENT SVCS INC
Chromalloy Connecticiut
601 Marshall Phelps Rd (06095-5716)
PHONE..................860 688-7798
Robert Jones, *Manager*
EMP: 140
SQ FT: 50,000
SALES (corp-wide): 2.4B **Publicly Held**
WEB: www.chromalloysatx.com
SIC: 3724 3812 2851 Aircraft engines & engine parts; search & navigation equipment; paints & allied products
HQ: Chromalloy Component Services, Inc.
 303 Industrial Park Rd
 San Antonio TX 78226
 210 331-2300

(G-10374)
CHROMALLOY GAS TURBINE LLC
Also Called: Chromalloy Connecticut
601 Marshall Phelps Rd (06095-5716)
P.O. Box 748, Wallingford (06492-0748)
PHONE..................860 688-7798
Clive Bailey, *Principal*
Darlene Reedy, *Controller*
Miguel Acevedo, *Manager*
EMP: 77
SALES (corp-wide): 2.4B **Publicly Held**
SIC: 3724 Aircraft engines & engine parts
HQ: Chromalloy Gas Turbine Llc
 3999 Rca Blvd
 Palm Beach Gardens FL 33410
 561 935-3571

(G-10375)
COLOUR TS LLC
167 Portman St (06095-3439)
PHONE..................860 298-0594
Jacob Trotman, *Principal*
EMP: 2
SALES (est): 141.1K **Privately Held**
SIC: 2759 Screen printing

(G-10376)
COMPUTER TECHNOLOGIES CORP
65 Tiffany Dr (06095-2471)
P.O. Box 357 (06095-0357)
PHONE..................860 683-4030
Carl Wrazien, *President*
EMP: 1
SALES (est): 119.5K **Privately Held**
WEB: www.ctceng.com
SIC: 8711 7372 Consulting engineer; prepackaged software

(G-10377)
COOPER CROUSE-HINDS LLC
Airport Lighting Division
1200 Kennedy Rd (06095-1384)
PHONE..................860 683-4300
Mike West, *Sales Mgr*
Jason Smith, *Manager*
Gerald Smith, *Bd of Directors*
Jacob Hicock, *Technician*
EMP: 92
SQ FT: 66,000 **Privately Held**
SIC: 3069 3648 Hard rubber & molded rubber products; airport lighting fixtures: runway approach, taxi or ramp
HQ: Cooper Crouse-Hinds, Llc
 1201 Wolf St
 Syracuse NY 13208
 315 477-7000

(G-10378)
COURTMAN ENTERPRISES LLC
33 Center St (06095-1403)
PHONE..................860 322-2837
Ramona Courtman,
Phillip Courtman,
EMP: 2
SALES (est): 219.9K **Privately Held**
SIC: 1799 3069 1761 Coating, caulking & weather, water & fireproofing; waterproofing; roofing, membrane rubber; roofing, siding & sheet metal work; roofing & gutter work; roofing contractor

(G-10379)
DARLY CUSTOM TECHNOLOGY INC
276 Addison Rd (06095-2334)
P.O. Box 527 (06095-0527)
PHONE..................860 298-7966
Yimou Yang, *President*
Stanley J Misunas, *Vice Pres*
Yao Kuang Yang, *Treasurer*
HEI-Ju Yang, *Shareholder*
Li-Chiung CHI Yang, *Shareholder*
▲ EMP: 12
SQ FT: 15,000
SALES (est): 1.8MM **Privately Held**
WEB: www.darlytech.com
SIC: 3599 Custom machinery

(G-10380)
DOUBLE BARREL DISTILLERY LLC
9 Shelley Ave (06095-3530)
PHONE..................860 285-0141
Mark Thomas, *Manager*
EMP: 2
SALES (est): 62.3K **Privately Held**
SIC: 2085 Distilled & blended liquors

(G-10381)
DOW DIV OF UTC
360 Bloomfield Ave (06095-2700)
PHONE..................860 683-7340
EMP: 3
SALES (est): 208.5K **Privately Held**
SIC: 3613 Mfg Switchgear/Switchboards

(G-10382)
EATON ELECTRIC HOLDINGS LLC
Crouse-Hinds Airport Lighting
1200 Kennedy Rd (06095-1384)
PHONE..................860 683-4300
Mark Guckin, *Engineer*
Kurt Foster, *Senior Engr*
Jack BAC, *Branch Mgr*
Dan Flanagan, *Manager*
EMP: 16 **Privately Held**
SIC: 3648 Airport lighting fixtures: runway approach, taxi or ramp
HQ: Eaton Electric Holdings Llc
 1000 Eaton Blvd
 Cleveland OH 44122
 440 523-5000

(G-10383)
EMHART GLASS INC (DH)
123 Great Pond Dr (06095-1569)
P.O. Box 220 (06095-0220)
PHONE..................860 298-7340
Joseph Laundry, *President*
Xu Ding, *Senior Engr*
Paula Messier, *Human Res Mgr*
Alan Batchelor, *Manager*
Walter E Lovell, *Info Tech Mgr*
◆ EMP: 65
SALES (est): 41.1MM
SALES (corp-wide): 3B **Privately Held**
SIC: 3559 Glass making machinery: blowing, molding, forming, etc.
HQ: Emhart Glass Sa
 Hinterbergstrasse 22
 Steinhausen ZG 6312
 417 494-200

(G-10384)
EMHART GLASS MANUFACTURING INC (DH)
123 Great Pond Dr (06095-1569)
P.O. Box 220 (06095-0220)
PHONE..................860 298-7340
Martin Jetter, *President*
William Grninger, *Vice Pres*
Jeffrey D Hartung, *Vice Pres*
Christer Hermannsson, *Vice Pres*
Matthias Kmmerle, *Vice Pres*
▲ EMP: 20
SALES (est): 32.3MM
SALES (corp-wide): 3B **Privately Held**
WEB: www.emhartglass.com
SIC: 3221 Glass containers
HQ: Emhart Glass Inc.
 123 Great Pond Dr
 Windsor CT 06095
 860 298-7340

(G-10385)
EUROPA SPORTS PRODUCTS INC
755 Rainbow Rd (06095-1024)
PHONE..................860 688-1110
Stan Schapp, *Manager*
EMP: 8
SALES (corp-wide): 296.1MM **Privately Held**
SIC: 3949 Sporting & athletic goods
PA: Europa Sports Products, Inc.
 11401 Granite St Ste H
 Charlotte NC 28273
 704 405-2022

(G-10386)
FIVE PONDS PRESS BOOKS INC
360 Bloomfield Ave (06095-2700)
PHONE..................877 833-0603
Lou Scolnik, *President*
EMP: 1
SALES (est): 33.3K **Privately Held**
SIC: 2731 Book publishing

(G-10387)
FOUNDATION CIGAR COMPANY LLC
110 Day Hill Rd (06095-1707)
PHONE..................203 738-9377
Michael Hyatt, *Opers Dir*
Nicholas Melillo, *Mng Member*
EMP: 11
SALES (est): 1.5MM **Privately Held**
SIC: 2121 5194 5993 Cigars; cigarettes; cigars; cigar store; cigarette store

(G-10388)
GE GRID SOLUTIONS LLC
175 Addison Rd (06095-2178)
PHONE..................425 250-2695
EMP: 3 EST: 2017
SALES (est): 267.4K **Privately Held**
SIC: 3613 Power circuit breakers

(G-10389)
GE STEAM POWER INC
Also Called: Alstom Power-Chattan Tubin Dis
200 Great Pond Dr (06095-1556)
PHONE..................423 648-4161
Marvin Smith III, *Principal*
EMP: 188
SALES (corp-wide): 121.6B **Publicly Held**
SIC: 8711 8731 3621 3564 Acoustical engineering; electronic research; armatures, industrial; air cleaning systems; air coolers, metal plate
HQ: Ge Steam Power, Inc.
 175 Addison Rd
 Windsor CT 06095
 866 257-8664

(G-10390)
GE STEAM POWER INC
3-4 Minatojima (06095)
PHONE..................860 688-1911
Tim Curran, *President*
EMP: 2
SALES (corp-wide): 121.6B **Publicly Held**
SIC: 3463 Pump, compressor, turbine & engine forgings, except auto
HQ: Ge Steam Power, Inc.
 175 Addison Rd
 Windsor CT 06095
 866 257-8664

(G-10391)
GE STEAM POWER INC
175 Addison Rd (06095-2178)
PHONE..................860 688-1911
Debbie Gee, *Buyer*
Nicholas Hauser, *Purchasing*
Marcela Gutierrez, *Business Anlyst*
Pierre Gauthier, *Branch Mgr*
Ian Brodie, *Manager*
EMP: 1
SALES (corp-wide): 121.6B **Publicly Held**
SIC: 3443 3564 3621 3823 Fabricated plate work (boiler shop); blowers & fans; motors & generators; industrial instrmnts msrmnt display/control process variable; engineering services
HQ: Ge Steam Power, Inc.
 175 Addison Rd
 Windsor CT 06095
 866 257-8664

(G-10392)
GET BAKED LLC
41 Mountain Rd (06095-2603)
PHONE..................860 688-0420
Emily Woodward, *Principal*
EMP: 1
SALES (est): 122.8K **Privately Held**
SIC: 3421 Table & food cutlery, including butchers'

(G-10393)
HFO CHICAGO LLC
910 Day Hill Rd (06095-5727)
PHONE..................860 285-0709
Bradley R Morris, *Manager*
EMP: 7
SALES (est): 994.4K **Privately Held**
SIC: 3599 Machine shop, jobbing & repair

(G-10394)
HIGHLANDER GROUP INC
24 Somerset Dr (06095-1479)
PHONE..................860 298-8618
Robert J Hartmann, *President*
Lenore M Hartmann, *Director*
EMP: 2 EST: 1995
SALES (est): 214.1K **Privately Held**
WEB: www.highlander-atlanta.com
SIC: 2221 Textile mills, broadwoven: silk & manmade, also glass

(G-10395)
HUBERGROUP USA INC
147 Addison Rd (06095-2102)
PHONE..................860 687-1617
Jeffrey Sorensen, *Manager*
EMP: 12
SALES (corp-wide): 355.8K **Privately Held**
WEB: www.hostmann-steinberg.com
SIC: 2893 Printing ink
HQ: Hubergroup Usa, Inc.
 1701 Golf Rd Ste 3-201
 Rolling Meadows IL 60008
 815 929-9293

(G-10396)
HW GRAPHICS
92 Wyndemere Ln (06095-1178)
PHONE..................860 278-2338
Hector V Webb, *Owner*
EMP: 3
SALES: 82K **Privately Held**
SIC: 2759 Commercial printing

(G-10397)
INTERSTATE ELEC SVCS CORP
800 Mrshll Phelps Rd 2 (06095-2143)
PHONE..................860 243-5644
Vincent Curro, *Purch Mgr*
Michael Perkins, *Buyer*
John Sloane, *Branch Mgr*
EMP: 20

▲ = Import ▼ = Export
◆ = Import/Export

Windsor - Hartford County (G-10426)

SALES (corp-wide): 132MM **Privately Held**
WEB: www.interelec.com
SIC: **1731** 3531 Electronic controls installation; communications specialization; cranes
PA: Interstate Electrical Services Corporation
70 Treble Cove Rd
North Billerica MA 01862
978 667-5200

(G-10398)
ITT STANDARD
1036 Poquonock Ave (06095-1860)
PHONE.................................860 683-2144
Debra Avenali, *Principal*
EMP: 3
SALES (est): 162.1K **Privately Held**
SIC: **3443** Heat exchangers, condensers & components

(G-10399)
JAZ INDUSTRIES LLC
25 Columbia Rd (06095-3811)
PHONE.................................860 243-9357
Jodi A Jones, *Principal*
EMP: 2
SALES (est): 204.2K **Privately Held**
SIC: **3999** Manufacturing industries

(G-10400)
JOHNSON CONTROLS INC
21 Griffin Rd N Ste 4 (06095-1512)
PHONE.................................860 688-7151
Donna Biaggiotti, *Manager*
EMP: 120 **Privately Held**
SIC: **3822** Energy cutoff controls, residential or commercial types
HQ: Johnson Controls, Inc.
5757 N Green Bay Ave
Milwaukee WI 53209
414 524-1200

(G-10401)
JPSEXTON LLC
460 Hayden Station Rd (06095-1367)
PHONE.................................860 748-2048
Davis Perlroth,
Davis B Perlroth,
EMP: 4 EST: 2012
SALES (est): 416K **Privately Held**
SIC: **3714** Oil strainers, motor vehicle

(G-10402)
KITCHEN KRAFTSMEN
77 Pierson Ln Ste A (06095-2000)
PHONE.................................860 616-1240
EMP: 3 EST: 2013
SALES (est): 190K **Privately Held**
SIC: **2434** Wood Kitchen Cabinets

(G-10403)
LAMAR ADVERTISING COMPANY
32 Midland St (06095-4334)
PHONE.................................860 246-6546
Steve Hebert, *Sales/Mktg Mgr*
Ellie Spear, *Admin Dir*
EMP: 25 **Publicly Held**
SIC: **7312** 3993 Outdoor advertising services; signs & advertising specialties
PA: Lamar Advertising Company
5321 Corporate Blvd
Baton Rouge LA 70808

(G-10404)
LEIPOLD INC
545 Marshall Phelps Rd (06095-1702)
PHONE.................................860 298-9791
Pascal Schiefer, *President*
Thomas Fees, *Vice Pres*
Ewa Boucher, *QC Mgr*
Lydia Blanche, *Sales Mgr*
Christoph Lange, *Admin Sec*
▲ EMP: 30 EST: 1997
SALES (est): 6.9MM
SALES (corp-wide): 775.7K **Privately Held**
WEB: www.leipold-inc.com
SIC: **3451** Screw machine products
HQ: Carl Leipold Gmbh
Schiltacher Str. 5
Wolfach 77709
783 483-950

(G-10405)
LONG ISLAND PIPE SUPPLY INC
Also Called: LONG ISLAND PIPE SUPPLY OF ALBANY, INC.
1220 Kennedy Rd (06095-1328)
PHONE.................................860 688-1780
Ryan Nicholson, *Opers Mgr*
Bryan Poresky, *Sales Staff*
Mark Krause, *Manager*
EMP: 6
SALES (corp-wide): 2.6B **Privately Held**
WEB: www.lipipe.com
SIC: **3498** Fabricated pipe & fittings
HQ: Miles Moss Of Albany, Inc.
586 Commercial Ave
Garden City NY 11530
516 222-8008

(G-10406)
MANUFACTURING PRODUCTIVI
910 Day Hill Rd (06095-5727)
PHONE.................................860 916-8189
Lee Morris, *Principal*
EMP: 3 EST: 2009
SALES (est): 196.7K **Privately Held**
SIC: **3999** Manufacturing industries

(G-10407)
MATERION LRGE AREA CATINGS LLC (DH)
300 Lamberton Rd (06095-2131)
PHONE.................................216 486-4200
Michael Giuliana, *CFO*
Bergeron Gerard, *Manager*
Lee Donohue, *Technology*
▲ EMP: 53
SQ FT: 30,000
SALES (est): 15MM
SALES (corp-wide): 1.2B **Publicly Held**
WEB: www.techni-met.com
SIC: **3479** Painting, coating & hot dipping
HQ: Materion Advanced Materials Technologies And Services Inc.
2978 Main St
Buffalo NY 14214
800 327-1355

(G-10408)
MEDIA LINKS INC
431-C Hayden Station Rd (06095)
PHONE.................................860 206-9163
Takatsugu Ono, *CEO*
John Dale III, *Vice Pres*
EMP: 14
SQ FT: 10,000
SALES: 24.4MM **Privately Held**
SIC: **3663** Television broadcasting & communications equipment
PA: Media Links Co., Ltd.
580-16, Horikawacho, Saiwai-Ku
Kawasaki KNG 212-0

(G-10409)
METAL IMPROVEMENT COMPANY LLC
145 Addison Rd (06095-2102)
PHONE.................................860 688-6201
Cesar Gonzales, *QC Mgr*
Kelly Hoffman, *Manager*
Nikia Wallace, *Executive*
EMP: 28
SALES (corp-wide): 2.4B **Publicly Held**
SIC: **3398** Shot peening (treating steel to reduce fatigue)
HQ: Metal Improvement Company, Llc
80 E Rte 4 Ste 310
Paramus NJ 07652
201 843-7800

(G-10410)
MHS INDUSTRIES
418 River St (06095-1321)
PHONE.................................860 798-7981
EMP: 1
SALES (est): 46.2K **Privately Held**
SIC: **3999** Mfg Misc Products

(G-10411)
MYTYME LLC
211 High Path Rd (06095-4112)
PHONE.................................860 327-2356
Marlene Gainey,
EMP: 1

SALES (est): 57.5K **Privately Held**
SIC: **5734** 7389 2211 2396 Software, business & non-game; ; apparel & outerwear fabrics, cotton; automotive & apparel trimmings

(G-10412)
NEL GROUP LLC
154 Broad St (06095-2944)
PHONE.................................860 683-0190
EMP: 10
SALES (corp-wide): 6MM **Privately Held**
SIC: **2066** 5149 5441 5199 Chocolate; chocolate; candy, nut & confectionery stores; gifts & novelties; gift shop; novelties & giftware, including trophies
PA: Nel Group Llc
32 Rainbow Rd
East Granby CT 06026
860 413-9042

(G-10413)
NEMFI PFS
60 Ezra Silva Ln (06095-2122)
PHONE.................................860 640-4600
Art French, *President*
EMP: 2
SALES (est): 113.2K **Privately Held**
SIC: **3471** Finishing, metals or formed products

(G-10414)
O S WALKER COMPANY INC (DH)
600 Day Hill Rd (06095-1703)
PHONE.................................508 853-3232
Richard Longo, *President*
Debra Krikorian, *Corp Secy*
Ken Wanko, *Director*
▲ EMP: 70
SALES (est): 15.5MM
SALES (corp-wide): 116.9MM **Privately Held**
WEB: www.speckvc.com
SIC: **3545** Chucks: drill, lathe or magnetic (machine tool accessories); drilling machine attachments & accessories
HQ: Walker Magnetics Group, Inc.
600 Day Hill Rd
Windsor CT 06095
508 853-3232

(G-10415)
OKAMOTO CORP
425 Hayden Station Rd (06095-1327)
PHONE.................................860 219-1006
EMP: 2
SALES (est): 139.2K **Privately Held**
SIC: **3541** Machine tools, metal cutting type

(G-10416)
OSF FLAVORS INC (PA)
40 Baker Hollow Rd (06095-2133)
P.O. Box 591 (06095-0591)
PHONE.................................860 298-8350
Olivier De Botton, *CEO*
Eduardo De Botao, *President*
Jim Bartlein, *Accounts Mgr*
Alan Ladd, *Manager*
▲ EMP: 15
SQ FT: 18,000
SALES (est): 4.2MM **Privately Held**
WEB: www.osfflavors.com
SIC: **2087** Flavoring extracts & syrups

(G-10417)
PEACHES PRINTS
16 Eagleton Dr (06095-3821)
PHONE.................................860 856-3525
EMP: 2
SALES (est): 83.9K **Privately Held**
SIC: **2752** Commercial printing, lithographic

(G-10418)
PEPSI-COLA METRO BTLG CO INC
Also Called: Pepsico
55 International Dr (06095-1062)
PHONE.................................860 688-6281
Mario Ramirez, *Project Mgr*
Doug Lord, *Opers Mgr*
Matt Karl, *Finance Mgr*
David Cronin, *Manager*
EMP: 125

SALES (corp-wide): 64.6B **Publicly Held**
WEB: www.pbg.com
SIC: **2086** Carbonated soft drinks, bottled & canned
HQ: Pepsi-Cola Metropolitan Bottling Company, Inc.
1111 Westchester Ave
White Plains NY 10604
914 767-6000

(G-10419)
PIONEER CAPITAL CORP
651 Day Hill Rd (06095-1798)
PHONE.................................860 683-2005
John Ferraro, *President*
Robert Lerman, *Treasurer*
EMP: 4 EST: 1988
SALES (est): 206.9K **Privately Held**
SIC: **3443** Heat exchangers, condensers & components

(G-10420)
PITNEY BOWES INC
2 Waterside Xing Ste 304 (06095-1588)
PHONE.................................860 285-7450
EMP: 2
SALES (corp-wide): 3.5B **Publicly Held**
SIC: **3579** Postage meters
PA: Pitney Bowes Inc.
3001 Summer St Ste 3
Stamford CT 06905
203 356-5000

(G-10421)
POLYTRONICS CORPORATION
800 Marshall Phelps Rd H (06095-2143)
PHONE.................................860 683-2442
Michael Serrano, *President*
▲ EMP: 5
SQ FT: 10,000
SALES (est): 248.9K **Privately Held**
SIC: **3089** Injection molding of plastics

(G-10422)
POQUONOCK SEWAGE PLANT
1222 Poquonock Ave (06095-1811)
PHONE.................................860 688-5420
Dave Arnett, *Principal*
EMP: 2
SALES (est): 106.4K **Privately Held**
SIC: **2899** Water treating compounds

(G-10423)
PRECISION E D M INC
775 Bloomfield Ave (06095-2322)
PHONE.................................413 733-2813
Keith Willis, *President*
Robert Learned, *QC Mgr*
EMP: 10
SQ FT: 15,000
SALES (est): 950.6K **Privately Held**
WEB: www.edmprecision.com
SIC: **3599** Electrical discharge machining (EDM); machine shop, jobbing & repair

(G-10424)
PRECISION FINISHING SVCS INC
60 Ezra Silva Ln (06095-2122)
P.O. Box 189, North Granby (06060-0189)
PHONE.................................860 882-1073
Arthur French, *President*
Linda Clark, *Admin Sec*
EMP: 20
SQ FT: 33,000
SALES (est): 2.2MM **Privately Held**
WEB: www.precisionfinishingservices.com
SIC: **3471** Plating of metals or formed products

(G-10425)
PRINT HUB
97 Pierson Ln (06095-2050)
PHONE.................................860 580-7907
EMP: 2
SALES (est): 83.9K **Privately Held**
SIC: **2752** Commercial printing, lithographic

(G-10426)
PROGRESSIVE PATTERN
245 Deerfield Rd (06095-4258)
PHONE.................................860 748-0088
Katherine Tolve, *Principal*
EMP: 1
SALES (est): 64.5K **Privately Held**
SIC: **3543** Industrial patterns

Windsor - Hartford County (G-10427) — GEOGRAPHIC SECTION

(G-10427)
PROLIANCE INTERNATIONAL INC
436 Hayden Station Rd (06095-1302)
PHONE 860 688-7644
Romero Rasho, *Principal*
EMP: 2
SALES (est): 87.2K Privately Held
SIC: 3714 Motor vehicle parts & accessories

(G-10428)
RAPIDEX
875 Marshall Phelps Rd (06095-2108)
PHONE 860 285-8818
Darek Luciarz, *Owner*
EMP: 6
SQ FT: 16,324
SALES (est): 721.6K Privately Held
SIC: 3599 Machine shop, jobbing & repair

(G-10429)
RD PRINTING LLC
138 Long Hill Rd (06095-2665)
PHONE 860 841-1397
Richard S Dean, *Principal*
EMP: 2
SALES (est): 145.2K Privately Held
SIC: 2752 Commercial printing, lithographic

(G-10430)
RELX INC
15 Cobbler Way (06095-1747)
PHONE 860 219-0733
EMP: 5
SALES (corp-wide): 9.6B Privately Held
SIC: 3541 Machine tools, metal cutting type
HQ: Relx Inc.
230 Park Ave Ste 700
New York NY 10169
212 309-8100

(G-10431)
SCA PHARMACEUTICALS LLC
755 Rainbow Rd Bldg 1 (06095-1024)
PHONE 501 312-2800
Roy Graves, *President*
Matthew Graves, *COO*
EMP: 7
SQ FT: 75,000
SALES (est): 1MM
SALES (corp-wide): 12.5MM Privately Held
SIC: 2834 Solutions, pharmaceutical
PA: Sca Pharmaceuticals, Llc
8821 Knoedl Ct
Little Rock AR 72205
501 312-2800

(G-10432)
SCAPA HOLDINGS INC (HQ)
111 Great Pond Dr (06095-1527)
PHONE 860 688-8000
Steve Lennon, *Chief*
EMP: 300
SALES (est): 91.9MM
SALES (corp-wide): 401.1MM Privately Held
SIC: 2672 Coated & laminated paper
PA: Scapa Group Public Limited Company
994 Manchester Road
Ashton-Under-Lyne LANCS OL7 0
161 301-7400

(G-10433)
SCAPA NORTH AMERICA INC (DH)
Also Called: Scapa Healthcare
111 Great Pond Dr (06095-1527)
PHONE 860 688-8000
Joe Davin, *President*
Margaret Gilmartin, *Vice Pres*
Shane Cote, *Receiver*
Michael Lostowski, *Receiver*
Sharon Floyd, *QC Mgr*
▼ EMP: 2 EST: 1955

SALES (est): 91.9MM
SALES (corp-wide): 401.1MM Privately Held
SIC: 2231 3069 2211 2824 Papermakers' felts, woven: wool, mohair or similar fibers; rubber rolls & roll coverings; printers' rolls & blankets: rubber or rubberized fabric; filter cloth, cotton; textured yarns, non-cellulosic; coated & laminated paper
HQ: Scapa Holdings Inc.
111 Great Pond Dr
Windsor CT 06095
860 688-8000

(G-10434)
SCAPA TAPES NORTH AMERICA LLC (DH)
Also Called: Finite Industries
111 Great Pond Dr (06095-1527)
PHONE 860 688-8000
Heejae Chae, *CEO*
Eric Springer, *President*
Margaret Gilmartin, *Vice Pres*
Joseph Brosseau, *Manager*
Rhonda Swearengen, *Manager*
◆ EMP: 138
SQ FT: 112,000
SALES (est): 61.1MM
SALES (corp-wide): 401.1MM Privately Held
WEB: www.scapa.com
SIC: 3842 Surgical appliances & supplies
HQ: Scapa North America Inc
111 Great Pond Dr
Windsor CT 06095
860 688-8000

(G-10435)
SECURITIES SOFTWARE & CONSULTI
80 Lamberton Rd (06095-2136)
PHONE 860 298-4500
William C Stone, *Principal*
Scott Whittle, *Sr Software Eng*
EMP: 9
SALES (est): 704.7K Privately Held
SIC: 7372 Prepackaged software

(G-10436)
SPENCER TURBINE COMPANY (HQ)
600 Day Hill Rd (06095-4706)
PHONE 860 688-8361
Antonio Mancini, *Exec VP*
Tony Mancini, *Exec VP*
Patti Mullins, *Plant Mgr*
Earle Fredericksen, *Buyer*
Jim Burns, *Engineer*
◆ EMP: 146
SQ FT: 200,000
SALES (est): 51.6MM
SALES (corp-wide): 116.9MM Privately Held
SIC: 3589 3564 3498 5084 Vacuum cleaners & sweepers, electric: industrial; turbo-blowers, industrial; tube fabricating (contract bending & shaping); compressors, except air conditioning
PA: Alliance Holdings, Inc.
100 Witmer Rd Ste 170
Horsham PA 19044
215 706-0873

(G-10437)
SS&C TECHNOLOGIES INC
261 Broad St (06095-2906)
PHONE 860 930-5882
EMP: 3
SALES (corp-wide): 3.4B Publicly Held
SIC: 7372 Prepackaged software
HQ: Ss&C Technologies, Inc.
80 Lamberton Rd
Windsor CT 06095
860 298-4500

(G-10438)
SS&C TECHNOLOGIES INC (HQ)
80 Lamberton Rd (06095-2136)
PHONE 860 298-4500
William C Stone, *Ch of Bd*
Normand A Boulanger, *President*
Campbell R Dyer, *President*
Marshall Pimenta, *Principal*
Claudius E Watts IV, *Principal*
EMP: 200
SQ FT: 73,000

SALES (est): 335.3MM
SALES (corp-wide): 3.4B Publicly Held
WEB: www.ssctech.com
SIC: 7372 7371 8741 Prepackaged software; custom computer programming services; management services
PA: Ss&C Technologies Holdings, Inc.
80 Lamberton Rd
Windsor CT 06095
860 298-4500

(G-10439)
SS&C TECHNOLOGIES HOLDINGS INC (PA)
Also Called: SS&C HOLDINGS
80 Lamberton Rd (06095-2136)
PHONE 860 298-4500
William C Stone, *Ch of Bd*
Normand A Boulanger, *Vice Ch Bd*
Craig Schachter, *Managing Dir*
Patrick J Pedonti, *CFO*
Joseph J Frank, *
EMP: 76
SQ FT: 93,500
SALES: 3.4B Publicly Held
SIC: 7372 7371 Prepackaged software; custom computer programming services

(G-10440)
STANADYNE INTRMDATE HLDNGS LLC (HQ)
92 Deerfield Rd (06095-4200)
PHONE 860 525-0821
David P Galuska, *CEO*
John A Pinson, *President*
Stephen S Langin, *CFO*
Steve Rodgers, *Treasurer*
▲ EMP: 250
SQ FT: 662,000
SALES (est): 210MM Privately Held
SIC: 3714 3492 Fuel systems & parts, motor vehicle; control valves, fluid power: hydraulic & pneumatic
PA: Stanadyne Parent Holdings, Inc.
92 Deerfield Rd
Windsor CT 06095
860 525-0821

(G-10441)
STANADYNE LLC (DH)
92 Deerfield Rd (06095-4200)
PHONE 860 525-0821
David P Galuska, *CEO*
Terrence Gilbert, *General Mgr*
Sanjay Chadda, *Managing Dir*
David Galuska, *COO*
Dave Vanderford, *Vice Pres*
◆ EMP: 950
SQ FT: 642,000
SALES (est): 209.8MM
SALES (corp-wide): 210MM Privately Held
SIC: 3714 Fuel pumps, motor vehicle; fuel systems & parts, motor vehicle
HQ: Stanadyne Intermediate Holdings, Llc
92 Deerfield Rd
Windsor CT 06095
860 525-0821

(G-10442)
STANADYNE PARENT HOLDINGS INC (PA)
92 Deerfield Rd (06095-4200)
PHONE 860 525-0821
David P Galuska, *CEO*
John A Pinson, *President*
Jerry Sweetland, *President*
David Zimmerman, *President*
Stephen S Langin, *CFO*
EMP: 2
SQ FT: 276,950
SALES (est): 210MM Privately Held
SIC: 3714 Fuel pumps, motor vehicle; fuel systems & parts, motor vehicle

(G-10443)
STAUFFER SHEET METAL LLC
56 Depot St (06006-0001)
PHONE 860 623-0518
Kenneth Stauffer, *Owner*
EMP: 9
SQ FT: 10,400
SALES (est): 961.5K Privately Held
SIC: 3444 Sheet metalwork

(G-10444)
STEPHEN HAWRYLIK
Also Called: Gemsco
462 Park Ave (06095-3289)
P.O. Box 280793, East Hartford (06128-0793)
PHONE 860 688-8651
Stephen Hawrylik, *Owner*
EMP: 1
SALES (est): 200K Privately Held
SIC: 5169 5033 3446 Industrial chemicals; insulation, thermal; partitions, ornamental metal

(G-10445)
SUBINAS USA LLC
4 Market Cir (06095-1422)
PHONE 860 298-0401
Daniel Herran, *Mng Member*
▲ EMP: 10
SALES (est): 1.9MM Privately Held
SIC: 2515 Mattresses, innerspring or box spring

(G-10446)
SWEET SPOT CUPCAKERY LLC
152 Mountain Rd (06095-2605)
PHONE 860 219-1123
Teneille McFarlane Smart, *Principal*
EMP: 2 EST: 2009
SALES (est): 75.9K Privately Held
SIC: 2051 Bread, cake & related products

(G-10447)
T & T AUTOMATION INC
88 Pierson Ln (06095-2049)
PHONE 860 683-8788
Ben Terkildsen, *President*
EMP: 12
SQ FT: 8,000
SALES: 1.2MM Privately Held
SIC: 3625 Control equipment, electric

(G-10448)
TAYLOR & FENN COMPANY
22 Deerfield Rd (06095-4237)
PHONE 860 219-9393
Edgar B Butler Jr, *Vice Ch Bd*
Brian Butler, *Chairman*
Rogers Sean, *Controller*
◆ EMP: 100 EST: 1834
SQ FT: 130,000
SALES (est): 12.2MM Privately Held
WEB: www.taylorfenn.com
SIC: 3321 Gray iron castings; ductile iron castings

(G-10449)
TELLING INDUSTRIES LLC
1050 Kennedy Rd (06095-1303)
PHONE 860 731-7975
Satrry Perleini, *General Mgr*
EMP: 1
SALES (corp-wide): 29.1MM Privately Held
SIC: 3316 Cold finishing of steel shapes
PA: Telling Industries, Llc
4420 Sherwin Rd
Willoughby OH 44094
440 974-3370

(G-10450)
TIMBER FRAME BARN CONVERSIONS
226 Rollingbrook (06095-1364)
PHONE 860 219-0519
Brian P Cigal, *Principal*
EMP: 4
SALES (est): 382.4K Privately Held
SIC: 2439 Timbers, structural: laminated lumber

(G-10451)
TIMBERWOLF LOGGING
416 Pigeon Hill Rd (06095-2157)
PHONE 860 683-0071
Ronnie Cranouski, *Principal*
EMP: 2
SALES (est): 244.4K Privately Held
SIC: 2411 Logging camps & contractors

(G-10452)
TLD ACE CORPORATION
805 Bloomfield Ave (06095-2341)
PHONE 860 602-3300

▲ = Import ▼ = Export
◆ = Import/Export

Mark Garlasco, *CEO*
Antoine Maguin, *President*
Peter Owitz, *COO*
Herve Criquillion, *Vice Pres*
Julian Stinton, *Vice Pres*
◆ **EMP:** 300 **EST:** 1953
SQ FT: 75,000
SALES: 165MM
SALES (corp-wide): 28.3MM **Privately Held**
WEB: www.tld-group.com
SIC: 3585 Refrigeration & heating equipment
HQ: Alvest (Usa) Inc.
812 Bloomfield Ave
Windsor CT 06095

(G-10453)
TLD AMERICA CORPORATION (DH)
Also Called: Tld Group
812 Bloomfield Ave (06095-2340)
PHONE..................................860 602-3400
Jean Marie Falconis, *Ch of Bd*
Mark L Garlasco, *President*
Walter Batchelor, *Buyer*
Peter Owitz, *Mktg Dir*
Janet Snarski, *Marketing Staff*
◆ **EMP:** 45
SQ FT: 20,000
SALES: 165MM
SALES (corp-wide): 28.3MM **Privately Held**
SIC: 5088 3728 7629 Aircraft & parts; aircraft equipment & supplies; aircraft parts & equipment; aircraft electrical equipment repair

(G-10454)
TOMMY LLC SOCK IT
4 Walters Way (06095-1071)
PHONE..................................860 688-2019
Thomas Defranzo, *Principal*
Thomas P Defranzo, *Principal*
EMP: 3
SALES (est): 162.3K **Privately Held**
SIC: 2252 Socks

(G-10455)
TRIUMPH ACTUATION SYSTEMS - CO (HQ)
175 Addison Rd Ste 4 (06095-2179)
PHONE..................................860 687-5412
Daniel Crowley, *CEO*
Richard C III, *Ch of Bd*
Jeffry D Frisby, *President*
Tom Holtzum, *President*
Tony Leblanc, *General Mgr*
▲ **EMP:** 85
SALES (est): 31.4MM **Publicly Held**
WEB: www.htdaerospace.com
SIC: 3728 Aircraft parts & equipment

(G-10456)
TURBINE SUPPORT SERVICES INC (PA)
344 Rainbow Rd (06095-1140)
PHONE..................................860 688-4800
Dean Angerami, *President*
EMP: 6
SQ FT: 4,700
SALES (est): 1.8MM **Privately Held**
WEB: www.turbinesupportservicesinc.com
SIC: 5088 3544 Aircraft engines & engine parts; special dies, tools, jigs & fixtures

(G-10457)
ULTRA FLOW DISPENSE LLC
820 Prospect Hill Rd (06095-1559)
PHONE..................................866 827-2534
Shelley Ogonoski,
Scott Ziskin,
EMP: 2 **EST:** 2013
SALES (est): 96.7K **Privately Held**
SIC: 3585 Beer dispensing equipment

(G-10458)
VELOCITY PRODUCTS
910 Day Hill Rd (06095-5727)
PHONE..................................860 687-3530
EMP: 2
SALES (est): 136.8K **Privately Held**
SIC: 3599 Machine shop, jobbing & repair

(G-10459)
VERTAFORE INC
5 Waterside Xing Fl 2 (06095-1577)
PHONE..................................860 602-6000
Johanna Carpino, *Branch Mgr*
Adrian Mayers, *Info Tech Dir*
EMP: 597
SALES (corp-wide): 243.9MM **Privately Held**
WEB: www.iix.com
SIC: 7371 8711 7373 7372 Computer software development; engineering services; computer integrated systems design; prepackaged software
PA: Vertafore, Inc.
999 18th St Ste 400
Denver CO 80202
800 444-4813

(G-10460)
VULCAN INDUSTRIES INC
651 Day Hill Rd (06095-1798)
PHONE..................................860 683-2005
Robert Lerman, *CEO*
Keith Briggs, *General Mgr*
John Ferarro, *Chairman*
John Hughes, *Director*
Fred Samuelson, *Director*
EMP: 142
SQ FT: 33,000
SALES (est): 12.1MM
SALES (corp-wide): 7.4MM **Publicly Held**
WEB: www.thermodynetics.com
SIC: 3714 3444 3443 Motor vehicle parts & accessories; sheet metalwork; fabricated plate work (boiler shop)
PA: Thermodynetics, Inc.
651 Day Hill Rd
Windsor CT 06095
860 683-2005

(G-10461)
WALKER MAGNETICS GROUP INC (HQ)
600 Day Hill Rd (06095-1703)
PHONE..................................508 853-3232
John Morissette, *President*
Jim Fitzgerald, *Regional Mgr*
Patricia Mullins, *Prdtn Mgr*
Debra Krikorian, *CFO*
Debra D Krikorian, *Treasurer*
◆ **EMP:** 45
SQ FT: 89,000
SALES: 20MM
SALES (corp-wide): 116.9MM **Privately Held**
WEB: www.walkermagnet.com
SIC: 3545 3559 3845 3535 Machine tool attachments & accessories; separation equipment, magnetic; electromedical equipment; conveyors & conveying equipment
PA: Alliance Holdings, Inc.
100 Witmer Rd Ste 170
Horsham PA 19044
215 706-0873

(G-10462)
WALTERS WOOD WORKING LLC
47 Old Kennedy Rd (06095-2020)
PHONE..................................860 683-8478
Kevin Walters, *Principal*
EMP: 2
SALES (est): 174.2K **Privately Held**
SIC: 2431 Millwork

(G-10463)
WESDYNE INTERNATIONAL LLC
Also Called: Wesdyne Amadata
20 International Dr (06095-1044)
PHONE..................................860 731-1683
Vincent Laduca, *Manager*
EMP: 2
SALES (est): 245.3K **Privately Held**
SIC: 3829 Testing equipment: abrasion, shearing strength, etc.

(G-10464)
WILSON WOODWORKS INC
100 Lamberton Rd (06095-2124)
PHONE..................................860 870-2500
Jonathan Boullay, *President*
EMP: 18
SALES (est): 3.2MM **Privately Held**
SIC: 2426 Flooring, hardwood

(G-10465)
WINDSOR MFG
169 Kennedy Rd (06095-2043)
PHONE..................................860 688-6411
Greg Milzcik, *President*
Jeff Buntin, *Engineer*
David Swearinger, *Manager*
Cindy Edwards, *Administration*
EMP: 2 **EST:** 2008
SALES (est): 130.1K **Privately Held**
SIC: 3999 Manufacturing industries

(G-10466)
WOODVIEW CONSTRUCTION SVCS LLC
11 Ashley Dr (06095-3420)
PHONE..................................860 402-9032
Anthony A Healis,
EMP: 1
SALES: 100K **Privately Held**
SIC: 1442 Construction sand & gravel

Windsor Locks
Hartford County

(G-10467)
ACCURATE WELDING SERVICES LLC
7 Industrial Rd (06096-1101)
PHONE..................................860 623-9500
Edward Loiseau, *Mng Member*
EMP: 10
SALES (est): 488K **Privately Held**
SIC: 7692 Welding repair

(G-10468)
AHLSTROM WINDSOR LOCKS LLC
3 Chirnside Rd (06096-1142)
PHONE..................................860 654-8629
◆ **EMP:** 11
SALES (est): 2.4MM **Privately Held**
SIC: 2621 Paper mills

(G-10469)
AHLSTROM-MUNKSJO NONWOVENS LLC (DH)
2 Elm St (06096-2335)
P.O. Box 270 (06096-0270)
PHONE..................................860 654-8300
Gary Blevins, *President*
Donna Decoteau, *Treasurer*
Leonard Mirahver, *Asst Treas*
Matthew Spaulding, *Asst Treas*
David Pluta, *Admin Sec*
◆ **EMP:** 264
SALES (est): 322.3MM
SALES (corp-wide): 2.7B **Privately Held**
SIC: 2591 3291 Drapery hardware & blinds & shades; abrasive products

(G-10470)
AHLSTROM-MUNKSJO USA INC (HQ)
2 Elm St (06096-2335)
P.O. Box 270 (06096-0270)
PHONE..................................860 654-8300
William Casey, *President*
Christopher Coates, *Vice Pres*
David T Pluta, *Vice Pres*
Leonard H Mirahver, *Treasurer*
Gustav Adlercreutz, *Asst Sec*
▼ **EMP:** 11
SALES (est): 461.7MM
SALES (corp-wide): 2.7B **Privately Held**
SIC: 2621 Specialty or chemically treated papers
PA: Ahlstrom-Munksjo Oyj
Alvar Aallon Katu 3c
Helsinki 00100
108 880-

(G-10471)
ALLEN PRECISION LLC
1 Northgate Dr (06096-1206)
PHONE..................................860 370-9881
Thomas A Pouliot, *Mng Member*
EMP: 3
SALES (est): 445.4K **Privately Held**
SIC: 3599 Machine shop, jobbing & repair

(G-10472)
ALTHOR PRODUCTS LLC
200 Old County Cir # 116 (06096-1599)
PHONE..................................860 386-6700
Matthew Anderson, *Mng Member*
Kelly E Anderson,
EMP: 3
SQ FT: 5,000
SALES: 750K **Privately Held**
WEB: www.althor.com
SIC: 3089 Boxes, plastic

(G-10473)
AWM LLC
Also Called: American Molding
100 D Neil Hagen Dr (06096-1595)
PHONE..................................860 386-1000
EMP: 55
SALES (corp-wide): 155.7MM **Privately Held**
SIC: 3089 5031 Mfg Plastic Products Whol Lumber/Plywood/Millwork
PA: Awm, Llc
1800 Washington Blvd # 140
Baltimore MD 21230
410 694-6802

(G-10474)
BROOME & COMPANY LLC
12 Copper Dr (06096-2624)
PHONE..................................860 623-0254
David A Broome,
Caroline Broome,
Catherine Broome,
Christopher Broome,
EMP: 4
SALES (est): 190K **Privately Held**
SIC: 3931 Pipes, organ

(G-10475)
BTI CCS
1000 Old County Cir (06096-1569)
PHONE..................................860 758-7644
EMP: 2
SALES (est): 158.7K **Privately Held**
SIC: 3843 Dental equipment & supplies

(G-10476)
C Q PUBLISHING
20 Church St (06096-2317)
PHONE..................................860 292-1566
EMP: 1
SALES (est): 57.8K **Privately Held**
SIC: 2741 Misc Publishing

(G-10477)
CBA LIGHTING AND CONTROLS INC
10 Northgate Dr (06096-1205)
P.O. Box 3220 (06096-3220)
PHONE..................................860 623-1924
Lawrence E Girard Jr, *President*
EMP: 2
SQ FT: 2,500
SALES: 300K **Privately Held**
WEB: www.rwylites.com
SIC: 3648 3679 Airport lighting fixtures: runway approach, taxi or ramp; antennas, receiving

(G-10478)
CHARLIES RIDE
389 North St (06096-1204)
PHONE..................................860 916-3637
Beth Hensel, *Principal*
EMP: 3 **EST:** 2011
SALES (est): 179.6K **Privately Held**
SIC: 3845 Pacemaker, cardiac

(G-10479)
CINDYS SOAP COTTAGE
82 Main St (06096-2325)
PHONE..................................860 370-9908
EMP: 2
SALES (est): 186.4K **Privately Held**
SIC: 2844 Toilet preparations

(G-10480)
COLONIAL PRINTERS OF WINDSOR
1 Concorde Way (06096-1533)
PHONE..................................860 627-5433
Gary Christensen, *President*
Margaret Christensen, *President*
Robert B Christensen, *Director*

Windsor Locks - Hartford County (G-10481)

EMP: 4
SQ FT: 3,200
SALES (est): 497.8K **Privately Held**
SIC: 2752 2759 Commercial printing, offset; letterpress printing

(G-10481)
DARCY SAW LLC
10 Canal Bank Rd (06096-2329)
PHONE...............................800 569-1264
John D'Arcy,
EMP: 3
SQ FT: 5,000
SALES: 1.2MM **Privately Held**
SIC: 3425 3546 Saw blades & handsaws; power-driven handtools

(G-10482)
DYNAMIC CONTROLS HS INC
1 Hamilton Rd (06096-1000)
PHONE...............................860 654-6000
Chester P Beach Jr, *Director*
Richard Burrell, *Director*
Charles E Hillman, *Director*
Raymond P Karlak, *Director*
EMP: 4
SALES (est): 252.4K
SALES (corp-wide): 66.5B **Publicly Held**
WEB: www.utc.com
SIC: 3812 3724 Aircraft control systems, electronic; aircraft engines & engine parts
PA: United Technologies Corporation
10 Farm Springs Rd
Farmington CT 06032
860 728-7000

(G-10483)
EMBRAER EXECUTIVE JET SVCS LLC
Also Called: Embraer Executive Jets
41 Perimeter Rd (06096-1069)
PHONE...............................860 804-4600
Eric Pettersen, *Manager*
EMP: 8 **Privately Held**
SIC: 3721 Aircraft
HQ: Embraer Executive Jet Services, Llc
2008 General Aviation Dr
Melbourne FL 32935
321 751-5050

(G-10484)
FLYING FUR LLC
592 Elm St (06096-1603)
PHONE...............................860 623-0450
Sandra Brengi, *Bd of Directors*
EMP: 2
SALES (est): 186K **Privately Held**
SIC: 3999 Furs

(G-10485)
G & D MACHINE CO
383 S Main St (06096-2839)
PHONE...............................860 623-2649
Geza Dobai, *Owner*
EMP: 1
SALES (est): 131.8K **Privately Held**
SIC: 3599 Machine shop, jobbing & repair

(G-10486)
GENUINE PARTS COMPANY
Also Called: NAPA Auto Parts
508 Spring St Ste 2 (06096-1148)
PHONE...............................860 623-4479
Don Wright, *General Mgr*
EMP: 13
SALES (corp-wide): 18.7B **Publicly Held**
SIC: 5531 5013 3714 Automobile & truck equipment & parts; automotive supplies & parts; motor vehicle parts & accessories
PA: Genuine Parts Company
2999 Wildwood Pkwy
Atlanta GA 30339
770 953-1700

(G-10487)
GIRARDIN MOULDING INC
564 Halfway House Rd (06096-1500)
P.O. Box 577 (06096-0577)
PHONE...............................860 623-4486
Gaston Girardin, *President*
Daniel Girardin, *Vice Pres*
Gail Girardin, *Admin Sec*
EMP: 15 EST: 1952
SQ FT: 55,000
SALES (est): 3MM **Privately Held**
WEB: www.girardinmoulding.com
SIC: 3442 Metal doors, sash & trim

(G-10488)
GREIF INC
491 North St (06096-1140)
PHONE...............................740 549-6000
Dave Brzezowski, *Plant Mgr*
Miles Withington, *Purchasing*
Dinal Patel, *Engineer*
Cristina Gonzalez, *Personnel*
David Russolski, *Manager*
EMP: 70
SALES (corp-wide): 3.8B **Publicly Held**
WEB: www.greif.com
SIC: 2655 Fiber cans, drums & similar products
PA: Greif, Inc.
425 Winter Rd
Delaware OH 43015
740 549-6000

(G-10489)
HAMILTON SNDSTRND SPACE
1 Hamilton Rd (06096-1000)
PHONE...............................860 654-6000
Edward Francis, *President*
Lawrence McNamara, *General Mgr*
Daneil Lee, *Dir Ops-Prd-Mfg*
Michael Randall, *Treasurer*
Paul Carew, *Asst Treas*
▲ EMP: 700
SQ FT: 230,000
SALES (est): 163MM **Privately Held**
SIC: 3841 3826 Diagnostic apparatus, medical; thermal analysis instruments, laboratory type

(G-10490)
HAMILTON STANDARD SPACE
1 Hamilton Rd (06096-1010)
PHONE...............................860 654-6000
Harry Garfinkel, *President*
Annemarie Orange, *General Mgr*
Robert Jenkins, *Opers Mgr*
Kristin Smith, *Export Mgr*
William Fiske, *Project Engr*
EMP: 24
SALES (est): 3.6MM **Privately Held**
SIC: 3822 3728 3842 3569 Auto controls regulating residntl & coml environmt & applncs; oxygen systems, aircraft; space suits; gas producers, generators & other gas related equipment

(G-10491)
HAMILTON SUNDSTRAND CORP (HQ)
Also Called: UTC Aerospace Systems
1 Hamilton Rd (06096-1000)
PHONE...............................860 654-6000
Kelly Ortberg, *CEO*
Robert Schechtman, *Business Mgr*
Usman Toor, *Project Mgr*
Tim Topitzer, *Opers Mgr*
Michael Cicero, *Engineer*
◆ EMP: 800 EST: 1910
SALES (est): 3.4B
SALES (corp-wide): 66.5B **Publicly Held**
WEB: www.hamilton-standard.com
SIC: 3621 3625 3728 3594 Frequency converters (electric generators); power generators; actuators, industrial; gears, aircraft power transmission; fluid power pumps & motors; auto controls regulating residntl & coml environmt & applncs; turbine flow meters, industrial process type
PA: United Technologies Corporation
10 Farm Springs Rd
Farmington CT 06032
860 728-7000

(G-10492)
JETSET INTERIORS LLC
Bradley Intl Bldg 85-173 (06096)
PHONE...............................860 292-7962
Ron Larabie, *Manager*
David Miller, *Manager*
EMP: 2 EST: 2013
SALES (est): 102K **Privately Held**
SIC: 2531 Seats, aircraft

(G-10493)
PINE MEADOW MACHINE CO INC
5 Webb St (06096-2500)
PHONE...............................860 623-4494
Thomas Bernadz, *President*
Paul Bernardz, *Vice Pres*
EMP: 6 EST: 1950
SQ FT: 35,000
SALES: 310K **Privately Held**
SIC: 3599 3545 Machine shop, jobbing & repair; tools & accessories for machine tools; gauges (machine tool accessories)

(G-10494)
PPG INDUSTRIES INC
565 Halfway House Rd (06096-1501)
PHONE...............................860 627-7401
Jeff Sommers, *Branch Mgr*
EMP: 2
SALES (corp-wide): 15.3B **Publicly Held**
SIC: 2851 Paints & allied products
PA: Ppg Industries, Inc.
1 Ppg Pl
Pittsburgh PA 15272
412 434-3131

(G-10495)
QUICK TURN MACHINE COMPANY INC
1000 Old County Cir # 105 (06096-1570)
PHONE...............................860 623-2569
Maria Rafalowski, *President*
Stanley Rafalowski, *Vice Pres*
Jessica Rafalowski, *Sales Staff*
EMP: 15
SQ FT: 21,000
SALES (est): 3MM **Privately Held**
WEB: www.quickturnmfg.com
SIC: 3599 Machine shop, jobbing & repair

(G-10496)
SINSIGALLI SIGNS & DESIGNS
445 Spring St Wndsor Lcks Windsor Locks (06096)
PHONE...............................860 627-8712
Christopher Sinsigalli, *Owner*
Susan Sinsigalli, *Co-Owner*
EMP: 2 EST: 1994
SQ FT: 2,000
SALES (est): 197.3K **Privately Held**
SIC: 3993 Signs, not made in custom sign painting shops

(G-10497)
SPECTRUM MACHINE & DESIGN LLC
800 Old County Cir (06096-1575)
P.O. Box 4144 (06096-4144)
PHONE...............................860 386-6490
Gary Poesnecker,
Connie Poesnecker,
EMP: 8
SQ FT: 4,000
SALES: 810K **Privately Held**
WEB: www.smd-llc.com
SIC: 3599 Machine shop, jobbing & repair

(G-10498)
STANDARD BELLOWS CO (PA)
375 Ella Grasso Tpke (06096-1003)
PHONE...............................860 623-2307
Stanley E Tkacz Jr, *President*
Theresa Miller, *General Mgr*
Thomas J Tkacz, *Corp Secy*
Stanley Tkacz, *CFO*
Thomas Tkacz, *CPA*
EMP: 20 EST: 1961
SQ FT: 18,400
SALES (est): 3.5MM **Privately Held**
WEB: www.std-bellows.com
SIC: 3599 Bellows, industrial: metal

(G-10499)
TWC TRANS WORLD CONSULTING
Also Called: Drainage Products
383 S Main St (06096-2839)
PHONE...............................860 668-5108
Paul Tarko Jr, *President*
Paul Tarko Sr, *CTO*
EMP: 5
SQ FT: 10,000
SALES: 500K **Privately Held**
WEB: www.drainaway.com
SIC: 3089 Injection molding of plastics

(G-10500)
ULITSCH MECHANICAL SVCS LLC
465 Spring St Ste H (06096-1157)
P.O. Box L, West Suffield (06093-0110)
PHONE...............................860 623-4223
Rachel Cormier, *Office Mgr*
Michael J Ulitsch,
EMP: 4
SALES (est): 756.3K **Privately Held**
SIC: 3585 3569 Refrigeration & heating equipment; testing chambers for altitude, temperature, ordnance, power

(G-10501)
VIJAY MANUFACTURING CO LLC
59 King Spring Rd Ste G (06096-1153)
PHONE...............................860 627-4901
Raj Kantesaria, *Owner*
EMP: 1
SALES (est): 45K **Privately Held**
SIC: 3999 Manufacturing industries

(G-10502)
YANKEE SIGNS
26 Preston Rd (06096-2821)
PHONE...............................860 623-8651
Robert Zdun, *Owner*
EMP: 1
SALES: 150K **Privately Held**
SIC: 3993 Signs, not made in custom sign painting shops

Windsorville
Hartford County

(G-10503)
CHRISTENSEN WOODWORKING
37 Rockville Rd (06016-9673)
PHONE...............................860 712-6166
EMP: 1 EST: 2017
SALES (est): 56.7K **Privately Held**
SIC: 2431 Millwork

Winsted
Litchfield County

(G-10504)
AMERICAN COLLARS COUPLINGS INC
88 Hubbard St (06098-1025)
PHONE...............................860 379-7043
Shirley A Clarke, *President*
Michael A Clarke, *Vice Pres*
Linda Stommel, *Vice Pres*
▲ EMP: 12
SQ FT: 8,000
SALES (est): 930K **Privately Held**
SIC: 3568 Collars, shaft (power transmission equipment)

(G-10505)
ARCONIC INC
145 Price Rd (06098-2237)
PHONE...............................860 379-3314
Richard Dellagnese, *Engineer*
Paul Masucci, *Engineer*
Klaus Kleinfield, *Branch Mgr*
EMP: 9
SALES (corp-wide): 14B **Publicly Held**
SIC: 3334 Primary aluminum
PA: Arconic Inc.
201 Isabella St Ste 200
New York NY 15212
412 553-1950

(G-10506)
ASAP MFG CO LLC
44 Taylor Rd (06063-3431)
PHONE...............................860 738-4831
David Fazzina, *Manager*
EMP: 2
SALES (est): 161.8K **Privately Held**
SIC: 3999 Manufacturing industries

GEOGRAPHIC SECTION — Winsted - Litchfield County (G-10537)

(G-10507)
ASSELIN ELECTRIC LLC
228 Smith Hill Rd (06098-2220)
PHONE..............................860 379-3056
Robert Michael Asselin, *Principal*
EMP: 2
SALES (est): 156.5K **Privately Held**
SIC: 3634 Electric housewares & fans

(G-10508)
B & M FABRICATION LLC
172 Florence St (06098-1312)
PHONE..............................860 379-5444
David B Brewer, *Principal*
EMP: 2 **EST:** 2008
SALES (est): 115.7K **Privately Held**
SIC: 3999 Manufacturing industries

(G-10509)
B E C MACHINETOOL INC
104 Groppo Dr (06098)
P.O. Box 1031 (06098-8031)
PHONE..............................860 738-9432
Bruce Babes, *President*
Barbara Babes, *Admin Sec*
EMP: 2
SQ FT: 5,000
SALES: 100K **Privately Held**
SIC: 3599 Machine shop, jobbing & repair

(G-10510)
BKMFG CORP
Also Called: Broil King
200 International Way (06098-2252)
PHONE..............................860 738-2200
Michael Shanahan, *President*
Michael Bosson, *Vice Pres*
▲ **EMP:** 35
SQ FT: 30,000
SALES (est): 7.3MM
SALES (corp-wide): 12.7MM **Privately Held**
WEB: www.broilking.com
SIC: 3634 Broilers, electric; fryers, electric: household
PA: Cadco, Ltd.
200 International Way
Winsted CT 06098
860 738-2500

(G-10511)
BROWSER DAILY
211 Spencer Hill Rd (06098-2214)
PHONE..............................860 469-5534
Jon Bishop, *Principal*
EMP: 5
SALES (est): 257.9K **Privately Held**
SIC: 2711 Newspapers, publishing & printing

(G-10512)
CABEA LLC
210 Holabird Ave Ste 8 (06098-1747)
PHONE..............................860 738-0819
Caroline W Christensen, *Principal*
EMP: 1 **EST:** 2007
SALES (est): 125.7K **Privately Held**
SIC: 2835 Pregnancy test kits

(G-10513)
CAINE MACHINING INC
43 Meadow St (06098-1419)
P.O. Box 293 (06098-0293)
PHONE..............................860 738-1619
Michael Sultaire, *President*
Robert Carpenter, *Admin Sec*
EMP: 4
SALES: 400K **Privately Held**
SIC: 3451 Screw machine products

(G-10514)
CONNECTCUT TMPRED GL DSTRS LLC
56 Torrington Rd (06098)
PHONE..............................860 379-5670
Shellie Poley,
EMP: 2
SALES (est): 152.1K **Privately Held**
SIC: 3231 Products of purchased glass

(G-10515)
DRT AEROSPACE LLC
Also Called: Drt Power Systems
200 Price Rd (06098-2236)
PHONE..............................860 379-0783
Gary Van Gundy, *CEO*
EMP: 16 **Privately Held**
SIC: 3728 5013 Aircraft parts & equipment; automotive engines & engine parts
HQ: Drt Aerospace, Llc
8694 Rite Track Way
West Chester OH 45069
937 298-7391

(G-10516)
DUFRANE NUCLEAR SHIELDING INC
150 Price Rd (06098-2265)
PHONE..............................860 379-2318
Joshua Brooks, *President*
Dusty McInturff, *Superintendent*
Dan Brooks, *Vice Pres*
Lena Neufeld, *Office Mgr*
EMP: 15
SQ FT: 2,000
SALES: 4.6MM **Privately Held**
WEB: www.dufrane.com
SIC: 7389 3444 3312 8711 Design services; metal housings, enclosures, casings & other containers; stainless steel; mechanical engineering; custom machinery; business consulting

(G-10517)
E & E TOOL & MANUFACTURING CO
100 International Way (06098-2251)
PHONE..............................860 738-8577
Edward Clark, *Partner*
Bill Clark, *Partner*
EMP: 10
SQ FT: 6,000
SALES: 1MM **Privately Held**
SIC: 3544 Special dies & tools

(G-10518)
EAST COAST LIGHTNING EQP INC
Also Called: East Coast Roof Specialties
24 Lanson Dr (06098-2072)
PHONE..............................860 379-9072
Mark P Morgan, *President*
Jennifer Morgan, *Corp Secy*
Anita Cassella, *Office Mgr*
EMP: 24
SQ FT: 20,000
SALES (est): 5.9MM **Privately Held**
WEB: www.eastcoastlightning.com
SIC: 3643 5072 Lightning protection equipment; miscellaneous fasteners

(G-10519)
EMBROIDERY WIZARD
141 E Mountain Ave (06098-1354)
PHONE..............................860 379-3294
Elaine Williams, *Owner*
EMP: 2
SALES: 65K **Privately Held**
SIC: 2395 7211 Embroidery & art needlework; power laundries, family & commercial

(G-10520)
FAIRCHILD AUTO-MATED PARTS INC
10 White St (06098-2132)
PHONE..............................860 379-2725
Norman F Thompson, *Ch of Bd*
Jonathan P Thompson, *President*
Linda Criss, *Manager*
EMP: 22 **EST:** 1944
SQ FT: 16,500
SALES (est): 3.9MM **Privately Held**
WEB: www.fairchildparts.com
SIC: 3599 Machine shop, jobbing & repair

(G-10521)
FLASHBACK WELDING
88 Torrington Rd (06098)
P.O. Box 91 (06098-0091)
PHONE..............................860 738-1122
Todd Hall, *Owner*
▲ **EMP:** 2
SALES (est): 260.3K **Privately Held**
SIC: 3441 Fabricated structural metal

(G-10522)
FRYS WELDING LLC
287 Gilbert Ave (06098-1350)
PHONE..............................860 944-2547
EMP: 1 **EST:** 2010
SALES (est): 62.6K **Privately Held**
SIC: 7692 Welding Repair

(G-10523)
H-O PRODUCTS CORPORATION
12 Munro St (06098-1423)
PHONE..............................860 379-9875
Chris Olson, *President*
Robert Carfiro, *Controller*
EMP: 26
SQ FT: 50,000
SALES (est): 4.7MM **Privately Held**
WEB: www.h-oproducts.com
SIC: 3069 3086 3053 2672 Weather strip, sponge rubber; rubber tape; insulation or cushioning material, foamed plastic; gaskets & sealing devices; adhesive papers, labels or tapes: from purchased material; narrow fabric mills

(G-10524)
HOWMET CASTINGS & SERVICES INC
Alcoa Howmet, Winsted
145 Price Rd (06098-2240)
PHONE..............................860 379-3314
Elmer Miller, *General Mgr*
Robert Beckquist, *Branch Mgr*
EMP: 270
SQ FT: 63,000
SALES (corp-wide): 14B **Publicly Held**
SIC: 3324 Commercial investment castings, ferrous
HQ: Howmet Castings & Services, Inc.
1616 Harvard Ave
Newburgh Heights OH 44105
216 641-4400

(G-10525)
J & G MACHINING COMPANY INC
100 Whiting St Ste 1 (06098-1878)
PHONE..............................860 379-7038
Robert Goulet, *President*
Lillian Goulet, *Treasurer*
Bob Goulet, *Data Proc Dir*
EMP: 6 **EST:** 1978
SQ FT: 1,500
SALES: 491K **Privately Held**
SIC: 3599 Machine shop, jobbing & repair

(G-10526)
KING OF COVERS INC (PA)
154 Torrington Rd (06098-2085)
PHONE..............................860 379-2427
Linwood Quinn, *President*
Constance Quinn, *Vice Pres*
EMP: 5 **EST:** 1970
SALES: 500K **Privately Held**
WEB: www.thekingofcovers.com
SIC: 3714 Motor vehicle parts & accessories

(G-10527)
LUCKY DUCK PRESS
9 Willow St (06098-2009)
PHONE..............................347 703-3984
EMP: 1 **EST:** 2011
SALES (est): 53.2K **Privately Held**
SIC: 2741 Miscellaneous publishing

(G-10528)
METAL PLUS LLC
214 Wallens Hill Rd (06098-1378)
PHONE..............................860 379-1327
Mario Lallier, *Principal*
EMP: 4
SALES (est): 609.4K **Privately Held**
SIC: 3531 Roofing equipment

(G-10529)
METAMORPHIC MATERIALS INC
122 Colebrook River Rd (06098)
PHONE..............................860 738-8638
Jay K Martin, *President*
▲ **EMP:** 10
SALES (est): 1.3MM **Privately Held**
SIC: 2819 2891 3479 Inorganic acids, except nitric & phosphoric; adhesives & sealants; etching & engraving

(G-10530)
MRC SPECIALTY BALLS
149 Colebrook River Rd (06098-2203)
PHONE..............................860 379-8511
David Brewer, *Principal*
EMP: 2
SALES (est): 107.4K **Privately Held**
SIC: 3562 Ball & roller bearings

(G-10531)
NARRAGANSETT SCREW CO
119 Rowley St (06098-2068)
PHONE..............................860 379-4059
Charlie Rhoades, *President*
EMP: 13 **EST:** 1960
SQ FT: 27,000
SALES (est): 1.3MM **Privately Held**
WEB: www.narragansettscrew.com
SIC: 3452 3364 3354 Screws, metal; non-ferrous die-castings except aluminum; aluminum extruded products

(G-10532)
PRECISION METALS AND PLASTICS
Also Called: Precision Metals and Plas Mfg
118 Colebrook River Rd # 7 (06098-2241)
P.O. Box 7264, Berlin (06037-7264)
PHONE..............................860 238-4320
William Bonk, *Principal*
EMP: 9
SALES (est): 1.1MM **Privately Held**
SIC: 3728 Aircraft assemblies, subassemblies & parts

(G-10533)
RED BARN WOODWORKERS
118 Laurel Way (06098-2532)
PHONE..............................860 379-3158
Waldo Placo, *Owner*
EMP: 3 **EST:** 1962
SALES (est): 170K **Privately Held**
SIC: 2431 Door frames, wood; door sashes, wood; doors, wood; window frames, wood

(G-10534)
SCHAEFFLER AEROSPACE USA CORP
Also Called: Winsted Precision Ball
159 Colebrook River Rd (06098-2203)
PHONE..............................860 379-7558
Roman Czarniecki, *General Mgr*
Charles Alicandro, *General Mgr*
Frank Nenninger, *Engineer*
EMP: 71
SALES (corp-wide): 68.1B **Privately Held**
SIC: 3562 3399 3229 Ball bearings & parts; steel balls; pressed & blown glass
HQ: Schaeffler Aerospace Usa Corporation
200 Park Ave
Danbury CT 06810
203 744-2211

(G-10535)
SKF SPECIALTY BALLS
149 Colebrook River Rd (06098-2203)
PHONE..............................860 379-8511
EMP: 3
SALES (est): 170.3K **Privately Held**
SIC: 3562 Ball & roller bearings

(G-10536)
SKF USA INC
149 Colebrook River Rd (06098-2203)
PHONE..............................860 379-8511
Frank Baker, *Branch Mgr*
EMP: 35
SALES (corp-wide): 9.5B **Privately Held**
WEB: www.skfusa.com
SIC: 3562 3053 Ball & roller bearings; gaskets & sealing devices
HQ: Skf Usa Inc.
890 Forty Foot Rd
Lansdale PA 19446
267 436-6000

(G-10537)
SMANTICS
19 Rock St (06098-1510)
PHONE..............................860 238-7714
Suzanne McDonald, *Owner*
EMP: 1

SALES (est): 63.2K **Privately Held**
WEB: www.smantics.com
SIC: 2741 Miscellaneous publishing

(G-10538)
SONCHIEF ELECTRICS INC
Also Called: Son-Chief Stampings
41 Meadow St Ste 1 (06098-1438)
P.O. Box 204, Harwinton (06791-0204)
PHONE...................................860 379-2741
Donal F Fitzgerald, *President*
Barbara Fitzgerald, *Admin Sec*
EMP: 5
SQ FT: 120,000
SALES (est): 727.2K **Privately Held**
SIC: 3469 Metal stampings

(G-10539)
SOUTHPORT PRODUCTS LLC
157 Colebrook River Rd (06098-2203)
PHONE...................................860 379-0761
John Auclair, *President*
Randolph Auclair,
EMP: 6
SQ FT: 10,000
SALES (est): 914.1K **Privately Held**
WEB: www.southportindustries.com
SIC: 3643 Electric connectors

(G-10540)
STERLING NAME TAPE COMPANY
9 Willow St (06098-2009)
P.O. Box 939 (06098-0939)
PHONE...................................860 379-5142
James P Barrett, *President*
Jonathan Ryan, *Vice Pres*
Paula Ryan-Richard, *Treasurer*
Daniel Barrett, *Admin Sec*
Virginia D Barrett, *Admin Sec*
EMP: 4 **EST:** 1901
SQ FT: 12,000
SALES (est): 639.8K **Privately Held**
WEB: www.sterlingtape.com
SIC: 2269 Labels, cotton: printed; printing of narrow fabrics

(G-10541)
SZEPANSKI MACHINE SERVICES LLC
48 Holabird Ave (06098-1616)
PHONE...................................860 738-9825
Felix Szepanski, *Principal*
EMP: 2
SALES (est): 108.4K **Privately Held**
SIC: 3599 Machine shop, jobbing & repair

(G-10542)
VIZ-PRO LLC
120 Colebrook River Rd (06098-2205)
PHONE...................................860 379-0055
Pan Haipo, *President*
EMP: 3
SQ FT: 4,000
SALES (est): 4MM **Privately Held**
SIC: 3931 Trombones & parts; trumpets & parts

(G-10543)
WESTWOOD PRODUCTS INC
167 Torrington Rd (06098-2087)
P.O. Box 933 (06098-0933)
PHONE...................................860 379-9401
Brian Tarbox, *President*
Sara Westervelt, *Office Mgr*
EMP: 16
SQ FT: 8,000
SALES: 2.3MM **Privately Held**
SIC: 2441 2448 2449 Boxes, wood; pallets, wood; wood containers

(G-10544)
WINCHESTER INDUSTRIES INC
106 Groppo Dr (06098)
P.O. Box 917 (06098-0917)
PHONE...................................860 379-5336
John Devanney, *President*
Linda Devanney, *Corp Secy*
Damien Devanney, *Vice Pres*
EMP: 7
SQ FT: 17,800
SALES (est): 1MM **Privately Held**
WEB: www.railroadgage.com
SIC: 3743 Railroad equipment

(G-10545)
WINCHESTER PRODUCTS INC
22 Lanson Dr (06098-2072)
PHONE...................................860 379-8590
Charles H Ackerman, *President*
Judy B Ackerman, *Vice Pres*
EMP: 6 **EST:** 1994
SQ FT: 5,000
SALES: 600K **Privately Held**
SIC: 3369 White metal castings (lead, tin, antimony), except die

(G-10546)
WINCHESTER STAIR & WOODWORKING
210 Holabird Ave Ste 6 (06098-1747)
PHONE...................................860 379-3194
George Majewski, *Manager*
EMP: 2
SALES (est): 183.5K **Privately Held**
SIC: 3446 Stairs, staircases, stair treads: prefabricated metal

(G-10547)
WINCHESTER WOODWORKS LLC
12 Munro St (06098-1423)
PHONE...................................860 379-9875
Chris Olson, *President*
EMP: 4
SALES (est): 327.5K **Privately Held**
SIC: 2431 Millwork

Wolcott
New Haven County

(G-10548)
ALDEN CORPORATION
Also Called: Drill-Out
1 Hillside Dr (06716-2403)
P.O. Box 6262 (06716-0262)
PHONE...................................203 879-8830
Yvon J Desaulniers, *President*
▲ **EMP:** 60
SQ FT: 40,000
SALES (est): 10.3MM **Privately Held**
WEB: www.aldencorporation.com
SIC: 3545 3546 Cutting tools for machine tools; drill attachments, portable

(G-10549)
BRASS CITY MUNITIONS LLC
1241 Spindle Hill Rd (06716-1200)
PHONE...................................203 509-7088
Lance M Walsh, *Principal*
EMP: 2
SALES (est): 175K **Privately Held**
SIC: 3482 Small arms ammunition

(G-10550)
BRUCE COREY ENTERPRISES INC
Also Called: Radon Systems of CT
40 Pratt Ln (06716-3013)
PHONE...................................203 272-3600
Bruce Corey, *President*
EMP: 2
SALES (est): 225.9K **Privately Held**
WEB: www.radonsystemsofct.com
SIC: 1389 Detection & analysis service, gas

(G-10551)
C & G PRECISIONS PRODUCTS INC
Also Called: C&G Precision Parts
14 Venus Dr (06716-2608)
PHONE...................................203 879-6989
Pat Guerrera, *President*
EMP: 5
SQ FT: 1,400
SALES: 600K **Privately Held**
SIC: 3549 Marking machines, metalworking

(G-10552)
C R SPRINGS INC
721 Bound Line Rd (06716-1541)
PHONE...................................203 879-3357
Greg Russak, *President*
EMP: 2

SALES (est): 147K **Privately Held**
SIC: 3496 Miscellaneous fabricated wire products

(G-10553)
CHILD EVNGELISM FELLOWSHIP INC
730 Bound Line Rd (06716-1556)
PHONE...................................203 879-2154
Daniel Guido, *Branch Mgr*
EMP: 41
SALES (corp-wide): 24.4MM **Privately Held**
SIC: 2752 Commercial printing, lithographic
PA: Child Evangelism Fellowship Incorporated
17482 Highway M
Warrenton MO 63383
636 456-4321

(G-10554)
CLEAR & COLORED COATINGS LLC
20 Swiss Ln (06716-2622)
PHONE...................................203 879-1379
Steven Bosse, *Branch Mgr*
EMP: 1
SALES (corp-wide): 680.6K **Privately Held**
SIC: 3471 Electroplating of metals or formed products
PA: Clear & Colored Coatings Llc
222 Spindle Hill Rd
Wolcott CT 06716
203 879-1379

(G-10555)
CLEAR & COLORED COATINGS LLC (PA)
222 Spindle Hill Rd (06716-1729)
PHONE...................................203 879-1379
Steven Chares Bosse, *Principal*
EMP: 8 **EST:** 2001
SALES (est): 680.6K **Privately Held**
SIC: 3479 Metal coating & allied service

(G-10556)
COILS PLUS INC
30 Town Line Rd (06716-2624)
PHONE...................................203 879-0755
Michael Mennillo, *President*
Daniel J Mennillo Jr, *Vice Pres*
Paul Jacovich, *Opers Staff*
EMP: 28
SQ FT: 13,000
SALES (est): 4.5MM **Privately Held**
WEB: www.coilsplus.com
SIC: 3621 3677 Coils, for electric motors or generators; electronic coils, transformers & other inductors

(G-10557)
COM TOWER
1140 Wolcott Rd (06716 1531)
P.O. Box 6059 (06716-0059)
PHONE...................................203 879-6568
Roger Levesque, *Owner*
EMP: 2
SALES (est): 160K **Privately Held**
SIC: 3441 Tower sections, radio & television transmission

(G-10558)
CREATIVE SOURCE LLC
32 Mountain View Dr (06716-2838)
P.O. Box 6161 (06716-0161)
PHONE...................................203 879-4005
Edwin Angulo,
EMP: 2
SALES (est): 499.8K **Privately Held**
WEB: www.creativesource.com
SIC: 2653 Boxes, corrugated: made from purchased materials

(G-10559)
CUSTOM SPORTSWEAR MFG
Also Called: Teta Actvwear By Cstm Sprtwear
14 Town Line Rd (06716-2635)
PHONE...................................203 879-4420
Mario Teta Jr, *President*
Sharon Gibson, *Corp Secy*
EMP: 6 **EST:** 1996
SQ FT: 3,500

SALES (est): 614.4K **Privately Held**
SIC: 2329 2339 Men's & boys' sportswear & athletic clothing; women's & misses' athletic clothing & sportswear

(G-10560)
DEVON PRECISION INDUSTRIES INC
Also Called: Devon Precision Industries.
251 Munson Rd (06716-2728)
P.O. Box 6555 (06716-0555)
PHONE...................................203 879-1437
Yvon J Desaulniers, *CEO*
David J Desaulniers, *President*
Lorraine Desaulniers, *Corp Secy*
Donald J Desaulniers, *Vice Pres*
John Trusch, *Project Mgr*
EMP: 65 **EST:** 1967
SQ FT: 55,000
SALES (est): 4.5MM **Privately Held**
WEB: www.devonp.com
SIC: 3451 Screw machine products

(G-10561)
DIECRAFT COMPACTING TOOL INC
36 James Pl (06716-1017)
PHONE...................................203 879-3019
James Mulvehill Sr, *President*
EMP: 5 **EST:** 1952
SQ FT: 6,800
SALES (est): 469.4K **Privately Held**
SIC: 3544 Special dies & tools

(G-10562)
DRAHER MACHINE COMPANY
30 Tosun Rd (06716-2629)
PHONE...................................203 753-0179
Robert Maton, *President*
Barbara Maton, *Admin Sec*
EMP: 6 **EST:** 1930
SQ FT: 9,000
SALES (est): 1.1MM **Privately Held**
SIC: 3599 Machine shop, jobbing & repair

(G-10563)
EDSON MANUFACTURING INC
10 Venus Dr (06716-2627)
P.O. Box 6211 (06716-0211)
PHONE...................................203 879-1411
Lee Gaw, *President*
John Famiglietti, *Admin Sec*
▲ **EMP:** 10
SQ FT: 6,200
SALES (est): 3.1MM **Privately Held**
WEB: www.edsonmfg.com
SIC: 3452 Rivets, metal

(G-10564)
EYELET TECH LLC
10 Venus Dr (06716-2627)
PHONE...................................203 879-5306
Scott Allen, *Mng Member*
EMP: 48
SALES (est): 5.3MM **Privately Held**
WEB: www.eyelettech.com
SIC: 3542 3965 3469 Brakes, metal forming; eyelets, metal: clothing, fabrics, boots or shoes; metal stampings

(G-10565)
FALLING HAMMER PRODUCTIONS LLC
10 Swiss Ln (06716-2622)
PHONE...................................203 879-1786
Jamie Lundell, *Manager*
EMP: 2
SALES (est): 235.7K **Privately Held**
SIC: 3446 Architectural metalwork

(G-10566)
GRANNYS GOT IT
724 Wolcott Rd Ste 3 (06716-2448)
PHONE...................................203 879-0042
Raeann Gugliotti, *Owner*
Regina Enbardo, *Office Mgr*
EMP: 3
SQ FT: 590
SALES (est): 275.8K **Privately Held**
SIC: 2782 5945 Scrapbooks; hobby & craft supplies

GEOGRAPHIC SECTION — Woodbridge - New Haven County (G-10597)

(G-10567)
GRAPHIC CNTRLS ACQISITION CORP
Also Called: Biomedical Innovations
1 Hillside Dr (06716-2403)
PHONE..................203 759-1020
EMP: 2 Privately Held
SIC: 3841 Surgical & medical instruments
HQ: Graphic Controls Acquisition Corp.
400 Exchange St
Buffalo NY 14204
716 853-7500

(G-10568)
HOB INDUSTRIES INC
750 Bound Line Rd (06716-1556)
PHONE..................203 879-3028
Francis X Macary Jr, CEO
Raymond R Macary, Vice Pres
Sarah Macary, Treasurer
Peter Macary, Admin Sec
EMP: 40 EST: 1975
SQ FT: 15,000
SALES (est): 7.6MM Privately Held
WEB: www.hobindustries.com
SIC: 3469 Stamping metal for the trade

(G-10569)
JAN MANUFACTURING INC
Also Called: Connecticut Cue Parts
14 Town Line Rd Ste 8 (06716-2635)
PHONE..................203 879-0580
John Ciavarella Jr, President
Nancy Ciavarella, Vice Pres
EMP: 7
SQ FT: 3,500
SALES (est): 1.1MM Privately Held
WEB: www.janmfg.com
SIC: 3599 7694 Machine shop, jobbing & repair; coil winding service

(G-10570)
JOVAN MACHINE CO INC
1133 Wolcott Rd Ste A (06716-1514)
P.O. Box 6171 (06716-0171)
PHONE..................203 879-2855
Daniel Brewster, President
EMP: 5
SQ FT: 5,000
SALES (est): 350K Privately Held
SIC: 3599 Machine shop, jobbing & repair

(G-10571)
LOUIS ELECTRIC CO INC
1584 Wolcott Rd (06716-1327)
P.O. Box 1781, Bristol (06011-1781)
PHONE..................203 879-5483
Louis R Duguette, President
Linda Duguette, Vice Pres
Louis R Duguette, Director
EMP: 3 EST: 1972
SALES (est): 456K Privately Held
SIC: 3823 1731 Controllers for process variables, all types; general electrical contractor

(G-10572)
M L GUERRERA WELDING
58 Averyll Ave (06716-1302)
P.O. Box 6012 (06716-0012)
PHONE..................203 879-6823
Mark Guerrera, Owner
EMP: 1
SALES (est): 125.7K Privately Held
SIC: 7692 Welding repair

(G-10573)
MAILLY MANUFACTURING COMPANY
54 Wakelee Rd (06716-2620)
P.O. Box 6143 (06716-0143)
PHONE..................203 879-1445
John Mailly, President
Richard Mailly, President
Janet Corden, Admin Sec
EMP: 7 EST: 1945
SQ FT: 8,000
SALES (est): 1.2MM Privately Held
SIC: 3451 Screw machine products

(G-10574)
MARK MACHINE TOOL LLC
72 Clark St (06716-1424)
PHONE..................203 910-5942
Madray Subramani,
EMP: 1
SQ FT: 2,000
SALES (est): 140K Privately Held
SIC: 3541 Machine tool replacement & repair parts, metal cutting types

(G-10575)
MUSANO INC
Also Called: NESLO MANUFACTURING
373 Woodtick Rd (06716-2824)
P.O. Box 6205 (06716-0205)
PHONE..................203 879-4651
Fred Musano Jr, President
Anthony Musano, Vice Pres
Tony Musano, Vice Pres
Patricia Musano, Admin Sec
EMP: 12
SQ FT: 10,000
SALES (est): 3.3MM Privately Held
WEB: www.neslo.com
SIC: 1542 2542 3446 Commercial & office buildings, renovation & repair; partitions for floor attachment, prefabricated: except wood; architectural metalwork

(G-10576)
NATIONAL DIE COMPANY
64 Wolcott Rd (06716-2612)
P.O. Box 6281 (06716-0281)
PHONE..................203 879-1408
John J Ernst, CEO
Paul Cote, President
EMP: 9 EST: 1945
SQ FT: 15,000
SALES (est): 1.8MM Privately Held
SIC: 3469 Stamping metal for the trade

(G-10577)
NATURALLY NUTRITOUS VEND LLC
23 Birch Ave (06716-3318)
PHONE..................860 416-9848
Carl Hyburg, Mng Member
EMP: 2
SALES (est): 103.3K Privately Held
SIC: 2824 Organic fibers, noncellulosic

(G-10578)
NUCAP US INC (DH)
238 Wolcott Rd (06716-2617)
PHONE..................203 879-1423
Roman Arbesman, President
John Diniz, CFO
Rick Tibau, Marketing Mgr
Robert Bosco, Manager
Sheila Tyson, Receptionist
▲ EMP: 30
SQ FT: 56,000
SALES (est): 18.3MM
SALES (corp-wide): 95MM Privately Held
WEB: www.anstroinc.com
SIC: 3965 3452 3469 3714 Eyelets, metal; clothing, fabrics, boots or shoes; rivets, metal; metal stampings; motor vehicle parts & accessories
HQ: Nucap Industries Inc
3370 Pharmacy Ave
Scarborough ON M1W 3
416 494-1444

(G-10579)
PRECISION CENTERLESS GRINDING
137 Tosun Rd (06716-2633)
PHONE..................203 879-1228
Roland Labonte, Principal
EMP: 2
SALES (est): 232.6K Privately Held
SIC: 3599 Grinding castings for the trade

(G-10580)
PRECISION METHODS INCORPORATED
Also Called: PMI
40 North St (06716-1332)
P.O. Box 6445 (06716-0445)
PHONE..................203 879-1429
C Thomas Accuosti, President
Thomas D Accuosti, Vice Pres
EMP: 19
SQ FT: 10,000
SALES (est): 1.5MM Privately Held
WEB: www.precisionmethods.com
SIC: 3451 Screw machine products

(G-10581)
PRINT SHOP OF WOLCOTT LLC
450 Wolcott Rd (06716-2639)
PHONE..................203 879-3353
Scott Little,
EMP: 3
SQ FT: 600
SALES (est): 379.4K Privately Held
SIC: 2752 7336 2759 Commercial printing, offset; graphic arts & related design; commercial printing

(G-10582)
PUPS IN A TUB
654 Wolcott Rd Ste 4 (06716-2445)
PHONE..................203 879-2947
Richard A Laferriere, Principal
EMP: 2
SALES (est): 121.6K Privately Held
SIC: 3999 Pet supplies

(G-10583)
RICHARDS METAL PRODUCTS INC
14 Swiss Ln (06716-2622)
P.O. Box 6290 (06716-0290)
PHONE..................203 879-2555
Christopher Cobb, President
Vezir Memeti, Mfg Staff
Fred Galarraga, Engineer
EMP: 12 EST: 1965
SQ FT: 10,000
SALES (est): 2.5MM Privately Held
WEB: www.richardsmetalproducts.com
SIC: 3469 Stamping metal for the trade

(G-10584)
ROGERS WOODSIDING
30 Cedar Ave (06716-1205)
PHONE..................203 879-9747
Roger Lamontagne, Owner
EMP: 1
SALES (est): 70.3K Privately Held
SIC: 2431 Panel work, wood

(G-10585)
SCHAEFER ROLLS INC
32 Bolduc Ct (06716-3146)
PHONE..................203 910-0224
EMP: 3
SALES (est): 148.8K Privately Held
SIC: 3724 Aircraft engines & engine parts

(G-10586)
SEAFOOD GOURMET INC
264 Lyman Rd Apt 3-13 (06716-2335)
PHONE..................203 272-1544
James L Romano, President
James Romano, President
Deborah Romano, Vice Pres
EMP: 12
SALES (est): 860K Privately Held
SIC: 2092 Chowders, fish & seafood: frozen

(G-10587)
SECONDARIES INC
19 Venus Dr (06716-2695)
PHONE..................203 879-4633
Robert A Ferry, President
John A Karas, Vice Pres
EMP: 7 EST: 1962
SQ FT: 6,400
SALES (est): 1MM Privately Held
WEB: www.secondariesinc.com
SIC: 3599 3462 Machine shop, jobbing & repair; flange, valve & pipe fitting forgings, ferrous

(G-10588)
SELECTCOM MFG CO INC
29 Nutmeg Valley Rd (06716-2621)
PHONE..................203 879-9900
Brian Lanese, President
Arthur Lanese Jr, Treasurer
Sheila Lanese, Admin Sec
EMP: 7 EST: 1970
SQ FT: 7,500
SALES (est): 430K Privately Held
SIC: 3451 Screw machine products

(G-10589)
SEQUEL SPECIAL PRODUCTS LLC
1 Hillside Dr (06716-2403)
PHONE..................203 759-1020
Adan Hernandez, Buyer
Scott Debisschop,
EMP: 25
SQ FT: 20,000
SALES (est): 5.8MM Privately Held
WEB: www.sequelmail.com
SIC: 3841 Surgical & medical instruments

(G-10590)
SILKSCREEN PLUS LLC
413 Wolcott Rd (06716-2613)
P.O. Box 6104 (06716-0104)
PHONE..................203 879-0345
James Briglia, President
EMP: 3
SALES (est): 290K Privately Held
WEB: www.silkscreenplus.com
SIC: 2759 Screen printing

(G-10591)
TETA ACTIVEWEAR BY CUSTOM
14 Town Line Rd Ste 1 (06716-2635)
PHONE..................203 879-4420
Mario Teta Jr, President
EMP: 3
SALES (est): 490K Privately Held
WEB: www.tetawear.com
SIC: 2339 Sportswear, women's

(G-10592)
TIMOTHY GRAY
Also Called: Versatile Machine
21 Porter Rd (06716-1414)
PHONE..................860 314-0863
Timothy Gray, Owner
Timothy JAS, Contractor
EMP: 1
SALES (est): 105.3K Privately Held
SIC: 3599 Machine shop, jobbing & repair

(G-10593)
YANKEE STEEL SERVICE LLC
9 Venus Dr (06716-2607)
PHONE..................203 879-5707
Fax: 203 879-5704
EMP: 4
SQ FT: 12,000
SALES: 500K Privately Held
SIC: 3312 Mfg Stainless Steel

Woodbridge
New Haven County

(G-10594)
BLUE BARN WORKS LLC
7 Pine Hill Rd (06525-1812)
PHONE..................203 389-0923
Tevin Abeshouse, Mng Member
EMP: 1
SALES (est): 63.7K Privately Held
SIC: 2869 Silicones

(G-10595)
BRYK MACHINE WORKS LLC
1125 Johnson Rd (06525-2630)
PHONE..................203 397-1405
Richard Bryk, Owner
EMP: 1
SALES (est): 76.9K Privately Held
SIC: 3599 Machine shop, jobbing & repair

(G-10596)
BUNSEN RUSH LABORATORIES INC
270 Amity Rd Ste 124 (06525-2236)
PHONE..................203 397-0820
Michael R Lerner, President
EMP: 6
SQ FT: 1,000
SALES (est): 616.4K Privately Held
SIC: 2844 Face creams or lotions

(G-10597)
CHASE CORPORATION
149 Amity Rd (06525-2244)
PHONE..................203 285-1244
EMP: 11

Woodbridge - New Haven County

SALES (corp-wide): 281.3MM **Publicly Held**
SIC: 3644 Noncurrent-carrying wiring services
PA: Chase Corporation
295 University Ave
Westwood MA 02090
781 332-0700

(G-10598)
CHEMIN PHARMA LLC
4 Research Dr (06525-2347)
PHONE...................203 208-2811
Uday R Khire, *Principal*
EMP: 6 EST: 2014
SALES (est): 579.1K **Privately Held**
SIC: 2834 Pharmaceutical preparations

(G-10599)
CLASSIC LABEL INC
10 Research Dr (06525-2347)
PHONE...................203 389-3535
Louis Fantarella, *President*
Dean J Fantarella, *Vice Pres*
Laura Fantarella, *Admin Sec*
▲ EMP: 9
SQ FT: 10,000
SALES (est): 1.8MM **Privately Held**
SIC: 2759 Commercial printing

(G-10600)
GALE THOMSON
12 Lunar Dr (06525-2322)
PHONE...................203 397-2600
EMP: 1
SALES (est): 37.5K **Privately Held**
SIC: 2741 Misc Publishing

(G-10601)
GR ENTERPRISES AND TECH
Also Called: Great
3 Penny Ln (06525-1531)
PHONE...................203 387-1430
Mark Gerber, *Partner*
Manny Ratafia,
EMP: 4 EST: 2013
SALES (est): 222.2K **Privately Held**
SIC: 3841 Surgical & medical instruments

(G-10602)
INTRACRANIAL BIOANALYTICS LLC
22 Richard Sweet Dr (06525-1126)
PHONE...................914 490-1524
Thomas Jasinski, *Mng Member*
Konstantine Drakonakis,
Mark Reed,
Dennise Spencer,
Hitten Zaveri,
EMP: 5
SALES (est): 198.4K **Privately Held**
SIC: 3845 Patient monitoring apparatus

(G-10603)
JOYCE PRINTERS INC
16 Research Dr (06525-2355)
PHONE...................203 389-4452
James F Scott, *President*
EMP: 3 EST: 1962
SQ FT: 4,000
SALES (est): 328.1K **Privately Held**
SIC: 2759 Commercial printing

(G-10604)
KIWI PUBLISHING INC
20 Manville Rd (06525-2025)
P.O. Box 3852 (06525-0852)
PHONE...................203 389-6220
Eitan Battat, *President*
EMP: 1
SALES (est): 95.2K **Privately Held**
SIC: 2741 Miscellaneous publishing

(G-10605)
KOL LLC
12 Cassway Rd (06525-1215)
PHONE...................203 393-2924
Christopher Neumann, *Mng Member*
Mark Schleimer, *Prgrmr*
Michael Toscani, *Director*
EMP: 25
SQ FT: 3,000
SALES (est): 2MM **Privately Held**
SIC: 7372 Business oriented computer software

(G-10606)
MANUFACTURERS SERVICE CO INC
Also Called: Air Handling Systems
5 Lunar Dr (06525-2320)
PHONE...................203 389-9595
David Edward Scott, *President*
Jamison Scott, *Vice Pres*
Patricia Scott, *Treasurer*
Curt Courm, *Technical Staff*
▼ EMP: 8
SQ FT: 12,800
SALES (est): 1.3MM **Privately Held**
WEB: www.airhand.com
SIC: 3444 Ducts, sheet metal

(G-10607)
MERRILL OIL LLC
517 Amity Rd (06525-1603)
PHONE...................203 387-1130
Christian Merrill, *Principal*
EMP: 3 EST: 2015
SALES (est): 99.1K **Privately Held**
SIC: 1311 Crude petroleum & natural gas

(G-10608)
NEW ENGLAND BREWING CO LLC
175 Amity Rd (06525-2201)
PHONE...................203 387-2222
Robert Leonard,
William Pastyrnak,
Matthew Westfall,
EMP: 6
SQ FT: 20,000
SALES (est): 1.1MM **Privately Held**
WEB: www.newenglandbrewing.com
SIC: 2082 Beer (alcoholic beverage)

(G-10609)
ODD JOBS HANDYMAN SERVICE LLC
19 Grouse Ln (06525-1452)
PHONE...................203 397-5275
Liliana Lara,
Alfonso Lara,
EMP: 4
SALES (est): 300K **Privately Held**
SIC: 2842 Specialty cleaning preparations

(G-10610)
OOSHEARS INC
214 Ansonia Rd (06525-2403)
PHONE...................415 230-0154
EMP: 2
SALES (est): 86.6K **Privately Held**
SIC: 3842 7371 Hearing aids; computer software development & applications

(G-10611)
P2 SCIENCE INC
4 Research Dr (06525-2347)
PHONE...................203 821-7457
Neil Burns, *CEO*
Patrick Foley, *Principal*
Rob Bettigole, *Chairman*
Ed Ogle, *Opers Mgr*
Tania Salam, *Technician*
EMP: 4
SALES (est): 670K **Privately Held**
SIC: 2879 3532 7353 Agricultural chemicals; drills & drilling equipment, mining (except oil & gas); oil field equipment, rental or leasing

(G-10612)
PETER DERMER CO
245 Amity Rd Ste 109 (06525-2288)
PHONE...................203 389-3297
EMP: 2
SALES (est): 200K **Privately Held**
SIC: 2311 Mfg Men's/Boy's Suits/Coats

(G-10613)
PLASTIC FORMING COMPANY INC (PA)
20 S Bradley Rd (06525-2330)
PHONE...................203 397-1338
John Womer, *President*
Peter T Schurman, *Vice President*
Gary Amatrudo, *Vice Pres*
Mike Warth, *Vice Pres*
Patrick Pietrantonio, *Design Engr*
▲ EMP: 25 EST: 1966
SQ FT: 60,000
SALES (est): 7.4MM **Privately Held**
WEB: www.plasticformingcompany.com
SIC: 3089 3086 Blow molded finished plastic products; plastics foam products

(G-10614)
PORTABLE GARAGE DEPOT LLC
73 Ford Rd (06525-1721)
PHONE...................203 397-1721
Norm Schaaf,
EMP: 2 EST: 2010
SALES (est): 167.7K **Privately Held**
SIC: 3448 Prefabricated metal buildings

(G-10615)
PRESCO INCORPORATED
Also Called: Presco Engineering
8 Lunar Dr Ste 4 (06525-2366)
PHONE...................203 397-8722
Phil Black, *President*
Jeff Gates, *Vice Pres*
Alan Katze, *Vice Pres*
Dan Kohler, *Vice Pres*
Daniel Kohler, *Vice Pres*
EMP: 12 EST: 1971
SQ FT: 5,000
SALES (est): 2.8MM **Privately Held**
WEB: www.prescoinc.com
SIC: 3699 7389 7371 Electrical equipment & supplies; design services; computer software development

(G-10616)
SCRY HEALTH INC
1 Bradley Rd Ste 404 (06525-2235)
PHONE...................203 936-8244
Kirk Mettler, *Principal*
EMP: 10
SALES (est): 432.4K **Privately Held**
SIC: 7372 8999 Business oriented computer software; scientific consulting

(G-10617)
SHELTERS OF AMERICA LLC
73 Ford Rd (06525-1721)
P.O. Box 3792, New Haven (06525-0792)
PHONE...................203 397-1037
Norm Schaaf, *Mng Member*
EMP: 3
SALES (est): 374.5K **Privately Held**
WEB: www.sheltersofamerica.com
SIC: 3448 Prefabricated metal buildings

(G-10618)
SPARROW WOODS CO LLC
21 Stewward Rd (06525-1850)
PHONE...................203 215-5200
Karen Hluchan,
Karen Hluschan,
EMP: 1
SALES (est): 162.7K **Privately Held**
WEB: www.sparrowwoods.com
SIC: 3827 Optical instruments & lenses

(G-10619)
TRANSATLANTIC BUBBLES LLC
935 Greenway Rd (06525-2412)
PHONE...................203 464-0051
Michael Carleton, *Principal*
EMP: 2
SALES (est): 103.2K **Privately Held**
SIC: 2087 Beverage bases

(G-10620)
UV INC
4 Jenick Ln (06525-1936)
PHONE...................203 333-1031
Vijay Mehan, *Ch of Bd*
EMP: 1 EST: 2013
SALES (est): 152.6K **Privately Held**
SIC: 3641 Ultraviolet lamps

(G-10621)
WARCO OF NE LLC
198 Newton Rd (06525-1245)
PHONE...................203 393-1691
Walter A Rish, *Principal*
EMP: 2
SALES (est): 94.3K **Privately Held**
SIC: 3069 Fabricated rubber products

Woodbury
Litchfield County

(G-10622)
A X M S INC
27 Woodside Cir (06798-1528)
PHONE...................203 263-5046
Emilia Corey, *President*
▲ EMP: 7
SALES (est): 672.8K **Privately Held**
SIC: 3199 Leather garments

(G-10623)
ACUFAB
137 Quassuk Rd (06798-2952)
PHONE...................203 263-3490
Fax: 203 263-0460
EMP: 2 EST: 2010
SALES (est): 130K **Privately Held**
SIC: 3599 Mfg Industrial Machinery

(G-10624)
ANDERSON MANUFACTURING COMPANY
337 Quassapaug Rd (06798-2306)
PHONE...................203 263-2318
Karen Anderson-Crimmins, *President*
Charles Whitcomb, *Vice Pres*
Denny Manders, *Engineer*
Mike Brady, *Director*
EMP: 4 EST: 1945
SQ FT: 5,000
SALES (est): 392.1K **Privately Held**
SIC: 3469 3728 Metal stampings; aircraft parts & equipment

(G-10625)
AXERRA NETWORKS INC
Also Called: Axerra Networks Limited
30 Bear Run (06798-3334)
PHONE...................203 906-3570
Hezi Lapid, *President*
EMP: 5
SALES (est): 422.8K **Privately Held**
SIC: 3663 Television broadcasting & communications equipment
PA: Axerra Networks Ltd
24 Wallenberg Raul
Tel Aviv-Jaffa
376 599-84

(G-10626)
BEARDSLEY PUBLISHING CORP
Also Called: Ski Area Management
45 Main St N (06798-2915)
P.O. Box 644 (06798-0644)
PHONE...................203 263-0888
Jennifer Rowan, *President*
Olivia Rowan, *Marketing Staff*
EMP: 6
SALES (est): 900K **Privately Held**
WEB: www.stablemanagement.com
SIC: 2741 Miscellaneous publishing

(G-10627)
BLESHUE LLC
4 Woods Way (06798-3229)
PHONE...................203 405-1034
Ian Solaski,
EMP: 1
SALES (est): 64.4K **Privately Held**
SIC: 2389 5651 7389 Apparel & accessories; family clothing stores;

(G-10628)
COGZ SYSTEMS LLC
58 Steeple View Ln (06798-3300)
PHONE...................203 263-7882
Jay Ambrose, *Owner*
EMP: 10
SALES (est): 1.4MM **Privately Held**
SIC: 3695 5961 Computer software tape & disks: blank, rigid & floppy; computer software, mail order

(G-10629)
COMPUWEIGH CORPORATION (PA)
50 Middle Quarter Rd (06798-3901)
PHONE...................203 262-9400
Robin B Sax, *CEO*
Harold Ecke, *President*

GEOGRAPHIC SECTION

Tim Ciucci, *VP Sales*
Chris Pack, *Prgrmr*
EMP: 20 **EST:** 1984
SQ FT: 15,000
SALES (est): 6.5MM **Privately Held**
SIC: 7371 3596 Computer software development; industrial scales

(G-10630)
CONNECTICUT OUTDOOR WOOD FRNCS
405 Grassy Hill Rd (06798-3129)
PHONE.................................203 263-0625
Jofh Sajmansky, *Owner*
EMP: 2
SALES (est): 50K **Privately Held**
SIC: 5712 2421 Outdoor & garden furniture; outdoor wood structural products

(G-10631)
COOLSPINE LLC
188 Hoop Pole Hill Rd (06798-1925)
PHONE.................................203 263-6188
EMP: 1
SALES (est): 91.6K **Privately Held**
SIC: 3845 Medical Device Manufacturing

(G-10632)
DALVENTO LLC
57 Old Grassy Hill Rd (06798-2621)
PHONE.................................203 263-6497
Marchello Chacchia, *Principal*
▲ **EMP:** 4 **EST:** 2012
SALES (est): 426.1K **Privately Held**
SIC: 2431 Millwork

(G-10633)
DENOMINATOR COMPANY INC
744 Main St S (06798-3732)
P.O. Box 5004 (06798-5004)
PHONE.................................203 263-3210
Thomas C Clark, *President*
EMP: 15 **EST:** 1961
SALES (est): 2.5MM **Privately Held**
WEB: www.denominatorcompany.com
SIC: 3824 Mechanical counters; tally counters

(G-10634)
DUDA AND GOODWIN INC
Also Called: Dg Precision Manufacturing
90 Washington Rd (06798-2804)
P.O. Box 349 (06798-0349)
PHONE.................................203 263-4353
David S Duda, *President*
Brian P Duda, *Vice Pres*
Brian Duda, *Mfg Staff*
Peggy Nelson, *Bookkeeper*
Patricia Sugden, *Office Mgr*
EMP: 10 **EST:** 1945
SQ FT: 8,000
SALES (est): 1.9MM **Privately Held**
WEB: www.dgprecision.com
SIC: 3451 Screw machine products

(G-10635)
EPILOG LASERS OF NEW ENGLAND
10 Applegate Ln (06798-3816)
PHONE.................................203 405-1124
Ryan C Sprole, *Owner*
EMP: 1
SALES (est): 117.5K **Privately Held**
SIC: 3699 Laser welding, drilling & cutting equipment

(G-10636)
EYE EAR IT LLC
19 Pomperaug Rd (06798-3714)
PHONE.................................203 487-8949
Sean Elwell, *Mng Member*
EMP: 18
SALES (est): 758.9K **Privately Held**
SIC: 2731 3577 5999 Book publishing; optical scanning devices; education aids, devices & supplies

(G-10637)
FOUR SEASONS COOLER EQP LLC
150 Brushy Hill Rd (06798-1606)
PHONE.................................203 263-0705
Toll Free:..........................877 -
Cheryl Korowotny,
EMP: 6

SALES (est): 470.7K **Privately Held**
SIC: 3585 Coolers, milk & water: electric

(G-10638)
HARD HILL WOODWORKING LLC
85 Hard Hill Rd (06798-2212)
PHONE.................................203 263-2820
EMP: 1
SALES (est): 75K **Privately Held**
SIC: 2431 Mfg Millwork

(G-10639)
J & H MOBILE MECHANIC LLC
241 Weekeepeemee Rd (06798-2029)
P.O. Box 37 (06798-0037)
PHONE.................................203 266-4748
Holly Talarico, *Treasurer*
Joseph Talarico,
EMP: 1
SALES (est): 120K **Privately Held**
SIC: 3462 Mechanical power transmission forgings, ferrous

(G-10640)
KEVIN G BARRY
Also Called: Woodbury At Mooer
47 Main St S (06798-3459)
PHONE.................................203 263-4948
Kevin G Barry, *Owner*
EMP: 2
SALES (est): 212.9K **Privately Held**
SIC: 3568 Power transmission equipment

(G-10641)
LINDEN SOAPS
41 Scuppo Rd A (06798-3812)
PHONE.................................563 552-2828
Ronald Lindblom, *Principal*
EMP: 1 **EST:** 2007
SALES (est): 50K **Privately Held**
SIC: 2841 Soap: granulated, liquid, cake, flaked or chip

(G-10642)
MC CLINTOCK MANUFACTURING
Also Called: M.C. Systems
237 Washington Rd (06798-2806)
PHONE.................................203 263-4743
E Christopher Kloss, *Vice Pres*
Richard McClintock, *Manager*
EMP: 2
SALES (est): 214.2K **Privately Held**
SIC: 2821 1796 8711 Thermoplastic materials; machinery installation; machine tool design

(G-10643)
MIDDLE QUARTER ANIMAL HOSPITAL
726 Main St S (06798-3701)
PHONE.................................203 263-4772
Jill Bogdan, *Principal*
EMP: 4
SALES (est): 613.3K **Privately Held**
SIC: 3131 Quarters

(G-10644)
MOONEY TIME INC
Also Called: Aerostar-Hot Air Balloons
72 Railtree Hill Rd (06798-2601)
PHONE.................................203 263-0167
Christopher Mooney, *President*
Cynthia Mooney, *Vice Pres*
EMP: 1
SALES (est): 250K **Privately Held**
SIC: 5599 3721 Hot air balloons & equipment; aircraft

(G-10645)
NATIONAL INSTITUTIONAL SUP LLC
235 Main St S (06798-3440)
P.O. Box 5008 (06798-5008)
PHONE.................................203 263-3455
Elaine C Kelemencky, *President*
EMP: 1
SALES: 75K **Privately Held**
SIC: 2099 Food preparations

(G-10646)
NATURAL SPRING VENTURES LLC
Also Called: Daily Nutmeg
68 Whittlesey Rd (06798-2537)
PHONE.................................203 556-2420
Stephen Mims, *Manager*
EMP: 2 **EST:** 2011
SALES (est): 157.6K **Privately Held**
SIC: 2711 7389 Newspapers;

(G-10647)
NIELSEN COMPANY
424 Washington Rd (06798-1904)
PHONE.................................203 586-1819
EMP: 2
SALES (est): 83.9K **Privately Held**
SIC: 2752 Commercial printing, lithographic

(G-10648)
NORTH FORTY PEST CTRL CO LLC
Also Called: Interquest
4 N Forty Rd (06798-2618)
PHONE.................................203 263-4551
Jon H Quint,
EMP: 1
SALES (est): 140K **Privately Held**
WEB: www.nfpestcont.com
SIC: 2499 Beekeeping supplies, wood

(G-10649)
PETAL PRFCTN & CONFECTION LLC
660 Main St S (06798-3433)
PHONE.................................203 263-0353
Michelle Gorey,
EMP: 2 **EST:** 2011
SALES (est): 85.4K **Privately Held**
SIC: 5992 2064 Flowers, fresh; candy & other confectionery products

(G-10650)
PEWTER HUTCH
860 Main St S (06798-3706)
PHONE.................................203 262-6181
EMP: 1
SALES (est): 68.4K **Privately Held**
SIC: 3421 Table & food cutlery, including butchers'

(G-10651)
POWER QUALITY AND DRIVES LLC
302 Tuttle Rd Apt 7g (06798-3633)
P.O. Box 83, Middlebury (06762-0083)
PHONE.................................203 217-2353
Francis Martino, *Mng Member*
EMP: 1 **EST:** 2003
SALES (est): 50K **Privately Held**
SIC: 5999 7694 7389 Motors, electric; electric motor repair;

(G-10652)
PROJECT GRAPHICS INC
41 Stone Pit Rd (06798-2717)
PHONE.................................802 488-8789
Andrew Riecker, *President*
Gregory McKim, *Vice Pres*
▲ **EMP:** 18
SQ FT: 19,000
SALES (est): 2.3MM **Privately Held**
WEB: www.projectgraphics.com
SIC: 7336 2752 3993 2396 Graphic arts & related design; commercial printing, lithographic; signs & advertising specialties; automotive & apparel trimmings

(G-10653)
RMS WOOD WORKS LLC
140 Old Town Farm Rd (06798-2232)
PHONE.................................203 405-3051
Robert M Schmidt, *Principal*
EMP: 1
SALES (est): 59.5K **Privately Held**
SIC: 2431 Millwork

(G-10654)
TOTAL PARTS SERVICES LLC
97 S Pomperaug Ave (06798-3711)
P.O. Box 696 (06798-0696)
PHONE.................................203 263-5619
Fred Plumb, *Principal*

EMP: 6
SALES (est): 1MM **Privately Held**
SIC: 3599 Machine shop, jobbing & repair

(G-10655)
WINDING DRIVE CORPORATION
744 Main St S (06798-3732)
PHONE.................................203 263-6961
Fran Adams, *President*
EMP: 3
SALES (est): 179.2K **Privately Held**
SIC: 2033 Marmalade: packaged in cans, jars, etc.

(G-10656)
WOODBURY PEWTERERS INC
860 Main St S (06798-3706)
P.O. Box 482 (06798-0482)
PHONE.................................203 263-2668
Paul Titcomb, *President*
Linda Charbonneau, *Vice Pres*
Brooks T Titcomb, *Plant Supt*
EMP: 32 **EST:** 1952
SQ FT: 10,000
SALES (est): 4.8MM **Privately Held**
WEB: www.woodburypewter.com
SIC: 3914 Pewter ware

Woodstock
Windham County

(G-10657)
BRIAN & SON POWERWASHING LLC
136 Harrisville Rd (06281-3417)
PHONE.................................860 963-1243
Brian Densmore, *Mng Member*
EMP: 2
SALES (est): 232.3K **Privately Held**
SIC: 3633 Washing machines, household: including coin-operated

(G-10658)
BRIGHTSIGHT LLC
9 Hebert Ln (06281-3502)
PHONE.................................860 208-0222
Heather Plummer, *President*
Scott Plummer, *Plant Mgr*
EMP: 3 **EST:** 2017
SALES (est): 154.9K **Privately Held**
SIC: 3827 Gun sights, optical

(G-10659)
BROOKE TAYLOR WINERY LLC (PA)
848 Route 171 (06281-2930)
PHONE.................................860 974-1263
Richard Auger,
EMP: 4
SALES: 370K **Privately Held**
SIC: 2084 Wines

(G-10660)
BUCKLES IN A SNAP LLC
27 Senexet Village Rd (06281-3132)
PHONE.................................774 452-5336
Erin Abrams,
EMP: 1
SALES (est): 71.3K **Privately Held**
SIC: 3965 Buckles & buckle parts

(G-10661)
CEDAR SWAMP LOG & LUMBER
45 Hager Rd (06281-1718)
PHONE.................................860 974-2344
John Rucki, *Owner*
EMP: 3
SALES (est): 260.4K **Privately Held**
SIC: 2421 Sawmills & planing mills, general

(G-10662)
CRABTREE & EVELYN LTD (DH)
102 Peake Brook Rd (06281-3429)
PHONE.................................800 272-2873
Kevin J Coen, *President*
Merrill Robbins, *Mfg Staff*
Koh Han Seow, *Treasurer*
Karen Barlow, *Asst Treas*
Christo Young, *Supervisor*
◆ **EMP:** 250
SQ FT: 80,000

Woodstock - Windham County (G-10663)

SALES (est): 299.3MM **Privately Held**
WEB: www.crabtree-evelyn.com
SIC: 5122 5149 2844 Toilet soap; toiletries; pickles, preserves, jellies & jams; specialty food items; toilet preparations

(G-10663)
DOUG HARTIN
353 Bungay Hill Rd (06281-2003)
PHONE.................860 377-4283
Doug Hartin, *Owner*
EMP: 1
SALES (est): 48.7K **Privately Held**
SIC: 0782 1442 Landscape contractors; construction sand & gravel

(G-10664)
DUHAMELS
40 Butts Rd (06281-3402)
PHONE.................860 928-4101
Edward Duhamel, *Owner*
EMP: 2
SALES: 90K **Privately Held**
SIC: 2441 Flats, wood: greenhouse

(G-10665)
FRANKLIN-HOWARD LLC
109 Converse Rd (06281-1445)
PHONE.................860 923-3343
Glenn H Converse, *Manager*
EMP: 2
SALES (est): 91.8K **Privately Held**
SIC: 1389 Oil field services

(G-10666)
GLOBAL MANUFACTURING
580 Brickyard Rd (06281-1508)
PHONE.................860 315-5502
Christopher Mark, *Principal*
EMP: 2
SALES (est): 168.3K **Privately Held**
SIC: 3999 Manufacturing industries

(G-10667)
HOLLOW FROST PUBLISHERS
411 Barlow Cemetery Rd (06281-2706)
PHONE.................860 974-2081
Leslie Roberts Holland, *Principal*
EMP: 4
SALES (est): 241.9K **Privately Held**
WEB: www.frosthollowpub.com
SIC: 2741 Miscellaneous publishing

(G-10668)
LANTERN LLC
Also Called: Lantern App
23 Senexet Village Rd (06281-3132)
PHONE.................866 203-5715
Justin Porter,
Craig Porter,
EMP: 2
SALES (est): 134.6K **Privately Held**
SIC: 3873 7389 Timers for industrial use, clockwork mechanism only;

(G-10669)
LINEMASTER SWITCH CORPORATION
29 Plaine Hill Rd (06281-2913)
P.O. Box 238 (06281-0238)
PHONE.................860 630-4920
Joseph J Carlone Jr, *President*
Jason Barnes, *Production*
Tammy Flores, *Purchasing*
Edward Ursillo, *QA Dir*
Mike Szostek, *Design Engr Mgr*
▲ EMP: 160 EST: 1952
SQ FT: 55,000
SALES (est): 45MM **Privately Held**
WEB: www.linemaster.com
SIC: 3625 Switches, electric power

(G-10670)
M J WILLIAMS HEATING AND AC
386 Dugg Hill Rd (06281-1611)
PHONE.................860 923-6991
Toll Free:.................877 -
Michael J Williams, *President*
Mary Williams, *Treasurer*
EMP: 2
SALES (est): 149.7K **Privately Held**
SIC: 3444 1711 7623 Sheet metalwork; heating & air conditioning contractors; air conditioning repair

(G-10671)
MARK A LITTLE
Also Called: Mark's Mechanical
402 Route 197 (06281-1638)
PHONE.................808 247-8604
Mark A Little, *Owner*
EMP: 1
SALES: 120K **Privately Held**
SIC: 3599 Machine shop, jobbing & repair

(G-10672)
MERIDIAN GROUP LLC
141 Lyon Hill Rd (06281-1539)
PHONE.................860 928-5266
Gary Garabrant, *Owner*
EMP: 1 EST: 1999
SALES: 350K **Privately Held**
SIC: 3843 Dental equipment & supplies

(G-10673)
MUDDY BROOK WOOD PRODUCTS
193 Woodstock Rd (06281-1814)
P.O. Box 105 (06281-0105)
PHONE.................860 928-2205
Bary Morgan, *Owner*
EMP: 1
SALES (est): 59K **Privately Held**
SIC: 2499 Decorative wood & woodwork

(G-10674)
OAK TREE MOULDING LLC
7 Pole Bridge Rd (06281-1203)
PHONE.................860 455-3056
Ranier E Landry,
Lorraine E Landry,
EMP: 3
SALES (est): 92.3K **Privately Held**
SIC: 3999 Manufacturing industries

(G-10675)
PARAMOUNT GLASSWORKS LLC
133 Lyon Hill Rd (06281-1539)
PHONE.................860 315-7624
Kenneth F Plouffe, *Mng Member*
EMP: 1
SALES: 400K **Privately Held**
SIC: 3827 Optical instruments & lenses

(G-10676)
PATRIOT OIL HEAT LLC
416 Senexet Rd (06281-2335)
PHONE.................860 928-4091
Matthew Tappins,
EMP: 2
SALES (est): 94.8K **Privately Held**
SIC: 1389 Oil consultants

(G-10677)
PEPPERL + FUCHS INC
Also Called: Sales Department
405 Dugg Hill Rd (06281-1609)
PHONE.................860 923-2703
Ron Burrell, *Manager*
EMP: 1
SALES (corp-wide): 744.1MM **Privately Held**
WEB: www.pepperlfuchs.com
SIC: 3625 Switches, electric power
HQ: Pepperl + Fuchs, Inc.
1600 Enterprise Pkwy
Twinsburg OH 44087
330 425-3555

(G-10678)
PERFORMANCE MACHINE INC
207 Center Rd (06281-1705)
PHONE.................860 974-3664
Shawn Wojciechowski, *President*
EMP: 1
SALES (est): 99.2K **Privately Held**
SIC: 3469 Machine parts, stamped or pressed metal

(G-10679)
QBA INC
24 Woodland Dr (06281-3032)
PHONE.................860 963-9438
Neil Brown, *President*
EMP: 6
SALES (est): 556.6K **Privately Held**
SIC: 2952 5033 7349 Roofing materials; roofing & siding materials; building maintenance, except repairs

(G-10680)
RICHMOND WOODWORKS LLC
321 Perrin Rd Apt C (06281-2727)
PHONE.................860 974-9995
Jeff Richmond, *Principal*
EMP: 2
SALES (est): 85.2K **Privately Held**
SIC: 2431 Millwork

(G-10681)
ROGERS CORPORATION
High Performance Foams Div
245 Woodstock Rd (06281-1815)
P.O. Box 188 (06281-0188)
PHONE.................860 928-3622
Peter Kaczmarek, *President*
EMP: 103
SALES (corp-wide): 879MM **Publicly Held**
WEB: www.rogers-corp.com
SIC: 3069 Reclaimed rubber & specialty rubber compounds
PA: Rogers Corporation
2225 W Chandler Blvd
Chandler AZ 85224
480 917-6000

(G-10682)
ROLAND A PARENT
Also Called: Parent Lea Farm
518 English Nghborhood Rd (06281-1317)
PHONE.................860 928-9158
Roland A Parent, *Owner*
EMP: 2
SALES (est): 90K **Privately Held**
SIC: 3999 Christmas tree ornaments, except electrical & glass

(G-10683)
SCOTT METAL PRODUCTS
Also Called: Scott Welding & Metal Products
30 Crabtree Ln (06281-3410)
PHONE.................860 928-4366
Norm Ruskin, *Owner*
EMP: 2
SQ FT: 12,000
SALES: 300K **Privately Held**
SIC: 3469 Machine parts, stamped or pressed metal

(G-10684)
SKYKO INTERNATIONAL LLC (PA)
243 New Sweden Rd (06281-3216)
P.O. Box 704, Putnam (06260-0704)
PHONE.................860 928-5170
Krista O Shultz, *Mng Member*
Preston Shultz,
EMP: 9
SALES (est): 2.8MM **Privately Held**
SIC: 3613 Power connectors, electric

(G-10685)
STEVEN ROSENDAHL INC
Also Called: Teagen and Ash Hand Painter
371 Route 197 (06281-1642)
PHONE.................860 928-3136
Steven Rosendahl, *President*
EMP: 2
SALES: 90K **Privately Held**
SIC: 2499 2621 3499 Picture & mirror frames, wood; specialty papers; picture frames, metal

(G-10686)
STILL RIVER SOFTWARE CO LLC
126 Crooked Trail Ext (06281-2502)
PHONE.................860 263-0396
Robert A Bazinet, *Principal*
EMP: 2
SALES (est): 109.7K **Privately Held**
SIC: 7372 Application computer software

(G-10687)
STILLWATER ARCHITECTURAL WOOD
510 Dugg Hill Rd (06281-1641)
P.O. Box 244, East Woodstock (06244-0244)
PHONE.................860 923-2858
Ronnie R Doros, *Principal*
EMP: 2
SALES (est): 109.2K **Privately Held**
SIC: 2431 Millwork

(G-10688)
STMICROELECTRONICS INC
118 English Nghborhood Rd (06281-1432)
PHONE.................860 928-7700
Walter Guntowski, *Branch Mgr*
EMP: 2
SALES (corp-wide): 64MM **Privately Held**
WEB: www.st.com
SIC: 3671 Electron beam (beta ray) generator tubes
HQ: Stmicroelectronics, Inc
750 Canyon Dr Ste 300
Coppell TX 75019
972 466-6000

(G-10689)
SYNERGY SALES LTD
50 Perrin Rd (06281-2714)
PHONE.................860 974-3288
EMP: 1
SALES (est): 170K **Privately Held**
SIC: 3559 Mfg Misc Industry Machinery

(G-10690)
WHITE BARRETTE MAIL LLC
274 Paine District Rd (06281-1623)
PHONE.................860 923-3183
Kevin White, *Principal*
EMP: 1 EST: 2015
SALES (est): 42.9K **Privately Held**
SIC: 3999 Barrettes

Woodstock Valley
Windham County

(G-10691)
BAY TACT CORPORATION
440 Route 198 (06282-2427)
PHONE.................860 315-7372
O Henry Grinde, *President*
Diane G Patterson, *Admin Sec*
EMP: 25
SQ FT: 9,000
SALES (est): 2.5MM **Privately Held**
WEB: www.prars.com
SIC: 2741 2721 2731 Miscellaneous publishing; periodicals; book publishing

(G-10692)
E & F WOOD LLC
28 Route 198 (06282-2424)
PHONE.................860 377-0601
Hans Frankhouser,
Michael Ernst,
EMP: 2
SALES (est): 1.2MM **Privately Held**
SIC: 2499 Saddle trees, wood

(G-10693)
PRESTIGE METAL FINISHING LLC
44 Bradford Corner Rd (06282-2001)
P.O. Box 97, Eastford (06242-0097)
PHONE.................860 974-1999
Cheryl Gillmore,
EMP: 3
SALES: 100K **Privately Held**
SIC: 3471 Plating of metals or formed products

Yalesville
New Haven County

(G-10694)
JOVAL MACHINE CO INC
Also Called: Pac Products
515 Main St (06492-1736)
PHONE.................203 284-0082
Gerald A Chase, *President*
Joyce Chase, *Corp Secy*
Jeffrey Chase, *Vice Pres*
Karen Madonna, *Bookkeeper*
EMP: 25
SQ FT: 25,000
SALES (est): 4.4MM **Privately Held**
WEB: www.jovalmachine.com
SIC: 3469 Machine parts, stamped or pressed metal

▲ = Import ▼=Export
◆ =Import/Export

Yantic
New London County

(G-10695)
AC/DC INDUSTRIAL ELECTRIC LLC
44 Yantic Flats Rd Ste 2 (06389-1005)
PHONE.................................860 886-2232
Charles Carroll, *Mng Member*
EMP: 8
SALES (est): 770K **Privately Held**
SIC: 3621 1731 5063 Generators & sets, electric; electric power systems contractors; generators

(G-10696)
AMERICAN VEHICLES SALES LLC
58 Yantic Flats Rd (06389-1020)
PHONE.................................860 886-0327
Scott Davis,
EMP: 3
SQ FT: 9,600
SALES: 1.5MM **Privately Held**
WEB: www.americanvehiclesales.com
SIC: 3711 5012 Buses, all types, assembly of; commercial vehicles

(G-10697)
CAMARO SIGNS INC (PA)
58 Yantic Flats Rd Unit 1 (06389-1019)
PHONE.................................860 886-1553
John Hansen, *President*
Erica Hansen, *Admin Sec*
Wayland James, *Graphic Designe*
Valerie Willey,
EMP: 7
SQ FT: 5,000
SALES (est): 1MM **Privately Held**
WEB: www.camarosigns.com
SIC: 3993 Electric signs

(G-10698)
MB CONSULTING LLC
39 Sunnyside St (06389-1010)
PHONE.................................860 889-7941
Mark Bialowans, *Mng Member*
EMP: 2
SQ FT: 1,600
SALES: 110K **Privately Held**
SIC: 3599 Machine & other job shop work

SIC INDEX

Standard Industrial Classification Alphabetical Index

SIC NO	PRODUCT

A

3291 Abrasive Prdts
2891 Adhesives & Sealants
3563 Air & Gas Compressors
3585 Air Conditioning & Heating Eqpt
3721 Aircraft
3724 Aircraft Engines & Engine Parts
3728 Aircraft Parts & Eqpt, NEC
2812 Alkalies & Chlorine
3363 Aluminum Die Castings
3354 Aluminum Extruded Prdts
3365 Aluminum Foundries
3355 Aluminum Rolling & Drawing, NEC
3353 Aluminum Sheet, Plate & Foil
3483 Ammunition, Large
3826 Analytical Instruments
2077 Animal, Marine Fats & Oils
1231 Anthracite Mining
2389 Apparel & Accessories, NEC
2387 Apparel Belts
3446 Architectural & Ornamental Metal Work
7694 Armature Rewinding Shops
3292 Asbestos products
2952 Asphalt Felts & Coatings
3822 Automatic Temperature Controls
3581 Automatic Vending Machines
3465 Automotive Stampings
2396 Automotive Trimmings, Apparel Findings, Related Prdts

B

2673 Bags: Plastics, Laminated & Coated
2674 Bags: Uncoated Paper & Multiwall
3562 Ball & Roller Bearings
2836 Biological Prdts, Exc Diagnostic Substances
1221 Bituminous Coal & Lignite: Surface Mining
1222 Bituminous Coal: Underground Mining
2782 Blankbooks & Looseleaf Binders
3312 Blast Furnaces, Coke Ovens, Steel & Rolling Mills
3564 Blowers & Fans
3732 Boat Building & Repairing
3452 Bolts, Nuts, Screws, Rivets & Washers
2732 Book Printing, Not Publishing
2789 Bookbinding
2731 Books: Publishing & Printing
3131 Boot & Shoe Cut Stock & Findings
2342 Brassieres, Girdles & Garments
2051 Bread, Bakery Prdts Exc Cookies & Crackers
3251 Brick & Structural Clay Tile
3991 Brooms & Brushes
3995 Burial Caskets
2021 Butter

C

3578 Calculating & Accounting Eqpt
2064 Candy & Confectionery Prdts
2033 Canned Fruits, Vegetables & Preserves
2032 Canned Specialties
2394 Canvas Prdts
3624 Carbon & Graphite Prdts
3955 Carbon Paper & Inked Ribbons
3592 Carburetors, Pistons, Rings & Valves
2273 Carpets & Rugs
3241 Cement, Hydraulic
3253 Ceramic Tile
2043 Cereal Breakfast Foods
2022 Cheese
2899 Chemical Preparations, NEC
2361 Children's & Infants' Dresses & Blouses
3261 China Plumbing Fixtures & Fittings
2066 Chocolate & Cocoa Prdts
2111 Cigarettes
2121 Cigars
2257 Circular Knit Fabric Mills
3255 Clay Refractories
1459 Clay, Ceramic & Refractory Minerals, NEC
1241 Coal Mining Svcs
3479 Coating & Engraving, NEC
2095 Coffee
3316 Cold Rolled Steel Sheet, Strip & Bars
3582 Commercial Laundry, Dry Clean & Pressing Mchs
2759 Commercial Printing
2754 Commercial Printing: Gravure
2752 Commercial Printing: Lithographic

3646 Commercial, Indl & Institutional Lighting Fixtures
3669 Communications Eqpt, NEC
3577 Computer Peripheral Eqpt, NEC
3572 Computer Storage Devices
3575 Computer Terminals
3271 Concrete Block & Brick
3272 Concrete Prdts
3531 Construction Machinery & Eqpt
1442 Construction Sand & Gravel
2679 Converted Paper Prdts, NEC
3535 Conveyors & Eqpt
2052 Cookies & Crackers
3366 Copper Foundries
1021 Copper Ores
2298 Cordage & Twine
2653 Corrugated & Solid Fiber Boxes
3961 Costume Jewelry & Novelties
2261 Cotton Fabric Finishers
2211 Cotton, Woven Fabric
2074 Cottonseed Oil Mills
3466 Crowns & Closures
1311 Crude Petroleum & Natural Gas
1423 Crushed & Broken Granite
1422 Crushed & Broken Limestone
1429 Crushed & Broken Stone, NEC
3643 Current-Carrying Wiring Devices
2391 Curtains & Draperies
3087 Custom Compounding Of Purchased Plastic Resins
3281 Cut Stone Prdts
3421 Cutlery
2865 Cyclic-Crudes, Intermediates, Dyes & Org Pigments

D

3843 Dental Eqpt & Splys
2835 Diagnostic Substances
2675 Die-Cut Paper & Board
3544 Dies, Tools, Jigs, Fixtures & Indl Molds
1411 Dimension Stone
2047 Dog & Cat Food
3942 Dolls & Stuffed Toys
2591 Drapery Hardware, Window Blinds & Shades
2381 Dress & Work Gloves
2034 Dried Fruits, Vegetables & Soup
1381 Drilling Oil & Gas Wells

E

3263 Earthenware, Whiteware, Table & Kitchen Articles
3634 Electric Household Appliances
3641 Electric Lamps
3694 Electrical Eqpt For Internal Combustion Engines
3629 Electrical Indl Apparatus, NEC
3699 Electrical Machinery, Eqpt & Splys, NEC
3845 Electromedical & Electrotherapeutic Apparatus
3313 Electrometallurgical Prdts
3675 Electronic Capacitors
3677 Electronic Coils & Transformers
3679 Electronic Components, NEC
3571 Electronic Computers
3678 Electronic Connectors
3676 Electronic Resistors
3471 Electroplating, Plating, Polishing, Anodizing & Coloring
3534 Elevators & Moving Stairways
3431 Enameled Iron & Metal Sanitary Ware
2677 Envelopes
2892 Explosives

F

2241 Fabric Mills, Cotton, Wool, Silk & Man-Made
3499 Fabricated Metal Prdts, NEC
3498 Fabricated Pipe & Pipe Fittings
3443 Fabricated Plate Work
3069 Fabricated Rubber Prdts, NEC
3441 Fabricated Structural Steel
2399 Fabricated Textile Prdts, NEC
2295 Fabrics Coated Not Rubberized
2297 Fabrics, Nonwoven
3523 Farm Machinery & Eqpt
3965 Fasteners, Buttons, Needles & Pins
2875 Fertilizers, Mixing Only
2655 Fiber Cans, Tubes & Drums
2091 Fish & Seafoods, Canned & Cured
2092 Fish & Seafoods, Fresh & Frozen
3211 Flat Glass
2087 Flavoring Extracts & Syrups

2045 Flour, Blended & Prepared
2041 Flour, Grain Milling
3824 Fluid Meters & Counters
3593 Fluid Power Cylinders & Actuators
3594 Fluid Power Pumps & Motors
3492 Fluid Power Valves & Hose Fittings
2657 Folding Paperboard Boxes
3556 Food Prdts Machinery
2099 Food Preparations, NEC
3149 Footwear, NEC
2053 Frozen Bakery Prdts
2037 Frozen Fruits, Juices & Vegetables
2038 Frozen Specialties
2371 Fur Goods
2599 Furniture & Fixtures, NEC

G

3944 Games, Toys & Children's Vehicles
3524 Garden, Lawn Tractors & Eqpt
3053 Gaskets, Packing & Sealing Devices
2369 Girls' & Infants' Outerwear, NEC
3221 Glass Containers
3231 Glass Prdts Made Of Purchased Glass
3321 Gray Iron Foundries
2771 Greeting Card Publishing
3769 Guided Missile/Space Vehicle Parts & Eqpt, NEC
3764 Guided Missile/Space Vehicle Propulsion Units & parts
3761 Guided Missiles & Space Vehicles
2861 Gum & Wood Chemicals
3275 Gypsum Prdts

H

3423 Hand & Edge Tools
3425 Hand Saws & Saw Blades
3171 Handbags & Purses
3429 Hardware, NEC
2426 Hardwood Dimension & Flooring Mills
2435 Hardwood Veneer & Plywood
2353 Hats, Caps & Millinery
3433 Heating Eqpt
3536 Hoists, Cranes & Monorails
2252 Hosiery, Except Women's
2392 House furnishings: Textile
3639 Household Appliances, NEC
3651 Household Audio & Video Eqpt
3631 Household Cooking Eqpt
2519 Household Furniture, NEC
3633 Household Laundry Eqpt
3632 Household Refrigerators & Freezers
3635 Household Vacuum Cleaners

I

2097 Ice
2024 Ice Cream
2819 Indl Inorganic Chemicals, NEC
3823 Indl Instruments For Meas, Display & Control
3569 Indl Machinery & Eqpt, NEC
3567 Indl Process Furnaces & Ovens
3537 Indl Trucks, Tractors, Trailers & Stackers
2813 Industrial Gases
2869 Industrial Organic Chemicals, NEC
3543 Industrial Patterns
1446 Industrial Sand
3491 Industrial Valves
2816 Inorganic Pigments
3825 Instrs For Measuring & Testing Electricity
3519 Internal Combustion Engines, NEC
3462 Iron & Steel Forgings
1011 Iron Ores

J

3915 Jewelers Findings & Lapidary Work
3911 Jewelry: Precious Metal

K

1455 Kaolin & Ball Clay
2253 Knit Outerwear Mills
2254 Knit Underwear Mills
2259 Knitting Mills, NEC

L

3821 Laboratory Apparatus & Furniture
2258 Lace & Warp Knit Fabric Mills
3952 Lead Pencils, Crayons & Artist's Mtrls
2386 Leather & Sheep Lined Clothing

SIC INDEX

SIC NO	PRODUCT
3199	Leather Goods, NEC
3111	Leather Tanning & Finishing
3648	Lighting Eqpt, NEC
3274	Lime
3996	Linoleum & Hard Surface Floor Coverings, NEC
2085	Liquors, Distilled, Rectified & Blended
2411	Logging
2992	Lubricating Oils & Greases
3161	Luggage

M

SIC NO	PRODUCT
2098	Macaroni, Spaghetti & Noodles
3545	Machine Tool Access
3541	Machine Tools: Cutting
3542	Machine Tools: Forming
3599	Machinery & Eqpt, Indl & Commercial, NEC
2082	Malt Beverages
2761	Manifold Business Forms
3999	Manufacturing Industries, NEC
3953	Marking Devices
2515	Mattresses & Bedsprings
3829	Measuring & Controlling Devices, NEC
3586	Measuring & Dispensing Pumps
2011	Meat Packing Plants
3568	Mechanical Power Transmission Eqpt, NEC
2833	Medicinal Chemicals & Botanical Prdts
2329	Men's & Boys' Clothing, NEC
2323	Men's & Boys' Neckwear
2325	Men's & Boys' Separate Trousers & Casual Slacks
2321	Men's & Boys' Shirts
2311	Men's & Boys' Suits, Coats & Overcoats
2326	Men's & Boys' Work Clothing
3143	Men's Footwear, Exc Athletic
3412	Metal Barrels, Drums, Kegs & Pails
3411	Metal Cans
3442	Metal Doors, Sash, Frames, Molding & Trim
3497	Metal Foil & Leaf
3398	Metal Heat Treating
2514	Metal Household Furniture
1081	Metal Mining Svcs
1099	Metal Ores, NEC
3469	Metal Stampings, NEC
3549	Metalworking Machinery, NEC
2026	Milk
2023	Milk, Condensed & Evaporated
2431	Millwork
3296	Mineral Wool
3295	Minerals & Earths: Ground Or Treated
3532	Mining Machinery & Eqpt
3496	Misc Fabricated Wire Prdts
2741	Misc Publishing
3449	Misc Structural Metal Work
1499	Miscellaneous Nonmetallic Mining
2451	Mobile Homes
3061	Molded, Extruded & Lathe-Cut Rubber Mechanical Goods
3716	Motor Homes
3714	Motor Vehicle Parts & Access
3711	Motor Vehicles & Car Bodies
3751	Motorcycles, Bicycles & Parts
3621	Motors & Generators
3931	Musical Instruments

N

SIC NO	PRODUCT
1321	Natural Gas Liquids
2711	Newspapers: Publishing & Printing
2873	Nitrogenous Fertilizers
3297	Nonclay Refractories
3644	Noncurrent-Carrying Wiring Devices
3364	Nonferrous Die Castings, Exc Aluminum
3463	Nonferrous Forgings
3369	Nonferrous Foundries: Castings, NEC
3357	Nonferrous Wire Drawing
3299	Nonmetallic Mineral Prdts, NEC
1481	Nonmetallic Minerals Svcs, Except Fuels

O

SIC NO	PRODUCT
2522	Office Furniture, Except Wood
3579	Office Machines, NEC
1382	Oil & Gas Field Exploration Svcs
1389	Oil & Gas Field Svcs, NEC
3533	Oil Field Machinery & Eqpt
3851	Ophthalmic Goods
3827	Optical Instruments
3489	Ordnance & Access, NEC
3842	Orthopedic, Prosthetic & Surgical Appliances/Splys

P

SIC NO	PRODUCT
3565	Packaging Machinery
2851	Paints, Varnishes, Lacquers, Enamels
2671	Paper Coating & Laminating for Packaging
2672	Paper Coating & Laminating, Exc for Packaging
3554	Paper Inds Machinery
2621	Paper Mills
2631	Paperboard Mills
2542	Partitions & Fixtures, Except Wood
2951	Paving Mixtures & Blocks
3951	Pens & Mechanical Pencils
2844	Perfumes, Cosmetics & Toilet Preparations
2721	Periodicals: Publishing & Printing
3172	Personal Leather Goods
2879	Pesticides & Agricultural Chemicals, NEC
2911	Petroleum Refining
2834	Pharmaceuticals
3652	Phonograph Records & Magnetic Tape
3861	Photographic Eqpt & Splys
2035	Pickled Fruits, Vegetables, Sauces & Dressings
3085	Plastic Bottles
3086	Plastic Foam Prdts
3083	Plastic Laminated Plate & Sheet
3084	Plastic Pipe
3088	Plastic Plumbing Fixtures
3089	Plastic Prdts
3082	Plastic Unsupported Profile Shapes
3081	Plastic Unsupported Sheet & Film
2821	Plastics, Mtrls & Nonvulcanizable Elastomers
2796	Platemaking & Related Svcs
2395	Pleating & Stitching For The Trade
3432	Plumbing Fixture Fittings & Trim, Brass
3264	Porcelain Electrical Splys
1474	Potash, Soda & Borate Minerals
2096	Potato Chips & Similar Prdts
3269	Pottery Prdts, NEC
2015	Poultry Slaughtering, Dressing & Processing
3546	Power Hand Tools
3612	Power, Distribution & Specialty Transformers
3448	Prefabricated Metal Buildings & Cmpnts
2452	Prefabricated Wood Buildings & Cmpnts
7372	Prepackaged Software
2048	Prepared Feeds For Animals & Fowls
3229	Pressed & Blown Glassware, NEC
3692	Primary Batteries: Dry & Wet
3399	Primary Metal Prdts, NEC
3339	Primary Nonferrous Metals, NEC
3334	Primary Production Of Aluminum
3331	Primary Smelting & Refining Of Copper
3672	Printed Circuit Boards
2893	Printing Ink
3555	Printing Trades Machinery & Eqpt
2999	Products Of Petroleum & Coal, NEC
2531	Public Building & Related Furniture
2611	Pulp Mills
3561	Pumps & Pumping Eqpt

R

SIC NO	PRODUCT
3663	Radio & T V Communications, Systs & Eqpt, Broadcast/Studio
3671	Radio & T V Receiving Electron Tubes
3743	Railroad Eqpt
3273	Ready-Mixed Concrete
2493	Reconstituted Wood Prdts
3695	Recording Media
3625	Relays & Indl Controls
3645	Residential Lighting Fixtures
2384	Robes & Dressing Gowns
3547	Rolling Mill Machinery & Eqpt
3351	Rolling, Drawing & Extruding Of Copper
3356	Rolling, Drawing-Extruding Of Nonferrous Metals
3021	Rubber & Plastic Footwear
3052	Rubber & Plastic Hose & Belting

S

SIC NO	PRODUCT
2068	Salted & Roasted Nuts & Seeds
2656	Sanitary Food Containers
2676	Sanitary Paper Prdts
2013	Sausages & Meat Prdts
2421	Saw & Planing Mills
3596	Scales & Balances, Exc Laboratory
3451	Screw Machine Prdts
3812	Search, Detection, Navigation & Guidance Systs & Instrs
3341	Secondary Smelting & Refining Of Nonferrous Metals
3674	Semiconductors
3589	Service Ind Machines, NEC
2652	Set-Up Paperboard Boxes
3444	Sheet Metal Work
3731	Shipbuilding & Repairing
2079	Shortening, Oils & Margarine
3993	Signs & Advertising Displays
2262	Silk & Man-Made Fabric Finishers
2221	Silk & Man-Made Fiber
3914	Silverware, Plated & Stainless Steel Ware
3484	Small Arms
3482	Small Arms Ammunition
2841	Soap & Detergents
2086	Soft Drinks
2842	Spec Cleaning, Polishing & Sanitation Preparations
3559	Special Ind Machinery, NEC
2429	Special Prdt Sawmills, NEC
3566	Speed Changers, Drives & Gears
3949	Sporting & Athletic Goods, NEC
2678	Stationery Prdts
3511	Steam, Gas & Hydraulic Turbines & Engines
3325	Steel Foundries, NEC
3324	Steel Investment Foundries
3317	Steel Pipe & Tubes
3493	Steel Springs, Except Wire
3315	Steel Wire Drawing & Nails & Spikes
3691	Storage Batteries
3259	Structural Clay Prdts, NEC
2439	Structural Wood Members, NEC
2063	Sugar, Beet
2062	Sugar, Cane Refining
2843	Surface Active & Finishing Agents, Sulfonated Oils
3841	Surgical & Medical Instrs & Apparatus
3613	Switchgear & Switchboard Apparatus
2824	Synthetic Organic Fibers, Exc Cellulosic
2822	Synthetic Rubber (Vulcanizable Elastomers)

T

SIC NO	PRODUCT
3795	Tanks & Tank Components
3661	Telephone & Telegraph Apparatus
2393	Textile Bags
2269	Textile Finishers, NEC
2299	Textile Goods, NEC
3552	Textile Machinery
2284	Thread Mills
2296	Tire Cord & Fabric
3011	Tires & Inner Tubes
2141	Tobacco Stemming & Redrying
2131	Tobacco, Chewing & Snuff
3799	Transportation Eqpt, NEC
3792	Travel Trailers & Campers
3713	Truck & Bus Bodies
3715	Truck Trailers
2791	Typesetting

U

SIC NO	PRODUCT
1094	Uranium, Radium & Vanadium Ores

V

SIC NO	PRODUCT
3494	Valves & Pipe Fittings, NEC
3647	Vehicular Lighting Eqpt

W

SIC NO	PRODUCT
3873	Watch & Clock Devices & Parts
2385	Waterproof Outerwear
3548	Welding Apparatus
7692	Welding Repair
2084	Wine & Brandy
3495	Wire Springs
2331	Women's & Misses' Blouses
2335	Women's & Misses' Dresses
2339	Women's & Misses' Outerwear, NEC
2337	Women's & Misses' Suits, Coats & Skirts
3144	Women's Footwear, Exc Athletic
2341	Women's, Misses' & Children's Underwear & Nightwear
2441	Wood Boxes
2449	Wood Containers, NEC
2511	Wood Household Furniture
2512	Wood Household Furniture, Upholstered
2434	Wood Kitchen Cabinets
2521	Wood Office Furniture
2448	Wood Pallets & Skids
2499	Wood Prdts, NEC
2491	Wood Preserving
2517	Wood T V, Radio, Phono & Sewing Cabinets
2541	Wood, Office & Store Fixtures
3553	Woodworking Machinery
2231	Wool, Woven Fabric

X

SIC NO	PRODUCT
3844	X-ray Apparatus & Tubes

Y

SIC NO	PRODUCT
2281	Yarn Spinning Mills
2282	Yarn Texturizing, Throwing, Twisting & Winding Mills

SIC INDEX

Standard Industrial Classification Numerical Index

SIC NO	PRODUCT

10 metal mining
1011 Iron Ores
1021 Copper Ores
1081 Metal Mining Svcs
1094 Uranium, Radium & Vanadium Ores
1099 Metal Ores, NEC

12 coal mining
1221 Bituminous Coal & Lignite: Surface Mining
1222 Bituminous Coal: Underground Mining
1231 Anthracite Mining
1241 Coal Mining Svcs

13 oil and gas extraction
1311 Crude Petroleum & Natural Gas
1321 Natural Gas Liquids
1381 Drilling Oil & Gas Wells
1382 Oil & Gas Field Exploration Svcs
1389 Oil & Gas Field Svcs, NEC

14 mining and quarrying of nonmetallic minerals, except fuels
1411 Dimension Stone
1422 Crushed & Broken Limestone
1423 Crushed & Broken Granite
1429 Crushed & Broken Stone, NEC
1442 Construction Sand & Gravel
1446 Industrial Sand
1455 Kaolin & Ball Clay
1459 Clay, Ceramic & Refractory Minerals, NEC
1474 Potash, Soda & Borate Minerals
1481 Nonmetallic Minerals Svcs, Except Fuels
1499 Miscellaneous Nonmetallic Mining

20 food and kindred products
2011 Meat Packing Plants
2013 Sausages & Meat Prdts
2015 Poultry Slaughtering, Dressing & Processing
2021 Butter
2022 Cheese
2023 Milk, Condensed & Evaporated
2024 Ice Cream
2026 Milk
2032 Canned Specialties
2033 Canned Fruits, Vegetables & Preserves
2034 Dried Fruits, Vegetables & Soup
2035 Pickled Fruits, Vegetables, Sauces & Dressings
2037 Frozen Fruits, Juices & Vegetables
2038 Frozen Specialties
2041 Flour, Grain Milling
2043 Cereal Breakfast Foods
2045 Flour, Blended & Prepared
2047 Dog & Cat Food
2048 Prepared Feeds For Animals & Fowls
2051 Bread, Bakery Prdts Exc Cookies & Crackers
2052 Cookies & Crackers
2053 Frozen Bakery Prdts
2062 Sugar, Cane Refining
2063 Sugar, Beet
2064 Candy & Confectionery Prdts
2066 Chocolate & Cocoa Prdts
2068 Salted & Roasted Nuts & Seeds
2074 Cottonseed Oil Mills
2077 Animal, Marine Fats & Oils
2079 Shortening, Oils & Margarine
2082 Malt Beverages
2084 Wine & Brandy
2085 Liquors, Distilled, Rectified & Blended
2086 Soft Drinks
2087 Flavoring Extracts & Syrups
2091 Fish & Seafoods, Canned & Cured
2092 Fish & Seafoods, Fresh & Frozen
2095 Coffee
2096 Potato Chips & Similar Prdts
2097 Ice
2098 Macaroni, Spaghetti & Noodles
2099 Food Preparations, NEC

21 tobacco products
2111 Cigarettes
2121 Cigars
2131 Tobacco, Chewing & Snuff
2141 Tobacco Stemming & Redrying

22 textile mill products
2211 Cotton, Woven Fabric
2221 Silk & Man-Made Fiber
2231 Wool, Woven Fabric
2241 Fabric Mills, Cotton, Wool, Silk & Man-Made
2252 Hosiery, Except Women's
2253 Knit Outerwear Mills
2254 Knit Underwear Mills
2257 Circular Knit Fabric Mills
2258 Lace & Warp Knit Fabric Mills
2259 Knitting Mills, NEC
2261 Cotton Fabric Finishers
2262 Silk & Man-Made Fabric Finishers
2269 Textile Finishers, NEC
2273 Carpets & Rugs
2281 Yarn Spinning Mills
2282 Yarn Texturizing, Throwing, Twisting & Winding Mills
2284 Thread Mills
2295 Fabrics Coated Not Rubberized
2296 Tire Cord & Fabric
2297 Fabrics, Nonwoven
2298 Cordage & Twine
2299 Textile Goods, NEC

23 apparel and other finished products made from fabrics and similar material
2311 Men's & Boys' Suits, Coats & Overcoats
2321 Men's & Boys' Shirts
2323 Men's & Boys' Neckwear
2325 Men's & Boys' Separate Trousers & Casual Slacks
2326 Men's & Boys' Work Clothing
2329 Men's & Boys' Clothing, NEC
2331 Women's & Misses' Blouses
2335 Women's & Misses' Dresses
2337 Women's & Misses' Suits, Coats & Skirts
2339 Women's & Misses' Outerwear, NEC
2341 Women's, Misses' & Children's Underwear & Nightwear
2342 Brassieres, Girdles & Garments
2353 Hats, Caps & Millinery
2361 Children's & Infants' Dresses & Blouses
2369 Girls' & Infants' Outerwear, NEC
2371 Fur Goods
2381 Dress & Work Gloves
2384 Robes & Dressing Gowns
2385 Waterproof Outerwear
2386 Leather & Sheep Lined Clothing
2387 Apparel Belts
2389 Apparel & Accessories, NEC
2391 Curtains & Draperies
2392 House furnishings: Textile
2393 Textile Bags
2394 Canvas Prdts
2395 Pleating & Stitching For The Trade
2396 Automotive Trimmings, Apparel Findings, Related Prdts
2399 Fabricated Textile Prdts, NEC

24 lumber and wood products, except furniture
2411 Logging
2421 Saw & Planing Mills
2426 Hardwood Dimension & Flooring Mills
2429 Special Prdt Sawmills, NEC
2431 Millwork
2434 Wood Kitchen Cabinets
2435 Hardwood Veneer & Plywood
2439 Structural Wood Members, NEC
2441 Wood Boxes
2448 Wood Pallets & Skids
2449 Wood Containers, NEC
2451 Mobile Homes
2452 Prefabricated Wood Buildings & Cmpnts
2491 Wood Preserving
2493 Reconstituted Wood Prdts
2499 Wood Prdts, NEC

25 furniture and fixtures
2511 Wood Household Furniture
2512 Wood Household Furniture, Upholstered
2514 Metal Household Furniture
2515 Mattresses & Bedsprings
2517 Wood T V, Radio, Phono & Sewing Cabinets
2519 Household Furniture, NEC
2521 Wood Office Furniture
2522 Office Furniture, Except Wood
2531 Public Building & Related Furniture
2541 Wood, Office & Store Fixtures
2542 Partitions & Fixtures, Except Wood
2591 Drapery Hardware, Window Blinds & Shades
2599 Furniture & Fixtures, NEC

26 paper and allied products
2611 Pulp Mills
2621 Paper Mills
2631 Paperboard Mills
2652 Set-Up Paperboard Boxes
2653 Corrugated & Solid Fiber Boxes
2655 Fiber Cans, Tubes & Drums
2656 Sanitary Food Containers
2657 Folding Paperboard Boxes
2671 Paper Coating & Laminating for Packaging
2672 Paper Coating & Laminating, Exc for Packaging
2673 Bags: Plastics, Laminated & Coated
2674 Bags: Uncoated Paper & Multiwall
2675 Die-Cut Paper & Board
2676 Sanitary Paper Prdts
2677 Envelopes
2678 Stationery Prdts
2679 Converted Paper Prdts, NEC

27 printing, publishing, and allied industries
2711 Newspapers: Publishing & Printing
2721 Periodicals: Publishing & Printing
2731 Books: Publishing & Printing
2732 Book Printing, Not Publishing
2741 Misc Publishing
2752 Commercial Printing: Lithographic
2754 Commercial Printing: Gravure
2759 Commercial Printing
2761 Manifold Business Forms
2771 Greeting Card Publishing
2782 Blankbooks & Looseleaf Binders
2789 Bookbinding
2791 Typesetting
2796 Platemaking & Related Svcs

28 chemicals and allied products
2812 Alkalies & Chlorine
2813 Industrial Gases
2816 Inorganic Pigments
2819 Indl Inorganic Chemicals, NEC
2821 Plastics, Mtrls & Nonvulcanizable Elastomers
2822 Synthetic Rubber (Vulcanizable Elastomers)
2824 Synthetic Organic Fibers, Exc Cellulosic
2833 Medicinal Chemicals & Botanical Prdts
2834 Pharmaceuticals
2835 Diagnostic Substances
2836 Biological Prdts, Exc Diagnostic Substances
2841 Soap & Detergents
2842 Spec Cleaning, Polishing & Sanitation Preparations
2843 Surface Active & Finishing Agents, Sulfonated Oils
2844 Perfumes, Cosmetics & Toilet Preparations
2851 Paints, Varnishes, Lacquers, Enamels
2861 Gum & Wood Chemicals
2865 Cyclic-Crudes, Intermediates, Dyes & Org Pigments
2869 Industrial Organic Chemicals, NEC
2873 Nitrogenous Fertilizers
2875 Fertilizers, Mixing Only
2879 Pesticides & Agricultural Chemicals, NEC
2891 Adhesives & Sealants
2892 Explosives
2893 Printing Ink
2899 Chemical Preparations, NEC

29 petroleum refining and related industries
2911 Petroleum Refining
2951 Paving Mixtures & Blocks
2952 Asphalt Felts & Coatings
2992 Lubricating Oils & Greases
2999 Products Of Petroleum & Coal, NEC

30 rubber and miscellaneous plastics products
3011 Tires & Inner Tubes
3021 Rubber & Plastic Footwear
3052 Rubber & Plastic Hose & Belting
3053 Gaskets, Packing & Sealing Devices
3061 Molded, Extruded & Lathe-Cut Rubber Mechanical Goods
3069 Fabricated Rubber Prdts, NEC
3081 Plastic Unsupported Sheet & Film
3082 Plastic Unsupported Profile Shapes
3083 Plastic Laminated Plate & Sheet
3084 Plastic Pipe
3085 Plastic Bottles
3086 Plastic Foam Prdts

SIC INDEX

SIC NO	PRODUCT
3087	Custom Compounding Of Purchased Plastic Resins
3088	Plastic Plumbing Fixtures
3089	Plastic Prdts

31 leather and leather products

SIC NO	PRODUCT
3111	Leather Tanning & Finishing
3131	Boot & Shoe Cut Stock & Findings
3143	Men's Footwear, Exc Athletic
3144	Women's Footwear, Exc Athletic
3149	Footwear, NEC
3161	Luggage
3171	Handbags & Purses
3172	Personal Leather Goods
3199	Leather Goods, NEC

32 stone, clay, glass, and concrete products

SIC NO	PRODUCT
3211	Flat Glass
3221	Glass Containers
3229	Pressed & Blown Glassware, NEC
3231	Glass Prdts Made Of Purchased Glass
3241	Cement, Hydraulic
3251	Brick & Structural Clay Tile
3253	Ceramic Tile
3255	Clay Refractories
3259	Structural Clay Prdts, NEC
3261	China Plumbing Fixtures & Fittings
3263	Earthenware, Whiteware, Table & Kitchen Articles
3264	Porcelain Electrical Splys
3269	Pottery Prdts, NEC
3271	Concrete Block & Brick
3272	Concrete Prdts
3273	Ready-Mixed Concrete
3274	Lime
3275	Gypsum Prdts
3281	Cut Stone Prdts
3291	Abrasive Prdts
3292	Asbestos products
3295	Minerals & Earths: Ground Or Treated
3296	Mineral Wool
3297	Nonclay Refractories
3299	Nonmetallic Mineral Prdts, NEC

33 primary metal industries

SIC NO	PRODUCT
3312	Blast Furnaces, Coke Ovens, Steel & Rolling Mills
3313	Electrometallurgical Prdts
3315	Steel Wire Drawing & Nails & Spikes
3316	Cold Rolled Steel Sheet, Strip & Bars
3317	Steel Pipe & Tubes
3321	Gray Iron Foundries
3324	Steel Investment Foundries
3325	Steel Foundries, NEC
3331	Primary Smelting & Refining Of Copper
3334	Primary Production Of Aluminum
3339	Primary Nonferrous Metals, NEC
3341	Secondary Smelting & Refining Of Nonferrous Metals
3351	Rolling, Drawing & Extruding Of Copper
3353	Aluminum Sheet, Plate & Foil
3354	Aluminum Extruded Prdts
3355	Aluminum Rolling & Drawing, NEC
3356	Rolling, Drawing-Extruding Of Nonferrous Metals
3357	Nonferrous Wire Drawing
3363	Aluminum Die Castings
3364	Nonferrous Die Castings, Exc Aluminum
3365	Aluminum Foundries
3366	Copper Foundries
3369	Nonferrous Foundries: Castings, NEC
3398	Metal Heat Treating
3399	Primary Metal Prdts, NEC

34 fabricated metal products, except machinery and transportation equipment

SIC NO	PRODUCT
3411	Metal Cans
3412	Metal Barrels, Drums, Kegs & Pails
3421	Cutlery
3423	Hand & Edge Tools
3425	Hand Saws & Saw Blades
3429	Hardware, NEC
3431	Enameled Iron & Metal Sanitary Ware
3432	Plumbing Fixture Fittings & Trim, Brass
3433	Heating Eqpt
3441	Fabricated Structural Steel
3442	Metal Doors, Sash, Frames, Molding & Trim
3443	Fabricated Plate Work
3444	Sheet Metal Work
3446	Architectural & Ornamental Metal Work
3448	Prefabricated Metal Buildings & Cmpnts
3449	Misc Structural Metal Work
3451	Screw Machine Prdts
3452	Bolts, Nuts, Screws, Rivets & Washers
3462	Iron & Steel Forgings
3463	Nonferrous Forgings
3465	Automotive Stampings
3466	Crowns & Closures
3469	Metal Stampings, NEC
3471	Electroplating, Plating, Polishing, Anodizing & Coloring
3479	Coating & Engraving, NEC
3482	Small Arms Ammunition
3483	Ammunition, Large
3484	Small Arms
3489	Ordnance & Access, NEC
3491	Industrial Valves
3492	Fluid Power Valves & Hose Fittings
3493	Steel Springs, Except Wire
3494	Valves & Pipe Fittings, NEC
3495	Wire Springs
3496	Misc Fabricated Wire Prdts
3497	Metal Foil & Leaf
3498	Fabricated Pipe & Pipe Fittings
3499	Fabricated Metal Prdts, NEC

35 industrial and commercial machinery and computer equipment

SIC NO	PRODUCT
3511	Steam, Gas & Hydraulic Turbines & Engines
3519	Internal Combustion Engines, NEC
3523	Farm Machinery & Eqpt
3524	Garden, Lawn Tractors & Eqpt
3531	Construction Machinery & Eqpt
3532	Mining Machinery & Eqpt
3533	Oil Field Machinery & Eqpt
3534	Elevators & Moving Stairways
3535	Conveyors & Eqpt
3536	Hoists, Cranes & Monorails
3537	Indl Trucks, Tractors, Trailers & Stackers
3541	Machine Tools: Cutting
3542	Machine Tools: Forming
3543	Industrial Patterns
3544	Dies, Tools, Jigs, Fixtures & Indl Molds
3545	Machine Tool Access
3546	Power Hand Tools
3547	Rolling Mill Machinery & Eqpt
3548	Welding Apparatus
3549	Metalworking Machinery, NEC
3552	Textile Machinery
3553	Woodworking Machinery
3554	Paper Inds Machinery
3555	Printing Trades Machinery & Eqpt
3556	Food Prdts Machinery
3559	Special Ind Machinery, NEC
3561	Pumps & Pumping Eqpt
3562	Ball & Roller Bearings
3563	Air & Gas Compressors
3564	Blowers & Fans
3565	Packaging Machinery
3566	Speed Changers, Drives & Gears
3567	Indl Process Furnaces & Ovens
3568	Mechanical Power Transmission Eqpt, NEC
3569	Indl Machinery & Eqpt, NEC
3571	Electronic Computers
3572	Computer Storage Devices
3575	Computer Terminals
3577	Computer Peripheral Eqpt, NEC
3578	Calculating & Accounting Eqpt
3579	Office Machines, NEC
3581	Automatic Vending Machines
3582	Commercial Laundry, Dry Clean & Pressing Mchs
3585	Air Conditioning & Heating Eqpt
3586	Measuring & Dispensing Pumps
3589	Service Ind Machines, NEC
3592	Carburetors, Pistons, Rings & Valves
3593	Fluid Power Cylinders & Actuators
3594	Fluid Power Pumps & Motors
3596	Scales & Balances, Exc Laboratory
3599	Machinery & Eqpt, Indl & Commercial, NEC

36 electronic and other electrical equipment and components, except computer

SIC NO	PRODUCT
3612	Power, Distribution & Specialty Transformers
3613	Switchgear & Switchboard Apparatus
3621	Motors & Generators
3624	Carbon & Graphite Prdts
3625	Relays & Indl Controls
3629	Electrical Indl Apparatus, NEC
3631	Household Cooking Eqpt
3632	Household Refrigerators & Freezers
3633	Household Laundry Eqpt
3634	Electric Household Appliances
3635	Household Vacuum Cleaners
3639	Household Appliances, NEC
3641	Electric Lamps
3643	Current-Carrying Wiring Devices
3644	Noncurrent-Carrying Wiring Devices
3645	Residential Lighting Fixtures
3646	Commercial, Indl & Institutional Lighting Fixtures
3647	Vehicular Lighting Eqpt
3648	Lighting Eqpt, NEC
3651	Household Audio & Video Eqpt
3652	Phonograph Records & Magnetic Tape
3661	Telephone & Telegraph Apparatus
3663	Radio & T V Communications, Systs & Eqpt, Broadcast/Studio
3669	Communications Eqpt, NEC
3671	Radio & T V Receiving Electron Tubes
3672	Printed Circuit Boards
3674	Semiconductors
3675	Electronic Capacitors
3676	Electronic Resistors
3677	Electronic Coils & Transformers
3678	Electronic Connectors
3679	Electronic Components, NEC
3691	Storage Batteries
3692	Primary Batteries: Dry & Wet
3694	Electrical Eqpt For Internal Combustion Engines
3695	Recording Media
3699	Electrical Machinery, Eqpt & Splys, NEC

37 transportation equipment

SIC NO	PRODUCT
3711	Motor Vehicles & Car Bodies
3713	Truck & Bus Bodies
3714	Motor Vehicle Parts & Access
3715	Truck Trailers
3716	Motor Homes
3721	Aircraft
3724	Aircraft Engines & Engine Parts
3728	Aircraft Parts & Eqpt, NEC
3731	Shipbuilding & Repairing
3732	Boat Building & Repairing
3743	Railroad Eqpt
3751	Motorcycles, Bicycles & Parts
3761	Guided Missiles & Space Vehicles
3764	Guided Missile/Space Vehicle Propulsion Units & parts
3769	Guided Missile/Space Vehicle Parts & Eqpt, NEC
3792	Travel Trailers & Campers
3795	Tanks & Tank Components
3799	Transportation Eqpt, NEC

38 measuring, analyzing and controlling instruments; photographic, medical an

SIC NO	PRODUCT
3812	Search, Detection, Navigation & Guidance Systs & Instrs
3821	Laboratory Apparatus & Furniture
3822	Automatic Temperature Controls
3823	Indl Instruments For Meas, Display & Control
3824	Fluid Meters & Counters
3825	Instrs For Measuring & Testing Electricity
3826	Analytical Instruments
3827	Optical Instruments
3829	Measuring & Controlling Devices, NEC
3841	Surgical & Medical Instrs & Apparatus
3842	Orthopedic, Prosthetic & Surgical Appliances/Splys
3843	Dental Eqpt & Splys
3844	X-ray Apparatus & Tubes
3845	Electromedical & Electrotherapeutic Apparatus
3851	Ophthalmic Goods
3861	Photographic Eqpt & Splys
3873	Watch & Clock Devices & Parts

39 miscellaneous manufacturing industries

SIC NO	PRODUCT
3911	Jewelry: Precious Metal
3914	Silverware, Plated & Stainless Steel Ware
3915	Jewelers Findings & Lapidary Work
3931	Musical Instruments
3942	Dolls & Stuffed Toys
3944	Games, Toys & Children's Vehicles
3949	Sporting & Athletic Goods, NEC
3951	Pens & Mechanical Pencils
3952	Lead Pencils, Crayons & Artist's Mtrls
3953	Marking Devices
3955	Carbon Paper & Inked Ribbons
3961	Costume Jewelry & Novelties
3965	Fasteners, Buttons, Needles & Pins
3991	Brooms & Brushes
3993	Signs & Advertising Displays
3995	Burial Caskets
3996	Linoleum & Hard Surface Floor Coverings, NEC
3999	Manufacturing Industries, NEC

73 business services

SIC NO	PRODUCT
7372	Prepackaged Software

76 miscellaneous repair services

SIC NO	PRODUCT
7692	Welding Repair
7694	Armature Rewinding Shops

SIC SECTION

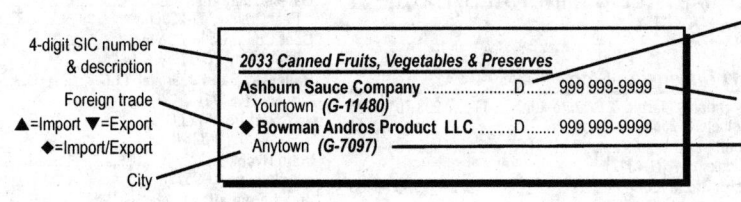

- 4-digit SIC number & description → **2033 Canned Fruits, Vegetables & Preserves**
- Foreign trade ▲=Import ▼=Export ◆=Import/Export
- City
- Indicates approximate employment figure A = Over 500 employees, B = 251-500 C = 101-250, D = 51-100, E = 20-50 F = 10-19, G = 1-9
- Business phone
- Geographic Section entry number where full company information appears.

Ashburn Sauce Company .... D 999 999-9999
Yourtown *(G-11480)*
◆ Bowman Andros Product LLC .... D 999 999-9999
Anytown *(G-7097)*

See footnotes for symbols and codes identification.

- The SIC codes in this section are from the latest Standard Industrial Classification manual published by the U.S. Government's Office of Management and Budget. For more information regarding SICs, see the Explanatory Notes.
- Companies may be listed under multiple classifications.

10 METAL MINING

1011 Iron Ores
◆ Farrel Corporation .... D 203 736-5500
Ansonia *(G-34)*
Iron Oxen Network Comm .... G 203 228-2556
Oxford *(G-6669)*

1021 Copper Ores
Baobab Asset Management LLC .... G 203 340-5700
Greenwich *(G-3129)*

1081 Metal Mining Svcs
Amci Capital LP .... G 203 625-9200
Greenwich *(G-3118)*
East Delta Resources Corp .... G 860 434-7750
Old Lyme *(G-6506)*
Imagin Minerals .... G 203 762-1249
Wilton *(G-10300)*

1094 Uranium, Radium & Vanadium Ores
Energy USA Incorporated .... G 203 791-2222
Danbury *(G-1811)*

1099 Metal Ores, NEC
Tronox Limited .... G 203 705-3800
Stamford *(G-8477)*

12 COAL MINING

1221 Bituminous Coal & Lignite: Surface Mining
Morning Sun of Trumbull LLC .... G 203 220-8509
Trumbull *(G-9050)*
Rhino Energy Holdings LLC .... A 203 862-7000
Greenwich *(G-3226)*
Wexford Capital LP .... D 203 862-7000
Greenwich *(G-3258)*

1222 Bituminous Coal: Underground Mining
▲ American Metals Coal Intl Inc .... F 203 625-9200
Greenwich *(G-3120)*
Rhino Energy Holdings LLC .... A 203 862-7000
Greenwich *(G-3226)*
Wexford Capital LP .... D 203 862-7000
Greenwich *(G-3258)*

1231 Anthracite Mining
Hartford Fire Equipment .... E 860 747-2757
Plainville *(G-6821)*

1241 Coal Mining Svcs
Buchanan Minerals LLC .... D 304 392-1000
Wilton *(G-10277)*
Coronado Group LLC .... G 203 761-1291
Wilton *(G-10282)*
Tronox LLC .... E 203 705-3800
Stamford *(G-8478)*

13 OIL AND GAS EXTRACTION

1311 Crude Petroleum & Natural Gas
Alternate Energy Futures .... G 917 745-7097
Danbury *(G-1738)*

Ammonite Corp .... G 203 972-1130
New Canaan *(G-5087)*
CCI Robinsons Bend LLC .... G 203 564-8571
Stamford *(G-8136)*
Country Oil LLC .... G 203 270-6439
Newtown *(G-5735)*
Dietze & Associates LLC .... F 203 762-3500
Wilton *(G-10289)*
▲ Direct Energy Inc .... F 800 260-0300
Stamford *(G-8186)*
Eazy Oil LLC .... G 860 426-3184
Plantsville *(G-6891)*
El Paso Prod Oil Gas Texas LP .... F 860 293-1990
Hartford *(G-3584)*
Fpr Pinedale LLC .... G 203 542-6000
Stamford *(G-8206)*
Frc Founders Corporation .... E 203 661-6601
Stamford *(G-8209)*
Gsv Inc .... G 203 221-2690
Westport *(G-10094)*
Kevin Field .... G 203 878-6339
Milford *(G-4564)*
Less Pay Oil LLC .... G 203 230-2568
Hamden *(G-3474)*
◆ Louis Dreyfus Holding Company .... B 203 761-2000
Wilton *(G-10310)*
McGuires Oil LLc .... G 860 889-2567
Preston *(G-6986)*
Merrill Oil LLC .... G 203 387-1130
Woodbridge *(G-10607)*
Oil Guy LLC .... G 203 910-2752
Watertown *(G-9717)*
Outpost Exploration LLC .... G 203 762-7206
Wilton *(G-10317)*
Petroglyph Energy Inc .... G 208 685-7600
Darien *(G-2038)*
Promise Propane .... G 860 685-0676
Newington *(G-5696)*
River Valley Oil Service LLC .... G 860 342-5670
Portland *(G-6973)*
Santa Energy Corporation .... G 800 937-2682
Bridgeport *(G-895)*
South Bend Ethanol LLC .... E 203 326-8132
Stamford *(G-8430)*
Viridian Energy LLC .... D 203 663-5089
Stamford *(G-8485)*
Winner Producing Co .... G 203 259-7576
Westport *(G-10176)*

1321 Natural Gas Liquids
Impact Nutraceuticals LLC .... G 203 493-4268
Greenwich *(G-3179)*
Servco Oil Inc .... G 203 762-7994
Wilton *(G-10328)*
Spicer Plus Inc .... G 860 445-2436
Groton *(G-3313)*

1381 Drilling Oil & Gas Wells
Aarons Enterprises .... G 203 762-9764
Wilton *(G-10266)*
Budget Oil .... G 860 649-1527
Bolton *(G-507)*
Coleman Drilling & Blasting .... G 860 376-3813
Voluntown *(G-9188)*
Concrete Coring Co Conn Inc .... G 203 287-8400
Hamden *(G-3430)*
D F Arszyla Well Drilling Inc .... G 860 628-6156
Southington *(G-7910)*
Directional Technologies Inc .... G 203 294-9200
Wallingford *(G-9250)*

Eows Midland Inc .... E 203 358-5705
Stamford *(G-8196)*
George Sima .... G 860 345-4660
Higganum *(G-3764)*
Louis E Allyn Sons Inc .... G 860 542-5741
Norfolk *(G-5825)*
Mercuria Energy Trading Inc .... G 203 413-3355
Greenwich *(G-3202)*
Millbrae Energy LLC .... F 203 742-2800
Greenwich *(G-3203)*
Rodger Craig .... G 203 264-8843
Southbury *(G-7876)*
Sterling Gas Drlg Fund 1982 LP .... G 203 358-5700
Stamford *(G-8442)*
Total Drilling Supply LLC .... G 860 923-1091
Thompson *(G-8844)*

1382 Oil & Gas Field Exploration Svcs
Ace Energy LLC .... G 860 623-3308
Broad Brook *(G-1143)*
Ammonite Corp .... G 203 972-1130
New Canaan *(G-5087)*
Bedrock Oil LLC .... G 860 295-8230
Marlborough *(G-4121)*
▲ Brownstone Exploration .... G 860 866-0208
Portland *(G-6954)*
Castleton Commodities .... G 203 564-8100
Stamford *(G-8131)*
CCI East Texas Upstream LLC .... G 203 564-8100
Stamford *(G-8135)*
El Paso Prod Oil Gas Texas LP .... F 860 293-1990
Hartford *(G-3584)*
Ellington Energy Inc .... G 860 872-9276
Ellington *(G-2588)*
Equinor Shipping Inc .... G 203 978-6900
Stamford *(G-8197)*
▲ Equinor US Holdings Inc .... C 203 978-6900
Stamford *(G-8198)*
Geosonics Inc .... F 203 271-2504
Cheshire *(G-1392)*
Jager Prof Gas Svcs LLC .... G 860 388-3422
Old Saybrook *(G-6546)*
Maine Power Express LLC .... G 203 661-0055
Greenwich *(G-3197)*
RTS Corporation .... G 203 459-9835
Trumbull *(G-9065)*
Seismic Monitoring Svcs LLC .... G 860 753-6363
Danielson *(G-2001)*
Vab Inc .... G 860 793-0246
Plainville *(G-6875)*

1389 Oil & Gas Field Svcs, NEC
A & C Connection Inspection .... G 203 287-8504
Hamden *(G-3408)*
Ace Servicing Co Inc .... G 203 795-1400
Orange *(G-6578)*
Acuren Inspection Inc .... A 203 702-8740
Danbury *(G-1731)*
Acuren Inspection Inc .... D 203 869-6734
Greenwich *(G-3116)*
Alliance Energy LLC .... G 203 933-2511
New Haven *(G-5223)*
Alterio Tractor Pulling LLC .... G 203 305-9812
Oxford *(G-6642)*
Artic Oil .... G 860 693-6925
Canton *(G-1305)*
Arts of Stone LLC .... G 860 355-9468
New Milford *(G-5507)*
Bruce Burgess .... G 860 510-9185
Middletown *(G-4328)*

13 OIL AND GAS EXTRACTION

Bruce Corey Enterprises Inc.................G....... 203 272-3600
  Wolcott (G-10550)
Buon Appetito From Italy LLC ....G....... 860 437-3668
  New London (G-5460)
Cameron International Corp ....F....... 860 633-0277
  Glastonbury (G-3018)
Cedar Ridge Oil Co ....G....... 860 435-9398
  Salisbury (G-7295)
Clean Ocean Technology ....G....... 401 212-8171
  Pawcatuck (G-6705)
Connectcut Shreline Developers............G....... 860 669-4424
  Clinton (G-1496)
Dimauro Oil Co LLC ....G....... 860 342-2969
  Portland (G-6958)
East Coast Pulling Parts LLC ....G....... 860 234-4285
  Danielson (G-1991)
East Mountain Oil Co LLC ....G....... 203 757-7774
  Prospect (G-7001)
Eastern Connecticut ....F....... 860 423-1972
  Willimantic (G-10226)
Franklin-Howard LLC ....G....... 860 923-3343
  Woodstock (G-10665)
Frc Founders Corporation ....E....... 203 661-6601
  Stamford (G-8209)
GE Oil & Gas Esp Inc ....E....... 405 670-1431
  Redding (G-7092)
High Fire Servicing LLC ....G....... 203 924-6562
  Shelton (G-7464)
J & M Plumbing & Cnstr LLC ....F....... 860 319-3082
  Norwich (G-6418)
J and R Shelter Rock Road LLC ....G....... 203 739-0697
  Danbury (G-1855)
James & Co LLC ....G....... 860 897-6242
  Bloomfield (G-426)
John Cutter ....G....... 860 749-0015
  Somers (G-7663)
Jonas Lieponis ....G....... 203 458-6912
  Guilford (G-3364)
Kafa Group LLC ....G....... 475 275-0090
  Bridgeport (G-812)
Kc Servicing LLC ....G....... 860 822-9766
  Preston (G-6985)
Kyung Pae Servicing Co LLC ....G....... 203 394-7472
  Fairfield (G-2807)
Loanworks Servicing LLC ....G....... 203 402-7304
  Shelton (G-7491)
Longview Holding Corporation ....G....... 203 869-6734
  Greenwich (G-3192)
Mid-Conn Testers LLC ....G....... 860 232-1943
  Newington (G-5677)
My Slide Lines LLC ....G....... 203 324-1642
  Norwalk (G-6267)
Nytex Petroleum Inc ....G....... 203 261-6329
  Westport (G-10131)
P J S Services ....G....... 860 345-4896
  Higganum (G-3774)
Palmieri Industries Inc. ....D....... 203 384-6020
  Bridgeport (G-859)
Patriot Oil Heat LLC ....G....... 860 928-4091
  Woodstock (G-10676)
Precision Servicing ....G....... 203 650-1392
  Easton (G-2562)
Pro Gas Installation & Svc LLC ....G....... 860 982-1370
  East Hampton (G-2275)
R&M Service ....G....... 860 645-7771
  Manchester (G-4080)
Reac Ready LLC ....G....... 860 760-8886
  Avon (G-103)
Rk Stucco LLC ....G....... 860 331-1791
  New Britain (G-5046)
Rockwood Service Corporation ....G....... 203 869-6734
  Greenwich (G-3230)
Santa Energy Corporation ....G....... 800 937-2682
  Bridgeport (G-895)
Sigma Tankers Inc ....F....... 203 662-2600
  Norwalk (G-6347)
Staxx Construction Svcs LLC ....G....... 860 259-5003
  Berlin (G-223)
Summit Birch Hill ....G....... 860 677-2763
  Farmington (G-2961)
Taylor Energy ....G....... 860 623-3309
  East Windsor (G-2526)
Tri State Maintenance Svcs LLC ....F....... 203 691-1343
  North Haven (G-6001)
W M G and Sons Inc ....G....... 860 584-0143
  Bristol (G-1136)
Weatherford International LLC ....E....... 203 294-0190
  Wallingford (G-9402)
Williams Oil Company ....G....... 860 664-9587
  Clinton (G-1534)

14 MINING AND QUARRYING OF NONMETALLIC MINERALS, EXCEPT FUELS

1411 Dimension Stone

▲ Academy Marble & Granite LLC ....G....... 203 791-2956
  Bethel (G-256)
Armetta LLC ....E....... 860 788-2369
  Middletown (G-4317)
Arts of Stone LLC ....G....... 860 355-9468
  New Milford (G-5507)
Coccomo Brothers Drilling LLC ....F....... 860 828-1632
  Berlin (G-171)
▲ Connecticut Stone Supplies Inc ....D....... 203 882-1000
  Milford (G-4499)
Exquisite Surfaces Inc ....G....... 203 866-9100
  Norwalk (G-6159)
GS Ruff Stuff ....G....... 860 859-9355
  Salem (G-7289)
Infinity Stone Inc ....F....... 203 575-9484
  Waterbury (G-9505)
Jf Granite & Marble ....G....... 860 355-4414
  New Milford (G-5550)
▲ LH Gault & Son Incorporated ....D....... 203 227-5181
  Westport (G-10112)
▲ Midwood Quarry and Cnstr Inc ....F....... 860 289-1414
  East Hartford (G-2345)
Stony Creek Quarry Corporation ....G....... 203 483-3904
  Branford (G-659)
West Hartford Stone Mulch LLC ....G....... 860 461-7616
  West Hartford (G-9872)

1422 Crushed & Broken Limestone

Allyndale Corporation ....F....... 860 824-7959
  East Canaan (G-2180)
Lime Rock Resources GP III LP ....G....... 203 293-2750
  Westport (G-10113)
Quarry Stone & Gravel LLC ....G....... 203 770-2664
  Danbury (G-1925)
Specialty Minerals Inc ....C....... 860 824-5435
  Canaan (G-1292)
Trap Rock Quarry..................................G....... 203 263-2195
  Southbury (G-7881)

1423 Crushed & Broken Granite

Mid-Island Aggregates/Distribu ....G....... 860 605-6753
  Sherman (G-7598)
Skyline Quarry ....E....... 860 875-3580
  Stafford Springs (G-8038)

1429 Crushed & Broken Stone, NEC

Galasso Materials LLC ....C....... 860 527-1825
  East Granby (G-2206)
Joe Passarelli & Co...............................G....... 203 877-1434
  Milford (G-4560)
Nu-Stone Mfg & Distrg LLC ....G....... 860 564-6555
  Sterling (G-8514)
Powder Hill Sand & Gravel LLC ....G....... 860 741-7274
  Enfield (G-2679)
York Hill Trap Rock Quarry Co...............F....... 203 237-8421
  Meriden (G-4270)

1442 Construction Sand & Gravel

Adelman Sand & Gravel Inc ....E....... 860 889-3394
  Bozrah (G-522)
Almond Sand Elephants........................G....... 860 232-4888
  West Hartford (G-9773)
B & C Sand & Gravel Company ....G....... 203 335-6640
  Bridgeport (G-706)
Bethel Sand & Gravel Co......................G....... 203 743-4469
  Bethel (G-264)
Brennan Realty LLC ....C....... 203 929-6314
  Shelton (G-7409)
Brooklyn Sand & Gravel LLC ....G....... 860 779-3980
  Danielson (G-1987)
Dan Beard Inc ....F....... 203 924-4346
  Shelton (G-7427)
Dens Sand & Gravel ....G....... 860 642-6478
  Lebanon (G-3853)
Desiato Sand & Gravel ....G....... 860 742-7573
  Coventry (G-1652)
Desiato Sand & Gravel Corp ....E....... 860 429-6479
  Storrs Mansfield (G-8555)
Doug Hartin ....G....... 860 377-4283
  Woodstock (G-10663)
Dunning Sand & Gravel Company ....G....... 860 677-1616
  Farmington (G-2899)
Freedom Properties ....G....... 860 508-3349
  West Hartford (G-9811)
Galasso Materials LLC ....C....... 860 527-1825
  East Granby (G-2206)
Geer Construction Co Inc ....G....... 860 376-5321
  Jewett City (G-3795)
Hathaway Sand & Gravel LLC ....G....... 860 647-7772
  Bolton (G-511)
Jn Construction LLC ....G....... 914 483-2998
  Stamford (G-8264)
John Hychko ....G....... 203 757-3458
  Waterbury (G-9512)
Judith Bennett ....G....... 203 729-6548
  Naugatuck (G-4895)
Judith Bennett......................................G....... 203 255-6363
  Fairfield (G-2804)
Kacerguis Farms Inc.............................G....... 203 405-1202
  Bethlehem (G-373)
Kobyluck Sand and Gravel Inc ....F....... 860 444-9600
  Waterford (G-9658)
Laurelbrook Ntral Rsources LLC ....F....... 860 824-5843
  East Canaan (G-2183)
▲ Midwood Quarry and Cnstr Inc ....F....... 860 289-1414
  East Hartford (G-2345)
O & G Industries Inc ....E....... 203 323-1111
  Stamford (G-8336)
Palumbo Sand & Gravel ....G....... 860 350-5322
  Sherman (G-7600)
Pine Ridge Gravel LLC ....G....... 860 873-2500
  East Haddam (G-2248)
Powder Hill Sand & Gravel LLC ....G....... 860 741-7274
  Enfield (G-2679)
Skyline Quarry ....E....... 860 875-3580
  Stafford Springs (G-8038)
Sterling Sand and Gravel LLC ....G....... 860 774-3985
  Sterling (G-8518)
Thomas Keegan & Sons Inc ....G....... 203 239-9248
  North Haven (G-5999)
Tilcon Connecticut Inc ....G....... 860 756-8016
  Newington (G-5712)
Tronox LLC ....E....... 203 705-3800
  Stamford (G-8478)
Turning Stone Sand & Grav LLC ....G....... 413 519-1560
  Enfield (G-2702)
Valley Sand & Gravel Corp ....E....... 203 562-3192
  North Haven (G-6010)
West Hartford Stone Mulch LLC ....G....... 860 461-7616
  West Hartford (G-9872)
Wfs Earth Materialsi LLC ....G....... 203 488-2055
  Branford (G-673)
Woodview Construction Svcs LLC ....G....... 203 402-9032
  Windsor (G-10466)

1446 Industrial Sand

Unimin Lime Corporation ....F....... 203 966-8880
  New Canaan (G-5155)

1455 Kaolin & Ball Clay

Sandballz International LLC ....G....... 860 465-9628
  Storrs Mansfield (G-8560)

1459 Clay, Ceramic & Refractory Minerals, NEC

◆ RT Vanderbilt Holding Co Inc ....F....... 203 295-2141
  Norwalk (G-6331)
◆ Vanderbilt Minerals LLC ....E....... 203 295-2140
  Norwalk (G-6384)

1474 Potash, Soda & Borate Minerals

◆ American Natural Soda Ash Corp .....E....... 203 226-9056
  Westport (G-10054)

1481 Nonmetallic Minerals Svcs, Except Fuels

Fred Rein ....G....... 860 460-8086
  Mystic (G-4818)
Haynes Aggregates - Deep River ....G....... 203 888-8100
  Seymour (G-7349)
New England Boring Contractors ....F....... 860 633-4649
  Glastonbury (G-3063)
Veronica Matthews Minerals ....G....... 860 399-0063
  Westbrook (G-10013)

1499 Miscellaneous Nonmetallic Mining

Galasso Materials LLC ....C....... 860 527-1825
  East Granby (G-2206)
◆ RT Vanderbilt Holding Co Inc ....F....... 203 295-2141
  Norwalk (G-6331)

Soapstone Landing LLC .... G 860 875-6200
Stafford Springs (G-8039)

20 FOOD AND KINDRED PRODUCTS

2011 Meat Packing Plants

E & J Andrychowski Farms .... G 860 423-4124
Windham (G-10345)
Frank Demartino and Sons .... G 203 734-1074
Seymour (G-7346)
▲ Grote & Weigel Inc .... E 860 242-8528
Bloomfield (G-415)
▲ Manchester Packing Company Inc ... D 860 646-5000
Manchester (G-4053)
Martin Rosols Inc .... E 860 223-2707
New Britain (G-5014)
Maurices Country Meat Mkt LLC .... G 860 546-9588
Canterbury (G-1300)
Noacks Meat Products .... G 203 235-7384
Meriden (G-4209)
Teys (usa) Inc .... G 203 227-0481
Westport (G-10166)

2013 Sausages & Meat Prdts

Baltasar & Sons Inc .... G 203 723-0425
Naugatuck (G-4860)
Baretta Provision Inc .... F 860 828-0802
East Berlin (G-2164)
Capitol Sausage & Provs Inc .... G 860 527-5510
Hartford (G-3562)
Cardoros Inc .... G 860 442-2907
Waterford (G-9644)
Chris & Zack Gourmet Foods .... G 203 912-7805
Orange (G-6591)
Custom Food Pdts Holdings LLC .... D 310 637-0900
Greenwich (G-3148)
Deyulio Sausage Company LLC .... F 203 348-1863
Bridgeport (G-750)
▲ Grote & Weigel Inc .... E 860 242-8528
Bloomfield (G-415)
Hummel Bros Inc .... D 203 787-4113
New Haven (G-5298)
Janik Sausage Co Inc .... G 860 749-4661
Enfield (G-2653)
Lamberti Packing Company .... G 203 562-0436
New Haven (G-5315)
Longhini LLC .... E 212 219-1230
New Haven (G-5320)
▲ Manchester Packing Company Inc ... D 860 646-5000
Manchester (G-4053)
Martin Rosols Inc .... E 860 223-2707
New Britain (G-5014)
Maurices Country Meat Mkt LLC .... G 860 546-9588
Canterbury (G-1300)
Mister BS Jerky Co .... G 203 631-2758
Meriden (G-4206)
Newington Meat Center .... F 860 666-3431
Newington (G-5686)

2015 Poultry Slaughtering, Dressing & Processing

Chris & Zack LLC .... G 203 298-0742
Orange (G-6592)
▲ Moark LLC .... E 951 332-3300
North Franklin (G-5876)
Phoenix Poultry Corporation .... E 413 732-1433
Enfield (G-2677)
Waybest Foods Inc .... G 860 289-7948
South Windsor (G-7839)
Whispering Winds Animal .... G 860 796-8098
Coventry (G-1682)

2021 Butter

Grass Roots Creamery .... G 860 653-6303
Granby (G-3108)
Redding Creamery LLC .... G 203 938-2766
Redding (G-7106)
Square Creamery LLC .... G 203 456-3490
Bethel (G-347)
Sweet Grass Creamery LLC .... G 860 887-8098
Preston (G-6989)
Whipstick Creamery LLC .... G 203 438-2203
Ridgefield (G-7184)

2022 Cheese

Chris & Zack LLC .... G 203 298-0742
Orange (G-6592)
Elm City Cheese Company Inc .... F 203 865-5768
Hamden (G-3443)
Mozzicato Fmly Investments LLC .... G 860 296-0426
Wethersfield (G-10213)
▲ Ndr Liuzzi Inc .... E 203 287-8477
Hamden (G-3487)
Nutty Cow Inc .... G 626 888-9269
West Hartford (G-9840)
Orange Cheese Company .... G 917 603-4378
Orange (G-6619)
▲ Red Apple Cheese LLC .... G 203 755-5579
Watertown (G-9730)

2023 Milk, Condensed & Evaporated

Bactana Corp .... G 203 716-1230
Farmington (G-2881)
Herbalife Distributor .... G 860 584-9721
Bristol (G-1048)
Inner Armour Black LLC .... G 860 656-7720
Berlin (G-190)
Kohler Mix Specialties LLC .... C 860 666-1511
Newington (G-5670)
▼ Natures First Inc .... G 203 795-8400
Orange (G-6614)
Nestle Usa Inc .... C 860 928-0082
Pomfret Center (G-6944)
Novogen Inc .... F 203 972-5901
New Canaan (G-5126)
Supplement Tech LLC .... G 203 377-5551
Stratford (G-8691)

2024 Ice Cream

Abbydabby .... G 860 586-8832
West Hartford (G-9771)
Angelas Italian Ice Inc .... G 860 536-9828
Mystic (G-4798)
B-Sweet LLC .... G 203 452-0499
Monroe (G-4695)
Ben & Jerrys Homemade Inc .... G 203 488-9666
Newington (G-5633)
Big Dipper Ice Cream Fctry Inc .... E 203 758-3200
Prospect (G-6994)
Bucks Spumoni Company Inc .... F 203 874-2007
Milford (G-4477)
Chip In A Bottle LLC .... G 203 460-0665
New Haven (G-5256)
Cold Stone Creamery .... G 860 669-7025
Clinton (G-1495)
Conopco Inc .... E 708 606-0540
Trumbull (G-9014)
Dari-Farms Ice Cream Co Inc .... F 860 872-8313
Tolland (G-8859)
Diversis Capital LLC .... G 860 872-8313
Tolland (G-8861)
Dr Mikes Ice Cream Inc .... G 203 792-4388
Bethel (G-282)
Fish Family Farm Inc .... G 860 646-9745
Bolton (G-509)
Gelato Giuliana LLC .... G 203 772-0607
New Haven (G-5285)
Greg Robbins and Associates .... G 888 699-8876
Branford (G-601)
HP Hood LLC .... C 860 623-4435
Suffield (G-8721)
J Foster Ice Cream .... G 860 651-1499
Simsbury (G-7631)
Jaksy 2 LLC .... G 203 371-4111
Fairfield (G-2799)
Kan Pak LLC .... G 203 933-6631
Southbury (G-7864)
Libbys Italian Pastry Shop .... G 203 234-2530
North Haven (G-5959)
Liberato Italian Ices Inc .... G 203 772-0381
New Haven (G-5318)
Longfords Ice Cream Ltd .... F 914 935-9469
Stamford (G-8288)
Lucille Piccirillo .... G 203 366-2353
Bridgeport (G-826)
Michaels Dairy Inc .... F 860 443-7617
New London (G-5479)
Mozzicato Pastry & Bake Shop .... E 860 296-0426
Hartford (G-3646)
New England Soft Serve .... G 860 537-5459
Colchester (G-1559)
Poppys LLC .... F 860 778-9044
Hartford (G-3667)
Pralines Inc .... F 203 284-8847
Wallingford (G-9338)
Pralines of Plainville .... G 860 410-1151
Plainville (G-6853)
Rbf Frozen Desserts LLC .... F 516 474-6488
West Hartford (G-9848)
◆ Reeds Inc .... E 203 890-0557
Norwalk (G-6318)
Rich Products Corporation .... B 860 827-8000
New Britain (G-5044)
Ritas of Milford .... F 203 301-4490
Milford (G-4630)
▲ Royal Ice Cream Company Inc .... F 860 649-5358
Manchester (G-4083)
Royal Ice Cream Company Inc .... G 860 649-5358
Manchester (G-4084)
Salem Vly Farms Ice Cream Inc .... G 860 859-2980
Salem (G-7291)
Sharon Masonry .... G 860 307-7427
Torrington (G-8970)
Smoothie King .... G 203 208-4098
Branford (G-653)
Smoothie King .... G 860 574-9382
Waterford (G-9671)
Sunny Daes of Fairfield .... G 203 372-3058
Fairfield (G-2851)
T & R Specialties LLC .... G 860 870-9684
Ellington (G-2605)
Tea-Rrific Ice Cream LLC .... G 203 354-9805
Bridgeport (G-921)
◆ Thomas J Lipton Inc .... A 206 381-3500
Trumbull (G-9081)
United Enterprises Inc .... G 860 225-9955
New Britain (G-5078)
Walnut Beach Creamery LLC .... G 203 878-7738
Milford (G-4679)
Wild-Froyo LLC .... G 860 739-6124
Niantic (G-5820)

2026 Milk

Guida-Seibert Dairy Company .... C 860 224-2404
New Britain (G-4994)
HP Hood LLC .... B 203 304-9151
Newtown (G-5747)
Kohler Mix Specialties LLC .... C 860 666-1511
Newington (G-5670)
Peachwave of Watertown .... G 203 942-4949
Watertown (G-9720)
R & D Services LLC .... G 860 628-5205
Southington (G-7964)
Swizzles of Greenwhich .... G 917 662-0080
Cos Cob (G-1642)
Willard J Stearns & Sons Inc .... E 860 423-9289
Storrs Mansfield (G-8561)
Yocrunch Co LLC .... G 866 963-7862
Naugatuck (G-4930)

2032 Canned Specialties

A S Fine Foods .... D 203 322-3899
Stamford (G-8052)
Cushs Homegrown LLC .... G 860 739-7373
Old Lyme (G-6501)
▲ D & M Packing LLC .... E 203 591-8986
Waterbury (G-9458)
Louis Rodriguz .... G 203 777-6937
New Haven (G-5321)
Sacla North America Inc .... G 203 855-1356
Norwalk (G-6335)
Shenondah Vly Specialty Foods .... G 203 348-0402
Stamford (G-8411)

2033 Canned Fruits, Vegetables & Preserves

Conant Valley Jams .... G 203 403-3811
Ridgefield (G-7129)
Conopco Inc .... E 708 606-0540
Trumbull (G-9014)
▲ Cosmos Food Products Inc .... E 800 942-6766
West Haven (G-9893)
Country Pure Foods Inc .... C 330 753-2293
Ellington (G-2583)
Fruitbud Juice LLC .... E 203 790-8200
Danbury (G-1830)
Guida-Seibert Dairy Company .... C 860 224-2404
New Britain (G-4994)
Herbs Farmstead & Goods .... G 860 876-3670
Old Saybrook (G-6540)
James P Smith .... G 203 744-1031
Danbury (G-1857)
Juice Press LLC .... G 212 777-0034
Greenwich (G-3185)
Nantucket Blonde LLC .... G 203 415-1522
Cheshire (G-1417)
Natural Country Farms Inc .... D 860 872-8346
Ellington (G-2597)

SIC

Employee Codes: A=Over 500 employees, B=251-500
C=101-250, D=51-100, E=20-50, F=10-19, G=1-9

20 FOOD AND KINDRED PRODUCTS

Omnomnom Jams and Jellies LLC ....G....... 203 630-6557
  Meriden (G-4213)
Onofrios Ultimate Foods Inc ....F 203 469-4014
  New Haven (G-5355)
Premier Foods Inc ....G....... 203 226-6577
  Westport (G-10143)
Ragozzino Foods Inc ....F 203 238-2553
  Meriden (G-4229)
▲ Sabatino North America LLC ....E 718 328-4120
  West Haven (G-9951)
Sweet Country Roads LLC ....G....... 860 537-0069
  Colchester (G-1578)
◆ Thomas J Lipton Inc ....A....... 206 381-3500
  Trumbull (G-9081)
Winding Drive Corporation ....G....... 203 263-6961
  Woodbury (G-10655)

2034 Dried Fruits, Vegetables & Soup

Conopco Inc ....E 708 606-0540
  Trumbull (G-9014)
◆ Thomas J Lipton Inc ....A....... 206 381-3500
  Trumbull (G-9081)
Zanni Ani Organic Snacks LLC ....G....... 203 214-2360
  Oxford (G-6702)

2035 Pickled Fruits, Vegetables, Sauces & Dressings

Da Silva Klanko Ltd ....G....... 203 756-4932
  Waterbury (G-9459)
Herbs Farmstead & Goods ....G....... 860 876-3670
  Old Saybrook (G-6540)
▼ JKL Specialty Foods Inc ....F 203 541-3990
  Stamford (G-8263)
Kerry R Wood ....G....... 203 221-7780
  Westport (G-10107)
Muggers Marrow LLC ....G....... 203 548-9566
  Bridgeport (G-845)
▼ Newmans Own Inc ....E 203 222-0136
  Westport (G-10128)
Onofrios Ultimate Foods Inc ....F 203 469-4014
  New Haven (G-5355)
◆ Thomas J Lipton Inc ....A....... 206 381-3500
  Trumbull (G-9081)
TSty Brands Inc ....G....... 203 609-4391
  Stamford (G-8479)

2037 Frozen Fruits, Juices & Vegetables

Conopco Inc ....D....... 203 381-3557
  Trumbull (G-9015)
Fruitbud Juice LLC ....E 203 790-8200
  Danbury (G-1830)
Fruta Juice Bar LLC ....G....... 203 690-9168
  Bridgeport (G-772)
Natureseal Inc ....E 203 454-1800
  Westport (G-10127)
Quality Kitchen Corp Delaware ....G....... 203 744-2000
  Danbury (G-1923)
Riverside Express ....G....... 203 326-1245
  Riverside (G-7201)
Santorini Breeze LLC ....G....... 203 640-3431
  Branford (G-646)

2038 Frozen Specialties

Flemming LLC ....G....... 818 746-6495
  Bloomfield (G-411)
Just Breakfast & Things ....G....... 860 376-4040
  Lisbon (G-3881)
Kohler Mix Specialties LLC ....C....... 860 666-1511
  Newington (G-5670)
Lucille Piccirillo ....G....... 203 366-2353
  Bridgeport (G-826)
Orange Cheese Company ....G....... 917 603-4378
  Orange (G-6619)
Ragozzino Foods Inc ....F 203 238-2553
  Meriden (G-4229)
Villarina Pasta & Fine Foods ....G....... 203 917-4463
  Danbury (G-1972)

2041 Flour, Grain Milling

Archer-Daniels-Midland Company ......G....... 203 966-4755
  New Canaan (G-5088)
Central Conn Cooperative Farme ....E 860 649-4523
  South Windsor (G-7727)
▲ Channel Alloys ....G....... 203 975-1404
  Norwalk (G-6112)
Lake House Brewing Company LLC ...G....... 917 620-6636
  Goshen (G-3102)
Michele Schiano Di Cola Inc ....G....... 203 265-5301
  Wallingford (G-9318)

Pelletier Millwrights LLC ....G....... 860 564-8936
  Danielson (G-2000)
Zeneli Pizzeria ....G....... 203 745-4194
  New Haven (G-5453)

2043 Cereal Breakfast Foods

Garden of Light Inc ....D....... 860 895-6622
  East Hartford (G-2330)
Granola Bar ....G....... 914 763-6320
  Greenwich (G-3170)
Kellogg Company ....A....... 860 665-9920
  Newington (G-5669)
Munk Pack Inc ....F 203 769-5005
  Greenwich (G-3207)
Rivera Marina ....G....... 917 676-4100
  New Haven (G-5381)

2045 Flour, Blended & Prepared

◆ Watson LLC ....B....... 203 932-3000
  West Haven (G-9960)

2047 Dog & Cat Food

◆ A L C Inovators Inc ....G....... 203 877-8526
  Milford (G-4436)
Blue Buffalo Company Ltd ....B....... 203 762-9751
  Wilton (G-10274)
Bravo LLC ....F 866 922-9222
  Manchester (G-3987)
Bravo LLC ....E 203 896-1899
  Vernon (G-9134)
CP Apn Inc ....G....... 330 682-3000
  Greenwich (G-3147)
Fine Pets LLC ....G....... 203 833-1517
  Greenwich (G-3160)
Joy Food Company ....G....... 917 549-6240
  Darien (G-2029)

2048 Prepared Feeds For Animals & Fowls

◆ A L C Inovators Inc ....G....... 203 877-8526
  Milford (G-4436)
ALC Sales Company LLC ....G....... 203 877-8526
  Milford (G-4445)
Bactana Corp ....G....... 203 716-1230
  Farmington (G-2881)
Blue Buffalo Pet Products Inc ....E 203 762-9751
  Wilton (G-10275)
Canidae Corp ....G....... 860 539-5307
  Plainville (G-6783)
Classic Brands LLC ....G....... 303 936-2444
  Plainfield (G-6744)
Earth Animal Ventures Inc ....E 717 271-6393
  Stamford (G-8190)
H J Baker & Brother Inc ....G....... 501 664-4870
  Shelton (G-7455)
◆ HJ Baker & Bro LLC ....E 203 682-9200
  Shelton (G-7465)
▲ Moark LLC ....E 951 332-3300
  North Franklin (G-5876)
◆ Source Inc ....G....... 203 488-6400
  North Branford (G-5858)

2051 Bread, Bakery Prdts Exc Cookies & Crackers

Abrantes Bakery & Pastry Shop ....G....... 860 232-1464
  Hartford (G-3544)
Amodios Inc ....F 203 573-1229
  Waterbury (G-9430)
Amoun Pita & Distribution LLC ....E 866 239-9990
  South Windsor (G-7708)
Apicellas Bakery Inc ....E 203 865-6204
  New Haven (G-5232)
Arabic Bread Bakery ....G....... 203 743-4743
  Danbury (G-1743)
Artisan Bread & Products LLC ....G....... 914 843-4401
  Norwalk (G-6074)
Atticus Bakery LLC ....C....... 203 562-9007
  New Haven (G-5237)
Bagel Boys Inc ....F 860 657-4400
  Glastonbury (G-3011)
Beans Inc ....G....... 860 945-9234
  Watertown (G-9683)
Beldotti Bakeries ....F 203 348-9029
  Stamford (G-8109)
Better Baking By Beth ....G....... 860 482-4706
  Torrington (G-8903)
Big Purple Cupcake LLC ....G....... 203 483-8738
  Branford (G-3399)
Bimbo Bakeries Usa Inc ....D....... 203 932-1000
  Orange (G-6586)

Bimbo Bakeries Usa Inc ....E 860 691-1180
  Portland (G-6953)
Boston Model Bakery ....E 203 562-9491
  New Haven (G-5250)
Chef J R ME Rest Group Corp ....G....... 860 940-8038
  New Britain (G-4960)
Congress Catering Inc ....E 860 291-8182
  East Hartford (G-2309)
D Rotondi LLC ....G....... 505 427-3233
  Bridgeport (G-741)
DAndrea Corporation ....F 203 932-6000
  West Haven (G-9895)
Darien Doughnut LLC ....G....... 203 656-2805
  Darien (G-2017)
Daybrake Donuts Inc ....F 203 368-4962
  Bridgeport (G-560)
DI Distributors LLC ....G....... 203 931-1724
  West Haven (G-9901)
Donut Stop ....G....... 203 924-7133
  Shelton (G-7433)
Dough Girl Baking Co LLC ....G....... 203 838-9695
  Norwalk (G-6148)
Elius Delight Snacks LLC ....G....... 646 302-4948
  Stratford (G-8608)
Foster Grandparent Program ....G....... 860 525-5437
  Hartford (G-3592)
Freihofer Charles Baking Co ....G....... 203 729-4545
  Naugatuck (G-4882)
Gracie Maes Kitchen LLC ....G....... 860 885-8250
  Griswold (G-3265)
Hardcore Sweet Cupcakes LLC ....G....... 203 808-5547
  Waterbury (G-9496)
Hartford Cpl Co-Op Inc ....C....... 860 296-5636
  Hartford (G-3610)
Haylons Market LLC ....G....... 860 739-9509
  Niantic (G-5808)
I and U LLC ....G....... 860 803-1491
  Waterbury (G-9502)
Izzi BS Allergy Free LLC ....G....... 203 810-4378
  Norwalk (G-6213)
Katona Bakery LLC ....E 203 337-5349
  Fairfield (G-2805)
Krafty Kakes Inc ....G....... 203 284-0299
  Wallingford (G-9299)
La Cayeyana Donis Bakery ....G....... 203 789-8030
  New Haven (G-5313)
Lupis Inc ....E 203 562-9491
  New Haven (G-5323)
Massconn Distribute Cpl ....D....... 860 882-0717
  South Windsor (G-7791)
Milite Bakery ....G....... 860 753-9451
  Waterbury (G-9543)
Modern Pastry Shop Inc ....E 860 296-7628
  Hartford (G-3645)
Mozzicato Pastry & Bake Shop ....E 860 296-0426
  Hartford (G-3646)
Northeast Foods Inc ....D....... 860 779-1117
  Dayville (G-2067)
Pastry Shop ....G....... 203 238-0483
  Meriden (G-4215)
Paulas Bakery ....G....... 203 743-9000
  Danbury (G-1903)
Pops Donuts ....G....... 203 876-1210
  Milford (G-4610)
Rafael Cakes & Sugar LLC ....G....... 203 642-4840
  Norwalk (G-6314)
Realejo Donuts Inc ....F 860 342-5120
  Portland (G-6971)
Red Rose Desserts ....G....... 860 603-2670
  Colchester (G-1571)
Riverside Baking Company LLC ....G....... 203 451-0331
  Fairfield (G-2837)
Shayna Bs & Pickle LLC ....G....... 860 428-3835
  Ashford (G-66)
Spencer Street Inc ....G....... 860 647-2955
  Manchester (G-4092)
Spinella Bakery ....F 860 753-9451
  Waterbury (G-9606)
Stonehouse Fine Cakes ....F 203 235-5091
  Meriden (G-4246)
Superior Bakery Inc ....E 860 923-9555
  North Grosvenordale (G-5892)
Sweet Peas Baking Company LLC .....G....... 203 637-4031
  Old Greenwich (G-6484)
Sweet Spot Cupcakery LLC ....G....... 860 219-1123
  Windsor (G-10446)
Take Cake LLC ....G....... 203 453-1896
  Guilford (G-3399)
TD's Acquisition LLC ....G....... 860 341-1001
  Middletown (G-4424)

Thadieo LLC ... G ... 860 621-4500
Southington *(G-7985)*
Tinas Heavenly Treats ... G ... 203 543-3560
Stratford *(G-8696)*
◆ Watson LLC ... B ... 203 932-3000
West Haven *(G-9960)*
Whole Donut ... F ... 860 745-3041
Enfield *(G-2706)*
Whole German Breads LLC ... G ... 203 507-0663
New Haven *(G-5432)*
Wildflour Cupcakes Sweets LLC ... G ... 203 828-6576
Seymour *(G-7373)*

2052 Cookies & Crackers

Bagelman III Inc ... F ... 203 792-0030
Danbury *(G-1749)*
Beldotti Bakeries ... F ... 203 348-9029
Stamford *(G-8109)*
Bimbo Bakeries Usa Inc ... D ... 203 932-1000
Orange *(G-6586)*
Bob The Baker LLC ... F ... 203 775-1032
Brookfield *(G-1162)*
Cherise Cpl LLC ... G ... 203 238-3482
Meriden *(G-4157)*
Elius Delight Snacks LLC ... G ... 646 302-4948
Stratford *(G-8608)*
Harsha Inc ... G ... 860 439-1466
Waterford *(G-9655)*
Modern Pastry Shop Inc ... E ... 860 296-7628
Hartford *(G-3645)*
Mozzicato Pastry & Bake Shop ... E ... 860 296-0426
Hartford *(G-3646)*
Pepperidge Farm Incorporated ... C ... 860 286-6400
Bloomfield *(G-463)*
R & K Cookies LLC ... G ... 860 613-2893
Cromwell *(G-1714)*

2053 Frozen Bakery Prdts

Chris & Zack Gourmet Foods ... G ... 203 912-7805
Orange *(G-6591)*
Cooper Marketing Group Inc ... G ... 203 797-9386
Danbury *(G-1774)*
Pepperidge Farm Incorporated ... C ... 860 286-6400
Bloomfield *(G-463)*
◆ Pepperidge Farm Incorporated ... A ... 203 846-7000
Norwalk *(G-6298)*
Rich Products Corporation ... A ... 866 737-8884
New Britain *(G-5042)*
Rich Products Corporation ... A ... 800 356-7094
New Britain *(G-5043)*
Something Sweet Inc ... E ... 203 603-9766
New Haven *(G-5399)*

2062 Sugar, Cane Refining

◆ CSC Sugar LLC ... F ... 203 846-5610
New Canaan *(G-5100)*
Imperial Sugar Company ... C ... 203 761-8474
Wilton *(G-10301)*
Jenkins Sugar Group Inc ... F ... 203 853-3000
Norwalk *(G-6221)*

2063 Sugar, Beet

◆ CSC Sugar LLC ... F ... 203 846-5610
New Canaan *(G-5100)*

2064 Candy & Confectionery Prdts

▲ Bridgewater Chocolate LLC ... G ... 203 775-2286
Brookfield *(G-1164)*
Cavegrl LLC ... G ... 914 261-5801
Stamford *(G-8132)*
Deborah Anns Hmmade Chocolates ... G ... 203 438-0065
Ridgefield *(G-7135)*
Emilys Sweet Confections LLC ... G ... 860 301-2586
Middletown *(G-4342)*
Fascias Chocolates Inc ... F ... 203 753-0515
Waterbury *(G-9480)*
Lollipop Kids LLC ... G ... 203 664-1799
Redding *(G-7098)*
▲ Mantrose-Haeuser Co Inc ... E ... 203 454-1800
Westport *(G-10117)*
Munsons Candy Kitchen Inc ... E ... 860 649-4332
Bolton *(G-517)*
OH Fudge and More LLC ... G ... 860 788-3839
Higganum *(G-3773)*
Penotti USA Inc ... G ... 203 341-9494
Westport *(G-10139)*
Petal Prfctn & Confection LLC ... G ... 203 263-0353
Woodbury *(G-10649)*
▲ Pez Candy Inc ... D ... 203 795-0531
Orange *(G-6622)*
▲ Pez Manufacturing Corp ... D ... 203 795-0531
Orange *(G-6623)*
◆ Reeds Inc ... E ... 203 890-0557
Norwalk *(G-6318)*
Sonias Chocolaterie Inc ... F ... 203 438-5965
Ridgefield *(G-7174)*
▲ Thompson Brands LLC ... D ... 203 235-2541
Meriden *(G-4254)*
Thompson Candy Company ... D ... 203 235-2541
Meriden *(G-4255)*
▲ Yummyearth LLC ... G ... 203 276-1259
Stamford *(G-8504)*

2066 Chocolate & Cocoa Prdts

Chip In A Bottle LLC ... G ... 203 460-0665
New Haven *(G-5256)*
Cote Dlvoire Imports ... G ... 203 243-4841
Stratford *(G-8600)*
CSC Cocoa LLC ... G ... 203 846-5611
New Canaan *(G-5099)*
Custom Chocolate Designs LLC ... G ... 203 886-6777
Meriden *(G-4164)*
Divine Treasure ... G ... 860 643-2552
Manchester *(G-4009)*
Green Tomatillo LLC ... G ... 860 749-0172
South Windsor *(G-7765)*
Hvc Lizard Chocolate LLC ... F ... 203 899-3075
Norwalk *(G-6203)*
▲ Mantrose-Haeuser Co Inc ... E ... 203 454-1800
Westport *(G-10117)*
Munsons Candy Kitchen Inc ... E ... 860 649-4332
Bolton *(G-517)*
Nel Group LLC ... G ... 860 413-9042
East Granby *(G-2216)*
Nel Group LLC ... F ... 860 683-0190
Windsor *(G-10412)*
Rosie Blakes Chocolates LLC ... G ... 732 604-3327
New Britain *(G-5048)*
▲ Thompson Brands LLC ... D ... 203 235-2541
Meriden *(G-4254)*

2068 Salted & Roasted Nuts & Seeds

Kathies Kitchen LLC ... G ... 203 407-0546
North Haven *(G-5956)*
Wizards Nuts Holdings LLC ... D ... 708 483-1315
Greenwich *(G-3260)*

2074 Cottonseed Oil Mills

O-Liminator LLc ... G ... 800 608-9541
Darien *(G-2036)*

2077 Animal, Marine Fats & Oils

Darling International Inc ... G ... 203 597-0773
Waterbury *(G-9462)*

2079 Shortening, Oils & Margarine

Devin David ... G ... 203 322-4000
Stamford *(G-8184)*
Essex Olive Oil Company LLC ... G ... 860 526-2205
Deep River *(G-2088)*
Lw Global LLC ... G ... 860 519-7134
Simsbury *(G-7632)*
New Canaan Olive Oil LLC ... G ... 845 240-3294
Stamford *(G-8322)*
Nsf Gourmet Products ... G ... 203 856-4995
Westport *(G-10129)*
Olive Capizzano Oils & Vinegar ... G ... 860 495-2187
Pawcatuck *(G-6721)*
Olive Chiappetta Oil LLC ... G ... 203 223-3655
Stamford *(G-8339)*
Olive Nutmeg Oil ... G ... 860 354-7300
New Milford *(G-5578)*
Olive Oil Factory LLC ... F ... 203 591-8986
Waterbury *(G-9570)*
Olive Oils and Balsamics LLC ... G ... 860 563-0105
Rocky Hill *(G-7260)*
Olive Sabor Oil Co ... G ... 860 922-7483
Somers *(G-7666)*
Shoreline Vine ... G ... 203 779-5331
Madison *(G-3957)*

2082 Malt Beverages

Alvarium Beer Company LLC ... G ... 860 306-3857
New Britain *(G-4943)*
Aspetuck Brew Lab LLC ... G ... 203 256-1902
Fairfield *(G-2749)*
Bear Hands Brewing Company ... G ... 860 576-5374
Central Village *(G-1336)*
Beerd Brewing Co LLC ... F ... 585 771-7428
Stonington *(G-8524)*
Brainard Brewing LLC ... G ... 860 324-5213
Mystic *(G-4802)*
Breakaway Brew Haus LLC ... G ... 860 647-9811
Bolton *(G-506)*
Brewery Legitimus LLC ... G ... 860 810-8894
Canton *(G-1307)*
British W Indies Trdg USA LLC ... G ... 704 451-8400
Litchfield *(G-3885)*
Brook Broad Brewing LLC ... F ... 860 623-1000
East Windsor *(G-2486)*
Cold Brew Coffee Company LLC ... G ... 860 250-4410
Cheshire *(G-1371)*
◆ Diageo Investment Corporation ... F ... 203 229-2100
Norwalk *(G-6139)*
East Rock Brewing Company LLC ... G ... 203 530-3484
New Haven *(G-5271)*
Easton Brewing Company LLC ... G ... 203 921-7263
Easton *(G-2550)*
Front Porch Brewing ... G ... 203 679-1096
Wallingford *(G-9272)*
▼ Guinness America Inc ... G ... 203 229-2100
Norwalk *(G-6188)*
Hamden Brewing Company LLC ... G ... 203 247-4677
Shelton *(G-7456)*
Kent Falls Brewing Company ... G ... 860 398-9645
Kent *(G-3823)*
New England Brewing Co LLC ... G ... 203 387-2222
Woodbridge *(G-10608)*
Nutmeg Brewing Rest Group LLC ... E ... 203 256-2337
Shelton *(G-7515)*
Outer Light Brewing Co LLC ... G ... 475 201-9972
Groton *(G-3302)*
Shoreline Brewing Company LLC ... G ... 203 225-7734
Shelton *(G-7554)*
Southport Brewing Co ... E ... 203 874-2337
Milford *(G-4649)*
Stetson Brewing Co Inc ... G ... 860 643-0257
Manchester *(G-4097)*
Swagnificent Ent LLC ... G ... 203 449-0124
Bridgeport *(G-918)*
Thimble Island Brewing Company ... E ... 203 208-2827
Branford *(G-663)*
▲ Thomas Hooker Brewing Co LLC ... E ... 860 242-3111
Bloomfield *(G-491)*
Willimantic Brewing Co LLC ... G ... 860 423-6777
Willimantic *(G-10239)*

2084 Wine & Brandy

Arrigoni Winery ... G ... 860 342-1999
Portland *(G-6950)*
Brignole Distillery LLC ... G ... 860 653-9463
East Granby *(G-2192)*
Brooke Taylor Winery LLC ... G ... 860 974-1263
Woodstock *(G-10659)*
Carlo Huber Selections Inc ... G ... 917 742-0601
Salisbury *(G-7294)*
Chamard Vineyards Inc ... G ... 860 664-0299
Clinton *(G-1493)*
Cocchia Norwalk Grape Co ... F ... 203 855-7911
Norwalk *(G-6119)*
Connecticut Valley Winery LLC ... G ... 860 489-9463
New Hartford *(G-5187)*
Connecticut Vineyard & Winery ... G ... 860 307-3550
West Hartford *(G-9794)*
Crush Club LLC ... G ... 203 626-9545
Wallingford *(G-9242)*
Di Grazia Vineyards Ltd ... G ... 203 775-1616
Brookfield *(G-1183)*
Diageo Americas Inc ... G ... 203 229-2100
Norwalk *(G-6137)*
◆ Diageo Americas Supply Inc ... G ... 203 229-2100
Norwalk *(G-6138)*
◆ Diageo North America Inc ... A ... 203 229-2100
Norwalk *(G-6140)*
Diageo PLC ... D ... 203 229-2100
Norwalk *(G-6141)*
▲ Edwards Wines LLC ... G ... 860 535-0202
North Stonington *(G-6023)*
Gouveia Vineyards LLC ... G ... 203 265-5526
Wallingford *(G-9277)*
Grapes of Norwalk ... G ... 203 845-9640
Norwalk *(G-6185)*
Haight Vineyard Inc ... G ... 860 567-4045
Litchfield *(G-3892)*
Hawk Ridge Winery LLC ... G ... 860 274-7440
Watertown *(G-9711)*

SIC

20 FOOD AND KINDRED PRODUCTS SIC SECTION

His Vineyard Inc....G....203 790-1600
Bethel (G-308)
▲ Horse Ridge Cellars LLC....G....860 763-5380
Somers (G-7661)
Kiro Bespoke LLC....G....203 981-4945
Middletown (G-4363)
Land of Nod Winery LLC....G....860 824-5225
East Canaan (G-2182)
Mattituck Vineyards LLC....G....203 637-4457
Riverside (G-7196)
Maugle Sierra Vineyards LLC....G....860 464-2987
Ledyard (G-3878)
Miranda Vineyard LLC....G....860 491-9906
Goshen (G-3103)
Northeast Vineyard Svcs LLC....G....860 872-8239
Tolland (G-8873)
Paradise Hlls Vnyrd Winery LLC....G....203 284-0123
Wallingford (G-9332)
Pozzi Fmly Wine & Spirits LLC....G....646 422-9134
Stamford (G-8369)
Preston Ridge Vineyard LLC....G....860 383-4278
Preston (G-6988)
Proof and Wood Ventures Inc....G....203 856-8680
New Canaan (G-5134)
Sharpe Hill Vineyard Inc....E....860 974-3549
Pomfret (G-6936)
Shelter Rock Winery....G....203 948-8235
Danbury (G-1945)
Stonington Vineyards Inc....G....860 535-1222
Stonington (G-8540)
Strawberry Ridge Vineyard Inc....G....860 868-0730
Cornwall Bridge (G-1621)
Sugar Creek Vineyard LLC....G....860 454-4219
Ellington (G-2603)
Sunset Hill Vineyard....G....860 598-9427
Lyme (G-3906)
Three Suns Ltd....G....860 233-7658
Hartford (G-3704)
Twelve Percent LLC....G....203 556-7024
North Haven (G-6002)
◆ UST LLC....G....203 817-3000
Stamford (G-8483)
Vineyard At Foxrun....G....860 779-0230
Brooklyn (G-1258)
Vineyard Brothers LLC....G....203 637-0381
Riverside (G-7204)
Vineyard Thimble....G....860 416-5115
Glastonbury (G-3093)
Vino Et Al LLC....G....203 405-3931
Stamford (G-8484)
White Silo Farm....G....860 355-0271
Sherman (G-7606)
Zoks Homebrewing & Winemaking....G....860 456-7704
Willimantic (G-10242)

2085 Liquors, Distilled, Rectified & Blended

American Distilling Inc....G....860 267-4444
Marlborough (G-4119)
▼ American Distilling Inc....D....860 267-4444
East Hampton (G-2253)
Asylum Distillery....G....203 209-0146
Southport (G-7999)
Cylinder Vodka Inc....G....203 979-0792
Stamford (G-8175)
Deep River Distillers LLC....G....860 788-6061
Cromwell (G-1700)
◆ Diageo North America Inc....A....203 229-2100
Norwalk (G-6140)
Diageo PLC....D....203 229-2100
Norwalk (G-6141)
Double Barrel Distillery LLC....G....860 285-0141
Windsor (G-10380)
Elm City Distillery LLC....G....203 285-8830
Ivoryton (G-3785)
Hartford Flavor Company LLC....G....860 604-9767
Hartford (G-3611)
Kra-Ze LLC....G....860 892-8025
Uncasville (G-9098)
Krystal Inc LLC....G....860 844-1267
Granby (G-3110)
Michael James Distler....G....203 241-4574
Redding (G-7102)
Millbrook Distillery LLC....G....203 637-2231
Cos Cob (G-1638)
Mine Hill Distillery....G....860 210-1872
Roxbury (G-7279)
Modern Distillery Age....G....203 971-8710
Norwalk (G-6263)
▲ Spirit of Hartford LLC....G....860 404-1776
Avon (G-115)

Waypoint Distillery....G....860 519-5390
Bloomfield (G-500)
Westford Hill Distillers LLC....G....860 429-0464
Ashford (G-69)

2086 Soft Drinks

Als Beverage Company Inc....E....860 627-7003
East Windsor (G-2480)
Als Holding Inc....G....860 627-7003
East Windsor (G-2481)
Averys Beverage LLC....G....860 224-0830
New Britain (G-4947)
B & E Juices Inc....E....203 333-1802
Bridgeport (G-707)
Bombadils Spirit Shop Inc....G....860 423-9661
Mansfield Center (G-4112)
Castle Beverages Inc....G....203 732-0883
Ansonia (G-27)
Cell Nique....G....888 417-9343
Weston (G-10022)
Coca-Cola Bottling....G....800 241-2653
East Hartford (G-2307)
Coca-Cola Company....G....860 443-2816
Waterford (G-9647)
Company of Coca-Cola Bottling....D....860 569-0037
East Hartford (G-2308)
Company of Coca-Cola Bottling....G....860 814-4241
Enfield (G-2630)
Company of Coca-Cola Bottling....D....203 905-3900
Stamford (G-8154)
▲ Crystal Rock Holdings Inc....E....860 945-0661
Watertown (G-9697)
▲ Crystal Rock Spring Water Co....B....860 945-0661
Watertown (G-9698)
Danone Holdings Inc....A....203 229-7000
Stamford (G-8179)
Derby Discount Liquor....G....203 732-0666
Derby (G-2111)
Drinking Water Div....G....860 509-7333
Hartford (G-3580)
Fishers Island Lemonade....G....860 306-3189
Mystic (G-4815)
Foxon Park Beverages Inc....G....203 467-7874
East Haven (G-2430)
Franklin Liquor Store....G....203 323-1356
Stamford (G-8208)
▲ G & G Beverage Distributors....D....203 949-6220
Wallingford (G-9273)
G I Package Store....G....203 624-4606
New Haven (G-5284)
Grand Fish Market LLC....G....203 691-8904
New Haven (G-5289)
Harvest Hill Holdings LLC....F....203 914-1620
Stamford (G-8230)
Hosmer Mountain Btlg Co Inc....G....860 643-6923
Manchester (G-4029)
Light Rock Spring Water Co....F....203 743-2251
Danbury (G-1874)
Miami Bay Beverage Company LLC....F....203 453-0090
Branford (G-626)
Natural Country Farms Inc....D....860 872-8346
Ellington (G-2597)
New Hartford Wine and Bev LLC....G....860 379-3764
New Hartford (G-5204)
▼ Newmans Own Inc....E....203 222-0136
Westport (G-10128)
Niagara Bottling LLC....G....909 226-7353
Bloomfield (G-450)
Pepsi Foods....G....860 567-5774
Litchfield (G-3898)
Pepsi-Cola Btlg of Wrcster Inc....E....860 774-4007
Dayville (G-2069)
Pepsi-Cola Metro Btlg Co Inc....B....203 375-2484
Stratford (G-8664)
Pepsi-Cola Metro Btlg Co Inc....E....860 848-1231
Uncasville (G-9102)
Pepsi-Cola Metro Btlg Co Inc....C....203 234-9014
North Haven (G-5975)
Pepsi-Cola Metro Btlg Co Inc....C....860 688-6281
Windsor (G-10418)
Pepsico....F....203 974-8912
New Haven (G-5360)
Pro Beverage Sales LLC....G....203 931-1029
New Haven (G-5372)
Red Bull LLC....G....860 519-1018
Bloomfield (G-474)
◆ Reeds Inc....E....203 890-0557
Norwalk (G-6318)
Shippan Liquors....G....203 348-0925
Stamford (G-8412)

▲ Sigg Switzerland (usa) Inc....G....203 321-1232
Stamford (G-8414)
Simply Originals LLC....G....203 273-3523
Norwalk (G-6351)
Subtle-T LLC....G....203 273-6061
Stamford (G-8447)
▲ Sweet Leaf Tea Company....F....203 863-0263
Stamford (G-8454)
Twelve Beverage LLC....G....203 256-8100
Fairfield (G-2859)
White Bridge Liquors Inc....G....203 655-0658
Darien (G-2051)

2087 Flavoring Extracts & Syrups

America Extract Corporation....F....860 267-4444
East Hampton (G-2252)
American Distilling Inc....G....860 267-4444
Marlborough (G-4119)
▼ American Distilling Inc....D....860 267-4444
East Hampton (G-2253)
Bep Flavor Holdings LLC....G....203 595-4520
Stamford (G-8110)
Brookside Flvors Ingrdents LLC....D....203 595-4520
Stamford (G-8120)
▲ Carrubba Incorporated....D....203 878-0605
Milford (G-4485)
◆ Charles Boggini Company LLC....G....860 742-2652
Coventry (G-1649)
Flavrz Organic Beverages LLC....G....203 716-8082
Darien (G-2026)
Focus Now Solutions LLC....G....203 247-9038
Fairfield (G-2786)
▲ Herbasway Laboratories LLC....E....203 269-6991
Wallingford (G-9280)
Jmf Group LLC....D....860 627-7003
East Windsor (G-2500)
K Chef Inc....G....646 778-8396
Waterbury (G-9514)
Metabev Inc....F....203 967-8502
Stamford (G-8307)
▲ Nobby Beverages Inc....G....860 747-3888
Plainville (G-6848)
▲ Osf Flavors Inc....F....860 298-8350
Windsor (G-10416)
Scitech International LLC....G....203 967-8502
Stamford (G-8404)
▲ Target Flavors Inc....F....203 775-4727
Brookfield (G-1228)
Transatlantic Bubbles LLC....G....203 464-0051
Woodbridge (G-10619)
◆ Watson LLC....B....203 932-3000
West Haven (G-9960)

2091 Fish & Seafoods, Canned & Cured

Bottarga Brothers LLC....G....203 355-1134
Stamford (G-8114)
Golden Oyster Company....G....203 929-3389
Shelton (G-7451)
◆ Greenport Foods LLC....F....203 221-2673
Westport (G-10093)
Tri-Union Seafoods LLC....G....203 426-1266
Newtown (G-5793)

2092 Fish & Seafoods, Fresh & Frozen

Coastal Seafoods Inc....F....203 431-0453
Fairfield (G-2765)
Rich Products Corporation....C....609 589-3049
New Britain (G-5045)
Saugatuck Kitchens LLC....G....203 334-1099
Stratford (G-8675)
Seafood Gourmet Inc....F....203 272-1544
Wolcott (G-10586)

2095 Coffee

Als Beverage Company Inc....E....860 627-7003
East Windsor (G-2480)
Ashlawn Farm Store....G....860 434-3636
Old Lyme (G-6490)
▲ B & B Ventures Ltd Lblty Co....E....203 481-1700
Branford (G-554)
Cote Dlvoire Imports....G....203 243-4841
Stratford (G-8600)
▲ Fjb America LLC....G....203 682-2424
Westport (G-10083)
Oasis Coffee Corp....E....203 847-0554
Norwalk (G-6283)
Omar Coffee Company....E....860 667-8889
Newington (G-5689)

SIC SECTION

Riseandshine Corporation ....F 917 599-7541
  Stamford (G-8393)
▲ Saccuzzo Company Inc ....G 860 665-1101
  Newington (G-5702)
Sacred Grunds Cof Roasters LLC ....G 860 717-2871
  Sherman (G-7604)
Tm Ward Co of Connecticut LLC ....G 203 866-9203
  Norwalk (G-6371)

2096 Potato Chips & Similar Prdts

Frito-Lay North America Inc ....A 860 412-1000
  Dayville (G-2063)
◆ Mediterranean Snack Fd Co LLC ......F 973 402-2644
  Stamford (G-8305)
▼ Old Lyme Gourmet Company ....E 860 434-7347
  Deep River (G-2097)
Severance Foods Inc ....E 860 724-7063
  Hartford (G-3684)
Smart Alex Foods LLC ....G 203 322-3368
  Stamford (G-8425)
U T Z ....G 860 383-4266
  North Franklin (G-5879)

2097 Ice

Dee Zee Ice LLC ....F 860 276-3500
  Southington (G-7912)
Dynaxa LLC ....G 203 300-5237
  Bethel (G-290)
Grotto Always Inc ....F 203 754-0295
  Waterbury (G-9491)
Leonard F Brooks ....G 203 335-4934
  Bridgeport (G-824)
▲ Olde Burnside Brewing Co LLC ....G 860 528-2200
  East Hartford (G-2349)
Twenty Five Commerce Inc ....G 203 866-0540
  Norwalk (G-6379)
◆ Vaporizer LLC ....E 860 564-7225
  Moosup (G-4784)

2098 Macaroni, Spaghetti & Noodles

▲ Carlas Pasta Inc ....C 860 436-4042
  South Windsor (G-7726)
Conopco Inc ....E 708 606-0540
  Trumbull (G-9014)
Grotto Always Inc ....F 203 754-0295
  Waterbury (G-9491)
Mecha Noodle Bar ....G 203 691-9671
  New Haven (G-5328)
Oasis Coffee Corp ....E 203 847-0554
  Norwalk (G-6283)
Roodle Rice & Noodle Bar ....G 203 269-9899
  Wallingford (G-9360)
◆ Thomas J Lipton Inc ....A 206 381-3500
  Trumbull (G-9081)
Villarina Pasta & Fine Foods ....G 203 917-4463
  Danbury (G-1972)

2099 Food Preparations, NEC

Amber Food Sales ....G 860 749-7272
  Enfield (G-2614)
Amodios Inc ....F 203 573-1229
  Waterbury (G-9430)
Atlantic Street Capitl MGT LLC ....E 203 428-3150
  Stamford (G-8098)
Balsam Woods Farm ....G 860 265-1800
  Stafford Springs (G-8018)
Bonney-Gee Cuisines ....G 203 372-3385
  Bridgeport (G-716)
Brothers & Sons Sugar House ....G 860 489-2719
  Torrington (G-8907)
Bureaus Sugar House ....G 860 434-5787
  Old Lyme (G-6492)
▲ Burlington Golf Center Inc ....G 860 675-7320
  Burlington (G-1262)
▲ Burnside Supermarket LLC ....G 860 291-9965
  East Hartford (G-2301)
Carriage House Companies Inc ....B 860 647-1909
  Manchester (G-3992)
Chen-Man Foods LLC ....G 860 659-9549
  Glastonbury (G-3020)
Chowder Pot of Hartford LLC ....G 860 244-3311
  Hartford (G-3566)
Clydes Cider Mill ....G 860 536-3354
  Mystic (G-4807)
Cofco Americas Resources Corp ....B 203 252-5200
  Stamford (G-8151)
Conopco Inc ....E 708 606-0540
  Trumbull (G-9014)

Crave Foods LLC ....G 203 227-6868
  Westport (G-10071)
Dp Foods L L C ....G 203 271-6212
  Cheshire (G-1382)
Dulcify LLC ....G 203 344-1671
  Riverside (G-7194)
Durantes Pasta Inc ....G 203 387-5560
  West Haven (G-9902)
Entrees Made Easy ....G 203 261-5777
  Monroe (G-4716)
Fabyan Sugar Shack LLC ....G 860 935-9281
  North Grosvenordale (G-5884)
Field Energy LLC ....G 860 817-2654
  West Hartford (G-9810)
Fine Food Services Inc ....E 860 445-5276
  Groton (G-3288)
First Chance Inc ....F 860 346-3663
  Middletown (G-4345)
Frescobene Foods LLC ....G 203 610-4688
  Fairfield (G-2788)
George Bailey ....G 860 423-2136
  Storrs (G-8549)
Global Palate Foods LLC ....G 203 543-3028
  Westport (G-10090)
Gracies Kitchens Inc ....F 203 773-0795
  New Haven (G-5288)
Grana Pastificio LLC ....G 203 979-2828
  Norwalk (G-6184)
Green Leaf Foods LLC ....G 860 657-4404
  Glastonbury (G-3043)
Guasa Salsa Vzla ....G 203 981-7011
  Norwalk (G-6187)
Harrison Farm ....G 203 488-7963
  North Branford (G-5842)
▲ Herbasway Laboratories LLC ....E 203 269-6991
  Wallingford (G-9280)
Hummel Bros Inc ....D 203 787-4113
  New Haven (G-5298)
Huntington Capital MGT LLC ....G 203 339-2126
  Shelton (G-7471)
Ikigai Foods LLC ....G 203 954-8083
  Shelton (G-7473)
Infinite Nutrition Inc ....G 203 940-1783
  Old Greenwich (G-6477)
Kerry R Wood ....G 203 221-7780
  Westport (G-10107)
Kohler Mix Specialties LLC ....C 860 666-1511
  Newington (G-5670)
Lawrence Mc Conney ....G 203 735-1133
  Derby (G-2118)
Lesser Evil ....G 203 529-3555
  Danbury (G-1872)
Loaves & Fishes Ministries ....G 860 524-1730
  Hartford (G-3630)
Local Traffic Fusion LLC ....G 203 938-8862
  Redding (G-7097)
Lyman Farm Incorporated ....C 860 349-1793
  Middlefield (G-4302)
Malta Food Pantry Inc ....G 860 725-0944
  Hartford (G-3632)
Maple Craft Foods LLC ....G 203 913-7066
  Sandy Hook (G-7321)
Mastriani Gourmet Food LLC ....G 203 368-9556
  Bridgeport (G-833)
Meals By Michael ....G 203 294-1770
  Wallingford (G-9316)
Mozzicato Pastry & Bake Shop ....E 860 296-0426
  Hartford (G-3646)
National Institutional Sup LLC ....G 203 263-3455
  Woodbury (G-10645)
◆ Nuovo Pasta Productions Ltd ....C 203 380-4090
  Stratford (G-8659)
Nutmeg Food Brokers LLC ....G 860 289-9566
  South Windsor (G-7797)
Nutriventus Inc ....G 860 990-9324
  Cromwell (G-1712)
Old Castle Foods LLC ....G 203 426-1344
  Newtown (G-5766)
Olive Flavored ....G 203 641-2086
  Meriden (G-4211)
Papas Maple Syrup ....G 860 379-0117
  New Hartford (G-5205)
Paridise Foods LLC ....G 203 283-3903
  Milford (G-4603)
Parma 1901 Usa Inc ....G 203 855-1356
  Norwalk (G-6291)
Peanut Butter and Jelly ....G 203 504-2280
  Stamford (G-8354)
Pepperidge Farm Incorporated ....C 860 286-6400
  Bloomfield (G-463)

◆ Pepperidge Farm Incorporated ....A 203 846-7000
  Norwalk (G-6298)
Podunk Popcorn ....G 860 648-9565
  South Windsor (G-7808)
Premiere Packg Partners LLC ....E 203 694-0003
  Waterbury (G-9586)
◆ RC Bigelow Inc ....C 888 244-3569
  Fairfield (G-2834)
Richard Walker ....G 860 267-7117
  East Hampton (G-2278)
Rivers Edge Sugar House ....G 860 429-1510
  Ashford (G-65)
Salsa Fresca New Haven ....G 301 675-6226
  New Haven (G-5386)
Skaarship Apiaries LLC ....G 203 805-9398
  Greenwich (G-3238)
Sodexo Inc ....E 860 679-2803
  Farmington (G-2958)
◆ Source Inc ....G 203 488-6400
  North Branford (G-5858)
Sovipe Food Distributors LLC ....G 203 648-2781
  Danbury (G-1954)
Supreme Storm Services LLC ....G 860 201-0642
  Southington (G-7983)
Swamp Yankee Products LLC ....G 203 720-1202
  Naugatuck (G-4923)
◆ Thomas J Lipton Inc ....A 206 381-3500
  Trumbull (G-9081)
Uncle Wileys Inc ....F 203 256-9313
  Fairfield (G-2860)
Unilever Ascc AG ....B 203 381-2482
  Shelton (G-7575)
Victors Hot House LLC ....G 203 264-0939
  Southbury (G-7882)
Vincent Jajer ....G 860 354-4747
  New Milford (G-5607)
Vinegar Syndrome LLC ....G 212 722-9755
  Bridgeport (G-934)
Vita Pasta Inc ....G 860 395-1452
  Old Saybrook (G-6577)
Whole G Food Intl Distrs LLC ....G 203 848-2136
  New Haven (G-5431)
Yumelish Food LLC ....G 203 522-6933
  Fairfield (G-2868)

21 TOBACCO PRODUCTS

2111 Cigarettes

Polep Distribution Services J ....G 203 378-2193
  Stratford (G-8666)
Smokey Mountain Chew Inc ....G 203 304-9200
  Sandy Hook (G-7330)

2121 Cigars

F D Grave & Son Inc ....G 203 239-9394
  North Haven (G-5939)
Foundation Cigar Company LLC ....F 203 738-9377
  Windsor (G-10387)
What A Life LLC ....G 860 632-1962
  Cromwell (G-1724)

2131 Tobacco, Chewing & Snuff

Bomboo LLC ....G 475 731-0865
  Norwalk (G-6096)
◆ Hay Island Holding Corporation ......C 203 656-8000
  Darien (G-2027)
Nordic American Smokeless Inc ....F 203 207-9977
  Danbury (G-1893)
◆ Nuway Tobacco Company ....D 860 289-6414
  South Windsor (G-7798)
Smokey Mountain Chew Inc ....G 203 656-1088
  Darien (G-2045)
US Smokeless Tobacco Co LLC ....D 203 661-1100
  Stamford (G-8482)
◆ UST LLC ....G 203 817-3000
  Stamford (G-8483)

2141 Tobacco Stemming & Redrying

Markowski Farm ....G 860 668-5033
  Suffield (G-8725)
UST ....F 203 661-1100
  Greenwich (G-3252)

22 TEXTILE MILL PRODUCTS

2211 Cotton, Woven Fabric

American Woolen Company Inc ....G 860 684-2766
  Stafford Springs (G-8017)

Employee Codes: A=Over 500 employees, B=251-500
C=101-250, D=51-100, E=20-50, F=10-19, G=1-9

Amy Coe Inc	G	203 227-9900	Norwalk *(G-6069)*
▲ Arnitex LLC	G	203 869-1406	Cos Cob *(G-1624)*
Atlantic Sail & Canvas Co	G	203 254-1315	Stratford *(G-8574)*
Baremore Canvas LLC	G	860 691-1402	East Lyme *(G-2463)*
Ben Barrett Canvas Service LLC	G	203 268-4315	Monroe *(G-4697)*
Blank Canvas Interiors LLC	G	203 226-5602	Weston *(G-10020)*
Coastal Canvas	G	203 270-7408	Sandy Hook *(G-7303)*
Creative Canvas LLC	G	860 559-8509	Lebanon *(G-3851)*
Custom Marine Canvas LLC	G	860 572-9547	Groton *(G-3281)*
D&R Marine Upholstery & Canvas	G	860 989-9646	Rocky Hill *(G-7232)*
◆ Dimension-Polyant Inc	E	860 928-8300	Putnam *(G-7039)*
Dominics Decorating Inc	G	203 838-1827	Norwalk *(G-6145)*
Donnas Canvas Creations	G	860 276-0327	Southington *(G-7916)*
Dune Denim LLC	G	203 241-5409	Bethel *(G-283)*
Eastern Canvas Works	G	860 245-9174	Willimantic *(G-10225)*
Exclusive Denim	G	203 549-9844	Fairfield *(G-2783)*
Island Style Mar Canvas Repr	G	707 338-8789	Norwalk *(G-6212)*
Janes Custom Canvas LLC	G	860 376-6778	Griswold *(G-3266)*
Lucky Enough Canvas	G	860 455-6994	Hampton *(G-3537)*
Mago Point Canvas	G	860 442-2111	Waterford *(G-9661)*
Marcia Jean Fabric and Cft LLC	G	203 273-1665	Old Greenwich *(G-6479)*
My Denim Queen	G	860 729-1142	Columbia *(G-1609)*
Mytyme LLC	G	860 327-2356	Windsor *(G-10411)*
Nautigirl Marine Canvas	G	203 891-8558	Orange *(G-6615)*
◆ North Sails Group LLC	D	203 874-7548	Milford *(G-4594)*
Offshore Canvas & Cushions LLC	G	860 442-7803	Waterford *(G-9665)*
Precision Canvas LLC	G	860 693-2353	Collinsville *(G-1600)*
▼ Scapa North America Inc	G	860 688-8000	Windsor *(G-10433)*
Seafarer Canvas	G	203 939-1872	Norwalk *(G-6338)*
Serge & Friends LLC	G	860 526-3882	Cromwell *(G-1718)*
Simply Canvas LLC	G	203 265-0659	Wallingford *(G-9368)*
Tassels	G	203 231-0973	Derby *(G-2128)*
Tom Voytek	G	203 367-3991	Bridgeport *(G-926)*
▲ Z-Medica LLC	D	203 294-0000	Wallingford *(G-9405)*

2221 Silk & Man-Made Fiber

A Wild Quilter	G	203 744-3405	Bethel *(G-255)*
Cap-Tech Products Inc	F	860 490-5078	Wethersfield *(G-10185)*
Challenge Sailcloth	G	860 871-8030	South Windsor *(G-7728)*
▼ Claremont Sales Corporation	E	860 349-4499	Durham *(G-2143)*
Deer Creek Fabrics Inc	G	203 964-0922	Stamford *(G-8183)*
◆ Deitsch Plastic Company Inc	D	203 934-6601	West Haven *(G-9896)*
◆ Dimension-Polyant Inc	E	860 928-8300	Putnam *(G-7039)*
Furs By Prezioso Ltd	G	203 230-2930	Hamden *(G-3449)*
G Thomas and Sons Inc	G	860 935-5174	North Grosvenordale *(G-5886)*
Hartford Artisans Weaving Ctr	G	860 727-5727	Hartford *(G-3605)*
Highlander Group Inc	G	860 298-8618	Windsor *(G-10394)*
▲ Nextec Applications Inc	G	203 661-1484	Greenwich *(G-3209)*
Noreaster Yachts Inc	G	203 877-4339	Milford *(G-4593)*
Peristere LLC	G	860 783-5301	Manchester *(G-4075)*
Sally Conant	F	203 878-3005	Orange *(G-6628)*
Satin Style LLC	G	203 287-5466	Hamden *(G-3507)*
Scarlethread LLC	G	860 528-0667	East Hartford *(G-2369)*
▲ Second Lac Inc	G	203 321-1221	Norwalk *(G-6341)*
▲ Swift Textile Metalizing LLC	D	860 243-1122	Bloomfield *(G-490)*
Top of Line Drapery & Uphl	G	203 348-0000	Stamford *(G-8470)*

2231 Wool, Woven Fabric

▲ Apparel Solutions Incorporated	G	203 226-8600	Bridgeport *(G-698)*
Bella Alpacas	G	860 946-3076	New Milford *(G-5510)*
Brook Burgis Alpacas LLC	G	203 605-0588	Canterbury *(G-1296)*
Chakana Sky Alpacas	G	860 204-1646	Chester *(G-1466)*
Chas W House & Sons Inc	D	860 673-2518	Unionville *(G-9112)*
Dominics Decorating Inc	G	203 838-1827	Norwalk *(G-6145)*
Drunk Alpaca LLC	G	646 415-4995	Riverside *(G-7193)*
Flatland Alpacas	G	860 376-4658	Griswold *(G-3264)*
Hidden Meadow Alpaca	G	203 262-1669	Southbury *(G-7856)*
Quinnipiac Valley Alpacas	G	203 271-0773	Cheshire *(G-1433)*
Roaring Acres Alpacas LLC	G	860 668-7075	Suffield *(G-8734)*
Round Hill Alpacas LLC	G	860 742-5195	Coventry *(G-1672)*
▼ Scapa North America Inc	G	860 688-8000	Windsor *(G-10433)*

2241 Fabric Mills, Cotton, Wool, Silk & Man-Made

◆ Brockway Ferry Corporation	G	860 767-8231	Essex *(G-2713)*
H-O Products Corporation	E	860 379-9875	Winsted *(G-10523)*
Mbs Web Creations	G	203 521-0642	Bridgeport *(G-834)*
National Ribbon LLC	G	860 742-6966	Coventry *(G-1664)*

2252 Hosiery, Except Women's

Human Interests LLC	G	203 270-9107	Newtown *(G-5749)*
Mosley Hosiery and Socks LLC	G	860 690-9227	Bloomfield *(G-447)*
Shock Sock Inc LLC	G	860 680-7252	Farmington *(G-2956)*
Soldier Socks	G	203 832-2005	Stamford *(G-8428)*
Tommy LLC Sock It	G	860 688-2019	Windsor *(G-10454)*

2253 Knit Outerwear Mills

Cozy Pants LLC	G	860 267-7507	Cobalt *(G-1537)*
Ida Dean	G	860 482-3589	Torrington *(G-8934)*
Kielo America Inc	G	203 431-3999	Ridgefield *(G-7153)*
Malia Mills Swim Wear	G	203 622-3137	Greenwich *(G-3198)*
Sophia Swim Wear LLC	G	203 481-9397	North Branford *(G-5857)*

2254 Knit Underwear Mills

Baby Knits and More	G	860 485-0146	Harwinton *(G-3721)*

2257 Circular Knit Fabric Mills

▲ Swift Textile Metalizing LLC	D	860 243-1122	Bloomfield *(G-490)*

2258 Lace & Warp Knit Fabric Mills

Lisas Clover Hill Quilts LLC	G	860 828-9325	Berlin *(G-195)*
Novelty Textile Mills LLC	G	860 774-5000	Waterford *(G-9664)*

2259 Knitting Mills, NEC

Cunningham Tech LLC	G	860 738-8759	Pine Meadow *(G-6733)*
Fashion Home Products	G	860 274-0824	Watertown *(G-9706)*

2261 Cotton Fabric Finishers

Bushy Hill Nature Center	G	860 767-2148	Ivoryton *(G-3784)*
To Give Is Better	G	860 261-5443	Bristol *(G-1129)*
Ultimate Ink LLC	G	203 762-0602	Wilton *(G-10339)*

2262 Silk & Man-Made Fabric Finishers

Lmj Designs Inc	G	845 363-1120	Norwalk *(G-6235)*
▲ Nextec Applications Inc	G	203 661-1484	Greenwich *(G-3209)*
Smyth Ink	G	203 801-4335	New Canaan *(G-5143)*
Tees & More LLC	G	860 244-2224	Hartford *(G-3700)*
Yankee Screen Printing	G	203 924-9926	Derby *(G-2133)*

2269 Textile Finishers, NEC

▲ Brookwood Laminating Inc	D	860 774-5001	Wauregan *(G-9752)*
Gorilla Graphics Inc	F	860 704-8208	Middletown *(G-4348)*
Grand Embroidery Inc	F	203 888-7484	Oxford *(G-6663)*
Sterling Name Tape Company	G	860 379-5142	Winsted *(G-10540)*

2273 Carpets & Rugs

Aj Mfg	G	860 963-7622	Thompson *(G-8828)*
▲ Alliance Carpet Cushion Co	D	860 489-4273	Torrington *(G-8889)*
American Veteran Textile LLC	G	203 583-0576	Ansonia *(G-19)*
▲ Apricot Home LLC	G	203 552-1791	Greenwich *(G-3121)*
◆ Ethan Allen Retail Inc	B	203 743-8000	Danbury *(G-1818)*
Graphic Memories By McKie	G	860 434-5222	Old Lyme *(G-6511)*
▲ Holland & Sherry Inc	F	212 628-1950	Norwalk *(G-6201)*
Joseph Cohn Son Tile Trazo LLC	E	203 772-2420	North Haven *(G-5955)*
Mohawk Industries Inc	C	203 739-0260	Danbury *(G-1888)*
Mohawk Industries Inc	G	706 629-7721	Torrington *(G-8950)*
New Haven Companies Inc	F	203 469-6421	East Haven *(G-2444)*
Rosemary Hallgarten Inc	G	203 259-1003	Fairfield *(G-2838)*
Rugsalecom LLC	G	860 756-0959	West Hartford *(G-9853)*
Srirret America	G	203 988-1852	Madison *(G-3961)*
Valentine Co LLC	G	203 245-9145	Madison *(G-3967)*
▲ Wool Solutions Inc	G	203 845-0921	Norwalk *(G-6400)*
Yankee Peddler	G	860 663-0526	Killingworth *(G-3840)*

2281 Yarn Spinning Mills

Buffalo Industrial Fabrics Inc	G	203 553-9400	Wilton *(G-10278)*

2282 Yarn Texturizing, Throwing, Twisting & Winding Mills

Altenergy LLC .... G 203 299-1400
  Norwalk *(G-6066)*
Dwelling LLC .... G 860 521-1935
  West Hartford *(G-9802)*
Personally Yours .... G 203 329-6645
  Stamford *(G-8358)*

2284 Thread Mills

J Arnold Mittleman .... E 860 346-6562
  Middletown *(G-4356)*
Terris Affordable Embroidery .... G 860 928-0552
  Putnam *(G-7073)*
Thread Mill Partners LLC .... G 860 495-5319
  Pawcatuck *(G-6727)*

2295 Fabrics Coated Not Rubberized

Advanced Def Slutions Tech LLC ... G 860 243-1122
  Bloomfield *(G-380)*
American Metaseal of Conn .... G 203 787-0281
  Hamden *(G-3414)*
◆ Au New Haven LLC .... C 203 468-0342
  New Haven *(G-5238)*
▲ Brookwood Laminating Inc .... D 860 774-5001
  Wauregan *(G-9752)*
Composites Inc .... G 860 646-1698
  Manchester *(G-3997)*
◆ Defender Industries Inc .... C 860 701-3400
  Waterford *(G-9652)*
◆ Deitsch Plastic Company Inc .... G 203 934-6601
  West Haven *(G-9896)*
Emson Inc .... G 860 489-6249
  Torrington *(G-8922)*
▲ Nextec Applications Inc .... G 203 661-1484
  Greenwich *(G-3209)*
▲ Second Lac Inc .... G 203 321-1221
  Norwalk *(G-6341)*
▲ Swift Textile Metalizing LLC .... D 860 243-1122
  Bloomfield *(G-490)*
Trelleborg Ctd Systems US Inc .... C 203 468-0342
  New Haven *(G-5421)*

2296 Tire Cord & Fabric

◆ United Abrasives Inc .... B 860 456-7131
  North Windham *(G-6040)*

2297 Fabrics, Nonwoven

Lydall Inc .... E 860 646-1233
  Manchester *(G-4050)*
Lydall Thermal Acoustical Inc ...... G 860 646-1233
  Manchester *(G-4051)*
New England Nonwovens LLC ..... F 203 891-0851
  West Haven *(G-9939)*
▼ Suominen US Holding Inc .... F 860 386-8001
  East Windsor *(G-2524)*
▲ Swift Textile Metalizing LLC ...... D 860 243-1122
  Bloomfield *(G-490)*
Web Industries Inc .... G 860 779-3403
  Dayville *(G-2079)*
◆ Windsor Locks Nonwovens Inc ... E 860 292-5600
  East Windsor *(G-2533)*
▲ Xamax Industries Inc .... E 203 888-7200
  Seymour *(G-7375)*

2298 Cordage & Twine

▲ Brownell & Company Inc .... F 860 873-8625
  Moodus *(G-4771)*
▲ Custom Plastic Distrs Inc .... G 860 779-5833
  Dayville *(G-2060)*
Detotec North America Inc .... G 860 230-0078
  Moosup *(G-4778)*
▲ Detotec North America Inc .... G 860 564-1012
  Sterling *(G-8509)*
East Shre Wre Rpe/Rggng Spply ... F 203 469-5204
  North Haven *(G-5934)*
◆ International Cordage East Ltd ... D 860 873-5000
  Colchester *(G-1555)*
◆ Loos & Co Inc .... B 860 928-7981
  Pomfret *(G-6933)*
Nca Inc .... G 860 974-2310
  Abington *(G-1)*
▲ Woodstock Line Co .... F 860 928-6557
  Putnam *(G-7080)*

2299 Textile Goods, NEC

A & P Coat Apron & Lin Sup Inc ... D 914 840-3200
  Hartford *(G-3542)*

A Al Harding .... G 203 238-1993
  Meriden *(G-4137)*
Advanced Linen Group .... F 203 877-3896
  Milford *(G-4441)*
Batters Box .... G 203 845-0212
  Norwalk *(G-6087)*
D & J Textile LLC .... G 203 569-7754
  Stamford *(G-8177)*
▲ Engineered Fibers Tech LLC .... F 203 922-1810
  Shelton *(G-7440)*
▼ H&H Engineered Solutions Inc ... G 860 575-0005
  Old Saybrook *(G-6537)*
Heidi M Greene Inc .... G 203 938-4132
  Redding *(G-7094)*
J & S Fashion .... G 203 572-0154
  Bridgeport *(G-795)*
New Haven Companies Inc .... F 203 469-6421
  East Haven *(G-2444)*
Wilhelm Gdale Elzabeth Designs ... G 203 371-8787
  Bridgeport *(G-937)*

23 APPAREL AND OTHER FINISHED PRODUCTS MADE FROM FABRICS AND SIMILAR MATERIAL

2311 Men's & Boys' Suits, Coats & Overcoats

▼ Bayer Clothing Group Inc .... D 203 661-4140
  Greenwich *(G-3131)*
Bella Hispaniola Entps LLC .... G 860 628-0105
  Southington *(G-7895)*
▲ Corinth Acquisition Corp .... G 203 504-6260
  Stamford *(G-8161)*
Front Line Apparel Group LLC ..... C 860 859-3524
  Hebron *(G-3749)*
Peter Dermer Co .... G 203 389-3297
  Woodbridge *(G-10612)*
Sassone Labwear LLC .... G 860 666-4484
  Bridgeport *(G-896)*
Shoreline Segway Inc .... G 203 453-6036
  Guilford *(G-3391)*
Stevens Industries Inc .... E 203 966-7555
  New Canaan *(G-5147)*

2321 Men's & Boys' Shirts

Fezza Inc .... G 203 222-9721
  Weston *(G-10026)*
Lawes International Group LLC ... G 860 808-4981
  Hartford *(G-3626)*
▲ MB Sport LLC .... F 203 966-1985
  New Canaan *(G-5118)*
Sportco Inc .... G 631 244-4513
  New Canaan *(G-5146)*

2323 Men's & Boys' Neckwear

Barnard-Maine Ltd .... G 860 535-9485
  Stonington *(G-8523)*
Xmi Corporation .... G 800 838-0424
  Greenwich *(G-3262)*

2325 Men's & Boys' Separate Trousers & Casual Slacks

▼ Bayer Clothing Group Inc .... D 203 661-4140
  Greenwich *(G-3131)*
Guess Inc .... G 860 629-0835
  Mashantucket *(G-4132)*
Lawes International Group LLC ... G 860 808-4981
  Hartford *(G-3626)*

2326 Men's & Boys' Work Clothing

A Gerber Corp .... G 203 918-1913
  Stamford *(G-8051)*
Childrens Medical Group .... E 860 242-8330
  Bloomfield *(G-402)*
Cintas Corporation .... F 203 272-2036
  Cheshire *(G-1370)*
▲ Dbebz Apparel LLC .... G 203 254-7356
  Fairfield *(G-2772)*
Doctors Clothes .... G 203 485-0494
  Greenwich *(G-3154)*
G&K Services LLC .... G 860 856-4400
  Hartford *(G-3596)*
Sassone Labwear LLC .... G 860 666-4484
  Bridgeport *(G-896)*
▲ Sewn In America Inc .... D 203 438-9149
  Ridgefield *(G-7172)*
Stevens Industries Inc .... E 203 966-7555
  New Canaan *(G-5147)*

2329 Men's & Boys' Clothing, NEC

Custom Sportswear Mfg .... G 203 879-4420
  Wolcott *(G-10559)*
◆ Cycling Sports Group Inc .... D 608 268-8916
  Wilton *(G-10287)*
Del Arbour LLC .... F 203 882-8501
  Milford *(G-4506)*
Everest Isles LLC .... G 203 561-5128
  Wallingford *(G-9259)*
Fiddle Horse Farm LLC .... G 203 557-3285
  Westport *(G-10080)*
Flemming LLC .... G 818 746-6495
  Bloomfield *(G-411)*
Gg Sportswear Inc .... E 860 296-4441
  Hartford *(G-3599)*
Gima LLC .... E 860 296-4441
  Hartford *(G-3600)*
▲ K&P Weaver LLC .... G 203 795-9024
  Orange *(G-6605)*
Marmot Mountain LLC .... G 203 869-0162
  Greenwich *(G-3199)*
Nomis Enterprises .... G 631 821-3120
  Wallingford *(G-9327)*
Shield Group .... G 203 981-6169
  Wilton *(G-10329)*
Tribal Wear .... G 203 637-7884
  Riverside *(G-7202)*
▲ Turq LLC .... G 203 344-1257
  Riverside *(G-7203)*
Under Armour Inc .... G 203 237-6031
  Mashantucket *(G-4133)*

2331 Women's & Misses' Blouses

Fyc Apparel Group LLC .... E 203 466-6525
  East Haven *(G-2432)*
▲ Fyc Apparel Group LLC .... D 203 481-2420
  Branford *(G-599)*
M S B International Ltd .... G 203 466-6525
  Branford *(G-620)*

2335 Women's & Misses' Dresses

▲ Fyc Apparel Group LLC .... D 203 481-2420
  Branford *(G-599)*
Kallai Designs .... G 860 653-6786
  Granby *(G-3109)*
Lady and The Leopard .... G 413 531-4811
  West Suffield *(G-9987)*
Lawes International Group LLC ... G 860 808-4981
  Hartford *(G-3626)*
M S B International Ltd .... G 203 466-6525
  Branford *(G-620)*
Nubridal .... G 860 768-5745
  Hartford *(G-3658)*
Runway Liquidation LLC .... G 202 865-3311
  Cromwell *(G-1716)*
Runway Liquidation LLC .... G 202 544-1900
  Brookfield *(G-1220)*
Runway Liquidation LLC .... G 202 466-2050
  Bristol *(G-1115)*
Runway Liquidation LLC .... G 239 337-2020
  Trumbull *(G-9067)*
Runway Liquidation LLC .... G 302 998-0551
  Bloomfield *(G-482)*
Runway Liquidation LLC .... G 561 391-3334
  Enfield *(G-2688)*
Runway Liquidation LLC .... G 561 279-4444
  Simsbury *(G-7643)*

2337 Women's & Misses' Suits, Coats & Skirts

▼ Bayer Clothing Group Inc .... D 203 661-4140
  Greenwich *(G-3131)*
▲ Fyc Apparel Group LLC .... D 203 481-2420
  Branford *(G-599)*
M S B International Ltd .... G 203 466-6525
  Branford *(G-620)*
▲ MB Sport LLC .... F 203 966-1985
  New Canaan *(G-5118)*
Nine West Holdings Inc .... G 860 669-3799
  Clinton *(G-1516)*
Sara Campbell Ltd .... G 203 966-5488
  New Canaan *(G-5139)*

2339 Women's & Misses' Outerwear, NEC

Blush By London .... G 860 610-9891
  Hartford *(G-3557)*
Cjbows .... G 860 287-5053
  Waterford *(G-9645)*

23 APPAREL AND OTHER FINISHED PRODUCTS MADE FROM FABRICS AND SIMILAR MATERIAL — SIC SECTION

Creative Enhancement Inc .... E 860 833-8493
  West Hartford (G-9795)
Custom Sportswear Mfg .... G 203 879-4420
  Wolcott (G-10559)
Del Arbour LLC .... F 203 882-8501
  Milford (G-4506)
Fiddle Horse Farm LLC .... G 203 557-3285
  Westport (G-10080)
Gg Sportswear Inc .... E 860 296-4441
  Hartford (G-3599)
Mangladesh LLC .... G 203 299-0697
  Fairfield (G-2812)
South Beach Inc .... G 860 953-0038
  West Hartford (G-9859)
Teta Activewear By Custom .... G 203 879-4420
  Wolcott (G-10591)
Tribal Wear .... G 203 637-7884
  Riverside (G-7202)

2341 Women's, Misses' & Children's Underwear & Nightwear

Arensky Group Inc .... G 203 919-1575
  Norwalk (G-6073)
M S B International Ltd .... G 203 466-6525
  Branford (G-620)

2342 Brassieres, Girdles & Garments

◆ Donghia Inc .... D 800 366-4442
  Milford (G-4514)

2353 Hats, Caps & Millinery

◆ 32 Degrees LLC .... G 978 602-2007
  West Hartford (G-9768)
April Rose Designs .... G 203 453-1797
  Guilford (G-3326)
Drinkin Hats LLC .... G 203 265-3489
  Wallingford (G-9253)
▲ Indigo Coast Inc .... G 860 592-0088
  Kent (G-3822)
Manup LLC .... G 203 588-9861
  Norwalk (G-6246)
New England Cap Company .... F 203 736-6184
  Seymour (G-7358)

2361 Children's & Infants' Dresses & Blouses

CPC Childrenswear Inc .... G 203 286-6204
  Norwalk (G-6131)
Crafty Baby Tm LLC .... G 203 921-1179
  Stamford (G-8164)

2369 Girls' & Infants' Outerwear, NEC

Aquatic Technologies Inc .... G 203 770-6791
  Brookfield (G-1160)
▲ One Kid LLC .... G 203 254-9978
  Westport (G-10132)
One Kid LLC .... G 203 254-9978
  Fairfield (G-2824)
WEI WEI Fashions Inc .... G 646 322-2599
  Greenwich (G-3256)

2371 Fur Goods

Sherwood Group Inc .... F 203 227-5288
  Westport (G-10156)
Varpro Inc .... E 203 227-6876
  Westport (G-10171)

2381 Dress & Work Gloves

Fabric Bty Inc .... G 203 845-7966
  Norwalk (G-6160)

2384 Robes & Dressing Gowns

◆ Graduation Solutions LLC .... E 914 934-5991
  Greenwich (G-3168)
Lawes International Group LLC .... G 860 808-4981
  Hartford (G-3626)
M S B International Ltd .... G 203 466-6525
  Branford (G-620)

2385 Waterproof Outerwear

Wrenfield Group Inc .... E 203 438-0090
  Ridgefield (G-7186)

2386 Leather & Sheep Lined Clothing

Dj Sportsware .... G 203 438-0078
  Ridgefield (G-7136)

2387 Apparel Belts

Boxtree Accessories Inc .... G 203 637-5794
  Old Greenwich (G-6468)
▲ Dooney & Bourke Inc .... E 203 853-7515
  Norwalk (G-6146)
Karen Callan Designs Inc .... G 203 762-9914
  Greenwich (G-3186)

2389 Apparel & Accessories, NEC

Alan M Crane .... G 860 608-2788
  Norwich (G-6405)
Benji Billionaire .... G 203 361-7744
  New Haven (G-5242)
Bleshue LLC .... G 203 405-1034
  Woodbury (G-10627)
Btf LLC .... G 860 354-8926
  Bridgewater (G-945)
Classic School Uniforms Ltd .... G 860 677-7207
  Farmington (G-2889)
De Muerte Usa LLC .... G 860 331-7085
  Hartford (G-3577)
▲ Fairway and Greene Inc .... G 203 926-1881
  Shelton (G-7443)
Hawie Manufacturing Company .... G 203 366-4303
  Bridgeport (G-783)
▲ Launell Inc .... G 203 340-2150
  Greenwich (G-3189)
M H Pierce & Co .... G 203 327-2970
  Stamford (G-8293)
Malabar Bay LLC .... G 203 359-9714
  Stamford (G-8294)
Mandee .... G 860 644-2128
  Manchester (G-4054)
Matrix Apparel Group LLC .... G 203 740-7837
  New Fairfield (G-5171)
Michael Kors .... G 203 748-4300
  Danbury (G-1884)
Mommy & ME .... G 860 269-6226
  Unionville (G-9121)
My Fair Lady .... G 860 322-4542
  Deep River (G-2095)
New Deal LLC .... G 860 648-9567
  Manchester (G-4060)
Ricco Vishnu .... G 203 449-0124
  Bridgeport (G-890)
Strapless Suspenders .... G 203 709-0992
  Waterbury (G-9608)
Style and Grace LLC .... G 917 751-2043
  Westport (G-10161)
▲ Tommys Supplies LLC .... G 860 265-2199
  Somers (G-7674)

2391 Curtains & Draperies

A Change of Scenery .... G 860 872-4435
  Ellington (G-2569)
Blue Lily Cotton LLC .... G 860 869-7734
  Milford (G-4473)
Byron Lord Inc .... G 203 287-9881
  Old Lyme (G-6493)
Chatham Drapery Co Inc .... G 860 267-7767
  East Hampton (G-2261)
Decorator Services Inc .... E 203 384-8144
  Bridgeport (G-743)
Dominics Decorating Inc .... G 203 838-1827
  Norwalk (G-6145)
Draperies Plus .... G 203 589-3634
  Bristol (G-1019)
Lyons Upholstery Shop Inc .... G 203 269-3782
  Wallingford (G-9308)
R L Fisher Inc .... D 860 951-8110
  Hartford (G-3674)
Scott C Parker .... G 860 355-9738
  Roxbury (G-7283)
Sew Beautiful Win Treatments .... G 203 598-0544
  Middlebury (G-4291)
Tetrault & Sons Inc .... G 860 872-9187
  Stafford Springs (G-8042)
Thomas W Raftery Inc .... E 860 278-9870
  Hartford (G-3703)
Threads of Evidence LLC .... G 203 929-5209
  Shelton (G-7566)
Top of Line Drapery & Uphl .... G 203 348-0000
  Stamford (G-8470)
Yard Stick Decore .... F 203 330-0360
  Bridgeport (G-943)

2392 House furnishings: Textile

Artemisia Inc .... G 917 797-7644
  Old Lyme (G-6489)
Beautiful Tables LLC .... G 203 602-9969
  Stamford (G-8108)
Dominics Decorating Inc .... G 203 838-1827
  Norwalk (G-6145)
▼ Hills Point Industries LLC .... G 917 515-8650
  Westport (G-10095)
◆ Latex Foam International LLC .... D 203 924-0700
  Shelton (G-7487)
Laura Spector Rustic Design .... G 203 254-3952
  Fairfield (G-2809)
Nesola Scarves LLC .... G 203 288-5058
  Cheshire (G-1419)
Patricia Spratt For Home LLC .... F 860 434-9291
  Old Lyme (G-6517)
R L Fisher Inc .... D 860 951-8110
  Hartford (G-3674)
Riverside Seat Cover Inc .... G 203 661-7893
  Cos Cob (G-1640)
Sammi Sleeping Systems LLC .... G 203 684-3131
  New Haven (G-5388)
Stephen Smith .... G 405 420-2226
  Eastford (G-2543)
Thomas W Raftery Inc .... E 860 278-9870
  Hartford (G-3703)
Upon A Once Pillow LLC .... G 203 222-1717
  Westport (G-10170)

2393 Textile Bags

American Marketing Group Inc .... G 203 367-2378
  Bridgeport (G-693)
Dayton Bag & Burlap Co .... G 860 653-8191
  East Granby (G-2202)
▲ Dow Cover Company Incorporated D 203 469-5394
  New Haven (G-5269)
Island Style Mar Canvas Repr .... G 707 338-8789
  Norwalk (G-6212)
Krutch Pack LLC .... G 860 836-1745
  Newington (G-5671)
Live and Dream Green LLC .... G 860 670-0870
  Avon (G-91)
Smiling Dog .... G 860 344-0707
  Middletown (G-4419)
Uninsred Alttude Cnnection Inc .... G 860 333-1461
  Brooklyn (G-1257)
Zhao LLC .... G 401 864-7186
  Stamford (G-8506)

2394 Canvas Prdts

3333 LLC .... G 860 643-1384
  Manchester (G-3971)
Ace Sailmakers .... G 860 739-5999
  East Lyme (G-2462)
American Sign Inc .... E 203 624-2991
  New Haven (G-5229)
Awnings Plus LLC .... G 860 496-7996
  Torrington (G-8899)
B and G Enterprise LLC .... G 203 562-7232
  New Haven (G-5239)
Branford Auto & Marine Center .... G 203 481-6572
  Branford (G-562)
Canvas LLC .... G 860 986-8553
  West Hartford (G-9784)
Canvas Products .... G 203 225-0507
  Shelton (G-7411)
▲ Commercial Sewing Inc .... C 860 482-5509
  Torrington (G-8913)
Connecticut Canvas Works .... G 860 295-9924
  Marlborough (G-4122)
Custom Covers .... G 860 669-4169
  Clinton (G-1499)
Custom Marine Canvas LLC .... G 860 572-9547
  Groton (G-3281)
◆ Defender Industries Inc .... C 860 701-3400
  Waterford (G-9652)
◆ Dimension-Polyant Inc .... E 860 928-8300
  Putnam (G-7039)
Economy Canvas Co .... G 860 289-5281
  Hartford (G-3582)
Evans Fabrication .... G 203 791-9517
  Bethel (G-298)
Fairclough Sailmakers Inc .... G 203 787-2322
  New Haven (G-5281)
Farrar Sails Inc .... G 860 447-0382
  New London (G-5471)
Fitzgerald-Norwalk Awning Co .... G 203 847-5858
  Norwalk (G-6169)
Genvario Awning Co .... G 203 847-5858
  Norwalk (G-6179)
Island Style Mar Canvas Repr .... G 707 338-8789
  Norwalk (G-6212)

SIC SECTION 23 APPAREL AND OTHER FINISHED PRODUCTS MADE FROM FABRICS AND SIMILAR MATERIAL

Kappa Sails LLC....G.... 860 399-8899
Gales Ferry *(G-2985)*
Liberty Services LLC....G.... 860 399-0077
Westbrook *(G-10002)*
▲ **Lubbert Supply Company LLC**....G.... 203 690-1105
Milford *(G-4570)*
Mbm Sales....F.... 203 866-3674
Norwalk *(G-6252)*
Meriden Awning & Decorating Co....G.... 203 634-0067
Meriden *(G-4194)*
Miller Marine Canvas....G.... 203 878-9291
Milford *(G-4582)*
New Haven Companies Inc....F.... 203 469-6421
East Haven *(G-2444)*
◆ **North Sails Group LLC**....D.... 203 874-7548
Milford *(G-4594)*
Rp3 Canvas LLC....G.... 860 225-7140
New Britain *(G-5050)*
Sail Spars Design LLC....G.... 860 429-9866
Storrs Mansfield *(G-8559)*
Seafarer Canvas....F.... 203 853-2624
Norwalk *(G-6339)*
▲ **Second Lac Inc**....G.... 203 321-1221
Norwalk *(G-6341)*
Sharp Canvas....G.... 860 526-2302
Chester *(G-1484)*
◆ **Shelterlogic Corp**....C.... 860 945-6442
Watertown *(G-9733)*
Slogic Holding Corp....G.... 203 966-2800
New Canaan *(G-5142)*
Soapstone Media Inc....G.... 860 749-0455
Somers *(G-7669)*
State Awning Company....G.... 860 246-2575
Hartford *(G-3692)*
Stonington Custom Canvas LLC....G.... 860 213-1240
Stonington *(G-8539)*
Tetrault & Sons Inc....G.... 860 872-9187
Stafford Springs *(G-8042)*
▲ **Toff Industry Inc**....G.... 860 378-0532
Milldale *(G-4689)*
Topside Canvas Upholstery....G.... 860 399-4845
Westbrook *(G-10011)*
W H Preuss Sons Incorporated....G.... 860 643-9492
Bolton *(G-521)*
Watertown Canvas and Awng LLC....G.... 860 274-0933
Oakville *(G-6467)*
William A Weinert Canvas....G.... 203 595-0580
Stamford *(G-8493)*
Window Pdts Awngs Blind Shade....G.... 203 481-9772
Branford *(G-676)*

2395 Pleating & Stitching For The Trade

A Dancing Thread....G.... 860 669-9094
Clinton *(G-1489)*
A2z Embroidery....G.... 860 747-9849
Plainville *(G-6762)*
Ad Embroidery LLC....G.... 860 653-9553
East Granby *(G-2187)*
Ad Embroidery LLC....G.... 860 651-4410
West Simsbury *(G-9971)*
Al-Lynn Sales LLC....G.... 203 922-7840
Shelton *(G-7390)*
All American Embroidery....G.... 203 906-9656
Monroe *(G-4691)*
All League Embroidery....G.... 203 377-7215
Stratford *(G-8567)*
American Eagle Embroidery LLC....G.... 203 239-7906
North Haven *(G-5901)*
American Embroidery....G.... 860 829-8586
Berlin *(G-156)*
American Stitch & Print Inc....G.... 203 239-5383
North Haven *(G-5902)*
ARC Services....G.... 203 264-0866
Southbury *(G-7844)*
Artwork Embroidery....G.... 860 620-0456
Southington *(G-7892)*
Baa Creations....G.... 860 464-1339
Ledyard *(G-3869)*
Bdg Embroidery....G.... 203 258-0175
Fairfield *(G-2751)*
Bruce Park Sports EMB LLC....G.... 203 853-4488
Norwalk *(G-6100)*
Cameo Embroidery....G.... 860 301-3123
Durham *(G-2140)*
Cjs Embroidery LLC....G.... 203 650-9066
Bridgeport *(G-735)*
CK Imaging and Embroidery....G.... 716 984-1957
Burlington *(G-1264)*
Connecticut Screen Print....G.... 203 877-6655
Milford *(G-4498)*
Cook Print....G.... 203 855-8785
Norwalk *(G-6129)*
Designs In Stitches Embroidery....G.... 203 730-1013
Danbury *(G-1793)*
Dr Stitch Seamstress To Stars....G.... 706 631-0859
New Britain *(G-4975)*
Earth Loving Stitches....G.... 405 833-9343
Bristol *(G-1025)*
Embroidery Wizard....G.... 860 379-3294
Winsted *(G-10519)*
Embroidery Works....G.... 800 681-0805
Berlin *(G-177)*
Embroidery World Inc....G.... 203 281-7303
Hamden *(G-3445)*
Expert Embroidery....F.... 203 269-9675
Wallingford *(G-9264)*
Eyelets For Industry Inc....G.... 203 754-6502
Waterbury *(G-9478)*
Fernellie LLC....G.... 860 799-7739
New Milford *(G-5534)*
Forsa Team Sports LLC....G.... 203 466-2890
East Haven *(G-2429)*
Gem Embroidery....G.... 860 326-0676
Ledyard *(G-3873)*
Gg Sportswear Inc....E.... 860 296-4441
Hartford *(G-3599)*
Grand Embroidery Inc....F.... 203 888-7484
Oxford *(G-6663)*
Guidera Marketing Services....E.... 860 599-8880
Pawcatuck *(G-6713)*
H J Hoffman Company....G.... 203 853-7740
Norwalk *(G-6189)*
Hilversum Embroidery....G.... 860 729-8532
Middletown *(G-4351)*
Hot Tops LLC....F.... 203 926-2067
Shelton *(G-7466)*
Initial Step Monogramming....G.... 860 665-0542
West Hartford *(G-9821)*
Ink and Stitch Solutions LLC....G.... 203 600-7161
Meriden *(G-4174)*
J & D Embroidering Co....G.... 860 822-9777
Baltic *(G-120)*
James Kingsley....G.... 203 458-6626
Guilford *(G-3363)*
Jane Sterry....G.... 860 342-4567
Portland *(G-6960)*
JC Embroidery....G.... 860 742-8686
Coventry *(G-1657)*
Jeffrey Morgan....G.... 860 583-2567
Bristol *(G-1054)*
Jennifers Tailor Shop....G.... 860 489-8968
Torrington *(G-8938)*
▲ **K&P Weaver LLC**....G.... 203 795-9024
Orange *(G-6605)*
Kadomar Krafts....G.... 860 346-2000
Middletown *(G-4359)*
Kamelot Kreations LLC....G.... 860 564-7399
Sterling *(G-8511)*
Keepsake Embroidery....G.... 203 503-1725
Orange *(G-6607)*
Lee Lowe & Stitch LLC....G.... 860 536-1392
Mystic *(G-4825)*
Logod Softwear Inc....E.... 203 272-4883
Cheshire *(G-1407)*
Lookers Embroidery....G.... 203 468-7262
East Haven *(G-2439)*
Mad Sportswear LLC....G.... 203 932-4868
West Haven *(G-9929)*
Mead Monogramming....G.... 203 618-0701
Cos Cob *(G-1637)*
Memory Lane Quilters LLC....G.... 203 272-1010
Cheshire *(G-1415)*
Michael Violano....G.... 203 934-3368
West Haven *(G-9937)*
Modern Stitch Company....G.... 860 927-5065
Kent *(G-3824)*
Monas Monograms....G.... 860 463-9530
Andover *(G-14)*
Monogram Mary LLC....G.... 203 536-9526
Riverside *(G-7197)*
Monogramit LLC....G.... 860 779-0694
Brooklyn *(G-1249)*
NCM Embroidery & Sportswear....G.... 860 223-1589
New Britain *(G-5020)*
New England Custom Built LLC....G.... 203 828-6480
Seymour *(G-7359)*
Nitch To Stitch LLC....G.... 203 948-9921
Brookfield *(G-1209)*
Personally Yours....G.... 860 537-2248
Colchester *(G-1564)*
Pink Fish Embroidery and D....G.... 860 339-5083
Old Saybrook *(G-6566)*
Pj Specialties....F.... 860 429-7626
Willington *(G-10254)*
Quilted Lizard....G.... 860 927-4296
Kent *(G-3825)*
R F H Company Inc....F.... 203 853-2863
Norwalk *(G-6313)*
Rainbow Graphics Inc....G.... 860 646-8997
Manchester *(G-4082)*
Ridgefeld Scrnprinting EMB LLC....G.... 203 438-1203
Ridgefield *(G-7167)*
▲ **Robert Audette**....G.... 203 872-3119
Cheshire *(G-1440)*
Rss Enterprises LLC....G.... 203 736-6220
Derby *(G-2124)*
S Tm Embroidery LLC....G.... 860 376-4537
Jewett City *(G-3800)*
S&V Screenprinting & Embroider....G.... 203 468-7538
East Haven *(G-2449)*
Scuttlebutt....G.... 860 572-3999
Mystic *(G-4843)*
Seems Inc....F.... 203 284-0259
Ansonia *(G-50)*
Sharon M Stinson....G.... 860 218-7282
Middletown *(G-4411)*
Shirt Graphix....G.... 203 294-1656
Wallingford *(G-9365)*
Silkscreening Plus Inc....G.... 203 622-6909
Greenwich *(G-3234)*
Son of A Stitch....G.... 203 527-3432
Waterbury *(G-9604)*
Son of A Stitch LLC....G.... 203 272-2548
Cheshire *(G-1450)*
Stitch In Time EMB Svcs LLC....G.... 860 496-0226
Torrington *(G-8973)*
Stitchers Hideaway LLC....G.... 860 268-4741
Manchester *(G-4098)*
Stitches & Seams Usa LLC....G.... 708 872-7326
Terryville *(G-8772)*
Stitches By ME....G.... 860 653-9701
Granby *(G-3115)*
Stitching On Maple Studio....G.... 860 480-2793
Norfolk *(G-5827)*
Straight Stitches....G.... 203 804-0409
Hamden *(G-3514)*
Terris Embroidery....G.... 860 928-0552
Putnam *(G-7074)*
Town Pride....G.... 860 664-0448
Clinton *(G-1532)*
Tri State Embroidery LLC....G.... 203 732-7636
Ansonia *(G-53)*
TSS & A Inc....F.... 800 633-3536
Prospect *(G-7027)*
Ulittlestitch....G.... 860 857-4066
East Lyme *(G-2477)*
Wild Bills Action Sports LLC....G.... 860 536-6648
Groton *(G-3319)*
Zuse Inc....F.... 203 458-3295
Guilford *(G-3402)*

2396 Automotive Trimmings, Apparel Findings, Related Prdts

3rd Half Productions....G.... 860 828-6929
Kensington *(G-3802)*
Ace Finishing Co LLC....G.... 860 582-4600
Bristol *(G-955)*
Advanced Graphics Inc....E.... 203 378-0471
Stratford *(G-8564)*
▲ **Allied Printing Services Inc**....B.... 860 643-1101
Manchester *(G-3980)*
Art Screen....G.... 203 744-1991
Bethel *(G-258)*
Bennettsville Holdings LLC....D.... 860 444-9400
Hebron *(G-3745)*
Byron Lord Inc....G.... 203 287-9881
Old Lyme *(G-6493)*
C Libby Leonard....G.... 203 375-6205
Stratford *(G-8591)*
▲ **Charles Clay Ltd**....G.... 203 662-0125
New Canaan *(G-5093)*
Concordia Ltd....G.... 203 483-0221
North Branford *(G-5832)*
Connecticut Screen Print....G.... 203 877-6655
Milford *(G-4498)*
Cook Print....G.... 203 855-8785
Norwalk *(G-6129)*
Fat City Screen Printers....G.... 860 354-4650
New Milford *(G-5533)*

S I C

23 APPAREL AND OTHER FINISHED PRODUCTS MADE FROM FABRICS AND SIMILAR MATERIAL SIC SECTION

Hi-Tech Fabricating Inc ....E 203 284-0894
Cheshire *(G-1396)*
Hot Tops LLC ....F 203 926-2067
Shelton *(G-7466)*
Images Unlimited ....G 860 350-6608
New Milford *(G-5545)*
J & D Embroidering Co ....G 860 822-9777
Baltic *(G-120)*
▲ **Jornik Man Corp** ....F 203 969-0500
Stamford *(G-8268)*
▲ **Kinamor Incorporated** ....E 203 269-0380
Wallingford *(G-9297)*
Logod Softwear Inc ....E 203 272-4883
Cheshire *(G-1407)*
Michael Violano ....G 203 934-3368
West Haven *(G-9937)*
Michael Zoppa ....G 860 289-5881
South Windsor *(G-7794)*
Mytyme LLC ....G 860 327-2356
Windsor *(G-10411)*
Pro Form Printed Bus Solutions ....G 203 266-5302
Bethlehem *(G-376)*
▲ **Project Graphics Inc** ....F 802 488-8789
Woodbury *(G-10652)*
▲ **Quality Name Plate Inc** ....D 860 633-9495
East Glastonbury *(G-2185)*
R F H Company Inc ....F 203 853-2863
Norwalk *(G-6313)*
Rainbow Graphics Inc ....G 860 646-8997
Manchester *(G-4082)*
▲ **Sam & Ty LLC** ....G 212 840-1871
Norwalk *(G-6337)*
Screen Designs ....G 203 797-9806
Bethel *(G-340)*
▲ **Second Lac Inc** ....G 203 321-1221
Norwalk *(G-6341)*
Seems Inc ....F 203 284-0259
Ansonia *(G-50)*
Systematic Automation Inc ....E 310 218-3361
Farmington *(G-2962)*
Tshirts Etc Inc ....G 860 657-3551
Glastonbury *(G-3090)*
Zuse Inc ....F 203 458-3295
Guilford *(G-3402)*

2399 Fabricated Textile Prdts, NEC

A Kick In Crochet ....G 413 210-7890
Enfield *(G-2610)*
Airborne Industries Inc ....F 203 315-0200
Branford *(G-538)*
Banner Works ....G 203 597-9999
Oakville *(G-6450)*
Bushy Hill Nature Center ....G 860 767-2148
Ivoryton *(G-3784)*
Cap-Tech Products Inc ....F 860 490-5078
Wethersfield *(G-10185)*
Crochet Away 203 ....G 203 690-7904
Weston *(G-10024)*
Crocheted By Bianca ....G 860 916-2925
Manchester *(G-4001)*
Cuvee 59 ....G 707 259-0559
Coventry *(G-1651)*
Dragon Hollow Design LLC ....G 860 861-6200
Norwich *(G-6411)*
DS Sewing Inc ....F 203 773-1344
New Haven *(G-5270)*
Encore Sales Corp ....G 203 301-4949
Milford *(G-4530)*
Flagman of America LLP ....G 860 678-0275
Avon *(G-81)*
Hooked On Fishing Charters ....G 203 257-3431
Fairfield *(G-2794)*
James Stenqvist ....G 203 339-6418
North Haven *(G-5950)*
John Demarchi ....G 860 649-9685
Willimantic *(G-10232)*
Judith Lynn Charters LLC ....G 203 246-6662
Norwalk *(G-6225)*
▲ **Kemper Manufacturing Corp** ....E 203 934-1600
West Haven *(G-9923)*
Kohinoor USA ....G 203 388-1850
Stamford *(G-8277)*
Lathrop Stables LLC ....G 860 230-9949
Plainfield *(G-6746)*
▲ **Lubbert Supply Company LLC** ....G 203 690-1105
Milford *(G-4570)*
Nomis Enterprises ....G 631 821-3120
Wallingford *(G-9327)*
Off The Hookhandmadecrochetllc ....G 203 912-1638
Sandy Hook *(G-7324)*
On Time Screen Printing & Embr ....F 203 874-4581
Derby *(G-2120)*
Pioneer Arspc Def Systems Corp ....G 860 528-0092
South Windsor *(G-7805)*
Power Cover Usa LLC ....G 203 755-2687
Waterbury *(G-9583)*
Puppy Hugger ....G 203 661-4858
Greenwich *(G-3219)*
Soapstone Media Inc ....G 860 749-0455
Somers *(G-7669)*
Taillon Auto Top Company ....G 860 583-5525
Bristol *(G-1125)*
Young Flan LLC ....G 203 878-0084
Derby *(G-2134)*

24 LUMBER AND WOOD PRODUCTS, EXCEPT FURNITURE

2411 Logging

B&B Logging LLC ....G 860 982-2425
Higganum *(G-3760)*
Brad Kettle ....G 860 546-9929
Canterbury *(G-1295)*
Brandy Hill Logging ....G 860 923-3175
Thompson *(G-8831)*
Brian Reynolds ....G 860 267-2021
East Hampton *(G-2259)*
Bryan Heavens Logging & Firewo ....G 860 485-1712
Harwinton *(G-3723)*
C & C Logging ....G 860 683-0071
Windsor *(G-10370)*
Can-AM Trading & Logistics LLC ....G 860 961-9932
Old Lyme *(G-6497)*
Chadbourne Woodshop ....G 203 468-4715
East Haven *(G-2415)*
Clover Hill Forest LLC ....G 860 672-0394
Cornwall *(G-1616)*
Cold River Logging LLC ....G 860 334-9506
North Windham *(G-6036)*
Daves Logging ....G 860 684-6533
Stafford Springs *(G-8025)*
Davis Tree & Logging LLC ....E 203 938-2153
Danbury *(G-1789)*
Fair Weather Logging LLC ....G 860 394-8217
Enfield *(G-2645)*
Fowler D J Log Land Clearing ....G 860 742-5842
Coventry *(G-1654)*
Guilford Logging ....G 203 453-5190
Guilford *(G-3357)*
Hancock Logging & Forestry MGT ....G 860 289-5647
South Windsor *(G-7767)*
Ibbitson Tree Service ....G 860 388-0624
Old Saybrook *(G-6541)*
Industrial Forrest Products LL ....G 203 863-9486
Greenwich *(G-3180)*
J and K Logging ....G 860 653-6165
East Hartland *(G-2403)*
James Callahan ....G 914 641-2852
Ridgefield *(G-7149)*
James M Munch ....G 802 353-3114
Sherman *(G-7596)*
L & M Logging LLC ....G 860 208-9884
Windham *(G-10349)*
Limb-It-Less Logging LLC ....G 860 227-0987
Essex *(G-2725)*
Luc-Tardiff Logging ....G 860 485-0693
Harwinton *(G-3733)*
Mud River Services ....G 860 767-0592
Essex *(G-2727)*
Nichols Forestry & Logging LLC ....G 860 642-4292
Lebanon *(G-3859)*
Northeast Logging Inc ....G 860 974-2959
Eastford *(G-2538)*
Oxford Outdoor Services LLC ....G 860 800-6260
Oxford *(G-6684)*
P&P Logging Co ....G 860 267-2176
East Hampton *(G-2272)*
Perry S Sawyer ....G 860 572-9473
Stonington *(G-8535)*
R & M Logging ....G 860 429-6209
Willington *(G-10255)*
R&J Harvesting LLC ....G 860 974-1323
Eastford *(G-2540)*
Rainbow Forest Log & Firewd ....G 860 455-1023
Hampton *(G-3539)*
Ralph B Fletcher Logging & Lan ....G 860 668-5404
Suffield *(G-8732)*
Riendeau & Sons Logging LLC ....G 860 429-7919
Ashford *(G-64)*
Rm Landclearing & Logging LLC ....G 860 228-1499
Columbia *(G-1611)*
Robert Downey Logging ....G 860 693-2914
Collinsville *(G-1602)*
Saugatuck Tree & Logging LLC ....G 203 470-9195
Brookfield *(G-1221)*
Saugatuck Tree & Logging LLC ....G 203 304-1326
Newtown *(G-5778)*
Sprague Logging LLC ....G 860 455-9768
Chaplin *(G-1342)*
Stanley Burr ....G 860 345-3578
Higganum *(G-3779)*
Thomas Carr III ....G 860 653-3431
North Granby *(G-5882)*
Timberwolf Logging ....G 860 683-0071
Windsor *(G-10451)*
Tr Landworks LLC ....G 860 402-6177
East Hartland *(G-2405)*
Trowbridge Forest Products LLC ....G 860 455-9931
Hampton *(G-3540)*
Wayne Horn ....G 860 491-3315
New Hartford *(G-5214)*
Witkowsky John ....G 203 483-0152
North Branford *(G-5868)*
Worthington Logging ....G 860 684-9605
Stafford Springs *(G-8047)*

2421 Saw & Planing Mills

A&D Enterprises ....G 860 779-9025
Danielson *(G-1985)*
Anstett Lumber Co ....G 860 491-3225
Goshen *(G-3095)*
Autumn Colors ....G 860 822-6568
Norwich *(G-6407)*
Biomass Energy LLC ....E 540 872-3300
Weatogue *(G-9755)*
Board Silly Custom Sawmill LLC ....G 203 438-3631
Ridgefield *(G-7119)*
Burell Bros Inc ....G 860 455-9681
Hampton *(G-3534)*
Cedar Swamp Log & Lumber ....G 860 974-2344
Woodstock *(G-10661)*
Charles Pike & Sons ....G 860 455-9968
Hampton *(G-3535)*
Connecticut Outdoor Wood Frncs ....G 203 263-0625
Woodbury *(G-10630)*
Dalla Corte Lumber ....G 860 875-9480
Stafford Springs *(G-8024)*
Davis Sawmill ....G 860 354-6008
New Milford *(G-5527)*
Decks R US ....G 860 505-0726
New Britain *(G-4973)*
E R Hinman & Sons Inc ....G 860 673-9170
Burlington *(G-1266)*
Edmund Price ....G 860 658-1441
West Simsbury *(G-9979)*
Ensign-Bickford Renewable Ener ....E 860 843-2000
Simsbury *(G-7623)*
Eylward Timber Co ....G 203 265-4276
Wallingford *(G-9265)*
Gebhardts Sawmill ....G 860 423-0123
Windham *(G-10346)*
Gregorys Sawmill LLC ....G 203 762-8298
Wilton *(G-10298)*
Hardwood Lumber Manufacturing ....E 860 423-2447
Scotland *(G-7332)*
Hedden Forest Products ....G 860 672-6023
West Cornwall *(G-9763)*
Henry W Zuwalick & Sons Inc ....G 203 488-3821
Branford *(G-604)*
◆ **Hull Forest Products Inc** ....E 860 974-0127
Pomfret Center *(G-6939)*
Interstate + Lakeland Lbr Corp ....F 203 531-8050
Greenwich *(G-3182)*
Jim N I LLC ....G 860 646-5155
Andover *(G-10)*
John J Pawloski Lumber Inc ....G 203 794-0737
Bethel *(G-316)*
Jordan Saw Mill L L C ....F 860 774-0247
Sterling *(G-8510)*
Mallery Lumber Inc ....G 860 632-3505
Cromwell *(G-1707)*
Moores Sawmill Inc ....G 860 242-3003
Bloomfield *(G-446)*
New England Forest Products ....G 203 457-0314
Guilford *(G-3379)*
Parker Septic Service ....F 860 749-8220
Somers *(G-7667)*
Ppk Inc ....G 203 376-9180
Branford *(G-636)*

- **Reusable Greenworks** G 203 745-3695 — New Haven *(G-5379)*
- **Saw Mill Capital LLC** G 203 662-0573 — Darien *(G-2043)*
- **Saw Miners Mill** G 860 599-5012 — Pawcatuck *(G-6724)*
- ▼ **Scotland Hardwoods LLC** E 860 423-1233 — Scotland *(G-7333)*
- **Sigfridson Wood Products LLC** G 860 774-2075 — Brooklyn *(G-1254)*
- **South Norfolk Lumber Co** G 860 542-5650 — Norfolk *(G-5826)*
- **Stuart Hardwood Corp** G 203 376-0036 — New Haven *(G-5402)*
- **Tallon Lumber Inc** E 860 824-0733 — Canaan *(G-1293)*
- ◆ **Tronox Incorporated** C 203 705-3800 — Stamford *(G-8476)*
- **Walker Industries LLC** G 860 455-3554 — Ashford *(G-67)*

2426 Hardwood Dimension & Flooring Mills

- **Artistic Hardwood Floors CT** G 860 537-5334 — Colchester *(G-1540)*
- **Ben Barretts LLC** G 860 928-9373 — Thompson *(G-8830)*
- **Caballros Hrdwood Flors Pntinc** G 914 312-0695 — Stamford *(G-8125)*
- **Carpet Products** G 860 278-6160 — Hartford *(G-3563)*
- ▲ **Conway Hardwood Products LLC** E 860 355-4030 — Gaylordsville *(G-2991)*
- **Custom Checkering** G 860 747-8035 — Plainville *(G-6794)*
- **Diamond Hrdwd Flrs of Fairfld** G 203 650-9192 — Bridgeport *(G-751)*
- **E R Hinman & Sons Inc** G 860 673-9170 — Burlington *(G-1266)*
- **GA Mals Woodwoorking LLC** G 860 747-4767 — Plainville *(G-6814)*
- ◆ **Hull Forest Products Inc** E 860 974-0127 — Pomfret Center *(G-6939)*
- **JC Turn Mfg** G 203 366-6164 — Bridgeport *(G-802)*
- **Jgf Hardwood Floor** G 203 650-9192 — Bridgeport *(G-805)*
- **Juan Gallegos** G 203 744-0575 — Danbury *(G-1866)*
- **Kellogg Hardwoods Inc** G 203 797-1992 — Bethel *(G-319)*
- **Stake Company LLC** G 860 623-2700 — East Windsor *(G-2523)*
- **Stepping Stones Marble** G 203 293-4796 — Westport *(G-10160)*
- **Tallon Lumber Inc** E 860 824-0733 — Canaan *(G-1293)*
- **Tg Floors** G 860 355-5660 — New Milford *(G-5595)*
- **Ultimate Hardwood Floors** G 203 746-9692 — New Fairfield *(G-5181)*
- **Wilson Woodworks Inc** F 860 870-2500 — Windsor *(G-10464)*

2429 Special Prdt Sawmills, NEC

- **Bonito Manufacturing Inc** D 203 234-8786 — North Haven *(G-5915)*
- **Epdm Coatings** G 203 225-0104 — Shelton *(G-7441)*

2431 Millwork

- **450 Woodworking LLC** G 860 350-0525 — New Milford *(G-5501)*
- **542 Rustic Woodworks** G 860 387-8680 — Norfolk *(G-5822)*
- ▲ **77 Mattatuck Heights LLC** E 203 597-9338 — Waterbury *(G-9420)*
- **AB Custom Woodwork LLC** G 203 334-7882 — Fairfield *(G-2742)*
- **Adam Fuller Woodworking** G 860 455-1296 — North Windham *(G-6033)*
- **AGA Mill Work LLC** G 860 426-9901 — Southington *(G-7888)*
- **Aj Wood Work LLC** G 203 826-9851 — Danbury *(G-1734)*
- **Alvarado Custom Cabinetry LLC** F 203 831-0181 — Norwalk *(G-6067)*
- **American Custom Fine Woodwrkng** G 860 871-8783 — Tolland *(G-8848)*
- **American Overhead Ret Div Inc** G 860 876-4552 — Middletown *(G-4316)*
- **Anchor Overhead Door Sales** G 860 651-6560 — Tariffville *(G-8743)*
- **Anchor Woodworking LLC** G 860 376-0795 — Jewett City *(G-3791)*
- **Anderson Stair & Railing** F 203 288-0117 — North Haven *(G-5904)*
- **Apex Cstm Cabinetry Wdwkg LLC** G 203 396-0496 — Bridgeport *(G-697)*
- **Apple Hill Woodworking LLC** G 860 945-6102 — Watertown *(G-9682)*
- **Arbon Equipment Corporation** G 410 796-5902 — Bloomfield *(G-388)*
- **Architectural Door Corp** G 203 255-3033 — Fairfield *(G-2748)*
- **Atlantic Woodcraft Inc** F 860 749-4887 — Enfield *(G-2616)*
- **Atlas Metal and Wood Works LLC** G 805 450-7031 — West Hartford *(G-9776)*
- **Axels Custom Woodworking LLC** G 203 869-1317 — Greenwich *(G-3126)*
- **AZ Woodworking LLC** G 203 595-9063 — Stamford *(G-8102)*
- **Aztec Woodworking** G 203 272-3814 — Cheshire *(G-1359)*
- **B & R Stair** G 860 582-6584 — Bristol *(G-970)*
- **B Douglass Custom Mllwk LLC** G 860 338-9305 — Glastonbury *(G-3010)*
- **B H Davis Co** G 860 923-2771 — Thompson *(G-8829)*
- **Belo Woodworking LLC** G 727 249-8514 — West Simsbury *(G-9972)*
- **Bergan Architectural Wdwkg Inc** E 860 346-0869 — Middletown *(G-4324)*
- **Best Built Custom Stair Buildi** G 203 488-8031 — North Branford *(G-5829)*
- **Birkett Woodworking LLC** G 860 361-9142 — Morris *(G-4787)*
- **Blais Woodworks LLC** G 860 274-2906 — Watertown *(G-9684)*
- **Blind Crafters** G 860 896-0366 — Vernon Rockville *(G-9162)*
- **Bonnieview Woodwork LLC** G 860 767-3299 — Ivoryton *(G-3783)*
- **Bradley Woodworking LLC** G 203 746-8357 — New Fairfield *(G-5162)*
- **Breakfast Woodworks Inc** G 203 458-8888 — Guilford *(G-3332)*
- **Brian Daigle** G 860 263-7831 — Hartford *(G-3559)*
- **Budget Woodworker LLC** G 860 468-5551 — Niantic *(G-5802)*
- **Built To Last Fine Wdwkg LLC** G 860 619-0119 — New Preston *(G-5611)*
- **Byrne Woodworking Inc** G 203 953-3205 — Bridgeport *(G-727)*
- **C J Cushing Woodworking** G 860 848-2746 — Old Lyme *(G-6494)*
- **C J S Millwork Inc** F 203 708-0080 — Stamford *(G-8124)*
- **C West Woodworks** G 860 309-7362 — Torrington *(G-8908)*
- **Cabin Woodworks** G 203 410-1073 — Hamden *(G-3421)*
- **Cambrdge Fine Wdwkg Renovation** G 860 583-7561 — Bristol *(G-998)*
- **Candle Woodworks** G 860 350-4390 — Sherman *(G-7591)*
- **Cavekraft Woodworking LLC** G 860 230-4480 — North Stonington *(G-6021)*
- **Cedar Woodworking** G 203 335-4108 — Bridgeport *(G-732)*
- **Century Woodworking Inc** F 860 379-7538 — Pleasant Valley *(G-6921)*
- **Chandler Furniture & Wdwrk LLC** G 203 895-6289 — Shelton *(G-7416)*
- **Chapman Lumber Inc** E 860 283-6213 — Thomaston *(G-8785)*
- **Charles A Boucher Co Inc** G 860 868-2881 — Washington *(G-9412)*
- **Charlys Custom Woodworking** G 860 227-2155 — Killingworth *(G-3829)*
- **Chesnut Woodworking** G 860 592-0383 — Kent *(G-3821)*
- **Chestnut Wdwkg & Antiq Flrg Co** G 860 672-4300 — West Cornwall *(G-9761)*
- **Chris Dedura** G 203 257-7304 — Trumbull *(G-9011)*
- **Chris Krawczyk Woodwork LLC** G 203 895-5785 — Shelton *(G-7417)*
- **Christensen Woodworking** G 860 712-6166 — Windsorville *(G-10503)*
- **Cko Woodworking** G 203 234-7156 — North Haven *(G-5920)*
- **Cko Woodworking LLC** G 203 815-3092 — Meriden *(G-4158)*
- **Clancy Woodworking LLC** G 860 355-3655 — Sherman *(G-7592)*
- **Colonial Wood Products Inc** F 203 932-9003 — West Haven *(G-9889)*
- **Colonial Woodworking Inc** F 203 866-5844 — Norwalk *(G-6120)*
- **Concept Woodworks LLC** G 860 746-4271 — Enfield *(G-2632)*
- **Connecticut Carpentry LLC** E 203 639-8585 — Meriden *(G-4161)*
- **Connecticut Custom Wdwrk LLC** G 203 888-3948 — Seymour *(G-7342)*
- **Connecticut Custom Woodwork** G 203 231-0097 — Milford *(G-4494)*
- **Connecticut Custom Woodworking** G 860 741-8946 — Somers *(G-7653)*
- **Connecticut Millwork Inc** G 860 875-2860 — Vernon *(G-9135)*
- **Connecticut Woodworks LLC** G 860 367-7449 — Waterford *(G-9648)*
- ▲ **Conway Hardwood Products LLC** E 860 355-4030 — Gaylordsville *(G-2991)*
- **Corgyn Woodworks** G 860 402-8273 — Manchester *(G-3999)*
- **Correia Wood Works LLC** G 203 515-7670 — Fairfield *(G-2769)*
- **CT Fine Woodworking** G 860 613-0856 — Cromwell *(G-1698)*
- **CT Moldings Inc** G 203 612-4922 — Bridgeport *(G-740)*
- **CT Woodworking LLC** G 860 884-9586 — North Franklin *(G-5872)*
- **Curtiss Woodworking Inc** F 203 527-9305 — Prospect *(G-6998)*
- **Custom Carpentry Unlimited** G 860 742-8932 — Coventry *(G-1650)*
- **Custom Design Woodworks LLC** G 860 434-0515 — Old Lyme *(G-6502)*
- **Custom Woodwork Etc** G 860 638-1006 — Middletown *(G-4334)*
- **Custom Woodworking** G 860 868-0257 — Washington Depot *(G-9417)*
- **Custom Woodworking** G 860 456-4466 — Lebanon *(G-3852)*
- **Custom Woodworking By Norman** G 860 663-3462 — Killingworth *(G-3831)*
- **Customized Woodworking LLC** G 860 274-4025 — Watertown *(G-9699)*
- **Dalbergia LLC** G 860 870-2500 — Tolland *(G-8858)*
- ▲ **Dalvento LLC** G 203 263-6497 — Woodbury *(G-10632)*
- **Danbury Stairs Corporation** G 203 743-5567 — Bethel *(G-278)*
- **Danchak Woodworks LLC** G 860 346-6057 — Durham *(G-2144)*
- **Daniel F Crapa** G 203 746-5706 — New Fairfield *(G-5167)*
- **Dante Ltd** G 860 376-0204 — Jewett City *(G-3793)*
- **Dante Ltd Liability Company** G 860 376-0204 — Griswold *(G-3263)*
- **David W Lintz Company** G 860 349-1392 — Middlefield *(G-4301)*
- **Defelice Woodworking Inc** G 203 445-0199 — Trumbull *(G-9019)*
- **Depercio Woodworking LLC** G 860 477-1051 — Ashford *(G-59)*
- **Deschenes & Cooper Architectur** G 860 599-2481 — Pawcatuck *(G-6709)*
- **Di Venere Co** G 860 582-0208 — Bristol *(G-1016)*
- **Dlz Architectural Mill Work** G 860 883-7562 — Hartford *(G-3578)*
- **Dooney Woodworks LLC** G 203 340-9770 — Cos Cob *(G-1631)*
- **Dooney Woodworks LLC** G 203 869-5457 — Greenwich *(G-3155)*
- **Drb Woodworks** G 203 216-7071 — Monroe *(G-4712)*
- **Dream Construction & Wdwkg** G 774 573-0495 — Eastford *(G-2535)*
- **East Coast Stairs Co Inc** G 860 528-7096 — South Windsor *(G-7744)*

Employee Codes: A=Over 500 employees, B=251-500 C=101-250, D=51-100, E=20-50, F=10-19, G=1-9

2020 Harris Connecticut Manufacturers Directory

383

24 LUMBER AND WOOD PRODUCTS, EXCEPT FURNITURE — SIC SECTION

Elite Woodworking LLC G 860 655-7806
Glastonbury ***(G-3033)***

End Grain Woodworks LLC G 203 817-7154
Wilton ***(G-10291)***

Errichetti Woodworks LLC G 203 528-3977
Prospect ***(G-7003)***

Esg Woodworking and Bldg LLC G 203 667-0811
Newtown ***(G-5737)***

Exterior Trim Specialities LLC G 860 261-5194
Terryville ***(G-8754)***

Fac Woodworking LLC G 203 469-1900
East Haven ***(G-2426)***

Fagan Design & Fabrication G 203 937-1874
West Haven ***(G-9907)***

Fairfield County Millwork F 203 393-9751
Bethany ***(G-241)***

Fairfield Wood Works G 203 838-6883
Norwalk ***(G-6161)***

Fairfield Woodworks LLC F 203 380-9842
Stratford ***(G-8609)***

Ferraro Custom Woodwork LLC G 203 876-1280
Milford ***(G-4536)***

Fine Lines Custom Cabinetry & G 860 729-6526
Plainville ***(G-6810)***

Fine Woodworker G 203 717-2444
Norwalk ***(G-6166)***

Fine Woodworking G 203 762-8197
Wilton ***(G-10296)***

Fineline Architechtural Wdwkg G 914 426-2648
Danbury ***(G-1825)***

First Class Custom Woodworking G 203 857-1000
Norwalk ***(G-6168)***

Freddie Nelson Woodworks G 203 378-2330
Stratford ***(G-8612)***

G M F Woodworking LLC G 203 788-8979
Norwalk ***(G-6172)***

G M Woodworking G 860 599-3781
North Stonington ***(G-6026)***

Gabriels Woodworking LLC G 860 263-7831
Hartford ***(G-3597)***

Gagne & Gagne Co G 860 742-5038
Andover ***(G-8)***

Gary D Kryszat G 860 526-3145
Chester ***(G-1473)***

Gideon S Fleece Woodworkin G 860 663-2757
Killingworth ***(G-3834)***

Gilbert G Fitch G 860 824-5832
Lakeville ***(G-3843)***

GNB Woodworking LLC G 860 282-0595
South Windsor ***(G-7761)***

Gngwoodworking G 203 996-5255
West Haven ***(G-9913)***

Good Earth Millwork LLC G 203 226-7958
Westport ***(G-10092)***

Gordon Woodworking LLC G 860 489-5445
Morris ***(G-4789)***

Gothers & Martin Wdwkg LLC G 860 982-4193
Wethersfield ***(G-10194)***

Grdn Woodworks G 203 814-6446
Trumbull ***(G-9031)***

Greenworks Woodworking G 203 886-8573
Bethel ***(G-305)***

Gregory Penta G 860 747-2681
Plainville ***(G-6819)***

Griffin Green G 203 266-5727
Bethlehem ***(G-371)***

H & S Woodworks L T D G 914 391-3926
New Milford ***(G-5544)***

Hard Hill Woodworking LLC G 203 263-2820
Woodbury ***(G-10638)***

Harris Enterprise Corp E 860 649-4663
Manchester ***(G-4025)***

Harry & Hios Woodworking LLC G 860 267-1535
East Hampton ***(G-2263)***

Head East Woodworking G 860 537-2072
Colchester ***(G-1553)***

Highland Woodworks G 203 758-6625
Prospect ***(G-7004)***

Hunt Architectural Wdwkg Inc G 203 947-1137
Danbury ***(G-1846)***

Hurley Woodworking LLC G 818 643-5809
Sandy Hook ***(G-7316)***

Indars Stairs LLC G 860 208-3826
Lebanon ***(G-3854)***

▲ Industrial Sales Corp F 203 227-5988
Westport ***(G-10099)***

Industrial Wood Product Co G 203 735-2374
Shelton ***(G-7475)***

Integrated Woodworks LLC G 860 563-4537
Wethersfield ***(G-10199)***

Integrity Custom Wdwkg LLC G 860 302-3726
Southington ***(G-7939)***

Iorfino Woodworking G 203 329-1075
Stamford ***(G-8257)***

Island View Woodworks LLC G 203 494-1760
Killingworth ***(G-3835)***

J & J Stairs G 860 793-8333
Plainville ***(G-6825)***

J G M Woodworks G 203 934-3726
West Haven ***(G-9917)***

Ja Custom Woodwork G 203 540-5747
Stratford ***(G-8635)***

Jacobsen Woodworking Co Inc G 203 531-9050
Greenwich ***(G-3183)***

Jakes Jr Lawrence E 860 974-3744
Pomfret Center ***(G-6940)***

James H Quinn G 203 809-6046
Wallingford ***(G-9293)***

James J Licari G 203 333-5000
Bridgeport ***(G-800)***

Jask Woodworking Inc G 954 766-7105
Bridgeport ***(G-801)***

Jjk Woodworking LLC G 203 224-0139
Bridgeport ***(G-806)***

Joe Salafia Woodworking LLC G 860 345-8657
Haddam ***(G-3405)***

John M Kriskey Carpentry G 203 531-0194
Greenwich ***(G-3184)***

Johnson Millwork Inc G 860 267-4693
East Hampton ***(G-2267)***

Jordan Woodworks G 203 512-3581
Bethel ***(G-317)***

Joshua Friedman & Co LLC F 860 439-1637
New London ***(G-5475)***

K L S Custom Wood Working G 203 520-5193
Monroe ***(G-4724)***

K Smith Custom Woodworking LLC G 203 981-4268
New Canaan ***(G-5113)***

K&M Woodworking LLC G 203 406-0694
Stamford ***(G-8273)***

Kariba Woodworks G 203 246-8917
Sandy Hook ***(G-7318)***

KB Custom Stair Builders Inc G 203 234-0836
North Haven ***(G-5957)***

Kenyon Woodworking G 860 432-4641
Manchester ***(G-4045)***

Kerry D Hogan G 203 213-4624
Wallingford ***(G-9296)***

Kingsland Co G 860 542-6981
Norfolk ***(G-5824)***

Kitchens By Deane Inc E 203 327-7008
Stamford ***(G-8276)***

Lagnese Woodworking G 203 426-6434
Newtown ***(G-5753)***

Lee & Sons Woodworkers G 860 742-7707
Andover ***(G-12)***

Legacy Woodworking LLC G 203 440-9710
Meriden ***(G-4186)***

Legere Group Ltd C 860 674-0392
Avon ***(G-89)***

Legno Bldrs & Fine Wdwkg LLC G 860 282-0091
Coventry ***(G-1660)***

Leos Kitchen & Stair Corp G 860 225-7363
New Britain ***(G-5010)***

Level Woodworks G 203 266-7153
Bethlehem ***(G-374)***

Lingard Cabinet Co LLC G 860 647-9886
Manchester ***(G-4048)***

Loranctis Orgnal Woodworks LLC G 860 924-8810
Terryville ***(G-8763)***

Lota Woodworking LLC G 203 978-0277
Norwalk ***(G-6239)***

Luckey LLC F 203 285-3819
New Haven ***(G-5322)***

M K M Woodworks LLC G 203 838-5605
Norwalk ***(G-6242)***

M Squared Woodworking LLC G 860 673-6079
Unionville ***(G-9118)***

Maclean Woodworking LLC G 203 452-8285
Monroe ***(G-4730)***

Maddog LLC G 203 878-0147
Milford ***(G-4572)***

Madigan Millwork Inc G 860 673-7601
Unionville ***(G-9119)***

Mars Architectural Millwork G 203 579-2632
Bridgeport ***(G-831)***

Martel Woodworking Co G 860 564-1983
Plainfield ***(G-6748)***

Matthew Ryan Woodworking LLC G 203 268-8469
Trumbull ***(G-9046)***

Maurer & Shepherd Joyners F 860 633-2383
Glastonbury ***(G-3057)***

Meadow Woodworking LLC G 203 213-3332
Cheshire ***(G-1414)***

Mh Woodworking Inc G 860 871-7321
Tolland ***(G-8870)***

Michaels Woodworking LLC G 203 470-0867
Southbury ***(G-7868)***

Miliard Custom Woodworks LLC G 860 621-5131
Plantsville ***(G-6903)***

Millwork Shop LLC G 860 489-8848
Torrington ***(G-8948)***

Mise En Place Wood Works Inc G 860 921-0208
New Hartford ***(G-5202)***

Mitchell Woodworking LLC G 203 878-4249
Milford ***(G-4583)***

Mitered Edge Woodworking G 860 576-6657
South Windham ***(G-7691)***

Modern Woodcrafts LLC D 860 677-7371
Plainville ***(G-6845)***

Morgan Woodworks LLC G 203 913-2489
Milford ***(G-4584)***

Morris Woodworking G 860 346-7500
Middletown ***(G-4382)***

Morton Wood Works G 203 594-6678
West Haven ***(G-9938)***

Mt Carmel Woodwork LLC G 203 230-8377
Hamden ***(G-3486)***

Mt Lebanon Joinery G 860 974-0896
Eastford ***(G-2537)***

Nancy R Marryat G 860 749-2632
Enfield ***(G-2666)***

Naugatuck Stair Company Inc F 203 729-7134
Naugatuck ***(G-4907)***

Nci Woodworking LLC LLC G 203 391-1614
Fairfield ***(G-2822)***

Ne Wood Works LLC G 860 883-3106
Manchester ***(G-4058)***

New England Cabinet Co Inc F 860 747-9995
New Britain ***(G-5021)***

New England Fine Woodworking G 860 526-5799
Chester ***(G-1475)***

New England Joinery Works Inc G 860 767-3377
Essex ***(G-2728)***

New England Stair Company Inc E 203 924-0606
Shelton ***(G-7509)***

New England Standard Corp G 203 876-7733
Milford ***(G-4589)***

New England Woodworking G 203 505-0830
Norwalk ***(G-6274)***

New England Woodworking LLC G 203 984-5032
Norwalk ***(G-6275)***

New Haven GL & Mirror Co LLC G 203 469-2440
New Haven ***(G-5344)***

Niantic Awning Company G 860 739-0161
Niantic ***(G-5813)***

Nichols Woodworking LLC G 860 350-4223
Washington Depot ***(G-9419)***

Nolan Woodworking LLC G 203 258-1538
Bridgeport ***(G-852)***

Nolan Woodworking LLC G 860 283-6000
Thomaston ***(G-8799)***

North Canton Custom Wdwkg G 508 451-5826
Canton ***(G-1320)***

North Hill Woodworking LLC G 203 985-0200
North Haven ***(G-5968)***

Northeast Stair Company LLC G 860 875-3358
Tolland ***(G-8872)***

Nutmeg Woodworks LLC G 203 980-5700
Milford ***(G-4596)***

Omondi Woodworking G 860 513-2292
Coventry ***(G-1667)***

Orion Manufacturing LLC G 860 572-2921
Mystic ***(G-4838)***

Owh LLC E 860 693-9464
Canton ***(G-1323)***

Oxford Woodworking LLC G 203 482-0982
Oxford ***(G-6687)***

Paco Assensio Woodworking LLC G 203 536-2608
Norwalk ***(G-6288)***

Pagoda Timber Frames G 860 526-3077
Chester ***(G-1477)***

Patalanos Woodworking LLC G 203 612-7537
Bridgeport ***(G-866)***

Patrick Odonoghue G 203 467-4041
East Haven ***(G-2446)***

Patriot Woodworking LLC G 860 653-4349
East Hartland ***(G-2404)***

Peter Arch Woodworking LLC G 203 374-9977
Fairfield ***(G-2827)***

Peter Conrad ..... G 860 673-3600
East Hampton *(G-2273)*
Petrunti Design & Wdwkg LLC ..... G 860 953-5332
West Hartford *(G-9844)*
Phoenix Woodworking ..... G 203 512-3521
New Fairfield *(G-5173)*
Pinkham Woodworking ..... G 860 733-3903
Torrington *(G-8958)*
Porta Door Co ..... E 203 888-6191
Seymour *(G-7362)*
Precision Mill LLC ..... G 860 357-4729
Berlin *(G-209)*
Precision Woodcraft Inc ..... G 860 693-3641
Canton *(G-1325)*
Premiere Kitchens & Wdwkg LLC ..... G 203 882-1745
Milford *(G-4615)*
Prescott Cabinet Co ..... G 860 495-0176
Pawcatuck *(G-6723)*
Proctor Woodworks LLC ..... G 860 767-9881
Essex *(G-2731)*
Qa Woodworking LLC ..... G 203 720-1781
Naugatuck *(G-4914)*
Quality Stairs Inc ..... E 203 367-8390
Bridgeport *(G-883)*
R Botsford Custom Wdwkg LLC ..... G 203 994-5302
Newtown *(G-5773)*
R D Woodwork LLC ..... G 203 947-9550
Danbury *(G-1926)*
R E S Woodworking LLC ..... G 860 664-9663
Clinton *(G-1519)*
R F Case ..... G 203 956-6348
Norwalk *(G-6312)*
R Woodworking Larson Inc ..... E 860 646-7904
Manchester *(G-4079)*
R&R Woodworking ..... G 508 202-3543
Thompson *(G-8842)*
Radius Mill Work ..... G 860 645-1036
Manchester *(G-4081)*
Red Barn Woodworkers ..... G 860 379-3158
Winsted *(G-10533)*
Renner Stairs ..... G 203 743-2452
Danbury *(G-1928)*
RG Woodworking LLC ..... G 860 742-0397
Coventry *(G-1671)*
Rgb Woodworking ..... G 203 537-1177
Meriden *(G-4232)*
Ribeiro Woodworking LLC ..... G 203 942-5838
Bethel *(G-335)*
Richard Woodworking ..... G 203 265-0887
Wallingford *(G-9354)*
Richmond Woodworks LLC ..... G 860 974-9995
Woodstock *(G-10680)*
Ridgefield Overhead Door LLC ..... G 203 431-3667
Ridgefield *(G-7168)*
River Mill Co ..... F 860 669-5915
Clinton *(G-1521)*
RMS Wood Works LLC ..... G 203 405-3051
Woodbury *(G-10653)*
Robert L Lovallo ..... G 203 324-6655
Stamford *(G-8396)*
Rogers Woodsiding ..... G 203 879-9747
Wolcott *(G-10584)*
Roman Woodworking ..... G 860 490-5989
New Britain *(G-5047)*
S G R Woodworks ..... G 203 216-3327
Trumbull *(G-9068)*
Sainte-Anne Custom Woodwork ..... G 203 961-9403
Stamford *(G-8401)*
Salisbury Artisans ..... G 860 435-0344
Salisbury *(G-7297)*
Saxony Wood Products Inc ..... G 203 869-3717
Greenwich *(G-3232)*
◆ Schuco USA Lllp ..... D 860 666-0505
Newington *(G-5703)*
Schwank Archtctural Woodworker ..... G 203 912-0109
Redding *(G-7107)*
Scott Wallace Woodworking ..... G 860 867-7229
Mystic *(G-4842)*
Select Woodworking LLC ..... G 203 743-1159
Danbury *(G-1943)*
Shelbrack Woodworking ..... G 860 431-5028
Simsbury *(G-7644)*
Sheldon Woodworks ..... G 203 260-2703
Fairfield *(G-2847)*
Silver Hill Woodworks LLC ..... G 860 318-1887
Cornwall Bridge *(G-1619)*
Smg Woodworking ..... G 203 804-1029
New Haven *(G-5396)*
Soja Woodworking LLC ..... G 860 345-3909
Higganum *(G-3778)*
Sound Custom Woodworking & Des ..... G 203 948-5594
Ridgefield *(G-7175)*
Splinters Woodworking LLC ..... G 203 272-1314
Cheshire *(G-1453)*
Spruce It Up Woodworking LLC ..... G 203 740-7975
Brookfield *(G-1226)*
St Johns Bridge LLC ..... G 860 927-3315
Kent *(G-3826)*
St Peter Woodworks ..... G 860 816-0455
Manchester *(G-4093)*
Stately Stair Co Inc ..... E 203 575-1966
Waterbury *(G-9607)*
Stephen Wenning ..... G 203 906-9273
Trumbull *(G-9077)*
Steven Vandermaelen LLC ..... G 203 457-0143
Guilford *(G-3393)*
Stillwater Architectural Wood ..... G 860 923-2858
Woodstock *(G-10687)*
Stonington Woodworks LLC ..... G 646 321-6412
Ledyard *(G-3880)*
Style Woodworking ..... G 860 944-7179
Coventry *(G-1677)*
Summit Atelier ..... G 646 284-0304
West Simsbury *(G-9983)*
Summit Stair Co Inc ..... F 203 778-2251
Bethel *(G-348)*
Sutters Mill ..... G 860 585-5333
Bristol *(G-1124)*
Swanhart Woodworking ..... G 203 746-1184
New Fairfield *(G-5178)*
Szostek Custom Woodworking LLC ..... G 203 891-9127
Orange *(G-6630)*
Thomas F Kyasky ..... G 860 567-4077
Litchfield *(G-3902)*
Thomas Townsend Custom Marine ..... G 860 536-9800
Mystic *(G-4849)*
Timbers Edge Woodworking ..... G 860 836-7328
Bozrah *(G-533)*
Tl Woodworking ..... G 203 787-9661
Hamden *(G-3519)*
Todd Lucien Mendes LLC ..... G 203 228-3134
Waterbury *(G-9612)*
Tolland Architectural Wdwkg LLC ..... G 860 875-9841
Tolland *(G-8882)*
Torrington Lumber Company ..... G 860 482-3529
Torrington *(G-8984)*
Tread Well Stair & Millwo ..... G 203 488-2146
North Branford *(G-5864)*
TS Whitman Custom Wdwkg LLC ..... G 860 575-1923
South Lyme *(G-7686)*
Ultimate Woodworking LLC ..... G 203 243-3367
Shelton *(G-7573)*
Unlimited Woodworking ..... G 203 380-2340
Stratford *(G-8700)*
Up & Down Overhead Door ..... G 203 876-8045
Milford *(G-4670)*
V & V Woodworking LLC ..... G 203 740-9494
Bethel *(G-360)*
V B Woodworking LLC ..... G 860 747-0228
Plainville *(G-6874)*
Valley Woodworking LLC ..... G 860 667-1241
Newington *(G-5719)*
Vision Kitchens and Mllwk LLC ..... G 203 775-0604
Brookfield *(G-1238)*
W G Woodworking ..... G 203 262-8308
Southbury *(G-7883)*
Walker Woodworking LLC ..... G 860 429-2644
Ashford *(G-68)*
Walpole Woodworkers Inc ..... G 203 595-9930
Stamford *(G-8488)*
Walston Inc ..... G 203 453-5929
Guilford *(G-3401)*
Walters Wood Working LLC ..... G 860 683-8478
Windsor *(G-10462)*
Warren Woodworking LLC ..... G 860 408-0030
West Simsbury *(G-9984)*
Wayne Woodworks ..... G 203 362-8084
Fairfield *(G-2866)*
Wesconn Stairs Inc ..... G 203 792-7367
Danbury *(G-1978)*
West Hrtford Stirs Cbinets Inc ..... D 860 953-9151
Newington *(G-5723)*
Wezenski Woodworking ..... G 203 488-3255
Branford *(G-672)*
Wheeler Woodworking ..... G 860 355-1638
Kent *(G-3827)*
White Dog Woodworking LLC ..... G 860 482-3776
Torrington *(G-8988)*
White Dove Woodworking LLC ..... G 860 268-4426
Coventry *(G-1683)*
Willis Mills House LLC ..... G 917 287-3260
New Canaan *(G-5159)*
Willow Woodworking Inc ..... G 203 426-8200
Newtown *(G-5798)*
Winchester Woodworking LLC ..... G 860 485-0742
Harwinton *(G-3743)*
Winchester Woodworks LLC ..... G 860 379-9875
Winsted *(G-10547)*
Window Master Real WD Pdts LLC ..... G 203 230-2638
North Haven *(G-6014)*
Windsor Woodworks ..... G 203 386-6975
New Haven *(G-5434)*
Windsors & Woodwork LLC ..... G 860 526-4092
Chester *(G-1487)*
Winters Group ..... G 860 749-3317
Enfield *(G-2707)*
Wood Works By Aranda LLC ..... G 203 908-3010
Stamford *(G-8499)*
Woodmsters Mllwk Rstration LLC ..... G 203 745-3165
North Haven *(G-6016)*
Woodwork Specialties Inc ..... G 860 583-4848
Bristol *(G-1141)*
Woodworkers ..... G 860 669-9113
Clinton *(G-1535)*
Woodworkers Club LLC ..... G 203 847-9663
Norwalk *(G-6399)*
Woodworking ..... G 860 354-6757
New Milford *(G-5608)*
Woodworking Plus LLC ..... G 203 393-1967
Bethany *(G-253)*
Woodworks of Connecticut Ltd ..... G 914 318-7970
Monroe *(G-4767)*
Yankee Woodworks LLC ..... G 860 933-9882
Mansfield Center *(G-4116)*
Yes Fine Woodworking LLC ..... G 203 255-6366
Southport *(G-8014)*
Yoguez Woodworking LLC ..... G 203 943-6956
Bridgeport *(G-944)*
York Millwork LLC ..... G 203 698-3460
Old Greenwich *(G-6485)*
Z & M Woodworking LLC ..... G 860 378-0563
Plantsville *(G-6919)*
Zander Wood Works LLC ..... G 203 493-5066
Ridgefield *(G-7188)*
Zavarella Woodworking Inc ..... G 860 666-6969
Newington *(G-5725)*

2434 Wood Kitchen Cabinets

A -Line Custom Counter Top ..... G 860 747-1917
Plainville *(G-6758)*
A Matter of Style LLC ..... G 203 272-1337
Cheshire *(G-1345)*
A S J Specialties LLC ..... G 203 284-8650
Wallingford *(G-9194)*
AB Custom Cabinetry LLC ..... G 203 367-5047
Fairfield *(G-2741)*
Affordable Cabinets ..... G 860 919-5204
Berlin *(G-152)*
Affordable Fine Cabinetry ..... G 860 919-5204
Plainville *(G-6767)*
Alfred Brown Cabinetry LLC ..... G 860 868-7261
Warren *(G-9406)*
Amelia Cabinet Co LLC ..... G 860 638-9047
Torrington *(G-8893)*
American Refacing Cstm Cab LLC ..... G 860 647-0868
Manchester *(G-3983)*
Axis Wood Works LLC ..... G 203 481-4946
Branford *(G-553)*
Bailey Avenue Kitchens ..... G 203 438-4868
Ridgefield *(G-7118)*
Belmont Corporation ..... E 860 589-5700
Bristol *(G-980)*
Bergan Architectural Wdwkg Inc ..... E 860 346-0869
Middletown *(G-4324)*
Beyond Forever Cabinetry LLC ..... G 203 427-7968
Bridgeport *(G-711)*
Bonito Manufacturing Inc ..... D 203 234-8786
North Haven *(G-5915)*
Boule LLC ..... G 860 267-8343
East Hampton *(G-2258)*
BP Countertop Design Co LLC ..... G 203 732-1620
Derby *(G-2110)*
C J Brand & Son ..... G 860 536-9266
Mystic *(G-4803)*
Cabinet Authority LLC ..... G 203 304-2010
Newtown *(G-5730)*
Cabinet Dreams LLC ..... G 203 558-4178
Oakville *(G-6451)*
Cabinet Harward Specialti ..... G 860 231-1192
West Hartford *(G-9782)*

SIC

Employee Codes: A=Over 500 employees, B=251-500
C=101-250, D=51-100, E=20-50, F=10-19, G=1-9
2020 Harris Connecticut
Manufacturers Directory
385

Cabinet Maker ..... G 860 933-0272
Dayville (G-2056)
Cabinet Resources Ct Inc ..... G 860 352-2030
Canton (G-1308)
Cabinet Specialties LLC ..... G 860 747-4114
Plainville (G-6781)
Cabinet Works LLC ..... G 860 450-0803
Storrs (G-8544)
Cabinetmakers Choice LLC ..... G 203 426-3247
Sandy Hook (G-7302)
Cabinets Kwik ..... G 860 538-5047
New Britain (G-4954)
Celtic Stoneworks ..... G 860 846-0279
Plainville (G-6786)
Chris Cross LLC ..... G 203 386-8426
Stratford (G-8595)
Chris Peterson Woodworks ..... G 860 542-0140
Norfolk (G-5823)
Christopher Peacock Homes ..... G 203 862-9333
Greenwich (G-3143)
Christopoulos Designs Inc ..... F 203 576-1110
Bridgeport (G-733)
Chunghua Cabinet CT Inc ..... G 718 886-4588
Stamford (G-8145)
Classic Cabinets ..... G 860 749-9743
Enfield (G-2625)
Clinton Babcock & Sons ..... G 860 887-9166
Ledyard (G-3871)
Connecticut Cabinet Distrs LLC ..... G 860 508-6240
Glastonbury (G-3024)
Connecticut Solid Surface LLC ..... E 860 410-9800
Plainville (G-6791)
▲ Conway Hardwood Products LLC ..... E 860 355-4030
Gaylordsville (G-2991)
Currie & Kingston LLC ..... G 203 698-9428
Riverside (G-7191)
Custom Cabinet & European ..... G 860 430-9396
Glastonbury (G-3026)
Custom Furniture & Design LLC ..... F 860 567-3519
Litchfield (G-3887)
Custom Interiors ..... G 860 738-8754
Winchester Center (G-10344)
Custom Stiles ..... G 203 410-2370
Milford (G-4503)
Cyr Woodworking Inc ..... G 860 232-1991
Newington (G-5646)
Dante Ltd ..... G 860 376-0204
Jewett City (G-3793)
David O Wells Custom Cabinetry ..... G 203 231-0280
Southbury (G-7851)
Design Shop Llc ..... G 203 937-1651
West Haven (G-9897)
Dj Cabinets ..... G 203 243-0032
West Haven (G-9900)
Domestic Kitchens Inc ..... E 203 368-1651
Fairfield (G-2776)
Dream Cabinets LLC ..... G 860 301-5625
Colchester (G-1547)
East Hartford Lamination Co ..... G 860 633-4637
Glastonbury (G-3029)
Edward Tomkievich ..... G 860 633 5811
Glastonbury (G-3032)
Farmington Valley Woodcrafts ..... G 860 793-9034
Plainville (G-6809)
Fdk Custom Cabinetry LLC ..... G 203 459-9909
Monroe (G-4717)
Focal Metals ..... G 203 743-4443
Bethel (G-300)
Forest Remodeling ..... G 413 222-7953
Somers (G-7659)
Golden Hill Cstm Cabinetry LLC ..... G 203 366-2222
Bridgeport (G-777)
Greenhaven Cabinetry & Millwor ..... G 860 535-1106
Stonington (G-8529)
Gregory Penta ..... G 860 747-2681
Plainville (G-6819)
Gridiron Capital LLC ..... D 203 972-1100
New Canaan (G-5108)
H & B Woodworking Co ..... G 860 793-6991
Plainville (G-6820)
Hanford Cabinet & Wdwkg Co ..... G 860 388-5055
Old Saybrook (G-6538)
Heartwood Cabinetry ..... G 860 295-0304
Marlborough (G-4124)
Holness Cabinetry LLC ..... G 203 598-0430
Middlebury (G-4279)
Homewood Cabinet Co Inc ..... G 860 599-2441
Pawcatuck (G-6715)
Hope Kit Cbinets Stone Sup LLC ..... G 203 504-3164
Stamford (G-8241)
▲ Hope Kit Cbinets Stone Sup LLC ..... G 203 610-6147
Bridgeport (G-786)
Industrial Wood Product Co ..... G 203 735-2374
Shelton (G-7475)
IS Cabinetry LLC ..... G 203 583-5857
Bridgeport (G-794)
J&A Woodworking Co Inc ..... G 203 287-1915
Hamden (G-3466)
John June Custom Cabinetry LLC ..... G 203 334-1720
Bridgeport (G-808)
John M Kriskey Carpentry ..... G 203 531-0194
Greenwich (G-3184)
Kingswood Kitchens Co Inc ..... D 203 792-8700
Danbury (G-1870)
Kit Architectural Designs LLC ..... G 203 378-6911
Stratford (G-8642)
Kitchen Cab Resurfacing LLC ..... F 203 334-2857
Bridgeport (G-818)
Kitchen Kraftsmen ..... G 860 616-1240
Windsor (G-10402)
Kitchen Living LLC ..... G 860 819-5847
East Hampton (G-2268)
Kitchenmax LLC ..... G 203 330-5041
Bridgeport (G-819)
Knb Design LLC ..... G 203 777-6661
New Haven (G-5310)
Kse Cabinets ..... G 860 754-7236
Middletown (G-4365)
Legere Group Ltd ..... C 860 674-0392
Avon (G-89)
Leos Kitchen & Stair Corp ..... G 860 225-7363
New Britain (G-5010)
Luchon Cabinet Woodwork ..... G 860 684-5037
Stafford Springs (G-8032)
Martin Cabinet Inc ..... E 860 747-5769
Plainville (G-6840)
Martin Cabinet Inc ..... D 860 747-5769
Bristol (G-1069)
Master Craft Kitchens ..... G 203 366-1461
Bridgeport (G-832)
Mj Martin Wood Working LLC ..... G 860 577-5311
Old Saybrook (G-6557)
Modern Classics ..... G 203 422-2862
Greenwich (G-3205)
Morris Woodworking ..... G 860 346-7500
Middletown (G-4382)
N Excellence Wood Inc ..... G 860 345-2050
Higganum (G-3770)
New England Kitchen Design Ctr ..... G 203 268-2626
Monroe (G-4742)
Northeast Cabinet Design ..... G 203 438-1709
Ridgefield (G-7158)
P L Woodworking ..... G 860 354-6855
Sherman (G-7599)
Peacock Cabinetry ..... G 203 862-9333
Norwalk (G-6293)
Pinhos Cabinets ..... G 860 274-1740
Oakville (G-6458)
Porta Door Co ..... E 203 888-6191
Seymour (G-7362)
Prescott Cabinet Co ..... G 860 495-0176
Pawcatuck (G-6723)
Prestige Cabinetry ..... G 860 558-2784
Stafford Springs (G-8034)
Privy Pine Products ..... G 203 272-6169
Cheshire (G-1432)
Quality Woodworks LLC ..... G 203 736-9200
Ansonia (G-48)
Ricci Cabinet &STair Co ..... G 203 889-6511
Wallingford (G-9353)
Rj Cabinetry LLC ..... G 203 515-8401
Westport (G-10149)
Robert L Lovallo ..... G 203 324-6655
Stamford (G-8396)
Ross Custom Cabinetry ..... G 203 913-2753
Milford (G-4633)
Roxbury Cabinet Co LLC ..... G 203 994-9855
Roxbury (G-7282)
Royal Woodcraft Inc ..... F 203 847-3461
Ansonia (G-49)
S J Pappas Inc ..... G 203 237-7701
Meriden (G-4236)
Schwank Archtctural Woodworker ..... G 203 912-0109
Redding (G-7107)
Sebastian Kitchen Cabinets ..... G 203 853-4411
Norwalk (G-6340)
Sharpline Cabinetry LLC ..... G 203 261-8454
Easton (G-2566)
▲ Song Bath LLC ..... G 800 353-0313
New Canaan (G-5144)
Specialty Shop Inc ..... G 860 647-1477
Manchester (G-4091)
St Johns Bridge LLC ..... G 860 927-3315
Kent (G-3826)
Star Woods Cabinet ..... G 203 546-8688
Brookfield (G-1227)
Sterling Custom Cabinetry LLC ..... G 203 335-5151
Bridgeport (G-913)
Steven Vandermaelen LLC ..... G 203 457-0143
Guilford (G-3393)
Stonewall Cabinetry LLC ..... G 860 803-7595
Enfield (G-2698)
Swan Cabinetry ..... G 203 667-7026
Trumbull (G-9079)
T C Kitchens Inc ..... G 203 375-4469
Stratford (G-8693)
Thornview Custom Cabinets ..... G 860 228-5054
Columbia (G-1613)
Timbercraft Cstm Dvtail Drwers ..... G 800 345-4930
New Milford (G-5596)
Tomkiel Furniture ..... G 860 871-7632
South Windsor (G-7834)
Top Sheft Cabinetry ..... G 203 345-0000
Bridgeport (G-928)
Viking Kitchen Cabinets LLC ..... E 860 223-7101
New Britain (G-5080)
West Hrtford Stirs Cbinets Inc ..... D 860 953-9151
Newington (G-5723)
West Mont Group ..... G 203 931-1033
West Haven (G-9963)
Westie Cabinetry LLC ..... G 860 873-8953
East Haddam (G-2250)
Wfv Cabinetmaker ..... G 203 761-9109
Wilton (G-10340)
Yankee Finishing ..... G 203 910-0645
Newington (G-5724)

2435 Hardwood Veneer & Plywood

Bergan Architectural Wdwkg Inc ..... E 860 346-0869
Middletown (G-4324)
Reis Floor Finishing ..... G 203 367-1273
Shelton (G-7546)
Thomas Bernhard Building Sys ..... E 203 925-0414
Southport (G-8013)

2439 Structural Wood Members, NEC

Country Carpenters Inc ..... G 860 228-2276
Hebron (G-3746)
Eastern Company ..... E 203 729-2255
Naugatuck (G-4878)
Richard G Swartwout Jr ..... G 860 377-2321
Andover (G-16)
Thomas Bernhard Building Sys ..... E 203 925-0414
Southport (G-8013)
Timber Frame Barn Conversions ..... G 860 219-0519
Windsor (G-10450)
Truss Manufacturing Inc ..... F 860 665-0000
Newington (G-5714)
Universal Component Corp ..... E 203 481-8787
East Haven (G-2458)

2441 Wood Boxes

Champlin-Packrite Inc ..... E 860 951-9217
Manchester (G-3994)
Coastal Pallet Corporation ..... E 203 333-1892
Bridgeport (G-737)
Colonial Wood Products Inc ..... F 203 932-9003
West Haven (G-9889)
Duhamels ..... G 860 928-4101
Woodstock (G-10664)
Eddinger Assoc LLC ..... G 860 344-0508
Middletown (G-4341)
Merrill Industries Inc ..... E 860 871-1888
Ellington (G-2595)
St Pierre Box and Lumber Co ..... G 860 413-9813
Canton (G-1326)
Vermont Pallet & Skid Shop ..... G 860 822-6949
Norwich (G-6437)
W R Hartigan & Son Inc ..... G 860 673-9203
Burlington (G-1278)
Westwood Products Inc ..... F 860 379-9401
Winsted (G-10543)

2448 Wood Pallets & Skids

Acm Warehouse & Distribution ..... G 203 239-9557
North Haven (G-5895)
Better Pallets Inc ..... G 203 230-9549
Branford (G-558)

SIC SECTION
24 LUMBER AND WOOD PRODUCTS, EXCEPT FURNITURE

Company	Code	Phone
Burn Time Enterprises LLC Plainville *(G-6780)*	G	860 410-0747
Central Pallet & Box New Britain *(G-4959)*	F	860 224-4416
Coastal Pallet Corporation Bridgeport *(G-737)*	E	203 333-1892
FCA LLC Norwalk *(G-6163)*	G	203 857-0825
Global Pallet Solutions LLC New Britain *(G-4992)*	G	860 826-5000
Guy Ravenelle Central Village *(G-1337)*	G	860 564-3200
HI-Tech Packaging Inc Stratford *(G-8626)*	E	203 378-2700
▲ Industrial Pallet LLC Eastford *(G-2536)*	E	860 974-0093
J J Box Co Inc Bridgeport *(G-796)*	G	203 367-1211
M & M Pallet Inc Waterbury *(G-9521)*	G	203 754-2606
Pallet Guys LLC North Haven *(G-5973)*	G	203 691-6716
Pallet Inc LLC Westport *(G-10137)*	G	203 227-8148
R & R Pallet Corp Cheshire *(G-1434)*	F	203 272-2784
Southern Conn Pallet Co Inc Wallingford *(G-9371)*	G	203 265-1313
St Pierre Box and Lumber Co Canton *(G-1326)*	G	860 413-9813
Talmadge & Valentine Co Inc New Milford *(G-5592)*	G	860 350-3534
Tcc Multi Kargo Norwalk *(G-6363)*	G	203 803-1462
Toy Pallet Ellington *(G-2607)*	G	860 803-9838
Vermont Pallet & Skid Shop Norwich *(G-6437)*	G	860 822-6949
Westwood Products Inc Winsted *(G-10543)*	F	860 379-9401

2449 Wood Containers, NEC

Company	Code	Phone
Champlin-Packrite Inc Manchester *(G-3994)*	E	860 951-9217
Indulge By Mersene LLC Westport *(G-10098)*	G	203 644-6172
Pith Products LLC Ashford *(G-63)*	F	860 487-4859
St Pierre Box and Lumber Co Canton *(G-1326)*	G	860 413-9813
Vermont Pallet & Skid Shop Norwich *(G-6437)*	G	860 822-6949
Westwood Products Inc Winsted *(G-10543)*	F	860 379-9401
Woodfree Crating Systems Inc Waterbury *(G-9636)*	F	203 759-1799

2451 Mobile Homes

Company	Code	Phone
Champion Enterprises Inc Storrs *(G-8545)*	G	860 429-3537
Old Coach Home Sales Sterling *(G-8515)*	E	860 774-1379
Rv Parts & Electric Inc Waterbury *(G-9595)*	G	203 754-5962

2452 Prefabricated Wood Buildings & Cmpnts

Company	Code	Phone
American Prefab Wood Pdts Co Bloomfield *(G-383)*	G	860 242-5468
Barcello Development Co Middletown *(G-4323)*	G	860 635-7676
Bond-Bilt Garages Inc Wallingford *(G-9221)*	G	203 269-3375
Carefree Building Co Inc Colchester *(G-1544)*	G	860 267-7600
Country Carpenters Inc Hebron *(G-3746)*	G	860 228-2276
Country Log Homes Canaan *(G-1285)*	G	413 229-8084
Country Log Homes Inc Goshen *(G-3097)*	F	413 229-8084
Design Ltd Sandy Hook *(G-7309)*	G	203 426-5539
Giuliano Construction LLC Hamden *(G-3451)*	G	203 230-3094
Heart Industrial Unions LLC Berlin *(G-187)*	G	800 769-0503
Nu Vision Homes LLC Middletown *(G-4388)*	G	860 209-8492
Post & Beam Homes Inc East Hampton *(G-2274)*	G	860 267-2060
Spedding Co New Milford *(G-5591)*	G	860 355-4076
Trigila Construction Inc Berlin *(G-228)*	E	860 828-8444
Walpole Woodworkers Inc Ridgefield *(G-7181)*	E	508 668-2800
Walpole Woodworkers Inc Westport *(G-10173)*	G	203 255-9010

2491 Wood Preserving

Company	Code	Phone
Amerifix LLC West Haven *(G-9883)*	G	203 931-7290
Bridgwell Rsources Holdings LLC Greenwich *(G-3137)*	G	203 622-9138
Country Carpenters Inc Hebron *(G-3746)*	G	860 228-2276
Techno Mtal Post Watertown LLC Waterbury *(G-9610)*	G	203 755-6403
Winthrop Construction LLC Deep River *(G-2106)*	G	860 322-4562

2493 Reconstituted Wood Prdts

Company	Code	Phone
Biofibers Capital Group LLC Ashford *(G-57)*	G	203 561-6133
Central Marble & Granite LLC Ansonia *(G-28)*	G	203 734-4644
Harris Wood Products Inc Manchester *(G-4026)*	G	860 649-7936
Mohegan Wood Pellets LLC Uncasville *(G-9099)*	G	860 862-6100
▲ Panolam Industries Intl Inc Shelton *(G-7523)*	E	203 925-1556
Robran Industries Inc Waterbury *(G-9594)*	G	203 510-6292
Stepping Stones MBL & Gran LLC Norwalk *(G-6357)*	G	203 854-0552

2499 Wood Prdts, NEC

Company	Code	Phone
111 Brentwood LLC Wallingford *(G-9192)*	G	203 284-5065
170 Mountainwood Road LLC Stamford *(G-8048)*	G	203 252-4284
227 Greenwood LLC Bethel *(G-254)*	G	203 798-9716
26 Beechwood Avenue LLC Milford *(G-4435)*	G	203 713-6425
29 Wychwood Road LLC Old Lyme *(G-6486)*	G	860 434-8078
6 Brookwood Drive LLC Watertown *(G-9678)*	G	860 945-3456
◆ Acme United Corporation Fairfield *(G-2743)*	C	203 254-6060
Agw Clssic Hardwood Floors LLC Westbrook *(G-9989)*	E	203 640-3106
Alpine Management Group LLC Westport *(G-10052)*	G	954 531-1692
American Metaseal of Conn Hamden *(G-3414)*	G	203 787-0281
Anne Queen Woodworking Naugatuck *(G-4858)*	F	203 720-1781
Aqua Design Kitchen and Bath S North Haven *(G-5908)*	G	203 773-1649
Artful Framer LLC Avon *(G-76)*	G	860 678-1321
Bender Management Inc Norwalk *(G-6091)*	G	203 847-3865
Brass City Tile Designs LLC Waterbury *(G-9443)*	G	203 597-8764
C N C Router Technologies Danbury *(G-1760)*	G	203 744-6651
Candlewood Boat Restoration New Fairfield *(G-5165)*	G	203 223-7893
▲ Carris Reels Connecticut Inc Enfield *(G-2621)*	D	860 749-8308
▲ Church Hill Classics Ltd Monroe *(G-4703)*	D	800 477-9005
Classic Framers Stonington *(G-8525)*	G	401 596-6820
Clint S Custom Woodworkin Jewett City *(G-3792)*	G	860 887-1476
Company of Craftsmen Mystic *(G-4808)*	G	860 536-4189
Connecticut Sign Service LLC Essex *(G-2714)*	G	860 767-7446
▲ Corktec Inc Stafford Springs *(G-8021)*	G	860 851-9417
Corts Custom Woodworking Bethlehem *(G-368)*	G	203 266-0146
Creative Woodworking LLC Waterbury *(G-9456)*	G	203 518-0336
D R Charles Envmtl Cnstr LLC Monroe *(G-4709)*	G	203 445-0412
DAngelo Woodcraft LLC Enfield *(G-2635)*	G	860 402-7175
Dante Ltd Jewett City *(G-3793)*	G	860 376-0204
Davenport Kitchen & Bath LLC West Simsbury *(G-9978)*	G	860 323-0630
Desjardins Woodworking Inc Goshen *(G-3098)*	G	860 491-9972
Devellis Woodworks LLC Kensington *(G-3809)*	G	203 610-4762
Diiorio Woodworks Norwalk *(G-6143)*	G	203 855-1331
Diy Awards LLC Stamford *(G-8187)*	G	800 810-1216
Dundorf Designs USA Inc Salem *(G-7288)*	G	860 859-2955
E & F Wood LLC Woodstock Valley *(G-10692)*	G	860 377-0601
Eastwoods Arms LLC Guilford *(G-3350)*	G	203 615-3476
Ebk Picture Framing & Gallery Hartford *(G-3581)*	G	860 523-9384
Edgewood Prospect LLC Unionville *(G-9114)*	G	860 255-7799
Elm City Manufacturing LLC North Haven *(G-5936)*	F	203 248-1969
Essex Wood Products Inc Colchester *(G-1550)*	G	860 537-3451
Fagan Design & Fabrication West Haven *(G-9907)*	G	203 937-1874
Finishing Solutions LLC Colchester *(G-1551)*	G	860 705-8231
Freezer Hill Mulch Company LLC Bethany *(G-242)*	G	203 758-3725
Greenwood Sub LLC East Hartford *(G-2332)*	G	860 291-8833
Harris Enterprise Corp Manchester *(G-4025)*	E	860 649-4663
Hydeville Manfacturing Inc Wallingford *(G-9285)*	G	203 265-0524
J & B Woodworking Stratford *(G-8634)*	G	203 377-4682
Jdm-Greenwood LLC Stamford *(G-8262)*	G	203 358-4816
Jim Kephart Woodturning Manchester *(G-4038)*	G	860 643-9431
Joe Charron Lebanon *(G-3855)*	G	860 423-2805
John M Kriskey Carpentry Greenwich *(G-3184)*	G	203 531-0194
Juan Gallegos Danbury *(G-1866)*	G	203 744-0575
Kensington Glass and Frmng Co Berlin *(G-192)*	G	860 828-9428
Legere Group Ltd Avon *(G-89)*	G	860 674-0392
Litchfield Windsors Harwinton *(G-3732)*	G	860 485-1019
LLC Wolff Woods Mystic *(G-4826)*	G	860 415-9089
Lundgren Eric Woodworking New Milford *(G-5559)*	G	860 350-5153
Luther Fence LLC Groton *(G-3298)*	G	860 445-5660
▲ Mc Cann Bros Inc Monroe *(G-4734)*	E	203 335-8630
Michael Shortell Hartford *(G-3642)*	G	860 236-4787
Muddy Brook Wood Products Woodstock *(G-10673)*	G	860 928-2205
Mulch Ferris Products LLC Danbury *(G-1889)*	G	203 790-1155
N A B Fine Woodworking LLC Stamford *(G-8317)*	G	203 667-3922
Nantz Woodcraft Colchester *(G-1558)*	G	860 267-8853
New England Joinery Works Inc Essex *(G-2728)*	G	203 767-3377
New England Tile & Stone Inc Stamford *(G-8323)*	F	914 481-4488
Nohha Inc Orange *(G-6616)*	G	203 687-6741
North Forty Pest Ctrl Co LLC Woodbury *(G-10648)*	G	203 263-4551
Northeast Wood Sales Marion *(G-4117)*	G	860 621-9613

Old Wood Workshop..................G....... 860 655-5259
Pomfret Center *(G-6945)*
Paul Dringoli..................G....... 203 248-0281
Hamden *(G-3496)*
Petrini Art & Frame LLC..................G....... 860 677-2747
Avon *(G-99)*
Pleasant Valley Fence Co Inc..................F....... 860 379-0088
Pleasant Valley *(G-6925)*
Purvins Woodcraft..................G....... 860 456-1933
Lebanon *(G-3860)*
Refined Designs..................G....... 860 535-7273
Stonington *(G-8537)*
Regional Stairs LLC..................G....... 860 290-1242
East Hartford *(G-2363)*
Renaissance Craftsmen LLC..................G....... 860 916-3583
Hartford *(G-3677)*
Rockwell Art & Framing LLC..................G....... 203 762-8311
Wilton *(G-10325)*
Saint Josephs Wood Pdts LLC..................G....... 203 787-5746
New Haven *(G-5385)*
Saints Woodworking LLC..................G....... 860 657-4733
Glastonbury *(G-3080)*
Sherwood Equine LLC..................G....... 860 653-3599
Granby *(G-3113)*
Smith Frame & Moulding LLC..................G....... 860 389-8871
Bozrah *(G-532)*
Steven Rosendahl Inc..................G....... 860 928-3136
Woodstock *(G-10685)*
Strouts Woodworking..................G....... 860 623-8445
Broad Brook *(G-1153)*
Sweet Peet North America Inc..................G....... 860 361-6444
Litchfield *(G-3901)*
Teak LLC..................G....... 203 845-0345
Norwalk *(G-6364)*
Thomas Delspina Fine Frames..................G....... 203 256-8628
Bridgeport *(G-924)*
Thomas Townsend Custom Marine..................G....... 860 536-9800
Mystic *(G-4849)*
Vacca Architectural Woodworkin..................G....... 860 599-3677
Pawcatuck *(G-6730)*
Vitale Woodworks LLC..................G....... 203 387-3565
Orange *(G-6633)*
W R Hartigan & Son Inc..................G....... 860 673-9203
Burlington *(G-1278)*
Walpole Woodworkers Inc..................E....... 508 668-2800
Ridgefield *(G-7181)*
Walpole Woodworkers Inc..................G....... 203 255-9010
Westport *(G-10173)*
Wood Creations & Graphics LLC..................G....... 203 271-3568
Cheshire *(G-1459)*
Wood Services LLC..................G....... 203 983-5752
Greenwich *(G-3261)*
Wood-N-Tap..................G....... 203 265-9663
Wallingford *(G-9404)*
Woodworkers Resource..................G....... 860 668-4100
Suffield *(G-8739)*
Woodys Wooden Wonders LLC..................G....... 860 669-5221
Clinton *(G-1536)*

25 FURNITURE AND FIXTURES

2511 Wood Household Furniture

Adirondack Wood Products LLC..................G....... 203 322-4518
Stamford *(G-8062)*
American Wood Products..................G....... 203 248-4433
North Haven *(G-5903)*
Andre Furniture Industries..................G....... 860 528-8826
South Windsor *(G-7709)*
Baldwin Lawn Furniture LLC..................F....... 860 347-1306
Middletown *(G-4322)*
Bolton Hill Industries Inc..................G....... 860 742-0311
Coventry *(G-1647)*
Bonito Manufacturing Inc..................D....... 203 234-8786
North Haven *(G-5915)*
Carefree Building Co Inc..................F....... 860 267-7600
Colchester *(G-1544)*
CB Seating Etc LLC..................G....... 203 359-3880
Norwalk *(G-6109)*
▲ Cherner Chair Company LLC..................G....... 203 894-4702
Ridgefield *(G-7127)*
Christopoulos Designs Inc..................F....... 203 576-1110
Bridgeport *(G-733)*
Connecticut Solid Surface LLC..................E....... 860 410-9800
Plainville *(G-6791)*
Craig Dascanio..................G....... 860 651-0466
West Simsbury *(G-9975)*
Custom Furniture & Design LLC..................F....... 860 567-3519
Litchfield *(G-3887)*
Daniel Richardson..................G....... 860 774-3675
Danielson *(G-1988)*
Designers Resource..................G....... 203 874-7731
Milford *(G-4509)*
Edko Cabinets LLC..................G....... 203 463-8346
Seymour *(G-7345)*
Ethan Allen Interiors Inc..................B....... 203 743-8000
Danbury *(G-1817)*
Finishing Touch Woodcraft..................G....... 860 916-2642
Canton *(G-1315)*
G A Mals Woodworking..................G....... 860 828-8702
Berlin *(G-183)*
Genie Shelf..................G....... 203 241-7523
Brookfield *(G-1190)*
Get Back Inc..................G....... 860 274-9991
Oakville *(G-6453)*
Hitchcock Chair Company Ltd..................G....... 860 738-0141
Riverton *(G-7208)*
Hitchcock Holding Company Inc..................G....... 860 738-0141
New Hartford *(G-5193)*
Home Sweeter HM Kit & Bath LLC..................G....... 203 948-6482
Bethel *(G-309)*
Ian Ingersoll Cabinetmaker..................F....... 860 672-6334
West Cornwall *(G-9764)*
Industrial Wood Product Co..................G....... 203 735-2374
Shelton *(G-7475)*
Kensington Woodworking Co..................G....... 860 828-4972
Kensington *(G-3812)*
L & L Capital Partners LLC..................F....... 203 834-6222
Wilton *(G-10307)*
Lookout Solutions LLC..................G....... 203 750-0307
Norwalk *(G-6237)*
Madigan Millwork Inc..................G....... 860 673-7601
Unionville *(G-9119)*
Moran Woodworking LLC..................G....... 203 438-0477
Ridgefield *(G-7156)*
Morris Woodworking..................G....... 860 346-7500
Middletown *(G-4382)*
Nap Brothers Parlor Frame Inc..................F....... 860 633-9998
Glastonbury *(G-3062)*
Nec A Nec Woods Inc..................G....... 203 431-0621
Redding *(G-7104)*
Old House Woodcraft LLC..................G....... 860 228-2174
Columbia *(G-1610)*
▼ Oomph LLC..................G....... 203 216-9848
New Canaan *(G-5128)*
▲ Parish Associates Inc..................G....... 203 335-4100
Fairfield *(G-2826)*
Paul Dringoli..................G....... 203 248-0281
Hamden *(G-3496)*
◆ Salamander Designs Ltd..................E....... 860 761-9500
Bloomfield *(G-484)*
Springbrook Woodcrafters LLC..................G....... 860 870-7303
Ellington *(G-2602)*
St Johns Bridge LLC..................G....... 860 927-3315
Kent *(G-3826)*
Thomas Lord Cabinet Maker..................G....... 860 546-9283
Canterbury *(G-1302)*
Transportable LLC..................G....... 860 455-9208
Chaplin *(G-1343)*
Tudor House Furniture Co Inc..................E....... 203 288-8451
Hamden *(G-3524)*
▲ USA Wood Incorporated..................G....... 203 238-4285
Meriden *(G-4262)*
Walpole Woodworkers Inc..................G....... 203 255-9010
Westport *(G-10173)*
Walpole Woodworkers Inc..................E....... 508 668-2800
Ridgefield *(G-7181)*
Western Conn Craftsmen LLC..................G....... 203 312-8167
New Fairfield *(G-5183)*
Woodworkers Heaven Inc..................F....... 203 333-2778
Bridgeport *(G-940)*
Woody Mosch Cabinet Makers..................G....... 203 266-7619
Bethlehem *(G-377)*

2512 Wood Household Furniture, Upholstered

C & D Upholstery..................G....... 203 838-1050
Norwalk *(G-6104)*
Cerrito Furniture Inds Inc..................F....... 203 481-2580
Branford *(G-573)*
Clark Manner Marguarite..................G....... 860 444-7679
New London *(G-5463)*
Craig Dascanio..................G....... 860 651-0466
West Simsbury *(G-9975)*
Da Cunha Woodworks..................G....... 860 529-3889
New Britain *(G-4970)*
Daniel Richardson..................G....... 860 774-3675
Danielson *(G-1988)*
Ethan Allen Interiors Inc..................B....... 203 743-8000
Danbury *(G-1817)*
Ethan Allen Retail Inc..................B....... 203 743-8600
Danbury *(G-1819)*
J G Taglieri..................G....... 860 645-1060
Manchester *(G-4037)*
Little Joes Upholstery..................G....... 203 975-2871
Stamford *(G-8286)*
Reborn House..................G....... 203 216-9874
Branford *(G-640)*
Reid Interiors..................G....... 860 569-1240
East Hartford *(G-2364)*
Tudor House Furniture Co Inc..................E....... 203 288-8451
Hamden *(G-3524)*
Weiss Sleep Shop Inc..................G....... 860 445-1219
Groton *(G-3317)*

2514 Metal Household Furniture

Advanced Prototype Development..................G....... 203 267-1262
Southbury *(G-7842)*
Bruce Kahn..................G....... 203 329-7441
Stamford *(G-8121)*
Columbia Mat & Upholstering Co..................G....... 203 789-1213
Hamden *(G-3429)*
CT Acquisitions LLC..................E....... 888 441-0537
Wallingford *(G-9243)*
◆ Durham Manufacturing Company..................D....... 860 349-3427
Durham *(G-2146)*
Get Back Inc..................G....... 860 274-9991
Oakville *(G-6453)*
Modern Objects Inc..................G....... 203 378-5785
Norwalk *(G-6264)*
Morris Woodworking..................G....... 860 346-7500
Middletown *(G-4382)*
Rj Kach Ltd..................G....... 203 457-1349
Madison *(G-3951)*
◆ Salamander Designs Ltd..................E....... 860 761-9500
Bloomfield *(G-484)*
Southern Almnum Intrmdte Hldin..................G....... 870 234-8660
New Canaan *(G-5145)*
Stonewall Kitchen LLC..................C....... 860 648-9215
South Windsor *(G-7831)*
Tailored Kitchens By Ann-Morin..................G....... 860 428-2397
Brooklyn *(G-1256)*

2515 Mattresses & Bedsprings

A&S Innersprings Usa LLC..................G....... 860 298-0401
Windsor *(G-10351)*
◆ Blue Bell Mattress Company LLC..................C....... 860 292-6372
East Windsor *(G-2484)*
Columbia Mat & Upholstering Co..................G....... 203 789-1213
Hamden *(G-3429)*
Demattia Charitable Found..................G....... 203 254-1558
Fairfield *(G-2773)*
J J Concrete Foundations..................G....... 203 798-8310
Bethel *(G-315)*
Ramdial Parts and Services LLC..................G....... 860 296-5175
Hartford *(G-3675)*
▲ Restopedic Inc..................G....... 203 393-1520
Bethany *(G-249)*
Saatva Inc..................E....... 877 672-2882
Westport *(G-10153)*
▲ Subinas USA LLC..................F....... 860 298-0401
Windsor *(G-10445)*
Symbol Mattress of New England..................B....... 860 779-3112
Dayville *(G-2075)*
Vijon Studios Inc..................G....... 860 399-7440
Old Saybrook *(G-6575)*
Water & Air Inc..................G....... 860 423-0234
South Windham *(G-7693)*

2517 Wood T V, Radio, Phono & Sewing Cabinets

Belmont Corporation..................E....... 860 589-5700
Bristol *(G-980)*
Christopoulos Designs Inc..................F....... 203 576-1110
Bridgeport *(G-733)*
St Johns Bridge LLC..................G....... 860 927-3315
Kent *(G-3826)*
These Guys..................G....... 860 344-0022
Middletown *(G-4426)*

2519 Household Furniture, NEC

Accolade Furniture LLC..................G....... 203 265-0524
Wallingford *(G-9196)*
Dbo Home LLC..................G....... 860 364-6008
Sharon *(G-7377)*
Ducduc LLC..................G....... 860 482-1322
Torrington *(G-8918)*
Lovesac Company..................G....... 888 636-1223
Stamford *(G-8290)*

SIC SECTION 25 FURNITURE AND FIXTURES

New Age Motorsports LLC ....G 203 268-1999
Monroe (G-4741)
▼ Oomph LLC ....G 203 216-9848
New Canaan (G-5128)

2521 Wood Office Furniture

Atlantic Group Connecticut LLC ....G 203 847-0000
Norwalk (G-6080)
Belmont Corporation ....E 860 589-5700
Bristol (G-980)
Bergan Architectural Wdwkg Inc ....E 860 346-0869
Middletown (G-4324)
Bloomfield Wood & Melamine Inc ....F 860 243-3226
Bloomfield (G-398)
▲ Bold Wood Interiors LLC ....F 203 907-4077
New Haven (G-5249)
Bolton Hill Industries Inc ....G 860 742-0311
Coventry (G-1647)
Clay Furniture Industries Inc ....F 860 643-7580
Manchester (G-3996)
Conco Wood Working Inc ....G 203 934-9665
West Haven (G-9890)
Cyr Woodworking Inc ....G 860 232-1991
Newington (G-5646)
G Woodcraft ....G 203 846-4168
Norwalk (G-6173)
Gregory Woodworks LLC ....G 203 794-0726
Bethel (G-306)
Innovant Inc ....G 203 594-7270
New Canaan (G-5111)
Knoll Inc ....E 860 395-2093
Old Saybrook (G-6550)
◆ Lesro Industries Inc ....D 800 275-7545
Bloomfield (G-442)
Neiss Corp ....F 860 872-8528
Vernon (G-9148)
Professional Trades Netwrk LLC ....G 860 567-0173
Watertown (G-9726)
S J Pappas Inc ....G 203 237-7701
Meriden (G-4236)
◆ Salamander Designs Ltd ....E 860 761-9500
Bloomfield (G-484)
Statham Woodwork ....G 203 831-0629
Norwalk (G-6355)

2522 Office Furniture, Except Wood

Bonito Manufacturing Inc ....D 203 234-8786
North Haven (G-5915)
Conco Wood Working Inc ....G 203 934-9665
West Haven (G-9890)
◆ Durham Manufacturing Company ....D 860 349-3427
Durham (G-2146)
Nutmeg Architectural Wdwrk Inc ....E 203 325-4434
Stamford (G-8333)
One and Co Inc ....F 860 892-5180
Norwich (G-6427)
Peristere LLC ....G 860 783-5301
Manchester (G-4075)
Sabon Industries Inc ....G 203 255-8880
Fairfield (G-2840)
Static Safe Products Company ....F 203 937-6391
Cornwall Bridge (G-1620)

2531 Public Building & Related Furniture

Air Cruisers Co ....G 732 681-3527
South Windsor (G-7703)
▲ FM Industries LLC ....G 860 610-0340
East Hartford (G-2327)
Halls Rental Service LLC ....G 203 488-0383
North Branford (G-5841)
Jetset Interiors LLC ....G 860 292-7962
Windsor Locks (G-10492)
Johnson Controls Inc ....G 860 887-7185
Norwich (G-6419)
Johnson Controls Inc ....D 860 886-9021
Ledyard (G-3875)
Johnson Controls Inc ....G 860 571-3300
Rocky Hill (G-7253)
Johnson Controls Inc ....D 678 297-4040
Meriden (G-4179)
Morris Woodworking ....G 860 346-7500
Middletown (G-4382)
▲ Torrington Distributors Inc ....E 860 482-4464
Torrington (G-8981)
Town of Vernon ....G 203 268-7200
Easton (G-2567)
Wepa Sports LLC ....G 203 971-9372
New London (G-5496)

2541 Wood, Office & Store Fixtures

A S J Specialties LLC ....G 203 284-8650
Wallingford (G-9194)
Absolute Countertops LLC ....G 203 395-8259
Derby (G-2107)
Ace Cabinet Company ....G 860 225-6111
New Britain (G-4933)
Bolton Hill Industries Inc ....G 860 742-0311
Coventry (G-1647)
BP Countertop Design Co LLC ....G 203 732-1620
Derby (G-2110)
C Mather Company Inc ....G 860 528-5667
South Windsor (G-7721)
▲ Creative Dimensions Inc ....E 203 250-6500
Cheshire (G-1376)
Custom Crft Ktchns By Rizio BR ....F 203 268-0271
Monroe (G-4708)
East Hartford Lamination Co ....G 860 633-4637
Glastonbury (G-3029)
Edko Cabinets LLC ....G 203 463-8346
Seymour (G-7345)
Edward Tomkievich ....G 860 633-5811
Glastonbury (G-3032)
Formatron Ltd ....F 860 676-0227
Farmington (G-2908)
Gambrel Acres ....G 860 774-3047
Danielson (G-1992)
Gregory Woodworks LLC ....G 203 794-0726
Bethel (G-306)
John M Kriskey Carpentry ....G 203 531-0194
Greenwich (G-3184)
Leos Kitchen & Stair Corp ....G 860 225-7363
New Britain (G-5010)
Lingard Cabinet Co LLC ....G 860 647-9886
Manchester (G-4048)
Michael Martinetto ....G 203 874-6114
Milford (G-4577)
Modern Woodcrafts LLC ....D 860 677-7371
Plainville (G-6845)
Morris Woodworking ....G 860 346-7500
Middletown (G-4382)
Mr Shower Door Inc ....G 203 838-3667
Norwalk (G-6265)
New England Cabinet Co Inc ....F 860 747-9995
New Britain (G-5021)
One and Co Inc ....F 860 892-5180
Norwich (G-6427)
Phone Booth Inc ....G 203 859-5389
New Haven (G-5364)
Premier Custom Cabinetry ....G 860 659-1863
Glastonbury (G-3073)
Premier Mfg Group Inc ....D 203 924-6617
Shelton (G-7539)
Pro Counters New England LLC ....G 203 347-8663
Ansonia (G-46)
Robert L Lovallo ....G 203 324-6655
Stamford (G-8396)
Specialty Shop Inc ....G 860 647-1477
Manchester (G-4091)
St Johns Bridge LLC ....G 860 927-3315
Kent (G-3826)
Stevenson Group Corporation ....F 860 689-0011
Harwinton (G-3740)
T C Kitchens Inc ....G 203 375-4469
Stratford (G-8693)
Tolland Architectural Wdwkg LLC ....G 860 875-9841
Tolland (G-8882)
Viking Kitchen Cabinets LLC ....E 860 223-7101
New Britain (G-5080)
W R Hartigan & Son Inc ....G 860 673-9203
Burlington (G-1278)

2542 Partitions & Fixtures, Except Wood

American Stonecrafters Inc ....G 203 514-9725
Wallingford (G-9202)
▲ Ardent Inc ....E 860 528-6000
East Hartford (G-2292)
Bethel Mail Service ....F 203 730-1399
Bethel (G-262)
Bull Metal Products Inc ....E 860 346-9691
Middletown (G-4329)
C Mather Company Inc ....G 860 528-5667
South Windsor (G-7721)
▼ Di-Cor Industries Inc ....F 860 585-5583
Bristol (G-1017)
▲ Displaycraft Inc ....E 860 747-9110
Plainville (G-6799)
◆ Durham Manufacturing Company ....D 860 349-3427
Durham (G-2146)
▲ In Store Experience Inc ....E 203 221-4777
Westport (G-10097)
Mitchell-Bate Company ....E 203 233-0862
Waterbury (G-9545)
Musano Inc ....F 203 879-4651
Wolcott (G-10575)
▲ Platt-Labonia of N Haven Inc ....D 203 239-5681
North Haven (G-5977)
Richard Riggio and Sons Inc ....E 860 767-0812
Ivoryton (G-3789)

2591 Drapery Hardware, Window Blinds & Shades

1st Vertical LLC ....G 860 458-0120
Willington (G-10243)
◆ Ahlstrom-Munksjo Nonwovens LLC ....B 860 654-8300
Windsor Locks (G-10469)
Arrow Window Shade Mfg Co ....G 860 956-3570
Wethersfield (G-10180)
Arrow Window Shade Mfg Co Mrdn ....F 860 563-4035
Wethersfield (G-10181)
Ben Baena & Son ....G 203 334-8568
Bridgeport (G-710)
Blinds Dept ....G 203 655-3378
Darien (G-2009)
Custom Upholstery Workshop ....G 203 367-4231
Fairfield (G-2770)
Debbie Pileika Interiors ....G 860 668-6324
West Suffield (G-9986)
Decorator Services Inc ....E 203 384-8144
Bridgeport (G-743)
Drapery Consultants ....G 203 855-0454
Norwalk (G-6150)
Guys Blind ....G 203 270-8977
Newtown (G-5741)
Kilcourse Specialty Products ....G 860 210-2075
New Milford (G-5555)
Middlesex Shades and Blinds ....G 860 346-7705
Middletown (G-4378)
Niantic Awning Company ....G 860 739-0161
Niantic (G-5813)
Porter Preston Inc ....E 203 753-1113
Waterbury (G-9582)
Prospect Flooring ....G 203 758-4207
Prospect (G-7017)
R & M Associates Inc ....F 860 633-0721
Glastonbury (G-3078)
◆ Rollease Acmeda Inc ....D 203 964-1573
Stamford (G-8397)
◆ Roto-Frank of America Inc ....D 860 526-4996
Chester (G-1482)
Thomas W Raftery Inc ....E 860 278-9870
Hartford (G-3703)
Vertical Development LLC ....G 203 208-0806
Branford (G-665)
Vertical Edge LLC ....G 203 513-2806
Shelton (G-7578)
Vertical Management LLC ....G 203 422-2547
Greenwich (G-3254)
Vertical Realms LLC ....G 860 508-5273
Tariffville (G-8745)
Vertical Studios LLC ....G 203 562-6542
North Haven (G-6012)
Vertical Ventures Intl LLC ....G 203 227-1364
Weston (G-10044)

2599 Furniture & Fixtures, NEC

▲ Brand Factory Agency ....G 203 984-6178
Southport (G-8000)
Copeland Latasha ....G 860 728-8289
Hartford (G-3570)
Curtiss Woodworking Inc ....F 203 527-9305
Prospect (G-6998)
DJS Campus Kitchen LLC ....G 860 439-1572
New London (G-5469)
General Seating Solutions LLC ....F 860 242-3307
South Windsor (G-7757)
JJ Greco Carting LLC ....G 203 661-4947
Cos Cob (G-1635)
Liberty Garage Inc ....G 203 778-0222
Danbury (G-1873)
Ordinary Joes ....G 860 945-1500
Watertown (G-9718)
River Mill Co ....F 860 669-5915
Clinton (G-1521)
Thames River Furniture LLC ....G 201 312-2050
Uncasville (G-9105)
Triple Play Sports ....F 860 417-2877
Watertown (G-9742)

S I C

Employee Codes: A=Over 500 employees, B=251-500
C=101-250, D=51-100, E=20-50, F=10-19, G=1-9
2020 Harris Connecticut
Manufacturers Directory
389

25 FURNITURE AND FIXTURES

Vazzanos Catering LLC .... F 203 378-3331
  Trumbull *(G-9091)*
Westmount Group LLC .... G 203 931-1033
  West Haven *(G-9964)*

26 PAPER AND ALLIED PRODUCTS

2611 Pulp Mills

Cellmark Pulp & Paper Inc .... F 203 299-5050
  Norwalk *(G-6111)*
▲ Eldorado Usa Inc .... G 203 208-2282
  Branford *(G-587)*
Heritage Newsprint LLC .... G 203 393-0567
  Bethany *(G-244)*
International Paper - 16 Inc .... G 203 329-8544
  Stamford *(G-8254)*
▲ Willimantic Waste Paper Co Inc .... C 860 423-4527
  Willimantic *(G-10240)*

2621 Paper Mills

◆ Ahlstrom Windsor Locks LLC .... F 860 654-8629
  Windsor Locks *(G-10468)*
▼ Ahlstrom-Munksjo USA Inc .... F 860 654-8300
  Windsor Locks *(G-10470)*
◆ American Banknote Corporation .... G 203 941-4090
  Stamford *(G-8074)*
American Kraft Paper Inds LLC .... G 203 323-1916
  Stamford *(G-8076)*
▲ Arrow Marketing Inc .... G 203 375-7541
  Stratford *(G-8570)*
◆ Brant Industries Inc .... F 203 661-3344
  Greenwich *(G-3136)*
Bristol Adult Resource Ctr Inc .... E 860 583-8721
  Bristol *(G-987)*
Bristol Bliss LLC .... G 203 704-0952
  Bristol *(G-988)*
Bristol Nitro Softball Corp .... G 860 940-1924
  Bristol *(G-990)*
Bristol Plaza .... G 617 553-1820
  Bristol *(G-991)*
Cifc Early Lrng Programs/Wic .... G 203 206-6341
  Danbury *(G-1768)*
Community Acpncture Brstol LLC .... G 860 833-9330
  Bristol *(G-1004)*
Coveris Advanced Coatings .... G 413 244-9685
  West Haven *(G-9894)*
D K Schulman .... G 860 868-4300
  New Preston *(G-5612)*
DAmbruoso Studios LLC .... G 203 758-9660
  Middlebury *(G-4276)*
Doubletree .... F 860 589-7766
  Bristol *(G-1018)*
Dunn Paper Holdings Inc .... D 860 289-7496
  East Hartford *(G-2316)*
Dynamic Printing .... G 203 459-8762
  Monroe *(G-4714)*
Finch Paper Holdings LLC .... G 203 622-9138
  Greenwich *(G-3159)*
First Papermill LLC .... G 203 740-1991
  Brookfield *(G-1188)*
Graphics Services Corporation .... G 203 270-7578
  Newtown *(G-5740)*
International Paper - 16 Inc .... G 203 329-8544
  Stamford *(G-8254)*
International Paper Company .... C 860 928-7901
  Putnam *(G-7047)*
JM Shea LLC .... G 203 431-4435
  Ridgefield *(G-7150)*
Kimberly-Clark Corporation .... A 860 210-1602
  New Milford *(G-5556)*
Kimberly-Clark Corporation .... C 973 986-8454
  Stratford *(G-8639)*
▲ Kiss-U Corps LLC .... G 203 226-7730
  Weston *(G-10031)*
LP Hometown Pizza LLC .... G 860 589-1208
  Bristol *(G-1064)*
Mafcote International Inc .... F 203 644-1200
  Norwalk *(G-6244)*
Magnificat Mother of Div Mrcy .... G 860 584-8803
  Bristol *(G-1067)*
McMullan Wall Coverings .... G 860 569-6260
  East Hartford *(G-2344)*
▲ Mega Sound and Light LLC .... G 203 743-4200
  Danbury *(G-1882)*
Montambault Riva .... G 203 758-4981
  Prospect *(G-7011)*
▲ Norcell Inc .... F 203 254-5292
  Shelton *(G-7513)*
Norton Paper Mill LLC .... G 860 861-9701
  Colchester *(G-1560)*

Resolute FP US Inc .... B 203 292-6560
  Southport *(G-8008)*
▲ Royal Consumer Products LLC .... E 203 847-8500
  Norwalk *(G-6330)*
Sheaffer Pen Corp .... B 203 783-2894
  Shelton *(G-7553)*
Smart Foods of Bristol .... G 860 582-8882
  Bristol *(G-1118)*
Smith Tia Custm Statnary Phot .... G 860 767-1976
  Essex *(G-2734)*
Sre Bristol 322 Park St LLC .... G 860 348-0198
  East Berlin *(G-2177)*
State of Connecticut Educ .... G 860 584-8433
  Bristol *(G-1123)*
Steven Rosendahl Inc .... G 860 928-3136
  Woodstock *(G-10685)*
Thomas Design Group LLC .... G 203 588-1910
  Stamford *(G-8466)*
Up With Paper .... G 203 453-3300
  Guilford *(G-3400)*
▲ UST LLC .... G 203 817-3000
  Stamford *(G-8483)*
Vanilla Politics LLC .... G 203 221-0895
  Weston *(G-10043)*
Web Industries Inc .... G 860 779-3403
  Dayville *(G-2079)*
▲ Xamax Industries Inc .... E 203 888-7200
  Seymour *(G-7375)*
Yale University .... G 203 432-2424
  New Haven *(G-5448)*
Yale University .... G 203 432-7494
  New Haven *(G-5451)*
Yourcover LLC .... G 203 563-9233
  Wilton *(G-10342)*

2631 Paperboard Mills

▲ Action Packaging Systems Inc .... G 860 222-9510
  Ellington *(G-2571)*
B-P Products Inc .... E 203 288-0200
  Hamden *(G-3416)*
◆ Connecticut Container Corp .... C 203 248-2161
  North Haven *(G-5924)*
Fluted Partition Inc .... C 203 368-2548
  Bridgeport *(G-770)*
Graphic Packaging Intl LLC .... G 860 567-4196
  Litchfield *(G-3890)*
Keystone Paper & Box Co Inc .... D 860 291-0027
  South Windsor *(G-7783)*
Lydall Inc .... E 860 646-1233
  Manchester *(G-4050)*
◆ Metsa Board Americas Corp .... D 203 229-0037
  Norwalk *(G-6256)*
▲ Millen Industries Inc .... G 203 847-8500
  Norwalk *(G-6259)*
Pact Inc .... F 203 759-1799
  Waterbury *(G-9573)*
Paper Alliance LLC .... G 203 315-3116
  Branford *(G-631)*
▲ Rice Packaging Inc .... D 860 870-7057
  Ellington *(G-2598)*
Risha Rishi LLC .... G 860 346-7645
  Middletown *(G-4405)*
Russell Partition Co Inc .... G 203 239-5749
  North Haven *(G-5988)*
Schrafel Paperboard Converting .... E 203 931-1700
  West Haven *(G-9953)*
Sonoco .... G 860 928-7795
  Putnam *(G-7067)*
Westrock Cp LLC .... C 860 848-1500
  Uncasville *(G-9108)*
Westrock Rkt Company .... C 860 284-9820
  Farmington *(G-2978)*

2652 Set-Up Paperboard Boxes

◆ Agi-Shorewood Group Us LLC ...... A 203 324-4839
  Stamford *(G-8067)*
Ehrlich & Company .... G 203 481-1999
  Branford *(G-586)*
▲ Hudson Paper Company .... E 203 378-8759
  Stratford *(G-8628)*
▲ Millen Industries Inc .... G 203 847-8500
  Norwalk *(G-6259)*
▲ Rice Packaging Inc .... D 860 870-7057
  Ellington *(G-2598)*
Rondo America Incorporated .... C 203 723-5831
  Naugatuck *(G-4917)*
Westrock Rkt Company .... C 860 284-9820
  Farmington *(G-2978)*

2653 Corrugated & Solid Fiber Boxes

▼ AP Disposition LLC .... D 860 889-1344
  Norwich *(G-6406)*
Cascades Holding US Inc .... D 203 426-5871
  Newtown *(G-5732)*
Champlin-Packrite Inc .... E 860 951-9217
  Manchester *(G-3994)*
Colonial Corrugated Pdts Inc .... E 203 597-1707
  Waterbury *(G-9453)*
Common Sense Engineered Pdts .. G 203 888-8695
  Beacon Falls *(G-132)*
◆ Connecticut Container Corp .... C 203 248-2161
  North Haven *(G-5924)*
Corr/Dis Incorporated .... G 203 838-6075
  Norwalk *(G-6130)*
Creative Source LLC .... G 203 879-4005
  Wolcott *(G-10558)*
Danbury Square Box Company ... E 203 744-4611
  Danbury *(G-1787)*
Fluted Partition Inc .... C 203 334-3500
  Bridgeport *(G-771)*
Fluted Partition Inc .... C 203 368-2548
  Bridgeport *(G-770)*
Fortis Solutions Group LLC .... E 860 872-6311
  Ellington *(G-2590)*
Gbc Marketing LLC .... G 860 739-8760
  Niantic *(G-5807)*
General Packaging Products Inc .. G 203 846-1340
  Norwalk *(G-6178)*
Hi-Tech Packaging Inc .... E 203 378-2700
  Stratford *(G-8626)*
Holm Corrugated Container Inc ... E 860 628-5559
  Southington *(G-7935)*
Jackson Corrugated Cont Corp .... E 860 767-3373
  Essex *(G-2720)*
Kapstone Paper and Packg Corp . G 860 928-2211
  Putnam *(G-7051)*
Knapp Container Inc .... E 203 888-0511
  Beacon Falls *(G-137)*
Merrill Industries Inc .... E 860 871-1888
  Ellington *(G-2595)*
Merrill Industries LLC .... E 860 871-1888
  Ellington *(G-2596)*
Nutmeg Container Corporation ... D 860 963-6727
  Putnam *(G-7054)*
Park City Packaging Inc .... F 203 579-1965
  Bridgeport *(G-862)*
R & R Corrugated Container Inc . D 860 584-1194
  Bristol *(G-1102)*
Rand-Whitney Group LLC .... D 203 426-5871
  Newtown *(G-5774)*
▲ Rice Packaging Inc .... D 860 870-7057
  Ellington *(G-2598)*
Russell Partition Co Inc .... G 203 239-5749
  North Haven *(G-5988)*
Skyline Exhibits & Graphics .... F 860 635-2400
  Middletown *(G-4417)*
Westrock Rkt Company .... F 203 739-0318
  Bethel *(G-365)*
Westrock Rkt Company .... C 860 284-9820
  Farmington *(G-2978)*
Windham Container Corporation . E 860 928-7934
  Putnam *(G-7079)*

2655 Fiber Cans, Tubes & Drums

Greif Inc .... D 740 549-6000
  Windsor Locks *(G-10488)*
Marshall Paper Tube .... G 860 245-5536
  North Stonington *(G-6029)*

2656 Sanitary Food Containers

James River Corp .... G 203 854-2328
  Norwalk *(G-6217)*

2657 Folding Paperboard Boxes

◆ Agi-Shorewood Group Us LLC . A 203 324-4839
  Stamford *(G-8067)*
B-P Products Inc .... E 203 288-0200
  Hamden *(G-3416)*
Clondalkin Pharma & Healthcare E 860 342-1987
  Portland *(G-6955)*
Curtis Corporation A Del Corp ... C 203 426-5861
  Sandy Hook *(G-7307)*
▲ Curtis Packaging Corporation . C 203 426-5861
  Sandy Hook *(G-7308)*
Keystone Paper & Box Co Inc ... D 860 291-0027
  South Windsor *(G-7783)*
▲ Rice Packaging Inc .... D 860 870-7057
  Ellington *(G-2598)*

SIC SECTION
27 PRINTING, PUBLISHING, AND ALLIED INDUSTRIES

Sdi Systems Development .... G 860 967-5464
  Avon *(G-109)*

2671 Paper Coating & Laminating for Packaging

◆ Agi-Shorewood Group Us LLC ...... A 203 324-4839
  Stamford *(G-8067)*
▲ Amgraph Packaging Inc .... C 860 822-2000
  Baltic *(G-118)*
Ansel Label and Packaging Corp ...... E 203 452-0311
  Trumbull *(G-8999)*
▼ Atlas Agi Holdings LLC .... A 203 622-9138
  Greenwich *(G-3125)*
Biomerics LLC .... D 203 268-7238
  Monroe *(G-4698)*
▲ Bollore Inc .... D 860 774-2930
  Dayville *(G-2054)*
CCL Label Inc .... C 203 926-1253
  Shelton *(G-7413)*
▲ Flagship Converters Inc .... D 203 792-0034
  Danbury *(G-1826)*
Fluted Partition Inc .... C 203 368-2548
  Bridgeport *(G-770)*
Fortis Solutions Group LLC .... E 860 872-6311
  Ellington *(G-2590)*
General Packaging Products Inc ...... G 203 846-1340
  Norwalk *(G-6178)*
Identification Products Corp .... G 203 331-0931
  Bridgeport *(G-790)*
Identification Products Corp .... F 203 334-5969
  Bridgeport *(G-791)*
◆ Knox Enterprises Inc .... G 203 226-6408
  Westport *(G-10108)*
◆ Koster Keunen LLC .... F 860 945-3333
  Watertown *(G-9715)*
Miami Wabash Paper LLC .... E 203 847-8500
  Norwalk *(G-6257)*
▲ Mid State Assembly & Packg Inc ... G 203 634-8740
  Meriden *(G-4202)*
Packaging and Crating Tech LLC ..... G 203 759-1799
  Waterbury *(G-9572)*
Paxxus Inc .... E 860 242-0663
  Bloomfield *(G-461)*
Penmar Industries Inc .... F 860 853-4868
  Stratford *(G-8663)*
Polymer Films Inc .... E 203 932-3000
  West Haven *(G-9946)*
▲ Polymeric Converting LLC .... E 860 623-1335
  Enfield *(G-2678)*
▲ Quality Name Plate Inc .... D 860 633-9495
  East Glastonbury *(G-2185)*
▲ Rol-Vac Limited Partnership .... F 860 928-9929
  Dayville *(G-2072)*
Sealed Air Corporation .... C 203 791-3648
  Danbury *(G-1942)*
Sonoco Prtective Solutions Inc .... E 860 928-7795
  Putnam *(G-7068)*
▲ Stora Enso N Amercn Sls Inc .... G 203 541-5178
  Stamford *(G-8444)*
Tht Inc .... G 203 226-6408
  Westport *(G-10167)*
Windham Container Corporation ..... E 860 928-7934
  Putnam *(G-7079)*

2672 Paper Coating & Laminating, Exc for Packaging

Alsip Acquisition LLC .... G 203 202-7777
  Westport *(G-10053)*
Beiersdorf Inc .... B 203 854-8000
  Norwalk *(G-6088)*
▲ Beiersdorf North America Inc ...... F 203 563-5800
  Wilton *(G-10272)*
Copy Cats Inc .... F 860 442-8424
  New London *(G-5465)*
Design Label Manufacturing Inc ...... E 860 739-6266
  Old Lyme *(G-6505)*
H-O Products Corporation .... E 860 379-9875
  Winsted *(G-10523)*
Illinois Tool Works Inc .... C 860 646-8153
  Manchester *(G-4031)*
Ipg (us) Holdings Inc .... G 813 621-8410
  Ansonia *(G-40)*
Lgl Group Inc .... G 407 298-2000
  Greenwich *(G-3191)*
Markal Finishing Co Inc .... E 203 384-8219
  Bridgeport *(G-830)*
Neato Products LLC .... G 203 466-5170
  Milford *(G-4587)*

Robinson Tape & Label Inc .... E 203 481-5581
  Branford *(G-643)*
Scapa Holdings Inc .... B 860 688-8000
  Windsor *(G-10432)*
▼ Scapa North America Inc .... G 860 688-8000
  Windsor *(G-10433)*
Securemark Decal Corp .... F 773 622-6815
  Trumbull *(G-9072)*
Specialty Printing LLC .... D 860 623-8870
  East Windsor *(G-2521)*
The E J Davis Company .... E 203 239-5391
  North Haven *(G-5998)*

2673 Bags: Plastics, Laminated & Coated

▲ Amgraph Packaging Inc .... C 860 822-2000
  Baltic *(G-118)*
Kage Poly Products LLC .... G 203 646-8228
  Manchester *(G-4043)*
Rbi Inc .... G 860 444-0534
  New London *(G-5486)*
Re-Style Your Closets LLC .... G 860 658-9450
  Simsbury *(G-7642)*
Safety Bags Inc .... G 203 242-0727
  Shelton *(G-7549)*

2674 Bags: Uncoated Paper & Multiwall

▲ Hudson Paper Company .... E 203 378-8759
  Stratford *(G-8628)*
Mettler Packaging LLC .... G 860 628-6193
  Southington *(G-7953)*

2675 Die-Cut Paper & Board

American CT Rng Bnder Index & .... F 860 868-7900
  Washington *(G-9411)*
B-P Products Inc .... E 203 288-0200
  Hamden *(G-3416)*
C & T Print Finishing Inc .... F 860 282-0616
  South Windsor *(G-7720)*
▲ Kiss-U Corps LLC .... G 203 226-7730
  Weston *(G-10031)*
▼ Liftline Capital LLC .... F 860 395-0150
  Old Saybrook *(G-6553)*
Makino Inc .... F 860 223-0236
  New Britain *(G-5012)*
▲ Walker Products Incorporated ..... F 860 659-3781
  Glastonbury *(G-3094)*

2676 Sanitary Paper Prdts

Aci Industries Converting Ltd .... G 740 368-4166
  Stamford *(G-8058)*
Alfa Nobel LLC .... G 203 876-2823
  Milford *(G-4447)*
Capricorn Investors II LP .... A 203 861-6600
  Greenwich *(G-3140)*
Dunn Paper LLC .... D 860 466-4141
  East Hartford *(G-2317)*
◆ Edgewell Per Care Brands LLC ..... B 203 944-5500
  Shelton *(G-7435)*
Georgia-Pacific LLC .... G 203 866-9774
  Norwalk *(G-6180)*
Kimberly-Clark Corporation .... A 860 210-1602
  New Milford *(G-5556)*
Kimberly-Clark Corporation .... G 973 986-8454
  Stratford *(G-8639)*
▼ Playtex Products LLC .... D 203 944-5500
  Shelton *(G-7531)*
Soundview Paper Mills LLC .... G 201 796-4000
  Greenwich *(G-3240)*
W2w Partners LLC .... G 781 424-7824
  Greenwich *(G-3255)*

2677 Envelopes

Cenveo Inc .... D 203 595-3000
  Stamford *(G-8138)*
Cenveo Corporation .... E 303 790-8023
  Stamford *(G-8139)*
Cenveo Enterprises Inc .... G 203 595-3000
  Stamford *(G-8140)*
Cenveo Worldwide Limited .... F 203 595-3000
  Stamford *(G-8141)*
Cwl Enterprises Inc .... G 303 790-8023
  Stamford *(G-8174)*

2678 Stationery Prdts

American CT Rng Bnder Index & .... F 860 868-7900
  Washington *(G-9411)*
Classic Images Inc .... G 860 243-8365
  Bloomfield *(G-403)*

Forgetful Gentleman LLC .... G 203 431-2486
  Ridgefield *(G-7141)*
Gleason Group Incorporated .... G 203 312-0683
  New Fairfield *(G-5168)*
Harpers Invitations .... G 860 257-4615
  Glastonbury *(G-3046)*
Panagrafix Inc .... E 203 691-5529
  West Haven *(G-9942)*
Professional Mktg Svcs Inc .... F 203 610-6222
  Stratford *(G-8669)*
▲ Pulp Paper Products Inc .... G 860 806-0143
  Torrington *(G-8961)*

2679 Converted Paper Prdts, NEC

Ambiance Painting LLC .... F 203 354-8689
  Norwalk *(G-6068)*
B 9 Air Quality Services LLC .... G 203 387-1709
  Wallingford *(G-9217)*
B-P Products Inc .... E 203 288-0200
  Hamden *(G-3416)*
Biomerics LLC .... D 203 268-7238
  Monroe *(G-4698)*
Cenveo Inc .... D 203 595-3000
  Stamford *(G-8138)*
Cenveo Enterprises Inc .... G 203 595-3000
  Stamford *(G-8140)*
Cenveo Worldwide Limited .... F 203 595-3000
  Stamford *(G-8141)*
Cwl Enterprises Inc .... G 303 790-8023
  Stamford *(G-8174)*
Dietzgen Corporation .... G 813 849-4334
  West Haven *(G-9899)*
▲ Eagle Tissue LLC .... F 860 282-2535
  South Windsor *(G-7742)*
Esten McGee Inc .... G 203 544-2000
  West Redding *(G-9969)*
Flat Vernacular .... G 347 457-6227
  Norwalk *(G-6170)*
Flexo Label Solutions LLC .... G 860 243-9300
  Deep River *(G-2089)*
Harrison Enterprise LLC .... G 914 665-8348
  Bridgeport *(G-781)*
Honey Cell Inc .... G 203 925-1818
  Bridgeport *(G-785)*
◆ Knox Industries Inc .... C 203 226-6408
  Westport *(G-10109)*
Meadwestvaco Packg Systems LLC ... G 409 276-3137
  Stamford *(G-8301)*
◆ Mercantile Development Inc .... E 203 922-8880
  Shelton *(G-7497)*
Over Moon .... G 203 853-2498
  Norwalk *(G-6287)*
Pactiv Corporation .... E 203 288-7722
  North Haven *(G-5972)*
Park City Packaging Inc .... E 203 378-7384
  Stratford *(G-8662)*
▲ Rand-Whitney Recycling LLC ...... D 860 848-1900
  Montville *(G-4770)*
▲ Royal Consumer Products LLC .... E 203 847-8500
  Norwalk *(G-6330)*
Schrafel Paperboard Converting .... E 203 931-1700
  West Haven *(G-9953)*
Specialty Printing LLC .... D 860 623-8870
  East Windsor *(G-2521)*
Stafford Paper Company .... G 860 749-0787
  Somers *(G-7671)*
▲ Surys Inc .... C 203 333-5503
  Trumbull *(G-9078)*
▲ Tudor Converted Products Inc .... G 203 304-1875
  Newtown *(G-5795)*
▲ Valley Container Inc .... E 203 368-6546
  Bridgeport *(G-933)*
▲ Yumi Ecosolutions Inc .... G 203 803-1880
  Westport *(G-10178)*

27 PRINTING, PUBLISHING, AND ALLIED INDUSTRIES

2711 Newspapers: Publishing & Printing

200 Mill Plain Road LLC .... G 203 254-0113
  Fairfield *(G-2740)*
21st Century Fox America Inc .... G 203 563-6600
  Wilton *(G-10263)*
8 Times LLC .... G 203 227-7575
  Westport *(G-10048)*
Advisor .... F 203 239-4121
  North Haven *(G-5896)*
Alm Media LLC .... E 860 527-7900
  Hartford *(G-3551)*

Employee Codes: A=Over 500 employees, B=251-500
C=101-250, D=51-100, E=20-50, F=10-19, G=1-9

2020 Harris Connecticut
Manufacturers Directory

391

27 PRINTING, PUBLISHING, AND ALLIED INDUSTRIES SIC SECTION

Amandas Daily Ideas LLC ....G.... 203 761-8599
Wilton *(G-10269)*
American-Republican Inc ....D.... 203 574-3636
Waterbury *(G-9429)*
American-Republican Inc ....C.... 860 496-9301
Torrington *(G-8894)*
Barbara Jones ....G.... 203 596-9219
Waterbury *(G-9437)*
Bargain News Free Classified A ....D.... 203 377-3000
Stratford *(G-8578)*
Brian and Brenda Basinger ....G.... 203 972-9407
New Canaan *(G-5089)*
Bristol Press ....D.... 860 584-0501
Torrington *(G-8906)*
Browser Daily ....G.... 860 469-5534
Winsted *(G-10511)*
C S M S-I P A ....G.... 203 562-7228
North Haven *(G-5917)*
Cantata Media LLC ....F.... 203 951-9885
Norwalk *(G-6106)*
Capital Cities Communications ....G.... 203 784-8800
New Haven *(G-5253)*
Car Buyers Market ....E.... 516 482-0292
Trumbull *(G-9010)*
Catholic Transcript Inc ....F.... 860 286-2828
Bloomfield *(G-401)*
CCC Media LLC ....G.... 860 225-4601
New Britain *(G-4957)*
Central Conn Cmmunications LLC ....D.... 860 225-4601
New Britain *(G-4958)*
Chase Media Group ....F.... 914 962-3871
Newtown *(G-5733)*
Chromatic Press US Inc ....G.... 860 796-7667
West Hartford *(G-9788)*
Chronicle Printing Company ....D.... 860 423-8466
Willimantic *(G-10222)*
Circle Publishing LLC ....G.... 516 459-5016
Fairfield *(G-2762)*
Citizen News ....G.... 203 746-4669
New Fairfield *(G-5166)*
Coffee News ....G.... 860 613-0796
Cromwell *(G-1696)*
Comunidade News ....G.... 203 730-0175
Danbury *(G-1772)*
Conn Daily Campus ....G.... 860 486-3407
Storrs Mansfield *(G-8553)*
Connecticut Newspapers Inc ....G.... 203 964-2200
Stamford *(G-8157)*
Courant Specialty Products Inc ....E.... 860 241-3795
Hartford *(G-3572)*
Cromwell Chronicle ....G.... 860 257-8715
Rocky Hill *(G-7229)*
Daily Fare LLC ....G.... 203 743-7300
Bethel *(G-277)*
Daily Impressions LLC ....G.... 203 508-5305
Hamden *(G-3439)*
Daily Mart ....G.... 860 529-5210
Rocky Hill *(G-7233)*
Day Publishing Company ....B.... 860 701-4200
New London *(G-5466)*
Day Trust ....G.... 860 442-2200
New London *(G-5467)*
Disco Chick ....G.... 860 788-6203
Middletown *(G-4336)*
Efitzgerald Publishing LLC ....G.... 860 904-7250
West Hartford *(G-9805)*
EPic Publishing Services LLC ....G.... 860 204-7450
East Haddam *(G-2241)*
Fairfield County Gazette ....G.... 203 929-1405
Shelton *(G-7442)*
Foothills Trader Classified ....G.... 860 489-3121
Torrington *(G-8925)*
Footnote Journal LLC ....G.... 203 924-0391
Shelton *(G-7446)*
Four County Catholic Newspaper ....G.... 860 886-1281
Norwich *(G-6413)*
Freemans News Service ....G.... 860 485-1000
Harwinton *(G-3731)*
Freshiana LLC ....G.... 800 301-8071
Greenwich *(G-3165)*
Gamut Publishing ....E.... 860 296-6128
Hartford *(G-3598)*
Gatehouse Media LLC ....C.... 860 886-0106
Norwich *(G-6414)*
Gatehouse Media Conn Holdings ....E.... 860 887-9211
Norwich *(G-6415)*
Glastonbury Citizen Inc ....E.... 860 633-4691
Glastonbury *(G-3040)*
GPA ....G.... 860 410-0624
Plainville *(G-6818)*
Green Manor Corporation ....B.... 860 643-8111
Manchester *(G-4023)*
Greenwich Gofer ....G.... 203 637-8425
Old Greenwich *(G-6473)*
Greenwich Sentinel ....G.... 203 883-1430
Greenwich *(G-3175)*
Greenwich Time ....G.... 203 253-2922
Stamford *(G-8221)*
Hamden Journal LLC ....G.... 203 668-6307
Hamden *(G-3456)*
Hamiltonbookcom LLC ....G.... 860 824-0275
Falls Village *(G-2871)*
Hamlethub LLC ....G.... 203 431-6400
Ridgefield *(G-7145)*
Hartford Courant Company ....G.... 860 678-1330
Avon *(G-83)*
Hartford Courant Company ....F.... 860 560-3747
West Hartford *(G-9816)*
Hartford Courant Company LLC ....A.... 860 241-6200
Hartford *(G-3608)*
Hartford Courant Company LLC ....F.... 860 525-5555
Hartford *(G-3609)*
Hartford Monthly Meeting ....G.... 860 232-3631
West Hartford *(G-9818)*
Hearst Communications Inc ....G.... 203 964-2200
Stamford *(G-8231)*
Hearst Corporation ....E.... 203 438-6544
New Canaan *(G-5109)*
Hearst Corporation ....G.... 203 926-2080
Shelton *(G-7463)*
Hearst Corporation ....E.... 203 625-4445
Norwalk *(G-6199)*
Hersam Acorn Cmnty Pubg LLC ....F.... 203 261-2548
Trumbull *(G-9034)*
Hersam Acorn Cmnty Pubg LLC ....F.... 203 438-6544
Ridgefield *(G-7146)*
Hersam Publishing Company ....B.... 203 966-9541
New Canaan *(G-5110)*
Hillside Capital Inc De Corp ....F.... 203 618-0202
Stamford *(G-8238)*
Hispanic Communications LLC ....G.... 203 674-6793
Stamford *(G-8239)*
Hispanic Communications LLC ....G.... 203 624-8007
New Haven *(G-5296)*
India Weekly Co ....G.... 203 699-8419
Cheshire *(G-1399)*
Inquiring News ....G.... 860 983-7587
Bloomfield *(G-422)*
Jewish Leader Newspaper ....G.... 860 442-7395
New London *(G-5474)*
Jj Portland News LLC ....G.... 860 342-1432
Middletown *(G-4358)*
Journal of Experimntal Scndary ....G.... 203 630-6508
Meriden *(G-4182)*
Journal Publishing Company Inc ....A.... 860 646-0500
Manchester *(G-4040)*
Journal Register East ....G.... 203 401-4004
New Haven *(G-5305)*
Judy Low ....G.... 860 491-9101
Goshen *(G-3099)*
Lakeville Journal Company LLC ....D.... 860 435-9873
Lakeville *(G-3845)*
Life Publications ....E.... 860 953-0444
West Hartford *(G-9831)*
Local Media Group Inc ....G.... 860 354-2273
New Milford *(G-5558)*
Los Angles Tmes Cmmnctions LLC ....C.... 203 965-6434
Stamford *(G-8289)*
M&G Berman Inc ....G.... 203 834-8754
Wilton *(G-10311)*
Meade Daily Group LLC ....G.... 860 399-7342
Westbrook *(G-10004)*
Medianews Group Inc ....F.... 203 333-0161
Norwalk *(G-6254)*
Middlbury Bee-Intelligencer-Ct ....G.... 203 577-6800
Middlebury *(G-4284)*
Miller Tina-Attorney ....G.... 203 938-8507
Redding *(G-7103)*
Minuteman Newspaper ....E.... 203 226-8877
Westport *(G-10121)*
Mkrs Corporation ....G.... 203 762-2662
Wilton *(G-10312)*
Morris Communications Co LLC ....D.... 203 458-4500
Guilford *(G-3377)*
My Citizens News ....G.... 203 729-2228
Waterbury *(G-9550)*
Natural Spring Ventures LLC ....G.... 203 556-2420
Woodbury *(G-10646)*
New England Theatre Conference ....G.... 203 288-8680
Hamden *(G-3490)*
▲ **New Haven Register LLC** ....A.... 203 789-5200
New Haven *(G-5346)*
New Mass Media Inc ....E.... 860 241-3617
Hartford *(G-3653)*
News 12 Connecticut ....E.... 203 849-1321
Norwalk *(G-6276)*
News Times ....G.... 203 744-5100
Danbury *(G-1892)*
Newspaper Space Buyers ....G.... 203 967-6452
Norwalk *(G-6277)*
Newtown Sports Group ....G.... 508 341-1238
Newtown *(G-5764)*
Northeast Minority News Inc ....G.... 860 249-6065
Hartford *(G-3655)*
Northend Agents LLC ....G.... 860 244-2445
Hartford *(G-3656)*
Northwest News Service ....G.... 860 567-4150
Bantam *(G-126)*
NRG Connecticut LLC ....E.... 860 231-2424
Hartford *(G-3657)*
Old Farmers Almanac ....G.... 860 862-9100
Uncasville *(G-9101)*
Online Journalism Project Inc ....G.... 203 668-5790
New Haven *(G-5354)*
Orange Democrat ....G.... 203 298-4575
Orange *(G-6620)*
Our Town Crier ....G.... 203 400-5000
Westport *(G-10135)*
Pages of Yesteryear ....G.... 203 426-0864
Newtown *(G-5767)*
Peaceful Daily Inc ....G.... 203 909-2961
Guilford *(G-3383)*
Penfield Communications Inc ....G.... 203 387-0354
New Haven *(G-5359)*
Pollinate News ....G.... 203 801-9623
New Canaan *(G-5132)*
Post Publishing Company ....G.... 203 333-0161
Bridgeport *(G-877)*
Prime Publishers Inc ....G.... 860 274-6721
Watertown *(G-9724)*
Printed Communications ....G.... 860 436-9619
South Windsor *(G-7812)*
Prospect Pages LLC ....G.... 203 758-6934
Prospect *(G-7020)*
Quinnipiac Valley Times ....G.... 203 675-9483
Hamden *(G-3500)*
▲ **Record-Journal Newspaper** ....C.... 203 235-1661
Meriden *(G-4230)*
Record-Journal Newspaper ....G.... 860 536-9577
Mystic *(G-4841)*
Reminder Broadcaster ....D.... 860 875-3366
Vernon *(G-9151)*
Rhode Island Beverage Journal ....G.... 203 288-3375
Hamden *(G-3505)*
Ritch Herald & Linda ....G.... 203 661-8634
Greenwich *(G-3227)*
Rmi Inc ....C.... 860 875-3366
Vernon Rockville *(G-9177)*
Second Wind Media Limited ....F.... 203 781-3480
New Haven *(G-5391)*
Shore Publishing LLC ....E.... 203 245-1877
Madison *(G-3956)*
Silver Arrow Publisher LLC ....G.... 203 265-4653
Wallingford *(G-9367)*
Sin Frntras Hspnic Newsppr LLC ....G.... 203 691-5986
New Haven *(G-5395)*
Southington Citizen ....G.... 860 620-5960
Meriden *(G-4243)*
Sports Department LLC ....G.... 860 872-0873
Ellington *(G-2601)*
Stella Press LLC ....G.... 203 661-2735
Greenwich *(G-3241)*
Suburban Voices Publishing LLC ....G.... 203 934-6397
West Haven *(G-9956)*
▲ **Swedish News Inc** ....G.... 203 299-0380
Norwalk *(G-6361)*
Ten 22 Inc ....G.... 860 963-1050
Putnam *(G-7072)*
The Around The Worlds Around ....G.... 860 871-7241
Ellington *(G-2606)*
▼ **The Bee Publishing Company** ....E.... 203 426-8036
Newtown *(G-5789)*
The Bee Publishing Company ....G.... 203 426-0178
Newtown *(G-5790)*
Thomson Reuters Risk MGT Inc ....G.... 203 539-8000
Stamford *(G-8467)*
Thomson Reuters US LLC ....E.... 203 539-8000
Stamford *(G-8468)*
Times Community News Group ....G.... 860 437-1150
New London *(G-5494)*

SIC SECTION

27 PRINTING, PUBLISHING, AND ALLIED INDUSTRIES

TLC Media LLC .... G 203 980-1361
  Hamden *(G-3520)*
Toms News .... G 860 535-1276
  Stonington *(G-8541)*
Town of Bridgewater .... F 860 354-5250
  Bridgewater *(G-947)*
Town Tribune LLC .... G 203 648-6085
  New Fairfield *(G-5179)*
Track180 LLC .... G 203 605-3540
  New Haven *(G-5418)*
▲ Tradewinds .... G 203 723-6966
  Beacon Falls *(G-148)*
Tradewinds .... G 203 324-2994
  Stamford *(G-8472)*
Tribuna Newspaper LLC .... G 203 730-0457
  Danbury *(G-1967)*
True Publishing Company .... F 203 272-5316
  Wallingford *(G-9392)*
Trumbull Transfer LLC .... G 203 377-2487
  Shelton *(G-7571)*
Twice Baked Twins LLC .... G 203 368-8841
  Trumbull *(G-9083)*
Unger Publishing LLC .... G 203 588-1363
  Stamford *(G-8480)*
Valley Independent Sentinel .... G 203 446-2335
  Ansonia *(G-55)*
Valley Publishing Company Inc .... F 203 735-6696
  Derby *(G-2129)*
Villager Newspapers .... G 860 928-1818
  Putnam *(G-7077)*
Weekly Retail Service LLC .... G 203 244-5150
  Ridgefield *(G-7183)*
Westerly Sun .... G 401 348-1000
  Pawcatuck *(G-6732)*
Wicks Business Information LLC .... F 203 334-2002
  Shelton *(G-7586)*
Wolcott Community News LL .... G 203 879-3900
  Waterbury *(G-9635)*
Woodbridge Town News .... G 203 298-4399
  Orange *(G-6635)*
Yale Daily News Publishing Co .... G 203 432-2400
  New Haven *(G-5440)*
Yale Law Journal Co Inc .... G 203 432-1666
  New Haven *(G-5441)*
Yale University .... G 203 432-2880
  New Haven *(G-5445)*
Yankee Delivery System .... G 860 243-1056
  Bloomfield *(G-503)*
Yankee Pennysaver Inc .... E 203 775-9122
  Brookfield *(G-1242)*

2721 Periodicals: Publishing & Printing

A Guideposts Church Corp .... B 203 749-0203
  Danbury *(G-1726)*
Aapi .... G 203 268-2450
  Monroe *(G-4690)*
Accent Magazine .... G 203 853-6015
  Norwalk *(G-6061)*
Access Intelligence .... G 203 854-6730
  Norwalk *(G-6062)*
Active Interest Media Inc .... G 860 767-3200
  Essex *(G-2710)*
Advantage Communications LLC ...... E 203 966-8390
  New Canaan *(G-5086)*
Air Age Inc .... E 203 431-9000
  Wilton *(G-10267)*
▲ Airtime Publishing Inc .... E 203 454-4773
  Westport *(G-10051)*
American Library Association .... E 860 347-6933
  Middletown *(G-4315)*
Aquastone Graphix LLC .... G 860 206-4935
  Hartford *(G-3552)*
Aquatic Mammals Journal Nfp .... G 860 514-4704
  Stonington *(G-8522)*
Artes Magazine LLC .... G 203 530-9811
  Branford *(G-547)*
Bargain News Free Classified A .... D 203 377-3000
  Stratford *(G-8578)*
Baxter Bros Inc .... G 203 637-4559
  Greenwich *(G-3130)*
Bay Tact Corporation .... E 860 315-7372
  Woodstock Valley *(G-10691)*
Belvoir Media Group LLC .... G 203 857-3128
  Norwalk *(G-6089)*
Beverage Publications Inc .... G 203 288-3375
  Hamden *(G-3418)*
Bff Holdings Inc .... C 860 510-0100
  Old Saybrook *(G-6523)*
Bottom Line Inc .... D 203 973-5900
  Stamford *(G-8115)*

Business Journals Inc .... D 203 853-6015
  Norwalk *(G-6102)*
Camarro Research .... G 203 254-1755
  Fairfield *(G-2757)*
Charting Economy .... G 860 667-9909
  Newington *(G-5640)*
Chief Executive Group LLC .... F 785 832-0303
  Stamford *(G-8143)*
Chief Executive Group LP .... E 203 930-2700
  Stamford *(G-8144)*
Circuit Cellar Inc .... F 860 289-0800
  East Hartford *(G-2305)*
Clemons Productions Inc .... G 203 316-9394
  Stamford *(G-8150)*
Comicana Inc .... G 203 968-0748
  Stamford *(G-8153)*
Commerce Connect Media Inc .... A 800 547-7377
  Westport *(G-10066)*
Connecticut Forest & Park Assn .... F 860 346-2372
  Rockfall *(G-7211)*
Corporate Connecticut Mag LLC .... G 860 257-0500
  Wethersfield *(G-10189)*
Creative Stone Group Inc .... G 203 554-7773
  Stamford *(G-8169)*
Domino Media Group Inc .... E 877 223-7844
  Westport *(G-10074)*
Donnin Publishing Inc .... G 203 453-8866
  Guilford *(G-3347)*
Douglas Moss .... G 203 854-5559
  Norwalk *(G-6149)*
Dulce Domum LLC .... E 203 227-1400
  Norwalk *(G-6151)*
Edible Nutmeg .... G 818 383-4603
  Washington *(G-9413)*
Editors Only .... G 860 881-2300
  New Britain *(G-4979)*
Evangelical Christian Center .... G 860 429-0856
  Ashford *(G-62)*
Evangelical Christian Center .... G 860 429-0856
  Ashford *(G-61)*
Fairfield County Look .... G 203 869-0077
  Greenwich *(G-3158)*
Fed Russell LLC .... G 203 934-2501
  West Haven *(G-9908)*
Financial Accnting Foundation .... C 203 847-0700
  Norwalk *(G-6165)*
Gamut Publishing .... E 860 296-6128
  Hartford *(G-3598)*
▲ Granta USA Ltd .... F 440 207-6051
  Danbury *(G-1837)*
Hartford Marathon Foundation .... G 860 652-8866
  Glastonbury *(G-3048)*
Ibnr LLC .... G 860 676-8600
  Farmington *(G-2916)*
Ida Publishing Co Inc .... G 203 661-9090
  Greenwich *(G-3178)*
Imani Magazine/Fmi .... G 203 809-2565
  West Haven *(G-9916)*
Informa Business Media Inc .... D 203 358-9900
  Stamford *(G-8248)*
Informa Business Media Inc .... C 203 358-9900
  Stamford *(G-8249)*
Informa Media Inc .... G 203 885-1045
  Danbury *(G-1850)*
Information Today Inc .... F 203 761-1466
  Wilton *(G-10302)*
International Mktg Strategies .... F 203 406-0106
  Stamford *(G-8253)*
Interstate Tax Corporation .... G 203 854-0704
  Norwalk *(G-6210)*
Joseph Malavenda .... G 203 746-4160
  New Fairfield *(G-5170)*
Karger S Publishers Inc .... G 860 675-7834
  Unionville *(G-9116)*
L M T Communications Inc .... F 203 426-4568
  Newtown *(G-5752)*
Legal Affairs Inc .... G 203 865-2520
  Hamden *(G-3473)*
Lighthouse Maps .... G 203 981-1090
  Brookfield *(G-1203)*
▲ Little India Publications Inc .... F 212 560-0608
  Torrington *(G-8943)*
Liturgical Publications Inc .... F 203 966-6470
  New Canaan *(G-5115)*
Liturgical Publications Inc .... G 860 635-9560
  Cromwell *(G-1706)*
Living Magazine .... G 203 283-5290
  Milford *(G-4569)*
Maplegate Media Group Inc .... E 203 826-7557
  Danbury *(G-1880)*

Mason Medical Communications ...... G 203 227-9252
  Westport *(G-10118)*
Matchbox USA .... G 860 349-1655
  Durham *(G-2152)*
Media Ventures Inc .... E 203 852-6570
  Norwalk *(G-6253)*
Merlin Associates Inc .... G 860 567-1620
  Litchfield *(G-3895)*
Moffly Publications Inc .... F 203 222-0600
  Westport *(G-10123)*
Moffly Publications Inc .... E 203 222-0600
  Westport *(G-10124)*
Morthanoscom LLC .... G 203 378-2414
  Stratford *(G-8651)*
Most Excllent Cmics Cllctibles .... G 860 741-0113
  Enfield *(G-2662)*
Motorcyclists Post .... G 203 929-9409
  Shelton *(G-7505)*
Naffa Inc .... G 203 562-3159
  New Haven *(G-5339)*
National Shooting Sports Found .... E 203 426-1320
  Newtown *(G-5762)*
Natural Nutmeg LLC .... G 860 206-9500
  Avon *(G-95)*
▲ Overseas Ministries Study Ctr .... F 203 624-6672
  New Haven *(G-5357)*
Park Group Solutions LLC .... G 203 459-8784
  Newtown *(G-5769)*
Penny Marketing Ltd Partnr .... E 203 866-6688
  Norwalk *(G-6295)*
Penny Press Inc .... C 203 866-6688
  Norwalk *(G-6296)*
Penny Press Inc .... E 203 866-6688
  Milford *(G-4605)*
Penny Publications LLC .... D 203 866-6688
  Norwalk *(G-6297)*
Ppc Books Ltd .... G 203 226-6644
  Westport *(G-10142)*
Premier Graphics LLC .... D 800 414-1624
  Stratford *(G-8668)*
Quad/Graphics Inc .... A 203 288-2468
  North Haven *(G-5985)*
R G L Inc .... E 860 653-7254
  East Granby *(G-2226)*
Racing Times .... E 203 298-2899
  Wallingford *(G-9347)*
Red 7 Media LLC .... E 203 853-2474
  Norwalk *(G-6316)*
Relocation Information Svc Inc .... E 203 855-1234
  Norwalk *(G-6319)*
Relx Inc .... A 203 840-4800
  Norwalk *(G-6320)*
Reserved Magazine .... G 860 560-9120
  Hartford *(G-3678)*
S Karger Publishers Inc .... G 860 675-7834
  Unionville *(G-9126)*
Sage Magazine .... G 347 452-3752
  New Haven *(G-5384)*
▲ Scholastic Library Pubg Inc .... A 203 797-3500
  Danbury *(G-1939)*
Scripture Research & Pubg Co .... G 203 272-1780
  Cheshire *(G-1443)*
Seasons Media LLC .... G 860 413-2022
  West Simsbury *(G-9982)*
Show Management Associates LLC .. G 203 939-9901
  Norwalk *(G-6345)*
Sixfurlongs LLC .... G 203 255-8553
  Fairfield *(G-2848)*
Snreview .... G 203 366-5991
  Fairfield *(G-2849)*
Society For Exprmntal McHanics ...... G 203 790-6373
  Bethel *(G-343)*
Society Plastics Engineers Inc .... E 203 740-5422
  Bethel *(G-344)*
Soundings Publications LLC .... E 860 767-8227
  Essex *(G-2735)*
Steed Read Horsemans Classifie ..... G 860 859-0770
  Salem *(G-7292)*
Strategic Insights Inc .... G 203 595-3200
  Stamford *(G-8446)*
Sumner Communications Inc .... E 203 748-2050
  Bethel *(G-349)*
Suzanne Ramljak .... G 203 792-5599
  Bethel *(G-350)*
Tam Communications Inc .... E 203 425-8777
  Norwalk *(G-6362)*
Taunton Inc .... A 203 426-8171
  Newtown *(G-5785)*
Taunton Press Inc .... B 203 426-8171
  Newtown *(G-5787)*

Employee Codes: A=Over 500 employees, B=251-500
C=101-250, D=51-100, E=20-50, F=10-19, G=1-9

▲ Tauton Press....G....203 304-3000
Newtown (G-5788)
This Old House Ventures LLC....E....475 209-8665
Stamford (G-8465)
Timer Digest Publishing Inc....G....203 629-2589
Greenwich (G-3245)
Toastmasters International....F....203 847-5667
Norwalk (G-6372)
Ubm LLC....G....203 662-6501
Darien (G-2048)
▲ Urban Exposition LLC....E....203 242-8717
Trumbull (G-9090)
Val Scansaroli Magazine Cnsltn....G....203 229-0256
Norwalk (G-6380)
▲ Venu Magazine LLC....G....203 259-2075
Fairfield (G-2863)
Westchester Forge Inc....G....914 584-2429
New Canaan (G-5158)
Wicks Business Information LLC....F....203 334-2002
Shelton (G-7586)
▼ Windhover Information Inc....E....203 838-4401
Norwalk (G-6396)
Wire Association Intl Inc....E....203 453-2777
Madison (G-3968)
Wire Journal Inc....E....203 453-2777
Madison (G-3969)
Woolworks International Ltd....G....203 661-7076
Stamford (G-8501)
▲ World Wrestling Entrmt Inc....C....203 352-8600
Stamford (G-8502)
Yale Alumni Publications Inc....G....203 432-0645
New Haven (G-5439)
Yale Law Journal Co Inc....G....203 432-1666
New Haven (G-5441)
Yale University....G....203 432-0499
New Haven (G-5450)
▲ Yale University....E....203 432-2550
New Haven (G-5443)
Yale University....D....203 764-4333
New Haven (G-5444)
Zackin Publications Inc....E....203 262-4670
Oxford (G-6701)

2731 Books: Publishing & Printing

A Guideposts Church Corp....B....203 749-0203
Danbury (G-1726)
African Link....G....203 925-1632
Shelton (G-7389)
Air Age Inc....E....203 431-9000
Wilton (G-10267)
AJK Publishing....G....203 259-8026
Fairfield (G-2746)
Andree Brooks....G....203 226-9834
Westport (G-10057)
Artchrist Com Inc....G....203 245-2246
Madison (G-3907)
Bay Tact Corporation....E....860 315-7372
Woodstock Valley (G-10691)
Begell House Inc....F....203 456-6161
Danbury (G-1751)
Belvoir Publications Inc....E....203 857-3100
Norwalk (G-6090)
Bff Holdings Inc....C....860 510-0100
Old Saybrook (G-6523)
Bick Publishing House....G....203 208-5253
Branford (G-559)
Biennix Corp....G....203 254-1727
Fairfield (G-2755)
Bigs Publishing LLC....G....203 249-1059
Greenwich (G-3133)
Birdtrack Press....G....203 389-7789
New Haven (G-5248)
Blauner Books....G....203 222-6042
Greenwich (G-3134)
Bosphorus Books....G....860 536-2540
Groton (G-3272)
Bradt Enterprises LLC....G....203 323-8501
Stamford (G-8116)
Bryan Doughty....G....860 536-2185
New London (G-5459)
Bunting & Lyon Inc....G....203 272-4623
Cheshire (G-1365)
Burns Walton....G....203 422-5222
Branford (G-566)
Calculator Training....G....860 355-8255
New Milford (G-5513)
Carala Ventures Ltd....E....800 483-6449
Stratford (G-8592)
Career Concepts....G....203 378-9943
Stratford (G-8594)

Charles Alain Publishing Ltd....G....203 226-2882
Westport (G-10063)
Charles McDougal....G....860 739-9952
Niantic (G-5803)
Chicory Blue Press Inc....G....860 491-2271
Goshen (G-3096)
Clear & Simple Inc....G....860 658-1204
West Simsbury (G-9974)
Clever Clover LLC....G....860 501-2800
Pawcatuck (G-6706)
Comicana Inc....G....203 968-0748
Stamford (G-8153)
Commandtech LLC....G....860 857-8502
Groton (G-3278)
Connectcut Acdemy Arts Scences....G....203 432-3113
New Haven (G-5259)
Connecticut Bass Guide....G....860 827-0787
New Britain (G-4962)
Connecticut Law Book Co Inc....F....203 458-8000
Guilford (G-3340)
Connecticut Parent Magazine....F....203 483-1700
Branford (G-576)
Cortina Learning Intl Inc....F....800 245-2145
Wilton (G-10283)
Creative Media Applications....F....203 226-0544
Weston (G-10023)
▲ Crown House Publishing Co LLC....G....203 778-1300
Bethel (G-274)
De Villiers Incorporated....G....203 966-9645
New Canaan (G-5101)
▲ Early Advantage LLC....F....203 259-6480
Fairfield (G-2778)
Editorial Directions Inc....G....203 245-2011
Madison (G-3919)
Educational Resources Network....G....203 866-9973
Ridgefield (G-7138)
Edward Fleur Fncl Educatn Corp....G....203 629-9333
Greenwich (G-3157)
EPic Publishing Services LLC....G....860 204-7450
East Haddam (G-2241)
Erinco Marketing....G....203 545-4550
Danbury (G-1816)
Eye Ear It LLC....F....203 487-8949
Woodbury (G-10636)
Five Ponds Press Books Inc....G....877 833-0603
Windsor (G-10386)
Flea Market Music Inc....G....860 664-1669
Clinton (G-1503)
Forecast International Inc....D....203 426-0800
Newtown (G-5739)
Fredercks Jnne Literarary Agcy....G....203 972-3011
New Canaan (G-5105)
Gamut Publishing....E....860 296-6128
Hartford (G-3598)
Glacier Publishing....G....860 621-7644
Southington (G-7928)
Godfrey Memorial Library....G....860 346-4375
Middletown (G-4347)
Graduate Group....G....860 233-2330
West Hartford (G-9813)
Graphics Press LLC....G....203 272 9187
Cheshire (G-1394)
Green Editorial....G....860 364-5100
Sharon (G-7379)
▲ Greenwich Workshop Inc....E....203 881-3336
Seymour (G-7348)
▲ Grolier Overseas Incorporated....G....203 797-3500
Danbury (G-1838)
▲ Industrial Press Inc....F....212 889-6330
Norwalk (G-6206)
Information Today Inc....F....203 761-1466
Wilton (G-10302)
Inside Track....G....203 431-4540
Ridgefield (G-7147)
Island Nation Press LLC....G....203 852-0028
Norwalk (G-6211)
K C K Publishing....G....203 924-1147
Shelton (G-7482)
Kendall Svengalis....G....860 535-0362
Guilford (G-3365)
Kieffer Associates Inc....G....203 323-3437
Stamford (G-8275)
Kirchoff Wohlberg Inc....F....212 644-2020
Madison (G-3934)
Konecky & Konecky LLC....G....860 388-0878
Old Saybrook (G-6551)
Life Study Fllwship Foundation....E....203 655-1436
Darien (G-2031)
Lindsay Graphics....G....860 355-8744
Sherman (G-7597)

Little Blue Book....G....860 409-7000
Avon (G-90)
Little Blue Insite LLC....G....203 202-7690
Darien (G-2032)
Marlin Company....D....203 294-9800
Wallingford (G-9312)
▲ McBooks Press Inc....G....607 272-2114
Guilford (G-3372)
Midnight Reader....G....860 643-4220
Bolton (G-516)
Millbrook Press Inc....E....203 740-2220
Brookfield (G-1206)
Mobius Press....G....860 767-0880
Essex (G-2726)
New England Publishing Assoc....G....860 345-7323
Higganum (G-3771)
Next Door Creations LLC....G....860 933-0366
Glastonbury (G-3064)
Nollysource Entertainment LLC....G....347 264-6655
Bridgeport (G-853)
Octavo Editions LLC....G....860 388-5772
Old Saybrook (G-6562)
Omicronworld Entertainment LLC....G....203 453-5700
Guilford (G-3381)
Orchard Press....G....860 672-4273
Cornwall Bridge (G-1618)
Originals LLC....G....203 421-4867
Madison (G-3944)
Pass Perfect LLC....G....203 629-9333
Greenwich (G-3214)
Paul D Wolff....G....203 319-7242
Easton (G-2560)
Peninsula Publishing....G....203 292-5621
Westport (G-10138)
Peter James Associates Inc....G....203 972-1070
New Canaan (G-5130)
Peter Kelsey Publishing Inc....G....860 231-9300
West Hartford (G-9843)
Pocket Parks Publishing LLC....G....203 499-7416
West Haven (G-9945)
Ppc Books Ltd....G....203 226-6644
Westport (G-10142)
R G L Inc....E....860 653-7254
East Granby (G-2226)
Real Sltons Edctl Cnslting Inc....G....203 220-2279
Trumbull (G-9062)
Robison Music Media & Pubg LLC....G....203 858-8106
Wallingford (G-9356)
▲ Rocket Books Inc....G....203 372-1818
Easton (G-2564)
Rothstein Associates Inc....G....203 740-7400
Brookfield (G-1219)
S Karger Publishers Inc....G....860 675-7834
Unionville (G-9126)
Sanguinaria Publishing Inc....G....203 576-9168
Bridgeport (G-894)
Sasc LLC....G....203 846-2274
Greenwich (G-3231)
▲ Scholastic Inc....G....212 343-6100
Danbury (G-1938)
▲ Scholastic Library Pubg Inc....A....203 797-3500
Danbury (G-1939)
Scholastic Library Pubg Inc....F....573 632-1762
Danbury (G-1940)
Scripture Research & Pubg Co....G....203 272-1780
Cheshire (G-1443)
Society For Exprmntal McHanics....G....203 790-6373
Bethel (G-343)
Society Plastics Engineers Inc....E....203 740-5422
Bethel (G-344)
Sourcebooks Inc....G....203 876-9790
Milford (G-4648)
Stamler Publishing Company....G....203 488-9808
Branford (G-655)
Stoneslide Media LLC....G....203 464-3471
Guilford (G-3395)
Summer Camp Stories LLC....G....203 705-1600
Stamford (G-8449)
Summer Street Press LLC....F....203 978-0098
Stamford (G-8450)
Sunday Paper....G....203 624-2520
New Haven (G-5403)
Symphonycs LLC....G....860 884-2308
Lisbon (G-3883)
▼ Tantor Media Incorporated....C....860 395-1155
Old Saybrook (G-6572)
Taunton Inc....A....203 426-8171
Newtown (G-5785)
Taunton Interactive Inc....G....203 426-8171
Newtown (G-5786)

SIC SECTION 27 PRINTING, PUBLISHING, AND ALLIED INDUSTRIES

Toni Leland.....G..... 860 892-8890
Uncasville *(G-9106)*
Two Ems Inc.....G..... 203 245-8211
Madison *(G-3965)*
Ubm LLC.....G..... 203 662-6501
Darien *(G-2048)*
Vital Health Publishing Inc.....G..... 203 438-3229
Ridgefield *(G-7180)*
Vocalis Limited.....G..... 203 753-5244
Waterbury *(G-9623)*
Weddles LLC.....G..... 203 964-1888
Stamford *(G-8489)*
Wesleyan University.....G..... 860 685-2980
Middletown *(G-4430)*
Wild Leaf Press Inc.....G..... 203 415-5309
Bethany *(G-252)*
Windcheck LLC.....G..... 203 332-7639
Bridgeport *(G-938)*
▼ Windhover Information Inc.....E..... 203 838-4401
Norwalk *(G-6396)*
Wood Pond Press.....G..... 860 521-0389
West Hartford *(G-9877)*
Writers Press LLC.....G..... 860 242-9271
Bloomfield *(G-502)*
Writestuff Creative Services L.....G..... 860 343-1919
Middletown *(G-4433)*
Yale Daily News Publishing Co.....G..... 203 432-2400
New Haven *(G-5440)*
▲ Yale University.....E..... 203 432-2550
New Haven *(G-5443)*
Yale University.....D..... 203 764-4333
New Haven *(G-5444)*
▲ Ziga Media LLC.....G..... 203 656-0076
Darien *(G-2052)*
Zp Couture LLC.....G..... 888 697-7239
North Haven *(G-6017)*

2732 Book Printing, Not Publishing

Bq Business Solutions.....G..... 203 268-3500
Monroe *(G-4701)*
Cagno Enterprises LLC.....G..... 203 729-3883
Naugatuck *(G-4867)*
M Baron Company.....G..... 860 536-1594
Mystic *(G-4827)*
Ppc Books Ltd.....G..... 203 226-6644
Westport *(G-10142)*
R R Donnelley & Sons Company.....F..... 860 649-5570
Manchester *(G-4078)*
Wesleyan University.....G..... 860 685-7727
Middletown *(G-4429)*

2741 Misc Publishing

12 Paws Publishing LLC.....G..... 203 232-4534
Seymour *(G-7334)*
3 Ethos LLC.....G..... 860 415-9191
Mystic *(G-4794)*
AAR Results LLC.....G..... 203 627-2193
Branford *(G-535)*
Accession Media.....G..... 203 702-4951
Brookfield *(G-1156)*
Action Media Inc.....G..... 203 466-5535
East Haven *(G-2407)*
Administrative Publications In.....G..... 860 747-6768
Plainville *(G-6766)*
Afroasia Publication LLC.....G..... 917 692-3937
Stamford *(G-8063)*
Alexander Street Press.....G..... 203 389-6881
New Haven *(G-5220)*
Algonquian Free Press LLC.....G..... 860 572-4811
Groton *(G-3270)*
Altare Publishing Inc.....G..... 860 490-6144
Avon *(G-75)*
American Art Heritage Pubg.....G..... 203 973-0564
Stamford *(G-8073)*
American Trade Fairs Org.....G..... 203 221-0114
Westport *(G-10055)*
Antrim House.....G..... 860 217-0023
Simsbury *(G-7611)*
Apple Publications.....G..... 860 392-8348
Tolland *(G-8849)*
Arcat Inc.....G..... 203 929-9444
Fairfield *(G-2747)*
Arp Publishing Inc.....G..... 888 503-6617
Middletown *(G-4318)*
Ashkaar Publishers LLC.....G..... 203 248-4804
North Haven *(G-5910)*
Audubon Copy Shppe of Firfield.....G..... 203 259-4311
Bridgeport *(G-705)*
Axol Media Inc.....G..... 650 315-1743
South Windsor *(G-7715)*
Bagogames LLC.....G..... 860 801-7462
Torrington *(G-8900)*
▲ Barker Advg Specialty Co Inc.....D..... 203 272-2222
Cheshire *(G-1360)*
Bay Tact Corporation.....E..... 860 315-7372
Woodstock Valley *(G-10691)*
Beardsley Publishing Corp.....G..... 203 263-0888
Woodbury *(G-10626)*
Beautiful Publications.....G..... 347 508-2798
Stratford *(G-8581)*
Bellable LLC.....G..... 800 212-2603
West Hartford *(G-9778)*
Belle Impression Pubg Inc.....G..... 203 826-5426
Danbury *(G-1755)*
Belvoir Publications.....G..... 203 422-7300
Greenwich *(G-3132)*
Bench Press 3 LLC.....G..... 203 848-5545
Fairfield *(G-2753)*
Bertram Sirkin.....G..... 860 656-7446
West Hartford *(G-9779)*
Betx LLC.....G..... 860 459-1681
New Hartford *(G-5186)*
Bff Holdings Inc.....C..... 860 510-0100
Old Saybrook *(G-6523)*
Biographical Publishing Co.....G..... 203 758-3661
Prospect *(G-6995)*
Black Crow Press LLC.....G..... 203 281-1034
Hamden *(G-3419)*
Bm Publishing LLC.....G..... 860 778-1583
Bristol *(G-984)*
BMHs Press Box.....G..... 203 810-4380
Norwalk *(G-6095)*
BNE Publishing Inc.....G..... 860 498-0032
Coventry *(G-1646)*
Brain Institute of America LLC.....G..... 860 967-5937
Groton *(G-3273)*
Brandon Nicholas Eza Pubg.....G..... 860 498-0032
Coventry *(G-1648)*
Broadcastmed Inc.....E..... 860 953-2900
Farmington *(G-2886)*
Brook & Whittle Holding Corp.....G..... 203 483-5602
Guilford *(G-3333)*
Btac Publications.....G..... 203 560-7742
Southbury *(G-7846)*
Burns Walton.....G..... 203 422-5222
Branford *(G-566)*
Business Journals Inc.....D..... 203 853-6015
Norwalk *(G-6102)*
Business Marketing & Pubg Inc.....G..... 203 834-9959
Wilton *(G-10279)*
Butterfly Press LLC.....G..... 860 621-2883
Southington *(G-7899)*
Butterfly Wings Pubg Co LLC.....G..... 203 642-4481
Norwalk *(G-6103)*
Bvc Publishing.....G..... 860 202-0704
Bristol *(G-995)*
Bwd Publishing LLC.....G..... 860 651-1966
West Simsbury *(G-9973)*
C Q Publishing.....G..... 860 292-1566
Windsor Locks *(G-10476)*
Calhoun Press Inc.....G..... 860 202-0998
Lebanon *(G-3849)*
Campbell Publicity LLC.....G..... 646 532-1512
Middlebury *(G-4274)*
Campus Yellow Pages LLC.....G..... 860 523-9909
West Hartford *(G-9783)*
Captive Global LLC.....G..... 860 302-6706
Southington *(G-7903)*
Cara C Andreoli.....G..... 860 888-6553
Glastonbury *(G-3019)*
Caribe House Press LLC.....G..... 812 320-5303
Guilford *(G-3337)*
Carlos Lee Publishing.....G..... 860 536-8450
Mystic *(G-4806)*
Cat Tales Press Inc.....G..... 203 268-3505
Easton *(G-2548)*
Cema Publishing LLC.....G..... 585 317-3724
Stamford *(G-8137)*
Charmed Press LLC.....G..... 203 877-3777
Milford *(G-4489)*
Chiara Publications.....G..... 203 797-1905
Bethel *(G-270)*
Chicken Soup For Soul LLC.....E..... 203 861-4000
Cos Cob *(G-1626)*
Chicken Soup For Soul Entrmt I.....G..... 855 398-0443
Cos Cob *(G-1627)*
Chicken Soup For Soul Pubg LLC.....G..... 203 861-4000
Cos Cob *(G-1628)*
Chicken Soup For The Soul.....G..... 855 398-0443
Cos Cob *(G-1629)*
Chief Executive Group LLC.....F..... 785 832-0303
Stamford *(G-8143)*
Childrens Health Market Inc.....G..... 203 762-2938
Wilton *(G-10280)*
Christian Science Committee On.....G..... 203 866-1200
Norwalk *(G-6113)*
Cimarron Music Press.....G..... 860 536-2185
Ledyard *(G-3870)*
Cimarron Music Press LLC.....G..... 860 859-3705
New London *(G-5462)*
Cisse Publications LLC.....G..... 203 685-4189
Shelton *(G-7420)*
Complimentary Healing.....G..... 203 622-1697
Cos Cob *(G-1630)*
Computer Xpress LLC.....G..... 203 469-6107
East Haven *(G-2419)*
▲ Connectcut Hspnic Yellow Pages.....F..... 860 560-8713
Hartford *(G-3569)*
Connecticut Digital Post Inc.....G..... 203 268-4554
Monroe *(G-4704)*
Connecticut Press.....G..... 203 257-6020
Cheshire *(G-1372)*
Connelly 3 Pubg Group Inc.....G..... 860 664-4988
Clinton *(G-1497)*
Corporate Express CT.....G..... 203 455-2500
Stratford *(G-8599)*
Cotton Press LLC.....G..... 203 257-7958
Wilton *(G-10284)*
Coupon Magazine Publishers Inc.....G..... 561 676-6498
Danbury *(G-1777)*
Crossfield Concepts Inc.....G..... 203 938-5667
Redding *(G-7091)*
Custom Publishing Design Group.....F..... 860 513-1213
Rocky Hill *(G-7231)*
Cygnal Publishing Co.....G..... 860 983-4757
Mystic *(G-4810)*
Db Press LLC.....G..... 203 699-9510
Cheshire *(G-1381)*
Debrasong Publishing LLC.....G..... 413 204-4682
Lyme *(G-3904)*
Directory Assistants Inc.....E..... 860 633-0122
Wethersfield *(G-10190)*
Dlpublshers Mystryntrtnmentllc.....G..... 203 556-4893
Bridgeport *(G-755)*
Dmb Publishing LLC.....G..... 203 798-9231
Bethel *(G-281)*
Dogwood Publishing LLC.....G..... 203 292-3815
Fairfield *(G-2775)*
Dollar Express LLC.....G..... 203 495-9209
New Haven *(G-5268)*
Doors To Explore Inc.....G..... 978 761-7210
Sandy Hook *(G-7310)*
Down Home Publishing.....G..... 860 521-6177
Newington *(G-5648)*
Duneland Press.....G..... 860 535-0362
Guilford *(G-3348)*
Dunnottar Publishing LLC.....G..... 203 488-0350
Branford *(G-581)*
Ecua Express.....G..... 860 344-1144
Middletown *(G-4340)*
Educational Reference Publishi.....G..... 203 797-1517
Danbury *(G-1804)*
Edwin Publishing Company.....G..... 203 228-9396
Waterbury *(G-9471)*
Ef Lee Publishing LLC.....G..... 203 546-7148
Brookfield *(G-1187)*
Ek Publishing LLC.....G..... 203 246-9683
Westport *(G-10077)*
Erielle Media LLC.....G..... 203 563-9159
Wilton *(G-10293)*
Essex Publishing Co.....G..... 314 627-0300
Branford *(G-590)*
Evertide Games Inc.....G..... 203 701-9145
New Canaan *(G-5104)*
▼ Executive Greetings Inc.....B..... 860 379-9911
New Hartford *(G-5190)*
Experience Publishing Inc.....G..... 203 637-2324
Riverside *(G-7195)*
Exponent Publishing Co.....G..... 203 264-1130
Southbury *(G-7852)*
Express Lab Service.....G..... 860 571-0355
Hartford *(G-3586)*
Express Lane Foods.....G..... 860 889-2266
North Franklin *(G-5873)*
Fayerweather Press LLC.....G..... 203 367-1601
Bridgeport *(G-768)*
Felk Publishing LLC.....G..... 203 421-3714
Madison *(G-3920)*
Flat Hammock Press.....G..... 860 572-2722
Mystic *(G-4816)*

S I C

Employee Codes: A=Over 500 employees, B=251-500
C=101-250, D=51-100, E=20-50, F=10-19, G=1-9
2020 Harris Connecticut
Manufacturers Directory
395

Floating World Editions.......G....... 860 868-0890
Warren *(G-9408)*
Floral Greens.......G....... 860 995-8772
Bloomfield *(G-412)*
Flying Aces Press LLC.......G....... 203 791-1172
Danbury *(G-1827)*
For Children With Love Public.......G....... 860 940-9878
Farmington *(G-2907)*
Four Winds Inc.......G....... 203 445-0733
Easton *(G-2554)*
Frank Alexander Weems Pubg LLC.......G....... 203 898-4654
Stamford *(G-8207)*
Frank Drago Custom Mapping.......G....... 203 483-7594
Branford *(G-596)*
Freedom Press.......G....... 860 599-5390
Pawcatuck *(G-6711)*
Frog Prints Publishing LLC.......G....... 610 425-0090
Shelton *(G-7447)*
Functional Concepts LLC.......G....... 203 813-0157
Stratford *(G-8614)*
Galassia Press LLC.......G....... 203 846-9075
Norwalk *(G-6174)*
Gale Thomson.......G....... 203 397-2600
Woodbridge *(G-10600)*
Gallagher Katie Publishers Rep.......G....... 203 221-7140
Westport *(G-10087)*
Gcn Publishing Inc.......F....... 203 665-6211
Norwalk *(G-6176)*
Gcooper Legacy Publishing LLC.......G....... 203 357-1483
Stamford *(G-8212)*
Get Go It Publishing.......G....... 203 772-9877
New Haven *(G-5286)*
Gettysburg Publishing LLC.......G....... 203 268-7111
Trumbull *(G-9029)*
Girl Cop Publishing LLC.......G....... 860 529-3424
Wethersfield *(G-10193)*
Global American Publishers LLC.......G....... 860 432-7589
Manchester *(G-4022)*
Global Publications & Mktg LLC.......G....... 860 676-9109
Farmington *(G-2913)*
Glorian Publishing Inc.......G....... 844 945-6742
Clinton *(G-1505)*
Gmq Publishing.......G....... 203 558-6142
Beacon Falls *(G-134)*
Goldpoint Publishing LLC.......G....... 860 432-8934
South Windsor *(G-7762)*
Grand Publications LLC.......G....... 203 288-5721
Hamden *(G-3453)*
Great American Publishing Soc.......G....... 203 531-9300
Greenwich *(G-3171)*
Greenwich Free Press LLC.......G....... 203 622-1731
Greenwich *(G-3174)*
Grey House Publishing Inc.......G....... 860 364-1444
Sharon *(G-7380)*
Greycourt Publishing LLC.......G....... 203 894-1535
Ridgefield *(G-7144)*
Halurgite Publishing LLC.......G....... 860 563-0372
Wethersfield *(G-10195)*
Harbor Publications Inc.......G....... 203 245-8009
Madison *(G-3925)*
Harvard Business School Pubg.......G....... 203 318 1234
New Haven *(G-5294)*
Hawkline Press.......G....... 203 248-4615
Hamden *(G-3461)*
Hawks Nest Publishing LLC.......G....... 860 536-5868
Madison *(G-3926)*
HB Publishing & Marketing.......G....... 203 852-9200
Norwalk *(G-6196)*
HB Publishing & Marketing Co.......G....... 203 852-1324
Norwalk *(G-6197)*
Healing Arts Press LLC.......G....... 203 374-2084
Fairfield *(G-2793)*
Hearst Corporation.......E....... 203 438-6544
New Canaan *(G-5109)*
Heartland Publications LLC.......G....... 860 388-3470
Old Saybrook *(G-6539)*
Helen Grace.......G....... 203 661-1927
Cos Cob *(G-1633)*
Hendrickson Group.......G....... 203 426-9266
Sandy Hook *(G-7315)*
Hersam Publishing Company.......B....... 203 966-9541
New Canaan *(G-5110)*
Hew Publishing LLC.......G....... 860 514-2045
Cromwell *(G-1704)*
Higher Consciousness LLC.......G....... 310 977-7541
Avon *(G-84)*
Hill House Press LLC.......G....... 203 405-1158
Southbury *(G-7857)*
Hilltop Publishing LLC.......G....... 203 426-8834
Newtown *(G-5743)*
Hiram Rock Publishing LLC.......G....... 203 453-0440
Guilford *(G-3360)*
Historical Art Prints.......G....... 203 262-6680
Southbury *(G-7858)*
HMS Publications Inc.......G....... 860 739-3187
Niantic *(G-5810)*
Hog River Music.......G....... 860 523-1820
Hartford *(G-3614)*
Hollow Frost Publishers.......G....... 860 974-2081
Woodstock *(G-10667)*
Hometown Publishing LLC.......G....... 203 426-5252
Newtown *(G-5744)*
Hotchkiss Publishing.......G....... 203 430-6289
Branford *(G-606)*
I3 Engineering Sciences LLC.......G....... 908 625-2347
Hartford *(G-3616)*
Industrial Press.......G....... 203 838-4080
Norwalk *(G-6205)*
Ink LLC.......G....... 860 581-0026
East Haddam *(G-2243)*
Ink Publishing LLC.......G....... 860 581-0026
Old Saybrook *(G-6542)*
Insight Media LLC.......G....... 203 831-8464
Norwalk *(G-6208)*
Intangible Matter LLC.......G....... 203 219-9619
Stamford *(G-8252)*
Intechs LLC.......G....... 203 260-8109
Monroe *(G-4721)*
Integer-Comfab Enterprises LLC.......G....... 646 620-9112
Westport *(G-10102)*
Iona Press.......G....... 860 841-5006
West Hartford *(G-9822)*
J C Publishing LLC.......G....... 860 525-7226
Hartford *(G-3619)*
Jacoby.......G....... 203 227-2220
Weston *(G-10030)*
James P King.......G....... 203 834-0050
Wilton *(G-10304)*
Jim Press Home Improvement.......G....... 860 416-4494
Manchester *(G-4039)*
JRC Publishing LLC.......G....... 203 942-2726
Ridgefield *(G-7152)*
Jsan Publishing LLC.......G....... 203 210-5495
Wilton *(G-10306)*
Juice Publishing LLC.......G....... 203 226-5715
Westport *(G-10106)*
Julie Wakely Enterprises LLC.......G....... 860 376-4515
Jewett City *(G-3797)*
Kanine Knits.......G....... 203 272-8548
Cheshire *(G-1402)*
Kathleen Parker OBeirne.......G....... 860 536-7179
Mystic *(G-4824)*
Kathy Pooler.......G....... 860 889-2893
Norwich *(G-6420)*
Kc Publishing.......G....... 203 318-8544
Madison *(G-3933)*
Keeper Press LLC.......G....... 860 810-9626
Glastonbury *(G-3054)*
Keiterbennett Publishers LLC.......G....... 860 308-2666
East Hartford *(G-2342)*
Kiera Publishing Inc.......G....... 203 838-5485
Norwalk *(G-6229)*
Kimberly Bon Publishing LLC.......G....... 203 258-9829
Trumbull *(G-9039)*
Kingsnake Publishing LLC.......G....... 860 865-0307
Groton *(G-3292)*
Kiwi Publishing Inc.......G....... 203 389-6220
Woodbridge *(G-10604)*
Labrador Press LLC.......G....... 860 887-0567
Bozrah *(G-526)*
Labrador Publishing LLC.......G....... 860 552-2564
Clinton *(G-1512)*
Langner Press LLC.......G....... 203 226-7752
Weston *(G-10032)*
Lasting Legacy Publishers LLC.......G....... 860 917-3545
Ledyard *(G-3876)*
Lda Publishers.......G....... 203 438-1484
Westport *(G-10111)*
Lead Dog Production.......G....... 203 732-4566
Oxford *(G-6672)*
Learners Dimension.......G....... 860 228-1236
Columbia *(G-1607)*
Leasefish LLC.......G....... 203 293-3603
Wilton *(G-10309)*
Lefora Publishing LLC.......G....... 860 845-8445
Bristol *(G-1063)*
Life Study Fllwship Foundation.......E....... 203 655-1436
Darien *(G-2031)*
Lindqist Historical Guides Inc.......G....... 203 335-8568
Bridgeport *(G-825)*
Little King Press.......G....... 203 981-2324
Fairfield *(G-2811)*
Liturgical Publications Inc.......F....... 203 966-6470
New Canaan *(G-5115)*
Lowencorp Publishing LLC.......G....... 203 966-3474
New Canaan *(G-5116)*
Lucky Duck Press.......G....... 347 703-3984
Winsted *(G-10527)*
Luxury Brand Network LLC.......G....... 203 930-2703
Greenwich *(G-3194)*
Malachite Publishing LLC.......G....... 860 495-5484
Pawcatuck *(G-6720)*
Mandel Vilar Press.......G....... 806 790-4731
Simsbury *(G-7633)*
Manuscritos Publishing LLC.......G....... 860 432-9519
Manchester *(G-4055)*
Mary Carroll.......G....... 860 543-0750
Andover *(G-13)*
Maryjanesfarm Publishing Group.......G....... 203 857-4880
Norwalk *(G-6249)*
Mason Press Inc.......G....... 860 625-3707
Waterford *(G-9662)*
Masters Publishing.......G....... 860 295-8454
Marlborough *(G-4126)*
Mathword Press LLC.......G....... 203 288-8114
Hamden *(G-3479)*
Mc Mahon Publishing Co.......G....... 203 544-8389
Redding *(G-7100)*
Medhumor Med Publications LLC.......G....... 203 550-9041
Stamford *(G-8302)*
Media Metrix LLC.......G....... 203 386-0228
Stratford *(G-8649)*
Media Ventures Inc.......E....... 203 852-6570
Norwalk *(G-6253)*
Metro Neighbors Publishing LLC.......G....... 203 494-3600
Madison *(G-3940)*
Ml Gente Express.......G....... 860 447-2525
New London *(G-5478)*
Militarylife Publishing LLC.......G....... 203 402-7234
Shelton *(G-7501)*
Millerwalk Publishing LLC.......G....... 203 397-8926
New Haven *(G-5332)*
Minuteman Press.......G....... 203 261-8318
Trumbull *(G-9049)*
Misfit Publishing Co LLC.......G....... 860 444-6796
Quaker Hill *(G-7083)*
Mlj Publishing Record Co LLC.......G....... 203 752-9021
New Haven *(G-5334)*
Mme Publishing LLC.......G....... 860 228-1369
Columbia *(G-1608)*
Mongillo Press.......G....... 203 467-1371
New Haven *(G-5336)*
More Than Asleep Pubg LLC.......G....... 860 872-5757
Vernon *(G-9145)*
Moriartys Desktop Publishing.......G....... 860 345-8063
Higganum *(G-3769)*
Move Books LLC.......G....... 203 709-0490
Beacon Falls *(G-144)*
Mowmedia LLC.......G....... 203 240-6416
Stamford *(G-8315)*
Mr Boltons Music Inc.......G....... 646 578-8081
Westport *(G-10125)*
Municipal Stadium.......G....... 203 755-4019
Waterbury *(G-9548)*
Music Together Fairfield Child.......G....... 203 256-1656
Fairfield *(G-2821)*
Musica Russica Inc.......G....... 203 458-3225
Guilford *(G-3378)*
MWK Publishing LLC.......G....... 860 675-6067
Hartford *(G-3647)*
Nancy Larson Publishers Inc.......E....... 860 434-0800
Old Lyme *(G-6515)*
Nancy Larson Publishers Hq.......G....... 860 598-9783
Old Lyme *(G-6516)*
National Shooting Sports Found.......E....... 203 426-1320
Newtown *(G-5762)*
Nelson & Miller Associates.......G....... 203 356-9694
Stamford *(G-8319)*
Nelson Publishing.......G....... 860 404-5292
Burlington *(G-1275)*
New Amrcan Political Press Inc.......G....... 860 747-2037
New Haven *(G-5341)*
New England Press Parts LLC.......G....... 203 623-7533
Cheshire *(G-1421)*
Newsbank Inc.......G....... 203 966-1100
New Canaan *(G-5125)*
Next Level Publishing LLC.......G....... 860 282-2428
East Hartford *(G-2347)*
Ninety-Nine Cent Pubg LLC.......G....... 203 922-9917
Shelton *(G-7512)*

SIC SECTION 27 PRINTING, PUBLISHING, AND ALLIED INDUSTRIES

Noroton Publishing Co..........G....... 203 655-1436
Darien *(G-2034)*
North Shore Publishing LLC..........G....... 860 561-8768
West Hartford *(G-9838)*
Northast Tnnis Pblications LLC..........G....... 203 984-1088
Weston *(G-10034)*
Northeast Publications LLC..........G....... 860 399-4801
Old Saybrook *(G-6560)*
Northern Wolf Press LLC..........G....... 860 227-0135
Middletown *(G-4387)*
Novanglus Publishing LLC..........G....... 203 885-7476
Greenwich *(G-3211)*
Odyssey Interactive LLC..........G....... 860 799-6088
New Milford *(G-5577)*
Office Insight..........G....... 203 966-5008
New Canaan *(G-5127)*
Open Science Publishing LLC..........G....... 860 568-4675
East Hartford *(G-2350)*
Organizational & Diversity Con..........G....... 203 777-3324
New Haven *(G-5356)*
Outer Office..........G....... 203 329-8600
Stamford *(G-8347)*
Owl King Publishing LLC..........G....... 203 530-6846
Orange *(G-6621)*
Pagani Publishing..........G....... 860 614-0303
Enfield *(G-2675)*
Palm Canyon Pictures..........G....... 203 853-1808
Norwalk *(G-6289)*
Paper and Prose Publishing LLC..........G....... 203 775-8228
Brookfield *(G-1210)*
Parkhill Publishing LLC..........G....... 203 938-9199
West Redding *(G-9970)*
Partner In Publishing LLC..........G....... 860 430-9440
Glastonbury *(G-3068)*
Passport Publications of..........G....... 631 736-6691
Middletown *(G-4390)*
Patrick Barrett DBA Lucky Duck..........G....... 347 703-3984
Canaan *(G-1290)*
Pattagansett Publishing Inc..........G....... 860 693-6156
Canton *(G-1324)*
Paw To Press..........G....... 303 709-2807
Groton *(G-3303)*
Pelican Island Publishing..........G....... 908 227-0991
Stamford *(G-8357)*
Pemberton Press Inc..........G....... 203 761-1466
Wilton *(G-10318)*
Penny Publications LLC..........E....... 203 866-6688
Milford *(G-4606)*
Pennycorner Press..........G....... 860 873-3545
East Haddam *(G-2247)*
Permanent Press LLC..........G....... 860 788-6001
Portland *(G-6967)*
Perry Heights Press LLC..........G....... 203 767-6509
Wilton *(G-10319)*
Pigeonhole Press LLC..........G....... 203 629-5754
Greenwich *(G-3215)*
Pine Bush Publishing LLC..........G....... 203 570-3523
Danbury *(G-1908)*
PINke&brown Publishing LLP..........G....... 860 798-9858
Avon *(G-100)*
Pinnacle Press LLC..........G....... 203 254-1947
Fairfield *(G-2828)*
Pinnacle Training and Publ..........G....... 203 691-6221
New Haven *(G-5365)*
Pixels 2 Press LLC..........G....... 203 642-3740
Norwalk *(G-6302)*
Pocket Parks Publishing LLC..........G....... 203 499-7416
West Haven *(G-9945)*
Podskoch Press..........G....... 860 267-2442
Colchester *(G-1567)*
Pointer Press..........G....... 203 355-0677
Stamford *(G-8366)*
Portfolio Arts Group Ltd..........F....... 203 661-2400
Norwalk *(G-6303)*
Premiere..........G....... 203 756-0178
Waterbury *(G-9585)*
Press Hartford..........G....... 860 216-6538
Hartford *(G-3669)*
Press On Sandwich Crafters..........G....... 860 694-9882
Groton *(G-3310)*
Press On Sandwich Crafters LLC..........G....... 860 415-9906
North Stonington *(G-6031)*
Primo Press LLC..........G....... 203 527-7904
Waterbury *(G-9588)*
Prison Publications Inc..........G....... 860 928-4055
Putnam *(G-7060)*
Proquest Inc..........G....... 860 644-2392
South Windsor *(G-7815)*
Prs Air Elite..........G....... 203 327-3500
New Canaan *(G-5135)*
Prs Mobile LLC..........G....... 203 909-5249
Prospect *(G-7022)*
Prs Woods LLC..........G....... 860 364-5173
Sharon *(G-7382)*
Publishing Dimensions LLC..........G....... 203 856-7716
Weston *(G-10037)*
Publishing Directions LLC..........G....... 860 673-7650
Avon *(G-101)*
Puddingstone Publishing LLC..........G....... 203 454-3939
Weston *(G-10038)*
Puppet Press..........G....... 203 838-3665
Norwalk *(G-6311)*
Pushpin Press..........G....... 203 797-8691
Danbury *(G-1922)*
Qmdi Press..........G....... 860 642-8074
North Franklin *(G-5878)*
Quantum Health Press..........G....... 203 396-0222
Trumbull *(G-9058)*
Quick & Dirty Press..........G....... 860 817-0912
Tolland *(G-8876)*
Quixpress Car Wash..........G....... 203 364-9777
Newtown *(G-5772)*
R and R Publishing LLC..........G....... 860 944-2085
Storrs Mansfield *(G-8558)*
R G L Inc..........E....... 860 653-7254
East Granby *(G-2226)*
Rambling Dog Publications LLC..........G....... 203 254-9230
Easton *(G-2563)*
Rand Media Co LLC..........G....... 203 226-8727
Westport *(G-10145)*
Rare Reminder Incorporated..........E....... 860 563-9386
Rocky Hill *(G-7264)*
Rcsi Publishing..........G....... 203 917-4223
Danbury *(G-1927)*
Real Data Inc..........G....... 203 255-2732
Southport *(G-8007)*
Red Beard Publishing LLC..........G....... 203 847-1655
Norwalk *(G-6317)*
Red Mat Media Inc..........G....... 203 283-5290
Milford *(G-4623)*
Register For Publications..........G....... 860 302-6706
Southington *(G-7966)*
Registrant James Trippe..........G....... 203 517-7567
Greenwich *(G-3224)*
Relocation Information Svc Inc..........E....... 203 855-1234
Norwalk *(G-6319)*
Remesas Express..........G....... 203 330-1444
Bridgeport *(G-889)*
Richmond Press..........G....... 860 649-0552
South Windsor *(G-7819)*
Ricia Mainhardt Agency..........G....... 718 434-1893
Meriden *(G-4234)*
Ridgetop Publishing LLC..........G....... 860 489-9555
New Hartford *(G-5210)*
Rockefeller Treasury Services..........G....... 203 264-8404
Southbury *(G-7875)*
Rotounderworld LLC..........G....... 202 236-7103
Fairfield *(G-2839)*
Rowayton Press LLC..........G....... 203 866-6646
Norwalk *(G-6329)*
Ruckus Media Group Inc..........G....... 203 939-1409
Norwalk *(G-6332)*
S & L Systems..........G....... 203 757-6159
Waterbury *(G-9596)*
Saltbox Press LLC..........G....... 203 762-9731
Wilton *(G-10327)*
▲ Sandvik Pubg Interactive Inc..........F....... 203 205-0188
Danbury *(G-1932)*
Savant Publishing LLC..........G....... 203 740-9850
Brookfield *(G-1222)*
Scene 1 Arts LLC..........G....... 203 748-0899
Bethel *(G-339)*
▲ Scholastic Inc..........G....... 212 343-6100
Danbury *(G-1938)*
Scott American LLC..........G....... 203 733-5512
Trumbull *(G-9071)*
Scriptural RES & Pubg Co Inc..........G....... 860 609-5138
Southington *(G-7972)*
Scripture Research & Pubg Co..........G....... 203 272-1780
Cheshire *(G-1443)*
Sea House Press LLC..........G....... 860 552-4141
Clinton *(G-1523)*
Senior Network Inc..........E....... 203 969-2700
Stamford *(G-8409)*
Senior Resource Publishing LLC..........G....... 203 295-3477
Stamford *(G-8410)*
Shiller and Company Inc..........D....... 203 210-5208
Wilton *(G-10330)*
Shop Smart Central Inc..........G....... 914 962-3871
Newtown *(G-5779)*
Shoppers-Turnpike Corporation..........F....... 860 928-3040
Putnam *(G-7065)*
Smantics..........G....... 860 238-7714
Winsted *(G-10537)*
Solana Publishing LLC..........G....... 203 380-2851
Trumbull *(G-9075)*
Solution Publishing..........G....... 203 758-9137
Middlebury *(G-4293)*
Somers Music Publications..........G....... 860 763-0366
Somers *(G-7670)*
Sound of Fury Publishing LLC..........G....... 860 803-0651
Coventry *(G-1675)*
South End Express 2..........G....... 203 720-2085
Naugatuck *(G-4920)*
South Wind Music Pubg LLC..........G....... 860 644-2357
South Windsor *(G-7825)*
Southern Neng Telecom Corp..........B....... 203 771-5200
New Haven *(G-5401)*
Stamford Capital Group Inc..........A....... 800 977-7837
Stamford *(G-8436)*
Stamler Publishing Company..........G....... 203 488-9808
Branford *(G-655)*
Starstatus Publishing..........G....... 877 453-9532
Derby *(G-2127)*
Step Saver Inc..........E....... 860 621-6751
Southington *(G-7982)*
Stonington Publications Inc..........G....... 860 599-2019
Pawcatuck *(G-6725)*
Summer Street Content LLC..........G....... 203 536-9895
Westport *(G-10162)*
Summit Ridge Publishing LLC..........G....... 860 689-3463
Harwinton *(G-3741)*
Sunny Publishing Company LLC..........G....... 203 619-3831
Vernon *(G-9153)*
Symmetry Press LLC..........G....... 203 988-2329
New Haven *(G-5409)*
Tab Brown Publishing LLC..........G....... 860 985-9621
Hartford *(G-3697)*
Tall Trees Press..........G....... 860 233-7024
West Hartford *(G-9864)*
Tam Communications Inc..........E....... 203 425-8777
Norwalk *(G-6362)*
Tax Tracker LLC..........G....... 860 296-8143
Hartford *(G-3698)*
Technical Brief..........G....... 203 432-8188
New Haven *(G-5411)*
Teed Off Publishing Inc..........G....... 561 266-0872
Greenwich *(G-3243)*
Tell ME Press LLC..........G....... 203 562-4215
New Haven *(G-5413)*
The Merrill Anderson Co Inc..........F....... 203 377-4996
Stratford *(G-8694)*
Think Big Publications LLC..........G....... 203 685-4957
Fairfield *(G-2855)*
Thirdshift Publishing..........G....... 860 521-6613
West Hartford *(G-9866)*
Thomson Reuters Corporation..........F....... 203 466-5055
East Haven *(G-2456)*
Three Poets Publishing Co LLC..........G....... 203 248-0200
Hamden *(G-3518)*
Thursdays Child Publishing LLC..........G....... 203 929-5080
Shelton *(G-7567)*
Tiffany Press Inc..........G....... 914 806-2245
Stamford *(G-8469)*
Times Publishing LLC..........G....... 860 349-8532
Middlefield *(G-4308)*
Tom Santos Publishing..........G....... 860 599-5067
Pawcatuck *(G-6729)*
Topaz Enterprise Sand Pubg..........G....... 203 449-1903
Norwalk *(G-6374)*
Topaz Enterprises & Pubg LLC..........G....... 203 993-9051
Norwalk *(G-6375)*
Tots411 LLP..........G....... 203 558-5369
Westport *(G-10168)*
Treble Clef Music Press..........G....... 919 932-5455
Niantic *(G-5818)*
Trusource Publications LLC..........G....... 860 350-6477
New Milford *(G-5602)*
Tune Door Inc..........G....... 914 713-0257
New Fairfield *(G-5180)*
Turkey Tail Publishing LLC..........G....... 860 671-0800
Washington *(G-9414)*
Twisko Press LLC..........G....... 203 938-3466
Redding *(G-7111)*
Ubm LLC..........G....... 203 662-6501
Darien *(G-2048)*
Unicorn Press LLC..........G....... 203 938-7405
Redding *(G-7112)*
Universe Publishing Co LLC..........G....... 203 283-5201
Milford *(G-4669)*

S I C

Employee Codes: A=Over 500 employees, B=251-500
C=101-250, D=51-100, E=20-50, F=10-19, G=1-9
2020 Harris Connecticut
Manufacturers Directory
397

27 PRINTING, PUBLISHING, AND ALLIED INDUSTRIES

University Hlth Pubg Group LLC .... G 203 791-0101
Bethel *(G-359)*

◆ **US Games Systems Inc** .... E 203 353-8400
Stamford *(G-8481)*

Valley Press Inc .... E 860 651-4700
Simsbury *(G-7650)*

Van Cott Rowe & Smith .... G 860 242-0707
Bloomfield *(G-497)*

Ventureout Publications LLC .... G 203 668-9162
Wallingford *(G-9400)*

Versimedia .... G 203 604-8094
Norwalk *(G-6386)*

Vitis Press .... G 860 921-8570
Watertown *(G-9747)*

Vocalis Limited .... G 203 753-5244
Waterbury *(G-9623)*

Wake Publishing .... G 860 559-2787
Monroe *(G-4763)*

Wakeen Gallery .... G 860 763-4565
Somers *(G-7676)*

Web Savvy Marketers LLC .... G 860 432-8756
East Hartford *(G-2401)*

Webwrite Publishing LLC .... G 203 544-9728
Weston *(G-10045)*

Weidner Publication Group .... G 203 272-2463
Cheshire *(G-1458)*

Wine Capp Inc .... G 860 355-0521
Sherman *(G-7607)*

Winespeak Press LLC .... G 203 968-8882
Stamford *(G-8496)*

Wizard Too LLC .... G 203 984-7180
Westport *(G-10177)*

Woodhall Press LLP .... G 203 428-1876
Norwalk *(G-6398)*

Word For Words LLC .... G 203 894-1908
Ridgefield *(G-7185)*

Wyndemere Publishing LLC .... G 860 868-1490
Warren *(G-9410)*

Yale Printing and Pubg Svcs .... G 203 432-6560
New Haven *(G-5442)*

▲ **Yale University** .... E 203 432-2550
New Haven *(G-5443)*

Yale University .... D 203 764-4333
New Haven *(G-5444)*

Yankee Delivery System .... G 860 243-1056
Bloomfield *(G-503)*

Yellow Girl Press LLC .... G 860 819-0260
Marlborough *(G-4131)*

▲ **Ziga Media LLC** .... G 203 656-0076
Darien *(G-2052)*

Zossima Press .... G 203 687-9385
Cheshire *(G-1461)*

2752 Commercial Printing: Lithographic

1 Way Custom Print .... G 860 712-0027
Manchester *(G-3970)*

24 Hours Design & Print .... G 347 350-4484
Bridgeport *(G-678)*

5 Star Printing .... G 203 975-1000
Stamford *(G-8050)*

A B C Printing Inc .... F 203 468-1245
East Haven *(G-2406)*

A Grey Soiree LLC .... G 203 530-0277
Branford *(G-534)*

A1 Commercial Printing Co LLC .... G 203 975-1000
Stamford *(G-8054)*

Abbey Printing .... G 860 745-0122
Enfield *(G-2611)*

Abbott Printing Company Inc .... G 203 562-5562
Hamden *(G-3410)*

Academy Printing Service .... G 860 828-5549
Kensington *(G-3803)*

Acme Press Inc .... G 203 334-8221
Milford *(G-4439)*

Acme Press Printers LLC .... G 203 237-2702
Meriden *(G-4140)*

Action Letter Inc .... E 203 323-2466
Stamford *(G-8061)*

Action Printing .... G 203 366-4413
Shelton *(G-7388)*

Adkins Printing Company .... E 800 228-9745
New Britain *(G-4938)*

Advance Images LLC .... G 860 749-1166
Enfield *(G-2613)*

Advanced Screen Printing LLC .... G 860 845-8337
Bristol *(G-959)*

Agjo Printing Service .... G 860 599-3143
Pawcatuck *(G-6703)*

Alexander and Mason .... G 860 349-0496
Durham *(G-2136)*

Alexander Hussey .... G 860 354-0118
New Milford *(G-5503)*

Alliance Graphics Inc .... F 860 666-7992
Newington *(G-5624)*

▲ **Allied Printing Services Inc** .... B 860 643-1101
Manchester *(G-3980)*

AlphaGraphics LLC .... G 203 230-0018
Hamden *(G-3413)*

◆ **American Banknote Corporation** .... G 203 941-4090
Stamford *(G-8074)*

American-Republican Inc .... D 203 574-3636
Waterbury *(G-9429)*

▲ **Amgraph Packaging Inc** .... C 860 822-2000
Baltic *(G-118)*

Amity Printing & Copy Ctr LLC .... G 860 828-0202
Berlin *(G-158)*

Ampco Publishing & Prtg Corp .... G 203 325-1509
Stamford *(G-8080)*

Anderson Publishing LLC .... G 860 621-2192
Southington *(G-7890)*

Anray Lithographers .... G 203 877-1000
Milford *(G-4453)*

Apb Associates LLC .... G 203 740-9792
Brookfield *(G-1159)*

Apps Screen Printing LLC .... G 860 938-7596
Waterbury *(G-9432)*

AR Robinson Printing .... G 203 961-1787
Stamford *(G-8089)*

Arcat Inc .... G 203 929-9444
Fairfield *(G-2747)*

Arch Parent Inc .... G 860 336-4856
Willimantic *(G-10221)*

Arrow Printers Inc .... G 203 734-7272
Ansonia *(G-21)*

Arrowhead Group LLC .... G 954 771-5115
Windsor *(G-10365)*

Audubon Copy Shppe of Firfield .... G 203 259-4311
Bridgeport *(G-705)*

Automated Mailing Services LLC .... G 203 439-2763
Cheshire *(G-1358)*

Back Country Graphics .... G 203 531-5878
Greenwich *(G-3128)*

Baker Graphics Corporation .... E 203 226-6928
Westport *(G-10059)*

Bam Custom Printing .... G 888 583-6690
Shelton *(G-7402)*

Barile Printers LLC .... G 860 224-0127
New Britain *(G-4950)*

Barron Print .... G 860 355-9535
New Milford *(G-5509)*

BCT Reporting LLC .... G 860 302-1876
Plainville *(G-6775)*

BCT-042 LLC .... G 203 331-0008
Bridgeport *(G-708)*

Benenson Family Realty LLC .... G 919 544-7839
Weston *(G-10019)*

Bethel Printing & Graphics .... G 203 748-7034
Bethel *(G-263)*

Bizcard Xpress LLC .... G 860 324-6840
Higganum *(G-3761)*

Bluc Print .... G 203 948-3883
Danbury *(G-1758)*

▼ **Boltprintingcom** .... G 203 885-0571
Brookfield *(G-1163)*

Brass City Custom .... G 860 995-9321
Waterbury *(G-9441)*

Brescias Printing Services Inc .... G 860 528-4254
East Hartford *(G-2300)*

Brian Berlepsch .... G 203 484-9799
North Branford *(G-5830)*

Briarwood Printing Company Inc .... F 860 747-6805
Plainville *(G-6778)*

Brody Printing Company Inc .... F 203 384-9313
Bridgeport *(G-724)*

Business Cards Tomorrow Inc .... G 203 723-5858
Naugatuck *(G-4864)*

Byrne Group Inc .... G 203 573-0100
Waterbury *(G-9444)*

Caco Print Productions LLC .... G 860 583-1223
Bristol *(G-996)*

Cadmus .... G 203 595-3000
Stamford *(G-8126)*

Cag Imaging LLC .... G 860 887-0836
Norwich *(G-6408)*

Cannelli Printing Co Inc .... G 203 932-1719
West Haven *(G-9886)*

Capitol Printing Co Inc .... G 860 522-1547
Hartford *(G-3561)*

Ceci Printer LLC .... G 203 994-6314
Danbury *(G-1764)*

Cenveo Corporation .... E 303 790-8023
Stamford *(G-8139)*

Chase Graphics Inc .... F 860 315-9006
Putnam *(G-7034)*

Child Evngelism Fellowship Inc .... E 203 879-2154
Wolcott *(G-10553)*

Clanol Systems Inc .... G 203 637-9909
Old Greenwich *(G-6469)*

Classic Ink .... G 860 225-3652
New Britain *(G-4961)*

Coastline Printing .... G 203 481-2744
Branford *(G-574)*

Colonial Printers of Windsor .... G 860 627-5433
Windsor Locks *(G-10480)*

Commercial Service .... G 203 755-0166
Waterbury *(G-9454)*

Compumail Corp .... G 860 583-1906
Bristol *(G-1005)*

Concord Litho .... G 203 866-9394
Norwalk *(G-6125)*

Connecticut Valley Litho Club .... G 203 234-0536
North Haven *(G-5925)*

Conner Printing .... G 203 929-2070
Shelton *(G-7423)*

Copy Stop Inc .... G 203 288-6401
Hamden *(G-3433)*

Copy-Rite Inc .... G 203 272-6923
Plantsville *(G-6889)*

Corporate Forms Printing .... G 800 840-9945
New Britain *(G-4967)*

Craftsmen Printing Group Inc .... G 203 327-2817
Stamford *(G-8163)*

Creative Printed Products LLC .... G 203 268-8980
Monroe *(G-4707)*

Cricket Press Inc .... G 860 521-9279
West Hartford *(G-9796)*

Critical Scrn Printg & EMB .... G 860 443-4327
Waterford *(G-9649)*

CT Prints .... G 203 281-6996
Hamden *(G-3435)*

CT Prints & More LLC .... G 860 604-5694
Hartford *(G-3573)*

Curry Printing & Copy Ctr LLC .... G 203 878-5767
Milford *(G-4502)*

Custom Printing & Copy Inc .... F 860 290-6890
Enfield *(G-2634)*

Custom Tee .... G 718 450-1210
Stamford *(G-8173)*

D & D Printing & Advertising .... G 860 871-7774
Vernon Rockville *(G-9166)*

D Cello Enterprises LLC .... G 860 659-0844
Glastonbury *(G-3027)*

D&D Printing Enterprises .... G 860 684-2023
Stafford Springs *(G-8023)*

Dane Millette .... G 860 635-6383
Cromwell *(G-1699)*

Das State of CT .... G 860 566-4718
Hartford *(G-3576)*

Data Management Incorporated .... E 860 677-8586
Unionville *(G-9113)*

Data Management Inc .... G 800 243-1969
Farmington *(G-2896)*

▲ **Data-Graphics Inc** .... D 860 667-0435
Newington *(G-5647)*

Del Printing LLC .... G 860 342-2959
Portland *(G-6957)*

Derosa Printing Company Inc .... F 860 646-1698
Manchester *(G-4005)*

Design & Print Interests LLC .... G 203 494-9072
Orange *(G-6596)*

Design Idea Printing .... G 860 896-0103
Ellington *(G-2586)*

Digital Imagining & Packaging .... G 203 458-3509
Guilford *(G-3345)*

Digitaldruker Inc .... G 203 888-6001
Oxford *(G-6656)*

Dlorio Printing Service .... G 203 656-0557
Darien *(G-2021)*

Dmjc Printing LLC .... G 860 502-4882
Hartford *(G-3579)*

Docuprint & Imaging Inc .... G 203 776-6000
New Haven *(G-5267)*

E R Hitchcock Company .... E 860 229-2024
New Britain *(G-4977)*

Eagle Printing Co .... G 860 953-2152
West Hartford *(G-9804)*

East Coast Name Plates Inc .... G 203 261-4347
Easton *(G-2549)*

East Coast Packaging LLC .... G 860 675-8500
Farmington *(G-2901)*

SIC SECTION 27 PRINTING, PUBLISHING, AND ALLIED INDUSTRIES

East Longmeadow Business Svcs........G 413 525-6111
Enfield (G-2637)
▲ Easy Graphics Inc.............................G 203 622-0001
Greenwich (G-3156)
Eccles-Lehman Inc ....G 203 268-0605
Easton (G-2551)
Economy Printing & Copy Center ....G 203 792-5610
Danbury (G-1803)
Economy Printing & Copy Center ....G 203 438-7401
Ridgefield (G-7137)
Edge Printing...G 609 707-4555
Norwalk (G-6155)
Ellington Printery Inc.............................G 860 875-3310
Ellington (G-2589)
Elm Press Incorporated.........................E 860 583-3600
Terryville (G-8752)
▲ Empire Printing Systems LLC ....G 860 633-3333
Glastonbury (G-3034)
Emulsion LLC...G 860 440-8685
Stonington (G-8527)
Enfield Printing Company.......................G 860 745-3600
Enfield (G-2639)
Entersport Management Inc...................G 203 972-9090
New Canaan (G-5103)
Evergreen Printing.................................G 203 323-4717
Stamford (G-8201)
Executive Office Services Inc ....E 203 373-1333
Bridgeport (G-765)
Executive Press Inc ....G 860 793-0060
Plainville (G-6807)
Executive Printing Darien LLC ....G 203 655-4691
Darien (G-2023)
Fairfield Marketing Group Inc ....F 203 261-0884
Easton (G-2552)
Fairfield Minuteman ....G 203 752-2711
New Haven (G-5282)
Falcon Press...G 860 763-2293
Enfield (G-2646)
Financial Prtg Solutions LLC.................G 860 886-9931
Preston (G-6983)
Fine Print New England Inc...................G 860 953-0660
Newington (G-5652)
Fleetprinters LLC ....G 860 684-2352
Stafford Springs (G-8030)
Flow Resources Inc ....E 860 666-1200
Newington (G-5653)
Fox Print ....G 860 485-0429
Harwinton (G-3729)
Framing and Printing Solu ....G 860 664-9679
Clinton (G-1504)
Frank Obuchowski..................................G 860 535-4739
Stonington (G-8528)
Franklin Print Shoppe Inc ....G 860 496-9516
Torrington (G-8926)
Fresh Prints of CT LLC ....G 860 398-4893
Rockfall (G-7212)
FSNB Enterprises Inc ....G 203 254-1947
Monroe (G-4718)
Fulcrum Promotions & Printing.............G 203 909-6362
Bridgeport (G-773)
Fusion Cross-Media LLC........................G 860 647-8367
Manchester (G-4020)
G & R Enterprises Incorporated ....G 860 549-6120
Hartford (G-3593)
Garcia Printing Inc.................................G 203 378-6200
Stratford (G-8615)
Garrett Printing & Graphics ....G 860 589-6710
Bristol (G-1045)
Gateway Digital Inc ....F 203 853-4929
Norwalk (G-6175)
George Bullock & Sons Inc....................G 860 355-1243
Roxbury (G-7277)
Ghp Media Inc ....C 203 479-7500
West Haven (G-9912)
Goodcopy Printing Center Inc ....E 203 624-0194
New Haven (G-5287)
Goulet Enterprises Inc...........................F 860 379-0793
Pleasant Valley (G-6922)
Grafik Print Shopp ....G 203 335-0777
Bridgeport (G-778)
Graphic Image Inc..................................E 203 877-8787
Milford (G-4542)
Graphic Plus...G 203 723-8387
Naugatuck (G-4885)
Gravelines Amercn Martial Arts.............G 860 753-1402
Brooklyn (G-1247)
Guilford Printing Inc ....G 203 453-5585
Guilford (G-3358)
Gulemo Inc ....G 860 456-1151
Willimantic (G-10229)

Hamden Press Inc..................................G 203 624-0554
Hamden (G-3458)
Hartford Business Supply Inc.................E 860 233-2138
Hartford (G-3607)
Hartford Prints LLC................................G 860 578-8447
Hartford (G-3613)
Harty Press Inc.......................................D 203 562-5112
New Haven (G-5293)
Hat Trick Graphics LLC ....G 203 748-1128
Danbury (G-1842)
Herff Jones LLC ....G 203 266-7170
Bethlehem (G-372)
High Ridge Copy Inc..............................F 203 329-1889
Stamford (G-8237)
Holly Press Inc ....G 203 846-1720
Norwalk (G-6202)
Ideal Printing Co Inc ....G 203 777-7626
New Haven (G-5299)
Ill Ink Graphic & Prtg Svcs ....G 203 748-0711
Danbury (G-1848)
Image Ink Inc..G 860 665-9792
Newington (G-5661)
Images Fine Print....................................G 203 482-1695
Brookfield (G-1196)
Imperial Grphic Cmmnctions Inc...........E 203 650-3478
Milford (G-4553)
Impression Point Inc...............................F 203 353-8800
Stamford (G-8246)
Imprint Printing ....G 203 794-1092
Bethel (G-310)
Inform Inc..G 203 924-9929
Shelton (G-7477)
Ink Well T-Shirts LLC ....G 860 355-3065
New Milford (G-5546)
Inkbyte LLC ....G 203 939-1140
Shelton (G-7478)
Inkwell...G 860 666-8312
Newington (G-5662)
Ins Sreen Printing & Air...........................G 860 779-0566
Danielson (G-1994)
Instant Replay ....G 203 264-1177
Oxford (G-6668)
Instant Style Home Staging ....G 203 417-0131
Weston (G-10029)
Instant Win Innovations ....G 203 648-4499
Newtown (G-5750)
Integrity Graphics Inc ....D 800 343-1248
Simsbury (G-7629)
Interctive Print Solutions LLC ....G 860 217-0412
Simsbury (G-7630)
J & T Printing LLC..................................G 860 529-4628
Wethersfield (G-10201)
Jerrys Printing & Graphics LLC ....G 203 384-0015
Bridgeport (G-803)
JMS Graphics Inc...................................G 203 598-7555
Middlebury (G-4280)
John L Prentis & Co Inc ....G 203 634-1266
Meriden (G-4178)
Jornik Screen Printing............................G 203 969-0500
Stamford (G-8269)
Joseph Merritt & Company Inc ....G 203 743-6734
Danbury (G-1863)
Joseph Merritt & Company Inc ....E 860 296-2500
Hartford (G-3620)
JS McCarthy Co Inc ....E 203 355-7600
Stamford (G-8270)
Jupiter Communications LLC.................F 475 238-7082
West Haven (G-9920)
K & G Graphics ....G 203 481-4884
Branford (G-614)
K&D Print LLC...G 203 483-1199
Branford (G-615)
Katahdin Printing....................................G 860 461-7037
Bloomfield (G-437)
Kathy Pooler...G 860 889-2893
Norwich (G-6420)
Kenny Kalipershad ....G 917 345-5038
Greenwich (G-3188)
Kingsley Printing Assoc LLC..................G 203 345-6046
Stratford (G-8641)
Kool Ink LLC..F 860 242-0303
Bloomfield (G-439)
Kramer Printing Company Inc ....F 203 933-5416
West Haven (G-9924)
Kris Squires Printing & P ....G 860 582-0782
Bristol (G-1059)
▲ L P Macadams Company Inc.............D 203 366-3647
Bridgeport (G-820)
Late Nite Printing Co ....G 203 374-9287
Bridgeport (G-823)

Leading Edge Printers LLC ....G 203 592-4477
Prospect (G-7007)
Liberty Screen Print Co LLC ....F 203 632-5449
Beacon Falls (G-140)
Lighthouse Printing LLC ....G 860 388-2677
Old Saybrook (G-6554)
Lithographics Inc ....D 860 678-1660
Farmington (G-2926)
Liturgical Publications Inc ....G 860 635-9560
Cromwell (G-1706)
Lone Wolfe Printing LLC ....G 203 444-5131
Hamden (G-3477)
Lowbrow ....G 203 518-4189
Bethel (G-324)
M Design & Printing Svcs LLC ....G 860 344-8289
Middletown (G-4372)
◆ Macdermid Incorporated ....C 203 575-5700
Waterbury (G-9522)
Magnani Press Incorporated..................G 860 236-2802
Hartford (G-3631)
Mainely Custom Carving........................G 203 426-8375
Newtown (G-5759)
Majestic Press ....G 860 673-2064
Unionville (G-9120)
Maple Print Services Inc.......................G 860 381-5470
Griswold (G-3267)
Maple Print Services Inc.......................G 860 381-5470
Jewett City (G-3799)
Mark Ramponi Printing...........................G 860 673-5507
Burlington (G-1272)
Marketing Sltons Unlimited LLC............E 860 523-0670
West Hartford (G-9834)
Massachusetts Envelope Co Inc ....E 860 727-9100
Hartford (G-3636)
Master Engrv & Printery Inc...................G 203 723-2779
Waterbury (G-9535)
Material Promotions Inc ....G 203 757-8900
Waterbury (G-9536)
Matthews Printing Co ....F 203 265-0363
Wallingford (G-9314)
Max Productions LLC ....G 203 838-2795
Norwalk (G-6250)
Melega Inc...G 203 961-8703
Stamford (G-8306)
Middletown Printing Co Inc....................F 860 347-5700
Middletown (G-4379)
Midnight Printing LLC ....G 203 257-3307
Monroe (G-4736)
Midstate Printing Group LLC ....G 203 998-7575
Stamford (G-8309)
Milestone Graphics.................................G 203 218-4528
Bridgeport (G-838)
Minit Print Inc..G 203 776-6000
New Haven (G-5333)
Minute Man Press ....G 203 891-6251
Hamden (G-3483)
Minuteman Arms LLC.............................G 203 268-4853
Trumbull (G-9048)
Minuteman Land Services Inc ....G 203 854-4949
Norwalk (G-6261)
Minuteman Press ....G 973 748-7160
Danbury (G-1885)
Minuteman Press ....G 203 445-6971
Shelton (G-7502)
Minuteman Press ....G 860 646-0601
Manchester (G-4057)
Minuteman Press ....G 860 646-0601
Hartford (G-3644)
Minuteman Press ....G 203 261-8318
Trumbull (G-9049)
Minuteman Press ....G 860 266-4154
Glastonbury (G-3059)
Minuteman Press ....G 860 529-4628
Wethersfield (G-10212)
Minuteman Press ....G 860 496-7525
Torrington (G-8949)
Minuteman Press ....G 203 261-9569
Newtown (G-5761)
Minuteman Press ....G 860 674-8700
Avon (G-93)
Minuteman Press LLC ....G 203 922-9228
Shelton (G-7503)
Minuteman Press of Bristol ....G 860 589-1100
Bristol (G-1072)
Minuteman Press of Danbury ....G 203 743-6755
Danbury (G-1886)
Misfit Prints LLC ....G 203 306-6322
Meriden (G-4205)
Mk & T Design & Print LLC ....G 203 295-8211
Norwalk (G-6262)

SIC

Employee Codes: A=Over 500 employees, B=251-500
C=101-250, D=51-100, E=20-50, F=10-19, G=1-9
2020 Harris Connecticut
Manufacturers Directory
399

27 PRINTING, PUBLISHING, AND ALLIED INDUSTRIES — SIC SECTION

Muir Envelope Plus Inc .... F 860 953-6847
　Newington *(G-5681)*
Murphy Boyz Printing Mark .... G 860 836-0829
　Litchfield *(G-3896)*
Murphy Boyz Prtg & Mktg LLC .... G 860 485-0607
　Harwinton *(G-3734)*
Napp Printing Plate Dist Inc .... G 203 575-5727
　Waterbury *(G-9552)*
Naugatuck Vly Photo Engrv Inc .... G 203 756-7345
　Waterbury *(G-9554)*
New England Info Districts .... G 860 446-1906
　Groton *(G-3300)*
New Fairfield Press Inc .... F 203 746-2700
　New Fairfield *(G-5172)*
▲ New Haven Register LLC .... A 203 789-5200
　New Haven *(G-5346)*
New Haven Rgster Fresh Air Fnd .... G 800 925-2509
　New Haven *(G-5347)*
New London Printing Co LLC .... G 860 701-9171
　New London *(G-5481)*
New Milford Print Works Inc .... G 860 799-0530
　New Milford *(G-5572)*
Nielsen Company .... G 203 586-1819
　Woodbury *(G-10647)*
Northeast Printing Networ .... G 860 788-3572
　Cromwell *(G-1710)*
Norwich Printing Co Inc .... G 860 745-3600
　Enfield *(G-2671)*
Oddo Print Shop Inc .... G 860 489-6585
　Torrington *(G-8953)*
Omniprint LLC .... G 203 881-9013
　Oxford *(G-6683)*
One Source Print and Promo LLC .... G 860 635-3257
　Cromwell *(G-1713)*
Optamark CT LLC .... G 203 325-1180
　Stamford *(G-8342)*
P & M Investments LLC .... G 860 745-3600
　Enfield *(G-2674)*
P & S Printing LLC .... G 203 327-9818
　Stamford *(G-8348)*
P C I Group .... F 203 327-0410
　Stamford *(G-8349)*
Paladin Commercial Prtrs LLC .... E 860 953-4900
　Newington *(G-5691)*
Palmisano Printing LLC .... G 860 582-6883
　Bristol *(G-1085)*
Pancoast Associates Inc .... G 203 377-6571
　Trumbull *(G-9054)*
Paper Mill Graphix Inc .... E 203 531-5904
　Greenwich *(G-3213)*
Parkway Printers Inc .... G 203 281-6773
　Hamden *(G-3494)*
Paul Dewitt .... F 203 792-5610
　Danbury *(G-1902)*
Paw Print Pantry LLC .... G 860 447-8442
　East Lyme *(G-2470)*
Paw Print Pantry LLC .... G 860 447-8442
　Niantic *(G-5815)*
Peach Printing Solutions .... G 203 793-7381
　Wallingford *(G-9334)*
Peaches Prints .... G 860 856 3525
　Windsor *(G-10417)*
Pequot Printing LLC .... G 860 381-5193
　Ledyard *(G-3879)*
Petes Print Shop .... G 860 581-8043
　Essex *(G-2729)*
Phoenix Memorial Printing LLC .... G 203 364-9617
　Sandy Hook *(G-7326)*
Phoenix Press Inc .... E 203 865-5555
　New Haven *(G-5363)*
Photo Arts Limited .... G 860 489-1170
　Torrington *(G-8957)*
Pinpoint Promotions & Prtg LLC .... F 203 301-4273
　West Haven *(G-9944)*
Play-It Productions Inc .... F 212 695-6530
　Colchester *(G-1566)*
Pointer Press .... G 650 269-3492
　New Canaan *(G-5131)*
Pony Express Print Co .... G 203 592-7095
　Waterbury *(G-9581)*
Precision Press LLC .... G 203 359-0211
　Stamford *(G-8371)*
Prentis Printing Solutions Inc .... G 203 634-1266
　Meriden *(G-4220)*
Prinertechs .... G 203 249-6646
　Stamford *(G-8373)*
Print B2b LLC .... G 203 744-5435
　Bethel *(G-333)*
Print House LLC .... G 860 652-0803
　Glastonbury *(G-3074)*

Print Hub .... G 860 580-7907
　Windsor *(G-10425)*
Print Indie LLC .... G 860 986-9446
　Plainville *(G-6854)*
Print Lab LLC .... G 860 410-6624
　New Britain *(G-5037)*
Print Master LLC .... G 860 482-8152
　Torrington *(G-8960)*
Print MGT & Consulting LLC .... G 860 521-7444
　West Hartford *(G-9847)*
▲ Print Promotions Inc .... G 203 778-2672
　Bethel *(G-334)*
Print Shop of Wolcott LLC .... G 860 879-3353
　Wolcott *(G-10581)*
Printer Source Inc .... G 800 788-5101
　Trumbull *(G-9057)*
Printer Techs LLC .... G 860 322-1160
　Stamford *(G-8374)*
Printers of Connecticut Inc .... G 203 852-0070
　Norwalk *(G-6306)*
Printing Services Inc .... G 860 584-9598
　Bristol *(G-1098)*
Printing Solutions LLC .... G 860 965-0090
　Riverside *(G-7200)*
Printing Solutions & Resources .... G 860 965-0090
　Stamford *(G-8375)*
Printing Solutions Group LLC .... G 860 647-0317
　Hebron *(G-3753)*
Pro Graphics Inc .... F 860 668-9067
　Suffield *(G-2693)*
Professional Graphics Inc .... G 203 846-4291
　Norwalk *(G-6307)*
Professional Print Graphics .... G 203 686-0151
　Meriden *(G-4222)*
▲ Project Graphics Inc .... F 802 488-8789
　Woodbury *(G-10652)*
Promos & Printing .... G 860 481-9212
　Pomfret Center *(G-6946)*
Pronto Printer of Newington .... G 860 666-2245
　Newington *(G-5697)*
Prospect Printing LLC .... F 203 758-6007
　Prospect *(G-7021)*
Prosperous Printing LLC .... G 203 834-1962
　Wilton *(G-10322)*
Protopac Inc .... G 860 274-6796
　Watertown *(G-9727)*
Pyne-Davidson Company .... E 860 522-9106
　Hartford *(G-3670)*
Qg Printing II Corp .... A 860 741-0150
　Enfield *(G-2685)*
Qmdi Press Services LLC .... G 860 942-8822
　Willimantic *(G-10235)*
Quad/Graphics Inc .... A 203 288-2468
　North Haven *(G-5985)*
Quality Printers Inc .... G 860 443-2800
　New London *(G-5484)*
Quebecor World (usa) Inc .... G 203 532-4200
　Greenwich *(G-3220)*
Quick Print .... G 860 425-5580
　Colchester *(G-1570)*
Quiet Corner Printing LLC .... G 860 753-0420
　Brooklyn *(G-1253)*
R R Donnelley & Sons Company .... F 860 649-5570
　Manchester *(G-4078)*
R R Donnelley & Sons Company .... E 860 773-6140
　Avon *(G-102)*
Rare Reminder Incorporated .... E 860 563-9386
　Rocky Hill *(G-7264)*
Rd Printing LLC .... G 860 841-1397
　Windsor *(G-10429)*
Ready4 Print LLC .... G 860 345-0376
　Bridgeport *(G-887)*
▲ Record-Journal Newspaper .... C 203 235-1661
　Meriden *(G-4230)*
Reliable Printing LLC .... G 203 261-8867
　Trumbull *(G-9064)*
Retail Print Solutions .... G 203 438-5457
　Ridgefield *(G-7166)*
Rf Printing LLC .... G 203 265-9939
　Wallingford *(G-9352)*
River Dog Prints LLC .... G 860 276-1578
　Avon *(G-105)*
RKP Printing Services LLC .... G 860 242-0131
　Bloomfield *(G-477)*
Rm Printing .... G 860 621-0498
　Plantsville *(G-6909)*
Rmi Inc .... C 860 875-3366
　Vernon Rockville *(G-9177)*
Rollins Printing Incorporated .... G 203 248-3200
　Hamden *(G-3506)*

Romark Printing Service .... G 860 691-0626
　East Lyme *(G-2474)*
Ronald Bottino .... G 860 585-9505
　Bristol *(G-1111)*
Ross Copy & Print LLC .... G 203 933-8732
　West Haven *(G-9950)*
Ross Type .... G 203 227-2007
　Westport *(G-10152)*
Ruiz Impress Scrn Printg & .... G 203 750-0050
　Norwalk *(G-6333)*
Ruiz Impressions Screen Prntg .... G 203 559-4865
　Norwalk *(G-6334)*
S and Z Graphics LLC .... G 203 783-9675
　Milford *(G-4637)*
Sabar Graphics LLC .... G 203 467-3016
　East Haven *(G-2450)*
Sarah May Block21prints .... G 860 604-4004
　Unionville *(G-9127)*
Savin Rock Printing .... G 203 500-1577
　West Haven *(G-9952)*
Savour Instant LLC .... G 203 374-4599
　Easton *(G-2565)*
Sazacks Inc .... G 860 647-8367
　Manchester *(G-4086)*
Screen Tek Printing Co Inc .... G 203 248-6248
　Hamden *(G-3508)*
Scripture Research & Pubg Co .... G 203 272-1780
　Cheshire *(G-1443)*
Seven Stitches Screen Prntng .... G 860 749-1166
　Enfield *(G-2693)*
Signature 22 Painting .... G 914 450-9780
　Danbury *(G-1951)*
Sir Speedy Printing .... E 203 346-0716
　Middlebury *(G-4292)*
Sir Speedy Prntng Ctr of N Bri .... G 860 826-1798
　New Britain *(G-5054)*
Sister Act Printing .... G 203 481-7171
　North Branford *(G-5856)*
Smoke & Print Universe .... G 203 540-5151
　Bridgeport *(G-910)*
Southbury Printing Centre Inc .... G 203 264-0102
　Southbury *(G-7878)*
Specialty Printing LLC .... F 860 654-1850
　East Windsor *(G-2520)*
Spectrum Press .... G 203 878-9090
　Milford *(G-4652)*
Speed Printing & Graphics Inc .... G 203 324-4000
　Stamford *(G-8433)*
Speedy Printing LLC .... G 860 445-8252
　Mystic *(G-4846)*
Step Saver Inc .... E 860 621-6751
　Southington *(G-7982)*
Stevens Printing .... G 203 245-3267
　Madison *(G-3962)*
Streamline Press .... G 203 484-9799
　North Branford *(G-5859)*
Streamline Press LLC .... G 203 484-9799
　North Branford *(G-5860)*
Success Printing & Mailing Inc .... F 203 847-1112
　Norwalk *(G-6359)*
Summit Promotional Printing LL .... G 860 666-1605
　Newington *(G-5707)*
Swipe Ink Screen Printing LLC .... G 203 783-0468
　Milford *(G-4659)*
System Intgrtion Cnsulting LLC .... G 203 926-9599
　Shelton *(G-7562)*
Tashua Litho .... G 203 268-5561
　Monroe *(G-4756)*
Team Destination Inc .... G 203 235-6000
　Meriden *(G-4251)*
Tech-Repro Inc .... F 203 348-8884
　Stamford *(G-8460)*
Technical Reproductions Inc .... F 203 849-9100
　Norwalk *(G-6365)*
Technique Printers Inc .... G 860 669-2516
　Clinton *(G-1529)*
Tektronix Graphics Printing .... G 203 359-8003
　Stamford *(G-8463)*
Testing Technologies Inc .... G 212 835-3617
　Wilton *(G-10337)*
Tfac LLC .... G 203 776-6000
　New Haven *(G-5414)*
Thelemic Printshop .... G 860 383-4014
　Plainfield *(G-6754)*
Three D Print LLC .... G 203 590-3463
　Monroe *(G-4760)*
Toto LLC .... F 203 776-6000
　New Haven *(G-5417)*
Tower Printing Inc .... G 203 757-1030
　Waterbury *(G-9615)*

27 PRINTING, PUBLISHING, AND ALLIED INDUSTRIES

▲ Transmonde USa Inc .... D 203 484-1528
  North Branford (G-5863)
Trend Offset Printing Svcs Inc .... G 860 773-6140
  Avon (G-117)
Tri-State EMB Screen Prtg LLC .... G 203 732-7636
  Ansonia (G-54)
Trumbull Printing Inc .... C 203 261-2548
  Trumbull (G-9082)
Turnstone Inc .... F 203 625-0000
  Greenwich (G-3250)
Typeisright .... G 860 564-0537
  Moosup (G-4783)
◆ US Games Systems Inc .... E 203 353-8400
  Stamford (G-8481)
Valley Press New Area Prtg Co .... G 860 526-5696
  Deep River (G-2105)
Value Print Incorporated .... F 203 265-1371
  Wallingford (G-9399)
Vernon Printing Co Inc .... G 860 872-1826
  Vernon Rockville (G-9186)
Versa Prints .... G 203 256-2342
  Fairfield (G-2864)
Versifi LLC .... G 860 890-1982
  Meriden (G-4263)
W B Mason Co Inc .... D 888 926-2766
  Meriden (G-4265)
W B Mason Co Inc .... E 888 926-2766
  Norwalk (G-6392)
W B Mason Co Inc .... D 888 926-2766
  Norwich (G-6439)
W B Mason Co Inc .... C 888 926-2766
  East Windsor (G-2530)
Walsh Prints .... G 860 829-5566
  Kensington (G-3820)
Warren Press Inc .... G 203 431-0011
  Ridgefield (G-7182)
Westrock Commercial LLC .... G 203 595-3130
  Stamford (G-8492)
Wethersfield Offset Inc .... G 860 721-8236
  Rocky Hill (G-7273)
Wethersfield Printing Co Inc .... F 860 721-8236
  Rocky Hill (G-7274)
Whhs B Wing Elevator .... G 203 288-5949
  West Haven (G-9965)
Wiki Community LLC .... G 860 582-3489
  Bristol (G-1139)
Wild Rver Cstm Screen Prtg LLC .... G 203 426-1500
  Newtown (G-5797)
Williams Printing Group LLC .... G 860 423-8779
  North Windham (G-6041)
Williams Printing LLC .... G 860 813-1717
  Manchester (G-4108)
Wing STC Revision Project .... G 203 432-1753
  New Haven (G-5435)
Woodway Print Inc .... G 203 323-6423
  Stamford (G-8500)
Yale-New Haven Hlth Svcs Corp .... D 203 688-2100
  New Haven (G-5452)
Yankee Screen Printing .... G 203 924-9926
  Derby (G-2133)
Youngs Communications Inc .... F 860 347-8567
  Middletown (G-4434)
▲ Ziga Media LLC .... G 203 656-0076
  Darien (G-2052)

2754 Commercial Printing: Gravure

A Flood of Paper .... G 203 529-3030
  Wilton (G-10265)
Aquastone Graphix LLC .... G 860 206-4935
  Hartford (G-3552)
▲ Brook & Whittle Limited .... C 203 483-5602
  Guilford (G-3334)
ECR Enterprises LLC .... G 860 426-3098
  Southington (G-7917)
Ideas Inc .... G 203 878-9686
  Milford (G-4551)
Jean Marie Papery LLC .... G 203 877-4299
  Milford (G-4559)
Massachusetts Envelope Co Inc .... E 860 727-9100
  Hartford (G-3636)
Mc Hugh Business Forms .... G 203 268-3500
  Monroe (G-4735)
Michael Lazorchak .... G 203 775-0608
  Brookfield (G-1205)
Montambault Riva .... G 203 758-4981
  Prospect (G-7011)
Naugatuck Vly Photo Engrv Inc .... G 203 756-7345
  Waterbury (G-9554)
Quad/Graphics Inc .... A 203 288-2468
  North Haven (G-5985)

R R Donnelley & Sons Company ...... F 860 649-5570
  Manchester (G-4078)
Roseville Designs LLC .... G 203 858-5744
  Darien (G-2042)
Rubber Labels USA LLC .... G 203 713-8059
  Milford (G-4635)
Simcha Designs .... G 203 273-1593
  Stamford (G-8422)
Sterling Forms and Cmpt Sups .... G 203 876-7337
  Milford (G-4653)
Sugarplums .... G 860 426-9945
  Middlebury (G-4296)
Trade Labels Inc .... G 860 535-4828
  Mystic (G-4850)
Tulaloo .... G 860 417-2587
  Oakville (G-6465)

2759 Commercial Printing

101 Business Solutions LLC .... G 860 774-6904
  Brooklyn (G-1243)
5 Star Printing .... G 203 975-1000
  Stamford (G-8050)
A 2 Z Screen Printing LLC .... G 860 526-9684
  Ivoryton (G-3782)
A 2 Z Screen Printing LLC .... G 860 526-9684
  Deep River (G-2081)
A To A Studio Solutions Ltd .... F 203 388-9050
  Stamford (G-8053)
Accent Screenprinting .... G 203 284-8601
  Wallingford (G-9195)
Acme Typesetting Service Co .... G 860 953-1470
  West Hartford (G-9772)
Action Printing .... G 203 366-4413
  Shelton (G-7388)
Ad Label Inc .... G 860 779-0513
  Brooklyn (G-1245)
Advanced Graphics Inc .... E 203 378-0471
  Stratford (G-8564)
Affordable Sign Co .... G 203 874-0875
  Milford (G-4443)
Alexander Hussey .... G 203 354-0118
  New Milford (G-5503)
▲ Allied Printing Services Inc .... B 860 643-1101
  Manchester (G-3980)
◆ American Banknote Corporation .... G 203 941-4090
  Stamford (G-8074)
American Silk Screening LLC .... G 203 828-5486
  Berlin (G-157)
American Solution For Business .... G 860 413-9415
  East Granby (G-2189)
American Stitch & Print Inc .... G 203 239-5383
  North Haven (G-5902)
▲ Amgraph Packaging Inc .... C 860 822-2000
  Baltic (G-118)
Amity Printing & Copy Ctr LLC .... G 860 828-0202
  Berlin (G-158)
Ansel Label and Packaging Corp ...... E 203 452-0311
  Trumbull (G-8999)
Anything Printed LLC .... G 860 429-1244
  Willington (G-10245)
Aquastone Graphix LLC .... G 860 206-4935
  Hartford (G-3552)
ARM Screen Printing .... G 860 649-6295
  Manchester (G-3984)
Arnow Silk Screening LLC .... G 203 964-1963
  Stamford (G-8093)
Art Screen .... G 203 744-1991
  Bethel (G-258)
▲ Autobond Eastern .... G 203 383-8982
  Pleasant Valley (G-6920)
Automated Graphic Systems Inc ...... G 860 659-1076
  South Glastonbury (G-7679)
AZ Copy Center Inc .... G 860 621-7325
  Southington (G-7893)
B T S Graphics LLC .... G 860 274-6422
  Oakville (G-6449)
B-P Products Inc .... E 203 288-0200
  Hamden (G-3416)
Barbara Garelick Enterprises .... G 203 855-9897
  Norwalk (G-6086)
Bardell Printing Corp .... G 203 469-2441
  East Haven (G-2413)
Baron Technology Inc .... E 203 452-0515
  Trumbull (G-9003)
Basement Screen Printing .... G 860 462-9103
  Broad Brook (G-1144)
Bayard Inc .... E 860 437-3012
  New London (G-5457)
Been Printed LLC .... G 860 618-3600
  Torrington (G-8901)

Benettieris Studio .... G 860 568-3590
  East Hartford (G-2297)
Beyond Invite .... G 203 219-9434
  Shelton (G-7405)
Biz Wiz Print & Copy Ctr LLC .... G 860 721-0040
  Rocky Hill (G-7224)
Biz Wiz Print & Copy Ctr LLC .... G 860 633-7446
  Glastonbury (G-3015)
Bl Printing Shop .... G 203 334-7779
  Bridgeport (G-713)
Blue Moon Printing LLC .... G 860 245-0827
  Mystic (G-4801)
Bread and Wine Publishing LLC .... G 860 649-3109
  Manchester (G-3988)
Britelite Promotions .... G 203 481-5755
  Branford (G-565)
C C and P .... G 203 222-8260
  Westport (G-10062)
C J Macsata LLC .... G 860 623-6755
  Enfield (G-2619)
C Libby Leonard .... G 203 375-6205
  Stratford (G-8591)
Cannelli Printing Co Inc .... G 203 932-1719
  West Haven (G-9886)
▲ CCL Industries Corporation .... D 203 926-1253
  Shelton (G-7412)
CCL Label Inc .... C 203 926-1253
  Shelton (G-7413)
▲ CCL Label (delaware) Inc .... G 203 926-1253
  Shelton (G-7414)
Cenveo Corporation .... E 303 790-8023
  Stamford (G-8139)
Christopher Condors .... G 203 852-8181
  Norwalk (G-6114)
Clanol Systems Inc .... G 203 637-9909
  Old Greenwich (G-6469)
▲ Classic Label Inc .... G 203 389-3535
  Woodbridge (G-10599)
Clicroi LLC .... G 203 599-1237
  Danbury (G-1769)
Collinsville Screen Printing .... G 860 693-2601
  Collinsville (G-1591)
Collinsville Screen/Embroidery .... G 860 693-2601
  Canton (G-1311)
Colonial Printers of Windsor .... G 860 627-5433
  Windsor Locks (G-10480)
Colorgraphix LLC .... G 203 264-5212
  Oxford (G-6652)
Colour TS LLC .... G 860 298-0594
  Windsor (G-10375)
Concordia Ltd .... G 203 483-0221
  North Branford (G-5832)
Copy Cats Inc .... F 860 442-8424
  New London (G-5465)
Core Studios .... G 203 364-9594
  Newtown (G-5734)
▲ Creative Envelope Inc .... G 860 963-1231
  Putnam (G-7038)
Crystal Labels Co .... G 860 870-8627
  Ellington (G-2585)
CT Thermography LLC .... G 860 415-1150
  Farmington (G-2894)
CT Thermography LLC .... G 860 690-9202
  Newington (G-5644)
Custom Tees Plus .... E 203 752-1071
  New Haven (G-5266)
Custom TS .... G 860 644-1514
  Manchester (G-4002)
Custom TS n More LLC .... G 203 438-1592
  Ridgefield (G-7133)
Cutting Edge Sgns Graphics LLC ...... G 203 758-7776
  Prospect (G-6999)
D Cello Enterprises LLC .... G 860 659-0844
  Glastonbury (G-3027)
Depaul Industries .... G 203 882-1331
  Milford (G-4508)
Desai Mukesh .... G 860 529-4141
  Rocky Hill (G-7234)
Design Label Manufacturing Inc .... E 860 739-6266
  Old Lyme (G-6505)
Digital Chameleon LLC .... G 203 354-4111
  Bridgeport (G-752)
Digital Copy LLC .... G 203 540-5181
  Bridgeport (G-753)
Diversified Printing Solutions .... G 203 826-7198
  Danbury (G-1796)
Doctor Stuff LLC .... G 203 785-8475
  Wallingford (G-9252)
Dst Output East LLC .... E 816 221-1234
  South Windsor (G-7740)

Employee Codes: A=Over 500 employees, B=251-500
C=101-250, D=51-100, E=20-50, F=10-19, G=1-9

27 PRINTING, PUBLISHING, AND ALLIED INDUSTRIES

E & A Enterprises Inc .... E 203 250-8050
  Wallingford *(G-9255)*
East Coast Name Plates Inc .... G 203 261-4347
  Easton *(G-2549)*
Eastwood Printing Inc .... F 860 529-6673
  Wethersfield *(G-10192)*
Eccles-Lehman Inc .... G 203 268-0605
  Easton *(G-2551)*
ECI Screen Print Inc .... F 860 283-9849
  Watertown *(G-9703)*
Elm Press Incorporated .... E 860 583-3600
  Terryville *(G-8752)*
Emulsion Apparel .... G 860 495-5792
  Pawcatuck *(G-6710)*
Encore Sales Corp .... G 203 301-4949
  Milford *(G-4530)*
Envelopes & More Inc .... F 860 286-7570
  Newington *(G-5651)*
Epic Printing Compny Inc .... G 203 469-3988
  East Haven *(G-2424)*
Ever Ready Press .... G 203 734-5157
  Ansonia *(G-33)*
Executive Graphic Systems LLC .... G 203 678-6432
  Wallingford *(G-9261)*
▼ Executive Greetings Inc .... B 860 379-9911
  New Hartford *(G-5190)*
Executive Office Services Inc .... E 203 373-1333
  Bridgeport *(G-765)*
Exhibitease LLC .... G 203 481-0792
  Branford *(G-592)*
Fairfield Marketing Group Inc .... F 203 261-0884
  Easton *(G-2552)*
Falcon Press .... G 860 763-2293
  Enfield *(G-2646)*
Fedex Office & Print Svcs Inc .... F 860 233-8245
  Hartford *(G-3588)*
Fit To A Tee Cstm Screen Prtg .... G 860 828-6632
  Kensington *(G-3810)*
Forsa Team Sports LLC .... G 203 466-2890
  East Haven *(G-2429)*
Four Color Inc .... G 860 691-1782
  Niantic *(G-5806)*
Frank Printing Co R .... G 203 265-6152
  Wallingford *(G-9270)*
Fresh Ink LLC .... G 860 656-7013
  West Hartford *(G-9812)*
Frontline Screen Printing & Em ...... G 860 749-0232
  Somers *(G-7660)*
G & R Enterprises Incorporated ..... G 860 549-6120
  Hartford *(G-3593)*
Gateway Digital Inc .... F 203 853-4929
  Norwalk *(G-6175)*
◆ George Schmitt & Co Inc .... D 203 453-4334
  Guilford *(G-3355)*
George Schmitt & Co Inc .... G 203 453-4334
  Guilford *(G-3356)*
Glenn Curtis .... G 860 349-8679
  Durham *(G-2147)*
Hampton Associates LLC .... G 203 817-0161
  Stamford *(G-8223)*
Hartford Toner & Cartridge Inc .... G 860 292 1280
  Broad Brook *(G-1150)*
Hat Trick Graphics LLC .... G 203 748-1128
  Danbury *(G-1842)*
Hawkeye Press Inc .... G 203 855-8580
  Norwalk *(G-6194)*
Hunt Printing Co .... G 203 891-5778
  Middletown *(G-4352)*
Hw Graphics .... G 860 278-2338
  Windsor *(G-10396)*
Ideal Printing Co Inc .... G 203 777-7626
  New Haven *(G-5299)*
Ideas Inc .... G 203 878-9686
  Milford *(G-4551)*
Identification Products Corp .... G 203 331-0931
  Bridgeport *(G-790)*
Identification Products Corp .... F 203 334-5969
  Bridgeport *(G-791)*
Image One Prtg & Graphics Inc ..... G 203 459-1880
  Monroe *(G-4720)*
Images Unlimited .... G 860 350-6608
  New Milford *(G-5545)*
Imperial Grphic Cmmnctions Inc .... E 203 650-3478
  Milford *(G-4553)*
Ink 13 LLC .... G 860 921-6910
  Burlington *(G-1270)*
▲ Integrated Print Solutions Inc .... F 203 330-0200
  Bridgeport *(G-793)*
International Comm Svcs Inc .... G 401 580-8888
  Guilford *(G-3362)*

▲ International Printing Access ..... G 860 599-8005
  Pawcatuck *(G-6717)*
Iovino Bros Sporting Goods .... G 203 790-5966
  Danbury *(G-1851)*
J & J Printing Co .... G 860 355-9535
  New Milford *(G-5548)*
Jb Muze Enterprises .... G 860 355-5949
  New Milford *(G-5549)*
Jeanann Stagnita .... G 860 516-4655
  Bristol *(G-1053)*
Jeffrey Morgan .... G 860 583-2567
  Bristol *(G-1054)*
JMS Graphics Inc .... G 203 598-7555
  Middlebury *(G-4280)*
Joyce Printers Inc .... G 203 389-4452
  Woodbridge *(G-10603)*
Jump 4 Tees .... G 860 228-4813
  Hebron *(G-3752)*
Kaibry Screen Printing .... G 860 774-0234
  Danielson *(G-1996)*
Keno Graphic Services Inc .... E 203 925-7722
  Shelton *(G-7483)*
Kool Ink LLC .... F 860 242-0303
  Bloomfield *(G-439)*
Korzon Screen Printing LLC .... G 203 729-1090
  Beacon Falls *(G-138)*
Korzon Silk Screening .... G 203 888-3273
  Beacon Falls *(G-139)*
Kramer Printing Company Inc .... F 203 933-5416
  West Haven *(G-9924)*
▲ L P Macadams Company Inc .... D 203 366-3647
  Bridgeport *(G-820)*
L R K Communications Inc .... G 203 372-1456
  Fairfield *(G-2808)*
Larkin Litho .... G 860 535-0116
  Stonington *(G-8534)*
Laser Engraved Services .... G 203 779-5116
  Madison *(G-3936)*
Ledgewood Publications .... G 860 693-9055
  Collinsville *(G-1597)*
Leonard Dongweck .... G 860 388-0700
  Old Saybrook *(G-6552)*
Liberty Screen Print Co LLC .... F 203 632-5449
  Beacon Falls *(G-140)*
Linda Case Writing Graphic .... G 860 563-5713
  Wethersfield *(G-10210)*
Living Word Imprints LLC .... G 860 882-1679
  Hartford *(G-3629)*
Logo Sportswear Inc .... G 203 678-4700
  Wallingford *(G-9306)*
Logod Softwear Inc .... E 203 272-4883
  Cheshire *(G-1407)*
Lorenco Industries Inc .... F 203 743-6962
  Bethel *(G-323)*
Lrp Conferences LLC .... E 203 663-0100
  Trumbull *(G-9044)*
Macwear LLC .... G 203 579-4277
  Southport *(G-8006)*
Mad Sportswear LLC .... G 203 932-4868
  West Haven *(G-9929)*
Mailourinvitationscom .... G 203 758-1860
  Middlebury *(G-4283)*
Majestic Press .... G 860 673-2064
  Unionville *(G-9120)*
Mallace Industries Corp .... G 800 521-0194
  Clinton *(G-1514)*
Master Engrv & Printery Inc .... G 203 723-2779
  Waterbury *(G-9535)*
Matthews Printing Co .... F 203 265-0363
  Wallingford *(G-9314)*
McLodesignscom .... G 203 296-1400
  Bridgeport *(G-835)*
McWeeney Marketing Group Inc .... G 203 891-8100
  Orange *(G-6613)*
Meco Precision Industries Inc .... G 860 210-1801
  Gaylordsville *(G-2994)*
Mediagraphicscom Inc .... F 203 404-7233
  Durham *(G-2153)*
Merrill Corporation .... D 860 249-7220
  Hartford *(G-3638)*
Mickey Herbst .... G 203 993-5879
  Fairfield *(G-2815)*
Micro Printing LLC .... G 203 265-5578
  Wallingford *(G-9319)*
Mlk Business Forms Inc .... F 203 624-6304
  New Haven *(G-5335)*
Moonlight Media LLC .... G 860 345-3595
  Haddam *(G-3407)*
Muir Envelope Plus Inc .... F 860 953-6847
  Newington *(G-5681)*

Multiprints Inc .... F 203 235-4409
  Meriden *(G-4207)*
New England Printing LLC .... G 860 745-3600
  Enfield *(G-2669)*
New Fairfield Press Inc .... F 203 746-2700
  New Fairfield *(G-5172)*
Nice T-Shirt .... G 860 349-0727
  Middletown *(G-4386)*
Norwalk Rutledge Printing Off .... G 203 956-5967
  Norwalk *(G-6281)*
Novel Tees Screen Prtg EMB LLC . F 860 643-6008
  Manchester *(G-4062)*
Novel-Tees Unlimited LLC .... G 860 643-6008
  Manchester *(G-4063)*
▲ O Berk Company Neng LLC ..... F 203 932-8000
  West Haven *(G-9940)*
Olde Tyme Graphics .... G 203 748-3360
  Danbury *(G-1898)*
◆ Omega Engineering Inc .... C 203 359-1660
  Norwalk *(G-6284)*
Omniprint LLC .... G 203 881-9013
  Oxford *(G-6683)*
On Time Screen Printing & Embr ... G 203 874-4581
  Derby *(G-2120)*
Online River LLC .... F 203 801-5900
  Westport *(G-10134)*
P M Hill .... G 860 242-2915
  Bloomfield *(G-457)*
Paper Station .... G 860 667-9087
  Newington *(G-5692)*
Paragon Publications .... G 860 875-4366
  Vernon *(G-9149)*
Parkway Printers Inc .... G 203 281-6773
  Hamden *(G-3494)*
Patriot Envelope LLC .... G 860 529-1553
  Wethersfield *(G-10214)*
Paul Dewitt .... F 203 792-5610
  Danbury *(G-1902)*
Phocuswright Inc .... E 860 350-4084
  Sherman *(G-7601)*
Picture Perfect Printing Inc .... G 203 386-9696
  Stratford *(G-8665)*
Pinpoint Thermography LLC .... G 203 546-8906
  New Fairfield *(G-5174)*
Pio Tee Gio LLC .... G 860 280-7073
  Vernon Rockville *(G-9174)*
Planes Road Assoc LLC .... G 860 469-3200
  Essex *(G-2730)*
Platt Brothers Realty II LLC .... G 203 562-5112
  New Haven *(G-5367)*
Popcorn Movie Poster Co LLC ...... F 860 610-0000
  East Hartford *(G-2356)*
▲ Practical Automation Inc .... D 203 882-5640
  Milford *(G-4611)*
◆ Prime Resources Corp .... B 203 331-9100
  Bridgeport *(G-880)*
Print & Post Services .... G 203 336-0055
  Bridgeport *(G-881)*
Print Producers LLC .... G 203 761-9877
  Wilton *(G-10321)*
Print Shop of Wolcott LLC .... G 203 879-3353
  Wolcott *(G-10581)*
Print Source Ltd .... G 203 876-1822
  Milford *(G-4617)*
Printing House The Inc .... G 203 869-1767
  Greenwich *(G-3218)*
Privateer Ltd .... F 860 526-1837
  Old Saybrook *(G-6568)*
Production Decorating Co Inc .... E 203 574-2975
  Waterbury *(G-9589)*
Psd Inc .... G 860 305-6346
  East Haven *(G-2448)*
Pushing Envelope LLC .... G 203 745-0988
  Hamden *(G-3498)*
▲ Quality Name Plate Inc .... D 860 633-9495
  East Glastonbury *(G-2185)*
Quinn and Gellar Marketing LLC ... G 860 444-0448
  New London *(G-5485)*
R & B Apparel Plus LLC .... G 860 333-1757
  Groton *(G-3311)*
R R Donnelley & Sons Company ... F 860 649-5570
  Manchester *(G-4078)*
R R Donnelley & Sons Company ... E 860 773-6140
  Avon *(G-102)*
Rainbow Graphics Inc .... G 860 646-8997
  Manchester *(G-4082)*
▲ Robert Audette .... G 203 872-3119
  Cheshire *(G-1440)*
Rosemarie Querns .... G 860 349-3315
  Durham *(G-2155)*

Roto-Die Company Inc F 860 292-7030 East Windsor *(G-2516)*
Royaltees LLC G 203 767-2808 Bridgeport *(G-893)*
S & V Screen Printing G 203 208-3112 Branford *(G-645)*
Saint Vincent De Paul Place G 860 889-7374 Norwich *(G-6430)*
Saybrook Press Incorporated F 203 458-3637 Guilford *(G-3388)*
Screen Designs G 203 797-9806 Bethel *(G-340)*
Scribbling Scribe G 203 329-7140 Stamford *(G-8405)*
Shadow Graphics G 203 590-3533 Trumbull *(G-9073)*
Sheila P Patrick G 203 575-1716 Waterbury *(G-9602)*
Shirt Graphix G 203 294-1656 Wallingford *(G-9365)*
Shirt Shark G 860 552-4197 Clinton *(G-1524)*
Sibtech Inc G 203 775-5677 Brookfield *(G-1223)*
Sigmawear G 860 924-2908 Berlin *(G-219)*
Signs Now LLC G 860 667-8339 Newington *(G-5705)*
Silkscreen Plus LLC G 203 879-0345 Wolcott *(G-10590)*
Silvermine Press Inc G 203 847-4368 Norwalk *(G-6350)*
Sirocco Screenprints Inc G 203 288-3565 North Haven *(G-5994)*
Snoogs & Wilde LLC G 860 824-9865 Falls Village *(G-2872)*
Special Events Screen Prtg LLC G 203 468-5453 East Haven *(G-2454)*
Specialty Printing LLC D 860 623-8870 East Windsor *(G-2521)*
Spectrum Mktg Cmmnications Inc G 203 853-4585 Norwalk *(G-6353)*
Speed Printing & Graphics Inc G 203 324-4000 Stamford *(G-8433)*
Speedi Sign G 203 431-0836 Bethel *(G-346)*
Speedy Printing LLC G 860 445-8252 Mystic *(G-4846)*
Sportees LLC G 860 440-3922 Waterford *(G-9673)*
STS Motorsports Graphics G 860 698-6697 Somers *(G-7673)*
▲ **Surys Inc** C 203 333-5503 Trumbull *(G-9078)*
Tee Squares G 844 669-8337 Bridgeport *(G-922)*
▲ **Tees Plus** F 800 782-8337 Bridgeport *(G-923)*
Tef LLC G 203 878-9740 Milford *(G-4662)*
Tex Elm Inc F 860 873-9715 East Haddam *(G-2249)*
Therma-Scan Inc G 860 872-9770 Vernon Rockville *(G-9181)*
Town Pride G 860 664-0448 Clinton *(G-1532)*
True Inspiration LLC G 860 635-7941 Cromwell *(G-1722)*
Tyco Printing & Copying G 203 562-2679 New Haven *(G-5424)*
Unique Graphics G 203 634-1932 Meriden *(G-4258)*
Up Top Screen Printing G 860 412-9798 Danielson *(G-2005)*
UPS Authorized Retailer G 203 256-9991 Fairfield *(G-2862)*
Varsity Imprints G 203 354-4371 Milford *(G-4672)*
Vios Sports Plus G 203 234-7231 North Haven *(G-6013)*
Vision Designs LLC F 203 778-9898 Brookfield *(G-1237)*
Visual Impact LLC G 203 790-9650 Danbury *(G-1973)*
Vp Printing G 203 736-1756 Ansonia *(G-56)*
Vrd Customs Ltd G 475 329-5184 Danbury *(G-1974)*
Wadsworth Press G 860 623-3820 East Windsor *(G-2531)*
Wallingford Prtg Bus Forms Inc F 203 481-1911 Branford *(G-669)*
Warren Press Inc G 203 431-0011 Ridgefield *(G-7182)*
Wink Ink LLC G 860 202-8709 Somers *(G-7677)*
Wm Corvo Consultants Inc G 860 346-6500 Middletown *(G-4432)*
Wolfe Promotional Services LLC G 203 452-7692 Monroe *(G-4766)*
Work n Gear LLC G 203 795-8998 Orange *(G-6636)*
Work n Gear LLC G 203 467-1156 East Haven *(G-2460)*
Xtreme Designs LLC G 203 773-9303 New Haven *(G-5437)*
Yale University E 203 737-1244 New Haven *(G-5446)*
Yankee Screen Printing G 203 924-9926 Derby *(G-2133)*
Yush Sign Display Co Inc G 860 289-1819 East Hartford *(G-2402)*

2761 Manifold Business Forms

Alicia Cersosimorathbun G 401 345-7097 Mystic *(G-4797)*
D Cello Enterprises LLC G 860 659-0844 Glastonbury *(G-3027)*
Federal Business Products Inc D 860 482-6231 Torrington *(G-8924)*
Mlk Business Forms Inc F 203 624-6304 New Haven *(G-5335)*
Occuptnal Trvl Mdcine Sups LLC G 866 206-4496 Fairfield *(G-2823)*
Taylor Communications Inc F 860 290-6851 East Hartford *(G-2382)*
Wallace Services Group LLC G 860 350-2992 Bloomfield *(G-499)*
Wallingford Prtg Bus Forms Inc F 203 481-1911 Branford *(G-669)*

2771 Greeting Card Publishing

Anothercreationbymichele G 203 322-4277 Stamford *(G-8087)*
Bella Ciao G 203 245-4433 Madison *(G-3911)*
C&S Collectibles G 860 872-6825 Tolland *(G-8853)*
◆ **Caspari Inc** F 203 888-1100 Seymour *(G-7338)*
▲ **Joy Carole Creations Inc** G 203 794-1401 Danbury *(G-1865)*
◆ **Olympia Sales Inc** D 860 749-0751 Enfield *(G-2672)*
Onion Hill Press Llc G 203 227-4895 Westport *(G-10133)*
Raven Ad Specialties G 203 521-8687 Stratford *(G-8673)*
Smiling Dog G 860 344-0707 Middletown *(G-4419)*
Stork N More G 203 746-7500 New Fairfield *(G-5177)*

2782 Blankbooks & Looseleaf Binders

American CT Rng Bnder Index & F 860 868-7900 Washington *(G-9411)*
Data Management Incorporated E 860 677-8586 Unionville *(G-9113)*
Grannys Got It G 203 879-0042 Wolcott *(G-10566)*
▲ **Mbsw Inc** D 860 243-0303 West Hartford *(G-9835)*
Pieces of Time Scrapbook G 203 879-2678 Waterbury *(G-9577)*
Scrapbook Clubhouse F 860 399-4443 Westbrook *(G-10007)*
Yolanda Dubose Records and F 203 823-6699 West Haven *(G-9967)*

2789 Bookbinding

Adkins Printing Company E 800 228-9745 New Britain *(G-4938)*
Agjo Printing Service G 860 599-3143 Pawcatuck *(G-6703)*
Alexander Hussey G 860 354-0118 New Milford *(G-5503)*
▲ **Allied Printing Services Inc** B 860 643-1101 Manchester *(G-3980)*
Blue Moon Bindery LLC G 860 435-9100 Lakeville *(G-3842)*
▲ **Book Automation Inc** G 860 354-7900 New Milford *(G-5512)*
Chapin Packaging LLC G 203 202-2747 Darien *(G-2011)*
▼ **Connecticut Valley Bindery** E 860 229-7637 New Britain *(G-4963)*
Conner Printing G 203 929-2070 Shelton *(G-7423)*
Desai Mukesh G 860 529-4141 Rocky Hill *(G-7234)*
E R Hitchcock Company E 860 229-2024 New Britain *(G-4977)*
Eccles-Lehman Inc G 203 268-0605 Easton *(G-2551)*
Elm Press Incorporated E 860 583-3600 Terryville *(G-8752)*
Falcon Press G 860 763-2293 Enfield *(G-2646)*
Fedex Office & Print Svcs Inc F 203 799-2679 Orange *(G-6601)*
Frank Obuchowski G 860 535-4739 Stonington *(G-8528)*
G & R Enterprises Incorporated G 860 549-6120 Hartford *(G-3593)*
Imperial Grphic Cmmnctions Inc E 203 650-3478 Milford *(G-4553)*
Jerrys Printing & Graphics LLC G 203 384-0015 Bridgeport *(G-803)*
Joseph Merritt & Company Inc G 203 743-6734 Danbury *(G-1863)*
Kool Ink LLC F 860 242-0303 Bloomfield *(G-439)*
Master Engrv & Printery Inc G 203 723-2779 Waterbury *(G-9535)*
Norwich Printing Company Inc F 860 887-7468 Norwich *(G-6425)*
Palmisano Printing LLC G 860 582-6883 Bristol *(G-1085)*
Pancoast Associates Inc G 203 377-6571 Trumbull *(G-9054)*
Paper Mill Graphix Inc E 203 531-5904 Greenwich *(G-3213)*
Paul Dewitt F 203 792-5610 Danbury *(G-1902)*
Phoenix Press Inc E 203 865-5555 New Haven *(G-5363)*
Prosperous Printing LLC G 203 834-1962 Wilton *(G-10322)*
Saybrook Press Incorporated F 203 458-3637 Guilford *(G-3388)*
Sinish Works G 860 693-0073 Collinsville *(G-1603)*
Speedy Printing LLC G 860 445-8252 Mystic *(G-4846)*
Step Saver Inc E 860 621-6751 Southington *(G-7982)*
STP Bindery Services Inc E 860 528-1430 East Hartford *(G-2378)*
Tech-Repro Inc F 203 348-8884 Stamford *(G-8460)*
Townsend John G 860 526-3896 Deep River *(G-2104)*
Vernon Printing Co Inc G 860 872-1826 Vernon Rockville *(G-9186)*
Warren Press Inc G 203 431-0011 Ridgefield *(G-7182)*

2791 Typesetting

A To A Studio Solutions Ltd F 203 388-9050 Stamford *(G-8053)*
A&V Typographics G 860 276-9060 Plantsville *(G-6880)*
Acme Typesetting Service Co G 860 953-1470 West Hartford *(G-9772)*
Action Letter Inc E 203 323-2466 Stamford *(G-8061)*
Action Printing G 203 366-4413 Shelton *(G-7388)*
▲ **Allied Printing Services Inc** B 860 643-1101 Manchester *(G-3980)*
Alphacom Inc G 203 637-7006 Greenwich *(G-3117)*
Arkettype G 860 350-4007 New Milford *(G-5504)*
Birdtrack Press G 203 389-7789 New Haven *(G-5248)*
Brenda Jubin G 203 393-2366 Bethany *(G-235)*

Employee Codes: A=Over 500 employees, B=251-500
C=101-250, D=51-100, E=20-50, F=10-19, G=1-9
2020 Harris Connecticut
Manufacturers Directory
403

Brescias Printing Services Inc ....G....... 860 528-4254
East Hartford *(G-2300)*

Childrens Press ....G....... 203 972-9404
New Canaan *(G-5094)*

Conner Printing ....G....... 203 929-2070
Shelton *(G-7423)*

Copy Stop Inc ....G....... 203 288-6401
Hamden *(G-3433)*

Criscola Design LLC ....G....... 203 248-4285
North Haven *(G-5932)*

Desai Mukesh ....G....... 860 529-4141
Rocky Hill *(G-7234)*

E R Hitchcock Company ....E....... 860 229-2024
New Britain *(G-4977)*

Eccles-Lehman Inc ....G....... 203 268-0605
Easton *(G-2551)*

Elm Press Incorporated ....E....... 860 583-3600
Terryville *(G-8752)*

Executive Office Services Inc ....E....... 203 373-1333
Bridgeport *(G-765)*

Fairfield Marketing Group Inc ....F....... 203 261-0884
Easton *(G-2552)*

Four Color Inc ....G....... 860 691-1782
Niantic *(G-5806)*

Franklin Print Shoppe Inc ....G....... 860 496-9516
Torrington *(G-8926)*

G & R Enterprises Incorporated ....G....... 860 549-6120
Hartford *(G-3593)*

Gateway Digital Inc ....F....... 203 853-4929
Norwalk *(G-6175)*

Guy Lindsay ....G....... 860 646-7865
Manchester *(G-4024)*

Hedges & Hedges Ltd ....G....... 860 257-3170
Wethersfield *(G-10196)*

IM Your Type LLC ....G....... 203 967-4063
Stamford *(G-8244)*

Image Processing ....E....... 203 488-3252
Guilford *(G-3361)*

Jerrys Printing & Graphics LLC ....G....... 203 384-0015
Bridgeport *(G-803)*

John Pecora ....G....... 860 677-9323
Farmington *(G-2920)*

Jupiter Communications LLC ....F....... 475 238-7082
West Haven *(G-9920)*

Kat Art Inc ....G....... 860 350-8016
New Milford *(G-5554)*

Kiagraphics ....G....... 203 261-4328
Monroe *(G-4726)*

Kool Ink LLC ....F....... 860 242-0303
Bloomfield *(G-439)*

Lettering Inc of New York ....E....... 203 329-7759
Stamford *(G-8283)*

Magnani Press Incorporated ....G....... 860 236-2802
Hartford *(G-3631)*

Master Engrv & Printery Inc ....G....... 203 723-2779
Waterbury *(G-9535)*

Meredith Graphics & Design ....G....... 203 375-1039
Stratford *(G-8650)*

Oddo Print Shop Inc ....G....... 860 489-6585
Torrington *(G-8953)*

Palmisano Printing LLC ....G....... 860 582-6883
Bristol *(G-1085)*

Pancoast Associates Inc ....G....... 203 377-6571
Trumbull *(G-9054)*

Paper Mill Graphix Inc ....E....... 203 531-5904
Greenwich *(G-3213)*

Paul Dewitt ....F....... 203 792-5610
Danbury *(G-1902)*

Phoenix Press Inc ....E....... 203 865-5555
New Haven *(G-5363)*

Professional Graphics Inc ....F....... 203 846-4291
Norwalk *(G-6307)*

Prosperous Printing LLC ....G....... 203 834-1962
Wilton *(G-10322)*

Quinn and Gellar Marketing LLC ....G....... 860 444-0448
New London *(G-5485)*

Saybrook Press Incorporated ....F....... 203 458-3637
Guilford *(G-3388)*

Sk Systems ....G....... 860 691-0366
East Lyme *(G-2475)*

Speedy Printing LLC ....G....... 860 445-8252
Mystic *(G-4846)*

Step Saver Inc ....E....... 860 621-6751
Southington *(G-7982)*

Supertype Inc ....G....... 216 816-8119
New Haven *(G-5405)*

Tech-Repro Inc ....F....... 203 348-8884
Stamford *(G-8460)*

Vernon Printing Co Inc ....G....... 860 872-1826
Vernon Rockville *(G-9186)*

Westchester Pubg Svcs LLC ....G....... 203 791-0080
Danbury *(G-1979)*

Westchster Bk/Rnsford Type Inc ....C....... 203 791-0080
Danbury *(G-1980)*

2796 Platemaking & Related Svcs

Baron Technology Inc ....E....... 203 452-0515
Trumbull *(G-9003)*

Cag Imaging ....G....... 203 632-5799
Naugatuck *(G-4866)*

Eccles-Lehman Inc ....G....... 203 268-0605
Easton *(G-2551)*

Endo Graphics Inc ....G....... 203 778-1557
Danbury *(G-1810)*

▼ **Exceptional Scratch Games LLC** ....G....... 203 526-8696
Bridgeport *(G-764)*

Four Color Ink LLC ....G....... 860 395-5471
Old Saybrook *(G-6534)*

Gateway Digital Inc ....F....... 203 853-4929
Norwalk *(G-6175)*

Ghp Media Inc ....C....... 203 479-7500
West Haven *(G-9912)*

Paul Dewitt ....F....... 203 792-5610
Danbury *(G-1902)*

Quinn and Gellar Marketing LLC ....G....... 860 444-0448
New London *(G-5485)*

Schrader Bellows ....E....... 860 749-2215
Enfield *(G-2689)*

Success Printing & Mailing Inc ....F....... 203 847-1112
Norwalk *(G-6359)*

Urg Graphics Inc ....E....... 860 928-0835
Stafford Springs *(G-8046)*

28 CHEMICALS AND ALLIED PRODUCTS

2812 Alkalies & Chlorine

Genesis Alkali LLC ....D....... 215 299-6773
Stamford *(G-8214)*

Kuehne New Haven LLC ....E....... 203 508-6703
New Haven *(G-5312)*

2813 Industrial Gases

A Helium Plus Balloons LLC ....G....... 860 833-1761
Wethersfield *(G-10179)*

Airgas Usa LLC ....G....... 203 729-2159
Naugatuck *(G-4856)*

Airgas Usa LLC ....E....... 860 442-0363
Waterford *(G-9641)*

Airgas Usa LLC ....C....... 203 792-1834
Danbury *(G-1733)*

Aldlab Chemicals LLC ....G....... 203 589-4934
North Haven *(G-5899)*

Boost Oxygen LLC ....G....... 203 331-8100
Milford *(G-4476)*

Haynes Hydrogen LLC ....G....... 203 605-2837
Meriden *(G-4172)*

Helium Plus Inc ....G....... 203 304-1880
Newtown *(G-5742)*

Hydrogen Highway LLC ....G....... 203 871-1000
North Branford *(G-5844)*

Just Neon Company ....G....... 860 881-7446
Vernon *(G-9142)*

New England Ortho Neuro LLC ....G....... 203 200-7228
Hamden *(G-3489)*

O2 Concepts LLC ....G....... 877 867-4008
Middlebury *(G-4286)*

Praxair Inc ....E....... 203 793-1200
Wallingford *(G-9339)*

Praxair Inc ....E....... 203 720-2477
Naugatuck *(G-4913)*

Praxair Inc ....D....... 860 292-5400
Suffield *(G-8729)*

◆ **Praxair Inc** ....B....... 203 837-2000
Danbury *(G-1913)*

Praxair Distribution Inc ....E....... 860 349-0305
Durham *(G-2154)*

▲ **Praxair Distribution Inc** ....F....... 203 837-2000
Danbury *(G-1914)*

Praxair Distribution Inc ....F....... 203 837-2162
Danbury *(G-1915)*

Tech Air Northern Cal LLC ....G....... 203 792-1834
Danbury *(G-1961)*

2816 Inorganic Pigments

Magneli Materials LLC ....G....... 203 644-8560
New Canaan *(G-5117)*

2819 Indl Inorganic Chemicals, NEC

Advanced Pwr Systems Intl Inc ....E....... 860 921-0009
New Hartford *(G-5184)*

Carbide Solutions LLC ....G....... 860 515-8665
Windsor *(G-10371)*

Carbide Technology Inc ....G....... 860 621-8981
Southington *(G-7904)*

Carbtrol Corporation ....E....... 203 337-4340
Stratford *(G-8593)*

▲ **CCL Industries Corporation** ....D....... 203 926-1253
Shelton *(G-7412)*

▲ **Chromatics Inc** ....F....... 203 743-6868
Bethel *(G-271)*

Composites Inc ....G....... 860 646-1698
Manchester *(G-3997)*

Demo Agent Sales LLC ....G....... 860 621-3303
Southington *(G-7913)*

Designing Element ....G....... 203 849-3076
Norwalk *(G-6135)*

Element One LLC ....G....... 203 344-1553
Norwalk *(G-6157)*

Elemental Mercury LLC ....G....... 860 355-9569
New Milford *(G-5531)*

Elements LLC ....G....... 860 231-8011
West Hartford *(G-9807)*

Fitness Elemnet ....G....... 860 670-2855
New Britain *(G-4989)*

Greek Elements LLC ....G....... 203 594-2022
New Canaan *(G-5107)*

H Krevit and Company Inc ....E....... 203 772-3350
New Haven *(G-5292)*

Innophase Corp ....G....... 860 399-2269
Westbrook *(G-9998)*

Integrated Chemical & Eqp Corp ....G....... 860 664-3951
Clinton *(G-1509)*

Joshua LLC ....E....... 203 624-0080
New Haven *(G-5304)*

Kwant Elements Intl LLC ....G....... 203 625-5553
Cos Cob *(G-1636)*

Meb Enterprises Inc ....G....... 203 599-0273
Meriden *(G-4193)*

▲ **Metamorphic Materials Inc** ....F....... 860 738-8638
Winsted *(G-10529)*

Modern Elements Products LLC ....G....... 860 667-4247
Newington *(G-5679)*

New Haven Chlor-Alkali LLC ....D....... 203 772-3350
New Haven *(G-5343)*

Perennial Elements LLC ....G....... 860 536-8593
Mystic *(G-4839)*

Redline Elements LLC ....G....... 860 305-0095
Marlborough *(G-4130)*

◆ **RT Vanderbilt Holding Co Inc** ....F....... 203 295-2141
Norwalk *(G-6331)*

Solidification Pdts Intl Inc ....G....... 203 484-9494
Northford *(G-6053)*

Solidification Products Intl ....F....... 203 484-9494
Northford *(G-6054)*

Specialty Minerals Inc ....C....... 860 824-5435
Canaan *(G-1292)*

▼ **Tiger-Sul Products LLC** ....E....... 251 202-3850
Shelton *(G-7568)*

◆ **Tronox Incorporated** ....C....... 203 705-3800
Stamford *(G-8476)*

◆ **Vanderbilt Chemicals LLC** ....D....... 203 295-2141
Norwalk *(G-6383)*

Vanderbilt Chemicals LLC ....E....... 203 744-3900
Bethel *(G-361)*

Vertech Inc ....G....... 203 876-1552
Milford *(G-4673)*

▲ **Yarmouth Materials Inc** ....G....... 203 739-0524
Danbury *(G-1984)*

2821 Plastics, Mtrls & Nonvulcanizable Elastomers

Age Plastics LLC ....G....... 860 502-0418
New Britain *(G-4940)*

Allnex USA Inc ....D....... 203 269-4481
Wallingford *(G-9199)*

Allread Products Co LLC ....F....... 860 589-3566
Terryville *(G-8747)*

Anapo Plastics Corp ....G....... 860 874-8174
Farmington *(G-2877)*

◆ **Axel Plastics RES Labs Inc** ....E....... 718 672-8300
Monroe *(G-4694)*

▲ **Bakelite N Sumitomo Amer Inc** ....D....... 860 645-3851
Manchester *(G-3985)*

C Mather Company Inc ....G....... 860 528-5667
South Windsor *(G-7721)*

▲ **Chessco Industries Inc** ....E....... 203 255-2804
Westport *(G-10064)*

SIC SECTION 28 CHEMICALS AND ALLIED PRODUCTS

Cytec Industries Inc............C....... 203 284-4334
Wallingford *(G-9245)*
Ditriorichard............G....... 203 531-0625
Greenwich *(G-3153)*
Dow Chemical Company............G....... 203 740-7510
Brookfield *(G-1184)*
▲ **Enflo Corporation**............E....... 860 589-0014
Bristol *(G-1029)*
▲ **Engineered Polymers Inds Inc**............G....... 203 272-2233
Cheshire *(G-1385)*
Fimor North America Inc............E....... 203 272-3219
Cheshire *(G-1389)*
Fimor North America Inc............G....... 941 921-5138
Cheshire *(G-1390)*
Forum Plastics LLC............E....... 203 754-0777
Waterbury *(G-9482)*
▲ **Galata Chemicals LLC**............F....... 203 236-9000
Southbury *(G-7854)*
▲ **Henkel of America Inc**............B....... 860 571-5100
Rocky Hill *(G-7246)*
◆ **Henkel US Operations Corp**............B....... 860 571-5100
Rocky Hill *(G-7247)*
Hexcel Corporation............G....... 203 969-0666
Stamford *(G-8234)*
Hexcel Corporation............E....... 203 969-0666
Stamford *(G-8233)*
JCB Plastics LLC............G....... 203 315-8154
North Branford *(G-5847)*
Lanxess Solutions US Inc............E....... 203 573-2000
Shelton *(G-7486)*
Line X of Western Connecticut............G....... 860 355-6997
Bridgewater *(G-946)*
Lumivisions Architectural Elem............G....... 203 529-3232
Norwalk *(G-6240)*
Mc Clintock Manufacturing............G....... 203 263-4743
Woodbury *(G-10642)*
Neu Spclty Engineered Mtls LLC............F....... 203 239-9629
North Haven *(G-5967)*
◆ **Osterman & Company Inc**............D....... 203 272-2233
Cheshire *(G-1426)*
Osterman & Company Inc............E....... 203 272-2233
Cheshire *(G-1427)*
▲ **Oxford Industries Conn Inc**............E....... 860 225-3700
New Britain *(G-5027)*
◆ **Oxford Performance Mtls Inc**............E....... 860 698-9300
South Windsor *(G-7801)*
Oxpekk Performance Mtls Inc............F....... 860 698-9300
South Windsor *(G-7802)*
Pastanch LLC............E....... 203 720-9478
Naugatuck *(G-4909)*
Pinnacle Polymers LLC............G....... 203 313-4116
Ridgefield *(G-7162)*
Plastics Color Corp Inc............G....... 800 922-9936
Dayville *(G-2070)*
▲ **Polar Industries Inc**............E....... 203 758-6651
Prospect *(G-7016)*
▲ **Polymer Resources Ltd**............D....... 203 324-3737
Farmington *(G-2949)*
Polyone Corporation............G....... 203 327-6010
Stamford *(G-8368)*
Precision Dip Coating LLC............G....... 203 805-4564
Waterbury *(G-9584)*
Presidium USA Inc............G....... 203 674-9374
Stamford *(G-8372)*
Ravago Americas LLC............E....... 203 855-6000
Wilton *(G-10324)*
▼ **Resinall Corp**............F....... 203 329-7100
Stamford *(G-8387)*
Roehm America LLC............E....... 203 269-4481
Wallingford *(G-9358)*
Seaview Plastic Recycling Inc............G....... 203 367-0070
Bridgeport *(G-899)*
SMS Machine Inc............G....... 860 829-0813
East Berlin *(G-2176)*
Sonoco Prtective Solutions Inc............E....... 860 928-7795
Putnam *(G-7068)*
Spartech LLC............C....... 203 327-6010
Stamford *(G-8432)*
Summit Plastics LLC............G....... 860 740-4482
Portland *(G-6975)*
◆ **Thornton and Company Inc**............F....... 860 628-6771
Southington *(G-7988)*
Total Ptrchemicals Ref USA Inc............E....... 203 375-0668
Stratford *(G-8698)*
Trinseo LLC............E....... 860 447-7298
Gales Ferry *(G-2989)*
Tyne Plastics LLC............G....... 860 673-7100
Burlington *(G-1277)*
W S Polymers............G....... 203 268-1557
Trumbull *(G-9093)*

2822 Synthetic Rubber (Vulcanizable Elastomers)

Fluoropolymer Resources Inc............G....... 860 291-9521
East Hartford *(G-2325)*
▼ **FMI Chemical Inc**............F....... 860 243-3222
Bloomfield *(G-413)*
Heaters Inc............G....... 860 739-5477
Niantic *(G-5809)*
◆ **Si Group USA (usaa) LLC**............C....... 203 702-6140
Danbury *(G-1946)*
Specialty Polymers Inc............G....... 203 575-5727
Waterbury *(G-9605)*

2824 Synthetic Organic Fibers, Exc Cellulosic

Age Plastics LLC............G....... 860 502-0418
New Britain *(G-4940)*
Atco Wire Rope and Indus Sup............G....... 203 239-1632
North Haven *(G-5911)*
▲ **Fairfield Processing Corp**............C....... 203 744-2090
Danbury *(G-1823)*
Naturally Nutritous Vend LLC............G....... 860 416-9848
Wolcott *(G-10577)*
Proteem LLC............G....... 203 787-2221
North Haven *(G-5982)*
R L Pritchard & Co Inc............G....... 203 393-0260
South Lyme *(G-7685)*
▼ **Scapa North America Inc**............G....... 860 688-8000
Windsor *(G-10433)*

2833 Medicinal Chemicals & Botanical Prdts

American Distilling Inc............G....... 860 267-4444
Marlborough *(G-4119)*
▼ **American Distilling Inc**............D....... 860 267-4444
East Hampton *(G-2253)*
Biomed Health Inc............F....... 860 657-2258
Glastonbury *(G-3014)*
Botanica Chachitas............G....... 860 247-5103
Hartford *(G-3558)*
Botanical Origins LLC............G....... 203 267-6061
Oxford *(G-6646)*
Candlewood Stars Inc............G....... 203 994-8826
Danbury *(G-1762)*
Effihealth LLC............G....... 888 435-3108
Stamford *(G-8193)*
Elementals LLC............G....... 203 438-1848
Ridgefield *(G-7139)*
▲ **Henkel of America Inc**............B....... 860 571-5100
Rocky Hill *(G-7246)*
◆ **Henkel US Operations Corp**............B....... 860 571-5100
Rocky Hill *(G-7247)*
▲ **Mantrose-Haeuser Co Inc**............E....... 203 454-1800
Westport *(G-10117)*
Modern Nutrition & Biotech............G....... 203 244-5830
Ridgefield *(G-7155)*
Nzymsys Inc............G....... 877 729-4190
Manchester *(G-4064)*
Optima Specialty Chemical............G....... 203 929-2031
Shelton *(G-7520)*
Pfizer Inc............G....... 860 441-4000
Groton *(G-3306)*
◆ **Watson LLC**............B....... 203 932-3000
West Haven *(G-9960)*
Yale University............G....... 203 432-6320
New Haven *(G-5449)*

2834 Pharmaceuticals

◆ **A & S Pharmaceutical Corp**............E....... 203 368-2538
Bridgeport *(G-679)*
Achillion Pharmaceuticals Inc............D....... 203 624-7000
New Haven *(G-5219)*
Actimus Inc............D....... 617 438-9968
Cromwell *(G-1685)*
Aeromics Inc............G....... 216 772-1004
Branford *(G-537)*
Alexion Pharma LLC............E....... 203 272-2596
New Haven *(G-5221)*
Aplicare Products LLC............C....... 203 630-0500
Meriden *(G-4145)*
Aptuit Global LLC............G....... 203 660-6000
Greenwich *(G-3122)*
▲ **Arkalon Chemical Tech LLC**............G....... 352 505-8098
Meriden *(G-4146)*
Arvinas Inc............F....... 203 535-1456
New Haven *(G-5234)*
Avara Pharmaceutical Svcs Inc............E....... 203 918-1659
Norwalk *(G-6084)*
Avara US Holdings LLC............G....... 203 655-1333
Norwalk *(G-6085)*
Avrio Health LP............A....... 888 827-0624
Stamford *(G-8101)*
◆ **Beta Pharma Inc**............F....... 203 315-5062
Shelton *(G-7403)*
Biohaven Pharmaceuticals Inc............D....... 203 404-0410
New Haven *(G-5245)*
Biohaven Phrm Holdg Co Ltd............E....... 203 404-0410
New Haven *(G-5246)*
Biomed Health Inc............F....... 860 657-2258
Glastonbury *(G-3014)*
Bioxcel Therapeutics Inc............F....... 475 238-6837
New Haven *(G-5247)*
◆ **Boehringer Ingelheim Corp**............A....... 203 798-9988
Ridgefield *(G-7120)*
▲ **Boehringer Ingelheim Pharma**............A....... 203 798-9988
Ridgefield *(G-7121)*
▲ **Boehringer Ingelheim USA Corp**............C....... 203 798-9988
Ridgefield *(G-7122)*
Boehrnger Ingelheim Roxane Inc............E....... 203 798-5555
Ridgefield *(G-7123)*
Brookfeld Mdcl/Srgical Sup Inc............F....... 203 775-0862
Brookfield *(G-1165)*
Cara Therapeutics Inc............E....... 203 406-3700
Stamford *(G-8127)*
Cardinal Health 414 LLC............G....... 860 291-9135
East Hartford *(G-2302)*
Cardioxyl Pharmaceuticals Inc............G....... 919 869-8586
Wallingford *(G-9225)*
Carigent Therapeutics Inc............G....... 203 887-2873
New Haven *(G-5255)*
Carogen Corporation............G....... 203 606-8796
Hamden *(G-3425)*
Celldex Therapeutics Inc............G....... 203 864-5771
Branford *(G-572)*
Chemin Pharma LLC............G....... 203 208-2811
Woodbridge *(G-10598)*
Cisen Usa Inc............G....... 203 706-9536
Middlebury *(G-4275)*
Condomdepot Co............G....... 860 747-1338
Plainville *(G-6789)*
Cytogel Pharma LLC............G....... 203 662-6617
Darien *(G-2016)*
Enw Pharma Writing LLC............G....... 860 663-0263
Killingworth *(G-3833)*
Evotec (us) Inc............E....... 650 228-1400
Branford *(G-591)*
Foster Delivery Science Inc............F....... 860 928-4102
Putnam *(G-7043)*
Foster Delivery Science Inc............F....... 860 630-4515
Putnam *(G-7044)*
▲ **Frederick Purdue Company Inc**............B....... 203 588-8000
Stamford *(G-8210)*
Frequency Therapeutics Inc............E....... 978 436-0704
Farmington *(G-2910)*
Gaia Chemical Corporation............G....... 860 355-2730
Gaylordsville *(G-2992)*
Glaxosmithkline LLC............E....... 203 232-5145
Southbury *(G-7855)*
Henry Thayer Company............G....... 203 226-0940
Easton *(G-2556)*
Hoffmann-La Roche Inc............A....... 203 871-2303
Branford *(G-605)*
▼ **Humphreys Pharmacal Inc**............F....... 860 267-8710
East Hampton *(G-2264)*
Infirst Healthcare Inc............G....... 203 222-1300
Westport *(G-10100)*
▼ **Innoteq Inc**............E....... 203 659-4444
Stratford *(G-8633)*
Intensity Therapeutics Inc............G....... 203 682-2434
Westport *(G-10103)*
Iterum Therapeutics Inc............G....... 860 391-8349
Old Saybrook *(G-6545)*
J & J Precision Eyelet Inc............D....... 860 283-8243
Thomaston *(G-8793)*
Kasten Inc............G....... 702 860-2407
Bridgeport *(G-813)*
Kinderma LLC............G....... 860 796-5503
Glastonbury *(G-3056)*
Kolltan Pharmaceuticals Inc............E....... 203 773-3000
New Haven *(G-5311)*
◆ **Koster Keunen LLC**............F....... 860 945-3333
Watertown *(G-9715)*
Lipid Genomics Inc............G....... 443 465-3495
Farmington *(G-2925)*
Loxo Oncology Inc............E....... 203 653-3880
Stamford *(G-8291)*
Mannkind Corporation............G....... 203 798-8000
Danbury *(G-1879)*

SIC

Employee Codes: A=Over 500 employees, B=251-500
C=101-250, D=51-100, E=20-50, F=10-19, G=1-9
2020 Harris Connecticut
Manufacturers Directory
405

28 CHEMICALS AND ALLIED PRODUCTS

Marinus Pharmaceuticals Inc .... G 484 801-4670
  New Haven (G-5325)
▲ MD Solarsciences Corporation .... F 203 857-0095
  Stamford (G-8300)
Medinstill LLC .... G 860 350-1900
  New Milford (G-5561)
Melinta Subsidiary Corp .... E 203 624-5606
  New Haven (G-5329)
Melinta Therapeutics Inc .... G 908 617-1309
  New Haven (G-5330)
Micro Source Discovery Systems ...... G 860 350-8078
  Gaylordsville (G-2995)
Mitchell Wods Phrmcuticals LLC ...... G 203 258-1305
  Shelton (G-7504)
Neurohydrate LLC .... G 203 799-7900
  Bridgeport (G-848)
New England Bphrmcuticals Corp ..... G 917 992-4250
  Darien (G-2033)
New England Dermatological .... G 203 432-0092
  New Haven (G-5342)
New Haven Naturopathic Center .... G 203 387-8661
  New Haven (G-5345)
New Leaf Pharmaceutical .... F 203 270-4167
  Newtown (G-5763)
Northstar Biosciences LLC .... G 203 689-5399
  Guilford (G-3380)
Novo Nordisk Pharmaceuticals .... G 860 779-2668
  Danielson (G-1999)
Novogen Inc .... F 203 972-5901
  New Canaan (G-5126)
Oncoarendi Therapeutics LLC .... G 609 571-0306
  Madison (G-3943)
Perosphere Inc .... F 203 885-1111
  Danbury (G-1905)
PF Laboratories Inc .... C 973 256-3100
  Stamford (G-8359)
Pfizer Inc .... G 860 389-7509
  Groton (G-3307)
Pfizer Inc .... G 860 441-4568
  Trumbull (G-9055)
Pfizer Inc .... G 203 401-0100
  New Haven (G-5361)
Pfizer Inc .... C 860 441-4100
  Groton (G-3308)
Pfizer Inc .... G 860 441-4000
  Groton (G-3306)
Pgxhealthholding Inc .... C 203 786-3400
  New Haven (G-5362)
Pharmaceutical Discovery Corp .... G 203 796-3425
  Danbury (G-1907)
Pharmaceutical RES Assoc Inc .... G 203 588-8000
  Stamford (G-8360)
Pharmavite Corp .... G 860 651-1885
  Simsbury (G-7639)
Pointpharma LLC .... G 203 668-8543
  Ridgefield (G-7164)
PRA Holdings Inc .... G 203 853-0123
  Stamford (G-8370)
Pre-Clinical Safety Inc .... G 860 739-9797
  East Lyme (G-2471)
Protein Sciences Corporation .... D 203 686-0800
  Meriden (G-4224)
Purdue Pharma Inc .... G 203 588-8000
  Stamford (G-8377)
▲ Purdue Pharma LP .... B 203 588-8000
  Stamford (G-8378)
▲ Purdue Pharma Manufacturing LP ... E 252 265-1924
  Stamford (G-8379)
Purdue Pharmaceutical Pdts LP .... G 203 588-5000
  Stamford (G-8380)
Purdue Pharmaceuticals LP .... F 252 265-1900
  Stamford (G-8381)
Pure Cycle Environmental LLC .... G 203 230-3631
  North Haven (G-5983)
Quality Care Drg/Cntrbrook LLC .... G 860 767-0206
  Centerbrook (G-1332)
Quanah Scents LLC .... G 888 849-2016
  Manchester (G-4077)
Renetx Bio Inc .... G 203 444-6642
  New Haven (G-5378)
Rx Analytic Inc .... G 203 733-0837
  Ridgefield (G-7170)
Sca Pharmaceuticals LLC .... G 501 312-2800
  Windsor (G-10431)
SDA Laboratories Inc .... G 203 861-0005
  Greenwich (G-3233)
Sheffield Pharmaceuticals LLC .... F 860 442-4451
  Norwich (G-6431)
Sherri Masinda .... G 860 429-4988
  Willington (G-10258)

Shire Rgenerative Medicine Inc .... G 877 422-4463
  Westport (G-10157)
Shore Therapeutics Inc .... G 646 562-1243
  Stamford (G-8413)
Sinol Usa Inc .... F 203 470-7404
  Newtown (G-5780)
Skyline Vet Pharma Inc .... G 860 625-0424
  Groton (G-3312)
Systamedic Inc .... G 860 912-6101
  Groton (G-3314)
Syzygy Halthcare Solutions LLC .... G 203 226-4449
  Wilton (G-10336)
Theracour Pharma Inc .... G 203 937-6137
  West Haven (G-9958)
Tower Laboratories Ltd .... E 860 669-7078
  Clinton (G-1531)
◆ Tower Laboratories Ltd .... D 860 767-2127
  Centerbrook (G-1334)
Trevi Therapeutics Inc .... F 203 304-2499
  New Haven (G-5422)
Unicorn Pharmaceuticals Inc .... G 973 699-3843
  Greenwich (G-3251)

2835 Diagnostic Substances

Applied Microbiology Services .... G 860 537-3118
  Lebanon (G-3847)
Bioarray Genetics Inc .... G 508 577-0205
  Farmington (G-2884)
Branford Open Mri & Diagnostic ...... G 203 481-7800
  Branford (G-563)
Cabea LLC .... G 860 738-0819
  Winsted (G-10512)
Cardinal Health 414 LLC .... G 860 291-9135
  East Hartford (G-2302)
Charles River Laboratories Inc .... E 860 429-7261
  Storrs (G-8546)
Lam Therapeutics Inc .... F 203 458-7100
  Guilford (G-3366)
Lucerion LLC .... G 203 699-8136
  Cheshire (G-1409)
Veterinary Medical Associates .... G 860 693-0214
  Canton (G-1327)

2836 Biological Prdts, Exc Diagnostic Substances

Alliances By Alisa LLC .... G 860 869-1509
  Simsbury (G-7610)
Axiomx Inc .... E 203 208-1034
  Branford (G-552)
Bactana Corp .... G 203 716-1230
  Farmington (G-2881)
Charles River Laboratories Inc .... E 860 376-1240
  Voluntown (G-9187)
Charles River Laboratories Inc .... E 860 889-1389
  Norwich (G-6409)
Charles River Laboratories Inc .... E 860 429-7261
  Storrs (G-8546)
Cold Plasma Neck .... G 203 935-0300
  Meriden (G-4160)
Coopersurgical Inc .... G 203 453-1700
  Guilford (G-3341)
Culture Media LLC .... G 203 470-5918
  Wilton (G-10286)
Evotec (us) Inc .... E 650 228-1400
  Branford (G-591)
Genx International Inc .... G 203 453-1700
  Guilford (G-3354)
Lifepharms Inc .... G 860 447-8583
  New London (G-5476)
Oncosynergy Inc .... G 617 755-9156
  Greenwich (G-3212)
Phoenixsongs Biologicals Inc .... G 203 433-4329
  Branford (G-635)
Plasma Coatings Inc .... G 203 598-3100
  Waterbury (G-9578)
Plasma Technology Incorporated ...... E 860 282-0659
  South Windsor (G-7807)
Protein Sciences Corporation .... D 203 686-0800
  Meriden (G-4224)
Serapure Technologies LLC .... G 203 972-0481
  New Canaan (G-5141)
Skin & Co North America LLC .... G 888 444-9971
  West Haven (G-9955)
Testing For Toxins .... G 203 972-6501
  New Canaan (G-5152)
▲ Vegware Us Inc .... G 860 779-7970
  Danielson (G-2006)
Westchester Pet Vaccines .... G 860 267-4554
  Colchester (G-1581)

2841 Soap & Detergents

Amodex Products Inc .... E 203 335-1255
  Bridgeport (G-696)
Bara Essentials LLC .... G 203 428-1786
  Stratford (G-8577)
Beiersdorf Inc .... B 203 854-8000
  Norwalk (G-6088)
▲ Beiersdorf North America Inc .... F 203 563-5800
  Wilton (G-10272)
Country Soap Samplers .... G 203 881-1986
  Oxford (G-6654)
Du-Lite Corporation .... G 860 347-2505
  Middletown (G-4337)
Goat Boy Soap .... G 860 350-0676
  New Milford (G-5539)
◆ Henkel Consumer Goods Inc .... A 475 210-0230
  Stamford (G-8232)
Henkel Corporation .... G 860 571-5100
  Rocky Hill (G-7244)
Integrity Industries Inc .... G 203 312-9788
  New Fairfield (G-5169)
Linden Soaps .... G 563 552-2828
  Woodbury (G-10641)
◆ Pharmaceal Research Labs Inc ..... E 203 755-4908
  Waterbury (G-9575)
Robert Chang .... G 203 737-2264
  Stamford (G-8395)
Robert Dinucci .... G 860 561-3730
  Hartford (G-3679)
▲ Simoniz Usa Inc .... C 860 646-0172
  Bolton (G-520)
Simply Soap .... G 860 347-4174
  Middletown (G-4416)
Unilever Ascc AG .... B 203 381-2482
  Shelton (G-7575)
◆ Unilever Home and Per Care NA ... D 203 502-0086
  Trumbull (G-9085)
▲ United States Chemical Corp .... G 860 621-6831
  Plantsville (G-6917)

2842 Spec Cleaning, Polishing & Sanitation Preparations

A Emergency Rooter Service .... G 860 582-3612
  Bristol (G-952)
Amodex Products Inc .... E 203 335-1255
  Bridgeport (G-696)
Armor All/STP Products Company .... G 203 205-2900
  Danbury (G-1745)
◆ Armor All/STP Products Company ... G 203 205-2900
  Danbury (G-1744)
Armored Autogroup Parent Inc .... G 203 205-2900
  Danbury (G-1747)
Barclay-Davis Enterprises LLC .... G 860 578-9563
  Hartford (G-3555)
Charles K White .... G 203 631-2540
  Hamden (G-3428)
Citra Solv LLC .... G 203 778-0881
  Ridgefield (G-7128)
Cloverdale Inc .... G 860 672-0216
  West Cornwall (G-9762)
Comanche Clean Energy Corp .... G 203 326-4570
  Stamford (G-8152)
Edsan Chemical Company Inc .... C 203 624-3123
  New Haven (G-5273)
F S P Research Inc .... G 203 874-3417
  Milford (G-4534)
Global Shield Solutions LLC .... G 860 983-3566
  Brookfield (G-1192)
◆ Great Lakes Chemical Corp .... E 203 573-2000
  Shelton (G-7454)
Griffith Company .... G 203 333-5557
  Bridgeport (G-780)
▲ Grill Daddy Brush Company .... E 888 840-7552
  Old Greenwich (G-6474)
▲ High-Tech Conversions Inc .... G 860 265-2633
  Enfield (G-2650)
◆ Hubbard-Hall Inc .... C 203 756-5521
  Waterbury (G-9501)
Hydrochemical Techniques Inc .... G 860 527-6350
  Hartford (G-3615)
Jimmys Cleaners & Alterations .... G 203 294-1006
  Wallingford (G-9295)
Korner Kare .... G 860 491-3731
  Goshen (G-3100)
◆ Koster Keunen LLC .... F 860 945-3333
  Watertown (G-9715)
Lanxess Solutions US Inc .... E 203 573-2000
  Shelton (G-7486)
▲ Lubbert Supply Company LLC ..... G 203 690-1105
  Milford (G-4570)

SIC SECTION

28 CHEMICALS AND ALLIED PRODUCTS

◆ Macdermid Incorporated ....C ... 203 575-5700
 Waterbury (G-9522)
Metal Works North ....G ... 203 723-9075
 Beacon Falls (G-143)
▲ Micro Care Corporation ....F ... 860 827-0626
 New Britain (G-5018)
Nature Plus Inc ....G ... 203 380-0316
 Stratford (G-8653)
NC Brands LP ....D ... 203 295-2300
 Norwalk (G-6269)
▲ Nci Holdings Inc ....E ... 203 295-2300
 Norwalk (G-6270)
Odd Jobs Handyman Service LLC ....G ... 203 397-5275
 Woodbridge (G-10609)
Pacific Engineering Inc ....G ... 860 677-0795
 Farmington (G-2944)
Richards Creative Interiors ....G ... 203 484-0361
 Wallingford (G-9355)
Roebic Laboratories Inc ....G ... 203 795-1283
 Orange (G-6626)
▲ Simoniz Usa Inc ....C ... 860 646-0172
 Bolton (G-520)
Suarez Services LLC ....G ... 203 895-0465
 Bridgeport (G-915)
Topcat LLC ....G ... 203 610-6544
 Stratford (G-8697)
Woods End Inc ....G ... 203 226-6303
 Weston (G-10047)
Xtreme Detail ....G ... 203 753-6608
 Waterbury (G-9637)

2843 Surface Active & Finishing Agents, Sulfonated Oils

Alternative Choice LLC ....G ... 860 875-7529
 Vernon Rockville (G-9159)
Chemloid Chemicals Inc ....G ... 203 255-7495
 Fairfield (G-2760)
▲ Henkel of America Inc ....B ... 860 571-5100
 Rocky Hill (G-7246)
◆ Henkel US Operations Corp ....B ... 860 571-5100
 Rocky Hill (G-7247)
Lanxess Solutions US Inc ....E ... 203 573-2000
 Shelton (G-7486)
Solidification Pdts Intl Inc ....G ... 203 484-9494
 Northford (G-6053)
Unimetal Surface Finishing LLC ....E ... 860 283-0271
 Thomaston (G-8816)

2844 Perfumes, Cosmetics & Toilet Preparations

▲ Albea Thomaston Inc ....B ... 860 283-2000
 Thomaston (G-8778)
Alexis Homemade Scrubs ....G ... 401 480-5074
 North Stonington (G-6018)
American Distilling Inc ....G ... 860 267-4444
 Marlborough (G-4119)
▼ American Distilling Inc ....D ... 860 267-4444
 East Hampton (G-2253)
Amodex Products Inc ....E ... 203 335-1255
 Bridgeport (G-696)
Angela Cosmai Inc ....G ... 203 329-7403
 Stamford (G-8085)
Bara Essentials LLC ....G ... 203 428-1786
 Stratford (G-8577)
▲ Bedoukian Research Inc ....E ... 203 830-4000
 Danbury (G-1750)
▲ Beiersdorf Inc ....G ... 203 563-5800
 Wilton (G-10271)
Beiersdorf Inc ....B ... 203 854-8000
 Norwalk (G-6088)
▲ Beiersdorf North America Inc ....F ... 203 563-5800
 Wilton (G-10272)
Black Pltnum MNS Essntials LLC .....G ... 203 501-3768
 Danbury (G-1757)
Blessed Creek ....G ... 860 416-3692
 Suffield (G-8715)
Browne Hansen LLC ....G ... 203 269-0557
 Wallingford (G-9224)
Bunsen Rush Laboratories Inc ....G ... 203 397-0820
 Woodbridge (G-10596)
▲ Carrubba Incorporated ....D ... 203 878-0605
 Milford (G-4485)
▲ Casaro Labs Ltd ....G ... 203 353-8500
 Stamford (G-8129)
▲ CCL Industries Corporation ....D ... 203 926-1253
 Shelton (G-7412)
Chemessence Inc ....G ... 860 355-4108
 New Milford (G-5519)

Cindys Soap Cottage ....G ... 860 370-9908
 Windsor Locks (G-10479)
Connecticut Crnial Fcial Imgery ....G ... 860 643-2940
 Manchester (G-3998)
Conopco Inc ....B ... 860 669-8601
 Clinton (G-1498)
◆ Crabtree & Evelyn Ltd ....C ... 800 272-2873
 Woodstock (G-10662)
Crystal Nails and Spa of Sh ....G ... 203 323-0551
 Stamford (G-8170)
D & F Scrubs & Gadgets LLC ....G ... 203 440-4666
 Meriden (G-4165)
Durol Laboratories LLC ....F ... 866 611-9694
 West Haven (G-9903)
▲ Ecometics Inc ....E ... 203 853-7856
 Norwalk (G-6154)
◆ Edgewell Per Care Brands LLC ....B ... 203 944-5500
 Shelton (G-7435)
Elizabeth Arden Inc ....G ... 203 905-1700
 Stamford (G-8194)
Essentalia LLC ....G ... 860 617-5106
 Storrs (G-8548)
Gillette Company ....G ... 203 796-4000
 Bethel (G-303)
▲ Golden Sun Inc ....F ... 800 575-7960
 Stamford (G-8217)
Harjani Hitesh ....G ... 860 913-6032
 Waterford (G-9654)
High Ridge Brands Co ....D ... 203 674-8080
 Stamford (G-8236)
In O Scents of Madison ....G ... 203 641-8910
 Madison (G-3929)
▲ Innarah Inc ....G ... 203 873-0015
 Stratford (G-8632)
Jolen Cream Bleach Corp ....F ... 203 259-8779
 Fairfield (G-2803)
Judith Jackson Inc ....G ... 203 698-3011
 Old Greenwich (G-6478)
K29 ....G ... 203 961-9662
 Stamford (G-8274)
Kims Nail Corporation ....G ... 203 380-8608
 Stratford (G-8640)
▲ Lady Anne Cosmetics Inc ....G ... 203 372-6972
 Trumbull (G-9041)
▲ Milbar Labs Inc ....F ... 203 467-1577
 East Haven (G-2442)
▲ Miyoshi America Inc ....D ... 860 779-3990
 Dayville (G-2064)
Miyoshi America Inc ....F ... 860 779-3990
 Dayville (G-2065)
Miyoshi America Inc ....G ... 860 779-3990
 Dayville (G-2066)
Naturally Relaxed LLC ....G ... 860 402-0613
 Milldale (G-4687)
Nina Nail Spa ....G ... 203 270-0777
 Newtown (G-5765)
Nutmeg Naturals LLC ....G ... 860 554-1272
 Higganum (G-3772)
Ozz ....G ... 203 318-5080
 Madison (G-3946)
◆ Parfums De Coeur Ltd ....E ... 203 655-8807
 Stamford (G-8350)
▼ Playtex Products LLC ....D ... 203 944-5500
 Shelton (G-7531)
Preferred Display Inc ....G ... 860 372-4653
 Enfield (G-2680)
Raffaele Ruberto LLC ....G ... 860 573-4094
 Wethersfield (G-10216)
Revive Beauty and Wellness LLC .....G ... 860 921-4952
 Brookfield (G-1218)
Rjtb Group LLC ....G ... 203 531-7216
 Greenwich (G-3228)
Rjtb Initiatives Inc ....G ... 203 531-7216
 Greenwich (G-3229)
◆ Russell Organics LLC ....G ... 203 285-6633
 Wallingford (G-9363)
Sallie Gawron ....G ... 203 258-9851
 Fairfield (G-2841)
◆ Sheffield Pharmaceuticals LLC ....C ... 860 442-4451
 New London (G-5488)
Skin & Co North America LLC ....G ... 888 444-9971
 West Haven (G-9955)
T N Dickinson Company ....F ... 860 267-2279
 East Hampton (G-2281)
◆ Unilever Home and Per Care NA ..D ... 203 502-0086
 Trumbull (G-9085)
Unilever Hpc USA ....G ... 203 381-3311
 Trumbull (G-9086)
◆ Unilever Trumbull RES Svcs Inc ..G ... 203 502-0086
 Trumbull (G-9087)

◆ Wenger Na Inc ....G ... 845 365-3500
 Monroe (G-4764)

2851 Paints, Varnishes, Lacquers, Enamels

A G C Incorporated ....C ... 203 235-3361
 Meriden (G-4138)
Air Born Coatings ....G ... 860 684-6762
 East Hartford (G-2289)
Albert Kemperle Inc ....F ... 860 727-0933
 Hartford (G-3550)
Brico LLC ....G ... 860 242-7068
 Bloomfield (G-399)
Chromalloy Component Svcs Inc .....C ... 860 688-7798
 Windsor (G-10373)
Clean Up Group ....G ... 203 668-8323
 Meriden (G-4159)
Colonial Coatings Inc ....E ... 203 783-9933
 Milford (G-4491)
Dumond Chemicals Inc ....G ... 609 655-7700
 Milford (G-4517)
Dumond Chemicals Inc ....G ... 609 655-7700
 Milford (G-4518)
Element 119 LLC ....F ... 860 358-0119
 Thomaston (G-8789)
Elena Dieck ....G ... 860 623-9872
 Broad Brook (G-1149)
▲ Five Star Products Inc ....G ... 203 336-7900
 Shelton (G-7444)
FMI Paint & Chemical Inc ....F ... 860 218-2210
 East Hartford (G-2328)
Fougera Pharmaceuticals Inc ....D ... 203 265-2086
 Wallingford (G-9269)
Greenmaker Industries Conn LLC ....F ... 860 761-2830
 West Hartford (G-9814)
Handyscape LLC ....G ... 860 318-1067
 Southington (G-7932)
ICI Dulux Paints ....G ... 860 621-8661
 Southington (G-7937)
Impermia Coatings Llc ....G ... 413 356-0077
 East Hartford (G-2338)
J + J Branford Inc ....G ... 203 488-5637
 Branford (G-611)
Jet Process Corporation ....G ... 203 985-6000
 North Haven (G-5953)
▲ M & D Coatings LLC ....G ... 203 380-9466
 Stratford (G-8644)
▲ Mantrose-Haeuser Co Inc ....E ... 203 454-1800
 Westport (G-10117)
Materials Proc Dev Group LLC ....G ... 203 269-6617
 Wallingford (G-9313)
Merrifield Paint Company Inc ....G ... 860 529-1583
 Rocky Hill (G-7257)
Minteq International Inc ....C ... 860 824-5435
 Canaan (G-1289)
Northeast Sealcoat Inc ....G ... 860 953-4400
 West Hartford (G-9839)
PPG Industries Inc ....G ... 203 750-9553
 Norwalk (G-6304)
PPG Industries Inc ....G ... 860 627-7401
 Windsor Locks (G-10494)
PPG Industries Inc ....G ... 203 562-5173
 New Haven (G-5369)
PPG Industries Inc ....G ... 203 744-4977
 Danbury (G-1911)
PPG Industries Inc ....G ... 203 522-9544
 Hartford (G-3668)
PPG Industries Inc ....G ... 860 953-1153
 West Hartford (G-9846)
▲ Tcg Green Technologies Inc ....F ... 860 364-4694
 Sharon (G-7384)

2861 Gum & Wood Chemicals

Sychron Inc ....G ... 860 953-8157
 Newington (G-5708)

2865 Cyclic-Crudes, Intermediates, Dyes & Org Pigments

Ethical Solutions LLC ....G ... 860 490-8124
 South Windsor (G-7752)
Jamilah Henna Creations ....G ... 860 365-9542
 East Hampton (G-2266)
Momentive Prfmce Mtls USA Inc .....G ... 203 240-5543
 Fairfield (G-2819)
TAR LLC ....G ... 203 449-4520
 Bridgeport (G-920)

2869 Industrial Organic Chemicals, NEC

Accustandard Inc ....D ... 203 786-5290
 New Haven (G-5218)

Advanced Fuel Co LLC .... G 860 642-4817
North Franklin *(G-5869)*
Advanced Pwr Systems Intl Inc .... E 860 921-0009
New Hartford *(G-5184)*
Ai Divestitures Inc .... G 203 575-5727
Waterbury *(G-9424)*
Alternative Fuel & Energy LLC .... G 860 537-5345
Colchester *(G-1539)*
American Greenfuels LLC .... F 203 672-9028
New Haven *(G-5227)*
Anthony s Fuel .... G 203 513-7400
Shelton *(G-7396)*
▲ Bedoukian Research Inc .... E 203 830-4000
Danbury *(G-1750)*
Bestway Food and Fuel .... G 860 447-0729
Waterford *(G-9643)*
Black Dog Fuel LLC .... G 860 489-0655
New Milford *(G-5511)*
Blue Barn Works LLC .... G 203 389-0923
Woodbridge *(G-10594)*
Brian Safa .... G 203 271-3499
Cheshire *(G-1363)*
▲ Carrubba Incorporated .... D 203 878-0605
Milford *(G-4485)*
Clearclad Coatings LLC .... G 860 945-9200
Watertown *(G-9693)*
Coastline Fuel Inc .... G 203 846-3601
Norwalk *(G-6117)*
Cobal-USA Altrnative Fuels LLC .... G 203 751-1974
Ansonia *(G-29)*
Connstem Inc .... G 203 558-4671
Cheshire *(G-1373)*
Crossroads Deli & Fuel LLC .... G 860 824-8474
Falls Village *(G-2869)*
CTS Services LLC .... G 203 268-5865
Shelton *(G-7424)*
Deep River Fuel Terminals LLC .... G 860 342-4619
Portland *(G-6956)*
▲ Dragonlab LLC .... G 860 436-9221
Rocky Hill *(G-7235)*
Dymax Corporation .... G 860 626-7006
Torrington *(G-8919)*
Dymax Materials Inc .... G 860 482-1010
Torrington *(G-8920)*
▲ Dymax Oligomers & Coatings .... F 860 626-7006
Torrington *(G-8921)*
E&S Automotive Operations LLC .... G 203 332-4555
Bridgeport *(G-759)*
Element Solutions Inc .... E 203 575-5850
Waterbury *(G-9475)*
Ethical Solutions LLC .... G 860 490-8124
South Windsor *(G-7752)*
Extra Fuel .... G 203 330-0613
Bridgeport *(G-766)*
Falls Fuel LLC .... G 203 744-3835
Bethel *(G-299)*
Firehouse Discount Oil LLC .... G 860 404-1827
Unionville *(G-9115)*
Fuel First .... G 203 735-5097
Ansonia *(G-35)*
Fuel For Humanity Inc .... G 203 255-5913
Westport *(G-10086)*
Fuel Lab .... G 860 677-4987
Farmington *(G-2911)*
Galaxy Fuel LLC .... G 203 878-8173
Milford *(G-4539)*
Greenleaf Bfuels New Haven LLC .... F 203 672-9028
New Haven *(G-5290)*
H Krevit and Company Inc .... E 203 772-3350
New Haven *(G-5292)*
Hajan LLC .... G 860 223-2005
New Britain *(G-4995)*
Hampford Research Inc .... G 203 380-2852
Stratford *(G-8621)*
▲ Hampford Research Inc .... E 203 375-1137
Stratford *(G-8622)*
▲ Henkel of America Inc .... B 860 571-5100
Rocky Hill *(G-7246)*
Hitbro Realty LLC .... G 860 824-1370
Canaan *(G-1286)*
Houston Macdermid Inc .... G 203 575-5700
Waterbury *(G-9500)*
Husky Fuel .... G 203 783-0783
Oxford *(G-6665)*
Ironic Chemicals LLC .... G 646 352-2692
Fairfield *(G-2798)*
Jsr Micro Inc .... G 203 426-7794
Newtown *(G-5751)*
Lanxess Solutions US Inc .... E 203 573-2000
Shelton *(G-7486)*
Lanxess Solutions US Inc .... G 203 605-5746
Naugatuck *(G-4900)*
Macdermid Anion Inc .... G 203 575-5700
Waterbury *(G-9527)*
Macdermid Brazil Inc .... G 203 575-5700
Waterbury *(G-9528)*
Macdermid South America Inc .... G 203 575-5700
Waterbury *(G-9531)*
Macdermid South Atlantic Inc .... G 203 575-5700
Waterbury *(G-9532)*
Med Opportunity Partners LLC .... G 203 622-1333
Greenwich *(G-3201)*
Mercury Fuel Co .... G 860 793-6602
Plainville *(G-6843)*
Mercury Fuel Service Inc .... G 203 291-0833
Westport *(G-10119)*
Metalast International In .... G 860 673-1725
Burlington *(G-1273)*
Midsun Group Inc .... G 860 378-0100
Southington *(G-7954)*
Miller Fuel LLC .... G 860 675-6121
Burlington *(G-1274)*
Nalas Engineering Services .... D 860 861-3691
Norwich *(G-6424)*
New England Fuels & Energy LLC .... G 860 585-5917
Terryville *(G-8766)*
Power Fuels LLC .... G 203 699-0099
Cheshire *(G-1431)*
Priced Right Fuel LLC .... G 203 856-7031
Norwalk *(G-6305)*
Pucks Putters & Fuel LLC .... F 203 877-5457
Milford *(G-4619)*
Pucks Putters & Fuel LLC .... G 203 494-3952
Shelton *(G-7540)*
▲ RSA Corp .... E 203 790-8100
Danbury *(G-1931)*
◆ RT Vanderbilt Holding Co Inc .... F 203 295-2141
Norwalk *(G-6331)*
Sanco Energy .... F 203 259-5914
Fairfield *(G-2842)*
◆ Si Group USA (usaa) LLC .... C 203 702-6140
Danbury *(G-1946)*
◆ Si Group USA Hldings Usha Corp .... E 203 702-6140
Danbury *(G-1947)*
Superior Fuel Co .... G 203 337-1213
Bridgeport *(G-917)*
Tylerville Technologies LLC .... G 860 798-0501
Higganum *(G-3780)*
Ultra Food and Fuel .... G 860 223-2005
New Britain *(G-5077)*
Uniroyal Chemical Corporation .... G 203 573-2000
Waterbury *(G-9620)*
◆ Vanderbilt Chemicals LLC .... D 203 295-2141
Norwalk *(G-6383)*
Vanderbilt Chemicals LLC .... E 203 744-3900
Bethel *(G-361)*
Victory Fuel LLC .... G 860 585-0532
Terryville *(G-8777)*
Waste Resource Recovery Inc .... G 860 287-3332
Lebanon *(G-3866)*
Waste To Green Fuel LLC .... G 203 536-5855
Bridgeport *(G-935)*
Wildcat Fuel Systems Conn LLC .... G 203 627-4310
Hamden *(G-3530)*
XCEL Fuel .... G 203 481-4510
Branford *(G-677)*
Yale University .... G 203 432-3916
New Haven *(G-5447)*

2873 Nitrogenous Fertilizers

Bobbex Inc .... G 800 792-4449
Monroe *(G-4700)*
▲ Good Earth Tree Care Inc .... G 203 375-7962
Stratford *(G-8619)*

2875 Fertilizers, Mixing Only

Blue Earth Compost Inc .... G 860 508-7114
Hartford *(G-3556)*
Clinton Nursery Products Inc .... C 860 399-3000
Westbrook *(G-9994)*
Collins Compost .... G 860 749-3416
Enfield *(G-2628)*
Curbside Compost LLC .... G 914 646-6890
Ridgefield *(G-7132)*
Grillo Services LLC .... E 203 877-5070
Milford *(G-4544)*
New Milford Farms Inc .... F 860 210-0250
New Milford *(G-5570)*
Scotts Company LLC .... D 860 642-7591
Lebanon *(G-3862)*
Siteone Landscape Supply LLC .... G 860 673-6912
Avon *(G-113)*

2879 Pesticides & Agricultural Chemicals, NEC

Adirondack Lkfront Retreat LLC .... G 203 267-5882
Southbury *(G-7841)*
Andrews Arboriculture LLC .... G 203 565-8570
Naugatuck *(G-4857)*
▲ Bedoukian Research Inc .... E 203 830-4000
Danbury *(G-1750)*
Chemtura Receivables LLC .... G 203 573-3327
Waterbury *(G-9449)*
Clinton Nursery Products Inc .... C 860 399-3000
Westbrook *(G-9994)*
Connecticut Tick Control LLC .... F 203 855-7849
Norwalk *(G-6128)*
Dupont .... G 860 368-0766
Middletown *(G-4338)*
Dupont De Nemours Inc .... G 203 330-6755
Bridgeport *(G-758)*
Dupont Guy Office .... G 203 679-0358
Wallingford *(G-9254)*
Ferrucci Services .... G 203 468-2319
East Haven *(G-2427)*
Healthy Harvest Inc .... G 203 245-3786
Madison *(G-3927)*
Lanxess Solutions US Inc .... D 203 723-2237
Naugatuck *(G-4899)*
Lenz Enterprises LLC .... G 860 961-2893
Middletown *(G-4368)*
Macdermid AG Solutions Inc .... F 203 575-5727
Waterbury *(G-9526)*
Michael Dupont .... G 203 434-0650
Redding *(G-7101)*
Mist Hill Property Maint LLC .... G 203 648-7434
Brookfield *(G-1207)*
Monsanto Mystic Research .... G 860 572-5200
Mystic *(G-4833)*
Nantucket Spider LLC .... G 203 423-3031
Wilton *(G-10315)*
P2 Science Inc .... G 203 821-7457
Woodbridge *(G-10611)*
Pamela Gordondupont Ms Ccca .... G 860 526-8686
Chester *(G-1478)*
Pic20 Group LLC .... F 203 957-3555
Norwalk *(G-6299)*
Tick Box Technology Corp .... G 203 852-7171
Norwalk *(G-6368)*

2891 Adhesives & Sealants

Advanced Adhesive Systems Inc .... E 860 953-4100
Newington *(G-5621)*
Apcm Manufacturing LLC .... G 860 564-7817
Plainfield *(G-6738)*
Babcock & King Incorporated .... G 203 336-7989
Fairfield *(G-2750)*
▲ Chessco Industries Inc .... E 203 255-2804
Westport *(G-10064)*
Conserv Epoxy LLC .... G 203 484-4123
Northford *(G-6044)*
Converting McHy Adhesives LLC .... G 860 561-0226
Newington *(G-5643)*
Ctech Adhesives .... G 860 482-5947
New Hartford *(G-5188)*
Cunningham Tech LLC .... G 860 738-8759
New Hartford *(G-5189)*
Cunningham Tech LLC .... G 860 738-8759
Pine Meadow *(G-6733)*
◆ Edison Coatings Inc .... F 860 747-2220
Plainville *(G-6804)*
▲ Five Star Products Inc .... E 203 336-7900
Shelton *(G-7444)*
Grafted Coatings Inc .... F 203 377-9979
Stratford *(G-8620)*
Henkel Corporation .... G 860 571-5100
Rocky Hill *(G-7244)*
◆ Henkel Loctite Corporation .... E 860 571-5100
Rocky Hill *(G-7245)*
▲ Henkel of America Inc .... B 860 571-5100
Rocky Hill *(G-7246)*
◆ Henkel US Operations Corp .... B 860 571-5100
Rocky Hill *(G-7247)*
Hexcel Corporation .... E 203 969-0666
Stamford *(G-8233)*
Incure Inc .... G 860 748-2979
New Britain *(G-4998)*
Laticrete International Inc .... G 203 393-0010
Bethany *(G-245)*

SIC SECTION

29 PETROLEUM REFINING AND RELATED INDUSTRIES

▲ Metamorphic Materials Inc ....F 860 738-8638
  Winsted *(G-10529)*
Panacol-Usa Inc ....F 860 738-7449
  Torrington *(G-8956)*
◆ Permatex Inc ....E 860 543-7500
  Hartford *(G-3663)*
S & S Sealcoating LLC ....G 203 284-0054
  Wallingford *(G-9364)*
Sealpro LLC ....G 860 289-0804
  East Hartford *(G-2370)*
Shurtape Specialty Coating LLC ....E 860 738-2600
  New Hartford *(G-5212)*
▲ Smarter Sealants LLC ....G 860 218-2210
  East Hartford *(G-2374)*
Synchron Inc ....G 860 953-8157
  Newington *(G-5709)*
Vanderbilt Chemicals LLC ....E 203 744-3900
  Bethel *(G-361)*
Xg Industries LLC ....F 475 282-4643
  Stratford *(G-8712)*

2892 Explosives

Austin Powder Company ....E 860 564-5466
  Sterling *(G-8507)*
Dyno Nobel Inc ....C 860 843-2000
  Simsbury *(G-7618)*
▲ Ensign-Bickford Arospc Def Co ....B 860 843-2289
  Simsbury *(G-7620)*
▲ Ensign-Bickford Company ....G 860 843-2001
  Simsbury *(G-7621)*
Ensign-Bickford Industries Inc ....E 860 658-4411
  Simsbury *(G-7622)*
Independent Explosives ....G 860 243-0137
  Bloomfield *(G-421)*
◆ Maxam Initiation Systems LLC ....F 860 774-3507
  Sterling *(G-8512)*
Maxam North America Inc ....G 860 774-2333
  Sterling *(G-8513)*
▲ Metal Finish Eqp & Sup Co Inc ....E 860 668-1050
  Suffield *(G-8726)*
Precision Explosives Inc ....G 860 567-4952
  Bantam *(G-127)*

2893 Printing Ink

Corporate Cartridge ....G 203 655-7197
  Darien *(G-2015)*
Hubergroup Usa Inc ....F 860 687-1617
  Windsor *(G-10395)*
Superior Printing Ink Co Inc ....E 203 281-1921
  Hamden *(G-3515)*

2899 Chemical Preparations, NEC

▲ 5n Plus Corp ....F 608 846-1357
  Trumbull *(G-8994)*
Advanced Pwr Systems Intl Inc ....E 860 921-0009
  New Hartford *(G-5184)*
Alent USA Holding Inc ....B 203 575-5727
  Waterbury *(G-9426)*
▲ All Power Manufacturing Co ....C 562 802-2640
  Oxford *(G-6641)*
Altasci LLC ....G 860 224-6668
  New Britain *(G-4942)*
Applied Immunotherapeutics Inc ....G 203 247-3895
  Morris *(G-4786)*
Aptex Corp ....G 203 743-6412
  Oxford *(G-6643)*
Armored Autogroup Parent Inc ....G 203 205-2900
  Danbury *(G-1747)*
Atlantic Coast Polymers Inc ....G 860 564-5641
  Plainfield *(G-6741)*
▲ Bic Consumer Products Mfg Co ....C 203 783-2000
  Milford *(G-4469)*
▲ Bic Corporation ....A 203 783-2000
  Shelton *(G-7407)*
▲ Bic USA Inc ....C 203 783-2000
  Shelton *(G-7408)*
◆ Brand-Nu Laboratories Inc ....E 203 235-7989
  Meriden *(G-4150)*
Brand-Nu Laboratories Inc ....G 203 235-7989
  Meriden *(G-4151)*
▲ Caap Co Inc ....E 203 877-0375
  Milford *(G-4478)*
Chad Labs Corporation ....G 203 877-3891
  Milford *(G-4487)*
Chemotex Protective Coatings ....F 860 349-0144
  Durham *(G-2142)*
▲ Chessco Industries Inc ....E 203 255-2804
  Westport *(G-10064)*
Concrete Supplement Co ....G 860 567-5556
  Litchfield *(G-3886)*
Constitution Sparkler Sales ....G 203 324-5159
  Stamford *(G-8158)*
▲ Crystal Rock Spring Water Co ....B 860 945-0661
  Watertown *(G-9698)*
Cytec Industries Inc ....D 203 321-2200
  Stamford *(G-8176)*
Cytec Industries Inc ....C 203 284-4334
  Wallingford *(G-9245)*
East Coast Insulation LLC ....G 302 685-3152
  Meriden *(G-4168)*
Eastern Salt Company ....G 203 466-6761
  New Haven *(G-5272)*
▲ Eastern Tech LLC ....G 203 877-5386
  Milford *(G-4524)*
Element Solutions Inc ....E 203 575-5850
  Waterbury *(G-9475)*
Evonik Tockhausen LLC ....G 860 530-1363
  Hebron *(G-3748)*
▲ Five Star Products Inc ....E 203 336-7900
  Shelton *(G-7444)*
Flottec International Sls Corp ....G 973 588-4717
  Westport *(G-10084)*
Gillette Company ....G 203 796-4000
  Bethel *(G-303)*
Globe Environmental Corp ....F 203 481-5586
  Branford *(G-600)*
Gotham Chemical Company Inc ....D 203 854-6644
  Norwalk *(G-6183)*
◆ Great Lakes Chemical Corp ....E 203 573-2000
  Shelton *(G-7454)*
H & M Systems ....G 860 445-2347
  Groton *(G-3290)*
◆ H Muehlstein & Co Inc ....G 800 257-3746
  Norwalk *(G-6190)*
▲ Henkel of America Inc ....B 860 571-5100
  Rocky Hill *(G-7246)*
◆ Henkel US Operations Corp ....B 860 571-5100
  Rocky Hill *(G-7271)*
◆ Hubbard-Hall Inc ....C 203 756-5521
  Waterbury *(G-9501)*
International Cnstr Pdts Res ....G 203 336-7900
  Fairfield *(G-2796)*
▲ Intersurface Dynamics Inc ....F 203 778-9995
  Bethel *(G-312)*
Inventec Prfmce Chem USA LLC ....E 860 526-8300
  Deep River *(G-2094)*
Joesjuicecom LLC ....G 203 824-1854
  Stamford *(G-8266)*
Kuehne New Haven LLC ....G 203 508-6703
  New Haven *(G-5312)*
Lanxess Solutions US Inc ....E 203 573-2000
  Shelton *(G-7486)*
Laticrete International Inc ....G 203 393-0010
  Bethany *(G-245)*
Lonza Wood Protection ....G 203 229-2900
  Norwalk *(G-6236)*
Lydall Inc ....E 860 646-1233
  Manchester *(G-4050)*
Macdermid Incorporated ....G 262 242-2892
  Waterbury *(G-9523)*
Macdermid Incorporated ....E 203 575-5700
  Waterbury *(G-9524)*
◆ Macdermid Incorporated ....C 203 575-5700
  Waterbury *(G-9522)*
Macdermid Acumen Inc ....G 203 575-5700
  Waterbury *(G-9525)*
◆ Macdermid Enthone Inc ....C 203 934-8611
  West Haven *(G-9928)*
Macdermid Overseas Asia Ltd ....G 203 575-5799
  Waterbury *(G-9529)*
Macdermid Printing Solutions ....G 203 575-5727
  Waterbury *(G-9530)*
Maps and More ....G 203 335-0556
  Bridgeport *(G-828)*
◆ Near Oak LLC ....G 203 329-6500
  Stamford *(G-8318)*
OMI International Corporation ....G 203 575-5727
  West Haven *(G-9941)*
Perfect Infinity Inc ....G 203 906-0442
  Milford *(G-4608)*
◆ Permatex Inc ....E 203 543-7500
  Hartford *(G-3663)*
Perricone Hydrogen Wtr Co LLC ....G 844 341-5941
  Meriden *(G-4217)*
Poquonock Sewage Plant ....G 860 688-5420
  Windsor *(G-10422)*
Prestone Products Corporation ....E 203 731-7880
  Danbury *(G-1919)*
▲ Pulse International Inc ....G 860 290-7878
  South Windsor *(G-7816)*
◆ Purification Technologies LLC ....F 860 526-7801
  Chester *(G-1480)*
Q Labtech LLC ....G 860 501-9119
  East Lyme *(G-2472)*
Rand Innovations LLC ....F 475 282-4643
  Bridgeport *(G-885)*
Recor Rust Solutions ....G 860 573-1942
  Hebron *(G-3755)*
▲ REM Chemicals Inc ....G 860 621-6755
  Southington *(G-7967)*
Russian Flare LLC ....G 860 404-1781
  Avon *(G-107)*
Southford Kindling Company LLC ....G 203 394-2148
  Southbury *(G-7879)*
Sparklers ....G 860 669-5110
  Clinton *(G-1527)*
Suez Wts Services Usa Inc ....E 860 291-9660
  East Hartford *(G-2380)*
▼ Swahili Aviation Aerospace LLC ....E 860 268-3639
  Tolland *(G-8879)*
▲ Three Kings Products LLC ....G 860 945-5294
  Watertown *(G-9740)*
▲ United States Chemical Corp ....G 860 621-6831
  Plantsville *(G-6917)*
Vichem Inc ....G 860 677-8133
  Farmington *(G-2975)*
W Canning Inc ....G 203 575-5727
  Waterbury *(G-9625)*

29 PETROLEUM REFINING AND RELATED INDUSTRIES

2911 Petroleum Refining

Annies Oil Co ....G 203 237-9276
  Meriden *(G-4143)*
App Polonia LLC ....G 860 747-3397
  Plainville *(G-6771)*
Armored Autogroup Parent Inc ....G 203 205-2900
  Danbury *(G-1747)*
CCI Corpus Christi LLC ....G 203 564-8100
  Stamford *(G-8133)*
▲ Chessco Industries Inc ....E 203 255-2804
  Westport *(G-10064)*
Du-Lite Corporation ....G 860 347-2505
  Middletown *(G-4337)*
G H Berlin Oil Company ....G 800 426-7754
  Hartford *(G-3594)*
Hart Technology LLC ....G 860 482-6160
  Torrington *(G-8932)*
Koster Keunen Inc ....G 860 945-3333
  Watertown *(G-9714)*
◆ Koster Keunen Mfg Inc ....D 860 945-3333
  Watertown *(G-9716)*
Lanxess Solutions US Inc ....E 203 573-2000
  Shelton *(G-7486)*
Leclaire Fuel Oil LLC ....G 203 922-1512
  Shelton *(G-7489)*
Madonna Black Buddist LLC ....G 203 589-9796
  Greenwich *(G-3196)*
Mercury Fuel Service Inc ....D 203 756-7284
  Waterbury *(G-9539)*
◆ Purification Technologies LLC ....F 860 526-7801
  Chester *(G-1480)*
▼ STP Products Manufacturing Co ....F 203 205-2900
  Danbury *(G-1957)*
US Chemicals Inc ....G 203 655-8878
  New Canaan *(G-5157)*

2951 Paving Mixtures & Blocks

A-1 Asphalt Paving ....G 860 436-6085
  Rocky Hill *(G-7217)*
AEN Asphalt Inc ....G 860 885-0500
  Bozrah *(G-523)*
All States Asphalt Inc ....G 860 774-7550
  Dayville *(G-2053)*
Betkoski Brothers LLC ....G 203 723-8262
  Beacon Falls *(G-131)*
Brico Inc ....G 203 693-0323
  Bloomfield *(G-400)*
Christopher Annelli ....G 860 537-4397
  Colchester *(G-1545)*
E B Asphalt & Landscaping LLC ....F 860 639-1921
  Norwich *(G-6412)*
Firestone Building Pdts Co LLC ....D 860 584-4516
  Bristol *(G-1039)*
L Suzio Asphalt Co Inc ....F 203 237-8421
  Meriden *(G-4185)*
O & G Industries Inc ....E 203 977-1618
  Stamford *(G-8335)*

Employee Codes: A=Over 500 employees, B=251-500
C=101-250, D=51-100, E=20-50, F=10-19, G=1-9

2020 Harris Connecticut Manufacturers Directory

29 PETROLEUM REFINING AND RELATED INDUSTRIES

O & G Industries Inc .... D 860 354-4438
  New Milford (G-5576)
O & G Industries Inc .... D 203 263-2195
  Southbury (G-7870)
O & G Industries Inc .... E 203 366-4586
  Bridgeport (G-854)
T D I Enterprises LLC .... G 203 630-1268
  Meriden (G-4249)
Tilcon Connecticut Inc .... G 860 342-6157
  Portland (G-6977)
▲ Tilcon Connecticut Inc .... D 860 224-6010
  New Britain (G-5074)
Tilcon Inc .... B 860 223-3651
  Newington (G-5713)
Wescon Corp of Conn .... G 860 599-2500
  Pawcatuck (G-6731)
Westchester Industries Inc .... F 203 661-0055
  Greenwich (G-3257)

2952 Asphalt Felts & Coatings

Epdm Coatings .... G 203 225-0104
  Shelton (G-7441)
Firestone Building Pdts Co LLC .... D 860 584-4516
  Bristol (G-1039)
Gorilla Sealcoating LLC .... G 475 218-3506
  Danbury (G-1836)
Neyra Industries Inc .... G 860 289-4359
  South Windsor (G-7796)
Qba Inc .... G 860 963-9438
  Woodstock (G-10679)
Roofing Solutions .... G 860 444-0486
  New London (G-5487)
Seal King Sealcoating .... G 203 871-1423
  Bethel (G-341)
Spectrum Powdercoating LLC .... G 860 591-1034
  Jewett City (G-3801)
TPC Replacement Window LLC .... G 860 274-6971
  Oakville (G-6464)
Westfort Construction Corp .... G 860 833-7970
  Hamden (G-3529)

2992 Lubricating Oils & Greases

◆ Artech Packaging LLC .... G 845 858-8558
  Bethel (G-259)
◆ Axel Plastics RES Labs Inc .... E 718 672-8300
  Monroe (G-4694)
Castrol Industrial N Amer Inc .... G 860 928-5100
  Putnam (G-7032)
▲ CCL Industries Corporation .... D 203 926-1253
  Shelton (G-7412)
▲ Chessco Industries Inc .... E 203 255-2804
  Westport (G-10064)
Fuchs Lubricants Co .... E 203 469-2336
  East Haven (G-2431)
Interflon of New England .... G 860 305-8976
  Wethersfield (G-10200)
◆ Macdermid Incorporated .... C 203 575-5700
  Waterbury (G-9522)
◆ Permatex Inc .... E 860 543-7500
  Hartford (G-3663)
Price-Driscoll Corporation .... G 860 442-3575
  Waterford (G-9666)
Safe Harbour Products Inc .... G 203 295-8377
  Norwalk (G-6336)
Sheldon Automotive Enterprises .... F 203 372-4948
  Fairfield (G-2846)

2999 Products Of Petroleum & Coal, NEC

◆ Koster Keunen LLC .... F 860 945-3333
  Watertown (G-9715)
Rain Cii Carbon LLC .... G 203 406-0535
  Stamford (G-8385)

30 RUBBER AND MISCELLANEOUS PLASTICS PRODUCTS

3011 Tires & Inner Tubes

Ace Tire & Auto Center Inc .... F 203 438-4042
  Ridgefield (G-7115)
BF Enterprises LLC .... G 860 693-8953
  Collinsville (G-1588)
BF Services LLC .... G 860 289-6929
  East Hartford (G-2299)
Edwards & Schmidt LLC .... G 203 393-5666
  Prospect (G-7002)
Major Tire Co LLC .... G 203 543-0334
  Stratford (G-8645)

▲ Toce Brothers Incorporated .... E 860 496-2080
  Torrington (G-8978)
Town Fair Tire Centers Inc .... F 860 646-2807
  Manchester (G-4103)

3021 Rubber & Plastic Footwear

▲ Inocraft Products Inc .... E 860 933-0485
  Tolland (G-8866)
Moda LLC .... G 203 302-2800
  Greenwich (G-3204)

3052 Rubber & Plastic Hose & Belting

▲ Kongsberg Actuation .... G 860 668-1285
  Suffield (G-8723)
Ram Belting Company Inc .... G 860 438-7029
  New Britain (G-5040)
Rubco Products Company .... G 860 496-1178
  Torrington (G-8965)

3053 Gaskets, Packing & Sealing Devices

A G C Incorporated .... C 203 235-3361
  Meriden (G-4138)
Alltop Ltd .... G 203 746-1509
  New Fairfield (G-5160)
American Seal and Engrg Co Inc .... E 203 789-8819
  Orange (G-6581)
Ametek Inc .... C 203 265-6731
  Wallingford (G-9203)
▲ Auburn Manufacturing Company .... E 860 346-6677
  Middletown (G-4319)
Beacon Group Inc .... C 860 594-5200
  Newington (G-5631)
Best Gaskets .... G 914 347-1971
  Stamford (G-8111)
Carem Assoc .... G 203 372-6788
  Fairfield (G-2758)
Chas W House & Sons Inc .... D 860 673-2518
  Unionville (G-9112)
Corru Seals Inc .... F 203 284-0319
  Wallingford (G-9241)
Derby Cellular Products Inc .... C 203 735-4661
  Shelton (G-7430)
EMR Global Inc .... G 203 452-8166
  East Hartford (G-2322)
H-O Products Corporation .... E 860 379-9875
  Winsted (G-10523)
Kenneth Industrial Pdts Inc .... G 860 349-7454
  Durham (G-2150)
Linda Hoagland .... G 203 878-7188
  Milford (G-4568)
Lydall Inc .... E 860 646-1233
  Manchester (G-4050)
Parker-Hannifin Corporation .... D 203 239-3341
  North Haven (G-5974)
Rubber Supplies Company Inc .... G 203 736-9995
  Derby (G-2125)
SKF USA Inc .... E 860 379-8511
  Winsted (G-10536)
▲ Spirol International Corp .... C 860 774-8571
  Danielson (G-2003)
Standard Washer & Mat Inc .... E 860 643-5125
  Manchester (G-4094)
Sur-Seal Holding LLC .... G 203 625-0770
  Norwalk (G-6360)
▲ Vanguard Products Corporation .... D 203 744-7265
  Danbury (G-1970)

3061 Molded, Extruded & Lathe-Cut Rubber Mechanical Goods

Acmt Inc .... D 860 645-0592
  Manchester (G-3977)
▲ Applied Rubber & Plastics Inc .... F 860 987-9018
  Windsor (G-10363)
Buestan Usa LLC .... G 203 954-8889
  Ansonia (G-25)
Jem Manufacturing Inc .... G 203 250-9404
  Wallingford (G-9294)
▲ Vanguard Products Corporation .... D 203 744-7265
  Danbury (G-1970)

3069 Fabricated Rubber Prdts, NEC

◆ Acme United Corporation .... C 203 254-6060
  Fairfield (G-2743)
American Roller Company LLC .... F 203 598-3100
  Middlebury (G-4273)
▲ Anchor Rubber Products LLC .... G 860 667-2628
  Newington (G-5627)

Apache Mill .... G 401 597-5580
  Branford (G-546)
Ascon Products Co .... G 860 439-1305
  New London (G-5456)
▲ Auburn Manufacturing Company .... E 860 346-6677
  Middletown (G-4319)
▼ Bite Tech Inc .... E 203 987-6898
  Norwalk (G-6093)
Buestan Usa LLC .... G 203 954-8889
  Ansonia (G-25)
Cooper Crouse-Hinds LLC .... D 860 683-4300
  Windsor (G-10377)
Courtman Enterprises LLC .... G 860 322-2837
  Windsor (G-10378)
Gordon Rubber and Pkg Co Inc .... G 203 735-7441
  Derby (G-2114)
▼ Griswold LLC .... D 860 564-3321
  Moosup (G-4779)
H-O Products Corporation .... E 860 379-9875
  Winsted (G-10523)
HI Tech Profiles Inc .... F 401 377-2040
  Pawcatuck (G-6714)
▼ Hutchinson Precision Ss Inc .... F 860 779-0300
  Danielson (G-1993)
▲ IR Industries Inc .... F 203 790-8273
  Bethel (G-313)
Jay Tee Corp .... G 203 732-5215
  Ansonia (G-41)
Jonal Laboratories Inc .... D 203 634-4444
  Meriden (G-4180)
Jump4fun USA LLC .... G 203 735-3702
  Ansonia (G-43)
▲ Klean Air Supplies Inc .... G 860 583-1589
  Bristol (G-1058)
▲ Ktt Enterprises LLC .... G 203 288-7883
  Hamden (G-3470)
▲ Latex Foam International LLC .... G 203 924-0700
  Shelton (G-7487)
▲ Latex Foam Intl Holdings Inc .... G 203 924-0700
  Shelton (G-7488)
Lord & Hodge Inc .... F 860 632-7006
  Middletown (G-4369)
▲ Mayborn Usa Inc .... F 781 269-7490
  Stamford (G-8298)
Meridian Operations LLC .... G 860 564-8811
  Plainfield (G-6749)
▲ Midsun Specialty Products Inc .... E 860 378-0111
  Berlin (G-200)
Nauta Roll Corporation .... G 860 267-2027
  East Hampton (G-2270)
New England Foam Products LLC .... E 860 524-0121
  Hartford (G-3650)
▼ Playtex Products LLC .... D 203 944-5500
  Shelton (G-7531)
Reilly Foam Corp .... E 860 243-8200
  Bloomfield (G-476)
Rogers Corporation .... C 860 928-3622
  Woodstock (G-10681)
Ross Enterprises .... G 860 308-2238
  Hartford (G-3682)
Rubberhouse .... G 860 646-3012
  Bolton (G-518)
▼ Scapa North America Inc .... G 860 688-8000
  Windsor (G-10433)
Standard Washer & Mat Inc .... E 860 643-5125
  Manchester (G-4094)
Sur-Seal Holding LLC .... G 203 625-0770
  Norwalk (G-6360)
Tellus Technology Inc .... G 646 265-7960
  Darien (G-2046)
◆ Universal Foam Products LLC .... F 860 216-3015
  Bloomfield (G-496)
Warco of Ne LLC .... G 203 393-1691
  Woodbridge (G-10621)

3081 Plastic Unsupported Sheet & Film

American Polyfilm Inc .... G 203 483-9797
  Branford (G-543)
▲ Apogee Corporation .... D 860 963-1976
  Putnam (G-7030)
Apogee Corporation .... D 860 632-3550
  Cromwell (G-1687)
▲ Atlas Metallizing Inc .... F 860 827-9777
  New Britain (G-4946)
Berry Global Inc .... G 413 529-7602
  East Hampton (G-2256)
Brushfoil LLC .... F 203 453-7403
  Guilford (G-3335)
Clopay Corporation .... C 203 230-9116
  North Haven (G-5921)

30 RUBBER AND MISCELLANEOUS PLASTICS PRODUCTS

◆ Engineering Services & Pdts Co ....D 860 528-1119
South Windsor (G-7750)
◆ Filmx Technologies ....G...... 860 779-3403
Dayville (G-2062)
▲ Flagship Converters Inc ....D...... 203 792-0034
Danbury (G-1826)
Grimco Inc ....G...... 800 542-9941
New Britain (G-4993)
Orafol Americas Inc ....C...... 860 676-7100
Avon (G-98)
Plastic Factory LLC ....G...... 203 908-3468
Bridgeport (G-874)
Polymer Films Inc ....E...... 203 932-3000
West Haven (G-9946)
◆ Rowland Technologies Inc ....D...... 203 269-9500
Wallingford (G-9361)
Spartech LLC ....C...... 203 327-6010
Stamford (G-8432)
Str Holdings Inc ....F...... 860 272-4235
Enfield (G-2699)
Superior Plas Extrusion Co Inc ....C...... 860 234-1864
Cromwell (G-1720)
▲ Superior Plas Extrusion Co Inc ....E...... 860 963-1976
Putnam (G-7071)
Vacumet Corp ....G...... 860 731-0860
East Hartford (G-2399)

3082 Plastic Unsupported Profile Shapes

Cebal Americas ....G...... 203 845-6356
Norwalk (G-6110)
East Coast Precision Mfg LLC ....G...... 978 887-5920
Killingworth (G-3832)
Plastic Factory LLC ....G...... 203 908-3468
Bridgeport (G-874)
Polymedex Discovery Group Inc ....F...... 860 928-4102
Putnam (G-7059)
Putnam Plastics Corporation ....C...... 860 774-1559
Dayville (G-2071)
▲ Web Industries Hartford Inc ....E...... 860 779-3197
Dayville (G-2078)

3083 Plastic Laminated Plate & Sheet

▲ Alcat Incorporated ....E...... 203 878-0648
Milford (G-4446)
Aptar Inc ....G...... 860 489-6249
Torrington (G-8897)
◆ Beckson Manufacturing Inc ....E...... 203 366-3644
Bridgeport (G-709)
CT Composites & Marine Svc LLC ....G...... 860 282-0100
South Windsor (G-7738)
Cytec Industries Inc ....C...... 203 284-4334
Wallingford (G-9245)
Diba Industries Inc ....C...... 203 744-0773
Danbury (G-1795)
▲ Hicks and Otis Prints Inc ....E...... 203 846-2087
Norwalk (G-6200)
New Precision Technology LLC ....G...... 800 243-4565
Madison (G-3941)
▲ Panolam Industries Inc ....E...... 203 925-1556
Shelton (G-7522)
◆ Pioneer Plastics Corporation ....D...... 203 925-1556
Shelton (G-7527)
Polymedex Discovery Group Inc ....F...... 860 928-4102
Putnam (G-7059)
▲ Quality Name Plate Inc ....D...... 860 633-9495
East Glastonbury (G-2185)
The E J Davis Company ....E...... 203 239-5391
North Haven (G-5998)

3084 Plastic Pipe

Advanced Drainage Systems Inc ....E...... 860 529-8188
Rocky Hill (G-7219)
Monarch Plastic LLC ....F...... 860 653-2000
Granby (G-3182)
▲ Virginia Industries Inc ....G...... 860 571-3600
Rocky Hill (G-7271)

3085 Plastic Bottles

Ansa Company Inc ....F...... 203 687-1664
Norwalk (G-6070)
Consolidated Container LP ....G...... 860 224-9381
New Britain (G-4964)
Green Egg Design LLC ....G...... 860 541-5411
Hartford (G-3602)
▲ Mayborn Usa Inc ....F...... 781 269-7490
Stamford (G-8298)
▲ Packaging Concepts Assoc LLC .....G...... 860 489-0480
Torrington (G-8955)

Silgan Holdings Inc ....C...... 203 975-7110
Stamford (G-8421)

3086 Plastic Foam Prdts

Ansonia Plastics LLC ....D...... 203 736-5200
Ansonia (G-20)
▼ Claremont Sales Corporation ....E...... 860 349-4499
Durham (G-2143)
▲ Covit America Inc ....B...... 203 274-6791
Watertown (G-9696)
Duz Manufacturing Inc ....G...... 203 874-1032
Milford (G-4519)
Extreme Foam Insulations LLC ....G...... 203 522-2207
Bridgeport (G-767)
Fc Meyer Packaging LLC ....D...... 203 847-8500
Norwalk (G-6162)
Foam Plastics New England Inc ....G...... 203 758-6651
Waterbury (G-9481)
General Packaging Products Inc ....G...... 203 846-1340
Norwalk (G-6178)
▼ Gilman Corporation ....E...... 860 887-7080
Gilman (G-3000)
H-O Products Corporation ....E...... 860 379-9875
Winsted (G-10523)
Hhc LLC ....E...... 860 456-0677
Manchester (G-4027)
HI-Tech Packaging Inc ....D...... 203 378-2700
Stratford (G-8626)
Hopp Companies Inc ....F...... 800 889-8425
Newtown (G-5746)
Hydrofera LLC ....D...... 860 456-0677
Manchester (G-4030)
Madison Polymeric Engrg Inc ....E...... 203 488-4554
Branford (G-622)
Merrill Industries Inc ....E...... 860 871-1888
Ellington (G-2595)
New England Foam Products LLC ....E...... 860 524-0121
Hartford (G-3650)
Paxxus Inc ....E...... 860 242-0663
Bloomfield (G-461)
▲ Plastic Forming Company Inc ....E...... 203 397-1338
Woodbridge (G-10613)
▲ Preferred Foam Products Inc ....G...... 860 669-3626
Clinton (G-1518)
Reilly Foam Corp ....G...... 860 243-8200
Bloomfield (G-476)
Sealed Air Corporation ....C...... 203 791-3648
Danbury (G-1942)
Sonoco Prtective Solutions Inc ....E...... 860 928-7795
Putnam (G-7068)
Sprayfoampolymerscom LLC ....G...... 800 853-1577
Wilton (G-10333)
◆ Universal Foam Products LLC ....F...... 860 216-3015
Bloomfield (G-496)
Vibrascience Inc ....G...... 203 483-6113
Branford (G-666)

3087 Custom Compounding Of Purchased Plastic Resins

◆ Electric Cable Compounds Inc ....D...... 203 723-2590
Naugatuck (G-4879)
▲ Foster Corporation ....D...... 860 928-4102
Putnam (G-7042)
Neu Spclty Engineered Mtls LLC ....F...... 203 239-9629
North Haven (G-5967)
New Polymer Systems ....G...... 203 594-7774
New Canaan (G-5124)
Performance Compounding Inc ....G...... 860 599-5616
Pawcatuck (G-6722)
◆ Pioneer Plastics Corporation ....D...... 203 925-1556
Shelton (G-7527)
Visual Polymer Tech LLC ....G...... 603 488-5263
Canton (G-1328)

3088 Plastic Plumbing Fixtures

▲ Neoperl Inc ....D...... 203 756-8891
Waterbury (G-9557)
▲ New Resources Group Inc ....G...... 203 366-1000
Bridgeport (G-850)
Syn-Mar Products Inc ....F...... 860 872-8505
Ellington (G-2604)
Trumbull Recreation Supply Co ....G...... 860 429-6604
Willington (G-10260)
▲ World Link Imports-Exports ....G...... 203 792-0281
Danbury (G-1983)

3089 Plastic Prdts

AA & B Co ....G...... 203 933-9110
West Haven (G-9879)

Aba-PGT Employee Medical Trust .....G...... 860 649-4591
Manchester (G-3973)
Aba-PGT Inc ....C...... 860 649-4591
Manchester (G-3974)
Aba-PGT Inc ....G...... 860 872-2058
Vernon Rockville (G-9158)
▼ Able Coil and Electronics Co ....E...... 860 646-5686
Bolton (G-504)
Accumold Technologies Inc ....G...... 203 384-9256
Bridgeport (G-681)
Accurate Mold Company Inc ....G...... 860 301-1988
Cromwell (G-1684)
Ace Technical Plastics Inc ....G...... 860 278-2444
Hartford (G-3545)
Advance Mold & Mfg Inc ....F...... 860 432-5887
Manchester (G-3979)
Advance Mold Mfg Inc ....G...... 860 783-5024
Ellington (G-2572)
Aero-Med Molding Technologies ....F...... 203 735-2331
Ansonia (G-17)
All-Time Manufacturing Co Inc ....F...... 860 848-9258
Montville (G-4768)
Althor Products LLC ....G...... 860 386-6700
Windsor Locks (G-10472)
American Metaseal of Conn ....G...... 203 787-0281
Hamden (G-3414)
American Molded Products Inc ....F...... 203 333-0183
Bridgeport (G-694)
American Plastic Products Inc ....C...... 203 596-2410
Waterbury (G-9428)
Anderson David C & Assoc LLC ....F...... 860 749-7547
Enfield (G-2615)
Apex Machine Tool Company Inc ......D...... 860 677-2884
Cheshire (G-1353)
Aptargroup Inc ....B...... 203 377-8100
Stratford (G-8569)
▲ Architectural Supplements LLC ......F...... 203 591-5505
Waterbury (G-9433)
Armor Box Company LLC ....G...... 860 242-9981
Bloomfield (G-389)
Asti Company Inc ....G...... 860 482-2675
Torrington (G-8898)
Atlas Hobbing and Tool Co Inc ....F...... 860 870-9226
Vernon Rockville (G-9160)
Awm LLC ....D...... 860 386-1000
Windsor Locks (G-10473)
Balfor Industries Inc ....F...... 203 828-6473
Oxford (G-6645)
Bennice Molding Co ....G...... 203 440-2543
Meriden (G-4149)
Berry Global Inc ....G...... 413 529-7602
East Hampton (G-2256)
Better Molded Products Inc ....F...... 860 589-0066
Bristol (G-982)
Betz Tool Company Inc ....G...... 203 878-1187
Milford (G-4468)
Bey-Low Molds ....G...... 860 482-6561
Torrington (G-8904)
Bidwell Industrial Group Inc ....E...... 860 346-9283
Middletown (G-4325)
Bprex Halthcare Brookville Inc ....C...... 203 754-4141
Waterbury (G-9440)
Brighton & Hove Mold Ltd ....G...... 203 264-3013
Oxford (G-6647)
Burteck LLC ....F...... 860 206-8872
Windsor (G-10369)
▲ C Cowles & Company ....D...... 203 865-3117
North Haven (G-5916)
Calanca & Assoc LLC ....G...... 203 972-6344
New Canaan (G-5092)
Canevari Plastics Inc ....G...... 203 878-4319
Milford (G-4482)
▲ Carpin Manufacturing Inc ....D...... 203 574-2556
Waterbury (G-9446)
Celeste Industries Corporation ....G...... 860 278-9800
Hartford (G-3565)
CKS Packaging Inc ....C...... 203 729-0716
Naugatuck (G-4868)
▲ Clean Holdings LLC ....G...... 203 466-3365
East Haven (G-2418)
Clearly Clean Products LLC ....F...... 860 646-1040
South Windsor (G-7729)
Coastline Environmental LLC ....G...... 203 483-6898
North Branford (G-5831)
Coating Design Group Inc ....E...... 203 878-3663
Stratford (G-8596)
▲ Colts Plastics Company Inc ....C...... 860 774-2277
Dayville (G-2058)
▲ Connecticut Laminating Co Inc ......D...... 203 787-2184
New Haven (G-5260)

30 RUBBER AND MISCELLANEOUS PLASTICS PRODUCTS

Connecticut Tool Co Inc .... E 860 928-0565
  Putnam *(G-7035)*
Connecticut Valley Packg LLC .... G 860 693-0776
  Collinsville *(G-1592)*
Cool-It LLC .... G 203 284-4848
  Wallingford *(G-9239)*
▲ Cowles Products Company Inc .... D 203 865-3110
  North Haven *(G-5930)*
Create A Castle LLC .... G 203 648-3553
  New Milford *(G-5524)*
Crown Molding Etc LLC .... G 203 287-9424
  Hamden *(G-3434)*
CT Organizer LLC .... G 203 858-5824
  Westport *(G-10072)*
▼ Cultec Inc .... F 203 775-4416
  Brookfield *(G-1176)*
◆ Davis-Standard LLC .... B 860 599-1010
  Pawcatuck *(G-6707)*
▲ Delmar Products Inc .... F 860 828-6501
  Berlin *(G-176)*
Dfs In-Home Services .... G 845 405-6464
  Danbury *(G-1794)*
Division X Specialties LLC .... G 860 402-7736
  Vernon *(G-9137)*
Djs Mobile Marine & Power Eqp .... G 203 331-9010
  Bridgeport *(G-754)*
Doss Corporation .... G 860 721-7384
  Wethersfield *(G-10191)*
Dymotek Corporation .... G 800 788-1984
  Somers *(G-7656)*
◆ Dymotek Corporation .... G 860 875-2868
  Ellington *(G-2587)*
East Branch Engrg & Mfg Inc .... F 860 355-9661
  New Milford *(G-5529)*
East Spring Obsolete Auto .... G 203 266-5488
  Bethlehem *(G-370)*
▲ Edco Industries Inc .... F 203 333-8982
  Bridgeport *(G-760)*
Empire Tool LLC .... G 203 735-7467
  Derby *(G-2113)*
Ensign-Bickford Industries Inc .... E 860 658-4411
  Simsbury *(G-7622)*
▲ Ensinger Prcsion Cmponents Inc ..... D 860 928-7911
  Putnam *(G-7040)*
Entegris Inc .... B 800 766-2681
  Danbury *(G-1814)*
▲ F F Screw Products Inc .... E 860 621-4567
  Southington *(G-7921)*
◆ Farrel Corporation .... D 203 736-5500
  Ansonia *(G-34)*
Fiberglass Engr & Design Co .... G 203 265-1644
  Wallingford *(G-9266)*
Fimor North America Inc .... E 203 272-3219
  Cheshire *(G-1389)*
Fimor North America Inc .... G 941 921-5138
  Cheshire *(G-1390)*
▲ Flagship Converters Inc .... D 203 792-0034
  Danbury *(G-1826)*
Fluoropolymer Resources LLC .... G 860 423-7622
  East Hartford *(G-2326)*
Form-All Plastics Corporation .... G 203 634 1137
  Meriden *(G-4171)*
Fred Radford .... G 203 377-6189
  Trumbull *(G-9027)*
▲ Fsm Plasticoid Mfg Inc .... F 860 623-1361
  East Windsor *(G-2493)*
Ginter Hill Corporation .... G 203 293-4301
  Westport *(G-10089)*
GP Industries .... G 860 859-9938
  Taftville *(G-8741)*
GP Industries Ltd LLC .... G 860 350-5400
  New Milford *(G-5540)*
Hartford Seamless Gutters .... G 860 266-2516
  West Hartford *(G-9819)*
Hawk Integrated Plastics LLC .... F 203 337-0310
  Columbia *(G-1606)*
Heck D Tool LLC .... G 860 935-9274
  Thompson *(G-8834)*
Hexcel Corporation .... E 203 969-0666
  Stamford *(G-8233)*
Homar Molds & Models Co .... G 203 753-9017
  Waterbury *(G-9498)*
Hosokawa Micron Intl Inc .... E 860 828-0541
  Berlin *(G-188)*
Idemia Identity & SEC USA LLC .... G 860 529-2559
  Rocky Hill *(G-7249)*
Idex Health & Science LLC .... C 860 314-2880
  Bristol *(G-1050)*
Illinois Tool Works Inc .... E 203 435-2574
  Lakeville *(G-3844)*

Injectech Engineering LLC .... G 860 379-9781
  New Hartford *(G-5199)*
◆ Inline Plastics Corp .... C 203 924-5933
  Shelton *(G-7479)*
J POMfret& Assoc Inc .... G 860 691-2149
  East Lyme *(G-2467)*
▲ J&L Plastic Molding LLC .... G 203 265-6237
  Wallingford *(G-9292)*
Jarden Corporation .... E 203 845-5300
  Norwalk *(G-6218)*
Jarden Corporation .... G 203 264-9717
  Oxford *(G-6670)*
Jor Services LLC .... G 203 594-7774
  New Canaan *(G-5112)*
Joseph Organek .... G 860 342-1906
  Portland *(G-6962)*
K-Tec LLC .... G 860 283-8875
  Thomaston *(G-8795)*
Kensco Inc .... F 203 734-8827
  Ansonia *(G-44)*
Keytag1 .... G 203 873-0749
  Bridgeport *(G-817)*
▲ Kinamor Incorporated .... E 203 269-0380
  Wallingford *(G-9297)*
▲ Lacey Manufacturing Co LLC .... B 203 336-7427
  Bridgeport *(G-821)*
Lawrence Holdings Inc .... F 203 949-1600
  Wallingford *(G-9301)*
▲ Lehvoss North America LLC .... F 860 495-2046
  Pawcatuck *(G-6718)*
Lingol Corporation .... G 203 265-3608
  Wallingford *(G-9303)*
Lisern Enterprises Inc .... G 203 426-9079
  Sandy Hook *(G-7319)*
Little Bits Manufacturing Inc .... G 860 923-2772
  North Grosvenordale *(G-5889)*
Lorex Plastics Co Inc .... G 203 286-0020
  Norwalk *(G-6238)*
Manchester Molding and Mfg Co .... E 860 643-2141
  Manchester *(G-4052)*
▲ Marlborough Plastics Inc .... G 860 295-9124
  Marlborough *(G-4125)*
▲ Mbsw Inc .... D 860 243-0303
  West Hartford *(G-9835)*
◆ Mdm Products LLC .... F 203 877-7070
  Milford *(G-4576)*
Meriden Precision Plastics LLC .... G 203 235-3261
  Meriden *(G-4198)*
Merritt Extruder Corp .... E 203 230-8100
  Hamden *(G-3481)*
▲ Mohawk Tool and Die Mfg Co Inc .... F 203 367-2181
  Bridgeport *(G-842)*
Mold Threads Inc .... G 203 483-1420
  Branford *(G-627)*
Molding Technologies LLC .... G 860 395-3230
  Old Saybrook *(G-6558)*
Monarch Plastic LLC .... F 860 653-2000
  Granby *(G-3112)*
▲ MPS Plastics Incorporated .... E 860 295-1161
  Marlborough *(G-4127)*
Nelcote Inc .... G 203 509-5247
  Waterbury *(G-9555)*
▲ Nevamar Company LLC .... B 203 925-1556
  Shelton *(G-7508)*
▲ New Star Mold Inc .... G 203 567-7760
  Bantam *(G-125)*
Newhart Plastics Inc .... G 203 877-5367
  Milford *(G-4591)*
Orban Designs LLC .... G 860 605-7975
  Torrington *(G-8954)*
Orbit Design LLC .... F 203 393-0171
  Meriden *(G-4214)*
Packaging and Crating Tech LLC ...... G 203 759-1799
  Waterbury *(G-9572)*
▲ Panolam Industries Inc .... E 203 925-1556
  Shelton *(G-7522)*
▲ Panolam Industries Intl Inc .... E 203 925-1556
  Shelton *(G-7523)*
Paragon Products Inc .... G 860 388-1363
  Old Saybrook *(G-6563)*
Pastanch LLC .... E 203 720-9478
  Naugatuck *(G-4909)*
Pel Associates LLC .... G 860 446-9921
  Groton *(G-3305)*
Phillips-Moldex Company .... E 860 928-0401
  Putnam *(G-7058)*
Plasco LLC .... G 860 217-1187
  Simsbury *(G-7640)*
▲ Plastic Design Intl Inc .... E 860 632-2001
  Middletown *(G-4393)*

▲ Plastic Forming Company Inc .... E 203 397-1338
  Woodbridge *(G-10613)*
Plastic Molding Technology .... G 203 881-1811
  Seymour *(G-7361)*
Plastic Solutions LLC .... G 203 266-5675
  Bethlehem *(G-375)*
▲ Plasticoid Manufacturing Inc .... E 860 623-1361
  East Windsor *(G-2514)*
Plastics and Concepts Conn Inc .... F 860 657-9655
  Glastonbury *(G-3072)*
Plastics Techniques .... G 203 335-8048
  Fairfield *(G-2829)*
▲ Polymer Engineered Pdts Inc .... D 203 324-3737
  Stamford *(G-8367)*
▲ Polymeric Converting LLC .... E 860 623-1335
  Enfield *(G-2678)*
Polymold Corp .... G 203 272-2622
  Cheshire *(G-1430)*
▲ Polytronics Corporation .... G 860 683-2442
  Windsor *(G-10421)*
Precision Engineered Pdts LLC .... E 203 265-3299
  Wallingford *(G-9341)*
Precision Plastic Fab .... G 203 775-7047
  Brookfield *(G-1215)*
▲ Precision Plastic Products Inc .... F 860 342-2233
  Portland *(G-6969)*
Precision Plastics Inc .... G 203 775-7047
  Brookfield *(G-1216)*
Prospect Products Incorporated .... E 203 666-0323
  Newington *(G-5698)*
Prototype Plastic Mold Co Inc .... E 203 632-2800
  Middletown *(G-4398)*
◆ Pucuda Inc .... F 860 526-8004
  Madison *(G-3949)*
Quatum Inc .... G 860 666-3464
  Hartford *(G-3673)*
Quest Plastics Inc .... F 860 489-1404
  Torrington *(G-8962)*
Rapid Slicer LLC .... G 203 610-3673
  Shelton *(G-7543)*
Reblee Inc .... G 203 372-3338
  Trumbull *(G-9063)*
Recognition Inc .... G 860 659-8629
  Glastonbury *(G-3079)*
RES-Tech Corporation .... D 860 828-1504
  Berlin *(G-216)*
▲ Rogers Manufacturing Company ..... D 860 346-8648
  Rockfall *(G-7215)*
Romano Construction LLC .... G 203 223-3136
  Southbury *(G-7877)*
Saltwater Usa LLC .... G 860 899-9240
  Bloomfield *(G-485)*
Savetime Corporation .... F 203 382-2991
  Bridgeport *(G-897)*
▲ Scan Tool & Mold Inc .... E 203 459-4950
  Trumbull *(G-9070)*
▲ Schaeffler Aerospace USA Corp ..... B 203 744-2211
  Danbury *(G-1936)*
▲ Seitz LLC .... E 860 489-0476
  Torrington *(G-8969)*
Select Plastics LLC .... G 203 866-3767
  Norwalk *(G-6342)*
Selectives LLC .... G 860 585-1956
  Thomaston *(G-8805)*
Shaeffer Plastic Mfg Corp .... G 860 537-5524
  Colchester *(G-1575)*
◆ Siemon Company .... A 860 945-4200
  Watertown *(G-9734)*
◆ Siftex Equipment Company .... E 860 289-8779
  South Windsor *(G-7821)*
Signs Unlimited Inc .... G 203 734-7446
  Derby *(G-2126)*
Silgan Holdings Inc .... C 203 975-7110
  Stamford *(G-8421)*
Silgan Plastics LLC .... C 860 526-6300
  Deep River *(G-2100)*
Somerset Plastics Company .... E 860 635-1601
  Middletown *(G-4421)*
Sound View Plastics LLC .... G 860 322-4139
  Deep River *(G-2102)*
Southpack LLC .... E 860 224-2242
  New Britain *(G-5057)*
Spartech LLC .... C 203 327-6010
  Stamford *(G-8432)*
Specialized Marketing Intl Inc .... G 860 779-3264
  Dayville *(G-2074)*
Specialty Sintered .... G 860 263-8332
  Hartford *(G-3691)*
Spectrum Marking Materials LLC ..... G 860 533-9533
  Glastonbury *(G-3083)*

Standard Washer & Mat Inc ... E ... 860 643-5125
Manchester *(G-4094)*

▲ Stelray Plastic Products Inc ... E ... 203 735-2331
Ansonia *(G-52)*

Summit Plastics LLC ... G ... 860 832-9730
New Britain *(G-5067)*

▲ Super Seal Corp ... F ... 203 378-5015
Stratford *(G-8690)*

Swpc Plastics LLC ... C ... 860 526-3200
Deep River *(G-2103)*

Technical Industries Inc ... D ... 860 489-2160
Torrington *(G-8976)*

▲ Technology Plastics LLC ... F ... 806 583-1590
Terryville *(G-8774)*

▲ Tops Manufacturing Co Inc ... G ... 203 655-9367
Darien *(G-2047)*

Trento Group LLC ... G ... 860 623-1361
East Windsor *(G-2528)*

Trinity Polymers LLC ... G ... 860 321-7209
Farmington *(G-2966)*

TWC Trans World Consulting ... G ... 860 668-5108
Windsor Locks *(G-10499)*

United Plastics Technologies ... F ... 860 224-1110
New Britain *(G-5079)*

Upc LLC ... G ... 877 466-1137
Meriden *(G-4261)*

▲ Vanguard Plastics Corporation ... E ... 860 628-4736
Southington *(G-7992)*

Vision Technical Molding ... G ... 860 783-5050
Manchester *(G-4105)*

Vivan Trucking LLC ... G ... 573 486-2811
Hartford *(G-3713)*

Watertown Plastics Inc ... E ... 860 274-7535
Watertown *(G-9749)*

Wayside Fence Co ... G ... 860 594-1090
Newington *(G-5722)*

Wepco Plastics Inc ... E ... 860 349-3407
Middlefield *(G-4309)*

Wilkinson Tool & Die Co ... G ... 860 599-5821
North Stonington *(G-6032)*

31 LEATHER AND LEATHER PRODUCTS

3111 Leather Tanning & Finishing

Buestan Usa LLC ... G ... 203 954-8889
Ansonia *(G-25)*

Cuero Operating ... G ... 203 253-8651
Westport *(G-10073)*

Cutter & Drill Parts LLC ... G ... 203 483-0876
North Branford *(G-5833)*

MGI usa Inc ... G ... 203 312-1200
Danbury *(G-1883)*

Patricia Poke ... G ... 860 354-4193
New Milford *(G-5580)*

Sean Christian Leather LLC ... G ... 787 690-7039
West Hartford *(G-9854)*

▲ Veto Pro Pac LLC ... G ... 203 847-0297
Norwalk *(G-6388)*

3131 Boot & Shoe Cut Stock & Findings

687 State Street Assoc LLC ... G ... 203 915-8469
North Haven *(G-5893)*

Bean Counters ... G ... 860 404-2930
Farmington *(G-2883)*

Catskill Gran Countertops Inc ... F ... 860 667-1555
Newington *(G-5637)*

Darlene Ann Miconi ... G ... 203 245-4127
Madison *(G-3917)*

Little T Qarter Midget CLB Inc ... G ... 860 823-7258
Thompson *(G-8839)*

Little T Quarter Midget Club ... G ... 860 885-1376
Oakdale *(G-6444)*

Middle Quarter Animal Hospital ... G ... 203 263-4772
Woodbury *(G-10643)*

Pace Chiropractic Wellness Ctr ... G ... 203 281-9635
Hamden *(G-3493)*

Quarter Mile ... G ... 203 438-9718
Ridgefield *(G-7165)*

Rand Newco LLC ... G ... 203 699-9125
Cheshire *(G-1436)*

Rand Whitney ... G ... 860 354-6063
New Milford *(G-5583)*

Top Source Inc ... G ... 203 753-6490
Waterbury *(G-9614)*

Wbcb Ventures LLC ... G ... 860 383-4203
Preston *(G-6991)*

3143 Men's Footwear, Exc Athletic

◆ B H Shoe Holdings Inc ... E ... 203 661-2424
Greenwich *(G-3127)*

Buestan Usa LLC ... G ... 203 954-8889
Ansonia *(G-25)*

▲ Fisher Footwear LLC ... F ... 203 302-2800
Greenwich *(G-3161)*

◆ HH Brown Shoe Company Inc ... E ... 203 661-2424
Greenwich *(G-3177)*

Kaufman Enterprises Inc ... F ... 203 777-2396
New Haven *(G-5307)*

▲ Mbf Holdings LLC ... F ... 203 302-2812
Greenwich *(G-3200)*

Vcs Group LLC ... G ... 203 413-6500
Greenwich *(G-3253)*

3144 Women's Footwear, Exc Athletic

▲ Aj Casey LLC ... G ... 203 226-5961
Norwalk *(G-6065)*

Buestan Usa LLC ... G ... 203 954-8889
Ansonia *(G-25)*

Cecelia New York LLC ... G ... 917 392-4536
Darien *(G-2010)*

▲ Dooney & Bourke Inc ... E ... 203 853-7515
Norwalk *(G-6146)*

▲ Fisher Footwear LLC ... F ... 203 302-2800
Greenwich *(G-3161)*

▲ Fisher Sigerson Morrison LLC ... E ... 203 302-2800
Greenwich *(G-3162)*

◆ HH Brown Shoe Company Inc ... E ... 203 661-2424
Greenwich *(G-3177)*

Kaufman Enterprises Inc ... F ... 203 777-2396
New Haven *(G-5307)*

Moda LLC ... G ... 203 302-2800
Greenwich *(G-3204)*

3149 Footwear, NEC

Buestan Usa LLC ... G ... 203 954-8889
Ansonia *(G-25)*

Dsw Inc ... F ... 860 644-6200
Manchester *(G-4012)*

Dsw Inc ... F ... 203 985-8241
North Haven *(G-5933)*

Kaufman Enterprises Inc ... F ... 203 777-2396
New Haven *(G-5307)*

3161 Luggage

2 Girl A Trunk ... G ... 203 762-0360
Wilton *(G-10262)*

Armor Box Company LLC ... G ... 860 242-9981
Bloomfield *(G-389)*

▲ Calzone Ltd ... E ... 203 367-5766
Bridgeport *(G-728)*

▲ Case Concepts Intl LLC ... F ... 203 883-8602
Stamford *(G-8130)*

▲ Commercial Sewing Inc ... C ... 860 482-5509
Torrington *(G-8913)*

▲ Dooney & Bourke Inc ... E ... 203 853-7515
Norwalk *(G-6146)*

▲ Fabrique Ltd ... F ... 203 481-5400
Branford *(G-593)*

Leader Management Corp ... G ... 860 643-4445
Bolton *(G-514)*

Leatherby ... G ... 860 658-6166
Weatogue *(G-9757)*

Manup LLC ... G ... 203 588-9861
Norwalk *(G-6246)*

Marc Johnson ... G ... 860 774-3315
Danielson *(G-1998)*

Michaels Finest LLC ... G ... 860 223-7671
New Britain *(G-5017)*

Prima Dona LLC ... G ... 203 820-9327
Bridgeport *(G-879)*

Tack Trunk ... G ... 203 880-9972
Monroe *(G-4754)*

Taylors Luggage Inc ... G ... 203 966-9961
New Canaan *(G-5150)*

3171 Handbags & Purses

Coach Inc ... F ... 203 372-0208
Trumbull *(G-9012)*

Dooney & Bourke ... G ... 203 795-3131
Orange *(G-6597)*

▲ Dooney & Bourke Inc ... E ... 203 853-7515
Norwalk *(G-6146)*

Its In Bag LLC ... G ... 860 229-6672
New Britain *(G-5004)*

Leatherby ... G ... 860 658-6166
Weatogue *(G-9757)*

Patricia Beavers ... G ... 860 233-4071
Hartford *(G-3662)*

3172 Personal Leather Goods

Boccelli ... G ... 860 862-9300
Uncasville *(G-9096)*

◆ Brockway Ferry Corporation ... G ... 860 767-8231
Essex *(G-2713)*

▲ Dooney & Bourke Inc ... E ... 203 853-7515
Norwalk *(G-6146)*

Ecoflik LLC ... G ... 860 460-4419
Old Lyme *(G-6507)*

Leatherby ... G ... 860 658-6166
Weatogue *(G-9757)*

Mayan Corporation ... F ... 203 854-4711
Norwalk *(G-6251)*

Old Leather Wallet Company LLC ... G ... 860 350-9868
Roxbury *(G-7280)*

▲ Putu LLC ... G ... 203 594-9700
New Canaan *(G-5136)*

Waterbury Leatherworks Co ... F ... 203 755-7789
Waterbury *(G-9627)*

3199 Leather Goods, NEC

▲ A X M S Inc ... G ... 203 263-5046
Woodbury *(G-10622)*

◆ Brockway Ferry Corporation ... G ... 860 767-8231
Essex *(G-2713)*

Can Straps LLC ... G ... 203 281-7333
Hamden *(G-3423)*

Equestrian Collection ... G ... 860 749-2964
Somers *(G-7657)*

Fiddle Horse Farm LLC ... G ... 203 557-3285
Westport *(G-10080)*

Grand View Stable LLC ... G ... 860 228-3791
Columbia *(G-1605)*

Leatherworks ... G ... 860 658-6178
Weatogue *(G-9758)*

Left Handed Holsters ... G ... 203 488-9654
Branford *(G-618)*

Mr Connecticut Leather Inc ... G ... 203 230-2166
Hamden *(G-3485)*

Pauls Leather Co ... G ... 203 871-7238
Branford *(G-632)*

▲ The Smith Worthington Sad Co ... G ... 860 527-9117
Hartford *(G-3702)*

Tillys Natural Blend LLC ... G ... 203 270-8406
Newtown *(G-5792)*

Triumph Consulting ... G ... 860 263-8335
Hartford *(G-3706)*

VO Leather Inc ... G ... 203 345-8442
Stratford *(G-8703)*

32 STONE, CLAY, GLASS, AND CONCRETE PRODUCTS

3211 Flat Glass

Glass Design Studio ... G ... 860 651-4233
Simsbury *(G-7627)*

▲ Insulpane Connecticut Inc ... D ... 800 922-3248
Hamden *(G-3465)*

Juanos Glass LLC ... G ... 203 449-5378
Bridgeport *(G-811)*

Laminated Glass Solutions LLC ... G ... 203 250-1025
Cheshire *(G-1404)*

Marilyn Gehring ... G ... 203 358-8700
Stamford *(G-8296)*

Onpoint Connections ... G ... 860 253-0489
Enfield *(G-2673)*

Paul Petrushonis Staind Glss ... G ... 203 878-0163
Milford *(G-4604)*

3221 Glass Containers

▲ Emhart Glass Manufacturing Inc ... E ... 860 298-7340
Windsor *(G-10384)*

Matthew Fisel ND ... G ... 203 453-0122
Guilford *(G-3371)*

Palmer Deep Draw Stamping LLC ... G ... 860 880-8022
Thomaston *(G-8800)*

3229 Pressed & Blown Glassware, NEC

Accuratus Optics Tech LLC ... G ... 213 344-9397
Cheshire *(G-1346)*

Artist and Craftsman ... G ... 203 330-0459
Bridgeport *(G-703)*

Bovano Industries Incorporated ... F ... 203 272-3208
Cheshire *(G-1361)*

Employee Codes: A=Over 500 employees, B=251-500
C=101-250, D=51-100, E=20-50, F=10-19, G=1-9
2020 Harris Connecticut
Manufacturers Directory
413

Bristow Studio Glass..........G....... 860 364-1670
Sharon *(G-7376)*
C C D Center..........G....... 203 348-0052
Stamford *(G-8123)*
Dbo Home LLC..........G....... 860 364-6008
Sharon *(G-7377)*
Fair Haven Glass..........G....... 203 773-3040
New Haven *(G-5280)*
Fiberglass Repairs &..........G....... 860 628-4962
Southington *(G-7923)*
Fiberoptics Technology Inc..........D....... 860 928-0443
Pomfret *(G-6932)*
▲ Flabeg Technical Glass US Corp......E....... 203 729-5227
Naugatuck *(G-4880)*
Flabeg US Holding Inc..........G....... 203 729-5227
Naugatuck *(G-4881)*
Fluid Coating Technology Inc..........G....... 860 963-2505
Putnam *(G-7041)*
G Schoepferinc..........F....... 203 250-7794
Cheshire *(G-1391)*
Greenwood Glass..........G....... 860 738-9464
Riverton *(G-7207)*
Greywall Inc..........G....... 860 267-6177
East Hampton *(G-2262)*
Incjet Inc..........F....... 860 823-3090
Norwich *(G-6417)*
Koninklijke Philips Elec NV..........F....... 860 886-2621
Norwich *(G-6421)*
Liberty Glass and Met Inds Inc..........E....... 860 923-3623
North Grosvenordale *(G-5888)*
Magic Industries Inc..........F....... 860 949-8380
Bozrah *(G-527)*
Marilyn Gehring..........G....... 203 358-8700
Stamford *(G-8296)*
▲ Medelco Inc..........G....... 203 275-8070
Bridgeport *(G-836)*
▲ Nufern..........D....... 860 408-5000
East Granby *(G-2220)*
O E M Controls Inc..........C....... 203 929-8431
Shelton *(G-7517)*
Periodic Tableware LLC..........F....... 310 428-4250
Shelton *(G-7524)*
Pioneer Optics Company Inc..........F....... 860 286-0071
Bloomfield *(G-465)*
PQ Optics..........G....... 860 582-2636
Bristol *(G-1094)*
Schaeffler Aerospace USA Corp..........D....... 860 379-7558
Winsted *(G-10534)*
Simon Pearce US Inc..........G....... 203 861-0780
Greenwich *(G-3236)*
▲ Tops Manufacturing Co Inc..........G....... 203 655-9367
Darien *(G-2047)*
Vitro Technology Ltd..........G....... 203 783-9566
Milford *(G-4676)*
Vogel Optics LLC..........G....... 203 925-9619
Shelton *(G-7582)*
Weekend Kitchen..........G....... 860 767-1010
Essex *(G-2737)*
West Rock Art Glass Inc..........G....... 203 488-8225
Branford *(G-671)*
▲ Whalley Glass Company..........D....... 203 735-9388
Derby *(G-2131)*
Woolworks Ltd..........G....... 860 963-1228
Putnam *(G-7081)*
Zsiba & Smolover Ltd..........G....... 860 354-5221
New Milford *(G-5610)*

3231 Glass Prdts Made Of Purchased Glass

Advanced Glass Design LLC..........G....... 860 426-0401
Plantsville *(G-6882)*
Ark Innovations LLC..........G....... 860 674-8800
Farmington *(G-2878)*
Baron Technology Inc..........E....... 203 452-0515
Trumbull *(G-9003)*
Bovano Industries Incorporated..........F....... 203 272-3208
Cheshire *(G-1361)*
Connectcut Tmpred GL Dstrs LLC..........G....... 860 379-5670
Winsted *(G-10514)*
▲ Flabeg Technical Glass US Corp......E....... 203 729-5227
Naugatuck *(G-4880)*
Garden Glass LLC..........G....... 203 330-8789
Fairfield *(G-2789)*
Glass Industries America LLC..........F....... 203 269-6700
Wallingford *(G-9276)*
Glass Master LLC..........G....... 860 658-0040
Simsbury *(G-7628)*
Glass Source LLC..........G....... 203 924-4368
Shelton *(G-7449)*
Glassworks..........G....... 860 673-1250
New Hartford *(G-5192)*
Legacy Corp..........G....... 860 236-6500
West Hartford *(G-9827)*
Marilyn Gehring..........G....... 203 358-8700
Stamford *(G-8296)*
National Picture Frame Inc..........G....... 860 774-5668
Brooklyn *(G-1251)*
Opera Glass Networks LLC..........G....... 203 919-2777
Norwalk *(G-6286)*
Peleganos Stained Glass Studio..........G....... 203 272-8067
Cheshire *(G-1428)*
Periodic Tableware LLC..........F....... 310 428-4250
Shelton *(G-7524)*
Renaissance Studio Inc..........G....... 203 226-9674
Westport *(G-10148)*
▲ U S Glass Distributors Inc..........E....... 860 741-3658
Enfield *(G-2703)*
Vijon Studios Inc..........G....... 860 399-7440
Old Saybrook *(G-6576)*

3241 Cement, Hydraulic

Beard Concrete Co Derby Inc..........F....... 203 735-4641
Derby *(G-2109)*
Gratton Concrete Sawingdri..........G....... 860 974-9127
Pomfret Center *(G-6938)*
Lafarge North America Inc..........G....... 203 468-6068
New Haven *(G-5314)*
McInnis USA Inc..........E....... 203 890-9950
Stamford *(G-8299)*

3251 Brick & Structural Clay Tile

K & G Corp..........F....... 860 643-1133
Manchester *(G-4041)*
Protiviti Inc..........G....... 203 371-5542
Fairfield *(G-2832)*
Redland Brick Inc..........C....... 860 528-1311
South Windsor *(G-7818)*

3253 Ceramic Tile

Arnold Trauth..........G....... 203 371-5624
Easton *(G-2546)*
Aspecta..........G....... 855 400-7732
Norwalk *(G-6077)*
Brass City Tile Designs LLC..........G....... 203 597-8764
Waterbury *(G-9443)*
Distributors of Standard Tile..........G....... 860 439-0627
New London *(G-5468)*
Michael Hurlburt..........G....... 860 745-0681
Enfield *(G-2660)*
Mohawk Industries Inc..........C....... 203 739-0260
Danbury *(G-1888)*
Painted Tiles Co..........G....... 860 658-7218
Simsbury *(G-7638)*
Porcelanosa New York Inc..........F....... 203 698-7618
Riverside *(G-7199)*
Quemere International LLC..........G....... 914 934-8366
Middletown *(G-4399)*

3255 Clay Refractories

Bonsal American Inc..........E....... 860 824-7733
Canaan *(G-1283)*
Harbisonwalker Intl Inc..........G....... 203 934-7960
West Haven *(G-9914)*
Redland Brick Inc..........C....... 860 528-1311
South Windsor *(G-7818)*
Zampell Refractories Inc..........F....... 860 564-2883
Plainfield *(G-6757)*

3259 Structural Clay Prdts, NEC

Eljen Corporation..........E....... 860 610-0426
East Hartford *(G-2321)*

3261 China Plumbing Fixtures & Fittings

Home Sweeter HM Kit & Bath LLC..........G....... 203 948-6482
Bethel *(G-309)*
Painted Tiles Co..........G....... 860 658-7218
Simsbury *(G-7638)*
Syn-Mar Products Inc..........F....... 860 872-8505
Ellington *(G-2604)*
◆ Water Works..........G....... 203 546-6000
Danbury *(G-1976)*

3263 Earthenware, Whiteware, Table & Kitchen Articles

Cornwall Bridge Pottery Inc..........G....... 860 672-6545
Warren *(G-9407)*
Express Cntertops Kit Flrg LLC..........G....... 203 283-4909
Orange *(G-6599)*

3264 Porcelain Electrical Splys

Coorstek Inc..........E....... 860 653-8071
East Granby *(G-2200)*
Newco Condenser Inc..........G....... 475 882-4000
Shelton *(G-7510)*

3269 Pottery Prdts, NEC

CJ Ceramics and More LLC..........G....... 203 246-2798
Darien *(G-2013)*
Company of Craftsmen..........G....... 860 536-4189
Mystic *(G-4808)*
Cornwall Bridge Pottery Inc..........G....... 860 672-6545
Warren *(G-9407)*
David Christian Ceramics LLC..........G....... 203 758-1532
Middlebury *(G-4278)*
Griffith & Parrott..........G....... 203 245-7837
Madison *(G-3924)*
Jean Elton Studios LLC..........G....... 917 287-0480
Fairfield *(G-2800)*
Jessica Howard Ceramics..........G....... 646 295-4778
Fairfield *(G-2801)*
Lilywork Ceramic Ornament LLC..........G....... 215 859-8753
Pawcatuck *(G-6719)*
▲ Mc Cann Bros Inc..........E....... 203 335-8630
Monroe *(G-4734)*
One Pair of Hands..........G....... 860 364-0027
Sharon *(G-7381)*
Salem Stone Design Inc..........F....... 860 439-1234
Waterford *(G-9668)*
▲ Tonmar LLC..........G....... 860 974-3714
Pomfret Center *(G-6947)*
Visionage..........G....... 203 787-0037
New Haven *(G-5429)*

3271 Concrete Block & Brick

Berlin Industries LLC..........G....... 860 819-9997
Berlin *(G-163)*
Central CT Snow LLC..........G....... 860 467-3107
East Hampton *(G-2260)*
City Cement Block-Del Corp Inc..........G....... 203 334-0702
Bridgeport *(G-734)*
Connecticut Concrete Form Inc..........F....... 860 674-1314
Farmington *(G-2892)*
Delvento Inc..........F....... 203 371-7279
Bridgeport *(G-748)*
Hatch and Bailey Company..........E....... 203 866-5515
Norwalk *(G-6193)*
Kobyluck Ready-Mix Inc..........F....... 860 444-9604
Waterford *(G-9657)*
Laydon Industries LLC..........D....... 203 562-7283
New Haven *(G-5317)*
Messiah Development LLC..........G....... 203 368-2405
Bridgeport *(G-837)*
New Milford Block & Supply..........F....... 860 355-1101
New Milford *(G-5568)*
Rahzel Enterprize LLC..........G....... 475 449-6561
Norwalk *(G-6315)*
Rockland Music LLC..........G....... 203 779-5299
Madison *(G-3952)*
Svl LLC..........G....... 860 819-9929
Avon *(G-116)*
Westbrook Con Block Co Inc..........E....... 860 399-6201
Westbrook *(G-10015)*

3272 Concrete Prdts

Advanced Drainage Systems Inc..........E....... 860 529-8188
Rocky Hill *(G-7219)*
▲ Arrow Concrete Products Inc..........E....... 860 653-5063
Granby *(G-3106)*
Artista Studio Monument..........G....... 203 333-9224
Bridgeport *(G-704)*
Atlantic Pipe Corporation..........D....... 860 747-5557
Plainville *(G-6772)*
Bella Pietra LLC..........G....... 203 655-1322
Darien *(G-2007)*
▲ Blakeslee Prestress Inc..........B....... 203 315-7090
Branford *(G-561)*
Bonsal American Inc..........G....... 860 824-7733
Canaan *(G-1282)*
Bonsal American Inc..........E....... 860 824-7733
Canaan *(G-1283)*
Bridgeport Burial Vault Co..........G....... 203 375-7375
Stratford *(G-8587)*
Capitol City Burial Vaults..........G....... 860 953-1060
West Hartford *(G-9785)*
Carpet Products..........G....... 860 278-6160
Hartford *(G-3563)*
Concrete Products..........G....... 860 423-4144
North Windham *(G-6037)*

SIC SECTION

32 STONE, CLAY, GLASS, AND CONCRETE PRODUCTS

Connecticut Precast Corp ....E..... 203 268-8688
Monroe (G-4705)
Coreslab Structures Conn Inc ....D..... 860 283-8281
Thomaston (G-8786)
▼ Dalton Enterprises Inc ....D..... 203 272-3221
Cheshire (G-1379)
David Shuck 860 434-8562
Old Lyme (G-6503)
◆ Dawn Enterprises LLC ....G..... 860 646-8200
Manchester (G-4004)
Direct Sales LLC ....G..... 203 371-2373
Fairfield (G-2774)
Eastern Precast Company Inc ....E..... 203 775-0230
Brookfield (G-1186)
Elm-Cap Industries Inc ....E..... 860 953-1060
West Hartford (G-9808)
Essex Concrete Products Inc 860 767-1768
Essex (G-2717)
Forterra Pipe & Precast LLC ....F..... 860 564-9000
Wauregan (G-9753)
Granite Hill Equity 203 801-4396
New Canaan (G-5106)
J B Concrete Products Inc ....G..... 860 928-9365
Putnam (G-7048)
Jolley Precast Inc 860 774-9066
Danielson (G-1995)
Lane Construction Corporation ....C..... 203 235-3351
Cheshire (G-1405)
Lane Industries Incorporated ....G..... 203 235-3351
Cheshire (G-1406)
M & M Precast Corp ....F..... 203 743-5559
Danbury (G-1878)
Mono Crete Step Co of CT LLC ....F..... 203 748-8419
Bethel (G-328)
Mt Hope Cemetery Association ....G..... 860 643-4264
Vernon (G-9146)
New England Cstm Concrete ....G..... 203 924-2142
Ansonia (G-45)
New Milford Block & Supply ....F..... 860 355-1101
New Milford (G-5568)
Nteco Inc ....E..... 203 656-1154
Darien (G-2035)
O & G Industries Inc ....E..... 203 323-1111
Stamford (G-8336)
Oldcastle Infrastructure Inc ....E..... 860 673-3291
Avon (G-97)
▲ Pauls Marble Depot LLC ....F..... 203 978-0669
Stamford (G-8352)
Plasticrete ....G..... 203 250-6700
Cheshire (G-1429)
Platt Brothers & Company ....D..... 203 753-4194
Waterbury (G-9580)
Robert J Ballas ....G..... 203 746-0506
New Fairfield (G-5175)
Rogers Septic Tanks Inc ....F..... 203 259-9947
Westport (G-10151)
Safety Tek Inc ....G..... 203 785-1808
New Haven (G-5383)
Salin-Mpregilo US Holdings Inc ....G..... 203 439-2900
Cheshire (G-1441)
Signature Pet Memorials ....G..... 860 455-0118
Chaplin (G-1341)
Snaplok Systems LLC ....G..... 888 570-5407
Bloomfield (G-487)
Stephanie Mark ....G..... 203 329-7562
Stamford (G-8441)
Steven Rosenburg ....G..... 203 329-8798
Stamford (G-8443)
Stone Image Custom Concrete ....G..... 860 668-2434
Suffield (G-8736)
Superior Concrete Products LLC ....G..... 860 342-0186
Portland (G-6976)
Superior Products Distrs Inc ....F..... 203 250-6700
Cheshire (G-1454)
Techno Mtal Post Watertown LLC ...G..... 203 755-6403
Waterbury (G-9610)
Tontine Partners L P ....G..... 203 769-2000
Greenwich (G-3247)
Torrington Industries Inc ....G..... 860 489-9261
Torrington (G-8983)
Traditional Bath and Tile ....G..... 347 539-2088
Bridgeport (G-929)
Washington Concrete Products ....F..... 860 747-5242
Plainville (G-6876)
West Hartford Stone Mulch LLC ....G..... 860 461-7616
West Hartford (G-9872)
WJ Kettleworks LLC ....G..... 203 377-5000
Stratford (G-8710)

3273 Ready-Mixed Concrete

A Aiudi & Sons LLC ....G..... 860 747-5534
Plainville (G-6759)
Aiudi Concrete Inc ....G..... 860 399-9289
Westbrook (G-9990)
Armed & Ready Alarm System ....F..... 203 596-0327
Waterbury (G-9434)
B&R Sand and Gravel ....G..... 860 464-5099
Gales Ferry (G-2981)
Barnes Concrete Co Inc ....E..... 860 928-7242
Putnam (G-7031)
Beard Concrete Co Derby Inc 203 874-2533
Milford (G-4467)
Bonsal American Inc ....E..... 860 824-7733
Canaan (G-1283)
Builders Concrete East LLC ....E..... 860 456-4111
North Windham (G-6035)
Century Acquisition ....G..... 518 758-7229
Canaan (G-1284)
Devine Brothers Incorporated ....E..... 203 866-4421
Norwalk (G-6136)
Enfield Transit Mix Inc ....F..... 860 763-0864
Enfield (G-2640)
Essex Concrete Products Inc ....F..... 860 767-1768
Essex (G-2717)
▲ Federici Brands LLC ....F..... 203 762-7667
Wilton (G-10295)
▲ Five Star Products Inc ....E..... 203 336-7900
Shelton (G-7444)
Iffland Lumber Company Inc ....E..... 860 489-9218
Torrington (G-8935)
Joe Kaulback ....G..... 860 742-0434
Andover (G-11)
Mix n Match LLC ....G..... 203 227-9588
Westport (G-10122)
Mohican Valley Concrete Corp ....E..... 203 254-7133
Fairfield (G-2817)
Mohican Vly Sand & Grav Corp ....F..... 203 254-7133
Fairfield (G-2818)
O & G Industries Inc ....E..... 203 366-4586
Bridgeport (G-854)
O & G Industries Inc ....E..... 203 748-5694
Danbury (G-1897)
O & G Industries Inc ....E..... 203 323-1111
Stamford (G-8336)
Pick & Mix Corp ....G..... 860 521-1521
West Hartford (G-9845)
Robert Ready ....G..... 203 853-0051
Norwalk (G-6326)
Sega Ready Mix Incorporated ....F..... 860 354-3969
New Milford (G-5589)
Sega Ready Mix Incorporated ....G..... 203 465-1052
Waterbury (G-9599)
Sterling Materials LLC ....G..... 203 315-6619
Branford (G-657)
Sutton Mix Avenue LLC ....G..... 203 288-8482
Hamden (G-3516)
Suzio York Hill Companies ....G..... 888 789-4626
Meriden (G-4248)
The L Suzio Concrete Co Inc ....E..... 203 237-8421
Meriden (G-4253)
Thomas Concrete ....G..... 860 628-4957
Southington (G-7986)
Tilcon Connecticut Inc ....G..... 860 224-6010
Enfield (G-2701)
Tilcon Connecticut Inc ....G..... 860 342-1096
Portland (G-6978)
Tilcon Connecticut Inc ....E..... 860 844-7000
East Granby (G-2232)
▲ Tilcon Connecticut Inc ....D..... 860 224-6010
New Britain (G-5074)
Tilcon Inc ....B..... 860 223-3651
Newington (G-5713)
Torrington Industries Inc ....G..... 860 489-9261
Torrington (G-8983)
Windham Materials LLC ....D..... 860 456-4111
Willimantic (G-10241)
Windham Sand and Stone Inc ....D..... 860 643-5578
Manchester (G-4110)

3274 Lime

Pink Lemon Blue Lime LLC ....G..... 203 521-2464
Norwalk (G-6301)

3275 Gypsum Prdts

Proudfoot Company Inc ....F..... 203 459-0031
Monroe (G-4750)

3281 Cut Stone Prdts

American Stonecrafters Inc ....G..... 203 514-9725
Wallingford (G-9202)
Architectural Stone Group LLC ....G..... 203 494-5451
Bridgeport (G-700)
Central Marble & Granite LLC ....G..... 203 734-4644
Ansonia (G-28)
Connecticut Solid Surface LLC ....E..... 860 410-9800
Plainville (G-6791)
▲ Connecticut Stone Supplies Inc ....D..... 203 882-1000
Milford (G-4499)
Core Site Services LLC ....G..... 475 227-9026
New Haven (G-5264)
Creative Stone LLC ....F..... 203 624-1882
East Haven (G-2420)
Dan Beard Inc ....F..... 203 924-4346
Shelton (G-7427)
▲ Eastern Marble & Granite LLC ....F..... 203 882-8221
Milford (G-4522)
French River Mtls Thompson LLC ...G..... 860 450-9574
North Grosvenordale (G-5885)
Godfrey Cemetary Maint LLC ....G..... 203 858-4035
Sherman (G-7595)
▲ Granite & Kitchen Studio LLC ....G..... 860 290-4444
South Windsor (G-7764)
Granite LLC ....G..... 860 586-8132
Newington (G-5657)
Granitech LLC ....G..... 860 620-1733
Plantsville (G-6895)
Hartford Stone Works Inc ....G..... 860 684-7995
Willington (G-10249)
Interntonal MBL Gran Entps Inc ......G..... 860 296-0741
Hartford (G-3618)
▲ Kenneth Lynch & Sons Inc ....G..... 203 762-8363
Oxford (G-6671)
Kwik Kerb Masters LLC ....G..... 860 653-8102
Granby (G-3111)
La Pietra Thinstone Veneer ....G..... 203 775-6162
Brookfield (G-1201)
Luis Raimundi ....G..... 860 294-1468
Pleasant Valley (G-6924)
Marble & Granite Creations LLC ......G..... 860 350-1306
New Milford (G-5560)
Mark Dzidzk ....E..... 860 793-2767
Plainville (G-6839)
New England Gran Cabinets LLC ....G..... 860 310-2981
West Hartford (G-9837)
New England Materials LLC ....G..... 203 261-5500
Monroe (G-4743)
▲ New England Stone Inc ....F..... 203 876-8606
Milford (G-4590)
O & G Industries Inc ....F..... 203 729-4529
Beacon Falls (G-146)
O & G Industries Inc ....E..... 203 323-1111
Stamford (G-8336)
Ontra Stone Concepts LLC ....G..... 203 371-8225
Bridgeport (G-856)
Paul H Gesswein & Company Inc ...G..... 860 388-0652
Old Saybrook (G-6565)
▲ Pistritto Marble Imports Inc ....G..... 860 296-5263
Hartford (G-3664)
Salem Stone Design Inc ....F..... 860 439-1234
Waterford (G-9668)
Signature Pet Memorials ....G..... 860 455-0118
Chaplin (G-1341)
Skyline Quarry ....E..... 860 875-3580
Stafford Springs (G-8038)
▲ Stone Workshop LLC ....G..... 203 362-1144
Bridgeport (G-914)
Stoneage LLC ....G..... 203 926-1133
Shelton (G-7559)
Surface Plate Co ....G..... 860 652-8905
Glastonbury (G-3084)
T B Marble Granite LLC ....G..... 860 443-0817
Oakdale (G-6447)
Timeless Stone Inc ....G..... 860 242-3300
Bloomfield (G-492)
Tri LLC ....G..... 203 353-8418
Stamford (G-8475)
Valley Marble and Slate Corp ....G..... 860 354-3955
New Milford (G-5606)

3291 Abrasive Prdts

◆ Ahlstrom-Munksjo Nonwovens LLC .B..... 860 654-8300
Windsor Locks (G-10469)
Associated Chemicals & Abr Inc .....G..... 203 481-7235
Branford (G-548)
▲ Avery Abrasives Inc ....E..... 203 372-3513
Trumbull (G-9001)

32 STONE, CLAY, GLASS, AND CONCRETE PRODUCTS

▲ Chessco Industries Inc .... E 203 255-2804
  Westport *(G-10064)*
Magcor Inc .... G 203 445-0302
  Monroe *(G-4731)*
Precision Dip Coating LLC .... G 203 805-4564
  Waterbury *(G-9584)*
Pressure Blast Mfg Co Inc .... F 800 722-5278
  South Windsor *(G-7811)*
Syncote Chemical Company Inc .... G 203 426-5526
  Newtown *(G-5784)*
▲ Tcg Green Technologies Inc .... F 860 364-4694
  Sharon *(G-7384)*
Triatic Incorporated .... F 203 236-2298
  West Hartford *(G-9868)*
◆ United Abrasives Inc .... B 860 456-7131
  North Windham *(G-6040)*

3292 Asbestos products

Zero Hazard LLC .... G 860 561-9879
  Farmington *(G-2979)*

3295 Minerals & Earths: Ground Or Treated

Miyoshi America Inc .... F 860 779-3990
  Dayville *(G-2065)*
Miyoshi America Inc .... F 860 779-3990
  Dayville *(G-2066)*
▲ Polstal Corporation .... G 203 849-7788
  Wilton *(G-10320)*
Ultimate Growers LLC .... G 203 269-9027
  Wallingford *(G-9394)*

3296 Mineral Wool

Ecologic Energy Solutions LLC .... E 203 889-0505
  Stamford *(G-8192)*
Installed Building Pdts Inc .... G 203 889-0505
  Stamford *(G-8251)*
▲ Leek Building Products Inc .... G 203 853-3883
  Norwalk *(G-6232)*
Realtraps LLC .... G 203 294-4285
  Wallingford *(G-9349)*
The E J Davis Company .... E 203 239-5391
  North Haven *(G-5998)*
Zampell Refractories Inc .... F 860 564-2883
  Plainfield *(G-6757)*

3297 Nonclay Refractories

HI Temp Electric Company .... E 661 259-9225
  Andover *(G-9)*
Joshua LLC .... E 203 624-0180
  New Haven *(G-5304)*
Specialty Minerals Inc .... C 860 824-5435
  Canaan *(G-1292)*

3299 Nonmetallic Mineral Prdts, NEC

AK Stucco LLC .... G 860 832-9589
  New Britain *(G-4941)*
Assoc Stucco .... G 860 221-5791
  Burlington *(G-1260)*
Brico Inc .... C 203 693 0323
  Bloomfield *(G-400)*
Connecticut Stucco LLC .... G 203 237-9500
  Hamden *(G-3431)*
CT Moldings Inc .... G 203 612-4922
  Bridgeport *(G-740)*
David Colbert .... G 860 672-0064
  Cornwall Bridge *(G-1617)*
Evolution Stucco LLC .... G 203 507-3639
  Wallingford *(G-9260)*
John Canning & Co Ltd .... E 203 272-9868
  Cheshire *(G-1401)*
Kelby Stucco LLC .... G 203 527-9501
  Prospect *(G-7005)*
Kenneth M Champlin & Assoc Inc .... F 203 562-8400
  New Haven *(G-5308)*
Lexo Group .... G 203 847-8293
  Norwalk *(G-6233)*
Luckey LLC .... F 203 285-3819
  New Haven *(G-5322)*
Nelson Archtctural Restoration .... G 860 429-3830
  Willington *(G-10252)*
Northeast Stucco LLC .... G 860 770-9473
  New Britain *(G-5024)*
Opal Manning Company Inc .... G 203 292-6981
  Fairfield *(G-2825)*
Riccio Artifacts .... G 860 267-6023
  East Hampton *(G-2277)*
S & J Stucco LLC .... G 203 260-1457
  Monroe *(G-4751)*

Stucco Depot LLC .... G 203 430-9186
  Wallingford *(G-9378)*
Tim Prentice .... G 860 672-6728
  West Cornwall *(G-9765)*
U S Stucco LLC .... G 860 667-1935
  Newington *(G-5715)*
Vincent Masonry .... G 860 836-5916
  New Britain *(G-5081)*

33 PRIMARY METAL INDUSTRIES

3312 Blast Furnaces, Coke Ovens, Steel & Rolling Mills

90 Arch St LLC .... G 860 881-2063
  Hartford *(G-3541)*
▲ American Standard Company .... E 860 628-9643
  Southington *(G-7889)*
Applied Diamond Coatings LLC .... G 860 349-3133
  Durham *(G-2137)*
Arnio Welding LLC .... F 860 564-7696
  Central Village *(G-1335)*
ATI Flat Rlled Pdts Hldngs LLC .... F 203 756-7414
  Waterbury *(G-9435)*
ATI New England .... G 860 358-9698
  Cromwell *(G-1689)*
Ball & Roller Bearing Co LLC .... F 860 355-4161
  New Milford *(G-5508)*
Boudreaus Welding Co Inc .... E 860 774-2771
  Dayville *(G-2055)*
Brookfield Stainless LLC .... G 203 987-6773
  Brookfield *(G-1166)*
Bushwick Metals LLC .... G 203 630-2459
  Meriden *(G-4152)*
▲ Ccr Products LLC .... E 860 953-0499
  West Hartford *(G-9786)*
▲ CMI Specialty Products Inc .... F 860 585-0409
  Bristol *(G-1003)*
DRM Associates LLC .... G 860 583-7744
  Bristol *(G-1020)*
Dufrane Nuclear Shielding Inc .... F 860 379-2318
  Winsted *(G-10516)*
Everything 2 Wheels LLC .... G 860 225-2453
  New Britain *(G-4986)*
Gerdau Ameristeel US Inc .... G 860 351-9029
  Plainville *(G-6817)*
H&A Detail On Wheels .... G 203 354-8845
  Norwalk *(G-6191)*
Industrial Flame Cutting Inc .... G 203 723-4897
  Beacon Falls *(G-136)*
J J Ryan Corporation .... C 860 628-0393
  Plantsville *(G-6897)*
Jo Vek Tool and Die Mfg Co .... G 203 755-1884
  Waterbury *(G-9511)*
Kimchuk Incorporated .... F 203 790-7800
  Danbury *(G-1868)*
Mark Tool Co .... G 860 673-5039
  Avon *(G-92)*
McCann Sales Inc .... G 860 614-0992
  West Simsbury *(G-9980)*
Microdyne Technologies .... G 860 747-9473
  Plainville *(G-6844)*
Mills On Wheels .... G 860 705-2903
  Norwich *(G-6423)*
Mott Corporation .... C 800 289-6688
  Farmington *(G-2932)*
National Integrated Inds Inc .... C 860 677-7995
  Farmington *(G-2933)*
▲ Nucor Steel Connecticut Inc .... C 203 265-0615
  Wallingford *(G-9330)*
Paoletti Fence Company Inc .... G 860 296-0396
  Hartford *(G-3660)*
Pequonnock Ironworks Inc .... F 203 336-2178
  Bridgeport *(G-7427)*
Portland Slitting Co Inc .... G 860 342-1500
  Portland *(G-6968)*
▲ Program Dynamix Inc .... G 860 282-0695
  South Windsor *(G-7813)*
Rcd LLC .... G 203 712-1900
  Shelton *(G-7544)*
▲ Redifoils LLC .... F 860 342-1500
  Portland *(G-6972)*
Sandvik Wire and Htg Tech Corp .... D 203 744-1440
  Bethel *(G-337)*
▲ Scp Management LLC .... G 860 738-2600
  New Hartford *(G-5211)*
▲ Thermo Conductor Services Inc ...... G 203 758-6611
  Prospect *(G-7026)*
Tinplex Corporation .... G 203 335-8217
  Fairfield *(G-2857)*

Tms International LLC .... G 203 629-8383
  Greenwich *(G-3246)*
▲ Ulbrich Stainless Steels .... D 203 239-4481
  North Haven *(G-6008)*
Ulbrich Stainless Steels .... G 203 269-2507
  Wallingford *(G-9393)*
Ultra Mfg LLC .... G 203 888-1180
  Seymour *(G-7371)*
Washburn Design LLC .... G 860 675-3215
  Burlington *(G-1279)*
Waterbury Rolling Mills Inc .... D 203 597-5000
  Waterbury *(G-9628)*
Wheels 45 .... G 203 762-8684
  Wilton *(G-10341)*
Wheels of Hope Inc .... G 203 305-5762
  Shelton *(G-7585)*
Yankee Steel Service LLC .... G 203 879-5707
  Wolcott *(G-10593)*

3313 Electrometallurgical Prdts

Alent USA Holding Inc .... B 203 575-5727
  Waterbury *(G-9426)*

3315 Steel Wire Drawing & Nails & Spikes

▲ Accel Intl Holdings Inc .... E 203 237-2700
  Meriden *(G-4139)*
Ametek Inc .... C 203 265-6731
  Wallingford *(G-9203)*
Atco Wire Rope and Indus Sup .... G 203 239-1632
  North Haven *(G-5911)*
Bridgeport Insulated Wire Co .... E 203 333-3191
  Bridgeport *(G-721)*
City Data Cable Co .... G 203 327-7917
  Stamford *(G-8149)*
Custom House LLC .... F 860 873-1259
  East Haddam *(G-2240)*
Federal Prison Industries .... F 203 743-6471
  Danbury *(G-1824)*
Graham Whitehead & Manger Co .... G 978 887-0430
  Shelton *(G-7452)*
Hamden Metal Service Company .... F 203 281-1522
  Hamden *(G-3457)*
Housatonic Wire Co .... G 203 888-9670
  Seymour *(G-7350)*
▼ International Pipe & Stl Corp .... G 203 481-7102
  North Branford *(G-5846)*
Lee Spring Company LLC .... E 860 584-0991
  Bristol *(G-1062)*
▲ Lex Products LLC .... C 203 363-3738
  Shelton *(G-7490)*
Loos & Co Inc .... F 860 928-6681
  Pomfret *(G-6934)*
◆ Loos & Co Inc .... B 860 928-7981
  Pomfret *(G-6933)*
◆ Marmon Utility LLC .... E 203 881-5358
  Seymour *(G-7354)*
Nutmeg Wire .... F 860 822-8616
  Baltic *(G-121)*
▲ Polstal Corporation .... G 203 849-7788
  Wilton *(G-10320)*
▲ Radcliff Wire Inc .... E 312 876-1754
  Bristol *(G-1103)*
▲ Rscc Wire & Cable LLC .... B 860 653-8300
  East Granby *(G-2228)*
◆ S A Candelora Enterprises .... F 203 484-2863
  North Branford *(G-5854)*
Sandvik Wire and Htg Tech Corp .... D 203 744-1440
  Bethel *(G-337)*
Shuster-Mettler Corp .... E 203 562-3178
  Plainville *(G-6861)*
▲ Siri Manufacturing Company .... E 860 236-5901
  Danielson *(G-2002)*
Specialty Cable Corp .... D 203 265-7126
  Wallingford *(G-9372)*
Stephens Pipe & Steel LLC .... F 877 777-8721
  Manchester *(G-4095)*
Tool Logistics II .... F 203 855-9754
  Norwalk *(G-6373)*
▲ Tsmc Inc .... B 860 283-8265
  Torrington *(G-8985)*
Ulbrich Solar Technologies Inc .... G 203 239-4481
  North Haven *(G-6006)*
UNI Machine & Mfg LLC .... G 860 485-0643
  Harwinton *(G-3742)*
◆ Wiremold Company .... A 860 233-6251
  West Hartford *(G-9874)*
Wiretek Inc .... F 860 242-9473
  Bloomfield *(G-501)*

SIC SECTION
33 PRIMARY METAL INDUSTRIES

3316 Cold Rolled Steel Sheet, Strip & Bars

▲ Channel Alloys .... G 203 975-1404
Norwalk *(G-6112)*
▼ Deringer-Ney Inc .... C 860 242-2281
Bloomfield *(G-407)*
Eastern Company .... E 203 729-2255
Naugatuck *(G-4878)*
▲ Feroleto Steel Company Inc .... D 203 366-3263
Bridgeport *(G-769)*
▲ North East Fasteners Corp .... E 860 589-3242
Terryville *(G-8767)*
Paradigm Manchester Inc .... C 860 649-2888
Manchester *(G-4069)*
▲ Sandvik Wire and Htg Tech Corp ..... D 203 744-1440
Bethel *(G-338)*
Sandvik Wire and Htg Tech Corp .... D 203 744-1440
Bethel *(G-337)*
Shepard Steel Co Inc .... E 860 525-4446
Newington *(G-5704)*
Telling Industries LLC .... G 860 731-7975
Windsor *(G-10449)*
◆ Theis Precision Steel USA Inc .... C 860 589-5511
Bristol *(G-1127)*
▲ Ulbrich Stainless Steels .... D 203 239-4481
North Haven *(G-6008)*
Ulbrich Stainless Steels .... C 203 269-2507
Wallingford *(G-9393)*

3317 Steel Pipe & Tubes

Gordon Corporation .... D 860 628-4775
Southington *(G-7931)*
▲ Litchfield International Inc .... G 860 567-8824
Litchfield *(G-3894)*
Piper .... G 860 405-1495
Groton *(G-3309)*

3321 Gray Iron Foundries

▲ Bingham & Taylor Corp .... G 540 825-8334
Rocky Hill *(G-7223)*
◆ Taylor & Fenn Company .... D 860 219-9393
Windsor *(G-10448)*
▲ Virginia Industries Inc .... G 860 571-3600
Rocky Hill *(G-7271)*

3324 Steel Investment Foundries

Doncasters Inc .... D 860 446-4803
Groton *(G-3282)*
Doncasters US Hldings 2018 Inc .... F 860 677-1376
Groton *(G-3284)*
Dundee Holding Inc .... B 860 677-1376
Farmington *(G-2898)*
Hexcel Corporation .... D 925 520-3232
South Windsor *(G-7770)*
Howmet Castings & Services Inc .... B 860 379-3314
Winsted *(G-10524)*
Howmet Corporation .... B 203 481-3451
Branford *(G-608)*
Integra-Cast Inc .... D 860 225-7600
New Britain *(G-4999)*
J & H Machine Company LLC .... G 860 643-6096
Manchester *(G-4035)*
JI Aerotech Inc .... G 860 248-8628
South Windsor *(G-7778)*
Miller Castings Inc .... C 860 822-9991
North Franklin *(G-5875)*
▲ Sturm Ruger & Company Inc .... B 203 259-7843
Southport *(G-8010)*
Tps Acquisition LLC .... G 860 589-5511
Waterbury *(G-9616)*

3325 Steel Foundries, NEC

Frank Roth Co Inc .... D 203 377-2155
Stratford *(G-8611)*
▲ Polstal Corporation .... G 203 849-7788
Wilton *(G-10320)*
Silicone Casting Technologies .... G 860 347-5227
Middletown *(G-4415)*
Tenova Inc .... E 203 265-5684
Wallingford *(G-9380)*

3331 Primary Smelting & Refining Of Copper

Ametek Inc .... C 203 265-6731
Wallingford *(G-9203)*

3334 Primary Production Of Aluminum

All Steel LLC .... G 860 871-6023
Ellington *(G-2574)*

Angelos Aluminum .... G 203 469-3117
East Haven *(G-2410)*
Arconic Inc .... G 860 379-3314
Winsted *(G-10505)*
Evergreen Aluminum LLC .... F 203 328-4900
Stamford *(G-8200)*
Wilson Partitions .... G 203 316-8033
Stamford *(G-8494)*
▼ Wilson Partitions Inc .... G 203 316-8033
Stamford *(G-8495)*

3339 Primary Nonferrous Metals, NEC

Alent USA Holding Inc .... B 203 575-5727
Waterbury *(G-9426)*
Amentos Gold Buyers and Secon .... G 203 691-1020
North Haven *(G-5900)*
Aztec Industries LLC .... E 860 343-1960
Middletown *(G-4321)*
Bal International Inc .... E 203 359-6775
Stamford *(G-8106)*
Elemetal Direct Usa LLC .... G 860 290-1701
East Hartford *(G-2320)*
Engelhard Surface Technologies .... G 203 623-9901
East Windsor *(G-2491)*
Judith E Goldstein Company .... G 860 644-4646
South Windsor *(G-7780)*
Northeastern Metals Corp .... G 203 348-8088
Stamford *(G-8330)*
R & A Precious Metals LLC .... G 203 220-8265
Trumbull *(G-9059)*
Reliable Silver Corporation .... F 203 574-7732
Naugatuck *(G-4916)*
Specialty Metls Smlters & Rfne .... G 203 366-2500
Fairfield *(G-2850)*
Ulbrich Stainless Steels .... C 203 269-2507
Wallingford *(G-9393)*

3341 Secondary Smelting & Refining Of Nonferrous Metals

▲ 5n Plus Wisconsin Inc .... F 203 384-0331
Trumbull *(G-8995)*
Alent USA Holding Inc .... B 203 575-5727
Waterbury *(G-9426)*
Lajoies Auto Wrecking Co Inc .... E 203 870-0641
Norwalk *(G-6230)*
▲ MJ Metal Inc .... E 203 334-3484
Bridgeport *(G-840)*
Paradigm Manchester Inc .... C 860 649-2888
Manchester *(G-4069)*
Smm New England Corporation .... F 203 777-7445
New Haven *(G-5397)*
Surf Metal Co Inc .... G 203 375-2211
Stratford *(G-8692)*
Thyssenkrupp Materials NA Inc .... E 610 586-1800
Wallingford *(G-9383)*
▲ Ulbrich Stainless Steels .... D 203 239-4481
North Haven *(G-6008)*
Utitec Inc .... D 860 945-0605
Watertown *(G-9744)*
Viking Platinum LLC .... F 203 574-7979
Waterbury *(G-9621)*
▲ Willimantic Waste Paper Co Inc .... C 860 423-4527
Willimantic *(G-10240)*

3351 Rolling, Drawing & Extruding Of Copper

▲ Alloy Metals Inc .... F 203 774-3270
Wallingford *(G-9200)*
▲ Global Brass & Copper LLC .... G 203 597-5000
Waterbury *(G-9488)*
Global Brass & Copper LLC .... G 203 597-5000
Waterbury *(G-9489)*
▲ Miller Company .... E 203 235-4474
Meriden *(G-4203)*
Specialty Wire & Cord Sets .... F 203 498-2932
Hamden *(G-3512)*
Waterbury Rolling Mills Inc .... D 203 597-5000
Waterbury *(G-9628)*

3353 Aluminum Sheet, Plate & Foil

◆ CMI Specialty Products Inc .... F 860 585-0409
Bristol *(G-1003)*
Panel Pro Technology .... G 203 333-0083
Bridgeport *(G-861)*

3354 Aluminum Extruded Prdts

Brynwood Partners V Ltd Partnr .... G 203 622-1790
Greenwich *(G-3138)*
Narragansett Screw Co .... F 860 379-4059
Winsted *(G-10531)*

▲ Unique Extrusions Incorporated ..... E 860 632-1314
Cromwell *(G-1723)*

3355 Aluminum Rolling & Drawing, NEC

▲ Acme Monaco Corporation .... C 860 224-1349
New Britain *(G-4934)*
◆ Alpha-Core Inc .... E 203 954-0050
Shelton *(G-7392)*
▲ Erickson Metals Corporation .... E 203 272-2918
Cheshire *(G-1386)*

3356 Rolling, Drawing-Extruding Of Nonferrous Metals

Aerospace Metals Inc .... C 860 522-3123
Hartford *(G-3548)*
Alent USA Holding Inc .... B 203 575-5727
Waterbury *(G-9426)*
Doncasters Inc .... D 860 446-4803
Groton *(G-3282)*
◆ Doncasters Inc .... D 860 449-1603
Groton *(G-3283)*
Magnesium Interactive LLC .... G 917 609-1306
Westport *(G-10115)*
Norilsk Nickel USA Inc .... G 203 730-0676
Ridgefield *(G-7157)*
Platt Brothers & Company .... D 203 753-4194
Waterbury *(G-9580)*
Precision Powders LLC .... G 203 748-7879
Danbury *(G-1917)*
▲ Tico Titanium Inc .... E 248 446-0400
Wallingford *(G-9384)*
Titanium Electric LLC .... G 203 810-4050
Norwalk *(G-6370)*
Titanium Industries Inc .... G 860 870-3939
Tolland *(G-8881)*
Titanium Metals Corporation .... G 860 627-7051
East Windsor *(G-2527)*
▲ Torrey S Crane Company .... E 860 628-4778
Plantsville *(G-6915)*
▲ Ulbrich Stainless Steels .... D 203 239-4481
North Haven *(G-6008)*
Ulbrich Stainless Steels .... C 203 269-2507
Wallingford *(G-9393)*
United Stts Sgn & Fbrction .... E 203 601-1000
Trumbull *(G-9088)*
Waterbury Rolling Mills Inc .... D 203 597-5000
Waterbury *(G-9628)*
Weldingrodscom LLC .... G 888 935-3703
Suffield *(G-8738)*

3357 Nonferrous Wire Drawing

A J R Inc .... F 203 384-0400
Bridgeport *(G-680)*
◆ Algonquin Industries Inc .... D 203 453-4348
Guilford *(G-3324)*
◆ Alpha-Core Inc .... E 203 954-0050
Shelton *(G-7392)*
▲ Altek Electronics Inc .... C 860 482-7626
Torrington *(G-8892)*
American Alloy Wire Corp .... G 203 426-3133
Newtown *(G-5726)*
American Imex Corporation .... G 203 261-5200
Monroe *(G-4693)*
American Wire Corporation .... F 203 426-3133
Newtown *(G-5727)*
Autac Incorporated .... G 203 481-3444
Branford *(G-550)*
Bridgeport Insulated Wire Co .... E 203 333-3191
Bridgeport *(G-721)*
Bridgeport Insulated Wire Co .... E 203 375-9579
Stratford *(G-8589)*
▲ Bridgeport Magnetics Group Inc ... E 203 954-0050
Shelton *(G-7410)*
Cable Technology Inc .... E 860 429-7889
Willington *(G-10246)*
DNE Systems Inc .... G 203 265-7151
Wallingford *(G-9251)*
▲ Fiberoptics Technology Inc .... C 860 928-0443
Pomfret *(G-6931)*
Fiberqa LLC .... G 860 739-8044
Old Lyme *(G-6508)*
General Cable Industries Inc .... C 860 456-8000
Willimantic *(G-10227)*
Hamden Metal Service Company ...... F 203 281-1522
Hamden *(G-3457)*
Insulated Wire Inc .... F 203 791-1999
Bethel *(G-311)*
◆ Loos & Co Inc .... B 860 928-7981
Pomfret *(G-6933)*

33 PRIMARY METAL INDUSTRIES

▲ Luvata Waterbury Inc .... D 203 753-5215
   Waterbury *(G-9519)*
◆ Marmon Utility LLC .... E 203 881-5358
   Seymour *(G-7354)*
Multi-Cable Corp .... F 860 589-9035
   Bristol *(G-1076)*
Norfield Data Products Inc .... F 203 849-0292
   Norwalk *(G-6280)*
Ofs Companies .... G 860 678-6574
   Bristol *(G-1082)*
Ofs Fitel LLC .... B 860 678-0371
   Avon *(G-96)*
Omerin Usa Inc .... E 475 343-3450
   Meriden *(G-4212)*
▲ Ortronics Inc .... D 860 445-3900
   New London *(G-5482)*
Ortronics Inc .... G 877 295-3472
   West Hartford *(G-9841)*
Platt Brothers & Company .... D 203 753-4194
   Waterbury *(G-9580)*
▲ Radcliff Wire Inc .... E 312 876-1754
   Bristol *(G-1103)*
REA Magnet Wire Company Inc .... D 203 738-6100
   Guilford *(G-3386)*
▲ Rscc Wire & Cable LLC .... B 860 653-8300
   East Granby *(G-2228)*
Sandvik Wire and Htg Tech Corp ..... D 203 744-1440
   Bethel *(G-337)*
▲ Sandvik Wire and Htg Tech Corp .. D 203 744-1440
   Bethel *(G-338)*
◆ Siemon Company .... A 860 945-4200
   Watertown *(G-9734)*
Specialty Cable Corp .... D 203 265-7126
   Wallingford *(G-9372)*
◆ Times Fiber Communications Inc .. D 203 265-8500
   Wallingford *(G-9385)*
▲ Times Microwave Systems Inc .... B 203 949-8400
   Wallingford *(G-9386)*
◆ Volpe Cable Corporation .... C 203 623-1818
   Branford *(G-667)*
Wiretek Inc .... F 860 242-9473
   Bloomfield *(G-501)*

3363 Aluminum Die Castings

Advanced Prcsion Castings Corp ...... G 203 736-9452
   Milford *(G-4442)*
Arrow Diversified Tooling Inc .... E 860 872-9072
   Ellington *(G-2576)*
▲ Custom Metal Crafters Inc .... D 860 953-4210
   Newington *(G-5645)*
McCann Sales Inc .... G 860 614-0992
   West Simsbury *(G-9980)*

3364 Nonferrous Die Castings, Exc Aluminum

▲ Custom Metal Crafters Inc .... D 860 953-4210
   Newington *(G-5645)*
Integra-Cast Inc .... D 860 225-7600
   New Britain *(G-4999)*
Narragansett Screw Co .... F 860 379-4059
   Winsted *(G-10531)*
▲ PCC Structurals Groton .... C 860 405-3700
   Groton *(G-3304)*

3365 Aluminum Foundries

Accu-Mill Technologies LLC .... G 860 747-3921
   Plainville *(G-6764)*
Aerocess Inc .... F 860 357-2451
   Berlin *(G-151)*
Charles W Simmons .... G 203 254-3388
   Fairfield *(G-2759)*
◆ Dwyer Aluminum Mast Company . F 203 484-0419
   North Branford *(G-5836)*
Integra-Cast Inc .... D 860 225-7600
   New Britain *(G-4999)*
JET Corporation .... F 203 334-3317
   Bridgeport *(G-804)*
Pyrotek Incorporated .... G 509 926-6212
   Killingworth *(G-3838)*
▲ Us-Malabar Company Inc .... G 203 226-1773
   Weston *(G-10041)*

3366 Copper Foundries

▲ American Sleeve Bearing LLC ..... E 860 684-8060
   Stafford Springs *(G-8016)*
Arctime LLC .... G 203 321-5628
   Norwalk *(G-6072)*
Fred Radford .... G 203 377-6189
   Trumbull *(G-9027)*

Mystic River Foundry LLC .... G 860 536-7634
   Mystic *(G-4835)*
Propeller LLC .... G 203 831-0877
   Norwalk *(G-6309)*
▲ Spirol International Corp .... G 203 774-8571
   Danielson *(G-2003)*

3369 Nonferrous Foundries: Castings, NEC

B H S Industries Ltd .... G 203 284-9764
   Wallingford *(G-9218)*
Carrier Manufacturing Inc .... G 860 223-2264
   New Britain *(G-4955)*
▲ Consoldted Inds Acqsition Corp .. D 203 272-5371
   Cheshire *(G-1374)*
▲ Custom Metal Crafters Inc .... D 860 953-4210
   Newington *(G-5645)*
Doncasters Inc .... D 860 446-4803
   Groton *(G-3282)*
Elm City Pttern Fndry Wrks Inc .... G 203 481-2518
   Branford *(G-588)*
F M Associates .... G 860 693-2263
   Canton *(G-1314)*
Fred Radford .... G 203 377-6189
   Trumbull *(G-9027)*
House of Bubba LLC .... G 860 429-4250
   Willington *(G-10250)*
Sycast Inc .... G 860 308-2122
   Hartford *(G-3696)*
Tighitco Inc .... C 860 828-0298
   Berlin *(G-225)*
Winchester Products Inc .... G 860 379-8590
   Winsted *(G-10545)*
Yankee Casting Co Inc .... D 860 749-6171
   Enfield *(G-2709)*

3398 Metal Heat Treating

A G C Incorporated .... C 203 235-3361
   Meriden *(G-4138)*
Accurate Brazing Corporation .... F 860 432-1840
   Manchester *(G-3976)*
Advance Heat Treating Co .... G 203 380-8898
   Bridgeport *(G-684)*
American Heat Treating Inc .... E 203 268-1750
   Monroe *(G-4692)*
Amk Welding Inc .... E 860 289-5634
   South Windsor *(G-7707)*
Anderson Specialty Company .... G 860 953-6630
   West Hartford *(G-9774)*
Aqua Blasting Corp .... F 860 242-8855
   Bloomfield *(G-387)*
Beehive Heat Treating Svcs Inc .... G 203 866-1635
   Fairfield *(G-2752)*
Blasting Techniques Inc .... G 860 528-4717
   South Windsor *(G-7718)*
Bodycote Thermal Proc Inc .... E 860 225-7691
   Berlin *(G-164)*
Bodycote Thermal Proc Inc .... E 860 282-1371
   South Windsor *(G-7719)*
Eastern Metal Treating Inc .... F 860 763-4311
   Enfield *(G-2638)*
General Heat Treating Co .... G 203 755-5441
   Waterbury *(G-9486)*
Hydro Honing Laboratories Inc .... E 860 289-4328
   East Hartford *(G-2335)*
▼ Johnstone Company Inc .... E 203 239-5834
   North Haven *(G-5954)*
Metal Improvement Company LLC .. E 860 635-9994
   Middletown *(G-4375)*
Metal Improvement Company LLC .. E 860 224-9148
   New Britain *(G-5015)*
Metal Improvement Company LLC .. E 860 688-6201
   Windsor *(G-10409)*
Metal Improvement Company LLC .. D 860 523-9901
   East Windsor *(G-2511)*
Nelson Heat Treating Co Inc .... F 203 754-0670
   Waterbury *(G-9556)*
New Britain Heat Treating Corp .... F 860 223-0684
   Enfield *(G-2667)*
O & W Heat Treat Inc .... F 860 528-9239
   South Windsor *(G-7799)*
O W Heat Treat Inc .... G 860 430-6709
   South Glastonbury *(G-7681)*
P&G Metal Components Corp .... F 860 243-2220
   Bloomfield *(G-458)*
Paradigm Manchester Inc .... F 860 649-2888
   Manchester *(G-4069)*
Peening Technologies Eqp LLC .... E 860 289-4328
   East Hartford *(G-2353)*
Sousa Corp .... F 860 523-9090
   Newington *(G-5706)*

Specialty Steel Treating Inc .... E 860 653-0061
   East Granby *(G-2231)*
Weld TEC LLC .... G 860 628-5750
   Plantsville *(G-6918)*

3399 Primary Metal Prdts, NEC

▲ Abbott Ball Company .... D 860 236-5901
   West Hartford *(G-9770)*
▲ Alinabal Inc .... C 203 877-3241
   Milford *(G-4448)*
▲ Alinabal Holdings Corporation ..... B 203 877-3241
   Milford *(G-4449)*
Allied Sinterings Incorporated .... E 203 743-7502
   Danbury *(G-1737)*
Allread Products Co LLC .... F 860 589-3566
   Terryville *(G-8747)*
Ametek Inc .... C 203 265-6731
   Wallingford *(G-9203)*
Ball Supply Corporation .... G 860 673-3364
   Avon *(G-77)*
▲ Ccr Products LLC .... E 860 953-0499
   West Hartford *(G-9786)*
Centritec Seals LLC .... G 860 594-7183
   East Hartford *(G-2304)*
▲ Conn Engineering Assoc Corp ..... F 203 426-4733
   Sandy Hook *(G-7305)*
Defabrications LLC .... G 203 791-1407
   Danbury *(G-1790)*
▲ Hartford Technologies Inc .... E 860 571-3602
   Rocky Hill *(G-7241)*
Kovacs Tamas .... G 860 738-8976
   Pine Meadow *(G-6734)*
Lisa Lee Creations Inc .... E 203 479-4462
   New Haven *(G-5319)*
Norwalk Powdered Metals Inc .... D 203 338-8000
   Stratford *(G-8657)*
Schaeffler Aerospace USA Corp ...... D 860 379-7558
   Winsted *(G-10534)*
▲ Schaeffler Aerospace USA Corp .. B 203 744-2211
   Danbury *(G-1936)*
Timber-Top Inc .... G 860 274-6706
   Watertown *(G-9741)*
▲ Trd Specialties Inc .... G 860 738-4505
   Pine Meadow *(G-6736)*
Wade R Moore .... G 203 767-6146
   Milford *(G-4678)*

34 FABRICATED METAL PRODUCTS, EXCEPT MACHINERY AND TRANSPORTATION EQUIPMENT

3411 Metal Cans

American Metaseal of Conn .... G 203 787-0281
   Hamden *(G-3414)*
▲ CCL Industries Corporation .... D 203 926-1253
   Shelton *(G-7412)*
CCL Label Inc .... G 203 926-1253
   Shelton *(G-7413)*
Crown Cork & Seal Usa Inc .... G 203 877-4131
   Milford *(G-4500)*
Inspired Brands Intl LLC .... G 203 722-5629
   Weston *(G-10028)*
Silgan Closures Intl Holdg Co .... G 203 975-7110
   Stamford *(G-8419)*
Silgan Containers Corporation .... F 203 975-7110
   Stamford *(G-8420)*
Silgan Holdings Inc .... C 203 975-7110
   Stamford *(G-8421)*

3412 Metal Barrels, Drums, Kegs & Pails

▲ Architectural Supplements LLC ... F 203 591-5505
   Waterbury *(G-9433)*
Champlin-Packrite Inc .... G 860 951-9217
   Manchester *(G-3994)*
◆ Connecticut Container Corp .... C 203 248-2161
   North Haven *(G-5924)*
Mobile Mini Inc .... G 860 668-1888
   Suffield *(G-8727)*

3421 Cutlery

49 High St LLC .... G 860 423-9496
   Willimantic *(G-10219)*
◆ Acme United Corporation .... C 203 254-6060
   Fairfield *(G-2743)*
Apizza Grande .... G 475 238-6928
   North Haven *(G-5905)*

34 FABRICATED METAL PRODUCTS, EXCEPT MACHINERY AND TRANSPORTATION EQUIPMENT

Arepas La Orquidea	G	203 275-8478
Bridgeport *(G-701)*
Baingan LLC ....G..... 203 924-2626
Shelton *(G-7399)*
Bella Nail & Spa LLC ....G..... 860 436-3119
Rocky Hill *(G-7222)*
▲ Bic Corporation ....A..... 203 783-2000
Shelton *(G-7407)*
▲ Bic USA Inc ....C..... 203 783-2000
Shelton *(G-7408)*
Calle Market ....G..... 203 789-0632
New Haven *(G-5252)*
Edgewell Per Care Brands LLC ....D..... 203 882-2300
Milford *(G-4526)*
◆ Edgewell Per Care Brands LLC .....B..... 203 944-5500
Shelton *(G-7435)*
Edgewell Personal Care Company ...E..... 203 882-2308
Milford *(G-4527)*
Get Baked LLC ....G..... 860 688-0420
Windsor *(G-10392)*
Gillette Company ....G..... 203 796-4000
Bethel *(G-303)*
Goong ....G..... 860 216-3041
East Hartford *(G-2331)*
Laylas Falafel ....G..... 203 685-2830
Stamford *(G-8280)*
Mexi-Grill LLC ....G..... 203 574-2127
Waterbury *(G-9541)*
New King of Hartford ....G..... 860 241-0664
Hartford *(G-3652)*
One Stop Jamacia ....G..... 203 507-2315
New Haven *(G-5353)*
Patty Mommys ....G..... 203 330-8575
Bridgeport *(G-867)*
Pewter Hutch ....G..... 203 262-6181
Woodbury *(G-10650)*
Relative Gourmet II ....G..... 203 358-4602
Stamford *(G-8386)*
◆ Schick Manufacturing Inc ....D..... 203 882-2100
Milford *(G-4639)*
▲ Tharavadu Cor ....G..... 203 852-1213
Norwalk *(G-6366)*
Veras Trattoria ....G..... 203 798-7800
Danbury *(G-1971)*
Waterbury Cpl LLC ....G..... 203 592-4069
Waterbury *(G-9626)*
◆ Wenger Na Inc ....G..... 845 365-3500
Monroe *(G-4764)*
Xin Yong Chen ....G..... 860 651-4937
Simsbury *(G-7651)*

3423 Hand & Edge Tools

A Line Design Inc ....G..... 203 294-0080
Wallingford *(G-9193)*
Ampol Tool Inc ....G..... 203 932-3161
West Haven *(G-9884)*
An Designs Inc ....G..... 860 618-0183
Torrington *(G-8895)*
Artisan Hand Tools Inc ....G..... 203 308-2063
Ansonia *(G-22)*
Atlantic Woodcraft Inc ....F..... 860 749-4887
Enfield *(G-2616)*
Bessette Holdings Inc ....E..... 860 289-6000
East Hartford *(G-2298)*
Better Lawns & Gardens ....G..... 203 735-5296
Ansonia *(G-23)*
Brimatco Corporation ....G..... 203 272-0044
Cheshire *(G-1364)*
Cambridge Specialty Co Inc ....D..... 860 828-3579
Berlin *(G-168)*
Changesurfer Consulting ....G..... 312 702-3742
Willington *(G-10247)*
Chapman Manufacturing Company .F..... 860 349-9228
Durham *(G-2141)*
Classic Trim LLC ....G..... 860 543-9102
Bristol *(G-1002)*
Conquip Systems LLC ....G..... 860 526-7883
Chester *(G-1468)*
Crrc LLC ....D..... 860 635-2200
Cromwell *(G-1697)*
E-Z Tools Inc ....G..... 203 838-2102
Norwalk *(G-6152)*
Edge Tool LLC ....G..... 860 747-1820
Plainville *(G-6803)*
Eds Jewelry LLC ....G..... 203 757-0018
Waterbury *(G-9470)*
◆ Fletcher-Terry Company LLC ....D..... 860 828-3400
East Berlin *(G-2169)*
H&H Tool LLC ....G..... 203 879-4519
Waterbury *(G-9493)*

Integrity Manufacturing LLC ....G..... 860 678-1599
Farmington *(G-2919)*
Ipt Technology ....G..... 860 395-1083
Old Saybrook *(G-6544)*
Irwin Industrial Tool Company ....G..... 860 438-3460
New Britain *(G-5003)*
J J Ryan Corporation ....C..... 860 628-0393
Plantsville *(G-6897)*
Kell-Strom Tool Co Inc ....E..... 860 529-6851
Wethersfield *(G-10206)*
Kell-Strom Tool Intl Inc ....E..... 860 529-6851
Wethersfield *(G-10207)*
▲ Lewmar Inc ....E..... 203 458-6200
Guilford *(G-3367)*
M G Solutions ....G..... 203 945-9615
Norwalk *(G-6241)*
Ngraver Company ....G..... 860 823-1533
Bozrah *(G-530)*
Online River LLC ....F..... 203 801-5900
Westport *(G-10134)*
Power-Dyne LLC ....E..... 860 346-9283
Middletown *(G-4395)*
Present Time Visions ....G..... 860 435-4997
Salisbury *(G-7296)*
▲ Rostra Tool Company ....E..... 203 488-8665
Branford *(G-644)*
Signature Gold ....G..... 860 523-0385
Hartford *(G-3688)*
Skillcraft Machine Tool Co ....F..... 860 953-1246
South Windsor *(G-7822)*
Southwire Company LLC ....F..... 203 324-0067
Stamford *(G-8431)*
Stanley Black & Decker Inc ....F..... 860 225-5111
Farmington *(G-2959)*
Stanley Black & Decker Inc ....C..... 860 225-5111
New Britain *(G-5061)*
Stanley Black & Decker Inc ....E..... 860 225-5111
New Britain *(G-5064)*
Stephen A Besade ....G..... 860 443-6033
New London *(G-5490)*
Sterling Jewelers Inc ....G..... 860 644-7207
Manchester *(G-4096)*
Tiger Enterprises Inc ....E..... 860 621-9155
Plantsville *(G-6914)*
Tool 2000 ....G..... 860 620-0020
Southington *(G-7989)*
Toolmax Designing Tooling Inc ....G..... 860 871-7265
Tolland *(G-8883)*
Triple Clover Products LLC ....G..... 475 558-9503
New Canaan *(G-5154)*
◆ Trumpf Inc ....B..... 860 255-6000
Farmington *(G-2967)*
Trumpf Inc ....B..... 860 255-6000
Farmington *(G-2968)*
Trumpf Inc ....B..... 860 255-6000
Plainville *(G-6872)*
Ttpockettools LLC ....G..... 860 642-6020
Lebanon *(G-3865)*
▲ Ullman Devices Corporation ....D..... 203 438-6577
Ridgefield *(G-7178)*
◆ Unger Enterprises LLC ....C..... 203 366-4884
Bridgeport *(G-930)*
Uniprise International Inc ....E..... 860 589-7262
Terryville *(G-8776)*
V Cannelli Co LLC ....G..... 203 421-4697
Madison *(G-3966)*
W J Savage Co Inc ....G..... 203 468-4100
East Haven *(G-2459)*
Wadsworth Falls Mfg Co ....F..... 860 346-3644
Rockfall *(G-7216)*

3425 Hand Saws & Saw Blades

▲ Blackstone Industries LLC ....D..... 203 792-8622
Bethel *(G-266)*
DArcy Saw LLC ....G..... 800 569-1264
Windsor Locks *(G-10481)*
Elka Precision ....G..... 860 526-1674
New Britain *(G-4981)*
Nesci Enterprises Inc ....G..... 860 267-2588
East Hampton *(G-2271)*
▲ Specialty Saw Inc ....E..... 860 658-4419
Simsbury *(G-7648)*

3429 Hardware, NEC

▲ Ador Inc ....G..... 860 583-2367
Bristol *(G-958)*
Air-Lock Incorporated ....E..... 203 878-4691
Milford *(G-4444)*
◆ Assa Inc ....B..... 203 624-5225
New Haven *(G-5235)*

▲ Assa Inc ....G..... 800 235-7482
New Haven *(G-5236)*
◆ Assa Abloy Accss & Edrss Hrdwr ..B..... 860 225-7411
Berlin *(G-160)*
◆ Beckson Manufacturing Inc ....E..... 203 366-3644
Bridgeport *(G-709)*
Bmr Associates ....G..... 203 453-1796
Guilford *(G-3330)*
▲ Bourdon Forge Co Inc ....C..... 860 632-2740
Middletown *(G-4326)*
Brookfield Industries Inc ....E..... 860 283-6211
Thomaston *(G-8782)*
◆ C Sherman Johnson Company ......F..... 860 873-8697
East Haddam *(G-2237)*
▲ Camlock Systems Inc ....G..... 860 378-0302
Southington *(G-7902)*
▲ Colonial Bronze Company ....D..... 860 489-9233
Torrington *(G-8912)*
Compair Inc ....G..... 860 635-8811
Middletown *(G-4331)*
Composite McHining Experts LLC ...G..... 203 624-0664
North Haven *(G-5923)*
▲ Connecticut Greenstar Inc ....G..... 203 368-1522
Fairfield *(G-2766)*
▲ Connecticut Trade Company Inc ..G..... 203 368-0398
Fairfield *(G-2767)*
Corbin Russwin ....G..... 860 225-7411
New Haven *(G-5263)*
▲ Cornell-Carr Co Inc ....E..... 203 261-2529
Monroe *(G-4706)*
Crrc LLC ....D..... 860 635-2200
Cromwell *(G-1697)*
D & B Tool Co LLC ....G..... 203 878-6026
Milford *(G-4504)*
D & M Screw Machine Pdts LLC .....G..... 860 410-9781
Plainville *(G-6795)*
Dimide Inc ....G..... 203 668-9621
Milford *(G-4510)*
Dsd Distributor LLC ....G..... 860 378-4487
Plainville *(G-6801)*
◆ Dwyer Aluminum Mast Company .F..... 203 484-0419
North Branford *(G-5836)*
Eastern Company ....E..... 203 729-2255
Naugatuck *(G-4878)*
Engineered Inserts & Systems ....F..... 203 301-3334
Milford *(G-4531)*
▲ Fsb Inc ....F..... 203 404-4700
Berlin *(G-182)*
GK Mechanical Systems LLC ....G..... 203 775-4970
Brookfield *(G-1191)*
Halls Edge Inc ....G..... 203 653-2281
Stamford *(G-8222)*
Hartford Aircraft Products ....E..... 860 242-8228
Bloomfield *(G-417)*
▲ Hicks and Otis Prints Inc ....E..... 203 846-2087
Norwalk *(G-6200)*
▲ Horton Brasses Inc ....G..... 860 635-4400
Cromwell *(G-1705)*
Industrial Shipg Entps MGT LLC .....G..... 203 504-5800
Stamford *(G-8247)*
J Ro Grounding Systems Inc ....G..... 860 747-2106
Plainville *(G-6827)*
James Ippolito & Co Conn Inc ....E..... 203 366-3840
Bridgeport *(G-799)*
James L Howard and Company Inc .E..... 860 242-3581
Bloomfield *(G-427)*
Kell-Strom Tool Co Inc ....E..... 860 529-6851
Wethersfield *(G-10206)*
Kell-Strom Tool Intl Inc ....E..... 860 529-6851
Wethersfield *(G-10207)*
▲ Lab Security Systems Corp ....E..... 860 589-6037
Bristol *(G-1060)*
Land Sea Air Inc ....G..... 860 448-9004
Groton *(G-3294)*
Lassy Tools Inc ....G..... 860 747-2748
Plainville *(G-6832)*
▲ Lewmar Inc ....E..... 203 458-6200
Guilford *(G-3367)*
Loctec Corporation ....E..... 203 364-1000
Newtown *(G-5755)*
Marine Fabricators ....G..... 203 488-7093
Branford *(G-624)*
◆ Mc Kinney Products Company ......C..... 800 346-7707
Berlin *(G-199)*
McMellon Associates LLC ....G..... 203 272-5859
Cheshire *(G-1413)*
Michael J Macisco ....G..... 203 924-0013
Shelton *(G-7499)*
Morning Star Tool LLC ....G..... 203 878-6026
Milford *(G-4585)*

Employee Codes: A=Over 500 employees, B=251-500
C=101-250, D=51-100, E=20-50, F=10-19, G=1-9

34 FABRICATED METAL PRODUCTS, EXCEPT MACHINERY AND TRANSPORTATION EQUIPMENT SIC SECTION

Nations Rent ......G 860 665-1489
Newington *(G-5683)*

Nielsen/Sessions ......G 860 522-8145
Hartford *(G-3654)*

Norse Inc ......G 860 482-1532
Torrington *(G-8952)*

Oslo Switch Inc ......E 203 272-2794
Cheshire *(G-1425)*

▲ Outland Engineering Inc ......F 800 797-3709
Milford *(G-4601)*

Paneloc Corporation ......E 860 677-6711
Farmington *(G-2945)*

Panza Woodwork & Supply LLC ......G 203 934-3430
West Haven *(G-9943)*

Paradigm Manchester Inc ......C 860 649-2888
Manchester *(G-4069)*

Pemko Manufacturing Co ......G 901 365-2160
New Haven *(G-5358)*

Peregrine Technical Svcs LLC ......G 813 469-9355
Colchester *(G-1563)*

Perry Technology Corporation ......D 860 738-2525
New Hartford *(G-5206)*

Pierce-Correll Corporation ......G 203 799-1208
Orange *(G-6624)*

Pro-Lock USA LLC ......G 203 382-3428
Monroe *(G-4748)*

Roller Bearing Co Amer Inc ......E 203 758-8272
Middlebury *(G-4289)*

◆ Sargent Manufacturing Company ......C 203 562-2151
New Haven *(G-5389)*

Specialized Marketing Intl Inc ......G 860 779-3264
Dayville *(G-2074)*

Specialty Products Mfg LLC ......G 860 621-6969
Southington *(G-7979)*

Stanley Black & Decker Inc ......C 860 225-5111
New Britain *(G-5061)*

Stanley Black & Decker Inc ......D 860 225-5111
New Britain *(G-5062)*

Stanley Black & Decker Inc ......E 860 225-5111
New Britain *(G-5064)*

Stanley Black & Decker Inc ......C 860 225-5111
New Britain *(G-5063)*

Stanley Industrial & Auto LLC ......E 800 800-8005
New Britain *(G-5066)*

▲ Thule Canada Holding LLC ......G 203 881-4919
Seymour *(G-7369)*

Tiger Enterprises Inc ......E 860 621-9155
Plantsville *(G-6914)*

Unger Industrial LLC ......G 203 336-3344
Bridgeport *(G-931)*

▼ Vector Engineering Inc ......F 860 572-0422
Mystic *(G-4851)*

▲ Walz & Krenzer Inc ......F 203 267-5712
Oxford *(G-6699)*

◆ Wind Corporation ......E 203 778-1001
Newtown *(G-5799)*

Wtm Company ......G 860 283-5871
Thomaston *(G-8826)*

Yacht Specialty Products ......G 203 565-5598
Hamden *(G-3532)*

Yale Security Inc ......B 865 986-7511
Berlin *(G-233)*

York Street Studio Inc ......G 203 266-9000
New Milford *(G-5609)*

▲ Zephyr Lock LLC ......F 866 937-4971
Newtown *(G-5800)*

3431 Enameled Iron & Metal Sanitary Ware

Kensco Inc ......F 203 734-8827
Ansonia *(G-44)*

3432 Plumbing Fixture Fittings & Trim, Brass

◆ Bead Industries Inc ......E 203 301-0270
Milford *(G-4466)*

Burt Process Equipment Inc ......E 203 287-1985
Hamden *(G-3420)*

Butler Irrigation ......G 203 877-2248
Orange *(G-6587)*

Butler Property Svc ......G 203 530-4554
Orange *(G-6588)*

▲ Colonial Bronze Company ......D 860 489-9233
Torrington *(G-8912)*

F W Webb Company ......F 203 865-6124
New Haven *(G-5279)*

Fitzgerald & Wood Inc ......G 203 488-2553
Branford *(G-594)*

Granite Group Wholesalers LLC ......G 860 537-7600
Colchester *(G-1552)*

▲ Macristy Industries Inc ......C 860 225-4637
Newington *(G-5674)*

▲ Mc Guire Manufacturing Co Inc ......D 203 699-1801
Cheshire *(G-1412)*

▲ Neoperl Inc ......D 203 756-8891
Waterbury *(G-9557)*

Plastic Assembly Systems LLC ......F 203 393-0639
Bethany *(G-248)*

▲ The Keeney Manufacturing Co ......C 603 239-6371
Newington *(G-5711)*

Thomas J Hunt Inc ......G 203 775-5050
Brookfield *(G-1230)*

Viking Supply Co ......G 860 886-0220
Norwich *(G-6438)*

3433 Heating Eqpt

Allgreenit LLC ......G 860 516-4948
Bristol *(G-961)*

American Radiant Technolo ......G 203 484-2888
Middlefield *(G-4299)*

Aquacomfort Solutions LLC ......G 203 265-0100
Wallingford *(G-9210)*

Carlin Combustion Tech Inc ......G 413 525-7700
North Haven *(G-5918)*

▲ Carlin Combustion Tech Inc ......D 203 680-9401
North Haven *(G-5919)*

Cheryl Aiudi & Son LLC ......G 860 575-8462
Westbrook *(G-9993)*

CP Solar Thermal LLC ......G 860 877-2238
Bristol *(G-1008)*

Dp2 LLC Head ......F 203 655-0747
Darien *(G-2022)*

▲ Enterex America LLC ......G 860 661-4635
Westbrook *(G-9996)*

Fives N Amercn Combustn Inc ......G 860 739-3466
East Lyme *(G-2465)*

Fives N Amercn Combustn Inc ......E 216 271-6000
Southington *(G-7925)*

Flabeg US Holding Inc ......G 203 729-5227
Naugatuck *(G-4881)*

▲ Hamworthy Peabody Combustn Inc E 203 922-1199
Shelton *(G-7457)*

▲ Hi-Temp Products Corp ......G 203 744-3025
Danbury *(G-1843)*

Hot Spot Stoves & Mech LLC ......G 860 829-7283
Berlin *(G-189)*

Jad LLC ......E 860 289-1551
South Windsor *(G-7776)*

John Zink Company LLC ......D 203 925-0380
Shelton *(G-7481)*

Kerigans Fuel Inc ......G 203 334-3646
Bridgeport *(G-815)*

Lewis R Martino ......G 203 463-4430
Oxford *(G-6673)*

▲ Macristy Industries Inc ......C 860 225-4637
Newington *(G-5674)*

Maxon Corporation ......G 860 571-6411
Rocky Hill *(G-7256)*

McDowell Group Inc ......G 203 494-4120
Guilford *(G-3373)*

▲ McIntire Company ......F 860 585-8559
Bristol *(G-1070)*

◆ Omega Engineering Inc ......C 203 359-1660
Norwalk *(G-6284)*

Optical Energy Technologies ......G 203 357-0626
Stamford *(G-8344)*

Preferred Utilities Mfg Corp ......D 203 743-6741
Danbury *(G-1918)*

Pumc Holding Corporation ......E 203 743-6741
Danbury *(G-1921)*

Red Barn Radiator Co ......G 860 829-2060
Berlin *(G-215)*

Saigeworks LLC ......G 203 767-1035
Trumbull *(G-9069)*

Schindler Combustion LLC ......G 203 371-5068
Fairfield *(G-2844)*

Shippee Solar and Cnstr LLC ......G 860 630-0322
Putnam *(G-7064)*

Zeeco Inc ......G 860 479-0999
Plainville *(G-6879)*

3441 Fabricated Structural Steel

▲ Accutron Inc ......C 860 683-8300
Windsor *(G-10354)*

Acquisitions Controlled Svcs ......G 203 327-6364
Stamford *(G-8060)*

▲ All Panel Systems LLC ......D 203 208-3142
Branford *(G-541)*

All Phase Steel Works LLC ......D 203 375-8881
New Haven *(G-5222)*

All Star Welding & Dem LLC ......G 203 948-0528
Danbury *(G-1735)*

Alloy Welding & Mfg Co Inc ......F 860 582-3638
Bristol *(G-962)*

Anco Engineering Inc ......D 203 925-9235
Shelton *(G-7395)*

▲ Andert Inc ......G 860 974-3893
Eastford *(G-2534)*

▲ Ansonia Stl Fabrication Co Inc ......E 203 888-4509
Beacon Falls *(G-129)*

Applied Laser Solutions Inc ......G 203 739-0179
Danbury *(G-1742)*

ARC Dynamics Inc ......G 860 563-1006
Rocky Hill *(G-7221)*

Atlantic Eqp Installers Inc ......E 203 284-0402
Wallingford *(G-9213)*

Atlantic Fabricating Co Inc ......F 860 291-9882
South Windsor *(G-7712)*

Atlas Metal Works LLC ......F 860 282-1030
South Windsor *(G-7713)*

Barzetti Welding LLC ......G 203 748-3200
Bethel *(G-261)*

▲ Berlin Steel Construction Co ......E 860 828-3531
Kensington *(G-3806)*

Bri Metal Works Inc ......G 203 368-1649
Bridgeport *(G-718)*

Capstan Inc ......G 508 384-3100
Weston *(G-10021)*

▲ Carpin Manufacturing Inc ......D 203 574-2556
Waterbury *(G-9446)*

Center Mass LLC ......G 860 350-0239
New Milford *(G-5518)*

Central Construction Inds LLC ......E 860 963-8902
Putnam *(G-7033)*

Cirillo Manufacturing Group ......G 203 484-5010
East Haven *(G-2416)*

Coastal Steel Corporation ......E 860 443-4073
Waterford *(G-9646)*

Colonial Iron Shop Inc ......G 860 763-0659
Enfield *(G-2629)*

Com Tower ......G 203 879-6568
Wolcott *(G-10557)*

Connecticut Iron Works Inc ......G 203 869-0657
Greenwich *(G-3144)*

Contractors Steel Supply ......F 203 782-1221
North Haven *(G-5926)*

Delany & Long Ltd ......G 203 532-0010
Greenwich *(G-3149)*

▼ Di-Cor Industries Inc ......F 860 585-5583
Bristol *(G-1017)*

Division 5 LLC ......G 860 752-4127
Stafford Springs *(G-8027)*

Eagle Manufacturing Co Inc ......F 860 537-3759
Colchester *(G-1549)*

East Windsor Metal Fabg Inc ......F 860 528-7107
South Windsor *(G-7745)*

Eastern Inc ......G 203 563-9535
New Canaan *(G-5102)*

Engineered Building Pdts Inc ......E 860 243-1110
Bloomfield *(G-409)*

▲ Engineers Welding LLC ......G 203 334-2492
Bridgeport *(G-763)*

Enginering Components Pdts LLC ......G 860 747-6222
Plainville *(G-6806)*

Equipment Works ......G 860 585-9686
Bristol *(G-1030)*

▲ ES Metal Fabrications Inc ......F 860 585-6067
Terryville *(G-8753)*

Esdras Steel Fabrication ......G 203 917-3053
Bethel *(G-297)*

▲ Flashback Welding ......G 860 738-1122
Winsted *(G-10521)*

Fox Steel Products LLC ......F 203 799-2356
Orange *(G-6602)*

Fox Steel Services LLC ......G 203 799-2356
Orange *(G-6603)*

Frank Porto ......G 203 596-0811
Watertown *(G-9707)*

Fwt4 LLC ......G 203 775-7087
Brookfield *(G-1189)*

George H Olson Steel Co Inc ......E 203 375-5656
Stratford *(G-8617)*

Grover D & Sons LLC ......G 860 429-9420
Willington *(G-10248)*

Gulf Manufacturing Inc ......E 860 529-8601
Rocky Hill *(G-7239)*

HRF Fastener Systems Inc ......E 860 589-0750
Bristol *(G-1049)*

Iron Craft Fabricating LLC ......G 860 923-9869
North Grosvenordale *(G-5887)*

Jwc Steel Co LLC ......E 860 296-5517
Hartford *(G-3621)*

SIC SECTION 34 FABRICATED METAL PRODUCTS, EXCEPT MACHINERY AND TRANSPORTATION EQUIPMENT

K J Welding ....G.... 860 345-8743
Haddam (G-3406)
▲ Kinamor Incorporated ....E.... 203 269-0380
Wallingford (G-9297)
Kostas Custom Ir Fabrications ....G.... 203 328-1308
Stamford (G-8279)
Lemac Iron Works Inc ....G.... 860 232-7380
West Hartford (G-9829)
▲ LH Gault & Son Incorporated ....D.... 203 227-5181
Westport (G-10112)
Logan Steel Inc ....E.... 203 235-0811
Meriden (G-4188)
Magna Steel Sales Inc ....F.... 203 888-0300
Beacon Falls (G-142)
Mayarc Industries Inc ....G.... 860 871-1872
Ellington (G-2594)
Metalpuck Co LLC ....G.... 860 561-5936
West Hartford (G-9836)
Mobile Mini Inc ....E.... 860 668-1888
Suffield (G-8727)
Mtj Manufacturing Inc ....G.... 203 334-4939
Bridgeport (G-844)
Mystic Stainless & Alum Inc ....G.... 860 536-2236
Mystic (G-4837)
Nesci Enterprises Inc ....G.... 860 267-2588
East Hampton (G-2271)
Northern Fabrication ....G.... 860 693-0635
Canton (G-1321)
Nutmeg Welding Company Inc ....G.... 203 756-7458
Waterbury (G-9564)
Ovl Manufacturing Inc LLC ....G.... 860 829-0271
Berlin (G-205)
Passion Engineering LLC ....G.... 203 204-3090
Guilford (G-3382)
Pcx Aerostructures LLC ....E.... 860 666-2471
Newington (G-5694)
Pds Engineering & Cnstr Inc ....E.... 860 242-8586
Bloomfield (G-462)
Pepin Steel and Iron Works LLC ....G.... 860 582-1852
Bristol (G-1090)
Pisani Steel Fabrication Inc ....G.... 203 720-0679
Naugatuck (G-4911)
Platt & Labonia Company LLC ....E.... 800 505-9099
North Haven (G-5976)
Putnam Welding & Eqp Repr Inc ....G.... 860 974-0292
Eastford (G-2539)
Qsr Steel Corporation LLC ....E.... 860 548-0248
Hartford (G-3671)
Quality Erectors LLC ....G.... 860 548-0248
Hartford (G-3672)
Reliable Welding & Speed LLC ....G.... 860 749-3977
Enfield (G-2687)
Remote Site Service LLC ....G.... 860 691-1911
Niantic (G-5816)
Romco Contractors Inc ....F.... 860 243-8872
Bloomfield (G-478)
Rwt Corporation ....E.... 203 245-2731
Madison (G-3953)
▲ Shepard Steel Co Inc ....D.... 860 525-4446
Hartford (G-3685)
Shepard Steel Co Inc ....E.... 860 525-4446
Newington (G-5704)
Stamford Iron & Stl Works Inc ....F.... 203 324-6751
Stamford (G-8438)
State Welding & Fabg Inc ....G.... 203 294-4071
Wallingford (G-9376)
Steeltech Building Pdts Inc ....D.... 860 290-8930
South Windsor (G-7829)
Steven Rosenburg ....G.... 203 329-8798
Stamford (G-8443)
Stratford Steel LLC ....E.... 203 612-7350
Stratford (G-8686)
Swift Innovations LLC ....G.... 860 572-8322
Mystic (G-4847)
Swift Innovations LLC ....G.... 860 710-2725
Preston (G-6990)
T Keefe and Sons ....G.... 203 457-0267
Guilford (G-3396)
Thomas La Ganga ....G.... 860 489-0920
Torrington (G-8977)
▲ Tico Titanium Inc ....E.... 248 446-0400
Wallingford (G-9384)
Tiger Fabrication LLC ....G.... 860 460-7600
Pawcatuck (G-6728)
▲ Tinsley GROup-Ps&w Inc ....D.... 919 742-5832
Milford (G-4665)
Total Fab LLC ....F.... 475 238-8176
East Haven (G-2457)
United Metal Solutions ....G.... 860 610-4026
East Hartford (G-2388)
United Steel Inc ....C.... 860 289-2323
East Hartford (G-2389)
Valley Welding Co Inc ....G.... 860 283-5768
Thomaston (G-8817)
Varnum Enterprises LLC ....F.... 203 743-4443
Bethel (G-362)
Vernier Metal Fabricating Inc ....D.... 203 881-3133
Seymour (G-7372)
Viking Enterprises Inc ....G.... 860 440-0728
Waterford (G-9675)
Web Industries Inc ....G.... 860 779-3403
Dayville (G-2079)
Yankee Metals LLC ....G.... 203 612-7470
Bridgeport (G-941)

3442 Metal Doors, Sash, Frames, Molding & Trim

2seal LLC ....G.... 860 227-6854
Old Lyme (G-6487)
Advanced Window Systems LLC ....F.... 800 841-6544
Berlin (G-150)
All-Time Manufacturing Co Inc ....F.... 860 848-9258
Montville (G-4768)
American Overhead Ret Div Inc ....G.... 860 876-4552
Middletown (G-4316)
◆ Arcadia Architectural Pdts Inc ....E.... 203 316-8000
Stamford (G-8090)
Brynwood Partners V Ltd Partnr ....G.... 203 622-1790
Greenwich (G-3138)
Carey Automatic Door LLC ....G.... 203 267-4278
Southbury (G-7847)
Ckh Industries Inc ....D.... 860 563-2999
Wethersfield (G-10187)
▲ Cornell-Carr Co Inc ....E.... 203 261-2529
Monroe (G-4706)
CT Moldings Inc ....G.... 203 612-4922
Bridgeport (G-740)
Cusson Sash Company ....G.... 860 659-0354
Glastonbury (G-3025)
Emhart Teknologies LLC ....G.... 877 364-2781
Danbury (G-1808)
Gagne & Gagne Co ....G.... 860 742-5038
Andover (G-8)
Girardin Moulding Inc ....F.... 860 623-4486
Windsor Locks (G-10487)
Gordon Corporation ....D.... 860 628-4775
Southington (G-7931)
Green Shutter Inc ....G.... 203 359-3863
Stamford (G-8220)
K H Cornell International Inc ....G.... 203 392-3660
New Haven (G-5306)
Ld Assoc LLC ....G.... 203 452-9393
Monroe (G-4727)
Lee Brown Co LLC ....F.... 860 379-4706
Riverton (G-7209)
Legere Group Ltd ....C.... 860 674-0392
Avon (G-89)
Liberty Glass and Met Inds Inc ....E.... 860 923-3623
North Grosvenordale (G-5888)
Odorox Iaq Inc ....G.... 203 541-5577
Stamford (G-8337)
Schoenrock Marine Door Systems ....G.... 203 600-8370
East Haven (G-2451)
Shutters & Sails LLC ....G.... 860 331-1510
Mystic (G-4845)
Stonington Services LLC ....E.... 860 464-1991
Gales Ferry (G-2987)

3443 Fabricated Plate Work

All Phase Dumpsters LLC ....G.... 203 778-9104
Bethel (G-257)
American Indus Acqisition Corp ....G.... 203 952-9212
Stamford (G-8075)
Angel Fuel LLC ....G.... 203 597-8759
Waterbury (G-9431)
Apcompower Inc ....E.... 860 688-1911
Windsor (G-10362)
B & C Industries ....G.... 203 572-0265
Stratford (G-8575)
Brian Arnio ....G.... 860 779-2983
Sterling (G-8508)
▲ C Cowles & Company ....D.... 203 865-3117
North Haven (G-5916)
Connectcut Boiler Repr Mfg Inc ....E.... 860 953-9117
West Hartford (G-9793)
Containment Solutions Inc ....C.... 860 651-4371
Simsbury (G-7614)
CT Dumpster LLC ....G.... 203 521-0779
Milford (G-4501)
▲ CTI Industries Inc ....E.... 203 795-0070
Orange (G-6593)
Dylans Dumpsters LLC ....G.... 860 455-9924
Chaplin (G-1339)
GE Steam Power Inc ....G.... 860 688-1911
Windsor (G-10391)
GE Steam Power Inc ....C.... 423 648-4161
Windsor (G-10389)
Hayes Services LLC ....G.... 860 739-2273
East Lyme (G-2466)
Hi-Tech Fabricating Inc ....E.... 203 284-0894
Cheshire (G-1396)
ITT Standard ....G.... 860 683-2144
Windsor (G-10398)
Jacob David Poppel ....G.... 860 904-3749
Burlington (G-1271)
JFd Tube & Coil Products Inc ....E.... 203 288-6941
Hamden (G-3468)
▼ Johnstone Company Inc ....E.... 203 239-5834
North Haven (G-5954)
L & L Mechanical LLC ....F.... 860 491-4007
Goshen (G-3101)
Linvar LLC ....G.... 860 951-3818
Rocky Hill (G-7254)
Mastercraft Tool and Mch Co ....F.... 860 628-5551
Southington (G-7950)
▲ Matias Importing & Distrg Corp ....G.... 860 666-5544
Newington (G-5675)
◆ Mimforms LLC ....G.... 800 445-1245
Norwalk (G-6260)
Mitchell-Bate Company ....E.... 203 233-0862
Waterbury (G-9545)
Mp Systems Inc ....F.... 860 687-3460
East Granby (G-2214)
New Haven Sheet Metal Co ....G.... 203 468-0341
New Haven (G-5348)
Performance Sheet Metal ....G.... 860 889-0550
Bozrah (G-531)
Pioneer Capital Corp ....G.... 860 683-2005
Windsor (G-10419)
Planit Manufacturing LLC ....G.... 203 641-6055
Bristol (G-1092)
◆ Porobond Products LLC ....F.... 203 234-7747
Hamden (G-3497)
PSI Plus Inc ....F.... 860 267-6667
East Hampton (G-2276)
Quality Tank Service LP ....G.... 203 792-9373
Danbury (G-1924)
Recon Tactical LLC ....G.... 860 677-8202
Farmington (G-2954)
Roll-Off Best Service LLC ....G.... 860 350-2378
New Milford (G-5586)
Safe-T-Tank Corp ....G.... 203 237-6320
Meriden (G-4239)
Same Day Dumpsters LLC ....G.... 203 676-1219
New Haven (G-5387)
SMR Metal Technology ....G.... 860 291-8259
South Windsor (G-7823)
SPX Corporation ....G.... 203 356-9308
Stamford (G-8435)
Stein Laboratories LLC ....G.... 203 853-9500
Norwalk (G-6356)
Tesco Resources Inc ....G.... 203 754-3900
Waterbury (G-9611)
Thermaxx LLC ....G.... 203 672-1021
West Haven (G-9959)
United Steel Inc ....C.... 860 289-2323
East Hartford (G-2389)
▼ Vitta Corporation ....E.... 203 790-8155
Bethel (G-364)
Vulcan Industries Inc ....C.... 860 683-2005
Windsor (G-10460)
Walz & Krenzer Inc ....G.... 203 267-5712
Oxford (G-6700)
▲ Wanho Manufacturing LLC ....E.... 203 759-3744
Cheshire (G-1457)
▲ Whitcraft LLC ....C.... 860 974-0786
Eastford (G-2544)
Whitcraft Scrborough/Tempe LLC ....C.... 860 974-0786
Eastford (G-2545)

3444 Sheet Metal Work

A B & F Sheet Metal ....G.... 203 272-9340
Cheshire (G-1344)
A G C Incorporated ....C.... 203 235-3361
Meriden (G-4138)
A-1 Seamless Gutters ....G.... 860 432-9118
Manchester (G-3972)
Acier Fab LLC ....G.... 860 282-1211
South Windsor (G-7700)

SIC

Employee Codes: A=Over 500 employees, B=251-500
C=101-250, D=51-100, E=20-50, F=10-19, G=1-9
2020 Harris Connecticut
Manufacturers Directory
421

34 FABRICATED METAL PRODUCTS, EXCEPT MACHINERY AND TRANSPORTATION EQUIPMENT SIC SECTION

Advanced Sheetmetal Assoc LLC........E....... 860 349-1644
Middlefield *(G-4298)*
Advantage Sheet Metal Mfg LLC..........E....... 203 720-0929
Naugatuck *(G-4854)*
Aerocor Inc..........F....... 860 281-9274
East Windsor *(G-2479)*
Airtech of Stamford Inc..........E....... 203 323-3959
Stamford *(G-8070)*
All Steel Fabricating Inc..........G....... 203 783-1860
Milford *(G-4450)*
American Cladding Technologies........G....... 860 413-3098
East Granby *(G-2188)*
American Performance Pdts LLC........G....... 203 269-4468
Wallingford *(G-9201)*
Anco Engineering Inc..........D....... 203 925-9235
Shelton *(G-7395)*
▲ **Ansonia Stl Fabrication Co Inc**........E....... 203 888-4509
Beacon Falls *(G-129)*
Atlantic Vent & Eqp Co Inc..........E....... 860 635-1300
Cromwell *(G-1690)*
Atlas Industrial Services LLC..........E....... 203 315-4538
Branford *(G-549)*
Axis Laser..........G....... 203 284-9455
Wallingford *(G-9216)*
B L C Investments Inc..........G....... 203 877-1888
Milford *(G-4464)*
Bantam Sheet Metal..........G....... 860 567-9690
Bantam *(G-123)*
Barzetti Welding LLC..........G....... 203 748-3200
Bethel *(G-261)*
Bills Sheet Metal..........G....... 860 859-2821
Oakdale *(G-6441)*
Brittany Company Inc..........G....... 203 269-7859
Wallingford *(G-9222)*
Buckley Associates Inc..........G....... 203 380-2405
Stratford *(G-8590)*
Bull Metal Products Inc..........E....... 860 346-9691
Middletown *(G-4329)*
C B S Contractors Inc..........F....... 203 734-8015
Ansonia *(G-26)*
Capstone Manufacturing Inc..........G....... 413 636-6170
South Windsor *(G-7723)*
Carlson Sheet Metal..........G....... 860 354-4660
New Milford *(G-5516)*
▲ **Chapco Inc**..........D....... 860 526-9535
Chester *(G-1467)*
Clemson Sheet Metal LLC..........G....... 860 871-9369
Vernon Rockville *(G-9164)*
Clemson Sheetmetal LLC..........G....... 860 721-7906
Ellington *(G-2581)*
Complete Sheet Metal LLC..........G....... 860 310-5447
Berlin *(G-172)*
Connecticut Fabricating Co Inc..........G....... 203 878-3465
Milford *(G-4496)*
Copperworks Inc..........G....... 203 248-3516
Hamden *(G-3432)*
Country Side Sheet Metal..........G....... 860 872-5729
Ellington *(G-2584)*
Croteau Development Group Inc..........G....... 860 684-3605
Stafford Springs *(G-8022)*
Custom & Precision Pdts Inc..........G....... 203 281-0818
Hamden *(G-3436)*
Dasco Welded Products Inc..........F....... 203 754-9353
Waterbury *(G-9463)*
DBA Ne Sheet Metal..........G....... 860 584-0362
Bristol *(G-1013)*
Denlar Fire Protection LLC..........G....... 860 526-9846
Chester *(G-1469)*
Ductco LLC..........E....... 860 243-0350
Bloomfield *(G-408)*
Dufrane Nuclear Shielding Inc..........F....... 860 379-2318
Winsted *(G-10516)*
Dyco Industries Inc..........E....... 860 289-4957
South Windsor *(G-7741)*
E&D Landscaping..........G....... 203 934-4088
West Haven *(G-9905)*
E-Skylight Inc..........G....... 203 208-1351
Branford *(G-584)*
East Coast Sheet Metal LLC..........F....... 860 283-1126
Litchfield *(G-3888)*
East Windsor Metal Fabg Inc..........F....... 860 528-7107
South Windsor *(G-7745)*
Engineered Building Pdts Inc..........E....... 860 243-1110
Bloomfield *(G-409)*
▲ **Erickson Metals Corporation**..........E....... 203 272-2918
Cheshire *(G-1386)*
Farrell Prcsion Mtalcraft Corp..........E....... 860 355-2651
New Milford *(G-5532)*
Fonda Fabricating & Welding Co..........G....... 860 793-0601
Plainville *(G-6812)*
G & R Welding..........G....... 860 526-3353
Deep River *(G-2090)*
General Dynamics Info Tech Inc..........D....... 860 441-2400
Pawcatuck *(G-6712)*
General Sheet Metal Works Inc..........F....... 203 333-6111
Bridgeport *(G-775)*
Gintys Welding Service Inc..........G....... 203 270-3399
Sandy Hook *(G-7314)*
Hamden Sheet Metal Inc..........G....... 203 776-1472
Hamden *(G-3459)*
Hartford Seamless Gutters..........G....... 860 266-2516
West Hartford *(G-9819)*
Hasson Sheet Metal LLC..........G....... 860 698-6951
Enfield *(G-2648)*
Hi-Tech Fabricating Inc..........E....... 203 284-0894
Cheshire *(G-1396)*
▼ **Highway Safety Corp**..........D....... 860 659-4330
Glastonbury *(G-3049)*
Hispanic Enterprises Inc..........E....... 203 588-9334
Bridgeport *(G-784)*
Hollums Sheet Metal LLC..........G....... 203 640-4970
West Haven *(G-9915)*
Illinois Tool Works Inc..........E....... 203 720-1676
Naugatuck *(G-4890)*
J M Sheet Metal LLC..........G....... 860 747-5537
Plainville *(G-6826)*
J OConnor LLC..........F....... 860 665-7702
Newington *(G-5666)*
Jared Manufacturing Co Inc..........F....... 203 846-1732
Norwalk *(G-6219)*
Jgs Properties LLC..........E....... 203 378-7508
Stratford *(G-8636)*
Jhs Restoration Inc..........F....... 860 757-3870
South Windsor *(G-7777)*
Jones Metal Products Co Inc..........G....... 860 289-8023
South Windsor *(G-7779)*
JV Sheet Metal..........G....... 203 540-0383
Stamford *(G-8271)*
Ken Hastedt..........G....... 203 268-6563
Monroe *(G-4725)*
Labco Welding Inc..........G....... 860 632-2625
Middletown *(G-4367)*
Lee Manufacturing Inc..........D....... 203 284-0466
Wallingford *(G-9302)*
▲ **Leek Building Products Inc**..........E....... 203 853-3883
Norwalk *(G-6232)*
Link Mechanical Services Inc..........E....... 860 826-5880
New Britain *(G-5011)*
Lostocco Refuse Service LLC..........E....... 203 748-9296
Danbury *(G-1877)*
Lyon Manufacturing LLC..........G....... 203 876-7386
Milford *(G-4571)*
Lyons Slitting Inc..........F....... 203 755-4564
Waterbury *(G-9520)*
M & O Corporation..........E....... 203 367-4292
Bridgeport *(G-827)*
M & W Sheet Metal LLC..........G....... 860 642-7748
North Franklin *(G-5874)*
▲ **M Cubed Technologies Inc**..........E....... 203 304-2940
Newtown *(G-5757)*
M J Boller Company..........G....... 860 738-8073
Pine Meadow *(G-6735)*
M J Williams Heating and AC..........G....... 860 923-6991
Woodstock *(G-10670)*
▼ **Manufacturers Service Co Inc**..........G....... 203 389-9595
Woodbridge *(G-10606)*
Marine Fabricators..........G....... 203 488-7093
Branford *(G-624)*
▲ **Marsco Sheetmetal LLC**..........G....... 203 459-2698
Monroe *(G-4733)*
McGill Airflow LLC..........G....... 860 653-8001
East Granby *(G-2213)*
McMullin Manufacturing Corp..........E....... 203 740-3360
Brookfield *(G-1204)*
Microfab Company..........G....... 203 267-1000
Oxford *(G-6677)*
Midget Louver Company Inc..........G....... 203 783-1444
Milford *(G-4578)*
Milford Fabricating Co Inc..........D....... 203 878-2476
Milford *(G-4579)*
Mrnd LLC..........G....... 860 749-0256
Enfield *(G-2663)*
Niantic Awning Company..........G....... 860 739-0161
Niantic *(G-5813)*
Niklyn Corp..........G....... 860 440-6244
New Haven *(G-5350)*
Northeast Panel Co LLC..........G....... 860 678-9078
Farmington *(G-2940)*
Northern Comfort Mech LLC..........G....... 203 456-5163
Danbury *(G-1895)*
Nt Lawn Service..........G....... 203 573-0285
Waterbury *(G-9563)*
Ovl Manufacturing Inc LLC..........G....... 860 829-0271
Berlin *(G-205)*
Panel Shop Inc..........G....... 203 377-6208
Stratford *(G-8661)*
Paradigm Manchester Inc..........D....... 860 646-4048
Manchester *(G-4066)*
Paradigm Manchester Inc..........C....... 860 646-4048
Manchester *(G-4067)*
Paradigm Manchester Inc..........C....... 860 649-2888
Manchester *(G-4069)*
Paradigm Manchester Inc..........G....... 860 646-4048
Manchester *(G-4070)*
Phoenix Sheet Metal LLC..........G....... 860 478-4579
Bloomfield *(G-464)*
Post Mortem Services LLC..........G....... 860 675-1103
Farmington *(G-2950)*
Precision Shtmtl Fabrication..........G....... 860 388-4466
Old Saybrook *(G-6567)*
Pro Forming Sheet Metal LLC..........G....... 860 886-9900
Norwich *(G-6428)*
Progressive Sheetmetal LLC..........E....... 860 436-9884
South Windsor *(G-7814)*
Quality Sheet Metal Inc..........F....... 203 729-2244
Naugatuck *(G-4915)*
R & D Precision Inc..........F....... 203 284-3396
Wallingford *(G-9346)*
R W E Inc..........E....... 860 974-1101
Putnam *(G-7061)*
R-D Mfg Inc..........F....... 860 739-3986
East Lyme *(G-2473)*
Rader Industries Inc..........G....... 203 334-6739
Bridgeport *(G-884)*
Reliable Welding & Speed LLC..........G....... 860 749-3977
Enfield *(G-2687)*
Richard Sadowski..........G....... 203 372-2151
Fairfield *(G-2836)*
Rissolo Precision Sheet Metal..........G....... 860 355-1949
New Milford *(G-5585)*
Saw Mill Sheet Metal LLC..........G....... 860 779-3194
Sterling *(G-8516)*
Seconn Automation Solutions..........F....... 860 442-4325
Waterford *(G-9669)*
Seconn Fabrication LLC..........D....... 860 443-0000
Waterford *(G-9670)*
Sheetmetal Systems Inc..........G....... 203 878-2633
Milford *(G-4642)*
Shoreline Metal Services LLC..........G....... 203 466-7372
East Haven *(G-2452)*
▲ **Sound Manufacturing Inc**..........D....... 860 388-4466
Old Saybrook *(G-6569)*
Statewide Sheet Metal LLC..........G....... 203 315-1159
Branford *(G-656)*
Stauffer Sheet Metal LLC..........G....... 860 623-0518
Windsor *(G-10443)*
Suraci Corp..........D....... 203 624-1345
New Haven *(G-5406)*
Target Custom Manufacturing Co..........G....... 860 388-5848
Old Saybrook *(G-6573)*
Tech-Air Incorporated..........E....... 860 848-1287
Uncasville *(G-9104)*
Tetrault & Sons Inc..........G....... 860 872-9187
Stafford Springs *(G-8042)*
Thomas La Ganga..........G....... 860 489-0920
Torrington *(G-8977)*
Thyssenkrupp Materials NA Inc..........E....... 203 265-1567
Wallingford *(G-9382)*
Toms Seamless Gutters Inc..........G....... 203 269-2296
Wallingford *(G-9389)*
Trumpf Photonics Inc..........G....... 860 255-6000
Farmington *(G-2969)*
U-Sealusa LLC..........D....... 860 667-0911
Newington *(G-5716)*
United Steel Inc..........C....... 860 289-2323
East Hartford *(G-2389)*
United Stts Sgn & Fbrction..........E....... 203 601-1000
Trumbull *(G-9088)*
Universal Metalworks LLC..........G....... 203 239-6349
North Haven *(G-6009)*
Vernier Metal Fabricating Inc..........D....... 203 881-3133
Seymour *(G-7372)*
Vulcan Industries Inc..........C....... 860 683-2005
Windsor *(G-10460)*
Wendon Technologies Inc..........D....... 203 348-6271
Stamford *(G-8491)*
▲ **Whitcraft LLC**..........C....... 860 974-0786
Eastford *(G-2544)*
Whitcraft Scrborough/Tempe LLC..........C....... 860 974-0786
Eastford *(G-2545)*

34 FABRICATED METAL PRODUCTS, EXCEPT MACHINERY AND TRANSPORTATION EQUIPMENT

White Welding Company Inc .... G 203 753-1197
  Waterbury *(G-9633)*
Yost Manufacturing & Supply .... F 860 447-9678
  Waterford *(G-9677)*

3446 Architectural & Ornamental Metal Work

All Star Welding & Dem LLC .... G 203 948-0528
  Danbury *(G-1735)*
American Iron Works .... G 203 624-7360
  New Haven *(G-5228)*
American Iron Works .... G 203 469-6117
  East Haven *(G-2409)*
ARC and Hammer .... G 860 605-0344
  Canton *(G-1304)*
Art Metal Industries LLC .... G 203 733-3092
  New Milford *(G-5505)*
Artistic Iron Works LLC .... G 203 838-9200
  Norwalk *(G-6075)*
Beckm LLC .... G 203 458-3800
  Guilford *(G-3327)*
Bhs .... G 860 585-0125
  Bristol *(G-983)*
Boudreaus Welding Co Inc .... E 860 774-2771
  Dayville *(G-2055)*
Burdon Enterprises LLC .... G 860 345-4882
  Higganum *(G-3762)*
Company of Craftsmen .... G 860 536-4189
  Mystic *(G-4808)*
Connecticut Iron Works Inc .... G 203 869-0657
  Greenwich *(G-3144)*
Dyco Industries Inc .... E 860 289-4957
  South Windsor *(G-7741)*
East Windsor Metal Fabg Inc .... F 860 528-7107
  South Windsor *(G-7745)*
▼ Eastern Metal Works Inc .... E 203 878-6995
  Milford *(G-4523)*
Edelman Metalworks Inc .... G 203 744-7331
  Newtown *(G-5736)*
Edi Landscape LLC .... F 860 216-6871
  Hartford *(G-3583)*
Engineered Building Pdts Inc .... E 860 243-1110
  Bloomfield *(G-409)*
Evans Fabrication .... G 203 791-9517
  Bethel *(G-298)*
F & L Iron Work Inc .... G 203 777-0751
  New Haven *(G-5278)*
Falling Hammer Productions LLC .... G 203 879-1786
  Wolcott *(G-10565)*
Future Swiss .... G 860 283-4358
  Thomaston *(G-8790)*
Garden Iron LLC .... G 860 767-9917
  Westbrook *(G-9997)*
Goodyfab Llc .... G 203 927-3059
  North Branford *(G-5839)*
H & D Ornamental Iron Works .... G 860 871-1708
  Ellington *(G-2591)*
Ida International Inc .... E 203 736-9249
  Derby *(G-2116)*
Imperial Metalworks LLC .... G 203 791-8567
  Stamford *(G-8245)*
▼ International Pipe & Stl Corp .... F 203 481-7102
  North Branford *(G-5846)*
Jacobs Ladder .... G 203 833-2227
  Naugatuck *(G-4894)*
Jeffrey Mingollello Backhoe Sr .... G 203 735-5458
  Ansonia *(G-42)*
▲ Jozef Custom Ironworks Inc .... F 203 384-6363
  Bridgeport *(G-810)*
Kammetal Inc .... E 718 722-9991
  Naugatuck *(G-4897)*
Ken Hastedt .... G 203 268-6563
  Monroe *(G-4725)*
▲ Kenneth Lynch & Sons Inc .... G 203 762-8363
  Oxford *(G-6671)*
Leed - Himmel Industries Inc .... D 203 288-8484
  Hamden *(G-3472)*
▲ Leek Building Products Inc .... E 203 853-3883
  Norwalk *(G-6232)*
Loyal Fence Company LLC .... G 203 530-7046
  Rockfall *(G-7214)*
Lpg Metal Crafts LLC .... G 860 982-3573
  Plainville *(G-6835)*
Luckey LLC .... F 203 285-3819
  New Haven *(G-5322)*
Magic Industries Inc .... G 860 949-8380
  Bozrah *(G-527)*
Metalcraft LLC .... G 860 361-6767
  Bantam *(G-124)*
Mono Crete Step Co of CT LLC .... F 203 748-8419
  Bethel *(G-328)*

Musano Inc .... F 203 879-4651
  Wolcott *(G-10575)*
Naugatuck Stair Company Inc .... F 203 729-7134
  Naugatuck *(G-4907)*
Patwil LLC .... G 860 589-9085
  Bristol *(G-1088)*
Pequonnock Ironworks Inc .... F 203 336-2178
  Bridgeport *(G-868)*
Quality Stairs Inc .... E 203 367-8390
  Bridgeport *(G-883)*
Richard Sadowski .... G 203 372-2151
  Fairfield *(G-2836)*
River Valley Stairs LLC .... G 860 767-7561
  Essex *(G-2732)*
Ryall Rbert Archtctral Ir Wrks .... G 203 458-1356
  Guilford *(G-3387)*
S M Churyk Iron Works Inc .... G 860 355-1777
  New Milford *(G-5588)*
Schiess John .... G 860 664-0336
  Clinton *(G-1522)*
▲ Shepard Steel Co Inc .... D 860 525-4446
  Hartford *(G-3685)*
Shepard Steel Co Inc .... E 860 525-4446
  Newington *(G-5704)*
Shoreline Stair & Millwork Co .... G 860 669-9591
  Clinton *(G-1525)*
Sorge Industries Inc .... G 203 924-8900
  Shelton *(G-7557)*
Southington Metal Fabg Co .... F 860 621-0149
  Southington *(G-7977)*
Specialty Stairs LLC .... G 203 484-2557
  Northford *(G-6055)*
Stamford Forge & Metal Cft Inc .... G 203 348-8290
  Stamford *(G-8437)*
Stately Stair Co Inc .... E 203 575-1966
  Waterbury *(G-9607)*
Stephen Hawrylik .... G 860 688-8651
  Windsor *(G-10444)*
Steve S Custom Ironworks LLC .... G 203 229-0612
  Norwalk *(G-6358)*
Steven Rosenburg .... G 203 329-8798
  Stamford *(G-8443)*
Susan Martovich .... G 203 881-1848
  Oxford *(G-6696)*
T Woodward Stair Building LLC .... G 860 664-0515
  North Branford *(G-5861)*
Teddy S Custom Metalworks Inc .... G 203 359-6927
  Stamford *(G-8462)*
United Metal Solutions .... G 860 610-4026
  East Hartford *(G-2388)*
United Steel Inc .... C 860 289-2323
  East Hartford *(G-2389)*
US Barricades LLC .... G 203 883-8660
  Darien *(G-2050)*
Washington Concrete Products .... F 860 747-5242
  Plainville *(G-6876)*
Winchester Stair & Woodworking .... G 860 379-3194
  Winsted *(G-10546)*

3448 Prefabricated Metal Buildings & Cmpnts

Brw Associates Inc .... G 203 426-3318
  Sandy Hook *(G-7301)*
Engineered Building Pdts Inc .... E 860 243-1110
  Bloomfield *(G-409)*
Illinois Tool Works Inc .... C 203 574-2119
  Waterbury *(G-9503)*
LLC Glass House .... G 860 974-1665
  Pomfret Center *(G-6941)*
◆ Mdm Products LLC .... F 203 877-7070
  Milford *(G-4576)*
Mobile Mini Inc .... E 860 668-1888
  Suffield *(G-8727)*
▲ Morin Corporation .... D 860 584-0900
  Bristol *(G-1074)*
Niantic Awning Company .... G 860 739-0161
  Niantic *(G-5813)*
Portable Garage Depot LLC .... G 203 397-1721
  Woodbridge *(G-10614)*
Readydock Inc .... G 860 523-9980
  Avon *(G-104)*
Rwt Corporation .... E 203 245-2731
  Madison *(G-3953)*
Shelters of America LLC .... G 203 397-1037
  Woodbridge *(G-10617)*
Star Steel Structures Inc .... G 860 763-5681
  Somers *(G-8574)*
Walpole Woodworkers Inc .... E 508 668-2800
  Ridgefield *(G-7181)*

3449 Misc Structural Metal Work

Aerospace Alloys Inc .... D 860 882-0019
  Bloomfield *(G-382)*
Barker Steel LLC .... E 860 282-1860
  South Windsor *(G-7717)*
C & S Engineering Inc .... E 203 235-5727
  Meriden *(G-4153)*
Cem Group LLC .... F 860 675-5000
  Burlington *(G-1263)*
▼ Eastern Metal Works Inc .... E 203 878-6995
  Milford *(G-4523)*
Engineered Building Pdts Inc .... E 860 243-1110
  Bloomfield *(G-409)*
Graycon Defense Industries LLC .... G 860 339-2505
  Chester *(G-1474)*
Helix Mooring Systems .... G 860 628-0933
  Southington *(G-7933)*
Met Tech Inc .... G 203 254-9319
  Fairfield *(G-2814)*
Michael Petruzzi .... G 860 621-7515
  Plantsville *(G-6902)*
▲ Nucor Steel Connecticut Inc .... C 203 265-0615
  Wallingford *(G-9330)*
Quality Engineering Svcs Inc .... E 203 269-5054
  Wallingford *(G-9345)*
Shamrock Sheet Metal .... G 860 537-4282
  Colchester *(G-1576)*
Simpson Strong-Tie Company Inc .. F 860 741-8923
  Enfield *(G-2697)*
Stephanie Mark .... G 203 329-7562
  Stamford *(G-8441)*
Supercool Metals LLC .... G 203 823-9032
  New Haven *(G-5404)*
United Metal Solutions .... G 860 610-4026
  East Hartford *(G-2388)*

3451 Screw Machine Prdts

Alinabal Inc .... F 860 828-9933
  Kensington *(G-3805)*
Atp Industries LLC .... F 860 479-5007
  Plainville *(G-6773)*
Automatic Machine Products .... G 860 346-7064
  Middletown *(G-4320)*
B&T Screw Machine Co Inc .... F 860 314-4410
  Bristol *(G-971)*
Bar Work Manufacturing Co Inc ...... F 203 753-4103
  Waterbury *(G-9436)*
Biedermann Mfg Inds Inc .... E 860 283-8268
  Thomaston *(G-8781)*
Bobken Automatics Inc .... G 203 757-5525
  Waterbury *(G-9439)*
Brass City Technologies LLC .... G 203 723-7021
  Naugatuck *(G-4863)*
Bristol Tool Works LLC .... G 860 585-7302
  Bristol *(G-994)*
Brophy Metal Products Inc .... G 860 621-3636
  Southington *(G-7898)*
C & A Machine Co Inc .... E 860 667-0605
  Newington *(G-5636)*
C C Precision Products Co Inc .... G 860 628-4403
  Southington *(G-7900)*
C-Tech Manufacturing Co LLC .... G 860 274-6879
  Watertown *(G-9689)*
Cadcom Inc .... F 203 877-0640
  Milford *(G-4479)*
Caine Machining Inc .... G 860 738-1619
  Winsted *(G-10513)*
Cole S Crew Machine Products ..... E 203 723-1418
  North Haven *(G-5922)*
▲ Creed-Monarch Inc .... B 860 225-7884
  New Britain *(G-4968)*
Curtis Products LLC .... F 203 754-4155
  Bristol *(G-1010)*
D & M Screw Machine Pdts LLC .... G 860 410-9781
  Plainville *(G-6795)*
Dacruz Manufacturing Inc .... E 860 584-5315
  Bristol *(G-1011)*
David Derewianka .... G 860 649-1983
  Manchester *(G-4003)*
Day Fred A Co LLC .... G 860 589-0531
  Bristol *(G-1012)*
Day Machine Systems Inc .... F 860 229-3440
  New Britain *(G-4971)*
Deco Products Inc .... G 860 528-4304
  East Hartford *(G-2312)*
Devon Precision Industries Inc ..... D 203 879-1437
  Wolcott *(G-10560)*
Don S Screw Machine Pdts LLC .... G 860 283-6448
  Thomaston *(G-8787)*

34 FABRICATED METAL PRODUCTS, EXCEPT MACHINERY AND TRANSPORTATION EQUIPMENT SIC SECTION

Duda and Goodwin Inc F 203 263-4353 — Woodbury (G-10634)
Durco Manufacturing Co Inc G 203 575-0446 — Waterbury (G-9467)
E P M Co Inc G 860 589-3233 — Bristol (G-1024)
Electro-Tech Inc E 203 271-1976 — Cheshire (G-1384)
▲ F F Screw Products Inc E 860 621-4567 — Southington (G-7921)
Fleetwood Industries Inc G 860 747-6750 — Plainville (G-6811)
▲ Forestville Machine Co Inc E 860 747-6000 — Plainville (G-6813)
G M T Manufacturing Co Inc G 860 628-6757 — Plantsville (G-6894)
Garmac Screw Machine Inc F 203 723-6911 — Naugatuck (G-4883)
Horst Engrg De Mexico LLC E 860 289-8209 — East Hartford (G-2334)
J & R Projects G 203 879-2347 — Waterbury (G-9507)
J J Ryan Corporation C 860 628-0393 — Plantsville (G-6897)
James Wright Precision Pdts F 860 928-7756 — Putnam (G-7049)
Jay Sons Screw Mch Pdts Inc F 860 621-0141 — Milldale (G-4684)
Jeskey LLC E 203 772-6675 — North Haven (G-5952)
Kamatics Corporation E 860 243-9704 — Bloomfield (G-435)
Kemby Manufacturing G 860 582-2850 — Terryville (G-8761)
▲ Leipold Inc E 860 298-9791 — Windsor (G-10404)
Mackson Mfg Co Inc F 860 589-4035 — Bristol (G-1065)
Mailly Manufacturing Company G 203 879-1445 — Wolcott (G-10573)
Manufacturers Associates Inc E 203 931-4344 — West Haven (G-9930)
Mario Precision Products G 203 758-3101 — Prospect (G-7009)
Matthew Warren Inc G 203 888-2133 — Seymour (G-7355)
Microbest Inc C 203 597-0355 — Waterbury (G-9542)
Mitchell Machine Screw Company G 860 633-7713 — Glastonbury (G-3061)
Multi-Metal Manufacturing Inc E 203 723-8887 — Naugatuck (G-4904)
▲ OEM Sources LLC G 203 283-5415 — Milford (G-4597)
Olson Brothers Company F 860 747-6844 — Plainville (G-6850)
Palladin Precision Pdts Inc E 203 574-0246 — Waterbury (G-9574)
Petron Automation Inc E 860 274-9091 — Watertown (G-9722)
Precision Methods Incorporated F 203 879-1429 — Wolcott (G-10580)
Prime Engneered Components Inc G 860 274-6773 — Watertown (G-9723)
Prime Screw Machine Pdts Inc D 860 274-6773 — Watertown (G-9725)
Pro-Manufactured Products Inc G 860 564-2197 — Plainfield (G-6750)
Quality Automatics Inc E 860 945-4795 — Oakville (G-6459)
Raypax Manufacturing Co Inc G 203 758-7416 — Waterbury (G-9592)
▲ Rgd Technologies Corp D 860 589-0756 — Bristol (G-1107)
Royal Screw Machine Pdts Co E 860 845-8920 — Bristol (G-1114)
S & M Swiss Products Inc G 860 283-4020 — Thomaston (G-8804)
Selectcom Mfg Co Inc G 203 879-9900 — Wolcott (G-10588)
Sga Components Group LLC G 203 758-3702 — Prospect (G-7024)
Sheldon Precision LLC G 203 758-4441 — Waterbury (G-9603)
Sheldon Precision LLC E 203 758-4441 — Prospect (G-7025)
Space Swiss Manufacturing Inc F 860 567-4341 — Litchfield (G-3900)
Specialty Products Mfg LLC G 860 621-6969 — Southington (G-7979)
Sperry Automatics Co Inc E 203 729-4589 — Naugatuck (G-4922)
Sun Corp G 860 567-0817 — Morris (G-4792)
▲ Supreme-Lake Mfg Inc D 860 621-8911 — Plantsville (G-6913)
T & J Screw Machine Pdts LLC G 860 417-3801 — Oakville (G-6463)
Thomastn-Mdtown Screw Mch Pdts F 860 283-9796 — Thomaston (G-8812)
Thomaston Industries Inc F 860 283-4358 — Thomaston (G-8813)
Tomz Corporation C 860 829-0670 — Berlin (G-226)
Tri-Star Industries Inc E 860 828-7570 — Berlin (G-227)
Tryon Manufacturing Company G 203 929-0464 — Shelton (G-7572)
Tyler Automatics Incorporated E 860 283-5878 — Thomaston (G-8815)
Ville Swiss Automatics Inc F 203 756-2825 — Waterbury (G-9622)
Waterbury Screw Machine G 203 756-8084 — Waterbury (G-9629)
Waterbury Screw Mch Pdts Co E 203 756-8084 — Waterbury (G-9630)
Waterbury Swiss Automatics E 203 573-8584 — Waterbury (G-9631)
Whiteledge Inc G 860 647-1883 — Manchester (G-4106)
Winslow Manufacturing Inc F 203 269-1977 — Wallingford (G-9403)
Wold Tool Engineering Inc G 860 564-8338 — Brooklyn (G-1259)

3452 Bolts, Nuts, Screws, Rivets & Washers

Aerotech Fasteners Inc F 860 928-6300 — Putnam (G-7028)
Ametek Inc C 203 265-6731 — Wallingford (G-9203)
Atp Industries LLC F 860 479-5007 — Plainville (G-6773)
◆ Bead Industries Inc E 203 301-0270 — Milford (G-4466)
Cast Global Manufacturing Corp F 203 828-6147 — Oxford (G-6648)
Click Bond Inc E 860 274-5435 — Watertown (G-9694)
Contorq Components LLC F 860 225-3366 — New Britain (G-4966)
Crescent Mnfacturing Operating E 860 673-1921 — Burlington (G-1265)
▼ Deringer-Ney Inc C 860 242-2281 — Bloomfield (G-407)
Eastern Company E 203 729-2255 — Naugatuck (G-4878)
▲ Edson Manufacturing Inc F 203 879-1411 — Wolcott (G-10563)
Hessel Industries Inc G 203 736-2317 — Derby (G-2115)
Holo-Krome USA E 800 879-6205 — Wallingford (G-9284)
Horberg Industries Inc F 203 334-9444 — Bridgeport (G-787)
Horst Engrg De Mexico LLC E 860 289-8209 — East Hartford (G-2334)
Howard Engineering LLC E 203 729-5213 — Naugatuck (G-4889)
Industrial Prssure Washers LLC G 860 608-6153 — Wethersfield (G-10197)
John C Green G 203 878-3781 — Milford (G-4561)
L & M Manufacturing Co Inc E 860 379-2751 — New Hartford (G-5201)
▲ Lab Security Systems Corp E 860 589-6037 — Bristol (G-1060)
Luis Pressure Washer G 203 706-7399 — Waterbury (G-9518)
Matthew Warren Inc G 203 888-2133 — Seymour (G-7355)
McMellon Bros Incorporated E 203 375-5685 — Stratford (G-8648)
Metalform Acquisition LLC F 860 224-2630 — New Britain (G-5016)
Miniature Nut & Screw Corp G 860 953-4490 — Newington (G-5678)
Mogo Rehab Incorporated G 860 673-5324 — Avon (G-94)
Narragansett Screw Co F 860 379-4059 — Winsted (G-10531)
Nelson Stud Welding Inc G 800 635-9353 — Farmington (G-2935)
▲ North East Fasteners Corp E 860 589-3242 — Terryville (G-8767)
▲ Nucap US Inc E 203 879-1423 — Wolcott (G-10578)
Plastic and Met Components Co F 203 877-2723 — Milford (G-4609)
▲ Progressive Stamping Co De Inc E 248 299-7100 — Farmington (G-2951)
▲ Rbc Prcision Pdts - Bremen Inc E 203 267-7001 — Oxford (G-6692)
▲ Spirol International Corp C 860 774-8571 — Danielson (G-2003)
▲ Spirol Intl Holdg Corp C 860 774-8571 — Danielson (G-2004)
Stanley Black & Decker Inc C 860 225-5111 — New Britain (G-5061)
Thread Rolling Inc F 860 528-1515 — East Hartford (G-2385)
▲ Tico Titanium Inc E 248 446-0400 — Wallingford (G-9384)
▲ Triem Industries LLC E 203 888-1212 — Terryville (G-8775)
United Thread Rolling LLC G 860 290-9349 — East Hartford (G-2397)
Universal Thread Grinding Co F 203 336-1849 — Fairfield (G-2861)
William Magenau & Company Inc G 860 423-7713 — Willimantic (G-10238)
Wilson Anchor Bolt Sleeve G 203 516-5260 — Derby (G-2132)
Wire Solutions LLC G 860 836-0787 — Plainville (G-6878)

3462 Iron & Steel Forgings

Afc Industries LLC G 860 246-7411 — Hartford (G-3549)
▲ Bourdon Forge Co Inc C 860 632-2740 — Middletown (G-4326)
Bristol Instrument Gears Inc F 860 583-1395 — Bristol (G-989)
Carlton Forge Works E 860 873-9730 — Moodus (G-4773)
▲ Consoldted Inds Acqsition Corp D 203 272-5371 — Cheshire (G-1374)
Cunningham Industries Inc G 203 324-2942 — Stamford (G-8171)
East Shore Wire Rope G 203 469-5204 — East Haven (G-2422)
Flange Lock LLC G 203 861-9400 — Greenwich (G-3163)
◆ Geneve Holdings Inc G 203 358-8000 — Stamford (G-8216)
Iron and Grain Co LLC G 860 840-2179 — West Hartford (G-9823)
J & H Mobile Mechanic LLC G 203 266-4748 — Woodbury (G-10639)
J J Ryan Corporation C 860 628-0393 — Plantsville (G-6897)
▲ OEM Sources LLC G 203 283-5415 — Milford (G-4597)
Paradigm Manchester Inc C 860 649-2888 — Manchester (G-4069)
Perry Technology Corporation D 860 738-2525 — New Hartford (G-5206)
Red Oak Stable LLC G 860 642-4671 — Lebanon (G-3861)
Roller Bearing Co Amer Inc E 203 758-8272 — Middlebury (G-4289)
Secondaries Inc G 203 879-4633 — Wolcott (G-10587)
United Gear & Machine Co Inc F 860 623-6618 — Suffield (G-8737)
White Bronze LLC G 214 605-7352 — Bridgeport (G-936)
William Martin G 860 355-1919 — Gaylordsville (G-2997)

3463 Nonferrous Forgings

GE Steam Power Inc G 860 688-1911 — Windsor (G-10390)

3465 Automotive Stampings

3M Company D 203 237-5541 — Meriden (G-4134)
Arthur G Byrne Co Inc G 203 461-8805 — Stamford (G-8096)
▲ C Cowles & Company D 203 865-3117 — North Haven (G-5916)

SIC SECTION 34 FABRICATED METAL PRODUCTS, EXCEPT MACHINERY AND TRANSPORTATION EQUIPMENT

CT Moldings Inc ....G....... 203 612-4922
Bridgeport *(G-740)*
Distinctive Steering Wheels ....G....... 860 274-9087
Watertown *(G-9702)*
Edison Atlas LLC ....G....... 860 335-6455
Rocky Hill *(G-7237)*
Inertia Dynamics Inc ....F....... 860 379-1252
New Hartford *(G-5198)*
Perrin Manufacturing ....G....... 203 265-1325
Wallingford *(G-9335)*
▲ **Progressive Stamping Co De Inc** .....E....... 248 299-7100
Farmington *(G-2951)*
Subimods LLC ....G....... 860 291-0015
Bloomfield *(G-489)*

3466 Crowns & Closures

Eyelet Design Inc ....D....... 203 754-4141
Waterbury *(G-9477)*
Orca Inc ....E....... 860 223-4180
New Britain *(G-5026)*

3469 Metal Stampings, NEC

A & D Components Inc ....G....... 860 582-9541
Bristol *(G-949)*
A G Russell Company Inc ....G....... 860 247-9093
Hartford *(G-3543)*
▲ **Acme Monaco Corporation** ....C....... 860 224-1349
New Britain *(G-4934)*
Addamo Manufacturing Inc ....G....... 860 667-2601
Newington *(G-5619)*
Alfro Custom Manufacturing Co ....G....... 203 264-6246
Southbury *(G-7843)*
▲ **Alinabal Inc** ....C....... 203 877-3241
Milford *(G-4448)*
▲ **Alinabal Holdings Corporation** ....B....... 203 877-3241
Milford *(G-4449)*
Alto Products Corp Al ....E....... 860 747-2736
Plainville *(G-6769)*
▲ **American Precision Product LLC** .....G....... 860 274-7301
Watertown *(G-9680)*
▲ **American Standard Company** ....E....... 860 628-9643
Southington *(G-7889)*
Anderson Manufacturing Company ......G....... 203 263-2318
Woodbury *(G-10624)*
Arcade Technology LLC ....E....... 203 366-3871
Bridgeport *(G-699)*
Arrow Manufacturing Company ....E....... 860 589-3900
Bristol *(G-966)*
Astro Industries Inc ....G....... 860 828-6304
Berlin *(G-161)*
Atlantic Precision Spring Inc ....E....... 860 583-1864
Bristol *(G-968)*
Atlas Stamping & Mfg Corp ....E....... 860 757-3233
Newington *(G-5629)*
B & G Forming Technology Inc ....G....... 203 235-2169
Meriden *(G-4147)*
Barlow Metal Stamping Inc ....E....... 860 583-1387
Bristol *(G-972)*
Barnes Group Inc ....D....... 860 582-9581
Bristol *(G-974)*
Barnes Group Inc ....G....... 860 298-7740
Farmington *(G-2882)*
▲ **Barnes Group Inc** ....B....... 860 583-7070
Bristol *(G-973)*
Bearicuda Inc ....G....... 860 361-6860
Litchfield *(G-3884)*
Ben Art Manufacturing Co Inc ....G....... 203 758-4435
Prospect *(G-6993)*
Bessette Holdings Inc ....E....... 860 289-6000
East Hartford *(G-2298)*
Beta Shim Co ....E....... 203 926-1150
Shelton *(G-7404)*
Birotech Inc ....G....... 203 968-5080
Stamford *(G-8112)*
Blase Manufacturing Company ....D....... 203 375-5646
Stratford *(G-8584)*
Bml Tool & Mfg Corp ....D....... 203 880-9485
Monroe *(G-4699)*
Bowden Engineering Co ....G....... 860 583-9585
Bristol *(G-985)*
Bracone Metal Spinning Inc ....E....... 860 628-5927
Southington *(G-7897)*
Bridgeport Tl & Stamping Corp ....E....... 203 336-2501
Bridgeport *(G-723)*
Bristol Tool & Die Company ....E....... 860 582-2577
Bristol *(G-993)*
C F D Engineering Company ....E....... 203 758-4148
Prospect *(G-6996)*
▲ **Carpin Manufacturing Inc** ....D....... 203 574-2556
Waterbury *(G-9446)*
Cee Orange LLC ....G....... 203 799-2665
Orange *(G-6590)*
Century Spring Mfg Co Inc ....E....... 860 582-3344
Bristol *(G-1000)*
Cgl Inc ....F....... 860 945-6166
Watertown *(G-9691)*
Cheshire Manufacturing Co Inc ....G....... 203 272-3586
Cheshire *(G-1369)*
▲ **Cly-Del Manufacturing Company** ......C....... 203 574-2100
Waterbury *(G-9452)*
Companion Industries Inc ....D....... 860 628-0504
Southington *(G-7907)*
◆ **Component Engineers Inc** ....D....... 203 269-0557
Wallingford *(G-9235)*
Conn Dept Motor Vehicles ....G....... 203 840-1993
Norwalk *(G-6126)*
▲ **Connectcut Spring Stmping Corp** ....B....... 860 677-1341
Farmington *(G-2891)*
Connecticut Fine Blanking ....G....... 203 925-0012
Shelton *(G-7422)*
Consulting Engrg Dev Svcs Inc ....D....... 203 828-6528
Oxford *(G-6653)*
▲ **Cowles Stamping Inc** ....E....... 203 865-3117
North Haven *(G-5931)*
Danco Manufacturing LLC ....G....... 860 870-1706
Vernon Rockville *(G-9167)*
Demsey Manufacturing Co Inc ....E....... 860 274-6209
Watertown *(G-9701)*
▼ **Deringer-Ney Inc** ....C....... 860 242-2281
Bloomfield *(G-407)*
Di-El Tool & Manufacturing ....G....... 203 235-2169
Meriden *(G-4166)*
◆ **Durham Manufacturing Company** .....D....... 860 349-3427
Durham *(G-2146)*
▼ **Dynamic Manufacturing Company** ...G....... 860 589-2751
Bristol *(G-1023)*
▲ **Empire Industries Inc** ....E....... 860 647-1431
Manchester *(G-4015)*
Excel Spring & Stamping LLC ....G....... 860 585-1495
Bristol *(G-1033)*
Eyelet Crafters Inc ....D....... 203 757-9221
Waterbury *(G-9476)*
Eyelet Design Inc ....D....... 203 754-4141
Waterbury *(G-9477)*
Eyelet Tech LLC ....E....... 203 879-5306
Wolcott *(G-10564)*
Eyelet Toolmakers Inc ....E....... 860 274-5423
Watertown *(G-9705)*
Fabor Fourslide Inc ....G....... 203 753-4380
Waterbury *(G-9479)*
Ferre Form Metal Products ....F....... 860 274-3280
Oakville *(G-6452)*
Finest Engraving LLC ....G....... 860 742-7579
Andover *(G-7)*
Forrest Machine Inc ....D....... 860 563-1796
Berlin *(G-180)*
Four Star Manufacturing Co ....E....... 860 583-1614
Bristol *(G-1041)*
Fourslide Spring Stamping Inc ....E....... 860 583-1688
Bristol *(G-1042)*
Fries Spinning & Stampings ....G....... 203 265-1678
Wallingford *(G-9271)*
◆ **Gem Manufacturing Co Inc** ....D....... 203 574-1466
Waterbury *(G-9485)*
Gemco Manufacturing Co Inc ....E....... 860 628-5529
Southington *(G-7926)*
Glen Manufacturing Co Inc ....G....... 860 589-0881
Terryville *(G-8758)*
Globe Tool & Met Stampg Co Inc ....E....... 860 621-6807
Southington *(G-7929)*
Government Surplus Sales Inc ....G....... 860 247-7787
Hartford *(G-3601)*
Guaranteed Quality Parts L L C ....G....... 860 450-0419
Willimantic *(G-10228)*
▲ **H&T Waterbury Inc** ....C....... 203 574-2240
Waterbury *(G-9494)*
Hessel Industries Inc ....G....... 203 736-2317
Derby *(G-2115)*
Hexcel Corporation ....E....... 203 969-0666
Stamford *(G-8233)*
Hi-Tech Fabricating Inc ....E....... 203 284-0894
Cheshire *(G-1396)*
Hob Industries Inc ....E....... 203 879-3028
Wolcott *(G-10568)*
Hobson and Motzer Incorporated ....C....... 860 349-1756
Durham *(G-2149)*
Howard Engineering LLC ....E....... 203 729-5213
Naugatuck *(G-4889)*
Hoyt Manufacturing Co Inc ....G....... 860 628-2050
Southington *(G-7936)*
Hurley Manufacturing Company ....E....... 860 379-8506
New Hartford *(G-5194)*
Hylie Products Incorporated ....F....... 203 439-8786
Cheshire *(G-1397)*
Illinois Tool Works Inc ....E....... 203 720-1676
Naugatuck *(G-4890)*
Illinois Tool Works Inc ....C....... 203 574-2119
Waterbury *(G-9503)*
▲ **Insulpane Connecticut Inc** ....D....... 800 922-3248
Hamden *(G-3465)*
ITW Drawform Inc ....E....... 203 574-3200
Waterbury *(G-9506)*
J & J Precision Eyelet Inc ....D....... 860 283-8243
Thomaston *(G-8793)*
J D Precision Machine Inc ....G....... 860 653-7787
East Granby *(G-2208)*
J T Tool Co Inc ....G....... 203 874-1234
Milford *(G-4558)*
Jennings Associates Inc ....G....... 860 749-4281
Somers *(G-7662)*
Jo Vek Tool and Die Mfg Co ....G....... 203 755-1884
Waterbury *(G-9511)*
▲ **Joma Incorporated** ....E....... 203 759-0848
Waterbury *(G-9513)*
Joval Machine Co Inc ....E....... 203 284-0082
Yalesville *(G-10694)*
Keberg LLC ....G....... 860 255-8135
Plainville *(G-6829)*
Lawrence Holdings Inc ....F....... 203 949-1600
Wallingford *(G-9301)*
Leelynd Corp ....G....... 203 753-9137
Waterbury *(G-9517)*
Lyons Tool and Die Company ....E....... 203 238-2689
Meriden *(G-4190)*
M & I Industries Inc ....G....... 860 747-6421
Plainville *(G-6837)*
▼ **Marion Manufacturing Company** ......E....... 203 272-5376
Cheshire *(G-1411)*
Mark Nicoletti ....G....... 860 582-5645
Bristol *(G-1068)*
Mastercraft Tool and Mch Co ....F....... 860 628-5551
Southington *(G-7950)*
McM Stamping Corporation ....E....... 203 792-3080
Danbury *(G-1881)*
McMullin Manufacturing Corp ....E....... 203 740-3360
Brookfield *(G-1204)*
Meriden Manufacturing Inc ....D....... 203 237-7481
Meriden *(G-4197)*
Metalform Acquisition LLC ....F....... 860 224-2630
New Britain *(G-5016)*
Metallon Inc ....E....... 860 283-8265
Thomaston *(G-8797)*
Midconn Precision Mfg LLC ....G....... 860 584-1340
Bristol *(G-1071)*
Minh Long Fine Porcelain ....G....... 860 586-8755
Hartford *(G-3643)*
MJM Marga LLC ....G....... 203 729-0600
Naugatuck *(G-4903)*
Mohawk Manufacturing Company ....F....... 860 632-2345
Middletown *(G-4381)*
National Die Company ....G....... 203 879-1408
Wolcott *(G-10576)*
National Spring & Stamping Inc ....E....... 860 283-0203
Thomaston *(G-8798)*
Nesci Enterprises Inc ....G....... 860 267-2588
East Hampton *(G-2271)*
New Hartford Industrial Park ....E....... 860 379-8506
New Hartford *(G-5203)*
▲ **No Butts Bin Company Inc** ....G....... 203 245-5924
Madison *(G-3942)*
▲ **Nucap US Inc** ....E....... 203 879-1423
Wolcott *(G-10578)*
▲ **OEM Sources LLC** ....G....... 203 283-5415
Milford *(G-4597)*
Okay Industries Inc ....G....... 860 225-8707
Berlin *(G-204)*
Oscar Jobs ....G....... 860 583-7834
Bristol *(G-1083)*
Owen Tool and Mfg Co Inc ....G....... 860 628-6540
Southington *(G-7961)*
P&G Metal Components Corp ....F....... 860 243-2220
Bloomfield *(G-458)*
Paradigm Prcision Holdings LLC ....G....... 860 649-2888
Manchester *(G-4071)*
Patriot Manufacturing LLC ....G....... 860 506-2213
Bristol *(G-1086)*
Performance Machine Inc ....G....... 860 974-3664
Woodstock *(G-10678)*
Platt Brothers & Company ....D....... 203 753-4194
Waterbury *(G-9580)*

SIC

Employee Codes: A=Over 500 employees, B=251-500
C=101-250, D=51-100, E=20-50, F=10-19, G=1-9
2020 Harris Connecticut
Manufacturers Directory
425

Pr-Mx Holdings Company LLC ....F 203 925-0012
Shelton (G-7532)
Pratt-Read Corporation ....F 860 625-3620
Branford (G-637)
▲ Precision Resource Inc ....C 203 925-0012
Shelton (G-7534)
Precision Rsurce Intl Sls Corp ....G 203 925-0012
Shelton (G-7535)
Preferred Tool & Die Inc ....D 203 925-8525
Shelton (G-7537)
Pressure Blast Mfg Co Inc ....F 800 722-5278
South Windsor (G-7811)
Preyco Mfg Co Inc ....G 203 574-4545
Waterbury (G-9587)
Prospect Machine Products Inc ....E 203 758-4448
Prospect (G-7019)
R A Tool Co ....G 203 877-2998
Milford (G-4622)
▲ Record Products America Inc ....F 203 248-6371
Hamden (G-3504)
Richards Metal Products Inc ....F 203 879-2555
Wolcott (G-10583)
Rowley Spring & Stamping Corp ....C 860 582-8175
Bristol (G-1113)
RTC Mfg Co Inc ....G 800 888-3701
Watertown (G-9731)
Satellite Aerospace Inc ....E 860 643-2771
Manchester (G-4085)
▲ Schaeffler Aerospace USA Corp ....B 203 744-2211
Danbury (G-1936)
Scott Metal Products ....G 860 928-4366
Woodstock (G-10683)
Semco Tool Manufacturing Co ....G 203 723-7411
Naugatuck (G-4918)
Seward Group LLC ....G 203 357-1900
Darien (G-2044)
◆ Siemon Company ....A 860 945-4200
Watertown (G-9734)
Solla Eyelet Products Inc ....E 860 274-5729
Watertown (G-9737)
Somers Tool & Weld Shop ....G 860 314-1075
Bristol (G-1120)
Sonchief Electrics Inc ....G 860 379-2741
Winsted (G-10538)
Southington Tool & Mfg Corp ....E 860 276-0021
Plantsville (G-6912)
Spartan Aerospace LLC ....D 860 533-7500
Manchester (G-4090)
▲ Spirol International Corp ....C 860 774-8571
Danielson (G-2003)
▲ Spirol Intl Holdg Corp ....C 860 774-8571
Danielson (G-2004)
▲ Stevens Company Incorporated ....D 860 283-8201
Thomaston (G-8806)
Stewart Efi LLC ....C 860 283-8213
Thomaston (G-8807)
Stewart Efi LLC ....E 860 283-2523
Thomaston (G-8808)
Stewart Efi Connecticut LLC ....C 860 283-8213
Thomaston (G-8809)
Stewart Efi Texas LLC ....G 860 283-8213
Thomaston (G-8810)
Taco Fasteners Inc ....F 860 747-5597
Plainville (G-6867)
Target Custom Manufacturing Co ....G 860 388-5848
Old Saybrook (G-6573)
Telke Tool & Die Mfg Co ....G 860 828-9955
Kensington (G-3819)
Tiger Enterprises Inc ....E 860 621-9155
Plantsville (G-6914)
▲ Tops Manufacturing Co Inc ....G 203 655-9367
Darien (G-2047)
▲ Truelove & Maclean Inc ....C 860 274-9600
Watertown (G-9743)
Truelove Maclean Inc ....G 203 574-2240
Waterbury (G-9619)
Tyger Tool Inc ....F 203 375-4344
Stratford (G-8699)
Utitec Inc ....D 860 945-0605
Watertown (G-9744)
Utitec Holdings Inc ....G 860 945-0601
Watertown (G-9745)
Washer Tech Inc ....G 203 886-0054
Meriden (G-4266)
Wces Inc ....F 203 573-1325
Waterbury (G-9632)
Weimann Brothers Mfg Co ....F 203 735-3311
Derby (G-2130)
West Shore Metals LLC ....G 860 749-8013
Enfield (G-2705)
Whitebeck John ....G 860 567-1398
Bantam (G-128)

3471 Electroplating, Plating, Polishing, Anodizing & Coloring

A & A Products and Services ....G 860 683-0879
Windsor (G-10350)
A&R Plating Services LLC ....G 860 274-9562
Oakville (G-6448)
A-1 Chrome and Polishing Corp ....F 860 666-4593
Newington (G-5616)
Accurate Burring Company ....F 860 747-8640
Plainville (G-6765)
Allied Metal Finishing L L C ....G 860 290-8865
South Windsor (G-7704)
Alpha Plating and Finishing Co ....F 860 747-5002
Plainville (G-6768)
Aluminum Finishing Company Inc ....E 203 333-1690
Bridgeport (G-689)
American Electro Products Inc ....C 203 756-7051
Waterbury (G-9427)
Anodic Incorporated ....F 203 268-9966
Stevenson (G-8520)
Anomatic Corporation ....G 203 720-2367
Naugatuck (G-4859)
Aqua Blasting Corp ....F 860 242-8855
Bloomfield (G-387)
Arrow Space Deburring ....G 860 683-0879
Windsor (G-10364)
B & P Plating Equipment LLC ....F 860 589-5799
Bristol (G-969)
Bar Plating Inc ....G 203 630-1046
Meriden (G-4148)
Baron & Young Co Inc ....G 860 589-3235
Bristol (G-976)
Bass Plating Company ....E 860 243-2557
Bloomfield (G-392)
Blasting Techniques Inc ....G 860 528-4717
South Windsor (G-7718)
Broad Peak Manufacturing LLC ....E 203 678-4664
Wallingford (G-9223)
C & S Engineering Inc ....E 203 235-5727
Meriden (G-4153)
Chemical-Electric Corporation ....G 203 743-5131
Danbury (G-1767)
Chicks Sandblasting ....G 860 334-0059
Preston (G-6982)
Chromalloy Component Svcs Inc ....G 203 924-1666
Shelton (G-7418)
Clear & Colored Coatings LLC ....G 203 879-1379
Wolcott (G-10554)
Colonial Coatings Inc ....E 203 783-9933
Milford (G-4491)
Color Ite Refinishing Co ....G 203 393-0240
Bethany (G-238)
Component Technologies Inc ....E 860 667-1065
Newington (G-5641)
▼ Composiclean LLC ....G 860 432-0067
Glastonbury (G-3021)
Concept Team Associates LLC ....G 203 269-5152
Wallingford (G-9236)
Connecticut Anodizing Finshg ....E 203 367-1765
Bridgeport (G-739)
Country Creations By Carol ....G 860 848-0276
Uncasville (G-9097)
CRC Chrome Corporation ....F 203 630-1008
Meriden (G-4163)
Custom Chrome Plating ....G 203 265-5667
Wallingford (G-9244)
D D M Metal Finishing Co Inc ....G 860 872-4683
Tolland (G-8857)
Danbury Metal Finishing Inc ....G 203 748-5044
Danbury (G-1784)
Dav-Co Finishing LLC ....G 860 828-5552
Berlin (G-175)
Deburr Co ....E 860 621-6634
Plantsville (G-6890)
Deburring House Inc ....E 860 828-0889
East Berlin (G-2165)
Deburring Laboratories Inc ....E 860 829-6300
New Britain (G-4972)
E & J Parts Cleaning Inc ....F 203 757-1716
Waterbury (G-9469)
EDS Perfect Polishing ....G 203 259-5187
Fairfield (G-2779)
▲ Ems International Inc ....G 860 526-2060
Chester (G-1472)
Etherington Brothers Inc ....G 860 585-5624
Bristol (G-1031)
Eyelet Crafters Inc ....D 203 757-9221
Waterbury (G-9476)
Gar Electro Forming ....G 203 885-1105
Danbury (G-1832)
Gybenorth Industries LLC ....F 203 876-9876
Milford (G-4546)
Halco Inc ....D 203 575-9450
Waterbury (G-9495)
Har-Conn Chrome Company ....D 860 236-6801
West Hartford (G-9815)
HI-Tech Polishing Inc ....F 860 665-1399
Newington (G-5659)
Hitech Chrome Pltg & Polsg Lc ....G 860 456-8070
North Windham (G-6038)
◆ Hubbard-Hall Inc ....C 203 756-5521
Waterbury (G-9501)
J H Metal Finishing Inc ....G 860 223-6412
New Britain (G-5005)
J M Compounds Inc ....G 203 376-9854
Meriden (G-4176)
Jarvis Precision Polishing ....F 860 589-5822
Bristol (G-1052)
K & K Black Oxide LLC ....G 860 223-1805
New Britain (G-5007)
Lake Grinding Company ....G 203 336-3767
Bridgeport (G-822)
Light Metals Coloring Co Inc ....D 860 621-0145
Southington (G-7947)
Logan Steel Inc ....E 203 235-0811
Meriden (G-4188)
M & Z Engineering Inc ....G 860 496-0282
Torrington (G-8945)
Marsam Metal Finishing Co ....E 860 826-5489
New Britain (G-5013)
Maryann D Langdon ....G 203 562-7161
New Haven (G-5326)
Mike Fineran ....G 860 974-3276
Pomfret Center (G-6942)
◆ Mirror Polishing & Pltg Co Inc ....E 203 574-5400
Waterbury (G-9544)
National Chromium Company Inc ....F 860 928-7965
Putnam (G-7052)
National Integrated Inds Inc ....C 860 677-7995
Farmington (G-2933)
National Integrated Inds Inc ....D 203 756-7051
Waterbury (G-9553)
Nemfi Pfs ....G 860 640-4600
Windsor (G-10413)
New England Chrome Plating ....G 860 528-7176
East Hartford (G-2346)
Niro Companies LLC ....G 860 982-5645
Berlin (G-203)
▲ Nylo Metal Finishing LLC ....G 203 574-5477
Waterbury (G-9565)
P&G Metal Components Corp ....F 860 243-2220
Bloomfield (G-458)
Plainville Electro Plating Co ....G 860 525-5328
Hartford (G-3665)
Plainville Plating Company Inc ....D 860 747-1624
Plainville (G-6852)
Plasma Technology Incorporated ....E 860 282-0659
South Windsor (G-7807)
◆ Praxair Inc ....B 203 837-2000
Danbury (G-1913)
Precision Deburring Inc ....G 860 583-4662
Bristol (G-1096)
Precision Finishing Svcs Inc ....E 860 882-1073
Windsor (G-10424)
Precision Plating Corp ....G 860 875-9267
Vernon (G-9150)
Prestige Metal Finishing LLC ....G 860 974-1999
Woodstock Valley (G-10693)
▲ Preventative Maintenance Corp ....F 860 683-1180
Poquonock (G-6948)
Quality Rolling Deburring Inc ....D 860 283-0271
Thomaston (G-8801)
Quicksand Blasting ....G 860 848-4482
Uncasville (G-9103)
R J Brass Inc ....F 860 793-2336
Plainville (G-6855)
Rader Industries Inc ....G 203 334-6739
Bridgeport (G-884)
Rayco Inc ....G 860 357-4693
New Britain (G-5041)
Rayco Metal Finishing Inc ....F 860 347-7434
Middletown (G-4402)
Reliable Plating & Polsg Co ....E 203 366-5261
Bridgeport (G-888)
Rollcorp LLC ....G 860 347-5227
Middletown (G-4406)

SIC SECTION — 34 FABRICATED METAL PRODUCTS, EXCEPT MACHINERY AND TRANSPORTATION EQUIPMENT

Scotts Metal Finishing LLC ....F 860 589-3778
  Bristol *(G-1116)*
Seaboard Metal Finishing Co ....E 203 933-1603
  New Britain *(G-5053)*
Seidel Inc ....D 203 757-7349
  Waterbury *(G-9600)*
▲ Seidel Inc ....D 203 757-7349
  Waterbury *(G-9601)*
Sifco Applied Srfc Cncepts LLC ....G 860 623-6006
  East Windsor *(G-2518)*
Silversmith Inc ....G 203 869-4244
  Greenwich *(G-3235)*
Smart Polishing ....G 203 559-1541
  Stamford *(G-8426)*
SMS Machine Inc ....G 860 829-0813
  East Berlin *(G-2176)*
Sousa Corp ....F 860 523-9090
  Newington *(G-5706)*
Spec Plating Inc ....F 203 366-3638
  Bridgeport *(G-911)*
▲ Summit Corporation of America ....D 860 283-4391
  Thomaston *(G-8811)*
Superior Plating Company ....D 203 255-1501
  Southport *(G-8011)*
Superior Technology Corp ....C 203 255-1501
  Southport *(G-8012)*
Suraci Metal Finishing LLC ....E 203 624-1345
  New Haven *(G-5407)*
Technical Metal Finishing Inc ....E 203 284-7825
  Wallingford *(G-9379)*
Unimetal Surface Finishing LLC ....E 203 729-8244
  Naugatuck *(G-4924)*
United States Fire Arms Mfg Co ....E 860 296-7441
  Hartford *(G-3708)*
Usc Technologies LLC ....G 203 378-9622
  Stratford *(G-8701)*
Vincent Jewelers ....G 203 882-8900
  Milford *(G-4674)*
Whyco Finishing Tech LLC ....E 860 283-5826
  Thomaston *(G-8824)*

3479 Coating & Engraving, NEC

A & E Engraving Service ....G 860 582-6503
  Bristol *(G-950)*
Ad Comm Ink ....G 860 824-7565
  Canaan *(G-1280)*
Advanced Graphics Inc ....E 203 378-0471
  Stratford *(G-8564)*
Advanced Powder Coating Techno ...G 860 612-0631
  New Britain *(G-4939)*
American Bus Tele & Tech LLC ....G 860 643-2200
  Manchester *(G-3982)*
American Metallizing ....G 860 289-1677
  South Windsor *(G-7706)*
American Metaseal of Conn ....G 203 787-0281
  Hamden *(G-3414)*
American Powdercoating LLC ....G 860 267-8870
  East Hampton *(G-2254)*
American Roller Company LLC ....F 203 598-3100
  Middlebury *(G-4273)*
American Rubber Stamp Company ...G 203 755-1135
  Cheshire *(G-1351)*
Ann S Davis ....F 860 642-7228
  Lebanon *(G-3846)*
Baron & Young Co Inc ....G 860 589-3235
  Bristol *(G-976)*
Biomerics LLC ....D 203 268-7238
  Monroe *(G-4698)*
Cametoid Technologies Inc ....F 860 646-4667
  Manchester *(G-3990)*
Central Connecticut Coating ....F 860 528-8281
  East Hartford *(G-2303)*
Chem-Tron Pntg Pwdr Cating Inc .....G 203 743-5131
  Danbury *(G-1766)*
Clear & Colored Coatings LLC ....G 203 879-1379
  Wolcott *(G-10555)*
Colonial Coatings Inc ....E 203 783-9933
  Milford *(G-4491)*
Competitive Edge Coatings LLC ....G 860 882-0762
  South Windsor *(G-7734)*
Competitive Edge Coatings LLC ....G 860 267-6255
  Colchester *(G-1546)*
▲ Conard Corporation ....E 860 659-0591
  Glastonbury *(G-3022)*
Connecticut Plasma Tech LLC ....F 860 289-5500
  South Windsor *(G-7735)*
Covalent Coating Tech LLC ....G 203 214-6452
  East Hartford *(G-2310)*
Dexter & Co ....G 860 536-9506
  Mystic *(G-4811)*

Distinctive Coating LLC ....G 860 530-1233
  Hebron *(G-3747)*
Donwell Company ....E 860 649-5374
  Manchester *(G-4010)*
Dynamic Coating Solutions LLC ....G 860 321-7483
  Bristol *(G-1022)*
Engineered Coatings Inc ....E 860 567-5556
  Litchfield *(G-3889)*
F J Weidner Inc ....G 203 469-4202
  East Haven *(G-2425)*
Farrell Prcsion Mtalcraft Corp ....E 860 355-2651
  New Milford *(G-5532)*
Final Liquid Coating LLC ....G 860 585-5625
  Bristol *(G-1038)*
Fonda Fabricating & Welding Co ......G 860 793-0601
  Plainville *(G-6812)*
Gybenorth Industries LLC ....F 203 876-9876
  Milford *(G-4546)*
Halco Inc ....D 203 575-9450
  Waterbury *(G-9495)*
Hartford Industrial Finshg Co ....G 860 243-2040
  Bloomfield *(G-418)*
High Grade Finishing Co LLC ....F 860 749-8883
  Enfield *(G-2649)*
▼ Highway Safety Corp ....D 860 659-4330
  Glastonbury *(G-3049)*
Identification Products Corp ....G 203 331-0931
  Bridgeport *(G-790)*
Identification Products Corp ....F 203 334-5969
  Bridgeport *(G-791)*
Immersive Custom Coatings ....G 401 636-1196
  Putnam *(G-7046)*
Imperial Metal Finishing Inc ....G 203 377-1229
  Stratford *(G-8631)*
Infante Coatings LLC ....G 203 252-6370
  Derby *(G-2117)*
Integrity Cylinder Sales LLC ....G 860 267-6667
  East Hampton *(G-2265)*
▲ ITW Hlographic Specialty Films ....G 860 243-0343
  Bloomfield *(G-424)*
Jet Process Corporation ....G 203 985-6000
  North Haven *(G-5953)*
Jonmandy Corporation ....G 860 482-2354
  Torrington *(G-8940)*
K & G Corp ....F 860 643-1133
  Manchester *(G-4041)*
Line-X of Hartford ....G 860 216-6180
  Hartford *(G-3628)*
▲ Marjan Inc ....F 203 573-1742
  Waterbury *(G-9534)*
▲ Materion Lrge Area Catings LLC ...D 216 486-4200
  Windsor *(G-10407)*
Metal Morphous ....G 203 239-0411
  North Haven *(G-5963)*
Metallizing Service Co Inc ....E 860 953-1144
  Hartford *(G-3641)*
▲ Metamorphic Materials Inc ....F 860 738-8638
  Winsted *(G-10529)*
Mitchell-Bate Company ....E 203 233-0862
  Waterbury *(G-9545)*
Modern Metal Finishing Inc ....F 203 267-1510
  Oxford *(G-6678)*
North East Powder Coating ....G 203 573-1543
  Waterbury *(G-9561)*
Paint & Powder Works LLC ....F 860 225-2019
  New Britain *(G-5028)*
Pauway Corp ....F 203 265-3939
  Wallingford *(G-9333)*
Pelegnos Stined GL Art Gallery ....G 860 621-2900
  Plantsville *(G-6907)*
Pioneer Coatings & Mfg LLC ....G 860 421-6086
  Madison *(G-3948)*
Plas-TEC Coatings Inc ....F 860 289-6029
  South Windsor *(G-7806)*
Plasti-Coat ....G 203 755-3741
  Waterbury *(G-9579)*
Plasti-Coat ....G 203 274-1234
  Middlebury *(G-4287)*
Plastonics Inc ....E 860 249-5455
  Hartford *(G-3666)*
◆ Praxair Inc ....B 203 837-2000
  Danbury *(G-1913)*
Praxair Surface Tech Inc ....G 203 837-2000
  Danbury *(G-1916)*
Praxair Surface Tech Inc ....D 860 646-0700
  Manchester *(G-4076)*
Pro Coatings LLC ....G 860 345-2107
  Higganum *(G-3776)*
Protective Home Coatings LLC ....G 203 410-5826
  Seymour *(G-7364)*

Pti Industries Inc ....G 860 698-9266
  Enfield *(G-2682)*
Pti Industries Inc ....E 800 318-8438
  Enfield *(G-2683)*
R and B Prtective Coatings LLC ....G 860 836-7854
  Middletown *(G-4400)*
Rdl Coatings LLC ....G 203 232-0411
  Oakville *(G-6461)*
▲ Robert Audette ....G 203 872-3119
  Cheshire *(G-1440)*
Rodriguez Ruiz Rosa Margarita ....G 860 840-0344
  Hartford *(G-3681)*
Shoreline Coatings LLC ....G 203 213-3471
  North Branford *(G-5855)*
Silver Lining Technologies LLC ....G 860 539-4182
  Vernon *(G-9152)*
Silversmith Inc ....G 203 869-4244
  Greenwich *(G-3235)*
▲ Summit Corporation of America ....D 860 283-4391
  Thomaston *(G-8811)*
Tetraflo ....G 860 575-0867
  Old Lyme *(G-6520)*
Tim Poloski ....G 860 508-6566
  Vernon Rockville *(G-9182)*
◆ U-Marq Usa LLC ....G 860 799-7800
  New Milford *(G-5603)*
Vitek ....G 203 351-1813
  Naugatuck *(G-4927)*
Vitek Research Corporation ....F 203 735-1813
  Naugatuck *(G-4928)*
Wired Inc ....G 601 992-0490
  Stratford *(G-8709)*
Zz Powder Coating ....G 860 917-7495
  Niantic *(G-5821)*

3482 Small Arms Ammunition

Brass City Munitions LLC ....G 203 509-7088
  Wolcott *(G-10549)*
Capstone Manufacturing Inc ....G 413 636-6170
  South Windsor *(G-7723)*
Classic Shotguns ....G 860 354-4648
  Roxbury *(G-7276)*
Fenrir Industries Inc ....F 203 977-0671
  Stamford *(G-8203)*
General Dynamics Ordnance ....F 860 404-0162
  Avon *(G-82)*
Illinois Tool Works Inc ....C 203 574-2119
  Waterbury *(G-9503)*
Independence Enterprises LLC ....G 774 549-8153
  Manchester *(G-4032)*
▲ Jkb Daira Inc ....G 203 642-4824
  Norwalk *(G-6223)*
Shell Shock Technologies Llc ....G 203 557-3256
  Westport *(G-10155)*

3483 Ammunition, Large

Buddy-Mentor Inc ....G 203 258-3871
  Bridgeport *(G-725)*
Ensign-Bickford Industries Inc ....E 860 658-4411
  Simsbury *(G-7622)*
Fenrir Industries Inc ....F 203 977-0671
  Stamford *(G-8203)*
Geneve Corporation ....E 203 358-8000
  Stamford *(G-8215)*
Glimmer of Light ....G 860 605-4086
  New Milford *(G-5537)*

3484 Small Arms

Colt Defense Emplye Pln ....G 860 232-4489
  West Hartford *(G-9789)*
Colt Defense LLC ....B 860 232-4489
  West Hartford *(G-9790)*
Colts Manufacturing Co LLC ....C 860 236-6311
  West Hartford *(G-9791)*
Continental Machine TI Co Inc ....D 860 223-2896
  New Britain *(G-4965)*
Deburring House Inc ....E 860 828-0889
  East Berlin *(G-2165)*
Dewey J Manufacturing Company ...G 203 264-3064
  Oxford *(G-6655)*
G W Elliot Inc ....G 860 528-6143
  East Hartford *(G-2329)*
Grimes Firearms LLC ....G 203 843-2271
  North Haven *(G-5944)*
Gunworks International L L C ....G 860 388-4591
  Old Saybrook *(G-6536)*
J & E Hidalgo Enterprises LLC ....G 203 246-2252
  Norwalk *(G-6214)*
▲ Jkb Daira Inc ....G 203 642-4824
  Norwalk *(G-6223)*

Employee Codes: A=Over 500 employees, B=251-500
C=101-250, D=51-100, E=20-50, F=10-19, G=1-9

34 FABRICATED METAL PRODUCTS, EXCEPT MACHINERY AND TRANSPORTATION EQUIPMENT

Kill Shot Precision LLC .... G 860 681-3162
  Bristol (G-1057)
Kinetic Development Group LLC .... G 203 888-4321
  Seymour (G-7353)
Lionheart Militaria Llc .... G 203 800-5759
  Guilford (G-3369)
M2 Tactical Solutions LLC .... G 203 247-3477
  Norwalk (G-6243)
Maverick Arms Inc .... G 203 230-5300
  North Haven (G-5961)
Mike Sadlak .... G 860 742-0227
  Coventry (G-1663)
▲ Mossberg Corporation .... G 203 230-5300
  North Haven (G-5966)
New Designz Inc .... F 860 384-1809
  Cheshire (G-1420)
▲ O F Mossberg & Sons Inc .... C 203 230-5300
  North Haven (G-5970)
Savage Arms Inc .... G 860 668-7049
  Suffield (G-8735)
Scott Olson Enterprises LLC .... G 860 482-4391
  Torrington (G-8967)
▲ Stag Arms LLC .... G 860 229-9994
  New Britain (G-5058)
Stag Arms LLC .... G 860 229-9994
  New Britain (G-5059)
▲ Sturm Ruger & Company Inc .... B 203 259-7843
  Southport (G-8010)
United States Fire Arms Mfg Co .... E 860 296-7441
  Hartford (G-3708)
US Firearms Manufacturing Co .... G 860 296-7441
  Hartford (G-3711)
Wilson Arms Company .... F 203 488-7297
  Branford (G-675)
Xavier Marcus .... G 203 543-2032
  Stratford (G-8711)

3489 Ordnance & Access, NEC

Capstone Manufacturing Inc .... G 413 636-6170
  South Windsor (G-7723)
Ensign-Bickford Industries Inc .... E 860 658-4411
  Simsbury (G-7622)
Fenrir Industries Inc .... F 203 977-0671
  Stamford (G-8203)
G W Elliot Inc .... G 860 528-6143
  East Hartford (G-2329)
Kaman Aerospace Corporation .... C 860 632-1000
  Middletown (G-4360)
Simulations LLC .... G 860 978-0772
  East Granby (G-2230)
Tek Arms Inc .... G 860 748-6289
  Hebron (G-3757)
United States Fire Arms Mfg Co .... E 860 296-7441
  Hartford (G-3708)

3491 Industrial Valves

BNL Industries Inc .... E 860 870-6222
  Vernon (G-9133)
Contemporary Products LLC .... E 860 346-9283
  Middletown (G-4332)
▲ Conval Inc .... C 860 749-0761
  Enfield (G-2633)
Cr-TEC Engineering Inc .... C 203 318-9500
  Madison (G-3914)
First Reserve Fund Viii LP .... G 203 661-6601
  Stamford (G-8205)
Fisher Controls Intl LLC .... C 860 599-1140
  North Stonington (G-6025)
Haltech Manufacturing Svcs LLC ...... G 860 625-0189
  New London (G-5473)
▲ Kip Inc .... C 860 677-0272
  Farmington (G-2922)
Logic Seal LLC .... G 203 598-3400
  Plainville (G-6834)
▼ Noank Controls LLC .... G 860 449-6776
  Groton (G-3301)
Northeast Pipeline Service LLC .... G 860 621-6921
  Southington (G-7960)
▲ Oventrop Corp .... E 860 413-9173
  East Granby (G-2222)
Parker-Hannifin Corporation .... C 860 827-2300
  New Britain (G-5030)
▲ Peter Paul Electronics Co Inc .... C 860 229-4884
  New Britain (G-5032)
▲ Rostra Vernatherm LLC .... E 860 582-6776
  Bristol (G-1112)
Ruby Automation LLC .... C 860 687-5000
  Bloomfield (G-479)
▲ Ruby Industrial Tech LLC .... D 860 687-5000
  Bloomfield (G-481)

Saf Industries LLC .... E 203 729-4900
  Meriden (G-4237)
Universal Building Contrls Inc .... F 203 235-1530
  Meriden (G-4260)
Watts .... G 203 230-8582
  Hamden (G-3528)

3492 Fluid Power Valves & Hose Fittings

American Metal Masters LLC .... G 860 621-6911
  Plantsville (G-6884)
Atp Industries LLC .... F 860 479-5007
  Plainville (G-6773)
◆ Clarcor Eng MBL Solutions LLC .... D 860 920-4200
  East Hartford (G-2306)
Crane Aerospace Inc .... C 203 363-7300
  Stamford (G-8165)
▲ Crane Co .... D 203 363-7300
  Stamford (G-8166)
Crane Controls Inc .... C 203 363-7300
  Stamford (G-8167)
Crane Intl Holdings Inc .... C 203 363-7300
  Stamford (G-8168)
▼ Enfield Technologies LLC .... F 203 375-3100
  Shelton (G-7439)
Faxon Engineering Company Inc ...... F 860 236-4266
  Bloomfield (G-410)
Fluid Dynamics LLC .... G 860 791-6325
  Manchester (G-4018)
Funkhouser Industrial Products .... G 860 653-1972
  East Granby (G-2205)
▲ Navtec Rigging Solutions Inc .... E 203 458-3163
  Clinton (G-1515)
Norgren Inc .... C 860 677-0272
  Farmington (G-2938)
Parker-Hannifin Corporation .... C 860 827-2300
  New Britain (G-5030)
Progressive Hydraulics Inc .... C 203 386-0885
  Stratford (G-8670)
Ruby Fluid Power LLC .... E 860 243-7100
  Bloomfield (G-480)
Saf Industries LLC .... E 203 729-4900
  Meriden (G-4237)
▲ Stanadyne Intrmdate Hldngs LLC .. C 860 525-0821
  Windsor (G-10440)

3493 Steel Springs, Except Wire

▲ Acme Monaco Corporation .... C 860 224-1349
  New Britain (G-4934)
American Specialty Co Inc .... F 203 929-5324
  Shelton (G-7393)
Arrow Manufacturing Company .... E 860 589-3900
  Bristol (G-966)
Atlantic Precision Spring Inc .... E 860 583-1864
  Bristol (G-968)
Century Spring Mfg Co Inc .... E 860 582-3344
  Bristol (G-1000)
▲ Connectcut Spring Stmping Corp .. B 860 677-1341
  Farmington (G-2891)
▲ Dayon Manufacturing Inc .... E 860 677-8561
  Farmington (G-2897)
▼ Dynamic Manufacturing Company .. G 860 589-2751
  Bristol (G-1023)
Excel Spring & Stamping LLC .... E 860 585-1495
  Bristol (G-1033)
Fourslide Spring Stamping Inc .... E 860 583-1688
  Bristol (G-1042)
Hurley Manufacturing Company .... E 860 379-8506
  New Hartford (G-5194)
Lee Spring Company LLC .... E 860 584-0991
  Bristol (G-1062)
Mark Nicoletti .... G 860 582-5645
  Bristol (G-1068)
Matthew Warren Inc .... D 860 621-7358
  Southington (G-7952)
Newcomb Spring Corp .... E 860 621-0111
  Southington (G-7957)
Oscar Jobs .... G 860 583-7834
  Bristol (G-1083)
Rowley Spring & Stamping Corp ...... C 860 582-8175
  Bristol (G-1113)
Spring Computerized Inds LLC .... G 860 605-9206
  Harwinton (G-3739)
Tollman Spring Company Inc .... G 860 583-4856
  Bristol (G-1130)
Triple A Spring Ltd Partnr .... E 860 589-3231
  Bristol (G-1132)

3494 Valves & Pipe Fittings, NEC

▲ Carten Controls Inc .... F 203 699-2100
  Cheshire (G-1366)

▲ Crane Co .... D 203 363-7300
  Stamford (G-8166)
Ctv Piping and Structural .... G 860 257-3027
  Hartford (G-3574)
▲ Dancar Corporation .... C 203 598-0205
  Middlebury (G-4277)
▼ Enfield Technologies LLC .... F 203 375-3100
  Shelton (G-7439)
Fisher Controls Intl LLC .... C 860 599-1140
  North Stonington (G-6025)
Genalco Inc .... G 203 932-5991
  West Haven (G-9911)
Houston Weber Systems Inc .... G 203 481-0115
  Branford (G-607)
▲ Hydrolevel Company .... F 203 776-0473
  North Haven (G-5946)
Hytek Plumbing and Heating LLC ..... G 860 389-1122
  Preston (G-6984)
Idex Health & Science LLC .... C 860 314-2880
  Bristol (G-1050)
Industrial Components CT LLC .... C 203 882-8201
  Milford (G-4555)
Saf Industries LLC .... E 203 729-4900
  Meriden (G-4237)

3495 Wire Springs

A & A Manufacturing Co Inc .... E 262 786-1500
  North Haven (G-5894)
Atlantic Precision Spring Inc .... E 860 583-1864
  Bristol (G-968)
Barnes Group Inc .... G 860 298-7740
  Farmington (G-2882)
▲ Barnes Group Inc .... B 860 583-7070
  Bristol (G-973)
Barnes Group Inc .... D 860 582-9581
  Bristol (G-974)
Century Spring Mfg Co Inc .... E 860 582-3344
  Bristol (G-1000)
▲ Connectcut Spring Stmping Corp .. B 860 677-1341
  Farmington (G-2891)
▲ Dayon Manufacturing Inc .... E 860 677-8561
  Farmington (G-2897)
Deka Enterprises .... G 860 582-6976
  Bristol (G-1014)
▼ DR Templeman Company .... F 860 747-2709
  Plainville (G-6800)
Excel Spring & Stamping LLC .... G 860 585-1495
  Bristol (G-1033)
Fourslide Spring Stamping Inc .... E 860 583-1688
  Bristol (G-1042)
Gemco Manufacturing Co Inc .... E 860 628-5529
  Southington (G-7926)
Lee Spring Company LLC .... E 860 584-0991
  Bristol (G-1062)
Mark Nicoletti .... G 860 582-5645
  Bristol (G-1068)
Matthew Warren Inc .... D 860 621-7358
  Southington (G-7952)
National Spring & Stamping Inc .... E 860 283-0203
  Thomaston (G-8798)
Newcomb Spring Corp .... E 860 621-0111
  Southington (G-7957)
Newcomb Springs Connecticut .... E 860 621-0111
  Southington (G-7958)
Oscar Jobs .... G 860 583-7834
  Bristol (G-1083)
Plymouth Spring Company Inc .... D 860 584-0594
  Bristol (G-1093)
Rowley Spring & Stamping Corp ...... C 860 582-8175
  Bristol (G-1113)
Southington Tool & Mfg Corp .... E 860 276-0021
  Plantsville (G-6912)
Spring Computerized Inds LLC .... G 860 605-9206
  Harwinton (G-3739)
Springfield Spring Corporation .... F 860 584-6560
  Bristol (G-1121)
Thomas Spring Co of Connenicut ..... G 203 874-7030
  Milford (G-4663)
U S Hairspring LLC .... G 860 747-9526
  Plainville (G-6873)
Ulbrich of Georgia Inc .... G 203 239-4481
  North Haven (G-6005)
Utica Spring Company Inc .... G 860 628-6165
  Southington (G-7991)

3496 Misc Fabricated Wire Prdts

▲ Acme Monaco Corporation .... C 860 224-1349
  New Britain (G-4934)
▲ Acme Wire Products Co Inc .... E 860 572-0511
  Mystic (G-4796)

35 INDUSTRIAL AND COMMERCIAL MACHINERY AND COMPUTER EQUIPMENT

Amtec Corporation .... E 860 230-0006
  Plainfield (G-6737)
Apco Products .... E 860 767-2108
  Centerbrook (G-1329)
▲ Armored Shield Technologies .... F 714 848-5796
  Redding (G-7090)
Arrow Manufacturing Company .... E 860 589-3900
  Bristol (G-966)
Bes Cu Inc .... E 860 582-8660
  Bristol (G-981)
Best In Backyards .... G 203 917-4381
  Danbury (G-1756)
Bridgeport Insulated Wire Co .... E 203 333-3191
  Bridgeport (G-721)
Bridgeport Insulated Wire Co .... E 203 375-9579
  Stratford (G-8589)
▲ C O Jelliff Corporation .... D 203 259-1615
  Southport (G-8001)
C R Springs Inc .... G 203 879-3357
  Wolcott (G-10552)
Cco Llc .... G 860 757-3434
  Rocky Hill (G-7226)
East Shre Wre Rpe/Rggng Spply .... F 203 469-5204
  North Haven (G-5934)
ERA Wire Inc .... F 203 933-0480
  West Haven (G-9906)
Excel Spring & Stamping LLC .... G 860 585-1495
  Bristol (G-1033)
Gemco Manufacturing Co Inc .... E 860 628-5529
  Southington (G-7926)
General Cable Industries Inc .... C 860 456-8000
  Willimantic (G-10227)
▲ Habasit Abt Inc .... C 860 632-2211
  Middletown (G-4349)
Habasit America Inc .... D 860 632-2211
  Middletown (G-4350)
Hessel Industries Inc .... G 203 736-2317
  Derby (G-2115)
▼ International Pipe & Stl Corp .... F 203 481-7102
  North Branford (G-5846)
John P Smith Co .... G 203 488-7226
  Branford (G-613)
◆ Knox Enterprises Inc .... G 203 226-6408
  Westport (G-10108)
Loos and Co Inc .... E 304 445-7820
  Pomfret (G-6935)
Meyer Wire & Cable Company LLC ...... E 203 281-0817
  Hamden (G-3482)
Miller Rebar LLC .... G 203 717-6645
  New Haven (G-5331)
Netsource Inc .... G 860 282-8994
  South Windsor (G-7795)
Netsource Inc .... D 860 649-6000
  Manchester (G-4059)
◆ Novo Precision LLC .... E 860 583-0517
  Bristol (G-1081)
▲ Nucor Steel Connecticut Inc .... C 203 265-0615
  Wallingford (G-9330)
Pauls Wire Rope & Sling Inc .... F 203 481-3469
  Branford (G-633)
Performance Fabrication .... G 860 678-8070
  Farmington (G-2948)
Protopac Inc .... G 860 274-6796
  Watertown (G-9727)
▲ Radcliff Wire Inc .... E 312 876-1754
  Bristol (G-1103)
▲ Redco Audio Inc .... F 203 502-7600
  Stratford (G-8674)
Rowley Spring & Stamping Corp .... C 860 582-8175
  Bristol (G-1113)
Tiger Enterprises Inc .... E 860 621-9155
  Plantsville (G-6914)
▲ U-Tech Wire Rope & Supply LLC ..... G 203 865-8885
  North Haven (G-6004)
Ultimate Wireforms Inc .... D 860 582-9111
  Bristol (G-1134)
Wire Design Originals .... G 203 795-3783
  Orange (G-6634)
Wire Solutions LLC .... G 860 836-0787
  Plainville (G-6878)
◆ Wiremold Company .... A 860 233-6251
  West Hartford (G-9874)

3497 Metal Foil & Leaf

▲ Dexmet Corporation .... D 203 294-4440
  Wallingford (G-9249)
Foilmark Inc .... F 860 243-0343
  Bloomfield (G-414)
PPG Industries Inc .... D 203 294-4440
  Wallingford (G-9337)

3498 Fabricated Pipe & Pipe Fittings

Carli Farm & Equipment LLC .... G 860 908-3227
  Salem (G-7287)
Clear Water Manufacturing Corp .... G 860 372-4907
  Wethersfield (G-10188)
Creative Rack Solutions Inc .... G 203 755-2102
  Waterbury (G-9455)
Diba Industries Inc .... C 203 744-0773
  Danbury (G-1795)
▼ EA Patten Co LLC .... D 860 649-2851
  Manchester (G-4013)
Farmington Mtal Fbrication LLC .... G 860 404-7415
  Bristol (G-1036)
Frank Porto .... G 203 596-0811
  Watertown (G-9707)
Harry Thommen Company .... G 203 333-3637
  Bridgeport (G-782)
JFd Tube & Coil Products Inc .... E 203 288-6941
  Hamden (G-3468)
L&P Aerospace Acquisition LLC .... D 860 635-8811
  Middletown (G-4366)
Long Island Pipe Supply Inc .... G 860 688-1780
  Windsor (G-10405)
▲ Macristy Industries Inc .... C 860 225-4637
  Newington (G-5674)
Plastics and Concepts Conn Inc .... F 860 657-9655
  Glastonbury (G-3072)
▲ Scantube Inc .... G 203 743-0908
  Danbury (G-1935)
◆ Spencer Turbine Company .... C 860 688-8361
  Windsor (G-10436)
Vas Integrated LLC .... G 860 748-4058
  Berlin (G-229)

3499 Fabricated Metal Prdts, NEC

Action Steel LLC .... G 860 216-6595
  Hartford (G-3546)
▲ Airpot Corporation .... E 800 848-7681
  Norwalk (G-6064)
Alvarez Industries LLC .... G 203 799-2356
  Orange (G-6580)
Alvarez Industries LLC .... G 203 401-1152
  New Haven (G-5226)
Aptargroup Inc .... B 203 377-8100
  Stratford (G-8569)
Artful Framer LLC .... G 203 678-1321
  Avon (G-76)
Beta Shim Co .... E 203 926-1150
  Shelton (G-7404)
Bob Worden .... G 203 567-4722
  Lakeside (G-3841)
Center Mass LLC .... G 860 350-0239
  New Milford (G-5518)
▲ Concord Industries Inc .... E 203 750-6060
  Norwalk (G-6124)
Cr Fabrication LLC .... G 860 377-1629
  South Windsor (G-7736)
Dangelo Family LLC .... G 203 235-1238
  Waterbury (G-9460)
Dcg-Pmi Inc .... E 203 743-5525
  Bethel (G-279)
▲ Farmington Engineering Inc .... G 800 428-7584
  North Haven (G-5940)
Farmington Mtal Fbrication LLC .... G 860 402-5148
  Bristol (G-1035)
Forgetful Gentleman LLC .... G 203 431-2486
  Ridgefield (G-7141)
Greco Industries Inc .... G 203 798-7804
  Bethel (G-304)
H G Steinmetz Machine Works .... F 203 794-1880
  Bethel (G-307)
Independent Metalworx Inc .... G 203 520-4089
  Ansonia (G-39)
J OConnor LLC .... F 860 665-7702
  Newington (G-5666)
K-Tech International .... E 860 489-9399
  Torrington (G-8941)
M & B Enterprise LLC .... F 203 298-9781
  Derby (G-2119)
M&M Metal Fabrication LLC .... G 203 889-6468
  East Haven (G-2440)
Mak Metal Fab .... G 203 213-0269
  Wallingford (G-9311)
Metalcraft LLC .... G 860 361-6767
  Bantam (G-124)
Metallon Inc .... G 203 437-8540
  Waterbury (G-9540)
National Picture Frame Inc .... G 860 774-5668
  Brooklyn (G-1251)
Nel Group LLC .... G 860 413-9042
  East Granby (G-2216)
Nel Group LLC .... F 860 683-0190
  Windsor (G-10412)
Oxford General Industries Inc .... F 203 758-4467
  Prospect (G-7013)
Performance Connection Systems .... G 203 868-5517
  Meriden (G-4216)
Recognition Inc .... G 860 659-8629
  Glastonbury (G-3079)
Royal Welding LLC .... G 860 232-5255
  Hartford (G-3683)
Specialty Metals and Fab .... G 203 509-5028
  Naugatuck (G-4921)
▲ Spirol International Corp .... C 860 774-8571
  Danielson (G-2003)
▲ Spirol Intl Holdg Corp .... C 860 774-8571
  Danielson (G-2004)
Steven Rosendahl Inc .... G 860 928-3136
  Woodstock (G-10685)
Sunnyside Fab & Welding Inc .... G 203 348-5040
  Stamford (G-8451)
Tek-Motive Inc .... D 203 468-2224
  Branford (G-662)
Tides Black Group LLC .... G 203 244-8433
  Monroe (G-4761)
◆ Torqmaster Inc .... E 203 326-5945
  Stamford (G-8471)
Victoria Art & Frame .... G 860 274-8222
  Watertown (G-9746)
Vintage Sheet Metal Fabg .... G 860 595-8423
  Berlin (G-230)
◆ Yarde Metals Inc .... B 860 406-6061
  Southington (G-7997)

35 INDUSTRIAL AND COMMERCIAL MACHINERY AND COMPUTER EQUIPMENT

3511 Steam, Gas & Hydraulic Turbines & Engines

American Metal Masters LLC .... G 860 621-6911
  Plantsville (G-6884)
American Wind Capital Co LLC .... G 860 767-1579
  Essex (G-2711)
Asea Brown Boveri Inc .... G 203 750-2200
  Norwalk (G-6076)
▲ Becon Incorporated .... D 860 243-1428
  Bloomfield (G-394)
Blastech Overhaul & Repair .... F 860 243-8811
  Bloomfield (G-396)
◆ Doncasters Inc .... D 860 449-1603
  Groton (G-3283)
▲ Gas Turbine Supply and Svc LLC .... G 860 254-5651
  Suffield (G-8719)
GE Transportation Parts LLC .... G 816 650-6171
  Fairfield (G-2791)
International Turbine Systems .... G 860 761-0358
  Bloomfield (G-423)
Northeast Wind Energy .... G 860 779-2179
  East Killingly (G-2461)
Pequot .... G 800 620-1492
  Bridgeport (G-869)
R&D Dynamics Corporation .... E 860 726-1204
  Bloomfield (G-472)
Winsol Clean Energy LLC .... G 203 216-1972
  Stamford (G-8497)
Winsol Economic Dev Corp .... G 203 216-1972
  Stamford (G-8498)

3519 Internal Combustion Engines, NEC

American Unmanned Systems LLC ..... G 203 406-7611
  Stamford (G-8079)
Atlantic Outboard Inc .... G 860 399-6773
  Westbrook (G-9991)
Automotive Machine .... G 860 627-9244
  East Windsor (G-2482)
▲ Bell Power Systems LLC .... D 860 767-7502
  Essex (G-2712)
Brash Engines Inc .... G 203 843-0757
  Branford (G-564)
CAM Group LLC .... F 860 646-2378
  Manchester (G-3989)
Cummins - Allison Corp .... G 203 794-9200
  Cheshire (G-1377)
Cummins Enviro Tech Inc .... F 860 388-6377
  Old Lyme (G-6499)

35 INDUSTRIAL AND COMMERCIAL MACHINERY AND COMPUTER EQUIPMENT — SIC SECTION

Cummins Envirotech .... G 860 598-9564
Old Lyme (G-6500)
Cummins Inc .... E 860 529-7474
Rocky Hill (G-7230)
Ex Model Engines .... G 860 681-2451
Southington (G-7919)
◆ Jacobs Vehicle Systems Inc .... B 860 243-5222
Bloomfield (G-425)
Johnson Marine .... G 860 536-8026
Mystic (G-4823)
Kco Numet Inc .... F 203 375-4995
Orange (G-6606)
▲ Liquidpiston Inc .... F 860 838-2677
Bloomfield (G-443)
Pmr Performance .... G 860 828-8828
Kensington (G-3817)
▲ Smith Hill of Delaware Inc .... E 860 767-7502
Essex (G-2733)
T/A Engines .... G 860 747-6713
Plainville (G-6866)
Terry Brick .... G 860 889-2232
Norwich (G-6436)

3523 Farm Machinery & Eqpt

16 Case LLC .... G 860 995-0555
Farmington (G-2873)
A Family Farm .... G 203 438-5497
Redding (G-7087)
Case Association .... G 860 989-6533
West Suffield (G-9985)
Comex Machinery .... G 203 334-2196
Bridgeport (G-738)
Connectcut Cswork Spclists LLC .... G 203 934-9665
West Haven (G-9891)
Domus VI LLC .... G 860 619-0707
Sharon (G-7378)
Double H Acres LLC .... G 860 250-3311
Broad Brook (G-1148)
◆ Engineering Services & Pdts Co .... D 860 528-1119
South Windsor (G-7750)
Grassy Meadows Lawn Care .... G 203 856-3823
Trumbull (G-9030)
Hunter Industries .... G 860 961-9646
Deep River (G-2092)
Latelier Bade LLC .... G 860 623-4661
Broad Brook (G-1151)
Stephens Pipe & Steel LLC .... F 877 777-8721
Manchester (G-4095)

3524 Garden, Lawn Tractors & Eqpt

Dirt Guy Topsoil .... G 860 303-0500
Durham (G-2145)
Fortified Holdings Corp .... G 203 594-1686
Norwalk (G-6171)
Greenscape of Clinton LLC .... G 860 669-1880
Clinton (G-1506)
Maltese Services LLC .... G 203 805-7669
Monroe (G-4732)
Mikes Plowing & Maintenance .... G 860 868-1413
Washington Depot (G-9418)
▲ Woodland Power Products Inc .... E 888 531-7253
West Haven (G-9966)
Worth Properties LLC .... G 203 281-1792
Hamden (G-3531)

3531 Construction Machinery & Eqpt

A & K Railroad Materials Inc .... G 203 495-8790
Hamden (G-3409)
▲ Bagela Usa LLC .... G 203 944-0525
Shelton (G-7398)
Bay Crane Service Conn Inc .... G 203 785-8000
North Haven (G-5913)
Calvin Brown .... G 860 536-6178
Gales Ferry (G-2982)
Canterbury Machinery Rnd Llc .... G 860 546-5000
Canterbury (G-1297)
▲ Capewell Aerial Systems LLC .... D 860 610-0700
South Windsor (G-7722)
Conair Corporation .... D 800 492-7464
Torrington (G-8914)
CT Crane and Hoist Service LLC .... G 860 283-4320
Plymouth (G-6928)
D R Charles Envmtl Cnstr LLC .... G 203 445-0412
Monroe (G-4709)
Daves Paving and Construction .... G 203 753-4992
Prospect (G-7000)
Double Diamond Construction .... G 203 357-7757
Stamford (G-8188)
Dp Marine LLC .... G 917 705-7435
Riverside (G-7192)
Drum Crane and Rigging LLC .... G 860 837-4517
East Hartford (G-2315)
Ezflow Limited Partnership .... E 860 577-7064
Old Saybrook (G-6533)
Fairfield Backhoe LLC .... G 203 247-4007
Fairfield (G-2784)
G L Yarocki & Company .... G 860 482-9215
Torrington (G-8928)
Green & Sons LLC .... G 860 459-4049
Litchfield (G-3891)
◆ H Barber & Sons Inc .... E 203 729-9000
Naugatuck (G-4886)
▲ Indeco North America Inc .... E 203 713-1030
Milford (G-4554)
Interstate Elec Svcs Corp .... E 860 243-5644
Windsor (G-10397)
K&L Enterprises .... G 860 645-7257
Manchester (G-4042)
▲ LH Gault & Son Incorporated .... D 203 227-5181
Westport (G-10112)
Logans Run Trnsp Svc LLC .... G 203 679-0870
Wallingford (G-9305)
▲ Maretron LLP .... F 602 861-1707
Plainville (G-6838)
Metal Plus LLC .... G 860 379-1327
Winsted (G-10528)
Michele Schiano Di Cola Inc .... G 203 265-5301
Wallingford (G-9318)
▲ Naiad Dynamics Us Inc .... E 203 929-6355
Shelton (G-7506)
Naiad Maritime Group Inc .... E 203 944-1932
Shelton (G-7507)
North America Overland LLC .... G 203 658-3697
Monroe (G-4744)
▼ Numa Tool Company .... D 860 923-9551
Thompson (G-8841)
Pavers of New England Inc .... G 860 289-7778
South Windsor (G-7804)
Rawson Manufacturing Inc .... F 860 928-4458
Putnam (G-7062)
Rayginn Mfg LLC .... G 860 243-2257
Bloomfield (G-473)
Robran Industries Inc .... G 203 510-6292
Waterbury (G-9594)
▲ Show Motion Inc .... E 203 866-1866
Milford (G-4643)
Spray Foam Outlets LLC .... G 631 291-9355
Norwalk (G-6354)
Steelwrist Inc .... G 225 936-1111
Berlin (G-224)
Tbs Adjusting Inc .... G 203 274-5525
Stamford (G-8459)
◆ Terex Corporation .... F 203 222-7170
Westport (G-10163)
Terex Utilities Inc .... G 860 436-3700
Hartford (G-3701)
▲ Tinsley GROup-Ps&w Inc .... D 919 742-5832
Milford (G-4665)
Town of Ledyard .... G 860 464-9060
Gales Ferry (G-2988)
Town of Wilton .... G 203 563-0152
Wilton (G-10338)

3532 Mining Machinery & Eqpt

▼ Numa Tool Company .... D 860 923-9551
Thompson (G-8841)
P2 Science Inc .... G 203 821-7457
Woodbridge (G-10611)
▲ Powerscreen Connecticut Inc .... F 860 627-6596
South Windsor (G-7810)
◆ Terex Usa LLC .... B 203 222-7170
Westport (G-10164)
Tipping Pt Resources Group LLC .... G 800 603-8902
New Haven (G-5415)

3533 Oil Field Machinery & Eqpt

First Reserve Fund Viii LP .... G 860 661-6601
Stamford (G-8205)
▼ Numa Tool Company .... D 860 923-9551
Thompson (G-8841)
▲ Oil Purification Systems Inc .... F 860 346-1800
Waterbury (G-9569)

3534 Elevators & Moving Stairways

◆ Ascend Elevator Inc .... C 215 703-0358
Bloomfield (G-391)
Bay State Elevator Company Inc .... F 860 243-9030
Bloomfield (G-393)
International Elevator Corp .... G 203 302-1023
Cos Cob (G-1634)
K-Tech International .... E 860 489-9399
Torrington (G-8941)
Netz New Haven Norton .... G 203 507-2108
New Haven (G-5340)
◆ Otis Elevator Company .... B 860 674-3000
Farmington (G-2942)
Otis Elevator Company .... G 860 290-3318
Farmington (G-2943)
Otis Elevator Company .... B 860 242-3632
Bloomfield (G-456)
Unitec Parts Co .... G 919 627-0192
Shelton (G-7576)
United Tech Advnced Prjcts Inc .... G 860 610-7159
East Hartford (G-2390)
United Technologies Corp .... G 860 292-3270
East Granby (G-2233)
▼ United Technologies Corp .... B 860 728-7000
Farmington (G-2972)

3535 Conveyors & Eqpt

Affordable Conveyors Svcs LLC .... F 860 582-1800
Bristol (G-960)
Alvest (usa) Inc .... G 860 602-3400
Windsor (G-10360)
CT Conveyor LLC .... G 860 637-2926
Bristol (G-1009)
Goldslager Conveyor Company .... G 203 795-9886
Hamden (G-3452)
Intelligrated Systems Ohio LLC .... G 203 938-8404
Redding (G-7095)
International Robotics Inc .... G 914 325-7773
Stamford (G-8255)
International Robotics Inc .... F 914 630-1060
Stamford (G-8256)
▲ National Conveyors Company Inc .... E 860 653-0374
East Granby (G-2215)
Nationwide Cnvyor Spclists LLC .... G 860 582-9816
Bristol (G-1077)
Production Equipment Company .... E 800 758-5697
Meriden (G-4221)
R & I Manufacturing Co .... F 860 589-6364
Terryville (G-8768)
Roller Bearing Co Amer Inc .... E 203 758-8272
Middlebury (G-4289)
Unimation .... G 203 792-3412
Bethel (G-358)
◆ Walker Magnetics Group Inc .... E 508 853-3232
Windsor (G-10461)
Z-Loda Systems Inc .... G 203 359-2991
Stamford (G-8505)

3536 Hoists, Cranes & Monorails

New England Lift Systems LLC .... G 860 372-4040
Newington (G-5685)
Production Equipment Company .... E 800 758-5697
Meriden (G-4221)

3537 Indl Trucks, Tractors, Trailers & Stackers

Automar Ne LLC .... G 203 793-7630
Wallingford (G-9215)
Dri-Air Industries Inc .... E 860 627-5110
East Windsor (G-2489)
L G Associates .... G 860 677-7167
Avon (G-87)
▼ Macton Corporation .... D 203 267-1500
Oxford (G-6674)
Marathon Enterprises LLC .... G 860 888-6294
West Hartford (G-9833)
New Haven Companies Inc .... F 203 469-6421
East Haven (G-2444)
Northside Minis LLC .... G 860 388-6871
Old Saybrook (G-6561)
Pierce-Correll Corporation .... G 203 799-1208
Orange (G-6624)
Power Cover Usa LLC .... G 203 755-2687
Waterbury (G-9583)
◆ Terex Corporation .... F 203 222-7170
Westport (G-10163)
Truth Trckg Expedited Svcs LLC .... G 860 306-5630
Hartford (G-3707)
Wet Crow Internet Inc .... G 860 919-0164
Middletown (G-4431)

3541 Machine Tools: Cutting

83 Erna Avenue LLC .... G 203 243-7426
Trumbull (G-8996)
American Automation .... G 203 556-7839
Bridgeport (G-690)

Company	Code	Phone	Location
AMR Machines LLC	G	860 336-6208	Putnam *(G-7029)*
Atp Industries LLC	F	860 479-5007	Plainville *(G-6773)*
B & L Tool and Machine Company	G	860 747-2721	Plainville *(G-6774)*
Baldwin Thread Rolling	G	860 283-4948	Thomaston *(G-8779)*
Benetec Inc	G	860 745-4455	Enfield *(G-2617)*
Bernell Tool & Mfg Co	G	203 756-4405	Waterbury *(G-9438)*
▲ Book Automation Inc	G	860 354-7900	New Milford *(G-5512)*
▲ Branson Ultrasonics Corp	B	203 796-0400	Danbury *(G-1759)*
Bryce Gear Inc	G	860 747-3341	Plainville *(G-6779)*
C V Tool Company Inc	E	978 353-7901	Southington *(G-7901)*
Ceda Company Inc	G	860 666-1593	Newington *(G-5638)*
Center Mass LLC	G	860 350-0239	New Milford *(G-5518)*
▲ Charter Oak Automation LLC	G	203 562-0699	Wallingford *(G-9226)*
Cnc Engineering Inc	E	860 749-1780	Enfield *(G-2627)*
Co-Op Jig Boring Jig Grinding	G	860 828-9882	Berlin *(G-170)*
Connecticut Tool & Cutter Co	E	860 314-1740	Bristol *(G-1006)*
CT Tool & Manufacturing LLC	G	860 846-0800	Farmington *(G-2895)*
D T Technologies Inc	G	203 312-3527	Ridgefield *(G-7134)*
Deburring Laboratories Inc	E	860 829-6300	New Britain *(G-4972)*
Denco Counter-Bore LLC	G	860 276-0782	Southington *(G-7914)*
Dennis Savela	G	860 774-3963	Danielson *(G-1989)*
Dunbar Commercial Enterprises	G	203 469-7575	East Haven *(G-2421)*
Edac Technologies LLC	F	860 789-2511	East Windsor *(G-2490)*
Edac Technologies LLC	C	203 806-2090	Cheshire *(G-1383)*
Emhart Teknologies LLC	E	203 790-5000	Danbury *(G-1807)*
Emhart Teknologies LLC	F	800 783-6427	New Britain *(G-4983)*
Enginering Components Pdts LLC	G	860 747-6222	Plainville *(G-6806)*
Farmington Machine Tools LLC	G	860 676-7736	Farmington *(G-2905)*
Finishers Technology Corp	F	860 829-1000	East Berlin *(G-2168)*
◆ Fletcher-Terry Company LLC	D	860 828-3400	East Berlin *(G-2169)*
Gary Tool Company	G	203 377-3077	Stratford *(G-8616)*
▲ Gmn Usa LLC	F	800 686-1679	Bristol *(G-1046)*
Guiseppe Mazzettini	G	203 597-9035	Waterbury *(G-9492)*
Hallden Shear Service of Amer	G	860 283-4386	Thomaston *(G-8791)*
Hata Hi-Tech Machining LLC	E	203 333-9139	Ansonia *(G-38)*
Iamaw	G	860 228-0049	Hebron *(G-3750)*
▲ JL Lucas Machinery Co Inc	F	203 597-1300	Waterbury *(G-9510)*
L C M Tool Co	G	203 757-1575	Waterbury *(G-9516)*
Laser Tool Company Inc	F	860 283-8284	Thomaston *(G-8796)*
Lefferts Brothers Vintage Mach	G	203-205-0500	Bethel *(G-322)*
Machine Builders Neng LLC	F	203 922-9446	Shelton *(G-7493)*
Machine Repair Services LLC	G	860 729-7410	Middletown *(G-4374)*
Magcor Inc	G	203 445-0302	Monroe *(G-4731)*
Marena Industries Inc	F	860 528-9701	East Hartford *(G-2343)*
Mark Machine Tool LLC	G	203 910-5942	Wolcott *(G-10574)*
▲ Max-Tek LLC	F	860 372-4900	Wallingford *(G-9315)*
Microbest Inc	C	203 597-0355	Waterbury *(G-9542)*
Mid-State Manufacturing Inc	F	860 621-6855	Milldale *(G-4686)*
Mikron Corp Monroe	G	203 261-3100	Monroe *(G-4737)*
Moon Cutter Co Inc	E	203 288-9249	Hamden *(G-3484)*
◆ Moore Tool Company Inc	D	203 366-3224	Bridgeport *(G-843)*
National Screw Manufacturing	F	203 469-7109	East Haven *(G-2443)*
Nemtec Inc	G	203 272-0788	Cheshire *(G-1418)*
New England Die Co Inc	F	203 574-5140	Waterbury *(G-9558)*
New England Plasma Dev Corp	F	860 928-6561	Putnam *(G-7053)*
New England Tooling Inc	F	800 866-5105	Killingworth *(G-3837)*
Nortek Gear and Machine LLC	G	860 355-5541	New Milford *(G-5574)*
North Haven Manufacturing Co	G	203 284-8578	Wallingford *(G-9328)*
Nowak Products Inc	G	860 666-9685	Newington *(G-5687)*
Okamoto Corp	G	860 219-1006	Windsor *(G-10415)*
◆ Pmt Group Inc	C	203 367-8675	Bridgeport *(G-875)*
Precision Deburring Inc	G	860 583-4662	Bristol *(G-1096)*
Producto Corporation	F	203 366-3224	Bridgeport *(G-882)*
Ramdy Corporation	E	860 274-3713	Oakville *(G-6460)*
Rbk Lathe LLC	G	860 321-7243	Farmington *(G-2953)*
Ready Tool Company	E	860 524-7811	West Hartford *(G-9849)*
Relx Inc	G	860 219-0733	Windsor *(G-10430)*
RWS Co Inc	G	860 434-2961	Old Lyme *(G-6518)*
Sadlak Industries LLC	E	860 742-0227	Coventry *(G-1673)*
Scott A Hebert	G	860 990-0793	Plainville *(G-6860)*
Secondary Operations Inc	F	203 288-8241	Hamden *(G-3509)*
Shuster-Mettler Corp	E	203 562-3178	Plainville *(G-6861)*
Sonitek Corporation	E	203 878-9321	Milford *(G-4647)*
Sperry Automatics Co Inc	E	203 729-4589	Naugatuck *(G-4922)*
Syman Machine LLC	G	860 747-8337	Plainville *(G-6865)*
Talk N Fix CT Inc	G	203 790-8905	Danbury *(G-1959)*
Tetco Inc	F	860 747-1280	Plainville *(G-6869)*
Tornos Technologies US Corp	G	203 775-4319	Brookfield *(G-1232)*
Turbine Controls Inc	D	860 242-0448	Bloomfield *(G-495)*
United Tool and Die Company	C	860 246-6531	West Hartford *(G-9871)*
US Avionics Inc / Superabr	G	860 528-1114	South Windsor *(G-7837)*
Viking Tool Company	E	203 929-1457	Shelton *(G-7579)*
W J Savage Co Inc	G	203 468-4100	East Haven *(G-2459)*
Watertown Jig Bore Service Inc	F	860 274-5898	Watertown *(G-9748)*

3542 Machine Tools: Forming

Company	Code	Phone	Location
A G Russell Company Inc	G	860 247-9093	Hartford *(G-3543)*
Accubend LLC	G	860 378-0303	Plantsville *(G-6881)*
Ace Finishing Co LLC	G	860 582-4600	Bristol *(G-955)*
Advanced Machine Services LLC	G	203 888-6600	Waterbury *(G-9423)*
American Actuator Corporation	F	203 324-6334	Redding *(G-7089)*
Arrow Diversified Tooling Inc	E	860 872-9072	Ellington *(G-2576)*
Cole S Crew Machine Products	E	203 723-1418	North Haven *(G-5922)*
▼ Deringer-Ney Inc	C	860 242-2281	Bloomfield *(G-407)*
Eyelet Tech LLC	E	203 879-5306	Wolcott *(G-10564)*
▲ Fenn LLC	E	860 259-6600	East Berlin *(G-2167)*
Grant Manufacturing & Mch Co	E	203 366-4557	Bridgeport *(G-779)*
J D & Associates	G	860 546-2112	Canterbury *(G-1299)*
Joshua LLC	E	203 624-0080	New Haven *(G-5304)*
L M Gill Welding and Mfr LLC	F	860 647-9931	Manchester *(G-4046)*
L R Brown Manufacturing Co	G	203 265-5639	Wallingford *(G-9300)*
Lou-Jan Tool & Die Inc	F	203 272-3536	Cheshire *(G-1408)*
Merritt Extruder Corp	E	203 230-8100	Hamden *(G-3481)*
New England PLC Systems LLC	G	860 793-2975	Southington *(G-7956)*
▲ OEM Sources LLC	G	203 283-5415	Milford *(G-4597)*
Okay Industries Inc	G	860 225-8707	Berlin *(G-204)*
Oxford General Industries Inc	F	203 758-4467	Prospect *(G-7013)*
Peter Hoelzel	G	860 749-4070	Enfield *(G-2676)*
Proiron LLC	G	203 934-7967	West Haven *(G-9948)*
Raymon Tool LLC	F	203 248-2199	Hamden *(G-3501)*
Richard Dahlen	G	860 584-8226	Bristol *(G-1108)*
Riveting Systems USA LLC	G	203 366-4557	Bridgeport *(G-891)*
Sandviks Inc	G	866 984-0188	Danbury *(G-1933)*
Savage Products LLC	G	203 440-1766	Meriden *(G-4240)*
Sirois Tool Company Inc	D	860 828-5327	Berlin *(G-220)*
▲ Stamptech Incorporated	F	860 628-9090	Southington *(G-7980)*
◆ Trumpf Inc	B	860 255-6000	Farmington *(G-2967)*
Trumpf Inc	B	860 255-6000	Plainville *(G-6872)*
Trumpf Inc	B	860 255-6000	Farmington *(G-2968)*
▲ Universal Storage Cntrs LLC	G	203 966-3043	New Canaan *(G-5156)*
US Product Mechanization Co	G	860 450-1139	Columbia *(G-1614)*
Vital Stretch LLC	G	203 847-4477	Norwalk *(G-6391)*

3543 Industrial Patterns

Company	Code	Phone	Location
Arrow Diversified Tooling Inc	E	860 872-9072	Ellington *(G-2576)*
Case Patterns Inc	G	860 445-6722	Groton *(G-3275)*
Equipment Designs Associate	G	860 217-1573	Simsbury *(G-7624)*
Pamelas Patterns	G	610 534-4182	Vernon Rockville *(G-9173)*
Pattern Genomics LLC	G	203 779-5470	Madison *(G-3947)*
Paw Patterns LLC	G	401 338-4723	Amston *(G-5)*
Pony Patterns LLC	G	203 535-0347	New Haven *(G-5368)*
Post Pattern	G	860 774-7911	Brooklyn *(G-1252)*
Progressive Pattern	G	860 748-0088	Windsor *(G-10426)*

3544 Dies, Tools, Jigs, Fixtures & Indl Molds

Company	Code	Phone	Location
A & H Tool Works	G	860 302-9284	Harwinton *(G-3717)*
A G M Tool	G	860 793-6808	Plainville *(G-6761)*
Aba-PGT Inc	C	860 649-4591	Manchester *(G-3974)*

SIC

35 INDUSTRIAL AND COMMERCIAL MACHINERY AND COMPUTER EQUIPMENT SIC SECTION

▲ **Accurate Tool & Die Inc** ....E....... 203 967-1200
Stamford *(G-8057)*
Acson Tool Company ....F....... 203 334-8050
Bridgeport *(G-682)*
Advance Mold & Mfg Inc ....C....... 860 432-5887
Manchester *(G-3979)*
Alberto Castillo ....G....... 203 834-1486
Wilton *(G-10268)*
▲ **Alinabal Inc** ....C....... 203 877-3241
Milford *(G-4448)*
▲ **All Five Tool Co Inc** ....E....... 860 583-1693
Berlin *(G-154)*
American Molded Products Inc ....F....... 203 333-0183
Bridgeport *(G-694)*
American Precision Mold Inc ....G....... 860 267-1356
East Hampton *(G-2255)*
Anderson Tool Company Inc ....G....... 203 777-4153
New Haven *(G-5231)*
Apex Machine Tool Company Inc ....D....... 860 677-2884
Cheshire *(G-1353)*
Arcade Technology LLC ....E....... 203 366-3871
Bridgeport *(G-699)*
Arrow Diversified Tooling Inc ....E....... 860 872-9072
Ellington *(G-2576)*
Astro Industries Inc ....G....... 860 828-6304
Berlin *(G-161)*
Atlas Stamping & Mfg Corp ....E....... 860 757-3233
Newington *(G-5629)*
B & D Machine Inc ....F....... 860 871-9226
Tolland *(G-8850)*
B & L Tool and Machine Company ....G....... 860 747-2721
Plainville *(G-6774)*
B & P Plating Equipment LLC ....F....... 860 589-5799
Bristol *(G-969)*
B-P Products Inc ....E....... 203 288-0200
Hamden *(G-3416)*
Bessette Holdings Inc ....E....... 860 289-6000
East Hartford *(G-2298)*
Better Molded Products Inc ....C....... 860 589-0066
Bristol *(G-982)*
Betz Tool Company Inc ....G....... 203 878-1187
Milford *(G-4468)*
Bml Tool & Mfg Corp ....D....... 203 880-9485
Monroe *(G-4699)*
Bremser Technologies Inc ....F....... 203 378-8486
Stratford *(G-8585)*
Bridgeport Tl & Stamping Corp ....E....... 203 336-2501
Bridgeport *(G-723)*
Bristol Tool & Die Company ....E....... 860 582-2577
Bristol *(G-993)*
C V Tool Company Inc ....E....... 978 353-7901
Southington *(G-7901)*
Cambridge Specialty Co Inc ....D....... 860 828-3579
Berlin *(G-168)*
Candlewood Tool & Machine Shop ....F....... 860 355-1892
Gaylordsville *(G-2990)*
Carnegie Tool Inc ....F....... 203 866-0744
Norwalk *(G-6108)*
Cas-Kel Manufacturing Co Inc ....G....... 860 693-8704
Canton *(G-1309)*
Castle Technologies Inc ....G....... 860 582-7299
Terryville *(G-8749)*
Century Tool Co Inc ....F....... 860 923-9523
Thompson *(G-8832)*
Cgl Inc ....F....... 860 945-6166
Watertown *(G-9691)*
Charles J Angelo Mfg Group LLC ....F....... 860 646-2378
Manchester *(G-3995)*
Classic Tool & Mfg Inc ....G....... 203 755-6313
Waterbury *(G-9450)*
Connecticut Tool Co Inc ....E....... 860 928-0565
Putnam *(G-7035)*
Country Tool & Die Inc ....G....... 860 429-7325
Ashford *(G-58)*
D & M Tool Company Inc ....G....... 860 236-6037
West Hartford *(G-9797)*
Diecraft Compacting Tool Inc ....G....... 203 879-3019
Wolcott *(G-10561)*
▲ **Drilling Dynamics LLC** ....G....... 203 783-1395
Milford *(G-4516)*
E & E Tool & Manufacturing Co ....F....... 860 738-8577
Winsted *(G-10517)*
E and S Gage Inc ....F....... 860 872-5917
Tolland *(G-8862)*
Edward D Segen Co ....G....... 203 929-8700
Shelton *(G-7436)*
F J Weidner Inc ....G....... 203 469-4202
East Haven *(G-2425)*
Fad Tool Company LLC ....E....... 860 582-7890
Bristol *(G-1034)*
Ferron Mold and Tool LLC ....G....... 860 774-5555
Dayville *(G-2061)*
Fly or Die Nation LLC ....G....... 860 218-3547
Hartford *(G-3590)*
Foilmark Inc ....F....... 860 243-0343
Bloomfield *(G-414)*
G P Tool Co Inc ....F....... 203 744-0310
Danbury *(G-1831)*
Gary Tool Company ....G....... 203 377-3077
Stratford *(G-8616)*
Globe Tool & Met Stampg Co Inc ....E....... 860 621-6807
Southington *(G-7929)*
Gordon Rubber and Pkg Co Inc ....E....... 203 735-7441
Derby *(G-2114)*
Hartford Gauge Co ....G....... 860 233-9619
West Hartford *(G-9817)*
Heck D Tool LLC ....G....... 860 935-9274
Thompson *(G-8834)*
Heise Industries Inc ....D....... 860 828-6538
East Berlin *(G-2170)*
Herman Schmidt Precision Workh ....G....... 860 289-3347
South Windsor *(G-7768)*
Highland Manufacturing Inc ....E....... 860 646-5142
Manchester *(G-4028)*
Hnat Mold & Die Inc ....G....... 860 537-0573
Colchester *(G-1554)*
Hobson and Motzer Incorporated ....C....... 860 349-1756
Durham *(G-2149)*
J & L Tool Company Inc ....E....... 203 265-6237
Wallingford *(G-9291)*
J F Tool Inc ....G....... 860 349-3063
Rockfall *(G-7213)*
J T Tool Co Inc ....G....... 203 874-1234
Milford *(G-4558)*
Jewett City Tool and Die Co ....G....... 860 376-0455
Voluntown *(G-9189)*
Joseph Organek ....G....... 860 342-1906
Portland *(G-6962)*
Jovek Tool and Die ....G....... 860 261-5020
Bristol *(G-1055)*
Kovacs Machine and Tool Co ....E....... 203 269-4949
Wallingford *(G-9298)*
Larosa Manufacturing LLC ....G....... 860 819-7066
Plainville *(G-6831)*
Lassy Tools Inc ....G....... 860 747-2748
Plainville *(G-6832)*
Laurel Tool & Manufacturing ....G....... 860 889-5354
Norwich *(G-6422)*
Lawrence Holdings Inc ....F....... 203 949-1600
Wallingford *(G-9301)*
Lou-Jan Tool & Die Inc ....F....... 203 272-3536
Cheshire *(G-1408)*
Lyons Tool and Die Company ....E....... 203 238-2689
Meriden *(G-4190)*
M & R Manufacturing Inc ....G....... 860 666-5066
Newington *(G-5673)*
M S Bickford LLC ....G....... 860 467-6937
East Hampton *(G-2269)*
Manchester Molding and Mfg Co ....E....... 860 643-2141
Manchester *(G-4052)*
Marc Tool & Die Inc ....G....... 203 758-5933
Prospect *(G-7008)*
Mastercraft Tool and Mch Co ....F....... 860 628-5551
Southington *(G-7950)*
Michaud Tool Co Inc ....G....... 860 582-6785
Terryville *(G-8765)*
Mid-State Manufacturing Inc ....F....... 860 621-6855
Milldale *(G-4686)*
▲ **Mohawk Tool and Die Mfg Co Inc** ....F....... 203 367-2181
Bridgeport *(G-842)*
Mold Threads Inc ....G....... 203 483-1420
Branford *(G-627)*
Moldvision LLC ....G....... 860 315-1025
Thompson *(G-8840)*
◆ **Moore Tool Company Inc** ....D....... 203 366-3224
Bridgeport *(G-843)*
My Tool Company Inc ....G....... 203 755-2333
Waterbury *(G-9551)*
Newhart Products Inc ....E....... 203 878-3546
Milford *(G-4592)*
Northeast Carbide Inc ....F....... 860 628-2515
Southington *(G-7959)*
Noujaim Tool Co Inc ....E....... 203 753-4441
Waterbury *(G-9562)*
Omni Mold Systems LLC ....G....... 888 666-4755
Lisbon *(G-3882)*
Oxford General Industries Inc ....F....... 203 758-4467
Prospect *(G-7013)*
P&G Metal Components Corp ....F....... 860 243-2220
Bloomfield *(G-458)*
Paragon Tool Company Inc ....G....... 860 647-9935
Manchester *(G-4072)*
Patriot Manufacturing LLC ....G....... 860 506-2213
Bristol *(G-1086)*
Plainville Machine & Tl Co Inc ....F....... 860 589-5595
Bristol *(G-1091)*
▲ **Plastic Design Intl Inc** ....E....... 860 632-2001
Middletown *(G-4393)*
◆ **Pmt Group Inc** ....C....... 203 367-8675
Bridgeport *(G-875)*
Precision Mold and Polsg LLC ....G....... 860 489-6249
Torrington *(G-8959)*
Precision Punch + Tooling Corp ....D....... 860 229-9902
Berlin *(G-210)*
Preferred Tool & Die Inc ....D....... 203 925-8525
Shelton *(G-7537)*
Producto Corporation ....F....... 203 366-3224
Bridgeport *(G-882)*
Proman Inc ....G....... 860 827-8778
New Britain *(G-5038)*
Prototype Plastic Mold Co Inc ....E....... 860 632-2800
Middletown *(G-4398)*
Quality Engineering Svcs Inc ....E....... 203 269-5054
Wallingford *(G-9345)*
Quality Wire Edm Inc ....G....... 860 583-9867
Bristol *(G-1101)*
R A Tool Co ....G....... 203 877-2998
Milford *(G-4622)*
R&R Tool & Die LLC ....G....... 860 627-9197
East Windsor *(G-2515)*
Ragis Fabrications Inc ....G....... 203 237-0424
Meriden *(G-4228)*
Ramar-Hall Inc ....E....... 860 349-1081
Middlefield *(G-4306)*
Ray Machine Corporation ....E....... 860 582-8202
Terryville *(G-8769)*
Reliable Tool & Die Inc ....E....... 203 877-3264
Milford *(G-4625)*
REm Tool & Die Llc ....G....... 860 582-7559
Bristol *(G-1106)*
▲ **Reno Machine Company Inc** ....D....... 860 666-5641
Newington *(G-5700)*
Reynolds Carbide Die Co Inc ....E....... 860 283-8246
Thomaston *(G-8802)*
Richards Machine Tool Co Inc ....F....... 860 436-2938
Newington *(G-5701)*
Rintec Corporation ....F....... 860 274-3697
Oakville *(G-6462)*
Roto-Die Company Inc ....F....... 860 292-7030
East Windsor *(G-2516)*
Royal Machine and Tool Corp ....E....... 860 828-6555
Berlin *(G-217)*
Sandur Tool Co ....G....... 203 753-0004
Waterbury *(G-9598)*
Savoir Consulting & Mfg Co LLC ....G....... 860 933-7614
Willington *(G-10257)*
▲ **Scan Tool & Mold Inc** ....E....... 203 459-4950
Trumbull *(G-9070)*
Sirois Tool Company Inc ....D....... 860 828-5327
Berlin *(G-220)*
Skico Manufacturing Co LLC ....G....... 203 230-1305
Hamden *(G-3510)*
Skillcraft Machine Tool Co ....F....... 860 953-1246
South Windsor *(G-7822)*
Somers Manufacturing Inc ....G....... 860 314-1075
Bristol *(G-1119)*
Somerset Plastics Company ....E....... 860 635-1601
Middletown *(G-4421)*
South Windsor Quality Black MO ....G....... 860 385-2740
South Windsor *(G-7827)*
Spartan Aerospace LLC ....D....... 860 533-7500
Manchester *(G-4090)*
Stafford Precision Tool LLC ....G....... 860 684-0471
Stafford Springs *(G-8040)*
Steel Rule Die Corp America ....G....... 860 621-5284
Milldale *(G-4688)*
Sterling Tool Die & Mfg Co ....G....... 203 378-0893
Stratford *(G-8685)*
Straton Industries Inc ....D....... 203 375-4488
Stratford *(G-8687)*
Superior Mold Corp ....G....... 860 225-7654
New Britain *(G-5069)*
Taco Fasteners Inc ....F....... 860 747-5597
Plainville *(G-6867)*
Tekcast Industries ....G....... 860 799-6464
Sherman *(G-7605)*
Telke Tool & Die Mfg Co ....G....... 860 828-9955
Kensington *(G-3819)*
Tmf Incorporated ....G....... 203 267-7364
Southbury *(G-7880)*

SIC SECTION
35 INDUSTRIAL AND COMMERCIAL MACHINERY AND COMPUTER EQUIPMENT

Total Concept Tool Inc ... G ... 203 483-1130
Branford *(G-664)*
Turbine Support Services Inc ... G ... 860 688-4800
Windsor *(G-10456)*
Upper Valley Mold LLC ... G ... 860 489-8282
Torrington *(G-8986)*
Victor Tool Co Inc ... G ... 203 634-8113
Meriden *(G-4264)*
Watertown Jig Bore Service Inc ... F ... 860 274-5898
Watertown *(G-9748)*
Watertown Plastics Inc ... E ... 860 274-7535
Watertown *(G-9749)*
Weimann Brothers Mfg Co ... F ... 203 735-3311
Derby *(G-2130)*
Wepco Plastics Inc ... E ... 860 349-3407
Middlefield *(G-4309)*
Wess Tool & Die Company Inc ... G ... 203 237-5277
Meriden *(G-4267)*
West Haven Tool & Mfg LLC ... G ... 203 932-1735
West Haven *(G-9962)*
West-Conn Tool and Die Inc ... F ... 203 538-5081
Shelton *(G-7584)*
Wilkinson Tool & Die Co ... G ... 860 599-5821
North Stonington *(G-6032)*
Winthrop Tool LLC ... G ... 860 526-9079
Essex *(G-2738)*

3545 Machine Tool Access

Accu-Rite Tool & Mfg Co ... F ... 860 688-4844
Tolland *(G-8847)*
Admill Machine Co ... G ... 860 667-3676
Newington *(G-5620)*
Advanced Torque Products LLC ... G ... 860 828-1523
Newington *(G-5622)*
▲ Advanced Vacuum Technology Inc ... G ... 860 653-4176
Simsbury *(G-7609)*
Aircraft Forged Tool Company ... G ... 860 347-3778
Rockfall *(G-7210)*
AKO Inc ... E ... 860 298-9765
Windsor *(G-10357)*
▲ Alden Corporation ... D ... 203 879-8830
Wolcott *(G-10548)*
Alden Tool Company Inc ... E ... 860 828-3556
Berlin *(G-153)*
▲ All Five Tool Co Inc ... E ... 860 583-1693
Berlin *(G-154)*
American Grippers Inc ... E ... 203 459-8345
Trumbull *(G-8997)*
Apex Machine Tool Company Inc ... D ... 860 677-2884
Cheshire *(G-1353)*
Arthur I Platt Inc ... G ... 203 874-0091
Milford *(G-4459)*
Blue Chip Tool ... G ... 860 875-7999
Tolland *(G-8852)*
Brass City Technologies LLC ... G ... 203 723-7021
Naugatuck *(G-4863)*
Byron Lord Inc ... G ... 203 287-9881
Old Lyme *(G-6493)*
Center Broach & Machine Co ... G ... 203 235-6329
Meriden *(G-4156)*
Century Tool and Design Inc ... F ... 860 621-6748
Milldale *(G-4683)*
Clear Site The Heated Wiper ... F ... 203 790-2100
Bethel *(G-272)*
Coastal Group Inc ... G ... 860 452-4148
Killingworth *(G-3830)*
Comex Machinery ... G ... 203 334-2196
Bridgeport *(G-738)*
Command Tooling Systems ... G ... 203 284-9615
Wallingford *(G-9234)*
D & M Tool Company Inc ... G ... 860 236-6037
West Hartford *(G-9797)*
Danco Manufacturing LLC ... G ... 860 870-1706
Vernon Rockville *(G-9167)*
Danjon Manufacturing Corp ... F ... 203 272-7258
Cheshire *(G-1380)*
Drill Rite Carbide Tool Co ... G ... 860 583-3200
Terryville *(G-8751)*
Durant Machine Inc ... G ... 860 572-8211
Mystic *(G-4814)*
E and S Gage Inc ... F ... 860 872-5917
Tolland *(G-8862)*
Eastern Broach Inc ... F ... 860 828-4800
Plainville *(G-6802)*
Edmunds Manufacturing Company ... D ... 860 677-2813
Farmington *(G-2903)*
Edrive Actuators Inc ... G ... 860 953-0588
Newington *(G-5650)*
Ewald Instruments Corp ... F ... 860 491-9042
Bristol *(G-1032)*

FDM LLC ... G ... 860 684-7466
Stafford Springs *(G-8029)*
◆ Fletcher-Terry Company LLC ... D ... 860 828-3400
East Berlin *(G-2169)*
▲ Goldenrod Corporation ... E ... 203 723-4400
Beacon Falls *(G-135)*
Guhring Inc ... C ... 860 216-5948
Bloomfield *(G-416)*
H & B Tool & Engineering Co ... E ... 860 528-9341
South Windsor *(G-7766)*
Haesche Machine Repair Service ... G ... 203 488-7271
Branford *(G-602)*
Hart Tool & Engineering ... G ... 203 264-9776
Oxford *(G-6664)*
Hartford Gauge Co ... G ... 860 233-9619
West Hartford *(G-9817)*
Hermann Schmidt Company Inc ... F ... 860 289-3347
South Windsor *(G-7769)*
Hgh Industries LLC ... G ... 860 644-1150
South Windsor *(G-7771)*
Highland Manufacturing Inc ... E ... 860 646-5142
Manchester *(G-4028)*
Integral Industries Inc ... F ... 860 953-0686
Newington *(G-5663)*
Iswiss Corporation ... G ... 860 327-4200
Manchester *(G-4034)*
J F Tool Inc ... G ... 860 349-3063
Rockfall *(G-7213)*
J J Industries Conn Inc ... F ... 860 628-4655
Southington *(G-7941)*
◆ James J Scott LLC ... G ... 860 571-9200
Rocky Hill *(G-7252)*
Jet Tool & Cutter Mfg Inc ... E ... 860 621-5381
Southington *(G-7943)*
Jims Machine Shop Inc ... G ... 860 928-5151
Putnam *(G-7050)*
▼ Johnson Gage Company ... E ... 860 242-5541
Bloomfield *(G-428)*
Juskhas Wp Co ... G ... 860 455-0502
Hampton *(G-3536)*
KB Services ... G ... 203 243-3594
Bridgeport *(G-814)*
Kinetic Tool Co Inc ... F ... 860 627-5882
East Windsor *(G-2505)*
Leeco Inc ... G ... 860 404-8876
Avon *(G-88)*
LLC Dow Gage ... E ... 860 828-5327
Berlin *(G-196)*
Lord & Hodge Inc ... F ... 860 632-7006
Middletown *(G-4369)*
Lyons Tool and Die Company ... E ... 203 238-2689
Meriden *(G-4190)*
M & M Carbide Inc ... G ... 860 628-2002
Southington *(G-7948)*
M & R Manufacturing Inc ... G ... 860 666-5066
Newington *(G-5673)*
M T S Tool LLC ... G ... 860 945-0875
Oakville *(G-6456)*
Mandrel ... G ... 410 507-7767
Shelton *(G-7495)*
Marena Industries Inc ... F ... 860 528-9701
East Hartford *(G-2343)*
MDN Assoc Inc ... G ... 203 758-6721
Prospect *(G-7010)*
Meadow Manufacturing Inc ... F ... 860 357-3785
Kensington *(G-3813)*
▲ Meyer Gage Co Inc ... F ... 860 528-6526
South Windsor *(G-7792)*
Micro Insert Inc ... G ... 860 621-5789
Milldale *(G-4685)*
Mid-State Manufacturing Inc ... F ... 860 621-6855
Milldale *(G-4686)*
Miracle Instruments Co ... F ... 860 642-7745
Lebanon *(G-3858)*
Moon Cutter Co Inc ... E ... 203 288-9249
Hamden *(G-3484)*
◆ Moore Tool Company Inc ... D ... 203 366-3224
Bridgeport *(G-843)*
Mrh Tool LLC ... G ... 203 878-3359
Milford *(G-4586)*
Nelson Apostle Inc ... G ... 860 953-4633
Hartford *(G-3649)*
North Haven Manufacturing Co ... G ... 203 284-8578
Wallingford *(G-9328)*
▲ O S Walker Company Inc ... D ... 508 853-3232
Windsor *(G-10414)*
Paradigm Prcision Holdings LLC ... D ... 860 829-3663
East Berlin *(G-2173)*
Perry Technology Corporation ... D ... 860 738-2525
New Hartford *(G-5206)*

Pine Meadow Machine Co Inc ... G ... 860 623-4494
Windsor Locks *(G-10493)*
◆ Pmt Group Inc ... C ... 203 367-8675
Bridgeport *(G-875)*
Powder Pushers ... G ... 860 295-6406
Marlborough *(G-4129)*
Powerhold Inc ... E ... 860 349-1044
Middlefield *(G-4304)*
Precision Punch + Tooling Corp ... G ... 860 225-4159
Berlin *(G-211)*
Preferred Tool & Die Inc ... E ... 203 925-8525
Shelton *(G-7538)*
Preferred Utilities Mfg Corp ... D ... 203 743-6741
Danbury *(G-1918)*
Producto Corporation ... F ... 203 366-3224
Bridgeport *(G-882)*
Q Alpha Inc ... E ... 860 357-7340
Colchester *(G-1569)*
R&R Tool & Die LLC ... G ... 860 627-9197
East Windsor *(G-2515)*
Ray Machine Corporation ... E ... 860 582-8202
Terryville *(G-8769)*
Royal Machine and Tool Corp ... E ... 860 828-6555
Berlin *(G-217)*
Sirois Tool Company Inc ... D ... 860 828-5327
Berlin *(G-220)*
Sjm Properties Inc ... G ... 860 979-0060
Ellington *(G-2600)*
Skico Manufacturing Co LLC ... G ... 203 230-1305
Hamden *(G-3510)*
Southwick & Meister Inc ... C ... 203 237-0000
Meriden *(G-4244)*
Space Electronics LLC ... E ... 860 829-0001
Berlin *(G-221)*
Swanson Tool Manufacturing Inc ... E ... 860 953-1641
West Hartford *(G-9863)*
Tool The Somma Company ... E ... 203 753-2114
Waterbury *(G-9613)*
Total Machine Co ... G ... 203 481-8780
Clinton *(G-1530)*
Universal Precision Mfg ... G ... 203 374-9809
Trumbull *(G-9089)*
Vertech Inc ... G ... 203 876-1552
Milford *(G-4673)*
Victor Tool Co Inc ... G ... 203 634-8113
Meriden *(G-4264)*
Viking Tool Company ... E ... 203 929-1457
Shelton *(G-7579)*
W J Savage Co Inc ... G ... 203 468-4100
East Haven *(G-2459)*
◆ Walker Magnetics Group Inc ... E ... 508 853-3232
Windsor *(G-10461)*
White Hills Tool ... G ... 203 590-3143
Monroe *(G-4765)*
Zero Check LLC ... G ... 860 283-5629
Thomaston *(G-8827)*

3546 Power Hand Tools

Air Tool Sales & Service Co ... G ... 860 673-2714
Unionville *(G-9110)*
▲ Alden Corporation ... D ... 203 879-8830
Wolcott *(G-10548)*
Amro Tool Co ... G ... 860 274-9766
Watertown *(G-9681)*
Apex Machine Tool Company Inc ... D ... 860 677-2884
Cheshire *(G-1353)*
Black & Decker (us) Inc ... G ... 860 563-5800
Wethersfield *(G-10184)*
Black & Decker (us) Inc ... G ... 860 225-5111
New Britain *(G-4951)*
◆ Black & Decker (us) Inc ... G ... 860 225-5111
New Britain *(G-4952)*
▲ Blackstone Industries LLC ... D ... 203 792-8622
Bethel *(G-266)*
DArcy Saw LLC ... G ... 800 569-1264
Windsor Locks *(G-10481)*
Darien Lawn Mower Repair ... G ... 203 656-1869
Darien *(G-2018)*
▲ Frasal Tool Co Inc ... F ... 860 666-3524
Newington *(G-5654)*
HRF Fastener Systems Inc ... E ... 860 589-0750
Bristol *(G-1049)*
Kucko Chain Saw Supplies ... G ... 860 684-3887
Willington *(G-10251)*
▲ Ridge View Associates Inc ... D ... 203 878-8560
Milford *(G-4628)*
Slater Hill Tool LLC ... G ... 860 963-0415
Putnam *(G-7066)*
Stanley Black & Decker Inc ... G ... 860 460-9122
Southington *(G-7981)*

S
I
C

Employee Codes: A=Over 500 employees, B=251-500
C=101-250, D=51-100, E=20-50, F=10-19, G=1-9
2020 Harris Connecticut
Manufacturers Directory
433

35 INDUSTRIAL AND COMMERCIAL MACHINERY AND COMPUTER EQUIPMENT SIC SECTION

Stanley Black & Decker Inc ....C 860 225-5111
New Britain *(G-5061)*
Stanley Black & Decker Inc ....E 860 225-5111
New Britain *(G-5064)*
Stihl Incorporated ....E 203 929-8488
Oxford *(G-6695)*
Trumpf Inc ....B 860 255-6000
Plainville *(G-6872)*
◆ **Trumpf Inc** ....B 860 255-6000
Farmington *(G-2967)*
Trumpf Inc ....B 860 255-6000
Farmington *(G-2968)*
Universal Precision Mfg ....G 203 374-9809
Trumbull *(G-9089)*
W J Savage Co Inc ....G 203 468-4100
East Haven *(G-2459)*

3547 Rolling Mill Machinery & Eqpt

Adam Z Golas ....G 860 224-7178
New Britain *(G-4936)*
Compass Group Management LLC ....F 203 221-1703
Westport *(G-10068)*
Technology In Controls Inc ....G 860 283-8405
Plymouth *(G-6929)*
Ulbrich Stainless Steels ....C 203 269-2507
Wallingford *(G-9393)*

3548 Welding Apparatus

▲ **Advanced Vacuum Technology Inc** ....G 860 653-4176
Simsbury *(G-7609)*
Air-Vac Engineering Co Inc ....E 203 888-9900
Seymour *(G-7335)*
Airgas Usa LLC ....G 860 442-0363
Waterford *(G-9640)*
▲ **Branson Ultrasonics Corp** ....B 203 796-0400
Danbury *(G-1759)*
▲ **Cadi Co Inc** ....E 203 729-1111
Naugatuck *(G-4865)*
Eastern Conectr Specialty Corp ....G 860 355-8100
New Milford *(G-5530)*
Industrial Prssure Washers LLC ....G 860 608-6153
Wethersfield *(G-10197)*
L & P Gate Company Inc ....G 860 296-8009
Hartford *(G-3623)*
▼ **Magnatech LLC** ....D 860 653-2573
East Granby *(G-2210)*
Nelson Stud Welding Inc ....G 800 635-9353
Farmington *(G-2935)*
New Hope Wldg Fabrication LLC ....G 203 357-0080
Stamford *(G-8324)*
Praxair Surface Tech Inc ....D 860 646-0700
Manchester *(G-4076)*
Quality Welding Service LLC ....G 860 342-7202
Portland *(G-6970)*
▲ **Sonics & Materials Inc** ....D 203 270-4600
Newtown *(G-5781)*
Sonitek Corporation ....E 203 878-9321
Milford *(G-4647)*
Systems and Tech Intl Inc ....G 860 871-0401
Tolland *(G-8880)*
Thermatool Mill Syst ....G 203 468-4178
Farmington *(G-2964)*
Tim Welder LLC ....G 860 646-1356
Manchester *(G-4101)*

3549 Metalworking Machinery, NEC

Adamczyk Enterprises Inc ....G 860 745-9830
Enfield *(G-2612)*
◆ **Alpha-Core Inc** ....E 203 954-0050
Shelton *(G-7392)*
C & G Precisions Products Inc ....G 203 879-6989
Wolcott *(G-10551)*
▲ **Charter Oak Automation LLC** ....G 203 562-0699
Wallingford *(G-9226)*
▲ **Clear Automation LLC** ....E 860 621-2955
Southington *(G-7906)*
◆ **Fletcher-Terry Company LLC** ....D 860 828-3400
East Berlin *(G-2169)*
Foilmark Inc ....F 860 243-0343
Bloomfield *(G-414)*
Force Automation Inc ....G 860 622-1618
New Britain *(G-4990)*
Hall Machine Systems Inc ....G 203 481-4275
North Branford *(G-5840)*
Herrick & Cowell Company Inc ....G 203 288-2578
Hamden *(G-3463)*
Jovil Universal LLC ....E 203 792-6700
Danbury *(G-1864)*
L M Gill Welding and Mfr LLC ....F 860 647-9931
Manchester *(G-4046)*

Merritt Extruder Corp ....E 203 230-8100
Hamden *(G-3481)*
MGS Manufacturing Inc ....G 203 481-4275
North Branford *(G-5849)*
Nielsen Consulting Inc ....G 914 831-1681
New Milford *(G-5573)*
Obi Laser Products ....G 860 305-0038
Canton *(G-1322)*
◆ **P/A Industries Inc** ....E 860 243-8306
Bloomfield *(G-459)*
Shuster-Mettler Corp ....E 203 562-3178
Plainville *(G-6861)*
Te Connectivity Corporation ....C 860 684-8000
Stafford Springs *(G-8041)*
Tmf Incorporated ....G 203 267-7364
Southbury *(G-7880)*
True Position Mfg LLC ....G 860 291-2987
South Windsor *(G-7835)*
Tyger Tool Inc ....F 203 375-4344
Stratford *(G-8699)*
Vangor Engineering Corporation ....G 203 267-4377
Oxford *(G-6698)*
Wtp Machine Robotics ....G 860 716-7281
Southington *(G-7996)*

3552 Textile Machinery

Advanced Machine Services LLC ....G 203 888-6600
Waterbury *(G-9423)*
Advanced Machine Services LLC ....G 203 888-6600
Oxford *(G-6638)*
Ehriched Stitch LLC ....G 203 210-5107
Wilton *(G-10290)*
▲ **France Voiles Co Inc** ....G 203 364-9454
Sandy Hook *(G-7311)*
Gros-Ite Precision Spindle ....G 860 679-7490
Farmington *(G-2915)*
Image Star LLC ....G 888 632-5515
Middletown *(G-4355)*
Monogram Studio Greenwich CT ....G 203 428-5700
Greenwich *(G-3206)*
Mp Impressions LLC ....G 860 873-1797
Moodus *(G-4774)*
Reynolds Carbide Die Co Inc ....E 860 283-8246
Thomaston *(G-8802)*
Screen-Tech Inc ....G 860 496-8016
Torrington *(G-8968)*
Sonic Corp ....F 203 375-0063
Stratford *(G-8683)*
Systematic Automation Inc ....E 310 218-3361
Farmington *(G-2962)*
Tri Star Graphics ....G 203 748-4792
Bethel *(G-355)*
Ultramatic West ....G 203 745-4688
Hamden *(G-3525)*

3553 Woodworking Machinery

Bakers Architectural Wdwkg LLC ....G 203 483-3173
Branford *(G-555)*
Bender Showroom ....G 860 618-2944
Torrington *(G-8902)*
Carls Closets LLC ....G 203 457-9401
Guilford *(G-3338)*
Cedar Accessories ....G 860 350-6969
New Milford *(G-5517)*
Cournoyer Flr Sanding Finshg ....G 860 963-7088
Thompson *(G-8833)*
Johns Floor Sanding ....G 860 423-3852
Windham *(G-10348)*
Northeast Cabinetry LLC ....G 860 216-0781
Bloomfield *(G-452)*
Patriotic Spirit ....G 704 239-4289
Suffield *(G-8728)*
◆ **United Abrasives Inc** ....B 860 456-7131
North Windham *(G-6040)*
Walsh Claim Services ....G 203 481-0680
North Branford *(G-5865)*

3554 Paper Inds Machinery

▲ **Andritz Shw Inc** ....E 860 496-8888
Torrington *(G-8896)*
▲ **Bar-Plate Manufacturing Co** ....F 203 397-0033
Hamden *(G-3417)*
▲ **Goldenrod Corporation** ....E 203 723-4400
Beacon Falls *(G-135)*
Lakeview Engineering & Mfg LLC ....G 860 490-2760
Higganum *(G-3767)*
Sonic Corp ....F 203 375-0063
Stratford *(G-8683)*
Zatorski Coating Company Inc ....F 860 267-9889
East Hampton *(G-2285)*

3555 Printing Trades Machinery & Eqpt

A & E Engraving Service ....G 860 582-6503
Bristol *(G-950)*
Arico Engineering Inc ....G 860 642-7040
North Franklin *(G-5870)*
Asml Us LLC ....A 203 761-4000
Wilton *(G-10270)*
Baldwin Graphic Systems Inc ....G 203 925-1100
Shelton *(G-7401)*
Davinci Technologies Inc ....G 860 265-3388
Enfield *(G-2636)*
I Q Technology LLC ....F 860 749-7255
Enfield *(G-2651)*
Image Star LLC ....G 888 632-5515
Middletown *(G-4355)*
Interpro LLC ....F 860 526-5869
Deep River *(G-2093)*
▲ **J-Teck Usa Inc** ....G 203 791-2121
Danbury *(G-1856)*
Santec Corporation ....F 203 878-1379
Milford *(G-4638)*
Systematic Automation Inc ....E 310 218-3361
Farmington *(G-2962)*
▲ **Verico Technology LLC** ....E 800 492-7286
Enfield *(G-2704)*

3556 Food Prdts Machinery

A & I Concentrate LLC ....F 203 447-1938
Shelton *(G-7385)*
Amt Micropure Inc ....G 203 226-7938
Weston *(G-10017)*
Bakery Engineering/Winkler Inc ....F 203 929-8630
Shelton *(G-7400)*
▼ **Capricorn Investors III LP** ....F 203 861-6600
Greenwich *(G-3141)*
▲ **Cimbali Usa Inc** ....G 203 254-6046
Fairfield *(G-2761)*
Conair Corporation ....D 800 492-7464
Torrington *(G-8914)*
Diamond Brewing Service ....G 860 508-0013
Manchester *(G-4008)*
EMI Inc ....G 860 669-1199
Clinton *(G-1502)*
◆ **Jarvis Products Corporation** ....F 860 347-7271
Middletown *(G-4357)*
Newgate Designs Co ....G 860 653-6991
East Granby *(G-2217)*
Penco Corporation ....C 860 347-7271
Middletown *(G-4392)*
Pro Scientific Inc ....F 203 267-4600
Oxford *(G-6689)*
Q-Jet DSI Inc ....G 203 230-4700
North Haven *(G-5984)*
Sonic Corp ....F 203 375-0063
Stratford *(G-8683)*
Sun Farm Corporation ....G 203 882-8000
Milford *(G-4657)*
Tasty Kale LLC ....G 203 560-9451
New Haven *(G-5410)*
Taylor Coml Foodservice Inc ....A 336 245-6400
Farmington *(G-2963)*
◆ **Treif USA Inc** ....F 203 929-9930
Shelton *(G-7569)*
Ventures LLC DOT Com LLC ....G 203 930-8972
Vernon *(G-9157)*
W J Savage Co Inc ....G 203 468-4100
East Haven *(G-2459)*

3559 Special Ind Machinery, NEC

Accurate Automation LLC ....G 203 988-9426
Wallingford *(G-9197)*
B & A Design Inc ....G 860 871-0134
Vernon Rockville *(G-9161)*
▲ **Bausch Advanced Tech Inc** ....E 860 669-7380
Clinton *(G-1492)*
Berkshire Photonics LLC ....G 860 868-0412
Washington Depot *(G-9416)*
Bg Machinery Services LLC ....G 203 374-4732
Fairfield *(G-2754)*
C&G Mfg ....G 860 274-9785
Watertown *(G-9688)*
Center Mass LLC ....G 860 350-0239
New Milford *(G-5518)*
Colmec Usa Inc ....G 203 502-8822
Trumbull *(G-9013)*
◆ **Davis-Standard Holdings Inc** ....B 860 599-1010
Pawcatuck *(G-6708)*
Day Machine Systems Inc ....F 860 229-3440
New Britain *(G-4971)*

E S Williams Co G 203 888-0093 Seymour *(G-7344)*
▲ **Edward Segal Inc** E 860 283-5821 Thomaston *(G-8788)*
◆ **Emhart Glass Inc** D 860 298-7340 Windsor *(G-10383)*
Emhart Teknologies LLC G 877 364-2781 Danbury *(G-1806)*
▼ **Evans Cooling Systems Inc** G 860 668-1114 Suffield *(G-8718)*
◆ **Farrel Corporation** D 203 736-5500 Ansonia *(G-34)*
Freds Auto Machine G 203 744-2950 Bethel *(G-302)*
◆ **Gerber Technology LLC** B 860 871-8082 Tolland *(G-8865)*
Hitek Electronics LLC G 203 982-4574 Naugatuck *(G-4888)*
Industrial Saws Inc G 860 496-7000 Torrington *(G-8936)*
International Plating Tech LLC G 860 589-2212 Southington *(G-7940)*
Jet Process Corporation G 203 985-6000 North Haven *(G-5953)*
▼ **Johnstone Company Inc** E 203 239-5834 North Haven *(G-5954)*
◆ **Lamor USA Corporation** G 203 888-7700 Shelton *(G-7485)*
◆ **Lyman Products Corporation** D 860 632-2020 Middletown *(G-4370)*
Lyman Products Corporation E 860 632-2020 Middletown *(G-4371)*
Lynch Corp G 203 452-3007 Greenwich *(G-3195)*
M I R Inc F 203 888-2541 Beacon Falls *(G-141)*
▲ **Medelco Inc** G 203 275-8070 Bridgeport *(G-836)*
Media One LLC E 203 745-5825 Hamden *(G-3480)*
Merritt Extruder Corp E 203 230-8100 Hamden *(G-3481)*
Mikro Industrial Finishing Co G 860 875-6357 Vernon *(G-9143)*
Nicholas Precision Pdts LLC G 518 428-8109 Portland *(G-6966)*
Omega Engineering Inc D 714 540-4914 Norwalk *(G-6285)*
Prospect Products Incorporated E 860 666-0323 Newington *(G-5698)*
▲ **Puritan Industries Inc** E 860 693-0791 Collinsville *(G-1601)*
PYC Deborring LLC F/K/A C & G 860 828-6806 Berlin *(G-213)*
Quest Plastics Inc F 860 489-1404 Torrington *(G-8962)*
Renewable Energy Natural RES G 860 923-1091 Thompson *(G-8843)*
Saf Industries LLC E 203 729-4900 Meriden *(G-4237)*
Single Load LLC G 860 944-7507 Bridgeport *(G-909)*
Snapwire Innovations LLC G 203 806-4773 Cheshire *(G-1448)*
Startech Environmental Corp F 203 762-2499 Wilton *(G-10334)*
Synergy Sales Ltd G 860 974-3288 Woodstock *(G-10689)*
Toppan Photomasks Inc E 203 775-9001 Brookfield *(G-1231)*
◆ **Walker Magnetics Group Inc** E 508 853-3232 Windsor *(G-10461)*
Windham Automated Machines Inc F 860 208-5297 South Windham *(G-7695)*
▲ **Wittmann Battenfeld Inc** D 860 496-9603 Torrington *(G-8991)*
Xavier Marcus G 203 543-2032 Stratford *(G-8711)*

3561 Pumps & Pumping Eqpt

◆ **A V I International Inc** G 860 482-8345 Torrington *(G-8885)*
◆ **Beckson Manufacturing Inc** E 203 366-3644 Bridgeport *(G-709)*
▲ **Bjm Pumps LLC** E 860 399-5937 Old Saybrook *(G-6524)*
Dpc Quality Pump Service G 203 874-6877 Milford *(G-4515)*
Flowserve Corporation E 203 877-4252 Milford *(G-4537)*
Foleys Pump Service Inc E 203 792-2236 Danbury *(G-1828)*
▲ **Gardner Denver Nash LLC** D 203 459-3923 Trumbull *(G-9028)*
▲ **Hamworthy Peabody Combustn Inc** E 203 922-1199 Shelton *(G-7457)*
Harrier Technologies Inc G 203 625-9700 Greenwich *(G-3176)*
▲ **Hisco Pump Incorporated** E 860 243-2705 Bloomfield *(G-420)*
Idex Health & Science LLC G 203 774-4422 Wallingford *(G-9286)*
Ingersoll-Rand Company D 860 616-6600 Rocky Hill *(G-7250)*
◆ **ITT Water & Wastewater USA Inc** D 262 548-8181 Shelton *(G-7480)*
Marsars Water Rescue Systems G 203 924-7315 Shelton *(G-7496)*
McVac Environmental Svcs Inc E 203 497-1960 New Haven *(G-5327)*
▼ **MSC Filtration Tech Inc** F 860 745-7475 Enfield *(G-2664)*
Omega Engineering Inc D 714 540-4914 Norwalk *(G-6285)*
Phillips Pump LLC F 203 576-6688 Bridgeport *(G-872)*
Preferred Utilities Mfg Corp D 203 743-6741 Danbury *(G-1918)*
Proflow Inc E 203 230-4700 North Haven *(G-5980)*
◆ **Pump Technology Incorporated** E 203 736-8890 Ansonia *(G-47)*
▲ **Sfc Koenig LLC** E 203 245-1100 North Haven *(G-5992)*
Sonic Corp F 203 375-0063 Stratford *(G-8683)*
◆ **Stancor LP** E 203 268-7513 Monroe *(G-4753)*
▲ **Sulzer Pump Solutions US Inc** E 203 238-2700 Meriden *(G-4247)*
▲ **Talcott Mountain Engineering** F 860 651-3141 Simsbury *(G-7649)*
Xylem Inc G 203 521-4934 Milford *(G-4682)*
Xylem Water Solutions USA Inc E 203 450-3715 Shelton *(G-7589)*

3562 Ball & Roller Bearings

▲ **Abek LLC** F 860 314-3905 Bristol *(G-953)*
Ball & Roller Bearing Co LLC F 860 355-4161 New Milford *(G-5508)*
Buswell Manufacturing Co Inc F 203 334-6069 Bridgeport *(G-726)*
C & S Engineering Inc E 203 235-5727 Meriden *(G-4153)*
Del-Tron Precision Inc E 203 778-2727 Bethel *(G-280)*
◆ **Fag Bearings LLC** D 203 790-5474 Danbury *(G-1821)*
◆ **FAg Holding Corporation** F 203 790-5474 Danbury *(G-1822)*
▲ **Gwilliam Company Inc** F 860 354-2884 New Milford *(G-5543)*
▲ **Hartford Technologies Inc** E 860 571-3602 Rocky Hill *(G-7241)*
K A F Manufacturing Co Inc E 203 324-3012 Stamford *(G-8272)*
Kamatics Corporation G 860 243-7230 Bloomfield *(G-436)*
Kamatics Corporation E 860 243-9704 Bloomfield *(G-435)*
MRC Specialty Balls G 860 379-8511 Winsted *(G-10530)*
Nn Inc G 203 793-7132 Wallingford *(G-9326)*
▲ **Pro-Tech Enterprises LLC** G 203 931-9668 West Haven *(G-9947)*
Rbc Bearings Incorporated B 203 267-7001 Oxford *(G-6691)*
Rbc Linear Precision Pdts Inc G 203 255-1511 Fairfield *(G-2833)*
Rollcorp LLC G 860 347-5227 Middletown *(G-4406)*
◆ **Roller Bearing Co Amer Inc** C 203 267-7001 Oxford *(G-6693)*
Roller Bearing Co Amer Inc E 203 267-7001 Oxford *(G-6694)*
▲ **Schaeffler Aerospace USA Corp** B 203 744-2211 Danbury *(G-1936)*
Schaeffler Aerospace USA Corp D 860 379-7558 Winsted *(G-10534)*
Schaeffler Group USA Inc B 203 790-5474 Danbury *(G-1937)*
SKF Specialty Balls G 860 379-8511 Winsted *(G-10535)*
SKF USA Inc E 860 379-8511 Winsted *(G-10536)*
Timken Company F 860 652-4630 Glastonbury *(G-3087)*
▲ **Virginia Industries Inc** G 860 571-3600 Rocky Hill *(G-7271)*

3563 Air & Gas Compressors

Afcon Products Inc F 203 393-9301 Bethany *(G-234)*
Bauer Compressors Inc G 203 445-9514 Monroe *(G-4696)*
▲ **Comvac Systems Inc** G 860 265-3658 Enfield *(G-2631)*
David H Johnson Inc G 860 677-5595 West Hartford *(G-9798)*
▲ **Gardner Denver Nash LLC** D 203 459-3923 Trumbull *(G-9028)*
▼ **Norwalk Compreseer Company** E 203 386-1234 Stratford *(G-8655)*
▲ **Norwalk Compressor Inc** G 203 386-1234 Stratford *(G-8656)*
P&G Metal Components Corp F 860 243-2220 Bloomfield *(G-458)*
Spfm Corp G 203 900-0005 Bridgeport *(G-912)*
Standard Pneumatic Products G 203 270-1400 Newtown *(G-5782)*
Stylair LLC F 860 747-4588 Plainville *(G-6863)*

3564 Blowers & Fans

Adk Pressure Equipment Corp G 860 585-0050 Bristol *(G-957)*
◆ **Anderson Technologies Inc** G 860 663-2100 Killingworth *(G-3828)*
Atlantic Vent & Eqp Co Inc E 860 635-1300 Cromwell *(G-1690)*
Clean Air Group Inc E 203 335-3700 Fairfield *(G-2764)*
▲ **EBM-Papst Inc** B 860 674-1515 Farmington *(G-2902)*
▼ **Environmental Monitor Service** G 203 935-0102 Meriden *(G-4169)*
GE Steam Power Inc G 860 688-1911 Windsor *(G-10391)*
GE Steam Power Inc C 423 648-4161 Windsor *(G-10389)*
Guardian Envmtl Tech Inc F 860 350-2200 New Milford *(G-5541)*
Kennedy Gustafson and Cole Inc E 860 828-2594 Berlin *(G-191)*
Lydall Inc E 860 646-1233 Manchester *(G-4050)*
▲ **McIntire Company** F 860 585-8559 Bristol *(G-1070)*
Mechancal Engnered Systems LLC G 203 400-4658 New Canaan *(G-5119)*
Microshield LLC G 800 553-1290 Stamford *(G-8308)*
Nidec America Corporation F 860 653-2144 East Granby *(G-2219)*
Novaerus US Inc F 813 304-2468 Stamford *(G-8331)*
▲ **Nq Industries Inc** G 860 258-3466 Rocky Hill *(G-7259)*
Planet Technologies Inc F 800 255-3749 Ridgefield *(G-7163)*
◆ **Spencer Turbine Company** C 860 688-8361 Windsor *(G-10436)*
Stylair LLC F 860 747-4588 Plainville *(G-6863)*
Treadwell Corporation E 860 283-7600 Thomaston *(G-8814)*

3565 Packaging Machinery

B & B Equipment LLC G 860 342-5773 Portland *(G-6951)*
▲ **Beardsworth Group Inc** G 860 283-4014 Thomaston *(G-8780)*
▲ **Gtrpet Smf LLC** G 203 661-1229 Cos Cob *(G-1632)*
Integrated Packg Systems Inc G 860 623-2623 East Windsor *(G-2499)*

Employee Codes: A=Over 500 employees, B=251-500 C=101-250, D=51-100, E=20-50, F=10-19, G=1-9
2020 Harris Connecticut Manufacturers Directory
435

James J Chasse .... G 860 572-0838
Stonington *(G-8531)*
Millwood Inc .... F 203 248-7902
North Haven *(G-5965)*
▲ **OEM Sources LLC** .... G 203 283-5415
Milford *(G-4597)*
Packard Inc .... E 203 758-6219
Prospect *(G-7014)*
PDC International Corp .... D 203 853-1516
Norwalk *(G-6292)*
RWS Co Inc .... G 860 434-2961
Old Lyme *(G-6518)*
Sanford Redmond Inc .... G 203 351-9800
Stamford *(G-8402)*
Staban Engineering Corp .... F 203 294-1997
Wallingford *(G-9375)*
▲ **Standard-Knapp Inc** .... D 860 342-1100
Portland *(G-6974)*

3566 Speed Changers, Drives & Gears

▼ **Carlyle Johnson Machine Co LLC** .... E 860 643-1531
Bolton *(G-508)*
◆ **Control Concepts Inc** .... F 860 928-6551
Putnam *(G-7037)*
Cunningham Industries Inc .... G 203 324-2942
Stamford *(G-8171)*
JET Corporation .... F 203 334-3317
Bridgeport *(G-804)*
Rexnord LLC .... G 860 355-0478
New Milford *(G-5584)*
Roller Bearing Co Amer Inc .... E 203 758-8272
Middlebury *(G-4289)*
So and Sew Plushies .... G 860 916-2918
Meriden *(G-4242)*

3567 Indl Process Furnaces & Ovens

American Catatech Inc .... G 203 483-6692
Branford *(G-542)*
▲ **Birk Manufacturing Inc** .... D 800 531-2070
East Lyme *(G-2464)*
Catelectric Corp .... G 860 912-0800
Groton *(G-3277)*
David Weisman LLC .... G 203 322-9978
Stamford *(G-8182)*
Dri-Air Industries Inc .... E 860 627-5110
East Windsor *(G-2489)*
▲ **Duralite Incorporated** .... F 860 379-3113
Riverton *(G-7206)*
Earth Engineered Systems .... G 203 231-4614
Derby *(G-2112)*
Envax Products Inc .... G 203 264-8181
Oxford *(G-6657)*
Furnace Concepts .... G 203 264-7856
Southbury *(G-7853)*
Furnace Source LLC .... F 860 582-4201
Terryville *(G-8755)*
▲ **Hamworthy Peabody Combustn Inc** E 203 922-1199
Shelton *(G-7457)*
HI Heat Company Inc .... G 860 528-9315
South Windsor *(G-7772)*
▼ **Industrial Heater Corp** .... D 203 250-0500
Cheshire *(G-1400)*
Jad LLC .... E 860 289-1551
South Windsor *(G-7776)*
Manufacturers Coml Fin LLC .... E 860 242-6287
West Hartford *(G-9832)*
Modean Industries Inc .... G 203 371-6625
Easton *(G-2559)*
Noble Fire Brick Company Inc .... G 860 623-9256
East Windsor *(G-2513)*
Preferred Utilities Mfg Corp .... D 203 743-6741
Danbury *(G-1918)*
Sandvik Wire and Htg Tech Corp .... D 203 744-1440
Bethel *(G-337)*
Sshc Inc .... F 860 399-5434
Westbrook *(G-10010)*
Thoughtventions Unlimited LLC .... G 860 657-9014
Glastonbury *(G-3086)*
Tvu Gold Coating Services .... G 860 657-2666
Glastonbury *(G-3092)*
▲ **Warmup Inc** .... F 203 791-0072
Danbury *(G-1975)*

3568 Mechanical Power Transmission Eqpt, NEC

A Papish Incorporated .... E 203 744-0323
Danbury *(G-1727)*
Altra Industrial Motion Corp .... G 860 379-1673
New Hartford *(G-5185)*
▲ **American Collars Couplings Inc** .... F 860 379-7043
Winsted *(G-10504)*
▲ **American Sleeve Bearing LLC** .... E 860 684-8060
Stafford Springs *(G-8016)*
Ball & Roller Bearing Co LLC .... F 860 355-4161
New Milford *(G-5508)*
◆ **Bead Industries Inc** .... E 203 301-0270
Milford *(G-4466)*
▼ **Carlyle Johnson Machine Co LLC** .... E 860 643-1531
Bolton *(G-508)*
Converter Consultants LLC .... G 203 729-1031
Naugatuck *(G-4873)*
Del-Tron Precision Inc .... E 203 778-2727
Bethel *(G-280)*
▲ **F K Bearings Inc** .... F 860 621-4567
Southington *(G-7922)*
▲ **Gwilliam Company Inc** .... F 860 354-2884
New Milford *(G-5543)*
Helander Products Inc .... F 860 669-7953
Clinton *(G-1507)*
▲ **Inertia Dynamics LLC** .... C 860 379-1252
New Hartford *(G-5197)*
Kasheta Power Equipment .... G 860 528-8421
South Windsor *(G-7782)*
Kevin G Barry .... G 203 263-4948
Woodbury *(G-10640)*
Perry Technology Corporation .... D 860 738-2525
New Hartford *(G-5206)*
◆ **Rollease Acmeda Inc** .... D 203 964-1573
Stamford *(G-8397)*
Roller Bearing Co Amer Inc .... E 203 758-8272
Middlebury *(G-4289)*
▲ **Virginia Industries Inc** .... G 860 571-3600
Rocky Hill *(G-7271)*

3569 Indl Machinery & Eqpt, NEC

▲ **3M Purification Inc** .... B 203 237-5541
Meriden *(G-4135)*
A F M Engineering Corp .... G 860 774-7518
Brooklyn *(G-1244)*
AAA Fire and Safety Inc .... G 860 267-1965
Bloomfield *(G-379)*
Act Robots Inc .... G 860 314-1557
Bristol *(G-956)*
Alstom Power Co .... F 860 688-1911
Windsor *(G-10358)*
American Kuhne .... G 401 326-6200
North Stonington *(G-6019)*
Andersen Laboratories Inc .... G 860 286-9090
Bloomfield *(G-385)*
▲ **Applied Porous Tech Inc** .... F 860 408-9793
Tariffville *(G-8744)*
◆ **Arthur G Russell Company Inc** .... D 860 583-4109
Bristol *(G-967)*
Automation Inc .... F 860 236-5991
West Hartford *(G-9777)*
Brown Larkin & Co LLC .... G 860 280-8858
Burlington *(G-1261)*
▲ **Cable Management LLC** .... E 860 670-1890
Meriden *(G-4154)*
Cold LLC .... G 203 543-6861
Milford *(G-4490)*
Connecticut Leaf Filter LLC .... G 203 857-0846
Norwalk *(G-6127)*
Csg Automation LLC .... G 860 691-1885
Niantic *(G-5804)*
Dynamic Bldg Engry Sltions LLC .... G 860 571-8590
Rocky Hill *(G-7236)*
Elmar Filter Corporation .... G 203 624-1708
New Haven *(G-5276)*
Environmantal Systems Cor .... F 860 953-5167
Hartford *(G-3585)*
Fire Technology Inc .... G 860 276-2181
Southington *(G-7924)*
GL and V .... G 203 876-5400
Milford *(G-4540)*
Gutter Filter New England LLC .... G 860 274-5943
Oakville *(G-6454)*
Hamilton Standard Space .... E 860 654-6000
Windsor Locks *(G-10490)*
Isopur Fluid Technologies Inc .... F 860 599-1872
North Stonington *(G-6027)*
Jones Fire Sprinkler Co LLC .... G 860 464-7284
Gales Ferry *(G-2984)*
Jpo Solutions Inc .... G 203 502-8609
Trumbull *(G-9038)*
Locking Filter LLC .... G 203 691-1221
Hamden *(G-3476)*
M P Robinson Production .... E 203 938-1336
Redding *(G-7099)*
▲ **Mid State Assembly & Packg Inc** .... G 203 634-8740
Meriden *(G-4202)*
▲ **Mott Corporation** .... C 860 793-6333
Farmington *(G-2931)*
▼ **MSC Filtration Tech Inc** .... F 860 745-7475
Enfield *(G-2664)*
▲ **Naiad Dynamics Us Inc** .... E 203 929-6355
Shelton *(G-7506)*
National Filter Media Corp .... E 203 741-2225
Wallingford *(G-9325)*
New England Machine Co LLC .... G 860 526-7844
Deep River *(G-2096)*
North Haven Eqp & Lsg LLC .... G 203 795-9494
Orange *(G-6617)*
Packard Inc .... E 203 758-6219
Prospect *(G-7014)*
▲ **Pallflex Products Company** .... E 860 928-7761
Putnam *(G-7057)*
Parts Feeders Inc .... G 860 528-9579
East Hartford *(G-2352)*
◆ **Praxair Inc** .... B 203 837-2000
Danbury *(G-1913)*
Prospect Industries LLC .... G 203 758-3736
Prospect *(G-7018)*
▲ **Proton Energy Systems Inc** .... D 203 678-2000
Wallingford *(G-9343)*
Qsonica LLC .... G 203 426-0101
Newtown *(G-5770)*
Red Barn Innovations .... G 203 393-0778
Prospect *(G-7023)*
Richard Dudgeon Inc .... G 203 336-4459
Waterbury *(G-9593)*
Rondo America Incorporated .... C 203 723-5831
Naugatuck *(G-4917)*
RWS Co Inc .... G 860 434-2961
Old Lyme *(G-6518)*
▼ **Schaefer Machine Company Inc** .... G 860 526-4000
Deep River *(G-2099)*
▲ **Sonics & Materials Inc** .... D 203 270-4600
Newtown *(G-5781)*
Stormwaterworkscom LLC .... G 203 324-0045
Stamford *(G-8445)*
▲ **Tinny Corporation** .... E 860 854-6121
Middletown *(G-4427)*
Triad Concepts Inc .... G 860 399-4045
Westbrook *(G-10012)*
Ulitsch Mechanical Svcs LLC .... G 860 623-4223
Windsor Locks *(G-10500)*
US Filter Surface Preparatio .... G 203 284-7825
Wallingford *(G-9397)*

3571 Electronic Computers

American Railway Technologies .... G 860 291-1170
East Hartford *(G-2290)*
Amsys Inc .... E 203 431-8814
Ridgefield *(G-7116)*
Apple John .... G 203 746-3459
New Fairfield *(G-5161)*
Apple Homecare Innovations LLC .... G 860 940-5005
Bloomfield *(G-386)*
Apple Leaf .... G 203 988-7262
North Haven *(G-5906)*
Aztech Engineering LLC .... G 860 659-8892
Glastonbury *(G-3009)*
Black Rock Tech Group LLC .... F 203 916-7200
Bridgeport *(G-714)*
Bristol Babcock Employees Fede .... G 860 945-2200
Watertown *(G-9687)*
Castle Systems Inc .... G 203 250-3140
Cheshire *(G-1368)*
Cls Design Group .... G 860 307-2810
Torrington *(G-8911)*
Cyclone Microsystems Inc .... E 203 786-5536
Hamden *(G-3437)*
Devrajan Govender .... G 678 429-3408
Manchester *(G-4007)*
Frontier Vision Tech Inc .... E 860 953-0240
Rocky Hill *(G-7238)*
General Digital Corp .... G 860 645-2200
Manchester *(G-4021)*
Glacier Computer LLC .... G 860 355-7552
New Milford *(G-5536)*
Hg Tech LLC .... G 203 632-5946
Naugatuck *(G-4887)*
Hoffman Engineering LLC .... D 203 425-8900
Stamford *(G-8240)*
Interactive Marketing Corp .... G 203 248-5324
North Haven *(G-5949)*
Kimchuk Incorporated .... C 203 798-0799
Danbury *(G-1869)*

35 INDUSTRIAL AND COMMERCIAL MACHINERY AND COMPUTER EQUIPMENT

Company	Code	Phone
Little Apple LLC	G	860 404-2833
Farmington (G-2927)		
Macworks LLC	G	860 377-1371
Durham (G-2151)		
Mark Fahey	G	203 686-0852
Meriden (G-4192)		
Mark Misercola	G	423 323-0183
Norwalk (G-6248)		
Modern Electronic Fax & Cmpt	G	203 292-6520
Fairfield (G-2816)		
Oracle America Inc	D	203 703-3000
Stamford (G-8345)		
Panboud Pierrot	G	203 296-4806
Bridgeport (G-860)		
Red Apple Creative US Inc	G	212 453-2540
Shelton (G-7545)		
Sandpiper Electronics Inc	G	860 364-5558
Sharon (G-7383)		
Seclingua Inc	G	203 922-4560
Stamford (G-8406)		
Sequent Consulting LLC	G	203 966-2340
New Canaan (G-5140)		
Snack Electronics	G	860 225-3714
New Britain (G-5056)		
Tapped Apple Winery	G	860 887-0727
Norwich (G-6435)		
Xiaohao Jia	G	203 866-3120
Norwalk (G-6403)		

3572 Computer Storage Devices

Company	Code	Phone
Clg Enterprises Inc	F	203 741-9300
Wallingford (G-9232)		
EMC Corporation	D	203 418-4500
Fairfield (G-2781)		
EMC Fun Factory Inc	G	914 837-2899
Danbury (G-1805)		
Emc7 LLC	G	203 429-4355
Fairfield (G-2782)		
Gaisertim	G	203 245-9276
Madison (G-3922)		
Image Graphics Inc	E	203 926-0100
Shelton (G-7474)		
Kaman Aerospace Corporation	C	860 632-1000
Middletown (G-4360)		
Mini LLC	G	203 464-5495
Naugatuck (G-4902)		
◆ Pexagon Technology Inc	E	203 458-3364
Branford (G-634)		
Quantum	G	732 407-1200
New Canaan (G-5137)		
Quantum Bpower Southington LLC	G	860 201-0621
Southington (G-7963)		
Quantum Circuits Inc	G	203 432-4289
Madison (G-3950)		
Quantum Circuits Inc	F	203 891-6216
New Haven (G-5373)		
Retech USA LLC	G	860 531-9653
Colchester (G-1573)		
Sequent Consulting LLC	G	203 966-2340
New Canaan (G-5140)		
Systematics Inc	F	860 721-0706
Rocky Hill (G-7267)		
Uchisearch LLC	G	203 268-9096
Trumbull (G-9084)		

3575 Computer Terminals

Company	Code	Phone
Computer Warehouse	G	203 426-1034
Sandy Hook (G-7304)		
◆ Omega Engineering Inc	C	203 359-1660
Norwalk (G-6284)		
Precision Electronic Assembly	F	203 452-1839
Monroe (G-4747)		

3577 Computer Peripheral Eqpt, NEC

Company	Code	Phone
▲ Alinabal Holdings Corporation	B	203 877-3241
Milford (G-4449)		
Arrayent Health LLC	G	973 568-0323
Stamford (G-8094)		
Associates Inc Bedford	G	203 846-0230
Norwalk (G-6078)		
Braxton Manufacturing Co Inc	C	860 274-6781
Watertown (G-9685)		
Bristol Babcock Employees Fede	G	860 945-2200
Watertown (G-9687)		
Cadesk Company LLC	G	203 268-8083
Trumbull (G-9008)		
Cisco Systems Inc	E	203 229-2300
Norwalk (G-6115)		
Cisco Systems Inc	A	860 284-5500
Farmington (G-2888)		

Company	Code	Phone
▲ Computer Express LLC	F	860 829-1310
Berlin (G-173)		
Contek International Corp	G	203 972-3406
New Canaan (G-5097)		
▲ Contek International Corp	F	203 972-7330
New Canaan (G-5098)		
Cyclone Pcie Systems LLC	G	203 786-5536
Hamden (G-3438)		
Dark Field Technologies Inc	F	203 298-0731
Shelton (G-7428)		
Data Technology Inc	E	860 871-8082
Tolland (G-8860)		
▲ Dictaphone Corporation	C	203 381-7000
Stratford (G-8606)		
Ebeam Film LLC	F	203 926-0100
Shelton (G-7434)		
Ellipson Data LLC	G	203 227-5520
Westport (G-10078)		
Eye Ear It LLC	F	203 487-8949
Woodbury (G-10636)		
▲ Flo-Tech LLC	D	860 613-3333
New Haven (G-5283)		
Fremco LLC	F	203 857-0522
Ridgefield (G-7142)		
Frontier Vision Tech Inc	E	860 953-0240
Rocky Hill (G-7238)		
◆ Gerber Scientific LLC	C	860 871-8082
Tolland (G-8864)		
Hint Peripherals Corp	G	203 634-4468
Meriden (G-4173)		
Image Graphics Inc	E	203 926-0100
Shelton (G-7474)		
▼ Interntnl Bar Code Systms	G	860 659-9660
Glastonbury (G-3051)		
Iwco Direct	G	203 557-4303
Westport (G-10105)		
◆ Macdermid Incorporated	C	203 575-5700
Waterbury (G-9522)		
Magnetec Corporation	D	203 949-9933
Wallingford (G-9310)		
Mannan 3d Innovations LLC	G	203 306-4203
Higganum (G-3768)		
Markany Na LLC	G	914 656-7073
South Windsor (G-7789)		
Measurement Systems Inc	E	203 949-3500
Wallingford (G-9317)		
▲ Morse Watchmans Inc	E	203 264-1108
Oxford (G-6679)		
Mumm Engineering Inc	G	203 445-9777
Monroe (G-4740)		
Newmack Inc	G	203 568-0443
Middlebury (G-4285)		
O E M Controls Inc	C	203 929-8431
Shelton (G-7517)		
OEM Design Services LLC	G	203 467-5993
East Haven (G-2445)		
◆ Omega Engineering Inc	C	203 359-1660
Norwalk (G-6284)		
Online River LLC	F	203 801-5900
Westport (G-10134)		
Optimized Micro Devices LLC	G	860 447-2142
East Lyme (G-2469)		
▲ Ortronics Inc	D	860 445-3900
New London (G-5482)		
Ortronics Inc	G	877 295-3472
West Hartford (G-9841)		
Ortronics Legrand	G	860 767-3515
Ivoryton (G-3788)		
Prolaser Prolaser	G	203 939-1750
Norwalk (G-6308)		
Recycle 4 Vets LLC	G	203 222-7300
Westport (G-10147)		
Red Rocket Site 2	G	860 581-8019
Centerbrook (G-1333)		
◆ Resavue Inc	F	203 878-0944
Orange (G-6625)		
Scan-Optics LLC	D	860 645-7878
Manchester (G-4087)		
Spectrum Virtual LLC	G	203 303-7540
Cheshire (G-1452)		
Sugar Run K9 LLC	G	860 591-4193
Voluntown (G-9191)		
Syferlock Technology Corp	G	203 292-5441
Shelton (G-7561)		
Technology Inf Parters	G	860 985-8760
Southington (G-7984)		
Tillerman	G	203 421-6643
Madison (G-3964)		
Transact Technologies Inc	C	203 859-6800
Hamden (G-3523)		

Company	Code	Phone
Ventus Technologies LLC	F	203 642-2800
Norwalk (G-6385)		
▲ Verico Technology LLC	E	800 492-7286
Enfield (G-2704)		
Xerox Corporation	B	203 968-3000
Norwalk (G-6401)		
Xerox Holdings Corporation	G	203 968-3000
Norwalk (G-6402)		
Xijet Corp	F	203 397-2800
New Haven (G-5436)		
Yellowfin Holdings Inc	E	866 341-0979
Ellington (G-2609)		

3578 Calculating & Accounting Eqpt

Company	Code	Phone
Barnum Wash & Dry	G	203 870-6099
Stratford (G-8580)		
Black Gold Enterprises	G	203 729-4444
Naugatuck (G-4862)		
▲ Blackwold Inc	D	860 526-0800
Chester (G-1464)		
Chestnut Shell	G	203 775-5067
Brookfield (G-1171)		
Hopp Companies Inc	F	800 889-8425
Newtown (G-5746)		
Marinero Express 809 East	G	203 487-0636
Stamford (G-8297)		
Positive Ventures LLC	G	860 499-0599
Bloomfield (G-468)		
Worldwide Products Inc	G	855 972-2867
Roxbury (G-7286)		

3579 Office Machines, NEC

Company	Code	Phone
A Westport Wordsmith	G	203 354-7309
Norwalk (G-6058)		
▲ Accu-Time Systems Inc	E	860 870-5000
Ellington (G-2570)		
◆ Acme United Corporation	C	203 254-6060
Fairfield (G-2743)		
Agissar Corporation	D	203 375-8662
Stratford (G-8565)		
Bell and Howell LLC	E	860 526-9561
Deep River (G-2085)		
Bidwell Industrial Group Inc	E	860 346-9283
Middletown (G-4325)		
▲ Dictaphone Corporation	C	203 381-7000
Stratford (G-8606)		
Energy Saving Products and Sls	E	860 675-6443
Burlington (G-1267)		
Hasler Inc	G	203 301-3400
Shelton (G-7461)		
Its New England Inc	G	203 265-8100
Wallingford (G-9290)		
Mailroom Finance Inc	G	203 301-3400
Milford (G-4574)		
▲ Neopost USA Inc	G	203 301-3400
Milford (G-4588)		
◆ Pitney Bowes Inc	A	203 356-5000
Stamford (G-8362)		
Pitney Bowes Inc	G	203 356-5000
Stamford (G-8363)		
Pitney Bowes Inc	E	203 792-1600
Shelton (G-7528)		
Pitney Bowes Inc	G	860 285-7450
Windsor (G-10420)		
Pitney Bowes Inc	E	203 922-4000
Shelton (G-7529)		
Pitney Bowes Inc	E	203 356-5000
Shelton (G-7530)		
▲ Pyramid Time Systems LLC	E	203 238-0550
Meriden (G-4225)		
Stanley Fastening Systems LP	G	860 225-5111
New Britain (G-5065)		
Xerox Corporation	B	203 968-3000
Norwalk (G-6401)		
Xerox Holdings Corporation	G	203 968-3000
Norwalk (G-6402)		

3581 Automatic Vending Machines

Company	Code	Phone
▲ Blackwold Inc	D	860 526-0800
Chester (G-1464)		
Bobs Vending	G	860 426-1232
Southington (G-7896)		
Eastern Company	D	860 526-0800
Chester (G-1471)		
Kk Manufacturing LLC	G	860 644-5330
South Windsor (G-7784)		
Smile Exchange LLC	G	860 342-0333
Middletown (G-4418)		
Waterside Vending LLC	G	860 399-6039
Westbrook (G-10014)		

Employee Codes: A=Over 500 employees, B=251-500, C=101-250, D=51-100, E=20-50, F=10-19, G=1-9

3582 Commercial Laundry, Dry Clean & Pressing Mchs

▲ **Edro Corporation** ....E 860 828-0311
East Berlin *(G-2166)*
▲ **Naugatuck Recovery Inc** ....E 203 723-1122
Naugatuck *(G-4906)*
▲ **Rema Dri-Vac Corp** ....F 203 847-2464
Norwalk *(G-6321)*
Rite Way Cleaner ....G 203 789-9561
New Haven *(G-5380)*
Sea-Lion America Company ....G 860 316-5563
Middletown *(G-4408)*
Stn Laundry Systems LLC ....G 203 887-8986
Hamden *(G-3513)*
Sumal Enterprises LLC ....G 860 945-3337
Watertown *(G-9739)*

3585 Air Conditioning & Heating Eqpt

261 Pascone Place LLC ....G 860 666-7845
Newington *(G-5614)*
ACR Technical Services ....G 860 225-0572
New Britain *(G-4935)*
Air Solutions East LLC ....G 860 883-4700
Avon *(G-73)*
All Phase Htg Coolg Contr LLC ....G 860 873-9680
East Haddam *(G-2235)*
Alteris Renewables Inc ....G 860 535-3370
Stonington *(G-8521)*
Alvest (usa) Inc ....E 860 602-3400
Windsor *(G-10360)*
AMS Strategic Management Inc ....G 845 500-5635
Stamford *(G-8083)*
Carrier Corporation ....G 860 728-7000
Farmington *(G-2887)*
Cascades Fine Papers ....G 860 870-7600
Ellington *(G-2580)*
Comfortable Environments ....G 203 876-2140
Milford *(G-4492)*
Croteau Development Group Inc ....G 860 684-3605
Stafford Springs *(G-8022)*
Dasco Supply LLC ....G 203 388-0095
Stamford *(G-8180)*
Demartino Fixture Co Inc ....E 203 269-3971
Wallingford *(G-9248)*
Dp2 LLC Head ....F 203 655-0747
Darien *(G-2022)*
Ductworx Unlimited LLC ....G 203 535-1425
Hamden *(G-3440)*
▲ **Enterex America LLC** ....G 860 661-4635
Westbrook *(G-9996)*
Four Seasons Cooler Eqp LLC ....G 203 263-0705
Woodbury *(G-10637)*
George Usaty Sons Heat ....G 860 350-2622
New Milford *(G-5535)*
Latin American Holding Inc ....G 860 674-3000
Farmington *(G-2924)*
Lenox Strategies LLC ....G 203 927-0871
East Haven *(G-2437)*
Lenox34 LLC ....G 203 869-6909
Greenwich *(G-3190)*
Mechancal Engnered Systems LLC ....G 203 400-4658
New Canaan *(G-5119)*
Nanocap Technologies LLC ....G 860 521-9743
Hartford *(G-3648)*
Novy International Inc ....G 203 743-7720
Danbury *(G-1896)*
▲ **Snowathome LLC** ....G 860 584-2991
Terryville *(G-8770)*
◆ **Tld Ace Corporation** ....B 860 602-3300
Windsor *(G-10452)*
Trane Inc ....D 203 866-7115
Norwalk *(G-6377)*
Trane Inc ....D 860 437-6208
New Haven *(G-5420)*
Trane US Inc ....G 203 295-2170
Stamford *(G-8473)*
Trane US Inc ....G 800 544-1642
Stamford *(G-8474)*
Trane US Inc ....D 860 437-6208
New London *(G-5495)*
Trane US Inc ....D 860 470-3901
Farmington *(G-2965)*
Trane US Inc ....G 860 541-1721
Hartford *(G-3705)*
Ulitsch Mechanical Svcs LLC ....G 860 623-4223
Windsor Locks *(G-10500)*
Ultra Flow Dispense LLC ....G 866 827-2534
Windsor *(G-10457)*
United Tech Advnced Prjcts Inc ....G 860 610-7159
East Hartford *(G-2390)*
United Tech Employee Sav Plan ....G 860 728-7000
Hartford *(G-3709)*
United Technologies Corp ....C 860 565-7622
East Hartford *(G-2392)*
United Technologies Corp ....B 860 767-9592
Essex *(G-2736)*
▼ **United Technologies Corp** ....B 860 728-7000
Farmington *(G-2972)*
▲ **Vector Controls LLC** ....F 203 749-0883
Bethel *(G-363)*
Waterlogic Usa Inc ....G 866 917-7873
Farmington *(G-2977)*
Wine Well Chiller Comp Inc ....G 203 878-2465
Milford *(G-4681)*

3586 Measuring & Dispensing Pumps

Innovationcooperative3d LLC ....G 860 540-4172
Farmington *(G-2918)*
Proflow Inc ....E 203 230-4700
North Haven *(G-5980)*

3589 Service Ind Machines, NEC

▲ **3M Purification Inc** ....B 203 237-5541
Meriden *(G-4135)*
Affordable Water Trtmnt ....G 860 423-3147
Mansfield Center *(G-4111)*
Alliance Water Treatment Co ....G 203 323-9968
Stamford *(G-8071)*
Aqualogic Inc ....E 203 248-8959
North Haven *(G-5909)*
Atlas Filtri North America LLC ....F 203 284-0080
Wallingford *(G-9214)*
Best Management Products Inc ....G 860 434-0277
East Haddam *(G-2236)*
Beyond Home Improvement ....G 203 859-0113
North Haven *(G-5914)*
Bobs Sandbox ....G 860 267-4530
Colchester *(G-1543)*
Brasco Technologies LLC ....G 203 484-4291
Northford *(G-6043)*
Clearwater Treatment Systems L ....G 860 799-0303
New Milford *(G-5520)*
Core Filtration LLC ....G 860 904-6640
Hartford *(G-3571)*
▲ **Crane Co** ....D 203 363-7300
Stamford *(G-8166)*
Creative Mobile Systems Inc ....G 860 649-6272
Manchester *(G-4000)*
▲ **Crystal Rock Holdings Inc** ....E 860 945-0661
Watertown *(G-9697)*
D P Engineering Inc ....G 203 421-7965
Madison *(G-3916)*
Ecochlor Inc ....G 203 915-4593
North Haven *(G-5935)*
Ecosystem Consulting Svc Inc ....G 860 742-0744
Coventry *(G-1653)*
Elegant Drycleaning ....G 203 849-1000
Norwalk *(G-6156)*
EMJ Contracting LLC ....G 475 449-7725
Bridgeport *(G-762)*
Erasable Images ....G 860 367-4545
Oakdale *(G-6442)*
Evoqua Water Technologies LLC ....E 860 528-6512
South Windsor *(G-7754)*
Fractal Water LLC ....G 888 897-6968
Harwinton *(G-3730)*
Guardian Envmtl Tech Inc ....F 860 350-2200
New Milford *(G-5541)*
H Krevit and Company Inc ....E 203 772-3350
New Haven *(G-5292)*
Hydro Service & Supplies Inc ....G 203 265-3995
Middletown *(G-4353)*
Jfj Services LLC ....G 860 395-1922
Old Saybrook *(G-6548)*
▲ **Kx Technologies LLC** ....F 203 799-9000
West Haven *(G-9925)*
Mardini Power Station ....G 203 576-8951
Bridgeport *(G-829)*
Meurer Industries ....G 303 279-8373
Meriden *(G-4200)*
Nalco Wtr Prtrtment Sltons LLC ....G 860 224-4443
New Britain *(G-5019)*
New Milford Commission ....F 860 354-3758
New Milford *(G-5569)*
Northeast Fluid Technology ....G 860 620-0393
Plantsville *(G-6906)*
Renewable Energy Natural RES ....G 860 923-1091
Thompson *(G-8843)*
Safe Water ....G 203 732-4806
Seymour *(G-7366)*
Shaws Pump Company Inc ....G 860 872-6891
Ellington *(G-2599)*
◆ **Spencer Turbine Company** ....C 860 688-8361
Windsor *(G-10436)*
Suez Wts Services Usa Inc ....E 860 291-9660
East Hartford *(G-2380)*
Town of Montville ....F 860 848-3830
Uncasville *(G-9107)*
Town of Vernon ....F 860 870-3545
Vernon *(G-9156)*
Town of Vernon ....G 860 870-3699
Vernon Rockville *(G-9183)*

3592 Carburetors, Pistons, Rings & Valves

Air Valves LLC ....G 203 266-7175
Bethlehem *(G-366)*
Caffeine and Carburetors ....G 203 966-2704
New Canaan *(G-5091)*
▲ **Carten Controls Inc** ....F 203 699-2100
Cheshire *(G-1366)*
◆ **James J Scott LLC** ....G 860 571-9200
Rocky Hill *(G-7252)*
Nutek Aerospace Corp ....G 860 355-3169
New Milford *(G-5575)*
Pearse Bertram LLC ....G 860 612-9060
New Britain *(G-5031)*
Saf Industries LLC ....E 203 729-4900
Meriden *(G-4237)*
Schwing Bioset Technologies ....E 203 744-2100
Danbury *(G-1941)*
Skinner Valve Division ....G 860 827-2300
New Britain *(G-5055)*

3593 Fluid Power Cylinders & Actuators

▲ **Airpot Corporation** ....E 800 848-7681
Norwalk *(G-6064)*
Durant Machine Inc ....G 860 536-7698
Mystic *(G-4813)*
Passion Engineering LLC ....G 203 204-3090
Guilford *(G-3382)*

3594 Fluid Power Pumps & Motors

▲ **Crane Co** ....D 203 363-7300
Stamford *(G-8166)*
Fluid Solutions LLC ....G 203 245-0708
Madison *(G-3921)*
◆ **Hamilton Sundstrand Corp** ....A 860 654-6000
Windsor Locks *(G-10491)*
▲ **Navtec Rigging Solutions Inc** ....E 203 458-3163
Clinton *(G-1515)*
Parker-Hannifin Corporation ....G 860 920-4231
East Hartford *(G-2351)*
▲ **Reidville Hydraulics & Mfg Inc** ....E 860 496-1133
Torrington *(G-8964)*
▲ **Sfc Koenig LLC** ....E 203 245-1100
North Haven *(G-5992)*

3596 Scales & Balances, Exc Laboratory

Able Scale & Equipment Corp ....G 860 646-6929
Manchester *(G-3975)*
Action Scale Service ....G 203 577-6420
Middlebury *(G-4271)*
Compuweigh Corporation ....E 203 262-9400
Woodbury *(G-10629)*
Kenneth Allevo ....G 860 745-0740
Enfield *(G-2654)*
North Eastern Scale Corp ....G 203 634-7942
Meriden *(G-4210)*
Reliable Scales & Systems LLC ....G 860 380-0600
Bristol *(G-1105)*
Rice Lake Weighing Systems Inc ....G 203 270-6012
Newtown *(G-5775)*

3599 Machinery & Eqpt, Indl & Commercial, NEC

3d Solutions LLC ....G 860 454-7302
Tolland *(G-8845)*
A & M Auto Machine Inc ....G 203 237-3502
Meriden *(G-4136)*
A C T Manufacturing LLC ....G 860 289-8837
South Windsor *(G-7696)*
A D Grinding ....F 860 747-6630
Plainville *(G-6760)*
A G M Tool ....G 860 793-6808
Plainville *(G-6761)*
A Hardiman Machine Co Inc ....G 860 623-8133
East Windsor *(G-2478)*
A J Tool Company Inc ....G 860 666-2883
Newington *(G-5615)*

Able Manufacturing Co LLC..........G....... 860 282-6108
South Windsor *(G-7698)*
Abstract Tool Inc..........F....... 860 526-4635
Deep River *(G-2082)*
Accupaulo Holding Corporation..........E....... 860 666-5621
Newington *(G-5617)*
Accurate Centerless Grinding..........G....... 860 747-9794
Bristol *(G-954)*
Accurate Threaded Products Co..........E....... 860 666-5621
Newington *(G-5618)*
▲ Accurate Tool & Die Inc..........E....... 203 967-1200
Stamford *(G-8057)*
Accutrol LLC..........E....... 203 445-9991
Danbury *(G-1730)*
Ace Industrial LLC..........G....... 203 272-7675
Cheshire *(G-1347)*
Ack Precision Machine Co..........G....... 860 664-0789
Clinton *(G-1490)*
Acucut Inc..........E....... 860 793-7012
Southington *(G-7887)*
Acufab..........G....... 203 263-3490
Woodbury *(G-10623)*
Addamo Manufacturing Inc..........G....... 860 667-2601
Newington *(G-5619)*
Advance Development & Mfg..........F....... 203 453-4325
Guilford *(G-3322)*
Advanced Machine Technology..........G....... 860 872-2664
Ellington *(G-2573)*
Aeroswiss LLC..........F....... 203 634-4545
Meriden *(G-4141)*
AJ Tuck Company..........E....... 203 775-1234
Brookfield *(G-1157)*
Albert E Erickson Co..........F....... 203 386-8931
Stratford *(G-8566)*
Allen Precision LLC..........G....... 860 370-9881
Windsor Locks *(G-10471)*
Allied Machining Co Inc..........G....... 860 665-1228
Newington *(G-5625)*
▲ Altek Electronics Inc..........C....... 860 482-7626
Torrington *(G-8892)*
Alto Products Corp Al..........E....... 860 747-2736
Plainville *(G-6769)*
AM Manufacturing LLC..........G....... 860 573-1987
Glastonbury *(G-3006)*
American Fnshg Specialists Inc..........G....... 203 367-0663
Bridgeport *(G-691)*
American Machining Tech Inc..........G....... 860 342-0005
Portland *(G-6949)*
American Metal Masters LLC..........G....... 860 621-6911
Plantsville *(G-6884)*
American Metallizing..........G....... 860 289-1677
South Windsor *(G-7706)*
American Precision Mfg LLC..........E....... 203 734-1800
Ansonia *(G-18)*
American Specialty Pdts LLC..........G....... 860 871-2279
Vernon *(G-9130)*
American Tool & Mfg Corp..........F....... 860 666-2255
Newington *(G-5626)*
▲ Anaconda Universal Assoc LLC..........G....... 203 699-9344
Cheshire *(G-1352)*
Andvic-Precision LLC..........G....... 860 836-7422
Newington *(G-5628)*
Andy Rakowicz..........G....... 860 828-1620
Berlin *(G-159)*
Apex Tool & Cutter Co Inc..........G....... 203 888-8970
Beacon Falls *(G-130)*
APS Robotics & Integration LLC..........G....... 860 526-1040
Deep River *(G-2084)*
Arcade Technology LLC..........E....... 203 366-3871
Bridgeport *(G-699)*
Arcor Systems LLC..........G....... 860 370-9780
Suffield *(G-8714)*
ASAP Machine Sp & Fabrication..........G....... 860 564-4114
Plainfield *(G-6740)*
Astro Aircom LLC..........G....... 860 688-3320
Windsor *(G-10366)*
At Industries LLC..........G....... 860 739-6639
Niantic *(G-5801)*
Atlantech Manufacturing Co Inc..........G....... 203 500-6880
Milford *(G-4460)*
Atlas Precision Mfg LLC..........E....... 860 290-9114
South Windsor *(G-7714)*
Automatic Machine Products..........G....... 860 346-7064
Middletown *(G-4320)*
B & A Company Inc..........E....... 203 876-7527
Milford *(G-4463)*
▲ B & F Machine Co Inc..........D....... 860 225-6349
New Britain *(G-4949)*
B & R Machine Works Inc..........G....... 203 798-0595
Bethel *(G-260)*
B & S Machine Inc..........G....... 860 829-0813
East Berlin *(G-2163)*
B E C Machinetool Inc..........G....... 860 738-9432
Winsted *(G-10509)*
Balding Precision Inc..........G....... 203 878-9135
Milford *(G-4465)*
Barlo Manufacturing..........G....... 203 481-3426
Branford *(G-556)*
Barnes Technical Products LLC..........G....... 203 931-8852
New Haven *(G-5240)*
Barre Precision Products Inc..........G....... 860 647-1913
Bolton *(G-505)*
▲ Barry E Leonard..........G....... 860 951-5105
Wethersfield *(G-10183)*
Bay State Machine Inc..........G....... 860 230-0054
Plainfield *(G-6743)*
Beck Industries LLC..........G....... 203 260-8864
Stratford *(G-8582)*
Bill Marlow..........G....... 860 829-1712
Portland *(G-6952)*
Bills Machine Shop..........G....... 860 875-6607
Ellington *(G-2578)*
Blahut Machine Co..........G....... 203 878-3643
Milford *(G-4472)*
Bmi Cad Services Inc..........F....... 860 658-0808
Simsbury *(G-7613)*
Boman Precision Tech Inc..........G....... 203 415-8350
Milford *(G-4475)*
Bomar Machine LLC..........G....... 860 505-7299
Berlin *(G-165)*
Bracone Metal Spinning Inc..........E....... 860 628-5927
Southington *(G-7897)*
Breisler Prcsion Machining LLC..........G....... 203 847-6614
Norwalk *(G-6099)*
Brings Machine Products..........G....... 860 346-0350
Middletown *(G-4327)*
Bristol Tool & Die Company..........E....... 860 582-2577
Bristol *(G-993)*
British Precision Inc..........E....... 860 633-3343
Glastonbury *(G-3016)*
Broadstripes LLC..........G....... 203 350-9824
New Haven *(G-5251)*
Bryk Machine Works LLC..........G....... 203 397-1405
Woodbridge *(G-10595)*
Bryt Manufacturing..........G....... 860 224-4772
New Britain *(G-4953)*
▲ Budney Overhaul & Repair Ltd..........C....... 860 828-0585
Berlin *(G-167)*
Budrad Engineering Co LLC..........G....... 203 452-7310
Monroe *(G-4702)*
Burke Precision Machine Co Inc..........G....... 860 408-1394
East Granby *(G-2195)*
Buswell Manufacturing Co Inc..........F....... 203 334-6069
Bridgeport *(G-726)*
C & A Machine Co Inc..........E....... 860 667-0605
Newington *(G-5636)*
C & L Automotive Machine Shop..........G....... 860 523-5268
West Hartford *(G-9781)*
C & W Manufacturing Co Inc..........E....... 860 633-4631
Glastonbury *(G-3017)*
C D Industries Inc..........G....... 203 966-4983
New Canaan *(G-5090)*
C V Tool Company Inc..........E....... 978 353-7901
Southington *(G-7901)*
C-B Manufacturing & Tool Co..........G....... 860 583-5402
Terryville *(G-8748)*
Cad CAM Machine LLC..........G....... 860 410-9788
Plainville *(G-6782)*
Canaan Custom Machine..........G....... 860 824-0674
East Canaan *(G-2181)*
Candlewood Machine Pdts LLC..........G....... 860 350-2211
New Milford *(G-5514)*
Candlewood Tool & Machine Shop..........F....... 860 355-1892
Gaylordsville *(G-2990)*
Capital Design & Engrg Inc..........G....... 203 798-6027
Danbury *(G-1763)*
Capitol Machine Inc Preci..........G....... 860 410-0758
Plainville *(G-6784)*
Carl Associates Inc..........G....... 860 749-7620
South Windsor *(G-7724)*
Carnegie Tool Inc..........F....... 203 866-0744
Norwalk *(G-6108)*
Carob Designs LLC..........G....... 203 630-9171
Meriden *(G-4155)*
Cavtech Industries..........G....... 203 437-8764
Waterbury *(G-9448)*
Central Connecticut Sls & Mfg..........G....... 860 667-1411
Newington *(G-5639)*
Central Connecticut Waterjet..........G....... 860 828-3877
Berlin *(G-169)*
Cgl Inc..........F....... 860 945-6166
Watertown *(G-9691)*
▲ Chapco Inc..........D....... 860 526-9535
Chester *(G-1467)*
Chip - Mar Inc..........G....... 860 355-4854
Roxbury *(G-7275)*
Cirillo Manufacturing Group..........G....... 203 484-5010
East Haven *(G-2416)*
Classic Jig Grinding..........G....... 860 870-4900
Tolland *(G-8854)*
Cnc Machine Tl Specialist LLC..........G....... 860 873-1816
East Haddam *(G-2239)*
Co-Op Jig Boring Jig Grinding..........G....... 860 828-9882
Berlin *(G-170)*
Compucision LLC..........G....... 860 355-9790
New Milford *(G-5523)*
Con-Tec Inc..........F....... 203 723-8942
Naugatuck *(G-4870)*
Connecticut Coining Inc..........D....... 203 743-3861
Bethel *(G-273)*
Connecticut Hone Incorporated..........G....... 860 747-3884
Plainville *(G-6790)*
Connecticut Machine & Marine..........G....... 860 446-8286
Groton *(G-3280)*
Connecticut Machine & Welding..........E....... 203 502-2605
Stratford *(G-8598)*
Connecticut Mch Tooling & Cast..........F....... 203 874-8300
Milford *(G-4497)*
Consulting Engrg Dev Svcs Inc..........D....... 203 828-6528
Oxford *(G-6653)*
Continental Machine Tl Co Inc..........D....... 860 223-2896
New Britain *(G-4965)*
Continuity Engine Inc..........G....... 203 907-4470
New Haven *(G-5262)*
Couturier Ino..........G....... 203 238-4555
Meriden *(G-4162)*
Crystal Tool and Machine Co..........G....... 860 870-7431
Vernon *(G-9136)*
D & L Engineering Company..........G....... 203 375-5856
Stratford *(G-8603)*
D & S Precision Turning LLC..........G....... 860 793-2640
Plainville *(G-6796)*
D F & B Precision Mfg Inc..........G....... 860 354-5663
New Milford *(G-5526)*
D S Manufacturing Co..........G....... 860 829-0334
Kensington *(G-3808)*
Daniel Dechamps..........G....... 860 463-3105
Plainville *(G-6797)*
▲ Darly Custom Technology Inc..........F....... 860 298-7966
Windsor *(G-10379)*
Dawid Manufacturing Inc..........G....... 203 734-1800
Ansonia *(G-31)*
Delltech Inc..........G....... 203 878-8266
Milford *(G-4507)*
Delta-Ray Corp..........G....... 203 367-6910
Bridgeport *(G-746)*
Dependable Repair Inc..........F....... 203 481-9706
North Branford *(G-5834)*
Dickson Product Development..........G....... 203 846-2128
Norwalk *(G-6142)*
Don Pomaski..........G....... 860 693-4469
Canton *(G-1313)*
Draher Machine Company..........G....... 203 753-0179
Wolcott *(G-10562)*
Dso Manufacturing Company Inc..........E....... 860 224-2641
New Britain *(G-4976)*
Dufrane Nuclear Shielding Inc..........F....... 860 379-2318
Winsted *(G-10516)*
Dundee Holding Inc..........G....... 860 677-1376
Farmington *(G-2898)*
Durbin Machine Inc..........G....... 860 342-1602
Portland *(G-6959)*
Durol Company..........F....... 203 288-3383
Hamden *(G-3441)*
Durstin Machine & Mfg..........G....... 860 485-1257
Harwinton *(G-3725)*
Dynamic Bldg Enrgy Sltions LLC..........F....... 860 599-1872
North Stonington *(G-6022)*
E & M Machine..........G....... 860 429-2427
Ashford *(G-60)*
E O Manufacturing Company Inc..........E....... 203 932-5981
West Haven *(G-9904)*
E S Custom Machining..........G....... 203 481-8653
Branford *(G-583)*
E-B Manufacturing Company Inc..........E....... 860 632-8563
Middletown *(G-4339)*
▼ EA Patten Co LLC..........D....... 860 649-2851
Manchester *(G-4013)*
▼ East Coast Metal Hose Inc..........G....... 203 723-7459
Naugatuck *(G-4877)*

Employee Codes: A=Over 500 employees, B=251-500
C=101-250, D=51-100, E=20-50, F=10-19, G=1-9
2020 Harris Connecticut
Manufacturers Directory
439

35 INDUSTRIAL AND COMMERCIAL MACHINERY AND COMPUTER EQUIPMENT SIC SECTION

East Coast Precision Grinding ....G 860 289-1010
South Windsor *(G-7743)*
Eastern Machine Co ....G 203 877-6308
Milford *(G-4521)*
Eastern Truck & Machine LLC ....G 860 528-0258
South Windsor *(G-7746)*
El Mar Inc ....G 860 729-7232
West Hartford *(G-9806)*
Elene A Moore ....G 203 377-0248
Trumbull *(G-9024)*
Empco Inc ....G 860 589-3233
Bristol *(G-1028)*
Esteem Manufacturing Corp ....E 860 282-9964
South Windsor *(G-7751)*
Excello Tool Engrg & Mfg Co ....E 203 878-4073
Milford *(G-4533)*
Experimental Prototype Pdts Co ....F 860 289-4948
South Windsor *(G-7755)*
Expressway Lube Centers ....F 203 744-2511
Danbury *(G-1820)*
Faille Precision Machining ....G 860 822-1964
Baltic *(G-119)*
Fairchild Auto-Mated Parts Inc ....E 860 379-2725
Winsted *(G-10520)*
Fairfield Cnty Stump Grinding ....G 203 261-7867
Trumbull *(G-9026)*
Filter Fab Inc ....G 860 749-6381
Somers *(G-7658)*
Fisher Mfg Systems Inc ....G 203 250-8033
Wallingford *(G-9267)*
Fisher Mfg Systems Inc ....F 203 269-3846
Wallingford *(G-9268)*
Flexco ....G 860 583-0219
Bristol *(G-1040)*
Focus Technologies Inc ....G 860 829-8998
Berlin *(G-179)*
Forrati Manufacturing & Tl LLC ....G 860 426-1105
Plantsville *(G-6892)*
Frank Roth Co Inc ....D 203 377-2155
Stratford *(G-8611)*
▲ Frasal Tool Co Inc ....F 860 666-3524
Newington *(G-5654)*
Fryer Corporation ....G 203 888-9944
Oxford *(G-6659)*
G & D Machine Co ....G 860 623-2649
Windsor Locks *(G-10485)*
G & M Tool Company ....G 203 888-9354
Seymour *(G-7347)*
G F Grinding Tool Mfg Co Inc ....G 203 757-6244
Waterbury *(G-9483)*
G H Tool Inc ....G 203 270-0566
Sandy Hook *(G-7313)*
Gen-El-Mec Associates Inc ....E 203 828-6566
Oxford *(G-6660)*
General Machine Company Inc ....F 860 426-9295
Southington *(G-7927)*
Genovese Manufacturing Co ....F 860 582-9944
Terryville *(G-8757)*
Georges Automotive Machine Sp ....G 860 223-6547
New Britain *(G-4991)*
Georgetown Machine ....G 203 544-8422
Georgetown *(G-2998)*
◆ Global Machine Movers LLC ....F 860 484-4449
Watertown *(G-9709)*
Golik Machine Co ....G 860 610-0095
South Windsor *(G-7763)*
Grace Machine Company LLC ....F 860 828-8789
Berlin *(G-184)*
Graham Tool and Machine LLC ....G 860 585-1261
Terryville *(G-8759)*
Gregor Technologies LLC ....E 860 482-2569
Torrington *(G-8930)*
Griswold Machine & Fabrication ....G 860 376-9891
Jewett City *(G-3796)*
Grotti Tool Company ....G 203 877-5570
Milford *(G-4545)*
Gulf Manufacturing Inc ....E 860 529-8601
Rocky Hill *(G-7239)*
Gypsum Systems LLC ....G 860 470-3916
Burlington *(G-1269)*
H & B Tool & Engineering Co ....E 860 528-9341
South Windsor *(G-7766)*
H & W Machine LLC ....G 860 828-7679
Berlin *(G-186)*
H G Steinmetz Machine Works ....F 203 794-1880
Bethel *(G-307)*
Harwest Holdings One Inc ....E 860 423-8334
South Windham *(G-7687)*
Hawthrn Smth Mfg & Cnsltng Srv ....G 203 866-2227
Norwalk *(G-6195)*
Herrick & Cowell Company Inc ....G 203 288-2578
Hamden *(G-3463)*
Hfo Chicago LLC ....G 860 285-0709
Windsor *(G-10393)*
High Tech Precision Mfg L L C ....G 860 621-7242
Southington *(G-7934)*
Houston Weber Systems Inc ....G 203 481-0115
Branford *(G-607)*
Hygrade Precision Tech Inc ....E 860 747-5773
Plainville *(G-6823)*
In Da Cut Music ....G 860 895-9445
East Hartford *(G-2339)*
Innovative Mechanics LLC ....G 203 530-6071
Milford *(G-4556)*
Inspired Machine Shop ....G 860 628-7822
Southington *(G-7938)*
Integra-Cast Inc ....D 860 225-7600
New Britain *(G-4999)*
▲ Integral Technologies Inc ....G 860 741-2281
Enfield *(G-2652)*
Interface Devices Incorporated ....G 203 878-4648
Milford *(G-4557)*
Intrasonics Inc ....G 860 283-8040
Thomaston *(G-8792)*
Intricut ....G 860 537-7766
Colchester *(G-1556)*
Irex Machine Inc ....G 860 870-1677
Vernon Rockville *(G-9170)*
Iskra John ....G 203 488-5402
Branford *(G-609)*
J & G Machining Company Inc ....G 860 379-7038
Winsted *(G-10525)*
J & L Machine Co Inc ....E 860 649-3539
Manchester *(G-4036)*
J P Fabrication and RPS LLC ....G 860 423-8993
Windham *(G-10347)*
Jan Manufacturing Inc ....G 203 879-0580
Wolcott *(G-10569)*
Janes Norman & Jacqueline Mach ....G 860 423-1932
South Windham *(G-7689)*
Jared Manufacturing Co Inc ....F 203 846-1732
Norwalk *(G-6219)*
Jaw Precision Machining LLC ....G 860 535-0615
Stonington *(G-8532)*
Jeff Manufacturing Co Inc ....F 860 482-8845
Torrington *(G-8937)*
JEM Precision Grinding Inc ....G 860 633-0152
Glastonbury *(G-3052)*
Jem Special Tool Co LLC ....G 860 276-9767
Southington *(G-7942)*
Jensen Machine Co ....G 860 666-5438
Newington *(G-5667)*
Jerome Ridel ....G 860 379-1774
West Granby *(G-9767)*
Jewett City Tool and Die Co ....G 860 376-0455
Voluntown *(G-9189)*
Jlp Machine Company ....G 860 649-5730
Bolton *(G-512)*
Joe Valentine Machine Company ....G 203 356-9776
Stamford *(G-8265)*
Joseph J McFadden Jr ....G 860 354-6794
New Milford *(G-5552)*
Joseph Rembock ....G 860 738-3981
Pleasant Valley *(G-6923)*
Jovan Machine Co Inc ....G 203 879-2855
Wolcott *(G-10570)*
JV Precision Machine Co ....E 203 888-0748
Seymour *(G-7352)*
K & E Auto Machine L L C ....G 203 723-7189
Naugatuck *(G-4896)*
K & K Precision Manufacturing ....G 860 828-7681
East Berlin *(G-2171)*
Kania Darius ....G 860 667-4400
Newington *(G-5668)*
Karas Engineering Co Inc ....G 860 355-3153
New Milford *(G-5553)*
Kbj Manufacturing Inc ....G 860 585-7257
Bristol *(G-1056)*
Kehl Technology & Prfmce LLC ....G 203 484-4808
Northford *(G-6049)*
Kell-Strom Tool Co Inc ....E 860 529-6851
Wethersfield *(G-10206)*
Kell-Strom Tool Intl Inc ....E 860 529-6851
Wethersfield *(G-10207)*
Keller Products Inc ....G 203 794-0075
Bethel *(G-318)*
Kenneth Leroux ....G 860 769-9800
Bloomfield *(G-438)*
Kevco ....G 860 747-4135
Plainville *(G-6830)*
Keyway Inc ....G 860 571-9181
Wethersfield *(G-10208)*
Kovacs Machine and Tool Co ....E 203 269-4949
Wallingford *(G-9298)*
Kovil Manufacturing LLC ....G 203 699-9425
Cheshire *(G-1403)*
L R Brown Manufacturing Co ....G 203 265-5639
Wallingford *(G-9300)*
Labco Welding Inc ....G 860 632-2625
Middletown *(G-4367)*
Larco Machines Co Inc ....G 860 647-9769
Bolton *(G-513)*
Larrys Auto Machine LLC ....G 860 449-9112
Groton *(G-3295)*
Lincoln Precision Machine Inc ....G 860 923-9358
Thompson *(G-8837)*
Loric Tool Inc ....F 860 928-0171
North Grosvenordale *(G-5890)*
Lundgren Centerless Grinding ....G 860 482-4927
Torrington *(G-8944)*
Lynn Welding Co Inc ....F 860 667-4400
Newington *(G-5672)*
M & A Turning Co LLC ....G 860 793-2774
Plainville *(G-6836)*
M & B Automotive Machine Shop ....G 203 348-6134
Stamford *(G-8292)*
M & S Products ....G 860 742-5141
Coventry *(G-1662)*
M & Z Engineering Inc ....G 860 496-0282
Torrington *(G-8945)*
M Cubed Technologies Inc ....G 203 452-2333
Monroe *(G-4729)*
▲ M Cubed Technologies Inc ....E 203 304-2940
Newtown *(G-5757)*
M K M Enterprises Inc ....G 203 250-7937
Cheshire *(G-1410)*
M T D Corporation ....F 203 261-3721
Trumbull *(G-9045)*
M-Fab LLC ....G 860 496-0055
Torrington *(G-8946)*
Macala Tool Inc ....G 860 763-2580
Enfield *(G-2656)*
Mackenzie Mch & Mar Works Inc ....G 203 777-3479
East Haven *(G-2441)*
Macton Oxford LLC ....G 203 267-1500
Oxford *(G-6675)*
Magna Standard Mfg Co Inc ....G 203 874-0444
Milford *(G-4573)*
Mahoney Machine & Fabrication ....G 203 722-4771
Old Saybrook *(G-6555)*
Mail Corecron ....G 860 342-1055
Portland *(G-6964)*
Malux Machine LLC ....G 203 526-1834
Stratford *(G-8646)*
Manchester Tl & Design ADP LLC ....G 860 296-6541
Hartford *(G-3633)*
Marc Bouley ....G 860 450-1713
Willimantic *(G-10233)*
Marenna Amusements LLC ....F 203 623-4386
Orange *(G-6612)*
Mark A Little ....G 808 247-8604
Woodstock *(G-10671)*
Master Tool & Machine Inc ....G 860 747-2581
Plainville *(G-6841)*
Master Tool and Machines LLC ....G 860 747-2581
Plainville *(G-6842)*
MB Consulting LLC ....G 860 889-7941
Yantic *(G-10698)*
Mega Manufacturing LLC ....G 860 666-5555
Newington *(G-5676)*
Mepp Tool Co Inc ....G 860 289-8230
Glastonbury *(G-3058)*
Merritt Machine Company ....G 860 257-4484
Wethersfield *(G-10211)*
Metal Industries Inc ....G 860 296-6228
Hartford *(G-3640)*
Metalpro Inc ....E 860 388-1811
Old Saybrook *(G-6556)*
MGS Manufacturing Inc ....G 203 484-9275
North Branford *(G-5850)*
Michaud Tool Co Inc ....G 860 582-6785
Terryville *(G-8765)*
Michele Pavisic ....G 860 876-2509
Kensington *(G-3814)*
Micro Precision LLC ....E 860 423-4575
South Windham *(G-7690)*
Mid-State Manufacturing Inc ....F 860 621-6855
Milldale *(G-4686)*
Mikco Manufacturing Inc ....F 203 269-2250
Wallingford *(G-9323)*

Milford Metal Products Inc....G.... 203 878-0148
Milford *(G-4580)*
Mill Machine Tool & Die Co....G.... 860 628-6700
Southington *(G-7955)*
Mill Manufacturing Inc....G.... 203 367-9572
Bridgeport *(G-839)*
Millturn Manufacturing Co....G.... 203 248-1602
North Haven *(G-5964)*
Mj Tool & Manufacturing Inc....G.... 860 352-2688
Simsbury *(G-7636)*
Mj Tool Mfg....G.... 860 352-2688
Canton *(G-1319)*
Mkb Machine & Tool Mfg....G.... 860 828-5728
Berlin *(G-201)*
Morris Precision Tool Inc....G.... 203 284-8488
Wallingford *(G-9324)*
Motherstar Online LLC....G.... 860 896-1869
Tolland *(G-8871)*
Mrh Tool LLC....G.... 203 878-3359
Milford *(G-4586)*
Mtr Precision Machining Inc....G.... 860 928-9440
Pomfret Center *(G-6943)*
Mvc Aquatic Machine Shop....G.... 203 598-5747
Waterbury *(G-9549)*
My Tool Company Inc....G.... 203 755-2333
Waterbury *(G-9551)*
Myco Tool & Manufacturing Inc....G.... 860 875-7340
Vernon *(G-9147)*
▲ Naiad Dynamics Us Inc....E.... 203 929-6355
Shelton *(G-7506)*
Nerjan Development Company....G.... 203 325-3228
Stamford *(G-8320)*
New Britain Saw Tech....G.... 860 410-1077
Plainville *(G-6846)*
New England Cnc Inc....F.... 203 288-8241
Hamden *(G-3488)*
New England Graphics Mtls LLC....F.... 860 210-2180
New Milford *(G-5566)*
New England Grinding and MA....G.... 203 333-1885
Bridgeport *(G-849)*
New England Honing LLC....G.... 860 712-6094
Coventry *(G-1665)*
New England Machining LLC....G.... 860 301-9434
Cromwell *(G-1708)*
New England Tool & Automtn Inc....G.... 860 827-9389
New Britain *(G-5022)*
New England Traveling Wire LLC....G.... 860 223-6297
New Britain *(G-5023)*
New Horizon Machine Co Inc....G.... 203 316-9355
Stamford *(G-8325)*
New Machine Products LLC....G.... 203 790-5520
Danbury *(G-1891)*
Niantic Tool Inc....G.... 860 739-2182
Niantic *(G-5814)*
Nicholas Melfi Jr....G.... 203 853-7235
Norwalk *(G-6278)*
Nolan Industries Inc....G.... 203 865-8160
New Haven *(G-5352)*
Normike Industries Inc....G.... 860 747-1110
Plainville *(G-6849)*
Northeast Double Disc Grind LL....G.... 860 643-6096
Manchester *(G-4061)*
▲ Northeast Quality Services LLC....E.... 860 632-7242
Cromwell *(G-1711)*
Northeast Tool Dist LLC....G.... 860 973-1455
Bristol *(G-1080)*
Northeast Waterjet Svcs LLC....G.... 203 794-0766
Danbury *(G-1894)*
Northwest Connecticut Mfg Co....G.... 860 379-1553
Colebrook *(G-1585)*
Noujaim Tool Co Inc....E.... 203 753-4441
Waterbury *(G-9562)*
Nova Machining LLC....G.... 860 223-9323
New Britain *(G-5025)*
Nova Machining LLC....G.... 860 675-8131
Unionville *(G-9123)*
Nyc Grind Sports Marketing LLC....G.... 917 513-0590
Stamford *(G-8334)*
Oakville Quality Products LLC....F.... 203 757-5525
Waterbury *(G-9567)*
P&P Tool & Die Corp....G.... 203 874-2571
Milford *(G-4602)*
Pal Corporation....G.... 860 666-9211
Newington *(G-5690)*
Pal Technologies LLC....G.... 860 953-1984
West Hartford *(G-9842)*
Par Manufacturing Inc....G.... 860 677-1797
Farmington *(G-2946)*
Paramount Machine Company Inc....E.... 860 643-5549
Manchester *(G-4073)*
Parason Machine Inc....F.... 860 526-3565
Deep River *(G-2098)*
Park Tool & Gage Co Inc....G.... 860 225-0187
New Britain *(G-5029)*
Parts Cutter Cnc....G.... 203 947-4407
Danbury *(G-1901)*
Pdq Inc....G.... 860 322-4412
Chester *(G-1479)*
Peening Technologies Eqp LLC....G.... 860 289-4328
East Hartford *(G-2354)*
Peter Tasi....G.... 203 732-6540
Derby *(G-2122)*
Peters Machine Company....G.... 860 529-3672
Rocky Hill *(G-7263)*
Phoenix Machine Inc....G.... 203 888-1135
Seymour *(G-7360)*
Pilot Machine Designers Inc....G.... 203 866-2227
Norwalk *(G-6300)*
Pine Meadow Machine Co Inc....G.... 860 623-4494
Windsor Locks *(G-10493)*
Pinto Manufacturing Llc....G.... 860 659-9543
Glastonbury *(G-3071)*
Pioneer Precision Products....F.... 860 828-5838
Berlin *(G-206)*
Poplar Tool & Mfg Co Inc....G.... 203 333-4369
Bridgeport *(G-876)*
Precision Centerless Grinding....G.... 203 879-1228
Wolcott *(G-10579)*
Precision Cut-Off Service Inc....G.... 860 582-7521
Bristol *(G-1095)*
Precision E D M Inc....F.... 413 733-2813
Windsor *(G-10423)*
Precision Grinding Company....F.... 860 229-9652
New Britain *(G-5036)*
Precision Machine and Gears....G.... 860 822-6993
North Franklin *(G-5877)*
Precision Manufacturing LLC....G.... 203 790-4663
Bethel *(G-332)*
Precision Metals and Plas....G.... 860 559-8843
Berlin *(G-208)*
Precision Products....G.... 203 265-2061
Wallingford *(G-9342)*
Precision Tool & Components....G.... 203 874-9215
Milford *(G-4614)*
Precision Wire Cutting....G.... 860 485-1494
Harwinton *(G-3736)*
Preferred Manufacturing Co....G.... 203 239-0727
North Haven *(G-5979)*
Preferred Products Co Inc....G.... 203 375-9139
Stratford *(G-8667)*
Prestige Tool Mfg LLC....G.... 203 874-0360
Milford *(G-4616)*
Pro Tool and Design Inc....F.... 860 828-4667
Berlin *(G-212)*
Progress Machining Co....G.... 860 763-1752
Enfield *(G-2681)*
Projects Inc....C.... 860 633-4615
Glastonbury *(G-3075)*
Proman Inc....G.... 860 827-8778
New Britain *(G-5038)*
Pulver Precision LLC....G.... 860 763-0763
Enfield *(G-2684)*
Pw Precision Machine LLC....G.... 203 889-8615
Higganum *(G-3777)*
Quality Machine Inc....G.... 860 354-6794
New Milford *(G-5581)*
Quality Wire Edm Inc....G.... 860 583-9867
Bristol *(G-1101)*
Quick Machine Services LLC....G.... 203 634-8822
Meriden *(G-4226)*
Quick Turn Machine Company Inc....F.... 860 623-2569
Windsor Locks *(G-10495)*
R C E Machine Works....G.... 860 354-6976
New Milford *(G-5582)*
R E F Machine Company Inc....G.... 860 349-9344
Middlefield *(G-4305)*
R K Machine Company LLC....G.... 860 224-7545
New Britain *(G-5039)*
▼ R L Turick Co Inc....G.... 860 693-2230
New Hartford *(G-5208)*
RA Senft Inc....G.... 860 399-5967
Westbrook *(G-10006)*
Rand Machine & Fabrication Co....F.... 203 272-1352
Cheshire *(G-1435)*
Rand Sheaves & Pulleys LLC....G.... 203 272-1352
Cheshire *(G-1437)*
Rapidex....G.... 860 285-8818
Windsor *(G-10428)*
Rayflex Company Inc....G.... 203 336-2173
Bridgeport *(G-886)*
Raym-Co Inc....E.... 860 678-8292
Farmington *(G-2952)*
Ready Tool LLC....G.... 860 436-2128
Wethersfield *(G-10217)*
▲ Reed & Stefanow Machine Tl Co....F.... 860 583-7834
Bristol *(G-1104)*
▲ Reidville Hydraulics & Mfg Inc....E.... 860 496-1133
Torrington *(G-8964)*
Renchel Tool Inc....F.... 860 315-9017
Putnam *(G-7063)*
▲ Reno Machine Company Inc....D.... 860 666-5641
Newington *(G-5700)*
Richard Dahlen....G.... 860 584-8226
Bristol *(G-1108)*
Richards Machine Tool Co Inc....F.... 860 436-2938
Newington *(G-5701)*
Richardson Machine....G.... 860 859-1458
Oakdale *(G-6446)*
Rick Bulach....G.... 860 875-7999
Hebron *(G-3756)*
◆ Riff Company Inc....G.... 203 272-4899
Cheshire *(G-1439)*
Riveal Technologies LLC....G.... 203 935-0997
Meriden *(G-4235)*
RK Manufacturing Corp Conn....D.... 203 797-8700
Danbury *(G-1930)*
Roma Tool & Machine Co....G.... 860 793-2315
Plainville *(G-6858)*
Ross Mfg & Design LLC....F.... 203 878-0187
Milford *(G-4634)*
RWK Tool Inc....E.... 860 635-0116
Cromwell *(G-1717)*
Rydz Engineering....G.... 203 878-5499
Milford *(G-4636)*
S & F Tools LLC....G.... 860 224-6839
New Britain *(G-5051)*
S A It Grind....G.... 860 903-1455
East Windsor *(G-2517)*
S P Johnson Inc....G.... 860 871-8664
Stafford Springs *(G-8036)*
S S Fabrications Inc....G.... 860 974-1910
Eastford *(G-2541)*
Salamon Industries LLC....G.... 860 612-8420
New Britain *(G-5052)*
Secondaries Inc....G.... 203 879-4633
Wolcott *(G-10587)*
Secondary Operations Inc....F.... 203 288-8241
Hamden *(G-3509)*
Senior Operations LLC....D.... 860 741-2546
Enfield *(G-2692)*
Setma Inc....G.... 409 833-9797
New Milford *(G-5590)*
Sharpac LLC....G.... 203 384-0568
Bridgeport *(G-901)*
Simsbury Precision Products....G.... 860 658-6909
Simsbury *(G-7647)*
Simson Products Co Inc....F.... 203 265-9882
Wallingford *(G-9369)*
Sirois Tool Company Inc....D.... 860 828-5327
Berlin *(G-220)*
Skico Manufacturing Co LLC....G.... 203 230-1305
Hamden *(G-3510)*
Skytech Machining Inc....G.... 203 378-9994
Stratford *(G-8681)*
Slater Hill Tool....G.... 860 377-5503
Dayville *(G-2073)*
Slater Hill Tool LLC....G.... 860 963-0415
Putnam *(G-7066)*
Sneham Manufacturing Inc....G.... 203 610-6669
Stratford *(G-8682)*
Soldream Spcial Process - Wldg....G.... 860 858-5247
Tolland *(G-8878)*
Soltis Speed Equipment....G.... 860 489-0119
Torrington *(G-8971)*
Somers Manufacturing Inc....G.... 860 314-1075
Bristol *(G-1119)*
Sonic Welding Co....G.... 203 348-8021
Stamford *(G-8429)*
Spa Machining Co....G.... 860 564-9584
Plainfield *(G-6753)*
Space Craft Mfg Inc....G.... 860 583-1387
Meriden *(G-4245)*
Space Tool & Machine Co Inc....G.... 860 290-8599
South Windsor *(G-7828)*
Spargo Machine Products Inc....F.... 860 583-3925
Terryville *(G-8771)*
Specialty Components Inc....G.... 203 284-9112
Wallingford *(G-9373)*
Spectrum Machine & Design LLC....G.... 860 386-6490
Windsor Locks *(G-10497)*

S I C

Employee Codes: A=Over 500 employees, B=251-500
C=101-250, D=51-100, E=20-50, F=10-19, G=1-9
2020 Harris Connecticut
Manufacturers Directory
441

Spin Shop ....G.... 860 349-1298
Durham *(G-2157)*
Ssi Manufacturing Tech Corp ....E.... 860 589-8004
Bristol *(G-1122)*
Stacy B Goff ....G.... 860 623-2547
East Windsor *(G-2522)*
Standard Bellows Co ....E.... 860 623-2307
Windsor Locks *(G-10498)*
State Cutter Grinding Svc Inc ....G.... 203 888-8821
Seymour *(G-7367)*
▲ **Sterling Engineering Corp** ....C.... 860 379-3366
Pleasant Valley *(G-6926)*
Sterling Precision Machining ....F.... 860 564-4043
Sterling *(G-8517)*
▲ **Stevens Manufacturing Co Inc** ....E.... 203 878-2328
Milford *(G-4654)*
Stickler Machine Company LLC ....G.... 860 267-8246
East Hampton *(G-2280)*
Straton Industries Inc ....D.... 203 375-4488
Stratford *(G-8687)*
Stump Grinding Plus ....G.... 860 884-6962
East Lyme *(G-2476)*
Sum Machine & Tool Co Inc ....G.... 860 742-6827
Coventry *(G-1678)*
Summit Screw Machine Corp ....G.... 203 693-2727
Milford *(G-4656)*
Swageco LLC ....G.... 860 331-3477
Coventry *(G-1679)*
Szepanski Machine Services LLC ....G.... 860 738-9825
Winsted *(G-10541)*
T & J Manufacturing LLP ....E.... 860 632-8655
Middletown *(G-4423)*
T G Industries Inc ....F.... 203 235-3239
Meriden *(G-4250)*
T L S Design & Manufacturing ....G.... 860 439-1414
New London *(G-5492)*
▲ **T M Industries Inc** ....D.... 860 828-0344
East Berlin *(G-2178)*
Tag Manufacturing LLC ....G.... 860 479-5120
Plainville *(G-6868)*
Target Machines Inc ....G.... 860 675-1539
Burlington *(G-1276)*
Technical Engineering ....G.... 860 645-9401
Manchester *(G-4100)*
TET Mfg Co Inc ....E.... 860 349-1004
Middlefield *(G-4307)*
Thavenet Machine Company Inc ....G.... 860 599-4495
Pawcatuck *(G-6726)*
◆ **Thermatool Corp** ....D.... 203 468-4100
East Haven *(G-2455)*
Tier One LLC ....D.... 203 426-3030
Newtown *(G-5791)*
Timna Manufacturing Inc ....G.... 203 265-4656
Wallingford *(G-9388)*
Timothy Gray ....G.... 860 314-0863
Wolcott *(G-10592)*
To The tenth Inc ....G.... 203 248-9437
Hamden *(G-3521)*
▲ **Tog Manufacturing Company Inc** ....E.... 413 663-5753
New Britain *(G-5075)*
Tolland Machine Co ....G.... 860 872-4863
Vernon *(G-9155)*
Tool Logistics II ....F.... 203 855-9754
Norwalk *(G-6373)*
Top Flight Machine Tool LLC ....G.... 860 747-4726
Plainville *(G-6870)*
Top Notch Manufacturing Co ....G.... 860 583-2080
Bristol *(G-1131)*
Top Priority Tool LLC ....G.... 860 665-1012
New Britain *(G-5076)*
Total Concept Tool Inc ....G.... 203 483-1130
Branford *(G-664)*
Total Machine Co ....G.... 203 481-8780
Clinton *(G-1530)*
Total Parts Services LLC ....G.... 203 263-5619
Woodbury *(G-10654)*
TP Cycle & Engineering Inc ....E.... 203 744-4960
Danbury *(G-1964)*
Transportation Conn Dept ....G.... 860 342-5996
Portland *(G-6979)*
Tri Mar Manufacturing Compan ....F.... 860 628-4791
Southington *(G-7990)*
Tri-County Mold & Machine ....G.... 860 642-7033
Lebanon *(G-3864)*
▲ **Triple A Manufacturing Company** ....G.... 203 743-9043
Newtown *(G-5794)*
Triumph Manufacturing Co Inc ....F.... 860 635-8811
Middletown *(G-4428)*
Tropax Precision Manufacturing ....F.... 203 794-0733
Danbury *(G-1968)*

Unas Grinding Corporation ....E.... 860 289-1538
East Hartford *(G-2387)*
Uniprise International Inc ....E.... 860 589-7262
Terryville *(G-8776)*
United Gear & Machine Co Inc ....F.... 860 623-6618
Suffield *(G-8737)*
US Product Mechanization Co ....G.... 860 450-1139
Columbia *(G-1614)*
Van Geldern Machine Company ....G.... 203 853-9402
Norwalk *(G-6382)*
Veeder-Root Co ....G.... 860 450-0895
Willimantic *(G-10237)*
Velocity Products ....G.... 860 687-3530
Windsor *(G-10458)*
Venture Tool and Manufacturing ....G.... 860 267-9647
East Hampton *(G-2283)*
Verzatec Inc ....G.... 860 628-0511
Southington *(G-7993)*
Vn Machine Co ....G.... 860 666-8797
Newington *(G-5721)*
Vortex Manufacturing ....G.... 860 749-9769
Somers *(G-7675)*
Voyteks Inc ....G.... 860 967-6558
East Windsor *(G-2529)*
Wallingford Industries Inc ....F.... 203 481-0359
Branford *(G-668)*
Warner Precision Machining & F ....G.... 203 281-3660
Hamden *(G-3527)*
Warrior Precision ....G.... 203 375-8154
Stratford *(G-8704)*
Watrous Brothers Machine Shop ....G.... 860 536-7014
Mystic *(G-4853)*
Wauregan Machine Shop ....G.... 860 774-0686
Wauregan *(G-9754)*
Wdss Corporation ....F.... 203 854-5930
Norwalk *(G-6393)*
Weld-All Inc ....F.... 860 621-3156
Southington *(G-7995)*
Welles Machine Shop ....G.... 860 536-8398
Groton *(G-3318)*
Wendon Company Inc ....F.... 203 348-6272
Stamford *(G-8490)*
Wentworth Manufacturing LLC ....E.... 860 423-4575
South Windham *(G-7694)*
▲ **Westminster Tool Inc** ....E.... 860 564-6966
Plainfield *(G-6756)*
Westminster Tool Inc ....G.... 860 317-1039
Sterling *(G-8519)*
Westport Precision LLC ....D.... 203 378-2175
Stratford *(G-8707)*
Wilde Manufacturing LLC ....G.... 203 693-3939
Milford *(G-4680)*
Williams Mold & Machine ....G.... 860 928-3522
Putnam *(G-7078)*
Willson Manufacturing of Conn ....G.... 860 643-8182
Manchester *(G-4109)*
Winthrop Tool LLC ....G.... 860 526-9079
Essex *(G-2738)*
Wire Cutting Precision ....G.... 860 496-9302
Torrington *(G-8990)*
Wire Tech LLC ....G.... 860 945-9473
Watertown *(G-9750)*
Xuare LLC ....G.... 860 383-8863
Norwich *(G-6440)*

36 ELECTRONIC AND OTHER ELECTRICAL EQUIPMENT AND COMPONENTS, EXCEPT COMPUTER

3612 Power, Distribution & Specialty Transformers

71 Pickett District Road LLC ....G.... 860 350-5964
New Milford *(G-5502)*
ABB Enterprise Software Inc ....D.... 203 790-8588
Danbury *(G-1728)*
ABB Enterprise Software Inc ....D.... 860 285-0183
Windsor *(G-10353)*
ABB Enterprise Software Inc ....F.... 203 329-8771
Stamford *(G-8055)*
▼ **Able Coil and Electronics Co** ....E.... 860 646-5686
Bolton *(G-504)*
Alpha-Core Corp ....G.... 203 335-6805
Bridgeport *(G-687)*
◆ **Alpha-Core Inc** ....E.... 203 954-0050
Shelton *(G-7392)*
Asea Brown Boveri Inc ....G.... 203 750-2200
Norwalk *(G-6076)*
◆ **Bicron Electronics Company** ....D.... 860 482-2524
Torrington *(G-8905)*
▲ **Bridgeport Magnetics Group Inc** ....E.... 203 954-0050
Shelton *(G-7410)*
▲ **Carling Technologies Inc** ....C.... 860 793-9281
Plainville *(G-6785)*
Diagnostic Devices Inc ....G.... 860 651-6583
Simsbury *(G-7616)*
Diagnostic Devices Inc ....G.... 860 651-6583
Simsbury *(G-7617)*
Emsc LLC ....G.... 203 268-5101
Stamford *(G-8195)*
K & D Precision Manufacturing ....G.... 203 931-9550
West Haven *(G-9922)*
Lighticians Inc ....G.... 203 494-2542
Clinton *(G-1513)*
◆ **Neeltran Inc** ....C.... 860 350-5964
New Milford *(G-5564)*
Neeltran International Inc ....G.... 860 350-5964
New Milford *(G-5565)*
▼ **Power Trans Co Inc** ....G.... 203 881-0314
Oxford *(G-6688)*
◆ **Pw Power Systems LLC** ....E.... 860 368-5900
Glastonbury *(G-3077)*
▲ **Superior Elc Holdg Group LLC** ....E.... 860 582-9561
Plainville *(G-6864)*
▲ **Transformer Technology Inc** ....F.... 860 349-1061
Durham *(G-2160)*
Universal Voltronics Corp ....E.... 203 740-8555
Brookfield *(G-1234)*

3613 Switchgear & Switchboard Apparatus

ABB Enterprise Software Inc ....A.... 860 747-7111
Plainville *(G-6763)*
ABB Finance (usa) Inc ....G.... 919 856-2360
Norwalk *(G-6059)*
▲ **Accutron Inc** ....C.... 860 683-8300
Windsor *(G-10354)*
Allied Controls Inc ....F.... 860 628-8443
Stamford *(G-8072)*
Asea Brown Boveri Inc ....G.... 203 750-2200
Norwalk *(G-6076)*
B & A Design Inc ....G.... 860 871-0134
Vernon Rockville *(G-9161)*
Bass Products LLC ....G.... 860 585-7923
Bristol *(G-977)*
Capitol Electronics Inc ....F.... 203 744-3300
Bethel *(G-268)*
▲ **Carling Technologies Inc** ....C.... 860 793-9281
Plainville *(G-6785)*
Connecticut Breaker Co Inc ....G.... 203 378-2240
Stratford *(G-8597)*
▲ **Connecticut Valley Inds LLC** ....G.... 860 388-0822
Old Saybrook *(G-6529)*
◆ **Control Concepts Inc** ....F.... 860 928-6551
Putnam *(G-7037)*
Corotec Corp ....F.... 860 678-0038
Farmington *(G-2893)*
Dow Div of UTC ....G.... 860 683-7340
Windsor *(G-10381)*
EC Holdings Inc ....G.... 203 846-1651
Norwalk *(G-6153)*
Ensign-Bickford Industries Inc ....E.... 860 658-4411
Simsbury *(G-7622)*
Fabcon Inc ....G.... 860 485-9019
Harwinton *(G-3728)*
▲ **Faria Beede Instruments Inc** ....C.... 860 848-9271
North Stonington *(G-6024)*
GE Grid Solutions LLC ....G.... 425 250-2695
Windsor *(G-10388)*
▲ **Gems Sensors Inc** ....B.... 860 747-3000
Plainville *(G-6815)*
◆ **General Electro Components** ....G.... 860 659-3573
Glastonbury *(G-3039)*
Industrial Cnnctons Sltons LLC ....E.... 860 747-7677
Plainville *(G-6824)*
J Ro Grounding Systems Inc ....G.... 860 747-2106
Plainville *(G-6827)*
John Olsen ....G.... 203 624-5544
Trumbull *(G-9037)*
Kilo Ampere Switch Corporation ....G.... 203 877-5994
Milford *(G-4565)*
La Chance Controls ....G.... 860 342-2212
Portland *(G-6963)*
▲ **Lex Products LLC** ....C.... 203 363-3738
Shelton *(G-7490)*
Madison Company ....E.... 203 488-4477
Branford *(G-621)*
▲ **MH Rhodes Cramer LLC** ....G.... 860 291-8402
South Windsor *(G-7793)*

Mil-Con Inc .... D 630 595-2366
Naugatuck ***(G-4901)***
Newco Condenser Inc .... G 475 882-4000
Shelton ***(G-7510)***
Omega Engineering Inc .... D 714 540-4914
Norwalk ***(G-6285)***
Oslo Switch Inc .... E 203 272-2794
Cheshire ***(G-1425)***
Precision Graphics Inc .... E 860 828-6561
East Berlin ***(G-2174)***
▲ Quality Name Plate Inc .... D 860 633-9495
East Glastonbury ***(G-2185)***
Reactel Inc .... G 203 773-0135
New Haven ***(G-5377)***
Satin American Corporation .... E 203 929-6363
Shelton ***(G-7551)***
◆ Siemon Company .... A 860 945-4200
Watertown ***(G-9734)***
Skyko International LLC .... G 860 928-5170
Woodstock ***(G-10684)***
Wiles Charles Preston M D .... G 203 562-7550
New Haven ***(G-5433)***

3621 Motors & Generators

▼ A-1 Machining Co .... D 860 223-6420
New Britain ***(G-4931)***
Ac/DC Industrial Electric LLC .... G 860 886-2232
Yantic ***(G-10695)***
Afcon Products Inc .... F 203 393-9301
Bethany ***(G-234)***
AKO Inc .... E 860 298-9765
Windsor ***(G-10357)***
Alstom Renewable US LLC .... G 860 688-1911
Windsor ***(G-10359)***
Autac Incorporated .... F 203 481-3444
Branford ***(G-551)***
Carter Inv Holdings Corp .... G 860 283-5801
Thomaston ***(G-8783)***
Coils Plus Inc .... E 203 879-0755
Wolcott ***(G-10556)***
Cramer Company .... G 860 291-8402
South Windsor ***(G-7737)***
Drs Naval Power Systems Inc .... B 203 366-5211
Bridgeport ***(G-756)***
Drs Naval Power Systems Inc .... E 203 366-5211
Bridgeport ***(G-757)***
Elinco International Inc .... G 203 275-8885
Fairfield ***(G-2780)***
Fuelcell Energy Inc .... E 860 496-1111
Torrington ***(G-8927)***
Gamma Ventures Inc .... G 860 653-2613
Granby ***(G-3107)***
GE Steam Power Inc .... C 423 648-4161
Windsor ***(G-10389)***
GE Steam Power Inc .... G 860 688-1911
Windsor ***(G-10391)***
Generators On Demand LLC .... F 860 662-4090
Old Lyme ***(G-6510)***
◆ Hamilton Sundstrand Corp .... A 860 654-6000
Windsor Locks ***(G-10491)***
Hydrotec Inc .... G 203 264-6700
Oxford ***(G-6666)***
Ktcr Holding .... G 203 227-4115
Westport ***(G-10110)***
Libby Power Systems LLC .... G 203 393-1239
Bethany ***(G-247)***
NGS Power LLC .... G 860 873-0100
Moodus ***(G-4775)***
Polaris Management Inc .... G 203 261-6399
Easton ***(G-2561)***
Power Strategies LLC .... G 203 254-9926
Fairfield ***(G-2831)***
Rowley Spring & Stamping Corp .... C 860 582-8175
Bristol ***(G-1113)***
Sandvik Wire and Htg Tech Corp .... D 203 744-1440
Bethel ***(G-337)***
Technipower Systems Inc .... G 203 748-7001
Brookfield ***(G-1229)***
Thomson Arpax Mechatronics LLC .... G 516 883-8000
Cheshire ***(G-1455)***
▲ Tritex Corporation .... C 203 756-7441
Waterbury ***(G-9618)***
◆ Ward Leonard CT LLC .... C 860 283-5801
Thomaston ***(G-8818)***
Ward Leonard CT LLC .... D 860 283-2294
Thomaston ***(G-8819)***
Ward Leonard Holdings LLC .... G 860 283-5801
Thomaston ***(G-8820)***
Ward Leonard Inv Holdings LLC .... G 860 283-5801
Thomaston ***(G-8821)***
Ward Leonard Operating LLC .... G 860 283-5801
Thomaston ***(G-8822)***
Ward Lonard Houma Holdings LLC .... G 860 283-5801
Thomaston ***(G-8823)***
WI Intermediate Holdings LLC .... G 860 283-5801
Thomaston ***(G-8825)***

3624 Carbon & Graphite Prdts

◆ Carbon Products Inc .... G 860 749-0614
Somersville ***(G-7678)***
Carbon Tools Inc .... G 860 228-9483
Amston ***(G-2)***
▲ Graphite Die Mold Inc .... G 860 349-4444
Durham ***(G-2148)***
Greenwich Carbon LLC .... G 203 531-7064
Greenwich ***(G-3173)***
Hexcel Corporation .... E 203 969-0666
Stamford ***(G-8233)***
Joshua LLC .... E 203 624-0080
New Haven ***(G-5304)***
Minteq International Inc .... C 860 824-5435
Canaan ***(G-1289)***
Rain Carbon Inc .... G 203 406-0535
Stamford ***(G-8384)***

3625 Relays & Indl Controls

(fast) International Inc .... G 203 380-3489
Stratford ***(G-8562)***
ABB Enterprise Software Inc .... E 203 798-6210
Danbury ***(G-1729)***
◆ Advanced Micro Controls Inc .... E 860 585-1254
Terryville ***(G-8746)***
Airflo Instrument Company .... G 860 633-9455
Glastonbury ***(G-3005)***
▲ Alinabal Inc .... C 203 877-3241
Milford ***(G-4448)***
Allied Controls Inc .... F 860 628-8443
Stamford ***(G-8072)***
Altek Company .... C 860 482-7626
Torrington ***(G-8891)***
▲ Altek Electronics Inc .... C 860 482-7626
Torrington ***(G-8892)***
Asea Brown Boveri Inc .... G 203 750-2200
Norwalk ***(G-6076)***
Ashcrft-Ngano Kiki Hldings Inc .... G 203 378-8281
Stratford ***(G-8571)***
◆ Ashcroft Inc .... B 203 378-8281
Stratford ***(G-8572)***
Automation & Servo Tech .... G 860 658-5172
Simsbury ***(G-7612)***
Automation Controls .... G 203 888-9330
Oxford ***(G-6644)***
▲ Baumer Ltd .... F 860 621-2121
Southington ***(G-7894)***
◆ Belimo Aircontrols (usa) Inc .... C 800 543-9038
Danbury ***(G-1752)***
▲ Belimo Customization USA Inc .... G 203 791-9915
Danbury ***(G-1754)***
Bristol Babcock Employees Fede .... G 860 945-2200
Watertown ***(G-9687)***
▼ Carlyle Johnson Machine Co LLC .... E 860 643-1531
Bolton ***(G-508)***
CET Inc .... G 203 882-8057
Milford ***(G-4486)***
Clarktron Products Inc .... G 203 333-6517
Fairfield ***(G-2763)***
Cogstate Inc .... G 203 773-5010
New Haven ***(G-5258)***
Component Concepts Inc .... G 860 523-4066
West Hartford ***(G-9792)***
Computer Components Inc .... F 860 653-9909
East Granby ***(G-2199)***
Conntrol International Inc .... F 860 928-0567
Putnam ***(G-7036)***
◆ Control Concepts Inc .... F 860 928-6551
Putnam ***(G-7037)***
Conveyco Technologies Inc .... E 860 589-8215
Bristol ***(G-1007)***
Das Distribution Inc .... G 860 844-3058
East Granby ***(G-2201)***
Delta Elevator Service Corp .... E 860 676-6152
Canton ***(G-1312)***
Devar Inc .... E 203 368-6751
Bridgeport ***(G-749)***
▲ Digatron Power Electronics Inc .... E 203 446-8000
Shelton ***(G-7432)***
Dynamic Bldg Enrgy Sltions LLC .... F 860 599-1872
North Stonington ***(G-6022)***
▲ E-Z Switch Manufacturing Inc .... F 203 874-7766
Milford ***(G-4520)***
Everlast Products LLC .... G 203 250-7111
Cheshire ***(G-1387)***
Ewald Instruments Corp .... F 860 491-9042
Bristol ***(G-1032)***
▲ Gems Sensors Inc .... B 860 747-3000
Plainville ***(G-6815)***
General Electric Company .... D 203 396-1572
Bridgeport ***(G-774)***
◆ General Electro Components .... G 860 659-3573
Glastonbury ***(G-3039)***
Gordon Products Incorporated .... E 203 775-4501
Brookfield ***(G-1194)***
◆ Hamilton Sundstrand Corp .... A 860 654-6000
Windsor Locks ***(G-10491)***
HI Tek Racing LLC .... G 203 378-5210
Stratford ***(G-8625)***
▲ Idevices LLC .... E 860 352-5252
Avon ***(G-85)***
In-Motion LLC .... G 860 742-3612
Coventry ***(G-1656)***
Independence Park .... G 203 421-9396
Madison ***(G-3930)***
▲ Inertia Dynamics LLC .... C 860 379-1252
New Hartford ***(G-5197)***
John Olsen .... G 203 624-5544
Trumbull ***(G-9037)***
Kc Crafts LLC .... G 860 426-9797
Plantsville ***(G-6898)***
Kimchuk Incorporated .... F 203 790-7800
Danbury ***(G-1868)***
▲ Linemaster Switch Corporation .... C 860 630-4920
Woodstock ***(G-10669)***
Measurement Systems Inc .... E 203 949-3500
Wallingford ***(G-9317)***
Micromod Automtn & Contrls LLC .... E 585 321-9200
Wallingford ***(G-9321)***
▲ Minarik Corporation .... C 860 687-5000
Bloomfield ***(G-445)***
▲ Naiad Dynamics Us Inc .... E 203 929-6355
Shelton ***(G-7506)***
New England Lift Systems LLC .... G 860 372-4040
Newington ***(G-5685)***
New Haven Companies Inc .... F 203 469-6421
East Haven ***(G-2444)***
▼ Noank Controls LLC .... G 860 449-6776
Groton ***(G-3301)***
North American Elev Svcs Co .... E 860 676-6000
Farmington ***(G-2939)***
O E M Controls Inc .... C 203 929-8431
Shelton ***(G-7517)***
▲ P-Q Controls Inc .... E 860 583-6994
Bristol ***(G-1084)***
◆ P/A Industries Inc .... E 860 243-8306
Bloomfield ***(G-459)***
Park Distributories Inc .... G 203 579-2140
Bridgeport ***(G-863)***
Park Distributories Inc .... F 203 366-7200
Bridgeport ***(G-864)***
Park Distributories Inc .... F 203 366-7200
Bridgeport ***(G-865)***
Pepperl + Fuchs Inc .... G 860 923-2703
Woodstock ***(G-10677)***
▲ Quality Name Plate Inc .... D 860 633-9495
East Glastonbury ***(G-2185)***
Safestart Systems LLC .... G 203 221-0652
Weston ***(G-10039)***
Saindon Crane Service .... G 860 505-7245
Berlin ***(G-218)***
Sound Construction & Engrg Co .... E 860 242-2109
Bloomfield ***(G-488)***
T & T Automation Inc .... F 860 683-8788
Windsor ***(G-10447)***
Thomas Products Ltd .... E 860 621-9101
Southington ***(G-7987)***
United Electric Controls Co .... D 203 877-2795
Milford ***(G-4668)***
Victory Controls LLC .... G 860 930-6226
Farmington ***(G-2976)***
◆ Ward Leonard CT LLC .... C 860 283-5801
Thomaston ***(G-8818)***

3629 Electrical Indl Apparatus, NEC

90 River Street LLC .... G 203 772-4700
New Haven ***(G-5216)***
Acceleron Inc .... E 860 651-9333
East Granby ***(G-2186)***
Advanced Sonics LLC .... G 203 266-4440
Oxford ***(G-6639)***
▲ B S T Systems Inc .... D 860 564-4078
Plainfield ***(G-6742)***

S I C

36 ELECTRONIC AND OTHER ELECTRICAL EQUIPMENT AND COMPONENTS, EXCEPT COMPUTER SIC SECTION

Charge Solutions Inc..........G....... 203 871-7282
Milford (G-4488)
Crystal Tool LLC..........G....... 860 510-0113
Old Saybrook (G-6530)
▲ **Digatron Power Electronics Inc**..........E....... 203 446-8000
Shelton (G-7432)
GE Enrgy Pwr Cnversion USA Inc..........G....... 203 373-2211
Fairfield (G-2790)
Harby Power Solutions LLC..........G....... 203 265-0012
Wallingford (G-9278)
High Voltage Outsourcing LLC..........G....... 203 456-3101
Danbury (G-1844)
Parmaco LLC..........G....... 860 573-7118
Glastonbury (G-3067)
Pressure Blast Mfg Co Inc..........F....... 800 722-5278
South Windsor (G-7811)
Prostaff Pro Shop..........G....... 203 239-3835
North Haven (G-5981)
Sober Touch Sensoring LLC..........G....... 203 540-2486
Ansonia (G-51)

3631 Household Cooking Eqpt

Airigan Solutions LLC..........G....... 203 594-7781
Southport (G-7998)
◆ **Conair Corporation**..........B....... 203 351-9000
Stamford (G-8156)
Kenyon International Inc..........G....... 860 664-4906
Clinton (G-1510)
◆ **Kenyon International Inc**..........E....... 860 664-4906
Clinton (G-1511)
South Windsor Golf Course LLC..........D....... 860 648-4653
South Windsor (G-7826)
Vigiroda Enterprises Inc..........G....... 203 268-6117
Trumbull (G-9092)
Vigiroda Products LLC..........G....... 860 391-8457
Old Saybrook (G-6574)

3632 Household Refrigerators & Freezers

▲ **Medelco Inc**..........G....... 203 275-8070
Bridgeport (G-836)
New Brnswick Scientific of Del..........G....... 732 287-1200
Enfield (G-2668)

3633 Household Laundry Eqpt

Brian & Son Powerwashing LLC..........G....... 860 963-1243
Woodstock (G-10657)
Instinctive Works LLC..........G....... 203 434-8094
Westport (G-10101)

3634 Electric Household Appliances

Alstrom Power..........G....... 203 783-1046
Milford (G-4451)
Asselin Electric LLC..........G....... 860 379-3056
Winsted (G-10507)
Betlan Corporation..........F....... 203 270-7898
Newtown (G-5729)
▲ **Bkmfg Corp**..........E....... 860 738-2200
Winsted (G-10510)
Black & Decker (us) Inc..........G....... 860 225-5111
New Britain (G-4951)
◆ **Black & Decker (us) Inc**..........G....... 860 225-5111
New Britain (G-4952)
Conair Corporation..........D....... 800 492-7464
Torrington (G-8914)
◆ **Conair Corporation**..........B....... 203 351-9000
Stamford (G-8156)
Crrc LLC..........D....... 860 635-2200
Cromwell (G-1697)
Dampits LLC..........G....... 203 210-7946
Wilton (G-10288)
Jarden Corporation..........E....... 203 845-5300
Norwalk (G-6218)
▲ **Mayborn Usa Inc**..........F....... 781 269-7490
Stamford (G-8298)
▲ **McIntire Company**..........F....... 860 585-8559
Bristol (G-1070)
Urban Antique Radio..........G....... 203 877-2409
Milford (G-4671)

3635 Household Vacuum Cleaners

A A Gentle House Washing..........G....... 860 243-8800
Bloomfield (G-378)
Matsutek Enterprises LLC..........G....... 860 276-2464
Southington (G-7951)
Stanley Steemer Intl Inc..........E....... 860 274-5540
Watertown (G-9738)
Traumaway LLC..........G....... 860 628-0706
Plantsville (G-6916)

3639 Household Appliances, NEC

A+ Plus Appliance..........G....... 860 878-9624
Harwinton (G-3718)
Clarke Distribution Corp..........G....... 203 838-9385
Norwalk (G-6116)
◆ **Conair Corporation**..........B....... 203 351-9000
Stamford (G-8156)
Demand Pro LLC..........G....... 860 438-8843
New Britain (G-4974)
▲ **Eemax Inc**..........D....... 203 267-7890
Waterbury (G-9472)

3641 Electric Lamps

Brian Cody..........G....... 203 331-7382
Stratford (G-8586)
Electro-Lite Corporation..........F....... 203 743-4059
Bethel (G-295)
Grigerek Co..........G....... 860 677-2560
Farmington (G-2914)
▲ **Lcd Lighting Inc**..........C....... 203 799-7877
Orange (G-6610)
▲ **Light Sources Inc**..........C....... 203 799-7877
Orange (G-6611)
Revolution Lighting..........G....... 203 504-1111
Stamford (G-8388)
Revolution Lighting Tech Inc..........C....... 203 504-1111
Stamford (G-8389)
Southern Neng Ultraviolet Inc..........G....... 203 483-5810
Branford (G-654)
Triton Thalassic Tech Inc..........G....... 203 438-0633
Ridgefield (G-7177)
Uv Inc..........G....... 203 333-1031
Woodbridge (G-10620)
Voltarc Technologies Inc..........G....... 203 753-6366
Waterbury (G-9624)
◆ **Whelen Engineering Company Inc**..........B....... 860 526-9504
Chester (G-1485)

3643 Current-Carrying Wiring Devices

ABB Enterprise Software Inc..........A....... 860 747-7111
Plainville (G-6763)
Allied Controls Inc..........F....... 860 628-8443
Stamford (G-8072)
American Specialty Pdts LLC..........G....... 860 871-2279
Vernon (G-9130)
Amphenol Corporation..........D....... 203 327-7300
Stamford (G-8081)
▼ **Amphenol Corporation**..........D....... 203 265-8900
Wallingford (G-9204)
Amphenol Nexus Technologies..........D....... 203 327-7300
Stamford (G-8082)
◆ **Bead Industries Inc**..........E....... 203 301-0270
Milford (G-4466)
Burndy LLC..........D....... 203 792-1115
Bethel (G-267)
▲ **Carling Technologies Inc**..........C....... 860 793-9281
Plainville (G-6785)
Dering-Ney Inc..........G....... 847 932-6782
Bloomfield (G-406)
▼ **Deringer-Ney Inc**..........C....... 860 242-2281
Bloomfield (G-407)
Dicon Connections Inc..........E....... 203 481-8080
North Branford (G-5835)
East Coast Lightning Eqp Inc..........E....... 860 379-9072
Winsted (G-10518)
Eaton Aerospace LLC..........E....... 203 796-6000
Bethel (G-292)
Eaton Corporation..........E....... 203 796-6000
Bethel (G-293)
Ek-Ris Cable Company Inc..........E....... 860 223-4327
New Britain (G-4980)
Everlast Products LLC..........G....... 203 250-7111
Cheshire (G-1387)
▲ **Faria Beede Instruments Inc**..........C....... 860 848-9271
North Stonington (G-6024)
Floodmaster LLC..........G....... 203 488-4477
Branford (G-595)
Gold Line Connector Inc..........E....... 203 938-2588
Redding (G-7093)
Gordon Products Incorporated..........E....... 203 775-4501
Brookfield (G-1194)
Hubbell Incorporated..........E....... 203 426-2555
Newtown (G-5748)
Hubbell Incorporated Delaware..........C....... 475 882-4800
Shelton (G-7469)
Hubbell Incorporated Delaware..........D....... 475 882-4000
Shelton (G-7470)
Hubbell Technical Ctr..........G....... 203 337-3333
Bridgeport (G-789)
◆ **Hubbell Wiring Device**..........F....... 203 882-4800
Milford (G-4549)
J Ro Grounding Systems Inc..........G....... 860 747-2106
Plainville (G-6827)
▲ **Legrand Holding Inc**..........E....... 860 233-6251
West Hartford (G-9828)
▲ **Lex Products LLC**..........C....... 203 363-3738
Shelton (G-7490)
M & I Industries Inc..........G....... 860 747-6421
Plainville (G-6837)
Northast Lghtning Prtction LLC..........F....... 860 243-0010
Bloomfield (G-451)
Old Cambridge Products Corp..........G....... 860 243-1761
Bloomfield (G-454)
Old Ni Incorporated..........G....... 203 327-7300
Stamford (G-8338)
On Line Building Systems LLC..........G....... 203 798-1194
Danbury (G-1899)
Oslo Switch Inc..........E....... 203 272-2794
Cheshire (G-1425)
Ripley Tools LLC..........E....... 860 635-2200
Cromwell (G-1715)
◆ **Siemon Company**..........A....... 860 945-4200
Watertown (G-9734)
Siemon Company..........E....... 860 945-4218
Watertown (G-9735)
Southport Products LLC..........G....... 860 379-0761
Winsted (G-10539)
Spectrum Associates Inc..........F....... 203 878-4618
Milford (G-4651)
Thomas Products Ltd..........E....... 860 621-9101
Southington (G-7987)
Times Wire and Cable Company..........G....... 203 949-8400
Wallingford (G-9387)
United Electric Controls Co..........D....... 203 877-2795
Milford (G-4668)
◆ **Wiremold Company**..........A....... 860 233-6251
West Hartford (G-9874)
Woods Lightning Protection..........G....... 203 929-1868
Shelton (G-7588)
▲ **World Cord Sets Inc**..........G....... 860 763-2100
Enfield (G-2708)

3644 Noncurrent-Carrying Wiring Devices

Arcade Technology LLC..........E....... 203 366-3871
Bridgeport (G-699)
▲ **Bridgeport Fittings LLC**..........C....... 203 377-5944
Stratford (G-8588)
Chase Corporation..........F....... 203 285-1244
Woodbridge (G-10597)
Family Raceway LLC..........G....... 860 896-0171
Vernon (G-9138)
Rhode Island Raceway LLC..........G....... 860 701-0192
Quaker Hill (G-7084)
Roaming Raceway and RR LLC..........G....... 413 531-3390
Suffield (G-8733)
Stamford RPM Raceway LLC..........G....... 203 323-7223
Stamford (G-8440)
Wiremold Company..........F....... 860 263-3115
West Hartford (G-9875)
◆ **Wiremold Company**..........A....... 860 233-6251
West Hartford (G-9874)
Wiremold Legrand Co Centerex..........E....... 877 295-3472
West Hartford (G-9876)

3645 Residential Lighting Fixtures

3t Lighting Inc..........G....... 203 775-1805
Brookfield (G-1154)
Bb Shades..........G....... 203 849-9345
Westport (G-10060)
E-Lite Technologies Inc..........F....... 203 371-2070
Trumbull (G-9022)
Electri-Cable Assemblies Inc..........G....... 203 924-6617
Shelton (G-7437)
Gs Thermal Solutions Inc..........G....... 475 289-4625
Danbury (G-1839)
Keeling Company Inc..........G....... 860 349-0916
Old Lyme (G-6514)
Keelings..........G....... 860 399-4527
Westbrook (G-9999)
▲ **Light Fantastic Realty Inc**..........C....... 203 934-3441
West Haven (G-9926)
Light Sources Inc..........C....... 203 799-7877
Milford (G-4567)
Lumivisions Architectural Elem..........G....... 203 529-3232
Norwalk (G-6240)
Premier Mfg Group Inc..........D....... 203 924-6617
Shelton (G-7539)
▲ **Seesmart Inc**..........E....... 203 504-1111
Stamford (G-8407)

36 ELECTRONIC AND OTHER ELECTRICAL EQUIPMENT AND COMPONENTS, EXCEPT COMPUTER

Siempre LLC .... G 203 873-0303
  Bridgeport *(G-902)*
Washington Copper Works Inc ..... F 860 868-7637
  Washington *(G-9415)*

3646 Commercial, Indl & Institutional Lighting Fixtures

3t Lighting Inc .... G 203 775-1805
  Brookfield *(G-1154)*
A&A Home Solutions .... G 203 993-1735
  Shelton *(G-7386)*
▲ C Cowles & Company .... D 203 865-3117
  North Haven *(G-5916)*
Green Ray Led Intl LLC .... G 203 485-1435
  Greenwich *(G-3172)*
▲ Innovative ARC Tubes Corp .... E 203 333-1031
  Bridgeport *(G-792)*
▲ Lcd Lighting Inc .... C 203 799-7877
  Orange *(G-6610)*
Led Lighting Solutions LLC .... G 860 770-6023
  Berlin *(G-193)*
Lighting Edge Inc .... G 860 767-8968
  Essex *(G-2724)*
Lumivisions Architectural Elem ..... G 203 529-3232
  Norwalk *(G-6240)*
Newco Lighting Inc .... G 475 882-4000
  Shelton *(G-7511)*
▲ Nutron Manufacturing Inc .... E 860 887-4550
  Norwich *(G-6426)*
▲ Pathway Lighting Products Inc ... D 860 388-6881
  Old Saybrook *(G-6564)*
Pegasus Capital Advisors LP .... E 203 869-4400
  Stamford *(G-8356)*
Prolume Inc .... G 203 268-7778
  Monroe *(G-4749)*
▲ Seesmart Inc .... E 203 504-1111
  Stamford *(G-8407)*
▲ Sylvan R Shemitz Designs LLC ... C 203 934-3441
  West Haven *(G-9957)*
The L C Doane Company .... F 860 767-8295
  Ivoryton *(G-3790)*
Top Priority Tool LLC .... G 860 665-1012
  New Britain *(G-5076)*
Tri-State Led Inc .... F 203 813-3791
  Greenwich *(G-3248)*
Whelen Engineering Company Inc ... F 860 526-9504
  Chester *(G-1486)*
◆ Whelen Engineering Company Inc ... B 860 526-9504
  Chester *(G-1485)*

3647 Vehicular Lighting Eqpt

Celb LLC .... G 203 739-0157
  Danbury *(G-1765)*
▲ Cornell-Carr Co Inc .... E 203 261-2529
  Monroe *(G-4706)*
Hoffman Engineering LLC .... D 203 425-8900
  Stamford *(G-8240)*
▲ Light Fantastic Realty Inc .... C 203 934-3441
  West Haven *(G-9926)*
Naugatuck Emergency Eqp LLC ..... G 203 228-7117
  Oakville *(G-6457)*
▲ Ridge View Associates Inc .... D 203 878-8560
  Milford *(G-4628)*
The L C Doane Company .... F 860 767-8295
  Ivoryton *(G-3790)*
Water Transit Services LLC .... G 860 625-3625
  Waterford *(G-9676)*
◆ Whelen Engineering Company Inc ... B 860 526-9504
  Chester *(G-1485)*

3648 Lighting Eqpt, NEC

Airflo Instrument Company .... G 860 633-9455
  Glastonbury *(G-3005)*
American Metaseal of Conn .... G 203 787-0281
  Hamden *(G-3414)*
American Solar & Altermative .... G 203 324-7186
  Stamford *(G-8078)*
Aqua Comfort Technologies LLC .... G 203 265-0100
  Wallingford *(G-9209)*
Aquacomfort Solutions LLC .... G 407 831-1941
  Cheshire *(G-1355)*
Architectural Outdoor Lighting ..... G 860 659-5795
  Glastonbury *(G-3007)*
▲ Astralite Inc .... G 203 775-0172
  Brookfield *(G-1161)*
CBA Lighting and Controls Inc .... G 860 623-1924
  Windsor Locks *(G-10477)*
▲ Connecticut Valley Inds LLC ...... G 860 388-0822
  Old Saybrook *(G-6529)*

Contemprary Lights Staging LLC ... G 203 359-8200
  Stamford *(G-8159)*
Cooper Crouse-Hinds LLC .... D 860 683-4300
  Windsor *(G-10377)*
Dave Ross .... G 203 775-4327
  Brookfield *(G-1177)*
Eaton Electric Holdings LLC .... F 860 683-4300
  Windsor *(G-10382)*
Elc Acquisition Corporation .... G 203 743-4059
  Bethel *(G-294)*
▲ Electrix LLC .... D 203 776-5577
  New Haven *(G-5274)*
▲ Fidelux Lighting LLC .... F 860 436-5000
  Hartford *(G-3589)*
Incure Inc .... G 860 748-2979
  New Britain *(G-4998)*
▲ Integro LLC .... E 860 832-8960
  New Britain *(G-5000)*
Jon Minard Lighting .... G 860 228-9069
  Amston *(G-3)*
Led Lighting Hub .... G 860 232-7141
  West Hartford *(G-9826)*
M & I Industries Inc .... G 860 747-6421
  Plainville *(G-6837)*
Macris Industries Inc .... G 860 514-7003
  Mystic *(G-4829)*
Malco Inc .... F 860 584-0446
  Terryville *(G-8764)*
Moonlighting LLC .... G 203 740-8964
  Brookfield *(G-1208)*
Mv Lighting .... G 203 856-3564
  Norwalk *(G-6266)*
Nova Electronics 860 537-3471
  Colchester *(G-1561)*
▲ Pathway Lighting Products Inc ... D 860 388-6881
  Old Saybrook *(G-6564)*
Pathway Lighting Source .... G 860 537-0600
  Colchester *(G-1562)*
Pegasus Capital Advisors LP .... E 203 869-4400
  Stamford *(G-8356)*
Pennsylvania Globe Gaslight Co .... E 203 484-7749
  North Branford *(G-5851)*
Point Lighting Corporation .... E 860 243-0600
  Bloomfield *(G-467)*
Reflex Ltg Group of CT LLC .... G 860 666-1548
  Wethersfield *(G-10218)*
Robin Reed Ltd LLC .... G 203 481-6378
  Branford *(G-642)*
Rsl Fiber Systems LLC .... F 860 282-4930
  East Hartford *(G-2367)*
Sapphire Mltnational Group Inc .... G 860 693-1233
  Torrington *(G-8966)*
Searchlight LLC .... G 203 577-4400
  Middlebury *(G-4290)*
Sensor Switch Inc .... E 203 265-2842
  New Haven *(G-5392)*
Smartcap Innovations LLC .... G 860 878-4688
  West Hartford *(G-9856)*
Snibbetts Inc .... G 860 526-5536
  Deep River *(G-2101)*
Solais Lighting Inc .... F 203 683-6222
  Stamford *(G-8427)*
▲ Sorenson Lighted Controls Inc ... D 860 527-3092
  West Hartford *(G-9858)*
Studio Steel Inc .... G 860 868-7305
  New Preston *(G-5613)*
◆ Whelen Engineering Company Inc ... B 860 526-9504
  Chester *(G-1485)*
Whiting Lighting LLC .... G 860 626-0734
  Torrington *(G-8989)*
York Street Studio Inc .... G 203 266-9000
  New Milford *(G-5609)*
Yourlightingsource Co LLC 917 439-6501
  West Haven *(G-9968)*

3651 Household Audio & Video Eqpt

Advanced HM Audio & Video LLC .. G 860 621-0631
  Plantsville *(G-6883)*
Alarmco .... G 203 458-2646
  Guilford *(G-3323)*
Audioworks Inc .... G 203 876-1133
  Milford *(G-4462)*
Colin Harrison LLC .... G 203 775-5035
  Brookfield *(G-1174)*
Color Film Media Group LLC .... G 203 202-2929
  Norwalk *(G-6121)*
David J Weber .... G 203 949-9198
  Wallingford *(G-9247)*
Harman Becker Automotive Syste .. G 203 328-3501
  Stamford *(G-8224)*

Harman Consumer Inc .... G 203 328-3500
  Stamford *(G-8225)*
▲ Harman International Inds Inc ... B 203 328-3500
  Stamford *(G-8226)*
Harman International Inds Inc 203 328-3500
  Stamford *(G-8227)*
Harman International Inds Inc ...... C 203 328-3500
  Stamford *(G-8228)*
Harman KG Holding LLC .... F 203 328-3500
  Stamford *(G-8229)*
Hatcams LLC .... G 203 303-7250
  Wallingford *(G-9279)*
Impact Sales & Marketing LLC ..... G 860 523-5366
  West Hartford *(G-9820)*
Infinite Audio LLC .... G 203 924-2558
  Shelton *(G-7476)*
Insight Plus Technology LLC .... G 860 930-4763
  Bristol *(G-1051)*
John Samuel Group .... G 860 806-5734
  Torrington *(G-8939)*
▲ Ki Inc .... E 203 641-5492
  Orange *(G-6608)*
Krell Industries LLC .... F 203 298-4000
  Orange *(G-6609)*
▲ Laufer Teknik .... G 860 355-4484
  Roxbury *(G-7278)*
Marathon Wood Work .... G 203 847-2800
  Norwalk *(G-6247)*
Microphase Corporation .... G 203 866-8000
  Shelton *(G-7500)*
Nollysource Entertainment LLC ... G 347 264-6655
  Bridgeport *(G-853)*
Omnicron Electronics 860 928-0377
  Putnam *(G-7055)*
PMC Technologies LLC .... G 203 222-0000
  Weston *(G-10036)*
Proxtalkercom LLC .... G 203 721-6074
  Waterbury *(G-9590)*
▲ Redco Audio Inc .... F 203 502-7600
  Stratford *(G-8674)*
Rossomano Pictures .... G 203 241-5087
  Sherman *(G-7603)*
Service Dept .... G 203 335-1491
  Bridgeport *(G-900)*
◆ Source Loudspeakers .... G 860 918-3088
  South Windsor *(G-7824)*
▲ Telefunken USA LLC .... F 860 882-5919
  South Windsor *(G-7832)*
Thor Audio .... G 203 373-9264
  Fairfield *(G-2856)*
Vintage Performance LLC .... G 860 542-5753
  Norfolk *(G-5828)*
Viola Audio Laboratories Inc .... G 203 772-0435
  New Haven *(G-5428)*
Visionpoint LLC .... E 860 436-9673
  Newington *(G-5720)*
◆ Whelen Engineering Company Inc ... B 860 526-9504
  Chester *(G-1485)*
Xintekidel Inc .... G 203 348-9229
  Stamford *(G-8503)*

3652 Phonograph Records & Magnetic Tape

American Melody Records .... G 203 457-0881
  Guilford *(G-3325)*
Bff Holdings Inc .... C 860 510-0100
  Old Saybrook *(G-6523)*
Mosaic Records Inc .... G 203 327-7111
  Stamford *(G-8314)*
Trod Nossel Prdctns & Rcrdng S ... G 203 269-4465
  Wallingford *(G-9391)*

3661 Telephone & Telegraph Apparatus

Ahead Communications Systems .. D 203 720-0227
  Naugatuck *(G-4855)*
▼ Amphenol Corporation .... D 203 265-8900
  Wallingford *(G-9204)*
Arris Technology Inc .... F 678 473-8493
  Wallingford *(G-9212)*
Avaya Inc .... G 203 234-9300
  North Haven *(G-5912)*
Canoga Perkins Corporation .... G 203 888-7914
  Seymour *(G-7337)*
Cardiophotonics LLC .... G 203 645-6077
  Bethany *(G-237)*
Carrier Access - Trin Networks ..... G 203 778-8222
  Brookfield *(G-1168)*
▲ Communication Networks LLC ... E 203 796-5300
  Danbury *(G-1771)*
Dac Systems Inc .... F 203 924-7000
  Shelton *(G-7426)*

36 ELECTRONIC AND OTHER ELECTRICAL EQUIPMENT AND COMPONENTS, EXCEPT COMPUTER

Daniel K Rogers .... G 860 455-0530
  Chaplin (G-1338)
Elot Inc .... G 203 388-1808
  Old Greenwich (G-6472)
Fibre Optic Plus Inc .... F 860 646-3581
  South Windsor (G-7756)
Freedom Technologies LLC .... G 860 633-0452
  Glastonbury (G-3037)
Gdc Federal Systems Inc .... G 203 729-0271
  Naugatuck (G-4884)
◆ General Datacomm Inc .... E 203 729-0271
  Oxford (G-6661)
General Datacomm Inds Inc .... E 203 729-0271
  Oxford (G-6662)
Hubbell Premise Wiring Inc .... F 860 535-8326
  Mystic (G-4821)
IPC Systems Inc .... F 203 339-7000
  Old Saybrook (G-6543)
IPC Systems Inc .... C 860 271-4100
  Fairfield (G-2797)
K-Tech International .... E 860 489-9399
  Torrington (G-8941)
Microphase Corporation 203 866-8000
  Shelton (G-7500)
Nutmeg Utility Products Inc .... E 203 250-8802
  Cheshire (G-1423)
Opticonx Inc 888 748-6855
  Putnam (G-7056)
Pamela D Siemon Lcsw LLC 203 232-8009
  Watertown (G-9719)
Photon Partners LLC 203 807-3623
  Darien (G-2039)
◆ Pitney Bowes Inc .... A 203 356-5000
  Stamford (G-8362)
Pitney Bowes Inc .... E 203 356-5000
  Shelton (G-7530)
◆ Radio Frequency Systems Inc .. E 203 630-3311
  Meriden (G-4227)
Ruckus Wireless Inc 203 303-6400
  Wallingford (G-9362)
Siemens AG 860 651-1399
  Simsbury (G-7645)
Sigmavoip Llc 203 541-5450
  Westport (G-10159)
▲ Sound Control Technologies 203 854-5701
  Norwalk (G-6352)
▲ Synectix LLC 203 283-0701
  Milford (G-4661)
Tango Modem LLC 203 421-2245
  Madison (G-3963)
Total Communications Inc .... D 860 282-9999
  East Hartford (G-2386)
Total Communications Inc .... E 203 882-0088
  Milford (G-4666)
United Photonics LLC 617 752-2073
  Vernon Rockville (G-9185)

3663 Radio & T V Communications, Systs & Eqpt, Broadcast/Studio

Advanced Receiver Research .... G 860 485-0310
  Harwinton (G-3719)
Ashcrft-Ngano Kiki Hldings Inc 203 378-8281
  Stratford (G-8571)
◆ Ashcroft Inc .... B 203 378-8281
  Stratford (G-8572)
Axerra Networks Inc 203 906-3570
  Woodbury (G-10625)
Commscope Technologies LLC .... F 203 699-4100
  Prospect (G-6997)
Comsat Inc .... F 203 264-4091
  Southbury (G-7848)
Connecticut Radio Inc .... G 860 563-4867
  Rocky Hill (G-7228)
Cuescript Inc 203 763-4030
  Stratford (G-8602)
Directv .... G 203 445-2876
  Trumbull (G-9021)
Fenton Corp .... F 203 221-2788
  Westport (G-10079)
Fisher Electronics 860 646-4779
  Vernon Rockville (G-9168)
Frontier Vision Tech Inc .... E 860 953-0240
  Rocky Hill (G-7238)
General Network Service Inc 203 359-5735
  Stamford (G-8213)
Gold Line Connector Inc .... E 203 938-2588
  Redding (G-7093)
I Tech Services Inc .... G 800 559-8991
  Danbury (G-1847)

Jk Antennas Inc .... G 845 228-8700
  Brookfield (G-1200)
Latino Multiservice LLC .... G 203 691-9715
  New Haven (G-5316)
Lf Engineering Co Inc .... G 860 526-4759
  East Haven (G-2438)
Mango Dsp Inc .... E 203 857-4008
  Norwalk (G-6245)
Matrixx Productions .... G 203 218-5565
  Hartford (G-3637)
Media Links Inc .... F 860 206-9163
  Windsor (G-10408)
Merl Inc .... G 203 237-8811
  Meriden (G-4199)
Microphase Corporation .... E 203 866-8000
  Shelton (G-7500)
Microtech Inc .... D 203 272-3234
  Cheshire (G-1416)
Newtec America Inc .... F 203 323-0042
  Stamford (G-8327)
Northastern Communications Inc .. F 203 381-9008
  Stratford (G-8654)
Peak Antennas .... G 203 268-3688
  Monroe (G-4745)
Peak Antennas LLC 203 268-3688
  Monroe (G-4746)
◆ Radio Frequency Systems Inc .. E 203 630-3311
  Meriden (G-4227)
◆ RFS Americas .... G 203 630-3311
  Meriden (G-4231)
Scinetx LLC 203 355-3676
  Stamford (G-8403)
Sonitor Technologies Inc .... G 727 466-4557
  Greenwich (G-3239)
Tactical Communications Inc .... F 203 453-2389
  Guilford (G-3398)
Titus Technological Labs .... G 860 633-5472
  Glastonbury (G-3088)
Video Automation Systems Inc 203 312-0152
  New Fairfield (G-5182)
Video Messengercom Corp 203 358-8842
  Stratford (G-8702)
Video Technologies Group LLC 203 341-0474
  Westport (G-10172)
Wagz Inc 203 553-9336
  Stamford (G-8487)
Xintekidel Inc 203 348-9229
  Stamford (G-8503)

3669 Communications Eqpt, NEC

Adam Bisson 203 861-8271
  Bridgeport (G-683)
Ademco Inc .... G 860 257-3266
  Rocky Hill (G-7218)
Ademco Inc .... G 203 877-2702
  Milford (G-4440)
Alarm One 203 239-1714
  North Haven (G-5898)
Allstate Fire Systems LLC .... E 860 246-7711
  Middletown (G-4314)
AMS Strategic Management Inc ... G 845 500-5635
  Stamford (G-8083)
Applied Physical Sciences Corp ... D 860 448-3253
  Groton (G-3271)
▲ Aquatic Sensor Netwrk Tech LLC .. F .. 860 429-4303
  Storrs Mansfield (G-8552)
Care Connection LLC .... G 860 274-1251
  Watertown (G-9690)
Colonial Metal Detectors .... G 860 317-1284
  Plainfield (G-6745)
Cord-Mate Inc .... G 203 272-8415
  Cheshire (G-1375)
Datacomm Management Svcs LLC ... G .. 203 858-9846
  Darien (G-2020)
Digital Bob .... G 203 322-5732
  Stamford (G-8185)
▲ Endoto Corp .... G 860 289-8033
  East Hartford (G-2323)
▲ Essential Trading Systems Corp .. F .. 860 295-8100
  Marlborough (G-4123)
Farmington River Holdings LLC .. G 203 777-2130
  Hamden (G-3447)
Gac Inc .... G 860 633-1768
  Glastonbury (G-3038)
Harris Security LLC .... G 860 583-6637
  Bristol (G-1047)
Lumentum Operations LLC .... F 408 546-5483
  Bloomfield (G-444)
M-Systems Inc .... G 203 270-8926
  Newtown (G-5758)

Mattatuck Alarm Co Inc .... G 203 754-0541
  Waterbury (G-9537)
Nutmeg Utility Products Inc .... E 203 250-8802
  Cheshire (G-1423)
Onsite Services Inc 203 669-3988
  Clinton (G-1517)
Preusser Research Group Inc .... E 203 459-8700
  Trumbull (G-9056)
Protection Industries Corp 203 375-9393
  Stratford (G-8671)
Q-Lane Turnstiles LLC .... F 860 410-1801
  Sandy Hook (G-7327)
▼ T-S Display Systems Inc .... G 203 964-0575
  Stamford (G-8456)
Trans-Tek Inc .... E 860 872-8351
  Ellington (G-2608)
United Technologies Corp .... B 954 485-6501
  Farmington (G-2973)
▼ United Technologies Corp .... B 860 728-7000
  Farmington (G-2972)
UTC Fire SEC Americas Corp Inc .. G .. 941 739-4200
  Farmington (G-2974)
UTC Fire SEC Americas Corp Inc .. C .. 203 426-1180
  Newtown (G-5796)
Victor F Leandri 860 345-8705
  Higganum (G-3781)
Visionpoint LLC .... G 860 436-9673
  Newington (G-5720)
▲ Voice Express Corp .... G 203 221-7799
  Fairfield (G-2865)

3671 Radio & T V Receiving Electron Tubes

Conklin-Sherman Company Incthe ... G .. 203 881-0190
  Beacon Falls (G-133)
Connecticut Coining Inc .... D 203 743-3861
  Bethel (G-273)
Stmicroelectronics Inc .... G 860 928-7700
  Woodstock (G-10688)
◆ Whelen Engineering Company Inc .. B .. 203 526-9504
  Chester (G-1485)

3672 Printed Circuit Boards

AB Electronics Inc .... E 203 740-2793
  Brookfield (G-1155)
▲ Accutron Inc .... C 860 683-8300
  Windsor (G-10354)
Advanced Product Solutions LLC .. G .. 203 745-4225
  Hamden (G-3412)
▲ Altek Electronics Inc .... C 860 482-7626
  Torrington (G-8892)
American Backplane Inc .... E 860 567-2360
  Morris (G-4785)
▲ Apct-Ct Inc .... C 203 284-1215
  Wallingford (G-9207)
Apct-Wallingford Inc .... E 203 269-3311
  Wallingford (G-9208)
◆ Carlton Industries Corp 203 288-5605
  Hamden (G-3424)
Custom Design Service Corp .... G 203 748-1105
  Danbury (G-1780)
Cyclone Microsystems Inc 203 786-5536
  Hamden (G-3437)
Eastern Company .... E 860 669-2233
  Clinton (G-1501)
Electronic Design Lab Inc 203 790-0500
  Bethel (G-296)
Electronic Spc Conn Inc .... E 203 288-1707
  Hamden (G-3442)
▲ Enhanced Mfg Solutions LLC ... F 203 488-5796
  Branford (G-589)
▲ Microboard Processing Inc .... C 203 881-4300
  Seymour (G-7357)
▲ Midstate Electronics Co .... F 203 265-9900
  Wallingford (G-9322)
Norfield Data Products Inc .... F 203 849-0292
  Norwalk (G-6280)
Northeast Circuit Tech LLC .... G 860 633-1967
  Glastonbury (G-3065)
▼ Power Trans Co Inc 203 881-0314
  Oxford (G-6688)
Precise Circuit Company Inc .... E 203 924-2512
  Shelton (G-7533)
Silicon Integration Inc 203 876-2844
  Milford (G-4645)
Te Connectivity Corporation .... C 860 684-8000
  Stafford Springs (G-8041)
Technical Manufacturing Corp ...... E 860 349-1735
  Durham (G-2158)
Tek Industries Inc .... E 860 870-0001
  Vernon (G-9154)

SIC SECTION 36 ELECTRONIC AND OTHER ELECTRICAL EQUIPMENT AND COMPONENTS, EXCEPT COMPUTER

Ttm Printed Circuit Group Inc...............C....... 860 684-8000
Stafford Springs *(G-8043)*
Ttm Technologies Inc...........................B....... 860 684-5881
Stafford Springs *(G-8044)*
Ttm Technologies Inc...........................D....... 860 684-8000
Stafford Springs *(G-8045)*

3674 Semiconductors

Advanced Semiconductor.....................G....... 860 349-1121
Durham *(G-2135)*
▲ Advanced Technology Mtls Inc.........G....... 203 794-1100
Danbury *(G-1732)*
▼ AG Semiconductor Services LLC....E....... 203 322-5300
Stamford *(G-8066)*
Alacrity Semiconductors Inc...............G....... 475 325-8435
Branford *(G-540)*
▲ Asct LLC..G....... 860 349-1121
Durham *(G-2139)*
Branbroks Dntl Stffing Sltions..............G....... 704 784-1056
Stamford *(G-8119)*
▲ Carten-Fujikin Incorporated.............G....... 203 699-2134
Cheshire *(G-1367)*
Convergent Solutions LLC....................G....... 203 293-3534
Westport *(G-10069)*
Delcom Products Inc............................G....... 914 934-5170
Danbury *(G-1792)*
◆ Doosan Fuel Cell America Inc..........C....... 860 727-2200
South Windsor *(G-7739)*
▲ Edal Industries Inc...........................E....... 203 467-2591
East Haven *(G-2423)*
Emosyn America Inc.............................E....... 203 794-1100
Danbury *(G-1809)*
◆ Entegris Prof Solutions Inc..............C....... 203 794-1100
Danbury *(G-1815)*
Fiber Mountain Inc................................E....... 203 806-4040
Cheshire *(G-1388)*
▲ Fidelux Lighting LLC........................F....... 860 436-5000
Hartford *(G-3589)*
Fuelcell Energy Inc...............................E....... 860 496-1111
Torrington *(G-8927)*
Gordon Products Incorporated............E....... 203 775-4501
Brookfield *(G-1194)*
Hi-Rel Group LLC.................................G....... 860 767-9031
Essex *(G-2718)*
Hi-Rel Products LLC............................E....... 860 767-9031
Essex *(G-2719)*
Hoffman Engineering LLC....................D....... 203 425-8900
Stamford *(G-8240)*
Liteideas LLC.......................................G....... 860 213-8311
Mansfield Center *(G-4114)*
LLC Dow Gage.....................................E....... 860 828-5327
Berlin *(G-197)*
Metis Microsystems LLC......................G....... 203 512-8453
Newtown *(G-5760)*
Micro-Probe Incorporated.....................G....... 203 267-6446
Southbury *(G-7869)*
Microphase Corporation.......................E....... 203 866-8000
Shelton *(G-7500)*
Newco Condenser Inc..........................G....... 475 882-4000
Shelton *(G-7510)*
▲ Opel Connecticut Solar LLC............E....... 203 612-2366
Shelton *(G-7519)*
Oracle America Inc..............................D....... 203 703-3000
Stamford *(G-8345)*
Paul Gaffney...G....... 203 221-1249
Weston *(G-10035)*
Pequot..G....... 800 620-1492
Bridgeport *(G-869)*
Photronics Inc......................................B....... 203 775-9000
Brookfield *(G-1211)*
Photronics Inc......................................C....... 203 740-5669
Brookfield *(G-1212)*
Photronics Texas Inc............................G....... 203 546-3039
Brookfield *(G-1213)*
Photronics Texas I LLC........................G....... 203 775-9000
Brookfield *(G-1214)*
▼ Radeco of Ct Inc...............................F....... 860 564-1220
Plainfield *(G-6751)*
Ray Green Corp....................................F....... 707 544-2662
Greenwich *(G-3222)*
Revolution Lighting...............................G....... 203 504-1111
Stamford *(G-8388)*
Revolution Lighting Tech Inc................C....... 203 504-1111
Stamford *(G-8389)*
Rmi Corporation...................................G....... 860 680-7368
Avon *(G-106)*
Saphlux Inc..G....... 475 221-8981
Branford *(G-647)*
Servers Storage Networking LLC..........G....... 203 433-0808
Norwalk *(G-6343)*
Silicon Catalyst LLC.............................G....... 203 240-0499
Ridgefield *(G-7173)*
Soluthin Inc..G....... 860 424-1228
Madison *(G-3958)*
Strain Measurement Devices Inc..........E....... 203 294-5800
Wallingford *(G-9377)*
T&K Technical Services LLC................G....... 860 235-5882
Quaker Hill *(G-7085)*
Trianja Technologies Inc......................G....... 203 775-9000
Brookfield *(G-1233)*
United Electric Controls Co..................D....... 203 877-2795
Milford *(G-4668)*
Viavi Solutions Inc................................G....... 860 243-6600
Bloomfield *(G-498)*
Vishay Americas Inc.............................B....... 203 452-5648
Shelton *(G-7580)*

3675 Electronic Capacitors

Electronic Film Capacitors....................E....... 203 755-5629
Waterbury *(G-9474)*
Glosystems Inc.....................................G....... 203 227-2464
Westport *(G-10091)*
Newco Condenser Inc...........................G....... 475 882-4000
Shelton *(G-7510)*

3676 Electronic Resistors

▼ Able Coil and Electronics Co............E....... 860 646-5686
Bolton *(G-504)*
▲ Prime Technology LLC.....................C....... 203 481-5721
North Branford *(G-5853)*
Vishay Americas Inc.............................B....... 203 452-5648
Shelton *(G-7580)*

3677 Electronic Coils & Transformers

3M Purification Inc................................C....... 860 684-8628
Stafford Springs *(G-8015)*
71 Pickett District Road LLC................G....... 860 350-5964
New Milford *(G-5502)*
▼ Able Coil and Electronics Co............E....... 860 646-5686
Bolton *(G-504)*
Aer Control Systems LLC.....................G....... 203 772-4700
North Haven *(G-5897)*
▲ Alpha Magnetics & Coils Inc............G....... 860 496-0122
Torrington *(G-8890)*
◆ Bicron Electronics Company............D....... 860 482-2524
Torrington *(G-8905)*
Cable Technology Inc...........................E....... 860 429-7889
Willington *(G-10246)*
▲ Classic Coil Company Inc................D....... 860 583-7600
Bristol *(G-1001)*
Coils Plus Inc.......................................E....... 203 879-0755
Wolcott *(G-10556)*
Future Manufacturing Inc.....................E....... 860 584-0685
Bristol *(G-1043)*
◆ Henkel Loctite Corporation..............E....... 860 571-5100
Rocky Hill *(G-7245)*
JB Filtration LLC..................................G....... 860 333-7962
Essex *(G-2721)*
Macneill Altrntive Cncepts LLC.............G....... 860 877-3968
Bristol *(G-1066)*
Microphase Corporation.......................E....... 203 866-8000
Shelton *(G-7500)*
Microtech Inc..D....... 203 272-3234
Cheshire *(G-1416)*
◆ Neeltran Inc......................................C....... 860 350-5964
New Milford *(G-5564)*
▼ New England Filter Company Inc.....G....... 203 531-0500
Greenwich *(G-3208)*
Omnicron Electronics...........................G....... 860 928-0377
Putnam *(G-7055)*
Pioneer Power Solutions Inc................G....... 203 782-4348
New Haven *(G-5366)*
Purfx Inc...G....... 860 399-4045
Westbrook *(G-10005)*
▲ Qtran Inc..E....... 203 367-8777
Milford *(G-4620)*
Quality Coils Incorporated...................C....... 860 584-0927
Bristol *(G-1099)*

3678 Electronic Connectors

Amphenol Corporation..........................C....... 203 743-9272
Danbury *(G-1739)*
▼ Amphenol Corporation.....................D....... 203 265-8900
Wallingford *(G-9204)*
Amphenol Corporation..........................D....... 203 287-2272
Hamden *(G-3415)*
Amphenol Funding Corp.......................G....... 203 265-8900
Wallingford *(G-9205)*
Amphenol International Ltd..................G....... 203 265-8900
Wallingford *(G-9206)*
◆ Bead Industries Inc..........................E....... 203 301-0270
Milford *(G-4466)*
Burndy LLC...D....... 203 792-1115
Bethel *(G-267)*
Component Concepts Inc.....................G....... 860 523-4066
West Hartford *(G-9792)*
Electro-Tech Inc....................................E....... 203 271-1976
Cheshire *(G-1384)*
▲ Fct Electronics LP............................D....... 860 482-2800
Torrington *(G-8923)*
Hubbell Incorporated............................D....... 475 882-4000
Shelton *(G-7468)*
Microtech Inc..D....... 203 272-3234
Cheshire *(G-1416)*
Molex LLC..G....... 860 482-2800
Torrington *(G-8951)*
▲ Phoenix Company of Chicago Inc....D....... 630 595-2300
Naugatuck *(G-4910)*
Radiall Usa Inc.....................................C....... 203 776-2813
New Haven *(G-5375)*
RC Connectors LLC.............................G....... 860 413-2196
Weatogue *(G-9759)*
Surface Mount Devices LLC.................G....... 203 322-8290
Stamford *(G-8452)*
▲ Times Microwave Systems Inc........B....... 203 949-8400
Wallingford *(G-9386)*
Winchester Interconnect Corp.............E....... 203 741-5400
Norwalk *(G-6395)*

3679 Electronic Components, NEC

71 Pickett District Road LLC................G....... 860 350-5964
New Milford *(G-5502)*
AB Electronics Inc................................E....... 203 740-2793
Brookfield *(G-1155)*
▼ Able Coil and Electronics Co............E....... 860 646-5686
Bolton *(G-504)*
◆ Alpha-Core Inc..................................E....... 203 954-0050
Shelton *(G-7392)*
Ambrosonics..G....... 860 752-9022
Windsor *(G-10361)*
Andrew Lambert....................................G....... 203 249-6310
Stamford *(G-8084)*
Arccos Golf LLC....................................E....... 844 692-7226
Stamford *(G-8091)*
Ashcrft-Ngano Kiki Hldings Inc............G....... 203 378-8281
Stratford *(G-8571)*
◆ Ashcroft Inc.......................................B....... 203 378-8281
Stratford *(G-8572)*
◆ Bead Industries Inc..........................E....... 203 301-0270
Milford *(G-4466)*
◆ Bicron Electronics Company............D....... 860 482-2524
Torrington *(G-8905)*
Bloomy Controls Inc.............................E....... 860 298-9925
Windsor *(G-10368)*
▲ Bridgeport Magnetics Group Inc......E....... 203 954-0050
Shelton *(G-7410)*
Cable Electronics Inc............................G....... 860 953-0300
Hartford *(G-3560)*
CBA Lighting and Controls Inc..............G....... 860 623-1924
Windsor Locks *(G-10477)*
Component Concepts Inc.....................G....... 860 523-4066
West Hartford *(G-9792)*
▼ Crystal Fairfield Tech LLC...............F....... 860 354-2111
New Milford *(G-5525)*
Data Signal Corporation.......................E....... 203 882-5393
Milford *(G-4505)*
Defense Cmmnications Solutions.........G....... 203 947-6283
Danbury *(G-1791)*
Doltronics LLC.....................................E....... 203 488-8766
Branford *(G-580)*
Dsaencore LLC.....................................D....... 203 740-4200
Brookfield *(G-1185)*
Eaton Aerospace LLC...........................E....... 203 796-6000
Bethel *(G-292)*
Ebl Products Inc...................................F....... 860 290-3737
East Hartford *(G-2319)*
▲ Edal Industries Inc...........................E....... 203 467-2591
East Haven *(G-2423)*
Electro-Tech Inc....................................E....... 203 271-1976
Cheshire *(G-1384)*
Electronic Connection Corp..................E....... 860 243-3356
Waterbury *(G-9473)*
Ens Microwave LLC..............................G....... 203 241-1888
Danbury *(G-1812)*
Ens Microwave LLC..............................G....... 203 794-7940
Danbury *(G-1813)*
Extreme Tech Pros LLC........................G....... 203 903-3050
Hamden *(G-3446)*

S I C

Employee Codes: A=Over 500 employees, B=251-500
C=101-250, D=51-100, E=20-50, F=10-19, G=1-9
2020 Harris Connecticut
Manufacturers Directory
447

36 ELECTRONIC AND OTHER ELECTRICAL EQUIPMENT AND COMPONENTS, EXCEPT COMPUTER

◆ General Electro Components ....G....... 860 659-3573
Glastonbury (G-3039)
Goodrich Corporation ....B....... 505 345-9031
Danbury (G-1834)
Hartford Electric Sup Co Inc ....F....... 860 760-4887
Rocky Hill (G-7240)
▲ Imperial Elctrnic Assembly Inc ....D....... 203 740-8425
Brookfield (G-1197)
Insys Micro Inc 917 566-5045
Norwalk (G-6209)
Ja Electronics LLC ....G....... 860 921-7549
Waterbury (G-9508)
Kbc Electronics Inc ....F....... 203 298-9654
Milford (G-4563)
▲ Linemaster Switch Corporation ......G....... 860 564-7713
Plainfield (G-6747)
▲ Lq Mechatronics Inc ....G....... 203 433-4430
Branford (G-619)
Lsr Electronic Assembly ....G....... 860 642-6883
Lebanon (G-3857)
Microtech Inc ....D....... 203 272-3234
Cheshire (G-1416)
Mil-Con Inc ....D....... 630 595-2366
Naugatuck (G-4901)
◆ Neeltran Inc ....C....... 860 350-5964
New Milford (G-5564)
▲ Northeast Electronics Corp ....G....... 203 878-3511
Milford (G-4595)
Osda Contract Services Inc ....E....... 203 878-2155
Milford (G-4599)
Osda Inc ....G....... 203 878-2155
Milford (G-4600)
Park Distributories Inc ....F....... 203 366-7200
Bridgeport (G-864)
Power Controls Inc ....F....... 203 284-0235
Wallingford (G-9336)
▼ Power Trans Co Inc ....G....... 203 881-0314
Oxford (G-6688)
Precision Electronic Assembly ....F....... 203 452-1839
Monroe (G-4747)
Preferred PDT & Mktg Group LLC ...G....... 203 567-0221
Shelton (G-7536)
▲ Prime Technology LLC ....C....... 203 481-5721
North Branford (G-5853)
Printed Prfmce Innovations LLC ......G....... 860 942-7338
Coventry (G-1669)
Protronix Inc ....F....... 203 269-5858
Wallingford (G-9344)
▲ Qtran Inc ....G....... 203 367-8777
Milford (G-4620)
Raman Power Technologies LLC ....G....... 203 695-4885
Wallingford (G-9348)
Rel-Tech Electronics Inc ....D....... 203 877-8770
Milford (G-4624)
Robert Warren LLC ....E....... 203 247-3347
Westport (G-10150)
◆ Royce Industries Inc ....F....... 203 674-2700
Southington (G-7969)
Sean Mecesery ....G....... 203 869-2277
Cos Cob (G-1641)
◆ Siemon Company ....A....... 860 945 4200
Watertown (G-9734)
Surface Mount Devices LLC ....G....... 203 322-8290
Stamford (G-8452)
▲ Sysdyne Technologies LLC ....F....... 203 327-3649
Stamford (G-8455)
T&K Technical Services LLC ....G....... 860 235-5882
Quaker Hill (G-7085)
Technical Manufacturing Corp ....E....... 860 349-1735
Durham (G-2158)
Tgs Cables ....G....... 203 668-6568
Meriden (G-4252)
▲ Times Microwave Systems Inc .....B....... 203 949-8400
Wallingford (G-9386)
Topex Inc ....F....... 203 748-5918
Danbury (G-1963)
▲ Tornik Inc ....C....... 860 282-6081
Rocky Hill (G-7269)
Transducer Products Inc ....G....... 860 824-1002
Canaan (G-1294)
▲ Transformer Technology Inc ....F....... 860 349-1061
Durham (G-2160)
Tri Source Inc ....F....... 203 924-7030
Shelton (G-7570)
▲ Tritex Corporation ....C....... 203 756-7441
Waterbury (G-9618)
USA Circuits LLC ....G....... 203 364-1378
Sandy Hook (G-7331)
Validus DC Systems LLC ....F....... 203 448-3600
Brookfield (G-1236)

Verotec Inc ....G....... 603 821-9921
North Haven (G-6011)
Winstanley Inc ....G....... 203 238-6614
Meriden (G-4269)

3691 Storage Batteries

▲ B S T Systems Inc ....D....... 860 564-4078
Plainfield (G-6742)
Duracell Company ....E....... 203 796-4000
Bethel (G-284)
Duracell Company ....A....... 203 796-4000
Bethel (G-285)
Duracell Manufacturing Inc ....G....... 203 796-4000
Bethel (G-286)
Duracell US Holding LLC ....F....... 203 796-4000
Bethel (G-288)
Duracell US Operations Inc ....G....... 203 796-4000
Bethel (G-289)
Evercel Inc ....D....... 781 741-8800
Stamford (G-8199)
◆ Hbl America Inc ....G....... 860 257-9800
Rocky Hill (G-7242)
Hbl America Inc ....G....... 860 257-9800
Rocky Hill (G-7243)
Interacter Inc ....G....... 203 949-0199
Wallingford (G-9289)
Johnson Controls Inc ....G....... 860 887-7185
Norwich (G-6419)
Johnson Controls Inc ....D....... 678 297-4040
Meriden (G-4179)
Nofet LLC ....F....... 203 848-9064
New Haven (G-5351)
Saft America Inc ....E....... 203 234-8333
North Haven (G-5990)

3692 Primary Batteries: Dry & Wet

▲ B S T Systems Inc ....D....... 860 564-4078
Plainfield (G-6742)
Duracell Manufacturing LLC ....G....... 203 796-4000
Bethel (G-287)
▲ Vitec Production Solutions Inc .....D....... 203 929-1100
Shelton (G-7581)

3694 Electrical Eqpt For Internal Combustion Engines

All Tech Auto/Truck Electric ....G....... 203 790-8990
Danbury (G-1736)
▲ Beede Electrical Instr Co Inc ....C....... 603 753-6362
North Stonington (G-6020)
E G Tech Solutions LLC ....G....... 203 200-7047
Old Greenwich (G-6471)
Merl Inc ....G....... 203 237-8811
Meriden (G-4199)
Simmonds Precision Pdts Inc ....E....... 203 797-5000
Danbury (G-1952)
West End Auto Parts ....G....... 203 453-9009
North Branford (G-5867)

3695 Recording Media

20/20 Software Inc ....G....... 203 316-5500
Stamford (G-8049)
American-Digital LLC ....G....... 203 838-0148
Bridgeport (G-695)
BEI Holdings Inc ....F....... 203 741-9300
Wallingford (G-9219)
Brain Parade Inc ....G....... 203 329-8136
Stamford (G-8117)
Cogz Systems LLC ....F....... 203 263-7882
Woodbury (G-10628)
Dataquest Korea Inc ....G....... 239 561-4862
Stamford (G-8181)
▲ Dictaphone Corporation ....C....... 203 381-7000
Stratford (G-8606)
Trod Nossel Prdctns & Rcrdng S ....G....... 203 269-4465
Wallingford (G-9391)
Video Outlet ....G....... 860 568-7473
East Hartford (G-2400)

3699 Electrical Machinery, Eqpt & Splys, NEC

A-1 Garage Door Co ....G....... 203 866-6620
Westport (G-10049)
Advanced Photonics Intl Inc ....G....... 203 259-0437
Fairfield (G-2745)
Aeroturn LLC ....G....... 203 262-8309
Oxford (G-6640)
Alent Inc ....D....... 203 575-5727
Waterbury (G-9425)
Alent USA Holding Inc ....B....... 203 575-5727
Waterbury (G-9426)

Arthur J Hurley Company ....G....... 860 257-5505
East Hartford (G-2293)
Ascentech LLC ....G....... 860 526-8903
Chester (G-1463)
◆ Assa Inc ....B....... 203 624-5225
New Haven (G-5235)
▲ Astrophonic Corp America ....G....... 203 853-9300
Norwalk (G-6079)
B & G Industries LLC ....G....... 203 571-8873
Wethersfield (G-10182)
Bam Electric LLC ....G....... 203 595-0008
Stamford (G-8107)
Bevin Bros Manufacturing Co ....E....... 860 267-4431
East Hampton (G-2257)
▲ Branson Ultrasonics Corp ....B....... 203 796-0400
Danbury (G-1759)
Brian Cheney ....G....... 203 734-4793
Seymour (G-7336)
Brookfield Industries Inc ....E....... 860 283-6211
Thomaston (G-8782)
C & E Electric ....G....... 203 546-7255
Brookfield (G-1167)
Cadence Ct Inc ....D....... 860 370-9780
Suffield (G-8716)
▲ Carey Manufacturing Co Inc ....E....... 860 829-1803
Cromwell (G-1694)
Carey Manufacturing Co Inc ....E....... 860 829-1803
Cromwell (G-1695)
Check It Darien LLC ....G....... 203 655-2036
Darien (G-2012)
Circuit Breaker Sales Ne Inc ....E....... 203 888-7500
Seymour (G-7340)
Clark Power Systems Inc ....G....... 203 775-8444
Brookfield (G-1172)
Coherent Inc ....C....... 860 243-9557
Bloomfield (G-404)
▲ Coherent-Deos LLC ....C....... 860 243-9557
Bloomfield (G-405)
Command Corporation ....F....... 800 851-6012
East Granby (G-2198)
Data Collection Dispersal Inc ....G....... 860 623-7364
Broad Brook (G-1146)
DC & D Inc ....G....... 860 623-2941
Broad Brook (G-1147)
Don Pomaski ....G....... 860 693-4469
Collinsville (G-1593)
Donald E Basil Inc ....G....... 203 574-0149
Waterbury (G-9466)
Donali Systems Integration Inc ....G....... 860 715-5432
Guilford (G-3346)
E-J Electric T & D LLC ....D....... 203 626-9625
Wallingford (G-9256)
Eagle Electric Service LLC ....F....... 860 868-9898
Bethlehem (G-369)
Eastern Electric Cnstr Co ....G....... 860 485-1100
Harwinton (G-3726)
Eastside Electric Inc ....F....... 860 485-0700
Harwinton (G-3727)
Electro Mech Specialists LLC ....G....... 860 887-2613
Bozrah (G-524)
Electrodes Incorporated ....E....... 203 878-7400
Milford (G-4528)
Epilog Lasers of New England ....G....... 203 405-1124
Woodbury (G-10635)
Eric Sapper ....G....... 203 239-6020
North Haven (G-5938)
Etron LLC ....G....... 860 673-0121
Burlington (G-1268)
Evse Llc ....G....... 860 745-2433
Enfield (G-2644)
Fuelcell Energy Inc ....E....... 860 496-1111
Torrington (G-8927)
Guest Co ....G....... 203 235-4421
Berlin (G-185)
Hamar Laser Instruments Inc ....E....... 203 730-4600
Danbury (G-1841)
Housatonic Mch & Prototype LLC ...G....... 203 922-2714
Shelton (G-7467)
Hubbell Incorporated ....D....... 475 882-4000
Shelton (G-7468)
Iemct ....G....... 203 683-4382
Milford (G-4552)
Insight Plus Technology LLC ....G....... 860 930-4763
Bristol (G-1051)
▲ Integral Technologies Inc ....G....... 860 741-2281
Enfield (G-2652)
Interior Plantworks Inc ....G....... 860 289-9499
South Windsor (G-7774)
Interior Plantworks Inc ....G....... 860 289-9499
South Windsor (G-7775)

Isupportws Inc....F....203 569-7600
Stamford (G-8260)
J Ro Grounding Systems Inc....G....860 747-2106
Plainville (G-6827)
▲ Jamieson Laser LLC....G....860 482-3375
Litchfield (G-3893)
Jared Manufacturing Co Inc....F....203 846-1732
Norwalk (G-6219)
Lighthouse Communications....G....203 445-9733
Monroe (G-4728)
▼ Magnatech LLC....D....860 653-2573
East Granby (G-2210)
Medical Laser Systems Inc....G....203 481-2395
Branford (G-625)
Miracle Instruments Co....F....860 642-7745
Lebanon (G-3858)
▲ Morse Watchmans Inc....E....203 264-1108
Oxford (G-6679)
Naugatuck Elec Indus Sup LLC....G....203 723-1082
Naugatuck (G-4905)
New Line USA Inc....G....860 498-0347
Coventry (G-1666)
Newco Condenser Inc....G....475 882-4000
Shelton (G-7510)
Power Up Electric....G....203 312-0601
Danbury (G-1910)
Presco Incorporated....F....203 397-8722
Woodbridge (G-10615)
Quality Scanning Solution....G....203 270-1833
Newtown (G-5771)
R K S Security LLC....G....860 749-4106
Enfield (G-2686)
Rexel....G....203 969-6601
Stamford (G-8391)
Richter Electric Inc....G....203 667-4644
Darien (G-2041)
▲ Rinco Ultrasonics USA Inc....G....203 744-4500
Danbury (G-1929)
Security Systems Inc....G....800 833-3211
Middletown (G-4409)
Sherric Group LLC....G....860 673-3924
Unionville (G-9128)
SOS Security Incorporated....G....860 563-2121
Rocky Hill (G-7265)
Stanley Black & Decker Inc....C....860 225-5111
New Britain (G-5063)
Stanley Black & Decker Inc....C....860 677-2861
Farmington (G-2960)
Stanley Black & Decker Inc....C....860 225-5111
New Britain (G-5061)
T J Russell Electric LLC....G....203 791-8950
Danbury (G-1958)
Technical Consulting....G....203 268-8890
Monroe (G-4757)
Thermal Fluidics....G....860 740-4880
Durham (G-2159)
Thomas Meade....G....203 209-7591
Shelton (G-7565)
▲ Total Register Inc....F....860 210-0465
New Milford (G-5600)
▲ Trine Access Technology Inc....F....203 730-1756
Bethel (G-356)
Ultra Clean Equipment Inc....G....860 669-1354
Clinton (G-1533)
United Technologies Corp....B....954 485-6501
Farmington (G-2973)
United Technologies Corp....B....860 610-7000
East Hartford (G-2395)
▼ United Technologies Corp....B....860 728-7000
Farmington (G-2972)
Varnum Enterprises LLC....F....203 743-4443
Bethel (G-362)
Westfair Electric Contractors....G....203 586-1760
Southbury (G-7885)
Williams Walter Ovrhd Door LLC....G....203 488-8620
Branford (G-674)
▲ World Cord Sets Inc....G....860 763-2100
Enfield (G-2708)

37 TRANSPORTATION EQUIPMENT

3711 Motor Vehicles & Car Bodies

911 Motorsports LLC....G....203 755-8405
Waterbury (G-9421)
Abair Manufacturing Company....F....203 757-0112
Waterbury (G-9422)
Airflow Truck Company....G....860 666-1977
Newington (G-5623)
American Vehicles Sales LLC....G....860 886-0327
Yantic (G-10696)
AMS Strategic Management Inc....G....845 500-5635
Stamford (G-8083)
Bloomfield Center Voluntee....G....860 242-1779
Bloomfield (G-397)
C B Fabrication....G....860 889-8030
Taftville (G-8740)
CD Racing Products....G....203 264-7822
Oxford (G-6650)
Chassis Dynamics Inc....G....203 262-6272
Oxford (G-6651)
Condon LLC....D....860 883-5416
Old Saybrook (G-6528)
Glastonbury Fire Training Ctr....G....860 633-3429
Glastonbury (G-3041)
M & J Bus Co....G....203 624-0836
North Haven (G-5960)
M & J Bus Co Inc....G....860 437-3721
Waterford (G-9660)
M & J Bus Inc....G....860 668-6526
Suffield (G-8724)
Markow Race Cars....G....860 610-0776
South Windsor (G-7790)
Meriden Fire Marshals Office....G....203 630-4010
Meriden (G-4196)
Mhq Inc....F....888 242-1118
Middletown (G-4376)
Motor Connections....G....860 583-3407
Bristol (G-1075)
Oshkosh Corporation....F....860 653-5548
East Granby (G-2221)
Puritan Lane LLC....G....203 602-5555
Stamford (G-8382)
Raceworks Inc....G....860 829-1312
Berlin (G-214)
Rock Hard Offroad LLC....G....860 919-3118
Wallingford (G-9357)
Rustic Rstrtions Race Cars LLC....G....203 929-4813
Shelton (G-7548)
Sharp Racing Enterprises....G....203 699-1191
Cheshire (G-1444)
Special Vhcl Developments Inc....G....203 272-7928
Cheshire (G-1451)
▲ Structured Solutions II LLC....G....203 972-5717
New Canaan (G-5148)
Triple D Transportation Inc....G....860 243-5057
Bloomfield (G-493)
Universal Body & Eqp Co LLC....F....860 274-7541
Oakville (G-6466)

3713 Truck & Bus Bodies

911 Motorsports LLC....G....203 755-8405
Waterbury (G-9421)
Alton Enterprises Inc....G....203 469-9719
East Haven (G-2408)
Boss Snowplows & Ice Control....G....860 886-7081
North Franklin (G-5871)
Composite Panel Tech Co....G....203 729-2255
Naugatuck (G-4869)
Composite Truck Body LLC....G....800 735-1668
Sherman (G-7593)
John Mezes & Sons Inc....G....203 255-6841
Bridgeport (G-809)
Lo Stocco Motors....G....203 797-9618
Danbury (G-1875)
Rj 15 Inc....F....860 585-0111
Bristol (G-1110)
Robert Kenneth Andrade LLC....G....203 937-8697
West Haven (G-9949)
Schwartz Body Company LLC....G....203 234-6046
North Haven (G-5991)
Sidney Dobson....G....203 255-5545
Westport (G-10158)
Sure Industries Inc....G....860 289-2522
East Hartford (G-2381)
Universal Body & Eqp Co LLC....F....860 274-7541
Oakville (G-6466)

3714 Motor Vehicle Parts & Access

AAM Welding + Fabrication LLC....G....203 479-4339
West Haven (G-9880)
▲ Airpot Corporation....E....800 848-7681
Norwalk (G-6064)
▲ Alinabal Inc....C....203 877-3241
Milford (G-4448)
▲ Alinabal Holdings Corporation....B....203 877-3241
Milford (G-4449)
All Tech Auto/Truck Electric....G....203 790-8990
Danbury (G-1736)
Anh Refractories....G....203 795-0597
Orange (G-6582)
◆ Armored Autogroup Inc....D....203 205-2900
Danbury (G-1746)
Armored Autogroup Sales Inc....C....203 205-2900
Danbury (G-1748)
Autopart International Inc....F....203 931-9189
West Haven (G-9885)
Beacon Group Inc....C....860 594-5200
Newington (G-5631)
Callaway Cars Inc....F....860 434-9002
Old Lyme (G-6495)
▲ Callaway Companies Inc....F....860 434-9002
Old Lyme (G-6496)
Cambridge Specialty Co Inc....D....860 828-3579
Berlin (G-168)
▲ Casco Products Corporation....F....203 922-3200
Bridgeport (G-731)
Cheshire Manufacturing Co Inc....G....203 272-3586
Cheshire (G-1369)
◆ Clarcor Eng MBL Solutions LLC....D....860 920-4200
East Hartford (G-2306)
Clayton Offroad Manufacturer....G....475 238-8251
East Haven (G-2417)
Competition Engineering Inc....C....203 453-5200
Guilford (G-3339)
Connecticut Axle Service LLC....G....860 872-3858
Ellington (G-2582)
Continental Machine Tl Co Inc....D....860 223-2896
New Britain (G-4965)
CT Drive-Shaft Service LLC....G....860 289-6459
East Hartford (G-2311)
Dearborn Deuce LLC....G....860 669-3232
Clinton (G-1500)
Defeo Manufacturaing....G....203 775-1950
Brookfield (G-1178)
Defeo Manufacturing....G....203 775-0254
Brookfield (G-1179)
Defeo Manufacturing Inc....G....203 775-0254
Brookfield (G-1180)
◆ Defeo Manufacturing Inc....E....203 775-0254
Brookfield (G-1181)
Dline LLC....G....860 984-2076
Old Saybrook (G-6531)
Dynamic Racing Transm LLC....G....203 315-0138
North Branford (G-5837)
ERA Replica Automobiles....G....860 229-7968
New Britain (G-4985)
Expressway Lube Centers....F....203 744-2511
Danbury (G-1820)
▼ Fram Group Operations LLC....E....203 830-7800
Danbury (G-1829)
Franks Performance....G....860 426-0439
Plantsville (G-6893)
G W P Inc....G....860 953-1153
Hartford (G-3595)
Genuine Parts Company....F....860 623-4479
Windsor Locks (G-10486)
◆ Global Steering Systems LLC....C....860 945-5400
Watertown (G-9710)
Hc Innovations Inc....G....203 925-9600
Shelton (G-7462)
International Automobile Entps....F....860 224-0253
New Britain (G-5001)
International Automobile Entps....F....860 224-0253
New Britain (G-5002)
Janus Motorsports LLC....G....860 857-6041
Niantic (G-5812)
Jk Motorsports....G....203 255-9120
Fairfield (G-2802)
Jobin Machine Inc....E....860 953-1631
West Hartford (G-9824)
Johnson Controls Inc....G....860 887-7185
Norwich (G-6419)
Johnson Controls Inc....D....678 297-4040
Meriden (G-4179)
JPsexton LLC....G....860 748-2048
Windsor (G-10401)
King of Covers Inc....G....860 379-2427
Winsted (G-10526)
Lac Landscaping LLC....F....203 807-1067
Milford (G-4566)
▲ Lee Company....A....860 399-6281
Westbrook (G-10000)
▲ Lewmar Inc....E....203 458-6200
Guilford (G-3367)
Lydall Inc....E....860 646-1233
Manchester (G-4050)
▲ Moroso Performance Pdts Inc....C....203 453-6571
Guilford (G-3376)
▲ Nathan Airchime Inc....G....860 423-4575
South Windham (G-7692)

Employee Codes: A=Over 500 employees, B=251-500
C=101-250, D=51-100, E=20-50, F=10-19, G=1-9
2020 Harris Connecticut
Manufacturers Directory
449

37 TRANSPORTATION EQUIPMENT

▲ Nickson Industries Inc .... E 860 747-1671
  Plainville (G-6847)
▲ Nucap US Inc .... E 203 879-1423
  Wolcott (G-10578)
Park Avenue Securities .... G 860 677-2600
  Farmington (G-2947)
Phillips Fuel Systems .... G 203 908-3323
  Bridgeport (G-871)
▲ Platt-Labonia of N Haven Inc .... D 203 239-5681
  North Haven (G-5977)
Pratt & Whitney Engine Svcs .... B 860 344-4000
  Middletown (G-4396)
Proliance International Inc .... G 860 688-7644
  Windsor (G-10427)
Russell Speeders Car Wash LLC .... G 203 925-0083
  Shelton (G-7547)
S Camerota & Sons Inc .... G 203 782-0360
  North Haven (G-5989)
Southington Transm Auto Repr .... G 860 329-0381
  Southington (G-7978)
Spectrum Brands Inc .... G 203 205-2900
  Danbury (G-1955)
▲ Stanadyne Intrmdate Hldngs LLC ...... C 860 525-0821
  Windsor (G-10440)
◆ Stanadyne LLC .... A 860 525-0821
  Windsor (G-10441)
Stanadyne Parent Holdings Inc .... G 860 525-0821
  Windsor (G-10442)
Swpci .... G 203 278-6400
  Shelton (G-7560)
Tek-Motive Inc .... D 203 468-2224
  Branford (G-662)
Thule Inc .... G 203 881-9600
  Milford (G-4664)
◆ Thule Inc .... C 203 881-9600
  Seymour (G-7368)
Thule Holding Inc .... F 203 881-9600
  Seymour (G-7370)
Tru Hitch Inc .... F 860 379-7772
  Pleasant Valley (G-6927)
Turbine Technologies Inc .... D 860 678-1642
  Farmington (G-2971)
Unitec .... G 203 778-0400
  Danbury (G-1969)
Vulcan Industries Inc .... C 860 683-2005
  Windsor (G-10460)
▲ Westfalia Inc .... E 860 314-2920
  Bristol (G-1137)

3715 Truck Trailers

All Star Welding & Dem LLC .... G 203 948-0528
  Danbury (G-1735)
Kensington Welding & Trlr Co .... G 860 828-3564
  Kensington (G-3811)
Mark Karotkin .... G 860 202-7821
  Hartford (G-3634)
Miller Professional Trans Svc .... G 860 871-6818
  Vernon (G-9144)
Webbers Truck Service Inc .... F 860 623-4554
  East Windsor (G-2532)

3716 Motor Homes

GM Home Solutions .... G 305 608-9721
  Waterbury (G-9490)

3721 Aircraft

Aircastle Advisor LLC .... D 203 504-1020
  Stamford (G-8069)
Amco Precision Tools Inc .... E 860 828-5640
  Berlin (G-155)
Antares Aerospace Inds LLC .... G 203 903-7531
  East Haven (G-2411)
Aquiline Drones LLC .... F 860 361-7958
  Hartford (G-3553)
Avolon Aerospace New York Inc .... G 203 663-5490
  Stamford (G-8100)
B & F Design Incorporated .... E 860 357-4317
  New Britain (G-4948)
Bae Systems Applied Intel Inc .... G 203 323-0066
  Stamford (G-8105)
Baghai Shahin .... G 203 268-6287
  Trumbull (G-9002)
Belair Aviation .... G 203 380-8993
  Stratford (G-8583)
Berkshire Balloons LLC .... G 203 250-8441
  Plantsville (G-6886)
CJ Aviation Services LLC .... G 860 741-6499
  Enfield (G-2624)
Connecticut Drone Services LLC .... G 203 966-7016
  New Canaan (G-5096)

Corporate Aircraft Svcs LLC .... G 203 730-2024
  Danbury (G-1775)
Drone Imaging LLC .... G 203 256-1151
  Fairfield (G-2777)
Dube Air LLC .... G 860 355-1705
  Sherman (G-7594)
Edac Nd Inc .... D 860 633-9474
  Glastonbury (G-3031)
Embraer Executive Jet Svcs LLC .... G 860 804-4600
  Windsor Locks (G-10483)
Four Six Juliet LLC .... G 203 227-1557
  Westport (G-10085)
Gateway Helicopter Service .... G 203 531-4395
  Greenwich (G-3166)
Gulfstream Aerospace Corp .... G 860 210-1469
  New Milford (G-5542)
Gulfstream Aerospace Corp .... G 912 965-3000
  East Granby (G-2207)
Hartford Jet Center LLC .... G 860 548-9334
  Hartford (G-3612)
Infocus Droneworx LLC .... G 860 499-0789
  Wethersfield (G-10198)
◆ Kaman Aerospace Corporation .... A 860 242-4461
  Bloomfield (G-430)
Kaman Aerospace Corporation .... E 860 242-4461
  Bloomfield (G-431)
Kaman Aerospace Corporation .... D 860 242-4461
  Bloomfield (G-432)
◆ Kaman Aerospace Group Inc .... F 860 243-7100
  Bloomfield (G-433)
Kaman Corporation .... D 860 243-7100
  Bloomfield (G-434)
KII Aerospace LLC .... G 860 806-8858
  Middlebury (G-4282)
MB Aerospace .... G 860 653-0569
  East Granby (G-2212)
Mooney Time Inc .... G 203 263-0167
  Woodbury (G-10644)
New England Airfoil Pdts Inc .... E 860 677-1376
  Farmington (G-2936)
Northeast Drone Services LLC .... G 203 220-6478
  Trumbull (G-9051)
Northeast Mfg Co LLC .... G 860 763-4000
  Enfield (G-2670)
P & S Manufacturing LLC .... G 203 685-2256
  Bridgeport (G-858)
▲ Riverside Aviation .... G 203 637-4231
  Old Greenwich (G-6483)
Santoto LLC .... G 203 984-2540
  Danbury (G-1934)
Shoreline Drone Solutions .... G 347 239-5636
  Guilford (G-3390)
Sikorsky Aircraft Corporation .... B 203 384-7532
  Bridgeport (G-907)
Sikorsky Aircraft Corporation .... A 203 386-7861
  Shelton (G-7556)
Sikorsky Aircraft Corporation .... F 516 228-2000
  North Haven (G-5993)
Sikorsky Aircraft Corporation .... C 203 386-4000
  Bridgeport (G-908)
◆ Sikorsky Aircraft Corporation .... A 203 386-4000
  Stratford (G-8678)
Sikorsky Aircraft Corporation .... E 610 644-4430
  Farmington (G-2957)
▼ Sikorsky Export Corporation .... B 203 386-4000
  Stratford (G-8679)
▼ Sikorsky International Product .... G 203 375-0095
  Stratford (G-8680)
Stonegate Capital Group .... G 860 899-1181
  Hartford (G-3694)
Straton Industries Inc .... D 203 375-4488
  Stratford (G-8687)
Swift Kathryn .... G 203 754-4150
  Moodus (G-4776)
Tag Manufacturing LLC .... G 860 479-5120
  Plainville (G-6868)
Target Marketing Assoc Inc .... G 860 571-7294
  Rocky Hill (G-7268)
Textron Aviation Inc .... A 203 262-9366
  Oxford (G-6697)
Tranquil Perspectives LLC .... G 860 919-9762
  North Haven (G-6000)
▼ United Technologies Corp .... B 860 728-7000
  Farmington (G-2972)
Vistar Foundation Inc .... G 203 968-1995
  Stamford (G-8486)

3724 Aircraft Engines & Engine Parts

▼ A-1 Machining Co .... D 860 223-6420
  New Britain (G-4931)

AAR Corp .... G 619 545-6129
  Windsor (G-10352)
Absolute Precision Co .... G 203 767-9066
  Southbury (G-7840)
Accupaulo Holding Corporation .... E 860 666-5621
  Newington (G-5617)
Acmt Inc .... D 860 645-0592
  Manchester (G-3977)
Aero Component Services LLC .... G 860 291-0417
  East Hartford (G-2288)
AGC Acquisition LLC .... C 203 639-7125
  Meriden (G-4142)
Alloy Specialties Incorporated .... E 860 646-4587
  Manchester (G-3981)
American Design & Mfg Inc .... E 860 282-2719
  South Windsor (G-7705)
American Unmanned Systems LLC ..... G 203 406-7611
  Stamford (G-8079)
Astralis Rocketry Corp .... G 203 254-0427
  Westport (G-10058)
ATI Ladish Machining Inc .... D 860 688-3688
  East Hartford (G-2295)
ATI Ladish Machining Inc .... D 860 688-3688
  South Windsor (G-7711)
ATI Ladish Machining Inc .... D 860 688-3688
  East Hartford (G-2296)
▲ Barnes Group Inc .... B 860 583-7070
  Bristol (G-973)
Barnes Group Inc .... A 860 298-7740
  Windsor (G-10367)
Barnes Group Inc .... G 860 653-5531
  East Granby (G-2191)
Barnes Group Inc .... A 513 759-3503
  Bristol (G-975)
Beacon Group Inc .... C 860 594-5200
  Newington (G-5631)
Birken Manufacturing Company .... D 860 242-2211
  Bloomfield (G-395)
Birotech Inc .... G 203 968-5080
  Stamford (G-8112)
Bolducs Machine Works Inc .... G 860 455-1232
  North Windham (G-6034)
Cambridge Specialty Co Inc .... D 860 828-3579
  Berlin (G-168)
Capstone Manufacturing Inc .... G 413 636-6170
  South Windsor (G-7723)
Carismo Productions .... G 203 334-8469
  Bridgeport (G-730)
CBS Manufacturing Company .... E 860 653-8100
  East Granby (G-2196)
Chromalloy Component Svcs Inc ...... C 860 688-7798
  Windsor (G-10373)
Chromalloy Gas Turbine LLC .... D 860 688-7798
  Windsor (G-10374)
▲ Columbia Manufacturing Inc .... D 860 228-2259
  Columbia (G-1604)
D & M Tool Company Inc .... G 860 236-6037
  West Hartford (G-9797)
Deburring House Inc .... E 860 828-0889
  East Berlin (G-2165)
Demusz Mfg Co Inc .... E 860 528-9845
  East Hartford (G-2313)
Drt Aerospace LLC .... E 203 781-8020
  Meriden (G-4167)
Dynamic Controls Hs Inc .... G 860 654-6000
  Windsor Locks (G-10482)
Edac Technologies LLC .... F 860 789-2511
  East Windsor (G-2490)
Edac Technologies LLC .... C 203 806-2090
  Cheshire (G-1383)
Electro-Methods Inc .... C 860 289-8661
  South Windsor (G-7747)
Electro-Methods Inc .... D 860 289-8661
  South Windsor (G-7748)
Engine Alliance LLC .... B 860 565-2239
  Glastonbury (G-3035)
Ethosenergy Component Repr LLC .... E 203 949-8144
  Wallingford (G-9258)
▼ Evans Cooling Systems Inc .... G 860 668-1114
  Suffield (G-8718)
First Aviation Services Inc .... G 203 291-3300
  Westport (G-10081)
First Equity Group Inc .... F 203 291-7700
  Westport (G-10082)
▼ Fredericks Jf Aero LLC .... D 860 677-2646
  Farmington (G-2909)
Gamma Ventures Inc .... G 860 653-2613
  Granby (G-3107)
Gay Tool & Machine .... G 860 668-5054
  Suffield (G-8720)

SIC SECTION
37 TRANSPORTATION EQUIPMENT

GKN Aerospace Newington LLC ....G....... 800 667-8502
Newington (G-5655)
▲ GKN Aerospace Newington LLC ......C....... 860 667-8502
Newington (G-5656)
GKN Arspace Svcs Strctures LLC.........C....... 860 613-0236
Cromwell (G-1702)
Global Trbine Cmpnent Tech LLC ....E....... 860 528-4722
South Windsor (G-7760)
Hartford Aviation Group Inc..................G....... 860 549-0096
Hartford (G-3606)
Heritage Custom Products LLC............G....... 860 292-1979
East Windsor (G-2495)
Honeywell International Inc ....D....... 203 484-7161
Northford (G-6045)
Honeywell International Inc ....B....... 203 484-7161
Northford (G-6046)
Honeywell International Inc ....B....... 203 484-6202
Northford (G-6047)
Honeywell International Inc ....A....... 203 484-7161
North Branford (G-5843)
Honeywell International Inc ....E....... 203 484-7161
Northford (G-6048)
Horst Engrg De Mexico LLC ....E....... 860 289-8209
East Hartford (G-2334)
Hsb Aircraft Components LLC ....F....... 860 505-7349
New Britain (G-4997)
▼ I & J Machine Tool Company ....F....... 203 877-5376
Milford (G-4550)
Iae International Aero Engs AG ....C....... 860 565-1773
East Hartford (G-2336)
International Aero Engines LLC ....E....... 860 565-5515
East Hartford (G-2340)
Intlaero Beta Corp.................................G....... 317 821-2000
East Hartford (G-2341)
Kaman Aerospace Corporation ....D....... 860 242-4461
Bloomfield (G-432)
◆ Kaman Aerospace Group Inc ....F....... 860 243-7100
Bloomfield (G-433)
Kamatics Corporation ....E....... 860 243-9704
Bloomfield (G-435)
Kenzinc LLC ....G....... 203 307-5369
Shelton (G-7484)
Lighthouse International LLC ....E....... 860 528-4722
South Windsor (G-7788)
Morning Star Tool LLC ....G....... 203 878-6026
Milford (G-4585)
Msj Investments Inc...............................F....... 860 684-9956
Stafford Springs (G-8033)
N & B Manufacturing Co Inc ....G....... 860 667-3204
Newington (G-5682)
New England Airfoil Pdts Inc ....E....... 860 677-1376
Farmington (G-2936)
▲ Numet Machining Techniques Inc ....E....... 203 375-4995
Orange (G-6618)
Palmer Manufacturing Co LLC ....G....... 860 828-0344
East Berlin (G-2172)
Pdq Inc...E....... 860 529-9051
Rocky Hill (G-7262)
Pinnacle Aerospace Mfg LLC ....F....... 203 258-3398
Greenwich (G-3216)
Point Machine Company ....E....... 860 828-6901
Berlin (G-207)
Polar Corp...G....... 860 225-6000
New Britain (G-5034)
Polar Corporation ....E....... 860 223-7891
New Britain (G-5035)
Pratt & Whitney Company Inc..............C....... 860 565-4321
East Hartford (G-2357)
Pratt & Whitney Eng Svcs Inc...............C....... 860 610-2631
East Hartford (G-2358)
Pratt & Whitney Engine Svcs................B....... 203 934-2806
North Haven (G-5978)
Pratt & Whitney Engine Svcs................E....... 860 565-4321
East Hartford (G-2359)
Pratt & Whitney Engine Svcs................B....... 860 344-4000
Middletown (G-4396)
Pratt & Whitney Services Inc ....E....... 860 565-5489
East Hartford (G-2360)
Precision Speed Mfg LLC......................E....... 860 635-8811
Middletown (G-4397)
Rimark Manufacturing LLC...................G....... 860 924-6222
East Granby (G-2227)
Saar Corporation....................................F....... 860 674-9440
Farmington (G-2955)
Scap Motors Inc.....................................C....... 203 384-0005
Fairfield (G-2843)
Schaefer Rolls Inc..................................G....... 203 910-0224
Wolcott (G-10585)
Sikorsky Aircraft Corporation...............A....... 203 386-4000
Stratford (G-8677)
Simmonds Precision Pdts Inc ....E....... 203 797-5000
Danbury (G-1952)
Soto Holdings Inc ....E....... 203 781-8020
New Haven (G-5400)
Spartan Aerospace LLC ....D....... 860 533-7500
Manchester (G-4090)
Specialty Tool Company USA LLC........F....... 203 874-2009
Milford (G-4650)
Tdy Industries LLC ....G....... 860 259-6346
New Britain (G-5072)
Time Aviation LLC..................................G....... 203 496-5716
Greenwich (G-3244)
Timken Arospc Drv Systems LLC ....C....... 860 649-0000
Manchester (G-4102)
Triumph Eng Ctrl Systems LLC ....A....... 860 236-0651
West Hartford (G-9869)
Turbine Kinetics Inc...............................F....... 860 633-8520
Glastonbury (G-3091)
Turbine Technologies Inc......................D....... 860 678-1642
Farmington (G-2971)
United Tech Advnced Prjcts Inc ....G....... 860 610-7159
East Hartford (G-2390)
▼ United Technologies Corp.................B....... 860 728-7000
Farmington (G-2972)
United Technologies Corp ....G....... 860 565-4321
East Hartford (G-2391)
United Technologies Corp ....B....... 860 727-2200
South Windsor (G-7836)
United Technologies Corp ....D....... 860 565-4321
East Hartford (G-2393)
United Technologies Corp ....G....... 860 565-4321
East Hartford (G-2394)
United Tool and Die Company..............C....... 860 246-6531
West Hartford (G-9871)
Wentworth Manufacturing LLC.............G....... 860 205-6437
New Britain (G-5082)
Westbrook Products LLC.......................G....... 860 205-6437
New Britain (G-5083)
Whitney Pratt..G....... 860 565-6431
Willington (G-10261)
Winslow Automatics Inc.........................D....... 860 225-6321
New Britain (G-5084)

3728 Aircraft Parts & Eqpt, NEC

A G C Incorporated ....C....... 203 235-3361
Meriden (G-4138)
▼ A-1 Machining Co...............................D....... 860 223-6420
New Britain (G-4931)
Acmt Inc..D....... 860 645-0592
Manchester (G-3977)
Advanced Def Slutions Tech LLC..........G....... 860 243-1122
Bloomfield (G-380)
◆ Aero Gear Incorporated ....C....... 860 688-0888
Windsor (G-10355)
Aero Tube Technologies LLC ....E....... 860 289-2520
South Windsor (G-7701)
Aerocision LLC ....D....... 860 526-9700
Chester (G-1462)
Aerocomposites Inc................................G....... 860 829-6809
Kensington (G-3804)
Aerospace Components Mfrs Inc..........G....... 860 513-3205
Rocky Hill (G-7220)
Air-Lock Incorporated ....E....... 203 878-4691
Milford (G-4444)
Airborne Industries Inc...........................F....... 203 315-0200
Branford (G-538)
Alexis Aerospace Inds LLC....................G....... 860 516-4602
Canton (G-1303)
▲ Alinabal Inc...C....... 203 877-3241
Milford (G-4448)
▲ All Power Manufacturing Co ....C....... 562 802-2640
Oxford (G-6641)
Anderson Manufacturing Company......G....... 203 263-2318
Woodbury (G-10624)
Arrow Diversified Tooling Inc ....E....... 860 872-9072
Ellington (G-2576)
Arthur Rodgers ....G....... 860 967-4598
Ledyard (G-3867)
Athens Industries Inc ....G....... 860 621-8957
Plantsville (G-6885)
Avalon Advanced Tech Repr Inc ....E....... 860 254-5442
East Windsor (G-2483)
Aviation Pro Pages LLC ....G....... 860 910-9336
Mystic (G-4800)
B&N Aerospace Inc................................E....... 860 665-0134
Newington (G-5630)
B/E Aerospace Inc ....G....... 203 380-5000
Stratford (G-8576)
▲ Beacon Industries Inc.........................C....... 860 594-5200
Newington (G-5632)
Birken Manufacturing Company............D....... 860 242-2211
Bloomfield (G-395)
▼ Brandstrom Instruments Inc..............E....... 203 544-9341
Ridgefield (G-7126)
Bryka Skystocks LLC ....G....... 845 507-8200
Newington (G-5635)
Budney Aerospace Inc ....D....... 860 828-0585
Berlin (G-166)
C & W Manufacturing Co Inc..................E....... 860 633-4631
Glastonbury (G-3017)
C V Tool Company Inc ....E....... 978 353-7901
Southington (G-7901)
Cambridge Specialty Co Inc ....D....... 860 828-3579
Berlin (G-168)
CBS Manufacturing Company ....E....... 860 653-8100
East Granby (G-2196)
Connecticut Advanced Products ....G....... 860 659-2260
Glastonbury (G-3023)
▲ Connecticut Tool & Mfg Co LLC ....D....... 860 846-0800
Plainville (G-6792)
Continental Machine Tl Co Inc...............D....... 860 223-2896
New Britain (G-4965)
▲ Crane Co...D....... 203 363-7300
Stamford (G-8166)
Dell Acquisition LLC...............................E....... 860 677-8545
Plainville (G-6798)
Delta-Ray Industries Inc.........................F....... 203 367-9903
Bridgeport (G-747)
◆ Doncasters Inc....................................D....... 860 449-1603
Groton (G-3283)
Drt Aerospace LLC ....F....... 860 379-0783
Winsted (G-10515)
Dynamic Flight Systems ....G....... 203 449-7211
Monroe (G-4713)
Edac Nd Inc ....D....... 860 633-9474
Glastonbury (G-3031)
Edac Technologies LLC ....C....... 860 667-2134
Newington (G-5649)
Electro-Methods Inc...............................C....... 860 289-8661
South Windsor (G-7747)
Enjet Aero New Britain LLC ....C....... 860 356-0330
New Britain (G-4984)
Evoaero Inc...D....... 860 289-2520
South Windsor (G-7753)
Faille Precision Machining.....................G....... 860 822-1964
Baltic (G-119)
First Aviation Services Inc ....G....... 203 291-3300
Westport (G-10081)
Flanagan Brothers Inc ....G....... 860 633-3558
Glastonbury (G-3036)
Flight Enhancements Corp ....G....... 912 257-0440
Oxford (G-6658)
Flight Support Inc ....E....... 203 562-1415
North Haven (G-5942)
Forrest Machine Inc ....D....... 860 563-1796
Berlin (G-180)
▲ GKN Aerospace Newington LLC ......C....... 860 667-8502
Newington (G-5656)
Global Trbine Cmpnent Tech LLC ....E....... 860 528-4722
South Windsor (G-7760)
Glyne Manufacturing Co Inc ....F....... 203 375-4495
Stratford (G-8618)
Goodrich Corporation ....B....... 203 797-5000
Danbury (G-1835)
H & B Tool & Engineering Co.................E....... 860 528-9341
South Windsor (G-7766)
Hamilton Standard Space ....E....... 860 654-6000
Windsor Locks (G-10490)
◆ Hamilton Sundstrand Corp.................A....... 860 654-6000
Windsor Locks (G-10491)
◆ Helicopter Support Inc........................B....... 203 416-4000
Trumbull (G-9033)
Hexcel Corporation.................................E....... 203 969-0666
Stamford (G-8233)
Hexcel Pottsville Corporation................G....... 203 969-0666
Stamford (G-8235)
▼ I & J Machine Tool Company ....F....... 203 877-5376
Milford (G-4550)
Isr (ntllgnce Srvllance Reconn ....G....... 203 797-5000
Danbury (G-1853)
Ithaco Space Systems Inc.....................D....... 607 272-7640
Danbury (G-1854)
▲ Jarvis Airfoil Inc ....D....... 860 342-5000
Portland (G-6961)
Jmk Tool Co..G....... 203 937-1229
West Haven (G-9919)
Jobin Machine Inc..................................E....... 860 953-1631
West Hartford (G-9824)
Jonal Labs Logistics LLC ....G....... 203 634-4444
Meriden (G-4181)

SIC

Employee Codes: A=Over 500 employees, B=251-500
C=101-250, D=51-100, E=20-50, F=10-19, G=1-9
2020 Harris Connecticut
Manufacturers Directory
451

Kaman Aerospace Corporation ....D....... 860 242-4461
Bloomfield *(G-432)*
◆ **Kaman Aerospace Corporation** ....A....... 860 242-4461
Bloomfield *(G-430)*
Kaman Aerospace Corporation ....E....... 860 242-4461
Bloomfield *(G-431)*
◆ **Kaman Aerospace Group Inc** ....F....... 860 243-7100
Bloomfield *(G-433)*
Kaman Corporation ....D....... 860 243-7100
Bloomfield *(G-434)*
Kamatics Corporation ....E....... 860 243-9704
Bloomfield *(G-435)*
Kirkhill Aircraft Parts Co ....E....... 860 581-5701
Centerbrook *(G-1330)*
L M Gill Welding and Mfr LLC ....E....... 860 647-9931
Manchester *(G-4047)*
Leading Edge Concepts Inc ....G....... 203 797-1200
Bethel *(G-321)*
▲ **Lee Company** ....A....... 860 399-6281
Westbrook *(G-10000)*
LM Gill Welding & Mfg LLC ....E....... 860 647-9931
Manchester *(G-4049)*
M & S Machine Tool Company ....G....... 203 933-8920
West Haven *(G-9927)*
McMellon Bros Incorporated ....E....... 203 375-5685
Stratford *(G-8648)*
Metallon Inc ....E....... 860 283-8265
Thomaston *(G-8797)*
Morning Star Tool LLC ....G....... 203 878-6026
Milford *(G-4585)*
Mtm Corporation ....G....... 860 742-9600
Andover *(G-15)*
▲ **Mtu Aero Engine Design Inc** ....G....... 860 667-2134
Newington *(G-5680)*
▲ **Naiad Dynamics Us Inc** ....E....... 203 929-6355
Shelton *(G-7506)*
Nalbor Mfg ....G....... 860 828-7676
Berlin *(G-202)*
Nelson Tool & Machine Co Inc ....G....... 860 589-8004
Bristol *(G-1078)*
Overhaul Support Services LLC ....G....... 860 653-1980
East Granby *(G-2223)*
Overhaul Support Services LLC ....E....... 860 264-2101
East Granby *(G-2224)*
▲ **Paradigm Manchester Inc** ....B....... 860 646-4048
Manchester *(G-4068)*
Paradigm Manchester Inc ....D....... 860 646-4048
Manchester *(G-4066)*
Paradigm Manchester Inc ....C....... 860 646-4048
Manchester *(G-4067)*
Paragon Tool Company Inc ....G....... 860 647-9935
Manchester *(G-4072)*
Pas Technologies Inc ....E....... 860 649-2727
Manchester *(G-4074)*
▲ **Pcx Aerostructures LLC** ....C....... 860 666-2471
Newington *(G-5695)*
Perry Technology Corporation ....D....... 860 738-2525
New Hartford *(G-5206)*
Polamer Precision Inc ....C....... 860 259-6200
New Britain *(G-5033)*
Polar Corporation ....E....... 860 223-7891
New Britain *(G-5035)*
Power Turbine Components LLC ....G....... 860 291-8885
South Windsor *(G-7809)*
Pratt & Whitney Engine Svcs ....B....... 860 344-4000
Middletown *(G-4396)*
Precision Aerospace Inc ....E....... 203 888-3022
Seymour *(G-7363)*
Precision Metals and Plastics ....G....... 860 238-4320
Winsted *(G-10532)*
Precision Speed Mfg LLC ....E....... 860 635-8811
Middletown *(G-4397)*
Ramar-Hall Inc ....E....... 860 349-1081
Middlefield *(G-4306)*
Richard Manufacturing Co Inc ....E....... 203 874-3617
Milford *(G-4627)*
Rotair Aerospace Corporation ....E....... 203 576-6545
Bridgeport *(G-892)*
Rotating Composite Tech LLC ....G....... 860 829-6809
Kensington *(G-3818)*
Rti Technologies LLC ....G....... 860 306-4772
Columbia *(G-1612)*
Saf Industries LLC ....E....... 203 729-4900
Meriden *(G-4238)*
Saf Industries LLC ....E....... 203 729-4900
Meriden *(G-4237)*
Saklax Manufacturing Company ....G....... 860 242-2538
Bloomfield *(G-483)*
Satellite Tool & Mch Co Inc ....E....... 860 290-8558
South Windsor *(G-7820)*
Senior Operations LLC ....D....... 860 741-2546
Enfield *(G-2691)*
Shari Goodstein Rossi ....G....... 914 485-1600
Danbury *(G-1944)*
Simmonds Precision Pdts Inc ....E....... 203 797-5000
Danbury *(G-1952)*
Sky Mfg Company ....G....... 203 439-7016
Cheshire *(G-1447)*
Solar Nebula LLC ....G....... 516 362-8048
North Granby *(G-5881)*
Straton Industries Inc ....D....... 203 375-4488
Stratford *(G-8687)*
Susan Martovich ....G....... 203 881-1848
Oxford *(G-6696)*
Tachwa Enterprises Inc ....G....... 203 691-5772
Hamden *(G-3517)*
Tachwa Enterprises Inc ....G....... 203 367-9903
Bridgeport *(G-919)*
Thompson Aerospace LLC ....F....... 860 516-0472
Bristol *(G-1128)*
Timken Arospc Drv Systems LLC ....C....... 860 649-0000
Manchester *(G-4102)*
◆ **TLD America Corporation** ....E....... 860 602-3400
Windsor *(G-10453)*
▲ **Triumph Actuation Systems - Co** ......D....... 860 687-5412
Windsor *(G-10455)*
Triumph Eng Ctrl Systems LLC ....A....... 860 236-0651
West Hartford *(G-9869)*
Triumph Group Inc ....G....... 860 726-9378
Bloomfield *(G-494)*
Unison Engine Components ....G....... 860 647-5586
Manchester *(G-4104)*
United Aero Group LLC ....G....... 203 283-9524
Shelton *(G-7577)*
United Avionics Inc ....E....... 203 723-1404
Naugatuck *(G-4925)*
United Technologies Corp ....D....... 860 557-3333
East Hartford *(G-2396)*
Valley Tool and Mfg LLC ....D....... 203 799-8800
Orange *(G-6632)*
W and G Machine Company Inc ....E....... 203 288-8772
Hamden *(G-3526)*
W&R Manufacturing Inc ....G....... 203 877-5955
Milford *(G-4677)*
Whitakers ....G....... 860 228-3762
Hebron *(G-3758)*
▲ **Whitcraft LLC** ....C....... 860 974-0786
Eastford *(G-2544)*
Whitcraft Scrborough/Tempe LLC ....C....... 860 974-0786
Eastford *(G-2545)*

3731 Shipbuilding & Repairing

Brewer Yacht Yards Inc ....G....... 860 399-5128
Old Saybrook *(G-6526)*
Bridgeport Boatwork Inc ....G....... 860 536-9651
Bridgeport *(G-719)*
Bridgeport Boatwork Inc ....G....... 860 536-9651
Groton *(G-3274)*
Connecticut Diesel and Marine ....G....... 203 481-1010
Milford *(G-4495)*
Dorado Tankers Pool Inc ....E....... 203 662-2600
Norwalk *(G-6147)*
Electric Boat Corporation ....D....... 860 433-0503
Groton *(G-3285)*
Electric Boat Corporation ....D....... 860 433-3000
Groton *(G-3286)*
◆ **Electric Boat Corporation** ....A....... 860 433-3000
Groton *(G-3287)*
Exocetus Atonomous Systems LLC ....G....... 860 512-7260
Wallingford *(G-9262)*
Exocetus Autonomous Systems ....G....... 860 512-7260
Wallingford *(G-9263)*
Globenix Inc ....G....... 203 740-7070
Norwalk *(G-6181)*
Igs-Med LLC ....G....... 203 698-0396
Old Greenwich *(G-6476)*
LM Gill Welding & Mfg LLC ....E....... 860 647-9931
Manchester *(G-4049)*
M Friedman Company ....G....... 860 447-9935
Mystic *(G-4828)*
Magnuss Services Inc ....G....... 347 703-0750
Westport *(G-10116)*
Mystic River Mar Surveyors LLC ....G....... 860 857-1798
Mystic *(G-4836)*
▲ **Naiad Dynamics Us Inc** ....E....... 203 929-6355
Shelton *(G-7506)*
Naiad Maritime Group Inc ....E....... 203 944-1932
Shelton *(G-7507)*
▲ **Navtec Rigging Solutions Inc** ....E....... 203 458-3163
Clinton *(G-1515)*
NGS Power LLC ....G....... 860 873-0100
East Haddam *(G-2246)*
Ocean Rigging LLC ....G....... 800 624-2101
Bridgeport *(G-855)*
Thames Shipyard & Repair Co ....D....... 860 442-5349
New London *(G-5493)*
Timbercraft LLC ....G....... 860 355-5538
New Milford *(G-5597)*

3732 Boat Building & Repairing

Ace Marine Service Inc ....G....... 860 489-5960
Torrington *(G-8886)*
Albin Manufacturing Corp ....G....... 203 661-4341
Cos Cob *(G-1622)*
Albin Marine Inc ....G....... 203 661-4341
Cos Cob *(G-1623)*
Arrigoni Distributors Ltd LLC ....G....... 860 669-6637
Clinton *(G-1491)*
Bills Boat Repair LLC ....G....... 203 804-8801
Guilford *(G-3328)*
Black Dog Boat Works LLC ....G....... 203 264-5823
Southbury *(G-7845)*
Brewer Yacht Yards Inc ....G....... 860 399-5128
Old Saybrook *(G-6526)*
Chester Boatworks ....G....... 860 526-2227
Deep River *(G-2086)*
Dinghy Pro LLC ....G....... 860 767-1596
Essex *(G-2715)*
Dp Custom Boat Repr Detail LLC ....G....... 203 536-3997
Monroe *(G-4711)*
Dutch Wharf Boat Yard & Marina ....F....... 203 488-9000
Branford *(G-582)*
Formula Boat Works LLC ....G....... 860 536-9309
Mystic *(G-4817)*
Grammas Hands LLC ....G....... 203 301-0791
Milford *(G-4541)*
Gregs Outboard Service LLC ....G....... 860 339-5139
Old Saybrook *(G-6535)*
Guillemot Kayaks ....G....... 860 659-8847
Glastonbury *(G-3044)*
Hbi Boat LLC ....G....... 860 536-7776
Groton *(G-3291)*
Housatonic Boat Works LLC ....G....... 203 375-3161
Stratford *(G-8627)*
Indikon Boatworks ....G....... 860 395-8297
Clinton *(G-1508)*
Jennings Yacht Services ....G....... 860 625-1368
Mystic *(G-4822)*
Kelsey Boat Yard ....G....... 203 488-9567
Branford *(G-616)*
Kiwanis Fndtion Middletown Inc ....G....... 860 638-8135
Middletown *(G-4364)*
Lbi Inc ....F....... 860 446-8058
Groton *(G-3296)*
Marine Fabricators ....G....... 203 488-7093
Branford *(G-624)*
McClave Philbrick & Giblin ....G....... 860 572-7710
Mystic *(G-4831)*
Montauk Pilots Inc ....G....... 860 535-3200
North Stonington *(G-6030)*
Narragansett Yacht Servic ....G....... 860 763-1980
Somers *(G-7665)*
New England Fiberglass Repair ....G....... 203 866-1690
Norwalk *(G-6272)*
Pmw Marine Repair ....G....... 860 535-3064
Stonington *(G-8536)*
RWS Marine Restoration ....G....... 860 350-4977
New Milford *(G-5587)*
Seabuzz Boatworks ....G....... 203 483-4576
Branford *(G-649)*
Seaport Marine Inc ....E....... 860 536-9651
Mystic *(G-4844)*
Shipstik LLC ....G....... 203 417-8022
Roxbury *(G-7284)*
Sound Yachts LLC ....G....... 860 399-8800
Westbrook *(G-10009)*
Stonington Boat Works LLC ....G....... 860 535-0332
Stonington *(G-8538)*
Sweetwater Boatworks LLC ....G....... 860 984-5118
New London *(G-5491)*
◆ **Vespoli Usa Inc** ....E....... 203 773-0311
New Haven *(G-5426)*
Vintage Boat Restorations LLC ....G....... 860 582-0774
Bristol *(G-1135)*

3743 Railroad Eqpt

Hammer Transport LLC ....G....... 860 338-0667
Chaplin *(G-1340)*
James L Howard and Company Inc ....E....... 860 242-3581
Bloomfield *(G-427)*

SIC SECTION

38 MEASURING, ANALYZING AND CONTROLLING INSTRUMENTS; PHOTOGRAPHIC, MEDICAL AN

L T A Group Inc ....E 860 291-9911
  South Windsor (G-7785)
Transit Systems Inc ....G 860 747-3669
  Plainville (G-6871)
Winchester Industries Inc ....G 860 379-5336
  Winsted (G-10544)
Winslow Automatics Inc ....D 860 225-6321
  New Britain (G-5084)

3751 Motorcycles, Bicycles & Parts

▲ Avalanche Downhill Racing Inc ....G 860 537-4306
  Colchester (G-1541)
▼ Cat LLC ....G 860 953-1807
  Hartford (G-3564)
◆ Cycling Sports Group Inc ....D 608 268-8916
  Wilton (G-10287)
Daads LLC ....G 860 274-1589
  Watertown (G-9700)
Frank Roth Co Inc ....D 203 377-2155
  Stratford (G-8611)
Fusion One Industries Inc ....G 860 992-4377
  Cromwell (G-1701)
Grasschoppers LLC ....G 860 294-1620
  Terryville (G-8760)
Kobuta Choppers LLC ....G 203 234-6047
  North Haven (G-5958)
Need For Speed Racing ....G 860 388-1204
  Old Saybrook (G-6559)
Pap Products LLC ....G 860 242-0415
  Bloomfield (G-460)
Tri State Choppers LLC ....G 860 210-1854
  New Milford (G-5601)

3761 Guided Missiles & Space Vehicles

Capstone Manufacturing Inc ....G 413 636-6170
  South Windsor (G-7723)
Singularity Space Systems LLC ....G 860 713-3626
  Granby (G-3114)

3764 Guided Missile/Space Vehicle Propulsion Units & parts

Atk Golf Services ....G 203 615-2099
  Trumbull (G-9000)

3769 Guided Missile/Space Vehicle Parts & Eqpt, NEC

Accupaulo Holding Corporation ....E 860 666-5621
  Newington (G-5617)
Aerocess Inc ....F 860 357-2451
  Berlin (G-151)
Braxton Manufacturing Co Inc ....C 860 274-6781
  Watertown (G-9685)
Edac Technologies LLC ....F 860 789-2511
  East Windsor (G-2490)
Edac Technologies LLC ....C 203 806-2090
  Cheshire (G-1383)
◆ Kaman Aerospace Group Inc ....F 860 243-7100
  Bloomfield (G-433)
Meriden Manufacturing Inc ....D 203 237-7481
  Meriden (G-4197)
Ramar-Hall Inc ....E 860 349-1081
  Middlefield (G-4306)
Spartan Aerospace LLC ....D 860 533-7500
  Manchester (G-4090)
▲ Sterling Engineering Corp ....C 860 379-3366
  Pleasant Valley (G-6926)
United Tool and Die Company ....C 860 246-6531
  West Hartford (G-9871)

3792 Travel Trailers & Campers

3333 LLC ....G 860 643-1384
  Manchester (G-3971)
Fiberglass Engr & Design Co ....G 203 265-1644
  Wallingford (G-9266)
Keystone Rv Company ....C 203 367-9847
  Bridgeport (G-816)
Thule Holding Inc ....F 203 881-9600
  Seymour (G-7370)

3795 Tanks & Tank Components

New England Airfoil Pdts Inc ....E 860 677-1376
  Farmington (G-2936)
Shawnee Chemical ....G 203 938-3003
  Redding (G-7109)

3799 Transportation Eqpt, NEC

Danbury Powersports Inc ....F 203 791-1310
  Danbury (G-1786)
Hoffman Towing & Transport ....G 860 627-0405
  East Windsor (G-2497)
New England Crrage Imports LLC ....G 860 889-6467
  Bozrah (G-529)
▲ On Track Karting Inc ....F 203 626-0464
  Wallingford (G-9331)
Pro Kart Racing Karts ....G 860 537-6900
  Colchester (G-1568)
Serafin Sulky Co ....G 860 684-2986
  Stafford Springs (G-8037)

38 MEASURING, ANALYZING AND CONTROLLING INSTRUMENTS; PHOTOGRAPHIC, MEDICAL AN

3812 Search, Detection, Navigation & Guidance Systs & Instrs

Accuturn Mfg Co LLC ....F 860 289-6355
  South Windsor (G-7699)
Airflo Instrument Company ....G 860 633-9455
  Glastonbury (G-3005)
Ais Global Holdings LLC ....A 203 250-3500
  Cheshire (G-1349)
Alternate Inc ....G 203 938-4125
  Redding (G-7088)
Amius Partners LLC ....G 203 526-5926
  New Haven (G-5230)
Apex Machine Tool Company Inc .....G 203 806-2090
  Cheshire (G-1354)
▲ Atlantic Inertial Systems Inc ....B 203 250-3500
  Cheshire (G-1356)
Atlantic Inertial Systems Inc ....A 203 250-3500
  Cheshire (G-1357)
Bae Systems Applied Intel Inc ....G 203 323-0066
  Stamford (G-8105)
Beacon Group Inc ....C 860 594-5200
  Newington (G-5631)
Boeing Company ....G 860 627-9393
  East Windsor (G-2485)
▼ Brandstrom Instruments Inc ....E 203 544-9341
  Ridgefield (G-7126)
Carl Perry ....G 860 834-4459
  Middletown (G-4330)
Carrier Corp ....G 860 728-7000
  Rocky Hill (G-7225)
Chromalloy Component Svcs Inc .....C 860 688-7798
  Windsor (G-10373)
Cloud Cap Technology Inc ....G 541 308-1089
  Danbury (G-1770)
Connecticut Aerospace Inc ....G 860 872-0036
  Vernon Rockville (G-9165)
Connecticut Analytical Corp ....F 203 393-9666
  Bethany (G-239)
Corporate Flight MGT Inc ....G 203 826-9224
  Danbury (G-1776)
Delta Level LLC ....G 203 919-1514
  Stratford (G-8605)
Drs Leonardo Inc ....E 203 798-3172
  Danbury (G-1799)
Drs Naval Power Systems Inc ....B 203 798-3000
  Danbury (G-1800)
Dynamic Controls Hs Inc ....G 860 654-6000
  Windsor Locks (G-10482)
Eaton Aerospace LLC ....E 203 796-6000
  Bethel (G-292)
Edac Nd Inc ....D 860 633-9474
  Glastonbury (G-3031)
Electro-Methods Inc ....C 860 289-8661
  South Windsor (G-7747)
Exocetus Autonomous Systems ....G 860 512-7260
  Wallingford (G-9263)
▲ Gems Sensors Inc ....B 860 747-3000
  Plainville (G-6815)
Hard-Core Self Defense ....G 203 231-2344
  Shelton (G-7459)
Hartford Aircraft Products ....E 860 242-8228
  Bloomfield (G-417)
Hermtech Inc ....G 860 758-7528
  East Windsor (G-2496)
Higgs Energy LLC ....G 860 213-5561
  Norwich (G-6416)
Integrated Systems Solutions ....G 860 665-1600
  Newington (G-5664)
Kaman Corporation ....C 860 632-1000
  Middletown (G-4361)

Kaman Precision Products Inc ....E 860 632-1000
  Middletown (G-4362)
Ladrdefense LLC ....G 860 637-8488
  Plantsville (G-6901)
▲ Lee Company ....A 860 399-6281
  Westbrook (G-10000)
Lockheed Martin Corporation ....G 860 447-8553
  New London (G-5477)
Max Padro ....G 203 530-0616
  West Haven (G-9933)
Meriden Electronics Corp ....G 203 237-8811
  Meriden (G-4195)
Meriden Manufacturing Inc ....D 203 237-7481
  Meriden (G-4197)
Msj Investments Inc ....F 860 684-9956
  Stafford Springs (G-8033)
Mtu Aero Engines N Amer Inc ....G 860 258-9700
  Rocky Hill (G-7258)
Northmen Defense LLC ....G 860 908-9308
  Oakdale (G-6445)
Northrop Grumman Corporation ....D 860 282-4461
  East Hartford (G-2348)
Passur Aerospace Inc ....E 203 622-4086
  Stamford (G-8351)
Polar Corporation ....E 860 223-7891
  New Britain (G-5035)
Raytheon Company ....E 860 446-4900
  Mystic (G-4840)
Real Manufacturing LLC ....G 860 757-3975
  South Windsor (G-7817)
Saf Industries LLC ....E 203 729-4900
  Meriden (G-4238)
Sensor Switch Inc ....E 203 265-2842
  New Haven (G-5392)
Sextant Btsllc ....G 203 500-3245
  Killingworth (G-3839)
Spectrogram Corporation ....G 203 245-2433
  Madison (G-3960)
Sperian Protectn Instrumentatn ....C 860 344-1079
  Middletown (G-4422)
▼ Swahili Aviation Aerospace LLC ....G 860 268-3639
  Tolland (G-8879)
Thayermahan Inc ....F 860 785-9994
  Groton (G-3315)
Triumph Eng Ctrl Systems LLC ....F 860 236-0651
  West Hartford (G-9870)
Triumph Eng Ctrl Systems LLC ....A 860 236-0651
  West Hartford (G-9869)
United States Dept of Navy ....G 860 694-3524
  Groton (G-3316)
United Technologies Corp ....G 860 595-4114
  Newington (G-5718)

3821 Laboratory Apparatus & Furniture

Ancera Inc ....G 203 819-2322
  Branford (G-544)
Bioclinica Inc ....G 860 701-0082
  New London (G-5458)
CFM Test & Balance Corp ....G 203 778-1900
  Bethel (G-269)
▲ Dragonlab LLC ....G 860 436-9221
  Rocky Hill (G-7235)
Environics Inc ....E 860 872-1111
  Tolland (G-8863)
▲ Eppendorf Inc ....B 732 287-1200
  Enfield (G-2641)
▲ Eppendorf Holding Inc ....E 860 253-3417
  Enfield (G-2642)
Fmp Products ....G 203 422-0686
  Greenwich (G-3164)
Idex Health & Science LLC ....C 860 314-2880
  Bristol (G-1050)
Mark V Laboratory Inc ....G 860 653-7201
  East Granby (G-2211)
▲ Mayborn Usa Inc ....F 781 269-7490
  Stamford (G-8298)
Novamont North America Inc ....F 203 744-8801
  Shelton (G-7514)
Novatech ....G 860 871-4180
  Tolland (G-8874)
◆ Origio Midatlantic Devices Inc ....E 856 762-2000
  Trumbull (G-9053)
Proteowise Inc ....G 203 430-4187
  Branford (G-638)
▲ Tomtec Inc ....D 203 281-6790
  Hamden (G-3522)
▲ Willoughby & Co LLC ....G 203 709-1464
  Southbury (G-7886)

Employee Codes: A=Over 500 employees, B=251-500
C=101-250, D=51-100, E=20-50, F=10-19, G=1-9

2020 Harris Connecticut Manufacturers Directory

453

3822 Automatic Temperature Controls

Ademco Inc....G....860 257-3266
Rocky Hill *(G-7218)*
Ademco Inc....G....203 877-2702
Milford *(G-4440)*
▲ Alloy Engineering Co Inc....E....203 366-5253
Bridgeport *(G-685)*
Alloy Engineering Co Inc....G....203 366-5253
Bridgeport *(G-686)*
◆ Belimo Aircontrols (usa) Inc....C....800 543-9038
Danbury *(G-1752)*
▲ Belimo Automation AG....F....203 749-3319
Danbury *(G-1753)*
▲ Belimo Customization USA Inc....G....203 791-9915
Danbury *(G-1754)*
Center For Discovery....E....203 955-1381
Southport *(G-8002)*
Emme Controls LLC....G....503 793-3792
Bristol *(G-1026)*
Emme E2ms LLC....F....860 845-8810
Bristol *(G-1027)*
◆ Food Atmtn - Svc Tchniques Inc....C....203 377-4414
Stratford *(G-8610)*
Graywolf Sensing Solutions LLC....G....203 402-0477
Shelton *(G-7453)*
Grove Systems Inc....G....860 663-2555
Deep River *(G-2091)*
Hamilton Standard Space....E....860 654-6000
Windsor Locks *(G-10490)*
◆ Hamilton Sundstrand Corp....A....860 654-6000
Windsor Locks *(G-10491)*
▲ Innovative Fusion Inc....E....203 729-3873
Naugatuck *(G-4891)*
J & B Service Company LLC....G....203 743-9357
Bethel *(G-314)*
Johnson Controls Inc....C....860 688-7151
Windsor *(G-10400)*
Johnson Controls Inc....G....860 887-7185
Norwich *(G-6419)*
Johnson Controls Inc....D....678 297-4040
Meriden *(G-4179)*
Johnson Goodyer II Inc....F....203 777-3424
New Haven *(G-5303)*
Kahn and Company Incorporated....G....860 529-8643
Wethersfield *(G-10203)*
▲ Lexa International Corporation....F....203 326-5200
Stamford *(G-8284)*
Mission Allergy Inc....G....203 364-1570
Hawleyville *(G-3744)*
Nats Inc....F....860 635-6820
Middletown *(G-4384)*
New Air Technologies Inc....G....860 767-1542
Ivoryton *(G-3787)*
Newgate Instruments LLC....G....860 784-1968
East Granby *(G-2218)*
Nurses Alarm Systems Inc....G....860 872-0025
Vernon Rockville *(G-9172)*
Omega Engineering Inc....D....714 540-4914
Norwalk *(G-6285)*
Process Automtn Solutions Inc....E....203 207-9917
Danbury *(G-1920)*
Rich Plastic Products Inc....G....203 235-4241
Meriden *(G-4233)*
▲ Tek-Air Systems Inc....E....203 791-1400
Monroe *(G-4758)*
Universal Building Contrls Inc....F....203 235-1530
Meriden *(G-4260)*
Whitman Controls LLC....F....800 233-4401
Bristol *(G-1138)*

3823 Indl Instruments For Meas, Display & Control

AKO Inc....E....860 298-9765
Windsor *(G-10357)*
▲ Alloy Engineering Co Inc....E....203 366-5253
Bridgeport *(G-685)*
Ametek Inc....C....203 265-6731
Wallingford *(G-9203)*
Appleton Grp LLC....E....860 653-1603
East Granby *(G-2190)*
Ashcrft-Ngano Kiki Hldings Inc....G....203 378-8281
Stratford *(G-8571)*
◆ Ashcroft Inc....B....203 378-8281
Stratford *(G-8572)*
▲ Bristol Inc....B....860 945-2200
Watertown *(G-9686)*
Bristol Babcock Employees Fede....G....860 945-2200
Watertown *(G-9687)*
Buck Scientific Inc....D....203 853-9444
Norwalk *(G-6101)*
C F D Engineering Company....F....203 754-2807
Waterbury *(G-9445)*
Cidra Chemical Management Inc....D....203 265-0035
Wallingford *(G-9227)*
Cidra Corporate Services Inc....D....203 265-0035
Wallingford *(G-9228)*
▼ Cidra Corporation....D....203 265-0035
Wallingford *(G-9229)*
Cidra Mineral Processing Inc....D....203 265-0035
Wallingford *(G-9230)*
Cidra Oilsands Inc....G....203 265-0035
Wallingford *(G-9231)*
Clinton Instrument Company....E....860 669-7548
Clinton *(G-1494)*
Danaher Tool Group....F....203 284-7000
Wallingford *(G-9246)*
Devar Inc....E....203 368-6751
Bridgeport *(G-749)*
Diba Industries Inc....C....203 744-0773
Danbury *(G-1795)*
Differential Pressure Plus....G....203 481-2545
Branford *(G-579)*
Drs Naval Power Systems Inc....B....203 798-3000
Danbury *(G-1801)*
Emerson Electric Co....G....203 891-1080
Orange *(G-6598)*
Environics Inc....E....860 872-1111
Tolland *(G-8863)*
▲ Faria Beede Instruments Inc....C....860 848-9271
North Stonington *(G-6024)*
Fleet Management LLC....G....800 722-6654
Enfield *(G-2647)*
Floodmaster LLC....G....203 488-4477
Branford *(G-595)*
◆ Food Atmtn - Svc Tchniques Inc....C....203 377-4414
Stratford *(G-8610)*
GE Steam Power Inc....G....860 688-1911
Windsor *(G-10391)*
Gordon Engineering Corp....F....203 775-4501
Brookfield *(G-1193)*
H & B Tool & Engineering Co....E....860 528-9341
South Windsor *(G-7766)*
◆ Hamilton Sundstrand Corp....A....860 654-6000
Windsor Locks *(G-10491)*
▲ Haydon Kerk Mtion Slutions Inc....C....203 756-7441
Waterbury *(G-9497)*
Idex Health & Science LLC....C....860 314-2880
Bristol *(G-1050)*
Innovative Components LLC....G....860 621-7220
Plantsville *(G-6896)*
Jad LLC....E....860 289-1551
South Windsor *(G-7776)*
▼ Johnson Gage Company....E....860 242-5541
Bloomfield *(G-428)*
Kahn and Company Incorporated....G....860 529-8643
Wethersfield *(G-10203)*
Kahn Instruments Incorporated....G....860 529-8643
Wethersfield *(G-10205)*
Kaman Aerospace Corporation....C....860 632-1000
Middletown *(G-4360)*
Kapcom LLC....G....203 891-5112
East Haven *(G-2436)*
Kde Instrumentation....G....860 657-2744
Glastonbury *(G-3053)*
Kulas Systems Inc....G....860 749-6645
Somers *(G-7664)*
Laticrete Supercap LLC....G....203 393-4558
Bethany *(G-246)*
▲ Lee Company....A....860 399-6281
Westbrook *(G-10000)*
Lee Company....C....860 399-6281
Essex *(G-2723)*
Lee Company....E....860 399-6281
Westbrook *(G-10001)*
Louis Electric Co Inc....G....203 879-5483
Wolcott *(G-10571)*
▲ Lq Mechatronics Inc....G....203 433-4430
Branford *(G-619)*
Madison Company....E....203 488-4477
Branford *(G-621)*
Micromod Automation & Controls....F....585 321-9209
Wallingford *(G-9320)*
Microtechnologies Inc....G....860 517-8314
Farmington *(G-2929)*
Minteq International Inc....C....860 824-5435
Canaan *(G-1289)*
Moeller Instrument Company Inc....E....800 243-9310
Ivoryton *(G-3786)*
National Magnetic Sensors Inc....G....860 621-6816
Plantsville *(G-6904)*
NDC Technologies Inc....G....860 635-2100
Middletown *(G-4385)*
North Controls Company LLC....G....860 584-8364
Bristol *(G-1079)*
◆ Omega Engineering Inc....C....203 359-1660
Norwalk *(G-6284)*
Omega Engineering Inc....G....203 359-7922
Stamford *(G-8340)*
Omega International Corp....G....203 359-1660
Stamford *(G-8341)*
Orange Research Inc....D....203 877-5657
Milford *(G-4598)*
PMC Engineering LLC....E....203 792-8686
Danbury *(G-1909)*
▼ Precision Sensors Inc....E....203 877-2795
Milford *(G-4613)*
▲ Prime Technology LLC....C....203 481-5721
North Branford *(G-5853)*
Proflow Inc....E....203 230-4700
North Haven *(G-5980)*
Projects Inc....C....860 633-4615
Glastonbury *(G-3075)*
Quad/Graphics Inc....A....203 288-2468
North Haven *(G-5985)*
RA Smythe LLC....G....860 398-5764
Middletown *(G-4401)*
Singularity Space Systems LLC....G....860 713-3626
Granby *(G-3114)*
▲ Solar Generations LLC....G....203 453-3920
Guilford *(G-3392)*
Sperian Protectn Instrumentatn....C....860 344-1079
Middletown *(G-4422)*
Syba Systems LLC....G....401 829-0822
Norwich *(G-6433)*
▲ Tek-Air Systems Inc....E....203 791-1400
Monroe *(G-4758)*
Underground Systems Inc....E....203 792-3444
Bethel *(G-357)*
United Electric Controls Co....D....203 877-2795
Milford *(G-4668)*
◆ Veeder-Root Company....D....860 651-2700
Weatogue *(G-9760)*
Vertiv Corporation....F....203 294-6020
Wallingford *(G-9401)*
Wentworth Laboratories Inc....G....203 775-9311
Brookfield *(G-1240)*
WMW LLC....G....203 227-4992
Weston *(G-10046)*

3824 Fluid Meters & Counters

▲ Alinabal Holdings Corporation....B....203 877-3241
Milford *(G-4449)*
▲ American Marine Inc....G....914 763-5367
Greenwich *(G-3119)*
Bidwell Industrial Group Inc....E....860 346-9283
Middletown *(G-4325)*
Denominator Company Inc....F....203 263-3210
Woodbury *(G-10633)*
Eastern Utility Products LLC....G....860 399-1724
Westbrook *(G-9995)*
▲ Faria Beede Instruments Inc....C....860 848-9271
North Stonington *(G-6024)*
▲ Gems Sensors Inc....B....860 747-3000
Plainville *(G-6815)*
Habco Industries LLC....E....860 682-6800
Glastonbury *(G-3045)*
Jedcontrol Corp....G....914 328-8593
Danbury *(G-1859)*
▲ Kongsberg Dgtal Simulation Inc....F....860 405-2300
Groton *(G-3293)*
▲ Lq Mechatronics Inc....G....203 433-4430
Branford *(G-619)*
◆ Veeder-Root Company....D....860 651-2700
Weatogue *(G-9760)*

3825 Instrs For Measuring & Testing Electricity

Advanced Business Group....G....203 881-9660
Oxford *(G-6637)*
AKO Inc....E....860 298-9765
Windsor *(G-10357)*
◆ All-Test Pro LLC....F....860 399-4222
Old Saybrook *(G-6522)*
▲ Altek Electronics Inc....C....860 482-7626
Torrington *(G-8892)*
AMS Strategic Management Inc....G....845 500-5635
Stamford *(G-8083)*
ARS Products LLC....E....860 564-0208
Plainfield *(G-6739)*

Ashcroft Inc ... E ... 203 378-8281
Stratford (G-8573)
Bloomy Controls Inc ... E ... 860 298-9925
Windsor (G-10368)
Bristol Babcock Employees Fede ... G ... 860 945-2200
Watertown (G-9687)
Carte Medical Corp ... G ... 860 258-1970
Wethersfield (G-10186)
Clinton Instrument Company ... E ... 860 669-7548
Clinton (G-1494)
▲ Dictaphone Corporation ... C ... 203 381-7000
Stratford (G-8606)
▲ Digatron Power Electronics Inc ... E ... 203 446-8000
Shelton (G-7432)
Dyadic Innovations LLC ... G ... 630 738-4113
Farmington (G-2900)
Energy Tech LLC ... G ... 860 345-3993
Haddam (G-3404)
Ets-Lindgren Inc ... G ... 203 838-4555
Norwalk (G-6158)
▲ Faria Beede Instruments Inc ... C ... 860 848-9271
North Stonington (G-6024)
Fitzhugh Electrical Corp ... G ... 203 453-3171
Guilford (G-3352)
▼ Forte Rts Inc ... G ... 860 464-5221
Ledyard (G-3872)
General Electric Company ... D ... 518 385-7164
Norwalk (G-6177)
Gold Line Connector Inc ... E ... 203 938-2588
Redding (G-7093)
Habco Industries LLC ... E ... 860 682-6800
Glastonbury (G-3045)
Hoffman Engineering LLC ... D ... 203 425-8900
Stamford (G-8240)
Image Graphics Inc ... E ... 203 926-0100
Shelton (G-7474)
Information Security Assoc LLC ... G ... 203 736-9587
Seymour (G-7351)
▲ International Contact Tech ... E ... 203 264-5757
Southbury (G-7862)
International Instruments Div ... G ... 203 481-3450
North Branford (G-5845)
Kahn and Company Incorporated ... G ... 860 529-8643
Wethersfield (G-10203)
KLA Kemp LLC ... G ... 860 464-6746
Gales Ferry (G-2986)
Madison Tstg Acqstion Svcs LLC ... G ... 203 421-9388
Madison (G-3938)
MB Systems LLC ... G ... 203 881-1583
Seymour (G-7356)
Microtools Inc ... G ... 860 651-6170
Simsbury (G-7635)
Nutmeg Energy Savers ... G ... 203 733-0147
Bethel (G-330)
Nutmeg Utility Products Inc ... E ... 203 250-8802
Cheshire (G-1423)
Omega Engineering Inc ... D ... 714 540-4914
Norwalk (G-6285)
Oslo Switch Inc ... E ... 203 272-2794
Cheshire (G-1425)
▲ Prime Technology LLC ... C ... 203 481-5721
North Branford (G-5853)
Solar Data Systems Inc ... F ... 203 702-7189
Bethel (G-345)
Space Electronics LLC ... E ... 860 829-0001
Berlin (G-221)
Technology Integrators Inc ... G ... 203 333-7185
Fairfield (G-2854)
Tektronix ... G ... 203 730-2730
Danbury (G-1962)
Test Logic Inc ... F ... 860 347-8378
Middletown (G-4425)
Trans-Tek Inc ... E ... 860 872-8351
Ellington (G-2608)
Uses Mfg Inc ... G ... 860 443-8737
Quaker Hill (G-7086)
Wentworth Laboratories Inc ... D ... 203 775-0448
Brookfield (G-1239)
Wentworth Laboratories Inc ... G ... 203 775-9311
Brookfield (G-1240)

3826 Analytical Instruments

A Douglas Thibodeau LLC ... G ... 860 295-9189
Marlborough (G-4118)
Albrayco Technologies Inc ... G ... 860 635-3369
Cromwell (G-1686)
Alpha 1c LLC ... G ... 860 354-7979
Sherman (G-7590)
American Ultraviolet ... G ... 203 926-0140
Shelton (G-7394)
Applied Biosystems LLC ... G ... 781 271-0045
Norwalk (G-6071)
Buck Scientific Inc ... D ... 203 853-9444
Norwalk (G-6101)
Cam2 Technologies LLC ... G ... 203 456-3025
Danbury (G-1761)
Carestream Health Molecular ... E ... 888 777-2072
New Haven (G-5254)
Connecticut Analytical Corp ... F ... 203 393-9666
Bethany (G-239)
Czitek LLC ... G ... 888 326-8186
Danbury (G-1781)
Designs & Prototypes Ltd ... G ... 860 658-0458
Simsbury (G-7615)
Dimension Zero Ltd ... G ... 860 325-7073
Willimantic (G-10224)
Energy Beam Sciences Inc ... F ... 860 653-0411
East Granby (G-2203)
G F E ... G ... 203 371-7334
Easton (G-2555)
▲ Hamilton Sndstrnd Space ... A ... 860 654-6000
Windsor Locks (G-10489)
Hoffman Engineering LLC ... D ... 203 425-8900
Stamford (G-8240)
Idex Health & Science LLC ... C ... 860 314-2880
Bristol (G-1050)
▼ Ihs Herold Inc ... D ... 203 857-0215
Norwalk (G-6204)
Industrial Analytics Corp ... G ... 203 245-0380
Madison (G-3931)
K A F Manufacturing Co Inc ... E ... 203 324-3012
Stamford (G-8272)
Kahn and Company Incorporated ... G ... 860 529-8643
Wethersfield (G-10203)
Macroscopic Solutions LLC ... G ... 410 870-5566
Tolland (G-8869)
Madison Technology Intl ... G ... 860 245-0245
Mystic (G-4830)
Max Analytical Tech Inc ... E ... 989 772-5088
East Windsor (G-2510)
Nats Inc ... F ... 860 635-6820
Middletown (G-4384)
◆ Omega Engineering Inc ... C ... 203 359-1660
Norwalk (G-6284)
Owlstone Inc ... G ... 203 908-4848
Westport (G-10136)
Perkinelmer Inc ... G ... 203 925-4600
Shelton (G-7525)
Perkinelmer Hlth Sciences Inc ... C ... 203 925-4600
Shelton (G-7526)
Precipio Inc ... G ... 203 907-2205
New Haven (G-5370)
▲ Precipio Inc ... E ... 402 452-5400
New Haven (G-5371)
Prospect Products Incorporated ... E ... 860 666-0323
Newington (G-5698)
Real-Time Analyzers Inc ... G ... 860 635-9800
Middletown (G-4403)
Scots Landing ... G ... 860 923-0437
Fabyan (G-2739)
▲ Spectral LLC ... G ... 860 928-7726
Putnam (G-7069)
Spectrogram Corporation ... G ... 203 245-2433
Madison (G-3960)
Swift Scientific LLC ... G ... 860 498-8577
Coventry (G-1680)
▲ Tomtec Inc ... D ... 203 281-6790
Hamden (G-3522)
Trajan Scientific Americas Inc ... G ... 203 830-4910
Bethel (G-354)
Wagner Instruments Inc ... G ... 203 869-9681
Cos Cob (G-1643)
Welch Materials Inc ... G ... 203 691-1721
West Haven (G-9961)
Wentworth Laboratories Inc ... G ... 203 775-9311
Brookfield (G-1240)

3827 Optical Instruments

4 D Technology Corporation ... G ... 860 365-0420
East Hampton (G-2251)
Abet Technologies Inc ... G ... 203 540-9990
Milford (G-4438)
Adaptive Optics Associates Inc ... F ... 860 282-4401
East Hartford (G-2287)
Advanced Photonics Intl Inc ... G ... 203 259-0437
Fairfield (G-2745)
Aecc/Pearlman Buying Group LLC ... F ... 203 598-3200
Middlebury (G-4272)
Aperture Optical Sciences Inc ... G ... 860 301-2589
Higganum (G-3759)
Aperture Optical Sciences Inc ... G ... 860 301-2372
Meriden (G-4144)
Argyle Optics LLC ... G ... 203 451-3320
Milford (G-4456)
Bradley Gun Sight Co Inc ... G ... 860 589-0531
Bristol (G-986)
Brightsight Llc ... G ... 860 208-0222
Woodstock (G-10658)
Ciaudelli Productions Inc ... G ... 860 848-0411
Montville (G-4769)
Coating Design Group Inc ... E ... 203 878-3663
Stratford (G-8596)
Coburn Technologies ... G ... 800 262-8761
South Windsor (G-7730)
◆ Coburn Technologies Inc ... C ... 860 648-6600
South Windsor (G-7731)
Coburn Technologies Intl Inc ... G ... 860 648-6600
South Windsor (G-7732)
Coburn Tecnologies Canada ... D ... 860 648-6710
South Windsor (G-7733)
Conoptics Inc ... F ... 203 743-3349
Danbury (G-1773)
CT Fiberoptics Inc ... F ... 860 763-4341
Somers (G-7654)
Data Technology Inc ... E ... 860 871-8082
Tolland (G-8860)
Doctors of Optometry ... G ... 203 743-9897
Danbury (G-1798)
Fedora Optical Inc ... G ... 860 646-3577
Manchester (G-4017)
▲ Flabeg Technical Glass US Corp ... E ... 203 729-5227
Naugatuck (G-4880)
◆ Gerber Coburn Optical Inc ... C ... 800 843-1479
South Windsor (G-7758)
Karl Stetson Associates LLC ... G ... 860 742-8414
Coventry (G-1659)
Macro Systems Inc ... G ... 203 225-6266
Shelton (G-7494)
Macroscopic Solutions LLC ... G ... 410 870-5566
Tolland (G-8869)
Mev Technologies LLC ... G ... 203 227-4723
Westport (G-10120)
Nntechnology Moore Systems LLC ... G ... 203 366-3224
Bridgeport (G-851)
Nvizix Corp ... G ... 203 222-8723
Westport (G-10130)
◆ Odis Inc ... G ... 860 450-8407
Storrs Mansfield (G-8557)
Optical Design Associates ... G ... 203 249-6408
Stamford (G-8343)
Optical Research Technologies ... G ... 203 762-9063
Wilton (G-10316)
Orafol Americas Inc ... C ... 860 676-7100
Avon (G-98)
Paramount Glassworks LLC ... G ... 860 315-7624
Woodstock (G-10675)
▲ Retina Systems Inc ... E ... 203 881-1311
Seymour (G-7365)
Scope Technology Inc ... F ... 860 963-1141
Plainfield (G-6752)
Sparrow Woods Co LLC ... G ... 203 215-5200
Woodbridge (G-10618)
Spectral Optics Inc ... G ... 978 682-1302
Putnam (G-7070)
Tower Optical Company Inc ... G ... 203 866-4535
Norwalk (G-6376)
UTC Fire SEC Americas Corp Inc ... C ... 203 426-1180
Newtown (G-5796)
▲ Zygo Corporation ... G ... 860 347-8506
Middlefield (G-4310)

3829 Measuring & Controlling Devices, NEC

AC Tek Instruments ... G ... 203 431-0825
Ridgefield (G-7114)
Aftel Corp ... G ... 203 329-2273
Stamford (G-8064)
▼ Ai-Tek Instruments LLC ... E ... 203 271-6927
Cheshire (G-1348)
Airflo Instrument Company ... G ... 860 633-9455
Glastonbury (G-3005)
American Design & Mfg Inc ... E ... 860 282-2719
South Windsor (G-7705)
Anchor Science LLC ... G ... 203 231-6181
Branford (G-545)
Array Systems LLC ... G ... 203 877-4625
Milford (G-4457)
Atlantic Sensors & Contrls LLC ... G ... 203 878-8118
Milford (G-4461)
▲ Bauer Inc ... D ... 860 583-9100
Bristol (G-978)

SIC

Employee Codes: A=Over 500 employees, B=251-500
C=101-250, D=51-100, E=20-50, F=10-19, G=1-9
2020 Harris Connecticut
Manufacturers Directory
455

Bojak Company.......G....... 203 378-5086
Milford *(G-4474)*
Boudreau Vasiliki.......G....... 203 734-6754
Ansonia *(G-24)*
Clinton Instrument Company.......E....... 860 669-7548
Clinton *(G-1494)*
CMI Time Management LLC.......G....... 800 722-6654
Enfield *(G-2626)*
◆ **Comet Technologies USA Inc**.......E....... 203 447-3200
Shelton *(G-7421)*
Connecticut Compass Service.......G....... 860 434-2019
Lyme *(G-3903)*
▲ **Cooper-Atkins Corporation**.......C....... 860 349-3473
Middlefield *(G-4300)*
Data Technology Inc.......E....... 860 871-8082
Tolland *(G-8860)*
Daybreak Nuclear & Med Systems.......G....... 203 453-3299
Guilford *(G-3343)*
Digysol LLC.......G....... 860 232-1614
West Hartford *(G-9800)*
Eastern Conn Hlth Netwrk.......G....... 860 652-3182
Glastonbury *(G-3030)*
Eastern Technology Corporation.......G....... 860 528-9821
East Hartford *(G-2318)*
Eaton Aerospace LLC.......E....... 203 796-6000
Bethel *(G-292)*
Edmunds Manufacturing Company.......D....... 860 677-2813
Farmington *(G-2903)*
Electro-Methods Inc.......C....... 860 289-8661
South Windsor *(G-7747)*
Gems Sensors Inc.......F....... 800 378-1600
Plainville *(G-6816)*
Gold Line Connector Inc.......E....... 203 938-2588
Redding *(G-7093)*
Habco Industries LLC.......E....... 860 682-6800
Glastonbury *(G-3045)*
Harcosemco LLC.......C....... 203 483-3700
Branford *(G-603)*
Hayward Turnstiles Inc.......G....... 203 877-7096
Milford *(G-4547)*
Hitachi Aloka Medical Ltd.......D....... 203 269-5088
Wallingford *(G-9282)*
Hitachi Aloka Medical Amer Inc.......D....... 203 269-5088
Wallingford *(G-9283)*
Image Insight Inc.......G....... 860 528-9806
East Hartford *(G-2337)*
◆ **Independent Repair Service**.......G....... 203 234-0218
North Haven *(G-5947)*
Interpace Diagnostics Corp.......G....... 855 776-6419
New Haven *(G-5302)*
Jovian Technologies.......G....... 860 896-1539
Ellington *(G-2593)*
Judge Tool & Gage Inc.......G....... 800 214-5990
Stratford *(G-8638)*
Jurman Metrics Inc.......F....... 203 261-9388
Monroe *(G-4723)*
Kahn and Company Incorporated.......G....... 860 529-8643
Wethersfield *(G-10203)*
▼ **Kahn Industries Inc**.......E....... 860 529-8643
Wethersfield *(G-10204)*
▲ **Lex Products LLC**.......C....... 203 363-3738
Shelton *(G-7490)*
Luxpoint Inc.......G....... 860 982-9588
Rocky Hill *(G-7255)*
Megasonics Inc.......G....... 203 966-3404
New Canaan *(G-5120)*
Microtechnologies Inc.......G....... 860 517-8314
Farmington *(G-2929)*
Miracle Instruments Co.......F....... 860 642-7745
Lebanon *(G-3858)*
▲ **Mirion Tech Canberra Inc**.......B....... 203 238-2351
Meriden *(G-4204)*
Mission Bmdical Scientific Inc.......G....... 860 941-8896
East Lyme *(G-2468)*
Mistras Group Inc.......E....... 860 447-2474
Waterford *(G-9663)*
Omega Engineering Inc.......D....... 714 540-4914
Norwalk *(G-6285)*
Online River LLC.......F....... 203 801-5900
Westport *(G-10134)*
Onsite Mammography.......G....... 860 254-5097
West Suffield *(G-9988)*
Owlstone Inc.......G....... 203 908-4848
Westport *(G-10136)*
OXY Couture LLC.......G....... 860 257-8750
Rocky Hill *(G-7261)*
Perey Turnstiles Inc.......E....... 203 333-9400
Bridgeport *(G-870)*
Perrella Specialties.......G....... 203 264-1758
Southbury *(G-7872)*
Pmd Scientific Inc.......G....... 860 242-8177
Bloomfield *(G-466)*
Power-Dyne LLC.......E....... 860 346-9283
Middletown *(G-4395)*
▲ **Pratt Whtney Msurement Systems**.......E....... 860 286-8181
Bloomfield *(G-469)*
Preferred Utilities Mfg Corp.......D....... 203 743-6741
Danbury *(G-1918)*
Projects Inc.......C....... 860 633-4615
Glastonbury *(G-3075)*
Q-Lane Turnstiles LLC.......F....... 860 410-1801
Sandy Hook *(G-7327)*
Radiation Safety Assoc Inc.......G....... 860 228-0721
Hebron *(G-3754)*
Semco Instruments Inc.......C....... 661 257-2000
Branford *(G-650)*
Semco Instruments Inc.......G....... 661 362-6117
Branford *(G-651)*
Sens All Inc.......G....... 860 628-8379
Southington *(G-7973)*
Simmonds Precision Pdts Inc.......E....... 203 797-5000
Danbury *(G-1952)*
Slide Rule Group LLC.......G....... 860 317-1624
Moosup *(G-4782)*
▼ **Soldream Inc**.......E....... 860 871-6883
Vernon Rockville *(G-9180)*
Specialist Sensor.......G....... 203 287-9699
Hamden *(G-3511)*
Specialty Components Inc.......G....... 203 284-9112
Wallingford *(G-9374)*
Sperian Protectn Instrumentatn.......C....... 860 344-1079
Middletown *(G-4422)*
Strain Measurement Devices Inc.......E....... 203 294-5800
Wallingford *(G-9377)*
Technisonic Research Inc.......G....... 203 368-3600
Fairfield *(G-2853)*
▲ **Tek-Air Systems Inc**.......E....... 203 791-1400
Monroe *(G-4758)*
TLC Ultrasound Inc.......G....... 860 354-6333
New Milford *(G-5599)*
Trans-Tek Inc.......E....... 860 872-8351
Ellington *(G-2608)*
▲ **Unholtz-Dickie Corporation**.......E....... 203 265-9875
Wallingford *(G-9395)*
▲ **Weigh & Test Systems Inc**.......F....... 203 698-9681
Riverside *(G-7205)*
Wesdyne International LLC.......G....... 860 731-1683
Windsor *(G-10463)*
Zactech Ultrasonics LLC.......G....... 203 438-0004
Ridgefield *(G-7187)*

3841 Surgical & Medical Instrs & Apparatus

109 Design LLC.......G....... 203 941-1812
New Haven *(G-5215)*
Abbott Associates Inc.......F....... 203 878-2370
Milford *(G-4437)*
▲ **Acme Monaco Corporation**.......C....... 860 224-1349
New Britain *(G-4934)*
All Cell Recovery LLC.......G....... 203 948-2566
Brookfield *(G-1158)*
AMG Development LLC.......G....... 203 292-8444
Westport *(G-10056)*
Ankleaid LLC.......G....... 860 305-5178
Ellington *(G-2575)*
Aplicare Products LLC.......C....... 203 630-0500
Meriden *(G-4145)*
Arm Medical Devices Inc.......G....... 860 583-5165
Bristol *(G-965)*
Auto Suture Company Australia.......G....... 203 845-1000
Norwalk *(G-6081)*
Auto Suture Company UK.......B....... 203 845-1000
Norwalk *(G-6082)*
Auto Suture Russia Inc.......G....... 203 845-1000
Norwalk *(G-6083)*
Becton Dickinson and Company.......B....... 860 824-5487
Canaan *(G-1281)*
Beekley Medical.......G....... 860 583-4700
Bristol *(G-979)*
▼ **Bio-Med Devices Inc**.......D....... 203 458-0202
Guilford *(G-3329)*
Biorasis Inc.......G....... 860 429-3592
Storrs *(G-8543)*
▲ **Blairden Precision Instrs Inc**.......G....... 203 799-2000
Trumbull *(G-9005)*
Boston Endo-Surgical Tech LLC.......D....... 203 336-6479
Bridgeport *(G-717)*
Boston Scientific Corporation.......B....... 860 673-2500
Avon *(G-78)*
Bridge Innvations Ventures LLC.......G....... 203 520-8241
Trumbull *(G-9007)*
Brown Larkin & Co LLC.......G....... 860 280-8858
Burlington *(G-1261)*
Butterfly Network Inc.......E....... 855 296-6188
Guilford *(G-3336)*
C & W Manufacturing Co Inc.......E....... 860 633-4631
Glastonbury *(G-3017)*
C3 Manufacturing LLC.......G....... 914 943-6877
New Fairfield *(G-5163)*
Calmare Therapeutics Inc.......G....... 203 368-6044
Fairfield *(G-2756)*
Campo Enterprises.......G....... 203 776-0664
Hamden *(G-3422)*
◆ **Carwild Corporation**.......E....... 860 442-4914
New London *(G-5461)*
Cas Medical Systems Inc.......G....... 203 488-1957
Branford *(G-568)*
Cas Medical Systems Inc.......G....... 203 315-6953
Branford *(G-569)*
Cas Medical Systems Inc.......D....... 203 488-6056
Branford *(G-570)*
▲ **Catachem Inc**.......G....... 203 262-0330
Oxford *(G-6649)*
Cirtec Medical Corp.......C....... 860 814-3973
Enfield *(G-2623)*
Clinical Dynamics Conn LLC.......G....... 203 269-0090
Plantsville *(G-6888)*
◆ **Connecticut Hypodermics Inc**.......D....... 203 265-4881
Wallingford *(G-9238)*
Convexity Scientific LLC.......G....... 949 637-1216
Fairfield *(G-2768)*
◆ **Coopersurgical Inc**.......C....... 203 601-5200
Trumbull *(G-9017)*
Covidien Holding Inc.......G....... 203 492-5000
North Haven *(G-5927)*
Covidien LP.......B....... 203 492-6332
North Haven *(G-5928)*
Covidien LP.......B....... 781 839-1722
New Haven *(G-5265)*
Covidien LP.......A....... 203 492-5000
North Haven *(G-5929)*
▲ **Cygnus Medical LLC**.......G....... 800 990-7489
Branford *(G-578)*
Dcg-Pmi Inc.......E....... 203 743-5525
Bethel *(G-279)*
Delfin Marketing Inc.......G....... 203 554-2707
Greenwich *(G-3150)*
E M M Inc.......E....... 203 245-0306
Madison *(G-3918)*
Elidah Inc.......G....... 978 435-4324
Monroe *(G-4715)*
◆ **Eppendorf Manufacturing Corp**.......C....... 860 253-3400
Enfield *(G-2643)*
First Airway LLC.......G....... 860 679-9285
Farmington *(G-2906)*
Frank Roth Co Inc.......D....... 203 377-2155
Stratford *(G-8611)*
Furnace Source LLC.......F....... 860 582-4201
Terryville *(G-8755)*
Fusion Medical Corporation.......G....... 860 906-7856
West Haven *(G-9910)*
Gr Enterprises and Tech.......G....... 203 387-1430
Woodbridge *(G-10601)*
Graphic Cntrls Acqisition Corp.......G....... 203 759-1020
Wolcott *(G-10567)*
Gynion LLC.......G....... 203 520-8241
Trumbull *(G-9032)*
▲ **Hamilton Sndstrnd Space**.......A....... 860 654-6000
Windsor Locks *(G-10489)*
Highland Medical Products Inc.......G....... 860 454-0625
Ellington *(G-2592)*
Hitachi Aloka Medical Ltd.......D....... 203 269-5088
Wallingford *(G-9282)*
Hitachi Aloka Medical Amer Inc.......D....... 203 269-5088
Wallingford *(G-9283)*
Hobbs Medical Inc.......E....... 860 684-5875
Stafford Springs *(G-8031)*
Hologic Inc.......C....... 203 790-1188
Danbury *(G-1845)*
Home Diagnostics Corp.......C....... 203 445-1170
Trumbull *(G-9035)*
Ipsogen.......G....... 203 504-8583
Stamford *(G-8258)*
Johnson & Johnson.......G....... 860 621-9111
Southington *(G-7945)*
Joseph L Gentile Entps LLC.......G....... 203 421-5144
Madison *(G-3932)*
Kbc Electronics Inc.......F....... 203 298-9654
Milford *(G-4563)*
Kenzinc LLC.......G....... 203 307-5369
Shelton *(G-7484)*

SIC SECTION 38 MEASURING, ANALYZING AND CONTROLLING INSTRUMENTS; PHOTOGRAPHIC, MEDICAL AN

▲ **Lacey Manufacturing Co LLC** .... B 203 336-7427
Bridgeport *(G-821)*
Lambdavision Incorporated .... G 860 486-6593
Farmington *(G-2923)*
▲ **Lee Company** .... A 860 399-6281
Westbrook *(G-10000)*
Lenses Only LLC .... F 860 769-2020
Bloomfield *(G-440)*
▲ **Liberty Products Inc** .... G 860 829-2122
Berlin *(G-194)*
Life Warmer Inc .... G 860 204-1711
Canton *(G-1317)*
▲ **Lorad Corporation** .... C 203 790-5544
Danbury *(G-1876)*
Lumendi LLC .... G 203 528-0316
Westport *(G-10114)*
M G M Instruments Inc .... E 203 248-4008
Hamden *(G-3478)*
Marel Corporation .... F 203 934-8187
West Haven *(G-9932)*
Medi Products .... G 203 324-3711
Stamford *(G-8303)*
Medtronic Inc .... E 203 492-5764
North Haven *(G-5962)*
Medtronic Xomed Inc .... E 860 572-9586
Mystic *(G-4832)*
Memry Corporation .... C 203 739-1100
Bethel *(G-326)*
Memry Corporation .... G 203 739-1146
Bethel *(G-327)*
Microspecialities Inc .... F 203 874-1832
Middletown *(G-4377)*
Monopol Corporation .... F 860 583-3852
Bristol *(G-1073)*
Natural Polymer Devices Inc .... G 860 679-7894
Farmington *(G-2934)*
▲ **New Wave Surgical Corp** .... E 954 796-4126
New Haven *(G-5349)*
Newmark Inc .... G 203 272-1158
Cheshire *(G-1422)*
Newmark Medical Components Inc .... F 203 753-1158
Waterbury *(G-9560)*
Novatek Medical Inc .... G 203 356-0156
Stamford *(G-8332)*
Oerlikon AM Medical Inc .... D 203 712-1030
Shelton *(G-7518)*
Opticare Health Systems Inc .... C 203 574-2020
Waterbury *(G-9571)*
Oral Fluid Dynamics LLC .... G 860 561-5036
Farmington *(G-2941)*
Orthozon Technologies LLC .... G 203 989-4937
Stamford *(G-8346)*
Oxford Science Inc .... F 203 881-3115
Oxford *(G-6685)*
Oxford Science Center LLC .... G 203 751-1912
Oxford *(G-6686)*
Perosphere Technologies Inc .... G 475 218-4600
Danbury *(G-1906)*
Precision Engineered Pdts LLC .... G 203 336-6479
Bridgeport *(G-878)*
Precision Metal Products Inc .... C 203 877-4258
Milford *(G-4612)*
Radx Cloud .... G 909 910-7434
New Haven *(G-5376)*
▲ **Respironics Novametrix LLC** .... C 203 697-6475
Wallingford *(G-9351)*
Retinographics Inc .... G 203 853-1735
Norwalk *(G-6322)*
▼ **S-Y-M Products Company LLC** .... F 203 329-2469
Litchfield *(G-3899)*
Saar Corporation .... F 860 674-9440
Farmington *(G-2955)*
Seclingua Inc .... G 203 922-4560
Stamford *(G-8406)*
SEI II Inc .... F 203 877-8488
Milford *(G-4641)*
Sekisui Diagnostics LLC .... G 203 602-7777
Stamford *(G-8408)*
Sequel Special Products LLC .... E 203 759-1020
Wolcott *(G-10589)*
Sleep Management Solutions LLC .... F 888 497-5337
Hartford *(G-3690)*
Smiths Medical Asd Inc .... B 860 621-9111
Southington *(G-7975)*
Soft Tissue Regeneration Inc .... G 973 879-6367
New Haven *(G-5398)*
Southington Tool & Mfg Corp .... E 860 276-0021
Plantsville *(G-6912)*
Spine Wave Inc .... D 203 944-9494
Shelton *(G-7558)*
Stryker Corporation .... F 860 528-1111
East Hartford *(G-2379)*
Summit Orthopedic Tech Inc .... E 203 693-2727
Milford *(G-4655)*
Supernova Diagnostics Inc .... G 301 792-4345
New Canaan *(G-5149)*
Surgiquest Inc .... D 203 799-2400
Milford *(G-4658)*
Synectic Engineering Inc .... F 203 877-8488
Milford *(G-4660)*
Tangen Biosciences Inc .... G 203 433-4045
Branford *(G-660)*
Tarry Medical Products Inc .... F 203 794-1438
Danbury *(G-1960)*
Tomtec .... G 203 795-5030
Orange *(G-6631)*
Tyco International MGT Co LLC .... G 203 492-5000
North Haven *(G-6003)*
Ultimate Wireforms Inc .... D 860 582-9111
Bristol *(G-1134)*
United Ophthalmics LLC .... G 203 745-8399
Meriden *(G-4259)*
▲ **United States Surgical Corp** .... A 203 845-1000
New Haven *(G-5425)*
Utitec Inc .... D 860 945-0605
Watertown *(G-9744)*
Utitec Holdings Inc .... G 860 945-0601
Watertown *(G-9745)*
Vivax Medical Corporation .... F 203 729-0514
Naugatuck *(G-4929)*
▲ **Wallach Surgical Devices Inc** .... E 203 799-2000
Trumbull *(G-9094)*
Wallach Surgical Devices Inc .... F 800 243-2463
Trumbull *(G-9095)*
Winslow Automatics Inc .... D 860 225-6321
New Britain *(G-5084)*

3842 Orthopedic, Prosthetic & Surgical Appliances/Splys

210 Innovation LLC .... G 860 444-1986
Waterford *(G-9638)*
Ability Prsthtics Orthtics LLC .... G 860 571-8979
Glastonbury *(G-3002)*
◆ **Acme United Corporation** .... C 203 254-6060
Fairfield *(G-2743)*
Adolf Gordon Corporation .... G 860 872-9037
Vernon *(G-9129)*
Advanced Hearing Solutions LLC .... F 860 674-8558
Avon *(G-72)*
Alternative Prosthetic Svcs .... G 203 367-1212
Bridgeport *(G-688)*
Auto Suture Company Australia .... G 203 845-1000
Norwalk *(G-6081)*
Auto Suture Company UK .... B 203 845-1000
Norwalk *(G-6082)*
Avitus Orthopaedics Inc .... F 860 637-9922
Farmington *(G-2880)*
Becton Dickinson and Company .... B 860 824-5487
Canaan *(G-1281)*
Beiersdorf Inc .... B 203 854-8000
Norwalk *(G-6088)*
▲ **Beiersdorf North America Inc** .... F 203 563-5800
Wilton *(G-10272)*
▼ **Bio Med Packaging Systems Inc** .... E 203 846-1923
Norwalk *(G-6092)*
Biometrics Inc .... G 203 261-1162
Trumbull *(G-9004)*
Brymill Corporation .... F 860 875-2460
Ellington *(G-2579)*
▲ **Cardiopulmonary Corp** .... E 203 877-1999
Milford *(G-4484)*
◆ **Carwild Corporation** .... E 860 442-4914
New London *(G-5461)*
Comprhnsive Prsthetic Svcs LLC .... G 203 315-1400
Branford *(G-575)*
Connecticut Brace and Limb LLC .... G 860 740-2154
Haddam *(G-3403)*
Contemporary Products LLC .... E 860 346-9283
Middletown *(G-4332)*
Coopersurgical Inc .... G 203 601-5200
Trumbull *(G-9016)*
◆ **Coopersurgical Inc** .... C 203 601-5200
Trumbull *(G-9017)*
Cranial Technologies Inc .... F 203 318-8739
Madison *(G-3915)*
Ctl Corporation .... G 860 651-9173
West Simsbury *(G-9976)*
Danbury Medi-Car Service Inc .... G 203 748-3433
Danbury *(G-1783)*
Danbury Ortho .... G 203 797-1500
Danbury *(G-1785)*
Dental Implant Services LLC .... G 203 720-1873
Naugatuck *(G-4876)*
Dermapac Inc .... G 203 924-7148
Shelton *(G-7431)*
Dougherty Sons Fur Stretchers .... G 860 839-0096
Suffield *(G-8717)*
▲ **Elvex Corporation** .... F 203 743-2488
Shelton *(G-7438)*
Enduro Wheelchair Company .... G 860 289-0374
East Hartford *(G-2324)*
Ethicon Inc .... B 860 621-9111
Southington *(G-7918)*
Ethicon Inc .... G 860 658-7653
Simsbury *(G-7625)*
Fire & Iron .... G 203 934-3756
West Haven *(G-9909)*
First Aid Bandage Co Inc .... F 860 443-8499
New London *(G-5472)*
Gordon Engineering Corp .... F 203 775-4501
Brookfield *(G-1193)*
GSC Orthotics Prosthetics LLC .... G 203 857-0887
Norwalk *(G-6186)*
Hamilton Standard Space .... E 860 654-6000
Windsor Locks *(G-10490)*
Hanger Prsthetcs & Ortho Inc .... G 860 482-5611
Torrington *(G-8931)*
Hanger Prsthetcs & Ortho Inc .... G 203 230-0667
North Haven *(G-5945)*
Hanger Prsthetcs & Ortho Inc .... G 860 667-5300
Cromwell *(G-1703)*
Hanger Prsthetcs & Ortho Inc .... F 860 545-9050
Hartford *(G-3604)*
Hanger Prsthetcs & Ortho Inc .... G 860 667-5370
Newington *(G-5658)*
Hanger Prsthetcs & Ortho Inc .... G 860 871-0905
Vernon *(G-9139)*
Hanger Prsthetcs & Ortho Inc .... G 203 377-8820
Stratford *(G-8623)*
▲ **Hermell Products Inc** .... E 860 242-6550
Bloomfield *(G-419)*
Ict Business .... G 203 595-9452
Stamford *(G-8243)*
Inka Inc .... G 212 475-2180
Greenwich *(G-3181)*
Johnson Meadows LLC .... G 860 642-0618
Lebanon *(G-3856)*
K W Griffen Company .... E 203 846-1923
Norwalk *(G-6226)*
Kaufman Enterprises Inc .... F 203 777-2396
New Haven *(G-5307)*
Kbc Electronics Inc .... F 203 298-9654
Milford *(G-4563)*
Kelyniam Global Inc .... F 800 280-8192
Collinsville *(G-1595)*
Kinetic Innvtive Sting Sys LLC .... G 203 488-1758
Branford *(G-617)*
Krutch Pack LLC .... G 860 836-1745
Newington *(G-5671)*
Leona Corp .... G 860 257-3840
Wethersfield *(G-10209)*
Limbkeepers LLC .... G 860 304-3250
Lyme *(G-3905)*
Lynne Marshall .... G 860 245-3645
Groton *(G-3299)*
▲ **McIntire Company** .... F 860 585-8559
Bristol *(G-1070)*
McNeil Healthcare Inc .... G 203 934-8187
West Haven *(G-9935)*
Medical Industries America LLC .... G 203 254-8080
Fairfield *(G-2813)*
Meditech LLC .... G 203 219-3688
Norwalk *(G-6255)*
Motiv Technology Inc .... G 203 371-7011
Fairfield *(G-2820)*
Nash Surgical Supply Co Inc .... G 203 828-6098
Oxford *(G-6681)*
New England Ctr For Hring Rhab .... G 860 455-1404
Hampton *(G-3538)*
New England Orthotic & Prost .... G 203 634-7566
Meriden *(G-4208)*
New England Orthotic & Prost .... G 860 967-0877
Hartford *(G-3651)*
New England Shoulder Elbow Soc .... G 860 679-6600
Farmington *(G-2937)*
Ooshears Inc .... G 415 230-0154
Woodbridge *(G-10610)*
Orchid Orthpd Solutions LLC .... G 203 922-0105
Shelton *(G-7521)*

S I C

Employee Codes: A=Over 500 employees, B=251-500
C=101-250, D=51-100, E=20-50, F=10-19, G=1-9

2020 Harris Connecticut
Manufacturers Directory

457

Orteoponix LLC....G....203 804-9775
Storrs (G-8550)
Out On A Limb....G....203 315-8977
Branford (G-630)
▼ Playtex Products LLC....D....203 944-5500
Shelton (G-7531)
Praxair Inc....D....800 772-9247
Danbury (G-1912)
Prospect Designs Inc....G....860 379-7858
New Hartford (G-5207)
Prosthetic and Orthotic....G....860 904-2419
Bloomfield (G-470)
Respironics Inc....C....203 697-6490
Wallingford (G-9350)
Safety Dispatch Inc....G....203 885-5722
Ridgefield (G-7171)
◆ Scapa Tapes North America LLC....C....860 688-8000
Windsor (G-10434)
▲ Schaeffler Aerospace USA Corp....B....203 744-2211
Danbury (G-1936)
Stride Inc....F....203 758-8307
Middlebury (G-4295)
Teleflex Incorporated....E....860 742-8821
Coventry (G-1681)
Tyco International MGT Co LLC....G....203 492-5000
North Haven (G-6003)
United Seating & Mobility LLC....G....860 761-0700
Rocky Hill (G-7270)
▲ United States Surgical Corp....A....203 845-1000
New Haven (G-5425)
Wellinks Inc....G....650 704-0714
New Haven (G-5430)
Westconn Orthopedic Laboratory....G....203 743-4420
Danbury (G-1981)
Yale Comfort Shoe Center Inc....G....203 338-8485
Stratford (G-8713)
Zenith-Omni Hearing Center....G....203 624-9857
New Haven (G-5454)

3843 Dental Eqpt & Splys

A & D Dental Innovations LLC....G....888 374-5134
Simsbury (G-7608)
▲ Acme Monaco Corporation....C....860 224-1349
New Britain (G-4934)
Aero-Med Ltd....G....860 659-2270
South Windsor (G-7702)
All Smiles Dental....G....860 450-9237
Willimantic (G-10220)
Anna M Chisilenco-Raho....G....203 877-0377
Milford (G-4452)
Bridgeport Dental LLC....G....203 384-2261
Bridgeport (G-720)
Bti CCS....G....860 758-7644
Windsor Locks (G-10475)
▲ Centrix Inc....C....203 929-5582
Shelton (G-7415)
Cristina Ilies....G....860 456-3153
Willimantic (G-10223)
Eagle Alloys....G....203 453-9910
Guilford (G-3349)
Essel Dental....C....860 254-6955
East Windsor (G-2492)
Gold Star Dental....G....860 445-1330
Groton (G-3289)
J S Dental Manufacturing Inc....G....203 438-8832
Ridgefield (G-7148)
▲ Jensen Industries Inc....D....203 285-1402
North Haven (G-5951)
Kinetic Instruments Inc....E....203 743-0080
Bethel (G-320)
Lloyd P McDonald....G....860 447-1787
Waterford (G-9659)
Mark D Tweedie DDS....G....860 649-0436
Manchester (G-4056)
Meridian Group LLC....G....860 928-5266
Woodstock (G-10672)
Nova Dental LLC....G....203 234-3900
North Haven (G-5969)
Orthotraction Pads LLC....G....203 698-0291
Old Greenwich (G-6482)
Palmero Healthcare LLC....F....203 377-6424
Stratford (G-8660)
Pbn LLC....G....860 582-9111
Bristol (G-1089)
▼ Pickadent Inc....G....203 431-8716
Ridgefield (G-7160)
Sabol Associates....G....203 762-2183
Wilton (G-10326)
Scott Woodford....G....203 245-4266
Madison (G-3955)
Ultimate Companies Inc....G....860 582-9111
Bristol (G-1133)
Ultimate Wireforms Inc....D....860 582-9111
Bristol (G-1134)
Uppercurve LLC....G....203 770-0223
New Milford (G-5604)
Winslow Automatics Inc....D....860 225-6321
New Britain (G-5084)

3844 X-ray Apparatus & Tubes

5w LLC....G....860 751-9209
Farmington (G-2874)
Associated X-Ray Corp....F....203 466-2446
East Haven (G-2412)
Bidwell Industrial Group Inc....E....860 346-9283
Middletown (G-4325)
Biowave Innovations LLC....C....203 982-8157
Wilton (G-10273)
◆ Comet Technologies USA Inc....E....203 447-3200
Shelton (G-7421)
High Energy X-Rays Intl Corp....G....203 909-9777
Wallingford (G-9281)
Hologic Inc....C....203 790-1188
Danbury (G-1845)
▼ Kub Technologies Inc....E....203 364-8544
Stratford (G-8643)
▲ Lorad Corporation....C....203 790-5544
Danbury (G-1876)
Parker Medical Inc....G....860 350-3446
New Milford (G-5579)
▲ Precision X-Ray Inc....F....203 484-2011
North Branford (G-5852)
Remote Technologies Inc....G....203 661-2798
Greenwich (G-3225)
Topex Inc....F....203 748-5918
Danbury (G-1963)

3845 Electromedical & Electrotherapeutic Apparatus

Abbey Aesthetics LLC....G....860 242-0497
Avon (G-71)
Amco Precision Tools Inc....E....860 828-5640
Berlin (G-155)
American Dream Unlimited LLC....G....860 742-5055
Andover (G-6)
Atlantic Inertial Systems Inc....A....203 250-3500
Cheshire (G-1357)
▼ Bio-Med Devices Inc....D....203 458-0202
Guilford (G-3329)
Charlies Ride....G....860 916-3637
Windsor Locks (G-10478)
Coherent Inc....E....860 243-9557
Bloomfield (G-404)
Coolspine LLC....G....203 263-6188
Woodbury (G-10631)
◆ Coopersurgical Inc....C....203 601-5200
Trumbull (G-9017)
Defibtech LLC....D....866 333-4248
Guilford (G-3344)
Door Step Prep LLC....G....860 550-0460
West Hartford (G-9801)
Dynamic Lasers LLC....G....866 731-9610
New Milford (G-5528)
Eclipse Systems Inc....G....203 483-0665
Branford (G-585)
Epicurean Feast Medtron O....G....203 492-5000
North Haven (G-5937)
Focus Medical LLC....G....203 730-8885
Bethel (G-301)
Heart Health Inc....G....800 692-7753
New Haven (G-5295)
Hobbs Medical Inc....E....860 684-5875
Stafford Springs (G-8031)
Home Diagnostics Corp....C....203 445-1170
Trumbull (G-9035)
Intracranial Bioanalytics LLC....G....914 490-1524
Woodbridge (G-10602)
▲ Ivy Biomedical Systems Inc....E....203 481-4183
Branford (G-610)
Jeffrey Gold....G....203 281-5737
Hamden (G-3467)
▲ Kent Scientific Corporation....F....860 626-1172
Torrington (G-8942)
Legnos Medical Inc....F....860 446-8058
Groton (G-3297)
Loon Medical Inc....G....860 373-0217
Tolland (G-8868)
Mobile Sense Technologies Inc....G....203 914-5375
Farmington (G-2930)
Non-Invasive Med Systems LLC....G....914 462-0701
Stamford (G-8329)
Novatek Medical Inc....G....203 356-0156
Stamford (G-8332)
Philips Ultrasound Inc....D....203 753-5215
Waterbury (G-9576)
Pioneer Optics Company Inc....F....860 286-0071
Bloomfield (G-465)
▲ Ram Technologies LLC....F....203 453-3916
Guilford (G-3385)
Razzberry Inc....G....510 495-5366
Hamden (G-3502)
Razzberry Operating Co Inc....G....510 495-5366
Hamden (G-3503)
▲ Respironics Novametrix LLC....C....203 697-6475
Wallingford (G-9351)
Respond Systems....F....203 481-2810
Branford (G-641)
Safe Laser Therapy LLC....G....203 261-4400
Stamford (G-8400)
Seclingua Inc....G....203 922-4560
Stamford (G-8406)
Star Tech Instruments Inc....G....203 312-0767
New Fairfield (G-5176)
Teclens LLC....G....919 824-5224
Stamford (G-8461)
Textspeak Corporation....F....203 803-1069
Westport (G-10165)
▲ Tomtec Inc....D....203 281-6790
Hamden (G-3522)
▲ United States Surgical Corp....A....203 845-1000
New Haven (G-5425)
Vesselon Inc....G....203 989-0500
Norwalk (G-6387)
Vital Hlthcare Cmmncations LLC....G....866 478-4825
Milford (G-4675)
◆ Walker Magnetics Group Inc....E....508 853-3232
Windsor (G-10461)
Wideband Solutions Inc....G....860 383-8918
Plainville (G-6877)

3851 Ophthalmic Goods

Cashon....G....786 325-4144
Groton (G-3276)
Central Optical....G....860 236-2329
West Hartford (G-9787)
◆ Coburn Technologies Inc....C....860 648-6600
South Windsor (G-7731)
▲ Encore Optics....F....860 282-0082
South Windsor (G-7749)
◆ Gerber Coburn Optical Inc....C....800 843-1479
South Windsor (G-7758)
◆ Gerber Scientific LLC....C....860 871-8082
Tolland (G-8864)
Hoya Corporation....B....860 289-5379
South Windsor (G-7773)
L A Vision LLC....G....860 523-0339
Hartford (G-3624)
Lens....G....203 426-8833
Newtown (G-5754)
Lenses Only....G....860 278-2020
Hartford (G-3627)
Lenses Only LLC....F....860 769-2020
Bloomfield (G-440)
Mager & Gougelman Inc....G....203 773-1753
New Haven (G-5324)
McLeod Optical Company Inc....G....203 754-2187
Waterbury (G-9538)
New England Quartz Co....G....203 846-9723
Norwalk (G-6273)
Opticare Eye Health & Vision....G....203 261-2619
Trumbull (G-9052)
Pilla Inc....G....203 894-3265
Ridgefield (G-7161)
Precision Optical Co....E....860 289-6023
East Hartford (G-2361)
Shari M Roth MD....G....860 676-2525
Avon (G-111)
University Optics LLC....G....860 779-6123
Dayville (G-2076)
Worldscreen Inc....G....860 274-9218
Watertown (G-9751)

3861 Photographic Eqpt & Splys

Aerial Imaging Solutions LLC....G....860 434-3637
Old Lyme (G-6488)
Bidwell Industrial Group Inc....E....860 346-9283
Middletown (G-4325)
Bpi Reprographics....F....203 866-5600
Norwalk (G-6097)

39 MISCELLANEOUS MANUFACTURING INDUSTRIES

Cag Imaging LLC .... G 860 887-0836
  Norwich (G-6408)
▲ Cine Magnetics Inc .... C 914 273-7600
  Stamford (G-8147)
CT Films LLC .... G 203 734-8307
  Seymour (G-7343)
Dan Chichester .... G 203 722-4619
  Stamford (G-8178)
Ebeam Film LLC .... F 203 926-0100
  Shelton (G-7434)
Flexxray LLC .... G 203 689-5435
  Guilford (G-3353)
Freedom Grafix LLC .... G 815 900-6189
  Fairfield (G-2787)
Fujifilm Elctrnic Mtls USA Inc .... G 203 363-3360
  Stamford (G-8211)
Image In Motion .... G 203 264-6784
  Southbury (G-7860)
Industrial Sensor Vision Inter .... G 203 592-8723
  Oxford (G-6667)
John Pecora .... G 860 677-9323
  Farmington (G-2920)
Kenyon Laboratories LLC .... G 860 345-2097
  Higganum (G-3766)
Kitty Guerrilla Films .... G 203 259-8395
  Fairfield (G-2806)
Laserman of Connecticut .... G 203 972-2887
  Norwalk (G-6231)
Macroscopic Solutions LLC .... G 410 870-5566
  Tolland (G-8869)
Medical Imaging Group Inc .... G 203 588-1921
  Stamford (G-8304)
Mid State ARC Inc .... E 203 238-9001
  Meriden (G-4201)
Nancy Tenenbaum Films .... G 203 221-6830
  Weston (G-10033)
Recycle 4 Vets LLC .... G 203 222-7300
  Westport (G-10147)
Reliance Business Systems Inc .... G 203 281-4407
  North Haven (G-5987)
River Valley Photographic LLC .... G 860 368-0882
  South Glastonbury (G-7682)
▲ Rosco Holdings Inc .... D 203 708-8900
  Stamford (G-8398)
▲ Rosco Laboratories Inc .... E 203 708-8900
  Stamford (G-8399)
▲ Verico Technology LLC .... E 800 492-7286
  Enfield (G-2704)
▲ Vitec Production Solutions Inc .... D 203 929-1100
  Shelton (G-7581)
Xerox Corporation .... B 203 968-3000
  Norwalk (G-6401)
Xerox Holdings Corporation .... G 203 968-3000
  Norwalk (G-6402)
Xerox Services .... G 860 883-8377
  Cromwell (G-1725)

3873 Watch & Clock Devices & Parts

A Telling Time Limited CB .... G 877 486-7865
  Colchester (G-1538)
▲ Accu-Time Systems Inc .... E 860 870-5000
  Ellington (G-2570)
Lantern LLC .... G 866 203-5715
  Woodstock (G-10668)
▲ Marhall Browing Intl Corp .... G 203 264-2702
  Oxford (G-6676)
▲ Morristown Star Struck LLC .... E 203 778-4925
  Bethel (G-329)
▲ Pyramid Time Systems LLC .... E 203 238-0550
  Meriden (G-4225)
Real Women International LLC .... G 212 719-3130
  Southbury (G-7874)
◆ Timex Group Usa Inc .... C 203 346-5000
  Middlebury (G-4297)
◆ Wenger Na Inc .... G 845 365-3500
  Monroe (G-4764)
West Hartford Lock Co LLC .... F 860 236-0671
  Hartford (G-3714)

39 MISCELLANEOUS MANUFACTURING INDUSTRIES

3911 Jewelry: Precious Metal

A&D Schneider LLC .... G 203 870-9474
  Stratford (G-8563)
AG Jewelry Designs LLC .... G 800 643-0978
  Stamford (G-8065)
AG Jewelry Designs LLC .... G 800 643-0978
  Norwalk (G-6063)

Arpie Krisie Gems & Jewelry .... G 203 799-8927
  Orange (G-6583)
Asha .... G 203 253-0146
  Greenwich (G-3124)
Beautybrain Bracelet LLC .... G 203 245-8913
  Madison (G-3910)
Brannkey Inc .... E 860 510-0501
  Old Saybrook (G-6525)
Carol Ackerman Designs .... G 860 693-1013
  Collinsville (G-1590)
Chainmail & More LLC .... G 860 741-2965
  Enfield (G-2622)
Dantes Jewelry & Repair .... G 860 346-4779
  Middletown (G-4335)
Dawn Hill Enterprises LLC .... G 860 496-9188
  Torrington (G-8917)
Elm City Mfg Jewelers Inc .... G 203 248-2195
  Hamden (G-3444)
Emilie Cohen .... G 860 693-9427
  Collinsville (G-1594)
Gabriel Inc .... G 203 824-1412
  Falls Village (G-2870)
Gemma Oro Inc .... G 203 227-0774
  Westport (G-10088)
George S Preisner Jewelers .... G 203 265-0057
  Wallingford (G-9275)
Goldworks .... G 203 743-9668
  Danbury (G-1833)
Gregmans Inc .... G 203 464-2530
  Milford (G-4543)
Herff Jones LLC .... F 203 368-9344
  Stratford (G-8624)
House of Bubba LLC .... G 860 429-4250
  Willington (G-10250)
J J Lane Designs .... G 860 849-0815
  Suffield (G-8722)
▲ Jewelry Designs Inc .... E 203 797-0389
  Danbury (G-1861)
Johannes Sulek Jewelry .... G 203 968-1729
  Stamford (G-8267)
Joseph A Cnte Mfg Jewelers Inc .... G 203 248-9853
  Hamden (G-3469)
Joseph Hannoush Family Inc .... F 860 561-4651
  Farmington (G-2921)
Karavas Fashions Ltd .... F 203 866-4000
  Norwalk (G-6228)
Kasson Jewelers of Southport .... G 203 319-0021
  Southport (G-8005)
Kenneth R Carson .... G 860 247-2707
  Manchester (G-4044)
▲ Lfbw LLC .... G 203 966-8499
  New Canaan (G-5114)
▲ Mrk Fine Arts LLC .... G 203 972-3115
  New Canaan (G-5122)
N Karpel Studio LLC .... G 203 782-9108
  New Haven (G-5338)
O C Tanner Company .... G 203 944-5430
  Shelton (G-7516)
Odyssey Jewelry .... G 203 574-4956
  Waterbury (G-9568)
Russell Amy Kahn .... F 203 438-2133
  Ridgefield (G-7169)
Silver Little Shop Inc .... G 860 678-1976
  Avon (G-112)
Silversmith Inc .... G 203 869-4244
  Greenwich (G-3235)
Swedes Jewelers Inc .... G 860 623-3916
  East Windsor (G-2525)
Tabar Designs .... G 203 453-8868
  Guilford (G-3397)

3914 Silverware, Plated & Stainless Steel Ware

Boardman Silversmiths Inc .... F 203 265-9978
  Wallingford (G-9220)
George S Preisner Jewelers .... G 203 265-0057
  Wallingford (G-9275)
House of Bubba LLC .... G 860 429-4250
  Willington (G-10250)
Silver Touch .... G 203 778-1778
  Bethel (G-342)
Silversmith Inc .... G 203 869-4244
  Greenwich (G-3235)
Ulbrich Solar Wire LLC .... F 203 239-4481
  North Haven (G-6007)
Woodbury Pewterers Inc .... E 203 263-2668
  Woodbury (G-10656)

3915 Jewelers Findings & Lapidary Work

Boxtree Accessories Inc .... G 203 637-5794
  Old Greenwich (G-6468)
International Mines Outlet .... G 203 264-9207
  Southbury (G-7863)
Ncc .... G 203 966-8307
  Sandy Hook (G-7323)
Opal Manning Company Inc .... G 203 292-6981
  Fairfield (G-2825)
Yankee Mineral & Gem Co .... G 860 267-0167
  East Hampton (G-2284)

3931 Musical Instruments

Acoustic Music .... G 203 458-2525
  Guilford (G-3321)
Alexander Tulchinsky Violins .... G 203 698-7844
  Riverside (G-7189)
Austin Organs Incorporated .... E 860 522-8293
  Hartford (G-3554)
Big City String Co .... G 203 371-8117
  Bridgeport (G-712)
Blu & Grae Music .... G 857 204-3095
  Stamford (G-8113)
Broome & Co LLC .... G 860 653-2106
  East Granby (G-2193)
Broome & Company LLC .... G 860 623-0254
  Windsor Locks (G-10474)
Dizzy Fish Music LLC .... G 203 599-5700
  Milford (G-4512)
Fender Musical Instrs Corp .... G 860 379-7575
  New Hartford (G-5191)
Jerry Freeman Pennywhistles .... G 860 498-0014
  Coventry (G-1658)
Jobo Enterprizes LLC .... G 203 367-7517
  Bridgeport (G-807)
Mary Jeans Musical Instrs LLC .... G 860 887-0633
  Salem (G-7290)
▲ Mountain Ocarinas .... G 860 242-6626
  Bloomfield (G-448)
Nollysource Entertainment LLC .... G 347 264-6655
  Bridgeport (G-853)
Sharps & Flats .... G 203 438-3300
  Redding (G-7108)
Strings By Aurora LLC .... G 203 583-9929
  Stratford (G-8688)
Sweetheart Flute Company LLC .... G 860 749-8514
  Enfield (G-2700)
Two Bsses & A Hrmonca Prdctns .... G 203 259-5916
  Easton (G-2568)
Ute Brinkmann Geigenbaumeister .... G 203 265-7456
  Wallingford (G-9398)
Violin Performance Co .... G 860 836-8647
  South Windsor (G-7838)
Vision Musical Instruments .... G 203 416-6359
  Norwalk (G-6390)
Viz-Pro LLC .... G 860 379-0055
  Winsted (G-10542)
Zuckerman Hrpsichords Intl LLC .... G 860 535-1715
  Stonington (G-8542)

3942 Dolls & Stuffed Toys

Anjar Co .... G 203 321-1023
  Stamford (G-8086)
▲ Cabin Critters Inc .... G 203 778-4552
  New Fairfield (G-5164)
Chantys Closet .... G 860 752-4512
  Windsor (G-10372)
▲ New England Toy LLC .... G 860 655-6089
  Simsbury (G-7637)
Next Door Creations LLC .... G 860 933-0366
  Glastonbury (G-3064)
Oskr Inc .... G 475 238-2634
  North Haven (G-5971)
Rags A Muffin .... G 203 377-7063
  Stratford (G-8672)
Tiny Woodshop .... G 203 866-6725
  Norwalk (G-6369)

3944 Games, Toys & Children's Vehicles

A Piece of Pzzle Bhvral Intrve .... G 860 250-8054
  West Hartford (G-9769)
AAA Distributors .... G 860 346-0230
  Middletown (G-4312)
Anjar Co .... G 203 321-1023
  Stamford (G-8086)
Bear Market .... G 860 379-8943
  Winchester Center (G-10343)
Bedard Puzzles .... G 860 657-3781
  Glastonbury (G-3013)

Berwick Industries LLC ....G.... 475 228-5822
Darien *(G-2008)*
Brainbeat Inc ....G.... 917 291-9747
Stamford *(G-8118)*
Card Carrier Games LLC ....G.... 203 521-0291
Milford *(G-4483)*
Col-Lar Enterprises Inc ....G.... 860 799-6970
Brookfield *(G-1173)*
▲ **Col-Lar Enterprises Inc** ....F.... 203 798-1786
New Milford *(G-5521)*
Crafty Creations ....G.... 860 673-6225
Avon *(G-79)*
E11even LLC ....G.... 855 246-6233
Westport *(G-10075)*
Eco Pallet World LLC ....G.... 203 343-9089
Milford *(G-4525)*
▲ **Enterplay LLC** ....F.... 203 458-1128
Guilford *(G-3351)*
Essex Wood Products Inc ....E.... 860 537-3451
Colchester *(G-1550)*
Game On LLC ....G.... 860 608-8931
East Haddam *(G-2242)*
◆ **Imagine 8 LLC** ....G.... 203 421-0905
Madison *(G-3928)*
Infinity Stone Inc ....F.... 203 575-9484
Waterbury *(G-9505)*
Keyes On Kites Tattoo Gallery ....G.... 203 387-5397
New Haven *(G-5309)*
Kite Business Solutions LLC ....G.... 860 302-0682
Plantsville *(G-6899)*
◆ **Lego Systems Inc** ....A.... 860 749-2291
Enfield *(G-2655)*
Mark Cappitellas Hnd-Cut Wden ....G.... 860 818-4334
East Haddam *(G-2244)*
Mark G Cappitella ....G.... 860 873-3093
East Haddam *(G-2245)*
Most Excllent Cmics Cllctibles ....G.... 860 741-0113
Enfield *(G-2662)*
Mwb Toy Company LLC ....G.... 212 598-4500
Danbury *(G-1890)*
Nancy Dighello ....G.... 860 763-4294
Enfield *(G-2665)*
New Beginnings Sea Glass ....G.... 203 329-7623
Stamford *(G-8321)*
One Piece of Puzzle LLC ....G.... 860 919-6956
Hartford *(G-3659)*
Pieces of Puzzle Daycare ....G.... 203 916-8332
Bridgeport *(G-873)*
Poof-Alex Holdings LLC ....G.... 203 930-7711
Greenwich *(G-3217)*
Pub Games Plus ....G.... 203 846-5991
Norwalk *(G-6310)*
Puzzle Rings Creations LLC ....G.... 203 550-1591
Stamford *(G-8383)*
Puzzlesocial LLC ....G.... 917 515-1030
Westport *(G-10144)*
Rocking Horse Saloon ....G.... 860 247-2566
Hartford *(G-3680)*
Rose To Occassion LLC ....G.... 860 628-6880
Southington *(G-7968)*
Ross Curtis Product Inc ....G.... 860 886-6800
Norwich *(G-6429)*
Roto-Die Company Inc ....F.... 860 292-7030
East Windsor *(G-2516)*
◆ **S & S Worldwide Inc** ....C.... 860 537-3451
Colchester *(G-1574)*
S&A Puzzle LLC ....G.... 860 675-0477
Avon *(G-108)*
▲ **Skydog Kites LLC** ....G.... 860 365-0600
Colchester *(G-1577)*
Spera Cottage Crafters ....G.... 860 738-2391
Colebrook *(G-1587)*
Spots and Ladybugs LLC ....G.... 203 378-8232
Trumbull *(G-9076)*
Tacdab LLC ....G.... 860 447-9023
Waterford *(G-9674)*
Team Walbern ....G.... 860 667-7627
Newington *(G-5710)*
Three Across LLC ....G.... 203 866-6688
Norwalk *(G-6367)*
Toddler Teams LLC ....G.... 203 972-7713
New Canaan *(G-5153)*
Tricycle Granola LLC ....G.... 203 861-1740
Greenwich *(G-3249)*
Tricycle Hill LLC ....G.... 203 895-2217
Fairfield *(G-2858)*
◆ **US Games Systems Inc** ....E.... 203 353-8400
Stamford *(G-8481)*
Walts Trooper Factory LLC ....G.... 203 871-9254
North Branford *(G-5866)*
Westport Model Works ....G.... 203 226-2798
Westport *(G-10175)*
World Wide Games Inc ....G.... 860 537-3451
Colchester *(G-1583)*
Worms Eye ....G.... 203 888-0895
Seymour *(G-7374)*
X44 LLC ....G.... 860 480-5560
Torrington *(G-8993)*

3949 Sporting & Athletic Goods, NEC

Ammunition Stor Components LLC ....G.... 860 225-3548
New Britain *(G-4945)*
▲ **Aqua Massage International Inc** ....F.... 860 536-3735
Mystic *(G-4799)*
Archers Only LLC ....G.... 860 689-0594
Harwinton *(G-3720)*
B & D Lures ....G.... 860 861-6530
Ledyard *(G-3868)*
Batrolling4u LLC ....G.... 860 439-1994
Waterford *(G-9642)*
Beckley Inc ....G.... 203 488-1019
Branford *(G-557)*
Bo-Dyn Bobsled Project Inc ....G.... 860 526-9504
Chester *(G-1465)*
Bob Vess Building LLC ....G.... 860 729-2536
Cromwell *(G-1693)*
Bonenfants Drv Your Auto Svc ....G.... 203 222-2239
Westport *(G-10061)*
Boomerang Consignment ....G.... 203 788-9002
South Kent *(G-7683)*
Boomerang Studio ....G.... 203 689-5155
Guilford *(G-3331)*
Brampton Technology Ltd ....G.... 860 667-7689
Newington *(G-5634)*
Brandmark Studios LLC ....G.... 203 438-9400
Ridgefield *(G-7125)*
Chromations LLC ....G.... 203 929-8007
Shelton *(G-7419)*
Coma Skateboards ....G.... 860 933-4830
Storrs *(G-8547)*
Compleat Angler ....G.... 203 655-9400
Darien *(G-2014)*
Creative Playthings Ltd ....G.... 203 748-7206
Brookfield *(G-1175)*
CT Amateur Jai Alai LLC ....G.... 860 357-2544
Berlin *(G-174)*
Danbury Grassroots Tennis Inc ....G.... 203 797-0500
Danbury *(G-1782)*
Demane Golf Inc ....G.... 203 531-9126
Greenwich *(G-3151)*
Dewey J Manufacturing Company ....G.... 203 264-3064
Oxford *(G-6655)*
East Coast Hockey Depot LLC ....G.... 203 247-3476
Stamford *(G-8191)*
▲ **Edgewater International LLC** ....F.... 860 851-9014
Stafford Springs *(G-8028)*
Ernest Ferraro ....G.... 914 921-4376
Weston *(G-10025)*
Europa Sports Products Inc ....G.... 860 688-1110
Windsor *(G-10385)*
Facet Skis ....G.... 203 529-3681
Wilton *(G-10294)*
Fairfield Pool & Equipment Co ....G.... 203 334-3600
Fairfield *(G-2785)*
Fishing Innovations LLC ....G.... 860 434-3974
Old Lyme *(G-6509)*
Force3 Pro Gear LLC ....G.... 315 367-2331
Milford *(G-4538)*
Frostbite LLC ....G.... 203 240-3449
Wilton *(G-10297)*
Gary Morris Clubmaker ....G.... 860 482-5929
Torrington *(G-8929)*
▼ **Gilman Corporation** ....E.... 860 887-7080
Gilman *(G-3000)*
Glovewhisperer Inc ....G.... 203 487-8997
Greenwich *(G-3167)*
Golf Galaxy LLC ....G.... 203 855-0500
Norwalk *(G-6182)*
Group Works ....G.... 203 834-7905
Wilton *(G-10299)*
Hamden Sports Center Inc ....G.... 203 248-9898
Hamden *(G-3460)*
High Hook Lures LLC ....G.... 860 334-2324
Old Lyme *(G-6513)*
Homeland Fundraising ....G.... 860 386-6698
East Windsor *(G-2498)*
Hoodlum Skateboard Company LLC ....G.... 860 690-6201
East Hartford *(G-2333)*
Impaled Longboards LLC ....G.... 860 379-1101
New Hartford *(G-5195)*
International Soccer & Rugby ....G.... 203 254-1979
Southport *(G-8004)*
Intersec LLC ....G.... 860 985-3158
Rocky Hill *(G-7251)*
Jacob Sportz LLC ....G.... 860 450-1073
Willimantic *(G-10231)*
Jammar Mfg Co Inc ....G.... 866 848-1113
Niantic *(G-5811)*
▲ **Jaypro Sports LLC** ....E.... 860 447-3001
Waterford *(G-9656)*
JW Gallas Rod Co ....G.... 203 790-4188
Danbury *(G-1867)*
K & D Business Ventures LLC ....G.... 860 237-1458
Jewett City *(G-3798)*
Lure of Cripple Creek ....G.... 860 564-5799
Moosup *(G-4781)*
Marty Gilman Incorporated ....D.... 860 889-7334
Gilman *(G-3001)*
Marty Gilman Incorporated ....G.... 860 889-7334
Bozrah *(G-528)*
MB Sports Training LLC ....G.... 203 269-1410
Northford *(G-6050)*
Mike Sadlak ....G.... 860 742-0227
Coventry *(G-1663)*
Montanas Board Sports ....G.... 860 537-2927
Colchester *(G-1557)*
NES Sports LLC ....G.... 765 532-2178
Bridgeport *(G-847)*
New Technologies Mfg Inc ....G.... 860 872-7605
Vernon Rockville *(G-9171)*
Paul Ramee LLC ....G.... 860 927-7135
South Kent *(G-7684)*
Pfd Studios ....G.... 860 295-8500
Marlborough *(G-4128)*
Physical Fitness Consultants ....G.... 860 653-4655
East Granby *(G-2225)*
Probatter Sports LLC ....G.... 203 874-2500
Milford *(G-4618)*
Protek Ski Racing Inc ....G.... 860 628-9643
Southington *(G-7962)*
Rampage LLC ....F.... 203 930-1022
Trumbull *(G-9061)*
Ransom Skateboards and App ....G.... 860 538-5577
Unionville *(G-9125)*
Recreational Equipment Inc ....G.... 860 313-0128
West Hartford *(G-9850)*
Road-Fit Enterprises LLC ....G.... 860 371-5137
Plainville *(G-6856)*
Robert Louis Company Inc ....G.... 203 270-1400
Newtown *(G-5776)*
Robert W Broska Enterprises ....G.... 203 846-0583
Norwalk *(G-6327)*
Roys Family Pools & Billiards ....G.... 860 546-0608
Canterbury *(G-1301)*
S Hassel Golf Works ....G.... 860 274-4011
Watertown *(G-9732)*
Sadlak Industries LLC ....E.... 860 742-0227
Coventry *(G-1673)*
Samsara Fitness LLC ....F.... 860 895-8533
Chester *(G-1483)*
Sfn LLC ....G.... 203 314-8436
Guilford *(G-3389)*
Soccer N More ....G.... 860 282-0224
East Hartford *(G-2375)*
Sports Center ....G.... 860 768-4650
West Hartford *(G-9860)*
Stone Innovations ....G.... 203 347-8536
Torrington *(G-8974)*
Swing Rite Golf ....G.... 203 748-4985
Bethel *(G-351)*
Swivel Machine Works Inc ....G.... 203 270-6343
Newtown *(G-5783)*
Tater Bats LLC ....G.... 203 510-4054
Waterbury *(G-9609)*
Toms Taz Lures ....G.... 860 429-0307
Willington *(G-10259)*
▲ **Trassig Corp** ....G.... 203 659-0456
Georgetown *(G-2999)*
Tucci Lumber Co LLC ....G.... 203 956-6181
Norwalk *(G-6378)*
Uniboard Corp ....G.... 860 428-5979
Putnam *(G-7075)*
Valley Golf Center CT LLC ....G.... 860 799-7605
New Milford *(G-5605)*
Warren Trading Company ....G.... 860 868-7848
Warren *(G-9409)*
Wasp Archery Products Inc ....G.... 860 283-0246
Plymouth *(G-6930)*
We String It ....G.... 203 512-4513
Danbury *(G-1977)*

39 MISCELLANEOUS MANUFACTURING INDUSTRIES

Wepa Sports LLC ....G..... 203 971-9372
  New London (G-5496)
Whalen Sticks LLC ....G..... 203 546-8515
  Brookfield (G-1241)
Wiffle Ball Incorporated ....F..... 203 924-4643
  Shelton (G-7587)
▲ Wild Card Golf LLC ....G..... 860 296-1661
  Hartford (G-3716)
◆ Wild Card Golf LLC ....G..... 860 296-1661
  Hartford (G-3715)
X44 LLC ....G..... 203 480-5560
  Torrington (G-8993)
Yakka LLC ....G..... 617 877-7553
  New Haven (G-5438)
Zombie Gang Skateboards LLC ....G..... 860 367-2650
  New London (G-5498)

3951 Pens & Mechanical Pencils

▲ Bic Consumer Pdts Mfg Co Inc ....G..... 203 783-2000
  Shelton (G-7406)
▲ Bic Consumer Products Mfg Co ....C..... 203 783-2000
  Milford (G-4469)
▲ Bic Corporation ....A..... 203 783-2000
  Shelton (G-7407)
Bic Corporation ....G..... 203 538-5028
  Milford (G-4470)
▲ Bic USA Inc ....C..... 203 783-2000
  Shelton (G-7408)
Carla Way ....G..... 203 351-7815
  Stamford (G-8128)
Gillette Company ....G..... 203 796-4000
  Bethel (G-303)
▲ Mega Sound and Light LLC ....G..... 203 743-4200
  Danbury (G-1882)

3952 Lead Pencils, Crayons & Artist's Mtrls

▲ Bic Corporation ....A..... 203 783-2000
  Shelton (G-7407)
Color Craft Ltd ....F..... 800 509-6563
  East Granby (G-2197)
Colors Ink ....G..... 203 269-4000
  Wallingford (G-9233)
Diiorios Custom Wdwkg LLC ....G..... 203 855-1635
  Norwalk (G-6144)
Explicit Airbrush ....G..... 860 582-6038
  Southington (G-7920)
Little Artist Paint Co LLC ....G..... 860 989-1996
  Plainville (G-6833)
Pastrana Unlimited LLC ....G..... 860 747-6633
  Plainville (G-6851)
Screening Ink LLC ....G..... 860 212-0475
  Enfield (G-2690)
Steve Cryan Studio ....G..... 860 388-5010
  Old Saybrook (G-6571)

3953 Marking Devices

A D Perkins Company ....G..... 203 777-3456
  New Haven (G-5217)
A G Russell Company Inc ....G..... 860 247-9093
  Hartford (G-3543)
Acme Sign Co ....F..... 203 324-2263
  Stamford (G-8059)
Allen of Ansonia Stamps ....G..... 203 736-2222
  Derby (G-2108)
American Rubber Stamp Company ....G..... 203 755-1135
  Cheshire (G-1351)
American Sign Inc ....E..... 203 624-2991
  New Haven (G-5229)
Arlene Lewis ....G..... 860 887-4265
  Preston (G-6981)
Biomerics LLC ....D..... 203 268-7238
  Monroe (G-4698)
D R S Desings ....G..... 203 744-2858
  Bethel (G-276)
First Place USA LLC ....G..... 203 777-5510
  Hamden (G-3448)
Gutkin Enterprises LLC ....G..... 203 777-5510
  Hamden (G-3454)
Hart Stamp & Seal LLC ....G..... 860 474-5382
  Bolton (G-510)
▼ Liftline Capital LLC ....F..... 860 395-0150
  Old Saybrook (G-6553)
▲ Mbsw Inc ....D..... 860 243-0303
  West Hartford (G-9835)
Schwerdtle Stamp Company ....E..... 203 330-2750
  Bridgeport (G-898)
Stampt By J ....G..... 860 995-3292
  East Hartford (G-2376)
United Stts Sgn & Fbrction ....E..... 203 601-1000
  Trumbull (G-9088)

Van Deusen & Levitt Assoc Inc ....E..... 203 445-6244
  Weston (G-10042)
William Korn Inc ....G..... 860 647-0284
  Manchester (G-4107)

3955 Carbon Paper & Inked Ribbons

Sandri Products ....G..... 860 824-0001
  Canaan (G-1291)

3961 Costume Jewelry & Novelties

A Capela Do Santo Antonio Inc ....G..... 860 447-3329
  New London (G-5455)
Beadazzle ....G..... 860 747-5101
  Plainville (G-6776)
Blue Lotus Bracelets ....G..... 203 858-6526
  Norwalk (G-6094)
Buisson Jewelers Inc ....G..... 203 869-8895
  Greenwich (G-3139)
Crista Grasso LLC ....G..... 347 946-2533
  Tolland (G-8856)
Dawn Hill Enterprises LLC ....G..... 860 496-9188
  Torrington (G-8917)
Designs By Diana ....G..... 860 649-1812
  Manchester (G-4006)
Gabriel Inc ....G..... 860 824-1412
  Falls Village (G-2870)
Glitzy Lady ....G..... 203 924-5663
  Shelton (G-7450)
Initial Reaction LLC ....G..... 203 255-1200
  Fairfield (G-2795)
K2steam ....G..... 860 251-9824
  Avon (G-86)
Mix Box ....G..... 203 591-8887
  Waterbury (G-9546)
Mystic Knotwork LLC ....F..... 860 889-3793
  Mystic (G-4834)
Potters Ink Inc ....G..... 860 896-5909
  Vernon Rockville (G-9176)
Smiling Dog ....G..... 860 344-0707
  Middletown (G-4419)
Swarovski North America Ltd ....G..... 203 462-3357
  Stamford (G-8453)
Swarovski North America Ltd ....G..... 203 372-0336
  Trumbull (G-9080)
The Did Collection ....G..... 203 807-4305
  Stamford (G-8464)
Wilhelm Gdale Elzabeth Designs ....G..... 203 371-8787
  Bridgeport (G-937)

3965 Fasteners, Buttons, Needles & Pins

588 Smainst LLC ....G..... 860 482-1625
  Torrington (G-8884)
Bees Knees Zipper Wax LLC ....G..... 203 521-5727
  Berlin (G-162)
Bernies Tool & Fastener Svcs ....G..... 203 466-5252
  Orange (G-6585)
Braxton Manufacturing Co Inc ....C..... 860 274-6781
  Watertown (G-9685)
Buckles In A Snap LLC ....G..... 774 452-5336
  Woodstock (G-10660)
Connectcut Prcsion Cmpnnts LLC ....G..... 860 489-8621
  Torrington (G-8915)
Eyelet Tech LLC ....E..... 203 879-5306
  Wolcott (G-10564)
Hawie Manufacturing Company ....G..... 203 366-4303
  Bridgeport (G-783)
Illinois Tool Works Inc ....E..... 203 720-1676
  Naugatuck (G-4890)
ITW Powertrain Fastening ....G..... 203 720-1676
  Naugatuck (G-4892)
J & J Precision Eyelet Inc ....D..... 860 283-8243
  Thomaston (G-8793)
Jo Vek Tool and Die Mfg Co ....G..... 203 755-1884
  Waterbury (G-9511)
Knight Inc ....G..... 203 754-6502
  Waterbury (G-9515)
Lord & Hodge Inc ....F..... 860 632-7006
  Middletown (G-4369)
Manchester Tl & Design ADP LLC ....G..... 860 296-6541
  Hartford (G-3633)
Metalform Acquisition LLC ....G..... 860 224-2630
  New Britain (G-5016)
▲ Nucap US Inc ....E..... 203 879-1423
  Wolcott (G-10578)
▲ Ogs Technologies Inc ....E..... 203 271-9055
  Cheshire (G-1424)
Paneloc Corporation ....E..... 860 677-6711
  Farmington (G-2945)
Platt Brothers & Company ....D..... 203 753-4194
  Waterbury (G-9580)

Rings Wire Inc ....E..... 203 874-6719
  Milford (G-4629)
▲ Rome Fastener Corporation ....E..... 203 874-6719
  Milford (G-4631)
Rome Fastener Sales Corp ....F..... 203 874-6719
  Milford (G-4632)
▲ Stevens Company Incorporated ....D..... 203 283-8201
  Thomaston (G-8806)
Timber-Top Inc ....G..... 860 274-6706
  Watertown (G-9741)
◆ US Button Corporation ....C..... 860 928-2707
  Putnam (G-7076)
Valley Eyelet Company ....F..... 203 729-4363
  Naugatuck (G-4926)

3991 Brooms & Brushes

Gros-Ite Industries Inc ....G..... 800 242-1790
  Cheshire (G-1395)
International Garrett-Hewitt ....G..... 203 761-1542
  Wilton (G-10303)
▼ Liftline Capital LLC ....F..... 860 395-0150
  Old Saybrook (G-6553)
Loos & Co Inc ....F..... 860 928-6681
  Pomfret (G-6934)
Torrington Brush Works Inc ....G..... 860 482-3517
  Torrington (G-8979)

3993 Signs & Advertising Displays

27 West Main Street LLC ....G..... 860 799-6494
  New Milford (G-5499)
420 Sign Design Inc ....G..... 203 852-1255
  Norwalk (G-6056)
A D Perkins Company ....G..... 203 777-3456
  New Haven (G-5217)
A To Z Signs ....G..... 203 840-0644
  Norwalk (G-6057)
ABC Sign Corporation ....E..... 203 513-8110
  Shelton (G-7387)
Accent Signs LLC ....G..... 203 975-8688
  Stamford (G-8056)
Acme Sign Co ....F..... 203 324-2263
  Stamford (G-8059)
Action Signs ....G..... 860 496-1232
  Torrington (G-8887)
Adamsahern Sign Solutions Inc ....F..... 860 523-8835
  Hartford (G-3547)
Affordable Sign Co ....G..... 203 874-0875
  Milford (G-4443)
Agjo Printing Service ....G..... 860 599-3143
  Pawcatuck (G-6703)
AIM Vinyl Signs ....G..... 203 868-1413
  Windsor (G-10356)
Albert Gramesty and Dawn Grame ....G..... 203 924-7947
  Shelton (G-7391)
All Tech Sign & Crane Service ....G..... 203 272-2207
  Cheshire (G-1350)
American Pront and Sign ....G..... 203 400-2155
  Trumbull (G-8998)
American Sign Inc ....E..... 203 624-2991
  New Haven (G-5229)
Applied Advertising Inc ....F..... 860 640-0800
  Danbury (G-1741)
Archambault Group LLC ....G..... 860 635-4006
  Cromwell (G-1688)
Archer Sign Service LLC ....G..... 203 882-8484
  Milford (G-4454)
Archer Sign Service LLC ....G..... 203 377-5362
  Milford (G-4455)
Arnco Sign Company ....E..... 203 238-1224
  Wallingford (G-9211)
Arrow Engraving & Sign LLC ....G..... 860 349-1788
  Durham (G-2138)
Art Craft Signs ....G..... 203 212-3980
  Bridgeport (G-702)
Art Q Tech Signs ....G..... 203 874-6504
  Milford (G-4458)
Art Signs ....G..... 860 871-8361
  Ellington (G-2577)
Arteffects Incorporated ....E..... 860 242-0031
  Bloomfield (G-390)
Artistic Sign Language LLC ....G..... 203 245-8213
  Madison (G-3909)
Artwork By Nora LLC ....G..... 860 963-0723
  Pomfret Center (G-6937)
Asi Sign Systems Inc ....G..... 860 828-3331
  East Berlin (G-2162)
Automotive Coop Couponing Inc ....G..... 203 227-2722
  Weston (G-10018)
Barneys Sign Service Inc ....G..... 203 878-3763
  Stratford (G-8579)

Employee Codes: A=Over 500 employees, B=251-500
C=101-250, D=51-100, E=20-50, F=10-19, G=1-9

2020 Harris Connecticut Manufacturers Directory

39 MISCELLANEOUS MANUFACTURING INDUSTRIES SIC SECTION

Baytek Sign Co....G....860 872-9279
Tolland (G-8851)
Belmeade Group LLC....G....860 413-3569
West Granby (G-9766)
Benoit Signs & Graphics....G....860 870-8300
Stafford Springs (G-8019)
Better Letters Signs....G....860 749-7235
Enfield (G-2618)
Big Prints LLC....G....203 469-1100
East Haven (G-2414)
Brass City Signs LLC....G....860 628-2046
Cheshire (G-1362)
Bristol Signart Inc....G....860 582-2577
Bristol (G-992)
Brushline Design....G....860 434-5055
Old Lyme (G-6491)
Camaro Signs Inc....G....860 886-1553
Yantic (G-10697)
Cameron Bortz....G....860 599-0477
Pawcatuck (G-6704)
Century Sign LLC....G....203 230-9000
Hamden (G-3427)
City Sign....G....860 232-4803
Hartford (G-3567)
Classic Sign & Graphics....G....203 834-1145
Wilton (G-10281)
Compu-Signs LLC....G....860 747-1985
Plainville (G-6788)
Computer Sgns Old Saybrook LLC....G....860 388-9773
Old Saybrook (G-6527)
▲ Concord Industries Inc....E....203 750-6060
Norwalk (G-6124)
Connectcut Dgital Graphics LLC....G....203 888-6509
Seymour (G-7341)
Connecticut Carved Sign Co LLC....G....860 274-2039
Watertown (G-9695)
◆ Connecticut Container Corp....C....203 248-2161
North Haven (G-5924)
Connecticut Sign Craft Inc....G....203 729-0706
Naugatuck (G-4872)
Connecticut Sign Factory....G....860 833-5689
Southington (G-7908)
Connecticut Sign Service LLC....G....860 391-9614
Old Lyme (G-6498)
Connecticut Sign Service LLC....G....860 767-7446
Essex (G-2714)
Copy Signs LLC....G....860 747-1985
Plainville (G-6793)
Corr/Dis Incorporated....G....203 838-6075
Norwalk (G-6130)
▲ Creative Dimensions Inc....E....203 250-6500
Cheshire (G-1376)
Creative Edge Solutions L....G....860 626-0007
Torrington (G-8916)
Critical Signs Graphics &....G....860 443-7446
Waterford (G-9650)
Critical Signs & Graphics....G....860 443-7446
Waterford (G-9651)
Crossroads Signs....G....203 894-5938
Ridgefield (G-7131)
CRS I Group Inc....G....860 593-4886
Southington (G-7909)
CT Sign Service LLC....G....860 322-3954
Deep River (G-2087)
Custom Art Sgns LLC....G....203 837-7674
Danbury (G-1779)
Custom Sign Solutions LLC....G....203 975-8344
Stamford (G-8172)
Cutting Edge Sgns Graphics LLC....G....203 758-7776
Prospect (G-6999)
David R Wttrwrth Son Signs LLC....G....203 753-3666
Waterbury (G-9464)
Davids Legal Signs....G....203 268-8943
Monroe (G-4710)
Defined Design Creative Art....G....203 378-2571
Stratford (G-8604)
Derrick Mason....G....413 527-4282
Norwich (G-6410)
Designs & Signs....G....203 775-0152
Brookfield (G-1182)
▲ Digit-X Inc....G....860 620-1221
Southington (G-7915)
▲ Displaycraft Inc....E....860 747-9110
Plainville (G-6799)
Douglas M Gagnon....G....860 779-2255
Danielson (G-1990)
Dundorf Designs USA Inc....G....860 859-2955
Salem (G-7288)
Eagle Signs LLC....G....860 227-1959
Essex (G-2716)
East Coast Name Plates Inc....G....203 261-4347
Easton (G-2549)
East Coast Sign and Supply Inc....G....203 791-8326
Bethel (G-291)
Elite Engraving & Awards....G....860 643-7459
Manchester (G-4014)
Executive Graphic Systems LLC....G....203 678-6432
Wallingford (G-9261)
Exhibitease LLC....G....203 481-0792
Branford (G-592)
▲ Farmington Displays Inc....E....860 677-2497
Farmington (G-2904)
Fast Sign....G....203 348-0222
Stamford (G-8202)
Fastsigns....G....203 298-4075
Milford (G-4535)
Fastsigns....G....860 437-7446
Waterford (G-9653)
Fastsigns....G....860 969-3030
Hartford (G-3587)
Fastsigns....G....860 470-7936
Avon (G-80)
Fastsigns....G....860 347-8569
Middletown (G-4343)
Fastsigns....G....860 347-8569
Middletown (G-4344)
Fastsigns....G....860 583-8000
Bristol (G-1037)
Fastsigns....G....203 239-9090
North Haven (G-5941)
Fastsigns of Hartford....G....860 644-5700
Manchester (G-4016)
Ferrucci Signs....G....203 469-0043
East Haven (G-2428)
Fit To A Tee Cstm Screen Prtg....G....860 828-6632
Kensington (G-3810)
Flag Store....G....203 237-8791
Meriden (G-4170)
Focus Sign Awning....G....860 890-6577
Hartford (G-3591)
Fs Signs LLC....G....203 612-4447
Stratford (G-8613)
◆ Gerber Scientific LLC....C....860 871-8082
Tolland (G-8864)
Ghezzi Enterprises Inc....G....860 787-5338
South Windsor (G-7759)
Gjg Signs Digital Signs....G....413 627-1852
East Windsor (G-2494)
Gorilla Signs & Wraps....G....203 439-8838
Cheshire (G-1393)
Graffeast Inc....G....203 622-1622
Greenwich (G-3169)
Granata Signs LLC....G....203 358-0780
Stamford (G-8219)
Grand Slam Signs....G....972 874-3658
Ledyard (G-3874)
Graphic Identity LLC....G....860 657-9755
Glastonbury (G-3042)
Graphica Sign Studios....G....203 619-2255
East Haven (G-2433)
Graphics Unlimited....G....860 928-1407
Putnam (G-7045)
Harry Tutunjian....G....203 944-9444
Shelton (G-7460)
Horizons Unlimited Inc....F....860 423-1931
Willimantic (G-10230)
Hot Tops LLC....F....203 926-2067
Shelton (G-7466)
I Level Sign and Graphics....G....203 256-9486
Shelton (G-7472)
I95 Signs LLC....G....203 296-2141
Stratford (G-8630)
Ignatowski John....G....203 452-9601
Monroe (G-4719)
Image 360....G....860 667-8339
Newington (G-5660)
Image Works Sign & Graph....G....860 569-7446
Coventry (G-1655)
Image360....F....203 949-0726
Wallingford (G-9287)
Innovative Signs LLC....G....860 870-7446
Vernon (G-9140)
J G Kurtzman....G....203 838-7791
Norwalk (G-6215)
J&R Signs....G....203 551-0781
Bridgeport (G-797)
Jaime M Camacho....G....203 846-8221
Norwalk (G-6216)
James Woznick....G....203 426-5585
Sandy Hook (G-7317)
Jason Kurtzman Signs....G....203 847-4397
Norwalk (G-6220)
Jill Ghi....G....860 824-7123
Canaan (G-1288)
Jk Sign & Stamp LLC....G....860 729-3860
Oakville (G-6455)
Jk Sign Company....G....203 544-7373
Norwalk (G-6222)
▲ John Oldham Studios Inc....E....860 529-3331
Wethersfield (G-10202)
John Rawlinson John Leary....G....203 882-8484
Milford (G-4562)
▲ Jornik Man Corp....F....203 969-0500
Stamford (G-8268)
Joseph Garrity....G....860 693-2134
Canton (G-1316)
Jvcart LLC....G....917 497-8791
Darien (G-2030)
Jyl LLP....G....860 767-7733
Essex (G-2722)
Kedo Koncepts LLC....G....860 315-7392
Thompson (G-8836)
Knight Lite Neon....G....203 238-4423
Meriden (G-4184)
Kyle C Niles....G....860 637-7625
Plantsville (G-6900)
Lamar Advertising Company....E....860 246-6546
Windsor (G-10403)
Landino Signs LLC....G....203 248-5437
Hamden (G-3471)
Landmark Sign Service....G....860 474-5305
South Windsor (G-7786)
Landmark Sign Service LLC....G....860 206-0643
Hartford (G-3625)
Lauretano Sign Group Inc....E....860 582-0233
Terryville (G-8762)
Leichsenring Studios LLC....G....203 452-7710
Trumbull (G-9043)
▲ Lewtan Industries Corporation....D....860 278-9800
West Hartford (G-9830)
Lifetime Acrylic Signs Inc....G....203 255-6751
Fairfield (G-2810)
Logod Softwear Inc....E....203 272-4883
Cheshire (G-1407)
Lorence Sign Works LLC....G....860 829-9999
Berlin (G-198)
Magic Signs....G....860 457-8940
Danielson (G-1997)
Margaret Witham....G....860 399-6403
Westbrook (G-10003)
McFigs Beyond Signs LLC....G....203 792-4057
Bethel (G-325)
▲ McIntire Company....F....860 585-8559
Bristol (G-1070)
Melvin Mayo....G....802 698-7635
Enfield (G-2658)
Merritt Sign....G....860 233-3557
Hartford (G-3639)
Metro Signs LLC....G....203 933-0333
West Haven (G-9936)
Michael Zoppa....G....860 289-5881
South Windsor (G-7794)
Mikes Sign Maintenance LLC....G....860 347-1462
Middletown (G-4380)
Millennium Shade & Sign LLC....G....203 968-5080
Stamford (G-8310)
Mkr Sign Company....G....860 265-7996
Enfield (G-2661)
Mr Skylight LLC....G....203 966-6005
New Canaan (G-5121)
Murdoch and Co....G....203 226-2800
Westport (G-10126)
Murray Signs & Designs Bob....G....203 375-7351
Stratford (G-8652)
Neonworks....G....203 335-6366
Bridgeport (G-846)
New England Post A Sign....G....203 635-3171
Waterbury (G-9559)
New England Sign Carvers....G....860 349-1669
Middlefield (G-4303)
New England Signal LLC....G....860 350-3212
New Milford (G-5567)
New Haven Sign Co....G....203 891-5710
Hamden (G-3491)
New Haven Sign Company....G....203 484-2777
Northford (G-6051)
Ninas Signs....G....315 963-2531
Morris (G-4791)
Nomis Enterprises....G....631 821-3120
Wallingford (G-9327)

Norwalk Sign Company Inc ....G....... 203 838-1942
Norwalk *(G-6282)*
Nu Line Design LLC ....G....... 203 949-0726
Wallingford *(G-9329)*
▲ **Ogs Technologies Inc** ....E....... 203 271-9055
Cheshire *(G-1424)*
One Look Sign Company ....G....... 860 581-8574
Centerbrook *(G-1331)*
Paper Mill Graphix Inc ....E....... 203 531-5904
Greenwich *(G-3213)*
Pariot Sign Company Llc ....G....... 203 364-9009
Newtown *(G-5768)*
Parking Lt Strpng & Asphlt Sgn ....G....... 203 648-6323
Danbury *(G-1900)*
Pattison Sign Group Inc ....G....... 860 583-3000
Bristol *(G-1087)*
Peter Ortali & Associates LLC ....G....... 203 571-8023
Sandy Hook *(G-7325)*
Picture This Hartford Inc ....G....... 860 528-1409
East Hartford *(G-2355)*
Point View Displays LLC ....G....... 203 468-0887
East Haven *(G-2447)*
Pop Graphics Inc ....G....... 203 639-1441
Meriden *(G-4218)*
Post Sign Specialists ....G....... 203 723-8448
Naugatuck *(G-4912)*
Precision Graphics Inc ....E....... 860 828-6561
East Berlin *(G-2174)*
◆ **Prime Resources Corp** ....B....... 203 331-9100
Bridgeport *(G-880)*
▲ **Project Graphics Inc** ....F....... 802 488-8789
Woodbury *(G-10652)*
Prokop Sign Co ....G....... 860 889-6265
Taftville *(G-8742)*
Quality Signs of Watertown ....G....... 860 274-4828
Watertown *(G-9728)*
Quinn and Gellar Marketing LLC ....G....... 860 444-0448
New London *(G-5485)*
R Way Signs LLC ....G....... 203 888-9709
Oxford *(G-6690)*
Ram Arts Signs ....G....... 860 274-6833
Watertown *(G-9729)*
Reflected Image ....G....... 203 484-0760
Northford *(G-6052)*
Revolution Lighting ....G....... 203 504-1111
Stamford *(G-8388)*
Revolution Lighting Tech Inc ....F....... 203 504-1111
Stamford *(G-8390)*
Revolution Lighting Tech Inc ....C....... 203 504-1111
Stamford *(G-8389)*
Rich Signs & Designs ....G....... 860 429-2165
Willington *(G-10256)*
Rising Sign Company Inc ....G....... 203 853-4155
Norwalk *(G-6325)*
Rokap Inc ....G....... 203 265-6895
Wallingford *(G-9359)*
Rossi Pter Signs Lettering LLC ....G....... 860 684-9229
Stafford Springs *(G-8035)*
Rykam LLC ....G....... 860 721-1411
East Hartford *(G-2368)*
S D & D Inc ....F....... 860 357-2603
East Berlin *(G-2175)*
Sam Augeri & Sons Signs ....G....... 860 346-1261
Middletown *(G-4407)*
Say It With Signs ....G....... 860 621-6535
Plantsville *(G-6910)*
Semiotics LLC ....G....... 860 644-5700
Manchester *(G-4088)*
Shiner Signs Inc ....E....... 203 634-4331
Meriden *(G-4241)*
Siam Valee ....G....... 203 269-6888
Wallingford *(G-9366)*
Sign A Rama ....G....... 860 870-7446
Vernon Rockville *(G-9178)*
Sign A Rama ....G....... 860 265-7996
Enfield *(G-2694)*
Sign A Rama ....G....... 860 443-9744
New London *(G-5489)*
Sign A Rama ....G....... 203 795-5450
Orange *(G-6629)*
Sign A Rama ....G....... 203 792-4091
Danbury *(G-1949)*
Sign A Rama Inc ....G....... 203 674-8900
Stamford *(G-8415)*
Sign and Wonders LLC ....G....... 860 274-8526
Watertown *(G-9736)*
Sign By Greubel ....G....... 860 632-2573
Cromwell *(G-1719)*
Sign Center Ltd Liability Co ....G....... 203 549-9820
Bridgeport *(G-903)*
Sign Connection Inc ....G....... 860 870-8855
Vernon Rockville *(G-9179)*
Sign Craft LLC ....G....... 860 739-2863
Niantic *(G-5817)*
Sign Creations ....G....... 203 259-8330
Southport *(G-8009)*
Sign Factory ....F....... 860 763-1085
Enfield *(G-2695)*
Sign Fast ....G....... 203 549-8500
Bridgeport *(G-904)*
Sign In Soft Inc ....G....... 203 216-3046
Shelton *(G-7555)*
Sign Language LLC ....G....... 203 778-2250
Danbury *(G-1950)*
Sign Maintenance Service Co ....G....... 203 336-1051
Bridgeport *(G-905)*
Sign of Flying Turtle LLC ....G....... 860 830-3132
West Hartford *(G-9855)*
Sign of Our Times ....G....... 860 669-4318
Clinton *(G-1526)*
Sign Pro Inc ....F....... 860 229-1812
Plantsville *(G-6911)*
Sign Professionals ....G....... 860 823-1122
Norwich *(G-6432)*
Sign Smarts LLC ....G....... 203 854-0808
Norwalk *(G-6348)*
Sign Solutions Inc ....G....... 860 583-8000
Bristol *(G-1117)*
Sign Stop Inc ....G....... 860 721-1411
East Hartford *(G-2371)*
Sign Wiz LLC ....G....... 860 351-5368
Plainville *(G-6862)*
Sign Wizard ....G....... 860 525-7729
Hartford *(G-3687)*
Sign-It LLC ....G....... 203 377-8831
Trumbull *(G-9074)*
Signature Signs ....G....... 860 704-0397
Middletown *(G-4412)*
Signature Signworks LLC ....G....... 860 646-4598
Bolton *(G-519)*
▲ **Signcenter LLC** ....G....... 800 269-2130
Milford *(G-4644)*
Signcrafters Inc ....G....... 203 353-9535
Stamford *(G-8416)*
Signman Signs LLC ....G....... 203 296-2846
Bridgeport *(G-906)*
Signmart LLC ....G....... 860 347-7446
Middletown *(G-4413)*
Signs By Anthony Inc ....G....... 203 866-1744
Norwalk *(G-6349)*
Signs By Autografix ....G....... 203 481-6502
Branford *(G-652)*
Signs By Flach ....G....... 203 881-0272
Beacon Falls *(G-147)*
Signs By MB ....G....... 203 710-9948
Cheshire *(G-1446)*
Signs By Scavotto ....G....... 860 745-5629
Enfield *(G-2696)*
Signs Direct Inc ....G....... 860 658-9589
Simsbury *(G-7646)*
Signs Now LLC ....G....... 860 667-8339
Newington *(G-5705)*
Signs of All Kinds ....G....... 860 649-1989
Manchester *(G-4089)*
Signs of America ....G....... 860 412-0054
Brooklyn *(G-1255)*
Signs of Success Inc ....G....... 203 329-3374
Stamford *(G-8417)*
Signs On Demand ....G....... 860 346-1720
Middletown *(G-4414)*
Signs Plus Inc ....G....... 860 653-0547
East Granby *(G-2229)*
Signs Plus LLC ....G....... 860 423-3048
Willimantic *(G-10236)*
Signs Pro LLC ....G....... 203 323-9994
Stamford *(G-8418)*
Signs Unlimited Inc ....G....... 203 734-7446
Derby *(G-2126)*
Signworks Studios LLC ....G....... 203 268-3993
Monroe *(G-4752)*
Simply Signs ....G....... 203 595-0123
Stamford *(G-8423)*
Sinsigalli Signs & Designs ....G....... 860 627-8712
Windsor Locks *(G-10496)*
Smart Signs LLC ....G....... 860 656-5257
East Hartford *(G-2373)*
Smart Signs Pro LLC ....G....... 203 684-9839
Milford *(G-4646)*
Sonalysts Inc ....B....... 860 442-4355
Waterford *(G-9672)*
Sons of Un Vtrans of Civil War ....G....... 816 241-5353
Avon *(G-114)*
Sound Marketing Concepts ....G....... 860 257-9367
Rocky Hill *(G-7266)*
South Paint and Sign Co ....G....... 203 245-7591
Madison *(G-3959)*
Specialty Sign Services LLC ....G....... 860 391-3291
Clinton *(G-1528)*
Speedi Sign LLC ....G....... 203 775-0700
Brookfield *(G-1225)*
Spooky Signs and Holiday Creat ....G....... 860 742-2805
Coventry *(G-1676)*
Spot-On Sign Solutions Inc ....G....... 860 584-9008
Berlin *(G-222)*
Stavola Signs ....G....... 860 395-0897
Old Saybrook *(G-6570)*
Sundance Signs LLC ....G....... 860 432-5760
Manchester *(G-4099)*
Swahn Engraving LLC ....G....... 860 657-4709
Glastonbury *(G-3085)*
Thirty Two Signs ....G....... 860 822-1132
Baltic *(G-122)*
Thirty Two Signs LLC ....G....... 860 564-0532
Plainfield *(G-6755)*
Tims Sign & Lighting Service ....G....... 203 634-8840
Meriden *(G-4256)*
Trophy Shop ....G....... 860 871-0867
Vernon Rockville *(G-9184)*
United Stts Sgn & Fbrction ....E....... 203 601-1000
Trumbull *(G-9088)*
Unlimited Signs Designs & Grap ....G....... 203 546-7267
Brookfield *(G-1235)*
US Highway Products Inc ....F....... 203 336-0332
Bridgeport *(G-932)*
Villano J Sign Company LLC ....G....... 203 624-7550
New Haven *(G-5427)*
Visual Impact Signs ....G....... 860 621-7446
Southington *(G-7994)*
Vital Signs & Graphic LLC ....G....... 860 829-7446
Berlin *(G-232)*
Vital Signs LLC ....G....... 860 365-0897
Colchester *(G-1580)*
Vital Signs Medical LLC ....G....... 860 563-4969
Rocky Hill *(G-7272)*
Wad Inc ....E....... 860 828-3331
East Berlin *(G-2179)*
Wesport Signs ....G....... 203 557-3668
Westport *(G-10174)*
Wesport Signs ....G....... 203 286-7710
Norwalk *(G-6394)*
Whats Your Sign LLC ....G....... 814 823-7807
Stratford *(G-8708)*
Wilbur Signs ....G....... 203 313-4950
Danbury *(G-1982)*
Window Tinting & Signs Inc ....G....... 203 336-5539
Bridgeport *(G-939)*
Write Way Signs & Design Inc ....G....... 860 482-8893
Torrington *(G-8992)*
X L Color Corp ....G....... 860 653-9705
East Granby *(G-2234)*
Yankee Plak Co Inc ....E....... 203 333-3168
Bridgeport *(G-942)*
Yankee Signs ....G....... 860 623-8651
Windsor Locks *(G-10502)*
Young Flan LLC ....G....... 203 878-0084
Derby *(G-2134)*
Yush Sign Display Co Inc ....G....... 860 289-1819
East Hartford *(G-2402)*

3995 Burial Caskets

Dignified Endings LLC ....D....... 860 291-0575
East Hartford *(G-2314)*

3996 Linoleum & Hard Surface Floor Coverings, NEC

Conformis Inc ....C....... 203 793-7178
Wallingford *(G-9237)*

3999 Manufacturing Industries, NEC

▲ **210 Innovations** ....G....... 860 445-0210
Groton *(G-3269)*
22 Candles ....G....... 203 577-5540
Wilton *(G-10264)*
283 Industries Inc ....G....... 203 276-8956
Ridgefield *(G-7113)*
A C Manufacturing ....G....... 860 314-8225
Bristol *(G-951)*
◆ **A L C Inovators Inc** ....G....... 203 877-8526
Milford *(G-4436)*

S
I
C

Employee Codes: A=Over 500 employees, B=251-500
C=101-250, D=51-100, E=20-50, F=10-19, G=1-9
2020 Harris Connecticut
Manufacturers Directory
463

A Little Soy Candle Co LLC ....G....... 860 877-6001
West Haven *(G-9878)*
AA Industries LLC....................G....... 860 291-8929
South Windsor *(G-7697)*
Aberdeen Mfg ....G....... 860 774-9679
Danielson *(G-1986)*
Ace Beauty Supply Inc ....G....... 203 488-2416
Branford *(G-536)*
Ace Beauty Systems New Britain..........G....... 860 224-2943
New Britain *(G-4932)*
Ace Wlding Fbrction Rstoration............G....... 203 758-3550
Prospect *(G-6992)*
Ack Industries LLC ....G....... 860 677-0056
Farmington *(G-2875)*
◆ Acme United Corporation ....C....... 203 254-6060
Fairfield *(G-2743)*
Action Industries....................G....... 860 644-3020
Manchester *(G-3978)*
Addison Industries LLC ....G....... 203 809-0254
West Haven *(G-9881)*
Additive Experts LLC....................G....... 860 351-3324
New Britain *(G-4937)*
Additive Manufacturing Neng................G....... 860 316-5946
Middletown *(G-4313)*
Advanced Golf Nutrition LLC................G....... 203 554-9120
Fairfield *(G-2744)*
▲ Advanced Specialist LLC ....G....... 860 945-9125
Watertown *(G-9679)*
Aero Precision Mfg LLC ....G....... 203 675-7625
Wallingford *(G-9198)*
AK Interactive USA LLC ....G....... 845 313-9380
Branford *(G-539)*
ALC Manufacturing LLC....................G....... 860 496-0883
Torrington *(G-8888)*
Alexis Aerospace Inds LLP....................G....... 860 673-6801
Avon *(G-74)*
Alpine Management Group LLC ....G....... 954 531-1692
Westport *(G-10052)*
American Hydrogen Northeast..............E....... 203 449-4614
Bridgeport *(G-692)*
American Industries ....G....... 860 381-5083
Gales Ferry *(G-2980)*
American Prototype Hob....................G....... 203 323-6832
Stamford *(G-8077)*
American Recreational Inds....................G....... 203 375-5900
Stratford *(G-8568)*
Andher Mfg LLC....................G....... 860 874-8816
East Hartford *(G-2291)*
Ann S Davis ....F....... 860 642-7228
Lebanon *(G-3846)*
Apiject Systems Corp....................G....... 203 461-7121
Stamford *(G-8088)*
Apple Valley Candle Company ....G....... 860 940-1176
Bristol *(G-963)*
Apricus Inc ....G....... 203 889-2667
North Haven *(G-5907)*
Aromalite Candle Co LLC....................G....... 860 872-1029
Vernon *(G-9131)*
Arrow Lock Manufacturing Co...............G....... 203 603-5959
New Haven *(G-5233)*
Art Metal Industries AMI....................G....... 860 799-5575
New Milford *(G-5506)*
Artemis Pine Candle Co LLC ....G....... 203 245-5170
Madison *(G-3908)*
Articrafts....................G....... 203 618-1715
Greenwich *(G-3123)*
ASAP Mfg Co LLC....................G....... 860 738-4831
Winsted *(G-10506)*
Atech Industries LLC....................G....... 203 887-4900
Orange *(G-6584)*
B & M Fabrication LLC ....G....... 860 379-5444
Winsted *(G-10508)*
B&D Industries LLC....................G....... 860 604-2404
Westbrook *(G-9992)*
B-E Industries....................G....... 203 357-8055
Stamford *(G-8104)*
Backyard Candles LLC....................G....... 860 644-9561
South Windsor *(G-7716)*
Bar Industries LLC....................G....... 203 729-4490
Naugatuck *(G-4861)*
Barco Industries New England..............G....... 860 798-8258
Glastonbury *(G-3012)*
Barn Beam Co of Neng LLC....................G....... 860 488-0317
Northfield *(G-6042)*
Barrette Mechanical....................G....... 860 774-0499
Brooklyn *(G-1246)*
Beelightful Candle LLC ....G....... 203 912-7122
Cos Cob *(G-1625)*
Belle Industries LLC ....G....... 203 245-0382
Madison *(G-3912)*

▲ Bic Corporation....................A....... 203 783-2000
Shelton *(G-7407)*
▲ Bic USA Inc....................C....... 203 783-2000
Shelton *(G-7408)*
Bill Hoagland....................G....... 203 877-0157
Milford *(G-4471)*
Biological Industries....................G....... 860 316-5197
Cromwell *(G-1692)*
Biomass Industries Inc....................G....... 203 207-9958
Bethel *(G-265)*
Bk Industries LLC ....G....... 832 744-3067
Vernon *(G-9132)*
Blackbird Manufacturing and De...........G....... 860 331-3477
Coventry *(G-1645)*
Blumen Laden Artificial Flower ....G....... 860 693-8600
Collinsville *(G-1589)*
Bolt Custom & Mfg LLC....................G....... 203 685-1840
Bridgeport *(G-715)*
Bomba Industries LLC....................G....... 203 304-9051
Sandy Hook *(G-7300)*
Boss Industries ....G....... 860 819-1637
Vernon Rockville *(G-9163)*
Boxtree Accessories Inc ....G....... 203 637-5794
Old Greenwich *(G-6468)*
BR Industries LLC....................G....... 203 216-3576
Norwalk *(G-6098)*
Bridgeport Proc & Mfg LLC....................G....... 203 612-7733
Bridgeport *(G-722)*
Bromley Industries ....G....... 860 370-9566
Broad Brook *(G-1145)*
Btx Industries ....G....... 203 359-4870
Stamford *(G-8122)*
▲ Bug Umbrella Gazebo LLC....................G....... 860 651-0030
East Granby *(G-2194)*
Bullie Industries LLC ....G....... 203 393-9763
Bethany *(G-236)*
Bunny Do LLC....................G....... 860 621-2365
Plantsville *(G-6887)*
C&G Mfg....................G....... 860 274-9785
Watertown *(G-9688)*
C&S Collectibles ....G....... 860 872-6825
Tolland *(G-8853)*
Cad/CAM Dntl Stdio Mil Ctr Inc.............G....... 203 733-3069
Newtown *(G-5731)*
CAM Industries....................G....... 860 738-8338
Colebrook *(G-1584)*
CAM Manufacturing Co LLC ....G....... 203 301-0153
Milford *(G-4480)*
CAM Manufacturing LLC....................G....... 203 415-0411
Milford *(G-4481)*
Candle Threads ....G....... 860 490-5890
Enfield *(G-2620)*
Candle Threads....................G....... 860 292-1667
East Windsor *(G-2488)*
Candles For A Cause USA ....G....... 860 912-3946
Bristol *(G-999)*
Canine Core Industries LLC....................G....... 203 459-1584
Trumbull *(G-9009)*
Cardinal Shehan Center Inc....................E....... 203 336-4468
Bridgeport *(G-729)*
Carin Industries Inc ....G....... 860 489-1122
Torrington *(G-8909)*
Carl Rizzo & Associates....................G....... 860 644-5849
South Windsor *(G-7725)*
Carlin Mfg Kitchens To Go....................G....... 413 519-2822
Mystic *(G-4805)*
Case Patterns Inc....................G....... 860 445-6722
Groton *(G-3275)*
Cash Time Industries LLC....................G....... 860 770-7192
New Britain *(G-4956)*
Castro Industries LLC ....G....... 203 249-9268
Greenwich *(G-3142)*
Cathys Country Scents Candles ....G....... 860 458-8219
Stafford Springs *(G-8020)*
Cavallo Manufacturing LLC ....G....... 203 596-8007
Waterbury *(G-9447)*
Cavar Industries LLC....................G....... 860 684-0706
Union *(G-9109)*
Cbd101 LLC....................G....... 203 273-9941
Orange *(G-6589)*
CCI Cyrus River Terminal LLC...............G....... 203 761-8000
Stamford *(G-8134)*
Chandler Industries LLC ....G....... 860 283-8147
Thomaston *(G-8784)*
Channys Candles LLC....................G....... 860 313-9139
Torrington *(G-8910)*
Charles Manufacturing Co....................G....... 860 747-3550
Plainville *(G-6787)*
Chef Gretchen LLC ....G....... 203 252-8892
Stamford *(G-8142)*

Christinas Creations....................G....... 203 605-2464
New Haven *(G-5257)*
Cicchetti & Co LLC ....G....... 860 945-0424
Watertown *(G-9692)*
Cigar World....................G....... 860 828-7870
Kensington *(G-3807)*
CJ First Candle....................G....... 203 966-1300
New Canaan *(G-5095)*
Classic Tool & Mfg LLC ....G....... 203 755-6313
Waterbury *(G-9451)*
Clean Tech Industries LLC....................G....... 860 447-1434
New London *(G-5464)*
Cleansource Industries ....G....... 203 401-1535
Madison *(G-3913)*
Coastal Industries LLC....................G....... 860 535-9043
Stonington *(G-8526)*
Components For Mfg LLC....................G....... 860 245-5326
Mystic *(G-4809)*
Components For Mfg LLC....................G....... 860 572-1671
Groton *(G-3279)*
◆ Conair Corporation ....B....... 203 351-9000
Stamford *(G-8156)*
Concentric Tool Mfg Co....................G....... 203 723-8846
Naugatuck *(G-4871)*
Connecticut Candle Group ....G....... 860 924-1766
Rocky Hill *(G-7227)*
Connecticut Candle LLC ....G....... 203 937-7330
West Haven *(G-9892)*
▲ Connecticut Components Inc...........G....... 860 633-0277
Tolland *(G-8855)*
◆ Connecticut Metal Industries ....G....... 203 736-0790
Ansonia *(G-30)*
Connecticut Mfg Svcs LLC ....G....... 860 667-8712
Newington *(G-5642)*
Controlled Interfaces LLC....................G....... 917 328-4471
Ridgefield *(G-7130)*
Corco Mfg....................G....... 203 284-1831
Wallingford *(G-9240)*
Corelli Industries LLC....................G....... 203 356-9058
Stamford *(G-8160)*
Countryside Crafts....................G....... 860 774-0446
Dayville *(G-2059)*
CPS Millworks LLC ....G....... 860 283-4276
Terryville *(G-8750)*
Creative Cupolas....................G....... 203 261-2178
Trumbull *(G-9018)*
Croton Industries East Africa ....G....... 407 947-4481
Wilton *(G-10285)*
▲ Crystal Journey Candles LLC...........E....... 203 433-4735
Branford *(G-577)*
CSS Industries LLC ....G....... 203 521-5246
Stratford *(G-8601)*
CT Pyro Mfg LLC....................G....... 203 856-8313
Sandy Hook *(G-7306)*
CT Sprayfoam Industries LLC..............G....... 203 232-0961
Southbury *(G-7849)*
Custom Creations LLC....................G....... 203 522-2113
Naugatuck *(G-4874)*
Customized Foods Mfg LLC ....G....... 203 759-1645
Waterbury *(G-9457)*
Cynful Scents....................G....... 860 866-7670
Morris *(G-4788)*
Cyro Industries....................G....... 203 269-4481
Orange *(G-6594)*
D & C Industries ....G....... 203 453-4424
Guilford *(G-3342)*
D E Sirman Specialty Company..............G....... 860 658-6336
West Simsbury *(G-9977)*
Damalias Candle and Body Bar.............G....... 860 725-2168
Hartford *(G-3575)*
Dangerous Industries Quality................G....... 860 986-0879
Waterbury *(G-9461)*
Dar More Mfg Co ....G....... 860 605-9164
Harwinton *(G-3724)*
Dash N Lash Extensions LLC................G....... 203 726-2952
Naugatuck *(G-4875)*
Ddk Industries LLC....................G....... 203 641-4218
Shelton *(G-7429)*
Delcon Industries....................G....... 203 371-5711
Trumbull *(G-9020)*
Delcon Industries....................G....... 203 540-5757
Bridgeport *(G-744)*
Delcon Industries LLC....................G....... 203 331-9720
Bridgeport *(G-745)*
Delta-Source LLC....................F....... 860 461-1600
West Hartford *(G-9799)*
Dexon Tech LLC....................G....... 860 584-1442
Bristol *(G-1015)*
Dianas Candles and Soap LLC ....G....... 203 527-4028
Waterbury *(G-9465)*

Dianna Blanchard.....G..... 860 684-4874
Stafford Springs *(G-8026)*
Diversified Manufact.....G..... 203 734-0379
Ansonia *(G-32)*
Docko Inc.....G..... 860 572-8939
Mystic *(G-4812)*
Dragon Hollow Design LLC.....G..... 860 861-6200
Norwich *(G-6411)*
Dt Manufacturing LLC.....G..... 860 384-8449
Bristol *(G-1021)*
Dythnam Industries LLC.....G..... 860 480-7980
Glastonbury *(G-3028)*
E6s Industries LLC.....G..... 512 920-3671
Colchester *(G-1548)*
East Coast Precision Mfg.....G..... 860 322-4624
Chester *(G-1470)*
East Lyme Puppetry Project.....G..... 860 739-7225
Niantic *(G-5805)*
Elevation Sells Group LLC.....G..... 203 871-7172
New Haven *(G-5275)*
Ellis Manufacturing LLC.....G..... 865 518-0531
Plainville *(G-6805)*
Elmo Nash Industries.....G..... 203 459-3648
Trumbull *(G-9025)*
Emdepoint Candles USA LLC.....G..... 860 205-8400
New Britain *(G-4982)*
Empty Cup Magic.....G..... 203 874-1093
Milford *(G-4529)*
Enaqua.....G..... 203 269-9890
Wallingford *(G-9257)*
Ensign Bickford Industries.....F..... 203 843-2126
Simsbury *(G-7619)*
Ether & Industries LLc.....G..... 475 224-0650
New Haven *(G-5277)*
Eye-Con Foods LLC.....G..... 203 752-7525
Bethany *(G-240)*
Eyelash Extensions and More.....F..... 860 951-9355
West Hartford *(G-9809)*
Ezee Fabricators LLC.....G..... 860 429-5664
Mansfield Center *(G-4113)*
Factor Industries LLC.....G..... 203 244-5429
Ridgefield *(G-7140)*
Farace Industries LLC.....G..... 203 315-1293
North Branford *(G-5838)*
Finn-Addict Manufacturing LLC.....G..... 860 464-2053
Gales Ferry *(G-2983)*
Fire Prevention Services.....F..... 203 866-6357
Norwalk *(G-6167)*
Flowe Manufacturing.....G..... 860 859-1573
Bozrah *(G-525)*
Flying Fur LLC.....G..... 860 623-0450
Windsor Locks *(G-10484)*
Formatron Ltd.....F..... 860 676-0227
Farmington *(G-2908)*
Four Twenty Industries LLC.....G..... 860 818-3334
Berlin *(G-181)*
Foxrun Danes.....G..... 860 685-8784
Higganum *(G-3763)*
Frates Custom Cabinetry.....G..... 203 994-1108
Sandy Hook *(G-7312)*
Fundrsing With Cndle Fndrisers.....G..... 860 384-3691
South Glastonbury *(G-7680)*
Fur Side LLC.....G..... 203 403-3369
Ridgefield *(G-7143)*
Fx Models LLC.....G..... 860 589-5279
Terryville *(G-8756)*
G A Industries.....G..... 860 261-5484
Bristol *(G-1044)*
G S S Industries.....G..... 203 755-6644
Waterbury *(G-9484)*
GA Remanufacturing LLC.....G..... 860 404-5186
Farmington *(G-2912)*
▲ Galata Chemicals LLC.....F..... 203 236-9000
Southbury *(G-7854)*
Garbeck Airflow Industries.....G..... 860 301-5032
Middletown *(G-4346)*
Garrett & Co Mfg LLC.....G..... 203 494-0935
Ansonia *(G-36)*
Global Manufacturing.....G..... 860 315-5502
Woodstock *(G-10666)*
▲ Global Scenic Services Inc.....E..... 203 334-2130
Bridgeport *(G-776)*
Go Green Industries LLC.....G..... 914 772-0026
New Milford *(G-5538)*
Goody Candles LLC.....G..... 860 426-9436
Southington *(G-7930)*
Gpk Mfg LLC.....G..... 860 536-2084
Mystic *(G-4819)*
Greenway Industries Inc.....G..... 203 885-1059
Brookfield *(G-1195)*
Greenwood Industries Inc.....G..... 203 234-2041
North Haven *(G-5943)*
Grinding System Services LLC.....G..... 860 208-5196
Storrs Mansfield *(G-8556)*
Grohe Manufacturing.....G..... 203 516-5536
Ansonia *(G-37)*
Gutkin Enterprises LLC.....G..... 203 777-5510
Hamden *(G-3454)*
H & K Industries LLC.....G..... 857 237-3944
Hartford *(G-3603)*
Hak Industries LLC.....G..... 860 572-7305
Mystic *(G-4820)*
Hamden Grinding.....G..... 203 288-2906
Hamden *(G-3455)*
Hannes Precision Industry Inc.....F..... 203 853-7276
Norwalk *(G-6192)*
Hardware Cy Soaps Candles LLC.....G..... 860 209-8494
New Britain *(G-4996)*
Harley Industries LLC.....G..... 860 951-5727
Higganum *(G-3765)*
Heatherwreath Partners LP.....G..... 203 662-1084
Darien *(G-2028)*
Hl Industries LLC.....G..... 203 783-1084
Milford *(G-4548)*
Hill Industries Llc.....G..... 860 747-6421
Plainville *(G-6822)*
Hopewell Harmony LLC.....G..... 203 222-2268
Newtown *(G-5745)*
▲ Hopewell Harmony LLC.....G..... 203 222-2268
Weston *(G-10027)*
Hpi Manufacturing Inc.....G..... 203 777-5395
Hamden *(G-3464)*
Hps Industries LLC.....G..... 203 915-5627
New Haven *(G-5297)*
Hub Industries.....G..... 203 803-8836
Bridgeport *(G-788)*
Hxb Industries LLC.....G..... 203 348-5922
Stamford *(G-8242)*
Hydro-Flex Inc.....G..... 203 269-5599
Stratford *(G-8629)*
ICC Wire Harness Mfg LLC.....G..... 203 469-8481
East Haven *(G-2435)*
Illicit Industries.....G..... 203 264-6293
Southbury *(G-7859)*
Incord Ltd.....G..... 860 537-1414
Oakdale *(G-6443)*
Ink Tank Industries LLC.....G..... 203 274-2717
Stamford *(G-8250)*
Innovative Industries LLC.....G..... 860 225-0000
Meriden *(G-4175)*
Innovative Mfg Systems LLC.....G..... 203 284-2605
Wallingford *(G-9288)*
Interior Plantworks Inc.....G..... 860 289-9499
South Windsor *(G-7775)*
Interspace Industries LLC.....G..... 203 814-1879
Brookfield *(G-1198)*
Ironhorse Industries LLC.....G..... 203 598-8720
Watertown *(G-9712)*
Isaac Industries.....G..... 203 778-3239
Danbury *(G-1852)*
J & S Industries LLC.....G..... 203 220-8970
Monroe *(G-4722)*
J&P Mfg LLC.....G..... 860 747-4790
Plainville *(G-6828)*
J&T Industries LLC.....G..... 203 375-8424
Bridgeport *(G-798)*
Jak Industries LLC.....G..... 877 964-2725
Stonington *(G-8530)*
Jam Industries LLC.....G..... 860 225-8862
New Britain *(G-5006)*
Jaz Industries LLC.....G..... 860 243-9357
Windsor *(G-10399)*
Jcm Industries.....G..... 203 748-1806
Danbury *(G-1858)*
Jeff Osborne Industries.....G..... 203 794-0863
Danbury *(G-1860)*
▲ Jenray Products Inc.....E..... 914 375-5596
Brookfield *(G-1199)*
Jfn Manufacturing LLC.....G..... 860 621-0069
Southington *(G-7944)*
Jfs Industries.....G..... 203 592-0754
Thomaston *(G-8794)*
Jimbpa Enterprises LLC.....G..... 203 755-9237
Waterbury *(G-9509)*
Jlc Industries.....G..... 315 761-8051
West Haven *(G-9918)*
Joseph Manufacturing Co.....G..... 203 431-6400
Ridgefield *(G-7151)*
Jra Industries LLC.....G..... 475 343-0262
Meriden *(G-4183)*
JS Industries.....G..... 860 928-0786
Thompson *(G-8835)*
Jungle Brew LLC.....G..... 860 335-4941
Bloomfield *(G-429)*
K and R Precision Grinding.....G..... 860 505-8030
New Britain *(G-5008)*
K F Machining.....G..... 860 292-6466
East Windsor *(G-2501)*
K2 Manufacturing Inc.....G..... 413 636-6170
South Windsor *(G-7781)*
K4 Industries LLC.....G..... 203 459-4992
Easton *(G-2558)*
Katy Industries Inc.....G..... 314 656-4321
Middlebury *(G-4281)*
Kaycandles.....G..... 860 794-3763
New Britain *(G-5009)*
Keith Reed Industries LLC.....G..... 860 677-7739
Unionville *(G-9117)*
Kellog Splitters Inc.....G..... 860 738-4986
New Hartford *(G-5200)*
Kelly Industries LLC.....G..... 860 388-5666
Old Saybrook *(G-6549)*
Kent Billings LLC.....G..... 860 659-1104
Glastonbury *(G-3055)*
Kh Industries LLC.....G..... 860 875-4779
Tolland *(G-8867)*
Kimlar Industries LLC.....G..... 203 220-2200
Trumbull *(G-9040)*
Kms Candle Company LLC.....G..... 203 758-3821
Prospect *(G-7006)*
Koster Keunen Manufacturing.....G..... 860 693-1295
Collinsville *(G-1596)*
Kpb Industries LLC.....G..... 203 687-7943
Madison *(G-3935)*
▲ La Care Industries LLC.....G..... 860 231-7772
West Hartford *(G-9825)*
Leaps & Bones LLC.....G..... 860 648-9708
South Windsor *(G-7787)*
▲ Leisure Learning Products Inc.....F..... 203 325-2800
Stamford *(G-8281)*
Lesco.....G..... 203 353-0061
Stamford *(G-8282)*
Lily Force Industries.....G..... 860 729-2458
Coventry *(G-1661)*
Lion Heart Industries LLC.....G..... 203 376-2212
Guilford *(G-3368)*
Liquid Sun.....G..... 860 254-5757
East Windsor *(G-2508)*
Lisa Barrette.....G..... 860 928-0599
Thompson *(G-8838)*
Ljs House of Candles.....G..... 203 464-5742
Meriden *(G-4187)*
Lombardo Industries LLC.....G..... 203 948-8562
Sandy Hook *(G-7320)*
Long FA Inc.....G..... 203 270-3878
Newtown *(G-5756)*
Lookingforsolutionscom LLC.....G..... 475 239-5773
Shelton *(G-7492)*
M & W Industries Inc.....G..... 860 621-7358
Southington *(G-7949)*
M P Robinson Production.....E..... 203 938-1336
Redding *(G-7099)*
MA & PA Fur LLC.....G..... 860 659-7766
Middletown *(G-4373)*
Madd Fiusch Industries.....G..... 203 982-8306
Madison *(G-3937)*
Magnum Industries.....G..... 860 490-9513
Enfield *(G-2657)*
Mak Industries LLC.....G..... 860 623-4911
East Windsor *(G-2509)*
Make A Candle.....G..... 203 871-8426
Branford *(G-623)*
Mandalay Industries LLC.....G..... 203 324-4033
Stamford *(G-8295)*
Manufacturing Assists.....G..... 203 934-6574
West Haven *(G-9931)*
Manufacturing Productivi.....G..... 860 916-8189
Windsor *(G-10406)*
Manufctring Alnce Svc Corp Inc.....G..... 203 596-1900
Waterbury *(G-9533)*
Marmon Engnered Wire Cable LLC.....G..... 860 653-8300
Hartford *(G-3635)*
Martin Mfg Services LLC.....G..... 860 663-1465
Killingworth *(G-3836)*
McGuire Manufacturing Co Inc.....G..... 203 301-0270
Milford *(G-4575)*
McGurk Industries.....G..... 917 524-5132
Trumbull *(G-9047)*
Metal Components Mfg.....G..... 203 267-5510
Southbury *(G-7867)*

SIC

Mf Industries....G.... 860 355-8188
New Milford (G-5562)
Mfg Directions....G.... 203 483-0797
North Branford (G-5848)
Mfg Service Co....G.... 860 749-8316
Enfield (G-2659)
MHS Industries....G.... 860 798-7981
Windsor (G-10410)
Michaud Industries LLC....G.... 860 408-0907
Simsbury (G-7634)
▲ Mikron Corp Stratford....G.... 203 261-3100
Monroe (G-4738)
Milford Smoke Junction LLC....G.... 203 301-9956
Milford (G-4581)
Mindscape Industries....G.... 860 574-9308
New London (G-5480)
MJM Marga LLC....G.... 203 597-9035
Waterbury (G-9547)
Mk Millwork LLC....G.... 860 567-0173
Morris (G-4790)
ML Industries....G.... 203 820-4922
Bridgeport (G-841)
MLS Acq Inc....F.... 860 386-6878
East Windsor (G-2512)
Mm Candles....G.... 203 205-0180
Danbury (G-1887)
Modelvision Inc....G.... 860 355-3884
New Milford (G-5563)
Mondo Sauce LLC....G.... 206 714-0390
Stamford (G-8313)
Motive Industries LLC....G.... 860 423-2064
North Windham (G-6039)
Murphy Industries LLC....G.... 203 426-1772
Sandy Hook (G-7322)
Mylo Industries LLC....G.... 860 228-1192
Amston (G-4)
Nac Industries Inc....G.... 845 214-0659
Oxford (G-6680)
▲ Nano Pet Products LLC....G.... 203 345-1330
Norwalk (G-6268)
New York Transit Shoes....G.... 203 968-6642
Stamford (G-8326)
Njd Enterprises....G.... 860 210-1113
Litchfield (G-3897)
Norfolk Industries LLC....G.... 860 618-8822
Greenwich (G-3210)
Northeast Wood Products LLC....E.... 860 862-6350
Uncasville (G-9100)
Nutmeg Industries LLC....G.... 860 436-6553
Newington (G-5688)
O & G Industries Inc....C.... 860 485-6600
Harwinton (G-3735)
O & G Industries Inc....C.... 203 881-5192
Beacon Falls (G-145)
▲ O Berk Company Neng LLC....F.... 203 932-8000
West Haven (G-9940)
Oak Hill Industries Inc....G.... 203 755-4400
Waterbury (G-9566)
Oak Tree Moulding LLC....G.... 860 455-3056
Woodstock (G-10674)
OConnell Industries Inc....G.... 860 508-7052
Manchester (G-4065)
Old Thyme Country Candles....G.... 860 655-2583
South Windsor (G-7800)
Olde Tyme Country Candles....G.... 860 673-5086
Unionville (G-9124)
Original Materials Inds LLC....G.... 203 535-1192
Hamden (G-3492)
Outdoor Industries LLC....G.... 203 350-2275
Madison (G-3945)
Parva Industries Inc....G.... 203 248-5553
Hamden (G-3495)
Parva Mfg Group Inc....G.... 860 828-6285
Kensington (G-3816)
Paul Maxx Industries LLC....G.... 203 417-2446
Southbury (G-7871)
PB&j Design Inc....G.... 203 332-4433
Derby (G-2121)
Peacock Manufacturing Co LLC....G.... 203 388-4100
Norwalk (G-6294)
Peaks Parrots....G.... 860 316-2788
Middletown (G-4391)
Perfex Manufacturing....G.... 203 739-0930
Danbury (G-1904)
Perry Industries LLC....G.... 203 505-5187
Cos Cob (G-1639)
Petro-Tech Industries LLC....G.... 860 881-5890
Willington (G-10253)
Picture This Hartford Inc....G.... 860 528-1409
East Hartford (G-2355)

Pleasant Valley Fence Co Inc....F.... 860 379-0088
Pleasant Valley (G-6925)
Polar Bear Industries LLC....G.... 203 858-4396
Westport (G-10141)
Polster Industries LLC....G.... 203 521-8517
Fairfield (G-2830)
Posh Pups LLC....G.... 860 454-4055
Vernon Rockville (G-9175)
Precision Express Mfg LLC....F.... 860 584-2627
Bristol (G-1097)
Precision Fire Fabrication LLC....G.... 203 706-0749
Plantsville (G-6908)
Precision Interface....G.... 203 235-2718
Meriden (G-4219)
Precision Metal Manufacturing....G.... 973 253-0500
Simsbury (G-7641)
Privateer Divers LLC....G.... 860 742-2699
Coventry (G-1670)
▲ Product Spring LLC....G.... 203 966-6766
New Canaan (G-5133)
Progress Manufacturing LLC....G.... 860 563-6254
Wethersfield (G-10215)
Pups In A Tub....G.... 203 879-2947
Wolcott (G-10582)
Purple Heart Industries LLC....G.... 203 655-5039
Darien (G-2040)
Qds LLC....G.... 203 338-9668
Shelton (G-7541)
Quality Bead Craft Inc....F.... 860 242-2167
Bloomfield (G-471)
Queenie Industries LLC....G.... 917 848-4490
Hamden (G-3499)
R and K Industries....G.... 860 289-3879
East Hartford (G-2362)
R S Industries LLC....G.... 203 261-1146
Trumbull (G-9060)
R Van Loan Custom Framing LLC....G.... 203 422-2881
Greenwich (G-3221)
▲ Raf Industries LLC....G.... 203 228-4290
Southbury (G-7873)
Raymond J Bykowski....G.... 203 271-2385
Cheshire (G-1438)
RC Fabrication and Off Rd LLC....G.... 203 500-7071
North Haven (G-5986)
Readydock Inc....G.... 860 523-9980
Avon (G-104)
Realizers Group LLC....G.... 203 253-9510
Westport (G-10146)
Red Door Industries....G.... 860 243-1960
Bloomfield (G-475)
Redco Industries LLC....G.... 860 537-2664
Colchester (G-1572)
Regional Industries LLC....G.... 860 227-3627
Clinton (G-1520)
Richard Batchelder....G.... 860 526-1614
Chester (G-1481)
Riopel Industries....G.... 860 384-9610
Bristol (G-1109)
Risdon Manufacturing Co....G.... 860 283-2000
Thomaston (G-8803)
▲ Rlp Inc....G.... 203 359-2504
Stamford (G-8394)
▲ Robert Audette....G.... 203 872-3119
Cheshire (G-1440)
Rockwood Manufacturing Co....G.... 800 582-2424
New Haven (G-5382)
Roland A Parent....G.... 860 928-9158
Woodstock (G-10682)
Rolling Motion Industries....G.... 860 846-0530
Plainville (G-6857)
▲ Rome Fastener Corporation....E.... 203 874-6719
Milford (G-4631)
Ronaco Industries Inc....G.... 203 979-7712
Roxbury (G-7281)
Roost Candle Co LLC....G.... 203 270-6577
Sandy Hook (G-7328)
Rooster Malt Company LLC....G.... 203 364-7612
Newtown (G-5777)
Ross Industries....G.... 203 838-6180
Norwalk (G-6328)
RR Design....G.... 203 792-3419
Bethel (G-336)
Ruch Industries LLC....G.... 203 268-6514
Trumbull (G-9066)
Ryan Industries LLC....G.... 860 716-0226
Broad Brook (G-1152)
Sabol Industries LLC....G.... 203 430-6502
Orange (G-6627)
Sadlak Manufacturing LLC....E.... 860 742-0227
Coventry (G-1674)

Sandra Mercier Procaccin....G.... 203 929-6968
Shelton (G-7550)
Sandy Brook Manufacturing LLC....G.... 860 205-4438
Colebrook (G-1586)
Scenic Route Candle Co LLC....G.... 203 606-7300
Branford (G-648)
Scrapeitrx LLC....G.... 203 918-8323
Fairfield (G-2845)
Seaboard Industries Inc....G.... 973 427-8500
Stratford (G-8676)
Seasaw LLC....G.... 203 815-9022
Milford (G-4640)
Seawolfs Products Co....G.... 203 225-0110
Shelton (G-7552)
Shimmer LLC....G.... 860 875-4701
Tolland (G-8877)
▲ Show Motion Inc....E.... 203 866-1866
Milford (G-4643)
Sideburnz....G.... 860 667-1900
Hartford (G-3686)
Sidel & McElwreath LLC....G.... 203 834-2946
Wilton (G-10331)
Sigma Engineering Tech LLC....G.... 508 243-2888
Durham (G-2156)
Simkins Industries....G.... 203 787-7171
East Haven (G-2453)
Siskin Agency....G.... 860 561-2937
Hartford (G-3689)
SJS Industries LLC....G.... 203 552-3001
Greenwich (G-3237)
Skyline Industries LLC....G.... 860 209-8013
East Hartford (G-2372)
Solidification Pdts Intl Inc....G.... 203 484-9494
Northford (G-6053)
Solon Manufacturing....G.... 203 230-5300
North Haven (G-5996)
Sparrow Industries....G.... 203 598-0034
Middlebury (G-4294)
Spartan Industries LLC....G.... 203 464-8600
North Haven (G-5997)
Specialty Paper Mfg LLC....G.... 860 654-8044
East Windsor (G-2519)
Spv Industries LLC....G.... 860 953-5928
West Hartford (G-9861)
Standard Manufacturing Co LLC....G.... 860 225-6581
New Britain (G-5060)
Step By Step Cnseling Svcs LLC....G.... 860 244-9836
Hartford (G-3693)
Stephanie Lauren LLC....G.... 203 938-0364
Redding (G-7110)
Stephen Mazzarelli....G.... 860 482-8200
Torrington (G-8972)
Sterling Industries LLC....G.... 860 434-6239
Old Lyme (G-6519)
Stevenson Prototype....G.... 203 245-0278
Guilford (G-3394)
Stm Industries LLC....G.... 860 785-8419
South Windsor (G-7830)
Stock Bar Candles LLC....G.... 860 805-1986
West Hartford (G-9862)
Suburban Industries Inc....G.... 203 716-8085
Stamford (G-8448)
Super Cell Industries Inc....G.... 203 393-1335
Bethany (G-250)
Swiss Tactics Industries LLC....G.... 203 974-3427
New Haven (G-5408)
Sylag Manufacturing LLC....G.... 860 832-8772
New Britain (G-5071)
T and A Industries LLC....G.... 860 309-9211
Torrington (G-8975)
▲ Tag Promotions Inc....G.... 800 909-4011
Monroe (G-4755)
Theresas Colorful Creations....G.... 860 726-6909
East Hartford (G-2384)
Thermal Energy Resource Mfg &....G.... 860 225-8792
New Britain (G-5073)
Thermospas Hot Tub Products....E.... 203 303-0005
Wallingford (G-9381)
Thomas Manufacturing LLC....G.... 203 209-4568
Stratford (G-8695)
Thomas S Klise Co....G.... 860 536-4200
Mystic (G-4848)
Thomaston Industries Inc....F.... 860 283-4358
Thomaston (G-8813)
Thommen Industries LLC....G.... 203 332-7999
Bridgeport (G-925)
Thorn Industries LLC....G.... 845 531-7767
Bethel (G-352)
▲ Three Kings Products LLC....G.... 860 945-5294
Watertown (G-9740)

SIC SECTION

73 BUSINESS SERVICES

Company	Code	Phone
Tired Mommy Candles	G	860 407-2002
Griswold *(G-3268)*		
Tjl Industries LLC	G	203 250-2187
Cheshire *(G-1456)*		
Tonys Smoke Shop Outlet LLC	G	203 367-8558
Bridgeport *(G-927)*		
Torq Industries LLC	G	860 537-8539
Colchester *(G-1579)*		
Total Industries LLC	G	203 624-0426
New Haven *(G-5416)*		
Total Quality & Mfg Assoc	G	203 261-3074
Monroe *(G-4762)*		
Tracy S Products	G	203 787-2013
New Haven *(G-5419)*		
Trades Industries	G	203 297-5648
Danbury *(G-1965)*		
Triangle Industries LLC	G	203 297-6255
Danbury *(G-1966)*		
Triton Excimer Group LLC	G	203 733-1063
Ridgefield *(G-7176)*		
UCI Sales Group LLC	G	860 667-4766
Newington *(G-5717)*		
Ultra Mfg LLC	G	203 888-1180
Seymour *(G-7371)*		
United-Bim Inc	G	860 289-1100
East Hartford *(G-2398)*		
◆ UST LLC	G	203 817-3000
Stamford *(G-8483)*		
Valkyrie Industries	G	860 518-5311
Hartford *(G-3712)*		
▲ Valore Inc	G	203 854-4799
Norwalk *(G-6381)*		
Vijay Manufacturing Co LLC	G	860 627-4901
Windsor Locks *(G-10501)*		
VIP Associates LLC	G	203 230-1878
Old Lyme *(G-6521)*		
Vr Industries LLC	G	860 618-2772
Torrington *(G-8987)*		
Waterfalls	G	203 377-1540
Stratford *(G-8705)*		
Watson Fabrication LLC	G	860 912-8778
Niantic *(G-5819)*		
Web Industries	G	860 779-3403
Dayville *(G-2077)*		
White Barrette Mail LLC	G	860 923-3183
Woodstock *(G-10690)*		
Wide Horizons Co Inc	G	203 661-9252
Greenwich *(G-3259)*		
Wilder Hill Farms	G	860 567-2459
Morris *(G-4793)*		
Wildside Fabrication LLC	G	860 585-0514
Bristol *(G-1140)*		
Windsor Mfg	G	860 688-6411
Windsor *(G-10465)*		
Wings N Things	G	860 859-9514
Salem *(G-7293)*		
Wire Burn Industries LLC	G	203 597-9424
Waterbury *(G-9634)*		
Wmb Industries LLC	G	860 927-2822
North Haven *(G-6015)*		
Wmo Industries LLC	G	203 246-2366
Norwalk *(G-6397)*		
Wraith Industries LLC	G	860 454-4003
Ashford *(G-70)*		
Wtf Mfg Co LLC	G	860 387-7472
Cheshire *(G-1460)*		
Yield Industries LLC	G	860 307-8202
Goshen *(G-3105)*		
▲ Z&Z Industries LLC	G	203 230-9533
Hamden *(G-3533)*		
Zachman Industries LLC	G	860 337-2234
New Britain *(G-5085)*		

73 BUSINESS SERVICES

7372 Prepackaged Software

Company	Code	Phone
2394 Berlin Turnpike Assoc LLC	G	860 347-1624
Middletown *(G-4311)*		
3 Story Software LLC	G	203 530-3224
New Milford *(G-5500)*		
360alumni Inc	G	203 253-5860
Weston *(G-10016)*		
Accessware	G	860 235-2982
Mystic *(G-4795)*		
Active Internet Tech LLC	C	800 592-2469
Glastonbury *(G-3003)*		
Actualmeds Corporation	G	888 838-9053
East Hartford *(G-2286)*		
Advance Software LLC	G	860 429-3721
Willington *(G-10244)*		
Advanced Decisions Inc	F	203 402-0603
Orange *(G-6579)*		
Advanced Reasoning	G	860 437-0508
Waterford *(G-9639)*		
Afficiency Inc	G	718 496-9071
Westport *(G-10050)*		
Agencyport Software Corp	G	860 674-6135
Farmington *(G-2876)*		
Agile Computer Systems	G	860 633-7807
Glastonbury *(G-3004)*		
Aicas Inc	G	203 359-5705
Stamford *(G-8068)*		
Al Huppenthal	G	203 364-1028
Sandy Hook *(G-7299)*		
Allexcel Inc	G	203 764-2036
West Haven *(G-9882)*		
Alva Health Inc	G	832 515-8235
New Haven *(G-5225)*		
Andeco Software LLC	G	225 229-2491
Danbury *(G-1740)*		
Aniyaq LLC	G	860 531-2835
Marlborough *(G-4120)*		
API Wizard LLC	G	914 764-5726
Ridgefield *(G-7117)*		
Applied Software	G	860 289-9153
South Windsor *(G-7710)*		
Appstract Ideas	G	860 857-1123
Bristol *(G-964)*		
Arbot Software	G	860 209-8460
West Hartford *(G-9775)*		
Aristo Data Systems	G	203 322-1113
Stamford *(G-8092)*		
Array Technologies Inc	G	860 657-8086
Glastonbury *(G-3008)*		
Arrochar Software LLC	G	203 987-5412
Newtown *(G-5728)*		
Art of Wellbeing LLC	G	917 453-3009
Stamford *(G-8095)*		
Asset Vantage Inc	G	475 218-2639
Stamford *(G-8097)*		
Auras Oracle	G	860 308-0893
Coventry *(G-1644)*		
Automatech Inc	F	860 673-5940
Unionville *(G-9111)*		
Avalon It Systems	G	203 323-7000
Stamford *(G-8099)*		
Becaid LLC	G	203 915-6914
New Haven *(G-5241)*		
Benedict M Lai	G	425 698-7267
Manchester *(G-3986)*		
Beverage Boss LLC	G	203 865-2240
New Haven *(G-5244)*		
Blackrock Media Inc	G	203 374-0369
Easton *(G-2547)*		
Blue Crystal Enterprises LLC	G	203 856-5397
Trumbull *(G-9006)*		
Blue Sky Studios Inc	C	203 992-6000
Greenwich *(G-3135)*		
Bottomline Technologies De Inc	G	203 761-1289
Wilton *(G-10276)*		
Bottomline Technologies De Inc	G	203 431-9787
Ridgefield *(G-7124)*		
Brass City Gamers Tournament	G	203 584-3359
Waterbury *(G-9442)*		
Breach Intelligence Inc	E	844 312-7001
Farmington *(G-2885)*		
Business & Prof Microcompter	G	860 231-7302
West Hartford *(G-9780)*		
C P I Computer Center Inc	G	203 483-8505
Branford *(G-567)*		
Ca Inc	E	800 225-5224
East Windsor *(G-2487)*		
Cadentia LLC	G	860 995-0173
Bristol *(G-997)*		
Calumma Technologies LLC	G	914 557-4562
Norwalk *(G-6105)*		
Capstone Software LLC	G	617 413-4444
Mystic *(G-4804)*		
Careerpath Mobile LLC	G	203 512-2379
New Milford *(G-5515)*		
CD Solutions Inc	E	203 481-5895
Branford *(G-571)*		
Center Road Software LLC	G	860 402-2767
East Haddam *(G-2238)*		
Century Software Systems	G	203 888-5233
Seymour *(G-7339)*		
Cerberus Enterprise Sftwr LLC	G	860 432-3861
Manchester *(G-3993)*		
Channel Sources LLC	F	203 775-6464
Brookfield *(G-1169)*		
Channel Sources Dist Co LLC	G	203 775-6464
Brookfield *(G-1170)*		
Cietrade Systems Inc	G	203 323-0074
Stamford *(G-8146)*		
Cita LLC	G	203 545-7035
Stamford *(G-8148)*		
Clg Solutions LLC	G	203 507-1105
West Haven *(G-9887)*		
Cliffside Entertainment LLC	G	203 290-7484
Bridgeport *(G-736)*		
Club Resource Inc	G	317 225-6940
Canton *(G-1310)*		
Coastalogix LLC	G	203 521-4770
Westport *(G-10065)*		
Cobra Green LLC	A	203 354-5000
Norwalk *(G-6118)*		
Codebridge Software Inc	G	203 535-0517
West Haven *(G-9888)*		
Community Brands Holdings LLC	F	203 227-1255
Westport *(G-10067)*		
Compart North America Inc	F	860 799-5612
New Milford *(G-5522)*		
Computer Prgrm & Systems Inc	G	203 324-9203
Stamford *(G-8155)*		
Computer Software Educ SE	G	860 677-4527
Farmington *(G-2890)*		
Computer Support People LLC	G	203 653-4643
Norwalk *(G-6122)*		
Computer Tech Express LLC	G	203 810-4932
Norwalk *(G-6123)*		
Computer Technologies Corp	G	860 683-4030
Windsor *(G-10376)*		
Connecticut Computer Svc Inc	G	860 276-1285
Milford *(G-4493)*		
Continuity Control	G	203 459-0155
New Haven *(G-5261)*		
Coss Systems Inc	G	800 961-0288
Greenwich *(G-3145)*		
Coss Systems Inc (not Inc)	G	732 447-7724
Old Greenwich *(G-6470)*		
Couponz Direct LLC	G	212 655-9615
Greenwich *(G-3146)*		
Coyote Software	G	203 227-6510
Westport *(G-10070)*		
CPC Software LLC	G	203 348-9684
Stamford *(G-8162)*		
Craig Keating	G	203 852-0571
Norwalk *(G-6132)*		
Criterion Inc	E	203 703-9000
Norwalk *(G-6133)*		
Cuprak Enterprises LLC	G	203 376-8789
Cheshire *(G-1378)*		
Custom Computer Systems	G	203 264-7808
Southbury *(G-7850)*		
Cya Technologies Inc	E	203 513-3111
Shelton *(G-7425)*		
Darien Technology Foundation I	G	203 655-5099
Darien *(G-2019)*		
Dataprep Inc	E	203 795-2095
Orange *(G-6595)*		
David Smith	G	860 877-3232
Southington *(G-7911)*		
Dayspring Communications LLC	G	336 775-2059
Fairfield *(G-2771)*		
Deep River LLC	G	860 388-9442
Old Lyme *(G-6504)*		
Dell Software Inc	G	203 259-0326
Southport *(G-8003)*		
Desrosier of Greenwich Inc	F	203 661-2334
Greenwich *(G-3152)*		
Device42 Inc	F	203 409-7242
West Haven *(G-9898)*		
Dirtcircle Media LLC	G	860 532-0674
Milford *(G-4511)*		
Dmt Solutions Global Corp	A	203 233-6231
Danbury *(G-1797)*		
Document Dynamics LLC	G	860 376-2944
Jewett City *(G-3794)*		
Dreamer Software LLC	G	860 645-1240
Manchester *(G-4011)*		
Drug Imprment Dtction Svcs LLC	G	203 616-3735
Danbury *(G-1802)*		
DSar Company	G	203 324-6456
Stamford *(G-8189)*		
Eagle Consulting LLC	G	203 445-1740
Trumbull *(G-9023)*		
Eagle Investment Systems LLC	F	860 561-4602
West Hartford *(G-9803)*		
Earnix Inc	F	203 557-8077
Westport *(G-10076)*		

Employee Codes: A=Over 500 employees, B=251-500
C=101-250, D=51-100, E=20-50, F=10-19, G=1-9

73 BUSINESS SERVICES

Eatzy LLC .... G 303 720-7532
  Old Saybrook (G-6532)
Enginuity Plm LLC .... F 203 218-7225
  Milford (G-4532)
Epath Learning Inc .... E 860 444-7900
  New London (G-5470)
Expansion Software LLC .... G 860 274-0338
  Watertown (G-9704)
Express Software Production .... G 860 844-0085
  East Granby (G-2204)
Fergtech Inc .... G 203 656-1139
  Darien (G-2024)
Fergtech Inc .... G 203 656-1139
  Darien (G-2025)
Fiduciaryai Inc .... G 203 724-7571
  Norwalk (G-6164)
Fieldstone Cnsulting Group LLC ... G 203 610-5592
  Easton (G-2553)
Financial Navigator Inc .... G 800 468-3636
  Stamford (G-8204)
First Light Software Inc .... G 860 217-0673
  Simsbury (G-7626)
Flagpole Software LLC .... G 203 426-5166
  Newtown (G-5738)
Flexiinternational Sftwr Inc .... E 203 925-3040
  Shelton (G-7445)
Freethink Technologies Inc .... F 860 237-5800
  Branford (G-597)
Frevvo Inc .... F 203 208-3117
  Branford (G-598)
Gamers That Lift LLC .... G 203 988-9211
  Orange (G-6604)
Genesis D T P .... G 860 350-2827
  Gaylordsville (G-2993)
◆ Gerber Scientific LLC .... C 860 871-8082
  Tolland (G-8864)
Golf Research Associates .... G 203 968-1608
  Stamford (G-8218)
Graybark Enterprises LLC .... G 203 255-4503
  Fairfield (G-2792)
Grayfin Security LLC .... G 203 800-6760
  Madison (G-3923)
Grey Wall Software LLC .... F 203 782-5944
  New Haven (G-5291)
Habanero Software Incorporated . G 203 453-5458
  Guilford (G-3359)
Handhold Adaptive LLC .... G 203 526-6313
  Shelton (G-7458)
Hanna RES & Consulting LLC ..... G 860 443-0443
  Quaker Hill (G-7082)
Harpoon Acquisition Corp .... A 860 815-5736
  Glastonbury (G-3047)
Healthper Inc .... G 203 506-0957
  Hamden (G-3462)
Healthprize Technologies LLC ..... G 203 957-3400
  Norwalk (G-6198)
Heckman Consulting LLC .... G 860 434-5877
  Old Lyme (G-6512)
Hexplora LLC .... G 860 760-7601
  Rocky Hill (G-7248)
Higgins Sftwr Consulting LLC ...... G 203 468-2350
  East Haven (G-2434)
Honeypotz Inc .... G 203 542-7891
  Old Greenwich (G-6475)
Horizon Software Inc .... G 860 633-2090
  Glastonbury (G-3050)
Hotseat Chassis Inc .... G 860 582-5031
  Waterbury (G-9499)
Hypack Inc .... F 860 635-1500
  Middletown (G-4354)
I-Logic Software .... G 860 875-7760
  Vernon Rockville (G-9169)
Illume Health LLC .... G 203 242-7801
  Westport (G-10096)
Imagine Software LLC .... G 203 271-0252
  Cheshire (G-1398)
Imprimi Fotos Ya LLC .... G 860 281-1787
  New Haven (G-5300)
Information Builders Inc .... F 860 249-7229
  Hartford (G-3617)
Information Resources Inc .... D 203 845-6400
  Norwalk (G-6207)
Information Tech Intl Corp .... G 860 648-2570
  Manchester (G-4033)
Inner Office Inc .... G 860 564-6777
  Moosup (G-4780)
Innovaticx LLC .... G 203 836-3501
  New Haven (G-5301)
Innovation Group .... E 860 674-2900
  Farmington (G-2917)

Innovative Software .... G 203 264-1564
  Southbury (G-7861)
Innovative Software LLC .... G 860 228-4144
  Hebron (G-3751)
Insight Enterprises Inc .... G 860 647-0848
  Vernon (G-9141)
Insight Enterprises Inc .... G 203 374-2013
  Easton (G-2557)
Intelium Software LLC .... G 860 667-4300
  Newington (G-5665)
Intellgent Clearing Netwrk Inc ..... G 203 972-0861
  North Haven (G-5948)
International Systems Cons .... G 203 268-1045
  Trumbull (G-9036)
Inverse Media LLC .... G 203 255-9620
  Westport (G-10104)
It Helps LLC .... G 860 799-8321
  New Milford (G-5547)
J H R Software .... G 203 723-4091
  Naugatuck (G-4893)
J Squared Software .... G 203 325-0275
  Stamford (G-8261)
Jcascio Software Inc .... G 860 535-2864
  Stonington (G-8533)
Jenkins Software Assoc LLC .... G 203 483-8386
  Branford (G-612)
Jmjp LLC .... G 888 737-7577
  Brooklyn (G-1248)
Jmp Software .... G 203 984-4096
  Norwalk (G-6224)
Jonathan David Humpherys .... G 415 847-3032
  Weatogue (G-9756)
Jpg Consulting Inc .... G 203 247-2730
  Wilton (G-10305)
▲ Kando Apps LLC .... G 203 722-4359
  Norwalk (G-6227)
Kaya Software LLC .... G 203 267-7817
  Southbury (G-7865)
Kenneth Finn .... G 914 764-4938
  Greenwich (G-3187)
Keypoint Forensics LLC .... G 860 877-6586
  Naugatuck (G-4898)
Kol LLC .... E 203 393-2924
  Woodbridge (G-10605)
Komputation Computer Services . G 203 744-3652
  Danbury (G-1871)
Lab Software Associates .... G 203 762-1342
  Wilton (G-10308)
Lablite LLC .... F 860 355-8817
  New Milford (G-5557)
Langlais Computer Cons LLC ..... G 860 589-0093
  Bristol (G-1061)
Lateral Thinking Software Sys .... G 203 452-9713
  Trumbull (G-9042)
Letout & Bliss LLC .... G 203 775-3548
  Brookfield (G-1202)
Light Speed LLC .... G 203 248-8550
  Hamden (G-3475)
Link Systems Inc .... F 203 274-9702
  Stamford (G-8285)
Litigation Analytics Inc .... F 203 431-0300
  Ridgefield (G-7154)
Littlefingers Software .... G 203 938-2684
  Redding (G-7096)
Living Abroad LLC .... G 203 221-1997
  Norwalk (G-6234)
Locallive Networks Inc .... G 877 355-6225
  Stamford (G-8287)
Loden Software .... G 203 949-9416
  Wallingford (G-9304)
Lost Code Software LLC .... G 203 626-9133
  Wallingford (G-9307)
Loving Life LLC .... G 860 326-1459
  Voluntown (G-9190)
Lu Lu Holdings LLC .... E 203 861-1988
  Greenwich (G-3193)
Management Hlth Solutions Inc .. E 888 647-4621
  Stratford (G-8647)
Management Software Inc .... G 860 536-5177
  Ledyard (G-3877)
Mannan 3d Innovations LLC .... G 203 306-4203
  Higganum (G-3768)
Market76 Inc .... G 866 808-5491
  Guilford (G-3370)
MB Software Development .... G 203 928-0436
  West Haven (G-9934)
Mbsiinet Inc .... F 888 466-2744
  Southbury (G-7866)
Mc Keon Computer Services ...... G 860 496-7171
  Torrington (G-8947)

Me2health LLC .... G 203 208-8927
  Guilford (G-3374)
Medpipes .... G 860 658-7300
  West Simsbury (G-9981)
Medpricercom Inc .... G 203 453-4554
  Guilford (G-3375)
Mental Canvas LLC .... G 475 329-0515
  Madison (G-3939)
Micro Training Associates Inc ..... F 860 693-7740
  Canton (G-1318)
Microsoft Corporation .... E 860 678-3100
  Farmington (G-2928)
Mind2mind Exchange LLC .... G 203 856-0981
  Stamford (G-8311)
Mindtrainr LLC .... G 914 799-1515
  Stamford (G-8312)
Mission Critical Software .... G 860 748-6946
  Glastonbury (G-3060)
Montage Software Systems Inc .. G 203 834-1144
  Wilton (G-10313)
Mpi Systems Inc .... G 203 762-2260
  Wilton (G-10314)
Mt Calvary Holy Church .... G 203 785-1253
  New Haven (G-5337)
Mvp Systems Software Inc .... F 860 269-3112
  Unionville (G-9122)
National Educ Suppt Trust US ... G 860 420-8008
  Branford (G-628)
National Instruments Corp .... G 203 661-6795
  Riverside (G-7198)
Navtech Systems Inc .... G 203 661-7800
  Old Greenwich (G-6480)
Neasi-Weber International .... G 203 857-4404
  Norwalk (G-6271)
Network Expert Sftwr Systems ... G 860 829-1427
  Kensington (G-3815)
New England Computer Svcs Inc E 475 221-8200
  Branford (G-629)
Newman Information Systems .... G 860 286-0540
  Bloomfield (G-449)
Nexvue Information Systems Inc F 203 327-0800
  Stamford (G-8328)
Nohtbook Inc .... G 203 493-1633
  Norwalk (G-6279)
Norfield Data Products Inc .... G 203 849-0292
  Norwalk (G-6280)
North Star Computing Svcs LLC G 860 635-7117
  Cromwell (G-1709)
Nuance Communications Inc 781 565-5000
  Stratford (G-8658)
Nupal LLC .... G 860 227-7964
  Chester (G-1476)
Nxtid Inc .... F 203 266-2103
  Oxford (G-6682)
O/D Dominion Software LLC ...... G 860 904-9261
  Bloomfield (G-453)
Old Road Software Inc .... G 914 755-1329
  Ridgefield (G-7159)
Only Queens LLC .... G 860 888-4413
  Bloomfield (G-455)
Open Solutions LLC .... C 860 815-5000
  Glastonbury (G-3066)
Open Water Development LLC .. G 646 883-2062
  Old Greenwich (G-6481)
Openiam Software LLC .... G 203 202-7186
  Redding (G-7105)
Oracle America Inc .... D 203 703-3000
  Stamford (G-8345)
Oracle Corporation .... B 860 632-8329
  Middletown (G-4389)
Orisha Oracle Inc .... G 203 612-8989
  Bridgeport (G-857)
Packrat Software .... G 860 774-1538
  Dayville (G-2068)
Paladin Software Inc .... G 203 966-0548
  New Canaan (G-5129)
Pallasian Software LLC .... G 203 758-5868
  Prospect (G-7015)
Parent Engagement Tracker LLC G 860 209-5522
  Hartford (G-3661)
Pawtrait Inc 848 992-4599
  Stamford (G-8353)
Peartree Point Software LLC ...... G 203 940-1069
  Darien (G-2037)
Peerless Systems Corporation ... F 203 350-0040
  Stamford (G-8355)
Penney Software Services .... G 860 870-3443
  Tolland (G-8875)
People Meeting LLC .... G 860 933-0366
  Glastonbury (G-3069)

76 MISCELLANEOUS REPAIR SERVICES

Pergenex Software LLC .... G 860 274-7318
  Watertown (G-9721)
Peter Hannan .... G 203 226-4335
  Westport (G-10140)
Phraction Management LLC .... G 860 531-9590
  Colchester (G-1565)
Pilot Software Inc .... G 203 252-2463
  Stamford (G-8361)
◆ Pitney Bowes Inc .... A 203 356-5000
  Stamford (G-8362)
Pitney Bowes Software Inc .... G 603 595-2060
  Stamford (G-8364)
Pmoys LLC .... G 203 541-0995
  Stamford (G-8365)
Polymath Software .... G 860 423-5823
  Willimantic (G-10234)
Pricing Excellence LLC .... G 866 557-8102
  Suffield (G-8730)
Prime Business Services .... G 203 453-1627
  Guilford (G-3384)
Private Communications Corp .... F 860 355-2718
  Sherman (G-7602)
Prolink Inc .... G 860 659-5928
  Glastonbury (G-3076)
Proserv Software & Support LLC ...... G 866 833-8999
  Meriden (G-4223)
Protegrity Usa Inc .... E 203 326-7200
  Stamford (G-8376)
Protoshield .... G 203 527-0321
  Middlebury (G-4288)
Psj Software LLC .... G 203 315-1523
  Branford (G-639)
Qdiscovery LLC .... E 860 271-7080
  New London (G-5483)
Qscend Technologies Inc .... E 203 757-6000
  Waterbury (G-9591)
Qualedi Inc .... G 203 538-5320
  Shelton (G-7542)
Qualedi Inc .... G 203 874-4334
  Milford (G-4621)
Racemyface LLC .... G 203 285-8090
  Wilton (G-10323)
Radical Computing Corporation .... G 860 953-0240
  Newington (G-5699)
Ramco Systems Corporation .... G 860 496-0099
  New Hartford (G-5209)
Reel Time LLC .... G 203 326-0664
  New Canaan (G-5138)
Regenerative Medicine LLC .... G 203 629-1438
  Greenwich (G-3223)
Relational Data Solutions LLC .... G 860 231-7682
  West Hartford (G-9851)
Relprog LLC .... G 203 734-7000
  Derby (G-2123)
Republic Systems Inc .... G 860 291-8832
  East Hartford (G-2365)
Results-Based Outsourcing Inc .... G 203 635-7600
  Fairfield (G-2835)
Reynolds and Reynolds Company ..... G 203 323-3748
  Stamford (G-8392)
Richard Breault .... G 203 876-2707
  Milford (G-4626)
Rindle LLC .... G 551 482-2037
  Norwalk (G-6324)
Robust Software LLC .... G 860 231-9880
  West Hartford (G-9852)
S-Frame Software LLC .... G 203 421-8527
  Madison (G-3954)
Saleschain LLC .... F 203 262-1611
  Waterbury (G-9597)
Sas Institute Inc .... E 860 633-4119
  Glastonbury (G-3081)
Satori Audio LLC .... G 203 571-6050
  Westport (G-10154)
Savin Rock Software LLC .... G 203 272-5039
  Cheshire (G-1442)
Schulz Consulting LLC .... G 860 657-4497
  Glastonbury (G-3082)
Scry Health Inc .... F 203 936-8244
  Woodbridge (G-10616)
Securities Software & Con .... G 860 242-7887
  Bloomfield (G-486)
Securities Software & Consulti .... G 860 298-4500
  Windsor (G-10435)
Sepdx .... G 803 479-6322
  New Haven (G-5393)
Sepsisdx .... G 856 359-5309
  New Haven (G-5394)
Servco Oil Inc .... G 203 762-7994
  Wilton (G-10328)

Servicetune Inc .... G 860 284-4445
  Avon (G-110)
Shagmeisters Enterprises .... G 203 937-5584
  West Haven (G-9954)
Shibumicom Inc .... F 855 744-2864
  Norwalk (G-6344)
Shiloh Software Inc .... G 203 272-8456
  Cheshire (G-1445)
Siggpay Inc .... G 203 957-8261
  Norwalk (G-6346)
Sigmund Software LLC .... F 800 448-6975
  Danbury (G-1948)
Skythink Inc .... G 203 324-1108
  Stamford (G-8424)
Slv Consulting Inc .... G 917 892-4034
  Wilton (G-10332)
Smartpay Solutions .... G 860 986-7659
  Southington (G-7974)
Snowdog Software LLC .... G 203 265-7116
  Wallingford (G-9370)
Sobrio LLC .... G 860 880-1990
  Storrs (G-8551)
Softstorms LLC .... G 860 578-8515
  West Hartford (G-9857)
Software By Design LLC .... G 203 271-1061
  Cheshire (G-1449)
Software Cnslting Rsources Inc .... G 860 491-2689
  Goshen (G-3104)
Software Establishment LLC .... G 860 426-2700
  Berlin (G-231)
Software Gallery Inc .... G 203 775-0520
  Brookfield (G-1224)
Software Matters .... G 860 354-8804
  Roxbury (G-7285)
Software Studios LLC .... G 203 288-3997
  North Haven (G-5995)
Software Systems & Support LLC ..... G 203 470-8482
  Middletown (G-4420)
Soundview Horizons Dgtl Ldrshp ...... G 203 292-0880
  Weston (G-10040)
SS&c Technologies Inc .... G 203 930-5882
  Windsor (G-10437)
SS&c Technologies Inc .... C 203 298-4500
  Windsor (G-10438)
SS&c Technologies Holdings Inc ...... D 203 298-4500
  Windsor (G-10439)
Stamford Risk Analytics LLC .... F 203 559-0883
  Stamford (G-8439)
Still River Software Co LLC .... G 860 263-0396
  Woodstock (G-10686)
Stony Creek Liquor LLC .... G 203 488-3318
  Branford (G-658)
Student Employment Sftwr LLC .... G 203 485-9417
  Greenwich (G-3242)
Success App .... G 203 218-6264
  Stratford (G-8689)
Swing By Swing Golf Inc .... G 310 922-8023
  Hartford (G-3695)
Synergy Solutions LLC .... G 203 762-1153
  Wilton (G-10335)
Syrver LLC .... G 203 598-5810
  Fairfield (G-2852)
Tagetik North America LLC .... G 203 391-7520
  Stamford (G-8457)
Tangoe Us Inc .... B 203 859-9300
  Shelton (G-7563)
Tangoe Us Inc .... C 973 257-0300
  Shelton (G-7564)
Tavisca LLC .... G 203 956-1000
  Stamford (G-8458)
Technology Group LLC .... G 860 524-4400
  Hartford (G-3699)
Technolutions Inc .... E 203 404-4835
  New Haven (G-5412)
Technosoft Solutions Inc .... E 203 676-8299
  Branford (G-661)
Telemark Systems Inc .... G 860 355-8001
  New Milford (G-5594)
Telenity Inc .... C 203 445-2000
  Monroe (G-4759)
Tenzingbrook Software LLC .... G 203 918-4500
  New Canaan (G-5151)
Thebeamer LLC .... F 860 212-5071
  East Hartford (G-2383)
Think Ahead Software LLC .... G 860 463-9786
  West Hartford (G-9865)
Ticket Software LLC .... G 860 644-0422
  South Windsor (G-7833)
Tiny B Code LLC .... G 617 308-9635
  West Hartford (G-9867)

Torrington Ig Partners LLC .... G 860 482-7868
  Torrington (G-8982)
Travers & Co LLC .... G 860 633-8586
  Glastonbury (G-3089)
Traxx Software LLC .... G 860 632-8712
  Cromwell (G-1721)
Trinity Mobile Networks Inc .... G 301 332-6401
  New Haven (G-5423)
Trycycle Data Systems US Inc .... G 860 558-1148
  Farmington (G-2970)
Turnkey Software LLC .... G 860 604-0837
  East Hampton (G-2282)
Tutors & Computers Inc .... G 203 393-3006
  Bethany (G-251)
Ultimate Interfaces Corp .... G 203 230-8184
  Milford (G-4667)
Ultra Golden Software LLC .... G 203 227-4009
  Westport (G-10169)
Unimelon Inc .... G 201 774-2786
  Ridgefield (G-7179)
Uniworld Bus Publications Inc .... G 201 384-4900
  Darien (G-2049)
Urise LLC .... G 860 833-3009
  Hartford (G-3710)
Vertafore Inc .... A 860 602-6000
  Windsor (G-10459)
Villa Ridge LLC .... G 303 330-9183
  Norwalk (G-6389)
Visual Software Systems LLC .... G 860 829-1223
  Berlin (G-231)
Voice Glance LLC .... F 800 260-3025
  Mystic (G-4852)
Warren Computer Services .... G 203 929-5725
  Shelton (G-7583)
Wdl Software Llc .... G 203 366-8640
  Fairfield (G-2867)
Web Charity LLC .... G 203 481-7600
  Branford (G-670)
Wipl-D (usa) LLC .... G 860 570-0678
  West Hartford (G-9873)
X Over Y Systems .... G 860 885-0034
  New London (G-5497)
Xolvi LLC .... G 339 222-3616
  Simsbury (G-7652)
Yourmembershipcom Inc .... G 860 271-7241
  Groton (G-3320)
Zillion Group Inc .... F 203 810-5400
  Norwalk (G-6404)

76 MISCELLANEOUS REPAIR SERVICES

7692 Welding Repair

A & A Welding LLC .... G 860 933-1284
  Moosup (G-4777)
A & L Welding Service .... G 860 664-1700
  Clinton (G-1488)
A Z Welding .... G 860 872-1301
  Tolland (G-8846)
AC Skips Welding Inc .... G 203 838-2089
  Norwalk (G-6060)
Accurate Welding Services LLC .... F 860 623-9500
  Windsor Locks (G-10467)
Ack Precision Machine Co .... G 860 664-0789
  Clinton (G-1490)
Advanced Welding & Repair Inc .... G 860 242-0400
  Bloomfield (G-381)
Aerotek Welding Co Inc .... G 860 653-0120
  North Granby (G-5880)
Alloy Welding .... G 203 737-5609
  New Haven (G-5224)
American Steel Fabricators Inc .... G 860 243-5005
  Bloomfield (G-384)
American Welding Service .... G 860 935-5314
  North Grosvenordale (G-5883)
American Wldg Fabrication LLC .... G 860 918-2094
  New Britain (G-4944)
Amk Welding Inc .... E 860 289-5634
  South Windsor (G-7707)
Anderson Tool Company Inc .... G 203 777-4153
  New Haven (G-5231)
▲ Ansonia Stl Fabrication Co Inc ...... E 203 888-4509
  Beacon Falls (G-129)
Anthony Da RE Welding .... G 860 526-2659
  Deep River (G-2083)
Apex Machine Tool Company Inc .... G 203 806-2090
  Cheshire (G-1354)
Arp Welding & Repair LLC .... G 203 924-6811
  Shelton (G-7397)

76 MISCELLANEOUS REPAIR SERVICES

Associated Welding Process .... G 860 677-0671
  Farmington (G-2879)
Astro Welding Inc .... G 860 289-6272
  East Hartford (G-2294)
▲ B & F Machine Co Inc .... D 860 225-6349
  New Britain (G-4949)
B T Welding .... G 860 537-6197
  Colchester (G-1542)
Bahres Welding .... G 860 693-4950
  Canton (G-1306)
Barzetti Welding LLC .... G 203 748-3200
  Bethel (G-261)
Bethany Welding .... G 203 393-0002
  New Haven (G-5243)
Bob Worden .... G 860 567-4722
  Lakeside (G-3841)
Bonati Brothers Welding & Fabr .... G 860 582-5000
  Plainville (G-6777)
Brazing Way LLC .... G 860 485-9337
  Harwinton (G-3722)
C and B Welding LLC .... G 860 423-9047
  Lebanon (G-3848)
C V Tool Company Inc .... E 978 353-7901
  Southington (G-7901)
Carlos Welding and Fab LLC .... G 860 647-8592
  Manchester (G-3991)
Carlson Welding & Fabrication .... G 860 788-3569
  Moodus (G-4772)
Carlucci Welding & Fabrication .... G 203 588-0746
  Norwalk (G-6107)
Carrano Railings .... G 203 248-7245
  Hamden (G-3426)
Cheshire Manufacturing Co Inc .... G 203 272-3586
  Cheshire (G-1369)
Chiappettas Welding .... G 203 637-1522
  Riverside (G-7190)
City Welding .... G 860 951-4714
  Hartford (G-3568)
Ckg Welding Fabrication LLC .... G 860 628-7129
  Southington (G-7905)
Crewelding .... G 855 204-7352
  Middletown (G-4333)
Ctr Welding .... G 704 473-1587
  Danbury (G-1778)
D and L Welding LLC .... G 860 429-8259
  Storrs Mansfield (G-8554)
D B F Industries Inc .... E 860 827-8283
  New Britain (G-4969)
Daigles Diversfd Wldg Svc LLC .... G 860 265-3024
  Somers (G-7655)
Danbury Welding LLC .... G 203 482-9306
  Danbury (G-1788)
Dark Moon Metals LLC .... G 203 858-3015
  Norwalk (G-6134)
Davco Systems .... G 860 546-9681
  Canterbury (G-1298)
Doctor Weld LLC .... G 203 877-3433
  Milford (G-4513)
Durant Machine Inc .... G 860 536-7698
  Mystic (G-4813)
Duros Welding Services .... G 203 982-6978
  Waterbury (G-9468)
Dyco Industries Inc .... E 860 289-4957
  South Windsor (G-7741)
East Side Car Clinic Corp .... G 860 223-2247
  New Britain (G-4978)
East Windsor Metal Fabg Inc .... F 860 528-7107
  South Windsor (G-7745)
Erection & Welding Contrs LLC .... G 860 828-9353
  Berlin (G-178)
Eric Nordlund Welding .... G 203 544-8293
  Wilton (G-10292)
EZ Welding LLC .... G 860 707-3099
  New Britain (G-4987)
EZ Welding LLC .... G 860 707-3100
  New Britain (G-4988)
F & W Rentals Inc .... F 203 795-0591
  Orange (G-6600)
Fabtron Incorporated .... G 860 410-1801
  Plainville (G-6808)
Farrell Prcsion Mtalcraft Corp .... E 860 355-2651
  New Milford (G-5532)
Fonda Fabricating & Welding Co .... G 860 793-0601
  Plainville (G-6812)
Fowlers Steel & Welding .... G 860 647-7641
  Manchester (G-4019)
Frank Porto .... G 203 596-0811
  Watertown (G-9707)
Frys Welding LLC .... G 860 944-2547
  Winsted (G-10522)

Gabbro Forge and Welding LLC .... G 617 699-0031
  Hamden (G-3450)
Gaida Welding Co & Mar Repr .... G 203 924-4868
  Shelton (G-7448)
Gardner Welding LLC .... G 203 265-1036
  Wallingford (G-9274)
Gavin Welding LLC .... G 203 393-9707
  Bethany (G-243)
General Welding Company Inc .... G 203 753-6988
  Waterbury (G-9487)
General Wldg & Fabrication Inc .... F 860 274-9668
  Watertown (G-9708)
Gintys Welding Service Inc .... G 203 270-3399
  Sandy Hook (G-7314)
Goodyfab Llc .... G 203 927-3059
  North Branford (G-5839)
Guy Montanari .... G 203 791-0642
  Danbury (G-1840)
H G Steinmetz Machine Works .... F 203 794-1880
  Bethel (G-307)
Harry Thommen Company .... G 203 333-3637
  Bridgeport (G-782)
Hs Welding LLC .... G 203 599-0372
  Pawcatuck (G-6716)
Hutch Welding Company .... G 860 496-9082
  Torrington (G-8933)
Independent Welding & Fabg .... G 860 605-4712
  New Hartford (G-5196)
▲ Innovative Fusion Inc .... E 203 729-3873
  Naugatuck (G-4891)
Ironman Welding L L C .... G 203 979-4063
  Stamford (G-8259)
Ives Welding Service .... G 860 423-6139
  South Windham (G-7688)
J T Fantozzi Co Inc .... G 203 238-7018
  Meriden (G-4177)
Jacquier Welding .... G 860 824-4182
  Canaan (G-1287)
Jakes Repair LLC .... G 203 627-8603
  Old Saybrook (G-6547)
James A Blazys .... G 860 274-3857
  Watertown (G-9713)
Jeff Manufacturing Co Inc .... F 860 482-8845
  Torrington (G-8937)
Jim Murray Wldg & Fabrication .... G 860 889-7777
  North Stonington (G-6028)
Jims Welding Service LLC .... G 203 744-2982
  Danbury (G-1862)
Jnt Welding Services LLC .... G 860 350-3957
  New Milford (G-5551)
Joe & Son Wldg Fabrication LLC .... G 203 380-2072
  Stratford (G-8637)
Joining Technologies Inc .... D 860 653-0111
  East Granby (G-2209)
Joseph Rembeck .... G 860 738-3981
  Pleasant Valley (G-6923)
K & L Welding LLC .... G 860 970-2390
  Hartford (G-3622)
K J Welding .... G 860 345-8743
  Haddam (G-3406)
K L & P Welding .... G 860 986-2518
  East Windsor (G-2502)
K T I Turbo-Tech Inc .... F 860 623-2511
  East Windsor (G-2503)
Kell-Strom Tool Intl Inc .... E 860 529-6851
  Wethersfield (G-10207)
Ken Hastedt .... G 203 268-6563
  Monroe (G-4725)
Kensington Welding & Trlr Co .... G 860 828-3564
  Kensington (G-3811)
Kin-Therm Inc .... F 860 623-2511
  East Windsor (G-2504)
Kordys Welding Inc .... G 860 621-2271
  Southington (G-7946)
Kostas Cstm Ir Fbrications LLC .... G 203 667-0881
  Stamford (G-8278)
KTI Bi-Metallix Inc .... F 860 623-2511
  East Windsor (G-2506)
KTI Inc .... F 860 623-2511
  East Windsor (G-2507)
L M Gill Welding and Mfr LLC .... E 860 647-9931
  Manchester (G-4047)
Labco Welding Inc .... G 860 632-2625
  Middletown (G-4367)
Lemac Iron Works Inc .... G 860 232-7380
  West Hartford (G-9829)
LM Gill Welding & Mfg LLC .... E 860 647-9931
  Manchester (G-4049)
Lostocco Refuse Service LLC .... E 203 748-9296
  Danbury (G-1877)

Louie S Welding .... G 203 634-0873
  Meriden (G-4189)
Lynn Welding Co Inc .... F 860 667-4400
  Newington (G-5672)
M D Welding & Fabricating LLC .... G 860 643-2448
  Bolton (G-515)
M L Guerrera Welding .... G 203 879-6823
  Wolcott (G-10572)
Mackenzie Mch & Mar Works Inc .... G 203 777-3479
  East Haven (G-2441)
Mainville Welding Co Inc .... G 203 237-3103
  Meriden (G-4191)
Marc Bouley .... G 860 450-1713
  Willimantic (G-10233)
Marks Construction Co LLC .... G 860 407-2391
  Portland (G-6965)
▲ Matias Importing & Distrg Corp .... G 860 666-5544
  Newington (G-5675)
Metal Industries Inc .... G 860 296-6228
  Hartford (G-3640)
Metals Edge Welding LLC .... G 203 500-5644
  Shelton (G-7498)
Mikes Welding .... G 203 855-9631
  Norwalk (G-6258)
Mobile Welding Repair .... G 203 459-2744
  Monroe (G-4739)
Modified Welding LLC .... G 860 428-3599
  North Grosvenordale (G-5891)
Msr Welding Service .... G 860 234-9949
  Brooklyn (G-1250)
Murphy & Sons Welding & Repair .... G 860 635-3372
  Stamford (G-8316)
National Welding LLC .... G 860 818-1240
  Middletown (G-4383)
Nct Inc .... F 860 666-8424
  Newington (G-5684)
New Canaan Forge LLC .... G 203 966-3858
  New Canaan (G-5123)
New England Welding Svcs LLC .... G 860 406-4030
  Plantsville (G-6905)
New Milford Foundry & Mch Co .... G 860 354-5561
  New Milford (G-5571)
Nutmeg Welding Company Inc .... G 203 756-7458
  Waterbury (G-9564)
On-Site Welding LLC .... G 860 662-6332
  Collinsville (G-1598)
Optimum Welding Solutions LLC .... G 203 598-8489
  Prospect (G-7012)
P & M Welding Co LLC .... G 860 528-2077
  South Windsor (G-7803)
Palladino Welding .... G 203 729-7542
  Naugatuck (G-4908)
Parama Corp .... F 203 790-8155
  Bethel (G-331)
Paul Welding Company Inc .... F 860 229-9945
  Newington (G-5693)
Pelchs Welding & Repair .... G 860 693-6328
  Collinsville (G-1599)
Perez Welding Services LLC .... G 203 876-1066
  Milford (G-4607)
Phils Welding .... G 860 685-1713
  Higganum (G-3775)
Phoenix Machine Inc .... G 203 888-1135
  Seymour (G-7360)
Phoenix Welding .... G 860 657-9481
  Glastonbury (G-3070)
Polish Welding LLC .... G 860 347-0368
  Middletown (G-4394)
Pop Moody Welding Services .... G 860 749-9537
  Somers (G-7668)
Precision Welding .... G 860 423-7772
  Mansfield Center (G-4115)
Precision Welding Services LLC .... G 860 268-0580
  Coventry (G-1668)
Quality Welding LLC .... G 860 585-1121
  Bristol (G-1100)
Quality Welding Service LLC .... G 860 342-7202
  Portland (G-6970)
R & F Welding Co .... G 203 393-2851
  New Haven (G-5374)
R Lange Welding-Fabrication .... G 203 994-5516
  Brookfield (G-1217)
Rapid Truck Service Inc .... G 860 482-5500
  Torrington (G-8963)
Recor Welding Center Inc .... G 860 573-1942
  Southington (G-7965)
Reliable Welding & Speed LLC .... G 860 749-3977
  Enfield (G-2687)
Reliant Services LLC .... G 860 346-6107
  Middletown (G-4404)

76 MISCELLANEOUS REPAIR SERVICES

▲ Reno Machine Company Inc..........D...... 860 666-5641
  Newington (G-5700)
Reyes Welding Svcs..........................G...... 203 505-1111
  Norwalk (G-6323)
Richies Automotive LLC..................G...... 860 482-0667
  Harwinton (G-3737)
Robert Schwartz.................................G...... 203 515-8162
  Gaylordsville (G-2996)
Rodney Tulba Welding & Fabg........G...... 860 442-9840
  Waterford (G-9667)
Ronald R Eschner..............................G...... 860 485-9373
  Harwinton (G-3738)
Rossitto Welding Inc.........................G...... 860 223-1598
  New Britain (G-5049)
Rozelle Specialty Processes............G...... 860 793-9400
  Plainville (G-6859)
S S Fabrications Inc.........................G...... 860 974-1910
  Eastford (G-2541)
Safin Wldg & Fabrication LLC.........G...... 860 974-3831
  Eastford (G-2542)
Sandy Hook Welding & Fabg...........G...... 203 731-9844
  Sandy Hook (G-7329)
Saucier Welding Services................G...... 860 747-4577
  Southington (G-7970)
Sauciers Misc Metal Works LLC.....G...... 860 747-4577
  Southington (G-7971)
Serena Granbery Welding................G...... 860 435-2322
  Salisbury (G-7298)
Shm Welding and Repair LLC.........G...... 860 267-4012
  East Hampton (G-2279)
Shoreline Boiler & Welding LLC.....G...... 860 575-0944
  Westbrook (G-10008)
Singers Welding Works....................G...... 203 743-9353
  Danbury (G-1953)
Solutions With Innovation LLC......G...... 203 729-3873
  Naugatuck (G-4919)
Somers Manufacturing Inc..............G...... 860 314-1075
  Bristol (G-1119)
Sonic Welding Co.............................G...... 203 348-8021
  Stamford (G-8429)
Sorge Industries Inc.........................G...... 203 924-8900
  Shelton (G-7557)
Spiers Welding Service....................G...... 203 322-1004
  Stamford (G-8434)
Spot Welders Inc..............................G...... 203 386-8938
  Stratford (G-8684)
Standard Welding Company Inc....G...... 860 528-9628
  East Hartford (G-2377)
State Welding & Fabg Inc................G...... 203 294-4071
  Wallingford (G-9376)
State Wide Welding Service............G...... 860 489-2465
  New Hartford (G-5213)
Sterzingers Welding LLC.................G...... 203 685-1575
  Danbury (G-1956)
Steven Sabo......................................G...... 860 642-6031
  Lebanon (G-3863)
Sunnyside Fab & Welding Inc........G...... 203 378-9515
  Bridgeport (G-916)
Superb Steel LLC..............................G...... 860 518-7281
  New Britain (G-5068)
Superior Welding..............................G...... 860 584-2632
  Terryville (G-8773)
Swistro Welding................................G...... 860 978-3238
  New Britain (G-5070)
Sylvia Engineering Wldg & Eqp......G...... 860 859-1791
  Norwich (G-6434)

Teck Welding & Fabrication LLC....G...... 860 584-1264
  Bristol (G-1126)
Ted Boccuzzi.....................................G...... 860 354-3799
  New Milford (G-5593)
Thomas La Ganga.............................G...... 860 489-0920
  Torrington (G-8977)
Tim Welding......................................G...... 203 488-3486
  North Branford (G-5862)
▲ Tinsley GROup-Ps&w Inc..............D...... 919 742-5832
  Milford (G-4665)
Tito Welding LLC..............................G...... 860 354-1536
  New Milford (G-5598)
Torrington Diesel Corporation.......G...... 860 496-9948
  Torrington (G-8980)
Total Fab LLC....................................F...... 475 238-8176
  East Haven (G-2457)
Trap Rock Ridge Welding LLC.......G...... 203 213-7578
  Meriden (G-4257)
Trico Welding Company LLC..........G...... 203 720-3782
  Beacon Falls (G-149)
Uneeda Welder..................................G...... 203 929-4507
  Shelton (G-7574)
United Steel Inc................................C...... 860 289-2323
  East Hartford (G-2389)
Upscale Welding & Fabrica.............G...... 203 265-0800
  Wallingford (G-9396)
Valley Welding Co Inc......................G...... 860 283-5768
  Thomaston (G-8817)
Wally-B Welding................................G...... 203 264-3853
  Southbury (G-7884)
Watchdog Welding LLC....................G...... 860 355-9549
  Bridgewater (G-948)
Weld TEC LLC....................................G...... 860 628-5750
  Plantsville (G-6918)
Weld-All Inc.......................................F...... 860 621-3156
  Southington (G-7995)
Welder Repair & Rental Svc Inc.....G...... 203 238-9284
  Durham (G-2161)
Welding On Wheels Services LLC..G...... 203 449-6273
  Stratford (G-8706)
WH Rose Inc......................................E...... 860 228-8258
  Columbia (G-1615)
Whatever Welding LLC.....................G...... 860 779-7703
  Dayville (G-2080)
White Welding Company Inc..........G...... 203 753-1197
  Waterbury (G-9633)
William Clark Welding Inc..............G...... 860 537-0122
  Colchester (G-1582)
William Linkovich.............................G...... 860 824-0298
  East Canaan (G-2184)
Willies Welding Inc..........................G...... 203 237-6235
  Meriden (G-4268)
WS Welding LLC...............................G...... 860 262-0214
  Portland (G-6980)
Yard Welding and Repair LLC........G...... 860 402-8321
  Bristol (G-1142)

7694 Armature Rewinding Shops

Accuwind Inc....................................G...... 203 287-9697
  Hamden (G-3411)
Andys Automotive Machine............G...... 860 793-2455
  Plainville (G-6770)
Aparos Electric Motor Service.......G...... 860 276-2044
  Southington (G-7891)
B & F Electric Motors LLC..............G...... 203 359-2626
  Stamford (G-8103)

Bemat TEC LLC.................................G...... 860 632-0049
  Cromwell (G-1691)
Canfield Electric..............................G...... 203 266-5290
  Bethlehem (G-367)
Carter Inv Holdings Corp................G...... 860 283-5801
  Thomaston (G-8783)
Central Electric Inc.........................G...... 860 774-3054
  Dayville (G-2057)
Central Electric Motor....................G...... 860 642-7421
  Lebanon (G-3850)
Cudzilo Enterprises Inc..................G...... 203 748-4694
  Bethel (G-275)
Electric Enterprise Inc...................F...... 203 378-7311
  Stratford (G-8607)
Electrical Maintenance Svc Co.....G...... 203 333-6163
  Bridgeport (G-761)
Industrial Drives Contrls Inc........F...... 203 753-5103
  Waterbury (G-9504)
Industrial Electric Motors..............G...... 203 743-9611
  Danbury (G-1849)
Jan Manufacturing Inc....................G...... 203 879-0580
  Wolcott (G-10569)
Just Call Jason LLC.........................G...... 203 934-3127
  West Haven (G-9921)
Leppert/Nutmeg Inc........................E...... 860 243-1737
  Bloomfield (G-441)
Magna-Wind Inc...............................G...... 203 269-4749
  Wallingford (G-9309)
Nicholas Melfi Jr..............................G...... 203 853-7235
  Norwalk (G-6278)
Palmers Elc Mtrs & Pumps Inc.....G...... 203 348-7378
  Norwalk (G-6290)
Piela Electric Inc.............................F...... 860 889-8476
  Preston (G-6987)
Power Quality and Drives LLC......G...... 203 217-2353
  Woodbury (G-10651)
Precision Devices Inc.....................F...... 203 265-9308
  Wallingford (G-9340)
Reliable Electric Motor Inc...........F...... 860 522-2257
  Hartford (G-3676)
Rite-Way Electric Motors Inc........G...... 860 528-8890
  East Hartford (G-2366)
SEC Electrical Inc............................F...... 203 562-5811
  New Haven (G-5390)
Servotech Inc....................................G...... 860 632-0164
  Middletown (G-4410)
Tibbys Electric Motor Service.......G...... 203 748-4694
  Bethel (G-353)
Total Control Inc.............................G...... 203 269-4749
  Wallingford (G-9390)
Traver Electric Motor Co Inc.........E...... 203 753-5103
  Waterbury (G-9617)
Ward Leonard Holdings LLC.........G...... 860 283-5801
  Thomaston (G-8820)
Ward Leonard Inv Holdings LLC...G...... 860 283-5801
  Thomaston (G-8821)
Ward Leonard Operating LLC.......G...... 860 283-5801
  Thomaston (G-8822)
Ward Lonard Houma Holdings LLC......G...... 860 283-5801
  Thomaston (G-8823)
WI Intermediate Holdings LLC.....G...... 860 283-5801
  Thomaston (G-8825)

ALPHABETIC SECTION

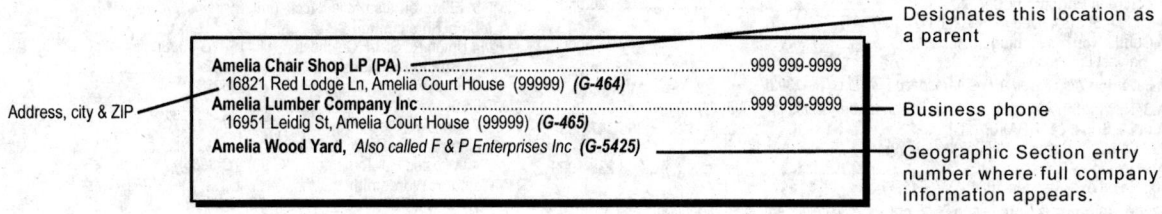

See footnotes for symbols and codes identification.
* Companies listed alphabetically.
* Complete physical or mailing address.

(fast) International Inc (PA) 203 380-3489
  905 Honeyspot Rd Stratford (06615) *(G-8562)*
1 Way Custom Print 860 712-0027
  61 Charter Oak St Apt D Manchester (06040) *(G-3970)*
101 Business Solutions LLC 860 774-6904
  128 Fitzgerald Rd Brooklyn (06234) *(G-1243)*
109 Design LLC (PA) 203 941-1812
  55 Whitney Ave Fl 2 New Haven (06510) *(G-5215)*
111 Brentwood LLC 203 284-5065
  15 Taylor Ln Wallingford (06492) *(G-9192)*
12 Paws Publishing LLC 203 232-4534
  78 Birchwood Rd Seymour (06483) *(G-7334)*
16 Case LLC 860 995-0555
  16 Case St Farmington (06032) *(G-2873)*
170 Mountainwood Road LLC 203 252-4284
  134 Forest St Stamford (06901) *(G-8048)*
1st Vertical LLC 860 458-0120
  65 Balazs Rd Willington (06279) *(G-10243)*
2 Girl A Trunk 203 762-0360
  35 Dudley Rd Wilton (06897) *(G-10262)*
20/20 Software Inc 203 316-5500
  2001 W Main St Ste 270 Stamford (06902) *(G-8049)*
200 Mill Plain Road LLC 203 254-0113
  1411 Cross Hwy Fairfield (06824) *(G-2740)*
210 Innovation LLC 860 444-1986
  4 Donna St Waterford (06385) *(G-9638)*
210 Innovations 860 445-0210
  210 Leonard Dr Groton (06340) *(G-3269)*
21st Century Fox America Inc 203 563-6600
  20 Westport Rd Wilton (06897) *(G-10263)*
22 Candles 203 577-5540
  188 Chestnut Hill Rd Wilton (06897) *(G-10264)*
227 Greenwood LLC 203 798-9716
  52 Sunset Hill Rd Bethel (06801) *(G-254)*
2394 Berlin Turnpike Assoc LLC 860 347-1624
  955 Washington St Middletown (06457) *(G-4311)*
24 Hours Design & Print 347 350-4484
  195 Garden Dr Bridgeport (06606) *(G-678)*
26 Beechwood Avenue LLC 203 713-6425
  34 Highwood Rd Milford (06460) *(G-4435)*
261 Pascone Place LLC 860 666-7845
  261 Pascone Pl Newington (06111) *(G-5614)*
27 West Main Street LLC 860 799-6494
  27 Main St New Milford (06776) *(G-5499)*
283 Industries Inc 203 276-8956
  3 Mallory Hill Rd Ridgefield (06877) *(G-7113)*
29 Wychwood Road LLC 860 434-8078
  13 Whippoorwill Rd Old Lyme (06371) *(G-6486)*
2seal LLC 860 227-6854
  6 Peppermint Rdg Old Lyme (06371) *(G-6487)*
3 Brothers EMB & Screen Prtg, Ansonia *Also called Seems Inc (G-50)*
3 Ethos LLC 860 415-9191
  169 Long Wharf Rd Mystic (06355) *(G-4794)*
3 Story Software LLC 203 530-3224
  63 Bridge St New Milford (06776) *(G-5500)*
32 Degrees LLC 978 602-2007
  216 South St West Hartford (06110) *(G-9768)*
3333 LLC 860 643-1384
  42 Hilliard St Manchester (06042) *(G-3971)*
360alumni Inc 203 253-5860
  1 Norfield Rd Weston (06883) *(G-10016)*
3d Solutions LLC 860 454-7302
  60 Industrial Park Rd W Tolland (06084) *(G-8845)*
3M Company 203 237-5541
  400 Research Pkwy Meriden (06450) *(G-4134)*
3M Purification Inc 860 684-8628
  32 River Rd Stafford Springs (06076) *(G-8015)*
3M Purification Inc (HQ) 203 237-5541
  400 Research Pkwy Meriden (06450) *(G-4135)*
3rd Half Productions 860 828-6929
  141 Carriage Dr Kensington (06037) *(G-3802)*

3t Lighting Inc 203 775-1805
  20 Pocono Rd Brookfield (06804) *(G-1154)*
4 D Technology Corporation 860 365-0420
  91 Daniel St East Hampton (06424) *(G-2251)*
420 Sign Design Inc 203 852-1255
  25 Commerce St Norwalk (06850) *(G-6056)*
450 Woodworking LLC 860 350-0525
  11 Heacock Ln New Milford (06776) *(G-5501)*
49 High St LLC 860 423-9496
  49 High St Willimantic (06226) *(G-10219)*
5 Star Printing 203 975-1000
  9 Old North Stamford Rd 35a Stamford (06905) *(G-8050)*
542 Rustic Woodworks 860 387-8680
  108 Sunset Ridge Rd Norfolk (06058) *(G-5822)*
588 Smainst LLC 860 482-1625
  588 S Main St Rear Torrington (06790) *(G-8884)*
5n Plus Corp 608 846-1357
  120 Corporate Dr Trumbull (06611) *(G-8994)*
5n Plus Wisconsin Inc 203 384-0331
  120 Corporate Dr Trumbull (06611) *(G-8995)*
5w LLC 860 751-9209
  222 Main St Ste 251 Farmington (06032) *(G-2874)*
6 Brookwood Drive LLC 860 945-3456
  329 Lovley Dr Watertown (06795) *(G-9678)*
687 State Street Assoc LLC 203 915-8469
  32 Windsor Rd E North Haven (06473) *(G-5893)*
71 Pickett District Road LLC 860 350-5964
  71 Pickett District Rd New Milford (06776) *(G-5502)*
77 Mattatuck Heights LLC 203 597-9338
  77 Mattatuck Heights Rd Waterbury (06705) *(G-9420)*
8 Times LLC 203 227-7575
  12 Juniper Rd Westport (06880) *(G-10048)*
83 Erna Avenue LLC 203 243-7426
  21 Blue Ridge Dr Trumbull (06611) *(G-8996)*
90 Arch St LLC 860 881-2063
  41 Crossroads Plz Ste 220 Hartford (06117) *(G-3541)*
90 River Street LLC 203 772-4700
  90 River St New Haven (06513) *(G-5216)*
911 Motorsports Inc 203 755-8405
  520 Watertown Ave Waterbury (06708) *(G-9421)*
A & A Manufacturing Co Inc 262 786-1500
  457 State St North Haven (06473) *(G-5894)*
A & A Products and Services 860 683-0879
  610 Hayden Station Rd Windsor (06095) *(G-10350)*
A & A Welding LLC 860 933-1284
  256 Moosup Pond Rd Moosup (06354) *(G-4777)*
A & B Ice Co, Bridgeport *Also called Leonard F Brooks (G-824)*
A & C Connection Inspection 203 287-8504
  30 Overlook Dr Hamden (06514) *(G-3408)*
A & D Components Inc 860 582-9541
  33 Stafford Ave Ste 2 Bristol (06010) *(G-949)*
A & D Dental Innovations LLC 888 374-5134
  40 Fawnbrook Ln Simsbury (06070) *(G-7608)*
A & E Engraving Service 860 582-6503
  37 Main St Bristol (06010) *(G-950)*
A & H Tool Works 860 302-9284
  101 Rocky Rd E Harwinton (06791) *(G-3717)*
A & I Concentrate LLC 203 447-1938
  2 Corporate Dr Ste 136 Shelton (06484) *(G-7385)*
A & K Railroad Materials Inc 203 495-8790
  200 Benton St Hamden (06517) *(G-3409)*
A & L Welding Service 860 664-1700
  14 Old Mill Rd Trlr 45 Clinton (06413) *(G-1488)*
A & M Auto Machine Inc 203 237-3502
  711 E Main St Meriden (06450) *(G-4136)*
A & P Coat Apron & Lin Sup Inc 914 840-3200
  420 Ledyard St Hartford (06114) *(G-3542)*
A & S Pharmaceutical Corp 203 368-2538
  480 Barnum Ave Ste 3 Bridgeport (06608) *(G-679)*
A -Line Custom Counter Top 860 747-1917
  7 Johnson Ave Plainville (06062) *(G-6758)*

A 2 Z Screen Printing LLC (PA) 860 526-9684
6 Pine Lake Rd Ivoryton (06442) **(G-3782)**
A 2 Z Screen Printing LLC 860 526-9684
500 Main St Ste 4 Deep River (06417) **(G-2081)**
A A Gentle House Washing 860 243-8800
11 Harvest Ln Bloomfield (06002) **(G-378)**
A A I, Canton *Also called Alexis Aerospace Inds LLC* **(G-1303)**
A A S, Newington *Also called Advanced Adhesive Systems Inc* **(G-5621)**
A Aiudi & Sons LLC (PA) 860 747-5534
190 Camp St Plainville (06062) **(G-6759)**
A Al Harding 203 238-1993
165 Eaton Ave Meriden (06451) **(G-4137)**
A American Stone & Countertop, Wallingford *Also called American Stonecrafters Inc* **(G-9202)**
A B & F Sheet Metal 203 272-9340
327 Sandbank Rd Cheshire (06410) **(G-1344)**
A B A Tool & Die Div, Manchester *Also called Aba-PGT Inc* **(G-3974)**
A B B Power Transmission, Norwalk *Also called Asea Brown Boveri Inc* **(G-6076)**
A B C Printing & Mailing, East Haven *Also called A B C Printing Inc* **(G-2406)**
A B C Printing Inc 203 468-1245
875 Foxon Rd East Haven (06513) **(G-2406)**
A Barney's Sign, Stratford *Also called Barneys Sign Service Inc* **(G-8579)**
A C A, Branford *Also called Associated Chemicals & Abr Inc* **(G-548)**
A C Manufacturing 860 314-8225
87 Mine Rd Bristol (06010) **(G-951)**
A C T Manufacturing LLC 860 289-8837
55 Glendale Rd South Windsor (06074) **(G-7696)**
A Capela Do Santo Antonio Inc 860 447-3329
35 Henry St New London (06320) **(G-5455)**
A Change of Scenery 860 872-4435
9 Benjamin Rd Ellington (06029) **(G-2569)**
A D Grinding 860 747-6630
54 Lewis St Plainville (06062) **(G-6760)**
A D Perkins Company 203 777-3456
43 Elm St New Haven (06510) **(G-5217)**
A Dancing Thread 860 669-9094
23 Riverside Dr Apt A13 Clinton (06413) **(G-1489)**
A Douglas Thibodeau LLC 860 295-9189
21 Portland Rd Marlborough (06447) **(G-4118)**
A Emergency Rooter Service 860 582-3612
116 Kilmartin Ave Bristol (06010) **(G-952)**
A F M Engineering Corp 860 774-7518
24 Woodward Rd Brooklyn (06234) **(G-1244)**
A Family Farm 203 438-5497
145 Mountain Rd Redding (06896) **(G-7087)**
A Flood of Paper 203 529-3030
94 Old Ridgefield Rd Wilton (06897) **(G-10265)**
A G C Incorporated (PA) 203 235-3361
106 Evansville Ave Meriden (06451) **(G-4138)**
A G I Automation, Trumbull *Also called American Grippers Inc* **(G-8997)**
A G M Tool 860 793-6808
15 Hultenius St Plainville (06062) **(G-6761)**
A G Russell Company Inc 860 247-9093
60 George St Hartford (06114) **(G-3543)**
A Gerber Corp 203 918-1913
110 Idlewood Dr Stamford (06905) **(G-8051)**
A Grey Soiree LLC 203 530-0277
65 Parish Farm Rd Branford (06405) **(G-534)**
A Guideposts Church Corp (PA) 203 749-0203
39 Old Ridgebury Rd # 27 Danbury (06810) **(G-1726)**
A Hardiman Machine Co Inc 860 623-8133
94 Newberry Rd East Windsor (06088) **(G-2478)**
A Helium Plus Balloons LLC 860 833-1761
94 Albert Ave Wethersfield (06109) **(G-10179)**
A J R Inc 203 384-0400
67 Poland St Bridgeport (06605) **(G-680)**
A J Tool Company Inc 860 666-2883
16 Progress Cir Bldg 2 Newington (06111) **(G-5615)**
A Kick In Crochet 413 210-7890
2 Guild St Enfield (06082) **(G-2610)**
A L C Inovators Inc 203 877-8526
230 Pepes Farm Rd Ste C Milford (06460) **(G-4436)**
A Line Design Inc 203 294-0080
18 Martin Trl Wallingford (06492) **(G-9193)**
A Little Soy Candle Co LLC 860 877-6001
30 Pauline Ave West Haven (06516) **(G-9878)**
A M C I, Greenwich *Also called American Metals Coal Intl Inc* **(G-3120)**
A M I, Mystic *Also called Aqua Massage International Inc* **(G-4799)**
A Matter of Style LLC 203 272-1337
680 S Main St Ste 201 Cheshire (06410) **(G-1345)**
A Matter Style Kitchens Baths, Cheshire *Also called A Matter of Style LLC* **(G-1345)**
A P S, Bridgeport *Also called Alternative Prosthetic Svcs* **(G-688)**
A Papish Incorporated (PA) 203 744-0323
21 Taylor St Danbury (06810) **(G-1727)**
A Piece of Pzzle Bhvral Intrve 860 250-8054
1100 New Britain Ave # 105 West Hartford (06110) **(G-9769)**
A R C O, Bridgeport *Also called Arcade Technology LLC* **(G-699)**
A R Tool, Berlin *Also called Andy Rakowicz* **(G-159)**
A S Fine Foods 203 322-3899
856 High Ridge Rd Stamford (06905) **(G-8052)**
A S J Specialties LLC 203 284-8650
2 Toms Dr Wallingford (06492) **(G-9194)**
A T S, Ellington *Also called Accu-Time Systems Inc* **(G-2570)**
A Telling Time Limited CB 877 486-7865
244 Upton Rd Ste 4 Colchester (06415) **(G-1538)**
A To A Studio Solutions Ltd 203 388-9050
47 Euclid Ave Stamford (06902) **(G-8053)**
A To Z Signs 203 840-0644
607 Main Ave Ste 3p Norwalk (06851) **(G-6057)**
A V I International Inc 860 482-8345
3240 Winsted Rd Torrington (06790) **(G-8885)**
A Westport Wordsmith 203 354-7309
101 Winfield St Norwalk (06855) **(G-6058)**
A Wild Quilter 203 744-3405
6 Taylor Ave Bethel (06801) **(G-255)**
A X M S Inc 203 263-5046
27 Woodside Cir Woodbury (06798) **(G-10622)**
A Z Copy Center, Southington *Also called AZ Copy Center Inc* **(G-7893)**
A Z Welding 860 872-1301
38 Goose Ln Tolland (06084) **(G-8846)**
A&A Home Solutions 203 993-1735
440 Nichols Ave Shelton (06484) **(G-7386)**
A&D Enterprises 860 779-9025
16 Basley Rd Danielson (06239) **(G-1985)**
A&D Schneider LLC 203 870-9474
111 Morningside Ter Stratford (06614) **(G-8563)**
A&R Plating Services LLC 860 274-9562
147 Riverside St Oakville (06779) **(G-6448)**
A&S Innersprings Usa LLC 860 298-0401
4 Market Cir Windsor (06095) **(G-10351)**
A&V Typographics 860 276-9060
36 Buckland St Unit 27 Plantsville (06479) **(G-6880)**
A+ Plus Appliance 860 878-9624
352 Scoville Hill Rd Harwinton (06791) **(G-3718)**
A-1 Asphalt Paving 860 436-6085
925 New Britain Ave Rocky Hill (06067) **(G-7217)**
A-1 Chrome and Polishing Corp 860 666-4593
125 Stamm Rd Newington (06111) **(G-5616)**
A-1 Garage Door Co 203 866-6620
8 Surf Rd Westport (06880) **(G-10049)**
A-1 Garage Door Specialties, Westport *Also called A-1 Garage Door Co* **(G-10049)**
A-1 Machining Co 860 223-6420
235 John Downey Dr New Britain (06051) **(G-4931)**
A-1 Seamless Gutters 860 432-9118
406 Oakland St Manchester (06042) **(G-3972)**
A-1 Stairs By Wesconn Stairs, Danbury *Also called Wesconn Stairs Inc* **(G-1978)**
A-S Catering, Stamford *Also called A S Fine Foods* **(G-8052)**
A1 Commercial Printing Co LLC 203 975-1000
9 Old North Stamford Rd 35a Stamford (06905) **(G-8054)**
A2z Embroidery 860 747-9849
433 East St Plainville (06062) **(G-6762)**
AA & B Co 203 933-9110
284 2nd Ave West Haven (06516) **(G-9879)**
AA Industries LLC 860 291-8929
223 Nutmeg Rd S South Windsor (06074) **(G-7697)**
AAA Distributors 860 346-0230
46 Sisk St Middletown (06457) **(G-4312)**
AAA Fire and Safety Inc (PA) 860 267-1965
67 Old Windsor Rd Bloomfield (06002) **(G-379)**
AAM Welding + Fabrication LLC 203 479-4339
67 Phillips Ter West Haven (06516) **(G-9880)**
Aapi 203 268-2450
593 M St Monroe (06468) **(G-4690)**
AAR Corp 619 545-6129
754 Rainbow Rd Windsor (06095) **(G-10352)**
AAR Results LLC 203 627-2193
80 S Montowese St Branford (06405) **(G-535)**
Aarons Enterprises 203 762-9764
24 Old Hwy Wilton (06897) **(G-10266)**
AB Custom Cabinetry LLC 203 367-5047
10 Vermont Ave Fairfield (06824) **(G-2741)**
AB Custom Woodwork LLC 203 334-7882
238 Roseville Ter Fairfield (06824) **(G-2742)**
AB Electronics Inc 203 740-2793
61 Commerce Dr Brookfield (06804) **(G-1155)**
AB&f Sheet Metal Products, Cheshire *Also called A B & F Sheet Metal* **(G-1344)**
Aba-PGT Employee Medical Trust 860 649-4591
10 Gear Dr Manchester (06042) **(G-3973)**
Aba-PGT Inc (PA) 860 649-4591
10 Gear Dr Manchester (06042) **(G-3974)**
Aba-PGT Inc 860 872-2058
140 Bolton Rd Vernon Rockville (06066) **(G-9158)**
Abair Assemblies, Waterbury *Also called Abair Manufacturing Company* **(G-9422)**
Abair Manufacturing Company 203 757-0112
250 Mill St Ste 2 Waterbury (06706) **(G-9422)**
ABB Enterprise Software Inc 860 747-7111
41 Woodford Ave Plainville (06062) **(G-6763)**
ABB Enterprise Software Inc 203 790-8588
24 Commerce Dr Danbury (06810) **(G-1728)**
ABB Enterprise Software Inc 203 798-6210
152 Deer Hill Ave Ste 304 Danbury (06810) **(G-1729)**

ABB Enterprise Software Inc 860 285-0183
5 Waterside Xing Fl 3-2 Windsor (06095) *(G-10353)*
ABB Enterprise Software Inc 203 329-8771
900 Long Ridge Rd Stamford (06902) *(G-8055)*
ABB Finance (usa) Inc 919 856-2360
501 Merritt 7 Ste 2 Norwalk (06851) *(G-6059)*
Abbey Aesthetics LLC 860 242-0497
135 Cold Spring Rd Avon (06001) *(G-71)*
Abbey Printing 860 745-0122
920 Enfield St Ste B Enfield (06082) *(G-2611)*
Abbott Associates Inc 203 878-2370
261a Pepes Farm Rd Milford (06460) *(G-4437)*
Abbott Ball Company 860 236-5901
19 Railroad Pl West Hartford (06110) *(G-9770)*
Abbott Manufacturing, West Hartford *Also called Lewtan Industries Corporation (G-9830)*
Abbott Printing Company Inc 203 562-5562
912 Dixwell Ave Hamden (06514) *(G-3410)*
Abbydabby 860 586-8832
2523 Albany Ave West Hartford (06117) *(G-9771)*
ABC Sign Corporation 203 513-8110
30 Controls Dr Ste 1 Shelton (06484) *(G-7387)*
Abcorp, Stamford *Also called American Banknote Corporation (G-8074)*
Abek LLC 860 314-3905
492 Birch St Bristol (06010) *(G-953)*
Aberdeen Mfg 860 774-9679
90 Wauregan Rd Danielson (06239) *(G-1986)*
Abet Technologies Inc 203 540-9990
168 Old Gate Ln Milford (06460) *(G-4438)*
Ability Prsthtics Orthtics LLC 860 571-8979
52 National Dr Ste 2 Glastonbury (06033) *(G-3002)*
Able Coil and Electronics Co 860 646-5686
25 Howard Rd Bolton (06043) *(G-504)*
Able Manufacturing Co LLC 860 282-6108
381 Governors Hwy Ste A South Windsor (06074) *(G-7698)*
Able Scale & Equipment Corp 860 646-6929
10 Hilliard St Manchester (06042) *(G-3975)*
Able To Cane, New Haven *Also called Maryann D Langdon (G-5326)*
Abrantes Bakery & Pastry Shop 860 232-1464
1851 Park St Hartford (06106) *(G-3544)*
Absnavigator.com, Deep River *Also called Townsend John (G-2104)*
Absolute Countertops LLC 203 395-8259
38 Commerce St Derby (06418) *(G-2107)*
Absolute Metrology Services, East Hampton *Also called Greywall Inc (G-2262)*
Absolute Precision Co 203 767-9066
234 Bates Rock Rd Southbury (06488) *(G-7840)*
Abstract Tool Inc 860 526-4635
500 Main St Ste 15 Deep River (06417) *(G-2082)*
AC Skips Welding Inc 203 838-2089
50 Commerce St Norwalk (06850) *(G-6060)*
AC Tek Instruments 203 431-0825
34 Loren Ln Ridgefield (06877) *(G-7114)*
Ac/DC Industrial Electric LLC 860 886-2232
44 Yantic Flats Rd Ste 2 Yantic (06389) *(G-10695)*
Acad24 / A-Nusign, Enfield *Also called Melvin Mayo (G-2658)*
Academy Marble & Granite LLC (PA) 203 791-2956
101 Wooster St Ste C Bethel (06801) *(G-256)*
Academy Printing Service 860 828-5549
900 Farmington Ave Ste 2 Kensington (06037) *(G-3803)*
Accel Intl Holdings Inc 203 237-2700
508 N Colony St Meriden (06450) *(G-4139)*
Acceleron Inc 860 651-9333
21 Lordship Rd Ste 1 East Granby (06026) *(G-2186)*
Accent Magazine 203 853-6015
535 Connecticut Ave # 300 Norwalk (06854) *(G-6061)*
Accent Screenprinting 203 284-8601
186 Center St Wallingford (06492) *(G-9195)*
Accent Signs LLC 203 975-8688
130 Lenox Ave Ste 21 Stamford (06906) *(G-8056)*
Access Intelligence 203 854-6730
761 Main Ave Ste 2 Norwalk (06851) *(G-6062)*
Accession Media 203 702-4951
51 Prange Rd Brookfield (06804) *(G-1156)*
Accessware 860 235-2982
93 High Meadow Ln Mystic (06355) *(G-4795)*
Accolade Furniture LLC 203 265-0524
340 Quinnipiac St Wallingford (06492) *(G-9196)*
Accu-Mill Technologies LLC 860 747-3921
161 Woodford Ave Ste 39 Plainville (06062) *(G-6764)*
Accu-Rite Tool & Mfg Co 860 688-4844
23 Industrial Park Rd W B Tolland (06084) *(G-8847)*
Accu-Time Systems Inc (HQ) 860 870-5000
420 Somers Rd Ellington (06029) *(G-2570)*
Accubend LLC 860 378-0303
1657 Mrden Wtrbury Tpke Plantsville (06479) *(G-6881)*
Accumold Technologies Inc 203 384-9256
52 Carroll Ave Bridgeport (06607) *(G-681)*
Accupaulo Holding Corporation (PA) 860 666-5621
280 Hartford Ave Newington (06111) *(G-5617)*
Accurate Automation LLC 203 988-9426
29 Pequot Rd Wallingford (06492) *(G-9197)*
Accurate Brazing Corporation 860 432-1840
4 Progress Dr Manchester (06042) *(G-3976)*
Accurate Burring Company 860 747-8640
161 Woodford Ave Ste 19 Plainville (06062) *(G-6765)*
Accurate Centerless Grinding 860 747-9794
43 Deer Park Rd Bristol (06010) *(G-954)*
Accurate Mold Company Inc 860 301-1988
64 Nooks Hill Rd Cromwell (06416) *(G-1684)*
Accurate Threaded Products, Newington *Also called Accupaulo Holding Corporation (G-5617)*
Accurate Threaded Products Co 860 666-5621
280 Hartford Ave Newington (06111) *(G-5618)*
Accurate Tool & Die Inc 203 967-1200
16 Leon Pl Stamford (06902) *(G-8057)*
Accurate Welding, Pleasant Valley *Also called Joseph Rembock (G-6923)*
Accurate Welding Services LLC 860 623-9500
7 Industrial Rd Windsor Locks (06096) *(G-10467)*
Accuratus Optics Tech LLC 213 344-9397
130 Rockview Dr Cheshire (06410) *(G-1346)*
Accustandard Inc 203 786-5290
125 Market St New Haven (06513) *(G-5218)*
Accutrol LLC 203 445-9991
21 Commerce Dr Danbury (06810) *(G-1730)*
Accutron Inc 860 683-8300
149 Addison Rd Windsor (06095) *(G-10354)*
Accuturn Mfg Co LLC 860 289-6355
100 Commerce Way South Windsor (06074) *(G-7699)*
Accuwind Inc 203 287-9697
1068 Sherman Ave Hamden (06514) *(G-3411)*
Ace Beauty Supply Inc 203 488-2416
937 W Main St Branford (06405) *(G-536)*
Ace Beauty Systems New Britain 860 224-2943
984 W Main St New Britain (06053) *(G-4932)*
Ace Cabinet Company 860 225-6111
321 Ellis St Ste 18 New Britain (06051) *(G-4933)*
Ace Energy LLC 860 623-3308
152 Broad Brook Rd Broad Brook (06016) *(G-1143)*
Ace Finishing Co LLC 860 582-4600
225 Terryville Rd Bristol (06010) *(G-955)*
Ace Industrial LLC 203 272-7675
108 Victoria Dr Cheshire (06410) *(G-1347)*
Ace Marine Service Inc 860 489-5960
511 Migeon Ave Torrington (06790) *(G-8886)*
Ace Sailmakers 860 739-5999
3 Colton Rd East Lyme (06333) *(G-2462)*
Ace Servicing Co Inc 203 795-1400
340 Edward Ct Orange (06477) *(G-6578)*
Ace Technical Plastics Inc 860 278-2444
122 Park Ave J Hartford (06108) *(G-3545)*
Ace Tire & Auto Center Inc 203 438-4042
861 Ethan Allen Hwy Ridgefield (06877) *(G-7115)*
Ace Wlding Fbrction Rstoration 203 758-3550
47 Sherwood Dr Prospect (06712) *(G-6992)*
Achillion Pharmaceuticals Inc 203 624-7000
300 George St Ste 801 New Haven (06511) *(G-5219)*
Aci Industries Converting Ltd 740 368-4166
1266 E Main St Ste 700r Stamford (06902) *(G-8058)*
Acier Fab LLC 860 282-1211
105 Edwin Rd South Windsor (06074) *(G-7700)*
Ack Industries LLC 860 677-0056
7 Belgravia Ter Farmington (06032) *(G-2875)*
Ack Precision Machine Co 860 664-0789
6 Old Post Rd Clinton (06413) *(G-1490)*
Acm Warehouse & Distribution 203 239-9557
77 Sackett Point Rd North Haven (06473) *(G-5895)*
Acme Monaco Corporation (PA) 860 224-1349
75 Winchell Rd New Britain (06052) *(G-4934)*
Acme Press Inc 203 334-8221
95 Erna Ave Milford (06461) *(G-4439)*
Acme Press Printers LLC 203 237-2702
1147 Hanover Ave Meriden (06451) *(G-4140)*
Acme Railing Company, Fairfield *Also called Richard Sadowski (G-2836)*
Acme Sign Co (PA) 203 324-2263
12 Research Dr Stamford (06906) *(G-8059)*
Acme Typesetting Service Co 860 953-1470
47 Cody St West Hartford (06110) *(G-9772)*
Acme United Corporation (PA) 203 254-6060
55 Walls Dr Ste 201 Fairfield (06824) *(G-2743)*
Acme Wire Products Co Inc 860 572-0511
1 Broadway Ave Mystic (06355) *(G-4796)*
Acmt Inc 860 645-0592
369 Progress Dr Manchester (06042) *(G-3977)*
Acoustic Music 203 458-2525
1238 Boston Post Rd Guilford (06437) *(G-3321)*
Acousticmusic.org, Guilford *Also called Acoustic Music (G-3321)*
Acquisitions Controlled Svcs 203 327-6364
55 Woodland Pl Apt 4 Stamford (06902) *(G-8060)*
ACR Technical Services 860 225-0572
27 Anise St New Britain (06053) *(G-4935)*
Acson Tool Company 203 334-8050
62 Carroll Ave Bridgeport (06607) *(G-682)*
Act Manufacturing, South Windsor *Also called A C T Manufacturing LLC (G-7696)*
Act Robots Inc 860 314-1557
95 Wooster Ct Bristol (06010) *(G-956)*

ALPHABETIC

(PA)=Parent Co (HQ)=Headquarters (DH)=Div Headquarters
2020 Harris Connecticut Manufacturers Directory
475

Actimus Inc ... 617 438-9968
189 Coles Rd Cromwell (06416) ***(G-1685)***
Action Industries ... 860 644-3020
164 E Center St Ste 8 Manchester (06040) ***(G-3978)***
Action Letter Inc (PA) ... 203 323-2466
11 Elm Ct Stamford (06902) ***(G-8061)***
Action Media Inc ... 203 466-5535
12 Baer Cir East Haven (06512) ***(G-2407)***
Action Packaging Systems Inc (PA) ... 860 222-9510
372 Somers Rd Ellington (06029) ***(G-2571)***
Action Printing ... 203 366-4413
415 Howe Ave Ste 328 Shelton (06484) ***(G-7388)***
Action Scale Service ... 203 577-6420
760 Whittemore Rd Middlebury (06762) ***(G-4271)***
Action Signs ... 860 496-1232
610 Migeon Ave Torrington (06790) ***(G-8887)***
Action Steel LLC ... 860 216-6595
55 Airport Rd Ste 104 Hartford (06114) ***(G-3546)***
Active Interest Media Inc ... 860 767-3200
10 Bokum Rd Essex (06426) ***(G-2710)***
Active Internet Tech LLC ... 800 592-2469
655 Winding Brook Dr # 100 Glastonbury (06033) ***(G-3003)***
Actualmeds Corporation ... 888 838-9053
222 Pitkin St Ste 107 East Hartford (06108) ***(G-2286)***
Actuaries Division, Stamford *Also called Computer Prgrm & Systems Inc* ***(G-8155)***
Acucut Inc ... 860 793-7012
200 Town Line Rd Southington (06489) ***(G-7887)***
Acufab ... 203 263-3490
137 Quassuk Rd Woodbury (06798) ***(G-10623)***
Acuren Inspection Inc (HQ) ... 203 702-8740
30 Main St Ste 402 Danbury (06810) ***(G-1731)***
Acuren Inspection Inc ... 203 869-6734
43 Arch St Greenwich (06830) ***(G-3116)***
Ad Comm Ink ... 860 824-7565
325 Ashley Falls Rd Canaan (06018) ***(G-1280)***
Ad Embroidery LLC ... 860 653-9553
186 Hartford Ave East Granby (06026) ***(G-2187)***
Ad Embroidery LLC ... 860 651-4410
350 W Mountain Rd West Simsbury (06092) ***(G-9971)***
Ad Label Inc ... 860 779-0513
59 N Society Rd Brooklyn (06234) ***(G-1245)***
Adam Bisson ... 203 861-8271
15 Janet Cir Unit A Bridgeport (06606) ***(G-683)***
Adam Fuller Woodworking ... 860 455-1296
143 S Brook Rd North Windham (06235) ***(G-6033)***
Adam Z Golas (PA) ... 860 224-7178
99 John Downey Dr New Britain (06051) ***(G-4936)***
Adamczyk Enterprises Inc ... 860 745-9830
3 Palomba Dr Enfield (06082) ***(G-2612)***
Adamsahern Sign Solutions Inc ... 860 523-8835
30 Arbor St Unit 208 Hartford (06106) ***(G-3547)***
Adaptive Optics Associates Inc ... 860 282-4401
121 Prestige Park Cir East Hartford (06108) ***(G-2287)***
Addamo Manufacturing Inc ... 860 667-2601
360 Stamm Rd Newington (06111) ***(G-5619)***
Addison Industries LLC ... 203 809-0254
23 Sarah Ct West Haven (06516) ***(G-9881)***
Additive Experts LLC ... 860 351-3324
1 Liberty Sq New Britain (06051) ***(G-4937)***
Additive Manufacturing Neng ... 860 316-5946
1270 Newfield St Middletown (06457) ***(G-4313)***
Addivant USA Holdings Corp., Danbury *Also called Si Group USA Hldings Usha Corp* ***(G-1947)***
Addivant Usa, LLC, Danbury *Also called Si Group USA (usaa) LLC* ***(G-1946)***
Address For Success, Prospect *Also called Montambault Riva* ***(G-7011)***
Adelman Sand & Gravel Inc ... 860 889-3394
34 Bozrah St Bozrah (06334) ***(G-522)***
Ademco Inc ... 860 257-3266
712 Brook St Rocky Hill (06067) ***(G-7218)***
Ademco Inc ... 203 877-2702
121 Woodmont Rd Milford (06460) ***(G-4440)***
Adhesives Prepregs, Plainfield *Also called Apcm Manufacturing LLC* ***(G-6738)***
ADI Global Distribution, Rocky Hill *Also called Ademco Inc* ***(G-7218)***
ADI Global Distribution, Milford *Also called Ademco Inc* ***(G-4440)***
Adirondack Lkfront Retreat LLC ... 203 267-5882
77 Main St N Southbury (06488) ***(G-7841)***
Adirondack Wood Products LLC ... 203 322-4518
174 Larkspur Rd Stamford (06903) ***(G-8062)***
Adk Pressure Equipment Corp (HQ) ... 860 585-0050
745 Clark Ave Bristol (06010) ***(G-957)***
Adkins Printing Company ... 800 228-9745
40 South St Ste 2 New Britain (06051) ***(G-4938)***
ADM, New Canaan *Also called Archer-Daniels-Midland Company* ***(G-5088)***
Admill Machine Co ... 860 667-3676
115 Pane Rd Newington (06111) ***(G-5620)***
Administrative Publications In ... 860 747-6768
6 Highland Dr Plainville (06062) ***(G-6766)***
Adolf Gordon Corporation ... 860 872-9037
142 Echo Dr Vernon (06066) ***(G-9129)***
Ador Inc ... 860 583-2367
210 Redstone Hill Rd # 5 Bristol (06010) ***(G-958)***
ADP Rivet, Hartford *Also called Manchester Tl & Design ADP LLC* ***(G-3633)***

Advance Affrdale Hring Sltions, Avon *Also called Advanced Hearing Solutions LLC* ***(G-72)***
Advance Development & Mfg ... 203 453-4325
325 Soundview Rd Guilford (06437) ***(G-3322)***
Advance Heat Treating Co ... 203 380-8898
147 West Ave Bridgeport (06604) ***(G-684)***
Advance Images LLC ... 860 749-1166
16 Grand View Dr Enfield (06082) ***(G-2613)***
Advance Mold & Mfg Inc ... 860 432-5887
71 Utopia Rd Manchester (06042) ***(G-3979)***
Advance Mold Mfg Inc ... 860 783-5024
15 Teaberry Ridge Rd Ellington (06029) ***(G-2572)***
Advance Software LLC ... 860 429-3721
65 Jared Sparks Rd Willington (06279) ***(G-10244)***
Advanced Adhesive Systems Inc ... 860 953-4100
681 N Mountain Rd Newington (06111) ***(G-5621)***
Advanced Business Group ... 203 881-9660
14 Douglas Rd Oxford (06478) ***(G-6637)***
Advanced Control Systems Div, East Haven *Also called Associated X-Ray Corp* ***(G-2412)***
Advanced Decisions Inc ... 203 402-0603
350 Woodland Ln Orange (06477) ***(G-6579)***
Advanced Def Slutions Tech LLC ... 860 243-1122
23 Britton Dr Bloomfield (06002) ***(G-380)***
Advanced Drainage Systems Inc ... 860 529-8188
520 Cromwell Ave Rocky Hill (06067) ***(G-7219)***
Advanced Fuel Co LLC ... 860 642-4817
126 Pleasure Hill Rd North Franklin (06254) ***(G-5869)***
Advanced Glass Design LLC ... 860 426-0401
30 Deer Run Plantsville (06479) ***(G-6882)***
Advanced Golf Nutrition LLC ... 203 554-9120
536 Hemlock Rd Fairfield (06824) ***(G-2744)***
Advanced Graphics Inc ... 203 378-0471
55 Old South Ave Stratford (06615) ***(G-8564)***
Advanced Hearing Solutions LLC ... 860 674-8558
47 W Main St Avon (06001) ***(G-72)***
Advanced HM Audio & Video LLC ... 860 621-0631
962 S Main St Apt 7 Plantsville (06479) ***(G-6883)***
Advanced Linen Group ... 203 877-3896
215 Pepes Farm Rd Milford (06460) ***(G-4441)***
Advanced Machine Services LLC (PA) ... 203 888-6600
2056 Thomaston Ave Waterbury (06704) ***(G-9423)***
Advanced Machine Services LLC ... 203 888-6600
55 Old State Rd Oxford (06478) ***(G-6638)***
Advanced Machine Technology ... 860 872-2664
5 Industrial Dr Ellington (06029) ***(G-2573)***
Advanced Micro Controls Inc ... 860 585-1254
20 Gear Dr Terryville (06786) ***(G-8746)***
Advanced Photonics Intl Inc ... 203 259-0437
96 Lamplighter Ln Fairfield (06825) ***(G-2745)***
Advanced Powder Coating Techno ... 860 612-0631
10 Harvard St New Britain (06051) ***(G-4939)***
Advanced Prcsion Castings Corp ... 203 736-9452
120 Pullman Dr Milford (06461) ***(G-4442)***
Advanced Precast Concrete, Old Lyme *Also called David Shuck* ***(G-6503)***
Advanced Product Solutions LLC ... 203 745-4225
555 Sherman Ave Unit C16 Hamden (06514) ***(G-3412)***
Advanced Products Operation, North Haven *Also called Parker-Hannifin Corporation* ***(G-5974)***
Advanced Prototype Development ... 203 267-1262
7 Stiles Rd Southbury (06488) ***(G-7842)***
Advanced Pwr Systems Intl Inc ... 860 921-0009
18 Hemlock Dr New Hartford (06057) ***(G-5184)***
Advanced Reasoning ... 860 437-0508
82 Boston Post Rd Ste 3 Waterford (06385) ***(G-9639)***
Advanced Receiver Research ... 860 485-0310
535 Burlington Rd Harwinton (06791) ***(G-3719)***
Advanced Screen Printing LLC ... 860 845-8337
75 Seneca Rd Bristol (06010) ***(G-959)***
Advanced Semiconductor ... 860 349-1121
30 Ozick Dr Durham (06422) ***(G-2135)***
Advanced Sheetmetal Assoc LLC ... 860 349-1644
52 Indstrial Pk Access Rd Middlefield (06455) ***(G-4298)***
Advanced Sonic Proc Systems, Oxford *Also called Advanced Sonics LLC* ***(G-6639)***
Advanced Sonics LLC ... 203 266-4440
324 Christian St Oxford (06478) ***(G-6639)***
Advanced Specialist LLC ... 860 945-9125
162 Commercial St Watertown (06795) ***(G-9679)***
Advanced Technology Mtls Inc (HQ) ... 203 794-1100
7 Commerce Dr Danbury (06810) ***(G-1732)***
Advanced Torque Products LLC ... 860 828-1523
56 Budney Rd Newington (06111) ***(G-5622)***
Advanced Vacuum Technology Inc ... 860 653-4176
7 Herman Dr Ste E Simsbury (06070) ***(G-7609)***
Advanced Welding & Repair Inc ... 860 242-0400
51 Old Windsor Rd Bloomfield (06002) ***(G-381)***
Advanced Window Systems LLC ... 800 841-6544
71 Deming Rd Berlin (06037) ***(G-150)***
Advantage Communications LLC ... 203 966-8390
43 Pine St New Canaan (06840) ***(G-5086)***
Advantage Sheet Metal Mfg LLC ... 203 720-0929
51 Elm St Naugatuck (06770) ***(G-4854)***
Advisor ... 203 239-4121
83 State St North Haven (06473) ***(G-5896)***

Aecc/Pearlman Buying Group LLC....203 598-3200
1255 Middlebury Rd Middlebury (06762) ***(G-4272)***
Aef Supply, Norwich *Also called Alan M Crane* ***(G-6405)***
AEN Asphalt Inc....860 885-0500
34 Bozrah St Bozrah (06334) ***(G-523)***
Aer Control Systems LLC....203 772-4700
36 Nettleton Ave North Haven (06473) ***(G-5897)***
Aerex Manufacturing, South Windsor *Also called ATI Ladish Machining Inc* ***(G-7711)***
Aerial Imaging Solutions LLC....860 434-3637
5 Myrica Way Old Lyme (06371) ***(G-6488)***
Aero Component Services LLC....860 291-0417
781 Goodwin St East Hartford (06108) ***(G-2288)***
Aero Gear Incorporated....860 688-0888
1050 Day Hill Rd Windsor (06095) ***(G-10355)***
Aero Precision Mfg LLC....203 675-7625
71 S Turnpike Rd Wallingford (06492) ***(G-9198)***
Aero Tube Technologies LLC....860 289-2520
425 Sullivan Ave Ste 8 South Windsor (06074) ***(G-7701)***
Aero-Med Ltd....860 659-2270
571 Nutmeg Rd N South Windsor (06074) ***(G-7702)***
Aero-Med Molding Technologies (PA)....203 735-2331
50 Westfield Ave Ansonia (06401) ***(G-17)***
Aerocess Inc....860 357-2451
500 Four Rod Rd Ste 110 Berlin (06037) ***(G-151)***
Aerocision LLC....860 526-9700
12a Inspiration Ln Chester (06412) ***(G-1462)***
Aerocomposites Inc....860 829-6809
49 Cambridge Hts Kensington (06037) ***(G-3804)***
Aerocor Inc....860 281-9274
59 Newberry Rd East Windsor (06088) ***(G-2479)***
Aeromics Inc....216 772-1004
11000 Cedar Ave Ste 270 Branford (06405) ***(G-537)***
Aerospace, Berlin *Also called Amco Precision Tools Inc* ***(G-155)***
Aerospace Alloys Inc....860 882-0019
11 Britton Dr Bloomfield (06002) ***(G-382)***
Aerospace Components Mfrs Inc....860 513-3205
1090 Elm St Ste 202 Rocky Hill (06067) ***(G-7220)***
Aerospace Metals Inc....860 522-3123
239 W Service Rd Hartford (06120) ***(G-3548)***
Aerospace Wndsor Airmotive Div, East Granby *Also called Barnes Group Inc* ***(G-2191)***
Aerostar-Hot Air Balloons, Woodbury *Also called Mooney Time Inc* ***(G-10644)***
Aeroswiss LLC....203 634-4545
20 Powers Dr Meriden (06451) ***(G-4141)***
Aerotech Fasteners Inc....860 928-6300
1 Ridge Rd Putnam (06260) ***(G-7028)***
Aerotek Welding Co Inc....860 653-0120
51 Loomis St North Granby (06060) ***(G-5880)***
Aeroturn LLC....203 262-8309
115 Hurley Rd Ste 2c Oxford (06478) ***(G-6640)***
Aesthetic Blacksmithing, Bridgeport *Also called Jozef Custom Ironworks Inc* ***(G-810)***
Afc Industries LLC....860 246-7411
80 Weston St Hartford (06120) ***(G-3549)***
Afcon Products Inc....203 393-9301
35 Sargent Dr Bethany (06524) ***(G-234)***
Afficiency Inc....718 496-9071
606 Post Rd E Westport (06880) ***(G-10050)***
Affordable Cabinets....860 919-5204
208 Beckley Rd Berlin (06037) ***(G-152)***
Affordable Conveyors Svcs LLC....860 582-1800
144 W Washington St Bristol (06010) ***(G-960)***
Affordable Fine Cabinetry....860 919-5204
143 Whiting St Plainville (06062) ***(G-6767)***
Affordable Sign Co....203 874-0875
467 Naugatuck Ave Milford (06460) ***(G-4443)***
Affordable Water Trtmnt....860 423-3147
498 Stafford Rd Mansfield Center (06250) ***(G-4111)***
African Link....203 925-1632
788 Long Hill Ave Shelton (06484) ***(G-7389)***
Afroasia Publication LLC....917 692-3937
132 Hope St Unit B Stamford (06906) ***(G-8063)***
Aftel Corp....203 329-2273
137 Big Oak Rd Stamford (06903) ***(G-8064)***
AG Jewelry Designs LLC (PA)....800 643-0978
1 Stamford Plz Stamford (06901) ***(G-8065)***
AG Jewelry Designs LLC....800 643-0978
314 Wilson Ave Norwalk (06854) ***(G-6063)***
AG Semiconductor Services LLC....203 322-5300
1111 Summer St Fl 4 Stamford (06905) ***(G-8066)***
AGA Mill Work LLC....860 426-9901
178 Newell St Southington (06489) ***(G-7888)***
AGC Acquisition LLC....203 639-7125
106 Evansville Ave Meriden (06451) ***(G-4142)***
Age Plastics LLC....860 502-0418
395 Brittany Farms Rd # 238 New Britain (06053) ***(G-4940)***
Agencyport Software Corp....860 674-6135
190 Farmington Ave Farmington (06032) ***(G-2876)***
Aggregate Products, Shelton *Also called Brennan Realty LLC* ***(G-7409)***
Agi-Shorewood Group Us LLC....203 324-4839
300 Atlantic St Ste 206 Stamford (06901) ***(G-8067)***
Agi-Shorewood U.S., Greenwich *Also called Atlas Agi Holdings LLC* ***(G-3125)***
Agile Computer Systems....860 633-7807
57 Littel Acres Rd Glastonbury (06033) ***(G-3004)***
Agio Printing Service, Pawcatuck *Also called Agjo Printing Service* ***(G-6703)***
Agissar Corporation....203 375-8662
526 Benton St Stratford (06615) ***(G-8565)***
Agjo Printing Service....860 599-3143
173 S Broad St Pawcatuck (06379) ***(G-6703)***
Agratoursim, Middletown *Also called Eddinger Assoc LLC* ***(G-4341)***
Agriphar Crop Solutions, Waterbury *Also called Macdermid AG Solutions Inc* ***(G-9526)***
Agw Clssic Hardwood Floors LLC....203 640-3106
1871 Boston Post Rd Westbrook (06498) ***(G-9989)***
Ahead Communications Systems....203 720-0227
6 Rubber Ave Naugatuck (06770) ***(G-4855)***
Ahlstrom Windsor Locks LLC....860 654-8629
3 Chirnside Rd Windsor Locks (06096) ***(G-10468)***
Ahlstrom-Munksjo Nonwovens LLC (HQ)....860 654-8300
2 Elm St Windsor Locks (06096) ***(G-10469)***
Ahlstrom-Munksjo USA Inc (HQ)....860 654-8300
2 Elm St Windsor Locks (06096) ***(G-10470)***
Ai Divestitures Inc....203 575-5727
245 Freight St Waterbury (06702) ***(G-9424)***
Ai-Tek Instruments LLC....203 271-6927
152 Knotter Dr Cheshire (06410) ***(G-1348)***
Aiac, Stamford *Also called American Indus Acqisition Corp* ***(G-8075)***
Aicas Inc....203 359-5705
6 Landmark Sq Ste 400 Stamford (06901) ***(G-8068)***
AIM Vinyl Signs....203 868-1413
105 Longview Dr Windsor (06095) ***(G-10356)***
Air Age Inc....203 431-9000
88 Danbury Rd Ste 2b Wilton (06897) ***(G-10267)***
Air Born Coatings....860 684-6762
52 Village St East Hartford (06108) ***(G-2289)***
Air Cruisers Co....732 681-3527
45 S Satellite Rd Ste 2 South Windsor (06074) ***(G-7703)***
Air Handling Systems, Woodbridge *Also called Manufacturers Service Co Inc* ***(G-10606)***
Air Solutions East LLC....860 883-4700
41 Brian Ln Avon (06001) ***(G-73)***
Air Tool Sales & Service Co (PA)....860 673-2714
1 Burnham Ave Unionville (06085) ***(G-9110)***
Air Valves LLC....203 266-7175
78 Thomson Rd Bethlehem (06751) ***(G-366)***
Air-Lock Incorporated....203 878-4691
108 Gulf St Milford (06460) ***(G-4444)***
Air-Vac Engineering Co Inc (PA)....203 888-9900
30 Progress Ave Ste 2 Seymour (06483) ***(G-7335)***
Airborne Industries Inc....203 315-0200
6 Sycamore Way Ste 2 Branford (06405) ***(G-538)***
Airbrush Studio's, Plainville *Also called Pastrana Unlimited LLC* ***(G-6851)***
Aircastle Advisor LLC....203 504-1020
201 Tresser Blvd Ste 400 Stamford (06901) ***(G-8069)***
Aircraft, Plainville *Also called Top Flight Machine Tool LLC* ***(G-6870)***
Aircraft Forged Tool Company....860 347-3778
98 Cedar St Rockfall (06481) ***(G-7210)***
Airfax R, Litchfield *Also called Merlin Associates Inc* ***(G-3895)***
Airflo Instrument Company....860 633-9455
53 Addison Rd Glastonbury (06033) ***(G-3005)***
Airflow Truck Company....860 666-1977
32 Old Musket Dr Newington (06111) ***(G-5623)***
Airgas Usa LLC....860 442-0363
130 Cross Rd Waterford (06385) ***(G-9640)***
Airgas Usa LLC....203 792-1834
50 Mill Plain Rd Danbury (06811) ***(G-1733)***
Airgas Usa LLC....203 729-2159
120 Rado Dr Naugatuck (06770) ***(G-4856)***
Airgas Usa LLC....860 442-0363
130 Cross Rd Waterford (06385) ***(G-9641)***
Airigan Solutions LLC....203 594-7781
107 John St Ste 1c Southport (06890) ***(G-7998)***
Airpot Corporation....800 848-7681
35 Lois St Norwalk (06851) ***(G-6064)***
Airtech of Stamford Inc....203 323-3959
21 Anthony St Stamford (06902) ***(G-8070)***
Airtime Publishing Inc....203 454-4773
191 Post Rd W Westport (06880) ***(G-10051)***
Ais Global Holdings LLC....203 250-3500
250 Knotter Dr Cheshire (06410) ***(G-1349)***
Aiudi Concrete Inc....860 399-9289
129 Norris Ave Westbrook (06498) ***(G-9990)***
Aj Casey LLC....203 226-5961
597 Westport Ave C363 Norwalk (06851) ***(G-6065)***
Aj Mfg....860 963-7622
999 Quaddick Town Farm Rd Thompson (06277) ***(G-8828)***
AJ Tuck Company....203 775-1234
32 Tucks Rd Brookfield (06804) ***(G-1157)***
Aj Wood Work LLC....203 826-9851
17 South Ave Apt A Danbury (06810) ***(G-1734)***
AJK Publishing....203 259-8026
296 Partridge Ln Fairfield (06824) ***(G-2746)***
AK Interactive USA LLC....845 313-9380
122 Monticello Dr Branford (06405) ***(G-539)***
AK Stucco LLC....860 832-9589
47 Hatch St New Britain (06053) ***(G-4941)***
Aki Computer, Norwalk *Also called Xiaohao Jia* ***(G-6403)***

ALPHABETIC

(PA)=Parent Co (HQ)=Headquarters (DH)=Div Headquarters
2020 Harris Connecticut
Manufacturers Directory
477

AKO Inc ... 860 298-9765
50 Baker Hollow Rd Windsor (06095) ***(G-10357)***
Al Huppenthal ... 203 364-1028
2 Hearthstone Ln Sandy Hook (06482) ***(G-7299)***
Al's Beverage Company, East Windsor *Also called Als Holding Inc* ***(G-2481)***
Al's Beverage Company, East Windsor *Also called Jmf Group LLC* ***(G-2500)***
Al-Lynn Sales LLC ... 203 922-7840
25 Brook St Ste 102 Shelton (06484) ***(G-7390)***
Alacrity Semiconductors Inc ... 475 325-8435
4 Pin Oak Dr Ste B Branford (06405) ***(G-540)***
Alan M Crane ... 860 608-2788
177 Maple St Norwich (06360) ***(G-6405)***
Alarm One ... 203 239-1714
142 Maple Ave North Haven (06473) ***(G-5898)***
Alarmco ... 203 458-2646
1 Bailey Dr Guilford (06437) ***(G-3323)***
Albe Furs, Westport *Also called Sherwood Group Inc* ***(G-10156)***
Albea Metal Americas, Watertown *Also called Covit America Inc* ***(G-9696)***
Albea Thomaston Inc ... 860 283-2000
60 Electric Ave Thomaston (06787) ***(G-8778)***
Albert E Erickson Co ... 203 386-8931
1111 Honeyspot Rd Ste 1 Stratford (06615) ***(G-8566)***
Albert Gramesty and Dawn Grame ... 203 924-7947
19 Wakeley St Shelton (06484) ***(G-7391)***
Albert Kemperle Inc ... 860 727-0933
141 Locust St Hartford (06114) ***(G-3550)***
Alberto Castillo ... 203 834-1486
7 Mather St Wilton (06897) ***(G-10268)***
Albin Manufacturing Corp ... 203 661-4341
143 River Rd Cos Cob (06807) ***(G-1622)***
Albin Marine Inc ... 203 661-4341
143 River Rd Cos Cob (06807) ***(G-1623)***
Albrayco Technologies Inc ... 860 635-3369
38 River Rd Cromwell (06416) ***(G-1686)***
ALC Manufacturing LLC ... 860 496-0883
323 Technology Park Dr Torrington (06790) ***(G-8888)***
ALC Sales Company LLC (PA) ... 203 877-8526
230 Pepes Farm Rd Ste C Milford (06460) ***(G-4445)***
Alcan Packaging, Norwalk *Also called Cebal Americas* ***(G-6110)***
Alcat Incorporated ... 203 878-0648
116 W Main St Milford (06460) ***(G-4446)***
Alden Corporation ... 203 879-8830
1 Hillside Dr Wolcott (06716) ***(G-10548)***
Alden Tool Company Inc ... 860 828-3556
199 New Park Dr Berlin (06037) ***(G-153)***
Aldlab Chemicals LLC ... 203 589-4934
410 Sackett Point Rd North Haven (06473) ***(G-5899)***
Alent Inc ... 203 575-5727
245 Freight St Waterbury (06702) ***(G-9425)***
Alent USA Holding Inc ... 203 575-5727
245 Freight St Waterbury (06702) ***(G-9426)***
Alexander and Mason ... 860 349-0496
151r Main St Durham (06422) ***(G-2136)***
Alexander Hussey ... 860 354-0118
221 Danbury Rd Ste D New Milford (06776) ***(G-5503)***
Alexander Street Press ... 203 389-6881
110 Curtis Dr New Haven (06515) ***(G-5220)***
Alexander Tulchinsky Violins ... 203 698-7844
35 Marks Rd Riverside (06878) ***(G-7189)***
Alexion Pharma LLC (HQ) ... 203 272-2596
100 College St New Haven (06510) ***(G-5221)***
Alexis Aerospace Inds LLC ... 860 516-4602
200 Smith Way Canton (06019) ***(G-1303)***
Alexis Aerospace Inds LLP ... 860 673-6801
94 Bronson Rd Avon (06001) ***(G-74)***
Alexis Homemade Scrubs ... 401 480-5074
25 Ella Wheeler Rd North Stonington (06359) ***(G-6018)***
Alfa Nobel LLC ... 203 876-2823
94 Utica St Milford (06461) ***(G-4447)***
Alfred Brown Cabinetry LLC (PA) ... 860 868-7261
24 Kent Rd Warren (06754) ***(G-9406)***
Alfro Custom Manufacturing Co ... 203 264-6246
99 Old Woodbury Rd Southbury (06488) ***(G-7843)***
Algonquian Free Press LLC ... 860 572-4811
230 Crosswinds Dr Groton (06340) ***(G-3270)***
Algonquin Industries Inc (HQ) ... 203 453-4348
129 Soundview Rd Guilford (06437) ***(G-3324)***
Alicia Cersosimorathbun ... 401 345-7097
84 Route 27 Mystic (06355) ***(G-4797)***
Alinabal Inc (HQ) ... 203 877-3241
28 Woodmont Rd Milford (06460) ***(G-4448)***
Alinabal Inc ... 860 828-9933
384 Christian Ln Kensington (06037) ***(G-3805)***
Alinabal Holdings Corporation (PA) ... 203 877-3241
28 Woodmont Rd Milford (06460) ***(G-4449)***
All American Embroidery ... 203 906-9656
92 Purdy Hill Rd Monroe (06468) ***(G-4691)***
All Cell Recovery LLC ... 203 948-2566
19 Logging Trail Ln Brookfield (06804) ***(G-1158)***
All Five Tool Co Inc ... 860 583-1693
169 White Oak Dr Berlin (06037) ***(G-154)***
All League Embroidery ... 203 377-7215
171 Bruce Ave Stratford (06615) ***(G-8567)***
All Panel Systems LLC ... 203 208-3142
9 Baldwin Dr Unit 1 Branford (06405) ***(G-541)***
All Phase Dumpsters LLC ... 203 778-9104
30 Wolfpits Rd Bethel (06801) ***(G-257)***
All Phase Htg Coolg Contr LLC ... 860 873-9680
500 Tater Hill Rd East Haddam (06423) ***(G-2235)***
All Phase Steel Works LLC ... 203 375-8881
57 Trumbull St New Haven (06510) ***(G-5222)***
All Power Manufacturing Co (HQ) ... 562 802-2640
1 Tribiology Ctr Oxford (06478) ***(G-6641)***
All Products Painting, Manchester *Also called American Bus Tele & Tech LLC* ***(G-3982)***
All Smiles Dental ... 860 450-9237
1003 Main St Willimantic (06226) ***(G-10220)***
All Star Welding & Dem LLC ... 203 948-0528
50 Shelter Rock Rd Danbury (06810) ***(G-1735)***
All States Asphalt Inc ... 860 774-7550
127 Attwaugan Crossing Rd Dayville (06241) ***(G-2053)***
All Steel LLC ... 860 871-6023
240 Crystal Lake Rd Ellington (06029) ***(G-2574)***
All Steel Fabricating Inc ... 203 783-1860
49 Higgins Dr Milford (06460) ***(G-4450)***
All Tech Auto/Truck Electric ... 203 790-8990
36 Kenosia Ave Ste B Danbury (06810) ***(G-1736)***
All Tech Sign & Crane Service ... 203 272-2207
128 Blacks Rd Ste A Cheshire (06410) ***(G-1350)***
All You Need For Sleep, South Windham *Also called Water & Air Inc* ***(G-7693)***
All-Test Pro LLC (PA) ... 860 399-4222
20 Research Pkwy Unit G&H Old Saybrook (06475) ***(G-6522)***
All-Time Manufacturing Co Inc ... 860 848-9258
Bridge St Montville (06353) ***(G-4768)***
Allard Electronics, Wallingford *Also called Raman Power Technologies LLC* ***(G-9348)***
Allegra Print & Imaging, Shelton *Also called System Intgrtion Cnsulting LLC* ***(G-7562)***
Allen of Ansonia Stamps ... 203 736-2222
16 Laurel Ave Derby (06418) ***(G-2108)***
Allen Precision LLC ... 860 370-9881
1 Northgate Dr Windsor Locks (06096) ***(G-10471)***
Allexcel Inc ... 203 764-2036
135 Wood St Ste 200 West Haven (06516) ***(G-9882)***
Allgreenit LLC ... 860 516-4948
123 Farmington Ave # 162 Bristol (06010) ***(G-961)***
Alliance Carpet Cushion Co (HQ) ... 860 489-4273
180 Church St Torrington (06790) ***(G-8889)***
Alliance Energy LLC ... 203 933-2511
Merritt Pkwy New Haven (06535) ***(G-5223)***
Alliance Graphics Inc ... 860 666-7992
16 Progress Cir Bldg 3 Newington (06111) ***(G-5624)***
Alliance Water Treatment Co ... 203 323-9968
28 Coachlamp Ln Stamford (06902) ***(G-8071)***
Alliance Welding Supplies, Danbury *Also called Tech Air Northern Cal LLC* ***(G-1961)***
Alliances By Alisa LLC ... 860 869-1509
14 Northgate Simsbury (06070) ***(G-7610)***
Allied Controls Inc ... 860 628-8443
25 Forest St Apt 14a Stamford (06901) ***(G-8072)***
Allied Engineering, Newington *Also called Allied Machining Co Inc* ***(G-5625)***
Allied Machining Co Inc ... 860 665-1228
50 Progress Cir Ste 3 Newington (06111) ***(G-5625)***
Allied Metal Finishing L L C ... 860 290-8865
379 Chapel Rd South Windsor (06074) ***(G-7704)***
Allied Printing Services Inc (PA) ... 860 643-1101
1 Allied Way Manchester (06042) ***(G-3980)***
Allied Sinterings Incorporated ... 203 743-7502
29 Briar Ridge Rd Danbury (06810) ***(G-1737)***
Allison Taylor, Branford *Also called Fyc Apparel Group LLC* ***(G-599)***
Allnex USA Inc ... 203 269-4481
528 S Cherry St Wallingford (06492) ***(G-9199)***
Alloy Engineering Co Inc (PA) ... 203 366-5253
304 Seaview Ave Bridgeport (06607) ***(G-685)***
Alloy Engineering Co Inc ... 203 366-5253
224 Dekalb Ave Bridgeport (06607) ***(G-686)***
Alloy Metals Inc (PA) ... 203 774-3270
34b Barnes Indus Rd S Wallingford (06492) ***(G-9200)***
Alloy Specialties Incorporated ... 860 646-4587
110 Batson Dr Manchester (06042) ***(G-3981)***
Alloy Welding ... 203 737-5609
85 Willow St New Haven (06511) ***(G-5224)***
Alloy Welding & Mfg Co Inc ... 860 582-3638
233 Riverside Ave Bristol (06010) ***(G-962)***
Allread Products Co LLC ... 860 589-3566
22 S Main St Terryville (06786) ***(G-8747)***
Allstar Welding and Demolition, Danbury *Also called All Star Welding & Dem LLC* ***(G-1735)***
Allstate Fire Systems LLC ... 860 246-7711
35 Phil Mack Dr Middletown (06457) ***(G-4314)***
Alltop Ltd ... 203 746-1509
13 Colonial Rd New Fairfield (06812) ***(G-5160)***
Allyndale Corporation ... 860 824-7959
40 Allyndale Rd East Canaan (06024) ***(G-2180)***
Alm Media LLC ... 860 527-7900
201 Ann Uccello St Fl 4 Hartford (06103) ***(G-3551)***
Almond Sand Elephants ... 860 232-4888
11 Craigmoor Rd West Hartford (06107) ***(G-9773)***
Alpha 1c LLC ... 860 354-7979
3 Leach Hollow Rd Sherman (06784) ***(G-7590)***

Alpha Magnetics & Coils Inc 860 496-0122
527 Westledge Dr Torrington (06790) ***(G-8890)***
Alpha Plating and Finishing Co 860 747-5002
169 W Main St Plainville (06062) ***(G-6768)***
Alpha-Core Corp 203 335-6805
915 Pembroke St Bridgeport (06608) ***(G-687)***
Alpha-Core Inc 203 954-0050
6 Waterview Dr Shelton (06484) ***(G-7392)***
Alphabet Publishing, Branford *Also called Burns Walton **(G-566)***
Alphacom Inc 203 637-7006
84 Havemeyer Pl Greenwich (06830) ***(G-3117)***
AlphaGraphics, Oxford *Also called Digitaldruker Inc **(G-6656)***
AlphaGraphics, Wallingford *Also called Rf Printing LLC **(G-9352)***
AlphaGraphics, Brookfield *Also called Apb Associates LLC **(G-1159)***
AlphaGraphics, Greenwich *Also called Turnstone Inc **(G-3250)***
AlphaGraphics, Stamford *Also called Melega Inc **(G-8306)***
AlphaGraphics LLC 203 230-0018
24 Rossotto Dr Hamden (06514) ***(G-3413)***
Alpine Art & Mirror, Westport *Also called Alpine Management Group LLC **(G-10052)***
Alpine Management Group LLC 954 531-1692
25 Sylvan Rd S Ste B Westport (06880) ***(G-10052)***
Alrite Manufacturing Company, Bloomfield *Also called Kenneth Leroux **(G-438)***
Als Beverage Company Inc 860 627-7003
13 Revay Rd East Windsor (06088) ***(G-2480)***
Als Holding Inc (PA) 860 627-7003
13 Revay Rd East Windsor (06088) ***(G-2481)***
Alsip Acquisition LLC 203 202-7777
315 Post Rd W Westport (06880) ***(G-10053)***
Alstom Power Co 860 688-1911
175 Addison Rd Windsor (06095) ***(G-10358)***
Alstom Power-Chattan Tubin Dis, Windsor *Also called GE Steam Power Inc **(G-10389)***
Alstom Renewable US LLC 860 688-1911
200 Great Pond Dr Windsor (06095) ***(G-10359)***
Alstrom Power 203 783-1046
55 Shelland St Milford (06461) ***(G-4451)***
Altare Publishing Inc 860 490-6144
79 Westbury Avon (06001) ***(G-75)***
Altasci LLC 860 224-6668
1 Hartford Sq Unit 230 New Britain (06052) ***(G-4942)***
Altek Company 860 482-7626
89 Commercial Blvd Ste 1 Torrington (06790) ***(G-8891)***
Altek Electronics Inc 860 482-7626
89 Commercial Blvd Torrington (06790) ***(G-8892)***
Altenergy LLC 203 299-1400
137 Rowayton Ave Norwalk (06853) ***(G-6066)***
Alterio Tractor Pulling LLC 203 305-9812
37 Cold Spring Dr Oxford (06478) ***(G-6642)***
Alteris Renewables Inc 860 535-3370
32 Taugwonk Spur Rd 12n Stonington (06378) ***(G-8521)***
Alternate Energy Futures 917 745-7097
3121 Avalon Valley Dr Danbury (06810) ***(G-1738)***
Alternate Inc 203 938-4125
30 Orchard Dr Redding (06896) ***(G-7088)***
Alternative Choice LLC 860 875-7529
5 Lawrence St Vernon Rockville (06066) ***(G-9159)***
Alternative Energy Retailer, Oxford *Also called Zackin Publications Inc **(G-6701)***
Alternative Fuel & Energy LLC 860 537-5345
31 Halls Hill Rd Colchester (06415) ***(G-1539)***
Alternative Prosthetic Svcs 203 367-1212
191 Bennett St Bridgeport (06605) ***(G-688)***
Althor Products LLC 860 386-6700
200 Old County Cir # 116 Windsor Locks (06096) ***(G-10472)***
Altman Orthotics & Prosthetics, Wethersfield *Also called Leona Corp **(G-10209)***
Alto Products Corp Al 860 747-2736
63 N Washington St Plainville (06062) ***(G-6769)***
Alton Enterprises Inc 203 469-9719
37 Panagrosi St East Haven (06512) ***(G-2408)***
Alton Truck & Trailer, East Haven *Also called Alton Enterprises Inc **(G-2408)***
Altra Industrial Motion Corp 860 379-1673
31 Industrial Park Rd New Hartford (06057) ***(G-5185)***
Alue Optics, Groton *Also called Cashon **(G-3276)***
Aluminum Finishing Company Inc 203 333-1690
1575 Railroad Ave Bridgeport (06605) ***(G-689)***
Alva Health Inc 832 515-8235
157 Church St Fl 19 New Haven (06510) ***(G-5225)***
Alvarado Custom Cabinetry LLC 203 831-0181
51 Midrocks Dr Norwalk (06851) ***(G-6067)***
Alvarez Industries LLC 203 799-2356
312 Boston Post Rd Orange (06477) ***(G-6580)***
Alvarez Industries LLC (PA) 203 401-1152
26 Brownell St Fl 3 New Haven (06511) ***(G-5226)***
Alvarium Beer Company LLC 860 306-3857
30 Biltmore St New Britain (06053) ***(G-4943)***
Alvest (usa) Inc (HQ) 860 602-3400
812 Bloomfield Ave Windsor (06095) ***(G-10360)***
AM Manufacturing LLC 860 573-1987
278 Oakwood Dr Ste 6 Glastonbury (06033) ***(G-3006)***
Amandas Daily Ideas LLC 203 761-8599
24 Glen Hill Rd Wilton (06897) ***(G-10269)***
Amatom Electronic Hardware, Cromwell *Also called Carey Manufacturing Co Inc **(G-1695)***
Amatom Electronic Hardwares, Cromwell *Also called Carey Manufacturing Co Inc **(G-1694)***
Amazing Signs, Sandy Hook *Also called James Woznick **(G-7317)***
Amazing Strawberries, New Haven *Also called Rivera Marina **(G-5381)***
Amber Food Sales 860 749-7272
10 Misty Meadow Rd Enfield (06082) ***(G-2614)***
Amber Synthetics, Stamford *Also called Near Oak LLC **(G-8318)***
Ambiance Painting LLC 203 354-8689
67 Murray St Norwalk (06851) ***(G-6068)***
Ambrosonics 860 752-9022
229 Rollingbrook Windsor (06095) ***(G-10361)***
Amci, Terryville *Also called Advanced Micro Controls Inc **(G-8746)***
Amci Capital LP 203 625-9200
600 Steamboat Rd Ste 3 Greenwich (06830) ***(G-3118)***
Amco Precision Tools Inc (PA) 860 828-5640
921 Farmington Ave Berlin (06037) ***(G-155)***
Amelia Cabinet Co LLC 860 638-9047
89 Colt Ave Torrington (06790) ***(G-8893)***
Amentos Gold Buyers and Secon 203 691-1020
140 Washington Ave Ste 1d North Haven (06473) ***(G-5900)***
America Extract Corporation 860 267-4444
31 E High St East Hampton (06424) ***(G-2252)***
American Actuator Corporation 203 324-6334
292 Newtown Tpke Redding (06896) ***(G-7089)***
American Alloy Wire Corp 203 426-3133
1 Wire Rd Newtown (06470) ***(G-5726)***
American Art Heritage Pubg 203 973-0564
66 Broad St Ste 4 Stamford (06901) ***(G-8073)***
American Automation 203 556-7839
540 Barnum Ave Bridgeport (06608) ***(G-690)***
American Backplane Inc 860 567-2360
355 Bantam Lake Rd Morris (06763) ***(G-4785)***
American Banknote Corporation (PA) 203 941-4090
1055 Washington Blvd Fl 6 Stamford (06901) ***(G-8074)***
American Bus Tele & Tech LLC 860 643-2200
1651 Tolland Tpke Manchester (06042) ***(G-3982)***
American Catalytic Tech, Branford *Also called American Catatech Inc **(G-542)***
American Catatech Inc 203 483-6692
209 Montowese St Ste 3 Branford (06405) ***(G-542)***
American Cladding Technologies 860 413-3098
15 International Dr East Granby (06026) ***(G-2188)***
American Collars Couplings Inc 860 379-7043
88 Hubbard St Winsted (06098) ***(G-10504)***
American CT Rng Bnder Index & 860 868-7900
42 Sabbaday Ln Washington (06793) ***(G-9411)***
American Custom Fine Woodwrkng 860 871-8783
714 Crystal Lake Rd 2b Tolland (06084) ***(G-8848)***
American Design & Mfg Inc 860 282-2719
145 Commerce Way South Windsor (06074) ***(G-7705)***
American Distilling Inc 860 267-4444
380 N Main St Marlborough (06447) ***(G-4119)***
American Distilling Inc (PA) 860 267-4444
31 E High St East Hampton (06424) ***(G-2253)***
American Dream Unlimited LLC 860 742-5055
212 Gilead Rd Andover (06232) ***(G-6)***
American Dry Stripping, Milford *Also called Gybenorth Industries LLC **(G-4546)***
American Eagle Embroidery LLC 203 239-7906
201 State St North Haven (06473) ***(G-5901)***
American Electro Products, Farmington *Also called National Integrated Inds Inc **(G-2933)***
American Electro Products Div, Waterbury *Also called National Integrated Inds Inc **(G-9553)***
American Electro Products Inc 203 756-7051
1358 Thomaston Ave Waterbury (06704) ***(G-9427)***
American Embroidery 860 829-8586
83 Vivian Dr Berlin (06037) ***(G-156)***
American Fiber Technologies, Bridgeport *Also called US Highway Products Inc **(G-932)***
American Fnshg Specialists Inc 203 367-0663
40 Cowles St Bridgeport (06607) ***(G-691)***
American Greenfuels LLC 203 672-9028
30 Waterfront St New Haven (06512) ***(G-5227)***
American Grippers Inc 203 459-8345
171 Spring Hill Rd Trumbull (06611) ***(G-8997)***
American Heat Treating Inc 203 268-1750
16 Commerce Dr Monroe (06468) ***(G-4692)***
American Hydrogen Northeast 203 449-4614
520 Savoy St Bridgeport (06606) ***(G-692)***
American Imex Corporation 203 261-5200
57 Maryanne Dr Monroe (06468) ***(G-4693)***
American Indus Acqisition Corp (PA) 203 952-9212
1 Harbor Point Rd # 1700 Stamford (06902) ***(G-8075)***
American Industrial Rbr Pdts, Wallingford *Also called Jem Manufacturing Inc **(G-9294)***
American Industries 860 381-5083
2 Chapman Ln Gales Ferry (06335) ***(G-2980)***
American Iron Works 203 624-7360
17 Morris St New Haven (06519) ***(G-5228)***
American Iron Works 203 469-6117
49 Old Town Hwy East Haven (06512) ***(G-2409)***
American Kraft Paper Inds LLC 203 323-1916
1 Harbor Point Rd # 1700 Stamford (06902) ***(G-8076)***
American Kuhne 401 326-6200
75 Frontage Rd 201 North Stonington (06359) ***(G-6019)***
American Library Association 860 347-6933
575 Main St Ste 300 Middletown (06457) ***(G-4315)***

ALPHABETIC

American Litho, Fairfield *Also called L R K Communications Inc* ***(G-2808)***
American Machining Tech Inc.......860 342-0005
141 Pickering St Portland (06480) ***(G-6949)***
American Mailing Depot, Cheshire *Also called American Rubber Stamp Company* ***(G-1351)***
American Marine Inc.......914 763-5367
40 High St Greenwich (06830) ***(G-3119)***
American Marketing Group Inc.......203 367-2378
51 Crescent Ave Bridgeport (06608) ***(G-693)***
American Melody Records.......203 457-0881
102 Wheeler Path Guilford (06437) ***(G-3325)***
American Metal Master Mch Tl, Plantsville *Also called American Metal Masters LLC* ***(G-6884)***
American Metal Masters LLC.......860 621-6911
141 Summer St Plantsville (06479) ***(G-6884)***
American Metalcrafters, Middletown *Also called Aztec Industries LLC* ***(G-4321)***
American Metallizing.......860 289-1677
401 Governors Hwy South Windsor (06074) ***(G-7706)***
American Metals Coal Intl Inc (HQ).......203 625-9200
475 Steamboat Rd Fl 2nd Greenwich (06830) ***(G-3120)***
American Metaseal of Conn.......203 787-0281
336 Putnam Ave Hamden (06517) ***(G-3414)***
American Molded Products Inc.......203 333-0183
130 Front St Bridgeport (06606) ***(G-694)***
American Molding, Windsor Locks *Also called Awm LLC* ***(G-10473)***
American Molding Product, Vernon Rockville *Also called Atlas Hobbing and Tool Co Inc* ***(G-9160)***
American Natural Soda Ash Corp (PA).......203 226-9056
15 Riverside Ave Ste 2 Westport (06880) ***(G-10054)***
American Overhead Ret Div Inc.......860 876-4552
1885 S Main St Middletown (06457) ***(G-4316)***
American Performance Pdts LLC.......203 269-4468
7 Atwater Pl Wallingford (06492) ***(G-9201)***
American Plastic Products Inc.......203 596-2410
2114 Thomaston Ave Waterbury (06704) ***(G-9428)***
American Polyfilm Inc (PA).......203 483-9797
15 Baldwin Dr Branford (06405) ***(G-543)***
American Powdercoating LLC.......860 267-8870
12 Summit St Ste 1 East Hampton (06424) ***(G-2254)***
American Precision Mfg LLC.......203 734-1800
26 Beaver St Ste 1 Ansonia (06401) ***(G-18)***
American Precision Mold Inc.......860 267-1356
58 E High St East Hampton (06424) ***(G-2255)***
American Precision Product LLC.......860 274-7301
81 Winding Brook Farm Rd Watertown (06795) ***(G-9680)***
American Prefab Wood Pdts Co.......860 242-5468
1217 Blue Hills Ave Bloomfield (06002) ***(G-383)***
American Pront and Sign.......203 400-2155
6 Gwendolyn Dr Trumbull (06611) ***(G-8998)***
American Prototype Hob.......203 323-6832
203 Sylvan Knoll Rd Stamford (06902) ***(G-8077)***
American Pulley Cover, South Windsor *Also called Siftex Equipment Company* ***(G-7821)***
American Radiant Technolo.......203 484-2888
67 Indstrial Pk Access Rd Middlefield (06455) ***(G-4299)***
American Railway Technologies.......860 291-1170
61 Alna Ln Ste 1 East Hartford (06108) ***(G-2290)***
American Recreational Inds.......203 375-5900
630 Surf Ave Stratford (06615) ***(G-8568)***
American Refacing Cstm Cab LLC.......860 647-0868
1 Mitchell Dr Manchester (06042) ***(G-3983)***
American Reprographics, Norwalk *Also called Bpi Reprographics* ***(G-6097)***
American Roller Company LLC.......203 598-3100
84 Turnpike Dr Middlebury (06762) ***(G-4273)***
American Rubber Stamp Company.......203 755-1135
35 Judson Ct Cheshire (06410) ***(G-1351)***
American Seal and Engrg Co Inc (HQ).......203 789-8819
295 Indian River Rd Orange (06477) ***(G-6581)***
American Sign Inc.......203 624-2991
614 Ferry St New Haven (06513) ***(G-5229)***
American Silk Screening LLC.......860 828-5486
386 Deming Rd Berlin (06037) ***(G-157)***
American Sleeve Bearing LLC.......860 684-8060
1 Spring St Stafford Springs (06076) ***(G-8016)***
American Solar & Alternative.......203 324-7186
2777 Summer St Ste 204 Stamford (06905) ***(G-8078)***
American Solution For Business.......860 413-9415
88 Kimberly Rd East Granby (06026) ***(G-2189)***
American Specialty Co Inc.......203 929-5324
762 River Rd Shelton (06484) ***(G-7393)***
American Specialty Pdts LLC.......860 871-2279
101 Industrial Park Rd Vernon (06066) ***(G-9130)***
American Standard Company.......860 628-9643
157 Water St Southington (06489) ***(G-7889)***
American Steel Fabricators Inc (PA).......860 243-5005
105 Old Windsor Rd Bloomfield (06002) ***(G-384)***
American Stitch & Print Inc.......203 239-5383
222 Elm St Ste 9 North Haven (06473) ***(G-5902)***
American Stonecrafters Inc.......203 514-9725
224 S Whittlesey Ave Wallingford (06492) ***(G-9202)***
American Tool & Mfg Corp.......860 666-2255
125 Rockwell Rd Newington (06111) ***(G-5626)***
American Trade Fairs Org.......203 221-0114
250 Main St Ste 101 Westport (06880) ***(G-10055)***
American Ultraviolet.......203 926-0140
22 Ivy Grove Ct Shelton (06484) ***(G-7394)***
American Unmanned Systems LLC.......203 406-7611
460 Summer St Stamford (06901) ***(G-8079)***
American Vehicles Sales LLC.......860 886-0327
58 Yantic Flats Rd Yantic (06389) ***(G-10696)***
American Veteran Textile LLC.......203 583-0576
674 Main St Fl 2 Ansonia (06401) ***(G-19)***
American Welding Service.......860 935-5314
214 Labby Rd North Grosvenordale (06255) ***(G-5883)***
American Wind Capital Co LLC (HQ).......860 767-1579
2 Essex Sq Unit 7 Essex (06426) ***(G-2711)***
American Wire Corporation.......203 426-3133
1 Wire Rd Newtown (06470) ***(G-5727)***
American Wldg Fabrication LLC.......860 918-2094
30 Precision Ct New Britain (06051) ***(G-4944)***
American Wood Products.......203 248-4433
301 State St North Haven (06473) ***(G-5903)***
American Woolen Company Inc.......860 684-2766
8 Furnace Ave Stafford Springs (06076) ***(G-8017)***
American-Digital LLC.......203 838-0148
135 Clarence St Bridgeport (06608) ***(G-695)***
American-Republican Inc (PA).......203 574-3636
389 Meadow St Waterbury (06702) ***(G-9429)***
American-Republican Inc.......860 496-9301
122 Franklin St Torrington (06790) ***(G-8894)***
Amerifix LLC.......203 931-7290
278 Washington Ave West Haven (06516) ***(G-9883)***
Ametek Inc.......203 265-6731
21 Toelles Rd Wallingford (06492) ***(G-9203)***
Ametek Specialty Metal Pdts, Wallingford *Also called Ametek Inc* ***(G-9203)***
AMG Development LLC.......203 292-8444
1698 Post Rd E Westport (06880) ***(G-10056)***
Amgraph Packaging Inc.......860 822-2000
90 Paper Mill Rd Baltic (06330) ***(G-118)***
Amity Printing & Copy Ctr LLC.......860 828-0202
947 Farmington Ave Berlin (06037) ***(G-158)***
Amius Partners LLC.......203 526-5926
180 E Rock Rd New Haven (06511) ***(G-5230)***
Amk Technical Services, South Windsor *Also called Amk Welding Inc* ***(G-7707)***
Amk Welding Inc (HQ).......860 289-5634
283 Sullivan Ave South Windsor (06074) ***(G-7707)***
Ammonite Corp.......203 972-1130
181 Mariomi Rd New Canaan (06840) ***(G-5087)***
Ammunition Stor Components LLC.......860 225-3548
206 Newington Ave New Britain (06051) ***(G-4945)***
Amodex Products Inc.......203 335-1255
1354 State St Bridgeport (06605) ***(G-696)***
Amodios Inc (PA).......203 573-1229
40 Falls Ave Ste 4 Waterbury (06708) ***(G-9430)***
Amoun Bakery & Distribution, South Windsor *Also called Amoun Pita & Distribution LLC* ***(G-7708)***
Amoun Pita & Distribution LLC.......866 239-9990
361 Pleasant Valley Rd South Windsor (06074) ***(G-7708)***
Ampco Publishing & Prtg Corp.......203 325-1509
130 Lenox Ave Ste 32 Stamford (06906) ***(G-8080)***
Amphenol, Wallingford *Also called Times Wire and Cable Company* ***(G-9387)***
Amphenol Corporation.......203 327-7300
50 Sunnyside Ave Stamford (06902) ***(G-8081)***
Amphenol Corporation.......203 743-9272
4 Old Newtown Rd Ste 2 Danbury (06810) ***(G-1739)***
Amphenol Corporation (PA).......203 265-8900
358 Hall Ave Wallingford (06492) ***(G-9204)***
Amphenol Corporation.......203 287-2272
720 Sherman Ave Hamden (06514) ***(G-3415)***
Amphenol Funding Corp.......203 265-8900
358 Hall Ave Wallingford (06492) ***(G-9205)***
Amphenol International Ltd (HQ).......203 265-8900
358 Hall Ave Wallingford (06492) ***(G-9206)***
Amphenol Nexus Technologies.......203 327-7300
50 Sunnyside Ave Stamford (06902) ***(G-8082)***
Amphenol Rf, Danbury *Also called Amphenol Corporation* ***(G-1739)***
Ampol Tool Inc.......203 932-3161
44 Hamilton St West Haven (06516) ***(G-9884)***
AMR Machines LLC.......860 336-6208
77 Industrial Park Rd # 6 Putnam (06260) ***(G-7029)***
Amro Tool Co.......860 274-9766
127 Echo Lake Rd Ste 26 Watertown (06795) ***(G-9681)***
AMS Strategic Management Inc.......845 500-5635
201 Commons Park S # 702 Stamford (06902) ***(G-8083)***
AMS Supply Management, Stamford *Also called AMS Strategic Management Inc* ***(G-8083)***
Amstep Products, Bristol *Also called Patwil LLC* ***(G-1088)***
Amsys Inc.......203 431-8814
900 Ethan Allen Hwy Ste 1 Ridgefield (06877) ***(G-7116)***
Amsys Computer, Ridgefield *Also called Amsys Inc* ***(G-7116)***
Amt Micropure Inc.......203 226-7938
14 Mountain View Dr Weston (06883) ***(G-10017)***
Amtec Corporation.......860 230-0006
30 Center Pkwy Plainfield (06374) ***(G-6737)***
Amusements Unlimited, Stamford *Also called Rlp Inc* ***(G-8394)***
Amy Coe Inc.......203 227-9900
20 Marshall St Ste 118 Norwalk (06854) ***(G-6069)***

An Designs Inc......860 618-0183
111 Putter Ln Torrington (06790) ***(G-8895)***
Anaconda Universal Assoc LLC......203 699-9344
76 Belridge Rd Cheshire (06410) ***(G-1352)***
Anapo Plastics Corp......860 874-8174
222 Main St 214 Farmington (06032) ***(G-2877)***
Ancera Inc......203 819-2322
15 Commercial St Branford (06405) ***(G-544)***
Anchor Overhead Door Sales......860 651-6560
24 Wooster Rd Tariffville (06081) ***(G-8743)***
Anchor Rubber Products LLC......860 667-2628
152 Rockwell Rd Ste C9 Newington (06111) ***(G-5627)***
Anchor Science LLC......203 231-6181
37 Victoria Dr Branford (06405) ***(G-545)***
Anchor Woodworking LLC......860 376-0795
494 Roode Rd Jewett City (06351) ***(G-3791)***
Anco Engineering Inc......203 925-9235
217 Long Hill Cross Rd Shelton (06484) ***(G-7395)***
Anco Tool & Manufacturing, Watertown *Also called Cgl Inc* ***(G-9691)***
Andeco Software LLC......225 229-2491
14 South St Unit 9 Danbury (06810) ***(G-1740)***
Andersen Laboratories Inc......860 286-9090
45 Old Iron Ore Rd Bloomfield (06002) ***(G-385)***
Anderson David C & Assoc LLC (PA)......860 749-7547
9 Moody Rd Ste 1 Enfield (06082) ***(G-2615)***
Anderson Group, Enfield *Also called Anderson David C & Assoc LLC* ***(G-2615)***
Anderson Manufacturing Company......203 263-2318
337 Quassapaug Rd Woodbury (06798) ***(G-10624)***
Anderson Publishing LLC......860 621-2192
24 Mooreland Dr Southington (06489) ***(G-7890)***
Anderson Specialty Company......860 953-6630
81 Custer St West Hartford (06110) ***(G-9774)***
Anderson Stair & Railing......203 288-0117
348 Sackett Point Rd North Haven (06473) ***(G-5904)***
Anderson Technologies Inc......860 663-2100
243 Roast Meat Hill Rd Killingworth (06419) ***(G-3828)***
Anderson Tool Company Inc......203 777-4153
85 Willow St Ste 3 New Haven (06511) ***(G-5231)***
Andert Inc......860 974-3893
39 Boston Tpke Eastford (06242) ***(G-2534)***
Andher Mfg LLC......860 874-8816
24 Emely St East Hartford (06108) ***(G-2291)***
Andre Furniture Industries......860 528-8826
55 Sandra Dr Ste 1 South Windsor (06074) ***(G-7709)***
Andree Brooks......203 226-9834
15 Hitchcock Rd Westport (06880) ***(G-10057)***
Andrew Lambert......203 249-6310
175 Atlantic St Stamford (06901) ***(G-8084)***
Andrews Arboriculture LLC......203 565-8570
860 Andrew Mountain Rd Naugatuck (06770) ***(G-4857)***
Andritz Shw Inc......860 496-8888
90 Commercial Blvd Torrington (06790) ***(G-8896)***
Andvic-Precision LLC......860 836-7422
11 Woodmere Rd Newington (06111) ***(G-5628)***
Andy Rakowicz......860 828-1620
600 Four Rod Rd Ste 4 Berlin (06037) ***(G-159)***
Andys Automotive Machine......860 793-2455
48 Lewis St Plainville (06062) ***(G-6770)***
Angel Fuel LLC......203 597-8759
56 Knoll St Waterbury (06705) ***(G-9431)***
Angela Cosmai Inc......203 329-7403
383 Janes Ln Stamford (06903) ***(G-8085)***
Angelas Italian Ice Inc......860 536-9828
16 Cottrell St Mystic (06355) ***(G-4798)***
Angelos Aluminum......203 469-3117
55 Thompson St Apt 14g East Haven (06513) ***(G-2410)***
Anh Refractories......203 795-0597
55 Connair Rd Orange (06477) ***(G-6582)***
Aniyaq LLC......860 531-2835
45 Hemlock Dr Marlborough (06447) ***(G-4120)***
Anjar Co......203 321-1023
42 Russet Rd Stamford (06903) ***(G-8086)***
Ankleaid LLC......860 305-5178
7 Jonathan Dr Ellington (06029) ***(G-2575)***
Ann S Davis......860 642-7228
754 Exeter Rd Lebanon (06249) ***(G-3846)***
Anna M Chisilenco-Raho......203 877-0377
67 Cherry St Ste 2 Milford (06460) ***(G-4452)***
Anne Queen Woodworking......203 720-1781
74 Great Hill Rd Naugatuck (06770) ***(G-4858)***
Annelli Paving, Colchester *Also called Christopher Annelli* ***(G-1545)***
Annies Oil Co......203 237-9276
10 Cooper St Meriden (06450) ***(G-4143)***
Anodic Incorporated......203 268-9966
1480 Monroe Tpke Stevenson (06491) ***(G-8520)***
Anodizing, Waterbury *Also called Seidel Inc* ***(G-9600)***
Anomatic Corporation......203 720-2367
50 Rado Dr Unit B Naugatuck (06770) ***(G-4859)***
Anothercreationbymichele......203 322-4277
1351 Riverbank Rd Stamford (06903) ***(G-8087)***
Anray Lithographers......203 877-1000
8 Parkway Ter Milford (06461) ***(G-4453)***
Ansa Company Inc......203 687-1664
130 Water St Norwalk (06854) ***(G-6070)***
Ansac, Westport *Also called American Natural Soda Ash Corp* ***(G-10054)***
Ansel Label and Packaging Corp......203 452-0311
204 Spring Hill Rd Ste 3 Trumbull (06611) ***(G-8999)***
Ansonia Plastics LLC......203 736-5200
401 Birmingham Blvd Ansonia (06401) ***(G-20)***
Ansonia Stl Fabrication Co Inc......203 888-4509
164 Pines Bridge Rd Beacon Falls (06403) ***(G-129)***
Anstett Lumber Co......860 491-3225
182 East St N Goshen (06756) ***(G-3095)***
Antares Aerospace Inds LLC......203 903-7531
90 Cosey Beach Ave East Haven (06512) ***(G-2411)***
Anthony Da RE Welding......860 526-2659
118 Stevenstown Rd Deep River (06417) ***(G-2083)***
Anthony s Fuel......203 513-7400
56 Great Oak Rd Shelton (06484) ***(G-7396)***
Antiqueweb.com, Middlefield *Also called Times Publishing LLC* ***(G-4308)***
Antrim House......860 217-0023
21 Goodrich Rd Simsbury (06070) ***(G-7611)***
Anything Goes, Durham *Also called Rosemarie Querns* ***(G-2155)***
Anything Printed LLC......860 429-1244
331 River Rd Willington (06279) ***(G-10245)***
Anything Printed Copy Center, Willington *Also called Anything Printed LLC* ***(G-10245)***
Aoa Xinetics, East Hartford *Also called Adaptive Optics Associates Inc* ***(G-2287)***
AP Disposition LLC......860 889-1344
387 N Main St Norwich (06360) ***(G-6406)***
Apache Mill......401 597-5580
491 Main St Branford (06405) ***(G-546)***
Aparo's Electric Motor Repair, Southington *Also called Aparos Electric Motor Service* ***(G-7891)***
Aparos Electric Motor Service......860 276-2044
134 Industrial Dr Southington (06489) ***(G-7891)***
Apb Associates LLC......203 740-9792
35 Obtuse Rocks Rd Brookfield (06804) ***(G-1159)***
Apcm Manufacturing LLC......860 564-7817
1366 Norwich Rd Plainfield (06374) ***(G-6738)***
Apco Products......860 767-2108
6 Essex Industrial Park Centerbrook (06409) ***(G-1329)***
Apcompower Inc (HQ)......860 688-1911
200 Great Pond Dr Windsor (06095) ***(G-10362)***
Apct Global, Wallingford *Also called Apct-Ct Inc* ***(G-9207)***
Apct-Ct Inc......203 284-1215
340 Quinnipiac St Unit 25 Wallingford (06492) ***(G-9207)***
Apct-Wallingford Inc......203 269-3311
340 Quinnipiac St Unit 25 Wallingford (06492) ***(G-9208)***
Aperture Optical Sciences Inc......860 301-2589
23 Soobitsky Rd Higganum (06441) ***(G-3759)***
Aperture Optical Sciences Inc......860 301-2372
170 Pond View Dr Meriden (06450) ***(G-4144)***
Apex Cstm Cabinetry Wdwkg LLC......203 396-0496
50 Lansing Pl Bridgeport (06606) ***(G-697)***
Apex Machine Tool Company Inc......860 677-2884
500 Knotter Dr Cheshire (06410) ***(G-1353)***
Apex Machine Tool Company Inc......203 806-2090
5 Mckee Pl Cheshire (06410) ***(G-1354)***
Apex Tool & Cutter Co Inc......203 888-8970
59 Old Turnpike Rd Beacon Falls (06403) ***(G-130)***
API, Branford *Also called American Polyfilm Inc* ***(G-543)***
API Wizard LLC......914 764-5726
10 Hamilton Rd Ridgefield (06877) ***(G-7117)***
Apicellas Bakery Inc......203 865-6204
365 Grand Ave New Haven (06513) ***(G-5232)***
Apiject Systems Corp (PA)......203 461-7121
2 High Ridge Park Stamford (06905) ***(G-8088)***
Apizza Grande......475 238-6928
630 Washington Ave Ste 1 North Haven (06473) ***(G-5905)***
Aplicare Products LLC (HQ)......203 630-0500
550 Research Pkwy Meriden (06450) ***(G-4145)***
Apogee Corporation (PA)......860 963-1976
5 Highland Dr Putnam (06260) ***(G-7030)***
Apogee Corporation......860 632-3550
154 West St Ste C Cromwell (06416) ***(G-1687)***
App Polonia LLC......860 747-3397
95 Metacomet Rd Plainville (06062) ***(G-6771)***
App Polonia Trading, Plainville *Also called App Polonia LLC* ***(G-6771)***
Apparel Solutions Incorporated......203 226-8600
67 Poland St Ste 4 Bridgeport (06605) ***(G-698)***
Apple John......203 746-3459
1 Hickory Ln New Fairfield (06812) ***(G-5161)***
Apple Hill Woodworking LLC......860 945-6102
155 Apple Hill Dr Watertown (06795) ***(G-9682)***
Apple Homecare Innovations LLC......860 940-5005
15 Beaudry Ln Ste 2 Bloomfield (06002) ***(G-386)***
Apple Leaf......203 988-7262
56 Laydon Ave North Haven (06473) ***(G-5906)***
Apple Publications......860 392-8348
105 Williams Way Tolland (06084) ***(G-8849)***
Apple Valley Candle Company......860 940-1176
25 Ingraham Pl Bristol (06010) ***(G-963)***
Appleton Grp LLC......860 653-1603
2 Connecticut South Dr East Granby (06026) ***(G-2190)***

ALPHABETIC

Applied Advertising Inc — 860 640-0800
71 Newtown Rd Ste 5 Danbury (06810) *(G-1741)*
Applied Biosystems LLC — 781 271-0045
301 Merritt 7 Ste 23 Norwalk (06851) *(G-6071)*
Applied Diamond Coatings LLC — 860 349-3133
30 Ozick Dr Durham (06422) *(G-2137)*
Applied Immunotherapeutics Inc — 203 247-3895
433 W Morris Rd Morris (06763) *(G-4786)*
Applied Laser Solutions Inc — 203 739-0179
28 Commerce Dr Danbury (06810) *(G-1742)*
Applied Microbiology Services — 860 537-3118
7 Deepwood Dr Lebanon (06249) *(G-3847)*
Applied Physical Sciences Corp (HQ) — 860 448-3253
475 Bridge St Ste 100 Groton (06340) *(G-3271)*
Applied Porous Tech Inc — 860 408-9793
2 Tunxis Rd Ste 103 Tariffville (06081) *(G-8744)*
Applied Rubber & Plastics Inc — 860 987-9018
100 Skitchewaug St Windsor (06095) *(G-10363)*
Applied Software — 860 289-9153
905 Main St South Windsor (06074) *(G-7710)*
Apps Screen Printing LLC — 860 938-7596
150 E Aurora St Ste D Waterbury (06708) *(G-9432)*
Appstract Ideas — 860 857-1123
81 Martin Rd Bristol (06010) *(G-964)*
Apricot Home LLC — 203 552-1791
15 Sheffield Way Greenwich (06831) *(G-3121)*
Apricus Inc — 203 889-2667
370 State St Ste 2 North Haven (06473) *(G-5907)*
April Rose Designs — 203 453-1797
69 Boston St Guilford (06437) *(G-3326)*
APS Robotics & Integration LLC — 860 526-1040
500 Main St Ste 9 Deep River (06417) *(G-2084)*
Aptar Inc — 860 489-6249
301 Ella Grasso Ave Torrington (06790) *(G-8897)*
Aptargroup Inc — 203 377-8100
125 Access Rd Stratford (06615) *(G-8569)*
Aptex Corp — 203 743-6412
6 Benson Rd Oxford (06478) *(G-6643)*
Aptuit Global LLC (PA) — 203 660-6000
2 Greenwich Office Park Greenwich (06831) *(G-3122)*
Aqua Blasting Corp — 860 242-8855
2 Northwood Dr Bloomfield (06002) *(G-387)*
Aqua Comfort Technologies LLC (PA) — 203 265-0100
8 Fairfield Blvd Ste 1 Wallingford (06492) *(G-9209)*
Aqua Design Kitchen and Bath S — 203 773-1649
222 Elm St Ste 1 North Haven (06473) *(G-5908)*
Aqua Massage International Inc — 860 536-3735
1101 Noank Ledyard Rd Mystic (06355) *(G-4799)*
Aquacomfort Solutions LLC — 203 265-0100
8 Fairfield Blvd Ste 5 Wallingford (06492) *(G-9210)*
Aquacomfort Solutions LLC — 407 831-1941
15 Burton Dr Cheshire (06410) *(G-1355)*
Aqualogic Inc — 203 248-8959
30 Devine St North Haven (06473) *(G-5909)*
Aquasent, Storrs Mansfield Also called Aquatic Sensor Netwrk Tech LLC *(G-8552)*
Aquastone Graphix Arts & Print, Hartford Also called Aquastone Graphix LLC *(G-3552)*
Aquastone Graphix LLC — 860 206-4935
1477 Park St Ste 8 Hartford (06106) *(G-3552)*
Aquatic Mammals Journal Nfp — 860 514-4704
222 Wolf Neck Rd Stonington (06378) *(G-8522)*
Aquatic Sensor Netwrk Tech LLC — 860 429-4303
30 Beacon Hill Dr Storrs Mansfield (06268) *(G-8552)*
Aquatic Technologies Inc — 203 770-6791
81 Whisconier Rd Brookfield (06804) *(G-1160)*
Aquiline Drones LLC — 860 361-7958
750 Main St Ste 319 Hartford (06103) *(G-3553)*
AR Robinson Printing — 203 961-1787
215 Lawn Ave Stamford (06902) *(G-8089)*
Arabic Bread Bakery — 203 743-4743
13 Well Ave Fl 2 Danbury (06810) *(G-1743)*
Arbon Equipment Corporation — 410 796-5902
29 Griffin Rd S Bloomfield (06002) *(G-388)*
Arbor Computer Systems, Westport Also called Peter Hannan *(G-10140)*
Arbot Software — 860 209-8460
1245 Farmington Ave Fl 2 West Hartford (06107) *(G-9775)*
ARC and Hammer — 860 605-0344
514 Cherry Brook Rd Canton (06019) *(G-1304)*
ARC Dynamics Inc — 860 563-1006
28 Belamose Ave Ste C Rocky Hill (06067) *(G-7221)*
ARC Services — 203 264-0866
190 High Meadow Dr Southbury (06488) *(G-7844)*
Arcade Technology LLC — 203 366-3871
38 Union Ave Bridgeport (06607) *(G-699)*
Arcadia, Stamford Also called Wilson Partitions Inc *(G-8495)*
Arcadia Architectural Pdts Inc — 203 316-8000
110 Viaduct Rd Stamford (06907) *(G-8090)*
Arcat Inc — 203 929-9444
173 Sherman St Fairfield (06824) *(G-2747)*
Arccos Golf LLC — 844 692-7226
700 Canal St Ste 19 Stamford (06902) *(G-8091)*
Arch Parent Inc — 860 336-4856
82 Storrs Rd Willimantic (06226) *(G-10221)*
Archambault Group LLC — 860 635-4006
9 Greenway Dr Cromwell (06416) *(G-1688)*
Archer Sign Service LLC — 203 882-8484
316 Boston Post Rd Milford (06460) *(G-4454)*
Archer Sign Service LLC — 203 377-5362
316 Boston Post Rd Milford (06460) *(G-4455)*
Archer Signs, Milford Also called Archer Sign Service LLC *(G-4454)*
Archer-Daniels-Midland Company — 203 966-4755
49 Locust Ave Ste 104 New Canaan (06840) *(G-5088)*
Archers Only LLC — 860 689-0594
194 Harmony Hill Rd Harwinton (06791) *(G-3720)*
Architectural Door Corp — 203 255-3033
75 N Pine Creek Rd Fairfield (06824) *(G-2748)*
Architectural Outdoor Lighting — 860 659-5795
199 Worthington Rd Glastonbury (06033) *(G-3007)*
Architectural Stone Group LLC — 203 494-5451
9 Island Brook Ave Bridgeport (06606) *(G-700)*
Architectural Supplements LLC — 203 591-5505
567 S Leonard St Bldg 1b Waterbury (06708) *(G-9433)*
Archstreet Designs, Greenwich Also called Alphacom Inc *(G-3117)*
Arconic Inc — 860 379-3314
145 Price Rd Winsted (06098) *(G-10505)*
Arcor Systems LLC — 860 370-9780
4 Kenny Roberts Mem Dr Suffield (06078) *(G-8714)*
Arctime LLC — 203 321-5628
23 W Rocks Rd Norwalk (06851) *(G-6072)*
Ardent Inc (PA) — 860 528-6000
95 Leggett St East Hartford (06108) *(G-2292)*
Ardent Displays & Packaging, East Hartford Also called Ardent Inc *(G-2292)*
Arensky Group Inc — 203 919-1575
12 Coventry Pl Norwalk (06854) *(G-6073)*
Arepas La Orquidea — 203 275-8478
1163 E Main St Bridgeport (06608) *(G-701)*
Argix Direct, South Windsor Also called L T A Group Inc *(G-7785)*
Argo Ems, Clinton Also called Eastern Company *(G-1501)*
Argyle Optics LLC — 203 451-3320
28 Tower St Milford (06460) *(G-4456)*
Arico Engineering Inc — 860 642-7040
841 Route 32 Ste 19 North Franklin (06254) *(G-5870)*
Aristo Data Systems — 203 322-1113
1010 Summer St Ste 102a Stamford (06905) *(G-8092)*
Ark Innovations LLC — 860 674-8800
4a Farmington Chase Cres Farmington (06032) *(G-2878)*
Arkalon Chemical Tech LLC — 352 505-8098
200 Carpenter Ave Ste 211 Meriden (06450) *(G-4146)*
Arkettype — 860 350-4007
221 Danbury Rd Ste L New Milford (06776) *(G-5504)*
Arlene Lewis — 860 887-4265
22 School House Rd Preston (06365) *(G-6981)*
Arm Medical Devices Inc — 860 583-5165
190 Dino Rd Bristol (06010) *(G-965)*
ARM Screen Printing — 860 649-6295
307 E Center St Manchester (06040) *(G-3984)*
Armed & Ready Alarm System — 203 596-0327
112 Fieldwood Rd Waterbury (06704) *(G-9434)*
Armetta LLC — 860 788-2369
90 Industrial Park Rd Middletown (06457) *(G-4317)*
Armor All/STP Products Company (HQ) — 203 205-2900
44 Old Ridgebury Rd # 300 Danbury (06810) *(G-1744)*
Armor All/STP Products Company — 203 205-2900
44 Old Ridgebury Rd Danbury (06810) *(G-1745)*
Armor Box Company LLC — 860 242-9981
29 Woods Rd Bloomfield (06002) *(G-389)*
Armored Auto Group, Danbury Also called Armored Autogroup Inc *(G-1746)*
Armored Autogroup Inc (HQ) — 203 205-2900
44 Old Ridgebury Rd # 300 Danbury (06810) *(G-1746)*
Armored Autogroup Parent Inc (HQ) — 203 205-2900
44 Old Ridgebury Rd # 300 Danbury (06810) *(G-1747)*
Armored Autogroup Sales Inc — 203 205-2900
44 Old Ridgebury Rd # 300 Danbury (06810) *(G-1748)*
Armored Shield Technologies — 714 848-5796
3655 W Mcfadden Ave Redding (06896) *(G-7090)*
Arnco Sign Company — 203 238-1224
1133 S Broad St Wallingford (06492) *(G-9211)*
Arnio Welding LLC — 860 564-7696
12 Water St Central Village (06332) *(G-1335)*
Arnitex LLC — 203 869-1406
110 Orchard St Cos Cob (06807) *(G-1624)*
Arnold Trauth — 203 371-5624
85 Asmara Way Easton (06612) *(G-2546)*
Arnow Silk Screening LLC — 203 964-1963
31 Viaduct Rd Ste 2 Stamford (06907) *(G-8093)*
Aromalite Candle Co LLC — 860 872-1029
242 Tlcttvlle Rd Unit 207 Vernon (06066) *(G-9131)*
Arp Publishing Inc — 888 503-6617
84 Mccormick Ln Middletown (06457) *(G-4318)*
Arp Welding & Repair LLC — 203 924-6811
38 Button Rd Shelton (06484) *(G-7397)*
Arpie Krisie Gems & Jewelry — 203 799-8927
438 Taulman Rd Orange (06477) *(G-6583)*
Arr, Harwinton Also called Advanced Receiver Research *(G-3719)*

Array Systems LLC 203 877-4625
205 Research Dr Ste 4 Milford (06460) ***(G-4457)***
Array Technologies Inc 860 657-8086
21 Sequin Dr Glastonbury (06033) ***(G-3008)***
Arrayent Health LLC 973 568-0323
1266 E Main St Ste 700r Stamford (06902) ***(G-8094)***
Arrigoni Design, Clinton *Also called Arrigoni Distributors Ltd LLC* ***(G-1491)***
Arrigoni Distributors Ltd LLC 860 669-6637
41 Commerce St Clinton (06413) ***(G-1491)***
Arrigoni Winery 860 342-1999
209 Sand Hill Rd Portland (06480) ***(G-6950)***
Arris Technology Inc 678 473-8493
15 Sterling Dr Wallingford (06492) ***(G-9212)***
Arrochar Software LLC 203 987-5412
45 Turkey Hill Rd Newtown (06470) ***(G-5728)***
Arrow Concrete Products Inc (PA) 860 653-5063
560 Salmon Brook St Granby (06035) ***(G-3106)***
Arrow Diversified Tooling Inc 860 872-9072
17 Pinney St Ellington (06029) ***(G-2576)***
Arrow Engraving & Sign LLC 860 349-1788
9 Commerce Cir Unit E Durham (06422) ***(G-2138)***
Arrow Lock Manufacturing Co 203 603-5959
110 Sargent Dr New Haven (06511) ***(G-5233)***
Arrow Manufacturing Company 860 589-3900
16 Jeannette St Bristol (06010) ***(G-966)***
Arrow Marketing Inc 203 375-7541
7365 Main St Ste 8 Stratford (06614) ***(G-8570)***
Arrow Printers Inc 203 734-7272
311 Main St Ansonia (06401) ***(G-21)***
Arrow Space Deburring 860 683-0879
610 Hayden Station Rd B Windsor (06095) ***(G-10364)***
Arrow Tool Division, Wethersfield *Also called Merritt Machine Company* ***(G-10211)***
Arrow Window Shade Mfg Co 860 956-3570
1252 Berlin Tpke Wethersfield (06109) ***(G-10180)***
Arrow Window Shade Mfg Co Mrdn 860 563-4035
47 Oxford St Wethersfield (06109) ***(G-10181)***
Arrowhead Group LLC 954 771-5115
159 Ethan Dr Windsor (06095) ***(G-10365)***
ARS Products LLC 860 564-0208
43 Lathrop Road Ext Plainfield (06374) ***(G-6739)***
Art Craft Signs 203 212-3980
1697 Barnum Ave Bridgeport (06610) ***(G-702)***
Art Metal Industries LLC 203 733-3092
564 Danbury Rd 1 New Milford (06776) ***(G-5505)***
Art Metal Industries AMI 860 799-5575
564 Danbury Rd New Milford (06776) ***(G-5506)***
Art of Perfection, Brookfield *Also called Revive Beauty and Wellness LLC* ***(G-1218)***
Art of Wellbeing LLC 917 453-3009
230 Saddle Hill Rd Stamford (06903) ***(G-8095)***
Art Q Tech Signs 203 874-6504
282 Woodmont Rd Ste J1 Milford (06460) ***(G-4458)***
Art Screen 203 744-1991
12 Francis J Clarke Cir Bethel (06801) ***(G-258)***
Art Signs 860 871-8361
8 Middle Butcher Rd Ellington (06029) ***(G-2577)***
Artchrist Com Inc 203 245-2246
70 Wall St Unit Rr Madison (06443) ***(G-3907)***
Artech Lubricants, Bethel *Also called Artech Packaging LLC* ***(G-259)***
Artech Packaging LLC 845 858-8558
18 Taylor Ave Ste 2 Bethel (06801) ***(G-259)***
Arteffects Incorporated 860 242-0031
27 Britton Dr Bloomfield (06002) ***(G-390)***
Artemis Pine Candle Co LLC 203 245-5170
182 Opening Hill Rd Madison (06443) ***(G-3908)***
Artemisia Inc 917 797-7644
35 Sill Ln Old Lyme (06371) ***(G-6489)***
Artes Magazine LLC 203 530-9811
242 Greens Farm Rd Branford (06405) ***(G-547)***
Artful Framer LLC 860 678-1321
195 W Main St Ste 15 Avon (06001) ***(G-76)***
Artfx Signs, Bloomfield *Also called Arteffects Incorporated* ***(G-390)***
Arthur G Byrne Co Inc 203 461-8805
88 Erskine Rd Stamford (06903) ***(G-8096)***
Arthur G Russell Company Inc 860 583-4109
750 Clark Ave Bristol (06010) ***(G-967)***
Arthur I Platt Inc 203 874-0091
160 Rock Ln Milford (06460) ***(G-4459)***
Arthur J Hurley Company 860 257-5505
60 Meadow St East Hartford (06108) ***(G-2293)***
Arthur Rodgers 860 967-4598
7 Jessica Ln Ledyard (06339) ***(G-3867)***
Artic Oil 860 693-6925
321 Albany Tpke Canton (06019) ***(G-1305)***
Articrafts 203 618-1715
3 Sound View Ter Greenwich (06830) ***(G-3123)***
Artisan Bread & Products LLC 914 843-4401
13 Dry Hill Rd Norwalk (06851) ***(G-6074)***
Artisan Hand Tools Inc 203 308-2063
4 Hershey Dr Ansonia (06401) ***(G-22)***
Artist and Craftsman 203 330-0459
1001 Main St Bridgeport (06604) ***(G-703)***
Artista Studio Monument 203 333-9224
500 Bostwick Ave Bridgeport (06605) ***(G-704)***
Artistic Hardwood Floors CT 860 537-5334
92 Pinebrook Rd Colchester (06415) ***(G-1540)***
Artistic Iron Works LLC 203 838-9200
11 Reynolds St Norwalk (06855) ***(G-6075)***
Artistic Sign Language LLC 203 245-8213
114 Bradley Rd Madison (06443) ***(G-3909)***
Arts In Architecture, New Milford *Also called Zsiba & Smolover Ltd* ***(G-5610)***
Arts of Stone LLC 860 355-9468
362 Danbury Rd New Milford (06776) ***(G-5507)***
Artscreen, Bethel *Also called Art Screen* ***(G-258)***
Arturo Milite and Spinella Bky, Waterbury *Also called Milite Bakery* ***(G-9543)***
Artwork By Nora LLC 860 963-0723
239 Kearney Rd Pomfret Center (06259) ***(G-6937)***
Artwork Embroidery 860 620-0456
36 Long Bottom Rd Southington (06489) ***(G-7892)***
Arvinas Inc (PA) 203 535-1456
395 Winchester Ave New Haven (06511) ***(G-5234)***
ASAP, Stamford *Also called American Solar & Altermative* ***(G-8078)***
ASAP Machine Sp & Fabrication 860 564-4114
89 Mill Brook Rd Plainfield (06374) ***(G-6740)***
ASAP Mfg Co LLC 860 738-4831
44 Taylor Rd Winsted (06063) ***(G-10506)***
Ascend Elevator Inc 215 703-0358
212 W Newberry Rd Bloomfield (06002) ***(G-391)***
Ascentech LLC 860 526-8903
127 Goose Hill Rd Chester (06412) ***(G-1463)***
Ascon Products Co 860 439-1305
2 Ferry St New London (06320) ***(G-5456)***
Ascon Products Co, The, New London *Also called Ascon Products Co* ***(G-5456)***
Asct LLC 860 349-1121
30 Ozick Dr Durham (06422) ***(G-2139)***
Ase, Orange *Also called American Seal and Engrg Co Inc* ***(G-6581)***
Asea Brown Boveri Inc (HQ) 203 750-2200
501 Merritt 7 Norwalk (06851) ***(G-6076)***
Asha 203 253-0146
9 Pecksland Rd Greenwich (06831) ***(G-3124)***
Ashcrft-Ngano Kiki Hldings Inc (HQ) 203 378-8281
250 E Main St Stratford (06614) ***(G-8571)***
Ashcroft Inc (HQ) 203 378-8281
250 E Main St Stratford (06614) ***(G-8572)***
Ashcroft Inc 203 378-8281
250 E Main St Stratford (06614) ***(G-8573)***
Ashkaar Publishers LLC 203 248-4804
325 Mansfield Rd North Haven (06473) ***(G-5910)***
Ashlawn Farm Store (PA) 860 434-3636
78 Bill Hill Rd Old Lyme (06371) ***(G-6490)***
Asi - A Soft Idea, Bridgeport *Also called Apparel Solutions Incorporated* ***(G-698)***
Asi Modulex, East Berlin *Also called Wad Inc* ***(G-2179)***
Asi Sign Systems Inc 860 828-3331
100 Clark Dr East Berlin (06023) ***(G-2162)***
Asml Us LLC 203 761-4000
77 Danbury Rd Wilton (06897) ***(G-10270)***
Aspecta 855 400-7732
15 Oakwood Ave Norwalk (06850) ***(G-6077)***
Aspetuck Brew Lab LLC 203 256-1902
167 Woods End Rd Fairfield (06824) ***(G-2749)***
Assa Inc (HQ) 203 624-5225
110 Sargent Dr New Haven (06511) ***(G-5235)***
Assa Inc (HQ) 800 235-7482
110 Sargent Dr New Haven (06511) ***(G-5236)***
Assa Abloy Accss & Edrss Hrdwr 860 225-7411
225 Episcopal Rd Berlin (06037) ***(G-160)***
Assa Abloy Inc., New Haven *Also called Assa Inc* ***(G-5235)***
Assa Abloy USA, New Haven *Also called Sargent Manufacturing Company* ***(G-5389)***
Assa High Security Locks, New Haven *Also called Assa Inc* ***(G-5236)***
Asselin Electric LLC 860 379-3056
228 Smith Hill Rd Winsted (06098) ***(G-10507)***
Asset Vantage Inc 475 218-2639
1 Dock St Ste 201 Stamford (06902) ***(G-8097)***
Assoc Stucco 860 221-5791
31 Wood Creek Rd Burlington (06013) ***(G-1260)***
Associated Chemicals & Abr Inc 203 481-7235
31 Business Park Dr Ste 3 Branford (06405) ***(G-548)***
Associated Welding & Radiator, Farmington *Also called Associated Welding Process* ***(G-2879)***
Associated Welding Process 860 677-0671
1091 Farmington Ave Farmington (06032) ***(G-2879)***
Associated X-Ray Corp (PA) 203 466-2446
246 Dodge Ave East Haven (06512) ***(G-2412)***
Associates Inc Bedford 203 846-0230
401 Merritt 7 Norwalk (06851) ***(G-6078)***
Asti Company Inc 860 482-2675
953 S Main St Torrington (06790) ***(G-8898)***
Astralis Rocketry Corp 203 254-0427
4 Davis Ln Westport (06880) ***(G-10058)***
Astralite Inc 203 775-0172
20 Pocono Rd Brookfield (06804) ***(G-1161)***
Astro Aircom LLC 860 688-3320
610 Hayden Station Rd Windsor (06095) ***(G-10366)***
Astro Industries Inc 860 828-6304
819 Farmington Ave Unit A Berlin (06037) ***(G-161)***

ALPHABETIC

Astro Welding Inc 860 289-6272
11 Oakland Ave East Hartford (06108) *(G-2294)*
Astrophonic Corp America 203 853-9300
149 Woodward Ave Norwalk (06854) *(G-6079)*
Asylum Distillery 203 209-0146
105 Waterville Rd Southport (06890) *(G-7999)*
At Industries LLC 860 739-6639
31 Greencliff Dr Niantic (06357) *(G-5801)*
AT&T, New Haven *Also called Southern Neng Telecom Corp (G-5401)*
Atco Wire Rope and Indus Sup 203 239-1632
11 Leonardo Dr North Haven (06473) *(G-5911)*
Atech Industries LLC 203 887-4900
879 Robert Treat Ext Orange (06477) *(G-6584)*
Atfo, Westport *Also called American Trade Fairs Org (G-10055)*
Athens Industries Inc 860 621-8957
220 West St Plantsville (06479) *(G-6885)*
ATI Flat Rlled Pdts Hldngs LLC 203 756-7414
271 Railroad Hill St Waterbury (06708) *(G-9435)*
ATI Forged Products, East Hartford *Also called ATI Ladish Machining Inc (G-2295)*
ATI Ladish Machining Inc (HQ) 860 688-3688
311 Prestige Park Rd East Hartford (06108) *(G-2295)*
ATI Ladish Machining Inc 860 688-3688
34 S Satellite Rd South Windsor (06074) *(G-7711)*
ATI Ladish Machining Inc 860 688-3688
311 Prestige Park Rd East Hartford (06108) *(G-2296)*
ATI New England 860 358-9698
14 Alcap Rdg Cromwell (06416) *(G-1689)*
ATI Specialty Materials, New Britain *Also called Tdy Industries LLC (G-5072)*
Atk Golf Services 203 615-2099
25 Hills Point Rd Trumbull (06611) *(G-9000)*
Atlantech Manufacturing Co Inc (PA) 203 500-6880
89 Eastern Steel Rd Milford (06460) *(G-4460)*
Atlantic Coast Polymers Inc 860 564-5641
12 East Pkwy Plainfield (06374) *(G-6741)*
Atlantic Eqp Installers Inc 203 284-0402
55 N Plains Industrial Rd Wallingford (06492) *(G-9213)*
Atlantic Fabricating Co Inc 860 291-9882
71 Edwin Rd South Windsor (06074) *(G-7712)*
Atlantic Group Connecticut LLC 203 847-0000
501 Merritt 7 Ste 1 Norwalk (06851) *(G-6080)*
Atlantic Inertial Systems, Cheshire *Also called Ais Global Holdings LLC (G-1349)*
Atlantic Inertial Systems Inc (HQ) 203 250-3500
250 Knotter Dr Cheshire (06410) *(G-1356)*
Atlantic Inertial Systems Inc 203 250-3500
250 Knotter Dr Cheshire (06410) *(G-1357)*
Atlantic Law Book Company, The, West Hartford *Also called Peter Kelsey Publishing Inc (G-9843)*
Atlantic Millwork, North Haven *Also called Elm City Manufacturing LLC (G-5936)*
Atlantic Outboard Inc 860 399-6773
475 Boston Post Rd Westbrook (06498) *(G-9991)*
Atlantic Pipe Corporation 860 747-5557
60 N Washington St Plainville (06062) *(G-6772)*
Atlantic Precision Spring Inc 860 583-1864
125 Ronzo Rd Bristol (06010) *(G-968)*
Atlantic Sail & Canvas Co 203 254-1315
1962 Elm St Stratford (06615) *(G-8574)*
Atlantic Sensors & Contrls LLC 203 878-8118
301 Brewster Rd Milford (06460) *(G-4461)*
Atlantic Street Capitl MGT LLC (PA) 203 428-3150
281 Tresser Blvd Fl 6 Stamford (06901) *(G-8098)*
Atlantic Vent & Eqp Co Inc 860 635-1300
125 Sebethe Dr Cromwell (06416) *(G-1690)*
Atlantic Woodcraft Inc 860 749-4887
199 Moody Rd Enfield (06082) *(G-2616)*
Atlas Agi Holdings LLC 203 622-9138
100 Northfield St Greenwich (06830) *(G-3125)*
Atlas Filtri North America LLC 203 284-0080
1068 N Farms Rd Ste 3 Wallingford (06492) *(G-9214)*
Atlas Hobbing and Tool Co Inc 860 870-9226
20 Mountain St Vernon Rockville (06066) *(G-9160)*
Atlas Industrial Services LLC 203 315-4538
30 Ne Industrial Rd Branford (06405) *(G-549)*
Atlas Metal and Wood Works LLC 805 450-7031
2 Auburn Rd West Hartford (06119) *(G-9776)*
Atlas Metal Works LLC 860 282-1030
48 Commerce Way South Windsor (06074) *(G-7713)*
Atlas Metallizing Inc 860 827-9777
5 East St New Britain (06051) *(G-4946)*
Atlas Precision Mfg LLC 860 290-9114
508 Burnham St South Windsor (06074) *(G-7714)*
Atlas Stamping & Mfg Corp 860 757-3233
729 N Mountain Rd Newington (06111) *(G-5629)*
Atmi, Inc., Danbury *Also called Entegris Prof Solutions Inc (G-1815)*
Atmosair, Fairfield *Also called Clean Air Group Inc (G-2764)*
Atp Industries LLC (PA) 860 479-5007
75 Northwest Dr Plainville (06062) *(G-6773)*
Atticus Bakery LLC 203 562-9007
360 James St New Haven (06513) *(G-5237)*
Au New Haven LLC 203 468-0342
30 Lenox St New Haven (06513) *(G-5238)*
Auburn Manufacturing Company 860 346-6677
29 Stack St Middletown (06457) *(G-4319)*
Audioworks Inc 203 876-1133
260 Old Gate Ln Milford (06460) *(G-4462)*
Audubon Copy Shppe of Firfield 203 259-4311
540 Barnum Ave Ste 4 Bridgeport (06608) *(G-705)*
Auras Oracle 860 308-0893
830 Boston Tpke Coventry (06238) *(G-1644)*
Austin Electronics, Chester *Also called Whelen Engineering Company Inc (G-1486)*
Austin Organs Incorporated 860 522-8293
156 Woodland St Hartford (06105) *(G-3554)*
Austin Powder Company 860 564-5466
332 Ekonk Hill Rd Sterling (06377) *(G-8507)*
Austin Rubber Stamps, Kensington *Also called Academy Printing Service (G-3803)*
Autac Incorporated (PA) 203 481-3444
25 Thompson Rd Branford (06405) *(G-550)*
Autac Incorporated 203 481-3444
25 Thompson Rd Branford (06405) *(G-551)*
Auto Merchandising Depot, Weston *Also called Automotive Coop Couponing Inc (G-10018)*
Auto Suture Company Australia 203 845-1000
150 Glover Ave Norwalk (06850) *(G-6081)*
Auto Suture Company UK 203 845-1000
150 Glover Ave Norwalk (06850) *(G-6082)*
Auto Suture Russia Inc 203 845-1000
150 Glover Ave Norwalk (06850) *(G-6083)*
Autobond Eastern 860 383-8982
60 Lavander Rd Pleasant Valley (06063) *(G-6920)*
Automar Ne LLC 203 793-7630
329 Main St Ste 108 Wallingford (06492) *(G-9215)*
Automatech Inc 860 673-5940
21 Westview Ter Unionville (06085) *(G-9111)*
Automated Graphic Systems Inc 860 659-1076
287 Great Pond Rd South Glastonbury (06073) *(G-7679)*
Automated Mailing Services LLC 203 439-2763
1687 Reinhard Rd Cheshire (06410) *(G-1358)*
Automatic Machine Products 860 346-7064
40 Liberty St Middletown (06457) *(G-4320)*
Automatic Rolls of New England, Dayville *Also called Northeast Foods Inc (G-2067)*
Automation Inc 860 236-5991
707 Oakwood Ave West Hartford (06110) *(G-9777)*
Automation & Servo Tech 860 658-5172
15 Hunting Ridge Dr Simsbury (06070) *(G-7612)*
Automation Controls 203 888-9330
127 Hogs Back Rd Oxford (06478) *(G-6644)*
Automotive Coop Couponing Inc 203 227-2722
27 Cardinal Rd Weston (06883) *(G-10018)*
Automotive Machine 860 627-9244
55 Newberry Rd East Windsor (06088) *(G-2482)*
Autopart International Inc 203 931-9189
732 Washington Ave West Haven (06516) *(G-9885)*
Autumn Colors 860 822-6568
453 Scotland Rd Norwich (06360) *(G-6407)*
Avalanche Downhill Racing Inc 860 537-4306
12 Davidson Rd Colchester (06415) *(G-1541)*
Avalon Advanced Tech Repr Inc 860 254-5442
59 Newberry Rd East Windsor (06088) *(G-2483)*
Avalon It Systems 203 323-7000
35 6th St Stamford (06905) *(G-8099)*
Avara Pharmaceutical Svcs Inc (HQ) 203 918-1659
401 Merritt 7 Norwalk (06851) *(G-6084)*
Avara US Holdings LLC (PA) 203 655-1333
101 Merritt 7 Norwalk (06851) *(G-6085)*
Avatar, East Windsor *Also called Avalon Advanced Tech Repr Inc (G-2483)*
Avaya Inc 203 234-9300
38 Brockett Farm Rd North Haven (06473) *(G-5912)*
Avenue Awards, Derby *Also called Young Flan LLC (G-2134)*
Avery Abrasives Inc 203 372-3513
2225 Reservoir Ave Ste 1 Trumbull (06611) *(G-9001)*
Averys Beverage LLC 860 224-0830
520 Corbin Ave New Britain (06052) *(G-4947)*
Aviation Pro Pages LLC 860 910-9336
3033 Gold Star Hwy Mystic (06355) *(G-4800)*
Avitus Orthopaedics Inc 860 637-9922
400 Farmington Ave R2826 Farmington (06032) *(G-2880)*
Avolon Aerospace New York Inc 203 663-5490
700 Canal St 2nd Stamford (06902) *(G-8100)*
Avrio Health LP 888 827-0624
201 Tresser Blvd Stamford (06901) *(G-8101)*
Avt, Simsbury *Also called Advanced Vacuum Technology Inc (G-7609)*
Awm LLC 860 386-1000
100 D Neil Hagen Dr Windsor Locks (06096) *(G-10473)*
Awnair, Stafford Springs *Also called Tetrault & Sons Inc (G-8042)*
Awnings Are US, Bethel *Also called Evans Fabrication (G-298)*
Awnings Plus LLC 860 496-7996
148 Sherwood Dr Torrington (06790) *(G-8899)*
Axel Plastics RES Labs Inc 718 672-8300
50 Cambridge Dr Monroe (06468) *(G-4694)*
Axels Custom Woodworking LLC 203 869-1317
45 Rodwell Ave Greenwich (06830) *(G-3126)*
Axerra Networks Inc 203 906-3570
30 Bear Run Woodbury (06798) *(G-10625)*
Axerra Networks Limited, Woodbury *Also called Axerra Networks Inc (G-10625)*
Axiomx Inc 203 208-1034
688 E Main St Branford (06405) *(G-552)*

Axis Laser ...203 284-9455
7 Atwater Pl Wallingford (06492) *(G-9216)*
Axis Wood Works LLC ...203 481-4946
41 Yowago Ave Branford (06405) *(G-553)*
Axol Media Inc ...650 315-1743
1502 Mill Pond Dr South Windsor (06074) *(G-7715)*
AZ Copy Center Inc ...860 621-7325
298 Captain Lewis Dr Southington (06489) *(G-7893)*
AZ Woodworking LLC ...203 595-9063
14 Dora St Apt 2 Stamford (06902) *(G-8102)*
Aztec Industries LLC ...860 343-1960
695 High St Middletown (06457) *(G-4321)*
Aztec Woodworking ...203 272-3814
384 Moss Farms Rd Cheshire (06410) *(G-1359)*
Aztech Engineering LLC ...860 659-8892
365 Weir St Glastonbury (06033) *(G-3009)*
B & A Company Inc ...203 876-7527
160 Wampus Ln Milford (06460) *(G-4463)*
B & A Design Inc ...860 871-0134
255 Bamforth Rd Vernon Rockville (06066) *(G-9161)*
B & B Equipment LLC ...860 342-5773
80 Main St Ste D Portland (06480) *(G-6951)*
B & B Ventures Ltd Lblty Co ...203 481-1700
550 E Main St Ste 27 Branford (06405) *(G-554)*
B & C Industries ...203 572-0265
3125 Broadbridge Ave Stratford (06614) *(G-8575)*
B & C Sand & Gravel Company ...203 335-6640
412 Housatonic Ave Bridgeport (06604) *(G-706)*
B & C Upholstery, East Hartford *Also called Reid Interiors* *(G-2364)*
B & D Lures ...860 861-6530
11 Hillcrest Ave Ledyard (06339) *(G-3868)*
B & D Machine Inc ...860 871-9226
30 Industrial Park Rd E Tolland (06084) *(G-8850)*
B & E Juices Inc ...203 333-1802
550 Knowlton St Bridgeport (06608) *(G-707)*
B & F Design Incorporated ...860 357-4317
120 Production Ct New Britain (06051) *(G-4948)*
B & F Electric Motors LLC ...203 359-2626
156 Magee Ave Stamford (06902) *(G-8103)*
B & F Machine Co Inc ...860 225-6349
145 Edgewood Ave New Britain (06051) *(G-4949)*
B & G Forming Technology Inc ...203 235-2169
956 Old Colony Rd Meriden (06451) *(G-4147)*
B & G Industries LLC ...860 571-8873
25 Knight St Wethersfield (06109) *(G-10182)*
B & L Tool and Machine Company ...860 747-2721
76 Northwest Dr Plainville (06062) *(G-6774)*
B & M Fabrication LLC ...860 379-5444
172 Florence St Winsted (06098) *(G-10508)*
B & P Plating Equipment LLC ...860 589-5799
74 Broderick Rd Bristol (06010) *(G-969)*
B & R Enterprises, Middletown *Also called Bruce Burgess* *(G-4328)*
B & R Machine Works Inc ...203 798-0595
23 Henry St Bethel (06801) *(G-260)*
B & R Stair ...860 582-6584
1 Glenn St Bristol (06010) *(G-970)*
B & S Machine Inc ...860 829-0813
54 Clark Dr Ste B East Berlin (06023) *(G-2163)*
B 9 Air Quality Services LLC ...203 387-1709
121 N Plains Industrial R Wallingford (06492) *(G-9217)*
B and G Enterprise LLC (PA) ...203 562-7232
178 Chapel St New Haven (06513) *(G-5239)*
B C T, Naugatuck *Also called Business Cards Tomorrow Inc* *(G-4864)*
B Douglass Custom Mllwk LLC ...860 338-9305
80 Great Swamp Rd Glastonbury (06033) *(G-3010)*
B E C Machinetool Inc ...860 738-9432
104 Groppo Dr Winsted (06098) *(G-10509)*
B H Davis Co ...860 923-2771
227 Riverside Dr Thompson (06277) *(G-8829)*
B H S Industries Ltd ...203 284-9764
23 N Plains Industrial Rd # 3 Wallingford (06492) *(G-9218)*
B H Shoe Holdings Inc (HQ) ...203 661-2424
124 W Putnam Ave Ste 1 Greenwich (06830) *(G-3127)*
B L C Investments Inc ...203 877-1888
228a Rowe Ave Milford (06461) *(G-4464)*
B L R, Old Saybrook *Also called Bff Holdings Inc* *(G-6523)*
B M I South, Thomaston *Also called Biedermann Mfg Inds Inc* *(G-8781)*
B P Mug, West Hartford *Also called Business & Prof Microcompter* *(G-9780)*
B S Clyde's Cider Mill, Mystic *Also called Clydes Cider Mill* *(G-4807)*
B S T Systems Inc ...860 564-4078
78 Plainfield Pike Plainfield (06374) *(G-6742)*
B T Building Systems, Southport *Also called Thomas Bernhard Building Sys* *(G-8013)*
B T S Graphics LLC ...860 274-6422
36 Zoar Ave Ste 2 Oakville (06779) *(G-6449)*
B T Welding ...860 537-6197
121 Van Cedarfield Rd Colchester (06415) *(G-1542)*
B&B Logging LLC ...860 982-2425
298 Brainard Hill Rd Higganum (06441) *(G-3760)*
B&C Kitchen and Bath, Enfield *Also called Atlantic Woodcraft Inc* *(G-2616)*
B&D Industries LLC ...860 604-2404
157 Lttle Stannard Bch Rd Westbrook (06498) *(G-9992)*
B&N Aerospace Inc ...860 665-0134
44 Rockwell Rd Newington (06111) *(G-5630)*
B&R Sand and Gravel ...860 464-5099
1358 Baldwin Hill Rd Gales Ferry (06335) *(G-2981)*
B&T Screw Machine Co Inc ...860 314-4410
571 Broad St Bristol (06010) *(G-971)*
B-E Industries ...203 357-8055
225 Pinewood Rd Stamford (06903) *(G-8104)*
B-P Products Inc ...203 288-0200
100 Sanford St Hamden (06514) *(G-3416)*
B-Sweet LLC ...203 452-0499
444 Main St Ste C Monroe (06468) *(G-4695)*
B/E Aerospace Inc ...203 380-5000
650 Long Beach Blvd Stratford (06615) *(G-8576)*
Baa Creations ...860 464-1339
13 Lambtown Rd Ledyard (06339) *(G-3869)*
Babcock & King Incorporated (PA) ...203 336-7989
750 Commerce Dr Fairfield (06825) *(G-2750)*
Baby Knits and More ...860 485-0146
121 Delay Rd Harwinton (06791) *(G-3721)*
Back Country Graphics ...203 531-5878
1147 King St Greenwich (06831) *(G-3128)*
Backyard Candles LLC ...860 644-9561
116 Debbie Dr South Windsor (06074) *(G-7716)*
Bactana Animal Health, Farmington *Also called Bactana Corp* *(G-2881)*
Bactana Corp ...203 716-1230
400 Farmington Ave Farmington (06032) *(G-2881)*
Bae Systems Applied Intel Inc ...203 323-0066
21 Harbor View Ave Stamford (06902) *(G-8105)*
Baena Ben & Matthew, Bridgeport *Also called Ben Baena & Son* *(G-710)*
Bagel Boys Inc (PA) ...860 657-4400
85 Nutmeg Ln Glastonbury (06033) *(G-3011)*
Bagela Usa LLC ...203 944-0525
70 Platt Rd Shelton (06484) *(G-7398)*
Bagelman III Inc ...203 792-0030
40 1/2 Padanaram Rd Danbury (06811) *(G-1749)*
Baghai Shahin ...203 268-6287
95 Cranbury Dr Trumbull (06611) *(G-9002)*
Bagogames LLC ...860 801-7462
79 Lewis St Torrington (06790) *(G-8900)*
Bahres Welding ...860 693-4950
248 Albany Tpke Canton (06019) *(G-1306)*
Bailey Avenue Kitchens ...203 438-4868
904 Ethan Allen Hwy Ridgefield (06877) *(G-7118)*
Baingan LLC ...203 924-2626
94 River Rd Shelton (06484) *(G-7399)*
Bakelite N Sumitomo Amer Inc (HQ) ...860 645-3851
24 Mill St Manchester (06042) *(G-3985)*
Baker Graphics Corporation ...203 226-6928
1753 Post Rd E Westport (06880) *(G-10059)*
Baker Grphics Reproduction Ctr, Westport *Also called Baker Graphics Corporation* *(G-10059)*
Bakers Architectural Wdwkg LLC ...203 483-3173
184 N Main St Branford (06405) *(G-555)*
Bakery Engineering/Winkler Inc ...203 929-8630
2 Trap Falls Rd Ste 105 Shelton (06484) *(G-7400)*
Bal International Inc ...203 359-6775
281 Tresser Blvd Fl 12 Stamford (06901) *(G-8106)*
Balding Precision Inc ...203 878-9135
61 Woodmont Rd Milford (06460) *(G-4465)*
Baldwin Cooke, New Hartford *Also called Executive Greetings Inc* *(G-5190)*
Baldwin Graphic Systems Inc ...203 925-1100
12 Commerce Dr Shelton (06484) *(G-7401)*
Baldwin Lawn Furniture LLC ...860 347-1306
440 Middlefield St Ste 1 Middletown (06457) *(G-4322)*
Baldwin Thread Rolling ...860 283-4948
40 Hillside Ave Thomaston (06787) *(G-8779)*
Balfor Industries Inc ...203 828-6473
327 Riggs St Oxford (06478) *(G-6645)*
Ball & Roller Bearing Co LLC ...860 355-4161
46 Old State Rd Ste 4 New Milford (06776) *(G-5508)*
Ball Supply Corporation ...860 673-3364
52 Old Mill Rd Avon (06001) *(G-77)*
Balsam Woods Farm ...860 265-1800
4 Clinton St Stafford Springs (06076) *(G-8018)*
Baltasar & Sons Inc ...203 723-0425
186 Sheridan Dr Naugatuck (06770) *(G-4860)*
Bam Custom Printing ...888 583-6690
51a Armstrong Rd Shelton (06484) *(G-7402)*
Bam Electric LLC ...203 595-0008
12 Sandy Ln Stamford (06905) *(G-8107)*
Bank Sails, Norwalk *Also called Mbm Sales* *(G-6252)*
Banner & Awning Works, Oakville *Also called Banner Works* *(G-6450)*
Banner Works ...203 597-9999
15 Rockland Ave Oakville (06779) *(G-6450)*
Bantam Manufacturing Company, Bantam *Also called Whitebeck John* *(G-128)*
Bantam Sheet Metal ...860 567-9690
1160 Bantam Rd Bantam (06750) *(G-123)*
Baobab Asset Management LLC ...203 340-5700
2 Greenwich Office Park # 300 Greenwich (06831) *(G-3129)*
Bar Co American, North Haven *Also called American Wood Products* *(G-5903)*

ALPHABETIC

Bar Industries LLC ALPHABETIC SECTION

Bar Industries LLC 203 729-4490
68 Radnor Ave Naugatuck (06770) ***(G-4861)***
Bar Plating Inc 203 630-1046
30 Powers Dr Ste 7 Meriden (06451) ***(G-4148)***
Bar Work Manufacturing Co Inc 203 753-4103
1198 Highland Ave Waterbury (06708) ***(G-9436)***
Bar-Plate Manufacturing Co 203 397-0033
1180 Sherman Ave Hamden (06514) ***(G-3417)***
Bara Essentials LLC 203 428-1786
3164 Broadbridge Ave Stratford (06614) ***(G-8577)***
Barbara Garelick Enterprises 203 855-9897
280 Richards Ave Norwalk (06850) ***(G-6086)***
Barbara Jones 203 596-9219
31 Granger St Waterbury (06705) ***(G-9437)***
Barbara McKie, Old Lyme *Also called Graphic Memories By McKie* ***(G-6511)***
Barcello Development Co 860 635-7676
160 Greenview Ter Middletown (06457) ***(G-4323)***
Barclay-Davis Enterprises LLC 860 578-9563
306 Sigourney St 2s Hartford (06105) ***(G-3555)***
Barco Industries New England 860 798-8258
224 Eastern Blvd Glastonbury (06033) ***(G-3012)***
Bardell Office Sty & Sups, East Haven *Also called Bardell Printing Corp* ***(G-2413)***
Bardell Printing Corp 203 469-2441
42 Michael St East Haven (06513) ***(G-2413)***
Barden Corporation, The, Danbury *Also called Schaeffler Aerospace USA Corp* ***(G-1936)***
Baremore Canvas LLC 860 691-1402
157 Chesterfield Rd East Lyme (06333) ***(G-2463)***
Baretta Provision Inc 860 828-0802
172 Commerce St East Berlin (06023) ***(G-2164)***
Bargain News Free Classified A 203 377-3000
720 Barnum Avenue Cutoff Stratford (06614) ***(G-8578)***
Barile Printers LLC 860 224-0127
43 Viets St New Britain (06053) ***(G-4950)***
Barker Advg Specialty Co Inc (PA) 203 272-2222
27 Realty Dr Cheshire (06410) ***(G-1360)***
Barker Screen Printers, Meriden *Also called Multiprints Inc* ***(G-4207)***
Barker Specialty Co, Cheshire *Also called Barker Advg Specialty Co Inc* ***(G-1360)***
Barker Steel LLC 860 282-1860
30 Talbot Ln South Windsor (06074) ***(G-7717)***
Barlo Manufacturing 203 481-3426
4 Beaver Rd Ste 1 Branford (06405) ***(G-556)***
Barlow Metal Stamping Inc 860 583-1387
2 Barlow St Bristol (06010) ***(G-972)***
Barn Beam Co of Neng LLC 860 488-0317
23 Old Northfield Rd Northfield (06778) ***(G-6042)***
Barnard-Maine Ltd 860 535-9485
1 Cross St Stonington (06378) ***(G-8523)***
Barnes Aerospace, Windsor *Also called Barnes Group Inc* ***(G-10367)***
Barnes Aerospace W Chester Div, Bristol *Also called Barnes Group Inc* ***(G-975)***
Barnes Concrete Co Inc 860 928-7242
873 Providence Pike Putnam (06260) ***(G-7031)***
Barnes Group Inc (PA) 860 583-7070
123 Main St Bristol (06010) ***(G-973)***
Barnes Group Inc 860 298-7740
169 Kennedy Rd Windsor (06095) ***(G-10367)***
Barnes Group Inc 860 582-9581
18 Main St Bristol (06010) ***(G-974)***
Barnes Group Inc 860 653-5531
7 Connecticut South Dr East Granby (06026) ***(G-2191)***
Barnes Group Inc 860 298-7740
80 Scott Swamp Rd Farmington (06032) ***(G-2882)***
Barnes Group Inc 513 759-3503
123 Main St Bristol (06010) ***(G-975)***
Barnes Technical Products LLC 203 931-8852
15 High St New Haven (06510) ***(G-5240)***
Barneys Sign Service Inc 203 878-3763
45 Seymour St Ste 3 Stratford (06615) ***(G-8579)***
Barnum Wash & Dry 203 870-6099
2370 Barnum Ave Stratford (06615) ***(G-8580)***
Baron & Young Co Inc 860 589-3235
400 Middle St Ste 13 Bristol (06010) ***(G-976)***
Baron Technology Inc 203 452-0515
62 Spring Hill Rd Trumbull (06611) ***(G-9003)***
Barre Precision Products Inc 860 647-1913
199 Hopriver Rd Bolton (06043) ***(G-505)***
Barrette Mechanical 860 774-0499
36 Bush Hill Rd Brooklyn (06234) ***(G-1246)***
Barron Print 860 355-9535
11 Howland Rd New Milford (06776) ***(G-5509)***
Barry E Leonard 860 951-5105
390 Nott St Wethersfield (06109) ***(G-10183)***
Barzetti Welding LLC 203 748-3200
143 Grassy Plain St Bethel (06801) ***(G-261)***
Barzettis Fabricating & Wldg, Bethel *Also called Barzetti Welding LLC* ***(G-261)***
Basement Screen Printing 860 462-9103
11 Lindsay Ln Broad Brook (06016) ***(G-1144)***
Bass Plating Company 860 243-2557
82 Old Windsor Rd Bloomfield (06002) ***(G-392)***
Bass Products LLC 860 585-7923
435 Lake Ave Bristol (06010) ***(G-977)***
Batrolling4u LLC 860 439-1994
40b Cross Rd Waterford (06385) ***(G-9642)***
Batters Box 203 845-0212
327 Main Ave Ste 2 Norwalk (06851) ***(G-6087)***
Bauer Inc 860 583-9100
175 Century Dr Bristol (06010) ***(G-978)***
Bauer Compressor North East, Monroe *Also called Bauer Compressors Inc* ***(G-4696)***
Bauer Compressors Inc 203 445-9514
60 Twin Brook Ter Monroe (06468) ***(G-4696)***
Baumer Electric, Southington *Also called Baumer Ltd* ***(G-7894)***
Baumer Ltd (HQ) 860 621-2121
122 Spring St Ste C6 Southington (06489) ***(G-7894)***
Bausch Advanced Tech Inc (PA) 860 669-7380
115 Nod Rd Clinton (06413) ***(G-1492)***
Baxter Bros Inc 203 637-4559
1030 E Putnam Ave Greenwich (06830) ***(G-3130)***
Baxter Investment Management, Greenwich *Also called Baxter Bros Inc* ***(G-3130)***
Bay Crane Service Conn Inc 203 785-8000
37 Nettleton Ave North Haven (06473) ***(G-5913)***
Bay State Elevator Company Inc 860 243-9030
105 W Ddley Town Rd Ste H Bloomfield (06002) ***(G-393)***
Bay State Machine Inc 860 230-0054
21 Center Pkwy Plainfield (06374) ***(G-6743)***
Bay Tact Corporation 860 315-7372
440 Route 198 Woodstock Valley (06282) ***(G-10691)***
Bayard Inc (HQ) 860 437-3012
1 Montauk Ave Ste 3 New London (06320) ***(G-5457)***
Bayer Clothing Group Inc (PA) 203 661-4140
503 Riversville Rd Greenwich (06831) ***(G-3131)***
Baynets Safety Systems, Colchester *Also called International Cordage East Ltd* ***(G-1555)***
Baytek Sign Co 860 872-9279
169 Goose Ln Tolland (06084) ***(G-8851)***
Bazzano, J Cedar Products, Pleasant Valley *Also called Pleasant Valley Fence Co Inc* ***(G-6925)***
Bb Shades 203 849-9345
62 Hills Ln Westport (06880) ***(G-10060)***
Bcbg, Cromwell *Also called Runway Liquidation LLC* ***(G-1716)***
Bcbg, Brookfield *Also called Runway Liquidation LLC* ***(G-1220)***
Bcbg, Bristol *Also called Runway Liquidation LLC* ***(G-1115)***
Bcbg, Trumbull *Also called Runway Liquidation LLC* ***(G-9067)***
Bcbg, Bloomfield *Also called Runway Liquidation LLC* ***(G-482)***
Bcbg, Enfield *Also called Runway Liquidation LLC* ***(G-2688)***
Bcbg, Simsbury *Also called Runway Liquidation LLC* ***(G-7643)***
BCT Reporting LLC 860 302-1876
55 Whiting St Ste 1a Plainville (06062) ***(G-6775)***
BCT-042 LLC 203 331-0008
42 Dean Pl Bridgeport (06610) ***(G-708)***
Bdg Embroidery 203 258-0175
206 Romanock Rd Fairfield (06825) ***(G-2751)***
Beacon Group Inc (PA) 860 594-5200
549 Cedar St Newington (06111) ***(G-5631)***
Beacon Industries Inc 860 594-5200
549 Cedar St Newington (06111) ***(G-5632)***
Bead Electronics, Milford *Also called Bead Industries Inc* ***(G-4466)***
Bead Industries Inc (PA) 203 301-0270
11 Cascade Blvd Milford (06460) ***(G-4466)***
Beadazzle 860 747-5101
31 Lincoln St Plainville (06062) ***(G-6776)***
Bean Counters 860 404-2930
1730 New Britain Ave Farmington (06032) ***(G-2883)***
Beans Inc 860 945-9234
2213 Litchfield Rd Watertown (06795) ***(G-9683)***
Bear Hands Brewing Company 860 576-5374
13 Palmer Ct Central Village (06332) ***(G-1336)***
Bear Market 860 379-8943
397 Colebrook River Rd Winchester Center (06098) ***(G-10343)***
Beard Concrete Co Derby Inc (PA) 203 874-2533
127 Boston Post Rd Milford (06460) ***(G-4467)***
Beard Concrete Co Derby Inc 203 735-4641
37 Main St Derby (06418) ***(G-2109)***
Beard Concrete Company, Milford *Also called Beard Concrete Co Derby Inc* ***(G-4467)***
Beardsley Publishing Corp 203 263-0888
45 Main St N Woodbury (06798) ***(G-10626)***
Beardsworth Group Inc 860 283-4014
1085 Waterbury Rd Thomaston (06787) ***(G-8780)***
Bearicuda Bins, Litchfield *Also called Bearicuda Inc* ***(G-3884)***
Bearicuda Inc 860 361-6860
3 West St Ste 3e Litchfield (06759) ***(G-3884)***
Beautiful Publications 347 508-2798
1345 Barnum Ave Ste 115 Stratford (06614) ***(G-8581)***
Beautiful Tables LLC 203 602-9969
53 W Bank Ln Stamford (06902) ***(G-8108)***
Beautybrain Bracelet LLC 203 245-8913
36 Kelsey Pl Madison (06443) ***(G-3910)***
Becaid LLC 203 915-6914
5 Science Park Ste 29 New Haven (06511) ***(G-5241)***
Beck Industries LLC 203 260-8864
103 Jamestown Rd Stratford (06614) ***(G-8582)***
Beckley Inc 203 488-1019
4 Sybil Ave Branford (06405) ***(G-557)***
Beckm LLC 203 458-3800
131 Nut Plains Rd Guilford (06437) ***(G-3327)***

Beckson Manufacturing Inc (PA) ... 203 366-3644
165 Holland Ave Bridgeport (06605) *(G-709)*
Becon Incorporated (PA) ... 860 243-1428
522 Cottage Grove Rd Bloomfield (06002) *(G-394)*
Becton Dickinson and Company ... 860 824-5487
Grace Way Rr 7 Canaan (06018) *(G-1281)*
Bedard Puzzles ... 860 657-3781
382 Great Swamp Rd Glastonbury (06033) *(G-3013)*
Bedoukian Research Inc (PA) ... 203 830-4000
6 Commerce Dr Danbury (06810) *(G-1750)*
Bedrock Oil LLC ... 860 295-8230
16 Parker Rd Marlborough (06447) *(G-4121)*
Bee-Commerce.com, Weston *Also called Woods End Inc (G-10047)*
Beebe Company, Westport *Also called Bb Shades (G-10060)*
Beede Electrical Instr Co Inc ... 603 753-6362
75 Frontage Rd 106 North Stonington (06359) *(G-6020)*
Beehive Heat Treating Svcs Inc ... 203 866-1635
373 Katona Dr Fairfield (06824) *(G-2752)*
Beekley Medical ... 860 583-4700
1 Prestige Ln Bristol (06010) *(G-979)*
Beelightful Candle LLC ... 203 912-7122
222 Cognewaugh Rd Cos Cob (06807) *(G-1625)*
Been Printed LLC ... 860 618-3600
66 Torrington Heights Rd Torrington (06790) *(G-8901)*
Been Printing, Torrington *Also called Been Printed LLC (G-8901)*
Beerd Brewing Co LLC ... 585 771-7428
22 Bayview Ave Stonington (06378) *(G-8524)*
Bees Knees Zipper Wax LLC ... 203 521-5727
3 Canoe Birch Ct Berlin (06037) *(G-162)*
Begell House Inc ... 203 456-6161
50 North St Danbury (06810) *(G-1751)*
BEI, Wallingford *Also called Clg Enterprises Inc (G-9232)*
BEI Holdings Inc ... 203 741-9300
6 Capital Dr Wallingford (06492) *(G-9219)*
Beiersdorf Inc (HQ) ... 203 563-5800
45 Danbury Rd Wilton (06897) *(G-10271)*
Beiersdorf Inc ... 203 854-8000
360 Dr Martin Luther King Norwalk (06854) *(G-6088)*
Beiersdorf North America Inc (HQ) ... 203 563-5800
45 Danbury Rd Wilton (06897) *(G-10272)*
Belair Aviation ... 203 380-8993
20 Wigwam Ln Stratford (06614) *(G-8583)*
Beldotti Bakeries ... 203 348-9029
605 Newfield Ave Stamford (06905) *(G-8109)*
Belimo Air Controls USA, Danbury *Also called Belimo Aircontrols (usa) Inc (G-1752)*
Belimo Aircontrols (usa) Inc (HQ) ... 800 543-9038
33 Turner Rd Danbury (06810) *(G-1752)*
Belimo Automation AG ... 203 749-3319
33 Turner Rd Danbury (06810) *(G-1753)*
Belimo Customization USA Inc ... 203 791-9915
33 Turner Rd Danbury (06810) *(G-1754)*
Bell and Howell LLC ... 860 526-9561
6 Winter Ave Deep River (06417) *(G-2085)*
Bell Power Systems LLC ... 860 767-7502
34 Plains Rd Essex (06426) *(G-2712)*
Bella Alpacas ... 860 946-3076
155 Squash Hollow Rd New Milford (06776) *(G-5510)*
Bella Ciao ... 203 245-4433
806 Green Hill Rd Madison (06443) *(G-3911)*
Bella Hispaniola Entps LLC ... 860 628-0105
384 Lazy Ln Southington (06489) *(G-7895)*
Bella Nail & Spa LLC ... 860 436-3119
945 Cromwell Ave Ste 19 Rocky Hill (06067) *(G-7222)*
Bella Pietra LLC ... 203 655-1322
110 Post Rd Ste A Darien (06820) *(G-2007)*
Bellable LLC ... 800 212-2603
1245 Farmington Ave Ste 1 West Hartford (06107) *(G-9778)*
Belle Impression Pubg Inc ... 203 826-5426
404 Larson Dr Danbury (06810) *(G-1755)*
Belle Industries LLC ... 203 245-0382
13 Corinth Dr Madison (06443) *(G-3912)*
Belmeade Group LLC ... 860 413-3569
46 Simsbury Rd West Granby (06090) *(G-9766)*
Belmeade Signs, West Granby *Also called Belmeade Group LLC (G-9766)*
Belmont Corporation ... 860 589-5700
60 Crystal Pond Pl Bristol (06010) *(G-980)*
Belo Woodworking LLC ... 727 249-8514
53 W Mountain Rd West Simsbury (06092) *(G-9972)*
Belvoir Media Group, Norwalk *Also called Belvoir Publications Inc (G-6090)*
Belvoir Media Group LLC ... 203 857-3128
535 Cnncticut Ave Ste 100 Norwalk (06854) *(G-6089)*
Belvoir Publications ... 203 422-7300
75 Holly Hill Ln Greenwich (06830) *(G-3132)*
Belvoir Publications Inc (PA) ... 203 857-3100
800 Connecticut Ave 4w02 Norwalk (06854) *(G-6090)*
Bemat TEC LLC ... 860 632-0049
114 West St Cromwell (06416) *(G-1691)*
Ben & Jerrys Homemade Inc ... 203 488-9666
120 Northwood Rd Newington (06111) *(G-5633)*
Ben Art Manufacturing Co Inc ... 203 758-4435
109 Waterbury Rd Prospect (06712) *(G-6993)*
Ben Baena & Son ... 203 334-8568
218 Charles St Bridgeport (06606) *(G-710)*
Ben Barrett Canvas Service LLC ... 203 268-4315
14 Patmar Ln Monroe (06468) *(G-4697)*
Ben Barretts LLC ... 860 928-9373
129 Robbins Rd Thompson (06277) *(G-8830)*
Bench Press 3 LLC ... 203 848-5545
340 Joan Dr Fairfield (06824) *(G-2753)*
Bender Management Inc ... 203 847-3865
235 Westport Ave Norwalk (06851) *(G-6091)*
Bender Showroom ... 860 618-2944
29 Main St Torrington (06790) *(G-8902)*
Bender Showrooms, Norwalk *Also called Bender Management Inc (G-6091)*
Benedict M Lai ... 425 698-7267
125 N School St Manchester (06042) *(G-3986)*
Benenson Family Realty LLC ... 919 544-7839
102 Ladder Hill Rd N Weston (06883) *(G-10019)*
Benetec Inc ... 860 745-4455
99 Phoenix Ave Enfield (06082) *(G-2617)*
Benettieris Studio ... 860 568-3590
115 Main St East Hartford (06118) *(G-2297)*
Benjamin Moore Authorized Ret, Thomaston *Also called Chapman Lumber Inc (G-8785)*
Benji Billionaire ... 203 361-7744
128 Carlisle St New Haven (06519) *(G-5242)*
Bennettisville Printing, Hebron *Also called Bennettsville Holdings LLC (G-3745)*
Bennettsville Holdings LLC ... 860 444-9400
33 Pendleton Dr A Hebron (06248) *(G-3745)*
Bennice Molding Co ... 203 440-2543
184 Gravel St Apt 42 Meriden (06450) *(G-4149)*
Benoit Signs & Graphics ... 860 870-8300
7 Hicks Ave Stafford Springs (06076) *(G-8019)*
Bep Flavor Holdings LLC (PA) ... 203 595-4520
201 Tresser Blvd Ste 320 Stamford (06901) *(G-8110)*
Bergan Architectural Wdwkg Inc ... 860 346-0869
55 N Main St Middletown (06457) *(G-4324)*
Berkshire Balloons LLC ... 203 250-8441
190 Tomlinson Ave Apt 12h Plantsville (06479) *(G-6886)*
Berkshire Photonics LLC ... 860 868-0412
88 Bee Brook Rd Washington Depot (06794) *(G-9416)*
Berlin Industries LLC ... 860 819-9997
84 Bernard Rd Berlin (06037) *(G-163)*
Berlin Operations, East Berlin *Also called Paradigm Prcision Holdings LLC (G-2173)*
Berlin Steel Construction Co (PA) ... 860 828-3531
76 Depot Rd Kensington (06037) *(G-3806)*
Bernell Tool & Mfg Co ... 203 756-4405
181 Mulloy Rd Waterbury (06705) *(G-9438)*
Bernies Tool & Fastener Svcs ... 203 466-5252
269 S Lambert Rd Orange (06477) *(G-6585)*
Berry Global Inc ... 413 529-7602
44o Niles St East Hampton (06424) *(G-2256)*
Bertram Sirkin ... 860 656-7446
200 Mohegan Dr West Hartford (06117) *(G-9779)*
Berwick Industries LLC ... 475 228-5822
366 Post Rd Darien (06820) *(G-2008)*
Bes Cu Inc ... 860 582-8660
400 Middle St Bristol (06010) *(G-981)*
Bessette Holdings Inc ... 860 289-6000
95 Leggett St East Hartford (06108) *(G-2298)*
Best Built Custom Stair Buildi ... 203 488-8031
2175 Maple Rd North Branford (06471) *(G-5829)*
Best Foods Baking Co. Now., Orange *Also called Bimbo Bakeries Usa Inc (G-6586)*
Best Gaskets ... 914 347-1971
41 Orange St Stamford (06902) *(G-8111)*
Best In Backyards (PA) ... 203 917-4381
66 Sugar Hollow Rd Danbury (06810) *(G-1756)*
Best Management Products Inc ... 860 434-0277
9 Matthews Dr Unit A1-A2 East Haddam (06423) *(G-2236)*
Best Manager Products, East Haddam *Also called Best Management Products Inc (G-2236)*
Bestway Food and Fuel ... 860 447-0729
6 Boston Post Rd Waterford (06385) *(G-9643)*
Beta Pharma Inc ... 203 315-5062
1 Enterprise Dr Ste 408 Shelton (06484) *(G-7403)*
Beta Shim Co ... 203 926-1150
11 Progress Dr Shelton (06484) *(G-7404)*
Bethany Welding ... 203 393-0002
793 Amity Rd New Haven (06524) *(G-5243)*
Bethel Division, Bethel *Also called Vanderbilt Chemicals LLC (G-361)*
Bethel Mail Service ... 203 730-1399
211 Greenwood Ave Ste 2 Bethel (06801) *(G-262)*
Bethel Mail Service Center, Bethel *Also called Bethel Mail Service (G-262)*
Bethel Printing & Graphics ... 203 748-7034
81 Greenwood Ave Ste 10 Bethel (06801) *(G-263)*
Bethel Sand & Gravel Co ... 203 743-4469
2 Maple Avenue Ext Bethel (06801) *(G-264)*
Betkoski Brothers LLC ... 203 723-8262
332 Bethany Rd Beacon Falls (06403) *(G-131)*
Betlan Corporation ... 203 270-7898
31 Pecks Ln Ste 7 Newtown (06470) *(G-5729)*
Betoel Publishers, Stamford *Also called Kieffer Associates Inc (G-8275)*
Better Baking By Beth ... 860 482-4706
270 W Hill Rd Torrington (06790) *(G-8903)*

Better Lawns & Gardens 203 735-5296
1 Chestnut St Bldg 5 Ansonia (06401) ***(G-23)***
Better Letters Signs 860 749-7235
11 Camelot Dr Enfield (06082) ***(G-2618)***
Better Molded Products Inc (PA) 860 589-0066
95 Valley St Ste 2 Bristol (06010) ***(G-982)***
Better Pallets Inc 203 230-9549
10 Corbin Cir Branford (06405) ***(G-558)***
Better Stones & Garden, East Hartford *Also called Midwood Quarry and Cnstr Inc* ***(G-2345)***
Betx LLC 860 459-1681
440 Cedar Ln New Hartford (06057) ***(G-5186)***
Betz Tool Company Inc 203 878-1187
70 Raton Rd Ste K Milford (06461) ***(G-4468)***
Beverage Boss LLC 203 865-2240
226 Whalley Ave New Haven (06511) ***(G-5244)***
Beverage Publications Inc 203 288-3375
2508 Whitney Ave Apt N Hamden (06518) ***(G-3418)***
Beverly Feldman, Norwalk *Also called Aj Casey LLC* ***(G-6065)***
Bevin Bells, East Hampton *Also called Bevin Bros Manufacturing Co* ***(G-2257)***
Bevin Bros Manufacturing Co 860 267-4431
17 Watrous St East Hampton (06424) ***(G-2257)***
Bey-Low Molds 860 482-6561
80 Sunrise Dr Torrington (06790) ***(G-8904)***
Beyond Forever Cabinetry LLC 203 427-7968
10 Gurdon St Bridgeport (06606) ***(G-711)***
Beyond Home Improvement 203 859-0113
30 Manor Dr North Haven (06473) ***(G-5914)***
Beyond Invite 203 219-9434
46 Brownson Dr Shelton (06484) ***(G-7405)***
BF Enterprises LLC 860 693-8953
241 Wright Rd Collinsville (06019) ***(G-1588)***
BF Services LLC 860 289-6929
44 Maplewood Ave East Hartford (06108) ***(G-2299)***
Bff Holdings Inc (HQ) 860 510-0100
141 Mill Rock Rd E Old Saybrook (06475) ***(G-6523)***
Bg Machinery Services LLC 203 374-4732
66 Lola St Fairfield (06825) ***(G-2754)***
Bhs 860 585-0125
43 Seminary St Bristol (06010) ***(G-983)***
Bhs-Torin, Manchester *Also called L M Gill Welding and Mfr LLC* ***(G-4046)***
Bi-Metalix, East Windsor *Also called KTI Bi-Metallix Inc* ***(G-2506)***
Bic Consumer Pdts Mfg Co Inc 203 783-2000
1 Bic Way Ste 1 # 1 Shelton (06484) ***(G-7406)***
Bic Consumer Products Mfg Co 203 783-2000
565 Bic Dr Milford (06461) ***(G-4469)***
Bic Corporation (HQ) 203 783-2000
1 Bic Way Ste 1 # 1 Shelton (06484) ***(G-7407)***
Bic Corporation 203 538-5028
95 Settlers Ridge Rd Milford (06460) ***(G-4470)***
Bic Graphic USA, Shelton *Also called Bic Corporation* ***(G-7407)***
Bic USA Inc (HQ) 203 783-2000
1 Bic Way Ste 1 # 1 Shelton (06484) ***(G-7408)***
Bick Publishing House 203 208-5253
16 Marion Rd Branford (06405) ***(G-559)***
Bicron Electronics Company (PA) 860 482-2524
427 Goshen Rd Torrington (06790) ***(G-8905)***
Bidwell Industrial Group Inc (PA) 860 346-9283
2055 S Main St Middletown (06457) ***(G-4325)***
Biedermann Mfg Inds Inc 860 283-8268
135 S Main St Thomaston (06787) ***(G-8781)***
Biennix Corp 203 254-1727
2490 Black Rock Tpke # 354 Fairfield (06825) ***(G-2755)***
Big City String Co 203 371-8117
820 Queen St Bridgeport (06606) ***(G-712)***
Big Dipper Ice Cream Fctry Inc 203 758-3200
91 Waterbury Rd Prospect (06712) ***(G-6994)***
Big Prints LLC 203 469-1100
15 Baer Cir Ste 2 East Haven (06512) ***(G-2414)***
Big Purple Cupcake LLC 203 483-8738
6 Conifer Dr Branford (06405) ***(G-560)***
Bigelow Tea, Fairfield *Also called RC Bigelow Inc* ***(G-2834)***
Bigs Publishing LLC 203 249-1059
22 Round Hill Club Rd Greenwich (06831) ***(G-3133)***
Bilbe Controls, Bristol *Also called Rostra Vernatherm LLC* ***(G-1112)***
Bill Hoagland 203 877-0157
250 Pond Point Ave Milford (06460) ***(G-4471)***
Bill Marlow 860 829-1712
228 Rose Hill Rd Portland (06480) ***(G-6952)***
Bills Boat Repair LLC 203 804-8801
44 Williamsburg Cir Guilford (06437) ***(G-3328)***
Bills Machine Shop 860 875-6607
2 Pinnacle Rd Ellington (06029) ***(G-2578)***
Bills Sheet Metal 860 859-2821
1451 Old Colchester Rd Oakdale (06370) ***(G-6441)***
Bimbo Bakeries Usa Inc 203 932-1000
284 Bull Hill Ln Orange (06477) ***(G-6586)***
Bimbo Bakeries Usa Inc 860 691-1180
9 Freedom Way Portland (06480) ***(G-6953)***
Bingham & Taylor Corp (HQ) 540 825-8334
1022 Elm St Rocky Hill (06067) ***(G-7223)***
Bio Med Packaging Systems Inc 203 846-1923
100 Pearl St Norwalk (06850) ***(G-6092)***
Bio Solutions, Meriden *Also called Brand-Nu Laboratories Inc* ***(G-4151)***
Bio-Med Devices Inc 203 458-0202
61 Soundview Rd Guilford (06437) ***(G-3329)***
Bioarray Genetics Inc 508 577-0205
400 Farmington Ave Farmington (06032) ***(G-2884)***
Bioclinica Inc 860 701-0082
234 Bank St New London (06320) ***(G-5458)***
Biofibers Capital Group LLC 203 561-6133
14 Amidon Dr Ashford (06278) ***(G-57)***
Biographical Publishing Co 203 758-3661
95 Sycamore Dr Prospect (06712) ***(G-6995)***
Biohaven Pharmaceuticals, New Haven *Also called Biohaven Phrm Holdg Co Ltd* ***(G-5246)***
Biohaven Pharmaceuticals Inc 203 404-0410
215 Church St New Haven (06510) ***(G-5245)***
Biohaven Phrm Holdg Co Ltd 203 404-0410
215 Church St New Haven (06510) ***(G-5246)***
Biological Industries 860 316-5197
100 Sebethe Dr Ste A3 Cromwell (06416) ***(G-1692)***
Biomass Energy LLC 540 872-3300
125 Powder Forest Dr Weatogue (06089) ***(G-9755)***
Biomass Industries Inc 203 207-9958
30 Henry St Bethel (06801) ***(G-265)***
Biomed Health Inc 860 657-2258
70 Oakwood Dr Ste 8 Glastonbury (06033) ***(G-3014)***
Biomed Packing Systems, Norwalk *Also called K W Griffen Company* ***(G-6226)***
Biomedical Innovations, Wolcott *Also called Graphic Cntrls Acqisition Corp* ***(G-10567)***
Biomerics LLC 203 268-7238
246 Main St Ste C Monroe (06468) ***(G-4698)***
Biometrics Inc (PA) 203 261-1162
115 Technology Dr Cp102 Trumbull (06611) ***(G-9004)***
Biorasis Inc 860 429-3592
23 Fellen Rd Storrs (06268) ***(G-8543)***
Biosolutions, Meriden *Also called Brand-Nu Laboratories Inc* ***(G-4150)***
Biowave Innovations LLC 203 982-8157
274 Ridgefield Rd Wilton (06897) ***(G-10273)***
Bioxcel Therapeutics Inc 475 238-6837
555 Long Wharf Dr New Haven (06511) ***(G-5247)***
Birdtrack Press 203 389-7789
26 Mckinley Ave New Haven (06515) ***(G-5248)***
Birk Manufacturing Inc 800 531-2070
14 Capitol Dr East Lyme (06333) ***(G-2464)***
Birken Manufacturing Company 860 242-2211
3 Old Windsor Rd Bloomfield (06002) ***(G-395)***
Birkett Woodworking LLC 860 361-9142
14 Benedict Rd Morris (06763) ***(G-4787)***
Birotech Inc 203 968-5080
29 Sunnyside Ave Ste 4 Stamford (06902) ***(G-8112)***
Bite Tech Inc 203 987-6898
20 Glover Ave Ste 1 Norwalk (06850) ***(G-6093)***
Biz Wiz Print & Copy Ctr LLC 860 633-7446
2341 Main St Glastonbury (06033) ***(G-3015)***
Biz Wiz Print & Copy Ctr LLC (PA) 860 721-0040
781 Cromwell Ave Ste E Rocky Hill (06067) ***(G-7224)***
Bizcard Xpress LLC 860 324-6840
26 Killingworth Rd Higganum (06441) ***(G-3761)***
Bjm Pumps LLC 860 399-5937
123 Spencer Plain Rd # 1 Old Saybrook (06475) ***(G-6524)***
Bk Industries LLC 832 744-3067
75 Hockanum Blvd Vernon (06066) ***(G-9132)***
Bkmfg Corp 860 738-2200
200 International Way Winsted (06098) ***(G-10510)***
Bl Printing Shop 203 334-7779
3442 Fairfield Ave Bridgeport (06605) ***(G-713)***
Black & Decker (us) Inc 860 563-5800
662 Silas Deane Hwy Wethersfield (06109) ***(G-10184)***
Black & Decker (us) Inc 860 225-5111
700 Stanley Dr New Britain (06053) ***(G-4951)***
Black & Decker (us) Inc (HQ) 860 225-5111
1000 Stanley Dr New Britain (06053) ***(G-4952)***
Black Crow Press LLC 203 281-1034
85 Spring Garden St Hamden (06517) ***(G-3419)***
Black Dog Boat Works LLC 203 264-5823
155 Lakemere Dr Southbury (06488) ***(G-7845)***
Black Dog Fuel LLC 860 489-0655
148 Candlewood Mtn Rd New Milford (06776) ***(G-5511)***
Black Gold Enterprises 203 729-4444
531 N Main St Naugatuck (06770) ***(G-4862)***
Black Pltnum MNS Essntials LLC 203 501-3768
47 Rocky Glen Rd Danbury (06810) ***(G-1757)***
Black Rock Tech Group LLC 203 916-7200
211 State St Ste 203 Bridgeport (06604) ***(G-714)***
Blackbird Manufacturing and De 860 331-3477
112 Gardner Tavern Ln Coventry (06238) ***(G-1645)***
Blackrock Media Inc 203 374-0369
112 Far Horizon Dr Easton (06612) ***(G-2547)***
Blackstone Industries LLC 203 792-8622
16 Stony Hill Rd Bethel (06801) ***(G-266)***
Blackwold Inc 860 526-0800
212 Middlesex Ave Chester (06412) ***(G-1464)***
Blahut Machine Co 203 878-3643
655 Plains Rd Unit I Milford (06461) ***(G-4472)***
Blairden Precision Instrs Inc 203 799-2000
95 Corporate Dr Trumbull (06611) ***(G-9005)***

Blais Woodworks LLC....860 274-2906
1216 Guernseytown Rd Watertown (06795) ***(G-9684)***
Blakeslee Prestress Inc (PA)....203 315-7090
At Mc Dermott Rd Rr 139 Branford (06405) ***(G-561)***
Blank Canvas Interiors LLC....203 226-5602
73 Norfield Rd Weston (06883) ***(G-10020)***
Blase Manufacturing Company (PA)....203 375-5646
60 Watson Blvd Ste 3 Stratford (06615) ***(G-8584)***
Blase Tool & Manufacturing Co, Stratford *Also called Blase Manufacturing Company* ***(G-8584)***
Blastech Overhaul & Repair....860 243-8811
86 W Dudley Town Rd Bloomfield (06002) ***(G-396)***
Blasting Techniques Inc....860 528-4717
350 Chapel Rd Ste A2 South Windsor (06074) ***(G-7718)***
Blauner Books....203 222-6042
19 Field Point Dr Greenwich (06830) ***(G-3134)***
Bleshue LLC....203 405-1034
4 Woods Way Woodbury (06798) ***(G-10627)***
Blessed Creek....860 416-3692
908 Overhill Dr Suffield (06078) ***(G-8715)***
Blind Crafters....860 896-0366
615 Talcottville Rd Vernon Rockville (06066) ***(G-9162)***
Blinds Dept....203 655-3378
366 Post Rd Darien (06820) ***(G-2009)***
Bloomfield Center Voluntee....860 242-1779
18 Wintonbury Ave Bloomfield (06002) ***(G-397)***
Bloomfield Wood & Melamine Inc....860 243-3226
1 Griffin Rd S Bloomfield (06002) ***(G-398)***
Bloomy Controls Inc (PA)....860 298-9925
839 Marshall Phelps Rd Windsor (06095) ***(G-10368)***
Bloomy Energy Systems, Windsor *Also called Bloomy Controls Inc* ***(G-10368)***
Blu & Grae Music....857 204-3095
1901 Long Ridge Rd Stamford (06903) ***(G-8113)***
Blue Barn Works LLC....203 389-0923
7 Pine Hill Rd Woodbridge (06525) ***(G-10594)***
Blue Bell Mattress Company LLC....860 292-6372
24 Thompson Rd East Windsor (06088) ***(G-2484)***
Blue Buffalo Company Ltd (HQ)....203 762-9751
11 River Rd Ste 200 Wilton (06897) ***(G-10274)***
Blue Buffalo Pet Products Inc (HQ)....203 762-9751
11 River Rd Ste 103 Wilton (06897) ***(G-10275)***
Blue Chip Tool, Hebron *Also called Rick Bulach* ***(G-3756)***
Blue Chip Tool....860 875-7999
40 Tolland Stage Rd D4 Tolland (06084) ***(G-8852)***
Blue Crystal Enterprises LLC....203 856-5397
43 Wedgewood Rd Trumbull (06611) ***(G-9006)***
Blue Earth Compost Inc....860 508-7114
3580 Main St Ste 10 Hartford (06120) ***(G-3556)***
Blue Lily Cotton LLC....860 869-7734
91 Governors Ave Milford (06460) ***(G-4473)***
Blue Lotus Bracelets....203 858-6526
175 Silvermine Ave Norwalk (06850) ***(G-6094)***
Blue Moon Bindery LLC....860 435-9100
206 Millerton Rd Lakeville (06039) ***(G-3842)***
Blue Moon Printing LLC....860 245-0827
44 Washington St Ste 5 Mystic (06355) ***(G-4801)***
Blue Print....203 948-3883
42 White St Danbury (06810) ***(G-1758)***
Blue Sky Studios Inc....203 992-6000
1 American Ln Ste 301 Greenwich (06831) ***(G-3135)***
Blue Sky/Vifx, Greenwich *Also called Blue Sky Studios Inc* ***(G-3135)***
Bluecrest, Danbury *Also called Dmt Solutions Global Corp* ***(G-1797)***
Bluewater Designs, Bristol *Also called Patriot Manufacturing LLC* ***(G-1086)***
Blumen Laden Artificial Flower....860 693-8600
41 Bridge St Collinsville (06019) ***(G-1589)***
Blush By London....860 610-9891
2 Fraser Pl Unit 2a Hartford (06105) ***(G-3557)***
Bm Publishing LLC....860 778-1583
557 Pine St Bristol (06010) ***(G-984)***
Bmd, Guilford *Also called Bio-Med Devices Inc* ***(G-3329)***
BMHs Press Box....203 810-4380
300 Highland Ave Norwalk (06854) ***(G-6095)***
Bmi Cad Services Inc....860 658-0808
8a Herman Dr Simsbury (06070) ***(G-7613)***
Bml Tool & Mfg Corp....203 880-9485
67 Enterprise Dr Monroe (06468) ***(G-4699)***
Bmr Associates....203 453-1796
45 Water St C Guilford (06437) ***(G-3330)***
BNE Publishing Inc....860 498-0032
3050 Main St Coventry (06238) ***(G-1646)***
BNL Industries Inc....860 870-6222
30 Industrial Park Rd Vernon (06066) ***(G-9133)***
Bo-Dyn Bobsled Project Inc....860 526-9504
51 Winthrop Rd Chester (06412) ***(G-1465)***
Board Silly Custom Sawmill LLC....203 438-3631
318 Ethan Allen Hwy Ridgefield (06877) ***(G-7119)***
Boardman Silversmiths Inc....203 265-9978
22 N Plains Industrial Rd 6c Wallingford (06492) ***(G-9220)***
Bob The Baker LLC....203 775-1032
594 Federal Rd Brookfield (06804) ***(G-1162)***
Bob Vess Building LLC....860 729-2536
605 Main St Cromwell (06416) ***(G-1693)***
Bob Worden....860 567-4722
53 Kenyon Rd Lakeside (06758) ***(G-3841)***
Bobbex Inc....800 792-4449
523 Pepper St Ste B Monroe (06468) ***(G-4700)***
Bobken Automatics, Waterbury *Also called Oakville Quality Products LLC* ***(G-9567)***
Bobken Automatics Inc....203 757-5525
1495 Thomaston Ave Ste 2 Waterbury (06704) ***(G-9439)***
Bobs Sandbox....860 267-4530
109 Westchester Rd Colchester (06415) ***(G-1543)***
Bobs Vending....860 426-1232
42 Vermont Ave Southington (06489) ***(G-7896)***
Boccelli....860 862-9300
1 Mohegan Sun Blvd 621c Uncasville (06382) ***(G-9096)***
Bodycote Thermal Proc Inc....860 225-7691
675 Christian Ln Berlin (06037) ***(G-164)***
Bodycote Thermal Proc Inc....860 282-1371
45 Connecticut Ave South Windsor (06074) ***(G-7719)***
Boehringer Ingelheim Corp (HQ)....203 798-9988
900 Ridgebury Rd Ridgefield (06877) ***(G-7120)***
Boehringer Ingelheim Pharma (HQ)....203 798-9988
900 Ridgebury Rd Ridgefield (06877) ***(G-7121)***
Boehringer Ingelheim USA Corp (HQ)....203 798-9988
900 Ridgebury Rd Ridgefield (06877) ***(G-7122)***
Boehrnger Ingelheim Roxane Inc....203 798-5555
175 Briar Ridge Rd Ridgefield (06877) ***(G-7123)***
Boeing Company....860 627-9393
1 Hartfield Blvd Ste 112 East Windsor (06088) ***(G-2485)***
Bogner's, Manchester *Also called Manchester Packing Company Inc* ***(G-4053)***
Bojak Company....203 378-5086
152 Old Gate Ln D Milford (06460) ***(G-4474)***
Bold Wood Interiors LLC....203 907-4077
138 Haven St New Haven (06513) ***(G-5249)***
Bolducs Machine Works Inc....860 455-1232
207 Miller Rd North Windham (06235) ***(G-6034)***
Bollore Inc....860 774-2930
60 Louisa Viens Dr Dayville (06241) ***(G-2054)***
Bolt Custom & Mfg LLC....203 685-1840
307 Remington St Bridgeport (06610) ***(G-715)***
Bolton Aerospace, Manchester *Also called Pas Technologies Inc* ***(G-4074)***
Bolton Hill Industries Inc (PA)....860 742-0311
65 Cedar Swamp Rd Coventry (06238) ***(G-1647)***
Bolton Hill Industries-Marine, Coventry *Also called Bolton Hill Industries Inc* ***(G-1647)***
Boltprintingcom....203 885-0571
20 Old Grays Bridge Rd Brookfield (06804) ***(G-1163)***
Boman Precision Tech Inc....203 415-8350
67 Erna Ave Milford (06461) ***(G-4475)***
Bomar Machine LLC....860 505-7299
600 Four Rod Rd Ste 7 Berlin (06037) ***(G-165)***
Bomba Industries LLC....203 304-9051
6 Crown Hill Dr Sandy Hook (06482) ***(G-7300)***
Bombadils Spirit Shop Inc....860 423-9661
135 Storrs Rd 8 Mansfield Center (06250) ***(G-4112)***
Bomboo LLC....475 731-0865
32 West Ave Norwalk (06854) ***(G-6096)***
Bonati Brothers Welding & Fabr....860 582-5000
26 S Canal St Plainville (06062) ***(G-6777)***
Bond-Bilt Garages Inc....203 269-3375
30 N Plains Industrial Rd # 16 Wallingford (06492) ***(G-9221)***
Bonenfants Drv Your Auto Svc....203 222-2239
23 Reichert Cir Westport (06880) ***(G-10061)***
Bonito Manufacturing Inc....203 234-8786
445 Washington Ave North Haven (06473) ***(G-5915)***
Bonney-Gee Cuisines....203 372-3385
957 Platt St Bridgeport (06606) ***(G-716)***
Bonnieview Woodwork LLC....860 767-3299
9 Westwood Rd Ivoryton (06442) ***(G-3783)***
Bonsal American Inc....860 824-7733
43 Clayton Rd Canaan (06018) ***(G-1282)***
Bonsal American Inc....860 824-7733
43 Clayton Rd Canaan (06018) ***(G-1283)***
Book Automation Inc....860 354-7900
458 Danbury Rd Ste B10 New Milford (06776) ***(G-5512)***
Book Mktg Works, Avon *Also called Publishing Directions LLC* ***(G-101)***
Boomerang Consignment....203 788-9002
90 S Kent Rd South Kent (06785) ***(G-7683)***
Boomerang Studio....203 689-5155
178 Denison Dr Guilford (06437) ***(G-3331)***
Boost Oxygen LLC....203 331-8100
92 Woodmont Rd Milford (06460) ***(G-4476)***
Bosphorus Books....860 536-2540
3 Ridge Rd Groton (06340) ***(G-3272)***
Boss Industries....860 819-1637
133 West St Vernon Rockville (06066) ***(G-9163)***
Boss Snowplows & Ice Control....860 886-7081
53 Lebanon Rd North Franklin (06254) ***(G-5871)***
Boston Endo-Surgical Tech, Bridgeport *Also called Precision Engineered Pdts LLC* ***(G-878)***
Boston Endo-Surgical Tech LLC....203 336-6479
1146 Barnum Ave Bridgeport (06610) ***(G-717)***
Boston Model Bakery....203 562-9491
169 Washington Ave New Haven (06519) ***(G-5250)***
Boston Scientific Corporation....860 673-2500
85 Bridgewater Dr Avon (06001) ***(G-78)***

Boswell's, Bethany *Also called Brenda Jubin* ***(G-235)***
Botanica Chachitas 860 247-5103
831 Park St Hartford (06106) ***(G-3558)***
Botanical Origins LLC 203 267-6061
341 Christian St Oxford (06478) ***(G-6646)***
Bottarga Brothers LLC 203 355-1134
263 Brookdale Rd Stamford (06903) ***(G-8114)***
Bottom Line Inc (PA) 203 973-5900
3 Landmark Sq Ste 230 Stamford (06901) ***(G-8115)***
Bottom Line Publications, Stamford *Also called Bottom Line Inc* ***(G-8115)***
Bottomline Technologies De Inc 203 761-1289
187 Danbury Rd Ste 204 Wilton (06897) ***(G-10276)***
Bottomline Technologies De Inc 203 431-9787
17 Weir Farm Ln Ridgefield (06877) ***(G-7124)***
Boudreau Vasiliki 203 734-6754
16 Reservoir Dr Ansonia (06401) ***(G-24)***
Boudreaus Welding Co Inc 860 774-2771
1029 N Main St Dayville (06241) ***(G-2055)***
Bouffard Metal Goods, Waterbury *Also called H&T Waterbury Inc* ***(G-9494)***
Boule LLC 860 267-8343
258 Injun Hollow Rd East Hampton (06424) ***(G-2258)***
Bourdon Forge Co Inc 860 632-2740
99 Tuttle Rd Middletown (06457) ***(G-4326)***
Bovano Industries Incorporated 203 272-3208
830 S Main St Ofc A Cheshire (06410) ***(G-1361)***
Bovano of Cheshire, Cheshire *Also called Bovano Industries Incorporated* ***(G-1361)***
Bowden Engineering Co 860 583-9585
88 Jeannette St Bristol (06010) ***(G-985)***
Boxtree Accessories Inc 203 637-5794
34 Lincoln Ave Old Greenwich (06870) ***(G-6468)***
BP Countertop Design Co LLC 203 732-1620
101 Elizabeth St Ste 1 Derby (06418) ***(G-2110)***
Bpi Reprographics 203 866-5600
87 Taylor Ave Norwalk (06854) ***(G-6097)***
Bprex Halthcare Brookville Inc 203 754-4141
574 E Main St Waterbury (06702) ***(G-9440)***
Bq Business Solutions 203 268-3500
93 Lazy Brook Rd Monroe (06468) ***(G-4701)***
BR Industries LLC 203 216-3576
16 Lakewood Dr Norwalk (06851) ***(G-6098)***
Bracone Metal Spinning Inc 860 628-5927
39 Depaolo Dr Southington (06489) ***(G-7897)***
Brad Kettle 860 546-9929
4 Howe Rd Canterbury (06331) ***(G-1295)***
Brad's Logging, Canterbury *Also called Brad Kettle* ***(G-1295)***
Bradley Gun Sight Co Inc 860 589-0531
300 Riverside Ave Bristol (06010) ***(G-986)***
Bradley Woodworking LLC 203 746-8357
276 State Route 39 New Fairfield (06812) ***(G-5162)***
Bradt Enterprises LLC 203 323-8501
200 W Hill Rd Stamford (06902) ***(G-8116)***
Brain Institute of America LLC 860 967-5937
93 Shennecossett Rd Groton (06340) ***(G-3273)***
Brain Parade LLC 203 329-8136
1177 High Ridge Rd Stamford (06905) ***(G-8117)***
Brainard Brewing LLC 860 324-5213
129 Irving St Mystic (06355) ***(G-4802)***
Brainbeat Inc 917 291-9747
6 Landmark Sq Fl 4 Stamford (06901) ***(G-8118)***
Brampton Technology Ltd 860 667-7689
61 Maselli Rd Newington (06111) ***(G-5634)***
Branbroks Dntl Stffing Sltions 704 784-1056
61 Quintard Ter Stamford (06902) ***(G-8119)***
Brand Factory Agency 203 984-6178
450 Center St Apt 9 Southport (06890) ***(G-8000)***
Brand Services, Gales Ferry *Also called Stonington Services LLC* ***(G-2987)***
Brand-Nu Laboratories Inc (PA) 203 235-7989
377 Research Pkwy Ste 2 Meriden (06450) ***(G-4150)***
Brand-Nu Laboratories Inc 203 235-7989
290 Pratt St Ofc Meriden (06450) ***(G-4151)***
Brandmark Studios LLC 203 438-9400
16 Whitewood Hollow Ct Ridgefield (06877) ***(G-7125)***
Brandon Nicholas Eza Pubg 860 498-0032
3050 Main St Coventry (06238) ***(G-1648)***
Brandstrom Instruments Inc 203 544-9341
85 Ethan Allen Hwy Ridgefield (06877) ***(G-7126)***
Brandy Hill Logging 860 923-3175
334 Brandy Hill Rd Thompson (06277) ***(G-8831)***
Branford Auto & Marine Center 203 481-6572
28 N Main St Branford (06405) ***(G-562)***
Branford Auto & Marine Cover, Branford *Also called Branford Auto & Marine Center* ***(G-562)***
Branford Open Mri & Diagnostic 203 481-7800
1208 Main St Branford (06405) ***(G-563)***
Brannkey Inc 860 510-0501
137 Mill Rock Rd E Old Saybrook (06475) ***(G-6525)***
Branson Ultrasonics Corp (HQ) 203 796-0400
41 Eagle Rd Ste 1 Danbury (06810) ***(G-1759)***
Brant Industries Inc (PA) 203 661-3344
80 Field Point Rd Ste 3 Greenwich (06830) ***(G-3136)***
Brasco Technologies LLC 203 484-4291
76 Woodland Dr Northford (06472) ***(G-6043)***
Brash Engines Inc 203 843-0757
34 Averill Pl Branford (06405) ***(G-564)***
Brass City Custom 860 995-9321
98 Glenstone Rd Waterbury (06705) ***(G-9441)***
Brass City Gamers Tournament 203 584-3359
300 Schraffts Dr Waterbury (06705) ***(G-9442)***
Brass City Munitions LLC 203 509-7088
1241 Spindle Hill Rd Wolcott (06716) ***(G-10549)***
Brass City Signs LLC 860 628-2046
1662 Musso View Ave Cheshire (06410) ***(G-1362)***
Brass City Technologies LLC (PA) 203 723-7021
1344 New Haven Rd Naugatuck (06770) ***(G-4863)***
Brass City Tile Designs LLC 203 597-8764
29 S Commons Rd Ste 3 Waterbury (06704) ***(G-9443)***
Brass Traditions, Terryville *Also called Malco Inc* ***(G-8764)***
Bravo LLC (PA) 866 922-9222
349 Wetherell St Manchester (06040) ***(G-3987)***
Bravo LLC 860 896-1899
1084 Hartford Tpke Vernon (06066) ***(G-9134)***
Bravo Pet Store, Manchester *Also called Bravo LLC* ***(G-3987)***
Braxton Manufacturing Co Inc 860 274-6781
858 Echo Lake Rd Watertown (06795) ***(G-9685)***
Brazing Way LLC 860 485-9337
25 Highview Dr Harwinton (06791) ***(G-3722)***
Breach Intelligence Inc 844 312-7001
6 S Ridge Rd Farmington (06032) ***(G-2885)***
Bread and Wine Publishing LLC 860 649-3109
220 Charter Oak St Manchester (06040) ***(G-3988)***
Bread Empire, Bridgeport *Also called D Rotondi LLC* ***(G-741)***
Breakaway Brew Haus LLC 860 647-9811
5 Steel Crossing Rd Bolton (06043) ***(G-506)***
Breakfast Woodworks Inc 203 458-8888
135 Leetes Island Rd Guilford (06437) ***(G-3332)***
Breisler Prcsion Machining LLC 203 847-6614
31 Ingleside Ave Norwalk (06850) ***(G-6099)***
Bremser Technologies Inc 203 378-8486
305 Sniffens Ln Stratford (06615) ***(G-8585)***
Brenda Jubin 203 393-2366
199 Wooding Hill Rd Bethany (06524) ***(G-235)***
Brennan Realty LLC (PA) 203 929-6314
70 Platt Rd Shelton (06484) ***(G-7409)***
Brescias Printing Services Inc 860 528-4254
66 Connecticut Blvd East Hartford (06108) ***(G-2300)***
Brewer Yacht Yards Inc 860 399-5128
333 Boston Post Rd Old Saybrook (06475) ***(G-6526)***
Brewery Legitimus LLC 860 810-8894
24 Shingel Mill Dr Canton Canton (06019) ***(G-1307)***
Bri Metal Works Inc 203 368-1649
105 Island Brook Ave Bridgeport (06606) ***(G-718)***
Brian & Son Powerwashing LLC 860 963-1243
136 Harrisville Rd Woodstock (06281) ***(G-10657)***
Brian and Brenda Basinger 203 972-9407
521 Brookside Rd New Canaan (06840) ***(G-5089)***
Brian Arnio 860 779-2983
556 Margaret Henry Rd Sterling (06377) ***(G-8508)***
Brian Arnio Welding and Fabg, Sterling *Also called Brian Arnio* ***(G-8508)***
Brian Berlepsch 203 484-9799
21 Commerce Dr Ste 2 North Branford (06471) ***(G-5830)***
Brian Cheney (PA) 203 734-4793
869 S Main St Seymour (06483) ***(G-7336)***
Brian Cody 203 331-7382
211 Plymouth St Stratford (06614) ***(G-8586)***
Brian Daigle 860 263-7831
158 Beacon St Hartford (06105) ***(G-3559)***
Brian Reynolds 860 267-2021
177 Hog Hill Rd East Hampton (06424) ***(G-2259)***
Brian Safa 203 271-3499
80 Royalwood Ct Cheshire (06410) ***(G-1363)***
Briarwood Printing Company Inc 860 747-6805
301 Farmington Ave Plainville (06062) ***(G-6778)***
Brico LLC 860 242-7068
6c Northwood Dr Bloomfield (06002) ***(G-399)***
Brico Inc 203 693-0323
185 W Newberry Rd Bloomfield (06002) ***(G-400)***
Bridge Innvations Ventures LLC 203 520-8241
286 Strobel Rd Trumbull (06611) ***(G-9007)***
Bridgeport Boatwork Inc (PA) 860 536-9651
837 Seaview Ave Bridgeport (06607) ***(G-719)***
Bridgeport Boatwork Inc 860 536-9651
145 Pearl St Groton (06340) ***(G-3274)***
Bridgeport Burial Vault Co 203 375-7375
544 Surf Ave Stratford (06615) ***(G-8587)***
Bridgeport Dental LLC 203 384-2261
633 Clinton Ave Bridgeport (06605) ***(G-720)***
Bridgeport Fittings LLC 203 377-5944
705 Lordship Blvd Stratford (06615) ***(G-8588)***
Bridgeport Insulated Wire Co (PA) 203 333-3191
51 Brookfield Ave Bridgeport (06610) ***(G-721)***
Bridgeport Insulated Wire Co 203 375-9579
514 Surf Ave Stratford (06615) ***(G-8589)***
Bridgeport Magnetics Group Inc 203 954-0050
6 Waterview Dr Shelton (06484) ***(G-7410)***
Bridgeport Plastics Co, Trumbull *Also called Reblee Inc* ***(G-9063)***

ALPHABETIC SECTION Built To Last Fine Wdwkg LLC

Bridgeport Proc & Mfg LLC 203 612-7733
155 Davenport St Bridgeport (06607) **(G-722)**
Bridgeport Tl & Stamping Corp.....203 336-2501
35 Burr Ct Bridgeport (06605) **(G-723)**
Bridgewater Chocolate LLC 203 775-2286
559 Federal Rd Brookfield (06804) **(G-1164)**
Bridgwell Rsurces Holdings LLC (HQ) 203 622-9138
1 Sound Shore Dr Ste 302 Greenwich (06830) **(G-3137)**
Brighton & Hove Mold Ltd 203 264-3013
115 Hurley Rd Ste 2c Oxford (06478) **(G-6647)**
Brightsight Llc 860 208-0222
9 Hebert Ln Woodstock (06281) **(G-10658)**
Brignole Distillery LLC.....860 653-9463
103 Hartford Ave East Granby (06026) **(G-2192)**
Brignole Vineyards, East Granby *Also called Brignole Distillery LLC* **(G-2192)**
Brimatco Corporation 203 272-0044
1486 Highland Ave Ste 10 Cheshire (06410) **(G-1364)**
Brings Machine Products 860 346-0350
50 Saint Johns St Middletown (06457) **(G-4327)**
Bristol Inc (HQ) 860 945-2200
1100 Buckingham St Watertown (06795) **(G-9686)**
Bristol Adult Resource Ctr Inc 860 583-8721
97 Peck Ln Bristol (06010) **(G-987)**
Bristol Babcock Employees Fede.....860 945-2200
1100 Buckingham St Watertown (06795) **(G-9687)**
Bristol Bliss LLC.....203 704-0952
229 Fall Mountain Rd Bristol (06010) **(G-988)**
Bristol Hydraulic Scaffolding, Bristol *Also called Bhs* **(G-983)**
Bristol Instrument Gears Inc 860 583-1395
164 Central St Ste 1 Bristol (06010) **(G-989)**
Bristol Nitro Softball Corp.....860 940-1924
104 Driftwood Rd Bristol (06010) **(G-990)**
Bristol Plaza 617 553-1820
576 Farmington Ave Bristol (06010) **(G-991)**
Bristol Press 860 584-0501
188 Main St Torrington (06790) **(G-8906)**
Bristol Signart Inc.....860 582-2577
550 Broad St Bristol (06010) **(G-992)**
Bristol Tool & Die Company 860 582-2577
550 Broad St Ste 13 Bristol (06010) **(G-993)**
Bristol Tool Works LLC.....860 585-7302
61 E Main St Bristol (06010) **(G-994)**
Bristow Studio Glass 860 364-1670
139 Sharon Valley Rd Sharon (06069) **(G-7376)**
Britelite Promotions 203 481-5755
1008 Main St Ste 1 Branford (06405) **(G-565)**
British Precision Inc.....860 633-3343
20 Sequin Dr Glastonbury (06033) **(G-3016)**
British W Indies Trdg USA LLC (PA).....704 451-8400
166 Town Farm Rd Litchfield (06759) **(G-3885)**
Brittany Company Inc 203 269-7859
193 S Cherry St Wallingford (06492) **(G-9222)**
Broad Peak Manufacturing LLC 203 678-4664
10 Beaumont Rd Ste 1 Wallingford (06492) **(G-9223)**
Broadband Communication Div, Wallingford *Also called Ruckus Wireless Inc* **(G-9362)**
Broadcastmed Inc 860 953-2900
195 Farmington Ave Farmington (06032) **(G-2886)**
Broadstripes LLC 203 350-9824
129 Church St Ste 805 New Haven (06510) **(G-5251)**
Brockway Ferry Corporation (PA).....860 767-8231
59 Plains Rd Essex (06426) **(G-2713)**
Brody Printing Company Inc 203 384-9313
265 Central Ave Bridgeport (06607) **(G-724)**
Broil King, Winsted *Also called Bkmfg Corp* **(G-10510)**
Bromley Industries.....860 370-9566
4 Plantation Rd Broad Brook (06016) **(G-1145)**
Brook & Whittle Holding Corp (PA).....203 483-5602
20 Carter Dr Guilford (06437) **(G-3333)**
Brook & Whittle Limited (HQ) 203 483-5602
20 Carter Dr Guilford (06437) **(G-3334)**
Brook Broad Brewing LLC.....860 623-1000
122 Prospect Hill Rd East Windsor (06088) **(G-2486)**
Brook Burgis Alpacas LLC 203 605-0588
44 N Canterbury Rd Canterbury (06331) **(G-1296)**
Brooke Taylor Winery LLC (PA).....860 974-1263
848 Route 171 Woodstock (06281) **(G-10659)**
Brookfeld Mdcl/Srgical Sup Inc.....203 775-0862
60 Old New Milford Rd Brookfield (06804) **(G-1165)**
Brookfield Industries Inc.....860 283-6211
99 W Hillside Ave Thomaston (06787) **(G-8782)**
Brookfield Phrm Compounding, Brookfield *Also called Brookfeld Mdcl/Srgical Sup Inc* **(G-1165)**
Brookfield Stainless LLC.....203 987-6773
12 Allen Rd Brookfield (06804) **(G-1166)**
Brookfield Tractor Prfmce Eqp, Brookfield *Also called Dave Ross* **(G-1177)**
Brooklyn Sand & Gravel LLC 860 779-3980
42 Junior Ave Danielson (06239) **(G-1987)**
Brookside Flvors Ingrdents LLC (HQ) 203 595-4520
201 Tresser Blvd Ste 320 Stamford (06901) **(G-8120)**
Brookwood Laminating Inc 860 774-5001
275 Putnam Rd Wauregan (06387) **(G-9752)**
Brookwood Roll Goods Group, Wauregan *Also called Brookwood Laminating Inc* **(G-9752)**
Broome & Co LLC.....860 653-2106
62 Turkey Hills Rd East Granby (06026) **(G-2193)**
Broome & Company LLC 860 623-0254
12 Copper Dr Windsor Locks (06096) **(G-10474)**
Brophy Metal Products Inc.....860 621-3636
364 Old Turnpike Rd Southington (06489) **(G-7898)**
Brothers & Sons Sugar House.....860 489-2719
998 Saw Mill Hill Rd Torrington (06790) **(G-8907)**
Brown House Communications, Wilton *Also called James P King* **(G-10304)**
Brown Larkin & Co LLC.....860 280-8858
63 Black Walnut Ln Burlington (06013) **(G-1261)**
Browne Hansen LLC 203 269-0557
44 School House Rd Wallingford (06492) **(G-9224)**
Brownell & Company Inc (PA).....860 873-8625
423 E Haddam Moodus Rd Moodus (06469) **(G-4771)**
Brownstone Exploration.....860 866-0208
161 Brownstone Ave Portland (06480) **(G-6954)**
Browser Daily.....860 469-5534
211 Spencer Hill Rd Winsted (06098) **(G-10511)**
Bruce Burgess.....860 510-9185
6303 Town Brooke Middletown (06457) **(G-4328)**
Bruce Corey Enterprises Inc.....203 272-3600
40 Pratt Ln Wolcott (06716) **(G-10550)**
Bruce Kahn 203 329-7441
225 Pinewood Rd Stamford (06903) **(G-8121)**
Bruce Park Sports EMB LLC 203 853-4488
20 Chatham Dr Norwalk (06854) **(G-6100)**
Brushfoil LLC.....203 453-7403
1 Shoreline Dr Ste 6 Guilford (06437) **(G-3335)**
Brushline Design.....860 434-5055
4 Jadon Dr Old Lyme (06371) **(G-6491)**
Brw Associates Inc.....203 426-3318
44 Great Ring Rd Sandy Hook (06482) **(G-7301)**
Bryan Doughty.....860 536-2185
975 Ocean Ave New London (06320) **(G-5459)**
Bryan Heavens Logging & Firewo 860 485-1712
50 Shingle Mill Rd Harwinton (06791) **(G-3723)**
Bryce Gear Inc 860 747-3341
11 N Washington St Plainville (06062) **(G-6779)**
Bryk Machine Works LLC.....203 397-1405
1125 Johnson Rd Woodbridge (06525) **(G-10595)**
Bryka Skystocks LLC.....845 507-8200
549 Cedar St Newington (06111) **(G-5635)**
Brymill Corporation (PA).....860 875-2460
105 Windermere Ave Ste 3b Ellington (06029) **(G-2579)**
Brymill Cryogenic Sys, Ellington *Also called Brymill Corporation* **(G-2579)**
Brynwood Partners V Ltd Partnr (PA).....203 622-1790
8 Sound Shore Dr Ste 265 Greenwich (06830) **(G-3138)**
Bryt Manufacturing.....860 224-4772
23 John St New Britain (06051) **(G-4953)**
Btac Publications 203 560-7742
391 Berkshire Rd Southbury (06488) **(G-7846)**
Btf LLC.....860 354-8926
236 Henry Sanford Rd Bridgewater (06752) **(G-945)**
Bti CCS.....860 758-7644
1000 Old County Cir Windsor Locks (06096) **(G-10475)**
Btx Industries.....203 359-4870
84 W Park Pl Stamford (06901) **(G-8122)**
Buchanan Minerals LLC (HQ).....304 392-1000
57 Danbury Rd Ste 201 Wilton (06897) **(G-10277)**
Buck Scientific Inc.....203 853-9444
58 Fort Point St Norwalk (06855) **(G-6101)**
Buck's Ice Cream, Milford *Also called Bucks Spumoni Company Inc* **(G-4477)**
Buckles In A Snap LLC 774 452-5336
27 Senexet Village Rd Woodstock (06281) **(G-10660)**
Buckley Associates Inc.....203 380-2405
350 Long Beach Blvd Stratford (06615) **(G-8590)**
Bucks Spumoni Company Inc.....203 874-2007
229 Pepes Farm Rd Milford (06460) **(G-4477)**
Bud's Bait Box, Branford *Also called Beckley Inc* **(G-557)**
Buddy-Mentor Inc.....203 258-3871
155 Brewster St Apt 4b Bridgeport (06605) **(G-725)**
Budget Oil 860 649-1527
271 Hopriver Rd Bolton (06043) **(G-507)**
Budget Woodworker LLC 860 468-5551
214 Pennsylvania Ave Niantic (06357) **(G-5802)**
Budney Aerospace Inc.....860 828-0585
131 New Park Dr Berlin (06037) **(G-166)**
Budney Overhaul & Repair Ltd 860 828-0585
131 New Park Dr Berlin (06037) **(G-167)**
Budrad Engineering Co LLC 203 452-7310
26 Patmar Cir Monroe (06468) **(G-4702)**
Buestan Usa LLC.....203 954-8889
5 Dorel Ter Ansonia (06401) **(G-25)**
Buffalo Industrial Fabrics Inc.....203 553-9400
372 Danbury Rd Ste 199 Wilton (06897) **(G-10278)**
Bug Umbrella Gazebo LLC 860 651-0030
48 Wynding Hills Rd East Granby (06026) **(G-2194)**
Builders Concrete East LLC.....860 456-4111
79 Boston Post Rd North Windham (06256) **(G-6035)**
Built To Last Fine Wdwkg LLC 860 619-0119
61 Christian St New Preston (06777) **(G-5611)**

ALPHABETIC

Buisson Jewelers Inc......203 869-8895
200 Railroad Ave Ste 201 Greenwich (06830) ***(G-3139)***
Bull Display, Middletown *Also called Bull Metal Products Inc* ***(G-4329)***
Bull Metal Products Inc......860 346-9691
191 Saybrook Rd Middletown (06457) ***(G-4329)***
Bullie Industries LLC......203 393-9763
21 Tollgate Rd Bethany (06524) ***(G-236)***
Bunny Do LLC......860 621-2365
634 Old Turnpike Rd Plantsville (06479) ***(G-6887)***
Bunsen Rush Laboratories Inc......203 397-0820
270 Amity Rd Ste 124 Woodbridge (06525) ***(G-10596)***
Bunting & Lyon Inc......203 272-4623
615 Broad Swamp Rd Cheshire (06410) ***(G-1365)***
Buon Appetito From Italy LLC......860 437-3668
15 Shaw St New London (06320) ***(G-5460)***
Burdon Enterprises LLC......860 345-4882
20 Reisman Trl Higganum (06441) ***(G-3762)***
Bureaus Sugar House......860 434-5787
60 Rowland Rd Old Lyme (06371) ***(G-6492)***
Burell Bros Inc......860 455-9681
Rr 97 Hampton (06247) ***(G-3534)***
Burke Precision Machine Co Inc......860 408-1394
7 Hatchett Hill Rd East Granby (06026) ***(G-2195)***
Burlington Golf Center Inc......860 675-7320
522 Spielman Hwy Burlington (06013) ***(G-1262)***
Burn Time Enterprises LLC......860 410-0747
15 Cronk Rd Ste 1 Plainville (06062) ***(G-6780)***
Burndy LLC......203 792-1115
185 Grassy Plain St Bethel (06801) ***(G-267)***
Burns Walton......203 422-5222
29 Milo Dr Branford (06405) ***(G-566)***
Burnside Supermarket LLC......860 291-9965
1150 Burnside Ave East Hartford (06108) ***(G-2301)***
Burt Process Equipment Inc (PA)......203 287-1985
100 Overlook Dr Hamden (06514) ***(G-3420)***
Burteck LLC......860 206-8872
863 Marshall Phelps Rd Windsor (06095) ***(G-10369)***
Bushwick Metals LLC......203 630-2459
130 Research Pkwy Ste 203 Meriden (06450) ***(G-4152)***
Bushy Hill Nature Center......860 767-2148
253 Bushy Hill Rd Ivoryton (06442) ***(G-3784)***
Business & Prof Microcompter......860 231-7302
15 Cassandra Blvd Apt 203 West Hartford (06107) ***(G-9780)***
Business Cards Tomorrow Inc......203 723-5858
69 Raytkwich Rd Naugatuck (06770) ***(G-4864)***
Business Journals Inc (PA)......203 853-6015
50 Day St Fl 3 Norwalk (06854) ***(G-6102)***
Business Marketing & Pubg Inc......203 834-9959
13 Silvermine Woods Wilton (06897) ***(G-10279)***
Business New Haven, New Haven *Also called Second Wind Media Limited* ***(G-5391)***
Buswell Manufacturing Co Inc......203 334-6069
229 Merriam St Bridgeport (06604) ***(G-726)***
Butler Irrigation......203 877-2248
85 Grannis Rd Orange (06477) ***(G-6587)***
Butler Property Svc......203 530-4554
85 Grannis Rd Orange (06477) ***(G-6588)***
Butterfly Network Inc (PA)......855 296-6188
530 Old Whitfield St Guilford (06437) ***(G-3336)***
Butterfly Press LLC......860 621-2883
229 Loper St Southington (06489) ***(G-7899)***
Butterfly Wings Pubg Co LLC......203 642-4481
2 Wildmere Ln Norwalk (06851) ***(G-6103)***
Bvc Publishing......860 202-0704
103 Harrison St Bristol (06010) ***(G-995)***
Bvd Press, New London *Also called Bryan Doughty* ***(G-5459)***
Bwd Publishing LLC......860 651-1966
11 Roswell Rd West Simsbury (06092) ***(G-9973)***
Byrne Group Inc......203 573-0100
170 Grand St Waterbury (06702) ***(G-9444)***
Byrne Woodworking Inc......203 953-3205
170 Herbert St Bridgeport (06604) ***(G-727)***
Byron Lord Inc......203 287-9881
18 Bailey Rd Old Lyme (06371) ***(G-6493)***
C & A Machine Co Inc......860 667-0605
49 Progress Cir Newington (06111) ***(G-5636)***
C & C Logging......860 683-0071
416 Pigeon Hill Rd Windsor (06095) ***(G-10370)***
C & D Upholstery......203 838-1050
234 East Ave Norwalk (06855) ***(G-6104)***
C & E Electric......203 546-7255
31 Old Route 7 Ste 5 Brookfield (06804) ***(G-1167)***
C & G Precisions Products Inc......203 879-6989
14 Venus Dr Wolcott (06716) ***(G-10551)***
C & L Automotive Machine Shop......860 523-5268
67 Grassmere Ave West Hartford (06110) ***(G-9781)***
C & R Printing, Bristol *Also called Ronald Bottino* ***(G-1111)***
C & S Engineering Inc......203 235-5727
956 Old Colony Rd Meriden (06451) ***(G-4153)***
C & T Print Finishing Inc......860 282-0616
67 Commerce Way South Windsor (06074) ***(G-7720)***
C & W Manufacturing Co Inc......860 633-4631
74 Eastern Blvd Glastonbury (06033) ***(G-3017)***
C and B Welding LLC......860 423-9047
20 Hillside Dr Lebanon (06249) ***(G-3848)***
C B Enterprises Division, Manchester *Also called Whiteledge Inc* ***(G-4106)***
C B Fabrication......860 889-8030
342 Norwich Ave Taftville (06380) ***(G-8740)***
C B S Contractors Inc......203 734-8015
1 Riverside Dr Ste D Ansonia (06401) ***(G-26)***
C C and P......203 222-8260
2 Fairview Dr Westport (06880) ***(G-10062)***
C C D Center......203 348-0052
24 Roxbury Rd Stamford (06902) ***(G-8123)***
C C I, East Hartford *Also called Circuit Cellar Inc* ***(G-2305)***
C C Precision Products Co Inc......860 628-4403
607 Old Turnpike Rd Southington (06489) ***(G-7900)***
C Cowles & Company (PA)......203 865-3117
126 Bailey Rd North Haven (06473) ***(G-5916)***
C D Industries Inc......203 966-4983
10 Hill St New Canaan (06840) ***(G-5090)***
C E D, Oxford *Also called Consulting Engrg Dev Svcs Inc* ***(G-6653)***
C E I, Wallingford *Also called Component Engineers Inc* ***(G-9235)***
C F D Engineering Company (PA)......203 758-4148
194 Cook Rd Prospect (06712) ***(G-6996)***
C F D Engineering Company......203 754-2807
105 Avenue Of Industry Waterbury (06705) ***(G-9445)***
C J Brand & Son......860 536-9266
9 Overlook Ave Mystic (06355) ***(G-4803)***
C J Cushing Woodworking......860 848-2746
4 Green Valley Lake Rd Old Lyme (06371) ***(G-6494)***
C J Macsata LLC......860 623-6755
115 Cottage Rd Enfield (06082) ***(G-2619)***
C J S Millwork Inc......203 708-0080
425 Fairfield Ave Ste 12 Stamford (06902) ***(G-8124)***
C Libby Leonard......203 375-6205
171 Bruce Ave Stratford (06615) ***(G-8591)***
C Mather Company Inc......860 528-5667
339 Chapel Rd South Windsor (06074) ***(G-7721)***
C N C Router Technologies......203 744-6651
4 Barnard Dr Danbury (06810) ***(G-1760)***
C O Jelliff Corporation (PA)......203 259-1615
354 Pequot Ave Ste 300 Southport (06890) ***(G-8001)***
C P D, Dayville *Also called Custom Plastic Distrs Inc* ***(G-2060)***
C P I Computer Center Inc......203 483-8505
1245 Main St Branford (06405) ***(G-567)***
C Q Publishing......860 292-1566
20 Church St Windsor Locks (06096) ***(G-10476)***
C R Springs Inc......203 879-3357
721 Bound Line Rd Wolcott (06716) ***(G-10552)***
C S I, Milford *Also called Charge Solutions Inc* ***(G-4488)***
C S M S-I P A......203 562-7228
127 Washington Ave Ste 3 North Haven (06473) ***(G-5917)***
C Sherman Johnson Company......860 873-8697
1 Matthews Dr East Haddam (06423) ***(G-2237)***
C V Tool Company Inc (PA)......978 353-7901
44 Robert Porter Rd Southington (06489) ***(G-7901)***
C West Woodworks......860 309-7362
143 Hoerle Blvd Torrington (06790) ***(G-8908)***
C&G Mfg......860 274-9785
126 Skilton Rd Watertown (06795) ***(G-9688)***
C&G Precision Parts, Wolcott *Also called C & G Precisions Products Inc* ***(G-10551)***
C&S Collectibles......860 872-6825
129 Torry Rd Tolland (06084) ***(G-8853)***
C-B Manufacturing & Tool Co......860 583-5402
118 Napco Dr Terryville (06786) ***(G-8748)***
C-Tech Manufacturing Co LLC......860 274-6879
27 Siemon Company Dr Watertown (06795) ***(G-9689)***
C3 Manufacturing LLC......914 943-6877
3a Pheasant Dr New Fairfield (06812) ***(G-5163)***
C8 Sciences, New Haven *Also called Becaid LLC* ***(G-5241)***
Ca Inc......800 225-5224
160 Bridge St Ste 300 East Windsor (06088) ***(G-2487)***
Caap Co Inc......203 877-0375
152 Pepes Farm Rd Milford (06460) ***(G-4478)***
Caballros Hrdwood Flors Pntinc......914 312-0695
2 Myano Ct Stamford (06902) ***(G-8125)***
Cabea LLC......860 738-0819
210 Holabird Ave Ste 8 Winsted (06098) ***(G-10512)***
Cabin Critters Inc......203 778-4552
3 Dunham Dr Ste A New Fairfield (06812) ***(G-5164)***
Cabin Woodworks......203 410-1073
280 Forest Street Ext Hamden (06518) ***(G-3421)***
Cabinet Authority LLC......203 304-2010
11 Overlook Dr Newtown (06470) ***(G-5730)***
Cabinet Dreams LLC......203 558-4178
158 Falls Ave Oakville (06779) ***(G-6451)***
Cabinet Harward Specialti......860 231-1192
50 Chelton Ave West Hartford (06110) ***(G-9782)***
Cabinet Maker......860 933-0272
119 Soap St Dayville (06241) ***(G-2056)***
Cabinet Resources Ct Inc......860 352-2030
180 Cherry Brook Rd Canton (06019) ***(G-1308)***
Cabinet Specialties LLC......860 747-4114
38 Neal Ct Plainville (06062) ***(G-6781)***

ALPHABETIC SECTION

Cabinet Works LLC 860 450-0803
  895 Mansfield City Rd Storrs (06268) *(G-8544)*
Cabinetmakers Choice LLC 203 426-3247
  32 Gelding Hill Rd Sandy Hook (06482) *(G-7302)*
Cabinets Kwik 860 538-5047
  1 Hartford Sq New Britain (06052) *(G-4954)*
Cable Electronics Inc 860 953-0300
  221 Newfield Ave Ste 2 Hartford (06106) *(G-3560)*
Cable Management LLC 860 670-1890
  290 Pratt St Ste 1108 Meriden (06450) *(G-4154)*
Cable Manufacturing Business, Redding Also called Armored Shield Technologies *(G-7090)*
Cable Technology Inc 860 429-7889
  73 River Rd Willington (06279) *(G-10246)*
Caco Print Productions LLC 860 583-1223
  132 Riverside Ave Bristol (06010) *(G-996)*
Cad CAM Machine LLC 860 410-9788
  150 Robert Jackson Way Plainville (06062) *(G-6782)*
Cad/CAM Dntl Stdio Mil Ctr Inc 203 733-3069
  184 Mount Pleasant Rd Newtown (06470) *(G-5731)*
Cadcom Inc 203 877-0640
  110 Raton Rd Milford (06461) *(G-4479)*
Cadence Ct Inc 860 370-9780
  4 Kenny Roberts Mem Dr Suffield (06078) *(G-8716)*
Cadentia LLC 860 995-0173
  136 Rockwell Ave Bristol (06010) *(G-997)*
Cadesk Company LLC (PA) 203 268-8083
  88 Cottage St Trumbull (06611) *(G-9008)*
Cadi Co Inc (PA) 203 729-1111
  60 Rado Dr Naugatuck (06770) *(G-4865)*
Cadi Company, Naugatuck Also called Cadi Co Inc *(G-4865)*
Cadmus 203 595-3000
  200 1st Stamford Pl Fl 2 Stamford (06902) *(G-8126)*
Caffeine and Carburetors 203 966-2704
  77 Pine St New Canaan (06840) *(G-5091)*
Cag Imaging 203 632-5799
  209 Great Hill Rd Naugatuck (06770) *(G-4866)*
Cag Imaging LLC 860 887-0836
  387 N Main St Norwich (06360) *(G-6408)*
Cagno Enterprises LLC 203 729-3883
  98 Morning Dove Rd Naugatuck (06770) *(G-4867)*
Caine Machining Inc 860 738-1619
  43 Meadow St Winsted (06098) *(G-10513)*
Cal Brown Paving, Gales Ferry Also called Calvin Brown *(G-2982)*
Calabria Granite & Stone, Pleasant Valley Also called Luis Raimundi *(G-6924)*
Calanca & Assoc LLC 203 972-6344
  40 Conrad Rd New Canaan (06840) *(G-5092)*
Calculator Training 860 355-8255
  94 Buckingham Rd New Milford (06776) *(G-5513)*
Calhoun Press Inc 860 202-0998
  205 Clarke Rd Lebanon (06249) *(G-3849)*
Callaway Cars Inc 860 434-9002
  3 High St Old Lyme (06371) *(G-6495)*
Callaway Companies Inc (PA) 860 434-9002
  3 High St Old Lyme (06371) *(G-6496)*
Calle Market 203 789-0632
  155 Kimberly Ave New Haven (06519) *(G-5252)*
Calmare Therapeutics Inc (PA) 203 368-6044
  1375 Kings Hwy Ste 400 Fairfield (06824) *(G-2756)*
Calumma Technologies LLC 914 557-4562
  11 Bedford Ave Apt H3 Norwalk (06850) *(G-6105)*
Calvin Brown 860 536-6178
  259 Gallup Hill Rd Gales Ferry (06339) *(G-2982)*
Calzone Ltd (PA) 203 367-5766
  225 Black Rock Ave Bridgeport (06605) *(G-728)*
Calzone Case Company, Bridgeport Also called Calzone Ltd *(G-728)*
CAM Group LLC 860 646-2378
  130 Chapel Rd Manchester (06042) *(G-3989)*
CAM Industries 860 738-8338
  8 Millbrook Rd Colebrook (06021) *(G-1584)*
CAM Manufacturing Co LLC 203 301-0153
  63 Whitney Ave Milford (06460) *(G-4480)*
CAM Manufacturing LLC 203 415-0411
  187 Rock Ln Milford (06460) *(G-4481)*
Cam2 Technologies LLC 203 456-3025
  6 Finance Dr Danbury (06810) *(G-1761)*
Camaro Signs Inc (PA) 860 886-1553
  58 Yantic Flats Rd Unit 1 Yantic (06389) *(G-10697)*
Camarro Research 203 254-1755
  345 Carroll Rd Fairfield (06824) *(G-2757)*
Cambrdge Fine Wdwkg Renovation 860 583-7561
  803 Wolcott St Bristol (06010) *(G-998)*
Cambridge Specialty Co Inc 860 828-3579
  588 Four Rod Rd Berlin (06037) *(G-168)*
Cameo Embroidery 860 301-3123
  34 School House Ln Durham (06422) *(G-2140)*
Cameron Bortz 860 599-0477
  256 S Broad St Pawcatuck (06379) *(G-6704)*
Cameron International Corp 860 633-0277
  256 Oakwood Dr Ste 1 Glastonbury (06033) *(G-3018)*
Camerota Truck Parts, North Haven Also called S Camerota & Sons Inc *(G-5989)*
Cametoid Technologies Inc 860 646-4667
  150 Colonial Rd Manchester (06042) *(G-3990)*
Camlock Systems Inc 860 378-0302
  109 Industrial Dr Southington (06489) *(G-7902)*
Campbell Publicity LLC 646 532-1512
  331 South St Middlebury (06762) *(G-4274)*
Campo Enterprises 203 776-0664
  1 Gallagher Rd Hamden (06517) *(G-3422)*
Campus Yellow Pages LLC 860 523-9909
  79 High Wood Rd West Hartford (06117) *(G-9783)*
Can Straps LLC 203 281-7333
  127 Woodlawn St Hamden (06517) *(G-3423)*
Can-AM Trading & Logistics LLC 860 961-9932
  2 Sands Dr Old Lyme (06371) *(G-6497)*
Canaan Custom Machine 860 824-0674
  351 Norfolk Rd East Canaan (06024) *(G-2181)*
Canberra Industries, Inc., Meriden Also called Mirion Tech Canberra Inc *(G-4204)*
Candle D' Lites, Stafford Springs Also called Dianna Blanchard *(G-8026)*
Candle Threads 860 490-5890
  20 Gem Grv Enfield (06082) *(G-2620)*
Candle Threads 860 292-1667
  33 S Main St East Windsor (06088) *(G-2488)*
Candle Woodworks 860 350-4390
  50 Route 37 E Sherman (06784) *(G-7591)*
Candles For A Cause USA 860 912-3946
  30 Summer St Apt 2 Bristol (06010) *(G-999)*
Candlewood Boat Restoration 203 223-7893
  10 Meetinghouse Hill Cir New Fairfield (06812) *(G-5165)*
Candlewood Machine Pdts LLC 860 350-2211
  46 Old State Rd Ste 6 New Milford (06776) *(G-5514)*
Candlewood Stars Inc 203 994-8826
  60 Newtown Rd Ste 32 Danbury (06810) *(G-1762)*
Candlewood Tool & Machine Shop 860 355-1892
  24 Martha Ln Gaylordsville (06755) *(G-2990)*
Canevari Plastics Inc 203 878-4319
  10 Furniture Row Milford (06460) *(G-4482)*
Canfield Electric 203 266-5290
  151 Hickory Ln Bethlehem (06751) *(G-367)*
Canidae Corp 860 539-5307
  1975 Tandem Way Plainville (06062) *(G-6783)*
Canine Core Industries LLC 203 459-1584
  232 Teller Rd Trumbull (06611) *(G-9009)*
Cannelli Printing Co Inc 203 932-1719
  39 Wood St West Haven (06516) *(G-9886)*
Cannondale Sports Group, Wilton Also called Cycling Sports Group Inc *(G-10287)*
Canoga Perkins Corporation 203 888-7914
  100 Bank St Seymour (06483) *(G-7337)*
Cantata Media LLC 203 951-9885
  132b Water St Norwalk (06854) *(G-6106)*
Canterbury Machinery Rnd Llc 860 546-5000
  22 N Society Rd Canterbury (06331) *(G-1297)*
Canton Sign Shop, Canton Also called Joseph Garrity *(G-1316)*
Canvas and Sail Repair Company, Westbrook Also called Liberty Services LLC *(G-10002)*
Canvas LLC 860 986-8553
  608 Park Rd West Hartford (06107) *(G-9784)*
Canvas Products 203 225-0507
  383 Isinglass Rd Shelton (06484) *(G-7411)*
Cap-Tech Products Inc 860 490-5078
  61 Arrow Rd Ste 11 Wethersfield (06109) *(G-10185)*
Capewell Aerial Systems LLC (PA) 860 610-0700
  105 Nutmeg Rd S South Windsor (06074) *(G-7722)*
Capital Cities Communications 203 784-8800
  8 Elm St New Haven (06510) *(G-5253)*
Capital Design & Engrg Inc 203 798-6027
  35 Eagle Rd Ste 2 Danbury (06810) *(G-1763)*
Capital Venture, Stamford Also called Scinetx LLC *(G-8403)*
Capitol City Burial Vaults 860 953-1060
  111 South St West Hartford (06110) *(G-9785)*
Capitol Electronics Inc 203 744-3300
  11 Francis J Clarke Cir Bethel (06801) *(G-268)*
Capitol Machine Inc Preci 860 410-0758
  30 Hayden Ave Ste B Plainville (06062) *(G-6784)*
Capitol Printing Co Inc 860 522-1547
  52 Pratt St Hartford (06103) *(G-3561)*
Capitol Sausage & Provs Inc 860 527-5510
  101 Reserve Rd Bldg 14 Hartford (06114) *(G-3562)*
Capricorn Investors II LP 203 861-6600
  30 E Elm St Greenwich (06830) *(G-3140)*
Capricorn Investors III LP (PA) 203 861-6600
  30 E Elm St Greenwich (06830) *(G-3141)*
Capstan Inc 508 384-3100
  263 Georgetown Rd Weston (06883) *(G-10021)*
Capstone Manufacturing Inc 413 636-6170
  1257 John Fitch Blvd 2 South Windsor (06074) *(G-7723)*
Capstone Software LLC 617 413-4444
  851 River Rd Mystic (06355) *(G-4804)*
Captive Global LLC 860 302-6706
  22 Summit Farms Rd Southington (06489) *(G-7903)*
Car Buyers Market 516 482-0292
  30 Nutmeg Dr Ste B Trumbull (06611) *(G-9010)*
Cara C Andreoli 860 888-6553
  41 Mockingbird Ln Glastonbury (06033) *(G-3019)*
Cara Therapeutics Inc 203 406-3700
  107 Elm St Fl 9 Stamford (06902) *(G-8127)*

Carala Ventures Ltd 800 483-6449
120 Research Dr Stratford (06615) **(G-8592)**
Carbide Solutions LLC 860 515-8665
800 Marshall Phelps Rd Windsor (06095) **(G-10371)**
Carbide Technology Inc 860 621-8981
55 Captain Lewis Dr Southington (06489) **(G-7904)**
Carbon Products Inc 860 749-0614
40 Scitico Rd Somersville (06072) **(G-7678)**
Carbon Tools Inc 860 228-9483
409 Church St Amston (06231) **(G-2)**
Carbtrol Corporation 203 337-4340
200 Benton St Stratford (06615) **(G-8593)**
Card Carrier Games LLC 203 521-0291
589 Bridgeport Ave # 17 Milford (06460) **(G-4483)**
Cardinal Health 414 LLC 860 291-9135
131 Hartland St Ste 8 East Hartford (06108) **(G-2302)**
Cardinal Shehan Center Inc 203 336-4468
1494 Main St Bridgeport (06604) **(G-729)**
Cardiophotonics LLC 203 645-6077
14 Lacey Rd Bethany (06524) **(G-237)**
Cardiopulmonary Corp 203 877-1999
200 Cascade Blvd Ste B Milford (06460) **(G-4484)**
Cardioxyl Pharmaceuticals Inc 919 869-8586
5 Research Pkwy Wallingford (06492) **(G-9225)**
Cardoros Inc 860 442-2907
5 Giovanni Dr Waterford (06385) **(G-9644)**
Care Connection LLC 860 274-1251
38 Breezy Knoll Dr Watertown (06795) **(G-9690)**
Career Concepts 203 378-9943
3841 Main St Stratford (06614) **(G-8594)**
Careerpath Mobile LLC 203 512-2379
8 Wildlife Dr New Milford (06776) **(G-5515)**
Carefree Building Co Inc (PA) 860 267-7600
48 Westchester Rd Colchester (06415) **(G-1544)**
Carefree Small Buildings, Colchester *Also called Carefree Building Co Inc* **(G-1544)**
Carem Assoc 203 372-6788
178 Autumn Ridge Rd Fairfield (06825) **(G-2758)**
Carestream Health Molecular 888 777-2072
4 Science Park New Haven (06511) **(G-5254)**
Carestream Molecular Imaging, New Haven *Also called Carestream Health Molecular* **(G-5254)**
Carey Automatic Door LLC 203 267-4278
35 Forest Rd Southbury (06488) **(G-7847)**
Carey Manufacturing Co Inc (PA) 860 829-1803
5 Pasco Hill Rd Unit A Cromwell (06416) **(G-1694)**
Carey Manufacturing Co Inc 860 829-1803
5 Pasco Hill Rd Unit B Cromwell (06416) **(G-1695)**
Caribe House Press LLC 812 320-5303
109 Bittersweet Cir Guilford (06437) **(G-3337)**
Carigent Therapeutics Inc 203 887-2873
5 Science Park Ste 10 New Haven (06511) **(G-5255)**
Carin Industries Inc 860 489-1122
78 N Elm St Torrington (06790) **(G-8909)**
Carismo Productions 203 334-8469
150 Scofield Ave Bridgeport (06605) **(G-730)**
Carl Associates Inc 860 749-7620
1257 John Fitch Blvd 3 South Windsor (06074) **(G-7724)**
Carl Perry 860 834-4459
91 Highview Ter Middletown (06457) **(G-4330)**
Carl Rizzo & Associates 860 644-5849
68 Mark Dr South Windsor (06074) **(G-7725)**
Carla Way 203 351-7815
65 High Ridge Rd 287 Stamford (06905) **(G-8128)**
Carlas Pasta Inc 860 436-4042
50 Talbot Ln South Windsor (06074) **(G-7726)**
Carli Farm & Equipment LLC 860 908-3227
40 Mill Ln Salem (06420) **(G-7287)**
Carlin Combustion Tech Inc 413 525-7700
126 Bailey Rd North Haven (06473) **(G-5918)**
Carlin Combustion Tech Inc (HQ) 203 680-9401
126 Bailey Rd North Haven (06473) **(G-5919)**
Carlin Mfg Kitchens To Go 413 519-2822
31 Masons Island Rd Mystic (06355) **(G-4805)**
Carling Technologies Inc (PA) 860 793-9281
60 Johnson Ave Plainville (06062) **(G-6785)**
Carlingswitch, Plainville *Also called Carling Technologies Inc* **(G-6785)**
Carlo Huber Selections Inc 917 742-0601
210 Between The Lakes Rd Salisbury (06068) **(G-7294)**
Carlos Lee Publishing 860 536-8450
202 Noank Ledyard Rd Mystic (06355) **(G-4806)**
Carlos Welding and Fab LLC 860 647-8592
74 Bretton Rd Manchester (06042) **(G-3991)**
Carls Closets LLC 203 457-9401
118 Williams Dr Guilford (06437) **(G-3338)**
Carlson Sheet Metal 860 354-4660
24 Bostwick Pl New Milford (06776) **(G-5516)**
Carlson Welding & Fabrication 860 788-3569
58 Great Hillwood Rd Moodus (06469) **(G-4772)**
Carlton Forge Works 860 873-9730
37 Eli Chapman Rd Moodus (06469) **(G-4773)**
Carlton Industries Corp 203 288-5605
33 Rossotto Dr Hamden (06514) **(G-3424)**
Carlucci Welding & Fabrication 203 588-0746
205 Wilson Ave Norwalk (06854) **(G-6107)**
Carlyle Johnson Machine Co LLC (PA) 860 643-1531
291 Boston Tpke Bolton (06043) **(G-508)**
Carnegie Tool Inc 203 866-0744
25 Perry Ave Ste 12 Norwalk (06850) **(G-6108)**
Carob Designs LLC 203 630-9171
290 Pratt St Ofc Meriden (06450) **(G-4155)**
Carogen Corporation 203 606-8796
295 Washington Ave Hamden (06518) **(G-3425)**
Carol Ackerman Designs 860 693-1013
107 Main St Collinsville (06019) **(G-1590)**
Carpet Products 860 278-6160
218 Murphy Rd Hartford (06114) **(G-3563)**
Carpin Manufacturing Inc 203 574-2556
411 Austin Rd Waterbury (06705) **(G-9446)**
Carrano Railings 203 248-7245
1130 Sherman Ave Hamden (06514) **(G-3426)**
Carriage House Companies Inc 860 647-1909
42 Steeplechase Dr Manchester (06040) **(G-3992)**
Carrier Access - Trin Networks 203 778-8222
61 Commerce Dr Brookfield (06804) **(G-1168)**
Carrier Corp 860 728-7000
175 Capital Blvd Ste 400 Rocky Hill (06067) **(G-7225)**
Carrier Corporation 860 728-7000
426 Colt Hwy Farmington (06032) **(G-2887)**
Carrier Manufacturing Inc 860 223-2264
70a Saint Claire Ave New Britain (06051) **(G-4955)**
Carris Reels Connecticut Inc 860 749-8308
11 Randolph St Enfield (06082) **(G-2621)**
Carrubba Incorporated 203 878-0605
70 Research Dr Milford (06460) **(G-4485)**
Carte Medical Corp 860 258-1970
850 Silas Deane Hwy Wethersfield (06109) **(G-10186)**
Carten Controls Inc 203 699-2100
604 W Johnson Ave Cheshire (06410) **(G-1366)**
Carten-Fujikin Incorporated 203 699-2134
604 W Johnson Ave Cheshire (06410) **(G-1367)**
Carter Inv Holdings Corp (HQ) 860 283-5801
401 Watertown Rd Thomaston (06787) **(G-8783)**
Carwild Corporation (PA) 860 442-4914
3 State Pier Rd New London (06320) **(G-5461)**
Cas Medical Systems Inc 203 488-1957
32 Park Dr E Branford (06405) **(G-568)**
Cas Medical Systems Inc 203 315-6953
32 E Industrial Rd Branford (06405) **(G-569)**
Cas Medical Systems Inc (HQ) 203 488-6056
44 E Industrial Rd Branford (06405) **(G-570)**
Cas-Kel Manufacturing Co Inc 860 693-8704
292 Albany Tpke Canton (06019) **(G-1309)**
Casaro Labs Ltd 203 353-8500
1100 Summer St Ste 203 Stamford (06905) **(G-8129)**
Cascades Fine Papers 860 870-7600
265 Windsorville Rd Ellington (06029) **(G-2580)**
Cascades Holding US Inc 203 426-5871
1 Edmund Rd Newtown (06470) **(G-5732)**
Casco Products Corporation (HQ) 203 922-3200
1000 Lafayette Blvd # 100 Bridgeport (06604) **(G-731)**
Case Association 860 989-6533
2750 Mountain Rd West Suffield (06093) **(G-9985)**
Case Concepts Intl LLC (PA) 203 883-8602
112 Prospect St Unit A Stamford (06901) **(G-8130)**
Case Patterns & Wood Products, Groton *Also called Case Patterns Inc* **(G-3275)**
Case Patterns Inc 860 445-6722
257 South Rd Groton (06340) **(G-3275)**
Caseysediblescom, Fairfield *Also called Sallie Gawron* **(G-2841)**
Cash Time Industries LLC 860 770-7192
522 Church St New Britain (06051) **(G-4956)**
Cashon 786 325-4144
350 W Shore Ave Groton (06340) **(G-3276)**
Casmed, Branford *Also called Cas Medical Systems Inc* **(G-569)**
Caspari Inc (PA) 203 888-1100
99 Cogwheel Ln Seymour (06483) **(G-7338)**
Cast Global Manufacturing Corp 203 828-6147
66 Prokop Rd Oxford (06478) **(G-6648)**
Casting Development Associates, Fairfield *Also called Charles W Simmons* **(G-2759)**
Castle Beverages Inc 203 732-0883
105 Myrtle Ave Ansonia (06401) **(G-27)**
Castle Systems Inc 203 250-3140
125 Commerce Ct Ste 4 Cheshire (06410) **(G-1368)**
Castle Technologies Inc 860 582-7299
5 Cross Rd Terryville (06786) **(G-8749)**
Castleton Commodities (HQ) 203 564-8100
2200 Atlantic St Ste 800 Stamford (06902) **(G-8131)**
Castro Industries LLC 203 249-9268
12 Joshua Ln Greenwich (06830) **(G-3142)**
Castrol Industrial N Amer Inc 860 928-5100
251 Kennedy Dr Putnam (06260) **(G-7032)**
Cat LLC 860 953-1807
819 N Mountain Rd Hartford (06111) **(G-3564)**
Cat Tales Press Inc 203 268-3505
61 Hall Rd Easton (06612) **(G-2548)**

Catachem Inc 203 262-0330
353 Christian St Ste 2 Oxford (06478) ***(G-6649)***
Catelectric Corp (PA) 860 912-0800
33 Island Cir S Groton (06340) ***(G-3277)***
Catera, The, Hartford *Also called Copeland Latasha* ***(G-3570)***
Catholic Transcript Inc 860 286-2828
467 Bloomfield Ave Bloomfield (06002) ***(G-401)***
Catholic Transcript Online, Bloomfield *Also called Catholic Transcript Inc* ***(G-401)***
Cathys Country Scents Candles 860 458-8219
100 Monson Rd Stafford Springs (06076) ***(G-8020)***
Catskill Gran Countertops Inc 860 667-1555
156 Pane Rd Ste A Newington (06111) ***(G-5637)***
Cavallo Manufacturing LLC 203 596-8007
289 Fairfield Ave Waterbury (06708) ***(G-9447)***
Cavar Industries LLC 860 684-0706
38 Mashapaug Rd Union (06076) ***(G-9109)***
Cavegrl LLC 914 261-5801
34 Clifford Ave Stamford (06905) ***(G-8132)***
Cavekraft Woodworking LLC 860 230-4480
155 Anna Farm Rd E North Stonington (06359) ***(G-6021)***
Cavtech Industries 203 437-8764
217 Interstate Ln Waterbury (06705) ***(G-9448)***
CB Seating Etc LLC (PA) 203 359-3880
324 Strawberry Hill Ave Norwalk (06851) ***(G-6109)***
CBA Lighting and Controls Inc 860 623-1924
10 Northgate Dr Windsor Locks (06096) ***(G-10477)***
Cbc Co, Coventry *Also called Charles Boggini Company LLC* ***(G-1649)***
Cbd101 LLC 203 273-9941
284 Racebrook Rd Orange (06477) ***(G-6589)***
Cbr, West Hartford *Also called Connectcut Boiler Repr Mfg Inc* ***(G-9793)***
CBS Contractors, Ansonia *Also called C B S Contractors Inc* ***(G-26)***
CBS Manufacturing Company 860 653-8100
35 Kripes Rd East Granby (06026) ***(G-2196)***
CBS Ne, Seymour *Also called Circuit Breaker Sales Ne Inc* ***(G-7340)***
CCC Media LLC 860 225-4601
1 Court St New Britain (06051) ***(G-4957)***
Cch Tagetik, Stamford *Also called Tagetik North America LLC* ***(G-8457)***
CCI, Putnam *Also called Central Construction Inds LLC* ***(G-7033)***
CCI Corpus Christi LLC 203 564-8100
2200 Atlantic St Ste 800 Stamford (06902) ***(G-8133)***
CCI Cyrus River Terminal LLC 203 761-8000
2200 Atlantic St Ste 800 Stamford (06902) ***(G-8134)***
CCI East Texas Upstream LLC 203 564-8100
2200 Atlantic St Ste 800 Stamford (06902) ***(G-8135)***
CCI Robinsons Bend LLC 203 564-8571
2200 Atlantic St Ste 800 Stamford (06902) ***(G-8136)***
Cciyes, Tolland *Also called Connecticut Components Inc* ***(G-8855)***
CCL Industries Corporation (HQ) 203 926-1253
15 Controls Dr Shelton (06484) ***(G-7412)***
CCL Label, Shelton *Also called CCL Industries Corporation* ***(G-7412)***
CCL Label Inc 203 926-1253
15 Controls Dr Shelton (06484) ***(G-7413)***
CCL Label (delaware) Inc (HQ) 203 926-1253
15 Controls Dr Shelton (06484) ***(G-7414)***
Cco Llc 860 757-3434
2138 Silas Deane Hwy # 101 Rocky Hill (06067) ***(G-7226)***
Ccr Products LLC 860 953-0499
167 South St West Hartford (06110) ***(G-9786)***
CD Racing Products 203 264-7822
91 Willenbrock Rd Ste B3 Oxford (06478) ***(G-6650)***
CD Solutions Inc 203 481-5895
420 E Main St Ste 16 Branford (06405) ***(G-571)***
Cde, Danbury *Also called Capital Design & Engrg Inc* ***(G-1763)***
Ceac, Sandy Hook *Also called Conn Engineering Assoc Corp* ***(G-7305)***
Cebal Americas (PA) 203 845-6356
101 Merritt 7 Ste 2 Norwalk (06851) ***(G-6110)***
Cecelia New York LLC 917 392-4536
23 Chestnut St Darien (06820) ***(G-2010)***
Ceci Printer LLC 203 994-6314
19 Germantown Rd Fl 2 Danbury (06810) ***(G-1764)***
Ceda Company Inc 860 666-1593
36 Holmes Rd Newington (06111) ***(G-5638)***
Cedar Accessories 860 350-6969
5 Old Town Park Rd New Milford (06776) ***(G-5517)***
Cedar Ridge Oil Co 860 435-9398
349 Taconic Rd Salisbury (06068) ***(G-7295)***
Cedar Swamp Log & Lumber 860 974-2344
45 Hager Rd Woodstock (06281) ***(G-10661)***
Cedar Woodworking 203 335-4108
65 Hawley Ave Bridgeport (06606) ***(G-732)***
Cedarapids, Westport *Also called Terex Usa LLC* ***(G-10164)***
Cee Orange LLC 203 799-2665
449 Boston Post Rd Orange (06477) ***(G-6590)***
Celb LLC 203 739-0157
11 Mountainville Ave Danbury (06810) ***(G-1765)***
Celeste Industries Corporation 860 278-9800
30 High St Hartford (06103) ***(G-3565)***
Cell Nique 888 417-9343
12 Old Stage Coach Rd Weston (06883) ***(G-10022)***
Celldex Therapeutics Inc 203 864-5771
688 E Main St Ste 1 Branford (06405) ***(G-572)***
Cellmark Pulp & Paper Inc 203 299-5050
80 Washington St Ste 1 Norwalk (06854) ***(G-6111)***
Celtic Co, West Hartford *Also called Component Concepts Inc* ***(G-9792)***
Celtic Stoneworks 860 846-0279
174 Whiting St Plainville (06062) ***(G-6786)***
Cem Group LLC (HQ) 860 675-5000
258 Spielman Hwy Ste 7 Burlington (06013) ***(G-1263)***
Cema Publishing LLC 585 317-3724
56 Maitland Rd Stamford (06906) ***(G-8137)***
Cemcolift Elevator Systems, Bloomfield *Also called Ascend Elevator Inc* ***(G-391)***
Center Broach & Machine Co 203 235-6329
525 N Colony St Meriden (06450) ***(G-4156)***
Center For Discovery 203 955-1381
1320 Mill Hill Rd Southport (06890) ***(G-8002)***
Center Mass LLC 860 350-0239
94 Town Farm Rd New Milford (06776) ***(G-5518)***
Center Road Software LLC 860 402-2767
1 Acorn Dr East Haddam (06423) ***(G-2238)***
Central Conn Cmmunications LLC 860 225-4601
1 Court St Fl 4 New Britain (06051) ***(G-4958)***
Central Conn Cooperative Farme 860 649-4523
1050 Sullivan Ave Ste A3 South Windsor (06074) ***(G-7727)***
Central Connecticut Coating 860 528-8281
52 Village St East Hartford (06108) ***(G-2303)***
Central Connecticut Sls & Mfg 860 667-1411
37 Stanwell Rd Newington (06111) ***(G-5639)***
Central Connecticut Waterjet 860 828-3877
194 Christian Ln Ste A Berlin (06037) ***(G-169)***
Central Construction Inds LLC 860 963-8902
30 Harris St Putnam (06260) ***(G-7033)***
Central CT Snow LLC 860 467-3107
85 Middletown Ave East Hampton (06424) ***(G-2260)***
Central Electric Inc 860 774-3054
364 Putnam Pike Dayville (06241) ***(G-2057)***
Central Electric Motor 860 642-7421
1378 Exeter Rd Lebanon (06249) ***(G-3850)***
Central Marble & Granite LLC 203 734-4644
22 Maple St Ansonia (06401) ***(G-28)***
Central Optical 860 236-2329
33 Lasalle Rd West Hartford (06107) ***(G-9787)***
Central Pallet & Box 860 224-4416
271 John Downey Dr New Britain (06051) ***(G-4959)***
Centritec Seals LLC 860 594-7183
222 Pitkin St Ste 104 East Hartford (06108) ***(G-2304)***
Centrix Inc 203 929-5582
770 River Rd Shelton (06484) ***(G-7415)***
Century Acquisition 518 758-7229
49 Clayton Rd Canaan (06018) ***(G-1284)***
Century Products, New Canaan *Also called Contek International Corp* ***(G-5098)***
Century Sign LLC 203 230-9000
2666 State St Hamden (06517) ***(G-3427)***
Century Software Systems 203 888-5233
26 Sagamore Dr Seymour (06483) ***(G-7339)***
Century Spring Mfg Co Inc 860 582-3344
100 Wooster Ct Bristol (06010) ***(G-1000)***
Century Tool and Design Inc 860 621-6748
260 Canal St Milldale (06467) ***(G-4683)***
Century Tool Co Inc 860 923-9523
753 Thompson Rd Thompson (06277) ***(G-8832)***
Century Woodworking Inc 860 379-7538
40 River Rd Pleasant Valley (06063) ***(G-6921)***
Cenveo Inc 203 595-3000
200 1st Stamford Pl Stamford (06902) ***(G-8138)***
Cenveo Corporation 303 790-8023
200 Frst Stamford Pl Fl 2 Stamford (06902) ***(G-8139)***
Cenveo Enterprises Inc (PA) 203 595-3000
200 First Stamford Pl # 2 Stamford (06902) ***(G-8140)***
Cenveo Worldwide Limited (HQ) 203 595-3000
200 First Stamford Pl # 2 Stamford (06902) ***(G-8141)***
Cerberus Enterprise Sftwr LLC 860 432-3861
180 Porter St Manchester (06040) ***(G-3993)***
Cerbone Bakery, Stamford *Also called Beldotti Bakeries* ***(G-8109)***
Cerrito Furniture Inds Inc 203 481-2580
7 Venice St Branford (06405) ***(G-573)***
Cerritos Upholstery Concepts, Branford *Also called Cerrito Furniture Inds Inc* ***(G-573)***
Cessna Aircraft, Oxford *Also called Textron Aviation Inc* ***(G-6697)***
CET Inc 203 882-8057
270 Rowe Ave Ste D Milford (06461) ***(G-4486)***
CFM Test & Balance Corp 203 778-1900
14 Depot Pl Ste 2 Bethel (06801) ***(G-269)***
CFPA, Rockfall *Also called Connecticut Forest & Park Assn* ***(G-7211)***
Cgl Inc 860 945-6166
1094 Echo Lake Rd Watertown (06795) ***(G-9691)***
Chabaso Bakery, New Haven *Also called Atticus Bakery LLC* ***(G-5237)***
Chachitas Chango, Hartford *Also called Botanica Chachitas* ***(G-3558)***
Chad Labs Corporation 203 877-3891
128 Research Dr Ste G Milford (06460) ***(G-4487)***
Chadbourne Woodshop 203 468-4715
190 Short Beach Rd East Haven (06512) ***(G-2415)***
Chainmail & More LLC 860 741-2965
54 Hazard Ave Ste 175 Enfield (06082) ***(G-2622)***

ALPHABETIC

Chakana Sky Alpacas ALPHABETIC SECTION

Chakana Sky Alpacas 860 204-1646
36a Turkey Hill Rd Chester (06412) ***(G-1466)***
Challenge Sailcloth 860 871-8030
560 Nutmeg Rd N South Windsor (06074) ***(G-7728)***
Chamard Vineyards Inc 860 664-0299
115 Cow Hill Rd Clinton (06413) ***(G-1493)***
Champion Enterprises Inc 860 429-3537
19 Greenfield Ln Storrs (06268) ***(G-8545)***
Champlin-Packrite Inc 860 951-9217
151 Batson Dr Manchester (06042) ***(G-3994)***
Chand Eisenmann Metallurgical, Burlington *Also called Cem Group LLC* ***(G-1263)***
Chandler Furniture & Wdwrk LLC 203 895-6289
17 Bonnie Brook Dr Shelton (06484) ***(G-7416)***
Chandler Industries LLC 860 283-8147
117 E Main St Thomaston (06787) ***(G-8784)***
Changesurfer Consulting 312 702-3742
56 Daleville School Rd Willington (06279) ***(G-10247)***
Channel Alloys 203 975-1404
301 Merritt 7 Ste 1 Norwalk (06851) ***(G-6112)***
Channel Sources LLC 203 775-6464
246 Federal Rd Ste A12-1 Brookfield (06804) ***(G-1169)***
Channel Sources Company, Brookfield *Also called Channel Sources LLC* ***(G-1169)***
Channel Sources Dist Co LLC 203 775-6464
246 Federal Rd Ste A12-1 Brookfield (06804) ***(G-1170)***
Channys Candles LLC 860 313-9139
62 Charles St Torrington (06790) ***(G-8910)***
Chantys Closet 860 752-4512
1210 Matianuck Ave Windsor (06095) ***(G-10372)***
Chapco Inc (PA) 860 526-9535
10 Denlar Dr Chester (06412) ***(G-1467)***
Chapin Packaging LLC 203 202-2747
1078 Post Rd Ste 1 Darien (06820) ***(G-2011)***
Chapin Printing Group, Darien *Also called Chapin Packaging LLC* ***(G-2011)***
Chapman Lumber Inc 860 283-6213
224 Watertown Rd Thomaston (06787) ***(G-8785)***
Chapman Manufacturing Company 860 349-9228
471 New Haven Rd Durham (06422) ***(G-2141)***
Charge Solutions Inc 203 871-7282
205 Research Dr Unit 1011 Milford (06460) ***(G-4488)***
Charles A Boucher Co Inc 860 868-2881
30 Dark Entry Rd Washington (06793) ***(G-9412)***
Charles Alain Publishing Ltd 203 226-2882
27 Cross Hwy Westport (06880) ***(G-10063)***
Charles Boggini Company LLC 860 742-2652
733 Bread And Milk St Coventry (06238) ***(G-1649)***
Charles Clay Ltd 203 662-0125
149 Cherry St New Canaan (06840) ***(G-5093)***
Charles J Angelo Mfg Group LLC 860 646-2378
130 Chapel Rd Manchester (06042) ***(G-3995)***
Charles J Sima & Son, Higganum *Also called George Sima* ***(G-3764)***
Charles K White 203 631-2540
2259 State St Hamden (06517) ***(G-3428)***
Charles Manufacturing Co 860 747-3550
161 Woodford Ave Plainville (06062) ***(G-6787)***
Charles McDougal 860 739-9952
61 White Birch Cir Niantic (06357) ***(G-5803)***
Charles Pike & Sons 860 455-9968
311 Providence Tpke Hampton (06247) ***(G-3535)***
Charles River Laboratories Inc 860 376-1240
425 Pendleton Hill Rd Voluntown (06384) ***(G-9187)***
Charles River Laboratories Inc 860 889-1389
1 Wisconsin Ave Ste 100 Norwich (06360) ***(G-6409)***
Charles River Laboratories Inc 860 429-7261
67 Baxter Rd Storrs (06268) ***(G-8546)***
Charles W Simmons 203 254-3388
640 Unquowa Rd Fairfield (06824) ***(G-2759)***
Charlies Ride 860 916-3637
389 North St Windsor Locks (06096) ***(G-10478)***
Charlys Custom Woodworking 860 227-2155
18 Rosemary Ln Killingworth (06419) ***(G-3829)***
Charmed Press LLC 203 877-3777
53 Jennifer Ln Milford (06461) ***(G-4489)***
Charter Oak Automation LLC 203 562-0699
340 Quinnipiac St Ste 19 Wallingford (06492) ***(G-9226)***
Charting Economy 860 667-9909
171 Market Sq Ste 213 Newington (06111) ***(G-5640)***
Chas W House & Sons Inc 860 673-2518
19 Perry St Unionville (06085) ***(G-9112)***
Chase Corporation 203 285-1244
149 Amity Rd Woodbridge (06525) ***(G-10597)***
Chase Graphics Inc 860 315-9006
124 School St Putnam (06260) ***(G-7034)***
Chase Media Group 914 962-3871
31 Pecks Ln Ste 3 Newtown (06470) ***(G-5733)***
Chase Press, Newtown *Also called Shop Smart Central Inc* ***(G-5779)***
Chassis Dynamics Inc 203 262-6272
91 Willenbrock Rd Ste A1 Oxford (06478) ***(G-6651)***
Chatham Drapery Co Inc 860 267-7767
59 Edgerton St East Hampton (06424) ***(G-2261)***
Check It Darien LLC 203 655-2036
40 Fairfield Ave Darien (06820) ***(G-2012)***
Chef Gretchen LLC 203 252-8892
1184 Newfield Ave Stamford (06905) ***(G-8142)***
Chef J R ME Rest Group Corp 860 940-8038
240 Newington Ave New Britain (06051) ***(G-4960)***
Chef's Equipment, Orange *Also called Cee Orange LLC* ***(G-6590)***
Chefs Equipment Emporium, Wallingford *Also called Demartino Fixture Co Inc* ***(G-9248)***
Chem-Tron, Danbury *Also called Chemical-Electric Corporation* ***(G-1767)***
Chem-Tron Pntg Pwdr Cating Inc 203 743-5131
92 Taylor St Danbury (06810) ***(G-1766)***
Chemessence Inc 860 355-4108
180 Sunny Valley Rd # 15 New Milford (06776) ***(G-5519)***
Chemical-Electric Corporation 203 743-5131
92 Taylor St Danbury (06810) ***(G-1767)***
Chemin Pharma LLC 203 208-2811
4 Research Dr Woodbridge (06525) ***(G-10598)***
Chemloid Chemicals Inc 203 255-7495
399 N Benson Rd Fairfield (06824) ***(G-2760)***
Chemotex Protective Coatings (PA) 860 349-0144
15 Commerce Cir Durham (06422) ***(G-2142)***
Chemtura Receivables LLC 203 573-3327
199 Benson Rd Waterbury (06749) ***(G-9449)***
Chemtura USA, Shelton *Also called Lanxess Solutions US Inc* ***(G-7486)***
Chen-Man Foods LLC 860 659-9549
110 Cedar Ridge Dr Glastonbury (06033) ***(G-3020)***
Cherise Cpl LLC 203 238-3482
57 S Broad St Meriden (06450) ***(G-4157)***
Cherner Chair Company LLC 203 894-4702
218 North St Ridgefield (06877) ***(G-7127)***
Cheryl Aiudi & Son LLC 860 575-8462
58 Sagamore Terrace Rd Westbrook (06498) ***(G-9993)***
Cheshire Division, Cheshire *Also called Atlantic Inertial Systems Inc* ***(G-1357)***
Cheshire Herald, Wallingford *Also called True Publishing Company* ***(G-9392)***
Cheshire Manufacturing Co Inc 203 272-3586
312 E Johnson Ave Ste 1 Cheshire (06410) ***(G-1369)***
Chesnut Woodworking 860 592-0383
5 Fulling Ln Kent (06757) ***(G-3821)***
Chessco Industries Inc (PA) 203 255-2804
1330 Post Rd E Ste 2 Westport (06880) ***(G-10064)***
Chester Boatworks 860 526-2227
444 Main St Deep River (06417) ***(G-2086)***
Chestnut Shell 203 775-5067
819 Federal Rd Brookfield (06804) ***(G-1171)***
Chestnut Wdwkg & Antiq Flrg Co 860 672-4300
14 Great Hollow Rd West Cornwall (06796) ***(G-9761)***
Chiappettas Welding 203 637-1522
21 Sheephill Rd Riverside (06878) ***(G-7190)***
Chiara Publications 203 797-1905
211 Greenwood Ave 22186 Bethel (06801) ***(G-270)***
Chicken of The Sea, Newtown *Also called Tri-Union Seafoods LLC* ***(G-5793)***
Chicken Soup For Soul LLC 203 861-4000
132 E Putnam Ave Ste 20 Cos Cob (06807) ***(G-1626)***
Chicken Soup For Soul Entrmt I (HQ) 855 398-0443
132 E Putnam Ave Fl 2w Cos Cob (06807) ***(G-1627)***
Chicken Soup For Soul Pubg LLC 203 861-4000
132 E Putnam Ave Cos Cob (06807) ***(G-1628)***
Chicken Soup For The Soul (PA) 855 398-0443
132 E Putnam Ave Ste 20 Cos Cob (06807) ***(G-1629)***
Chicks Sandblasting 860 334-0059
101 Pierce Rd Preston (06365) ***(G-6982)***
Chicory Blue Press Inc 860 491-2271
795 East St N Goshen (06756) ***(G-3096)***
Chief Executive Group LLC (PA) 785 832-0303
9 W Broad St Ste 430 Stamford (06902) ***(G-8143)***
Chief Executive Group LP (PA) 203 930-2700
9 W Broad St Ste 430 Stamford (06902) ***(G-8144)***
Chief Executive Magazine, Stamford *Also called Chief Executive Group LP* ***(G-8144)***
Child Evngelism Fellowship Inc 203 879-2154
730 Bound Line Rd Wolcott (06716) ***(G-10553)***
Childrens Health Market Inc 203 762-2938
27 Cannon Rd Ste 1b Wilton (06897) ***(G-10280)***
Childrens Medical Group (PA) 860 242-8330
6 Northwestern Dr Ste 101 Bloomfield (06002) ***(G-402)***
Childrens Press 203 972-9404
795 Carter St New Canaan (06840) ***(G-5094)***
Chip - Mar Inc 860 355-4854
2 Moosehorn Rd Roxbury (06783) ***(G-7275)***
Chip In A Bottle LLC 203 460-0665
837 Whalley Ave Ste 1 New Haven (06515) ***(G-5256)***
Choice Magazine, Middletown *Also called American Library Association* ***(G-4315)***
Chowder Pot of Hartford LLC 860 244-3311
165 Brainard Rd Hartford (06114) ***(G-3566)***
Chris & Zack Gourmet Foods 203 912-7805
383 Boston Post Rd Orange (06477) ***(G-6591)***
Chris & Zack LLC 203 298-0742
385 Boston Post Rd Orange (06477) ***(G-6592)***
Chris Cross LLC 203 386-8426
294 Benton St Stratford (06615) ***(G-8595)***
Chris Dedura 203 257-7304
33 Hillside Ave Trumbull (06611) ***(G-9011)***
Chris Krawczyk Woodwork LLC 203 895-5785
105 Toas St Shelton (06484) ***(G-7417)***
Chris Peterson Woodworks 860 542-0140
44 Ashpohtag Rd Norfolk (06058) ***(G-5823)***

Christensen Woodworking 860 712-6166
37 Rockville Rd Windsorville (06016) ***(G-10503)***
Christian Science Committee On 203 866-1200
50 Washington St Norwalk (06854) ***(G-6113)***
Christinas Creations 203 605-2464
395 Howard Ave New Haven (06519) ***(G-5257)***
Christopher Annelli 860 537-4397
448 New London Rd Colchester (06415) ***(G-1545)***
Christopher Condors 203 852-8181
23 1st St Ste 1 Norwalk (06855) ***(G-6114)***
Christopher Peacock Homes 203 862-9333
2 Dearfield Dr Ste 1 Greenwich (06831) ***(G-3143)***
Christopoulos Designs Inc 203 576-1110
195 Dewey St Bridgeport (06605) ***(G-733)***
Chromalloy Component Svcs Inc 203 924-1666
415 Howe Ave Shelton (06484) ***(G-7418)***
Chromalloy Component Svcs Inc 860 688-7798
601 Marshall Phelps Rd Windsor (06095) ***(G-10373)***
Chromalloy Connecticut, Windsor *Also called Chromalloy Gas Turbine LLC* ***(G-10374)***
Chromalloy Gas Turbine LLC 860 688-7798
601 Marshall Phelps Rd Windsor (06095) ***(G-10374)***
Chromatic Press US Inc 860 796-7667
84 Woodrow St West Hartford (06107) ***(G-9788)***
Chromatics Inc 203 743-6868
19 Francis J Clarke Cir Bethel (06801) ***(G-271)***
Chromations LLC 203 929-8007
20 Elderberry Ln Shelton (06484) ***(G-7419)***
Chronicle Printing Company 860 423-8466
1 Chronicle Rd Willimantic (06226) ***(G-10222)***
Chronicle, The, Willimantic *Also called Chronicle Printing Company* ***(G-10222)***
Chunghua Cabinet CT Inc 718 886-4588
120 Viaduct Rd Stamford (06907) ***(G-8145)***
Church Hill Classics Ltd 800 477-9005
594 Pepper St Monroe (06468) ***(G-4703)***
Churyk, Stefan M, New Milford *Also called S M Churyk Iron Works Inc* ***(G-5588)***
Ciaudelli Productions Inc 860 848-0411
14 Bridge St Montville (06353) ***(G-4769)***
Cicchetti & Co LLC 860 945-0424
124 Winding Brook Farm Rd Watertown (06795) ***(G-9692)***
Cico, Norwalk *Also called Twenty Five Commerce Inc* ***(G-6379)***
Cidra Chemical Management Inc (HQ) 203 265-0035
50 Barnes Park Rd N # 103 Wallingford (06492) ***(G-9227)***
Cidra Corporate Services Inc 203 265-0035
50 Barnes Park Rd N Wallingford (06492) ***(G-9228)***
Cidra Corporation 203 265-0035
50 Barnes Park Rd N # 103 Wallingford (06492) ***(G-9229)***
Cidra Mineral Processing Inc 203 265-0035
50 Barnes Park Rd N Wallingford (06492) ***(G-9230)***
Cidra Oilsands Inc (HQ) 203 265-0035
50 Barnes Park Rd N Wallingford (06492) ***(G-9231)***
Cietrade Systems Inc 203 323-0074
263 Tresser Blvd Ste 1030 Stamford (06901) ***(G-8146)***
Cifc Early Lrng Programs/Wic 203 206-6341
80 Main St Danbury (06810) ***(G-1768)***
Cigar World 860 828-7870
126 Mill St Kensington (06037) ***(G-3807)***
Cimarron Music Press 860 536-2185
79 Meeting House Ln Ledyard (06339) ***(G-3870)***
Cimarron Music Press LLC 860 859-3705
975 Ocean Ave New London (06320) ***(G-5462)***
Cimbali Usa Inc 203 254-6046
418 Meadow St Ste 203 Fairfield (06824) ***(G-2761)***
Cindys Soap Cottage 860 370-9908
82 Main St Windsor Locks (06096) ***(G-10479)***
Cine Magnetics Inc (PA) 914 273-7600
9 W Broad St Ste 250 Stamford (06902) ***(G-8147)***
Cine Research Laboratory, New Fairfield *Also called Joseph Malavenda* ***(G-5170)***
Cintas Corporation 203 272-2036
10 Diana Ct Cheshire (06410) ***(G-1370)***
Cira, New Haven *Also called Yale University* ***(G-5444)***
Circle Publishing LLC 516 459-5016
1525 Kings Hwy Fairfield (06824) ***(G-2762)***
Circuit Breaker Sales Ne Inc 203 888-7500
79 Main St Seymour (06483) ***(G-7340)***
Circuit Cellar Inc 860 289-0800
111 Founders Plz Ste 904 East Hartford (06108) ***(G-2305)***
Cirillo Manufacturing Group 203 484-5010
34 Panagrosi St East Haven (06512) ***(G-2416)***
Cirtec Medical Corp 860 814-3973
99 Print Shop Rd Enfield (06082) ***(G-2623)***
Cisco Systems Inc 203 229-2300
383 Main Ave Ste 7 Norwalk (06851) ***(G-6115)***
Cisco Systems Inc 860 284-5500
50 Stanford Dr Farmington (06032) ***(G-2888)***
Cisen Usa Inc (PA) 203 706-9536
4 Colonial Ct Middlebury (06762) ***(G-4275)***
Cisse Publications LLC 203 685-4189
18 Kimberly Dr Shelton (06484) ***(G-7420)***
Cita LLC 203 545-7035
25 Forest St Apt 6k Stamford (06901) ***(G-8148)***
Citizen News 203 746-4669
Candle Wood Cor Rm 39 New Fairfield (06812) ***(G-5166)***
Citra Solv LLC 203 778-0881
188 Shadow Lake Rd Ridgefield (06877) ***(G-7128)***
City Cement Block-Del Corp Inc 203 334-0702
83 North Ave Bridgeport (06606) ***(G-734)***
City Data Cable Co 203 327-7917
34 Parker Ave Stamford (06906) ***(G-8149)***
City Sign 860 232-4803
1811 Park St Hartford (06106) ***(G-3567)***
City Stitchers, Derby *Also called Rss Enterprises LLC* ***(G-2124)***
City Welding 860 951-4714
84 Wellington St Hartford (06106) ***(G-3568)***
CJ Aviation Services LLC 860 741-6499
4 Lovely Dr Enfield (06082) ***(G-2624)***
CJ Ceramics and More LLC 203 246-2798
11 Homewood Ln Darien (06820) ***(G-2013)***
CJ First Candle 203 966-1300
49 Locust Ave New Canaan (06840) ***(G-5095)***
Cjbows 860 287-5053
35 Yorkshire Dr Waterford (06385) ***(G-9645)***
Cjmco, Bolton *Also called Carlyle Johnson Machine Co LLC* ***(G-508)***
Cjs Embroidery LLC 203 650-9066
119 Lee Ave Bridgeport (06605) ***(G-735)***
CK Imaging and Embroidery 716 984-1957
3 Northridge Dr Burlington (06013) ***(G-1264)***
Ckg Welding Fabrication LLC 860 628-7129
217 Flanders Rd Southington (06489) ***(G-7905)***
Ckh Industries Inc 860 563-2999
365 Silas Deane Hwy Ste 1 Wethersfield (06109) ***(G-10187)***
Cko Woodworking 203 234-7156
33 Laydon Ave North Haven (06473) ***(G-5920)***
Cko Woodworking LLC 203 815-3092
85 Tremont St Meriden (06450) ***(G-4158)***
CKS Packaging Inc 203 729-0716
10 Great Hill Rd Naugatuck (06770) ***(G-4868)***
Clancy Woodworking LLC 860 355-3655
12 Anderson Rd E Sherman (06784) ***(G-7592)***
Clanol Systems Inc 203 637-9909
1374 E Putnam Ave Old Greenwich (06870) ***(G-6469)***
Clarcor Eng MBL Solutions LLC (HQ) 860 920-4200
60 Prestige Park Rd East Hartford (06108) ***(G-2306)***
Claremont Sales Corporation 860 349-4499
35 Winsome Rd Durham (06422) ***(G-2143)***
Clarion Ux, Trumbull *Also called Urban Exposition LLC* ***(G-9090)***
Clark Manner Marguarite 860 444-7679
601 Broad St New London (06320) ***(G-5463)***
Clark Power Systems Inc 203 775-8444
7 Premium Point Ln Brookfield (06804) ***(G-1172)***
Clarke Distribution Corp 203 838-9385
64 S Main St Norwalk (06854) ***(G-6116)***
Clarktron Products Inc 203 333-6517
1525 Kings Hwy Ste 7 Fairfield (06824) ***(G-2763)***
Classic Brands LLC 303 936-2444
55 Lathrop Road Ext Plainfield (06374) ***(G-6744)***
Classic Cabinets 860 749-9743
44 N Maple St Enfield (06082) ***(G-2625)***
Classic Coil Company Inc 860 583-7600
205 Century Dr Bristol (06010) ***(G-1001)***
Classic Framers 401 596-6820
211 Cove Rd Stonington (06378) ***(G-8525)***
Classic Images Inc 860 243-8365
16 Walts Hl Bloomfield (06002) ***(G-403)***
Classic Ink 860 225-3652
104 Country Club Rd New Britain (06053) ***(G-4961)***
Classic Jig Grinding 860 870-4900
38 Gerber Dr Tolland (06084) ***(G-8854)***
Classic Label Inc 203 389-3535
10 Research Dr Woodbridge (06525) ***(G-10599)***
Classic School Uniforms Ltd 860 677-7207
15 Salisbury Way Farmington (06032) ***(G-2889)***
Classic Shotguns 860 354-4648
58 Garnet Rd Roxbury (06783) ***(G-7276)***
Classic Sign & Graphics 203 834-1145
23 Gaylord Dr N Wilton (06897) ***(G-10281)***
Classic Sign Company, Wilton *Also called Classic Sign & Graphics* ***(G-10281)***
Classic Tool & Mfg Inc 203 755-6313
112 Porter St Waterbury (06708) ***(G-9450)***
Classic Tool & Mfg LLC 203 755-6313
112 Porter St Waterbury (06708) ***(G-9451)***
Classic Trim LLC 860 543-9102
70 Maple Ave Bristol (06010) ***(G-1002)***
Classics of Golf, Stratford *Also called Carala Ventures Ltd* ***(G-8592)***
Clay Furniture Industries Inc 860 643-7580
41 Chapel St Manchester (06042) ***(G-3996)***
Clayton Offroad Manufacturer 475 238-8251
99 Commerce St East Haven (06512) ***(G-2417)***
Clean Air Group Inc 203 335-3700
418 Meadow St Ste 204 Fairfield (06824) ***(G-2764)***
Clean Cut Logging, East Hampton *Also called Brian Reynolds* ***(G-2259)***
Clean Holdings LLC 203 466-3365
47 Redfield Ave East Haven (06512) ***(G-2418)***
Clean Ocean Technology 401 212-8171
113 Greenhaven Rd Pawcatuck (06379) ***(G-6705)***

Clean Tech Industries LLC 860 447-1434
16 Elm St New London (06320) ***(G-5464)***
Clean Up Group 203 668-8323
82 Jodi Dr Meriden (06450) ***(G-4159)***
Cleansource Industries 203 401-1535
126 Green Hill Rd Madison (06443) ***(G-3913)***
Clear & Colored Coatings LLC 203 879-1379
20 Swiss Ln Wolcott (06716) ***(G-10554)***
Clear & Colored Coatings LLC (PA) 203 879-1379
222 Spindle Hill Rd Wolcott (06716) ***(G-10555)***
Clear & Simple Inc 860 658-1204
5 Notch Rd West Simsbury (06092) ***(G-9974)***
Clear Automation LLC 860 621-2955
85 Robert Porter Rd Southington (06489) ***(G-7906)***
Clear Site The Heated Wiper 203 790-2100
4 Paul St Bethel (06801) ***(G-272)***
Clear Water Manufacturing Corp (PA) 860 372-4907
900 Wells Rd Wethersfield (06109) ***(G-10188)***
Clearclad Coatings LLC 860 945-9200
11 Pepperidge Tree Rd Watertown (06795) ***(G-9693)***
Clearly Clean Products LLC (PA) 860 646-1040
225 Oakland Rd Ste 401 South Windsor (06074) ***(G-7729)***
Clearspan, South Windsor *Also called Engineering Services & Pdts Co* ***(G-7750)***
Clearwater Treatment Systems L 860 799-0303
446 W Meetinghouse Rd New Milford (06776) ***(G-5520)***
Clemons Productions Inc 203 316-9394
875 Westover Rd Stamford (06902) ***(G-8150)***
Clemson Sheet Metal LLC 860 871-9369
344 Somers Rd Unit 1 Vernon Rockville (06066) ***(G-9164)***
Clemson Sheetmetal LLC 860 721-7906
24 Ladd Rd Ellington (06029) ***(G-2581)***
Clever Clover LLC 860 501-2800
72 Greenhaven Rd Pawcatuck (06379) ***(G-6706)***
Clg Enterprises Inc 203 741-9300
6 Capital Dr Wallingford (06492) ***(G-9232)***
Clg Solutions LLC 203 507-1105
123 Dogburn Rd West Haven (06516) ***(G-9887)***
Click Bond Inc 860 274-5435
18 Park Rd Watertown (06795) ***(G-9694)***
Clicroi LLC 203 599-1237
13 Caldwell Ter Danbury (06810) ***(G-1769)***
Cliffside Entertainment LLC 203 290-7484
1355 Fairfield Ave Bridgeport (06605) ***(G-736)***
Cliggott Publishing, Darien *Also called Ubm LLC* ***(G-2048)***
Clinical Dynamics Conn LLC 203 269-0090
1210 Mrden Waterbury Tpke Plantsville (06479) ***(G-6888)***
Clint S Custom Woodworkin 860 887-1476
628 River Rd Jewett City (06351) ***(G-3792)***
Clint's Cabinets, Ledyard *Also called Clinton Babcock & Sons* ***(G-3871)***
Clinton Babcock & Sons 860 887-9166
54 Silas Deane Rd Ledyard (06339) ***(G-3871)***
Clinton Instrument Company 860 669-7548
295 E Main St Clinton (06413) ***(G-1494)***
Clinton Nursery Products Inc (PA) 860 399-3000
517 Pond Meadow Rd Westbrook (06498) ***(G-9994)***
Clondalkin Pharma & Healthcare 860 342-1987
264 Freestone Ave Portland (06480) ***(G-6955)***
Cloodloc, Stamford *Also called Novatek Medical Inc* ***(G-8332)***
Clopay Corporation 203 230-9116
285 State St Ste 4 North Haven (06473) ***(G-5921)***
Close To Home, Glastonbury *Also called R & M Associates Inc* ***(G-3078)***
Cloud Cap Technology Inc 541 308-1089
100 Wooster Hts Danbury (06810) ***(G-1770)***
Clover Hill Forest LLC 860 672-0394
20 Hurlburt Pl Cornwall (06753) ***(G-1616)***
Cloverdale Cleaner, West Cornwall *Also called Cloverdale Inc* ***(G-9762)***
Cloverdale Inc 860 672-0216
5 Smith Pl West Cornwall (06796) ***(G-9762)***
Cls Design Group 860 307-2810
131 Lawrence Ln Torrington (06790) ***(G-8911)***
Club Resource Inc 317 225-6940
10 Andrew Dr Canton (06019) ***(G-1310)***
Cly-Del Manufacturing Company 203 574-2100
151 Sharon Rd Waterbury (06705) ***(G-9452)***
Clydes Cider Mill 860 536-3354
129 N Stonington Rd Mystic (06355) ***(G-4807)***
CMI Media Management, Stamford *Also called Cine Magnetics Inc* ***(G-8147)***
CMI Specialty Products Inc 860 585-0409
105 Redstone Hill Rd Bristol (06010) ***(G-1003)***
CMI Time Management LLC 800 722-6654
89 Phoenix Ave Enfield (06082) ***(G-2626)***
CMS Automation, Prospect *Also called Prospect Industries LLC* ***(G-7018)***
Cnc Engineering Inc 860 749-1780
19 Bacon Rd Enfield (06082) ***(G-2627)***
Cnc Machine Tl Specialist LLC 860 873-1816
55 Warner Rd East Haddam (06423) ***(G-2239)***
Co-Op Jig Boring Jig Grinding 860 828-9882
1152 Worthington Rdg Berlin (06037) ***(G-170)***
Coach Inc 203 372-0208
5065 Main St Ste P2114 Trumbull (06611) ***(G-9012)***
Coastal Canvas 203 270-7408
24 Poplar Dr Sandy Hook (06482) ***(G-7303)***
Coastal Group Inc 860 452-4148
145 Chestnut Hill Rd Killingworth (06419) ***(G-3830)***
Coastal Industries LLC 860 535-9043
3 Walnut St Stonington (06378) ***(G-8526)***
Coastal Pallet Corporation 203 333-1892
135 E Washington Ave Bridgeport (06604) ***(G-737)***
Coastal Seafoods Inc (PA) 203 431-0453
35 Brentwood Ave Ste 4 Fairfield (06825) ***(G-2765)***
Coastal Steel Corporation 860 443-4073
10 Mallard Ln Waterford (06385) ***(G-9646)***
Coastal Tooling, Killingworth *Also called Coastal Group Inc* ***(G-3830)***
Coastalogix LLC 203 521-4770
1771 Post Rd E 205 Westport (06880) ***(G-10065)***
Coastline Environmental LLC 203 483-6898
12 Ridgetop Ln North Branford (06471) ***(G-5831)***
Coastline Fuel Inc 203 846-3601
3 Van Zant St Norwalk (06855) ***(G-6117)***
Coastline Printing 203 481-2744
11 Briarwood Ln Branford (06405) ***(G-574)***
Coating Design Group Inc 203 878-3663
430 Sniffens Ln Stratford (06615) ***(G-8596)***
Cobal-USA Altrnative Fuels LLC 203 751-1974
40 James St Ansonia (06401) ***(G-29)***
Cobra Green LLC 203 354-5000
50 N Water St Norwalk (06854) ***(G-6118)***
Coburn Technologies 800 262-8761
83 Gerber Rd W South Windsor (06074) ***(G-7730)***
Coburn Technologies Inc (PA) 860 648-6600
83 Gerber Rd W South Windsor (06074) ***(G-7731)***
Coburn Technologies Intl Inc (HQ) 860 648-6600
55 Gerber Rd E South Windsor (06074) ***(G-7732)***
Coburn Tecnologies Canada 860 648-6710
55 Gerber Rd E South Windsor (06074) ***(G-7733)***
Coca-Cola Bottling 800 241-2653
475 Main St East Hartford (06118) ***(G-2307)***
Coca-Cola Company 860 443-2816
150 Parkway S Waterford (06385) ***(G-9647)***
Cocchia Norwalk Grape Co 203 855-7911
25 Ely Ave Norwalk (06854) ***(G-6119)***
Coccomo Brothers Drilling LLC 860 828-1632
1897 Berlin Tpke Berlin (06037) ***(G-171)***
Codebridge Software Inc 203 535-0517
91 Honor Rd West Haven (06516) ***(G-9888)***
Cofco Americas Resources Corp (PA) 203 252-5200
4 Stamford Plz Stamford (06902) ***(G-8151)***
Cofco-Agri Coffee Cotton Grain, Stamford *Also called Cofco Americas Resources Corp* ***(G-8151)***
Coffee News 860 613-0796
271 Main St Cromwell (06416) ***(G-1696)***
Cofmic Computers, Norwalk *Also called Norfield Data Products Inc* ***(G-6280)***
Cogstate Inc (HQ) 203 773-5010
195 Church St Ste 1004 New Haven (06510) ***(G-5258)***
Cogz Systems LLC 203 263-7882
58 Steeple View Ln Woodbury (06798) ***(G-10628)***
Coherent Inc 860 243-9557
1280 Blue Hills Ave Ste A Bloomfield (06002) ***(G-404)***
Coherent Bloomfield, Bloomfield *Also called Coherent Inc* ***(G-404)***
Coherent-Deos LLC 860 243-9557
1280 Blue Hills Ave Ste A Bloomfield (06002) ***(G-405)***
Coils Plus Inc 203 879-0755
30 Town Line Rd Wolcott (06716) ***(G-10556)***
Col Lar Enterprises, Brookfield *Also called Col-Lar Enterprises Inc* ***(G-1173)***
Col-Lar Enterprises Inc 860 799-6970
4 Chelsea Ct Brookfield (06804) ***(G-1173)***
Col-Lar Enterprises Inc (PA) 203 798-1786
37 S End Plz New Milford (06776) ***(G-5521)***
Colchester Bulletin Bulletin, Norwich *Also called Gatehouse Media Conn Holdings* ***(G-6415)***
Cold Brew Coffee Company LLC 860 250-4410
27 E Ridge Ct Cheshire (06410) ***(G-1371)***
Cold LLC 203 543-6861
393 Naugatuck Ave Milford (06460) ***(G-4490)***
Cold Plasma Neck 203 935-0300
639 Research Pkwy Meriden (06450) ***(G-4160)***
Cold River Logging LLC 860 334-9506
195 Tuckie Rd North Windham (06256) ***(G-6036)***
Cold Stone Creamery, Fairfield *Also called Jaksy 2 LLC* ***(G-2799)***
Cold Stone Creamery (PA) 860 669-7025
7 Glenwood Rd Unit F Clinton (06413) ***(G-1495)***
Cole S Crew Machine Products 203 723-1418
69 Dodge Ave North Haven (06473) ***(G-5922)***
Coleman Drilling & Blasting 860 376-3813
1458 Hopeville Rd Voluntown (06384) ***(G-9188)***
Colin Harrison LLC 203 775-5035
16 Cove Rd Brookfield (06804) ***(G-1174)***
Collins Compost 860 749-3416
11 Powder Hill Rd Enfield (06082) ***(G-2628)***
Collinsville Screen Printing 860 693-2601
30 Depot St Collinsville (06019) ***(G-1591)***
Collinsville Screen/Embroidery 860 693-2601
35 Secret Lake Rd Canton (06019) ***(G-1311)***
Colmec Usa Inc 203 502-8822
35 Nutmeg Dr Trumbull (06611) ***(G-9013)***

Colonial Bronze Company 860 489-9233
511 Winsted Rd Torrington (06790) ***(G-8912)***
Colonial Coatings Inc 203 783-9933
66 Erna Ave Milford (06461) ***(G-4491)***
Colonial Corrugated Pdts Inc 203 597-1707
118 Railroad Hill St Waterbury (06708) ***(G-9453)***
Colonial Iron Shop Inc 860 763-0659
15 Dust House Rd Enfield (06082) ***(G-2629)***
Colonial Metal Detectors 860 317-1284
299 Gendron Rd Plainfield (06374) ***(G-6745)***
Colonial Print & Imaging, Old Greenwich *Also called Clanol Systems Inc* ***(G-6469)***
Colonial Printers of Windsor 860 627-5433
1 Concorde Way Windsor Locks (06096) ***(G-10480)***
Colonial Spring Company, Bristol *Also called Triple A Spring Ltd Partnr* ***(G-1132)***
Colonial Welding Service, Torrington *Also called Thomas La Ganga* ***(G-8977)***
Colonial Wood Products Inc 203 932-9003
250 Callegari Dr West Haven (06516) ***(G-9889)***
Colonial Wood Turning, Danbury *Also called Juan Gallegos* ***(G-1866)***
Colonial Woodworking Inc 203 866-5844
145 Water St Norwalk (06854) ***(G-6120)***
Color Craft Ltd 800 509-6563
14 Airport Park Rd East Granby (06026) ***(G-2197)***
Color Film Media Group LLC (PA) 203 202-2929
45 Keeler Ave Norwalk (06854) ***(G-6121)***
Color Ite Refinishing Co 203 393-0240
868 Carrington Rd Bethany (06524) ***(G-238)***
Colorgraphix LLC 203 264-5212
91 Willenbrock Rd Ste B5 Oxford (06478) ***(G-6652)***
Colorite Refinishing, Bethany *Also called Color Ite Refinishing Co* ***(G-238)***
Colors Ink 203 269-4000
40 Capital Dr Wallingford (06492) ***(G-9233)***
Colour TS LLC 860 298-0594
167 Portman St Windsor (06095) ***(G-10375)***
Colt Defense Emplye Pln (HQ) 860 232-4489
547 New Park Ave West Hartford (06110) ***(G-9789)***
Colt Defense Holding, West Hartford *Also called Colt Defense LLC* ***(G-9790)***
Colt Defense LLC (HQ) 860 232-4489
547 New Park Ave West Hartford (06110) ***(G-9790)***
Colts Manufacturing Co LLC (HQ) 860 236-6311
547 New Park Ave West Hartford (06110) ***(G-9791)***
Colts Plastics Company Inc 860 774-2277
969 N Main St Dayville (06241) ***(G-2058)***
Columbia Manufacturing Inc 860 228-2259
165 Route 66 E Columbia (06237) ***(G-1604)***
Columbia Mat & Upholstering Co 203 789-1213
824 Dixwell Ave Hamden (06514) ***(G-3429)***
Columbia Mattress Co, Hamden *Also called Columbia Mat & Upholstering Co* ***(G-3429)***
Com Tower 203 879-6568
1140 Wolcott Rd Wolcott (06716) ***(G-10557)***
Coma Skateboards 860 933-4830
10 Fern Rd Storrs (06268) ***(G-8547)***
Comanche Clean Energy Corp 203 326-4570
1 Dock St Ste 101 Stamford (06902) ***(G-8152)***
Comet Technologies USA Inc (HQ) 203 447-3200
100 Trap Falls Road Ext Shelton (06484) ***(G-7421)***
Comex Machinery 203 334-2196
145 Front St Bridgeport (06606) ***(G-738)***
Comfortable Environments 203 876-2140
11 Terrell Dr Milford (06461) ***(G-4492)***
Comicana Inc 203 968-0748
61 Studio Rd Stamford (06903) ***(G-8153)***
Command Corporation 800 851-6012
59 Rainbow Rd East Granby (06026) ***(G-2198)***
Command Tooling Systems 203 284-9615
16 Cliffside Dr Wallingford (06492) ***(G-9234)***
Commandtech LLC 860 857-8502
404 Thames St Ste C Groton (06340) ***(G-3278)***
Commerce Connect Media Inc 800 547-7377
830 Post Rd E Fl 2 Westport (06880) ***(G-10066)***
Commercial Service 203 755-0166
45 Freight St Rm 1 Waterbury (06702) ***(G-9454)***
Commercial Sewing Inc 860 482-5509
65 Grant St Torrington (06790) ***(G-8913)***
Common Sense Engineered Pdts 203 888-8695
164 Pines Bridge Rd Beacon Falls (06403) ***(G-132)***
Commscope Technologies LLC 203 699-4100
33 Union City Rd Ste 2 Prospect (06712) ***(G-6997)***
Communication Networks LLC 203 796-5300
3 Corporate Dr Danbury (06810) ***(G-1771)***
Community Acpncture Brstol LLC 860 833-9330
25 Newell Rd Bristol (06010) ***(G-1004)***
Community Brands Holdings LLC 203 227-1255
180 Post Rd E Ste 200 Westport (06880) ***(G-10067)***
Compair Inc 860 635-8811
422 Timber Ridge Rd Middletown (06457) ***(G-4331)***
Companion Industries Inc 860 628-0504
891 W Queen St Southington (06489) ***(G-7907)***
Company of Coca-Cola Bottling 860 569-0037
471 Main St 471 # 471 East Hartford (06118) ***(G-2308)***
Company of Coca-Cola Bottling 860 814-4241
100 Print Shop Rd Enfield (06082) ***(G-2630)***
Company of Coca-Cola Bottling 203 905-3900
333 Ludlow St Ste 8 Stamford (06902) ***(G-8154)***
Company of Craftsmen 860 536-4189
43 W Main St Mystic (06355) ***(G-4808)***
Compart North America Inc 860 799-5612
30 Bridge St Ste 2 New Milford (06776) ***(G-5522)***
Compass Group Management LLC (PA) 203 221-1703
301 Riverside Ave Westport (06880) ***(G-10068)***
Competition Engineering Inc 203 453-5200
80 Carter Dr Guilford (06437) ***(G-3339)***
Competitive Edge Coatings LLC 860 882-0762
185 Nutmeg Rd S South Windsor (06074) ***(G-7734)***
Competitive Edge Coatings LLC 860 267-6255
164 Bull Hill Rd Colchester (06415) ***(G-1546)***
Compleat Angler 203 655-9400
541 Post Rd Darien (06820) ***(G-2014)***
Complete Sheet Metal LLC 860 310-5447
500 Four Rod Rd Ste 122 Berlin (06037) ***(G-172)***
Complimentary Healing 203 622-1697
45 Valleywood Rd Cos Cob (06807) ***(G-1630)***
Component Concepts Inc 860 523-4066
26 Hammick Rd West Hartford (06107) ***(G-9792)***
Component Engineers Inc 203 269-0557
108 N Plains Indus Rd Wallingford (06492) ***(G-9235)***
Component Technologies Inc (PA) 860 667-1065
68 Holmes Rd Newington (06111) ***(G-5641)***
Components For Mfg LLC (PA) 860 245-5326
800 Flanders Rd Unit 3-5 Mystic (06355) ***(G-4809)***
Components For Mfg LLC 860 572-1671
26 High St Groton (06340) ***(G-3279)***
Composiclean LLC 860 432-0067
75 Hope Ln Glastonbury (06033) ***(G-3021)***
Composlte McHining Experts LLC 203 624-0664
222 Universal Dr Bldg 1 North Haven (06473) ***(G-5923)***
Composite Panel Tech Co 203 729-2255
112 Bridge St Naugatuck (06770) ***(G-4869)***
Composite Truck Body LLC 800 735-1668
3 Nutmeg Ln Sherman (06784) ***(G-7593)***
Composites Inc 860 646-1698
485 Middle Tpke E Manchester (06040) ***(G-3997)***
Comprhnsive Prsthetic Svcs LLC 203 315-1400
21 Business Park Dr Branford (06405) ***(G-575)***
Compu-Signs LLC 860 747-1985
105 E Main St Plainville (06062) ***(G-6788)***
Compucision LLC 860 355-9790
29 S End Plz New Milford (06776) ***(G-5523)***
Compumail Corp 860 583-1906
135 Cross St Bristol (06010) ***(G-1005)***
Computer Components Inc 860 653-9909
18 Kripes Rd East Granby (06026) ***(G-2199)***
Computer Express LLC 860 829-1310
365 New Britain Rd Ste D Berlin (06037) ***(G-173)***
Computer Playscapes, Branford *Also called C P I Computer Center Inc* ***(G-567)***
Computer Prgrm & Systems Inc (PA) 203 324-9203
1011 High Ridge Rd # 208 Stamford (06905) ***(G-8155)***
Computer Sgns Old Saybrook LLC 860 388-9773
460 Boston Post Rd Old Saybrook (06475) ***(G-6527)***
Computer Software Educ SE 860 677-4527
19 Salisbury Way Farmington (06032) ***(G-2890)***
Computer Support People LLC 203 653-4643
16 River St Ste 1 Norwalk (06850) ***(G-6122)***
Computer Tech Express LLC 203 810-4932
95 New Canaan Ave Norwalk (06850) ***(G-6123)***
Computer Technologies Corp 860 683-4030
65 Tiffany Dr Windsor (06095) ***(G-10376)***
Computer Warehouse 203 426-1034
42 Valley Field Rd S Sandy Hook (06482) ***(G-7304)***
Computer Xpress LLC 203 469-6107
16 River Rd East Haven (06512) ***(G-2419)***
Computing and Media Center, New Haven *Also called Yale University* ***(G-5446)***
Compuweigh Corporation (PA) 203 262-9400
50 Middle Quarter Rd Woodbury (06798) ***(G-10629)***
Comsat Inc 203 264-4091
2120 River Rd Southbury (06488) ***(G-7848)***
Comunidade News 203 730-0175
4 Laurel St Danbury (06810) ***(G-1772)***
Comvac Systems Inc 860 265-3658
3 Peerless Way Ste U Enfield (06082) ***(G-2631)***
Con-Tec Inc 203 723-8942
41 Raytkwich Rd Naugatuck (06770) ***(G-4870)***
Conair Corporation 800 492-7464
314 Ella Grasso Ave Torrington (06790) ***(G-8914)***
Conair Corporation (PA) 203 351-9000
1 Cummings Point Rd Stamford (06902) ***(G-8156)***
Conant Valley Jams 203 403-3811
11 Wilton Rd W Ridgefield (06877) ***(G-7129)***
Conard Corporation 860 659-0591
101 Commerce St Glastonbury (06033) ***(G-3022)***
Concentric Tool Mfg Co 203 723-8846
360 Prospect St Naugatuck (06770) ***(G-4871)***
Concept Team Associates LLC 203 269-5152
41 Hill Ave Wallingford (06492) ***(G-9236)***

ALPHABETIC

Concept Woodworks LLC **ALPHABETIC SECTION**

Concept Woodworks LLC 860 746-4271
30 Oakwood St Enfield (06082) ***(G-2632)***
Conco Wood Working Inc 203 934-9665
755 1st Ave West Haven (06516) ***(G-9890)***
Concord Distributing, Norwalk *Also called Concord Industries Inc* ***(G-6124)***
Concord Industries Inc 203 750-6060
19 Willard Rd Norwalk (06851) ***(G-6124)***
Concord Litho 203 866-9394
9 Walnut Ave Norwalk (06851) ***(G-6125)***
Concordia Ltd 203 483-0221
5 Enterprise Dr North Branford (06471) ***(G-5832)***
Concrete Coring Co Conn Inc 203 287-8400
34 Raccio Park Rd Ste 2 Hamden (06514) ***(G-3430)***
Concrete Products 860 423-4144
356 Tuckie Rd North Windham (06256) ***(G-6037)***
Concrete Supplement Co 860 567-5556
272 Norfolk Rd Litchfield (06759) ***(G-3886)***
Condec, Newtown *Also called Rice Lake Weighing Systems Inc* ***(G-5775)***
Condomdepot Co 860 747-1338
186 Camp St Plainville (06062) ***(G-6789)***
Condon LLC 860 883-5416
33 Main St Ste P Old Saybrook (06475) ***(G-6528)***
Condor Press, Norwalk *Also called Christopher Condors* ***(G-6114)***
Conformis Inc 203 793-7178
10 Beaumont Rd Ste 4 Wallingford (06492) ***(G-9237)***
Congress Catering Inc 860 291-8182
53 Cherry St East Hartford (06108) ***(G-2309)***
Congress Rotisserie, East Hartford *Also called Congress Catering Inc* ***(G-2309)***
Conklin-Sherman Company Incthe 203 881-0190
59 Old Turnpike Rd Beacon Falls (06403) ***(G-133)***
Conn Daily Campus 860 486-3407
11 Dog Ln Storrs Mansfield (06268) ***(G-8553)***
Conn Dept Motor Vehicles 203 840-1993
540 Main Ave Norwalk (06851) ***(G-6126)***
Conn Engineering Assoc Corp 203 426-4733
27 Philo Curtis Rd Sandy Hook (06482) ***(G-7305)***
Connectcut Acdemy Arts Scences 203 432-3113
310 Prospect St New Haven (06511) ***(G-5259)***
Connectcut Boiler Repr Mfg Inc 860 953-9117
694 Oakwood Ave West Hartford (06110) ***(G-9793)***
Connectcut Crnial Fcial Imgery 860 643-2940
483 Middle Tpke W Ste 102 Manchester (06040) ***(G-3998)***
Connectcut Cswork Spclists LLC 203 934-9665
755 1st Ave Ste B West Haven (06516) ***(G-9891)***
Connectcut Dgital Graphics LLC 203 888-6509
100 S Main St Seymour (06483) ***(G-7341)***
Connectcut Hspnic Yellow Pages 860 560-8713
2074 Park St Ste 2 Hartford (06106) ***(G-3569)***
Connectcut Prcsion Cmpnnts LLC 860 489-8621
588 S Main St Rear Torrington (06790) ***(G-8915)***
Connectcut Shreline Developers 860 669-4424
10 Long Hill Rd Clinton (06413) ***(G-1496)***
Connectcut Spring Stmping Corp 860 677-1341
48 Spring Ln Farmington (06032) ***(G-2891)***
Connectcut Tmpred GL Dstrs LLC 860 379-5670
56 Torrington Rd Winsted (06098) ***(G-10514)***
Connecticut Advanced Products 860 659-2260
41c New London Tpke Glastonbury (06033) ***(G-3023)***
Connecticut Aerospace Inc 860 872-0036
101 Industrial Park Rd Vernon Rockville (06066) ***(G-9165)***
Connecticut Analytical Corp 203 393-9666
696 Amity Rd Ste 13 Bethany (06524) ***(G-239)***
Connecticut Anodizing Finshg 203 367-1765
128 Logan St Bridgeport (06607) ***(G-739)***
Connecticut Axle Service LLC 860 872-3858
94 Muddy Brook Rd Ellington (06029) ***(G-2582)***
Connecticut Bass Guide 860 827-0787
891 Slater Rd New Britain (06053) ***(G-4962)***
Connecticut Beverage Journal, Hamden *Also called Beverage Publications Inc* ***(G-3418)***
Connecticut Brace and Limb LLC 860 740-2154
59 Timms Hill Rd Haddam (06438) ***(G-3403)***
Connecticut Breaker Co Inc 203 378-2240
680 Surf Ave Stratford (06615) ***(G-8597)***
Connecticut Cabinet Distrs LLC 860 508-6240
27 Kreiger Ln Glastonbury (06033) ***(G-3024)***
Connecticut Candle Group 860 924-1766
19a Carillon Dr Rocky Hill (06067) ***(G-7227)***
Connecticut Candle LLC 203 937-7330
25 Ranchwood Dr West Haven (06516) ***(G-9892)***
Connecticut Canvas Works 860 295-9924
27 Standish Dr Marlborough (06447) ***(G-4122)***
Connecticut Carpentry LLC 203 639-8585
290 Pratt St Ofc Meriden (06450) ***(G-4161)***
Connecticut Carved Sign Co LLC 860 274-2039
140 Circuit Ave Watertown (06795) ***(G-9695)***
Connecticut Coining Inc 203 743-3861
10 Trowbridge Dr Bethel (06801) ***(G-273)***
Connecticut Compass Service 860 434-2019
301 Grassy Hill Rd Lyme (06371) ***(G-3903)***
Connecticut Components Inc 860 633-0277
60 Industrial Park Rd W # 2 Tolland (06084) ***(G-8855)***
Connecticut Computer Svc Inc 860 276-1285
344 W Main St Milford (06460) ***(G-4493)***
Connecticut Concrete Form Inc 860 674-1314
168 Brickyard Rd Farmington (06032) ***(G-2892)***
Connecticut Container Corp (PA) 203 248-2161
455 Sackett Point Rd North Haven (06473) ***(G-5924)***
Connecticut Cue Parts, Wolcott *Also called Jan Manufacturing Inc* ***(G-10569)***
Connecticut Custom Wdwrk LLC 203 888-3948
57 Botsford Rd Seymour (06483) ***(G-7342)***
Connecticut Custom Woodwork 203 231-0097
15 Monroe St Apt B Milford (06460) ***(G-4494)***
Connecticut Custom Woodworking 860 741-8946
31 Pine Knob Rd Somers (06071) ***(G-7653)***
Connecticut Die Cutting Svc, East Hartford *Also called Bessette Holdings Inc* ***(G-2298)***
Connecticut Diesel and Marine 203 481-1010
287 Woodmont Rd Milford (06460) ***(G-4495)***
Connecticut Digital Post Inc 203 268-4554
66 Grindstone Ln Monroe (06468) ***(G-4704)***
Connecticut Dist Svcs Ltd, East Hartford *Also called Burnside Supermarket LLC* ***(G-2301)***
Connecticut Drone Services LLC 203 966-7016
125 Forest St New Canaan (06840) ***(G-5096)***
Connecticut Engravers, Milford *Also called Ideas Inc* ***(G-4551)***
Connecticut Fabricating Co Inc 203 878-3465
15 Warfield St Milford (06461) ***(G-4496)***
Connecticut Fine Blanking 203 925-0012
25 Forest Pkwy Shelton (06484) ***(G-7422)***
Connecticut Forest & Park Assn 860 346-2372
16 Meriden Rd Rockfall (06481) ***(G-7211)***
CONNECTICUT GALVANIZING, Glastonbury *Also called Highway Safety Corp* ***(G-3049)***
Connecticut Greenstar Inc 203 368-1522
1157 Melville Ave Fairfield (06825) ***(G-2766)***
Connecticut Hone Incorporated 860 747-3884
9 Grace Ave Plainville (06062) ***(G-6790)***
Connecticut Hypodermics Inc 203 265-4881
519 Main St Wallingford (06492) ***(G-9238)***
Connecticut Iron Works Inc 203 869-0657
59 Davenport Ave Greenwich (06830) ***(G-3144)***
Connecticut Java User Group, Cheshire *Also called Cuprak Enterprises LLC* ***(G-1378)***
Connecticut Laminating Co Inc 203 787-2184
162 James St New Haven (06513) ***(G-5260)***
Connecticut Law Book Co Inc 203 458-8000
39 Chaffinch Island Rd Guilford (06437) ***(G-3340)***
Connecticut Leaf Filter LLC 203 857-0846
288 East Ave Apt 2 Norwalk (06855) ***(G-6127)***
Connecticut Machine & Marine 860 446-8286
266 Bridge St Ste 4 Groton (06340) ***(G-3280)***
Connecticut Machine & Welding 203 502-2605
425 Harding Ave Stratford (06615) ***(G-8598)***
Connecticut Mch Tooling & Cast 203 874-8300
93 Research Dr Milford (06460) ***(G-4497)***
Connecticut Metal Industries 203 736-0790
1 Riverside Dr Ste G Ansonia (06401) ***(G-30)***
Connecticut Metalworks, Newington *Also called J OConnor LLC* ***(G-5666)***
Connecticut Mfg Svcs LLC 860 667-8712
631 Church St Newington (06111) ***(G-5642)***
Connecticut Millwork Inc 860 875-2860
80 Spring St Vernon (06066) ***(G-9135)***
Connecticut Newspapers Inc 203 964-2200
75 Tresser Blvd Stamford (06901) ***(G-8157)***
Connecticut Outdoor Wood Frncs 203 263-0625
405 Grassy Hill Rd Woodbury (06798) ***(G-10630)***
Connecticut Parent Magazine 203 483-1700
420 E Main St Ste 18 Branford (06405) ***(G-576)***
Connecticut Plasma Tech LLC 860 289-5500
273 Chapel Rd South Windsor (06074) ***(G-7735)***
Connecticut Post, Norwalk *Also called Medianews Group Inc* ***(G-6254)***
Connecticut Precast Corp 203 268-8688
555 Fan Hill Rd Monroe (06468) ***(G-4705)***
Connecticut Press 203 257-6020
36 Wildlife Ct Cheshire (06410) ***(G-1372)***
Connecticut Radio Inc 860 563-4867
1208 Cromwell Ave Ste C Rocky Hill (06067) ***(G-7228)***
Connecticut Refining Co, New Haven *Also called Alliance Energy LLC* ***(G-5223)***
Connecticut School Jewelry Art, Collinsville *Also called Emilie Cohen* ***(G-1594)***
Connecticut Screen Print 203 877-6655
215 Research Dr Ste 1 Milford (06460) ***(G-4498)***
Connecticut Sign Craft Inc 203 729-0706
47 Cherry St Naugatuck (06770) ***(G-4872)***
Connecticut Sign Factory 860 833-5689
11 Hart St Southington (06489) ***(G-7908)***
Connecticut Sign Service LLC 860 767-7446
25 Saybrook Rd Ste 6 Essex (06426) ***(G-2714)***
Connecticut Sign Service LLC 860 391-9614
5 Chadwick Dr Old Lyme (06371) ***(G-6498)***
Connecticut Solid Surface LLC 860 410-9800
361 East St Plainville (06062) ***(G-6791)***
Connecticut Spring & Stamping, Farmington *Also called Connectcut Spring Stmping Corp* ***(G-2891)***
Connecticut Stone Supplies Inc (PA) 203 882-1000
138 Woodmont Rd Milford (06460) ***(G-4499)***
Connecticut Stucco LLC 203 237-9500
82 Leo Rd Hamden (06517) ***(G-3431)***

ALPHABETIC SECTION

Connecticut Tick Control LLC ... 203 855-7849
  15 Chapel St Norwalk (06850) *(G-6128)*
Connecticut Tool & Cutter Co ... 860 314-1740
  280 Redstone Hill Rd # 1 Bristol (06010) *(G-1006)*
Connecticut Tool & Mfg Co LLC ... 860 846-0800
  35 Corp Ave Plainville (06062) *(G-6792)*
Connecticut Tool Co Inc ... 860 928-0565
  6 Highland Dr Putnam (06260) *(G-7035)*
Connecticut Trade Company Inc ... 203 368-0398
  1157 Melville Ave Fairfield (06825) *(G-2767)*
Connecticut Valley Bindery ... 860 229-7637
  1 Hartford Sq Ste 28w New Britain (06052) *(G-4963)*
Connecticut Valley Inds LLC ... 860 388-0822
  8 Center Rd Old Saybrook (06475) *(G-6529)*
Connecticut Valley Litho Club ... 203 234-0536
  190 Clintonville Rd North Haven (06473) *(G-5925)*
Connecticut Valley Packg LLC ... 860 693-0776
  20 Country Ln Collinsville (06019) *(G-1592)*
Connecticut Valley Winery LLC ... 860 489-9463
  1480 Litchfield Tpke New Hartford (06057) *(G-5187)*
Connecticut Vineyard & Winery ... 860 307-3550
  433 S Main St Ste 309 West Hartford (06110) *(G-9794)*
Connecticut Woodworks LLC ... 860 367-7449
  39 Braman Rd Waterford (06385) *(G-9648)*
Connelly 3 Pubg Group Inc ... 860 664-4988
  10 W Main St Fl 2 Clinton (06413) *(G-1497)*
Conner Printing ... 203 929-2070
  226 Leavenworth Rd Shelton (06484) *(G-7423)*
Conner, James A Printer, Shelton *Also called Conner Printing (G-7423)*
Connstem Inc ... 203 558-4671
  505 Highland Ave Cheshire (06410) *(G-1373)*
Conntrol International Inc ... 860 928-0567
  135 Park Rd Putnam (06260) *(G-7036)*
Conopco Inc ... 708 606-0540
  75 Merritt Blvd Trumbull (06611) *(G-9014)*
Conopco Inc ... 860 669-8601
  1 John St Clinton (06413) *(G-1498)*
Conopco Inc ... 203 381-3557
  75 Merritt Blvd Trumbull (06611) *(G-9015)*
Conoptics Inc ... 203 743-3349
  19 Eagle Rd Danbury (06810) *(G-1773)*
Conquip Systems LLC ... 860 526-7883
  78 Turkey Hill Rd Chester (06412) *(G-1468)*
Conserv Epoxy LLC ... 203 484-4123
  49 Old Post Rd Northford (06472) *(G-6044)*
Consoldted Inds Acqsition Corp ... 203 272-5371
  677 Mixville Rd Cheshire (06410) *(G-1374)*
Consolidated Container LP ... 860 224-9381
  90 Pleasant St New Britain (06051) *(G-4964)*
Constitution Sparkler Sales ... 203 324-5159
  505 W Hill Rd Stamford (06902) *(G-8158)*
Consulting Engrg Dev Svcs Inc ... 203 828-6528
  3 Fox Hollow Rd Oxford (06478) *(G-6653)*
Containment Solutions Inc ... 860 651-4371
  35 Ichabod Rd Simsbury (06070) *(G-7614)*
Contek International Corp ... 203 972-3406
  93 Cherry St New Canaan (06840) *(G-5097)*
Contek International Corp ... 203 972-7330
  60 Field Crest Rd New Canaan (06840) *(G-5098)*
Contemporary Products LLC ... 860 346-9283
  2055 S Main St Middletown (06457) *(G-4332)*
Contemprary Lights Staging LLC ... 203 359-8200
  425 Fairfield Ave Ste 4 Stamford (06902) *(G-8159)*
Continental Machine TI Co Inc ... 860 223-2896
  533 John Downey Dr New Britain (06051) *(G-4965)*
Continental Marble & Granite, Plainville *Also called Mark Dzidzk (G-6839)*
Continuity Control (PA) ... 203 459-0155
  59 Elm St Ste 300 New Haven (06510) *(G-5261)*
Continuity Engine Inc ... 203 907-4470
  59 Elm St New Haven (06510) *(G-5262)*
Contorq Components LLC ... 860 225-3366
  433 John Downey Dr New Britain (06051) *(G-4966)*
Contractors Steel Supply ... 203 782-1221
  111 Quinnipiac Ave North Haven (06473) *(G-5926)*
Control Concepts Inc (PA) ... 860 928-6551
  100 Park St Putnam (06260) *(G-7037)*
Controlled Interfaces LLC ... 917 328-4471
  34 Farm Hill Rd Ridgefield (06877) *(G-7130)*
Conval Inc ... 860 749-0761
  96 Phoenix Ave Enfield (06082) *(G-2633)*
Convergent Solutions LLC ... 203 293-3534
  3 Baywood Ln Westport (06880) *(G-10069)*
Converter Consultants LLC ... 203 729-1031
  1058 Rubber Ave Naugatuck (06770) *(G-4873)*
Converting McHy Adhesives LLC ... 860 561-0226
  50 Sleepy Hollow Rd Newington (06111) *(G-5643)*
Convexity Scientific LLC ... 949 637-1216
  418 Meadow St Fairfield (06824) *(G-2768)*
Conveyco Technologies Inc (PA) ... 860 589-8215
  47 Commerce Dr Bristol (06010) *(G-1007)*
Conway Hardwood Products LLC ... 860 355-4030
  37 Gaylord Rd Gaylordsville (06755) *(G-2991)*
Conway, Jeremiah, Gaylordsville *Also called Conway Hardwood Products LLC (G-2991)*

Cook Print ... 203 855-8785
  35 Van Zant St Norwalk (06855) *(G-6129)*
Cool-It LLC ... 203 284-4848
  340 Quinnipiac St Wallingford (06492) *(G-9239)*
Coolspine LLC ... 203 263-6188
  188 Hoop Pole Hill Rd Woodbury (06798) *(G-10631)*
Cooper Crouse-Hinds LLC ... 860 683-4300
  1200 Kennedy Rd Windsor (06095) *(G-10377)*
Cooper Marketing Group Inc ... 203 797-9386
  41 Eagle Rd Ste 2 Danbury (06810) *(G-1774)*
Cooper Surgical, Trumbull *Also called Blairden Precision Instrs Inc (G-9005)*
Cooper-Atkins Corporation (HQ) ... 860 349-3473
  33 Reeds Gap Rd Middlefield (06455) *(G-4300)*
Coopersurgical Inc ... 203 601-5200
  120 Corporate Dr Trumbull (06611) *(G-9016)*
Coopersurgical Inc ... 203 453-1700
  393 Soundview Rd Guilford (06437) *(G-3341)*
Coopersurgical Inc (HQ) ... 203 601-5200
  95 Corporate Dr Trumbull (06611) *(G-9017)*
Coorstek Inc ... 860 653-8071
  10 Airport Park Rd East Granby (06026) *(G-2200)*
Coorstek East Granby, East Granby *Also called Coorstek Inc (G-2200)*
Copar Industries, Middletown *Also called Armetta LLC (G-4317)*
Copeland Latasha ... 860 728-8289
  354 Woodland St Hartford (06112) *(G-3570)*
Copies Now, Wethersfield *Also called Hedges & Hedges Ltd (G-10196)*
Copper and Brass Sales Div, Wallingford *Also called Thyssenkrupp Materials NA Inc (G-9382)*
Copperworks Inc (PA) ... 203 248-3516
  277 Still Hill Rd Hamden (06518) *(G-3432)*
Copy Cats Inc ... 860 442-8424
  458 Williams St Ste 1 New London (06320) *(G-5465)*
Copy Signs LLC ... 860 747-1985
  105 E Main St Plainville (06062) *(G-6793)*
Copy Stop Inc ... 203 288-6401
  2371 Whitney Ave Hamden (06518) *(G-3433)*
Copy-Rite Inc ... 203 272-6923
  384 Old Turnpike Rd # 2 Plantsville (06479) *(G-6889)*
Corbin Russwin ... 860 225-7411
  110 Sargent Dr New Haven (06511) *(G-5263)*
Corbin Russwin Arch Hdwr, Berlin *Also called Assa Abloy Accss & Edrss Hrdwr (G-160)*
Corco Mfg ... 203 284-1831
  550 Woodhouse Ave Wallingford (06492) *(G-9240)*
Cord Industries, Milford *Also called John C Green (G-4561)*
Cord-Mate Inc ... 203 272-8415
  705 Wallingford Rd Cheshire (06410) *(G-1375)*
Core Filtration LLC ... 860 904-6640
  30 Arbor St Ste 210b Hartford (06106) *(G-3571)*
Core Site Services LLC ... 475 227-9026
  470 James St Ste 7 New Haven (06513) *(G-5264)*
Core Studios ... 203 364-9594
  117 Mount Pleasant Rd Newtown (06470) *(G-5734)*
Corelli Industries LLC ... 203 356-9058
  94 Elaine Dr Stamford (06902) *(G-8160)*
Corerepro, Newtown *Also called Core Studios (G-5734)*
Coreslab Structures Conn Inc ... 860 283-8281
  1023 Waterbury Rd Thomaston (06787) *(G-8786)*
Corgyn Woodworks ... 860 402-8273
  152 Hawthorne St Manchester (06042) *(G-3999)*
Corinth Acquisition Corp (PA) ... 203 504-6260
  2777 Summer St Ste 206 Stamford (06905) *(G-8161)*
Corktec Inc ... 860 851-9417
  17 Middle River Dr Stafford Springs (06076) *(G-8021)*
Cornell-Carr Co Inc ... 203 261-2529
  626 Main St Monroe (06468) *(G-4706)*
Cornwall & Patterson Div, Branford *Also called Pratt-Read Corporation (G-637)*
Cornwall Bridge Pottery Inc ... 860 672-6545
  69 Kent Rd Warren (06754) *(G-9407)*
Coronado Group LLC (PA) ... 203 761-1291
  57 Danbury Rd Ste 201 Wilton (06897) *(G-10282)*
Corotec Corp ... 860 678-0038
  145 Hyde Rd Farmington (06032) *(G-2893)*
Corporate, Windsor *Also called ABB Enterprise Software Inc (G-10353)*
Corporate Aircraft Svcs LLC ... 203 730-2024
  38 Maplewood Dr Danbury (06811) *(G-1775)*
Corporate Cartridge ... 203 655-7197
  145 Raymond St Darien (06820) *(G-2015)*
Corporate Connecticut Mag LLC ... 860 257-0500
  912 Silas Deane Hwy Wethersfield (06109) *(G-10189)*
Corporate Express CT ... 203 455-2500
  400 Long Beach Blvd Ste 1 Stratford (06615) *(G-8599)*
Corporate Flight MGT Inc ... 203 826-9224
  53 Miry Brook Rd Danbury (06810) *(G-1776)*
Corporate Forms Printing ... 800 840-9945
  80 Kent Rd New Britain (06052) *(G-4967)*
Corr/Dis Incorporated ... 203 838-6075
  38 Burchard Ln Norwalk (06853) *(G-6130)*
Correia Wood Works LLC ... 203 515-7670
  79 Parkwood Rd Fairfield (06824) *(G-2769)*
Corru Seals Inc ... 203 284-0319
  24 Capital Dr Wallingford (06492) *(G-9241)*

Cortina Famous Schools, Wilton *Also called Cortina Learning Intl Inc* ***(G-10283)***
Cortina Learning Intl Inc (PA)....800 245-2145
33 Catalpa Rd Wilton (06897) ***(G-10283)***
Corts Custom Woodworking....203 266-0146
154 Town Line Hwy S Bethlehem (06751) ***(G-368)***
Cos Cob T V & Video, Cos Cob *Also called Sean Mecesery* ***(G-1641)***
Cosmos Food Products Inc....800 942-6766
200 Callegari Dr West Haven (06516) ***(G-9893)***
Coss Systems Inc....800 961-0288
8 Fairview Ter Greenwich (06831) ***(G-3145)***
Coss Systems Inc (not Inc)....732 447-7724
26 Arcadia Rd Old Greenwich (06870) ***(G-6470)***
Cote Dlvoire Imports....203 243-4841
260 Prayer Spring Rd Stratford (06614) ***(G-8600)***
Cottages & Grdns Publications, Norwalk *Also called Dulce Domum LLC* ***(G-6151)***
Cotton Press LLC....203 257-7958
596 Nod Hill Rd Wilton (06897) ***(G-10284)***
Counters, Newington *Also called Catskill Gran Countertops Inc* ***(G-5637)***
Country Carpenters Inc....860 228-2276
326 Gilead St Hebron (06248) ***(G-3746)***
Country Creations By Carol....860 848-0276
103 Moxley Rd Uncasville (06382) ***(G-9097)***
Country Log Homes....413 229-8084
77 Clayton Rd Canaan (06018) ***(G-1285)***
Country Log Homes Inc....413 229-8084
27 Rockwall Ct Goshen (06756) ***(G-3097)***
Country Oil LLC....203 270-6439
3 Bentagrass Ln Newtown (06470) ***(G-5735)***
Country Pure Foods, Ellington *Also called Natural Country Farms Inc* ***(G-2597)***
Country Pure Foods Inc....330 753-2293
58 West Rd Ellington (06029) ***(G-2583)***
Country Side Sheet Metal....860 872-5729
182 Jobs Hill Rd Ellington (06029) ***(G-2584)***
Country Soap Samplers....203 881-1986
156 Punkup Rd Oxford (06478) ***(G-6654)***
Country Tool & Die Inc....860 429-7325
278 Pumpkin Hill Rd Ashford (06278) ***(G-58)***
Countryside Crafts....860 774-0446
517 Chestnut Hill Rd Dayville (06241) ***(G-2059)***
Countryside Sheet Metal, Ellington *Also called Country Side Sheet Metal* ***(G-2584)***
Coupon Magazine Publishers Inc....561 676-6498
31 Corn Tassle Rd Danbury (06811) ***(G-1777)***
Couponz Direct LLC....212 655-9615
25 Lewis St Ste 303 Greenwich (06830) ***(G-3146)***
Courant Specialty Products Inc....860 241-3795
285 Broad St Hartford (06115) ***(G-3572)***
Cournoyer Flr Sanding Finshg....860 963-7088
424 Quaddick Rd Thompson (06277) ***(G-8833)***
Courtman Enterprises LLC....860 322-2837
33 Center St Windsor (06095) ***(G-10378)***
Couturier Ino....203 238-4555
5 Cross St Meriden (06451) ***(G-4162)***
Covalent Coating Tech LLC....860 214-6452
222 Pitkin St East Hartford (06108) ***(G-2310)***
Cove Press, Stamford *Also called US Games Systems Inc* ***(G-8481)***
Cove Shoe Company Division, Greenwich *Also called HH Brown Shoe Company Inc* ***(G-3177)***
Coveris Advanced Coatings....413 244-9685
351 Morgan Ln West Haven (06516) ***(G-9894)***
Covidien Holding Inc....203 492-5000
195 Mcdermott Rd North Haven (06473) ***(G-5927)***
Covidien LP....203 492-6332
195 Mcdermott Rd North Haven (06473) ***(G-5928)***
Covidien LP....781 839-1722
555 Long Wharf Dr Fl 4 New Haven (06511) ***(G-5265)***
Covidien LP....203 492-5000
60 Middletown Ave North Haven (06473) ***(G-5929)***
Covit America Inc....860 274-6791
1 Seemar Rd Watertown (06795) ***(G-9696)***
Cowles Products Company Inc....203 865-3110
126 Bailey Rd North Haven (06473) ***(G-5930)***
Cowles Stamping Inc....203 865-3117
126 Bailey Rd North Haven (06473) ***(G-5931)***
Coyote Software....203 227-6510
53 Cross Hwy Westport (06880) ***(G-10070)***
Cozy Pants LLC....860 267-7507
6 Stagecoach Run Cobalt (06414) ***(G-1537)***
CP, Torrington *Also called Connectcut Prcsion Cmpnnts LLC* ***(G-8915)***
CP Apn Inc....330 682-3000
599 W Putnam Ave Greenwich (06830) ***(G-3147)***
CP Solar Thermal LLC....860 877-2238
210 Century Dr Bristol (06010) ***(G-1008)***
CPC Childrenswear Inc....203 286-6204
6 Logan Pl Norwalk (06853) ***(G-6131)***
CPC Software LLC....203 348-9684
197 Lawn Ave Stamford (06902) ***(G-8162)***
CPS Millworks LLC....860 283-4276
5 Katy Ct Terryville (06786) ***(G-8750)***
CPT, Naugatuck *Also called Composite Panel Tech Co* ***(G-4869)***
Cr Fabrication LLC....860 377-1629
10 Thomas St South Windsor (06074) ***(G-7736)***
Cr-TEC Engineering Inc....203 318-9500
15 Orchard Park Rd A20 Madison (06443) ***(G-3914)***
Crabtree & Evelyn Ltd (HQ)....800 272-2873
102 Peake Brook Rd Woodstock (06281) ***(G-10662)***
Craftline, North Haven *Also called Platt-Labonia of N Haven Inc* ***(G-5977)***
Craftsmen Printing Group Inc....203 327-2817
104 Lincoln Ave Stamford (06902) ***(G-8163)***
Crafty Baby Tm LLC....203 921-1179
193 Minivale Rd Stamford (06907) ***(G-8164)***
Crafty Creations....860 673-6225
55 Sunnybrook Dr Avon (06001) ***(G-79)***
Craig Dascanio....860 651-0466
250 Farms Village Rd Rear West Simsbury (06092) ***(G-9975)***
Craig Keating....203 852-0571
39 Fairfield Ave Rear D Norwalk (06854) ***(G-6132)***
Cramer Company....860 291-8402
105 Nutmeg Rd S South Windsor (06074) ***(G-7737)***
Crane Aerospace Inc (HQ)....203 363-7300
100 Stamford Pl Stamford (06902) ***(G-8165)***
Crane Co (PA)....203 363-7300
100 1st Stamford Pl # 300 Stamford (06902) ***(G-8166)***
Crane Controls Inc (HQ)....203 363-7300
100 Stamford Pl Stamford (06902) ***(G-8167)***
Crane Intl Holdings Inc (HQ)....203 363-7300
100 Stamford Pl Stamford (06902) ***(G-8168)***
Cranial Technologies Inc....203 318-8739
1343 Boston Post Rd Madison (06443) ***(G-3915)***
Crave Foods LLC....203 227-6868
33 Danbury Ave Westport (06880) ***(G-10071)***
CRC Chrome Corporation....203 630-1008
169 Pratt St R Meriden (06450) ***(G-4163)***
Create A Castle LLC....203 648-3553
15 Glenbrook Dr New Milford (06776) ***(G-5524)***
Createx Colors, East Granby *Also called Color Craft Ltd* ***(G-2197)***
Creative Canvas LLC....860 559-8509
89 Madley Rd Lebanon (06249) ***(G-3851)***
Creative Communications, New London *Also called Bayard Inc* ***(G-5457)***
Creative Cupolas....203 261-2178
10 Sutton Pl Trumbull (06611) ***(G-9018)***
Creative Dimensions Inc....203 250-6500
345 Mccausland Ct Cheshire (06410) ***(G-1376)***
Creative Edge Solutions L....860 626-0007
960 Migeon Ave Torrington (06790) ***(G-8916)***
Creative Enhancement Inc....860 833-8493
1028 Boulevard Ste 243 West Hartford (06119) ***(G-9795)***
Creative Envelope Inc....860 963-1231
26 Highland Dr Putnam (06260) ***(G-7038)***
Creative Media Applications....203 226-0544
22 Old Orchard Dr Weston (06883) ***(G-10023)***
Creative Mobile Systems Inc....860 649-6272
189 Adams St Manchester (06042) ***(G-4000)***
Creative Playthings Ltd....203 748-7206
559a Federal Rd Ste 4 Brookfield (06804) ***(G-1175)***
Creative Printed Products LLC....203 268-8980
446 Main St Fl 1 Monroe (06468) ***(G-4707)***
Creative Rack Solutions Inc....203 755-2102
365 Thomaston Ave Waterbury (06702) ***(G-9455)***
Creative Source LLC....203 879-4005
32 Mountain View Dr Wolcott (06716) ***(G-10558)***
Creative Stone LLC....203 624-1882
42 Vista Dr East Haven (06512) ***(G-2420)***
Creative Stone & Tile, East Haven *Also called Creative Stone LLC* ***(G-2420)***
Creative Stone Group Inc....203 554-7773
444 Bedford St Apt 4e Stamford (06901) ***(G-8169)***
Creative Woodworking LLC....203 518-0336
515 Pierpont Rd Waterbury (06705) ***(G-9456)***
Creed-Monarch Inc....860 225-7884
1 Pucci Park New Britain (06051) ***(G-4968)***
Crescent Mnfacturing Operating....860 673-1921
700 George Wash Tpke Burlington (06013) ***(G-1265)***
Crewelding....855 204-7352
50 Walnut St Middletown (06457) ***(G-4333)***
Cricket Press Inc....860 521-9279
236 Park Rd West Hartford (06119) ***(G-9796)***
Criscara, Tolland *Also called Crista Grasso LLC* ***(G-8856)***
Criscola Design LLC....203 248-4285
1477 Ridge Rd North Haven (06473) ***(G-5932)***
Crista Grasso LLC....347 946-2533
55 Kendall Mountain Rd Tolland (06084) ***(G-8856)***
Cristina Ilies....860 456-3153
1671 Main St Willimantic (06226) ***(G-10223)***
Criterion Inc....203 703-9000
501 Merritt 7 Ste 1 Norwalk (06851) ***(G-6133)***
Critical Scrn Printg & EMB....860 443-4327
82 Boston Post Rd Waterford (06385) ***(G-9649)***
Critical Signs Graphics &....860 443-7446
1068 Hartford Tpke Ste 4 Waterford (06385) ***(G-9650)***
Critical Signs & Graphics....860 443-7446
106 Boston Post Rd Waterford (06385) ***(G-9651)***
Crochet Away 203....203 690-7904
159 Georgetown Rd Weston (06883) ***(G-10024)***
Crocheted By Bianca....860 916-2925
7 Pine Hill St Manchester (06042) ***(G-4001)***

Cromwell Chronicle 860 257-8715
222 Dividend Rd Rocky Hill (06067) *(G-7229)*
Crossfield Concepts Inc 203 938-5667
105 Cross Hwy Redding (06896) *(G-7091)*
Crossgrain Wood Products, Madison *Also called Darlene Ann Miconi (G-3917)*
Crossroads Deli & Fuel LLC 860 824-8474
123 Johnson Rd Falls Village (06031) *(G-2869)*
Crossroads Signs 203 894-5938
679 Danbury Rd Ste 2 Ridgefield (06877) *(G-7131)*
Croteau Development Group Inc 860 684-3605
25 West St Stafford Springs (06076) *(G-8022)*
Croton Industries East Africa 407 947-4481
18 Banks Dr Wilton (06897) *(G-10285)*
Crown Cork & Seal Usa Inc 203 877-4131
86 Victory Cres Milford (06460) *(G-4500)*
Crown House Publishing Co LLC 203 778-1300
6 Trowbridge Dr Ste 5 Bethel (06801) *(G-274)*
Crown Molding Etc LLC 203 287-9424
148 Gillies Rd Hamden (06517) *(G-3434)*
Crrc LLC 860 635-2200
46 Nooks Hill Rd Cromwell (06416) *(G-1697)*
CRS I Group Inc 860 593-4886
130 Ciccolella Ct Southington (06489) *(G-7909)*
Crush Club LLC 203 626-9545
65 S Colony St Wallingford (06492) *(G-9242)*
Crystal Fairfield Tech LLC 860 354-2111
8 S End Plz New Milford (06776) *(G-5525)*
Crystal Journey Candles LLC 203 433-4735
69 N Branford Rd Branford (06405) *(G-577)*
Crystal Labels Co 860 870-8627
116 Stafford Rd Ellington (06029) *(G-2585)*
Crystal Nails and Spa of Sh 203 323-0551
20 Magee Ave Stamford (06902) *(G-8170)*
Crystal Rock Holdings Inc (HQ) 860 945-0661
1050 Buckingham St Watertown (06795) *(G-9697)*
Crystal Rock Spring Water Co 860 945-0661
1050 Buckingham St Watertown (06795) *(G-9698)*
Crystal Rock Water & Coffee Co, Watertown *Also called Crystal Rock Spring Water Co (G-9698)*
Crystal Tool and Machine Co 860 870-7431
114 Brooklyn St Vernon (06066) *(G-9136)*
Crystal Tool LLC 860 510-0113
50 Connally Dr Old Saybrook (06475) *(G-6530)*
CSC Cocoa LLC 203 846-5611
36 Grove St New Canaan (06840) *(G-5099)*
CSC El Paso, New Canaan *Also called CSC Sugar LLC (G-5100)*
CSC Sugar LLC (PA) 203 846-5610
36 Grove St Ste 2 New Canaan (06840) *(G-5100)*
Csg Automation LLC 860 691-1885
36 Industrial Park Rd Niantic (06357) *(G-5804)*
Csi, Harwinton *Also called Spring Computerized Inds LLC (G-3739)*
CSS Industries LLC 203 521-5246
220 Whippoorwill Ln Stratford (06614) *(G-8601)*
CT Acquisitions LLC 888 441-0537
1 Grand St Wallingford (06492) *(G-9243)*
CT Amateur Jai Alai LLC 860 357-2544
500 Four Rod Rd Ste 119 Berlin (06037) *(G-174)*
CT Composites & Marine Svc LLC 860 282-0100
620 Sullivan Ave South Windsor (06074) *(G-7738)*
CT Conveyor LLC 860 637-2926
320 Terryville Rd Bristol (06010) *(G-1009)*
CT Crane and Hoist Service LLC 860 283-4320
19 Burr Rd Plymouth (06782) *(G-6928)*
CT Drive-Shaft Service LLC 860 289-6459
77 Cherry St East Hartford (06108) *(G-2311)*
CT Dumpster LLC 203 521-0779
32 Birch Ave Milford (06460) *(G-4501)*
CT Fiberoptics Inc 860 763-4341
64 Field Rd Ste 11 Somers (06071) *(G-7654)*
CT Films LLC 203 734-8307
38 N Benham Rd Seymour (06483) *(G-7343)*
CT Fine Woodworking 860 613-0856
211 Shunpike Rd Ste 4 Cromwell (06416) *(G-1698)*
CT Moldings Inc 203 612-4922
308 Bishop Ave Bridgeport (06610) *(G-740)*
CT Organizer LLC 203 858-5824
8 Washington Ave Westport (06880) *(G-10072)*
CT Pellet, Torrington *Also called Scott Olson Enterprises LLC (G-8967)*
CT Precast, Monroe *Also called Connecticut Precast Corp (G-4705)*
CT Prints 203 281-6996
3000 Whitney Ave Hamden (06518) *(G-3435)*
CT Prints & More LLC 860 604-5694
100 Margarita Dr Hartford (06106) *(G-3573)*
CT Pyro Mfg LLC 203 856-8313
15 Glen Rd Sandy Hook (06482) *(G-7306)*
CT Sign Service LLC 860 322-3954
500 Industrial Park Rd Deep River (06417) *(G-2087)*
CT Sprayfoam Industries LLC 203 232-0961
571 Main St N Southbury (06488) *(G-7849)*
CT Thermography LLC 860 415-1150
2 Forest Park Dr Farmington (06032) *(G-2894)*
CT Thermography LLC 860 690-9202
70 Golf St Newington (06111) *(G-5644)*
CT Tool, Plainville *Also called Connecticut Tool & Mfg Co LLC (G-6792)*
CT Tool & Manufacturing LLC 860 846-0800
4 Right Ln Farmington (06032) *(G-2895)*
CT Woodworking LLC 860 884-9586
438 Route 32 North Franklin (06254) *(G-5872)*
Ctech, Pine Meadow *Also called Cunningham Tech LLC (G-6733)*
Ctech Adhesives 860 482-5947
39 Maple Hollow Rd New Hartford (06057) *(G-5188)*
CTI, Newington *Also called Component Technologies Inc (G-5641)*
CTI Industries Inc (HQ) 203 795-0070
283 Indian River Rd Orange (06477) *(G-6593)*
Ctl Corporation 860 651-9173
10 Rocklyn Ct West Simsbury (06092) *(G-9976)*
Ctr, Bridgeport *Also called Palmieri Industries Inc (G-859)*
Ctr Welding 704 473-1587
39 Padanaram Rd Danbury (06811) *(G-1778)*
CTS Services LLC 203 268-5865
15 Rayo Dr Shelton (06484) *(G-7424)*
Ctv Piping and Structural 860 257-3027
407 Goff Rd Hartford (06109) *(G-3574)*
Cudzilo Enterprises Inc 203 748-4694
40 Taylor Ave Bethel (06801) *(G-275)*
Cuero Operating 203 253-8651
34 Meeker Rd Westport (06880) *(G-10073)*
Cuescript Inc 203 763-4030
555 Lordship Blvd Unit F Stratford (06615) *(G-8602)*
Cultec Inc 203 775-4416
878 Federal Rd Brookfield (06804) *(G-1176)*
Culture Media LLC 203 470-5918
944 Danbury Rd Wilton (06897) *(G-10286)*
Cummins - Allison Corp 203 794-9200
125 Commerce Ct Ste 6 Cheshire (06410) *(G-1377)*
Cummins Allison, Cheshire *Also called Cummins - Allison Corp (G-1377)*
Cummins Enviro Tech Inc 860 388-6377
29 Mile Creek Rd Old Lyme (06371) *(G-6499)*
Cummins Envirotech 860 598-9564
61 Buttonball Rd Old Lyme (06371) *(G-6500)*
Cummins Inc 860 529-7474
914 Cromwell Ave Rocky Hill (06067) *(G-7230)*
Cunningham Industries Inc 203 324-2942
102 Lincoln Ave Ste 3 Stamford (06902) *(G-8171)*
Cunningham Tech LLC 860 738-8759
10 Wickett St Pine Meadow (06061) *(G-6733)*
Cunningham Tech LLC (PA) 860 738-8759
39 Maple Hollow Rd New Hartford (06057) *(G-5189)*
Cuprak Enterprises LLC 203 376-8789
150 N Timber Ln Cheshire (06410) *(G-1378)*
Curbside Compost LLC 914 646-6890
65 Spring Valley Rd Ridgefield (06877) *(G-7132)*
Currie & Kingston LLC 203 698-9428
1111 E Putnam Ave Riverside (06878) *(G-7191)*
Curry Printing & Copy Ctr LLC 203 878-5767
878 Boston Post Rd Milford (06460) *(G-4502)*
Curtis Corporation A Del Corp 203 426-5861
44 Berkshire Rd Sandy Hook (06482) *(G-7307)*
Curtis Packaging Corporation 203 426-5861
44 Berkshire Rd Sandy Hook (06482) *(G-7308)*
Curtis Products LLC 203 754-4155
70 Halcyon Dr Bristol (06010) *(G-1010)*
Curtis Studio, Durham *Also called Glenn Curtis (G-2147)*
Curtiss Woodworking Inc 203 527-9305
123 Union City Rd Prospect (06712) *(G-6998)*
Curved Glass Distributors, Derby *Also called Whalley Glass Company (G-2131)*
Cushs Homegrown LLC 860 739-7373
4 Green Valley Lake Rd Old Lyme (06371) *(G-6501)*
Cusson Sash Company 860 659-0354
128 Addison Rd Glastonbury (06033) *(G-3025)*
Custom & Precision Pdts Inc 203 281-0818
2893 State St Rear Hamden (06517) *(G-3436)*
Custom Art Sgns LLC 203 837-7674
34 Tamarack Ave Danbury (06811) *(G-1779)*
Custom Cabinet & European 860 430-9396
2934 Main St Glastonbury (06033) *(G-3026)*
Custom Carpentry Unlimited 860 742-8932
82 Woodbridge Rd Coventry (06238) *(G-1650)*
Custom Checkering 860 747-8035
46 Spring St Plainville (06062) *(G-6794)*
Custom Chocolate Designs LLC 203 886-6777
16 Welles Ter Meriden (06450) *(G-4164)*
Custom Chrome Plating 203 265-5667
400 S Orchard St Wallingford (06492) *(G-9244)*
Custom Computer Systems 203 264-7808
250 Main St S Southbury (06488) *(G-7850)*
Custom Covers 860 669-4169
20 Riverside Dr Clinton (06413) *(G-1499)*
Custom Creations LLC 203 522-2113
89 Beebe St Naugatuck (06770) *(G-4874)*
Custom Crft Ktchns By Rizio BR 203 268-0271
8 Maple Dr Monroe (06468) *(G-4708)*

A L P H A B E T I C

Custom Design Service Corp 203 748-1105
6 Ohehyahtah Pl Danbury (06810) *(G-1780)*
Custom Design Woodworks LLC 860 434-0515
10 Maywood Dr Old Lyme (06371) *(G-6502)*
Custom Food Pdts Holdings LLC 310 637-0900
411 W Putnam Ave Greenwich (06830) *(G-3148)*
Custom Furniture & Design LLC 860 567-3519
601 Bantam Rd Litchfield (06759) *(G-3887)*
Custom House LLC 860 873-1259
8 Matthews Dr Ste 3 East Haddam (06423) *(G-2240)*
Custom Interiors 860 738-8754
152 Colebrook River Rd Winchester Center (06098) *(G-10344)*
Custom Marine Canvas LLC 860 572-9547
71 Marsh Rd Groton (06340) *(G-3281)*
Custom Marine Woodworking, Mystic *Also called Thomas Townsend Custom Marine (G-4849)*
Custom Metal Crafters Inc 860 953-4210
815 N Mountain Rd Newington (06111) *(G-5645)*
Custom Metal Crafters CMC, Newington *Also called Custom Metal Crafters Inc (G-5645)*
Custom Plastic Distrs Inc 860 779-5833
364 Putnam Pike Dayville (06241) *(G-2060)*
Custom Printing & Copy Inc (PA) 860 290-6890
16 Debra St Enfield (06082) *(G-2634)*
Custom Publishing Design Group 860 513-1213
35 Cold Spring Rd Ste 321 Rocky Hill (06067) *(G-7231)*
Custom Sign Solutions LLC 203 975-8344
93 Prospect St Stamford (06901) *(G-8172)*
Custom Sportswear Mfg 203 879-4420
14 Town Line Rd Wolcott (06716) *(G-10559)*
Custom Stiles 203 410-2370
18 Cleveland Ave Milford (06460) *(G-4503)*
Custom Tee 718 450-1210
400 Main St Ste 510 Stamford (06901) *(G-8173)*
Custom Tees Plus 203 752-1071
365 Whalley Ave New Haven (06511) *(G-5266)*
Custom TS 860 644-1514
194 Bucklnd Hills Dr 10 Ste 1018 Manchester (06042) *(G-4002)*
Custom TS n More LLC 203 438-1592
135 Ethan Allen Hwy Ridgefield (06877) *(G-7133)*
Custom Upholstery Workshop 203 367-4231
10 Greenfield St Fairfield (06825) *(G-2770)*
Custom Woodwork Etc 860 638-1006
789 Saybrook Rd Middletown (06457) *(G-4334)*
Custom Woodworking 860 868-0257
3 Church Hill Rd Washington Depot (06794) *(G-9417)*
Custom Woodworking 860 456-4466
54 Pigeon Swamp Rd Lebanon (06249) *(G-3852)*
Custom Woodworking By Norman 860 663-3462
15 Goldfield Rd Killingworth (06419) *(G-3831)*
Customized Foods Mfg LLC 203 759-1645
8 S Commons Rd Waterbury (06704) *(G-9457)*
Customized Woodworking LLC 860 274-4025
109 Skilton Rd Watertown (06795) *(G-9699)*
Cutter & Drill Parts LLC 203 483-0876
31 Ciro Rd North Branford (06471) *(G-5833)*
Cutting Edge Sgns Graphics LLC 203 758-7776
21a Gramar Ave Prospect (06712) *(G-6999)*
Cuvee 59 .... 707 259-0559
3718 South St Coventry (06238) *(G-1651)*
Cwl Enterprises Inc (HQ) 303 790-8023
200 First Stamford Pl # 2 Stamford (06902) *(G-8174)*
Cya Technologies Inc 203 513-3111
3 Enterprise Dr Ste 408 Shelton (06484) *(G-7425)*
Cycling Sports Group Inc (HQ) 608 268-8916
1 Cannondale Way Wilton (06897) *(G-10287)*
Cyclone Microsystems Inc 203 786-5536
25 Marne St Hamden (06514) *(G-3437)*
Cyclone Pcie Systems LLC 203 786-5536
25 Marne St Hamden (06514) *(G-3438)*
Cygnal Publishing Co 860 983-4757
116 Godfrey Rd Mystic (06355) *(G-4810)*
Cygnus Business Media, Westport *Also called Commerce Connect Media Inc (G-10066)*
Cygnus Medical LLC 800 990-7489
965 W Main St Ste 2 Branford (06405) *(G-578)*
Cylinder Vodka Inc 203 979-0792
101 Washington Blvd # 1223 Stamford (06902) *(G-8175)*
Cynful Scents 860 866-7670
26 Isaiah Smith Ln N Morris (06763) *(G-4788)*
Cyr Woodworking Inc 860 232-1991
139 Summit St Newington (06111) *(G-5646)*
Cyro Industries 203 269-4481
25 Executive Blvd 1 Orange (06477) *(G-6594)*
Cytec Industries Inc 203 284-4334
5 S Cherry St Wallingford (06492) *(G-9245)*
Cytec Industries Inc 203 321-2200
1937 W Main St Ste 1 Stamford (06902) *(G-8176)*
Cytogel Pharma LLC (PA) 203 662-6617
3 Thorndal Cir Darien (06820) *(G-2016)*
Czitek LLC 888 326-8186
4 Ford Ln Danbury (06811) *(G-1781)*
D & B Tool Co LLC 203 878-6026
83 Erna Ave Milford (06461) *(G-4504)*
D & C Industries 203 453-4424
282 Stepstone Hill Rd Guilford (06437) *(G-3342)*
D & D Printing & Advertising 860 871-7774
1264 Hartford Tpke Vernon Rockville (06066) *(G-9166)*
D & D Refuse, Westport *Also called Sidney Dobson (G-10158)*
D & F Scrubs & Gadgets LLC 203 440-4666
235 Hanover St Meriden (06451) *(G-4165)*
D & J Textile LLC 203 569-7754
31 Congress St Ste 2 Stamford (06902) *(G-8177)*
D & L Engineering Company 203 375-5856
564 Surf Ave Stratford (06615) *(G-8603)*
D & M Packing LLC 203 591-8986
407 Brookside Rd Ste 1 Waterbury (06708) *(G-9458)*
D & M Screw Machine Pdts LLC 860 410-9781
97 Forestville Ave Plainville (06062) *(G-6795)*
D & M Tool Company Inc 860 236-6037
17 Grassmere Ave West Hartford (06110) *(G-9797)*
D & P Instruments, Simsbury *Also called Designs & Prototypes Ltd (G-7615)*
D & S Precision Turning LLC 860 793-2640
57 Brussel Ave Plainville (06062) *(G-6796)*
D and L Welding LLC 860 429-8259
309 S Eagleville Rd Storrs Mansfield (06268) *(G-8554)*
D B F Industries Inc 860 827-8283
145 Edgewood Ave New Britain (06051) *(G-4969)*
D C D, Broad Brook *Also called Data Collection Dispersal Inc (G-1146)*
D C Hall Rental Service, North Branford *Also called Halls Rental Service LLC (G-5841)*
D Cello Enterprises LLC 860 659-0844
98 Newell Ln Glastonbury (06033) *(G-3027)*
D D I, Simsbury *Also called Diagnostic Devices Inc (G-7616)*
D D I, Simsbury *Also called Diagnostic Devices Inc (G-7617)*
D D M Metal Finishing Co Inc 860 872-4683
25 Industrial Park Rd W Tolland (06084) *(G-8857)*
D E Sirman Specialty Company 860 658-6336
111 Westledge Rd West Simsbury (06092) *(G-9977)*
D F & B Precision Mfg Inc 860 354-5663
180 Sunny Valley Rd Ste 3 New Milford (06776) *(G-5526)*
D F Arszyla Well Drilling Inc 860 628-6156
1255 East St Southington (06489) *(G-7910)*
D Heck Tool, Thompson *Also called Heck D Tool LLC (G-8834)*
D K Schulman 860 868-4300
239 New Milford Tpke New Preston (06777) *(G-5612)*
D L A Disposition Services, Groton *Also called United States Dept of Navy (G-3316)*
D P Engineering Inc 203 421-7965
211 Summer Hill Rd Madison (06443) *(G-3916)*
D R Charles Envmtl Cnstr LLC 203 445-0412
189 Monroe Tpke Monroe (06468) *(G-4709)*
D R S Desings 203 744-2858
217 Greenwood Ave Bethel (06801) *(G-276)*
D Rotondi LLC 505 427-3233
480 Barnum Ave Ste 4 Bridgeport (06608) *(G-741)*
D S Manufacturing Co 860 829-0334
806 Four Rod Rd Kensington (06037) *(G-3808)*
D T Technologies Inc 203 312-3527
139 Sleepy Hollow Rd Ridgefield (06877) *(G-7134)*
D&B Tool Co., Milford *Also called Morning Star Tool LLC (G-4585)*
D&D Printing Enterprises (PA) 860 684-2023
30 Conklin Rd Stafford Springs (06076) *(G-8023)*
D&R Marine Upholstery & Canvas 860 989-9646
369 Old Main St Rocky Hill (06067) *(G-7232)*
D'Andrea USA, Berlin *Also called Delmar Products Inc (G-176)*
D.R. Charles Envmtl Excav, Monroe *Also called D R Charles Envmtl Cnstr LLC (G-4709)*
Da Cunha Woodworks 860 529-3889
45 Noble St New Britain (06051) *(G-4970)*
Da Silva Klanko Ltd 203 756-4932
70 Deerwood Ln Unit 8 Waterbury (06704) *(G-9459)*
Daad Motorcyle Emporuim, Watertown *Also called Daads LLC (G-9700)*
Daads LLC 860 274-1589
1376 Main St Watertown (06795) *(G-9700)*
Dac Systems Inc 203 924-7000
4 Armstrong Rd Ste 12 Shelton (06484) *(G-7426)*
Dacruz Manufacturing Inc 860 584-5315
100 Broderick Rd Bristol (06010) *(G-1011)*
Daigles Diversfd Wldg Svc LLC 860 265-3024
19 Haystack Ln Somers (06071) *(G-7655)*
Daily Campus, The, Storrs Mansfield *Also called Conn Daily Campus (G-8553)*
Daily Fare LLC 203 743-7300
13 Durant Ave Bethel (06801) *(G-277)*
Daily Impressions LLC 203 508-5305
60 Village Cir Hamden (06514) *(G-3439)*
Daily Mart 860 529-5210
2204 Silas Deane Hwy Rocky Hill (06067) *(G-7233)*
Daily Nutmeg, Woodbury *Also called Natural Spring Ventures LLC (G-10646)*
Daily Voice, Norwalk *Also called Cantata Media LLC (G-6106)*
Dakota Life Sciences, Bridgeport *Also called Kasten Inc (G-813)*
Dalbergia LLC (PA) 860 870-2500
58 Gerber Dr Tolland (06084) *(G-8858)*
Dalla Corte Lumber 860 875-9480
12 Minor Rd Stafford Springs (06076) *(G-8024)*
Dalton Enterprises Inc (PA) 203 272-3221
131 Willow St Cheshire (06410) *(G-1379)*

ALPHABETIC SECTION

Dalvento LLC 203 263-6497
57 Old Grassy Hill Rd Woodbury (06798) *(G-10632)*
Damalias Candle and Body Bar 860 725-2168
3580 Main St Hartford (06120) *(G-3575)*
DAmbruoso Studios LLC 203 758-9660
67 Richardson Dr Middlebury (06762) *(G-4276)*
Dampits LLC 203 210-7946
98 Ridgefield Rd Wilton (06897) *(G-10288)*
Dan Beard Inc 203 924-4346
64 Hawthorne Ave Shelton (06484) *(G-7427)*
Dan Chichester 203 722-4619
104 Soundview Ave Stamford (06902) *(G-8178)*
Danaher Tool Group 203 284-7000
61 Barnes Industrial Park Wallingford (06492) *(G-9246)*
Danbury Aviation, Danbury Also called Santoto LLC *(G-1934)*
Danbury Grassroots Tennis Inc 203 797-0500
196 Main St Danbury (06810) *(G-1782)*
Danbury Medi-Car Service Inc 203 748-3433
14 Walnut St Danbury (06811) *(G-1783)*
Danbury Metal Finishing Inc 203 748-5044
124 West St Danbury (06810) *(G-1784)*
Danbury Ortho 203 797-1500
2 Riverview Dr Danbury (06810) *(G-1785)*
Danbury Powersports Inc 203 791-1310
41 Lake Avenue Ext Danbury (06811) *(G-1786)*
Danbury Sheet Metal, Bethel Also called Varnum Enterprises LLC *(G-362)*
Danbury Square Box Company 203 744-4611
1a Broad St Danbury (06810) *(G-1787)*
Danbury Stairs Corporation 203 743-5567
25 Francis J Clarke Cir # 1 Bethel (06801) *(G-278)*
Danbury Welding LLC 203 482-9306
26 New St Apt 1 Danbury (06810) *(G-1788)*
Dancar Corporation 203 598-0205
145 N Benson Rd Unit 2 Middlebury (06762) *(G-4277)*
Danchak Woodworks LLC 860 346-6057
339 Oxbow Rd Durham (06422) *(G-2144)*
Danco Manufacturing LLC 860 870-1706
77 Industrial Park Rd # 13 Vernon Rockville (06066) *(G-9167)*
DAndrea Corporation 203 932-6000
985 Boston Post Rd West Haven (06516) *(G-9895)*
Dane Millette 860 635-6383
15 Robertson Rd Cromwell (06416) *(G-1699)*
Dangelo Family LLC 203 235-1238
460 Fairfield Ave Waterbury (06708) *(G-9460)*
DAngelo Woodcraft LLC 860 402-7175
32 Fairview Ave Enfield (06082) *(G-2635)*
Dangerous Industries Quality 860 986-0879
13 Harriet Ave Fl 3 Waterbury (06708) *(G-9461)*
Daniel Dechamps 860 463-3105
50 Corporate Ave Plainville (06062) *(G-6797)*
Daniel F Crapa 203 746-5706
17 Calverton Dr New Fairfield (06812) *(G-5167)*
Daniel K Rogers 860 455-0530
25 Nutmeg Ln Chaplin (06235) *(G-1338)*
Daniel Richardson 860 774-3675
482 Westcott Rd Danielson (06239) *(G-1988)*
Danjon Manufacturing Corp 203 272-7258
1075 S Main St Cheshire (06410) *(G-1380)*
Danone Holdings Inc 203 229-7000
208 Harbor Dr Fl 3 Stamford (06902) *(G-8179)*
Dante Ltd 860 376-0204
633 Plainfield Rd Jewett City (06351) *(G-3793)*
Dante Ltd Liability Company 860 376-0204
633 Plainfield Rd Griswold (06351) *(G-3263)*
Dante's Jewelry and Repairs, Middletown Also called Dantes Jewelry & Repair *(G-4335)*
Dantes Jewelry & Repair 860 346-4779
871b Newfield St Middletown (06457) *(G-4335)*
Danver, Wallingford Also called CT Acquisitions LLC *(G-9243)*
Dar More Mfg Co 860 605-9164
601 Hill Rd Harwinton (06791) *(G-3724)*
DArcy Saw LLC 800 569-1264
10 Canal Bank Rd Windsor Locks (06096) *(G-10481)*
Dari-Farms Ice Cream, Tolland Also called Diversis Capital LLC *(G-8861)*
Dari-Farms Ice Cream Co Inc 860 872-8313
55 Gerber Dr Tolland (06084) *(G-8859)*
Darien Doughnut LLC 203 656-2805
364 Heights Rd Darien (06820) *(G-2017)*
Darien Lawn Mower Repair 203 656-1869
126 Post Rd Darien (06820) *(G-2018)*
Darien Technology Foundation I 203 655-5099
5 Brook St Ste G Darien (06820) *(G-2019)*
Darien Times, New Canaan Also called Hersam Publishing Company *(G-5110)*
Dark Field Technologies Inc 203 298-0731
5 Research Dr Shelton (06484) *(G-7428)*
Dark Moon Metals LLC 203 858-3015
38 Creeping Hemlock Dr Norwalk (06851) *(G-6134)*
Darlene Ann Miconi 203 245-4127
615 Horse Pond Rd Madison (06443) *(G-3917)*
Darling International Inc 203 597-0773
172 E Aurora St Waterbury (06708) *(G-9462)*
Darly Custom Technology Inc 860 298-7966
276 Addison Rd Windsor (06095) *(G-10379)*

Dart Products Screen Printing, Bridgeport Also called BI Printing Shop *(G-713)*
Das Distribution Inc 860 844-3058
66e Floydville Rd East Granby (06026) *(G-2201)*
Das State of CT 860 566-4718
18-20 Trinity St Hartford (06106) *(G-3576)*
Dasco Supply LLC 203 388-0095
43 Homestead Ave Stamford (06902) *(G-8180)*
Dasco Welded Products Inc 203 754-9353
2038 Thomaston Ave Waterbury (06704) *(G-9463)*
Dash N Lash Extensions LLC 203 726-2952
18 Davin Dr Naugatuck (06770) *(G-4875)*
Data Collection Dispersal Inc 860 623-7364
42 Skinner Rd Broad Brook (06016) *(G-1146)*
Data Ladder, Suffield Also called Pricing Excellence LLC *(G-8730)*
Data Management Incorporated 860 677-8586
557 New Britain Ave Unionville (06085) *(G-9113)*
Data Management Inc 800 243-1969
557 New Britain Ave Farmington (06032) *(G-2896)*
Data Signal Corporation 203 882-5393
16 Higgins Dr Milford (06460) *(G-4505)*
Data Technology Inc 860 871-8082
24 Industrial Park Rd W Tolland (06084) *(G-8860)*
Data-Graphics Inc 203 667-0435
240 Hartford Ave Newington (06111) *(G-5647)*
Datacomm Management Svcs LLC 203 858-9846
245 Noroton Ave Darien (06820) *(G-2020)*
Dataprep Inc 203 795-2095
109 Boston Post Rd Ste 2 Orange (06477) *(G-6595)*
Dataquest Korea Inc 239 561-4862
56 Top Gallant Rd Stamford (06902) *(G-8181)*
Datex Microcomputer Service, Milford Also called Richard Breault *(G-4626)*
Dav-Co Finishing LLC 860 828-5552
1082 Farmington Ave Berlin (06037) *(G-175)*
Davco Systems 860 546-9681
383 Brooklyn Rd Canterbury (06331) *(G-1298)*
Dave Ross 203 775-4327
92 S Lake Shore Dr Brookfield (06804) *(G-1177)*
Dave's Storage Train, Colebrook Also called Spera Cottage Crafters *(G-1587)*
Davenport Kitchen & Bath LLC 860 323-0630
20 Mountain View Rd West Simsbury (06092) *(G-9978)*
Daves Logging 860 684-6533
252 Hydeville Rd Stafford Springs (06076) *(G-8025)*
Daves Paving and Construction 203 753-4992
105 Waterbury Rd Ste 5 Prospect (06712) *(G-7000)*
David Christian Ceramics LLC 203 758-1532
35 George St Middlebury (06762) *(G-4278)*
David Colbert 860 672-0064
76 Warren Hill Rd Cornwall Bridge (06754) *(G-1617)*
David Derewianka 860 649-1983
459 Dennison Rdg Manchester (06040) *(G-4003)*
David H Johnson Inc 860 677-5595
137 Woodpond Rd West Hartford (06107) *(G-9798)*
David J Weber 203 949-9198
131 N Colony St Wallingford (06492) *(G-9247)*
David O Wells Custom Cabinetry 203 231-0280
172 Jacob Rd Southbury (06488) *(G-7851)*
David R Wttrwrth Son Signs LLC 203 753-3666
71 Mountain View Dr Waterbury (06706) *(G-9464)*
David Shuck 860 434-8562
Hatchetts Hill Rd Old Lyme (06371) *(G-6503)*
David Smith 860 877-3232
66 N Summit St Southington (06489) *(G-7911)*
David W Lintz Company 860 349-1392
24 West St Middlefield (06455) *(G-4301)*
David W Lintz Woodworking, Middlefield Also called David W Lintz Company *(G-4301)*
David Weisman LLC 203 322-9978
30 Mill Valley Ln Stamford (06903) *(G-8182)*
Davids Legal Signs 203 268-8943
384 Hammertown Rd Monroe (06468) *(G-4710)*
Davinci Technologies Inc 860 265-3388
1 Corporate Rd Enfield (06082) *(G-2636)*
Davis Sawmill 860 354-6008
28 Squash Hollow Rd New Milford (06776) *(G-5527)*
Davis Tree & Logging LLC 203 938-2153
57 North St Ste 209 Danbury (06810) *(G-1789)*
Davis-Standard LLC (HQ) 860 599-1010
1 Extrusion Dr Pawcatuck (06379) *(G-6707)*
Davis-Standard Holdings Inc (PA) 860 599-1010
1 Extrusion Dr Pawcatuck (06379) *(G-6708)*
Dawid Manufacturing Inc 203 734-1800
26 Beaver St Ansonia (06401) *(G-31)*
Dawn Enterprises LLC 860 646-8200
275 Progress Dr Ste B Manchester (06042) *(G-4004)*
Dawn Hill Designs, Torrington Also called Dawn Hill Enterprises LLC *(G-8917)*
Dawn Hill Enterprises LLC 860 496-9188
66 Elmwood Ter Torrington (06790) *(G-8917)*
Day Fred A Co LLC 860 589-0531
11 Commerce Dr Bristol (06010) *(G-1012)*
Day Machine Systems Inc 860 229-3440
221 South St Bldg F2 New Britain (06051) *(G-4971)*
Day Publishing Company (HQ) 860 701-4200
47 Eugene Oneill Dr New London (06320) *(G-5466)*

Day Trust (PA) 860 442-2200
47 Eugene Oneill Dr New London (06320) ***(G-5467)***
Day, The, New London *Also called Day Publishing Company* ***(G-5466)***
Daybrake Donuts Inc 203 368-4962
941 Madison Ave Bridgeport (06606) ***(G-742)***
Daybreak Nuclear & Med Systems 203 453-3299
50 Denison Dr Guilford (06437) ***(G-3343)***
Dayon Manufacturing Inc 860 677-8561
1820 New Britain Ave Farmington (06032) ***(G-2897)***
Dayspring Communications LLC 336 775-2059
1220 Unquowa Rd W Fairfield (06824) ***(G-2771)***
Dayton Bag & Burlap Co 860 653-8191
10 Hazelwood Rd Ste A5 East Granby (06026) ***(G-2202)***
Db Press LLC 203 699-9510
14 Bradford Dr Cheshire (06410) ***(G-1381)***
DB&f Industries, New Britain *Also called D B F Industries Inc* ***(G-4969)***
DBA Ne Sheet Metal 860 584-0362
385 King St Bristol (06010) ***(G-1013)***
Dbebz Apparel LLC 203 254-7356
432 Old Post Rd Fairfield (06824) ***(G-2772)***
Dbo Home LLC 860 364-6008
25 Millerton Rd Sharon (06069) ***(G-7377)***
DC & D Inc 860 623-2941
42 Skinner Rd Broad Brook (06016) ***(G-1147)***
Dcci, New Haven *Also called Dow Cover Company Incorporated* ***(G-5269)***
Dcg Precision Manufacturing, Bethel *Also called Dcg-Pmi Inc* ***(G-279)***
Dcg-Pmi Inc 203 743-5525
9 Trowbridge Dr Bethel (06801) ***(G-279)***
Ddk Industries LLC 203 641-4218
70 Center St Shelton (06484) ***(G-7429)***
De Muerte Usa LLC 860 331-7085
73 Morningside St W Hartford (06112) ***(G-3577)***
De Villiers Incorporated 203 966-9645
194 Putnam Rd New Canaan (06840) ***(G-5101)***
Dearborn Deuce LLC 860 669-3232
28 Cream Pot Rd Clinton (06413) ***(G-1500)***
Debbie Pileika Interiors 860 668-6324
30 Chestnut Cir West Suffield (06093) ***(G-9986)***
Deborah Anns Hmmade Chocolates 203 438-0065
453 Main St Ridgefield (06877) ***(G-7135)***
Debrasong Publishing LLC 413 204-4682
82-3 Mount Archer Rd Lyme (06371) ***(G-3904)***
Deburr Co 860 621-6634
201 Atwater St Plantsville (06479) ***(G-6890)***
Deburring House Inc 860 828-0889
230 Berlin St East Berlin (06023) ***(G-2165)***
Deburring Laboratories Inc 860 829-6300
206 Newington Ave New Britain (06051) ***(G-4972)***
Decks R US 860 505-0726
35 Carlton St Fl 2 New Britain (06053) ***(G-4973)***
Deco Products Inc 860 528-4304
34 Nelson St Ste C East Hartford (06108) ***(G-2312)***
Decorator Services Inc 203 384-8144
25 Wells St Ste 1 Bridgeport (06604) ***(G-743)***
Dee Zee Ice LLC 860 276-3500
93 Industrial Dr Southington (06489) ***(G-7912)***
Deep River Distillers LLC 860 788-6061
10 Bellaire Mnr Cromwell (06416) ***(G-1700)***
Deep River Fuel Terminals LLC 860 342-4619
29 Myrtle Rd Portland (06480) ***(G-6956)***
Deep River LLC 860 388-9442
1 Davis Rd W Old Lyme (06371) ***(G-6504)***
Deep River Snacks, Deep River *Also called Old Lyme Gourmet Company* ***(G-2097)***
Deer Creek Fabrics Inc 203 964-0922
509 Glenbrook Rd Stamford (06906) ***(G-8183)***
Defabrications LLC 203 791-1407
39 Rockwood Ln Danbury (06811) ***(G-1790)***
Defelice Woodworking Inc 203 445-0199
50 Oakland Dr Trumbull (06611) ***(G-9019)***
Defender Industries Inc 860 701-3400
42 Great Neck Rd Waterford (06385) ***(G-9652)***
Defender Warehouse Outlet Str, Waterford *Also called Defender Industries Inc* ***(G-9652)***
Defense Cmmnications Solutions 203 947-6283
11 Autumn Dr Danbury (06811) ***(G-1791)***
Defeo Manufacturaing 203 775-1950
115 Commerce Dr Brookfield (06804) ***(G-1178)***
Defeo Manufacturing 203 775-0254
559 Federal Rd Brookfield (06804) ***(G-1179)***
Defeo Manufacturing Inc 203 775-0254
57 Commerce Dr Brookfield (06804) ***(G-1180)***
Defeo Manufacturing Inc 203 775-0254
115 Commerce Dr Brookfield (06804) ***(G-1181)***
Defibtech LLC (PA) 866 333-4248
741 Boston Post Rd # 201 Guilford (06437) ***(G-3344)***
Defined Design Creative Art 203 378-2571
2505 Main St Ste 226b Stratford (06615) ***(G-8604)***
Deitsch Plastic Company Inc 203 934-6601
14 Farwell St West Haven (06516) ***(G-9896)***
Deka Enterprises 860 582-6976
200 Central St Bristol (06010) ***(G-1014)***
Del Arbour LLC 203 882-8501
152 Old Gate Ln Milford (06460) ***(G-4506)***
Del Printing LLC 860 342-2959
42 Gospel Ln Portland (06480) ***(G-6957)***
Del-Tron Precision Inc 203 778-2727
5 Trowbridge Dr Ste 1 Bethel (06801) ***(G-280)***
Delany & Long Ltd 203 532-0010
41 Chestnut St Greenwich (06830) ***(G-3149)***
Delcom Products Inc 914 934-5170
45 Backus Ave Danbury (06810) ***(G-1792)***
Delcon Industries 203 371-5711
31 Frenchtown Rd Trumbull (06611) ***(G-9020)***
Delcon Industries 203 540-5757
480 Barnum Ave Ste 4 Bridgeport (06608) ***(G-744)***
Delcon Industries LLC 203 331-9720
560 N Washington Ave # 4 Bridgeport (06604) ***(G-745)***
Delfin Marketing Inc 203 554-2707
500 W Putnam Ave Ste 400 Greenwich (06830) ***(G-3150)***
Dell Acquisition LLC 860 677-8545
35 Corporate Ave Plainville (06062) ***(G-6798)***
Dell Manufacturing, Plainville *Also called Dell Acquisition LLC* ***(G-6798)***
Dell Software Inc 203 259-0326
49 John St Southport (06890) ***(G-8003)***
Delltech Inc 203 878-8266
175 Buckingham Ave Milford (06460) ***(G-4507)***
Delmar Products Inc 860 828-6501
400 Christian Ln Berlin (06037) ***(G-176)***
Delta Elevator Service, Farmington *Also called North American Elev Svcs Co* ***(G-2939)***
Delta Elevator Service Corp (HQ) 860 676-6152
1 Farm Springs Rd Canton (06019) ***(G-1312)***
Delta Level Defense, Stratford *Also called Delta Level LLC* ***(G-8605)***
Delta Level LLC 203 919-1514
40 Embree St Stratford (06615) ***(G-8605)***
Delta-Ray Corp 203 367-6910
805 Housatonic Ave Bridgeport (06604) ***(G-746)***
Delta-Ray Industries Inc 203 367-9903
805 Housatonic Ave Bridgeport (06604) ***(G-747)***
Delta-Source LLC 860 461-1600
138 Beacon Hill Dr West Hartford (06117) ***(G-9799)***
Delvento Inc (PA) 203 371-7279
83 North Ave Bridgeport (06606) ***(G-748)***
Demand Pro LLC 860 438-8843
120 Dogwood Dr New Britain (06052) ***(G-4974)***
Demane Golf Inc 203 531-9126
35 Chapel St Greenwich (06831) ***(G-3151)***
Demartino Fixture Co Inc 203 269-3971
920 S Colony Rd Wallingford (06492) ***(G-9248)***
Demartino Packing, Seymour *Also called Frank Demartino and Sons* ***(G-7346)***
Demattia Charitable Found 203 254-1558
163 Mistywood Ln Fairfield (06824) ***(G-2773)***
Demo Agent Sales LLC 860 621-3303
312 Mill St Southington (06489) ***(G-7913)***
Demsey Manufacturing Co Inc 860 274-6209
78 New Wood Rd Watertown (06795) ***(G-9701)***
Demusz Mfg Co Inc 860 528-9845
303 Burnham St East Hartford (06108) ***(G-2313)***
Denco Counter-Bore LLC 860 276-0782
30 Peters Cir Southington (06489) ***(G-7914)***
Denlar Fire Protection LLC 860 526-9846
20 Denlar Dr Chester (06412) ***(G-1469)***
Dennis Savela 860 774-3963
35 Margaret Henry Rd Danielson (06239) ***(G-1989)***
Denominator Company Inc 203 263-3210
744 Main St S Woodbury (06798) ***(G-10633)***
Dens Sand & Gravel 860 642-6478
970 Goshen Hill Rd Ext Lebanon (06249) ***(G-3853)***
Dental Implant Services LLC 203 720-1873
10 Peppermill Ct Naugatuck (06770) ***(G-4876)***
Depaul Industries 203 882-1331
6 Drexel Rd Milford (06460) ***(G-4508)***
Dependable Hydraulics, North Branford *Also called Dependable Repair Inc* ***(G-5834)***
Dependable Repair Inc 203 481-9706
2110 Foxon Rd North Branford (06471) ***(G-5834)***
Depercio Woodworking LLC 860 477-1051
136 Moon Rd Ashford (06278) ***(G-59)***
Derby Cellular Products Inc 203 735-4661
680 Bridgeport Ave Ste 3 Shelton (06484) ***(G-7430)***
Derby Discount Liquor 203 732-0666
441 Roosevelt Dr Derby (06418) ***(G-2111)***
Dering-Ney Inc 847 932-6782
353 Woodland Ave Bloomfield (06002) ***(G-406)***
Deringer-Ney Inc (PA) 860 242-2281
353 Woodland Ave Bloomfield (06002) ***(G-407)***
Dermapac Inc 203 924-7148
33 Hull St Ste 4 Shelton (06484) ***(G-7431)***
Derosa Printing Company Inc 860 646-1698
485 Middle Tpke E Manchester (06040) ***(G-4005)***
Derrick Mason (PA) 413 527-4282
2 Nelson St Norwich (06360) ***(G-6410)***
Desai Mukesh 860 529-4141
632 Cromwell Ave Rocky Hill (06067) ***(G-7234)***
Deschenes & Cooper Architectur 860 599-2481
25 White Rock Bridge Rd Pawcatuck (06379) ***(G-6709)***
Desiato Sand & Gravel 860 742-7573
245 Brigham Rd Coventry (06238) ***(G-1652)***

Desiato Sand & Gravel Corp 860 429-6479
999 Stafford Rd Storrs Mansfield (06268) *(G-8555)*
Design & Print Interests LLC 203 494-9072
719 Derby Ave Orange (06477) *(G-6596)*
Design Books, Sharon *Also called Green Editorial* *(G-7379)*
Design Idea Printing 860 896-0103
344 Somers Rd Ellington (06029) *(G-2586)*
Design Label Manufacturing Inc (PA) 860 739-6266
12 Nottingham Dr Old Lyme (06371) *(G-6505)*
Design Ltd 203 426-5539
62 Underhill Rd Sandy Hook (06482) *(G-7309)*
Design Shop Llc 203 937-1651
170 Wood St West Haven (06516) *(G-9897)*
Designers Resource 203 874-7731
116 Research Dr Ste G Milford (06460) *(G-4509)*
Designing Element 203 849-3076
6 Barnum Ave Norwalk (06851) *(G-6135)*
Designs & Prototypes Ltd 860 658-0458
1280 Hopmeadow St Ste E Simsbury (06070) *(G-7615)*
Designs & Signs 203 775-0152
20 Beverly Dr Brookfield (06804) *(G-1182)*
Designs By Diana 860 649-1812
14 Ensign St Manchester (06040) *(G-4006)*
Designs In Stitches Embroidery 203 730-1013
11 Frandon Dr Danbury (06811) *(G-1793)*
Desjardins Woodworking Inc 860 491-9972
211 East St N Goshen (06756) *(G-3098)*
Desrosier of Greenwich Inc 203 661-2334
103 Mason St Greenwich (06830) *(G-3152)*
Detotec North America Inc 860 230-0078
363 Ekonk Hill Rd Moosup (06354) *(G-4778)*
Detotec North America Inc 860 564-1012
401 Snake Meadow Hill Rd Sterling (06377) *(G-8509)*
Devar Inc 203 368-6751
706 Bostwick Ave Bridgeport (06605) *(G-749)*
Devellis Woodworks LLC 203 610-4762
763 Orchard Rd Kensington (06037) *(G-3809)*
Device42 Inc 203 409-7242
600 Saw Mill Rd West Haven (06516) *(G-9898)*
Devin David 203 322-4000
12 Long Ridge Rd Stamford (06905) *(G-8184)*
Devine Brothers Incorporated 203 866-4421
38 Commerce St Norwalk (06850) *(G-6136)*
Devon Precision Industries Inc 203 879-1437
251 Munson Rd Wolcott (06716) *(G-10560)*
Devon Precision Industries., Wolcott *Also called Devon Precision Industries Inc* *(G-10560)*
Devrajan Govender 678 429-3408
190 John Olds Dr Apt 112 Manchester (06042) *(G-4007)*
Dewalt Service Center 050, Wethersfield *Also called Black & Decker (us) Inc* *(G-10184)*
Dewey J Manufacturing Company 203 264-3064
112 Willenbrock Rd Oxford (06478) *(G-6655)*
Dexmet Corporation 203 294-4440
22 Barnes Industrial Rd S Wallingford (06492) *(G-9249)*
Dexon Tech LLC 860 584-1442
550 Broad St Unit H Bristol (06010) *(G-1015)*
Dexter & Co 860 536-9506
3 Pearl St Ste 1 Mystic (06355) *(G-4811)*
Deyulio Sausage Company LLC 203 348-1863
1501 State St Bridgeport (06605) *(G-750)*
Dfs In-Home Services 845 405-6464
15 Great Pasture Rd Danbury (06810) *(G-1794)*
Dg Precision Manufacturing, Woodbury *Also called Duda and Goodwin Inc* *(G-10634)*
Dge, Norwalk *Also called Barbara Garelick Enterprises* *(G-6086)*
Di Grazia Vineyards Ltd 203 775-1616
131 Tower Rd Brookfield (06804) *(G-1183)*
Di Venere Co 860 582-0208
35 Wooster Ct Ste 1 Bristol (06010) *(G-1016)*
Di-Cor Industries Inc 860 585-5583
139 Center St Bristol (06010) *(G-1017)*
Di-El Tool & Manufacturing 203 235-2169
69 Research Pkwy Ste 1 Meriden (06450) *(G-4166)*
Diageo Americas Inc 203 229-2100
801 Main Ave Norwalk (06851) *(G-6137)*
Diageo Americas Supply Inc 203 229-2100
801 Main Ave Norwalk (06851) *(G-6138)*
Diageo Investment Corporation 203 229-2100
801 Main Ave Norwalk (06851) *(G-6139)*
Diageo North America Inc (HQ) 203 229-2100
801 Main Ave Norwalk (06851) *(G-6140)*
Diageo PLC 203 229-2100
801 Main Ave Norwalk (06851) *(G-6141)*
Diagnostic Devices Inc 860 651-6583
11 Windham Dr Simsbury (06070) *(G-7616)*
Diagnostic Devices Inc (PA) 860 651-6583
50 Wolcott Rd Simsbury (06070) *(G-7617)*
Diamond Brewing Service 860 508-0013
52 Hilltop Dr Manchester (06042) *(G-4008)*
Diamond Hrdwd Flrs of Fairfld 203 650-9192
40 Hillside Ave Bridgeport (06604) *(G-751)*
Dianas Candles and Soap LLC 203 527-4028
206 Long Hill Rd Waterbury (06704) *(G-9465)*
Dianna Blanchard 860 684-4874
4 Spellman Rd Stafford Springs (06076) *(G-8026)*
Diba Industries Inc (HQ) 203 744-0773
4 Precision Rd Danbury (06810) *(G-1795)*
Dickinson's Cosmetics, East Hampton *Also called T N Dickinson Company* *(G-2281)*
Dickson Product Development 203 846-2128
14 Perry Ave Norwalk (06850) *(G-6142)*
Dicon Connections Inc 203 481-8080
33 Fowler Rd North Branford (06471) *(G-5835)*
Dictaphone Corporation (HQ) 203 381-7000
3191 Broadbridge Ave Stratford (06614) *(G-8606)*
Diecraft Compacting Tool Inc 203 879-3019
36 James Pl Wolcott (06716) *(G-10561)*
Dietze & Associates LLC 203 762-3500
88 Danbury Rd Ste 1a Wilton (06897) *(G-10289)*
Dietze Associates, Wilton *Also called Dietze & Associates LLC* *(G-10289)*
Dietzgen Corporation 813 849-4334
351 Morgan Ln West Haven (06516) *(G-9899)*
Differential Pressure Plus 203 481-2545
67 N Branford Rd Ste 4 Branford (06405) *(G-579)*
Digatron Power Electronics Inc 203 446-8000
50 Waterview Dr Shelton (06484) *(G-7432)*
Digit-X Inc 860 620-1221
173 Hart St Southington (06489) *(G-7915)*
Digital Bob 203 322-5732
51 Northwood Ln Stamford (06903) *(G-8185)*
Digital Chameleon LLC 203 354-4111
55 Hawley Ave Bridgeport (06606) *(G-752)*
Digital Copy LLC 203 540-5181
3076 Fairfield Ave Bridgeport (06605) *(G-753)*
Digital Imagining & Packaging 203 458-3509
761 Goose Ln Guilford (06437) *(G-3345)*
Digitaldruker Inc 203 888-6001
11 Old Farm Rd Oxford (06478) *(G-6656)*
Dignified Endings LLC 860 291-0575
15 Stanley St East Hartford (06108) *(G-2314)*
Digrazia Vineyards & Winery, Brookfield *Also called Di Grazia Vineyards Ltd* *(G-1183)*
Digysol LLC 860 232-1614
34 Miamis Rd West Hartford (06117) *(G-9800)*
Diiorio Woodworks 203 855-1331
304 Wilson Ave Norwalk (06854) *(G-6143)*
Diiorios Custom Wdwkg LLC 203 855-1635
32 Triangle St Norwalk (06855) *(G-6144)*
Dilorio Woodworks, Norwalk *Also called Diiorio Woodworks* *(G-6143)*
Dimauro Oil Co LLC 860 342-2969
48 Gospel Ln Portland (06480) *(G-6958)*
Dimension Zero Ltd 860 325-7073
52 Prospect St Willimantic (06226) *(G-10224)*
Dimension-Polyant Inc 860 928-8300
78 Highland Dr Putnam (06260) *(G-7039)*
Dimide Inc 203 668-9621
252 Depot Rd Milford (06460) *(G-4510)*
Dinghy Pro LLC 860 767-1596
46 Plains Rd Ste 10 Essex (06426) *(G-2715)*
Dlorio Printing Service 203 656-0557
14 Center St Darien (06820) *(G-2021)*
Diplomaframe.com, Monroe *Also called Church Hill Classics Ltd* *(G-4703)*
Direct Energy Inc (HQ) 800 260-0300
263 Tresser Blvd Fl 8 Stamford (06901) *(G-8186)*
Direct Sales LLC (PA) 203 371-2373
440 Sky Top Dr Fairfield (06825) *(G-2774)*
Directional Technologies Inc 203 294-9200
89 N Main St Wallingford (06492) *(G-9250)*
Directory Assistants Inc 860 633-0122
1321 Silas Deane Hwy 2f Wethersfield (06109) *(G-10190)*
Directv 203 445-2876
6058 Main St Trumbull (06611) *(G-9021)*
Dirt Guy Topsoil 860 303-0500
601 Guilford Rd Durham (06422) *(G-2145)*
Dirtcircle Media LLC 860 532-0674
141 Welchs Point Rd Milford (06460) *(G-4511)*
Disco Chick 860 788-6203
170 Main St Middletown (06457) *(G-4336)*
Displaycraft Inc 860 747-9110
335 S Washington St Plainville (06062) *(G-6799)*
Distinctive Coating LLC 860 530-1233
42 Knollwood Dr Hebron (06248) *(G-3747)*
Distinctive Designs USA, Salem *Also called Dundorf Designs USA Inc* *(G-7288)*
Distinctive Steering Wheels 860 274-9087
189 Chimney Rd Watertown (06795) *(G-9702)*
Distributors of Standard Tile 860 439-0627
531 Broad St New London (06320) *(G-5468)*
Ditriorichard 203 531-0625
21 Grey Rock Dr Greenwich (06831) *(G-3153)*
Diversified Manufact 203 734-0379
1 Riverside Dr Ste H Ansonia (06401) *(G-32)*
Diversified Printing Solutions 203 826-7198
128 E Liberty St Danbury (06810) *(G-1796)*
Diversis Capital LLC 860 872-8313
1 Dari Farms Way Tolland (06084) *(G-8861)*
Divine Treasure 860 643-2552
404 Middle Tpke W Manchester (06040) *(G-4009)*
Division 5 LLC 860 752-4127
99 Cooper Ln Stafford Springs (06076) *(G-8027)*

ALPHABETIC

Division X Specialties LLC 860 402-7736
75 Diane Dr Vernon (06066) *(G-9137)*
Diy Awards LLC (PA) 800 810-1216
1 Atlantic St Ste 705 Stamford (06901) *(G-8187)*
Dizzy Fish Music LLC 203 599-5700
910 E Broadway Milford (06460) *(G-4512)*
Dj Cabinets 203 243-0032
627 Main St West Haven (06516) *(G-9900)*
Dj Sportsware 203 438-0078
17 Woodstone Rd Ridgefield (06877) *(G-7136)*
DJS Campus Kitchen LLC 860 439-1572
405 Williams St New London (06320) *(G-5469)*
Djs Mobile Marine & Power Eqp 203 331-9010
141 Wilmot Ave Bridgeport (06607) *(G-754)*
Dl Distributors LLC 203 931-1724
343 Beach St West Haven (06516) *(G-9901)*
Dline LLC 860 984-2076
57 Fenwood Grove Rd Old Saybrook (06475) *(G-6531)*
Dlpublshers Mystryntrtnmentllc 203 556-4893
390 Charles St Apt 216 Bridgeport (06606) *(G-755)*
Dlz Architectural Mill Work 860 883-7562
510 Ledyard St Hartford (06114) *(G-3578)*
Dmb Publishing LLC 203 798-9231
5 Kingswood Dr Bethel (06801) *(G-281)*
Dmjc Printing LLC 860 502-4882
579 New Britain Ave Hartford (06106) *(G-3579)*
Dmt Solutions Global Corp 203 233-6231
37 Executive Dr Danbury (06810) *(G-1797)*
DNE Systems Inc (HQ) 203 265-7151
50 Barnes Industrial Park Wallingford (06492) *(G-9251)*
Docko Inc 860 572-8939
14 Holmes St Ste 5 Mystic (06355) *(G-4812)*
Doctor Stuff LLC 203 785-8475
20 N Plains Industrial Rd # 1 Wallingford (06492) *(G-9252)*
Doctor Weld LLC 203 877-3433
170 Eastern Pkwy Milford (06460) *(G-4513)*
Doctors Clothes 203 485-0494
67 Church St Greenwich (06830) *(G-3154)*
Doctors of Optometry 203 743-9897
7 Backus Ave Danbury (06810) *(G-1798)*
Document Dynamics LLC 860 376-2944
178 Preston Rd Jewett City (06351) *(G-3794)*
Docuprint & Imaging Inc 203 776-6000
27 Whitney Ave New Haven (06510) *(G-5267)*
Docuprintnow, New Haven *Also called Docuprint & Imaging Inc* *(G-5267)*
Dog Gone Smart, Norwalk *Also called Nano Pet Products LLC* *(G-6268)*
Dogwood Publishing LLC 203 292-3815
117 Deepwood Rd Fairfield (06824) *(G-2775)*
Dollar Express LLC 203 495-9209
690 Washington Ave New Haven (06519) *(G-5268)*
Doltronics LLC 203 488-8766
65-4 N Branford Rd Branford (06405) *(G-580)*
Domestic Kitchens Inc 203 368-1651
515 Commerce Dr Fairfield (06825) *(G-2776)*
Dominics Decorating Inc 203 838-1827
6 Allen Ct Norwalk (06851) *(G-6145)*
Domino Media Group Inc 877 223-7844
16 Taylor Pl Westport (06880) *(G-10074)*
Domino.com, Westport *Also called Domino Media Group Inc* *(G-10074)*
Domus VI LLC 860 619-0707
85 Herb Rd Sharon (06069) *(G-7378)*
Don Pomaski (PA) 860 693-4469
2 Highfields Dr Canton (06019) *(G-1313)*
Don Pomaski 860 693-4469
10 Front St Collinsville (06019) *(G-1593)*
Don S Screw Machine Pdts LLC 860 283-6448
247 Old Northfield Rd Thomaston (06787) *(G-8787)*
Donald E Basil Inc 203 574-0149
76 Sabal Dr Waterbury (06708) *(G-9466)*
Donali Systems Integration Inc 860 715-5432
128 Tanner Marsh Rd Guilford (06437) *(G-3346)*
Donavita International, Bridgeport *Also called Prima Dona LLC* *(G-879)*
Doncasters Inc 860 446-4803
835 Poquonnock Rd Groton (06340) *(G-3282)*
Doncasters Inc (HQ) 860 449-1603
835 Poquonnock Rd Groton (06340) *(G-3283)*
Doncasters Precision Castings-, Groton *Also called Doncasters Inc* *(G-3282)*
Doncasters US Hldings 2018 Inc 860 677-1376
835 Poquonnock Rd Groton (06340) *(G-3284)*
Donghia Inc (PA) 800 366-4442
500 Bic Dr Gate 1 Ste 200 1 Gate Milford (06461) *(G-4514)*
Donghia Furniture and Textiles, Milford *Also called Donghia Inc* *(G-4514)*
Donham Crafts, Naugatuck *Also called Unimetal Surface Finishing LLC* *(G-4924)*
Donnas Canvas Creations 860 276-0327
100 Forest Ln Southington (06489) *(G-7916)*
Donnin Publishing Inc 203 453-8866
800 Village Walk Guilford (06437) *(G-3347)*
Donut Stop 203 924-7133
368 Howe Ave Shelton (06484) *(G-7433)*
Donwell Company 860 649-5374
130 Sheldon Rd Manchester (06042) *(G-4010)*
Dooney & Bourke 203 795-3131
22 Marsh Hill Rd Orange (06477) *(G-6597)*
Dooney & Bourke Inc (PA) 203 853-7515
1 Regent St Norwalk (06855) *(G-6146)*
Dooney Woodworks LLC 203 340-9770
105 River Rd Cos Cob (06807) *(G-1631)*
Dooney Woodworks LLC 203 869-5457
55 Conyers Farm Dr Greenwich (06831) *(G-3155)*
Door Step Prep LLC 860 550-0460
51 Thomson Rd West Hartford (06107) *(G-9801)*
Doors To Explore Inc 978 761-7210
16 Chestnut Hill Rd Sandy Hook (06482) *(G-7310)*
Doosan Fuel Cell America Inc (HQ) 860 727-2200
195 Governors Hwy South Windsor (06074) *(G-7739)*
Dorado Tankers Pool Inc 203 662-2600
20 Glover Ave Norwalk (06850) *(G-6147)*
Doss Corporation 860 721-7384
102 Orchard Hill Dr Wethersfield (06109) *(G-10191)*
Double Barrel Distillery LLC 860 285-0141
9 Shelley Ave Windsor (06095) *(G-10380)*
Double Diamond Construction 203 357-7757
11 Deleo Dr Stamford (06906) *(G-8188)*
Double H Acres LLC 860 250-3311
47 Broad Brook Rd Broad Brook (06016) *(G-1148)*
Doubletree 860 589-7766
42 Century Dr Bristol (06010) *(G-1018)*
Doug Hartin 860 377-4283
353 Bungay Hill Rd Woodstock (06281) *(G-10663)*
Dough Girl Baking Co LLC 203 838-9695
50 Sammis St Norwalk (06853) *(G-6148)*
Dougherty Sons Fur Stretchers 860 839-0096
878 North St Suffield (06078) *(G-8717)*
Douglas M Gagnon 860 779-2255
666 Upper Maple St Danielson (06239) *(G-1990)*
Douglas Moss 203 854-5559
28 Knight St Ste 5 Norwalk (06851) *(G-6149)*
Dow Chemical Company 203 740-7510
9 Meadowview Dr Brookfield (06804) *(G-1184)*
Dow Cover Company Incorporated 203 469-5394
373 Lexington Ave New Haven (06513) *(G-5269)*
Dow Div of UTC 860 683-7340
360 Bloomfield Ave Windsor (06095) *(G-10381)*
Down Home Publishing 860 521-6177
46 Dover Rd Newington (06111) *(G-5648)*
Dp Custom Boat Repr Detail LLC 203 536-3997
483 Monroe Tpke Ste 167 Monroe (06468) *(G-4711)*
Dp Foods L L C 203 271-6212
152 Knotter Dr Cheshire (06410) *(G-1382)*
Dp Marine LLC 917 705-7435
34 Lockwood Ln Riverside (06878) *(G-7192)*
Dp2 LLC Head 203 655-0747
25 Old Kings Hwy N Darien (06820) *(G-2022)*
Dpc Quality Pump Service 203 874-6877
544 Bridgeport Ave Milford (06460) *(G-4515)*
Dr Mike's Ice Cream Shop, Bethel *Also called Dr Mikes Ice Cream Inc* *(G-282)*
Dr Mikes Ice Cream Inc 203 792-4388
158 Greenwood Ave Bethel (06801) *(G-282)*
Dr Stitch Seamstress To Stars 706 631-0859
21 Arch St New Britain (06051) *(G-4975)*
DR Templeman Company 860 747-2709
1 Northwest Dr Plainville (06062) *(G-6800)*
Dragon Hollow Design LLC 860 861-6200
230 Dunham St Norwich (06360) *(G-6411)*
Dragon Hollow Promotions, Norwich *Also called Dragon Hollow Design LLC* *(G-6411)*
Dragonlab LLC 860 436-9221
1275 Cromwell Ave Ste C6 Rocky Hill (06067) *(G-7235)*
Draher Machine Company 203 753-0179
30 Tosun Rd Wolcott (06716) *(G-10562)*
Drainage Products, Windsor Locks *Also called TWC Trans World Consulting* *(G-10499)*
Draperies Plus 860 589-3634
31 Ridgecrest Ln Bristol (06010) *(G-1019)*
Drapery Consultants 203 855-0454
88 Old Saugatuck Rd Norwalk (06855) *(G-6150)*
Drb Woodworks 203 216-7071
285 Wheeler Rd Monroe (06468) *(G-4712)*
Dream Cabinets LLC 860 301-5625
25 Pickeral Dr Colchester (06415) *(G-1547)*
Dream Construction & Wdwkg 774 573-0495
28 Hall Rd Eastford (06242) *(G-2535)*
Dreamer Software LLC 860 645-1240
17 Mckinley St Manchester (06040) *(G-4011)*
Dri-Air Industries Inc 860 627-5110
16 Thompson Rd East Windsor (06088) *(G-2489)*
Dried Materials Unlimited, Cheshire *Also called Raymond J Bykowski* *(G-1438)*
Drill Rite Carbide Tool Co 860 583-3200
6 Orchard St Terryville (06786) *(G-8751)*
Drill-Out, Wolcott *Also called Alden Corporation* *(G-10548)*
Drilling Dynamics LLC 203 783-1395
336 Boston Post Rd Milford (06460) *(G-4516)*
Drinkin Hats LLC 203 265-3489
10 Huntington Ridge Rd Wallingford (06492) *(G-9253)*
Drinking Water Div 860 509-7333
410 Capitol Ave Hartford (06106) *(G-3580)*

ALPHABETIC SECTION

DRM Associates LLC 860 583-7744
  21 Yale Dr Bristol (06010) *(G-1020)*
Drone Imaging LLC 203 256-1151
  195 Wood House Rd Fairfield (06824) *(G-2777)*
Drs Leonardo Inc 203 798-3172
  21 South St Nn Danbury (06810) *(G-1799)*
Drs Naval Power Systems Inc 203 366-5211
  141 North Ave Bridgeport (06606) *(G-756)*
Drs Naval Power Systems Inc 203 798-3000
  21 South St Danbury (06810) *(G-1800)*
Drs Naval Power Systems Inc 203 798-3000
  21 South St Danbury (06810) *(G-1801)*
Drs Naval Power Systems Inc 203 366-5211
  206 Island Brook Ave Bridgeport (06606) *(G-757)*
Drt Aerospace LLC 203 781-8020
  620 Research Pkwy Meriden (06450) *(G-4167)*
Drt Aerospace LLC 860 379-0783
  200 Price Rd Winsted (06098) *(G-10515)*
Drt Power Systems, Winsted Also called Drt Aerospace LLC *(G-10515)*
Drug Imprment Dtction Svcs LLC 203 616-3735
  71 Newtown Rd Danbury (06810) *(G-1802)*
Drum Crane and Rigging LLC 860 837-4517
  324 Governor St East Hartford (06108) *(G-2315)*
Drunk Alpaca LLC 646 415-4995
  23 Hoover Rd Riverside (06878) *(G-7193)*
DS Sewing Inc 203 773-1344
  260 Wolcott St New Haven (06513) *(G-5270)*
Dsaencore LLC (PA) 203 740-4200
  50 Pocono Rd Brookfield (06804) *(G-1185)*
DSar Company 203 324-6456
  3 Nash Pl Ste 7 Stamford (06906) *(G-8189)*
Dsd Distributor LLC 860 378-4487
  27 E Maple St Plainville (06062) *(G-6801)*
Dso Manufacturing Company Inc 860 224-2641
  390 John Downey Dr New Britain (06051) *(G-4976)*
Dst Output East LLC (HQ) 816 221-1234
  125 Ellington Rd South Windsor (06074) *(G-7740)*
Dsw Inc 860 644-6200
  120 Slater St Manchester (06042) *(G-4012)*
Dsw Inc 203 985-8241
  410 Universal Dr N North Haven (06473) *(G-5933)*
Dt Manufacturing LLC 860 384-8449
  550 Broad St Unit P Bristol (06010) *(G-1021)*
Du-Lite Corporation 860 347-2505
  171 River Rd Middletown (06457) *(G-4337)*
Dube Air LLC 860 355-1705
  8 Brookside Ln Sherman (06784) *(G-7594)*
Ducduc LLC 860 482-1322
  100 Lawton St Torrington (06790) *(G-8918)*
Ducksworth Antq Vintage & Cstm, New Milford Also called Ted Boccuzzi *(G-5593)*
Ducky O Soat Company, Uncasville Also called Country Creations By Carol *(G-9097)*
Ductco LLC 860 243-0350
  13 Britton Dr Bloomfield (06002) *(G-408)*
Ductworx Unlimited LLC 203 535-1425
  62 Crestway Hamden (06514) *(G-3440)*
Duda and Goodwin Inc 203 263-4353
  90 Washington Rd Woodbury (06798) *(G-10634)*
Dufrane Nuclear Shielding Inc 860 379-2318
  150 Price Rd Winsted (06098) *(G-10516)*
Duhamels 860 928-4101
  40 Butts Rd Woodstock (06281) *(G-10664)*
Dulce Domum LLC 203 227-1400
  40 Richards Ave Ste 4 Norwalk (06854) *(G-6151)*
Dulcify LLC 203 344-1671
  175 Riverside Ave Riverside (06878) *(G-7194)*
Dumond Chemicals Inc 609 655-7700
  620 West Ave Milford (06461) *(G-4517)*
Dumond Chemicals Inc 609 655-7700
  695 West Ave Milford (06461) *(G-4518)*
Dunbar Commercial Enterprises 203 469-7575
  372 Cosey Beach Ave East Haven (06512) *(G-2421)*
Dundee Holding Inc (HQ) 860 677-1376
  36 Spring Ln Farmington (06032) *(G-2898)*
Dundorf Designs USA Inc 860 859-2955
  426 Forsyth Rd Salem (06420) *(G-7288)*
Dune Denim LLC 203 241-5409
  6 Meadow Ln Bethel (06801) *(G-283)*
Duneland Press 860 535-0362
  3 Rockland Rd Guilford (06437) *(G-3348)*
Dunkin' Donuts, Portland Also called Realejo Donuts Inc *(G-6971)*
Dunkin' Donuts, Manchester Also called Spencer Street Inc *(G-4092)*
Dunkin' Donuts, West Haven Also called DAndrea Corporation *(G-9895)*
Dunn Paper Holdings Inc 860 289-7496
  2 Forbes St East Hartford (06108) *(G-2316)*
Dunn Paper LLC 860 466-4141
  2 Forbes St East Hartford (06108) *(G-2317)*
Dunning Sand & Gravel Company 860 677-1616
  105 Brickyard Rd Farmington (06032) *(G-2899)*
Dunnottar Publishing LLC 203 488-0350
  3 Lakeview Ter Branford (06405) *(G-581)*
Dunphey Associates Supply Co, Stamford Also called Dasco Supply LLC *(G-8180)*

Dupont 860 368-0766
  1075 Newfield St Middletown (06457) *(G-4338)*
Dupont De Nemours Inc 203 330-6755
  615 Asylum St Bridgeport (06610) *(G-758)*
Dupont Guy Office 203 679-0358
  21 Cassella Dr Wallingford (06492) *(G-9254)*
Dur-Mate, Mystic Also called Durant Machine Inc *(G-4813)*
Duracell Company (HQ) 203 796-4000
  14 Research Dr Bethel (06801) *(G-284)*
Duracell Company 203 796-4000
  Berkshire Corporate Bldg Bethel (06801) *(G-285)*
Duracell Manufacturing Inc 203 796-4000
  15 Research Dr Bethel (06801) *(G-286)*
Duracell Manufacturing LLC 203 796-4000
  14 Research Dr Bethel (06801) *(G-287)*
Duracell US Holding LLC (HQ) 203 796-4000
  14 Research Dr Bethel (06801) *(G-288)*
Duracell US Operations Inc 203 796-4000
  14 Research Dr Bethel (06801) *(G-289)*
Duralite Incorporated 860 379-3113
  15 School St Riverton (06065) *(G-7206)*
Durant Machine Inc (PA) 860 536-7698
  664 Noank Rd Mystic (06355) *(G-4813)*
Durant Machine Inc 860 572-8211
  Broadway Ext Mystic (06355) *(G-4814)*
Durantes Pasta Inc 203 387-5560
  78 Fenwick St West Haven (06516) *(G-9902)*
Durbin Machine Inc 860 342-1602
  101 Airline Ave Portland (06480) *(G-6959)*
Durco Manufacturing Co Inc 203 575-0446
  493 S Leonard St Waterbury (06708) *(G-9467)*
Durham Manufacturing Company (PA) 860 349-3427
  201 Main St Durham (06422) *(G-2146)*
Durol Company 203 288-3383
  2580 State St Hamden (06517) *(G-3441)*
Durol Cosmetic Laboratories, West Haven Also called Durol Laboratories LLC *(G-9903)*
Durol Laboratories LLC 866 611-9694
  5 Knight Ln West Haven (06516) *(G-9903)*
Duros Welding Services 203 982-6978
  353 Highland Dr Waterbury (06708) *(G-9468)*
Durstin Machine & Mfg 860 485-1257
  57 Westleigh Dr Harwinton (06791) *(G-3725)*
Dutch Wharf Boat Yard & Marina 203 488-9000
  70 Maple St Branford (06405) *(G-582)*
Duz Manufacturing Inc 203 874-1032
  87 Opal St Milford (06461) *(G-4519)*
Dwelling LLC 860 521-1935
  149 Raymond Rd West Hartford (06107) *(G-9802)*
Dwyer Aluminum Mast Company 203 484-0419
  2 Commerce Dr Ste 1 North Branford (06471) *(G-5836)*
Dyadic Innovations LLC 630 738-4113
  400 Farmington Ave R1844 Farmington (06032) *(G-2900)*
Dyco Industries Inc 860 289-4957
  229 S Satellite Rd South Windsor (06074) *(G-7741)*
Dylans Dumpsters LLC 860 455-9924
  84 Scotland Rd Chaplin (06235) *(G-1339)*
Dymax Corporation 860 626-7006
  51 Greenwoods Rd Torrington (06790) *(G-8919)*
Dymax Materials Inc (HQ) 860 482-1010
  51 Greenwoods Rd Torrington (06790) *(G-8920)*
Dymax Oligomers & Coatings, Torrington Also called Dymax Corporation *(G-8919)*
Dymax Oligomers & Coatings 860 626-7006
  318 Industrial Ln Torrington (06790) *(G-8921)*
Dymco, Bristol Also called Dynamic Manufacturing Company *(G-1023)*
Dymotek Corporation 800 788-1984
  24 Scitico Rd Somers (06071) *(G-7656)*
Dymotek Corporation 860 875-2868
  7 Main St Ellington (06029) *(G-2587)*
Dynamic Bldg Enrgy Sltions LLC 860 571-8590
  70 Inwood Rd Rocky Hill (06067) *(G-7236)*
Dynamic Bldg Enrgy Sltions LLC (PA) 860 599-1872
  183 Provdnc New London North Stonington (06359) *(G-6022)*
Dynamic Coating Solutions LLC 860 321-7483
  26 Columbus Ave Bristol (06010) *(G-1022)*
Dynamic Controls Hs Inc 860 654-6000
  1 Hamilton Rd Windsor Locks (06096) *(G-10482)*
Dynamic Flight Systems 203 449-7211
  303 Stanley Rd Monroe (06468) *(G-4713)*
Dynamic Gunver Technologies, Manchester Also called Paradigm Manchester Inc *(G-4069)*
Dynamic Lasers LLC 866 731-9610
  324 Candlewood Mtn Rd New Milford (06776) *(G-5528)*
Dynamic Manufacturing Company 860 589-2751
  95 Valley St Ste 5 Bristol (06010) *(G-1023)*
Dynamic Print Management, Cromwell Also called Dane Millette *(G-1699)*
Dynamic Printing 203 459-8762
  91 Main St Monroe (06468) *(G-4714)*
Dynamic Racing Transm LLC 203 315-0138
  104-5 Enterprise Dr North Branford (06471) *(G-5837)*
Dynawash, East Berlin Also called Edro Corporation *(G-2166)*
Dynaxa LLC 203 300-5237
  211 Greenwood Ave Ste 2 Bethel (06801) *(G-290)*

Dyno Nobel Inc 860 843-2000
  660 Hopmeadow St Simsbury (06070) *(G-7618)*
Dythnam Industries LLC 860 480-7980
  529 Thompson St Glastonbury (06033) *(G-3028)*
E & A Enterprises Inc 203 250-8050
  10 Capital Dr A Wallingford (06492) *(G-9255)*
E & E Tool & Manufacturing Co 860 738-8577
  100 International Way Winsted (06098) *(G-10517)*
E & F Wood LLC 860 377-0601
  28 Route 198 Woodstock Valley (06282) *(G-10692)*
E & J Andrychowski Farms 860 423-4124
  257 Brick Top Rd Windham (06280) *(G-10345)*
E & J Parts Cleaning Inc 203 757-1716
  1669 Thomaston Ave Waterbury (06704) *(G-9469)*
E & M Machine 860 429-2427
  358 Westford Rd Ashford (06278) *(G-60)*
E & S Gauge Company, Tolland Also called E and S Gage Inc *(G-8862)*
E and S Gage Inc 860 872-5917
  38 Gerber Dr Tolland (06084) *(G-8862)*
E B Asphalt & Landscaping LLC 860 639-1921
  60 Terminal Way Norwich (06360) *(G-6412)*
E B Buffing, Bristol Also called Etherington Brothers Inc *(G-1031)*
E G Tech Solutions LLC 203 200-7047
  6 Ledge Rd Old Greenwich (06870) *(G-6471)*
E M M Inc 203 245-0306
  8 Bishop Ln Madison (06443) *(G-3918)*
E M S, Bridgeport Also called Electrical Maintenance Svc Co *(G-761)*
E Magazine, Norwalk Also called Douglas Moss *(G-6149)*
E O Manufacturing Company Inc 203 932-5981
  474 Frontage Rd West Haven (06516) *(G-9904)*
E P M Co Inc 860 589-3233
  147 Terryville Rd Bristol (06010) *(G-1024)*
E R Hinman & Sons Inc 860 673-9170
  77 Milford St Burlington (06013) *(G-1266)*
E R Hitchcock Company 860 229-2024
  191 John Downey Dr New Britain (06051) *(G-4977)*
E S Custom Machining 203 481-8653
  195 N Main St Apt A Branford (06405) *(G-583)*
E S Williams Co 203 888-0093
  61 Washington Ave Seymour (06483) *(G-7344)*
E T I, Cheshire Also called Electro-Tech Inc *(G-1384)*
E&D Landscaping 203 934-4088
  91 Cynthia Dr West Haven (06516) *(G-9905)*
E&S Automotive Operations LLC 203 332-4555
  425 Boston Ave Bridgeport (06610) *(G-759)*
E-B Manufacturing Company Inc 860 632-8563
  825 Middle St Middletown (06457) *(G-4339)*
E-J Electric T & D LLC 203 626-9625
  53 N Plains Industrial Rd Wallingford (06492) *(G-9256)*
E-Lite Technologies Inc 203 371-2070
  2285 Reservoir Ave Trumbull (06611) *(G-9022)*
E-Skylight Inc 203 208-1351
  66 N Main St Branford (06405) *(G-584)*
E-Z Switch Manufacturing Inc 203 874-7766
  463 Naugatuck Ave Milford (06460) *(G-4520)*
E-Z Tools Inc 203 838-2102
  5 Poplar St Norwalk (06855) *(G-6152)*
E11even LLC 855 246-6233
  35 Post Rd W Westport (06880) *(G-10075)*
E6s Industries LLC 512 920-3671
  38 Scott Hill Rd Colchester (06415) *(G-1548)*
EA Patten Co LLC 860 649-2851
  303 Wetherell St Manchester (06040) *(G-4013)*
Eagle Alloys 203 453-9910
  2514 Boston Post Rd 6c Guilford (06437) *(G-3349)*
Eagle Consulting LLC 203 445-1740
  180 Merrimac Dr Trumbull (06611) *(G-9023)*
Eagle Electric Service LLC 860 868-9898
  145 Flanders Rd Bethlehem (06751) *(G-369)*
Eagle Investment Systems LLC 860 561-4602
  65 Lasalle Rd Ste 305 West Hartford (06107) *(G-9803)*
Eagle Manufacturing Co Inc 860 537-3759
  13 Homonick Rd Colchester (06415) *(G-1549)*
Eagle Printing Co 860 953-2152
  7a Andover Dr West Hartford (06110) *(G-9804)*
Eagle Signs LLC 860 227-1959
  50 West Ave Essex (06426) *(G-2716)*
Eagle Tissue LLC 860 282-2535
  70 Bidwell Rd South Windsor (06074) *(G-7742)*
Early Advantage LLC 203 259-6480
  426 Mine Hill Rd Fairfield (06824) *(G-2778)*
Earmark, Hamden Also called Farmington River Holdings LLC *(G-3447)*
Earnix Inc 203 557-8077
  191 Post Rd W Westport (06880) *(G-10076)*
Earth Animal Ventures Inc 717 271-6393
  49 John St Stamford (06902) *(G-8190)*
Earth Engineered Systems 203 231-4614
  630 Hawthorne Ave Derby (06418) *(G-2112)*
Earth Loving Stitches 405 833-9343
  60 Leominster Rd Bristol (06010) *(G-1025)*
East Branch Engrg & Mfg Inc 860 355-9661
  57 S End Plz New Milford (06776) *(G-5529)*

East Canaan Equipment Repair, East Canaan Also called William Linkovich *(G-2184)*
East Coast Hockey Depot LLC 203 247-3476
  3 Old Long Ridge Rd Stamford (06903) *(G-8191)*
East Coast Insulation LLC 302 685-3152
  657 E Main St Apt A12 Meriden (06450) *(G-4168)*
East Coast Lightning Eqp Inc 860 379-9072
  24 Lanson Dr Winsted (06098) *(G-10518)*
East Coast Metal Hose Inc 203 723-7459
  41 Raytkwich Rd Naugatuck (06770) *(G-4877)*
East Coast Name Plates Inc 203 261-4347
  884 Black Rock Tpke Easton (06612) *(G-2549)*
East Coast Packaging LLC (PA) 860 675-8500
  210 Main St Unit 1182 Farmington (06034) *(G-2901)*
East Coast Precision Grinding 860 289-1010
  259 Sullivan Ave Ste D South Windsor (06074) *(G-7743)*
East Coast Precision Mfg 860 322-4624
  221 Middlesex Ave Chester (06412) *(G-1470)*
East Coast Precision Mfg LLC 978 887-5920
  63 Pond Meadow Rd Killingworth (06419) *(G-3832)*
East Coast Pulling Parts LLC 860 234-4285
  80 Tillinghast Rd Danielson (06239) *(G-1991)*
East Coast Roof Specialties, Winsted Also called East Coast Lightning Eqp Inc *(G-10518)*
East Coast Sheet Metal LLC 860 283-1126
  141 Woodruff St Litchfield (06759) *(G-3888)*
East Coast Sign and Supply Inc 203 791-8326
  11 Francis J Clarke Cir Bethel (06801) *(G-291)*
East Coast Stairs Co Inc 860 528-7096
  125 Bidwell Rd South Windsor (06074) *(G-7744)*
East Delta Resources Corp 860 434-7750
  76 Lyme St Old Lyme (06371) *(G-6506)*
East Hartford Lamination Co 860 633-4637
  110 Commerce St Glastonbury (06033) *(G-3029)*
East Hartford Operations, East Hartford Also called ATI Ladish Machining Inc *(G-2296)*
East Longmeadow Business Svcs 413 525-6111
  25 Lake Dr Enfield (06082) *(G-2637)*
East Lyme Puppetry Project 860 739-7225
  11 Lake Avenue Ext Niantic (06357) *(G-5805)*
East Mountain Oil Co LLC 203 757-7774
  21 Gramar Ave Prospect (06712) *(G-7001)*
East Rock Brewing Company LLC 203 530-3484
  285 Nicoll St New Haven (06511) *(G-5271)*
East Shore Wire Rope 203 469-5204
  5 Old Bradley St East Haven (06512) *(G-2422)*
East Shre Wre Rpe/Rggng Spply 203 469-5204
  78 Rebeschi Dr North Haven (06473) *(G-5934)*
East Side Car Clinic Corp 860 223-2247
  1181 East St New Britain (06051) *(G-4978)*
East Side Welding, New Britain Also called East Side Car Clinic Corp *(G-4978)*
East Spring Obsolete Auto 203 266-5488
  60 Woodland Rd Bethlehem (06751) *(G-370)*
East Windsor Metal Fabg Inc 860 528-7107
  91 Glendale Rd South Windsor (06074) *(G-7745)*
Eastern Broach Inc 860 828-4800
  10 Sparks St Plainville (06062) *(G-6802)*
Eastern Canvas Works 860 245-9174
  88 Windham Rd Willimantic (06226) *(G-10225)*
Eastern Company (PA) 203 729-2255
  112 Bridge St Naugatuck (06770) *(G-4878)*
Eastern Company 860 526-0800
  212 Middlesex Ave Chester (06412) *(G-1471)*
Eastern Company 860 669-2233
  1 Heritage Park Rd Clinton (06413) *(G-1501)*
Eastern Conectr Specialty Corp 860 355-8100
  566 Danbury Rd Ste 3 New Milford (06776) *(G-5530)*
Eastern Conn Hlth Netwrk 860 652-3182
  628 Hebron Ave Ste 104b Glastonbury (06033) *(G-3030)*
Eastern Connecticut 860 423-1972
  42 Boston Post Rd Willimantic (06226) *(G-10226)*
Eastern Electric Cnstr Co 860 485-1100
  75 North Rd Harwinton (06791) *(G-3726)*
Eastern Inc 203 563-9535
  95 Locust Ave New Canaan (06840) *(G-5102)*
Eastern Machine Co 203 877-6308
  655 Plains Rd Unit I Milford (06461) *(G-4521)*
Eastern Marble & Granite LLC 203 882-8221
  201 Buckingham Ave Milford (06460) *(G-4522)*
Eastern Metal Treating Inc 860 763-4311
  28 Bacon Rd Enfield (06082) *(G-2638)*
Eastern Metal Works Inc 203 878-6995
  333 Woodmont Rd Milford (06460) *(G-4523)*
Eastern Plastics, Bristol Also called Idex Health & Science LLC *(G-1050)*
Eastern Precast Company Inc 203 775-0230
  1 Commerce Dr Brookfield (06804) *(G-1186)*
Eastern Salt Company 203 466-6761
  400 Waterfront St New Haven (06512) *(G-5272)*
Eastern Tech LLC 203 877-5386
  55 Old Gate Ln Milford (06460) *(G-4524)*
Eastern Technology Corporation 860 528-9821
  42 Nelson St East Hartford (06108) *(G-2318)*
Eastern Trading, Milford Also called Eastern Tech LLC *(G-4524)*
Eastern Truck & Machine LLC 860 528-0258
  23 Barbara Rd South Windsor (06074) *(G-7746)*

Eastern Utility Products LLC....860 399-1724
246 Toby Hill Rd Westbrook (06498) ***(G-9995)***
Easton Brewing Company LLC....203 921-7263
53 Ridgeway Rd Easton (06612) ***(G-2550)***
Eastside Electric Inc....860 485-0700
178 Birge Park Rd Harwinton (06791) ***(G-3727)***
Eastwood Printing Inc....860 529-6673
501 Middletown Ave Wethersfield (06109) ***(G-10192)***
Eastwoods Arms LLC....203 615-3476
37 Orcutt Dr Guilford (06437) ***(G-3350)***
Easy Graphics Inc....203 622-0001
31 Saint Roch Ave Ste 1 Greenwich (06830) ***(G-3156)***
Easy Powerful Innovations Co, Manchester *Also called Benedict M Lai* ***(G-3986)***
Eaton Aerospace LLC....203 796-6000
15 Durant Ave Bethel (06801) ***(G-292)***
Eaton Corporation....203 796-6000
15 Durant Ave Bethel (06801) ***(G-293)***
Eaton Electric Holdings LLC....860 683-4300
1200 Kennedy Rd Windsor (06095) ***(G-10382)***
Eatzy LLC....303 720-7532
38 Pond Rd Old Saybrook (06475) ***(G-6532)***
Eazy Oil LLC....860 426-3184
415 Marion Ave Plantsville (06479) ***(G-6891)***
EBA&d, Simsbury *Also called Ensign-Bickford Arospc Def Co* ***(G-7620)***
Ebeam Film LLC....203 926-0100
240 Long Hill Cross Rd Shelton (06484) ***(G-7434)***
Ebk Picture Framing & Gallery....860 523-9384
30 Bartholomew Ave Hartford (06106) ***(G-3581)***
Ebl Products Inc....860 290-3737
22 Prestige Park Cir East Hartford (06108) ***(G-2319)***
EBM-Papst Inc (HQ)....860 674-1515
100 Hyde Rd Farmington (06032) ***(G-2902)***
EC Holdings Inc....203 846-1651
2 Muller Ave Norwalk (06851) ***(G-6153)***
Eccles Carleton, Easton *Also called Eccles-Lehman Inc* ***(G-2551)***
Eccles-Lehman Inc....203 268-0605
44 Sanford Dr Easton (06612) ***(G-2551)***
ECI Screen Print Inc....860 283-9849
15 Mountain View Rd Watertown (06795) ***(G-9703)***
Eclipse Systems Inc....203 483-0665
14 Commercial St Ub Branford (06405) ***(G-585)***
Eco Pallet World LLC....203 343-9089
5 Chapel St Milford (06460) ***(G-4525)***
Ecochlor Inc....203 915-4593
285 State St Ste 12 North Haven (06473) ***(G-5935)***
Ecoflik LLC....860 460-4419
1 Old Bridge Rd Old Lyme (06371) ***(G-6507)***
Ecogenics, Trumbull *Also called Lady Anne Cosmetics Inc* ***(G-9041)***
Ecologic Energy Solutions LLC....203 889-0505
48 Union St Ste 14 Stamford (06906) ***(G-8192)***
Ecometics Inc....203 853-7856
19 Concord St Norwalk (06854) ***(G-6154)***
Economy Canvas, Hartford *Also called Econony Canvas Co* ***(G-3582)***
Economy Printing, Danbury *Also called Paul Dewitt* ***(G-1902)***
Economy Printing & Copy Center (PA)....203 792-5610
128 E Liberty St Ste 4 Danbury (06810) ***(G-1803)***
Economy Printing & Copy Center....203 438-7401
971 Ethan Allen Hwy Ridgefield (06877) ***(G-7137)***
Economy Spring, Southington *Also called Matthew Warren Inc* ***(G-7952)***
Econony Canvas Co....860 289-5281
115 Hamilton St Hartford (06106) ***(G-3582)***
Ecosystem Consulting Svc Inc....860 742-0744
30 Mason St Coventry (06238) ***(G-1653)***
ECR Enterprises LLC....860 426-3098
77 Knollwood Rd Southington (06489) ***(G-7917)***
Ecua Express....860 344-1144
470 Main St Middletown (06457) ***(G-4340)***
Edac Aero Components, Newington *Also called Mtu Aero Engine Design Inc* ***(G-5680)***
Edac Nd Inc....860 633-9474
81 National Dr Glastonbury (06033) ***(G-3031)***
Edac Technologies, Cheshire *Also called Apex Machine Tool Company Inc* ***(G-1354)***
Edac Technologies LLC....860 789-2511
68 Prospect Hill Rd East Windsor (06088) ***(G-2490)***
Edac Technologies LLC (HQ)....203 806-2090
5 Mckee Pl Cheshire (06410) ***(G-1383)***
Edac Technologies LLC....860 667-2134
275 Richard St Newington (06111) ***(G-5649)***
Edal Industries Inc....203 467-2591
51 Commerce St East Haven (06512) ***(G-2423)***
Edco Industries Inc....203 333-8982
203 Dekalb Ave Bridgeport (06607) ***(G-760)***
Eddinger Assoc LLC....860 344-0508
278 Chamberlain Rd Middletown (06457) ***(G-4341)***
Edelman Metalworks Inc....203 744-7331
36 Butterfield Rd Newtown (06470) ***(G-5736)***
Edge Printing....609 707-4555
6 Bayberry Ln Norwalk (06851) ***(G-6155)***
Edge Tool LLC....860 747-1820
163 Stillwell Dr Plainville (06062) ***(G-6803)***
Edgewater International LLC....860 851-9014
17 Middle River Dr Stafford Springs (06076) ***(G-8028)***
Edgewell Per Care Brands LLC....203 882-2300
10 Leighton Rd Milford (06460) ***(G-4526)***
Edgewell Per Care Brands LLC (HQ)....203 944-5500
6 Research Dr Shelton (06484) ***(G-7435)***
Edgewell Personal Care Company....203 882-2308
10 Leighton Rd Milford (06460) ***(G-4527)***
Edgewood Prospect LLC....860 255-7799
15 Edgewood St Unionville (06085) ***(G-9114)***
Edi Landscape LLC....860 216-6871
32 Belmont St Hartford (06106) ***(G-3583)***
Edible Nutmeg....818 383-4603
90 Old Litchfield Rd Washington (06793) ***(G-9413)***
Edison Atlas LLC....860 335-6455
1275 Cromwell Ave Ste F1 Rocky Hill (06067) ***(G-7237)***
Edison Coatings Inc....860 747-2220
3 Northwest Dr Plainville (06062) ***(G-6804)***
Editorial Directions Inc....203 245-2011
46 Brookview Ter Madison (06443) ***(G-3919)***
Editors Only....860 881-2300
275 Batterson Dr New Britain (06053) ***(G-4979)***
Edko Cabinets LLC....203 463-8346
101 Derby Ave Apt 1 Seymour (06483) ***(G-7345)***
Edmund Price....860 658-1441
78 Woodchuck Hill Rd West Simsbury (06092) ***(G-9979)***
Edmunds Gages, Farmington *Also called Edmunds Manufacturing Company* ***(G-2903)***
Edmunds Manufacturing Company (PA)....860 677-2813
45 Spring Ln Farmington (06032) ***(G-2903)***
Edrive Actuators Inc....860 953-0588
385 Stamm Rd Newington (06111) ***(G-5650)***
Edro Corporation....860 828-0311
37 Commerce St East Berlin (06023) ***(G-2166)***
Eds Jewelry LLC....203 757-0018
625 Wolcott St Ste 14 Waterbury (06705) ***(G-9470)***
EDS Perfect Polishing....203 259-5187
256 Pratt St Fairfield (06824) ***(G-2779)***
Edsan Chemical Company Inc....203 624-3123
150 Whittier Rd New Haven (06515) ***(G-5273)***
Edson Manufacturing Inc....203 879-1411
10 Venus Dr Wolcott (06716) ***(G-10563)***
Educational Reference Publishi....203 797-1517
13 Lindencrest Dr Danbury (06811) ***(G-1804)***
Educational Resources Network....203 866-9973
4 Sarah Bishop Rd Ridgefield (06877) ***(G-7138)***
Edward D Segen Co....203 929-8700
100 Trap Falls Road Ext Shelton (06484) ***(G-7436)***
Edward Fleur Fncl Educatn Corp....203 629-9333
176 Bedford Rd Greenwich (06831) ***(G-3157)***
Edward Segal Inc....860 283-5821
360 Reynolds Bridge Rd Thomaston (06787) ***(G-8788)***
Edward Tomkievich....860 633-5811
65 Griswold St Glastonbury (06033) ***(G-3032)***
Edwards & Schmidt LLC....203 393-5666
16 Waterbury Rd Prospect (06712) ***(G-7002)***
Edwards Detection & Alarm, Farmington *Also called UTC Fire SEC Americas Corp Inc* ***(G-2974)***
Edwards Wines LLC....860 535-0202
74 Chester Maine Rd North Stonington (06359) ***(G-6023)***
Edwards, Jonathan Winery, North Stonington *Also called Edwards Wines LLC* ***(G-6023)***
Edwin Publishing Company....203 228-9396
70 Edwin Ave Waterbury (06708) ***(G-9471)***
Eemax Inc (HQ)....203 267-7890
400 Captain Neville Dr Waterbury (06705) ***(G-9472)***
Ef Lee Publishing LLC....203 546-7148
44 Whisconier Rd Brookfield (06804) ***(G-1187)***
EFC, Waterbury *Also called Electronic Film Capacitors* ***(G-9474)***
Effihealth LLC....888 435-3108
259 Main St Apt 3 Stamford (06901) ***(G-8193)***
Efitzgerald Publishing LLC....860 904-7250
319 Ridgewood Rd West Hartford (06107) ***(G-9805)***
Egan, Sterling, Nrm, Brookes, Pawcatuck *Also called Davis-Standard Holdings Inc* ***(G-6708)***
Egs Electrcl Grp Nelson Heat T, East Granby *Also called Appleton Grp LLC* ***(G-2190)***
Ehl Kitchens, Glastonbury *Also called East Hartford Lamination Co* ***(G-3029)***
Ehriched Stitch LLC....203 210-5107
196 Danbury Rd Wilton (06897) ***(G-10290)***
Ehrlich & Company....203 481-1999
3 Wellsweep Rd Branford (06405) ***(G-586)***
Eis, Milford *Also called Engineered Inserts & Systems* ***(G-4531)***
Ek Publishing LLC....203 246-9683
88 Compo Rd S Westport (06880) ***(G-10077)***
Ek-Ris Cable Company Inc....860 223-4327
503 Burritt St Apt 7 New Britain (06053) ***(G-4980)***
El Mar Inc....860 729-7232
38 Cody St 2 West Hartford (06110) ***(G-9806)***
El Paso Prod Oil Gas Texas LP....860 293-1990
490 Capitol Ave Hartford (06106) ***(G-3584)***
Elc Acquisition Corporation....203 743-4059
6 Trowbridge Dr Bethel (06801) ***(G-294)***
Eldorado Usa Inc....203 208-2282
322 E Main St Ste 2 Branford (06405) ***(G-587)***
Electri-Cable Assemblies, Shelton *Also called Premier Mfg Group Inc* ***(G-7539)***
Electri-Cable Assemblies Inc....203 924-6617
70 Shelton Technology Ctr Shelton (06484) ***(G-7437)***

ALPHABETIC

Electric Boat Corporation.......860 433-0503
210 Mitchell St Groton (06340) **(G-3285)**
Electric Boat Corporation.......860 433-3000
75 Eastern Point Rd Groton (06340) **(G-3286)**
Electric Boat Corporation (HQ).......860 433-3000
75 Eastern Point Rd Groton (06340) **(G-3287)**
Electric Boat Fairwater Div, Groton *Also called Electric Boat Corporation* **(G-3286)**
Electric Cable Compounds Inc.......203 723-2590
108 Rado Dr Naugatuck (06770) **(G-4879)**
Electric Enterprise Inc.......203 378-7311
1410 Stratford Ave Stratford (06615) **(G-8607)**
Electrical Maintenance Svc Co.......203 333-6163
143 Bennett St Bridgeport (06605) **(G-761)**
Electrix LLC.......203 776-5577
45 Spring St New Haven (06519) **(G-5274)**
Electro Mech Specialists LLC.......860 887-2613
6 Commerce Park Rd Bozrah (06334) **(G-524)**
Electro-Flex Heat, West Hartford *Also called Manufacturers Coml Fin LLC* **(G-9832)**
Electro-Lite Corporation.......203 743-4059
6 Trowbridge Dr Bethel (06801) **(G-295)**
Electro-Methods Inc (PA).......860 289-8661
330 Governors Hwy South Windsor (06074) **(G-7747)**
Electro-Methods Inc.......860 289-8661
525 Nutmeg Rd N South Windsor (06074) **(G-7748)**
Electro-Tech Inc.......203 271-1976
408 Sandbank Rd Cheshire (06410) **(G-1384)**
Electrodes Incorporated.......203 878-7400
160 Cascade Blvd Milford (06460) **(G-4528)**
Electronic Connection Corp.......860 243-3356
112 Porter St Waterbury (06708) **(G-9473)**
Electronic Design Lab Inc.......203 790-0500
23 Francis J Clarke Cir 1b Bethel (06801) **(G-296)**
Electronic Film Capacitors.......203 755-5629
41 Interstate Ln Waterbury (06705) **(G-9474)**
Electronic Finishing Company, Bridgeport *Also called Park Distributories Inc* **(G-864)**
Electronic Magazine, Stamford *Also called Informa Business Media Inc* **(G-8248)**
Electronic Spc Conn Inc.......203 288-1707
19 Hamden Park Dr Hamden (06517) **(G-3442)**
Elegant Drycleaning.......203 849-1000
388 Westport Ave Norwalk (06851) **(G-6156)**
Element 119 LLC.......860 358-0119
296 Reynolds Bridge Rd Thomaston (06787) **(G-8789)**
Element One LLC.......203 344-1553
1 N Water St Ste 100 Norwalk (06854) **(G-6157)**
Element Solutions Inc.......203 575-5850
245 Freight St Waterbury (06702) **(G-9475)**
Elemental Mercury LLC.......860 355-9569
22 Howland Rd New Milford (06776) **(G-5531)**
Elementals LLC.......203 438-1848
158 Main St Ridgefield (06877) **(G-7139)**
Elements LLC.......860 231-8011
945 Farmington Ave West Hartford (06107) **(G-9807)**
Elemetal Direct Usa LLC.......860 290-1701
210 Roberts St Ste B East Hartford (06108) **(G-2320)**
Elena Dieck.......860 623-9872
7 Eastwood Dr Broad Brook (06016) **(G-1149)**
Elene A Moore.......203 377-0248
400 Booth Hill Rd Trumbull (06611) **(G-9024)**
Elevation Sells Group LLC.......203 871-7172
120 Curtis Dr New Haven (06515) **(G-5275)**
Elidah Inc.......978 435-4324
810 Main St Ste C Monroe (06468) **(G-4715)**
Elinco International Inc (PA).......203 275-8885
1525 Kings Hwy Fairfield (06824) **(G-2780)**
Elite Electronics, Ledyard *Also called Arthur Rodgers* **(G-3867)**
Elite Engraving & Awards.......860 643-7459
71 Woodland St B Manchester (06042) **(G-4014)**
Elite Woodworking LLC.......860 655-7806
23 Chestnut Hill Rd Glastonbury (06033) **(G-3033)**
Elius Delight Snacks LLC.......646 302-4948
1915 Stratford Ave Stratford (06615) **(G-8608)**
Elizabeth Arden Inc.......203 905-1700
300 Main St Ste 800 Stamford (06901) **(G-8194)**
Elizabeth Eakins, Norwalk *Also called Holland & Sherry Inc* **(G-6201)**
Eljen Corporation.......860 610-0426
125 Mckee St East Hartford (06108) **(G-2321)**
Elka Precision.......860 526-1674
124 Pennsylvania Ave New Britain (06052) **(G-4981)**
Ellen and Crafts, Enfield *Also called Nancy Dighello* **(G-2665)**
Ellignton Energy Inc.......860 872-9276
263 Crystal Lake Rd Ellington (06029) **(G-2588)**
Ellington Printery Inc.......860 875-3310
25 West Rd Ste B Ellington (06029) **(G-2589)**
Ellipson Data LLC.......203 227-5520
21 Bridge Sq Westport (06880) **(G-10078)**
Ellis Manufacturing LLC.......865 518-0531
161 Woodford Ave Ste 62 Plainville (06062) **(G-6805)**
Elm City Cheese Company Inc.......203 865-5768
2240 State St Hamden (06517) **(G-3443)**
Elm City Distillery LLC.......203 285-8830
7 Read St Ivoryton (06442) **(G-3785)**
Elm City Manufacturing LLC.......203 248-1969
370 Sackett Point Rd North Haven (06473) **(G-5936)**
Elm City Mfg Jewelers Inc.......203 248-2195
29 Marne St Hamden (06514) **(G-3444)**
Elm City Pttern Fndry Wrks Inc.......203 481-2518
14 Griffing Pond Rd Branford (06405) **(G-588)**
Elm Press Incorporated.......860 583-3600
16 Tremco Dr Terryville (06786) **(G-8752)**
Elm-Cap Industries Inc.......860 953-1060
111 South St West Hartford (06110) **(G-9808)**
Elmar Filter Corporation.......203 624-1708
72 Blatchley Ave New Haven (06513) **(G-5276)**
Elmo Nash Industries.......203 459-3648
9 Trefoil Dr Trumbull (06611) **(G-9025)**
Elot Inc (PA).......203 388-1808
51 Forest Ave Apt 117 Old Greenwich (06870) **(G-6472)**
Elottery, Old Greenwich *Also called Elot Inc* **(G-6472)**
Elvex Corporation.......203 743-2488
2 Mountain View Dr Shelton (06484) **(G-7438)**
Embraer Executive Jet Svcs LLC.......860 804-4600
41 Perimeter Rd Windsor Locks (06096) **(G-10483)**
Embraer Executive Jets, Windsor Locks *Also called Embraer Executive Jet Svcs LLC* **(G-10483)**
Embroidery By Sharon, Middletown *Also called Sharon M Stinson* **(G-4411)**
Embroidery Wizard.......860 379-3294
141 E Mountain Ave Winsted (06098) **(G-10519)**
Embroidery Works.......800 681-0805
1083 Farmington Ave Berlin (06037) **(G-177)**
Embroidery World Inc.......203 281-7303
62 Bagley Ave Hamden (06514) **(G-3445)**
EMC Corporation.......203 418-4500
2150 Post Rd Fl 5 Fairfield (06824) **(G-2781)**
EMC Fun Factory Inc.......914 837-2899
7 Backus Ave Danbury (06810) **(G-1805)**
Emc7 LLC.......203 429-4355
149 Brookview Ave Fairfield (06825) **(G-2782)**
Emdepoint Candles USA LLC.......860 205-8400
334 Lewis Rd New Britain (06053) **(G-4982)**
Emerson Electric Co.......203 891-1080
58 Robinson Blvd Ste C Orange (06477) **(G-6598)**
Emerson Rmote Automtn Solution, Watertown *Also called Bristol Inc* **(G-9686)**
Emhart Glass Inc (HQ).......860 298-7340
123 Great Pond Dr Windsor (06095) **(G-10383)**
Emhart Glass Manufacturing Inc (HQ).......860 298-7340
123 Great Pond Dr Windsor (06095) **(G-10384)**
Emhart Teknologies LLC (HQ).......800 783-6427
480 Myrtle St New Britain (06053) **(G-4983)**
Emhart Teknologies LLC.......877 364-2781
4 Shelter Rock Rd Danbury (06810) **(G-1806)**
Emhart Teknologies LLC.......203 790-5000
Shelter Rock Danbury (06810) **(G-1807)**
Emhart Teknologies LLC.......877 364-2781
4 Shelter Rock Ln Danbury (06810) **(G-1808)**
EMI Inc.......860 669-1199
4 Heritage Park Rd Clinton (06413) **(G-1502)**
Emilee's Italian Ice, Hartford *Also called Poppys LLC* **(G-3667)**
Emilie Cohen.......860 693-9427
51 Bridge St Collinsville (06019) **(G-1594)**
Emilys Sweet Confections LLC.......860 301-2586
680 Ridge Rd Middletown (06457) **(G-4342)**
EMJ Contracting LLC.......475 449-7725
695 Beechwood Ave Bridgeport (06605) **(G-762)**
Emme Controls LLC.......503 793-3792
32 Valley St Fl C Bristol (06010) **(G-1026)**
Emme E2ms LLC.......860 845-8810
32 Valley St Fl C Bristol (06010) **(G-1027)**
Emosyn America Inc.......203 794-1100
7 Commerce Dr Danbury (06810) **(G-1809)**
Emotion Printing, Pawcatuck *Also called Emulsion Apparel* **(G-6710)**
Empco Inc (PA).......860 589-3233
147 Terryville Rd Bristol (06010) **(G-1028)**
Empco Prcision Swiss Screw Mch, Bristol *Also called Empco Inc* **(G-1028)**
Empire Industries Inc.......860 647-1431
180 Olcott St Manchester (06040) **(G-4015)**
Empire Printing Systems LLC.......860 633-3333
63 Hebron Ave Ste C Glastonbury (06033) **(G-3034)**
Empire Tool LLC.......203 735-7467
259 Roosevelt Dr Derby (06418) **(G-2113)**
Empty Cup Magic.......203 874-1093
46 Whalley Ave Milford (06460) **(G-4529)**
EMR Global Inc.......203 452-8166
265 Prestige Park Rd East Hartford (06108) **(G-2322)**
Ems International Inc.......860 526-2060
244 Middlesex Ave Chester (06412) **(G-1472)**
Emsc LLC.......203 268-5101
2009 Summer St Ste 201 Stamford (06905) **(G-8195)**
Emson Inc.......860 489-6249
301 Ella Grasso Ave Torrington (06790) **(G-8922)**
Emtec Metal Products, Bridgeport *Also called Hispanic Enterprises Inc* **(G-784)**
Emulsion Apparel.......860 495-5792
21 River Rd Pawcatuck (06379) **(G-6710)**

Emulsion LLC 860 440-8685
34 Taugwonk Spur Rd # 3 Stonington (06378) *(G-8527)*
Enaqua 203 269-9890
57 Grieb Trl Wallingford (06492) *(G-9257)*
Encarnation Center The, Ivoryton *Also called Bushy Hill Nature Center (G-3784)*
Encore Optics 860 282-0082
140 Commerce Way South Windsor (06074) *(G-7749)*
Encore Sales Corp 203 301-4949
500 Bic Dr Ste 102 Milford (06461) *(G-4530)*
End Grain Woodworks LLC 203 817-7154
73 Old Driftway Wilton (06897) *(G-10291)*
Endo Graphics Inc 203 778-1557
41 Kenosia Ave Ste 102 Danbury (06810) *(G-1810)*
Endoto Corp 860 289-8033
43 Franklin St East Hartford (06108) *(G-2323)*
Enduro Wheelchair Company 860 289-0374
750 Tolland St East Hartford (06108) *(G-2324)*
Energizer, Shelton *Also called Edgewell Per Care Brands LLC (G-7435)*
Energy Beam Sciences Inc 860 653-0411
29 Kripes Rd Ste B East Granby (06026) *(G-2203)*
Energy Saving Products and Sls 860 675-6443
713 George Washington Tpk Burlington (06013) *(G-1267)*
Energy Tech LLC 860 345-3993
63 Church Hill Rd Haddam (06438) *(G-3404)*
Energy USA Incorporated (HQ) 203 791-2222
83 Wooster Hts Danbury (06810) *(G-1811)*
Enfield Collision, Enfield *Also called Adamczyk Enterprises Inc (G-2612)*
Enfield Printing Company 860 745-3600
1 Anngina Dr Enfield (06082) *(G-2639)*
Enfield Stationers, Enfield *Also called Olympia Sales Inc (G-2672)*
Enfield Technologies LLC 203 375-3100
50 Waterview Dr Ste 120 Shelton (06484) *(G-7439)*
Enfield Transit Mix Inc 860 763-0864
84 Broadbrook Rd Enfield (06082) *(G-2640)*
Enflo Corporation (PA) 860 589-0014
315 Lake Ave Bristol (06010) *(G-1029)*
Engelhard Surface Technologies 860 623-9901
12 Thompson Rd East Windsor (06088) *(G-2491)*
Engine Alliance LLC 860 565-2239
124 Hebron Ave Ste 200 Glastonbury (06033) *(G-3035)*
Engineered Building Pdts Inc 860 243-1110
18 Southwood Dr Bloomfield (06002) *(G-409)*
Engineered Coatings Inc 860 567-5556
272 Norfolk Rd Litchfield (06759) *(G-3889)*
Engineered Fibers Tech LLC 203 922-1810
88 Long Hill Cross Rd # 4 Shelton (06484) *(G-7440)*
Engineered Inserts & Systems (PA) 203 301-3334
26 Quirk Rd Milford (06460) *(G-4531)*
Engineered Polymer Industries, Cheshire *Also called Osterman & Company Inc (G-1427)*
Engineered Polymers Inds Inc 203 272-2233
726 S Main St Cheshire (06410) *(G-1385)*
Engineering Division, Dayville *Also called Web Industries Inc (G-2079)*
Engineering Services & Pdts Co (PA) 860 528-1119
1395 John Fitch Blvd South Windsor (06074) *(G-7750)*
Engineers Welding LLC 203 334-2492
425 Kossuth St Bridgeport (06608) *(G-763)*
Enginering Components Pdts LLC 860 747-6222
35 Forshaw Ave Plainville (06062) *(G-6806)*
Enginuity Plm LLC (HQ) 203 218-7225
440 Wheelers Farms Rd Milford (06461) *(G-4532)*
Enhanced Mfg Solutions LLC 203 488-5796
33 Business Park Dr Ste 4 Branford (06405) *(G-589)*
Enjet Aero New Britain LLC 860 356-0330
150 John Downey Dr New Britain (06051) *(G-4984)*
Ens Microwave LLC 203 241-1888
37 Ironwood Dr Danbury (06811) *(G-1812)*
Ens Microwave LLC 203 794-7940
14 Commerce Dr Danbury (06810) *(G-1813)*
Ensign Bickford Industries 203 843-2126
100 Grist Mill Ln Simsbury (06070) *(G-7619)*
Ensign-Bickford Arospc Def Co (HQ) 860 843-2289
640 Hopmeadow St Simsbury (06070) *(G-7620)*
Ensign-Bickford Company (HQ) 860 843-2001
125 Powder Forest Dr Simsbury (06070) *(G-7621)*
Ensign-Bickford Industries Inc 860 658-4411
630 Hopmeadow St Rm 20 Simsbury (06070) *(G-7622)*
Ensign-Bickford Renewable Ener 860 843-2000
125 Powder Forest Dr Simsbury (06070) *(G-7623)*
Ensinger Prcsion Cmponents Inc 860 928-7911
11 Danco Rd Putnam (06260) *(G-7040)*
Entegris Inc 800 766-2681
7 Commerce Dr Danbury (06810) *(G-1814)*
Entegris Prof Solutions Inc (HQ) 203 794-1100
7 Commerce Dr Danbury (06810) *(G-1815)*
Enterex America LLC 860 661-4635
2046 Boston Post Rd Ste 2 Westbrook (06498) *(G-9996)*
Enterplay LLC 203 458-1128
800 Village Walk Ste 307 Guilford (06437) *(G-3351)*
Entersport Management Inc 203 972-9090
128 Heather Dr New Canaan (06840) *(G-5103)*
Entrees Made Easy 203 261-5777
100 Cross Hill Rd Monroe (06468) *(G-4716)*
Envax Products Inc 203 264-8181
349 Christian St Oxford (06478) *(G-6657)*
Envelopes & More Inc 860 286-7570
124 Francis Ave Newington (06111) *(G-5651)*
Environics Inc 860 872-1111
69 Industrial Park Rd E Tolland (06084) *(G-8863)*
Environmantal Systems Cor 860 953-5167
18 Jansen Ct Hartford (06110) *(G-3585)*
Environmental Monitor Service 203 935-0102
87 Gypsy Ln Meriden (06450) *(G-4169)*
Enw Pharma Writing LLC 860 663-0263
181 N Chestnut Hill Rd Killingworth (06419) *(G-3833)*
Eon Designs, Norwich *Also called One and Co Inc (G-6427)*
Eows Midland Inc 203 358-5705
1 Landmark Sq Fl 11 Stamford (06901) *(G-8196)*
Epath Learning Inc 860 444-7900
300 State St Ste 400 New London (06320) *(G-5470)*
Epdm Coatings 203 225-0104
15 Rushbrooke Ln Shelton (06484) *(G-7441)*
Epic By Nextec, Greenwich *Also called Nextec Applications Inc (G-3209)*
Epic Printing Compny Inc 203 469-3988
699 Silver Sands Rd East Haven (06512) *(G-2424)*
EPic Publishing Services LLC 860 204-7450
1c Honey Hill Rd East Haddam (06423) *(G-2241)*
Epicurean Feast Medtron O 203 492-5000
195 Mcdermott Rd North Haven (06473) *(G-5937)*
Epilog Lasers of New England 203 405-1124
10 Applegate Ln Woodbury (06798) *(G-10635)*
Eppendorf Inc (HQ) 732 287-1200
175 Freshwater Blvd Enfield (06082) *(G-2641)*
Eppendorf Holding Inc (HQ) 860 253-3417
175 Freshwater Blvd Enfield (06082) *(G-2642)*
Eppendorf Manufacturing Corp 860 253-3400
175 Freshwater Blvd Enfield (06082) *(G-2643)*
Equestrian Collection 860 749-2964
62 South Rd Somers (06071) *(G-7657)*
Equine Graphics, Uncasville *Also called Toni Leland (G-9106)*
Equinor Shipping Inc 203 978-6900
120 Long Ridge Rd 3eo1 Stamford (06902) *(G-8197)*
Equinor US Holdings Inc (HQ) 203 978-6900
120 Long Ridge Rd 3eo1 Stamford (06902) *(G-8198)*
Equipment Designs Associate 860 217-1573
11 Long View Dr Simsbury (06070) *(G-7624)*
Equipment Works 860 585-9686
542 Jerome Ave Bristol (06010) *(G-1030)*
ERA Replica Automobiles, New Britain *Also called International Automobile Entps (G-5001)*
ERA Replica Automobiles 860 229-7968
24 Dewey St New Britain (06051) *(G-4985)*
ERA Wire Inc 203 933-0480
19 Locust St West Haven (06516) *(G-9906)*
Erasable Images 860 367-4545
450 Oxoboxo Dam Rd Oakdale (06370) *(G-6442)*
Erection & Welding Contrs LLC 860 828-9353
190 New Park Dr Berlin (06037) *(G-178)*
Eric Lindquist Photography, South Glastonbury *Also called River Valley Photographic LLC (G-7682)*
Eric Nordlund Welding 203 544-8293
140 Old Mill Rd Wilton (06897) *(G-10292)*
Eric Sapper 203 239-6020
55 Beach Ln North Haven (06473) *(G-5938)*
Erickson Metals Corporation (PA) 203 272-2918
25 Knotter Dr Cheshire (06410) *(G-1386)*
Erielle Media LLC 203 563-9159
341 Newtown Tpke Wilton (06897) *(G-10293)*
Erinco Marketing 203 545-4550
7 Olympic Dr Danbury (06810) *(G-1816)*
Ernest Ferraro 914 921-4376
2 High Noon Rd Weston (06883) *(G-10025)*
Errichetti Woodworks LLC 203 528-3977
15 Bronson Rd Prospect (06712) *(G-7003)*
ES Metal Fabrications Inc 860 585-6067
11 Allread Dr Terryville (06786) *(G-8753)*
Esdras Steel Fabrication 203 917-3053
9 Francis J Clarke Cir Bethel (06801) *(G-297)*
Esg Woodworking and Bldg LLC 203 667-0811
24 Park Ln Newtown (06470) *(G-5737)*
Essel Dental 860 254-6955
44 S Main St Ste 14 East Windsor (06088) *(G-2492)*
Essentalia LLC 860 617-5106
69 Summit Rd Storrs (06268) *(G-8548)*
Essential Trading Systems Corp 860 295-8100
9 Austin Dr Ste 3 Marlborough (06447) *(G-4123)*
Essex Concrete Products Inc 860 767-1768
141 Westbrook Rd Essex (06426) *(G-2717)*
Essex Mail Mart, Essex *Also called Jyl LLP (G-2722)*
Essex Motorsports Int'l, Chester *Also called Ems International Inc (G-1472)*
Essex Olive Oil Company LLC 860 526-2205
39 Winthrop Rd Deep River (06417) *(G-2088)*
Essex Publishing Co 314 627-0300
130 Montowese St Ste B Branford (06405) *(G-590)*
Essex Wood Products Inc 860 537-3451
75 Mill St Colchester (06415) *(G-1550)*

A L P H A B E T I C

(PA)=Parent Co (HQ)=Headquarters (DH)=Div Headquarters
2020 Harris Connecticut Manufacturers Directory
513

Esteem Manufacturing Corp 860 282-9964
  175 S Satellite Rd South Windsor (06074) *(G-7751)*
Esten McGee Inc 203 544-2000
  4 Old Mill Rd West Redding (06896) *(G-9969)*
Etc, Marlborough *Also called Essential Trading Systems Corp (G-4123)*
Ethan Allen Interiors Inc (PA) 203 743-8000
  25 Lake Avenue Ext Danbury (06811) *(G-1817)*
Ethan Allen Retail Inc (HQ) 203 743-8000
  25 Lake Avenue Ext Danbury (06811) *(G-1818)*
Ethan Allen Retail Inc 203 743-8600
  25 Lake Avenue Ext Danbury (06811) *(G-1819)*
Ether & Industries LLc 475 224-0650
  40 Walnut St New Haven (06511) *(G-5277)*
Etherington Brothers Inc 860 585-5624
  33 Stafford Ave Ste 2 Bristol (06010) *(G-1031)*
Ethical Solutions LLC 860 490-8124
  177 Governors Hwy South Windsor (06074) *(G-7752)*
Ethicalchem, South Windsor *Also called Ethical Solutions LLC (G-7752)*
Ethicon Endo - Surgery, Southington *Also called Ethicon Inc (G-7918)*
Ethicon Inc 860 621-9111
  201 W Queen St Southington (06489) *(G-7918)*
Ethicon Inc 860 658-7653
  31 Pine Glen Rd Simsbury (06070) *(G-7625)*
Ethosenergy Component Repr LLC 203 949-8144
  34 Capital Dr Wallingford (06492) *(G-9258)*
Etron LLC 860 673-0121
  9 Hunters Xing Burlington (06013) *(G-1268)*
Ets-Lindgren Inc 203 838-4555
  97 Richards Ave Apt A11 Norwalk (06854) *(G-6158)*
Europa Sports Products Inc 860 688-1110
  755 Rainbow Rd Windsor (06095) *(G-10385)*
Evangelical Baptist Center, Ashford *Also called Evangelical Christian Center (G-61)*
Evangelical Christian Center (PA) 860 429-0856
  574 Ashford Center Rd Ashford (06278) *(G-61)*
Evangelical Christian Center 860 429-0856
  574 Ashfor Center Rd Ashford (06278) *(G-62)*
Evans Cooling Systems Inc (PA) 860 668-1114
  1 Mountain Rd Ste 1 # 1 Suffield (06078) *(G-8718)*
Evans Fabrication 203 791-9517
  184 Grassy Plain St Bethel (06801) *(G-298)*
Ever Ready Press 203 734-5157
  78 Clifton Ave Ansonia (06401) *(G-33)*
Evercel Inc (PA) 781 741-8800
  1055 Washington Blvd Fl 8 Stamford (06901) *(G-8199)*
Everest Isles LLC 203 561-5128
  616 N Elm St Wallingford (06492) *(G-9259)*
Everett Print, Bridgeport *Also called Integrated Print Solutions Inc (G-793)*
Evergreen Aluminum LLC 203 328-4900
  301 Tresser Blvd Ste 1500 Stamford (06901) *(G-8200)*
Evergreen Printing 203 323-4717
  61 Seaview Ave Stamford (06902) *(G-8201)*
Everlast Products LLC 203 250-7111
  150 Knotter Dr Cheshire (06410) *(G-1387)*
Evertide Games Inc 203 701-9145
  459 Old Stamford Rd New Canaan (06840) *(G-5104)*
Everything 2 Wheels LLC 860 225-2453
  230 South St New Britain (06051) *(G-4986)*
Evoaero Inc 860 289-2520
  425 Sullivan Ave Ste 5 South Windsor (06074) *(G-7753)*
Evogence, Rocky Hill *Also called Frontier Vision Tech Inc (G-7238)*
Evolution Stucco LLC 203 507-3639
  35 Old Colony Rd Wallingford (06492) *(G-9260)*
Evonic Cyro, Wallingford *Also called Allnex USA Inc (G-9199)*
Evonik Tockhausen LLC 860 530-1363
  25 Wildflower Dr Hebron (06248) *(G-3748)*
Evoqua Water Technologies LLC 860 528-6512
  88 Nutmeg Rd S South Windsor (06074) *(G-7754)*
Evotec (us) Inc 650 228-1400
  33 Business Park Dr # 6 Branford (06405) *(G-591)*
Evse Llc 860 745-2433
  89 Phoenix Ave Enfield (06082) *(G-2644)*
Ewald Instruments Corp 860 491-9042
  95 Wooster Ct Ste 3 Bristol (06010) *(G-1032)*
Ewp, Colchester *Also called Essex Wood Products Inc (G-1550)*
Ex Model Engines 860 681-2451
  39 Amato Cir Southington (06489) *(G-7919)*
Exact Printing & Graphics, Trumbull *Also called Pancoast Associates Inc (G-9054)*
Excel Spring & Stamping LLC 860 585-1495
  61 E Main St Ste 2 Bristol (06010) *(G-1033)*
Excello Tool Engrg & Mfg Co 203 878-4073
  37 Warfield St Milford (06461) *(G-4533)*
Exceptional Scratch Games LLC 203 526-8696
  348 Harmony St Bridgeport (06606) *(G-764)*
Exclusive Denim 203 549-9844
  64 Grasmere Ave Fairfield (06824) *(G-2783)*
Executive Graphic Systems LLC 203 678-6432
  61 N Plains Industrial Rd # 184 Wallingford (06492) *(G-9261)*
Executive Greetings Inc (HQ) 860 379-9911
  120 Industrial Park Rd New Hartford (06057) *(G-5190)*
Executive Office Services Inc 203 373-1333
  2085 Madison Ave Bridgeport (06606) *(G-765)*
Executive Press Inc 860 793-0060
  27 East St Plainville (06062) *(G-6807)*
Executive Printing Darien LLC 203 655-4691
  1082 Post Rd Darien (06820) *(G-2023)*
Exhibitease LLC 203 481-0792
  1204 Main St Unit 207 Branford (06405) *(G-592)*
Exocetus Atonomous Systems LLC 860 512-7260
  7 Laser Ln Wallingford (06492) *(G-9262)*
Exocetus Autonomous Systems 860 512-7260
  7 Laser Ln Wallingford (06492) *(G-9263)*
Expansion Software LLC 860 274-0338
  1064 Middlebury Rd Watertown (06795) *(G-9704)*
Exper-Tees, Bristol *Also called Jeffrey Morgan (G-1054)*
Experience Publishing Inc 203 637-2324
  4 William St Riverside (06878) *(G-7195)*
Experimental Prototype Pdts Co 860 289-4948
  248 Chapel Rd South Windsor (06074) *(G-7755)*
Expert Embroidery 203 269-9675
  121 N Plains Indus Ste G Wallingford (06492) *(G-9264)*
Explicit Airbrush 860 582-6038
  45 Railroad Ave Southington (06489) *(G-7920)*
Exponent Publishing Co 203 264-1130
  949a Heritage Vlg Southbury (06488) *(G-7852)*
Express Cntertops Kit Flrg LLC 203 283-4909
  303 Boston Post Rd Orange (06477) *(G-6599)*
Express Lab Service 860 571-0355
  286 Silas Deane Hwy Hartford (06109) *(G-3586)*
Express Lane Foods 860 889-2266
  96 Route 32 North Franklin (06254) *(G-5873)*
Express Software Production 860 844-0085
  99 Newgate Rd East Granby (06026) *(G-2204)*
Expressway Lube Centers 203 744-2511
  225 White St Danbury (06810) *(G-1820)*
Exquisite Surfaces Inc 203 866-9100
  139 Woodward Ave Norwalk (06854) *(G-6159)*
Exterior Trim Specialities LLC 860 261-5194
  84 Napco Dr Terryville (06786) *(G-8754)*
Extile.com, Stamford *Also called Pauls Marble Depot LLC (G-8352)*
Extra Fuel 203 330-0613
  540 Boston Ave Bridgeport (06610) *(G-766)*
Extreme Foam Insulations LLC 203 522-2207
  47 Scofield Ave Bridgeport (06605) *(G-767)*
Extreme Tech Pros LLC 203 903-3050
  10 Collins St Hamden (06514) *(G-3446)*
Eye Ear It LLC 203 487-8949
  19 Pomperaug Rd Woodbury (06798) *(G-10636)*
Eye-Con Foods LLC 203 752-7525
  7 Green Hill Rd Bethany (06524) *(G-240)*
Eyelash Extensions and More 860 951-9355
  998 Farmington Ave West Hartford (06107) *(G-9809)*
Eyelet Crafters Inc 203 757-9221
  2712 S Main St Waterbury (06706) *(G-9476)*
Eyelet Design Inc 203 754-4141
  574 E Main St Waterbury (06702) *(G-9477)*
Eyelet Tech LLC 203 879-5306
  10 Venus Dr Wolcott (06716) *(G-10564)*
Eyelet Toolmakers Inc 860 274-5423
  40 Callender Rd Watertown (06795) *(G-9705)*
Eyelets For Industry Inc 203 754-6502
  47 Stevens St Waterbury (06704) *(G-9478)*
Eylward Timber Co 203 265-4276
  13 Quince St Wallingford (06492) *(G-9265)*
EZ Welding LLC 860 707-3099
  47 Saint Claire Ave New Britain (06051) *(G-4987)*
EZ Welding LLC 860 707-3100
  244 Garry Dr New Britain (06052) *(G-4988)*
Ezee Fabricators LLC 860 429-5664
  221 Wormwood Hill Rd Mansfield Center (06250) *(G-4113)*
Ezflow Limited Partnership (HQ) 860 577-7064
  4 Business Park Rd Old Saybrook (06475) *(G-6533)*
F & L Iron Work Inc 203 777-0751
  105 Barclay St New Haven (06519) *(G-5278)*
F & W Rentals Inc 203 795-0591
  164 Boston Post Rd Orange (06477) *(G-6600)*
F A D C O, Bristol *Also called Day Fred A Co LLC (G-1012)*
F D Grave & Son Inc 203 239-9394
  85 State St Ste C North Haven (06473) *(G-5939)*
F D I, Farmington *Also called Farmington Displays Inc (G-2904)*
F F Screw Products Inc 860 621-4567
  888 W Queen St Southington (06489) *(G-7921)*
F J Weidner Inc 203 469-4202
  34 Tyler Street Ext East Haven (06512) *(G-2425)*
F K Bearings Inc 860 621-4567
  865 W Queen St Southington (06489) *(G-7922)*
F M, Cheshire *Also called Fiber Mountain Inc (G-1388)*
F M Associates 860 693-2263
  17 Blueberry Ln Canton (06019) *(G-1314)*
F R C, Stamford *Also called Frc Founders Corporation (G-8209)*
F S P Research Inc 203 874-3417
  148 Research Dr Ste F Milford (06460) *(G-4534)*
F W Webb Company 203 865-6124
  650 Boulevard New Haven (06519) *(G-5279)*

ALPHABETIC SECTION — Ferre Form Metal Products

Fabco Wrap, New London Also called First Aid Bandage Co Inc (G-5472)
Fabcon Inc 860 485-9019
  141 Terryville Rd Harwinton (06791) (G-3728)
Fabor Fourslide Inc 203 753-4380
  44 Railroad Hill St Waterbury (06708) (G-9479)
Fabric Bty Inc 203 845-7966
  179 Westport Ave Norwalk (06851) (G-6160)
Fabricgraphics, Pawcatuck Also called Guidera Marketing Services (G-6713)
Fabrique Ltd 203 481-5400
  28 School St Branford (06405) (G-593)
Fabtron Incorporated 860 410-1801
  80 Farmington Valley Dr Plainville (06062) (G-6808)
Fabyan Sugar Shack LLC 860 935-9281
  384 Fabyan Rd North Grosvenordale (06255) (G-5884)
Fac Woodworking LLC 203 469-1900
  67 Wood Ter East Haven (06513) (G-2426)
Facet Skis 203 529-3681
  46 Mollbrook Dr Wilton (06897) (G-10294)
Factor Industries LLC 203 244-5429
  68 Topstone Rd Ridgefield (06877) (G-7140)
Fad Tool Company LLC 860 582-7890
  95 Valley St Ste 7 Bristol (06010) (G-1034)
Fag Bearings LLC (HQ) 203 790-5474
  200 Park Ave Danbury (06810) (G-1821)
FAg Holding Corporation (HQ) 203 790-5474
  200 Park Ave Danbury (06810) (G-1822)
Fagan Design & Fabrication 203 937-1874
  44 Railroad Ave West Haven (06516) (G-9907)
Fahren Heit Book, Guilford Also called Omicronworld Entertainment LLC (G-3381)
Faille Precision Machining 860 822-1964
  118 W Main St Baltic (06330) (G-119)
Fair Haven Glass 203 773-3040
  103 Clinton Ave New Haven (06513) (G-5280)
Fair Weather Logging LLC 860 394-8217
  33 School St Enfield (06082) (G-2645)
Fairchild Auto-Mated Parts Inc 860 379-2725
  10 White St Winsted (06098) (G-10520)
Fairclough Sailmakers Inc 203 787-2322
  620 Ella T Grasso Blvd New Haven (06519) (G-5281)
Fairfield Backhoe LLC 203 247-4007
  1055 Old Academy Rd Fairfield (06824) (G-2784)
Fairfield Cnty Stump Grinding 203 261-7867
  35 Corporate Dr Ste 1045 Trumbull (06611) (G-9026)
Fairfield County Gazette 203 929-1405
  11 Woodlawn Ter Shelton (06484) (G-7442)
Fairfield County Look 203 869-0077
  6 Wyckham Hill Ln Greenwich (06831) (G-3158)
Fairfield County Millwork 203 393-9751
  20 Sargent Dr Bethany (06524) (G-241)
Fairfield Marketing Group Inc (PA) 203 261-0884
  830 Sport Hill Rd Easton (06612) (G-2552)
Fairfield Minuteman 203 752-2711
  40 Sargent Dr New Haven (06511) (G-5282)
Fairfield Pool & Equipment Co (PA) 203 334-3600
  278 Meadow St Fairfield (06824) (G-2785)
Fairfield Processing Corp (PA) 203 744-2090
  88 Rose Hill Ave Danbury (06810) (G-1823)
Fairfield Wood Works, Stratford Also called Fairfield Woodworks LLC (G-8609)
Fairfield Wood Works 203 838-6883
  7 Lexington Ave Norwalk (06854) (G-6161)
Fairfield Woodworks LLC 203 380-9842
  365 Sniffens Ln Stratford (06615) (G-8609)
Fairway and Greene Inc 203 926-1881
  2 Enterprise Dr Ste 505 Shelton (06484) (G-7443)
Falcon Press 860 763-2293
  13 Rockland Dr Enfield (06082) (G-2646)
Falling Hammer Productions LLC 203 879-1786
  10 Swiss Ln Wolcott (06716) (G-10565)
Falls Fuel LLC 203 744-3835
  5 Laughlin Rd Bethel (06801) (G-299)
Family Raceway LLC 860 896-0171
  11 Earl St Vernon (06066) (G-9138)
Farace Industries LLC 203 315-1293
  21 Ciro Rd North Branford (06471) (G-5838)
Faria Beede Instruments Inc 860 848-9271
  75 Frontage Rd Ste 106 North Stonington (06359) (G-6024)
Faria Marine Instruments, North Stonington Also called Faria Beede Instruments Inc (G-6024)
Farmington Displays Inc 860 677-2497
  21 Hyde Rd Ste 2 Farmington (06032) (G-2904)
Farmington Engineering Inc 800 428-7584
  73 Defco Park Rd North Haven (06473) (G-5940)
Farmington Machine Tools LLC 860 676-7736
  81 Spring Ln Farmington (06032) (G-2905)
Farmington Mtal Fbrication LLC 860 402-5148
  26 Lewis St Bristol (06010) (G-1035)
Farmington Mtal Fbrication LLC 860 404-7415
  139 Center St Ste 2001 Bristol (06010) (G-1036)
Farmington River Holdings LLC 203 777-2130
  1125 Dixwell Ave Hamden (06514) (G-3447)
Farmington Valley Woodcrafts 860 793-9034
  119 Williams St Plainville (06062) (G-6809)

Farmstead Goods, Old Saybrook Also called Herbs Farmstead & Goods (G-6540)
Farrar Sails Inc 860 447-0382
  6 Union St Ste 6 # 6 New London (06320) (G-5471)
Farrel Corporation (HQ) 203 736-5500
  1 Farrel Blvd Ansonia (06401) (G-34)
Farrel Pomini, Ansonia Also called Farrel Corporation (G-34)
Farrell Prcsion Mtalcraft Corp 860 355-2651
  192 Danbury Rd New Milford (06776) (G-5532)
Fasanella, Frank T, Norwalk Also called Drapery Consultants (G-6150)
Fascias Chocolates Inc 203 753-0515
  44 Chase River Rd Waterbury (06704) (G-9480)
Fashion Home Products 860 274-0824
  604 Guernseytown Rd Watertown (06795) (G-9706)
Fast, Stratford Also called Food Atmtn - Svc Tchniques Inc (G-8610)
Fast Sign 203 348-0222
  95 Atlantic St Stamford (06901) (G-8202)
Fastserv/Northeast, Norwalk Also called Corr/Dis Incorporated (G-6130)
FASTSIGNS, Manchester Also called Semiotics LLC (G-4088)
Fastsigns 203 298-4075
  1015 Bridgeport Ave Milford (06460) (G-4535)
Fastsigns 860 437-7446
  40 Boston Post Rd Waterford (06385) (G-9653)
Fastsigns 860 969-3030
  942 Main St Hartford (06103) (G-3587)
Fastsigns 860 470-7936
  11 E Main St Avon (06001) (G-80)
Fastsigns 860 347-8569
  182 Court St Middletown (06457) (G-4343)
Fastsigns 860 347-8569
  182 Court St Middletown (06457) (G-4344)
Fastsigns 860 583-8000
  1290 Farmington Ave Bristol (06010) (G-1037)
Fastsigns 203 239-9090
  310 Washington Ave Ste 1 North Haven (06473) (G-5941)
Fastsigns of Hartford 860 644-5700
  1540 Pleasant Valley Rd D Manchester (06042) (G-4016)
Fat City Screen Printers 860 354-4650
  180 Sunny Valley Rd Ste 9 New Milford (06776) (G-5533)
Fat City Sports, New Milford Also called Jb Muze Enterprises (G-5549)
Faxon Engineering Company Inc (PA) 860 236-4266
  17 Britton Dr Bloomfield (06002) (G-410)
Fayerweather Press LLC 203 367-1601
  2 Seabright Ave Bridgeport (06605) (G-768)
Fc Meyer Packaging LLC (HQ) 203 847-8500
  108 Main St Ste 3 Norwalk (06851) (G-6162)
FCA LLC 203 857-0825
  26 2nd St Norwalk (06855) (G-6163)
Fct Electronics LP 860 482-2800
  187 Commercial Blvd Torrington (06790) (G-8923)
Fdk Custom Cabinetry LLC 203 459-9909
  25 Lanthorne Rd Monroe (06468) (G-4717)
FDM LLC 860 684-7466
  16 Woodland Dr Stafford Springs (06076) (G-8029)
Fed Russell LLC 203 934-2501
  52 Collis St West Haven (06516) (G-9908)
Fedco, Wallingford Also called Fiberglass Engr & Design Co (G-9266)
Federal Business Products Inc 860 482-6231
  368 Ella Grasso Ave Torrington (06790) (G-8924)
Federal Prison Industries 203 743-6471
  Rr 37 Danbury (06811) (G-1824)
Federici Brands LLC 203 762-7667
  195 Danbury Rd Wilton (06897) (G-10295)
Fedex Authorized Ship Center, Bridgeport Also called American-Digital LLC (G-695)
Fedex Office & Print Svcs Inc 860 233-8245
  544 Farmington Ave Hartford (06105) (G-3588)
Fedex Office & Print Svcs Inc 203 799-2679
  400 Boston Post Rd Ste 1 Orange (06477) (G-6601)
Fedora Optical Inc 860 646-3577
  236 N Main St Manchester (06042) (G-4017)
Felk Publishing LLC 203 421-3714
  15 Sheffield Ln Madison (06443) (G-3920)
Fender Musical Instrs Corp 860 379-7575
  37 Greenwoods Rd New Hartford (06057) (G-5191)
Fenn LLC 860 259-6600
  80 Clark Dr Unit 5d East Berlin (06023) (G-2167)
Fenrir Industries Inc 203 977-0671
  652 Glenbrook Rd 6-202 Stamford (06906) (G-8203)
Fenton Corp 203 221-2788
  191 Post Rd W Westport (06880) (G-10079)
Fergtech Inc 203 656-1139
  28 Thorndal Cir Ste 1 Darien (06820) (G-2024)
Fergtech Inc (PA) 203 656-1139
  19 Wilson Ridge Rd Darien (06820) (G-2025)
Fernellie LLC 860 799-7739
  5 Church St New Milford (06776) (G-5534)
Feroleto Steel Company Inc (HQ) 203 366-3263
  300 Scofield Ave Bridgeport (06605) (G-769)
Ferraro Custom Woodwork LLC 203 876-1280
  29 Eastern Steel Rd Milford (06460) (G-4536)
Ferre Form Metal Products 860 274-3280
  25 Falls Ave Oakville (06779) (G-6452)

Ferron Mold and Tool LLC 860 774-5555
154 Louisa Viens Dr Dayville (06241) *(G-2061)*
Ferrucci Services 203 468-2319
46 Gene St East Haven (06513) *(G-2427)*
Ferrucci Signs 203 469-0043
641 Main St East Haven (06512) *(G-2428)*
Fezza Inc 203 222-9721
14 Riverfield Dr Weston (06883) *(G-10026)*
Ff Screw Products, Southington *Also called F F Screw Products Inc (G-7921)*
Fiber Mountain Inc 203 806-4040
700 W Johnson Ave Ste 100 Cheshire (06410) *(G-1388)*
Fiberglass Engr & Design Co 203 265-1644
25 N Plains Industrial Hw Wallingford (06492) *(G-9266)*
Fiberglass Repairs & 860 628-4962
209 Meriden Ave Southington (06489) *(G-7923)*
Fiberoptics Technology Inc (PA) 860 928-0443
1 Quasset Rd Pomfret (06258) *(G-6931)*
Fiberoptics Technology Inc 860 928-0443
1 Fiber Rd Pomfret (06258) *(G-6932)*
Fiberqa LLC 860 739-8044
10 Vista Dr Old Lyme (06371) *(G-6508)*
Fibre Optic Plus Inc 860 646-3581
585 Nutmeg Rd N South Windsor (06074) *(G-7756)*
Fiddle Horse Farm LLC 203 557-3285
95 Bayberry Ln Westport (06880) *(G-10080)*
Fidelux Lighting LLC (HQ) 860 436-5000
100 Great Meadow Rd # 600 Hartford (06109) *(G-3589)*
Fiduciaryai Inc 203 724-7571
13 N Main St Norwalk (06854) *(G-6164)*
Field Energy LLC 860 817-2654
17 Fawn Brk West Hartford (06117) *(G-9810)*
Fieldstone Cnsulting Group LLC 203 610-5592
50 Fieldstone Dr Easton (06612) *(G-2553)*
Fife, Westport *Also called Flottec International Sls Corp (G-10084)*
Filmx Technologies 860 779-3403
20 Louisa Viens Dr Dayville (06241) *(G-2062)*
Filter Fab Inc 860 749-6381
23b Eleanor Rd Somers (06071) *(G-7658)*
Filter Fabrication, Somers *Also called Filter Fab Inc (G-7658)*
Fimor North America Inc (HQ) 203 272-3219
50 Grandview Ct Cheshire (06410) *(G-1389)*
Fimor North America Inc 941 921-5138
30 Grandview Ct Cheshire (06410) *(G-1390)*
Final Liquid Coating LLC 860 585-5625
134 Mcintosh Dr Bristol (06010) *(G-1038)*
Finalsite, Glastonbury *Also called Active Internet Tech LLC (G-3003)*
Financial Accnting Foundation (PA) 203 847-0700
401 Merritt 7 Ste 5 Norwalk (06851) *(G-6165)*
Financial Accnting Stndards Bd, Norwalk *Also called Financial Accnting Foundation (G-6165)*
Financial Navigator Inc 800 468-3636
1 Dock St Ste 200 Stamford (06902) *(G-8204)*
Financial Prtg Solutions LLC 860 886-9931
21a River Rd Preston (06365) *(G-6983)*
Finch Paper Holdings LLC (PA) 203 622-9138
1 Sound Shore Dr Ste 302 Greenwich (06830) *(G-3159)*
Fine Food Services Inc 860 445-5276
223 Thames St Groton (06340) *(G-3288)*
Fine Lines Custom Cabinetry & 860 729-6526
16 Unionville Ave Plainville (06062) *(G-6810)*
Fine Pets LLC 203 833-1517
229 Stanwich Rd Greenwich (06830) *(G-3160)*
Fine Print New England Inc 860 953-0660
711 N Mountain Rd Newington (06111) *(G-5652)*
Fine Woodworker 203 717-2444
20 Fitch St Norwalk (06855) *(G-6166)*
Fine Woodworking 203 762-8197
143 Cheesespring Rd Wilton (06897) *(G-10296)*
Fineline Architechtural Wdwkg 914 426-2648
1 Mannions Ln Danbury (06810) *(G-1825)*
Fineran's Finishing, Pomfret Center *Also called Mike Fineran (G-6942)*
Finest Engraving LLC 860 742-7579
5 Bunker Hill Rd Andover (06232) *(G-7)*
Finest Kind Signs, Pawcatuck *Also called Cameron Bortz (G-6704)*
Finishers Technology Corp 860 829-1000
319 Main St East Berlin (06023) *(G-2168)*
Finishing Solutions LLC 860 705-8231
28 Jurach Rd Colchester (06415) *(G-1551)*
Finishing Touch Woodcraft 860 916-2642
3 Noja Trl Canton (06019) *(G-1315)*
Finite Industries, Windsor *Also called Scapa Tapes North America LLC (G-10434)*
Finn-Addict Manufacturing LLC 860 464-2053
940 Long Cove Rd Trlr 2 Gales Ferry (06335) *(G-2983)*
Fire & Iron 203 934-3756
298 Platt Ave West Haven (06516) *(G-9909)*
Fire Prevention Services 203 866-6357
13 Winfield St Norwalk (06855) *(G-6167)*
Fire Technology Inc 860 276-2181
122 Spring St Southington (06489) *(G-7924)*
Firehouse Discount Oil LLC (PA) 860 404-1827
17 Depot Pl Ste C Unionville (06085) *(G-9115)*
Firestone Building Pdts Co LLC 860 584-4516
780 James P Casey Rd # 4 Bristol (06010) *(G-1039)*
First Aid Bandage Co Inc 860 443-8499
3 State Pier Rd New London (06320) *(G-5472)*
First Airway LLC 860 679-9285
6 Hartfield Ln Farmington (06032) *(G-2906)*
First Aviation Services Inc (PA) 203 291-3300
15 Riverside Ave Westport (06880) *(G-10081)*
First Chance Inc 860 346-3663
598 Washington St Middletown (06457) *(G-4345)*
First Class Custom Woodworking 203 857-1000
4 Wilton Ave Norwalk (06851) *(G-6168)*
First Equity Group Inc (PA) 203 291-7700
15 Riverside Ave Ste 1 Westport (06880) *(G-10082)*
First Light Software Inc 860 217-0673
6 Deepwood Rd Simsbury (06070) *(G-7626)*
First Papermill LLC 203 740-1991
2 Old New Milford Rd 1f Brookfield (06804) *(G-1188)*
First Place USA, Hamden *Also called Gutkin Enterprises LLC (G-3454)*
First Place USA LLC 203 777-5510
1349 Dixwell Ave Ste 1 Hamden (06514) *(G-3448)*
First Reserve Fund Viii LP 203 661-6601
290 Harbor Dr Stamford (06902) *(G-8205)*
Fish Family Farm Inc 860 646-9745
20 Dimock Ln Bolton (06043) *(G-509)*
Fisher Controls Intl LLC 860 599-1140
95 Pendleton Hill Rd North Stonington (06359) *(G-6025)*
Fisher Electronics 860 646-7779
6 Brighton Ln Vernon Rockville (06066) *(G-9168)*
Fisher Footwear LLC 203 302-2800
777 W Putnam Ave Greenwich (06830) *(G-3161)*
Fisher Mfg Systems Inc 203 250-8033
20 N Plains Industrial Rd # 12 Wallingford (06492) *(G-9267)*
Fisher Mfg Systems Inc (PA) 203 269-3846
20 N Plains Industrial Rd # 12 Wallingford (06492) *(G-9268)*
Fisher Products, Wallingford *Also called Fisher Mfg Systems Inc (G-9268)*
Fisher Sigerson Morrison LLC 203 302-2800
777 W Putnam Ave Greenwich (06830) *(G-3162)*
Fishers Island Lemonade 860 306-3189
8 Summit St Mystic (06355) *(G-4815)*
Fishing Innovations LLC 860 434-3974
2 Dogwood Dr Old Lyme (06371) *(G-6509)*
Fit To A Tee Cstm Screen Prtg 860 828-6632
95 Four Rod Rd Kensington (06037) *(G-3810)*
Fitness Elemnet 860 670-2855
267 Chapman St New Britain (06051) *(G-4989)*
Fitzgerald & Wood Inc 203 488-2553
85 Rogers St Ste 3 Branford (06405) *(G-594)*
Fitzgerald-Norwalk Awning Co 203 847-5858
131 Main St Norwalk (06851) *(G-6169)*
Fitzhugh Electrical Corp 203 453-3171
361 Long Hill Rd Guilford (06437) *(G-3352)*
Five Ponds Press Books Inc 877 833-0603
360 Bloomfield Ave Windsor (06095) *(G-10386)*
Five Star Products Inc 203 336-7900
60 Parrott Dr Shelton (06484) *(G-7444)*
Fives N Amercn Combustn Inc 860 739-3466
287 Boston Post Rd East Lyme (06333) *(G-2465)*
Fives N Amercn Combustn Inc 216 271-6000
999 Andrews St Southington (06489) *(G-7925)*
Fjb America LLC 203 682-2424
8 Wright St Ste 107 Westport (06880) *(G-10083)*
Flabeg Technical Glass US Corp 203 729-5227
451 Church St Naugatuck (06770) *(G-4880)*
Flabeg US Holding Inc (HQ) 203 729-5227
1000 Church St Naugatuck (06770) *(G-4881)*
Flag Store 203 237-8791
186 Hall Ave Meriden (06450) *(G-4170)*
Flag Store of Conn The, Meriden *Also called Flag Store (G-4170)*
Flagman of America LLP 860 678-0275
22 E Main St Avon (06001) *(G-81)*
Flagpole Software LLC 203 426-5166
19 Scudder Rd Newtown (06470) *(G-5738)*
Flagship Converters Inc 203 792-0034
205 Shelter Rock Rd Danbury (06810) *(G-1826)*
Flanagan Brothers Inc 860 633-3558
25 Mill St Glastonbury (06033) *(G-3036)*
Flanagan Brothers, Inc, Glastonbury *Also called Edac Nd Inc (G-3031)*
Flange Lock LLC 203 861-9400
57 Old Post Rd No 2 Ste 3 Greenwich (06830) *(G-3163)*
Flashback Welding 860 738-1122
88 Torrington Rd Winsted (06098) *(G-10521)*
Flat Hammock Press 860 572-2722
5 Church St Mystic (06355) *(G-4816)*
Flat Vernacular 347 457-6227
173 Ponus Ave Norwalk (06850) *(G-6170)*
Flatland Alpacas 860 376-4658
285 Sam Chikan Rd Griswold (06351) *(G-3264)*
Flavrz Organic Beverages LLC 203 716-8082
25 Hamilton Ln Darien (06820) *(G-2026)*
Flea Market Music Inc 860 664-1669
22 Pratt Rd Clinton (06413) *(G-1503)*

ALPHABETIC SECTION — Fram Group Operations LLC

Fleet Management LLC 800 722-6654
  89 Phoenix Ave Enfield (06082) *(G-2647)*
Fleetprinters LLC 860 684-2352
  163 Diamond Ledge Rd Stafford Springs (06076) *(G-8030)*
Fleetwood Industries Inc 860 747-6750
  4 Northwest Dr Plainville (06062) *(G-6811)*
Flemming LLC 818 746-6495
  9 Jonathan Pl Bloomfield (06002) *(G-411)*
Fletcher-Terry Company LLC (PA) 860 828-3400
  91 Clark Dr East Berlin (06023) *(G-2169)*
Fleur, East Haddam Also called EPic Publishing Services LLC *(G-2241)*
Flexco 860 583-0219
  95 Rossi Dr Bristol (06010) *(G-1040)*
Flexiinternational Sftwr Inc (PA) 203 925-3040
  2 Trap Falls Rd Ste 501 Shelton (06484) *(G-7445)*
Flexo Label Solutions LLC 860 243-9300
  500 Main St Ste 6 Deep River (06417) *(G-2089)*
Flexxray LLC 203 689-5435
  320 Soundview Rd Guilford (06437) *(G-3353)*
Flight Enhancements Corp 912 257-0440
  47 Oakcrest Rd Oxford (06478) *(G-6658)*
Flight Support Inc 203 562-1415
  101 Sackett Point Rd North Haven (06473) *(G-5942)*
Flo-Tech LLC (PA) 860 613-3333
  545 Long Wharf Dr Ste 602 New Haven (06511) *(G-5283)*
Floating World Editions 860 868-0890
  26 Jack Corner Rd Warren (06777) *(G-9408)*
Floodmaster LLC 203 488-4477
  27 Business Park Dr Branford (06405) *(G-595)*
Floral Greens 860 995-8772
  31 Revere Dr Apt 1 Bloomfield (06002) *(G-412)*
Florian Tools, Southington Also called American Standard Company *(G-7889)*
Flottec International Sls Corp 973 588-4717
  3 Meeker Rd Westport (06880) *(G-10084)*
Flow Resources Inc (HQ) 860 666-1200
  135 Day St Ste 1 Newington (06111) *(G-5653)*
Flowe Manufacturing 860 859-1573
  12 Stockhouse Rd Bozrah (06334) *(G-525)*
Flowserve Corporation 203 877-4252
  408 Woodmont Rd Milford (06460) *(G-4537)*
Fluid Coating Technology Inc 860 963-2505
  48 Industrial Park Rd Putnam (06260) *(G-7041)*
Fluid Controls Division, New Britain Also called Parker-Hannifin Corporation *(G-5030)*
Fluid Dynamics LLC (PA) 860 791-6325
  192 Sheldon Rd Manchester (06042) *(G-4018)*
Fluid Solutions LLC 203 245-0708
  18 Johns Path Madison (06443) *(G-3921)*
Fluoropolymer Resources Inc 860 291-9521
  99 E River Dr East Hartford (06108) *(G-2325)*
Fluoropolymer Resources LLC (PA) 860 423-7622
  99 Erver Dr Rvrview Sq Ii Riverview East Hartford (06108) *(G-2326)*
Fluted Partition Inc (PA) 203 368-2548
  850 Union Ave Bridgeport (06607) *(G-770)*
Fluted Partition Inc 203 334-3500
  850 Union Ave Bridgeport (06607) *(G-771)*
Fly or Die Nation LLC 860 218-3547
  166 Cleveland Ave Hartford (06120) *(G-3590)*
Flying Aces Press LLC 203 791-1172
  25 Sunrise Rd Danbury (06810) *(G-1827)*
Flying Fur LLC 860 623-0450
  592 Elm St Windsor Locks (06096) *(G-10484)*
FM Industries LLC (PA) 860 610-0340
  166 Prestige Park Rd East Hartford (06108) *(G-2327)*
FMI Chemical Inc 860 243-3222
  4 Northwood Dr Bloomfield (06002) *(G-413)*
FMI Paint & Chemical Inc 860 218-2210
  14 Eastern Park Rd East Hartford (06108) *(G-2328)*
Fmp Products 203 422-0686
  100 Melrose Ave Ste 206 Greenwich (06830) *(G-3164)*
Foam Plastics New England Inc 203 758-6651
  32 Gramar Ave Waterbury (06712) *(G-9481)*
Focal Metals 203 743-4443
  11 Trowbridge Dr Bethel (06801) *(G-300)*
Focus Medical LLC 203 730-8885
  23 Francis J Clarke Cir Bethel (06801) *(G-301)*
Focus Now Solutions LLC 203 247-9038
  1140 Post Rd Fairfield (06824) *(G-2786)*
Focus Sign Awning 860 890-6577
  83 Meadow St Ste G Hartford (06114) *(G-3591)*
Focus Technologies Inc 860 829-8998
  600 Four Rod Rd Ste 5 Berlin (06037) *(G-179)*
Foilmark Inc 860 243-0343
  40 E Newberry Rd Bloomfield (06002) *(G-414)*
Foleys Pump Service Inc 203 792-2236
  30 Miry Brook Rd Danbury (06810) *(G-1828)*
Fonda Fabricating & Welding Co 860 793-0601
  50 Milford Street Ext Plainville (06062) *(G-6812)*
Food Atmtn - Svc Tchniques Inc (PA) 203 377-4414
  905 Honeyspot Rd Stratford (06615) *(G-8610)*
Foothills Trader Classified 860 489-3121
  59 Field St Torrington (06790) *(G-8925)*
Footnote Journal LLC 203 924-0391
  87 Ten Coat Ln Shelton (06484) *(G-7446)*

For Children With Love Public 860 940-9878
  290 Mountain Spring Rd Farmington (06032) *(G-2907)*
Force Automation Inc 860 622-1618
  100 Production Ct Ste 2 New Britain (06051) *(G-4990)*
Force3 Pro Gear LLC 315 367-2331
  45 Banner Dr 1 Milford (06460) *(G-4538)*
Forecast International Inc 203 426-0800
  22 Commerce Rd Ste 1 Newtown (06470) *(G-5739)*
Foredom Electric Co, Bethel Also called Blackstone Industries LLC *(G-266)*
Forensicon, New London Also called Qdiscovery LLC *(G-5483)*
Forest Remodeling 413 222-7953
  122 Hampden Rd Somers (06071) *(G-7659)*
Forestville Machine Co Inc 860 747-6000
  355 S Washington St Plainville (06062) *(G-6813)*
Forgetful Gentleman LLC 203 431-2486
  54 Hobby Dr Ridgefield (06877) *(G-7141)*
Form Factor, Southbury Also called Micro-Probe Incorporated *(G-7869)*
Form-All Plastics Corporation 203 634-1137
  104 Gracey Ave Meriden (06451) *(G-4171)*
Formatron Ltd 860 676-0227
  21 Hyde Rd Farmington (06032) *(G-2908)*
Formula Boat Works LLC 860 536-9309
  565 Noank Ledyard Rd Mystic (06355) *(G-4817)*
Forrati Manufacturing & TI LLC 860 426-1105
  411 Summer St Plantsville (06479) *(G-6892)*
Forrest Machine Inc 860 563-1796
  236 Christian Ln Berlin (06037) *(G-180)*
Forsa Team Sports LLC 203 466-2890
  920 Foxon Rd Ste 1 East Haven (06513) *(G-2429)*
Forte Carbon Fiber Products, Ledyard Also called Forte Rts Inc *(G-3872)*
Forte Rts Inc 860 464-5221
  14 Lorenz Industrial Pkwy Ledyard (06339) *(G-3872)*
Forterra Pipe & Precast LLC 860 564-9000
  174 All Hallows Rd Wauregan (06387) *(G-9753)*
Fortified Holdings Corp 203 594-1686
  40 Richards Ave Ste 3 Norwalk (06854) *(G-6171)*
Fortis Solutions Group LLC 860 872-6311
  374 Somers Rd Ellington (06029) *(G-2590)*
Forum Plastics LLC 203 754-0777
  105 Progress Ln Waterbury (06705) *(G-9482)*
Foster Corporation (HQ) 860 928-4102
  45 Ridge Rd Putnam (06260) *(G-7042)*
Foster Delivery Science, Putnam Also called Foster Corporation *(G-7042)*
Foster Delivery Science Inc (HQ) 860 928-4102
  36 Ridge Rd Putnam (06260) *(G-7043)*
Foster Delivery Science Inc 860 630-4515
  45 Ridge Rd Putnam (06260) *(G-7044)*
Foster Grandparent Program 860 525-5437
  30 Laurel St Ste 3 Hartford (06106) *(G-3592)*
Fougera Pharmaceuticals Inc 203 265-2086
  524 S Cherry St Wallingford (06492) *(G-9269)*
Foundation Cigar Company LLC 203 738-9377
  110 Day Hill Rd Windsor (06095) *(G-10387)*
Four Color Inc 860 691-1782
  10 Liberty Way Unit A8 Niantic (06357) *(G-5806)*
Four Color Ink LLC 860 395-5471
  2 Business Park Rd Old Saybrook (06475) *(G-6534)*
Four County Catholic Newspaper 860 886-1281
  31 Perkins Ave Norwich (06360) *(G-6413)*
Four Seasons Cooler Eqp LLC 203 263-0705
  150 Brushy Hill Rd Woodbury (06798) *(G-10637)*
Four Six Juliet LLC 203 227-1557
  11 Bermuda Rd Westport (06880) *(G-10085)*
Four Star Manufacturing Co 860 583-1614
  400 Riverside Ave Bristol (06010) *(G-1041)*
Four Twenty Industries LLC 860 818-3334
  314 Deming Rd Berlin (06037) *(G-181)*
Four Winds Inc 203 445-0733
  45 Kellers Farm Rd Easton (06612) *(G-2554)*
Fourslide Spring Stamping Inc 860 583-1688
  87 Cross St Bristol (06010) *(G-1042)*
Fowler D J Log Land Clearing 860 742-5842
  150 Plains Rd Coventry (06238) *(G-1654)*
Fowler's Steel Store, Manchester Also called Fowlers Steel & Welding *(G-4019)*
Fowlers Steel & Welding 860 647-7641
  405 New State Rd Manchester (06042) *(G-4019)*
Fox Print 860 485-0429
  48 Lake Harwinton Rd Harwinton (06791) *(G-3729)*
Fox Steel Products LLC 203 799-2356
  312 Boston Post Rd Orange (06477) *(G-6602)*
Fox Steel Services LLC 203 799-2356
  312 Boston Post Rd Orange (06477) *(G-6603)*
Foxon Park Beverages Inc 203 467-7874
  103 Foxon Blvd East Haven (06513) *(G-2430)*
Foxrun Danes 860 685-8784
  17 Hickory Ln Higganum (06441) *(G-3763)*
Fpr Pinedale LLC 203 542-6000
  58 Commerce Rd Stamford (06902) *(G-8206)*
Fractal Water LLC 888 897-6968
  18 Burlington Rd Harwinton (06791) *(G-3730)*
Fram Group Operations LLC 203 830-7800
  39 Old Ridgebury Rd Danbury (06810) *(G-1829)*

(PA)=Parent Co (HQ)=Headquarters (DH)=Div Headquarters

Framatone Connectors USA, Bethel *Also called Burndy LLC* ***(G-267)***
Framing and Printing Solu..........860 664-9679
11 Davis Farm Rd Clinton (06413) ***(G-1504)***
France Voiles Co Inc..........203 364-9454
75 Glen Rd Ste 300 Sandy Hook (06482) ***(G-7311)***
Frank Alexander Weems Pubg LLC..........203 898-4654
261 Montauk Dr Apt 212 Stamford (06902) ***(G-8207)***
Frank Demartino and Sons..........203 734-1074
66 Old Ansonia Rd Seymour (06483) ***(G-7346)***
Frank Drago Custom Mapping..........203 483-7594
94 Ivy St Fl 1 Branford (06405) ***(G-596)***
Frank Obuchowski..........860 535-4739
50 Ashworth Ave Stonington (06378) ***(G-8528)***
Frank Porto..........203 596-0811
27 Walnut St Watertown (06795) ***(G-9707)***
Frank Printing Co R..........203 265-6152
184 Center St Wallingford (06492) ***(G-9270)***
Frank Roth Co Inc..........203 377-2155
1795 Stratford Ave Stratford (06615) ***(G-8611)***
Franklin Liquor Store..........203 323-1356
99 North St Stamford (06902) ***(G-8208)***
Franklin Print Shoppe Inc..........860 496-9516
48 Main St Torrington (06790) ***(G-8926)***
Franklin-Howard LLC..........860 923-3343
109 Converse Rd Woodstock (06281) ***(G-10665)***
Franks Performance..........860 426-0439
131 W Main St Plantsville (06479) ***(G-6893)***
Fraqtir, West Haven *Also called Light Fantastic Realty Inc* ***(G-9926)***
Frasal Tool Co Inc..........860 666-3524
14 Foster St Newington (06111) ***(G-5654)***
Frates Custom Cabinetry..........203 994-1108
6a Russett Rd Sandy Hook (06482) ***(G-7312)***
Frc Founders Corporation (PA)..........203 661-6601
290 Harbor Dr Stamford (06902) ***(G-8209)***
Fred Radford..........203 377-6189
135 Pinewood Trl Trumbull (06611) ***(G-9027)***
Fred Rein..........860 460-8086
4 Marjorie St Mystic (06355) ***(G-4818)***
Freddie Nelson Woodworks..........203 378-2330
493 Sedgewick Ave Stratford (06615) ***(G-8612)***
Fredercks Jnne Literarary Agcy..........203 972-3011
221 Benedict Hill Rd New Canaan (06840) ***(G-5105)***
Frederick Purdue Company Inc (PA)..........203 588-8000
201 Tresser Blvd Stamford (06901) ***(G-8210)***
Fredericks Jf Aero LLC..........860 677-2646
25 Spring Ln Farmington (06032) ***(G-2909)***
Freds Auto Machine..........203 744-2950
151 Grassy Plain St C2 Bethel (06801) ***(G-302)***
Freedom Grafix LLC..........815 900-6189
457 Castle Ave Fairfield (06825) ***(G-2787)***
Freedom Press..........860 599-5390
30 Sunrise Ave Pawcatuck (06379) ***(G-6711)***
Freedom Properties..........860 508-3349
1865 Boulevard West Hartford (06107) ***(G-9811)***
Freedom Technologies LLC..........860 633-0452
80 Timrod Trl Glastonbury (06033) ***(G-3037)***
Freemans News Service..........860 485-1000
75 Westleigh Dr Harwinton (06791) ***(G-3731)***
Freethink Technologies Inc..........860 237-5800
35 Ne Industrial Rd # 201 Branford (06405) ***(G-597)***
Freezer Concepts, Southbury *Also called Furnace Concepts* ***(G-7853)***
Freezer Hill Mulch Company LLC..........203 758-3725
845 Carrington Rd Bethany (06524) ***(G-242)***
Freihofer Charles Baking Co..........203 729-4545
1041 New Haven Rd Naugatuck (06770) ***(G-4882)***
Fremco LLC..........203 857-0522
8 Redwood Ln Ridgefield (06877) ***(G-7142)***
French River Mtls Thompson LLC..........860 450-9574
307 Reardon Rd North Grosvenordale (06255) ***(G-5885)***
Frequency Therapeutics Inc..........978 436-0704
400 Farmington Ave Farmington (06032) ***(G-2910)***
Frescobene Foods LLC..........203 610-4688
185 Red Oak Rd Fairfield (06824) ***(G-2788)***
Fresh Ink LLC..........860 656-7013
216 Park Rd West Hartford (06119) ***(G-9812)***
Fresh Prints of CT LLC..........860 398-4893
21 Cedar St Rockfall (06481) ***(G-7212)***
Freshiana LLC..........800 301-8071
375 Greenwich Ave Apt 6 Greenwich (06830) ***(G-3165)***
Frevvo Inc..........203 208-3117
500 E Main St Ste 330 Branford (06405) ***(G-598)***
Friction Force, Prospect *Also called Red Barn Innovations* ***(G-7023)***
Fries Spinning & Stampings..........203 265-1678
65 Washington St Wallingford (06492) ***(G-9271)***
Frito-Lay North America Inc..........860 412-1000
1886 Upper Maple St Dayville (06241) ***(G-2063)***
Frog Prints Publishing LLC..........610 425-0090
22 Cold Spring Cir Shelton (06484) ***(G-7447)***
Front Line Apparel Group LLC..........860 859-3524
33 Pendleton Dr Hebron (06248) ***(G-3749)***
Front Line Group, The, Hebron *Also called Front Line Apparel Group LLC* ***(G-3749)***
Front Porch Brewing..........203 679-1096
226 N Plins Ind Rd Unit 4 Wallingford (06492) ***(G-9272)***
Frontier Vision Tech Inc..........860 953-0240
2080 Silas Deane Hwy # 203 Rocky Hill (06067) ***(G-7238)***
Frontline Screen Printing & Em..........860 749-0232
19 Bradfield Dr Somers (06071) ***(G-7660)***
Frostbite LLC..........203 240-3449
46 Mollbrook Dr Wilton (06897) ***(G-10297)***
Fruitbud Juice LLC..........203 790-8200
131 West St Danbury (06810) ***(G-1830)***
Fruta Juice Bar LLC..........203 690-9168
295 Fairfield Ave Bridgeport (06604) ***(G-772)***
Fryer Corporation..........203 888-9944
43 Old State Road 67 Oxford (06478) ***(G-6659)***
Frys Welding LLC..........860 944-2547
287 Gilbert Ave Winsted (06098) ***(G-10522)***
Fs Signs LLC..........203 612-4447
1895 Stratford Ave Stratford (06615) ***(G-8613)***
Fsb Inc..........203 404-4700
24 New Park Dr Berlin (06037) ***(G-182)***
Fsb North America, Berlin *Also called Fsb Inc* ***(G-182)***
Fsm Plasticoid Mfg Inc..........860 623-1361
32 North Rd East Windsor (06088) ***(G-2493)***
FSNB Enterprises Inc..........203 254-1947
12 Woodacre Ln Monroe (06468) ***(G-4718)***
Fuchs Lubricants Co..........203 469-2336
281 Silver Sands Rd East Haven (06512) ***(G-2431)***
Fuchs Northeast Division, East Haven *Also called Fuchs Lubricants Co* ***(G-2431)***
Fuel Cell Manufacturing, Torrington *Also called Fuelcell Energy Inc* ***(G-8927)***
Fuel First..........203 735-5097
575 Main St Ansonia (06401) ***(G-35)***
Fuel For Humanity Inc..........203 255-5913
11 Hedley Farms Rd Westport (06880) ***(G-10086)***
Fuel Lab..........860 677-4987
20 Burnt Hill Rd Farmington (06032) ***(G-2911)***
Fuelcell Energy Inc..........860 496-1111
539 Technology Park Dr Torrington (06790) ***(G-8927)***
Fujifilm Elctrnic Mtls USA Inc..........203 363-3360
419 West Ave Stamford (06902) ***(G-8211)***
Fujifilm NDT Systems, Stamford *Also called Fujifilm Elctrnic Mtls USA Inc* ***(G-8211)***
Fulcrum Promotions & Printing..........203 909-6362
75 Wheeler Ave Apt 102 Bridgeport (06606) ***(G-773)***
Functional Concepts LLC..........203 813-0157
166 Holmes St Stratford (06615) ***(G-8614)***
Fundrsing With Cndle Fndrisers..........860 384-3691
97 Overshot Dr South Glastonbury (06073) ***(G-7680)***
Funkhouser Industrial Products..........860 653-1972
10 Hazelwood Rd Ste 3b East Granby (06026) ***(G-2205)***
Fur Side LLC..........203 403-3369
622 Main St Ridgefield (06877) ***(G-7143)***
Furnace Concepts..........203 264-7856
186 Beecher Dr Southbury (06488) ***(G-7853)***
Furnace Source LLC..........860 582-4201
99 Agney Ave Terryville (06786) ***(G-8755)***
Furs By Prezioso Ltd..........203 230-2930
2969 Whitney Ave Ste 201 Hamden (06518) ***(G-3449)***
Fusion Cross-Media LLC..........860 647-8367
520 Center St Manchester Manchester (06040) ***(G-4020)***
Fusion Medical Corporation..........860 906-7856
44 Church St West Haven (06516) ***(G-9910)***
Fusion One Industries Inc..........860 992-4377
6 Sydney Ln Cromwell (06416) ***(G-1701)***
Future Manufacturing Inc..........860 584-0685
75 Center St Bristol (06010) ***(G-1043)***
Future Swiss..........860 283-4358
41 Electric Ave Thomaston (06787) ***(G-8790)***
Fwt4 LLC..........203 775-7087
12 Jason Ct Brookfield (06804) ***(G-1189)***
Fx Models LLC..........860 589-5279
111 Seymour Rd Terryville (06786) ***(G-8756)***
Fyc Apparel Group LLC..........203 466-6525
158 Commerce St East Haven (06512) ***(G-2432)***
Fyc Apparel Group LLC (PA)..........203 481-2420
30 Thompson Rd Branford (06405) ***(G-599)***
G & D Machine Co..........860 623-2649
383 S Main St Windsor Locks (06096) ***(G-10485)***
G & G Beverage Distributors..........203 949-6220
207 Church St Wallingford (06492) ***(G-9273)***
G & G Recycling Center, Wallingford *Also called G & G Beverage Distributors* ***(G-9273)***
G & M Tool Company..........203 888-9354
45 Highland Rd Seymour (06478) ***(G-7347)***
G & R Enterprises Incorporated..........860 549-6120
101 Kinsley St Hartford (06103) ***(G-3593)***
G & R Welding..........860 526-3353
537 Winthrop Rd Deep River (06417) ***(G-2090)***
G A Industries..........860 261-5484
630 Emmett St Unit 1 Bristol (06010) ***(G-1044)***
G A Mals Woodworking..........860 828-8702
77 Willow Brook Dr Berlin (06037) ***(G-183)***
G F E..........203 371-7334
11 Birch Dr Easton (06612) ***(G-2555)***
G F Grinding Tool Mfg Co Inc..........203 757-6244
649 Captain Neville Dr Waterbury (06705) ***(G-9483)***
G H Berlin Oil Company..........800 426-7754
155 W Service Rd Hartford (06120) ***(G-3594)***

ALPHABETIC SECTION General Dynamics Info Tech Inc

G H Tool Inc...203 270-0566
26 Berkshire Rd Sandy Hook (06482) ***(G-7313)***
G I Package Store...203 624-4606
282 Ferry St New Haven (06513) ***(G-5284)***
G K Services, Hartford *Also called G&K Services LLC* ***(G-3596)***
G L Yarocki & Company...860 482-9215
679 Riverside Ave Torrington (06790) ***(G-8928)***
G M F Woodworking LLC...203 788-8979
22 Sunset Hill Ave Norwalk (06851) ***(G-6172)***
G M T Manufacturing Co Inc...860 628-6757
220 West St Plantsville (06479) ***(G-6894)***
G M Woodworking...860 599-3781
490a Prov Nl Tpke North Stonington (06359) ***(G-6026)***
G P Tool Co Inc...203 744-0310
59 James St Danbury (06810) ***(G-1831)***
G S S, Watertown *Also called Global Steering Systems LLC* ***(G-9710)***
G S S Industries...203 755-6644
44 Railroad Hill St Waterbury (06708) ***(G-9484)***
G Schoepferinc...203 250-7794
460 Cook Hill Rd Cheshire (06410) ***(G-1391)***
G Thomas and Sons Inc...860 935-5174
573 Fabyan Rd North Grosvenordale (06255) ***(G-5886)***
G W Elliot Inc...860 528-6143
95 Rene Ct East Hartford (06108) ***(G-2329)***
G W P Inc...860 953-1153
141 South St Ste E Hartford (06110) ***(G-3595)***
G Woodcraft...203 846-4168
11 Ruby St Norwalk (06850) ***(G-6173)***
G&K Services LLC...860 856-4400
96 Murphy Rd Hartford (06114) ***(G-3596)***
G-Force Signs & Graphics, South Windsor *Also called Ghezzi Enterprises Inc* ***(G-7759)***
GA Mals Woodwoorking LLC...860 747-4767
20 Ciccio Ct Plainville (06062) ***(G-6814)***
GA Remanufacturing LLC...860 404-5186
298 Scott Swamp Rd Farmington (06032) ***(G-2912)***
Gabbro Forge and Welding LLC...617 699-0031
93 Quaker Rd Hamden (06517) ***(G-3450)***
Gabriel Inc...860 824-1412
Rr 126 Falls Village (06031) ***(G-2870)***
Gabriels Woodworking LLC...860 263-7831
158 Beacon St Hartford (06105) ***(G-3597)***
Gac Inc...860 633-1768
160 Oak St Ste 412 Glastonbury (06033) ***(G-3038)***
Gagne & Gagne Co...860 742-5038
3 Lindholms Cor Andover (06232) ***(G-8)***
Gagnon Sign Studio, Danielson *Also called Douglas M Gagnon* ***(G-1990)***
Gaia Chemical Corporation...860 355-2730
23 George Washington Plz Gaylordsville (06755) ***(G-2992)***
Gaida Welding Co & Mar Repr...203 924-4868
57 West St Shelton (06484) ***(G-7448)***
Gaisertim...203 245-9276
11 Soundview Ave Madison (06443) ***(G-3922)***
Galassia Press LLC...203 846-9075
17 Ponus Ave Norwalk (06850) ***(G-6174)***
Galasso Materials LLC...860 527-1825
60 S Main St East Granby (06026) ***(G-2206)***
Galata Chemicals LLC (HQ)...203 236-9000
464 Heritage Rd Ste A1 Southbury (06488) ***(G-7854)***
Galaxy Fuel LLC...203 878-8173
180 New Haven Ave Milford (06460) ***(G-4539)***
Gale Thomson...203 397-2600
12 Lunar Dr Woodbridge (06525) ***(G-10600)***
Gallagher Katie Publishers Rep...203 221-7140
3 Ridgewood Ln Westport (06880) ***(G-10087)***
Gambrel Acres...860 774-3047
195 Terwilleger Rd Danielson (06239) ***(G-1992)***
Game On LLC...860 608-8931
112 Shanaghans Rd East Haddam (06423) ***(G-2242)***
Gamers That Lift LLC...203 988-9211
530 Ridge Rd Orange (06477) ***(G-6604)***
Gamma Ventures Inc...860 653-2613
11 Rondure Rd Granby (06035) ***(G-3107)***
Gamut Publishing...860 296-6128
563 Franklin Ave Hartford (06114) ***(G-3598)***
Gar Electro Forming...203 885-1105
3 Commerce Dr Danbury (06810) ***(G-1832)***
Gar Kenyon Aerospace & Defense, Meriden *Also called Saf Industries LLC* ***(G-4238)***
Garage Door Center, Fairfield *Also called Architectural Door Corp* ***(G-2748)***
Garbeck Airflow Industries...860 301-5032
442 Arbutus St Middletown (06457) ***(G-4346)***
Garcia Printing Inc...203 378-6200
860 Honeyspot Rd Stratford (06615) ***(G-8615)***
Garden Glass LLC...203 330-8789
578 Stratfield Rd Fairfield (06825) ***(G-2789)***
Garden Iron LLC...860 767-9917
47 Westbrook Indust Pk Rd Westbrook (06498) ***(G-9997)***
Garden Light Natural Foods Mkt, East Hartford *Also called Garden of Light Inc* ***(G-2330)***
Garden of Light Inc (PA)...860 895-6622
127 Park Ave Ste 100 East Hartford (06108) ***(G-2330)***
Gardner Denver Nash LLC (HQ)...203 459-3923
2 Trefoil Dr Trumbull (06611) ***(G-9028)***
Gardner Welding LLC...203 265-1036
850 S Colony Rd Wallingford (06492) ***(G-9274)***
Garmac Screw Machine Inc...203 723-6911
70 Great Hill Rd Naugatuck (06770) ***(G-4883)***
Garrett & Co Mfg LLC...203 494-0935
16 Ells St Ansonia (06401) ***(G-36)***
Garrett Printing & Graphics...860 589-6710
331 Riverside Ave Bristol (06010) ***(G-1045)***
Gary D Kryszat...860 526-3145
194 Middlesex Ave Chester (06412) ***(G-1473)***
Gary Morris Clubmaker...860 482-5929
475 Harwinton Ave Torrington (06790) ***(G-8929)***
Gary Tool Company...203 377-3077
26 Grant St Stratford (06615) ***(G-8616)***
Gas Turbine Supply and Svc LLC...860 254-5651
120 Barndoor Hills Rd Suffield (06078) ***(G-8719)***
Gatehouse Media LLC...860 886-0106
10 Railroad Ave Norwich (06360) ***(G-6414)***
Gatehouse Media Conn Holdings...860 887-9211
10 Railroad Ave Norwich (06360) ***(G-6415)***
Gateway Digital Inc...203 853-4929
16 Testa Pl Norwalk (06854) ***(G-6175)***
Gateway Helicopter Service...203 531-4395
34 Bedford Rd Greenwich (06831) ***(G-3166)***
Gateway Helicopters, Greenwich *Also called Gateway Helicopter Service* ***(G-3166)***
Gavin Welding LLC...203 393-9707
290 Bear Hill Rd Bethany (06524) ***(G-243)***
Gay Tool & Machine...860 668-5054
129 Kent Ave Suffield (06078) ***(G-8720)***
Gbc Marketing LLC...860 739-8760
13 Saunders Dr Niantic (06357) ***(G-5807)***
Gcn Media Services, Norwalk *Also called Gcn Publishing Inc* ***(G-6176)***
Gcn Publishing Inc...203 665-6211
194 Main St Ste 2nw Norwalk (06851) ***(G-6176)***
Gcooper Legacy Publishing LLC...203 357-1483
65 Judy Ln Stamford (06906) ***(G-8212)***
Gdc Federal Systems Inc...203 729-0271
6 Rubber Ave Naugatuck (06770) ***(G-4884)***
GE, Plainville *Also called ABB Enterprise Software Inc* ***(G-6763)***
GE Enrgy Pwr Cnversion USA Inc...203 373-2211
3135 Eon Tpke Fairfield (06828) ***(G-2790)***
GE Grid Solutions LLC...425 250-2695
175 Addison Rd Windsor (06095) ***(G-10388)***
GE Oil & Gas Esp Inc...405 670-1431
78 Black Rock Tpke Redding (06896) ***(G-7092)***
GE Renewable Energy USA, Windsor *Also called Alstom Renewable US LLC* ***(G-10359)***
GE Steam Power Inc...423 648-4161
200 Great Pond Dr Windsor (06095) ***(G-10389)***
GE Steam Power Inc...860 688-1911
3-4 Minatojima Windsor (06095) ***(G-10390)***
GE Steam Power Inc...860 688-1911
175 Addison Rd Windsor (06095) ***(G-10391)***
GE Transportation Parts LLC...816 650-6171
3135 Easton Tpke Fairfield (06828) ***(G-2791)***
Gebhardts Sawmill...860 423-0123
101 Ballamahack Rd Windham (06280) ***(G-10346)***
Geer Construction Co Inc...860 376-5321
852 Voluntown Rd Jewett City (06351) ***(G-3795)***
Geer Sand & Gravel, Jewett City *Also called Geer Construction Co Inc* ***(G-3795)***
Gelato Giuliana LLC...203 772-0607
240 Sargent Dr Ste 9 New Haven (06511) ***(G-5285)***
Gem Embroidery...860 326-0676
227 Haley Rd Ledyard (06339) ***(G-3873)***
Gem Manufacturing Co Inc (PA)...203 574-1466
78 Brookside Rd Waterbury (06708) ***(G-9485)***
Gemco Manufacturing Co Inc...860 628-5529
555 W Queen St Southington (06489) ***(G-7926)***
Gemini Group, Greenwich *Also called Kenneth Finn* ***(G-3187)***
Gemma Oro Inc...203 227-0774
2 Coach Ln Westport (06880) ***(G-10088)***
Gems Sensors & Controls, Plainville *Also called Gems Sensors Inc* ***(G-6815)***
Gems Sensors Inc (HQ)...860 747-3000
1 Cowles Rd Plainville (06062) ***(G-6815)***
Gems Sensors Inc...800 378-1600
1 Cowles Rd Plainville (06062) ***(G-6816)***
Gemsco, Windsor *Also called Stephen Hawrylik* ***(G-10444)***
Gen-El-Mec Associates Inc...203 828-6566
2 Fox Hollow Rd Oxford (06478) ***(G-6660)***
Genalco Inc...203 932-5991
44 W Clark St West Haven (06516) ***(G-9911)***
General Cable Industries Inc...860 456-8000
1600 Main St Willimantic (06226) ***(G-10227)***
General Datacomm Inc (HQ)...203 729-0271
353 Christian St Ste 4 Oxford (06478) ***(G-6661)***
General Datacomm Inds Inc (PA)...203 729-0271
353 Christian St Ste 4 Oxford (06478) ***(G-6662)***
General Digital Corp...860 645-2200
160 Chapel Rd Manchester (06042) ***(G-4021)***
General Dynamics Electric Boat, Groton *Also called Electric Boat Corporation* ***(G-3287)***
General Dynamics Info Tech Inc...860 441-2400
100 Mechanic St Pawcatuck (06379) ***(G-6712)***

ALPHABETIC

General Dynamics Ordnance 860 404-0162
65 Sandscreen Rd Avon (06001) *(G-82)*
General Electric Company 203 396-1572
1285 Boston Ave Bridgeport (06610) *(G-774)*
General Electric Company 518 385-7164
901 Main Ave Ste 103 Norwalk (06851) *(G-6177)*
General Electro Components 860 659-3573
122 Naubuc Ave Ste A7 Glastonbury (06033) *(G-3039)*
General Heat Treating Co 203 755-5441
80 Fulkerson Dr Waterbury (06708) *(G-9486)*
General Machine Company Inc 860 426-9295
1223 Mount Vernon Rd Southington (06489) *(G-7927)*
General Network Service Inc 203 359-5735
6 Landmark Sq Ste 400 Stamford (06901) *(G-8213)*
General Packaging Products Inc 203 846-1340
3 Valley View Rd Apt 9 Norwalk (06851) *(G-6178)*
General Pneumatics, Meriden *Also called Saf Industries LLC (G-4237)*
General Seating Solutions LLC 860 242-3307
45 S Satellite Rd Ste 5 South Windsor (06074) *(G-7757)*
General Sheet Metal Works Inc 203 333-6111
120 Silliman Ave Bridgeport (06605) *(G-775)*
General Welding Company Inc 203 753-6988
28 Broadway St Waterbury (06705) *(G-9487)*
General Wldg & Fabrication Inc 860 274-9668
977 Echo Lake Rd Watertown (06795) *(G-9708)*
Generators On Demand LLC 860 662-4090
61-1 Buttonball Rd Old Lyme (06371) *(G-6510)*
Genesis Alkali LLC 215 299-6773
1 Stamford Plz 263 Stamford (06901) *(G-8214)*
Genesis D T P 860 350-2827
36 Cedar Hill Rd Gaylordsville (06755) *(G-2993)*
Geneve Corporation (HQ) 203 358-8000
96 Cummings Point Rd Stamford (06902) *(G-8215)*
Geneve Holdings Inc (PA) 203 358-8000
96 Cummings Point Rd Stamford (06902) *(G-8216)*
Genie Shelf 203 241-7523
16 S Lake Shore Dr Brookfield (06804) *(G-1190)*
Genovese Manufacturing Co 860 582-9944
8 Bombard Ct Terryville (06786) *(G-8757)*
Genuine Parts Company 860 623-4479
508 Spring St Ste 2 Windsor Locks (06096) *(G-10486)*
Genvario Awning Co 203 847-5858
131 Main St Norwalk (06851) *(G-6179)*
Genx International Inc (PA) 203 453-1700
393 Soundview Rd Guilford (06437) *(G-3354)*
Geographics Australia, Norwalk *Also called Royal Consumer Products LLC (G-6330)*
George Bailey 860 423-2136
75 Crane Hill Rd Storrs (06268) *(G-8549)*
George Bullock & Sons Inc 860 355-1243
28 Minor Bridge Rd Roxbury (06783) *(G-7277)*
George H Olson Steel Co Inc 203 375-5656
245 Access Rd Stratford (06615) *(G-8617)*
George S Preisner Jewelers 203 265-0057
150 Center St Wallingford (06492) *(G-9275)*
George Schmithet and Company, Guilford *Also called George Schmitt & Co Inc (G-3356)*
George Schmitt & Co Inc (PA) 203 453-4334
251 Boston Post Rd Guilford (06437) *(G-3355)*
George Schmitt & Co Inc 203 453-4334
251 Boston Post Rd Guilford (06437) *(G-3356)*
George Sima 860 345-4660
863 Killingworth Rd Higganum (06441) *(G-3764)*
George Usaty Sons Heat 860 350-2622
67 Bonnie Vu Ln New Milford (06776) *(G-5535)*
Georges Automotive Machine Sp 860 223-6547
158 Dwight St New Britain (06051) *(G-4991)*
Georgetown Machine 203 544-8422
16 Sunset Hill Rd Georgetown (06829) *(G-2998)*
Georgia-Pacific LLC 203 866-9774
19 Meadow St Norwalk (06854) *(G-6180)*
Geosonics Inc 203 271-2504
416 Highland Ave Ste D Cheshire (06410) *(G-1392)*
Gerber Coburn Optical Inc (HQ) 800 843-1479
55 Gerber Rd E South Windsor (06074) *(G-7758)*
Gerber Scientific LLC (PA) 860 871-8082
24 Indl Pk Rd W Tolland (06084) *(G-8864)*
Gerber Technology LLC (HQ) 860 871-8082
24 Industrial Park Rd W Tolland (06084) *(G-8865)*
Gerdau Ameristeel US Inc 860 351-9029
75 Neal Ct Plainville (06062) *(G-6817)*
Get Back Inc 860 274-9991
27 Main St Ste 4 Oakville (06779) *(G-6453)*
Get Baked LLC 860 688-0420
41 Mountain Rd Windsor (06095) *(G-10392)*
Get Go It Publishing 203 772-9877
69 Rock Creek Rd New Haven (06515) *(G-5286)*
Gettysburg Publishing LLC 203 268-7111
192 Edison Rd Trumbull (06611) *(G-9029)*
Gg Sportswear Inc 860 296-4441
241 Ledyard St Ste B10 Hartford (06114) *(G-3599)*
Ghezzi Enterprises Inc 860 787-5338
52 Connecticut Ave Ste B South Windsor (06074) *(G-7759)*
Ghi Sign Service, Canaan *Also called Jill Ghi (G-1288)*
Ghp Media Inc (PA) 203 479-7500
475 Heffernan Dr West Haven (06516) *(G-9912)*
Gideon S Fleece Woodworkin 860 663-2757
42 Kenilworth Dr Killingworth (06419) *(G-3834)*
Gilbert Fitch Woodworking, Lakeville *Also called Gilbert G Fitch (G-3843)*
Gilbert G Fitch 860 824-5832
352 Millerton Rd Lakeville (06039) *(G-3843)*
Gillette Company 203 796-4000
14 Research Dr Bethel (06801) *(G-303)*
Gilman Corporation 860 887-7080
1 Polly Ln Gilman (06336) *(G-3000)*
Gilman Gear, Gilman *Also called Marty Gilman Incorporated (G-3001)*
Gilman Gear, Bozrah *Also called Marty Gilman Incorporated (G-528)*
Gima LLC 860 296-4441
241 Ledyard St Ste B10 Hartford (06114) *(G-3600)*
Gimasport, Hartford *Also called Gima LLC (G-3600)*
Ginter Hill Corporation 203 293-4301
1 Flower Farm Ln Westport (06880) *(G-10089)*
Ginty's, Sandy Hook *Also called Gintys Welding Service Inc (G-7314)*
Gintys Welding Service Inc 203 270-3399
29 Philo Curtis Rd Sandy Hook (06482) *(G-7314)*
Girardin Moulding Inc 860 623-4486
564 Halfway House Rd Windsor Locks (06096) *(G-10487)*
Girl Cop Publishing LLC 860 529-3424
45 Prospect St Wethersfield (06109) *(G-10193)*
Giuliano Construction LLC 203 230-3094
730 Still Hill Rd Hamden (06518) *(G-3451)*
Gjg Signs Digital Signs 413 627-1852
250 S Main St East Windsor (06088) *(G-2494)*
GK Mechanical Systems LLC 203 775-4970
934 Federal Rd Ste 1b Brookfield (06804) *(G-1191)*
GKN Aerospace Newington LLC 800 667-8502
183 Louis St Newington (06111) *(G-5655)*
GKN Aerospace Newington LLC (HQ) 860 667-8502
183 Louis St Newington (06111) *(G-5656)*
GKN Arspace Svcs Strctures LLC 860 613-0236
1000 Corporate Row Cromwell (06416) *(G-1702)*
GL and V 203 876-5400
612 Wheelers Farms Rd # 1 Milford (06461) *(G-4540)*
Glacier Computer LLC (PA) 860 355-7552
46 Bridge St Ste 1 New Milford (06776) *(G-5536)*
Glacier Publishing 860 621-7644
40 Oak St Southington (06489) *(G-7928)*
Glass Design Studio 860 651-4233
2 Mathers Xing Simsbury (06070) *(G-7627)*
Glass Industries America LLC 203 269-6700
340 Quinnipiac St Unit 9 Wallingford (06492) *(G-9276)*
Glass Master LLC 860 658-0040
24 Deepwood Rd Simsbury (06070) *(G-7628)*
Glass Source LLC 203 924-4368
410 Howe Ave Shelton (06484) *(G-7449)*
Glasshouse, Pomfret Center *Also called LLC Glass House (G-6941)*
Glassworks 860 673-1250
790 Litchfield Tpke New Hartford (06057) *(G-5192)*
Glastonbury Cabinets, Glastonbury *Also called Edward Tomkievich (G-3032)*
Glastonbury Citizen Inc 860 633-4691
87 Nutmeg Ln Glastonbury (06033) *(G-3040)*
Glastonbury Dianostic Center, Glastonbury *Also called Eastern Conn Hlth Netwrk (G-3030)*
Glastonbury Fire Training Ctr 860 633-3429
87 Orchard St Glastonbury (06033) *(G-3041)*
Glastonbury Southern Gage Div, Colchester *Also called Q Alpha Inc (G-1569)*
Glaxosmithkline LLC 203 232-5145
186 Beecher Dr Southbury (06488) *(G-7855)*
Gleason Group Incorporated 203 312-0683
5 Fox Hollow Rd New Fairfield (06812) *(G-5168)*
Glen Manufacturing Co Inc 860 589-0881
19 Church St Terryville (06786) *(G-8758)*
Glencore, Eaar, Switzerland, Stamford *Also called Evergreen Aluminum LLC (G-8200)*
Glenn Curtis (PA) 860 349-8679
105 Oak Ter Durham (06422) *(G-2147)*
Glimmer of Light 860 605-4086
56 Danbury Rd Ste 10 New Milford (06776) *(G-5537)*
Glitzy Lady 203 924-5663
255 Kneen St Unit 20 Shelton (06484) *(G-7450)*
Global American Publishers LLC 860 432-7589
5 Orchard St Manchester (06040) *(G-4022)*
Global Brass & Copper LLC (PA) 203 597-5000
215 Piedmont St Waterbury (06706) *(G-9488)*
Global Brass & Copper LLC 203 597-5000
94 Baldwin Ave Waterbury (06706) *(G-9489)*
Global E.D.M. Supplies, New Britain *Also called Makino Inc (G-5012)*
Global Machine Movers LLC 860 484-4449
58 Commercial St Watertown (06795) *(G-9709)*
Global Manufacturing 860 315-5502
580 Brickyard Rd Woodstock (06281) *(G-10666)*
Global Palate Foods LLC 203 543-3028
161 Cross Hwy Westport (06880) *(G-10090)*
Global Pallet Solutions LLC 860 826-5000
271 John Downey Dr New Britain (06051) *(G-4992)*
Global Publications & Mktg LLC 860 676-9109
222 Main St Ste 156 Farmington (06032) *(G-2913)*

Global Scenic Services Inc..........203 334-2130
46 Brookfield Ave Bridgeport (06610) *(G-776)*
Global Shield Solutions LLC..........860 983-3566
22 Westview Ln Brookfield (06804) *(G-1192)*
Global Steering Systems LLC (PA)..........860 945-5400
156 Park Rd Watertown (06795) *(G-9710)*
Global Trbine Cmpnent Tech LLC..........860 528-4722
125 S Satellite Rd South Windsor (06074) *(G-7760)*
Globe Environmental Corp..........203 481-5586
131 Commercial Pkwy 1b Branford (06405) *(G-600)*
Globe Pequot Press, Guilford *Also called Morris Communications Co LLC (G-3377)*
Globe Tool & Met Stampg Co Inc..........860 621-6807
95 Robert Porter Rd Southington (06489) *(G-7929)*
Globenix Inc..........203 740-7070
9 Lois St Norwalk (06851) *(G-6181)*
Glorian Publishing Inc..........844 945-6742
455 Boston Post Rd Ste 9 Clinton (06413) *(G-1505)*
Glosystems Inc..........203 227-2464
3 Tarone Dr Westport (06880) *(G-10091)*
Glovewhisperer Inc..........203 487-8997
22 Hartford Ave Greenwich (06830) *(G-3167)*
Glyne Manufacturing Co Inc..........203 375-4495
380 E Main St Stratford (06614) *(G-8618)*
GM Home Solutions..........305 608-9721
59 Fairview St Waterbury (06710) *(G-9490)*
Gmb, Watertown *Also called Global Machine Movers LLC (G-9709)*
Gmn Usa LLC..........800 686-1679
181 Business Park Dr Bristol (06010) *(G-1046)*
Gmq Publishing..........203 558-6142
375 Bethany Rd Beacon Falls (06403) *(G-134)*
Gmt Mfg, Plantsville *Also called G M T Manufacturing Co Inc (G-6894)*
GNB Woodworking LLC..........860 282-0595
381 Governors Hwy South Windsor (06074) *(G-7761)*
Gngwoodworking..........203 996-5255
39 Carlson Rd West Haven (06516) *(G-9913)*
Go Green Industries LLC..........914 772-0026
23 Meredith Ln New Milford (06776) *(G-5538)*
Goat Boy Soap..........860 350-0676
1 Murphys Way New Milford (06776) *(G-5539)*
Godfrey Cemetary Maint LLC..........203 858-4035
4 Briarwood Dr Sherman (06784) *(G-7595)*
Godfrey Memorial Library..........860 346-4375
134 Newfield St Middletown (06457) *(G-4347)*
Gold Line Connector Inc (PA)..........203 938-2588
40 Great Pasture Rd Redding (06896) *(G-7093)*
Gold Star Dental..........860 445-1330
491 Gold Star Hwy Ste 300 Groton (06340) *(G-3289)*
Golden Hill Cstm Cabinetry LLC..........203 366-2222
315 Harral Ave Bridgeport (06604) *(G-777)*
Golden Oyster Company..........203 929-3389
9 Pueblo Trl Shelton (06484) *(G-7451)*
Golden Sun Inc..........800 575-7960
5 High Ridge Park Ste 200 Stamford (06905) *(G-8217)*
Goldenrod Corporation..........203 723-4400
25 Lancaster Dr Beacon Falls (06403) *(G-135)*
Goldpoint Publishing LLC..........860 432-8934
258 Lefoll Blvd South Windsor (06074) *(G-7762)*
Goldslager Conveyor Company..........203 795-9886
73 Fernwood Rd Hamden (06517) *(G-3452)*
Goldworks..........203 743-9668
5 Locust Ave Danbury (06810) *(G-1833)*
Golf Galaxy LLC..........203 855-0500
595 Connecticut Ave Ste 4 Norwalk (06854) *(G-6182)*
Golf Research Associates..........203 968-1608
2810 High Ridge Rd Stamford (06903) *(G-8218)*
Golfsmith, Norwalk *Also called Golf Galaxy LLC (G-6182)*
Golik Machine Co..........860 610-0095
154 Commerce Way South Windsor (06074) *(G-7763)*
Good Earth Millwork LLC..........203 226-7958
292 Post Rd E Westport (06880) *(G-10092)*
Good Earth Tree Care Inc..........203 375-7962
540 Longbrook Ave Stratford (06614) *(G-8619)*
Goodcopy Printing & Graphics, New Haven *Also called Goodcopy Printing Center Inc (G-5287)*
Goodcopy Printing Center Inc..........203 624-0194
110 Hamilton St New Haven (06511) *(G-5287)*
Goodrich, West Hartford *Also called Triumph Eng Ctrl Systems LLC (G-9869)*
Goodrich Corporation..........505 345-9031
100 Wooster Hts Danbury (06810) *(G-1834)*
Goodrich Corporation..........203 797-5000
100 Wooster Hts Danbury (06810) *(G-1835)*
Goodrich Sensors and Integrate, Cheshire *Also called Atlantic Inertial Systems Inc (G-1356)*
Goody Candles LLC..........860 426-9436
434 Pleasant St Southington (06489) *(G-7930)*
Goodyfab Llc..........203 927-3059
88 Totoket Rd North Branford (06471) *(G-5839)*
Goong..........860 216-3041
798 Silver Ln East Hartford (06118) *(G-2331)*
Gordon Corporation..........860 628-4775
170 Spring St Unit 3 Southington (06489) *(G-7931)*
Gordon Engineering Corp..........203 775-4501
67 Del Mar Dr Brookfield (06804) *(G-1193)*
Gordon Products Incorporated..........203 775-4501
67 Del Mar Dr Brookfield (06804) *(G-1194)*
Gordon Rubber and Pkg Co Inc..........203 735-7441
10 Cemetery Ave Derby (06418) *(G-2114)*
Gordon Woodworking LLC..........860 489-5445
499 W Morris Rd Morris (06763) *(G-4789)*
Gorilla Graphics Inc..........860 704-8208
52 N Main St Middletown (06457) *(G-4348)*
Gorilla Sealcoating LLC..........475 218-3506
38 Balmforth Ave Apt 3 Danbury (06810) *(G-1836)*
Gorilla Signs & Wraps..........203 439-8838
182 Sandbank Rd Cheshire (06410) *(G-1393)*
Gotham Chemical Company Inc..........203 854-6644
21 South St Norwalk (06854) *(G-6183)*
Gothers & Martin Wdwkg LLC..........860 982-4193
16 State St Wethersfield (06109) *(G-10194)*
Goulet Enterprises Inc..........860 379-0793
115 New Hartford Rd Pleasant Valley (06063) *(G-6922)*
Goulet Printery, Pleasant Valley *Also called Goulet Enterprises Inc (G-6922)*
Gouveia Vineyards LLC..........203 265-5526
1339 Whirlwind Hill Rd Wallingford (06492) *(G-9277)*
Government Sales, Hartford *Also called Government Surplus Sales Inc (G-3601)*
Government Sourcing Group, Guilford *Also called Medpricercom Inc (G-3375)*
Government Surplus Sales Inc..........860 247-7787
69 Francis Ave Hartford (06106) *(G-3601)*
GP Industries..........860 859-9938
500 Norwich Ave Ste 7 Taftville (06380) *(G-8741)*
GP Industries Ltd LLC (PA)..........860 350-5400
106 Fort Hill Rd New Milford (06776) *(G-5540)*
GPA..........860 410-0624
10 Farmington Valley Dr # 5 Plainville (06062) *(G-6818)*
Gpk Mfg LLC..........860 536-2084
178 Colonel Ledyard Hwy Mystic (06355) *(G-4819)*
Gqp, Willimantic *Also called Guaranteed Quality Parts L L C (G-10228)*
Gr Enterprises and Tech..........203 387-1430
3 Penny Ln Woodbridge (06525) *(G-10601)*
Grace Machine Company LLC..........860 828-8789
46 Woodlawn Rd Ste A Berlin (06037) *(G-184)*
Gracie Maes Kitchen LLC..........860 885-8250
383 Bethel Rd Griswold (06351) *(G-3265)*
Gracies Kitchens Inc..........203 773-0795
211 Food Terminal Plz New Haven (06511) *(G-5288)*
Gradar Metals, Milford *Also called B L C Investments Inc (G-4464)*
Graduate Group..........860 233-2330
25 Norwood Rd West Hartford (06117) *(G-9813)*
Graduate Group Booksellers, West Hartford *Also called Graduate Group (G-9813)*
Graduation Solutions LLC..........914 934-5991
200 Pemberwick Rd Greenwich (06831) *(G-3168)*
Graduation Source, Greenwich *Also called Graduation Solutions LLC (G-3168)*
Graffeast Inc..........203 622-1622
25 Sherwood Pl Greenwich (06830) *(G-3169)*
Grafik Print Shopp..........203 335-0777
378 Granfield Ave Bridgeport (06610) *(G-778)*
Grafted Coatings Inc..........203 377-9979
400 Surf Ave Stratford (06615) *(G-8620)*
Graham Tool and Machine LLC..........860 585-1261
9 Container Dr Terryville (06786) *(G-8759)*
Graham Whitehead & Manger Co..........978 887-0430
431 Howe Ave Shelton (06484) *(G-7452)*
Grammas Hands LLC..........203 301-0791
655 West Ave Milford (06461) *(G-4541)*
Grana Pastificio LLC..........203 979-2828
23 Sachem St Norwalk (06850) *(G-6184)*
Granata Sign Co, Stamford *Also called Granata Signs LLC (G-8219)*
Granata Signs LLC..........203 358-0780
80 Lincoln Ave 90 Stamford (06902) *(G-8219)*
Grand Embroidery Inc..........203 888-7484
225 Christian St Oxford (06478) *(G-6663)*
Grand Fish Market LLC..........203 691-8904
353 Grand Ave New Haven (06513) *(G-5289)*
Grand Imprints, Oxford *Also called Grand Embroidery Inc (G-6663)*
Grand Publications LLC..........203 288-5721
95 Brooksvale Ave Hamden (06518) *(G-3453)*
Grand Slam Signs..........972 874-3658
15 Tuckers Run Ledyard (06339) *(G-3874)*
Grand View Stable LLC..........860 228-3791
42 Pine St Columbia (06237) *(G-1605)*
Granite & Kitchen Studio LLC..........860 290-4444
313 Pleasant Valley Rd South Windsor (06074) *(G-7764)*
Granite Group Wholesalers LLC..........860 537-7600
464 S Main St Ste 1 Colchester (06415) *(G-1552)*
Granite Group, The, Colchester *Also called Granite Group Wholesalers LLC (G-1552)*
Granite Hill Equity..........203 801-4396
280 New Norwalk Rd New Canaan (06840) *(G-5106)*
Granite LLC..........860 586-8132
116 Willard Ave Newington (06111) *(G-5657)*
Granitech LLC..........860 620-1733
409 Canal St Ste 4 Plantsville (06479) *(G-6895)*
Grannick's Bitter Apple Co, Norwalk *Also called Valore Inc (G-6381)*
Grannys Got It..........203 879-0042
724 Wolcott Rd Ste 3 Wolcott (06716) *(G-10566)*

ALPHABETIC

Granola Bar 914 763-6320
41 Greenwich Ave Greenwich (06830) *(G-3170)*
Grant Manufacturing & Mch Co 203 366-4557
90 Silliman Ave Bridgeport (06605) *(G-779)*
Grant Riveters USA, Bridgeport *Also called Riveting Systems USA LLC* *(G-891)*
Granta USA Ltd 440 207-6051
62 E Starrs Plain Rd Danbury (06810) *(G-1837)*
Grapes of Norwalk 203 845-9640
10 Cross St Norwalk (06851) *(G-6185)*
Graphic Cntrls Acqisition Corp 203 759-1020
1 Hillside Dr Wolcott (06716) *(G-10567)*
Graphic Identity LLC 860 657-9755
36 Kreiger Ln Ste G Glastonbury (06033) *(G-3042)*
Graphic Image Inc 203 877-8787
561 Boston Post Rd Milford (06460) *(G-4542)*
Graphic Memories By McKie 860 434-5222
40 Bill Hill Rd Old Lyme (06371) *(G-6511)*
Graphic Packaging Intl LLC 860 567-4196
133 Goodhouse Rd Litchfield (06759) *(G-3890)*
Graphic Plus 203 723-8387
99 Evening Star Dr Naugatuck (06770) *(G-4885)*
Graphica Sign Studios 203 619-2255
140 Hunt Ln 2 East Haven (06512) *(G-2433)*
Graphics Press LLC 203 272-9187
1161 Sperry Rd Cheshire (06410) *(G-1394)*
Graphics Services Corporation 203 270-7578
153 S Main St Newtown (06470) *(G-5740)*
Graphics Unlimited 860 928-1407
445 School St Putnam (06260) *(G-7045)*
Graphik Identities, Glastonbury *Also called Graphic Identity LLC* *(G-3042)*
Graphite Die Mold Inc 860 349-4444
18 Airline Rd Durham (06422) *(G-2148)*
Grass Roots Creamery 860 653-6303
4 Park Pl Granby (06035) *(G-3108)*
Grasschoppers LLC 860 294-1620
29 Hillside Ave Terryville (06786) *(G-8760)*
Grassy Meadows Lawn Care 203 856-3823
849 Plattsville Rd Trumbull (06611) *(G-9030)*
Gratton Concrete Sawingdri 860 974-9127
677 Hampton Rd Pomfret Center (06259) *(G-6938)*
Gravelines Amercn Martial Arts 860 753-1402
12 Providence Rd Brooklyn (06234) *(G-1247)*
Graybark Enterprises LLC 203 255-4503
20 Governors Ln Fairfield (06824) *(G-2792)*
Graycon Defense Industries LLC 860 339-2505
71 Goose Hill Rd Chester (06412) *(G-1474)*
Grayfin Micro, Madison *Also called Grayfin Security LLC* *(G-3923)*
Grayfin Security LLC 203 800-6760
82 Bradley Rd Madison (06443) *(G-3923)*
Graywolf Sensing Solutions LLC (PA) 203 402-0477
6 Research Dr Ste 110 Shelton (06484) *(G-7453)*
Grdn Woodworks 203 814-6446
3 Raynor Ave Trumbull (06611) *(G-9031)*
Great, Woodbridge *Also called Gr Enterprises and Tech* *(G-10601)*
Great American Publishing Soc 203 531-9300
219 Pemberwick Rd Greenwich (06831) *(G-3171)*
Great Lakes Chemical Corp (HQ) 203 573-2000
2 Armstrong Rd Ste 101 Shelton (06484) *(G-7454)*
Greater New Milford Spectrum, New Milford *Also called Local Media Group Inc* *(G-5558)*
Greco Industries Inc 203 798-7804
14 Trowbridge Dr Bethel (06801) *(G-304)*
Greek Elements LLC 203 594-2022
49 Journeys End Rd New Canaan (06840) *(G-5107)*
Green & Sons LLC 860 459-4049
19 Little Pitch Rd Litchfield (06759) *(G-3891)*
Green and Sons, Litchfield *Also called Green & Sons LLC* *(G-3891)*
Green Editorial 860 364-5100
139 Calkinstown Rd Sharon (06069) *(G-7379)*
Green Egg Design LLC 860 541-5411
750 Main St Ste 506 Hartford (06103) *(G-3602)*
Green Leaf Foods LLC 860 657-4404
703 Hebron Ave Glastonbury (06033) *(G-3043)*
Green Manor Corporation (PA) 860 643-8111
306 Progress Dr Manchester (06042) *(G-4023)*
Green Ray Led Intl LLC (PA) 203 485-1435
115 E Putnam Ave Ste 3 Greenwich (06830) *(G-3172)*
Green Shutter Inc 203 359-3863
439 Courtland Ave Stamford (06906) *(G-8220)*
Green Tomatillo LLC 860 749-0172
935 Sullivan Pl Ctr South Windsor (06074) *(G-7765)*
Greenhaven Cabinetry & Millwor 860 535-1106
338 Elm St Stonington (06378) *(G-8529)*
Greenleaf Bfuels New Haven LLC 203 672-9028
100 Waterfront St New Haven (06512) *(G-5290)*
Greenmaker Industries Conn LLC 860 761-2830
697 Oakwood Ave West Hartford (06110) *(G-9814)*
Greenport Foods LLC 203 221-2673
191 Post Rd W Westport (06880) *(G-10093)*
Greenscape of Clinton LLC 860 669-1880
13 Janes Ln Clinton (06413) *(G-1506)*
Greenwald Industries, Chester *Also called Blackwold Inc* *(G-1464)*

Greenway Industries Inc 203 885-1059
150 Laurel Hill Rd Brookfield (06804) *(G-1195)*
Greenwich Carbon LLC 203 531-7064
500 W Putnam Ave Ste 400 Greenwich (06830) *(G-3173)*
Greenwich Free Press LLC 203 622-1731
21 Lincoln Ave Greenwich (06830) *(G-3174)*
Greenwich Gofer 203 637-8425
56 Halsey Dr Old Greenwich (06870) *(G-6473)*
Greenwich Magazine, Westport *Also called Moffly Publications Inc* *(G-10124)*
Greenwich Sentinel 203 883-1430
28 Bruce Park Ave Greenwich (06830) *(G-3175)*
Greenwich Time, Norwalk *Also called Hearst Corporation* *(G-6199)*
Greenwich Time 203 253-2922
44 Columbus Pl Apt 9 Stamford (06907) *(G-8221)*
Greenwich Workshop Inc (PA) 203 881-3336
151 Main St Seymour (06483) *(G-7348)*
Greenwood Glass 860 738-9464
3 Robertsville Rd 242 Riverton (06065) *(G-7207)*
Greenwood Industries Inc 203 234-2041
88 Leonardo Dr North Haven (06473) *(G-5943)*
Greenwood Sub LLC 860 291-8833
162 Governor St East Hartford (06108) *(G-2332)*
Greenworks Woodworking 203 886-8573
72 Turkey Plain Rd Bethel (06801) *(G-305)*
Greg Robbins and Associates 888 699-8876
15 Park Pl Branford (06405) *(G-601)*
Gregmans Inc 203 464-2530
167 Cherry St Milford (06460) *(G-4543)*
Gregor Technologies LLC 860 482-2569
529 Technology Park Dr Torrington (06790) *(G-8930)*
Gregory Penta 860 747-2681
111 Laurel Ct Plainville (06062) *(G-6819)*
Gregory Woodworks LLC 203 794-0726
6 Sympaug Park Rd Bethel (06801) *(G-306)*
Gregorys Sawmill LLC 203 762-8298
3 Pimpewaug Rd Wilton (06897) *(G-10298)*
Gregs Outboard Service LLC 860 339-5139
304 Boston Post Rd Old Saybrook (06475) *(G-6535)*
Greif Inc 740 549-6000
491 North St Windsor Locks (06096) *(G-10488)*
Grey House Publishing Inc 860 364-1444
23 N Main St Sharon (06069) *(G-7380)*
Grey Wall Software LLC 203 782-5944
195 Church St Fl 14 New Haven (06510) *(G-5291)*
Greycourt Publishing LLC 203 894-1535
11 Conant Rd Ridgefield (06877) *(G-7144)*
Greywall Inc 860 267-6177
144 Bear Swamp Rd East Hampton (06424) *(G-2262)*
Gridiron Capital LLC (PA) 203 972-1100
220 Elm St Fl 2 New Canaan (06840) *(G-5108)*
Griffin Green 203 266-5727
190 Hard Hill Rd N Bethlehem (06751) *(G-371)*
Griffith & Parrott 203 245-7837
120 Acorn Rd Madison (06443) *(G-3924)*
Griffith Company 203 333-5557
239 Asylum St Bridgeport (06610) *(G-780)*
Grigerek Co 860 677-2560
11 Oakland Ave Farmington (06032) *(G-2914)*
Grill Daddy Brush Company 888 840-7552
29 Arcadia Rd Old Greenwich (06870) *(G-6474)*
Grillo Services LLC 203 877-5070
1183 Oronoque Rd Milford (06461) *(G-4544)*
Grimco Inc 800 542-9941
221 South St Unit G1 New Britain (06051) *(G-4993)*
Grimes Firearms LLC 203 843-2271
3132 Avalon Haven Dr North Haven (06473) *(G-5944)*
Grinding System Services LLC 860 208-5196
673 Chaffeeville Rd Storrs Mansfield (06268) *(G-8556)*
Griswold LLC 860 564-3321
1 River St Moosup (06354) *(G-4779)*
Griswold Machine & Fabrication 860 376-9891
8 Sheldon Rd Jewett City (06351) *(G-3796)*
Griswold Rubber Company, Moosup *Also called Griswold LLC* *(G-4779)*
Grohe Manufacturing 203 516-5536
26 Beaver St Ste 2 Ansonia (06401) *(G-37)*
Grolier Overseas Incorporated (HQ) 203 797-3500
90 Sherman Tpke Danbury (06816) *(G-1838)*
Gros-Ite Industries Inc 800 242-1790
5 Mckee Pl Cheshire (06410) *(G-1395)*
Gros-Ite Precision Spindle 860 679-7490
21 Spring Ln Farmington (06032) *(G-2915)*
Grote & Weigel Inc (PA) 860 242-8528
76 Granby St Bloomfield (06002) *(G-415)*
Grotti Tool Company 203 877-5570
80 Erna Ave Milford (06461) *(G-4545)*
Grotto Always Inc 203 754-0295
634 Watertown Ave Waterbury (06708) *(G-9491)*
Group Works 203 834-7905
50 Powder Horn Hill Rd Wilton (06897) *(G-10299)*
Grove Systems Inc 860 663-2555
572 Route 148 Deep River (06419) *(G-2091)*
Grover D & Sons LLC 860 429-9420
156 Old Farms Rd Willington (06279) *(G-10248)*

ALPHABETIC SECTION

GS Ruff Stuff 860 859-9355
  49 Rattlesnake Ledge Rd Salem (06420) *(G-7289)*
Gs Thermal Solutions Inc 475 289-4625
  144 Old Brookfield Rd C Danbury (06811) *(G-1839)*
GSC Orthotics Prosthetics LLC 203 857-0887
  37 Hunt St Norwalk (06853) *(G-6186)*
Gsv Inc 203 221-2690
  191 Post Rd W Westport (06880) *(G-10094)*
Gtrpet Smf LLC 203 661-1229
  10 Mead Ave Unit B Cos Cob (06807) *(G-1632)*
Guaranteed Quality Parts L L C 860 450-0419
  120 Union St Willimantic (06226) *(G-10228)*
Guardian Envmtl Tech Inc 860 350-2200
  208 Sawyer Hill Rd New Milford (06776) *(G-5541)*
Guasa Salsa Vzla 203 981-7011
  9 Rainbow Rd Norwalk (06851) *(G-6187)*
Guess Inc 860 629-0835
  455 Trolley Line Blvd # 780 Mashantucket (06338) *(G-4132)*
Guest Co 203 235-4421
  24 New Park Dr Berlin (06037) *(G-185)*
Guhring Inc 860 216-5948
  121 W Ddley Town Rd Ste C Bloomfield (06002) *(G-416)*
Guida's Milk & Ice Cream, New Britain Also called Guida-Seibert Dairy Company *(G-4994)*
Guida-Seibert Dairy Company (PA) 860 224-2404
  433 Park St New Britain (06051) *(G-4994)*
Guidera Marketing Services 860 599-8880
  21 Pawcatuck Ave Pawcatuck (06379) *(G-6713)*
Guilford Logging 203 453-5190
  484 Goose Ln Guilford (06437) *(G-3357)*
Guilford Printing Inc 203 453-5585
  74 Wildrose Ave Guilford (06437) *(G-3358)*
Guilford Printworks, Guilford Also called Guilford Printing Inc *(G-3358)*
Guillemot Kayaks 860 659-8847
  10 Ash Swamp Rd Glastonbury (06033) *(G-3044)*
Guinness America Inc 203 229-2100
  801 Main Ave Norwalk (06851) *(G-6188)*
Guiseppe Mazzettini 203 597-9035
  270 Bradley Ave Waterbury (06708) *(G-9492)*
Gulemo Inc 860 456-1151
  2 Birch St Willimantic (06226) *(G-10229)*
Gulf Manufacturing Inc 860 529-8601
  645 Cromwell Ave Rocky Hill (06067) *(G-7239)*
Gulfstream Aerospace Corp 860 210-1469
  142 Second Hill Rd New Milford (06776) *(G-5542)*
Gulfstream Aerospace Corp 912 965-3000
  95 Old County Rd East Granby (06026) *(G-2207)*
Gunworks International L L C 860 388-4591
  4 Center Rd Old Saybrook (06475) *(G-6536)*
Gutkin Enterprises LLC 203 777-5510
  1349 Dixwell Ave Ste 1 Hamden (06514) *(G-3454)*
Gutter Filter New England LLC 860 274-5943
  51 Ice House Rd Oakville (06779) *(G-6454)*
Guy Lindsay 860 646-7865
  307 E Center St Manchester (06040) *(G-4024)*
Guy Montanari 203 791-0642
  82 Payne Rd Danbury (06810) *(G-1840)*
Guy Ravenelle 860 564-3200
  71 Black Hill Rd Central Village (06332) *(G-1337)*
Guys Blind 203 270-8977
  37 Mount Pleasant Rd Newtown (06470) *(G-5741)*
Gwilliam Company Inc 860 354-2884
  46 Old State Rd New Milford (06776) *(G-5543)*
Gws Marketing Associates, Seymour Also called Greenwich Workshop Inc *(G-7348)*
Gybenorth Industries LLC 203 876-9876
  80 Wampus Ln Ste 13 Milford (06460) *(G-4546)*
Gynion LLC 203 520-8241
  286 Strobel Rd Trumbull (06611) *(G-9032)*
Gypsum Systems LLC 860 470-3916
  11 Hinman Meadow Rd Burlington (06013) *(G-1269)*
H & B Tool & Engineering Co 860 528-9341
  481 Sullivan Ave South Windsor (06074) *(G-7766)*
H & B Woodworking Co 860 793-6991
  105 E Main St Plainville (06062) *(G-6820)*
H & D Ornamental Iron Works 860 871-1708
  295 Somers Rd Ellington (06029) *(G-2591)*
H & K Industries LLC 857 237-3944
  200 Nutmeg Ln Apt 119 Hartford (06118) *(G-3603)*
H & M Systems 860 445-2347
  34 Pegasus Dr Groton (06340) *(G-3290)*
H & S Woodworks L T D 914 391-3926
  161 Merryall Rd New Milford (06776) *(G-5544)*
H & W Machine LLC 860 828-7679
  37 Willow Brook Dr Berlin (06037) *(G-186)*
H Barber & Sons Inc 203 729-9000
  15 Raytkwich Rd Naugatuck (06770) *(G-4886)*
H G Steinmetz Machine Works 203 794-1880
  2 Turnage Ln Bethel (06801) *(G-307)*
H J Baker & Brother Inc 501 664-4870
  2 Corporate Dr Ste 545 Shelton (06484) *(G-7455)*
H J Hoffman Company 203 853-7740
  25 Hanford Pl Norwalk (06854) *(G-6189)*
H Krevit and Company Inc 203 772-3350
  73 Welton St New Haven (06511) *(G-5292)*

H Muehlstein & Co Inc 800 257-3746
  800 Connecticut Ave 5n01 Norwalk (06854) *(G-6190)*
H&A Detail On Wheels 203 354-8845
  7 Testa Pl Norwalk (06854) *(G-6191)*
H&H Engineered Solutions Inc 860 575-0005
  20 N Cove Rd Old Saybrook (06475) *(G-6537)*
H&H Tool LLC 203 879-4519
  59 Nichols Rd Waterbury (06716) *(G-9493)*
H&T Waterbury Inc 203 574-2240
  984 Waterville St Waterbury (06710) *(G-9494)*
H-O Products Corporation 860 379-9875
  12 Munro St Winsted (06098) *(G-10523)*
H.krevit, New Haven Also called New Haven Chlor-Alkali LLC *(G-5343)*
Habanero Software Incorporated 203 453-5458
  281 Durham Rd Guilford (06437) *(G-3359)*
Habasit Abt Inc 860 632-2211
  150 Industrial Park Rd Middletown (06457) *(G-4349)*
Habasit America Inc 860 632-2211
  150 Industrial Park Rd Middletown (06457) *(G-4350)*
Habco Industries LLC 860 682-6800
  172 Oak St Glastonbury (06033) *(G-3045)*
Haesche Machine Repair Service 203 488-7271
  422 Shore Dr Branford (06405) *(G-602)*
Haight Vineyard Inc (PA) 860 567-4045
  29 Chestnut Hill Rd Litchfield (06759) *(G-3892)*
Hajan LLC 860 223-2005
  788 W Main St New Britain (06053) *(G-4995)*
Hak Industries LLC 860 572-7305
  56 Washington St Mystic (06355) *(G-4820)*
Halco Inc 203 575-9450
  114 Porter St Waterbury (06708) *(G-9495)*
Hall Industries, North Branford Also called Hall Machine Systems Inc *(G-5840)*
Hall Machine Systems Inc (HQ) 203 481-4275
  8c Commerce Dr North Branford (06471) *(G-5840)*
Hallden America, Thomaston Also called Hallden Shear Service of Amer *(G-8791)*
Hallden Shear Service of Amer 860 283-4386
  290 Reynolds Bridge Rd Thomaston (06787) *(G-8791)*
Halls Edge Inc 203 653-2281
  420 Fairfield Ave Ste 3 Stamford (06902) *(G-8222)*
Halls Rental Service LLC 203 488-0383
  45 Cedar Lake Rd North Branford (06471) *(G-5841)*
Haltech Manufacturing Svcs LLC 860 625-0189
  100 Blinman St New London (06320) *(G-5473)*
Halurgite Publishing LLC 860 563-0372
  108 Round Hill Rd Wethersfield (06109) *(G-10195)*
Hamar Laser Instruments Inc 203 730-4600
  5 Ye Olde Rd Danbury (06810) *(G-1841)*
Hamden Brewing Company LLC 203 247-4677
  819 Bridgeport Ave Shelton (06484) *(G-7456)*
Hamden Grinding 203 288-2906
  555 Sherman Ave Ste 11 Hamden (06514) *(G-3455)*
Hamden Journal LLC 203 668-6307
  99 Burke St Hamden (06514) *(G-3456)*
Hamden Metal Service Company 203 281-1522
  2 Broadway Hamden (06518) *(G-3457)*
Hamden Press Inc 203 624-0554
  1054 Dixwell Ave Hamden (06514) *(G-3458)*
Hamden Sheet Metal Inc 203 776-1472
  1079 Dixwell Ave Hamden (06514) *(G-3459)*
Hamden Sports Center Inc 203 248-9898
  2858 Whitney Ave Hamden (06518) *(G-3460)*
Hamilton Sndstrnd Space 860 654-6000
  1 Hamilton Rd Windsor Locks (06096) *(G-10489)*
Hamilton Standard Space 860 654-6000
  1 Hamilton Rd Windsor Locks (06096) *(G-10490)*
Hamilton Sundstrand Corp (HQ) 860 654-6000
  1 Hamilton Rd Windsor Locks (06096) *(G-10491)*
Hamiltonbookcom LLC 860 824-0275
  147 Route 7 S Falls Village (06031) *(G-2871)*
Hamlethub LLC 203 431-6400
  37 Danbury Rd Ste 202 Ridgefield (06877) *(G-7145)*
Hammer Transport LLC 860 338-0667
  9 Mansure Rd Chaplin (06235) *(G-1340)*
Hammersmith, Stamford Also called Steven Rosenburg *(G-8443)*
Hampford Research Inc 203 380-2852
  1255 W Broad St Stratford (06615) *(G-8621)*
Hampford Research Inc (PA) 203 375-1137
  54 Veterans Blvd Stratford (06615) *(G-8622)*
Hampton Associates LLC 203 817-0161
  287 Hamilton Ave Apt 4c Stamford (06902) *(G-8223)*
Hamworthy Peabody Combustn Inc (HQ) 203 922-1199
  6 Armstrong Rd Ste 2 Shelton (06484) *(G-7457)*
Hancock Logging & Forestry MGT 860 289-5647
  147 Foster Rd South Windsor (06074) *(G-7767)*
Handhold Adaptive LLC 203 526-6313
  2 Arden Ln Shelton (06484) *(G-7458)*
Handyscape LLC 860 318-1067
  43 Sandy Pine Dr Southington (06489) *(G-7932)*
Hanford Cabinet & Wdwkg Co 860 388-5055
  102 Ingham Hill Rd Old Saybrook (06475) *(G-6538)*
Hanger Prsthetcs & Ortho Inc 860 482-5611
  811 E Main St Ste B Torrington (06790) *(G-8931)*

Hanger Prsthetcs & Ortho Inc 203 230-0667
260 State St North Haven (06473) ***(G-5945)***
Hanger Prsthetcs & Ortho Inc 860 667-5300
10 Countyline Dr Cromwell (06416) ***(G-1703)***
Hanger Prsthetcs & Ortho Inc 860 545-9050
282 Washington St 1b Hartford (06106) ***(G-3604)***
Hanger Prsthetcs & Ortho Inc 860 667-5370
181 Patricia M Genova Dr Newington (06111) ***(G-5658)***
Hanger Prsthetcs & Ortho Inc 860 871-0905
428 Hartford Tpke Ste 103 Vernon (06066) ***(G-9139)***
Hanger Prsthetcs & Ortho Inc 203 377-8820
1985 Barnum Ave Stratford (06615) ***(G-8623)***
Hanna RES & Consulting LLC 860 443-0443
72 Old Colchester Rd Quaker Hill (06375) ***(G-7082)***
Hannes Precision Industry Inc 203 853-7276
74 Fort Point St Norwalk (06855) ***(G-6192)***
Hannoush Jewelers, Farmington *Also called Joseph Hannoush Family Inc* ***(G-2921)***
Har-Conn Chrome Company (PA) 860 236-6801
603 New Park Ave West Hartford (06110) ***(G-9815)***
Harbisonwalker Intl Inc 203 934-7960
163 Boston Post Rd West Haven (06516) ***(G-9914)***
Harbor Publications Inc 203 245-8009
1 Orchard Park Rd Ste 8 Madison (06443) ***(G-3925)***
Harby Power Solutions LLC 203 265-0012
105 S Elm St Wallingford (06492) ***(G-9278)***
Harcosemco, Branford *Also called Semco Instruments Inc* ***(G-650)***
Harcosemco, Branford *Also called Semco Instruments Inc* ***(G-651)***
Harcosemco LLC 203 483-3700
186 Cedar St Branford (06405) ***(G-603)***
Hard Hill Woodworking LLC 203 263-2820
85 Hard Hill Rd Woodbury (06798) ***(G-10638)***
Hard-Core Self Defense 203 231-2344
500 River Rd Shelton (06484) ***(G-7459)***
Hardcore Sweet Cupcakes LLC 203 808-5547
784 Cooke St Waterbury (06710) ***(G-9496)***
Harding, A C Company, Meriden *Also called A Al Harding* ***(G-4137)***
Hardware Cy Soaps Candles LLC 860 209-8494
14 Dorman Rd New Britain (06053) ***(G-4996)***
Hardwood Lumber Manufacturing 860 423-2447
111 Ziegler Rd Scotland (06264) ***(G-7332)***
Harjani Hitesh 860 913-6032
850 Hartford Tpke H109 Waterford (06385) ***(G-9654)***
Harkness Industries, Inc., Cheshire *Also called Fimor North America Inc* ***(G-1389)***
Harley Industries LLC 860 951-5727
34 Foxglove Cir Higganum (06441) ***(G-3765)***
Harman Becker Automotive Syste 203 328-3501
400 Atlantic St Ste 15 Stamford (06901) ***(G-8224)***
Harman Consumer Inc 203 328-3500
400 Atlantic St Ste 1500 Stamford (06901) ***(G-8225)***
Harman Consumer Group Division, Stamford *Also called Harman International Inds Inc* ***(G-8227)***
Harman International Inds Inc (HQ) 203 328-3500
400 Atlantic St Ste 15 Stamford (06901) ***(G-8226)***
Harman International Inds Inc 203 328-3500
400 Atlantic St Ste 15 Stamford (06901) ***(G-8227)***
Harman International Inds Inc 203 328-3500
400 Atlantic St Fl 5 Stamford (06901) ***(G-8228)***
Harman KG Holding LLC (HQ) 203 328-3500
400 Atlantic St Ste 1500 Stamford (06901) ***(G-8229)***
Harmonics Limited, New Haven *Also called Pioneer Power Solutions Inc* ***(G-5366)***
Harpers Invitations 860 257-4615
22 Kreiger Ln Ste 18 Glastonbury (06033) ***(G-3046)***
Harpoon Acquisition Corp 860 815-5736
455 Winding Brook Dr Glastonbury (06033) ***(G-3047)***
Harrel, Pawcatuck *Also called Davis-Standard LLC* ***(G-6707)***
Harrier Technologies Inc 203 625-9700
67 Holly Hill Ln Ste 301 Greenwich (06830) ***(G-3176)***
Harris Enterprise Corp 860 649-4663
80 Colonial Rd Manchester (06042) ***(G-4025)***
Harris Security LLC 860 583-6637
34 4th St Bristol (06010) ***(G-1047)***
Harris Wood Products Inc 860 649-7936
35 Country Club Dr Manchester (06040) ***(G-4026)***
Harris Woodworking, Manchester *Also called Harris Enterprise Corp* ***(G-4025)***
Harrison Enterprise LLC 914 665-8348
237 Asylum St Bridgeport (06610) ***(G-781)***
Harrison Farm 203 488-7963
95 North St North Branford (06471) ***(G-5842)***
Harry & Hios Woodworking LLC 860 267-1535
35 Stevenson Rd East Hampton (06424) ***(G-2263)***
Harry Thommen Company 203 333-3637
3404 Fairfield Ave Bridgeport (06605) ***(G-782)***
Harry Tutunjian 203 944-9444
44 Ridgewood Ct Shelton (06484) ***(G-7460)***
Harsha Inc 860 439-1466
850 Hartford Tpke Waterford (06385) ***(G-9655)***
Hart Stamp & Seal LLC 860 474-5382
22 Westridge Dr Bolton (06043) ***(G-510)***
Hart Technology LLC 860 482-6160
70 Suncrest Ct Torrington (06790) ***(G-8932)***
Hart Tool & Engineering 203 264-9776
339 Christian St Oxford (06478) ***(G-6664)***
Hartford Advocate, Hartford *Also called New Mass Media Inc* ***(G-3653)***
Hartford Aircraft Products 860 242-8228
94 Old Poquonock Rd Bloomfield (06002) ***(G-417)***
Hartford Artisans Weaving Ctr 860 727-5727
42 Woodland St Hartford (06105) ***(G-3605)***
Hartford Aviation Group Inc (PA) 860 549-0096
1 Gold St Apt 18a Hartford (06103) ***(G-3606)***
Hartford Business Supply Inc 860 233-2138
1718 Park St Hartford (06106) ***(G-3607)***
Hartford Courant Company 860 678-1330
80 Darling Dr Avon (06001) ***(G-83)***
Hartford Courant Company 860 560-3747
141 South St Ste E West Hartford (06110) ***(G-9816)***
Hartford Courant Company LLC (HQ) 860 241-6200
285 Broad St Hartford (06115) ***(G-3608)***
Hartford Courant Company LLC 860 525-5555
121 Wawarme Ave Hartford (06114) ***(G-3609)***
Hartford Courant South BR Off, Hartford *Also called Hartford Courant Company LLC* ***(G-3609)***
Hartford Cpl Co-Op Inc 860 296-5636
75 Airport Rd Hartford (06114) ***(G-3610)***
Hartford Division, Hartford *Also called Terex Utilities Inc* ***(G-3701)***
Hartford Electric Sup Co Inc 860 760-4887
70 Inwood Rd Rocky Hill (06067) ***(G-7240)***
Hartford Fine Art & Framing Co, East Hartford *Also called Picture This Hartford Inc* ***(G-2355)***
Hartford Fire Equipment 860 747-2757
394 East St Plainville (06062) ***(G-6821)***
Hartford Flavor Company LLC 860 604-9767
30 Arbor St Unit 107 Hartford (06106) ***(G-3611)***
Hartford Gauge Co 860 233-9619
23 Brook St West Hartford (06110) ***(G-9817)***
Hartford Industrial Finshg Co 860 243-2040
25 Northwood Dr Bloomfield (06002) ***(G-418)***
Hartford Jet Center LLC 860 548-9334
20 Lindbergh Dr Hartford (06114) ***(G-3612)***
Hartford Marathon Foundation 860 652-8866
41 Sequin Dr Ste 1 Glastonbury (06033) ***(G-3048)***
Hartford Monthly Meeting 860 232-3631
144 Quaker Ln S West Hartford (06119) ***(G-9818)***
Hartford Prints LLC 860 578-8447
42 1/2 Pratt St Hartford (06103) ***(G-3613)***
Hartford Seamless Gutters 860 266-2516
41 Crossroads Plz West Hartford (06117) ***(G-9819)***
Hartford Stone Works Inc 860 684-7995
3 Lisa Ln Willington (06279) ***(G-10249)***
Hartford Technologies Inc 860 571-3602
1022 Elm St Rocky Hill (06067) ***(G-7241)***
Hartford Toner & Cartridge Inc (PA) 860 292-1280
6 Wapping Rd Broad Brook (06016) ***(G-1150)***
Harty Integrated Solutions, New Haven *Also called Harty Press Inc* ***(G-5293)***
Harty Press Inc 203 562-5112
25 James St New Haven (06513) ***(G-5293)***
Harvard Business School Pubg 203 318-1234
1050 State St Apt 202 New Haven (06511) ***(G-5294)***
Harvest Hill Holdings LLC (PA) 203 914-1620
1 High Ridge Park Fl 2 Stamford (06905) ***(G-8230)***
Harwest Holdings One Inc 860 423-8334
1102 Windham Rd South Windham (06266) ***(G-7687)***
Hasler Inc 203 301-3400
19 Forest Pkwy Shelton (06484) ***(G-7461)***
Hasson Sheet Metal LLC 860 698-6951
36 Ridge Rd Enfield (06082) ***(G-2648)***
Hat Trick Graphics LLC 203 748-1128
87 Sand Pit Rd Ste 1 Danbury (06810) ***(G-1842)***
Hata Hi-Tech Machining LLC 203 333-9139
1 Riverside Dr Ste E Ansonia (06401) ***(G-38)***
Hatcams LLC 203 303-7250
168 N Plains Industrial Wallingford (06492) ***(G-9279)***
Hatch and Bailey Company (PA) 203 866-5515
1 Meadow Street Ext Norwalk (06854) ***(G-6193)***
Hatchway Corals, Bloomfield *Also called Saltwater Usa LLC* ***(G-485)***
Hathaway Sand & Gravel LLC 860 647-7772
10 Quarry Rd Bolton (06043) ***(G-511)***
Hawie Manufacturing Company 203 366-4303
73 River St Bridgeport (06604) ***(G-783)***
Hawk Integrated Plastics LLC 860 337-0310
1 Commerce Dr Columbia (06237) ***(G-1606)***
Hawk Ridge Winery LLC 860 274-7440
28 Plungis Rd Watertown (06795) ***(G-9711)***
Hawkeye Press Inc 203 855-8580
8 Day St Norwalk (06854) ***(G-6194)***
Hawkline Press 203 248-4615
50 Ives St Hamden (06518) ***(G-3461)***
Hawks Nest Publishing LLC 860 536-5868
194 Opening Hill Rd Madison (06443) ***(G-3926)***
Hawthrn Smth Mfg & Cnsltng Srv 203 866-2227
32 Hemlock Pl Norwalk (06854) ***(G-6195)***
Hay Island Holding Corporation (PA) 203 656-8000
20 Thorndal Cir Darien (06820) ***(G-2027)***
Haydon Kerk Mtion Slutions Inc 203 756-7441
1500 Meriden Rd Waterbury (06705) ***(G-9497)***
Haydon Motion Europe, Waterbury *Also called Tritex Corporation* ***(G-9618)***

Hayes Services LLC 860 739-2273
15 Colton Rd East Lyme (06333) ***(G-2466)***
Haylons Market LLC 860 739-9509
157 W Main St Ste 1 Niantic (06357) ***(G-5808)***
Haynes Aggregates - Deep River 203 888-8100
30d Progress Ave Seymour (06483) ***(G-7349)***
Haynes Hydrogen LLC 203 605-2837
48 Whitney Dr Meriden (06450) ***(G-4172)***
Hayward Turnstiles Inc 203 877-7096
160 Wampus Ln Milford (06460) ***(G-4547)***
HB Publishing & Marketing 203 852-9200
50 Washington St Fl 7 Norwalk (06854) ***(G-6196)***
HB Publishing & Marketing Co 203 852-1324
4 Top Sail Rd Norwalk (06853) ***(G-6197)***
Hbi Boat LLC 860 536-7776
145 Pearl St Groton (06340) ***(G-3291)***
Hbl America Inc (HQ) 860 257-9800
712 Brook St Ste 107 Rocky Hill (06067) ***(G-7242)***
Hbl America Inc 860 257-9800
712 Brook St Ste 107 Rocky Hill (06067) ***(G-7243)***
Hbl Batteries, Rocky Hill *Also called Hbl America Inc* ***(G-7242)***
Hbl Power Systems Limited, Rocky Hill *Also called Hbl America Inc* ***(G-7243)***
Hc Innovations Inc 203 925-9600
10 Progress Dr 200 Shelton (06484) ***(G-7462)***
Head East Woodworking 860 537-2072
90 Davidson Rd Colchester (06415) ***(G-1553)***
Healing Arts Press LLC 203 374-2084
432 Lockwood Rd Fairfield (06825) ***(G-2793)***
Health Monitor, Newtown *Also called The Bee Publishing Company* ***(G-5789)***
Healthper Inc 203 506-0957
24 Guenevere Ct Hamden (06518) ***(G-3462)***
Healthprize Technologies LLC 203 957-3400
230 East Ave Ste 101 Norwalk (06855) ***(G-6198)***
Healthy Harvest Inc 203 245-3786
42 Godman Rd Madison (06443) ***(G-3927)***
Hearst Communications Inc 203 964-2200
9a Riverbend Dr S Stamford (06907) ***(G-8231)***
Hearst Corporation 203 438-6544
42 Vitti St New Canaan (06840) ***(G-5109)***
Hearst Corporation 203 926-2080
1000 Bridgeport Ave Shelton (06484) ***(G-7463)***
Hearst Corporation 203 625-4445
301 Merritt 7 Ste 1 Norwalk (06851) ***(G-6199)***
Heart Health Inc 800 692-7753
1440 Whalley Ave New Haven (06515) ***(G-5295)***
Heart Industrial Unions LLC 800 769-0503
870a Four Rod Rd Berlin (06037) ***(G-187)***
Heartland Publications LLC 860 388-3470
20 Research Pkwy Ste G Old Saybrook (06475) ***(G-6539)***
Heartwood Cabinetry 860 295-0304
345 N Main St Marlborough (06447) ***(G-4124)***
Heat Treating, East Granby *Also called Specialty Steel Treating Inc* ***(G-2231)***
Heaters Inc 860 739-5477
11 Freedom Way Unit D5 Niantic (06357) ***(G-5809)***
Heatherwreath Partners LP 203 662-1084
282 Noroton Ave Darien (06820) ***(G-2028)***
Hebert Tool, Plainville *Also called Scott A Hebert* ***(G-6860)***
Heck D Tool LLC 860 935-9274
1250 Thompson Rd Thompson (06277) ***(G-8834)***
Heckman Consulting LLC 860 434-5877
21-3 Library Ln Old Lyme (06371) ***(G-6512)***
Hedden Forest Products 860 672-6023
87 Cream Hill Rd West Cornwall (06796) ***(G-9763)***
Hedges & Hedges Ltd 860 257-3170
1155 Silas Deane Hwy # 3 Wethersfield (06109) ***(G-10196)***
Heidi M Greene Inc 203 938-4132
18 Lonetown Rd Redding (06896) ***(G-7094)***
Heise Industries Inc (PA) 860 828-6538
196 Commerce St East Berlin (06023) ***(G-2170)***
Helander Products Inc 860 669-7953
26 Knollwood Dr Clinton (06413) ***(G-1507)***
Helen Grace 203 661-1927
25 Dartmouth Rd Cos Cob (06807) ***(G-1633)***
Helicopter Support Inc (HQ) 203 416-4000
124 Quarry Rd Trumbull (06611) ***(G-9033)***
Helium Plus Inc 203 304-1880
17 Pebble Rd Newtown (06470) ***(G-5742)***
Helix Mooring Systems 860 628-0933
170 Spring St Southington (06489) ***(G-7933)***
Hellier, Danbury *Also called Acuren Inspection Inc* ***(G-1731)***
Henderson Trumbull Supply Co, Bridgeport *Also called Delvento Inc* ***(G-748)***
Hendrickson Group 203 426-9266
11 Washington Ave Sandy Hook (06482) ***(G-7315)***
Henkel Consumer Goods Inc (HQ) 475 210-0230
200 Elm St Stamford (06902) ***(G-8232)***
Henkel Corporation (HQ) 860 571-5100
1 Henkel Way Rocky Hill (06067) ***(G-7244)***
Henkel Loctite Corporation (HQ) 860 571-5100
1 Henkel Way Rocky Hill (06067) ***(G-7245)***
Henkel of America Inc (HQ) 860 571-5100
1 Henkel Way Rocky Hill (06067) ***(G-7246)***
Henkel US Operations Corp (HQ) 860 571-5100
1 Henkel Way Rocky Hill (06067) ***(G-7247)***
Henry Thayer Company 203 226-0940
65 Adams Rd Easton (06612) ***(G-2556)***
Henry W Zuwalick & Sons Inc 203 488-3821
36 Zuwallack Ln Branford (06405) ***(G-604)***
Herbalife Distributor 860 584-9721
607 King St Bristol (06010) ***(G-1048)***
Herbasway Laboratories LLC 203 269-6991
101 N Plains Indstrl Rd Wallingford (06492) ***(G-9280)***
Herbs Farmstead & Goods 860 876-3670
155 Ingham Hill Rd Old Saybrook (06475) ***(G-6540)***
Herff Jones LLC 203 266-7170
39 Terrell Farm Rd Bethlehem (06751) ***(G-372)***
Herff Jones LLC 203 368-9344
71 Vought Pl Stratford (06614) ***(G-8624)***
Heritage Custom Products LLC 860 292-1979
8 Thompson Rd Ste 6 East Windsor (06088) ***(G-2495)***
Heritage Newsprint LLC 203 393-0567
68 Anthony Ct Bethany (06524) ***(G-244)***
Heritage Printers, Hartford *Also called G & R Enterprises Incorporated* ***(G-3593)***
Herman Schmidt Precision Workh 860 289-3347
26 Sea Pave Rd South Windsor (06074) ***(G-7768)***
Hermann Schmidt Company Inc 860 289-3347
26 Sea Pave Rd South Windsor (06074) ***(G-7769)***
Hermell Products Inc 860 242-6550
9 Britton Dr Bloomfield (06002) ***(G-419)***
Hermtech Inc 860 758-7528
8 Thompson Rd Ste 9 East Windsor (06088) ***(G-2496)***
Herrick & Cowell Company Inc 203 288-2578
839 Sherman Ave Hamden (06514) ***(G-3463)***
Hersam Acorn Cmnty Pubg LLC 203 261-2548
205 Spring Hill Rd Trumbull (06611) ***(G-9034)***
Hersam Acorn Cmnty Pubg LLC (HQ) 203 438-6544
16 Bailey Ave Ridgefield (06877) ***(G-7146)***
Hersam Publishing Company 203 966-9541
42 Vitti St New Canaan (06840) ***(G-5110)***
Hessel Industries Inc 203 736-2317
95 Roosevelt Dr Derby (06418) ***(G-2115)***
Hew Publishing LLC 860 514-2045
5 Redwood Ct Cromwell (06416) ***(G-1704)***
Hexcel Corporation (PA) 203 969-0666
281 Tresser Blvd Ste 1503 Stamford (06901) ***(G-8233)***
Hexcel Corporation 203 969-0666
281 Tresser Blvd Ste 1503 Stamford (06901) ***(G-8234)***
Hexcel Corporation 925 520-3232
250 Nutmeg Rd S South Windsor (06074) ***(G-7770)***
Hexcel Pottsville Corporation 203 969-0666
2 Stamford Plz 16thf Stamford (06901) ***(G-8235)***
Hexi, Wallingford *Also called High Energy X-Rays Intl Corp* ***(G-9281)***
Hexplora LLC 860 760-7601
10 Waterchase Dr Iii Fl Rocky Hill (06067) ***(G-7248)***
Hfo Chicago LLC 860 285-0709
910 Day Hill Rd Windsor (06095) ***(G-10393)***
Hg Tech LLC 203 632-5946
162 Spencer St Naugatuck (06770) ***(G-4887)***
Hgh Industries LLC 860 644-1150
43 Sally Dr South Windsor (06074) ***(G-7771)***
HH Brown Shoe Company Inc (HQ) 203 661-2424
124 W Putnam Ave Ste 1a Greenwich (06830) ***(G-3177)***
Hhc LLC 860 456-0677
340 Progress Dr Manchester (06042) ***(G-4027)***
Hht, Ansonia *Also called Hata Hi-Tech Machining LLC* ***(G-38)***
HI Heat Company Inc 860 528-9315
32 Glendale Rd South Windsor (06074) ***(G-7772)***
HI Industries LLC 203 783-1084
55 Oak Ridge Ln Milford (06461) ***(G-4548)***
HI Tech Profiles Inc 401 377-2040
185 S Broad St Ste 301 Pawcatuck (06379) ***(G-6714)***
HI Tek Racing LLC 203 378-5210
7365 Main St Ste 8 Stratford (06614) ***(G-8625)***
HI Temp Electric Company 661 259-9225
102 Hendee Rd Andover (06232) ***(G-9)***
Hi-Rel Group LLC 860 767-9031
16 Plains Rd Essex (06426) ***(G-2718)***
Hi-Rel Products LLC 860 767-9031
16 Plains Rd Essex (06426) ***(G-2719)***
Hi-Tech Fabricating Inc 203 284-0894
30 Knotter Dr Cheshire (06410) ***(G-1396)***
HI-Tech Packaging Inc 203 378-2700
1 Bruce Ave Stratford (06615) ***(G-8626)***
HI-Tech Polishing Inc 860 665-1399
50 Progress Cir Ste 3 Newington (06111) ***(G-5659)***
Hi-Temp Products Corp 203 744-3025
88 Taylor St Danbury (06810) ***(G-1843)***
Hicks and Otis Prints Inc 203 846-2087
9 Wilton Ave Norwalk (06851) ***(G-6200)***
Hidden Meadow Alpaca 203 262-1669
901 Kettletown Rd Southbury (06488) ***(G-7856)***
Higgins Sftwr Consulting LLC 203 468-2350
20 Hunt Ln East Haven (06512) ***(G-2434)***
Higgs Energy LLC 860 213-5561
66 Franklin St Norwich (06360) ***(G-6416)***

ALPHABETIC

(PA)=Parent Co (HQ)=Headquarters (DH)=Div Headquarters
2020 Harris Connecticut Manufacturers Directory
525

High Energy X-Rays Intl Corp 203 909-9777
57 N Plains Industrial Rd B Wallingford (06492) ***(G-9281)***
High Fire Servicing LLC 203 924-6562
63 Cranston Ave Shelton (06484) ***(G-7464)***
High Grade Finishing Co LLC 860 749-8883
6 Print Shop Rd Enfield (06082) ***(G-2649)***
High Grade Furnishing, Enfield *Also called High Grade Finishing Co LLC* ***(G-2649)***
High Hook Lures LLC 860 334-2324
25 Noyes Rd Old Lyme (06371) ***(G-6513)***
High Ridge Brands Co (PA) 203 674-8080
333 Ludlow St Ste 2 Stamford (06902) ***(G-8236)***
High Ridge Copy Inc 203 329-1889
1009 High Ridge Rd Stamford (06905) ***(G-8237)***
High Ridge Printing & Copy Ctr, Stamford *Also called High Ridge Copy Inc* ***(G-8237)***
High School Counselor Connect, West Hartford *Also called Campus Yellow Pages LLC* ***(G-9783)***
High Tech Precision Mfg L L C 860 621-7242
43 Aircraft Rd Southington (06489) ***(G-7934)***
High Voltage Outsourcing LLC 203 456-3101
1 Corporate Dr Danbury (06810) ***(G-1844)***
High-Tech Conversions Inc (PA) 860 265-2633
1699 King St Ste 104 Enfield (06082) ***(G-2650)***
Higher Consciousness LLC 310 977-7541
10 Templeton Ct Avon (06001) ***(G-84)***
Highland Manufacturing Inc 860 646-5142
5 Glen Rd Ste 4 Manchester (06040) ***(G-4028)***
Highland Medical Products Inc 860 454-0625
24 Highland Ave Ellington (06029) ***(G-2592)***
Highland Woodworks 203 758-6625
21 Gramar Ave Prospect (06712) ***(G-7004)***
Highlander Group Inc 860 298-8618
24 Somerset Dr Windsor (06095) ***(G-10394)***
Highway Safety Corp (PA) 860 659-4330
239 Commerce St Ste C Glastonbury (06033) ***(G-3049)***
Highway Vehicle/Safety Report, Branford *Also called Stamler Publishing Company* ***(G-655)***
Hill House Press LLC 203 405-1158
327 Turrill Brook Dr Southbury (06488) ***(G-7857)***
Hill Industries Llc 860 747-6421
15 N Washington St Plainville (06062) ***(G-6822)***
Hills Point Industries LLC (PA) 917 515-8650
191 Post Rd W Westport (06880) ***(G-10095)***
Hillside Capital Inc De Corp (HQ) 203 618-0202
201 Tresser Blvd Ste 200 Stamford (06901) ***(G-8238)***
Hilltop Publishing LLC 203 426-8834
10 The Old Rd Newtown (06470) ***(G-5743)***
Hilversum Embroidery 860 729-8532
85 Barbara Rd Middletown (06457) ***(G-4351)***
Hinman Lumber, Burlington *Also called E R Hinman & Sons Inc* ***(G-1266)***
Hint Peripherals Corp 203 634-4468
46 Gracey Ave Meriden (06451) ***(G-4173)***
Hiram Rock Publishing LLC 203 453-0440
359 Willow Rd Guilford (06437) ***(G-3360)***
His Vineyard Inc 203 790-1600
2 Vail Rd Bethel (06801) ***(G-308)***
Hisco Pump Incorporated (PA) 860 243-2705
4 Mosey Dr Bloomfield (06002) ***(G-420)***
Hispanic Communications LLC 203 674-6793
400 Main St Stamford (06901) ***(G-8239)***
Hispanic Communications LLC 203 624-8007
51 Elm St New Haven (06510) ***(G-5296)***
Hispanic Enterprises Inc 203 588-9334
200 Cogswell St Bridgeport (06610) ***(G-784)***
Historical Art Prints 203 262-6680
464 Burr Rd Southbury (06488) ***(G-7858)***
Hitachi Aloka Medical Ltd 203 269-5088
10 Fairfield Blvd Wallingford (06492) ***(G-9282)***
Hitachi Aloka Medical Amer Inc 203 269-5088
10 Fairfield Blvd Wallingford (06492) ***(G-9283)***
Hitbro Realty LLC 860 824-1370
78 High St Canaan (06018) ***(G-1286)***
Hitchcock Chair Company Ltd (HQ) 860 738-0141
13 Riverton Rd Riverton (06065) ***(G-7208)***
Hitchcock Holding Company Inc (HQ) 860 738-0141
31 Industrial Park Rd New Hartford (06057) ***(G-5193)***
Hitchcock Printers, New Britain *Also called E R Hitchcock Company* ***(G-4977)***
Hitech Chrome Pltg & Polsg Lc 860 456-8070
30 Baker Rd North Windham (06256) ***(G-6038)***
Hitek Electronics LLC 203 982-4574
27 Pleasant View St Naugatuck (06770) ***(G-4888)***
HJ Baker & Bro LLC (PA) 203 682-9200
2 Corporate Dr Ste 545 Shelton (06484) ***(G-7465)***
HMS Publications Inc 860 739-3187
2 Louise Dr Niantic (06357) ***(G-5810)***
Hnat Mold & Die Inc 860 537-0573
14 Scott Hill Rd Colchester (06415) ***(G-1554)***
Hob Industries Inc 203 879-3028
750 Bound Line Rd Wolcott (06716) ***(G-10568)***
Hobbs Medical Inc 860 684-5875
8 Spring St Stafford Springs (06076) ***(G-8031)***
Hobson and Motzer Incorporated (PA) 860 349-1756
30 Airline Rd Durham (06422) ***(G-2149)***
Hoffman Engineering LLC (HQ) 203 425-8900
8 Riverbend Dr Stamford (06907) ***(G-8240)***
Hoffman Towing & Transport 860 627-0405
219 Scantic Rd East Windsor (06088) ***(G-2497)***
Hoffmann-La Roche Inc 203 871-2303
15 Commercial St Branford (06405) ***(G-605)***
Hog River Music 860 523-1820
1800 Albany Ave Hartford (06105) ***(G-3614)***
Hogan's Cider Mill, Burlington *Also called Burlington Golf Center Inc* ***(G-1262)***
Holland & Sherry Inc (PA) 212 628-1950
5 Taft St Norwalk (06854) ***(G-6201)***
Hollow Frost Publishers 860 974-2081
411 Barlow Cemetery Rd Woodstock (06281) ***(G-10667)***
Hollums Sheet Metal LLC 203 640-4970
47 Dana St West Haven (06516) ***(G-9915)***
Holly Press Inc 203 846-1720
8 College St Norwalk (06851) ***(G-6202)***
Holm Corrugated Container Inc 860 628-5559
Metals Dr Southington (06489) ***(G-7935)***
Holness Cabinetry LLC 203 598-0430
395 Shadduck Rd Middlebury (06762) ***(G-4279)***
Holo-Krome USA 800 879-6205
61 Barnes Industrial Park Wallingford (06492) ***(G-9284)***
Hologic Inc 203 790-1188
36 Apple Ridge Rd Danbury (06810) ***(G-1845)***
Holometrology, Coventry *Also called Karl Stetson Associates LLC* ***(G-1659)***
Homa Pump Technology, Ansonia *Also called Pump Technology Incorporated* ***(G-47)***
Homar Molds & Models Co 203 753-9017
64 Diane Ter Waterbury (06705) ***(G-9498)***
Home Diagnostics Corp 203 445-1170
1 Trefoil Dr Trumbull (06611) ***(G-9035)***
Home Sweeter HM Kit & Bath LLC 203 948-6482
8 Topstone Dr Bethel (06801) ***(G-309)***
Homeland Fundraising 860 386-6698
38 Borrup Rd East Windsor (06088) ***(G-2498)***
Homemade Lbtons By Ccchia Sons, Norwalk *Also called Cocchia Norwalk Grape Co* ***(G-6119)***
Hometown Publishing LLC 203 426-5252
87 S Main St Ste 13 Newtown (06470) ***(G-5744)***
Homewood Cabinet Co Inc 860 599-2441
262 S Broad St Pawcatuck (06379) ***(G-6715)***
Honey Cell Inc (PA) 203 925-1818
850 Union Ave Bridgeport (06607) ***(G-785)***
Honeypotz Inc 203 542-7891
1465 E Putnam Ave Apt 604 Old Greenwich (06870) ***(G-6475)***
Honeywell Authorized Dealer, New Milford *Also called George Usaty Sons Heat* ***(G-5535)***
Honeywell Authorized Dealer, New Britain *Also called Link Mechanical Services Inc* ***(G-5011)***
Honeywell International Inc 203 484-7161
12 Clintonville Rd Northford (06472) ***(G-6045)***
Honeywell International Inc 203 484-7161
12 Clintonville Rd Northford (06472) ***(G-6046)***
Honeywell International Inc 203 484-6202
12 Clintonville Rd Northford (06472) ***(G-6047)***
Honeywell International Inc 203 484-7161
12 Clintonville Rd North Branford (06471) ***(G-5843)***
Honeywell International Inc 203 484-7161
1 Fire Lite Pl 4 Northford (06472) ***(G-6048)***
Hood Sailmakers, Groton *Also called Custom Marine Canvas LLC* ***(G-3281)***
Hoodlum Skateboard Company LLC 860 690-6201
609 Oak St East Hartford (06118) ***(G-2333)***
Hooked On Fishing Charters 203 257-3431
15 Verna Hill Rd Fairfield (06824) ***(G-2794)***
Hope Kit Cbinets Stone Sup LLC 203 504-3164
308 Hope St Stamford (06906) ***(G-8241)***
Hope Kit Cbinets Stone Sup LLC (PA) 203 610-6147
1901 Commerce Dr Bridgeport (06605) ***(G-786)***
Hopewell Harmony LLC 203 222-2268
8 Hopewell Rd Newtown (06470) ***(G-5745)***
Hopewell Harmony LLC 203 222-2268
11 Lilac Ln Weston (06883) ***(G-10027)***
Hopp Companies Inc 800 889-8425
3 Simm Ln Ste 2 Newtown (06470) ***(G-5746)***
Horberg Industries Inc 203 334-9444
19 Staples St Bridgeport (06604) ***(G-787)***
Horizon Software Inc 860 633-2090
148 Eastern Blvd Ste 208 Glastonbury (06033) ***(G-3050)***
Horizons Unlimited Inc 860 423-1931
90 S Park St Ste 1 Willimantic (06226) ***(G-10230)***
Horse Ridge Cellars LLC (PA) 860 763-5380
11 South Rd Somers (06071) ***(G-7661)***
Horst Engrg De Mexico LLC 860 289-8209
36 Cedar St East Hartford (06108) ***(G-2334)***
Horton Brasses Inc 860 635-4400
49 Nooks Hill Rd Cromwell (06416) ***(G-1705)***
Hosmer Mountain Btlg Co Inc 860 643-6923
15 Spencer St Manchester (06040) ***(G-4029)***
Hosmer Mountain Soda Shack, Manchester *Also called Hosmer Mountain Btlg Co Inc* ***(G-4029)***
Hosokawa Micron Intl Inc 860 828-0541
63 Fuller Way Berlin (06037) ***(G-188)***

Hosokawa Polymer Systems Div, Berlin *Also called Hosokawa Micron Intl Inc* ***(G-188)***
Hot Spot Stoves & Mech LLC 860 829-7283
4 Lower Ln Berlin (06037) ***(G-189)***
Hot Tops LLC 203 926-2067
240 Long Hill Cross Rd # 4 Shelton (06484) ***(G-7466)***
Hotchkiss Publishing 203 430-6289
17 Frank St Branford (06405) ***(G-606)***
Hotseat Chassis Inc 860 582-5031
20 S Commons Rd Waterbury (06704) ***(G-9499)***
Housatonic Boat Works LLC 203 375-3161
485 Chapel St Stratford (06614) ***(G-8627)***
Housatonic Mch & Prototype LLC 203 922-2714
14 Audubon Ln Shelton (06484) ***(G-7467)***
Housatonic Wire Co 203 888-9670
109 River St Seymour (06483) ***(G-7350)***
House of Bubba LLC 860 429-4250
106 Clint Eldredge Rd Willington (06279) ***(G-10250)***
Houston Macdermid Inc 203 575-5700
245 Freight St Waterbury (06702) ***(G-9500)***
Houston Weber Systems Inc 203 481-0115
31 Business Park Dr Ste 3 Branford (06405) ***(G-607)***
Howard Engineering LLC 203 729-5213
687 Wooster St Naugatuck (06770) ***(G-4889)***
Howmet Castings & Services Inc 860 379-3314
145 Price Rd Winsted (06098) ***(G-10524)***
Howmet Corporation 203 481-3451
4 Commercial St Branford (06405) ***(G-608)***
Hoya Corporation 860 289-5379
580 Nutmeg Rd N South Windsor (06074) ***(G-7773)***
Hoya Optcal Labs Amrc-Hartford, South Windsor *Also called Hoya Corporation* ***(G-7773)***
Hoyt Manufacturing Co Inc 860 628-2050
37 W Center St Ste Ll1 Southington (06489) ***(G-7936)***
HP Hood LLC 860 623-4435
1250 East St S Suffield (06078) ***(G-8721)***
HP Hood LLC 203 304-9151
153 S Main St Newtown (06470) ***(G-5747)***
Hpi Manufacturing Inc 203 777-5395
375 Morse St Hamden (06517) ***(G-3464)***
Hps Industries LLC 203 915-5627
33 Long Hill Ter New Haven (06515) ***(G-5297)***
HRF Fastener Systems Inc 860 589-0750
70 Horizon Dr Bristol (06010) ***(G-1049)***
Hs Welding LLC 860 599-0372
879 Stonington Rd Pawcatuck (06379) ***(G-6716)***
Hsb Aircraft Components LLC 860 505-7349
80 Production Ct New Britain (06051) ***(G-4997)***
Hub Industries 203 803-8836
209 Center St Bridgeport (06604) ***(G-788)***
Hubbard-Hall Inc (PA) 203 756-5521
563 S Leonard St Waterbury (06708) ***(G-9501)***
Hubbell Incorporated (PA) 475 882-4000
40 Waterview Dr Shelton (06484) ***(G-7468)***
Hubbell Incorporated 203 426-2555
14 Prospect Dr Newtown (06470) ***(G-5748)***
Hubbell Incorporated Delaware 475 882-4800
40 Waterview Dr Shelton (06484) ***(G-7469)***
Hubbell Incorporated Delaware (HQ) 475 882-4000
40 Waterview Dr Shelton (06484) ***(G-7470)***
Hubbell Premise Wiring Inc 860 535-8326
23 Clara Dr Ste 103 Mystic (06355) ***(G-4821)***
Hubbell Technical Ctr 203 337-3333
1613 State St Bridgeport (06605) ***(G-789)***
Hubbell Wiring Device 203 882-4800
185 Plains Rd Milford (06461) ***(G-4549)***
Hubergroup Usa Inc 860 687-1617
147 Addison Rd Windsor (06095) ***(G-10395)***
Hudson Paper Company (PA) 203 378-8759
1341 W Broad St Ste 4 Stratford (06615) ***(G-8628)***
Hugger Design, Greenwich *Also called Puppy Hugger* ***(G-3219)***
Hull Forest Products Inc 860 974-0127
101 Hampton Rd Pomfret Center (06259) ***(G-6939)***
Human Interests LLC 203 270-9107
22 Whitewood Rd Newtown (06470) ***(G-5749)***
Hummel Bros Inc 203 787-4113
180 Sargent Dr New Haven (06511) ***(G-5298)***
Humphreys Pharmacal Inc 860 267-8710
31 E High St East Hampton (06424) ***(G-2264)***
Hunt Architectural Wdwkg Inc 203 947-1137
5 Robinson Ave Danbury (06810) ***(G-1846)***
Hunt Printing Co 203 891-5778
675 Newfield St Apt 2 Middletown (06457) ***(G-4352)***
Hunter Industries 860 961-9646
17 Everett Ln Deep River (06417) ***(G-2092)***
Huntington Capital MGT LLC 203 339-2126
41 Patricia Dr Shelton (06484) ***(G-7471)***
Hupaco, Stratford *Also called Hudson Paper Company* ***(G-8628)***
Hurley Manufacturing, New Hartford *Also called New Hartford Industrial Park* ***(G-5203)***
Hurley Manufacturing Company 860 379-8506
37 Greenwoods Rd New Hartford (06057) ***(G-5194)***
Hurley Woodworking LLC 818 643-5809
68 Jeremiah Rd Sandy Hook (06482) ***(G-7316)***
Husky Fuel 203 783-0783
62 Larkey Rd Oxford (06478) ***(G-6665)***
Husky Meadows Farm, Greenwich *Also called Norfolk Industries LLC* ***(G-3210)***
Hutch Welding Company 860 496-9082
153 Durand St Torrington (06790) ***(G-8933)***
Hutchinson Precision Ss Inc 860 779-0300
39 Wauregan Rd Danielson (06239) ***(G-1993)***
Hvc Brands, Norwalk *Also called Hvc Lizard Chocolate LLC* ***(G-6203)***
Hvc Lizard Chocolate LLC 203 899-3075
13 Marshall St Ste 100 Norwalk (06854) ***(G-6203)***
Hvo, Danbury *Also called High Voltage Outsourcing LLC* ***(G-1844)***
Hw Graphics 860 278-2338
92 Wyndemere Ln Windsor (06095) ***(G-10396)***
Hxb Industries LLC 203 348-5922
7 Bend Of River Ln Stamford (06902) ***(G-8242)***
Hyde Clothes Div, Greenwich *Also called Bayer Clothing Group Inc* ***(G-3131)***
Hydeville Manfacturing Inc 203 265-0524
340 Quinnipiac St Wallingford (06492) ***(G-9285)***
Hydro Honing Laboratories Inc (PA) 860 289-4328
8 Eastern Park Rd East Hartford (06108) ***(G-2335)***
Hydro Service & Supplies Inc 203 265-3995
975 Middle St Ste K Middletown (06457) ***(G-4353)***
Hydro-Flex Inc 203 269-5599
534 Surf Ave Stratford (06615) ***(G-8629)***
Hydrochemical Techniques Inc 860 527-6350
253 Locust St Hartford (06114) ***(G-3615)***
Hydroclean Rstrtn Clng Systms, Hartford *Also called Hydrochemical Techniques Inc* ***(G-3615)***
Hydrofera, Manchester *Also called Hhc LLC* ***(G-4027)***
Hydrofera LLC 860 456-0677
340 Progress Dr Manchester (06042) ***(G-4030)***
Hydrogen Highway LLC 203 871-1000
242 Branford Rd North Branford (06471) ***(G-5844)***
Hydrolevel Company 203 776-0473
126 Bailey Rd North Haven (06473) ***(G-5946)***
Hydrolevel Div, North Haven *Also called C Cowles & Company* ***(G-5916)***
Hydrotec Inc 203 264-6700
115 Hurley Rd Ste 7a Oxford (06478) ***(G-6666)***
Hygrade Precision Tech Inc 860 747-5773
329 Cooke St Plainville (06062) ***(G-6823)***
Hylie Products Incorporated 203 439-8786
30 Grandview Ct Cheshire (06410) ***(G-1397)***
Hypack Inc (PA) 860 635-1500
56 Bradley St Middletown (06457) ***(G-4354)***
Hytek Plumbing and Heating LLC 860 389-1122
241 Krug Rd Preston (06365) ***(G-6984)***
I & J Machine Tool Company 203 877-5376
230 Woodmont Rd Ste V Milford (06460) ***(G-4550)***
I and U LLC 860 803-1491
66 Mattatuck Heights Rd Waterbury (06705) ***(G-9502)***
I C T, Southbury *Also called International Contact Tech* ***(G-7862)***
I E A, Brookfield *Also called Imperial Elctrnic Assembly Inc* ***(G-1197)***
I Level Sign and Graphics 203 256-9486
42 New Castle Dr Shelton (06484) ***(G-7472)***
I Level Sign Company, Shelton *Also called I Level Sign and Graphics* ***(G-7472)***
I Q Technology LLC 860 749-7255
9 Moody Rd Ste 18 Enfield (06082) ***(G-2651)***
I T C, Bridgeport *Also called Innovative ARC Tubes Corp* ***(G-792)***
I Tech Services Inc (PA) 800 559-8991
39 Old Ridgebury Rd D1-1 Danbury (06810) ***(G-1847)***
I-Logic Software 860 875-7760
655 Talcottville Rd Vernon Rockville (06066) ***(G-9169)***
I3 Engineering Sciences LLC 908 625-2347
1 Linden Pl Apt 300 Hartford (06106) ***(G-3616)***
I95 Signs LLC 203 296-2141
300 Honeyspot Rd Stratford (06615) ***(G-8630)***
Iae, East Hartford *Also called International Aero Engines LLC* ***(G-2340)***
Iae International Aero Engs AG 860 565-1773
400 Main St Ms121-10 East Hartford (06108) ***(G-2336)***
Iamaw 860 228-0049
249 East St Hebron (06248) ***(G-3750)***
Ian Ingersoll Cabinetmaker 860 672-6334
422 Sharon Goshen Tpke West Cornwall (06796) ***(G-9764)***
Ibbitson Tree Service 860 388-0624
5 Hilltop Dr Old Saybrook (06475) ***(G-6541)***
Ibnr LLC 860 676-8600
190 Farmington Ave Farmington (06032) ***(G-2916)***
IC&e, Clinton *Also called Integrated Chemical & Eqp Corp* ***(G-1509)***
ICC Wire Harness Mfg LLC 203 469-8481
46 Hobson St East Haven (06512) ***(G-2435)***
ICI Dulux Paints 860 621-8661
320 Queen St Southington (06489) ***(G-7937)***
Iconotech, Clinton *Also called Mallace Industries Corp* ***(G-1514)***
Ics, Guilford *Also called International Comm Svcs Inc* ***(G-3362)***
Ict Business 203 595-9452
17 Bridge St Stamford (06905) ***(G-8243)***
Ida Dean 860 482-3589
98 Main St Torrington (06790) ***(G-8934)***
Ida International Inc 203 736-9249
200 Roosevelt Dr Derby (06418) ***(G-2116)***
Ida Publishing Co Inc 203 661-9090
282 Railroad Ave Ste 4 Greenwich (06830) ***(G-3178)***

Ida's Bridal Suite, Torrington *Also called Ida Dean* ***(G-8934)***
Ideal Printing Co Inc 203 777-7626
228 Food Terminal Plz New Haven (06511) ***(G-5299)***
Ideas Inc 203 878-9686
80a Rowe Ave Milford (06461) ***(G-4551)***
Idemia Identity & SEC USA LLC 860 529-2559
101 Hammer Mill Rd Rocky Hill (06067) ***(G-7249)***
Identification Products Corp 203 331-0931
104 Silliman Ave Bridgeport (06605) ***(G-790)***
Identification Products Corp 203 334-5969
1073 State St Bridgeport (06605) ***(G-791)***
Idevices LLC 860 352-5252
50 Tower Ln Avon (06001) ***(G-85)***
Idex Health & Science LLC 203 774-4422
50 Barnes Park Rd N Wallingford (06492) ***(G-9286)***
Idex Health & Science LLC 860 314-2880
110 Halcyon Dr Bristol (06010) ***(G-1050)***
IDI, Milford *Also called Interface Devices Incorporated* ***(G-4557)***
Iemct 203 683-4382
205 Research Dr Ste 8 Milford (06460) ***(G-4552)***
Iffland Lumber Company Inc 860 489-9218
747 S Main St Torrington (06790) ***(G-8935)***
Ignatowski John 203 452-9601
232 Main St Ste D Monroe (06468) ***(G-4719)***
Igs-Med LLC 203 698-0396
7 Ferris Dr Old Greenwich (06870) ***(G-6476)***
Ihs Herold Inc (HQ) 203 857-0215
200 Connecticut Ave Ste 8 Norwalk (06854) ***(G-6204)***
Ikigai Foods LLC 203 954-8083
19 Beverly Hill Dr Shelton (06484) ***(G-7473)***
Ill Ink Graphic & Prtg Svcs 203 748-0711
258 Main St Danbury (06810) ***(G-1848)***
Illicit Industries 203 264-6293
325 Berkshire Rd Southbury (06488) ***(G-7859)***
Illinois Tool Works Inc 860 646-8153
375 New State Rd Manchester (06042) ***(G-4031)***
Illinois Tool Works Inc 203 720-1676
29 Rado Dr Naugatuck (06770) ***(G-4890)***
Illinois Tool Works Inc 203 574-2119
1240 Wolcott St Waterbury (06705) ***(G-9503)***
Illinois Tool Works Inc 860 435-2574
14 Brook St Lakeville (06039) ***(G-3844)***
Illume Health LLC 203 242-7801
20 Ketchum St Westport (06880) ***(G-10096)***
IM Your Type LLC 203 967-4063
10 Reynolds Ave Stamford (06905) ***(G-8244)***
Image 360 .... 860 667-8339
2434 Berlin Tpke Newington (06111) ***(G-5660)***
Image Graphics Inc 203 926-0100
240 Long Hill Croct Rd Shelton (06484) ***(G-7474)***
Image In Motion 203 264-6784
679 Jacob Rd Southbury (06488) ***(G-7860)***
Image Ink Inc 860 665-9792
102 Pane Rd Ste A Newington (06111) ***(G-5661)***
Image Insight Inc 860 528-9806
87 Church St East Hartford (06108) ***(G-2337)***
Image One Prtg & Graphics Inc 203 459-1880
838 Main St Ste L Monroe (06468) ***(G-4720)***
Image Processing 203 488-3252
251 Boston Post Rd Guilford (06437) ***(G-3361)***
Image Star LLC 888 632-5515
35 Phil Mack Dr Middletown (06457) ***(G-4355)***
Image Works Sign & Graph 860 569-7446
200 Brewster St Coventry (06238) ***(G-1655)***
Image360 .... 203 949-0726
163 N Plains Indus Rd Wallingford (06492) ***(G-9287)***
Images Fine Print 203 482-1695
594 Federal Rd Ste 5 Brookfield (06804) ***(G-1196)***
Images Unlimited 860 350-6608
38 Old State Rd New Milford (06776) ***(G-5545)***
Imagin Minerals 203 762-1249
32 Bryant Wilton (06897) ***(G-10300)***
Imagine 8 LLC 203 421-0905
26 Eagle Meadow Rd Madison (06443) ***(G-3928)***
Imagine Software LLC 203 271-0252
60 Frances Ct Cheshire (06410) ***(G-1398)***
Imani Magazine/Fmi 203 809-2565
15 Boylston St West Haven (06516) ***(G-9916)***
IMC Internet, North Haven *Also called Interactive Marketing Corp* ***(G-5949)***
IMI Precision Engineering, Farmington *Also called Norgren Inc* ***(G-2938)***
Immersive Custom Coatings 401 636-1196
30 Chassey St Putnam (06260) ***(G-7046)***
Impact Nutraceuticals LLC 203 493-4268
401 Riversville Rd Greenwich (06831) ***(G-3179)***
Impact Plastics, Putnam *Also called Apogee Corporation* ***(G-7030)***
Impact Plastics, Cromwell *Also called Apogee Corporation* ***(G-1687)***
Impact Sales & Marketing LLC 860 523-5366
48 Carlyle Rd West Hartford (06117) ***(G-9820)***
Impaled Longboards LLC 860 379-1101
298 Niles Rd New Hartford (06057) ***(G-5195)***
Imperial Elctrnic Assembly Inc 203 740-8425
1000 Federal Rd Brookfield (06804) ***(G-1197)***
Imperial Graphics, Milford *Also called Imperial Grphic Cmmnctions Inc* ***(G-4553)***
Imperial Grphic Cmmnctions Inc 203 650-3478
22 Way St Milford (06460) ***(G-4553)***
Imperial Metal Finishing Inc 203 377-1229
920 Honeyspot Rd Stratford (06615) ***(G-8631)***
Imperial Metalworks LLC 203 791-8567
92 Coolidge Ave Stamford (06906) ***(G-8245)***
Imperial Sugar Company 203 761-8474
40 Danbury Rd Wilton (06897) ***(G-10301)***
Impermia Coatings Llc 413 356-0077
222 Pitkin St East Hartford (06108) ***(G-2338)***
Imposition Graphics, North Branford *Also called Brian Berlepsch* ***(G-5830)***
Impression Point Inc 203 353-8800
500 West Ave Ste 4 Stamford (06902) ***(G-8246)***
Imprimi Fotos Ya LLC 860 628-1787
66 Lyon St New Haven (06511) ***(G-5300)***
Imprint Printing 203 794-1092
17 Francis J Clarke Cir Bethel (06801) ***(G-310)***
IMS, Milford *Also called Enginuity Plm LLC* ***(G-4532)***
In Da Cut Music 860 895-9445
108 Jessica Dr East Hartford (06118) ***(G-2339)***
In O Scents of Madison 203 641-8910
837 Boston Post Rd Madison (06443) ***(G-3929)***
In Store Experience Inc 203 221-4777
49 Richmondville Ave # 102 Westport (06880) ***(G-10097)***
In Style Fragrances, Waterford *Also called Harjani Hitesh* ***(G-9654)***
In-Motion LLC 860 742-3612
55 Pine Knoll Rd Coventry (06238) ***(G-1656)***
Inc, Waterbury, Waterbury *Also called Wces Inc* ***(G-9632)***
Incjet Inc 860 823-3090
31 Clinton Ave Ste 2 Norwich (06360) ***(G-6417)***
Incord Ltd 860 537-1414
430 Chapel Hill Rd Oakdale (06370) ***(G-6443)***
Incure Inc 860 748-2979
1 Hartford Sq Ste 16w New Britain (06052) ***(G-4998)***
Indars Stairs LLC 860 208-3826
39 W Town St Lebanon (06249) ***(G-3854)***
Indeco North America Inc 203 713-1030
135 Research Dr Milford (06460) ***(G-4554)***
Independence Enterprises LLC 774 549-8153
235 Cougar Dr Manchester (06040) ***(G-4032)***
Independence Park 203 421-9396
38 Sheffield Ln Madison (06443) ***(G-3930)***
Independent Explosives 860 243-0137
103 Old Windsor Rd Bloomfield (06002) ***(G-421)***
Independent Machine, Danielson *Also called Dennis Savela* ***(G-1989)***
Independent Metalworx Inc 203 520-4089
4 Hershey Dr Ste 1a Ansonia (06401) ***(G-39)***
Independent Repair Service 203 234-0218
156 State St North Haven (06473) ***(G-5947)***
Independent Welding & Fabg 860 605-4712
171 Dings Rd New Hartford (06057) ***(G-5196)***
India Weekly Co 203 699-8419
328 Industrial Ave Cheshire (06410) ***(G-1399)***
Indigo Coast Inc 860 592-0088
17 Meadow St Kent (06757) ***(G-3822)***
Indikon Boatworks 860 395-8297
11 Bright Hill Dr Clinton (06413) ***(G-1508)***
Indulge By Mersene LLC 203 644-6172
20 Railroad Pl Westport (06880) ***(G-10098)***
Industrial Analytics Corp 203 245-0380
1 Orchard Park Rd Ste 10 Madison (06443) ***(G-3931)***
Industrial Automation, Plainville *Also called Enginering Components Pdts LLC* ***(G-6806)***
Industrial Cnnctons Sltons LLC 860 747-7677
41 Woodford Ave Plainville (06062) ***(G-6824)***
Industrial Components CT LLC 203 882-8201
270 Rowe Ave Milford (06461) ***(G-4555)***
Industrial Drives Contrls Inc (PA) 203 753-5103
165 Homer St Waterbury (06704) ***(G-9504)***
Industrial Electric Motors 203 743-9611
85 Shelter Rock Rd Danbury (06810) ***(G-1849)***
Industrial Flame Cutting Inc 203 723-4897
45 Lancaster Dr Beacon Falls (06403) ***(G-136)***
Industrial Forrest Products LL 203 863-9486
21 Stanwich Rd Greenwich (06830) ***(G-3180)***
Industrial Heater Corp 203 250-0500
30 Knotter Dr Cheshire (06410) ***(G-1400)***
Industrial Pallet LLC 860 974-0093
27 Chaplin Rd Eastford (06242) ***(G-2536)***
Industrial Prcision Components, Bridgeport *Also called Comex Machinery* ***(G-738)***
Industrial Press 203 838-4080
32 Haviland St Norwalk (06854) ***(G-6205)***
Industrial Press Inc 212 889-6330
32 Haviland St 3 Norwalk (06854) ***(G-6206)***
Industrial Prssure Washers LLC 860 608-6153
500 Ridge Rd Wethersfield (06109) ***(G-10197)***
Industrial Sales Corp (PA) 203 227-5988
727 Post Rd E Westport (06880) ***(G-10099)***
Industrial Sales Supply, Westport *Also called Industrial Sales Corp* ***(G-10099)***
Industrial Saws Inc 860 496-7000
105 Summer St Torrington (06790) ***(G-8936)***
Industrial Scale Service, Enfield *Also called Kenneth Allevo* ***(G-2654)***

Industrial Sensor Vision Inter......203 592-8723
3 Morse Rd Ste 2a Oxford (06478) *(G-6667)*
Industrial Shipg Entps MGT LLC......203 504-5800
2187 Atlantic St Stamford (06902) *(G-8247)*
Industrial Wood Product Co......203 735-2374
84 Platt Rd Shelton (06484) *(G-7475)*
Industronics Service, South Windsor *Also called Jad LLC (G-7776)*
Inertia Dynamics LLC......860 379-1252
31 Industrial Park Rd New Hartford (06057) *(G-5197)*
Inertia Dynamics Inc......860 379-1252
31 Industrial Park Rd New Hartford (06057) *(G-5198)*
Infante Coatings LLC......203 252-6370
142 New Haven Ave Derby (06418) *(G-2117)*
Infinite Audio LLC......203 924-2558
61 Montgomery St Shelton (06484) *(G-7476)*
Infinite Nutrition Inc......203 940-1783
3 Nimitz Pl Old Greenwich (06870) *(G-6477)*
Infinity Printing, Danbury *Also called Hat Trick Graphics LLC (G-1842)*
Infinity Stone Inc......203 575-9484
1261 Meriden Rd Waterbury (06705) *(G-9505)*
Infirst Healthcare Inc......203 222-1300
8 Church Ln Westport (06880) *(G-10100)*
Infocus Droneworx LLC......860 499-0789
1077 Silas Deane Hwy Wethersfield (06109) *(G-10198)*
Inform Inc......203 924-9929
25 Brook St Ste 200 Shelton (06484) *(G-7477)*
Informa Business Media Inc......203 358-9900
11 Riverbend Dr S Stamford (06907) *(G-8248)*
Informa Business Media Inc......203 358-9900
11 River Band Dry S Stamford (06906) *(G-8249)*
Informa Media Inc......203 885-1045
252 Great Plain Rd Danbury (06811) *(G-1850)*
Information Builders Inc......860 249-7229
100 Pearl St Fl 14 Hartford (06103) *(G-3617)*
Information Resources Inc......203 845-6400
383 Main Ave Ste 20 Norwalk (06851) *(G-6207)*
Information Security Assoc LLC......203 736-9587
6 Spruce Brook Rd Seymour (06483) *(G-7351)*
Information Tech Intl Corp......860 648-2570
440 Oakland St Manchester (06042) *(G-4033)*
Information Today Inc......203 761-1466
88 Danbury Rd Ste 2c Wilton (06897) *(G-10302)*
Ingersoll-Rand Company......860 616-6600
716 Brook St Ste 130 Rocky Hill (06067) *(G-7250)*
Initial Reaction LLC......203 255-1200
303 Linwood Ave Ste 3 Fairfield (06824) *(G-2795)*
Initial Step Monogramming......860 665-0542
635 New Park Ave Ste 2a West Hartford (06110) *(G-9821)*
Injectech Engineering LLC (PA)......860 379-9781
19 Pioneer Rd New Hartford (06057) *(G-5199)*
Ink 13 LLC......860 921-6910
9 Deerfield Trce Burlington (06013) *(G-1270)*
Ink and Stitch Solutions LLC......203 600-7161
88 Laurel Hts Meriden (06451) *(G-4174)*
Ink LLC......860 581-0026
107 Hemlock Valley Rd East Haddam (06423) *(G-2243)*
Ink Publishing LLC......860 581-0026
71 Maple Ave Old Saybrook (06475) *(G-6542)*
Ink Tank Industries LLC......203 274-2717
1069 E Main St Stamford (06902) *(G-8250)*
Ink Well T-Shirts LLC......860 355-3065
7 Mill Ln New Milford (06776) *(G-5546)*
Inka Inc......212 475-2180
390 Lake Ave Greenwich (06830) *(G-3181)*
Inkbyte LLC......203 939-1140
35 Nutmeg Ln Shelton (06484) *(G-7478)*
Inkwell......860 666-8312
18 Kinnear Ave Newington (06111) *(G-5662)*
Inline Plastics Corp (PA)......203 924-5933
42 Canal St Shelton (06484) *(G-7479)*
Innarah Inc......203 873-0015
838 Woodend Rd Stratford (06615) *(G-8632)*
Inner Armour Black LLC......860 656-7720
83 White Oak Dr Berlin (06037) *(G-190)*
Inner City Newspaper Group, New Haven *Also called Penfield Communications Inc (G-5359)*
Inner Office Inc......860 564-6777
49 Daggett St Moosup (06354) *(G-4780)*
Innophase Corp......860 399-2269
18 Sea Scape Dr Westbrook (06498) *(G-9998)*
Innoteq Inc (PA)......203 659-4444
555 Lordship Blvd Stratford (06615) *(G-8633)*
Innova Motors, Unionville *Also called Sherric Group LLC (G-9128)*
Innovant Inc......203 594-7270
21 Locust Ave Ste 2d New Canaan (06840) *(G-5111)*
Innovant Group, New Canaan *Also called Innovant Inc (G-5111)*
Innovaticx LLC......203 836-3501
50 Fitch St New Haven (06515) *(G-5301)*
Innovation Group......860 674-2900
76 Batterson Park Rd Farmington (06032) *(G-2917)*
Innovationcooperative3d LLC......860 540-4172
400 Farmington Ave Farmington (06032) *(G-2918)*
Innovative ARC Tubes Corp......203 333-1031
1240 Central Ave Bridgeport (06607) *(G-792)*
Innovative Components LLC......860 621-7220
635 Old Turnpike Rd Plantsville (06479) *(G-6896)*
Innovative Designs, Ivoryton *Also called Richard Riggio and Sons Inc (G-3789)*
Innovative Fusion Inc......203 729-3873
60 Great Hill Rd Naugatuck (06770) *(G-4891)*
Innovative Industries LLC......860 225-0000
290 Pratt St Unit 1321 Meriden (06450) *(G-4175)*
Innovative Mechanics LLC......203 530-6071
11 Wilshire Blvd Milford (06460) *(G-4556)*
Innovative Mfg Systems LLC......203 284-2605
53 High Hill Rd Wallingford (06492) *(G-9288)*
Innovative Signs LLC......860 870-7446
536 Talcottville Rd Vernon (06066) *(G-9140)*
Innovative Software......203 264-1564
134 Lower Fish Rock Rd Southbury (06488) *(G-7861)*
Innovative Software LLC......860 228-4144
94 Country Ln Hebron (06248) *(G-3751)*
Innovative Systems, Meriden *Also called Southwick & Meister Inc (G-4244)*
Inocraft Products Inc......860 933-0485
77 Bucks Xing Tolland (06084) *(G-8866)*
Inotec, Middletown *Also called Carl Perry (G-4330)*
Inquiring News......860 983-7587
51 Gilbert Ave Bloomfield (06002) *(G-422)*
Ins Sreen Printing & Air......860 779-0566
150 Main St Danielson (06239) *(G-1994)*
Inside Track......203 431-4540
18 Lost Mine Pl Ridgefield (06877) *(G-7147)*
Insight Enterprises Inc......860 647-0848
32 Lily Ln Vernon (06066) *(G-9141)*
Insight Enterprises Inc......203 374-2013
78 Gate Ridge Rd Easton (06612) *(G-2557)*
Insight Media LLC......203 831-8464
3 Morgan Ave Ste 2 Norwalk (06851) *(G-6208)*
Insight Plus Technology LLC......860 930-4763
191 Redstone Hill Rd Bristol (06010) *(G-1051)*
Inspired Brands Intl LLC......203 722-5629
25 Lords Hwy Weston (06883) *(G-10028)*
Inspired Machine Shop......860 628-7822
122 Spring St Ste D3 Southington (06489) *(G-7938)*
Insrcd, Manchester *Also called Cerberus Enterprise Sftwr LLC (G-3993)*
Installed Building Pdts Inc......203 889-0505
43 Crescent St Apt 19 Stamford (06906) *(G-8251)*
Instant Imprints, Meriden *Also called Team Destination Inc (G-4251)*
Instant Imprints, Enfield *Also called Advance Images LLC (G-2613)*
Instant Replay......203 264-1177
83 Hawley Rd Oxford (06478) *(G-6668)*
Instant Style Home Staging......203 417-0131
1 Meadowbrook Ln Weston (06883) *(G-10029)*
Instant Win Innovations......203 648-4499
32 Butterfield Rd Newtown (06470) *(G-5750)*
Instinctive Works LLC......203 434-8094
5 Spicer Ct Westport (06880) *(G-10101)*
Insulated Wire Inc......203 791-1999
2c Park Lawn Dr Bethel (06801) *(G-311)*
Insulpane Connecticut Inc......800 922-3248
30 Edmund St Hamden (06517) *(G-3465)*
Insys Micro Inc......917 566-5045
40 Richards Ave Ste 3 Norwalk (06854) *(G-6209)*
Intangible Matter LLC......203 219-9619
151 Courtland Ave Stamford (06902) *(G-8252)*
Intechs LLC......203 260-8109
17 Bittersweet Cir Monroe (06468) *(G-4721)*
Integ Systems, Danbury *Also called On Line Building Systems LLC (G-1899)*
Integer Confab, Westport *Also called Integer-Comfab Enterprises LLC (G-10102)*
Integer-Comfab Enterprises LLC......646 620-9112
1771 Post Rd E 21 Westport (06880) *(G-10102)*
Integra-Cast Inc......860 225-7600
265 Newington Ave New Britain (06051) *(G-4999)*
Integral Industries Inc......860 953-0686
111 Holmes Rd Newington (06111) *(G-5663)*
Integral Technologies Inc (HQ)......860 741-2281
120 Post Rd Enfield (06082) *(G-2652)*
Integrated Chemical & Eqp Corp......860 664-3951
22 Jefferson Cir Clinton (06413) *(G-1509)*
Integrated Packg Systems Inc......860 623-2623
256 Main St Ste D East Windsor (06088) *(G-2499)*
Integrated Print Solutions Inc......203 330-0200
35 Benham Ave Ste 2 Bridgeport (06605) *(G-793)*
Integrated Systems Solutions......860 665-1600
25 Holly Dr Newington (06111) *(G-5664)*
Integrated Woodworks LLC......860 563-4537
140 Carriage Hill Dr Wethersfield (06109) *(G-10199)*
Integrity Custom Wdwkg LLC......860 302-3726
137 Walnut St Southington (06489) *(G-7939)*
Integrity Cylinder Sales LLC......860 267-6667
17 Watrous St East Hampton (06424) *(G-2265)*
Integrity Graphics Inc......800 343-1248
42 Carver Cir Simsbury (06070) *(G-7629)*
Integrity Industries Inc......203 312-9788
1 Saw Mill Rd Ste 7 New Fairfield (06812) *(G-5169)*
Integrity Manufacturing LLC......860 678-1599
1451 New Britain Ave # 1 Farmington (06032) *(G-2919)*

ALPHABETIC

Integro LLC 860 832-8960
30 Peter Ct New Britain (06051) ***(G-5000)***
Intelium Software LLC 860 667-4300
80 Forest Dr Newington (06111) ***(G-5665)***
Intellgent Clearing Netwrk Inc 203 972-0861
110 Washington Ave North Haven (06473) ***(G-5948)***
Intelligrated Systems Ohio LLC 203 938-8404
3 Costa Ln Redding (06896) ***(G-7095)***
Intelvideo, Stamford *Also called Xintekidel Inc* ***(G-8503)***
Intensity Therapeutics Inc 203 682-2434
61 Wilton Rd Ste 3 Westport (06880) ***(G-10103)***
Interacter Inc 203 949-0199
10 Beaumont Rd Ste 1 Wallingford (06492) ***(G-9289)***
Interactive Marketing Corp 203 248-5324
399 Sackett Point Rd North Haven (06473) ***(G-5949)***
Interctive Print Solutions LLC 860 217-0412
411 Bushy Hill Rd Simsbury (06070) ***(G-7630)***
Interface Devices Incorporated 203 878-4648
230 Depot Rd Milford (06460) ***(G-4557)***
Interface Technology, Bridgeport *Also called A J R Inc* ***(G-680)***
Interflon of New England 860 305-8976
310 Forest Dr Wethersfield (06109) ***(G-10200)***
Interior Plantworks Inc 860 289-9499
369 Main St South Windsor (06074) ***(G-7774)***
Interior Plantworks Inc (PA) 860 289-9499
52 Oakwood Dr South Windsor (06074) ***(G-7775)***
International Aero Engines LLC 860 565-5515
400 Main St East Hartford (06108) ***(G-2340)***
International Automobile Entps (PA) 860 224-0253
608 E Main St Ste 612 New Britain (06051) ***(G-5001)***
International Automobile Entps 860 224-0253
608 E Main St New Britain (06051) ***(G-5002)***
International Bky Waterberry, Danbury *Also called Paulas Bakery* ***(G-1903)***
International Cnstr Pdts Res 203 336-7900
750 Commerce Dr Fairfield (06825) ***(G-2796)***
International Comm Svcs Inc 401 580-8888
2 Burgis Ln Guilford (06437) ***(G-3362)***
International Contact Tech 203 264-5757
1432 Old Waterbury Rd # 6 Southbury (06488) ***(G-7862)***
International Cordage East Ltd 860 873-5000
226 Upton Rd Colchester (06415) ***(G-1555)***
International Elevator Corp 203 302-1023
97 Valley Rd Cos Cob (06807) ***(G-1634)***
International Energy MGT, Milford *Also called Iemct* ***(G-4552)***
International Garrett-Hewitt 203 761-1542
228 Danbury Rd Wilton (06897) ***(G-10303)***
International Instruments Div 203 481-3450
344 Twin Lakes Rd North Branford (06471) ***(G-5845)***
International Mines Outlet 203 264-9207
351 Peter Rd Southbury (06488) ***(G-7863)***
International Mktg Strategies 203 406-0106
1 Stamford Lndg Stamford (06902) ***(G-8253)***
International Paper - 16 Inc (HQ) 203 329-8544
281 Tresser Blvd Stamford (06901) ***(G-8254)***
International Paper Company 860 928-7901
175 Park Rd Putnam (06260) ***(G-7047)***
International Pipe & Stl Corp 203 481-7102
4 Enterprise Dr North Branford (06471) ***(G-5846)***
International Plating Tech LLC 860 589-2212
75 Aircraft Rd Ste 3 Southington (06489) ***(G-7940)***
International Printing Access 860 599-8005
113 Liberty St Pawcatuck (06379) ***(G-6717)***
International Robotics Inc 914 325-7773
1074 Hope St Ste 206 Stamford (06907) ***(G-8255)***
International Robotics Inc 914 630-1060
761 Stillwater Rd Stamford (06902) ***(G-8256)***
International Soccer & Rugby 203 254-1979
3683 Post Rd Southport (06890) ***(G-8004)***
International Systems Cons 203 268-1045
58 Firehouse Rd Trumbull (06611) ***(G-9036)***
International Turbine Systems 860 761-0358
131 W Dudley Town Rd Bloomfield (06002) ***(G-423)***
Interntnl Bar Code Systms 860 659-9660
160 Oak St Ste 1a Glastonbury (06033) ***(G-3051)***
Interntonal MBL Gran Entps Inc 860 296-0741
110 Airport Rd Hartford (06114) ***(G-3618)***
Interpace Diagnostics Corp 855 776-6419
2 Church St S Ste B-05b New Haven (06519) ***(G-5302)***
Interpro LLC 860 526-5869
630 Industrial Park Rd Deep River (06417) ***(G-2093)***
Interpro Rapid Technology, Deep River *Also called Interpro LLC* ***(G-2093)***
Interquest, Woodbury *Also called North Forty Pest Ctrl Co LLC* ***(G-10648)***
Intersec LLC 860 985-3158
1275 Cromwell Ave Ste B3 Rocky Hill (06067) ***(G-7251)***
Interspace Industries LLC 203 814-1879
72 Grays Bridge Rd Ste 1c Brookfield (06804) ***(G-1198)***
Interstate + Lakeland Lbr Corp 203 531-8050
184 S Water St Greenwich (06830) ***(G-3182)***
Interstate Elec Svcs Corp 860 243-5644
800 Mrshll Phelps Rd 2 Windsor (06095) ***(G-10397)***
Interstate Tax Corporation 203 854-0704
83 East Ave Ste 110 Norwalk (06851) ***(G-6210)***
Intersurface Dynamics Inc 203 778-9995
21 Francis J Clarke Cir Bethel (06801) ***(G-312)***
Intlaero Beta Corp 317 821-2000
400 Main St East Hartford (06108) ***(G-2341)***
Intracranial Bioanalytics LLC 914 490-1524
22 Richard Sweet Dr Woodbridge (06525) ***(G-10602)***
Intrasonics Inc 860 283-8040
1401 Waterbury Rd Thomaston (06787) ***(G-8792)***
Intricut 860 537-7766
199 Upton Rd Colchester (06415) ***(G-1556)***
Inventec Prfmce Chem USA LLC 860 526-8300
500 Main St Ste 18 Deep River (06417) ***(G-2094)***
Inverse Media LLC 203 255-9620
2 Evergreen Ave Westport (06880) ***(G-10104)***
Iona Press 860 841-5006
1245 Farmington Ave West Hartford (06107) ***(G-9822)***
Iorfino Woodworking 203 329-1075
97 Blue Ridge Dr Stamford (06903) ***(G-8257)***
Iovino Bros Sporting Goods 203 790-5966
2 Lee Mac Ave Ste 2 # 2 Danbury (06810) ***(G-1851)***
IPC Information Systems, Old Saybrook *Also called IPC Systems Inc* ***(G-6543)***
IPC Information Systems, Fairfield *Also called IPC Systems Inc* ***(G-2797)***
IPC Systems Inc 203 339-7000
8 Custom Dr Old Saybrook (06475) ***(G-6543)***
IPC Systems Inc 860 271-4100
777 Commerce Dr Ste 100 Fairfield (06825) ***(G-2797)***
Ipg (us) Holdings Inc 813 621-8410
4 Hershey Dr Ansonia (06401) ***(G-40)***
Ipsogen 203 504-8583
700 Canal St Ste 5 Stamford (06902) ***(G-8258)***
Ipt Technology 860 395-1083
119 Ayers Point Rd Old Saybrook (06475) ***(G-6544)***
IR Industries Inc 203 790-8273
21 Francis J Clarke Cir Bethel (06801) ***(G-313)***
Irex Machine Inc 860 870-1677
77 Industrial Park Rd Vernon Rockville (06066) ***(G-9170)***
Iron and Grain Co LLC 860 840-2179
183 Webster Hill Blvd West Hartford (06107) ***(G-9823)***
Iron Craft Fabricating LLC 860 923-9869
34 Corttiss Rd North Grosvenordale (06255) ***(G-5887)***
Iron Oxen Network Comm 203 228-2556
51 Old Good Hill Rd Oxford (06478) ***(G-6669)***
Ironhorse Industries LLC 203 598-8720
11 Vista Dr Watertown (06795) ***(G-9712)***
Ironic Chemicals LLC 646 352-2692
252 Old Oaks Rd Fairfield (06825) ***(G-2798)***
Ironman Welding L L C 203 979-4063
420 Courtland Ave Stamford (06906) ***(G-8259)***
Irwin Industrial Tool Company 860 438-3460
700 Stanley Dr Fl 2 New Britain (06053) ***(G-5003)***
IS Cabinetry LLC 203 583-5857
141 Arcadia Ave Bridgeport (06604) ***(G-794)***
ISA, Seymour *Also called Information Security Assoc LLC* ***(G-7351)***
Isaac Industries 203 778-3239
108 Stadley Rough Rd Danbury (06811) ***(G-1852)***
Iskra John 203 488-5402
2 Research Dr Ste 8 Branford (06405) ***(G-609)***
Island Design, New London *Also called Quinn and Gellar Marketing LLC* ***(G-5485)***
Island Nation Press LLC 203 852-0028
144 Rowayton Woods Dr Norwalk (06854) ***(G-6211)***
Island Sand & Gravel Pit, Shelton *Also called Dan Beard Inc* ***(G-7427)***
Island Style Mar Canvas Repr 707 338-8789
49 Myrtle Street Ext Norwalk (06855) ***(G-6212)***
Island View Woodworks LLC 203 494-1760
259 Route 81 Killingworth (06419) ***(G-3835)***
Isopur Fluid Technologies Inc 860 599-1872
183 Provi New Londo Tpke North Stonington (06359) ***(G-6027)***
Isr (ntllgnce Srvllance Reconn 203 797-5000
100 Wooster Hts Danbury (06810) ***(G-1853)***
Isr Systems, Danbury *Also called Cloud Cap Technology Inc* ***(G-1770)***
Isupportws Inc 203 569-7600
65 High Ridge Rd Stamford (06905) ***(G-8260)***
Iswiss Corporation 860 327-4200
161 Sanrico Dr Manchester (06042) ***(G-4034)***
It Helps LLC 860 799-8321
54 Boxwood Ln New Milford (06776) ***(G-5547)***
Iterum Therapeutics Inc 860 391-8349
20 Research Pkwy Old Saybrook (06475) ***(G-6545)***
Ithaca Peripherals Div, Wallingford *Also called Magnetec Corporation* ***(G-9310)***
Ithaco Space Systems Inc 607 272-7640
100 Wooster Hts Danbury (06810) ***(G-1854)***
Its In Bag LLC 860 229-6672
15 Parkmore St New Britain (06051) ***(G-5004)***
Its New England Inc 203 265-8100
8 Capital Dr Wallingford (06492) ***(G-9290)***
ITT Standard 860 683-2144
1036 Poquonock Ave Windsor (06095) ***(G-10398)***
ITT Water & Wastewater USA Inc (HQ) 262 548-8181
1 Greenwich Pl Ste 2 Shelton (06484) ***(G-7480)***
ITW Drawform Inc 203 574-3200
1240 Wolcott St Waterbury (06705) ***(G-9506)***
ITW Foilmark, Bloomfield *Also called Foilmark Inc* ***(G-414)***

ALPHABETIC SECTION James J Licari (PA)

ITW Hlographic Specialty Films...860 243-0343
40 E Newberry Rd Bloomfield (06002) ***(G-424)***
ITW Nutmeg, Naugatuck *Also called Illinois Tool Works Inc* ***(G-4890)***
ITW Powertrain Fastening...203 720-1676
29 Rado Dr Naugatuck (06770) ***(G-4892)***
Ives Welding Service...860 423-6139
299 Old S Windham Rd South Windham (06266) ***(G-7688)***
Ivy Biomedical Systems Inc...203 481-4183
11 Business Park Dr # 10 Branford (06405) ***(G-610)***
Iwco Direct...203 557-4303
1276 Post Rd E Westport (06880) ***(G-10105)***
Izzi B'S Allergen Free Cupcake, Norwalk *Also called Izzi BS Allergy Free LLC* ***(G-6213)***
Izzi BS Allergy Free LLC...203 810-4378
22 Knight St Norwalk (06851) ***(G-6213)***
J & B Service Company LLC...203 743-9357
12 Trowbridge Dr Bethel (06801) ***(G-314)***
J & B Woodworking...203 377-4682
55 Anson St Stratford (06614) ***(G-8634)***
J & D Embroidering Co...860 822-9777
26 Bushnell Hollow Rd A Baltic (06330) ***(G-120)***
J & E Hidalgo Enterprises LLC...203 246-2252
59 Wolfpit Ave Norwalk (06851) ***(G-6214)***
J & G Machining Company Inc...860 379-7038
100 Whiting St Ste 1 Winsted (06098) ***(G-10525)***
J & H Machine Company LLC...860 643-6096
31 Mitchell Dr Manchester (06042) ***(G-4035)***
J & H Mobile Mechanic LLC...203 266-4748
241 Weekeepeemee Rd Woodbury (06798) ***(G-10639)***
J & J Moulding, Pomfret Center *Also called Jakes Jr Lawrence* ***(G-6940)***
J & J Precision Eyelet Inc...860 283-8243
116 Waterbury Rd Thomaston (06787) ***(G-8793)***
J & J Printing Co...860 355-9535
11 Howland Rd New Milford (06776) ***(G-5548)***
J & J Stairs...860 793-8333
230 S Washington St # 11 Plainville (06062) ***(G-6825)***
J & L Machine Co Inc...860 649-3539
62 Batson Dr Manchester (06042) ***(G-4036)***
J & L Tool Company Inc...203 265-6237
368 N Cherry Street Ext Wallingford (06492) ***(G-9291)***
J & M Plumbing & Cnstr LLC...860 319-3082
16 West St Norwich (06360) ***(G-6418)***
J & R Projects...203 879-2347
1509 Wolcott Rd Waterbury (06716) ***(G-9507)***
J & S Fashion...203 572-0154
762 Boston Ave Bridgeport (06610) ***(G-795)***
J & S Industries LLC...203 220-8970
17 Enterprise Dr Monroe (06468) ***(G-4722)***
J & T Printing LLC...860 529-4628
46 2 Silas Deane Hwy Wethersfield (06109) ***(G-10201)***
J + J Branford Inc (PA)...203 488-5637
145 N Mn St Branford (06405) ***(G-611)***
J and K Logging...860 653-6165
26 Westwoods Rd East Hartland (06027) ***(G-2403)***
J and R Shelter Rock Road LLC...203 739-0697
2 Old Shelter Rock Rd Danbury (06810) ***(G-1855)***
J Arnold Mittleman...860 346-6562
29 Stack St Middletown (06457) ***(G-4356)***
J B Concrete Products Inc...860 928-9365
1 Arch St Putnam (06260) ***(G-7048)***
J B Silk Screen Printing, North Branford *Also called Concordia Ltd* ***(G-5832)***
J Burdon Division, Milford *Also called Ridge View Associates Inc* ***(G-4628)***
J C Publishing LLC...860 525-7226
132 Adams St Hartford (06112) ***(G-3619)***
J D & Associates...860 546-2112
115 John Brook Rd Canterbury (06331) ***(G-1299)***
J D Precision Machine Inc...860 653-7787
1 School St East Granby (06026) ***(G-2208)***
J F Tool Inc...860 349-3063
205 Main St Ste C Rockfall (06481) ***(G-7213)***
J Foster Ice Cream...860 651-1499
894 Hopmeadow St Simsbury (06070) ***(G-7631)***
J Furano Trucking, Norwalk *Also called Coastline Fuel Inc* ***(G-6117)***
J G Kurtman Sign Shop, Norwalk *Also called J G Kurtzman* ***(G-6215)***
J G Kurtzman...203 838-7791
97 Taylor Ave Ste 1 Norwalk (06854) ***(G-6215)***
J G M Woodworks...203 934-3726
190 Jaffrey St West Haven (06516) ***(G-9917)***
J G Taglieri...860 645-1060
825 Main St Manchester (06040) ***(G-4037)***
J H Metal Finishing Inc (PA)...860 223-6412
1146 East St New Britain (06051) ***(G-5005)***
J H R Software...203 723-4091
82 Nicole Dr Naugatuck (06770) ***(G-4893)***
J J Box Co Inc...203 367-1211
25 Admiral St Bridgeport (06605) ***(G-796)***
J J Concrete Foundations...203 798-8310
15 Stony Hill Rd Bethel (06801) ***(G-315)***
J J Industries Conn Inc...860 628-4655
125 W Queen St Southington (06489) ***(G-7941)***
J J Lane Designs...860 849-0815
45 Shad Row Suffield (06078) ***(G-8722)***
J J Ryan Corporation...860 628-0393
355 Atwater St Plantsville (06479) ***(G-6897)***
J M Compounds Inc...203 376-9854
290 Pratt St Ofc Meriden (06450) ***(G-4176)***
J M Shea Assc, Ridgefield *Also called JM Shea LLC* ***(G-7150)***
J M Sheet Metal LLC...860 747-5537
161 Woodford Ave Ste 11 Plainville (06062) ***(G-6826)***
J OConnor LLC...860 665-7702
309 Pane Rd Ste 1 Newington (06111) ***(G-5666)***
J P Fabrication and RPS LLC...860 423-8993
622 Jerusalem Rd Windham (06280) ***(G-10347)***
J POMfret& Assoc Inc...860 691-2149
39 Plants Dam Rd East Lyme (06333) ***(G-2467)***
J Ro Grounding Systems Inc (PA)...860 747-2106
161 Woodford Ave Ste 39 Plainville (06062) ***(G-6827)***
J S Dental, Ridgefield *Also called J S Dental Manufacturing Inc* ***(G-7148)***
J S Dental Manufacturing Inc...203 438-8832
196 N Salem Rd Ridgefield (06877) ***(G-7148)***
J S Jewelry, Stamford *Also called Johannes Sulek Jewelry* ***(G-8267)***
J Squared Software...203 325-0275
1127 High Ridge Rd Stamford (06905) ***(G-8261)***
J T Fantozzi Co Inc...203 238-7018
95 Fair St Meriden (06451) ***(G-4177)***
J T Tool Co Inc...203 874-1234
57 Buckingham Ave Milford (06460) ***(G-4558)***
J&A Woodworking Co Inc...203 287-1915
90 Chatterton Way Hamden (06518) ***(G-3466)***
J&L Plastic Molding LLC...203 265-6237
368 N Cherry Street Ext Wallingford (06492) ***(G-9292)***
J&P Mfg LLC...860 747-4790
125 Robert Jackson Way F Plainville (06062) ***(G-6828)***
J&R Signs...203 551-0781
172 Dover St Bridgeport (06610) ***(G-797)***
J&T Industries LLC...203 375-8424
876 Huntington Rd Bridgeport (06610) ***(G-798)***
J-Ro Tool & Die Co, Plainville *Also called J Ro Grounding Systems Inc* ***(G-6827)***
J-Teck Usa Inc...203 791-2121
50 Miry Brook Rd Danbury (06810) ***(G-1856)***
J.C. Engineering & Project MGT, Stonington *Also called James J Chasse* ***(G-8531)***
Ja Custom Woodwork...203 540-5747
35 Soundview Ave Stratford (06615) ***(G-8635)***
Ja Electronics LLC...860 921-7549
121 Bennett Ave Waterbury (06708) ***(G-9508)***
Jackson Corrugated Cont Corp...860 767-3373
45 River Rd Essex (06426) ***(G-2720)***
Jacob David Poppel...860 904-3749
35 Gilbert Ln Burlington (06013) ***(G-1271)***
Jacob Sportz LLC...860 450-1073
28 Ash Ave Willimantic (06226) ***(G-10231)***
Jacobs Ladder...203 833-2227
1395 New Haven Rd Naugatuck (06770) ***(G-4894)***
Jacobs Vehicle Systems Inc...860 243-5222
22 E Dudley Town Rd Bloomfield (06002) ***(G-425)***
Jacobsen Woodworking Co Inc...203 531-9050
3 Oak St W Greenwich (06830) ***(G-3183)***
Jacoby...203 227-2220
11 Blueberry Hill Rd Weston (06883) ***(G-10030)***
Jacquier Welding...860 824-4182
213 Daisy Hill Rd Canaan (06018) ***(G-1287)***
Jad LLC...860 289-1551
489 Sullivan Ave South Windsor (06074) ***(G-7776)***
Jager Prof Gas Svcs LLC...860 388-3422
93 Elm St Apt E Old Saybrook (06475) ***(G-6546)***
Jagtar, Cos Cob *Also called Arnitex LLC* ***(G-1624)***
Jaime M Camacho...203 846-8221
345 Main Ave Norwalk (06851) ***(G-6216)***
Jak Industries LLC...877 964-2725
493 Pequot Trl Stonington (06378) ***(G-8530)***
Jake Brake, Bloomfield *Also called Jacobs Vehicle Systems Inc* ***(G-425)***
Jakes Jr Lawrence...860 974-3744
405 Brooklyn Rd Pomfret Center (06259) ***(G-6940)***
Jakes Repair LLC...203 627-8603
251 School House Rd Old Saybrook (06475) ***(G-6547)***
Jaksy 2 LLC...203 371-4111
2323 Black Rock Tpke Fairfield (06825) ***(G-2799)***
Jam Industries LLC...860 225-8862
226 Grove St New Britain (06053) ***(G-5006)***
James & Co LLC...860 897-6242
2 Wyndemere Rd Bloomfield (06002) ***(G-426)***
James A Blazys...860 274-3857
280 Lake Winnemaug Rd Watertown (06795) ***(G-9713)***
James Callahan...914 641-2852
55 Buck Hill Rd Ridgefield (06877) ***(G-7149)***
James H Quinn...203 809-6046
60 Lee Ave Wallingford (06492) ***(G-9293)***
James Hunt, Coventry *Also called Custom Carpentry Unlimited* ***(G-1650)***
James Ippolito & Co Conn Inc...203 366-3840
1069 Conn Ave Ste 16 Bridgeport (06607) ***(G-799)***
James J Chasse...860 572-0838
578 New London Tpke Stonington (06378) ***(G-8531)***
James J Licari (PA)...203 333-5000
300 N Washington Ave Bridgeport (06604) ***(G-800)***

ALPHABETIC

James J Scott LLC 860 571-9200
38 New Britain Ave Ste 3 Rocky Hill (06067) *(G-7252)*
James Kingsley 203 458-6626
1250 Boston Post Rd Ste 5 Guilford (06437) *(G-3363)*
James L Howard and Company Inc 860 242-3581
10 Britton Dr Bloomfield (06002) *(G-427)*
James M Munch 802 353-3114
48 Route 37 S Sherman (06784) *(G-7596)*
James Manufacturing, North Haven *Also called Jeskey LLC (G-5952)*
James P King 203 834-0050
108 Pond Rd Wilton (06897) *(G-10304)*
James P Smith 203 744-1031
156 Long Ridge Rd Danbury (06810) *(G-1857)*
James River Corp 203 854-2328
800 Connecticut Ave 4w01 Norwalk (06854) *(G-6217)*
James Stenqvist 203 339-6418
18 Larson Dr North Haven (06473) *(G-5950)*
James Woznick 203 426-5585
2 Rocky Wood Dr Sandy Hook (06482) *(G-7317)*
James Wright Precision Pdts 860 928-7756
20 Mechanics St Putnam (06260) *(G-7049)*
Jamieson Laser LLC 860 482-3375
50 Thomaston Rd Litchfield (06759) *(G-3893)*
Jamilah Henna Creations 860 365-9542
29 Peach Farm Rd East Hampton (06424) *(G-2266)*
Jammar Mfg Co Inc 866 848-1113
26 Industrial Park Rd Niantic (06357) *(G-5811)*
Jan Manufacturing Inc 203 879-0580
14 Town Line Rd Ste 8 Wolcott (06716) *(G-10569)*
Jane Sterry 860 342-4567
216 Main St Portland (06480) *(G-6960)*
Janes Custom Canvas LLC 860 376-6778
201 Slater Ave Griswold (06351) *(G-3266)*
Janes Norman & Jacqueline Mach 860 423-1932
74 Machine Shop Hill Rd South Windham (06266) *(G-7689)*
Janik Sausage Co Inc 860 749-4661
136 Hazard Ave Enfield (06082) *(G-2653)*
Janitorial Commercial Gen Svc, Hamden *Also called Daily Impressions LLC (G-3439)*
Janus Motorsports LLC 860 857-6041
22 Park Pl Niantic (06357) *(G-5812)*
Jarden Corporation 203 845-5300
301 Merritt 7 Ste 5 Norwalk (06851) *(G-6218)*
Jarden Corporation 203 264-9717
288 Christian St Ste 11 Oxford (06478) *(G-6670)*
Jared Manufacturing Co Inc 203 846-1732
25 Perry Ave Norwalk (06850) *(G-6219)*
Jarvis Airfoil Inc 860 342-5000
528 Glastonbury Tpke Portland (06480) *(G-6961)*
Jarvis Precision Polishing 860 589-5822
190 Century Dr Bristol (06010) *(G-1052)*
Jarvis Products, Middletown *Also called Penco Corporation (G-4392)*
Jarvis Products Corporation (HQ) 860 347-7271
33 Anderson Rd Middletown (06457) *(G-4357)*
Jask Woodworking Inc 954 766-7105
209 Center St Bridgeport (06604) *(G-801)*
Jason Kurtzman Signs 203 847-4397
3 Devon Ave Norwalk (06850) *(G-6220)*
Jaw Precision Machining LLC 860 535-0615
44 Taugwonk Spur Rd # 1 Stonington (06378) *(G-8532)*
Jay Sons Screw Mch Pdts Inc 860 621-0141
197 Burritt St Milldale (06467) *(G-4684)*
Jay Tee Corp 203 732-5215
7 Pin Oak Ln Ansonia (06401) *(G-41)*
Jaye's Studio, Stamford *Also called Malabar Bay LLC (G-8294)*
Jaypro Sports LLC 860 447-3001
976 Hartford Tpke Ste B Waterford (06385) *(G-9656)*
Jaz Industries LLC 860 243-9357
25 Columbia Rd Windsor (06095) *(G-10399)*
JB Filtration LLC 860 333-7962
18 River Road Dr Essex (06426) *(G-2721)*
Jb Muze Enterprises 860 355-5949
180 Sunny Valley Rd Ste 9 New Milford (06776) *(G-5549)*
Jbl, Stamford *Also called Harman Consumer Inc (G-8225)*
JC Embroidery 860 742-8686
2508 Boston Tpke Coventry (06238) *(G-1657)*
JC Turn Mfg 203 366-6164
86 Willow St Bridgeport (06610) *(G-802)*
Jcascio Software Inc 860 535-2864
10 Juniper Ln Stonington (06378) *(G-8533)*
JCB Plastics LLC 203 315-8154
437 Sea Hill Rd North Branford (06471) *(G-5847)*
Jcm Industries 203 748-1806
2 Westwood Dr Danbury (06811) *(G-1858)*
Jdm-Greenwood LLC 203 358-4816
50 Glenbrook Rd Apt 5a Stamford (06902) *(G-8262)*
Jean Elton Studios LLC 917 287-0480
1305 Round Hill Rd Fairfield (06824) *(G-2800)*
Jean Marie Papery LLC 203 877-4299
61 Shelter Cove Rd Milford (06460) *(G-4559)*
Jeanann Stagnita 860 516-4655
44 Rita Dr Bristol (06010) *(G-1053)*
Jeanne Crscola Crscola Design, North Haven *Also called Criscola Design LLC (G-5932)*
Jedcontrol Corp 914 328-8593
4 Mill Plain Rd Danbury (06811) *(G-1859)*
Jeep, Fairfield *Also called Scap Motors Inc (G-2843)*
Jeff Manufacturing Co Inc 860 482-8845
679 Riverside Ave Torrington (06790) *(G-8937)*
Jeff Osborne Industries 203 794-0863
3 Sunset Rdg Danbury (06811) *(G-1860)*
Jeffrey Gold 203 281-5737
2440 Whitney Ave Ste 6 Hamden (06518) *(G-3467)*
Jeffrey Mingollello Backhoe Sr 203 735-5458
33 N Coe Ln Ansonia (06401) *(G-42)*
Jeffrey Morgan 860 583-2567
61 E Main St Ste 1 Bristol (06010) *(G-1054)*
Jem Manufacturing Inc 203 250-9404
20 N Plains Industrial Rd # 12 Wallingford (06492) *(G-9294)*
JEM Precision Grinding Inc 860 633-0152
35 Nutmeg Ln Glastonbury (06033) *(G-3052)*
Jem Special Tool Co LLC 860 276-9767
116 N Star Dr Southington (06489) *(G-7942)*
Jenkins Software Assoc LLC 203 483-8386
60 Averill Pl Branford (06405) *(G-612)*
Jenkins Sugar Group Inc 203 853-3000
16 S Main St Ste 202 Norwalk (06854) *(G-6221)*
Jennifers Tailor Shop 860 489-8968
539 Main St Torrington (06790) *(G-8938)*
Jennings Associates Inc 860 749-4281
541 Main St Somers (06071) *(G-7662)*
Jennings Yacht Services 860 625-1368
800 Flanders Rd Mystic (06355) *(G-4822)*
Jenray Products Inc 914 375-5596
4 Production Dr Brookfield (06804) *(G-1199)*
Jensen Dental, North Haven *Also called Jensen Industries Inc (G-5951)*
Jensen Industries Inc (PA) 203 285-1402
50 Stillman Rd North Haven (06473) *(G-5951)*
Jensen Machine Co 860 666-5438
721 Russell Rd Newington (06111) *(G-5667)*
Jerome Ridel 860 379-1774
15 Hampsted Rd West Granby (06090) *(G-9767)*
Jerry Freeman Pennywhistles 860 498-0014
500 Flanders Rd Coventry (06238) *(G-1658)*
Jerrys Printing & Graphics LLC 203 384-0015
1183 Broad St Bridgeport (06604) *(G-803)*
Jeskey LLC 203 772-6675
69 Dodge Ave North Haven (06473) *(G-5952)*
Jessica Howard Ceramics 646 295-4778
457 Wilson St Fairfield (06825) *(G-2801)*
JET Corporation 203 334-3317
146 Davis Ave Bridgeport (06605) *(G-804)*
Jet Process Corporation 203 985-6000
57 Dodge Ave North Haven (06473) *(G-5953)*
Jet Tool & Cutter Mfg Inc 860 621-5381
125 W Queen St Southington (06489) *(G-7943)*
Jetset Interiors LLC 860 292-7962
Bradley Intl Bldg 85-173 Windsor Locks (06096) *(G-10492)*
Jewelry Designs Inc 203 797-0389
86 Mill Plain Rd Danbury (06811) *(G-1861)*
Jewett City Tool and Die Co 860 376-0455
576 Beach Pond Rd Voluntown (06384) *(G-9189)*
Jewish Leader Newspaper 860 442-7395
28 Channing St New London (06320) *(G-5474)*
Jewish Ledger, Hartford *Also called NRG Connecticut LLC (G-3657)*
Jf Granite & Marble 860 355-4414
190 Danbury Rd New Milford (06776) *(G-5550)*
JFd Tube & Coil Products Inc 203 288-6941
7 Hamden Park Dr Hamden (06517) *(G-3468)*
Jfj Services LLC 860 395-1922
17 Forest Glen Rd Old Saybrook (06475) *(G-6548)*
Jfn Manufacturing LLC 860 621-0069
76 Berlin St Southington (06489) *(G-7944)*
Jfs Industries 203 592-0754
90 Walnut St Apt B Thomaston (06787) *(G-8794)*
Jgf Hardwood Floor 203 650-9192
40 Quarry St Apt C Bridgeport (06606) *(G-805)*
Jgs Properties LLC 203 378-7508
1805 Stratford Ave Stratford (06615) *(G-8636)*
Jhs Restoration Inc 860 757-3870
170 Strong Rd South Windsor (06074) *(G-7777)*
Jill Ghi 860 824-7123
532 Ashley Falls Rd Canaan (06018) *(G-1288)*
Jim Hanson Building, Mystic *Also called Formula Boat Works LLC (G-4817)*
Jim Kephart Woodturning 860 643-9431
85 Hilliard St Manchester (06042) *(G-4038)*
Jim Murray Wldg & Fabrication 860 889-7777
294b Cossaduck Hill Rd North Stonington (06359) *(G-6028)*
Jim N I LLC 860 646-5155
36 Oak Farms Rd Andover (06232) *(G-10)*
Jim Press Home Improvement 860 416-4494
47 Dougherty St Manchester (06040) *(G-4039)*
Jimbpa Enterprises LLC 203 755-9237
36 Wheeler St Waterbury (06704) *(G-9509)*
Jimmys Cleaners & Alterations 203 294-1006
200 Church St Ste 9 Wallingford (06492) *(G-9295)*

Jims Machine Shop Inc....860 928-5151
475 School St Putnam (06260) *(G-7050)*
Jims Welding Service LLC....203 744-2982
18 Finance Dr Danbury (06810) *(G-1862)*
JJ Greco Carting LLC....203 661-4947
40 Gregory Rd Cos Cob (06807) *(G-1635)*
Jj Portland News LLC....860 342-1432
264 Main St Middletown (06457) *(G-4358)*
Jjk Woodworking LLC....203 224-0139
230 5th St Bridgeport (06607) *(G-806)*
Jk Antennas Inc....845 228-8700
72 Grays Bridge Rd Ste D Brookfield (06804) *(G-1200)*
Jk Motorsports....203 255-9120
500 Grasmere Ave Fairfield (06824) *(G-2802)*
Jk Sign & Stamp LLC....860 729-3860
63 Capewell Ave Oakville (06779) *(G-6455)*
Jk Sign Company....203 544-7373
3 Devon Ave Norwalk (06850) *(G-6222)*
Jkb Daira Inc....203 642-4824
22 S Smith St Norwalk (06855) *(G-6223)*
JKL Specialty Foods Inc....203 541-3990
417 Shippan Ave Ste 2 Stamford (06902) *(G-8263)*
Jl Aerotech Inc....860 248-8628
475 Buckland Rd Ste 103 South Windsor (06074) *(G-7778)*
JL Lucas Machinery Co Inc....203 597-1300
429 Brookside Rd Waterbury (06708) *(G-9510)*
Jl Services, Stamford *Also called Isupportws Inc (G-8260)*
Jlc Industries....315 761-8051
362 2nd Ave West Haven (06516) *(G-9918)*
Jlp Machine Company....860 649-5730
115 Cidermill Rd Bolton (06043) *(G-512)*
JM Logging Forestry, Sherman *Also called James M Munch (G-7596)*
JM Shea LLC....203 431-4435
25 Hessian Dr Ridgefield (06877) *(G-7150)*
Jmf Group LLC....860 627-7003
13 Revay Rd East Windsor (06088) *(G-2500)*
Jmjp LLC....888 737-7577
18 Suzanne Ln Brooklyn (06234) *(G-1248)*
Jmk Tool Co....203 937-1229
184 Forest Rd West Haven (06516) *(G-9919)*
Jmp Software....203 984-4096
98 Spring Hill Ave Norwalk (06850) *(G-6224)*
JMS Graphics Inc....203 598-7555
850 Straits Tpke Ste 204 Middlebury (06762) *(G-4280)*
Jn Construction LLC....914 483-2998
341 Shippan Ave Apt 2 Stamford (06902) *(G-8264)*
Jnt Welding Services LLC....860 350-3957
32 New St New Milford (06776) *(G-5551)*
Jo Vek Tool and Die Mfg Co....203 755-1884
2121 Thomaston Ave Waterbury (06704) *(G-9511)*
Jobin Machine Inc....860 953-1631
37 Custer St West Hartford (06110) *(G-9824)*
Jobo Enterprizes LLC....203 367-7517
608 N Summerfield Ave Bridgeport (06610) *(G-807)*
Joe & Son Wldg Fabrication LLC....203 380-2072
7 Raven Ter Stratford (06614) *(G-8637)*
Joe Charron....860 423-2805
43 Pigeon Swamp Rd Lebanon (06249) *(G-3855)*
Joe Kaulback....860 742-0434
405 Route 6 Andover (06232) *(G-11)*
Joe Passarelli & Co....203 877-1434
67 Andrews Ave Milford (06460) *(G-4560)*
Joe Salafia Woodworking LLC....860 345-8657
152 Old Cart Rd Haddam (06438) *(G-3405)*
Joe Valentine Machine Company....203 356-9776
77 Southfield Ave Ste 2 Stamford (06902) *(G-8265)*
Joe's Paint Center, Branford *Also called J + J Branford Inc (G-611)*
Joesjuicecom LLC....203 824-1854
25 Elmbrook Dr Stamford (06906) *(G-8266)*
Johannes Sulek Jewelry....203 968-1729
13 Opper Rd Stamford (06903) *(G-8267)*
John C Green....203 878-3781
21 Roselle St Milford (06461) *(G-4561)*
John Canning & Co Ltd....203 272-9868
150 Commerce Ct Cheshire (06410) *(G-1401)*
John Cutter....860 749-0015
14 Olmsted Manor Dr Somers (06071) *(G-7663)*
John Deere Authorized Dealer, Essex *Also called Bell Power Systems LLC (G-2712)*
John Demarchi....860 649-9685
23 Potter St Willimantic (06226) *(G-10232)*
John Hychko....203 757-3458
299 Sheffield St Waterbury (06704) *(G-9512)*
John J Pawloski Lumber Inc....203 794-0737
4 Pleasantview Ter Bethel (06801) *(G-316)*
John June Custom Cabinetry LLC....203 334-1720
541 Fairfield Ave Bridgeport (06604) *(G-808)*
John L Prentis & Co Inc....203 634-1266
35 Pratt St Meriden (06450) *(G-4178)*
John M Kriskey Carpentry....203 531-0194
129 N Water St Greenwich (06830) *(G-3184)*
John Mezes & Sons Inc....203 255-6841
322 Dewey St Bridgeport (06605) *(G-809)*
John Oldham Studios Inc....860 529-3331
888 Wells Rd Wethersfield (06109) *(G-10202)*
John Olsen....203 624-5544
19 Meadow Rd Trumbull (06611) *(G-9037)*
John P Smith Co....203 488-7226
20 Baldwin Dr Branford (06405) *(G-613)*
John Pecora....860 677-9323
21 Hyde Rd Ste 4 Farmington (06032) *(G-2920)*
John Pecora Photography, Farmington *Also called John Pecora (G-2920)*
John Rawlinson John Leary....203 882-8484
316 Boston Post Rd Milford (06460) *(G-4562)*
John Samuel Group....860 806-5734
25 Fairview St Torrington (06790) *(G-8939)*
John Zink -Todd Combustn Group, Shelton *Also called John Zink Company LLC (G-7481)*
John Zink Company, Shelton *Also called Hamworthy Peabody Combustn Inc (G-7457)*
John Zink Company LLC....203 925-0380
2 Armstrong Rd Fl 3 Shelton (06484) *(G-7481)*
Johns Floor Sanding....860 423-3852
75 Mullen Hill Rd Windham (06280) *(G-10348)*
Johnson & Johnson....860 621-9111
201 W Queen St Southington (06489) *(G-7945)*
Johnson Contrls Authorized Dlr, New Haven *Also called F W Webb Company (G-5279)*
Johnson Controls Inc....860 887-7185
100 Winnenden Rd Norwich (06360) *(G-6419)*
Johnson Controls Inc....860 886-9021
39 Route 2 Ledyard (06339) *(G-3875)*
Johnson Controls Inc....860 571-3300
27 Inwood Rd Rocky Hill (06067) *(G-7253)*
Johnson Controls Inc....860 688-7151
21 Griffin Rd N Ste 4 Windsor (06095) *(G-10400)*
Johnson Controls Inc....678 297-4040
71 Deerfield Ln Meriden (06450) *(G-4179)*
Johnson Gage Company....860 242-5541
534 Cottage Grove Rd Bloomfield (06002) *(G-428)*
Johnson Goodyer II Inc....203 777-3424
199 Terminal Ln New Haven (06519) *(G-5303)*
Johnson Marine, East Haddam *Also called C Sherman Johnson Company (G-2237)*
Johnson Marine....860 536-8026
16 Fort Rachel Pl Mystic (06355) *(G-4823)*
Johnson Meadows LLC....860 642-0618
779 Exeter Rd Lebanon (06249) *(G-3856)*
Johnson Millwork Inc....860 267-4693
222 Quarry Hill Rd East Hampton (06424) *(G-2267)*
Johnson-Goodyear, New Haven *Also called Johnson Goodyer II Inc (G-5303)*
Johnstone Company Inc....203 239-5834
222 Sackett Point Rd North Haven (06473) *(G-5954)*
Joining Technologies Inc....860 653-0111
17 Connecticut South Dr B East Granby (06026) *(G-2209)*
Jolen Cream Bleach Corp....203 259-8779
25 Walls Dr Fairfield (06824) *(G-2803)*
Jolie Montre, Southbury *Also called Real Women International LLC (G-7874)*
Jolley Precast Inc....860 774-9066
463 Putnam Rd Danielson (06239) *(G-1995)*
Joma Incorporated....203 759-0848
185 Interstate Ln Waterbury (06705) *(G-9513)*
Jon Minard Lighting....860 228-9069
283 Hope Valley Rd Amston (06231) *(G-3)*
Jonal Laboratories Inc....203 634-4444
456 Center St Meriden (06450) *(G-4180)*
Jonal Labs Logistics LLC....203 634-4444
468 Center St Meriden (06450) *(G-4181)*
Jonas Lieponis....203 458-6912
461 Vineyard Point Rd Guilford (06437) *(G-3364)*
Jonathan David Humphreys....415 847-3032
78 Simsbury Manor Dr Weatogue (06089) *(G-9756)*
Jones Fire Sprinkler Co LLC....860 464-7284
1360 Baldwin Hill Rd Gales Ferry (06335) *(G-2984)*
Jones Metal Products Co Inc....860 289-8023
22 Schwier Rd Ste 1 South Windsor (06074) *(G-7779)*
Jonmandy Corporation....860 482-2354
151 Ella Grasso Ave Ste 3 Torrington (06790) *(G-8940)*
Jor Services LLC....203 594-7774
4 Parting Brook Rd New Canaan (06840) *(G-5112)*
Jordan Saw Mill L L C....860 774-0247
201 Saw Mill Hill Rd Sterling (06377) *(G-8510)*
Jordan Sawmill, Sterling *Also called Jordan Saw Mill L L C (G-8510)*
Jordan Woodworks....203 512-3581
24 Wolfpits Rd Bethel (06801) *(G-317)*
Jornik Man Corp....203 969-0500
652 Glenbrook Rd Ste 2 Stamford (06906) *(G-8268)*
Jornik Screen Printing....203 969-0500
652 Glenbrook Rd 8-201 Stamford (06906) *(G-8269)*
Joseph A Cnte Mfg Jewelers Inc....203 248-9853
2582 Whitney Ave Hamden (06518) *(G-3469)*
Joseph Cohn Son Tile Trazo LLC....203 772-2420
50 Devine St North Haven (06473) *(G-5955)*
Joseph Garrity....860 693-2134
5 Old Albany Tpke Canton (06019) *(G-1316)*
Joseph Hannoush Family Inc....860 561-4651
500 Westfarms Mall Farmington (06032) *(G-2921)*
Joseph J McFadden Jr....860 354-6794
87 Danbury Rd New Milford (06776) *(G-5552)*

ALPHABETIC

Joseph L Gentile Entps LLC 203 421-5144
28 Lenore Dr Madison (06443) **(G-3932)**
Joseph Malavenda 203 746-4160
15 Mill Pond Rd New Fairfield (06812) **(G-5170)**
Joseph Manufacturing Co 203 431-6400
18 Thunder Hill Ln Ridgefield (06877) **(G-7151)**
Joseph Merritt & Company Inc (PA) 860 296-2500
650 Franklin Ave Ste 3 Hartford (06114) **(G-3620)**
Joseph Merritt & Company Inc 203 743-6734
4c Chrstpher Columbus Ave Danbury (06810) **(G-1863)**
Joseph Organek 860 342-1906
151 Freestone Ave Portland (06480) **(G-6962)**
Joseph Rembock 860 738-3981
7 Old County Rd Pleasant Valley (06063) **(G-6923)**
Joshua Friedman & Co LLC 860 439-1637
49 Jay St New London (06320) **(G-5475)**
Joshua LLC (PA) 203 624-0080
90 Hamilton St New Haven (06511) **(G-5304)**
Journal Inquirer, Manchester *Also called Green Manor Corporation* **(G-4023)**
Journal Inquirer, Manchester *Also called Journal Publishing Company Inc* **(G-4040)**
Journal of Experimntal Scndary 203 630-6508
234 Debbie Dr Meriden (06451) **(G-4182)**
Journal Publishing Company Inc 860 646-0500
306 Progress Dr Manchester (06042) **(G-4040)**
Journal Register East 203 401-4004
100 Gando Dr New Haven (06513) **(G-5305)**
Joval Machine Co Inc 203 284-0082
515 Main St Yalesville (06492) **(G-10694)**
Jovan Machine Co Inc 203 879-2855
1133 Wolcott Rd Ste A Wolcott (06716) **(G-10570)**
Jovek Tool and Die 860 261-5020
474 Birch St Bristol (06010) **(G-1055)**
Jovian Technologies 860 896-1539
115 West Rd Apt 206 Ellington (06029) **(G-2593)**
Jovil Universal LLC 203 792-6700
10 Precision Rd Danbury (06810) **(G-1864)**
Joy Carole Creations Inc 203 794-1401
42 Mill Plain Rd Danbury (06811) **(G-1865)**
Joy Food Company 917 549-6240
138 Goodwives River Rd Darien (06820) **(G-2029)**
Joyce Printers Inc 203 389-4452
16 Research Dr Woodbridge (06525) **(G-10603)**
Jozef Custom Ironworks Inc 203 384-6363
250 Smith St Bridgeport (06607) **(G-810)**
Jpg Consulting Inc 203 247-2730
65 Heather Ln Wilton (06897) **(G-10305)**
Jpo Absorbents, Trumbull *Also called Jpo Solutions Inc* **(G-9038)**
Jpo Solutions Inc 203 502-8609
30 Nutmeg Dr Ste F Trumbull (06611) **(G-9038)**
JPsexton LLC 860 748-2048
460 Hayden Station Rd Windsor (06095) **(G-10401)**
Jra Industries LLC 475 343-0262
159 Springdale Ave 1 Meriden (06451) **(G-4183)**
JRC Publishing LLC 203 942-2726
20 Mckeon Pl Ridgefield (06877) **(G-7152)**
JS Industries 860 928-0786
526 Quaddick Rd Thompson (06277) **(G-8835)**
JS McCarthy Co Inc 203 355-7600
652 Glenbrook Rd 4-101 Stamford (06906) **(G-8270)**
Jsan Publishing LLC 203 210-5495
14 Woodway Ln Wilton (06897) **(G-10306)**
Jsr Micro Inc 203 426-7794
3 Taunton Lake Dr Newtown (06470) **(G-5751)**
Juan Gallegos 203 744-0575
29 Benson Dr Danbury (06810) **(G-1866)**
Juanos Glass LLC 203 449-5378
56 Davis Ave Bridgeport (06605) **(G-811)**
Judge Tool & Gage Inc 800 214-5990
555 Lordship Blvd Unit A Stratford (06615) **(G-8638)**
Judge Tool Sales Company, Stratford *Also called Judge Tool & Gage Inc* **(G-8638)**
Judith Bennett (PA) 203 255-6363
27 Noyes Rd Fairfield (06824) **(G-2804)**
Judith Bennett 203 729-6548
1236 New Haven Rd Naugatuck (06770) **(G-4895)**
Judith E Goldstein Company 860 644-4646
66 Windshire Dr South Windsor (06074) **(G-7780)**
Judith Jackson Inc 203 698-3011
1535 E Putnam Ave Apt 406 Old Greenwich (06870) **(G-6478)**
Judith Lynn Charters LLC 203 246-6662
29 Starlight Dr Norwalk (06851) **(G-6225)**
Judy Low 860 491-9101
192 5 1/2 Mile Rd Goshen (06756) **(G-3099)**
Juice Press LLC 212 777-0034
360 Greenwich Ave Greenwich (06830) **(G-3185)**
Juice Publishing LLC 203 226-5715
80 Compo Rd N Westport (06880) **(G-10106)**
Julie Wakely Enterprises LLC 860 376-4515
31 Bushnell Rd Jewett City (06351) **(G-3797)**
Jump 4 Tees 860 228-4813
33 Scarboro Rd Hebron (06248) **(G-3752)**
Jump4fun USA LLC 203 735-3702
96 Garden St Ansonia (06401) **(G-43)**
Jungle Brew LLC 860 335-4941
125 Duncaster Rd Bloomfield (06002) **(G-429)**
Jupiter Communications LLC 475 238-7082
755 1st Ave West Haven (06516) **(G-9920)**
Jurman Metrics Inc 203 261-9388
555 Hammertown Rd Monroe (06468) **(G-4723)**
Juskhas Wp Co 860 455-0502
632 Brook Rd Hampton (06247) **(G-3536)**
Just Breakfast & Things 860 376-4040
15 River Rd Lisbon (06351) **(G-3881)**
Just Call Jason LLC 203 934-3127
44 Tyler St West Haven (06516) **(G-9921)**
Just Neon Company 860 881-7446
37 Oxbow Dr Vernon (06066) **(G-9142)**
JV Precision Machine Co 203 888-0748
71 Cogwheel Ln Seymour (06483) **(G-7352)**
JV Sheet Metal 203 540-0383
58 East Ave Stamford (06902) **(G-8271)**
Jvcart LLC 917 497-8791
10 Birch Rd Darien (06820) **(G-2030)**
JW Gallas Rod Co 203 790-4188
7 Mirijo Rd Danbury (06811) **(G-1867)**
Jwc Steel Co LLC 860 296-5517
540 Ledyard St Hartford (06114) **(G-3621)**
Jyl LLP 860 767-7733
12 Plains Rd Essex (06426) **(G-2722)**
K & D Business Ventures LLC 860 237-1458
39 1/2 Wedgewood Dr Jewett City (06351) **(G-3798)**
K & D Precision Manufacturing 203 931-9550
25 High St West Haven (06516) **(G-9922)**
K & E Auto Machine L L C 203 723-7189
628 Prospect St Naugatuck (06770) **(G-4896)**
K & G Corp 860 643-1133
219 Adams St Manchester (06042) **(G-4041)**
K & G Graphics 203 481-4884
540 E Main St Ste 7 Branford (06405) **(G-614)**
K & K Black Oxide LLC 860 223-1805
50 Peter Ct New Britain (06051) **(G-5007)**
K & K Precision Manufacturing 860 828-7681
54 Clark Dr Ste F East Berlin (06023) **(G-2171)**
K & L Welding LLC 860 970-2390
87 Campfield Ave Hartford (06114) **(G-3622)**
K A F Manufacturing Co Inc 203 324-3012
14 Fahey St Stamford (06907) **(G-8272)**
K A Switch, Milford *Also called Kilo Ampere Switch Corporation* **(G-4565)**
K and R Precision Grinding 860 505-8030
39 John St New Britain (06051) **(G-5008)**
K C K Publishing 203 924-1147
127 Toas St Shelton (06484) **(G-7482)**
K Chef Inc 646 778-8396
108 Edwin Ave Waterbury (06708) **(G-9514)**
K F Brick Plant, South Windsor *Also called Redland Brick Inc* **(G-7818)**
K F Machining 860 292-6466
36 Newberry Rd East Windsor (06088) **(G-2501)**
K H Cornell International Inc 203 392-3660
59 Amity Rd New Haven (06515) **(G-5306)**
K J Welding 860 345-8743
116 Filley Rd Haddam (06438) **(G-3406)**
K L & P Welding 860 986-2518
8 Thompson Rd East Windsor (06088) **(G-2502)**
K L S Custom Wood Working 203 520-5193
88 Twin Brook Ter Monroe (06468) **(G-4724)**
K Smith Custom Woodworking LLC 203 981-4268
33 Fitch Ln New Canaan (06840) **(G-5113)**
K T I, East Windsor *Also called Kin-Therm Inc* **(G-2504)**
K T I Kin Therm, East Windsor *Also called KTI Inc* **(G-2507)**
K T I Turbo-Tech Inc 860 623-2511
3 Thompson Rd East Windsor (06088) **(G-2503)**
K W Griffen Company 203 846-1923
100 Pearl St Norwalk (06850) **(G-6226)**
K&D Print LLC 203 483-1199
33 Beechwood Rd Branford (06405) **(G-615)**
K&L Enterprises 860 645-7257
25 Raymond Rd Manchester (06040) **(G-4042)**
K&M Woodworking LLC 203 406-0694
25 E Walnut St Stamford (06902) **(G-8273)**
K&P Weaver LLC 203 795-9024
527 Carriage Dr Orange (06477) **(G-6605)**
K-Tec LLC 860 283-8875
33 River St Ste 2 Thomaston (06787) **(G-8795)**
K-Tech International 860 489-9399
56 Ella Grasso Ave Torrington (06790) **(G-8941)**
K2 Manufacturing Inc 413 636-6170
1257 John Fitch Blvd South Windsor (06074) **(G-7781)**
K29 203 961-9662
149 Emery Dr E Stamford (06902) **(G-8274)**
K2steam 860 251-9824
5 Delbon Ln Avon (06001) **(G-86)**
K4 Industries LLC 203 459-4992
15 Adirondack Trl Easton (06612) **(G-2558)**
Kacerguis Farms Inc 203 405-1202
78 Crane Hollow Rd Bethlehem (06751) **(G-373)**

Kadomar Krafts 860 346-2000
398 Wadsworth St Middletown (06457) *(G-4359)*
Kafa Group LLC 475 275-0090
800 Union Ave Bridgeport (06607) *(G-812)*
Kage Co, Manchester Also called Kage Poly Products LLC *(G-4043)*
Kage Poly Products LLC 860 646-8228
96 Elm St Manchester (06040) *(G-4043)*
Kahn and Company Incorporated 860 529-8643
885 Wells Rd Wethersfield (06109) *(G-10203)*
Kahn Industries Inc 860 529-8643
885 Wells Rd Wethersfield (06109) *(G-10204)*
Kahn Instruments Incorporated 860 529-8643
885 Wells Rd Wethersfield (06109) *(G-10205)*
Kaibry Screen Printing 860 774-0234
17 Colleen St Danielson (06239) *(G-1996)*
Kallai Designs 860 653-6786
1 Granby Farms Rd Granby (06035) *(G-3109)*
Kaman Aerospace Corporation (HQ) 860 242-4461
1332 Blue Hills Ave Bloomfield (06002) *(G-430)*
Kaman Aerospace Corporation 860 242-4461
30 Old Windsor Rd Bloomfield (06002) *(G-431)*
Kaman Aerospace Corporation 860 242-4461
30 Old Windsor Rd Bloomfield (06002) *(G-432)*
Kaman Aerospace Corporation 860 632-1000
217 Smith St Middletown (06457) *(G-4360)*
Kaman Aerospace Group Inc (HQ) 860 243-7100
1332 Blue Hills Ave Bloomfield (06002) *(G-433)*
Kaman Automation, Inc., Bloomfield Also called Ruby Automation LLC *(G-479)*
Kaman Corporation (PA) 860 243-7100
1332 Blue Hills Ave Bloomfield (06002) *(G-434)*
Kaman Corporation 860 632-1000
217 Smith St Middletown (06457) *(G-4361)*
Kaman Fluid Power, LLC, Bloomfield Also called Ruby Fluid Power LLC *(G-480)*
Kaman Precision Products Inc 860 632-1000
217 Smith St Middletown (06457) *(G-4362)*
Kamatics Corporation (HQ) 860 243-9704
1330 Blue Hills Ave Bloomfield (06002) *(G-435)*
Kamatics Corporation 860 243-7230
1331 Blue Hills Ave Bloomfield (06002) *(G-436)*
Kamelot Kreations LLC 860 564-7399
50 Hungry Hill Rd Sterling (06377) *(G-8511)*
Kammetal Inc (PA) 718 722-9991
300 Great Hill Rd Naugatuck (06770) *(G-4897)*
Kan Pak LLC 203 933-6731
425 Main St N Southbury (06488) *(G-7864)*
Kando Apps LLC 203 722-4359
9 Country Club Rd Norwalk (06851) *(G-6227)*
Kania Darius 860 667-4400
75 Rockwell Rd Newington (06111) *(G-5668)*
Kanine Knits 203 272-8548
877 Marion Rd Cheshire (06410) *(G-1402)*
Kapco Valtec, Centerbrook Also called Kirkhill Aircraft Parts Co *(G-1330)*
Kapcom LLC 203 891-5112
86 John St East Haven (06513) *(G-2436)*
Kaplan Tarps & Cargo Controls, Manchester Also called 3333 LLC *(G-3971)*
Kappa Sails LLC 860 399-8899
25 Whippoorwill Dr Gales Ferry (06335) *(G-2985)*
Kapstone Paper and Packg Corp 860 928-2211
25 Intervale St Putnam (06260) *(G-7051)*
Karas Engineering Co Inc 860 355-3153
20 Old Route 7 Plz New Milford (06776) *(G-5553)*
Karavas Fashions Ltd 203 866-4000
17 Wall St Norwalk (06850) *(G-6228)*
Karen Callan Designs Inc 203 762-9914
30 Field Point Dr Greenwich (06830) *(G-3186)*
Karger S Publishers Inc 860 675-7834
26 W Avon Rd Unionville (06085) *(G-9116)*
Kariba Woodworks 203 246-8917
25 Riverside Rd Sandy Hook (06482) *(G-7318)*
Karl Stetson Associates LLC 860 742-8414
2060 South St Coventry (06238) *(G-1659)*
Karpel N Studio, New Haven Also called N Karpel Studio LLC *(G-5338)*
Kasanof Bread, North Grosvenordale Also called Superior Bakery Inc *(G-5892)*
Kasheta Power Equipment 860 528-8421
1275 John Fitch Blvd South Windsor (06074) *(G-7782)*
Kasper, Clinton Also called Nine West Holdings Inc *(G-1516)*
Kasson Jewelers of Southport 203 319-0021
393 Pequot Ave Southport (06890) *(G-8005)*
Kasten Inc 702 860-2407
304 Bishop Ave Bridgeport (06610) *(G-813)*
Kat Art Inc 860 350-8016
458 Danbury Rd Ste B17 New Milford (06776) *(G-5554)*
Katahdin Printing 860 461-7037
23 Old Windsor Rd Ste D Bloomfield (06002) *(G-437)*
Katart Graphics, New Milford Also called Kat Art Inc *(G-5554)*
Kathies Kitchen LLC 203 407-0546
50 Devine St North Haven (06473) *(G-5956)*
Kathleen Parker OBeirne 860 536-7179
32 New London Rd Mystic (06355) *(G-4824)*
Kathy Pooler 860 889-2893
5 Melody Ln Norwich (06360) *(G-6420)*

Katona Bakery LLC 203 337-5349
1189 Post Rd Ste 3b Fairfield (06824) *(G-2805)*
Katy Industries Inc 314 656-4321
765 Straits Tpke Bldg 2 Middlebury (06762) *(G-4281)*
Kaufman Enterprises Inc 203 777-2396
627 Chapel St 629 New Haven (06511) *(G-5307)*
Kaya Software LLC 203 267-7817
19 Greenwood Dr Southbury (06488) *(G-7865)*
Kaycandles 860 794-3763
82 Judd Ave New Britain (06051) *(G-5009)*
KB Custom Stair Builders Inc 203 234-0836
101 Powdered Metal Rd # 1 North Haven (06473) *(G-5957)*
KB Services 203 243-3594
1 Bostwick Ave Bridgeport (06605) *(G-814)*
Kbc Electronics Inc 203 298-9654
273 Pepes Farm Rd Milford (06460) *(G-4563)*
Kbj Manufacturing Inc 860 585-7257
137 Stafford Ave Bristol (06010) *(G-1056)*
Kc Crafts LLC 860 426-9797
384 Old Turnpike Rd Plantsville (06479) *(G-6898)*
Kc Publishing 203 318-8544
67 Flintlock Rd Madison (06443) *(G-3933)*
Kc Servicing LLC 860 822-9766
461 Route 164 Preston (06365) *(G-6985)*
Kco Numet Inc (PA) 203 375-4995
235 Edison Rd Orange (06477) *(G-6606)*
Kdc Mobile Mix, Andover Also called Joe Kaulback *(G-11)*
Kde Instrumentation 860 657-2744
20 Coltsfoot Cir Glastonbury (06033) *(G-3053)*
Kdg, Seymour Also called Kinetic Development Group LLC *(G-7353)*
Keberg LLC 860 255-8135
45 Tyler Farms Rd Plainville (06062) *(G-6829)*
Kedo Koncepts LLC 860 315-7392
310 W Thompson Rd Thompson (06277) *(G-8836)*
Keegan Construction, North Haven Also called Thomas Keegan & Sons Inc *(G-5999)*
Keeling Company Inc 860 349-0916
107 Shore Dr Old Lyme (06371) *(G-6514)*
Keeling's, Old Lyme Also called Keeling Company Inc *(G-6514)*
Keelings 860 399-4545
1566 Boston Post Rd Westbrook (06498) *(G-9999)*
Keeper Press LLC 860 810-9626
218 Conestoga Way Glastonbury (06033) *(G-3054)*
Keepsake Embroidery 203 503-1725
46 Sunset Dr Orange (06477) *(G-6607)*
Kehl Technology & Prfmce LLC 203 484-4808
1831 Middletown Ave L6 Northford (06472) *(G-6049)*
Keiterbennett Publishers LLC 860 308-2666
118 Oxford Dr East Hartford (06118) *(G-2342)*
Keith Reed Industries LLC 860 677-7739
22 Stonegate Unionville (06085) *(G-9117)*
Kelby Stucco LLC 203 527-9501
5 Barry Ln Prospect (06712) *(G-7005)*
Kell-Strom Tool Co Inc (PA) 860 529-6851
214 Church St Wethersfield (06109) *(G-10206)*
Kell-Strom Tool Intl Inc 860 529-6851
214 Church St Wethersfield (06109) *(G-10207)*
Kelleher Marketing, East Windsor Also called Homeland Fundraising *(G-2498)*
Keller Products Inc 203 794-0075
26 Old Hawleyville Rd Bethel (06801) *(G-318)*
Kellog Splitters Inc 860 738-4986
224 Bruning Rd New Hartford (06057) *(G-5200)*
Kellogg Company 860 665-9920
52 Hollow Tree Ln Newington (06111) *(G-5669)*
Kellogg Hardwoods Inc 203 797-1992
11 Diamond Ave Bethel (06801) *(G-319)*
Kelly Industries LLC 860 388-5666
2 Center Rd Old Saybrook (06475) *(G-6549)*
Kelsey Boat Yard 203 488-9567
1 Paynes Pt Branford (06405) *(G-616)*
Kelsey Mfg Division, East Berlin Also called Finishers Technology Corp *(G-2168)*
Kelyniam Global Inc 800 280-8192
97 River Rd Ste A Collinsville (06019) *(G-1595)*
Kemby Manufacturing 860 582-2850
56 E Orchard St Terryville (06786) *(G-8761)*
Kemper Manufacturing Corp 203 934-1600
5 Clinton Pl West Haven (06516) *(G-9923)*
Ken Hastedt 203 268-6563
33 W Maiden Ln Monroe (06468) *(G-4725)*
Ken-Labs, Higganum Also called Kenyon Laboratories LLC *(G-3766)*
Kendall Svengalis 860 535-0362
3 Rockland Rd Guilford (06437) *(G-3365)*
Kennedy Gustafson and Cole Inc 860 828-2594
100 White Oak Dr Berlin (06037) *(G-191)*
Kenneth Allevo 860 745-0740
18 Hudson St Enfield (06082) *(G-2654)*
Kenneth Finn 914 764-4938
422 W Lyon Farm Dr Greenwich (06831) *(G-3187)*
Kenneth Industrial Pdts Inc 860 349-7454
35 Winsome Rd Durham (06422) *(G-2150)*
Kenneth Leroux 860 769-9800
105 Filley St Unit C Bloomfield (06002) *(G-438)*

Kenneth Lynch & Sons Inc 203 762-8363
114 Willenbrock Rd Oxford (06478) *(G-6671)*
Kenneth M Champlin & Assoc Inc 203 562-8400
85 Willow St Ste 6 New Haven (06511) *(G-5308)*
Kenneth R Carson 860 247-2707
34 Cole St Manchester (06042) *(G-4044)*
Kenny Kalipershad 917 345-5038
12 Wessels Pl Greenwich (06830) *(G-3188)*
Keno Graphic Services Inc 203 925-7722
1 Parrott Dr Ste 100 Shelton (06484) *(G-7483)*
Kensco Inc (PA) 203 734-8827
41 Clifton Ave Ansonia (06401) *(G-44)*
Kensington Glass and Frmng Co 860 828-9428
124 Woodlawn Rd Berlin (06037) *(G-192)*
Kensington Welding & Trlr Co 860 828-3564
1114 Farmington Ave Kensington (06037) *(G-3811)*
Kensington Woodworking Co 860 828-4972
430 New Britain Rd Kensington (06037) *(G-3812)*
Kent Billings LLC 860 659-1104
320 Spring Street Ext Glastonbury (06033) *(G-3055)*
Kent Falls Brewing Company 860 398-9645
33 Camps Rd Kent (06757) *(G-3823)*
Kent Scientific Corporation 860 626-1172
1116 Litchfield St Torrington (06790) *(G-8942)*
Kenyon International Inc 860 664-4906
11 Heritage Park Rd Clinton (06413) *(G-1510)*
Kenyon International Inc 860 664-4906
8 Heritage Park Rd Clinton (06413) *(G-1511)*
Kenyon Laboratories LLC 860 345-2097
12 Scovil Rd Higganum (06441) *(G-3766)*
Kenyon Woodworking 860 432-4641
85 Hilliard St Manchester (06042) *(G-4045)*
Kenzinc LLC 203 307-5369
7 Acadia Ln Unit 5303 Shelton (06484) *(G-7484)*
Keola Sandals, Tolland *Also called Inocraft Products Inc* *(G-8866)*
Kerigans Fuel Inc 203 334-3646
258 Dekalb Ave Bridgeport (06607) *(G-815)*
Kerite, Seymour *Also called Marmon Utility LLC* *(G-7354)*
Kerry D Hogan 203 213-4624
7 Morgan Dr Wallingford (06492) *(G-9296)*
Kerry R Wood 203 221-7780
2 Hideaway Ln Westport (06880) *(G-10107)*
Kevco 860 747-4135
63 Bartlett St Plainville (06062) *(G-6830)*
Kevin Field 203 878-6339
321 Rock Ln Milford (06460) *(G-4564)*
Kevin G Barry 203 263-4948
47 Main St S Woodbury (06798) *(G-10640)*
Keyes On Kites Tattoo Gallery 203 387-5397
869 Whalley Ave Fl 1 New Haven (06515) *(G-5309)*
Keypoint Forensics LLC 860 877-6586
505 N Main St 1440 Naugatuck (06770) *(G-4898)*
Keys-Plus, Shelton *Also called Michael J Macisco* *(G-7499)*
Keystone Paper & Box Co Inc 860 291-0027
31 Edwin Rd South Windsor (06074) *(G-7783)*
Keystone Rv Company 203 367-9847
2660 North Ave Bridgeport (06604) *(G-816)*
Keytag1 ....203 873-0749
955 Conn Ave Ste 1306 Bridgeport (06607) *(G-817)*
Keyway Inc 860 571-9181
3 Wells Rd Wethersfield (06109) *(G-10208)*
Kgc, Berlin *Also called Kennedy Gustafson and Cole Inc* *(G-191)*
Kh Industries LLC 860 875-4779
30 White Birch Dr Tolland (06084) *(G-8867)*
Ki Inc 203 641-5492
342 Cedarwood Dr Orange (06477) *(G-6608)*
Kiagraphics 203 261-4328
189 Josies Ring Rd Monroe (06468) *(G-4726)*
Kieffer Associates Inc 203 323-3437
86 Wallacks Dr Stamford (06902) *(G-8275)*
Kielo America Inc 203 431-3999
163 Branchville Rd Ridgefield (06877) *(G-7153)*
Kiera Publishing Inc 203 838-5485
161 East Ave Norwalk (06851) *(G-6229)*
Kilcourse Specialty Products 860 210-2075
46 Old State Rd Ste 3 New Milford (06776) *(G-5555)*
Kill Shot Precision LLC 860 681-3162
43 Elm St Bristol (06010) *(G-1057)*
Killingly Asphalt Products, Dayville *Also called All States Asphalt Inc* *(G-2053)*
Kilo Ampere Switch Corporation 203 877-5994
230 Woodmont Rd Ste 27 Milford (06460) *(G-4565)*
Kim Machine, Kensington *Also called Michele Pavisic* *(G-3814)*
Kim's Nail Salon, Stratford *Also called Kims Nail Corporation* *(G-8640)*
Kimberly Bon Publishing LLC 203 258-9829
655 Booth Hill Rd Trumbull (06611) *(G-9039)*
Kimberly-Clark Corporation 860 210-1602
58 Pickett District Rd New Milford (06776) *(G-5556)*
Kimberly-Clark Corporation 973 986-8454
137 Ryegate Ter Stratford (06615) *(G-8639)*
Kimchuk Incorporated (PA) 203 790-7800
1 Corporate Dr Ste 1 # 1 Danbury (06810) *(G-1868)*
Kimchuk Incorporated 203 798-0799
4 Finance Dr Danbury (06810) *(G-1869)*
Kimlar Industries LLC 203 220-2200
53 Flint St Trumbull (06611) *(G-9040)*
Kims Nail Corporation 203 380-8608
7365 Main St Ste 11 Stratford (06614) *(G-8640)*
Kin-Therm Inc 860 623-2511
3 Thompson Rd East Windsor (06088) *(G-2504)*
Kinamor Incorporated 203 269-0380
63 N Plains Industrial Rd Wallingford (06492) *(G-9297)*
Kinamor Plastics, Wallingford *Also called Kinamor Incorporated* *(G-9297)*
Kinderma LLC 860 796-5503
55 Village Pl Glastonbury (06033) *(G-3056)*
Kinetic Development Group LLC 203 888-4321
71 Cogwheel Ln Seymour (06483) *(G-7353)*
Kinetic Innvtive Sting Sys LLC 203 488-1758
26 N Main St Ofc Bldg Branford (06405) *(G-617)*
Kinetic Instruments Inc 203 743-0080
17 Berkshire Blvd Bethel (06801) *(G-320)*
Kinetic Tool Co Inc 860 627-5882
5 Craftsman Rd Ste 7 East Windsor (06088) *(G-2505)*
King Koil Northeast, East Windsor *Also called Blue Bell Mattress Company LLC* *(G-2484)*
King of Covers Inc (PA) 860 379-2427
154 Torrington Rd Winsted (06098) *(G-10526)*
Kingsland Co 860 542-6981
7 Colebrook Rd Norfolk (06058) *(G-5824)*
Kingsley Printing Assoc LLC 203 345-6046
4883 Main St Stratford (06614) *(G-8641)*
Kingsnake Publishing LLC 860 865-0307
149 Buckeye Rd Groton (06340) *(G-3292)*
Kingswood Kitchens Co Inc 203 792-8700
70 Beaver St Danbury (06810) *(G-1870)*
Kip Inc 860 677-0272
72 Spring Ln Farmington (06032) *(G-2922)*
Kirchoff Wohlberg Inc 212 644-2020
897 Boston Post Rd Madison (06443) *(G-3934)*
Kirkhill Aircraft Parts Co 860 581-5701
1 Industrial Park Rd Centerbrook (06409) *(G-1330)*
Kiro Bespoke LLC 203 981-4945
23 Roberts St Middletown (06457) *(G-4363)*
Kiss, Branford *Also called Kinetic Innvtive Sting Sys LLC* *(G-617)*
Kiss-U Corps LLC 203 226-7730
14 Lilac Ln Weston (06883) *(G-10031)*
Kiss-U Tissue, Weston *Also called Kiss-U Corps LLC* *(G-10031)*
Kit Architectural Designs LLC 203 378-6911
825 Barnum Avenue Cutoff Stratford (06614) *(G-8642)*
Kitchen Brains, Stratford *Also called (fast) International Inc* *(G-8562)*
Kitchen Cab Resurfacing LLC 203 334-2857
136 Merriam St Bridgeport (06604) *(G-818)*
Kitchen Kraftsmen 860 616-1240
77 Pierson Ln Ste A Windsor (06095) *(G-10402)*
Kitchen Living LLC 860 819-5847
21 Main St East Hampton (06424) *(G-2268)*
Kitchenmax LLC 203 330-5041
198 Knowlton St Bridgeport (06608) *(G-819)*
Kitchens By Deane Inc 203 327-7008
1267 E Main St Stamford (06902) *(G-8276)*
Kite Business Solutions LLC 860 302-0682
95 Great Pine Path Plantsville (06479) *(G-6899)*
Kitty Guerrilla Films 203 259-8395
25 Brett Rd Fairfield (06824) *(G-2806)*
Kiwanis Fndtion Middletown Inc 860 638-8135
340 Chamberlain Hill Rd Middletown (06457) *(G-4364)*
Kiwi Publishing Inc 203 389-6220
20 Manville Rd Woodbridge (06525) *(G-10604)*
Kk Manufacturing LLC 860 644-5330
27 Stonehenge Rd South Windsor (06074) *(G-7784)*
KLA Kemp LLC 860 464-6746
34 Osprey Dr Gales Ferry (06335) *(G-2986)*
Klean Air Supplies Inc 860 583-1589
32 Valley St Bristol (06010) *(G-1058)*
Kline Chemistry Laboratory, New Haven *Also called Yale University* *(G-5447)*
Kll Aerospace LLC 860 806-8858
116 Breakneck Hill Rd Middlebury (06762) *(G-4282)*
Klx Aerospace Solutions, Stratford *Also called B/E Aerospace Inc* *(G-8576)*
Kms Candle Company LLC 203 758-3821
10 Birchwood Ter Prospect (06712) *(G-7006)*
Knapp Container Inc 203 888-0511
17 Old Turnpike Rd Beacon Falls (06403) *(G-137)*
Knb Design LLC 203 777-6661
91 Shelton Ave New Haven (06511) *(G-5310)*
Knight Inc 203 754-6502
47 Stevens St Waterbury (06704) *(G-9515)*
Knight Light Neon, Meriden *Also called Knight Lite Neon* *(G-4184)*
Knight Lite Neon 203 238-4423
763 Hanover Rd Meriden (06451) *(G-4184)*
Knight Manufacturing, Waterbury *Also called Knight Inc* *(G-9515)*
Knits For Baby, Harwinton *Also called Baby Knits and More* *(G-3721)*
Knoll Inc 860 395-2093
5 Connolly Dr Old Saybrook (06475) *(G-6550)*
Knox Enterprises Inc (PA) 203 226-6408
830 Post Rd E Ste 205 Westport (06880) *(G-10108)*

Knox Industries Inc 203 226-6408
830 Post Rd E Ste 205 Westport (06880) ***(G-10109)***
Kobuta Choppers LLC 203 234-6047
439 Washington Ave North Haven (06473) ***(G-5958)***
Kobyluck Ready-Mix Inc 860 444-9604
24 Industrial Dr Waterford (06385) ***(G-9657)***
Kobyluck Sand and Gravel Inc 860 444-9600
24 Industrial Dr Waterford (06385) ***(G-9658)***
Koffee Karousel, South Windsor *Also called Kk Manufacturing LLC* ***(G-7784)***
Kohinoor USA 203 388-1850
46 Southfield Ave Stamford (06902) ***(G-8277)***
Kohler Mix Specialties LLC 860 666-1511
100 Milk Ln Newington (06111) ***(G-5670)***
Kol LLC 203 393-2924
12 Cassway Rd Woodbridge (06525) ***(G-10605)***
Kolltan Pharmaceuticals Inc (HQ) 203 773-3000
300 George St Ste 530 New Haven (06511) ***(G-5311)***
Komputation Computer Services 203 744-3652
5 Windaway Rd Danbury (06810) ***(G-1871)***
Konecky & Konecky LLC 860 388-0878
72 Ayers Point Rd Old Saybrook (06475) ***(G-6551)***
Kongsberg Actuation (HQ) 860 668-1285
1 Firestone Dr Suffield (06078) ***(G-8723)***
Kongsberg Automotive, Suffield *Also called Kongsberg Actuation* ***(G-8723)***
Kongsberg Dgtal Simulation Inc 860 405-2300
170 Leonard Dr Groton (06340) ***(G-3293)***
Koninklijke Philips Elec NV 860 886-2621
40 Wisconsin Ave Norwich (06360) ***(G-6421)***
Kool Ink LLC 860 242-0303
21 Old Windsor Rd Ste B Bloomfield (06002) ***(G-439)***
Koolart USA, Haddam *Also called Moonlight Media LLC* ***(G-3407)***
Kordys Welding Inc 860 621-2271
162 Pratt St Southington (06489) ***(G-7946)***
Korner Kare 860 491-3731
175 North St Goshen (06756) ***(G-3100)***
Korzon Screen Printing LLC 203 729-1090
53a Lancaster Dr Beacon Falls (06403) ***(G-138)***
Korzon Silk Screening 203 888-3273
49 Rimmon Hill Rd Beacon Falls (06403) ***(G-139)***
Kostas Cstm Ir Fbrications LLC 203 667-0881
21 Judy Ln Stamford (06906) ***(G-8278)***
Kostas Custom Ir Fabrications 203 328-1308
42 Lockwood Ave Stamford (06902) ***(G-8279)***
Koster Keunen Inc 860 945-3333
1021 Echo Lake Rd Watertown (06795) ***(G-9714)***
Koster Keunen LLC (PA) 860 945-3333
1021 Echo Lake Rd Watertown (06795) ***(G-9715)***
Koster Keunen Manufacturing 860 693-1295
13 Sweetheart Mountain Rd Collinsville (06019) ***(G-1596)***
Koster Keunen Mfg Inc 860 945-3333
1021 Echo Lake Rd Watertown (06795) ***(G-9716)***
Kovacs Machine and Tool Co 203 269-4949
50 N Plains Industrial Rd Wallingford (06492) ***(G-9298)***
Kovacs Tamas 860 738-8976
63 Industrial Park Rd Pine Meadow (06061) ***(G-6734)***
Kovil Manufacturing LLC 203 699-9425
1486 Highland Ave Ste 2 Cheshire (06410) ***(G-1403)***
Kpb Industries LLC 203 687-7943
71 Deepwood Dr Madison (06443) ***(G-3935)***
Kra-Ze LLC 860 892-8025
32 Cedar Ln Uncasville (06382) ***(G-9098)***
Krafty Kakes Inc 203 284-0299
39 N Plains Industrial Rd E Wallingford (06492) ***(G-9299)***
Kramer Printing Company Inc 203 933-5416
270 Front Ave West Haven (06516) ***(G-9924)***
Krav Maga Southington, Plantsville *Also called Ladrdefense LLC* ***(G-6901)***
Krell Industries LLC 203 298-4000
45 Connair Rd Ste 1 Orange (06477) ***(G-6609)***
Kris Squires Printing & P 860 582-0782
21 Lexington St Bristol (06010) ***(G-1059)***
Krutch Pack LLC 860 836-1745
56 Forest Dr Newington (06111) ***(G-5671)***
Krystal Inc LLC 860 844-1267
9a Bank St Granby (06035) ***(G-3110)***
Krystal Restaurant, Granby *Also called Krystal Inc LLC* ***(G-3110)***
Kse Cabinets 860 754-7236
129 Highland Ave Middletown (06457) ***(G-4365)***
Ktcr Holding 203 227-4115
4 Pheasant Ln Westport (06880) ***(G-10110)***
KTI Bi-Metallix Inc 860 623-2511
3 Thompson Rd East Windsor (06088) ***(G-2506)***
KTI Inc (HQ) 860 623-2511
3 Thompson Rd East Windsor (06088) ***(G-2507)***
Ktt Enterprises LLC 203 288-7883
15 Marne St Hamden (06514) ***(G-3470)***
Kub Technologies Inc 203 364-8544
111 Research Dr Stratford (06615) ***(G-8643)***
Kubtec, Stratford *Also called Kub Technologies Inc* ***(G-8643)***
Kucko Chain Saw Supplies 860 684-3887
65 Kucko Rd Willington (06279) ***(G-10251)***
Kuehne New Haven LLC 203 508-6703
71 Welton St New Haven (06511) ***(G-5312)***
Kulas Systems Inc 860 749-6645
64 Field Rd Ste 2d Somers (06071) ***(G-7664)***
Kwant Elements Intl LLC 203 625-5553
464 Valley Rd Cos Cob (06807) ***(G-1636)***
Kwik Kerb Masters LLC 860 653-8102
45 Old Stagecoach Rd Granby (06035) ***(G-3111)***
Kx Technologies LLC (HQ) 203 799-9000
55 Railroad Ave West Haven (06516) ***(G-9925)***
Kyle C Niles 860 637-7625
116 Mount Vernon Rd Plantsville (06479) ***(G-6900)***
Kyung Pae Servicing Co LLC 203 394-7472
1910 Black Rock Tpke Fairfield (06825) ***(G-2807)***
L & L Capital Partners LLC 203 834-6222
57 Danbury Rd Ste 3 Wilton (06897) ***(G-10307)***
L & L Mechanical LLC 860 491-4007
28 Pie Hill Rd Goshen (06756) ***(G-3101)***
L & M Logging LLC 860 208-9884
5 George St Windham (06280) ***(G-10349)***
L & M Manufacturing Co Inc 860 379-2751
37 Greenwoods Rd New Hartford (06057) ***(G-5201)***
L & P Gate Company Inc 860 296-8009
83 Meadow St Hartford (06114) ***(G-3623)***
L 'espoir, Stratford *Also called Xavier Marcus* ***(G-8711)***
L A B, Bristol *Also called Lab Security Systems Corp* ***(G-1060)***
L A Vision LLC 860 523-0339
112 S Whitney St Ste 1 Hartford (06105) ***(G-3624)***
L C M Tool Co 203 757-1575
68 Diane Ter Waterbury (06705) ***(G-9516)***
L D G, Avon *Also called Live and Dream Green LLC* ***(G-91)***
L G Associates 860 677-7167
2 Farmstead Ln Avon (06001) ***(G-87)***
L M C, Southington *Also called Light Metals Coloring Co Inc* ***(G-7947)***
L M Gill Welding and Mfr LLC (PA) 860 647-9931
1422 Tolland Tpke Manchester (06042) ***(G-4046)***
L M Gill Welding and Mfr LLC 860 647-9931
1422 Tolland Tpke Manchester (06042) ***(G-4047)***
L M T Communications Inc 203 426-4568
84 S Main St Newtown (06470) ***(G-5752)***
L M T Magazine, Newtown *Also called L M T Communications Inc* ***(G-5752)***
L P Macadams Company Inc 203 366-3647
50 Austin St Bridgeport (06604) ***(G-820)***
L R Brown Manufacturing Co 203 265-5639
53 Prince St Wallingford (06492) ***(G-9300)***
L R K Communications Inc 203 372-1456
96 Toll House Ln Fairfield (06825) ***(G-2808)***
L S I, Orange *Also called Light Sources Inc* ***(G-6611)***
L Suzio Asphalt Co Inc 203 237-8421
975 Westfield Rd Meriden (06450) ***(G-4185)***
L T A Group Inc 860 291-9911
694 Nutmeg Rd N South Windsor (06074) ***(G-7785)***
L&P Aerospace Acquisition LLC 860 635-8811
422 Timber Ridge Rd Middletown (06457) ***(G-4366)***
La Care Industries LLC 860 231-7772
54 W Ridge Dr West Hartford (06117) ***(G-9825)***
La Cayeyana Donis Bakery 203 789-8030
188 Lamberton St New Haven (06519) ***(G-5313)***
La Chance Controls 860 342-2212
175 Penfield Hill Rd Portland (06480) ***(G-6963)***
La Joies Auto Scrap & Recycl, Norwalk *Also called Lajoies Auto Wrecking Co Inc* ***(G-6230)***
La Pietra Custom Marble & Gran, Brookfield *Also called La Pietra Thinstone Veneer* ***(G-1201)***
La Pietra Thinstone Veneer 203 775-6162
1106 Federal Rd Brookfield (06804) ***(G-1201)***
La Voz Hispana De Connecticut, New Haven *Also called Hispanic Communications LLC* ***(G-5296)***
Lab Security Systems Corp 860 589-6037
700 Emmett St Bristol (06010) ***(G-1060)***
Lab Software Associates 203 762-1342
48 Old Driftway Wilton (06897) ***(G-10308)***
Labco Welding Inc 860 632-2625
129 Industrial Park Rd Middletown (06457) ***(G-4367)***
Label One, Old Saybrook *Also called Privateer Ltd* ***(G-6568)***
Lablite LLC 860 355-8817
8 S Main St New Milford (06776) ***(G-5557)***
Labpulse Medical, East Granby *Also called Energy Beam Sciences Inc* ***(G-2203)***
Labrador Press LLC 860 887-0567
107 Bashon Hill Rd Bozrah (06334) ***(G-526)***
Labrador Publishing LLC 860 552-2564
24 W Main St Ste 330 Clinton (06413) ***(G-1512)***
Labwear.com, Bridgeport *Also called Sassone Labwear LLC* ***(G-896)***
Lac Landscaping LLC 203 807-1067
60 Country Ln Milford (06461) ***(G-4566)***
Lacey Manufacturing Co LLC 203 336-7427
1146 Barnum Ave Bridgeport (06610) ***(G-821)***
Ladrdefense LLC 860 637-8488
243 Canal St Plantsville (06479) ***(G-6901)***
Lady and The Leopard 413 531-4811
935 N Grand St West Suffield (06093) ***(G-9987)***
Lady Anne Cosmetics Inc 203 372-6972
78 Russ Rd Trumbull (06611) ***(G-9041)***

ALPHABETIC

(PA)=Parent Co (HQ)=Headquarters (DH)=Div Headquarters
2020 Harris Connecticut Manufacturers Directory
537

Lafarge North America Inc — 203 468-6068
410 Waterfront St New Haven (06512) (G-5314)

Lagnese Woodworking — 203 426-6434
9 Pebble Rd Newtown (06470) (G-5753)

Lajoies Auto Wrecking Co Inc — 203 870-0641
40 Meadow St Norwalk (06854) (G-6230)

Lake Grinding Company — 203 336-3767
231 Asylum St Bridgeport (06610) (G-822)

Lake House Brewing Company LLC — 917 620-6636
287 W Hyerdale Dr Goshen (06756) (G-3102)

Lakeview Engineering & Mfg LLC — 860 490-2760
420 Hidden Lake Rd Higganum (06441) (G-3767)

Lakeville Journal Company LLC (PA) — 860 435-9873
33 Bissell St Lakeville (06039) (G-3845)

Lakeville Journal, The, Lakeville Also called Lakeville Journal Company LLC (G-3845)

Lam Therapeutics Inc — 203 458-7100
530 Old Whitfield St Guilford (06437) (G-3366)

Lamar Advertising Company — 860 246-6546
32 Midland St Windsor (06095) (G-10403)

Lambdavision Incorporated — 860 486-6593
400 Farmington Ave Mc6409 Farmington (06032) (G-2923)

Lamberti Packing Company — 203 562-0436
207 Food Terminal Plz # 207 New Haven (06511) (G-5315)

Laminated Glass Solutions LLC — 203 250-1025
270 Oregon Rd Cheshire (06410) (G-1404)

Lamor USA Corporation — 203 888-7700
2 Enterprise Dr Ste 404 Shelton (06484) (G-7485)

Lance International, Westport Also called Robert Warren LLC (G-10150)

Land Sea Air Inc — 860 448-9004
108 Fort Hill Rd Groton (06340) (G-3294)

Land of Nod Winery LLC — 860 824-5225
99 Lower Rd East Canaan (06024) (G-2182)

Landino Signs LLC — 203 248-5437
15 Corporate Ridge Rd # 11 Hamden (06514) (G-3471)

Landmark Sign Service — 860 474-5305
123 Pine Knob Dr South Windsor (06074) (G-7786)

Landmark Sign Service LLC — 860 206-0643
111 Amherst St Hartford (06106) (G-3625)

Lane Construction Corporation (HQ) — 203 235-3351
90 Fieldstone Ct Cheshire (06410) (G-1405)

Lane Industries Incorporated (HQ) — 203 235-3351
90 Fieldstone Ct Cheshire (06410) (G-1406)

Langlais Computer Cons LLC — 860 589-0093
67 Posa Dr Bristol (06010) (G-1061)

Langner Press LLC — 203 226-7752
31 Langner Ln Weston (06883) (G-10032)

Lantern LLC — 866 203-5715
23 Senexet Village Rd Woodstock (06281) (G-10668)

Lantern App, Woodstock Also called Lantern LLC (G-10668)

Lanxess Solutions US Inc — 203 723-2237
400 Elm St Naugatuck (06770) (G-4899)

Lanxess Solutions US Inc (HQ) — 203 573-2000
2 Armstrong Rd Ste 101 Shelton (06484) (G-7486)

Lanxess Solutions US Inc — 203 605-5746
12 Spencer St Naugatuck (06770) (G-4900)

Larco Machines Co Inc — 860 647-9769
239 Hopriver Rd Bolton (06043) (G-513)

Larkin Litho — 860 535-0116
131 Elm St Stonington (06378) (G-8534)

Larosa Manufacturing LLC — 860 819-7066
15 Hultenius St Plainville (06062) (G-6831)

Larry's Auto Machine & Supply, Groton Also called Larrys Auto Machine LLC (G-3295)

Larrys Auto Machine LLC — 860 449-9112
175 Leonard Dr Groton (06340) (G-3295)

Laser Body Solutions, Hamden Also called Jeffrey Gold (G-3467)

Laser Engraved Services — 203 779-5116
164b Horse Pond Rd Madison (06443) (G-3936)

Laser Tool Company Inc — 860 283-8284
98 N Main St Thomaston (06787) (G-8796)

Laserman of Connecticut — 203 972-2887
168 East Ave Norwalk (06851) (G-6231)

Lassy Tools Inc — 860 747-2748
96 Bohemia St Plainville (06062) (G-6832)

Lasting Impressions, Bethel Also called D R S Desings (G-276)

Lasting Legacy Publishers LLC — 860 917-3545
57 Coachman Pike Ledyard (06339) (G-3876)

Late Nite Printing Co — 203 374-9287
97 Travis Dr Bridgeport (06606) (G-823)

Latelier Bade LLC — 860 623-4661
6 Old Ellington Rd Broad Brook (06016) (G-1151)

Lateral Thinking Software Sys — 203 452-9713
835 Daniels Farm Rd Trumbull (06611) (G-9042)

Latex Foam International LLC (HQ) — 203 924-0700
510 River Rd Shelton (06484) (G-7487)

Latex Foam Intl Holdings Inc (PA) — 203 924-0700
510 River Rd Shelton (06484) (G-7488)

Latex Foam Products, Shelton Also called Latex Foam International LLC (G-7487)

Lathrop Stables LLC — 860 230-9949
427 Lathrop Rd Plainfield (06374) (G-6746)

Laticrete International Inc — 203 393-0010
91 Amity Rd Bethany (06524) (G-245)

Laticrete Supercap LLC — 203 393-4558
91 Amity Rd Bethany (06524) (G-246)

Latin American Holding Inc (HQ) — 860 674-3000
1 Carrier Pl Farmington (06032) (G-2924)

Latino Multiservice LLC — 203 691-9715
552 Ferry St New Haven (06513) (G-5316)

Laufer Teknik — 860 355-4484
360 Southbury Rd Roxbury (06783) (G-7278)

Launell Group, The, Greenwich Also called Launell Inc (G-3189)

Launell Inc — 203 340-2150
24 Spring St Unit 2 Greenwich (06830) (G-3189)

Laura Spector Rustic Design — 203 254-3952
786 Westport Tpke Fairfield (06824) (G-2809)

Laurel Tool & Manufacturing — 860 889-5354
177 Franklin St Norwich (06360) (G-6422)

Laurelbrook Ntral Rsources LLC — 860 824-5843
12 Casey Hill Rd East Canaan (06024) (G-2183)

Lauretano Sign Group Inc — 860 582-0233
1 Tremco Dr Terryville (06786) (G-8762)

Lawes International Group LLC — 860 808-4981
1465 Albany Ave Fl 2 Hartford (06112) (G-3626)

Lawrence Holdings Inc (PA) — 203 949-1600
34b Barnes Indus Rd S Wallingford (06492) (G-9301)

Lawrence Mc Conney — 203 735-1133
795 Roosevelt Dr Derby (06418) (G-2118)

Laydon Industries LLC (PA) — 203 562-7283
51 Longhini Ln New Haven (06519) (G-5317)

Laylas Falafel — 203 685-2830
936 High Ridge Rd Stamford (06905) (G-8280)

Lbi Inc — 860 446-8058
973 North Rd Groton (06340) (G-3296)

Lcd Lighting Inc — 203 799-7877
37 Robinson Blvd Orange (06477) (G-6610)

Ld Assoc LLC — 203 452-9393
16 Georges Ln Monroe (06468) (G-4727)

Lda Publishers — 203 438-1484
12 Little Fox Ln Westport (06880) (G-10111)

Lead Dog Production — 203 732-4566
235 Freeman Rd Oxford (06478) (G-6672)

Leader Management Corp — 860 643-4445
282 Hebron Rd Bolton (06043) (G-514)

Leading Edge Concepts Inc — 203 797-1200
15 Berkshire Blvd Ste A Bethel (06801) (G-321)

Leading Edge Printers LLC — 203 592-4477
27 Cornwall Ave Prospect (06712) (G-7007)

Leading Edge Safety Systems, Madison Also called Pucuda Inc (G-3949)

Leaps & Bones LLC — 860 648-9708
81 Evergreen Way South Windsor (06074) (G-7787)

Learners Dimension — 860 228-1236
7 Lakeview Dr Columbia (06237) (G-1607)

Leasefish LLC — 203 293-3603
11 Bayberry Ln Wilton (06897) (G-10309)

Leather Man Limited, Essex Also called Brockway Ferry Corporation (G-2713)

Leatherby — 860 658-6166
19 Deer Park Rd Weatogue (06089) (G-9757)

Leatherworks — 860 658-6178
18 Butternut Ln Weatogue (06089) (G-9758)

Leclaire Fuel Oil LLC — 203 922-1512
97 Unit 3 Bridgeport Ave Shelton (06484) (G-7489)

Led Lighting Hub — 860 232-7141
193 Simsbury Rd West Hartford (06117) (G-9826)

Led Lighting Solutions LLC — 860 770-6023
169 Circlewood Dr Berlin (06037) (G-193)

Ledgewood Publications — 860 693-9055
3 Mountain Laurel Ct Collinsville (06019) (G-1597)

Lee Lowe & Stitch LLC — 860 536-1392
60 Hyde Pond Ct Mystic (06355) (G-4825)

Lee & Sons Woodworkers — 860 742-7707
475 Lake Rd Andover (06232) (G-12)

Lee Brown Co LLC — 860 379-4706
91 Old Forge Rd Riverton (06065) (G-7209)

Lee Company (PA) — 860 399-6281
2 Pettipaug Rd Westbrook (06498) (G-10000)

Lee Company — 860 399-6281
55 Bokum Rd Essex (06426) (G-2723)

Lee Company — 860 399-6281
22 Pequot Park Rd Westbrook (06498) (G-10001)

Lee Manufacturing Inc — 203 284-0466
46 Barnes Industrial Rd S Wallingford (06492) (G-9302)

Lee Rail Embroidery, Guilford Also called James Kingsley (G-3363)

Lee Spring Company LLC — 860 584-0991
245 Lake Ave Bristol (06010) (G-1062)

Leeco Inc — 860 404-8876
5 Alexandra Ln Avon (06001) (G-88)

Leed - Himmel Industries Inc — 203 288-8484
75 Leeder Hill Dr Hamden (06517) (G-3472)

Leek Building Products Inc — 203 853-3883
205 Wilson Ave Ste 3 Norwalk (06854) (G-6232)

Leelynd Corp — 203 753-9137
546 S Main St Waterbury (06706) (G-9517)

Lefferts Brothers Vintage Mach — 203 205-0500
20 Henry St Bethel (06801) (G-322)

Lefora Publishing LLC 860 845-8445
18 Chimney Crest Ln Bristol (06010) ***(G-1063)***
Left Handed Holsters 203 488-9654
8 7th Ave Branford (06405) ***(G-618)***
Legacy Corp 860 236-6500
555 New Park Ave West Hartford (06110) ***(G-9827)***
Legacy Woodworking LLC 203 440-9710
912 Old Colony Rd Meriden (06451) ***(G-4186)***
Legal Affairs Inc 203 865-2520
115 Blake Rd Hamden (06517) ***(G-3473)***
LEGAL AFFAIRS MAGAZINE, Hamden *Also called Legal Affairs Inc* ***(G-3473)***
Legere Group Ltd 860 674-0392
80 Darling Dr Avon (06001) ***(G-89)***
Legere Woodworking, Avon *Also called Legere Group Ltd* ***(G-89)***
Legno Bldrs & Fine Wdwkg LLC 860 282-0091
35 Ross Ave Coventry (06238) ***(G-1660)***
Legnos Boat Industries, Groton *Also called Lbi Inc* ***(G-3296)***
Legnos Medical Inc 860 446-8058
973 North Rd Groton (06340) ***(G-3297)***
Lego Brand Retail, Enfield *Also called Lego Systems Inc* ***(G-2655)***
Lego Systems Inc (HQ) 860 749-2291
555 Taylor Rd Enfield (06082) ***(G-2655)***
Legrand, West Hartford *Also called Ortronics Inc* ***(G-9841)***
Legrand Holding Inc (HQ) 860 233-6251
60 Woodlawn St West Hartford (06110) ***(G-9828)***
Lehvoss North America LLC 860 495-2046
185 S Broad St Ste 2b Pawcatuck (06379) ***(G-6718)***
Leichsenring Studios LLC 203 452-7710
9 Oxen Hill Rd Trumbull (06611) ***(G-9043)***
Leipold Inc 860 298-9791
545 Marshall Phelps Rd Windsor (06095) ***(G-10404)***
Leisure Group, Stamford *Also called Leisure Learning Products Inc* ***(G-8281)***
Leisure Learning Products Inc 203 325-2800
652 Glenbrook Rd Bldg 8 Stamford (06906) ***(G-8281)***
Lemac Iron Works Inc 860 232-7380
18 Brainard Rd West Hartford (06117) ***(G-9829)***
Lenox Strategies LLC 203 927-0871
28 Ozone Rd East Haven (06512) ***(G-2437)***
Lenox34 LLC 203 869-6909
66 Milbank Ave Greenwich (06830) ***(G-3190)***
Lens 203 426-8833
33 Currituck Rd Newtown (06470) ***(G-5754)***
Lenses Only 860 278-2020
42 Pratt St Hartford (06103) ***(G-3627)***
Lenses Only LLC 860 769-2020
812 Park Ave Bloomfield (06002) ***(G-440)***
Lenz Enterprises LLC 860 961-2893
180 Johnson St Middletown (06457) ***(G-4368)***
Leon's Upholstery, New London *Also called Clark Manner Marguarite* ***(G-5463)***
Leona Corp 860 257-3840
638 Silas Deane Hwy Wethersfield (06109) ***(G-10209)***
Leonard Dongweck 860 388-0700
23 School House Rd Old Saybrook (06475) ***(G-6552)***
Leonard F Brooks (PA) 203 335-4934
199 Asylum St Bridgeport (06610) ***(G-824)***
Leos Kitchen & Stair Corp 860 225-7363
48 John St New Britain (06051) ***(G-5010)***
Leppert/Nutmeg Inc 860 243-1737
113 W Dudley Town Rd Bloomfield (06002) ***(G-441)***
Lesco 203 353-0061
52b Poplar St Stamford (06907) ***(G-8282)***
Lesro Industries Inc 800 275-7545
1 Griffin Rd S Bloomfield (06002) ***(G-442)***
Less Pay Oil LLC 203 230-2568
78 Linden Ave Hamden (06518) ***(G-3474)***
Lesser Evil 203 529-3555
18 Finance Dr Danbury (06810) ***(G-1872)***
Letout & Bliss LLC 203 775-3548
246 Federal Rd Brookfield (06804) ***(G-1202)***
Lettering Inc of New York (PA) 203 329-7759
255 Mill Rd Stamford (06903) ***(G-8283)***
Level Woodworks 203 266-7153
7 White Birch Ln Bethlehem (06751) ***(G-374)***
Lewis R Martino 203 463-4430
328 Oxford Rd Oxford (06478) ***(G-6673)***
Lewmar Inc (HQ) 203 458-6200
351 New Whitfield St Guilford (06437) ***(G-3367)***
Lewmar Marine, Guilford *Also called Lewmar Inc* ***(G-3367)***
Lewtan Industries Corporation 860 278-9800
57 Loomis Dr Apt A1 West Hartford (06107) ***(G-9830)***
Lex Products LLC (PA) 203 363-3738
15 Progress Dr Shelton (06484) ***(G-7490)***
Lexa International Corporation (PA) 203 326-5200
1 Landmark Sq Ste 407 Stamford (06901) ***(G-8284)***
Lexo Group 203 847-8293
241 New Canaan Ave Norwalk (06850) ***(G-6233)***
Lf Engineering Co Inc 860 526-4759
17 Jeffrey Rd East Haven (06513) ***(G-2438)***
Lf Engineering Co., East Haven *Also called Lf Engineering Co Inc* ***(G-2438)***
Lfbw LLC 203 966-8499
137 Llewellyn Dr New Canaan (06840) ***(G-5114)***

Lgl Group Inc 407 298-2000
140 Greenwich Ave Ste 4 Greenwich (06830) ***(G-3191)***
LH Gault & Son Incorporated 203 227-5181
11 Ferry Ln W Westport (06880) ***(G-10112)***
Lhi Metals, Wallingford *Also called Tico Titanium Inc* ***(G-9384)***
Libby Power Systems LLC (PA) 203 393-1239
35 Sargent Dr Bethany (06524) ***(G-247)***
Libbys Italian Pastry Shop 203 234-2530
310 Washington Ave North Haven (06473) ***(G-5959)***
Liberato Italian Ices Inc 203 772-0381
139 Wooster St Ste 141 New Haven (06511) ***(G-5318)***
Liberty Garage Inc 203 778-0222
51 Sugar Hollow Rd Ste 1 Danbury (06810) ***(G-1873)***
Liberty Glass and Met Inds Inc 860 923-3623
339 Riverside Dr North Grosvenordale (06255) ***(G-5888)***
Liberty Products Inc 860 829-2122
598 Deming Rd Berlin (06037) ***(G-194)***
Liberty Screen Print Co LLC 203 632-5449
141 S Main St Beacon Falls (06403) ***(G-140)***
Liberty Services LLC 860 399-0077
790 Boston Post Rd Westbrook (06498) ***(G-10002)***
Licari Woodworking, Bridgeport *Also called James J Licari* ***(G-800)***
Life Global, Guilford *Also called Genx International Inc* ***(G-3354)***
Life Publications 860 953-0444
106 South St Ste 5 West Hartford (06110) ***(G-9831)***
Life Study Fllwship Foundation 203 655-1436
90 Heights Rd Darien (06820) ***(G-2031)***
Life Warmer Inc 860 204-1711
336 E Hill Rd Canton (06019) ***(G-1317)***
Lifeglobal Group, The, Guilford *Also called Coopersurgical Inc* ***(G-3341)***
Lifepharms Inc 860 447-8583
143 Shaw St New London (06320) ***(G-5476)***
Lifescape Enterprises, Mystic *Also called Kathleen Parker OBeirne* ***(G-4824)***
Lifetime Acrylic Signs Inc 203 255-6751
593 Cascade Dr Fairfield (06825) ***(G-2810)***
Liftline Capital LLC 860 395-0150
7 Center Rd W Old Saybrook (06475) ***(G-6553)***
Light Fantastic Realty Inc 203 934-3441
114 Boston Post Rd West Haven (06516) ***(G-9926)***
Light Metals Coloring Co Inc 860 621-0145
270 Spring St Southington (06489) ***(G-7947)***
Light Rock Beverage, Danbury *Also called Light Rock Spring Water Co* ***(G-1874)***
Light Rock Spring Water Co 203 743-2251
9 Balmforth Ave Danbury (06810) ***(G-1874)***
Light Sources Inc (PA) 203 799-7877
37 Robinson Blvd Orange (06477) ***(G-6611)***
Light Sources Inc 203 799-7877
70 Cascade Blvd Milford (06460) ***(G-4567)***
Light Speed LLC 203 248-8550
653 Gaylord Mountain Rd Hamden (06518) ***(G-3475)***
Lighthouse Communications 203 445-9733
47 Flint Ridge Rd Monroe (06468) ***(G-4728)***
Lighthouse International LLC 860 528-4722
125 S Satellite Rd South Windsor (06074) ***(G-7788)***
Lighthouse Maps 203 981-1090
20 Obtuse Rocks Rd Brookfield (06804) ***(G-1203)***
Lighthouse Printing LLC 860 388-2677
315 Boston Post Rd Ste 3 Old Saybrook (06475) ***(G-6554)***
Lighthouse Signs, Westbrook *Also called Margaret Witham* ***(G-10003)***
Lighthouse Technology Partners, Greenwich *Also called Desrosier of Greenwich Inc* ***(G-3152)***
Lighticians Inc 203 494-2542
80 Waterside Ln Clinton (06413) ***(G-1513)***
Lighting Edge Inc 860 767-8968
50 West Ave Ste 4 Essex (06426) ***(G-2724)***
Lighting Quotient, The, West Haven *Also called Sylvan R Shemitz Designs LLC* ***(G-9957)***
Lightninglabel.com, Stamford *Also called Cenveo Worldwide Limited* ***(G-8141)***
Lily Force Industries 860 729-2458
65 Cedar Swamp Ext Coventry (06238) ***(G-1661)***
Lilywork Ceramic Ornament LLC 215 859-8753
42 Palmer St Pawcatuck (06379) ***(G-6719)***
Limb-It-Less Logging LLC 860 227-0987
182 Saybrook Rd Essex (06426) ***(G-2725)***
Limbkeepers LLC 860 304-3250
25 Joshuatown Rd Lyme (06371) ***(G-3905)***
Lime Rock Resources GP III LP 203 293-2750
274 Riverside Ave Westport (06880) ***(G-10113)***
Lincoln Precision Machine Inc 860 923-9358
923 Thompson Rd Thompson (06277) ***(G-8837)***
Linda Case Writing Graphic 860 563-5713
103 Park Ave Wethersfield (06109) ***(G-10210)***
Linda Hoagland 203 878-7188
19 Pine Knob Ter Milford (06461) ***(G-4568)***
Linden Soaps 563 552-2828
41 Scuppo Rd A Woodbury (06798) ***(G-10641)***
Lindqist Historical Guides Inc 203 335-8568
119 Midland St Bridgeport (06605) ***(G-825)***
Lindsay Graphics 860 355-8744
9 Partridge Trl Sherman (06784) ***(G-7597)***
Lindsay Total Graphics, Manchester *Also called Guy Lindsay* ***(G-4024)***
Line Electric, Glastonbury *Also called General Electro Components* ***(G-3039)***

ALPHABETIC

(PA)=Parent Co (HQ)=Headquarters (DH)=Div Headquarters
2020 Harris Connecticut Manufacturers Directory
539

Line X of Western Connecticut 860 355-6997
26 New Milford Rd E Bridgewater (06752) *(G-946)*
Line-X of Hartford 860 216-6180
192 Ledyard St Hartford (06114) *(G-3628)*
Linemaster Switch Corporation 860 630-4920
29 Plaine Hill Rd Woodstock (06281) *(G-10669)*
Linemaster Switch Corporation 860 564-7713
16 Center Pkwy Plainfield (06374) *(G-6747)*
Lingard Cabinet Co LLC 860 647-9886
540 N Main St Ste 2 Manchester (06042) *(G-4048)*
Lingol Corporation 203 265-3608
415 S Cherry St Wallingford (06492) *(G-9303)*
Link AKC, Stamford Also called Wagz Inc *(G-8487)*
Link Mechanical Services Inc 860 826-5880
34 Walnut St New Britain (06051) *(G-5011)*
Link Systems Inc 203 274-9702
1 Dock St Ste 200 Stamford (06902) *(G-8285)*
Linvar LLC 860 951-3818
2189 Silas Deane Hwy # 15 Rocky Hill (06067) *(G-7254)*
Lion Cords Division, Norwalk Also called Astrophonic Corp America *(G-6079)*
Lion Heart Industries LLC 203 376-2212
1809 Little Meadow Rd Guilford (06437) *(G-3368)*
Lionheart Militaria Llc 203 800-5759
2458 Boston Post Rd Ste 5 Guilford (06437) *(G-3369)*
Lipid Genomics Inc 443 465-3495
400 Farmington Ave R1718 Farmington (06032) *(G-2925)*
Liquid Sun 860 254-5757
10 S Main St East Windsor (06088) *(G-2508)*
Liquidpiston Inc 860 838-2677
1292a Blue Hills Ave Bloomfield (06002) *(G-443)*
Lisa Barrette 860 928-0599
38 Ballard Rd Thompson (06277) *(G-8838)*
Lisa Lee Creations Inc 203 479-4462
10 Selden St New Haven (06525) *(G-5319)*
Lisas Clover Hill Quilts LLC 860 828-9325
27 Webster Square Rd Berlin (06037) *(G-195)*
Lisern Enterprises Inc 203 426-9079
57 Lakeview Ter Sandy Hook (06482) *(G-7319)*
Litchfield International Inc 860 567-8824
457 Bantam Rd Ste 12 Litchfield (06759) *(G-3894)*
Litchfield Windsors 860 485-1019
10 Robinwood Ln Harwinton (06791) *(G-3732)*
Liteideas LLC (PA) 860 213-8311
417 Mulberry Rd Mansfield Center (06250) *(G-4114)*
Lithographics Inc 860 678-1660
55 Spring Ln Farmington (06032) *(G-2926)*
Litigation Analytics Inc (PA) 203 431-0300
127 Main St Bldg Ii Ridgefield (06877) *(G-7154)*
Little Apple LLC 860 404-2833
5 Blackberry Rdg Farmington (06032) *(G-2927)*
Little Artist Paint Co LLC 860 989-1996
8 Race Ave Plainville (06062) *(G-6833)*
Little Bits Manufacturing Inc 860 923-2772
694 Riverside Dr North Grosvenordale (06255) *(G-5889)*
Little Blue Book 860 409-7000
302 W Main St Ste 206 Avon (06001) *(G-90)*
Little Blue Insite LLC 203 202-7690
9 Old Kings Hwy S Fl 4 Darien (06820) *(G-2032)*
Little Honey's Bakery, Middletown Also called TD&s Acquisition LLC *(G-4424)*
Little India Publications Inc 212 560-0608
408 Windtree St Torrington (06790) *(G-8943)*
Little Joe Upholstery, Stamford Also called Little Joes Upholstery *(G-8286)*
Little Joes Upholstery 203 975-2871
94 Franklin St Stamford (06901) *(G-8286)*
Little John's Sign Factory, Enfield Also called Sign Factory *(G-2695)*
Little King Press 203 981-2324
15 May St Fairfield (06825) *(G-2811)*
Little T Qarter Midget CLB Inc 860 823-7258
205 E Thompson Rd Thompson (06277) *(G-8839)*
Little T Quarter Midget Club 860 885-1376
32 Georgia Rd Oakdale (06370) *(G-6444)*
Littlefingers Software 203 938-2684
5 Chapman Pl Redding (06896) *(G-7096)*
Liturgical Publications Inc 203 966-6470
87 Lambert Rd New Canaan (06840) *(G-5115)*
Liturgical Publications Inc 860 635-9560
5 Progress Dr Cromwell (06416) *(G-1706)*
Liuzzi Cheese, Hamden Also called Ndr Liuzzi Inc *(G-3487)*
Live and Dream Green LLC 860 670-0870
4 Orchard Farms Ln Avon (06001) *(G-91)*
Living Abroad LLC 203 221-1997
501 Westport Ave Norwalk (06851) *(G-6234)*
Living Magazine 203 283-5290
162 Bridgeport Ave Milford (06460) *(G-4569)*
Living Word Imprints LLC 860 882-1679
450 Homestead Ave Hartford (06112) *(G-3629)*
Ljs House of Candles 203 464-5742
49 Old Gate Rd Meriden (06451) *(G-4187)*
LLC Dow Gage 860 828-5327
169 White Oak Rd 6037 Berlin (06037) *(G-196)*
LLC Dow Gage 860 828-5327
169 White Oak Dr Berlin (06037) *(G-197)*

LLC Glass House 860 974-1665
50 Swedetown Rd Pomfret Center (06259) *(G-6941)*
LLC Wolff Woods 860 415-9089
12 Ivy Rd Mystic (06355) *(G-4826)*
Lloyd P McDonald 860 447-1787
112 Cross Rd Waterford (06385) *(G-9659)*
Lm Gill Welding & Mfg, Manchester Also called L M Gill Welding and Mfr LLC *(G-4047)*
LM Gill Welding & Mfg LLC 860 647-9931
1422 Tolland Tpke Manchester (06042) *(G-4049)*
Lmj Designs Inc 845 363-1120
345 Wilson Ave Ste 1 Norwalk (06854) *(G-6235)*
Lo Stocco Motors 203 797-9618
19 Chestnut St Danbury (06810) *(G-1875)*
Loanworks Servicing LLC 203 402-7304
3 Corporate Dr Ste 208 Shelton (06484) *(G-7491)*
Loaves & Fishes Ministries 860 524-1730
646 Prospect Ave Hartford (06105) *(G-3630)*
Local Media Group Inc 860 354-2273
45 Main St New Milford (06776) *(G-5558)*
Local Traffic Fusion LLC 203 938-8862
431 Newtown Tpke Redding (06896) *(G-7097)*
Locallive Networks Inc 877 355-6225
175 Atlantic St Ste 2 Stamford (06901) *(G-8287)*
Lockheed Martin Corporation 860 447-8553
18 4th St New London (06320) *(G-5477)*
Locking Filter LLC 203 691-1221
151 Sandquist Cir Hamden (06514) *(G-3476)*
Loctec Corporation 203 364-1000
15 Commerce Rd Ste 2 Newtown (06470) *(G-5755)*
Loden Software 203 949-9416
37 Jamestown Cir Wallingford (06492) *(G-9304)*
Logan Sandblasting, Meriden Also called Logan Steel Inc *(G-4188)*
Logan Steel Inc (PA) 203 235-0811
119 Empire Ave Meriden (06450) *(G-4188)*
Logans Run Trnsp Svc LLC 203 679-0870
226 N Plains Industrl 8 Wallingford (06492) *(G-9305)*
Logantech, Waterbury Also called Proxtalkercom LLC *(G-9590)*
Logic Seal LLC 203 598-3400
10 Sparks St Plainville (06062) *(G-6834)*
Logo Sportswear Inc 203 678-4700
12 Beaumont Rd Wallingford (06492) *(G-9306)*
Logod Softwear Inc 203 272-4883
500 Cornwall Ave Ste 3 Cheshire (06410) *(G-1407)*
Lollipop Kids LLC 203 664-1799
13 Woodland Drive Ext Redding (06896) *(G-7098)*
Lolo Bags, New Canaan Also called Putu LLC *(G-5136)*
Lombardo Industries LLC 203 948-8562
42 Berkshire Rd Sandy Hook (06482) *(G-7320)*
Lone Wolfe Printing LLC 203 444-5131
740 Mix Ave Unit 102 Hamden (06514) *(G-3477)*
Long FA Inc 203 270-3878
228 S Main St Newtown (06470) *(G-5756)*
Long Island Pipe Supply Inc 860 688-1780
1220 Kennedy Rd Windsor (06095) *(G-10405)*
LONG ISLAND PIPE SUPPLY OF ALBANY, INC., Windsor Also called Long Island Pipe Supply Inc *(G-10405)*
Longford's Own, Stamford Also called Longfords Ice Cream Ltd *(G-8288)*
Longfords Ice Cream Ltd 914 935-9469
425 Fairfield Ave Ste 25 Stamford (06902) *(G-8288)*
Longhini LLC 212 219-1230
41 Longhini Ln New Haven (06519) *(G-5320)*
Longview Holding Corporation (HQ) 203 869-6734
43 Arch St Greenwich (06830) *(G-3192)*
Lonza Wood Protection 203 229-2900
501 Merritt 7 Norwalk (06851) *(G-6236)*
Lookers Embroidery 203 468-7262
15 Wheelbarrow Ln East Haven (06513) *(G-2439)*
Lookingforsolutionscom LLC 475 239-5773
4 Research Dr Ste 402 Shelton (06484) *(G-7492)*
Lookout Solutions LLC 203 750-0307
7 Lookout Rd Norwalk (06850) *(G-6237)*
Loon Medical Inc 860 373-0217
1 Technology Dr Tolland (06084) *(G-8868)*
Loos & Co Inc (PA) 860 928-7981
16b Mashamoquet Rd Pomfret (06258) *(G-6933)*
Loos & Co Inc 860 928-6681
Rr 101 Pomfret (06258) *(G-6934)*
Loos and Co Inc 304 445-7820
1 Cable Rd Pomfret (06258) *(G-6935)*
Lorad Corporation 203 790-5544
36 Apple Ridge Rd Danbury (06810) *(G-1876)*
Lorad Medical Systems, Danbury Also called Lorad Corporation *(G-1876)*
Loranctis Orgnal Woodworks LLC 860 924-8810
78 Allen St Terryville (06786) *(G-8763)*
Lord & Hodge Inc 860 632-7006
362 Industrial Park Rd # 4 Middletown (06457) *(G-4369)*
Lorence Sign Works LLC 860 829-9999
55 Willow Brook Dr Berlin (06037) *(G-198)*
Lorence Signworks, Berlin Also called Lorence Sign Works LLC *(G-198)*
Lorenco Industries Inc 203 743-6962
25 Henry St Bethel (06801) *(G-323)*

Lorex Plastics Co Inc 203 286-0020
221 Wilson Ave Norwalk (06854) **(G-6238)**
Loric Tool Inc 860 928-0171
95 Gaumond Rd North Grosvenordale (06255) **(G-5890)**
Los Angles Tmes Cmmnctions LLC 203 965-6434
250 Harbor Dr Stamford (06902) **(G-8289)**
Lost Code Software LLC 203 626-9133
49 Hanover St Wallingford (06492) **(G-9307)**
Lostocco Refuse Service LLC 203 748-9296
79 Beaver Brook Rd Danbury (06810) **(G-1877)**
Lostocco Services, Danbury *Also called Lostocco Refuse Service LLC* **(G-1877)**
Lota Woodworking LLC 203 978-0277
15 Styles Ln Norwalk (06850) **(G-6239)**
Lou-Jan Tool & Die Inc 203 272-3536
161 E Johnson Ave Cheshire (06410) **(G-1408)**
Louie S Welding 203 634-0873
55 Cooper St Meriden (06451) **(G-4189)**
Louis Dreyfus Holding Company (HQ) 203 761-2000
40 Danbury Rd Wilton (06897) **(G-10310)**
Louis E Allyn Sons Inc 860 542-5741
270 Ashpohtag Rd Norfolk (06058) **(G-5825)**
Louis Electric Co Inc 203 879-5483
1584 Wolcott Rd Wolcott (06716) **(G-10571)**
Louis Rodriguz 203 777-6937
145 Adeline St New Haven (06519) **(G-5321)**
Love 'n Herbs, Waterbury *Also called Da Silva Klanko Ltd* **(G-9459)**
Lovesac Company (PA) 888 636-1223
2 Landmark Sq Ste 300 Stamford (06901) **(G-8290)**
Loving Life LLC 860 326-1459
363 Rockville Rd Voluntown (06384) **(G-9190)**
Lowbrow 203 518-4189
103 Greenwood Ave Bethel (06801) **(G-324)**
Lowe Manufacturing, Plainville *Also called D & M Screw Machine Pdts LLC* **(G-6795)**
Lowencorp Publishing LLC 203 966-3474
82 Puddin Hill Rd New Canaan (06840) **(G-5116)**
Loxo Oncology Inc (HQ) 203 653-3880
281 Tresser Blvd Fl 9 Stamford (06901) **(G-8291)**
Loyal Fence Company LLC 203 530-7046
1 Lorraine Ter Rockfall (06481) **(G-7214)**
LP Hometown Pizza LLC 860 589-1208
90 Burlington Ave Bristol (06010) **(G-1064)**
Lpg Metal Crafts LLC 860 982-3573
54 Carol Dr Plainville (06062) **(G-6835)**
Lq Mechatronics Inc 203 433-4430
2 Sycamore Way Branford (06405) **(G-619)**
Lrp Conferences LLC 203 663-0100
35 Nutmeg Dr Trumbull (06611) **(G-9044)**
Lsr Electronic Assembly 860 642-6883
99 Old Colchester Rd Lebanon (06249) **(G-3857)**
Lu Lu Holdings LLC 203 861-1988
55 Lewis St Greenwich (06830) **(G-3193)**
Lubbert Supply Company LLC 203 690-1105
89 Eastern Steel Rd Milford (06460) **(G-4570)**
Lubrication Management, Danbury *Also called Expressway Lube Centers* **(G-1820)**
Luc-Tardiff Logging 860 485-0693
112 Valley Rd Harwinton (06791) **(G-3733)**
Lucerion LLC 203 699-8136
10 Teds Ct Cheshire (06410) **(G-1409)**
Luchon Cabinet Woodwork 860 684-5037
140 Buckley Hwy Stafford Springs (06076) **(G-8032)**
Lucille Piccirillo 203 366-2353
712 Madison Ave Bridgeport (06606) **(G-826)**
Luckey LLC 203 285-3819
184 Chapel St New Haven (06513) **(G-5322)**
Lucky Duck Press 347 703-3984
9 Willow St Winsted (06098) **(G-10527)**
Lucky Enough Canvas 860 455-6994
453 Brook St Hampton (06247) **(G-3537)**
Luis Pressure Washer 203 706-7399
47 Esther Ave Waterbury (06708) **(G-9518)**
Luis Raimundi 860 294-1468
64 Ratlum Rd Pleasant Valley (06063) **(G-6924)**
Luke's Toy Factory, Danbury *Also called Mwb Toy Company LLC* **(G-1890)**
Lumendi LLC 203 528-0316
253 Post Rd W Westport (06880) **(G-10114)**
Lumentum Operations LLC 408 546-5483
45 Griffin Rd S Bloomfield (06002) **(G-444)**
Lumivisions Architectural Elem 203 529-3232
300 Wilson Ave Ste 202 Norwalk (06854) **(G-6240)**
Lundgren Centerless Grinding 860 482-4927
3263 Torringford St Torrington (06790) **(G-8944)**
Lundgren Eric Woodworking 860 350-5153
89 Cherniske Rd New Milford (06776) **(G-5559)**
Lundgren Woodworking, New Milford *Also called Lundgren Eric Woodworking* **(G-5559)**
Lupi-Marchigiano Bakery, New Haven *Also called Boston Model Bakery* **(G-5250)**
Lupis Inc 203 562-9491
169 Washington Ave New Haven (06519) **(G-5323)**
Lure of Cripple Creek 860 564-5799
147 Ekonk Hill Rd Moosup (06354) **(G-4781)**
Luther Fence Inc 860 445-5660
145 Leonard Dr Unit A Groton (06340) **(G-3298)**
Luvata Waterbury Inc 203 753-5215
2121 Thomaston Ave Ste 1 Waterbury (06704) **(G-9519)**
Luxpoint Inc 860 982-9588
101 Hammer Mill Rd Ste K Rocky Hill (06067) **(G-7255)**
Luxury Brand Network LLC 203 930-2703
35 Anderson Rd Greenwich (06830) **(G-3194)**
Lw Global LLC 860 519-7134
36 Metacom Dr Simsbury (06070) **(G-7632)**
Lydall Inc (PA) 860 646-1233
1 Colonial Rd Manchester (06042) **(G-4050)**
Lydall Thermal Acoustical Inc 860 646-1233
1 Colonial Rd Manchester (06042) **(G-4051)**
Lyman Farm Incorporated 860 349-1793
7 Lyman Rd Middlefield (06455) **(G-4302)**
Lyman Orchards, Middlefield *Also called Lyman Farm Incorporated* **(G-4302)**
Lyman Products Corporation (PA) 860 632-2020
475 Smith St Middletown (06457) **(G-4370)**
Lyman Products Corporation 860 632-2020
475 Smith St Middletown (06457) **(G-4371)**
Lynch Corp 203 452-3007
140 Greenwich Ave Ste 3 Greenwich (06830) **(G-3195)**
Lynn Welding Co Inc 860 667-4400
75 Rockwell Rd Ste 1 Newington (06111) **(G-5672)**
Lynne Marshall 860 245-3645
118 Pearl St Groton (06340) **(G-3299)**
Lyon Manufacturing LLC 203 876-7386
215 Research Dr Ste 4 Milford (06460) **(G-4571)**
Lyons Slitting Inc 203 755-4564
46 Mattatuck Heights Rd Waterbury (06705) **(G-9520)**
Lyons Tool and Die Company 203 238-2689
185 Research Pkwy Meriden (06450) **(G-4190)**
Lyons Upholstery & Carpet Shop, Wallingford *Also called Lyons Upholstery Shop Inc* **(G-9308)**
Lyons Upholstery Shop Inc 203 269-3782
864 N Colony Rd Wallingford (06492) **(G-9308)**
M & A Turning Co LLC 860 793-2774
15 Hultenius St Ste 3a Plainville (06062) **(G-6836)**
M & B Automotive Machine Shop 203 348-6134
443 Elm St Stamford (06902) **(G-8292)**
M & B Enterprise LLC 203 298-9781
155 New Haven Ave Derby (06418) **(G-2119)**
M & D Coatings LLC 203 380-9466
167 Avon St Stratford (06615) **(G-8644)**
M & I Industries Inc 860 747-6421
15 N Washington St Plainville (06062) **(G-6837)**
M & J Bus Co 203 624-0836
121 Quinnipiac Ave North Haven (06473) **(G-5960)**
M & J Bus Co Inc 860 437-3721
30 Fargo Rd Waterford (06385) **(G-9660)**
M & J Bus Inc 860 668-6526
1353 South St Suffield (06078) **(G-8724)**
M & M Carbide Inc 860 628-2002
290 Center St Southington (06489) **(G-7948)**
M & M Pallet Inc 203 754-2606
360 Baldwin St Waterbury (06706) **(G-9521)**
M & M Precast Corp 203 743-5559
39 Padanaram Rd Danbury (06811) **(G-1878)**
M & O Corporation 203 367-4292
164 Alex St Bridgeport (06607) **(G-827)**
M & R Manufacturing Inc 860 666-5066
111 Carr Ave Newington (06111) **(G-5673)**
M & S Machine Tool Company 203 933-8920
744 Washington Ave Ste 8 West Haven (06516) **(G-9927)**
M & S Products 860 742-5141
24 Brigham Tavern Rd Ext Coventry (06238) **(G-1662)**
M & W Industries Inc 860 621-7358
29 Depaolo Dr Southington (06489) **(G-7949)**
M & W Sheet Metal LLC 860 642-7748
841 Route 32 Ste 7 North Franklin (06254) **(G-5874)**
M & Z Engineering Inc 860 496-0282
643 Riverside Ave Torrington (06790) **(G-8945)**
M B Machine, Willimantic *Also called Marc Bouley* **(G-10233)**
M Baron Company 860 536-1594
26 Packer Ln Mystic (06355) **(G-4827)**
M Cubed Technologies Inc (HQ) 203 304-2940
31 Pecks Ln Ste 8 Newtown (06470) **(G-5757)**
M Cubed Technologies Inc 203 452-2333
921 Main St Monroe (06468) **(G-4729)**
M D Welding & Fabricating LLC 860 643-2448
112 French Rd Bolton (06043) **(G-515)**
M Design & Printing Svcs LLC 860 344-8289
163 Newtown St Middletown (06457) **(G-4372)**
M Friedman Company 860 447-9935
25 Willow St Mystic (06355) **(G-4828)**
M G M Instruments Inc (PA) 203 248-4008
925 Sherman Ave Hamden (06514) **(G-3478)**
M G Solutions 203 945-9615
285 W Cedar St Norwalk (06854) **(G-6241)**
M H Pierce & Co 203 327-2970
11 Ledge Ter Stamford (06905) **(G-8293)**
M I R Inc 203 888-2541
103 Breault Rd Beacon Falls (06403) **(G-141)**

ALPHABETIC

(PA)=Parent Co (HQ)=Headquarters (DH)=Div Headquarters
2020 Harris Connecticut
Manufacturers Directory
541

M J Boller Company 860 738-8073
  8 Wickett St Pine Meadow (06061) *(G-6735)*
M J Williams Heating and AC 860 923-6991
  386 Dugg Hill Rd Woodstock (06281) *(G-10670)*
M K M Enterprises Inc 203 250-7937
  758 Jarvis St Cheshire (06410) *(G-1410)*
M K M Woodworks LLC 203 838-5605
  20 Nostrum Rd Norwalk (06850) *(G-6242)*
M L Guerrera Welding 203 879-6823
  58 Averyll Ave Wolcott (06716) *(G-10572)*
M Martinetto & Sons Cnstr, Milford Also called Michael Martinetto *(G-4577)*
M P E, Branford Also called Madison Polymeric Engrg Inc *(G-622)*
M P I, Seymour Also called Microboard Processing Inc *(G-7357)*
M P Robinson Production 203 938-1336
  77 Topstone Rd Redding (06896) *(G-7099)*
M S B International Ltd 203 466-6525
  30 Thompson Rd Branford (06405) *(G-620)*
M S Bickford LLC 860 467-6937
  19 Crows Nest Ln East Hampton (06424) *(G-2269)*
M S C, Enfield Also called MSC Filtration Tech Inc *(G-2664)*
M Squared Woodworking LLC 860 673-6079
  66 Litchfield Rd Unionville (06085) *(G-9118)*
M T D Corporation 203 261-3721
  171 Spring Hill Rd Trumbull (06611) *(G-9045)*
M T I, Mystic Also called Madison Technology Intl *(G-4830)*
M T S Tool LLC 860 945-0875
  27 Main St Ste 2 Oakville (06779) *(G-6456)*
M&G Berman Inc 203 834-8754
  67 Pond Rd Wilton (06897) *(G-10311)*
M&M Metal Fabrication LLC 203 889-6468
  105 Foxon Rd East Haven (06513) *(G-2440)*
M-Fab LLC 860 496-0055
  52 Norwood St Torrington (06790) *(G-8946)*
M-Systems Inc 203 270-8926
  12 Valley View Rd Newtown (06470) *(G-5758)*
M.C. Systems, Woodbury Also called Mc Clintock Manufacturing *(G-10642)*
M2 Tactical Solutions LLC 203 247-3477
  12 Rainbow Rd Norwalk (06851) *(G-6243)*
M3di, Higganum Also called Mannan 3d Innovations LLC *(G-3768)*
MA & PA Fur LLC 860 659-7766
  746 Long Hill Rd Middletown (06457) *(G-4373)*
Mac Dermid Elec Solution, Waterbury Also called Macdermid Incorporated *(G-9524)*
Macala Tool Inc 860 763-2580
  7 Moody Rd Bldg 5 Enfield (06082) *(G-2656)*
Macdermid Incorporated (HQ) 203 575-5700
  245 Freight St Waterbury (06702) *(G-9522)*
Macdermid Incorporated 262 242-2892
  245 Freight St Waterbury (06702) *(G-9523)*
Macdermid Incorporated 203 575-5700
  245 Freight St Waterbury (06702) *(G-9524)*
Macdermid Acumen Inc 203 575-5700
  245 Freight St Waterbury (06702) *(G-9525)*
Macdermid AG Solutions Inc 203 575-5727
  245 Freight St Waterbury (06702) *(G-9526)*
Macdermid Anion Inc 203 575-5700
  245 Freight St Waterbury (06702) *(G-9527)*
Macdermid Brazil Inc 203 575-5700
  245 Freight St Waterbury (06702) *(G-9528)*
Macdermid Enthone Inc (HQ) 203 934-8611
  350 Frontage Rd West Haven (06516) *(G-9928)*
Macdermid Overseas Asia Ltd (HQ) 203 575-5799
  245 Freight St Waterbury (06702) *(G-9529)*
Macdermid Prfmce Solutions, Waterbury Also called Macdermid Incorporated *(G-9522)*
Macdermid Printing Solutions 203 575-5727
  245 Freight St Waterbury (06702) *(G-9530)*
Macdermid South America Inc 203 575-5700
  245 Freight St Waterbury (06702) *(G-9531)*
Macdermid South Atlantic Inc 203 575-5700
  245 Freight St Waterbury (06702) *(G-9532)*
Machine Builders Neng LLC 203 922-9446
  33 Hull St Ste 6a Shelton (06484) *(G-7493)*
Machine Repair Services LLC 860 729-7410
  142 Freeman Rd Middletown (06457) *(G-4374)*
Machine Shop, Niantic Also called Niantic Tool Inc *(G-5814)*
Mackenzie Mch & Mar Works Inc 203 777-3479
  36 Morgan Ter East Haven (06512) *(G-2441)*
Mackson Mfg Co Inc 860 589-4035
  139 Center St Ste 2002 Bristol (06010) *(G-1065)*
Maclean Woodworking LLC 203 452-8285
  696 Main St Monroe (06468) *(G-4730)*
Macneill Altrntive Cncepts LLC 860 877-3968
  47 Colony St Bristol (06010) *(G-1066)*
Macris Industries Inc 860 514-7003
  8 Summit St Mystic (06355) *(G-4829)*
Macristy Industries Inc (PA) 860 225-4637
  610 N Mountain Rd Newington (06111) *(G-5674)*
Macro Systems Inc 203 225-6266
  20 Hubbell Ln Shelton (06484) *(G-7494)*
Macroscopic Solutions LLC 410 870-5566
  1 Technology Dr Tolland (06084) *(G-8869)*
Macton Corporation 203 267-1500
  116 Willenbrock Rd Oxford (06478) *(G-6674)*

Macton Oxford LLC 203 267-1500
  116 Willenbrock Rd Oxford (06478) *(G-6675)*
Macwear Athletic Apparel & Eqp, Southport Also called Macwear LLC *(G-8006)*
Macwear LLC (PA) 203 579-4277
  3300 Post Rd Southport (06890) *(G-8006)*
Macworks LLC 860 377-1371
  230 Parmelee Hill Rd Durham (06422) *(G-2151)*
Mad Sportswear LLC 203 932-4868
  100 Putney Dr West Haven (06516) *(G-9929)*
Madd Fiusch Industries 203 982-8306
  1085 Durham Rd Madison (06443) *(G-3937)*
Maddog LLC 203 878-0147
  33 Tall Pine Rd Milford (06461) *(G-4572)*
Madigan Millwork Inc 860 673-7601
  150 New Britain Ave Unionville (06085) *(G-9119)*
Madison Company (PA) 203 488-4477
  27 Business Park Dr Branford (06405) *(G-621)*
Madison Polymeric Engrg Inc 203 488-4554
  965 W Main St Ste 2 Branford (06405) *(G-622)*
Madison Technology Intl 860 245-0245
  375 Allyn St Unit 1 Mystic (06355) *(G-4830)*
Madison Tstg Acqstion Svcs LLC 203 421-9388
  899 Durham Rd Madison (06443) *(G-3938)*
Madonna Black Buddist LLC 203 589-9796
  32 Greenwich Ave 3 Greenwich (06830) *(G-3196)*
Mafcote International Inc (HQ) 203 644-1200
  108 Main St Ste 3 Norwalk (06851) *(G-6244)*
Magcor Inc 203 445-0302
  14 Wrabel Cir Monroe (06468) *(G-4731)*
Mager & Gougelman Inc 203 773-1753
  200 Orchard St Ste 305 New Haven (06511) *(G-5324)*
Magic Industries Inc 860 949-8380
  140 Bozrah St Bozrah (06334) *(G-527)*
Magic Signs 860 457-8940
  75 Connecticut Mills Ave Danielson (06239) *(G-1997)*
Magivac Sales, Seymour Also called Brian Cheney *(G-7336)*
Magna Standard Mfg Co Inc 203 874-0444
  122 Cascade Blvd Milford (06460) *(G-4573)*
Magna Steel Sales Inc 203 888-0300
  2 Alliance Cir Beacon Falls (06403) *(G-142)*
Magna-Wind Inc 203 269-4749
  130 S Turnpike Rd Wallingford (06492) *(G-9309)*
Magna-Wind Electric Motor Repr, Wallingford Also called Magna-Wind Inc *(G-9309)*
Magnani Press Incorporated 860 236-2802
  120 New Park Ave Hartford (06106) *(G-3631)*
Magnatech LLC 860 653-2573
  6 Kripes Rd East Granby (06026) *(G-2210)*
Magnatech Dsd Co, The, East Granby Also called Magnatech LLC *(G-2210)*
Magneli Materials LLC 203 644-8560
  33 Weeburn Dr New Canaan (06840) *(G-5117)*
Magnesium Interactive LLC 917 609-1306
  171 Roseville Rd Westport (06880) *(G-10115)*
Magnetec Corporation 203 949-9933
  7 Laser Ln Wallingford (06492) *(G-9310)*
Magnificat Mother of Div Mrcy 860 584-8803
  12 Pleasant St Bristol (06010) *(G-1067)*
Magnum Industries 860 490-9513
  6 Harrison Ave Enfield (06082) *(G-2657)*
Magnuss Services Inc 347 703-0750
  580 Riverside Ave Apt 104 Westport (06880) *(G-10116)*
Mago Point Canvas 860 442-2111
  362 Mago Point Way Waterford (06385) *(G-9661)*
Mahoney Machine & Fabrication 203 722-4771
  341 Boston Post Rd 2s Old Saybrook (06475) *(G-6555)*
Mail Corecron 860 342-1055
  80 Main St Portland (06480) *(G-6964)*
Mail-A-Map, Madison Also called Harbor Publications Inc *(G-3925)*
Mailly Manufacturing Company 203 879-1445
  54 Wakelee Rd Wolcott (06716) *(G-10573)*
Mailourinvitationscom 203 758-1860
  896 Middlebury Rd Middlebury (06762) *(G-4283)*
Mailroom Finance Inc (HQ) 203 301-3400
  478 Wheelers Farms Rd Milford (06461) *(G-4574)*
Maine Power Express LLC 203 661-0055
  485 W Putnam Ave Greenwich (06830) *(G-3197)*
Mainely Custom Carving 203 426-8375
  9 Cobblestone Ln Newtown (06470) *(G-5759)*
Mainville Welding Co Inc 203 237-3103
  55 Goffe St Meriden (06451) *(G-4191)*
Majestic Press 860 673-2064
  55 Railroad Ave Unionville (06085) *(G-9120)*
Majilly, Pomfret Center Also called Tonmar LLC *(G-6947)*
Major Tire Co LLC 203 543-0334
  80 Century Dr Ste 2 Stratford (06615) *(G-8645)*
Mak Industries LLC 860 623-4911
  40 Tromley Rd East Windsor (06088) *(G-2509)*
Mak Metal Fab 203 213-0269
  89 N Plains Industrial Rd Wallingford (06492) *(G-9311)*
Make A Candle 203 871-8426
  11 Rose St Branford (06405) *(G-623)*
Makino Inc 860 223-0236
  255 Myrtle St New Britain (06053) *(G-5012)*

ALPHABETIC SECTION

Malabar Bay LLC 203 359-9714
1127 High Ridge Rd # 159 Stamford (06905) *(G-8294)*

Malachite Publishing LLC 860 495-5484
15 Croft Ct Pawcatuck (06379) *(G-6720)*

Malco Inc 860 584-0446
38 Napco Dr Terryville (06786) *(G-8764)*

Malia Mills Swim Wear 203 622-3137
16 Greenwich Ave Greenwich (06830) *(G-3198)*

Mallace Industries Corp 800 521-0194
2 Heritage Park Rd Clinton (06413) *(G-1514)*

Mallery Lumber Inc 860 632-3505
162 West St Cromwell (06416) *(G-1707)*

Malta Food Pantry Inc 860 725-0944
19 Woodland St Ste 37 Hartford (06105) *(G-3632)*

Maltese Services LLC 203 805-7669
27 Diane Dr Monroe (06468) *(G-4732)*

Malux Machine LLC 203 526-1834
360 Sniffens Ln Stratford (06615) *(G-8646)*

Management Hlth Solutions Inc (PA) 888 647-4621
99 Hawley Ln Ste 1201 Stratford (06614) *(G-8647)*

Management Software Inc 860 536-5177
547 Colonel Ledyard Hwy Ledyard (06339) *(G-3877)*

Manchester Molding and Mfg Co 860 643-2141
96 Sheldon Rd Manchester (06042) *(G-4052)*

Manchester Packing, Vernon Also called Bravo LLC *(G-9134)*

Manchester Packing Company Inc 860 646-5000
349 Wetherell St Manchester (06040) *(G-4053)*

Manchester TI & Design ADP LLC 860 296-6541
465 Ledyard St Hartford (06114) *(G-3633)*

Mandalay Industries LLC 203 324-4033
82 Akbar Rd Stamford (06902) *(G-8295)*

Mandee 860 644-2128
194 Buckland Hills Dr Manchester (06042) *(G-4054)*

Mandel Vilar Press 806 790-4731
19 Oxford Ct Simsbury (06070) *(G-7633)*

Mandrel 410 507-7767
65 Philip Dr Shelton (06484) *(G-7495)*

Mangladesh LLC 203 299-0697
172 Forest Ave Fairfield (06824) *(G-2812)*

Mango Dsp Inc 203 857-4008
83 East Ave Ste 115 Norwalk (06851) *(G-6245)*

Mango Intlgent Vdeo Solutions, Norwalk Also called Mango Dsp Inc *(G-6245)*

Mannan 3d Innovations LLC 860 306-4203
35 Country Walk Higganum (06441) *(G-3768)*

Manning International, Fairfield Also called Opal Manning Company Inc *(G-2825)*

Mannkind Biopharm, Danbury Also called Mannkind Corporation *(G-1879)*

Mannkind Corporation 203 798-8000
1 Casper St Danbury (06810) *(G-1879)*

Mantrose-Haeuser Co Inc (HQ) 203 454-1800
100 Nyala Farms Rd Westport (06880) *(G-10117)*

Manufacturers Associates Inc 203 931-4344
45 Railroad Ave West Haven (06516) *(G-9930)*

Manufacturers Coml Fin LLC 860 242-6287
1022 Boulevard West Hartford (06119) *(G-9832)*

Manufacturers Service Co Inc 203 389-9595
5 Lunar Dr Woodbridge (06525) *(G-10606)*

Manufacturing, Meriden Also called Savage Products LLC *(G-4240)*

Manufacturing Assists 203 934-6574
36 Hillside Ave West Haven (06516) *(G-9931)*

Manufacturing Productivi 860 916-8189
910 Day Hill Rd Windsor (06095) *(G-10406)*

Manufctring Alnce Svc Corp Inc 203 596-1900
173 Interstate Ln Waterbury (06705) *(G-9533)*

Manup LLC 203 588-9861
345 Wilson Ave Norwalk (06854) *(G-6246)*

Manuscritos Publishing LLC 860 432-9519
9 Coughlin Rd Manchester (06040) *(G-4055)*

Mapeco Products, Oxford Also called Walz & Krenzer Inc *(G-6699)*

Maple Craft Foods LLC 203 913-7066
6 Cider Mill Rd Sandy Hook (06482) *(G-7321)*

Maple Print Services Inc 860 381-5470
92 Osga Ln Griswold (06351) *(G-3267)*

Maple Print Services Inc 860 381-5470
39 Wedgewood Dr Jewett City (06351) *(G-3799)*

Maple Slope Creations, Lebanon Also called Joe Charron *(G-3855)*

Maple Syrup, Old Lyme Also called Bureaus Sugar House *(G-6492)*

Maplegate Media Group Inc 203 826-7557
1503 Sienna Dr Danbury (06810) *(G-1880)*

Maps and More 203 335-0556
226 Sampson St Bridgeport (06606) *(G-828)*

Marathon Enterprises LLC 860 888-6294
9 Rushleigh Rd West Hartford (06117) *(G-9833)*

Marathon Speaker System, Norwalk Also called Marathon Wood Work *(G-6247)*

Marathon Wood Work 203 847-2800
327 Main Ave Ste 2 Norwalk (06851) *(G-6247)*

Marble & Granite Creations LLC 860 350-1306
469 Danbury Rd Ste 4 New Milford (06776) *(G-5560)*

Marc Bouley 860 450-1713
28 Young St Willimantic (06226) *(G-10233)*

Marc Johnson 860 774-3315
16 Depot Rd Danielson (06239) *(G-1998)*

Marc Tool & Die Inc 203 758-5933
23 Oak Ln Prospect (06712) *(G-7008)*

Marcia Jean Fabric and Cft LLC 203 273-1665
35 Lincoln Ave Old Greenwich (06870) *(G-6479)*

Mardini Power Station 203 576-8951
1267 Fairfield Ave Bridgeport (06605) *(G-829)*

Marel Corporation 203 934-8187
5 Saw Mill Rd West Haven (06516) *(G-9932)*

Marena Industries Inc 860 528-9701
433 School St East Hartford (06108) *(G-2343)*

Marena Machinery Sales Div, East Hartford Also called Marena Industries Inc *(G-2343)*

Marenna Amusements LLC 203 623-4386
88 Marsh Hill Rd Orange (06477) *(G-6612)*

Maretron LLP 602 861-1707
60 Johnson Ave Plainville (06062) *(G-6838)*

Margaret Witham 860 399-6403
662 Boston Post Rd Westbrook (06498) *(G-10003)*

Marhall Browing Intl Corp 203 264-2702
353 Christian St Ste 3 Oxford (06478) *(G-6676)*

Marilyn Gehring 203 358-8700
496 Glenbrook Rd Stamford (06906) *(G-8296)*

Marine Fabricators 203 488-7093
145 S Montowese St Branford (06405) *(G-624)*

Marine Money, Stamford Also called International Mktg Strategies *(G-8253)*

Marinero Express 809 East 203 487-0636
809 E Main St Stamford (06902) *(G-8297)*

Marinus Pharmaceuticals Inc 484 801-4670
8 Mansion St New Haven (06512) *(G-5325)*

Mario Precision Products 203 758-3101
19 Wihbey Dr Prospect (06712) *(G-7009)*

Marion Manufacturing Company 203 272-5376
1675 Reinhard Rd Cheshire (06410) *(G-1411)*

Marjan Inc 203 573-1742
44 Railroad Hill St Waterbury (06708) *(G-9534)*

Mark A Little 808 247-8604
402 Route 197 Woodstock (06281) *(G-10671)*

Mark Cappitellas Hnd-Cut Wden 860 818-4334
58 Schulman Veslak Rd East Haddam (06423) *(G-2244)*

Mark D Tweedie DDS 860 649-0436
566 Center St Manchester (06040) *(G-4056)*

Mark Dzidzk 860 793-2767
20k Hultenius St Plainville (06062) *(G-6839)*

Mark Fahey 203 686-0852
64 Nutmeg Dr Apt B Meriden (06451) *(G-4192)*

Mark G Cappitella (PA) 860 873-3093
31 Bogue Ln East Haddam (06423) *(G-2245)*

Mark Karotkin 860 202-7821
17 Grassmere Ave Hartford (06110) *(G-3634)*

Mark Machine Tool LLC 203 910-5942
72 Clark St Wolcott (06716) *(G-10574)*

Mark Misercola 423 323-0183
105 Silvermine Ave Norwalk (06850) *(G-6248)*

Mark Nicoletti 860 582-5645
33 Stafford Ave Ste 2 Bristol (06010) *(G-1068)*

Mark Ramponi Printing 860 673-5507
28 Covey Rd Burlington (06013) *(G-1272)*

Mark Tool Co 860 673-5039
88 Tamara Cir Avon (06001) *(G-92)*

Mark V Laboratory Inc 860 653-7201
18 Kripes Rd East Granby (06026) *(G-2211)*

Mark's Mechanical, Woodstock Also called Mark A Little *(G-10671)*

Markal Finishing Co Inc 203 384-8219
400 Bostwick Ave Bridgeport (06605) *(G-830)*

Markany Na LLC 914 656-7073
152 Deming St South Windsor (06074) *(G-7789)*

Market76 Inc 866 808-5491
58 Boston St Guilford (06437) *(G-3370)*

Marketing Sltons Unlimited LLC 860 523-0670
109 Talcott Rd West Hartford (06110) *(G-9834)*

Markow Race Cars 860 610-0776
701 Nutmeg Rd N Ste 1 South Windsor (06074) *(G-7790)*

Markowski Farm 860 668-5033
101 3rd St Suffield (06078) *(G-8725)*

Marks Construction Co LLC (PA) 860 407-2391
201 Marlborough St Portland (06480) *(G-6965)*

Marlborough Plastics Inc 860 295-9124
350 N Main St Marlborough (06447) *(G-4125)*

Marlin Company (PA) 203 294-9800
10 Research Pkwy Ste 4 Wallingford (06492) *(G-9312)*

Marlow Tool Co, Portland Also called Bill Marlow *(G-6952)*

Marmon Engnered Wire Cable LLC 860 653-8300
280 Trumbull St Fl 23 Hartford (06103) *(G-3635)*

Marmon Utility LLC 203 881-5358
49 Day St Seymour (06483) *(G-7354)*

Marmot Mountain LLC 203 869-0162
165 Greenwich Ave Greenwich (06830) *(G-3199)*

Mars Architectural Millwork 203 579-2632
55 Randall Ave Ste A Bridgeport (06606) *(G-831)*

Marsam Metal Finishing Co 860 826-5489
206 Newington Ave New Britain (06051) *(G-5013)*

Marsars Water Rescue Systems 203 924-7315
8 Algonkin Rd Shelton (06484) *(G-7496)*

Marsco Sheetmetal LLC 203 459-2698
474 Pepper St Monroe (06468) ***(G-4733)***
Marsh Botanical Garden, New Haven *Also called Yale University* ***(G-5449)***
Marshall Paper Tube 860 245-5536
159 Babcock Rd North Stonington (06359) ***(G-6029)***
Martel Woodworking Co 860 564-1983
196 Black Hill Rd Plainfield (06374) ***(G-6748)***
Martin Cabinet Inc (PA) 860 747-5769
336 S Washington St Ste 2 Plainville (06062) ***(G-6840)***
Martin Cabinet Inc 860 747-5769
500 Broad St Bristol (06010) ***(G-1069)***
Martin Mfg Services LLC 860 663-1465
96 Cow Hill Rd Killingworth (06419) ***(G-3836)***
Martin Rosols Inc 860 223-2707
45 Grove St New Britain (06053) ***(G-5014)***
Marty Gilman Incorporated (PA) 860 889-7334
30 Gilman Rd Gilman (06336) ***(G-3001)***
Marty Gilman Incorporated 860 889-7334
1 Commerce Park Rd Bozrah (06334) ***(G-528)***
Mary Carroll 860 543-0750
22 Bailey Rd Andover (06232) ***(G-13)***
Mary Jeans Musical Instrs LLC 860 887-0633
204 West Rd Salem (06420) ***(G-7290)***
Maryann D Langdon 203 562-7161
178 E Rock Rd New Haven (06511) ***(G-5326)***
Maryjanesfarm Publishing Group 203 857-4880
535 Cnncticut Ave Ste 100 Norwalk (06854) ***(G-6249)***
Mason Medical Communications 203 227-9252
10 Covlee Dr Westport (06880) ***(G-10118)***
Mason Press Inc 860 625-3707
139 Oswegatchie Rd Waterford (06385) ***(G-9662)***
Massachusetts Envelope Co Inc 860 727-9100
10 Midland St Hartford (06120) ***(G-3636)***
Massconn Distribute Cpl 860 882-0717
12 Commerce Way South Windsor (06074) ***(G-7791)***
Master Craft Kitchens 203 366-1461
2397 E Main St Bridgeport (06610) ***(G-832)***
Master Engrv & Printery Inc (PA) 203 723-2779
45 Westridge Dr Waterbury (06708) ***(G-9535)***
Master Tool & Machine Inc 860 747-2581
13 Grace Ave Plainville (06062) ***(G-6841)***
Master Tool and Machines LLC 860 747-2581
13 Grace Ave Plainville (06062) ***(G-6842)***
Mastercraft Tool and Mch Co 860 628-5551
100 Newell St Southington (06489) ***(G-7950)***
Masterman & Kovil, Cheshire *Also called Kovil Manufacturing LLC* ***(G-1403)***
Masters Publishing 860 295-8454
52 Keirstead Cir Marlborough (06447) ***(G-4126)***
Mastriani Gourmet Food LLC 203 368-9556
570 Barnum Ave Bridgeport (06608) ***(G-833)***
Matchbox USA 860 349-1655
62 Saw Mill Rd Durham (06422) ***(G-2152)***
Material Promotions Inc 203 757-8900
145 Railroad Hill St Waterbury (06708) ***(G-9536)***
Materials Proc Dev Group LLC 203 269-6617
7 Swan Ave Wallingford (06492) ***(G-9313)***
Materion Lrge Area Catings LLC (HQ) 216 486-4200
300 Lamberton Rd Windsor (06095) ***(G-10407)***
Mathertops, South Windsor *Also called C Mather Company Inc* ***(G-7721)***
Mathword Press LLC 203 288-8114
97 Fennbrook Dr Hamden (06517) ***(G-3479)***
Matias Importing & Distrg Co, Newington *Also called Matias Importing & Distrg Corp* ***(G-5675)***
Matias Importing & Distrg Corp 860 666-5544
135 Fenn Rd Newington (06111) ***(G-5675)***
Matrix Apparel Group LLC 203 740-7837
29 Candlewood Dr New Fairfield (06812) ***(G-5171)***
Matrixx Productions 860 218-5565
232 Farmington Ave Hartford (06105) ***(G-3637)***
Matsutek Enterprises LLC 860 276-2464
213 Wedgewood Rd Southington (06489) ***(G-7951)***
Mattatuck Alarm Co Inc 203 754-0541
161 Fairfield Ave Waterbury (06708) ***(G-9537)***
Matthew Fisel ND 203 453-0122
20 Dunk Rock Rd Guilford (06437) ***(G-3371)***
Matthew Ryan Woodworking LLC 203 268-8469
5778 Main St Trumbull (06611) ***(G-9046)***
Matthew Warren Inc 860 621-7358
29 Depaolo Dr Southington (06489) ***(G-7952)***
Matthew Warren Inc 203 888-2133
95 Silvermine Rd Ste 1 Seymour (06483) ***(G-7355)***
Matthews Printing Co 203 265-0363
10 Marshall St Wallingford (06492) ***(G-9314)***
Mattituck Vineyards LLC 203 637-4457
33 Gilliam Ln Riverside (06878) ***(G-7196)***
Maugle Sierra Vineyards LLC 860 464-2987
825 Colonel Ledyard Hwy # 827 Ledyard (06339) ***(G-3878)***
Maurer & Shepherd Joyners 860 633-2383
122 Naubuc Ave Ste B4 Glastonbury (06033) ***(G-3057)***
Maurices Country Meat Mkt LLC 860 546-9588
155 Gooseneck Hill Rd Canterbury (06331) ***(G-1300)***
Maverick Arms Inc 203 230-5300
7 Grasso Ave North Haven (06473) ***(G-5961)***
Max Analytical Tech Inc 989 772-5088
32 North Rd East Windsor (06088) ***(G-2510)***
Max Padro 203 530-0616
13 Cullen Ave West Haven (06516) ***(G-9933)***
Max Productions LLC 203 838-2795
167 Main St Ste 1 Norwalk (06851) ***(G-6250)***
Max-Tek LLC 860 372-4900
48 N Plains Industrial Rd # 1 Wallingford (06492) ***(G-9315)***
Max-Tek Ue Superabrasive Mch, Wallingford *Also called Max-Tek LLC* ***(G-9315)***
Maxam Initiation Systems LLC 860 774-3507
74 Dixon Rd Sterling (06377) ***(G-8512)***
Maxam North America Inc 860 774-2333
74 Dixon Rd Sterling (06377) ***(G-8513)***
Maxon Corporation 860 571-6411
712 Brook St Ste 106 Rocky Hill (06067) ***(G-7256)***
Mayan Corporation 203 854-4711
79 Day St Norwalk (06854) ***(G-6251)***
Mayarc Industries Inc 860 871-1872
54 Minor Hill Rd Ellington (06029) ***(G-2594)***
Mayborn Group, Stamford *Also called Mayborn Usa Inc* ***(G-8298)***
Mayborn Usa Inc 781 269-7490
1010 Washington Blvd # 11 Stamford (06901) ***(G-8298)***
MB Aerospace 860 653-0569
99 Rainbow Rd East Granby (06026) ***(G-2212)***
MB Consulting LLC 860 889-7941
39 Sunnyside St Yantic (06389) ***(G-10698)***
MB Software Development 203 928-0436
109 Coleman St West Haven (06516) ***(G-9934)***
MB Sport LLC (PA) 203 966-1985
31 Grove St New Canaan (06840) ***(G-5118)***
MB Sports Training LLC 203 269-1410
24 Fire Lite Pl Northford (06472) ***(G-6050)***
MB Systems LLC 203 881-1583
9 Old Town Rd Seymour (06483) ***(G-7356)***
Mbf Holdings LLC 203 302-2812
777 W Putnam Ave Greenwich (06830) ***(G-3200)***
Mbm Sales 203 866-3674
40 Quintard Ave Norwalk (06854) ***(G-6252)***
Mbs Web Creations 203 521-0642
432 Indian Ave Bridgeport (06606) ***(G-834)***
Mbsiinet Inc 888 466-2744
194 Main St N Southbury (06488) ***(G-7866)***
Mbsw Inc 860 243-0303
41 Plainfield Rd West Hartford (06117) ***(G-9835)***
Mc Cann Bros Inc 203 335-8630
490 Pepper St Monroe (06468) ***(G-4734)***
Mc Cann Brothers Baskets, Monroe *Also called Mc Cann Bros Inc* ***(G-4734)***
Mc Clintock Manufacturing 203 263-4743
237 Washington Rd Woodbury (06798) ***(G-10642)***
Mc Conney's Farm, Derby *Also called Lawrence Mc Conney* ***(G-2118)***
Mc Guire Manufacturing Co Inc 203 699-1801
60 Grandview Ct Cheshire (06410) ***(G-1412)***
Mc Hugh Business Forms 203 268-3500
93 Lazy Brook Rd Monroe (06468) ***(G-4735)***
Mc Keon Computer Services 860 496-7171
142 Cedar Ln Torrington (06790) ***(G-8947)***
Mc Kinney Products Company 800 346-7707
225 Episcopal Rd 1 Berlin (06037) ***(G-199)***
Mc Mahon Publishing Co 203 544-8389
83 Peaceable St Redding (06896) ***(G-7100)***
McBooks Press Inc 607 272-2114
246 Goose Ln Ste 200 Guilford (06437) ***(G-3372)***
McCann Sales Inc 860 614-0992
9 Case Cir West Simsbury (06092) ***(G-9980)***
McClave Philbrick & Giblin 860 572-7710
929 Flanders Rd Mystic (06355) ***(G-4831)***
McDowell Group Inc 203 494-4120
107 River St Guilford (06437) ***(G-3373)***
McFigs Beyond Signs LLC 203 792-4057
61 Quaker Ridge Rd Bethel (06801) ***(G-325)***
McGill Airflow LLC 860 653-8001
99 Rainbow Rd Ste E East Granby (06026) ***(G-2213)***
McGuire Manufacturing Co Inc 203 301-0270
11 Cascade Blvd Milford (06460) ***(G-4575)***
McGuires Oil LLc 860 889-2567
19 Burdick Rd Preston (06365) ***(G-6986)***
McGurk Industries 917 524-5132
49 Meadow Rd Trumbull (06611) ***(G-9047)***
McInnis USA Inc 203 890-9950
850 Canal St Stamford (06902) ***(G-8299)***
McIntire Company (HQ) 860 585-8559
745 Clark Ave Bristol (06010) ***(G-1070)***
McLeod Optical Company Inc 203 754-2187
451 Meriden Rd Ste 3 Waterbury (06705) ***(G-9538)***
McLodesignscom 203 296-1400
1138 Hancock Ave Bridgeport (06605) ***(G-835)***
McM Stamping Corporation 203 792-3080
66 Beaver Brook Rd Danbury (06810) ***(G-1881)***
McMellon Associates LLC 203 272-5859
510 Cornwall Ave Ste 4 Cheshire (06410) ***(G-1413)***
McMellon Bros Incorporated 203 375-5685
915 Honeyspot Rd Stratford (06615) ***(G-8648)***

McMullan Wall Coverings 860 569-6260
105 Huckleberry Rd East Hartford (06118) *(G-2344)*
McMullin Manufacturing Corp 203 740-3360
70 Pocono Rd Brookfield (06804) *(G-1204)*
McNeil Healthcare Inc 203 934-8187
5 Saw Mill Rd West Haven (06516) *(G-9935)*
McVac Environmental Svcs Inc 203 497-1960
481 Grand Ave New Haven (06513) *(G-5327)*
McWeeney Marketing Group Inc 203 891-8100
53 Robinson Blvd Orange (06477) *(G-6613)*
MD Solarsciences Corporation 203 857-0095
9 W Broad St Ste 320 Stamford (06902) *(G-8300)*
Mdm Products LLC 203 877-7070
105 Woodmont Rd Milford (06460) *(G-4576)*
MDN Assoc Inc 203 758-6721
18 Robindale Dr Prospect (06712) *(G-7010)*
Me2health LLC 203 208-8927
253 Village Pond Rd Guilford (06437) *(G-3374)*
Mead Monogramming 203 618-0701
9 Mead Ave Cos Cob (06807) *(G-1637)*
Meade Computer Services, Shelton *Also called Thomas Meade (G-7565)*
Meade Daily Group LLC 860 399-7342
103 Cold Spring Dr Westbrook (06498) *(G-10004)*
Meadow Manufacturing Inc 860 357-3785
120 Old Brickyard Ln Kensington (06037) *(G-3813)*
Meadow Woodworking LLC 203 213-3332
22 Cedar Ln Cheshire (06410) *(G-1414)*
Meadwestvaco Packg Systems LLC 409 276-3137
1 High Ridge Park Stamford (06905) *(G-8301)*
Meadwestvaco Texas, Stamford *Also called Meadwestvaco Packg Systems LLC (G-8301)*
Meals By Michael 203 294-1770
8 Mulligan Dr Wallingford (06492) *(G-9316)*
Measurement Systems, Glastonbury *Also called Cameron International Corp (G-3018)*
Measurement Systems Inc 203 949-3500
50 Barnes Park Rd N # 102 Wallingford (06492) *(G-9317)*
Meb Enterprises Inc 203 599-0273
496 S Broad St Meriden (06450) *(G-4193)*
Mecha Noodle Bar 203 691-9671
201 Crown St New Haven (06510) *(G-5328)*
Mechancal Engnered Systems LLC 203 400-4658
180 Jonathan Rd New Canaan (06840) *(G-5119)*
Meco Precision Industries Inc 860 210-1801
523 River Rd Gaylordsville (06755) *(G-2994)*
Med Opportunity Partners LLC (PA) 203 622-1333
1 Roger Dr Greenwich (06831) *(G-3201)*
Med Print, Ellington *Also called Ellington Printery Inc (G-2589)*
Medelco Inc 203 275-8070
54 Washburn St Bridgeport (06605) *(G-836)*
Medex Southington, Southington *Also called Smiths Medical Asd Inc (G-7975)*
Medhumor Med Publications LLC 203 550-9041
1127 High Ridge Rd # 332 Stamford (06905) *(G-8302)*
Medi Products 203 324-3711
30 Nurney St Stamford (06902) *(G-8303)*
Media Links Inc 860 206-9163
431-C Hayden Station Rd Windsor (06095) *(G-10408)*
Media Metrix LLC 203 386-0228
999 Oronoque Ln Ste 3b Stratford (06614) *(G-8649)*
Media One LLC 203 745-5825
44 Hawley Rd Hamden (06517) *(G-3480)*
Media Ventures Inc 203 852-6570
200 Connecticut Ave # 23 Norwalk (06854) *(G-6253)*
Mediagraphicscom Inc 203 404-7233
9 Commerce Cir Durham (06422) *(G-2153)*
Medianews Group Inc 203 333-0161
301 Merritt 7 Ste 1 Norwalk (06851) *(G-6254)*
Medical Imaging Group Inc (PA) 203 588-1921
216 Cascade Rd Stamford (06903) *(G-8304)*
Medical Industries America LLC 203 254-8080
1735 Post Rd Ste 6 Fairfield (06824) *(G-2813)*
Medical Laser Systems Inc 203 481-2395
20 Baldwin Dr Branford (06405) *(G-625)*
Medinstill LLC 860 350-1900
201 Housatonic Ave New Milford (06776) *(G-5561)*
Meditech LLC 203 219-3688
2 Farm House Ln Norwalk (06851) *(G-6255)*
Mediterranean Snack Fd Co LLC 973 402-2644
1111 Summer St Ste 5a Stamford (06905) *(G-8305)*
Medpipes 860 658-7300
19 Drumlin Rd West Simsbury (06092) *(G-9981)*
Medpricercom Inc 203 453-4554
2346 Boston Post Rd Ste 2 Guilford (06437) *(G-3375)*
Medtronic Inc 203 492-5764
60 Middletown Ave North Haven (06473) *(G-5962)*
Medtronic Xomed Inc 860 572-9586
950 Flanders Rd Mystic (06355) *(G-4832)*
Mega Manufacturing LLC 860 666-5555
115 Pane Rd Newington (06111) *(G-5676)*
Mega Resveratrol, Danbury *Also called Candlewood Stars Inc (G-1762)*
Mega Sound and Light LLC 203 743-4200
36 Mill Plain Rd Ste 312 Danbury (06811) *(G-1882)*
Megasonics Inc 203 966-3404
205 Benedict Hill Rd New Canaan (06840) *(G-5120)*
Melco, Meriden *Also called Meriden Electronics Corp (G-4195)*
Melega Inc 203 961-8703
47 W Main St Stamford (06902) *(G-8306)*
Melinta Subsidiary Corp (HQ) 203 624-5606
300 George St Ste 301 New Haven (06511) *(G-5329)*
Melinta Therapeutics Inc (PA) 908 617-1309
300 George St Ste 301 New Haven (06511) *(G-5330)*
Melvin Mayo 802 698-7635
46 Sword Ave Enfield (06082) *(G-2658)*
Memory Lane Collections, Danbury *Also called Visual Impact LLC (G-1973)*
Memory Lane Quilters LLC 203 272-1010
330 Towpath Ln Cheshire (06410) *(G-1415)*
Memry Corporation (HQ) 203 739-1100
3 Berkshire Blvd Bethel (06801) *(G-326)*
Memry Corporation 203 739-1146
8 Berkshire Blvd Bethel (06801) *(G-327)*
Mental Canvas LLC 475 329-0515
61 Hartford Ave Madison (06443) *(G-3939)*
Mepp Tool Co Inc 860 289-8230
81 Commerce St Glastonbury (06033) *(G-3058)*
Mercantile Development Inc 203 922-8880
10 Waterview Dr Shelton (06484) *(G-7497)*
Mercuria Energy Trading Inc 203 413-3355
33 Benedict Pl Ste 1 Greenwich (06830) *(G-3202)*
Mercury Fuel Co 860 793-6602
301 East St Plainville (06062) *(G-6843)*
Mercury Fuel Service Inc (PA) 203 756-7284
43 Lafayette St Waterbury (06708) *(G-9539)*
Mercury Fuel Service Inc 203 291-0833
322 Post Rd E Westport (06880) *(G-10119)*
Meredith Graphics & Design 203 375-1039
375 N Abram St Stratford (06614) *(G-8650)*
Meriden Awning & Decorating Co 203 634-0067
336 Hanover St Meriden (06451) *(G-4194)*
Meriden Electronics Corp 203 237-8811
1777 N Colony Rd Meriden (06450) *(G-4195)*
Meriden Fire Marshals Office 203 630-4010
142 E Main St Meriden (06450) *(G-4196)*
Meriden Manufacturing Inc 203 237-7481
230 State Street Ext Meriden (06450) *(G-4197)*
Meriden Precision Plastics LLC 203 235-3261
290 Pratt St Ste 18 Meriden (06450) *(G-4198)*
Meridian Group LLC 860 928-5266
141 Lyon Hill Rd Woodstock (06281) *(G-10672)*
Meridian Operations LLC 860 564-8811
1414 Norwich Rd Plainfield (06374) *(G-6749)*
Meritronics, Oxford *Also called Power Trans Co Inc (G-6688)*
Merl Inc 203 237-8811
1777 N Colony Rd Meriden (06450) *(G-4199)*
Merlin Associates Inc 860 567-1620
457 Bantam Rd Ste 5 Litchfield (06759) *(G-3895)*
Merlyn, Putnam *Also called Control Concepts Inc (G-7037)*
Merrifield Paint Company Inc 860 529-1583
47 Inwood Rd Rocky Hill (06067) *(G-7257)*
Merrill Corporation 860 249-7220
100 Pearl St Fl 14 Hartford (06103) *(G-3638)*
Merrill Industries Inc 860 871-1888
26 Village St Ellington (06029) *(G-2595)*
Merrill Industries LLC 860 871-1888
26 Village St Ellington (06029) *(G-2596)*
Merrill Oil LLC 203 387-1130
517 Amity Rd Woodbridge (06525) *(G-10607)*
Merritt Extruder Corp 203 230-8100
15 Marne St Hamden (06514) *(G-3481)*
Merritt Machine Company 860 257-4484
61 Arrow Rd Ste 5 Wethersfield (06109) *(G-10211)*
Merritt Sign 860 233-3557
143 Quaker Ln S Hartford (06119) *(G-3639)*
Merritt, Joseph & Company, Danbury *Also called Joseph Merritt & Company Inc (G-1863)*
Mery Manufacturing, Rockfall *Also called Rogers Manufacturing Company (G-7215)*
Messiah Development LLC 203 368-2405
210 Congress St Bridgeport (06604) *(G-837)*
Met Tech Inc 203 254-9319
1901 Post Rd Fairfield (06824) *(G-2814)*
Met-Craft, Oxford *Also called Cast Global Manufacturing Corp (G-6648)*
Metabev Inc (PA) 203 967-8502
50 Soundview Dr Stamford (06902) *(G-8307)*
Metal Components Mfg 203 267-5510
43 Bagley Rd Southbury (06488) *(G-7867)*
Metal Finish Eqp & Sup Co Inc 860 668-1050
19 Kenny Roberts Mem Dr Suffield (06078) *(G-8726)*
Metal Improvement Company LLC 860 635-9994
20 Tuttle Pl Ste 6 Middletown (06457) *(G-4375)*
Metal Improvement Company LLC 860 224-9148
1 John Downey Dr New Britain (06051) *(G-5015)*
Metal Improvement Company LLC 860 688-6201
145 Addison Rd Windsor (06095) *(G-10409)*
Metal Improvement Company LLC 860 523-9901
12 Thompson Rd East Windsor (06088) *(G-2511)*
Metal Industries Inc 860 296-6228
806r Wethersfield Ave Hartford (06114) *(G-3640)*

ALPHABETIC

Metal Morphous 203 239-0411
 222 Elm St Ste 11 North Haven (06473) *(G-5963)*
Metal Perfection, Hamden Also called Charles K White *(G-3428)*
Metal Plus LLC 860 379-1327
 214 Wallens Hill Rd Winsted (06098) *(G-10528)*
Metal Works North 203 723-9075
 141 S Main St Beacon Falls (06403) *(G-143)*
Metalast International In 860 673-1725
 12 Stanwich Ln Burlington (06013) *(G-1273)*
Metalcraft LLC 860 361-6767
 607 Bantam Rd Ste D Bantam (06750) *(G-124)*
Metalform Acquisition LLC (PA) 860 224-2630
 555 John Downey Dr New Britain (06051) *(G-5016)*
Metalform Company, New Britain Also called Metalform Acquisition LLC *(G-5016)*
Metallizing Service Co Inc (PA) 860 953-1144
 11 Cody St Hartford (06110) *(G-3641)*
Metallon Inc 860 283-8265
 1415 Waterbury Rd Thomaston (06787) *(G-8797)*
Metallon Inc 203 437-8540
 2120 Thomaston Ave Waterbury (06704) *(G-9540)*
Metalpro Inc 860 388-1811
 50 School House Rd Old Saybrook (06475) *(G-6556)*
Metalpuck Co LLC 860 561-5936
 25 Common Dr West Hartford (06107) *(G-9836)*
Metals Edge Welding LLC 203 500-5644
 135 Big Horn Rd Shelton (06484) *(G-7498)*
Metamorphic Materials Inc 860 738-8638
 122 Colebrook River Rd Winsted (06098) *(G-10529)*
Metfin Shot Blast Systems, Suffield Also called Metal Finish Eqp & Sup Co Inc *(G-8726)*
Metis Microsystems LLC 203 512-8453
 48 Farrell Rd Newtown (06470) *(G-5760)*
Metro Neighbors Publishing LLC 203 494-3600
 22 Esterly Farms Rd Madison (06443) *(G-3940)*
Metro Signs LLC 203 933-0333
 912 Boston Post Rd West Haven (06516) *(G-9936)*
Metropower, Rocky Hill Also called Cummins Inc *(G-7230)*
Metsa Board Americas Corp 203 229-0037
 301 Merritt 7 Ste 2 Norwalk (06851) *(G-6256)*
Mettler Packaging LLC 860 628-6193
 100 Queen St Ste 5 Southington (06489) *(G-7953)*
Meurer Industries 303 279-8373
 400 Research Pkwy Meriden (06450) *(G-4200)*
Mev Photonics, Westport Also called Mev Technologies LLC *(G-10120)*
Mev Technologies LLC 203 227-4723
 9 Janson Dr Westport (06880) *(G-10120)*
Mexi-Grill LLC 203 574-2127
 495 Union St Waterbury (06706) *(G-9541)*
Meyer Gage Co Inc 860 528-6526
 230 Burnham St South Windsor (06074) *(G-7792)*
Meyer Wire & Cable Company LLC 203 281-0817
 1072 Sherman Ave Hamden (06514) *(G-3482)*
Mezes J & Sons, Bridgeport Also called John Mezes & Sons Inc *(G-809)*
Mf Industries 860 355-8188
 5 Old Town Park Rd New Milford (06776) *(G-5562)*
Mfg Directions 203 483-0797
 31 Ciro Rd North Branford (06471) *(G-5848)*
Mfg Service Co 860 749-8316
 10 Dust House Rd Enfield (06082) *(G-2659)*
MGA Emblem Co, Cheshire Also called Robert Audette *(G-1440)*
Mgc's Cstm Made Wooden, East Haddam Also called Mark G Cappitella *(G-2245)*
MGI usa Inc 203 312-1200
 23 Forest Ave Danbury (06810) *(G-1883)*
Mgs Group-Hall Industries The, North Branford Also called MGS Manufacturing Inc *(G-5849)*
MGS Manufacturing Inc 203 481-4275
 8c Commerce Dr North Branford (06471) *(G-5849)*
MGS Manufacturing Inc 203 484-9275
 8 Commerce Dr North Branford (06471) *(G-5850)*
MH Rhodes Cramer LLC 860 291-8402
 105 Nutmeg Rd S South Windsor (06074) *(G-7793)*
Mh Woodworking Inc 860 871-7321
 327 Sugar Hill Rd Tolland (06084) *(G-8870)*
Mhq Inc 888 242-1118
 750 Newfield St Middletown (06457) *(G-4376)*
MHS Industries 860 798-7981
 418 River St Windsor (06095) *(G-10410)*
MI Gente Express 860 447-2525
 130 Bank St New London (06320) *(G-5478)*
Miami Bay Beverage Company LLC 203 453-0090
 7 Sycamore Way Unit 3 Branford (06405) *(G-626)*
Miami Wabash Paper LLC (HQ) 203 847-8500
 108 Main St Ste 3 Norwalk (06851) *(G-6257)*
Micalizzi Ice Cream, Bridgeport Also called Lucille Piccirillo *(G-826)*
Michael Dupont 203 434-0650
 1 Beeholm Rd Redding (06896) *(G-7101)*
Michael Hurlburt 860 745-0681
 155 Pearl St Enfield (06082) *(G-2660)*
Michael J Macisco 203 924-0013
 318 Meadowridge Rd Shelton (06484) *(G-7499)*
Michael James Distler 203 241-4574
 34 Wagon Wheel Rd Redding (06896) *(G-7102)*

Michael Kors 203 748-4300
 7 Backus Ave Ste H102 Danbury (06810) *(G-1884)*
Michael Lazorchak 203 775-0608
 35 Mist Hill Dr Brookfield (06804) *(G-1205)*
Michael Martinetto (PA) 203 874-6114
 170 Walnut St Milford (06461) *(G-4577)*
Michael Petruzzi 860 621-7515
 39 Crescent St Plantsville (06479) *(G-6902)*
Michael Shortell 860 236-4787
 30 Arbor St Ste 2 Hartford (06106) *(G-3642)*
Michael Violano 203 934-3368
 487 Campbell Ave West Haven (06516) *(G-9937)*
Michael Zoppa 860 289-5881
 23 Sea Pave Rd South Windsor (06074) *(G-7794)*
Michaels Dairy Inc 860 443-7617
 11 Harbor Ln New London (06320) *(G-5479)*
Michaels Finest LLC 860 223-7671
 19 Vibberts Ave New Britain (06051) *(G-5017)*
Michaels Woodworking LLC 203 470-0867
 474 S Flat Hill Rd Southbury (06488) *(G-7868)*
Michaud Industries LLC 860 408-0907
 72 Riverside Rd Simsbury (06070) *(G-7634)*
Michaud Tool Co Inc 860 582-6785
 122 Napco Dr Terryville (06786) *(G-8765)*
Michele Pavisic 860 876-2509
 37 Willow Brook Dr Kensington (06037) *(G-3814)*
Michele Schiano Di Cola Inc 203 265-5301
 11 S Colony St Wallingford (06492) *(G-9318)*
Mickey Herbst 203 993-5879
 32 Laurel St Fairfield (06825) *(G-2815)*
Micro Care Corporation (PA) 860 827-0626
 595 John Downey Dr New Britain (06051) *(G-5018)*
Micro Care Marketing Svcs Div, New Britain Also called Micro Care Corporation *(G-5018)*
Micro Insert Inc 860 621-5789
 183 Clark St Milldale (06467) *(G-4685)*
Micro Matic, Naugatuck Also called Advantage Sheet Metal Mfg LLC *(G-4854)*
Micro Precision LLC 860 423-4575
 1102 Windham Rd South Windham (06266) *(G-7690)*
Micro Printing LLC 203 265-5578
 216 Center St Wallingford (06492) *(G-9319)*
Micro Source Discovery Systems 860 350-8078
 11 George Washington Plz Gaylordsville (06755) *(G-2995)*
Micro Training Associates Inc 860 693-7740
 320 Albany Tpke Canton (06019) *(G-1318)*
Micro-Probe Incorporated 203 267-6446
 2 Pomperaug Office Park # 103 Southbury (06488) *(G-7869)*
Microbest Inc 203 597-0355
 670 Captain Neville Dr # 1 Waterbury (06705) *(G-9542)*
Microboard Processing Inc 203 881-4300
 36 Cogwheel Ln Seymour (06483) *(G-7357)*
Microdisplay Report, Norwalk Also called Insight Media LLC *(G-6208)*
Microdyne Technologies 860 747-9473
 64 Neal Ct Plainville (06062) *(G-6844)*
Microfab Company 203 267-1000
 339 Christian St Oxford (06478) *(G-6677)*
Micromod Automation & Controls 585 321-9209
 10 Capital Dr Wallingford (06492) *(G-9320)*
Micromod Automtn & Contrls LLC 585 321-9200
 10 Capital Dr Wallingford (06492) *(G-9321)*
Microphase Corporation 203 866-8000
 100 Trap Falls Road Ext # 400 Shelton (06484) *(G-7500)*
Microshield LLC 800 553-1290
 200 Henry St Stamford (06902) *(G-8308)*
Microsoft Corporation 860 678-3100
 74 Batterson Park Rd # 100 Farmington (06032) *(G-2928)*
Microspecialities Inc 203 874-1832
 430 Smith St Middletown (06457) *(G-4377)*
Microtech Inc 203 272-3234
 1425 Highland Ave Cheshire (06410) *(G-1416)*
Microtechnologies Inc 860 517-8314
 128 Garden St Farmington (06032) *(G-2929)*
Microtools Inc 860 651-6170
 714 Hopmeadow St Ste 14 Simsbury (06070) *(G-7635)*
Mid State ARC Inc 203 238-9001
 20 Powers Dr Meriden (06451) *(G-4201)*
Mid State Assembly & Packg Inc 203 634-8740
 604 Pomeroy Ave Meriden (06450) *(G-4202)*
Mid-Conn Testers LLC 860 232-1943
 269 W Hill Rd Newington (06111) *(G-5677)*
Mid-Island Aggregates/Distribu 860 605-6753
 5 Highview Ln Sherman (06784) *(G-7598)*
Mid-State Manufacturing Inc 860 621-6855
 1610 Mriden Waterburytpke Milldale (06467) *(G-4686)*
Midconn Precision Mfg LLC 860 584-1340
 190 Century Dr Ste 9 Bristol (06010) *(G-1071)*
Middlbury Bee-Intelligencer-Ct 203 577-6800
 2030 Straits Tpke Middlebury (06762) *(G-4284)*
Middle Quarter Animal Hospital 203 263-4772
 726 Main St S Woodbury (06798) *(G-10643)*
Middlesex Shades and Blinds 860 346-7705
 386 Main St Middletown (06457) *(G-4378)*
Middletown Engine Center, East Hartford Also called Pratt & Whitney Company Inc *(G-2357)*

Middletown Printing Co Inc 860 347-5700
512 Main St Middletown (06457) ***(G-4379)***
Midget Louver Company Inc 203 783-1444
671 Naugatuck Ave Milford (06461) ***(G-4578)***
Midnight Printing LLC 203 257-3307
241 Monroe Tpke Monroe (06468) ***(G-4736)***
Midnight Reader 860 643-4220
11 Green Hill Dr Bolton (06043) ***(G-516)***
Midstate Electronics Co 203 265-9900
71 S Turnpike Rd Ste 2 Wallingford (06492) ***(G-9322)***
Midstate Printing Group LLC 203 998-7575
1 Bank St Ste 401 Stamford (06901) ***(G-8309)***
Midsun Group Inc (PA) 860 378-0100
135 Redstone St Southington (06489) ***(G-7954)***
Midsun Specialty Products Inc 860 378-0111
378 Four Rod Rd Berlin (06037) ***(G-200)***
Midwood Quarry and Cnstr Inc (PA) 860 289-1414
200 Tolland St East Hartford (06108) ***(G-2345)***
Mikco Manufacturing Inc 203 269-2250
14 Village Ln Wallingford (06492) ***(G-9323)***
Mike Fineran 860 974-3276
280 Hampton Rd Pomfret Center (06259) ***(G-6942)***
Mike Sadlak 860 742-0227
712 Bread Milk St Unit A6 Coventry (06238) ***(G-1663)***
Mike's Engine Stand, Naugatuck *Also called K & E Auto Machine L L C* ***(G-4896)***
Mikes Plowing & Maintenance 860 868-1413
41 W Morris Rd Washington Depot (06794) ***(G-9418)***
Mikes Sign Maintenance LLC 860 347-1462
35 Sisk St Middletown (06457) ***(G-4380)***
Mikes Welding 203 855-9631
124 Lexington Ave Norwalk (06854) ***(G-6258)***
Mikro Industrial Finishing Co 860 875-6357
170 W Main St Vernon (06066) ***(G-9143)***
Mikron Corp Monroe 203 261-3100
200 Main St Ste D Monroe (06468) ***(G-4737)***
Mikron Corp Stratford 203 261-3100
600a Pepper St # 1 Monroe (06468) ***(G-4738)***
Mil-Con Inc 630 595-2366
22 Great Hill Rd Naugatuck (06770) ***(G-4901)***
Milbar Labs Inc 203 467-1577
20 Commerce St East Haven (06512) ***(G-2442)***
Milestone Graphics 203 218-4528
434 Grand St Bridgeport (06604) ***(G-838)***
Milford Fabricating Co Inc 203 878-2476
500 Bic Dr Bldg 2 Milford (06461) ***(G-4579)***
Milford Metal Products Inc 203 878-0148
394 Oronoque Rd Milford (06461) ***(G-4580)***
Milford Mirror, The, Shelton *Also called Hearst Corporation* ***(G-7463)***
Milford Smoke Junction LLC 203 301-9956
487a Bridgeport Ave Milford (06460) ***(G-4581)***
Miliard Custom Woodworks LLC 860 621-5131
60 Hacienda Cir Plantsville (06479) ***(G-6903)***
Militarylife Publishing LLC 203 402-7234
4 Research Dr Shelton (06484) ***(G-7501)***
Milite Bakery 203 753-9451
53 Interstate Ln Waterbury (06705) ***(G-9543)***
Mill Machine Tool & Die Co 860 628-6700
280 Mill St Southington (06489) ***(G-7955)***
Mill Manufacturing Inc 203 367-9572
105 Willow St Bridgeport (06610) ***(G-839)***
Millbrae Energy LLC (PA) 203 742-2800
500 W Putnam Ave Ste 400 Greenwich (06830) ***(G-3203)***
Millbrook Distillery LLC 203 637-2231
687 River Rd Cos Cob (06807) ***(G-1638)***
Millbrook Press Inc 203 740-2220
2 Old New Milford Rd 2e Brookfield (06804) ***(G-1206)***
Millen Industries Inc (PA) 203 847-8500
108 Main St Ste 4 Norwalk (06851) ***(G-6259)***
Millennium Shade & Sign LLC 203 968-5080
29 Sunnyside Ave Ste 2 Stamford (06902) ***(G-8310)***
Miller Castings Inc 860 822-9991
30 Pautipaug Hill Rd North Franklin (06254) ***(G-5875)***
Miller Company 203 235-4474
275 Pratt St Meriden (06450) ***(G-4203)***
Miller Fuel LLC 860 675-6121
28 Monce Rd Burlington (06013) ***(G-1274)***
Miller Marine Canvas 203 878-9291
282 Woodmont Rd Ste 36 Milford (06460) ***(G-4582)***
Miller Professional Trans Svc 860 871-6818
8 Bancroft Rd Vernon (06066) ***(G-9144)***
Miller Rebar LLC 203 717-6645
157 Church St Fl 19 New Haven (06510) ***(G-5331)***
Miller Tina-Attorney 203 938-8507
81 Seventy Acre Rd Redding (06896) ***(G-7103)***
Millerwalk Publishing LLC 203 397-8926
221 W Rock Ave New Haven (06515) ***(G-5332)***
Mills On Wheels 860 705-2903
30 Forest St Norwich (06360) ***(G-6423)***
Millturn Manufacturing Co 203 248-1602
1203 Ridge Rd North Haven (06473) ***(G-5964)***
Millwood Inc 203 248-7902
33 Stiles Ln North Haven (06473) ***(G-5965)***
Millwork Shop LLC 860 489-8848
39 Putter Ln Torrington (06790) ***(G-8948)***
Mimforms LLC 800 445-1245
50 Washington St Fl 7 Norwalk (06854) ***(G-6260)***
Minarik Automation & Control, Bloomfield *Also called Minarik Corporation* ***(G-445)***
Minarik Corporation 860 687-5000
1 Vision Way Bloomfield (06002) ***(G-445)***
Mind2mind Exchange LLC 203 856-0981
32 Mill Brook Rd Stamford (06902) ***(G-8311)***
Mindscape Industries 860 574-9308
159 Hawthorne Dr New London (06320) ***(G-5480)***
Mindtrainr LLC 914 799-1515
107 Revonah Cir Stamford (06905) ***(G-8312)***
Mine Hill Distillery 860 210-1872
5 Mine Hill Rd Roxbury (06783) ***(G-7279)***
Mineral Technology, Canaan *Also called Minteq International Inc* ***(G-1289)***
Minh Long Fine Porcelain 860 586-8755
635 New Park Ave Hartford (06110) ***(G-3643)***
Mini LLC 203 464-5495
66 Church St Naugatuck (06770) ***(G-4902)***
Miniature Nut & Screw Corp 860 953-4490
820 N Mountain Rd Newington (06111) ***(G-5678)***
Minit Print Inc 203 776-6000
27 Whitney Ave New Haven (06510) ***(G-5333)***
Minteq International Inc 860 824-5435
30 Daisy Hill Rd Canaan (06018) ***(G-1289)***
Minute Man Press 203 891-6251
5 Hamden Park Dr Hamden (06517) ***(G-3483)***
Minuteman Arms LLC 203 268-4853
35 Washington St Trumbull (06611) ***(G-9048)***
Minuteman Land Services Inc 203 854-4949
377 Highland Ave Norwalk (06854) ***(G-6261)***
Minuteman Newspaper (PA) 203 226-8877
1175 Post Rd E Ste 3e Westport (06880) ***(G-10121)***
Minuteman Press, Hamden *Also called Minute Man Press* ***(G-3483)***
Minuteman Press, Enfield *Also called P & M Investments LLC* ***(G-2674)***
Minuteman Press, Milford *Also called S and Z Graphics LLC* ***(G-4637)***
Minuteman Press, East Haven *Also called Sabar Graphics LLC* ***(G-2450)***
Minuteman Press, Greenwich *Also called Easy Graphics Inc* ***(G-3156)***
Minuteman Press, Enfield *Also called Enfield Printing Company* ***(G-2639)***
Minuteman Press, Monroe *Also called FSNB Enterprises Inc* ***(G-4718)***
Minuteman Press, Middletown *Also called Middletown Printing Co Inc* ***(G-4379)***
Minuteman Press, Stamford *Also called P & S Printing LLC* ***(G-8348)***
Minuteman Press, Hartford *Also called Capitol Printing Co Inc* ***(G-3561)***
Minuteman Press, Vernon Rockville *Also called Vernon Printing Co Inc* ***(G-9186)***
Minuteman Press, Norwalk *Also called Max Productions LLC* ***(G-6250)***
Minuteman Press, Norwich *Also called Norwich Printing Company Inc* ***(G-6425)***
Minuteman Press, New London *Also called New London Printing Co LLC* ***(G-5481)***
Minuteman Press 973 748-7160
12 Mill Plain Rd Ste 1 Danbury (06811) ***(G-1885)***
Minuteman Press 203 445-6971
42 Bridgeport Ave Shelton (06484) ***(G-7502)***
Minuteman Press 860 646-0601
757 Main St Manchester (06040) ***(G-4057)***
Minuteman Press 860 646-0601
52 Pratt St Hartford (06103) ***(G-3644)***
Minuteman Press 203 261-8318
14 Kitcher Ct Trumbull (06611) ***(G-9049)***
Minuteman Press 860 266-4154
63 Hebron Ave Ste B Glastonbury (06033) ***(G-3059)***
Minuteman Press 860 529-4628
462 Silas Deane Hwy Wethersfield (06109) ***(G-10212)***
Minuteman Press 860 496-7525
257 Main St Bsmt A Torrington (06790) ***(G-8949)***
Minuteman Press 203 261-9569
123 S Main St Ste 210 Newtown (06470) ***(G-5761)***
Minuteman Press 860 674-8700
195 W Main St Ste E Avon (06001) ***(G-93)***
Minuteman Press LLC 203 922-9228
427b Howe Ave Shelton (06484) ***(G-7503)***
Minuteman Press of Bristol 860 589-1100
98 Farmington Ave Bristol (06010) ***(G-1072)***
Minuteman Press of Danbury 203 743-6755
12 Mill Plain Rd Ste 10 Danbury (06811) ***(G-1886)***
Minuteman Tress, Waterbury *Also called Byrne Group Inc* ***(G-9444)***
Miracle Instruments Co 860 642-7745
1667 Exeter Rd Lebanon (06249) ***(G-3858)***
Miranda Vineyard LLC 860 491-9906
42 Ives Rd Goshen (06756) ***(G-3103)***
Mirion Tech Canberra Inc (HQ) 203 238-2351
800 Research Pkwy Meriden (06450) ***(G-4204)***
Mirror Go Round, Farmington *Also called Ark Innovations LLC* ***(G-2878)***
Mirror Polishing & Pltg Co Inc 203 574-5400
346 Huntingdon Ave Waterbury (06708) ***(G-9544)***
Mise En Place Wood Works Inc 860 921-0208
135 Whitbeck Rd New Hartford (06057) ***(G-5202)***
Misfit Prints LLC 203 306-6322
161 State St Apt 315 Meriden (06450) ***(G-4205)***
Misfit Publishing Co LLC 860 444-6796
11 Totoket Rd Quaker Hill (06375) ***(G-7083)***

ALPHABETIC

Miss Speedy Printing Center, Mystic *Also called Speedy Printing LLC* ***(G-4846)***
Mission Allergy Inc....203 364-1570
28 Hawleyville Rd Hawleyville (06440) ***(G-3744)***
Mission Bmdical Scientific Inc....860 941-8896
99 Arbor Xing East Lyme (06333) ***(G-2468)***
Mission Critical Software....860 748-6946
146 Shagbark Rd Glastonbury (06033) ***(G-3060)***
Mist Hill Property Maint LLC....203 648-7434
32 Mist Hill Dr Brookfield (06804) ***(G-1207)***
Mister BS Jerky Co....203 631-2758
25 Harness Dr Meriden (06450) ***(G-4206)***
Mistras Group Inc....860 447-2474
6 Mill Ln Waterford (06385) ***(G-9663)***
Mitchell Machine Screw Company....860 633-7713
167 Oak St Glastonbury (06033) ***(G-3061)***
Mitchell Wods Phrmcuticals LLC....203 258-1305
4 Corporate Dr Ste 287 Shelton (06484) ***(G-7504)***
Mitchell Woodworking LLC....203 878-4249
72 Maple St Milford (06460) ***(G-4583)***
Mitchell-Bate Company....203 233-0862
365 Thomaston Ave Waterbury (06702) ***(G-9545)***
Mitered Edge Woodworking....860 576-6657
186 Babcock Hill Rd South Windham (06266) ***(G-7691)***
Mix Box....203 591-8887
495 Union St Ste 1024 Waterbury (06706) ***(G-9546)***
Mix n Match LLC....203 227-9588
19 Pequot Trl Westport (06880) ***(G-10122)***
Miyoshi America Inc (HQ)....860 779-3990
110 Louisa Viens Dr Dayville (06241) ***(G-2064)***
Miyoshi America Inc....860 779-3990
313 Lake Rd Dayville (06241) ***(G-2065)***
Miyoshi America Inc....860 779-3990
90 Louisa Viens Dr Dayville (06241) ***(G-2066)***
Mj Martin Wood Working LLC....860 577-5311
851 Middlesex Tpke Old Saybrook (06475) ***(G-6557)***
MJ Metal Inc....203 334-3484
225 Howard Ave Bridgeport (06605) ***(G-840)***
Mj Tool & Manufacturing Inc....860 352-2688
11 Herman Dr Ste B Simsbury (06070) ***(G-7636)***
Mj Tool Mfg....860 352-2688
359 E Hill Rd Canton (06019) ***(G-1319)***
MJM Islet, Waterbury *Also called Guiseppe Mazzettini* ***(G-9492)***
MJM Marga LLC....203 729-0600
28 Raytkwich Rd Naugatuck (06770) ***(G-4903)***
MJM Marga LLC....203 597-9035
561 Sylvan Ave Waterbury (06706) ***(G-9547)***
Mk & T Design & Print LLC....203 295-8211
250 Westport Ave Norwalk (06851) ***(G-6262)***
Mk Manufacturing, Bristol *Also called Mark Nicoletti* ***(G-1068)***
Mk Millwork LLC....860 567-0173
234 Thomaston Rd Morris (06763) ***(G-4790)***
Mkb Machine & Tool Mfg....860 828-5728
600 Four Rod Rd Ste 3 Berlin (06037) ***(G-201)***
Mkr Sign Company....860 265-7996
3 Peerless Way Ste V Enfield (06082) ***(G-2661)***
Mkrs Corporation....203 762-2662
32 Blueberry Hill Pl Wilton (06897) ***(G-10312)***
ML Industries....203 820-4922
312 Cambridge St Bridgeport (06606) ***(G-841)***
Mlj Publishing Record Co LLC....203 752-9021
385 Peck St New Haven (06513) ***(G-5334)***
Mlk Business Forms Inc....203 624-6304
25 James St New Haven (06513) ***(G-5335)***
MLS Acq Inc....860 386-6878
32 North Rd East Windsor (06088) ***(G-2512)***
Mm Candles....203 205-0180
119 Carol St Danbury (06810) ***(G-1887)***
Mme Publishing LLC....860 228-1369
15 Homestead Ln Columbia (06237) ***(G-1608)***
Moark LLC (HQ)....951 332-3300
28 Under The Mountain Rd North Franklin (06254) ***(G-5876)***
Mobile Asset Solutions, Danbury *Also called I Tech Services Inc* ***(G-1847)***
Mobile Mini Inc....860 668-1888
911 S St Mach 1 Indus Par 1 Mach Suffield (06078) ***(G-8727)***
Mobile Sense Technologies Inc....203 914-5375
400 Farmington Ave # 2858 Farmington (06032) ***(G-2930)***
Mobile Welding Repair....203 459-2744
639 Wheeler Rd Monroe (06468) ***(G-4739)***
Mobius Press....860 767-0880
23 Eagle Ridge Dr Essex (06426) ***(G-2726)***
Moda LLC....203 302-2800
777 W Putnam Ave Ste 10 Greenwich (06830) ***(G-3204)***
Modean Industries Inc....203 371-6625
15 Lucielle Dr Easton (06612) ***(G-2559)***
Model Works, Newington *Also called Pal Corporation* ***(G-5690)***
Modelvision Inc....860 355-3884
566 Danbury Rd Ste 4 New Milford (06776) ***(G-5563)***
Modern Classics....203 422-2862
1049 North St Greenwich (06831) ***(G-3205)***
Modern Distillery Age....203 971-8710
228 Silvermine Ave Norwalk (06850) ***(G-6263)***
Modern Elec Fax & Computers, Fairfield *Also called Modern Electronic Fax & Cmpt* ***(G-2816)***
Modern Electronic Fax & Cmpt....203 292-6520
65 Milton St Fairfield (06824) ***(G-2816)***
Modern Elements Products LLC....860 667-4247
141 Superior Ave Newington (06111) ***(G-5679)***
Modern Metal Finishing Inc....203 267-1510
110 Willenbrock Rd Oxford (06478) ***(G-6678)***
Modern Nutrition & Biotech....203 244-5830
61 Overlook Dr Ridgefield (06877) ***(G-7155)***
Modern Objects Inc....203 378-5785
5 River Dr Norwalk (06855) ***(G-6264)***
Modern Pastry Shop Inc....860 296-7628
422 Franklin Ave Hartford (06114) ***(G-3645)***
Modern Stitch Company....860 927-5065
13 Railroad St Kent (06757) ***(G-3824)***
Modern Woodcrafts LLC....860 677-7371
72 Northwest Dr Plainville (06062) ***(G-6845)***
Modified Welding LLC....860 428-3599
90 Rich Rd North Grosvenordale (06255) ***(G-5891)***
Moeller Instrument Company Inc....800 243-9310
126 Main St Ivoryton (06442) ***(G-3786)***
Moffly Publications Inc....203 222-0600
205 Main St Ste 1 Westport (06880) ***(G-10123)***
Moffly Publications Inc (PA)....203 222-0600
205 Main St Ste 1 Westport (06880) ***(G-10124)***
Mogo Rehab Incorporated....860 673-5324
193 W Avon Rd Avon (06001) ***(G-94)***
Mohawk Industries Inc....203 739-0260
4 Nabby Rd Danbury (06811) ***(G-1888)***
Mohawk Industries Inc....706 629-7721
180 Church St Torrington (06790) ***(G-8950)***
Mohawk Manufacturing Company....860 632-2345
1270 Newfield St Middletown (06457) ***(G-4381)***
Mohawk Tool and Die Mfg Co Inc....203 367-2181
25 Wells St Ste 4 Bridgeport (06604) ***(G-842)***
Mohegan Wood Pellets LLC....860 862-6100
13 Crow Hill Rd Uncasville (06382) ***(G-9099)***
Mohican Valley Concrete Corp....203 254-7133
195 Ardmore St Fairfield (06824) ***(G-2817)***
Mohican Vly Sand & Grav Corp....203 254-7133
195 Ardmore St Fairfield (06824) ***(G-2818)***
Mold Threads Inc....203 483-1420
21 W End Ave Branford (06405) ***(G-627)***
Mold-Craft Plastics, Portland *Also called Joseph Organek* ***(G-6962)***
Molding Technologies LLC....860 395-3230
304 Boston Post Rd Ste 1 Old Saybrook (06475) ***(G-6558)***
Moldvision LLC....860 315-1025
316 County Home Rd Thompson (06277) ***(G-8840)***
Molex LLC....860 482-2800
187 Commercial Blvd Torrington (06790) ***(G-8951)***
Momentive Prfmce Mtls USA Inc....203 240-5543
385 Lockwood Rd Fairfield (06825) ***(G-2819)***
Mommy & ME....860 269-6226
9 School St Unionville (06085) ***(G-9121)***
Monarch Plastic LLC....860 653-2000
514r Salmon Brook St Granby (06035) ***(G-3112)***
Monas Monograms....860 463-9530
902 East St Andover (06232) ***(G-14)***
Mondo Sauce LLC....206 714-0390
151 Courtland Ave Apt 5e Stamford (06902) ***(G-8313)***
Mongillo Press....203 467-1371
16 Alfred St New Haven (06512) ***(G-5336)***
Mono Crete Step Co of CT LLC....203 748-8419
12 Trowbridge Dr Bethel (06801) ***(G-328)***
Monogram Mary LLC....203 536-9526
8 Somerset Ln Riverside (06878) ***(G-7197)***
Monogram Studio Greenwich CT....203 428-5700
222 Pemberwick Rd Greenwich (06831) ***(G-3206)***
Monogramit LLC....860 779-0694
9 S Main St Brooklyn (06234) ***(G-1249)***
Monopol Corporation....860 583-3852
394 Riverside Ave Bristol (06010) ***(G-1073)***
Monsanto Mystic Research....860 572-5200
62 Maritime Dr Mystic (06355) ***(G-4833)***
Montage Software Systems Inc....203 834-1144
76 Hillbrook Rd Wilton (06897) ***(G-10313)***
Montambault Riva....203 758-4981
25 Luke St Prospect (06712) ***(G-7011)***
Montanari Repair, Danbury *Also called Guy Montanari* ***(G-1840)***
Montanas Board Sports....860 537-2927
32 Bruce Cir Colchester (06415) ***(G-1557)***
Montauk Pilots Inc....860 535-3200
90 Wintechog Hill Rd North Stonington (06359) ***(G-6030)***
Montville Sewer Plant, Uncasville *Also called Town of Montville* ***(G-9107)***
Moon Cutter Co Inc....203 288-9249
2969 State St Hamden (06517) ***(G-3484)***
Mooney Time Inc....203 263-0167
72 Railtree Hill Rd Woodbury (06798) ***(G-10644)***
Moonlight Media LLC....860 345-3595
95 Bridge Rd Bldg 4b Haddam (06438) ***(G-3407)***
Moonlighting LLC....203 740-8964
4 Jackson Dr Brookfield (06804) ***(G-1208)***
Moore Precisionworks, Trumbull *Also called Elene A Moore* ***(G-9024)***

Moore Tool Company Inc (HQ) 203 366-3224
800 Union Ave Bridgeport (06607) ***(G-843)***
Moores Sawmill Inc 860 242-3003
171 Mountain Ave Bloomfield (06002) ***(G-446)***
Mople Home Xixit, Waterbury *Also called Rv Parts & Electric Inc* ***(G-9595)***
Moran Tool & Die, Bolton *Also called Barre Precision Products Inc* ***(G-505)***
Moran Woodworking LLC 203 438-0477
636 Ethan Allen Hwy Ridgefield (06877) ***(G-7156)***
More Than Asleep Pubg LLC 860 872-5757
38 Zoey Dr Vernon (06066) ***(G-9145)***
Morgan Woodworks LLC 203 913-2489
169 Clark St Milford (06460) ***(G-4584)***
Moriartys Desktop Publishing 860 345-8063
39 Little Fawn Trl Higganum (06441) ***(G-3769)***
Morin Corporation (HQ) 860 584-0900
685 Middle St Bristol (06010) ***(G-1074)***
Morin East, Bristol *Also called Morin Corporation* ***(G-1074)***
Morning Star Tool LLC 203 878-6026
83 Erna Ave Milford (06461) ***(G-4585)***
Morning Sun of Trumbull LLC 203 220-8509
98 Cottage St Trumbull (06611) ***(G-9050)***
Moroso Performance Pdts Inc (PA) 203 453-6571
80 Carter Dr Guilford (06437) ***(G-3376)***
Morris Communications Co LLC 203 458-4500
246 Goose Ln Ste 200 Guilford (06437) ***(G-3377)***
Morris Precision Tool Inc 203 284-8488
50 N Plains Industrial Rd Wallingford (06492) ***(G-9324)***
Morris Woodworking 860 346-7500
75 Pease Ave Middletown (06457) ***(G-4382)***
Morristown Star Struck LLC 203 778-4925
8 Francis J Clarke Cir Bethel (06801) ***(G-329)***
Morse Watchmans Inc 203 264-1108
2 Morse Rd Oxford (06478) ***(G-6679)***
Morthanoscom LLC 203 378-2414
4 Ocean Ave Stratford (06615) ***(G-8651)***
Morton Wood Works 203 594-6678
362 2nd Ave West Haven (06516) ***(G-9938)***
Mosaic Records Inc 203 327-7111
425 Fairfield Ave Ste 1 Stamford (06902) ***(G-8314)***
Mosley Hosiery and Socks LLC 860 690-9227
71 Prospect St Bloomfield (06002) ***(G-447)***
Mossberg Corporation (PA) 203 230-5300
7 Grasso Ave North Haven (06473) ***(G-5966)***
Most Excllent Cmics Cllctibles 860 741-0113
481 Enfield St Enfield (06082) ***(G-2662)***
Mother's Kitchen, New Britain *Also called Rich Products Corporation* ***(G-5045)***
Motherstar Online LLC 860 896-1869
103 Mountain Spring Rd Tolland (06084) ***(G-8871)***
Motiv Technology Inc 203 371-7011
145 Ridgeview Ave Fairfield (06825) ***(G-2820)***
Motive Industries LLC 860 423-2064
356 Tuckie Rd North Windham (06256) ***(G-6039)***
Motor Connections 860 583-3407
225 Terryville Rd Bristol (06010) ***(G-1075)***
Motorcyclists Post 203 929-9409
11 Haven Ln Shelton (06484) ***(G-7505)***
Mott Corporation (PA) 860 793-6333
84 Spring Ln Farmington (06032) ***(G-2931)***
Mott Corporation 800 289-6688
75 Spring Ln Farmington (06032) ***(G-2932)***
Mountain Dairy, Storrs Mansfield *Also called Willard J Stearns & Sons Inc* ***(G-8561)***
Mountain Ocarinas 860 242-6626
323 Tunxis Ave Bloomfield (06002) ***(G-448)***
Move Books LLC 203 709-0490
10 N Main St Apt S103 Beacon Falls (06403) ***(G-144)***
Mowmedia LLC 203 240-6416
85 Camp Ave Apt 10l Stamford (06907) ***(G-8315)***
Mozzicato Fmly Investments LLC 860 296-0426
631 Ridge Rd Wethersfield (06109) ***(G-10213)***
Mozzicato Pastry & Bake Shop 860 296-0426
329 Franklin Ave Hartford (06114) ***(G-3646)***
Mozzict-De Psqale Bky Pstry Sp, Hartford *Also called Mozzicato Pastry & Bake Shop* ***(G-3646)***
Mp Impressions LLC 860 873-1797
25 Salls Rd Moodus (06469) ***(G-4774)***
Mp Systems Inc 860 687-3460
34 Bradley Park Rd East Granby (06026) ***(G-2214)***
Mpi Systems Inc 203 762-2260
28 Powder Horn Hill Rd Wilton (06897) ***(G-10314)***
MPS Plastics Incorporated 860 295-1161
351 N Main St Marlborough (06447) ***(G-4127)***
Mr Boltons Music Inc 646 578-8081
31 Kings Hwy N Westport (06880) ***(G-10125)***
Mr Connecticut Leather Inc 203 230-2166
30 Rossotto Dr Hamden (06514) ***(G-3485)***
Mr Shower Door Inc 203 838-3667
651 Connecticut Ave Ste 1 Norwalk (06854) ***(G-6265)***
Mr Skylight LLC 203 966-6005
411 South Ave New Canaan (06840) ***(G-5121)***
MRC Specialty Balls 860 379-8511
149 Colebrook River Rd Winsted (06098) ***(G-10530)***
Mrh Tool LLC 203 878-3359
124 Research Dr Ste A Milford (06460) ***(G-4586)***
Mrk Fine Arts LLC 203 972-3115
65 Locust Ave Ste 301 New Canaan (06840) ***(G-5122)***
Mrnd LLC 860 749-0256
75 Hazard Ave Ste 1 Enfield (06082) ***(G-2663)***
Ms Design CT, Oxford *Also called Susan Martovich* ***(G-6696)***
MSC Filtration Tech Inc 860 745-7475
198 Freshwater Blvd Enfield (06082) ***(G-2664)***
MSI, Ledyard *Also called Management Software Inc* ***(G-3877)***
Msj Investments Inc 860 684-9956
72 W Stafford Rd Ste 3 Stafford Springs (06076) ***(G-8033)***
Msr Welding Service 860 234-9949
158 Providence Rd Brooklyn (06234) ***(G-1250)***
Mt Calvary Holy Church 203 785-1253
392 Legion Ave New Haven (06519) ***(G-5337)***
Mt Carmel Woodwork LLC 203 230-8377
770 Evergreen Ave Hamden (06518) ***(G-3486)***
Mt Hope Cemetery Association 860 643-4264
41 Elm Hill Rd Vernon (06066) ***(G-9146)***
Mt Lebanon Joinery 860 974-0896
89 John Perry Rd Eastford (06242) ***(G-2537)***
Mtaas, Madison *Also called Madison Tstg Acqstion Svcs LLC* ***(G-3938)***
Mtj Manufacturing Inc 203 334-4939
127 Wilmot Ave Bridgeport (06607) ***(G-844)***
Mtm Corporation 860 742-9600
643 Route 6 Andover (06232) ***(G-15)***
Mtr Precision Machining Inc 860 928-9440
60a Bradley Rd Pomfret Center (06259) ***(G-6943)***
Mtu Aero Engine Design Inc 860 667-2134
275 Richard St Newington (06111) ***(G-5680)***
Mtu Aero Engines N Amer Inc 860 258-9700
795 Brook St 5 Rocky Hill (06067) ***(G-7258)***
Mud River Services 860 767-0592
37 Bokum Rd Essex (06426) ***(G-2727)***
Muddy Brook Wood Products 860 928-2205
193 Woodstock Rd Woodstock (06281) ***(G-10673)***
Muggers Marrow LLC 203 548-9566
150 Shelton St Bridgeport (06608) ***(G-845)***
Muir Envelope Div, Newington *Also called Muir Envelope Plus Inc* ***(G-5681)***
Muir Envelope Plus Inc 860 953-6847
124 Francis Ave Newington (06111) ***(G-5681)***
Mulch Ferris Products LLC 203 790-1155
6 Plumtrees Rd Danbury (06810) ***(G-1889)***
Multi-Cable Corp 860 589-9035
37 Horizon Dr Bristol (06010) ***(G-1076)***
Multi-Metal Manufacturing Inc 203 723-8887
550 Spring St Naugatuck (06770) ***(G-4904)***
Multiprints Inc 203 235-4409
812 Old Colony Rd Meriden (06451) ***(G-4207)***
Mumm Engineering Inc 203 445-9777
57 Wells Rd Monroe (06468) ***(G-4740)***
Municipal Stadium 203 755-4019
1200 Watertown Ave Waterbury (06708) ***(G-9548)***
Munk Pack Inc 203 769-5005
222 Railroad Ave Ste 2 Greenwich (06830) ***(G-3207)***
Munson's Chocolates, Bolton *Also called Munsons Candy Kitchen Inc* ***(G-517)***
Munsons Candy Kitchen Inc (PA) 860 649-4332
174 Hopriver Rd Bolton (06043) ***(G-517)***
Murdoch and Co 203 226-2800
3 Sniffen Rd Westport (06880) ***(G-10126)***
Murphy & Sons Welding & Repair 203 635-3372
117 North St Stamford (06901) ***(G-8316)***
Murphy Boyz Printing Mark 860 836-0829
110 Richards Rd Litchfield (06759) ***(G-3896)***
Murphy Boyz Prtg & Mktg LLC 860 485-0607
271 North Rd Harwinton (06791) ***(G-3734)***
Murphy Industries LLC 203 426-1772
37 Great Ring Rd Sandy Hook (06482) ***(G-7322)***
Murray Signs & Designs Bob 203 375-7351
118 Winter St Stratford (06614) ***(G-8652)***
Musano Inc 203 879-4651
373 Woodtick Rd Wolcott (06716) ***(G-10575)***
Music Together Fairfield Child 203 256-1656
76 Walbin Ct Fairfield (06824) ***(G-2821)***
Musica Russica Inc 203 458-3225
310 Glenwood Dr Guilford (06437) ***(G-3378)***
Mv Lighting 203 856-3564
228 Newtown Ave Norwalk (06851) ***(G-6266)***
Mvc Aquatic Machine Shop 203 598-5747
17 Highview St Waterbury (06708) ***(G-9549)***
Mvp Systems Software Inc 860 269-3112
29 Mill St Ste 8 Unionville (06085) ***(G-9122)***
Mvp Visuals, Somers *Also called Soapstone Media Inc* ***(G-7669)***
Mwb Toy Company LLC 212 598-4500
128 E Liberty St Danbury (06810) ***(G-1890)***
MWK Publishing LLC 860 675-6067
2446 Albany Ave Ste 3 Hartford (06117) ***(G-3647)***
My Citizens News 203 729-2228
389 Meadow St Waterbury (06702) ***(G-9550)***
My Denim Queen 860 729-1142
23 Yeomans Rd Columbia (06237) ***(G-1609)***

ALPHABETIC

My Fair Lady.....860 322-4542
246 Main St Deep River (06417) ***(G-2095)***
My Slide Lines LLC.....203 324-1642
173 Main St Norwalk (06851) ***(G-6267)***
My Tool Company Inc.....203 755-2333
1212 S Main St Waterbury (06706) ***(G-9551)***
Myco Tool & Manufacturing Inc.....860 875-7340
176 Bolton Rd Ste 6 Vernon (06066) ***(G-9147)***
Mylo Industries LLC.....860 228-1192
49 Northam Rd Amston (06231) ***(G-4)***
Mystic Knotwork LLC.....860 889-3793
25 Cottrell St Ste 1 Mystic (06355) ***(G-4834)***
Mystic River Foundry LLC.....860 536-7634
2 Broadway Ave Mystic (06355) ***(G-4835)***
Mystic River Mar Surveyors LLC.....860 857-1798
16 Whitehall Pond Mystic (06355) ***(G-4836)***
Mystic River Press, Mystic *Also called Record-Journal Newspaper* ***(G-4841)***
Mystic Stainless & Alum Inc.....860 536-2236
23 Jackson Ave Mystic (06355) ***(G-4837)***
Mytyme LLC.....860 327-2356
211 High Path Rd Windsor (06095) ***(G-10411)***
N & B Manufacturing Co Inc.....860 667-3204
215 Pascone Pl Newington (06111) ***(G-5682)***
N A B Fine Woodworking LLC.....203 667-3922
50 Euclid Ave Apt 2 Stamford (06902) ***(G-8317)***
N E C H E A R, Hampton *Also called New England Ctr For Hring Rhab* ***(G-3538)***
N Excellence Wood Inc.....860 345-2050
323 Hidden Lake Rd Higganum (06441) ***(G-3770)***
N Karpel Studio LLC.....203 782-9108
87 Willow St Bldg A New Haven (06511) ***(G-5338)***
Nac Industries Inc.....845 214-0659
112 Hurley Rd Oxford (06478) ***(G-6680)***
Naffa Inc.....203 562-3159
315 Whitney Ave Ste 8 New Haven (06511) ***(G-5339)***
Naiad Dynamics, Shelton *Also called Naiad Maritime Group Inc* ***(G-7507)***
Naiad Dynamics Us Inc (HQ).....203 929-6355
50 Parrott Dr Shelton (06484) ***(G-7506)***
Naiad Marine Systems, Shelton *Also called Naiad Dynamics Us Inc* ***(G-7506)***
Naiad Maritime Group Inc (PA).....203 944-1932
50 Parrott Dr Shelton (06484) ***(G-7507)***
Nalas Engineering Services.....860 861-3691
1 Winnenden Rd Norwich (06360) ***(G-6424)***
Nalbor Mfg.....860 828-7676
872 Four Rod Rd Ste C Berlin (06037) ***(G-202)***
Nalco Wtr Prtrtment Sltons LLC.....860 224-4443
255 Myrtle St New Britain (06053) ***(G-5019)***
Nancy Dighello.....860 763-4294
4 Welch Dr Enfield (06082) ***(G-2665)***
Nancy Larson Publishers Inc.....860 434-0800
27 Talcott Farm Rd Old Lyme (06371) ***(G-6515)***
Nancy Larson Publishers Hq.....860 598-9783
120 Boston Post Rd Old Lyme (06371) ***(G-6516)***
Nancy R Marryat.....860 749-2632
63 Post Rd Enfield (06082) ***(G-2666)***
Nancy Tenenbaum Films.....203 221-6830
41 Lyons Plain Rd Weston (06883) ***(G-10033)***
Nano Pet Products LLC.....203 345-1330
10 Hoyt St Norwalk (06851) ***(G-6268)***
Nanocap Technologies LLC (PA).....860 521-9743
17 Morningcrest Dr Hartford (06117) ***(G-3648)***
Nantucket Blonde LLC.....203 415-1522
131 Paulney Rd Cheshire (06410) ***(G-1417)***
Nantucket Spider LLC.....203 423-3031
49 Liberty St Wilton (06897) ***(G-10315)***
Nantz Woodcraft.....860 267-8853
608 Westchester Rd Colchester (06415) ***(G-1558)***
Nap Brothers Parlor Frame Inc.....860 633-9998
122 Naubuc Ave Ste B3 Glastonbury (06033) ***(G-3062)***
NAPA Auto Parts, Windsor Locks *Also called Genuine Parts Company* ***(G-10486)***
Napp Printing Plate Dist Inc.....203 575-5727
245 Freight St Waterbury (06702) ***(G-9552)***
Narragansett Screw Co.....860 379-4059
119 Rowley St Winsted (06098) ***(G-10531)***
Narragansett Yacht Servic.....860 763-1980
200 Battle St Somers (06071) ***(G-7665)***
Nash Surgical Supply Co Inc.....203 828-6098
10 Tall Pines Dr Oxford (06478) ***(G-6681)***
Nathan Airchime Inc.....860 423-4575
1102 Windham Rd South Windham (06266) ***(G-7692)***
Natick Auto Sales, Middletown *Also called Mhq Inc* ***(G-4376)***
National Chromium Company Inc.....860 928-7965
10 Senexet Rd Putnam (06260) ***(G-7052)***
National Conveyors Company Inc.....860 653-0374
33 Nicholson Rd Ste 2 East Granby (06026) ***(G-2215)***
National Die Company.....203 879-1408
64 Wolcott Rd Wolcott (06716) ***(G-10576)***
National Educ Suppt Trust US.....860 420-8008
1204 Main St Ste 535 Branford (06405) ***(G-628)***
National Filter Media Corp.....203 741-2225
9 Fairfield Blvd Wallingford (06492) ***(G-9325)***
National Institutional Sup LLC.....203 263-3455
235 Main St S Woodbury (06798) ***(G-10645)***
National Instruments Corp.....203 661-6795
1117 E Putnam Ave Ste 240 Riverside (06878) ***(G-7198)***
National Integrated Inds Inc (PA).....860 677-7995
322 Main St Farmington (06032) ***(G-2933)***
National Integrated Inds Inc.....203 756-7051
1358 Thomaston Ave Waterbury (06704) ***(G-9553)***
National Magnetic Sensors Inc.....860 621-6816
141 Summer St Ste 3 Plantsville (06479) ***(G-6904)***
National Picture Frame Inc.....860 774-5668
9 Whitebrook Dr Brooklyn (06234) ***(G-1251)***
National Relocation & RE Mag, Norwalk *Also called Relocation Information Svc Inc* ***(G-6319)***
National Ribbon LLC.....860 742-6966
1159 Main St Coventry (06238) ***(G-1664)***
National Screw Manufacturing.....203 469-7109
259 Commerce St East Haven (06512) ***(G-2443)***
National Shooting Sports Found.....203 426-1320
11 Mile Hill Rd Ste A Newtown (06470) ***(G-5762)***
National Spring & Stamping Inc.....860 283-0203
135 S Main St Ste 8 Thomaston (06787) ***(G-8798)***
National Tool & CAM, Newington *Also called M & R Manufacturing Inc* ***(G-5673)***
National Welding LLC.....860 818-1240
27 Clinton Ave Middletown (06457) ***(G-4383)***
Nations Rent.....860 665-1489
2258 Berlin Tpke Newington (06111) ***(G-5683)***
Nationwide Cnvyor Spclists LLC.....860 582-9816
340 Maple Ave Bristol (06010) ***(G-1077)***
Nats Inc.....860 635-6820
511 Centerpoint Dr Middletown (06457) ***(G-4384)***
Natural Country Farms Inc.....860 872-8346
58 West Rd Ellington (06029) ***(G-2597)***
Natural Nutmeg LLC.....860 206-9500
53 Mountain View Ave Avon (06001) ***(G-95)***
Natural Polymer Devices Inc.....860 679-7894
400 Farmington Ave Mc6409 Farmington (06032) ***(G-2934)***
Natural Spring Ventures LLC.....203 556-2420
68 Whittlesey Rd Woodbury (06798) ***(G-10646)***
Naturalase, Bethel *Also called Focus Medical LLC* ***(G-301)***
Naturally Nutritous Vend LLC.....860 416-9848
23 Birch Ave Wolcott (06716) ***(G-10577)***
Naturally Relaxed LLC.....860 402-0613
183 Clark St Milldale (06467) ***(G-4687)***
Nature Plus Inc.....203 380-0316
55 Rachel Dr Stratford (06615) ***(G-8653)***
Natures First Inc (PA).....203 795-8400
58 Robinson Blvd Ste C Orange (06477) ***(G-6614)***
Natureseal Inc.....203 454-1800
1175 Post Rd E Ste 3b Westport (06880) ***(G-10127)***
Naugatuck Elec Indus Sup LLC.....203 723-1082
68 Radnor Ave Naugatuck (06770) ***(G-4905)***
Naugatuck Emergency Eqp LLC.....203 228-7117
54 Ridgeway Ave Oakville (06779) ***(G-6457)***
Naugatuck Recovery Inc (HQ).....203 723-1122
300 Great Hill Rd Naugatuck (06770) ***(G-4906)***
Naugatuck Stair Company Inc.....203 729-7134
51 Elm St Naugatuck (06770) ***(G-4907)***
Naugatuck Vly Photo Engrv Inc.....203 756-7345
2148 S Main St Waterbury (06706) ***(G-9554)***
Nauta Roll Corporation.....860 267-2027
7 Whippoorwill Hollow Rd East Hampton (06424) ***(G-2270)***
Nautigirl Marine Canvas.....203 891-8558
598 High Ridge Rd Orange (06477) ***(G-6615)***
Navtec Rigging Solutions Inc.....203 458-3163
37 Stanton Rd Clinton (06413) ***(G-1515)***
Navtech Systems Inc.....203 661-7800
322 Sound Beach Ave Old Greenwich (06870) ***(G-6480)***
NC Brands LP.....203 295-2300
40 Richards Ave Ste 2 Norwalk (06854) ***(G-6269)***
Nca Inc.....860 974-2310
500 Hampton Rd Abington (06230) ***(G-1)***
Ncc.....203 966-8307
14 Osborne Hill Rd Sandy Hook (06482) ***(G-7323)***
Nci Holdings Inc (PA).....203 295-2300
40 Richards Ave Ste 2 Norwalk (06854) ***(G-6270)***
Nci Woodworking LLC LLC.....203 391-1614
230 Hollydale Rd Fairfield (06824) ***(G-2822)***
NCM Embroidery & Sportswear.....860 223-1589
203 Oakland Ave New Britain (06053) ***(G-5020)***
Nct Inc.....860 666-8424
20 Holmes Rd Newington (06111) ***(G-5684)***
NDC Technologies Inc.....860 635-2100
454 Smith St Middletown (06457) ***(G-4385)***
Ndr Liuzzi Inc.....203 287-8477
86 Rossotto Dr Hamden (06514) ***(G-3487)***
Ndz Performance, Cheshire *Also called New Designz Inc* ***(G-1420)***
Ne Wood Works LLC.....860 883-3106
79 Lockwood St Manchester (06042) ***(G-4058)***
Near Oak LLC.....203 329-6500
1011 High Ridge Rd Stamford (06905) ***(G-8318)***
Neasi-Weber International.....203 857-4404
17 Little Fox Ln Norwalk (06850) ***(G-6271)***
Neato Products LLC.....203 466-5170
37 Eastern Steel Rd Milford (06460) ***(G-4587)***

Nec A Nec Woods Inc 203 431-0621
57 Seventy Acre Rd Redding (06896) ***(G-7104)***
Necs, Branford *Also called New England Computer Svcs Inc* ***(G-629)***
Necs, Stratford *Also called Hydro-Flex Inc* ***(G-8629)***
Need For Speed Racing 860 388-1204
1383 Boston Post Rd 3 Old Saybrook (06475) ***(G-6559)***
Neeltran Inc 860 350-5964
71 Pickett District Rd New Milford (06776) ***(G-5564)***
Neeltran International Inc 860 350-5964
71 Pickett District Rd New Milford (06776) ***(G-5565)***
Negg Maker, The, Southport *Also called Airigan Solutions LLC* ***(G-7998)***
Neid Printing, Groton *Also called New England Info Districts* ***(G-3300)***
Neiss Corp 860 872-8528
29 Naek Rd Vernon (06066) ***(G-9148)***
Nel Group LLC (PA) 860 413-9042
32 Rainbow Rd East Granby (06026) ***(G-2216)***
Nel Group LLC 860 683-0190
154 Broad St Windsor (06095) ***(G-10412)***
Nelcote Inc 203 509-5247
172 E Aurora St Ste A Waterbury (06708) ***(G-9555)***
Nelson & Miller Associates 203 356-9694
5 Hillandale Ave Ste F Stamford (06902) ***(G-8319)***
Nelson Apostle Inc 860 953-4633
11 Sherman St Hartford (06110) ***(G-3649)***
Nelson Archtctural Restoration 860 429-3830
40 Fisher Hill Rd Willington (06279) ***(G-10252)***
Nelson Heat Treating Co Inc 203 754-0670
2046 N Main St Waterbury (06704) ***(G-9556)***
Nelson Publishing 860 404-5292
479 Spielman Hwy Burlington (06013) ***(G-1275)***
Nelson Stud Welding Inc 800 635-9353
36 Spring Ln Farmington (06032) ***(G-2935)***
Nelson Tool & Machine Co Inc 860 589-8004
675 Emmett St Bristol (06010) ***(G-1078)***
Nemfi Pfs 860 640-4600
60 Ezra Silva Ln Windsor (06095) ***(G-10413)***
Nemtec Inc 203 272-0788
B 8 Trackside Cheshire (06410) ***(G-1418)***
Neonworks 203 335-6366
125 Front St Bridgeport (06606) ***(G-846)***
Neoperl Inc 203 756-8891
171 Mattatuck Heights Rd Waterbury (06705) ***(G-9557)***
Neopost USA, Milford *Also called Mailroom Finance Inc* ***(G-4574)***
Neopost USA Inc (HQ) 203 301-3400
478 Wheelers Farms Rd Milford (06461) ***(G-4588)***
Nerjan Development Company 203 325-3228
101 West Ave Stamford (06902) ***(G-8320)***
NES Sports LLC 765 532-2178
456 Ruth St Bridgeport (06606) ***(G-847)***
Nesci Enterprises Inc 860 267-2588
12 Summit St East Hampton (06424) ***(G-2271)***
Nesci Factory Store, East Hampton *Also called Nesci Enterprises Inc* ***(G-2271)***
Neses, Farmington *Also called New England Shoulder Elbow Soc* ***(G-2937)***
NESLO MANUFACTURING, Wolcott *Also called Musano Inc* ***(G-10575)***
Nesola Scarves LLC 203 288-5058
309 Old Lane Rd Cheshire (06410) ***(G-1419)***
Nessen Lighting, Brookfield *Also called 3t Lighting Inc* ***(G-1154)***
Nestle Usa Inc 860 928-0082
151 Mashamoquet Rd Pomfret Center (06259) ***(G-6944)***
Netsource Inc 860 282-8994
350 Pleasant Valley Rd South Windsor (06074) ***(G-7795)***
Netsource Inc (PA) 860 649-6000
260 Progress Dr Manchester (06042) ***(G-4059)***
Netw, New Britain *Also called New England Traveling Wire LLC* ***(G-5023)***
Network Expert Sftwr Systems 860 829-1427
110 E Shore Ave Kensington (06037) ***(G-3815)***
Netz New Haven Norton 203 507-2108
66 Norton St New Haven (06511) ***(G-5340)***
Neu Spclty Engineered Mtls LLC 203 239-9629
15 Corporate Dr North Haven (06473) ***(G-5967)***
Neurohydrate LLC 203 799-7900
4637 Main St Unit 5 Bridgeport (06606) ***(G-848)***
Nevamar Company LLC (HQ) 203 925-1556
1 Corporate Dr Ste 725 Shelton (06484) ***(G-7508)***
Nevamar Distributors, Shelton *Also called Nevamar Company LLC* ***(G-7508)***
New Age Motorsports LLC 203 268-1999
501 Pepper St Monroe (06468) ***(G-4741)***
New Air Technologies Inc 860 767-1542
65 N Main St Ivoryton (06442) ***(G-3787)***
New Amrcan Political Press Inc 860 747-2037
100 York St Apt 8o New Haven (06511) ***(G-5341)***
New Beginnings Sea Glass 203 329-7623
40 Club Cir Stamford (06905) ***(G-8321)***
New Britain Heat Treating Corp 860 223-0684
5 Grant Ave Enfield (06082) ***(G-2667)***
New Britain Herald , The, New Britain *Also called Central Conn Cmmunications LLC* ***(G-4958)***
New Britain Saw Tech 860 410-1077
161 Woodford Ave Ste 62a Plainville (06062) ***(G-6846)***
New Brnswick Scientific of Del 732 287-1200
175 Freshwater Blvd Enfield (06082) ***(G-2668)***
New Canaan Advertiser, New Canaan *Also called Hearst Corporation* ***(G-5109)***
New Canaan Forge LLC (PA) 203 966-3858
26 Burtis Ave New Canaan (06840) ***(G-5123)***
New Canaan Olive Oil LLC 845 240-3294
47 Blachley Rd Stamford (06902) ***(G-8322)***
New Christie Ventures, Naugatuck *Also called Pastanch LLC* ***(G-4909)***
New Deal LLC 860 648-9567
194 Buckland Hills Dr # 2225 Manchester (06042) ***(G-4060)***
New Designz Inc 860 384-1809
278 Sanbank Rd Cheshire (06410) ***(G-1420)***
New England Airfoil Pdts Inc 860 677-1376
36 Spring Ln Farmington (06032) ***(G-2936)***
New England Boring Contractors 860 633-4649
129 Kreiger Ln Ste A Glastonbury (06033) ***(G-3063)***
New England Bphrmcuticals Corp 917 992-4250
10 Five Mile River Rd Darien (06820) ***(G-2033)***
New England Brewing Co LLC 203 387-2222
175 Amity Rd Woodbridge (06525) ***(G-10608)***
New England Cabinet Co Inc 860 747-9995
580 E Main St New Britain (06051) ***(G-5021)***
New England Cap Company 203 736-6184
756 Derby Ave Seymour (06483) ***(G-7358)***
New England Chrome Plating 860 528-7176
63 Thomas St East Hartford (06108) ***(G-2346)***
New England Clock, North Haven *Also called Bonito Manufacturing Inc* ***(G-5915)***
New England Cnc Inc 203 288-8241
46 Manila Ave Hamden (06514) ***(G-3488)***
New England Computer Svcs Inc 475 221-8200
322 E Main St Branford (06405) ***(G-629)***
New England Crrage Imports LLC 860 889-6467
279 Bozrah St Bozrah (06334) ***(G-529)***
New England Cstm Concrete 203 924-2142
112 Pershing Dr Ste 5 Ansonia (06401) ***(G-45)***
New England Ctr For Hring Rhab 860 455-1404
354 Hartford Tpke Hampton (06247) ***(G-3538)***
New England Custom Built LLC 203 828-6480
133 West St Apt 29g Seymour (06483) ***(G-7359)***
New England Dermatological 203 432-0092
333 Cedar St New Haven (06510) ***(G-5342)***
New England Die Co Inc 203 574-5140
48 Ford Ave Waterbury (06708) ***(G-9558)***
New England Fiberglass Repair (PA) 203 866-1690
144 Water St Norwalk (06854) ***(G-6272)***
New England Filter Company Inc (PA) 203 531-0500
21 S Water St Ste 2a Greenwich (06830) ***(G-3208)***
New England Fine Woodworking 860 526-5799
37 Castle View Dr Chester (06412) ***(G-1475)***
New England Foam Products LLC (PA) 860 524-0121
760 Windsor St Hartford (06120) ***(G-3650)***
New England Forest Products 203 457-0314
564 Great Hill Rd Guilford (06437) ***(G-3379)***
New England Fuels & Energy LLC 860 585-5917
86 Allen St Terryville (06786) ***(G-8766)***
New England Gran Cabinets LLC 860 310-2981
8 Cody St West Hartford (06110) ***(G-9837)***
New England Graphics Mtls LLC (PA) 860 210-2180
312 Danbury Rd New Milford (06776) ***(G-5566)***
New England Grinding and MA 203 333-1885
30 Radel St Bridgeport (06607) ***(G-849)***
New England Honing LLC 860 712-6094
151 Barnsbee Ln Coventry (06238) ***(G-1665)***
New England Info Districts 860 446-1906
15 Chicago Ave Groton (06340) ***(G-3300)***
New England Joinery Works Inc 860 767-3377
19 Bokum Rd Essex (06426) ***(G-2728)***
New England Kitchen Design Ctr 203 268-2626
401 Monroe Tpke Ste 4 Monroe (06468) ***(G-4742)***
New England Lawpress, Guilford *Also called Kendall Svengalis* ***(G-3365)***
New England Lift Systems LLC 860 372-4040
714 N Mountain Rd Newington (06111) ***(G-5685)***
New England Machine Co LLC 860 526-7844
10 Spring St Deep River (06417) ***(G-2096)***
New England Machining LLC 860 301-9434
18 Senator Dr Cromwell (06416) ***(G-1708)***
New England Materials LLC 203 261-5500
64 Cambridge Dr Monroe (06468) ***(G-4743)***
New England Nonwovens LLC 203 891-0851
283 Dogburn Rd West Haven (06516) ***(G-9939)***
New England Ortho Neuro LLC 203 200-7228
2080 Whitney Ave Ste 290 Hamden (06518) ***(G-3489)***
New England Orthotic & Prost 203 634-7566
61 Pomeroy Ave Unit 2a Meriden (06450) ***(G-4208)***
New England Orthotic & Prost 860 967-0877
100 Retreat Ave Ste 805 Hartford (06106) ***(G-3651)***
New England Plasma Dev Corp 860 928-6561
14 Highland Dr Putnam (06260) ***(G-7053)***
New England PLC Systems LLC 860 793-2975
453 N Main St Pmb 364 Southington (06489) ***(G-7956)***
New England Post A Sign 203 635-3171
215 Oakville Ave Waterbury (06708) ***(G-9559)***
New England Press Parts LLC 203 623-7533
124 Belridge Rd Cheshire (06410) ***(G-1421)***
New England Printing LLC 860 745-3600
1 Anngina Dr Enfield (06082) ***(G-2669)***

ALPHABETIC

(PA)=Parent Co (HQ)=Headquarters (DH)=Div Headquarters
2020 Harris Connecticut Manufacturers Directory
551

New England Publishing Assoc (PA) 860 345-7323
  59 Parker Hill Rd Higganum (06441) *(G-3771)*
New England Quartz Co 203 846-9723
  270 Main Ave Norwalk (06851) *(G-6273)*
New England Shoulder Elbow Soc 860 679-6600
  232 Farmington Ave Farmington (06030) *(G-2937)*
New England Sign Carvers 860 349-1669
  25 Lyman Rd Middlefield (06455) *(G-4303)*
New England Signal LLC 860 350-3212
  10 Bridge St New Milford (06776) *(G-5567)*
New England Soft Serve 860 537-5459
  56 School Rd Colchester (06415) *(G-1559)*
New England Stair Company Inc 203 924-0606
  1 White St Shelton (06484) *(G-7509)*
New England Standard Corp 203 876-7733
  16 Honey St Milford (06461) *(G-4589)*
New England Stone Inc 203 876-8606
  35 Higgins Dr Milford (06460) *(G-4590)*
New England Theatre Conference 203 288-8680
  215 Knob Hill Dr Hamden (06518) *(G-3490)*
New England Tile & Stone Inc 914 481-4488
  85 Old Long Ridge Rd # 2 Stamford (06903) *(G-8323)*
New England Tool & Automtn Inc 860 827-9389
  321 Ellis St Ste 17 New Britain (06051) *(G-5022)*
New England Tooling Inc 800 866-5105
  145 Chestnut Hill Rd Killingworth (06419) *(G-3837)*
New England Toy LLC 860 655-6089
  4 Mclean St Simsbury (06070) *(G-7637)*
New England Traffic Solutions, Glastonbury Also called Gac Inc *(G-3038)*
New England Traveling Wire LLC 860 223-6297
  162 Whiting St New Britain (06051) *(G-5023)*
New England Welding Svcs LLC 860 406-4030
  47 West St Plantsville (06479) *(G-6905)*
New England Woodturners, Andover Also called Richard G Swartwout Jr *(G-16)*
New England Woodworking 203 505-0830
  190 Fillow St Norwalk (06850) *(G-6274)*
New England Woodworking LLC 203 984-5032
  1 Burlington Ct Norwalk (06851) *(G-6275)*
New ERA Printing Co, Deep River Also called Valley Press New Area Prtg Co *(G-2105)*
New Fairfield Press Inc 203 746-2700
  3 Dunham Dr New Fairfield (06812) *(G-5172)*
New Hartford Industrial Park 860 379-8506
  37 Greenwoods Rd New Hartford (06057) *(G-5203)*
New Hartford Wine and Bev LLC 860 379-3764
  516 Main St New Hartford (06057) *(G-5204)*
New Haven Awning Co, New Haven Also called B and G Enterprise LLC *(G-5239)*
New Haven Chlor-Alkali LLC 203 772-3350
  73 Welton St New Haven (06511) *(G-5343)*
New Haven Companies Inc 203 469-6421
  41 Washington Ave East Haven (06512) *(G-2444)*
New Haven GL & Mirror Co LLC 203 469-2440
  40 Edgemere Rd New Haven (06512) *(G-5344)*
New Haven Glass and Mirror, New Haven Also called New Haven GL & Mirror Co LLC *(G-5344)*
NEW HAVEN INDEPENDENT, New Haven Also called Online Journalism Project Inc *(G-5354)*
New Haven Naturopathic Center 203 387-8661
  14 Judwin Ave New Haven (06515) *(G-5345)*
New Haven Register LLC 203 789-5200
  100 Gando Dr New Haven (06513) *(G-5346)*
New Haven Rgster Fresh Air Fnd 800 925-2509
  100 Gando Dr New Haven (06513) *(G-5347)*
New Haven Sheet Metal Co 203 468-0341
  42 Foxon St New Haven (06513) *(G-5348)*
New Haven Sign Co 203 891-5710
  264 Morse St Hamden (06517) *(G-3491)*
New Haven Sign Company 203 484-2777
  1831 Middletown Ave Northford (06472) *(G-6051)*
New Hope Wldg Fabrication LLC 203 357-0080
  914 E Main St Ste 9 Stamford (06902) *(G-8324)*
New Horizon Machine Co Inc 203 316-9355
  36 Ludlow St Stamford (06902) *(G-8325)*
New King of Hartford 860 241-0664
  102 Weston St Hartford (06120) *(G-3652)*
New Leaf Pharmaceutical 203 270-4167
  77 S Main St Newtown (06470) *(G-5763)*
New Line USA Inc 860 498-0347
  247 Brigham Tavern Rd Coventry (06238) *(G-1666)*
New London Printing Co LLC 860 701-9171
  147 State St Ste 1 New London (06320) *(G-5481)*
New Machine Products LLC 203 790-5520
  81 Beaver Brook Rd Ste B Danbury (06810) *(G-1891)*
New Mass Media Inc 860 241-3617
  285 Broad St Hartford (06115) *(G-3653)*
New Milford Block & Supply 860 355-1101
  574 Danbury Rd New Milford (06776) *(G-5568)*
New Milford Commission 860 354-3758
  123 West St New Milford (06776) *(G-5569)*
New Milford Farms Inc 860 210-0250
  60 Boardman Rd New Milford (06776) *(G-5570)*
New Milford Foundry & Mch Co 860 354-5561
  84 West St New Milford (06776) *(G-5571)*

New Milford Print Works Inc 860 799-0530
  481 Danbury Rd Ste 3 New Milford (06776) *(G-5572)*
New Milford Printing, New Milford Also called Alexander Hussey *(G-5503)*
New Milfrd Water Pollutn Cntrl, New Milford Also called New Milford Commission *(G-5569)*
New Polymer Systems 203 594-7774
  4 Parting Brook Rd New Canaan (06840) *(G-5124)*
New Precision Technology LLC 800 243-4565
  98 Fort Path Rd Ste B Madison (06443) *(G-3941)*
New Resources Group Inc 203 366-1000
  955 Conn Ave Ste 1211 Bridgeport (06607) *(G-850)*
New Star Mold Inc 860 567-7760
  607 Bantam Rd Ste B Bantam (06750) *(G-125)*
New Tech Replacement Part Co, Bristol Also called Rgd Technologies Corp *(G-1107)*
New Technologies Mfg Inc 860 872-7605
  63 Duncaster Ln Vernon Rockville (06066) *(G-9171)*
New Wave Surgical Corp 954 796-4126
  555 Long Wharf Dr Fl 2 New Haven (06511) *(G-5349)*
New York City Blouse Co, Branford Also called M S B International Ltd *(G-620)*
New York Graphic Society, Norwalk Also called Portfolio Arts Group Ltd *(G-6303)*
New York Transit Shoes 203 968-6642
  2828 High Ridge Rd Stamford (06903) *(G-8326)*
Newco Condenser Inc 475 882-4000
  40 Waterview Dr Shelton (06484) *(G-7510)*
Newco Lighting Inc (HQ) 475 882-4000
  40 Waterview Dr Shelton (06484) *(G-7511)*
Newcomb Spring Corp 860 621-0111
  235 Spring St Southington (06489) *(G-7957)*
Newcomb Springs Connecticut 860 621-0111
  235 Spring St Southington (06489) *(G-7958)*
Newgate Designs Co 860 653-6991
  101 Newgate Rd East Granby (06026) *(G-2217)*
Newgate Instruments LLC 860 784-1968
  17 Connecticut South Dr B East Granby (06026) *(G-2218)*
Newhall Labs, Stamford Also called Golden Sun Inc *(G-8217)*
Newhart Plastics Inc 203 877-5367
  10 Furniture Row Milford (06460) *(G-4591)*
Newhart Products Inc 203 878-3546
  80 Collingsdale Dr Milford (06461) *(G-4592)*
Newington Meat Center 860 666-3431
  847 Main St Newington (06111) *(G-5686)*
Newmack Inc 203 568-0443
  209 Munson Rd Middlebury (06762) *(G-4285)*
Newman Information Systems 860 286-0540
  37 Jerome Ave Bloomfield (06002) *(G-449)*
Newman's Own Organics, Westport Also called Newmans Own Inc *(G-10128)*
Newmans Own Inc (PA) 203 222-0136
  1 Morningside Dr N Ste 1 # 1 Westport (06880) *(G-10128)*
Newmark Inc 203 272-1158
  182 Sandbank Rd Cheshire (06410) *(G-1422)*
Newmark Medical Components Inc 203 753-1158
  2670 S Main St Waterbury (06706) *(G-9560)*
Newport Electronics, Norwalk Also called Omega Engineering Inc *(G-6285)*
News 12 Connecticut 203 849-1321
  28 Cross St Norwalk (06851) *(G-6276)*
News Times 203 744-5100
  333 Main St Danbury (06810) *(G-1892)*
Newsbank Inc 203 966-1100
  58 Pine St Ste 1 New Canaan (06840) *(G-5125)*
Newspaper, Goshen Also called Judy Low *(G-3099)*
Newspaper Space Buyers 203 967-6452
  149 Rowayton Ave Ste 2 Norwalk (06853) *(G-6277)*
Newtec America Inc 203 323-0042
  1055 Washington Blvd Fl 6 Stamford (06901) *(G-8327)*
Newtown Sports Group 508 341-1238
  15 Anthony Ridge Rd Newtown (06470) *(G-5764)*
Next Door Creations LLC 860 933-0366
  15 Conestoga Way Glastonbury (06033) *(G-3064)*
Next Level Publishing LLC 860 282-2428
  46 Leverich Dr East Hartford (06108) *(G-2347)*
Nextec Applications Inc (PA) 203 661-1484
  11 Turner Dr Greenwich (06831) *(G-3209)*
Nexvue Information Systems Inc 203 327-0800
  65 Broad St Stamford (06901) *(G-8328)*
Neyra Industries Inc 860 289-4359
  239 Sullivan Ave South Windsor (06074) *(G-7796)*
Ngraver Company 860 823-1533
  67 Wawecus Hill Rd Bozrah (06334) *(G-530)*
NGS Power LLC 860 873-0100
  385 Town St East Haddam (06423) *(G-2246)*
NGS Power LLC (PA) 860 873-0100
  25 Falls Rd Moodus (06469) *(G-4775)*
Niagara Bottling LLC 909 226-7353
  380 Woodland Ave Bloomfield (06002) *(G-450)*
Niantic Awning & Sunroom Co, Niantic Also called Niantic Awning Company *(G-5813)*
Niantic Awning Company 860 739-0161
  193 Pennsylvania Ave Niantic (06357) *(G-5813)*
Niantic Tool Inc 860 739-2182
  32 Industrial Park Rd Niantic (06357) *(G-5814)*
Nice T-Shirt 860 349-0727
  180 Johnson St Ste 1 Middletown (06457) *(G-4386)*
Nicholas Melfi Jr 203 853-7235
  41 Commerce St Norwalk (06850) *(G-6278)*

ALPHABETIC SECTION — Northeast Wind Energy

Nicholas Precision Pdts LLC 518 428-8109
  136 Marlborough St Unit F Portland (06480) *(G-6966)*
Nichols Forestry & Logging LLC 860 642-4292
  151 Exeter Rd Lebanon (06249) *(G-3859)*
Nichols Woodworking LLC (PA) 860 350-4223
  136 Walker Brook Rd S Washington Depot (06794) *(G-9419)*
Nicholsons, Wallingford Also called Corru Seals Inc *(G-9241)*
Nickson Industries Inc 860 747-1671
  336 Woodford Ave Plainville (06062) *(G-6847)*
Nidec America Corporation 860 653-2144
  16 International Dr East Granby (06026) *(G-2219)*
Nielsen Company 203 586-1819
  424 Washington Rd Woodbury (06798) *(G-10647)*
Nielsen Consulting Inc (PA) 914 831-1681
  186 Pickett District Rd New Milford (06776) *(G-5573)*
Nielsen/Sessions 860 522-8145
  770 Wethersfield Ave Hartford (06114) *(G-3654)*
Niklyn Corp 860 440-6244
  90 River St Ste A New Haven (06513) *(G-5350)*
Nina Nail Spa 203 270-0777
  14 Church Hill Rd Ste A2 Newtown (06470) *(G-5765)*
Ninas Signs 315 963-2531
  90 Curtiss Hill Rd Morris (06763) *(G-4791)*
Nine West Holdings Inc 860 669-3799
  20 Killingworth Tpke # 125 Clinton (06413) *(G-1516)*
Ninety-Nine Cent Pubg LLC 203 922-9917
  132 New St Shelton (06484) *(G-7512)*
Niro Companies LLC 860 982-5645
  100 Harding St Berlin (06037) *(G-203)*
Nis, Bloomfield Also called Newman Information Systems *(G-449)*
Nitch To Stitch LLC 203 948-9921
  419 Federal Rd Brookfield (06804) *(G-1209)*
Njd Enterprises 860 210-1113
  15 Bigos Rd Litchfield (06759) *(G-3897)*
Nn Inc 203 793-7132
  6 Northrop Indus Pk Rd W Wallingford (06492) *(G-9326)*
Nntechnology Moore Systems LLC 203 366-3224
  800 Union Ave Bridgeport (06607) *(G-851)*
No Butts Bin Company Inc 203 245-5924
  16 Birch Ln Madison (06443) *(G-3942)*
Noacks Meat Products 203 235-7384
  1112 E Main St Meriden (06450) *(G-4209)*
Noank Controls LLC (PA) 860 449-6776
  195 Leonard Dr Unit 6 Groton (06340) *(G-3301)*
Nobby Beverages Inc 860 747-3888
  30 Hayden Ave Ste E Plainville (06062) *(G-6848)*
Noble Army, The, Manchester Also called Independence Enterprises LLC *(G-4032)*
Noble Fire Brick Company Inc (PA) 860 623-9256
  40 Woolam Rd East Windsor (06088) *(G-2513)*
Noble Industrial Furnace Co, East Windsor Also called Noble Fire Brick Company Inc *(G-2513)*
Noble Publishing, Torrington Also called Little India Publications Inc *(G-8943)*
Nofet LLC 203 848-9064
  227 Church St Apt 5j New Haven (06510) *(G-5351)*
Nohha Inc 203 687-6741
  109 Cummings Dr Orange (06477) *(G-6616)*
Nohtbook Inc 203 493-1633
  597 Westport Ave B521 Norwalk (06851) *(G-6279)*
Nolan Industries Inc 203 865-8160
  67 Mill River St New Haven (06511) *(G-5352)*
Nolan Woodworking LLC 203 258-1538
  187 Monroe St Bridgeport (06605) *(G-852)*
Nolan Woodworking LLC 860 283-6000
  135 S Main St Ste 14 Thomaston (06787) *(G-8799)*
Nollysource Entertainment LLC 347 264-6655
  1455 Penboke Ln Bridgeport (06608) *(G-853)*
Nomis Enterprises 631 821-3120
  90 Northford Rd Wallingford (06492) *(G-9327)*
Non-Invasive Med Systems LLC 914 462-0701
  1 Harbor Point Rd # 2050 Stamford (06902) *(G-8329)*
Nootelligence, Fairfield Also called Focus Now Solutions LLC *(G-2786)*
Norcell Inc (HQ) 203 254-5292
  2 Corporate Dr Fl 5 Shelton (06484) *(G-7513)*
Nordic American Smokeless Inc 203 207-9977
  100 Mill Plain Rd Ste 115 Danbury (06811) *(G-1893)*
Noreaster Yachts Inc 203 877-4339
  29 Roselle St Milford (06461) *(G-4593)*
Norfield Data Products Inc 203 849-0292
  181 Main St Ste 2 Norwalk (06851) *(G-6280)*
Norfolk Industries LLC 860 618-8822
  21 Deer Park Dr Greenwich (06830) *(G-3210)*
Norgren, Farmington Also called Kip Inc *(G-2922)*
Norgren Inc 860 677-0272
  72 Spring Ln Farmington (06032) *(G-2938)*
Norilsk Nickel USA Inc 203 730-0676
  3 Turtle Ridge Ct Ridgefield (06877) *(G-7157)*
Normike Industries Inc 860 747-1110
  1 Town Line Rd Ste 6 Plainville (06062) *(G-6849)*
Noroton Publishing Co 203 655-1436
  100 Heights Rd Darien (06820) *(G-2034)*
Norse Inc 860 482-1532
  100 South Rd Torrington (06790) *(G-8952)*

Nortek Gear and Machine LLC 860 355-5541
  5 Old Town Park Rd 18 New Milford (06776) *(G-5574)*
North Amercn Spring Tl Co Div, Berlin Also called All Five Tool Co Inc *(G-154)*
North America Overland LLC 203 658-3697
  181 Hattertown Rd Monroe (06468) *(G-4744)*
North American Elev Svcs Co (HQ) 860 676-6000
  1 Farm Springs Rd Farmington (06032) *(G-2939)*
North American Technical Svcs, Middletown Also called Nats Inc *(G-4384)*
North Canton Custom Wdwkg 508 451-5826
  760 Cherry Brook Rd Canton (06019) *(G-1320)*
North Controls Company LLC 860 584-8364
  75 Julia Rd Bristol (06010) *(G-1079)*
North East Fasteners Corp 860 589-3242
  8 Tremco Dr Terryville (06786) *(G-8767)*
North East Powder Coating 203 573-1543
  112 Porter St Waterbury (06708) *(G-9561)*
North Eastern Scale Corp 203 634-7942
  201 4th St Meriden (06451) *(G-4210)*
North Forty Pest Ctrl Co LLC 203 263-4551
  4 N Forty Rd Woodbury (06798) *(G-10648)*
North Haven Eqp & Lsg LLC 203 795-9494
  212 Argyle Rd Orange (06477) *(G-6617)*
North Haven Manufacturing Co 203 284-8578
  25 George St Wallingford (06492) *(G-9328)*
North Hill Woodworking LLC 203 985-0200
  117 N Hill Rd North Haven (06473) *(G-5968)*
North Sails Group LLC (HQ) 203 874-7548
  125 Old Gate Ln Ste 7 Milford (06460) *(G-4594)*
North Shannon, Norwalk Also called Swedish News Inc *(G-6361)*
North Shore Door, North Haven Also called Eric Sapper *(G-5938)*
North Shore Publishing LLC 860 561-8768
  111 Stoner Dr West Hartford (06107) *(G-9838)*
North Star Computing Svcs LLC 860 635-7117
  288 Skyview Dr Cromwell (06416) *(G-1709)*
North Technology Group, Milford Also called North Sails Group LLC *(G-4594)*
Northast Lghtning Prtction LLC 860 243-0010
  10 Peters Rd Bloomfield (06002) *(G-451)*
Northast Tnnis Pblications LLC 203 984-1088
  17 Walnut Ln Weston (06883) *(G-10034)*
Northastern Communications Inc 203 381-9008
  255 Hathaway Dr Ste 3 Stratford (06615) *(G-8654)*
Northeast Cabinet Design 203 438-1709
  18 Bailey Ave Ridgefield (06877) *(G-7158)*
Northeast Cabinetry LLC 860 216-0781
  111 W Dudley Town Rd Bloomfield (06002) *(G-452)*
Northeast Carbide Inc 860 628-2515
  525 W Queen St Southington (06489) *(G-7959)*
Northeast Circuit Tech LLC 860 633-1967
  112 Sherwood Dr Glastonbury (06033) *(G-3065)*
Northeast Double Disc Grind LL 860 643-6096
  31 Mitchell Dr Manchester (06042) *(G-4061)*
Northeast Drone Services LLC 203 220-6478
  115 Technology Dr A201 Trumbull (06611) *(G-9051)*
Northeast Electronics Corp 203 878-3511
  455 Bic Dr Milford (06461) *(G-4595)*
Northeast Fluid Technology 860 620-0393
  161 Atwater St Plantsville (06479) *(G-6906)*
Northeast Foods Inc 860 779-1117
  328 Lake Rd Dayville (06241) *(G-2067)*
Northeast Logging Inc 860 974-2959
  153 Pomfret Rd Eastford (06242) *(G-2538)*
Northeast Mfg Co LLC 860 763-4000
  3 Peerless Way Ste D Enfield (06082) *(G-2670)*
Northeast Minority News Inc 860 249-6065
  3580 Main St Ste 1 Hartford (06120) *(G-3655)*
Northeast Panel Co LLC 860 678-9078
  325 Main St Ste 3 Farmington (06032) *(G-2940)*
Northeast Pipeline Service LLC 860 621-6921
  156 Old Turnpike Rd Southington (06489) *(G-7960)*
Northeast Printing Networ 860 788-3572
  135 Sebethe Dr 8 Cromwell (06416) *(G-1710)*
Northeast Publications LLC 860 399-4801
  5 Thompson Ln Old Saybrook (06475) *(G-6560)*
Northeast Quality Services LLC 860 632-7242
  14 Alcap Rdg Cromwell (06416) *(G-1711)*
Northeast Sealcoat Inc 860 953-4400
  38 Jansen Ct West Hartford (06110) *(G-9839)*
Northeast Stair Company LLC 860 875-3358
  185 Buff Cap Rd Tolland (06084) *(G-8872)*
Northeast Stihl, Oxford Also called Stihl Incorporated *(G-6695)*
Northeast Stucco LLC 860 770-9473
  14 Beatty St New Britain (06051) *(G-5024)*
Northeast Thermography, Wallingford Also called E & A Enterprises Inc *(G-9255)*
Northeast Tool Dist LLC 860 973-1455
  280 Morningside Dr E Bristol (06010) *(G-1080)*
Northeast Vineyard Svcs LLC 860 872-8239
  66 Shanda Ln Tolland (06084) *(G-8873)*
Northeast Waterjet Svcs LLC 203 794-0766
  24 Finance Dr Danbury (06810) *(G-1894)*
Northeast Wind Energy 860 779-2179
  225 Bear Hill Rd East Killingly (06243) *(G-2461)*

(PA)=Parent Co (HQ)=Headquarters (DH)=Div Headquarters

Northeast Wood Products LLC 860 862-6350
13 Crow Hill Rd Uncasville (06382) *(G-9100)*
Northeast Wood Sales 860 621-9613
1146 Marion Ave Marion (06444) *(G-4117)*
Northeastern Metals Corp 203 348-8088
130 Lenox Ave Ste 23 Stamford (06906) *(G-8330)*
Northend Agents LLC 860 244-2445
150 Trumbull St Fl 4 Hartford (06103) *(G-3656)*
Northern Comfort Mech LLC 203 456-5163
178 Osborne St Danbury (06810) *(G-1895)*
Northern Fabrication 860 693-0635
382 Cherry Brook Rd Canton (06019) *(G-1321)*
Northern Wolf Press LLC 860 227-0135
1189 Washington St E19 Middletown (06457) *(G-4387)*
Northmen Defense LLC 860 908-9308
24 Old Colchester Rd Ext Oakdale (06370) *(G-6445)*
Northrop Grumman Corporation 860 282-4461
121 Prestige Park Cir East Hartford (06108) *(G-2348)*
Northside Minis LLC 860 388-6871
27 Bellaire Dr Old Saybrook (06475) *(G-6561)*
Northstar Biosciences LLC 203 689-5399
2514 Boston Post Rd 4r Guilford (06437) *(G-3380)*
Northville Horseshoe Supply, Gaylordsville *Also called William Martin (G-2997)*
Northwest Connecticut Mfg Co 860 379-1553
95 Beech Hill Rd Colebrook (06021) *(G-1585)*
Northwest News Service 860 567-4150
33 Trumbull St Bantam (06750) *(G-126)*
Norton Paper Mill LLC 860 861-9701
167 Marvin Rd Colchester (06415) *(G-1560)*
Norwalk Awning Company, Norwalk *Also called Fitzgerald-Norwalk Awning Co (G-6169)*
Norwalk Compreseer Company 203 386-1234
1650 Stratford Ave Stratford (06615) *(G-8655)*
Norwalk Compressor Inc 203 386-1234
1650 Stratford Ave Stratford (06615) *(G-8656)*
Norwalk Electric Mtrs & Pumps, Norwalk *Also called Nicholas Melfi Jr (G-6278)*
Norwalk Powdered Metals Inc 203 338-8000
30 Moffitt St Stratford (06615) *(G-8657)*
Norwalk Rutledge Printing Off 203 956-5967
28 Cross St Norwalk (06851) *(G-6281)*
Norwalk Sign Company Inc 203 838-1942
19 Fitch St Norwalk (06855) *(G-6282)*
Norwich Printing Co Inc 860 745-3600
1 Anngina Dr Enfield (06082) *(G-2671)*
Norwich Printing Company Inc 860 887-7468
595 W Main St Ste 2 Norwich (06360) *(G-6425)*
Noujaim Tool Co Inc 203 753-4441
412 Chase River Rd Waterbury (06704) *(G-9562)*
Nova Dental LLC (PA) 203 234-3900
41 Middletown Ave Ste 2 North Haven (06473) *(G-5969)*
Nova Electronics 860 537-3471
36 Dr Foote Rd Ste A Colchester (06415) *(G-1561)*
Nova Machining LLC 860 223-9323
56 Saint Claire Ave New Britain (06051) *(G-5025)*
Nova Machining LLC 860 675-8131
16 E Shore Blvd Unionville (06085) *(G-9123)*
Novaerus US Inc (PA) 813 304-2468
35 Melrose Pl Stamford (06902) *(G-8331)*
Novamont North America Inc 203 744-8801
1000 Bridgeport Ave # 304 Shelton (06484) *(G-7514)*
Novanglus Publishing LLC 203 885-7476
16 Dingletown Rd Greenwich (06830) *(G-3211)*
Novatech 860 871-4180
184 Goose Ln Tolland (06084) *(G-8874)*
Novatek Medical Inc 203 356-0156
1 Strawberry Hill Ave Stamford (06902) *(G-8332)*
Novel Tees Screen Prtg EMB LLC 860 643-6008
81 Tolland Tpke Manchester (06042) *(G-4062)*
Novel-Tees Unlimited LLC 860 643-6008
81 Tolland Tpke Manchester (06042) *(G-4063)*
Novelty Textile Mills LLC 860 774-5000
24 Spithead Rd Waterford (06385) *(G-9664)*
Novo Nordisk Pharmaceuticals 860 779-2668
31 King St Danielson (06239) *(G-1999)*
Novo Precision LLC 860 583-0517
150 Dolphin Rd Bristol (06010) *(G-1081)*
Novogen Inc 203 972-5901
262 Marvin Ridge Rd New Canaan (06840) *(G-5126)*
Novy International Inc 203 743-7720
6 Abbott St Danbury (06810) *(G-1896)*
Nowak Products Inc 860 666-9685
101 Rockwell Rd Newington (06111) *(G-5687)*
Npi Medical, Ansonia *Also called Ansonia Plastics LLC (G-20)*
Npm, Stratford *Also called Norwalk Powdered Metals Inc (G-8657)*
Nq Industries Inc 860 258-3466
1275 Cromwell Ave Ste A9 Rocky Hill (06067) *(G-7259)*
NRG Connecticut LLC 860 231-2424
36 Woodland St Ste 1 Hartford (06105) *(G-3657)*
Nsf Gourmet Products 203 856-4995
940 Post Rd E Westport (06880) *(G-10129)*
Nt Lawn Service 203 573-0285
142 Fillmore St Waterbury (06705) *(G-9563)*
Nteco Inc 203 656-1154
10 Center St Darien (06820) *(G-2035)*
Nu Line Design LLC 203 949-0726
21 N Plains Industrial Rd Wallingford (06492) *(G-9329)*
Nu Line Signs, Wallingford *Also called Nu Line Design LLC (G-9329)*
Nu Vision Homes LLC 860 209-8492
110 Court St Middletown (06457) *(G-4388)*
Nu-Stone Mfg & Distrg LLC 860 564-6555
160 Sterling Rd Sterling (06377) *(G-8514)*
Nuance Communications Inc 781 565-5000
3191 Broadbridge Ave Fl 2 Stratford (06614) *(G-8658)*
Nubridal 860 768-5745
655 Garden St Apt 3 Hartford (06112) *(G-3658)*
Nucap US Inc (HQ) 203 879-1423
238 Wolcott Rd Wolcott (06716) *(G-10578)*
Nucor Bar Mill Group, Wallingford *Also called Nucor Steel Connecticut Inc (G-9330)*
Nucor Steel Connecticut Inc 203 265-0615
35 Toelles Rd Wallingford (06492) *(G-9330)*
Nufern 860 408-5000
7 Airport Park Rd East Granby (06026) *(G-2220)*
Numa Tool Company (PA) 860 923-9551
646 Thompson Rd Thompson (06277) *(G-8841)*
Numerical Control Technology, Newington *Also called Nct Inc (G-5684)*
Numet Machining Techniques Inc 203 375-4995
235 Edison Rd Orange (06477) *(G-6618)*
Numotion, Rocky Hill *Also called United Seating & Mobility LLC (G-7270)*
Nuovo Pasta Productions Ltd 203 380-4090
1330 Honeyspot Road Ext Stratford (06615) *(G-8659)*
Nupal LLC 860 227-7964
49 Parkers Point Rd Chester (06412) *(G-1476)*
Nurses Alarm Systems Inc 860 872-0025
27 Naek Rd Ste 6 Vernon Rockville (06066) *(G-9172)*
Nutek Aerospace Corp 860 355-3169
180 Sunny Valley Rd Ste 2 New Milford (06776) *(G-5575)*
Nutmeg Architectural Wdwrk Inc 203 325-4434
48 Union St Ste 14 Stamford (06906) *(G-8333)*
Nutmeg Brewing Rest Group LLC 203 256-2337
819 Bridgeport Ave Shelton (06484) *(G-7515)*
Nutmeg Container Corporation (HQ) 860 963-6727
100 Canal St Putnam (06260) *(G-7054)*
Nutmeg Energy Savers 203 733-0147
35 Hickok Ave Bethel (06801) *(G-330)*
Nutmeg Food Brokers LLC 860 289-9566
130 Mcgrath Rd South Windsor (06074) *(G-7797)*
Nutmeg Industries LLC 860 436-6553
354 Main St Ste 5 Newington (06111) *(G-5688)*
Nutmeg Naturals LLC 860 554-1272
67 Parker Hill Rd Higganum (06441) *(G-3772)*
Nutmeg Printers, Naugatuck *Also called Cagno Enterprises LLC (G-4867)*
Nutmeg Utility Products Inc (PA) 203 250-8802
1755 Highland Ave Cheshire (06410) *(G-1423)*
Nutmeg Welding Company Inc 203 756-7458
92 Rockaway Ave Waterbury (06705) *(G-9564)*
Nutmeg Wire 860 822-8616
14 Main St Baltic (06330) *(G-121)*
Nutmeg Woodworking, Danielson *Also called Daniel Richardson (G-1988)*
Nutmeg Woodworks LLC 203 980-5700
36 Castle Ln Milford (06460) *(G-4596)*
Nutrition Matters, Glastonbury *Also called Cara C Andreoli (G-3019)*
Nutriventus Inc 860 990-9324
8 Elm Rd Cromwell (06416) *(G-1712)*
Nutron Manufacturing Inc 860 887-4550
5 Wisconsin Ave Norwich (06360) *(G-6426)*
Nutty Cow Inc 626 888-9269
126 Brewster Rd West Hartford (06117) *(G-9840)*
Nuway Tobacco Company 860 289-6414
200 Sullivan Ave Ste 2 South Windsor (06074) *(G-7798)*
Nvizix Corp 203 222-8723
381 Main St Westport (06880) *(G-10130)*
Nxtid Inc 203 266-2103
288 Christian St Oxford (06478) *(G-6682)*
Nyc Grind Sports Marketing LLC 917 513-0590
1127 High Ridge Rd Stamford (06905) *(G-8334)*
Nylo Metal Finishing LLC 203 574-5477
730 N Main St Ste 1 Waterbury (06704) *(G-9565)*
Nytex Petroleum Inc 203 261-6329
1771 Post Rd E Ste 133 Westport (06880) *(G-10131)*
Nzymsys Inc 877 729-4190
642 Hilliard St Ste 1208 Manchester (06042) *(G-4064)*
O & G Industries Inc 860 485-6600
255 Lower Bogue Rd Harwinton (06791) *(G-3735)*
O & G Industries Inc 203 977-1618
686 Canal St Stamford (06902) *(G-8335)*
O & G Industries Inc 203 881-5192
105 Breault Rd Beacon Falls (06403) *(G-145)*
O & G Industries Inc 203 366-4586
240 Bostwick Ave Bridgeport (06605) *(G-854)*
O & G Industries Inc 203 263-2195
236 Roxbury Rd Southbury (06488) *(G-7870)*
O & G Industries Inc 203 748-5694
9 Segar St Danbury (06810) *(G-1897)*
O & G Industries Inc 203 323-1111
40 Meadow St Stamford (06902) *(G-8336)*

O & G Industries Inc 203 729-4529
Railroad Ave Ext Beacon Falls (06403) *(G-146)*
O & G Industries Inc 860 354-4438
271 Danbury Rd New Milford (06776) *(G-5576)*
O & W Heat Treat Inc 860 528-9239
1 Bidwell Rd South Windsor (06074) *(G-7799)*
O Berk Company Neng LLC 203 932-8000
300 Callegari Dr West Haven (06516) *(G-9940)*
O Beverages, Fairfield *Also called Twelve Beverage LLC* *(G-2859)*
O C Tanner Company 203 944-5430
2 Corporate Dr Ste 935 Shelton (06484) *(G-7516)*
O E M Controls Inc (PA) 203 929-8431
10 Controls Dr Shelton (06484) *(G-7517)*
O F Mossberg & Sons Inc (HQ) 203 230-5300
7 Grasso Ave North Haven (06473) *(G-5970)*
O S C, Oxford *Also called Oxford Science Center LLC* *(G-6686)*
O S Walker Company Inc (HQ) 508 853-3232
600 Day Hill Rd Windsor (06095) *(G-10414)*
O W Heat Treat Inc 860 430-6709
77 Great Pond Rd South Glastonbury (06073) *(G-7681)*
O-Liminator LLc 800 608-9541
137 Hollow Tree Ridge Rd Darien (06820) *(G-2036)*
O/D Dominion Software LLC 860 904-9261
21 High Wood Rd Bloomfield (06002) *(G-453)*
O2 Concepts LLC 877 867-4008
199 Park Road Ext Ste B Middlebury (06762) *(G-4286)*
Oak Hill Industries Inc 203 755-4400
2457 E Main St Ste 1j Waterbury (06705) *(G-9566)*
Oak Tree Moulding LLC 860 455-3056
7 Pole Bridge Rd Woodstock (06281) *(G-10674)*
Oakville Quality Products LLC 203 757-5525
1495 Thomaston Ave Ste 2 Waterbury (06704) *(G-9567)*
Oasis Coffee Corp 203 847-0554
327 Main Ave Norwalk (06851) *(G-6283)*
Obi Laser Products 860 305-0038
45 Bristol Dr Canton (06019) *(G-1322)*
Observer, The, Southington *Also called Step Saver Inc* *(G-7982)*
Occuptnal Trvl Mdcine Sups LLC 866 206-4496
2490 Black Rock Tpke Fairfield (06825) *(G-2823)*
Ocean Rigging LLC 800 624-2101
1 Bostwick Ave Bridgeport (06605) *(G-855)*
OConnell Industries Inc 860 508-7052
20 Tolland Tpke Manchester (06042) *(G-4065)*
Octavo Editions LLC 860 388-5772
72 Ayers Point Rd Old Saybrook (06475) *(G-6562)*
Odd Jobs Handyman Service LLC 203 397-5275
19 Grouse Ln Woodbridge (06525) *(G-10609)*
Oddo Print Shop & Copy Center, Torrington *Also called Oddo Print Shop Inc* *(G-8953)*
Oddo Print Shop Inc 860 489-6585
142 E Main St Torrington (06790) *(G-8953)*
Odis Inc 860 450-8407
22 Quail Run Rd Storrs Mansfield (06268) *(G-8557)*
Odorox Iaq Inc 203 541-5577
1266 E Main St Ste 700r Stamford (06902) *(G-8337)*
Odyssey Interactive LLC 860 799-6088
126 Aspetuck Vlg New Milford (06776) *(G-5577)*
Odyssey Jewelry 203 574-4956
495 Union St Ofc Waterbury (06706) *(G-9568)*
OEM Design Services LLC 203 467-5993
34 Panagrosi St East Haven (06512) *(G-2445)*
OEM Sources LLC 203 283-5415
214 Broadway Milford (06460) *(G-4597)*
Oerlikon AM Medical Inc 203 712-1030
10 Constitution Blvd S Shelton (06484) *(G-7518)*
Off The Hookhandmadecrochetllc 203 912-1638
96 High Rock Rd Sandy Hook (06482) *(G-7324)*
Office Insight 203 966-5008
24 East Ave New Canaan (06840) *(G-5127)*
Offshore Canvas & Cushions LLC 860 442-7803
249 Shore Rd Waterford (06385) *(G-9665)*
Ofs Companies 860 678-6574
180 Pondview Ln Bristol (06010) *(G-1082)*
Ofs Fitel LLC 860 678-0371
55 Darling Dr Avon (06001) *(G-96)*
Ofs Specialty Photonics Div, Avon *Also called Ofs Fitel LLC* *(G-96)*
Ogle Specialty, Meriden *Also called Couturier Ino* *(G-4162)*
Ogs Technologies Inc 203 271-9055
1855 Peck Ln Cheshire (06410) *(G-1424)*
OH Fudge and More LLC 860 788-3839
19 Larkspur Dr Higganum (06441) *(G-3773)*
Ohlheiser, H R Jr Pe, South Windsor *Also called O & W Heat Treat Inc* *(G-7799)*
Oil Guy LLC 203 910-2752
70 Farmdale Rd Watertown (06795) *(G-9717)*
Oil Purification Systems Inc 203 346-1800
2176 Thomaston Ave Waterbury (06704) *(G-9569)*
Okamoto Corp 860 219-1006
425 Hayden Station Rd Windsor (06095) *(G-10415)*
Okay Industries Inc 860 225-8707
245 New Park Dr Berlin (06037) *(G-204)*
Okay Medical Products Mfg, Berlin *Also called Okay Industries Inc* *(G-204)*
Old Cambridge Products Corp 860 243-1761
244 Woodland Ave Bloomfield (06002) *(G-454)*
Old Castle Foods LLC 203 426-1344
13 Old Castle Dr Newtown (06470) *(G-5766)*
Old Coach Home Sales 860 774-1379
242 Harris Rd Sterling (06377) *(G-8515)*
Old Farmers Almanac 860 862-9100
1 Mohegan Sun Blvd Uncasville (06382) *(G-9101)*
Old Harbor Fine Handcrafted, Watertown *Also called James A Blazys* *(G-9713)*
Old House Woodcraft LLC 860 228-2174
77 Johnson Rd Columbia (06237) *(G-1610)*
Old Leather Wallet Company LLC 860 350-9868
8 Wellers Bridge Rd Roxbury (06783) *(G-7280)*
Old Lyme Gourmet Company 860 434-7347
16 Grove St Deep River (06417) *(G-2097)*
Old Ni Incorporated 203 327-7300
50 Sunnyside Ave Stamford (06902) *(G-8338)*
Old Road Software Inc 914 755-1329
87 Grandview Dr Ridgefield (06877) *(G-7159)*
Old Thyme Country Candles 860 655-2583
807 Twin Circle Dr South Windsor (06074) *(G-7800)*
Old Wood Workshop 860 655-5259
193 Hampton Rd Pomfret Center (06259) *(G-6945)*
Oldcastle Infrastructure Inc 860 673-3291
151 Old Farms Rd Avon (06001) *(G-97)*
Olde Burnside Brewing Co LLC 860 528-2200
780 Tolland St East Hartford (06108) *(G-2349)*
Olde Tyme Country Candles 860 673-5086
8 Mohawk Dr Unionville (06085) *(G-9124)*
Olde Tyme Graphics 203 748-3360
4 Starr Rd Danbury (06810) *(G-1898)*
Olive Capizzano Oils & Vinegar 860 495-2187
5 Coggswell St Ste 1 Pawcatuck (06379) *(G-6721)*
Olive Chiappetta Oil LLC 203 223-3655
50 Mathews St Stamford (06902) *(G-8339)*
Olive Flavored 203 641-2086
167 Cobblestone Ln Meriden (06450) *(G-4211)*
Olive Nutmeg Oil 860 354-7300
25 Main St New Milford (06776) *(G-5578)*
Olive Oil Factory LLC 203 591-8986
197 Huntingdon Ave Waterbury (06708) *(G-9570)*
Olive Oil Mediterranean, Stamford *Also called Devin David* *(G-8184)*
Olive Oils and Balsamics LLC 860 563-0105
35 New Rd Rocky Hill (06067) *(G-7260)*
Olive Sabor Oil Co 860 922-7483
22 Brookford Rd Somers (06071) *(G-7666)*
Oliver Poons Children's Brand, Glastonbury *Also called Next Door Creations LLC* *(G-3064)*
Olson Brothers Company 860 747-6844
272 Camp St Plainville (06062) *(G-6850)*
Olson, G H Steel, Stratford *Also called George H Olson Steel Co Inc* *(G-8617)*
Olympia Sales Inc 860 749-0751
215 Moody Rd Ste 3 Enfield (06082) *(G-2672)*
Olympic STEel-Ps&w, Milford *Also called Tinsley GROup-Ps&w Inc* *(G-4665)*
Om Cass Swiss, Seymour *Also called New England Cap Company* *(G-7358)*
Omar Coffee Company 860 667-8889
41 Commerce Ct Newington (06111) *(G-5689)*
Omega Engineering Inc (HQ) 203 359-1660
800 Connecticut Ave 5n01 Norwalk (06854) *(G-6284)*
Omega Engineering Inc 714 540-4914
800 Cnncticut Ave Ste 5n1 Norwalk (06854) *(G-6285)*
Omega Engineering Inc 203 359-7922
1 Omega Dr Stamford (06907) *(G-8340)*
Omega International Corp 203 359-1660
1 Omega Dr Stamford (06907) *(G-8341)*
Omegadyne, Norwalk *Also called Omega Engineering Inc* *(G-6284)*
Omerin Usa Inc 475 343-3450
95 Research Pkwy Meriden (06450) *(G-4212)*
OMI International Corporation 203 575-5727
350 Frontage Rd West Haven (06516) *(G-9941)*
Omicronworld Entertainment LLC 203 453-5700
29 Horseshoe Rd Guilford (06437) *(G-3381)*
Omni Mold Systems LLC 888 666-4755
21 Kimball Heights Ln Lisbon (06351) *(G-3882)*
Omnicron Electronics 860 928-0377
554 Liberty Hwy Ste 2 Putnam (06260) *(G-7055)*
Omniprint LLC 203 881-9013
160 Christian St Oxford (06478) *(G-6683)*
Omnomnom Jams and Jellies LLC 203 630-6557
31 Orient St Meriden (06450) *(G-4213)*
Omondi Woodworking 860 513-2292
2690 Boston Tpke Coventry (06238) *(G-1667)*
OMSC, New Haven *Also called Overseas Ministries Study Ctr* *(G-5357)*
On Line Building Systems LLC 203 798-1194
22 Shelter Rock Ln Unit 4 Danbury (06810) *(G-1899)*
On Time Screen Printing & Embr 203 874-4581
155 New Haven Ave Derby (06418) *(G-2120)*
On Track Karting Inc (PA) 203 626-0464
984 N Colony Rd Wallingford (06492) *(G-9331)*
On-Site Welding LLC 860 662-6332
106 Dunne Ave Collinsville (06019) *(G-1598)*
Oncoarendi Therapeutics LLC 609 571-0306
125 Devonshire Ln Madison (06443) *(G-3943)*
Oncosynergy Inc 617 755-9156
380 Greenwich Ave Greenwich (06830) *(G-3212)*

ALPHABETIC

One and Co Inc 860 892-5180
154 N Main St Norwich (06360) *(G-6427)*
One Kid LLC (PA) 203 254-9978
188 Compo Rd S Westport (06880) *(G-10132)*
One Kid LLC 203 254-9978
160 Carter Henry Dr Fairfield (06824) *(G-2824)*
One Look Sign Company 860 581-8574
17 Industrial Park Rd # 7 Centerbrook (06409) *(G-1331)*
One Pair of Hands 860 364-0027
79 Gay St Sharon (06069) *(G-7381)*
One Piece of Puzzle LLC 860 919-6956
122 Grant St Hartford (06106) *(G-3659)*
One Source Print and Promo LLC 860 635-3257
150 Salem Dr Cromwell (06416) *(G-1713)*
One Stop Jamacia 203 507-2315
117 Whalley Ave New Haven (06511) *(G-5353)*
Onion Hill Press Llc 203 227-4895
17 Buena Vista Dr Westport (06880) *(G-10133)*
Online Journalism Project Inc 203 668-5790
493 Central Ave New Haven (06515) *(G-5354)*
Online River LLC 203 801-5900
606 Post Rd E Ste 723 Westport (06880) *(G-10134)*
Only Queens LLC 860 888-4413
21 Barry Cir Bloomfield (06002) *(G-455)*
Onofrios Ultimate Foods Inc 203 469-4014
35 Wheeler St New Haven (06512) *(G-5355)*
Onpoint Connections 860 253-0489
780 Enfield St Enfield (06082) *(G-2673)*
Onsite Mammography 860 254-5097
70 Sunset Dr West Suffield (06093) *(G-9988)*
Onsite Services Inc 860 669-3988
23 Meadow Rd Clinton (06413) *(G-1517)*
Ontra Stone Concepts LLC 203 371-8225
541 Central Ave Bridgeport (06607) *(G-856)*
Oomph LLC 203 216-9848
5 Elm St New Canaan (06840) *(G-5128)*
Ooshears Inc 415 230-0154
214 Ansonia Rd Woodbridge (06525) *(G-10610)*
Opal Manning Company Inc 203 292-6981
195 Grovers Ave Fairfield (06824) *(G-2825)*
Opel Connecticut Solar LLC 203 612-2366
3 Corporate Dr Ste 204 Shelton (06484) *(G-7519)*
Open Science Publishing LLC 860 568-4675
41 Applegate Ln Apt 217 East Hartford (06118) *(G-2350)*
Open Solutions LLC (HQ) 860 815-5000
455 Winding Brook Dr # 101 Glastonbury (06033) *(G-3066)*
Open Water Development LLC 646 883-2062
14 Cove Ridge Ln Old Greenwich (06870) *(G-6481)*
Openiam Software LLC 203 202-7186
49 Whortleberry Rd Redding (06896) *(G-7105)*
Opera Glass Networks LLC 203 919-2777
597 Westport Ave C261 Norwalk (06851) *(G-6286)*
Optamark CT LLC 203 325-1180
15 Bank St Ste 1 Stamford (06901) *(G-8342)*
Optical Design Associates 203 249-6408
600 Summer St Stamford (06901) *(G-8343)*
Optical Energy Technologies 203 357-0626
472 Westover Rd Stamford (06902) *(G-8344)*
Optical Research Technologies 203 762-9063
310 Hurlbutt St Wilton (06897) *(G-10316)*
Opticare Eye Health & Vision 203 261-2619
925 White Plains Rd Ste 5 Trumbull (06611) *(G-9052)*
Opticare Health Systems Inc (HQ) 203 574-2020
87 Grandview Ave Ste A Waterbury (06708) *(G-9571)*
Opticonx Inc 888 748-6855
45 Danco Rd Putnam (06260) *(G-7056)*
Optima Specialty Chemical 203 929-2031
8 Huntington St 332 Shelton (06484) *(G-7520)*
Optimized Micro Devices LLC 860 447-2142
184 Chesterfield Rd East Lyme (06333) *(G-2469)*
Optimum Welding Solutions LLC 203 598-8489
25 Gramar Ave Unit B Prospect (06712) *(G-7012)*
Or-Live, Inc., Farmington Also called Broadcastmed Inc *(G-2886)*
Oracle America Inc 203 703-3000
900 Long Ridge Rd Bldg 1 Stamford (06902) *(G-8345)*
Oracle Corporation 860 632-8329
54 Shady Hill Ln Middletown (06457) *(G-4389)*
Orafol Americas Inc 860 676-7100
120 Darling Dr Avon (06001) *(G-98)*
Oral Fluid Dynamics LLC 860 561-5036
400 Farmington Ave R1844 Farmington (06032) *(G-2941)*
Orange Cheese Company 917 603-4378
5 Hampton Close Orange (06477) *(G-6619)*
Orange Democrat 203 298-4575
297 Boston Post Rd Orange (06477) *(G-6620)*
Orange Research Inc 203 877-5657
140 Cascade Blvd Milford (06460) *(G-4598)*
Orange Restoration Labs, Orange Also called Sally Conant *(G-6628)*
Orban Designs LLC 860 605-7975
339 Allison Dr Torrington (06790) *(G-8954)*
Orbit Design LLC 203 393-0171
290 Pratt St Meriden (06450) *(G-4214)*

Orca Inc 860 223-4180
199 Whiting St New Britain (06051) *(G-5026)*
Orchard Press 860 672-4273
78 Popple Swamp Rd Cornwall Bridge (06754) *(G-1618)*
Orchid Design, Shelton Also called Orchid Orthpd Solutions LLC *(G-7521)*
Orchid Orthpd Solutions LLC 203 922-0105
80 Shelton Technology Ctr Shelton (06484) *(G-7521)*
Ordinary Joes 860 945-1500
253 Buckingham St Watertown (06779) *(G-9718)*
Organic Project The, Greenwich Also called W2w Partners LLC *(G-3255)*
Organizational & Diversity Con 203 777-3324
66 Colony Rd New Haven (06511) *(G-5356)*
Original Materials Inds LLC 203 535-1192
94 Squire Ln Hamden (06518) *(G-3492)*
Originals LLC 203 421-4867
2096 Durham Rd Madison (06443) *(G-3944)*
Origio Midatlantic Devices Inc 856 762-2000
75 Corporate Dr Trumbull (06611) *(G-9053)*
Orion Manufacturing LLC 860 572-2921
800 Flanders Rd Unit 4-8 Mystic (06355) *(G-4838)*
Orisha Oracle Inc 203 612-8989
59 Regent St Bridgeport (06606) *(G-857)*
Orsini's Sausages, Waterford Also called Cardoros Inc *(G-9644)*
Orteoponix LLC 203 804-9775
22 Scottron Dr Storrs (06268) *(G-8550)*
Orthotraction Pads LLC 203 698-0291
3 Old Club House Rd Old Greenwich (06870) *(G-6482)*
Orthozon Technologies LLC 203 989-4937
175 Atlantic St Ste 206 Stamford (06901) *(G-8346)*
Ortronics Inc (HQ) 860 445-3900
125 Eugene Oneill Dr # 140 New London (06320) *(G-5482)*
Ortronics Inc 877 295-3472
60 Woodlawn St West Hartford (06110) *(G-9841)*
Ortronics Legrand 860 767-3515
14 Windermere Way Ivoryton (06442) *(G-3788)*
Oscar Jobs 860 583-7834
165 Riverside Ave Bristol (06010) *(G-1083)*
Osda Contract Services Inc 203 878-2155
291 Pepes Farm Rd Milford (06460) *(G-4599)*
Osda Inc 203 878-2155
98 Quirk Rd Milford (06460) *(G-4600)*
Osf Flavors Inc (PA) 860 298-8350
40 Baker Hollow Rd Windsor (06095) *(G-10416)*
Oshkosh Corporation 860 653-5548
35 Nicholson Rd East Granby (06026) *(G-2221)*
Oskr Inc 475 238-2634
14a Buell St North Haven (06473) *(G-5971)*
Oslo Switch Inc 203 272-2794
30 Diana Ct Cheshire (06410) *(G-1425)*
Oslo Switches, Cheshire Also called Oslo Switch Inc *(G-1425)*
Osterman & Company Inc (PA) 203 272-2233
726 S Main St Cheshire (06410) *(G-1426)*
Osterman & Company Inc 203 272-2233
726 S Main St Cheshire (06410) *(G-1427)*
Osterman Trading Div, Cheshire Also called Osterman & Company Inc *(G-1426)*
Otis Elevator Company, Canton Also called Delta Elevator Service Corp *(G-1312)*
Otis Elevator Company (HQ) 860 674-3000
1 Carrier Pl Farmington (06032) *(G-2942)*
Otis Elevator Company 860 290-3318
5 Farm Springs Rd Farmington (06032) *(G-2943)*
Otis Elevator Company 860 242-3632
212 W Newberry Rd Bloomfield (06002) *(G-456)*
Our Town Crier 203 400-5000
36 Lyons Plains Rd Westport (06880) *(G-10135)*
Out On A Limb 203 315-8977
51 Mill Plain Rd Branford (06405) *(G-630)*
Outdoor Industries LLC 203 350-2275
80 Devonshire Ln Madison (06443) *(G-3945)*
Outdoor Life Channel, Stamford Also called Los Angles Tmes Cmmnctions LLC *(G-8289)*
Outer Light Brewing Co LLC 475 201-9972
266 Bridge St Ste 1 Groton (06340) *(G-3302)*
Outer Office 203 329-8600
218 Quarry Rd Stamford (06903) *(G-8347)*
Outland Engineering Inc 800 797-3709
167 Cherry St Pmb 280 Milford (06460) *(G-4601)*
Outpost Exploration LLC 203 762-7206
7 Broad Axe Ln Wilton (06897) *(G-10317)*
Oventrop Corp 860 413-9173
29 Kripes Rd East Granby (06026) *(G-2222)*
Over Moon 203 853-2498
35 Lenox Ave Norwalk (06854) *(G-6287)*
Overhaul Support Services LLC 860 653-1980
18 Connecticut South Dr East Granby (06026) *(G-2223)*
Overhaul Support Services LLC (PA) 860 264-2101
5 Connecticut South Dr East Granby (06026) *(G-2224)*
Overseas Ministries Study Ctr 203 624-6672
490 Prospect St Ste A New Haven (06511) *(G-5357)*
Ovl Manufacturing Inc LLC 860 829-0271
49 Cambridge Hts Berlin (06037) *(G-205)*
Owen Tool and Mfg Co Inc 860 628-6540
149 Aircraft Rd Southington (06489) *(G-7961)*

ALPHABETIC SECTION

Owh LLC 860 693-9464
  50 Albany Tpke Canton (06019) *(G-1323)*
Owl King Publishing LLC 203 530-6846
  119 Kennedy Dr Orange (06477) *(G-6621)*
Owlstone Inc (PA) 203 908-4848
  19 Ludlow Rd Ste 202 Westport (06880) *(G-10136)*
Oxford General Industries Inc 203 758-4467
  3 Gramar Ave Prospect (06712) *(G-7013)*
Oxford Industries Conn Inc 860 225-3700
  221 South St Bldg H New Britain (06051) *(G-5027)*
Oxford Outdoor Services LLC 860 800-6260
  2 Little Valley Rd Oxford (06478) *(G-6684)*
Oxford Performance Mtls Inc 860 698-9300
  30 S Satellite Rd South Windsor (06074) *(G-7801)*
Oxford Polymers, New Britain Also called Oxford Industries Conn Inc *(G-5027)*
Oxford Science Inc 203 881-3115
  178 Christian St Oxford (06478) *(G-6685)*
Oxford Science Center LLC 203 751-1912
  Iii One American Way Oxford (06478) *(G-6686)*
Oxford Woodworking LLC 203 482-0982
  133 Moose Hill Rd Oxford (06478) *(G-6687)*
Oxpekk Performance Mtls Inc 860 698-9300
  30 S Satellite Rd South Windsor (06074) *(G-7802)*
OXY Couture LLC 860 257-8750
  228 Raymond Rd Rocky Hill (06067) *(G-7261)*
Ozz 203 318-5080
  33 Seaview Ave Madison (06443) *(G-3946)*
P & M Investments LLC 860 745-3600
  1 Anngina Dr Enfield (06082) *(G-2674)*
P & M Welding Co LLC 860 528-2077
  38 Edwin Rd South Windsor (06074) *(G-7803)*
P & S Manufacturing LLC 203 685-2256
  225 Wheeler Ave Bridgeport (06606) *(G-858)*
P & S Printing LLC 203 327-9818
  513 Summer St Stamford (06901) *(G-8348)*
P C I Group 203 327-0410
  652 Glenbrook Rd 3-201 Stamford (06906) *(G-8349)*
P D M Company, Trumbull Also called John Olsen *(G-9037)*
P J S Services 860 345-4896
  135 Skunk Misery Rd Higganum (06441) *(G-3774)*
P L Woodworking 860 354-6855
  4 Deer Hill Rd Sherman (06784) *(G-7599)*
P M Hill 860 242-2915
  60 Loeffler Rd Bloomfield (06002) *(G-457)*
P M I, East Windsor Also called Plasticoid Manufacturing Inc *(G-2514)*
P T I, Enfield Also called Pti Industries Inc *(G-2683)*
P T Tool & Machine, Derby Also called Peter Tasi *(G-2122)*
P&G Metal Components Corp 860 243-2220
  98 Filley St Bloomfield (06002) *(G-458)*
P&M Welding, South Windsor Also called P & M Welding Co LLC *(G-7803)*
P&P Logging Co 860 267-2176
  38 Lakewood Rd East Hampton (06424) *(G-2272)*
P&P Tool & Die Corp 203 874-2571
  72 Erna Ave Milford (06461) *(G-4602)*
P-Q Controls Inc (PA) 860 583-6994
  95 Dolphin Rd Bristol (06010) *(G-1084)*
P.M.c, Danbury Also called PMC Engineering LLC *(G-1909)*
P/A Industries Inc (PA) 860 243-8306
  522 Cottage Grove Rd B Bloomfield (06002) *(G-459)*
P2 Science Inc 203 821-7457
  4 Research Dr Woodbridge (06525) *(G-10611)*
Pac Products, Yalesville Also called Joval Machine Co Inc *(G-10694)*
Pace Chiropractic Wellness Ctr 203 281-9635
  3154 Whitney Ave Hamden (06518) *(G-3493)*
Pacific Engineering Inc 860 677-0795
  24 Colton St Farmington (06032) *(G-2944)*
Pack Center , The, Stratford Also called Park City Packaging Inc *(G-8662)*
Packaging and Crating Tech LLC 203 759-1799
  150 Mattatuck Heights Rd Waterbury (06705) *(G-9572)*
Packaging Concepts Assoc LLC 860 489-0480
  230 Ella Grasso Ave Torrington (06790) *(G-8955)*
Packaging Displays, Hamden Also called American Metaseal of Conn *(G-3414)*
Packard Inc 203 758-6219
  6 Industrial Rd Prospect (06712) *(G-7014)*
Packard Specialties, Prospect Also called Packard Inc *(G-7014)*
Packrat Software 860 774-1538
  5 Conrad Park Dayville (06241) *(G-2068)*
Paco Assensio Woodworking LLC 203 536-2608
  15 Meadow St Norwalk (06854) *(G-6288)*
Pact Inc 203 759-1799
  150 Mattatuck Heights Rd Waterbury (06705) *(G-9573)*
Pactiv Corporation 203 288-7722
  458 Sackett Point Rd North Haven (06473) *(G-5972)*
Pagani Publishing 860 614-0303
  47 Bernardino Ave Enfield (06082) *(G-2675)*
Pages of Yesteryear 203 426-0864
  9 Old Hawleyville Rd Newtown (06470) *(G-5767)*
Pagoda Timber Frames 860 526-3077
  8 Butter Jones Rd Chester (06412) *(G-1477)*
Paint & Powder Works LLC 860 225-2019
  35 M And S Ct New Britain (06051) *(G-5028)*

Painted Tiles Co 860 658-7218
  58 Laurel Ln Simsbury (06070) *(G-7638)*
Pal Corporation 860 666-9211
  45 Maselli Rd Newington (06111) *(G-5690)*
Pal Technologies LLC 860 953-1984
  9 Tolles St West Hartford (06110) *(G-9842)*
Paladin Commercial Prtrs LLC 860 953-4900
  300 Hartford Ave Newington (06111) *(G-5691)*
Paladin Software Inc 203 966-0548
  379 South Ave New Canaan (06840) *(G-5129)*
Palladin Precision Pdts Inc 203 574-0246
  57 Bristol St Waterbury (06708) *(G-9574)*
Palladino Welding 203 729-7542
  270 City Hill St Naugatuck (06770) *(G-4908)*
Pallasian Software LLC 203 758-5868
  6 Rolling Ridge Ct Prospect (06712) *(G-7015)*
Pallet Guys LLC 203 691-6716
  102 Bailey Rd North Haven (06473) *(G-5973)*
Pallet Inc LLC 203 227-8148
  41 Charcoal Hill Rd Westport (06880) *(G-10137)*
Palliflex Products Company 860 928-7761
  125 Kennedy Dr Putnam (06260) *(G-7057)*
Palm Canyon Pictures 203 853-1808
  24 Crockett St Norwalk (06853) *(G-6289)*
Palmer Deep Draw Stamping LLC 860 880-8022
  135 S Main St Thomaston (06787) *(G-8800)*
Palmer Manufacturing Co LLC 860 828-0344
  134 Commerce St East Berlin (06023) *(G-2172)*
Palmero Healthcare LLC 203 377-6424
  120 Goodwin Pl Stratford (06615) *(G-8660)*
Palmers Elc Mtrs & Pumps Inc 203 348-7378
  40 Osborne Ave Norwalk (06855) *(G-6290)*
Palmieri Industries Inc 203 384-6020
  118 Burr Ct Ste 1 Bridgeport (06605) *(G-859)*
Palmisano Printing LLC 860 582-6883
  319 Queen St Bristol (06010) *(G-1085)*
Palumbo Sand & Gravel 860 350-5322
  4 Old Greenwoods Rd Sherman (06784) *(G-7600)*
Pamela D Siemon Lcsw LLC 203 232-8009
  51 Depot St Ste 207 Watertown (06795) *(G-9719)*
Pamela Gordondupont Ms Ccca 860 526-8686
  38 Gilbert Hill Rd Chester (06412) *(G-1478)*
Pamelas Patterns 610 534-4182
  613 Talcottville Rd Vernon Rockville (06066) *(G-9173)*
Pan De Oro Brand, Hartford Also called Severance Foods Inc *(G-3684)*
Pan Del Cielo, Waterbury Also called I and U LLC *(G-9502)*
Panacol-Usa Inc 860 738-7449
  142 Industrial Ln Torrington (06790) *(G-8956)*
Panagrafix Inc 203 691-5529
  50 Fresh Meadow Rd West Haven (06516) *(G-9942)*
Panboud Pierrot 203 296-4806
  240 William St Bridgeport (06608) *(G-860)*
Pancoast Associates Inc 203 377-6571
  25 Mariner Cir Trumbull (06611) *(G-9054)*
Panel Pro Technology 203 333-0083
  104 Silliman Ave Bridgeport (06605) *(G-861)*
Panel Shop Inc 203 377-6208
  100 Lupes Dr Stratford (06615) *(G-8661)*
Paneloc Corporation 860 677-6711
  142 Brickyard Rd Farmington (06032) *(G-2945)*
Panolam Industries Inc (HQ) 203 925-1556
  1 Corporate Dr Ste 725 Shelton (06484) *(G-7522)*
Panolam Industries Intl Inc (PA) 203 925-1556
  1 Corporate Dr Ste 725 Shelton (06484) *(G-7523)*
Panolam Surface System, Shelton Also called Panolam Industries Inc *(G-7522)*
Panolam Surface Systems, Shelton Also called Panolam Industries Intl Inc *(G-7523)*
Panza Woodwork & Supply LLC 203 934-3430
  4 Hugo St West Haven (06516) *(G-9943)*
Paoletti Fence Company Inc 860 296-0396
  241 Ledyard St Ste B8 Hartford (06114) *(G-3660)*
Pap Products LLC 860 242-0415
  14 Griffin Rd S Bloomfield (06002) *(G-460)*
Papaer Mill Graphix, Greenwich Also called Paper Mill Graphix Inc *(G-3213)*
Papas Maple Syrup 860 379-0117
  624 Niles Rd New Hartford (06057) *(G-5205)*
Paper Alliance LLC 203 315-3116
  45 Ne Industrial Rd Branford (06405) *(G-631)*
Paper and Prose Publishing LLC 203 775-8228
  9 Willow Run Brookfield (06804) *(G-1210)*
Paper Mill Graphix Inc 203 531-5904
  2 Armonk St Greenwich (06830) *(G-3213)*
Paper Station 860 667-9087
  29 E Cedar St Newington (06111) *(G-5692)*
Papish, Leo & Company, Danbury Also called A Papish Incorporated *(G-1727)*
Par Manufacturing Inc 860 677-1797
  1824 New Britain Ave Farmington (06032) *(G-2946)*
Par Thread Grinding, Farmington Also called Par Manufacturing Inc *(G-2946)*
Parachute Indust Engrg Consult, Colchester Also called Peregrine Technical Svcs LLC *(G-1563)*
Paradigm Manchester Inc 860 646-4048
  203 Sheldon Rd Bldg 2 Manchester (06042) *(G-4066)*

Paradigm Manchester Inc ... 860 646-4048
 186 Adams St S Bldg 3 Manchester (06040) *(G-4067)*
Paradigm Manchester Inc (HQ) ... 860 646-4048
 967 Parker St Manchester (06042) *(G-4068)*
Paradigm Manchester Inc ... 860 649-2888
 255 Sheldon Rd Bldg 4 Manchester (06042) *(G-4069)*
Paradigm Manchester Inc ... 860 646-4048
 151 Sheldon Rd Manchester (06042) *(G-4070)*
Paradigm Prcision Holdings LLC ... 860 829-3663
 134 Commerce St East Berlin (06023) *(G-2173)*
Paradigm Prcision Holdings LLC ... 860 649-2888
 967 Parker St Manchester (06042) *(G-4071)*
Paradigm Precision, Manchester Also called Paradigm Manchester Inc *(G-4066)*
Paradigm Precision, Manchester Also called Paradigm Manchester Inc *(G-4067)*
Paradigm Precision, Manchester Also called Paradigm Manchester Inc *(G-4068)*
Paradise Hlls Vnyrd Winery LLC ... 203 284-0123
 15 Windswept Hill Rd Wallingford (06492) *(G-9332)*
Paragon Products Inc ... 860 388-1363
 175 Elm St Ste 1 Old Saybrook (06475) *(G-6563)*
Paragon Publications ... 860 875-4366
 124 Rollingview Dr Vernon (06066) *(G-9149)*
Paragon Tool Company Inc ... 860 647-9935
 121 Adams St S Manchester (06040) *(G-4072)*
Parama Corp ... 203 790-8155
 7 Trowbridge Dr Bethel (06801) *(G-331)*
Paramount Glassworks LLC ... 860 315-7624
 133 Lyon Hill Rd Woodstock (06281) *(G-10675)*
Paramount Machine Company Inc ... 860 643-5549
 138 Sanrico Dr Manchester (06042) *(G-4073)*
Parason Machine Inc ... 860 526-3565
 1000 Industrial Park Rd Deep River (06417) *(G-2098)*
Parent Engagement Tracker LLC ... 860 209-5522
 126 Yale St Hartford (06106) *(G-3661)*
Parent Lea Farm, Woodstock Also called Roland A Parent *(G-10682)*
Parfums De Coeur Ltd (PA) ... 203 655-8807
 750 E Main St Stamford (06902) *(G-8350)*
Paridise Foods LLC ... 203 283-3903
 828 New Haven Ave Milford (06460) *(G-4603)*
Pariot Sign Company Llc ... 203 364-9009
 78 Main St Newtown (06470) *(G-5768)*
Parish Associates Inc ... 203 335-4100
 1383 Kings Hwy Fairfield (06824) *(G-2826)*
Parish Publishing, New Canaan Also called Liturgical Publications Inc *(G-5115)*
Park Avenue Securities ... 860 677-2600
 197 Scott Swamp Rd Farmington (06032) *(G-2947)*
Park City Packaging Inc (PA) ... 203 378-7384
 480 Sniffens Ln Stratford (06615) *(G-8662)*
Park City Packaging Inc ... 203 579-1965
 1069 Conn Ave Ste 22 Bridgeport (06607) *(G-862)*
Park Distributories Inc (PA) ... 203 579-2140
 347 Railroad Ave Bridgeport (06604) *(G-863)*
Park Distributories Inc ... 203 366-7200
 347 Railroad Ave Bridgeport (06604) *(G-864)*
Park Distributories Inc ... 203 366-7200
 347 Railroad Ave Bridgeport (06604) *(G-865)*
Park Group Solutions LLC ... 203 459-8784
 8 Pecks Ln Ste A2 Newtown (06470) *(G-5769)*
Park Lane Cider Mill, New Milford Also called Vincent Jajer *(G-5607)*
Park Tool & Gage Co Inc ... 860 225-0187
 56 Saint Claire Ave New Britain (06051) *(G-5029)*
Parker, East Hartford Also called Clarcor Eng MBL Solutions LLC *(G-2306)*
Parker Medical Inc ... 860 350-3446
 5 Old Town Park Rd # 34 New Milford (06776) *(G-5579)*
Parker Saw Mill, Somers Also called Parker Septic Service *(G-7667)*
Parker Septic Service ... 860 749-8220
 77 South Rd Somers (06071) *(G-7667)*
Parker-Hannifin Corporation ... 860 827-2300
 95 Edgewood Ave New Britain (06051) *(G-5030)*
Parker-Hannifin Corporation ... 860 920-4231
 60 Prestige Park Rd East Hartford (06108) *(G-2351)*
Parker-Hannifin Corporation ... 203 239-3341
 33 Defco Park Rd North Haven (06473) *(G-5974)*
Parkhill Publishing LLC ... 203 938-9199
 32 Drummer Ln West Redding (06896) *(G-9970)*
Parking Lt Strpng & Asphlt Sgn ... 203 648-6323
 4 Liberty Ave Danbury (06810) *(G-1900)*
Parkway Printers Inc ... 203 281-6773
 60 Connolly Pkwy Hamden (06514) *(G-3494)*
Parma 1901 Usa Inc ... 203 855-1356
 1 Selleck St Fl 2 Norwalk (06855) *(G-6291)*
Parmaco LLC ... 860 573-7118
 111 Warner Ct Glastonbury (06033) *(G-3067)*
Partner In Publishing LLC ... 860 430-9440
 947 Neipsic Rd Glastonbury (06033) *(G-3068)*
Parts Cutter Cnc ... 203 947-4407
 78 Triangle St Danbury (06810) *(G-1901)*
Parts Feeders Inc ... 860 528-9579
 22 John St East Hartford (06108) *(G-2352)*
Parva Industries Inc ... 203 248-5553
 2974 Whitney Ave Hamden (06518) *(G-3495)*
Parva Mfg Group Inc ... 860 828-6285
 101 Alling St Kensington (06037) *(G-3816)*

Pas, Bethany Also called Plastic Assembly Systems LLC *(G-248)*
Pas Technologies Inc ... 860 649-2727
 321 Progress Dr Manchester (06042) *(G-4074)*
Pass Perfect LLC ... 203 629-9333
 176 Bedford Rd Greenwich (06831) *(G-3214)*
Pass Perfect Associates, Greenwich Also called Edward Fleur Fncl Educatn Corp *(G-3157)*
Passion Engineering LLC ... 203 204-3090
 579 Lake Dr Guilford (06437) *(G-3382)*
Passport Publications of ... 631 736-6691
 1099 Arbutus St Middletown (06457) *(G-4390)*
Passur Aerospace Inc (PA) ... 203 622-4086
 1 Landmark Sq Ste 1900 Stamford (06901) *(G-8351)*
Pastanch LLC ... 203 720-9478
 31 Sheridan Dr Naugatuck (06770) *(G-4909)*
Pastrana Unlimited LLC ... 860 747-6633
 131 Whiting St Ste 1 Plainville (06062) *(G-6851)*
Pastry Shop ... 203 238-0483
 31 Main St Meriden (06451) *(G-4215)*
Patalanos Woodworking LLC ... 203 612-7537
 53 Arthur St Bridgeport (06605) *(G-866)*
Patches and Patchwork, Portland Also called Jane Sterry *(G-6960)*
Pathway Lighting Products Inc ... 860 388-6881
 175 Elm St 5 Old Saybrook (06475) *(G-6564)*
Pathway Lighting Source ... 860 537-0600
 226 Upton Rd Colchester (06415) *(G-1562)*
Pathway The Lighting Source, Old Saybrook Also called Pathway Lighting Products Inc *(G-6564)*
Patricia Beavers ... 860 233-4071
 48 Beacon St Hartford (06105) *(G-3662)*
Patricia Poke ... 860 354-4193
 20 Maple Ln New Milford (06776) *(G-5580)*
Patricia Spratt For Home LLC ... 860 434-9291
 60 Lyme St Old Lyme (06371) *(G-6517)*
Patricias Presents, New Milford Also called Patricia Poke *(G-5580)*
Patrick Barrett DBA Lucky Duck ... 347 703-3984
 79 Old Turnpike Rd Canaan (06018) *(G-1290)*
Patrick Odonoghue ... 203 467-4041
 8 Wood Ter East Haven (06513) *(G-2446)*
Patriot Envelope LLC ... 860 529-1553
 501 Middletown Ave Wethersfield (06109) *(G-10214)*
Patriot Manufacturing Inc ... 860 506-2213
 205 Cross St Bristol (06010) *(G-1086)*
Patriot Oil Heat LLC ... 860 928-4091
 416 Senexet Rd Woodstock (06281) *(G-10676)*
Patriot Woodworking LLC ... 860 653-4349
 261 South Rd East Hartland (06027) *(G-2404)*
Patriotic Spirit ... 704 239-4289
 251 Hill St Suffield (06078) *(G-8728)*
Pattaconk Millwork, Chester Also called Gary D Kryszat *(G-1473)*
Pattagansett Publishing Inc ... 860 693-6156
 176 Morgan Rd Canton (06019) *(G-1324)*
Pattern Genomics LLC ... 203 779-5470
 22 Alex Dr Madison (06443) *(G-3947)*
Pattison Sign Group Inc ... 860 583-3000
 2074 Perkins St Bristol (06010) *(G-1087)*
Patty Mommys ... 203 330-8575
 578 Boston Ave Bridgeport (06610) *(G-867)*
Patwil LLC ... 860 589-9085
 190 Century Dr Ste 102 Bristol (06010) *(G-1088)*
Paul D Wolff ... 203 319-7242
 77 Mile Common Rd Easton (06612) *(G-2560)*
Paul Dewitt ... 203 792-5610
 128 E Liberty St Ste 4 Danbury (06810) *(G-1902)*
Paul Dringoli ... 203 248-0281
 3569 Whitney Ave Hamden (06518) *(G-3496)*
Paul Gaffney ... 203 221-1249
 8 Brookwood Ln Weston (06883) *(G-10035)*
Paul H Gesswein & Company Inc ... 860 388-0652
 40 River St Old Saybrook (06475) *(G-6565)*
Paul Maxx Industries LLC ... 203 417-2446
 6 Freedom Cir Southbury (06488) *(G-7871)*
Paul Petrushonis Staind Glss ... 203 878-0163
 400 Boston Post Rd Milford (06460) *(G-4604)*
Paul Ramee LLC ... 860 927-7135
 71 Bulls Bridge Rd South Kent (06785) *(G-7684)*
Paul Welding Company Inc ... 860 229-9945
 157 Kelsey St Newington (06111) *(G-5693)*
Paul's Pasta Shop, Groton Also called Fine Food Services Inc *(G-3288)*
Paul's Prosperous Printing, Wilton Also called Prosperous Printing LLC *(G-10322)*
Paulas Bakery ... 203 743-9000
 54 Liberty St Ste 1 Danbury (06810) *(G-1903)*
Pauls Leather Co ... 203 871-7238
 7 Bryan Rd Branford (06405) *(G-632)*
Pauls Marble Depot LLC ... 203 978-0669
 40 Warshaw Pl Ste 1 Stamford (06902) *(G-8352)*
Pauls Wire Rope & Sling Inc ... 203 481-3469
 4 Indian Neck Ave Branford (06405) *(G-633)*
Pauway Corp ... 203 265-3939
 63 N Cherry St Ste 2 Wallingford (06492) *(G-9333)*
Pavers of New England Inc ... 860 289-7778
 1370 John Fitch Blvd South Windsor (06074) *(G-7804)*

ALPHABETIC SECTION

Paw Patterns LLC 401 338-4723
   157 Cannon Dr Amston (06231) *(G-5)*
Paw Print Pantry LLC (PA) 860 447-8442
   33 Gurley Rd East Lyme (06333) *(G-2470)*
Paw Print Pantry LLC 860 447-8442
   214 Flanders Rd Ste A Niantic (06357) *(G-5815)*
Paw To Press 303 709-2807
   224 Thames St Groton (06340) *(G-3303)*
Pawtrait Inc 848 992-4599
   38 Pine Hill Ter Stamford (06903) *(G-8353)*
Paxxus Inc 860 242-0663
   16 Southwood Dr Bloomfield (06002) *(G-461)*
PB&j Design Inc 203 332-4433
   251 Roosevelt Dr Derby (06418) *(G-2121)*
PBM Printers & Copy Center, Rocky Hill *Also called Desai Mukesh* *(G-7234)*
Pbn LLC 860 582-9111
   200 Central St Bristol (06010) *(G-1089)*
PCA, Torrington *Also called Packaging Concepts Assoc LLC* *(G-8955)*
PCC Structurals Groton (HQ) 860 405-3700
   839 Poquonnock Rd Groton (06340) *(G-3304)*
Pcx Aerostructures LLC 860 666-2471
   300 Fenn Rd Newington (06111) *(G-5694)*
Pcx Aerostructures LLC (PA) 860 666-2471
   300 Fenn Rd Newington (06111) *(G-5695)*
PDC Brands, Stamford *Also called Parfums De Coeur Ltd* *(G-8350)*
PDC International Corp 203 853-1516
   8 Sheehan Ave Norwalk (06854) *(G-6292)*
PDI, Middletown *Also called Plastic Design Intl Inc* *(G-4393)*
Pdq Inc 860 322-4412
   65 Airport Industrial Rd Chester (06412) *(G-1479)*
Pdq Inc (PA) 860 529-9051
   24 Evans Rd Rocky Hill (06067) *(G-7262)*
Pds Engineering & Cnstr Inc 860 242-8586
   107 Old Windsor Rd Bloomfield (06002) *(G-462)*
Peaceful Daily Inc 203 909-2961
   800 Village Walk Ste 103 Guilford (06437) *(G-3383)*
Peach Printing Solutions 203 793-7381
   18 Chimney Sweep Rd Wallingford (06492) *(G-9334)*
Peaches Prints 860 856-3525
   16 Eagleton Dr Windsor (06095) *(G-10417)*
Peachwave of Watertown 203 942-4949
   1156 Main St Watertown (06795) *(G-9720)*
Peacock Cabinetry 203 862-9333
   9 Bettswood Rd Norwalk (06851) *(G-6293)*
Peacock Manufacturing Co LLC 203 388-4100
   9 Bettswood Rd Norwalk (06851) *(G-6294)*
Peak Antennas 203 268-3688
   200 Main St Unit 3a Monroe (06468) *(G-4745)*
Peak Antennas LLC 203 268-3688
   200 Main St Unit 3a Monroe (06468) *(G-4746)*
Peaks Parrots 860 316-2788
   749 Saybrook Rd Ste 2 Middletown (06457) *(G-4391)*
Peale Ctr For Christn Living, Danbury *Also called A Guideposts Church Corp* *(G-1726)*
Peanut Butter and Jelly 203 504-2280
   500 Bedford St Apt 227 Stamford (06901) *(G-8354)*
Pearse Bertram LLC 860 612-9060
   595 John Downey Dr New Britain (06051) *(G-5031)*
Peartree Point Software LLC 203 940-1069
   45 Edgerton St Darien (06820) *(G-2037)*
Peekaboopumpkin.com, Stamford *Also called Thomas Design Group LLC* *(G-8466)*
Peening Technologies Conn, East Hartford *Also called Hydro Honing Laboratories Inc* *(G-2335)*
Peening Technologies Eqp LLC 860 289-4328
   8 Eastern Park Rd East Hartford (06108) *(G-2353)*
Peening Technologies Eqp LLC 860 289-4328
   261 Burnham St East Hartford (06108) *(G-2354)*
Peerless Systems Corporation (HQ) 203 350-0040
   1055 Washington Blvd Fl 8 Stamford (06901) *(G-8355)*
Pegasus Capital Advisors LP (PA) 203 869-4400
   750 E Main St Stamford (06902) *(G-8356)*
Pegasus Manufacturing, Middletown *Also called L&P Aerospace Acquisition LLC* *(G-4366)*
Pegasus Productions, Redding *Also called A Family Farm* *(G-7087)*
Pel Associates LLC (PA) 860 446-9921
   187 Ledgewood Rd Apt 407 Groton (06340) *(G-3305)*
Pelchs Auto Repair, Collinsville *Also called Pelchs Welding & Repair* *(G-1599)*
Pelchs Welding & Repair 860 693-6328
   40 Ramp Rd Collinsville (06019) *(G-1599)*
Peleganos Stained Glass Studio 203 272-8067
   83 Saint Joseph St Cheshire (06410) *(G-1428)*
Pelegnos Stined GL Art Gallery 860 621-2900
   1241 Mrden Waterbury Tpke Plantsville (06479) *(G-6907)*
Pelican Island Publishing 908 227-0991
   41 Foxwood Rd Stamford (06903) *(G-8357)*
Pelletier Millwrights LLC 860 564-8936
   161 Moosup Pond Rd Danielson (06239) *(G-2000)*
Pemberton Press Inc 203 761-1466
   462 Danbury Rd Wilton (06897) *(G-10318)*
Pemko Manufacturing Co 901 365-2160
   110 Sargent Dr New Haven (06511) *(G-5358)*
Penco Corporation 860 347-7271
   33 Anderson Rd Middletown (06457) *(G-4392)*

Penfield Communications Inc 203 387-0354
   50 Fitch St New Haven (06515) *(G-5359)*
Peninsula Publishing 203 292-5621
   1630 Post Rd E Unit 312 Westport (06880) *(G-10138)*
Penmar Industries Inc 203 853-4868
   35 Ontario St Stratford (06615) *(G-8663)*
Penney Software Services 860 870-3443
   84 Angela Dr Tolland (06084) *(G-8875)*
Pennsylvania Globe Gaslight Co 203 484-7749
   300 Shaw Rd North Branford (06471) *(G-5851)*
Penny Marketing Ltd Partnr (PA) 203 866-6688
   6 Prowitt St Norwalk (06855) *(G-6295)*
Penny Press Inc (PA) 203 866-6688
   6 Prowitt St Norwalk (06855) *(G-6296)*
Penny Press Inc 203 866-6688
   185 Plains Rd Ste 100e Milford (06461) *(G-4605)*
Penny Publications LLC 203 866-6688
   185 Plains Rd Ste 201e Milford (06461) *(G-4606)*
Penny Publications LLC (PA) 203 866-6688
   6 Prowitt St Norwalk (06855) *(G-6297)*
Pennycorner Press 860 873-3545
   382 Town St East Haddam (06423) *(G-2247)*
Penotti USA Inc 203 341-9494
   4 Maple Grove Ave Westport (06880) *(G-10139)*
Penta Woodworking Shop, Plainville *Also called Gregory Penta* *(G-6819)*
People Meeting LLC (PA) 860 933-0366
   15 Conestoga Way Glastonbury (06033) *(G-3069)*
Pep Be-St, Bridgeport *Also called Boston Endo-Surgical Tech LLC* *(G-717)*
Pep Connecticut Plastics, Wallingford *Also called Precision Engineered Pdts LLC* *(G-9341)*
Pepin Steel and Iron Works LLC 860 582-1852
   47 Old Waterbury Rd Bristol (06010) *(G-1090)*
Pepperidge Farm Incorporated 860 286-6400
   1414 Blue Hills Ave Bloomfield (06002) *(G-463)*
Pepperidge Farm Incorporated (HQ) 203 846-7000
   595 Westport Ave Norwalk (06851) *(G-6298)*
Pepperl + Fuchs Inc 860 923-2703
   405 Dugg Hill Rd Woodstock (06281) *(G-10677)*
Pepsi Foods 860 567-5774
   143 Northfield Rd Litchfield (06759) *(G-3898)*
Pepsi-Cola Btlg of Wrcster Inc 860 774-4007
   135 Louisa Viens Dr Dayville (06241) *(G-2069)*
Pepsi-Cola Metro Btlg Co Inc 203 375-2484
   355 Benton St Stratford (06615) *(G-8664)*
Pepsi-Cola Metro Btlg Co Inc 860 848-1231
   260 Gallivan Ln Uncasville (06382) *(G-9102)*
Pepsi-Cola Metro Btlg Co Inc 203 234-9014
   27 Leonardo Dr North Haven (06473) *(G-5975)*
Pepsi-Cola Metro Btlg Co Inc 860 688-6281
   55 International Dr Windsor (06095) *(G-10418)*
Pepsico, Stratford *Also called Pepsi-Cola Metro Btlg Co Inc* *(G-8664)*
Pepsico, Litchfield *Also called Pepsi Foods* *(G-3898)*
Pepsico, Dayville *Also called Pepsi-Cola Btlg of Wrcster Inc* *(G-2069)*
Pepsico, North Haven *Also called Pepsi-Cola Metro Btlg Co Inc* *(G-5975)*
Pepsico, Windsor *Also called Pepsi-Cola Metro Btlg Co Inc* *(G-10418)*
Pepsico 203 974-8912
   150 Munson St New Haven (06511) *(G-5360)*
Pequonnock Ironworks Inc 203 336-2178
   621 Knowlton St Bridgeport (06608) *(G-868)*
Pequot 800 620-1492
   1000 Lafayette Blvd # 1100 Bridgeport (06604) *(G-869)*
Pequot Printing LLC 860 381-5193
   1 Windward Ln Ledyard (06339) *(G-3879)*
Peregrine Manufacturing, Brooklyn *Also called Uninsred Alttude Cnnection Inc* *(G-1257)*
Peregrine Technical Svcs LLC 813 469-9355
   87 Brookstone Dr Colchester (06415) *(G-1563)*
Perennial Elements LLC 860 536-8593
   15 Mystic Hill Rd Mystic (06355) *(G-4839)*
Perey Turnstiles Inc 203 333-9400
   308 Bishop Ave Bridgeport (06610) *(G-870)*
Perez Welding Services LLC 203 876-1066
   25 Belfast St Milford (06460) *(G-4607)*
Perfect Infinity Inc 203 906-0442
   167 Cherry St Ste 145 Milford (06460) *(G-4608)*
Perfectsoftware, Norwalk *Also called Criterion Inc* *(G-6133)*
Perfex Manufacturing 203 739-0930
   30 Commerce Dr Danbury (06810) *(G-1904)*
Performance Compounding Inc 860 599-5616
   185 S Broad St Ste 2a Pawcatuck (06379) *(G-6722)*
Performance Connection Systems 203 868-5517
   599 W Main St Meriden (06451) *(G-4216)*
Performance Fabrication 860 678-8070
   799 New Britain Ave Farmington (06032) *(G-2948)*
Performance Machine Inc 860 974-3664
   207 Center Rd Woodstock (06281) *(G-10678)*
Performance Sheet Metal 860 889-0550
   57 Bishop Rd Bozrah (06334) *(G-531)*
Pergenex Software LLC 860 274-7318
   410 Winding Brook Farm Rd Watertown (06795) *(G-9721)*
Periodic Tableware LLC 310 428-4250
   415 Howe Ave Ste 110 Shelton (06484) *(G-7524)*
Peristere LLC 860 783-5301
   95 Hilliard St Manchester (06042) *(G-4075)*

Perkinelmer Inc...203 925-4600
710 Bridgeport Ave Shelton (06484) ***(G-7525)***
Perkinelmer Hlth Sciences Inc...203 925-4600
710 Bridgeport Ave Shelton (06484) ***(G-7526)***
Permanent Press LLC...860 788-6001
86 Appletree Ln Portland (06480) ***(G-6967)***
Permatex Inc (PA)...860 543-7500
10 Columbus Blvd Ste 1 Hartford (06106) ***(G-3663)***
Permatex, Inc./ A Division ITW, Hartford *Also called Permatex Inc* ***(G-3663)***
Perosphere Inc...203 885-1111
20 Kenosia Ave Danbury (06810) ***(G-1905)***
Perosphere Technologies Inc...475 218-4600
108 Mill Plain Rd Ste 301 Danbury (06811) ***(G-1906)***
Perrella Guide Service, Southbury *Also called Perrella Specialties* ***(G-7872)***
Perrella Specialties...203 264-1758
278 W Purchase Rd Southbury (06488) ***(G-7872)***
Perricone Hydrogen Wtr Co LLC...844 341-5941
639 Research Pkwy Meriden (06450) ***(G-4217)***
Perrin Manufacturing...203 265-1325
102 Liney Hall Ln Wallingford (06492) ***(G-9335)***
Perry Heights Press LLC...203 767-6509
610 Nod Hill Rd Wilton (06897) ***(G-10319)***
Perry Industries LLC...203 505-5187
41 Sundance Dr Cos Cob (06807) ***(G-1639)***
Perry S Sawyer...860 572-9473
1307 Pequot Trl Stonington (06378) ***(G-8535)***
Perry Technology Corporation...860 738-2525
120 Industrial Park Rd New Hartford (06057) ***(G-5206)***
Personal Care Appliances Div, Stamford *Also called Conair Corporation* ***(G-8156)***
Personal Service, Wallingford *Also called Meals By Michael* ***(G-9316)***
Personally Yours...860 537-2248
83 Oconnell Rd Colchester (06415) ***(G-1564)***
Personally Yours...203 329-6645
45 Idlewood Pl Stamford (06905) ***(G-8358)***
Petal Prfctn & Confection LLC...203 263-0353
660 Main St S Woodbury (06798) ***(G-10649)***
Peter Arch Woodworking LLC...203 374-9977
611 Church Hill Rd Fairfield (06825) ***(G-2827)***
Peter Conrad...860 673-3600
3 Raymond Rd East Hampton (06424) ***(G-2273)***
Peter Dermer Co...203 389-3297
245 Amity Rd Ste 109 Woodbridge (06525) ***(G-10612)***
Peter Hannan...203 226-4335
117 Weston Rd Westport (06880) ***(G-10140)***
Peter Hoelzel...860 749-4070
31 Taft Ln Enfield (06082) ***(G-2676)***
Peter James Associates Inc...203 972-1070
296 Old Norwalk Rd New Canaan (06840) ***(G-5130)***
Peter Kelsey Publishing Inc...860 231-9300
22 Grassmere Ave West Hartford (06110) ***(G-9843)***
Peter Ortali & Associates LLC...203 571-8023
45 New Lebbon Rd Sandy Hook (06482) ***(G-7325)***
Peter Paul Electronics Co Inc...860 229-4884
480 John Downey Dr New Britain (06051) ***(G-5032)***
Peter Tasi...203 732-6540
10 Francis St Derby (06418) ***(G-2122)***
Peters Machine Company...860 529-3672
1275 Cromwell Ave Ste B8 Rocky Hill (06067) ***(G-7263)***
Petes Print Shop...860 581-8043
46 Plains Rd Essex (06426) ***(G-2729)***
Petrini Art & Frame LLC (PA)...860 677-2747
35 E Main St Avon (06001) ***(G-99)***
Petro-Tech Industries LLC...860 881-5890
16 Laurel Dr Willington (06279) ***(G-10253)***
Petroglyph Energy Inc (PA)...208 685-7600
1 Thorndal Cir Ste 3 Darien (06820) ***(G-2038)***
Petron Automation Inc...860 274-9091
65 Mountain View Rd Watertown (06795) ***(G-9722)***
Petrunti Design & Wdwkg LLC...860 953-5332
23c Andover Dr West Hartford (06110) ***(G-9844)***
Pewter Hutch...203 262-6181
860 Main St S Woodbury (06798) ***(G-10650)***
Pexagon Technology Inc...203 458-3364
14 Business Park Dr Ste E Branford (06405) ***(G-634)***
Pez Candy Inc (HQ)...203 795-0531
35 Prindle Hill Rd Orange (06477) ***(G-6622)***
Pez Manufacturing Corp...203 795-0531
35 Prindle Hill Rd Orange (06477) ***(G-6623)***
PF Laboratories Inc (HQ)...973 256-3100
201 Tresser Blvd Ste 324 Stamford (06901) ***(G-8359)***
Pfd Studios...860 295-8500
213 Flood Rd Marlborough (06447) ***(G-4128)***
Pfizer Inc...860 441-4000
445 Eastern Point Rd Groton (06340) ***(G-3306)***
Pfizer Inc...860 389-7509
156a Eastern Point Rd Groton (06340) ***(G-3307)***
Pfizer Inc...860 441-4568
9 Pinehurst St Trumbull (06611) ***(G-9055)***
Pfizer Inc...203 401-0100
1 Howe St New Haven (06511) ***(G-5361)***
Pfizer Inc...860 441-4100
100 Eastern Point Rd Groton (06340) ***(G-3308)***
Pgxhealthholding Inc (PA)...203 786-3400
5 Science Park New Haven (06511) ***(G-5362)***
Pharmacal Research Labs Inc...203 755-4908
562 Captain Neville Dr # 1 Waterbury (06705) ***(G-9575)***
Pharmaceutical Discovery Corp...203 796-3425
1 Casper St Danbury (06810) ***(G-1907)***
Pharmaceutical RES Assoc Inc (HQ)...203 588-8000
201 Tresser Blvd Stamford (06901) ***(G-8360)***
Pharmavite Corp...860 651-1885
10 Station St Simsbury (06070) ***(G-7639)***
Philip Cups, Bridgeport *Also called Harrison Enterprise LLC* ***(G-781)***
Philips Ultrasound Inc...203 753-5215
1875 Thomaston Ave Ste 5 Waterbury (06704) ***(G-9576)***
Phillips Fuel Systems...203 908-3323
109 Holland Ave Bridgeport (06605) ***(G-871)***
Phillips Pump LLC...203 576-6688
661 Lindley St Bridgeport (06606) ***(G-872)***
Phillips Pumps, Bridgeport *Also called Phillips Pump LLC* ***(G-872)***
Phillips, R J Associates, Bozrah *Also called Ngraver Company* ***(G-530)***
Phillips-Moldex Company...860 928-0401
161 Park Rd Putnam (06260) ***(G-7058)***
Phils Welding...860 685-1713
6 Soobitsky Rd Higganum (06441) ***(G-3775)***
Phocuswright Inc (PA)...860 350-4084
1 Route 37 E Ste 200 Sherman (06784) ***(G-7601)***
Phoenix Company of Chicago Inc (PA)...630 595-2300
22 Great Hill Rd Naugatuck (06770) ***(G-4910)***
Phoenix Machine Inc...203 888-1135
279 Pearl St Seymour (06483) ***(G-7360)***
Phoenix Memorial Printing LLC...203 364-9617
18 Evergreen Rd Sandy Hook (06482) ***(G-7326)***
Phoenix Poultry Corporation...413 732-1433
8 Wheeler Dr Enfield (06082) ***(G-2677)***
Phoenix Press Inc...203 865-5555
15 James St New Haven (06513) ***(G-5363)***
Phoenix Sheet Metal LLC...860 478-4579
16 Joyce St Bloomfield (06002) ***(G-464)***
Phoenix Welding...860 657-9481
122 Naubuc Ave Ste A3 Glastonbury (06033) ***(G-3070)***
Phoenix Woodworking...203 512-3521
141 Pine Hill Rd New Fairfield (06812) ***(G-5173)***
Phoenixsongs Biologicals Inc...203 433-4329
33 Business Park Dr 1a Branford (06405) ***(G-635)***
Phone Booth Inc...203 859-5389
14 Kimberly Ave New Haven (06519) ***(G-5364)***
Photo Arts Limited...860 489-1170
44 Putter Ln Torrington (06790) ***(G-8957)***
Photobert Cheatsheets, West Hartford *Also called Bertram Sirkin* ***(G-9779)***
Photon Partners LLC...203 807-3623
366 Hollow Tree Ridge Rd Darien (06820) ***(G-2039)***
Photronics Inc (PA)...203 775-9000
15 Secor Rd Brookfield (06804) ***(G-1211)***
Photronics Inc...203 740-5669
15 Secor Rd Brookfield (06804) ***(G-1212)***
Photronics Texas Inc...203 546-3039
15 Secor Rd Brookfield (06804) ***(G-1213)***
Photronics Texas I LLC...203 775-9000
15 Secor Rd Brookfield (06804) ***(G-1214)***
Phraction Management LLC...860 531-9590
288 Old Hebron Rd Colchester (06415) ***(G-1565)***
Physical Fitness Consultants...860 653-4655
169 Newgate Rd East Granby (06026) ***(G-2225)***
Pic20 Group LLC...203 957-3555
155 Woodward Ave Ste 3 Norwalk (06854) ***(G-6299)***
Pick & Mix Corp...860 521-1521
1234 Farmington Ave Ste 3 West Hartford (06107) ***(G-9845)***
Pickadent Inc...203 431-8716
196 N Salem Rd Ste 2 Ridgefield (06877) ***(G-7160)***
Picture Perfect Printing Inc...203 386-9696
335 Sniffens Ln Stratford (06615) ***(G-8665)***
Picture This Hartford Inc...860 528-1409
80 Pitkin St East Hartford (06108) ***(G-2355)***
Pieces of Puzzle Daycare...203 916-8332
160 Wake St Bridgeport (06610) ***(G-873)***
Pieces of Time Scrapbook...203 879-2678
32 Devonshire Rd Waterbury (06716) ***(G-9577)***
Piela Electric Inc...860 889-8476
16 Halls Mill Rd Preston (06365) ***(G-6987)***
Pierce-Correll Corporation...203 799-1208
168 Christian Cir Orange (06477) ***(G-6624)***
Pigeonhole Press LLC...203 629-5754
368 Davis Ave Greenwich (06830) ***(G-3215)***
Pilgrim Nuts, Oxford *Also called Walz & Krenzer Inc* ***(G-6700)***
Pilla Inc...203 894-3265
908 Ethan Allen Hwy Ridgefield (06877) ***(G-7161)***
Pilot Machine Designers Inc...203 866-2227
32 Hemlock Pl Norwalk (06854) ***(G-6300)***
Pilot Seasonings, Waterbury *Also called Amodios Inc* ***(G-9430)***
Pilot Software Inc...203 252-2463
144 Morgan St Ste 1 Stamford (06905) ***(G-8361)***
Pine Bush Publishing LLC...203 570-3523
33 Crestview Ln Danbury (06810) ***(G-1908)***

Pine Meadow Machine Co Inc 860 623-4494
5 Webb St Windsor Locks (06096) ***(G-10493)***
Pine Ridge Gravel LLC 860 873-2500
24 Mount Parnassus Rd East Haddam (06423) ***(G-2248)***
Pinhos Cabinets 860 274-1740
158 Falls Ave Oakville (06779) ***(G-6458)***
Pink Fish Embroidery and D 860 339-5083
41 Great Hammock Rd Old Saybrook (06475) ***(G-6566)***
Pink Lemon Blue Lime LLC 203 521-2464
64 Wall St Norwalk (06850) ***(G-6301)***
PINke&brown Publishing LLP 860 798-9858
35 E Main St Ste 373 Avon (06001) ***(G-100)***
Pinkham Woodworking 860 733-3903
239 Dorothy Dr Torrington (06790) ***(G-8958)***
Pinnacl X, Moodus *Also called Swift Kathryn* ***(G-4776)***
Pinnacle Aerospace Mfg LLC 203 258-3398
361 Field Point Rd Greenwich (06830) ***(G-3216)***
Pinnacle Polymers LLC 203 313-4116
31 Bailey Ave Ste 4 Ridgefield (06877) ***(G-7162)***
Pinnacle Press LLC 203 254-1947
1700 Post Rd Fairfield (06824) ***(G-2828)***
Pinnacle Training and Publ 203 691-6221
470 Quinnipiac Ave New Haven (06513) ***(G-5365)***
Pinpoint Promotions & Prtg LLC 203 301-4273
45 Railroad Ave West Haven (06516) ***(G-9944)***
Pinpoint Thermography LLC 203 546-8906
32 Windmill Rd New Fairfield (06812) ***(G-5174)***
Pinto Manufacturing Llc 860 659-9543
122 Naubuc Ave Ste A6 Glastonbury (06033) ***(G-3071)***
Pio Tee Gio LLC 860 280-7073
482 Talcottville Rd Vernon Rockville (06066) ***(G-9174)***
Pioneer Arspc Def Systems Corp 860 528-0092
45 S Satellite Rd South Windsor (06074) ***(G-7805)***
Pioneer Capital Corp 860 683-2005
651 Day Hill Rd Windsor (06095) ***(G-10419)***
Pioneer Coatings & Mfg LLC 203 421-6086
188 Warpas Rd Madison (06443) ***(G-3948)***
Pioneer Optics Company Inc 860 286-0071
35 Griffin Rd S Bloomfield (06002) ***(G-465)***
Pioneer Plastics Corporation (HQ) 203 925-1556
1 Corporate Dr Ste 725 Shelton (06484) ***(G-7527)***
Pioneer Power Solutions Inc 203 782-4348
900 Chapel St Fl 10 New Haven (06510) ***(G-5366)***
Pioneer Precision Products (PA) 860 828-5838
2311 Chamberlain Hwy Berlin (06037) ***(G-206)***
Pionite Decorative Surfaces, Shelton *Also called Pioneer Plastics Corporation* ***(G-7527)***
PIP Printing, Manchester *Also called Sazacks Inc* ***(G-4086)***
Piper 860 405-1495
63 Elderberry Rd Groton (06340) ***(G-3309)***
Pisani Steel Fabrication Inc 203 720-0679
360 Prospect St Ste 1 Naugatuck (06770) ***(G-4911)***
Pistritto Marble Imports Inc 860 296-5263
97 Airport Rd Hartford (06114) ***(G-3664)***
Pith Products LLC 860 487-4859
39 Nott Hwy Unit 1 Ashford (06278) ***(G-63)***
Pitney Bowes Inc (PA) 203 356-5000
3001 Summer St Ste 3 Stamford (06905) ***(G-8362)***
Pitney Bowes Inc 203 356-5000
300 Stamford Pl Ste 200 Stamford (06902) ***(G-8363)***
Pitney Bowes Inc 203 792-1600
27 Waterview Dr Shelton (06484) ***(G-7528)***
Pitney Bowes Inc 860 285-7450
2 Waterside Xing Ste 304 Windsor (06095) ***(G-10420)***
Pitney Bowes Inc 203 922-4000
27 Waterview Dr Shelton (06484) ***(G-7529)***
Pitney Bowes Inc 203 356-5000
27 Waterview Dr Shelton (06484) ***(G-7530)***
Pitney Bowes Software Inc 603 595-2060
3001 Summer St Ste 3 Stamford (06905) ***(G-8364)***
Pixels 2 Press LLC 203 642-3740
26 Pearl St Ste 8 Norwalk (06850) ***(G-6302)***
Pj Specialties 860 429-7626
7 Luchon Rd Willington (06279) ***(G-10254)***
Pjtrepanier Tktechserv.com, Quaker Hill *Also called T&K Technical Services LLC* ***(G-7085)***
Plainville Electro Plating Co 860 525-5328
21 Forest Hills Dr Hartford (06117) ***(G-3665)***
Plainville Machine & Tl Co Inc 860 589-5595
65 Ronzo Rd Bristol (06010) ***(G-1091)***
Plainville Plating Company Inc 860 747-1624
21 Forestville Ave Plainville (06062) ***(G-6852)***
Plainville Special Tool, Plainville *Also called Alto Products Corp Al* ***(G-6769)***
Plan & Sponsor, Stamford *Also called Strategic Insights Inc* ***(G-8446)***
Planes Road Assoc LLC 860 469-3200
38 Plains Rd Essex (06426) ***(G-2730)***
Planet Technologies Inc 800 255-3749
96 Danbury Rd Ridgefield (06877) ***(G-7163)***
Planit Manufacturing LLC 203 641-6055
515 Broad St Unit D Bristol (06010) ***(G-1092)***
Plas-TEC Coatings Inc 860 289-6029
68 Mascolo Rd South Windsor (06074) ***(G-7806)***
Plasco LLC 860 217-1187
3 Pennington Dr Simsbury (06070) ***(G-7640)***
Plasma Coatings, Middlebury *Also called American Roller Company LLC* ***(G-4273)***
Plasma Coatings Inc 203 598-3100
758 E Main St Waterbury (06702) ***(G-9578)***
Plasma Technology Incorporated 860 282-0659
70 Rye St South Windsor (06074) ***(G-7807)***
Plastech Manufacturing, East Windsor *Also called Trento Group LLC* ***(G-2528)***
Plasti-Coat 203 755-3741
137 Brookside Rd Waterbury (06708) ***(G-9579)***
Plasti-Coat 860 274-1234
80 Turnpike Dr Ste 4 Middlebury (06762) ***(G-4287)***
Plastic and Met Components Co 203 877-2723
381 Bridgeport Ave Milford (06460) ***(G-4609)***
Plastic Assembly Systems LLC 203 393-0639
19 Sargent Dr Bethany (06524) ***(G-248)***
Plastic Design Intl Inc (PA) 860 632-2001
111 Industrial Park Rd Middletown (06457) ***(G-4393)***
Plastic Factory LLC 203 908-3468
678 Howard Ave Bridgeport (06605) ***(G-874)***
Plastic Forming Company Inc (PA) 203 397-1338
20 S Bradley Rd Woodbridge (06525) ***(G-10613)***
Plastic Molding Technology 203 881-1811
92 Cogwheel Ln Seymour (06483) ***(G-7361)***
Plastic Solutions LLC 203 266-5675
263 Hickory Ln Bethlehem (06751) ***(G-375)***
Plasticoid Manufacturing Inc 860 623-1361
32 North Rd Rear East Windsor (06088) ***(G-2514)***
Plasticrete 203 250-6700
210 Realty Dr Cheshire (06410) ***(G-1429)***
Plastics and Concepts Conn Inc 860 657-9655
101 Laurel Trl Glastonbury (06033) ***(G-3072)***
Plastics Color Corp Inc 800 922-9936
349 Lake Rd Dayville (06241) ***(G-2070)***
Plastics Techniques 203 335-8048
160 Castle Ave Fairfield (06825) ***(G-2829)***
Plastock, Putnam *Also called Ensinger Prcsion Cmponents Inc* ***(G-7040)***
Plastonics Inc 860 249-5455
230 Locust St Hartford (06114) ***(G-3666)***
Platt & Labonia Company LLC 800 505-9099
70-80 Stoddard Ave North Haven (06473) ***(G-5976)***
Platt Brothers & Company (PA) 203 753-4194
2670 S Main St Waterbury (06706) ***(G-9580)***
Platt Brothers Realty II LLC 203 562-5112
25 James St New Haven (06513) ***(G-5367)***
Platt-Labonia of N Haven Inc 203 239-5681
70 Stoddard Ave North Haven (06473) ***(G-5977)***
Play-It Productions Inc 212 695-6530
167b Lebanon Ave Colchester (06415) ***(G-1566)***
Playtex Products LLC (HQ) 203 944-5500
6 Research Dr Ste 400 Shelton (06484) ***(G-7531)***
Pleasant Valley Fence Co Inc 860 379-0088
Rr 181 Pleasant Valley (06063) ***(G-6925)***
Plumb Pak Medical, Newington *Also called The Keeney Manufacturing Co* ***(G-5711)***
Plymouth Spring Company Inc 860 584-0594
281 Lake Ave Bristol (06010) ***(G-1093)***
PMC Engineering LLC 203 792-8686
11 Old Sugar Hollow Rd Danbury (06810) ***(G-1909)***
PMC Technologies LLC 203 222-0000
31 Glenwood Rd Weston (06883) ***(G-10036)***
Pmd Scientific Inc 860 242-8177
105 W Ddley Town Rd Ste F Bloomfield (06002) ***(G-466)***
PMG, Kensington *Also called Parva Mfg Group Inc* ***(G-3816)***
PMI, Wolcott *Also called Precision Methods Incorporated* ***(G-10580)***
Pmoys LLC 203 541-0995
Soundview Plz Stamford (06902) ***(G-8365)***
Pmr Performance 860 828-8828
114 Burnham St Kensington (06037) ***(G-3817)***
Pmsi, Stratford *Also called Professional Mktg Svcs Inc* ***(G-8669)***
Pmt Group Inc (PA) 203 367-8675
800 Union Ave Bridgeport (06607) ***(G-875)***
Pmw Marine Repair 860 535-3064
228 N Water St Stonington (06378) ***(G-8536)***
Pnb Designs, Hartford *Also called Patricia Beavers* ***(G-3662)***
Pocket Parks Publishing LLC 203 499-7416
116 Cherry Ln West Haven (06516) ***(G-9945)***
Podskoch Press 860 267-2442
36 Waterhole Rd Colchester (06415) ***(G-1567)***
Podunk Popcorn 860 648-9565
245 Barber Hill Rd South Windsor (06074) ***(G-7808)***
Point Lighting Corporation 860 243-0600
61-65 W Dudley Town Rd Bloomfield (06002) ***(G-467)***
Point Machine Company 860 828-6901
588 Four Rod Rd Berlin (06037) ***(G-207)***
Point View Displays LLC 203 468-0887
200 Morgan Ave East Haven (06512) ***(G-2447)***
Pointer Press 203 355-0677
41 Minivale Rd Stamford (06907) ***(G-8366)***
Pointer Press 650 269-3492
57 Holly Rd New Canaan (06840) ***(G-5131)***
Pointpharma LLC 203 668-8543
127 Rising Ridge Rd Ridgefield (06877) ***(G-7164)***
Polamer Precision Inc 860 259-6200
105 Alton Brooks Way New Britain (06053) ***(G-5033)***

ALPHABETIC

Polar Bear Industries LLC 203 858-4396
2 Plunkett Pl Westport (06880) *(G-10141)*
Polar Corp 860 225-6000
33 Columbus Blvd New Britain (06051) *(G-5034)*
Polar Corporation 860 223-7891
59 High St Ste 11 New Britain (06051) *(G-5035)*
Polar Industries Inc (PA) 203 758-6651
32 Gramar Ave Prospect (06712) *(G-7016)*
Polaris Management Inc 203 261-6399
30 Silver Hill Rd Easton (06612) *(G-2561)*
Polarity, Farmington Also called Breach Intelligence Inc *(G-2885)*
Polep Distribution Services J 203 378-2193
1075 Honeyspot Rd Stratford (06615) *(G-8666)*
Polish Welding LLC 860 347-0368
476 Long Hill Rd Middletown (06457) *(G-4394)*
Pollinate News 203 801-9623
4 Holmewood Ln New Canaan (06840) *(G-5132)*
Polstal Corporation 203 849-7788
10 Admiral Ln Wilton (06897) *(G-10320)*
Polster Industries LLC 203 521-8517
115 Verna Hill Rd Fairfield (06824) *(G-2830)*
Poly Mold Inc Building 1, Cheshire Also called Polymold Corp *(G-1430)*
Polycast, Stamford Also called Spartech LLC *(G-8432)*
Polymath Software 860 423-5823
42 Carey St Willimantic (06226) *(G-10234)*
Polymedex Discovery Group Inc (PA) 860 928-4102
45 Ridge Rd Putnam (06260) *(G-7059)*
Polymer Engineered Pdts Inc (PA) 203 324-3737
595 Summer St Ste 2 Stamford (06901) *(G-8367)*
Polymer Films Inc 203 932-3000
301 Heffernan Dr West Haven (06516) *(G-9946)*
Polymer Resources Ltd (PA) 203 324-3737
656 New Britain Ave Farmington (06032) *(G-2949)*
Polymeric Converting LLC 860 623-1335
5 Old Depot Hill Rd Enfield (06082) *(G-2678)*
Polymold Corp 203 272-2622
951 S Meriden Rd Cheshire (06410) *(G-1430)*
Polyone Corporation 203 327-6010
70 Carlisle Pl Stamford (06902) *(G-8368)*
Polypolish Products Div, Bethel Also called Intersurface Dynamics Inc *(G-312)*
Polytronics Corporation 860 683-2442
800 Marshall Phelps Rd H Windsor (06095) *(G-10421)*
Pomaski Tool & Mfg Co, Canton Also called Don Pomaski *(G-1313)*
Pony Express Print Co 203 592-7095
51 Newport Dr Waterbury (06705) *(G-9581)*
Pony Patterns LLC 203 535-0347
56 W Hills Rd New Haven (06515) *(G-5368)*
Poof-Alex Holdings LLC (PA) 203 930-7711
10 Glenville St Ste 1 Greenwich (06831) *(G-3217)*
Pop Graphics Inc 203 639-1441
38 Elm St Meriden (06450) *(G-4218)*
Pop Moody Welding Services 860 749-9537
712 Stafford Rd Somers (06071) *(G-7668)*
Popcorn Movie Poster Co LLC 860 610-0000
1 Cherry St East Hartford (06108) *(G-2356)*
Poplar Tool & Mfg Co Inc 203 333-4369
420 Poplar St Bridgeport (06605) *(G-876)*
Poppys LLC 860 778-9044
260 Steele Rd Hartford (06117) *(G-3667)*
Pops Donuts 203 876-1210
587 New Haven Ave Milford (06460) *(G-4610)*
Poquonock Sewage Plant 860 688-5420
1222 Poquonock Ave Windsor (06095) *(G-10422)*
Porcelanosa New York Inc 203 698-7618
1063 E Putnam Ave Riverside (06878) *(G-7199)*
Porobond Products LLC 203 234-7747
80 Sanford St Hamden (06514) *(G-3497)*
Porta Door Co 203 888-6191
65 Cogwheel Ln Seymour (06483) *(G-7362)*
Portable Garage Depot LLC 203 397-1721
73 Ford Rd Woodbridge (06525) *(G-10614)*
Porter Preston Inc 203 753-1113
61 Mattatuck Heights Rd # 2 Waterbury (06705) *(G-9582)*
Portfolio Arts Group Ltd 203 661-2400
129 Glover Ave Norwalk (06850) *(G-6303)*
Portland Connecticut Mch Sp, Portland Also called Transportation Conn Dept *(G-6979)*
Portland Slitting Co Inc 860 342-1500
193 Pickering St Portland (06480) *(G-6968)*
Posh Pups LLC 860 454-4055
56 Hyde Ave Vernon Rockville (06066) *(G-9175)*
Positive Pos, Bloomfield Also called Positive Ventures LLC *(G-468)*
Positive Ventures LLC 860 499-0599
244 Woodland Ave Bloomfield (06002) *(G-468)*
Post & Beam Homes Inc 860 267-2060
4 Sexton Hill Rd East Hampton (06424) *(G-2274)*
Post Mortem Services LLC 860 675-1103
82 Knollwood Rd Farmington (06032) *(G-2950)*
Post Pattern 860 774-7911
100 Tatnic Rd Brooklyn (06234) *(G-1252)*
Post Publishing Company 203 333-0161
410 State St Bridgeport (06604) *(G-877)*
Post Sign Specialists 203 723-8448
25 Cedar St Naugatuck (06770) *(G-4912)*
Potters Ink Inc 860 896-5909
84 Grove St C Vernon Rockville (06066) *(G-9176)*
Powder Hill Sand & Gravel LLC (PA) 860 741-7274
38 Post Office Rd Enfield (06082) *(G-2679)*
Powder Pushers 860 295-6406
49 S Main St Marlborough (06447) *(G-4129)*
Power Controls Inc 203 284-0235
801 N Main Street Ext Wallingford (06492) *(G-9336)*
Power Cover Usa LLC 203 755-2687
37 Commons Ct Ste 3 Waterbury (06704) *(G-9583)*
Power Fuels LLC 203 699-0099
143 Main St Cheshire (06410) *(G-1431)*
Power Quality and Drives LLC 203 217-2353
302 Tuttle Rd Apt 7g Woodbury (06798) *(G-10651)*
Power Strategies LLC 203 254-9926
2384 Redding Rd Fairfield (06824) *(G-2831)*
Power Systems Division, South Windsor Also called United Technologies Corp *(G-7836)*
Power Trans Co Inc 203 881-0314
315 Riggs St Ste 2 Oxford (06478) *(G-6688)*
Power Turbine Components LLC 860 291-8885
125 S Satellite Rd South Windsor (06074) *(G-7809)*
Power Up Electric 203 312-0601
48 Pembroke Rd Danbury (06811) *(G-1910)*
Power-Dyne LLC 860 346-9283
2055 S Main St Middletown (06457) *(G-4395)*
Power-Dyne LLC/Bidwll Indstrl, Middletown Also called Power-Dyne LLC *(G-4395)*
Powerhold Inc 860 349-1044
63 Old Indian Trl Middlefield (06455) *(G-4304)*
Powers Industries & Laserpro, Meriden Also called Mid State ARC Inc *(G-4201)*
Powerscreen Connecticut Inc 860 627-6596
140 Nutmeg Rd S South Windsor (06074) *(G-7810)*
Powerscreen England, South Windsor Also called Powerscreen Connecticut Inc *(G-7810)*
Pozzi Fmly Wine & Spirits LLC 646 422-9134
37 Old Well Rd Stamford (06907) *(G-8369)*
Ppc Books Ltd 203 226-6644
335 Post Rd W Westport (06880) *(G-10142)*
PPG 9431, Hartford Also called PPG Industries Inc *(G-3668)*
PPG Industries Inc 203 750-9553
106 Main St Norwalk (06851) *(G-6304)*
PPG Industries Inc 860 627-7401
565 Halfway House Rd Windsor Locks (06096) *(G-10494)*
PPG Industries Inc 203 562-5173
390 East St New Haven (06511) *(G-5369)*
PPG Industries Inc 203 744-4977
211 White St Danbury (06810) *(G-1911)*
PPG Industries Inc 203 294-4440
22 Barnes Industrial Rd S Wallingford (06492) *(G-9337)*
PPG Industries Inc 860 522-9544
292 Murphy Rd Hartford (06114) *(G-3668)*
PPG Industries Inc 860 953-1153
141 South St West Hartford (06110) *(G-9846)*
PPG Painters Supply, Norwalk Also called PPG Industries Inc *(G-6304)*
PPG Painters Supply, New Haven Also called PPG Industries Inc *(G-5369)*
PPG Painters Supply, Danbury Also called PPG Industries Inc *(G-1911)*
Ppk Inc 203 376-9180
41 Montoya Dr Branford (06405) *(G-636)*
PQ Optics 860 582-2636
63 Saw Mill Rd Bristol (06010) *(G-1094)*
Pr-Mx Holdings Company LLC (HQ) 203 925-0012
25 Forest Pkwy Shelton (06484) *(G-7532)*
PRA Holdings Inc 203 853-0123
1 Stamford Forum Stamford (06901) *(G-8370)*
Practical Automation Inc (HQ) 203 882-5640
45 Woodmont Rd Milford (06460) *(G-4611)*
Pralines Central, Wallingford Also called Pralines Inc *(G-9338)*
Pralines Inc 203 284-8847
30 N Plains Industrial Rd # 12 Wallingford (06492) *(G-9338)*
Pralines of Plainville 860 410-1151
107 New Britain Ave Plainville (06062) *(G-6853)*
Pratt & Whitney, East Hartford Also called United Technologies Corp *(G-2391)*
Pratt & Whitney, East Hartford Also called United Technologies Corp *(G-2393)*
Pratt & Whitney Company Inc (HQ) 860 565-4321
400 Main St East Hartford (06108) *(G-2357)*
Pratt & Whitney Eng Svcs Inc 860 610-2631
126 Silver Ln Apt 19 East Hartford (06118) *(G-2358)*
Pratt & Whitney Engine Svcs 203 934-2806
415 Washington Ave North Haven (06473) *(G-5978)*
Pratt & Whitney Engine Svcs 860 344-4000
1 Aircraft Rd Middletown (06457) *(G-4396)*
Pratt & Whitney Engine Svcs 860 565-4321
400 Main St Ste 1 East Hartford (06118) *(G-2359)*
Pratt & Whitney Services Inc 860 565-5489
400 Main St East Hartford (06108) *(G-2360)*
Pratt & Whitneys Repair &, East Hartford Also called United Technologies Corp *(G-2396)*
Pratt Whitney-Spare Parts Div, East Hartford Also called United Technologies Corp *(G-2394)*
Pratt Whtney Cstmer Trning Ctr, East Hartford Also called Pratt & Whitney Engine Svcs *(G-2359)*

Pratt Whtney Msurement Systems 860 286-8181
66 Douglas St Bloomfield (06002) *(G-469)*
Pratt-Read Corporation (PA) 860 625-3620
193 Turtle Bay Dr Branford (06405) *(G-637)*
Praxair Inc 800 772-9247
10 Riverview Dr Danbury (06810) *(G-1912)*
Praxair Inc 203 793-1200
10 Research Pkwy Wallingford (06492) *(G-9339)*
Praxair Inc 203 720-2477
120 Rado Dr Naugatuck (06770) *(G-4913)*
Praxair Inc 860 292-5400
1 U Car St Suffield (06078) *(G-8729)*
Praxair Inc (HQ) 203 837-2000
10 Riverview Dr Danbury (06810) *(G-1913)*
Praxair Distribution Inc 860 349-0305
89 Commerce Cir Durham (06422) *(G-2154)*
Praxair Distribution Inc (HQ) 203 837-2000
10 Riverview Dr Danbury (06810) *(G-1914)*
Praxair Distribution Inc 203 837-2162
55 Old Ridgebury Rd Danbury (06810) *(G-1915)*
Praxair Surface Tech Inc 203 837-2000
39 Old Ridgebury Rd Danbury (06810) *(G-1916)*
Praxair Surface Tech Inc 860 646-0700
1366 Tolland Tpke Manchester (06042) *(G-4076)*
Pre -Clinical Safety Inc 860 739-9797
69 Quarry Dock Rd East Lyme (06333) *(G-2471)*
Precipio Inc 203 907-2205
5 Science Park New Haven (06511) *(G-5370)*
Precipio Inc (PA) 402 452-5400
4 Science Park Ste 3 New Haven (06511) *(G-5371)*
Precise Circuit Company Inc 203 924-2512
155 Myrtle St Shelton (06484) *(G-7533)*
Precision Aerospace Inc 203 888-3022
88 Cogwheel Ln Seymour (06483) *(G-7363)*
Precision Canvas LLC 860 693-2353
20 Collins Rd Collinsville (06019) *(G-1600)*
Precision Centerless Grinding 203 879-1228
137 Tosun Rd Wolcott (06716) *(G-10579)*
Precision Cut-Off Service Inc 860 582-7521
625 Emmett St Bristol (06010) *(G-1095)*
Precision Deburring Inc 860 583-4662
139 Center St Ste 5002 Bristol (06010) *(G-1096)*
Precision Devices Inc (PA) 203 265-9308
55 N Plains Industrial Rd Wallingford (06492) *(G-9340)*
Precision Dip Coating LLC 203 805-4564
176 Chase River Rd Waterbury (06704) *(G-9584)*
Precision E D M Inc 413 733-2813
775 Bloomfield Ave Windsor (06095) *(G-10423)*
Precision Electronic Assembly 203 452-1839
133 Bart Rd Monroe (06468) *(G-4747)*
Precision Electronic Hardware, Naugatuck *Also called Multi-Metal Manufacturing Inc (G-4904)*
Precision Engineered Pdts LLC 203 336-6479
1146 Barnum Ave Bridgeport (06610) *(G-878)*
Precision Engineered Pdts LLC 203 265-3299
6 Northrop Indus Pk Rd W Wallingford (06492) *(G-9341)*
Precision Explosives Inc 860 567-4952
28 Countryside Ln Bantam (06750) *(G-127)*
Precision Express Mfg LLC 860 584-2627
630 Emmett St Unit 3 Bristol (06010) *(G-1097)*
Precision Finishing Svcs Inc 860 882-1073
60 Ezra Silva Ln Windsor (06095) *(G-10424)*
Precision Fire Fabrication LLC 203 706-0749
8 West St Plantsville (06479) *(G-6908)*
Precision Graphics Inc 860 828-6561
10 Clark Dr East Berlin (06023) *(G-2174)*
Precision Grinding Company 860 229-9652
33 Charles St New Britain (06051) *(G-5036)*
Precision Interface 203 235-2718
40 Hampshire Rd Meriden (06450) *(G-4219)*
Precision Machine and Gears 860 822-6993
21 Country Club Dr North Franklin (06254) *(G-5877)*
Precision Manufacturing LLC 203 790-4663
153 Gracty Plain St A12 Bethel (06801) *(G-332)*
Precision Metal Manufacturing 973 253-0500
34 Northgate Simsbury (06070) *(G-7641)*
Precision Metal Products Inc 203 877-4258
307 Pepes Farm Rd Milford (06460) *(G-4612)*
Precision Metals and Plas 860 559-8843
758 Four Rod Rd Berlin (06037) *(G-208)*
Precision Metals and Plas Mfg, Winsted *Also called Precision Metals and Plastics (G-10532)*
Precision Metals and Plastics 860 238-4320
118 Colebrook River Rd # 7 Winsted (06098) *(G-10532)*
Precision Methods Incorporated 203 879-1429
40 North St Wolcott (06716) *(G-10580)*
Precision Mfg Tool & Tl Design, Bethel *Also called Precision Manufacturing LLC (G-332)*
Precision Mill LLC 860 357-4729
872 Four Rod Rd Ste B Berlin (06037) *(G-209)*
Precision Mold and Polsg LLC 860 489-6249
301 Ella Grasso Ave Torrington (06790) *(G-8959)*
Precision Optical Co 860 289-6023
351 Burnham St East Hartford (06108) *(G-2361)*
Precision Plastic Fab 203 775-7047
5d Del Mar Dr Brookfield (06804) *(G-1215)*
Precision Plastic Products Inc 860 342-2233
151 Freestone Ave Portland (06480) *(G-6969)*
Precision Plating Corp 860 875-9267
1050 Hartford Tpke Vernon (06066) *(G-9150)*
Precision Powders LLC 203 748-7879
9 Flintlock Dr Danbury (06811) *(G-1917)*
Precision Press LLC 203 359-0211
149 Skyview Dr Stamford (06902) *(G-8371)*
Precision Products 203 265-2061
8 Enterprise Rd Wallingford (06492) *(G-9342)*
Precision Punch + Tooling Corp (PA) 860 229-9902
304 Christian Ln Berlin (06037) *(G-210)*
Precision Punch + Tooling Corp 860 225-4159
304 Christian Ln Berlin (06037) *(G-211)*
Precision Resource Inc (PA) 203 925-0012
25 Forest Pkwy Shelton (06484) *(G-7534)*
Precision Resource Mexico, Shelton *Also called Pr-Mx Holdings Company LLC (G-7532)*
Precision Rsurce Intl Sls Corp 203 925-0012
25 Forest Pkwy Shelton (06484) *(G-7535)*
Precision Sensors, Milford *Also called United Electric Controls Co (G-4668)*
Precision Sensors Inc 203 877-2795
340 Woodmont Rd Milford (06460) *(G-4613)*
Precision Servicing 203 650-1392
242 Everett Rd Easton (06612) *(G-2562)*
Precision Shtmtl Fabrication 860 388-4466
51 Donnelly Rd Old Saybrook (06475) *(G-6567)*
Precision Speed Mfg LLC 860 635-8811
422 Timber Ridge Rd Middletown (06457) *(G-4397)*
Precision Swiss Screw Machine, Bristol *Also called E P M Co Inc (G-1024)*
Precision Threaded Products, Bristol *Also called Thompson Aerospace LLC (G-1128)*
Precision Tool & Components 203 874-9215
195 Rock Ln Milford (06460) *(G-4614)*
Precision Welding, Watertown *Also called Frank Porto (G-9707)*
Precision Welding 860 423-7772
15 Buckingham Rd Mansfield Center (06250) *(G-4115)*
Precision Welding Services LLC 860 268-0580
30 Babcock Hill Road Ext Coventry (06238) *(G-1668)*
Precision Wire Cutting 860 485-1494
9 Windmill Rd Harwinton (06791) *(G-3736)*
Precision Woodcraft Inc 860 693-3641
16 Cheryl Dr Canton (06019) *(G-1325)*
Precision Woodcraft ME, Canton *Also called Precision Woodcraft Inc (G-1325)*
Precision X-Ray Inc 203 484-2011
15 Comm Dr Unit 1 North Branford (06471) *(G-5852)*
Predcision Plastics Inc 203 775-7047
150 Laurel Hill Rd Brookfield (06804) *(G-1216)*
Preferred Display Inc 860 372-4653
215 Moody Rd Ste 1 Enfield (06082) *(G-2680)*
Preferred Foam Products Inc 860 669-3626
140 Killingworth Tpke Clinton (06413) *(G-1518)*
Preferred Instruments, Danbury *Also called Preferred Utilities Mfg Corp (G-1918)*
Preferred Manufacturing Co 203 239-0727
68 Old Broadway E North Haven (06473) *(G-5979)*
Preferred PDT & Mktg Group LLC 203 567-0221
415 Howe Ave Ste 103 Shelton (06484) *(G-7536)*
Preferred Precision, Shelton *Also called Preferred Tool & Die Inc (G-7537)*
Preferred Products Co Inc 203 375-9139
55 Browning St Ste 1 Stratford (06615) *(G-8667)*
Preferred Tool & Die Inc (PA) 203 925-8525
30 Forest Pkwy Shelton (06484) *(G-7537)*
Preferred Tool & Die Inc 203 925-8525
19 Forest Pkwy Shelton (06484) *(G-7538)*
Preferred Utilities Mfg Corp (HQ) 203 743-6741
31-35 South St Danbury (06810) *(G-1918)*
Preisner, George S Pewter Co, Wallingford *Also called George S Preisner Jewelers (G-9275)*
Premier Custom Cabinetry 860 659-1863
22 Kreiger Ln Glastonbury (06033) *(G-3073)*
Premier Foods Inc 203 226-6577
31 Imperial Ave Westport (06880) *(G-10143)*
Premier Graphics LLC 800 414-1624
860 Honeyspot Rd Ste 1 Stratford (06615) *(G-8668)*
Premier Mfg Group Inc 203 924-6617
10 Mountain View Dr Shelton (06484) *(G-7539)*
Premier Prtg Mailing Solutions, Stratford *Also called Premier Graphics LLC (G-8668)*
Premiere 203 756-0178
1159 Highland Ave Waterbury (06708) *(G-9585)*
Premiere Kitchens & Wdwkg LLC 203 882-1745
111 Pepes Farm Rd Milford (06460) *(G-4615)*
Premiere Packg Partners LLC 203 694-0003
197 Huntingdon Ave Waterbury (06708) *(G-9586)*
Prentis Printing Solutions Inc 203 634-1266
35 Pratt St Meriden (06450) *(G-4220)*
Presco Incorporated 203 397-8722
8 Lunar Dr Ste 4 Woodbridge (06525) *(G-10615)*
Presco Engineering, Woodbridge *Also called Presco Incorporated (G-10615)*
Prescott Cabinet Co 860 495-0176
31 Buckingham St Pawcatuck (06379) *(G-6723)*
Present Perfect, Essex *Also called Mobius Press (G-2726)*

ALPHABETIC

(PA)=Parent Co (HQ)=Headquarters (DH)=Div Headquarters
2020 Harris Connecticut Manufacturers Directory 563

Present Time Visions...860 435-4997
12 Slater Rd Salisbury (06068) ***(G-7296)***
Presidium USA Inc...203 674-9374
100 Stamford Pl Stamford (06902) ***(G-8372)***
Press Hartford...860 216-6538
187 Allyn St Hartford (06103) ***(G-3669)***
Press On Sandwich Crafters...860 694-9882
136 Mitchell St Groton (06340) ***(G-3310)***
Press On Sandwich Crafters LLC...860 415-9906
391 Norwich Westerly Rd North Stonington (06359) ***(G-6031)***
Pressure Blast Mfg Co Inc...800 722-5278
205 Nutmeg Rd S Ste E South Windsor (06074) ***(G-7811)***
Prestige Cabinetry...860 558-2784
2 Rice Rd Stafford Springs (06076) ***(G-8034)***
Prestige Metal Finishing LLC...860 974-1999
44 Bradford Corner Rd Woodstock Valley (06282) ***(G-10693)***
Prestige Remodeling, Stratford *Also called Chris Cross LLC* ***(G-8595)***
Prestige Tool Mfg LLC...203 874-0360
154 Old Gate Ln Milford (06460) ***(G-4616)***
Prestige Tournament Supplies, Norwalk *Also called Robert W Broska Enterprises* ***(G-6327)***
Prestige Welding & Fabrication, Monroe *Also called Ken Hastedt* ***(G-4725)***
Preston Engravers, East Windsor *Also called Roto-Die Company Inc* ***(G-2516)***
Preston Ridge Vineyard LLC...860 383-4278
26 Miller Rd Preston (06365) ***(G-6988)***
Prestone Products Corporation...203 731-7880
55 Federal Rd Danbury (06810) ***(G-1919)***
Preusser Research Group Inc (PA)...203 459-8700
7100 Main St Trumbull (06611) ***(G-9056)***
Preventative Maintenance Corp...860 683-1180
55 Tunxis St Poquonock (06064) ***(G-6948)***
Preyco Mfg Co Inc...203 574-4545
1184 N Main St Waterbury (06704) ***(G-9587)***
Prezioso Furs, Hamden *Also called Furs By Prezioso Ltd* ***(G-3449)***
Price-Driscoll Corporation...860 442-3575
17 Industrial Dr Waterford (06385) ***(G-9666)***
Priced Right Fuel LLC...203 856-7031
29 Golden Hill St Norwalk (06854) ***(G-6305)***
Pricing Excellence LLC...866 557-8102
68 Bridge St Unit 304 Suffield (06078) ***(G-8730)***
Prima Dona LLC...203 820-9327
80 Bywatyr Ln Bridgeport (06605) ***(G-879)***
Prime Business Services...203 453-1627
40 Stillmeadow Dr Guilford (06437) ***(G-3384)***
Prime Engineered Components, Watertown *Also called Prime Screw Machine Pdts Inc* ***(G-9725)***
Prime Engneered Components Inc...860 274-6773
1012 Buckingham St Watertown (06795) ***(G-9723)***
Prime Line, Bridgeport *Also called Prime Resources Corp* ***(G-880)***
Prime Publishers Inc...860 274-6721
449 Main St Watertown (06795) ***(G-9724)***
Prime Resources Corp...203 331-9100
1100 Boston Ave Bldg 1 Bridgeport (06610) ***(G-880)***
Prime Screw Machine Pdts Inc (PA)...860 274-6773
1012 Buckingham St Watertown (06795) ***(G-9725)***
Prime Technology LLC...203 481-5721
344 Twin Lakes Rd North Branford (06471) ***(G-5853)***
Primo Press LLC...203 527-7904
67 Meriden Rd Waterbury (06705) ***(G-9588)***
Prinertechs...203 249-6646
255 Strawberry Hill Ave Stamford (06902) ***(G-8373)***
Print & Post Services...203 336-0055
1 Seaview Ave Bridgeport (06607) ***(G-881)***
Print B2b LLC...203 744-5435
3 Hillcrest Rd Bethel (06801) ***(G-333)***
Print House LLC...860 652-0803
22 Kreiger Ln Ste 6 Glastonbury (06033) ***(G-3074)***
Print Hub...860 580-7907
97 Pierson Ln Windsor (06095) ***(G-10425)***
Print Indie LLC...860 986-9446
56 Neal Ct Ste 2 Plainville (06062) ***(G-6854)***
Print Lab LLC...860 410-6624
125 Carlton St New Britain (06053) ***(G-5037)***
Print Master LLC...860 482-8152
1219 E Main St Torrington (06790) ***(G-8960)***
Print Media Specialist, Mystic *Also called Alicia Cersosimorathbun* ***(G-4797)***
Print MGT & Consulting LLC...860 521-7444
26 Westland Ave West Hartford (06107) ***(G-9847)***
Print Producers LLC...203 761-9877
1042 Ridgefield Rd Wilton (06897) ***(G-10321)***
Print Promotions Inc...203 778-2672
50 Oak Ridge Rd Bethel (06801) ***(G-334)***
Print Shop of Wolcott LLC...203 879-3353
450 Wolcott Rd Wolcott (06716) ***(G-10581)***
Print Source Ltd...203 876-1822
116a Research Dr Ste D Milford (06460) ***(G-4617)***
Printech, Stamford *Also called JS McCarthy Co Inc* ***(G-8270)***
Printed Communications...860 436-9619
400 Chapel Rd Ste L1 South Windsor (06074) ***(G-7812)***
Printed Prfmce Innovations LLC...860 942-7338
362 S River Rd Coventry (06238) ***(G-1669)***
Printer Source Inc...800 788-5101
101 Merritt Blvd Ste 21 Trumbull (06611) ***(G-9057)***
Printer Techs LLC...203 322-1160
44 Commerce Rd Stamford (06902) ***(G-8374)***
Printers, Hartford *Also called Hartford Business Supply Inc* ***(G-3607)***
Printers of Connecticut Inc...203 852-0070
89 Taylor Ave Fl 1 Norwalk (06854) ***(G-6306)***
Printing & Graphic Services, New Haven *Also called Yale University* ***(G-5445)***
Printing House The Inc...203 869-1767
11 Carissa Ln Greenwich (06830) ***(G-3218)***
Printing Plus, Waterbury *Also called Sheila P Patrick* ***(G-9602)***
Printing Services Inc...860 584-9598
889 Farmington Ave Ste A Bristol (06010) ***(G-1098)***
Printing Solutions LLC...203 965-0090
1117 E Putnam Ave Ste 249 Riverside (06878) ***(G-7200)***
Printing Solutions & Resources...203 965-0090
16 Dyke Ln Stamford (06902) ***(G-8375)***
Printing Solutions Group LLC...860 647-0317
210 Skinner Ln Hebron (06248) ***(G-3753)***
Printing Store, The, Hamden *Also called Copy Stop Inc* ***(G-3433)***
Priority Press, Enfield *Also called East Longmeadow Business Svcs* ***(G-2637)***
Prison Publications Inc...860 928-4055
107 Providence St Putnam (06260) ***(G-7060)***
Private Communications Corp...860 355-2718
39 Holiday Point Rd Sherman (06784) ***(G-7602)***
Private Wifi, Sherman *Also called Private Communications Corp* ***(G-7602)***
Privateer Ltd...860 526-1837
5 Center Rd W Old Saybrook (06475) ***(G-6568)***
Privateer Divers LLC...860 742-2699
425 Geraldine Dr Coventry (06238) ***(G-1670)***
Privy Pine Products...203 272-6169
180 Brentwood Dr Cheshire (06410) ***(G-1432)***
Pro Beverage Sales LLC...203 931-1029
5 Clinton Pl New Haven (06513) ***(G-5372)***
Pro Coatings LLC...860 345-2107
47 Boulder Dell Rd Higganum (06441) ***(G-3776)***
Pro Counters New England LLC...203 347-8663
1 Chestnut St Ansonia (06401) ***(G-46)***
Pro Form Printed Bus Solutions...203 266-5302
246 Magnolia Hill Rd Bethlehem (06751) ***(G-376)***
Pro Forming Sheet Metal LLC...860 886-9900
31 Connecticut Ave Ste 3 Norwich (06360) ***(G-6428)***
Pro Gas Installation & Svc LLC...860 982-1370
176 Tartia Rd East Hampton (06424) ***(G-2275)***
Pro Graphics Inc...860 668-9067
378 Thompsonville Rd Suffield (06078) ***(G-8731)***
Pro Kart Racing Karts...860 537-6900
483 Lebanon Ave Colchester (06415) ***(G-1568)***
Pro Line Sports Design, Stratford *Also called C Libby Leonard* ***(G-8591)***
Pro Scientific Inc...203 267-4600
99 Willenbrock Rd Oxford (06478) ***(G-6689)***
Pro Tool and Design Inc...860 828-4667
230 Deming Rd Berlin (06037) ***(G-212)***
Pro-Lock USA LLC...203 382-3428
62 Church St Monroe (06468) ***(G-4748)***
Pro-Manufactured Products Inc...860 564-2197
29 Center Pkwy Plainfield (06374) ***(G-6750)***
Pro-Tech Enterprises LLC...203 931-9668
375 Morgan Ln Ste 102 West Haven (06516) ***(G-9947)***
Probatter Sports LLC...203 874-2500
49 Research Dr Ste 1 Milford (06460) ***(G-4618)***
Process Automtn Solutions Inc (HQ)...203 207-9917
107 Mill Plain Rd Ste 301 Danbury (06811) ***(G-1920)***
Proctor Woodworks LLC...860 767-9881
53 Grandview Ter Essex (06426) ***(G-2731)***
Product Spring LLC...203 966-6766
30 Butler Ln New Canaan (06840) ***(G-5133)***
Production Decorating Co Inc...203 574-2975
184 Railroad Hill St Waterbury (06708) ***(G-9589)***
Production Equipment Company...800 758-5697
401 Liberty St Meriden (06450) ***(G-4221)***
Producto Corporation (HQ)...203 366-3224
800 Union Ave Bridgeport (06607) ***(G-882)***
Producto Machine Company, The, Bridgeport *Also called Producto Corporation* ***(G-882)***
Professional Graphics Inc...203 846-4291
25 Perry Ave Norwalk (06850) ***(G-6307)***
Professional Media Group, Trumbull *Also called Lrp Conferences LLC* ***(G-9044)***
Professional Mktg Svcs Inc...203 610-6222
300 Long Beach Blvd Ste 6 Stratford (06615) ***(G-8669)***
Professional Print Graphics...203 686-0151
40 Edgewood Pl Meriden (06451) ***(G-4222)***
Professional Trades Netwrk LLC...860 567-0173
1100 Buckingham St Watertown (06795) ***(G-9726)***
Proflow Inc...203 230-4700
303 State St North Haven (06473) ***(G-5980)***
Proflow Process Equipment, North Haven *Also called Proflow Inc* ***(G-5980)***
Proforma/Graphicworks, Glastonbury *Also called D Cello Enterprises LLC* ***(G-3027)***
Program Dynamix Inc...860 282-0695
1155 Main St South Windsor (06074) ***(G-7813)***
Progress Machining Co...860 763-1752
15a Dust House Rd Enfield (06082) ***(G-2681)***
Progress Manufacturing LLC...860 563-6254
334 Back Ln Wethersfield (06109) ***(G-10215)***

Progressive Hydraulics Inc 203 386-0885
590 Lordship Blvd Unit 1 Stratford (06615) ***(G-8670)***
Progressive Pattern 860 748-0088
245 Deerfield Rd Windsor (06095) ***(G-10426)***
Progressive Sheetmetal LLC 860 436-9884
36 Mascolo Rd South Windsor (06074) ***(G-7814)***
Progressive Stamping Co De Inc 248 299-7100
36 Spring Ln Farmington (06032) ***(G-2951)***
Proiron LLC 203 934-7967
1 Calgery Dr West Haven (06516) ***(G-9948)***
Project Graphics Inc 802 488-8789
41 Stone Pit Rd Woodbury (06798) ***(G-10652)***
Projects Inc 860 633-4615
65 Sequin Dr Glastonbury (06033) ***(G-3075)***
Prokop Sign Co 860 889-6265
338 Norwich Ave Taftville (06380) ***(G-8742)***
Prokop Signs & Graphics, Taftville *Also called Prokop Sign Co* ***(G-8742)***
Prolaser Prolaser 203 939-1750
83 N Main St Norwalk (06854) ***(G-6308)***
Prolease, Stamford *Also called Link Systems Inc* ***(G-8285)***
Proliance International Inc 860 688-7644
436 Hayden Station Rd Windsor (06095) ***(G-10427)***
Prolink Inc 860 659-5928
148 Eastern Blvd Ste 104 Glastonbury (06033) ***(G-3076)***
Prolume Inc 203 268-7778
525 Fan Hill Rd Ste E Monroe (06468) ***(G-4749)***
Proman Inc 860 827-8778
60 Saint Claire Ave Ste 2 New Britain (06051) ***(G-5038)***
Promec, Columbia *Also called US Product Mechanization Co* ***(G-1614)***
Promise Propane 860 685-0676
110 Holmes Rd Newington (06111) ***(G-5696)***
Promos & Printing 860 481-9212
61 Wrights Crossing Rd Pomfret Center (06259) ***(G-6946)***
Pronto Printer of Newington 860 666-2245
2406 Berlin Tpke Newington (06111) ***(G-5697)***
Proof and Wood Ventures Inc 203 856-8680
365 West Rd New Canaan (06840) ***(G-5134)***
Propeller LLC 203 831-0877
24 Meridian Rd Norwalk (06853) ***(G-6309)***
Proquest Inc 860 644-2392
171 Trumbull Ln South Windsor (06074) ***(G-7815)***
Proserv Software & Support LLC 866 833-8999
69 Research Pkwy Meriden (06450) ***(G-4223)***
Prospect Designs Inc 860 379-7858
11 Prospect St New Hartford (06057) ***(G-5207)***
Prospect Flooring 203 758-4207
19a Scott Rd Prospect (06712) ***(G-7017)***
Prospect Industries LLC 203 758-3736
4 Catherine Dr Prospect (06712) ***(G-7018)***
Prospect Machine Products Inc 203 758-4448
139 Union City Rd Prospect (06712) ***(G-7019)***
Prospect Pages LLC 203 758-6934
50 Waterbury Rd Ste C Prospect (06712) ***(G-7020)***
Prospect Printing LLC 203 758-6007
16 Waterbury Rd Prospect (06712) ***(G-7021)***
Prospect Products Incorporated 860 666-0323
43 Kelsey St Newington (06111) ***(G-5698)***
Prosperous Printing LLC 203 834-1962
35 Danbury Rd Ste 4 Wilton (06897) ***(G-10322)***
Prostaff Pro Shop 203 239-3835
156 State St North Haven (06473) ***(G-5981)***
Prosthetic and Orthotic 860 904-2419
45 Wintonbury Ave Bloomfield (06002) ***(G-470)***
Protac, New Haven *Also called Arvinas Inc* ***(G-5234)***
Protection Industries Corp (PA) 203 375-9393
2897 Main St Stratford (06614) ***(G-8671)***
Protective Home Coatings LLC 203 410-5826
18 Buckingham Rd Seymour (06483) ***(G-7364)***
Proteem LLC 203 787-2221
9 Wilson Ave North Haven (06473) ***(G-5982)***
Protegrity Usa Inc (PA) 203 326-7200
333 Ludlow St Ste 8 Stamford (06902) ***(G-8376)***
Protein Sciences Corporation (HQ) 203 686-0800
1000 Research Pkwy Meriden (06450) ***(G-4224)***
Protek Ski Racing Inc 860 628-9643
85 Ladyslipper Ln Southington (06489) ***(G-7962)***
Proteowise Inc 203 430-4187
34 Bryan Rd Branford (06405) ***(G-638)***
Protiviti Inc 203 371-5542
401 Fairfield Woods Rd Fairfield (06825) ***(G-2832)***
Proto Industrial Tools, New Britain *Also called Stanley Industrial & Auto LLC* ***(G-5066)***
Proton Energy Systems Inc 203 678-2000
10 Technology Dr Wallingford (06492) ***(G-9343)***
Proton Onsite, Wallingford *Also called Proton Energy Systems Inc* ***(G-9343)***
Protopac Inc 860 274-6796
120 Echo Lake Rd Watertown (06795) ***(G-9727)***
Protopac Printing Services, Watertown *Also called Protopac Inc* ***(G-9727)***
Protoshield 203 527-0321
140 Christian Rd Middlebury (06762) ***(G-4288)***
Protoshield.com, Middlebury *Also called Protoshield* ***(G-4288)***
Prototype Plastic Mold Co Inc 860 632-2800
35 Industrial Park Pl Middletown (06457) ***(G-4398)***
Protronix Inc 203 269-5858
28 Parker St Wallingford (06492) ***(G-9344)***
Proudfoot Company Inc 203 459-0031
588 Pepper St Monroe (06468) ***(G-4750)***
Proxtalkercom LLC (PA) 203 721-6074
327 Huntingdon Ave Waterbury (06708) ***(G-9590)***
Prs Air Elite 203 327-3500
19 Gray Squirrel Dr New Canaan (06840) ***(G-5135)***
Prs Mobile LLC 203 909-5249
2 New Haven Rd Prospect (06712) ***(G-7022)***
Prs Woods LLC 860 364-5173
94 Lambert Rd Sharon (06069) ***(G-7382)***
Psd Inc 860 305-6346
80 Caroline Rd East Haven (06512) ***(G-2448)***
PSI Plus Inc 860 267-6667
17 Watrous St East Hampton (06424) ***(G-2276)***
Psj Software LLC 203 315-1523
60 Jerimoth Dr Branford (06405) ***(G-639)***
Pti Industries Inc 860 698-9266
5 Pearson Way Enfield (06082) ***(G-2682)***
Pti Industries Inc (HQ) 800 318-8438
2 Peerless Way Enfield (06082) ***(G-2683)***
Pub Games Plus 203 846-5991
176 Main St Ste 2 Norwalk (06851) ***(G-6310)***
Public Works Dept, Wilton *Also called Town of Wilton* ***(G-10338)***
Publications Plus, Norwich *Also called Kathy Pooler* ***(G-6420)***
Publishing Dimensions LLC 203 856-7716
15 Treadwell Ln Weston (06883) ***(G-10037)***
Publishing Directions LLC 860 673-7650
50 Lovely St Avon (06001) ***(G-101)***
Publishing Packagers, Westport *Also called Ppc Books Ltd* ***(G-10142)***
Pucks Putters & Fuel LLC 203 877-5457
10 Robert Dennis Dr Milford (06461) ***(G-4619)***
Pucks Putters & Fuel LLC (PA) 203 494-3952
784 River Rd Shelton (06484) ***(G-7540)***
Pucuda Inc 860 526-8004
14 New Rd Madison (06443) ***(G-3949)***
Puddingstone Publishing LLC 203 454-3939
163 Weston Rd Weston (06883) ***(G-10038)***
Pulp Paper Products Inc 860 806-0143
30 Norwood St Torrington (06790) ***(G-8961)***
Pulse International Inc 860 290-7878
2 Jeffrey Rd South Windsor (06074) ***(G-7816)***
Pulver Precision LLC 860 763-0763
38 Bacon Rd Enfield (06082) ***(G-2684)***
Pumc Holding Corporation (PA) 203 743-6741
31-35 South St Danbury (06810) ***(G-1921)***
Pump Technology Incorporated 203 736-8890
390 Birmingham Blvd Ansonia (06401) ***(G-47)***
Puppet Press 203 838-3665
162 Strawberry Hill Ave Norwalk (06851) ***(G-6311)***
Puppy Hugger 203 661-4858
121 North St Greenwich (06830) ***(G-3219)***
Pups In A Tub 203 879-2947
654 Wolcott Rd Ste 4 Wolcott (06716) ***(G-10582)***
Purdue Pharma, Stamford *Also called Frederick Purdue Company Inc* ***(G-8210)***
Purdue Pharma Inc 203 588-8000
201 Tresser Blvd Fl 1 Stamford (06901) ***(G-8377)***
Purdue Pharma LP (PA) 203 588-8000
201 Tresser Blvd Fl 1 Stamford (06901) ***(G-8378)***
Purdue Pharma Manufacturing LP 252 265-1924
1 Stamford Forum 201 Stamford (06901) ***(G-8379)***
Purdue Pharmaceutical Pdts LP 203 588-5000
1 Stamford Forum Stamford (06901) ***(G-8380)***
Purdue Pharmaceuticals LP 252 265-1900
1 Stamford Forum Stamford (06901) ***(G-8381)***
Pure Cycle Environmental LLC 203 230-3631
30 Devine St North Haven (06473) ***(G-5983)***
Purfx Inc 860 399-4045
51 Brookwood Dr Westbrook (06498) ***(G-10005)***
Purification Technologies LLC (HQ) 860 526-7801
67 Winthrop Rd Chester (06412) ***(G-1480)***
Puritan Industries Inc 860 693-0791
122 Powder Mill Rd Collinsville (06019) ***(G-1601)***
Puritan Lane LLC 203 602-5555
59 Puritan Ln Stamford (06906) ***(G-8382)***
Purple Heart Industries LLC 203 655-5039
25 Salt Box Ln Darien (06820) ***(G-2040)***
Purvins Woodcraft 860 456-1933
333 Trumbull Hwy Lebanon (06249) ***(G-3860)***
Pushing Envelope LLC 203 745-0988
2315 Whitney Ave Hamden (06518) ***(G-3498)***
Pushpin Press 203 797-8691
209 Long Ridge Rd Danbury (06810) ***(G-1922)***
Putnam Plastics Corporation 860 774-1559
40 Louisa Viens Dr Dayville (06241) ***(G-2071)***
Putnam Town Crier & N E Ledger, Putnam *Also called Ten 22 Inc* ***(G-7072)***
Putnam Welding & Eqp Repr Inc 860 974-0292
144 Eastford Rd Eastford (06242) ***(G-2539)***
Putu LLC 203 594-9700
48 Elm St New Canaan (06840) ***(G-5136)***
Puzzle Rings Creations LLC 203 550-1591
6 Donata Ln Stamford (06905) ***(G-8383)***

ALPHABETIC

(PA)=Parent Co (HQ)=Headquarters (DH)=Div Headquarters
2020 Harris Connecticut Manufacturers Directory
565

Puzzlesocial LLC 917 515-1030
29 W Parish Rd Westport (06880) *(G-10144)*
Pw Power Systems LLC (HQ) 860 368-5900
628 Hebron Ave Ste 400 Glastonbury (06033) *(G-3077)*
Pw Power Systems, Inc., Glastonbury Also called Pw Power Systems LLC *(G-3077)*
Pw Precision Machine LLC 203 889-8615
12 Scovil Rd Unit B Higganum (06441) *(G-3777)*
PYC Deborring LLC F/K/A C & 860 828-6806
500 Four Rod Rd Ste 114 Berlin (06037) *(G-213)*
Pyne-Davidson Company 860 522-9106
237 Weston St Hartford (06120) *(G-3670)*
Pyramid Productions, Danbury Also called Joy Carole Creations Inc *(G-1865)*
Pyramid Time Systems LLC 203 238-0550
45 Gracey Ave Meriden (06451) *(G-4225)*
Pyridiam Block, Stamford Also called Stephanie Mark *(G-8441)*
Pyrotek Incorporated 509 926-6212
66 Lovers Ln Killingworth (06419) *(G-3838)*
Q Alpha Inc 860 357-7340
87 Upton Rd Colchester (06415) *(G-1569)*
Q Labtech LLC 860 501-9119
94 Arbor Xing East Lyme (06333) *(G-2472)*
Q-Jet DSI Inc 203 230-4700
303 State St North Haven (06473) *(G-5984)*
Q-Lane Turnstiles LLC 860 410-1801
52 Riverside Rd Sandy Hook (06482) *(G-7327)*
Qa Woodworking LLC 203 720-1781
74 Great Hill Rd Naugatuck (06770) *(G-4914)*
Qba Inc 860 963-9438
24 Woodland Dr Woodstock (06281) *(G-10679)*
Qdiscovery LLC (HQ) 860 271-7080
125 Eugene Oneill Dr # 140 New London (06320) *(G-5483)*
Qds LLC 203 338-9668
120 Long Hill Cross Rd Shelton (06484) *(G-7541)*
Qg Printing II Corp 860 741-0150
96 Phoenix Ave Enfield (06082) *(G-2685)*
Qmdi Press 860 642-8074
841 Route 32 Ste 19 North Franklin (06254) *(G-5878)*
Qmdi Press Services LLC (PA) 860 942-8822
322 Main St Ste 1 Willimantic (06226) *(G-10235)*
Qnp Technologies, East Glastonbury Also called Quality Name Plate Inc *(G-2185)*
Qs Tehcnoligies Divison, Meriden Also called Omerin Usa Inc *(G-4212)*
Qscend Technologies Inc 203 757-6000
231 Bank St Waterbury (06702) *(G-9591)*
Qsonica LLC 203 426-0101
53 Church Hill Rd Newtown (06470) *(G-5770)*
Qsr Steel Corporation LLC 860 548-0248
121 Elliott St E Hartford (06114) *(G-3671)*
Qtran Inc 203 367-8777
155 Hill St Ste 3 Milford (06460) *(G-4620)*
Quad/Graphics Inc 203 288-2468
291 State St North Haven (06473) *(G-5985)*
Qualedi Inc 203 538-5320
1 Trap Falls Rd Ste 206 Shelton (06484) *(G-7542)*
Qualedi Inc (PA) 203 874-4334
121 W Main St Ste 4 Milford (06460) *(G-4621)*
Quality Automatics Inc (PA) 860 945-4795
15 Mclennan Dr Oakville (06779) *(G-6459)*
Quality Bead Craft Inc 860 242-2167
25 Northwood Dr Bloomfield (06002) *(G-471)*
Quality Care Drg/Cntrbrook LLC 860 767-0206
33 Main St Centerbrook (06409) *(G-1332)*
Quality Coils Incorporated (PA) 860 584-0927
748 Middle St Bristol (06010) *(G-1099)*
Quality Engineering Svcs Inc 203 269-5054
122 N Plains Indus Rd Wallingford (06492) *(G-9345)*
Quality Erectors LLC 860 548-0248
300 Locust St Hartford (06114) *(G-3672)*
Quality Kitchen Corp Delaware 203 744-2000
131 West St Ste 1 Danbury (06810) *(G-1923)*
Quality Machine, New Milford Also called Joseph J McFadden Jr *(G-5552)*
Quality Machine Inc 860 354-6794
87 Danbury Rd New Milford (06776) *(G-5581)*
Quality Name Plate Inc 860 633-9495
22 Fisher Hill Rd East Glastonbury (06025) *(G-2185)*
Quality Printers Inc 860 443-2800
141 Shaw St New London (06320) *(G-5484)*
Quality Printing & Graphics, Fairfield Also called Mickey Herbst *(G-2815)*
Quality Rolling Deburring Inc 860 283-0271
135 S Main St Ste 3 Thomaston (06787) *(G-8801)*
Quality Scanning Solution 203 270-1833
5 Ferris Rd Newtown (06470) *(G-5771)*
Quality Sheet Metal Inc 203 729-2244
17 Clark Rd Naugatuck (06770) *(G-4915)*
Quality Sign Crafters, Willimantic Also called Horizons Unlimited Inc *(G-10230)*
Quality Signs of Watertown 860 274-4828
140 Circuit Ave Watertown (06795) *(G-9728)*
Quality Stairs Inc 203 367-8390
70 Logan St Bridgeport (06607) *(G-883)*
Quality Tank Service LP 203 792-9373
16 Driftway Rd Danbury (06811) *(G-1924)*
Quality Welding LLC 860 585-1121
61 E Main St Bldg C Bristol (06010) *(G-1100)*
Quality Welding Service LLC 860 342-7202
265 Brownstone Ave Portland (06480) *(G-6970)*
Quality Wire Edm Inc 860 583-9867
329 Redstone Hill Rd Bristol (06010) *(G-1101)*
Quality Woodworks LLC 203 736-9200
1 Riverside Dr Ansonia (06401) *(G-48)*
Quanah Scents LLC 888 849-2016
147 Tonica Spring Trl Manchester (06040) *(G-4077)*
Quantum 732 407-1200
192 Cross Ridge Rd New Canaan (06840) *(G-5137)*
Quantum Bpower Southington LLC 860 201-0621
49 Depaolo Dr Southington (06489) *(G-7963)*
Quantum Circuits Inc 203 432-4289
44 Northwood Rd Madison (06443) *(G-3950)*
Quantum Circuits Inc 203 891-6216
25 Science Park Ste 203 New Haven (06511) *(G-5373)*
Quantum Health Press 203 396-0222
5520 Park Ave Ste 301 Trumbull (06611) *(G-9058)*
Quarry Stone & Gravel LLC 203 770-2664
4 Ridgewood St Danbury (06811) *(G-1925)*
Quarter Mile 203 438-9718
91 Peaceable St Ridgefield (06877) *(G-7165)*
Quatum Inc 860 666-3464
43 Maselli Rd Hartford (06111) *(G-3673)*
Quebecor World (usa) Inc 203 532-4200
340 Pemberwick Rd Greenwich (06831) *(G-3220)*
Queenie Industries LLC 917 848-4490
50 Harrison Dr Hamden (06514) *(G-3499)*
Quemere International LLC 914 934-8366
234 Middle St Middletown (06457) *(G-4399)*
Quero Shoes, Westport Also called Cuero Operating *(G-10073)*
Quest Plastics Inc 860 489-1404
89 Commercial Blvd Ste 3 Torrington (06790) *(G-8962)*
Quest Software, Southport Also called Dell Software Inc *(G-8003)*
Quick & Dirty Press 860 817-0912
16 Wonderview Dr Tolland (06084) *(G-8876)*
Quick Machine Services LLC 203 634-8822
290 Pratt St Ste 4 Meriden (06450) *(G-4226)*
Quick Print 860 425-5580
48 Main St Colchester (06415) *(G-1570)*
Quick Turn Machine Company Inc 860 623-2569
1000 Old County Cir # 105 Windsor Locks (06096) *(G-10495)*
Quicksand Blasting 860 848-4482
107 Jerome Rd Uncasville (06382) *(G-9103)*
Quiet Corner Printing LLC 860 753-0420
200 Bailey Woods Rd Brooklyn (06234) *(G-1253)*
Quilted Lizard 860 927-4296
19 South Rd Kent (06757) *(G-3825)*
Quinn and Gellar Marketing LLC 860 444-0448
147 State St New London (06320) *(G-5485)*
Quinn Capentry & Painting, Wallingford Also called James H Quinn *(G-9293)*
Quinnipiac Valley Alpacas 203 271-0773
30 Homestead Pl Cheshire (06410) *(G-1433)*
Quinnipiac Valley Times 203 675-9483
2301 State St Hamden (06517) *(G-3500)*
Quixpress Car Wash 203 364-9777
1 Simm Ln Newtown (06470) *(G-5772)*
R & A Precious Metals LLC 203 220-8265
3 Plumb Creek Rd Trumbull (06611) *(G-9059)*
R & B Apparel Plus LLC 860 333-1757
78 Plaza Ct Groton (06340) *(G-3311)*
R & D Precision Inc 203 284-3396
63 N Cherry St Ste 1 Wallingford (06492) *(G-9346)*
R & D Services LLC 860 628-5205
45 Old Turnpike Rd Southington (06489) *(G-7964)*
R & F Welding Co 203 393-2851
51 Ructell Rd Ste 3 New Haven (06524) *(G-5374)*
R & I Manufacturing Co 860 589-6364
118 Napco Dr Terryville (06786) *(G-8768)*
R & K Cookies LLC 860 613-2893
9 Smith Farm Rd Cromwell (06416) *(G-1714)*
R & M Associates Inc 860 633-0721
277 Hebron Ave Glastonbury (06033) *(G-3078)*
R & M Logging 860 429-6209
268 River Rd Willington (06279) *(G-10255)*
R & R Corrugated Container Inc 860 584-1194
360 Minor St Bristol (06010) *(G-1102)*
R & R Fabricaton, Cheshire Also called Sharp Racing Enterprises *(G-1444)*
R & R McHy & Rebuilding Co, Bristol Also called Richard Dahlen *(G-1108)*
R & R Pallet Corp 203 272-2784
120 Schoolhouse Rd Cheshire (06410) *(G-1434)*
R & T Manufacturing, Newington Also called Team Walbern *(G-5710)*
R A Lalli, Stratford Also called Jgs Properties LLC *(G-8636)*
R A Tool Co 203 877-2998
230 Woodmont Rd Ste Y Milford (06460) *(G-4622)*
R and B Prtective Coatings LLC 860 836-7854
29 Copper Beech Dr Middletown (06457) *(G-4400)*
R and K Industries 860 289-3879
24 Arbutus St East Hartford (06108) *(G-2362)*
R and R Publishing LLC 860 944-2085
42 Fern Rd Storrs Mansfield (06268) *(G-8558)*
R B C, Oxford Also called Roller Bearing Co Amer Inc *(G-6693)*

R Botsford Custom Wdwkg LLC 203 994-5302
171 Brushy Hill Rd Newtown (06470) ***(G-5773)***
R C E Machine Works 860 354-6976
39 Old Route 7 Plz New Milford (06776) ***(G-5582)***
R D Woodwork LLC 203 947-9550
29 Morris St Danbury (06810) ***(G-1926)***
R E F Machine Company Inc 860 349-9344
24 West St Middlefield (06455) ***(G-4305)***
R E M, Southington *Also called REM Chemicals Inc* ***(G-7967)***
R E S Woodworking LLC 860 664-9663
22 Nod Pl Clinton (06413) ***(G-1519)***
R F Case 203 956-6348
178 Flax Hill Rd Apt C101 Norwalk (06854) ***(G-6312)***
R F H Company Inc 203 853-2863
79 Rockland Rd Ste 3 Norwalk (06854) ***(G-6313)***
R G L Inc 860 653-7254
121 Rainbow Rd East Granby (06026) ***(G-2226)***
R J Brass Inc 860 793-2336
26 Ashford Rd Plainville (06062) ***(G-6855)***
R K Machine Company LLC 860 224-7545
200 Myrtle St New Britain (06053) ***(G-5039)***
R K S Security LLC 860 749-4106
4 Cleveland St Enfield (06082) ***(G-2686)***
R L Fisher Inc 860 951-8110
30 Bartholomew Ave Hartford (06106) ***(G-3674)***
R L Pritchard & Co Inc 203 393-0260
1 North Rd South Lyme (06376) ***(G-7685)***
R L Turick Co Inc 860 693-2230
186 Main St New Hartford (06057) ***(G-5208)***
R Lange Welding-Fabrication 203 994-5516
114 Candlewood Lake Rd Brookfield (06804) ***(G-1217)***
R P A, Hamden *Also called Record Products America Inc* ***(G-3504)***
R R Donnelley & Sons Company 860 649-5570
151 Redstone Rd Manchester (06042) ***(G-4078)***
R R Donnelley & Sons Company 860 773-6140
60 Security Dr Avon (06001) ***(G-102)***
R S Enterprise, West Granby *Also called Jerome Ridel* ***(G-9767)***
R S Industries LLC 203 261-1146
51 Bassick Rd Trumbull (06611) ***(G-9060)***
R T G, Manchester *Also called K & G Corp* ***(G-4041)***
R Tulba Welding, Waterford *Also called Rodney Tulba Welding & Fabg* ***(G-9667)***
R Van Loan Custom Framing LLC 203 422-2881
115 Mason St Ste 6 Greenwich (06830) ***(G-3221)***
R W E Inc 860 974-1101
91 Highland Dr Putnam (06260) ***(G-7061)***
R Way Signs LLC 203 888-9709
18 Bowers Hill Rd Oxford (06478) ***(G-6690)***
R Woodworking Larson Inc 860 646-7904
192 Sheldon Rd Manchester (06042) ***(G-4079)***
R&D Dynamics Corporation 860 726-1204
49 W Dudley Town Rd Bloomfield (06002) ***(G-472)***
R&J Harvesting LLC 860 974-1323
54 Hartford Tpke Eastford (06242) ***(G-2540)***
R&M Service 860 645-7771
1 Shady Ln Manchester (06042) ***(G-4080)***
R&R Tool & Die LLC 860 627-9197
94 Newberry Rd East Windsor (06088) ***(G-2515)***
R&R Woodworking 508 202-3543
11 Lakeside Dr Thompson (06277) ***(G-8842)***
R-D Mfg Inc 860 739-3986
6 Colton Rd East Lyme (06333) ***(G-2473)***
R4v, Westport *Also called Recycle 4 Vets LLC* ***(G-10147)***
RA Senft Inc 860 399-5967
159 Wesley Ave Westbrook (06498) ***(G-10006)***
RA Smythe LLC 860 398-5764
439 Higby Rd Middletown (06457) ***(G-4401)***
Race Works, Berlin *Also called Raceworks Inc* ***(G-214)***
Racemyface LLC 203 285-8090
82 Village Ct Wilton (06897) ***(G-10323)***
Raceworks Inc 860 829-1312
55 Willow Brook Dr Berlin (06037) ***(G-214)***
Racing Times 203 298-2899
428 Main St Wallingford (06492) ***(G-9347)***
Radcliff Wire Inc 312 876-1754
97 Ronzo Rd Bristol (06010) ***(G-1103)***
Radeco of Ct Inc 860 564-1220
17 West Pkwy Plainfield (06374) ***(G-6751)***
Rader Industries Inc 203 334-6739
115 Island Brook Ave Bridgeport (06606) ***(G-884)***
Radford, F Castings Plastic ML, Trumbull *Also called Fred Radford* ***(G-9027)***
Radiall Usa Inc 203 776-2813
104 John W Murphy Dr New Haven (06513) ***(G-5375)***
Radiation Safety Assoc Inc 860 228-0721
19 Pendleton Dr Hebron (06248) ***(G-3754)***
Radical Computing Corporation 860 953-0240
705 N Mountain Rd A210 Newington (06111) ***(G-5699)***
Radio Frequency Systems, Meriden *Also called RFS Americas* ***(G-4231)***
Radio Frequency Systems Inc (HQ) 203 630-3311
200 Pond View Dr Meriden (06450) ***(G-4227)***
Radius Mill Work 860 645-1036
22 Olcott Dr Manchester (06040) ***(G-4081)***
Radius Millworks, Manchester *Also called Radius Mill Work* ***(G-4081)***
Radon Systems of CT, Wolcott *Also called Bruce Corey Enterprises Inc* ***(G-10550)***
Radx Cloud 909 910-7434
123 York St Apt 11a New Haven (06511) ***(G-5376)***
Raf Electronic Hardware, Seymour *Also called Matthew Warren Inc* ***(G-7355)***
Raf Industries LLC 203 228-4290
257 Strongtown Rd Southbury (06488) ***(G-7873)***
Rafael Cakes & Sugar LLC 203 642-4840
77 N Main St 79 Norwalk (06854) ***(G-6314)***
Raffaele Ruberto LLC 860 573-4094
214 Amherst St Wethersfield (06109) ***(G-10216)***
Ragis Fabrications Inc 203 237-0424
250 Goodspeed Ave Meriden (06451) ***(G-4228)***
Ragozzino Foods Inc (PA) 203 238-2553
10 Ames Ave Meriden (06451) ***(G-4229)***
Rags A Muffin 203 377-7063
120 Kings Row Stratford (06614) ***(G-8672)***
Rahzel Enterprize LLC 475 449-6561
15 Madison St Apt C8 Norwalk (06854) ***(G-6315)***
Rain Carbon Inc 203 406-0535
10 Signal Rd Stamford (06902) ***(G-8384)***
Rain Cii Carbon LLC 203 406-0535
10 Signal Rd Stamford (06902) ***(G-8385)***
Rainbow Forest Log & Firewd 860 455-1023
88 Old Canterbury Rd Hampton (06247) ***(G-3539)***
Rainbow Graphics Inc 860 646-8997
118 Adams St S Manchester (06040) ***(G-4082)***
Rally For A Cure, Ridgefield *Also called Wrenfield Group Inc* ***(G-7186)***
Ralph B Fletcher Logging & Lan 860 668-5404
834 East St S Suffield (06078) ***(G-8732)***
Ram Arts Signs 860 274-6833
24 Ledgewood Rd Watertown (06795) ***(G-9729)***
Ram Belting Company Inc 860 438-7029
100 Production Ct Ste 3 New Britain (06051) ***(G-5040)***
Ram Technologies LLC 203 453-3916
29 Soundview Rd Ste 12 Guilford (06437) ***(G-3385)***
Raman Power Technologies LLC 203 695-4885
46 Capital Dr Wallingford (06492) ***(G-9348)***
Ramar-Hall Inc 860 349-1081
26 Old Indian Trl Middlefield (06455) ***(G-4306)***
Rambling Dog Publications LLC 203 254-9230
229 Mile Common Rd Easton (06612) ***(G-2563)***
Ramco Systems Corporation 860 496-0099
30 Kinsey Rd New Hartford (06057) ***(G-5209)***
Ramdial Parts and Services LLC 860 296-5175
18 Adelaide St Hartford (06114) ***(G-3675)***
Ramdy Corporation 860 274-3713
40 Mclennan Dr Oakville (06779) ***(G-6460)***
Rampage LLC 203 930-1022
38 Palisade Ave Trumbull (06611) ***(G-9061)***
Rand Brands, Bridgeport *Also called Rand Innovations LLC* ***(G-885)***
Rand Innovations LLC 475 282-4643
3389 Fairfield Ave Bridgeport (06605) ***(G-885)***
Rand Machine & Fabrication Co 203 272-1352
1486 Highland Ave Ste 2 Cheshire (06410) ***(G-1435)***
Rand Media Co LLC 203 226-8727
265 Post Rd W Westport (06880) ***(G-10145)***
Rand Newco LLC 203 699-9125
151 Moss Farms Rd Cheshire (06410) ***(G-1436)***
Rand Sheaves & Pulleys LLC 203 272-1352
1486 Highland Ave Cheshire (06410) ***(G-1437)***
Rand Whitney 860 354-6063
7 Nutmeg Dr New Milford (06776) ***(G-5583)***
Rand-Whitney Container Newtown, Newtown *Also called Rand-Whitney Group LLC* ***(G-5774)***
Rand-Whitney Group LLC 203 426-5871
1 Edmund Rd Newtown (06470) ***(G-5774)***
Rand-Whitney Recycling LLC 860 848-1900
370 Route 163 Montville (06353) ***(G-4770)***
Ranger Ready Repellents, Norwalk *Also called Pic20 Group LLC* ***(G-6299)***
Ransom Skateboards and App 860 538-5577
178 Plainville Ave Unionville (06085) ***(G-9125)***
Rapid Press, Stamford *Also called Tech-Repro Inc* ***(G-8460)***
Rapid Slicer LLC 203 610-3673
16 Crystal Ln Shelton (06484) ***(G-7543)***
Rapid Truck Service Inc 860 482-5500
1745 Torringford West St Torrington (06790) ***(G-8963)***
Rapidex 860 285-8818
875 Marshall Phelps Rd Windsor (06095) ***(G-10428)***
Rapidprint, Middletown *Also called Bidwell Industrial Group Inc* ***(G-4325)***
Rare Reminder Incorporated 860 563-9386
222 Dividend Rd Rocky Hill (06067) ***(G-7264)***
Ravago Americas LLC 203 855-6000
10 Westport Rd Wilton (06897) ***(G-10324)***
Ravco Wood Products, Central Village *Also called Guy Ravenelle* ***(G-1337)***
Raven Ad Specialties 203 521-8687
52 Raven Ter Stratford (06614) ***(G-8673)***
Rawson Manufacturing Inc (PA) 860 928-4458
99 Canal St Putnam (06260) ***(G-7062)***
Ray Green Corp 707 544-2662
115 E Putnam Ave Ste 1 Greenwich (06830) ***(G-3222)***
Ray Machine Corporation 860 582-8202
84 Town Hill Rd Terryville (06786) ***(G-8769)***

ALPHABETIC

(PA)=Parent Co (HQ)=Headquarters (DH)=Div Headquarters
2020 Harris Connecticut Manufacturers Directory
567

Ray Proof Shielding Systems, Norwalk *Also called Ets-Lindgren Inc* ***(G-6158)***
Rayco Inc....860 357-4693
206 Newington Ave Fl 2 New Britain (06051) ***(G-5041)***
Rayco Metal Finishing Inc....860 347-7434
134 Mill St Middletown (06457) ***(G-4402)***
Rayflex Company Inc....203 336-2173
1061 Howard Ave Bridgeport (06605) ***(G-886)***
Rayginn Mfg LLC....860 243-2257
109 W Ddley Town Rd Ste J Bloomfield (06002) ***(G-473)***
Raym-Co Inc....860 678-8292
62 Spring Ln Farmington (06032) ***(G-2952)***
Raymon Tool LLC....203 248-2199
79 Rossotto Dr Hamden (06514) ***(G-3501)***
Raymond J Bykowski....203 271-2385
1685 Reinhard Rd Cheshire (06410) ***(G-1438)***
Raypax Manufacturing Co Inc....203 758-7416
21 Tremont St Waterbury (06708) ***(G-9592)***
Raytech Industries Div, Middletown *Also called Lyman Products Corporation* ***(G-4370)***
Raytheon Company....860 446-4900
11 Main St Ste 3 Mystic (06355) ***(G-4840)***
Rayvel, Montville *Also called Ciaudelli Productions Inc* ***(G-4769)***
Razzberry Inc....510 495-5366
2228 Shepard Ave Hamden (06518) ***(G-3502)***
Razzberry Operating Co Inc....510 495-5366
2228 Shepard Ave Hamden (06518) ***(G-3503)***
Rbc Bearings Incorporated (PA)....203 267-7001
102 Willenbrock Rd Oxford (06478) ***(G-6691)***
Rbc Linear Precision Pdts Inc....203 255-1511
60 Round Hill Rd Fairfield (06824) ***(G-2833)***
Rbc Prcision Pdts - Bremen Inc (HQ)....203 267-7001
102 Willenbrock Rd Oxford (06478) ***(G-6692)***
Rbf Frozen Desserts LLC....516 474-6488
240 Park Rd Ste 3 West Hartford (06119) ***(G-9848)***
Rbi Inc....860 444-0534
30 Plant St New London (06320) ***(G-5486)***
Rbk Lathe LLC....860 321-7243
1451 New Britain Ave # 1 Farmington (06032) ***(G-2953)***
RC Bigelow Inc (PA)....888 244-3569
201 Black Rock Tpke Fairfield (06825) ***(G-2834)***
RC Connectors LLC....860 413-2196
146 Hopmeadow St Weatogue (06089) ***(G-9759)***
RC Fabrication and Off Rd LLC....203 500-7071
96 Pond Hill Rd Unit 24 North Haven (06473) ***(G-5986)***
Rcd LLC....203 712-1900
230 Long Hill Cross Rd Shelton (06484) ***(G-7544)***
Rcsi Publishing....203 917-4223
114 Westville Ave Danbury (06810) ***(G-1927)***
Rd Printing LLC....860 841-1397
138 Long Hill Rd Windsor (06095) ***(G-10429)***
Rdl Coatings LLC....203 232-0411
28 Main St Oakville (06779) ***(G-6461)***
Re-Style Your Closets LLC....860 658-9450
86 E Weatogue St Simsbury (06070) ***(G-7642)***
REA Magnet Wire Company Inc....203 738-6100
129 Soundview Rd Guilford (06437) ***(G-3386)***
Reac Ready LLC (PA)....860 760-8886
1 Darling Dr Avon (06001) ***(G-103)***
Reactel Inc....203 773-0135
315 Peck St Fl 3 New Haven (06513) ***(G-5377)***
Readily Apparent, Wilton *Also called Perry Heights Press LLC* ***(G-10319)***
Ready Tool Company (HQ)....860 524-7811
1 Carney Rd West Hartford (06110) ***(G-9849)***
Ready Tool LLC....860 436-2128
6 Palomina Way Wethersfield (06109) ***(G-10217)***
Ready4 Print LLC....203 345-0376
2051 Main St Bridgeport (06604) ***(G-887)***
Readydock Inc....860 523-9980
46 W Avon Rd Ste 302 Avon (06001) ***(G-104)***
Real Data Inc....203 255-2732
657 Mill Hill Rd Southport (06890) ***(G-8007)***
Real Estate Valuation Magazine, New Haven *Also called Naffa Inc* ***(G-5339)***
Real Manufacturing LLC....860 757-3975
524 Sullivan Ave Ste 8 South Windsor (06074) ***(G-7817)***
Real Sltons Edctl Cnslting Inc....203 220-2279
67 Driftwood Ln Trumbull (06611) ***(G-9062)***
Real Women International LLC....212 719-3130
385 Main St S Ste 404 Southbury (06488) ***(G-7874)***
Real-Time Analyzers Inc....860 635-9800
362 Industrial Park Rd # 8 Middletown (06457) ***(G-4403)***
Realejo Donuts Inc....860 342-5120
860 Portland Cobalt Rd Portland (06480) ***(G-6971)***
Realizers Group LLC....203 253-9510
15 Danbury Ave Westport (06880) ***(G-10146)***
Realmaplesyrup.com, Stafford Springs *Also called Balsam Woods Farm* ***(G-8018)***
Realtraps LLC....203 294-4285
47 N Plains Industrial Rd F Wallingford (06492) ***(G-9349)***
Realtraps Manufacturing, Wallingford *Also called Realtraps LLC* ***(G-9349)***
Reblee Inc (PA)....203 372-3338
27 Bonazzo Dr Trumbull (06611) ***(G-9063)***
Reborn House....203 216-9874
204 Damascus Rd Branford (06405) ***(G-640)***
Rec Components, Stafford Springs *Also called Edgewater International LLC* ***(G-8028)***
Recognition Inc....860 659-8629
77 Kreiger Ln Ste 810 Glastonbury (06033) ***(G-3079)***
Recognition Products, Lebanon *Also called Ann S Davis* ***(G-3846)***
Recon Tactical LLC....860 677-8202
30 Lakeshore Dr Apt B2 Farmington (06032) ***(G-2954)***
Recor Rust Solutions....860 573-1942
246 Wall St Hebron (06248) ***(G-3755)***
Recor Welding Center Inc....860 573-1942
86 Gannet Dr Southington (06489) ***(G-7965)***
Record Journal, The, Meriden *Also called Southington Citizen* ***(G-4243)***
Record Products America Inc....203 248-6371
700 Sherman Ave Hamden (06514) ***(G-3504)***
Record-Journal Newspaper (PA)....203 235-1661
500 S Broad St Ste 2 Meriden (06450) ***(G-4230)***
Record-Journal Newspaper....860 536-9577
15 Holmes St Ste 3 Mystic (06355) ***(G-4841)***
Recovery Zone, Manchester *Also called Peristere LLC* ***(G-4075)***
Recreational Equipment Inc....860 313-0128
1417 New Britain Ave West Hartford (06110) ***(G-9850)***
Recycle 4 Vets LLC....203 222-7300
518 Riverside Ave Ste 1 Westport (06880) ***(G-10147)***
Red 7 Media LLC (HQ)....203 853-2474
10 Norden Pl Ste 202 Norwalk (06855) ***(G-6316)***
Red Apple Cheese LLC (PA)....203 755-5579
27 Siemon Co Dr Ste 231w Watertown (06795) ***(G-9730)***
Red Apple Creative US Inc....212 453-2540
38 Ann Ave Shelton (06484) ***(G-7545)***
Red Barn Innovations....203 393-0778
8 Tress Rd Prospect (06712) ***(G-7023)***
Red Barn Radiator Co....860 829-2060
54 Fuller Way Berlin (06037) ***(G-215)***
Red Barn Woodworkers....860 379-3158
118 Laurel Way Winsted (06098) ***(G-10533)***
Red Beard Publishing LLC....203 847-1655
22 France St Norwalk (06851) ***(G-6317)***
Red Bull LLC....860 519-1018
460 Woodland Ave Bloomfield (06002) ***(G-474)***
Red Coach Sand & Gravel, Naugatuck *Also called Judith Bennett* ***(G-4895)***
Red Coach Sand & Stone, Fairfield *Also called Judith Bennett* ***(G-2804)***
Red Door Industries....860 243-1960
96 Old Windsor Rd Bloomfield (06002) ***(G-475)***
Red Mat Media Inc....203 283-5290
162 Bridgeport Ave Milford (06460) ***(G-4623)***
Red Oak Stable LLC....860 642-4671
4 Oliver Rd Lebanon (06249) ***(G-3861)***
Red Rocket Site 2....860 581-8019
47 Industrial Park Rd Centerbrook (06409) ***(G-1333)***
Red Rose Desserts....860 603-2670
125 Lebanon Ave Colchester (06415) ***(G-1571)***
Redco Audio Inc....203 502-7600
1701 Stratford Ave Stratford (06615) ***(G-8674)***
Redco Industries LLC....860 537-2664
15 Sashel Ln Colchester (06415) ***(G-1572)***
Redding Creamery LLC....203 938-2766
2 Marli Ln Redding (06896) ***(G-7106)***
Redifoils LLC....860 342-1500
193 Pickering St Portland (06480) ***(G-6972)***
Redland Brick Inc....860 528-1311
1440 John Fitch Blvd South Windsor (06074) ***(G-7818)***
Redline Elements LLC....860 305-0095
70 Finley Hill Rd Marlborough (06447) ***(G-4130)***
Reed & Stefanow Machine Tl Co....860 583-7834
165 Riverside Ave Bristol (06010) ***(G-1104)***
Reeds Inc....203 890-0557
201 Merritt 7 Norwalk (06851) ***(G-6318)***
Reel Time LLC....203 326-0664
43 Green Meadow Ln New Canaan (06840) ***(G-5138)***
Refined Designs....860 535-7273
779 Stonington Rd Stonington (06378) ***(G-8537)***
Reflected Image....203 484-0760
21 Westwind Dr Northford (06472) ***(G-6052)***
Reflex Ltg Group of CT LLC....860 666-1548
1290 Silas Deane Hwy 1a Wethersfield (06109) ***(G-10218)***
Regen Med, Greenwich *Also called Regenerative Medicine LLC* ***(G-3223)***
Regenerative Medicine LLC (PA)....203 629-1438
68 Doubling Rd Greenwich (06830) ***(G-3223)***
Regional Industries LLC....860 227-3627
41 Commerce St Clinton (06413) ***(G-1520)***
Regional Stairs LLC....860 290-1242
183 Prestige Park Rd East Hartford (06108) ***(G-2363)***
Register For Publications....860 302-6706
22 Summit Farms Rd Southington (06489) ***(G-7966)***
Registrant James Trippe....203 517-7567
137 Valley Dr Greenwich (06831) ***(G-3224)***
Reid Interiors....860 569-1240
200 Burnside Ave East Hartford (06108) ***(G-2364)***
Reidville Hydraulics & Mfg Inc....860 496-1133
175 Industrial Ln Torrington (06790) ***(G-8964)***
Reilly Foam Corp....860 243-8200
16 Britton Dr Bloomfield (06002) ***(G-476)***
Reis Floor Finishing....203 367-1273
46 Cathy Dr Shelton (06484) ***(G-7546)***

ALPHABETIC SECTION
Richard Woodworking

Rel-Tech Electronics Inc 203 877-8770
215 Pepes Farm Rd Milford (06460) ***(G-4624)***
Relational Data Solutions LLC 860 231-7682
123 Thomas St West Hartford (06119) ***(G-9851)***
Relative Gourmet II 203 358-4602
30 Spring St Stamford (06901) ***(G-8386)***
Relays Unlimited, East Granby *Also called Computer Components Inc* ***(G-2199)***
Reliable Electric Motor Inc 860 522-2257
285 Murphy Rd Hartford (06114) ***(G-3676)***
Reliable Plating & Polsg Co 203 366-5261
80 Bishop Ave Bridgeport (06607) ***(G-888)***
Reliable Printing LLC 203 261-8867
4 Daniels Farm Rd Ste 268 Trumbull (06611) ***(G-9064)***
Reliable Scales & Systems LLC 860 380-0600
150 Village St Bristol (06010) ***(G-1105)***
Reliable Silver Corporation 203 574-7732
302 Platts Mill Rd Naugatuck (06770) ***(G-4916)***
Reliable Spring Company, Bristol *Also called Oscar Jobs* ***(G-1083)***
Reliable Tool & Die Inc 203 877-3264
435 Woodmont Rd Milford (06460) ***(G-4625)***
Reliable Welding & Speed LLC 860 749-3977
85 North St Enfield (06082) ***(G-2687)***
Reliance Business Systems Inc 203 281-4407
420 Sackett Point Rd # 8 North Haven (06473) ***(G-5987)***
Reliant Services LLC 860 346-6107
100 Saddle Hill Dr Middletown (06457) ***(G-4404)***
Relocation Information Svc Inc 203 855-1234
69 East Ave Ste 4 Norwalk (06851) ***(G-6319)***
Relprog LLC 203 734-7000
174 Hawthorne Ave Derby (06418) ***(G-2123)***
Relx Inc 860 219-0733
15 Cobbler Way Windsor (06095) ***(G-10430)***
Relx Inc 203 840-4800
383 Main Ave Fl 3 Norwalk (06851) ***(G-6320)***
REM Chemicals Inc (PA) 860 621-6755
325 W Queen St Southington (06489) ***(G-7967)***
REm Tool & Die Llc 860 582-7559
550 Broad St Bristol (06010) ***(G-1106)***
Rema Dri-Vac Corp 203 847-2464
45 Ruby St Norwalk (06850) ***(G-6321)***
Remesas Express 203 330-1444
1213 North Ave Bridgeport (06604) ***(G-889)***
Reminder Broadcaster 860 875-3366
130 Old Town Rd Vernon (06066) ***(G-9151)***
Reminder Media, Vernon *Also called Reminder Broadcaster* ***(G-9151)***
Remote Site Service LLC 860 691-1911
46 Old Black Point Rd Niantic (06357) ***(G-5816)***
Remote Technologies Inc (PA) 203 661-2798
57 Old Mill Rd Greenwich (06831) ***(G-3225)***
Renaissance Craftsmen LLC 860 916-3583
263 Simsbury Rd Hartford (06117) ***(G-3677)***
Renaissance Studio Inc 203 226-9674
188 Imperial Ave Westport (06880) ***(G-10148)***
Renchel Tool Inc 860 315-9017
51 Ridge Rd Putnam (06260) ***(G-7063)***
Renetx Bio Inc 203 444-6642
157 Church St Fl 19 New Haven (06510) ***(G-5378)***
Renewable Energy Natural RES 860 923-1091
144 New Rd Thompson (06277) ***(G-8843)***
Renner Stairs 203 743-2452
92 Sand Pit Rd Danbury (06810) ***(G-1928)***
Reno Machine Company Inc 860 666-5641
170 Pane Rd Ste 1 Newington (06111) ***(G-5700)***
Republic Systems Inc 860 291-8832
222 Pitkin St Ste 117 East Hartford (06108) ***(G-2365)***
Republican-American, Waterbury *Also called American-Republican Inc* ***(G-9429)***
RES-Tech Corporation 860 828-1504
114 New Park Dr Berlin (06037) ***(G-216)***
Resavue Inc 203 878-0944
48 Grannis Rd Orange (06477) ***(G-6625)***
Resavue Exhibits, Orange *Also called Resavue Inc* ***(G-6625)***
Reserved Magazine 860 560-9120
99 Pratt St Hartford (06103) ***(G-3678)***
Resinall Corp (HQ) 203 329-7100
3065 High Ridge Rd Stamford (06903) ***(G-8387)***
Resolute FP US Inc 203 292-6560
97 Village Ln Southport (06890) ***(G-8008)***
Respironics Inc 203 697-6490
5 Technology Dr Wallingford (06492) ***(G-9350)***
Respironics Novametrix LLC 203 697-6475
5 Technology Dr Wallingford (06492) ***(G-9351)***
Respond Systems 203 481-2810
20 Baldwin Dr Branford (06405) ***(G-641)***
Restech Plastic Molding, Berlin *Also called RES-Tech Corporation* ***(G-216)***
Restopedic Inc 203 393-1520
695 Amity Rd Bethany (06524) ***(G-249)***
Results-Based Outsourcing Inc 203 635-7600
2490 Blck Rock Tpke # 344 Fairfield (06825) ***(G-2835)***
Retail Print Solutions 203 438-5457
300 West Ln Ridgefield (06877) ***(G-7166)***
Retech USA LLC 860 531-9653
12 Esther Ln Colchester (06415) ***(G-1573)***
Retina Systems Inc 203 881-1311
146 Day St Seymour (06483) ***(G-7365)***
Retinographics Inc 203 853-1735
9 Dock Rd Norwalk (06854) ***(G-6322)***
Reusable Greenworks 203 745-3695
192 Forbes Ave New Haven (06512) ***(G-5379)***
Revive Beauty and Wellness LLC 860 921-4952
2 Old New Milford Rd 3d Brookfield (06804) ***(G-1218)***
Revolution Lighting, Stamford *Also called Seesmart Inc* ***(G-8407)***
Revolution Lighting (HQ) 203 504-1111
177 Broad St Fl 12 Stamford (06901) ***(G-8388)***
Revolution Lighting Tech Inc (PA) 203 504-1111
177 Broad St Fl 12 Stamford (06901) ***(G-8389)***
Revolution Lighting Tech Inc 203 504-1111
177 Broad St Fl 12 Stamford (06901) ***(G-8390)***
Rex Forge Div, Plantsville *Also called J J Ryan Corporation* ***(G-6897)***
Rex Precast Systems, Cheshire *Also called Superior Products Distrs Inc* ***(G-1454)***
Rexel 203 969-6601
390 Fairfield Ave Stamford (06902) ***(G-8391)***
Rexnord LLC 860 355-0478
14 Crescent Ln New Milford (06776) ***(G-5584)***
Reyes Welding Svcs 203 505-1111
46 Elmwood Ave Norwalk (06854) ***(G-6323)***
Reynolds and Reynolds Company 203 323-3748
102 Fieldstone Ter Stamford (06902) ***(G-8392)***
Reynolds Carbide Die Co Inc 860 283-8246
27 Reynolds Bridge Rd Thomaston (06787) ***(G-8802)***
Rf Printing LLC 203 265-9939
200 Church St Ste 5 Wallingford (06492) ***(G-9352)***
RFS Americas 203 630-3311
175 Corporate Ct Meriden (06450) ***(G-4231)***
RG Woodworking LLC 860 742-0397
327 Dunn Rd Coventry (06238) ***(G-1671)***
Rgb Woodworking 203 537-1177
730 Allen Ave Meriden (06451) ***(G-4232)***
Rgd Technologies Corp 860 589-0756
50 Emmett St Bristol (06010) ***(G-1107)***
Rh Rosen Group, Trumbull *Also called Eagle Consulting LLC* ***(G-9023)***
Rhino Energy Holdings LLC 203 862-7000
411 W Putnam Ave Ste 125 Greenwich (06830) ***(G-3226)***
Rhino Shelters, Milford *Also called Mdm Products LLC* ***(G-4576)***
Rhode Island Beverage Journal 203 288-3375
2508 Whitney Ave Hamden (06518) ***(G-3505)***
Rhode Island Raceway LLC 860 701-0192
846 Vauxhall Street Ext Quaker Hill (06375) ***(G-7084)***
Ribeiro Woodworking LLC 203 942-5838
19 Putnam Park Rd Bethel (06801) ***(G-335)***
Ricci Cabinet &STair Co 203 889-6511
110 Constitution St Wallingford (06492) ***(G-9353)***
Riccio Artifacts 860 267-6023
18 Abbey Rd East Hampton (06424) ***(G-2277)***
Ricco Vishnu 203 449-0124
79 Sage Ave Bridgeport (06610) ***(G-890)***
Ricco Vishnu Brew House, Bridgeport *Also called Swagnificent Ent LLC* ***(G-918)***
Rice Lake Weighing Systems Inc 203 270-6012
3 Simm Ln Ste 2a Newtown (06470) ***(G-5775)***
Rice Packaging Inc 860 870-7057
356 Somers Rd Ellington (06029) ***(G-2598)***
Rich Plastic Products Inc 203 235-4241
57 High St Meriden (06450) ***(G-4233)***
Rich Products Corporation 866 737-8884
263 Myrtle St New Britain (06053) ***(G-5042)***
Rich Products Corporation 800 356-7094
263 Myrtle St New Britain (06053) ***(G-5043)***
Rich Products Corporation 860 827-8000
1 Celebration Way New Britain (06053) ***(G-5044)***
Rich Products Corporation 609 589-3049
263 Myrtle St New Britain (06053) ***(G-5045)***
Rich Signs & Designs 860 429-2165
55 Timber Ln Willington (06279) ***(G-10256)***
Rich Snob Fashions, Bridgeport *Also called Ricco Vishnu* ***(G-890)***
Richard Batchelder 860 526-1614
61 Winthrop Rd Chester (06412) ***(G-1481)***
Richard Breault 203 876-2707
117 North St Milford (06460) ***(G-4626)***
Richard Dahlen 860 584-8226
350 Riverside Ave Bristol (06010) ***(G-1108)***
Richard Dudgeon Inc 203 336-4459
24 Swift Pl Waterbury (06710) ***(G-9593)***
Richard G Swartwout Jr 860 377-2321
627 Route 6 Andover (06232) ***(G-16)***
Richard Manufacturing Co Inc 203 874-3617
250 Rock Ln Milford (06460) ***(G-4627)***
Richard Riggio and Sons Inc 860 767-0812
90 Pond Meadow Rd Ivoryton (06442) ***(G-3789)***
Richard Sadowski 203 372-2151
290 Euclid Ave Fairfield (06825) ***(G-2836)***
Richard Walker 860 267-7117
69 Collie Brook Rd East Hampton (06424) ***(G-2278)***
Richard Woodworking 203 265-0887
7 Sunny Ct Wallingford (06492) ***(G-9354)***

ALPHABETIC

(PA)=Parent Co (HQ)=Headquarters (DH)=Div Headquarters
2020 Harris Connecticut
Manufacturers Directory
569

Richards Creative Interiors.......203 484-0361
1060 S Colony Rd Wallingford (06492) ***(G-9355)***
Richards Machine Tool Co Inc.......860 436-2938
187 Stamm Rd Newington (06111) ***(G-5701)***
Richards Metal Products Inc.......203 879-2555
14 Swiss Ln Wolcott (06716) ***(G-10583)***
Richardson Machine.......860 859-1458
162 Connecticut Blvd Oakdale (06370) ***(G-6446)***
Richies Automotive LLC.......860 482-0667
205 Birge Park Rd Harwinton (06791) ***(G-3737)***
Richmond Press.......860 649-0552
676 Main St South Windsor (06074) ***(G-7819)***
Richmond Woodworks LLC.......860 974-9995
321 Perrin Rd Apt C Woodstock (06281) ***(G-10680)***
Richter Electric Inc.......203 667-4644
27 Middlesex Rd Darien (06820) ***(G-2041)***
Ricia Mainhardt Agency.......718 434-1893
85 Lincoln St Apt 1 Meriden (06451) ***(G-4234)***
Rick Bulach.......860 875-7999
36 Cone Rd Hebron (06248) ***(G-3756)***
Rick's Sugar Shack, East Hampton *Also called Richard Walker* ***(G-2278)***
Ridge View Associates Inc.......203 878-8560
122 Cascade Blvd Milford (06460) ***(G-4628)***
Ridgefeld Scrnprinting EMB LLC.......203 438-1203
71 Hussars Camp Pl Ridgefield (06877) ***(G-7167)***
Ridgefield Overhead Door LLC.......203 431-3667
703 Danbury Rd Ste 4 Ridgefield (06877) ***(G-7168)***
Ridgetop Publishing LLC.......860 489-9555
37 Richards Rd New Hartford (06057) ***(G-5210)***
Ridgeway Racing, Vernon *Also called Crystal Tool and Machine Co* ***(G-9136)***
Riendeau & Sons Logging LLC.......860 429-7919
109 Supina Rd Ashford (06278) ***(G-64)***
Riff Company Inc.......203 272-4899
1484 Highland Ave Ste 7 Cheshire (06410) ***(G-1439)***
Rimark Manufacturing LLC.......860 924-6222
6 Talcott Range Dr East Granby (06026) ***(G-2227)***
Rinco Ultrasonics USA Inc.......203 744-4500
87 Sand Pit Rd Ste 1b Danbury (06810) ***(G-1929)***
Rindle LLC.......551 482-2037
3 Richards Ave Norwalk (06854) ***(G-6324)***
Rings Wire Inc (PA).......203 874-6719
257 Depot Rd Milford (06460) ***(G-4629)***
Rintec Corporation.......860 274-3697
30 Mclennan Dr Oakville (06779) ***(G-6462)***
Riopel Industries.......860 384-9610
31 Dipietro Ln Bristol (06010) ***(G-1109)***
Ripley, Cromwell *Also called Crrc LLC* ***(G-1697)***
Ripley Tools LLC (PA).......860 635-2200
46 Nooks Hill Rd Cromwell (06416) ***(G-1715)***
Risdon Manufacturing Co.......860 283-2000
60 Electric Ave Thomaston (06787) ***(G-8803)***
Rise Brewing Co, Stamford *Also called Riseandshine Corporation* ***(G-8393)***
Riseandshine Corporation (PA).......917 599-7541
425 Fairfield Ave 1a11 Stamford (06902) ***(G-8393)***
Risha Rishi LLC.......860 346-7645
596 Washington St Middletown (06457) ***(G-4405)***
Rising Sign Company Inc.......203 853-4155
50 Commerce St Ste 1 Norwalk (06850) ***(G-6325)***
Rissolo Precision Sheet Metal.......860 355-1949
22 Palomino Dr New Milford (06776) ***(G-5585)***
Ritas of Milford.......203 301-4490
175 Boston Post Rd Milford (06460) ***(G-4630)***
Ritch Herald & Linda.......203 661-8634
10 Fort Hill Ln Greenwich (06831) ***(G-3227)***
Rite Way Cleaner.......203 789-9561
192 Dixwell Ave Ste 1 New Haven (06511) ***(G-5380)***
Rite-Way Cleaners & Tailors, New Haven *Also called Rite Way Cleaner* ***(G-5380)***
Rite-Way Electric Motors Inc.......860 528-8890
27 Franklin St East Hartford (06108) ***(G-2366)***
Riveal Technologies LLC.......203 935-0997
74 Hillwood Ln Meriden (06450) ***(G-4235)***
River Dog Prints LLC.......860 276-1578
50 Forge Dr Avon (06001) ***(G-105)***
River Mill Co.......860 669-5915
43 River Rd Clinton (06413) ***(G-1521)***
River Valley Oil Service LLC.......860 342-5670
695 Portland Cobalt Rd Portland (06480) ***(G-6973)***
River Valley Photographic LLC.......860 368-0882
908 Main St 2ff South Glastonbury (06073) ***(G-7682)***
River Valley Stairs LLC.......860 767-7561
21 Main St Essex (06426) ***(G-2732)***
Rivera Marina.......917 676-4100
1290 Townsend Ave Apt 2 New Haven (06513) ***(G-5381)***
Rivers Edge Sugar House.......860 429-1510
326 Mansfield Rd Ashford (06278) ***(G-65)***
Riverside Aviation.......203 637-4231
8 Rocky Point Rd Old Greenwich (06870) ***(G-6483)***
Riverside Baking Company LLC.......203 451-0331
1891 Post Rd Fairfield (06824) ***(G-2837)***
Riverside Boat Covers Cushions, Cos Cob *Also called Riverside Seat Cover Inc* ***(G-1640)***
Riverside Express.......203 326-1245
1117 E Putnam Ave Ste 264 Riverside (06878) ***(G-7201)***
Riverside Seat Cover Inc.......203 661-7893
535 E Putnam Ave Cos Cob (06807) ***(G-1640)***
Riveting Systems USA LLC.......203 366-4557
90 Silliman Ave Bridgeport (06605) ***(G-891)***
Rj 15 Inc.......860 585-0111
115 Cross St Bristol (06010) ***(G-1110)***
Rj Cabinetry LLC.......203 515-8401
943 Post Rd E Westport (06880) ***(G-10149)***
Rj Kach Ltd.......203 457-1349
21 Old Toll Rd Madison (06443) ***(G-3951)***
Rjtb Group LLC.......203 531-7216
253 Mill St Greenwich (06830) ***(G-3228)***
Rjtb Initiatives Inc.......203 531-7216
253 Mill St Greenwich (06830) ***(G-3229)***
Rk Machine, New Britain *Also called R K Machine Company LLC* ***(G-5039)***
RK Manufacturing Corp Conn.......203 797-8700
34 Executive Dr Ste 2 Danbury (06810) ***(G-1930)***
Rk Stucco LLC.......860 331-1791
29 Curtin Ave New Britain (06053) ***(G-5046)***
RKP Printing Services LLC.......860 242-0131
79 W Eggleston St Bloomfield (06002) ***(G-477)***
Rlf Homes, Hartford *Also called R L Fisher Inc* ***(G-3674)***
Rlp Inc.......203 359-2504
12 Magee Ave Stamford (06902) ***(G-8394)***
Rm Landclearing & Logging LLC.......860 228-1499
10 Pine St Columbia (06237) ***(G-1611)***
Rm Printing.......860 621-0498
384 Old Turnpike Rd Plantsville (06479) ***(G-6909)***
Rmi, Stafford Springs *Also called Msj Investments Inc* ***(G-8033)***
Rmi Inc.......860 875-3366
130 Old Town Rd Vernon Rockville (06066) ***(G-9177)***
Rmi Corporation.......860 680-7368
20 Tower Ln Avon (06001) ***(G-106)***
RMS Wood Works LLC.......203 405-3051
140 Old Town Farm Rd Woodbury (06798) ***(G-10653)***
Road Bike, Norwalk *Also called Tam Communications Inc* ***(G-6362)***
Road-Fit Enterprises LLC.......860 371-5137
98 Whiting St Plainville (06062) ***(G-6856)***
Roaming Raceway and RR LLC.......413 531-3390
755 Sheldon St Suffield (06078) ***(G-8733)***
Roaring Acres Alpacas LLC.......860 668-7075
685 Hale St Suffield (06078) ***(G-8734)***
Roaring Brook Veterenary Hosp, Canton *Also called Veterinary Medical Associates* ***(G-1327)***
Robert Audette (PA).......203 872-3119
1732 S Main St Cheshire (06410) ***(G-1440)***
Robert Chang.......203 737-2264
1500 Bedford St Apt 203 Stamford (06905) ***(G-8395)***
Robert Dinucci.......860 561-3730
469 Mountain Rd Hartford (06117) ***(G-3679)***
Robert Downey Logging.......860 693-2914
31 Wright Rd Collinsville (06019) ***(G-1602)***
Robert J Ballas.......203 746-0506
14 Jeremy Dr New Fairfield (06812) ***(G-5175)***
Robert Kenneth Andrade LLC.......203 937-8697
975 Campbell Ave West Haven (06516) ***(G-9949)***
Robert L Lovallo.......203 324-6655
127 Myrtle Ave Stamford (06902) ***(G-8396)***
Robert Louis Company Inc.......203 270-1400
31 Shepard Hill Rd Newtown (06470) ***(G-5776)***
Robert Ready.......203 853-0051
11 Woodland Rd Norwalk (06854) ***(G-6326)***
Robert Schwartz.......203 515-8162
6 Buckingham Ln Gaylordsville (06755) ***(G-2996)***
Robert W Broska Enterprises.......203 846-0583
11 Assisi Way Norwalk (06851) ***(G-6327)***
Robert Warren LLC (PA).......203 247-3347
1 Sprucewood Ln Westport (06880) ***(G-10150)***
Robin Reed Ltd LLC.......203 481-6378
175 E Main St Branford (06405) ***(G-642)***
Robinson Tape & Label Inc.......203 481-5581
32 Park Dr E Ste 1 Branford (06405) ***(G-643)***
Robison Music Media & Pubg LLC.......203 858-8106
15 Sullivan Rd Wallingford (06492) ***(G-9356)***
Roblo Woodworks, Stamford *Also called Robert L Lovallo* ***(G-8396)***
Robran Industries Inc.......203 510-6292
15 Palma Cir Waterbury (06704) ***(G-9594)***
Robust Software LLC.......860 231-9880
64 Whitehill Dr West Hartford (06117) ***(G-9852)***
Rock Hard Offroad LLC.......860 919-3118
168 N Plains Indus Rd Wallingford (06492) ***(G-9357)***
Rockefeller Treasury Services.......203 264-8404
905 Georges Hill Rd Southbury (06488) ***(G-7875)***
Rocket Books Inc.......203 372-1818
34 Ridgeway Rd Easton (06612) ***(G-2564)***
Rockhouse, West Haven *Also called Fed Russell LLC* ***(G-9908)***
Rocking Horse Saloon.......860 247-2566
181 Ann Uccello St Hartford (06103) ***(G-3680)***
Rockland Music LLC.......203 779-5299
130 Fort Path Rd Ste 11 Madison (06443) ***(G-3952)***
Rockwell Art & Framing LLC (PA).......203 762-8311
151 Old Ridgefield Rd # 101 Wilton (06897) ***(G-10325)***

Rockwood Manufacturing Co....800 582-2424
100 Sargent Dr New Haven (06511) ***(G-5382)***
Rockwood Service Corporation (PA)....203 869-6734
43 Arch St Greenwich (06830) ***(G-3230)***
Rodger Craig....203 264-8843
380 Old Waterbury Rd # 12 Southbury (06488) ***(G-7876)***
Rodney Tulba Welding & Fabg....860 442-9840
1 Myrock Ave Waterford (06385) ***(G-9667)***
Rodriguez Ruiz Rosa Margarita....860 840-0344
336 Jefferson St Hartford (06106) ***(G-3681)***
Roebic Laboratories Inc (PA)....203 795-1283
25 Connair Rd Orange (06477) ***(G-6626)***
Roehm America LLC....203 269-4481
528 S Cherry St Wallingford (06492) ***(G-9358)***
Roetech, Orange *Also called Roebic Laboratories Inc* ***(G-6626)***
Rogers Corporation....860 928-3622
245 Woodstock Rd Woodstock (06281) ***(G-10681)***
Rogers Fiber Optics, Chaplin *Also called Daniel K Rogers* ***(G-1338)***
Rogers Manufacturing Company....860 346-8648
72 Main St Rockfall (06481) ***(G-7215)***
Rogers Septic Tanks Inc....203 259-9947
1480 Post Rd E Westport (06880) ***(G-10151)***
Rogers Woodsiding....203 879-9747
30 Cedar Ave Wolcott (06716) ***(G-10584)***
Rokap Inc....203 265-6895
1002 Yale Ave Wallingford (06492) ***(G-9359)***
Rol-Vac Limited Partnership....860 928-9929
207 Tracy Rd Dayville (06241) ***(G-2072)***
Roland A Parent....860 928-9158
518 English Nghborhood Rd Woodstock (06281) ***(G-10682)***
Roll-Off Best Service LLC....860 350-2378
36 S End Plz New Milford (06776) ***(G-5586)***
Rollcorp LLC....860 347-5227
9 Red Orange Rd Middletown (06457) ***(G-4406)***
Rollease Acmeda Inc (PA)....203 964-1573
750 E Main St 7 Stamford (06902) ***(G-8397)***
Roller Bearing Co Amer Inc (HQ)....203 267-7001
102 Willenbrock Rd Oxford (06478) ***(G-6693)***
Roller Bearing Co Amer Inc....203 758-8272
86 Benson Rd Middlebury (06762) ***(G-4289)***
Roller Bearing Co Amer Inc....203 267-7001
1 Tribiology Ctr Oxford (06478) ***(G-6694)***
Rolling Motion Industries....860 846-0530
75 Northwest Dr Plainville (06062) ***(G-6857)***
Rollins Printing Incorporated....203 248-3200
3281 Whitney Ave Hamden (06518) ***(G-3506)***
Rollins Transmission Service, Stratford *Also called Connecticut Machine & Welding* ***(G-8598)***
Rollprint Packaging, Bloomfield *Also called Paxxus Inc* ***(G-461)***
Roma Tool & Machine Co....860 793-2315
65 Robert Jackson Way Plainville (06062) ***(G-6858)***
Roman Woodworking....860 490-5989
1181 East St New Britain (06051) ***(G-5047)***
Romano Construction LLC....203 223-3136
315 Old Waterbury Rd Southbury (06488) ***(G-7877)***
Romark Printing Service....860 691-0626
39 Webster Rd East Lyme (06333) ***(G-2474)***
Romco Contractors Inc....860 243-8872
12 E Newberry Rd Bloomfield (06002) ***(G-478)***
Rome Fastener Corporation....203 874-6719
257 Depot Rd Milford (06460) ***(G-4631)***
Rome Fastener Sales Corp....203 874-6719
257 Depot Rd Milford (06460) ***(G-4632)***
Ronaco Industries Inc....203 979-7712
141 Bacon Rd Roxbury (06783) ***(G-7281)***
Ronald Bottino....860 585-9505
381 Riverside Ave Bristol (06010) ***(G-1111)***
Ronald R Eschner....860 485-9373
283 Terryville Rd Harwinton (06791) ***(G-3738)***
Rondo America Incorporated....203 723-5831
209 Great Hill Rd Naugatuck (06770) ***(G-4917)***
Rondo Packaging Systems, Naugatuck *Also called Rondo America Incorporated* ***(G-4917)***
Roodle Rice & Noodle Bar....203 269-9899
1263 S Broad St Wallingford (06492) ***(G-9360)***
Roofing Solutions....860 444-0486
45 Bank St New London (06320) ***(G-5487)***
Roost Candle Co LLC....203 270-6577
16 Gelding Hill Rd Sandy Hook (06482) ***(G-7328)***
Rooster Malt Company LLC....203 364-7612
21 Plumtrees Rd Newtown (06470) ***(G-5777)***
Rosco Holdings Inc (PA)....203 708-8900
52 Harbor View Ave Stamford (06902) ***(G-8398)***
Rosco Laboratories Inc (HQ)....203 708-8900
52 Harbor View Ave Stamford (06902) ***(G-8399)***
Rose To Occassion LLC....860 628-6880
92 Monarch Dr Southington (06489) ***(G-7968)***
Rose To The Occasion Florist, Southington *Also called Rose To Occassion LLC* ***(G-7968)***
Rosemarie Querns....860 349-3315
66 Middlefield Rd Durham (06422) ***(G-2155)***
Rosemary Hallgarten Inc....203 259-1003
116 Sherman St Fairfield (06824) ***(G-2838)***
Roseville Designs LLC (PA)....203 858-5744
3 Cliff Ave Darien (06820) ***(G-2042)***
Rosie Blakes Chocolates LLC....732 604-3327
200 Myrtle St New Britain (06053) ***(G-5048)***
Ross Copy & Print LLC....203 933-8732
611 Campbell Ave West Haven (06516) ***(G-9950)***
Ross Curtis Product Inc....860 886-6800
45 Church St Norwich (06360) ***(G-6429)***
Ross Custom Cabinetry....203 913-2753
179 Buckingham Ave Milford (06460) ***(G-4633)***
Ross Custom Switches, Norwich *Also called Ross Curtis Product Inc* ***(G-6429)***
Ross Enterprises....860 308-2238
23 Edgewood St Apt 2s Hartford (06112) ***(G-3682)***
Ross Industries....203 838-6180
15 Rolling Ln Norwalk (06851) ***(G-6328)***
Ross Mfg & Design LLC....203 878-0187
124 Research Dr Ste A Milford (06460) ***(G-4634)***
Ross Type....203 227-2007
7 Lincoln St Westport (06880) ***(G-10152)***
Rossi Pter Signs Lettering LLC....860 684-9229
34 West St Stafford Springs (06076) ***(G-8035)***
Rossitto Welding Inc....860 223-1598
395 Allen St New Britain (06053) ***(G-5049)***
Rossomano Pictures....203 241-5087
35 Route 37 S Sherman (06784) ***(G-7603)***
Rostra Tool Company....203 488-8665
30 E Industrial Rd Branford (06405) ***(G-644)***
Rostra Vernatherm LLC....860 582-6776
106 Enterprise Dr Bristol (06010) ***(G-1112)***
Rotair Aerospace Corporation....203 576-6545
964 Crescent Ave Bridgeport (06607) ***(G-892)***
Rotating Composite Tech LLC....860 829-6809
49 Cambridge Hts Kensington (06037) ***(G-3818)***
Rothstein Associates Inc....203 740-7400
4 Arapaho Rd Brookfield (06804) ***(G-1219)***
Rothstein Ctlg On Distr Recvry, Brookfield *Also called Rothstein Associates Inc* ***(G-1219)***
Roto Hardware Systems, Chester *Also called Roto-Frank of America Inc* ***(G-1482)***
Roto-Die Company Inc....860 292-7030
7d Pasco Dr East Windsor (06088) ***(G-2516)***
Roto-Frank of America Inc....860 526-4996
14 Inspiration Ln Chester (06412) ***(G-1482)***
Rotondo Precast, Avon *Also called Oldcastle Infrastructure Inc* ***(G-97)***
Rotounderworld LLC....202 236-7103
2490 Black Rock Tpke Fairfield (06825) ***(G-2839)***
Round Hill Alpacas LLC....860 742-5195
56 Round Hill Rd Coventry (06238) ***(G-1672)***
Rovic, Oxford *Also called Marhall Browing Intl Corp* ***(G-6676)***
Rowayton Press LLC....203 866-6646
108 Witch Ln Norwalk (06853) ***(G-6329)***
Rowland Technologies Inc....203 269-9500
320 Barnes Rd Wallingford (06492) ***(G-9361)***
Rowley Spring & Stamping Corp....860 582-8175
210 Redstone Hill Rd # 2 Bristol (06010) ***(G-1113)***
Roxbury Cabinet Co LLC....203 994-9855
16 Evergreen Ln Roxbury (06783) ***(G-7282)***
Roy Tech, Meriden *Also called S J Pappas Inc* ***(G-4236)***
Royal Consumer Products LLC (HQ)....203 847-8500
108 Main St Ste 3 Norwalk (06851) ***(G-6330)***
Royal Ice Cream Company Inc (PA)....860 649-5358
27 Warren St Manchester (06040) ***(G-4083)***
Royal Ice Cream Company Inc....860 649-5358
16 Warren St Manchester (06040) ***(G-4084)***
Royal Machine and Tool Corp....860 828-6555
4 Willow Brook Dr Berlin (06037) ***(G-217)***
Royal Screw Machine Pdts Co....860 845-8920
409 Lake Ave Bristol (06010) ***(G-1114)***
Royal Welding LLC....860 232-5255
50 Francis Ave Ste 4 Hartford (06106) ***(G-3683)***
Royal Woodcraft Inc....203 847-3461
1 Riverside Dr Ansonia (06401) ***(G-49)***
Royaltees LLC....203 767-2808
1645 Chopsey Hill Rd Bridgeport (06606) ***(G-893)***
Royce Industries Inc (PA)....860 674-2700
357 Captain Lewis Dr Southington (06489) ***(G-7969)***
Roys Family Pools & Billiards....860 546-0608
7 Plainfield Rd Canterbury (06331) ***(G-1301)***
Rozelle Specialty Processes....860 793-9400
123 Whiting St Ste G Plainville (06062) ***(G-6859)***
Rp3 Canvas LLC....860 225-7140
105 Jubilee St New Britain (06051) ***(G-5050)***
RR Design....203 792-3419
13 Hearthstone Dr Bethel (06801) ***(G-336)***
Rs Tutoring, Trumbull *Also called Real Sltons Edctl Cnslting Inc* ***(G-9062)***
RSA Corp....203 790-8100
36 Old Sherman Tpke Danbury (06810) ***(G-1931)***
Rsa Laboratories, Hebron *Also called Radiation Safety Assoc Inc* ***(G-3754)***
Rscc Wire & Cable LLC (HQ)....860 653-8300
20 Bradley Park Rd East Granby (06026) ***(G-2228)***
Rsl Fiber Systems LLC....860 282-4930
473 Silver Ln East Hartford (06118) ***(G-2367)***
Rss Enterprises LLC....203 736-6220
101 Elizabeth St Ste 7 Derby (06418) ***(G-2124)***

ALPHABETIC

RT Vanderbilt Holding Co Inc (PA)   ALPHABETIC SECTION

RT Vanderbilt Holding Co Inc (PA) 203 295-2141
  30 Winfield St Norwalk (06855) *(G-6331)*
RTC Mfg Co Inc 800 888-3701
  1094 Echo Lake Rd Watertown (06795) *(G-9731)*
Rti Technologies LLC (PA) 860 306-4772
  32 Lake Rd Columbia (06237) *(G-1612)*
RTS Corporation 203 459-9835
  115 Technology Dr A201 Trumbull (06611) *(G-9065)*
Rubber Fabricators, Ansonia Also called Jay Tee Corp *(G-41)*
Rubber Labels USA LLC 203 713-8059
  500 Bic Dr Bldg 2 Milford (06461) *(G-4635)*
Rubber Supplies Company Inc 203 736-9995
  1 Park Ave Ste 1 # 1 Derby (06418) *(G-2125)*
Rubberhouse 860 646-3012
  29 Mount Sumner Dr Bolton (06043) *(G-518)*
Rubco Products Company 860 496-1178
  1697 E Main St Torrington (06790) *(G-8965)*
Ruby Automation Inc (HQ) 860 687-5000
  1 Vision Way Bloomfield (06002) *(G-479)*
Ruby Fluid Power LLC (HQ) 860 243-7100
  1 Vision Way Bloomfield (06002) *(G-480)*
Ruby Industrial Tech LLC (PA) 860 687-5000
  1 Vision Way Bloomfield (06002) *(G-481)*
Ruch Industries LLC 203 268-6514
  686 Fairchild Rd Trumbull (06611) *(G-9066)*
Ruckus Media Group Inc 203 939-1409
  55 Tory Hill Ln Norwalk (06853) *(G-6332)*
Ruckus Wireless Inc 203 303-6400
  15 Sterling Dr Wallingford (06492) *(G-9362)*
Rugsalecom LLC 860 756-0959
  17 S Main St West Hartford (06107) *(G-9853)*
Ruiz Impress Scrn Printg & 203 750-0050
  430 Main Ave Norwalk (06851) *(G-6333)*
Ruiz Impressions Screen Prntg 203 559-4865
  31 N Taylor Ave Norwalk (06854) *(G-6334)*
Runway Liquidation LLC 202 865-3311
  2510 E 15th St Cromwell (06416) *(G-1716)*
Runway Liquidation LLC 202 544-1900
  2812 N Univisity Dr Brookfield (06804) *(G-1220)*
Runway Liquidation LLC 202 466-2050
  112 S 42nd St Bristol (06010) *(G-1115)*
Runway Liquidation LLC 239 337-2020
  15 Corporate Dr Trumbull (06611) *(G-9067)*
Runway Liquidation LLC 302 998-0551
  3033 W Jefferson St Bloomfield (06002) *(G-482)*
Runway Liquidation LLC 561 391-3334
  3802 A Britton Plz Enfield (06082) *(G-2688)*
Runway Liquidation LLC 561 279-4444
  2320 Gala St Simsbury (06070) *(G-7643)*
Russell Amy Kahn (PA) 203 438-2133
  225 S Salem Rd Ridgefield (06877) *(G-7169)*
Russell Organics LLC 203 285-6633
  329 Main St Ste 208 Wallingford (06492) *(G-9363)*
Russell Partition Co Inc 203 239-5749
  20 Dodge Ave North Haven (06473) *(G-5988)*
Russell Speeders Car Wash LLC 203 925-0083
  811 River Rd Shelton (06484) *(G-7547)*
Russian Flare LLC 860 404-1781
  24 Brentwood Dr Avon (06001) *(G-107)*
Rustic Rstrtions Race Cars LLC 203 929-4813
  3 Spoke Dr Shelton (06484) *(G-7548)*
Rv Parts & Electric Inc 203 754-5962
  385 S Leonard St Waterbury (06708) *(G-9595)*
RWK Tool Inc 860 635-0116
  200 Corporate Row Cromwell (06416) *(G-1717)*
RWS Co Inc 860 434-2961
  41 Brockway Ferry Rd Old Lyme (06371) *(G-6518)*
RWS Marine Restoration 860 350-4977
  26 Old Route 7 Plz New Milford (06776) *(G-5587)*
Rwt Corporation 203 245-2731
  32 New Rd Madison (06443) *(G-3953)*
Rx Analytic Inc 203 733-0837
  6 Bob Hill Rd Ridgefield (06877) *(G-7170)*
Ryall Rbert Archtctral Ir Wrks 203 458-1356
  1352 Little Meadow Rd Guilford (06437) *(G-3387)*
Ryan Industries LLC 860 716-0226
  95 Rye St Broad Brook (06016) *(G-1152)*
Rydz Engineering 203 878-5499
  136 Research Dr Ste H Milford (06460) *(G-4636)*
Rykam LLC 860 721-1411
  657 Main St East Hartford (06108) *(G-2368)*
S & F Tools LLC 860 224-6839
  551 Stanley St New Britain (06051) *(G-5051)*
S & J Stucco LLC 203 260-1457
  454 Moose Hill Rd Monroe (06468) *(G-4751)*
S & L Systems 203 757-6159
  60 Fiske St Waterbury (06710) *(G-9596)*
S & M Swiss Products Inc 860 283-4020
  135 S Main St Ste 7 Thomaston (06787) *(G-8804)*
S & S Sealcoating LLC 203 284-0054
  5 Barker Dr Wallingford (06492) *(G-9364)*
S & S Worldwide Inc 860 537-3451
  75 Mill St Colchester (06415) *(G-1574)*

S & V Screen Printing 203 208-3112
  288 E Main St Apt 4 Branford (06405) *(G-645)*
S A Candelora Enterprises 203 484-2863
  250 Totoket Rd North Branford (06471) *(G-5854)*
S A It Grind 860 903-1455
  2 North Rd East Windsor (06088) *(G-2517)*
S and Z Graphics LLC 203 783-9675
  415 Boston Post Rd Ste 7 Milford (06460) *(G-4637)*
S C T, Norwalk Also called Sound Control Technologies *(G-6352)*
S Camerota & Sons Inc 203 782-0360
  166 Universal Dr Unit 2 North Haven (06473) *(G-5989)*
S D & D Inc 860 357-2603
  99 Clark Dr 1 East Berlin (06023) *(G-2175)*
S G R Woodworks 203 216-3327
  2 Woodfield Dr Trumbull (06611) *(G-9068)*
S Hassel Golf Works 860 274-4011
  55 Morehouse Rd Watertown (06795) *(G-9732)*
S J Pappas Inc 203 237-7701
  718 Old Colony Rd Meriden (06451) *(G-4236)*
S Karger Publishers Inc 860 675-7834
  26 W Avon Rd Unionville (06085) *(G-9126)*
S M Churyk Iron Works Inc 860 355-1777
  539 Danbury Rd New Milford (06776) *(G-5588)*
S M D, Stamford Also called Surface Mount Devices LLC *(G-8452)*
S P, East Windsor Also called Specialty Printing LLC *(G-2521)*
S P & G, Stamford Also called Speed Printing & Graphics Inc *(G-8433)*
S P E, Bethel Also called Society Plastics Engineers Inc *(G-344)*
S P Johnson Inc 860 871-8664
  20 Bowles Rd Stafford Springs (06076) *(G-8036)*
S S Fabrications Inc 860 974-1910
  82 County Rd Eastford (06242) *(G-2541)*
S Tm Embroidery LLC 860 376-4537
  290 Preston Rd Jewett City (06351) *(G-3800)*
S&A Puzzle LLC 860 675-0477
  468 Lovely St Avon (06001) *(G-108)*
S&V Screenprinting & Embroider 203 468-7538
  121 Vista Dr East Haven (06512) *(G-2449)*
S-Frame Software LLC 203 421-8527
  7 Carmel Ct Madison (06443) *(G-3954)*
S-Y-M Products Company LLC 203 329-2469
  49 Clark Rd Litchfield (06759) *(G-3899)*
Saar Corporation 860 674-9440
  81 Spring Ln Farmington (06032) *(G-2955)*
Saatva Inc 877 672-2882
  8 Wright St Ste 108 Westport (06880) *(G-10153)*
Sabar Graphics LLC (PA) 203 467-3016
  330 Main St East Haven (06512) *(G-2450)*
Sabatino North America LLC (PA) 718 328-4120
  135 Front Ave West Haven (06516) *(G-9951)*
Sabol Associates 203 762-2183
  50 Village Walk Wilton (06897) *(G-10326)*
Sabol Industries LLC 203 430-6502
  349 W River Rd Orange (06477) *(G-6627)*
Sabon Industries Inc 203 255-8880
  150 Jennie Ln Fairfield (06824) *(G-2840)*
Saccuzzo Company Inc 860 665-1101
  149 Louis St Newington (06111) *(G-5702)*
Sacla North America Inc 203 855-1356
  1 Selleck St Fl 2 Norwalk (06855) *(G-6335)*
Sacred Grunds Cof Roasters LLC 860 717-2871
  1 Route 37 E Ste 1 # 1 Sherman (06784) *(G-7604)*
Sadlak Industries LLC 860 742-0227
  712 Bread And Milk St A9 Coventry (06238) *(G-1673)*
Sadlak Innovative Design, Coventry Also called Mike Sadlak *(G-1663)*
Sadlak Manufacturing LLC 860 742-0227
  712 Bread And Milk St # 7 Coventry (06238) *(G-1674)*
Saes Memry, Bethel Also called Memry Corporation *(G-326)*
Saf Industries LLC 203 729-4900
  106 Evansville Ave Meriden (06451) *(G-4237)*
Saf Industries LLC (HQ) 203 729-4900
  106 Evansville Ave Meriden (06451) *(G-4238)*
Safe Harbour Products Inc 203 295-8377
  1 Selleck St Ste 3e Norwalk (06855) *(G-6336)*
Safe Laser Therapy LLC 203 261-4400
  1747 Summer St Ste 4 Stamford (06905) *(G-8400)*
Safe Water 203 732-4806
  371 Roosevelt Dr Seymour (06483) *(G-7366)*
Safe-T-Tank Corp 203 237-6320
  25 Powers Dr Meriden (06451) *(G-4239)*
Safestart Systems LLC 203 221-0652
  80 Wells Hill Rd Weston (06883) *(G-10039)*
Safety Bags Inc 203 242-0727
  2 Corporate Dr Ste 250 Shelton (06484) *(G-7549)*
Safety Dispatch Inc 203 885-5722
  57 Jefferson Dr Ridgefield (06877) *(G-7171)*
Safety Tek Inc 203 785-1808
  28 Rockview Ter New Haven (06511) *(G-5383)*
Safin Wldg & Fabrication LLC 860 974-3831
  278 Eastford Rd Eastford (06242) *(G-2542)*
Saft America Inc 203 234-8333
  3 Powdered Metal Rd North Haven (06473) *(G-5990)*

ALPHABETIC SECTION

Sage Magazine 347 452-3752
  205 Prospect St New Haven (06511) *(G-5384)*
Saigeworks LLC 203 767-1035
  138 Chestnut Hill Rd Trumbull (06611) *(G-9069)*
Sail Spars Design LLC 860 429-9866
  455 Gurleyville Rd Storrs Mansfield (06268) *(G-8559)*
Saindon Crane Service 860 505-7245
  1830 Berlin Tpke Berlin (06037) *(G-218)*
Saint Cloud Mining, Wilton Also called Imagin Minerals *(G-10300)*
Saint Josephs Wood Pdts LLC 203 787-5746
  80 Middletown Ave New Haven (06513) *(G-5385)*
Saint Vincent De Paul Place 860 889-7374
  120 Cliff St Norwich (06360) *(G-6430)*
Sainte-Anne Custom Woodwork 203 961-9403
  50 Euclid Ave Stamford (06902) *(G-8401)*
Saints Woodworking LLC 860 657-4733
  111 Forest Ln Glastonbury (06033) *(G-3080)*
Saklax Manufacturing Company 860 242-2538
  1346 Blue Hills Ave Ste B Bloomfield (06002) *(G-483)*
Salamander Designs Ltd 860 761-9500
  811 Blue Hills Ave Bloomfield (06002) *(G-484)*
Salamon Industries LLC 860 612-8420
  250 John Downey Dr New Britain (06051) *(G-5052)*
Salem Stone Design Inc 860 439-1234
  18a Industrial Dr Waterford (06385) *(G-9668)*
Salem Vly Farms Ice Cream Inc 860 859-2980
  20 Darling Rd Salem (06420) *(G-7291)*
Sales Department, Woodstock Also called Pepperl + Fuchs Inc *(G-10677)*
Saleschain LLC 203 262-1611
  61 Mattatuck Heights Rd # 201 Waterbury (06705) *(G-9597)*
Salin-Mpregilo US Holdings Inc (HQ) 203 439-2900
  90 Fieldstone Ct Cheshire (06410) *(G-1441)*
Salisbury Artisans 860 435-0344
  80 Factory St Salisbury (06068) *(G-7297)*
Sallie Gawron 203 258-9851
  105 Blaine St Fairfield (06824) *(G-2841)*
Sally Conant 203 878-3005
  454 Old Cellar Rd Orange (06477) *(G-6628)*
Salsa Fresca New Haven 301 675-6226
  51 Broadway New Haven (06511) *(G-5386)*
Saltbox Press LLC 203 762-9731
  522 Ridgefield Rd Wilton (06897) *(G-10327)*
Saltwater Usa LLC 860 899-9240
  214 Cottage Grove Rd Bloomfield (06002) *(G-485)*
Sam & Ty LLC (PA) 212 840-1871
  12 S Main St Ste 403 Norwalk (06854) *(G-6337)*
Sam Augeri & Sons Signs 860 346-1261
  695 High St Ste A Middletown (06457) *(G-4407)*
Sam Maulucci & Sons, Wethersfield Also called Mozzicato Fmly Investments LLC *(G-10213)*
Same Day Dumpsters LLC 203 676-1219
  225 Quinnipiac Ave New Haven (06513) *(G-5387)*
Sammi Sleeping Systems LLC 203 684-3131
  5 Science Park New Haven (06511) *(G-5388)*
Sams Food Stores, Rocky Hill Also called Cco Llc *(G-7226)*
Samsara Fitness LLC 860 895-8533
  10 Denlar Dr Chester (06412) *(G-1483)*
Sanco Energy 203 259-5914
  41 Riders Ln Fairfield (06824) *(G-2842)*
Sandballz International LLC 860 465-9628
  832 Stafford Rd Storrs Mansfield (06268) *(G-8560)*
Sandpiper Electronics Inc 860 364-5558
  95 Westwoods Road 1 Sharon (06069) *(G-7383)*
Sandra Mercier Procaccin 203 929-6968
  234 Deer Run Shelton (06484) *(G-7550)*
Sandri Products 860 824-0001
  24 Sand Rd Canaan (06018) *(G-1291)*
Sandur Tool Co 203 753-0004
  853 Hamilton Ave Waterbury (06706) *(G-9598)*
Sandvik Heating Technogy USA, Bethel Also called Sandvik Wire and Htg Tech Corp *(G-338)*
Sandvik Pubg Interactive Inc (PA) 203 205-0188
  83 Wooster Hts Ste 208 Danbury (06810) *(G-1932)*
Sandvik Wire and Htg Tech Corp 203 744-1440
  119 Wooster St Bethel (06801) *(G-337)*
Sandvik Wire and Htg Tech Corp (HQ) 203 744-1440
  119 Wooster St Bethel (06801) *(G-338)*
Sandviks Inc (PA) 866 984-0188
  83 Wooster Hts Ste 110 Danbury (06810) *(G-1933)*
Sandy Brook Manufacturing LLC 860 205-4438
  12 Riverton Rd Colebrook (06021) *(G-1586)*
Sandy Hook Welding & Fabg 203 731-9844
  4 Forest Dr Sandy Hook (06482) *(G-7329)*
Sanford Redmond Inc 203 351-9800
  746 Riverbank Rd Stamford (06903) *(G-8402)*
Sangari Active Science, Greenwich Also called Sasc LLC *(G-3231)*
Sanguinaria Publishing Inc 203 576-9168
  85 Ferris St Bridgeport (06605) *(G-894)*
Santa Energy Corporation 800 937-2682
  154 Admiral St Bridgeport (06605) *(G-895)*
Santec Corporation 203 878-1379
  84 Old Gate Ln Milford (06460) *(G-4638)*
Santorini Breeze LLC 203 640-3431
  374 E Main St Branford (06405) *(G-646)*

Santoto LLC 203 984-2540
  Danbury Municipal Danbury (06810) *(G-1934)*
Saphlux Inc 475 221-8981
  4 Pin Oak Dr Branford (06405) *(G-647)*
Sapphire Mltnational Group Inc 860 693-1233
  21 Prospect St Ste B Torrington (06790) *(G-8966)*
Sara Campbell Ltd 203 966-5488
  137 Elm St New Canaan (06840) *(G-5139)*
Sarah May Block21prints 860 604-4004
  39 Forest St Unionville (06085) *(G-9127)*
Sargent Manufacturing Company 203 562-2151
  100 Sargent Dr New Haven (06511) *(G-5389)*
Sargent Quality Tools, Branford Also called Rostra Tool Company *(G-644)*
Sas Institute Inc 860 633-4119
  95 Glastonbury Blvd # 301 Glastonbury (06033) *(G-3081)*
Sasc LLC (PA) 203 846-2274
  44 Amogerone Crossway Greenwich (06830) *(G-3231)*
Sassone Labwear LLC 860 666-4484
  480 Barnum Ave Ste 5 Bridgeport (06608) *(G-896)*
Satellite Aerospace Inc 860 643-2771
  240 Chapel Rd Manchester (06042) *(G-4085)*
Satellite Tool & Mch Co Inc 860 290-8558
  185 Commerce Way Ste 1 South Windsor (06074) *(G-7820)*
Satin American Corporation 203 929-6363
  40 Oliver Ter Shelton (06484) *(G-7551)*
Satin Style LLC 203 287-5466
  331 Deerfield Dr Hamden (06518) *(G-3507)*
Satori Audio LLC 203 571-6050
  180 Post Rd E Ste 201 Westport (06880) *(G-10154)*
Satori Nyc, Westport Also called Satori Audio LLC *(G-10154)*
Saucier Welding Services 860 747-4577
  252 Washington Dr Southington (06489) *(G-7970)*
Sauciers Misc Metal Works LLC 860 747-4577
  89 Birch St Southington (06489) *(G-7971)*
Saugatuck Kitchens LLC 203 334-1099
  125 Bruce Ave Stratford (06615) *(G-8675)*
Saugatuck Tree & Logging LLC 203 470-9195
  117 Whisconier Rd Brookfield (06804) *(G-1221)*
Saugatuck Tree & Logging LLC (PA) 203 304-1326
  309 S Main St Newtown (06470) *(G-5778)*
Savage Arms Inc 860 668-7049
  118 Mountain Rd Suffield (06078) *(G-8735)*
Savage Products LLC 203 440-1766
  197 Pratt St Meriden (06450) *(G-4240)*
Savage Saws, East Haven Also called W J Savage Co Inc *(G-2459)*
Savant Publishing LLC 203 740-9850
  1 Deer Trail Dr Brookfield (06804) *(G-1222)*
Savetime Corporation 203 382-2991
  2710 North Ave Ste 105b Bridgeport (06604) *(G-897)*
Savin Rock Printing 203 500-1577
  145 Boston Post Rd West Haven (06516) *(G-9952)*
Savin Rock Software LLC 203 272-5039
  129 Crescent Cir Cheshire (06410) *(G-1442)*
Savoir Consulting & Mfg Co LLC 860 933-7614
  102 Latham Rd Willington (06279) *(G-10257)*
Savour Instant LLC 203 374-4599
  41 Flat Rock Rd Easton (06612) *(G-2565)*
Saw Mill Capital LLC 203 662-0573
  137 Hollow Tree Ridge Rd # 303 Darien (06820) *(G-2043)*
Saw Mill Sheet Metal LLC 860 779-3194
  143 Saw Mill Hill Rd Sterling (06377) *(G-8516)*
Saw Miners Mill 860 599-5012
  153 N Anguilla Rd Pawcatuck (06379) *(G-6724)*
Saxony Wood Products Inc 203 869-3717
  18 Beech St Greenwich (06830) *(G-3232)*
Say It With Signs 860 621-6535
  216 Summer St Plantsville (06479) *(G-6910)*
Saybrook Press Incorporated 203 458-3637
  39 Chaffinch Island Rd Guilford (06437) *(G-3388)*
Sazacks Inc 860 647-8367
  520 Center St Manchester (06040) *(G-4086)*
Sb USA, Southbury Also called Willoughby & Co LLC *(G-7886)*
Sca Pharmaceuticals LLC 501 312-2800
  755 Rainbow Rd Bldg 1 Windsor (06095) *(G-10431)*
Scan Tool & Mold Inc 203 459-4950
  2 Trefoil Dr Trumbull (06611) *(G-9070)*
Scan-Optics LLC 860 645-7878
  169 Progress Dr Manchester (06042) *(G-4087)*
Scantube Inc 203 743-0908
  22 Shelter Rock Ln # 24 Danbury (06810) *(G-1935)*
Scap Motors Inc 203 384-0005
  421 Tunxis Hill Rd Fairfield (06825) *(G-2843)*
Scapa Healthcare, Windsor Also called Scapa North America Inc *(G-10433)*
Scapa Holdings Inc (HQ) 860 688-8000
  111 Great Pond Dr Windsor (06095) *(G-10432)*
Scapa North America Inc (HQ) 860 688-8000
  111 Great Pond Dr Windsor (06095) *(G-10433)*
Scapa Tapes North America LLC (HQ) 860 688-8000
  111 Great Pond Dr Windsor (06095) *(G-10434)*
Scarlethread LLC 860 528-0667
  34 Laraia Ave East Hartford (06108) *(G-2369)*
Scene 1 Arts LLC 203 748-0899
  10 Library Pl Bethel (06801) *(G-339)*

(PA)=Parent Co (HQ)=Headquarters (DH)=Div Headquarters

Scenic Route Candle Co LLC 203 606-7300
67 S Montowese St Branford (06405) **(G-648)**
Schaefer Machine Company Inc 860 526-4000
200 Commercial Dr Deep River (06417) **(G-2099)**
Schaefer Rolls Inc 203 910-0224
32 Bolduc Ct Wolcott (06716) **(G-10585)**
Schaeffler Aerospace USA Corp (HQ) 203 744-2211
200 Park Ave Danbury (06810) **(G-1936)**
Schaeffler Aerospace USA Corp 860 379-7558
159 Colebrook River Rd Winsted (06098) **(G-10534)**
Schaeffler Group USA Inc 203 790-5474
200 Park Ave Danbury (06810) **(G-1937)**
Schick Manufacturing Inc (HQ) 203 882-2100
10 Leighton Rd Milford (06460) **(G-4639)**
Schick-Wilkinson Sword, Milford *Also called Schick Manufacturing Inc* **(G-4639)**
Schiess John 860 664-0336
100 Cow Hill Rd Clinton (06413) **(G-1522)**
Schindler Combustion LLC 203 371-5068
159 Tahmore Dr Fairfield (06825) **(G-2844)**
Schoenrock Marine Door Systems 203 600-8370
29 Massachusetts Ave East Haven (06512) **(G-2451)**
Scholastic Inc (HQ) 212 343-6100
90 Old Sherman Tpke Danbury (06810) **(G-1938)**
Scholastic Library Pubg Inc (HQ) 203 797-3500
90 Sherman Tpke Danbury (06816) **(G-1939)**
Scholastic Library Pubg Inc 573 632-1762
90 Old Sherman Tpke Danbury (06810) **(G-1940)**
Schrader Bellows 860 749-2215
80 Shaker Rd Enfield (06082) **(G-2689)**
Schrafel Paperboard Converting 203 931-1700
82 W Clark St Ste 1 West Haven (06516) **(G-9953)**
Schuco International, Newington *Also called Schuco USA Lllp* **(G-5703)**
Schuco USA Lllp (HQ) 860 666-0505
240 Pane Rd Newington (06111) **(G-5703)**
Schulz Consulting LLC 860 657-4497
160 Oak St Ste 1b Glastonbury (06033) **(G-3082)**
Schwank Archtctural Woodworker 203 912-0109
111 Redding Rd Redding (06896) **(G-7107)**
Schwartz Body Company LLC 203 234-6046
89 Stoddard Ave North Haven (06473) **(G-5991)**
Schwerdtle Stamp Company 203 330-2750
41 Benham Ave Bridgeport (06605) **(G-898)**
Schwing Bioset Technologies 203 744-2100
98 Mill Plain Rd Ste A Danbury (06811) **(G-1941)**
Scinetx LLC 203 355-3676
1836 Long Ridge Rd Stamford (06903) **(G-8403)**
Scitech Ingredients, Stamford *Also called Scitech International LLC* **(G-8404)**
Scitech International LLC 203 967-8502
50 Soundview Dr Stamford (06902) **(G-8404)**
Scope Technology Inc 860 963-1141
8 Center Pkwy Plainfield (06374) **(G-6752)**
Scotland Hardwoods, Scotland *Also called Hardwood Lumber Manufacturing* **(G-7332)**
Scotland Hardwoods LLC 860 423-1233
117 Ziegler Rd Scotland (06264) **(G-7333)**
Scots Landing 860 923-0437
929 Riverside Dr Fabyan (06245) **(G-2739)**
Scott A Hebert 860 990-0793
230 East St Plainville (06062) **(G-6860)**
Scott American LLC 203 733-5512
6 Regency Cir Trumbull (06611) **(G-9071)**
Scott C Parker 860 355-9738
80 Transylvania Rd Roxbury (06783) **(G-7283)**
Scott Metal Finishing, Bristol *Also called Scotts Metal Finishing LLC* **(G-1116)**
Scott Metal Products 860 928-4366
30 Crabtree Ln Woodstock (06281) **(G-10683)**
Scott Olson Enterprises LLC 860 482-4391
1707 E Main St Torrington (06790) **(G-8967)**
Scott Wallace Woodworking 860 867-7229
54 Boulder Ct Mystic (06355) **(G-4842)**
Scott Welding & Metal Products, Woodstock *Also called Scott Metal Products* **(G-10683)**
Scott Woodford 203 245-4266
817 Boston Post Rd Madison (06443) **(G-3955)**
Scotts Company LLC 860 642-7591
20 Industrial Rd Lebanon (06249) **(G-3862)**
Scotts Metal Finishing LLC 860 589-3778
310 Birch St Bristol (06010) **(G-1116)**
Scp Management LLC 860 738-2600
29 Industrial Park Rd New Hartford (06057) **(G-5211)**
Scrapbook Clubhouse 860 399-4443
20 Westbrook Pl Westbrook (06498) **(G-10007)**
Scrapeitrx LLC 203 918-8323
363 Hemlock Rd Fairfield (06824) **(G-2845)**
Screen Designs 203 797-9806
81 Codfish Hill Rd Bethel (06801) **(G-340)**
Screen Tek Printing Co Inc 203 248-6248
130 Welton St Hamden (06517) **(G-3508)**
Screen-Tech Inc 860 496-8016
230 Ella Grasso Ave Torrington (06790) **(G-8968)**
Screening Ink LLC 860 212-0475
39 Celtic Ct Enfield (06082) **(G-2690)**
Scribbling Scribe 203 329-7140
79 Hickory Rd Stamford (06903) **(G-8405)**
Scriptural RES & Pubg Co Inc 860 609-5138
550 N Main St Southington (06489) **(G-7972)**
SCRIPTURAL RESEARCH PUBG CO, Cheshire *Also called Scripture Research & Pubg Co* **(G-1443)**
Scripture Research & Pubg Co 203 272-1780
344 E Johnson Ave Ste 4 Cheshire (06410) **(G-1443)**
Scry Health Inc 203 936-8244
1 Bradley Rd Ste 404 Woodbridge (06525) **(G-10616)**
Scuttlebutt 860 572-3999
10 Cottrell St Mystic (06355) **(G-4843)**
SD Labs, Brookfield *Also called Global Shield Solutions LLC* **(G-1192)**
SDA Laboratories Inc 203 861-0005
280 Railroad Ave Ste 207 Greenwich (06830) **(G-3233)**
Sdi Systems Development 860 967-5464
13 Francis St Avon (06001) **(G-109)**
Sea House Press LLC 860 552-4141
155 Shore Rd Clinton (06413) **(G-1523)**
Sea-Lion America Company 860 316-5563
800 Plaza Middlesex 1 Middletown (06457) **(G-4408)**
Seaboard Industries Inc 973 427-8500
100 Benton St Unit A Stratford (06615) **(G-8676)**
Seaboard Metal Finishing Co 203 933-1603
410 John Downey Dr New Britain (06051) **(G-5053)**
Seaboard Plating, New Britain *Also called Seaboard Metal Finishing Co* **(G-5053)**
Seabuzz Boatworks 203 483-4576
15 Swift St Branford (06405) **(G-649)**
Seafarer Canvas 203 939-1872
45 Calf Pasture Beach Rd Norwalk (06855) **(G-6338)**
Seafarer Canvas (PA) 203 853-2624
144 Water St Norwalk (06854) **(G-6339)**
Seafood Gourmet Inc 203 272-1544
264 Lyman Rd Apt 3-13 Wolcott (06716) **(G-10586)**
Seal King Sealcoating 203 871-1423
11 Old Town Rd Bethel (06801) **(G-341)**
Sealed Air Corporation 203 791-3648
10 Old Sherman Tpke Danbury (06810) **(G-1942)**
Sealpro LLC 860 289-0804
721 Burnham St East Hartford (06108) **(G-2370)**
Sean Christian Leather LLC 787 690-7039
134 Abbotsford Ave West Hartford (06110) **(G-9854)**
Sean Mecesery 203 869-2277
5 Strickland Rd Cos Cob (06807) **(G-1641)**
Seaport Marine Inc 860 536-9651
2 Washington St Mystic (06355) **(G-4844)**
Searchlight LLC 203 577-4400
271 Southford Rd Middlebury (06762) **(G-4290)**
Seasaw LLC 203 815-9022
16 Fenway St N Milford (06460) **(G-4640)**
Seasons Media LLC 860 413-2022
6 Sharlin Dr West Simsbury (06092) **(G-9982)**
Seatek Wireless, Stamford *Also called Southwire Company LLC* **(G-8431)**
Seaview Plastic Recycling Inc 203 367-0070
938 Crescent Ave Bridgeport (06607) **(G-899)**
Seawolfs Products Co 203 225-0110
18 Longview Rd Shelton (06484) **(G-7552)**
Sebastian Kitchen Cabinets 203 853-4411
4 Taft St Ste B1 Norwalk (06854) **(G-6340)**
SEC Electrical Inc 203 562-5811
30 Gando Dr New Haven (06513) **(G-5390)**
Seclingua Inc 203 922-4560
52 Mill Valley Ln Stamford (06903) **(G-8406)**
Second Lac Inc (PA) 203 321-1221
401 Merritt 7 Ste 1 Norwalk (06851) **(G-6341)**
Second Wind Media Limited 203 781-3480
315 Front St New Haven (06513) **(G-5391)**
Secondaries Inc 203 879-4633
19 Venus Dr Wolcott (06716) **(G-10587)**
Secondary Operations Inc 203 288-8241
46 Manila Ave Hamden (06514) **(G-3509)**
Seconn Automation Solutions 860 442-4325
147 Cross Rd Waterford (06385) **(G-9669)**
Seconn Fabrication LLC 860 443-0000
180 Cross Rd Waterford (06385) **(G-9670)**
Sector 1 Defense, West Haven *Also called Max Padro* **(G-9933)**
Securemark Decal Corp 773 622-6815
20 Nutmeg Dr Trumbull (06611) **(G-9072)**
Securities Software & Con 860 242-7887
705 Bloomfield Ave Bloomfield (06002) **(G-486)**
Securities Software & Consulti 860 298-4500
80 Lamberton Rd Windsor (06095) **(G-10435)**
Security Systems Inc 800 833-3211
1125 Middle St Middletown (06457) **(G-4409)**
Seems Inc 203 284-0259
26 East St Ansonia (06401) **(G-50)**
Seesmart Inc 203 504-1111
177 Broad St Fl 12 Stamford (06901) **(G-8407)**
Sega Ready Mix Incorporated (PA) 860 354-3969
519 Danbury Rd New Milford (06776) **(G-5589)**
Sega Ready Mix Incorporated 203 465-1052
310 Chase River Rd Waterbury (06704) **(G-9599)**
SEI II Inc 203 877-8488
60 Commerce Park Ste 1 Milford (06460) **(G-4641)**

Seidel Inc ... 203 757-7349
1883 Thomaston Ave Waterbury (06704) *(G-9600)*
Seidel Inc ... 203 757-7349
2223 Thomaston Ave Waterbury (06704) *(G-9601)*
Seismic Monitoring Svcs LLC ... 860 753-6363
70 Black Rock Ave Danielson (06239) *(G-2001)*
Seitz LLC ... 860 489-0476
212 Industrial Ln Torrington (06790) *(G-8969)*
Sekisui Diagnostics LLC ... 203 602-7777
500 West Ave Stamford (06902) *(G-8408)*
Select Plastics LLC ... 203 866-3767
219 Liberty Sq Norwalk (06855) *(G-6342)*
Select Woodworking LLC ... 203 743-1159
11 Farm St Danbury (06811) *(G-1943)*
Selectcom Mfg Co Inc ... 203 879-9900
29 Nutmeg Valley Rd Wolcott (06716) *(G-10588)*
Selectives LLC ... 860 585-1956
166 Litchfield St Thomaston (06787) *(G-8805)*
Semco Instruments Inc (HQ) ... 661 257-2000
186 Cedar St Branford (06405) *(G-650)*
Semco Instruments Inc ... 661 362-6117
186 Cedar St Branford (06405) *(G-651)*
Semco Tool Manufacturing Co ... 203 723-7411
30 Naugatuck Dr Naugatuck (06770) *(G-4918)*
Seminar Services, Bethel *Also called Crown House Publishing Co LLC* *(G-274)*
Semiotics LLC ... 860 644-5700
1540 Pleasant Valley Rd D Manchester (06042) *(G-4088)*
Semipilot, Waterbury *Also called Hotseat Chassis Inc* *(G-9499)*
Senior Aerospace Connecticut, Enfield *Also called Senior Operations LLC* *(G-2691)*
Senior Network Inc ... 203 969-2700
777 Summer St Ste 103 Stamford (06901) *(G-8409)*
Senior Operations LLC ... 860 741-2546
4 Peerless Way Enfield (06082) *(G-2691)*
Senior Operations LLC ... 860 741-2546
4 Peerless Way Enfield (06082) *(G-2692)*
Senior Resource Publishing LLC ... 203 295-3477
27 5th St Stamford (06905) *(G-8410)*
Sens All Inc ... 860 628-8379
85 Water St Southington (06489) *(G-7973)*
Sensor Switch Inc (HQ) ... 203 265-2842
265 Church St Fl 15 New Haven (06510) *(G-5392)*
Sepdx ... 803 479-6332
291 Humphrey St Unit 1 New Haven (06511) *(G-5393)*
Sepsisdx ... 856 359-5309
291 Humphrey St Unit 1 New Haven (06511) *(G-5394)*
Sequel Special Products LLC ... 203 759-1020
1 Hillside Dr Wolcott (06716) *(G-10589)*
Sequent Consulting LLC ... 203 966-2340
925 Oenoke Rdg New Canaan (06840) *(G-5140)*
Serafin Sulky Co ... 860 684-2986
65 Buckley Hwy Stafford Springs (06076) *(G-8037)*
Serapure Technologies LLC ... 203 972-0481
17 Autumn Ln New Canaan (06840) *(G-5141)*
Serena Granbery Welding ... 860 435-2322
82 Indian Cave Rd Salisbury (06068) *(G-7298)*
Serge & Friends LLC ... 860 526-3882
34 Winthrop Blvd Cromwell (06416) *(G-1718)*
Servco Oil Inc ... 203 762-7994
387 Danbury Rd Wilton (06897) *(G-10328)*
Servers Storage Networking LLC ... 203 433-0808
25 Perry Ave Norwalk (06850) *(G-6343)*
Service Dept ... 203 335-1491
30 Unquowa Hill St Bridgeport (06604) *(G-900)*
Servicetune Inc ... 860 284-4445
107 Cider Brook Rd Avon (06001) *(G-110)*
Servotech Inc ... 860 632-0164
478 Timber Ridge Rd Middletown (06457) *(G-4410)*
Setma Inc ... 409 833-9797
458 Danbury Rd Ste A2 New Milford (06776) *(G-5590)*
Seven Stitches Screen Prntng ... 860 749-1166
9 Moody Rd Unit C-13 Enfield (06082) *(G-2693)*
Severance Foods Inc ... 860 724-7063
3478 Main St Hartford (06120) *(G-3684)*
Sew Beautiful Win Treatments ... 203 598-0544
203 Burr Hall Rd Middlebury (06762) *(G-4291)*
Seward Group LLC ... 203 357-1900
6 Oakshade Ave Darien (06820) *(G-2044)*
Sewn In America Inc (PA) ... 203 438-9149
54 Danbury Rd Ste 240 Ridgefield (06877) *(G-7172)*
Sextant Btsllc ... 203 500-3245
166 Route 81 Killingworth (06419) *(G-3839)*
Sfc Koenig LLC ... 203 245-1100
73 Defco Park Rd North Haven (06473) *(G-5992)*
Sfn LLC ... 203 314-8436
340 Boston St Guilford (06437) *(G-3389)*
Sga Components Group LLC ... 203 758-3702
13 Gramar Ave Prospect (06712) *(G-7024)*
Shadow Graphics ... 203 590-3533
21 Cottage St Trumbull (06611) *(G-9073)*
Shaeffer Plastic Mfg Corp ... 860 537-5524
523 Old Hartford Rd Colchester (06415) *(G-1575)*
Shagmeisters Enterprises ... 203 937-5584
94 4th Ave West Haven (06516) *(G-9954)*
Shamrock Sheet Metal ... 860 537-4282
23 Briarwood Dr Colchester (06415) *(G-1576)*
Shari Goodstein Rossi ... 914 485-1600
81 Kenosia Ave Danbury (06810) *(G-1944)*
Shari M Roth MD ... 860 676-2525
100 Simsbury Rd Ste 210 Avon (06001) *(G-111)*
Sharon M Stinson ... 860 218-7282
60 Ferry St Apt 2c Middletown (06457) *(G-4411)*
Sharon Masonry ... 860 307-7427
55 Norton St Torrington (06790) *(G-8970)*
Sharp Canvas ... 860 526-2302
22 Denlar Dr Apt D Chester (06412) *(G-1484)*
Sharp Racing Enterprises ... 203 699-1191
128 Blacks Rd Cheshire (06410) *(G-1444)*
Sharpac Cutter Grinding & Sls, Bridgeport *Also called Sharpac LLC* *(G-901)*
Sharpac LLC ... 203 384-0568
114 Miles St Bridgeport (06607) *(G-901)*
Sharpe Hill Vineyard Inc ... 860 974-3549
108 Wade Rd Pomfret (06258) *(G-6936)*
Sharpline Cabinetry LLC ... 203 261-8454
533 Sport Hill Rd Easton (06612) *(G-2566)*
Sharps & Flats ... 203 438-3300
16 Sullivan Dr Redding (06896) *(G-7108)*
Sharwood's, Westport *Also called Premier Foods Inc* *(G-10143)*
Shawnee Chemical ... 203 938-3003
429 Rock House Rd Redding (06896) *(G-7109)*
Shaws Pump Company Inc ... 860 872-6891
37 Windermere Ave Ellington (06029) *(G-2599)*
Shayna Bs & Pickle LLC ... 860 428-3835
627 Westford Rd Ashford (06278) *(G-66)*
Sheaffer Pen Corp ... 203 783-2894
1 Bic Way Ste 1 Shelton (06484) *(G-7553)*
Sheet Metal Systems, Milford *Also called Sheetmetal Systems Inc* *(G-4642)*
Sheetmetal Systems Inc ... 203 878-2633
30 Stran Rd Milford (06461) *(G-4642)*
Sheffield Pharmaceuticals LLC ... 860 442-4451
9 Wisconsin Ave Norwich (06360) *(G-6431)*
Sheffield Pharmaceuticals LLC (PA) ... 860 442-4451
170 Broad St New London (06320) *(G-5488)*
Sheila P Patrick ... 203 575-1716
179 Dwight St Waterbury (06704) *(G-9602)*
Shelbrack Woodworking ... 860 431-5028
15 Nod Brook Dr Simsbury (06070) *(G-7644)*
Shelco Filters Division, Middletown *Also called Tinny Corporation* *(G-4427)*
Sheldon Automotive Enterprises ... 203 372-4948
273 Wheeler Park Ave Fairfield (06825) *(G-2846)*
Sheldon Precision LLC ... 203 758-4441
10 Industrial Rd Waterbury (06712) *(G-9603)*
Sheldon Precision LLC ... 203 758-4441
10 Industrial Rd Prospect (06712) *(G-7025)*
Sheldon Woodworks ... 203 260-2703
895 Galloping Hill Rd Fairfield (06824) *(G-2847)*
Shelfgenie, Norwalk *Also called Lookout Solutions LLC* *(G-6237)*
Shell Shock Technologies Llc ... 203 557-3256
38 Owenoke Park Westport (06880) *(G-10155)*
Shelter Rock Winery ... 203 948-8235
5 Shelter Rock Rd Danbury (06810) *(G-1945)*
Shelterlogic Corp (HQ) ... 860 945-6442
150 Callender Rd Watertown (06795) *(G-9733)*
Shelters of America LLC ... 203 397-1037
73 Ford Rd Woodbridge (06525) *(G-10617)*
Shenondah Vly Specialty Foods ... 203 348-0402
28 Intervale Rd Stamford (06905) *(G-8411)*
Shepard Steel Co Inc (PA) ... 860 525-4446
110 Meadow St Hartford (06114) *(G-3685)*
Shepard Steel Co Inc ... 860 525-4446
55 Shepard Dr Newington (06111) *(G-5704)*
Sherri Masinda ... 860 429-4988
216 Luchon Rd Willington (06279) *(G-10258)*
Sherric Group LLC ... 860 673-3924
77 Lido Rd Unionville (06085) *(G-9128)*
Sherwood Equine LLC ... 860 653-3599
2 Hayfield Ln Granby (06035) *(G-3113)*
Sherwood Group Inc (PA) ... 203 227-5288
286 Post Rd E Westport (06880) *(G-10156)*
Shibumicom Inc ... 855 744-2864
50 Washington St Ste 302e Norwalk (06854) *(G-6344)*
Shield Group ... 203 981-6169
64 Danbury Rd Ste 700 Wilton (06897) *(G-10329)*
Shiller and Company Inc ... 203 210-5208
258 Thunder Lake Rd Wilton (06897) *(G-10330)*
Shillermath, Wilton *Also called Shiller and Company Inc* *(G-10330)*
Shiloh Software Inc ... 203 272-8456
718 Cortland Cir Cheshire (06410) *(G-1445)*
Shimmer LLC ... 860 875-4701
443 Buff Cap Rd Tolland (06084) *(G-8877)*
Shiner Signs Inc ... 203 634-4331
38 Elm St Ste 3 Meriden (06450) *(G-4241)*
Shippan Liquors ... 203 348-0925
316 Shippan Ave Stamford (06902) *(G-8412)*
Shippee Solar and Cnstr LLC ... 860 630-0322
111 Sabin St Putnam (06260) *(G-7064)*

ALPHABETIC

Shipstik LLC 203 417-8022
30 Sentry Hill Rd Roxbury (06783) *(G-7284)*
Shire Rgenerative Medicine Inc (HQ) 877 422-4463
36 Church Ln Westport (06880) *(G-10157)*
Shirt Graphix 203 294-1656
198 Center St Wallingford (06492) *(G-9365)*
Shirt Shark 860 552-4197
87 W Main St Clinton (06413) *(G-1524)*
Shm Welding and Repair LLC 860 267-4012
328 Moodus Rd East Hampton (06424) *(G-2279)*
Shock Sock Inc LLC 860 680-7252
409 Colt Hwy Farmington (06032) *(G-2956)*
Shop Smart Central Inc 914 962-3871
31 Pecks Ln Newtown (06470) *(G-5779)*
Shoppers Guide, Putnam *Also called Shoppers-Turnpike Corporation (G-7065)*
Shoppers-Turnpike Corporation 860 928-3040
70 Main St Putnam (06260) *(G-7065)*
Shore Publishing LLC 203 245-1877
724 Boston Post Rd Madison (06443) *(G-3956)*
Shore Therapeutics Inc 646 562-1243
177 Broad St Ste 1101 Stamford (06901) *(G-8413)*
Shoreline Boiler & Welding LLC 860 575-0944
43 Pepperidge Ave Westbrook (06498) *(G-10008)*
Shoreline Brewing Company LLC 203 225-7734
819 Bridgeport Ave Shelton (06484) *(G-7554)*
Shoreline Coatings LLC 203 213-3471
14 Commerce Dr Ste 1 North Branford (06471) *(G-5855)*
Shoreline Drone Solutions 347 239-5636
151 Flat Iron Rd Guilford (06437) *(G-3390)*
Shoreline Metal Services LLC 203 466-7372
250 Dodge Ave East Haven (06512) *(G-2452)*
Shoreline Segway Inc 203 453-6036
1310 Boston Post Rd Ste 5 Guilford (06437) *(G-3391)*
Shoreline Stair & Millwork Co 860 669-9591
10 Robin Ln Clinton (06413) *(G-1525)*
Shoreline Vine 203 779-5331
724 Boston Post 105a Madison (06443) *(G-3957)*
Shortell Framing, Hartford *Also called Michael Shortell (G-3642)*
Shotbyshop.com, Stamford *Also called Golf Research Associates (G-8218)*
Show Management Associates LLC 203 939-9901
8 Knight St Ste 205 Norwalk (06851) *(G-6345)*
Show Motion Inc 203 866-1866
1034 Bridgeport Ave Milford (06460) *(G-4643)*
Shurtape Specialty Coating LLC (HQ) 860 738-2600
29 Industrial Park Rd New Hartford (06057) *(G-5212)*
Shuster Machines, Plainville *Also called Shuster-Mettler Corp (G-6861)*
Shuster-Mettler Corp 203 562-3178
10 Sparks St Plainville (06062) *(G-6861)*
Shutters & Sails LLC 860 331-1510
31 Water St Mystic (06355) *(G-4845)*
Si Group USA (usaa) LLC (HQ) 203 702-6140
4 Mountainview Ter Danbury (06810) *(G-1946)*
Si Group USA Hldings Usha Corp (HQ) 203 702-6140
4 Mountainview Ter Danbury (06810) *(G-1947)*
Sia, Ridgefield *Also called Sewn In America Inc (G-7172)*
Siam Valee 203 269-6888
20 Ives Rd Wallingford (06492) *(G-9366)*
Sibtech Inc 203 775-5677
115 Commerce Dr Ste A Brookfield (06804) *(G-1223)*
Sideburnz 860 667-1900
87 Market Sq Hartford (06111) *(G-3686)*
Sidel & McElwreath LLC 203 834-2946
142 Old Kings Hwy Wilton (06897) *(G-10371)*
Sidney Dobson 203 255-5545
7 Palmieri Rd Westport (06880) *(G-10158)*
Siemens AG 860 651-1399
24 Old Barge Rd Simsbury (06070) *(G-7645)*
Siemon Company (PA) 860 945-4200
101 Siemon Company Dr Watertown (06795) *(G-9734)*
Siemon Company 860 945-4218
101 Siemon Company Dr Watertown (06795) *(G-9735)*
Siemon Global Project Services, Watertown *Also called Siemon Company (G-9734)*
Siempre LLC 203 873-0303
3360 Fairfield Ave Bridgeport (06605) *(G-902)*
Sifco Applied Srfc Cncepts LLC 860 623-6006
22 Thompson Rd Ste 2 East Windsor (06088) *(G-2518)*
Siftex Equipment Company 860 289-8779
52 Connecticut Ave Ste D South Windsor (06074) *(G-7821)*
Sigfridson Wood Products LLC 860 774-2075
125 Fitzgerald Rd Brooklyn (06234) *(G-1254)*
Sigg Switzerland (usa) Inc 203 321-1232
1177 High Ridge Rd Stamford (06905) *(G-8414)*
Siggpay Inc 203 957-8261
50 Water St Rear B Norwalk (06854) *(G-6346)*
Sigma Engineering Tech LLC 508 243-2888
19 Old Powder Hill Rd Durham (06422) *(G-2156)*
Sigma Tankers Inc 203 662-2600
20 Glover Ave Ste 5 Norwalk (06850) *(G-6347)*
Sigmavoip Llc 203 541-5450
980 Post Rd E Ste 3 Westport (06880) *(G-10159)*
Sigmawear 860 924-2908
202 New Britain Rd Berlin (06037) *(G-219)*

Sigmund Software LLC 800 448-6975
83 Wooster Hts Ste 210 Danbury (06810) *(G-1948)*
Sign A Rama 860 870-7446
536 Talcottville Rd Vernon Rockville (06066) *(G-9178)*
Sign A Rama 860 265-7996
3 Peerless Way Ste V Enfield (06082) *(G-2694)*
Sign A Rama 860 443-9744
365 Broad St New London (06320) *(G-5489)*
Sign A Rama 203 795-5450
553 Boston Post Rd Orange (06477) *(G-6629)*
Sign A Rama 203 792-4091
35 Eagle Rd Danbury (06810) *(G-1949)*
Sign A Rama Inc 203 674-8900
854 High Ridge Rd Stamford (06905) *(G-8415)*
Sign and Wonders LLC 860 274-8526
98 Birch St Watertown (06795) *(G-9736)*
Sign By Greubel 860 632-2573
1100 Corporate Row Cromwell (06416) *(G-1719)*
Sign Center Ltd Liability Co 203 549-9820
140 North Ave Bridgeport (06606) *(G-903)*
Sign Connection Inc 860 870-8855
101 West St Vernon Rockville (06066) *(G-9179)*
Sign Craft LLC 860 739-2863
5 Black Point Rd Niantic (06357) *(G-5817)*
Sign Creations 203 259-8330
89 Arbor Dr Southport (06890) *(G-8009)*
Sign Design & Display, East Berlin *Also called S D & D Inc (G-2175)*
Sign Factory 860 763-1085
25 Dust House Rd Enfield (06082) *(G-2695)*
Sign Fast 203 549-8500
3841 Main St Bridgeport (06606) *(G-904)*
Sign In Soft Inc 203 216-3046
1 Waterview Dr Shelton (06484) *(G-7555)*
Sign Language LLC 203 778-2250
71 Newtown Rd Ste 6 Danbury (06810) *(G-1950)*
Sign Maintenance Service Co 203 336-1051
24 Wallace St Bridgeport (06604) *(G-905)*
Sign of Flying Turtle LLC 860 830-3132
68 Kingswood Rd West Hartford (06119) *(G-9855)*
Sign of Our Times 860 669-4318
232 E Main St Clinton (06413) *(G-1526)*
Sign Pro Inc 860 229-1812
60 Westfield Dr Plantsville (06479) *(G-6911)*
Sign Professionals 860 823-1122
303 W Main St Norwich (06360) *(G-6432)*
Sign Smarts LLC (PA) 203 854-0808
2 Fair St Norwalk (06851) *(G-6348)*
Sign Solutions Inc 860 583-8000
1290 Farmington Ave Bristol (06010) *(G-1117)*
Sign Stop, East Hartford *Also called Rykam LLC (G-2368)*
Sign Stop, Wallingford *Also called Rokap Inc (G-9359)*
Sign Stop Inc 860 721-1411
657 Main St East Hartford (06108) *(G-2371)*
Sign Wiz LLC 860 351-5368
452 East St Ste 1r Plainville (06062) *(G-6862)*
Sign Wizard 860 525-7729
1 Union Pl Hartford (06103) *(G-3687)*
Sign-A-Rama, Vernon Rockville *Also called Sign A Rama (G-9178)*
Sign-A-Rama, Stamford *Also called Sign A Rama Inc (G-8415)*
Sign-A-Rama, Enfield *Also called Sign A Rama (G-2694)*
Sign-A-Rama, New London *Also called Sign A Rama (G-5489)*
Sign-A-Rama, Orange *Also called Sign A Rama (G-6629)*
Sign-A-Rama, Norwalk *Also called Jaime M Camacho (G-6216)*
Sign-A-Rama, Danbury *Also called Sign A Rama (G-1949)*
Sign-Grafx Group, Norwich *Also called Derrick Mason (G-6410)*
Sign-It LLC 203 377-8831
672 White Plains Rd Trumbull (06611) *(G-9074)*
Signage US, Meriden *Also called Shiner Signs Inc (G-4241)*
Signal Graphics Printing, Glastonbury *Also called Empire Printing Systems LLC (G-3034)*
Signature 22 Painting 914 450-9780
4 Driftway Rd Unit C2 Danbury (06811) *(G-1951)*
Signature Gold 860 523-0385
698 Park St Hartford (06106) *(G-3688)*
Signature Pet Memorials 860 455-0118
187 Federal Rd Chaplin (06235) *(G-1341)*
Signature Signs 860 704-0397
22 Green Briar Cir Middletown (06457) *(G-4412)*
Signature Signworks LLC 860 646-4598
10 Garth Ln Bolton (06043) *(G-519)*
Signcenter LLC 800 269-2130
333 Quarry Rd Milford (06460) *(G-4644)*
Signcrafters Inc 203 353-9535
874 E Main St Stamford (06902) *(G-8416)*
Signman Signs LLC 203 296-2846
775 Wood Ave Bridgeport (06604) *(G-906)*
Signmart LLC 860 347-7446
471 Washington St Middletown (06457) *(G-4413)*
Signs & Shirts, Prospect *Also called Cutting Edge Sgns Graphics LLC (G-6999)*
Signs By Anthony Inc 203 866-1744
19 Fitch St Norwalk (06855) *(G-6349)*

ALPHABETIC SECTION
Slater Hill Tool

Signs By Art Vassilopoulos, Ellington *Also called Art Signs* ***(G-2577)***
Signs By Autografix 203 481-6502
7 Svea Ave Branford (06405) ***(G-652)***
Signs By Flach 203 881-0272
59 Old Turnpike Rd Beacon Falls (06403) ***(G-147)***
Signs By MB 203 710-9948
202 Mixville Rd Cheshire (06410) ***(G-1446)***
Signs By Scavotto 860 745-5629
5 Whitewood St Enfield (06082) ***(G-2696)***
Signs By Tomorrow, Wallingford *Also called Image360* ***(G-9287)***
Signs Direct Inc 860 658-9589
4 Woods Ln Simsbury (06070) ***(G-7646)***
Signs Now LLC 860 667-8339
2434 Berlin Tpke Ste 14 Newington (06111) ***(G-5705)***
Signs of All Kinds 860 649-1989
227 Progress Dr Ste A Manchester (06042) ***(G-4089)***
Signs of America 860 412-0054
59 N Society Rd Brooklyn (06234) ***(G-1255)***
Signs of Success Inc 203 329-3374
1084 Hope St Stamford (06907) ***(G-8417)***
Signs On Demand 860 346-1720
777 Laurel Grove Rd Middletown (06457) ***(G-4414)***
Signs Plus Inc (PA) 860 653-0547
3 Turkey Hills Rd East Granby (06026) ***(G-2229)***
Signs Plus LLC 860 423-3048
700 Main St Willimantic (06226) ***(G-10236)***
Signs Pro LLC 203 323-9994
100 Research Dr Stamford (06906) ***(G-8418)***
Signs Unlimited Inc 203 734-7446
2 Francis St Derby (06418) ***(G-2126)***
Signworks Studios LLC 203 268-3993
86 Field Rock Rd Monroe (06468) ***(G-4752)***
Sikorsky Aircraft Corporation 203 384-7532
1201 South Ave Bridgeport (06604) ***(G-907)***
Sikorsky Aircraft Corporation 203 386-7861
1 Far Mill Xing Shelton (06484) ***(G-7556)***
Sikorsky Aircraft Corporation 516 228-2000
1 N Frontage Rd North Haven (06473) ***(G-5993)***
Sikorsky Aircraft Corporation 203 386-4000
1825 Main St Stratford (06615) ***(G-8677)***
Sikorsky Aircraft Corporation 203 386-4000
1210 South Ave Bridgeport (06604) ***(G-908)***
Sikorsky Aircraft Corporation (HQ) 203 386-4000
6900 Main St Stratford (06614) ***(G-8678)***
Sikorsky Aircraft Corporation 610 644-4430
9 Farm Springs Rd Ste 3 Farmington (06032) ***(G-2957)***
Sikorsky Commercial, Trumbull *Also called Helicopter Support Inc* ***(G-9033)***
Sikorsky Export Corporation 203 386-4000
6900 Main St Stratford (06614) ***(G-8679)***
Sikorsky International Product 203 375-0095
6900 Main St Stratford (06614) ***(G-8680)***
Silgan Closures Intl Holdg Co 203 975-7110
4 Landmark Sq Stamford (06901) ***(G-8419)***
Silgan Containers Corporation 203 975-7110
4 Landmark Sq Stamford (06901) ***(G-8420)***
Silgan Holdings Inc (PA) 203 975-7110
4 Landmark Sq Ste 400 Stamford (06901) ***(G-8421)***
Silgan Plastics LLC 860 526-6300
38 Bridge St Deep River (06417) ***(G-2100)***
Silicon Catalyst LLC 203 240-0499
258 W Mountain Rd Ridgefield (06877) ***(G-7173)***
Silicon Integration Inc 203 876-2844
241 Research Dr Ste 9 Milford (06460) ***(G-4645)***
Silicone Casting Technologies 860 347-5227
9 Red Orange Rd Middletown (06457) ***(G-4415)***
Silkscreen Plus LLC 203 879-0345
413 Wolcott Rd Wolcott (06716) ***(G-10590)***
Silkscreening Plus Inc 203 622-6909
175 Hamilton Ave Greenwich (06830) ***(G-3234)***
Silver Arrow Publisher LLC 203 265-4653
71 Curtis Ave Apt 3 Wallingford (06492) ***(G-9367)***
Silver Hill Woodworks LLC 860 318-1887
150 Kent Rd S Cornwall Bridge (06754) ***(G-1619)***
Silver Lining Technologies LLC 860 539-4182
48 Rainbow Trl Vernon (06066) ***(G-9152)***
Silver Little Shop Inc 860 678-1976
23 E Main St Avon (06001) ***(G-112)***
Silver Touch 203 778-1778
211 Greenwood Ave Ste 6 Bethel (06801) ***(G-342)***
Silvermine Press Inc 203 847-4368
4 Van Tassell Ct Norwalk (06851) ***(G-6350)***
Silversmith Inc 203 869-4244
392 W Putnam Ave Greenwich (06830) ***(G-3235)***
Simcha Designs 203 273-1593
53 Boxwood Dr Stamford (06906) ***(G-8422)***
Simkins Industries 203 787-7171
317 Foxon Rd Ste 3 East Haven (06513) ***(G-2453)***
Simmonds Precision Pdts Inc 203 797-5000
100 Wooster Hts Danbury (06810) ***(G-1952)***
Simon Pearce US Inc 203 861-0780
125 E Putnam Ave Greenwich (06830) ***(G-3236)***
Simoniz Usa Inc (PA) 860 646-0172
201 Boston Tpke Bolton (06043) ***(G-520)***

Simple Card Sort, Weatogue *Also called Jonathan David Humpherys* ***(G-9756)***
Simply Canvas LLC 203 265-0659
39 Reynolds Dr Wallingford (06492) ***(G-9368)***
Simply Originals LLC 203 273-3523
14 Crest Rd Norwalk (06853) ***(G-6351)***
Simply Signs 203 595-0123
48 Putter Dr Stamford (06907) ***(G-8423)***
Simply Soap 860 347-4174
86 Plumb Rd Middletown (06457) ***(G-4416)***
Simpson Strong-Tie Company Inc 860 741-8923
7 Pearson Way Enfield (06082) ***(G-2697)***
Simsbury Precision Products 860 658-6909
11 Herman Dr Ste C Simsbury (06070) ***(G-7647)***
Simson Products Co Inc 203 265-9882
50 N Plains Industrial Rd Wallingford (06492) ***(G-9369)***
Simulations LLC 860 978-0772
133 Hartford Ave Ste 3 East Granby (06026) ***(G-2230)***
Simunition Operations, Avon *Also called General Dynamics Ordnance* ***(G-82)***
Sin Frntras Hspnic Newsppr LLC 203 691-5986
266 Grand Ave New Haven (06513) ***(G-5395)***
Singers Welding Works 203 743-9353
44 Payne Rd Danbury (06810) ***(G-1953)***
Single Load LLC 860 944-7507
2056 Main St Bridgeport (06604) ***(G-909)***
Singularity Space Systems LLC 860 713-3626
33 Wolcott Dr Granby (06035) ***(G-3114)***
Sinish Works 860 693-0073
20 Dyer Ave Collinsville (06019) ***(G-1603)***
Sinol Usa Inc 203 470-7404
77 S Main St Newtown (06470) ***(G-5780)***
Sinsigalli Signs & Designs 860 627-8712
445 Spring St Wndsor Lcks Windsor Locks Windsor Locks (06096) ***(G-10496)***
Sir Speedy, Bloomfield *Also called Kool Ink LLC* ***(G-439)***
Sir Speedy Printing 203 346-0716
199 Park Road Ext Ste D Middlebury (06762) ***(G-4292)***
Sir Speedy Prntng Ctr of N Bri 860 826-1798
200 Main St New Britain (06051) ***(G-5054)***
Siri Manufacturing Company 860 236-5901
90 Wauregan Rd Danielson (06239) ***(G-2002)***
Sirocco Screenprints Inc 203 288-3565
376 State St North Haven (06473) ***(G-5994)***
Sirois Tool Company Inc (PA) 860 828-5327
169 White Oak Dr Berlin (06037) ***(G-220)***
Siskin Agency 860 561-2937
33 Quincy Ln Hartford (06111) ***(G-3689)***
Sister Act Printing 203 481-7171
229 Branford Rd Unit 455 North Branford (06471) ***(G-5856)***
Siteone Landscape Supply LLC 860 673-6912
15 Industrial Dr Avon (06001) ***(G-113)***
Sixfurlongs LLC 203 255-8553
382 Round Hill Rd Fairfield (06824) ***(G-2848)***
Sjm Properties Inc 860 979-0060
164 Maple St Ellington (06029) ***(G-2600)***
SJS Industries LLC 203 552-3001
21 Wilshire Rd Greenwich (06831) ***(G-3237)***
Sk Systems 860 691-0366
231 Boston Post Rd # 16 East Lyme (06333) ***(G-2475)***
Skaarship Apiaries LLC 860 805-9398
50 Hunting Ridge Rd Greenwich (06831) ***(G-3238)***
SKF Specialty Balls 860 379-8511
149 Colebrook River Rd Winsted (06098) ***(G-10535)***
SKF USA Inc 860 379-8511
149 Colebrook River Rd Winsted (06098) ***(G-10536)***
Ski Area Management, Woodbury *Also called Beardsley Publishing Corp* ***(G-10626)***
Skico Manufacturing Co LLC 203 230-1305
3 Industrial Cir Hamden (06517) ***(G-3510)***
Skillcraft Machine Tool Co 860 953-1246
255 Nutmeg Rd S South Windsor (06074) ***(G-7822)***
Skin & Co North America LLC 888 444-9971
135 Front Ave West Haven (06516) ***(G-9955)***
Skinner Valve Division 860 827-2300
95 Edgewood Ave New Britain (06051) ***(G-5055)***
Sky Mfg Company 203 439-7016
268 Sandbank Rd Cheshire (06410) ***(G-1447)***
Skyart Studio and Gallery, Meriden *Also called Carob Designs LLC* ***(G-4155)***
Skydog Kites LLC 860 365-0600
220 Westchester Rd Colchester (06415) ***(G-1577)***
Skyko International LLC (PA) 860 928-5170
243 New Sweden Rd Woodstock (06281) ***(G-10684)***
Skyline Exhibits & Graphics 860 635-2400
362 Industrial Park Rd # 6 Middletown (06457) ***(G-4417)***
Skyline Industries LLC 860 209-8013
362 Tolland St East Hartford (06108) ***(G-2372)***
Skyline Quarry 860 875-3580
110 Conklin Rd Stafford Springs (06076) ***(G-8038)***
Skyline Vet Pharma Inc 860 625-0424
37 Skyline Dr Groton (06340) ***(G-3312)***
Skytech Machining Inc 203 378-9994
765 Woodend Rd Stratford (06615) ***(G-8681)***
Skythink Inc 203 324-1108
1 Rock Spring Rd Apt 4 Stamford (06906) ***(G-8424)***
Slater Hill Tool 860 377-5503
134 Slater Hill Rd Dayville (06241) ***(G-2073)***

ALPHABETIC

Slater Hill Tool LLC ... 860 963-0415
  77 Industrial Park Rd Putnam (06260) *(G-7066)*
Sleep Management Solutions LLC (HQ) ... 888 497-5337
  20 Church St Ste 900 Hartford (06103) *(G-3690)*
Slide Rule Group LLC ... 860 317-1624
  25 Mortimer Rd Moosup (06354) *(G-4782)*
Slim-Fast Foods Company, Trumbull *Also called Conopco Inc* *(G-9015)*
Slinky, Greenwich *Also called Poof-Alex Holdings LLC* *(G-3217)*
Slogic Holding Corp (PA) ... 203 966-2800
  36 Grove St New Canaan (06840) *(G-5142)*
Slv Consulting Inc ... 917 892-4034
  6 Forest Ln Wilton (06897) *(G-10332)*
Small Black Dog, Bridgeport *Also called American Marketing Group Inc* *(G-693)*
Smantics ... 860 238-7714
  19 Rock St Winsted (06098) *(G-10537)*
Smart Alex Foods LLC ... 203 322-3368
  41 Shelter Rock Rd Stamford (06903) *(G-8425)*
Smart Foods of Bristol ... 860 582-8882
  63 Middle St Bristol (06010) *(G-1118)*
Smart Polishing ... 203 559-1541
  24 Betts Ave Stamford (06902) *(G-8426)*
Smart Signs LLC ... 860 656-5257
  470 Burnside Ave East Hartford (06108) *(G-2373)*
Smart Signs Pro LLC ... 203 684-9839
  225 Research Dr Unit 13 Milford (06460) *(G-4646)*
Smartcap Innovations LLC ... 860 878-4688
  121 Walbridge Rd West Hartford (06119) *(G-9856)*
Smarter Sealants LLC ... 860 218-2210
  14 Eastern Park Rd East Hartford (06108) *(G-2374)*
Smartpay Solutions ... 860 986-7659
  200 Executive Blvd Ste 3a Southington (06489) *(G-7974)*
Smg Woodworking ... 203 804-1029
  425 W Rock Ave New Haven (06515) *(G-5396)*
SMI, Dayville *Also called Specialized Marketing Intl Inc* *(G-2074)*
Smile Exchange LLC ... 860 342-0333
  839 Long Hill Rd Apt C Middletown (06457) *(G-4418)*
Smiling Dog ... 860 344-0707
  77 Arbutus St Middletown (06457) *(G-4419)*
Smith Bros Woodland Mgmt LLC, Newtown *Also called Saugatuck Tree & Logging LLC* *(G-5778)*
Smith Frame & Moulding LLC ... 860 389-8871
  112 Stockhouse Rd Bozrah (06334) *(G-532)*
Smith Hill of Delaware Inc ... 860 767-7502
  34 Plains Rd Essex (06426) *(G-2733)*
Smith Tia Custm Statnary Phot ... 860 767-1976
  7 Hudson Ln Essex (06426) *(G-2734)*
Smiths Medical Asd Inc ... 860 621-9111
  201 W Queen St Southington (06489) *(G-7975)*
Smm New England Corporation ... 203 777-7445
  808 Washington Ave New Haven (06519) *(G-5397)*
Smoke & Print Universe ... 203 540-5151
  4106 Main St Bridgeport (06606) *(G-910)*
Smokey Mountain Chew Inc (PA) ... 203 656-1088
  1 Center St Fl 2 Darien (06820) *(G-2045)*
Smokey Mountain Chew Inc ... 203 304-9200
  107 Church Hill Rd Sandy Hook (06482) *(G-7330)*
Smoothie King, Waterford *Also called Smoothie King* *(G-9671)*
Smoothie King ... 203 208-4098
  847 W Main St Ste 3 Branford (06405) *(G-653)*
Smoothie King ... 860 574-9382
  106 Boston Post Rd Ste A Waterford (06385) *(G-9671)*
SMR Metal Technology ... 860 291-8259
  524 Sullivan Ave Ste 15 South Windsor (06074) *(G-7823)*
SMS Machine Inc ... 860 829-0813
  54 Clark Dr Ste A East Berlin (06023) *(G-2176)*
Smsc Flags and Flagpoles, Bridgeport *Also called Sign Maintenance Service Co* *(G-905)*
Smyth Ink ... 203 801-4335
  128 Putnam Rd New Canaan (06840) *(G-5143)*
Snack Electronics ... 860 225-3714
  180 Broad St New Britain (06053) *(G-5056)*
Snaplok Systems LLC ... 888 570-5407
  24 Tobey Rd Bloomfield (06002) *(G-487)*
Snapple Juices, Bridgeport *Also called B & E Juices Inc* *(G-707)*
Snapwire Innovations LLC ... 203 806-4773
  125 Commerce Ct Ste 11 Cheshire (06410) *(G-1448)*
Sneham Manufacturing Inc ... 203 610-6669
  727 Honeyspot Rd Ste 99 Stratford (06615) *(G-8682)*
Snibbetts Inc ... 860 526-5536
  58 Warsaw St Deep River (06417) *(G-2101)*
Snoogs & Wilde LLC ... 860 824-9865
  25 Main St Falls Village (06031) *(G-2872)*
Snowathome LLC ... 860 584-2991
  84 Napco Dr Ste 6 Terryville (06786) *(G-8770)*
Snowdog Software LLC ... 203 265-7116
  32 Southview Dr Wallingford (06492) *(G-9370)*
Snreview ... 203 366-5991
  197 Fairchild Ave Fairfield (06825) *(G-2849)*
So and Sew Plushies ... 860 916-2918
  104 Elm St Meriden (06450) *(G-4242)*
So-Lo Marine Division, Bridgeport *Also called Hawie Manufacturing Company* *(G-783)*
Soapstone Landing LLC ... 860 875-6200
  32 Gulf Rd Stafford Springs (06076) *(G-8039)*

Soapstone Media Inc ... 860 749-0455
  27 Quality Ave Ste B Somers (06071) *(G-7669)*
Sober Touch Sensoring LLC ... 203 540-2486
  182 N State St Ansonia (06401) *(G-51)*
Sobrio LLC ... 860 880-1990
  Longley 270 Mid Trnpk 203 Storrs (06269) *(G-8551)*
Soccer N More ... 860 282-0224
  525 Burnside Ave East Hartford (06108) *(G-2375)*
Society For Exprmntal McHanics ... 203 790-6373
  7 School St Bethel (06801) *(G-343)*
Society Plastics Engineers Inc (PA) ... 203 740-5422
  6 Berkshire Blvd Ste 306 Bethel (06801) *(G-344)*
Sodexo Inc ... 860 679-2803
  263 Farmington Ave Farmington (06032) *(G-2958)*
Sofrito Ponce, New Haven *Also called Louis Rodriguz* *(G-5321)*
Soft Tissue Regeneration Inc ... 973 879-6367
  470 James St Ste 14 New Haven (06513) *(G-5398)*
Softstorms LLC ... 860 578-8515
  35 Hollywood Ave West Hartford (06110) *(G-9857)*
Software By Design LLC ... 203 271-1061
  15 Kelly Ct Cheshire (06410) *(G-1449)*
Software Cnslting Rsources Inc ... 860 491-2689
  9 Valcove Ct Goshen (06756) *(G-3104)*
Software Establishment LLC ... 860 426-2700
  42 Clearview Ct Southington (06489) *(G-7976)*
Software Gallery Inc ... 203 775-0520
  86 Ironworks Hill Rd Brookfield (06804) *(G-1224)*
Software Matters ... 860 354-8804
  38 River Rd Roxbury (06783) *(G-7285)*
Software Studios LLC ... 203 288-3997
  26 Grandview Ter North Haven (06473) *(G-5995)*
Software Systems & Support LLC ... 203 470-8482
  194 Rising Trail Dr Middletown (06457) *(G-4420)*
Soja Woodworking LLC ... 860 345-3909
  548 Killingworth Rd Higganum (06441) *(G-3778)*
Solais Lighting Inc ... 203 683-6222
  650 West Ave Stamford (06902) *(G-8427)*
Solana Publishing LLC ... 203 380-2851
  2361 Huntington Rd Trumbull (06611) *(G-9075)*
Solar Data Systems Inc ... 203 702-7189
  23 Francis J Clarke Cir Bethel (06801) *(G-345)*
Solar Generations LLC ... 203 453-3920
  741 Podunk Rd Guilford (06437) *(G-3392)*
Solar Nebula LLC ... 516 362-8048
  7 Dara Ln North Granby (06060) *(G-5881)*
Solar Seal of Connecticut, Hamden *Also called Insulpane Connecticut Inc* *(G-3465)*
Soldier Socks ... 203 832-2005
  90 Fairfield Ave Stamford (06902) *(G-8428)*
Soldream Inc ... 860 871-6883
  129 Reservoir Rd Vernon Rockville (06066) *(G-9180)*
Soldream Spcial Process - Wldg ... 860 858-5247
  203 Hartford Tpke Tolland (06084) *(G-8878)*
Solico, West Hartford *Also called Sorenson Lighted Controls Inc* *(G-9858)*
Solid State Heating, Westbrook *Also called Sshc Inc* *(G-10010)*
Solidification Pdts Intl Inc ... 203 484-9494
  524 Forest Rd Northford (06472) *(G-6053)*
Solidification Products Intl, Northford *Also called Solidification Products Intl* *(G-6054)*
Solidification Products Intl ... 203 484-9494
  215 Village St Northford (06472) *(G-6054)*
Solla Eyelet Products Inc ... 860 274-5729
  50 Seemar Rd Watertown (06795) *(G-9737)*
Solon Manufacturing ... 203 230-5300
  7 Grasso Ave North Haven (06473) *(G-5996)*
Soltis Speed Equipment ... 860 489-0119
  186 N Elm St Torrington (06790) *(G-8971)*
Soluthin Inc ... 860 424-1228
  30 Renees Way Madison (06443) *(G-3958)*
Solution Publishing ... 203 758-9137
  177 Falcon Crest Rd Middlebury (06762) *(G-4293)*
Solutions With Innovation LLC ... 203 729-3873
  60 Great Hill Rd Naugatuck (06770) *(G-4919)*
Somers Manufacturing Inc ... 860 314-1075
  165 Riverside Ave Bristol (06010) *(G-1119)*
Somers Music Publications ... 860 763-0366
  45 Kibbe Dr Somers (06071) *(G-7670)*
Somers Thin Strip, Waterbury *Also called Global Brass & Copper LLC* *(G-9488)*
Somers Thin Strip, Waterbury *Also called Global Brass & Copper LLC* *(G-9489)*
Somers Tool & Weld Shop ... 860 314-1075
  165 Riverside Ave Bristol (06010) *(G-1120)*
Somerset Plastics Company ... 860 635-1601
  454 Timber Ridge Rd Middletown (06457) *(G-4421)*
Something Sweet Inc (PA) ... 203 603-9766
  724 Grand Ave New Haven (06511) *(G-5399)*
Son of A Stitch ... 203 527-3432
  28 E Main St Waterbury (06702) *(G-9604)*
Son of A Stitch LLC ... 203 272-2548
  78 George Ave Cheshire (06410) *(G-1450)*
Son-Chief Stampings, Winsted *Also called Sonchief Electrics Inc* *(G-10538)*
Sonalysts Inc (PA) ... 860 442-4355
  215 Parkway N Waterford (06385) *(G-9672)*
Sonchief Electrics Inc ... 860 379-2741
  41 Meadow St Ste 1 Winsted (06098) *(G-10538)*

ALPHABETIC SECTION Specialty Stairs LLC

Song Bath LLC.......800 353-0313
146 Old Kings Hwy New Canaan (06840) ***(G-5144)***
Sonias Chocolaterie Inc.......203 438-5965
6 Ascot Way Ridgefield (06877) ***(G-7174)***
Sonic Corp.......203 375-0063
1 Research Dr Stratford (06615) ***(G-8683)***
Sonic Welding Co.......203 348-8021
18 West Ave Stamford (06902) ***(G-8429)***
Sonicators, Newtown *Also called Qsonica LLC* ***(G-5770)***
Sonics & Materials Inc (PA).......203 270-4600
53 Church Hill Rd Newtown (06470) ***(G-5781)***
Sonitek Corporation.......203 878-9321
84 Research Dr Milford (06460) ***(G-4647)***
Sonitor Technologies Inc.......727 466-4557
37 Brookside Dr Greenwich (06830) ***(G-3239)***
Sonoco.......860 928-7795
29 Park Rd Putnam (06260) ***(G-7067)***
Sonoco Prtective Solutions Inc.......860 928-7795
29 Park Rd Putnam (06260) ***(G-7068)***
Sons of Un Vtrans of Civil War.......816 241-5353
4 Raven Cir Avon (06001) ***(G-114)***
Sophia Swim Wear LLC.......203 481-9397
115 Crossfield Rd North Branford (06471) ***(G-5857)***
Sorenson Lighted Controls Inc (PA).......860 527-3092
100 Shield St West Hartford (06110) ***(G-9858)***
Sorge Industries Inc.......203 924-8900
289 Coram Rd Shelton (06484) ***(G-7557)***
SOS Security Incorporated.......860 563-2121
2264 Silas Deane Hwy Rocky Hill (06067) ***(G-7265)***
Soto Holdings Inc.......203 781-8020
300 East St New Haven (06511) ***(G-5400)***
Sound Construction & Engrg Co.......860 242-2109
522 Cottage Grove Rd H Bloomfield (06002) ***(G-488)***
Sound Control Technologies.......203 854-5701
22 S Smith St Norwalk (06855) ***(G-6352)***
Sound Custom Woodworking & Des.......203 948-5594
260 North St Ridgefield (06877) ***(G-7175)***
Sound Manufacturing Inc.......860 388-4466
1 Williams Ln Old Saybrook (06475) ***(G-6569)***
Sound Marketing Concepts.......860 257-9367
1800 Silas Deane Hwy # 7 Rocky Hill (06067) ***(G-7266)***
Sound of Fury Publishing LLC.......860 803-0651
600 Hop River Rd Coventry (06238) ***(G-1675)***
Sound View Plastics LLC.......860 322-4139
500 Main St Ste 25a Deep River (06417) ***(G-2102)***
Sound View Press, Madison *Also called Artchrist Com Inc* ***(G-3907)***
Sound Yachts LLC.......860 399-8800
333 Boston Post Rd Fl 2 Westbrook (06498) ***(G-10009)***
Soundings Publications LLC.......860 767-8227
10 Bokum Rd Essex (06426) ***(G-2735)***
Soundview Horizons Dgtl Ldrshp.......203 292-0880
26 Soundview Farm Weston (06883) ***(G-10040)***
Soundview Paper Mills LLC (HQ).......201 796-4000
1 Sound Shore Dr Ste 203 Greenwich (06830) ***(G-3240)***
Source Inc (PA).......203 488-6400
101 Fowler Rd North Branford (06471) ***(G-5858)***
Source Loudspeakers.......860 918-3088
701 Nutmeg Rd N Ste 2 South Windsor (06074) ***(G-7824)***
Source Technologies, South Windsor *Also called Source Loudspeakers* ***(G-7824)***
Sourcebooks Inc.......203 876-9790
18 Cherry St Ste 1 Milford (06460) ***(G-4648)***
Sousa Corp.......860 523-9090
565 Cedar St Newington (06111) ***(G-5706)***
South Beach Inc.......860 953-0038
12 Cody St West Hartford (06110) ***(G-9859)***
South Beach Swimsuits, West Hartford *Also called South Beach Inc* ***(G-9859)***
South Bend Ethanol LLC.......203 326-8132
107 Elm St Stamford (06902) ***(G-8430)***
South End Express 2.......203 720-2085
921 New Haven Rd Naugatuck (06770) ***(G-4920)***
South Norfolk Lumber Co.......860 542-5650
1117 Litchfield Rd Norfolk (06058) ***(G-5826)***
South Paint and Sign Co.......203 245-7591
96 Robin Ridge Dr Madison (06443) ***(G-3959)***
South Wind Music Pubg LLC.......860 644-2357
40 Steep Rd South Windsor (06074) ***(G-7825)***
South Windsor Golf Course LLC.......860 648-4653
516 Griffin Rd South Windsor (06074) ***(G-7826)***
South Windsor Quality Black MO.......860 385-2740
287 Oakland Rd South Windsor (06074) ***(G-7827)***
Southbury Printing Centre Inc.......203 264-0102
385 Main St S Ste 107 Southbury (06488) ***(G-7878)***
Southern Almnum Intrmdte Hldin (PA).......870 234-8660
130 Main St New Canaan (06840) ***(G-5145)***
Southern Conn Pallet Co Inc.......203 265-1313
346 Quinnipiac St Wallingford (06492) ***(G-9371)***
Southern Neng Telecom Corp (HQ).......203 771-5200
2 Science Park New Haven (06511) ***(G-5401)***
Southern Neng Ultraviolet Co, Branford *Also called Southern Neng Ultraviolet Inc* ***(G-654)***
Southern Neng Ultraviolet Inc.......203 483-5810
55029 E Main St Branford (06405) ***(G-654)***
Southford Kindling Company LLC.......203 394-2148
94 Bridle Path Rd Southbury (06488) ***(G-7879)***
Southington Citizen.......860 620-5960
500 S Broad St Ste 1 Meriden (06450) ***(G-4243)***
Southington Metal Fabg Co.......860 621-0149
95 Corporate Dr Southington (06489) ***(G-7977)***
Southington Tool & Mfg Corp.......860 276-0021
300 Atwater St Plantsville (06479) ***(G-6912)***
Southington Transm Auto Repr.......860 329-0381
1900 West St Southington (06489) ***(G-7978)***
Southpack LLC.......860 224-2242
1 Hartford Sq New Britain (06052) ***(G-5057)***
Southport Brewing Co.......203 874-2337
33 New Haven Ave Milford (06460) ***(G-4649)***
Southport Brewing Company, Shelton *Also called Nutmeg Brewing Rest Group LLC* ***(G-7515)***
Southport Products LLC.......860 379-0761
157 Colebrook River Rd Winsted (06098) ***(G-10539)***
Southside Media, Hartford *Also called Gamut Publishing* ***(G-3598)***
Southwick & Meister Inc.......203 237-0000
1455 N Colony Rd Meriden (06450) ***(G-4244)***
Southwire Company LLC.......203 324-0067
392 Pacific St Stamford (06902) ***(G-8431)***
Sovipe Food Distributors LLC.......203 648-2781
87 E Liberty St Danbury (06810) ***(G-1954)***
Spa Machining Co.......860 564-9584
31 Center Pkwy Plainfield (06374) ***(G-6753)***
Space Craft Mfg Inc.......860 583-1387
620 Research Pkwy Meriden (06450) ***(G-4245)***
Space Electronics LLC.......860 829-0001
81 Fuller Way Berlin (06037) ***(G-221)***
Space Swiss Manufacturing Inc.......860 567-4341
428 Maple St Litchfield (06759) ***(G-3900)***
Space Tool & Machine Co Inc.......860 290-8599
130 Commerce Way Ste 1 South Windsor (06074) ***(G-7828)***
Spargo Machine Products Inc.......860 583-3925
6 Gear Dr Terryville (06786) ***(G-8771)***
Spark Manufacturing, Branford *Also called Iskra John* ***(G-609)***
Sparklers.......860 669-5110
307 E Main St Clinton (06413) ***(G-1527)***
Sparrow Industries.......203 598-0034
162 Old Watertown Rd Middlebury (06762) ***(G-4294)***
Sparrow Woods Co LLC.......203 215-5200
21 Westward Rd Woodbridge (06525) ***(G-10618)***
Spartan Aerospace LLC.......860 533-7500
41 Progress Dr Manchester (06042) ***(G-4090)***
Spartan Industries LLC.......203 464-8600
58 Summer Ln North Haven (06473) ***(G-5997)***
Spartech LLC.......203 327-6010
69 Southfield Ave Stamford (06902) ***(G-8432)***
Speakeasy Ai, Old Greenwich *Also called Open Water Development LLC* ***(G-6481)***
Spec Label Systems, Stratford *Also called Penmar Industries Inc* ***(G-8663)***
Spec Plating Inc.......203 366-3638
740 Seaview Ave Bridgeport (06607) ***(G-911)***
Special Events Screen Prtg LLC.......203 468-5453
35 Washington Ave East Haven (06512) ***(G-2454)***
Special Vhcl Developments Inc.......203 272-7928
337 Blacks Rd Cheshire (06410) ***(G-1451)***
Specialist Sensor.......203 287-9699
47 Park Ave Hamden (06517) ***(G-3511)***
Specialized Marketing Intl Inc.......860 779-3264
505 Hartford Pike Dayville (06241) ***(G-2074)***
Specialty Cable Corp.......203 265-7126
2 Tower Dr Wallingford (06492) ***(G-9372)***
Specialty Components Inc (PA).......203 284-9112
14 Village Ln Ste 1 Wallingford (06492) ***(G-9373)***
Specialty Components Inc.......203 284-9112
14 Village Ln Wallingford (06492) ***(G-9374)***
Specialty Metals and Fab.......203 509-5028
51 Elm St Naugatuck (06770) ***(G-4921)***
Specialty Metls Smlters & Rfne.......203 366-2500
2490 Black Rock Tpke Fairfield (06825) ***(G-2850)***
Specialty Minerals Inc.......860 824-5435
30 Daisy Hill Rd Canaan (06018) ***(G-1292)***
Specialty Paper Mfg LLC.......860 654-8044
7b Pasco Dr East Windsor (06088) ***(G-2519)***
Specialty Polymers Inc.......203 575-5727
245 Freight St Waterbury (06702) ***(G-9605)***
Specialty Printing LLC.......860 654-1850
15 Thompson Rd East Windsor (06088) ***(G-2520)***
Specialty Printing LLC (PA).......860 623-8870
4 Thompson Rd East Windsor (06088) ***(G-2521)***
Specialty Products Mfg LLC.......860 621-6969
251 Captain Lewis Dr Southington (06489) ***(G-7979)***
Specialty Saw Inc.......860 658-4419
30 Wolcott Rd Simsbury (06070) ***(G-7648)***
Specialty Shop Inc.......860 647-1477
18 Sanrico Dr Manchester (06042) ***(G-4091)***
Specialty Sign Services LLC.......860 391-3291
24 W Main St Clinton (06413) ***(G-1528)***
Specialty Sintered.......860 263-8332
3580 Main St Bldg 11 Hartford (06120) ***(G-3691)***
Specialty Stairs LLC.......203 484-2557
58 Lanes Pond Rd Northford (06472) ***(G-6055)***

ALPHABETIC

(PA)=Parent Co (HQ)=Headquarters (DH)=Div Headquarters
2020 Harris Connecticut
Manufacturers Directory
579

Specialty Steel Treating Inc...860 653-0061
12 Kripes Rd East Granby (06026) *(G-2231)*
Specialty Tool Company USA LLC...203 874-2009
61 Erna Ave Milford (06461) *(G-4650)*
Specialty Wire & Cord Sets...203 498-2932
1 Gallagher Rd Hamden (06517) *(G-3512)*
Spectral LLC (PA)...860 928-7726
111 Highland Dr Putnam (06260) *(G-7069)*
Spectral Optics Inc...978 682-1302
111 Highland Dr Putnam (06260) *(G-7070)*
Spectral Products, Putnam *Also called Spectral LLC (G-7069)*
Spectrogram Corporation...203 245-2433
287 Boston Post Rd Madison (06443) *(G-3960)*
Spectrum Associates Inc...203 878-4618
440 New Haven Ave Ste 1 Milford (06460) *(G-4651)*
Spectrum Brands Inc...203 205-2900
44 Old Ridgebury Rd # 300 Danbury (06810) *(G-1955)*
Spectrum Graphix, Milford *Also called Spectrum Press (G-4652)*
Spectrum Machine & Design LLC...860 386-6490
800 Old County Cir Windsor Locks (06096) *(G-10497)*
Spectrum Marking Materials LLC...860 533-9533
128 Addison Rd Glastonbury (06033) *(G-3083)*
Spectrum Mktg Cmmnications Inc...203 853-4585
30 Osborne Ave Norwalk (06855) *(G-6353)*
Spectrum Powdercoating LLC...860 591-1034
1131 Voluntown Rd Jewett City (06351) *(G-3801)*
Spectrum Press...203 878-9090
354 Woodmont Rd Ste 15 Milford (06460) *(G-4652)*
Spectrum Virtual LLC...203 303-7540
55 Realty Dr Ste 315 Cheshire (06410) *(G-1452)*
Spedding Co...860 355-4076
315 Litchfield Rd New Milford (06776) *(G-5591)*
Speed Printing & Graphics Inc...203 324-4000
330 Fairfield Ave Ste 3 Stamford (06902) *(G-8433)*
Speedi Sign...203 431-0836
3 Reservoir St Bethel (06801) *(G-346)*
Speedi Sign LLC...203 775-0700
770 Federal Rd Brookfield (06804) *(G-1225)*
Speedy Food Group USA, West Haven *Also called Sabatino North America LLC (G-9951)*
Speedy Printing LLC...860 445-8252
8 Forest Ave Mystic (06355) *(G-4846)*
Speedy Sign Design, Shelton *Also called Harry Tutunjian (G-7460)*
Spencer Street Inc...860 647-2955
1205 Tolland Tpke Manchester (06042) *(G-4092)*
Spencer Turbine Company (HQ)...860 688-8361
600 Day Hill Rd Windsor (06095) *(G-10436)*
Spera Cottage Crafters...860 738-2391
65 Stillman Hill Rd Colebrook (06021) *(G-1587)*
Sperian Protectn Instrumentatn...860 344-1079
651 S Main St Middletown (06457) *(G-4422)*
Sperry Automatics Co Inc...203 729-4589
1372 New Haven Rd Naugatuck (06770) *(G-4922)*
Spfm Corp...203 900-0005
330 Pine St Bridgeport (06605) *(G-912)*
Spicer Advanced Gas, Groton *Also called Spicer Plus Inc (G-3313)*
Spicer Plus Inc (PA)...860 445-2436
36 Thames St Groton (06340) *(G-3313)*
Spiers Welding Service...203 322-1004
1277 Long Ridge Rd Stamford (06903) *(G-8434)*
Spin Shop...860 349-1298
36 Commerce Cir Durham (06422) *(G-2157)*
Spine Wave Inc...203 944-9494
3 Enterprise Dr Ste 210 Shelton (06484) *(G-7558)*
Spinella Bakery...203 753-9451
53 Interstate Ln Waterbury (06705) *(G-9606)*
Spirit of Hartford LLC...860 404-1776
45 Crocus Ln Avon (06001) *(G-115)*
Spirol International Corp (HQ)...860 774-8571
30 Rock Ave Danielson (06239) *(G-2003)*
Spirol Intl Holdg Corp (PA)...860 774-8571
30 Rock Ave Danielson (06239) *(G-2004)*
Splinters Woodworking LLC...203 272-1314
40 Copper Valley Ct Cheshire (06410) *(G-1453)*
Spooky Signs and Holiday Creat...860 742-2805
23 Leslie Ln Coventry (06238) *(G-1676)*
Sportco Inc...631 244-4513
75 Parish Rd New Canaan (06840) *(G-5146)*
Sportees LLC...860 440-3922
262 Boston Post Rd Unit 8 Waterford (06385) *(G-9673)*
Sports Center...860 768-4650
200 Bloomfield Ave West Hartford (06117) *(G-9860)*
Sports Department LLC...860 872-0873
18 Brookfield Dr Ellington (06029) *(G-2601)*
Spot Welders Inc...203 386-8938
1021 Honeyspot Rd Stratford (06615) *(G-8684)*
Spot-On Sign Solutions Inc...860 584-9008
67 Burgundy Dr Berlin (06037) *(G-222)*
Spots and Ladybugs LLC...203 378-8232
45 Hilltop Dr Trumbull (06611) *(G-9076)*
Sprague Logging LLC...860 455-9768
138 Bujak Rd Chaplin (06235) *(G-1342)*
Spray Foam Outlets LLC...631 291-9355
30 Muller Ave Unit 19 Norwalk (06851) *(G-6354)*
Spray Market, The, Bridgeport *Also called Spfm Corp (G-912)*
Sprayfoampolymerscom LLC...800 853-1577
134 Old Ridgefield Rd # 3 Wilton (06897) *(G-10333)*
Spring Computerized Inds LLC...860 605-9206
93 Oakwood Dr Harwinton (06791) *(G-3739)*
Springbrook Woodcrafters LLC...860 870-7303
469 Somers Rd Ellington (06029) *(G-2602)*
Springfield Spring Corporation...860 584-6560
24 Dell Manor Dr Bristol (06010) *(G-1121)*
Springs Manufacturer Supply Co, Southington *Also called Northeast Carbide Inc (G-7959)*
Spruce It Up Woodworking LLC...203 740-7975
1 Richards Rd Brookfield (06804) *(G-1226)*
Spv Industries LLC...860 953-5928
9 Tolles St West Hartford (06110) *(G-9861)*
SPX Corporation...203 356-9308
2001 W Main St Ste 222 Stamford (06902) *(G-8435)*
Square Creamery LLC...203 456-3490
7 P T Barnum Sq Bethel (06801) *(G-347)*
Sre Bristol 322 Park St LLC...860 348-0198
129 Ice Pond Ln East Berlin (06023) *(G-2177)*
Srirret America...203 988-1852
20 Maplewood Ln Madison (06443) *(G-3961)*
Srk9, Voluntown *Also called Sugar Run K9 LLC (G-9191)*
SS&C HOLDINGS, Windsor *Also called SS&c Technologies Holdings Inc (G-10439)*
SS&c Technologies Inc...860 930-5882
261 Broad St Windsor (06095) *(G-10437)*
SS&c Technologies Inc (HQ)...860 298-4500
80 Lamberton Rd Windsor (06095) *(G-10438)*
SS&c Technologies Holdings Inc (PA)...860 298-4500
80 Lamberton Rd Windsor (06095) *(G-10439)*
Sshc Inc...860 399-5434
1244 Old Clinton Rd Westbrook (06498) *(G-10010)*
Ssi Manufacturing Tech Corp...860 589-8004
675 Emmett St Bristol (06010) *(G-1122)*
SSS, Granby *Also called Singularity Space Systems LLC (G-3114)*
St Johns Bridge LLC...860 927-3315
25 Railroad St Kent (06757) *(G-3826)*
St Peter Woodworks...860 816-0455
120 Waddell Rd Manchester (06040) *(G-4093)*
St Pierre Box and Lumber Co...860 413-9813
66 Lovely St Canton (06019) *(G-1326)*
Staban Engineering Corp...203 294-1997
65 N Plains Industrial Rd Wallingford (06492) *(G-9375)*
Stace Welding, East Windsor *Also called Stacy B Goff (G-2522)*
Stacy B Goff...860 623-2547
100 Newberry Rd East Windsor (06088) *(G-2522)*
Stacy Lawes International, Hartford *Also called Lawes International Group LLC (G-3626)*
Stafford Paper Company...860 749-0787
34 Egypt Rd Ste D Somers (06071) *(G-7671)*
Stafford Precision Tool LLC...860 684-0471
25 West St Stafford Springs (06076) *(G-8040)*
Stafford Reminder, Vernon Rockville *Also called Rmi Inc (G-9177)*
Stag Arms LLC...860 229-9994
515 John Downey Dr New Britain (06051) *(G-5058)*
Stag Arms LLC...860 229-9994
515 John Downey Dr New Britain (06051) *(G-5059)*
Stained Glass Apple, The, Stamford *Also called Marilyn Gehring (G-8296)*
Stake Company LLC...860 623-2700
22 Thompson Rd Ste 7 East Windsor (06088) *(G-2523)*
Stamford Capital Group Inc (PA)...800 977-7837
1266 E Main St Stamford (06902) *(G-8436)*
Stamford Fabricating, Stamford *Also called Wendon Technologies Inc (G-8491)*
Stamford Forge & Metal Cft Inc...203 348-8290
63 Victory St Stamford (06902) *(G-8437)*
Stamford Iron & Stl Works Inc...203 324-6751
347 Courtland Ave Stamford (06906) *(G-8438)*
Stamford Risk Analytics LLC...203 559-0883
263 Tresser Blvd Fl 9 Stamford (06901) *(G-8439)*
Stamford RPM Raceway LLC...203 323-7223
600 West Ave Stamford (06902) *(G-8440)*
Stamler Publishing Company...203 488-9808
178 Thimble Island Rd Branford (06405) *(G-655)*
Stampt By J...860 995-3292
9 Glenn Rd East Hartford (06118) *(G-2376)*
Stamptech Incorporated...860 628-9090
445 W Queen St Ste 100 Southington (06489) *(G-7980)*
Stampworks, The, Preston *Also called Arlene Lewis (G-6981)*
Stanadyne Intrmdate Hldngs LLC (HQ)...860 525-0821
92 Deerfield Rd Windsor (06095) *(G-10440)*
Stanadyne LLC (HQ)...860 525-0821
92 Deerfield Rd Windsor (06095) *(G-10441)*
Stanadyne Parent Holdings Inc (PA)...860 525-0821
92 Deerfield Rd Windsor (06095) *(G-10442)*
Stancor LP...203 268-7513
515 Fan Hill Rd Monroe (06468) *(G-4753)*
Stancor Pumps, Monroe *Also called Stancor LP (G-4753)*
Standard Bellows Co (PA)...860 623-2307
375 Ella Grasso Tpke Windsor Locks (06096) *(G-10498)*
Standard Manufacturing Co LLC...860 225-6581
100 Burritt St New Britain (06053) *(G-5060)*

Standard Pneumatic Products 203 270-1400
31 Shepard Hill Rd Newtown (06470) ***(G-5782)***
Standard Washer & Mat Inc 860 643-5125
299 Progress Dr Manchester (06042) ***(G-4094)***
Standard Welding Company Inc 860 528-9628
212 Prospect St East Hartford (06108) ***(G-2377)***
Standard-Knapp Inc 860 342-1100
63 Pickering St Portland (06480) ***(G-6974)***
Stanley Access Technologies, Farmington *Also called Stanley Black & Decker Inc* ***(G-2960)***
Stanley Black & Decker Inc (PA) 860 225-5111
1000 Stanley Dr New Britain (06053) ***(G-5061)***
Stanley Black & Decker Inc 860 225-5111
100 Curtis St New Britain (06052) ***(G-5062)***
Stanley Black & Decker Inc 860 225-5111
65 Spot Swamp Rd Farmington (06032) ***(G-2959)***
Stanley Black & Decker Inc 860 460-9122
400 Executive Blvd Southington (06489) ***(G-7981)***
Stanley Black & Decker Inc 860 225-5111
480 Myrtle St New Britain (06053) ***(G-5063)***
Stanley Black & Decker Inc 860 225-5111
480 Myrtle St New Britain (06053) ***(G-5064)***
Stanley Black & Decker Inc 860 677-2861
65 Scott Swamp Rd Farmington (06032) ***(G-2960)***
Stanley Black and Decker, New Britain *Also called Black & Decker (us) Inc* ***(G-4951)***
Stanley Burr 860 345-3578
46 Jackson Rd Higganum (06441) ***(G-3779)***
Stanley Engineered Fastening, New Britain *Also called Emhart Teknologies LLC* ***(G-4983)***
Stanley Engineered Fastening, Danbury *Also called Emhart Teknologies LLC* ***(G-1808)***
Stanley Fastening Systems LP 860 225-5111
480 Myrtle St New Britain (06053) ***(G-5065)***
Stanley Industrial & Auto LLC 800 800-8005
480 Myrtle St New Britain (06053) ***(G-5066)***
Stanley Steemer Intl Inc 860 274-5540
46 Meadow Ln Watertown (06795) ***(G-9738)***
Stanley-Bostitch, New Britain *Also called Stanley Fastening Systems LP* ***(G-5065)***
Star Steel Structures Inc 860 763-5681
392 Four Bridges Rd Somers (06071) ***(G-7672)***
Star Tech Instruments Inc 203 312-0767
3 State Route 39 New Fairfield (06812) ***(G-5176)***
Star Woods Cabinet 203 546-8688
132 Federal Rd Brookfield (06804) ***(G-1227)***
Starstatus Publishing 877 453-9532
195 Caroline St Derby (06418) ***(G-2127)***
Startech Environmental Corp (PA) 203 762-2499
88 Danbury Rd Ste 2b Wilton (06897) ***(G-10334)***
State Awning Company 860 246-2575
100 Cedar St Hartford (06106) ***(G-3692)***
State Cutter Grinding Svc Inc 203 888-8821
481 N Main St Seymour (06483) ***(G-7367)***
State of Connecticut Educ 860 584-8433
431 Minor St Bristol (06010) ***(G-1123)***
State Welding & Fabg Inc 203 294-4071
107 N Cherry St Wallingford (06492) ***(G-9376)***
State Wide Welding Service 860 489-2465
110 Whitbeck Rd New Hartford (06057) ***(G-5213)***
Stately Stair Co Inc 203 575-1966
3810 E Main St Waterbury (06705) ***(G-9607)***
Statewide Sheet Metal LLC 203 315-1159
92 Sunny Meadow Rd Branford (06405) ***(G-656)***
Statham Woodwork 203 831-0629
38 Hemlock Pl Norwalk (06854) ***(G-6355)***
Static Safe Products Company 203 937-6391
8 Cook Rd Cornwall Bridge (06754) ***(G-1620)***
Stauffer Sheet Metal LLC 860 623-0518
56 Depot St Windsor (06006) ***(G-10443)***
Stavola Signs 860 395-0897
14 Riverside Ave Old Saybrook (06475) ***(G-6570)***
Staxx Construction Svcs LLC 860 259-5003
84 Bernard Rd Berlin (06037) ***(G-223)***
Steed Read Horsemans Classifie 860 859-0770
16b Mill Ln Salem (06420) ***(G-7292)***
Steel Rule Die Corp America 860 621-5284
289 Clark Street Ext Milldale (06467) ***(G-4688)***
Steeltech Building Pdts Inc 860 290-8930
636 Nutmeg Rd N South Windsor (06074) ***(G-7829)***
Steelwrist Inc 225 936-1111
576 Christian Ln Berlin (06037) ***(G-224)***
Stein Laboratories LLC 203 853-9500
46 Chestnut St Norwalk (06854) ***(G-6356)***
Stella Press LLC 203 661-2735
58 Brookridge Dr Greenwich (06830) ***(G-3241)***
Stelray Plastic Products Inc 203 735-2331
50 Westfield Ave Ansonia (06401) ***(G-52)***
Stencil Ease, Old Saybrook *Also called Liftline Capital LLC* ***(G-6553)***
Step By Step Cnseling Svcs LLC 860 244-9836
3580 Main St Hartford (06120) ***(G-3693)***
Step Saver Inc 860 621-6751
213 Spring St Southington (06489) ***(G-7982)***
Stephanie Lauren LLC 203 938-0364
32 High Ridge Rd Redding (06896) ***(G-7110)***
Stephanie Mark 203 329-7562
181 Turn Of River Rd Stamford (06905) ***(G-8441)***
Stephen A Besade 860 443-6033
11 Konomoc St New London (06320) ***(G-5490)***
Stephen Hawrylik 860 688-8651
462 Park Ave Windsor (06095) ***(G-10444)***
Stephen Mazzarelli 860 482-8200
1880 Mountain Rd Torrington (06790) ***(G-8972)***
Stephen Smith 405 420-2226
226 Old Colony Rd Eastford (06242) ***(G-2543)***
Stephen Wenning 203 906-9273
43 Clemens Ave Trumbull (06611) ***(G-9077)***
Stephens Pipe & Steel LLC 877 777-8721
776 N Main St Manchester (06042) ***(G-4095)***
Stepping Stones Marble 203 293-4796
420 Post Rd W Westport (06880) ***(G-10160)***
Stepping Stones MBL & Gran LLC (PA) 203 854-0552
4 Taft St Ste D1 Norwalk (06854) ***(G-6357)***
Sterling Custom Cabinetry LLC 203 335-5151
323 North Ave Bridgeport (06606) ***(G-913)***
Sterling Engineering Corp 860 379-3366
236 New Hartford Rd Pleasant Valley (06063) ***(G-6926)***
Sterling Forms and Cmpt Sups 203 876-7337
326 W Main St Ste 106 Milford (06460) ***(G-4653)***
Sterling Gas Drlg Fund 1982 LP 203 358-5700
1 Landmark Sq Stamford (06901) ***(G-8442)***
Sterling Industries LLC 860 434-6239
41 Sterling Hill Rd Old Lyme (06371) ***(G-6519)***
Sterling Jewelers Inc 860 644-7207
194 Bucklnd Hills Dr 10 Manchester (06042) ***(G-4096)***
Sterling Machine Division, Enfield *Also called Senior Operations LLC* ***(G-2692)***
Sterling Materials LLC 203 315-6619
17 Tanglewood Dr Branford (06405) ***(G-657)***
Sterling Name Tape Company 860 379-5142
9 Willow St Winsted (06098) ***(G-10540)***
Sterling Precision Machining 860 564-4043
112 Industrial Park Rd Sterling (06377) ***(G-8517)***
Sterling Printing & Graphics, Milford *Also called Sterling Forms and Cmpt Sups* ***(G-4653)***
Sterling Sand and Gravel LLC 860 774-3985
485 Saw Mill Hill Rd Sterling (06377) ***(G-8518)***
Sterling Screw Machine Div, Milford *Also called Alinabal Inc* ***(G-4448)***
Sterling Screw Machine Pdts, Kensington *Also called Alinabal Inc* ***(G-3805)***
Sterling Tool Die & Mfg Co 203 378-0893
1135 James Farm Rd Stratford (06614) ***(G-8685)***
Sterzingers Welding LLC 203 685-1575
28 Alan Rd Danbury (06810) ***(G-1956)***
Stetson Brewing Co Inc 860 643-0257
22 Fleming Rd Manchester (06042) ***(G-4097)***
Steve Cryan Studio 860 388-5010
30 Howard St Old Saybrook (06475) ***(G-6571)***
Steve H Smith Cabinetmaker, Eastford *Also called Stephen Smith* ***(G-2543)***
Steve S Custom Ironworks LLC 203 229-0612
176 Main St Rear Rear Norwalk (06851) ***(G-6358)***
Steven Rosenburg 203 329-8798
148 Old Long Ridge Rd Stamford (06903) ***(G-8443)***
Steven Rosendahl Inc 860 928-3136
371 Route 197 Woodstock (06281) ***(G-10685)***
Steven Sabo 860 642-6031
636 Trumbull Hwy Lebanon (06249) ***(G-3863)***
Steven Vandermaelen LLC 203 457-0143
709 County Rd Guilford (06437) ***(G-3393)***
Stevens Company Incorporated 860 283-8201
1085 Waterbury Rd 1 Thomaston (06787) ***(G-8806)***
Stevens Industries Inc 203 966-7555
585 Old Stamford Rd New Canaan (06840) ***(G-5147)***
Stevens Manufacturing Co Inc 203 878-2328
220 Rock Ln Milford (06460) ***(G-4654)***
Stevens Printing 203 245-3267
289 Horse Pond Rd Madison (06443) ***(G-3962)***
Stevenson Group Corporation 860 689-0011
120 Wilson Pond Rd Harwinton (06791) ***(G-3740)***
Stevenson Prototype 203 245-0278
77 Fair St Guilford (06437) ***(G-3394)***
Stewart Efi LLC (PA) 860 283-8213
45 Old Waterbury Rd Thomaston (06787) ***(G-8807)***
Stewart Efi LLC 860 283-2523
332 Reynolds Bridge Rd Thomaston (06787) ***(G-8808)***
Stewart Efi Connecticut LLC 860 283-8213
45 Old Waterbury Rd Thomaston (06787) ***(G-8809)***
Stewart Efi Texas LLC 860 283-8213
45 Old Waterbury Rd Thomaston (06787) ***(G-8810)***
Stickler Machine Company LLC 860 267-8246
4 N Main St Ste 1 East Hampton (06424) ***(G-2280)***
Stihl Incorporated 203 929-8488
2 Patriot Way Oxford (06478) ***(G-6695)***
Still River Software Co LLC 860 263-0396
126 Crooked Trail Ext Woodstock (06281) ***(G-10686)***
Stillwater Architectural Wood 860 923-2858
510 Dugg Hill Rd Woodstock (06281) ***(G-10687)***
Stitch In Time EMB Svcs LLC 860 496-0226
80 Culvert St Torrington (06790) ***(G-8973)***
Stitchers Hideaway LLC 860 268-4741
172 Birch St Manchester (06040) ***(G-4098)***
Stitches & Seams Usa LLC 708 872-7326
412 Main St Apt 16 Terryville (06786) ***(G-8772)***

ALPHABETIC

Stitches By ME............860 653-9701
10 Hartford Ave Granby (06035) ***(G-3115)***
Stitching On Maple Studio............860 480-2793
48 Maple Ave Norfolk (06058) ***(G-5827)***
Stm Industries LLC............860 785-8419
185 Commerce Way South Windsor (06074) ***(G-7830)***
Stmc, Plantsville *Also called Southington Tool & Mfg Corp* ***(G-6912)***
Stmicroelectronics Inc............860 928-7700
118 English Nghborhood Rd Woodstock (06281) ***(G-10688)***
Stn Laundry Systems LLC............203 887-8986
844 W Woods Rd Hamden (06518) ***(G-3513)***
Stock Bar Candles LLC............860 805-1986
105 Beechwood Rd West Hartford (06107) ***(G-9862)***
Stone Image Custom Concrete............860 668-2434
1186 Old Coach Xing Suffield (06078) ***(G-8736)***
Stone Innovations............203 347-8536
47 Hitchcock Way Torrington (06790) ***(G-8974)***
Stone Workshop LLC............203 362-1144
1108 Railroad Ave Bridgeport (06605) ***(G-914)***
Stoneage LLC............203 926-1133
36 Narragansett Trl Shelton (06484) ***(G-7559)***
Stonegate Capital Group............860 899-1181
100 Pearl St Fl 12 Hartford (06103) ***(G-3694)***
Stonehouse Fine Cakes............203 235-5091
61 N 1st St Meriden (06451) ***(G-4246)***
Stoneslide Media LLC............203 464-3471
4 Elm St Guilford (06437) ***(G-3395)***
Stonewall Cabinetry LLC............860 803-7595
3 Peerless Way Enfield (06082) ***(G-2698)***
Stonewall Kitchen LLC............860 648-9215
400 Evergreen Way # 408 South Windsor (06074) ***(G-7831)***
Stonington Boat Works LLC............860 535-0332
228 N Water St Stonington (06378) ***(G-8538)***
Stonington Custom Canvas LLC............860 213-1240
501 Stonington Rd Stonington (06378) ***(G-8539)***
Stonington Publications Inc............860 599-2019
12 Stillman Ave Pawcatuck (06379) ***(G-6725)***
Stonington Services LLC (PA)............860 464-1991
39 Kings Hwy Ste 1 Gales Ferry (06335) ***(G-2987)***
Stonington Vineyards Inc............860 535-1222
523 Taugwonk Rd Stonington (06378) ***(G-8540)***
Stonington Woodworks LLC............646 321-6412
272 Gallup Hill Rd Ledyard (06339) ***(G-3880)***
Stony Creek Liquor LLC............203 488-3318
3 Thimble Island Rd Branford (06405) ***(G-658)***
Stony Creek Package Store, Branford *Also called Stony Creek Liquor LLC* ***(G-658)***
Stony Creek Quarry Corporation............203 483-3904
7 Business Park Dr Ste A Branford (06405) ***(G-659)***
Stora Enso N Amercn Sls Inc (HQ)............203 541-5178
201 Broad St Stamford (06901) ***(G-8444)***
Stork N More............203 746-7500
1 Penney Ln New Fairfield (06812) ***(G-5177)***
Stormwaterworkscom LLC............203 324-0045
48 Union St Ste M Stamford (06906) ***(G-8445)***
Stovewood Acres, South Windsor *Also called Hancock Logging & Forestry MGT* ***(G-7767)***
STP Bindery Services Inc............860 528-1430
265 Prestige Park Rd # 2 East Hartford (06108) ***(G-2378)***
STP Products Manufacturing Co (HQ)............203 205-2900
44 Old Ridgebury Rd # 300 Danbury (06810) ***(G-1957)***
Str Holdings Inc (PA)............860 272-4235
1559 King St Enfield (06082) ***(G-2699)***
Straight Stitches............203 804-0409
198 Sandquist Cir Hamden (06514) ***(G-3514)***
Strain Measurement Devices Inc............203 294-5800
55 Barnes Park Rd N Wallingford (06492) ***(G-9377)***
Strapless Suspenders............203 709-0992
16 Pleasant St Waterbury (06706) ***(G-9608)***
Strategic Insights Inc............203 595-3200
1055 Washington Blvd # 400 Stamford (06901) ***(G-8446)***
Stratford Steel LLC............203 612-7350
185 Masarik Ave Stratford (06615) ***(G-8686)***
Straton Industries Inc............203 375-4488
180 Surf Ave Stratford (06615) ***(G-8687)***
Strawberry Ridge Vineyard Inc............860 868-0730
23 Strawbery Ridge Rd Cornwall Bridge (06754) ***(G-1621)***
Streamline Press............203 484-9799
21 Commerce Dr Ste 2 North Branford (06471) ***(G-5859)***
Streamline Press LLC............203 484-9799
21 Commerce Dr Ste 2 North Branford (06471) ***(G-5860)***
Streetime Technologies, Danbury *Also called Drug Imprment Dtction Svcs LLC* ***(G-1802)***
Stride Inc............203 758-8307
80 Turnpike Dr Ste 1 Middlebury (06762) ***(G-4295)***
Strings By Aurora LLC............203 583-9929
514 Surf Ave Stratford (06615) ***(G-8688)***
Strout Custom Millwork, Broad Brook *Also called Strouts Woodworking* ***(G-1153)***
Strouts Woodworking............860 623-8445
45 Plantation Rd Broad Brook (06016) ***(G-1153)***
Structured Solutions II LLC............203 972-5717
55 Saint Johns Pl Ste 201 New Canaan (06840) ***(G-5148)***
Stryker Corporation............860 528-1111
155 Founders Plz East Hartford (06108) ***(G-2379)***
STS Motorsports Graphics............860 698-6697
16 Egypt Rd Somers (06071) ***(G-7673)***
STS Special Technology & Svcs, New Canaan *Also called De Villiers Incorporated* ***(G-5101)***
Stuart Hardwood Corp............203 376-0036
32 Old Amity Rd New Haven (06524) ***(G-5402)***
Stuart Xlan, New Haven *Also called Stuart Hardwood Corp* ***(G-5402)***
Stucco Depot LLC............203 430-9186
150 N Plains Indus Rd Wallingford (06492) ***(G-9378)***
Student Employment Sftwr LLC............203 485-9417
107 Maple Ave Greenwich (06830) ***(G-3242)***
Studio Steel Inc............860 868-7305
159 New Milford Tpke New Preston (06777) ***(G-5613)***
Stump Grinding Plus............860 884-6962
19 Heritage Rd East Lyme (06333) ***(G-2476)***
Sturm Ruger & Company Inc (PA)............203 259-7843
1 Lacey Pl Southport (06890) ***(G-8010)***
Stylair LLC............860 747-4588
161 Woodford Ave Plainville (06062) ***(G-6863)***
Style and Grace LLC............917 751-2043
101 Franklin St Ste 3 Westport (06880) ***(G-10161)***
Style Woodworking............860 944-7179
199 Nathan Hale Rd Coventry (06238) ***(G-1677)***
Suarez Services LLC............203 895-0465
47 Cityview Ave Bridgeport (06606) ***(G-915)***
Subimods LLC............860 291-0015
9 Old Windsor Rd Ste B Bloomfield (06002) ***(G-489)***
Subinas USA LLC............860 298-0401
4 Market Cir Windsor (06095) ***(G-10445)***
Subtle-T LLC............203 273-6061
225 Greenwich Ave Stamford (06902) ***(G-8447)***
Suburban Industries Inc............203 716-8085
1 Shore Rd Unit 14 Stamford (06902) ***(G-8448)***
Suburban Voices Publishing LLC............203 934-6397
840 Boston Post Rd Ste 2 West Haven (06516) ***(G-9956)***
Success App............203 218-6264
54 Melville St Stratford (06615) ***(G-8689)***
Success Printing & Mailing Inc............203 847-1112
10 Pearl St Norwalk (06850) ***(G-6359)***
Sue's Shirt Creations, Somers *Also called Wink Ink LLC* ***(G-7677)***
Suez Wts Services Usa Inc............860 291-9660
405 School St East Hartford (06108) ***(G-2380)***
Sugar Creek Vineyard LLC............860 454-4219
20 Wheelock Rd Ellington (06029) ***(G-2603)***
Sugar Run K9 LLC............860 591-4193
43 Valley Dr Voluntown (06384) ***(G-9191)***
Sugarplums............860 426-9945
93 Fenn Rd Middlebury (06762) ***(G-4296)***
Suisman & Blumenthal, Hartford *Also called Aerospace Metals Inc* ***(G-3548)***
Sulas, Hartford *Also called Rodriguez Ruiz Rosa Margarita* ***(G-3681)***
Sulzer Pump Solutions US Inc (PA)............203 238-2700
140 Pond View Dr Meriden (06450) ***(G-4247)***
Sum Machine & Tool Co Inc............860 742-6827
156 Mark Dr Coventry (06238) ***(G-1678)***
Sumal Enterprises LLC............860 945-3337
620 Main St Watertown (06795) ***(G-9739)***
Summer Camp Stories LLC............203 705-1600
35 Toilsome Brook Rd Stamford (06905) ***(G-8449)***
Summer Street Content LLC............203 536-9895
1771 Post Rd E Westport (06880) ***(G-10162)***
Summer Street Press LLC............203 978-0098
460 Summer St Stamford (06901) ***(G-8450)***
Summit Atelier............646 284-0304
2 Old Stone Xing West Simsbury (06092) ***(G-9983)***
Summit Birch Hill............860 677-2763
271 Main St Farmington (06032) ***(G-2961)***
Summit Corporation of America............860 283-4391
1430 Waterbury Rd Thomaston (06787) ***(G-8811)***
Summit Finishing Division, Thomaston *Also called Summit Corporation of America* ***(G-8811)***
Summit Orthopedic Tech Inc............203 693-2727
294 Quarry Rd Milford (06460) ***(G-4655)***
Summit Plastics LLC............860 740-4482
91 Main St Portland (06480) ***(G-6975)***
Summit Plastics LLC............860 832-9730
100 Production Ct New Britain (06051) ***(G-5067)***
Summit Promotional Printing LL............860 666-1605
100 School House Rd Newington (06111) ***(G-5707)***
Summit Ridge Publishing LLC............860 689-3463
421 Hill Rd Harwinton (06791) ***(G-3741)***
Summit Screw Machine Corp............203 693-2727
49 Research Dr Ste 3 Milford (06460) ***(G-4656)***
Summit Stair Co Inc............203 778-2251
101 Wooster St Bethel (06801) ***(G-348)***
Sumner Communications Inc............203 748-2050
24 Stony Hill Rd Ste 5 Bethel (06801) ***(G-349)***
Sun Corp............860 567-0817
27 Anderson Road Ext Morris (06763) ***(G-4792)***
Sun Farm Corporation............203 882-8000
75 Woodmont Rd Milford (06460) ***(G-4657)***
Sundance Signs LLC............860 432-5760
118 Adams St Manchester (06042) ***(G-4099)***
Sunday Paper............203 624-2520
19 Colony Rd New Haven (06511) ***(G-5403)***
Sunny Daes of Fairfield............203 372-3058
2505 Black Rock Tpke # 4 Fairfield (06825) ***(G-2851)***

Sunny Publishing Company LLC....203 619-3831
1134 Hartford Tpke Vernon (06066) **(G-9153)**
Sunnyside Fab & Welding Inc....203 348-5040
55 Sunnyside Ave Stamford (06902) **(G-8451)**
Sunnyside Fab & Welding Inc....203 378-9515
1146 E Main St Bridgeport (06608) **(G-916)**
Sunset Hill Vineyard....860 598-9427
5 Elys Ferry Rd Lyme (06371) **(G-3906)**
Suominen Nonwoven, East Windsor *Also called Windsor Locks Nonwovens Inc* **(G-2533)**
Suominen US Holding Inc (HQ)....860 386-8001
1 Hartfield Blvd Ste 101 East Windsor (06088) **(G-2524)**
Super Cell Industries Inc....203 393-1335
229 Hatfield Hill Rd Bethany (06524) **(G-250)**
Super Coups, Bethel *Also called Print Promotions Inc* **(G-334)**
Super Seal Corp....203 378-5015
45 Seymour St Stratford (06615) **(G-8690)**
Superb Steel LLC....860 518-7281
40 Harvard St New Britain (06051) **(G-5068)**
Supercool Metals LLC....203 823-9032
5 Science Park Ste 2 New Haven (06511) **(G-5404)**
Superior Bakery Inc....860 923-9555
72 Main St North Grosvenordale (06255) **(G-5892)**
Superior Concrete Products LLC....860 342-0186
830 Portland Cobalt Rd Portland (06480) **(G-6976)**
Superior Elc Holdg Group LLC (HQ)....860 582-9561
1 Cowles Rd Plainville (06062) **(G-6864)**
Superior Fuel Co....203 337-1213
154 Admiral St Bridgeport (06605) **(G-917)**
Superior Mold Corp....860 225-7654
206 South St New Britain (06051) **(G-5069)**
Superior Plas Extrusion Co Inc....860 234-1864
154 West St Cromwell (06416) **(G-1720)**
Superior Plas Extrusion Co Inc (PA)....860 963-1976
5 Highland Dr Putnam (06260) **(G-7071)**
Superior Plating Company....203 255-1501
2 Lacey Pl Southport (06890) **(G-8011)**
Superior Printing Ink Co Inc....203 281-1921
750 Sherman Ave Hamden (06514) **(G-3515)**
Superior Products Distrs Inc....203 250-6700
210 Realty Dr Cheshire (06410) **(G-1454)**
Superior Signs, Monroe *Also called Ignatowski John* **(G-4719)**
Superior Technology Corp (PA)....203 255-1501
Lacey Pl Southport (06890) **(G-8012)**
Superior Welding....860 584-2632
15 Ridge Rd Terryville (06786) **(G-8773)**
Supernova Diagnostics Inc....301 792-4345
36 Richmond Hill Rd New Canaan (06840) **(G-5149)**
Superseedz, North Haven *Also called Kathies Kitchen LLC* **(G-5956)**
Supertype Inc....216 816-8119
1275 Chapel St Apt 15 New Haven (06511) **(G-5405)**
Supplement Tech LLC....203 377-5551
1625 Main St Stratford (06615) **(G-8691)**
Supplements Unlimited, Stratford *Also called Supplement Tech LLC* **(G-8691)**
Supreme Storm Services LLC....860 201-0642
49 Depaolo Dr Southington (06489) **(G-7983)**
Supreme-Lake Mfg Inc....860 621-8911
455 Atwater St Plantsville (06479) **(G-6913)**
Sur-Seal Holding LLC (PA)....203 625-0770
301 Merritt 7 Norwalk (06851) **(G-6360)**
Suraci Corp....203 624-1345
90 River St Ste 2 New Haven (06513) **(G-5406)**
Suraci Metal Finishing LLC....203 624-1345
90 River St Ste 2 New Haven (06513) **(G-5407)**
Suraci Paint & Powder Coating, New Haven *Also called Suraci Corp* **(G-5406)**
Sure Industries Inc....860 289-2522
122 Park Ave Ste C East Hartford (06108) **(G-2381)**
Surelock Division, Shelton *Also called Inline Plastics Corp* **(G-7479)**
Surf Metal Co Inc....203 375-2211
460 Lordship Blvd Stratford (06615) **(G-8692)**
Surface Mount Devices LLC....203 322-8290
16 Acre View Dr Stamford (06903) **(G-8452)**
Surface Plate Co....860 652-8905
23 Pearl St Glastonbury (06033) **(G-3084)**
Surgical Devices, New Haven *Also called Covidien LP* **(G-5265)**
Surgical Devices, North Haven *Also called Covidien LP* **(G-5929)**
Surgiquest Inc....203 799-2400
488 Wheelers Farms Rd # 3 Milford (06461) **(G-4658)**
Surys Inc....203 333-5503
20 Nutmeg Dr Trumbull (06611) **(G-9078)**
Susan Martovich....203 881-1848
118 Bowers Hill Rd Oxford (06478) **(G-6696)**
Sutters Mill....860 585-5333
1142 Hill St Bristol (06010) **(G-1124)**
Sutton Mix Avenue LLC....203 288-8482
760 Mix Ave Apt 1s Hamden (06514) **(G-3516)**
Suzanne Ramljak....203 792-5599
22 Rockwell Rd Bethel (06801) **(G-350)**
Suzio York Hill Companies....888 789-4626
975 Westfield Rd Meriden (06450) **(G-4248)**
Svl LLC....860 819-9929
369 W Main St Ste 4d Avon (06001) **(G-116)**
Swageco LLC....860 331-3477
112 Gardner Tavern Ln Coventry (06238) **(G-1679)**
Swagnificent Ent LLC....203 449-0124
79 Sage Ave Bridgeport (06610) **(G-918)**
Swahili Aviation Aerospace LLC....860 268-3639
3 Charlotte Dr Tolland (06084) **(G-8879)**
Swahn Engraving LLC....860 657-4709
1207 Main St Glastonbury (06033) **(G-3085)**
Swamp Yankee Products LLC....203 720-1202
43 General Patton Dr Naugatuck (06770) **(G-4923)**
Swan Cabinetry....203 667-7026
844 Daniels Farm Rd Trumbull (06611) **(G-9079)**
Swanhart Woodworking....203 746-1184
5 Bayberry Ln New Fairfield (06812) **(G-5178)**
Swanson Tool Manufacturing Inc....860 953-1641
71 Custer St West Hartford (06110) **(G-9863)**
Swarovski North America Ltd....203 462-3357
100 Greyrock Pl Stamford (06901) **(G-8453)**
Swarovski North America Ltd....203 372-0336
5065 Main St Trumbull (06611) **(G-9080)**
SWC, Hamden *Also called Specialty Wire & Cord Sets* **(G-3512)**
Swedes Jewelers Inc....860 623-3916
98 Bridge St East Windsor (06088) **(G-2525)**
Swedish News Inc....203 299-0380
268 Fillow St Norwalk (06850) **(G-6361)**
Sweet Country Roads LLC....860 537-0069
180 Mcdonald Rd Colchester (06415) **(G-1578)**
Sweet Grass Creamery LLC....860 887-8098
51 Mattern Rd Preston (06365) **(G-6989)**
Sweet Leaf Tea Company (HQ)....203 863-0263
900 Long Ridge Rd Bldg 2 Stamford (06902) **(G-8454)**
Sweet Peas Baking Company LLC....203 637-4031
6 Highview Ave Old Greenwich (06870) **(G-6484)**
Sweet Peet North America Inc....860 361-6444
3 West St Ste 3 Litchfield (06759) **(G-3901)**
Sweet Spot Cupcakery LLC....860 219-1123
152 Mountain Rd Windsor (06095) **(G-10446)**
Sweetheart Flute Company LLC....860 749-8514
32 S Maple St Enfield (06082) **(G-2700)**
Sweetwater Boatworks LLC....860 984-5118
18 Smith St New London (06320) **(G-5491)**
Swift Kathryn....860 754-4150
16 W Cove Rd Moodus (06469) **(G-4776)**
Swift Innovations LLC....860 572-8322
800 Flanders Rd Bldg 5 Mystic (06355) **(G-4847)**
Swift Innovations LLC....860 710-2725
166 Watson Rd Preston (06365) **(G-6990)**
Swift Scientific LLC....860 498-8577
89 S River Rd Coventry (06238) **(G-1680)**
Swift Textile Metalizing LLC (PA)....860 243-1122
23 Britton Dr Bloomfield (06002) **(G-490)**
Swing By Swing Golf Inc....310 922-8023
80 State House Sq # 158 Hartford (06123) **(G-3695)**
Swing Rite Golf....203 748-4985
3 Ridge Rd Bethel (06801) **(G-351)**
Swipe Ink Screen Printing LLC....203 783-0468
233 Research Dr Ste 5 Milford (06460) **(G-4659)**
Swiss Army Parfums, Monroe *Also called Wenger Na Inc* **(G-4764)**
Swiss Tactics Industries LLC....203 974-3427
157 Church St Fl 19 New Haven (06510) **(G-5408)**
Swistro Welding....860 978-3238
115 Paul Manafort Dr New Britain (06053) **(G-5070)**
Swivel Machine Works Inc....203 270-6343
11 Monitor Hill Rd Newtown (06470) **(G-5783)**
Swizzles of Greenwhich....917 662-0080
207 E Putnam Ave Cos Cob (06807) **(G-1642)**
Sword-Agencyport, Farmington *Also called Agencyport Software Corp* **(G-2876)**
Swpc Plastics LLC....860 526-3200
12 Bridge St Deep River (06417) **(G-2103)**
Swpci....203 278-6400
18 Longview Rd Shelton (06484) **(G-7560)**
Syba Systems LLC....401 829-0822
20 Huntington Pl Norwich (06360) **(G-6433)**
Sycast Inc....860 308-2122
148 Bartholomew Ave Hartford (06106) **(G-3696)**
Sychron Inc....860 953-8157
683 N Mountain Rd Newington (06111) **(G-5708)**
Syferlock Technology Corp....203 292-5441
917 Bridgeport Ave Ste 5 Shelton (06484) **(G-7561)**
Syft, Stratford *Also called Management Hlth Solutions Inc* **(G-8647)**
Sykies Diagnostics, Ansonia *Also called Boudreau Vasiliki* **(G-24)**
Sylag Manufacturing LLC....860 832-8772
365 John Downey Dr Ste 2 New Britain (06051) **(G-5071)**
Sylvan R Shemitz Designs LLC....203 934-3441
114 Boston Post Rd West Haven (06516) **(G-9957)**
Sylvia Engineering Wldg & Eqp....860 859-1791
42 Case St Norwich (06360) **(G-6434)**
Syman Machine LLC....860 747-8337
161 Woodford Ave Ste 5b Plainville (06062) **(G-6865)**
Symbol Mattress of New England....860 779-3112
312 Lake Rd Dayville (06241) **(G-2075)**
Symmetry Press LLC....203 988-2329
17 Pine St New Haven (06513) **(G-5409)**

(PA)=Parent Co (HQ)=Headquarters (DH)=Div Headquarters
2020 Harris Connecticut Manufacturers Directory
583

Symphonycs LLC 860 884-2308
210 S Burnham Hwy Lisbon (06351) ***(G-3883)***
Syn-Mar Products Inc 860 872-8505
5 Nutmeg Dr Ellington (06029) ***(G-2604)***
Synchron Inc 860 953-8157
683 N Mountain Rd Ste 2 Newington (06111) ***(G-5709)***
Syncote Chemical Company Inc 203 426-5526
16 Greenbriar Ln Newtown (06470) ***(G-5784)***
Synectic Engineering Inc 203 877-8488
60 Commerce Park Ste 1 Milford (06460) ***(G-4660)***
Synectix LLC 203 283-0701
291 Pepes Farm Rd Milford (06460) ***(G-4661)***
Synergy Sales Ltd 860 974-3288
50 Perrin Rd Woodstock (06281) ***(G-10689)***
Synergy Solutions LLC 203 762-1153
276 Newtown Tpke Wilton (06897) ***(G-10335)***
Syntac Coated Products, New Hartford *Also called Scp Management LLC* ***(G-5211)***
Syrver LLC 203 598-5810
501 Kings Hwy E Ste 201 Fairfield (06825) ***(G-2852)***
Syrver.com, Fairfield *Also called Syrver LLC* ***(G-2852)***
Sysdyne Technologies LLC 203 327-3649
9 Riverbend Dr S Stamford (06907) ***(G-8455)***
Systamedic Inc 860 912-6101
1084 Shennecossett Rd Groton (06340) ***(G-3314)***
System Intgrtion Cnsulting LLC 203 926-9599
1000 Bridgeport Ave 1-3 Shelton (06484) ***(G-7562)***
Systematic Automation Inc 310 218-3361
20 Executive Dr Farmington (06032) ***(G-2962)***
Systematics Inc 860 721-0706
1275 Cromwell Ave Ste B1 Rocky Hill (06067) ***(G-7267)***
Systems and Tech Intl Inc 860 871-0401
24 Goose Ln Ste 5 Tolland (06084) ***(G-8880)***
Syzygy Halthcare Solutions LLC 203 226-4449
33 Cannon Rd Wilton (06897) ***(G-10336)***
Szepanski Machine Services LLC 860 738-9825
48 Holabird Ave Winsted (06098) ***(G-10541)***
Szostek Custom Woodworking LLC 203 891-9127
366 Coachmans Ln Orange (06477) ***(G-6630)***
T & J Manufacturing LLP 860 632-8655
1385 Newfield St Middletown (06457) ***(G-4423)***
T & J Screw Machine Pdts LLC 860 417-3801
27 Main St Oakville (06779) ***(G-6463)***
T & R Specialties LLC 860 870-9684
20 Ridgeview Dr Ellington (06029) ***(G-2605)***
T & T Automation Inc 860 683-8788
88 Pierson Ln Windsor (06095) ***(G-10447)***
T and A Industries LLC 860 309-9211
134 New Harwinton Rd Torrington (06790) ***(G-8975)***
T and G Floors, New Milford *Also called Tg Floors* ***(G-5595)***
T B Marble Granite LLC 860 443-0817
1404 Hartfrd New Lndn Tpk Oakdale (06370) ***(G-6447)***
T C Kitchens Inc 203 375-4469
416 Jackson Ave Stratford (06615) ***(G-8693)***
T D I Enterprises LLC 203 630-1268
22 Gypsy Ln Meriden (06451) ***(G-4249)***
T G Industries Inc 203 235-3239
361 S Colony St Ste 1 Meriden (06451) ***(G-4250)***
T J Russell Electric LLC 203 791-8950
15 Connecticut Ave Danbury (06810) ***(G-1958)***
T Keefe and Sons 203 457-0267
1790 Little Meadow Rd Guilford (06437) ***(G-3396)***
T L S Design & Manufacturing 860 439-1414
100 Blinman St New London (06320) ***(G-5492)***
T M C, Durham *Also called Technical Manufacturing Corp* ***(G-2158)***
T M F, Wallingford *Also called Technical Metal Finishing Inc* ***(G-9379)***
T M Industries Inc 860 828-0344
134 Commerce St East Berlin (06023) ***(G-2178)***
T Murphy Auto Repair, Stamford *Also called Murphy & Sons Welding & Repair* ***(G-8316)***
T N Dickinson Company 860 267-2279
31 E High St East Hampton (06424) ***(G-2281)***
T N T Logging, North Granby *Also called Thomas Carr III* ***(G-5882)***
T P Engineering, Danbury *Also called TP Cycle & Engineering Inc* ***(G-1964)***
T R D Specialities, Pine Meadow *Also called Trd Specialties Inc* ***(G-6736)***
T Woodward Stair Building LLC 860 664-0515
10 Bailey Dr North Branford (06471) ***(G-5861)***
T&J Manufacturing, Middletown *Also called T & J Manufacturing LLP* ***(G-4423)***
T&K Technical Services LLC 860 235-5882
26 Upper Bartlett Rd Quaker Hill (06375) ***(G-7085)***
T-S Display Systems Inc 203 964-0575
76 Progress Dr Stamford (06902) ***(G-8456)***
T/A Engines 860 747-6713
124 Hilltop Rd Plainville (06062) ***(G-6866)***
Tab Brown Publishing LLC 860 985-9621
49 Girard Ave Hartford (06105) ***(G-3697)***
Tabar Designs 203 453-8868
71 Whitfield St Ste 204 Guilford (06437) ***(G-3397)***
Tacdab LLC 860 447-9023
611 Vauxhall Street Ext Waterford (06385) ***(G-9674)***
Tachwa Enterprises Inc 203 691-5772
4 Industrial Cir Hamden (06517) ***(G-3517)***
Tachwa Enterprises Inc 203 367-9903
805 Housatonic Ave Bridgeport (06604) ***(G-919)***
Tack Trunk 203 880-9972
444 Main St Ste B Monroe (06468) ***(G-4754)***
Taco Fasteners Inc 860 747-5597
71 Northwest Dr Plainville (06062) ***(G-6867)***
Taconic Wire, North Branford *Also called S A Candelora Enterprises* ***(G-5854)***
Tactical Communications Inc 203 453-2389
29 Soundview Rd Guilford (06437) ***(G-3398)***
Tag Manufacturing LLC 860 479-5120
161 Woodford Ave Ste 49 Plainville (06062) ***(G-6868)***
Tag Promotions Inc 800 909-4011
500 Purdy Hill Rd Ste 9 Monroe (06468) ***(G-4755)***
Tagetik North America LLC 203 391-7520
9 W Broad St Ste 400 Stamford (06902) ***(G-8457)***
Taillon Auto Top Company 860 583-5525
334 West St Ste 1 Bristol (06010) ***(G-1125)***
Tailor Vintage, Norwalk *Also called Sam & Ty LLC* ***(G-6337)***
Tailored Kitchens By Ann-Morin 860 428-2397
33 Grand View Ter Brooklyn (06234) ***(G-1256)***
Take Cake LLC 203 453-1896
2458 Boston Post Rd Ste 2 Guilford (06437) ***(G-3399)***
Talalay Global, Shelton *Also called Latex Foam Intl Holdings Inc* ***(G-7488)***
Talcott Mountain Engineering 860 651-3141
22 Talcott Mountain Rd Simsbury (06070) ***(G-7649)***
Talk N Fix CT Inc 203 790-8905
7 Backus Ave Fl 2 Danbury (06810) ***(G-1959)***
Tall Trees Press 860 233-7024
54 Henley Way West Hartford (06117) ***(G-9864)***
Tallon Lumber Inc 860 824-0733
2 Tallon Dr Canaan (06018) ***(G-1293)***
Talmadge & Valentine Co Inc 860 350-3534
85 Danbury Rd New Milford (06776) ***(G-5592)***
Tam Communications Inc 203 425-8777
37 North Ave Ste 208 Norwalk (06851) ***(G-6362)***
Tangen Biosciences Inc 203 433-4045
780r E Main St Ste 1 Branford (06405) ***(G-660)***
Tango Modem LLC 203 421-2245
303 Race Hill Rd Madison (06443) ***(G-3963)***
Tangoe Us Inc 203 859-9300
1 Waterview Dr Ste 200 Shelton (06484) ***(G-7563)***
Tangoe Us Inc (HQ) 973 257-0300
1 Waterview Dr Ste 200 Shelton (06484) ***(G-7564)***
Tantor Media Incorporated 860 395-1155
6 Business Park Rd Old Saybrook (06475) ***(G-6572)***
Tapped Apple Winery 860 887-0727
32 Perkins Ave Norwich (06360) ***(G-6435)***
TAR LLC 203 449-4520
2209 Main St Bridgeport (06606) ***(G-920)***
Target Custom Manufacturing Co 860 388-5848
164 Old Boston Post Rd Old Saybrook (06475) ***(G-6573)***
Target Flavors Inc 203 775-4727
7 Del Mar Dr Brookfield (06804) ***(G-1228)***
Target Machines Inc 860 675-1539
713 George Wash Tpke Burlington (06013) ***(G-1276)***
Target Marketing Assoc Inc 860 571-7294
35 Cold Spring Rd Ste 224 Rocky Hill (06067) ***(G-7268)***
Taroli Chris, New Canaan *Also called Eastern Inc* ***(G-5102)***
Tarry Manufacturing, Danbury *Also called Tarry Medical Products Inc* ***(G-1960)***
Tarry Medical Products Inc 203 794-1438
22 Shelter Rock Ln Unit 7 Danbury (06810) ***(G-1960)***
Tashua Litho 203 268-5561
79 Old Newtown Rd Monroe (06468) ***(G-4756)***
Tassels 203 231-0973
17 Cedric Ave Derby (06418) ***(G-2128)***
Tasteful Gift Baskets By Mrs G, Waterbury *Also called Grotto Always Inc* ***(G-9491)***
Tasty Kale LLC 203 560-9451
65 Mckinley Ave New Haven (06515) ***(G-5410)***
Tater Bats LLC 203 510-4054
82 Woodhaven St Waterbury (06708) ***(G-9609)***
Taunton Inc 203 426-8171
63 S Main St Newtown (06470) ***(G-5785)***
Taunton Interactive Inc 203 426-8171
63 S Main St Newtown (06470) ***(G-5786)***
Taunton Press, Newtown *Also called Taunton Inc* ***(G-5785)***
Taunton Press Inc 203 426-8171
191 S Main St Newtown (06470) ***(G-5787)***
Tauton Press 203 304-3000
52 Church Hill Rd Newtown (06470) ***(G-5788)***
Tavisca LLC 203 956-1000
6 High Ridge Park Stamford (06905) ***(G-8458)***
Tax Tracker LLC 860 296-8143
380 Ranklin Ave Hartford (06114) ***(G-3698)***
Taylor & Fenn Company 860 219-9393
22 Deerfield Rd Windsor (06095) ***(G-10448)***
Taylor Coml Foodservice Inc 336 245-6400
3 Farm Glen Blvd Ste 301 Farmington (06032) ***(G-2963)***
Taylor Communications Inc 860 290-6851
800 Connecticut Blvd East Hartford (06108) ***(G-2382)***
Taylor Energy 860 623-3309
152 Broad Brook Rd East Windsor (06088) ***(G-2526)***
Taylors Luggage Inc 203 966-9961
8 Elm St New Canaan (06840) ***(G-5150)***

ALPHABETIC SECTION

Tbs Adjusting Inc 203 274-5525
  35 Lawton Ave Stamford (06907) *(G-8459)*
Tca, Darien Also called Compleat Angler *(G-2014)*
Tcc Multi Kargo 203 803-1462
  349 Dr Mrtin L King Jr Dr Norwalk (06854) *(G-6363)*
Tcg Green Technologies Inc 860 364-4694
  1 Skiff Mountain Rd Sharon (06069) *(G-7384)*
Tcsp, Norwalk Also called Computer Support People LLC *(G-6122)*
TD&s Acquisition LLC 860 341-1001
  180 Johnson St Middletown (06457) *(G-4424)*
Tdi, Torrington Also called Torrington Distributors Inc *(G-8981)*
Tdy Industries LLC 860 259-6346
  33 John St Ste 39 New Britain (06051) *(G-5072)*
Te Connectivity Corporation 860 684-8000
  15 Tyco Dr Stafford Springs (06076) *(G-8041)*
Tea-Rrific Ice Cream LLC 203 354-9805
  480 Barnum Ave Ste 3 Bridgeport (06608) *(G-921)*
Teagen and Ash Hand Painter, Woodstock Also called Steven Rosendahl Inc *(G-10685)*
Teak LLC 203 845-0345
  215 Westport Ave Norwalk (06851) *(G-6364)*
Teakflex Products, Pawcatuck Also called International Printing Access *(G-6717)*
Team Destination Inc 203 235-6000
  477 S Broad St Ste 14 Meriden (06450) *(G-4251)*
Team Walbern 860 667-7627
  37 Stanwell Rd Newington (06111) *(G-5710)*
Tech Air, Naugatuck Also called Airgas Usa LLC *(G-4856)*
Tech Air Northern Cal LLC (PA) 203 792-1834
  50 Mill Plain Rd Danbury (06811) *(G-1961)*
Tech Circuits, Wallingford Also called Apct-Wallingford Inc *(G-9208)*
Tech-Air Incorporated 860 848-1287
  152 Route 163 Uncasville (06382) *(G-9104)*
Tech-Repro Inc 203 348-8884
  555 Summer St Ste 1 Stamford (06901) *(G-8460)*
Technical Brief 203 432-8188
  222 York St New Haven (06511) *(G-5411)*
Technical Consulting 203 268-8890
  17 Westview Dr Monroe (06468) *(G-4757)*
Technical Engineering 860 645-9401
  100 Chapel Rd Manchester (06042) *(G-4100)*
Technical Industries Inc (PA) 860 489-2160
  336 Pinewoods Rd Torrington (06790) *(G-8976)*
Technical Manufacturing Corp 860 349-1735
  645 New Haven Rd Durham (06422) *(G-2158)*
Technical Metal Finishing Inc 203 284-7825
  29 Capital Dr Wallingford (06492) *(G-9379)*
Technical Reproductions Inc 203 849-9100
  326 Main Ave Norwalk (06851) *(G-6365)*
Technipower Systems Inc (HQ) 203 748-7001
  57 Commerce Dr Brookfield (06804) *(G-1229)*
Technique Printers Inc 860 669-2516
  36 Old Post Rd Clinton (06413) *(G-1529)*
Technisonic Research Inc 203 368-3600
  328 Commerce Dr Fairfield (06825) *(G-2853)*
Techno Mtal Post Watertown LLC 203 755-6403
  88 Meadowbrook Dr Waterbury (06706) *(G-9610)*
Technology Group LLC 860 524-4400
  280 Trumbull St Fl 24 Hartford (06103) *(G-3699)*
Technology In Controls Inc 860 283-8405
  390 South St Plymouth (06782) *(G-6929)*
Technology Inf Parters 860 985-8760
  302 Stonegate Rd Southington (06489) *(G-7984)*
Technology Integrators Inc 203 333-7185
  136 Szost Dr Fairfield (06824) *(G-2854)*
Technology Plastics LLC 806 583-1590
  75 Napco Dr Terryville (06786) *(G-8774)*
Technolutions Inc 203 404-4835
  234 Church St Fl 15 New Haven (06510) *(G-5412)*
Technosoft Solutions Inc 203 676-8299
  87 Florence Rd Unit 1a Branford (06405) *(G-661)*
Techwear USA, New Canaan Also called Sportco Inc *(G-5146)*
Teck Welding & Fabrication LLC 860 584-1264
  52 Carmelo Rd Bristol (06010) *(G-1126)*
Teclens LLC 919 824-5224
  9 Riverbend Dr S Ste C Stamford (06907) *(G-8461)*
Ted Boccuzzi 860 354-3799
  64 Sunny Valley Ln New Milford (06776) *(G-5593)*
Teddy S Custom Metalworks Inc 203 359-6927
  100 Research Dr Ste 1 Stamford (06906) *(G-8462)*
Tee Squares 844 669-8337
  672 Lakeside Dr Bridgeport (06606) *(G-922)*
Teed Off Publishing Inc 561 266-0872
  48 Nicholas Ave Greenwich (06831) *(G-3243)*
Tees & More LLC 860 244-2224
  306 Murphy Rd Hartford (06114) *(G-3700)*
Tees Plus 800 782-8337
  850 Main St Fl 6 Bridgeport (06604) *(G-923)*
Tef LLC 203 878-9740
  65 Centennial Dr Milford (06461) *(G-4662)*
Tek Arms Inc 860 748-6289
  282 Jagger Ln Hebron (06248) *(G-3757)*
Tek Industries Inc 860 870-0001
  48 Hockanum Blvd Unit 1 Vernon (06066) *(G-9154)*

Tek-Air Systems Inc 203 791-1400
  600 Pepper St Monroe (06468) *(G-4758)*
Tek-Motive Inc 203 468-2224
  171 Turtle Bay Dr Branford (06405) *(G-662)*
Tekcast Industries 860 799-6464
  6 Oak Dr Sherman (06784) *(G-7605)*
Tektronix 203 730-2730
  100 Wooster Hts Danbury (06810) *(G-1962)*
Tektronix Graphics Printing 203 359-8003
  456 Glenbrook Rd Ste 2 Stamford (06906) *(G-8463)*
Tele-Spot Systems, Stamford Also called T-S Display Systems Inc *(G-8456)*
Teleboardusa.com, Putnam Also called Uniboard Corp *(G-7075)*
Teleflex Incorporated 860 742-8821
  1295 Main St Coventry (06238) *(G-1681)*
Teleflight Stair System, Guilford Also called Beckm LLC *(G-3327)*
Telefunken Elektro Acoustic, South Windsor Also called Telefunken USA LLC *(G-7832)*
Telefunken USA LLC 860 882-5919
  300 Pleasant Valley Rd E South Windsor (06074) *(G-7832)*
Telemark Systems Inc 860 355-8001
  42 Squire Hill Rd New Milford (06776) *(G-5594)*
Telenity Inc 203 445-2000
  755 Main St Ste 7 Monroe (06468) *(G-4759)*
Telic Manufacturing, Milford Also called Linda Hoagland *(G-4568)*
Telke Tool & Die Mfg Co 860 828-9955
  47 Cambridge Hts Kensington (06037) *(G-3819)*
Tell ME Press LLC 203 562-4215
  98 Mansfield St New Haven (06511) *(G-5413)*
Telling Industries LLC 860 731-7975
  1050 Kennedy Rd Windsor (06095) *(G-10449)*
Tellus Technology Inc (PA) 646 265-7960
  10 Corbin Dr Ste 210 Darien (06820) *(G-2046)*
Temperature Guard, Farmington Also called Microtechnologies Inc *(G-2929)*
Ten 22 Inc 860 963-1050
  158 Main St Ste 9 Putnam (06260) *(G-7072)*
Tenova Inc 203 265-5684
  1070 N Farms Rd Ste 3b Wallingford (06492) *(G-9380)*
Tenzingbrook Software LLC 203 918-4500
  887 Weed St New Canaan (06840) *(G-5151)*
Terex Corporation (PA) 203 222-7170
  200 Nyala Farms Rd Ste 2 Westport (06880) *(G-10163)*
Terex Usa LLC (HQ) 203 222-7170
  200 Nyala Farms Rd Westport (06880) *(G-10164)*
Terex Utilities Inc 860 436-3700
  61 Arrow Rd Ste 12 Hartford (06109) *(G-3701)*
Terris Affordable Embroidery 860 928-0552
  144 Providence St Putnam (06260) *(G-7073)*
Terris Embroidery 860 928-0552
  96 Front St Putnam (06260) *(G-7074)*
Terry Brick 860 889-2232
  77 Clinton Ave Norwich (06360) *(G-6436)*
Tesco Resources Inc 203 754-3900
  170 Freight St Waterbury (06702) *(G-9611)*
Test Logic Inc 860 347-8378
  17 Kenneth Dooley Dr Middletown (06457) *(G-4425)*
Testing For Toxins 203 972-6501
  159 Lost District Dr New Canaan (06840) *(G-5152)*
Testing Technologies Inc 212 835-3617
  30 Spoonwood Rd Wilton (06897) *(G-10337)*
TET Mfg Co Inc 860 349-1004
  2 Old Indian Trl Middlefield (06455) *(G-4307)*
Tet Mfg Co/Machine Shop, Middlefield Also called TET Mfg Co Inc *(G-4307)*
Teta Activewear By Custom 203 879-4420
  14 Town Line Rd Ste 1 Wolcott (06716) *(G-10591)*
Teta Actvwear By Cstm Sprtwear, Wolcott Also called Custom Sportswear Mfg *(G-10559)*
Tetco Inc 860 747-1280
  4 Northwest Dr Plainville (06062) *(G-6869)*
Tetraflo 860 575-0867
  100 Halls Rd Old Lyme (06371) *(G-6520)*
Tetrault & Sons Inc 860 872-9187
  75 Tetrault Rd Stafford Springs (06076) *(G-8042)*
Tex Elm Inc 860 873-9715
  136 Town St East Haddam (06423) *(G-2249)*
Textron Aviation Inc 203 262-9366
  288 Christian St Oxford (06478) *(G-6697)*
Textspeak Corporation 203 803-1069
  55 Greens Farms Rd Westport (06880) *(G-10165)*
Textspeak Design, Westport Also called Textspeak Corporation *(G-10165)*
Teys (usa) Inc 203 227-0481
  191 Post Rd W Westport (06880) *(G-10166)*
Tfac LLC 203 776-6000
  27 Whitney Ave New Haven (06510) *(G-5414)*
Tg Floors 860 355-5660
  63 Heacock Crossbrook Rd New Milford (06776) *(G-5595)*
Tgs Cables 203 668-6568
  290 Pratt St Meriden (06450) *(G-4252)*
Thadieo Inc 860 621-4500
  405 Queen St Ste M Southington (06489) *(G-7985)*
Thames River Furniture LLC 201 312-2050
  5 Red Cedar Ave Uncasville (06382) *(G-9105)*
Thames Shipyard & Repair Co 860 442-5349
  50 Farnsworth St New London (06320) *(G-5493)*

(PA)=Parent Co (HQ)=Headquarters (DH)=Div Headquarters

Tharavadu Cor 203 852-1213
86 Washington St Norwalk (06854) *(G-6366)*
Thavenet Machine Company Inc 860 599-4495
12 Chase St Ste 14 Pawcatuck (06379) *(G-6726)*
Thayermahan Inc 860 785-9994
120b Leonard Dr Groton (06340) *(G-3315)*
Thayers Natural Remedies, Easton *Also called Henry Thayer Company (G-2556)*
The Around The Worlds Around 860 871-7241
126 Windermere Ave Ellington (06029) *(G-2606)*
The Bee Publishing Company (PA) 203 426-8036
5 Church Hill Rd Newtown (06470) *(G-5789)*
The Bee Publishing Company 203 426-0178
17 Commerce Rd Newtown (06470) *(G-5790)*
The Connecticut Law Tribune, Hartford *Also called Alm Media LLC (G-3551)*
The Did Collection 203 807-4305
42 Van Buskirk Ave Stamford (06902) *(G-8464)*
The E J Davis Company 203 239-5391
10 Dodge Ave North Haven (06473) *(G-5998)*
The Keeney Manufacturing Co (PA) 603 239-6371
1170 Main St Newington (06111) *(G-5711)*
The L C Doane Company (PA) 860 767-8295
110 Pond Meadow Rd Ivoryton (06442) *(G-3790)*
The L Suzio Concrete Co Inc (PA) 203 237-8421
975 Westfield Rd Meriden (06450) *(G-4253)*
The Merrill Anderson Co Inc 203 377-4996
1166 Barnum Ave Stratford (06614) *(G-8694)*
The Real Estate Book, Guilford *Also called Donnin Publishing Inc (G-3347)*
The Smith Worthington Sad Co 860 527-9117
275 Homestead Ave Hartford (06112) *(G-3702)*
Thebeamer LLC 860 212-5071
87 Church St East Hartford (06108) *(G-2383)*
Theis Precision Steel USA Inc (HQ) 860 589-5511
300 Broad St Bristol (06010) *(G-1127)*
Thelemic Printshop 860 383-4014
13 West Pkwy Plainfield (06374) *(G-6754)*
Theracour Pharma Inc 203 937-6137
135 Wood St Ste 8 West Haven (06516) *(G-9958)*
Theresas Colorful Creations 860 726-6909
15 Myrtle St East Hartford (06108) *(G-2384)*
Therma-Scan Inc 860 872-9770
43 Claire Rd Vernon Rockville (06066) *(G-9181)*
Thermaglo, Uncasville *Also called Northeast Wood Products LLC (G-9100)*
Thermal Energy Resource Mfg & 860 225-8792
312 Monroe St New Britain (06052) *(G-5073)*
Thermal Fluidics 860 740-4880
42 Ozick Dr Ste 5 Durham (06422) *(G-2159)*
Thermatool Corp (HQ) 203 468-4100
31 Commerce St East Haven (06512) *(G-2455)*
Thermatool Mill Syst 203 468-4178
15 Michael Dr Farmington (06032) *(G-2964)*
Thermaxx LLC (PA) 203 672-1021
14 Farwell St West Haven (06516) *(G-9959)*
Thermo Conductor Services Inc 203 758-6611
3 Industrial Rd Prospect (06712) *(G-7026)*
Thermospas Hot Tub Products 203 303-0005
10 Research Pkwy Ste 300 Wallingford (06492) *(G-9381)*
These Guys 860 344-0022
32 Washington St Ste 5 Middletown (06457) *(G-4426)*
Thimble Island Brewing Company 203 208-2827
16 Business Park Dr Branford (06405) *(G-663)*
Think Ahead Software LLC (PA) 860 463-9786
30 Wardwell Rd West Hartford (06107) *(G-9865)*
Think Big Publications LLC 203 685-4957
44 Moody Ave Fairfield (06825) *(G-2855)*
Thirdshift Publishing 860 521-6613
215 Raymond Rd West Hartford (06107) *(G-9866)*
Thirty Two Signs 860 822-1132
220 Main St Baltic (06330) *(G-122)*
Thirty Two Signs LLC 860 564-0532
13 West Pkwy Plainfield (06374) *(G-6755)*
This Old House Ventures LLC 475 209-8665
2 Harbor Dr Stamford (06902) *(G-8465)*
Thomas Bernhard Building Sys 203 925-0414
281 Pequot Ave Southport (06890) *(G-8013)*
Thomas Carr III 860 653-3431
52 Cooley Rd North Granby (06060) *(G-5882)*
Thomas Concrete 860 628-4957
111 Ciccio Rd Southington (06489) *(G-7986)*
Thomas Delspina Fine Frames 203 256-8628
67 Poland St Bridgeport (06605) *(G-924)*
Thomas Design Group LLC 203 588-1910
360 Fairfield Ave Stamford (06902) *(G-8466)*
Thomas F Kyasky 860 567-4077
442 Milton Rd Litchfield (06759) *(G-3902)*
Thomas Hooker Brewing Co LLC 860 242-3111
16 Tobey Rd Rear Bloomfield (06002) *(G-491)*
Thomas J Hunt Inc 203 775-5050
317 Federal Rd Ste A Brookfield (06804) *(G-1230)*
Thomas J Lipton, Trumbull *Also called Conopco Inc (G-9014)*
Thomas J Lipton Inc 206 381-3500
75 Merritt Blvd Trumbull (06611) *(G-9081)*
Thomas Keegan & Sons Inc (PA) 203 239-9248
75 Valley Service Rd North Haven (06473) *(G-5999)*

Thomas La Ganga 860 489-0920
612 S Main St Torrington (06790) *(G-8977)*
Thomas Lord Cabinet Maker 860 546-9283
68 N Society Rd Canterbury (06331) *(G-1302)*
Thomas Manufacturing LLC 203 209-4568
378 Highland Ave Stratford (06614) *(G-8695)*
Thomas Meade 203 209-7591
40 Beacon Hill Ter Shelton (06484) *(G-7565)*
Thomas Products Ltd 860 621-9101
987 West St Southington (06489) *(G-7987)*
Thomas S Klise Co 860 536-4200
42 Denison Ave Mystic (06355) *(G-4848)*
Thomas Spring Co of Conneticut 203 874-7030
29 Seemans Ln Milford (06460) *(G-4663)*
Thomas Townsend Custom Marine 860 536-9800
100 Essex St Mystic (06355) *(G-4849)*
Thomas W Raftery Inc 860 278-9870
1055 Broad St Hartford (06106) *(G-3703)*
Thomastn-Mdtown Screw Mch Pdts 860 283-9796
550 N Main St Thomaston (06787) *(G-8812)*
Thomaston Express, The Div, Torrington *Also called Bristol Press (G-8906)*
Thomaston Industries Inc 860 283-4358
41 Electric Ave Thomaston (06787) *(G-8813)*
Thomaston Swiss, Thomaston *Also called Tyler Automatics Incorporated (G-8815)*
Thommen Industries LLC 203 332-7999
450 Lake Ave Bridgeport (06605) *(G-925)*
Thommen, Harry Co, Bridgeport *Also called Harry Thommen Company (G-782)*
Thompson Aerospace LLC 860 516-0472
220 Business Park Dr Bristol (06010) *(G-1128)*
Thompson Brands LLC 203 235-2541
80 S Vine St Meriden (06451) *(G-4254)*
Thompson Candy Company 203 235-2541
80 S Vine St Meriden (06451) *(G-4255)*
Thomson Arpax Mechatronics LLC 516 883-8000
7 Mckee Pl Cheshire (06410) *(G-1455)*
Thomson Reuters Corporation 203 466-5055
250 Dodge Ave East Haven (06512) *(G-2456)*
Thomson Reuters Risk MGT Inc 203 539-8000
1 Station Pl Stamford (06902) *(G-8467)*
Thomson Reuters US LLC (HQ) 203 539-8000
1 Station Pl Ste 6 Stamford (06902) *(G-8468)*
Thor Audio 203 373-9264
315 Palamar Dr Fairfield (06825) *(G-2856)*
Thorn Industries LLC 845 531-7767
81 Milwaukee Ave Apt 3 Bethel (06801) *(G-352)*
Thornton and Company Inc 860 628-6771
132 Main St Ste 2a 3 Southington (06489) *(G-7988)*
Thornview Custom Cabinets 860 228-5054
186 Pine St Columbia (06237) *(G-1613)*
Thought For The Week, Stamford *Also called Clemons Productions Inc (G-8150)*
Thoughtventions Unlimited LLC 860 657-9014
40 Nutmeg Ln Glastonbury (06033) *(G-3086)*
Thread Mill Partners LLC 860 495-5319
12 River Rd Pawcatuck (06379) *(G-6727)*
Thread Rolling Inc 860 528-1515
41 Cedar St East Hartford (06108) *(G-2385)*
Threads of Evidence LLC 203 929-5209
52 Oronoque Trl Shelton (06484) *(G-7566)*
Three Across LLC 203 866-6688
6 Prowitt St Norwalk (06855) *(G-6367)*
Three D Print LLC 203 590-3463
31 Scenic Hill Ln Monroe (06468) *(G-4760)*
Three Kings Products LLC 860 945-5294
1021 Echo Lake Rd Watertown (06795) *(G-9740)*
Three Poets Publishing Co LLC 203 248-0200
900 Mix Ave U64 Hamden (06514) *(G-3518)*
Three Suns Ltd 860 233-7658
157 Robin Rd Hartford (06119) *(G-3704)*
Threshold, Unionville *Also called Data Management Incorporated (G-9113)*
Tht Inc 203 226-6408
33 Riverside Ave Ste 506 Westport (06880) *(G-10167)*
Thule Inc 203 881-9600
40 Pepes Farm Rd Milford (06460) *(G-4664)*
Thule Inc (HQ) 203 881-9600
42 Silvermine Rd Seymour (06483) *(G-7368)*
Thule Canada Holding LLC 203 881-4919
42 Silvermine Rd Seymour (06483) *(G-7369)*
Thule Holding Inc (HQ) 203 881-9600
42 Silvermine Rd Seymour (06483) *(G-7370)*
Thursdays Child Publishing LLC 203 929-5080
7 Tulip Ln Shelton (06484) *(G-7567)*
Thyssenkrupp Materials NA Inc 203 265-1567
5 Sterling Dr Wallingford (06492) *(G-9382)*
Thyssenkrupp Materials NA Inc 610 586-1800
5 Sterling Dr Wallingford (06492) *(G-9383)*
Tibby's Electric Motor Service, Bethel *Also called Cudzilo Enterprises Inc (G-275)*
Tibbys Electric Motor Service 203 748-4694
40 Taylor Ave Bethel (06801) *(G-353)*
Tick Box Technology Corp 203 852-7171
15 Chapel St Norwalk (06850) *(G-6368)*
Ticket Software LLC 860 644-0422
83 Gerber Rd W South Windsor (06074) *(G-7833)*

ALPHABETIC SECTION

Tico Titanium Inc (PA) 248 446-0400
34b Barnes Indus Rd S Wallingford (06492) *(G-9384)*
Tides Black Group LLC 203 244-8433
8 Diane Dr Monroe (06468) *(G-4761)*
Tier One LLC 203 426-3030
31 Pecks Ln Ste 1 Newtown (06470) *(G-5791)*
Tiffany Press Inc 914 806-2245
68 Saddle Hill Rd Stamford (06903) *(G-8469)*
Tiger Enterprises Inc 860 621-9155
379 Summer St Plantsville (06479) *(G-6914)*
Tiger Fabrication LLC 860 460-7600
12 Alice Ct Ste 3 Pawcatuck (06379) *(G-6728)*
Tiger-Sul Products LLC 251 202-3850
4 Armstrong Rd Ste 220 Shelton (06484) *(G-7568)*
Tighitco Inc 860 828-0298
245 Old Brickyard Ln Berlin (06037) *(G-225)*
Tilcon Bituminous Concrete, Portland *Also called Tilcon Connecticut Inc (G-6977)*
Tilcon Connecticut Inc (HQ) 860 224-6010
642 Black Rock Ave New Britain (06052) *(G-5074)*
Tilcon Connecticut Inc 860 342-6157
231 Airline Ave Portland (06480) *(G-6977)*
Tilcon Connecticut Inc 860 756-8016
301 Harford Ave Unit 301 Newington (06111) *(G-5712)*
Tilcon Connecticut Inc 860 224-6010
245 Shaker Rd Enfield (06082) *(G-2701)*
Tilcon Connecticut Inc 860 844-7000
60 S Main St East Granby (06026) *(G-2232)*
Tilcon Connecticut Inc 860 342-1096
Black Rock Ave Portland (06480) *(G-6978)*
Tilcon Connecticut Portland, Portland *Also called Tilcon Connecticut Inc (G-6978)*
Tilcon Inc (HQ) 860 223-3651
301 Hartford Ave Newington (06111) *(G-5713)*
Tillerman 203 421-6643
28 Field Brook Rd Madison (06443) *(G-3964)*
Tillys Natural Blend LLC 203 270-8406
32 Old Farm Hill Rd Newtown (06470) *(G-5792)*
Tim Poloski 860 508-6566
38 Risley Rd Vernon Rockville (06066) *(G-9182)*
Tim Prentice 860 672-6728
129 Lake Rd West Cornwall (06796) *(G-9765)*
Tim Welder LLC 860 646-1356
37 Cook St Manchester (06040) *(G-4101)*
Tim Welding 203 488-3486
107 W Pond Rd North Branford (06471) *(G-5862)*
Timber Frame Barn Conversions 860 219-0519
226 Rollingbrook Windsor (06095) *(G-10450)*
Timber-Top Inc 860 274-6706
210 Hopkins Rd Watertown (06795) *(G-9741)*
Timbercraft Cstm Dvtail Drwers 800 345-4930
5 Old Town Park Rd New Milford (06776) *(G-5596)*
Timbercraft LLC 860 355-5538
70 S End Plz New Milford (06776) *(G-5597)*
Timbers Edge Woodworking 860 836-7328
24 Goshen Rd Bozrah (06334) *(G-533)*
Timberwolf Logging 860 683-0071
416 Pigeon Hill Rd Windsor (06095) *(G-10451)*
Timco Instruments Div, Guilford *Also called Fitzhugh Electrical Corp (G-3352)*
Time Aviation LLC 203 496-5716
75 Holly Hill Ln Ste 100 Greenwich (06830) *(G-3244)*
Timeless Stone Inc 860 242-3300
21b E Dudley Town Rd Bloomfield (06002) *(G-492)*
Timer Digest Publishing Inc 203 629-2589
268 Round Hill Rd Greenwich (06831) *(G-3245)*
Times Community News Group 860 437-1150
47 Eugene Oneill Dr New London (06320) *(G-5494)*
Times Fiber Communications Inc (HQ) 203 265-8500
358 Hall Ave Wallingford (06492) *(G-9385)*
Times Microwave Systems Inc (HQ) 203 949-8400
358 Hall Ave Wallingford (06492) *(G-9386)*
Times Publishing LLC 860 349-8532
491 Main St Middlefield (06455) *(G-4308)*
Times Wire and Cable Company (HQ) 203 949-8400
358 Hall Ave Wallingford (06492) *(G-9387)*
Timet, East Windsor *Also called Titanium Metals Corporation (G-2527)*
Timex Group Usa Inc (HQ) 203 346-5000
555 Christian Rd Middlebury (06762) *(G-4297)*
Timken Arospc Drv Systems LLC 860 649-0000
586 Hilliard St Manchester (06042) *(G-4102)*
Timken Company 860 652-4630
701 Hebron Ave Ste 2 Glastonbury (06033) *(G-3087)*
Timna Manufacturing Inc 203 265-4656
204 N Plains Indus Rd Wallingford (06492) *(G-9388)*
Timothy Gray 860 314-0863
21 Porter Rd Wolcott (06716) *(G-10592)*
Tims Sign & Lighting Service 203 634-8840
38 Elm St Ste 2 Meriden (06450) *(G-4256)*
Tinas Heavenly Treats 203 543-3560
35 Meadowview Ave Stratford (06615) *(G-8696)*
Tinny Corporation 860 854-6121
100 Bradley St Middletown (06457) *(G-4427)*
Tinplex Corporation 203 335-8217
210 Stillson Rd Fairfield (06825) *(G-2857)*
Tinsley GROup-Ps&w Inc (HQ) 919 742-5832
1 Eastern Steel Rd Milford (06460) *(G-4665)*
Tiny B Code LLC 617 308-9635
38 N Main St Apt 30 West Hartford (06107) *(G-9867)*
Tiny Woodshop 203 866-6725
123 Stuart Ave Norwalk (06850) *(G-6369)*
Tiny-Clutch, Clinton *Also called Helander Products Inc (G-1507)*
Tipping Pt Resources Group LLC 800 603-8902
100 Waterfront St New Haven (06512) *(G-5415)*
Tired Mommy Candles 860 407-2002
52 Bergendahl Dr Griswold (06351) *(G-3268)*
Titanium Electric LLC 203 810-4050
15 Arbor Dr Norwalk (06854) *(G-6370)*
Titanium Industries Inc 860 870-3939
362 Mile Hill Rd Tolland (06084) *(G-8881)*
Titanium Metals Corporation 860 627-7051
7 Craftsman Rd East Windsor (06088) *(G-2527)*
Tito Welding LLC 860 354-1536
2 Tito Ln New Milford (06776) *(G-5598)*
Titus Technological Labs 860 633-5472
77 Kreiger Ln Ste 914 Glastonbury (06033) *(G-3088)*
Tjl Industries LLC 203 250-2187
19 Willow St Cheshire (06410) *(G-1456)*
Tl Woodworking 203 787-9661
299 Welton St Hamden (06517) *(G-3519)*
Tlb Auto Machine, Norwich *Also called Terry Brick (G-6436)*
TLC Media LLC 203 980-1361
900 Mix Ave Apt 22 Hamden (06514) *(G-3520)*
TLC Ultrasound Inc 860 354-6333
143 West St Ste V New Milford (06776) *(G-5599)*
Tld Ace Corporation 860 602-3300
805 Bloomfield Ave Windsor (06095) *(G-10452)*
TLD America Corporation (HQ) 860 602-3400
812 Bloomfield Ave Windsor (06095) *(G-10453)*
Tld Group, Windsor *Also called TLD America Corporation (G-10453)*
Tm Ward Co of Connecticut LLC 203 866-9203
5 Wilbur St Norwalk (06854) *(G-6371)*
Tmf Incorporated 203 267-7364
1266 Main St S Ste 3 Southbury (06488) *(G-7880)*
Tms International LLC 203 629-8383
165 W Putnam Ave Greenwich (06830) *(G-3246)*
Tna Records & Studios, Wallingford *Also called Trod Nossel Prdctns & Rcrdng S (G-9391)*
To Give Is Better 860 261-5443
139 Center St Ste 5007 Bristol (06010) *(G-1129)*
To The tenth Inc 203 248-9437
60 Connolly Pkwy 15b-101 Hamden (06514) *(G-3521)*
Toastmasters International 203 847-5667
10 Maher Dr Norwalk (06850) *(G-6372)*
Toce Brothers Incorporated (PA) 860 496-2080
145 E Main St Torrington (06790) *(G-8978)*
Todd Lucien Mendes LLC 203 228-3134
63 Tracy Ave Waterbury (06706) *(G-9612)*
Toddler Teams LLC 203 972-7713
5 Southwood Dr New Canaan (06840) *(G-5153)*
Toff Industry Inc 860 378-0532
323 Clark St Milldale (06467) *(G-4689)*
Tog Manufacturing Company Inc 413 663-5753
1000 Stanley Dr New Britain (06053) *(G-5075)*
Tolland Architectural Wdwkg, Tolland *Also called Tolland Archtectural Wdwkg LLC (G-8882)*
Tolland Architectural Wdwkg LLC 860 875-9841
526 Tolland Stage Rd Tolland (06084) *(G-8882)*
Tolland Machine Co 860 872-4863
1050 Hartford Tpke Vernon (06066) *(G-9155)*
Tollman Spring Company Inc 860 583-4856
560 Birch St Bristol (06010) *(G-1130)*
Tom Santos Publishing 860 599-5067
107-3 Brookside Ln Pawcatuck (06379) *(G-6729)*
Tom Voytek 203 367-3991
186 Bradley St Bridgeport (06610) *(G-926)*
Tomkiel Furniture 860 871-7632
84 Jessica Dr South Windsor (06074) *(G-7834)*
Tommy LLC Sock It 860 688-2019
4 Walters Way Windsor (06095) *(G-10454)*
Tommy Tape, Berlin *Also called Midsun Specialty Products Inc (G-200)*
Tommys Supplies LLC 860 265-2199
34 Egypt Rd Unit A Somers (06071) *(G-7674)*
Toms News 860 535-1276
133 Water St Stonington (06378) *(G-8541)*
Toms Seamless Gutters Inc 203 269-2296
54 Ridgewood Rd Wallingford (06492) *(G-9389)*
Toms Taz Lures 860 429-0307
245 River Rd Willington (06279) *(G-10259)*
Tomtec 203 795-5030
607 Harborview Rd Orange (06477) *(G-6631)*
Tomtec Inc 203 281-6790
1000 Sherman Ave Hamden (06514) *(G-3522)*
Tomz Corporation 860 829-0670
47 Episcopal Rd Berlin (06037) *(G-226)*
Toni Leland 860 892-8890
58 Indian Hill Rd Uncasville (06382) *(G-9106)*
Tonmar LLC 860 974-3714
56 Babbitt Hill Rd Pomfret Center (06259) *(G-6947)*

(PA)=Parent Co (HQ)=Headquarters (DH)=Div Headquarters

Tontine Partners L P...203 769-2000
55 Railroad Ave Fl 3 Greenwich (06830) ***(G-3247)***
Tonys Smoke Shop Outlet LLC...203 367-8558
2738 Main St Bridgeport (06606) ***(G-927)***
Tool 2000...860 620-0020
327 Captain Lewis Dr Southington (06489) ***(G-7989)***
Tool Clip, Milford *Also called Arthur I Platt Inc* ***(G-4459)***
Tool Logistics II...203 855-9754
46 Chestnut St Norwalk (06854) ***(G-6373)***
Tool The Somma Company...203 753-2114
109 Scott Rd Waterbury (06705) ***(G-9613)***
Toolmax Designing Tooling Inc...860 871-7265
69 Industrial Park Rd E A Tolland (06084) ***(G-8883)***
Top Flight Machine Tool LLC...860 747-4726
90 Robert Jackson Way Plainville (06062) ***(G-6870)***
Top Notch Manufacturing Co...860 583-2080
130 Enterprise Dr Bristol (06010) ***(G-1131)***
Top of Line Drapery & Uphl...203 348-0000
90 Lincoln Ave Stamford (06902) ***(G-8470)***
Top Priority Tool LLC...860 665-1012
321 Ellis St Ste 8 New Britain (06051) ***(G-5076)***
Top Sheft Cabinetry...203 345-0000
955 Connecticut Ave Bridgeport (06607) ***(G-928)***
Top Source Inc...203 753-6490
490 S Main St Waterbury (06706) ***(G-9614)***
Topaz Enterprise Sand Pubg...203 449-1903
304 Main Ave Norwalk (06851) ***(G-6374)***
Topaz Enterprises & Pubg LLC...203 993-9051
26 Monroe St Norwalk (06854) ***(G-6375)***
Topcat LLC...203 610-6544
120 Goodwin Pl Stratford (06615) ***(G-8697)***
Topex Inc...203 748-5918
10 Precision Rd Fl 2 Danbury (06810) ***(G-1963)***
Toppan Photomasks Inc...203 775-9001
246 Federal Rd Ste C22 Brookfield (06804) ***(G-1231)***
Tops Manufacturing Co Inc (PA)...203 655-9367
83 Salisbury Rd Darien (06820) ***(G-2047)***
Topside Canvas Upholstery...860 399-4845
768 Boston Post Rd Westbrook (06498) ***(G-10011)***
Topstone Golf Course, South Windsor *Also called South Windsor Golf Course LLC* ***(G-7826)***
Tornik Inc...860 282-6081
16 Old Forge Rd B Rocky Hill (06067) ***(G-7269)***
Tornos Technologies US Corp...203 775-4319
70 Pocono Rd Brookfield (06804) ***(G-1232)***
Torq Industries LLC...860 537-8539
38 Skinner Rd Colchester (06415) ***(G-1579)***
Torqmaster Inc...203 326-5945
200 Harvard Ave Stamford (06902) ***(G-8471)***
Torqmaster International, Stamford *Also called Torqmaster Inc* ***(G-8471)***
Torque Specialties, Windsor *Also called AKO Inc* ***(G-10357)***
Torrey S Crane Company...860 628-4778
492 Summer St Plantsville (06479) ***(G-6915)***
Torrington Brush Works Inc...860 482-3517
63 Avenue A Torrington (06790) ***(G-8979)***
Torrington Diesel Corporation...860 496-9948
287 Old Winsted Rd Torrington (06790) ***(G-8980)***
Torrington Distributors Inc (PA)...860 482-4464
43 Norfolk St Torrington (06790) ***(G-8981)***
Torrington Ig Partners LLC...860 482-7868
59 Field St Torrington (06790) ***(G-8982)***
Torrington Industries Inc (PA)...860 489-9261
112 Wall St Torrington (06790) ***(G-8983)***
Torrington Lumber Company...860 482-3529
281 Church St Torrington (06790) ***(G-8984)***
Torrington Ready-Mix, Torrington *Also called Torrington Industries Inc* ***(G-8983)***
Total Communications Inc (PA)...860 282-9999
333 Burnham St East Hartford (06108) ***(G-2386)***
Total Communications Inc...203 882-0088
500 Bic Dr Bldg 2 Milford (06461) ***(G-4666)***
Total Concept Tool Inc...203 483-1130
2 Research Dr Ste 1 Branford (06405) ***(G-664)***
Total Control Inc...203 269-4749
130 S Turnpike Rd Wallingford (06492) ***(G-9390)***
Total Drilling Supply LLC...860 923-1091
144 New Rd Thompson (06277) ***(G-8844)***
Total Fab LLC...475 238-8176
140 Commerce St East Haven (06512) ***(G-2457)***
Total Food Service, Greenwich *Also called Ida Publishing Co Inc* ***(G-3178)***
Total Industries LLC...203 624-0426
81 Howard Ave New Haven (06519) ***(G-5416)***
Total Machine Co...203 481-8780
6 Walkley Ml Clinton (06413) ***(G-1530)***
Total Parts Services LLC...203 263-5619
97 S Pomperaug Ave Woodbury (06798) ***(G-10654)***
Total Printing Center, The, Norwalk *Also called Printers of Connecticut Inc* ***(G-6306)***
Total Ptrchemicals Ref USA Inc...203 375-0668
125 Ontario St Stratford (06615) ***(G-8698)***
Total Quality & Mfg Assoc...203 261-3074
76 Holly Pl Monroe (06468) ***(G-4762)***
Total Register Inc...860 210-0465
180 Sunny Valley Rd Ste 1 New Milford (06776) ***(G-5600)***

Toto LLC...203 776-6000
27 Whitney Ave New Haven (06510) ***(G-5417)***
Tots411 LLP...203 558-5369
8 Carolyn Pl Westport (06880) ***(G-10168)***
Tower Brands, Centerbrook *Also called Tower Laboratories Ltd* ***(G-1334)***
Tower Laboratories Ltd...860 669-7078
7 Heritage Park Rd Clinton (06413) ***(G-1531)***
Tower Laboratories Ltd (PA)...860 767-2127
8 Industrial Park Rd Centerbrook (06409) ***(G-1334)***
Tower Optical Company Inc...203 866-4535
275 East Ave Fl 2 Norwalk (06855) ***(G-6376)***
Tower Printing Inc...203 757-1030
1713 Thomaston Ave Waterbury (06704) ***(G-9615)***
Town & Country Cleaners & Tlrs, Watertown *Also called Sumal Enterprises LLC* ***(G-9739)***
Town Fair Tire Centers Inc...860 646-2807
328 Middle Tpke W Manchester (06040) ***(G-4103)***
Town of Bridgewater...860 354-5250
44 Main St Bridgewater (06752) ***(G-947)***
Town of Ledyard...860 464-9060
889 Colonel Ledyard Hwy Gales Ferry (06339) ***(G-2988)***
Town of Medyard, The, Gales Ferry *Also called Town of Ledyard* ***(G-2988)***
Town of Montville...860 848-3830
83 Pink Row Uncasville (06382) ***(G-9107)***
Town of Putnam, Putnam *Also called Superior Plas Extrusion Co Inc* ***(G-7071)***
Town of Vernon...203 268-7200
366 Sport Hill Rd Easton (06612) ***(G-2567)***
Town of Vernon...860 870-3545
100 Windsorville Rd Vernon (06066) ***(G-9156)***
Town of Vernon...860 870-3699
5 Park St Fl 2 Vernon Rockville (06066) ***(G-9183)***
Town of Wilton...203 563-0152
238 Danbury Rd Wilton (06897) ***(G-10338)***
Town Planner, Cos Cob *Also called Helen Grace* ***(G-1633)***
Town Pride...860 664-0448
201 Cow Hill Rd Clinton (06413) ***(G-1532)***
Town Times, Meriden *Also called Record-Journal Newspaper* ***(G-4230)***
Town Times, Watertown *Also called Prime Publishers Inc* ***(G-9724)***
Town Tribune LLC...203 648-6085
10 Sleepy Hollow Rd New Fairfield (06812) ***(G-5179)***
Townhall Bridgewater Selectman, Bridgewater *Also called Town of Bridgewater* ***(G-947)***
Townsend John...860 526-3896
132 Hemlock Dr Deep River (06417) ***(G-2104)***
Toy Pallet...860 803-9838
11 Rothe Ln Ellington (06029) ***(G-2607)***
TP Cycle & Engineering Inc...203 744-4960
4 Finance Dr Danbury (06810) ***(G-1964)***
TPC Replacement Window LLC...860 274-6971
122 Capewell Ave Oakville (06779) ***(G-6464)***
Tps Acquisition LLC (PA)...860 589-5511
151 Sharon Rd Waterbury (06705) ***(G-9616)***
Tr Landworks LLC...860 402-6177
36 Kensington Acres Rd East Hartland (06027) ***(G-2405)***
Track Fresh, Shelton *Also called Swpci* ***(G-7560)***
Track180 LLC...203 605-3540
900 Chapel St Fl 10 New Haven (06510) ***(G-5418)***
Tracy S Products...203 787-2013
300 Whalley Ave Ste 2 New Haven (06511) ***(G-5419)***
Tracy's Products, New Haven *Also called Tracy S Products* ***(G-5419)***
Trade Labels Inc...860 535-4828
28 Cottrell St Ste 28e Mystic (06355) ***(G-4850)***
Trades Industries...203 297-5648
20 Mountainville Ave Danbury (06810) ***(G-1965)***
Tradewinds...203 723-6966
274 Bethany Rd Beacon Falls (06403) ***(G-148)***
Tradewinds...203 324-2994
1010 Washington Blvd # 3 Stamford (06901) ***(G-8472)***
Traditional Bath and Tile...347 539-2088
435 Dogwood Dr Bridgeport (06606) ***(G-929)***
Trailheads, Kent *Also called Indigo Coast Inc* ***(G-3822)***
Trajan Scientific Americas Inc...203 830-4910
21 Berkshire Blvd Bethel (06801) ***(G-354)***
Trajan Scientific and Medical, Bethel *Also called Trajan Scientific Americas Inc* ***(G-354)***
Trane Inc...203 866-7115
145 Main St Norwalk (06851) ***(G-6377)***
Trane Inc...860 437-6208
178 Wallace St New Haven (06511) ***(G-5420)***
Trane Supply, New Haven *Also called Trane Inc* ***(G-5420)***
Trane US Inc...203 295-2170
47 Harbor View Ave Stamford (06902) ***(G-8473)***
Trane US Inc...800 544-1642
390 Fairfield Ave Stamford (06902) ***(G-8474)***
Trane US Inc...860 437-6208
571 Broad St New London (06320) ***(G-5495)***
Trane US Inc...860 470-3901
135 South Rd Ste 1 Farmington (06032) ***(G-2965)***
Trane US Inc...860 541-1721
485 Ledyard St Hartford (06114) ***(G-3705)***
Tranquil Perspectives LLC...860 919-9762
46 Blakeslee Ave North Haven (06473) ***(G-6000)***
Trans-Tek Inc...860 872-8351
10 Industrial Dr Ellington (06029) ***(G-2608)***

ALPHABETIC SECTION

Transact Technologies Inc (PA) 203 859-6800
2319 Whitney Ave Ste 3b Hamden (06518) *(G-3523)*
Transatlantic Bubbles LLC 203 464-0051
935 Greenway Rd Woodbridge (06525) *(G-10619)*
Transducer Products Inc 860 824-1002
4 Gandolfo Dr Canaan (06018) *(G-1294)*
Transformer Technology Inc 860 349-1061
60 Commerce Cir Durham (06422) *(G-2160)*
Transit Systems Inc 860 747-3669
161 Woodford Ave Ste 34 Plainville (06062) *(G-6871)*
Transmode USA, North Branford Also called Transmonde USa Inc *(G-5863)*
Transmonde USa Inc 203 484-1528
100 Shaw Rd North Branford (06471) *(G-5863)*
Transportable LLC 860 455-9208
851 Phoenixville Rd Chaplin (06235) *(G-1343)*
Transportation Conn Dept 860 342-5996
263 Freestone Ave Portland (06480) *(G-6979)*
Trap Rock Quarry 203 263-2195
236 Roxbury Rd Southbury (06488) *(G-7881)*
Trap Rock Ridge Welding LLC 203 213-7578
513 High Hill Rd Meriden (06450) *(G-4257)*
Trassig Corp 203 659-0456
65 Redding Rd Unit 874 Georgetown (06829) *(G-2999)*
Traumaway LLC 860 628-0706
82 Parkview Dr Plantsville (06479) *(G-6916)*
Travel Wear, Norwalk Also called Business Journals Inc *(G-6102)*
Traver Electric Motor Co Inc 203 753-5103
151 Homer St Waterbury (06704) *(G-9617)*
Travers & Co LLC 860 633-8586
311 Woodhaven Rd Glastonbury (06033) *(G-3089)*
Travers Macintosh Consulting, Glastonbury Also called Travers & Co LLC *(G-3089)*
Traxx Software LLC 860 632-8712
1 Pleasant St Cromwell (06416) *(G-1721)*
Trd Specialties Inc 860 738-4505
8 Wickett St Pine Meadow (06061) *(G-6736)*
Tread Well Stair & Millwo 203 488-2146
26 Altieri Rd North Branford (06471) *(G-5864)*
Treadwell Corporation 860 283-7600
341 Railroad St Thomaston (06787) *(G-8814)*
Treasury & Risk Management, Shelton Also called Wicks Business Information LLC *(G-7586)*
Treble Clef Music Press 919 932-5455
14 N Washington Ave Niantic (06357) *(G-5818)*
Treif USA Inc 203 929-9930
50 Waterview Dr Ste 130 Shelton (06484) *(G-7569)*
Trelleborg Ctd Systems US Inc 203 468-0342
30 Lenox St New Haven (06513) *(G-5421)*
Trend Offset Printing Svcs Inc 860 773-6140
60 Security Dr Avon (06001) *(G-117)*
Trento Group LLC 860 623-1361
32 North Rd East Windsor (06088) *(G-2528)*
Trevi Therapeutics Inc 203 304-2499
195 Church St Fl 14 New Haven (06510) *(G-5422)*
Tri LLC 203 353-8418
34 Crescent St Apt 1i Stamford (06906) *(G-8475)*
Tri Mar Manufacturing Compan 860 628-4791
191 Captain Lewis Dr Southington (06489) *(G-7990)*
Tri Source Inc 203 924-7030
84 Platt Rd Shelton (06484) *(G-7570)*
Tri Star Graphics 203 748-4792
274 Greenwood Ave Bethel (06801) *(G-355)*
Tri State Choppers LLC 860 210-1854
30 Old Route 7 Plz New Milford (06776) *(G-5601)*
Tri State Embroidery LLC 203 732-7636
26 East St Ansonia (06401) *(G-53)*
Tri State Maintenance Svcs LLC 203 691-1343
356 Old Maple Ave North Haven (06473) *(G-6001)*
Tri Town Precision Plastics, Deep River Also called Swpc Plastics LLC *(G-2103)*
Tri-County Mold & Machine 860 642-7033
1912 Exeter Rd Lebanon (06249) *(G-3864)*
Tri-County Power Sled, Lebanon Also called Tri-County Mold & Machine *(G-3864)*
Tri-Star Industries Inc 860 828-7570
101 Massirio Dr Berlin (06037) *(G-227)*
Tri-State EMB Screen Prtg LLC 203 732-7636
26 East St Ansonia (06401) *(G-54)*
Tri-State Led Inc 203 813-3791
255 Mill St Greenwich (06830) *(G-3248)*
Tri-Union Seafoods Inc 203 426-1266
16 Palestine Rd Newtown (06470) *(G-5793)*
Triad Concepts Inc 860 399-4045
51 Brookwood Dr Westbrook (06498) *(G-10012)*
Triangle Industries LLC 203 297-6255
64 Triangle St Ste 1 Danbury (06810) *(G-1966)*
Trianja Technologies Inc 203 775-9000
15 Secor Rd Brookfield (06804) *(G-1233)*
Triatic Incorporated 860 236-2298
22 Grassmere Ave West Hartford (06110) *(G-9868)*
Tribal Wear 203 637-7884
27 Summit Rd Riverside (06878) *(G-7202)*
Tribuna Newspaper LLC 203 730-0457
32 Farview Ave 3 Danbury (06810) *(G-1967)*
Trico Welding Company LLC 203 720-3782
84 Feldspar Ave Beacon Falls (06403) *(G-149)*

Tricycle Granola LLC 203 861-1740
27 Meadow Wood Dr Greenwich (06830) *(G-3249)*
Tricycle Hill LLC 203 895-2217
461 Riverside Dr Fairfield (06824) *(G-2858)*
Triem Industries LLC 203 888-1212
105 Napco Dr Terryville (06786) *(G-8775)*
Trigila Construction Inc 860 828-8444
30 And A Half Ripple Ct Berlin (06037) *(G-228)*
Trimino, Branford Also called Miami Bay Beverage Company LLC *(G-626)*
Trine Access Technology Inc 203 730-1756
2 Park Lawn Dr Bethel (06801) *(G-356)*
Trinity Mobile Networks Inc 301 332-6401
770 Chapel St Ste 2 New Haven (06510) *(G-5423)*
Trinity Polymers LLC 860 321-7209
39 Robin Rd Farmington (06032) *(G-2966)*
Trinseo LLC 860 447-7298
1761 Route 12 Bldg 21 Gales Ferry (06335) *(G-2989)*
Tripbuilder Media, Westport Also called Community Brands Holdings LLC *(G-10067)*
Triple A Manufacturing Company 203 743-9043
1 Brookwood Dr Newtown (06470) *(G-5794)*
Triple A Spring Ltd Partnr 860 589-3231
95 Valley St Ste 1 Bristol (06010) *(G-1132)*
Triple Clover Products LLC 475 558-9503
4 Smith Ridge Ln New Canaan (06840) *(G-5154)*
Triple D Transportation Inc 860 243-5057
129 W Dudley Town Rd Bloomfield (06002) *(G-493)*
Triple Play Sports 860 417-2877
16 Straits Tpke Watertown (06795) *(G-9742)*
Triple Stitch Sportswear, Prospect Also called TSS & A Inc *(G-7027)*
Tritex Corporation 203 756-7441
1500 Meriden Rd Waterbury (06705) *(G-9618)*
Triton Excimer Group LLC 203 733-1063
241 Ethan Allen Hwy Ridgefield (06877) *(G-7176)*
Triton Thalassic Tech Inc (PA) 203 438-0633
241 Ethan Allen Hwy Ridgefield (06877) *(G-7177)*
Triumph Actuation Systems - Co (HQ) 860 687-5412
175 Addison Rd Ste 4 Windsor (06095) *(G-10455)*
Triumph Consulting 860 263-8335
75 Tremont St Hartford (06105) *(G-3706)*
Triumph Eng Ctrl Systems LLC 860 236-0651
1 Charter Oak Blvd West Hartford (06110) *(G-9869)*
Triumph Eng Ctrl Systems LLC 860 236-0651
1 Talcott Rd West Hartford (06110) *(G-9870)*
Triumph Group Inc 860 726-9378
1395 Blue Hills Ave Bloomfield (06002) *(G-494)*
Triumph Manufacturing Co Inc 860 635-8811
422 Timber Ridge Rd Middletown (06457) *(G-4428)*
Trod Nossel Prdctns & Rcrdng S 203 269-4465
10 George St Wallingford (06492) *(G-9391)*
Tronox Incorporated (HQ) 203 705-3800
1 Stamford Plz Stamford (06901) *(G-8476)*
Tronox Limited 203 705-3800
1 Stamford Plz Stamford (06901) *(G-8477)*
Tronox LLC (PA) 203 705-3800
263 Tresser Blvd Ste 1100 Stamford (06901) *(G-8478)*
Tropax Precision Manufacturing 203 794-0733
10 Precision Rd Danbury (06810) *(G-1968)*
Trophy Shop 860 871-0867
214 Hartford Tpke Vernon Rockville (06066) *(G-9184)*
Trophy Shop, The, Ashford Also called Wraith Industries LLC *(G-70)*
Trowbridge Forest Products LLC (PA) 860 455-9931
136 Lewis Rd Hampton (06247) *(G-3540)*
Tru Hitch Inc 860 379-7772
16 W West Hill Rd Pleasant Valley (06063) *(G-6927)*
True Inspiration LLC 860 635-7941
20 Timber Hill Rd Cromwell (06416) *(G-1722)*
True Position Mfg LLC 860 291-2987
40 Sandra Dr Ste 3 South Windsor (06074) *(G-7835)*
True Publishing Company 203 272-5316
125 Grandview Ave Wallingford (06492) *(G-9392)*
Trueform Runner, Chester Also called Samsara Fitness LLC *(G-1483)*
Truelove & Maclean Inc 860 274-9600
57 Callender Rd Watertown (06795) *(G-9743)*
Truelove Maclean Inc 203 574-2240
984 Waterville St Waterbury (06710) *(G-9619)*
Trumbull Printing, Trumbull Also called Hersam Acorn Cmnty Pubg LLC *(G-9034)*
Trumbull Printing Inc 203 261-2548
205 Spring Hill Rd Trumbull (06611) *(G-9082)*
Trumbull Recreation Supply Co 860 429-6604
148 River Rd Willington (06279) *(G-10260)*
Trumbull Transfer LLC 203 377-2487
12 Commerce Dr Shelton (06484) *(G-7571)*
Trumpf Inc (HQ) 860 255-6000
111 Hyde Rd Farmington (06032) *(G-2967)*
Trumpf Inc 860 255-6000
3 Johnson Ave Plainville (06062) *(G-6872)*
Trumpf Inc 860 255-6000
1 Johnson Ave Farmington (06032) *(G-2968)*
Trumpf Photonics Inc 860 255-6000
111 Hyde Rd Farmington (06032) *(G-2969)*
Trusource Publications LLC 860 350-6477
7 Elbo Dr New Milford (06776) *(G-5602)*

(PA)=Parent Co (HQ)=Headquarters (DH)=Div Headquarters

Truss Manufacturing Inc 860 665-0000
97 Stanwell Rd Newington (06111) *(G-5714)*
Truth Trckg Expedited Svcs LLC 860 306-5630
2015 Main St Hartford (06120) *(G-3707)*
Trycycle Data Systems US Inc 860 558-1148
400 Farmington Ave # 1844 Farmington (06032) *(G-2970)*
Tryon Manufacturing Company 203 929-0464
30 Oliver Ter Shelton (06484) *(G-7572)*
TS Whitman Custom Wdwkg LLC 860 575-1923
389 Shore Rd South Lyme (06376) *(G-7686)*
Tsg Web Plus, Brookfield *Also called Software Gallery Inc (G-1224)*
Tshirts Etc Inc 860 657-3551
74 Kreiger Ln Ste 1 Glastonbury (06033) *(G-3090)*
Tsmc Inc 860 283-8265
100 Lawton St Torrington (06790) *(G-8985)*
TSS & A Inc 800 633-3536
115 Waterbury Rd Prospect (06712) *(G-7027)*
TSty Brands Inc 203 609-4391
155 Frederick St Apt 2l Stamford (06902) *(G-8479)*
Ttm, Pine Meadow *Also called Kovacs Tamas (G-6734)*
Ttm Printed Circuit Group Inc 860 684-8000
15 Industrial Park Dr Stafford Springs (06076) *(G-8043)*
Ttm Technologies Inc 860 684-5881
4 Old Monson Rd Stafford Springs (06076) *(G-8044)*
Ttm Technologies Inc 860 684-8000
20 Industrial Park Dr Stafford Springs (06076) *(G-8045)*
Ttpockettools LLC 860 642-6020
266 Clubhouse Rd Lebanon (06249) *(G-3865)*
Tub's & Stuff Plumbing Supply, Ansonia *Also called Kensco Inc (G-44)*
Tucci Lumber Co LLC 203 956-6181
227 Wilson Ave Norwalk (06854) *(G-6378)*
Tudor Converted Products Inc (PA) 203 304-1875
22 Main St Unit 1b Newtown (06470) *(G-5795)*
Tudor House Furniture Co Inc 203 288-8451
929 Sherman Ave Hamden (06514) *(G-3524)*
Tulaloo 860 417-2587
72 Parkman St Oakville (06779) *(G-6465)*
Tune Door Inc 914 713-0257
19 Joels Dr New Fairfield (06812) *(G-5180)*
Turbine Controls Inc (PA) 860 242-0448
5 Old Windsor Rd Bloomfield (06002) *(G-495)*
Turbine Kinetics Inc 860 633-8520
60 Sequin Dr Ste 2 Glastonbury (06033) *(G-3091)*
Turbine Support Services Inc (PA) 860 688-4800
344 Rainbow Rd Windsor (06095) *(G-10456)*
Turbine Technologies Inc (PA) 860 678-1642
126 Hyde Rd Farmington (06032) *(G-2971)*
Turkey Tail Publishing LLC 860 671-0800
68 Carmel Hill Rd Washington (06793) *(G-9414)*
Turning Stone Sand & Grav LLC 413 519-1560
128 Moody Rd Enfield (06082) *(G-2702)*
Turnkey Software LLC 860 604-0837
18 Quiet Woods Rd East Hampton (06424) *(G-2282)*
Turnstone Inc 203 625-0000
154 Prospect St Greenwich (06830) *(G-3250)*
Turq LLC 203 344-1257
123 Lockwood Rd Riverside (06878) *(G-7203)*
Turtle Clan Global, Sharon *Also called Tcg Green Technologies Inc (G-7384)*
Tutors & Computers Inc 203 393-3006
36 Perkins Rd Bethany (06524) *(G-251)*
Tvu Gold Coating Services 860 657-2666
40 Nutmeg Ln Glastonbury (06033) *(G-3092)*
TWC Trans World Consulting 860 668-5108
383 S Main St Windsor Locks (06096) *(G-10499)*
Tweedie Dental Arts, Manchester *Also called Mark D Tweedie DDS (G-4056)*
Twelve Beverage LLC 203 256-8100
1552 Post Rd Fairfield (06824) *(G-2859)*
Twelve Percent LLC 203 556-7024
341 State St North Haven (06473) *(G-6002)*
Twenty Five Commerce Inc 203 866-0540
25 Commerce St Norwalk (06850) *(G-6379)*
Twice Baked Twins LLC 203 368-8841
6486 Main St Trumbull (06611) *(G-9083)*
Twisko Press LLC 203 938-3466
331 Redding Rd Redding (06896) *(G-7111)*
Two Bsses & A Hrmonca Prdctns 203 259-5916
135 Mile Common Rd Easton (06612) *(G-2568)*
Two Ems Inc 203 245-8211
782 Boston Post Rd Ste 2 Madison (06443) *(G-3965)*
Tyco International MGT Co LLC 203 492-5000
195 Mcdermott Rd North Haven (06473) *(G-6003)*
Tyco Printing & Copying 203 562-2679
262 Elm St New Haven (06511) *(G-5424)*
Tyger Tool Inc 203 375-4344
45 Sperry Ave Stratford (06615) *(G-8699)*
Tylaska Marine Hardware, Mystic *Also called Vector Engineering Inc (G-4851)*
Tyler Automatics Incorporated 860 283-5878
437 S Main St Thomaston (06787) *(G-8815)*
Tyler's Total Truck Service, Wallingford *Also called Logans Run Trnsp Svc LLC (G-9305)*
Tylerville Technologies LLC 860 798-0501
67 Bartman Rd Higganum (06441) *(G-3780)*
Tyne Plastics LLC (PA) 860 673-7100
252 Spielman Hwy Ste B Burlington (06013) *(G-1277)*
Type Is Right The, Moosup *Also called Typeisright (G-4783)*
Typeisright 860 564-0537
11 E Main St Moosup (06354) *(G-4783)*
U S C, New Canaan *Also called Universal Storage Cntrs LLC (G-5156)*
U S Glass Distributors Inc 860 741-3658
7 Niblick Rd Enfield (06082) *(G-2703)*
U S Hairspring LLC 860 747-9526
47 Reliance Rd Plainville (06062) *(G-6873)*
U S Stucco LLC 860 667-1935
28 Costello Pl Newington (06111) *(G-5715)*
U T Z 860 383-4266
140 Route 32 North Franklin (06254) *(G-5879)*
U-Marq Usa LLC 860 799-7800
137 Danbury Rd New Milford (06776) *(G-5603)*
U-Sealusa LLC 860 667-0911
56 Fenn Rd Newington (06111) *(G-5716)*
U-Tech Wire Rope & Supply LLC 203 865-8885
222 Universal Dr Bldg 9 North Haven (06473) *(G-6004)*
U.s Surgical, New Haven *Also called United States Surgical Corp (G-5425)*
Ua, Naugatuck *Also called United Avionics Inc (G-4925)*
Ubm LLC 203 662-6501
330 Post Rd Fl 2 Darien (06820) *(G-2048)*
Uchisearch LLC 203 268-9096
15 Wedgewood Rd Trumbull (06611) *(G-9084)*
UCI Sales Group LLC 860 667-4766
22 Whiteside St Newington (06111) *(G-5717)*
Uh Motor Sports, Monroe *Also called New Age Motorsports LLC (G-4741)*
Ulbrich of Georgia Inc 203 239-4481
153 Washington Ave North Haven (06473) *(G-6005)*
Ulbrich Solar Technologies Inc 203 239-4481
153 Washington Ave North Haven (06473) *(G-6006)*
Ulbrich Solar Wire LLC 203 239-4481
153 Washington Ave North Haven (06473) *(G-6007)*
Ulbrich Stainless Steels (PA) 203 239-4481
153 Washington Ave North Haven (06473) *(G-6008)*
Ulbrich Stainless Steels 203 269-2507
1 Dudley Ave Wallingford (06492) *(G-9393)*
Ulbrich Steel, Wallingford *Also called Ulbrich Stainless Steels (G-9393)*
Ulitsch Mechanical Svcs LLC 860 623-4223
465 Spring St Ste H Windsor Locks (06096) *(G-10500)*
Ulittlestitch 860 857-4066
451 Boston Post Rd East Lyme (06333) *(G-2477)*
Ullman Devices Corporation 203 438-6577
664 Danbury Rd Ridgefield (06877) *(G-7178)*
Ultimate Companies Inc (PA) 860 582-9111
200 Central St Bristol (06010) *(G-1133)*
Ultimate Growers LLC 203 269-9027
30 Mapleview Rd Wallingford (06492) *(G-9394)*
Ultimate Hardwood Floors 203 746-9692
119 Shortwoods Rd New Fairfield (06812) *(G-5181)*
Ultimate Ink LLC 203 762-0602
681 Danbury Rd Ste 1 Wilton (06897) *(G-10339)*
Ultimate Interfaces Corp 203 230-8184
96 Salem Walk Milford (06460) *(G-4667)*
Ultimate Wireforms Inc 860 582-9111
200 Central St Bristol (06010) *(G-1134)*
Ultimate Woodworking LLC 203 243-3367
16 Fair Oaks Dr Shelton (06484) *(G-7573)*
Ultra Clean Equipment Inc 860 669-1354
112 Nod Rd Ste 9 Clinton (06413) *(G-1533)*
Ultra Elec Measurement Systems, Wallingford *Also called Measurement Systems Inc (G-9317)*
Ultra Flow Dispense LLC 866 827-2534
820 Prospect Hill Rd Windsor (06095) *(G-10457)*
Ultra Food and Fuel 860 223-2005
788 W Main St New Britain (06053) *(G-5077)*
Ultra Golden Software LLC 203 227-4009
35 Narrow Rocks Rd Westport (06880) *(G-10169)*
Ultra Mfg LLC 203 888-1180
43 Patton Ave Seymour (06483) *(G-7371)*
Ultra Sonic Seal Co, Newtown *Also called Sonics & Materials Inc (G-5781)*
Ultramatic West 203 745-4688
87 Beechwood Ave Hamden (06514) *(G-3525)*
Unas Grinding Corporation 860 289-1538
28 Cherry St East Hartford (06108) *(G-2387)*
Uncle Bill's Tweezers, West Hartford *Also called El Mar Inc (G-9806)*
Uncle Wileys Inc 203 256-9313
1220 Post Rd Ste 2 Fairfield (06824) *(G-2860)*
Under Armour Inc 860 237-6031
455 Trolley Line Blvd # 760 Mashantucket (06338) *(G-4133)*
Underground Systems Inc (PA) 203 792-3444
3a Trowbridge Dr Bethel (06801) *(G-357)*
Uneeda Welder 203 929-4507
25 Oak Hill Ln Shelton (06484) *(G-7574)*
Unger Enterprises LLC 203 366-4884
425 Asylum St Bridgeport (06610) *(G-930)*
Unger Industrial LLC 203 336-3344
425 Asylum St Bridgeport (06610) *(G-931)*
Unger Publishing LLC 203 588-1363
700 Canal St Ste 4 Stamford (06902) *(G-8480)*

ALPHABETIC SECTION

Unholtz-Dickie Corporation (PA) 203 265-9875
  6 Brookside Dr Wallingford (06492) *(G-9395)*
UNI Machine & Mfg LLC 860 485-0643
  72 Orchard Hill Rd Harwinton (06791) *(G-3742)*
Uniboard Corp 860 428-5979
  570 River Rd Putnam (06260) *(G-7075)*
Unicast Development Co., New Haven *Also called Joshua LLC (G-5304)*
Unicor, Danbury *Also called Federal Prison Industries (G-1824)*
Unicorn Pharmaceuticals Inc 973 699-3843
  181 Milbank Ave Ste W Greenwich (06830) *(G-3251)*
Unicorn Press LLC 203 938-7405
  17 Church Hill Rd Redding (06896) *(G-7112)*
Unicorr Group, North Haven *Also called Connecticut Container Corp (G-5924)*
Unilever Ascc AG 203 381-2482
  3 Corporate Dr Shelton (06484) *(G-7575)*
Unilever Foods Chill, Trumbull *Also called Thomas J Lipton Inc (G-9081)*
Unilever Home and Per Care NA 203 502-0086
  75 Merritt Blvd Trumbull (06611) *(G-9085)*
Unilever Hpc NA, Trumbull *Also called Unilever Home and Per Care NA (G-9085)*
Unilever Hpc USA, Trumbull *Also called Unilever Trumbull RES Svcs Inc (G-9087)*
Unilever Hpc USA 203 381-3311
  45 Commerce Dr Trumbull (06611) *(G-9086)*
Unilever Trumbull RES Svcs Inc (HQ) 203 502-0086
  40 Merritt Blvd Trumbull (06611) *(G-9087)*
Unimation 203 792-3412
  102 Wooster St Ste 4a Bethel (06801) *(G-358)*
Unimelon Inc 201 774-2786
  5 Taylor Ct Ridgefield (06877) *(G-7179)*
Unimetal Surface Finishing LLC 203 729-8244
  15 E Waterbury Rd Naugatuck (06770) *(G-4924)*
Unimetal Surface Finishing LLC (PA) 860 283-0271
  135 S Main St Thomaston (06787) *(G-8816)*
Unimin Lime Corporation (HQ) 203 966-8880
  258 Elm St New Canaan (06840) *(G-5155)*
Uninsred Altitude Cnnection Inc 860 333-1461
  330 Day St Brooklyn (06234) *(G-1257)*
Uniprise International Inc 860 589-7262
  50 Napco Dr Terryville (06786) *(G-8776)*
Uniprise Sales, Terryville *Also called Uniprise International Inc (G-8776)*
Unique Extrusions Incorporated 860 632-1314
  10 Countyline Dr Cromwell (06416) *(G-1723)*
Unique Graphics 203 634-1932
  905 Hanover Rd Meriden (06451) *(G-4258)*
Uniroyal Chemical Corporation 203 573-2000
  Benson Road Waterbury (06749) *(G-9620)*
Unison Engine Components 860 647-5586
  171 Utopia Rd Manchester (06042) *(G-4104)*
Unitec 203 778-0400
  4 Larson Dr Danbury (06810) *(G-1969)*
Unitec Parts Co 919 627-0192
  1 Enterprise Dr Ste 205 Shelton (06484) *(G-7576)*
United Abrasives Inc (PA) 860 456-7131
  185 Boston Post Rd North Windham (06256) *(G-6040)*
United Aero Group LLC 203 283-9524
  12 Commerce Dr Shelton (06484) *(G-7577)*
United Avionics Inc 203 723-1404
  38 Great Hill Rd Naugatuck (06770) *(G-4925)*
United Electric Controls Co 203 877-2795
  340 Woodmont Rd Milford (06460) *(G-4668)*
United Enterprises Inc 860 225-9955
  264 Broad St New Britain (06053) *(G-5078)*
United Gear & Machine Co Inc 860 623-6618
  1087 East St S Suffield (06078) *(G-8737)*
United Metal Solutions 860 610-4026
  164 School St East Hartford (06108) *(G-2388)*
United Ophthalmics LLC 203 745-8399
  430 Smith St Meriden (06451) *(G-4259)*
United Photonics LLC 617 752-2073
  42 Diane Dr Vernon Rockville (06066) *(G-9185)*
United Pioneer Company, Stamford *Also called Corinth Acquisition Corp (G-8161)*
United Plastics Technologies 860 224-1110
  163 John Downey Dr New Britain (06051) *(G-5079)*
United Seating & Mobility LLC (PA) 860 761-0700
  1111 Cromwell Ave Rocky Hill (06067) *(G-7270)*
United States Chemical Corp 860 621-6831
  609 Old Turnpike Rd Plantsville (06479) *(G-6917)*
United States Dept of Navy 860 694-3524
  33 Grayback Ave Bldg 33 Groton (06349) *(G-3316)*
United States Fire Arms Mfg Co 860 296-7441
  445 Ledyard St Ste 453 Hartford (06114) *(G-3708)*
United States Surgical Corp (HQ) 203 845-1000
  555 Long Wharf Dr Fl 4 New Haven (06511) *(G-5425)*
United Steel Inc 860 289-2323
  164 School St East Hartford (06108) *(G-2389)*
United Steel Inc., East Hartford *Also called United Metal Solutions (G-2388)*
United Stts Sgn & Fbrction 203 601-1000
  1 Trefoil Dr Ste 2 Trumbull (06611) *(G-9088)*
United Tech Advnced Prjcts Inc 860 610-7159
  411 Silver Ln East Hartford (06118) *(G-2390)*
United Tech Employee Sav Plan 860 728-7000
  1 Financial Plz Hartford (06103) *(G-3709)*

United Technologies Corp (PA) 860 728-7000
  10 Farm Springs Rd Farmington (06032) *(G-2972)*
United Technologies Corp 860 565-4321
  400 Main St East Hartford (06118) *(G-2391)*
United Technologies Corp 860 565-7622
  400 Main St East Hartford (06108) *(G-2392)*
United Technologies Corp 860 727-2200
  Governors Hwy South Windsor (06074) *(G-7836)*
United Technologies Corp 860 767-9592
  10 Curiosity Ln Essex (06426) *(G-2736)*
United Technologies Corp 954 485-6501
  9 Farm Springs Rd Ste 3 Farmington (06032) *(G-2973)*
United Technologies Corp 860 565-4321
  400 Main St East Hartford (06108) *(G-2393)*
United Technologies Corp 860 595-4114
  25 Holly Dr Newington (06111) *(G-5718)*
United Technologies Corp 860 565-4321
  400 Main St East Hartford (06118) *(G-2394)*
United Technologies Corp 860 292-3270
  200 Signature Way East Granby (06026) *(G-2233)*
United Technologies Corp 860 610-7000
  411 Silver Ln East Hartford (06118) *(G-2395)*
United Technologies Corp 860 557-3333
  400 Main St East Hartford (06108) *(G-2396)*
United Thread Rolling LLC 860 290-9349
  25 Rosenthal St East Hartford (06108) *(G-2397)*
United Tool and Die Company (PA) 860 246-6531
  1 Carney Rd West Hartford (06110) *(G-9871)*
United-Bim Inc 860 289-1100
  1111 Main St East Hartford (06108) *(G-2398)*
Unitex Textile Rental Service, Hartford *Also called A & P Coat Apron & Lin Sup Inc (G-3542)*
Universal Body & Eqp Co LLC 860 274-7541
  17 Di Nunzio Rd Oakville (06779) *(G-6466)*
Universal Building Contrls Inc 203 235-1530
  170 Research Pkwy Ste 1 Meriden (06450) *(G-4260)*
Universal Component Corp 203 481-8787
  193 Silver Sands Rd East Haven (06512) *(G-2458)*
Universal Foam Products LLC 860 216-3015
  101 W Dudley Town Rd Bloomfield (06002) *(G-496)*
Universal Metalworks LLC 203 239-6349
  5 Philip Pl North Haven (06473) *(G-6009)*
Universal Precision Mfg 203 374-9809
  21 Leffert Rd Trumbull (06611) *(G-9089)*
Universal Relay Company, Bridgeport *Also called Park Distributories Inc (G-863)*
Universal Relays, Bridgeport *Also called Park Distributories Inc (G-865)*
Universal Storage Cntrs LLC 203 966-3043
  146 Old Kings Hwy New Canaan (06840) *(G-5156)*
Universal Thread Grinding Co 203 336-1849
  30 Chambers St Fairfield (06825) *(G-2861)*
Universal Voltronics Corp 203 740-8555
  57 Commerce Dr Brookfield (06804) *(G-1234)*
Universe Publishing Co LLC 203 283-5201
  167 Cherry St Ste 261 Milford (06460) *(G-4669)*
University Hlth Pubg Group LLC 203 791-0101
  6 Trowbridge Dr Ste 1 Bethel (06801) *(G-359)*
University Opticians, Dayville *Also called University Optics LLC (G-2076)*
University Optics LLC 860 779-6123
  791 Hartford Pike Dayville (06241) *(G-2076)*
Uniworld Bus Publications Inc 201 384-4900
  35 Kensett Ln Darien (06820) *(G-2049)*
Unlimited Signs Designs & Grap 203 546-7267
  72 Grays Bridge Rd Ste F Brookfield (06804) *(G-1235)*
Unlimited Woodworking 203 380-2340
  205 York St Stratford (06615) *(G-8700)*
Up & Down Overhead Door 203 876-8045
  181 Research Dr Ste 1 Milford (06460) *(G-4670)*
Up In Smoke, Cromwell *Also called What A Life LLC (G-1724)*
Up Top Screen Printing 860 412-9798
  106 Main St Danielson (06239) *(G-2005)*
Up With Paper 203 453-3300
  34 York St Ste 3 Guilford (06437) *(G-3400)*
Upc LLC 877 466-1137
  170 Research Pkwy Meriden (06450) *(G-4261)*
Upon A Once Pillow LLC 203 222-1717
  4 Sunnyside Ln Westport (06880) *(G-10170)*
Upper Valley Mold LLC 860 489-8282
  481 Guerdat Rd Torrington (06790) *(G-8986)*
Uppercurve LLC 203 770-0223
  143 West St Ste T New Milford (06776) *(G-5604)*
UPS Authorized Retailer 203 256-9991
  857 Post Rd Fairfield (06824) *(G-2862)*
Upscale Welding & Fabrica 203 265-0800
  418 S Cherry St Wallingford (06492) *(G-9396)*
Urban Antique Radio 203 877-2409
  58 Naugatuck Ave Milford (06460) *(G-4671)*
Urban Exposition LLC (HQ) 203 242-8717
  35 Nutmeg Dr Ste 125 Trumbull (06611) *(G-9090)*
Urban Reach Institute, Hartford *Also called Urise LLC (G-3710)*
Uretek, New Haven *Also called Trelleborg Ctd Systems US Inc (G-5421)*
Urg Graphics Inc (PA) 860 928-0835
  12 Fox Hill Dr Stafford Springs (06076) *(G-8046)*

ALPHABETIC SECTION

Urise LLC 860 833-3009
  15 Lewis St Ste 302 Hartford (06103) *(G-3710)*
US Athletic Equipment, Waterford Also called Jaypro Sports LLC *(G-9656)*
US Avionics, South Windsor Also called US Avionics Inc / Superabr *(G-7837)*
US Avionics Inc / Superabr 860 528-1114
  1265 John Fitch Blvd # 3 South Windsor (06074) *(G-7837)*
US Barricades LLC 203 883-8660
  30 Old Kings Hwy S Ste 10 Darien (06820) *(G-2050)*
US Button Corporation 860 928-2707
  328 Kennedy Dr Putnam (06260) *(G-7076)*
US Chemicals Inc 203 655-8878
  280 Elm St New Canaan (06840) *(G-5157)*
US Filter Surface Preparatio 203 284-7825
  29 Capital Dr Wallingford (06492) *(G-9397)*
US Firearms Manufacturing Co 860 296-7441
  453 Ledyard St Hartford (06114) *(G-3711)*
US Games Systems Inc 203 353-8400
  179 Ludlow St Stamford (06902) *(G-8481)*
US Highway Products Inc 203 336-0332
  500 Bostwick Ave Bridgeport (06605) *(G-932)*
US Product Mechanization Co 860 450-1139
  21 Route 87 Columbia (06237) *(G-1614)*
US Sign, Trumbull Also called United Stts Sgn & Fbrction *(G-9088)*
US Smokeless Tobacco Co LLC 203 661-1100
  6 High Ridge Park Bldg A Stamford (06905) *(G-8482)*
Us-Malabar Company Inc 203 226-1773
  25 Timber Mill Ln Weston (06883) *(G-10041)*
USA Circuits LLC 203 364-1378
  114 Lakeview Ter Sandy Hook (06482) *(G-7331)*
USA Notepads, West Haven Also called Panagrafix Inc *(G-9942)*
USA Wood Incorporated 203 238-4285
  998 N Colony Rd Meriden (06450) *(G-4262)*
Usc Technologies LLC 203 378-9622
  175 Garfield Ave Stratford (06615) *(G-8701)*
Uses Mfg Inc 860 443-8737
  152 Old Colchester Rd Quaker Hill (06375) *(G-7086)*
USI, Bethel Also called Underground Systems Inc *(G-357)*
USI Education & Government Sls, Madison Also called New Precision Technology LLC *(G-3941)*
UST 203 661-1100
  100 W Putnam Ave Greenwich (06830) *(G-3252)*
UST LLC (HQ) 203 817-3000
  6 High Ridge Park Bldg A Stamford (06905) *(G-8483)*
UTC, Farmington Also called United Technologies Corp *(G-2972)*
UTC Aerospace Systems, Danbury Also called Simmonds Precision Pdts Inc *(G-1952)*
UTC Aerospace Systems, Windsor Locks Also called Hamilton Sundstrand Corp *(G-10491)*
UTC Climate Controls & SEC, Farmington Also called United Technologies Corp *(G-2973)*
UTC Fire SEC Americas Corp Inc 941 739-4200
  30 Batterson Park Rd # 100 Farmington (06032) *(G-2974)*
UTC Fire SEC Americas Corp Inc 203 426-1180
  16 Commerce Rd Newtown (06470) *(G-5796)*
Ute Brinkmann Geigenbaumeister 203 265-7456
  84 S Orchard St Wallingford (06492) *(G-9398)*
Utica Spring Company Inc 860 628-6165
  474 Churchill St Southington (06489) *(G-7991)*
Utitec Inc (HQ) 860 945-0605
  169 Callender Rd Watertown (06795) *(G-9744)*
Utitec Holdings Inc (PA) 860 945-0601
  169 Callender Rd Watertown (06795) *(G-9745)*
Utrc, East Hartford Also called United Technologies Corp *(G-2395)*
Uv Inc 203 333-1031
  4 Jenick Ln Woodbridge (06525) *(G-10620)*
V & V Woodworking LLC 203 740-9494
  107 Wooster St Bethel (06801) *(G-360)*
V B Woodworking LLC 203 747-0228
  13 Spring St Plainville (06062) *(G-6874)*
V Cannelli Co LLC 203 421-4697
  120 Genesee Ln Madison (06443) *(G-3966)*
V M F, Seymour Also called Vernier Metal Fabricating Inc *(G-7372)*
Vab Inc 860 793-0246
  49 Johnson Ave Plainville (06062) *(G-6875)*
Vacca Architectural Woodworkin 860 599-3677
  9 Coggswell St Pawcatuck (06379) *(G-6730)*
Vacumet Corp 860 731-0860
  300 Prestige Park Rd East Hartford (06108) *(G-2399)*
Val Scansaroli Magazine Cnsltn 203 229-0256
  603 Foxboro Dr Norwalk (06851) *(G-6380)*
Valentine Co LLC 203 245-9145
  60 Boston Post Rd Madison (06443) *(G-3967)*
Validus DC Systems LLC 203 448-3600
  50 Pocono Rd Brookfield (06804) *(G-1236)*
Valkyrie Industries 860 518-5311
  114 Waverly St Hartford (06112) *(G-3712)*
Valley Container Inc 203 368-6546
  850 Union Ave Bridgeport (06607) *(G-933)*
Valley Eyelet Company 203 729-4363
  10 E Waterbury Rd Naugatuck (06770) *(G-4926)*
Valley Golf Center CT LLC 860 799-7605
  562 Danbury Rd New Milford (06776) *(G-5605)*
Valley Independent Sentinel 203 446-2335
  158 Main St Ansonia (06401) *(G-55)*

Valley Marble and Slate Corp 860 354-3955
  15 Valmar Dr New Milford (06776) *(G-5606)*
Valley of Mexico, Stamford Also called Shenondah Vly Specialty Foods *(G-8411)*
Valley Press Inc 860 651-4700
  540 1/2 Hopmeadow St Simsbury (06070) *(G-7650)*
Valley Press New Area Prtg Co 860 526-5696
  169 Main St Ste 1 Deep River (06417) *(G-2105)*
Valley Publishing Company Inc 203 735-6696
  7 Francis St Derby (06418) *(G-2129)*
Valley Sand & Gravel Corp 203 562-3192
  400 N Frontage Rd North Haven (06473) *(G-6010)*
Valley Times, Derby Also called Valley Publishing Company Inc *(G-2129)*
Valley Tool and Mfg LLC 203 799-8800
  22 Prindle Hill Rd Orange (06477) *(G-6632)*
Valley Truckstop, Waterbury Also called John Hychko *(G-9512)*
Valley Welding Co Inc 203 283-5768
  164 S Main St Thomaston (06787) *(G-8817)*
Valley Woodworking LLC 860 667-1241
  22 Styles Ave Newington (06111) *(G-5719)*
Valore Inc 203 854-4799
  2 Academy St Norwalk (06850) *(G-6381)*
Value Print Incorporated 203 265-1371
  34 Mellor Dr Wallingford (06492) *(G-9399)*
Van Cott Rowe & Smith 860 242-0707
  60 Hoskins Rd Bloomfield (06002) *(G-497)*
Van Deusen & Levitt Assoc Inc 203 445-6244
  14 Wood Hill Rd Weston (06883) *(G-10042)*
Van Geldern Machine Company 203 853-9402
  151 Rowayton Ave Norwalk (06853) *(G-6382)*
Vanderbilt Chemicals LLC 203 744-3900
  31 Taylor Ave Bethel (06801) *(G-361)*
Vanderbilt Chemicals LLC (HQ) 203 295-2141
  30 Winfield St Norwalk (06855) *(G-6383)*
Vanderbilt Minerals LLC (HQ) 203 295-2140
  33 Winfield St Norwalk (06855) *(G-6384)*
Vangor Engineering Corporation 203 267-4377
  115 Hurley Rd Ste 7f Oxford (06478) *(G-6698)*
Vanguard Plastics Corporation 860 628-4736
  100 Robert Porter Rd Southington (06489) *(G-7992)*
Vanguard Products Corporation 203 744-7265
  87 Newtown Rd Danbury (06810) *(G-1970)*
Vanilla Politics LLC 203 221-0895
  203 Godfrey Rd E Weston (06883) *(G-10043)*
Vaporizer LLC 860 564-7225
  245 Main St Moosup (06354) *(G-4784)*
Varnum Enterprises LLC 203 743-4443
  11 Trowbridge Dr Bethel (06801) *(G-362)*
Varpro Inc 203 227-6876
  4 Shadbush Ln Pmb 2224 Westport (06880) *(G-10171)*
Varsity Imprints 203 354-4371
  22 Roller Ter Milford (06461) *(G-4672)*
Vas Integrated LLC 860 748-4058
  600 Four Rod Rd Ste 9 Berlin (06037) *(G-229)*
Vazzanos Catering LLC 203 378-3331
  2456 Huntington Tpke Trumbull (06611) *(G-9091)*
Vcs Group LLC 203 413-6500
  411 W Putnam Ave Fl 2 Greenwich (06830) *(G-3253)*
Vector Contrls & Automtn Group, Bethel Also called Vector Controls LLC *(G-363)*
Vector Controls LLC (PA) 203 749-0883
  17 Francis J Clarke Cir Bethel (06801) *(G-363)*
Vector Engineering Inc 860 572-0422
  800 Flanders Rd Unit 1-4 Mystic (06355) *(G-4851)*
Veeder-Root Co 860 450-0895
  407 Jackson St Willimantic (06226) *(G-10237)*
Veeder-Root Company (HQ) 860 651-2700
  125 Powder Forest Dr Fl 1 Weatogue (06089) *(G-9760)*
Vegware Us Inc 860 779-7970
  90 Wauregan Rd Danielson (06239) *(G-2006)*
Velocity Print Solution, Middlebury Also called JMS Graphics Inc *(G-4280)*
Velocity Products 860 687-3530
  910 Day Hill Rd Windsor (06095) *(G-10458)*
Venture Tool and Manufacturing 860 267-9647
  12 Summit St East Hampton (06424) *(G-2283)*
Ventureout Publications LLC 203 668-9162
  19 Country Way Wallingford (06492) *(G-9400)*
Ventures LLC DOT Com LLC 203 930-8972
  35-31 Tlcottville Rd 23 Vernon (06066) *(G-9157)*
Ventus Technologies LLC 203 642-2800
  10 Norden Pl Ste 8 Norwalk (06855) *(G-6385)*
Venu Magazine LLC 203 259-2075
  840 Reef Rd Fairfield (06824) *(G-2863)*
Veoci.com, New Haven Also called Grey Wall Software LLC *(G-5291)*
Veras Trattoria 203 798-7800
  33 Mill Plain Rd Ste 400 Danbury (06811) *(G-1971)*
Verico Technology LLC (HQ) 800 492-7286
  230 Shaker Rd Enfield (06082) *(G-2704)*
Vermont Pallet & Skid Shop 860 822-6949
  104 Baltic Rd Norwich (06360) *(G-6437)*
Vernier Metal Fabricating Inc 203 881-3133
  26 Progress Ave Seymour (06483) *(G-7372)*
Vernon Printing Co Inc 860 872-1826
  352 Hartford Tpke Ste 9 Vernon Rockville (06066) *(G-9186)*

Veronica Matthews Minerals....860 399-0063
287 Hammock Rd N Westbrook (06498) *(G-10013)*
Verotec Inc....603 821-9921
473 Washington Ave Unit E North Haven (06473) *(G-6011)*
Versa Prints....203 256-2342
136 Papermill Ln Fairfield (06824) *(G-2864)*
Versatile Machine, Wolcott *Also called Timothy Gray (G-10592)*
Versifi LLC....860 890-1982
380 S Curtis St Meriden (06450) *(G-4263)*
Versimedia....203 604-8094
117 Glover Ave Norwalk (06850) *(G-6386)*
Vertafore Inc....860 602-6000
5 Waterside Xing Fl 2 Windsor (06095) *(G-10459)*
Vertech Inc....203 876-1552
181 Research Dr Ste 5 Milford (06460) *(G-4673)*
Vertical Development LLC....203 208-0806
20 Commercial St Branford (06405) *(G-665)*
Vertical Edge LLC....203 513-2806
283 Eagles Lndg Shelton (06484) *(G-7578)*
Vertical Management LLC....203 422-2547
110 Patterson Ave Greenwich (06830) *(G-3254)*
Vertical Realms LLC....860 508-5273
38 White Water Turn Tariffville (06081) *(G-8745)*
Vertical Studios LLC....203 562-6542
18 Montowese Ave North Haven (06473) *(G-6012)*
Vertical Ventures Intl LLC....203 227-1364
40 Hackberry Hill Rd Weston (06883) *(G-10044)*
Vertiv Corporation....203 294-6020
8 Fairfield Blvd Ste 4 Wallingford (06492) *(G-9401)*
Verzatec Inc....860 628-0511
119 Sabina Dr Southington (06489) *(G-7993)*
Vespoli Usa Inc....203 773-0311
385 Clinton Ave New Haven (06513) *(G-5426)*
Vesselon Inc....203 989-0500
101 Merritt 7 Ste 300 Norwalk (06851) *(G-6387)*
Veterinary Medical Associates....860 693-0214
60 Lovely St Canton (06019) *(G-1327)*
Veto Pro Pac LLC....203 847-0297
3 Morgan Ave Ste 4 Norwalk (06851) *(G-6388)*
Viavi Solutions Inc....860 243-6600
45 Griffin Rd S Bloomfield (06002) *(G-498)*
Vibrascience Inc....203 483-6113
186 N Main St Branford (06405) *(G-666)*
Vichem Inc....860 677-8133
16 Evergreen Trl Farmington (06032) *(G-2975)*
Victor F Leandri....860 345-8705
286 Killingworth Rd Higganum (06441) *(G-3781)*
Victor Tool Co Inc....203 634-8113
290 Pratt St Ste 7 Meriden (06450) *(G-4264)*
Victoria Art & Frame....860 274-8222
81 Winding Brook Farm Rd Watertown (06795) *(G-9746)*
Victors Hot House LLC....203 264-0939
101 Pomperaug Trl Southbury (06488) *(G-7882)*
Victory Controls LLC....860 930-6226
222 Main St Ste 261 Farmington (06032) *(G-2976)*
Victory Fuel LLC....860 585-0532
248 Main St Terryville (06786) *(G-8777)*
Video Automation Systems Inc....203 312-0152
13 Arrow Meadow Rd New Fairfield (06812) *(G-5182)*
Video Messenger Co, Stratford *Also called Video Messengercom Corp (G-8702)*
Video Messengercom Corp....203 358-8842
862 Judson Pl Stratford (06615) *(G-8702)*
Video Outlet....860 568-7473
775 Silver Ln East Hartford (06118) *(G-2400)*
Video Technologies Group LLC....203 341-0474
21 Charles St Ste 116 Westport (06880) *(G-10172)*
Vigiroda Enterprises Inc....203 268-6117
104 Garwood Rd Trumbull (06611) *(G-9092)*
Vigiroda Products LLC....860 391-8457
6 Business Park Rd Ste 2 Old Saybrook (06475) *(G-6574)*
Vijay Manufacturing Co LLC....860 627-4901
59 King Spring Rd Ste G Windsor Locks (06096) *(G-10501)*
Vijon Stdios Stined GL Sup Ctr, Old Saybrook *Also called Vijon Studios Inc (G-6576)*
Vijon Studios Inc....860 399-7440
97a Spencer Plain Rd Old Saybrook (06475) *(G-6575)*
Vijon Studios Inc....860 399-7440
97 Spencer Plain Rd Ste A Old Saybrook (06475) *(G-6576)*
Viking Automation, New Milford *Also called Nielsen Consulting Inc (G-5573)*
Viking Enterprises Inc....860 440-0728
41 Millstone Rd Waterford (06385) *(G-9675)*
Viking Kitchen Cabinets LLC (PA)....860 223-7101
33-39 John St New Britain (06051) *(G-5080)*
Viking Platinum LLC....203 574-7979
46 Municipal Rd Waterbury (06708) *(G-9621)*
Viking Supply Co....860 886-0220
31 Connecticut Ave Norwich (06360) *(G-6438)*
Viking Tool Company....203 929-1457
435 Access Rd Shelton (06484) *(G-7579)*
Villa Ridge LLC....303 330-9183
9 Ridge St Norwalk (06854) *(G-6389)*
Village Cabinets, Bristol *Also called Belmont Corporation (G-980)*
Village Printer, Ridgefield *Also called Economy Printing & Copy Center (G-7137)*
Village Printers, Ridgefield *Also called Warren Press Inc (G-7182)*
Villager Newspapers....860 928-1818
107 Providence St Putnam (06260) *(G-7077)*
Villano J Sign Company LLC....203 624-7550
414 East St New Haven (06511) *(G-5427)*
Villarina Pasta & Fine Foods (PA)....203 917-4463
22 Shelter Rock Ln Unit 4 Danbury (06810) *(G-1972)*
Ville Swiss Automatics Inc....203 756-2825
205 Cherry St Waterbury (06702) *(G-9622)*
Vincent Jajer....860 354-4747
4 Chestnut Land Rd New Milford (06776) *(G-5607)*
Vincent Jewelers....203 882-8900
23 New Haven Ave Milford (06460) *(G-4674)*
Vincent Masonry....860 836-5916
332 Barbour Rd New Britain (06053) *(G-5081)*
Vincent Masonry & Chimney, New Britain *Also called Vincent Masonry (G-5081)*
Vinegar Syndrome LLC....212 722-9755
100 Congress St Bridgeport (06604) *(G-934)*
Vineyard At Foxrun....860 779-0230
580 Pomfret Rd Brooklyn (06234) *(G-1258)*
Vineyard At Strawberry Ridge, Cornwall Bridge *Also called Strawberry Ridge Vineyard Inc (G-1621)*
Vineyard Brothers LLC....203 637-0381
29 Normandy Ln Riverside (06878) *(G-7204)*
Vineyard Thimble....860 416-5115
808 Thompson St Glastonbury (06033) *(G-3093)*
Vino Et Al LLC....203 405-3931
53 Wire Mill Rd Stamford (06903) *(G-8484)*
Vintage Boat Restorations LLC....860 582-0774
201 Terryville Rd Ste 1 Bristol (06010) *(G-1135)*
Vintage Performance LLC....860 542-5753
7 Terrace Vw Norfolk (06058) *(G-5828)*
Vintage Sheet Metal Fabg....860 595-8423
44 Washington Ave Ste 7 Berlin (06037) *(G-230)*
Vio's Sport Shack West Haven, West Haven *Also called Michael Violano (G-9937)*
Viola Audio Laboratories Inc....203 772-0435
446a Blake St Ste 220 New Haven (06515) *(G-5428)*
Violin Performance Co....860 836-8647
677 Rye St South Windsor (06074) *(G-7838)*
Vios Sports Plus....203 234-7231
117 Washington Ave Ste 6 North Haven (06473) *(G-6013)*
VIP Associates LLC....203 230-1878
16 Oak Tree Ln Old Lyme (06371) *(G-6521)*
Virginia Industries Inc (PA)....860 571-3600
1022 Elm St Rocky Hill (06067) *(G-7271)*
Viridian Energy LLC....203 663-5089
1055 Washington Blvd Fl 7 Stamford (06901) *(G-8485)*
Vishay Americas Inc (HQ)....203 452-5648
1 Greenwich Pl Shelton (06484) *(G-7580)*
Visible Record Systems, Shelton *Also called Inform Inc (G-7477)*
Vision Designs LLC....203 778-9898
1120 Federal Rd Ste 2 Brookfield (06804) *(G-1237)*
Vision Kitchens and Mllwk LLC....203 775-0604
3 Production Dr Ste 4 Brookfield (06804) *(G-1238)*
Vision Musical Instruments....203 416-6359
20 Fitch St Norwalk (06855) *(G-6390)*
Vision Technical Molding, Manchester *Also called Advance Mold & Mfg Inc (G-3979)*
Vision Technical Molding....860 783-5050
20 Utopia Rd Manchester (06042) *(G-4105)*
Visionage....203 787-0037
131 Cottage St New Haven (06511) *(G-5429)*
Visionpoint LLC....860 436-9673
152 Rockwell Rd Ste B6 Newington (06111) *(G-5720)*
Vistar Foundation Inc....203 968-1995
75 Ridge Brook Dr Stamford (06903) *(G-8486)*
Visual Impact LLC....203 790-9650
12 Finance Dr Danbury (06810) *(G-1973)*
Visual Impact Signs....860 621-7446
115 Meeker Rd Southington (06489) *(G-7994)*
Visual Polymer Tech LLC....603 488-5263
34 Westwood Dr Canton (06019) *(G-1328)*
Visual Software Systems LLC....860 829-1223
32 Maryann Ct Berlin (06037) *(G-231)*
Vita Pasta Inc....860 395-1452
225 Elm St Old Saybrook (06475) *(G-6577)*
Vital Eyes, Greenwich *Also called Inka Inc (G-3181)*
Vital Health Publishing Inc....203 438-3229
149 Old Branchville Rd Ridgefield (06877) *(G-7180)*
Vital Hlthcare Cmmncations LLC....866 478-4825
661 West Ave Apt 16 Milford (06461) *(G-4675)*
Vital Signs & Graphic LLC....860 829-7446
873 Farmington Ave Ste B Berlin (06037) *(G-232)*
Vital Signs LLC....860 365-0897
56 Stoneridge Rd Colchester (06415) *(G-1580)*
Vital Signs Medical LLC....860 563-4969
318 Old Main St Rocky Hill (06067) *(G-7272)*
Vital Stretch LLC....203 847-4477
112 Main St Norwalk (06851) *(G-6391)*
Vitale Woodworks LLC....203 387-3565
842 Alling Rd Orange (06477) *(G-6633)*
Vitec Production Solutions Inc (HQ)....203 929-1100
14 Progress Dr Shelton (06484) *(G-7581)*

ALPHABETIC

Vitek
ALPHABETIC SECTION

Vitek.....203 351-1813
33 Sheridan Dr Ste 1 Naugatuck (06770) ***(G-4927)***
Vitek Research Corporation.....203 735-1813
33 Sheridan Dr Naugatuck (06770) ***(G-4928)***
Vitis Press.....860 921-8570
1083 Bunker Hill Rd Watertown (06795) ***(G-9747)***
Vitro Technology Ltd.....203 783-9566
205 Research Dr Ste 12 Milford (06460) ***(G-4676)***
Vitta Corporation.....203 790-8155
7 Trowbridge Dr Ste 2 Bethel (06801) ***(G-364)***
Vivan Trucking LLC.....573 486-2811
67 E Morningside St Hartford (06112) ***(G-3713)***
Vivax Medical Corporation.....203 729-0514
54 Great Hill Rd Naugatuck (06770) ***(G-4929)***
Viz-Pro LLC.....860 379-0055
120 Colebrook River Rd Winsted (06098) ***(G-10542)***
Vn Machine Co.....860 666-8797
57 Maselli Rd Newington (06111) ***(G-5721)***
VO Leather Inc.....203 345-8442
489a Commanche Ln Stratford (06614) ***(G-8703)***
Vocalis Limited.....203 753-5244
100 Avalon Cir Waterbury (06710) ***(G-9623)***
Vogel Optics LLC.....203 925-9619
12 Old Coram Rd Shelton (06484) ***(G-7582)***
Voice Express Corp.....203 221-7799
1525 Kings Hwy Ste 1 Fairfield (06824) ***(G-2865)***
Voice Glance LLC.....800 260-3025
12 Roosevelt Ave Mystic (06355) ***(G-4852)***
Volpe Cable Corporation.....203 623-1818
201 Linden Ave Branford (06405) ***(G-667)***
Voltarc, Orange *Also called Lcd Lighting Inc* ***(G-6610)***
Voltarc Technologies Inc.....203 753-6366
400 Captain Neville Dr Waterbury (06705) ***(G-9624)***
Vortex Manufacturing.....860 749-9769
60 Sunshine Farms Dr Somers (06071) ***(G-7675)***
Voyteks Inc.....860 967-6558
7 Thompson Rd East Windsor (06088) ***(G-2529)***
Vp Printing.....203 736-1756
2 N Westwood Rd Ansonia (06401) ***(G-56)***
Vr Industries LLC.....860 618-2772
27 Elton St Torrington (06790) ***(G-8987)***
Vrd Customs Ltd.....475 329-5184
50 Beaver Brook Rd Ste 1 Danbury (06810) ***(G-1974)***
Vulcan Industries Inc.....860 683-2005
651 Day Hill Rd Windsor (06095) ***(G-10460)***
W A M, South Windham *Also called Windham Automated Machines Inc* ***(G-7695)***
W and G Machine Company Inc.....203 288-8772
4 Hamden Park Dr Hamden (06517) ***(G-3526)***
W B Mason Co Inc.....888 926-2766
194 Research Pkwy Meriden (06450) ***(G-4265)***
W B Mason Co Inc.....888 926-2766
151 Woodward Ave Ste 1 Norwalk (06854) ***(G-6392)***
W B Mason Co Inc.....888 926-2766
2 Consumers Ave Norwich (06360) ***(G-6439)***
W B Mason Co Inc.....888 926-2766
43 North Rd East Windsor (06088) ***(G-2530)***
W Canning Inc.....203 575-5727
245 Freight St Waterbury (06702) ***(G-9625)***
W G Woodworking.....203 262-8308
1370 Kettletown Rd Southbury (06488) ***(G-7883)***
W H Preuss Sons Incorporated.....860 643-9492
228 Boston Tpke Bolton (06043) ***(G-521)***
W J Savage Co Inc.....203 468-4100
31 Commerce St East Haven (06512) ***(G-2459)***
W M G and Sons Inc.....860 584-0143
8 Summerberry Rd Bristol (06010) ***(G-1136)***
W R Hartigan & Son Inc.....860 673-9203
10 Spielman Hwy Burlington (06013) ***(G-1278)***
W S Polymers.....203 268-1557
93 Calhoun Ave Trumbull (06611) ***(G-9093)***
W&R Manufacturing Inc.....203 877-5955
230 Woodmont Rd Ste U Milford (06460) ***(G-4677)***
W2w Partners LLC.....781 424-7824
125 Greenwich Ave Ste 3 Greenwich (06830) ***(G-3255)***
Wad Inc.....860 828-3331
100 Clark Dr East Berlin (06023) ***(G-2179)***
Wade R Moore.....203 767-6146
124 Research Dr Ste C Milford (06460) ***(G-4678)***
Wadsworth Falls Mfg Co.....860 346-3644
72 Main St Rockfall (06481) ***(G-7216)***
Wadsworth Press.....860 623-3820
182 Main St East Windsor (06088) ***(G-2531)***
Wagner Instruments, Riverside *Also called Weigh & Test Systems Inc* ***(G-7205)***
Wagner Instruments Inc.....203 869-9681
88 River Rd Cos Cob (06807) ***(G-1643)***
Wagz Inc.....203 553-9336
1 Landmark Sq Ste 505 Stamford (06901) ***(G-8487)***
Wai, Madison *Also called Wire Association Intl Inc* ***(G-3968)***
Wake Publishing.....860 559-2787
1318 Monroe Tpke Monroe (06468) ***(G-4763)***
Wakeen Gallery.....860 763-4565
128 Parker Rd Somers (06071) ***(G-7676)***
Walker Industries LLC.....860 455-3554
464 Zaicek Rd Ashford (06278) ***(G-67)***
Walker Magnetics Group Inc (HQ).....508 853-3232
600 Day Hill Rd Windsor (06095) ***(G-10461)***
Walker Products Incorporated.....860 659-3781
80 Commerce St Ste C Glastonbury (06033) ***(G-3094)***
Walker Woodworking LLC.....860 429-2644
18 Cotswold Dr Ashford (06278) ***(G-68)***
Wallace Services Group LLC.....860 350-2992
6 Biltmore Park Bloomfield (06002) ***(G-499)***
Wallach Surgical, Trumbull *Also called Coopersurgical Inc* ***(G-9016)***
Wallach Surgical Devices Inc (PA).....203 799-2000
75 Corporate Dr Trumbull (06611) ***(G-9094)***
Wallach Surgical Devices Inc.....800 243-2463
95 Corporate Dr Trumbull (06611) ***(G-9095)***
Wallingford Industries Inc.....203 481-0359
31 Business Park Dr Ste 3 Branford (06405) ***(G-668)***
Wallingford Prtg Bus Forms Inc.....203 481-1911
758 E Main St Branford (06405) ***(G-669)***
Wally-B Welding.....203 264-3853
556 Berkshire Rd Southbury (06488) ***(G-7884)***
Walnut Beach Creamery LLC.....203 878-7738
17 Broadway 19 Milford (06460) ***(G-4679)***
Walpole Fence Company, Ridgefield *Also called Walpole Woodworkers Inc* ***(G-7181)***
Walpole Outdoors, Westport *Also called Walpole Woodworkers Inc* ***(G-10173)***
Walpole Woodworkers Inc.....508 668-2800
346 Ethan Allen Hwy Ridgefield (06877) ***(G-7181)***
Walpole Woodworkers Inc.....203 595-9930
129 Interlaken Rd Stamford (06903) ***(G-8488)***
Walpole Woodworkers Inc.....203 255-9010
1835 Post Rd E Ste 6 Westport (06880) ***(G-10173)***
Walsh Claim Services.....203 481-0680
6 Enterprise Dr North Branford (06471) ***(G-5865)***
Walsh Prints.....860 829-5566
143 Winding Meadow Dr Kensington (06037) ***(G-3820)***
Walston Inc.....203 453-5929
131 Nut Plains Rd Guilford (06437) ***(G-3401)***
Walters Wood Working LLC.....860 683-8478
47 Old Kennedy Rd Windsor (06095) ***(G-10462)***
Walts Trooper Factory LLC.....203 871-9254
44 Circle Dr North Branford (06471) ***(G-5866)***
Walz & Krenzer Inc (PA).....203 267-5712
91 Willenbrock Rd Ste B4 Oxford (06478) ***(G-6699)***
Walz & Krenzer Inc.....203 267-5712
91 Willenbrock Rd Ste B4 Oxford (06478) ***(G-6700)***
Wanho Manufacturing LLC.....203 759-3744
154 Knotter Dr Cheshire (06410) ***(G-1457)***
Warco of Ne LLC.....203 393-1691
198 Newton Rd Woodbridge (06525) ***(G-10621)***
Ward Leonard CT LLC (HQ).....860 283-5801
401 Watertown Rd Thomaston (06787) ***(G-8818)***
Ward Leonard CT LLC.....860 283-2294
401 Watertown Rd Thomaston (06787) ***(G-8819)***
Ward Leonard Holdings LLC (PA).....860 283-5801
401 Watertown Rd Thomaston (06787) ***(G-8820)***
Ward Leonard Inv Holdings LLC (HQ).....860 283-5801
401 Watertown Rd Thomaston (06787) ***(G-8821)***
Ward Leonard Operating LLC (HQ).....860 283-5801
401 Watertown Rd Thomaston (06787) ***(G-8822)***
Ward Lonard Houma Holdings LLC.....860 283-5801
401 Watertown Rd Thomaston (06787) ***(G-8823)***
Warehouse Dept, Hartford *Also called G W P Inc* ***(G-3595)***
Waring Products Division, Torrington *Also called Conair Corporation* ***(G-8914)***
Warmup Inc.....203 791-0072
52 Federal Rd Ste 1b Danbury (06810) ***(G-1975)***
Warner Precision Machining & F.....203 281-3660
875 Shepard Ave Hamden (06514) ***(G-3527)***
Warren Computer Services.....203 929-5725
79 Fairlane Dr Shelton (06484) ***(G-7583)***
Warren Press Inc.....203 431-0011
470 Main St Ste 1 Ridgefield (06877) ***(G-7182)***
Warren Trading Company.....860 868-7848
14 Brick School Rd Warren (06754) ***(G-9409)***
Warren Woodworking LLC.....860 408-0030
31 Canton Rd West Simsbury (06092) ***(G-9984)***
Warrior Precision.....203 375-8154
264 Seymour St Stratford (06615) ***(G-8704)***
Washburn Design LLC.....860 675-3215
148 Jerome Ave Burlington (06013) ***(G-1279)***
Washer Tech Inc.....203 886-0054
956 Old Colony Rd Meriden (06451) ***(G-4266)***
Washington Concrete Products.....860 747-5242
328 S Washington St Plainville (06062) ***(G-6876)***
Washington Copper Works Inc.....860 868-7637
49 South St Washington (06793) ***(G-9415)***
Wasp Archery Products Inc.....860 283-0246
707 Main St Plymouth (06782) ***(G-6930)***
Waste Resource Recovery Inc (PA).....860 287-3332
505 Exeter Rd Lebanon (06249) ***(G-3866)***
Waste To Green Fuel LLC.....203 536-5855
1376 Chopsey Hill Rd Bridgeport (06606) ***(G-935)***
Watchdog Welding LLC.....860 355-9549
26 New Milford Rd E Bridgewater (06752) ***(G-948)***

ALPHABETIC SECTION

Water & Air Inc (PA) 860 423-0234
  885 Windham Rd South Windham (06266) *(G-7693)*
Water Pollution Control Dept, Vernon Rockville Also called Town of Vernon *(G-9183)*
Water Transit Services LLC 860 625-3625
  22 Prindiville Ave Waterford (06385) *(G-9676)*
Water Treatment Plant, Vernon Also called Town of Vernon *(G-9156)*
Water Works 203 546-6000
  60 Backus Ave Danbury (06810) *(G-1976)*
Waterbury Button Company, Cheshire Also called Ogs Technologies Inc *(G-1424)*
Waterbury Cpl LLC 203 592-4069
  535 Watertown Ave Waterbury (06708) *(G-9626)*
Waterbury Leatherworks Co 203 755-7789
  1691 Thomaston Ave Ste 3 Waterbury (06704) *(G-9627)*
Waterbury Plating, Waterbury Also called Halco Inc *(G-9495)*
Waterbury Printing, Waterbury Also called Master Engrv & Printery Inc *(G-9535)*
Waterbury Rolling Mills Inc 203 597-5000
  215 Piedmont St Waterbury (06706) *(G-9628)*
Waterbury Screw Machine 203 756-8084
  319 Thomaston Ave Waterbury (06702) *(G-9629)*
Waterbury Screw Mch Pdts Co 203 756-8084
  311 Thomaston Ave Ste 319 Waterbury (06702) *(G-9630)*
Waterbury Swiss Automatics 203 573-8584
  43 Mattatuck Heights Rd Waterbury (06705) *(G-9631)*
Waterfalls 203 377-1540
  296 1st Ave Stratford (06615) *(G-8705)*
Waterlogic Usa Inc 866 917-7873
  8 Two Mile Rd Ste 200 Farmington (06032) *(G-2977)*
Waterside Vending LLC 860 399-6039
  643 Old Clinton Rd Westbrook (06498) *(G-10014)*
Watertown Canvas and Awng LLC 860 274-0933
  98 Falls Ave Oakville (06779) *(G-6467)*
Watertown Jig Bore Service Inc 860 274-5898
  29 New Wood Rd Watertown (06795) *(G-9748)*
Watertown Plastics Inc 860 274-7535
  830 Echo Lake Rd Watertown (06795) *(G-9749)*
Watrous Brothers Machine Shop 860 536-7014
  137 Fishtown Rd Mystic (06355) *(G-4853)*
Watson Fabrication LLC 860 912-8778
  15 E Pattagansett Rd Niantic (06357) *(G-5819)*
Watson LLC (HQ) 203 932-3000
  301 Heffernan Dr West Haven (06516) *(G-9960)*
Watts 203 230-8582
  11 Quarry Ln Hamden (06518) *(G-3528)*
Wauregan Machine Shop 860 774-0686
  51 S Walnut St Wauregan (06387) *(G-9754)*
Waybest Foods Inc 860 289-7948
  1510 John Fitch Blvd South Windsor (06074) *(G-7839)*
Wayne Horn 860 491-3315
  308 Cedar Ln New Hartford (06057) *(G-5214)*
Wayne Woodworks 203 362-8084
  1680 Cross Hwy Fairfield (06824) *(G-2866)*
Waypoint Distillery 860 519-5390
  410 Woodland Ave Bloomfield (06002) *(G-500)*
Wayside Fence Co 860 594-1090
  56 Fenn Rd Newington (06111) *(G-5722)*
Wbcb Ventures LLC 860 383-4203
  88 Hollowell Rd Preston (06365) *(G-6991)*
Wces Inc 203 573-1325
  225 S Leonard St Waterbury (06708) *(G-9632)*
Wdl Software Llc 203 366-8640
  131 Vesper St Fairfield (06825) *(G-2867)*
Wdss Corporation 203 854-5930
  7 Old Well Ct Norwalk (06855) *(G-6393)*
We Make Paint, Stratford Also called Grafted Coatings Inc *(G-8620)*
We String It 203 512-4513
  89 Hayestown Rd Danbury (06811) *(G-1977)*
Weatherford International LLC 203 294-0190
  8 Enterprise Rd Wallingford (06492) *(G-9402)*
Web Charity LLC 203 481-7600
  36 Park Dr E Branford (06405) *(G-670)*
Web Industries 860 779-3403
  312 Lake Rd Dayville (06241) *(G-2077)*
Web Industries Hartford Inc (HQ) 860 779-3197
  20 Louisa Viens Dr Dayville (06241) *(G-2078)*
Web Industries Inc 860 779-3403
  154 Louisa Viens Dr Dayville (06241) *(G-2079)*
Web Savvy Marketers LLC 860 432-8756
  222 Pitkin St Ste 5 East Hartford (06108) *(G-2401)*
Webbers Truck Service Inc 860 623-4554
  27 Depot Hill Rd East Windsor (06088) *(G-2532)*
Weber Audio Systems, Wallingford Also called David J Weber *(G-9247)*
Webwrite Publishing LLC 203 544-9728
  134 Georgetown Rd Weston (06883) *(G-10045)*
Weddles LLC 203 964-1888
  2052 Shippan Ave Stamford (06902) *(G-8489)*
Weekend Kitchen 860 767-1010
  16 Main St Essex (06426) *(G-2737)*
Weekly Retail Service LLC 203 244-5150
  94 Cooper Rd Ridgefield (06877) *(G-7183)*
WEI WEI Fashions Inc 646 322-2599
  58 Washington Ave Greenwich (06830) *(G-3256)*

Weidner Publication Group 203 272-2463
  490 Cornwall Ave Cheshire (06410) *(G-1458)*
Weigh & Test Systems Inc 203 698-9681
  17 Wilmot Ln Ste 2 Riverside (06878) *(G-7205)*
Weimann Brothers Mfg Co 203 735-3311
  247 Roosevelt Dr Derby (06418) *(G-2130)*
Weiss Sleep Shop Inc 860 445-1219
  740 Long Hill Rd Groton (06340) *(G-3317)*
Weiss Sleep Shop Outlet, Groton Also called Weiss Sleep Shop Inc *(G-3317)*
Welch Materials Inc 203 691-1721
  334 Main St West Haven (06516) *(G-9961)*
Weld TEC LLC 860 628-5750
  245 Summer St Plantsville (06479) *(G-6918)*
Weld-All Inc 860 621-3156
  987 West St Southington (06489) *(G-7995)*
Weld-TEC, Plantsville Also called Weld TEC LLC *(G-6918)*
Welder Repair & Rental Svc Inc 203 238-9284
  37 Commerce Cir Durham (06422) *(G-2161)*
Welding On Wheels Services LLC 203 449-6273
  163 Jackson Ave Stratford (06615) *(G-8706)*
Welding Works, Madison Also called Rwt Corporation *(G-3953)*
Weldingrodscom LLC 888 935-3703
  1242 South St Suffield (06078) *(G-8738)*
Welles Machine Shop 860 536-8398
  61 Wells St Groton (06340) *(G-3318)*
Wellinks Inc 650 704-0714
  770 Chapel St Ste 2d New Haven (06510) *(G-5430)*
Wendon Company Inc 203 348-6272
  17 Irving Ave Stamford (06902) *(G-8490)*
Wendon Technologies Inc 203 348-6271
  17 Irving Ave Stamford (06902) *(G-8491)*
Wenger Na Inc (HQ) 845 365-3500
  7 Victoria Dr Monroe (06468) *(G-4764)*
Wentworth Laboratories Inc (PA) 203 775-0448
  1087 Federal Rd Ste 4 Brookfield (06804) *(G-1239)*
Wentworth Laboratories Inc 203 775-9311
  500 Federal Rd Brookfield (06804) *(G-1240)*
Wentworth Manufacturing LLC 860 205-6437
  623 E Main St New Britain (06051) *(G-5082)*
Wentworth Manufacturing LLC (PA) 860 423-4575
  1102 Windham Rd South Windham (06266) *(G-7694)*
Wepa Sports LLC 203 971-9372
  39 W High St New London (06320) *(G-5496)*
Wepco Plastics Inc 860 349-3407
  27 Indstrial Pk Access Rd Middlefield (06455) *(G-4309)*
Wes Press, Middletown Also called Wesleyan University *(G-4430)*
Wescon Corp of Conn 860 599-2500
  Elmata Ave Pawcatuck (06379) *(G-6731)*
Wesconn Stairs Inc 203 792-7367
  2 Mill Plain Rd Danbury (06811) *(G-1978)*
Wesdyne Amadata, Windsor Also called Wesdyne International LLC *(G-10463)*
Wesdyne International LLC 860 731-1683
  20 International Dr Windsor (06095) *(G-10463)*
Wesleyan University 860 685-7727
  215 Long Ln Middletown (06457) *(G-4429)*
Wesleyan University 860 685-2980
  110 Mount Vernon St Middletown (06457) *(G-4430)*
Wesleyan University Press, Middletown Also called Wesleyan University *(G-4429)*
Wesport Signs 203 557-3668
  1761 Post Rd E Westport (06880) *(G-10174)*
Wesport Signs 203 286-7710
  17 Linden St Norwalk (06851) *(G-6394)*
Wess Tool & Die Company Inc 203 237-5277
  140 Research Pkwy Ste 2 Meriden (06450) *(G-4267)*
West and Package, Middletown Also called Risha Rishi LLC *(G-4405)*
West End Auto Parts 203 453-9009
  797 Foxon Rd North Branford (06471) *(G-5867)*
West Hartford Lock Co LLC 860 236-0671
  360 Prospect Ave Hartford (06105) *(G-3714)*
West Hartford Stone Mulch LLC 860 461-7616
  154 Reed Ave West Hartford (06110) *(G-9872)*
West Haven Tool & Mfg, West Haven Also called West Haven Tool & Mfg LLC *(G-9962)*
West Haven Tool & Mfg LLC 203 932-1735
  1 Hart St West Haven (06516) *(G-9962)*
West Haven Voice, West Haven Also called Suburban Voices Publishing LLC *(G-9956)*
West Hrtford Stirs Cbinets Inc 860 953-9151
  17 Main St Newington (06111) *(G-5723)*
West Mont Group 203 931-1033
  14 Gilbert St Ste 202 West Haven (06516) *(G-9963)*
West Rock Art Glass Inc 203 488-8225
  11 Sycamore Way Ste 106 Branford (06405) *(G-671)*
West Shore Metals LLC 860 749-8013
  28 W Shore Dr Enfield (06082) *(G-2705)*
West-Conn Tool and Die Inc 203 538-5081
  128 Long Hill Cross Rd Shelton (06484) *(G-7584)*
Westbrook Con Block Co Inc 860 399-6201
  Cold Spring Brook Ind Par Westbrook (06498) *(G-10015)*
Westbrook Products LLC 860 205-6437
  623 E Main St New Britain (06051) *(G-5083)*
Westchester Book Group, Danbury Also called Westchester Pubg Svcs LLC *(G-1979)*
Westchester Forge Inc 914 584-2429
  28 Benedict Hill Rd New Canaan (06840) *(G-5158)*

Westchester Industries Inc 203 661-0055
485 W Putnam Ave Greenwich (06830) ***(G-3257)***
Westchester Pet Vaccines 860 267-4554
111 Loomis Rd Ste 1 Colchester (06415) ***(G-1581)***
Westchester Pubg Svcs LLC (PA) 203 791-0080
4 Old Newtown Rd Danbury (06810) ***(G-1979)***
Westchster Bk/Rnsford Type Inc 203 791-0080
4 Old Newtown Rd Danbury (06810) ***(G-1980)***
Westconn Orthopedic Laboratory 203 743-4420
52 Federal Rd Ste 2 Danbury (06810) ***(G-1981)***
Westerly Sun 401 348-1000
99 Mechanic St Ste C Pawcatuck (06379) ***(G-6732)***
Western Conn Craftsmen LLC 203 312-8167
246 Pine Hill Rd New Fairfield (06812) ***(G-5183)***
Western Progress, Bristol *Also called McIntire Company* ***(G-1070)***
Westfair Electric Contractors 203 586-1760
1181 Main St S Southbury (06488) ***(G-7885)***
Westfalia Inc 860 314-2920
625 Middle St Bristol (06010) ***(G-1137)***
Westford Hill Distillers LLC 860 429-0464
196 Chatey Rd Ashford (06278) ***(G-69)***
Westfort Construction Corp 860 833-7970
3000 Whitney Ave Hamden (06518) ***(G-3529)***
Westie Cabinetry LLC 860 873-8953
15 Main St East Haddam (06423) ***(G-2250)***
Westminster Tool Inc 860 564-6966
5 East Pkwy Plainfield (06374) ***(G-6756)***
Westminster Tool Inc 860 317-1039
51 Industrial Park Rd Sterling (06377) ***(G-8519)***
Westmount Group LLC 203 931-1033
14b Gilbert St M202 West Haven (06516) ***(G-9964)***
Westport Magazine, Westport *Also called Moffly Publications Inc* ***(G-10123)***
Westport Model Works 203 226-2798
24 Cob Dr Westport (06880) ***(G-10175)***
Westport Precision LLC 203 378-2175
280 Hathaway Dr Stratford (06615) ***(G-8707)***
Westrock Commercial LLC 203 595-3130
1635 Coining Dr Stamford (06902) ***(G-8492)***
Westrock Cp LLC 860 848-1500
125 Depot Rd Uncasville (06382) ***(G-9108)***
WESTROCK RKT COMPANY, Bethel *Also called Westrock Rkt Company* ***(G-365)***
Westrock Rkt Company 203 739-0318
2 Research Dr Bethel (06801) ***(G-365)***
Westrock Rkt Company 860 284-9820
33 Skyview Dr Farmington (06032) ***(G-2978)***
Westwood Products Inc 860 379-9401
167 Torrington Rd Winsted (06098) ***(G-10543)***
Wet Crow Internet Inc 860 919-0164
515 Centerpoint Dr 703 Middletown (06457) ***(G-4431)***
Wethersfield Offset Inc 860 721-8236
1795 Silas Deane Hwy Rocky Hill (06067) ***(G-7273)***
Wethersfield Printing Co Inc 860 721-8236
1795 Silas Deane Hwy Rocky Hill (06067) ***(G-7274)***
Wexford Capital LP (PA) 203 862-7000
411 W Putnam Ave Ste 125 Greenwich (06830) ***(G-3258)***
Wezenski Woodworking 203 488-3255
214 Crosswoods Rd Branford (06405) ***(G-672)***
Wfs Earth Materialsi LLC 203 488-2055
11 Business Park Dr Branford (06405) ***(G-673)***
Wfv Cabinetmaker 203 761-9109
760 Ridgefield Rd Wilton (06897) ***(G-10340)***
WH Rose Inc 860 228-8258
9 Route 66 E Columbia (06237) ***(G-1615)***
Whalen Sticks LLC 203 546-8515
518 Federal Rd Brookfield (06804) ***(G-1241)***
Whalley Glass Company (PA) 203 735-9388
72 Chapel St Derby (06418) ***(G-2131)***
What A Life LLC 860 632-1962
136 Berlin Rd Ste 118 Cromwell (06416) ***(G-1724)***
Whatever Welding LLC 860 779-7703
510 Putnam Pike Dayville (06241) ***(G-2080)***
Whats Your Sign LLC 814 823-7807
1097 Hillside Ave Stratford (06614) ***(G-8708)***
Wheeler Woodworking 860 355-1638
415 Kent Hollow Rd Kent (06757) ***(G-3827)***
Wheels 45 ......203 762-8684
386 Danbury Rd Wilton (06897) ***(G-10341)***
Wheels of Hope Inc 203 305-5762
44 Brownson Dr Shelton (06484) ***(G-7585)***
Whelen Engineering Company Inc (PA) 860 526-9504
51 Winthrop Rd Chester (06412) ***(G-1485)***
Whelen Engineering Company Inc 860 526-9504
Rr 145 Chester (06412) ***(G-1486)***
Whhs B Wing Elevator 203 288-5949
1 Circle St West Haven (06516) ***(G-9965)***
Whipstick Creamery LLC 203 438-2203
43 Whipstick Rd Ridgefield (06877) ***(G-7184)***
Whispering Winds Animal 860 796-8098
178 Nathan Hale Rd Coventry (06238) ***(G-1682)***
Whitakers 860 228-3762
58 Indian Field Rd Hebron (06248) ***(G-3758)***
Whitcraft LLC (PA) 860 974-0786
76 County Rd Eastford (06242) ***(G-2544)***
Whitcraft Scrborough/Tempe LLC (HQ) 860 974-0786
76 County Rd Eastford (06242) ***(G-2545)***
White Barrette Mail LLC 860 923-3183
274 Paine District Rd Woodstock (06281) ***(G-10690)***
White Birch Paper Company, Greenwich *Also called Brant Industries Inc* ***(G-3136)***
White Bride Wines, Darien *Also called White Bridge Liquors Inc* ***(G-2051)***
White Bridge Liquors Inc 203 655-0658
284 Tokeneke Rd Ste 3 Darien (06820) ***(G-2051)***
White Bronze LLC 214 605-7352
60 Wordin Ave Bridgeport (06605) ***(G-936)***
White Dog Woodworking LLC 860 482-3776
199 W Pearl Rd Torrington (06790) ***(G-8988)***
White Dove Woodworking LLC 860 268-4426
117 Eastview Dr Coventry (06238) ***(G-1683)***
White Eagle Printing Co, Stonington *Also called Frank Obuchowski* ***(G-8528)***
White Hills Tool 203 590-3143
8 Maple Dr Monroe (06468) ***(G-4765)***
White Publishing, West Hartford *Also called Life Publications* ***(G-9831)***
White Silo Farm 860 355-0271
32 Route 37 E Sherman (06784) ***(G-7606)***
White Welding Company Inc 203 753-1197
44 N Elm St Waterbury (06702) ***(G-9633)***
Whitebeck John 860 567-1398
931 Bantam Rd Bantam (06750) ***(G-128)***
Whitehawk Construction Svcs, Canton *Also called Owh LLC* ***(G-1323)***
Whiteledge Inc 860 647-1883
134 Pine St Manchester (06040) ***(G-4106)***
Whiting Lighting LLC 860 626-0734
839 Main St Apt 79 Torrington (06790) ***(G-8989)***
Whitman Controls LLC 800 233-4401
201 Dolphin Rd Bristol (06010) ***(G-1138)***
Whitney Pratt 860 565-6431
64 Cemetery Rd Willington (06279) ***(G-10261)***
Whole Donut 860 745-3041
920 Enfield St Ste A Enfield (06082) ***(G-2706)***
Whole G Food Intl Distrs LLC 203 848-2136
105 Hamilton St New Haven (06511) ***(G-5431)***
Whole German Breads LLC 203 507-0663
85 Willow St New Haven (06511) ***(G-5432)***
Wholesale Poster Frames, Derby *Also called M & B Enterprise LLC* ***(G-2119)***
Whyco Finishing Tech LLC 860 283-5826
670 Waterbury Rd Thomaston (06787) ***(G-8824)***
Wicks Business Information LLC (PA) 203 334-2002
4 Research Dr Ste 402 Shelton (06484) ***(G-7586)***
Wide Horizons Co Inc 203 661-9252
18 Huckleberry Ln Greenwich (06831) ***(G-3259)***
Wideband Solutions Inc 860 383-8918
37 Northwest Dr Plainville (06062) ***(G-6877)***
Wiffle Ball Incorporated 203 924-4643
275 Bridgeport Ave Shelton (06484) ***(G-7587)***
Wiki Community LLC 860 582-3489
35 Drayla Dr Bristol (06010) ***(G-1139)***
Wilbur Signs 203 313-4950
32 Concord Rd Danbury (06810) ***(G-1982)***
Wild Bills Action Sports LLC 860 536-6648
93 Marsh Rd Groton (06340) ***(G-3319)***
Wild Card Golf LLC 860 296-1661
394 Ledyard St Hartford (06114) ***(G-3715)***
Wild Card Golf LLC 860 296-1661
222 Murphy Rd Hartford (06114) ***(G-3716)***
Wild Leaf Press Inc 203 415-5309
12 Fatima Dr Bethany (06524) ***(G-252)***
Wild Rver Cstm Screen Prtg LLC 203 426-1500
3 Simm Ln Ste 2e1 Newtown (06470) ***(G-5797)***
Wild-Froyo LLC 860 739-6124
16 Town Rd Niantic (06357) ***(G-5820)***
Wildcat Fuel Systems Conn LLC 203 627-4310
36 Vantage Rd Hamden (06514) ***(G-3530)***
Wilde Manufacturing LLC 203 693-3939
80 Wampus Ln Ste 4 Milford (06460) ***(G-4680)***
Wilder Hill Farms 860 567-2459
84 Platt Farm Rd Morris (06763) ***(G-4793)***
Wildflour Cupcakes Sweets LLC 203 828-6576
18 Bank St Seymour (06483) ***(G-7373)***
Wildside Fabrication LLC 860 585-0514
625 N Main St Bristol (06010) ***(G-1140)***
Wiles Charles Preston M D 203 562-7550
291 Whitney Ave Ste 303 New Haven (06511) ***(G-5433)***
Wilhelm Gdale Elzabeth Designs 203 371-8787
333 Vincellette St # 37 Bridgeport (06606) ***(G-937)***
Wilkinson Tool & Die Co 860 599-5821
55 Stillman Rd North Stonington (06359) ***(G-6032)***
Willard J Stearns & Sons Inc 860 423-9289
50 Stearns Rd Storrs Mansfield (06268) ***(G-8561)***
William A Weinert Canvas 203 595-0580
98 Pinewood Rd Stamford (06903) ***(G-8493)***
William Clark Welding Inc 860 537-0122
248 Boretz Rd Colchester (06415) ***(G-1582)***
William Korn Inc 860 647-0284
132 1/2 Pine St Manchester (06040) ***(G-4107)***
William Linkovich 860 824-0298
41 Trescott Hill Rd East Canaan (06024) ***(G-2184)***

William Magenau & Company Inc 860 423-7713
42 Walnut St Willimantic (06226) *(G-10238)*
William Martin 860 355-1919
157 Gaylord Rd Gaylordsville (06755) *(G-2997)*
Williams Mold & Machine 860 928-3522
407 Chase Rd Putnam (06260) *(G-7078)*
Williams Oil Company 860 664-9587
1 Walnut Hill Rd Clinton (06413) *(G-1534)*
Williams Printing Group LLC 860 423-8779
387 Tuckie Rd Ste G North Windham (06256) *(G-6041)*
Williams Printing LLC 860 813-1717
1131 Tolland Tpke 0-134 Manchester (06042) *(G-4108)*
Williams Walter Ovrhd Door LLC 203 488-8620
10 Vineyard Rd Branford (06405) *(G-674)*
Willies Welding Inc 203 237-6235
313 Spring St Meriden (06451) *(G-4268)*
Willimantic Brewing Co LLC 860 423-6777
967 Main St Willimantic (06226) *(G-10239)*
Willimantic Waste Paper Co Inc (PA) 860 423-4527
185 Recycling Way Willimantic (06226) *(G-10240)*
Willimantic, CT Plant, Willimantic *Also called General Cable Industries Inc (G-10227)*
Willimatic Instant Print, Willimantic *Also called Gulemo Inc (G-10229)*
Willis Mills House LLC 917 287-3260
1380 Ponus Rdg New Canaan (06840) *(G-5159)*
Willoughby & Co LLC 203 709-1464
427 Old Poverty Rd Southbury (06488) *(G-7886)*
Willoughby's Coffee & Tea, Branford *Also called B & B Ventures Ltd Lblty Co (G-554)*
Willow Woodworking Inc 203 426-8200
36 Maltbie Rd Newtown (06470) *(G-5798)*
Willson Manufacturing of Conn 860 643-8182
71 Batson Dr Manchester (06042) *(G-4109)*
Wilson Anchor Bolt Sleeve 203 516-5260
259 Roosevelt Dr Derby (06418) *(G-2132)*
Wilson Arms Company 203 488-7297
97 Leetes Island Rd 101 Branford (06405) *(G-675)*
Wilson Partitions 203 316-8033
110 Viaduct Rd Stamford (06907) *(G-8494)*
Wilson Partitions Inc 203 316-8033
120 Viaduct Rd Stamford (06907) *(G-8495)*
Wilson Woodworks Inc 860 870-2500
100 Lamberton Rd Windsor (06095) *(G-10464)*
Wilton Art Framing, Wilton *Also called Rockwell Art & Framing LLC (G-10325)*
Winchester Industries Inc 860 379-5336
106 Groppo Dr Winsted (06098) *(G-10544)*
Winchester Interconnect Corp (PA) 203 741-5400
68 Water St Norwalk (06854) *(G-6395)*
Winchester Products Inc 860 379-8590
22 Lanson Dr Winsted (06098) *(G-10545)*
Winchester Stair & Woodworking 860 379-3194
210 Holabird Ave Ste 6 Winsted (06098) *(G-10546)*
Winchester Woodworking LLC 860 485-0742
243 Woodchuck Ln Harwinton (06791) *(G-3743)*
Winchester Woodworks LLC 860 379-9875
12 Munro St Winsted (06098) *(G-10547)*
Wind Corporation 203 778-1001
30 Pecks Ln Newtown (06470) *(G-5799)*
Wind Hardware & Engineering, Newtown *Also called Wind Corporation (G-5799)*
Windcheck LLC 203 332-7639
110 Chapel St Bridgeport (06604) *(G-938)*
Windfall Woodworking, West Simsbury *Also called Craig Dascanio (G-9975)*
Windham Automated Machines Inc 860 208-5297
1102 Windham Rd South Windham (06266) *(G-7695)*
Windham Container Corporation 860 928-7934
30 Park Rd Putnam (06260) *(G-7079)*
Windham Materials LLC (PA) 860 456-4111
79 Boston Post Rd Willimantic (06226) *(G-10241)*
Windham Sand and Stone Inc 860 643-5578
60 Adams St S Manchester (06040) *(G-4110)*
Windhover Information Inc (HQ) 203 838-4401
383 Main Ave Norwalk (06851) *(G-6396)*
Windhver Rvw-Emerging Med Vent, Norwalk *Also called Windhover Information Inc (G-6396)*
Winding Drive Corporation 203 263-6961
744 Main St S Woodbury (06798) *(G-10655)*
Window Master Real WD Pdts LLC 203 230-2638
400 Sackett Point Rd North Haven (06473) *(G-6014)*
Window Pdts Awngs Blind Shade 203 481-9772
11 Business Park Dr Branford (06405) *(G-676)*
Window Tinting & Signs Inc 203 336-5539
68 Elizabeth St Bridgeport (06610) *(G-939)*
Windsor Locks Nonwovens Inc (HQ) 860 292-5600
1 Hartfield Blvd Ste 101 East Windsor (06088) *(G-2533)*
Windsor Mfg 860 688-6411
169 Kennedy Rd Windsor (06095) *(G-10465)*
Windsor Woodworks 203 386-6975
53 Chamberlain St New Haven (06512) *(G-5434)*
Windsors & Woodwork LLC 860 526-4092
12 Brooks Ln Chester (06412) *(G-1487)*
Wine Capp Inc 860 355-0521
35 Mauweehoo Hl Sherman (06784) *(G-7607)*
Wine Well Chiller Comp Inc 203 878-2465
301 Brewster Rd Ste 3 Milford (06460) *(G-4681)*
Winespeak Press LLC 203 968-8882
38 Janice Rd Stamford (06905) *(G-8496)*
Wing STC Revision Project 203 432-1753
120 High St Rm 607 New Haven (06511) *(G-5435)*
Wings, New Haven *Also called Wing STC Revision Project (G-5435)*
Wings N Things 860 859-9514
26 New London Rd Ste 1 Salem (06420) *(G-7293)*
Wink Ink LLC 860 202-8709
154 Main St Somers (06071) *(G-7677)*
Winkler USA, Shelton *Also called Bakery Engineering/Winkler Inc (G-7400)*
Winner Producing Co 203 259-7576
31 Bulkley Ave N Westport (06880) *(G-10176)*
Winslow Automatics Inc 860 225-6321
23 Saint Claire Ave New Britain (06051) *(G-5084)*
Winslow Manufacturing Inc 203 269-1977
68 N Plains Indus Hwy Wallingford (06492) *(G-9403)*
Winsol Clean Energy LLC 203 216-1972
112 Prospect St Fl 3 Stamford (06901) *(G-8497)*
Winsol Economic Dev Corp (PA) 203 216-1972
112 Prospect St Fl 3 Stamford (06901) *(G-8498)*
Winstanley Inc 203 238-6614
321 Research Pkwy Meriden (06450) *(G-4269)*
Winsted Precision Ball, Winsted *Also called Schaeffler Aerospace USA Corp (G-10534)*
Winters Group 860 749-3317
150 Hazard Ave Ste C1 Enfield (06082) *(G-2707)*
Winthrop Construction LLC 860 322-4562
10 Woodbury Rd Deep River (06417) *(G-2106)*
Winthrop Tool LLC 860 526-9079
55 Plains Rd Essex (06426) *(G-2738)*
Wiperbooties, Bristol *Also called Cadentia LLC (G-997)*
Wipl-D (usa) LLC 860 570-0678
103 High Ridge Rd West Hartford (06117) *(G-9873)*
Wire Association Intl Inc (PA) 203 453-2777
71 Bradley Rd Unit 9 Madison (06443) *(G-3968)*
Wire Burn Industries LLC 203 597-9424
546 S Main St Waterbury (06706) *(G-9634)*
Wire Cutting Precision 860 496-9302
30 Norwood St Torrington (06790) *(G-8990)*
Wire Design Originals 203 795-3783
985 Garden Rd Orange (06477) *(G-6634)*
Wire Journal Inc 203 453-2777
71 Bradley Rd Unit 9 Madison (06443) *(G-3969)*
Wire Rope Div, Pomfret *Also called Loos & Co Inc (G-6933)*
Wire Solutions LLC 860 836-0787
138 Farmington Ave Plainville (06062) *(G-6878)*
Wire Tech LLC 860 945-9473
1094 Echo Lake Rd Watertown (06795) *(G-9750)*
Wired Inc 601 992-0490
3010 Huntington Rd Stratford (06614) *(G-8709)*
Wiremold Company (HQ) 860 233-6251
60 Woodlawn St West Hartford (06110) *(G-9874)*
Wiremold Company 860 263-3115
21 Railroad Pl West Hartford (06110) *(G-9875)*
Wiremold Legrand Co Centerex 877 295-3472
60 Woodlawn St West Hartford (06110) *(G-9876)*
Wiretek Inc 860 242-9473
48 E Newberry Rd Bloomfield (06002) *(G-501)*
Witkowsky John 203 483-0152
73 Branford Rd North Branford (06471) *(G-5868)*
Wittmann Battenfeld Inc (HQ) 860 496-9603
1 Technology Park Dr Torrington (06790) *(G-8991)*
Wizard Too LLC 203 984-7180
34 Little Fox Ln Westport (06880) *(G-10177)*
Wizards Nuts Holdings LLC (PA) 708 483-1315
100 Northfield St Greenwich (06830) *(G-3260)*
WJ Kettleworks LLC 203 377-5000
55 Sperry Ave Stratford (06615) *(G-8710)*
Wl Intermediate Holdings LLC (HQ) 860 283-5801
401 Watertown Rd Thomaston (06787) *(G-8825)*
Wm Corvo Consultants Inc 860 346-6500
769 Newfield St Middletown (06457) *(G-4432)*
Wmb Industries LLC 203 927-2822
62 Pool Rd North Haven (06473) *(G-6015)*
Wmo Industries LLC 203 246-2366
58 Ponus Ave Norwalk (06850) *(G-6397)*
WMW LLC 203 227-4992
13 Scatacook Trl Weston (06883) *(G-10046)*
Wolcott Community News LL 203 879-3900
18 Hilltop Dr Waterbury (06716) *(G-9635)*
Wold Tool Engineering Inc 860 564-8338
7 Commonway Dr Brooklyn (06234) *(G-1259)*
Wolf Colorprint, Newington *Also called Flow Resources Inc (G-5653)*
Wolfe Promotional Services LLC 203 452-7692
56 Far Horizon Dr Monroe (06468) *(G-4766)*
Wolfpit Silencer Solutions, Norwalk *Also called J & E Hidalgo Enterprises LLC (G-6214)*
Wood Creations & Graphics LLC 203 271-3568
41 Willow St Cheshire (06410) *(G-1459)*
Wood Group Component Repair, Wallingford *Also called Ethosenergy Component Repr LLC (G-9258)*
Wood N Excellence Cab Refacing, Higganum *Also called N Excellence Wood Inc (G-3770)*
Wood Pond Press 860 521-0389
365 Ridgewood Rd West Hartford (06107) *(G-9877)*

ALPHABETIC

(PA)=Parent Co (HQ)=Headquarters (DH)=Div Headquarters
2020 Harris Connecticut Manufacturers Directory
597

Wood Services LLC 203 983-5752
1 Sound Shore Dr Ste 203 Greenwich (06830) ***(G-3261)***
Wood Works By Aranda LLC 203 908-3010
652 Glenbrook Rd 3-301 Stamford (06906) ***(G-8499)***
Wood-N-Tap 203 265-9663
970 N Colony Rd Ste 2 Wallingford (06492) ***(G-9404)***
Woodbridge Town News 203 298-4399
653 Orange Center Rd Orange (06477) ***(G-6635)***
Woodbury At Mooer, Woodbury *Also called Kevin G Barry* ***(G-10640)***
Woodbury Pewterers Inc 203 263-2668
860 Main St S Woodbury (06798) ***(G-10656)***
Woodfree Crating Systems Inc 203 759-1799
150 Mattatuck Heights Rd Waterbury (06705) ***(G-9636)***
Woodhall Press LLP 203 428-1876
81 Old Saugatuck Rd Norwalk (06855) ***(G-6398)***
Woodland Power Products Inc 888 531-7253
72 Acton St West Haven (06516) ***(G-9966)***
Woodmsters Mllwk Rstration LLC 203 745-3165
119 Patten Rd North Haven (06473) ***(G-6016)***
Woods End Inc 203 226-6303
11 Lilac Ln Weston (06883) ***(G-10047)***
Woods Lightning Protection 203 929-1868
31 School St Shelton (06484) ***(G-7588)***
Woodshop News Magazine, Essex *Also called Soundings Publications LLC* ***(G-2735)***
Woodstock Line Co 860 928-6557
91 Canal St Putnam (06260) ***(G-7080)***
Woodview Construction Svcs LLC 860 402-9032
11 Ashley Dr Windsor (06095) ***(G-10466)***
Woodway Print Inc 203 323-6423
48 Union St Ste 21 Stamford (06906) ***(G-8500)***
Woodwork Specialties Inc 860 583-4848
123 New St Bristol (06010) ***(G-1141)***
Woodworkers 860 669-9113
7 Oakwood Ln Clinton (06413) ***(G-1535)***
Woodworkers Club LLC 203 847-9663
215 Westport Ave Norwalk (06851) ***(G-6399)***
Woodworkers Heaven Inc 203 333-2778
955 Conn Ave Ste 4106 Bridgeport (06607) ***(G-940)***
Woodworkers Resource 860 668-4100
10 Wren Dr Suffield (06078) ***(G-8739)***
Woodworking 860 354-6757
89 Cherniske Rd New Milford (06776) ***(G-5608)***
Woodworking Plus LLC 203 393-1967
375 Bethmour Rd Bethany (06524) ***(G-253)***
Woodworks of Connecticut Ltd 914 318-7970
83 Purdy Hill Rd Monroe (06468) ***(G-4767)***
Woody Mosch Cabinet Makers 203 266-7619
23 Wood Creek Rd Bethlehem (06751) ***(G-377)***
Woodys Wooden Wonders LLC 860 669-5221
80 Olde Orchard Rd Clinton (06413) ***(G-1536)***
Wool Solutions Inc 203 845-0921
57 Cranbury Rd Norwalk (06851) ***(G-6400)***
Woolworks International Ltd (PA) 203 661-7076
379 Old Long Ridge Rd Stamford (06903) ***(G-8501)***
Woolworks Ltd 860 963-1228
154 Main St B Putnam (06260) ***(G-7081)***
Word For Words LLC 203 894-1908
12 Abbott Ave Ridgefield (06877) ***(G-7185)***
Worden's Welding, Lakeside *Also called Bob Worden* ***(G-3841)***
Work 'n Gear 8061, Orange *Also called Work n Gear LLC* ***(G-6636)***
Work n Gear LLC 203 795-8998
440 Boston Post Rd Ste A Orange (06477) ***(G-6636)***
Work n Gear LLC 203 467-1156
52 Frontage Rd East Haven (06512) ***(G-2460)***
Work'n Gear 8014, East Haven *Also called Work n Gear LLC* ***(G-2460)***
World Cord Sets Inc 860 763-2100
210 Moody Rd Enfield (06082) ***(G-2708)***
World Link Imports-Exports 203 792-0281
14 Chelsea Dr Danbury (06811) ***(G-1983)***
World Wide Games Inc 860 537-3451
10 Mill St Colchester (06415) ***(G-1583)***
World Wrestling Entrmt Inc (PA) 203 352-8600
1241 E Main St Stamford (06902) ***(G-8502)***
Worldscreen Inc 860 274-9218
843 Echo Lake Rd Watertown (06795) ***(G-9751)***
Worldwide Products Inc 855 972-2867
58 Mallory Rd Roxbury (06783) ***(G-7286)***
Worms Eye 203 888-0895
66 Briarwood Dr Seymour (06483) ***(G-7374)***
Worth Properties LLC 203 281-1792
27 Spring Glen Ter Hamden (06517) ***(G-3531)***
Worthington Logging 860 684-9605
6 Crow Hill Rd Stafford Springs (06076) ***(G-8047)***
Wraith Industries LLC (PA) 860 454-4003
9 Hillside Rd Ashford (06278) ***(G-70)***
Wrenfield Group Inc 203 438-0090
27 Governor St Ridgefield (06877) ***(G-7186)***
Write Way Signs & Design Inc 860 482-8893
73 Migeon Ave Torrington (06790) ***(G-8992)***
Writers Press LLC 860 242-9271
1010 Kensington Park Bloomfield (06002) ***(G-502)***
Writestuff Creative Services L 860 343-1919
32 Andrew St Middletown (06457) ***(G-4433)***
WS Welding LLC 860 262-0214
121 Rose Hill Rd Portland (06480) ***(G-6980)***
Wtf Mfg Co LLC 860 387-7472
523 W Main St Cheshire (06410) ***(G-1460)***
Wtm Company 860 283-5871
135 S Main St Ste 12 Thomaston (06787) ***(G-8826)***
Wtp Machine Robotics 860 716-7281
41 Water St Southington (06489) ***(G-7996)***
Wyndemere Publishing LLC 860 868-1490
22 Partridge Rd Warren (06754) ***(G-9410)***
X L Color Corp 860 653-9705
3 Turkey Hills Rd East Granby (06026) ***(G-2234)***
X Over Y Systems 860 885-0034
35 Neptune Ave New London (06320) ***(G-5497)***
X44 LLC 860 480-5560
23 Pershing St Torrington (06790) ***(G-8993)***
X44 Project, The, Torrington *Also called X44 LLC* ***(G-8993)***
Xamax Industries Inc 203 888-7200
63 Silvermine Rd Seymour (06483) ***(G-7375)***
Xavier Marcus 203 543-2032
25 Washburn Dr Stratford (06614) ***(G-8711)***
XCEL Fuel 203 481-4510
501 Main St Branford (06405) ***(G-677)***
Xerox Corporation (HQ) 203 968-3000
201 Merritt 7 Norwalk (06851) ***(G-6401)***
Xerox Holdings Corporation (PA) 203 968-3000
201 Merritt 7 Norwalk (06851) ***(G-6402)***
Xerox Services 860 883-8377
73 Court St Cromwell (06416) ***(G-1725)***
Xg Industries LLC 475 282-4643
53 Hancock St Stratford (06615) ***(G-8712)***
Xiaohao Jia 203 866-3120
97 Taylor Ave Ste 2 Norwalk (06854) ***(G-6403)***
Xijet Corp 203 397-2800
8 Lunar Dr Ste 3 New Haven (06525) ***(G-5436)***
Xin Yong Chen 860 651-4937
773 Hopmeadow St Simsbury (06070) ***(G-7651)***
Xintekidel Inc 203 348-9229
56 W Broad St Stamford (06902) ***(G-8503)***
Xmi Corporation 800 838-0424
140 Greenwich Ave Greenwich (06830) ***(G-3262)***
Xolvi LLC 339 222-3616
207 Great Pond Rd Simsbury (06070) ***(G-7652)***
Xtreme Designs LLC 203 773-9303
192 Forbes Ave New Haven (06512) ***(G-5437)***
Xtreme Detail 203 753-6608
600 Meriden Rd Waterbury (06705) ***(G-9637)***
Xuare LLC 860 383-8863
471 N Main St Norwich (06360) ***(G-6440)***
Xylem Inc 203 521-4934
94 Midwood Rd Milford (06460) ***(G-4682)***
Xylem Water Solutions USA Inc 203 450-3715
1000 Bridgeport Ave # 402 Shelton (06484) ***(G-7589)***
Yacht Specialty Products 203 565-5598
86 Birchwood Dr Hamden (06518) ***(G-3532)***
Yakka LLC 617 877-7553
24 Dixwell Ave New Haven (06511) ***(G-5438)***
Yale Alumni Publications Inc 203 432-0645
149 York St Fl 2 New Haven (06511) ***(G-5439)***
Yale Comfort Shoe Center Inc 203 338-8485
305 Boston Ave Fl 1 Stratford (06614) ***(G-8713)***
Yale Commercial Locks & Hdwr, Berlin *Also called Yale Security Inc* ***(G-233)***
Yale Daily News, New Haven *Also called Yale University* ***(G-5448)***
Yale Daily News Publishing Co 203 432-2400
212 York St New Haven (06511) ***(G-5440)***
Yale Herald, New Haven *Also called Yale University* ***(G-5451)***
Yale Law Journal Co Inc 203 432-1666
127 Wall St Rm 452 New Haven (06511) ***(G-5441)***
Yale Law Journal, The, New Haven *Also called Yale Law Journal Co Inc* ***(G-5441)***
Yale Printing and Pubg Svcs 203 432-6560
344 Winchester Ave New Haven (06511) ***(G-5442)***
Yale Review, The, New Haven *Also called Yale University* ***(G-5450)***
Yale Security Inc 865 986-7511
225 Episcopal Rd Berlin (06037) ***(G-233)***
Yale Surgical Company, New Haven *Also called Kaufman Enterprises Inc* ***(G-5307)***
Yale University (PA) 203 432-2550
105 Wall St New Haven (06511) ***(G-5443)***
Yale University 203 764-4333
135 College St Ste 200 New Haven (06510) ***(G-5444)***
Yale University 203 432-2880
149 York St New Haven (06511) ***(G-5445)***
Yale University 203 737-1244
333 Cedar St le90shm New Haven (06510) ***(G-5446)***
Yale University 203 432-3916
225 Prospect St Rm 1 New Haven (06511) ***(G-5447)***
Yale University 203 432-2424
202 York St New Haven (06511) ***(G-5448)***
Yale University 203 432-6320
285 Mansfield St New Haven (06511) ***(G-5449)***
Yale University 203 432-0499
314 Prospect St New Haven (06511) ***(G-5450)***

ALPHABETIC SECTION — Zz Powder Coating

Yale University 203 432-7494
  305 Crown St New Haven (06511) *(G-5451)*
Yale-New Haven Hlth Svcs Corp 203 688-2100
  789 Howard Ave New Haven (06519) *(G-5452)*
Yankee Casting Co Inc 860 749-6171
  243 Shaker Rd Enfield (06082) *(G-2709)*
Yankee Delivery System 860 243-1056
  1 Flyer Row Bloomfield (06002) *(G-503)*
Yankee Finishing 203 910-0645
  700 N Mountain Rd Ste 3 Newington (06111) *(G-5724)*
Yankee Metals LLC 203 612-7470
  76 Knowlton St Bridgeport (06608) *(G-941)*
Yankee Mineral & Gem Co 860 267-0167
  22 E Hayes Rd East Hampton (06424) *(G-2284)*
Yankee Peddler 860 663-0526
  267 Route 81 Killingworth (06419) *(G-3840)*
Yankee Pennysaver Inc 203 775-9122
  246 Federal Rd Ste D15 Brookfield (06804) *(G-1242)*
Yankee Photo Service, Bridgeport Also called Yankee Plak Co Inc *(G-942)*
Yankee Plak Co Inc 203 333-3168
  240 Alice St Bridgeport (06606) *(G-942)*
Yankee Screen Printing 203 924-9926
  15 Kings Ct Derby (06418) *(G-2133)*
Yankee Signs 860 623-8651
  26 Preston Rd Windsor Locks (06096) *(G-10502)*
Yankee Steel Service LLC 203 879-5707
  9 Venus Dr Wolcott (06716) *(G-10593)*
Yankee Woodcraft, Hamden Also called Paul Dringoli *(G-3496)*
Yankee Woodworks LLC 860 933-9882
  91 Pleasant Valley Rd Mansfield Center (06250) *(G-4116)*
Yard Stick Decore 203 330-0360
  145 Hart St # 1 Bridgeport (06606) *(G-943)*
Yard Welding and Repair LLC 860 402-8321
  96 Chestnut St Bristol (06010) *(G-1142)*
Yarde Metals Inc (HQ) 860 406-6061
  45 Newell St Southington (06489) *(G-7997)*
Yarmouth Materials Inc 203 739-0524
  28 Shelter Rock Rd Ste 2 Danbury (06810) *(G-1984)*
Yellow Girl Press LLC 860 819-0260
  315 Jones Hollow Rd Marlborough (06447) *(G-4131)*
Yellowfin Holdings Inc 866 341-0979
  160 West Rd Ellington (06029) *(G-2609)*
Yes Fine Woodworking LLC 203 255-6366
  183 Barberry Rd Southport (06890) *(G-8014)*
Yield Industries LLC 860 307-8202
  209 Milton Rd Goshen (06756) *(G-3105)*
Yocrunch Co LLC 866 963-7862
  141 Sheridan Dr Ste A Naugatuck (06770) *(G-4930)*
Yoguez Woodworking LLC 203 943-6956
  22 Colorado Ave Bridgeport (06605) *(G-944)*
Yolanda Dubose Records and 203 823-6699
  105 W Prospect St West Haven (06516) *(G-9967)*
York Hill Trap Rock Quarry Co 203 237-8421
  975 Westfield Rd Meriden (06450) *(G-4270)*
York Millwork LLC 203 698-3460
  210 Sound Beach Ave Old Greenwich (06870) *(G-6485)*
York Street Studio Inc 203 266-9000
  143 West St Ste Y New Milford (06776) *(G-5609)*
Yorkstreet.com, New Milford Also called York Street Studio Inc *(G-5609)*
Yost Manufacturing & Supply 860 447-9678
  1018 Hartford Tpke Waterford (06385) *(G-9677)*
Young Flan LLC 203 878-0084
  155 New Haven Ave Derby (06418) *(G-2134)*
Youngs Communications Inc 860 347-8567
  182 Court St Middletown (06457) *(G-4434)*
Youngs Printing, Middletown Also called Youngs Communications Inc *(G-4434)*
Your Membership.com, Groton Also called Yourmembershipcom Inc *(G-3320)*
Yourcover LLC 203 563-9233
  11 Grumman Hill Rd Ste 2 Wilton (06897) *(G-10342)*
Yourlightingsource Co LLC 917 439-6501
  17 Ivy St West Haven (06516) *(G-9968)*
Yourmembershipcom Inc 860 271-7241
  541 Eastern Point Rd Groton (06340) *(G-3320)*
Yumearth, Stamford Also called Yummyearth LLC *(G-8504)*
Yumelish Food LLC 203 522-6933
  90 Harvester Rd Fairfield (06825) *(G-2868)*
Yumi Ecosolutions Inc 203 803-1880
  4 Bruce Ln Westport (06880) *(G-10178)*
Yummyearth LLC (PA) 203 276-1259
  9 W Broad St Ste 440 Stamford (06902) *(G-8504)*
Yush Sign Display Co Inc 860 289-1819
  42 Thomas St East Hartford (06108) *(G-2402)*
Yuya Paperie, Southington Also called ECR Enterprises LLC *(G-7917)*
Yxlon International, Shelton Also called Comet Technologies USA Inc *(G-7421)*
Z & M Woodworking LLC 860 378-0563
  118 Old Mill Rd Plantsville (06479) *(G-6919)*
Z&Z Industries LLC 203 230-9533
  30 Glen Ridge Rd Hamden (06518) *(G-3533)*
Z-Loda Systems Inc 203 359-2991
  111 Prospect St Stamford (06901) *(G-8505)*
Z-Medica LLC 203 294-0000
  4 Fairfield Blvd Ste 1 Wallingford (06492) *(G-9405)*
Zachman Industries LLC 860 337-2234
  30 Alexander Rd New Britain (06053) *(G-5085)*
Zackin Publications Inc 203 262-4670
  100 Willenbrock Rd Oxford (06478) *(G-6701)*
Zactech Ultrasonics LLC 203 438-0004
  199 Ethan Allen Hwy Ridgefield (06877) *(G-7187)*
Zag Machine & Tool Co, New Britain Also called Adam Z Golas *(G-4936)*
Zampell Refractories Inc 860 564-2883
  1370 Norwich Rd Plainfield (06374) *(G-6757)*
Zander Wood Works LLC 203 493-5066
  137 Ethan Allen Hwy Ridgefield (06877) *(G-7188)*
Zanni Ani Organic Snacks LLC 203 214-2360
  586 Oxford Rd Oxford (06478) *(G-6702)*
Zara Tool & Die Co, Wilton Also called Alberto Castillo *(G-10268)*
Zatorski Coating Company Inc 860 267-9889
  77 Wopowog Rd East Hampton (06424) *(G-2285)*
Zavarella Woodworking Inc 860 666-6969
  48 Commerce Ct Newington (06111) *(G-5725)*
Zeeco Inc 860 479-0999
  80 Spring Ln Plainville (06062) *(G-6879)*
Zeneli Pizzeria 203 745-4194
  138 Wooster St New Haven (06511) *(G-5453)*
Zenith Hearing Aid, New Haven Also called Zenith-Omni Hearing Center *(G-5454)*
Zenith-Omni Hearing Center (PA) 203 624-9857
  111 Park St Ste 1k New Haven (06511) *(G-5454)*
Zephyr Lock LLC 866 937-4971
  30 Pecks Ln Newtown (06470) *(G-5800)*
Zero Check LLC 860 283-5629
  297 Reynolds Bridge Rd Thomaston (06787) *(G-8827)*
Zero Hazard LLC 860 561-9879
  38 Pembroke Hl Farmington (06032) *(G-2979)*
Zhao LLC 401 864-7186
  28 Glenbrook Rd Unit 28 # 28 Stamford (06902) *(G-8506)*
Ziga Media LLC 203 656-0076
  5 Overbrook Ln Darien (06820) *(G-2052)*
Zillion Group Inc 203 810-5400
  501 Merritt 7 Norwalk (06851) *(G-6404)*
Zoks Homebrewing & Winemaking 860 456-7704
  18 North St Willimantic (06226) *(G-10242)*
Zombie Gang Skateboards LLC 860 367-2650
  176 State St New London (06320) *(G-5498)*
Zoppa Studio, South Windsor Also called Michael Zoppa *(G-7794)*
Zossima Press 203 687-9385
  366 S Brooksvale Rd Cheshire (06410) *(G-1461)*
Zp Couture LLC 888 697-7239
  410 State St Rm 6 North Haven (06473) *(G-6017)*
Zsiba & Smolover Ltd 860 354-5221
  87 Danbury Rd New Milford (06776) *(G-5610)*
Zuckerman Hrpsichords Intl LLC 860 535-1715
  65 Cutler St Stonington (06378) *(G-8542)*
Zuse Inc 203 458-3295
  727 Boston Post Rd Ste 1 Guilford (06437) *(G-3402)*
Zygo Corporation (HQ) 860 347-8506
  21 Laurel Brook Rd Middlefield (06455) *(G-4310)*
Zz Powder Coating 860 917-7495
  13 Roxbury Ct Niantic (06357) *(G-5821)*

PRODUCT INDEX

- Product categories are listed in alphabetical order.

A

ABRASIVES
ABRASIVES: Artificial
ABRASIVES: Coated
ACADEMIC TUTORING SVCS
ACCELERATION INDICATORS & SYSTEM COMPONENTS: Aerospace
ACCOUNTING SVCS, NEC
ACIDS: Hydrofluoric
ACIDS: Inorganic
ACOUSTICAL BOARD & TILE
ACRYLIC RESINS
ACTUATORS: Indl, NEC
ADHESIVES
ADHESIVES & SEALANTS
ADHESIVES: Epoxy
ADVERTISING AGENCIES
ADVERTISING AGENCIES: Consultants
ADVERTISING DISPLAY PRDTS
ADVERTISING REPRESENTATIVES: Magazine
ADVERTISING REPRESENTATIVES: Media
ADVERTISING REPRESENTATIVES: Printed Media
ADVERTISING SPECIALTIES, WHOLESALE
ADVERTISING SVCS, NEC
ADVERTISING SVCS: Direct Mail
ADVERTISING SVCS: Display
ADVERTISING SVCS: Outdoor
ADVERTISING SVCS: Transit
AERIAL WORK PLATFORMS
AGENTS, BROKERS & BUREAUS: Personal Service
AGRICULTURAL DISINFECTANTS
AGRICULTURAL EQPT: Curers, Tobacco
AGRICULTURAL EQPT: Fertilizing Machinery
AGRICULTURAL EQPT: Tractors, Farm
AGRICULTURAL LIMESTONE: Ground
AGRICULTURAL MACHINERY & EQPT REPAIR
AIR CLEANING SYSTEMS
AIR CONDITIONERS: Motor Vehicle
AIR CONDITIONING & VENTILATION EQPT & SPLYS: Wholesales
AIR CONDITIONING EQPT
AIR CONDITIONING REPAIR SVCS
AIR CONDITIONING UNITS: Complete, Domestic Or Indl
AIR COOLERS: Metal Plate
AIR POLLUTION MEASURING SVCS
AIR PURIFICATION EQPT
AIRCRAFT & AEROSPACE FLIGHT INSTRUMENTS & GUIDANCE SYSTEMS
AIRCRAFT & HEAVY EQPT REPAIR SVCS
AIRCRAFT ASSEMBLY PLANTS
AIRCRAFT CONTROL SYSTEMS:
AIRCRAFT CONTROL SYSTEMS: Electronic Totalizing Counters
AIRCRAFT DEALERS
AIRCRAFT ELECTRICAL EQPT REPAIR SVCS
AIRCRAFT ENGINES & ENGINE PARTS: Airfoils
AIRCRAFT ENGINES & ENGINE PARTS: Cooling Systems
AIRCRAFT ENGINES & ENGINE PARTS: Mount Parts
AIRCRAFT ENGINES & ENGINE PARTS: Pumps
AIRCRAFT ENGINES & ENGINE PARTS: Research & Development, Mfr
AIRCRAFT ENGINES & ENGINE PARTS: Rocket Motors
AIRCRAFT ENGINES & PARTS
AIRCRAFT EQPT & SPLYS WHOLESALERS
AIRCRAFT LIGHTING
AIRCRAFT MAINTENANCE & REPAIR SVCS
AIRCRAFT PARTS & AUX EQPT: Panel Assy/Hydro Prop Test Stands
AIRCRAFT PARTS & AUXILIARY EQPT: Accumulators, Propeller
AIRCRAFT PARTS & AUXILIARY EQPT: Ailerons
AIRCRAFT PARTS & AUXILIARY EQPT: Assys, Subassemblies/Parts
AIRCRAFT PARTS & AUXILIARY EQPT: Body & Wing Assys & Parts
AIRCRAFT PARTS & AUXILIARY EQPT: Body Assemblies & Parts
AIRCRAFT PARTS & AUXILIARY EQPT: Gears, Power Transmission
AIRCRAFT PARTS & AUXILIARY EQPT: Lighting/Landing Gear Assy
AIRCRAFT PARTS & AUXILIARY EQPT: Military Eqpt & Armament
AIRCRAFT PARTS & AUXILIARY EQPT: Oxygen Systems
AIRCRAFT PARTS & AUXILIARY EQPT: Research & Development, Mfr
AIRCRAFT PARTS & EQPT, NEC
AIRCRAFT PARTS WHOLESALERS
AIRCRAFT PARTS/AUX EQPT: Airframe Assy, Exc Guided Missiles
AIRCRAFT PROPELLERS & PARTS
AIRCRAFT SEATS
AIRCRAFT SERVICING & REPAIRING
AIRCRAFT TURBINES
AIRCRAFT: Airplanes, Fixed Or Rotary Wing
AIRCRAFT: Autogiros
AIRCRAFT: Motorized
AIRCRAFT: Nonmotorized & Lighter-Than-air
AIRCRAFT: Research & Development, Manufacturer
AIRPORTS, FLYING FIELDS & SVCS
ALARMS: Burglar
ALARMS: Fire
ALLOYS: Additive, Exc Copper Or Made In Blast Furnaces
ALUMINUM
ALUMINUM PRDTS
ALUMINUM: Pigs
ALUMINUM: Rolling & Drawing
AMBULANCE SVCS
AMMUNITION
AMMUNITION: Cartridges Case, 30 mm & Below
AMMUNITION: Components
AMMUNITION: Small Arms
AMPLIFIERS
AMPLIFIERS: RF & IF Power
AMUSEMENT & RECREATION SVCS: Art Gallery, Commercial
AMUSEMENT & RECREATION SVCS: Fishing Boat Operations, Party
AMUSEMENT & RECREATION SVCS: Golf Club, Membership
AMUSEMENT & RECREATION SVCS: Golf Professionals
AMUSEMENT & RECREATION SVCS: Hot Air Balloon Rides
AMUSEMENT & RECREATION SVCS: Physical Fitness Instruction
AMUSEMENT & RECREATION SVCS: Recreation Center
AMUSEMENT & RECREATION SVCS: Tennis Courts, Non-Member
AMUSEMENT & RECREATION SVCS: Yoga Instruction
AMUSEMENT MACHINES: Coin Operated
AMUSEMENT PARK DEVICES & RIDES
AMUSEMENT PARK DEVICES & RIDES: Carnival Mach & Eqpt, NEC
ANALYZERS: Blood & Body Fluid
ANALYZERS: Network
ANIMAL FEED & SUPPLEMENTS: Livestock & Poultry
ANIMAL FOOD & SUPPLEMENTS: Dog
ANIMAL FOOD & SUPPLEMENTS: Dog & Cat
ANIMAL FOOD & SUPPLEMENTS: Feed Supplements
ANIMAL FOOD & SUPPLEMENTS: Pet, Exc Dog & Cat, Canned
ANIMAL FOOD & SUPPLEMENTS: Poultry
ANODIZING SVC
ANTENNAS: Radar Or Communications
ANTENNAS: Receiving
ANTI-OXIDANTS
ANTIFREEZE
ANTIQUE & CLASSIC AUTOMOBILE RESTORATION
ANTIQUE FURNITURE RESTORATION & REPAIR
ANTIQUE REPAIR & RESTORATION SVCS, EXC FURNITURE & AUTOS
ANTISEPTICS, MEDICINAL
APPAREL DESIGNERS: Commercial
APPLIANCE CORDS: Household Electrical Eqpt
APPLIANCES, HOUSEHOLD: Kitchen, Major, Exc Refrigs & Stoves
APPLIANCES, HOUSEHOLD: Refrigs, Mechanical & Absorption
APPLIANCES: Household, NEC
APPLIANCES: Household, Refrigerators & Freezers
APPLIANCES: Major, Cooking
APPLIANCES: Small, Electric
APPRAISAL SVCS, EXC REAL ESTATE
ARCHITECT'S SUPPLIES WHOLESALERS
ARCHITECTURAL PANELS OR PARTS: Porcelain Enameled
ARCHITECTURAL SVCS
ARCHITECTURAL SVCS: Engineering
ARCHITECTURAL SVCS: Engineering
ARMATURE REPAIRING & REWINDING SVC
ARMATURES: Ind
ART & ORNAMENTAL WARE: Pottery
ART DEALERS & GALLERIES
ART GALLERIES
ART GOODS & SPLYS WHOLESALERS
ART GOODS, WHOLESALE
ART MARBLE: Concrete
ART RELATED SVCS
ART RESTORATION SVC
ARTIST'S MATERIALS & SPLYS
ARTISTS' AGENTS & BROKERS
ARTISTS' MATERIALS, WHOLESALE
ARTISTS' MATERIALS: Brushes, Air
ARTISTS' MATERIALS: Chalks, Carpenters', Blackboard, Etc
ARTISTS' MATERIALS: Easels
ARTISTS' MATERIALS: Ink, Drawing, Black & Colored
ARTISTS' MATERIALS: Tables, Drawing
ARTISTS' MATERIALS: Water Colors
ARTS & CRAFTS SCHOOL
ARTWORK: Framed
ASBESTOS PRODUCTS
ASBESTOS REMOVAL EQPT
ASH TRAYS: Stamped Metal
ASPHALT & ASPHALT PRDTS
ASPHALT COATINGS & SEALERS
ASPHALT MINING & BITUMINOUS STONE QUARRYING SVCS
ASPHALT MIXTURES WHOLESALERS
ASSEMBLING & PACKAGING SVCS: Cosmetic Kits
ASSEMBLING SVC: Plumbing Fixture Fittings, Plastic
ASSOCIATIONS: Business
ASSOCIATIONS: Engineering
ASSOCIATIONS: Real Estate Management
ASSOCIATIONS: Trade
ATHLETIC CLUB & GYMNASIUMS, MEMBERSHIP
ATOMIZERS
AUCTION SVCS: Livestock
AUDIO & VIDEO EQPT, EXC COMMERCIAL
AUDIO COMPONENTS
AUDIO ELECTRONIC SYSTEMS
AUDIO-VISUAL PROGRAM PRODUCTION SVCS
AUDIOLOGICAL EQPT: Electronic
AUTHORS' AGENTS & BROKERS
AUTO & HOME SUPPLY STORES: Auto & Truck Eqpt & Parts
AUTO & HOME SUPPLY STORES: Automotive Access
AUTO & HOME SUPPLY STORES: Automotive parts
AUTO & HOME SUPPLY STORES: Speed Shops, Incl Race Car Splys
AUTO & HOME SUPPLY STORES: Truck Eqpt & Parts
AUTO SPLYS & PARTS, NEW, WHSLE: Exhaust Sys, Mufflers, Etc
AUTOMATIC REGULATING CNTRLS: Liq Lvl, Residential/Comm Heat
AUTOMATIC REGULATING CONTROL: Building Svcs Monitoring, Auto
AUTOMATIC REGULATING CONTROLS: AC & Refrigeration
AUTOMATIC REGULATING CONTROLS: Energy Cutoff, Residtl/Comm
AUTOMATIC REGULATING CONTROLS: Hydronic Pressure Or Temp
AUTOMATIC REGULATING CONTROLS: Limit, Heating, Residtl/Comm
AUTOMATIC REGULATING CONTROLS: Refrig/Air-Cond Defrost
AUTOMATIC TELLER MACHINES

PRODUCT INDEX

AUTOMOBILES & OTHER MOTOR VEHICLES WHOLESALERS
AUTOMOTIVE & TRUCK GENERAL REPAIR SVC
AUTOMOTIVE BODY SHOP
AUTOMOTIVE LETTERING & PAINTING SVCS
AUTOMOTIVE PAINT SHOP
AUTOMOTIVE PARTS, ACCESS & SPLYS
AUTOMOTIVE PARTS: Plastic
AUTOMOTIVE RADIATOR REPAIR SHOPS
AUTOMOTIVE REPAIR SHOPS: Auto Front End Repair
AUTOMOTIVE REPAIR SHOPS: Engine Rebuilding
AUTOMOTIVE REPAIR SHOPS: Machine Shop
AUTOMOTIVE REPAIR SHOPS: Truck Engine Repair, Exc Indl
AUTOMOTIVE SPLYS & PARTS, NEW, WHOLESALE: Engines/Eng Parts
AUTOMOTIVE SPLYS & PARTS, NEW, WHOLESALE: Trailer Parts
AUTOMOTIVE SPLYS & PARTS, USED, WHOLESALE
AUTOMOTIVE SPLYS & PARTS, WHOLESALE, NEC
AUTOMOTIVE SVCS, EXC REPAIR & CARWASHES: Glass Tinting
AUTOMOTIVE SVCS, EXC REPAIR & CARWASHES: Trailer Maintenance
AUTOMOTIVE SVCS, EXC REPAIR: Washing & Polishing
AUTOMOTIVE SVCS, EXC RPR/CARWASHES: High Perf Auto Rpr/Svc
AUTOMOTIVE TOPS INSTALLATION OR REPAIR: Canvas Or Plastic
AUTOMOTIVE UPHOLSTERY SHOPS
AUTOMOTIVE WELDING SVCS
AUTOMOTIVE: Bodies
AUTOMOTIVE: Seating
AVIATION PROPELLER & BLADE REPAIR SVCS
AWNINGS & CANOPIES
AWNINGS & CANOPIES: Awnings, Fabric, From Purchased Matls
AWNINGS & CANOPIES: Canopies, Fabric, From Purchased Matls
AWNINGS & CANOPIES: Fabric
AWNINGS: Fiberglass
AWNINGS: Metal
AXES & HATCHETS

B

BABY PACIFIERS: Rubber
BACKHOES
BADGES: Identification & Insignia
BAGS & CONTAINERS: Textile, Exc Sleeping
BAGS: Canvas
BAGS: Duffle, Canvas, Made From Purchased Materials
BAGS: Flour, Fabric, Made From Purchased Materials
BAGS: Paper
BAGS: Plastic
BAGS: Plastic, Made From Purchased Materials
BAGS: Textile
BAGS: Wardrobe, Closet Access, Made From Purchased Materials
BAIT, FISHING, WHOLESALE
BAKERIES, COMMERCIAL: On Premises Baking Only
BAKERIES: On Premises Baking & Consumption
BAKERY PRDTS: Bagels, Fresh Or Frozen
BAKERY PRDTS: Bakery Prdts, Partially Cooked, Exc frozen
BAKERY PRDTS: Bread, All Types, Fresh Or Frozen
BAKERY PRDTS: Cakes, Bakery, Exc Frozen
BAKERY PRDTS: Cakes, Bakery, Frozen
BAKERY PRDTS: Cookies
BAKERY PRDTS: Cookies & crackers
BAKERY PRDTS: Doughnuts, Exc Frozen
BAKERY PRDTS: Dry
BAKERY PRDTS: Frozen
BAKERY PRDTS: Pastries, Exc Frozen
BAKERY PRDTS: Wholesalers
BAKERY: Wholesale Or Wholesale & Retail Combined
BALLOONS: Toy & Advertising, Rubber
BALLS: Steel
BANNERS: Fabric
BARBECUE EQPT
BARRETTES
BARRICADES: Metal
BARS, COLD FINISHED: Steel, From Purchased Hot-Rolled
BARS: Concrete Reinforcing, Fabricated Steel
BASES, BEVERAGE
BATHROOM ACCESS & FITTINGS: Vitreous China & Earthenware

BATTERIES, EXC AUTOMOTIVE: Wholesalers
BATTERIES: Alkaline, Cell Storage
BATTERIES: Dry
BATTERIES: Lead Acid, Storage
BATTERIES: Rechargeable
BATTERIES: Storage
BATTERIES: Wet
BATTERY CASES: Plastic Or Plastics Combination
BATTERY CHARGERS
BEADS: Unassembled
BEARINGS
BEARINGS & PARTS Ball
BEARINGS: Ball & Roller
BEARINGS: Plastic
BEARINGS: Roller & Parts
BEAUTY & BARBER SHOP EQPT
BEAUTY & BARBER SHOP EQPT & SPLYS WHOLESALERS
BEAUTY SALONS
BEDDING, BEDSPREADS, BLANKETS & SHEETS
BEEKEEPERS' SPLYS
BEER & ALE WHOLESALERS
BEER & ALE, WHOLESALE: Beer & Other Fermented Malt Liquors
BEER, WINE & LIQUOR STORES
BEER, WINE & LIQUOR STORES: Beer, Packaged
BEER, WINE & LIQUOR STORES: Wine
BEER, WINE & LIQUOR STORES: Wine & Beer
BEESWAX PROCESSING
BELLOWS
BELLS: Electric
BELT LOADERS: Passenger Baggage
BELTS & BELT PRDTS
BELTS: Conveyor, Made From Purchased Wire
BENTONITE MINING
BEVERAGE BASES & SYRUPS
BEVERAGE PRDTS: Brewers' Grain
BEVERAGE STORES
BEVERAGE, NONALCOHOLIC: Iced Tea/Fruit Drink, Bottled/Canned
BEVERAGES, ALCOHOLIC: Beer
BEVERAGES, ALCOHOLIC: Beer & Ale
BEVERAGES, ALCOHOLIC: Bourbon Whiskey
BEVERAGES, ALCOHOLIC: Cordials
BEVERAGES, ALCOHOLIC: Distilled Liquors
BEVERAGES, ALCOHOLIC: Near Beer
BEVERAGES, ALCOHOLIC: Neutral Spirits, Exc Fruit
BEVERAGES, ALCOHOLIC: Vodka
BEVERAGES, ALCOHOLIC: Wines
BEVERAGES, MALT
BEVERAGES, NONALCOHOLIC: Bottled & canned soft drinks
BEVERAGES, NONALCOHOLIC: Carbonated
BEVERAGES, NONALCOHOLIC: Carbonated, Canned & Bottled, Etc
BEVERAGES, NONALCOHOLIC: Cider
BEVERAGES, NONALCOHOLIC: Flavoring extracts & syrups, nec
BEVERAGES, NONALCOHOLIC: Fruit Drnks, Under 100% Juice, Can
BEVERAGES, NONALCOHOLIC: Lemonade, Bottled & Canned, Etc
BEVERAGES, NONALCOHOLIC: Soft Drinks, Canned & Bottled, Etc
BEVERAGES, WINE & DISTILLED ALCOHOLIC, WHOLESALE: Wine
BEVERAGES, WINE/DISTILLED ALCOHOLIC, WHOL: Bttlg Wine/Liquor
BICYCLES, PARTS & ACCESS
BILLIARD & POOL TABLES & SPLYS
BINDING SVC: Books & Manuals
BINDING SVC: Trade
BINOCULARS
BINS: Prefabricated, Metal Plate
BIOLOGICAL PRDTS: Exc Diagnostic
BIOLOGICAL PRDTS: Serums
BIOLOGICAL PRDTS: Toxins
BIOLOGICAL PRDTS: Vaccines
BIOLOGICAL PRDTS: Veterinary
BLACKSMITH SHOP
BLADES: Saw, Hand Or Power
BLANKBOOKS: Account
BLANKBOOKS: Albums, Record
BLANKBOOKS: Scrapbooks
BLANKETING, FROM MANMADE FIBER
BLASTING SVC: Sand, Metal Parts

BLINDS & SHADES: Porch, Wood Slat
BLINDS & SHADES: Vertical
BLINDS : Window
BLINDS, WOOD
BLOCKS & BRICKS: Concrete
BLOCKS: Landscape Or Retaining Wall, Concrete
BLOCKS: Paving, Concrete
BLOCKS: Paving, Cut Stone
BLOCKS: Standard, Concrete Or Cinder
BLOOD RELATED HEALTH SVCS
BLOWERS & FANS
BLOWERS & FANS
BLOWERS, TURBO: Indl
BLUEPRINTING SVCS
BOAT BUILDING & REPAIR
BOAT BUILDING & REPAIRING: Fiberglass
BOAT BUILDING & REPAIRING: Motorboats, Inboard Or Outboard
BOAT BUILDING & REPAIRING: Motorized
BOAT BUILDING & REPAIRING: Non-Motorized
BOAT BUILDING & REPAIRING: Tenders, Small Motor Craft
BOAT BUILDING & REPAIRING: Yachts
BOAT DEALERS
BOAT DEALERS: Outboard
BOAT DEALERS: Sails & Eqpt
BOAT REPAIR SVCS
BOAT YARD: Boat yards, storage & incidental repair
BOATS & OTHER MARINE EQPT: Plastic
BODIES: Truck & Bus
BODY PARTS: Automobile, Stamped Metal
BOILER REPAIR SHOP
BOILERS: Low-Pressure Heating, Steam Or Hot Water
BOLTS: Metal
BOOK STORES
BOOKS, WHOLESALE
BOOTS: Women's
BORING MILL
BOTTLE CAPS & RESEALERS: Plastic
BOTTLED GAS DEALERS: Liquefied Petro, Dlvrd To Customers
BOTTLED WATER DELIVERY
BOTTLES: Plastic
BOULDER: Crushed & Broken
BOXES & CRATES: Rectangular, Wood
BOXES & SHOOK: Nailed Wood
BOXES: Corrugated
BOXES: Filing, Paperboard Made From Purchased Materials
BOXES: Mail Or Post Office, Collection/Storage, Sheet Metal
BOXES: Paperboard, Folding
BOXES: Paperboard, Set-Up
BOXES: Plastic
BOXES: Solid Fiber
BOXES: Stamped Metal
BOXES: Wooden
BRAKES & BRAKE PARTS
BRAKES: Electromagnetic
BRAKES: Metal Forming
BRAKES: Press
BRAZING SVCS
BRAZING: Metal
BREAD WRAPPERS: Waxed Or Laminated, Made From Purchased Matl
BRICK, STONE & RELATED PRDTS WHOLESALERS
BRIDAL SHOPS
BROADCASTING & COMMS EQPT: Antennas, Transmitting/Comms
BROADCASTING & COMMUNICATION EQPT: Transmit-Receiver, Radio
BROADCASTING & COMMUNICATIONS EQPT: Transmitting, Radio/TV
BROADCASTING STATIONS, RADIO: Sports
BROKERS' SVCS
BROKERS: Business
BROKERS: Printing
BRONZE FOUNDRY, NEC
BRONZE ROLLING & DRAWING
BROOMS
BROOMS & BRUSHES
BROOMS & BRUSHES: Hair Pencils Or Artists' Brushes
BROOMS & BRUSHES: Paintbrushes
BUCKLES & PARTS
BUFFING FOR THE TRADE
BUILDING & STRUCTURAL WOOD MBRS: Timbers, Struct, Lam Lumber
BUILDING & STRUCTURAL WOOD MEMBERS

PRODUCT INDEX

BUILDING COMPONENTS: Structural Steel
BUILDING EXTERIOR CLEANING SVCS
BUILDING ITEM REPAIR SVCS, MISCELLANEOUS
BUILDING MAINTENANCE SVCS, EXC REPAIRS
BUILDING PRDTS & MATERIALS DEALERS
BUILDING PRDTS: Concrete
BUILDING PRDTS: Stone
BUILDING STONE, ARTIFICIAL: Concrete
BUILDINGS & COMPONENTS: Prefabricated Metal
BUILDINGS: Portable
BUILDINGS: Prefabricated, Wood
BUILDINGS: Prefabricated, Wood
BURGLAR ALARM MAINTENANCE & MONITORING SVCS
BURIAL VAULTS: Concrete Or Precast Terrazzo
BURIAL VAULTS: Stone
BURNERS: Gas, Indl
BURNERS: Oil, Domestic Or Indl
BURNT WOOD ARTICLES
BUSES: Wholesalers
BUSINESS ACTIVITIES: Non-Commercial Site
BUSINESS FORMS: Printed, Continuous
BUSINESS FORMS: Printed, Manifold
BUSINESS MACHINE REPAIR, ELECTRIC
BUSINESS SUPPORT SVCS
BUTTONS

C

CABINETS & CASES: Show, Display & Storage, Exc Wood
CABINETS: Bathroom Vanities, Wood
CABINETS: Entertainment
CABINETS: Entertainment Units, Household, Wood
CABINETS: Factory
CABINETS: Kitchen, Metal
CABINETS: Kitchen, Wood
CABINETS: Office, Metal
CABINETS: Office, Wood
CABINETS: Show, Display, Etc, Wood, Exc Refrigerated
CABLE & OTHER PAY TELEVISION DISTRIBUTION
CABLE TELEVISION PRDTS
CABLE: Coaxial
CABLE: Fiber
CABLE: Fiber Optic
CABLE: Noninsulated
CABLE: Steel, Insulated Or Armored
CAGES: Wire
CALCULATING & ACCOUNTING EQPT
CALIPERS & DIVIDERS
CAMERA REPAIR SHOP
CAMERAS & RELATED EQPT: Photographic
CAMERAS: Microfilm
CAMSHAFTS
CANDLES
CANDY & CONFECTIONS: Chocolate Candy, Exc Solid Chocolate
CANDY & CONFECTIONS: Fudge
CANDY, NUT & CONFECTIONERY STORES: Candy
CANDY, NUT & CONFECTIONERY STORES: Confectionery
CANDY, NUT & CONFECTIONERY STORES: Produced For Direct Sale
CANDY: Hard
CANNED SPECIALTIES
CANS: Aluminum
CANS: Garbage, Stamped Or Pressed Metal
CANS: Metal
CANS: Tin
CANVAS PRDTS
CANVAS PRDTS: Boat Seats
CANVAS PRDTS: Convertible Tops, Car/Boat, Fm Purchased Mtrl
CAPACITORS: NEC
CAPS: Plastic
CAR WASH EQPT
CARBIDES
CARBON & GRAPHITE PRDTS, NEC
CARBON SPECIALTIES Electrical Use
CARBURETORS
CARDIOVASCULAR SYSTEM DRUGS, EXC DIAGNOSTIC
CARDS: Color
CARDS: Greeting
CARDS: Identification
CARPET & UPHOLSTERY CLEANING SVCS: Carpet/Furniture, On Loc
CARPETS & RUGS: Tufted
CARPETS, RUGS & FLOOR COVERING
CARPETS: Axminster

CARPETS: Hand & Machine Made
CARPETS: Textile Fiber
CARRIAGES: Horse Drawn
CARTS: Grocery
CASEIN PRDTS
CASEMENTS: Aluminum
CASES, WOOD
CASES: Attache'
CASES: Carrying
CASES: Carrying, Clothing & Apparel
CASES: Packing, Nailed Or Lock Corner, Wood
CASH REGISTERS WHOLESALERS
CASINGS: Sheet Metal
CASKETS & ACCESS
CAST STONE: Concrete
CASTINGS GRINDING: For The Trade
CASTINGS: Aerospace Investment, Ferrous
CASTINGS: Aerospace, Aluminum
CASTINGS: Aerospace, Nonferrous, Exc Aluminum
CASTINGS: Aluminum
CASTINGS: Brass, Bronze & Copper
CASTINGS: Commercial Investment, Ferrous
CASTINGS: Die, Aluminum
CASTINGS: Die, Nonferrous
CASTINGS: Gray Iron
CASTINGS: Precision
CASTINGS: Steel
CASTINGS: Titanium
CATALOG & MAIL-ORDER HOUSES
CATALOG SALES
CATALYSTS: Chemical
CATAPULTS
CEILING SYSTEMS: Luminous, Commercial
CEMENT ROCK: Crushed & Broken
CEMENT, EXC LINOLEUM & TILE
CEMENT: Hydraulic
CEMETERY MEMORIAL DEALERS
CERAMIC FLOOR & WALL TILE WHOLESALERS
CHAINS: Forged
CHARCOAL: Activated
CHART & GRAPH DESIGN SVCS
CHASSIS: Motor Vehicle
CHEESE WHOLESALERS
CHEMICAL ELEMENTS
CHEMICAL INDICATORS
CHEMICAL PROCESSING MACHINERY & EQPT
CHEMICAL SPLYS FOR FOUNDRIES
CHEMICAL: Sodm Compnds/Salts, Inorg, Exc Rfnd Sodm Chloride
CHEMICALS & ALLIED PRDTS WHOLESALERS, NEC
CHEMICALS & ALLIED PRDTS, WHOL: Chemical, Organic, Synthetic
CHEMICALS & ALLIED PRDTS, WHOLESALE: Acids
CHEMICALS & ALLIED PRDTS, WHOLESALE: Adhesives
CHEMICALS & ALLIED PRDTS, WHOLESALE: Chemicals, Indl
CHEMICALS & ALLIED PRDTS, WHOLESALE: Chemicals, Indl & Heavy
CHEMICALS & ALLIED PRDTS, WHOLESALE: Essential Oils
CHEMICALS & ALLIED PRDTS, WHOLESALE: Manmade Fibers
CHEMICALS & ALLIED PRDTS, WHOLESALE: Plastics Film
CHEMICALS & ALLIED PRDTS, WHOLESALE: Plastics Materials, NEC
CHEMICALS & ALLIED PRDTS, WHOLESALE: Plastics Prdts, NEC
CHEMICALS & ALLIED PRDTS, WHOLESALE: Plastics Sheets & Rods
CHEMICALS & ALLIED PRDTS, WHOLESALE: Resin, Synthetic Rubber
CHEMICALS & ALLIED PRDTS, WHOLESALE: Resins
CHEMICALS & ALLIED PRDTS, WHOLESALE: Rubber, Synthetic
CHEMICALS & ALLIED PRDTS, WHOLESALE: Sanitation Preparations
CHEMICALS & ALLIED PRDTS, WHOLESALE: Silicon Lubricants
CHEMICALS & ALLIED PRDTS, WHOLESALE: Spec Clean/Sanitation
CHEMICALS & ALLIED PRDTS, WHOLESALE: Syn Resin, Rub/Plastic
CHEMICALS: Agricultural
CHEMICALS: Alkali Metals, Lithium, Cesium, Francium/Rubidium
CHEMICALS: Boron Compounds, Not From Mines, NEC

CHEMICALS: Fire Retardant
CHEMICALS: Hydrogen Peroxide
CHEMICALS: Inorganic, NEC
CHEMICALS: Medicinal
CHEMICALS: Metal Compounds Or Salts, Inorganic, NEC
CHEMICALS: NEC
CHEMICALS: Organic, NEC
CHEMICALS: Sodium Bicarbonate
CHEMICALS: Sulfur, Incl Rcvrd/Refined, Fm Sour Natural Gas
CHEMICALS: Water Treatment
CHILDREN'S & INFANTS' CLOTHING STORES
CHIROPRACTORS' OFFICES
CHLORINE
CHOCOLATE, EXC CANDY FROM BEANS: Chips, Powder, Block, Syrup
CHOCOLATE, EXC CANDY FROM PURCH CHOC: Chips, Powder, Block
CHRISTMAS TREE ORNAMENTS: Electric
CHROMATOGRAPHY EQPT
CHUCKS
CHURCHES
CHUTES: Mail, Sheet Metal
CIGAR STORES
CIGARETTE & CIGAR PRDTS & ACCESS
CIGARETTE LIGHTERS
CIRCUIT BOARD REPAIR SVCS
CIRCUIT BOARDS, PRINTED: Television & Radio
CIRCUIT BREAKERS
CIRCUIT BREAKERS: Air
CIRCUITS, INTEGRATED: Hybrid
CIRCUITS: Electronic
CLAMPS: Ground, Electric-Wiring Devices
CLAMPS: Metal
CLAY MINING, COMMON
CLEANING & DESCALING SVC: Metal Prdts
CLEANING & DYEING PLANTS, EXC RUGS
CLEANING EQPT: Commercial
CLEANING EQPT: High Pressure
CLEANING OR POLISHING PREPARATIONS, NEC
CLEANING PRDTS: Automobile Polish
CLEANING PRDTS: Drain Pipe Solvents Or Cleaners
CLEANING PRDTS: Drycleaning Preparations
CLEANING PRDTS: Dusting Cloths, Chemically Treated
CLEANING PRDTS: Floor Waxes
CLEANING PRDTS: Furniture Polish Or Wax
CLEANING PRDTS: Metal Polish
CLEANING PRDTS: Polishing Preparations & Related Prdts
CLEANING PRDTS: Sanitation Preparations
CLEANING PRDTS: Sanitation Preps, Disinfectants/Deodorants
CLEANING PRDTS: Specialty
CLEANING PRDTS: Stain Removers
CLEANING PRDTS: Window Cleaning Preparations
CLEANING SVCS
CLEANING SVCS: Industrial Or Commercial
CLIPPERS: Fingernail & Toenail
CLOSURES: Closures, Stamped Metal
CLOSURES: Plastic
CLOTHING & ACCESS STORES
CLOTHING & ACCESS, WOMEN, CHILD & INFANT, WHOLESALE: Under
CLOTHING & ACCESS, WOMEN, CHILD/INFANT, WHOLESALE: Child
CLOTHING & ACCESS, WOMENS, CHILDREN & INFANTS, WHOL: Hats
CLOTHING & ACCESS: Garters
CLOTHING & ACCESS: Handicapped
CLOTHING & ACCESS: Men's Miscellaneous Access
CLOTHING & ACCESS: Suspenders
CLOTHING & APPAREL STORES: Custom
CLOTHING & FURNISHINGS, MEN'S & BOYS', WHOLESALE: Gloves
CLOTHING & FURNISHINGS, MEN/BOY, WHOL: Hats, Scarves/Gloves
CLOTHING ACCESS STORES: Umbrellas
CLOTHING STORES, NEC
CLOTHING STORES: Leather
CLOTHING STORES: Lingerie, Outerwear
CLOTHING STORES: T-Shirts, Printed, Custom
CLOTHING STORES: Work
CLOTHING: Access
CLOTHING: Access, Women's & Misses'
CLOTHING: Athletic & Sportswear, Men's & Boys'
CLOTHING: Athletic & Sportswear, Women's & Girls'

PRODUCT INDEX

CLOTHING: Bathing Suits & Swimwear, Girls, Children & Infant
CLOTHING: Bathing Suits & Swimwear, Knit
CLOTHING: Belts
CLOTHING: Blouses, Women's & Girls'
CLOTHING: Bridal Gowns
CLOTHING: Children & Infants'
CLOTHING: Children's, Girls'
CLOTHING: Clergy Vestments
CLOTHING: Coats & Suits, Men's & Boys'
CLOTHING: Coats, Overcoats & Vests
CLOTHING: Corset Access, Clasps & Stays
CLOTHING: Dresses
CLOTHING: Dresses & Skirts
CLOTHING: Dressing Gowns, Mens/Womens, From Purchased Matls
CLOTHING: Garments, Indl, Men's & Boys
CLOTHING: Gloves & Mittens, Knit
CLOTHING: Gowns & Dresses, Wedding
CLOTHING: Hospital, Men's
CLOTHING: Leather
CLOTHING: Men's & boy's clothing, nec
CLOTHING: Mens & Boys Jackets, Sport, Suede, Leatherette
CLOTHING: Neckwear
CLOTHING: Outerwear, Women's & Misses' NEC
CLOTHING: Raincoats, Exc Vulcanized Rubber, Purchased Matls
CLOTHING: Robes & Dressing Gowns
CLOTHING: Shirts
CLOTHING: Shirts, Dress, Men's & Boys'
CLOTHING: Shirts, Sports & Polo, Men's & Boys'
CLOTHING: Socks
CLOTHING: Sportswear, Women's
CLOTHING: Suits & Skirts, Women's & Misses'
CLOTHING: Suits, Men's & Boys', From Purchased Materials
CLOTHING: Sweaters & Sweater Coats, Knit
CLOTHING: Sweatshirts & T-Shirts, Men's & Boys'
CLOTHING: Swimwear, Men's & Boys'
CLOTHING: Swimwear, Women's & Misses'
CLOTHING: Tailored Dress/Sport Coats, Mens & Boys
CLOTHING: Ties, Bow, Men's & Boys', From Purchased Materials
CLOTHING: Trousers & Slacks, Men's & Boys'
CLOTHING: Tuxedos, From Purchased Materials
CLOTHING: Underwear, Knit
CLOTHING: Underwear, Women's & Children's
CLOTHING: Uniforms & Vestments
CLOTHING: Uniforms, Military, Men/Youth, Purchased Materials
CLOTHING: Uniforms, Team Athletic
CLOTHING: Uniforms, Work
CLOTHING: Work Apparel, Exc Uniforms
CLOTHING: Work, Men's
CLUTCHES, EXC VEHICULAR
COAL & OTHER MINERALS & ORES WHOLESALERS
COAL MINING SERVICES
COAL MINING: Anthracite
COAL MINING: Bituminous & Lignite Surface
COAL MINING: Bituminous Coal & Lignite-Surface Mining
COAL MINING: Bituminous Underground
COAL, MINERALS & ORES, WHOLESALE: Coal
COAL, MINERALS & ORES, WHOLESALE: Sulfur
COATED OR PLATED PRDTS
COATERS: High Vacuum, Metal Plate
COATING COMPOUNDS: Tar
COATING SVC
COATING SVC: Aluminum, Metal Prdts
COATING SVC: Hot Dip, Metals Or Formed Prdts
COATING SVC: Metals & Formed Prdts
COATING SVC: Metals, With Plastic Or Resins
COATINGS: Air Curing
COIL WINDING SVC
COILS & TRANSFORMERS
COILS: Electric Motors Or Generators
COILS: Pipe
COKE: Calcined Petroleum, Made From Purchased Materials
COLLETS
COLOR SEPARATION: Photographic & Movie Film
COLORS IN OIL, EXC ARTISTS'
COLORS: Pigments, Organic
COMFORTERS & QUILTS, FROM MANMADE FIBER OR SILK
COMMERCIAL & OFFICE BUILDINGS RENOVATION & REPAIR
COMMERCIAL ART & GRAPHIC DESIGN SVCS
COMMERCIAL ART & ILLUSTRATION SVCS
COMMERCIAL EQPT WHOLESALERS, NEC
COMMERCIAL EQPT, WHOLESALE: Coffee Brewing Eqpt & Splys
COMMERCIAL EQPT, WHOLESALE: Comm Cooking & Food Svc Eqpt
COMMERCIAL EQPT, WHOLESALE: Display Eqpt, Exc Refrigerated
COMMERCIAL EQPT, WHOLESALE: Scales, Exc Laboratory
COMMERCIAL LAUNDRY EQPT
COMMERCIAL PHOTOGRAPHIC STUDIO
COMMERCIAL PRINTING & NEWSPAPER PUBLISHING COMBINED
COMMODITY INVESTORS
COMMON SAND MINING
COMMUNICATIONS EQPT & SYSTEMS, NEC
COMMUNICATIONS EQPT WHOLESALERS
COMMUNICATIONS EQPT: Microwave
COMMUNICATIONS SVCS: Cellular
COMMUNICATIONS SVCS: Data
COMMUNICATIONS SVCS: Electronic Mail
COMMUNICATIONS SVCS: Facsimile Transmission
COMMUNICATIONS SVCS: Internet Host Svcs
COMMUNICATIONS SVCS: Online Svc Providers
COMMUNICATIONS SVCS: Signal Enhancement Network Svcs
COMMUNICATIONS SVCS: Telephone, Local & Long Distance
COMMUNICATIONS SVCS: Telephone, Voice
COMMUNITY DEVELOPMENT GROUPS
COMMUTATORS: Electronic
COMPACT DISC PLAYERS
COMPARATORS: Optical
COMPASSES & ACCESS
COMPOST
COMPRESSORS, AIR CONDITIONING: Wholesalers
COMPRESSORS: Air & Gas
COMPRESSORS: Air & Gas, Including Vacuum Pumps
COMPRESSORS: Wholesalers
COMPUTER & COMPUTER SOFTWARE STORES
COMPUTER & COMPUTER SOFTWARE STORES: Printers & Plotters
COMPUTER & COMPUTER SOFTWARE STORES: Software & Access
COMPUTER & COMPUTER SOFTWARE STORES: Software, Bus/Non-Game
COMPUTER & OFFICE MACHINE MAINTENANCE & REPAIR
COMPUTER FACILITIES MANAGEMENT SVCS
COMPUTER GRAPHICS SVCS
COMPUTER HARDWARE REQUIREMENTS ANALYSIS
COMPUTER PERIPHERAL EQPT REPAIR & MAINTENANCE
COMPUTER PERIPHERAL EQPT, NEC
COMPUTER PERIPHERAL EQPT, WHOLESALE
COMPUTER PERIPHERAL EQPT: Graphic Displays, Exc Terminals
COMPUTER PERIPHERAL EQPT: Input Or Output
COMPUTER PERIPHERAL EQPT: Output To Microfilm Units
COMPUTER PROCESSING SVCS
COMPUTER PROGRAMMING SVCS
COMPUTER PROGRAMMING SVCS: Custom
COMPUTER RELATED MAINTENANCE SVCS
COMPUTER SOFTWARE DEVELOPMENT
COMPUTER SOFTWARE DEVELOPMENT & APPLICATIONS
COMPUTER SOFTWARE SYSTEMS ANALYSIS & DESIGN: Custom
COMPUTER SOFTWARE WRITERS: Freelance
COMPUTER STORAGE DEVICES, NEC
COMPUTER STORAGE UNITS: Auxiliary
COMPUTER SYSTEMS ANALYSIS & DESIGN
COMPUTER TERMINALS
COMPUTER TRAINING SCHOOLS
COMPUTER-AIDED DESIGN SYSTEMS SVCS
COMPUTER-AIDED SYSTEM SVCS
COMPUTERS, NEC
COMPUTERS, PERIPHERALS & SOFTWARE, WHOLESALE: Printers
COMPUTERS, PERIPHERALS & SOFTWARE, WHOLESALE: Software
COMPUTERS: Indl, Process, Gas Flow
COMPUTERS: Mini
COMPUTERS: Personal
CONCENTRATES, FLAVORING, EXC DRINK
CONCRETE BUILDING PRDTS WHOLESALERS
CONCRETE CURING & HARDENING COMPOUNDS
CONCRETE PRDTS
CONCRETE PRDTS, PRECAST, NEC
CONCRETE REINFORCING MATERIAL
CONCRETE: Bituminous
CONCRETE: Ready-Mixed
CONDUITS & FITTINGS: Electric
CONFECTIONS & CANDY
CONNECTORS & TERMINALS: Electrical Device Uses
CONNECTORS: Cord, Electric
CONNECTORS: Electrical
CONNECTORS: Electronic
CONNECTORS: Power, Electric
CONSTRUCTION & MINING MACHINERY WHOLESALERS
CONSTRUCTION & ROAD MAINTENANCE EQPT: Drags, Road
CONSTRUCTION EQPT: Attachments
CONSTRUCTION EQPT: Attachments, Backhoe Mounted, Hyd Pwrd
CONSTRUCTION EQPT: Backhoes, Tractors, Cranes & Similar Eqpt
CONSTRUCTION EQPT: Cranes
CONSTRUCTION EQPT: Hammer Mills, Port, Incl Rock/Ore Crush
CONSTRUCTION EQPT: Roofing Eqpt
CONSTRUCTION EQPT: Trucks, Off-Highway
CONSTRUCTION MATERIALS, WHOL: Concrete/Cinder Bldg Prdts
CONSTRUCTION MATERIALS, WHOLESALE: Block, Concrete & Cinder
CONSTRUCTION MATERIALS, WHOLESALE: Blocks, Building, NEC
CONSTRUCTION MATERIALS, WHOLESALE: Building Stone
CONSTRUCTION MATERIALS, WHOLESALE: Building Stone, Marble
CONSTRUCTION MATERIALS, WHOLESALE: Building, Exterior
CONSTRUCTION MATERIALS, WHOLESALE: Cement
CONSTRUCTION MATERIALS, WHOLESALE: Concrete Mixtures
CONSTRUCTION MATERIALS, WHOLESALE: Fiberglass Building Mat
CONSTRUCTION MATERIALS, WHOLESALE: Glass
CONSTRUCTION MATERIALS, WHOLESALE: Insulation, Thermal
CONSTRUCTION MATERIALS, WHOLESALE: Limestone
CONSTRUCTION MATERIALS, WHOLESALE: Millwork
CONSTRUCTION MATERIALS, WHOLESALE: Molding, All Materials
CONSTRUCTION MATERIALS, WHOLESALE: Paneling, Wood
CONSTRUCTION MATERIALS, WHOLESALE: Paving Materials
CONSTRUCTION MATERIALS, WHOLESALE: Prefabricated Structures
CONSTRUCTION MATERIALS, WHOLESALE: Roof, Asphalt/Sheet Metal
CONSTRUCTION MATERIALS, WHOLESALE: Roofing & Siding Material
CONSTRUCTION MATERIALS, WHOLESALE: Sand
CONSTRUCTION MATERIALS, WHOLESALE: Stone, Crushed Or Broken
CONSTRUCTION MATL, WHOLESALE: Structural Assy, Prefab, Wood
CONSTRUCTION MATLS, WHOL: Lumber, Rough, Dressed/Finished
CONSTRUCTION SITE PREPARATION SVCS
CONSTRUCTION: Airport Runway
CONSTRUCTION: Athletic & Recreation Facilities
CONSTRUCTION: Commercial & Institutional Building
CONSTRUCTION: Commercial & Office Building, New
CONSTRUCTION: Curb
CONSTRUCTION: Drainage System
CONSTRUCTION: Elevated Highway
CONSTRUCTION: Guardrails, Highway
CONSTRUCTION: Heavy Highway & Street
CONSTRUCTION: Indl Buildings, New, NEC
CONSTRUCTION: Institutional Building
CONSTRUCTION: Oil & Gas Line & Compressor Station
CONSTRUCTION: Power Plant
CONSTRUCTION: Residential, Nec
CONSTRUCTION: Single-Family Housing
CONSTRUCTION: Single-family Housing, New

PRODUCT INDEX

CONSTRUCTION: Subway
CONSTRUCTION: Swimming Pools
CONSTRUCTION: Utility Line
CONSTRUCTION: Water & Sewer Line
CONSULTING SVC: Actuarial
CONSULTING SVC: Business, NEC
CONSULTING SVC: Chemical
CONSULTING SVC: Computer
CONSULTING SVC: Data Processing
CONSULTING SVC: Educational
CONSULTING SVC: Engineering
CONSULTING SVC: Financial Management
CONSULTING SVC: Human Resource
CONSULTING SVC: Management
CONSULTING SVC: Marketing Management
CONSULTING SVC: Telecommunications
CONSULTING SVCS, BUSINESS: Communications
CONSULTING SVCS, BUSINESS: Economic
CONSULTING SVCS, BUSINESS: Energy Conservation
CONSULTING SVCS, BUSINESS: Environmental
CONSULTING SVCS, BUSINESS: Publishing
CONSULTING SVCS, BUSINESS: Safety Training Svcs
CONSULTING SVCS, BUSINESS: Sys Engnrg, Exc Computer/Prof
CONSULTING SVCS, BUSINESS: Traffic
CONSULTING SVCS: Oil
CONSULTING SVCS: Scientific
CONSUMER ELECTRONICS STORE: Video & Disc Recorder/Player
CONTACT LENSES
CONTACTS: Electrical
CONTAINERS, GLASS: Cosmetic Jars
CONTAINERS, GLASS: Medicine Bottles
CONTAINERS: Cargo, Wood & Metal Combination
CONTAINERS: Corrugated
CONTAINERS: Food & Beverage
CONTAINERS: Glass
CONTAINERS: Metal
CONTAINERS: Plastic
CONTAINERS: Sanitary, Food
CONTAINERS: Shipping, Wood
CONTAINERS: Wood
CONTRACTORS: Asphalt
CONTRACTORS: Awning Installation
CONTRACTORS: Blasting, Exc Building Demolition
CONTRACTORS: Boiler & Furnace
CONTRACTORS: Building Eqpt & Machinery Installation
CONTRACTORS: Building Front Installation, Metal
CONTRACTORS: Building Sign Installation & Mntnce
CONTRACTORS: Carpentry Work
CONTRACTORS: Carpentry, Cabinet & Finish Work
CONTRACTORS: Carpentry, Cabinet Building & Installation
CONTRACTORS: Chimney Construction & Maintenance
CONTRACTORS: Closed Circuit Television Installation
CONTRACTORS: Coating, Caulking & Weather, Water & Fire
CONTRACTORS: Commercial & Office Building
CONTRACTORS: Communications Svcs
CONTRACTORS: Computer Installation
CONTRACTORS: Computer Power Conditioning Svcs
CONTRACTORS: Concrete
CONTRACTORS: Construction Site Cleanup
CONTRACTORS: Countertop Installation
CONTRACTORS: Demolition, Building & Other Structures
CONTRACTORS: Directional Oil & Gas Well Drilling Svc
CONTRACTORS: Electric Power Systems
CONTRACTORS: Electrical
CONTRACTORS: Electronic Controls Installation
CONTRACTORS: Energy Management Control
CONTRACTORS: Excavating
CONTRACTORS: Exterior Concrete Stucco
CONTRACTORS: Fence Construction
CONTRACTORS: Floor Laying & Other Floor Work
CONTRACTORS: Flooring
CONTRACTORS: Garage Doors
CONTRACTORS: Gas Detection & Analysis Svcs
CONTRACTORS: Gas Field Svcs, NEC
CONTRACTORS: General Electric
CONTRACTORS: Glass Tinting, Architectural & Automotive
CONTRACTORS: Glass, Glazing & Tinting
CONTRACTORS: Grave Excavation
CONTRACTORS: Gutters & Downspouts
CONTRACTORS: Heating & Air Conditioning
CONTRACTORS: Heating Systems Repair & Maintenance Svc
CONTRACTORS: Highway & Street Paving
CONTRACTORS: Highway Sign & Guardrail Construction & Install
CONTRACTORS: Home & Office Intrs Finish, Furnish/Remodel
CONTRACTORS: Hydraulic Eqpt Installation & Svcs
CONTRACTORS: Insulation Installation, Building
CONTRACTORS: Kitchen & Bathroom Remodeling
CONTRACTORS: Lighting Conductor Erection
CONTRACTORS: Machinery Installation
CONTRACTORS: Marble Installation, Interior
CONTRACTORS: Marble Masonry, Exterior
CONTRACTORS: Masonry & Stonework
CONTRACTORS: Mechanical
CONTRACTORS: Oil & Gas Well Drilling Svc
CONTRACTORS: Oil Field Lease Tanks: Erectg, Clng/Rprg Svcs
CONTRACTORS: Oil Field Pipe Testing Svcs
CONTRACTORS: Oil/Gas Well Construction, Rpr/Dismantling Svcs
CONTRACTORS: On-Site Welding
CONTRACTORS: Ornamental Metal Work
CONTRACTORS: Painting, Commercial
CONTRACTORS: Painting, Residential
CONTRACTORS: Patio & Deck Construction & Repair
CONTRACTORS: Petroleum Storage Tank Install, Underground
CONTRACTORS: Plumbing
CONTRACTORS: Power Generating Eqpt Installation
CONTRACTORS: Prefabricated Window & Door Installation
CONTRACTORS: Refrigeration
CONTRACTORS: Rigging, Theatrical
CONTRACTORS: Roustabout Svcs
CONTRACTORS: Safety & Security Eqpt
CONTRACTORS: Sandblasting Svc, Building Exteriors
CONTRACTORS: Seismograph Survey Svcs
CONTRACTORS: Sheet Metal Work, NEC
CONTRACTORS: Single-family Home General Remodeling
CONTRACTORS: Skylight Installation
CONTRACTORS: Special Trades, NEC
CONTRACTORS: Sprinkler System
CONTRACTORS: Structural Iron Work, Structural
CONTRACTORS: Structural Steel Erection
CONTRACTORS: Svc Well Drilling Svcs
CONTRACTORS: Tile Installation, Ceramic
CONTRACTORS: Ventilation & Duct Work
CONTRACTORS: Warm Air Heating & Air Conditioning
CONTRACTORS: Water Intake Well Drilling Svc
CONTRACTORS: Water Well Drilling
CONTRACTORS: Windows & Doors
CONTRACTORS: Wood Floor Installation & Refinishing
CONTRACTORS: Wrecking & Demolition
CONTROL EQPT: Electric
CONTROL PANELS: Electrical
CONTROLS & ACCESS: Indl, Electric
CONTROLS: Adjustable Speed Drive
CONTROLS: Air Flow, Refrigeration
CONTROLS: Automatic Temperature
CONTROLS: Crane & Hoist, Including Metal Mill
CONTROLS: Electric Motor
CONTROLS: Environmental
CONTROLS: Marine & Navy, Auxiliary
CONTROLS: Nuclear Reactor
CONTROLS: Relay & Ind
CONTROLS: Remote, Boat
CONTROLS: Resistance Welder
CONTROLS: Thermostats
CONVENTION & TRADE SHOW SVCS
CONVERTERS: Data
CONVERTERS: Frequency
CONVERTERS: Power, AC to DC
CONVEYOR SYSTEMS
CONVEYOR SYSTEMS: Robotic
CONVEYORS & CONVEYING EQPT
CONVEYORS: Overhead
COOKING & FOODWARMING EQPT: Coffee Brewing
COOKWARE, STONEWARE: Coarse Earthenware & Pottery
COOLING TOWERS: Metal
COPPER ORES
COPPER: Rolling & Drawing
CORD & TWINE
CORD: Braided
CORES: Magnetic
CORK & CORK PRDTS
CORK & CORK PRDTS: Tiles
CORRECTION FLUID
CORRECTIONAL INSTITUTIONS
CORRESPONDENCE SCHOOLS
COSMETIC PREPARATIONS
COSMETICS & TOILETRIES
COSMETICS WHOLESALERS
COSTUME JEWELRY & NOVELTIES: Apparel, Exc Precious Metals
COSTUME JEWELRY & NOVELTIES: Bracelets, Exc Precious Metals
COSTUME JEWELRY & NOVELTIES: Exc Semi & Precious
COSTUME JEWELRY & NOVELTIES: Ornament, Exc Precious Mtl/Gem
COSTUME JEWELRY STORES
COUNTER & SINK TOPS
COUNTERS & COUNTING DEVICES
COUNTERS OR COUNTER DISPLAY CASES, EXC WOOD
COUNTERS OR COUNTER DISPLAY CASES, WOOD
COUNTERS: Mechanical
COUNTING DEVICES: Controls, Revolution & Timing
COUNTING DEVICES: Electromechanical
COUNTING DEVICES: Tachometer, Centrifugal
COUNTRY MUSIC GROUPS OR ARTIST
COUPLINGS, EXC PRESSURE & SOIL PIPE
COUPLINGS: Hose & Tube, Hydraulic Or Pneumatic
COURIER SVCS: Package By Vehicle
COVERS: Automobile Seat
COVERS: Automotive, Exc Seat & Tire
COVERS: Canvas
CRANE & AERIAL LIFT SVCS
CRANES: Overhead
CRANKSHAFTS & CAMSHAFTS: Machining
CREDIT INSTITUTIONS: Short-Term Business
CREDIT UNIONS: Federally Chartered
CROWNS & CLOSURES
CRUDE PETROLEUM & NATURAL GAS PRODUCTION
CRUDE PETROLEUM & NATURAL GAS PRODUCTION
CRUDE PETROLEUM PRODUCTION
CRYSTALS
CRYSTALS: Piezoelectric
CULTURE MEDIA
CUPS: Paper
CURBING: Granite Or Stone
CURRENT TAPS: Attachment Plug & Screw Shell Types
CURTAIN & DRAPERY FIXTURES: Poles, Rods & Rollers
CURTAIN WALLS: Building, Steel
CURTAINS & BEDDING: Knit
CURTAINS: Window, From Purchased Materials
CUSHIONS & PILLOWS
CUSHIONS & PILLOWS: Boat
CUSHIONS: Carpet & Rug, Foamed Plastics
CUSTOM COMPOUNDING OF RUBBER MATERIALS
CUT STONE & STONE PRODUCTS
CUTLERY
CUTOUTS: Distribution
CUTTING EQPT: Milling
CYLINDER & ACTUATORS: Fluid Power
CYLINDERS: Pressure

D

DAIRY EQPT
DAIRY PRDTS STORE: Ice Cream, Packaged
DAIRY PRDTS WHOLESALERS: Fresh
DAIRY PRDTS: Butter
DAIRY PRDTS: Cheese
DAIRY PRDTS: Dairy Based Desserts, Frozen
DAIRY PRDTS: Dietary Supplements, Dairy & Non-Dairy Based
DAIRY PRDTS: Evaporated Milk
DAIRY PRDTS: Frozen Desserts & Novelties
DAIRY PRDTS: Ice Cream & Ice Milk
DAIRY PRDTS: Ice Cream, Bulk
DAIRY PRDTS: Ice Cream, Packaged, Molded, On Sticks, Etc.
DAIRY PRDTS: Imitation Cheese
DAIRY PRDTS: Milk, Condensed & Evaporated
DAIRY PRDTS: Milk, Fluid
DAIRY PRDTS: Milk, Processed, Pasteurized, Homogenized/Btld
DAIRY PRDTS: Natural Cheese
DAIRY PRDTS: Yogurt, Exc Frozen
DAIRY PRDTS: Yogurt, Frozen
DATA PROCESSING & PREPARATION SVCS
DATA PROCESSING SVCS
DATABASE INFORMATION RETRIEVAL SVCS
DEALERS: Commodity Contracts

PRODUCT INDEX

DECORATIVE WOOD & WOODWORK
DEFENSE SYSTEMS & EQPT
DEHYDRATION EQPT
DELIVERY SVCS, BY VEHICLE
DENTAL EQPT
DENTAL EQPT & SPLYS
DENTAL EQPT & SPLYS WHOLESALERS
DENTAL EQPT & SPLYS: Alloys, For Amalgams
DENTAL EQPT & SPLYS: Dental Materials
DENTAL EQPT & SPLYS: Drills, Bone
DENTAL EQPT & SPLYS: Enamels
DENTAL EQPT & SPLYS: Gold
DENTAL EQPT & SPLYS: Metal
DENTAL EQPT & SPLYS: Orthodontic Appliances
DENTISTS' OFFICES & CLINICS
DEODORANTS: Personal
DEPARTMENT STORES
DERMATOLOGICALS
DESIGN SVCS, NEC
DESIGN SVCS: Commercial & Indl
DESIGN SVCS: Computer Integrated Systems
DESIGN SVCS: Hand Tools
DETONATORS & DETONATING CAPS
DIAGNOSTIC SUBSTANCES
DIAGNOSTIC SUBSTANCES OR AGENTS: In Vitro
DIAGNOSTIC SUBSTANCES OR AGENTS: In Vivo
DIAGNOSTIC SUBSTANCES OR AGENTS: Microbiology & Virology
DIAGNOSTIC SUBSTANCES OR AGENTS: Radioactive
DIAGNOSTIC SUBSTANCES OR AGENTS: Veterinary
DIAPERS: Disposable
DIE CUTTING SVC: Paper
DIE SETS: Presses, Metal Stamping
DIES & TOOLS: Special
DIES: Cutting, Exc Metal
DIES: Plastic Forming
DIES: Steel Rule
DIET & WEIGHT REDUCING CENTERS
DIODES: Light Emitting
DIRECT SELLING ESTAB: Coffee, Soda/Beer, Etc, Door-To-Door
DIRECT SELLING ESTABLISHMENTS: Encyclopedias, House-To-House
DIRECT SELLING ESTABLISHMENTS: Food Svcs
DIRECT SELLING ESTABLISHMENTS: Telemarketing
DISC JOCKEYS
DISKETTE DUPLICATING SVCS
DISKETTE OR KEY-DISK EQPT
DISPENSERS, TISSUE: Plastic
DISPENSING EQPT & PARTS, BEVERAGE: Beer
DISPENSING EQPT & PARTS, BEVERAGE: Coolers, Milk/Water, Elec
DISPENSING EQPT & PARTS, BEVERAGE: Fountain/Other Beverage
DISPLAY FIXTURES: Wood
DISPLAY ITEMS: Corrugated, Made From Purchased Materials
DISPLAY LETTERING SVCS
DISTILLERS DRIED GRAIN & SOLUBLES
DOCK EQPT & SPLYS, INDL
DOCK OPERATION SVCS, INCL BLDGS, FACILITIES, OPERS & MAINT
DOCKS: Prefabricated Metal
DOCUMENT DESTRUCTION SVC
DOOR & WINDOW REPAIR SVCS
DOOR FRAMES: Wood
DOOR OPERATING SYSTEMS: Electric
DOORS & WINDOWS WHOLESALERS: All Materials
DOORS & WINDOWS: Screen & Storm
DOORS & WINDOWS: Storm, Metal
DOORS: Combination Screen & Storm, Wood
DOORS: Fiberglass
DOORS: Fire, Metal
DOORS: Garage, Overhead, Metal
DOORS: Garage, Overhead, Wood
DOORS: Hangar, Metal
DOORS: Rolling, Indl Building Or Warehouse, Metal
DOORS: Wooden
DRAFTING SVCS
DRAINAGE PRDTS: Concrete
DRAPERIES & CURTAINS
DRAPERIES & DRAPERY FABRICS, COTTON
DRAPERIES: Plastic & Textile, From Purchased Materials
DRAPERY & UPHOLSTERY STORES: Draperies
DRESSMAKERS: Custom
DRILLS & DRILLING EQPT: Mining
DRINKING PLACES: Alcoholic Beverages
DRINKING PLACES: Bars & Lounges
DRINKING WATER COOLERS WHOLESALERS: Mechanical
DRUG TESTING KITS: Blood & Urine
DRUGS & DRUG PROPRIETARIES, WHOLESALE: Antiseptics
DRUGS & DRUG PROPRIETARIES, WHOLESALE: Pharmaceuticals
DRUGS ACTING ON THE CENTRAL NERVOUS SYSTEM & SENSE ORGANS
DRUMS: Shipping, Metal
DRYCLEANING & LAUNDRY SVCS: Commercial & Family
DRYCLEANING EQPT & SPLYS: Commercial
DRYERS & REDRYERS: Indl
DUCTING: Metal Plate
DUCTING: Plastic
DUCTS: Sheet Metal
DUMPSTERS: Garbage
DURABLE GOODS WHOLESALERS, NEC
DYNAMOMETERS

E

EARTH SCIENCE SVCS
EATING PLACES
EDITORIAL SVCS
EDUCATIONAL SVCS, NONDEGREE GRANTING: Continuing Education
EFFERVESCENT SALTS
EGG WHOLESALERS
ELASTOMERS
ELECTRIC MOTOR REPAIR SVCS
ELECTRIC SERVICES
ELECTRIC SVCS, NEC: Power Generation
ELECTRIC TOOL REPAIR SVCS
ELECTRICAL APPARATUS & EQPT WHOLESALERS
ELECTRICAL APPLIANCES, TELEVISIONS & RADIOS WHOLESALERS
ELECTRICAL CURRENT CARRYING WIRING DEVICES
ELECTRICAL DISCHARGE MACHINING, EDM
ELECTRICAL EQPT & SPLYS
ELECTRICAL EQPT FOR ENGINES
ELECTRICAL EQPT REPAIR & MAINTENANCE
ELECTRICAL EQPT REPAIR SVCS
ELECTRICAL EQPT: Automotive, NEC
ELECTRICAL GOODS, WHOLESALE: Burglar Alarm Systems
ELECTRICAL GOODS, WHOLESALE: Cable Conduit
ELECTRICAL GOODS, WHOLESALE: Connectors
ELECTRICAL GOODS, WHOLESALE: Electronic Parts
ELECTRICAL GOODS, WHOLESALE: Flashlights
ELECTRICAL GOODS, WHOLESALE: Generators
ELECTRICAL GOODS, WHOLESALE: Irons
ELECTRICAL GOODS, WHOLESALE: Lighting Fixtures, Comm & Indl
ELECTRICAL GOODS, WHOLESALE: Motor Ctrls, Starters & Relays
ELECTRICAL GOODS, WHOLESALE: Motors
ELECTRICAL GOODS, WHOLESALE: Security Control Eqpt & Systems
ELECTRICAL GOODS, WHOLESALE: Sound Eqpt
ELECTRICAL GOODS, WHOLESALE: Telephone Eqpt
ELECTRICAL GOODS, WHOLESALE: Transformer & Transmission Eqpt
ELECTRICAL GOODS, WHOLESALE: Wire & Cable
ELECTRICAL GOODS, WHOLESALE: Wire & Cable, Ctrl & Sig
ELECTRICAL GOODS, WHOLESALE: Wire & Cable, Electronic
ELECTRICAL HOUSEHOLD APPLIANCE REPAIR
ELECTRICAL INDL APPARATUS, NEC
ELECTRICAL SPLYS
ELECTRICAL SUPPLIES: Porcelain
ELECTRODES: Thermal & Electrolytic
ELECTROMEDICAL EQPT
ELECTRON BEAM: Cutting, Forming, Welding
ELECTRON TUBES
ELECTRONIC COMPONENTS
ELECTRONIC DEVICES: Solid State, NEC
ELECTRONIC EQPT REPAIR SVCS
ELECTRONIC LOADS & POWER SPLYS
ELECTRONIC PARTS & EQPT WHOLESALERS
ELECTRONIC SHOPPING
ELECTROPLATING & PLATING SVC
ELEMENTARY & SECONDARY SCHOOLS, SPECIAL EDUCATION
ELEVATORS & EQPT
ELEVATORS WHOLESALERS
ELEVATORS: Installation & Conversion
EMBLEMS: Embroidered
EMBROIDERING & ART NEEDLEWORK FOR THE TRADE
EMBROIDERING SVC
EMBROIDERY ADVERTISING SVCS
EMERGENCY ALARMS
EMPLOYMENT AGENCY SVCS
EMPLOYMENT SVCS: Teachers' Registry
ENAMELING SVC: Metal Prdts, Including Porcelain
ENCODERS: Digital
ENCRYPTION EQPT & DEVICES
ENERGY MEASUREMENT EQPT
ENGINE REBUILDING: Gas
ENGINEERING SVCS
ENGINEERING SVCS: Acoustical
ENGINEERING SVCS: Aviation Or Aeronautical
ENGINEERING SVCS: Building Construction
ENGINEERING SVCS: Construction & Civil
ENGINEERING SVCS: Electrical Or Electronic
ENGINEERING SVCS: Energy conservation
ENGINEERING SVCS: Heating & Ventilation
ENGINEERING SVCS: Industrial
ENGINEERING SVCS: Machine Tool Design
ENGINEERING SVCS: Marine
ENGINEERING SVCS: Mechanical
ENGINEERING SVCS: Professional
ENGINES: Diesel & Semi-Diesel Or Duel Fuel
ENGINES: Internal Combustion, NEC
ENGINES: Jet Propulsion
ENGINES: Marine
ENGRAVING SVC, NEC
ENGRAVING SVC: Jewelry & Personal Goods
ENGRAVING SVCS
ENGRAVINGS: Plastic
ENTERTAINERS & ENTERTAINMENT GROUPS
ENTERTAINMENT GROUP
ENTERTAINMENT SVCS
ENVELOPES
ENVELOPES WHOLESALERS
ENVIRONMENTAL QUALITY PROGS ADMIN, GOVT: Recreational
EPOXY RESINS
EQUIPMENT: Pedestrian Traffic Control
EQUIPMENT: Rental & Leasing, NEC
ERASERS: Rubber Or Rubber & Abrasive Combined
ETCHING & ENGRAVING SVC
ETCHING SVC: Metal
ETHYLENE-PROPYLENE RUBBERS: EPDM Polymers
EXCAVATING EQPT
EXHAUST SYSTEMS: Eqpt & Parts
EXPLOSIVES
EXTRACTS, FLAVORING
EYEGLASSES
EYEGLASSES: Sunglasses
EYELASHES, ARTIFICIAL

F

FABRIC STORES
FABRICATED METAL PRODUCTS, NEC
FABRICS & CLOTH: Quilted
FABRICS & YARN: Plastic Coated
FABRICS: Alpacas, Mohair, Woven
FABRICS: Apparel & Outerwear, Cotton
FABRICS: Apparel & Outerwear, From Manmade Fiber Or Silk
FABRICS: Blankets & Blanketing, Wool Or Similar Fibers
FABRICS: Broadwoven, Synthetic Manmade Fiber & Silk
FABRICS: Canvas
FABRICS: Card Roll, Cotton
FABRICS: Coated Or Treated
FABRICS: Denims
FABRICS: Dress, From Manmade Fiber Or Silk
FABRICS: Fiberglass, Broadwoven
FABRICS: Filter Cloth, Cotton
FABRICS: Fur-Type, From Manmade Fiber
FABRICS: Glass & Fiberglass, Broadwoven
FABRICS: Jean
FABRICS: Laminated
FABRICS: Metallized
FABRICS: Nonwoven
FABRICS: Papermakers Felt, Woven, Wool, Mohair/Similar Fiber
FABRICS: Resin Or Plastic Coated
FABRICS: Sail Cloth

PRODUCT INDEX

FABRICS: Satin
FABRICS: Slip Cover, Cotton
FABRICS: Specialty Including Twisted Weaves, Broadwoven
FABRICS: Stretch, Cotton
FABRICS: Trimmings
FABRICS: Upholstery, Cotton
FABRICS: Upholstery, Wool
FABRICS: Warp Knit, Lace & Netting
FABRICS: Weft Or Circular Knit
FABRICS: Woven, Narrow Cotton, Wool, Silk
FACILITIES SUPPORT SVCS
FACSIMILE COMMUNICATION EQPT
FAMILY CLOTHING STORES
FANS, EXHAUST: Indl Or Commercial
FARM & GARDEN MACHINERY WHOLESALERS
FARM PRDTS, RAW MATERIALS, WHOLESALE: Sugar
FARM SPLYS, WHOLESALE: Equestrian Eqpt
FARM SPLYS, WHOLESALE: Feed
FARM SPLYS, WHOLESALE: Garden Splys
FARM SPLYS, WHOLESALE: Insecticides
FARM SPLYS, WHOLESALE: Soil, Potting & Planting
FASTENERS WHOLESALERS
FASTENERS: Brads, Alum, Brass/Other Nonferrous Metal/Wire
FASTENERS: Metal
FASTENERS: Metal
FASTENERS: Notions, Hooks & Eyes
FASTENERS: Notions, NEC
FASTENERS: Notions, Snaps
FASTENERS: Notions, Zippers
FATTY ACID ESTERS & AMINOS
FELT PARTS
FELT: Acoustic
FENCES OR POSTS: Ornamental Iron Or Steel
FENCING DEALERS
FENCING MADE IN WIREDRAWING PLANTS
FENCING MATERIALS: Plastic
FENCING MATERIALS: Wood
FENCING: Chain Link
FERTILIZER, AGRICULTURAL: Wholesalers
FERTILIZERS: NEC
FIBER & FIBER PRDTS: Organic, Noncellulose
FIBER & FIBER PRDTS: Polyester
FIBER & FIBER PRDTS: Vinyl
FIBER OPTICS
FIBER PRDTS: Pressed, Wood Pulp, From Purchased Materials
FIBERS: Carbon & Graphite
FILM & SHEET: Unsuppported Plastic
FILM: Motion Picture
FILTERS
FILTERS & SOFTENERS: Water, Household
FILTERS & STRAINERS: Pipeline
FILTERS: Air
FILTERS: Air Intake, Internal Combustion Engine, Exc Auto
FILTERS: General Line, Indl
FILTERS: Motor Vehicle
FILTERS: Oil, Internal Combustion Engine, Exc Auto
FILTRATION DEVICES: Electronic
FINANCIAL INVESTMENT ADVICE
FINDINGS & TRIMMINGS: Fabric
FINISHING AGENTS
FINISHING SVCS
FIRE ARMS, SMALL: Guns Or Gun Parts, 30 mm & Below
FIRE ARMS, SMALL: Machine Guns/Machine Gun Parts, 30mm/below
FIRE ARMS, SMALL: Pellet & BB guns
FIRE ARMS, SMALL: Pistols Or Pistol Parts, 30 mm & below
FIRE ARMS, SMALL: Revolvers Or Revolver Parts, 30 mm & Below
FIRE ARMS, SMALL: Rifles Or Rifle Parts, 30 mm & below
FIRE ARMS, SMALL: Shotguns Or Shotgun Parts, 30 mm & Below
FIRE DETECTION SYSTEMS
FIRE ESCAPES
FIRE EXTINGUISHERS: Portable
FIRE PROTECTION EQPT
FIREARMS & AMMUNITION, EXC SPORTING, WHOLESALE
FIREARMS: Large, Greater Than 30mm
FIREARMS: Small, 30mm or Less
FIREPLACE & CHIMNEY MATERIAL: Concrete
FIREWOOD, WHOLESALE
FIREWORKS
FISH & SEAFOOD PROCESSORS: Canned Or Cured
FISH & SEAFOOD PROCESSORS: Fresh Or Frozen

FISH & SEAFOOD WHOLESALERS
FISHING EQPT: Lures
FITTINGS & ASSEMBLIES: Hose & Tube, Hydraulic Or Pneumatic
FITTINGS & SPECIALTIES: Steam
FITTINGS: Pipe
FLAGS: Fabric
FLARES
FLAT GLASS: Construction
FLAT GLASS: Laminated
FLAT GLASS: Window, Clear & Colored
FLAVORS OR FLAVORING MATERIALS: Synthetic
FLOOR COVERING STORES
FLOOR COVERING STORES: Carpets
FLOOR COVERING STORES: Rugs
FLOOR COVERINGS WHOLESALERS
FLOOR COVERINGS: Art Squares, Textile Fiber
FLOOR COVERINGS: Textile Fiber
FLOOR COVERINGS: Twisted Paper, Grass, Reed, Coir, Etc
FLOORING: Hard Surface
FLOORING: Hardwood
FLOORING: Rubber
FLORAL ARRANGEMENT INSTRUCTION
FLORIST: Flowers, Fresh
FLORISTS
FLORISTS' SPLYS, WHOLESALE
FLOWER ARRANGEMENTS: Artificial
FLOWER POTS: Red Earthenware
FLOWERS, ARTIFICIAL, WHOLESALE
FLOWERS: Artificial & Preserved
FLUID METERS & COUNTING DEVICES
FLUID POWER PUMPS & MOTORS
FLUID POWER VALVES & HOSE FITTINGS
FLUXES
FOAM RUBBER
FOIL & LEAF: Metal
FOOD PRDTS, BREAKFAST: Cereal, Granola & Muesli
FOOD PRDTS, BREAKFAST: Cereal, Oatmeal
FOOD PRDTS, BREAKFAST: Cereal, Rye
FOOD PRDTS, CANNED OR FRESH PACK: Fruit Juices
FOOD PRDTS, CANNED: Barbecue Sauce
FOOD PRDTS, CANNED: Ethnic
FOOD PRDTS, CANNED: Fruit Juices, Fresh
FOOD PRDTS, CANNED: Fruits
FOOD PRDTS, CANNED: Italian
FOOD PRDTS, CANNED: Jams, Jellies & Preserves
FOOD PRDTS, CANNED: Marmalade
FOOD PRDTS, CANNED: Mushrooms
FOOD PRDTS, CANNED: Spaghetti & Other Pasta Sauce
FOOD PRDTS, CANNED: Spanish
FOOD PRDTS, CONFECTIONERY, WHOLESALE: Candy
FOOD PRDTS, CONFECTIONERY, WHOLESALE: Snack Foods
FOOD PRDTS, DAIRY, WHOLESALE: Frozen Dairy Desserts
FOOD PRDTS, FISH & SEAFOOD, WHOLESALE: Seafood
FOOD PRDTS, FISH & SEAFOOD: Canned & Jarred, Etc
FOOD PRDTS, FISH & SEAFOOD: Chowders, Frozen
FOOD PRDTS, FISH & SEAFOOD: Crab cakes, Frozen
FOOD PRDTS, FISH & SEAFOOD: Fish, Cured, NEC
FOOD PRDTS, FISH & SEAFOOD: Oysters, Preserved & Cured
FOOD PRDTS, FROZEN: Breakfasts, Packaged
FOOD PRDTS, FROZEN: Fruit Juice, Concentrates
FOOD PRDTS, FROZEN: Fruits, Juices & Vegetables
FOOD PRDTS, FROZEN: NEC
FOOD PRDTS, FROZEN: Snack Items
FOOD PRDTS, FROZEN: Soups
FOOD PRDTS, FRUITS & VEGETABLES, FRESH, WHOLESALE
FOOD PRDTS, MEAT & MEAT PRDTS, WHOLESALE: Cured Or Smoked
FOOD PRDTS, MEAT & MEAT PRDTS, WHOLESALE: Fresh
FOOD PRDTS, WHOLESALE: Beverages, Exc Coffee & Tea
FOOD PRDTS, WHOLESALE: Chocolate
FOOD PRDTS, WHOLESALE: Cocoa
FOOD PRDTS, WHOLESALE: Condiments
FOOD PRDTS, WHOLESALE: Flavorings & Fragrances
FOOD PRDTS, WHOLESALE: Food Gift Baskets
FOOD PRDTS, WHOLESALE: Grains
FOOD PRDTS, WHOLESALE: Health
FOOD PRDTS, WHOLESALE: Juices
FOOD PRDTS, WHOLESALE: Organic & Diet
FOOD PRDTS, WHOLESALE: Pasta & Rice
FOOD PRDTS, WHOLESALE: Sauces
FOOD PRDTS, WHOLESALE: Sugar, Refined

FOOD PRDTS, WHOLESALE: Water, Mineral Or Spring, Bottled
FOOD PRDTS, WHOLESALE: Wine Makers' Eqpt & Splys
FOOD PRDTS: Bread Crumbs, Exc Made In Bakeries
FOOD PRDTS: Cereals
FOOD PRDTS: Chocolate Liquor
FOOD PRDTS: Cocoa, Instant
FOOD PRDTS: Cocoa, Powdered
FOOD PRDTS: Coconut, Desiccated & Shredded
FOOD PRDTS: Coffee
FOOD PRDTS: Coffee Roasting, Exc Wholesale Grocers
FOOD PRDTS: Cooking Oils, Refined Vegetable, Exc Corn
FOOD PRDTS: Cottonseed Oil, Deodorized
FOOD PRDTS: Dips, Exc Cheese & Sour Cream Based
FOOD PRDTS: Dough, Pizza, Prepared
FOOD PRDTS: Dressings, Salad, Raw & Cooked Exc Dry Mixes
FOOD PRDTS: Eggs, Processed
FOOD PRDTS: Flavored Ices, Frozen
FOOD PRDTS: Flour & Other Grain Mill Products
FOOD PRDTS: Flour Mixes & Doughs
FOOD PRDTS: Fresh Vegetables, Peeled Or Processed
FOOD PRDTS: Fruit Juices
FOOD PRDTS: Fruits, Freeze-Dried
FOOD PRDTS: Granola & Energy Bars, Nonchocolate
FOOD PRDTS: Honey
FOOD PRDTS: Ice, Cubes
FOOD PRDTS: Instant Coffee
FOOD PRDTS: Macaroni, Noodles, Spaghetti, Pasta, Etc
FOOD PRDTS: Nuts & Seeds
FOOD PRDTS: Oils & Fats, Animal
FOOD PRDTS: Olive Oil
FOOD PRDTS: Pasta, Rice/Potatoes, Uncooked, Pkgd
FOOD PRDTS: Pasta, Uncooked, Packaged With Other Ingredients
FOOD PRDTS: Peanut Butter
FOOD PRDTS: Potato & Corn Chips & Similar Prdts
FOOD PRDTS: Potato Chips & Other Potato-Based Snacks
FOOD PRDTS: Poultry Sausage, Lunch Meats/Other Poultry Prdts
FOOD PRDTS: Preparations
FOOD PRDTS: Prepared Meat Sauces Exc Tomato & Dry
FOOD PRDTS: Salads
FOOD PRDTS: Sandwiches
FOOD PRDTS: Seasonings & Spices
FOOD PRDTS: Soup Mixes
FOOD PRDTS: Soy Sauce
FOOD PRDTS: Spices, Including Ground
FOOD PRDTS: Sugar
FOOD PRDTS: Sugar, Cane
FOOD PRDTS: Sugar, Granulated Cane, Purchd Raw Sugar/Syrup
FOOD PRDTS: Sugar, Liquid Sugar Beet
FOOD PRDTS: Sugar, Maple, Indl
FOOD PRDTS: Sugar, Refined Cane, Purchased Raw Sugar/Syrup
FOOD PRDTS: Syrup, Maple
FOOD PRDTS: Syrups
FOOD PRDTS: Tea
FOOD PRDTS: Tortilla Chips
FOOD PRDTS: Vegetables, Brined
FOOD PRDTS: Vinegar
FOOD PRODUCTS MACHINERY
FOOD STORES: Convenience, Chain
FOOD STORES: Convenience, Independent
FOOD STORES: Supermarkets
FOOD WARMING EQPT: Commercial
FOOTWEAR, WHOLESALE: Boots
FOOTWEAR, WHOLESALE: Shoe Access
FOOTWEAR: Cut Stock
FOOTWEAR: Except Rubber, NEC
FORGINGS
FORGINGS: Aircraft, Ferrous
FORGINGS: Iron & Steel
FORGINGS: Mechanical Power Transmission, Ferrous
FORGINGS: Ordnance, Ferrous
FORMS HANDLING EQPT
FOUNDRIES: Aluminum
FOUNDRIES: Brass, Bronze & Copper
FOUNDRIES: Nonferrous
FOUNDRIES: Steel
FOUNDRIES: Steel Investment
FOUNDRY MACHINERY & EQPT
FRACTIONATION PRDTS OF CRUDE PETROLEUM, HYDROCARBONS, NEC

PRODUCT INDEX

FRAMES: Handbag & Pocketbook
FRANCHISES, SELLING OR LICENSING
FREIGHT FORWARDING ARRANGEMENTS
FRICTION MATERIAL, MADE FROM POWDERED METAL
FRUIT & VEGETABLE MARKETS
FRUIT STANDS OR MARKETS
FRUITS & VEGETABLES WHOLESALERS: Fresh
FUEL ADDITIVES
FUEL CELLS: Solid State
FUEL DEALERS: Wood
FUEL OIL DEALERS
FUELS: Diesel
FUELS: Ethanol
FUELS: Jet
FUELS: Oil
FUNDRAISING SVCS
FUNERAL HOMES & SVCS
FUR: Apparel
FUR: Coats & Other Apparel
FURNACES & OVENS: Indl
FURNACES & OVENS: Vacuum
FURNITURE & CABINET STORES: Cabinets, Custom Work
FURNITURE & CABINET STORES: Custom
FURNITURE & FIXTURES Factory
FURNITURE COMPONENTS: Porcelain Enameled
FURNITURE REPAIR & MAINTENANCE SVCS
FURNITURE STOCK & PARTS: Carvings, Wood
FURNITURE STOCK & PARTS: Turnings, Wood
FURNITURE STORES
FURNITURE STORES: Custom Made, Exc Cabinets
FURNITURE STORES: Office
FURNITURE STORES: Outdoor & Garden
FURNITURE UPHOLSTERY REPAIR SVCS
FURNITURE WHOLESALERS
FURNITURE, BARBER & BEAUTY SHOP
FURNITURE, HOUSEHOLD: Wholesalers
FURNITURE, OUTDOOR & LAWN: Wholesalers
FURNITURE, WHOLESALE: Racks
FURNITURE: Assembly Hall
FURNITURE: Bean Bag Chairs
FURNITURE: Bedroom, Wood
FURNITURE: Bookcases, Wood
FURNITURE: Cabinets & Vanities, Medicine, Metal
FURNITURE: Chairs, Household Wood
FURNITURE: End Tables, Wood
FURNITURE: Foundations & Platforms
FURNITURE: Household, Metal
FURNITURE: Household, NEC
FURNITURE: Household, Novelty, Metal
FURNITURE: Household, Upholstered, Exc Wood Or Metal
FURNITURE: Household, Wood
FURNITURE: Institutional, Exc Wood
FURNITURE: Juvenile, Wood
FURNITURE: Kitchen & Dining Room
FURNITURE: Kitchen & Dining Room, Metal
FURNITURE: Lawn, Wood
FURNITURE: Living Room, Upholstered On Wood Frames
FURNITURE: Mattresses & Foundations
FURNITURE: Mattresses, Box & Bedsprings
FURNITURE: Mattresses, Innerspring Or Box Spring
FURNITURE: NEC
FURNITURE: Office Panel Systems, Wood
FURNITURE: Office, Exc Wood
FURNITURE: Office, Wood
FURNITURE: Outdoor, Wood
FURNITURE: Picnic Tables Or Benches, Park
FURNITURE: Rattan
FURNITURE: Restaurant
FURNITURE: Studio Couches
FURNITURE: Table Tops, Marble
FURNITURE: Television, Wood
FURNITURE: Unfinished, Wood
FURNITURE: Upholstered
FURNITURE: Wall Cases, Office, Exc Wood
FURRIERS
Furs

G

GAMES & TOYS: Automobiles & Trucks
GAMES & TOYS: Baby Carriages & Restraint Seats
GAMES & TOYS: Blocks
GAMES & TOYS: Board Games, Children's & Adults'
GAMES & TOYS: Craft & Hobby Kits & Sets
GAMES & TOYS: Darts & Dart Games
GAMES & TOYS: Dolls & Doll Clothing
GAMES & TOYS: Dolls, Exc Stuffed Toy Animals
GAMES & TOYS: Electronic
GAMES & TOYS: Erector Sets
GAMES & TOYS: Game Machines, Exc Coin-Operated
GAMES & TOYS: Marbles
GAMES & TOYS: Models, Railroad, Toy & Hobby
GAMES & TOYS: Puzzles
GAMES & TOYS: Rocking Horses
GAMES & TOYS: Structural Toy Sets
GAMES & TOYS: Trains & Eqpt, Electric & Mechanical
GAMES & TOYS: Tricycles
GARAGES: Portable, Prefabricated Metal
GARMENT: Pressing & cleaners' agents
GAS & OIL FIELD EXPLORATION SVCS
GAS & OIL FIELD SVCS, NEC
GAS STATIONS
GASES: Helium
GASES: Hydrogen
GASES: Indl
GASES: Neon
GASES: Oxygen
GASKET MATERIALS
GASKETS
GASKETS & SEALING DEVICES
GASOLINE FILLING STATIONS
GASOLINE WHOLESALERS
GASTROINTESTINAL OR GENITOURINARY SYSTEM DRUGS
GATES: Ornamental Metal
GAUGES
GAUGES: Pressure
GEARS
GEARS: Power Transmission, Exc Auto
GENERATING APPARATUS & PARTS: Electrical
GENERATION EQPT: Electronic
GENERATOR REPAIR SVCS
GENERATORS SETS: Steam
GENERATORS: Automotive & Aircraft
GENERATORS: Electric
GENERATORS: Ultrasonic
GIFT SHOP
GIFT, NOVELTY & SOUVENIR STORES: Artcraft & carvings
GIFT, NOVELTY & SOUVENIR STORES: Gift Baskets
GIFT, NOVELTY & SOUVENIR STORES: Party Favors
GIFT, NOVELTY & SOUVENIR STORES: Trading Cards, Sports
GIFTS & NOVELTIES: Wholesalers
GLASS & GLASS CERAMIC PRDTS, PRESSED OR BLOWN: Tableware
GLASS FABRICATORS
GLASS PRDTS, FROM PURCHASED GLASS: Art
GLASS PRDTS, FROM PURCHASED GLASS: Enameled
GLASS PRDTS, FROM PURCHASED GLASS: Glassware
GLASS PRDTS, FROM PURCHASED GLASS: Mirrors, Framed
GLASS PRDTS, PRESSED OR BLOWN: Furnishings & Access
GLASS PRDTS, PRESSED OR BLOWN: Glass Fibers, Textile
GLASS PRDTS, PRESSED OR BLOWN: Glassware, Art Or Decorative
GLASS PRDTS, PRESSED OR BLOWN: Lighting Eqpt Parts
GLASS PRDTS, PRESSED OR BLOWN: Optical
GLASS PRDTS, PRESSED OR BLOWN: Stationers Glassware
GLASS PRDTS, PRESSED OR BLOWN: Yarn, Fiberglass
GLASS PRDTS, PRESSED/BLOWN: Glassware, Art, Decor/Novelty
GLASS STORE: Leaded Or Stained
GLASS: Fiber
GLASS: Flat
GLASS: Indl Prdts
GLASS: Insulating
GLASS: Pressed & Blown, NEC
GLASS: Stained
GLASSWARE STORES
GLASSWARE WHOLESALERS
GLASSWARE: Laboratory
GLOBAL POSITIONING SYSTEMS & EQPT
GLOVES: Fabric
GLOVES: Safety
GOLD STAMPING, EXC BOOKS
GOLF CLUB & EQPT REPAIR SVCS
GOLF COURSES: Public
GOLF DRIVING RANGES
GOLF EQPT
GOLF GOODS & EQPT
GOVERNMENT, LEGISLATIVE BODIES: Town Council
GRAIN & FIELD BEANS WHOLESALERS
GRANITE: Crushed & Broken
GRANITE: Cut & Shaped
GRANITE: Dimension
GRANITE: Dimension
GRAPHIC ARTS & RELATED DESIGN SVCS
GRAPHIC LAYOUT SVCS: Printed Circuitry
GRAVE MARKERS: Concrete
GREENHOUSES: Prefabricated Metal
GREETING CARDS WHOLESALERS
GRILLS & GRILLWORK: Woven Wire, Made From Purchased Wire
GRINDING SVC: Precision, Commercial Or Indl
GRINDING SVCS: Ophthalmic Lens, Exc Prescription
GRITS: Crushed & Broken
GROCERIES WHOLESALERS, NEC
GROMMETS: Rubber
GUARDRAILS
GUIDED MISSILES & SPACE VEHICLES
GUN SIGHTS: Optical
GUN STOCKS: Wood
GUTTERS
GUTTERS: Sheet Metal
GYROSCOPES

H

HAIR & HAIR BASED PRDTS
HAIR CARE PRDTS
HAIR DRESSING, FOR THE TRADE
HAMPERS: Solid Fiber, Made From Purchased Materials
HAND TOOLS, NEC: Wholesalers
HANDBAG STORES
HANDBAGS
HANDBAGS: Men's
HANDBAGS: Women's
HANDYMAN SVCS
HANGERS: Garment, Plastic
HARDWARE
HARDWARE & BUILDING PRDTS: Plastic
HARDWARE STORES
HARDWARE STORES: Pumps & Pumping Eqpt
HARDWARE STORES: Tools
HARDWARE STORES: Tools, Hand
HARDWARE WHOLESALERS
HARDWARE, WHOLESALE: Builders', NEC
HARDWARE, WHOLESALE: Chains
HARDWARE, WHOLESALE: Furniture, NEC
HARDWARE, WHOLESALE: Power Tools & Access
HARDWARE, WHOLESALE: Security Devices, Locks
HARDWARE: Aircraft
HARDWARE: Aircraft & Marine, Incl Pulleys & Similar Items
HARDWARE: Builders'
HARDWARE: Cabinet
HARDWARE: Door Opening & Closing Devices, Exc Electrical
HARDWARE: Furniture, Builders' & Other Household
HARDWARE: Parachute
HARDWARE: Plastic
HARNESS ASSEMBLIES: Cable & Wire
HARNESSES, HALTERS, SADDLERY & STRAPS
HEALTH & ALLIED SERVICES, NEC
HEALTH AIDS: Exercise Eqpt
HEALTH FOOD & SUPPLEMENT STORES
HEARING AID REPAIR SVCS
HEARING AIDS
HEAT EXCHANGERS: After Or Inter Coolers Or Condensers, Etc
HEAT TREATING: Metal
HEATERS: Space, Exc Electric
HEATERS: Swimming Pool, Oil Or Gas
HEATING & AIR CONDITIONING UNITS, COMBINATION
HEATING EQPT & SPLYS
HEATING EQPT: Complete
HEATING UNITS & DEVICES: Indl, Electric
HELICOPTERS
HELMETS: Steel
HIGHWAY SIGNALS: Electric
HOBBY & CRAFT SPLY STORES
HOBBY, TOY & GAME STORES: Arts & Crafts & Splys
HOBBY, TOY & GAME STORES: Children's Toys & Games, Exc Dolls
HOLDERS, PAPER TOWEL, GROCERY BAG, ETC: Plastic
HOLDING COMPANIES: Investment, Exc Banks
HOLDING COMPANIES: Personal, Exc Banks

PRODUCT INDEX

HOME CENTER STORES
HOME ENTERTAINMENT EQPT: Electronic, NEC
HOME FURNISHINGS WHOLESALERS
HOME HEALTH CARE SVCS
HOME IMPROVEMENT & RENOVATION CONTRACTOR AGENCY
HOMEBUILDERS & OTHER OPERATIVE BUILDERS
HOMEFURNISHING STORE: Bedding, Sheet, Blanket,Spread/Pillow
HOMEFURNISHING STORES: Lighting Fixtures
HOMEFURNISHING STORES: Mirrors
HOMEFURNISHING STORES: Pictures & Mirrors
HOMEFURNISHING STORES: Pottery
HOMEFURNISHING STORES: Venetian Blinds
HOMEFURNISHING STORES: Window Furnishings
HOMEFURNISHING STORES: Window Shades, NEC
HOMEFURNISHINGS & SPLYS, WHOLESALE: Decorative
HOMEFURNISHINGS, WHOLESALE: Blinds, Vertical
HOMEFURNISHINGS, WHOLESALE: Carpets
HOMEFURNISHINGS, WHOLESALE: Kitchenware
HOMEFURNISHINGS, WHOLESALE: Mirrors/Pictures, Framed/Unframd
HOMEFURNISHINGS, WHOLESALE: Wood Flooring
HOMES FOR THE ELDERLY
HOMES, MODULAR: Wooden
HOMES: Log Cabins
HONEYCOMB CORE & BOARD: Made From Purchased Materials
HOODS: Range, Sheet Metal
HORSE & PET ACCESSORIES: Textile
HORSE DRAWN VEHICLE REPAIR SVCS
HORSESHOES
HOSE: Flexible Metal
HOSE: Rubber
HOSES & BELTING: Rubber & Plastic
HOSPITALS: Rehabilitation, Drug Addiction
HOT AIR BALLOONS & EQPT DEALERS
HOT TUBS
HOUSEHOLD APPLIANCE STORES
HOUSEHOLD APPLIANCE STORES: Air Cond Rm Units, Self-Contnd
HOUSEHOLD APPLIANCE STORES: Electric
HOUSEHOLD APPLIANCE STORES: Electric Household, Major
HOUSEHOLD ARTICLES: Metal
HOUSEHOLD FURNISHINGS, NEC
HOUSEKEEPING & MAID SVCS
HOUSEWARES, ELECTRIC: Appliances, Personal
HOUSEWARES, ELECTRIC: Blowers, Portable
HOUSEWARES, ELECTRIC: Bottle Warmers
HOUSEWARES, ELECTRIC: Broilers
HOUSEWARES, ELECTRIC: Cooking Appliances
HOUSEWARES, ELECTRIC: Fans, Exhaust & Ventilating
HOUSEWARES: Dishes, Earthenware
HOUSEWARES: Pots & Pans, Glass
HUB CAPS: Automobile, Stamped Metal
HYDRAULIC EQPT REPAIR SVC
HYDRAULIC FLUIDS: Synthetic Based
HYDROFLUORIC ACID COMPOUND: Etching Or Polishing Glass
HYDROPONIC EQPT
Hard Rubber & Molded Rubber Prdts

I

ICE
IDENTIFICATION TAGS, EXC PAPER
IGNEOUS ROCK: Crushed & Broken
IGNITION SYSTEMS: High Frequency
INCENSE
INDL & PERSONAL SVC PAPER, WHOL: Bags, Paper/Disp Plastic
INDL & PERSONAL SVC PAPER, WHOLESALE: Boxes & Containers
INDL & PERSONAL SVC PAPER, WHOLESALE: Disposable
INDL & PERSONAL SVC PAPER, WHOLESALE: Shipping Splys
INDL EQPT SVCS
INDL GASES WHOLESALERS
INDL MACHINERY & EQPT WHOLESALERS
INDL MACHINERY REPAIR & MAINTENANCE
INDL PROCESS INSTRUMENTS: Absorp Analyzers, Infrared, X-Ray
INDL PROCESS INSTRUMENTS: Control
INDL PROCESS INSTRUMENTS: Controllers, Process Variables
INDL PROCESS INSTRUMENTS: Digital Display, Process Variables
INDL PROCESS INSTRUMENTS: Fluidic Devices, Circuit & Systems
INDL PROCESS INSTRUMENTS: Indl Flow & Measuring
INDL PROCESS INSTRUMENTS: Moisture Meters
INDL PROCESS INSTRUMENTS: Temperature
INDL PROCESS INSTRUMENTS: Water Quality Monitoring/Cntrl Sys
INDL SPLYS WHOLESALERS
INDL SPLYS, WHOL: Fasteners, Incl Nuts, Bolts, Screws, Etc
INDL SPLYS, WHOLESALE: Abrasives
INDL SPLYS, WHOLESALE: Bearings
INDL SPLYS, WHOLESALE: Bottler Splys
INDL SPLYS, WHOLESALE: Filters, Indl
INDL SPLYS, WHOLESALE: Fittings
INDL SPLYS, WHOLESALE: Gears
INDL SPLYS, WHOLESALE: Power Transmission, Eqpt & Apparatus
INDL SPLYS, WHOLESALE: Rubber Goods, Mechanical
INDL SPLYS, WHOLESALE: Signmaker Eqpt & Splys
INDL SPLYS, WHOLESALE: Springs
INDL SPLYS, WHOLESALE: Tools, NEC
INDL SPLYS, WHOLESALE: Valves & Fittings
INDL TOOL GRINDING SVCS
INDUCTORS
INDUSTRIAL & COMMERCIAL EQPT INSPECTION SVCS
INFORMATION RETRIEVAL SERVICES
INFRARED OBJECT DETECTION EQPT
INK OR WRITING FLUIDS
INK: Duplicating
INK: Printing
INSECTICIDES
INSECTICIDES & PESTICIDES
INSPECTION & TESTING SVCS
INSTRUMENTS & ACCESSORIES: Surveying
INSTRUMENTS & METERS: Measuring, Electric
INSTRUMENTS, LABORATORY: Analyzers, Elemental
INSTRUMENTS, LABORATORY: Analyzers, Thermal
INSTRUMENTS, LABORATORY: Flame Photometers
INSTRUMENTS, LABORATORY: Infrared Analytical
INSTRUMENTS, LABORATORY: Magnetic/Elec Properties Measuring
INSTRUMENTS, LABORATORY: Mass Spectroscopy
INSTRUMENTS, LABORATORY: Photometers
INSTRUMENTS, LABORATORY: Ultraviolet Analytical
INSTRUMENTS, MEASURING & CNTRL: Auto Turnstiles
INSTRUMENTS, MEASURING & CNTRL: Geophysical & Meteorological
INSTRUMENTS, MEASURING & CNTRL: Radiation & Testing, Nuclear
INSTRUMENTS, MEASURING & CNTRL: Tester, Acft Hydc Ctrl Test
INSTRUMENTS, MEASURING & CNTRL: Testing, Abrasion, Etc
INSTRUMENTS, MEASURING & CNTRLG: Aircraft & Motor Vehicle
INSTRUMENTS, MEASURING & CNTRLG: Thermometers/Temp Sensors
INSTRUMENTS, MEASURING & CNTRLNG: Levels & Tapes, Surveying
INSTRUMENTS, MEASURING & CNTRLNG: Nuclear Instrument Modules
INSTRUMENTS, MEASURING & CONTROLLING: Breathalyzers
INSTRUMENTS, MEASURING & CONTROLLING: Gas Detectors
INSTRUMENTS, MEASURING & CONTROLLING: Ultrasonic Testing
INSTRUMENTS, MEASURING/CNTRL: Compasses, Magnetic, Portable
INSTRUMENTS, MEASURING/CNTRL: Gauging, Ultrasonic Thickness
INSTRUMENTS, MEASURING/CNTRLG: Fire Detect Sys, Non-Electric
INSTRUMENTS, MEASURING/CNTRLNG: Med Diagnostic Sys, Nuclear
INSTRUMENTS, OPTICAL: Elements & Assemblies, Exc Ophthalmic
INSTRUMENTS, OPTICAL: Gratings, Diffraction
INSTRUMENTS, OPTICAL: Lenses, All Types Exc Ophthalmic
INSTRUMENTS, OPTICAL: Magnifying, NEC
INSTRUMENTS, OPTICAL: Mirrors
INSTRUMENTS, OPTICAL: Sighting & Fire Control
INSTRUMENTS, OPTICAL: Test & Inspection
INSTRUMENTS, SURGICAL & MED: Needles & Syringes, Hypodermic
INSTRUMENTS, SURGICAL & MEDI: Knife Blades/Handles, Surgical
INSTRUMENTS, SURGICAL & MEDICAL: Biopsy
INSTRUMENTS, SURGICAL & MEDICAL: Blood & Bone Work
INSTRUMENTS, SURGICAL & MEDICAL: Blood Pressure
INSTRUMENTS, SURGICAL & MEDICAL: Blood Transfusion
INSTRUMENTS, SURGICAL & MEDICAL: Catheters
INSTRUMENTS, SURGICAL & MEDICAL: Inhalators
INSTRUMENTS, SURGICAL & MEDICAL: Plates & Screws, Bone
INSTRUMENTS, SURGICAL & MEDICAL: Stapling Devices, Surgical
INSTRUMENTS, SURGICAL/MED: Bronchoscopes, Exc Electromedical
INSTRUMENTS: Airspeed
INSTRUMENTS: Analytical
INSTRUMENTS: Analyzers, Radio Apparatus, NEC
INSTRUMENTS: Colonoscopes, Electromedical
INSTRUMENTS: Combustion Control, Indl
INSTRUMENTS: Electrolytic Conductivity, Laboratory
INSTRUMENTS: Electron Test Tube
INSTRUMENTS: Electronic, Analog-Digital Converters
INSTRUMENTS: Endoscopic Eqpt, Electromedical
INSTRUMENTS: Eye Examination
INSTRUMENTS: Flow, Indl Process
INSTRUMENTS: Humidity, Indl Process
INSTRUMENTS: Indicating, Electric
INSTRUMENTS: Indl Process Control
INSTRUMENTS: Infrared, Indl Process
INSTRUMENTS: Laser, Scientific & Engineering
INSTRUMENTS: Liquid Level, Indl Process
INSTRUMENTS: Measuring & Controlling
INSTRUMENTS: Measuring Electricity
INSTRUMENTS: Measuring, Electrical Power
INSTRUMENTS: Medical & Surgical
INSTRUMENTS: Meteorological
INSTRUMENTS: Meters, Integrating Electricity
INSTRUMENTS: Nautical
INSTRUMENTS: Photographic, Electronic
INSTRUMENTS: Power Measuring, Electrical
INSTRUMENTS: Pressure Measurement, Indl
INSTRUMENTS: Radar Testing, Electric
INSTRUMENTS: Radio Frequency Measuring
INSTRUMENTS: Temperature Measurement, Indl
INSTRUMENTS: Test, Electrical, Engine
INSTRUMENTS: Test, Electronic & Electric Measurement
INSTRUMENTS: Test, Electronic & Electrical Circuits
INSTRUMENTS: Testing, Semiconductor
INSTRUMENTS: Thermal Conductive, Indl
INSTRUMENTS: Transducers, Volts, Amperes, Watts, VARs & Freq
INSTRUMENTS: Vibration
INSULATING COMPOUNDS
INSULATION & CUSHIONING FOAM: Polystyrene
INSULATION MATERIALS WHOLESALERS
INSULATION: Fiberglass
INSULATORS, PORCELAIN: Electrical
INSURANCE CARRIERS: Dental
INTEGRATED CIRCUITS, SEMICONDUCTOR NETWORKS, ETC
INTERCOMMUNICATIONS SYSTEMS: Electric
INTERIOR DECORATING SVCS
INTERIOR DESIGN SVCS, NEC
INVERTERS: Nonrotating Electrical
INVESTMENT ADVISORY SVCS
INVESTMENT BANKERS
INVESTMENT COUNSELORS
INVESTMENT FUNDS, NEC
INVESTMENT FUNDS: Open-Ended
INVESTMENT RESEARCH SVCS
INVESTORS, NEC
IRON & STEEL PRDTS: Hot-Rolled
IRON ORE PELLETIZING
IRON ORES

J

JACKETS: Indl, Metal Plate
JACKS: Hydraulic
JANITORIAL & CUSTODIAL SVCS
JANITORIAL EQPT & SPLYS WHOLESALERS
JARS: Plastic
JEWELRY & PRECIOUS STONES WHOLESALERS

PRODUCT INDEX

JEWELRY APPAREL
JEWELRY FINDINGS & LAPIDARY WORK
JEWELRY REPAIR SVCS
JEWELRY STORES
JEWELRY STORES: Clocks
JEWELRY STORES: Precious Stones & Precious Metals
JEWELRY STORES: Silverware
JEWELRY, PRECIOUS METAL: Cases
JEWELRY, PRECIOUS METAL: Pearl, Natural Or Cultured
JEWELRY, WHOLESALE
JEWELRY: Decorative, Fashion & Costume
JEWELRY: Precious Metal
JIGS & FIXTURES
JOB PRINTING & NEWSPAPER PUBLISHING COMBINED
JOB TRAINING & VOCATIONAL REHABILITATION SVCS
JOB TRAINING SVCS

K

KAOLIN & BALL CLAY MINING
KEYBOARDS: Computer Or Office Machine
KITCHEN & COOKING ARTICLES: Pottery
KITCHEN ARTICLES: Semivitreous Earthenware
KITCHEN CABINET STORES, EXC CUSTOM
KITCHEN CABINETS WHOLESALERS
KITCHEN TOOLS & UTENSILS WHOLESALERS
KITCHEN UTENSILS: Market Baskets, Wood
KITCHENWARE: Plastic
KNIT GOODS, WHOLESALE

L

LABELS: Cotton, Printed
LABELS: Paper, Made From Purchased Materials
LABORATORIES, TESTING: Metallurgical
LABORATORIES, TESTING: Pollution
LABORATORIES, TESTING: Product Testing
LABORATORIES, TESTING: Product Testing, Safety/Performance
LABORATORIES, TESTING: Radiation
LABORATORIES, TESTING: Soil Analysis
LABORATORIES: Biological Research
LABORATORIES: Biotechnology
LABORATORIES: Commercial Nonphysical Research
LABORATORIES: Dental
LABORATORIES: Electronic Research
LABORATORIES: Noncommercial Research
LABORATORIES: Physical Research, Commercial
LABORATORIES: Testing
LABORATORIES: Testing
LABORATORY APPARATUS & FURNITURE
LABORATORY APPARATUS: Calibration Tapes, Phy Testing Mach
LABORATORY APPARATUS: Shakers & Stirrers
LABORATORY CHEMICALS: Organic
LABORATORY EQPT: Balances
LABORATORY EQPT: Centrifuges
LABORATORY EQPT: Chemical
LABORATORY EQPT: Clinical Instruments Exc Medical
LABORATORY EQPT: Measuring
LABORATORY EQPT: Sterilizers
LACQUERING SVC: Metal Prdts
LADDERS: Permanent Installation, Metal
LAMINATED PLASTICS: Plate, Sheet, Rod & Tubes
LAMINATING SVCS
LAMP & LIGHT BULBS & TUBES
LAMP BULBS & TUBES, ELECTRIC: For Specialized Applications
LAMP BULBS & TUBES, ELECTRIC: Light, Complete
LAMP BULBS & TUBES/PARTS, ELECTRIC: Generalized Applications
LAMP FIXTURES: Ultraviolet
LAMP SHADES: Metal
LAMP STORES
LAMPS: Ultraviolet
LAND SUBDIVISION & DEVELOPMENT
LAPIDARY WORK: Contract Or Other
LAPIDARY WORK: Jewel Cut, Drill, Polish, Recut/Setting
LASER SYSTEMS & EQPT
LASERS: Welding, Drilling & Cutting Eqpt
LATEX: Foamed
LATHES
LAUNDRY & GARMENT SVCS, NEC: Garment Alteration & Repair
LAUNDRY EQPT: Commercial
LAUNDRY EQPT: Household
LAUNDRY SVCS: Indl

LAWN & GARDEN EQPT
LAWN & GARDEN EQPT: Lawnmowers, Residential, Hand Or Power
LAWN MOWER REPAIR SHOP
LEAD
LEAD PENCILS & ART GOODS
LEAF TOBACCO WHOLESALERS
LEASING & RENTAL SVCS: Oil Field Eqpt
LEASING & RENTAL: Computers & Eqpt
LEASING & RENTAL: Construction & Mining Eqpt
LEASING & RENTAL: Medical Machinery & Eqpt
LEASING & RENTAL: Trucks, Without Drivers
LEASING: Shipping Container
LEATHER GOODS: Belting & Strapping
LEATHER GOODS: Cigarette & Cigar Cases
LEATHER GOODS: Cosmetic Bags
LEATHER GOODS: Garments
LEATHER GOODS: Holsters
LEATHER GOODS: Mill Strapping, Textile Mills
LEATHER GOODS: NEC
LEATHER GOODS: Personal
LEATHER GOODS: Riding Crops
LEATHER GOODS: Wallets
LEATHER TANNING & FINISHING
LEATHER: Accessory Prdts
LEATHER: Bag
LEATHER: Bookbinders'
LEATHER: Processed
LEATHER: Shoe
LEGAL OFFICES & SVCS
LICENSE TAGS: Automobile, Stamped Metal
LIFTS & TRUCKS: Bomb
LIGHT SENSITIVE DEVICES
LIGHTING EQPT: Locomotive & Railroad Car Lights
LIGHTING EQPT: Motor Vehicle, Dome Lights
LIGHTING EQPT: Motor Vehicle, NEC
LIGHTING EQPT: Motor Vehicle, Parking Lights
LIGHTING EQPT: Outdoor
LIGHTING EQPT: Searchlights
LIGHTING EQPT: Spotlights
LIGHTING FIXTURES WHOLESALERS
LIGHTING FIXTURES, NEC
LIGHTING FIXTURES: Airport
LIGHTING FIXTURES: Decorative Area
LIGHTING FIXTURES: Fluorescent, Commercial
LIGHTING FIXTURES: Indl & Commercial
LIGHTING FIXTURES: Marine
LIGHTING FIXTURES: Motor Vehicle
LIGHTING FIXTURES: Residential
LIGHTING FIXTURES: Street
LIGHTING FIXTURES: Swimming Pool
LIGHTING MAINTENANCE SVC
LIME
LIME ROCK: Ground
LIMESTONE: Crushed & Broken
LIMESTONE: Dimension
LINEN SPLY SVC: Uniform
LINENS: Table & Dresser Scarves, From Purchased Materials
LINENS: Tablecloths, From Purchased Materials
LINERS & COVERS: Fabric
LININGS: Apparel, Made From Purchased Materials
LIP BALMS
LOADS: Electronic
LOCKS
LOCKSMITHS
LOGGING
LOGGING CAMPS & CONTRACTORS
LOGGING: Stump Harvesting
LOGGING: Timber, Cut At Logging Camp
LOGGING: Wooden Logs
LOOSELEAF BINDERS
LOTIONS OR CREAMS: Face
LOTIONS: SHAVING
LOUDSPEAKERS
LOZENGES: Pharmaceutical
LUBRICANTS: Corrosion Preventive
LUBRICATING EQPT: Indl
LUBRICATING OIL & GREASE WHOLESALERS
LUGGAGE & BRIEFCASES
LUGGAGE & LEATHER GOODS STORES
LUGGAGE & LEATHER GOODS STORES: Luggage, Exc Footlckr/Trunk
LUGGAGE: Traveling Bags
LUMBER & BLDG MATLS DEALER, RET: Garage Doors, Sell/Install

LUMBER & BLDG MATRLS DEALERS, RET: Bath Fixtures, Eqpt/Sply
LUMBER & BLDG MATRLS DEALERS, RETAIL: Doors, Wood/Metal
LUMBER & BLDG MTRLS DEALERS, RET: Doors, Storm, Wood/Metal
LUMBER & BLDG MTRLS DEALERS, RET: Insultn & Energy Consrvtn
LUMBER & BLDG MTRLS DEALERS, RET: Planing Mill Prdts/Lumber
LUMBER & BUILDING MATERIALS DEALER, RET: Door & Window Prdts
LUMBER & BUILDING MATERIALS DEALER, RET: Masonry Matls/Splys
LUMBER & BUILDING MATERIALS DEALERS, RETAIL: Brick
LUMBER & BUILDING MATERIALS DEALERS, RETAIL: Countertops
LUMBER & BUILDING MATERIALS DEALERS, RETAIL: Flooring, Wood
LUMBER & BUILDING MATERIALS DEALERS, RETAIL: Sand & Gravel
LUMBER & BUILDING MATERIALS DEALERS, RETAIL: Tile, Ceramic
LUMBER & BUILDING MATERIALS RET DEALERS: Millwork & Lumber
LUMBER & BUILDING MATLS DEALERS, RET: Concrete/Cinder Block
LUMBER: Box
LUMBER: Cut Stock, Softwood
LUMBER: Hardwood Dimension
LUMBER: Hardwood Dimension & Flooring Mills
LUMBER: Piles, Foundation & Marine Construction, Treated
LUMBER: Plywood, Hardwood
LUMBER: Plywood, Prefinished, Hardwood

M

MACHINE PARTS: Stamped Or Pressed Metal
MACHINE SHOPS
MACHINE TOOL ACCESS: Balancing Machines
MACHINE TOOL ACCESS: Broaches
MACHINE TOOL ACCESS: Cams
MACHINE TOOL ACCESS: Cutting
MACHINE TOOL ACCESS: Diamond Cutting, For Turning, Etc
MACHINE TOOL ACCESS: Pushers
MACHINE TOOL ACCESS: Threading Tools
MACHINE TOOL ACCESS: Tool Holders
MACHINE TOOL ACCESS: Tools & Access
MACHINE TOOL ATTACHMENTS & ACCESS
MACHINE TOOLS & ACCESS
MACHINE TOOLS, METAL CUTTING: Exotic, Including Explosive
MACHINE TOOLS, METAL CUTTING: Jig, Boring & Grinding
MACHINE TOOLS, METAL CUTTING: Robot, Drilling, Cutting, Etc
MACHINE TOOLS, METAL CUTTING: Sawing & Cutoff
MACHINE TOOLS, METAL CUTTING: Saws, Power
MACHINE TOOLS, METAL CUTTING: Screw & Thread
MACHINE TOOLS, METAL CUTTING: Tool Replacement & Rpr Parts
MACHINE TOOLS, METAL CUTTING: Ultrasonic
MACHINE TOOLS, METAL CUTTING: Vertical Turning & Boring
MACHINE TOOLS, METAL FORMING: Bending
MACHINE TOOLS, METAL FORMING: Container, Metal Incl Cans
MACHINE TOOLS, METAL FORMING: Die Casting & Extruding
MACHINE TOOLS, METAL FORMING: Forming, Metal Deposit
MACHINE TOOLS, METAL FORMING: Marking
MACHINE TOOLS, METAL FORMING: Rebuilt
MACHINE TOOLS, METAL FORMING: Robots, Pressing, Extrudg, Etc
MACHINE TOOLS, METAL FORMING: Spinning, Spline Rollg/Windg
MACHINE TOOLS, METAL FORMING: Spring Winding & Forming
MACHINE TOOLS, METAL FORMING: Stretching
MACHINE TOOLS: Metal Cutting
MACHINE TOOLS: Metal Forming
MACHINERY & EQPT FINANCE LEASING
MACHINERY & EQPT, AGRICULTURAL, WHOLESALE: Landscaping Eqpt
MACHINERY & EQPT, AGRICULTURAL, WHOLESALE: Poultry Eqpt

PRODUCT INDEX

MACHINERY & EQPT, INDL, WHOL: Brewery Prdts Mfrg, Commercial
MACHINERY & EQPT, INDL, WHOL: Controlling Instruments/Access
MACHINERY & EQPT, INDL, WHOLESALE: Cement Making
MACHINERY & EQPT, INDL, WHOLESALE: Cranes
MACHINERY & EQPT, INDL, WHOLESALE: Engines, Gasoline
MACHINERY & EQPT, INDL, WHOLESALE: Engs/Transportation Eqpt
MACHINERY & EQPT, INDL, WHOLESALE: Fans
MACHINERY & EQPT, INDL, WHOLESALE: Hydraulic Systems
MACHINERY & EQPT, INDL, WHOLESALE: Indl Machine Parts
MACHINERY & EQPT, INDL, WHOLESALE: Instruments & Cntrl Eqpt
MACHINERY & EQPT, INDL, WHOLESALE: Machine Tools & Access
MACHINERY & EQPT, INDL, WHOLESALE: Machine Tools & Metalwork
MACHINERY & EQPT, INDL, WHOLESALE: Measure/Test, Electric
MACHINERY & EQPT, INDL, WHOLESALE: Packaging
MACHINERY & EQPT, INDL, WHOLESALE: Petroleum Industry
MACHINERY & EQPT, INDL, WHOLESALE: Pneumatic Tools
MACHINERY & EQPT, INDL, WHOLESALE: Processing & Packaging
MACHINERY & EQPT, INDL, WHOLESALE: Safety Eqpt
MACHINERY & EQPT, INDL, WHOLESALE: Sewing
MACHINERY & EQPT, INDL, WHOLESALE: Threading Tools
MACHINERY & EQPT, INDL, WHOLESALE: Water Pumps
MACHINERY & EQPT, WHOLESALE: Construction, General
MACHINERY & EQPT: Farm
MACHINERY & EQPT: Gas Producers, Generators/Other Rltd Eqpt
MACHINERY & EQPT: Liquid Automation
MACHINERY & EQPT: Metal Finishing, Plating Etc
MACHINERY BASES
MACHINERY, COMMERCIAL LAUNDRY: Washing, Incl Coin-Operated
MACHINERY, EQPT & SUPPLIES: Parking Facility
MACHINERY, FOOD PRDTS: Beverage
MACHINERY, FOOD PRDTS: Homogenizing, Dairy, Fruit/Vegetable
MACHINERY, FOOD PRDTS: Mills, Food
MACHINERY, FOOD PRDTS: Mixers, Commercial
MACHINERY, FOOD PRDTS: Mixers, Feed, Exc Agricultural
MACHINERY, FOOD PRDTS: Ovens, Bakery
MACHINERY, FOOD PRDTS: Roasting, Coffee, Peanut, Etc.
MACHINERY, FOOD PRDTS: Slicers, Commercial
MACHINERY, MAILING: Mailing
MACHINERY, MAILING: Postage Meters
MACHINERY, METALWORKING: Assembly, Including Robotic
MACHINERY, METALWORKING: Coil Winding, For Springs
MACHINERY, METALWORKING: Coiling
MACHINERY, METALWORKING: Cutting & Slitting
MACHINERY, OFFICE: Dictating
MACHINERY, OFFICE: Duplicating
MACHINERY, OFFICE: Paper Handling
MACHINERY, OFFICE: Pencil Sharpeners
MACHINERY, OFFICE: Stapling, Hand Or Power
MACHINERY, OFFICE: Time Clocks &Time Recording Devices
MACHINERY, OFFICE: Typing & Word Processing
MACHINERY, PACKAGING: Packing & Wrapping
MACHINERY, PAPER INDUSTRY: Coating & Finishing
MACHINERY, PAPER INDUSTRY: Converting, Die Cutting & Stampng
MACHINERY, PRINTING TRADES: Lithographic Stones
MACHINERY, PRINTING TRADES: Plates
MACHINERY, PRINTING TRADES: Printing Trade Parts & Attchts
MACHINERY, SERVICING: Coin-Operated, Exc Dry Clean & Laundry
MACHINERY, SEWING: Buttonhole/Eyelet Mach/Attachments, Indl
MACHINERY, SEWING: Sewing & Hat & Zipper Making
MACHINERY, TEXTILE: Embroidery
MACHINERY, TEXTILE: Printing
MACHINERY, TEXTILE: Silk Screens
MACHINERY, WOODWORKING: Bandsaws
MACHINERY, WOODWORKING: Cabinet Makers'
MACHINERY, WOODWORKING: Jointers
MACHINERY, WOODWORKING: Sanding, Exc Portable Floor Sanders
MACHINERY/EQPT, INDL, WHOL: Cleaning, High Press, Sand/Steam
MACHINERY: Ammunition & Explosives Loading
MACHINERY: Assembly, Exc Metalworking
MACHINERY: Automotive Related
MACHINERY: Blasting, Electrical
MACHINERY: Brewery & Malting
MACHINERY: Construction
MACHINERY: Cryogenic, Industrial
MACHINERY: Custom
MACHINERY: Deburring
MACHINERY: Die Casting
MACHINERY: Electrical Discharge Erosion
MACHINERY: Electronic Component Making
MACHINERY: Electronic Teaching Aids
MACHINERY: Fiber Optics Strand Coating
MACHINERY: Gas Producers
MACHINERY: Gear Cutting & Finishing
MACHINERY: General, Industrial, NEC
MACHINERY: Glassmaking
MACHINERY: Grinding
MACHINERY: Ice Cream
MACHINERY: Ice Making
MACHINERY: Industrial, NEC
MACHINERY: Jack Screws
MACHINERY: Jewelers
MACHINERY: Labeling
MACHINERY: Marking, Metalworking
MACHINERY: Metalworking
MACHINERY: Milling
MACHINERY: Optical Lens
MACHINERY: Packaging
MACHINERY: Paper Industry Miscellaneous
MACHINERY: Pharmaciutical
MACHINERY: Photographic Reproduction
MACHINERY: Plastic Working
MACHINERY: Printing Presses
MACHINERY: Recycling
MACHINERY: Road Construction & Maintenance
MACHINERY: Robots, Molding & Forming Plastics
MACHINERY: Rubber Working
MACHINERY: Semiconductor Manufacturing
MACHINERY: Separation Eqpt, Magnetic
MACHINERY: Sheet Metal Working
MACHINERY: Snow Making
MACHINERY: Specialty
MACHINERY: Swaging
MACHINERY: Textile
MACHINERY: Thread Rolling
MACHINERY: Tobacco Prdts
MACHINERY: Woodworking
MACHINES: Forming, Sheet Metal
MACHINISTS' TOOLS: Measuring, Precision
MACHINISTS' TOOLS: Precision
MAGNESIUM
MAGNETIC INK & OPTICAL SCANNING EQPT
MAIL-ORDER HOUSE, NEC
MAIL-ORDER HOUSES: Arts & Crafts Eqpt & Splys
MAIL-ORDER HOUSES: Books, Exc Book Clubs
MAIL-ORDER HOUSES: Clothing, Exc Women's
MAIL-ORDER HOUSES: Collectibles & Antiques
MAIL-ORDER HOUSES: Computer Software
MAIL-ORDER HOUSES: Educational Splys & Eqpt
MAIL-ORDER HOUSES: Novelty Merchandise
MAIL-ORDER HOUSES: Order Taking Office Only
MAILBOX RENTAL & RELATED SVCS
MAILING LIST: Compilers
MAILING SVCS, NEC
MANAGEMENT CONSULTING SVCS: Automation & Robotics
MANAGEMENT CONSULTING SVCS: Business
MANAGEMENT CONSULTING SVCS: Business Planning & Organizing
MANAGEMENT CONSULTING SVCS: Construction Project
MANAGEMENT CONSULTING SVCS: Food & Beverage
MANAGEMENT CONSULTING SVCS: Hospital & Health
MANAGEMENT CONSULTING SVCS: Industrial
MANAGEMENT CONSULTING SVCS: Industrial & Labor
MANAGEMENT CONSULTING SVCS: Industry Specialist
MANAGEMENT CONSULTING SVCS: Training & Development
MANAGEMENT SERVICES
MANAGEMENT SVCS, FACILITIES SUPPORT: Environ Remediation
MANAGEMENT SVCS: Business
MANAGEMENT SVCS: Financial, Business
MANAGEMENT SVCS: Hospital
MANDRELS
MANICURE PREPARATIONS
MANIFOLDS: Pipe, Fabricated From Purchased Pipe
MANPOWER TRAINING
MANUFACTURING INDUSTRIES, NEC
MAPS
MARBLE BOARD
MARBLE, BUILDING: Cut & Shaped
MARBLE: Dimension
MARINAS
MARINE CARGO HANDLING SVCS
MARINE CARGO HANDLING SVCS: Marine Terminal
MARINE HARDWARE
MARINE RELATED EQPT
MARINE SPLY DEALERS
MARINE SPLYS WHOLESALERS
MARKING DEVICES
MARKING DEVICES: Date Stamps, Hand, Rubber Or Metal
MARKING DEVICES: Embossing Seals & Hand Stamps
MARKING DEVICES: Irons, Marking Or Branding
MARKING DEVICES: Pads, Inking & Stamping
MARKING DEVICES: Printing Dies, Marking Mach, Rubber/Plastic
MARKING DEVICES: Textile Making Stamps, Hand, Rubber/Metal
MASQUERADE OR THEATRICAL COSTUMES STORES
MASSAGE THERAPIST
MASTIC ROOFING COMPOSITION
MASTS: Cast Aluminum
MATERIAL GRINDING & PULVERIZING SVCS NEC
MATERIALS HANDLING EQPT WHOLESALERS
MATS OR MATTING, NEC: Rubber
MATS, MATTING & PADS: Bathmats & Sets, Textile
MATTRESS STORES
MEAT & FISH MARKETS: Fish
MEAT & FISH MARKETS: Food & Freezer Plans, Meat
MEAT & MEAT PRDTS WHOLESALERS
MEAT CUTTING & PACKING
MEAT MARKETS
MEAT PRDTS: Bologna, From Purchased Meat
MEAT PRDTS: Prepared Beef Prdts From Purchased Beef
MEAT PRDTS: Sausages & Related Prdts, From Purchased Meat
MEAT PRDTS: Sausages, From Purchased Meat
MEAT PRDTS: Snack Sticks, Incl Jerky, From Purchased Meat
MEAT PROCESSED FROM PURCHASED CARCASSES
MECHANISMS: Coin-Operated Machines
MEDIA BUYING AGENCIES
MEDIA: Magnetic & Optical Recording
MEDICAL & HOSPITAL EQPT WHOLESALERS
MEDICAL & SURGICAL SPLYS: Bandages & Dressings
MEDICAL & SURGICAL SPLYS: Clothing, Fire Resistant & Protect
MEDICAL & SURGICAL SPLYS: Cosmetic Restorations
MEDICAL & SURGICAL SPLYS: Crutches & Walkers
MEDICAL & SURGICAL SPLYS: Dressings, Surgical
MEDICAL & SURGICAL SPLYS: Ear Plugs
MEDICAL & SURGICAL SPLYS: Grafts, Artificial
MEDICAL & SURGICAL SPLYS: Gynecological Splys & Appliances
MEDICAL & SURGICAL SPLYS: Ligatures
MEDICAL & SURGICAL SPLYS: Limbs, Artificial
MEDICAL & SURGICAL SPLYS: Orthopedic Appliances
MEDICAL & SURGICAL SPLYS: Personal Safety Eqpt
MEDICAL & SURGICAL SPLYS: Prosthetic Appliances
MEDICAL & SURGICAL SPLYS: Respiratory Protect Eqpt, Personal
MEDICAL & SURGICAL SPLYS: Stretchers
MEDICAL & SURGICAL SPLYS: Tape, Adhesive, Non/Medicated
MEDICAL & SURGICAL SPLYS: Technical Aids, Handicapped
MEDICAL & SURGICAL SPLYS: Welders' Hoods
MEDICAL EQPT: Cardiographs
MEDICAL EQPT: Defibrillators
MEDICAL EQPT: Diagnostic
MEDICAL EQPT: Electromedical Apparatus
MEDICAL EQPT: Electrotherapeutic Apparatus
MEDICAL EQPT: Laser Systems
MEDICAL EQPT: MRI/Magnetic Resonance Imaging Devs, Nuclear
MEDICAL EQPT: Pacemakers

PRODUCT INDEX

MEDICAL EQPT: Patient Monitoring
MEDICAL EQPT: Ultrasonic Scanning Devices
MEDICAL EQPT: Ultrasonic, Exc Cleaning
MEDICAL EQPT: X-Ray Apparatus & Tubes, Radiographic
MEDICAL FIELD ASSOCIATION
MEDICAL HELP SVCS
MEDICAL PHOTOGRAPHY & ART SVCS
MEDICAL SVCS ORGANIZATION
MEDICAL X-RAY MACHINES & TUBES WHOLESALERS
MEDICAL, DENTAL & HOSPITAL EQPT, WHOL: Hospital Eqpt & Splys
MEDICAL, DENTAL & HOSPITAL EQPT, WHOL: Hosptl Eqpt/Furniture
MEDICAL, DENTAL & HOSPITAL EQPT, WHOL: Surgical Eqpt & Splys
MEDICAL, DENTAL & HOSPITAL EQPT, WHOLESALE: Med Eqpt & Splys
MEDICAL, DENTAL & HOSPITAL EQPT, WHOLESALE: Medical Lab
MEDICAL, DENTAL & HOSPITAL EQPT, WHOLESALE: Orthopedic
MEMBERSHIP ORGANIZATIONS, NEC: Charitable
MEMBERSHIP ORGANIZATIONS, PROFESSIONAL: Accounting Assoc
MEMBERSHIP ORGANIZATIONS, REL: Churches, Temples & Shrines
MEMBERSHIP ORGANIZATIONS, RELIGIOUS: Assembly Of God Church
MEMBERSHIP ORGS, BUSINESS: Growers' Marketing Advisory Svc
MEMBERSHIP SPORTS & RECREATION CLUBS
MEMORIALS, MONUMENTS & MARKERS
MEN'S & BOYS' HATS STORES
MEN'S & BOYS' SPORTSWEAR WHOLESALERS
MEN'S CLOTHING STORES: Everyday, Exc Suits & Sportswear
METAL COMPONENTS: Prefabricated
METAL CUTTING SVCS
METAL DETECTORS
METAL FABRICATORS: Architechtural
METAL FABRICATORS: Plate
METAL FABRICATORS: Sheet
METAL FABRICATORS: Structural, Ship
METAL FINISHING SVCS
METAL MINING SVCS
METAL RESHAPING & REPLATING SVCS
METAL SERVICE CENTERS & OFFICES
METAL SLITTING & SHEARING
METAL SPINNING FOR THE TRADE
METAL STAMPING, FOR THE TRADE
METAL STAMPINGS: Perforated
METAL TREATING COMPOUNDS
METALS SVC CENTERS & WHOL: Structural Shapes, Iron Or Steel
METALS SVC CENTERS & WHOLESALERS: Bars, Metal
METALS SVC CENTERS & WHOLESALERS: Cable, Wire
METALS SVC CENTERS & WHOLESALERS: Nonferrous Sheets, Etc
METALS SVC CENTERS & WHOLESALERS: Pipe & Tubing, Steel
METALS SVC CENTERS & WHOLESALERS: Reinforcement Mesh, Wire
METALS SVC CENTERS & WHOLESALERS: Rope, Wire, Exc Insulated
METALS SVC CENTERS & WHOLESALERS: Sheets, Metal
METALS SVC CENTERS & WHOLESALERS: Stampings, Metal
METALS SVC CENTERS & WHOLESALERS: Steel
METALS SVC CENTERS & WHOLESALERS: Strip, Metal
METALS SVC CNTRS & WHOL: Metal Wires, Ties, Cables/Screening
METALS SVC CTRS & WHOLESALERS: Aluminum Bars, Rods, Etc
METALS: Honeycombed
METALS: Precious NEC
METALS: Precious, Secondary
METALS: Primary Nonferrous, NEC
METALWORK: Miscellaneous
METALWORK: Ornamental
METERING DEVICES: Measuring, Mechanical
METERING DEVICES: Water Quality Monitoring & Control Systems
METERS: Liquid
METERS: Turbine Flow, Indl Process

MGMT CONSULTING SVCS: Matls, Incl Purch, Handle & Invntry
MICA PRDTS
MICROCIRCUITS, INTEGRATED: Semiconductor
MICROPHONES
MICROPROCESSORS
MICROSCOPES
MICROSCOPES: Electron & Proton
MICROWAVE COMPONENTS
MILITARY GOODS & REGALIA STORES
MILITARY INSIGNIA, TEXTILE
MILL PRDTS: Structural & Rail
MILLING: Chemical
MILLING: Corn Grits & Flakes, For Brewers' Use
MILLWORK
MINE & QUARRY SVCS: Nonmetallic Minerals
MINERAL WOOL
MINERALS: Ground Or Otherwise Treated
MINERALS: Ground or Treated
MINING EXPLORATION & DEVELOPMENT SVCS
MINING MACHINES & EQPT: Sedimentation, Mineral
MINING SVCS, NEC: Bituminous
MIXTURES & BLOCKS: Asphalt Paving
MOBILE COMMUNICATIONS EQPT
MOBILE HOMES
MOBILE HOMES: Indl Or Commercial Use
MODELS
MODELS: Airplane, Exc Toy
MODELS: General, Exc Toy
MODULES: Solid State
MOLDED RUBBER PRDTS
MOLDING COMPOUNDS
MOLDINGS & TRIM: Metal, Exc Automobile
MOLDINGS & TRIM: Wood
MOLDINGS OR TRIM: Automobile, Stamped Metal
MOLDINGS, ARCHITECTURAL: Plaster Of Paris
MOLDINGS: Picture Frame
MOLDS: Indl
MOLDS: Plastic Working & Foundry
MONUMENTS & GRAVE MARKERS, EXC TERRAZZO
MORTAR: High Temperature, Nonclay
MOTION PICTURE & VIDEO PRODUCTION SVCS
MOTION PICTURE & VIDEO PRODUCTION SVCS: Indl
MOTION PICTURE EQPT
MOTOR HOMES
MOTOR REBUILDING SVCS, EXC AUTOMOTIVE
MOTOR REPAIR SVCS
MOTOR VEHICLE ASSEMBLY, COMPLETE: Autos, Incl Specialty
MOTOR VEHICLE ASSEMBLY, COMPLETE: Buses, All Types
MOTOR VEHICLE ASSEMBLY, COMPLETE: Cars, Armored
MOTOR VEHICLE ASSEMBLY, COMPLETE: Fire Department Vehicles
MOTOR VEHICLE ASSEMBLY, COMPLETE: Military Motor Vehicle
MOTOR VEHICLE ASSEMBLY, COMPLETE: Patrol Wagons
MOTOR VEHICLE ASSEMBLY, COMPLETE: Road Oilers
MOTOR VEHICLE ASSEMBLY, COMPLETE: Snow Plows
MOTOR VEHICLE DEALERS: Automobiles, New & Used
MOTOR VEHICLE PARTS & ACCESS: Bearings
MOTOR VEHICLE PARTS & ACCESS: Body Components & Frames
MOTOR VEHICLE PARTS & ACCESS: Electrical Eqpt
MOTOR VEHICLE PARTS & ACCESS: Engines & Parts
MOTOR VEHICLE PARTS & ACCESS: Engs & Trans,Factory, Rebuilt
MOTOR VEHICLE PARTS & ACCESS: Fifth Wheels
MOTOR VEHICLE PARTS & ACCESS: Fuel Pumps
MOTOR VEHICLE PARTS & ACCESS: Fuel Systems & Parts
MOTOR VEHICLE PARTS & ACCESS: Horns
MOTOR VEHICLE PARTS & ACCESS: Lifting Mechanisms, Dump Truck
MOTOR VEHICLE PARTS & ACCESS: Lubrication Systems & Parts
MOTOR VEHICLE PARTS & ACCESS: Oil Strainers
MOTOR VEHICLE PARTS & ACCESS: Tie Rods
MOTOR VEHICLE PARTS & ACCESS: Tops
MOTOR VEHICLE PARTS & ACCESS: Transmission Housings Or Parts
MOTOR VEHICLE PARTS & ACCESS: Transmissions
MOTOR VEHICLE SPLYS & PARTS WHOLESALERS: New
MOTOR VEHICLE: Hardware
MOTOR VEHICLES & CAR BODIES
MOTOR VEHICLES, WHOLESALE: Commercial
MOTOR VEHICLES, WHOLESALE: Motorized Cycles

MOTOR VEHICLES, WHOLESALE: Truck bodies
MOTORCYCLE ACCESS
MOTORCYCLE DEALERS
MOTORCYCLE DEALERS
MOTORCYCLE PARTS & ACCESS DEALERS
MOTORCYCLE REPAIR SHOPS
MOTORCYCLES & RELATED PARTS
MOTORS: Electric
MOTORS: Generators
MOTORS: Pneumatic
MOTORS: Torque
MOUNTING SVC: Map
MOUTHPIECES, PIPE & CIGARETTE HOLDERS: Rubber
MOVING SVC: Local
MULTIPLEXERS: Telephone & Telegraph
MUSIC ARRANGING & COMPOSING SVCS
MUSIC DISTRIBUTION APPARATUS
MUSIC RECORDING PRODUCER
MUSIC SCHOOLS
MUSIC VIDEO PRODUCTION SVCS
MUSICAL INSTRUMENT PARTS & ACCESS, WHOLESALE
MUSICAL INSTRUMENTS & ACCESS: NEC
MUSICAL INSTRUMENTS & ACCESS: Pipe Organs
MUSICAL INSTRUMENTS & SPLYS STORES
MUSICAL INSTRUMENTS & SPLYS STORES: String instruments
MUSICAL INSTRUMENTS: Flutes & Parts
MUSICAL INSTRUMENTS: Guitars & Parts, Electric & Acoustic
MUSICAL INSTRUMENTS: Harmonicas
MUSICAL INSTRUMENTS: Harpsichords
MUSICAL INSTRUMENTS: Ocarinas
MUSICAL INSTRUMENTS: Organs
MUSICAL INSTRUMENTS: Recorders, Musical
MUSICAL INSTRUMENTS: Trombones & Parts
MUSICAL INSTRUMENTS: Violins & Parts
MUTUAL ACCIDENT & HEALTH ASSOCIATIONS

N

NAILS: Steel, Wire Or Cut
NAME PLATES: Engraved Or Etched
NAMEPLATES
NATURAL GAS LIQUIDS PRODUCTION
NATURAL GAS PRODUCTION
NATURAL GAS TRANSMISSION & DISTRIBUTION
NATURAL PROPANE PRODUCTION
NATURAL RESOURCE PRESERVATION SVCS
NAUTICAL REPAIR SVCS
NAVIGATIONAL SYSTEMS & INSTRUMENTS
NEEDLES
NETTING: Cargo
NETTING: Plastic
NICKEL ALLOY
NIPPLES: Rubber
NONCURRENT CARRYING WIRING DEVICES
NONDURABLE GOODS WHOLESALERS, NEC
NONFERROUS: Rolling & Drawing, NEC
NONMETALLIC MINERALS: Support Activities, Exc Fuels
NOVELTIES
NOVELTIES, DURABLE, WHOLESALE
NOVELTIES: Plastic
NOVELTY SHOPS
NOZZLES & SPRINKLERS Lawn Hose
NUCLEAR REACTORS: Military Or Indl
NURSERIES & LAWN & GARDEN SPLY STORES, RETAIL: Top Soil
NURSERIES & LAWN/GARDEN SPLY STORE, RET: Lawnmowers/Tractors
NURSERIES & LAWN/GARDEN SPLY STORES, RET: Garden Splys/Tools
NURSERY & GARDEN CENTERS
NURSERY STOCK, WHOLESALE
NUTS: Metal
NYLON FIBERS

O

OFFICE EQPT WHOLESALERS
OFFICE FIXTURES: Wood
OFFICE HELP SPLY SVCS
OFFICE MACHINES, NEC
OFFICE SPLY & STATIONERY STORES
OFFICE SPLY & STATIONERY STORES: Office Forms & Splys
OFFICE SPLYS, NEC, WHOLESALE
OFFICES & CLINICS OF DENTISTS: Dental Clinic

PRODUCT INDEX

OFFICES & CLINICS OF DENTISTS: Dental Clinics & Offices
OFFICES & CLINICS OF DOCTORS OF MEDICINE: Ophthalmologist
OFFICES & CLINICS OF DOCTORS OF MEDICINE: Pediatrician
OFFICES & CLINICS OF DOCTORS OF MEDICINE: Radiologist
OFFICES & CLINICS OF DRS OF MED: Clinic, Op by Physicians
OFFICES & CLINICS OF HEALTH PRACTITIONERS: Physical Therapy
OIL & GAS FIELD MACHINERY
OIL FIELD MACHINERY & EQPT
OIL FIELD SVCS, NEC
OILS & GREASES: Lubricating
OILS: Cutting
OILS: Lubricating
OILS: Lubricating
OPERATOR: Nonresidential Buildings
OPHTHALMIC GOODS
OPHTHALMIC GOODS WHOLESALERS
OPHTHALMIC GOODS, NEC, WHOLESALE: Contact Lenses
OPHTHALMIC GOODS: Lenses, Intraocular
OPHTHALMIC GOODS: Lenses, Ophthalmic
OPHTHALMIC GOODS: Protectors, Eye
OPTICAL GOODS STORES
OPTICAL GOODS STORES: Contact Lenses, Prescription
OPTICAL GOODS STORES: Opticians
OPTICAL INSTRUMENT REPAIR SVCS
OPTICAL INSTRUMENTS & APPARATUS
OPTICAL INSTRUMENTS & LENSES
OPTICAL SCANNING SVCS
OPTOMETRISTS' OFFICES
ORAL PREPARATIONS
ORDNANCE
ORDNANCE: Flame Throwers
ORGANIZATIONS: Biotechnical Research, Noncommercial
ORGANIZATIONS: Medical Research
ORGANIZATIONS: Physical Research, Noncommercial
ORGANIZATIONS: Professional
ORGANIZATIONS: Religious
ORGANIZERS, CLOSET & DRAWER Plastic
ORNAMENTS: Christmas Tree, Exc Electrical & Glass
OUTBOARD MOTOR DEALERS
OUTBOARD MOTORS: Electric
OUTREACH PROGRAM

P

PACKAGE DESIGN SVCS
PACKAGING & LABELING SVCS
PACKAGING MATERIALS, WHOLESALE
PACKAGING MATERIALS: Paper
PACKAGING MATERIALS: Paper, Coated Or Laminated
PACKAGING MATERIALS: Plastic Film, Coated Or Laminated
PACKAGING MATERIALS: Polystyrene Foam
PACKAGING: Blister Or Bubble Formed, Plastic
PACKING MATERIALS: Mechanical
PACKING SVCS: Shipping
PAINT & PAINTING SPLYS STORE
PAINT STORE
PAINTING SVC: Metal Prdts
PAINTING: Hand, Textiles
PAINTS & ADDITIVES
PAINTS & ALLIED PRODUCTS
PAINTS, VARNISHES & SPLYS, WHOLESALE: Paints
PAINTS: Lead-In-Oil
PAINTS: Waterproof
PALLETS
PALLETS & SKIDS: Wood
PALLETS: Wooden
PANELS: Building, Plastic, NEC
PANELS: Electric Metering
PAPER & BOARD: Die-cut
PAPER CONVERTING
PAPER MANUFACTURERS: Exc Newsprint
PAPER PRDTS
PAPER PRDTS: Feminine Hygiene Prdts
PAPER PRDTS: Infant & Baby Prdts
PAPER PRDTS: Sanitary
PAPER PRDTS: Sanitary Tissue Paper
PAPER PRDTS: Tampons, Sanitary, Made From Purchased Material
PAPER PRDTS: Towels, Napkins/Tissue Paper, From Purchd Mtrls
PAPER PRDTS: Wrappers, Blank, Made From Purchased Materials
PAPER: Adhesive
PAPER: Bristols
PAPER: Building, Insulating & Packaging
PAPER: Card
PAPER: Cigarette
PAPER: Coated & Laminated, NEC
PAPER: Corrugated
PAPER: Cover
PAPER: Greeting Card
PAPER: Insulation Siding
PAPER: Kraft
PAPER: Newsprint
PAPER: Packaging
PAPER: Poster & Art
PAPER: Printer
PAPER: Specialty
PAPER: Specialty Or Chemically Treated
PAPER: Wallpaper
PAPER: Writing
PAPERBOARD
PAPERBOARD CONVERTING
PAPERBOARD PRDTS: Automobile Board
PAPERBOARD PRDTS: Container Board
PAPERBOARD PRDTS: Folding Boxboard
PAPERBOARD PRDTS: Packaging Board
PAPERBOARD: Boxboard
PAPERBOARD: Corrugated
PARACHUTES
PARTICLEBOARD
PARTITIONS & FIXTURES: Except Wood
PARTITIONS WHOLESALERS
PARTITIONS: Metal, Ornamental
PARTITIONS: Nonwood, Floor Attached
PARTITIONS: Wood & Fixtures
PARTS: Metal
PARTY & SPECIAL EVENT PLANNING SVCS
PATENT OWNERS & LESSORS
PATIENT MONITORING EQPT WHOLESALERS
PATTERNS: Indl
PAVERS
PAVING MATERIALS: Prefabricated, Concrete
PENCILS & PENS WHOLESALERS
PENS & PARTS: Ball Point
PENS & PENCILS: Mechanical, NEC
PENS: Meter
PERFORMANCE RIGHTS, PUBLISHING & LICENSING
PERFUME: Concentrated
PERFUME: Perfumes, Natural Or Synthetic
PERFUMES
PERSONAL DOCUMENT & INFORMATION SVCS
PEST CONTROL IN STRUCTURES SVCS
PET COLLARS, LEASHES, MUZZLES & HARNESSES: Leather
PET FOOD WHOLESALERS
PET SPLYS
PETROLEUM & PETROLEUM PRDTS, WHOLESALE Crude Oil
PETROLEUM & PETROLEUM PRDTS, WHOLESALE Fuel Oil
PETROLEUM & PETROLEUM PRDTS, WHOLESALE: Bulk Stations
PEWTER WARE
PHARMACEUTICAL PREPARATIONS: Druggists' Preparations
PHARMACEUTICAL PREPARATIONS: Medicines, Capsule Or Ampule
PHARMACEUTICAL PREPARATIONS: Pills
PHARMACEUTICAL PREPARATIONS: Powders
PHARMACEUTICAL PREPARATIONS: Proprietary Drug PRDTS
PHARMACEUTICAL PREPARATIONS: Solutions
PHARMACEUTICAL PREPARATIONS: Tablets
PHARMACEUTICALS
PHARMACEUTICALS: Medicinal & Botanical Prdts
PHONOGRAPH RECORDS: Prerecorded
PHOTOCOPY MACHINES
PHOTOCOPYING & DUPLICATING SVCS
PHOTOFINISHING LABORATORIES
PHOTOGRAPH DEVELOPING & RETOUCHING SVCS
PHOTOGRAPH ENLARGING SVCS
PHOTOGRAPHIC EQPT & SPLYS
PHOTOGRAPHIC EQPT & SPLYS WHOLESALERS
PHOTOGRAPHIC EQPT & SPLYS, WHOLESALE: Printing Apparatus
PHOTOGRAPHIC EQPT & SPLYS: Cameras, Aerial
PHOTOGRAPHIC EQPT & SPLYS: Enlargers
PHOTOGRAPHIC EQPT & SPLYS: Graphic Arts Plates, Sensitized
PHOTOGRAPHIC EQPT & SPLYS: Lantern Slide Plates, Sensitized
PHOTOGRAPHIC EQPT & SPLYS: Stands, Camera & Projector
PHOTOGRAPHIC EQPT & SPLYS: Toners, Prprd, Not Chem Plnts
PHOTOGRAPHIC EQPT & SPLYS: X-Ray Film
PHOTOGRAPHIC PEOCESSING CHEMICALS
PHOTOGRAPHY SVCS: Commercial
PHOTOGRAPHY SVCS: Home
PHOTOGRAPHY SVCS: Still Or Video
PHOTOGRAPHY: Aerial
PHOTOTYPESETTING SVC
PHOTOVOLTAIC Solid State
PICTURE FRAMES: Metal
PICTURE FRAMES: Wood
PICTURE FRAMING SVCS, CUSTOM
PIECE GOODS, NOTIONS & DRY GOODS, WHOLESALE: Sewing Access
PIECE GOODS, NOTIONS & OTHER DRY GOODS, WHOL: Flags/Banners
PIECE GOODS, NOTIONS & OTHER DRY GOODS, WHOLESALE: Fabrics
PIECE GOODS, NOTIONS/DRY GOODS, WHOL: Fabrics, Synthetic
PIECE GOODS, NOTIONS/DRY GOODS, WHOL: Linen Piece, Woven
PINS
PINS: Dowel
PIPE & FITTING: Fabrication
PIPE & FITTINGS: Cast Iron
PIPE CLEANERS
PIPE FITTINGS: Plastic
PIPE: Concrete
PIPE: Plastic
PIPE: Sheet Metal
PIPES & TUBES: Steel
PISTONS & PISTON RINGS
PLANT HORMONES
PLAQUES: Picture, Laminated
PLASMAS
PLASTER WORK: Ornamental & Architectural
PLASTER, ACOUSTICAL: Gypsum
PLASTIC COLORING & FINISHING
PLASTIC PRDTS
PLASTICIZERS, ORGANIC: Cyclic & Acyclic
PLASTICS FILM & SHEET
PLASTICS FILM & SHEET: Polyethylene
PLASTICS FILM & SHEET: Vinyl
PLASTICS FINISHED PRDTS: Laminated
PLASTICS FOAM, WHOLESALE
PLASTICS MATERIAL & RESINS
PLASTICS MATERIALS, BASIC FORMS & SHAPES WHOLESALERS
PLASTICS PROCESSING
PLASTICS: Blow Molded
PLASTICS: Extruded
PLASTICS: Finished Injection Molded
PLASTICS: Injection Molded
PLASTICS: Molded
PLASTICS: Polystyrene Foam
PLASTICS: Thermoformed
PLATEMAKING SVC: Color Separations, For The Printing Trade
PLATEMAKING SVC: Gravure, Plates Or Cylinders
PLATES
PLATFORMS: Cargo
PLATING & FINISHING SVC: Decorative, Formed Prdts
PLATING & POLISHING SVC
PLATING COMPOUNDS
PLATING SVC: Chromium, Metals Or Formed Prdts
PLATING SVC: Electro
PLATING SVC: Gold
PLATING SVC: NEC
PLAYGROUND EQPT
PLEATING & STITCHING FOR THE TRADE: Appliqueing
PLEATING & STITCHING FOR THE TRADE: Decorative & Novelty
PLEATING & STITCHING FOR THE TRADE: Eyelets

PRODUCT INDEX

PLEATING & STITCHING FOR THE TRADE: Lace, Burnt-Out
PLEATING & STITCHING SVC
PLUGS: Drain, Magnetic, Metal
PLUMBING & HEATING EQPT & SPLY, WHOL: Htg Eqpt/Panels, Solar
PLUMBING & HEATING EQPT & SPLYS WHOLESALERS
PLUMBING & HEATING EQPT & SPLYS, WHOL: Pipe/Fitting, Plastic
PLUMBING & HEATING EQPT & SPLYS, WHOL: Plumbing Fitting/Sply
PLUMBING & HEATING EQPT & SPLYS, WHOL: Water Purif Eqpt
PLUMBING & HEATING EQPT & SPLYS, WHOLESALE: Brass/Fittings
PLUMBING & HEATING EQPT & SPLYS, WHOLESALE: Oil Burners
PLUMBING & HEATING EQPT & SPLYS, WHOLESALE: Pwr Indl Boiler
PLUMBING FIXTURES
PLUMBING FIXTURES: Brass, Incl Drain Cocks, Faucets/Spigots
PLUMBING FIXTURES: Plastic
POINT OF SALE DEVICES
POLES & POSTS: Concrete
POLISHING SVC: Metals Or Formed Prdts
POLYCARBONATE RESINS
POLYETHYLENE RESINS
POLYSTYRENE RESINS
POLYVINYL CHLORIDE RESINS
PORCELAIN ENAMELED PRDTS & UTENSILS
POTTERY
POTTING SOILS
POULTRY & SMALL GAME SLAUGHTERING & PROCESSING
POWDER: Iron
POWDER: Metal
POWER GENERATORS
POWER SPLY CONVERTERS: Static, Electronic Applications
POWER SUPPLIES: All Types, Static
POWER TOOL REPAIR SVCS
POWER TOOLS, HAND: Cartridge-Activated
POWER TOOLS, HAND: Drill Attachments, Portable
POWER TOOLS, HAND: Drills & Drilling Tools
POWER TRANSMISSION EQPT: Mechanical
POWER TRANSMISSION EQPT: Vehicle
PRECAST TERRAZZO OR CONCRETE PRDTS
PRECIOUS METALS WHOLESALERS
PRECIOUS STONES WHOLESALERS
PRECISION INSTRUMENT REPAIR SVCS
PREFABRICATED BUILDING DEALERS
PRESSURE COOKERS: Stamped Or Drawn Metal
PRESTRESSED CONCRETE PRDTS
PRIMARY METAL PRODUCTS
PRINT CARTRIDGES: Laser & Other Computer Printers
PRINTED CIRCUIT BOARDS
PRINTERS & PLOTTERS
PRINTERS' SVCS: Folding, Collating, Etc
PRINTERS: Computer
PRINTERS: Magnetic Ink, Bar Code
PRINTING & BINDING: Books
PRINTING & BINDING: Textbooks
PRINTING & ENGRAVING: Card, Exc Greeting
PRINTING & ENGRAVING: Financial Notes & Certificates
PRINTING & ENGRAVING: Invitation & Stationery
PRINTING & ENGRAVING: Poster & Decal
PRINTING & STAMPING: Fabric Articles
PRINTING & WRITING PAPER WHOLESALERS
PRINTING INKS WHOLESALERS
PRINTING MACHINERY
PRINTING MACHINERY, EQPT & SPLYS: Wholesalers
PRINTING, COMMERCIAL: Business Forms, NEC
PRINTING, COMMERCIAL: Cards, Souvenir, NEC
PRINTING, COMMERCIAL: Cards, Visiting, Incl Business, NEC
PRINTING, COMMERCIAL: Envelopes, NEC
PRINTING, COMMERCIAL: Imprinting
PRINTING, COMMERCIAL: Invitations, NEC
PRINTING, COMMERCIAL: Labels & Seals, NEC
PRINTING, COMMERCIAL: Letterpress & Screen
PRINTING, COMMERCIAL: Literature, Advertising, NEC
PRINTING, COMMERCIAL: Magazines, NEC
PRINTING, COMMERCIAL: Periodicals, NEC
PRINTING, COMMERCIAL: Promotional
PRINTING, COMMERCIAL: Publications
PRINTING, COMMERCIAL: Screen

PRINTING, COMMERCIAL: Tags, NEC
PRINTING, COMMERCIAL: Wrappers, NEC
PRINTING, LITHOGRAPHIC: Calendars
PRINTING, LITHOGRAPHIC: Calendars & Cards
PRINTING, LITHOGRAPHIC: Forms, Business
PRINTING, LITHOGRAPHIC: Offset & photolithographic printing
PRINTING, LITHOGRAPHIC: Promotional
PRINTING, LITHOGRAPHIC: Publications
PRINTING: Book Music
PRINTING: Books
PRINTING: Commercial, NEC
PRINTING: Engraving & Plate
PRINTING: Flexographic
PRINTING: Gravure, Announcements
PRINTING: Gravure, Cards, Exc Greeting
PRINTING: Gravure, Catalogs, No Publishing On-Site
PRINTING: Gravure, Forms, Business
PRINTING: Gravure, Invitations
PRINTING: Gravure, Labels
PRINTING: Gravure, Rotogravure
PRINTING: Gravure, Stationery & Invitation
PRINTING: Laser
PRINTING: Letterpress
PRINTING: Lithographic
PRINTING: Manmade Fiber & Silk, Broadwoven Fabric
PRINTING: Offset
PRINTING: Photo-Offset
PRINTING: Screen, Broadwoven Fabrics, Cotton
PRINTING: Screen, Fabric
PRINTING: Screen, Manmade Fiber & Silk, Broadwoven Fabric
PRINTING: Thermography
PROFESSIONAL EQPT & SPLYS, WHOLESALE: Engineers', NEC
PROFESSIONAL EQPT & SPLYS, WHOLESALE: Optical Goods
PROFESSIONAL EQPT & SPLYS, WHOLESALE: Scientific & Engineerg
PROFESSIONAL INSTRUMENT REPAIR SVCS
PROFILE SHAPES: Unsupported Plastics
PROMOTION SVCS
PROPELLERS: Boat & Ship, Cast
PROPULSION UNITS: Guided Missiles & Space Vehicles
PROTECTION EQPT: Lightning
PUBLIC LIBRARY
PUBLIC RELATIONS SVCS
PUBLISHERS: Art Copy
PUBLISHERS: Art Copy & Poster
PUBLISHERS: Book
PUBLISHERS: Book Clubs, No Printing
PUBLISHERS: Books, No Printing
PUBLISHERS: Comic Books, No Printing
PUBLISHERS: Directories, NEC
PUBLISHERS: Guides
PUBLISHERS: Magazines, No Printing
PUBLISHERS: Maps
PUBLISHERS: Miscellaneous
PUBLISHERS: Music Book
PUBLISHERS: Music Book & Sheet Music
PUBLISHERS: Music, Sheet
PUBLISHERS: Newsletter
PUBLISHERS: Newspaper
PUBLISHERS: Newspapers, No Printing
PUBLISHERS: Pamphlets, No Printing
PUBLISHERS: Periodical, With Printing
PUBLISHERS: Periodicals, Magazines
PUBLISHERS: Periodicals, No Printing
PUBLISHERS: Racing Forms & Programs
PUBLISHERS: Sheet Music
PUBLISHERS: Technical Manuals
PUBLISHERS: Technical Manuals & Papers
PUBLISHERS: Telephone & Other Directory
PUBLISHERS: Textbooks, No Printing
PUBLISHERS: Trade journals, No Printing
PUBLISHING & BROADCASTING: Internet Only
PUBLISHING & PRINTING: Art Copy
PUBLISHING & PRINTING: Book Music
PUBLISHING & PRINTING: Books
PUBLISHING & PRINTING: Catalogs
PUBLISHING & PRINTING: Comic Books
PUBLISHING & PRINTING: Directories, NEC
PUBLISHING & PRINTING: Directories, Telephone
PUBLISHING & PRINTING: Guides
PUBLISHING & PRINTING: Magazines: publishing & printing

PUBLISHING & PRINTING: Newsletters, Business Svc
PUBLISHING & PRINTING: Newspapers
PUBLISHING & PRINTING: Pamphlets
PUBLISHING & PRINTING: Patterns, Paper
PUBLISHING & PRINTING: Shopping News
PUBLISHING & PRINTING: Technical Papers
PUBLISHING & PRINTING: Textbooks
PUBLISHING & PRINTING: Trade Journals
PULP MILLS
PUMPS
PUMPS & PARTS: Indl
PUMPS & PUMPING EQPT REPAIR SVCS
PUMPS & PUMPING EQPT WHOLESALERS
PUMPS: Domestic, Water Or Sump
PUMPS: Hydraulic Power Transfer
PUMPS: Measuring & Dispensing
PUMPS: Vacuum, Exc Laboratory
PUNCHES: Forming & Stamping
PUPPETS & MARIONETTES

Q

QUILTING SVC & SPLYS, FOR THE TRADE
QUILTING: Individuals

R

RACEWAYS
RACKS: Bicycle, Automotive
RACKS: Display
RADIATORS, EXC ELECTRIC
RADIO & TELEVISION COMMUNICATIONS EQUIPMENT
RADIO & TELEVISION REPAIR
RADIO BROADCASTING & COMMUNICATIONS EQPT
RADIO BROADCASTING STATIONS
RADIO EQPT: Citizens Band
RADIO REPAIR & INSTALLATION SVCS
RADIO REPAIR SHOP, NEC
RADIO, TELEVISION & CONSUMER ELECTRONICS STORES: Antennas
RADIO, TELEVISION & CONSUMER ELECTRONICS STORES: Eqpt, NEC
RADIO, TV/CONSUMER ELEC STORES: Antennas, Satellite Dish
RAILINGS: Prefabricated, Metal
RAILROAD CARGO LOADING & UNLOADING SVCS
RAILROAD EQPT
RAILROAD EQPT & SPLYS WHOLESALERS
RAILROAD EQPT: Brakes, Air & Vacuum
RAILROAD EQPT: Cars & Eqpt, Dining
RAILROAD EQPT: Cars & Eqpt, Interurban
RAILROAD EQPT: Cars & Eqpt, Train, Freight Or Passenger
RAILROAD RELATED EQPT: Ballast Distributors
RAILROAD RELATED EQPT: Laying Eqpt, Rail
RAILROAD TIES: Wood
RAILS: Steel Or Iron
RAZORS, RAZOR BLADES
REAL ESTATE AGENTS & MANAGERS
REAL ESTATE APPRAISERS
REAL ESTATE OPERATORS, EXC DEVELOPERS: Commercial/Indl Bldg
REAL ESTATE OPERATORS, EXC DEVELOPERS: Property, Retail
RECLAIMED RUBBER: Reworked By Manufacturing Process
RECORDERS: Sound
RECORDERS: Tape, Computer Data
RECORDS & TAPES: Prerecorded
RECORDS OR TAPES: Masters
RECOVERY SVC: Iron Ore, From Open Hearth Slag
RECREATIONAL CAMPS
RECREATIONAL VEHICLE PARTS & ACCESS STORES
RECREATIONAL VEHICLE REPAIRS
RECTIFIERS: Electronic, Exc Semiconductor
RECYCLING: Paper
REFINERS & SMELTERS: Copper
REFINERS & SMELTERS: Gold
REFINERS & SMELTERS: Lead, Secondary
REFINERS & SMELTERS: Nonferrous Metal
REFINERS & SMELTERS: Platinum Group Metals, Secondary
REFINING LUBRICATING OILS & GREASES, NEC
REFINING: Petroleum
REFRACTORIES: Brick
REFRACTORIES: Clay
REFRACTORIES: Nonclay
REFRIGERATION & HEATING EQUIPMENT
REFRIGERATION EQPT & SPLYS WHOLESALERS

PRODUCT INDEX

REFRIGERATION EQPT & SPLYS, WHOLESALE: Beverage Coolers
REFRIGERATION EQPT & SPLYS, WHOLESALE: Beverage Dispensers
REFRIGERATION EQPT: Complete
REFUSE SYSTEMS
REGULATORS: Line Voltage
REHABILITATION CENTER, OUTPATIENT TREATMENT
RELAYS: Electronic Usage
REMOVERS & CLEANERS
RENTAL SVCS: Aircraft
RENTAL SVCS: Beach & Water Sports Eqpt
RENTAL SVCS: Business Machine & Electronic Eqpt
RENTAL SVCS: Home Cleaning & Maintenance Eqpt
RENTAL SVCS: Recreational Vehicle
RENTAL SVCS: Saddle Horse
RENTAL SVCS: Tent & Tarpaulin
RENTAL SVCS: Video Disk/Tape, To The General Public
RENTAL: Video Tape & Disc
REPRODUCTION SVCS: Video Tape Or Disk
RESEARCH, DEVELOPMENT & TEST SVCS, COMM: Business Analysis
RESEARCH, DEVELOPMENT & TEST SVCS, COMM: Cmptr Hardware Dev
RESEARCH, DEVELOPMENT & TEST SVCS, COMM: Research, Exc Lab
RESEARCH, DEVELOPMENT & TESTING SVCS, COMM: Research Lab
RESEARCH, DEVELOPMENT & TESTING SVCS, COMMERCIAL: Business
RESEARCH, DEVELOPMENT & TESTING SVCS, COMMERCIAL: Education
RESEARCH, DEVELOPMENT & TESTING SVCS, COMMERCIAL: Energy
RESEARCH, DEVELOPMENT & TESTING SVCS, COMMERCIAL: Medical
RESEARCH, DEVELOPMENT & TESTING SVCS, COMMERCIAL: Physical
RESEARCH, DEVELOPMENT SVCS, COMMERCIAL: Indl Lab
RESEARCH, DVLPT & TEST SVCS, COMM: Mkt Analysis or Research
RESIDENTIAL REMODELERS
RESIDUES
RESINS: Custom Compound Purchased
RESISTORS
RESPIRATORY SYSTEM DRUGS
RESTAURANT EQPT: Carts
RESTAURANT EQPT: Food Wagons
RESTAURANTS: Delicatessen
RESTAURANTS:Full Svc, American
RESTAURANTS:Full Svc, Chinese
RESTAURANTS:Full Svc, Ethnic Food
RESTAURANTS:Full Svc, Family
RESTAURANTS:Full Svc, Italian
RESTAURANTS:Limited Svc, Coffee Shop
RESTAURANTS:Limited Svc, Ice Cream Stands Or Dairy Bars
RESTAURANTS:Ltd Svc, Ice Cream, Soft Drink/Fountain Stands
RETAIL BAKERY: Bread
RETAIL BAKERY: Cakes
RETAIL BAKERY: Doughnuts
RETAIL LUMBER YARDS
RETAIL STORES, NEC
RETAIL STORES: Architectural Splys
RETAIL STORES: Audio-Visual Eqpt & Splys
RETAIL STORES: Awnings
RETAIL STORES: Banners
RETAIL STORES: Canvas Prdts
RETAIL STORES: Concrete Prdts, Precast
RETAIL STORES: Cosmetics
RETAIL STORES: Educational Aids & Electronic Training Mat
RETAIL STORES: Electronic Parts & Eqpt
RETAIL STORES: Flags
RETAIL STORES: Hearing Aids
RETAIL STORES: Insecticides
RETAIL STORES: Mobile Telephones & Eqpt
RETAIL STORES: Monuments, Finished To Custom Order
RETAIL STORES: Motors, Electric
RETAIL STORES: Orthopedic & Prosthesis Applications
RETAIL STORES: Plumbing & Heating Splys
RETAIL STORES: Police Splys
RETAIL STORES: Rubber Stamps
RETAIL STORES: Safety Splys & Eqpt
RETAIL STORES: Telephone & Communication Eqpt
RETAIL STORES: Training Materials, Electronic
RETAIL STORES: Water Purification Eqpt
RETAIL STORES: Welding Splys
RETREADING MATERIALS: Tire
REUPHOLSTERY & FURNITURE REPAIR
REUPHOLSTERY SVCS
RIBBONS & BOWS
RIBBONS, NEC
RIDING APPAREL STORES
RIVETS: Metal
ROBOTS: Assembly Line
RODS: Plastic
RODS: Steel & Iron, Made In Steel Mills
RODS: Welding
ROLLERS: Wooden
ROLLING MILL EQPT: Rod Mills
ROLLING MILL MACHINERY
ROLLING MILL ROLLS: Cast Steel
ROLLS & ROLL COVERINGS: Rubber
ROLLS: Rubber, Solid Or Covered
ROOF DECKS
ROOFING MATERIALS: Asphalt
ROOFING MATERIALS: Sheet Metal
ROOFING MEMBRANE: Rubber
RUBBER PRDTS
RUBBER PRDTS: Mechanical
RUBBER PRDTS: Reclaimed
RUBBER PRDTS: Silicone
RUBBER PRDTS: Sponge
RUBBER STAMP, WHOLESALE
RUGS : Hand & Machine Made
RULES: Slide

S

SADDLERY STORES
SAFE DEPOSIT BOXES
SAFETY EQPT & SPLYS WHOLESALERS
SAILBOAT BUILDING & REPAIR
SAILS
SALES PROMOTION SVCS
SALT
SAND & GRAVEL
SAND MINING
SAND: Hygrade
SANDBLASTING EQPT
SANITARY SVCS: Dumps, Operation Of
SANITARY SVCS: Environmental Cleanup
SANITARY SVCS: Rubbish Collection & Disposal
SANITARY SVCS: Waste Materials, Recycling
SANITATION CHEMICALS & CLEANING AGENTS
SASHES: Door Or Window, Metal
SATCHELS
SATELLITE COMMUNICATIONS EQPT
SATELLITES: Communications
SAW BLADES
SAWDUST & SHAVINGS
SAWING & PLANING MILLS
SAWING & PLANING MILLS: Custom
SAWS & SAWING EQPT
SCAFFOLDS: Mobile Or Stationary, Metal
SCALE REPAIR SVCS
SCALES & BALANCES, EXC LABORATORY
SCALES: Indl
SCANNING DEVICES: Optical
SCHOOL SPLYS, EXC BOOKS: Wholesalers
SCIENTIFIC EQPT REPAIR SVCS
SCISSORS: Hand
SCRAP & WASTE MATERIALS, WHOLESALE: Auto Wrecking For Scrap
SCRAP & WASTE MATERIALS, WHOLESALE: Ferrous Metal
SCRAP & WASTE MATERIALS, WHOLESALE: Metal
SCRAP & WASTE MATERIALS, WHOLESALE: Paper
SCRAP STEEL CUTTING
SCREW MACHINE PRDTS
SCREW MACHINES
SCREWS: Metal
SCREWS: Wood
SEALANTS
SEALS: Hermetic
SEARCH & DETECTION SYSTEMS, EXC RADAR
SEARCH & NAVIGATION SYSTEMS
SEATING: Chairs, Table & Arm
SECRETARIAL & COURT REPORTING
SECRETARIAL SVCS
SECURE STORAGE SVC: Document
SECURITY CONTROL EQPT & SYSTEMS
SECURITY DEVICES
SECURITY DISTRIBUTORS
SECURITY EQPT STORES
SECURITY PROTECTIVE DEVICES MAINTENANCE & MONITORING SVCS
SECURITY SYSTEMS SERVICES
SEMICONDUCTOR CIRCUIT NETWORKS
SEMICONDUCTOR DEVICES: Wafers
SEMICONDUCTORS & RELATED DEVICES
SENSORS: Radiation
SENSORS: Temperature, Exc Indl Process
SEPTIC TANK CLEANING SVCS
SEPTIC TANKS: Concrete
SEWAGE & WATER TREATMENT EQPT
SEWER CLEANING & RODDING SVC
SEWING CONTRACTORS
SEWING MACHINE REPAIR SHOP
SEWING MACHINES & PARTS: Indl
SEWING, NEEDLEWORK & PIECE GOODS STORE: Needlework Gds/Sply
SEWING, NEEDLEWORK & PIECE GOODS STORES
SEWING, NEEDLEWORK & PIECE GOODS STORES: Knitting Splys
SEXTANTS
SHADES: Window
SHAFTS: Shaft Collars
SHAPES & PILINGS, STRUCTURAL: Steel
SHEET METAL SPECIALTIES, EXC STAMPED
SHEETS & STRIPS: Aluminum
SHELLAC
SHIMS: Metal
SHIP BLDG/RPRG: Submersible Marine Robots, Manned/Unmanned
SHIP BUILDING & REPAIRING: Cargo Vessels
SHIP BUILDING & REPAIRING: Cargo, Commercial
SHIP BUILDING & REPAIRING: Ferryboats
SHIP BUILDING & REPAIRING: Military
SHIP BUILDING & REPAIRING: Rigging, Marine
SHIP BUILDING & REPAIRING: Trawlers
SHIPBUILDING & REPAIR
SHOCK ABSORBERS: Indl
SHOE MATERIALS: Counters
SHOE MATERIALS: Quarters
SHOE MATERIALS: Rands
SHOE STORES
SHOE STORES: Children's
SHOE STORES: Custom & Orthopedic
SHOES: Athletic, Exc Rubber Or Plastic
SHOES: Men's
SHOES: Men's, Dress
SHOES: Men's, Work
SHOES: Orthopedic, Children's
SHOES: Orthopedic, Men's
SHOES: Orthopedic, Women's
SHOES: Plastic Or Rubber
SHOES: Women's
SHOES: Women's, Dress
SHOT PEENING SVC
SHOWER STALLS: Plastic & Fiberglass
SHUTTERS, DOOR & WINDOW: Metal
SIDING & STRUCTURAL MATERIALS: Wood
SIGN LETTERING & PAINTING SVCS
SIGN PAINTING & LETTERING SHOP
SIGNALING APPARATUS: Electric
SIGNALS: Traffic Control, Electric
SIGNALS: Transportation
SIGNS & ADVERTISING SPECIALTIES
SIGNS & ADVERTISING SPECIALTIES: Artwork, Advertising
SIGNS & ADVERTISING SPECIALTIES: Displays, Paint Process
SIGNS & ADVERTISING SPECIALTIES: Letters For Signs, Metal
SIGNS & ADVERTISING SPECIALTIES: Novelties
SIGNS & ADVERTISING SPECIALTIES: Signs
SIGNS & ADVERTSG SPECIALTIES: Displays/Cutouts Window/Lobby
SIGNS, ELECTRICAL: Wholesalers
SIGNS, EXC ELECTRIC, WHOLESALE
SIGNS: Electrical
SIGNS: Neon
SILICONE RESINS
SILICONES
SILK SCREEN DESIGN SVCS

PRODUCT INDEX

SILVERSMITHS
SILVERWARE
SILVERWARE & PLATED WARE
SILVERWARE, STERLING SILVER
SINK TOPS, PLASTIC LAMINATED
SINKS: Vitreous China
SIRENS: Vehicle, Marine, Indl & Warning
SKIN CARE PRDTS: Suntan Lotions & Oils
SKYLIGHTS
SLAB & TILE, ROOFING: Concrete
SLAUGHTERING & MEAT PACKING
SLINGS: Lifting, Made From Purchased Wire
SLINGS: Rope
SLIPCOVERS & PADS
SNOW PLOWING SVCS
SNOW REMOVAL EQPT: Residential
SOAPS & DETERGENTS
SOAPS & DETERGENTS: Textile
SOAPSTONE MINING
SOCIAL SVCS CENTER
SOCIAL SVCS, HANDICAPPED
SOCIAL SVCS: Individual & Family
SOCKETS: Electronic Tube
SODA ASH MINING: Natural
SODIUM CHLORIDE: Refined
SOFT DRINKS WHOLESALERS
SOFTWARE PUBLISHERS: Application
SOFTWARE PUBLISHERS: Business & Professional
SOFTWARE PUBLISHERS: Computer Utilities
SOFTWARE PUBLISHERS: Education
SOFTWARE PUBLISHERS: Home Entertainment
SOFTWARE PUBLISHERS: NEC
SOFTWARE PUBLISHERS: Operating Systems
SOFTWARE PUBLISHERS: Publisher's
SOFTWARE TRAINING, COMPUTER
SOLAR CELLS
SOLAR HEATING EQPT
SOLDERING EQPT: Electrical, Exc Handheld
SOLDERS
SOLENOIDS
SOLVENTS
SONAR SYSTEMS & EQPT
SOUND RECORDING STUDIOS
SPACE FLIGHT OPERATIONS, EXC GOVERNMENT
SPACE SUITS
SPACE VEHICLE EQPT
SPACE VEHICLES
SPAS
SPEAKER SYSTEMS
SPECIAL EVENTS DECORATION SVCS
SPECIALTY FOOD STORES: Coffee
SPECIALTY FOOD STORES: Food Gift Baskets
SPECIALTY FOOD STORES: Soft Drinks
SPEED CHANGERS
SPINDLES: Textile
SPONGES: Plastic
SPORTING & ATHLETIC GOODS: Arrows, Archery
SPORTING & ATHLETIC GOODS: Bobsleds
SPORTING & ATHLETIC GOODS: Boomerangs
SPORTING & ATHLETIC GOODS: Bowling Balls
SPORTING & ATHLETIC GOODS: Driving Ranges, Golf, Electronic
SPORTING & ATHLETIC GOODS: Dumbbells & Other Weight Eqpt
SPORTING & ATHLETIC GOODS: Fencing Eqpt
SPORTING & ATHLETIC GOODS: Fishing Eqpt
SPORTING & ATHLETIC GOODS: Gymnasium Eqpt
SPORTING & ATHLETIC GOODS: Hockey Eqpt & Splys, NEC
SPORTING & ATHLETIC GOODS: Pools, Swimming, Exc Plastic
SPORTING & ATHLETIC GOODS: Rods & Rod Parts, Fishing
SPORTING & ATHLETIC GOODS: Shafts, Golf Club
SPORTING & ATHLETIC GOODS: Shooting Eqpt & Splys, General
SPORTING & ATHLETIC GOODS: Skateboards
SPORTING & ATHLETIC GOODS: Snow Skiing Eqpt & Sply, Exc Skis
SPORTING & ATHLETIC GOODS: Snow Skis
SPORTING & ATHLETIC GOODS: Snowshoes
SPORTING & ATHLETIC GOODS: Soccer Eqpt & Splys
SPORTING & ATHLETIC GOODS: Targets, Archery & Rifle Shooting
SPORTING & ATHLETIC GOODS: Team Sports Eqpt
SPORTING & ATHLETIC GOODS: Tennis Eqpt & Splys
SPORTING & ATHLETIC GOODS: Track & Field Athletic Eqpt
SPORTING & ATHLETIC GOODS: Treadmills
SPORTING & ATHLETIC GOODS: Water Sports Eqpt
SPORTING & ATHLETIC GOODS: Winter Sports
SPORTING & REC GOODS, WHOLESALE: Camping Eqpt & Splys
SPORTING & RECREATIONAL GOODS & SPLYS WHOLESALERS
SPORTING & RECREATIONAL GOODS, WHOLESALE: Fishing Tackle
SPORTING & RECREATIONAL GOODS, WHOLESALE: Fitness
SPORTING & RECREATIONAL GOODS, WHOLESALE: Golf
SPORTING & RECREATIONAL GOODS, WHOLESALE: Watersports
SPORTING GOODS
SPORTING GOODS STORES, NEC
SPORTING GOODS STORES: Archery Splys
SPORTING GOODS STORES: Bait & Tackle
SPORTING GOODS STORES: Baseball Eqpt
SPORTING GOODS STORES: Firearms
SPORTING GOODS STORES: Skating Eqpt
SPORTING GOODS STORES: Skiing Eqpt
SPORTING GOODS STORES: Specialty Sport Splys, NEC
SPORTING GOODS STORES: Team sports Eqpt
SPORTING GOODS: Archery
SPORTING GOODS: Fishing Nets
SPORTS APPAREL STORES
SPORTS PROMOTION SVCS
SPRAYS: Artificial & Preserved
SPRINGS: Clock, Precision
SPRINGS: Coiled Flat
SPRINGS: Instrument, Precision
SPRINGS: Mechanical, Precision
SPRINGS: Precision
SPRINGS: Steel
SPRINGS: Wire
SPRINKLING SYSTEMS: Fire Control
STACKS: Smoke
STAGE LIGHTING SYSTEMS
STAINLESS STEEL
STAINLESS STEEL WARE
STAIRCASES & STAIRS, WOOD
STAMPINGS: Automotive
STAMPINGS: Metal
STATIONERY & OFFICE SPLYS WHOLESALERS
STATIONERY PRDTS
STATORS REWINDING SVCS
STEAM HEATING SYSTEMS SPLY SVCS
STEAM, HEAT & AIR CONDITIONING DISTRIBUTION SVC
STEEL & ALLOYS: Tool & Die
STEEL FABRICATORS
STEEL MILLS
STEEL, COLD-ROLLED: Sheet Or Strip, From Own Hot-Rolled
STEEL, COLD-ROLLED: Strip NEC, From Purchased Hot-Rolled
STEEL, COLD-ROLLED: Strip Or Wire
STEEL: Cold-Rolled
STEEL: Laminated
STEERING SYSTEMS & COMPONENTS
STENCILS
STENCILS & LETTERING MATERIALS: Die-Cut
STITCHING SVCS
STITCHING SVCS: Custom
STONE: Cast Concrete
STONE: Dimension, NEC
STONE: Quarrying & Processing, Own Stone Prdts
STONES, SYNTHETIC: Gem Stone & Indl Use
STONEWARE PRDTS: Pottery
STORE FIXTURES: Exc Wood
STORE FIXTURES: Wood
STORES: Auto & Home Supply
STORES: Drapery & Upholstery
STOVES: Wood & Coal Burning
STRAIN GAGES: Solid State
STRAINERS: Line, Piping Systems
STRAPPING
STRAPS: Beltings, Woven or Braided
STRIPS: Copper & Copper Alloy
STRUCTURAL SUPPORT & BUILDING MATERIAL: Concrete
STUCCO
STUDIOS: Artist
SUBMARINE BUILDING & REPAIR
SUBSCRIPTION FULFILLMENT SVCS: Magazine, Newspaper, Etc
SUITCASES
SUNROOMS: Prefabricated Metal
SUPERMARKETS & OTHER GROCERY STORES
SURFACE ACTIVE AGENTS
SURFACE ACTIVE AGENTS: Oils & Greases
SURFACE ACTIVE AGENTS: Processing Assistants
SURFACE ACTIVE AGENTS: Textile Processing Assistants
SURGICAL & MEDICAL INSTRUMENTS WHOLESALERS
SURGICAL APPLIANCES & SPLYS
SURGICAL APPLIANCES & SPLYS
SURGICAL EQPT: See Also Instruments
SURGICAL IMPLANTS
SVC ESTABLISHMENT EQPT & SPLYS WHOLESALERS
SVC ESTABLISHMENT EQPT, WHOL: Cleaning & Maint Eqpt & Splys
SVC ESTABLISHMENT EQPT, WHOLESALE: Beauty Parlor Eqpt & Sply
SVC ESTABLISHMENT EQPT, WHOLESALE: Shredders, Indl & Comm
SWAGE BLOCKS
SWITCHBOARDS & PARTS: Power
SWITCHES
SWITCHES: Electric Power
SWITCHES: Electric Power, Exc Snap, Push Button, Etc
SWITCHES: Electronic
SWITCHES: Electronic Applications
SWITCHES: Flow Actuated, Electrical
SWITCHES: Stepping
SWITCHES: Time, Electrical Switchgear Apparatus
SWITCHGEAR & SWITCHBOARD APPARATUS
SWITCHGEAR & SWITCHGEAR ACCESS, NEC
SYRUPS, DRINK
SYSTEMS ENGINEERING: Computer Related
SYSTEMS INTEGRATION SVCS
SYSTEMS INTEGRATION SVCS: Local Area Network
SYSTEMS INTEGRATION SVCS: Office Computer Automation
SYSTEMS SOFTWARE DEVELOPMENT SVCS

T

TABLE OR COUNTERTOPS, PLASTIC LAMINATED
TABLECLOTHS & SETTINGS
TABLETS & PADS: Book & Writing, Made From Purchased Material
TACKS: Nonferrous Metal Or Wire
TAGS & LABELS: Paper
TAILORS: Custom
TALC MINING
TANKS & OTHER TRACKED VEHICLE CMPNTS
TANKS: Concrete
TANKS: Fuel, Including Oil & Gas, Metal Plate
TANKS: Standard Or Custom Fabricated, Metal Plate
TANKS: Water, Metal Plate
TAPE MEASURES
TAPE: Rubber
TAPES, ADHESIVE: MedicaL
TAPES: Plastic Coated
TAPES: Pressure Sensitive
TAPES: Pressure Sensitive, Rubber
TAR
TAX RETURN PREPARATION SVCS
TELECOMMUNICATION EQPT REPAIR SVCS, EXC TELEPHONES
TELECOMMUNICATION SYSTEMS & EQPT
TELECOMMUNICATIONS CARRIERS & SVCS: Wired
TELECOMMUNICATIONS CARRIERS & SVCS: Wireless
TELEPHONE EQPT: Modems
TELEPHONE EQPT: NEC
TELEPHONE EQPT: PBX, Manual & Automatic
TELEPHONE SET REPAIR SVCS
TELEPHONE SVCS
TELEPHONE: Fiber Optic Systems
TELEVISION BROADCASTING & COMMUNICATIONS EQPT
TELEVISION FILM PRODUCTION SVCS
TENTS: All Materials
TERRAZZO PRECAST PRDTS
TEST BORING SVCS: Nonmetallic Minerals
TEST KITS: Pregnancy
TESTERS: Battery
TESTERS: Environmental
TESTERS: Gas, Exc Indl Process
TESTERS: Spark Plug
TEXTILE DESIGNERS
TEXTILE FABRICATORS

PRODUCT INDEX

TEXTILE FINISHING: Chem Coat/Treat, Man, Broadwoven, Cotton
TEXTILE FINISHING: Dyeing, Finishing & Printng, Linen Fabric
TEXTILE PRDTS: Hand Woven & Crocheted
TEXTILE: Finishing, Raw Stock NEC
TEXTILES
TEXTILES: Crash, Linen
TEXTILES: Fibers, Textile, Rcvrd From Mill Waste/Rags
TEXTILES: Flock
TEXTILES: Jute & Flax Prdts
TEXTILES: Mill Waste & Remnant
THEATRICAL PRODUCERS & SVCS
THEATRICAL SCENERY
THERMOCOUPLES
THERMOCOUPLES: Indl Process
THERMOMETERS: Medical, Digital
THERMOPLASTIC MATERIALS
THERMOSETTING MATERIALS
THIN FILM CIRCUITS
THREAD: All Fibers
THREAD: Embroidery
TIES, FORM: Metal
TILE: Brick & Structural, Clay
TILE: Clay, Drain & Structural
TILE: Fireproofing, Clay
TILE: Precast Terrazzo, Floor
TILE: Stamped Metal, Floor Or Wall
TILE: Terrazzo Or Concrete, Precast
TILE: Wall & Floor, Ceramic
TIMERS: Indl, Clockwork Mechanism Only
TIMING DEVICES: Cycle & Program Controllers
TIMING DEVICES: Electronic
TINPLATE
TIRE & INNER TUBE MATERIALS & RELATED PRDTS
TIRE CORD & FABRIC
TIRE DEALERS
TIRE RECAPPING & RETREADING
TIRES & INNER TUBES
TIRES & TUBES WHOLESALERS
TIRES: Auto
TITANIUM MILL PRDTS
TITANIUM ORE MINING
TOBACCO & PRDTS, WHOLESALE: Cigarettes
TOBACCO & PRDTS, WHOLESALE: Smoking
TOBACCO & TOBACCO PRDTS WHOLESALERS
TOBACCO LEAF PROCESSING
TOBACCO: Chewing
TOBACCO: Chewing & Snuff
TOBACCO: Cigarettes
TOBACCO: Cigars
TOBACCO: Smoking
TOILET PREPARATIONS
TOILETRIES, COSMETICS & PERFUME STORES
TOILETRIES, WHOLESALE: Toilet Soap
TOILETRIES, WHOLESALE: Toiletries
TOILETS: Portable Chemical, Plastics
TOOL & DIE STEEL
TOOL REPAIR SVCS
TOOLS: Carpenters', Including Levels & Chisels, Exc Saws
TOOLS: Hand
TOOLS: Hand, Engravers'
TOOLS: Hand, Ironworkers'
TOOLS: Hand, Jewelers'
TOOLS: Hand, Mechanics
TOOLS: Hand, Plumbers'
TOOLS: Hand, Power
TOOLS: Hand, Stonecutters'
TOOLS: Soldering
TOOTHPASTES, GELS & TOOTHPOWDERS
TOUR OPERATORS
TOWERS, SECTIONS: Transmission, Radio & Television
TOYS
TOYS & HOBBY GOODS & SPLYS, WHOLESALE: Model Kits
TOYS & HOBBY GOODS & SPLYS, WHOLESALE: Playing Cards
TOYS & HOBBY GOODS & SPLYS, WHOLESALE: Toys & Games
TOYS & HOBBY GOODS & SPLYS, WHOLESALE: Video Games
TOYS, HOBBY GOODS & SPLYS WHOLESALERS
TOYS: Dolls, Stuffed Animals & Parts
TOYS: Electronic
TOYS: Kites

TRADE SHOW ARRANGEMENT SVCS
TRADERS: Commodity, Contracts
TRAILERS & PARTS: Truck & Semi's
TRANSDUCERS: Electrical Properties
TRANSDUCERS: Pressure
TRANSFORMERS: Coupling
TRANSFORMERS: Electric
TRANSFORMERS: Electronic
TRANSFORMERS: Fluorescent Lighting
TRANSFORMERS: Power Related
TRANSFORMERS: Specialty
TRANSPORTATION EPQT & SPLYS, WHOL: Aircraft Engs/Eng Parts
TRANSPORTATION EPQT & SPLYS, WHOLESALE: Helicopter Parts
TRANSPORTATION EPQT & SPLYS, WHOLESALE: Marine Crafts/Splys
TRANSPORTATION EQPT & SPLYS WHOLESALERS, NEC
TRANSPORTATION EQUIPMENT, NEC
TRANSPORTATION PROGRAMS REGULATION & ADMINISTRATION SVCS
TRANSPORTATION SVCS, WATER: Surveyors, Marine
TRAP ROCK: Crushed & Broken
TRAVEL TRAILERS & CAMPERS
TRAVELER ACCOMMODATIONS, NEC
TRAYS: Cable, Metal Plate
TRAYS: Greenhouse Flats, Wood
TRAYS: Plastic
TROPHIES: Metal, Exc Silver
TROPHY & PLAQUE STORES
TRUCK & BUS BODIES: Automobile Wrecker Truck
TRUCK & BUS BODIES: Garbage Or Refuse Truck
TRUCK & BUS BODIES: Truck Cabs, Motor Vehicles
TRUCK & BUS BODIES: Truck, Motor Vehicle
TRUCK & BUS BODIES: Utility Truck
TRUCK GENERAL REPAIR SVC
TRUCK PAINTING & LETTERING SVCS
TRUCK PARTS & ACCESSORIES: Wholesalers
TRUCKING & HAULING SVCS: Contract Basis
TRUCKING & HAULING SVCS: Furniture, Local W/out Storage
TRUCKING & HAULING SVCS: Heavy, NEC
TRUCKING & HAULING SVCS: Lumber & Log, Local
TRUCKING, AUTOMOBILE CARRIER
TRUCKING, DUMP
TRUCKING: Local, Without Storage
TRUCKS & TRACTORS: Industrial
TRUCKS: Forklift
TRUNKS
TRUSSES: Wood, Floor
TRUSSES: Wood, Roof
TUB CONTAINERS: Plastic
TUBE & TUBING FABRICATORS
TUBES: Generator, Electron Beam, Beta Ray
TUBING: Flexible, Metallic
TUBING: Plastic
TUMBLING
TURBINES & TURBINE GENERATOR SET UNITS, COMPLETE
TURBINES & TURBINE GENERATOR SETS
TURBINES & TURBINE GENERATOR SETS & PARTS
TURNKEY VENDORS: Computer Systems
TURNSTILES
TWINE
TYPESETTING SVC
TYPESETTING SVC: Computer
TYPESETTING SVC: Hand Composition
TYPOGRAPHY

U

ULTRASONIC EQPT: Cleaning, Exc Med & Dental
UMBRELLAS: Garden Or Wagon
UNDERCOATINGS: Paint
UNIFORM STORES
UNIVERSITY
UPHOLSTERY MATERIAL
UPHOLSTERY WORK SVCS
USED CAR DEALERS
USED MERCHANDISE STORES: Art Objects, Antique
USED MERCHANDISE STORES: Rare Books
UTENSILS: Household, Cooking & Kitchen, Metal

V

VACUUM CLEANER STORES
VACUUM CLEANERS: Household

VACUUM CLEANERS: Indl Type
VALUE-ADDED RESELLERS: Computer Systems
VALVES
VALVES & PIPE FITTINGS
VALVES & REGULATORS: Pressure, Indl
VALVES Solenoid
VALVES: Aerosol, Metal
VALVES: Aircraft
VALVES: Aircraft, Control, Hydraulic & Pneumatic
VALVES: Aircraft, Fluid Power
VALVES: Control, Automatic
VALVES: Fluid Power, Control, Hydraulic & pneumatic
VALVES: Indl
VALVES: Plumbing & Heating
VALVES: Regulating & Control, Automatic
VALVES: Regulating, Process Control
VALVES: Water Works
VEHICLES: All Terrain
VENDING MACHINES & PARTS
VENETIAN BLINDS & SHADES
VENTILATING EQPT: Metal
VENTURE CAPITAL COMPANIES
VETERINARY PHARMACEUTICAL PREPARATIONS
VIDEO & AUDIO EQPT, WHOLESALE
VIDEO EQPT
VIDEO PRODUCTION SVCS
VIDEO TAPE PRODUCTION SVCS
VISES: Machine
VISUAL COMMUNICATIONS SYSTEMS
VITAMINS: Natural Or Synthetic, Uncompounded, Bulk
VITAMINS: Pharmaceutical Preparations

W

WALL COVERINGS WHOLESALERS
WALLPAPER & WALL COVERINGS
WALLPAPER STORE
WAREHOUSE CLUBS STORES
WAREHOUSING & STORAGE FACILITIES, NEC
WAREHOUSING & STORAGE, REFRIGERATED: Cold Storage Or Refrig
WAREHOUSING & STORAGE: General
WAREHOUSING & STORAGE: Refrigerated
WARM AIR HEATING/AC EQPT/SPLY, WHOL Humidifier, Exc Portable
WARM AIR HEATING/AC EQPT/SPLYS, WHOL Warm Air Htg Eqpt/Splys
WARP KNIT FABRIC FINISHING
WASHERS
WASHERS: Plastic
WASHERS: Rubber
WASHING MACHINES: Household
WATCHES
WATER HEATERS
WATER PURIFICATION EQPT: Household
WATER PURIFICATION PRDTS: Chlorination Tablets & Kits
WATER SOFTENER SVCS
WATER TREATMENT EQPT: Indl
WATER: Distilled
WATER: Mineral, Carbonated, Canned & Bottled, Etc
WATER: Pasteurized & Mineral, Bottled & Canned
WATER: Pasteurized, Canned & Bottled, Etc
WATERPROOFING COMPOUNDS
WAVEGUIDES & FITTINGS
WAXES: Mineral, Natural
WAXES: Petroleum, Not Produced In Petroleum Refineries
WEATHER STRIP: Sponge Rubber
WEATHER VANES
WELDING & CUTTING APPARATUS & ACCESS, NEC
WELDING EQPT
WELDING EQPT & SPLYS WHOLESALERS
WELDING EQPT & SPLYS: Arc Welders, Transformer-Rectifier
WELDING EQPT & SPLYS: Electrode Holders, Electric Welding
WELDING EQPT REPAIR SVCS
WELDING EQPT: Electric
WELDING EQPT: Electrical
WELDING MACHINES & EQPT: Ultrasonic
WELDING REPAIR SVC
WELDING SPLYS, EXC GASES: Wholesalers
WELDING TIPS: Heat Resistant, Metal
WELDMENTS
WELL CURBING: Concrete
WHEELCHAIRS
WHEELS

PRODUCT INDEX

WHEELS: Abrasive
WINCHES
WINDINGS: Coil, Electronic
WINDMILLS: Electric Power Generation
WINDOW & DOOR FRAMES
WINDOW BLIND REPAIR SVCS
WINDOW FRAMES & SASHES: Plastic
WINDOWS: Frames, Wood
WINDOWS: Louver, Glass, Wood Framed
WINDOWS: Wood
WINDSHIELD WIPER SYSTEMS
WINE CELLARS, BONDED: Wine, Blended
WIRE
WIRE & CABLE: Aluminum
WIRE & CABLE: Nonferrous, Aircraft
WIRE & CABLE: Nonferrous, Automotive, Exc Ignition Sets
WIRE & CABLE: Nonferrous, Building
WIRE & WIRE PRDTS
WIRE FABRIC: Welded Steel
WIRE MATERIALS: Copper
WIRE MATERIALS: Steel
WIRE PRDTS: Ferrous Or Iron, Made In Wiredrawing Plants
WIRE PRDTS: Steel & Iron
WIRE WINDING OF PURCHASED WIRE
WIRE: Communication
WIRE: Magnet
WIRE: Mesh
WIRE: Nonferrous
WIRE: Steel, Insulated Or Armored
WIRE: Wire, Ferrous Or Iron
WIRING DEVICES WHOLESALERS
WOMEN'S & CHILDREN'S CLOTHING WHOLESALERS, NEC
WOMEN'S & GIRLS' SPORTSWEAR WHOLESALERS
WOMEN'S CLOTHING STORES
WOMEN'S CLOTHING STORES: Ready-To-Wear
WOMEN'S KNITWEAR STORES
WOOD CHIPS, PRODUCED AT THE MILL
WOOD EXTRACT PRDTS
WOOD PRDTS
WOOD PRDTS: Applicators
WOOD PRDTS: Barrels & Barrel Parts
WOOD PRDTS: Baskets, Fruit & Veg, Round Stave, Till, Etc
WOOD PRDTS: Beekeeping Splys
WOOD PRDTS: Engraved
WOOD PRDTS: Moldings, Unfinished & Prefinished
WOOD PRDTS: Mulch Or Sawdust
WOOD PRDTS: Mulch, Wood & Bark
WOOD PRDTS: Novelties, Fiber
WOOD PRDTS: Outdoor, Structural
WOOD PRDTS: Panel Work
WOOD PRDTS: Plugs
WOOD PRDTS: Rulers & Rules
WOOD PRDTS: Saddle Trees
WOOD PRDTS: Signboards
WOOD PRDTS: Stepladders
WOOD PRDTS: Trim
WOOD PRDTS: Trophy Bases
WOOD PRODUCTS: Reconstituted
WOOD SHAVINGS BALES, MULCH TYPE, WHOLESALE
WOOD TREATING: Millwork
WOOD TREATING: Wood Prdts, Creosoted
WOODWORK & TRIM: Exterior & Ornamental
WOODWORK & TRIM: Interior & Ornamental
WOODWORK: Carved & Turned
WOODWORK: Interior & Ornamental, NEC
WOODWORK: Ornamental, Cornices, Mantels, Etc.
WORD PROCESSING SVCS
WOVEN WIRE PRDTS, NEC
WREATHS: Artificial
WRENCHES
WRITING FOR PUBLICATION SVCS

X

X-RAY EQPT & TUBES

Y

YARN MILLS: Texturizing, Throwing & Twisting
YARN, ORGANIC SYNTHETIC
YARN: Specialty & Novelty
YARN: Weaving, Spun

PRODUCT SECTION

Product category → BOXES: Folding
Edgar & Son Paperboard .... G 999 999-9999
Yourtown (G-11480)
Ready Box Co .... E 999 999-9999
City → Anytown (G-7097)

Indicates approximate employment figure
A = Over 500 employees, B = 251-500
C = 101-250, D = 51-100, E = 20-50
F = 10-19, G = 1-9
Business phone
Geographic Section entry number where full company information appears.

See footnotes for symbols and codes identification.
• Refer to the Industrial Product Index preceding this section to locate product headings.

ABRASIVES

Ahlstrom-Munksjo Nonwovens LLC .....B....... 860 654-8300
Windsor Locks (G-10469)
Associated Chemicals & Abr Inc...........G....... 203 481-7235
Branford (G-548)
Chessco Industries Inc............................E....... 203 255-2804
Westport (G-10064)
Pressure Blast Mfg Co Inc ....F....... 800 722-5278
South Windsor (G-7811)
Syncote Chemical Company Inc ....G....... 203 426-5526
Newtown (G-5784)
Tcg Green Technologies Inc ....F....... 860 364-4694
Sharon (G-7384)

ABRASIVES: Artificial

Triatic Incorporated ....F....... 860 236-2298
West Hartford (G-9868)

ABRASIVES: Coated

Precision Dip Coating LLC.....................G....... 203 805-4564
Waterbury (G-9584)

ACADEMIC TUTORING SVCS

Real Sltons Edctl Cnslting Inc................G....... 203 220-2279
Trumbull (G-9062)

ACCELERATION INDICATORS & SYSTEM COMPONENTS: Aerospace

Accuturn Mfg Co LLC..............................F....... 860 289-6355
South Windsor (G-7699)
Carl Perry..G....... 860 834-4459
Middletown (G-4330)
Eaton Aerospace LLC...............................E....... 203 796-6000
Bethel (G-292)
Hermtech Inc..G....... 860 758-7528
East Windsor (G-2496)
Kaman Corporation ....C....... 860 632-1000
Middletown (G-4361)
Kaman Precision Products Inc ....E....... 860 632-1000
Middletown (G-4362)
Real Manufacturing LLC..........................G....... 860 757-3975
South Windsor (G-7817)
Saf Industries LLC ....E....... 203 729-4900
Meriden (G-4238)

ACCOUNTING SVCS, NEC

Eagle Investment Systems LLC...............F....... 860 561-4602
West Hartford (G-9803)

ACIDS: Hydrofluoric

New Haven Chlor-Alkali LLC...................D....... 203 772-3350
New Haven (G-5343)

ACIDS: Inorganic

Metamorphic Materials Inc.......................F....... 860 738-8638
Winsted (G-10529)

ACOUSTICAL BOARD & TILE

Realtraps LLC..G....... 203 294-4285
Wallingford (G-9349)

ACRYLIC RESINS

Pinnacle Polymers LLC............................G....... 203 313-4116
Ridgefield (G-7162)

ACTUATORS: Indl, NEC

Das Distribution Inc.................................G....... 860 844-3058
East Granby (G-2201)
Hamilton Sundstrand Corp ....A....... 860 654-6000
Windsor Locks (G-10491)

ADHESIVES

Advanced Adhesive Systems Inc.............E....... 860 953-4100
Newington (G-5621)
Apcm Manufacturing LLC ....G....... 860 564-7817
Plainfield (G-6738)
Converting McHy Adhesives LLC ....G....... 860 561-0226
Newington (G-5643)
Ctech Adhesives......................................G....... 860 482-5947
New Hartford (G-5188)
Edison Coatings Inc ....F....... 860 747-2220
Plainville (G-6804)
Henkel Loctite Corporation......................E....... 860 571-5100
Rocky Hill (G-7245)
Henkel of America Inc ....B....... 860 571-5100
Rocky Hill (G-7246)
Henkel US Operations Corp ....B....... 860 571-5100
Rocky Hill (G-7247)
Hexcel Corporation..................................E....... 203 969-0666
Stamford (G-8233)
Permatex Inc..E....... 860 543-7500
Hartford (G-3663)
Shurtape Specialty Coating LLC ....E....... 860 738-2600
New Hartford (G-5212)
Synchron Inc ....G....... 860 953-8157
Newington (G-5709)

ADHESIVES & SEALANTS

Chessco Industries Inc............................E....... 203 255-2804
Westport (G-10064)
Cunningham Tech LLC............................G....... 860 738-8759
New Hartford (G-5189)
Cunningham Tech LLC............................G....... 860 738-8759
Pine Meadow (G-6733)
Five Star Products Inc ....E....... 203 336-7900
Shelton (G-7444)
Henkel Corporation..................................G....... 860 571-5100
Rocky Hill (G-7244)
Incure Inc...G....... 860 748-2979
New Britain (G-4998)
Metamorphic Materials Inc.......................F....... 860 738-8638
Winsted (G-10529)
Panacol-Usa Inc.......................................F....... 860 738-7449
Torrington (G-8956)
S & S Sealcoating LLC ....G....... 203 284-0054
Wallingford (G-9364)
Vanderbilt Chemicals LLC........................E....... 203 744-3900
Bethel (G-361)
Xg Industries LLC....................................F....... 475 282-4643
Stratford (G-8712)

ADHESIVES: Epoxy

Conserv Epoxy LLC.................................G....... 203 484-4123
Northford (G-6044)
Laticrete International Inc ....G....... 203 393-0010
Bethany (G-245)

ADVERTISING AGENCIES

Automotive Coop Couponing Inc.............G....... 203 227-2722
Weston (G-10018)
Cls Design Group.....................................G....... 860 307-2810
Easton (G-8911)
Criscola Design LLC................................G....... 203 248-4285
North Haven (G-5932)
Media Metrix LLC....................................G....... 203 386-0228
Stratford (G-8649)
Peter Ortali & Associates LLC ....G....... 203 571-8023
Sandy Hook (G-7325)

ADVERTISING AGENCIES: Consultants

Applied Advertising Inc...........................F....... 860 640-0800
Danbury (G-1741)
Directory Assistants Inc..........................E....... 860 633-0122
Wethersfield (G-10190)
Park Group Solutions LLC......................G....... 203 459-8784
Newtown (G-5769)
PB&j Design Inc......................................G....... 203 332-4433
Derby (G-2121)
Web Savvy Marketers LLC......................G....... 860 432-8756
East Hartford (G-2401)

ADVERTISING DISPLAY PRDTS

Connecticut Components Inc..................G....... 860 633-0277
Tolland (G-8855)
Product Spring LLC................................G....... 203 966-6766
New Canaan (G-5133)
Tag Promotions Inc.................................G....... 800 909-4011
Monroe (G-4755)

ADVERTISING REPRESENTATIVES: Magazine

Sixfurlongs LLC.......................................G....... 203 255-8553
Fairfield (G-2848)

ADVERTISING REPRESENTATIVES: Media

Morthanoscom LLC..................................G....... 203 378-2414
Stratford (G-8651)

ADVERTISING REPRESENTATIVES: Printed Media

Educational Resources Network..............G....... 203 866-9973
Ridgefield (G-7138)

ADVERTISING SPECIALTIES, WHOLESALE

Ciaudelli Productions Inc........................G....... 860 848-0411
Montville (G-4769)
D&D Printing Enterprises.......................G....... 860 684-2023
Stafford Springs (G-8023)
Encore Sales Corp..................................G....... 203 301-4949
Milford (G-4530)
McWeeney Marketing Group Inc ....G....... 203 891-8100
Orange (G-6613)
Professional Mktg Svcs Inc ....F....... 203 610-6222
Stratford (G-8669)
R & B Apparel Plus LLC ....G....... 860 333-1757
Groton (G-3311)

ADVERTISING SVCS, NEC

AAR Results LLC.....................................G....... 203 627-2193
Branford (G-535)
Britelite Promotions.................................G....... 203 481-5755
Branford (G-565)

ADVERTISING SVCS: Direct Mail

Automotive Coop Couponing Inc.............G....... 203 227-2722
Weston (G-10018)
Fairfield Marketing Group Inc ....F....... 203 261-0884
Easton (G-2552)
Joseph Merritt & Company Inc...............E....... 860 296-2500
Hartford (G-3620)

ADVERTISING SVCS: Direct Mail

L P Macadams Company Inc ....D....... 203 366-3647
  Bridgeport *(G-820)*
Life Study Fllwship Foundation............E....... 203 655-1436
  Darien *(G-2031)*
R R Donnelley & Sons Company ....F....... 860 649-5570
  Manchester *(G-4078)*
Transmonde USa Inc ....D....... 203 484-1528
  North Branford *(G-5863)*

ADVERTISING SVCS: Display

Murdoch and Co..…….. 203 226-2800
  Westport *(G-10126)*
Pop Graphics Inc ....G....... 203 639-1441
  Meriden *(G-4218)*
Resavue Inc ....F....... 203 878-0944
  Orange *(G-6625)*
Valley Container Inc ....E....... 203 368-6546
  Bridgeport *(G-933)*

ADVERTISING SVCS: Outdoor

D Cello Enterprises LLC ....…….. 860 659-0844
  Glastonbury *(G-3027)*
Lamar Advertising Company ....E....... 860 246-6546
  Windsor *(G-10403)*

ADVERTISING SVCS: Transit

Applied Advertising Inc ....F....... 860 640-0800
  Danbury *(G-1741)*

AERIAL WORK PLATFORMS

Capewell Aerial Systems LLC ....D....... 860 610-0700
  South Windsor *(G-7722)*

AGENTS, BROKERS & BUREAUS: Personal Service

Advanced HM Audio & Video LLC........G....... 860 621-0631
  Plantsville *(G-6883)*
Federal Business Products Inc ....D....... 860 482-6231
  Torrington *(G-8924)*

AGRICULTURAL DISINFECTANTS

Healthy Harvest Inc..................................G....... 203 245-3786
  Madison *(G-3927)*

AGRICULTURAL EQPT: Curers, Tobacco

Latelier Bade LLC ....G....... 860 623-4661
  Broad Brook *(G-1151)*

AGRICULTURAL EQPT: Fertilizing Machinery

Grassy Meadows Lawn Care ....G....... 203 856-3823
  Trumbull *(G-9030)*

AGRICULTURAL EQPT: Tractors, Farm

Domus VI LLC ....G....... 860 619-0707
  Sharon *(G-7378)*

AGRICULTURAL LIMESTONE: Ground

Allyndale Corporation ....F....... 860 824-7959
  East Canaan *(G-2180)*

AGRICULTURAL MACHINERY & EQPT REPAIR

William Linkovich.......................................G....... 860 824-0298
  East Canaan *(G-2184)*

AIR CLEANING SYSTEMS

GE Steam Power Inc ....C....... 423 648-4161
  Windsor *(G-10389)*
Novaerus US Inc ....F....... 813 304-2468
  Stamford *(G-8331)*
Nq Industries Inc ....G....... 860 258-3466
  Rocky Hill *(G-7259)*
Planet Technologies Inc ....F....... 800 255-3749
  Ridgefield *(G-7163)*

AIR CONDITIONERS: Motor Vehicle

United Tech Employee Sav Plan.............G....... 860 728-7000
  Hartford *(G-3709)*

AIR CONDITIONING & VENTILATION EQPT & SPLYS: Wholesales

Outland Engineering Inc ....F....... 800 797-3709
  Milford *(G-4601)*

AIR CONDITIONING EQPT

Alvest (usa) Inc ....E....... 860 602-3400
  Windsor *(G-10360)*
Carrier Corporation...................................G....... 860 728-7000
  Farmington *(G-2887)*
Dp2 LLC Head ....F....... 203 655-0747
  Darien *(G-2022)*
Enterex America LLC...............................G....... 860 661-4635
  Westbrook *(G-9996)*

AIR CONDITIONING REPAIR SVCS

M J Williams Heating and AC.................G....... 860 923-6991
  Woodstock *(G-10670)*

AIR CONDITIONING UNITS: Complete, Domestic Or Indl

Dasco Supply LLC ....G....... 203 388-0095
  Stamford *(G-8180)*
Nanocap Technologies LLC....................G....... 860 521-9743
  Hartford *(G-3648)*
Trane Inc ....D....... 203 866-7115
  Norwalk *(G-6377)*

AIR COOLERS: Metal Plate

GE Steam Power Inc ....C....... 423 648-4161
  Windsor *(G-10389)*
Mastercraft Tool and Mch Co ....F....... 860 628-5551
  Southington *(G-7950)*

AIR POLLUTION MEASURING SVCS

Environmental Monitor Service...............G....... 203 935-0102
  Meriden *(G-4169)*

AIR PURIFICATION EQPT

Clean Air Group Inc ....E....... 203 335-3700
  Fairfield *(G-2764)*
Environmental Monitor Service...............G....... 203 935-0102
  Meriden *(G-4169)*
Treadwell Corporation..............................E....... 860 283-7600
  Thomaston *(G-8814)*

AIRCRAFT & AEROSPACE FLIGHT INSTRUMENTS & GUIDANCE SYSTEMS

Apex Machine Tool Company Inc..........G....... 203 806-2090
  Cheshire *(G-1354)*
Bae Systems Applied Intel Inc ....G....... 203 323-0066
  Stamford *(G-8105)*
Connecticut Aerospace Inc....................G....... 860 872-0036
  Vernon Rockville *(G-9165)*
Corporate Flight MGT Inc.......................G....... 203 826-9224
  Danbury *(G-1776)*
Higgs Energy LLC.....................................G....... 860 213-5561
  Norwich *(G-6416)*
Integrated Systems Solutions ....G....... 860 665-1600
  Newington *(G-5664)*
Msj Investments Inc ....F....... 860 684-9956
  Stafford Springs *(G-8033)*
United Technologies Corp ....G....... 860 595-4114
  Newington *(G-5718)*

AIRCRAFT & HEAVY EQPT REPAIR SVCS

Aviation Pro Pages LLC ....G....... 860 910-9336
  Mystic *(G-4800)*
Doncasters Inc ....D....... 860 449-1603
  Groton *(G-3283)*
Guy Montanari..G....... 203 791-0642
  Danbury *(G-1840)*
Sign Maintenance Service Co................G....... 203 336-1051
  Bridgeport *(G-905)*
Skico Manufacturing Co LLC ....G....... 203 230-1305
  Hamden *(G-3510)*

AIRCRAFT ASSEMBLY PLANTS

Aircastle Advisor LLC ....D....... 203 504-1020
  Stamford *(G-8069)*
Amco Precision Tools Inc ....E....... 860 828-5640
  Berlin *(G-155)*

Antares Aerospace Inds LLC.................G....... 203 903-7531
  East Haven *(G-2411)*
Avolon Aerospace New York Inc ....G....... 203 663-5490
  Stamford *(G-8100)*
B & F Design Incorporated.....................E....... 860 357-4317
  New Britain *(G-4948)*
Baghai Shahin ....G....... 203 268-6287
  Trumbull *(G-9002)*
Belair Aviation ....G....... 203 380-8993
  Stratford *(G-8583)*
Berkshire Balloons LLC ....G....... 203 250-8441
  Plantsville *(G-6886)*
CJ Aviation Services LLC ....G....... 203 741-6499
  Enfield *(G-2624)*
Dube Air LLC ....G....... 860 355-1705
  Sherman *(G-7594)*
Edac Nd Inc ....D....... 860 633-9474
  Glastonbury *(G-3031)*
Embraer Executive Jet Svcs LLC ....G....... 860 804-4600
  Windsor Locks *(G-10483)*
Four Six Juliet LLC ....G....... 203 227-1557
  Westport *(G-10085)*
Gateway Helicopter Service ....G....... 203 531-4395
  Greenwich *(G-3166)*
Gulfstream Aerospace Corp ....G....... 860 210-1469
  New Milford *(G-5542)*
Gulfstream Aerospace Corp ....G....... 912 965-3000
  East Granby *(G-2207)*
Hartford Jet Center LLC..........................G....... 860 548-9334
  Hartford *(G-3612)*
Kaman Aerospace Corporation..............A....... 860 242-4461
  Bloomfield *(G-430)*
Kaman Aerospace Corporation..............D....... 860 242-4461
  Bloomfield *(G-432)*
Kaman Aerospace Group Inc ....F....... 860 243-7100
  Bloomfield *(G-433)*
KII Aerospace LLC ....G....... 860 806-8858
  Middlebury *(G-4282)*
MB Aerospace ....G....... 860 653-0569
  East Granby *(G-2212)*
Mooney Time Inc.......................................G....... 203 263-0167
  Woodbury *(G-10644)*
New England Airfoil Pdts Inc ....E....... 860 677-1376
  Farmington *(G-2936)*
P & S Manufacturing LLC ....G....... 203 685-2256
  Bridgeport *(G-858)*
Santoto LLC...G....... 203 984-2540
  Danbury *(G-1934)*
Sikorsky Aircraft Corporation.................F....... 516 228-2000
  North Haven *(G-5993)*
Sikorsky Aircraft Corporation.................C....... 203 386-4000
  Bridgeport *(G-908)*
Stonegate Capital Group ....G....... 860 899-1181
  Hartford *(G-3694)*
Tag Manufacturing LLC ....G....... 860 479-5120
  Plainville *(G-6868)*
Target Marketing Assoc Inc ....G....... 860 571-7294
  Rocky Hill *(G-7268)*
Textron Aviation Inc ....A....... 203 262-9366
  Oxford *(G-6697)*
United Technologies Corp ....B....... 860 728-7000
  Farmington *(G-2972)*

AIRCRAFT CONTROL SYSTEMS:

Triumph Eng Ctrl Systems LLC ....F....... 860 236-0651
  West Hartford *(G-9870)*
Triumph Eng Ctrl Systems LLC ....A....... 860 236-0651
  West Hartford *(G-9869)*

AIRCRAFT CONTROL SYSTEMS: Electronic Totalizing Counters

Dynamic Controls Hs Inc ....G....... 860 654-6000
  Windsor Locks *(G-10482)*
Swahili Aviation Aerospace LLC ....G....... 860 268-3639
  Tolland *(G-8879)*

AIRCRAFT DEALERS

Sikorsky Aircraft Corporation.................A....... 203 386-4000
  Stratford *(G-8678)*

AIRCRAFT ELECTRICAL EQPT REPAIR SVCS

Electro-Methods Inc.................................C....... 860 289-8661
  South Windsor *(G-7747)*
TLD America Corporation ....E....... 860 602-3400
  Windsor *(G-10453)*

AIRCRAFT ENGINES & ENGINE PARTS: Airfoils

Hartford Aviation Group Inc .... G 860 549-0096
  Hartford *(G-3606)*

AIRCRAFT ENGINES & ENGINE PARTS: Cooling Systems

Evans Cooling Systems Inc .... G 860 668-1114
  Suffield *(G-8718)*

AIRCRAFT ENGINES & ENGINE PARTS: Mount Parts

Bolducs Machine Works Inc .... G 860 455-1232
  North Windham *(G-6034)*

AIRCRAFT ENGINES & ENGINE PARTS: Pumps

Columbia Manufacturing Inc .... D 860 228-2259
  Columbia *(G-1604)*

AIRCRAFT ENGINES & ENGINE PARTS: Research & Development, Mfr

Pratt & Whitney Eng Svcs Inc .... C 860 610-2631
  East Hartford *(G-2358)*

AIRCRAFT ENGINES & ENGINE PARTS: Rocket Motors

Astralis Rocketry Corp .... G 203 254-0427
  Westport *(G-10058)*

AIRCRAFT ENGINES & PARTS

A-1 Machining Co .... D 860 223-6420
  New Britain *(G-4931)*
AAR Corp .... G 619 545-6129
  Windsor *(G-10352)*
Absolute Precision Co .... G 203 767-9066
  Southbury *(G-7840)*
Accupaulo Holding Corporation .... E 860 666-5621
  Newington *(G-5617)*
Acmt Inc .... D 860 645-0592
  Manchester *(G-3977)*
Aero Component Services LLC .... G 860 291-0417
  East Hartford *(G-2288)*
AGC Acquisition LLC .... C 203 639-7125
  Meriden *(G-4142)*
Alloy Specialties Incorporated .... E 860 646-4587
  Manchester *(G-3981)*
American Design & Mfg Inc .... E 860 282-2719
  South Windsor *(G-7705)*
American Unmanned Systems LLC .. G 203 406-7611
  Stamford *(G-8079)*
ATI Ladish Machining Inc .... D 860 688-3688
  East Hartford *(G-2295)*
ATI Ladish Machining Inc .... D 860 688-3688
  South Windsor *(G-7711)*
ATI Ladish Machining Inc .... D 860 688-3688
  East Hartford *(G-2296)*
Barnes Group Inc .... B 860 583-7070
  Bristol *(G-973)*
Barnes Group Inc .... A 860 298-7740
  Windsor *(G-10367)*
Barnes Group Inc .... G 860 653-5531
  East Granby *(G-2191)*
Barnes Group Inc .... A 513 759-3503
  Bristol *(G-975)*
Beacon Group Inc .... C 860 594-5200
  Newington *(G-5631)*
Birken Manufacturing Company .... D 860 242-2211
  Bloomfield *(G-395)*
Birotech Inc .... G 203 968-5080
  Stamford *(G-8112)*
Cambridge Specialty Co Inc .... D 860 828-3579
  Berlin *(G-168)*
Carismo Productions .... G 203 334-8469
  Bridgeport *(G-730)*
CBS Manufacturing Company .... E 860 653-8100
  East Granby *(G-2196)*
Chromalloy Component Svcs Inc ..... C 860 688-7798
  Windsor *(G-10373)*
Chromalloy Gas Turbine LLC .... D 860 688-7798
  Windsor *(G-10374)*
D & M Tool Company Inc .... G 860 236-6037
  West Hartford *(G-9797)*

Deburring House Inc .... E 860 828-0889
  East Berlin *(G-2165)*
Demusz Mfg Co Inc .... E 860 528-9845
  East Hartford *(G-2313)*
Drt Aerospace LLC .... E 203 781-8020
  Meriden *(G-4167)*
Dynamic Controls Hs Inc .... G 860 654-6000
  Windsor Locks *(G-10482)*
Edac Technologies LLC .... F 860 789-2511
  East Windsor *(G-2490)*
Edac Technologies LLC .... C 203 806-2090
  Cheshire *(G-1383)*
Electro-Methods Inc .... C 860 289-8661
  South Windsor *(G-7747)*
Electro-Methods Inc .... D 860 289-8661
  South Windsor *(G-7748)*
Engine Alliance LLC .... B 860 565-2239
  Glastonbury *(G-3035)*
First Aviation Services Inc .... G 203 291-3300
  Westport *(G-10081)*
First Equity Group Inc .... F 203 291-7700
  Westport *(G-10082)*
Fredericks Jf Aero LLC .... D 860 677-2646
  Farmington *(G-2909)*
Gay Tool & Machine .... G 860 668-5054
  Suffield *(G-8720)*
GKN Aerospace Newington LLC ...... G 800 667-8502
  Newington *(G-5655)*
GKN Aerospace Newington LLC ...... C 800 667-8502
  Newington *(G-5656)*
GKN Arspace Svcs Strctures LLC .... C 860 613-0236
  Cromwell *(G-1702)*
Global Trbine Cmpnent Tech LLC ... E 860 528-4722
  South Windsor *(G-7760)*
Heritage Custom Products LLC .... G 860 292-1979
  East Windsor *(G-2495)*
Honeywell International Inc .... D 203 484-7161
  Northford *(G-6045)*
Honeywell International Inc .... B 203 484-7161
  Northford *(G-6046)*
Honeywell International Inc .... B 203 484-6202
  Northford *(G-6047)*
Honeywell International Inc .... A 203 484-7161
  North Branford *(G-5843)*
Honeywell International Inc .... E 203 484-7161
  Northford *(G-6048)*
Horst Engrg De Mexico LLC .... E 860 289-8209
  East Hartford *(G-2334)*
Hsb Aircraft Components LLC .... F 860 505-7349
  New Britain *(G-4997)*
I & J Machine Tool Company .... F 203 877-5376
  Milford *(G-4550)*
Iae International Aero Engs AG .... C 860 565-1773
  East Hartford *(G-2336)*
International Aero Engines LLC .... E 860 565-5515
  East Hartford *(G-2340)*
Intlaero Beta Corp .... G 317 821-2000
  East Hartford *(G-2341)*
Kaman Aerospace Corporation .... D 860 242-4461
  Bloomfield *(G-432)*
Kaman Aerospace Group Inc .... F 860 243-7100
  Bloomfield *(G-433)*
Kamatics Corporation .... E 860 243-9704
  Bloomfield *(G-435)*
Kenzinc LLC .... G 203 307-5369
  Shelton *(G-7484)*
Lighthouse International LLC .... E 860 528-4722
  South Windsor *(G-7788)*
Morning Star Tool LLC .... G 203 878-6026
  Milford *(G-4585)*
Msj Investments Inc .... F 860 684-9956
  Stafford Springs *(G-8033)*
N & B Manufacturing Co Inc .... G 860 667-3204
  Windsor *(G-5682)*
New England Airfoil Pdts Inc .... E 860 677-1376
  Farmington *(G-2936)*
Numet Machining Techniques Inc .... E 203 375-4995
  Orange *(G-6618)*
Palmer Manufacturing Co LLC .... G 860 828-0344
  East Berlin *(G-2172)*
Pdq Inc .... E 860 529-9051
  Rocky Hill *(G-7262)*
Pinnacle Aerospace Mfg LLC .... F 203 258-3398
  Greenwich *(G-3216)*
Point Machine Company .... E 860 828-6901
  Berlin *(G-207)*
Polar Corp .... G 860 225-6000
  New Britain *(G-5034)*
Polar Corporation .... E 860 223-7891
  New Britain *(G-5035)*

Pratt & Whitney Company Inc .... C 860 565-4321
  East Hartford *(G-2357)*
Pratt & Whitney Engine Svcs .... B 203 934-2806
  North Haven *(G-5978)*
Pratt & Whitney Engine Svcs .... E 860 565-4321
  East Hartford *(G-2359)*
Pratt & Whitney Engine Svcs .... B 860 344-4000
  Middletown *(G-4396)*
Pratt & Whitney Services Inc .... E 860 565-5489
  East Hartford *(G-2360)*
Precision Speed Mfg LLC .... E 860 635-8811
  Middletown *(G-4397)*
Rimark Manufacturing LLC .... G 860 924-6222
  East Granby *(G-2227)*
Saar Corporation .... F 860 674-9440
  Farmington *(G-2955)*
Scap Motors Inc .... C 203 384-0005
  Fairfield *(G-2843)*
Schaefer Rolls Inc .... G 203 910-0224
  Wolcott *(G-10585)*
Sikorsky Aircraft Corporation .... A 203 386-4000
  Stratford *(G-8677)*
Simmonds Precision Pdts Inc .... E 203 797-5000
  Danbury *(G-1952)*
Soto Holdings Inc .... E 203 781-8020
  New Haven *(G-5400)*
Spartan Aerospace LLC .... D 860 533-7500
  Manchester *(G-4090)*
Specialty Tool Company USA LLC ... F 203 874-2009
  Milford *(G-4650)*
Tdy Industries LLC .... G 860 259-6346
  New Britain *(G-5072)*
Time Aviation LLC .... G 203 496-5716
  Greenwich *(G-3244)*
Timken Arospc Drv Systems LLC ... G 860 649-0000
  Manchester *(G-4102)*
Triumph Eng Ctrl Systems LLC .... A 860 236-0651
  West Hartford *(G-9869)*
Turbine Kinetics Inc .... F 860 633-8520
  Glastonbury *(G-3091)*
Turbine Technologies Inc .... D 860 678-1642
  Farmington *(G-2971)*
United Tech Advnced Prjcts Inc .... G 860 610-7159
  East Hartford *(G-2390)*
United Technologies Corp .... B 860 728-7000
  Farmington *(G-2972)*
United Technologies Corp .... C 860 565-4321
  East Hartford *(G-2391)*
United Technologies Corp .... B 860 727-2200
  South Windsor *(G-7836)*
United Technologies Corp .... C 860 565-4321
  East Hartford *(G-2393)*
United Technologies Corp .... G 860 565-4321
  East Hartford *(G-2394)*
United Tool and Die Company .... C 860 246-6531
  West Hartford *(G-9871)*
Wentworth Manufacturing LLC .... G 860 205-6437
  New Britain *(G-5082)*
Westbrook Products LLC .... G 860 205-6437
  New Britain *(G-5083)*
Whitney Pratt .... G 860 565-6431
  Willington *(G-10261)*
Winslow Automatics Inc .... D 860 225-6321
  New Britain *(G-5084)*

AIRCRAFT EQPT & SPLYS WHOLESALERS

Connecticut Advanced Products .... G 860 659-2260
  Glastonbury *(G-3023)*

AIRCRAFT LIGHTING

Hoffman Engineering LLC .... D 203 425-8900
  Stamford *(G-8240)*

AIRCRAFT MAINTENANCE & REPAIR SVCS

Gulfstream Aerospace Corp .... G 860 210-1469
  New Milford *(G-5542)*
Helicopter Support Inc .... B 203 416-4000
  Trumbull *(G-9033)*
Sikorsky Aircraft Corporation .... A 203 386-4000
  Stratford *(G-8678)*
Swahili Aviation Aerospace LLC .... G 860 268-3639
  Tolland *(G-8879)*
Turbine Controls Inc .... D 860 242-0448
  Bloomfield *(G-495)*

Employee Codes: A=Over 500 employees, B=251-500, C=101-250, D=51-100, E=20-50, F=10-19, G=1-9

AIRCRAFT PARTS & AUX EQPT: Panel Assy/Hydro Prop Test Stands

AIRCRAFT PARTS & AUX EQPT: Panel Assy/Hydro Prop Test Stands

Electro-Methods Inc .... C 860 289-8661
South Windsor *(G-7747)*

AIRCRAFT PARTS & AUXILIARY EQPT: Accumulators, Propeller

Saf Industries LLC .... E 203 729-4900
Meriden *(G-4237)*

AIRCRAFT PARTS & AUXILIARY EQPT: Ailerons

Pas Technologies Inc .... E 860 649-2727
Manchester *(G-4074)*

AIRCRAFT PARTS & AUXILIARY EQPT: Assys, Subassemblies/Parts

A G C Incorporated .... C 203 235-3361
Meriden *(G-4138)*
All Power Manufacturing Co .... C 562 802-2640
Oxford *(G-6641)*
Athens Industries Inc .... G 860 621-8957
Plantsville *(G-6885)*
B&N Aerospace Inc .... E 860 665-0134
Newington *(G-5630)*
Budney Aerospace Inc .... D 860 828-0585
Berlin *(G-166)*
Connecticut Tool & Mfg Co LLC .... D 860 846-0800
Plainville *(G-6792)*
Edac Nd Inc .... D 860 633-9474
Glastonbury *(G-3031)*
Flanagan Brothers Inc .... G 860 633-3558
Glastonbury *(G-3036)*
Jarvis Airfoil Inc .... G 860 342-5000
Portland *(G-6961)*
Metallon Inc .... E 860 283-8265
Thomaston *(G-8797)*
Paradigm Manchester Inc .... B 860 646-4048
Manchester *(G-4068)*
Pcx Aerostructures LLC .... C 860 666-2471
Newington *(G-5695)*
Pratt & Whitney Engine Svcs .... B 860 344-4000
Middletown *(G-4396)*
Precision Metals and Plastics .... G 860 238-4320
Winsted *(G-10532)*
Richard Manufacturing Co Inc .... E 203 874-3617
Milford *(G-4627)*
Saf Industries LLC .... E 203 729-4900
Meriden *(G-4238)*
Tachwa Enterprises Inc .... E 203 691-5772
Hamden *(G-3517)*

AIRCRAFT PARTS & AUXILIARY EQPT: Body & Wing Assys & Parts

Triumph Eng Ctrl Systems LLC .... A 860 236-0651
West Hartford *(G-9869)*

AIRCRAFT PARTS & AUXILIARY EQPT: Body Assemblies & Parts

Airborne Industries Inc .... F 203 315-0200
Branford *(G-538)*
I & J Machine Tool Company .... F 203 877-5376
Milford *(G-4550)*
Timken Arospc Drv Systems LLC .... C 860 649-0000
Manchester *(G-4102)*
United Technologies Corp .... D 860 557-3333
East Hartford *(G-2396)*

AIRCRAFT PARTS & AUXILIARY EQPT: Gears, Power Transmission

Aero Gear Incorporated .... C 860 688-0888
Windsor *(G-10355)*
Hamilton Sundstrand Corp .... A 860 654-6000
Windsor Locks *(G-10491)*
Perry Technology Corporation .... D 860 738-2525
New Hartford *(G-5206)*

AIRCRAFT PARTS & AUXILIARY EQPT: Lighting/Landing Gear Assy

Straton Industries Inc .... D 203 375-4488
Stratford *(G-8687)*

AIRCRAFT PARTS & AUXILIARY EQPT: Military Eqpt & Armament

Faille Precision Machining .... G 860 822-1964
Baltic *(G-119)*
Morning Star Tool LLC 203 878-6026
Milford *(G-4585)*
Rti Technologies LLC .... G 860 306-4772
Columbia *(G-1612)*

AIRCRAFT PARTS & AUXILIARY EQPT: Oxygen Systems

Hamilton Standard Space .... E 860 654-6000
Windsor Locks *(G-10490)*

AIRCRAFT PARTS & AUXILIARY EQPT: Research & Development, Mfr

Delta-Ray Industries Inc .... F 203 367-9903
Bridgeport *(G-747)*

AIRCRAFT PARTS & EQPT, NEC

A-1 Machining Co .... D 860 223-6420
New Britain *(G-4931)*
Acmt Inc .... D 860 645-0592
Manchester *(G-3977)*
Advanced Def Slutions Tech LLC 860 243-1122
Bloomfield *(G-380)*
Aero Tube Technologies LLC .... E 860 289-2520
South Windsor *(G-7701)*
Aerocision LLC .... D 860 526-9700
Chester *(G-1462)*
Aerospace Components Mfrs Inc .... G 860 513-3205
Rocky Hill *(G-7220)*
Air-Lock Incorporated .... E 203 878-4691
Milford *(G-4444)*
Alexis Aerospace Inds LLC .... G 860 516-4602
Canton *(G-1303)*
Alinabal Inc .... C 203 877-3241
Milford *(G-4448)*
Anderson Manufacturing Company 203 263-2318
Woodbury *(G-10624)*
Arrow Diversified Tooling Inc .... E 860 872-9072
Ellington *(G-2576)*
Arthur Rodgers .... G 860 967-4598
Ledyard *(G-3867)*
Avalon Advanced Tech Repr Inc .... E 860 254-5442
East Windsor *(G-2483)*
Aviation Pro Pages LLC .... G 860 910-9336
Mystic *(G-4800)*
B/E Aerospace Inc .... E 203 380-5000
Stratford *(G-8576)*
Beacon Industries Inc .... C 860 594-5200
Newington *(G-5632)*
Birken Manufacturing Company .... D 860 242-2211
Bloomfield *(G-395)*
Brandstrom Instruments Inc .... E 203 544-9341
Ridgefield *(G-7126)*
Bryka Skystocks LLC .... G 845 507-8200
Newington *(G-5635)*
C & W Manufacturing Co Inc .... E 860 633-4631
Glastonbury *(G-3017)*
C V Tool Company Inc .... E 978 353-7901
Southington *(G-7901)*
Cambridge Specialty Co Inc .... D 860 828-3579
Berlin *(G-168)*
CBS Manufacturing Company .... E 860 653-8100
East Granby *(G-2196)*
Connecticut Advanced Products .... G 860 659-2260
Glastonbury *(G-3023)*
Continental Machine TI Co Inc .... E 860 223-2896
New Britain *(G-4965)*
Crane Co .... D 203 363-7300
Stamford *(G-8166)*
Dell Acquisition LLC .... E 860 677-8545
Plainville *(G-6798)*
Doncasters Inc .... D 860 449-1603
Groton *(G-3283)*
Drt Aerospace LLC .... F 860 379-0783
Winsted *(G-10515)*
Dynamic Flight Systems .... G 203 449-7211
Monroe *(G-4713)*
Edac Technologies LLC .... C 860 667-2134
Newington *(G-5649)*
Enjet Aero New Britain LLC .... C 860 356-0330
New Britain *(G-4984)*
Evoaero Inc 860 289-2520
South Windsor *(G-7753)*

First Aviation Services Inc .... G 203 291-3300
Westport *(G-10081)*
Flight Enhancements Corp .... G 912 257-0440
Oxford *(G-6658)*
Flight Support Inc .... E 203 562-1415
North Haven *(G-5942)*
Forrest Machine Inc .... D 860 563-1796
Berlin *(G-180)*
GKN Aerospace Newington LLC .... C 860 667-8502
Newington *(G-5656)*
Global Trbine Cmpnent Tech LLC .... E 860 528-4722
South Windsor *(G-7760)*
Glyne Manufacturing Co Inc .... F 203 375-4495
Stratford *(G-8618)*
Goodrich Corporation .... B 203 797-5000
Danbury *(G-1835)*
H & B Tool & Engineering Co .... E 860 528-9341
South Windsor *(G-7766)*
Helicopter Support Inc .... B 203 416-4000
Trumbull *(G-9033)*
Hexcel Corporation .... E 203 969-0666
Stamford *(G-8233)*
Hexcel Pottsville Corporation .... G 203 969-0666
Stamford *(G-8235)*
Isr (ntllgnce Srvllance Reconn .... G 203 797-5000
Danbury *(G-1853)*
Ithaco Space Systems Inc .... D 607 272-7640
Danbury *(G-1854)*
Jmk Tool Co .... G 203 937-1229
West Haven *(G-9919)*
Jobin Machine Inc .... E 860 953-1631
West Hartford *(G-9824)*
Jonal Labs Logistics LLC 203 634-4444
Meriden *(G-4181)*
Kaman Aerospace Corporation .... A 860 242-4461
Bloomfield *(G-430)*
Kaman Aerospace Corporation .... E 860 242-4461
Bloomfield *(G-431)*
Kaman Aerospace Group Inc .... F 860 243-7100
Bloomfield *(G-433)*
Kaman Corporation 860 243-7100
Bloomfield *(G-434)*
Kamatics Corporation .... E 860 243-9704
Bloomfield *(G-435)*
Kirkhill Aircraft Parts Co .... E 860 581-5701
Centerbrook *(G-1330)*
L M Gill Welding and Mfr LLC .... E 860 647-9931
Manchester *(G-4047)*
Lee Company .... A 860 399-6281
Westbrook *(G-10000)*
LM Gill Welding & Mfg LLC .... E 860 647-9931
Manchester *(G-4049)*
M & S Machine Tool Company .... G 203 933-8920
West Haven *(G-9927)*
McMellon Bros Incorporated .... E 203 375-5685
Stratford *(G-8648)*
Mtm Corporation 860 742-9600
Andover *(G-15)*
Mtu Aero Engine Design Inc .... G 860 667-2134
Newington *(G-5680)*
Naiad Dynamics Us Inc .... E 203 929-6355
Shelton *(G-7506)*
Nalbor Mfg .... G 860 828-7676
Berlin *(G-202)*
Nelson Tool & Machine Co Inc .... G 860 589-8004
Bristol *(G-1078)*
Overhaul Support Services LLC .... G 860 653-1980
East Granby *(G-2223)*
Overhaul Support Services LLC .... E 860 264-2101
East Granby *(G-2224)*
Paradigm Manchester Inc .... D 860 646-4048
Manchester *(G-4066)*
Paradigm Manchester Inc .... C 860 646-4048
Manchester *(G-4067)*
Paragon Tool Company Inc .... G 860 647-9935
Manchester *(G-4072)*
Polamer Precision Inc .... E 860 259-6200
New Britain *(G-5033)*
Polar Corporation .... G 860 223-7891
New Britain *(G-5035)*
Power Turbine Components LLC .... G 860 291-8885
South Windsor *(G-7809)*
Precision Aerospace Inc .... E 203 888-3022
Seymour *(G-7363)*
Precision Speed Mfg LLC .... E 860 635-8811
Middletown *(G-4397)*
Ramar-Hall Inc .... E 860 349-1081
Middlefield *(G-4306)*
Rotair Aerospace Corporation .... E 203 576-6545
Bridgeport *(G-892)*

PRODUCT SECTION

AMUSEMENT & RECREATION SVCS: Golf Club, Membership

Rotating Composite Tech LLC............G...... 860 829-6809
 Kensington (G-3818)
Saklax Manufacturing Company ....G...... 860 242-2538
 Bloomfield (G-483)
Satellite Tool & Mch Co Inc ....E...... 860 290-8558
 South Windsor (G-7820)
Senior Operations LLC ....D...... 860 741-2546
 Enfield (G-2691)
Shari Goodstein Rossi ....G...... 914 485-1600
 Danbury (G-1944)
Simmonds Precision Pdts Inc ....E...... 203 797-5000
 Danbury (G-1952)
Sky Mfg Company ....G...... 203 439-7016
 Cheshire (G-1447)
Solar Nebula LLC ....G...... 516 362-8048
 North Granby (G-5881)
Susan Martovich ....G...... 203 881-1848
 Oxford (G-6696)
Tachwa Enterprises Inc ....G...... 203 367-9903
 Bridgeport (G-919)
Thompson Aerospace LLC ....F...... 860 516-0472
 Bristol (G-1128)
TLD America Corporation ....E...... 860 602-3400
 Windsor (G-10453)
Triumph Actuation Systems - Co ....D...... 860 687-5412
 Windsor (G-10455)
Triumph Group Inc ....G...... 860 726-9378
 Bloomfield (G-494)
Unison Engine Components ....G...... 860 647-5586
 Manchester (G-4104)
United Aero Group LLC ....G...... 203 283-9524
 Shelton (G-7577)
United Avionics Inc ....E...... 203 723-1404
 Naugatuck (G-4925)
Valley Tool and Mfg LLC ....D...... 203 799-8800
 Orange (G-6632)
W and G Machine Company Inc ....E...... 203 288-8772
 Hamden (G-3526)
W&R Manufacturing Inc ....G...... 203 877-5955
 Milford (G-4677)
Whitakers ....G...... 860 228-3762
 Hebron (G-3758)
Whitcraft LLC ....C...... 860 974-0786
 Eastford (G-2544)
Whitcraft Scrborough/Tempe LLC......C...... 860 974-0786
 Eastford (G-2545)

AIRCRAFT PARTS WHOLESALERS

James J Scott LLC ....G...... 860 571-9200
 Rocky Hill (G-7252)
Kirkhill Aircraft Parts Co ....E...... 860 581-5701
 Centerbrook (G-1330)
TLD America Corporation ....E...... 860 602-3400
 Windsor (G-10453)

AIRCRAFT PARTS/AUX EQPT: Airframe Assy, Exc Guided Missiles

Kaman Aerospace Corporation ....D...... 860 242-4461
 Bloomfield (G-432)

AIRCRAFT PROPELLERS & PARTS

Aerocomposites Inc ....G...... 860 829-6809
 Kensington (G-3804)
Leading Edge Concepts Inc ....G...... 203 797-1200
 Bethel (G-321)

AIRCRAFT SEATS

Jetset Interiors LLC ....G...... 860 292-7962
 Windsor Locks (G-10492)
Torrington Distributors Inc ....E...... 860 482-4464
 Torrington (G-8981)

AIRCRAFT SERVICING & REPAIRING

Sikorsky International Product...........G...... 203 375-0095
 Stratford (G-8680)

AIRCRAFT TURBINES

Capstone Manufacturing Inc ....G...... 413 636-6170
 South Windsor (G-7723)
Ethosenergy Component Repr LLC ...E...... 203 949-8144
 Wallingford (G-9258)
Gamma Ventures Inc ....G...... 860 653-2613
 Granby (G-3107)

AIRCRAFT: Airplanes, Fixed Or Rotary Wing

Northeast Mfg Co LLC........................G...... 860 763-4000
 Enfield (G-2670)
Riverside Aviation ....G...... 203 637-4231
 Old Greenwich (G-6483)

AIRCRAFT: Autogiros

Corporate Aircraft Svcs LLC................G...... 203 730-2024
 Danbury (G-1775)

AIRCRAFT: Motorized

Connecticut Drone Services LLC ....G...... 203 966-7016
 New Canaan (G-5096)
Drone Imaging LLC..............................G...... 203 256-1151
 Fairfield (G-2777)
Infocus Droneworx LLC ....G...... 860 499-0789
 Wethersfield (G-10198)
Northeast Drone Services LLC ....G...... 203 220-6478
 Trumbull (G-9051)
Shoreline Drone Solutions ....G...... 347 239-5636
 Guilford (G-3390)

AIRCRAFT: Nonmotorized & Lighter-Than-air

Aquiline Drones LLC ....F...... 860 361-7958
 Hartford (G-3553)
Bae Systems Applied Intel Inc.............G...... 203 323-0066
 Stamford (G-8105)

AIRCRAFT: Research & Development, Manufacturer

Straton Industries Inc ....D...... 203 375-4488
 Stratford (G-8687)
Swift Kathryn ....G...... 860 754-4150
 Moodus (G-4776)
Tranquil Perspectives LLC ....G...... 860 919-9762
 North Haven (G-6000)
Vistar Foundation Inc ....G...... 203 968-1995
 Stamford (G-8486)

AIRPORTS, FLYING FIELDS & SVCS

United Technologies Corp ....F...... 860 292-3270
 East Granby (G-2233)

ALARMS: Burglar

Alarm One...G...... 203 239-1714
 North Haven (G-5898)
Mattatuck Alarm Co Inc ....G...... 203 754-0541
 Waterbury (G-9537)
UTC Fire SEC Americas Corp Inc ....G...... 941 739-4200
 Farmington (G-2974)
UTC Fire SEC Americas Corp Inc ....C...... 203 426-1180
 Newtown (G-5796)

ALARMS: Fire

Allstate Fire Systems LLC ....E...... 860 246-7711
 Middletown (G-4314)

ALLOYS: Additive, Exc Copper Or Made In Blast Furnaces

Alent USA Holding Inc ....B...... 203 575-5727
 Waterbury (G-9426)

ALUMINUM

Angelos Aluminum ....G...... 203 469-3117
 East Haven (G-2410)
Arconic Inc ....G...... 860 379-3314
 Winsted (G-10505)
Evergreen Aluminum LLC ....F...... 203 328-4900
 Stamford (G-8200)
Wilson Partitions ....G...... 203 316-8033
 Stamford (G-8494)
Wilson Partitions Inc ....F...... 203 316-8033
 Stamford (G-8495)

ALUMINUM PRDTS

Brynwood Partners V Ltd Partnr ....G...... 203 622-1790
 Greenwich (G-3138)
Narragansett Screw Co ....F...... 860 379-4059
 Winsted (G-10531)
Unique Extrusions Incorporated ....E...... 860 632-1314
 Cromwell (G-1723)

ALUMINUM: Pigs

All Steel LLC ....G...... 860 871-6023
 Ellington (G-2574)

ALUMINUM: Rolling & Drawing

Acme Monaco Corporation ....C...... 860 224-1349
 New Britain (G-4934)
Alpha-Core Inc ....E...... 203 954-0050
 Shelton (G-7392)
Erickson Metals Corporation ....E...... 203 272-2918
 Cheshire (G-1386)

AMBULANCE SVCS

Danbury Medi-Car Service Inc ....G...... 203 748-3433
 Danbury (G-1783)

AMMUNITION

Buddy-Mentor Inc ....G...... 203 258-3871
 Bridgeport (G-725)
Ensign-Bickford Industries Inc ....E...... 860 658-4411
 Simsbury (G-7622)
Fenrir Industries Inc ....F...... 203 977-0671
 Stamford (G-8203)
Glimmer of Light ....G...... 860 605-4086
 New Milford (G-5537)

AMMUNITION: Cartridges Case, 30 mm & Below

Shell Shock Technologies Llc ....G...... 203 557-3256
 Westport (G-10155)

AMMUNITION: Components

Geneve Corporation ....E...... 203 358-8000
 Stamford (G-8215)

AMMUNITION: Small Arms

Brass City Munitions LLC ....G...... 203 509-7088
 Wolcott (G-10549)
Capstone Manufacturing Inc................G...... 413 636-6170
 South Windsor (G-7723)
Fenrir Industries Inc ....F...... 203 977-0671
 Stamford (G-8203)
General Dynamics Ordnance ....F...... 860 404-0162
 Avon (G-82)
Illinois Tool Works Inc ....C...... 203 574-2119
 Waterbury (G-9503)
Independence Enterprises LLC ....G...... 774 549-8153
 Manchester (G-4032)
Jkb Daira Inc ....G...... 203 642-4824
 Norwalk (G-6223)

AMPLIFIERS

Ki Inc ....E...... 203 641-5492
 Orange (G-6608)
Krell Industries LLC ....F...... 203 298-4000
 Orange (G-6609)

AMPLIFIERS: RF & IF Power

Advanced Receiver Research..............G...... 860 485-0310
 Harwinton (G-3719)

AMUSEMENT & RECREATION SVCS: Art Gallery, Commercial

Pelegnos Stined GL Art Gallery............G...... 860 621-2900
 Plantsville (G-6907)
Petrini Art & Frame LLC ....G...... 860 677-2747
 Avon (G-99)

AMUSEMENT & RECREATION SVCS: Fishing Boat Operations, Party

Montauk Pilots Inc ....G...... 860 535-3200
 North Stonington (G-6030)

AMUSEMENT & RECREATION SVCS: Golf Club, Membership

South Windsor Golf Course LLC ....D...... 860 648-4653
 South Windsor (G-7826)

Employee Codes: A=Over 500 employees, B=251-500
C=101-250, D=51-100, E=20-50, F=10-19, G=1-9

AMUSEMENT & RECREATION SVCS: Golf Professionals
S Hassel Golf Works .... G 860 274-4011
  Watertown *(G-9732)*

AMUSEMENT & RECREATION SVCS: Hot Air Balloon Rides
Berkshire Balloons LLC .... G 203 250-8441
  Plantsville *(G-6886)*

AMUSEMENT & RECREATION SVCS: Physical Fitness Instruction
Safe Laser Therapy LLC .... G 203 261-4400
  Stamford *(G-8400)*

AMUSEMENT & RECREATION SVCS: Recreation Center
Lyman Farm Incorporated .... C 860 349-1793
  Middlefield *(G-4302)*

AMUSEMENT & RECREATION SVCS: Tennis Courts, Non-Member
Danbury Grassroots Tennis Inc .... G 203 797-0500
  Danbury *(G-1782)*

AMUSEMENT & RECREATION SVCS: Yoga Instruction
Vanilla Politics LLC .... G 203 221-0895
  Weston *(G-10043)*

AMUSEMENT MACHINES: Coin Operated
Rlp Inc .... G 203 359-2504
  Stamford *(G-8394)*

AMUSEMENT PARK DEVICES & RIDES
EA Patten Co LLC .... D 860 649-2851
  Manchester *(G-4013)*
Kevco .... G 860 747-4135
  Plainville *(G-6830)*
MGS Manufacturing Inc .... G 203 484-9275
  North Branford *(G-5850)*

AMUSEMENT PARK DEVICES & RIDES: Carnival Mach & Eqpt, NEC
Marenna Amusements LLC .... F 203 623-4386
  Orange *(G-6612)*

ANALYZERS: Blood & Body Fluid
Razzberry Inc .... G 510 495-5366
  Hamden *(G-3502)*

ANALYZERS: Network
Advanced Business Group .... G 203 881-9660
  Oxford *(G-6637)*
Carte Medical Corp .... G 860 258-1970
  Wethersfield *(G-10186)*
Technology Integrators Inc .... G 203 333-7185
  Fairfield *(G-2854)*

ANIMAL FEED & SUPPLEMENTS: Livestock & Poultry
Classic Brands LLC .... G 303 936-2444
  Plainfield *(G-6744)*
H J Baker & Brother Inc .... G 501 664-4870
  Shelton *(G-7455)*

ANIMAL FOOD & SUPPLEMENTS: Dog
A L C Inovators Inc .... G 203 877-8526
  Milford *(G-4436)*
Bravo LLC .... F 866 922-9222
  Manchester *(G-3987)*
Bravo LLC .... E 860 896-1899
  Vernon *(G-9134)*
CP Apn Inc .... G 330 682-3000
  Greenwich *(G-3147)*
Joy Food Company .... G 917 549-6240
  Darien *(G-2029)*

ANIMAL FOOD & SUPPLEMENTS: Dog & Cat
Blue Buffalo Company Ltd .... B 203 762-9751
  Wilton *(G-10274)*
Fine Pets LLC .... G 203 833-1517
  Greenwich *(G-3160)*

ANIMAL FOOD & SUPPLEMENTS: Feed Supplements
A L C Inovators Inc .... G 203 877-8526
  Milford *(G-4436)*
ALC Sales Company LLC .... G 203 877-8526
  Milford *(G-4445)*
Bactana Corp .... G 203 716-1230
  Farmington *(G-2881)*
Earth Animal Ventures Inc 717 271-6393
  Stamford *(G-8190)*
Source Inc .... G 203 488-6400
  North Branford *(G-5858)*

ANIMAL FOOD & SUPPLEMENTS: Pet, Exc Dog & Cat, Canned
Blue Buffalo Pet Products Inc .... E 203 762-9751
  Wilton *(G-10275)*
Canidae Corp .... G 860 539-5307
  Plainville *(G-6783)*

ANIMAL FOOD & SUPPLEMENTS: Poultry
HJ Baker & Bro LLC .... E 203 682-9200
  Shelton *(G-7465)*
Moark LLC .... E 951 332-3300
  North Franklin *(G-5876)*

ANODIZING SVC
Aluminum Finishing Company Inc ..... E 203 333-1690
  Bridgeport *(G-689)*
Anomatic Corporation .... G 203 720-2367
  Naugatuck *(G-4859)*
Chemical-Electric Corporation .... G 203 743-5131
  Danbury *(G-1767)*
Light Metals Coloring Co Inc .... D 860 621-0145
  Southington *(G-7947)*
Maryann D Langdon .... G 203 562-7161
  New Haven *(G-5326)*

ANTENNAS: Radar Or Communications
Meriden Electronics Corp .... G 203 237-8811
  Meriden *(G-4195)*

ANTENNAS: Receiving
CBA Lighting and Controls Inc .... G 860 623-1924
  Windsor Locks *(G-10477)*

ANTI-OXIDANTS
Si Group USA (usaa) LLC .... C 203 702-6140
  Danbury *(G-1946)*
Si Group USA Hldings Usha Corp ..... E 203 702-6140
  Danbury *(G-1947)*

ANTIFREEZE
Prestone Products Corporation .... E 203 731-7880
  Danbury *(G-1919)*

ANTIQUE & CLASSIC AUTOMOBILE RESTORATION
Ems International Inc .... G 860 526-2060
  Chester *(G-1472)*

ANTIQUE FURNITURE RESTORATION & REPAIR
Reborn House .... G 203 216-9874
  Branford *(G-640)*
Urban Antique Radio .... G 203 877-2409
  Milford *(G-4671)*

ANTIQUE REPAIR & RESTORATION SVCS, EXC FURNITURE & AUTOS
McMellon Associates LLC .... G 203 272-5859
  Cheshire *(G-1413)*

ANTISEPTICS, MEDICINAL
Aplicare Products LLC .... C 203 630-0500
  Meriden *(G-4145)*

APPAREL DESIGNERS: Commercial
House of Bubba LLC .... G 860 429-4250
  Willington *(G-10250)*
Mangladesh LLC .... G 203 299-0697
  Fairfield *(G-2812)*

APPLIANCE CORDS: Household Electrical Eqpt
Naugatuck Elec Indus Sup LLC .... G 203 723-1082
  Naugatuck *(G-4905)*
World Cord Sets Inc .... G 860 763-2100
  Enfield *(G-2708)*

APPLIANCES, HOUSEHOLD: Kitchen, Major, Exc Refrigs & Stoves
Clarke Distribution Corp .... G 203 838-9385
  Norwalk *(G-6116)*
Conair Corporation .... B 203 351-9000
  Stamford *(G-8156)*

APPLIANCES, HOUSEHOLD: Refrigs, Mechanical & Absorption
Medelco Inc .... G 203 275-8070
  Bridgeport *(G-836)*

APPLIANCES: Household, NEC
A+ Plus Appliance .... G 860 878-9624
  Harwinton *(G-3718)*
Demand Pro LLC .... G 860 438-8843
  New Britain *(G-4974)*

APPLIANCES: Household, Refrigerators & Freezers
New Brnswick Scientific of Del ...... G 732 287-1200
  Enfield *(G-2668)*

APPLIANCES: Major, Cooking
Airigan Solutions LLC .... G 203 594-7781
  Southport *(G-7998)*
Conair Corporation .... B 203 351-9000
  Stamford *(G-8156)*
Kenyon International Inc .... G 860 664-4906
  Clinton *(G-1510)*

APPLIANCES: Small, Electric
Alstrom Power .... G 203 783-1046
  Milford *(G-4451)*
Asselin Electric LLC .... G 860 379-3056
  Winsted *(G-10507)*
Conair Corporation .... D 800 492-7464
  Torrington *(G-8914)*
Conair Corporation .... B 203 351-9000
  Stamford *(G-8156)*
Dampits LLC .... G 203 210-7946
  Wilton *(G-10288)*
Jarden Corporation .... E 203 845-5300
  Norwalk *(G-6218)*
McIntire Company .... F 860 585-8559
  Bristol *(G-1070)*

APPRAISAL SVCS, EXC REAL ESTATE
Murdoch and Co .... G 203 226-2800
  Westport *(G-10126)*

ARCHITECT'S SUPPLIES WHOLESALERS
Technical Reproductions Inc .... F 203 849-9100
  Norwalk *(G-6365)*

ARCHITECTURAL PANELS OR PARTS: Porcelain Enameled
Insulpane Connecticut Inc .... D 800 922-3248
  Hamden *(G-3465)*

ARCHITECTURAL SVCS
Coreslab Structures Conn Inc .... D 860 283-8281
  Thomaston *(G-8786)*

PRODUCT SECTION

AUDIO & VIDEO EQPT, EXC COMMERCIAL

Hydeville Manfacturing Inc .... G 203 265-0524
  Wallingford (G-9285)
Nelson Archtctural Restoration .... G 860 429-3830
  Willington (G-10252)

ARCHITECTURAL SVCS: Engineering
United-Bim Inc .... G 860 289-1100
  East Hartford (G-2398)

ARCHITECTURAL SVCS: Engineering
Kenneth M Champlin & Assoc Inc .... F 203 562-8400
  New Haven (G-5308)

ARMATURE REPAIRING & REWINDING SVC
Carter Inv Holdings Corp .... G 860 283-5801
  Thomaston (G-8783)
Ward Leonard Holdings LLC .... G 860 283-5801
  Thomaston (G-8820)
Ward Leonard Inv Holdings LLC .... G 860 283-5801
  Thomaston (G-8821)
Ward Leonard Operating LLC .... G 860 283-5801
  Thomaston (G-8822)
Ward Lonard Houma Holdings LLC .... G 860 283-5801
  Thomaston (G-8823)
WI Intermediate Holdings LLC .... G 860 283-5801
  Thomaston (G-8825)

ARMATURES: Ind
GE Steam Power Inc .... C 423 648-4161
  Windsor (G-10389)

ART & ORNAMENTAL WARE: Pottery
Company of Craftsmen .... G 860 536-4189
  Mystic (G-4808)
Jean Elton Studios LLC .... G 917 287-0480
  Fairfield (G-2800)

ART DEALERS & GALLERIES
Artful Framer LLC .... G 860 678-1321
  Avon (G-76)
Greenwich Workshop Inc .... E 203 881-3336
  Seymour (G-7348)

ART GALLERIES
Greenwich Workshop Inc .... E 203 881-3336
  Seymour (G-7348)

ART GOODS & SPLYS WHOLESALERS
Exhibitease LLC .... G 203 481-0792
  Branford (G-592)

ART GOODS, WHOLESALE
Greenwich Workshop Inc .... E 203 881-3336
  Seymour (G-7348)
S & S Worldwide Inc .... C 860 537-3451
  Colchester (G-1574)

ART MARBLE: Concrete
Bella Pietra LLC .... G 203 655-1322
  Darien (G-2007)

ART RELATED SVCS
Elena Dieck .... G 860 623-9472
  Broad Brook (G-1149)

ART RESTORATION SVC
John Canning & Co Ltd .... E 203 272-9868
  Cheshire (G-1401)

ARTIST'S MATERIALS & SPLYS
Color Craft Ltd .... F 800 509-6563
  East Granby (G-2197)

ARTISTS' AGENTS & BROKERS
Kirchoff Wohlberg Inc .... F 212 644-2020
  Madison (G-3934)

ARTISTS' MATERIALS, WHOLESALE
Color Craft Ltd .... F 800 509-6563
  East Granby (G-2197)

ARTISTS' MATERIALS: Brushes, Air
Explicit Airbrush .... G 860 582-6038
  Southington (G-7920)

ARTISTS' MATERIALS: Chalks, Carpenters', Blackboard, Etc
Diiorios Custom Wdwkg LLC .... G 203 855-1635
  Norwalk (G-6144)

ARTISTS' MATERIALS: Easels
Pastrana Unlimited LLC .... G 860 747-6633
  Plainville (G-6851)

ARTISTS' MATERIALS: Ink, Drawing, Black & Colored
Colors Ink .... G 203 269-4000
  Wallingford (G-9233)
Screening Ink LLC .... G 860 212-0475
  Enfield (G-2690)

ARTISTS' MATERIALS: Tables, Drawing
Little Artist Paint Co LLC .... G 860 989-1996
  Plainville (G-6833)

ARTISTS' MATERIALS: Water Colors
Steve Cryan Studio .... G 860 388-5010
  Old Saybrook (G-6571)

ARTS & CRAFTS SCHOOL
Hartford Artisans Weaving Ctr .... G 860 727-5727
  Hartford (G-3605)
Pelegnos Stined GL Art Gallery .... G 860 621-2900
  Plantsville (G-6907)

ARTWORK: Framed
Alpine Management Group LLC .... G 954 531-1692
  Westport (G-10052)
K F Machining .... G 860 292-6466
  East Windsor (G-2501)
Picture This Hartford Inc .... G 860 528-1409
  East Hartford (G-2355)
R Van Loan Custom Framing LLC .... G 203 422-2881
  Greenwich (G-3221)

ASBESTOS PRODUCTS
Zero Hazard LLC .... G 860 561-9879
  Farmington (G-2979)

ASBESTOS REMOVAL EQPT
D P Engineering Inc .... G 203 421-7965
  Madison (G-3916)

ASH TRAYS: Stamped Metal
No Butts Bin Company Inc .... G 203 245-5924
  Madison (G-3942)

ASPHALT & ASPHALT PRDTS
AEN Asphalt Inc .... G 860 885-0500
  Bozrah (G-523)
Betkoski Brothers LLC .... G 203 723-8262
  Beacon Falls (G-131)
L Suzio Asphalt Co Inc .... F 203 237-8421
  Meriden (G-4185)
T D I Enterprises LLC .... G 203 630-1268
  Meriden (G-4249)
Wescon Corp of Conn .... G 860 599-2500
  Pawcatuck (G-6731)
Westchester Industries Inc .... F 203 661-0055
  Greenwich (G-3257)

ASPHALT COATINGS & SEALERS
Firestone Building Pdts Co LLC .... D 860 584-4516
  Bristol (G-1039)
Gorilla Sealcoating LLC .... G 475 218-3506
  Danbury (G-1836)
Seal King Sealcoating .... G 203 871-1423
  Bethel (G-341)
TPC Replacement Window LLC .... G 860 274-6971
  Oakville (G-6464)

ASPHALT MINING & BITUMINOUS STONE QUARRYING SVCS
Galasso Materials LLC .... C 860 527-1825
  East Granby (G-2206)

ASPHALT MIXTURES WHOLESALERS
Suzio York Hill Companies .... G 888 789-4626
  Meriden (G-4248)

ASSEMBLING & PACKAGING SVCS: Cosmetic Kits
Madonna Black Buddist LLC .... G 203 589-9796
  Greenwich (G-3196)
Skin & Co North America LLC .... G 888 444-9971
  West Haven (G-9955)

ASSEMBLING SVC: Plumbing Fixture Fittings, Plastic
Plastic Assembly Systems LLC .... F 203 393-0639
  Bethany (G-248)

ASSOCIATIONS: Business
Chief Executive Group LLC .... F 785 832-0303
  Stamford (G-8143)
Prime Business Services .... G 203 453-1627
  Guilford (G-3384)
Ram Belting Company Inc .... G 860 438-7029
  New Britain (G-5040)

ASSOCIATIONS: Engineering
Society For Exprmntal McHanics .... G 203 790-6373
  Bethel (G-343)
Society Plastics Engineers Inc .... E 203 740-5422
  Bethel (G-344)

ASSOCIATIONS: Real Estate Management
Louis Dreyfus Holding Company .... B 203 761-2000
  Wilton (G-10310)
Triumph Consulting .... G 860 263-8335
  Hartford (G-3706)

ASSOCIATIONS: Trade
National Shooting Sports Found .... E 203 426-1320
  Newtown (G-5762)

ATHLETIC CLUB & GYMNASIUMS, MEMBERSHIP
Barclay-Davis Enterprises LLC .... G 860 578-9563
  Hartford (G-3555)

ATOMIZERS
B&D Industries LLC .... G 860 604-2404
  Westbrook (G-9992)
Galata Chemicals LLC .... F 203 236-9000
  Southbury (G-7854)
Marmon Engnered Wire Cable LLC .... G 860 653-8300
  Hartford (G-3635)
Norfolk Industries LLC .... G 860 618-8822
  Greenwich (G-3210)
O & G Industries Inc .... C 860 485-6600
  Harwinton (G-3735)
O & G Industries Inc .... C 203 881-5192
  Beacon Falls (G-145)
Solidification Pdts Intl Inc .... G 203 484-9494
  Northford (G-6053)

AUCTION SVCS: Livestock
Frank Demartino and Sons .... G 203 734-1074
  Seymour (G-7346)

AUDIO & VIDEO EQPT, EXC COMMERCIAL
Harman Becker Automotive Syste .... G 203 328-3501
  Stamford (G-8224)
Hatcams LLC .... G 203 303-7250
  Wallingford (G-9279)
Impact Sales & Marketing LLC .... G 860 523-5366
  West Hartford (G-9820)
Infinite Audio LLC .... G 203 924-2558
  Shelton (G-7476)
Insight Plus Technology LLC .... G 860 930-4763
  Bristol (G-1051)

Employee Codes: A=Over 500 employees, B=251-500
C=101-250, D=51-100, E=20-50, F=10-19, G=1-9

AUDIO & VIDEO EQPT, EXC COMMERCIAL

Microphase Corporation .... E 203 866-8000
  Shelton *(G-7500)*
PMC Technologies LLC .... G 203 222-0000
  Weston *(G-10036)*
Whelen Engineering Company Inc .... B 860 526-9504
  Chester *(G-1485)*
Xintekidel Inc .... G 203 348-9229
  Stamford *(G-8503)*

AUDIO COMPONENTS

Harman International Inds Inc .... B 203 328-3500
  Stamford *(G-8226)*
Harman International Inds Inc .... G 203 328-3500
  Stamford *(G-8227)*
Harman KG Holding LLC .... F 203 328-3500
  Stamford *(G-8229)*
Redco Audio Inc .... F 203 502-7600
  Stratford *(G-8674)*
Thor Audio .... G 203 373-9264
  Fairfield *(G-2856)*

AUDIO ELECTRONIC SYSTEMS

Advanced HM Audio & Video LLC .... G 860 621-0631
  Plantsville *(G-6883)*
Alarmco .... G 203 458-2646
  Guilford *(G-3323)*
David J Weber .... G 203 949-9198
  Wallingford *(G-9247)*
Harman Consumer Inc .... G 203 328-3500
  Stamford *(G-8225)*
John Samuel Group .... G 860 806-5734
  Torrington *(G-8939)*
Laufer Teknik .... G 860 355-4484
  Roxbury *(G-7278)*
Proxtalkercom LLC .... G 203 721-6074
  Waterbury *(G-9590)*
Service Dept .... G 203 335-1491
  Bridgeport *(G-900)*
Vintage Performance LLC .... G 860 542-5753
  Norfolk *(G-5828)*
Visionpoint LLC .... E 860 436-9673
  Newington *(G-5720)*

AUDIO-VISUAL PROGRAM PRODUCTION SVCS

Play-It Productions Inc .... F 212 695-6530
  Colchester *(G-1566)*

AUDIOLOGICAL EQPT: Electronic

Textspeak Corporation .... F 203 803-1069
  Westport *(G-10165)*
Wideband Solutions Inc .... G 203 383-8918
  Plainville *(G-6877)*

AUTHORS' AGENTS & BROKERS

New England Publishing Assoc .... G 860 345-7323
  Higganum *(G-3771)*

AUTO & HOME SUPPLY STORES: Auto & Truck Eqpt & Parts

Autopart International Inc .... F 203 931-9189
  West Haven *(G-9885)*
Genuine Parts Company .... F 860 623-4479
  Windsor Locks *(G-10486)*

AUTO & HOME SUPPLY STORES: Automotive Access

Ems International Inc .... G 860 526-2060
  Chester *(G-1472)*

AUTO & HOME SUPPLY STORES: Automotive parts

C B Fabrication .... G 860 889-8030
  Taftville *(G-8740)*
Freds Auto Machine .... G 203 744-2950
  Bethel *(G-302)*
Soltis Speed Equipment .... G 860 489-0119
  Torrington *(G-8971)*

AUTO & HOME SUPPLY STORES: Speed Shops, Incl Race Car Splys

Reliable Welding & Speed LLC .... G 860 749-3977
  Enfield *(G-2687)*

AUTO & HOME SUPPLY STORES: Truck Eqpt & Parts

Lo Stocco Motors .... G 203 797-9618
  Danbury *(G-1875)*
S Camerota & Sons Inc .... G 203 782-0360
  North Haven *(G-5989)*

AUTO SPLYS & PARTS, NEW, WHSLE: Exhaust Sys, Mufflers, Etc

Autopart International Inc .... F 203 931-9189
  West Haven *(G-9885)*

AUTOMATIC REGULATING CNTRLS: Liq Lvl, Residential/Comm Heat

Center For Discovery .... E 203 955-1381
  Southport *(G-8002)*
Innovative Fusion Inc .... E 203 729-3873
  Naugatuck *(G-4891)*

AUTOMATIC REGULATING CONTROL: Building Svcs Monitoring, Auto

Johnson Controls Inc .... G 860 887-7185
  Norwich *(G-6419)*
Johnson Controls Inc .... D 678 297-4040
  Meriden *(G-4179)*
Newgate Instruments LLC .... G 860 784-1968
  East Granby *(G-2218)*
Nurses Alarm Systems Inc .... G 860 872-0025
  Vernon Rockville *(G-9172)*
Process Automtn Solutions Inc .... E 203 207-9917
  Danbury *(G-1920)*
Universal Building Contrls Inc .... F 203 235-1530
  Meriden *(G-4260)*

AUTOMATIC REGULATING CONTROLS: AC & Refrigeration

New Air Technologies Inc .... G 860 767-1542
  Ivoryton *(G-3787)*

AUTOMATIC REGULATING CONTROLS: Energy Cutoff, Residtl/Comm

Johnson Controls Inc .... C 860 688-7151
  Windsor *(G-10400)*

AUTOMATIC REGULATING CONTROLS: Hydronic Pressure Or Temp

J & B Service Company LLC .... G 203 743-9357
  Bethel *(G-314)*

AUTOMATIC REGULATING CONTROLS: Limit, Heating, Residtl/Comm

Emme E2ms LLC .... F 860 845-8810
  Bristol *(G-1027)*

AUTOMATIC REGULATING CONTROLS: Refrig/Air-Cond Defrost

Belimo Aircontrols (usa) Inc .... C 800 543-9038
  Danbury *(G-1752)*
Belimo Automation AG .... F 203 749-3319
  Danbury *(G-1753)*
Belimo Customization USA Inc .... G 203 791-9915
  Danbury *(G-1754)*

AUTOMATIC TELLER MACHINES

Barnum Wash & Dry .... G 203 870-6099
  Stratford *(G-8580)*
Black Gold Enterprises .... G 203 729-4444
  Naugatuck *(G-4862)*
Chestnut Shell .... G 203 775-5067
  Brookfield *(G-1171)*
Marinero Express 809 East .... G 203 487-0636
  Stamford *(G-8297)*

AUTOMOBILES & OTHER MOTOR VEHICLES WHOLESALERS

New Haven Companies Inc .... F 203 469-6421
  East Haven *(G-2444)*

AUTOMOTIVE & TRUCK GENERAL REPAIR SVC

All Tech Auto/Truck Electric .... G 203 790-8990
  Danbury *(G-1736)*
Bonenfants Drv Your Auto Svc .... G 203 222-2239
  Westport *(G-10061)*
G W P Inc .... G 860 953-1153
  Hartford *(G-3595)*
Richies Automotive LLC .... G 860 482-0667
  Harwinton *(G-3737)*

AUTOMOTIVE BODY SHOP

Alton Enterprises Inc .... G 203 469-9719
  East Haven *(G-2408)*
John Mezes & Sons Inc .... G 203 255-6841
  Bridgeport *(G-809)*

AUTOMOTIVE LETTERING & PAINTING SVCS

911 Motorsports LLC .... G 203 755-8405
  Waterbury *(G-9421)*

AUTOMOTIVE PAINT SHOP

Color Ite Refinishing Co .... G 203 393-0240
  Bethany *(G-238)*

AUTOMOTIVE PARTS, ACCESS & SPLYS

AAM Welding + Fabrication LLC .... G 203 479-4339
  West Haven *(G-9880)*
Airpot Corporation .... E 800 848-7681
  Norwalk *(G-6064)*
Armored Autogroup Inc .... D 203 205-2900
  Danbury *(G-1746)*
Armored Autogroup Sales Inc .... C 203 205-2900
  Danbury *(G-1748)*
Beacon Group Inc .... C 860 594-5200
  Newington *(G-5631)*
Cambridge Specialty Co Inc .... D 860 828-3579
  Berlin *(G-168)*
Cheshire Manufacturing Co Inc .... G 203 272-3586
  Cheshire *(G-1369)*
Clayton Offroad Manufacturer .... G 475 238-8251
  East Haven *(G-2417)*
Competition Engineering Inc .... C 203 453-5200
  Guilford *(G-3339)*
Connecticut Axle Service LLC .... G 860 872-3858
  Ellington *(G-2582)*
Continental Machine TI Co Inc .... D 860 223-2896
  New Britain *(G-4965)*
CT Drive-Shaft Service LLC .... G 860 289-6459
  East Hartford *(G-2311)*
Dearborn Deuce LLC .... G 860 669-3232
  Clinton *(G-1500)*
Defeo Manufacturaing .... G 203 775-1950
  Brookfield *(G-1178)*
Defeo Manufacturing .... G 203 775-0254
  Brookfield *(G-1179)*
Defeo Manufacturing Inc .... G 203 775-0254
  Brookfield *(G-1180)*
Dline LLC .... G 860 984-2076
  Old Saybrook *(G-6531)*
ERA Replica Automobiles .... G 860 229-7968
  New Britain *(G-4985)*
Expressway Lube Centers .... F 203 744-2511
  Danbury *(G-1820)*
Fram Group Operations LLC .... E 203 830-7800
  Danbury *(G-1829)*
Genuine Parts Company .... F 860 623-4479
  Windsor Locks *(G-10486)*
Hc Innovations Inc .... G 203 925-9600
  Shelton *(G-7462)*
International Automobile Entps .... F 860 224-0253
  New Britain *(G-5001)*
International Automobile Entps .... F 860 224-0253
  New Britain *(G-5002)*
Janus Motorsports LLC .... G 860 857-6041
  Niantic *(G-5812)*
Jk Motorsports .... G 203 255-9120
  Fairfield *(G-2802)*
Jobin Machine Inc .... E 860 953-1631
  West Hartford *(G-9824)*
King of Covers Inc .... G 860 379-2427
  Winsted *(G-10526)*
Lee Company .... A 860 399-6281
  Westbrook *(G-10000)*
Nickson Industries Inc .... E 860 747-1671
  Plainville *(G-6847)*

PRODUCT SECTION

Nucap US Inc ....E...... 203 879-1423
  Wolcott *(G-10578)*
Park Avenue Securities ....G...... 860 677-2600
  Farmington *(G-2947)*
Platt-Labonia of N Haven Inc ....D...... 203 239-5681
  North Haven *(G-5977)*
Pratt & Whitney Engine Svcs ....B...... 860 344-4000
  Middletown *(G-4396)*
Proliance International Inc ....G...... 860 688-7644
  Windsor *(G-10427)*
S Camerota & Sons Inc ....G...... 203 782-0360
  North Haven *(G-5989)*
Spectrum Brands Inc ....G...... 203 205-2900
  Danbury *(G-1955)*
Swpci ....G...... 203 278-6400
  Shelton *(G-7560)*
Thule Inc ....G...... 203 881-9600
  Milford *(G-4664)*
Turbine Technologies Inc ....G...... 860 678-1642
  Farmington *(G-2971)*
Unitec ....G...... 203 778-0400
  Danbury *(G-1969)*
Vulcan Industries Incl ....C...... 860 683-2005
  Windsor *(G-10460)*

AUTOMOTIVE PARTS: Plastic

East Spring Obsolete Auto ....G...... 203 266-5488
  Bethlehem *(G-370)*
Jor Services LLC ....G...... 203 594-7774
  New Canaan *(G-5112)*
Lawrence Holdings Inc ....F...... 203 949-1600
  Wallingford *(G-9301)*
Specialty Sintered ....G...... 860 263-8332
  Hartford *(G-3691)*

AUTOMOTIVE RADIATOR REPAIR SHOPS

Associated Welding Process ....G...... 860 677-0671
  Farmington *(G-2879)*

AUTOMOTIVE REPAIR SHOPS: Auto Front End Repair

WH Rose Inc ....E...... 860 228-8258
  Columbia *(G-1615)*

AUTOMOTIVE REPAIR SHOPS: Engine Rebuilding

A & M Auto Machine Inc ....G...... 203 237-3502
  Meriden *(G-4136)*
RA Senft Inc ....G...... 860 399-5967
  Westbrook *(G-10006)*

AUTOMOTIVE REPAIR SHOPS: Machine Shop

A & M Auto Machine Inc ....G...... 203 237-3502
  Meriden *(G-4136)*
Accu-Mill Technologies LLC ....G...... 860 747-3921
  Plainville *(G-6764)*
Andys Automotive Machine ....G...... 860 793-2455
  Plainville *(G-6770)*
Dennis Savela ....G...... 860 774-3963
  Danielson *(G-1989)*
Kehl Technology & Prfmce LLC ....G...... 203 484-4808
  Northford *(G-6049)*
M & B Automotive Machine Shop ....G...... 203 348-6134
  Stamford *(G-8292)*
M K M Enterprises Inc ....G...... 203 250-7937
  Cheshire *(G-1410)*
RA Senft Inc ....G...... 860 399-5967
  Westbrook *(G-10006)*

AUTOMOTIVE REPAIR SHOPS: Truck Engine Repair, Exc Indl

Lo Stocco Motors ....G...... 203 797-9618
  Danbury *(G-1875)*

AUTOMOTIVE SPLYS & PARTS, NEW, WHOLESALE: Engines/Eng Parts

Drt Aerospace LLC ....F...... 860 379-0783
  Winsted *(G-10515)*

AUTOMOTIVE SPLYS & PARTS, NEW, WHOLESALE: Trailer Parts

Kensington Welding & Trlr Co ....G...... 860 828-3564
  Kensington *(G-3811)*

AUTOMOTIVE SPLYS & PARTS, USED, WHOLESALE

Cadentia LLC ....G...... 860 995-0173
  Bristol *(G-997)*

AUTOMOTIVE SPLYS & PARTS, WHOLESALE, NEC

Genuine Parts Company ....F...... 860 623-4479
  Windsor Locks *(G-10486)*
Tek-Motive Inc ....D...... 203 468-2224
  Branford *(G-662)*

AUTOMOTIVE SVCS, EXC REPAIR & CARWASHES: Glass Tinting

Window Tinting & Signs Inc ....G...... 203 336-5539
  Bridgeport *(G-939)*

AUTOMOTIVE SVCS, EXC REPAIR & CARWASHES: Trailer Maintenance

Standard Welding Company Inc ....G...... 860 528-9628
  East Hartford *(G-2377)*

AUTOMOTIVE SVCS, EXC REPAIR: Washing & Polishing

Russell Speeders Car Wash LLC ....G...... 203 925-0083
  Shelton *(G-7547)*

AUTOMOTIVE SVCS, EXC RPR/CARWASHES: High Perf Auto Rpr/Svc

T/A Engines ....G...... 860 747-6713
  Plainville *(G-6866)*

AUTOMOTIVE TOPS INSTALLATION OR REPAIR: Canvas Or Plastic

Taillon Auto Top Company ....G...... 860 583-5525
  Bristol *(G-1125)*

AUTOMOTIVE UPHOLSTERY SHOPS

Branford Auto & Marine Center ....G...... 203 481-6572
  Branford *(G-562)*

AUTOMOTIVE WELDING SVCS

A & L Welding Service ....G...... 860 664-1700
  Clinton *(G-1488)*
Associated Welding Process ....G...... 860 677-0671
  Farmington *(G-2879)*
East Side Car Clinic Corp ....G...... 860 223-2247
  New Britain *(G-4978)*
Richies Automotive LLC ....G...... 860 482-0667
  Harwinton *(G-3737)*
WH Rose Inc ....E...... 860 228-8258
  Columbia *(G-1615)*

AUTOMOTIVE: Bodies

911 Motorsports LLC ....G...... 203 755-8405
  Waterbury *(G-9421)*

AUTOMOTIVE: Seating

Johnson Controls Inc ....G...... 860 887-7185
  Norwich *(G-6419)*
Johnson Controls Inc ....D...... 860 886-9021
  Ledyard *(G-3875)*
Johnson Controls Inc ....G...... 860 571-3300
  Rocky Hill *(G-7253)*
Johnson Controls Inc ....D...... 678 297-4040
  Meriden *(G-4179)*

AVIATION PROPELLER & BLADE REPAIR SVCS

Amk Welding Inc ....E...... 860 289-5634
  South Windsor *(G-7707)*

AWNINGS & CANOPIES

Niantic Awning Company ....G...... 860 739-0161
  Niantic *(G-5813)*

AWNINGS & CANOPIES: Awnings, Fabric, From Purchased Matls

Awnings Plus LLC ....G...... 860 496-7996
  Torrington *(G-8899)*
B and G Enterprise LLC ....G...... 203 562-7232
  New Haven *(G-5239)*
Canvas Products ....G...... 203 225-0507
  Shelton *(G-7411)*
Economy Canvas Co ....G...... 860 289-5281
  Hartford *(G-3582)*
Evans Fabrication ....G...... 203 791-9517
  Bethel *(G-298)*
Fitzgerald-Norwalk Awning Co ....G...... 203 847-5858
  Norwalk *(G-6169)*
Meriden Awning & Decorating Co ....G...... 203 634-0067
  Meriden *(G-4194)*
Miller Marine Canvas ....G...... 203 878-9291
  Milford *(G-4582)*
State Awning Company ....G...... 860 246-2575
  Hartford *(G-3692)*
Stonington Custom Canvas LLC ....G...... 860 213-1240
  Stonington *(G-8539)*
Tetrault & Sons Inc ....G...... 860 872-9187
  Stafford Springs *(G-8042)*
Toff Industry Inc ....G...... 860 378-0532
  Milldale *(G-4689)*
W H Preuss Sons Incorporated ....G...... 860 643-9492
  Bolton *(G-521)*

AWNINGS & CANOPIES: Canopies, Fabric, From Purchased Matls

Soapstone Media Inc ....G...... 860 749-0455
  Somers *(G-7669)*

AWNINGS & CANOPIES: Fabric

Genvario Awning Co ....G...... 203 847-5858
  Norwalk *(G-6179)*
Window Pdts Awngs Blind Shade ....G...... 203 481-9772
  Branford *(G-676)*

AWNINGS: Fiberglass

Signs Unlimited Inc ....G...... 203 734-7446
  Derby *(G-2126)*

AWNINGS: Metal

Tetrault & Sons Inc ....G...... 860 872-9187
  Stafford Springs *(G-8042)*

AXES & HATCHETS

Lewmar Inc ....E...... 203 458-6200
  Guilford *(G-3367)*

BABY PACIFIERS: Rubber

Mayborn Usa Inc ....F...... 781 269-7490
  Stamford *(G-8298)*

BACKHOES

Fairfield Backhoe LLC ....G...... 203 247-4007
  Fairfield *(G-2784)*

BADGES: Identification & Insignia

D E Sirman Specialty Company ....G...... 860 658-6336
  West Simsbury *(G-9977)*
Parva Mfg Group Inc ....G...... 860 828-6285
  Kensington *(G-3816)*

BAGS & CONTAINERS: Textile, Exc Sleeping

Krutch Pack LLC ....G...... 860 836-1745
  Newington *(G-5671)*
Uninsred Alttude Cnnection Inc ....G...... 860 333-1461
  Brooklyn *(G-1257)*

BAGS: Canvas

American Marketing Group Inc ....G...... 203 367-2378
  Bridgeport *(G-693)*

BAGS: Duffle, Canvas, Made From Purchased Materials

Island Style Mar Canvas Repr..........G........707 338-8789
Norwalk *(G-6212)*

BAGS: Flour, Fabric, Made From Purchased Materials

Live and Dream Green LLC..........G........860 670-0870
Avon *(G-91)*

BAGS: Paper

Hudson Paper Company..........E........203 378-8759
Stratford *(G-8628)*
Mettler Packaging LLC..........G........860 628-6193
Southington *(G-7953)*

BAGS: Plastic

Amgraph Packaging Inc..........C........860 822-2000
Baltic *(G-118)*

BAGS: Plastic, Made From Purchased Materials

Kage Poly Products LLC..........G........860 646-8228
Manchester *(G-4043)*
Rbi Inc..........G........860 444-0534
New London *(G-5486)*
Safety Bags Inc..........G........203 242-0727
Shelton *(G-7549)*

BAGS: Textile

Dayton Bag & Burlap Co..........G........860 653-8191
East Granby *(G-2202)*
Dow Cover Company Incorporated..........D........203 469-5394
New Haven *(G-5269)*
Smiling Dog..........G........860 344-0707
Middletown *(G-4419)*
Zhao LLC..........G........401 864-7186
Stamford *(G-8506)*

BAGS: Wardrobe, Closet Access, Made From Purchased Materials

Re-Style Your Closets LLC..........G........860 658-9450
Simsbury *(G-7642)*

BAIT, FISHING, WHOLESALE

Compleat Angler..........G........203 655-9400
Darien *(G-2014)*

BAKERIES, COMMERCIAL: On Premises Baking Only

Abrantes Bakery & Pastry Shop..........G........860 232-1464
Hartford *(G-3544)*
Amodios Inc..........F........203 573-1229
Waterbury *(G-9430)*
Amoun Pita & Distribution LLC..........E........866 239-9990
South Windsor *(G-7708)*
Apicellas Bakery Inc..........E........203 865-6204
New Haven *(G-5232)*
Atticus Bakery LLC..........C........203 562-9007
New Haven *(G-5237)*
Better Baking By Beth..........G........860 482-4706
Torrington *(G-8903)*
Big Purple Cupcake LLC..........G........203 483-8738
Branford *(G-560)*
Boston Model Bakery..........E........203 562-9491
New Haven *(G-5250)*
D Rotondi LLC..........G........505 427-3233
Bridgeport *(G-741)*
Dough Girl Baking Co LLC..........G........203 838-9695
Norwalk *(G-6148)*
Foster Grandparent Program..........G........860 525-5437
Hartford *(G-3592)*
Freihofer Charles Baking Co..........G........203 729-4545
Naugatuck *(G-4882)*
Hardcore Sweet Cupcakes LLC..........G........203 808-5547
Waterbury *(G-9496)*
I and U LLC..........G........860 803-1491
Waterbury *(G-9502)*
Katona Bakery LLC..........E........203 337-5349
Fairfield *(G-2805)*
La Cayeyana Donis Bakery..........G........203 789-8030
New Haven *(G-5313)*
Modern Pastry Shop Inc..........E........860 296-7628
Hartford *(G-3645)*
Mozzicato Pastry & Bake Shop..........E........860 296-0426
Hartford *(G-3646)*
Pastry Shop..........G........203 238-0483
Meriden *(G-4215)*
Paulas Bakery..........G........203 743-9000
Danbury *(G-1903)*
Red Rose Desserts..........G........860 603-2670
Colchester *(G-1571)*
Riverside Baking Company LLC..........G........203 451-0331
Fairfield *(G-2837)*
Spinella Bakery..........F........203 753-9451
Waterbury *(G-9606)*
Superior Bakery Inc..........E........860 923-9555
North Grosvenordale *(G-5892)*
Sweet Spot Cupcakery LLC..........G........860 219-1123
Windsor *(G-10446)*
Thadieo LLC..........G........860 621-4500
Southington *(G-7985)*
Tinas Heavenly Treats..........G........203 543-3560
Stratford *(G-8696)*
Watson LLC..........B........203 932-3000
West Haven *(G-9960)*
Whole German Breads LLC..........G........203 507-0663
New Haven *(G-5432)*
Wildflour Cupcakes Sweets LLC..........G........203 828-6576
Seymour *(G-7373)*

BAKERIES: On Premises Baking & Consumption

Abrantes Bakery & Pastry Shop..........G........860 232-1464
Hartford *(G-3544)*
Capricorn Investors II LP..........A........203 861-6600
Greenwich *(G-3140)*
Libbys Italian Pastry Shop..........G........203 234-2530
North Haven *(G-5959)*
Lupis Inc..........E........203 562-9491
New Haven *(G-5323)*
Milite Bakery..........G........203 753-9451
Waterbury *(G-9543)*
Pepperidge Farm Incorporated..........C........860 286-6400
Bloomfield *(G-463)*
Pepperidge Farm Incorporated..........A........203 846-7000
Norwalk *(G-6298)*

BAKERY PRDTS: Bagels, Fresh Or Frozen

Bagel Boys Inc..........F........860 657-4400
Glastonbury *(G-3011)*

BAKERY PRDTS: Bakery Prdts, Partially Cooked, Exc frozen

Haylons Market LLC..........G........860 739-9509
Niantic *(G-5808)*

BAKERY PRDTS: Bread, All Types, Fresh Or Frozen

Arabic Bread Bakery..........G........203 743-4743
Danbury *(G-1743)*
Krafty Kakes Inc..........G........203 284-0299
Wallingford *(G-9299)*
Lupis Inc..........E........203 562-9491
New Haven *(G-5323)*
Milite Bakery..........G........203 753-9451
Waterbury *(G-9543)*

BAKERY PRDTS: Cakes, Bakery, Exc Frozen

Bimbo Bakeries Usa Inc..........D........203 932-1000
Orange *(G-6586)*
Izzi BS Allergy Free LLC..........G........203 810-4378
Norwalk *(G-6213)*
TD&s Acquisition LLC..........G........860 341-1001
Middletown *(G-4424)*

BAKERY PRDTS: Cakes, Bakery, Frozen

Chris & Zack Gourmet Foods..........G........203 912-7805
Orange *(G-6591)*
Something Sweet Inc..........E........203 603-9766
New Haven *(G-5399)*

BAKERY PRDTS: Cookies

Bimbo Bakeries Usa Inc..........D........203 932-1000
Orange *(G-6586)*
Pepperidge Farm Incorporated..........C........860 286-6400
Bloomfield *(G-463)*
R & K Cookies LLC..........G........860 613-2893
Cromwell *(G-1714)*

BAKERY PRDTS: Cookies & crackers

Beldotti Bakeries..........F........203 348-9029
Stamford *(G-8109)*
Bob The Baker LLC..........F........203 775-1032
Brookfield *(G-1162)*
Elius Delight Snacks LLC..........G........646 302-4948
Stratford *(G-8608)*
Modern Pastry Shop Inc..........E........860 296-7628
Hartford *(G-3645)*
Mozzicato Pastry & Bake Shop..........E........860 296-0426
Hartford *(G-3646)*

BAKERY PRDTS: Doughnuts, Exc Frozen

DAndrea Corporation..........F........203 932-6000
West Haven *(G-9895)*
Darien Doughnut LLC..........G........203 656-2805
Darien *(G-2017)*
Daybrake Donuts Inc..........F........203 368-4962
Bridgeport *(G-742)*
Donut Stop..........G........203 924-7133
Shelton *(G-7433)*
Hartford Cpl Co-Op Inc..........C........860 296-5636
Hartford *(G-3610)*
Massconn Distribute Cpl..........D........860 882-0717
South Windsor *(G-7791)*
Pops Donuts..........G........203 876-1210
Milford *(G-4610)*
Realejo Donuts Inc..........F........860 342-5120
Portland *(G-6971)*
Spencer Street Inc..........G........203 647-2955
Manchester *(G-4092)*
Whole Donut..........F........860 745-3041
Enfield *(G-2706)*

BAKERY PRDTS: Dry

Bagelman III Inc..........F........203 792-0030
Danbury *(G-1749)*
Cherise Cpl LLC..........G........203 238-3482
Meriden *(G-4157)*
Harsha Inc..........G........860 439-1466
Waterford *(G-9655)*

BAKERY PRDTS: Frozen

Cooper Marketing Group Inc..........G........203 797-9386
Danbury *(G-1774)*
Pepperidge Farm Incorporated..........C........860 286-6400
Bloomfield *(G-463)*
Pepperidge Farm Incorporated..........A........203 846-7000
Norwalk *(G-6298)*
Rich Products Corporation..........A........866 737-8884
New Britain *(G-5042)*
Rich Products Corporation..........A........800 356-7094
New Britain *(G-5043)*

BAKERY PRDTS: Pastries, Exc Frozen

Take Cake LLC..........G........203 453-1896
Guilford *(G-3399)*

BAKERY PRDTS: Wholesalers

Apicellas Bakery Inc..........E........203 865-6204
New Haven *(G-5232)*
D Rotondi LLC..........G........505 427-3233
Bridgeport *(G-741)*
Mozzicato Pastry & Bake Shop..........E........860 296-0426
Hartford *(G-3646)*
Superior Bakery Inc..........E........860 923-9555
North Grosvenordale *(G-5892)*

BAKERY: Wholesale Or Wholesale & Retail Combined

Artisan Bread & Products LLC..........G........914 843-4401
Norwalk *(G-6074)*
Beans Inc..........G........860 945-9234
Watertown *(G-9683)*
Beldotti Bakeries..........F........203 348-9029
Stamford *(G-8109)*
Bimbo Bakeries Usa Inc..........E........860 691-1180
Portland *(G-6953)*
Chef J R ME Rest Group Corp..........G........860 940-8038
New Britain *(G-4960)*
Congress Catering Inc..........G........860 291-8182
East Hartford *(G-2309)*

PRODUCT SECTION

DI Distributors LLC .... G 203 931-1724
West Haven *(G-9901)*
Gracie Maes Kitchen LLC .... G 860 885-8250
Griswold *(G-3265)*
Northeast Foods Inc .... D 860 779-1117
Dayville *(G-2067)*
Shayna Bs & Pickle LLC .... G 860 428-3835
Ashford *(G-66)*
Stonehouse Fine Cakes .... F 203 235-5091
Meriden *(G-4246)*
Sweet Peas Baking Company LLC .... G 203 637-4031
Old Greenwich *(G-6484)*

BALLOONS: Toy & Advertising, Rubber

Jump4fun USA LLC .... G 203 735-3702
Ansonia *(G-43)*

BALLS: Steel

Abbott Ball Company .... D 860 236-5901
West Hartford *(G-9770)*
Ball Supply Corporation .... G 860 673-3364
Avon *(G-77)*
Hartford Technologies Inc .... E 860 571-3602
Rocky Hill *(G-7241)*
Schaeffler Aerospace USA Corp .... D 860 379-7558
Winsted *(G-10534)*
Schaeffler Aerospace USA Corp .... B 203 744-2211
Danbury *(G-1936)*
Trd Specialties Inc .... G 860 738-4505
Pine Meadow *(G-6736)*

BANNERS: Fabric

Banner Works .... G 203 597-9999
Oakville *(G-6450)*
DS Sewing Inc .... F 203 773-1344
New Haven *(G-5270)*
Young Flan LLC .... G 203 878-0084
Derby *(G-2134)*

BARBECUE EQPT

Kenyon International Inc .... E 860 664-4906
Clinton *(G-1511)*
South Windsor Golf Course LLC .... D 860 648-4653
South Windsor *(G-7826)*
Vigiroda Enterprises Inc .... G 203 268-6117
Trumbull *(G-9092)*
Vigiroda Products LLC .... G 860 391-8457
Old Saybrook *(G-6574)*

BARRETTES

Barrette Mechanical .... G 860 774-0499
Brooklyn *(G-1246)*
Lisa Barrette .... G 860 928-0599
Thompson *(G-8838)*
White Barrette Mail LLC .... G 860 923-3183
Woodstock *(G-10690)*

BARRICADES: Metal

K-Tech International .... E 860 489-9399
Torrington *(G-8941)*

BARS, COLD FINISHED: Steel, From Purchased Hot-Rolled

Channel Alloys .... G 203 975-1404
Norwalk *(G-6112)*

BARS: Concrete Reinforcing, Fabricated Steel

Barker Steel LLC .... E 860 282-1860
South Windsor *(G-7717)*
Eastern Metal Works Inc .... E 203 878-6995
Milford *(G-4523)*
Nucor Steel Connecticut Inc .... C 203 265-0615
Wallingford *(G-9330)*

BASES, BEVERAGE

K Chef Inc .... G 646 778-8396
New Haven *(G-9514)*
Transatlantic Bubbles LLC .... G 203 464-0051
Woodbridge *(G-10619)*

BATHROOM ACCESS & FITTINGS: Vitreous China & Earthenware

Home Sweeter HM Kit & Bath LLC .... G 203 948-6482
Bethel *(G-309)*
Water Works .... G 203 546-6000
Danbury *(G-1976)*

BATTERIES, EXC AUTOMOTIVE: Wholesalers

Interacter Inc .... G 203 949-0199
Wallingford *(G-9289)*

BATTERIES: Alkaline, Cell Storage

Duracell Company .... E 203 796-4000
Bethel *(G-284)*
Duracell US Holding LLC .... F 203 796-4000
Bethel *(G-288)*
Duracell US Operations Inc .... G 203 796-4000
Bethel *(G-289)*
Evercel Inc .... D 781 741-8800
Stamford *(G-8199)*

BATTERIES: Dry

Duracell Manufacturing LLC .... C 203 796-4000
Bethel *(G-287)*

BATTERIES: Lead Acid, Storage

Johnson Controls Inc .... G 860 887-7185
Norwich *(G-6419)*
Johnson Controls Inc .... D 678 297-4040
Meriden *(G-4179)*

BATTERIES: Rechargeable

Nofet LLC .... F 203 848-9064
New Haven *(G-5351)*

BATTERIES: Storage

B S T Systems Inc .... D 860 564-4078
Plainfield *(G-6742)*
Duracell Company .... A 203 796-4000
Bethel *(G-285)*
Duracell Manufacturing Inc .... G 203 796-4000
Bethel *(G-286)*
Hbl America Inc .... G 860 257-9800
Rocky Hill *(G-7242)*
Hbl America Inc .... G 860 257-9800
Rocky Hill *(G-7243)*
Interacter Inc .... G 203 949-0199
Wallingford *(G-9289)*
Saft America Inc .... E 203 234-8333
North Haven *(G-5990)*

BATTERIES: Wet

B S T Systems Inc .... D 860 564-4078
Plainfield *(G-6742)*
Vitec Production Solutions Inc .... D 203 929-1100
Shelton *(G-7581)*

BATTERY CASES: Plastic Or Plastics Combination

GP Industries .... G 860 859-9938
Taftville *(G-8741)*

BATTERY CHARGERS

Charge Solutions Inc .... G 203 871-7282
Milford *(G-4488)*
Crystal Tool LLC .... G 860 510-0113
Old Saybrook *(G-6530)*
Digatron Power Electronics Inc .... E 203 446-8000
Shelton *(G-7432)*

BEADS: Unassembled

Quality Bead Craft Inc .... F 860 242-2167
Bloomfield *(G-471)*

BEARINGS

A Papish Incorporated .... E 203 744-0323
Danbury *(G-1727)*
American Sleeve Bearing LLC .... E 860 684-8060
Stafford Springs *(G-8016)*
Ball & Roller Bearing Co LLC .... F 860 355-4161
New Milford *(G-5508)*
Virginia Industries Inc .... G 860 571-3600
Rocky Hill *(G-7271)*

BEARINGS & PARTS Ball

Abek LLC .... F 860 314-3905
Bristol *(G-953)*
Buswell Manufacturing Co Inc .... F 203 334-6069
Bridgeport *(G-726)*
Fag Bearings LLC .... F 203 790-5474
Danbury *(G-1821)*
FAg Holding Corporation .... F 203 790-5474
Danbury *(G-1822)*
Gwilliam Company Inc .... F 860 354-2884
New Milford *(G-5543)*
Nn Inc .... G 203 793-7132
Wallingford *(G-9326)*
Rbc Bearings Incorporated .... B 203 267-7001
Oxford *(G-6691)*
Schaeffler Aerospace USA Corp .... B 203 744-2211
Danbury *(G-1936)*
Schaeffler Aerospace USA Corp .... D 860 379-7558
Winsted *(G-10534)*

BEARINGS: Ball & Roller

Ball & Roller Bearing Co LLC .... F 860 355-4161
New Milford *(G-5508)*
C & S Engineering Inc .... E 203 235-5727
Meriden *(G-4153)*
Hartford Technologies Inc .... E 860 571-3602
Rocky Hill *(G-7241)*
K A F Manufacturing Co Inc .... E 203 324-3012
Stamford *(G-8272)*
Kamatics Corporation .... G 860 243-7230
Bloomfield *(G-436)*
Kamatics Corporation .... G 860 243-9704
Bloomfield *(G-435)*
MRC Specialty Balls .... G 860 379-8511
Winsted *(G-10530)*
Pro-Tech Enterprises LLC .... G 203 931-9668
West Haven *(G-9947)*
Rbc Linear Precision Pdts Inc .... G 203 255-1511
Fairfield *(G-2833)*
Roller Bearing Co Amer Inc .... E 203 267-7001
Oxford *(G-6694)*
SKF Specialty Balls .... G 860 379-8511
Winsted *(G-10535)*
SKF USA Inc .... E 860 379-8511
Winsted *(G-10536)*
Timken Company .... F 860 652-4630
Glastonbury *(G-3087)*
Virginia Industries Inc .... G 860 571-3600
Rocky Hill *(G-7271)*

BEARINGS: Plastic

Asti Company Inc .... G 860 482-2675
Torrington *(G-8898)*

BEARINGS: Roller & Parts

Del-Tron Precision Inc .... E 203 778-2727
Bethel *(G-280)*
Rollcorp LLC .... G 860 347-5227
Middletown *(G-4406)*
Roller Bearing Co Amer Inc .... C 203 267-7001
Oxford *(G-6693)*
Schaeffler Group USA Inc .... B 203 790-5474
Danbury *(G-1937)*

BEAUTY & BARBER SHOP EQPT

Ace Beauty Supply Inc .... G 203 488-2416
Branford *(G-536)*
Ace Beauty Systems New Britain .... G 860 224-2943
New Britain *(G-4932)*
Advanced Golf Nutrition LLC .... G 203 554-9120
Fairfield *(G-2744)*
Bridgeport Proc & Mfg LLC .... G 203 612-7733
Bridgeport *(G-722)*
Components For Mfg LLC .... G 860 572-1671
Groton *(G-3279)*
Conair Corporation .... B 203 351-9000
Stamford *(G-8156)*
Ether & Industries LLc .... G 475 224-0650
New Haven *(G-5277)*
Frates Custom Cabinetry .... G 203 994-1108
Sandy Hook *(G-7312)*
G S S Industries .... G 203 755-6644
Waterbury *(G-9484)*
Grohe Manufacturing .... G 203 516-5536
Ansonia *(G-37)*

Employee Codes: A=Over 500 employees, B=251-500
C=101-250, D=51-100, E=20-50, F=10-19, G=1-9

BEAUTY & BARBER SHOP EQPT

Hannes Precision Industry Inc ....F 203 853-7276
  Norwalk (G-6192)
Kent Billings LLC ....G 860 659-1104
  Glastonbury (G-3055)
M & W Industries Inc ....G 860 621-7358
  Southington (G-7949)
Mandalay Industries LLC ....G 203 324-4033
  Stamford (G-8295)
Michaud Industries LLC ....G 860 408-0907
  Simsbury (G-7634)
Nutmeg Industries LLC ....G 860 436-6553
  Newington (G-5688)
Peacock Manufacturing Co LLC ....G 203 388-4100
  Norwalk (G-6294)
Sideburnz ....G 860 667-1900
  Hartford (G-3686)
Thomaston Industries Inc ....F 203 283-4358
  Thomaston (G-8813)

BEAUTY & BARBER SHOP EQPT & SPLYS WHOLESALERS

Ace Beauty Systems New Britain ....G 860 224-2943
  New Britain (G-4932)

BEAUTY SALONS

Ace Beauty Systems New Britain ....G 860 224-2943
  New Britain (G-4932)

BEDDING, BEDSPREADS, BLANKETS & SHEETS

Thomas W Raftery Inc ....E 860 278-9870
  Hartford (G-3703)

BEEKEEPERS' SPLYS

Hopewell Harmony LLC ....G 203 222-2268
  Weston (G-10027)

BEER & ALE WHOLESALERS

A & I Concentrate LLC ....F 203 447-1938
  Shelton (G-7385)

BEER & ALE, WHOLESALE: Beer & Other Fermented Malt Liquors

G & G Beverage Distributors ....D 203 949-6220
  Wallingford (G-9273)
Matias Importing & Distrg Corp ....G 860 666-5544
  Newington (G-5675)

BEER, WINE & LIQUOR STORES

Derby Discount Liquor ....G 203 732-0666
  Derby (G-2111)
New Hartford Wine and Bev LLC ....G 860 379-3764
  New Hartford (G-5204)
Shippan Liquors ....G 203 348-0925
  Stamford (G-8412)
Spirit of Hartford LLC ....G 860 404-1776
  Avon (G-115)
Stony Creek Liquor LLC ....G 203 488-3318
  Branford (G-658)
White Bridge Liquors Inc ....G 203 655-0658
  Darien (G-2051)

BEER, WINE & LIQUOR STORES: Beer, Packaged

Franklin Liquor Store ....G 203 323-1356
  Stamford (G-8208)
G I Package Store ....G 203 624-4606
  New Haven (G-5284)

BEER, WINE & LIQUOR STORES: Wine

Haight Vineyard Inc ....G 860 567-4045
  Litchfield (G-3892)
Kiro Bespoke LLC ....G 203 981-4945
  Middletown (G-4363)

BEER, WINE & LIQUOR STORES: Wine & Beer

Alvarium Beer Company LLC ....G 860 306-3857
  New Britain (G-4943)

BEESWAX PROCESSING

Woods End Inc ....G 203 226-6303
  Weston (G-10047)

BELLOWS

Standard Bellows Co ....E 860 623-2307
  Windsor Locks (G-10498)

BELLS: Electric

Bevin Bros Manufacturing Co ....E 860 267-4431
  East Hampton (G-2257)

BELT LOADERS: Passenger Baggage

Nationwide Cnvyor Spclists LLC ....G 860 582-9816
  Bristol (G-1077)

BELTS & BELT PRDTS

Kemper Manufacturing Corp ....E 203 934-1600
  West Haven (G-9923)
Lubbert Supply Company LLC ....G 203 690-1105
  Milford (G-4570)

BELTS: Conveyor, Made From Purchased Wire

Habasit Abt Inc ....C 860 632-2211
  Middletown (G-4349)

BENTONITE MINING

Vanderbilt Minerals LLC ....E 203 295-2140
  Norwalk (G-6384)

BEVERAGE BASES & SYRUPS

Flavrz Organic Beverages LLC ....G 203 716-8082
  Darien (G-2026)
Focus Now Solutions LLC ....G 203 247-9038
  Fairfield (G-2786)
Jmf Group LLC ....D 860 627-7003
  East Windsor (G-2500)

BEVERAGE PRDTS: Brewers' Grain

Kent Falls Brewing Company ....G 860 398-9645
  Kent (G-3823)

BEVERAGE STORES

Beverage Boss LLC ....G 203 865-2240
  New Haven (G-5244)
Miami Bay Beverage Company LLC ....F 203 453-0090
  Branford (G-626)
Smoothie King ....G 203 208-4098
  Branford (G-653)
Twelve Beverage LLC ....G 203 256-8100
  Fairfield (G-2859)

BEVERAGE, NONALCOHOLIC: Iced Tea/Fruit Drink, Bottled/Canned

Subtle-T LLC ....G 203 273-6061
  Stamford (G-8447)
Sweet Leaf Tea Company ....F 203 863-0263
  Stamford (G-8454)

BEVERAGES, ALCOHOLIC: Beer

Beerd Brewing Co LLC ....F 585 771-7428
  Stonington (G-8524)
Brainard Brewing LLC ....G 860 324-5213
  Mystic (G-4802)
Brewery Legitimus LLC ....G 860 810-8894
  Canton (G-1307)
British W Indies Trdg USA LLC ....G 704 451-8400
  Litchfield (G-3885)
East Rock Brewing Company LLC ....G 203 530-3484
  New Haven (G-5271)
Easton Brewing Company LLC ....G 203 921-7263
  Easton (G-2550)
Front Porch Brewing ....G 203 679-1096
  Wallingford (G-9272)
Guinness America Inc ....G 203 229-2100
  Norwalk (G-6188)
New England Brewing Co LLC ....G 203 387-2222
  Woodbridge (G-10608)
Nutmeg Brewing Rest Group LLC ....E 203 256-2337
  Shelton (G-7515)

PRODUCT SECTION

Shoreline Brewing Company LLC ....G 203 225-7734
  Shelton (G-7554)
Southport Brewing Co ....E 203 874-2337
  Milford (G-4649)
Thomas Hooker Brewing Co LLC ....E 860 242-3111
  Bloomfield (G-491)
Willimantic Brewing Co LLC ....G 860 423-6777
  Willimantic (G-10239)

BEVERAGES, ALCOHOLIC: Beer & Ale

Aspetuck Brew Lab LLC ....G 203 256-1902
  Fairfield (G-2749)
Bear Hands Brewing Company ....G 860 576-5374
  Central Village (G-1336)
Breakaway Brew Haus LLC ....G 860 647-9811
  Bolton (G-506)
Brook Broad Brewing LLC ....F 860 623-1000
  East Windsor (G-2486)
Cold Brew Coffee Company LLC ....G 860 250-4410
  Cheshire (G-1371)
Diageo Investment Corporation ....F 203 229-2100
  Norwalk (G-6139)
Hamden Brewing Company LLC ....G 203 247-4677
  Shelton (G-7456)
Stetson Brewing Co Inc ....G 860 643-0257
  Manchester (G-4097)
Swagnificent Ent LLC ....G 203 449-0124
  Bridgeport (G-918)

BEVERAGES, ALCOHOLIC: Bourbon Whiskey

Kra-Ze LLC ....G 860 892-8025
  Uncasville (G-9098)

BEVERAGES, ALCOHOLIC: Cordials

Diageo North America Inc ....A 203 229-2100
  Norwalk (G-6140)

BEVERAGES, ALCOHOLIC: Distilled Liquors

Asylum Distillery ....G 203 209-0146
  Southport (G-7999)
Deep River Distillers LLC ....G 860 788-6061
  Cromwell (G-1700)
Diageo PLC ....D 203 229-2100
  Norwalk (G-6141)
Double Barrel Distillery LLC ....G 860 285-0141
  Windsor (G-10380)
Elm City Distillery LLC ....G 203 285-8830
  Ivoryton (G-3785)
Hartford Flavor Company LLC ....G 860 604-9767
  Hartford (G-3611)
Michael James Distler ....G 203 241-4574
  Redding (G-7102)
Millbrook Distillery LLC ....G 203 637-2231
  Cos Cob (G-1638)
Mine Hill Distillery ....G 860 210-1872
  Roxbury (G-7279)
Modern Distillery Age ....G 203 971-8710
  Norwalk (G-6263)
Spirit of Hartford LLC ....G 860 404-1776
  Avon (G-115)
Waypoint Distillery ....G 860 519-5390
  Bloomfield (G-500)
Westford Hill Distillers LLC ....G 860 429-0464
  Ashford (G-69)

BEVERAGES, ALCOHOLIC: Near Beer

Alvarium Beer Company LLC ....G 860 306-3857
  New Britain (G-4943)
Thimble Island Brewing Company ....E 203 208-2827
  Branford (G-663)

BEVERAGES, ALCOHOLIC: Neutral Spirits, Exc Fruit

Krystal Inc LLC ....G 860 844-1267
  Granby (G-3110)

BEVERAGES, ALCOHOLIC: Vodka

Cylinder Vodka Inc ....G 203 979-0792
  Stamford (G-8175)

BEVERAGES, ALCOHOLIC: Wines

Arrigoni Winery ....G 860 342-1999
  Portland (G-6950)

PRODUCT SECTION

BINDING SVC: Books & Manuals

Brignole Distillery LLC ....G...... 860 653-9463
  East Granby (G-2192)
Brooke Taylor Winery LLC ....G...... 860 974-1263
  Woodstock (G-10659)
Carlo Huber Selections Inc ....G...... 917 742-0601
  Salisbury (G-7294)
Chamard Vineyards Inc ....G...... 860 664-0299
  Clinton (G-1493)
Cocchia Norwalk Grape Co ....F...... 203 855-7911
  Norwalk (G-6119)
Connecticut Valley Winery LLC ....G...... 860 489-9463
  New Hartford (G-5187)
Connecticut Vineyard & Winery ....G...... 860 307-3550
  West Hartford (G-9794)
Crush Club LLC ....G...... 203 626-9545
  Wallingford (G-9242)
Edwards Wines LLC ....G...... 860 535-0202
  North Stonington (G-6023)
Gouveia Vineyards LLC ....G...... 203 265-5526
  Wallingford (G-9277)
Grapes of Norwalk ....G...... 203 845-9640
  Norwalk (G-6185)
Haight Vineyard Inc ....G...... 860 567-4045
  Litchfield (G-3892)
Hawk Ridge Winery LLC ....G...... 860 274-7440
  Watertown (G-9711)
Kiro Bespoke LLC ....G...... 203 981-4945
  Middletown (G-4363)
Land of Nod Winery LLC ....G...... 860 824-5225
  East Canaan (G-2182)
Maugle Sierra Vineyards LLC ....G...... 860 464-2987
  Ledyard (G-3878)
Miranda Vineyard LLC ....G...... 860 491-9906
  Goshen (G-3103)
Northeast Vineyard Svcs LLC ....G...... 860 872-8239
  Tolland (G-8873)
Paradise Hlls Vnyrd Winery LLC ....G...... 203 284-0123
  Wallingford (G-9332)
Pozzi Fmly Wine & Spirits LLC ....G...... 646 422-9134
  Stamford (G-8369)
Preston Ridge Vineyard LLC ....G...... 860 383-4278
  Preston (G-6988)
Sharpe Hill Vineyard Inc ....E...... 860 974-3549
  Pomfret (G-6936)
Shelter Rock Winery ....G...... 203 948-8235
  Danbury (G-1945)
Stonington Vineyards Inc ....G...... 860 535-1222
  Stonington (G-8540)
Strawberry Ridge Vineyard Inc ....G...... 860 868-0730
  Cornwall Bridge (G-1621)
Sugar Creek Vineyard LLC ....G...... 860 454-4219
  Ellington (G-2603)
Three Suns Ltd ....G...... 860 233-7658
  Hartford (G-3704)
Vineyard Brothers LLC ....G...... 203 637-0381
  Riverside (G-7204)
Vineyard Thimble ....G...... 860 416-5115
  Glastonbury (G-3093)
White Silo Farm ....G...... 860 355-0271
  Sherman (G-7606)
Zoks Homebrewing & Winemaking ......G...... 860 456-7704
  Willimantic (G-10242)

BEVERAGES, MALT

Outer Light Brewing Co LLC ....G...... 475 201-9972
  Groton (G-3302)

BEVERAGES, NONALCOHOLIC: Bottled & canned soft drinks

B & E Juices Inc ....E...... 203 333-1802
  Bridgeport (G-707)
Bombadils Spirit Shop Inc ....G...... 860 423-9661
  Mansfield Center (G-4112)
Cell Nique ....G...... 888 417-9343
  Weston (G-10022)
Coca-Cola Bottling ....G...... 800 241-2653
  East Hartford (G-2307)
Coca-Cola Company ....G...... 860 443-2816
  Waterford (G-9647)
Company of Coca-Cola Bottling ....D...... 860 569-0037
  East Hartford (G-2308)
Company of Coca-Cola Bottling ....G...... 860 814-4241
  Enfield (G-2630)
Company of Coca-Cola Bottling ....D...... 203 905-3900
  Stamford (G-8154)
Crystal Rock Spring Water Co ....B...... 860 945-0661
  Watertown (G-9698)
Derby Discount Liquor ....G...... 203 732-0666
  Derby (G-2111)

Franklin Liquor Store ....G...... 203 323-1356
  Stamford (G-8208)
G & G Beverage Distributors ....D...... 203 949-6220
  Wallingford (G-9273)
G I Package Store ....G...... 203 624-4606
  New Haven (G-5284)
Natural Country Farms Inc ....D...... 860 872-8346
  Ellington (G-2597)
New Hartford Wine and Bev LLC ....G...... 860 379-3764
  New Hartford (G-5204)
Niagara Bottling LLC ....G...... 909 226-7353
  Bloomfield (G-450)
Pro Beverage Sales LLC ....G...... 203 931-1029
  New Haven (G-5372)
Red Bull LLC ....G...... 860 519-1018
  Bloomfield (G-474)
Shippan Liquors ....G...... 203 348-0925
  Stamford (G-8412)
Sigg Switzerland (usa) Inc ....G...... 203 321-1232
  Stamford (G-8414)
White Bridge Liquors Inc ....G...... 203 655-0658
  Darien (G-2051)

BEVERAGES, NONALCOHOLIC: Carbonated

Pepsi Foods ....G...... 860 567-5774
  Litchfield (G-3898)
Pepsi-Cola Btlg of Wrcster Inc ....E...... 860 774-4007
  Dayville (G-2069)
Pepsi-Cola Metro Btlg Co Inc ....B...... 203 375-2484
  Stratford (G-8664)
Pepsi-Cola Metro Btlg Co Inc ....E...... 860 848-1231
  Uncasville (G-9102)
Pepsi-Cola Metro Btlg Co Inc ....C...... 860 688-6281
  Windsor (G-10418)
Pepsico ....F...... 203 974-8912
  New Haven (G-5360)

BEVERAGES, NONALCOHOLIC: Carbonated, Canned & Bottled, Etc

Als Beverage Company Inc ....E...... 860 627-7003
  East Windsor (G-2480)
Als Holding Inc ....G...... 860 627-7003
  East Windsor (G-2481)
Castle Beverages Inc ....G...... 203 732-0883
  Ansonia (G-27)
Grand Fish Market LLC ....G...... 203 691-8904
  New Haven (G-5289)
Miami Bay Beverage Company LLC ....F...... 203 453-0090
  Branford (G-626)
Simply Originals LLC ....G...... 203 273-3523
  Norwalk (G-6351)
Twelve Beverage LLC ....G...... 203 256-8100
  Fairfield (G-2859)

BEVERAGES, NONALCOHOLIC: Cider

Burlington Golf Center Inc ....G...... 860 675-7320
  Burlington (G-1262)
Clydes Cider Mill ....G...... 860 536-3354
  Mystic (G-4807)
Lyman Farm Incorporated ....C...... 860 349-1793
  Middlefield (G-4302)
Vincent Jajer ....G...... 860 354-4747
  New Milford (G-5607)

BEVERAGES, NONALCOHOLIC: Flavoring extracts & syrups, nec

American Distilling Inc ....G...... 860 267-4444
  Marlborough (G-4119)
American Distilling Inc ....D...... 860 267-4444
  East Hampton (G-2253)
Bep Flavor Holdings LLC ....G...... 203 595-4520
  Stamford (G-8110)
Brookside Flvors Ingrdents LLC ....D...... 203 595-4520
  Stamford (G-8120)
Carrubba Incorporated ....D...... 203 878-0605
  Milford (G-4485)
Herbasway Laboratories LLC ....E...... 203 269-6991
  Wallingford (G-9280)
Metabev Inc ....F...... 203 967-8502
  Stamford (G-8307)
Osf Flavors Inc ....F...... 860 298-8350
  Windsor (G-10416)
Scitech International LLC ....G...... 203 967-8502
  Stamford (G-8404)
Watson LLC ....B...... 203 932-3000
  West Haven (G-9960)

BEVERAGES, NONALCOHOLIC: Fruit Drnks, Under 100% Juice, Can

Harvest Hill Holdings LLC ....F...... 203 914-1620
  Stamford (G-8230)

BEVERAGES, NONALCOHOLIC: Lemonade, Bottled & Canned, Etc

Fishers Island Lemonade ....G...... 860 306-3189
  Mystic (G-4815)
Newmans Own Inc ....E...... 203 222-0136
  Westport (G-10128)

BEVERAGES, NONALCOHOLIC: Soft Drinks, Canned & Bottled, Etc

Averys Beverage LLC ....G...... 860 224-0830
  New Britain (G-4947)
Foxon Park Beverages Inc ....G...... 203 467-7874
  East Haven (G-2430)
Light Rock Spring Water Co ....F...... 203 743-2251
  Danbury (G-1874)
Pepsi-Cola Metro Btlg Co Inc ....C...... 203 234-9014
  North Haven (G-5975)
Reeds Inc ....E...... 203 890-0557
  Norwalk (G-6318)

BEVERAGES, WINE & DISTILLED ALCOHOLIC, WHOLESALE: Wine

De Villiers Incorporated ....G...... 203 966-9645
  New Canaan (G-5101)
Di Grazia Vineyards Ltd ....G...... 203 775-1616
  Brookfield (G-1183)
Matias Importing & Distrg Corp ....G...... 860 666-5544
  Newington (G-5675)

BEVERAGES, WINE/DISTILLED ALCOHOLIC, WHOL: Bttlg Wine/Liquor

Kiro Bespoke LLC ....G...... 203 981-4945
  Middletown (G-4363)

BICYCLES, PARTS & ACCESS

Avalanche Downhill Racing Inc ....G...... 860 537-4306
  Colchester (G-1541)
Cycling Sports Group Inc ....D...... 608 268-8916
  Wilton (G-10287)

BILLIARD & POOL TABLES & SPLYS

Pfd Studios ....G...... 860 295-8500
  Marlborough (G-4128)
Roys Family Pools & Billiards ....G...... 860 546-0608
  Canterbury (G-1301)

BINDING SVC: Books & Manuals

Adkins Printing Company ....E...... 800 228-9745
  New Britain (G-4938)
Alexander Hussey ....G...... 860 354-0118
  New Milford (G-5503)
Allied Printing Services Inc ....B...... 860 643-1101
  Manchester (G-3980)
Blue Moon Bindery LLC ....G...... 860 435-9100
  Lakeville (G-3842)
Chapin Packaging LLC ....G...... 203 202-2747
  Darien (G-2011)
Conner Printing ....G...... 203 929-2070
  Shelton (G-7423)
Desai Mukesh ....G...... 860 529-4141
  Rocky Hill (G-7234)
E R Hitchcock Company ....E...... 860 229-2024
  New Britain (G-4977)
Eccles-Lehman Inc ....G...... 203 268-0605
  Easton (G-2551)
Elm Press Incorporated ....E...... 860 583-3600
  Terryville (G-8752)
Falcon Press ....G...... 860 763-2293
  Enfield (G-2646)
Fedex Office & Print Svcs Inc ....F...... 203 799-2679
  Orange (G-6601)
Frank Obuchowski ....G...... 860 535-4739
  Stonington (G-8528)
G & R Enterprises Incorporated ....G...... 860 549-6120
  Hartford (G-3593)
Imperial Grphic Cmmnctions Inc ....E...... 203 650-3478
  Milford (G-4553)

Employee Codes: A=Over 500 employees, B=251-500
C=101-250, D=51-100, E=20-50, F=10-19, G=1-9

2020 Harris Connecticut
Manufacturers Directory

631

BINDING SVC: Books & Manuals

Jerrys Printing & Graphics LLC .... G 203 384-0015
  Bridgeport *(G-803)*
Joseph Merritt & Company Inc .... G 203 743-6734
  Danbury *(G-1863)*
Kool Ink LLC .... F 860 242-0303
  Bloomfield *(G-439)*
Master Engrv & Printery Inc .... G 203 723-2779
  Waterbury *(G-9535)*
Norwich Printing Company Inc .... F 860 887-7468
  Norwich *(G-6425)*
Palmisano Printing LLC .... G 860 582-6883
  Bristol *(G-1085)*
Pancoast Associates Inc .... G 203 377-6571
  Trumbull *(G-9054)*
Paper Mill Graphix Inc .... E 203 531-5904
  Greenwich *(G-3213)*
Paul Dewitt .... G 203 792-5610
  Danbury *(G-1902)*
Phoenix Press Inc .... E 203 865-5555
  New Haven *(G-5363)*
Prosperous Printing LLC .... G 203 834-1962
  Wilton *(G-10322)*
Speedy Printing LLC .... G 860 445-8252
  Mystic *(G-4846)*
Step Saver Inc .... E 860 621-6751
  Southington *(G-7982)*
Tech-Repro Inc .... F 203 348-8884
  Stamford *(G-8460)*
Townsend John .... G 860 526-3896
  Deep River *(G-2104)*
Vernon Printing Co Inc .... G 860 872-1826
  Vernon Rockville *(G-9186)*
Warren Press Inc .... G 203 431-0011
  Ridgefield *(G-7182)*

BINDING SVC: Trade

Agjo Printing Service .... G 860 599-3143
  Pawcatuck *(G-6703)*

BINOCULARS

Tower Optical Company Inc .... G 203 866-4535
  Norwalk *(G-6376)*

BINS: Prefabricated, Metal Plate

Linvar LLC .... G 860 951-3818
  Rocky Hill *(G-7254)*

BIOLOGICAL PRDTS: Exc Diagnostic

Axiomx Inc .... E 203 208-1034
  Branford *(G-552)*
Charles River Laboratories Inc .... E 860 376-1240
  Voluntown *(G-9187)*
Coopersurgical Inc .... E 203 453-1700
  Guilford *(G-3341)*
Evotec (us) Inc .... E 650 228-1400
  Branford *(G-591)*
Genx International Inc .... E 203 453-1700
  Guilford *(G-3354)*
Lifepharms Inc .... E 860 447-8583
  New London *(G-5476)*
Oncosynergy Inc .... E 617 755-9156
  Greenwich *(G-3212)*
Phoenixsongs Biologicals Inc .... E 203 433-4329
  Branford *(G-635)*
Serapure Technologies LLC .... E 203 972-0481
  New Canaan *(G-5141)*
Vegware Us Inc .... G 860 779-7970
  Danielson *(G-2006)*

BIOLOGICAL PRDTS: Serums

Skin & Co North America LLC .... G 888 444-9971
  West Haven *(G-9955)*

BIOLOGICAL PRDTS: Toxins

Testing For Toxins .... G 203 972-6501
  New Canaan *(G-5152)*

BIOLOGICAL PRDTS: Vaccines

Charles River Laboratories Inc .... E 860 429-7261
  Storrs *(G-8546)*
Protein Sciences Corporation .... D 203 686-0800
  Meriden *(G-4224)*
Westchester Pet Vaccines .... G 860 267-4554
  Colchester *(G-1581)*

BIOLOGICAL PRDTS: Veterinary

Bactana Corp .... G 203 716-1230
  Farmington *(G-2881)*
Charles River Laboratories Inc .... E 860 889-1389
  Norwich *(G-6409)*

BLACKSMITH SHOP

Wide Horizons Co Inc .... G 203 661-9252
  Greenwich *(G-3259)*

BLADES: Saw, Hand Or Power

Blackstone Industries LLC .... D 203 792-8622
  Bethel *(G-266)*
Specialty Saw Inc .... E 860 658-4419
  Simsbury *(G-7648)*

BLANKBOOKS: Account

Data Management Incorporated .... E 860 677-8586
  Unionville *(G-9113)*

BLANKBOOKS: Albums, Record

Yolanda Dubose Records and .... F 203 823-6699
  West Haven *(G-9967)*

BLANKBOOKS: Scrapbooks

Grannys Got It .... G 203 879-0042
  Wolcott *(G-10566)*
Pieces of Time Scrapbook .... G 203 879-2678
  Waterbury *(G-9577)*
Scrapbook Clubhouse .... F 860 399-4443
  Westbrook *(G-10007)*

BLANKETING, FROM MANMADE FIBER

Peristere LLC .... G 860 783-5301
  Manchester *(G-4075)*

BLASTING SVC: Sand, Metal Parts

Logan Steel Inc .... E 203 235-0811
  Meriden *(G-4188)*
Quicksand Blasting .... G 860 848-4482
  Uncasville *(G-9103)*

BLINDS & SHADES: Porch, Wood Slat

Niantic Awning Company .... G 860 739-0161
  Niantic *(G-5813)*

BLINDS & SHADES: Vertical

1st Vertical LLC .... G 860 458-0120
  Willington *(G-10243)*
Decorator Services Inc .... E 203 384-8144
  Bridgeport *(G-743)*
Kilcourse Specialty Products .... G 860 210-2075
  New Milford *(G-5555)*
Prospect Flooring .... G 203 758-4207
  Prospect *(G-7017)*
Vertical Development LLC .... G 203 208-0806
  Branford *(G-665)*
Vertical Edge LLC .... G 203 513-2806
  Shelton *(G-7578)*
Vertical Management LLC .... G 203 422-2547
  Greenwich *(G-3254)*
Vertical Realms LLC .... G 860 508-5273
  Tariffville *(G-8745)*
Vertical Studios LLC .... G 203 562-6542
  North Haven *(G-6012)*

BLINDS: Window

Custom Upholstery Workshop .... G 203 367-4231
  Fairfield *(G-2770)*
Guys Blind .... G 203 270-8977
  Newtown *(G-5741)*
Middlesex Shades and Blinds .... G 860 346-7705
  Middletown *(G-4378)*
Porter Preston Inc .... F 203 753-1118
  Waterbury *(G-9582)*
Roto-Frank of America Inc .... D 860 526-4996
  Chester *(G-1482)*

BLINDS, WOOD

Blind Crafters .... G 860 896-0366
  Vernon Rockville *(G-9162)*

BLOCKS & BRICKS: Concrete

Delvento Inc .... F 203 371-7279
  Bridgeport *(G-748)*
Messiah Development LLC .... G 203 368-2405
  Bridgeport *(G-837)*

BLOCKS: Landscape Or Retaining Wall, Concrete

Berlin Industries LLC .... G 860 819-9997
  Berlin *(G-163)*
Central CT Snow LLC .... G 860 467-3107
  East Hampton *(G-2260)*
Rahzel Enterprize LLC .... G 475 449-6561
  Norwalk *(G-6315)*
Rockland Music LLC .... G 203 779-5299
  Madison *(G-3952)*
Svl LLC .... G 860 819-9929
  Avon *(G-116)*

BLOCKS: Paving, Concrete

Laydon Industries LLC .... D 203 562-7283
  New Haven *(G-5317)*

BLOCKS: Paving, Cut Stone

Connecticut Stone Supplies Inc .... D 203 882-1000
  Milford *(G-4499)*

BLOCKS: Standard, Concrete Or Cinder

City Cement Block-Del Corp Inc .... G 203 334-0702
  Bridgeport *(G-734)*
Connecticut Concrete Form Inc .... F 860 674-1314
  Farmington *(G-2892)*
Hatch and Bailey Company .... E 203 866-5515
  Norwalk *(G-6193)*
Kobyluck Ready-Mix Inc .... F 860 444-9604
  Waterford *(G-9657)*
New Milford Block & Supply .... G 860 355-1101
  New Milford *(G-5568)*
Westbrook Con Block Co Inc .... E 860 399-6201
  Westbrook *(G-10015)*

BLOOD RELATED HEALTH SVCS

New England Ctr For Hring Rhab .... G 860 455-1404
  Hampton *(G-3538)*

BLOWERS & FANS

Adk Pressure Equipment Corp .... G 860 585-0050
  Bristol *(G-957)*
Anderson Technologies Inc .... G 860 663-2100
  Killingworth *(G-3828)*
Atlantic Vent & Eqp Co Inc .... E 860 635-1300
  Cromwell *(G-1690)*
EBM-Papst Inc .... B 860 674-1515
  Farmington *(G-2902)*
GE Steam Power Inc .... G 860 688-1911
  Windsor *(G-10391)*
Nidec America Corporation .... F 860 653-2144
  East Granby *(G-2219)*
Stylair LLC .... F 860 747-4588
  Plainville *(G-6863)*

BLOWERS & FANS

McIntire Company .... F 860 585-8559
  Bristol *(G-1070)*

BLOWERS, TURBO: Indl

Mechancal Engnered Systems LLC .... G 203 400-4658
  New Canaan *(G-5119)*
Spencer Turbine Company .... C 860 688-8361
  Windsor *(G-10436)*

BLUEPRINTING SVCS

Bpi Reprographics .... F 203 866-5600
  Norwalk *(G-6097)*
John L Prentis & Co Inc .... G 203 634-1266
  Meriden *(G-4178)*
Technical Reproductions Inc .... F 203 849-9100
  Norwalk *(G-6365)*

BOAT BUILDING & REPAIR

Albin Manufacturing Corp .... G 203 661-4341
  Cos Cob *(G-1622)*

Arrigoni Distributors Ltd LLC ....G....... 860 669-6637
  Clinton (G-1491)
Bills Boat Repair LLC ....G....... 203 804-8801
  Guilford (G-3328)
Black Dog Boat Works LLC ....G....... 203 264-5823
  Southbury (G-7845)
Brewer Yacht Yards Inc ....G....... 860 399-5128
  Old Saybrook (G-6526)
Dp Custom Boat Repr Detail LLC ....G....... 203 536-3997
  Monroe (G-4711)
Dutch Wharf Boat Yard & Marina ....F....... 203 488-9000
  Branford (G-582)
Formula Boat Works LLC ....G....... 860 536-9309
  Mystic (G-4817)
Guillemot Kayaks ....G....... 860 659-8847
  Glastonbury (G-3044)
Hbi Boat LLC ....G....... 860 536-7776
  Groton (G-3291)
Housatonic Boat Works LLC ....G....... 203 375-3161
  Stratford (G-8627)
Indikon Boatworks ....G....... 860 395-8297
  Clinton (G-1508)
Kelsey Boat Yard ....G....... 203 488-9567
  Branford (G-616)
Kiwanis Fndtion Middletown Inc ....G....... 860 638-8135
  Middletown (G-4364)
Marine Fabricators ....G....... 203 488-7093
  Branford (G-624)
Montauk Pilots Inc ....G....... 860 535-3200
  North Stonington (G-6030)
Narragansett Yacht Servic ....G....... 860 763-1980
  Somers (G-7665)
Pmw Marine Repair ....G....... 860 535-3064
  Stonington (G-8536)
RWS Marine Restoration ....G....... 860 350-4977
  New Milford (G-5587)
Seabuzz Boatworks ....G....... 203 483-4576
  Branford (G-649)
Shipstik LLC ....G....... 203 417-8022
  Roxbury (G-7284)

BOAT BUILDING & REPAIRING: Fiberglass

Chester Boatworks ....G....... 860 526-2227
  Deep River (G-2086)
Lbi Inc ....F....... 860 446-8058
  Groton (G-3296)
New England Fiberglass Repair ....G....... 203 866-1690
  Norwalk (G-6272)
Stonington Boat Works LLC ....G....... 860 535-0332
  Stonington (G-8538)
Sweetwater Boatworks LLC ....G....... 860 984-5118
  New London (G-5491)
Vespoli Usa Inc ....E....... 203 773-0311
  New Haven (G-5426)
Vintage Boat Restorations LLC ....G....... 860 582-0774
  Bristol (G-1135)

BOAT BUILDING & REPAIRING: Motorboats, Inboard Or Outboard

Ace Marine Service Inc ....G....... 860 489-5960
  Torrington (G-8886)
Albin Marine Inc ....G....... 203 661-4341
  Cos Cob (G-1623)

BOAT BUILDING & REPAIRING: Motorized

Seaport Marine Inc ....E....... 860 536-9651
  Mystic (G-4844)

BOAT BUILDING & REPAIRING: Non-Motorized

Gregs Outboard Service LLC ....G....... 860 339-5139
  Old Saybrook (G-6535)

BOAT BUILDING & REPAIRING: Tenders, Small Motor Craft

Dinghy Pro LLC ....G....... 860 767-1596
  Essex (G-2715)
Grammas Hands LLC ....G....... 203 301-0791
  Milford (G-4541)

BOAT BUILDING & REPAIRING: Yachts

Jennings Yacht Services ....G....... 860 625-1368
  Mystic (G-4822)
Sound Yachts LLC ....G....... 860 399-8800
  Westbrook (G-10009)

BOAT DEALERS

Marine Fabricators ....G....... 203 488-7093
  Branford (G-624)

BOAT DEALERS: Outboard

Atlantic Outboard Inc ....G....... 860 399-6773
  Westbrook (G-9991)

BOAT DEALERS: Sails & Eqpt

Vespoli Usa Inc ....E....... 203 773-0311
  New Haven (G-5426)

BOAT REPAIR SVCS

Atlantic Outboard Inc ....G....... 860 399-6773
  Westbrook (G-9991)
Gaida Welding Co & Mar Repr ....G....... 203 924-4868
  Shelton (G-7448)
Jason Kurtzman Signs ....G....... 203 847-4397
  Norwalk (G-6220)
Rokap Inc ....G....... 203 265-6895
  Wallingford (G-9359)
Water Transit Services LLC ....G....... 860 625-3625
  Waterford (G-9676)

BOAT YARD: Boat yards, storage & incidental repair

Kelsey Boat Yard ....G....... 203 488-9567
  Branford (G-616)
Nu Line Design LLC ....G....... 203 949-0726
  Wallingford (G-9329)

BOATS & OTHER MARINE EQPT: Plastic

Djs Mobile Marine & Power Eqp ....G....... 203 331-9010
  Bridgeport (G-754)

BODIES: Truck & Bus

911 Motorsports LLC ....G....... 203 755-8405
  Waterbury (G-9421)
Boss Snowplows & Ice Control ....G....... 860 886-7081
  North Franklin (G-5871)
John Mezes & Sons Inc ....G....... 203 255-6841
  Bridgeport (G-809)
Rj 15 Inc ....F....... 860 585-0111
  Bristol (G-1110)

BODY PARTS: Automobile, Stamped Metal

Arthur G Byrne Co Inc ....G....... 203 461-8805
  Stamford (G-8096)
Inertia Dynamics Inc ....F....... 860 379-1252
  New Hartford (G-5198)
Perrin Manufacturing ....G....... 203 265-1325
  Wallingford (G-9335)
Subimods LLC ....G....... 860 291-0015
  Bloomfield (G-489)

BOILER REPAIR SHOP

Bri Metal Works Inc ....G....... 203 368-1649
  Bridgeport (G-718)
Connectcut Boiler Repr Mfg Inc ....E....... 860 953-9117
  West Hartford (G-9793)
Shoreline Boiler & Welding LLC ....G....... 860 575-0944
  Westbrook (G-10008)

BOILERS: Low-Pressure Heating, Steam Or Hot Water

Saigeworks LLC ....G....... 203 767-1035
  Trumbull (G-9069)

BOLTS: Metal

Ametek Inc ....C....... 203 265-6731
  Wallingford (G-9203)
Click Bond Inc ....E....... 860 274-5435
  Watertown (G-9694)
Industrial Prssure Washers LLC ....G....... 860 608-6153
  Wethersfield (G-10197)

BOOK STORES

Charles Alain Publishing Ltd ....G....... 203 226-2882
  Westport (G-10063)
Townsend John ....G....... 860 526-3896
  Deep River (G-2104)

BOOKS, WHOLESALE

Pages of Yesteryear ....G....... 203 426-0864
  Newtown (G-9843)
Peter Kelsey Publishing Inc ....G....... 860 231-9300
  West Hartford (G-9843)
Scholastic Inc ....G....... 212 343-6100
  Danbury (G-1938)
Scholastic Library Pubg Inc ....A....... 203 797-3500
  Danbury (G-1939)

BOOTS: Women's

Cecelia New York LLC ....G....... 917 392-4536
  Darien (G-2010)

BORING MILL

National Screw Manufacturing ....F....... 203 469-7109
  East Haven (G-2443)

BOTTLE CAPS & RESEALERS: Plastic

Berry Global Inc ....G....... 413 529-7602
  East Hampton (G-2256)

BOTTLED GAS DEALERS: Liquefied Petro, Dlvrd To Customers

Spicer Plus Inc ....G....... 860 445-2436
  Groton (G-3313)

BOTTLED WATER DELIVERY

Averys Beverage LLC ....G....... 860 224-0830
  New Britain (G-4947)

BOTTLES: Plastic

Ansa Company Inc ....F....... 203 687-1664
  Norwalk (G-6070)
Consolidated Container LP ....G....... 860 224-9381
  New Britain (G-4964)
Green Egg Design LLC ....G....... 860 541-5411
  Hartford (G-3602)
Mayborn Usa Inc ....F....... 781 269-7490
  Stamford (G-8298)
Packaging Concepts Assoc LLC ....G....... 860 489-0480
  Torrington (G-8955)
Silgan Holdings Inc ....C....... 203 975-7110
  Stamford (G-8421)

BOULDER: Crushed & Broken

Powder Hill Sand & Gravel LLC ....G....... 860 741-7274
  Enfield (G-2679)

BOXES & CRATES: Rectangular, Wood

Pith Products LLC ....F....... 860 487-4859
  Ashford (G-63)
St Pierre Box and Lumber Co ....G....... 860 413-9813
  Canton (G-1326)
Woodfree Crating Systems Inc ....F....... 203 759-1799
  Waterbury (G-9636)

BOXES & SHOOK: Nailed Wood

Coastal Pallet Corporation ....E....... 203 333-1892
  Bridgeport (G-737)

BOXES: Corrugated

AP Disposition LLC ....D....... 860 889-1344
  Norwich (G-6406)
Champlin-Packrite Inc ....E....... 860 951-9217
  Manchester (G-3994)
Colonial Corrugated Pdts Inc ....E....... 203 597-1707
  Waterbury (G-9453)
Connecticut Container Corp ....C....... 203 248-2161
  North Haven (G-5924)
Creative Source LLC ....G....... 203 879-4005
  Wolcott (G-10558)
Danbury Square Box Company ....E....... 203 744-4611
  Danbury (G-1787)
General Packaging Products Inc ....G....... 203 846-1340
  Norwalk (G-6178)
HI-Tech Packaging Inc ....E....... 203 378-2700
  Stratford (G-8626)
Holm Corrugated Container Inc ....E....... 860 628-5559
  Southington (G-7935)
Jackson Corrugated Cont Corp ....E....... 860 767-3373
  Essex (G-2720)

BOXES: Corrugated

Knapp Container Inc .... G 203 888-0511
  Beacon Falls *(G-137)*
Merrill Industries Inc .... E 860 871-1888
  Ellington *(G-2595)*
Merrill Industries LLC .... E 860 871-1888
  Ellington *(G-2596)*
Nutmeg Container Corporation .... D 860 963-6727
  Putnam *(G-7054)*
Park City Packaging Inc .... F 203 579-1965
  Bridgeport *(G-862)*
R & R Corrugated Container Inc .... D 860 584-1194
  Bristol *(G-1102)*
Rand-Whitney Group LLC .... D 203 426-5871
  Newtown *(G-5774)*
Windham Container Corporation .... E 860 928-7934
  Putnam *(G-7079)*

BOXES: Filing, Paperboard Made From Purchased Materials

Westrock Rkt Company .... C 860 284-9820
  Farmington *(G-2978)*

BOXES: Mail Or Post Office, Collection/Storage, Sheet Metal

Post Mortem Services LLC .... G 860 675-1103
  Farmington *(G-2950)*

BOXES: Paperboard, Folding

Agi-Shorewood Group Us LLC .... A 203 324-4839
  Stamford *(G-8067)*
B-P Products Inc .... E 203 288-0200
  Hamden *(G-3416)*
Clondalkin Pharma & Healthcare .... E 860 342-1987
  Portland *(G-6955)*
Curtis Corporation A Del Corp .... C 203 426-5861
  Sandy Hook *(G-7307)*
Curtis Packaging Corporation .... C 203 426-5861
  Sandy Hook *(G-7308)*
Keystone Paper & Box Co Inc .... D 860 291-0027
  South Windsor *(G-7783)*
Rice Packaging Inc .... D 860 870-7057
  Ellington *(G-2598)*
Sdi Systems Development .... G 860 967-5464
  Avon *(G-109)*

BOXES: Paperboard, Set-Up

Agi-Shorewood Group Us LLC .... A 203 324-4839
  Stamford *(G-8067)*
Ehrlich & Company .... G 203 481-1999
  Branford *(G-586)*
Millen Industries Inc .... G 203 847-8500
  Norwalk *(G-6259)*
Rice Packaging Inc .... D 860 870-7057
  Ellington *(G-2598)*
Rondo America Incorporated .... C 203 723-5831
  Naugatuck *(G-4917)*

BOXES: Plastic

Althor Products LLC .... G 860 386-6700
  Windsor Locks *(G-10472)*

BOXES: Solid Fiber

Common Sense Engineered Pdts .... G 203 888-8695
  Beacon Falls *(G-132)*

BOXES: Stamped Metal

Durham Manufacturing Company .... D 860 349-3427
  Durham *(G-2146)*

BOXES: Wooden

Colonial Wood Products Inc .... F 203 932-9003
  West Haven *(G-9889)*
Merrill Industries Inc .... E 860 871-1888
  Ellington *(G-2595)*
St Pierre Box and Lumber Co .... G 860 413-9813
  Canton *(G-1326)*
Vermont Pallet & Skid Shop .... G 860 822-6949
  Norwich *(G-6437)*
Westwood Products Inc .... F 860 379-9401
  Winsted *(G-10543)*

BRAKES & BRAKE PARTS

Tek-Motive Inc .... D 203 468-2224
  Branford *(G-662)*

BRAKES: Electromagnetic

Carlyle Johnson Machine Co LLC .... E 860 643-1531
  Bolton *(G-508)*
Inertia Dynamics LLC .... C 860 379-1252
  New Hartford *(G-5197)*

BRAKES: Metal Forming

Eyelet Tech LLC .... E 203 879-5306
  Wolcott *(G-10564)*

BRAKES: Press

J D & Associates .... G 860 546-2112
  Canterbury *(G-1299)*

BRAZING SVCS

Brazing Way LLC .... G 860 485-9337
  Harwinton *(G-3722)*
D B F Industries Inc .... E 860 827-8283
  New Britain *(G-4969)*
Parama Corp .... F 203 790-8155
  Bethel *(G-331)*

BRAZING: Metal

Accurate Brazing Corporation .... F 860 432-1840
  Manchester *(G-3976)*
Bodycote Thermal Proc Inc .... E 860 282-1371
  South Windsor *(G-7719)*
O & W Heat Treat Inc .... E 860 528-9239
  South Windsor *(G-7799)*

BREAD WRAPPERS: Waxed Or Laminated, Made From Purchased Matl

Koster Keunen LLC .... F 860 945-3333
  Watertown *(G-9715)*

BRICK, STONE & RELATED PRDTS WHOLESALERS

Aarons Enterprises .... G 203 762-9764
  Wilton *(G-10266)*
Dan Beard Inc .... F 203 924-4346
  Shelton *(G-7427)*
Desiato Sand & Gravel Corp .... E 860 429-6479
  Storrs Mansfield *(G-8555)*
Mid-Island Aggregates/Distribu .... G 860 605-6753
  Sherman *(G-7598)*
Midwood Quarry and Cnstr Inc .... F 860 289-1414
  East Hartford *(G-2345)*

BRIDAL SHOPS

Ida Dean .... G 860 482-3589
  Torrington *(G-8934)*

BROADCASTING & COMMS EQPT: Antennas, Transmitting/Comms

Jk Antennas Inc .... G 845 228-8700
  Brookfield *(G-1200)*
Peak Antennas .... G 203 268-3688
  Monroe *(G-4745)*
Radio Frequency Systems Inc .... E 203 630-3311
  Meriden *(G-4227)*

BROADCASTING & COMMUNICATION EQPT: Transmit-Receiver, Radio

Ashcrft-Ngano Kiki Hldings Inc .... G 203 378-8281
  Stratford *(G-8571)*
Ashcroft Inc .... B 203 378-8281
  Stratford *(G-8572)*

BROADCASTING & COMMUNICATIONS EQPT: Transmitting, Radio/TV

Video Automation Systems Inc .... G 203 312-0152
  New Fairfield *(G-5182)*

BROADCASTING STATIONS, RADIO: Sports

Rotounderworld LLC .... G 202 236-7103
  Fairfield *(G-2839)*

BROKERS' SVCS

M G Solutions .... G 203 945-9615
  Norwalk *(G-6241)*

BROKERS: Business

First Equity Group Inc .... F 203 291-7700
  Westport *(G-10082)*

BROKERS: Printing

Alicia Cersosimorathbun .... G 401 345-7097
  Mystic *(G-4797)*
Omniprint LLC .... G 203 881-9013
  Oxford *(G-6683)*
Sterling Forms and Cmpt Sups .... G 203 876-7337
  Milford *(G-4653)*

BRONZE FOUNDRY, NEC

Arctime LLC .... G 203 321-5628
  Norwalk *(G-6072)*

BRONZE ROLLING & DRAWING

Waterbury Rolling Mills Inc .... D 203 597-5000
  Waterbury *(G-9628)*

BROOMS

International Garrett-Hewitt .... G 203 761-1542
  Wilton *(G-10303)*

BROOMS & BRUSHES

Loos & Co Inc .... F 860 928-6681
  Pomfret *(G-6934)*
Torrington Brush Works Inc .... G 860 482-3517
  Torrington *(G-8979)*

BROOMS & BRUSHES: Hair Pencils Or Artists' Brushes

Gros-Ite Industries Inc .... G 800 242-1790
  Cheshire *(G-1395)*

BROOMS & BRUSHES: Paintbrushes

Liftline Capital LLC .... F 860 395-0150
  Old Saybrook *(G-6553)*

BUCKLES & PARTS

Buckles In A Snap LLC .... G 774 452-5336
  Woodstock *(G-10660)*
Hawie Manufacturing Company .... G 203 366-4303
  Bridgeport *(G-783)*

BUFFING FOR THE TRADE

Baron & Young Co Inc .... G 860 589-3235
  Bristol *(G-976)*
D D M Metal Finishing Co Inc .... G 860 872-4683
  Tolland *(G-8857)*
Deburring House Inc .... E 860 828-0889
  East Berlin *(G-2165)*
J M Compounds Inc .... G 203 376-9854
  Meriden *(G-4176)*
Precision Plating Corp .... G 860 875-9267
  Vernon *(G-9150)*
R J Brass Inc .... F 860 793-2336
  Plainville *(G-6855)*

BUILDING & STRUCTURAL WOOD MBRS: Timbers, Struct, Lam Lumber

Timber Frame Barn Conversions .... G 860 219-0519
  Windsor *(G-10450)*

BUILDING & STRUCTURAL WOOD MEMBERS

Country Carpenters Inc .... G 860 228-2276
  Hebron *(G-3746)*
Eastern Company .... E 203 729-2255
  Naugatuck *(G-4878)*
Richard G Swartwout Jr .... G 860 377-2321
  Andover *(G-16)*

BUILDING COMPONENTS: Structural Steel

All Phase Steel Works LLC .... D 203 375-8881
  New Haven *(G-5222)*
Engineers Welding LLC .... G 203 334-2492
  Bridgeport *(G-763)*
Esdras Steel Fabrication .... G 203 917-3053
  Bethel *(G-297)*

PRODUCT SECTION

BUSINESS ACTIVITIES: Non-Commercial Site

Pds Engineering & Cnstr Inc .... E 860 242-8586
  Bloomfield *(G-462)*
Pisani Steel Fabrication Inc .... G 203 720-0679
  Naugatuck *(G-4911)*
Qsr Steel Corporation LLC .... E 860 548-0248
  Hartford *(G-3671)*
Shepard Steel Co Inc .... D 860 525-4446
  Hartford *(G-3685)*
State Welding & Fabg Inc .... G 203 294-4071
  Wallingford *(G-9376)*
T Keefe and Sons .... G 203 457-0267
  Guilford *(G-3396)*

BUILDING EXTERIOR CLEANING SVCS

Beyond Home Improvement .... G 203 859-0113
  North Haven *(G-5914)*

BUILDING ITEM REPAIR SVCS, MISCELLANEOUS

Otis Elevator Company .... B 860 674-3000
  Farmington *(G-2942)*

BUILDING MAINTENANCE SVCS, EXC REPAIRS

Qba Inc .... G 860 963-9438
  Woodstock *(G-10679)*

BUILDING PRDTS & MATERIALS DEALERS

Brian Cheney .... G 203 734-4793
  Seymour *(G-7336)*
Davis Sawmill .... G 860 354-6008
  New Milford *(G-5527)*
Delvento Inc .... F 203 371-7279
  Bridgeport *(G-748)*
Drapery Consultants .... G 203 855-0454
  Norwalk *(G-6150)*
Eric Sapper .... G 203 239-6020
  North Haven *(G-5938)*
Gregory Penta .... G 860 747-2681
  Plainville *(G-6819)*
Homewood Cabinet Co Inc .... G 860 599-2441
  Pawcatuck *(G-6715)*
Moores Sawmill Inc .... G 860 242-3003
  Bloomfield *(G-446)*
Viking Kitchen Cabinets LLC .... E 860 223-7101
  New Britain *(G-5080)*

BUILDING PRDTS: Concrete

Direct Sales LLC .... G 203 371-2373
  Fairfield *(G-2774)*
Lane Construction Corporation .... C 203 235-3351
  Cheshire *(G-1405)*
Lane Industries Incorporated .... G 203 235-3351
  Cheshire *(G-1406)*
Salin-Mpregilo US Holdings Inc .... G 203 439-2900
  Cheshire *(G-1441)*

BUILDING PRDTS: Stone

Mark Dzidzk .... E 860 793-2767
  Plainville *(G-6839)*
Ontra Stone Concepts LLC .... G 203 371-8225
  Bridgeport *(G-856)*

BUILDING STONE, ARTIFICIAL: Concrete

Torrington Industries Inc .... G 860 489-9261
  Torrington *(G-8983)*
West Hartford Stone Mulch LLC .... G 860 461-7616
  West Hartford *(G-9872)*

BUILDINGS & COMPONENTS: Prefabricated Metal

Engineered Building Pdts Inc .... E 860 243-1110
  Bloomfield *(G-409)*
Illinois Tool Works Inc .... C 203 574-2119
  Waterbury *(G-9503)*
Morin Corporation .... D 860 584-0900
  Bristol *(G-1074)*
Portable Garage Depot LLC .... G 203 397-1721
  Woodbridge *(G-10614)*
Shelters of America LLC .... G 203 397-1037
  Woodbridge *(G-10617)*
Walpole Woodworkers Inc .... E 508 668-2800
  Ridgefield *(G-7181)*

BUILDINGS: Portable

Mobile Mini Inc .... E 860 668-1888
  Suffield *(G-8727)*

BUILDINGS: Prefabricated, Wood

Barcello Development Co .... G 860 635-7676
  Middletown *(G-4323)*
Country Carpenters Inc .... G 860 228-2276
  Hebron *(G-3746)*
Heart Industrial Unions LLC .... G 800 769-0503
  Berlin *(G-187)*
Spedding Co .... G 860 355-4076
  New Milford *(G-5591)*
Trigila Construction Inc .... E 860 828-8444
  Berlin *(G-228)*
Walpole Woodworkers Inc .... E 508 668-2800
  Ridgefield *(G-7181)*
Walpole Woodworkers Inc .... E 203 255-9010
  Westport *(G-10173)*

BUILDINGS: Prefabricated, Wood

American Prefab Wood Pdts Co .... G 860 242-5468
  Bloomfield *(G-383)*
Bond-Bilt Garages Inc .... G 203 269-3375
  Wallingford *(G-9221)*
Carefree Building Co Inc .... F 860 267-7600
  Colchester *(G-1544)*

BURGLAR ALARM MAINTENANCE & MONITORING SVCS

Grayfin Security LLC .... G 203 800-6760
  Madison *(G-3923)*

BURIAL VAULTS: Concrete Or Precast Terrazzo

Bridgeport Burial Vault Co .... G 203 375-7375
  Stratford *(G-8587)*
Capitol City Burial Vaults .... G 860 953-1060
  West Hartford *(G-9785)*
Elm-Cap Industries Inc .... E 860 953-1060
  West Hartford *(G-9808)*

BURIAL VAULTS: Stone

Godfrey Cemetary Maint LLC .... G 203 858-4035
  Sherman *(G-7595)*

BURNERS: Gas, Indl

Carlin Combustion Tech Inc .... D 203 680-9401
  North Haven *(G-5919)*
Hamworthy Peabody Combustn Inc .... E 203 922-1199
  Shelton *(G-7457)*
Preferred Utilities Mfg Corp .... D 203 743-6741
  Danbury *(G-1918)*
Pumc Holding Corporation .... E 203 743-6741
  Danbury *(G-1921)*
Zeeco Inc .... G 860 479-0999
  Plainville *(G-6879)*

BURNERS: Oil, Domestic Or Indl

John Zink Company LLC .... D 203 925-0380
  Shelton *(G-7481)*

BURNT WOOD ARTICLES

Northeast Wood Products LLC .... E 860 862-6350
  Uncasville *(G-9100)*

BUSES: Wholesalers

M & J Bus Co .... G 203 624-0836
  North Haven *(G-5960)*
M & J Bus Co Inc .... G 860 437-3721
  Waterford *(G-9660)*
M & J Bus Inc .... G 860 668-6526
  Suffield *(G-8724)*

BUSINESS ACTIVITIES: Non-Commercial Site

32 Degrees LLC .... G 978 602-2007
  West Hartford *(G-9768)*
A&D Schneider LLC .... G 203 870-9474
  Stratford *(G-8563)*
Actimus Inc .... D 617 438-9968
  Cromwell *(G-1685)*
Alternate Energy Futures .... G 917 745-7097
  Danbury *(G-1738)*
Alva Health Inc .... G 832 515-8235
  New Haven *(G-5225)*
Aniyaq LLC .... G 860 531-2835
  Marlborough *(G-4120)*
API Wizard LLC .... G 914 764-5726
  Ridgefield *(G-7117)*
Art of Wellbeing LLC .... G 917 453-3009
  Stamford *(G-8095)*
Bara Essentials LLC .... G 203 428-1786
  Stratford *(G-8577)*
Biofibers Capital Group LLC .... G 203 561-6133
  Ashford *(G-57)*
Bleshue LLC .... G 203 405-1034
  Woodbury *(G-10627)*
Blue Crystal Enterprises LLC .... G 203 856-5397
  Trumbull *(G-9006)*
Brass City Gamers Tournament .... G 203 584-3359
  Waterbury *(G-9442)*
Bridge Innvations Ventures LLC .... G 203 520-8241
  Trumbull *(G-9007)*
Cagno Enterprises LLC .... G 203 729-3883
  Naugatuck *(G-4867)*
Calumma Technologies LLC .... G 914 557-4562
  Norwalk *(G-6105)*
Cara C Andreoli .... G 860 888-6553
  Glastonbury *(G-3019)*
Careerpath Mobile LLC .... G 203 512-2379
  New Milford *(G-5515)*
Celb LLC .... G 203 739-0157
  Danbury *(G-1765)*
Central CT Snow LLC .... G 860 467-3107
  East Hampton *(G-2260)*
Clever Clover LLC .... G 860 501-2800
  Pawcatuck *(G-6706)*
Cliffside Entertainment LLC .... G 203 290-7484
  Bridgeport *(G-736)*
Cold LLC .... G 203 543-6861
  Milford *(G-4490)*
Composite Truck Body LLC .... G 800 735-1668
  Sherman *(G-7593)*
Connecticut Trade Company Inc .... G 203 368-0398
  Fairfield *(G-2767)*
Creative Stone Group Inc .... G 203 554-7773
  Stamford *(G-8169)*
Crista Grasso LLC .... G 347 946-2533
  Tolland *(G-8856)*
D Cello Enterprises LLC .... G 860 659-0844
  Glastonbury *(G-3027)*
Datacomm Management Svcs LLC .... G 203 858-9846
  Darien *(G-2020)*
Dbo Home LLC .... G 860 364-6008
  Sharon *(G-7377)*
Dirtcircle Media LLC .... G 860 532-0674
  Milford *(G-4511)*
Dlpublshers Mystryntrtnmentllc .... G 203 556-4893
  Bridgeport *(G-755)*
Donali Systems Integration Inc .... G 860 715-5432
  Guilford *(G-3346)*
Dragon Hollow Design LLC .... G 860 861-6200
  Norwich *(G-6411)*
Drug Imprment Dtction Svcs LLC .... G 203 616-3735
  Danbury *(G-1802)*
Elidah Inc .... G 978 435-4324
  Monroe *(G-4715)*
EPic Publishing Services LLC .... G 860 204-7450
  East Haddam *(G-2241)*
Frostbite LLC .... G 203 240-3449
  Wilton *(G-10297)*
Graycon Defense Industries LLC .... G 860 339-2505
  Chester *(G-1474)*
Hart Stamp & Seal LLC .... G 860 474-5382
  Bolton *(G-510)*
Higher Consciousness LLC .... G 310 977-7541
  Avon *(G-84)*
Imprimi Fotos Ya LLC .... G 860 628-1787
  New Haven *(G-5300)*
Integer-Comfab Enterprises LLC .... G 646 620-9112
  Westport *(G-10102)*
J & E Hidalgo Enterprises LLC .... G 203 246-2252
  Norwalk *(G-6214)*
Kamelot Kreations LLC .... G 860 564-7399
  Sterling *(G-8511)*
Kando Apps LLC .... G 203 722-4359
  Norwalk *(G-6227)*
Kanine Knits .... G 203 272-8548
  Cheshire *(G-1402)*
Kimberly Bon Publishing LLC .... G 203 258-9829
  Trumbull *(G-9039)*

Employee Codes: A=Over 500 employees, B=251-500
C=101-250, D=51-100, E=20-50, F=10-19, G=1-9

Lantern LLC ......G....... 866 203-5715
Woodstock *(G-10668)*
Leader Management Corp ......G....... 860 643-4445
Bolton *(G-514)*
Led Lighting Solutions LLC ......G....... 860 770-6023
Berlin *(G-193)*
Live and Dream Green LLC ......G....... 860 670-0870
Avon *(G-91)*
Loving Life LLC ......G....... 860 326-1459
Voluntown *(G-9190)*
Mindtrainr LLC ......G....... 914 799-1515
Stamford *(G-8312)*
Muggers Marrow LLC ......G....... 203 548-9566
Bridgeport *(G-845)*
Mytyme LLC ......G....... 860 327-2356
Windsor *(G-10411)*
Nalco Wtr Prtrtment Sltons LLC ......G....... 860 224-4443
New Britain *(G-5019)*
Natural Spring Ventures LLC ......G....... 203 556-2420
Woodbury *(G-10646)*
Nesola Scarves LLC ......G....... 203 288-5058
Cheshire *(G-1419)*
New Beginnings Sea Glass ......G....... 203 329-7623
Stamford *(G-8321)*
New England Toy LLC ......G....... 860 655-6089
Simsbury *(G-7637)*
Nofet LLC ......F....... 203 848-9064
New Haven *(G-5351)*
Only Queens LLC ......G....... 860 888-4413
Bloomfield *(G-455)*
People Meeting LLC ......G....... 860 933-0366
Glastonbury *(G-3069)*
Perosphere Inc ......F....... 203 885-1111
Danbury *(G-1905)*
Pmoys LLC ......G....... 203 541-0995
Stamford *(G-8365)*
Power Quality and Drives LLC ......G....... 203 217-2353
Woodbury *(G-10651)*
Pro Gas Installation & Svc LLC ......G....... 860 982-1370
East Hampton *(G-2275)*
Rahzel Enterprize LLC ......G....... 475 449-6561
Norwalk *(G-6315)*
Regenerative Medicine LLC ......G....... 203 629-1438
Greenwich *(G-3223)*
Robison Music Media & Pubg LLC ......G....... 203 858-8106
Wallingford *(G-9356)*
Rodriguez Ruiz Rosa Margarita ......G....... 860 840-0344
Hartford *(G-3681)*
Rotounderworld LLC ......G....... 202 236-7103
Fairfield *(G-2839)*
Rubberhouse ......G....... 860 646-3012
Bolton *(G-518)*
Sean Christian Leather LLC ......G....... 787 690-7039
West Hartford *(G-9854)*
Seasons Media LLC ......G....... 860 413-2022
West Simsbury *(G-9982)*
Single Load LLC ......G....... 860 944-7507
Bridgeport *(G-909)*
Soundview Horizons Dgtl Ldrshp ......G....... 203 292-0880
Weston *(G-10040)*
Spots and Ladybugs LLC ......G....... 203 378-8232
Trumbull *(G-9076)*
Suarez Services LLC ......G....... 203 895-0465
Bridgeport *(G-915)*
Swift Scientific LLC ......G....... 860 498-8577
Coventry *(G-1680)*
Target Machines Inc ......G....... 860 675-1539
Burlington *(G-1276)*
Tillys Natural Blend LLC ......G....... 203 270-8406
Newtown *(G-5792)*
Triple Clover Products LLC ......G....... 475 558-9503
New Canaan *(G-5154)*
Ultimate Interfaces Corp ......G....... 203 230-8184
Milford *(G-4667)*
Uniworld Bus Publications Inc ......G....... 201 384-4900
Darien *(G-2049)*
Us-Malabar Company Inc ......G....... 203 226-1773
Weston *(G-10041)*
Utica Spring Company Inc ......G....... 860 628-6165
Southington *(G-7991)*
Westfort Construction Corp ......G....... 860 833-7970
Hamden *(G-3529)*
X44 LLC ......G....... 860 480-5560
Torrington *(G-8993)*
Xolvi LLC ......G....... 339 222-3616
Simsbury *(G-7652)*
Yakka LLC ......G....... 617 877-7553
New Haven *(G-5438)*
Yard Welding and Repair LLC ......G....... 860 402-8321
Bristol *(G-1142)*
Yolanda Dubose Records and ......F....... 203 823-6699
West Haven *(G-9967)*

BUSINESS FORMS: Printed, Continuous

Alicia Cersosimorathbun ......G....... 401 345-7097
Mystic *(G-4797)*

BUSINESS FORMS: Printed, Manifold

D Cello Enterprises LLC ......G....... 860 659-0844
Glastonbury *(G-3027)*
Federal Business Products Inc ......D....... 860 482-6231
Torrington *(G-8924)*
Mlk Business Forms Inc ......F....... 203 624-6304
New Haven *(G-5335)*
Occuptnal Trvl Mdcine Sups LLC ......G....... 866 206-4496
Fairfield *(G-2823)*
Taylor Communications Inc ......F....... 860 290-6851
East Hartford *(G-2382)*
Wallace Services Group LLC ......G....... 860 350-2992
Bloomfield *(G-499)*
Wallingford Prtg Bus Forms Inc ......F....... 203 481-1911
Branford *(G-669)*

BUSINESS MACHINE REPAIR, ELECTRIC

Agissar Corporation ......D....... 203 375-8662
Stratford *(G-8565)*
Neopost USA Inc ......C....... 203 301-3400
Milford *(G-4588)*
Xerox Corporation ......B....... 203 968-3000
Norwalk *(G-6401)*
Xerox Holdings Corporation ......G....... 203 968-3000
Norwalk *(G-6402)*

BUSINESS SUPPORT SVCS

Bellable LLC ......G....... 800 212-2603
West Hartford *(G-9778)*
Indigo Coast Inc ......G....... 860 592-0088
Kent *(G-3822)*
Mc Keon Computer Services ......G....... 860 496-7171
Torrington *(G-8947)*

BUTTONS

Ogs Technologies Inc ......E....... 203 271-9055
Cheshire *(G-1424)*
US Button Corporation ......C....... 860 928-2707
Putnam *(G-7076)*

CABINETS & CASES: Show, Display & Storage, Exc Wood

Bull Metal Products Inc ......E....... 860 346-9691
Middletown *(G-4329)*
Platt-Labonia of N Haven Inc ......D....... 203 239-5681
North Haven *(G-5977)*

CABINETS: Bathroom Vanities, Wood

Christopoulos Designs Inc ......F....... 203 576-1110
Bridgeport *(G-733)*
Kingswood Kitchens Co Inc ......D....... 203 792-8700
Danbury *(G-1870)*
Knb Design LLC ......G....... 203 777-6661
New Haven *(G-5310)*
Martin Cabinet Inc ......D....... 860 747-5769
Bristol *(G-1069)*
Privy Pine Products ......G....... 203 272-6169
Cheshire *(G-1432)*
Royal Woodcraft Inc ......F....... 203 847-3461
Ansonia *(G-49)*
S J Pappas Inc ......G....... 203 237-7701
Meriden *(G-4236)*
Sebastian Kitchen Cabinets ......G....... 203 853-4411
Norwalk *(G-6340)*

CABINETS: Entertainment

Belmont Corporation ......E....... 860 589-5700
Bristol *(G-980)*
St Johns Bridge LLC ......G....... 860 927-3315
Kent *(G-3826)*

CABINETS: Entertainment Units, Household, Wood

These Guys ......G....... 860 344-0022
Middletown *(G-4426)*

CABINETS: Factory

Curtiss Woodworking Inc ......F....... 203 527-9305
Prospect *(G-6998)*
Liberty Garage Inc ......G....... 203 778-0222
Danbury *(G-1873)*
River Mill Co ......F....... 860 669-5915
Clinton *(G-1521)*
Westmount Group LLC ......G....... 203 931-1033
West Haven *(G-9964)*

CABINETS: Kitchen, Metal

CT Acquisitions LLC ......E....... 888 441-0537
Wallingford *(G-9243)*
Tailored Kitchens By Ann-Morin ......G....... 860 428-2397
Brooklyn *(G-1256)*

CABINETS: Kitchen, Wood

A -Line Custom Counter Top ......G....... 860 747-1917
Plainville *(G-6758)*
A Matter of Style LLC ......G....... 203 272-1337
Cheshire *(G-1345)*
A S J Specialties LLC ......G....... 203 284-8650
Wallingford *(G-9194)*
AB Custom Cabinetry LLC ......G....... 203 367-5047
Fairfield *(G-2741)*
Affordable Cabinets ......G....... 860 919-5204
Berlin *(G-152)*
Affordable Fine Cabinetry ......G....... 860 919-5204
Plainville *(G-6767)*
Alfred Brown Cabinetry LLC ......G....... 860 868-7261
Warren *(G-9406)*
Amelia Cabinet Co LLC ......G....... 860 638-9047
Torrington *(G-8893)*
American Refacing Cstm Cab LLC ......G....... 860 647-0868
Manchester *(G-3983)*
Axis Wood Works LLC ......G....... 203 481-4946
Branford *(G-553)*
Bailey Avenue Kitchens ......G....... 203 438-4868
Ridgefield *(G-7118)*
Belmont Corporation ......E....... 860 589-5700
Bristol *(G-980)*
Bergan Architectural Wdwkg Inc ......E....... 860 346-0869
Middletown *(G-4324)*
Beyond Forever Cabinetry LLC ......G....... 203 427-7968
Bridgeport *(G-711)*
Bonito Manufacturing Inc ......D....... 203 234-8786
North Haven *(G-5915)*
Boule LLC ......G....... 860 267-8343
East Hampton *(G-2258)*
BP Countertop Design Co LLC ......G....... 203 732-1620
Derby *(G-2110)*
C J Brand & Son ......G....... 860 536-9266
Mystic *(G-4803)*
Cabinet Authority LLC ......G....... 203 304-2010
Newtown *(G-5730)*
Cabinet Dreams LLC ......G....... 203 558-4178
Oakville *(G-6451)*
Cabinet Harward Specialti ......G....... 860 231-1192
West Hartford *(G-9782)*
Cabinet Maker ......G....... 860 933-0272
Dayville *(G-2056)*
Cabinet Resources Ct Inc ......G....... 860 352-2030
Canton *(G-1308)*
Cabinet Specialties LLC ......G....... 860 747-4114
Plainville *(G-6781)*
Cabinet Works LLC ......G....... 860 450-0803
Storrs *(G-8544)*
Cabinetmakers Choice LLC ......G....... 203 426-3247
Sandy Hook *(G-7302)*
Cabinets Kwik ......G....... 860 538-5047
New Britain *(G-4954)*
Celtic Stoneworks ......G....... 860 846-0279
Plainville *(G-6786)*
Chris Cross LLC ......G....... 203 386-8426
Stratford *(G-8595)*
Chris Peterson Woodworks ......G....... 860 542-0140
Norfolk *(G-5823)*
Christopher Peacock Homes ......G....... 203 862-9333
Greenwich *(G-3143)*
Chunghua Cabinet CT Inc ......G....... 718 886-4588
Stamford *(G-8145)*
Classic Cabinets ......G....... 860 749-9743
Enfield *(G-2625)*
Clinton Babcock & Sons ......G....... 860 887-9166
Ledyard *(G-3871)*
Connecticut Cabinet Distrs LLC ......G....... 860 508-6240
Glastonbury *(G-3024)*
Connecticut Solid Surface LLC ......E....... 860 410-9800
Plainville *(G-6791)*

CAMERAS & RELATED EQPT: Photographic

Conway Hardwood Products LLC .... E 860 355-4030
  Gaylordsville (G-2991)
Currie & Kingston LLC .... G 203 698-9428
  Riverside (G-7191)
Custom Cabinet & European .... G 860 430-9396
  Glastonbury (G-3026)
Custom Furniture & Design LLC .... F 860 567-3519
  Litchfield (G-3887)
Custom Interiors .... G 860 738-8754
  Winchester Center (G-10344)
Custom Stiles .... G 203 410-2370
  Milford (G-4503)
Cyr Woodworking Inc .... G 860 232-1991
  Newington (G-5646)
Dante Ltd .... G 860 376-0204
  Jewett City (G-3793)
David O Wells Custom Cabinetry .... G 203 231-0280
  Southbury (G-7851)
Design Shop Llc .... G 203 937-1651
  West Haven (G-9897)
Dj Cabinets .... G 203 243-0032
  West Haven (G-9900)
Domestic Kitchens Inc .... E 203 368-1651
  Fairfield (G-2776)
Dream Cabinets LLC .... G 860 301-5625
  Colchester (G-1547)
East Hartford Lamination Co .... G 860 633-4637
  Glastonbury (G-3029)
Edward Tomkievich .... G 860 633-5811
  Glastonbury (G-3032)
Farmington Valley Woodcrafts .... G 860 793-9034
  Plainville (G-6809)
Fdk Custom Cabinetry LLC .... G 203 459-9909
  Monroe (G-4717)
Focal Metals .... G 203 743-4443
  Bethel (G-300)
Forest Remodeling .... G 413 222-7953
  Somers (G-7659)
Golden Hill Cstm Cabinetry LLC .... G 203 366-2222
  Bridgeport (G-777)
Greenhaven Cabinetry & Millwor .... G 860 535-1106
  Stonington (G-8529)
Gregory Penta .... G 860 747-2681
  Plainville (G-6819)
Gridiron Capital LLC .... D 203 972-1100
  New Canaan (G-5108)
H & B Woodworking Co .... G 860 793-6991
  Plainville (G-6820)
Hanford Cabinet & Wdwkg Co .... G 860 388-5055
  Old Saybrook (G-6538)
Heartwood Cabinetry .... G 860 295-0304
  Marlborough (G-4124)
Holness Cabinetry LLC .... G 203 598-0430
  Middlebury (G-4279)
Homewood Cabinet Co Inc .... G 860 599-2441
  Pawcatuck (G-6715)
Hope Kit Cbinets Stone Sup LLC .... G 203 504-3164
  Stamford (G-8241)
Hope Kit Cbinets Stone Sup LLC .... G 203 610-6147
  Bridgeport (G-786)
Industrial Wood Product Co .... G 203 735-2374
  Shelton (G-7475)
IS Cabinetry LLC .... G 203 583-5857
  Bridgeport (G-794)
J&A Woodworking Co Inc .... G 203 287-1915
  Hamden (G-3466)
John June Custom Cabinetry LLC .... G 203 334-1720
  Bridgeport (G-808)
John M Kriskey Carpentry .... G 203 531-0194
  Greenwich (G-3184)
Kit Architectural Designs LLC .... G 203 378-6911
  Stratford (G-8642)
Kitchen Cab Resurfacing LLC .... F 203 334-2857
  Bridgeport (G-818)
Kitchen Kraftsmen .... G 860 616-1240
  Windsor (G-10402)
Kitchen Living LLC .... G 860 819-5847
  East Hampton (G-2268)
Kitchenmax LLC .... G 203 330-5041
  Bridgeport (G-819)
Kse Cabinets .... G 860 754-7236
  Middletown (G-4365)
Legere Group Ltd .... C 860 674-0392
  Avon (G-89)
Leos Kitchen & Stair Corp .... G 203 225-7363
  New Britain (G-5010)
Luchon Cabinet Woodwork .... G 860 684-5037
  Stafford Springs (G-8032)
Martin Cabinet Inc .... E 860 747-5769
  Plainville (G-6840)
Master Craft Kitchens .... G 203 366-1461
  Bridgeport (G-832)
Mj Martin Wood Working LLC .... G 860 577-5311
  Old Saybrook (G-6557)
Modern Classics .... G 203 422-2862
  Greenwich (G-3205)
Morris Woodworking .... G 860 346-7500
  Middletown (G-4382)
N Excellence Wood Inc .... G 860 345-2050
  Higganum (G-3770)
New England Kitchen Design Ctr .... G 203 268-2626
  Monroe (G-4742)
Northeast Cabinet Design .... G 203 438-1709
  Ridgefield (G-7158)
P L Woodworking .... G 860 354-6855
  Sherman (G-7599)
Peacock Cabinetry .... G 203 862-9333
  Norwalk (G-6293)
Pinhos Cabinets .... G 860 274-1740
  Oakville (G-6458)
Porta Door Co .... E 203 888-6191
  Seymour (G-7362)
Prescott Cabinet Co .... G 860 495-0176
  Pawcatuck (G-6723)
Prestige Cabinetry .... G 860 558-2784
  Stafford Springs (G-8034)
Quality Woodworks LLC .... G 203 736-9200
  Ansonia (G-48)
Ricci Cabinet &STair Co .... G 203 889-6511
  Wallingford (G-9353)
Rj Cabinetry LLC .... G 203 515-8401
  Westport (G-10149)
Robert L Lovallo .... G 203 324-6655
  Stamford (G-8396)
Ross Custom Cabinetry .... G 203 913-2753
  Milford (G-4633)
Roxbury Cabinet Co LLC .... G 203 994-9855
  Roxbury (G-7282)
Schwank Archtctural Woodworker .... G 203 912-0109
  Redding (G-7107)
Sharpline Cabinetry LLC .... G 203 261-8454
  Easton (G-2566)
Song Bath LLC .... G 800 353-0313
  New Canaan (C-5144)
Specialty Shop Inc .... G 860 647-1477
  Manchester (G-4091)
St Johns Bridge LLC .... G 860 927-3315
  Kent (G-3826)
Star Woods Cabinet .... G 203 546-8688
  Brookfield (G-1227)
Sterling Custom Cabinetry LLC .... G 203 335-5151
  Bridgeport (G-913)
Steven Vandermaelen LLC .... G 203 457-0143
  Guilford (G-3393)
Stonewall Cabinetry LLC .... G 860 803-7595
  Enfield (G-2698)
Swan Cabinetry .... G 203 667-7026
  Trumbull (G-9079)
T C Kitchens Inc .... G 203 375-4469
  Stratford (G-8693)
Thornview Custom Cabinets .... G 860 228-5054
  Columbia (G-1613)
Timbercraft Cstm Dvtail Drwers .... G 800 345-4930
  New Milford (G-5596)
Tomkiel Furniture .... G 860 871-7632
  South Windsor (G-7834)
Top Sheft Cabinetry .... G 203 345-0000
  Bridgeport (G-928)
Viking Kitchen Cabinets LLC .... E 860 223-7101
  New Britain (G-5080)
West Hrtford Stirs Cbinets Inc .... D 860 953-9151
  Newington (G-5723)
West Mont Group .... G 203 931-1033
  West Haven (G-9963)
Westie Cabinetry LLC .... G 860 873-8953
  East Haddam (G-2250)
Wfv Cabinetmaker .... G 203 761-9109
  Wilton (G-10340)
Yankee Finishing .... G 203 910-0645
  Newington (G-5724)

CABINETS: Office, Metal

Nutmeg Architectural Wdwrk Inc .... E 203 325-4434
  Stamford (G-8333)

CABINETS: Office, Wood

Clay Furniture Industries Inc .... F 860 643-7580
  Manchester (G-3996)
G Woodcraft .... G 203 846-4168
  Norwalk (G-6173)
Gregory Woodworks LLC .... G 203 794-0726
  Bethel (G-306)
Statham Woodwork .... G 203 831-0629
  Norwalk (G-6355)

CABINETS: Show, Display, Etc, Wood, Exc Refrigerated

Bolton Hill Industries Inc .... G 860 742-0311
  Coventry (G-1647)
Lingard Cabinet Co LLC .... G 860 647-9886
  Manchester (G-4048)
Michael Martinetto .... G 203 874-6114
  Milford (G-4577)
New England Cabinet Co Inc .... F 860 747-9995
  New Britain (G-5021)
Premier Custom Cabinetry .... G 860 659-1863
  Glastonbury (G-3073)

CABLE & OTHER PAY TELEVISION DISTRIBUTION

Ripley Tools LLC .... E 860 635-2200
  Cromwell (G-1715)

CABLE TELEVISION PRDTS

RFS Americas .... G 203 630-3311
  Meriden (G-4231)

CABLE: Coaxial

A J R Inc .... F 203 384-0400
  Bridgeport (G-680)
Times Fiber Communications Inc .... D 203 265-8500
  Wallingford (G-9385)
Volpe Cable Corporation .... C 203 623-1818
  Branford (G-667)

CABLE: Fiber

Custom Plastic Distrs Inc .... G 860 779-5833
  Dayville (G-2060)
Nca Inc .... G 860 974-2310
  Abington (G-1)

CABLE: Fiber Optic

Fiberqa LLC .... G 860 739-8044
  Old Lyme (G-6508)

CABLE: Noninsulated

Armored Shield Technologies .... F 714 848-5796
  Redding (G-7090)
Redco Audio Inc .... F 203 502-7600
  Stratford (G-8674)

CABLE: Steel, Insulated Or Armored

Custom House LLC .... F 860 873-1259
  East Haddam (G-2240)
Federal Prison Industries .... F 203 743-6471
  Danbury (G-1824)
Lex Products LLC .... C 203 363-3738
  Shelton (G-7490)
Rscc Wire & Cable LLC .... B 860 653-8300
  East Granby (G-2228)
Specialty Cable Corp .... D 203 265-7126
  Wallingford (G-9372)

CAGES: Wire

Excel Spring & Stamping LLC .... G 860 585-1495
  Bristol (G-1033)

CALCULATING & ACCOUNTING EQPT

Blackwold Inc .... D 860 526-0800
  Chester (G-1464)

CALIPERS & DIVIDERS

KB Services .... G 203 243-3594
  Bridgeport (G-814)

CAMERA REPAIR SHOP

Quality Scanning Solution .... G 203 270-1833
  Newtown (G-5771)

CAMERAS & RELATED EQPT: Photographic

Vitec Production Solutions Inc .... D 203 929-1100
  Shelton (G-7581)

CAMERAS: Microfilm

Ebeam Film LLC .... F 203 926-0100
  Shelton *(G-7434)*

CAMSHAFTS

Westfalia Inc .... E 860 314-2920
  Bristol *(G-1137)*

CANDLES

22 Candles .... G 203 577-5540
  Wilton *(G-10264)*
A Little Soy Candle Co LLC .... G 860 877-6001
  West Haven *(G-9878)*
Apple Valley Candle Company .... G 860 940-1176
  Bristol *(G-963)*
Aromalite Candle Co LLC .... G 860 872-1029
  Vernon *(G-9131)*
Artemis Pine Candle Co LLC .... G 203 245-5170
  Madison *(G-3908)*
Backyard Candles LLC .... G 860 644-9561
  South Windsor *(G-7716)*
Beelightful Candle LLC .... G 860 912-7122
  Cos Cob *(G-1625)*
Candle Threads .... G 860 490-5890
  Enfield *(G-2620)*
Candle Threads .... G 860 292-1667
  East Windsor *(G-2488)*
Candles For A Cause USA .... G 860 912-3946
  Bristol *(G-999)*
Cathys Country Scents Candles .... G 860 458-8219
  Stafford Springs *(G-8020)*
Chandler Industries LLC .... G 860 283-8147
  Thomaston *(G-8784)*
Channys Candles LLC .... G 860 313-9139
  Torrington *(G-8910)*
Christinas Creations .... G 203 605-2464
  New Haven *(G-5257)*
CJ First Candle .... G 203 966-1300
  New Canaan *(G-5095)*
Connecticut Candle Group .... G 860 924-1766
  Rocky Hill *(G-7227)*
Connecticut Candle LLC .... G 860 937-7330
  West Haven *(G-9892)*
Crystal Journey Candles LLC .... E 203 433-4735
  Branford *(G-577)*
Cynful Scents .... G 860 866-7670
  Morris *(G-4788)*
Damalias Candle and Body Bar .... G 860 725-2168
  Hartford *(G-3575)*
Dianas Candles and Soap LLC .... G 203 527-4028
  Waterbury *(G-9465)*
Dianna Blanchard .... G 860 684-4874
  Stafford Springs *(G-8026)*
Emdepoint Candles USA LLC .... G 860 205-8400
  New Britain *(G-4982)*
Fundrsing With Cndle Fndrisers .... G 860 384-3691
  South Glastonbury *(G-7680)*
Goody Candles LLC .... G 860 426-9436
  Southington *(G-7930)*
Hardware Cy Soaps Candles LLC ..... G 860 209-8494
  New Britain *(G-4996)*
Kaycandles .... G 860 794-3763
  New Britain *(G-5009)*
Kms Candle Company LLC .... G 203 758-3821
  Prospect *(G-7006)*
Ljs House of Candles .... G 203 464-5742
  Meriden *(G-4187)*
Make A Candle .... G 203 871-8426
  Branford *(G-623)*
Mm Candles .... G 203 205-0180
  Danbury *(G-1887)*
Nac Industries Inc .... G 845 214-0659
  Oxford *(G-6680)*
Old Thyme Country Candles .... G 860 655-2583
  South Windsor *(G-7800)*
Olde Tyme Country Candles .... G 860 673-5086
  Unionville *(G-9124)*
Roost Candle Co LLC .... G 203 270-6577
  Sandy Hook *(G-7328)*
Scenic Route Candle Co LLC .... G 203 606-7300
  Branford *(G-648)*
Shimmer LLC .... G 860 875-4701
  Tolland *(G-8877)*
Step By Step Cnseling Svcs LLC ...... G 860 244-9836
  Hartford *(G-3693)*
Stock Bar Candles LLC .... G 860 805-1986
  West Hartford *(G-9862)*
Theresas Colorful Creations .... G 860 726-6909
  East Hartford *(G-2384)*
Tired Mommy Candles .... G 860 407-2002
  Griswold *(G-3268)*
Wilder Hill Farms .... G 860 567-2459
  Morris *(G-4793)*

CANDY & CONFECTIONS: Chocolate Candy, Exc Solid Chocolate

Deborah Anns Hmmade Chocolates .... G 203 438-0065
  Ridgefield *(G-7135)*
Penotti USA Inc .... G 203 341-9494
  Westport *(G-10139)*

CANDY & CONFECTIONS: Fudge

OH Fudge and More LLC .... G 860 788-3839
  Higganum *(G-3773)*

CANDY, NUT & CONFECTIONERY STORES: Candy

Bridgewater Chocolate LLC .... G 203 775-2286
  Brookfield *(G-1164)*
Munsons Candy Kitchen Inc .... E 860 649-4332
  Bolton *(G-517)*
Thompson Brands LLC .... D 203 235-2541
  Meriden *(G-4254)*
Thompson Candy Company .... D 203 235-2541
  Meriden *(G-4255)*

CANDY, NUT & CONFECTIONERY STORES: Confectionery

Chip In A Bottle LLC .... G 203 460-0665
  New Haven *(G-5256)*
Elius Delight Snacks LLC .... G 646 302-4948
  Stratford *(G-8608)*

CANDY, NUT & CONFECTIONERY STORES: Produced For Direct Sale

Fascias Chocolates Inc .... F 203 753-0515
  Waterbury *(G-9480)*

CANDY: Hard

Lollipop Kids LLC .... G 203 664-1799
  Redding *(G-7098)*
Yummyearth LLC .... G 203 276-1259
  Stamford *(G-8504)*

CANNED SPECIALTIES

Cushs Homegrown LLC .... G 860 739-7373
  Old Lyme *(G-6501)*
Shenondah Vly Specialty Foods .... G 203 348-0402
  Stamford *(G-8411)*

CANS: Aluminum

CCL Industries Corporation .... D 203 926-1253
  Shelton *(G-7412)*
CCL Label Inc .... C 203 926-1253
  Shelton *(G-7413)*

CANS: Garbage, Stamped Or Pressed Metal

Bearicuda Inc .... G 860 361-6860
  Litchfield *(G-3884)*

CANS: Metal

Crown Cork & Seal Usa Inc .... G 203 877-4131
  Milford *(G-4500)*
Silgan Closures Intl Holdg Co .... G 203 975-7110
  Stamford *(G-8419)*
Silgan Containers Corporation .... F 203 975-7110
  Stamford *(G-8420)*

CANS: Tin

American Metaseal of Conn .... G 203 787-0281
  Hamden *(G-3414)*

CANVAS PRDTS

American Sign Inc .... E 203 624-2991
  New Haven *(G-5229)*
Canvas LLC .... G 860 986-8553
  West Hartford *(G-9784)*
Connecticut Canvas Works .... G 860 295-9924
  Marlborough *(G-4122)*
Custom Marine Canvas LLC .... G 860 572-9547
  Groton *(G-3281)*
Defender Industries Inc .... C 860 701-3400
  Waterford *(G-9652)*
Dimension-Polyant Inc .... G 860 928-8300
  Putnam *(G-7039)*
New Haven Companies Inc .... F 203 469-6421
  East Haven *(G-2444)*
Rp3 Canvas LLC .... G 860 225-7140
  New Britain *(G-5050)*
Seafarer Canvas .... F 203 853-2624
  Norwalk *(G-6339)*
Second Lac Inc .... G 203 321-1221
  Norwalk *(G-6341)*
Sharp Canvas .... G 860 526-2302
  Chester *(G-1484)*
Topside Canvas Upholstery .... G 860 399-4845
  Westbrook *(G-10011)*
Watertown Canvas and Awng LLC ..... G 860 274-0933
  Oakville *(G-6467)*
William A Weinert Canvas .... G 203 595-0580
  Stamford *(G-8493)*

CANVAS PRDTS: Boat Seats

Branford Auto & Marine Center .... G 203 481-6572
  Branford *(G-562)*

CANVAS PRDTS: Convertible Tops, Car/Boat, Fm Purchased Mtrl

Island Style Mar Canvas Repr 707 338-8789
  Norwalk *(G-6212)*

CAPACITORS: NEC

Electronic Film Capacitors .... E 203 755-5629
  Waterbury *(G-9474)*
Newco Condenser Inc .... G 475 882-4000
  Shelton *(G-7510)*

CAPS: Plastic

Bprex Halthcare Brookville Inc .... C 203 754-4141
  Waterbury *(G-9440)*

CAR WASH EQPT

Mardini Power Station .... G 203 576-8951
  Bridgeport *(G-829)*

CARBIDES

Carbide Solutions LLC .... G 860 515-8665
  Windsor *(G-10371)*
Carbide Technology Inc .... G 860 621-8981
  Southington *(G-7904)*

CARBON & GRAPHITE PRDTS, NEC

Carbon Products Inc .... G 860 749-0614
  Somersville *(G-7678)*
Graphite Die Mold Inc .... G 860 349-4444
  Durham *(G-2148)*
Joshua LLC .... E 203 624-0080
  New Haven *(G-5304)*
Minteq International Inc .... C 860 824-5435
  Canaan *(G-1289)*
Rain Carbon Inc .... G 203 406-0535
  Stamford *(G-8384)*

CARBON SPECIALTIES Electrical Use

Greenwich Carbon LLC .... G 203 531-7064
  Greenwich *(G-3173)*

CARBURETORS

Caffeine and Carburetors .... G 203 966-2704
  New Canaan *(G-5091)*

CARDIOVASCULAR SYSTEM DRUGS, EXC DIAGNOSTIC

Boehringer Ingelheim Pharma .... A 203 798-9988
  Ridgefield *(G-7121)*

CARDS: Color

American Banknote Corporation .... G 203 941-4090
  Stamford *(G-8074)*

PRODUCT SECTION

CARDS: Greeting

Anothercreationbymichele ....G....... 203 322-4277
  Stamford *(G-8087)*
Bella Ciao ....G....... 203 245-4433
  Madison *(G-3911)*
C&S Collectibles ....G....... 860 872-6825
  Tolland *(G-8853)*
Caspari Inc ....F....... 203 888-1100
  Seymour *(G-7338)*
Joy Carole Creations Inc ....G....... 203 794-1401
  Danbury *(G-1865)*
Olympia Sales Inc ....D....... 860 749-0751
  Enfield *(G-2672)*
Onion Hill Press Llc ....G....... 203 227-4895
  Westport *(G-10133)*
Raven Ad Specialties ....G....... 203 521-8687
  Stratford *(G-8673)*
Smiling Dog ....G....... 860 344-0707
  Middletown *(G-4419)*
Stork N More ....G....... 203 746-7500
  New Fairfield *(G-5177)*

CARDS: Identification

Connecticut Laminating Co Inc ....D....... 203 787-2184
  New Haven *(G-5260)*
Idemia Identity & SEC USA LLC ....G....... 860 529-2559
  Rocky Hill *(G-7249)*
Keytag1 ....G....... 203 873-0749
  Bridgeport *(G-817)*

CARPET & UPHOLSTERY CLEANING SVCS: Carpet/Furniture, On Loc

Stanley Steemer Intl Inc ....E....... 860 274-5540
  Watertown *(G-9738)*

CARPETS & RUGS: Tufted

Mohawk Industries Inc ....C....... 203 739-0260
  Danbury *(G-1888)*
Mohawk Industries Inc ....G....... 706 629-7721
  Torrington *(G-8950)*

CARPETS, RUGS & FLOOR COVERING

Alliance Carpet Cushion Co ....D....... 860 489-4273
  Torrington *(G-8889)*
Apricot Home LLC ....G....... 203 552-1791
  Greenwich *(G-3121)*
Ethan Allen Retail Inc ....B....... 203 743-8000
  Danbury *(G-1818)*
New Haven Companies Inc ....F....... 203 469-6421
  East Haven *(G-2444)*
Rosemary Hallgarten Inc ....G....... 203 259-1003
  Fairfield *(G-2838)*
Yankee Peddler ....G....... 860 663-0526
  Killingworth *(G-3840)*

CARPETS: Axminster

Wool Solutions Inc ....G....... 203 845-0921
  Norwalk *(G-6400)*

CARPETS: Hand & Machine Made

Holland & Sherry Inc ....F....... 212 628-1950
  Norwalk *(G-6201)*

CARPETS: Textile Fiber

Valentine Co LLC ....G....... 203 245-9145
  Madison *(G-3967)*

CARRIAGES: Horse Drawn

Serafin Sulky Co ....G....... 860 684-2986
  Stafford Springs *(G-8037)*

CARTS: Grocery

Cco Llc ....G....... 860 757-3434
  Rocky Hill *(G-7226)*

CASEIN PRDTS

Armor Box Company LLC ....G....... 860 242-9981
  Bloomfield *(G-389)*

CASEMENTS: Aluminum

Cusson Sash Company ....G....... 860 659-0354
  Glastonbury *(G-3025)*

CASES, WOOD

W R Hartigan & Son Inc ....G....... 860 673-9203
  Burlington *(G-1278)*

CASES: Attache'

Case Concepts Intl LLC ....F....... 203 883-8602
  Stamford *(G-8130)*
Taylors Luggage Inc ....G....... 203 966-9961
  New Canaan *(G-5150)*

CASES: Carrying

Armor Box Company LLC ....G....... 860 242-9981
  Bloomfield *(G-389)*
Calzone Ltd ....E....... 203 367-5766
  Bridgeport *(G-728)*
Fabrique Ltd ....F....... 203 481-5400
  Branford *(G-593)*

CASES: Carrying, Clothing & Apparel

Michaels Finest LLC ....G....... 860 223-7671
  New Britain *(G-5017)*

CASES: Packing, Nailed Or Lock Corner, Wood

Champlin-Packrite Inc ....E....... 860 951-9217
  Manchester *(G-3994)*

CASH REGISTERS WHOLESALERS

Tutors & Computers Inc ....G....... 203 393-3006
  Bethany *(G-251)*

CASINGS: Sheet Metal

Capstone Manufacturing Inc ....G....... 413 636-6170
  South Windsor *(G-7723)*

CASKETS & ACCESS

Dignified Endings LLC ....D....... 860 291-0575
  East Hartford *(G-2314)*

CAST STONE: Concrete

Dawn Enterprises LLC ....G....... 860 646-8200
  Manchester *(G-4004)*
Granite Hill Equity ....G....... 203 801-4396
  New Canaan *(G-5106)*
Stone Image Custom Concrete ....G....... 860 668-2434
  Suffield *(G-8736)*
Tontine Partners L P ....G....... 203 769-2000
  Greenwich *(G-3247)*

CASTINGS GRINDING: For The Trade

A D Grinding ....F....... 860 747-6630
  Plainville *(G-6760)*
Accurate Centerless Grinding ....G....... 860 747-9794
  Bristol *(G-954)*
Classic Jig Grinding ....G....... 860 870-4900
  Tolland *(G-8854)*
East Coast Precision Grinding ....G....... 860 289-1010
  South Windsor *(G-7743)*
Fairfield Cnty Stump Grinding ....G....... 203 261-7867
  Trumbull *(G-9026)*
JEM Precision Grinding Inc ....G....... 860 633-0152
  Glastonbury *(G-3052)*
Lundgren Centerless Grinding ....G....... 860 482-4927
  Torrington *(G-8944)*
New England Honing LLC ....G....... 860 712-6094
  Coventry *(G-1665)*
Northeast Double Disc Grind LL ....G....... 860 643-6096
  Manchester *(G-4061)*
Nyc Grind Sports Marketing LLC ....G....... 917 513-0590
  Stamford *(G-8334)*
Precision Centerless Grinding ....G....... 203 879-1228
  Wolcott *(G-10579)*
S A lt Grind ....G....... 860 903-1455
  East Windsor *(G-2517)*
Stump Grinding Plus ....G....... 860 884-6962
  East Lyme *(G-2476)*
Unas Grinding Corporation ....E....... 860 289-1538
  East Hartford *(G-2387)*

CASTINGS: Aerospace Investment, Ferrous

Doncasters US Hldings 2018 Inc ....F....... 860 677-1376
  Groton *(G-3284)*

CASTINGS: Aerospace, Aluminum

Accu-Mill Technologies LLC ....G....... 860 747-3921
  Plainville *(G-6764)*
Aerocess Inc ....F....... 860 357-2451
  Berlin *(G-151)*
Integra-Cast Inc ....D....... 860 225-7600
  New Britain *(G-4999)*

CASTINGS: Aerospace, Nonferrous, Exc Aluminum

Carrier Manufacturing Inc ....G....... 860 223-2264
  New Britain *(G-4955)*
Consoldted Inds Acqsition Corp ....D....... 203 272-5371
  Cheshire *(G-1374)*

CASTINGS: Aluminum

Us-Malabar Company Inc ....G....... 203 226-1773
  Weston *(G-10041)*

CASTINGS: Brass, Bronze & Copper

Fred Radford ....G....... 203 377-6189
  Trumbull *(G-9027)*

CASTINGS: Commercial Investment, Ferrous

Howmet Castings & Services Inc ....B....... 860 379-3314
  Winsted *(G-10524)*
Howmet Corporation ....B....... 203 481-3451
  Branford *(G-608)*
Sturm Ruger & Company Inc ....B....... 203 259-7843
  Southport *(G-8010)*

CASTINGS: Die, Aluminum

Advanced Prcsion Castings Corp ....G....... 203 736-9452
  Milford *(G-4442)*
Arrow Diversified Tooling Inc ....E....... 860 872-9072
  Ellington *(G-2576)*
Custom Metal Crafters Inc ....D....... 860 953-4210
  Newington *(G-5645)*
McCann Sales Inc ....G....... 860 614-0992
  West Simsbury *(G-9980)*

CASTINGS: Die, Nonferrous

Custom Metal Crafters Inc ....D....... 860 953-4210
  Newington *(G-5645)*
Integra-Cast Inc ....D....... 860 225-7600
  New Britain *(G-4999)*
Narragansett Screw Co ....F....... 860 379-4059
  Winsted *(G-10531)*
PCC Structurals Groton ....C....... 860 405-3700
  Groton *(G-3304)*

CASTINGS: Gray Iron

Taylor & Fenn Company ....D....... 860 219-9393
  Windsor *(G-10448)*

CASTINGS: Precision

B H S Industries Ltd ....G....... 203 284-9764
  Wallingford *(G-9218)*
Fred Radford ....G....... 203 377-6189
  Trumbull *(G-9027)*
House of Bubba LLC ....G....... 860 429-4250
  Willington *(G-10250)*
Sycast Inc ....G....... 860 308-2122
  Hartford *(G-3696)*
Yankee Casting Co Inc ....D....... 860 749-6171
  Enfield *(G-2709)*

CASTINGS: Steel

Frank Roth Co Inc ....D....... 203 377-2155
  Stratford *(G-8611)*
Silicone Casting Technologies ....G....... 860 347-5227
  Middletown *(G-4415)*

CASTINGS: Titanium

Hexcel Corporation ....D....... 925 520-3232
  South Windsor *(G-7770)*
J & H Machine Company LLC ....G....... 860 643-6096
  Manchester *(G-4035)*
JI Aerotech Inc ....G....... 860 248-8628
  South Windsor *(G-7778)*
Tightco Inc ....C....... 860 828-0298
  Berlin *(G-225)*

CATALOG & MAIL-ORDER HOUSES

Brico Inc .... G 203 693-0323
  Bloomfield *(G-400)*
Logod Softwear Inc .... E 203 272-4883
  Cheshire *(G-1407)*

CATALOG SALES

Connecticut Advanced Products .... G 860 659-2260
  Glastonbury *(G-3023)*

CATALYSTS: Chemical

Advanced Pwr Systems Intl Inc .... E 860 921-0009
  New Hartford *(G-5184)*
Joshua LLC .... E 203 624-0080
  New Haven *(G-5304)*

CATAPULTS

Soltis Speed Equipment .... G 860 489-0119
  Torrington *(G-8971)*

CEILING SYSTEMS: Luminous, Commercial

C Cowles & Company .... D 203 865-3117
  North Haven *(G-5916)*

CEMENT ROCK: Crushed & Broken

Quarry Stone & Gravel LLC .... G 203 770-2664
  Danbury *(G-1925)*

CEMENT, EXC LINOLEUM & TILE

Babcock & King Incorporated .... G 203 336-7989
  Fairfield *(G-2750)*

CEMENT: Hydraulic

Beard Concrete Co Derby Inc .... F 203 735-4641
  Derby *(G-2109)*
Gratton Concrete Sawingdri .... G 860 974-9127
  Pomfret Center *(G-6938)*
Lafarge North America Inc .... G 203 468-6068
  New Haven *(G-5314)*
McInnis USA Inc .... E 203 890-9950
  Stamford *(G-8299)*

CEMETERY MEMORIAL DEALERS

American Stonecrafters Inc .... G 203 514-9725
  Wallingford *(G-9202)*
Bella Pietra LLC .... G 203 655-1322
  Darien *(G-2007)*
Pistritto Marble Imports Inc .... G 860 296-5263
  Hartford *(G-3664)*

CERAMIC FLOOR & WALL TILE WHOLESALERS

Brass City Tile Designs LLC .... G 203 597-8764
  Waterbury *(G-9443)*
Distributors of Standard Tile .... G 860 439-0627
  New London *(G-5468)*
Porcelanosa New York Inc .... F 203 698-7618
  Riverside *(G-7199)*

CHAINS: Forged

Afc Industries LLC .... G 860 246-7411
  Hartford *(G-3549)*

CHARCOAL: Activated

Carbtrol Corporation .... E 203 337-4340
  Stratford *(G-8593)*

CHART & GRAPH DESIGN SVCS

Frank Drago Custom Mapping .... G 203 483-7594
  Branford *(G-596)*

CHASSIS: Motor Vehicle

Chassis Dynamics Inc .... G 203 262-6272
  Oxford *(G-6651)*

CHEESE WHOLESALERS

Mozzicato Fmly Investments LLC .... G 860 296-0426
  Wethersfield *(G-10213)*
Ndr Liuzzi Inc .... E 203 287-8477
  Hamden *(G-3487)*

CHEMICAL ELEMENTS

Designing Element .... G 203 849-3076
  Norwalk *(G-6135)*
Element One LLC .... G 203 344-1553
  Norwalk *(G-6157)*
Elemental Mercury LLC .... G 860 355-9569
  New Milford *(G-5531)*
Fitness Elemnet .... G 860 670-2855
  New Britain *(G-4989)*
Meb Enterprises Inc .... G 203 599-0273
  Meriden *(G-4193)*
Modern Elements Products LLC .... G 860 667-4247
  Newington *(G-5679)*
Perennial Elements LLC .... G 860 536-8593
  Mystic *(G-4839)*

CHEMICAL INDICATORS

Ethical Solutions LLC .... G 860 490-8124
  South Windsor *(G-7752)*
Momentive Prfmce Mtls USA Inc .... G 203 240-5543
  Fairfield *(G-2819)*

CHEMICAL PROCESSING MACHINERY & EQPT

Lamor USA Corporation .... G 203 888-7700
  Shelton *(G-7485)*

CHEMICAL SPLYS FOR FOUNDRIES

Swahili Aviation Aerospace LLC .... G 860 268-3639
  Tolland *(G-8879)*

CHEMICAL: Sodm Compnds/Salts, Inorg, Exc Rfnd Sodm Chloride

Tronox Incorporated .... C 203 705-3800
  Stamford *(G-8476)*

CHEMICALS & ALLIED PRDTS WHOLESALERS, NEC

Airgas Usa LLC .... C 203 792-1834
  Danbury *(G-1733)*
Cloverdale Inc .... G 860 672-0216
  West Cornwall *(G-9762)*
Hydrochemical Techniques Inc .... G 860 527-6350
  Hartford *(G-3615)*
Midsun Group Inc .... G 860 378-0100
  Southington *(G-7954)*
Miyoshi America Inc .... D 860 779-3990
  Dayville *(G-2064)*
Miyoshi America Inc .... F 860 779-3990
  Dayville *(G-2065)*
Miyoshi America Inc .... G 860 779-3990
  Dayville *(G-2066)*
Sheldon Automotive Enterprises .... F 203 372-4948
  Fairfield *(G-2846)*
Vanderbilt Chemicals LLC .... D 203 295-2141
  Norwalk *(G-6383)*

CHEMICALS & ALLIED PRDTS, WHOL: Chemical, Organic, Synthetic

Galata Chemicals LLC .... F 203 236-9000
  Southbury *(G-7854)*
Integrated Chemical & Eqp Corp .... G 203 664-3951
  Clinton *(G-1509)*
Optima Specialty Chemical .... G 203 929-2031
  Shelton *(G-7520)*

CHEMICALS & ALLIED PRDTS, WHOLESALE: Acids

US Chemicals Inc .... G 203 655-8878
  New Canaan *(G-5157)*

CHEMICALS & ALLIED PRDTS, WHOLESALE: Adhesives

Ethical Solutions LLC .... G 860 490-8124
  South Windsor *(G-7752)*

CHEMICALS & ALLIED PRDTS, WHOLESALE: Chemicals, Indl

Stephen Hawrylik .... G 860 688-8651
  Windsor *(G-10444)*

CHEMICALS & ALLIED PRDTS, WHOLESALE: Chemicals, Indl & Heavy

Hubbard-Hall Inc .... C 203 756-5521
  Waterbury *(G-9501)*
Near Oak LLC .... G 203 329-6500
  Stamford *(G-8318)*
RT Vanderbilt Holding Co Inc .... F 203 295-2141
  Norwalk *(G-6331)*

CHEMICALS & ALLIED PRDTS, WHOLESALE: Essential Oils

Field Energy LLC .... G 860 817-2654
  West Hartford *(G-9810)*

CHEMICALS & ALLIED PRDTS, WHOLESALE: Manmade Fibers

Engineered Fibers Tech LLC .... F 203 922-1810
  Shelton *(G-7440)*

CHEMICALS & ALLIED PRDTS, WHOLESALE: Plastics Film

Orafol Americas Inc .... C 860 676-7100
  Avon *(G-98)*
Web Industries Hartford Inc .... E 860 779-3197
  Dayville *(G-2078)*

CHEMICALS & ALLIED PRDTS, WHOLESALE: Plastics Materials, NEC

Edco Industries Inc .... F 203 333-8982
  Bridgeport *(G-760)*
Spectrum Marking Materials LLC .... G 860 533-9533
  Glastonbury *(G-3083)*

CHEMICALS & ALLIED PRDTS, WHOLESALE: Plastics Prdts, NEC

Brighton & Hove Mold Ltd .... G 203 264-3013
  Oxford *(G-6647)*
Thornton and Company Inc .... F 860 628-6771
  Southington *(G-7988)*

CHEMICALS & ALLIED PRDTS, WHOLESALE: Plastics Sheets & Rods

Delmar Products Inc .... F 860 828-6501
  Berlin *(G-176)*
Thyssenkrupp Materials NA Inc .... E 203 265-1567
  Wallingford *(G-9382)*

CHEMICALS & ALLIED PRDTS, WHOLESALE: Resin, Synthetic Rubber

Age Plastics LLC .... G 860 502-0418
  New Britain *(G-4940)*

CHEMICALS & ALLIED PRDTS, WHOLESALE: Resins

Neu Spclty Engineered Mtls LLC .... F 203 239-9629
  North Haven *(G-5967)*

CHEMICALS & ALLIED PRDTS, WHOLESALE: Rubber, Synthetic

Auburn Manufacturing Company .... E 860 346-6677
  Middletown *(G-4319)*

CHEMICALS & ALLIED PRDTS, WHOLESALE: Sanitation Preparations

High-Tech Conversions Inc .... G 860 265-2633
  Enfield *(G-2650)*

CHEMICALS & ALLIED PRDTS, WHOLESALE: Silicon Lubricants

Advanced Machine Services LLC .... G 203 888-6600
  Oxford *(G-6638)*

CHEMICALS & ALLIED PRDTS, WHOLESALE: Spec Clean/Sanitation

Klean Air Supplies Inc .... G 860 583-1589
  Bristol *(G-1058)*

Richards Creative Interiors ......G....... 203 484-0361
Wallingford *(G-9355)*

CHEMICALS & ALLIED PRDTS, WHOLESALE: Syn Resin, Rub/Plastic

Seaview Plastic Recycling Inc ......G....... 203 367-0070
Bridgeport *(G-899)*

CHEMICALS: Agricultural

Adirondack Lkfront Retreat LLC ......G....... 203 267-5882
Southbury *(G-7841)*
Clinton Nursery Products Inc ......C....... 860 399-3000
Westbrook *(G-9994)*
Dupont ......G....... 860 368-0766
Middletown *(G-4338)*
Dupont De Nemours Inc ......G....... 203 330-6755
Bridgeport *(G-758)*
Dupont Guy Office ......G....... 203 679-0358
Wallingford *(G-9254)*
Ferrucci Services ......G....... 203 468-2319
East Haven *(G-2427)*
Lanxess Solutions US Inc ......D....... 203 723-2237
Naugatuck *(G-4899)*
Lenz Enterprises LLC ......G....... 860 961-2893
Middletown *(G-4368)*
Macdermid AG Solutions Inc ......F....... 203 575-5727
Waterbury *(G-9526)*
Michael Dupont ......G....... 203 434-0650
Redding *(G-7101)*
Monsanto Mystic Research ......G....... 860 572-5200
Mystic *(G-4833)*
P2 Science Inc ......G....... 203 821-7457
Woodbridge *(G-10611)*
Pamela Gordondupont Ms Ccca ......G....... 860 526-8686
Chester *(G-1478)*

CHEMICALS: Alkali Metals, Lithium, Cesium, Francium/Rubidium

Vertech Inc ......G....... 203 876-1552
Milford *(G-4673)*

CHEMICALS: Boron Compounds, Not From Mines, NEC

Composites Inc ......G....... 860 646-1698
Manchester *(G-3997)*

CHEMICALS: Fire Retardant

Great Lakes Chemical Corp ......E....... 203 573-2000
Shelton *(G-7454)*
Lanxess Solutions US Inc ......E....... 203 573-2000
Shelton *(G-7486)*

CHEMICALS: Hydrogen Peroxide

Integrated Chemical & Eqp Corp ......G....... 860 664-3951
Clinton *(G-1509)*

CHEMICALS: Inorganic, NEC

CCL Industries Corporation ......D....... 203 926-1253
Shelton *(G-7412)*
Chromatics Inc ......F....... 203 743-6868
Bethel *(G-271)*
Demo Agent Sales LLC ......G....... 860 621-3303
Southington *(G-7913)*
Elements LLC ......G....... 860 231-8011
West Hartford *(G-9807)*
Greek Elements LLC ......G....... 203 594-2022
New Canaan *(G-5107)*
H Krevit and Company Inc ......E....... 203 772-3350
New Haven *(G-5292)*
Innophase Corp ......G....... 860 399-2269
Westbrook *(G-9998)*
Kwant Elements Intl LLC ......G....... 203 625-5553
Cos Cob *(G-1636)*
Redline Elements LLC ......G....... 860 305-0095
Marlborough *(G-4130)*
RT Vanderbilt Holding Co Inc ......F....... 203 295-2141
Norwalk *(G-6331)*
Solidification Pdts Intl Inc ......G....... 203 484-9494
Northford *(G-6053)*
Solidification Products Intl ......F....... 203 484-9494
Northford *(G-6054)*
Specialty Minerals Inc ......C....... 860 824-5435
Canaan *(G-1292)*
Vanderbilt Chemicals LLC ......D....... 203 295-2141
Norwalk *(G-6383)*
Vanderbilt Chemicals LLC ......E....... 203 744-3900
Bethel *(G-361)*

CHEMICALS: Medicinal

Nzymsys Inc ......G....... 877 729-4190
Manchester *(G-4064)*

CHEMICALS: Metal Compounds Or Salts, Inorganic, NEC

Yarmouth Materials Inc ......G....... 203 739-0524
Danbury *(G-1984)*

CHEMICALS: NEC

5n Plus Corp ......F....... 608 846-1357
Trumbull *(G-8994)*
Advanced Pwr Systems Intl Inc ......E....... 860 921-0009
New Hartford *(G-5184)*
All Power Manufacturing Co ......C....... 562 802-2640
Oxford *(G-6641)*
Aptex Corp ......G....... 203 743-6412
Oxford *(G-6643)*
Armored Autogroup Parent Inc ......G....... 203 205-2900
Danbury *(G-1747)*
Atlantic Coast Polymers Inc ......G....... 860 564-5641
Plainfield *(G-6741)*
Brand-Nu Laboratories Inc ......E....... 203 235-7989
Meriden *(G-4150)*
Brand-Nu Laboratories Inc ......G....... 203 235-7989
Meriden *(G-4151)*
Chemotex Protective Coatings ......F....... 860 349-0144
Durham *(G-2142)*
Chessco Industries Inc ......E....... 203 255-2804
Westport *(G-10064)*
Crystal Rock Spring Water Co ......B....... 860 945-0661
Watertown *(G-9698)*
Cytec Industries Inc ......D....... 203 321-2200
Stamford *(G-8176)*
Element Solutions Inc ......E....... 203 575-5850
Waterbury *(G-9475)*
Evonik Tockhausen LLC ......G....... 860 530-1363
Hebron *(G-3748)*
Five Star Products Inc ......E....... 203 336-7900
Shelton *(G-7444)*
Flottec International Sls Corp ......G....... 973 588-4717
Westport *(G-10084)*
H & M Systems ......G....... 860 445-2347
Groton *(G-3290)*
H Muehlstein & Co Inc ......G....... 800 257-3746
Norwalk *(G-6190)*
Henkel of America Inc ......B....... 860 571-5100
Rocky Hill *(G-7246)*
Henkel US Operations Corp ......B....... 860 571-5100
Rocky Hill *(G-7247)*
Hubbard-Hall Inc ......C....... 203 756-5521
Waterbury *(G-9501)*
Intersurface Dynamics Inc ......F....... 203 778-9995
Bethel *(G-312)*
Laticrete International Inc ......G....... 203 393-0010
Bethany *(G-245)*
Lonza Wood Protection ......G....... 203 229-2900
Norwalk *(G-6236)*
Macdermid Incorporated ......G....... 262 242-2892
Waterbury *(G-9523)*
Macdermid Acumen Inc ......G....... 203 575-5700
Waterbury *(G-9525)*
Macdermid Enthone Inc ......C....... 203 934-8611
West Haven *(G-9928)*
Macdermid Overseas Asia Ltd ......G....... 203 575-5799
Waterbury *(G-9529)*
Macdermid Printing Solutions ......G....... 203 575-5727
Waterbury *(G-9530)*
Near Oak LLC ......G....... 203 329-6500
Stamford *(G-8318)*
OMI International Corporation ......G....... 203 575-5727
West Haven *(G-9941)*
Permatex Inc ......E....... 860 543-7500
Hartford *(G-3663)*
Purification Technologies LLC ......F....... 860 526-7801
Chester *(G-1480)*
Q Labtech LLC ......G....... 860 501-9119
East Lyme *(G-2472)*
Recor Rust Solutions ......G....... 860 573-1942
Hebron *(G-3755)*
REM Chemicals Inc ......F....... 860 621-6755
Southington *(G-7967)*
Southford Kindling Company LLC ......G....... 203 394-2148
Southbury *(G-7879)*
Vichem Inc ......G....... 860 677-8133
Farmington *(G-2975)*
W Canning Inc ......G....... 203 575-5727
Waterbury *(G-9625)*

CHEMICALS: Organic, NEC

Accustandard Inc ......D....... 203 786-5290
New Haven *(G-5218)*
Advanced Pwr Systems Intl Inc ......E....... 860 921-0009
New Hartford *(G-5184)*
Brian Safa ......G....... 203 271-3499
Cheshire *(G-1363)*
Clearclad Coatings LLC ......G....... 860 945-9200
Watertown *(G-9693)*
Coastline Fuel Inc ......G....... 203 846-3601
Norwalk *(G-6117)*
Connstem Inc ......G....... 203 558-4671
Cheshire *(G-1373)*
Dymax Corporation ......G....... 860 626-7006
Torrington *(G-8919)*
Dymax Materials Inc ......G....... 860 482-1010
Torrington *(G-8920)*
Dymax Oligomers & Coatings ......F....... 860 626-7006
Torrington *(G-8921)*
Ethical Solutions LLC ......G....... 860 490-8124
South Windsor *(G-7752)*
Greenleaf Bfuels New Haven LLC ......F....... 203 672-9028
New Haven *(G-5290)*
H Krevit and Company Inc ......E....... 203 772-3350
New Haven *(G-5292)*
Hajan LLC ......G....... 860 223-2005
New Britain *(G-4995)*
Hampford Research Inc ......G....... 203 380-2852
Stratford *(G-8621)*
Hampford Research Inc ......E....... 203 375-1137
Stratford *(G-8622)*
Ironic Chemicals LLC ......G....... 646 352-2692
Fairfield *(G-2798)*
Jsr Micro Inc ......G....... 203 426-7794
Newtown *(G-5751)*
Lanxess Solutions US Inc ......E....... 203 573-2000
Shelton *(G-7486)*
Lanxess Solutions US Inc ......G....... 203 605-5746
Naugatuck *(G-4900)*
Med Opportunity Partners LLC ......G....... 203 622-1333
Greenwich *(G-3201)*
Metalast International In ......G....... 860 673-1725
Burlington *(G-1273)*
Nalas Engineering Services ......D....... 860 861-3691
Norwich *(G-6424)*
Sanco Energy ......F....... 203 259-5914
Fairfield *(G-2842)*
Tylerville Technologies LLC ......G....... 860 798-0501
Higganum *(G-3780)*
Uniroyal Chemical Corporation ......G....... 203 573-2000
Waterbury *(G-9620)*
Vanderbilt Chemicals LLC ......D....... 203 295-2141
Norwalk *(G-6383)*
Vanderbilt Chemicals LLC ......E....... 203 744-3900
Bethel *(G-361)*

CHEMICALS: Sodium Bicarbonate

Genesis Alkali LLC ......D....... 215 299-6773
Stamford *(G-8214)*

CHEMICALS: Sulfur, Incl Rcvrd/Refined, Fm Sour Natural Gas

Tiger-Sul Products LLC ......E....... 251 202-3850
Shelton *(G-7568)*

CHEMICALS: Water Treatment

Globe Environmental Corp ......F....... 203 481-5586
Branford *(G-600)*
Gotham Chemical Company Inc ......D....... 203 854-6644
Norwalk *(G-6183)*
Joesjuicecom LLC ......G....... 203 824-1854
Stamford *(G-8266)*
Poquonock Sewage Plant ......G....... 860 688-5420
Windsor *(G-10422)*
Suez Wts Services Usa Inc ......E....... 860 291-9660
East Hartford *(G-2380)*

CHILDREN'S & INFANTS' CLOTHING STORES

One Kid LLC ......G....... 203 254-9978
Fairfield *(G-2824)*

Employee Codes: A=Over 500 employees, B=251-500
C=101-250, D=51-100, E=20-50, F=10-19, G=1-9

CHIROPRACTORS' OFFICES
Respond Systems .... F 203 481-2810
  Branford *(G-641)*

CHLORINE
Kuehne New Haven LLC .... E 203 508-6703
  New Haven *(G-5312)*

CHOCOLATE, EXC CANDY FROM BEANS: Chips, Powder, Block, Syrup
Divine Treasure .... G 860 643-2552
  Manchester *(G-4009)*
Hvc Lizard Chocolate LLC .... F 203 899-3075
  Norwalk *(G-6203)*
Mantrose-Haeuser Co Inc .... E 203 454-1800
  Westport *(G-10117)*
Munsons Candy Kitchen Inc .... E 860 649-4332
  Bolton *(G-517)*
Thompson Brands LLC .... D 203 235-2541
  Meriden *(G-4254)*

CHOCOLATE, EXC CANDY FROM PURCH CHOC: Chips, Powder, Block
Chip In A Bottle LLC .... G 203 460-0665
  New Haven *(G-5256)*
Custom Chocolate Designs LLC .... G 203 886-6777
  Meriden *(G-4164)*
Nel Group LLC .... G 860 413-9042
  East Granby *(G-2216)*
Nel Group LLC .... F 860 683-0190
  Windsor *(G-10412)*
Rosie Blakes Chocolates LLC .... G 732 604-3327
  New Britain *(G-5048)*

CHRISTMAS TREE ORNAMENTS: Electric
Interior Plantworks Inc .... G 860 289-9499
  South Windsor *(G-7774)*
Interior Plantworks Inc .... G 860 289-9499
  South Windsor *(G-7775)*

CHROMATOGRAPHY EQPT
Welch Materials Inc .... G 203 691-1721
  West Haven *(G-9961)*

CHUCKS
Miracle Instruments Co .... F 860 642-7745
  Lebanon *(G-3858)*
O S Walker Company Inc .... D 508 853-3232
  Windsor *(G-10414)*
Royal Machine and Tool Corp .... E 860 828-6555
  Berlin *(G-217)*

CHURCHES
Mt Calvary Holy Church .... G 203 785-1253
  New Haven *(G-5337)*

CHUTES: Mail, Sheet Metal
E&D Landscaping .... G 203 934-4088
  West Haven *(G-9905)*

CIGAR STORES
Foundation Cigar Company LLC .... F 203 738-9377
  Windsor *(G-10387)*

CIGARETTE & CIGAR PRDTS & ACCESS
Cigar World .... G 860 828-7870
  Kensington *(G-3807)*
Milford Smoke Junction LLC .... G 203 301-9956
  Milford *(G-4581)*
Tonys Smoke Shop Outlet LLC .... G 203 367-8558
  Bridgeport *(G-927)*

CIGARETTE LIGHTERS
Bic Corporation .... A 203 783-2000
  Shelton *(G-7407)*
Bic USA Inc .... C 203 783-2000
  Shelton *(G-7408)*

CIRCUIT BOARD REPAIR SVCS
Microboard Processing Inc .... C 203 881-4300
  Seymour *(G-7357)*

CIRCUIT BOARDS, PRINTED: Television & Radio
Apct-Wallingford Inc .... E 203 269-3311
  Wallingford *(G-9208)*
Microboard Processing Inc .... C 203 881-4300
  Seymour *(G-7357)*
Power Trans Co Inc .... G 203 881-0314
  Oxford *(G-6688)*
Precise Circuit Company Inc .... E 203 924-2512
  Shelton *(G-7533)*
Silicon Integration Inc .... E 203 876-2844
  Milford *(G-4645)*

CIRCUIT BREAKERS
Bass Products LLC .... G 860 585-7923
  Bristol *(G-977)*
Carling Technologies Inc .... C 860 793-9281
  Plainville *(G-6785)*
GE Grid Solutions LLC .... G 425 250-2695
  Windsor *(G-10388)*

CIRCUIT BREAKERS: Air
Connecticut Breaker Co Inc .... G 203 378-2240
  Stratford *(G-8597)*
EC Holdings Inc .... G 203 846-1651
  Norwalk *(G-6153)*

CIRCUITS, INTEGRATED: Hybrid
Hi-Rel Group LLC .... G 860 767-9031
  Essex *(G-2718)*
Hi-Rel Products LLC .... E 860 767-9031
  Essex *(G-2719)*

CIRCUITS: Electronic
AB Electronics Inc .... E 203 740-2793
  Brookfield *(G-1155)*
Ambrosonics .... G 860 752-9022
  Windsor *(G-10361)*
Andrew Lambert .... G 203 249-6310
  Stamford *(G-8084)*
Arccos Golf LLC .... E 844 692-7226
  Stamford *(G-8091)*
Bead Industries Inc .... E 203 301-0270
  Milford *(G-4466)*
Cable Electronics Inc .... G 860 953-0300
  Hartford *(G-3560)*
Doltronics LLC .... E 203 488-8766
  Branford *(G-580)*
Electro-Tech Inc .... E 203 271-1976
  Cheshire *(G-1384)*
General Electro Components .... G 860 659-3573
  Glastonbury *(G-3039)*
Goodrich Corporation .... B 505 345-9031
  Danbury *(G-1834)*
Imperial Elctrnc Assembly Inc .... D 203 740-8425
  Brookfield *(G-1197)*
Kbc Electronics Inc .... F 203 298-9654
  Milford *(G-4563)*
Lsr Electronic Assembly .... G 860 642-6883
  Lebanon *(G-3857)*
Mil-Con Inc .... D 630 595-2366
  Naugatuck *(G-4901)*
Osda Contract Services Inc .... E 203 878-2155
  Milford *(G-4599)*
Osda Inc .... G 203 878-2155
  Milford *(G-4600)*
Park Distributories Inc .... F 203 366-7200
  Bridgeport *(G-864)*
Printed Prfmce Innovations LLC .... G 860 942-7338
  Coventry *(G-1669)*
Protronix Inc .... F 203 269-5858
  Wallingford *(G-9344)*
Qtran Inc .... E 203 367-8777
  Milford *(G-4620)*
Sean Mecesery .... G 203 869-2277
  Cos Cob *(G-1641)*
Tgs Cables .... G 203 668-6568
  Meriden *(G-4252)*
USA Circuits LLC .... G 203 364-1378
  Sandy Hook *(G-7331)*
Verotec Inc .... G 603 821-9921
  North Haven *(G-6011)*

CLAMPS: Ground, Electric-Wiring Devices
J Ro Grounding Systems Inc .... G 860 747-2106
  Plainville *(G-6827)*

CLAMPS: Metal
Dimide Inc .... G 203 668-9621
  Milford *(G-4510)*
Lassy Tools Inc .... G 860 747-2748
  Plainville *(G-6832)*

CLAY MINING, COMMON
RT Vanderbilt Holding Co Inc .... F 203 295-2141
  Norwalk *(G-6331)*

CLEANING & DESCALING SVC: Metal Prdts
Composiclean LLC .... G 860 432-0067
  Glastonbury *(G-3021)*
E & J Parts Cleaning Inc .... F 203 757-1716
  Waterbury *(G-9469)*
Preventative Maintenance Corp .... F 860 683-1180
  Poquonock *(G-6948)*

CLEANING & DYEING PLANTS, EXC RUGS
Elegant Drycleaning .... G 203 849-1000
  Norwalk *(G-6156)*

CLEANING EQPT: Commercial
EMJ Contracting LLC .... G 475 449-7725
  Bridgeport *(G-762)*
Jfj Services LLC .... G 860 395-1922
  Old Saybrook *(G-6548)*

CLEANING EQPT: High Pressure
Beyond Home Improvement .... G 203 859-0113
  North Haven *(G-5914)*
Erasable Images .... G 860 367-4545
  Oakdale *(G-6442)*

CLEANING OR POLISHING PREPARATIONS, NEC
Grill Daddy Brush Company .... E 888 840-7552
  Old Greenwich *(G-6474)*
Hydrochemical Techniques Inc .... G 860 527-6350
  Hartford *(G-3615)*
Macdermid Incorporated .... C 203 575-5700
  Waterbury *(G-9522)*
Nature Plus Inc .... G 203 380-0316
  Stratford *(G-8653)*
Simoniz Usa Inc .... G 860 646-0172
  Bolton *(G-520)*

CLEANING PRDTS: Automobile Polish
Armor All/STP Products Company .... G 203 205-2900
  Danbury *(G-1745)*
Armor All/STP Products Company .... G 203 205-2900
  Danbury *(G-1744)*
Armored Autogroup Parent Inc .... G 203 205-2900
  Danbury *(G-1747)*
Xtreme Detail .... G 203 753-6608
  Waterbury *(G-9637)*

CLEANING PRDTS: Drain Pipe Solvents Or Cleaners
A Emergency Rooter Service .... G 860 582-3612
  Bristol *(G-952)*

CLEANING PRDTS: Drycleaning Preparations
Jimmys Cleaners & Alterations .... G 203 294-1006
  Wallingford *(G-9295)*

CLEANING PRDTS: Dusting Cloths, Chemically Treated
High-Tech Conversions Inc .... G 860 265-2633
  Enfield *(G-2650)*

CLEANING PRDTS: Floor Waxes
Koster Keunen LLC .... F 860 945-3333
  Watertown *(G-9715)*

CLEANING PRDTS: Furniture Polish Or Wax
Pacific Engineering Inc .... G 860 677-0795
  Farmington *(G-2944)*

PRODUCT SECTION

CLEANING PRDTS: Metal Polish
Charles K White .... G 203 631-2540
  Hamden *(G-3428)*
Metal Works North .... G 203 723-9075
  Beacon Falls *(G-143)*

CLEANING PRDTS: Polishing Preparations & Related Prdts
F S P Research Inc .... G 203 874-3417
  Milford *(G-4534)*

CLEANING PRDTS: Sanitation Preparations
Roebic Laboratories Inc .... G 203 795-1283
  Orange *(G-6626)*

CLEANING PRDTS: Sanitation Preps, Disinfectants/Deodorants
Great Lakes Chemical Corp .... E 203 573-2000
  Shelton *(G-7454)*
Lanxess Solutions US Inc .... E 203 573-2000
  Shelton *(G-7486)*
Topcat LLC .... G 203 610-6544
  Stratford *(G-8697)*

CLEANING PRDTS: Specialty
Barclay-Davis Enterprises LLC .... G 860 578-9563
  Hartford *(G-3555)*
Cloverdale Inc .... G 860 672-0216
  West Cornwall *(G-9762)*
Comanche Clean Energy Corp .... G 203 326-4570
  Stamford *(G-8152)*
Korner Kare .... G 860 491-3731
  Goshen *(G-3100)*
Micro Care Corporation .... F 860 827-0626
  New Britain *(G-5018)*
Odd Jobs Handyman Service LLC .... G 203 397-5275
  Woodbridge *(G-10609)*
Suarez Services LLC .... G 203 895-0465
  Bridgeport *(G-915)*

CLEANING PRDTS: Stain Removers
Amodex Products Inc .... E 203 335-1255
  Bridgeport *(G-696)*

CLEANING PRDTS: Window Cleaning Preparations
Richards Creative Interiors .... G 203 484-0361
  Wallingford *(G-9355)*

CLEANING SVCS
B 9 Air Quality Services LLC .... G 203 387-1709
  Wallingford *(G-9217)*
Domus VI LLC .... G 860 619-0707
  Sharon *(G-7378)*

CLEANING SVCS: Industrial Or Commercial
E & J Parts Cleaning Inc .... F 203 757-1716
  Waterbury *(G-9469)*
Hartford Fire Equipment .... E 860 747-2757
  Plainville *(G-6821)*

CLIPPERS: Fingernail & Toenail
Bella Nail & Spa LLC .... G 860 436-3119
  Rocky Hill *(G-7222)*

CLOSURES: Closures, Stamped Metal
Orca Inc .... E 860 223-4180
  New Britain *(G-5026)*

CLOSURES: Plastic
Aptargroup Inc .... B 203 377-8100
  Stratford *(G-8569)*

CLOTHING & ACCESS STORES
Emulsion Apparel .... G 860 495-5792
  Pawcatuck *(G-6710)*
Equestrian Collection .... G 860 749-2964
  Somers *(G-7657)*

CLOTHING & ACCESS, WOMEN, CHILD & INFANT, WHOLESALE: Under
Arensky Group Inc .... G 203 919-1575
  Norwalk *(G-6073)*

CLOTHING & ACCESS, WOMEN, CHILD/INFANT, WHOLESALE: Child
One Kid LLC .... G 203 254-9978
  Fairfield *(G-2824)*

CLOTHING & ACCESS, WOMENS, CHILDREN & INFANTS, WHOL: Hats
32 Degrees LLC .... G 978 602-2007
  West Hartford *(G-9768)*

CLOTHING & ACCESS: Garters
Hawie Manufacturing Company .... G 203 366-4303
  Bridgeport *(G-783)*

CLOTHING & ACCESS: Handicapped
Tommys Supplies LLC .... G 860 265-2199
  Somers *(G-7674)*

CLOTHING & ACCESS: Men's Miscellaneous Access
Btf LLC .... G 860 354-8926
  Bridgewater *(G-945)*
De Muerte Usa LLC .... G 860 331-7085
  Hartford *(G-3577)*
Launell Inc .... G 203 340-2150
  Greenwich *(G-3189)*
Malabar Bay LLC .... G 203 359-9714
  Stamford *(G-8294)*
Matrix Apparel Group LLC .... G 203 740-7837
  New Fairfield *(G-5171)*
Style and Grace LLC .... G 917 751-2043
  Westport *(G-10161)*

CLOTHING & ACCESS: Suspenders
Strapless Suspenders .... G 203 709-0992
  Waterbury *(G-9608)*

CLOTHING & APPAREL STORES: Custom
Logo Sportswear Inc .... G 203 678-4700
  Wallingford *(G-9306)*
Macwear LLC .... G 203 579-4277
  Southport *(G-8006)*
Raven Ad Specialties .... G 203 521-8687
  Stratford *(G-8673)*
Team Destination Inc .... G 203 235-6000
  Meriden *(G-4251)*

CLOTHING & FURNISHINGS, MEN'S & BOYS', WHOLESALE: Gloves
Gima LLC .... E 860 296-4441
  Hartford *(G-3600)*

CLOTHING & FURNISHINGS, MEN/BOY, WHOL: Hats, Scarves/Gloves
32 Degrees LLC .... G 978 602-2007
  West Hartford *(G-9768)*
Nesola Scarves LLC .... G 203 288-5058
  Cheshire *(G-1419)*

CLOTHING ACCESS STORES: Umbrellas
Bug Umbrella Gazebo LLC .... G 860 651-0030
  East Granby *(G-2194)*
Taylors Luggage Inc .... G 203 966-9961
  New Canaan *(G-5150)*

CLOTHING STORES, NEC
Malabar Bay LLC .... G 203 359-9714
  Stamford *(G-8294)*

CLOTHING STORES: Leather
Prima Dona LLC .... G 203 820-9327
  Bridgeport *(G-879)*

CLOTHING STORES: Lingerie, Outerwear
South Beach Inc .... G 860 953-0038
  West Hartford *(G-9859)*

CLOTHING STORES: T-Shirts, Printed, Custom
Cook Print .... G 203 855-8785
  Norwalk *(G-6129)*
Garrett Printing & Graphics .... G 860 589-6710
  Bristol *(G-1045)*
Jeffrey Morgan .... G 860 583-2567
  Bristol *(G-1054)*
Kaibry Screen Printing .... G 860 774-0234
  Danielson *(G-1996)*
Sam Augeri & Sons Signs .... G 860 346-1261
  Middletown *(G-4407)*
Yankee Screen Printing .... G 203 924-9926
  Derby *(G-2133)*
Young Flan LLC .... G 203 878-0084
  Derby *(G-2134)*

CLOTHING STORES: Work
Air Tool Sales & Service Co .... G 860 673-2714
  Unionville *(G-9110)*

CLOTHING: Access
Alan M Crane .... G 860 608-2788
  Norwich *(G-6405)*
Benji Billionaire .... G 203 361-7744
  New Haven *(G-5242)*
Bleshue LLC .... G 203 405-1034
  Woodbury *(G-10627)*
Fairway and Greene Inc .... G 203 926-1881
  Shelton *(G-7443)*
Mandee .... G 860 644-2128
  Manchester *(G-4054)*
Michael Kors .... G 203 748-4300
  Danbury *(G-1884)*
Mommy & ME .... G 860 269-6226
  Unionville *(G-9121)*
My Fair Lady .... G 860 322-4542
  Deep River *(G-2095)*
New Deal LLC .... G 860 648-9567
  Manchester *(G-4060)*
Ricco Vishnu .... G 203 449-0124
  Bridgeport *(G-890)*

CLOTHING: Access, Women's & Misses'
Cjbows .... G 860 287-5053
  Waterford *(G-9645)*

CLOTHING: Athletic & Sportswear, Men's & Boys'
Custom Sportswear Mfg .... G 203 879-4420
  Wolcott *(G-10559)*
Cycling Sports Group Inc .... D 608 268-8916
  Wilton *(G-10287)*
Flemming LLC .... G 818 746-6495
  Bloomfield *(G-411)*
Gg Sportswear Inc .... E 860 296-4441
  Hartford *(G-3599)*
Gima LLC .... E 860 296-4441
  Hartford *(G-3600)*
Marmot Mountain LLC .... G 203 869-0162
  Greenwich *(G-3199)*
Turq LLC .... G 203 344-1257
  Riverside *(G-7203)*
Under Armour Inc .... G 860 237-6031
  Mashantucket *(G-4133)*

CLOTHING: Athletic & Sportswear, Women's & Girls'
Custom Sportswear Mfg .... G 203 879-4420
  Wolcott *(G-10559)*

CLOTHING: Bathing Suits & Swimwear, Girls, Children & Infant
Aquatic Technologies Inc .... G 203 770-6791
  Brookfield *(G-1160)*
WEI WEI Fashions Inc .... G 646 322-2599
  Greenwich *(G-3256)*

CLOTHING: Bathing Suits & Swimwear, Knit

Malia Mills Swim Wear .... G 203 622-3137
  Greenwich (G-3198)
Sophia Swim Wear LLC .... G 203 481-9397
  North Branford (G-5857)

CLOTHING: Belts

Boxtree Accessories Inc .... G 203 637-5794
  Old Greenwich (G-6468)
Dooney & Bourke Inc .... E 203 853-7515
  Norwalk (G-6146)
Karen Callan Designs Inc .... G 203 762-9914
  Greenwich (G-3186)

CLOTHING: Blouses, Women's & Girls'

Fyc Apparel Group LLC .... E 203 466-6525
  East Haven (G-2432)
Fyc Apparel Group LLC .... D 203 481-2420
  Branford (G-599)
M S B International Ltd .... G 203 466-6525
  Branford (G-620)

CLOTHING: Bridal Gowns

Lawes International Group LLC .... G 860 808-4981
  Hartford (G-3626)
Nubridal .... G 860 768-5745
  Hartford (G-3658)

CLOTHING: Children & Infants'

CPC Childrenswear Inc .... G 203 286-6204
  Norwalk (G-6131)

CLOTHING: Children's, Girls'

One Kid LLC .... G 203 254-9978
  Westport (G-10132)
One Kid LLC .... G 203 254-9978
  Fairfield (G-2824)

CLOTHING: Clergy Vestments

M H Pierce & Co .... G 203 327-2970
  Stamford (G-8293)

CLOTHING: Coats & Suits, Men's & Boys'

Bella Hispaniola Entps LLC .... G 860 628-0105
  Southington (G-7895)
Sassone Labwear LLC .... G 860 666-4484
  Bridgeport (G-896)

CLOTHING: Coats, Overcoats & Vests

Corinth Acquisition Corp .... G 203 504-6260
  Stamford (G-8161)

CLOTHING: Corset Access, Clasps & Stays

Donghia Inc .... D 800 366-4442
  Milford (G-4514)

CLOTHING: Dresses

Fyc Apparel Group LLC .... D 203 481-2420
  Branford (G-599)
M S B International Ltd .... G 203 466-6525
  Branford (G-620)
Runway Liquidation LLC .... G 202 865-3311
  Cromwell (G-1716)
Runway Liquidation LLC .... G 202 544-1900
  Brookfield (G-1220)
Runway Liquidation LLC .... G 202 466-2050
  Bristol (G-1115)
Runway Liquidation LLC .... G 239 337-2020
  Trumbull (G-9067)
Runway Liquidation LLC .... G 302 998-0551
  Bloomfield (G-482)
Runway Liquidation LLC .... G 561 391-3334
  Enfield (G-2688)
Runway Liquidation LLC .... G 561 279-4444
  Simsbury (G-7643)

CLOTHING: Dresses & Skirts

Ida Dean .... G 860 482-3589
  Torrington (G-8934)

CLOTHING: Dressing Gowns, Mens/Womens, From Purchased Matls

Lawes International Group LLC .... G 860 808-4981
  Hartford (G-3626)

CLOTHING: Garments, Indl, Men's & Boys

A Gerber Corp .... G 203 918-1913
  Stamford (G-8051)

CLOTHING: Gloves & Mittens, Knit

Cunningham Tech LLC .... G 860 738-8759
  Pine Meadow (G-6733)

CLOTHING: Gowns & Dresses, Wedding

Kallai Designs .... G 860 653-6786
  Granby (G-3109)

CLOTHING: Hospital, Men's

Doctors Clothes .... G 203 485-0494
  Greenwich (G-3154)
Sassone Labwear LLC .... G 860 666-4484
  Bridgeport (G-896)

CLOTHING: Leather

Dj Sportsware .... G 203 438-0078
  Ridgefield (G-7136)

CLOTHING: Men's & boy's clothing, nec

Shield Group .... G 203 981-6169
  Wilton (G-10329)

CLOTHING: Mens & Boys Jackets, Sport, Suede, Leatherette

Tribal Wear .... G 203 637-7884
  Riverside (G-7202)

CLOTHING: Neckwear

Xmi Corporation .... G 800 838-0424
  Greenwich (G-3262)

CLOTHING: Outerwear, Women's & Misses' NEC

Blush By London .... G 860 610-9891
  Hartford (G-3557)
Creative Enhancement Inc .... E 860 833-8493
  West Hartford (G-9795)

CLOTHING: Raincoats, Exc Vulcanized Rubber, Purchased Matls

Wrenfield Group Inc .... E 203 438-0090
  Ridgefield (G-7186)

CLOTHING: Robes & Dressing Gowns

Graduation Solutions LLC .... E 914 934-5991
  Greenwich (G-3168)
M S B International Ltd .... G 203 466-6525
  Branford (G-620)

CLOTHING: Shirts

Fezza Inc .... G 203 222-9721
  Weston (G-10026)

CLOTHING: Shirts, Dress, Men's & Boys'

Lawes International Group LLC .... G 860 808-4981
  Hartford (G-3626)

CLOTHING: Shirts, Sports & Polo, Men's & Boys'

Sportco Inc .... G 631 244-4513
  New Canaan (G-5146)

CLOTHING: Socks

Human Interests LLC .... G 203 270-9107
  Newtown (G-5749)
Mosley Hosiery and Socks LLC .... G 860 690-9227
  Bloomfield (G-447)
Shock Sock Inc LLC .... G 860 680-7252
  Farmington (G-2956)
Soldier Socks .... G 203 832-2005
  Stamford (G-8428)
Tommy LLC Sock It .... G 860 688-2019
  Windsor (G-10454)

CLOTHING: Sportswear, Women's

Gg Sportswear Inc .... E 860 296-4441
  Hartford (G-3599)
Teta Activewear By Custom .... G 203 879-4420
  Wolcott (G-10591)

CLOTHING: Suits & Skirts, Women's & Misses'

Fyc Apparel Group LLC .... D 203 481-2420
  Branford (G-599)

CLOTHING: Suits, Men's & Boys', From Purchased Materials

Bayer Clothing Group Inc .... D 203 661-4140
  Greenwich (G-3131)

CLOTHING: Sweaters & Sweater Coats, Knit

Kielo America Inc .... G 203 431-3999
  Ridgefield (G-7153)

CLOTHING: Sweatshirts & T-Shirts, Men's & Boys'

MB Sport LLC .... F 203 966-1985
  New Canaan (G-5118)

CLOTHING: Swimwear, Men's & Boys'

Everest Isles LLC .... G 203 561-5128
  Wallingford (G-9259)

CLOTHING: Swimwear, Women's & Misses'

Mangladesh LLC .... G 203 299-0697
  Fairfield (G-2812)
South Beach Inc .... G 860 953-0038
  West Hartford (G-9859)

CLOTHING: Tailored Dress/Sport Coats, Mens & Boys

Peter Dermer Co .... G 203 389-3297
  Woodbridge (G-10612)

CLOTHING: Ties, Bow, Men's & Boys', From Purchased Materials

Barnard-Maine Ltd .... G 860 535-9485
  Stonington (G-8523)

CLOTHING: Trousers & Slacks, Men's & Boys'

Guess Inc .... G 860 629-0835
  Mashantucket (G-4132)

CLOTHING: Tuxedos, From Purchased Materials

Shoreline Segway Inc .... G 203 453-6036
  Guilford (G-3391)

CLOTHING: Underwear, Knit

Baby Knits and More .... G 860 485-0146
  Harwinton (G-3721)

CLOTHING: Underwear, Women's & Children's

M S B International Ltd .... G 203 466-6525
  Branford (G-620)

CLOTHING: Uniforms & Vestments

Classic School Uniforms Ltd .... G 860 677-7207
  Farmington (G-2889)

CLOTHING: Uniforms, Military, Men/Youth, Purchased Materials

Front Line Apparel Group LLC .... C 860 859-3524
  Hebron (G-3749)

PRODUCT SECTION

COILS: Pipe

Stevens Industries Inc .... E 203 966-7555
  New Canaan *(G-5147)*

CLOTHING: Uniforms, Team Athletic

Nomis Enterprises .... G 631 821-3120
  Wallingford *(G-9327)*

CLOTHING: Uniforms, Work

Cintas Corporation .... F 203 272-2036
  Cheshire *(G-1370)*

CLOTHING: Work Apparel, Exc Uniforms

Dbebz Apparel LLC .... G 203 254-7356
  Fairfield *(G-2772)*

CLOTHING: Work, Men's

Childrens Medical Group .... E 860 242-8330
  Bloomfield *(G-402)*
G&K Services LLC .... G 860 856-4400
  Hartford *(G-3596)*
Sewn In America Inc .... D 203 438-9149
  Ridgefield *(G-7172)*
Stevens Industries Inc .... E 203 966-7555
  New Canaan *(G-5147)*

CLUTCHES, EXC VEHICULAR

Carlyle Johnson Machine Co LLC .... E 860 643-1531
  Bolton *(G-508)*
Helander Products Inc .... F 860 669-7953
  Clinton *(G-1507)*
Inertia Dynamics LLC .... C 860 379-1252
  New Hartford *(G-5197)*
Rollease Acmeda Inc .... D 203 964-1573
  Stamford *(G-8397)*

COAL & OTHER MINERALS & ORES WHOLESALERS

De Villiers Incorporated .... G 203 966-9645
  New Canaan *(G-5101)*
Thyssenkrupp Materials NA Inc .... E 610 586-1800
  Wallingford *(G-9383)*

COAL MINING SERVICES

Coronado Group LLC .... G 203 761-1291
  Wilton *(G-10282)*
Tronox LLC .... E 203 705-3800
  Stamford *(G-8478)*

COAL MINING: Anthracite

Hartford Fire Equipment .... E 860 747-2757
  Plainville *(G-6821)*

COAL MINING: Bituminous & Lignite Surface

Rhino Energy Holdings LLC .... A 203 862-7000
  Greenwich *(G-3226)*
Wexford Capital LP .... D 203 862-7000
  Greenwich *(G-3258)*

COAL MINING: Bituminous Coal & Lignite-Surface Mining

Morning Sun of Trumbull LLC .... G 203 220-8509
  Trumbull *(G-9050)*

COAL MINING: Bituminous Underground

American Metals Coal Intl Inc .... F 203 625-9200
  Greenwich *(G-3120)*
Rhino Energy Holdings LLC .... A 203 862-7000
  Greenwich *(G-3226)*
Wexford Capital LP .... D 203 862-7000
  Greenwich *(G-3258)*

COAL, MINERALS & ORES, WHOLESALE: Coal

American Metals Coal Intl Inc .... F 203 625-9200
  Greenwich *(G-3120)*

COAL, MINERALS & ORES, WHOLESALE: Sulfur

HJ Baker & Bro LLC .... E 203 682-9200
  Shelton *(G-7465)*

COATED OR PLATED PRDTS

Applied Diamond Coatings LLC .... G 860 349-3133
  Durham *(G-2137)*
Scp Management LLC .... E 860 738-2600
  New Hartford *(G-5211)*

COATERS: High Vacuum, Metal Plate

Stein Laboratories LLC .... G 203 853-9500
  Norwalk *(G-6356)*

COATING COMPOUNDS: Tar

Neyra Industries Inc .... G 860 289-4359
  South Windsor *(G-7796)*
Spectrum Powdercoating LLC .... G 860 591-1034
  Jewett City *(G-3801)*

COATING SVC

Advanced Powder Coating Techno .... G 860 612-0631
  New Britain *(G-4939)*
Clear & Colored Coatings LLC .... G 203 879-1379
  Wolcott *(G-10555)*
Competitive Edge Coatings LLC .... G 860 267-6255
  Colchester *(G-1546)*
Distinctive Coating LLC .... G 860 530-1233
  Hebron *(G-3747)*
Dynamic Coating Solutions LLC .... G 860 321-7483
  Bristol *(G-1022)*
Final Liquid Coating LLC .... G 860 585-5625
  Bristol *(G-1038)*
Immersive Custom Coatings .... G 401 636-1196
  Putnam *(G-7046)*
Infante Coatings LLC .... G 203 252-6370
  Derby *(G-2117)*
ITW Hlographic Specialty Films .... G 860 243-0343
  Bloomfield *(G-424)*
Line-X of Hartford .... G 860 216-6180
  Hartford *(G-3628)*
Pioneer Coatings & Mfg LLC .... G 203 421-6086
  Madison *(G-3948)*
Plasti-Coat .... G 203 755-3741
  Waterbury *(G-9579)*
Plasti-Coat .... G 860 274-1234
  Middlebury *(G-4287)*
Pro Coatings LLC .... G 860 345-2107
  Higganum *(G-3776)*
Protective Home Coatings LLC .... G 203 410-5826
  Seymour *(G-7364)*
R and B Prtective Coatings LLC .... G 860 836-7854
  Middletown *(G-4400)*
Rdl Coatings LLC .... G 203 232-0411
  Oakville *(G-6461)*
Silver Lining Technologies LLC .... G 860 539-4182
  Vernon *(G-9152)*
Tetraflo .... G 860 575-0867
  Old Lyme *(G-6520)*
Tim Poloski .... G 860 508-6566
  Vernon Rockville *(G-9182)*
Wired Inc .... G 601 992-0490
  Stratford *(G-8709)*

COATING SVC: Aluminum, Metal Prdts

Gybenorth Industries LLC .... F 203 876-9876
  Milford *(G-4546)*

COATING SVC: Hot Dip, Metals Or Formed Prdts

Marjan Inc .... F 203 573-1742
  Waterbury *(G-9534)*
Paint & Powder Works LLC .... F 860 225-2019
  New Britain *(G-5028)*

COATING SVC: Metals & Formed Prdts

American Metallizing .... G 860 289-1677
  South Windsor *(G-7706)*
American Metaseal of Conn .... G 203 787-0281
  Hamden *(G-3414)*
American Powdercoating LLC .... G 860 267-8870
  East Hampton *(G-2254)*
Cametoid Technologies Inc .... F 860 646-4667
  Manchester *(G-3990)*
Central Connecticut Coating .... F 860 528-8281
  East Hartford *(G-2303)*
Chem-Tron Pntg Pwdr Cating Inc .... G 860 743-5131
  Danbury *(G-1766)*
Colonial Coatings Inc .... E 203 783-9933
  Milford *(G-4491)*
Competitive Edge Coatings LLC .... G 860 882-0762
  South Windsor *(G-7734)*
Connecticut Plasma Tech LLC .... F 860 289-5500
  South Windsor *(G-7735)*
Covalent Coating Tech LLC .... G 860 214-6452
  East Hartford *(G-2310)*
Engineered Coatings Inc .... E 860 567-5556
  Litchfield *(G-3889)*
Integrity Cylinder Sales LLC .... G 860 267-6667
  East Hampton *(G-2265)*
K & G Corp .... F 860 643-1133
  Manchester *(G-4041)*
Metal Morphous .... G 203 239-0411
  North Haven *(G-5963)*
Metallizing Service Co Inc .... E 860 953-1144
  Hartford *(G-3641)*
North East Powder Coating .... G 203 573-1543
  Waterbury *(G-9561)*
Plas-TEC Coatings Inc .... F 860 289-6029
  South Windsor *(G-7806)*
Praxair Inc .... B 203 837-2000
  Danbury *(G-1913)*
Praxair Surface Tech Inc .... D 860 646-0700
  Manchester *(G-4076)*
Pti Industries Inc .... G 860 698-9266
  Enfield *(G-2682)*
Pti Industries Inc .... E 800 318-8438
  Enfield *(G-2683)*
Shoreline Coatings LLC .... E 203 213-3471
  North Branford *(G-5855)*
Vitek Research Corporation .... F 203 735-1813
  Naugatuck *(G-4928)*
Zz Powder Coating .... G 860 917-7495
  Niantic *(G-5821)*

COATING SVC: Metals, With Plastic Or Resins

American Roller Company LLC .... F 203 598-3100
  Middlebury *(G-4273)*
Donwell Company .... E 860 649-5374
  Manchester *(G-4010)*
Mitchell-Bate Company .... E 203 233-0862
  Waterbury *(G-9545)*
Plastonics Inc .... E 860 249-5455
  Hartford *(G-3666)*

COATINGS: Air Curing

Tcg Green Technologies Inc .... F 860 364-4694
  Sharon *(G-7384)*

COIL WINDING SVC

Jan Manufacturing Inc .... G 203 879-0580
  Wolcott *(G-10569)*

COILS & TRANSFORMERS

Bicron Electronics Company .... D 860 482-2524
  Torrington *(G-8905)*
Cable Technology Inc .... E 860 429-7889
  Willington *(G-10246)*
Coils Plus Inc .... E 203 879-0755
  Wolcott *(G-10556)*
Future Manufacturing Inc .... E 860 584-0685
  Bristol *(G-1043)*
Microphase Corporation .... E 203 866-8000
  Shelton *(G-7500)*
Microtech Inc .... D 203 272-3234
  Cheshire *(G-1416)*
Pioneer Power Solutions Inc .... G 203 782-4348
  New Haven *(G-5366)*
Qtran Inc .... E 203 367-8777
  Milford *(G-4620)*

COILS: Electric Motors Or Generators

Autac Incorporated .... F 203 481-3444
  Branford *(G-551)*
Coils Plus Inc .... E 203 879-0755
  Wolcott *(G-10556)*

COILS: Pipe

JFd Tube & Coil Products Inc .... E 203 288-6941
  Hamden *(G-3468)*

Employee Codes: A=Over 500 employees, B=251-500
C=101-250, D=51-100, E=20-50, F=10-19, G=1-9

COKE: Calcined Petroleum, Made From Purchased Materials
Rain Cii Carbon LLC .... F 203 406-0535
  Stamford *(G-8385)*

COLLETS
Iswiss Corporation .... G 860 327-4200
  Manchester *(G-4034)*

COLOR SEPARATION: Photographic & Movie Film
Cag Imaging LLC .... G 860 887-0836
  Norwich *(G-6408)*

COLORS IN OIL, EXC ARTISTS'
Elena Dieck .... G 860 623-9872
  Broad Brook *(G-1149)*

COLORS: Pigments, Organic
Jamilah Henna Creations .... G 860 365-9542
  East Hampton *(G-2266)*

COMFORTERS & QUILTS, FROM MANMADE FIBER OR SILK
A Wild Quilter .... G 203 744-3405
  Bethel *(G-255)*

COMMERCIAL & OFFICE BUILDINGS RENOVATION & REPAIR
Musano Inc .... F 203 879-4651
  Wolcott *(G-10575)*

COMMERCIAL ART & GRAPHIC DESIGN SVCS
Creative Stone Group Inc .... G 203 554-7773
  Stamford *(G-8169)*
Criscola Design LLC .... G 203 248-4285
  North Haven *(G-5932)*
Fusion Cross-Media LLC .... G 860 647-8367
  Manchester *(G-4020)*
Garrett Printing & Graphics .... G 860 589-6710
  Bristol *(G-1045)*
Gerber Scientific LLC .... C 860 871-8082
  Tolland *(G-8864)*
Intechs LLC .... G 203 260-8109
  Monroe *(G-4721)*
John Pecora .... G 860 677-9323
  Farmington *(G-2920)*
Lettering Inc of New York .... E 203 329-7759
  Stamford *(G-8283)*
Melvin Mayo .... G 802 698-7635
  Enfield *(G-2658)*
Print Source Ltd .... G 203 876-1822
  Milford *(G-4617)*
Renaissance Studio Inc .... G 203 226-9674
  Westport *(G-10148)*
S and Z Graphics LLC .... G 203 783-9675
  Milford *(G-4637)*
Sk Systems .... G 860 691-0366
  East Lyme *(G-2475)*
Success Printing & Mailing Inc ... F 203 847-1112
  Norwalk *(G-6359)*
Zp Couture LLC .... G 888 697-7239
  North Haven *(G-6017)*

COMMERCIAL ART & ILLUSTRATION SVCS
Designs & Signs .... G 203 775-0152
  Brookfield *(G-1182)*
Omniprint LLC .... G 203 881-9013
  Oxford *(G-6683)*

COMMERCIAL EQPT WHOLESALERS, NEC
Capricorn Investors III LP .... F 203 861-6600
  Greenwich *(G-3141)*
Cummins - Allison Corp .... G 203 794-9200
  Cheshire *(G-1377)*
Treif USA Inc .... F 203 929-9930
  Shelton *(G-7569)*

COMMERCIAL EQPT, WHOLESALE: Coffee Brewing Eqpt & Splys
Saccuzzo Company Inc .... G 860 665-1101
  Newington *(G-5702)*

COMMERCIAL EQPT, WHOLESALE: Comm Cooking & Food Svc Eqpt
Milford Metal Products Inc .... G 203 878-0148
  Milford *(G-4580)*

COMMERCIAL EQPT, WHOLESALE: Display Eqpt, Exc Refrigerated
Ardent Inc .... E 860 528-6000
  East Hartford *(G-2292)*

COMMERCIAL EQPT, WHOLESALE: Scales, Exc Laboratory
Kenneth Allevo .... G 860 745-0740
  Enfield *(G-2654)*

COMMERCIAL LAUNDRY EQPT
Naugatuck Recovery Inc .... E 203 723-1122
  Naugatuck *(G-4906)*
Stn Laundry Systems LLC .... G 203 887-8986
  Hamden *(G-3513)*

COMMERCIAL PHOTOGRAPHIC STUDIO
John Pecora .... G 860 677-9323
  Farmington *(G-2920)*

COMMERCIAL PRINTING & NEWSPAPER PUBLISHING COMBINED
Bristol Press .... D 860 584-0501
  Torrington *(G-8906)*
Chronicle Printing Company .... D 860 423-8466
  Willimantic *(G-10222)*
Day Publishing Company .... B 860 701-4200
  New London *(G-5466)*
Gatehouse Media Conn Holdings .. E 860 887-9211
  Norwich *(G-6415)*
GPA .... G 860 410-0624
  Plainville *(G-6818)*
Green Manor Corporation .... B 860 643-8111
  Manchester *(G-4023)*
Hersam Publishing Company ..... B 203 966-9541
  New Canaan *(G-5110)*
Hillside Capital Inc De Corp .... F 203 618-0202
  Stamford *(G-8238)*
New Haven Register LLC .... A 203 789-5200
  New Haven *(G-5346)*
Printed Communications .... G 860 436-9619
  South Windsor *(G-7812)*
Record-Journal Newspaper .... C 203 235-1661
  Meriden *(G-4230)*
Shore Publishing LLC .... E 203 245-1877
  Madison *(G-3956)*
The Bee Publishing Company .... E 203 426-8036
  Newtown *(G-5789)*
Villager Newspapers .... G 860 928-1818
  Putnam *(G-7077)*
Wolcott Community News LL ..... G 203 879-3900
  Waterbury *(G-9635)*

COMMODITY INVESTORS
Castleton Commodities .... G 203 564-8100
  Stamford *(G-8131)*
CCI East Texas Upstream LLC .. G 203 564-8100
  Stamford *(G-8135)*

COMMON SAND MINING
Dunning Sand & Gravel Company .. F 860 677-1616
  Farmington *(G-2899)*
Kacerguis Farms Inc .... G 203 405-1202
  Bethlehem *(G-373)*
Kobyluck Sand and Gravel Inc ... F 860 444-9600
  Waterford *(G-9658)*
Laurelbrook Ntral Rsources LLC .. F 860 824-5843
  East Canaan *(G-2183)*

COMMUNICATIONS EQPT & SYSTEMS, NEC
Adam Bisson .... G 203 861-8271
  Bridgeport *(G-683)*
Digital Bob .... G 203 322-5732
  Stamford *(G-8185)*
Harris Security LLC .... G 860 583-6637
  Bristol *(G-1047)*

COMMUNICATIONS EQPT WHOLESALERS
Connecticut Radio Inc .... G 860 563-4867
  Rocky Hill *(G-7228)*
Fenton Corp .... F 203 221-2788
  Westport *(G-10079)*
Globenix Inc .... G 203 740-7070
  Norwalk *(G-6181)*

COMMUNICATIONS EQPT: Microwave
Microphase Corporation .... E 203 866-8000
  Shelton *(G-7500)*
Scinetx LLC .... G 203 355-3676
  Stamford *(G-8403)*

COMMUNICATIONS SVCS: Cellular
Southern Neng Telecom Corp .... B 203 771-5200
  New Haven *(G-5401)*

COMMUNICATIONS SVCS: Data
I Tech Services Inc .... G 800 559-8991
  Danbury *(G-1847)*

COMMUNICATIONS SVCS: Electronic Mail
Southern Neng Telecom Corp .... B 203 771-5200
  New Haven *(G-5401)*

COMMUNICATIONS SVCS: Facsimile Transmission
Jyl LLP .... G 860 767-7733
  Essex *(G-2722)*
Two Ems Inc .... G 203 245-8211
  Madison *(G-3965)*

COMMUNICATIONS SVCS: Internet Host Svcs
20/20 Software Inc .... G 203 316-5500
  Stamford *(G-8049)*
Drug Imprment Dtction Svcs LLC .. G 203 616-3735
  Danbury *(G-1802)*
Villa Ridge LLC .... G 303 330-9183
  Norwalk *(G-6389)*

COMMUNICATIONS SVCS: Online Svc Providers
Amsys Inc .... E 203 431-8814
  Ridgefield *(G-7116)*
Topcat LLC .... G 203 610-6544
  Stratford *(G-8697)*

COMMUNICATIONS SVCS: Signal Enhancement Network Svcs
Textspeak Corporation .... F 203 803-1069
  Westport *(G-10165)*

COMMUNICATIONS SVCS: Telephone, Local & Long Distance
Southern Neng Telecom Corp .... B 203 771-5200
  New Haven *(G-5401)*

COMMUNICATIONS SVCS: Telephone, Voice
Mirion Tech Canberra Inc .... B 203 238-2351
  Meriden *(G-4204)*
Sigmavoip Llc 203 541-5450
  Westport *(G-10159)*

COMMUNITY DEVELOPMENT GROUPS
Dimension Zero Ltd .... G 860 325-7073
  Willimantic *(G-10224)*

COMMUTATORS: Electronic
Sysdyne Technologies LLC .... F 203 327-3649
  Stamford *(G-8455)*

PRODUCT SECTION

COMPACT DISC PLAYERS

Colin Harrison LLC .... G 203 775-5035
  Brookfield *(G-1174)*
Color Film Media Group LLC .... G 203 202-2929
  Norwalk *(G-6121)*

COMPARATORS: Optical

Macro Systems Inc .... G 203 225-6266
  Shelton *(G-7494)*

COMPASSES & ACCESS

Alternate Inc .... G 203 938-4125
  Redding *(G-7088)*

COMPOST

Blue Earth Compost Inc .... G 860 508-7114
  Hartford *(G-3556)*
Collins Compost .... G 860 749-3416
  Enfield *(G-2628)*
Curbside Compost LLC .... G 914 646-6890
  Ridgefield *(G-7132)*
New Milford Farms Inc .... F 860 210-0250
  New Milford *(G-5570)*

COMPRESSORS, AIR CONDITIONING: Wholesalers

David H Johnson Inc .... G 860 677-5595
  West Hartford *(G-9798)*

COMPRESSORS: Air & Gas

Afcon Products Inc .... F 203 393-9301
  Bethany *(G-234)*
Bauer Compressors Inc .... G 203 445-9514
  Monroe *(G-4696)*
David H Johnson Inc .... G 860 677-5595
  West Hartford *(G-9798)*
Norwalk Compreseer Company .... E 203 386-1234
  Stratford *(G-8655)*
Norwalk Compressor Inc .... G 203 386-1234
  Stratford *(G-8656)*
Spfm Corp .... G 203 900-0005
  Bridgeport *(G-912)*
Standard Pneumatic Products .... G 203 270-1400
  Newtown *(G-5782)*
Stylair LLC .... F 860 747-4588
  Plainville *(G-6863)*

COMPRESSORS: Air & Gas, Including Vacuum Pumps

Gardner Denver Nash LLC .... D 203 459-3923
  Trumbull *(G-9028)*
P&G Metal Components Corp .... F 860 243-2220
  Bloomfield *(G-458)*

COMPRESSORS: Wholesalers

David H Johnson Inc .... G 860 677-5595
  West Hartford *(G-9798)*
Gardner Denver Nash LLC .... D 203 459-3923
  Trumbull *(G-9028)*
Leppert/Nutmeg Inc .... E 860 243-1737
  Bloomfield *(G-441)*
Spencer Turbine Company .... C 860 688-8361
  Windsor *(G-10436)*

COMPUTER & COMPUTER SOFTWARE STORES

Advanced Business Group .... G 203 881-9660
  Oxford *(G-6637)*
Jimbpa Enterprises LLC .... G 203 755-9237
  Waterbury *(G-9509)*
Littlefingers Software .... G 203 938-2684
  Redding *(G-7096)*
S & L Systems .... G 203 757-6159
  Waterbury *(G-9596)*
Tutors & Computers Inc .... G 203 393-3006
  Bethany *(G-251)*

COMPUTER & COMPUTER SOFTWARE STORES: Printers & Plotters

Hartford Toner & Cartridge Inc .... G 860 292-1280
  Broad Brook *(G-1150)*

Tyco Printing & Copying .... G 203 562-2679
  New Haven *(G-5424)*

COMPUTER & COMPUTER SOFTWARE STORES: Software & Access

Gleason Group Incorporated .... G 203 312-0683
  New Fairfield *(G-5168)*

COMPUTER & COMPUTER SOFTWARE STORES: Software, Bus/Non-Game

Cunningham Industries Inc .... G 203 324-2942
  Stamford *(G-8171)*
Mytyme LLC .... G 860 327-2356
  Windsor *(G-10411)*

COMPUTER & OFFICE MACHINE MAINTENANCE & REPAIR

Amsys Inc .... E 203 431-8814
  Ridgefield *(G-7116)*
Computer Support People LLC .... G 203 653-4643
  Norwalk *(G-6122)*
Frontier Vision Tech Inc .... G 860 953-0240
  Rocky Hill *(G-7238)*
Jimbpa Enterprises LLC .... G 203 755-9237
  Waterbury *(G-9509)*
Laserman of Connecticut .... G 203 972-2887
  Norwalk *(G-6231)*
Mackenzie Mch & Mar Works Inc .... G 203 777-3479
  East Haven *(G-2441)*
Modern Electronic Fax & Cmpt .... G 203 292-6520
  Fairfield *(G-2816)*
Servotech Inc .... G 860 632-0164
  Middletown *(G-4410)*

COMPUTER FACILITIES MANAGEMENT SVCS

Computer Support People LLC .... G 203 653-4643
  Norwalk *(G-6122)*

COMPUTER GRAPHICS SVCS

A To A Studio Solutions Ltd .... F 203 388-9050
  Stamford *(G-8053)*
Aquastone Graphix LLC .... G 860 206-4935
  Hartford *(G-3552)*
Club Resource Inc .... G 317 225-6940
  Canton *(G-1310)*
Inverse Media LLC .... G 203 255-9620
  Westport *(G-10104)*
Joseph Merritt & Company Inc .... E 860 296-2500
  Hartford *(G-3620)*
Kiagraphics .... G 203 261-4328
  Monroe *(G-4726)*

COMPUTER HARDWARE REQUIREMENTS ANALYSIS

Advanced Decisions Inc .... F 203 402-0603
  Orange *(G-6579)*

COMPUTER PERIPHERAL EQPT REPAIR & MAINTENANCE

Transact Technologies Inc .... C 203 859-6800
  Hamden *(G-3523)*
Xerox Corporation .... B 203 968-3000
  Norwalk *(G-6401)*
Xerox Holdings Corporation .... G 203 968-3000
  Norwalk *(G-6402)*

COMPUTER PERIPHERAL EQPT, NEC

Arrayent Health LLC .... G 973 568-0323
  Stamford *(G-8094)*
Associates Inc Bedford .... G 203 846-0230
  Norwalk *(G-6078)*
Braxton Manufacturing Co Inc .... C 860 274-6781
  Watertown *(G-9685)*
Bristol Babcock Employees Fede .... G 860 945-2200
  Watertown *(G-9687)*
Cadesk Company LLC .... G 203 268-8083
  Trumbull *(G-9008)*
Computer Express LLC .... F 860 829-1310
  Berlin *(G-173)*
Contek International Corp .... G 203 972-3406
  New Canaan *(G-5097)*

COMPUTER PROGRAMMING SVCS

Contek International Corp .... F 203 972-7330
  New Canaan *(G-5098)*
Data Technology Inc .... E 860 871-8082
  Tolland *(G-8860)*
Dictaphone Corporation .... C 203 381-7000
  Stratford *(G-8606)*
Ellipson Data LLC .... G 203 227-5520
  Westport *(G-10078)*
Hint Peripherals Corp .... G 203 634-4468
  Meriden *(G-4173)*
Image Graphics Inc .... E 203 926-0100
  Shelton *(G-7474)*
Markany Na LLC .... G 914 656-7073
  South Windsor *(G-7789)*
Measurement Systems Inc .... E 203 949-3500
  Wallingford *(G-9317)*
Morse Watchmans Inc .... E 203 264-1108
  Oxford *(G-6679)*
Newmack Inc .... G 203 568-0443
  Middlebury *(G-4285)*
O E M Controls Inc .... C 203 929-8431
  Shelton *(G-7517)*
Online River LLC .... G 203 801-5900
  Westport *(G-10134)*
Optimized Micro Devices LLC .... G 860 447-2142
  East Lyme *(G-2469)*
Ortronics Inc .... D 860 445-3900
  New London *(G-5482)*
Ortronics Inc .... G 877 295-3472
  West Hartford *(G-9841)*
Ortronics Legrand .... G 860 767-3515
  Ivoryton *(G-3788)*
Syferlock Technology Corp .... G 203 292-5441
  Shelton *(G-7561)*
Technology Inf Parters .... G 860 985-8760
  Southington *(G-7984)*
Tillerman .... G 203 421-6643
  Madison *(G-3964)*
Ventus Technologies LLC .... F 203 642-2800
  Norwalk *(G-6385)*
Xerox Corporation .... B 203 968-3000
  Norwalk *(G-6401)*
Xerox Holdings Corporation .... G 203 968-3000
  Norwalk *(G-6402)*

COMPUTER PERIPHERAL EQPT, WHOLESALE

W R Hartigan & Son Inc .... G 860 673-9203
  Burlington *(G-1278)*

COMPUTER PERIPHERAL EQPT: Graphic Displays, Exc Terminals

Frontier Vision Tech Inc .... E 860 953-0240
  Rocky Hill *(G-7238)*
Resavue Inc .... F 203 878-0944
  Orange *(G-6625)*

COMPUTER PERIPHERAL EQPT: Input Or Output

Cyclone Pcie Systems LLC .... G 203 786-5536
  Hamden *(G-3438)*
OEM Design Services LLC .... G 203 467-5993
  East Haven *(G-2445)*

COMPUTER PERIPHERAL EQPT: Output To Microfilm Units

Ebeam Film LLC .... F 203 926-0100
  Shelton *(G-7434)*

COMPUTER PROCESSING SVCS

Image Graphics Inc .... E 203 926-0100
  Shelton *(G-7474)*

COMPUTER PROGRAMMING SVCS

Ancera Inc .... G 203 819-2322
  Branford *(G-544)*
Functional Concepts LLC .... G 203 813-0157
  Stratford *(G-8614)*
Intangible Matter LLC .... G 203 219-9619
  Stamford *(G-8252)*
Kat Art Inc .... G 860 350-8016
  New Milford *(G-5554)*
Kimchuk Incorporated .... F 203 790-7800
  Danbury *(G-1868)*

Employee Codes: A=Over 500 employees, B=251-500
C=101-250, D=51-100, E=20-50, F=10-19, G=1-9

COMPUTER PROGRAMMING SVCS

Peerless Systems Corporation .... F 203 350-0040
  Stamford *(G-8355)*

COMPUTER PROGRAMMING SVCS: *Custom*

Criscola Design LLC .... G 203 248-4285
  North Haven *(G-5932)*
Gerber Technology LLC .... B 860 871-8082
  Tolland *(G-8865)*
Intechs LLC .... G 203 260-8109
  Monroe *(G-4721)*
SS&c Technologies Inc .... C 860 298-4500
  Windsor *(G-10438)*
SS&c Technologies Holdings Inc .... D 860 298-4500
  Windsor *(G-10439)*
Visionpoint LLC .... E 860 436-9673
  Newington *(G-5720)*

COMPUTER RELATED MAINTENANCE SVCS

General Dynamics Info Tech Inc .... D 860 441-2400
  Pawcatuck *(G-6712)*
Norfield Data Products Inc .... F 203 849-0292
  Norwalk *(G-6280)*

COMPUTER SOFTWARE DEVELOPMENT

Active Internet Tech LLC .... C 800 592-2469
  Glastonbury *(G-3003)*
American-Digital LLC .... G 203 838-0148
  Bridgeport *(G-695)*
Clear & Simple Inc .... G 860 658-1204
  West Simsbury *(G-9974)*
Cnc Engineering Inc .... E 860 749-1780
  Enfield *(G-2627)*
Compuweigh Corporation .... E 203 262-9400
  Woodbury *(G-10629)*
Cuprak Enterprises LLC .... G 203 376-8789
  Cheshire *(G-1378)*
Desrosier of Greenwich Inc .... F 203 661-2334
  Greenwich *(G-3152)*
Document Dynamics LLC .... G 860 376-2944
  Jewett City *(G-3794)*
Electronic Design Lab Inc .... G 203 790-0500
  Bethel *(G-296)*
Financial Navigator Inc .... G 800 468-3636
  Stamford *(G-8204)*
Link Systems Inc .... F 203 274-9702
  Stamford *(G-8285)*
Microtools Inc .... G 860 651-6170
  Simsbury *(G-7635)*
Montage Software Systems Inc .... G 203 834-1144
  Wilton *(G-10313)*
Presco Incorporated .... F 203 397-8722
  Woodbridge *(G-10615)*
Pricing Excellence LLC .... G 866 557-8102
  Suffield *(G-8730)*
Real Data Inc .... G 203 255-2732
  Southport *(G-8007)*
Republic Systems Inc .... G 860 291-8832
  East Hartford *(G-2365)*
Scholastic Library Pubg Inc .... A 203 797-3500
  Danbury *(G-1939)*
Vertafore Inc .... A 860 602-6000
  Windsor *(G-10459)*

COMPUTER SOFTWARE DEVELOPMENT & APPLICATIONS

Aicas Inc .... G 203 359-5705
  Stamford *(G-8068)*
Betx LLC .... G 860 459-1681
  New Hartford *(G-5186)*
Blackrock Media Inc .... G 203 374-0369
  Easton *(G-2547)*
Broadstripes LLC .... G 203 350-9824
  New Haven *(G-5251)*
Cantata Media LLC .... F 203 951-9885
  Norwalk *(G-6106)*
Evertide Games Inc .... G 203 701-9145
  New Canaan *(G-5104)*
Fergtech Inc .... G 203 656-1139
  Darien *(G-2025)*
Fidelux Lighting LLC .... F 860 436-5000
  Hartford *(G-3589)*
Gamers That Lift LLC .... G 203 988-9211
  Orange *(G-6604)*
General Network Service Inc .... G 203 359-5735
  Stamford *(G-8213)*
Isupportws Inc .... F 203 569-7600
  Stamford *(G-8260)*

Ladrdefense LLC .... G 860 637-8488
  Plantsville *(G-6901)*
Mannan 3d Innovations LLC .... G 860 306-4203
  Higganum *(G-3768)*
Ooshears Inc .... G 415 230-0154
  Woodbridge *(G-10610)*
Rotounderworld LLC .... G 202 236-7103
  Fairfield *(G-2839)*
W R Hartigan & Son Inc .... G 860 673-9203
  Burlington *(G-1278)*

COMPUTER SOFTWARE SYSTEMS ANALYSIS & DESIGN: *Custom*

Amsys Inc .... E 203 431-8814
  Ridgefield *(G-7116)*
Dataprep Inc .... E 203 795-2095
  Orange *(G-6595)*
Grayfin Security LLC .... G 203 800-6760
  Madison *(G-3923)*
Innovation Group .... E 860 674-2900
  Farmington *(G-2917)*
Mc Keon Computer Services .... G 860 496-7171
  Torrington *(G-8947)*
Pacific Engineering Inc .... G 860 677-0795
  Farmington *(G-2944)*
Prime Business Services .... G 203 453-1627
  Guilford *(G-3384)*
Technosoft Solutions Inc .... E 203 676-8299
  Branford *(G-661)*
Tutors & Computers Inc .... G 203 393-3006
  Bethany *(G-251)*
Unimelon Inc .... G 201 774-2786
  Ridgefield *(G-7179)*

COMPUTER SOFTWARE WRITERS: *Freelance*

Robison Music Media & Pubg LLC .... G 203 858-8106
  Wallingford *(G-9356)*

COMPUTER STORAGE DEVICES, NEC

EMC Corporation .... D 203 418-4500
  Fairfield *(G-2781)*
EMC Fun Factory Inc .... G 914 837-2899
  Danbury *(G-1805)*
Emc7 LLC .... G 203 429-4355
  Fairfield *(G-2782)*
Gaisertim .... G 203 245-9276
  Madison *(G-3922)*
Image Graphics Inc .... E 203 926-0100
  Shelton *(G-7474)*
Kaman Aerospace Corporation .... C 860 632-1000
  Middletown *(G-4360)*
Pexagon Technology Inc .... E 203 458-3364
  Branford *(G-634)*
Quantum .... G 732 407-1200
  New Canaan *(G-5137)*
Quantum Bpower Southington LLC .... G 860 201-0621
  Southington *(G-7963)*
Quantum Circuits Inc .... G 203 432-4289
  Madison *(G-3950)*
Quantum Circuits Inc .... F 203 891-6216
  New Haven *(G-5373)*
Retech USA LLC .... G 860 531-9653
  Colchester *(G-1573)*
Sequent Consulting LLC .... G 203 966-2340
  New Canaan *(G-5140)*
Systematics Inc .... F 860 721-0706
  Rocky Hill *(G-7267)*
Uchisearch LLC .... G 203 268-9096
  Trumbull *(G-9084)*

COMPUTER STORAGE UNITS: *Auxiliary*

Mini LLC .... G 203 464-5495
  Naugatuck *(G-4902)*

COMPUTER SYSTEMS ANALYSIS & DESIGN

Intechs LLC .... G 203 260-8109
  Monroe *(G-4721)*

COMPUTER TERMINALS

Omega Engineering Inc .... C 203 359-1660
  Norwalk *(G-6284)*

COMPUTER TRAINING SCHOOLS

Tutors & Computers Inc .... G 203 393-3006
  Bethany *(G-251)*

COMPUTER-AIDED DESIGN SYSTEMS SVCS

House of Bubba LLC .... G 860 429-4250
  Willington *(G-10250)*

COMPUTER-AIDED SYSTEM SVCS

Bpi Reprographics .... F 203 866-5600
  Norwalk *(G-6097)*

COMPUTERS, NEC

American Railway Technologies .... G 860 291-1170
  East Hartford *(G-2290)*
Amsys Inc .... E 203 431-8814
  Ridgefield *(G-7116)*
Aztech Engineering LLC .... G 860 659-8892
  Glastonbury *(G-3009)*
Black Rock Tech Group LLC .... F 203 916-7200
  Bridgeport *(G-714)*
Bristol Babcock Employees Fede .... G 860 945-2200
  Watertown *(G-9687)*
Castle Systems Inc .... G 203 250-3140
  Cheshire *(G-1368)*
Devrajan Govender .... G 678 429-3408
  Manchester *(G-4007)*
General Digital Corp .... G 860 645-2200
  Manchester *(G-4021)*
Glacier Computer LLC .... G 860 355-7552
  New Milford *(G-5536)*
Hg Tech LLC .... G 203 632-5946
  Naugatuck *(G-4887)*
Hoffman Engineering LLC .... D 203 425-8900
  Stamford *(G-8240)*
Kimchuk Incorporated .... C 203 798-0799
  Danbury *(G-1869)*
Macworks LLC .... G 860 377-1371
  Durham *(G-2151)*
Mark Fahey .... G 203 686-0852
  Meriden *(G-4192)*
Mark Misercola .... G 423 323-0183
  Norwalk *(G-6248)*
Modern Electronic Fax & Cmpt .... G 203 292-6520
  Fairfield *(G-2816)*
Panboud Pierrot .... G 203 296-4806
  Bridgeport *(G-860)*
Sandpiper Electronics Inc .... G 860 364-5558
  Sharon *(G-7383)*
Seclingua Inc .... G 203 922-4560
  Stamford *(G-8406)*
Sequent Consulting LLC .... G 203 966-2340
  New Canaan *(G-5140)*
Snack Electronics .... G 860 225-3714
  New Britain *(G-5056)*
Xiaohao Jia .... G 203 866-3120
  Norwalk *(G-6403)*

COMPUTERS, PERIPHERALS & SOFTWARE, WHOLESALE: *Printers*

Flo-Tech LLC .... D 860 613-3333
  New Haven *(G-5283)*

COMPUTERS, PERIPHERALS & SOFTWARE, WHOLESALE: *Software*

Compart North America Inc .... F 860 799-5612
  New Milford *(G-5522)*
Interntnl Bar Code Systms .... G 860 659-9660
  Glastonbury *(G-3051)*
Online River LLC .... F 203 801-5900
  Westport *(G-10134)*
Richard Breault .... G 203 876-2707
  Milford *(G-4626)*
Sign In Soft Inc .... G 203 216-3046
  Shelton *(G-7555)*
Syferlock Technology Corp .... G 203 292-5441
  Shelton *(G-7561)*

COMPUTERS: *Indl, Process, Gas Flow*

Cidra Oilsands Inc .... G 203 265-0035
  Wallingford *(G-9231)*
Environics Inc .... E 860 872-1111
  Tolland *(G-8863)*

PRODUCT SECTION

COMPUTERS: Mini
Oracle America Inc ....D...... 203 703-3000
  Stamford (G-8345)

COMPUTERS: Personal
Apple John ....G...... 203 746-3459
  New Fairfield (G-5161)
Apple Homecare Innovations LLC ......G...... 860 940-5005
  Bloomfield (G-386)
Apple Leaf ....G...... 203 988-7262
  North Haven (G-5906)
Cls Design Group ....G...... 860 307-2810
  Torrington (G-8911)
Cyclone Microsystems Inc ....E...... 203 786-5536
  Hamden (G-3437)
Interactive Marketing Corp ....G...... 203 248-5324
  North Haven (G-5949)
Little Apple LLC ....G...... 860 404-2833
  Farmington (G-2927)
Red Apple Creative US Inc ....G...... 212 453-2540
  Shelton (G-7545)
Tapped Apple Winery ....G...... 860 887-0727
  Norwich (G-6435)

CONCENTRATES, FLAVORING, EXC DRINK
Target Flavors Inc ....F...... 203 775-4727
  Brookfield (G-1228)

CONCRETE BUILDING PRDTS WHOLESALERS
Lemac Iron Works Inc ....G...... 860 232-7380
  West Hartford (G-9829)

CONCRETE CURING & HARDENING COMPOUNDS
Concrete Supplement Co ....G...... 860 567-5556
  Litchfield (G-3886)
International Cnstr Pdts Res ....G...... 203 336-7900
  Fairfield (G-2796)

CONCRETE PRDTS
Bonsal American Inc ....G...... 860 824-7733
  Canaan (G-1282)
Bonsal American Inc ....E...... 860 824-7733
  Canaan (G-1283)
New England Cstm Concrete ....G...... 203 924-2142
  Ansonia (G-45)
O & G Industries Inc ....E...... 203 323-1111
  Stamford (G-8336)
Oldcastle Infrastructure Inc ....E...... 860 673-3291
  Avon (G-97)
Plasticrete ....G...... 203 250-6700
  Cheshire (G-1429)
Robert J Ballas ....G...... 203 746-0506
  New Fairfield (G-5175)
Safety Tek Inc ....G...... 203 785-1808
  New Haven (G-5383)
Steven Rosenburg ....G...... 203 329-8798
  Stamford (G-8443)
Superior Products Distrs Inc ....F...... 203 250-6700
  Cheshire (G-1454)
Washington Concrete Products ....F...... 860 747-5242
  Plainville (G-6876)

CONCRETE PRDTS, PRECAST, NEC
Concrete Products ....G...... 860 423-4144
  North Windham (G-6037)
Eastern Precast Company Inc ....E...... 203 775-0230
  Brookfield (G-1186)
Essex Concrete Products Inc ....F...... 860 767-1768
  Essex (G-2717)
Forterra Pipe & Precast LLC ....F...... 860 564-9000
  Wauregan (G-9753)
New Milford Block & Supply ....F...... 860 355-1101
  New Milford (G-5568)

CONCRETE REINFORCING MATERIAL
Miller Rebar LLC ....G...... 203 717-6645
  New Haven (G-5331)

CONCRETE: Bituminous
Tilcon Connecticut Inc ....G...... 860 342-6157
  Portland (G-6977)

CONCRETE: Ready-Mixed
A Aiudi & Sons LLC ....G...... 860 747-5534
  Plainville (G-6759)
Aiudi Concrete Inc ....G...... 860 399-9289
  Westbrook (G-9990)
Armed & Ready Alarm System ....F...... 203 596-0327
  Waterbury (G-9434)
B&R Sand and Gravel ....G...... 860 464-5099
  Gales Ferry (G-2981)
Barnes Concrete Co Inc ....E...... 860 928-7242
  Putnam (G-7031)
Beard Concrete Co Derby Inc ....G...... 203 874-2533
  Milford (G-4467)
Bonsal American Inc ....E...... 860 824-7733
  Canaan (G-1283)
Builders Concrete East LLC ....E...... 860 456-4111
  North Windham (G-6035)
Century Acquisition ....G...... 518 758-7229
  Canaan (G-1284)
Devine Brothers Incorporated ....E...... 203 866-4421
  Norwalk (G-6136)
Enfield Transit Mix Inc ....F...... 860 763-0864
  Enfield (G-2640)
Essex Concrete Products Inc ....F...... 203 767-1768
  Essex (G-2717)
Federici Brands LLC ....F...... 203 762-7667
  Wilton (G-10295)
Five Star Products Inc ....E...... 203 336-7900
  Shelton (G-7444)
Iffland Lumber Company Inc ....E...... 860 489-9218
  Torrington (G-8935)
Joe Kaulbach ....G...... 203 742-0434
  Andover (G-11)
Mix n Match LLC ....G...... 203 227-9588
  Westport (G-10122)
Mohican Valley Concrete Corp ....E...... 203 254-7133
  Fairfield (G-2817)
Mohican Vly Sand & Grav Corp ....F...... 203 254-7133
  Fairfield (G-2818)
O & G Industries Inc ....E...... 203 366-4586
  Bridgeport (G-854)
O & G Industries Inc ....E...... 203 748-5694
  Danbury (G-1897)
O & G Industries Inc ....E...... 203 323-1111
  Stamford (G-8336)
Pick & Mix Corp ....G...... 860 521-1521
  West Hartford (G-9845)
Robert Ready ....G...... 203 853-0051
  Norwalk (G-6326)
Sega Ready Mix Incorporated ....F...... 860 354-3969
  New Milford (G-5589)
Sega Ready Mix Incorporated ....G...... 203 465-1052
  Waterbury (G-9599)
Sterling Materials LLC ....G...... 203 315-6619
  Branford (G-657)
Sutton Mix Avenue LLC ....G...... 203 288-8482
  Hamden (G-3516)
Suzio York Hill Companies ....G...... 888 789-4626
  Meriden (G-4248)
The L Suzio Concrete Co Inc ....G...... 203 237-8421
  Meriden (G-4253)
Thomas Concrete ....G...... 860 628-4957
  Southington (G-7986)
Tilcon Connecticut Inc ....G...... 860 224-6010
  Enfield (G-2701)
Tilcon Connecticut Inc ....G...... 860 342-1096
  Portland (G-6978)
Tilcon Connecticut Inc ....E...... 860 844-7000
  East Granby (G-2232)
Tilcon Connecticut Inc ....D...... 860 224-6010
  New Britain (G-5074)
Tilcon Inc ....B...... 860 223-3651
  Newington (G-5713)
Torrington Industries Inc ....G...... 860 489-9261
  Torrington (G-8983)
Windham Materials LLC ....D...... 860 456-4111
  Willimantic (G-10241)
Windham Sand and Stone Inc ....D...... 860 643-5578
  Manchester (G-4110)

CONDUITS & FITTINGS: Electric
Bridgeport Fittings LLC ....C...... 203 377-5944
  Stratford (G-8588)

CONFECTIONS & CANDY
Bridgewater Chocolate LLC ....G...... 203 775-2286
  Brookfield (G-1164)
Emilys Sweet Confections LLC ....G...... 860 301-2586
  Middletown (G-4342)
Fascias Chocolates Inc ....F...... 203 753-0515
  Waterbury (G-9480)
Mantrose-Haeuser Co Inc ....E...... 203 454-1800
  Westport (G-10117)
Munsons Candy Kitchen Inc ....E...... 860 649-4332
  Bolton (G-517)
Petal Prfctn & Confection LLC ....G...... 203 263-0353
  Woodbury (G-10649)
Pez Candy Inc ....E...... 203 795-0531
  Orange (G-6622)
Pez Manufacturing Corp ....D...... 203 795-0531
  Orange (G-6623)
Reeds Inc ....E...... 203 890-0557
  Norwalk (G-6318)
Sonias Chocolaterie Inc ....F...... 203 438-5965
  Ridgefield (G-7174)
Thompson Brands LLC ....D...... 203 235-2541
  Meriden (G-4254)
Thompson Candy Company ....D...... 203 235-2541
  Meriden (G-4255)

CONNECTORS & TERMINALS: Electrical Device Uses
Amphenol Corporation ....D...... 203 265-8900
  Wallingford (G-9204)
Hubbell Incorporated ....E...... 203 426-2555
  Newtown (G-5748)

CONNECTORS: Cord, Electric
Gold Line Connector Inc ....E...... 203 938-2588
  Redding (G-7093)

CONNECTORS: Electrical
Amphenol Nexus Technologies ....D...... 203 327-7300
  Stamford (G-8082)
Siemon Company ....A...... 860 945-4200
  Watertown (G-9734)
Southport Products LLC ....G...... 860 379-0761
  Winsted (G-10539)

CONNECTORS: Electronic
Amphenol Corporation ....C...... 203 743-9272
  Danbury (G-1739)
Amphenol Corporation ....D...... 203 265-8900
  Wallingford (G-9204)
Amphenol Corporation ....D...... 203 287-2272
  Hamden (G-3415)
Amphenol Funding Corp ....G...... 203 265-8900
  Wallingford (G-9205)
Amphenol International Ltd ....D...... 203 265-8900
  Wallingford (G-9206)
Bead Industries Inc ....E...... 203 301-0270
  Milford (G-4466)
Burndy LLC ....D...... 203 792-1115
  Bethel (G-267)
Component Concepts Inc ....G...... 860 523-4066
  West Hartford (G-9792)
Electro-Tech Inc ....E...... 203 271-1976
  Cheshire (G-1384)
Fct Electronics LP ....D...... 860 482-2800
  Torrington (G-8923)
Hubbell Incorporated ....D...... 475 882-4000
  Shelton (G-7468)
Microtech Inc ....D...... 203 272-3234
  Cheshire (G-1416)
Molex LLC ....G...... 860 482-2800
  Torrington (G-8951)
Phoenix Company of Chicago Inc .....D...... 630 595-2300
  Naugatuck (G-4910)
Radiall Usa Inc ....E...... 203 776-2813
  New Haven (G-5375)
RC Connectors LLC ....G...... 860 413-2196
  Weatogue (G-9759)
Surface Mount Devices LLC ....G...... 203 322-8290
  Stamford (G-8452)
Times Microwave Systems Inc ....B...... 203 949-8400
  Wallingford (G-9386)
Winchester Interconnect Corp ....E...... 203 741-5400
  Norwalk (G-6395)

CONNECTORS: Power, Electric
Skyko International LLC ....G...... 860 928-5170
  Woodstock (G-10684)

CONSTRUCTION & MINING MACHINERY WHOLESALERS | PRODUCT SECTION

CONSTRUCTION & MINING MACHINERY WHOLESALERS

Bell Power Systems LLC .... D 860 767-7502
   Essex *(G-2712)*

CONSTRUCTION & ROAD MAINTENANCE EQPT: Drags, Road

Town of Wilton .... G 203 563-0152
   Wilton *(G-10338)*

CONSTRUCTION EQPT: Attachments

G L Yarocki & Company .... G 860 482-9215
   Torrington *(G-8928)*
Steelwrist Inc .... G 225 936-1111
   Berlin *(G-224)*

CONSTRUCTION EQPT: Attachments, Backhoe Mounted, Hyd Pwrd

Indeco North America Inc .... E 203 713-1030
   Milford *(G-4554)*

CONSTRUCTION EQPT: Backhoes, Tractors, Cranes & Similar Eqpt

CT Crane and Hoist Service LLC ...... G 860 283-4320
   Plymouth *(G-6928)*
Drum Crane and Rigging LLC .... G 860 837-4517
   East Hartford *(G-2315)*

CONSTRUCTION EQPT: Cranes

Bay Crane Service Conn Inc .... G 203 785-8000
   North Haven *(G-5913)*
Interstate Elec Svcs Corp .... E 860 243-5644
   Windsor *(G-10397)*
Terex Corporation .... F 203 222-7170
   Westport *(G-10163)*

CONSTRUCTION EQPT: Hammer Mills, Port, Incl Rock/Ore Crush

Numa Tool Company .... D 860 923-9551
   Thompson *(G-8841)*

CONSTRUCTION EQPT: Roofing Eqpt

Metal Plus LLC .... G 860 379-1327
   Winsted *(G-10528)*

CONSTRUCTION EQPT: Trucks, Off-Highway

Logans Run Trnsp Svc LLC .... G 203 679-0870
   Wallingford *(G-9305)*

CONSTRUCTION MATERIALS, WHOL: Concrete/Cinder Bldg Prdts

Washington Concrete Products .... F 860 747-5242
   Plainville *(G-6876)*

CONSTRUCTION MATERIALS, WHOLESALE: Block, Concrete & Cinder

New Milford Block & Supply .... F 860 355-1101
   New Milford *(G-5568)*

CONSTRUCTION MATERIALS, WHOLESALE: Blocks, Building, NEC

Hatch and Bailey Company .... E 203 866-5515
   Norwalk *(G-6193)*

CONSTRUCTION MATERIALS, WHOLESALE: Building Stone

Connecticut Stone Supplies Inc .... D 203 882-1000
   Milford *(G-4499)*
Hartford Stone Works Inc .... G 860 684-7995
   Willington *(G-10249)*
LH Gault & Son Incorporated .... D 203 227-5181
   Westport *(G-10112)*
Skyline Quarry .... G 860 875-3580
   Stafford Springs *(G-8038)*

CONSTRUCTION MATERIALS, WHOLESALE: Building Stone, Marble

American Stonecrafters Inc .... G 203 514-9725
   Wallingford *(G-9202)*
Pauls Marble Depot LLC .... F 203 978-0669
   Stamford *(G-8352)*
Pistritto Marble Imports Inc .... G 860 296-5263
   Hartford *(G-3664)*

CONSTRUCTION MATERIALS, WHOLESALE: Building, Exterior

Delvento Inc .... F 203 371-7279
   Bridgeport *(G-748)*
Devine Brothers Incorporated .... E 203 866-4421
   Norwalk *(G-6136)*

CONSTRUCTION MATERIALS, WHOLESALE: Cement

Lafarge North America Inc .... G 203 468-6068
   New Haven *(G-5314)*

CONSTRUCTION MATERIALS, WHOLESALE: Concrete Mixtures

Babcock & King Incorporated .... G 203 336-7989
   Fairfield *(G-2750)*
Devine Brothers Incorporated .... E 203 866-4421
   Norwalk *(G-6136)*

CONSTRUCTION MATERIALS, WHOLESALE: Fiberglass Building Mat

A Al Harding .... G 203 238-1993
   Meriden *(G-4137)*

CONSTRUCTION MATERIALS, WHOLESALE: Glass

Liberty Glass and Met Inds Inc .... E 860 923-3623
   North Grosvenordale *(G-5888)*
New Milford Block & Supply .... F 860 355-1101
   New Milford *(G-5568)*
U S Glass Distributors Inc .... E 860 741-3658
   Enfield *(G-2703)*

CONSTRUCTION MATERIALS, WHOLESALE: Insulation, Thermal

Stephen Hawrylik .... G 860 688-8651
   Windsor *(G-10444)*

CONSTRUCTION MATERIALS, WHOLESALE: Limestone

New England Stone Inc .... F 203 876-8606
   Milford *(G-4590)*

CONSTRUCTION MATERIALS, WHOLESALE: Millwork

Gary D Kryszat .... G 860 526-3145
   Chester *(G-1473)*

CONSTRUCTION MATERIALS, WHOLESALE: Molding, All Materials

Stelray Plastic Products Inc .... E 203 735-2331
   Ansonia *(G-52)*

CONSTRUCTION MATERIALS, WHOLESALE: Paneling, Wood

Bridgwell Rsurces Holdings LLC ...... G 203 622-9138
   Greenwich *(G-3137)*

CONSTRUCTION MATERIALS, WHOLESALE: Paving Materials

Lane Construction Corporation .... C 203 235-3351
   Cheshire *(G-1405)*
Lane Industries Incorporated .... G 203 235-3351
   Cheshire *(G-1406)*
Salin-Mpregilo US Holdings Inc ...... G 203 439-2900
   Cheshire *(G-1441)*

CONSTRUCTION MATERIALS, WHOLESALE: Prefabricated Structures

Bridgwell Rsurces Holdings LLC ...... G 203 622-9138
   Greenwich *(G-3137)*
Laydon Industries LLC .... D 203 562-7283
   New Haven *(G-5317)*

CONSTRUCTION MATERIALS, WHOLESALE: Roof, Asphalt/Sheet Metal

Epdm Coatings .... G 203 225-0104
   Shelton *(G-7441)*

CONSTRUCTION MATERIALS, WHOLESALE: Roofing & Siding Material

Dfs In-Home Services .... G 845 405-6464
   Danbury *(G-1794)*
Qba Inc .... G 860 963-9438
   Woodstock *(G-10679)*
Roofing Solutions .... G 860 444-0486
   New London *(G-5487)*

CONSTRUCTION MATERIALS, WHOLESALE: Sand

Adelman Sand & Gravel Inc .... E 860 889-3394
   Bozrah *(G-522)*
O & G Industries Inc .... D 203 263-2195
   Southbury *(G-7870)*
Tilcon Connecticut Inc .... G 860 224-6010
   New Britain *(G-5074)*
Tilcon Inc .... B 860 223-3651
   Newington *(G-5713)*
Windham Materials LLC .... G 860 456-4111
   Willimantic *(G-10241)*

CONSTRUCTION MATERIALS, WHOLESALE: Stone, Crushed Or Broken

Powder Hill Sand & Gravel LLC ...... G 860 741-7274
   Enfield *(G-2679)*
Tilcon Connecticut Inc .... E 860 844-7000
   East Granby *(G-2232)*

CONSTRUCTION MATL, WHOLESALE: Structural Assy, Prefab, Wood

Metalcraft LLC .... G 860 361-6767
   Bantam *(G-124)*

CONSTRUCTION MATLS, WHOL: Lumber, Rough, Dressed/Finished

Anstett Lumber Co .... G 860 491-3225
   Goshen *(G-3095)*
Hardwood Lumber Manufacturing .... E 860 423-2447
   Scotland *(G-7332)*
Hull Forest Products Inc .... E 860 974-0127
   Pomfret Center *(G-6939)*
River Mill Co .... F 860 669-5915
   Clinton *(G-1521)*

CONSTRUCTION SITE PREPARATION SVCS

Brian Reynolds .... G 860 267-2021
   East Hampton *(G-2259)*
Mud River Services .... G 860 767-0592
   Essex *(G-2727)*
Saugatuck Tree & Logging LLC ...... G 203 470-9195
   Brookfield *(G-1221)*
Saugatuck Tree & Logging LLC ...... G 203 304-1326
   Newtown *(G-5778)*

CONSTRUCTION: Airport Runway

Lane Construction Corporation .... C 203 235-3351
   Cheshire *(G-1405)*
Lane Industries Incorporated .... G 203 235-3351
   Cheshire *(G-1406)*
Salin-Mpregilo US Holdings Inc ...... G 203 439-2900
   Cheshire *(G-1441)*

CONSTRUCTION: Athletic & Recreation Facilities

Quicksand Blasting .... G 860 848-4482
   Uncasville *(G-9103)*

CONSTRUCTION: Commercial & Institutional Building

Central Construction Inds LLC..............E...... 860 963-8902
  Putnam (G-7033)
Mud River Services..................................G...... 860 767-0592
  Essex (G-2727)

CONSTRUCTION: Commercial & Office Building, New

Brennan Realty LLC................................C...... 203 929-6314
  Shelton (G-7409)
Charles A Boucher Co Inc.......................G...... 860 868-2881
  Washington (G-9412)
Edward Tomkievich..................................G...... 860 633-5811
  Glastonbury (G-3032)
Kafa Group LLC..G...... 475 275-0090
  Bridgeport (G-812)
O & G Industries Inc...............................E...... 203 748-5694
  Danbury (G-1897)
O & G Industries Inc...............................F...... 203 729-4529
  Beacon Falls (G-146)
O & G Industries Inc...............................D...... 860 354-4438
  New Milford (G-5576)
O & G Industries Inc...............................D...... 203 263-2195
  Southbury (G-7870)
O & G Industries Inc...............................E...... 203 323-1111
  Stamford (G-8336)
O & G Industries Inc...............................E...... 203 366-4586
  Bridgeport (G-854)
Pds Engineering & Cnstr Inc...................E...... 860 242-8586
  Bloomfield (G-462)
Xavier Marcus..G...... 203 543-2032
  Stratford (G-8711)

CONSTRUCTION: Curb

Winthrop Construction LLC....................G...... 860 322-4562
  Deep River (G-2106)

CONSTRUCTION: Drainage System

LH Gault & Son Incorporated.................D...... 203 227-5181
  Westport (G-10112)

CONSTRUCTION: Elevated Highway

Lane Construction Corporation..............C...... 203 235-3351
  Cheshire (G-1405)
Lane Industries Incorporated.................G...... 203 235-3351
  Cheshire (G-1406)
Salin-Mpregilo US Holdings Inc.............G...... 203 439-2900
  Cheshire (G-1441)

CONSTRUCTION: Guardrails, Highway

Atlas Industrial Services LLC................E...... 203 315-4538
  Branford (G-549)

CONSTRUCTION: Heavy Highway & Street

Berlin Industries LLC..............................G...... 860 819-9997
  Berlin (G-163)
Winthrop Construction LLC....................G...... 860 322-4562
  Deep River (G-2106)

CONSTRUCTION: Indl Buildings, New, NEC

Division X Specialties LLC.....................G...... 860 402-7736
  Vernon (G-9137)
Kafa Group LLC..G...... 475 275-0090
  Bridgeport (G-812)
Pds Engineering & Cnstr Inc...................E...... 860 242-8586
  Bloomfield (G-462)

CONSTRUCTION: Institutional Building

Windham Materials LLC..........................D...... 860 456-4111
  Willimantic (G-10241)

CONSTRUCTION: Oil & Gas Line & Compressor Station

Marks Construction Co LLC....................G...... 860 407-2391
  Portland (G-6965)

CONSTRUCTION: Power Plant

Apcompower Inc.......................................E...... 860 688-1911
  Windsor (G-10362)

CONSTRUCTION: Residential, Nec

Charles A Boucher Co Inc.......................G...... 860 868-2881
  Washington (G-9412)
Connectcut Shreline Developers............G...... 860 669-4424
  Clinton (G-1496)
Interntonal MBL Gran Entps Inc.............G...... 860 296-0741
  Hartford (G-3618)
Rk Stucco LLC..G...... 860 331-1791
  New Britain (G-5046)
United-Bim Inc..G...... 860 289-1100
  East Hartford (G-2398)

CONSTRUCTION: Single-Family Housing

Bhs...G...... 860 585-0125
  Bristol (G-983)
C J Brand & Son.......................................G...... 860 536-9266
  Mystic (G-4803)
Central Construction Inds LLC..............E...... 860 963-8902
  Putnam (G-7033)
Country Carpenters Inc............................G...... 860 228-2276
  Hebron (G-3746)
Country Log Homes Inc...........................F...... 413 229-8084
  Goshen (G-3097)
Eastern Electric Cnstr Co........................G...... 860 485-1100
  Harwinton (G-3726)
Edward Tomkievich..................................G...... 860 633-5811
  Glastonbury (G-3032)
Hanford Cabinet & Wdwkg Co................G...... 860 388-5055
  Old Saybrook (G-6538)
United-Bim Inc..G...... 860 289-1100
  East Hartford (G-2398)
Winthrop Construction LLC....................G...... 860 322-4562
  Deep River (G-2106)

CONSTRUCTION: Single-family Housing, New

B & R Stair..G...... 860 582-6584
  Bristol (G-970)
Michael Martinetto...................................G...... 203 874-6114
  Milford (G-4577)
Post & Beam Homes Inc..........................G...... 860 267-2060
  East Hampton (G-2274)
Richard Riggio and Sons Inc..................E...... 860 767-0812
  Ivoryton (G-3789)

CONSTRUCTION: Subway

Lane Construction Corporation..............C...... 203 235-3351
  Cheshire (G-1405)
Lane Industries Incorporated.................G...... 203 235-3351
  Cheshire (G-1406)
Salin-Mpregilo US Holdings Inc.............G...... 203 439-2900
  Cheshire (G-1441)

CONSTRUCTION: Swimming Pools

Fairfield Pool & Equipment Co...............G...... 203 334-3600
  Fairfield (G-2785)
Group Works..G...... 203 834-7905
  Wilton (G-10299)

CONSTRUCTION: Utility Line

Brennan Realty LLC................................C...... 203 929-6314
  Shelton (G-7409)

CONSTRUCTION: Water & Sewer Line

Ecosystem Consulting Svc Inc...............G...... 860 742-0744
  Coventry (G-1653)

CONSULTING SVC: Actuarial

Computer Prgrm & Systems Inc............G...... 203 324-9203
  Stamford (G-8155)

CONSULTING SVC: Business, NEC

Anchor Science LLC................................G...... 203 231-6181
  Branford (G-545)
Anderson David C & Assoc LLC............F...... 860 749-7547
  Enfield (G-2615)
Childrens Health Market Inc...................G...... 203 762-2938
  Wilton (G-10280)
Cobra Green LLC.....................................A...... 203 354-5000
  Norwalk (G-6118)
DAmbruoso Studios LLC.........................G...... 203 758-9660
  Middlebury (G-4276)
Dufrane Nuclear Shielding Inc................F...... 860 379-2318
  Winsted (G-10516)

Eagle Consulting LLC..............................G...... 203 445-1740
  Trumbull (G-9023)
Etron LLC..G...... 860 673-0121
  Burlington (G-1268)
Fabcon Inc...G...... 860 485-9019
  Harwinton (G-3728)
Fieldstone Cnsulting Group LLC............G...... 203 610-5592
  Easton (G-2553)
Kathleen Parker OBeirne........................G...... 860 536-7179
  Mystic (G-4824)
KB Services..G...... 203 243-3594
  Bridgeport (G-814)
Learners Dimension................................G...... 860 228-1236
  Columbia (G-1607)
Light Speed LLC......................................G...... 203 248-8550
  Hamden (G-3475)
Mc Keon Computer Services..................G...... 860 496-7171
  Torrington (G-8947)
Octavo Editions LLC................................G...... 860 388-5772
  Old Saybrook (G-6562)
Vertech Inc..G...... 203 876-1552
  Milford (G-4673)
Video Automation Systems Inc..............G...... 203 312-0152
  New Fairfield (G-5182)

CONSULTING SVC: Chemical

Innophase Corp..G...... 860 399-2269
  Westbrook (G-9998)

CONSULTING SVC: Computer

Aerial Imaging Solutions LLC.................G...... 203 434-3637
  Old Lyme (G-6488)
Alphacom Inc..G...... 203 637-7006
  Greenwich (G-3117)
Amsys Inc..E...... 203 431-8814
  Ridgefield (G-7116)
Blackrock Media Inc................................G...... 203 374-0369
  Easton (G-2547)
Brown Larkin & Co LLC..........................G...... 860 280-8858
  Burlington (G-1261)
Clear & Simple Inc..................................G...... 860 658-1204
  West Simsbury (G-9974)
Computer Support People LLC..............G...... 203 653-4643
  Norwalk (G-6122)
David Smith...G...... 860 877-3232
  Southington (G-7911)
E G Tech Solutions LLC..........................G...... 203 200-7047
  Old Greenwich (G-6471)
Fieldstone Cnsulting Group LLC............G...... 203 610-5592
  Easton (G-2553)
Information Tech Intl Corp......................G...... 860 648-2570
  Manchester (G-4033)
Isupportws Inc..F...... 203 569-7600
  Stamford (G-8260)
Link Systems Inc.....................................F...... 203 274-9702
  Stamford (G-8285)
Management Software Inc......................G...... 860 536-5177
  Ledyard (G-3877)
Oracle America Inc.................................D...... 203 703-3000
  Stamford (G-8345)
Process Automtn Solutions Inc..............E...... 203 207-9917
  Danbury (G-1920)
Schulz Consulting LLC............................G...... 860 657-4497
  Glastonbury (G-3082)
Technical Consulting...............................G...... 203 268-8890
  Monroe (G-4757)
Thomas Meade...G...... 203 209-7591
  Shelton (G-7565)
Travers & Co LLC....................................G...... 860 633-8586
  Glastonbury (G-3089)
Woods End Inc..G...... 203 226-6303
  Weston (G-10047)

CONSULTING SVC: Data Processing

Advanced Sonics LLC.............................G...... 203 266-4440
  Oxford (G-6639)
DSar Company...G...... 203 324-6456
  Stamford (G-8189)
Mc Keon Computer Services..................G...... 860 496-7171
  Torrington (G-8947)
Shiloh Software Inc.................................G...... 203 272-8456
  Cheshire (G-1445)

CONSULTING SVC: Educational

Bunting & Lyon Inc..................................G...... 203 272-4623
  Cheshire (G-1365)

CONSULTING SVC: Engineering

- Applied Physical Sciences Corp ....D....... 860 448-3253
  Groton *(G-3271)*
- Cloud Cap Technology Inc ....G....... 541 308-1089
  Danbury *(G-1770)*
- Computer Technologies Corp ....G....... 860 683-4030
  Windsor *(G-10376)*
- Cummins Enviro Tech Inc ....F....... 860 388-6377
  Old Lyme *(G-6499)*
- Doctor Stuff LLC ....G....... 203 785-8475
  Wallingford *(G-9252)*
- Faxon Engineering Company Inc ....F....... 860 236-4266
  Bloomfield *(G-410)*
- Pacific Engineering Inc ....G....... 860 677-0795
  Farmington *(G-2944)*
- Peregrine Technical Svcs LLC ....G....... 813 469-9355
  Colchester *(G-1563)*
- SEI II Inc ....F....... 203 877-8488
  Milford *(G-4641)*
- Sonalysts Inc ....B....... 860 442-4355
  Waterford *(G-9672)*
- TP Cycle & Engineering Inc ....E....... 203 744-4960
  Danbury *(G-1964)*

CONSULTING SVC: Financial Management

- Pricing Excellence LLC ....G....... 866 557-8102
  Suffield *(G-8730)*

CONSULTING SVC: Human Resource

- Fieldstone Cnsulting Group LLC ....G....... 203 610-5592
  Easton *(G-2553)*

CONSULTING SVC: Management

- American Marketing Group Inc ....G....... 203 367-2378
  Bridgeport *(G-693)*
- Blackrock Media Inc ....G....... 203 374-0369
  Easton *(G-2547)*
- Brown Larkin & Co LLC ....G....... 860 280-8858
  Burlington *(G-1261)*
- Ca Inc ....E....... 800 225-5224
  East Windsor *(G-2487)*
- Chief Executive Group LLC ....F....... 785 832-0303
  Stamford *(G-8143)*
- Chief Executive Group LP ....E....... 203 930-2700
  Stamford *(G-8144)*
- Computer Prgrm & Systems Inc ....G....... 203 324-9203
  Stamford *(G-8155)*
- DAmbruoso Studios LLC ....G....... 203 758-9660
  Middlebury *(G-4276)*
- De Villiers Incorporated ....G....... 203 966-9645
  New Canaan *(G-5101)*
- Enginuity Plm LLC ....F....... 203 218-7225
  Milford *(G-4532)*
- Ensign-Bickford Industries Inc ....E....... 860 658-4411
  Simsbury *(G-7622)*
- Forecast International Inc ....D....... 203 426-0800
  Newtown *(G-5739)*
- O & W Heat Treat Inc ....F....... 860 528-9239
  South Windsor *(G-7799)*
- Peter Ortali & Associates LLC ....G....... 203 571-8023
  Sandy Hook *(G-7325)*
- Rothstein Associates Inc ....G....... 203 740-7400
  Brookfield *(G-1219)*
- Stonington Services LLC ....E....... 860 464-1991
  Gales Ferry *(G-2987)*
- Varpro Inc ....E....... 203 227-6876
  Westport *(G-10171)*

CONSULTING SVC: Marketing Management

- AAR Results LLC ....G....... 203 627-2193
  Branford *(G-535)*
- Fairfield Marketing Group Inc ....F....... 203 261-0884
  Easton *(G-2552)*
- Fusion Cross-Media LLC ....G....... 860 647-8367
  Manchester *(G-4020)*
- Ihs Herold Inc ....D....... 203 857-0215
  Norwalk *(G-6204)*
- Intersec LLC ....G....... 860 985-3158
  Rocky Hill *(G-7251)*
- Kenneth Finn ....G....... 914 764-4938
  Greenwich *(G-3187)*
- Park Group Solutions LLC ....G....... 203 459-8784
  Newtown *(G-5769)*
- Phocuswright Inc ....E....... 860 350-4084
  Sherman *(G-7601)*
- Sabol Associates ....G....... 203 762-2183
  Wilton *(G-10326)*

- The Merrill Anderson Co Inc ....F....... 203 377-4996
  Stratford *(G-8694)*
- Web Savvy Marketers LLC ....G....... 860 432-8756
  East Hartford *(G-2401)*
- Wrenfield Group Inc ....E....... 203 438-0090
  Ridgefield *(G-7186)*

CONSULTING SVC: Telecommunications

- Positive Ventures LLC ....G....... 860 499-0599
  Bloomfield *(G-468)*

CONSULTING SVCS, BUSINESS: Communications

- Joseph Merritt & Company Inc ....E....... 860 296-2500
  Hartford *(G-3620)*
- Marlin Company ....D....... 203 294-9800
  Wallingford *(G-9312)*

CONSULTING SVCS, BUSINESS: Economic

- Park Group Solutions LLC ....G....... 203 459-8784
  Newtown *(G-5769)*

CONSULTING SVCS, BUSINESS: Energy Conservation

- New Resources Group Inc ....G....... 203 366-1000
  Bridgeport *(G-850)*

CONSULTING SVCS, BUSINESS: Environmental

- Cummins Envirotech ....G....... 860 598-9564
  Old Lyme *(G-6500)*
- Ecosystem Consulting Svc Inc ....G....... 860 742-0744
  Coventry *(G-1653)*
- Max Analytical Tech Inc ....E....... 989 772-5088
  East Windsor *(G-2510)*
- Rain Cii Carbon LLC ....F....... 203 406-0535
  Stamford *(G-8385)*

CONSULTING SVCS, BUSINESS: Publishing

- Editors Only ....G....... 860 881-2300
  New Britain *(G-4979)*
- Gleason Group Incorporated ....G....... 203 312-0683
  New Fairfield *(G-5168)*
- New England Publishing Assoc ....G....... 860 345-7323
  Higganum *(G-3771)*
- Toni Leland ....G....... 860 892-8890
  Uncasville *(G-9106)*
- Ubm LLC ....E....... 203 662-6501
  Darien *(G-2048)*

CONSULTING SVCS, BUSINESS: Safety Training Svcs

- Sugar Run K9 LLC ....G....... 860 591-4193
  Voluntown *(G-9191)*

CONSULTING SVCS, BUSINESS: Sys Engnrg, Exc Computer/Prof

- E G Tech Solutions LLC ....G....... 203 200-7047
  Old Greenwich *(G-6471)*
- High Voltage Outsourcing LLC ....G....... 203 456-3101
  Danbury *(G-1844)*
- Sonalysts Inc ....B....... 860 442-4355
  Waterford *(G-9672)*

CONSULTING SVCS, BUSINESS: Traffic

- Preusser Research Group Inc ....F....... 203 459-8700
  Trumbull *(G-9056)*

CONSULTING SVCS: Oil

- Clean Ocean Technology ....G....... 401 212-8171
  Pawcatuck *(G-6705)*
- Nytex Petroleum Inc ....G....... 203 261-6329
  Westport *(G-10131)*
- Patriot Oil Heat LLC ....G....... 860 928-4091
  Woodstock *(G-10676)*
- Taylor Energy ....G....... 860 623-3309
  East Windsor *(G-2526)*

CONSULTING SVCS: Scientific

- Scry Health Inc ....F....... 203 936-8244
  Woodbridge *(G-10616)*

- Stein Laboratories LLC ....G....... 203 853-9500
  Norwalk *(G-6356)*

CONSUMER ELECTRONICS STORE: Video & Disc Recorder/Player

- Krystal Inc LLC ....G....... 860 844-1267
  Granby *(G-3110)*

CONTACT LENSES

- Opticare Eye Health & Vision ....G....... 203 261-2619
  Trumbull *(G-9052)*

CONTACTS: Electrical

- Deringer-Ney Inc ....C....... 860 242-2281
  Bloomfield *(G-407)*

CONTAINERS, GLASS: Cosmetic Jars

- Palmer Deep Draw Stamping LLC ....G....... 860 880-8022
  Thomaston *(G-8800)*

CONTAINERS, GLASS: Medicine Bottles

- Matthew Fisel ND ....G....... 203 453-0122
  Guilford *(G-3371)*

CONTAINERS: Cargo, Wood & Metal Combination

- Tcc Multi Kargo ....G....... 203 803-1462
  Norwalk *(G-6363)*

CONTAINERS: Corrugated

- Cascades Holding US Inc ....D....... 203 426-5871
  Newtown *(G-5732)*
- Fortis Solutions Group LLC ....G....... 860 872-6311
  Ellington *(G-2590)*
- Gbc Marketing LLC ....G....... 860 739-8760
  Niantic *(G-5807)*
- Kapstone Paper and Packg Corp ....G....... 860 928-2211
  Putnam *(G-7051)*
- Rice Packaging Inc ....D....... 860 870-7057
  Ellington *(G-2598)*
- Westrock Rkt Company ....F....... 203 739-0318
  Bethel *(G-365)*

CONTAINERS: Food & Beverage

- Inspired Brands Intl LLC ....G....... 203 722-5629
  Weston *(G-10028)*
- Silgan Holdings Inc ....C....... 203 975-7110
  Stamford *(G-8421)*

CONTAINERS: Glass

- Emhart Glass Manufacturing Inc ....E....... 860 298-7340
  Windsor *(G-10384)*

CONTAINERS: Metal

- Architectural Supplements LLC ....F....... 203 591-5505
  Waterbury *(G-9433)*
- Champlin-Packrite Inc ....F....... 860 951-9217
  Manchester *(G-3994)*
- Connecticut Container Corp ....C....... 203 248-2161
  North Haven *(G-5924)*

CONTAINERS: Plastic

- American Metaseal of Conn ....G....... 203 787-0281
  Hamden *(G-3414)*
- Architectural Supplements LLC ....F....... 203 591-5505
  Waterbury *(G-9433)*
- CKS Packaging Inc ....D....... 203 729-0716
  Naugatuck *(G-4868)*
- Clearly Clean Products LLC ....F....... 860 646-1040
  South Windsor *(G-7729)*
- Cool-It LLC ....G....... 203 284-4848
  Wallingford *(G-9239)*
- Jarden Corporation ....E....... 203 845-5300
  Norwalk *(G-6218)*
- Jarden Corporation ....G....... 203 264-9717
  Oxford *(G-6670)*
- Select Plastics LLC ....G....... 203 866-3767
  Norwalk *(G-6342)*
- Silgan Holdings Inc ....C....... 203 975-7110
  Stamford *(G-8421)*
- Silgan Plastics LLC ....C....... 860 526-6300
  Deep River *(G-2100)*

PRODUCT SECTION

CONTRACTORS: Floor Laying & Other Floor Work

Upc LLC .... G 877 466-1137
  Meriden *(G-4261)*

CONTAINERS: Sanitary, Food
James River Corp .... G 203 854-2328
  Norwalk *(G-6217)*

CONTAINERS: Shipping, Wood
Champlin-Packrite Inc .... E 860 951-9217
  Manchester *(G-3994)*

CONTAINERS: Wood
Vermont Pallet & Skid Shop .... G 860 822-6949
  Norwich *(G-6437)*
Westwood Products Inc .... F 860 379-9401
  Winsted *(G-10543)*

CONTRACTORS: Asphalt
Christopher Annelli .... G 860 537-4397
  Colchester *(G-1545)*
O & G Industries Inc .... E 203 366-4586
  Bridgeport *(G-854)*

CONTRACTORS: Awning Installation
Fitzgerald-Norwalk Awning Co .... G 203 847-5858
  Norwalk *(G-6169)*
Tetrault & Sons Inc .... G 860 872-9187
  Stafford Springs *(G-8042)*

CONTRACTORS: Blasting, Exc Building Demolition
Coleman Drilling & Blasting .... G 860 376-3813
  Voluntown *(G-9188)*

CONTRACTORS: Boiler & Furnace
Connectcut Boiler Repr Mfg Inc .... E 860 953-9117
  West Hartford *(G-9793)*

CONTRACTORS: Building Eqpt & Machinery Installation
Atlantic Eqp Installers Inc .... E 203 284-0402
  Wallingford *(G-9213)*

CONTRACTORS: Building Front Installation, Metal
All Phase Steel Works LLC .... D 203 375-8881
  New Haven *(G-5222)*

CONTRACTORS: Building Sign Installation & Mntnce
Adamsahern Sign Solutions Inc .... F 860 523-8835
  Hartford *(G-3547)*
Archer Sign Service LLC .... G 203 882-8484
  Milford *(G-4454)*
Derrick Mason .... G 413 527-4282
  Norwich *(G-6410)*
Post Sign Specialists .... G 203 723-8448
  Naugatuck *(G-4912)*
Tims Sign & Lighting Service .... G 203 634-8840
  Meriden *(G-4256)*
Wad Inc .... E 860 828-3331
  East Berlin *(G-2179)*

CONTRACTORS: Carpentry Work
Agw Clssic Hardwood Floors LLC .... E 203 640-3106
  Westbrook *(G-9989)*
Diiorio Woodworks .... G 203 855-1331
  Norwalk *(G-6143)*
Owh LLC .... E 860 693-9464
  Canton *(G-1323)*

CONTRACTORS: Carpentry, Cabinet & Finish Work
Custom Woodwork Etc .... G 860 638-1006
  Middletown *(G-4334)*
Frates Custom Cabinetry .... G 203 994-1108
  Sandy Hook *(G-7312)*
Industrial Wood Product Co .... G 203 735-2374
  Shelton *(G-7475)*
Martel Woodworking Co .... G 860 564-1983
  Plainfield *(G-6748)*

St Johns Bridge LLC .... G 860 927-3315
  Kent *(G-3826)*

CONTRACTORS: Carpentry, Cabinet Building & Installation
Custom Crft Ktchns By Rizio BR .... F 203 268-0271
  Monroe *(G-4708)*
Daniel Richardson .... G 860 774-3675
  Danielson *(G-1988)*
S J Pappas Inc .... G 203 237-7701
  Meriden *(G-4236)*

CONTRACTORS: Chimney Construction & Maintenance
Vincent Masonry .... G 860 836-5916
  New Britain *(G-5081)*

CONTRACTORS: Closed Circuit Television Installation
Command Corporation .... F 800 851-6012
  East Granby *(G-2198)*

CONTRACTORS: Coating, Caulking & Weather, Water & Fire
Courtman Enterprises LLC .... G 860 322-2837
  Windsor *(G-10378)*
Northeast Sealcoat Inc .... G 860 953-4400
  West Hartford *(G-9839)*

CONTRACTORS: Commercial & Office Building
EMJ Contracting LLC .... G 475 449-7725
  Bridgeport *(G-762)*
United-Bim Inc .... G 860 289-1100
  East Hartford *(G-2398)*

CONTRACTORS: Communications Svcs
General Datacomm Inc .... E 203 729-0271
  Oxford *(G-6661)*

CONTRACTORS: Computer Installation
Brian Cheney .... G 203 734-4793
  Seymour *(G-7336)*

CONTRACTORS: Computer Power Conditioning Svcs
On Line Building Systems LLC .... G 203 798-1194
  Danbury *(G-1899)*

CONTRACTORS: Concrete
A Aiudi & Sons LLC .... G 860 747-5534
  Plainville *(G-6759)*
Concrete Coring Co Conn Inc .... G 203 287-8400
  Hamden *(G-3430)*
Coreslab Structures Conn Inc .... D 860 283-8281
  Thomaston *(G-8786)*
J J Concrete Foundations .... G 203 798-8310
  Bethel *(G-315)*

CONTRACTORS: Construction Site Cleanup
J & M Plumbing & Cnstr LLC .... F 860 319-3082
  Norwich *(G-6418)*

CONTRACTORS: Countertop Installation
Custom Crft Ktchns By Rizio BR .... F 203 268-0271
  Monroe *(G-4708)*
Jf Granite & Marble .... G 860 355-4414
  New Milford *(G-5550)*
Salem Stone Design Inc .... F 860 439-1234
  Waterford *(G-9668)*

CONTRACTORS: Demolition, Building & Other Structures
Laydon Industries LLC .... D 203 562-7283
  New Haven *(G-5317)*
Owh LLC .... E 860 693-9464
  Canton *(G-1323)*

CONTRACTORS: Directional Oil & Gas Well Drilling Svc
Directional Technologies Inc .... G 203 294-9200
  Wallingford *(G-9250)*
Millbrae Energy LLC .... F 203 742-2800
  Greenwich *(G-3203)*

CONTRACTORS: Electric Power Systems
Ac/DC Industrial Electric LLC .... G 860 886-2232
  Yantic *(G-10695)*

CONTRACTORS: Electrical
American Railway Technologies .... G 860 291-1170
  East Hartford *(G-2290)*
C & E Electric .... G 203 546-7255
  Brookfield *(G-1167)*
Carter Inv Holdings Corp .... G 860 283-5801
  Thomaston *(G-8783)*
E-J Electric T & D LLC .... D 203 626-9625
  Wallingford *(G-9256)*
Eastern Electric Cnstr Co .... G 860 485-1100
  Harwinton *(G-3726)*
Eastside Electric Inc .... F 860 485-0700
  Harwinton *(G-3727)*
Modern Electronic Fax & Cmpt .... G 203 292-6520
  Fairfield *(G-2816)*
Power Up Electric .... G 203 312-0601
  Danbury *(G-1910)*
T J Russell Electric LLC .... G 203 791-8950
  Danbury *(G-1958)*
Ward Leonard Holdings LLC .... G 860 283-5801
  Thomaston *(G-8820)*
Ward Leonard Inv Holdings LLC .... G 860 283-5801
  Thomaston *(G-8821)*
Ward Leonard Operating LLC .... G 860 283-5801
  Thomaston *(G-8822)*
Ward Lonard Houma Holdings LLC ... G 860 283-5801
  Thomaston *(G-8823)*
Wl Intermediate Holdings LLC .... G 860 283-5801
  Thomaston *(G-8825)*

CONTRACTORS: Electronic Controls Installation
Interstate Elec Svcs Corp .... E 860 243-5644
  Windsor *(G-10397)*

CONTRACTORS: Energy Management Control
Universal Building Contrls Inc .... F 203 235-1530
  Meriden *(G-4260)*

CONTRACTORS: Excavating
Core Site Services LLC .... G 475 227-9026
  New Haven *(G-5264)*
Desiato Sand & Gravel Corp .... E 860 429-6479
  Storrs Mansfield *(G-8555)*
Svl LLC .... G 860 819-9929
  Avon *(G-116)*
Thomas Keegan & Sons Inc .... G 203 239-9248
  North Haven *(G-5999)*

CONTRACTORS: Exterior Concrete Stucco
Vincent Masonry .... G 860 836-5916
  New Britain *(G-5081)*

CONTRACTORS: Fence Construction
E&D Landscaping .... G 203 934-4088
  West Haven *(G-9905)*
Paoletti Fence Company Inc .... G 860 296-0396
  Hartford *(G-3660)*
Wayside Fence Co .... G 860 594-1090
  Newington *(G-5722)*

CONTRACTORS: Floor Laying & Other Floor Work
Artistic Hardwood Floors CT .... G 860 537-5334
  Colchester *(G-1540)*
Diamond Hrdwd Flrs of Fairfld .... G 203 650-9192
  Bridgeport *(G-751)*
Interntonal MBL Gran Entps Inc .... G 860 296-0741
  Hartford *(G-3618)*
Jgf Hardwood Floor .... G 203 650-9192
  Bridgeport *(G-805)*

Employee Codes: A=Over 500 employees, B=251-500
C=101-250, D=51-100, E=20-50, F=10-19, G=1-9

2020 Harris Connecticut Manufacturers Directory

CONTRACTORS: Floor Laying & Other Floor Work

Ultimate Hardwood Floors ....G....... 203 746-9692
 New Fairfield *(G-5181)*

CONTRACTORS: Flooring

Alliance Carpet Cushion Co..................D....... 860 489-4273
 Torrington *(G-8889)*
Artistic Hardwood Floors CT ....G....... 860 537-5334
 Colchester *(G-1540)*
Diamond Hrdwd Flrs of Fairfld ....G....... 203 650-9192
 Bridgeport *(G-751)*
Jgf Hardwood Floor ....G....... 203 650-9192
 Bridgeport *(G-805)*
Ultimate Hardwood Floors ....G....... 203 746-9692
 New Fairfield *(G-5181)*

CONTRACTORS: Garage Doors

Eric Sapper..G....... 203 239-6020
 North Haven *(G-5938)*

CONTRACTORS: Gas Detection & Analysis Svcs

Bruce Corey Enterprises Inc................G....... 203 272-3600
 Wolcott *(G-10550)*

CONTRACTORS: Gas Field Svcs, NEC

Pro Gas Installation & Svc LLC ....G....... 860 982-1370
 East Hampton *(G-2275)*

CONTRACTORS: General Electric

Louis Electric Co Inc ....G....... 203 879-5483
 Wolcott *(G-10571)*
Richter Electric Inc ....G....... 203 667-4644
 Darien *(G-2041)*
Tri State Maintenance Svcs LLC..........F....... 203 691-1343
 North Haven *(G-6001)*

CONTRACTORS: Glass Tinting, Architectural & Automotive

Onpoint Connections ....G....... 860 253-0489
 Enfield *(G-2673)*

CONTRACTORS: Glass, Glazing & Tinting

Kensington Glass and Frmng Co ....G....... 860 828-9428
 Berlin *(G-192)*
Liberty Glass and Met Inds Inc ....E....... 860 923-3623
 North Grosvenordale *(G-5888)*
New Haven GL & Mirror Co LLC ....G....... 203 469-2440
 New Haven *(G-5344)*

CONTRACTORS: Grave Excavation

Core Site Services LLC ....G....... 475 227-9026
 New Haven *(G-5264)*

CONTRACTORS: Gutters & Downspouts

Toms Seamless Gutters Inc................G....... 203 269-2296
 Wallingford *(G-9389)*

CONTRACTORS: Heating & Air Conditioning

Airtech of Stamford Inc ....E....... 203 323-3959
 Stamford *(G-8070)*
East Coast Sheet Metal LLC ....F....... 860 283-1126
 Litchfield *(G-3888)*
M J Williams Heating and AC ....G....... 860 923-6991
 Woodstock *(G-10670)*
McVac Environmental Svcs Inc ....E....... 203 497-1960
 New Haven *(G-5327)*
Northern Comfort Mech LLC..............G....... 203 456-5163
 Danbury *(G-1895)*

CONTRACTORS: Heating Systems Repair & Maintenance Svc

Zampell Refractories Inc ....F....... 860 564-2883
 Plainfield *(G-6757)*

CONTRACTORS: Highway & Street Paving

Tilcon Connecticut Inc ....D....... 860 224-6010
 New Britain *(G-5074)*
Tilcon Inc ....B....... 860 223-3651
 Newington *(G-5713)*
Westchester Industries Inc ....F....... 203 661-0055
 Greenwich *(G-3257)*

CONTRACTORS: Highway Sign & Guardrail Construction & Install

Laydon Industries LLC ....D....... 203 562-7283
 New Haven *(G-5317)*

CONTRACTORS: Home & Office Intrs Finish, Furnish/Remodel

Rahzel Enterprize LLC ....G....... 475 449-6561
 Norwalk *(G-6315)*

CONTRACTORS: Hydraulic Eqpt Installation & Svcs

B L C Investments Inc ....G....... 203 877-1888
 Milford *(G-4464)*

CONTRACTORS: Insulation Installation, Building

Ecologic Energy Solutions LLC ....E....... 203 889-0505
 Stamford *(G-8192)*

CONTRACTORS: Kitchen & Bathroom Remodeling

Bender Management Inc ....G....... 203 847-3865
 Norwalk *(G-6091)*
Fiberglass Repairs & ....G....... 860 628-4962
 Southington *(G-7923)*
New England Stone Inc ....F....... 203 876-8606
 Milford *(G-4590)*
Roman Woodworking ....G....... 860 490-5989
 New Britain *(G-5047)*

CONTRACTORS: Lighting Conductor Erection

Woods Lightning Protection ....G....... 203 929-1868
 Shelton *(G-7588)*

CONTRACTORS: Machinery Installation

Mc Clintock Manufacturing ....G....... 203 263-4743
 Woodbury *(G-10642)*

CONTRACTORS: Marble Installation, Interior

Arts of Stone LLC ....G....... 860 355-9468
 New Milford *(G-5507)*

CONTRACTORS: Marble Masonry, Exterior

Mike Fineran ....G....... 860 974-3276
 Pomfret Center *(G-6942)*

CONTRACTORS: Masonry & Stonework

John Canning & Co Ltd ....E....... 203 272-9868
 Cheshire *(G-1401)*

CONTRACTORS: Mechanical

Link Mechanical Services Inc ....E....... 860 826-5880
 New Britain *(G-5011)*

CONTRACTORS: Oil & Gas Well Drilling Svc

Coleman Drilling & Blasting...............G....... 860 376-3813
 Voluntown *(G-9188)*
Eows Midland Inc ....E....... 203 358-5705
 Stamford *(G-8196)*
Louis E Allyn Sons Inc ....G....... 860 542-5741
 Norfolk *(G-5825)*
Mercuria Energy Trading Inc..............G....... 203 413-3355
 Greenwich *(G-3202)*
Sterling Gas Drlg Fund 1982 LP ....G....... 203 358-5700
 Stamford *(G-8442)*
Total Drilling Supply LLC ....G....... 860 923-1091
 Thompson *(G-8844)*

CONTRACTORS: Oil Field Lease Tanks: Erectg, Clng/Rprg Svcs

Palmieri Industries Inc......................D....... 203 384-6020
 Bridgeport *(G-859)*

CONTRACTORS: Oil Field Pipe Testing Svcs

A & C Connection Inspection ....G....... 203 287-8504
 Hamden *(G-3408)*

CONTRACTORS: Oil/Gas Well Construction, Rpr/Dismantling Svcs

Alliance Energy LLC ....G....... 203 933-2511
 New Haven *(G-5223)*
Alterio Tractor Pulling LLC ....G....... 203 305-9812
 Oxford *(G-6642)*
Arts of Stone LLC ....G....... 860 355-9468
 New Milford *(G-5507)*
Bruce Burgess ....G....... 860 510-9185
 Middletown *(G-4328)*
Buon Appetito From Italy LLC ....G....... 860 437-3668
 New London *(G-5460)*
Connectcut Shreline Developers..........G....... 860 669-4424
 Clinton *(G-1496)*
East Coast Pulling Parts LLC ....G....... 860 234-4285
 Danielson *(G-1991)*
J & M Plumbing & Cnstr LLC ....F....... 860 319-3082
 Norwich *(G-6418)*
James & Co LLC ....G....... 860 897-6242
 Bloomfield *(G-426)*
John Cutter......................................G....... 860 749-0015
 Somers *(G-7663)*
Kafa Group LLC ....G....... 475 275-0090
 Bridgeport *(G-812)*
My Slide Lines LLC ....G....... 203 324-1642
 Norwalk *(G-6267)*
Reac Ready LLC ....G....... 860 760-8886
 Avon *(G-103)*
Rk Stucco LLC ....G....... 860 331-1791
 New Britain *(G-5046)*
Staxx Construction Svcs LLC..............G....... 860 259-5003
 Berlin *(G-223)*
Summit Birch Hill ....G....... 860 677-2763
 Farmington *(G-2961)*
Tri State Maintenance Svcs LLC..........F....... 203 691-1343
 North Haven *(G-6001)*
W M G and Sons Inc ....G....... 860 584-0143
 Bristol *(G-1136)*

CONTRACTORS: On-Site Welding

All Star Welding & Dem LLC ....G....... 203 948-0528
 Danbury *(G-1735)*
Alloy Welding & Mfg Co Inc ....F....... 860 582-3638
 Bristol *(G-962)*
Arnio Welding LLC ....F....... 860 564-7696
 Central Village *(G-1335)*
Engineers Welding LLC ....G....... 203 334-2492
 Bridgeport *(G-763)*
G & R Welding ....G....... 860 526-3353
 Deep River *(G-2090)*
Gaida Welding Co & Mar Repr ....G....... 203 924-4868
 Shelton *(G-7448)*
Gardner Welding LLC ....G....... 203 265-1036
 Wallingford *(G-9274)*
H & D Ornamental Iron Works ....G....... 860 871-1708
 Ellington *(G-2591)*
Hamden Sheet Metal Inc..................G....... 203 776-1472
 Hamden *(G-3459)*
Innovative Fusion Inc ....E....... 203 729-3873
 Naugatuck *(G-4891)*
J T Fantozzi Co Inc ....G....... 203 238-7018
 Meriden *(G-4177)*
Ken Hastedt.....................................G....... 203 268-6563
 Monroe *(G-4725)*
Pelchs Welding & Repair ....G....... 860 693-6328
 Collinsville *(G-1599)*
Pop Moody Welding Services ....G....... 860 749-9537
 Somers *(G-7668)*
R & F Welding Co ....G....... 203 393-2851
 New Haven *(G-5374)*
Weld TEC LLC ....G....... 860 628-5750
 Plantsville *(G-6918)*

CONTRACTORS: Ornamental Metal Work

Garden Iron LLC ....G....... 860 767-9917
 Westbrook *(G-9997)*
Jacob David Poppel ....G....... 860 904-3749
 Burlington *(G-1271)*
Richard Sadowski.............................G....... 203 372-2151
 Fairfield *(G-2836)*
Spiers Welding Service ....G....... 203 322-1004
 Stamford *(G-8434)*
Teddy S Custom Metalworks Inc ....G....... 203 359-6927
 Stamford *(G-8462)*

CONTRACTORS: Painting, Commercial

John Canning & Co Ltd ....E....... 203 272-9868
 Cheshire *(G-1401)*

PRODUCT SECTION

Rahzel Enterprize LLC..................G...... 475 449-6561
Norwalk (G-6315)

CONTRACTORS: Painting, Residential

Beyond Home Improvement...............G...... 203 859-0113
North Haven (G-5914)
Vanilla Politics LLC........................G...... 203 221-0895
Weston (G-10043)

CONTRACTORS: Patio & Deck Construction & Repair

Rk Stucco LLC..................................G...... 860 331-1791
New Britain (G-5046)
Tetrault & Sons Inc.........................G...... 860 872-9187
Stafford Springs (G-8042)

CONTRACTORS: Petroleum Storage Tank Install, Underground

Foleys Pump Service Inc...................E...... 203 792-2236
Danbury (G-1828)

CONTRACTORS: Plumbing

A Emergency Rooter Service...............G...... 860 582-3612
Bristol (G-952)
Clearwater Treatment Systems L.........G...... 860 799-0303
New Milford (G-5520)
Double Diamond Construction...........G...... 203 357-7757
Stamford (G-8188)
J & M Plumbing & Cnstr LLC.............F...... 860 319-3082
Norwich (G-6418)
New Milford Foundry & Mch Co..........G...... 860 354-5561
New Milford (G-5571)

CONTRACTORS: Power Generating Eqpt Installation

Renewable Energy Natural RES..........G...... 860 923-1091
Thompson (G-8843)

CONTRACTORS: Prefabricated Window & Door Installation

All-Time Manufacturing Co Inc...........F...... 860 848-9258
Montville (G-4768)
Cusson Sash Company.....................G...... 860 659-0354
Glastonbury (G-3025)

CONTRACTORS: Refrigeration

Waterlogic Usa Inc..........................G...... 866 917-7873
Farmington (G-2977)

CONTRACTORS: Rigging, Theatrical

Show Motion Inc..............................E...... 203 866-1866
Milford (G-4643)

CONTRACTORS: Roustabout Svcs

Ace Servicing Co Inc........................G...... 203 795-1400
Orange (G-6578)
High Fire Servicing LLC....................G...... 203 924-6562
Shelton (G-7464)
Kyung Pae Servicing Co LLC.............G...... 203 394-7472
Fairfield (G-2807)
Loanworks Servicing LLC..................G...... 203 402-7304
Shelton (G-7491)
Precision Servicing..........................G...... 203 650-1392
Easton (G-2562)

CONTRACTORS: Safety & Security Eqpt

Q-Lane Turnstiles LLC......................F...... 860 410-1801
Sandy Hook (G-7327)

CONTRACTORS: Sandblasting Svc, Building Exteriors

Blasting Techniques Inc...................G...... 860 528-4717
South Windsor (G-7718)
Glass Source LLC............................G...... 203 924-4368
Shelton (G-7449)
Peleganos Stained Glass Studio.........G...... 203 272-4067
Cheshire (G-1428)

CONTRACTORS: Seismograph Survey Svcs

Geosonics Inc.................................F...... 203 271-2504
Cheshire (G-1392)

Seismic Monitoring Svcs LLC............G...... 860 753-6363
Danielson (G-2001)

CONTRACTORS: Sheet Metal Work, NEC

Airtech of Stamford Inc....................E...... 203 323-3959
Stamford (G-8070)
Copperworks Inc.............................G...... 203 248-3516
Hamden (G-3432)
Country Side Sheet Metal................G...... 860 872-5729
Ellington (G-2584)
Fabtron Incorporated.......................G...... 860 410-1801
Plainville (G-6808)
Redco Audio Inc.............................F...... 203 502-7600
Stratford (G-8674)
Sheetmetal Systems Inc..................G...... 860 878-2633
Milford (G-4642)
Tech-Air Incorporated......................E...... 860 848-1287
Uncasville (G-9104)

CONTRACTORS: Single-family Home General Remodeling

A&A Home Solutions........................G...... 203 993-1735
Shelton (G-7386)
Adam Fuller Woodworking................G...... 860 455-1296
North Windham (G-6033)
Cusson Sash Company.....................G...... 860 659-0354
Glastonbury (G-3025)
Deschenes & Cooper Architectur........G...... 860 599-2481
Pawcatuck (G-6709)
Gregory Penta................................G...... 860 747-2681
Plainville (G-6819)
J&A Woodworking Co Inc.................G...... 203 287-1915
Hamden (G-3466)
Rahzel Enterprize LLC......................G...... 475 449-6561
Norwalk (G-6315)
Trigila Construction Inc....................E...... 860 828-8444
Berlin (G-228)

CONTRACTORS: Skylight Installation

E-Skylight Inc.................................G...... 203 208-1351
Branford (G-584)

CONTRACTORS: Special Trades, NEC

Cummins Envirotech.........................G...... 860 598-9564
Old Lyme (G-6500)
J & J Stairs...................................G...... 860 793-8333
Plainville (G-6825)
Lundgren Eric Woodworking..............G...... 860 350-5153
New Milford (G-5559)
Renner Stairs.................................G...... 203 743-2452
Danbury (G-1928)
Saints Woodworking LLC..................G...... 860 657-4733
Glastonbury (G-3080)

CONTRACTORS: Sprinkler System

Allstate Fire Systems LLC.................E...... 860 246-7711
Middletown (G-4314)

CONTRACTORS: Structural Iron Work, Structural

Marks Construction Co LLC...............G...... 860 407-2391
Portland (G-6965)

CONTRACTORS: Structural Steel Erection

Berlin Steel Construction Co.............E...... 860 828-3531
Kensington (G-3806)
Colonial Iron Shop Inc.....................G...... 860 763-0659
Enfield (G-2629)
Engineered Building Pdts Inc............E...... 860 243-1110
Bloomfield (G-409)
George H Olson Steel Co Inc............E...... 203 375-5656
Stratford (G-8617)
Jwc Steel Co LLC............................E...... 860 296-5517
Hartford (G-3621)
New Canaan Forge LLC...................G...... 203 966-3858
New Canaan (G-5123)
Steeltech Building Pdts Inc..............D...... 860 290-8930
South Windsor (G-7829)
United Steel Inc..............................C...... 860 289-2323
East Hartford (G-2389)

CONTRACTORS: Svc Well Drilling Svcs

Aarons Enterprises..........................G...... 203 762-9764
Wilton (G-10266)

CONTROL EQPT: Electric

Budget Oil......................................G...... 860 649-1527
Bolton (G-507)
Concrete Coring Co Conn Inc............G...... 203 287-8400
Hamden (G-3430)
D F Arszyla Well Drilling Inc..............G...... 860 628-6156
Southington (G-7910)
Rodger Craig..................................G...... 203 264-8843
Southbury (G-7876)

CONTRACTORS: Tile Installation, Ceramic

Distributors of Standard Tile.............G...... 860 439-0627
New London (G-5468)
Joseph Cohn Son Tile Trazo LLC.......E...... 203 772-2420
North Haven (G-5955)
New England Stone Inc...................F...... 203 876-8606
Milford (G-4590)

CONTRACTORS: Ventilation & Duct Work

Atlantic Vent & Eqp Co Inc...............E...... 860 635-1300
Cromwell (G-1690)
Betlan Corporation..........................F...... 203 270-7898
Newtown (G-5729)
L & L Mechanical LLC......................F...... 860 491-4007
Goshen (G-3101)

CONTRACTORS: Warm Air Heating & Air Conditioning

C B S Contractors Inc......................F...... 203 734-8015
Ansonia (G-26)
Hamden Sheet Metal Inc..................G...... 203 776-1472
Hamden (G-3459)
J & B Service Company LLC.............G...... 203 743-9357
Bethel (G-314)
M & O Corporation..........................E...... 203 367-4292
Bridgeport (G-827)
Mercury Fuel Service Inc..................D...... 203 756-7284
Waterbury (G-9539)

CONTRACTORS: Water Intake Well Drilling Svc

George Sima..................................G...... 860 345-4660
Higganum (G-3764)

CONTRACTORS: Water Well Drilling

D F Arszyla Well Drilling Inc..............G...... 860 628-6156
Southington (G-7910)

CONTRACTORS: Windows & Doors

Brynwood Partners V Ltd Partnr........G...... 203 622-1790
Greenwich (G-3138)
Stanley Black & Decker Inc..............C...... 860 677-2861
Farmington (G-2960)
Tetrault & Sons Inc.........................G...... 860 872-9187
Stafford Springs (G-8042)

CONTRACTORS: Wood Floor Installation & Refinishing

Agw Clssic Hardwood Floors LLC.......E...... 203 640-3106
Westbrook (G-9989)

CONTRACTORS: Wrecking & Demolition

All Star Welding & Dem LLC..............G...... 203 948-0528
Danbury (G-1735)
Oxford Outdoor Services LLC............G...... 860 800-6260
Oxford (G-6684)

CONTROL EQPT: Electric

Altek Electronics Inc........................C...... 860 482-7626
Torrington (G-8892)
CET Inc...G...... 203 882-8057
Milford (G-4486)
Conveyco Technologies Inc...............E...... 860 589-8215
Bristol (G-1007)
Delta Elevator Service Corp..............E...... 860 676-6152
Canton (G-1312)
Kimchuk Incorporated......................F...... 203 790-7800
Danbury (G-1868)
New Haven Companies Inc...............F...... 203 469-6421
East Haven (G-2444)
North American Elev Svcs Co...........E...... 860 676-6000
Farmington (G-2939)
P-Q Controls Inc.............................E...... 860 583-6994
Bristol (G-1084)

Employee Codes: A=Over 500 employees, B=251-500
C=101-250, D=51-100, E=20-50, F=10-19, G=1-9

CONTROL EQPT: Electric

T & T Automation Inc ....F 860 683-8788
Windsor *(G-10447)*

CONTROL PANELS: Electrical

Accutron Inc ....C 860 683-8300
Windsor *(G-10354)*
B & A Design Inc ....G 860 871-0134
Vernon Rockville *(G-9161)*
Connecticut Valley Inds LLC ....G 860 388-0822
Old Saybrook *(G-6529)*
Corotec Corp ....F 860 678-0038
Farmington *(G-2893)*
Fabcon Inc ....G 860 485-9019
Harwinton *(G-3728)*
Industrial Cnnctons Sltons LLC ....E 860 747-7677
Plainville *(G-6824)*
La Chance Controls ....G 860 342-2212
Portland *(G-6963)*
Precision Graphics Inc ....E 860 828-6561
East Berlin *(G-2174)*

CONTROLS & ACCESS: Indl, Electric

Alinabal Inc ....C 203 877-3241
Milford *(G-4448)*
Clarktron Products Inc ....G 203 333-6517
Fairfield *(G-2763)*
Devar Inc ....E 203 368-6751
Bridgeport *(G-749)*
Gordon Products Incorporated ....E 203 775-4501
Brookfield *(G-1194)*
Measurement Systems Inc ....E 203 949-3500
Wallingford *(G-9317)*
O E M Controls Inc ....E 203 929-8431
Shelton *(G-7517)*

CONTROLS: Adjustable Speed Drive

Advanced Micro Controls Inc ....E 860 585-1254
Terryville *(G-8746)*

CONTROLS: Air Flow, Refrigeration

Emme Controls LLC ....G 503 793-3792
Bristol *(G-1026)*

CONTROLS: Automatic Temperature

Food Atmtn - Svc Tchniques Inc ....C 203 377-4414
Stratford *(G-8610)*
Grove Systems Inc ....G 860 663-2555
Deep River *(G-2091)*
Johnson Goodyer II Inc ....F 203 777-3424
New Haven *(G-5303)*
Omega Engineering Inc ....D 714 540-4914
Norwalk *(G-6285)*

CONTROLS: Crane & Hoist, Including Metal Mill

New England Lift Systems LLC ....G 860 372-4040
Newington *(G-5685)*
Saindon Crane Service ....G 860 505-7245
Berlin *(G-218)*

CONTROLS: Electric Motor

ABB Enterprise Software Inc ....E 203 798-6210
Danbury *(G-1729)*
Automation & Servo Tech ....G 860 658-5172
Simsbury *(G-7612)*
Digatron Power Electronics Inc ....E 203 446-8000
Shelton *(G-7432)*
Ward Leonard CT LLC ....C 860 283-5801
Thomaston *(G-8818)*

CONTROLS: Environmental

Ademco Inc ....G 860 257-3266
Rocky Hill *(G-7218)*
Ademco Inc ....G 203 877-2702
Milford *(G-4440)*
Alloy Engineering Co Inc ....E 203 366-5253
Bridgeport *(G-685)*
Alloy Engineering Co Inc ....G 203 366-5253
Bridgeport *(G-686)*
Graywolf Sensing Solutions LLC ....G 203 402-0477
Shelton *(G-7453)*
Hamilton Standard Space ....E 860 654-6000
Windsor Locks *(G-10490)*
Hamilton Sundstrand Corp ....A 860 654-6000
Windsor Locks *(G-10491)*

Kahn and Company Incorporated ....G 860 529-8643
Wethersfield *(G-10203)*
Lexa International Corporation ....F 203 326-5200
Stamford *(G-8284)*
Mission Allergy Inc ....G 203 364-1570
Hawleyville *(G-3744)*
Nats Inc ....F 860 635-6820
Middletown *(G-4384)*
Tek-Air Systems Inc ....E 203 791-1400
Monroe *(G-4758)*
Whitman Controls LLC ....F 800 233-4401
Bristol *(G-1138)*

CONTROLS: Marine & Navy, Auxiliary

Naiad Dynamics Us Inc ....E 203 929-6355
Shelton *(G-7506)*

CONTROLS: Nuclear Reactor

Drs Naval Power Systems Inc ....B 203 798-3000
Danbury *(G-1801)*

CONTROLS: Relay & Ind

Altek Company ....C 860 482-7626
Torrington *(G-8891)*
Asea Brown Boveri Inc ....G 203 750-2200
Norwalk *(G-6076)*
Automation Controls ....G 203 888-9330
Oxford *(G-6644)*
Belimo Aircontrols (usa) Inc ....C 800 543-9038
Danbury *(G-1752)*
Belimo Customization USA Inc ....G 203 791-9915
Danbury *(G-1754)*
Bristol Babcock Employees Fede ....G 860 945-2200
Watertown *(G-9687)*
Conntrol International Inc ....F 860 928-0567
Putnam *(G-7036)*
Everlast Products LLC ....G 203 250-7111
Cheshire *(G-1387)*
Gems Sensors Inc ....B 860 747-3000
Plainville *(G-6815)*
General Electric Company ....D 203 396-1572
Bridgeport *(G-774)*
In-Motion LLC ....G 860 742-3612
Coventry *(G-1656)*
Independence Park ....G 203 421-9396
Madison *(G-3930)*
John Olsen ....G 203 624-5544
Trumbull *(G-9037)*
Minarik Corporation ....C 860 687-5000
Bloomfield *(G-445)*
P/A Industries Inc ....E 860 243-8306
Bloomfield *(G-459)*
Park Distributories Inc ....G 203 579-2140
Bridgeport *(G-863)*
Park Distributories Inc ....F 203 366-7200
Bridgeport *(G-864)*
Park Distributories Inc ....F 203 366-7200
Bridgeport *(G-865)*
Quality Name Plate Inc ....D 860 633-9495
East Glastonbury *(G-2185)*
Safestart Systems LLC ....G 203 221-0652
Weston *(G-10039)*
Sound Construction & Engrg Co ....E 203 242-2109
Bloomfield *(G-488)*
United Electric Controls Co ....D 203 877-2795
Milford *(G-4668)*
Victory Controls LLC ....G 860 930-6226
Farmington *(G-2976)*

CONTROLS: Remote, Boat

American Unmanned Systems LLC .....G 203 406-7611
Stamford *(G-8079)*

CONTROLS: Resistance Welder

Ewald Instruments Corp ....F 860 491-9042
Bristol *(G-1032)*

CONTROLS: Thermostats

Rich Plastic Products Inc ....G 203 235-4241
Meriden *(G-4233)*

CONVENTION & TRADE SHOW SVCS

Information Today Inc ....F 203 761-1466
Wilton *(G-10302)*
Urban Exposition LLC ....E 203 242-8717
Trumbull *(G-9090)*

CONVERTERS: Data

Cisco Systems Inc ....E 203 229-2300
Norwalk *(G-6115)*
Cisco Systems Inc ....A 860 284-5500
Farmington *(G-2888)*
Spectrum Virtual LLC ....G 203 303-7540
Cheshire *(G-1452)*
Sugar Run K9 LLC ....G 860 591-4193
Voluntown *(G-9191)*

CONVERTERS: Frequency

Hamilton Sundstrand Corp ....A 860 654-6000
Windsor Locks *(G-10491)*

CONVERTERS: Power, AC to DC

GE Enrgy Pwr Cnversion USA Inc ....G 203 373-2211
Fairfield *(G-2790)*
High Voltage Outsourcing LLC ....G 203 456-3101
Danbury *(G-1844)*
Prostaff Pro Shop ....G 203 239-3835
North Haven *(G-5981)*

CONVEYOR SYSTEMS

Alvest (usa) Inc ....E 860 602-3400
Windsor *(G-10360)*

CONVEYOR SYSTEMS: Robotic

International Robotics Inc ....G 914 325-7773
Stamford *(G-8255)*
International Robotics Inc ....F 914 630-1060
Stamford *(G-8256)*
R & I Manufacturing Co ....F 860 589-6364
Terryville *(G-8768)*
Unimation ....E 203 792-3412
Bethel *(G-358)*

CONVEYORS & CONVEYING EQPT

Affordable Conveyors Svcs LLC ....F 860 582-1800
Bristol *(G-960)*
CT Conveyor LLC ....G 860 637-2926
Bristol *(G-1009)*
Goldslager Conveyor Company ....E 203 795-9886
Hamden *(G-3452)*
Intelligrated Systems Ohio LLC ....G 203 938-8404
Redding *(G-7095)*
National Conveyors Company Inc ......E 860 653-0374
East Granby *(G-2215)*
Roller Bearing Co Amer Inc ....E 203 758-8272
Middlebury *(G-4289)*
Walker Magnetics Group Inc ....E 508 853-3232
Windsor *(G-10461)*
Z-Loda Systems Inc ....G 203 359-2991
Stamford *(G-8505)*

CONVEYORS: Overhead

Production Equipment Company ....E 800 758-5697
Meriden *(G-4221)*

COOKING & FOODWARMING EQPT: Coffee Brewing

Crystal Rock Holdings Inc ....E 860 945-0661
Watertown *(G-9697)*

COOKWARE, STONEWARE: Coarse Earthenware & Pottery

Salem Stone Design Inc ....F 860 439-1234
Waterford *(G-9668)*

COOLING TOWERS: Metal

SPX Corporation ....G 203 356-9308
Stamford *(G-8435)*

COPPER ORES

Baobab Asset Management LLC ....G 203 340-5700
Greenwich *(G-3129)*

COPPER: Rolling & Drawing

Global Brass & Copper LLC ....G 203 597-5000
Waterbury *(G-9488)*
Global Brass & Copper LLC ....G 203 597-5000
Waterbury *(G-9489)*

PRODUCT SECTION

CORD & TWINE
Detotec North America Inc ....G...... 860 230-0078
  Moosup (G-4778)
Detotec North America Inc ....G...... 860 564-1012
  Sterling (G-8509)
Loos & Co Inc ....B...... 860 928-7981
  Pomfret (G-6933)

CORD: Braided
Woodstock Line Co ....F...... 860 928-6557
  Putnam (G-7080)

CORES: Magnetic
Alpha-Core Inc ....E...... 203 954-0050
  Shelton (G-7392)
Bridgeport Magnetics Group Inc ......E...... 203 954-0050
  Shelton (G-7410)

CORK & CORK PRDTS
Corktec Inc ....G...... 860 851-9417
  Stafford Springs (G-8021)

CORK & CORK PRDTS: Tiles
Brass City Tile Designs LLC ....G...... 203 597-8764
  Waterbury (G-9443)
New England Tile & Stone Inc ....F...... 914 481-4488
  Stamford (G-8323)

CORRECTION FLUID
Bic Consumer Products Mfg Co ....C...... 203 783-2000
  Milford (G-4469)
Bic Corporation ....A...... 203 783-2000
  Shelton (G-7407)
Bic USA Inc ....C...... 203 783-2000
  Shelton (G-7408)
Gillette Company ....G...... 203 796-4000
  Bethel (G-303)

CORRECTIONAL INSTITUTIONS
Federal Prison Industries ....F...... 203 743-6471
  Danbury (G-1824)

CORRESPONDENCE SCHOOLS
Cortina Learning Intl Inc ....F...... 800 245-2145
  Wilton (G-10283)

COSMETIC PREPARATIONS
Albea Thomaston Inc ....B...... 860 283-2000
  Thomaston (G-8778)
Amodex Products Inc ....E...... 203 335-1255
  Bridgeport (G-696)
Casaro Labs Ltd ....G...... 203 353-8500
  Stamford (G-8129)
CCL Industries Corporation ....D...... 203 926-1253
  Shelton (G-7412)
Ecometics Inc ....E...... 203 853-7856
  Norwalk (G-6154)
Innarah Inc ....G...... 203 873-0015
  Stratford (G-8632)
Judith Jackson Inc ....G...... 203 698-3011
  Old Greenwich (G-6478)
Milbar Labs Inc ....F...... 203 467-1577
  East Haven (G-2442)
Miyoshi America Inc ....D...... 860 779-3990
  Dayville (G-2064)
Naturally Relaxed LLC ....G...... 860 402-0613
  Milldale (G-4687)
Preferred Display Inc ....G...... 860 372-4653
  Enfield (G-2680)
Revive Beauty and Wellness LLC ....G...... 860 921-4952
  Brookfield (G-1218)
Russell Organics LLC ....G...... 203 285-6633
  Wallingford (G-9363)

COSMETICS & TOILETRIES
Alexis Homemade Scrubs ....G...... 401 480-5074
  North Stonington (G-6018)
Blessed Creek ....G...... 860 416-3692
  Suffield (G-8715)
Carrubba Incorporated ....D...... 203 878-0605
  Milford (G-4485)
Cindys Soap Cottage ....G...... 860 370-9908
  Windsor Locks (G-10479)

Crabtree & Evelyn Ltd ....C...... 800 272-2873
  Woodstock (G-10662)
D & F Scrubs & Gadgets LLC ....G...... 203 440-4666
  Meriden (G-4165)
Elizabeth Arden Inc ....G...... 203 905-1700
  Stamford (G-8194)
Essentalia LLC ....G...... 860 617-5106
  Storrs (G-8548)
Harjani Hitesh ....G...... 860 913-6032
  Waterford (G-9654)
High Ridge Brands Co ....D...... 203 674-8080
  Stamford (G-8236)
In O Scents of Madison ....G...... 203 641-8910
  Madison (G-3929)
K29 ....G...... 203 961-9662
  Stamford (G-8274)
Miyoshi America Inc ....F...... 860 779-3990
  Dayville (G-2065)
Miyoshi America Inc ....G...... 860 779-3990
  Dayville (G-2066)
Nutmeg Naturals LLC ....G...... 860 554-1272
  Higganum (G-3772)
Ozz ....G...... 203 318-5080
  Madison (G-3946)
Rjtb Group LLC ....G...... 203 531-7216
  Greenwich (G-3228)
Rjtb Initiatives Inc ....G...... 203 531-7216
  Greenwich (G-3229)
Sallie Gawron ....G...... 203 258-9851
  Fairfield (G-2841)
T N Dickinson Company ....F...... 860 267-2279
  East Hampton (G-2281)
Unilever Trumbull RES Svcs Inc .....G...... 203 502-0086
  Trumbull (G-9087)
Wenger Na Inc ....G...... 845 365-3500
  Monroe (G-4764)

COSMETICS WHOLESALERS
Optima Specialty Chemical ....G...... 203 929-2031
  Shelton (G-7520)

COSTUME JEWELRY & NOVELTIES: Apparel, Exc Precious Metals
Initial Reaction LLC ....G...... 203 255-1200
  Fairfield (G-2795)
The Did Collection ....G...... 203 807-4305
  Stamford (G-8464)

COSTUME JEWELRY & NOVELTIES: Bracelets, Exc Precious Metals
Blue Lotus Bracelets ....G...... 203 858-6526
  Norwalk (G-6094)
Mystic Knotwork LLC ....F...... 860 889-3793
  Mystic (G-4834)
Wilhelm Gdale Elzabeth Designs ....G...... 203 371-8787
  Bridgeport (G-937)

COSTUME JEWELRY & NOVELTIES: Exc Semi & Precious
Dawn Hill Enterprises LLC ....G...... 860 496-9188
  Torrington (G-8917)

COSTUME JEWELRY & NOVELTIES: Ornament, Exc Precious Mtl/Gem
A Capela Do Santo Antonio Inc .....G...... 860 447-3329
  New London (G-5455)

COSTUME JEWELRY STORES
K2steam ....G...... 860 251-9824
  Avon (G-86)
Rodriguez Ruiz Rosa Margarita .....G...... 860 840-0444
  Hartford (G-3681)

COUNTER & SINK TOPS
Custom Crft Ktchns By Rizio BR ....F...... 203 268-0271
  Monroe (G-4708)
Pro Counters New England LLC ....G...... 203 347-8663
  Ansonia (G-46)
Specialty Shop Inc ....G...... 860 647-1477
  Manchester (G-4091)

COUNTERS & COUNTING DEVICES
Alinabal Holdings Corporation ....B...... 203 877-3241
  Milford (G-4449)

COUNTERS OR COUNTER DISPLAY CASES, EXC WOOD
American Stonecrafters Inc ....G...... 203 514-9725
  Wallingford (G-9202)
C Mather Company Inc ....G...... 860 528-5667
  South Windsor (G-7721)
Richard Riggio and Sons Inc ....E...... 860 767-0812
  Ivoryton (G-3789)

COUNTERS OR COUNTER DISPLAY CASES, WOOD
T C Kitchens Inc ....G...... 203 375-4469
  Stratford (G-8693)

COUNTERS: Mechanical
Denominator Company Inc ....F...... 203 263-3210
  Woodbury (G-10633)

COUNTING DEVICES: Controls, Revolution & Timing
Kongsberg Dgtal Simulation Inc .....F...... 860 405-2300
  Groton (G-3293)

COUNTING DEVICES: Electromechanical
Bidwell Industrial Group Inc ....E...... 860 346-9283
  Middletown (G-4325)
Lq Mechatronics Inc ....G...... 203 433-4430
  Branford (G-619)

COUNTING DEVICES: Tachometer, Centrifugal
Faria Beede Instruments Inc ....C...... 860 848-9271
  North Stonington (G-6024)

COUNTRY MUSIC GROUPS OR ARTIST
Nesola Scarves LLC ....G...... 203 288-5058
  Cheshire (G-1419)

COUPLINGS, EXC PRESSURE & SOIL PIPE
Saf Industries LLC ....E...... 203 729-4900
  Meriden (G-4237)

COUPLINGS: Hose & Tube, Hydraulic Or Pneumatic
Progressive Hydraulics Inc ....G...... 203 386-0885
  Stratford (G-8670)

COURIER SVCS: Package By Vehicle
Meadwestvaco Packg Systems LLC ...G...... 409 276-3137
  Stamford (G-8301)

COVERS: Automobile Seat
Taillon Auto Top Company ....G...... 860 583-5525
  Bristol (G-1125)

COVERS: Automotive, Exc Seat & Tire
Power Cover Usa LLC ....G...... 203 755-2687
  Waterbury (G-9583)

COVERS: Canvas
3333 LLC ....G...... 860 643-1384
  Manchester (G-3971)

CRANE & AERIAL LIFT SVCS
Arnco Sign Company ....E...... 203 238-1224
  Wallingford (G-9211)
Tims Sign & Lighting Service ....G...... 203 634-8840
  Meriden (G-4256)

CRANES: Overhead
Production Equipment Company .....E...... 800 758-5697
  Meriden (G-4221)

CRANKSHAFTS & CAMSHAFTS: Machining
Co-Op Jig Boring Jig Grinding ....G...... 860 828-9882
  Berlin (G-170)

Employee Codes: A=Over 500 employees, B=251-500
C=101-250, D=51-100, E=20-50, F=10-19, G=1-9

CREDIT INSTITUTIONS: Short-Term Business

CREDIT INSTITUTIONS: Short-Term Business

Capricorn Investors III LP .... F 203 861-6600
  Greenwich *(G-3141)*

CREDIT UNIONS: Federally Chartered

Bristol Babcock Employees Fede .... G 860 945-2200
  Watertown *(G-9687)*

CROWNS & CLOSURES

Eyelet Design Inc .... D 203 754-4141
  Waterbury *(G-9477)*

CRUDE PETROLEUM & NATURAL GAS PRODUCTION

Ammonite Corp .... G 203 972-1130
  New Canaan *(G-5087)*

CRUDE PETROLEUM & NATURAL GAS PRODUCTION

Alternate Energy Futures .... G 917 745-7097
  Danbury *(G-1738)*
CCI Robinsons Bend LLC .... G 203 564-8571
  Stamford *(G-8136)*
Country Oil LLC .... G 203 270-6439
  Newtown *(G-5735)*
Dietze & Associates LLC .... F 203 762-3500
  Wilton *(G-10289)*
Frc Founders Corporation .... E 203 661-6601
  Stamford *(G-8209)*
Gsv Inc .... G 203 221-2690
  Westport *(G-10094)*
Kevin Field .... G 203 878-6339
  Milford *(G-4564)*
Less Pay Oil LLC .... G 203 230-2568
  Hamden *(G-3474)*
McGuires Oil LLc .... G 860 889-2567
  Preston *(G-6986)*
Merrill Oil LLC .... G 203 387-1130
  Woodbridge *(G-10607)*
Oil Guy LLC .... G 203 910-2752
  Watertown *(G-9717)*
Outpost Exploration LLC .... G 203 762-7206
  Wilton *(G-10317)*
Promise Propane .... G 860 685-0676
  Newington *(G-5696)*
River Valley Oil Service LLC .... G 860 342-5670
  Portland *(G-6973)*
Santa Energy Corporation .... G 800 937-2682
  Bridgeport *(G-895)*
Winner Producing Co .... G 203 259-7576
  Westport *(G-10176)*

CRUDE PETROLEUM PRODUCTION

Eazy Oil LLC .... G 860 426-3184
  Plantsville *(G-6891)*
El Paso Prod Oil Gas Texas LP .... F 860 293-1990
  Hartford *(G-3584)*
Petroglyph Energy Inc .... G 208 685-7600
  Darien *(G-2038)*

CRYSTALS

Crystal Fairfield Tech LLC .... F 860 354-2111
  New Milford *(G-5525)*
Transducer Products Inc .... G 860 824-1002
  Canaan *(G-1294)*

CRYSTALS: Piezoelectric

Ebl Products Inc .... F 860 290-3737
  East Hartford *(G-2319)*

CULTURE MEDIA

Alliances By Alisa LLC .... G 860 869-1509
  Simsbury *(G-7610)*
Culture Media LLC .... G 203 470-5918
  Wilton *(G-10286)*

CUPS: Paper

Harrison Enterprise LLC .... G 914 665-8348
  Bridgeport *(G-781)*

CURBING: Granite Or Stone

Central Marble & Granite LLC .... G 203 734-4644
  Ansonia *(G-28)*
Granite & Kitchen Studio LLC .... G 860 290-4444
  South Windsor *(G-7764)*
Granite LLC .... G 860 586-8132
  Newington *(G-5657)*
Luis Raimundi .... G 860 294-1468
  Pleasant Valley *(G-6924)*
New England Gran Cabinets LLC .... G 860 310-2981
  West Hartford *(G-9837)*

CURRENT TAPS: Attachment Plug & Screw Shell Types

M & I Industries Inc .... G 860 747-6421
  Plainville *(G-6837)*

CURTAIN & DRAPERY FIXTURES: Poles, Rods & Rollers

Ahlstrom-Munksjo Nonwovens LLC ..... B 860 654-8300
  Windsor Locks *(G-10469)*
Ben Baena & Son .... G 203 334-8568
  Bridgeport *(G-710)*
Blinds Dept .... G 203 655-3378
  Darien *(G-2009)*
Drapery Consultants .... G 203 855-0454
  Norwalk *(G-6150)*
R & M Associates Inc .... F 860 633-0721
  Glastonbury *(G-3078)*
Rollease Acmeda Inc .... D 203 964-1573
  Stamford *(G-8397)*
Thomas W Raftery Inc .... G 860 278-9870
  Hartford *(G-3703)*
Vertical Ventures Intl LLC .... G 203 227-1364
  Weston *(G-10044)*

CURTAIN WALLS: Building, Steel

Stephanie Mark .... G 203 329-7562
  Stamford *(G-8441)*

CURTAINS & BEDDING: Knit

Fashion Home Products .... G 860 274-0824
  Watertown *(G-9706)*

CURTAINS: Window, From Purchased Materials

R L Fisher Inc .... D 860 951-8110
  Hartford *(G-3674)*

CUSHIONS & PILLOWS

Artemisia Inc .... G 917 797-7644
  Old Lyme *(G-6489)*
Sammi Sleeping Systems LLC .... G 203 684-3131
  New Haven *(G-5388)*
Upon A Once Pillow LLC .... G 203 222-1717
  Westport *(G-10170)*

CUSHIONS & PILLOWS: Boat

Riverside Seat Cover Inc .... G 203 661-7893
  Cos Cob *(G-1640)*

CUSHIONS: Carpet & Rug, Foamed Plastics

HI-Tech Packaging Inc .... E 203 378-2700
  Stratford *(G-8626)*

CUSTOM COMPOUNDING OF RUBBER MATERIALS

Jonal Laboratories Inc .... D 203 634-4444
  Meriden *(G-4180)*

CUT STONE & STONE PRODUCTS

American Stonecrafters Inc .... G 203 514-9725
  Wallingford *(G-9202)*
Architectural Stone Group LLC .... G 203 494-5451
  Bridgeport *(G-700)*
Connecticut Solid Surface LLC .... E 860 410-9800
  Plainville *(G-6791)*
Dan Beard Inc .... F 203 924-4346
  Shelton *(G-7427)*
Interntonal MBL Gran Entps Inc .... G 860 296-0741
  Hartford *(G-3618)*

O & G Industries Inc .... E 203 323-1111
  Stamford *(G-8336)*
T B Marble Granite LLC .... G 860 443-0817
  Oakdale *(G-6447)*
Tri LLC .... G 203 353-8418
  Stamford *(G-8475)*
Valley Marble and Slate Corp .... G 860 354-3955
  New Milford *(G-5606)*

CUTLERY

Wenger Na Inc .... G 845 365-3500
  Monroe *(G-4764)*

CUTOUTS: Distribution

Dow Div of UTC .... G 860 683-7340
  Windsor *(G-10381)*

CUTTING EQPT: Milling

Clear Site The Heated Wiper .... F 203 790-2100
  Bethel *(G-272)*

CYLINDER & ACTUATORS: Fluid Power

Airpot Corporation .... E 800 848-7681
  Norwalk *(G-6064)*

CYLINDERS: Pressure

PSI Plus Inc .... F 860 267-6667
  East Hampton *(G-2276)*

DAIRY EQPT

Engineering Services & Pdts Co .... D 860 528-1119
  South Windsor *(G-7750)*

DAIRY PRDTS STORE: Ice Cream, Packaged

Cold Stone Creamery .... G 860 669-7025
  Clinton *(G-1495)*
Fish Family Farm Inc .... G 860 646-9745
  Bolton *(G-509)*

DAIRY PRDTS WHOLESALERS: Fresh

Guida-Seibert Dairy Company .... C 860 224-2404
  New Britain *(G-4994)*
Longfords Ice Cream Ltd .... F 914 935-9469
  Stamford *(G-8288)*

DAIRY PRDTS: Butter

Grass Roots Creamery .... G 860 653-6303
  Granby *(G-3108)*
Redding Creamery LLC .... G 203 938-2766
  Redding *(G-7106)*
Square Creamery LLC .... G 203 456-3490
  Bethel *(G-347)*
Sweet Grass Creamery LLC .... G 860 887-8098
  Preston *(G-6989)*
Whipstick Creamery LLC .... G 203 438-2203
  Ridgefield *(G-7184)*

DAIRY PRDTS: Cheese

Chris & Zack LLC .... G 203 298-0742
  Orange *(G-6592)*
Mozzicato Fmly Investments LLC .... G 860 296-0426
  Wethersfield *(G-10213)*
Ndr Liuzzi Inc .... E 203 287-8477
  Hamden *(G-3487)*
Red Apple Cheese LLC .... G 203 755-5579
  Watertown *(G-9730)*

DAIRY PRDTS: Dairy Based Desserts, Frozen

Gelato Giuliana LLC .... G 203 772-0607
  New Haven *(G-5285)*
Poppys LLC .... F 860 778-9044
  Hartford *(G-3667)*

DAIRY PRDTS: Dietary Supplements, Dairy & Non-Dairy Based

Bactana Corp .... G 203 716-1230
  Farmington *(G-2881)*
Inner Armour Black LLC .... G 860 656-7720
  Berlin *(G-190)*
Natures First Inc .... G 203 795-8400
  Orange *(G-6614)*
Novogen Inc .... F 203 972-5901
  New Canaan *(G-5126)*

PRODUCT SECTION

DEFENSE SYSTEMS & EQPT

Supplement Tech LLC ....G...... 203 377-5551
  Stratford *(G-8691)*

DAIRY PRDTS: Evaporated Milk

Nestle Usa Inc ....C...... 860 928-0082
  Pomfret Center *(G-6944)*

DAIRY PRDTS: Frozen Desserts & Novelties

Angelas Italian Ice Inc ....G...... 860 536-9828
  Mystic *(G-4798)*
Big Dipper Ice Cream Fctry Inc ....E...... 203 758-3200
  Prospect *(G-6994)*
Chip In A Bottle LLC ....G...... 203 460-0665
  New Haven *(G-5256)*
Cold Stone Creamery ....G...... 860 669-7025
  Clinton *(G-1495)*
Dari-Farms Ice Cream Co Inc ....F...... 860 872-8313
  Tolland *(G-8859)*
Diversis Capital LLC ....G...... 860 872-8313
  Tolland *(G-8861)*
Dr Mikes Ice Cream Inc ....G...... 203 792-4388
  Bethel *(G-282)*
Fish Family Farm Inc ....G...... 860 646-9745
  Bolton *(G-509)*
Greg Robbins and Associates ....G...... 888 699-8876
  Branford *(G-601)*
HP Hood LLC ....C...... 860 623-4435
  Suffield *(G-8721)*
J Foster Ice Cream ....G...... 860 651-1499
  Simsbury *(G-7631)*
Jaksy 2 LLC ....G...... 203 371-4111
  Fairfield *(G-2799)*
Kan Pak LLC ....G...... 203 933-6631
  Southbury *(G-7864)*
Libbys Italian Pastry Shop ....G...... 203 234-2530
  North Haven *(G-5959)*
Longfords Ice Cream Ltd ....F...... 914 935-9469
  Stamford *(G-8288)*
Mozzicato Pastry & Bake Shop ....E...... 860 296-0426
  Hartford *(G-3646)*
Rbf Frozen Desserts LLC ....F...... 516 474-6488
  West Hartford *(G-9848)*
Rich Products Corporation ....B...... 860 827-8000
  New Britain *(G-5044)*
Smoothie King ....G...... 203 208-4098
  Branford *(G-653)*
Smoothie King ....G...... 860 574-9382
  Waterford *(G-9671)*
Sunny Daes of Fairfield ....G...... 203 372-3058
  Fairfield *(G-2851)*
T & R Specialties LLC ....G...... 860 870-9684
  Ellington *(G-2605)*
United Enterprises Inc ....G...... 860 225-9955
  New Britain *(G-5078)*

DAIRY PRDTS: Ice Cream & Ice Milk

Lucille Piccirillo ....G...... 203 366-2353
  Bridgeport *(G-826)*
Michaels Dairy Inc ....F...... 860 443-7617
  New London *(G-5479)*
New England Soft Serve ....G...... 860 537-5459
  Colchester *(G-1559)*
Reeds Inc ....E...... 203 890-0557
  Norwalk *(G-6318)*
Royal Ice Cream Company Inc .....F...... 860 649-5358
  Manchester *(G-4083)*
Royal Ice Cream Company Inc .....G...... 860 649-5358
  Manchester *(G-4084)*

DAIRY PRDTS: Ice Cream, Bulk

Abbydabby ....G...... 860 586-8832
  West Hartford *(G-9771)*
B-Sweet LLC ....G...... 203 452-0499
  Monroe *(G-4695)*
Ben & Jerrys Homemade Inc ....G...... 203 488-9666
  Newington *(G-5633)*
Bucks Spumoni Company Inc .....F...... 203 874-2007
  Milford *(G-4477)*
Pralines Inc ....F...... 203 284-8847
  Wallingford *(G-9338)*
Pralines of Plainville ....G...... 860 410-1151
  Plainville *(G-6853)*
Ritas of Milford ....F...... 203 301-4490
  Milford *(G-4630)*
Salem Vly Farms Ice Cream Inc ....G...... 860 859-2980
  Salem *(G-7291)*
Tea-Rrific Ice Cream LLC ....G...... 203 354-9805
  Bridgeport *(G-921)*

Walnut Beach Creamery LLC ....G...... 203 878-7738
  Milford *(G-4679)*

DAIRY PRDTS: Ice Cream, Packaged, Molded, On Sticks, Etc.

Conopco Inc ....E...... 708 606-0540
  Trumbull *(G-9014)*
Thomas J Lipton Inc ....A...... 206 381-3500
  Trumbull *(G-9081)*

DAIRY PRDTS: Imitation Cheese

Nutty Cow Inc ....G...... 626 888-9269
  West Hartford *(G-9840)*

DAIRY PRDTS: Milk, Condensed & Evaporated

Herbalife Distributor ....G...... 860 584-9721
  Bristol *(G-1048)*

DAIRY PRDTS: Milk, Fluid

HP Hood LLC ....B...... 203 304-9151
  Newtown *(G-5747)*
Kohler Mix Specialties LLC ....C...... 860 666-1511
  Newington *(G-5670)*
Willard J Stearns & Sons Inc ....E...... 860 423-9289
  Storrs Mansfield *(G-8561)*

DAIRY PRDTS: Milk, Processed, Pasteurized, Homogenized/Btld

Guida-Seibert Dairy Company ......C...... 860 224-2404
  New Britain *(G-4994)*

DAIRY PRDTS: Natural Cheese

Elm City Cheese Company Inc .....F...... 203 865-5768
  Hamden *(G-3443)*
Orange Cheese Company ....G...... 917 603-4378
  Orange *(G-6619)*

DAIRY PRDTS: Yogurt, Exc Frozen

Peachwave of Watertown ....G...... 203 942-4949
  Watertown *(G-9720)*
R & D Services LLC ....G...... 860 628-5205
  Southington *(G-7964)*
Swizzles of Greenwhich ....G...... 917 662-0080
  Cos Cob *(G-1642)*
Yocrunch Co LLC ....G...... 866 963-7862
  Naugatuck *(G-4930)*

DAIRY PRDTS: Yogurt, Frozen

Sharon Masonry ....G...... 860 307-7427
  Torrington *(G-8970)*
Wild-Froyo LLC ....G...... 860 739-6124
  Niantic *(G-5820)*

DATA PROCESSING & PREPARATION SVCS

Custom Computer Systems ....G...... 203 264-7808
  Southbury *(G-7850)*
Medpricercom Inc ....G...... 860 453-4554
  Guilford *(G-3375)*
Shibumicom Inc ....F...... 855 744-2864
  Norwalk *(G-6344)*
Spectrum Virtual LLC ....G...... 203 303-7540
  Cheshire *(G-1452)*
Warren Computer Services ....G...... 203 929-5725
  Shelton *(G-7583)*
Xerox Corporation ....B...... 203 968-3000
  Norwalk *(G-6401)*

DATA PROCESSING SVCS

Campus Yellow Pages LLC ....G...... 860 523-9909
  West Hartford *(G-9783)*
Creative Stone Group Inc ....G...... 203 554-7773
  Stamford *(G-8169)*
Dataprep Inc ....E...... 203 795-2095
  Orange *(G-6595)*
Hexplora LLC ....G...... 860 760-7601
  Rocky Hill *(G-7248)*
Intechs LLC ....G...... 203 260-8109
  Norwalk *(G-4721)*
Mc Keon Computer Services ....G...... 860 496-7171
  Torrington *(G-8947)*

DATABASE INFORMATION RETRIEVAL SVCS

Windhover Information Inc ....E...... 203 838-4401
  Norwalk *(G-6396)*

DEALERS: Commodity Contracts

Cofco Americas Resources Corp ...B...... 203 252-5200
  Stamford *(G-8151)*

DECORATIVE WOOD & WOODWORK

Agw Clssic Hardwood Floors LLC ..E...... 203 640-3106
  Westbrook *(G-9989)*
Anne Queen Woodworking ....F...... 203 720-1781
  Naugatuck *(G-4858)*
C N C Router Technologies ....G...... 203 744-6651
  Danbury *(G-1760)*
Clint S Custom Woodworkin ....G...... 860 887-1476
  Jewett City *(G-3792)*
Company of Craftsmen ....G...... 860 536-4189
  Mystic *(G-4808)*
Corts Custom Woodworking ....G...... 203 266-0146
  Bethlehem *(G-368)*
Desjardins Woodworking Inc ....G...... 860 491-9972
  Goshen *(G-3098)*
Diiorio Woodworks ....G...... 203 855-1331
  Norwalk *(G-6143)*
Elm City Manufacturing LLC ....F...... 203 248-1969
  North Haven *(G-5936)*
Finishing Solutions LLC ....G...... 860 705-8231
  Colchester *(G-1551)*
Harris Enterprise Corp ....E...... 860 649-4663
  Manchester *(G-4025)*
Hydeville Manfacturing Inc ....G...... 203 265-0524
  Wallingford *(G-9285)*
J & B Woodworking ....G...... 203 377-4682
  Stratford *(G-8634)*
Joe Charron ....G...... 860 423-2805
  Lebanon *(G-3855)*
John M Kriskey Carpentry ....G...... 203 531-0194
  Greenwich *(G-3184)*
Legere Group Ltd ....C...... 860 674-0392
  Avon *(G-89)*
Litchfield Windsors ....G...... 860 485-1019
  Harwinton *(G-3732)*
Lundgren Eric Woodworking ....G...... 860 350-5153
  New Milford *(G-5559)*
Muddy Brook Wood Products ....G...... 860 928-2205
  Woodstock *(G-10673)*
New England Joinery Works Inc ....G...... 203 767-3377
  Essex *(G-2728)*
Old Wood Workshop ....G...... 860 655-5259
  Pomfret Center *(G-6945)*
Refined Designs ....G...... 860 535-7273
  Stonington *(G-8537)*
Saints Woodworking LLC ....G...... 860 657-4733
  Glastonbury *(G-3080)*
Smith Frame & Moulding LLC ....G...... 203 389-8871
  Bozrah *(G-532)*
Strouts Woodworking ....G...... 860 623-8445
  Broad Brook *(G-1153)*
Teak LLC ....G...... 203 845-0345
  Norwalk *(G-6364)*
Thomas Townsend Custom Marine ..G...... 860 536-9800
  Mystic *(G-4849)*
Vacca Architectural Woodworkin ...G...... 860 599-3677
  Pawcatuck *(G-6730)*
Wood Creations & Graphics LLC ..G...... 203 271-3568
  Cheshire *(G-1459)*
Wood Services LLC ....G...... 203 983-5752
  Greenwich *(G-3261)*
Woodworkers Resource ....G...... 860 668-4100
  Suffield *(G-8739)*

DEFENSE SYSTEMS & EQPT

Amius Partners LLC ....G...... 203 526-5926
  New Haven *(G-5230)*
Delta Level LLC ....G...... 203 919-1514
  Stratford *(G-8605)*
Hard-Core Self Defense ....G...... 203 231-2344
  Shelton *(G-7459)*
Ladrdefense LLC ....G...... 860 637-8488
  Plantsville *(G-6901)*
Max Padro ....G...... 203 530-0616
  West Haven *(G-9933)*
Northmen Defense LLC ....G...... 860 908-9308
  Oakdale *(G-6445)*
United States Dept of Navy ....G...... 860 694-3524
  Groton *(G-3316)*

Employee Codes: A=Over 500 employees, B=251-500
C=101-250, D=51-100, E=20-50, F=10-19, G=1-9

2020 Harris Connecticut
Manufacturers Directory

DEHYDRATION EQPT

Q-Jet DSI Inc .... G 203 230-4700
  North Haven *(G-5984)*
Tasty Kale LLC .... G 203 560-9451
  New Haven *(G-5410)*

DELIVERY SVCS, BY VEHICLE

Congress Catering Inc .... E 860 291-8182
  East Hartford *(G-2309)*
Lu Lu Holdings LLC .... E 203 861-1988
  Greenwich *(G-3193)*

DENTAL EQPT

Centrix Inc .... C 203 929-5582
  Shelton *(G-7415)*
J S Dental Manufacturing Inc ..... G 203 438-8832
  Ridgefield *(G-7148)*
Kinetic Instruments Inc .... E 203 743-0080
  Bethel *(G-320)*
Nova Dental LLC .... G 203 234-3900
  North Haven *(G-5969)*
Uppercurve LLC .... G 203 770-0223
  New Milford *(G-5604)*

DENTAL EQPT & SPLYS

A & D Dental Innovations LLC .... G 888 374-5134
  Simsbury *(G-7608)*
Aero-Med Ltd .... G 860 659-2270
  South Windsor *(G-7702)*
Bti CCS .... G 860 758-7644
  Windsor Locks *(G-10475)*
Mark D Tweedie DDS .... G 860 649-0436
  Manchester *(G-4056)*
Meridian Group LLC .... G 860 928-5266
  Woodstock *(G-10672)*
Orthotraction Pads LLC .... G 203 698-0291
  Old Greenwich *(G-6482)*
Palmero Healthcare LLC .... F 203 377-6424
  Stratford *(G-8660)*
Pickadent Inc .... G 203 431-8716
  Ridgefield *(G-7160)*
Sabol Associates .... G 203 762-2183
  Wilton *(G-10326)*
Ultimate Companies Inc .... G 860 582-9111
  Bristol *(G-1133)*
Ultimate Wireforms Inc .... D 860 582-9111
  Bristol *(G-1134)*
Winslow Automatics Inc .... D 860 225-6321
  New Britain *(G-5084)*

DENTAL EQPT & SPLYS WHOLESALERS

Orthotraction Pads LLC .... G 203 698-0291
  Old Greenwich *(G-6482)*

DENTAL EQPT & SPLYS: Alloys, For Amalgams

Jensen Industries Inc .... D 203 285-1402
  North Haven *(G-5951)*

DENTAL EQPT & SPLYS: Dental Materials

Eagle Alloys .... G 203 453-9910
  Guilford *(G-3349)*

DENTAL EQPT & SPLYS: Drills, Bone

Essel Dental .... G 860 254-6955
  East Windsor *(G-2492)*

DENTAL EQPT & SPLYS: Enamels

All Smiles Dental .... G 860 450-9237
  Willimantic *(G-10220)*
Anna M Chisilenco-Raho .... G 203 877-0377
  Milford *(G-4452)*
Bridgeport Dental LLC .... G 203 384-2261
  Bridgeport *(G-720)*
Cristina Ilies .... G 203 456-3153
  Willimantic *(G-10223)*
Lloyd P McDonald .... G 860 447-1787
  Waterford *(G-9659)*
Scott Woodford .... G 203 245-4266
  Madison *(G-3955)*

DENTAL EQPT & SPLYS: Gold

Gold Star Dental .... G 860 445-1330
  Groton *(G-3289)*

DENTAL EQPT & SPLYS: Metal

Pbn LLC .... G 860 582-9111
  Bristol *(G-1089)*

DENTAL EQPT & SPLYS: Orthodontic Appliances

Acme Monaco Corporation .... C 860 224-1349
  New Britain *(G-4934)*

DENTISTS' OFFICES & CLINICS

Ultimate Wireforms Inc .... D 860 582-9111
  Bristol *(G-1134)*

DEODORANTS: Personal

Unilever Hpc USA .... G 203 381-3311
  Trumbull *(G-9086)*

DEPARTMENT STORES

Editorial Directions Inc .... G 203 245-2011
  Madison *(G-3919)*

DERMATOLOGICALS

Kinderma LLC .... G 860 796-5503
  Glastonbury *(G-3056)*
New England Dermatological ..... G 203 432-0092
  New Haven *(G-5342)*

DESIGN SVCS, NEC

20/20 Software Inc .... G 203 316-5500
  Stamford *(G-8049)*
Aerospace Alloys Inc .... D 860 882-0019
  Bloomfield *(G-382)*
Aquastone Graphix LLC .... G 860 206-4935
  Hartford *(G-3552)*
Century Tool and Design Inc ...... F 860 621-6748
  Milldale *(G-4683)*
Dawn Hill Enterprises LLC .... G 860 496-9188
  Torrington *(G-8917)*
Dufrane Nuclear Shielding Inc .... F 860 379-2318
  Winsted *(G-10516)*
ECR Enterprises LLC .... G 860 426-3098
  Southington *(G-7917)*
Fusion Cross-Media LLC .... G 860 647-8367
  Manchester *(G-4020)*
John Oldham Studios Inc .... E 860 529-3331
  Wethersfield *(G-10202)*
Karen Callan Designs Inc .... G 203 762-9914
  Greenwich *(G-3186)*
Presco Incorporated .... F 203 397-8722
  Woodbridge *(G-10615)*
Simulations LLC .... G 860 978-0772
  East Granby *(G-2230)*
West Mont Group .... G 203 931-1033
  West Haven *(G-9963)*

DESIGN SVCS: Commercial & Indl

Kimchuk Incorporated .... F 203 790-7800
  Danbury *(G-1868)*
On Line Building Systems LLC ... G 203 798-1194
  Danbury *(G-1899)*
Zsiba & Smolover Ltd .... G 860 354-5221
  New Milford *(G-5610)*

DESIGN SVCS: Computer Integrated Systems

Agile Computer Systems .... G 860 633-7807
  Glastonbury *(G-3004)*
Castle Systems Inc .... G 203 250-3140
  Cheshire *(G-1368)*
Computer Support People LLC .. G 203 653-4643
  Norwalk *(G-6122)*
General Dynamics Info Tech Inc . D 860 441-2400
  Pawcatuck *(G-6712)*
Insys Micro Inc .... G 917 566-5045
  Norwalk *(G-6209)*
Kimchuk Incorporated .... F 203 790-7800
  Danbury *(G-1868)*
Perry Heights Press LLC .... G 203 767-6509
  Wilton *(G-10319)*
Vertafore Inc .... A 860 602-6000
  Windsor *(G-10459)*

DESIGN SVCS: Hand Tools

B & F Design Incorporated .... E 860 357-4317
  New Britain *(G-4948)*
Cas-Kel Manufacturing Co Inc .... G 860 693-8704
  Canton *(G-1309)*
Tool 2000 .... G 860 620-0020
  Southington *(G-7989)*

DETONATORS & DETONATING CAPS

Dyno Nobel Inc .... C 860 843-2000
  Simsbury *(G-7618)*
Ensign-Bickford Arospc Def Co .. B 860 843-2289
  Simsbury *(G-7620)*
Ensign-Bickford Company .... G 860 843-2001
  Simsbury *(G-7621)*

DIAGNOSTIC SUBSTANCES

Bioarray Genetics Inc .... G 508 577-0205
  Farmington *(G-2884)*
Branford Open Mri & Diagnostic . G 203 481-7800
  Branford *(G-563)*
Charles River Laboratories Inc ... E 860 429-7261
  Storrs *(G-8546)*

DIAGNOSTIC SUBSTANCES OR AGENTS: In Vitro

Lucerion LLC .... G 203 699-8136
  Cheshire *(G-1409)*

DIAGNOSTIC SUBSTANCES OR AGENTS: In Vivo

Lam Therapeutics Inc .... F 203 458-7100
  Guilford *(G-3366)*

DIAGNOSTIC SUBSTANCES OR AGENTS: Microbiology & Virology

Applied Microbiology Services .... G 860 537-3118
  Lebanon *(G-3847)*

DIAGNOSTIC SUBSTANCES OR AGENTS: Radioactive

Cardinal Health 414 LLC .... G 860 291-9135
  East Hartford *(G-2302)*

DIAGNOSTIC SUBSTANCES OR AGENTS: Veterinary

Veterinary Medical Associates .... G 860 693-0214
  Canton *(G-1327)*

DIAPERS: Disposable

Capricorn Investors II LP .... A 203 861-6600
  Greenwich *(G-3140)*

DIE CUTTING SVC: Paper

C & T Print Finishing Inc .... F 860 282-0616
  South Windsor *(G-7720)*

DIE SETS: Presses, Metal Stamping

Globe Tool & Met Stampg Co Inc . E 860 621-6807
  Southington *(G-7929)*
P&G Metal Components Corp .... F 860 243-2220
  Bloomfield *(G-458)*

DIES & TOOLS: Special

Accurate Tool & Die Inc .... E 203 967-1200
  Stamford *(G-8057)*
Alberto Castillo .... G 203 834-1486
  Wilton *(G-10268)*
All Five Tool Co Inc .... E 860 583-1693
  Berlin *(G-154)*
Anderson Tool Company Inc .... G 203 777-4153
  New Haven *(G-5231)*
Arrow Diversified Tooling Inc ...... E 860 872-9072
  Ellington *(G-2576)*
B & L Tool and Machine Company . G 860 747-2721
  Plainville *(G-6774)*
B & P Plating Equipment LLC ..... F 860 589-5799
  Bristol *(G-969)*
Bremser Technologies Inc .... F 203 378-8486
  Stratford *(G-8585)*

PRODUCT SECTION

Bridgeport TI & Stamping Corp .... E 203 336-2501
  Bridgeport (G-723)
Bristol Tool & Die Company .... E 860 582-2577
  Bristol (G-993)
Candlewood Tool & Machine Shop ...... F 860 355-1892
  Gaylordsville (G-2990)
Carnegie Tool Inc .... F 203 866-0744
  Norwalk (G-6108)
Cas-Kel Manufacturing Co Inc .... G 860 693-8704
  Canton (G-1309)
Cgl Inc .... F 860 945-6166
  Watertown (G-9691)
Country Tool & Die Inc .... G 860 429-7325
  Ashford (G-58)
Diecraft Compacting Tool Inc .... G 203 879-3019
  Wolcott (G-10561)
Drilling Dynamics LLC .... G 203 783-1395
  Milford (G-4516)
E & E Tool & Manufacturing Co .... F 860 738-8577
  Winsted (G-10517)
Fad Tool Company LLC .... E 860 582-7890
  Bristol (G-1034)
Fly or Die Nation LLC .... G 860 218-3547
  Hartford (G-3590)
G P Tool Co Inc .... F 203 744-0310
  Danbury (G-1831)
Highland Manufacturing Inc .... E 860 646-5142
  Manchester (G-4028)
Hnat Mold & Die Inc .... G 860 537-0573
  Colchester (G-1554)
Hobson and Motzer Incorporated .... C 860 349-1756
  Durham (G-2149)
J T Tool Co Inc .... G 203 874-1234
  Milford (G-4558)
Jewett City Tool & Die Co .... G 860 376-0455
  Voluntown (G-9189)
Jovek Tool and Die .... G 860 261-5020
  Bristol (G-1055)
Lassy Tools Inc .... G 860 747-2748
  Plainville (G-6832)
Laurel Tool & Manufacturing .... G 860 889-5354
  Norwich (G-6422)
Lou-Jan Tool & Die Inc .... F 203 272-3536
  Cheshire (G-1408)
Lyons Tool and Die Company .... E 203 238-2689
  Meriden (G-4190)
Manchester Molding and Mfg Co .... E 860 643-2141
  Manchester (G-4052)
Marc Tool & Die Inc .... G 203 758-5933
  Prospect (G-7008)
Mastercraft Tool and Mch Co .... F 860 628-5551
  Southington (G-7950)
Michaud Tool Co Inc .... G 860 582-6785
  Terryville (G-8765)
Mid-State Manufacturing Inc .... F 860 621-6855
  Milldale (G-4686)
Northeast Carbide Inc .... F 860 628-2515
  Southington (G-7959)
Paragon Tool Company Inc .... G 860 647-9935
  Manchester (G-4072)
Plainville Machine & TI Co Inc .... F 860 589-5595
  Bristol (G-1091)
Preferred Tool & Die Inc .... D 203 925-8525
  Shelton (G-7537)
Quality Wire Edm Inc .... G 860 583-9867
  Bristol (G-1101)
R A Tool Co .... G 203 877-2998
  Milford (G-4622)
Ramar-Hall Inc .... E 860 349-1081
  Middlefield (G-4306)
Ray Machine Corporation .... E 860 582-8202
  Terryville (G-8769)
Reliable Tool & Die Inc .... E 203 877-3264
  Milford (G-4625)
REm Tool & Die Llc .... G 860 582-7559
  Bristol (G-1106)
Reynolds Carbide Die Co Inc .... E 860 283-8246
  Thomaston (G-8802)
Richards Machine Tool Co Inc .... F 860 436-2938
  Newington (G-5701)
Rintec Corporation .... F 860 274-3697
  Oakville (G-6462)
Sandur Tool Co .... G 203 753-0004
  Waterbury (G-9598)
Skico Manufacturing Co LLC .... G 203 230-1305
  Hamden (G-3510)
Skillcraft Machine Tool Co .... F 860 953-1246
  South Windsor (G-7822)
Spartan Aerospace LLC .... D 860 533-7500
  Manchester (G-4090)

Steel Rule Die Corp America .... G 860 621-5284
  Milldale (G-4688)
Straton Industries Inc .... D 203 375-4488
  Stratford (G-8687)
Taco Fasteners Inc .... F 860 747-5597
  Plainville (G-6867)
Telke Tool & Die Mfg Co .... G 860 828-9955
  Kensington (G-3819)
Total Concept Tool Inc .... G 203 483-1130
  Branford (G-664)
Victor Tool Co Inc .... G 203 634-8113
  Meriden (G-4264)
Watertown Jig Bore Service Inc .... F 860 274-5898
  Watertown (G-9748)
Weimann Brothers Mfg Co .... F 203 735-3311
  Derby (G-2130)
Wess Tool & Die Company Inc .... G 203 237-5277
  Meriden (G-4267)
West-Conn Tool and Die Inc .... F 203 538-5081
  Shelton (G-7584)
Wilkinson Tool & Die Co .... G 860 599-5821
  North Stonington (G-6032)

DIES: Cutting, Exc Metal

Bessette Holdings Inc .... E 860 289-6000
  East Hartford (G-2298)

DIES: Plastic Forming

Aba-PGT Inc .... C 860 649-4591
  Manchester (G-3974)
Acson Tool Company .... F 203 334-8050
  Bridgeport (G-682)

DIES: Steel Rule

B-P Products Inc .... E 203 288-0200
  Hamden (G-3416)
Bessette Holdings Inc .... E 860 289-6000
  East Hartford (G-2298)

DIET & WEIGHT REDUCING CENTERS

Barclay-Davis Enterprises LLC .... G 860 578-9563
  Hartford (G-3555)

DIODES: Light Emitting

Liteideas LLC .... G 860 213-8311
  Mansfield Center (G-4114)
Ray Green Corp .... F 707 544-2662
  Greenwich (G-3222)
Revolution Lighting .... G 203 504-1111
  Stamford (G-8388)
Revolution Lighting Tech Inc .... C 203 504-1111
  Stamford (G-8389)

DIRECT SELLING ESTAB: Coffee, Soda/Beer, Etc, Door-To-Door

Alvarium Beer Company LLC .... G 860 306-3857
  New Britain (G-4943)

DIRECT SELLING ESTABLISHMENTS: Encyclopedias, House-To-House

Scholastic Library Pubg Inc .... A 203 797-3500
  Danbury (G-1939)

DIRECT SELLING ESTABLISHMENTS: Food Svcs

Chef Gretchen LLC .... G 203 252-8892
  Stamford (G-8142)
Sodexo Inc .... E 860 679-2803
  Farmington (G-2958)

DIRECT SELLING ESTABLISHMENTS: Telemarketing

Mediagraphicscom Inc .... F 203 404-7233
  Durham (G-2153)
Taunton Inc .... A 203 426-8171
  Newtown (G-5785)

DISC JOCKEYS

Sign Craft LLC .... G 860 739-2863
  Niantic (G-5817)

DOCUMENT DESTRUCTION SVC

DISKETTE DUPLICATING SVCS

Computer Tech Express LLC .... G 203 810-4932
  Norwalk (G-6123)

DISKETTE OR KEY-DISK EQPT

Mumm Engineering Inc .... G 203 445-9777
  Monroe (G-4740)

DISPENSERS, TISSUE: Plastic

Clean Holdings LLC .... G 203 466-3365
  East Haven (G-2418)

DISPENSING EQPT & PARTS, BEVERAGE: Beer

Ultra Flow Dispense LLC .... G 866 827-2534
  Windsor (G-10457)

DISPENSING EQPT & PARTS, BEVERAGE: Coolers, Milk/Water, Elec

Four Seasons Cooler Eqp LLC .... G 203 263-0705
  Woodbury (G-10637)
Waterlogic Usa Inc .... G 866 917-7873
  Farmington (G-2977)

DISPENSING EQPT & PARTS, BEVERAGE: Fountain/Other Beverage

261 Pascone Place LLC .... G 860 666-7845
  Newington (G-5614)
Cascades Fine Papers .... G 860 870-7600
  Ellington (G-2580)

DISPLAY FIXTURES: Wood

W R Hartigan & Son Inc .... G 860 673-9203
  Burlington (G-1278)

DISPLAY ITEMS: Corrugated, Made From Purchased Materials

Corr/Dis Incorporated .... G 203 838-6075
  Norwalk (G-6130)
Skyline Exhibits & Graphics .... F 860 635-2400
  Middletown (G-4417)

DISPLAY LETTERING SVCS

Action Signs .... G 860 496-1232
  Torrington (G-8887)
Norwalk Sign Company Inc .... G 203 838-1942
  Norwalk (G-6282)

DISTILLERS DRIED GRAIN & SOLUBLES

American Distilling Inc .... G 860 267-4444
  Marlborough (G-4119)
American Distilling Inc .... D 860 267-4444
  East Hampton (G-2253)

DOCK EQPT & SPLYS, INDL

CCI Cyrus River Terminal LLC .... G 203 761-8000
  Stamford (G-8134)
Docko Inc .... G 860 572-8939
  Mystic (G-4812)
Kelly Industries LLC .... G 860 388-5666
  Old Saybrook (G-6549)
Readydock Inc .... G 860 523-9980
  Avon (G-104)

DOCK OPERATION SVCS, INCL BLDGS, FACILITIES, OPERS & MAINT

Docko Inc .... G 860 572-8939
  Mystic (G-4812)

DOCKS: Prefabricated Metal

Readydock Inc .... G 860 523-9980
  Avon (G-104)

DOCUMENT DESTRUCTION SVC

Joseph Merritt & Company Inc .... E 860 296-2500
  Hartford (G-3620)

DOOR & WINDOW REPAIR SVCS

Stanley Black & Decker Inc .... C 860 677-2861
  Farmington *(G-2960)*

DOOR FRAMES: Wood

Patrick Odonoghue .... G 203 467-4041
  East Haven *(G-2446)*
Red Barn Woodworkers .... G 860 379-3158
  Winsted *(G-10533)*
River Mill Co .... F 860 669-5915
  Clinton *(G-1521)*

DOOR OPERATING SYSTEMS: Electric

A-1 Garage Door Co .... G 203 866-6620
  Westport *(G-10049)*
Brian Cheney .... G 203 734-4793
  Seymour *(G-7336)*
Eric Sapper .... G 203 239-6020
  North Haven *(G-5938)*
Miracle Instruments Co .... F 860 642-7745
  Lebanon *(G-3858)*
Williams Walter Ovrhd Door LLC .... G 203 488-8620
  Branford *(G-674)*

DOORS & WINDOWS WHOLESALERS: All Materials

Advanced Window Systems LLC .... F 800 841-6544
  Berlin *(G-150)*
Hatch and Bailey Company .... E 203 866-5515
  Norwalk *(G-6193)*

DOORS & WINDOWS: Screen & Storm

2seal LLC .... G 860 227-6854
  Old Lyme *(G-6487)*
Ld Assoc LLC .... G 203 452-9393
  Monroe *(G-4727)*

DOORS & WINDOWS: Storm, Metal

All-Time Manufacturing Co Inc .... F 860 848-9258
  Montville *(G-4768)*

DOORS: Combination Screen & Storm, Wood

Salisbury Artisans .... G 860 435-0344
  Salisbury *(G-7297)*

DOORS: Fiberglass

Hexcel Corporation .... E 203 969-0666
  Stamford *(G-8233)*

DOORS: Fire, Metal

Stonington Services LLC .... E 860 464-1991
  Gales Ferry *(G-2987)*

DOORS: Garage, Overhead, Metal

American Overhead Ret Div Inc .... G 860 876-4552
  Middletown *(G-4316)*

DOORS: Garage, Overhead, Wood

American Overhead Ret Div Inc .... G 860 876-4552
  Middletown *(G-4316)*
Anchor Overhead Door Sales .... G 860 651-6560
  Tariffville *(G-8743)*
New England Standard Corp .... G 203 876-7733
  Milford *(G-4589)*
Ridgefield Overhead Door LLC .... G 203 431-3667
  Ridgefield *(G-7168)*
Up & Down Overhead Door .... G 203 876-8045
  Milford *(G-4670)*

DOORS: Hangar, Metal

Schoenrock Marine Door Systems .... G 203 600-8370
  East Haven *(G-2451)*

DOORS: Rolling, Indl Building Or Warehouse, Metal

Emhart Teknologies LLC .... G 877 364-2781
  Danbury *(G-1808)*

DOORS: Wooden

Adam Fuller Woodworking .... G 860 455-1296
  North Windham *(G-6033)*

Deschenes & Cooper Architectur .... G 860 599-2481
  Pawcatuck *(G-6709)*
Gagne & Gagne Co .... G 860 742-5038
  Andover *(G-8)*

DRAFTING SVCS

Melvin Mayo .... G 802 698-7635
  Enfield *(G-2658)*

DRAINAGE PRDTS: Concrete

Atlantic Pipe Corporation .... D 860 747-5557
  Plainville *(G-6772)*

DRAPERIES & CURTAINS

A Change of Scenery .... G 860 872-4435
  Ellington *(G-2569)*
Blue Lily Cotton LLC .... G 860 869-7734
  Milford *(G-4473)*
Dominics Decorating Inc .... G 203 838-1827
  Norwalk *(G-6145)*
Lyons Upholstery Shop Inc .... G 203 269-3782
  Wallingford *(G-9308)*
Scott C Parker .... G 860 355-9738
  Roxbury *(G-7283)*
Sew Beautiful Win Treatments .... G 203 598-0544
  Middlebury *(G-4291)*
Tetrault & Sons Inc .... G 860 872-9187
  Stafford Springs *(G-8042)*
Threads of Evidence LLC .... G 203 929-5209
  Shelton *(G-7566)*
Top of Line Drapery & Uphl .... G 203 348-0000
  Stamford *(G-8470)*
Yard Stick Decore .... F 203 330-0360
  Bridgeport *(G-943)*

DRAPERIES & DRAPERY FABRICS, COTTON

Tassels .... G 203 231-0973
  Derby *(G-2128)*

DRAPERIES: Plastic & Textile, From Purchased Materials

Byron Lord Inc .... G 203 287-9881
  Old Lyme *(G-6493)*
Chatham Drapery Co Inc .... G 860 267-7767
  East Hampton *(G-2261)*
Decorator Services Inc .... E 203 384-8144
  Bridgeport *(G-743)*
Draperies Plus .... G 860 589-3634
  Bristol *(G-1019)*
Thomas W Raftery Inc .... E 860 278-9870
  Hartford *(G-3703)*

DRAPERY & UPHOLSTERY STORES: Draperies

Draperies Plus .... G 860 589-3634
  Bristol *(G-1019)*

DRESSMAKERS: Custom

Jennifers Tailor Shop .... G 860 489-8968
  Torrington *(G-8938)*

DRILLS & DRILLING EQPT: Mining

Numa Tool Company .... D 860 923-9551
  Thompson *(G-8841)*
P2 Science Inc .... G 203 821-7457
  Woodbridge *(G-10611)*

DRINKING PLACES: Alcoholic Beverages

Congress Catering Inc .... E 860 291-8182
  East Hartford *(G-2309)*

DRINKING PLACES: Bars & Lounges

Swagnificent Ent LLC .... G 203 449-0124
  Bridgeport *(G-918)*
Thimble Island Brewing Company .... E 203 208-2827
  Branford *(G-663)*

DRINKING WATER COOLERS WHOLESALERS: Mechanical

Waterlogic Usa Inc .... G 866 917-7873
  Farmington *(G-2977)*

DRUG TESTING KITS: Blood & Urine

Altasci LLC .... G 860 224-6668
  New Britain *(G-4942)*
Maps and More .... G 203 335-0556
  Bridgeport *(G-828)*

DRUGS & DRUG PROPRIETARIES, WHOLESALE: Antiseptics

Beiersdorf Inc .... B 203 854-8000
  Norwalk *(G-6088)*
Beiersdorf North America Inc .... F 203 563-5800
  Wilton *(G-10272)*

DRUGS & DRUG PROPRIETARIES, WHOLESALE: Pharmaceuticals

Frederick Purdue Company Inc .... B 203 588-8000
  Stamford *(G-8210)*
Pharmaceutical RES Assoc Inc .... G 203 588-8000
  Stamford *(G-8360)*
PRA Holdings Inc .... G 203 853-0123
  Stamford *(G-8370)*
Purdue Pharma Inc .... G 203 588-8000
  Stamford *(G-8377)*
Purdue Pharma LP .... B 203 588-8000
  Stamford *(G-8378)*
Purdue Pharmaceuticals LP .... F 252 265-1900
  Stamford *(G-8381)*
Sheffield Pharmaceuticals LLC .... C 860 442-4451
  New London *(G-5488)*

DRUGS ACTING ON THE CENTRAL NERVOUS SYSTEM & SENSE ORGANS

Biohaven Phrm Holdg Co Ltd .... E 203 404-0410
  New Haven *(G-5246)*
Neurohydrate LLC .... G 203 799-7900
  Bridgeport *(G-848)*

DRUMS: Shipping, Metal

Mobile Mini Inc .... E 860 668-1888
  Suffield *(G-8727)*

DRYCLEANING & LAUNDRY SVCS: Commercial & Family

Embroidery Wizard .... G 860 379-3294
  Winsted *(G-10519)*
Sally Conant .... F 203 878-3005
  Orange *(G-6628)*

DRYCLEANING EQPT & SPLYS: Commercial

Rema Dri-Vac Corp .... F 203 847-2464
  Norwalk *(G-6321)*
Rite Way Cleaner .... G 203 789-9561
  New Haven *(G-5380)*

DRYERS & REDRYERS: Indl

Dri-Air Industries Inc .... E 860 627-5110
  East Windsor *(G-2489)*

DUCTING: Metal Plate

L & L Mechanical LLC .... F 860 491-4007
  Goshen *(G-3101)*
New Haven Sheet Metal Co .... G 203 468-0341
  New Haven *(G-5348)*
Performance Sheet Metal .... G 860 889-0550
  Bozrah *(G-531)*

DUCTING: Plastic

Siftex Equipment Company .... E 860 289-8779
  South Windsor *(G-7821)*

DUCTS: Sheet Metal

Buckley Associates Inc .... G 203 380-2405
  Stratford *(G-8590)*
General Sheet Metal Works Inc .... F 203 333-6111
  Bridgeport *(G-775)*
M & O Corporation .... E 203 367-4292
  Bridgeport *(G-827)*
Manufacturers Service Co Inc .... G 203 389-9595
  Woodbridge *(G-10606)*
McGill Airflow LLC .... G 860 653-8001
  East Granby *(G-2213)*

PRODUCT SECTION

DUMPSTERS: Garbage

All Phase Dumpsters LLC ....G...... 203 778-9104
  Bethel *(G-257)*
B & C Industries ....G...... 203 572-0265
  Stratford *(G-8575)*
CT Dumpster LLC ....G...... 203 521-0779
  Milford *(G-4501)*
Dylans Dumpsters LLC ....G...... 860 455-9924
  Chaplin *(G-1339)*
Hayes Services LLC ....G...... 860 739-2273
  East Lyme *(G-2466)*
Roll-Off Best Service LLC ....G...... 860 350-2378
  New Milford *(G-5586)*
Same Day Dumpsters LLC ....G...... 203 676-1219
  New Haven *(G-5387)*

DURABLE GOODS WHOLESALERS, NEC

AAA Distributors ....G...... 860 346-0230
  Middletown *(G-4312)*
Polep Distribution Services J ....G...... 203 378-2193
  Stratford *(G-8666)*

DYNAMOMETERS

Kahn Industries Inc ....E...... 860 529-8643
  Wethersfield *(G-10204)*

EARTH SCIENCE SVCS

Coastline Environmental LLC ....G...... 203 483-6898
  North Branford *(G-5831)*

EATING PLACES

Baltasar & Sons Inc ....G...... 203 723-0425
  Naugatuck *(G-4860)*
Capricorn Investors III LP ....F...... 203 861-6600
  Greenwich *(G-3141)*
Fine Food Services Inc ....E...... 860 445-5276
  Groton *(G-3288)*
Olive Oil Factory LLC ....F...... 203 591-8986
  Waterbury *(G-9570)*
Sharpe Hill Vineyard Inc ....E...... 860 974-3549
  Pomfret *(G-6936)*
Southport Brewing Co ....E...... 203 874-2337
  Milford *(G-4649)*

EDITORIAL SVCS

Editorial Directions Inc ....G...... 203 245-2011
  Madison *(G-3919)*

EDUCATIONAL SVCS, NONDEGREE GRANTING: Continuing Education

Overseas Ministries Study Ctr ....F...... 203 624-6672
  New Haven *(G-5357)*
Toastmasters International ....F...... 203 847-5667
  Norwalk *(G-6372)*

EFFERVESCENT SALTS

Tower Laboratories Ltd ....D...... 860 767-2127
  Centerbrook *(G-1334)*

EGG WHOLESALERS

Moark LLC ....E...... 951 332-3300
  North Franklin *(G-5876)*

ELASTOMERS

Pastanch LLC ....E...... 203 720-9478
  Naugatuck *(G-4909)*

ELECTRIC MOTOR REPAIR SVCS

Accuwind Inc ....G...... 203 287-9697
  Hamden *(G-3411)*
Aparos Electric Motor Service ....G...... 860 276-2044
  Southington *(G-7891)*
B & F Electric Motors LLC ....G...... 203 359-2626
  Stamford *(G-8103)*
Canfield Electric ....G...... 203 266-5290
  Bethlehem *(G-367)*
Central Electric Inc ....G...... 860 774-3054
  Dayville *(G-2057)*
Central Electric Motor ....G...... 860 642-7421
  Lebanon *(G-3850)*
Cudzilo Enterprises Inc ....G...... 203 748-4694
  Bethel *(G-275)*

Electric Enterprise Inc ....F...... 203 378-7311
  Stratford *(G-8607)*
Electrical Maintenance Svc Co ....G...... 203 333-6163
  Bridgeport *(G-761)*
Industrial Drives Contrls Inc ....F...... 203 753-5103
  Waterbury *(G-9504)*
Industrial Electric Motors ....G...... 203 743-9611
  Danbury *(G-1849)*
Just Call Jason LLC ....G...... 203 934-3127
  West Haven *(G-9921)*
Leppert/Nutmeg Inc ....E...... 860 243-1737
  Bloomfield *(G-441)*
Magna-Wind Inc ....G...... 203 269-4749
  Wallingford *(G-9309)*
Nicholas Melfi Jr ....G...... 203 853-7235
  Norwalk *(G-6278)*
Palmers Elc Mtrs & Pumps Inc ....G...... 203 348-7378
  Norwalk *(G-6290)*
Power Quality and Drives LLC ....G...... 203 217-2353
  Woodbury *(G-10651)*
Precision Devices Inc ....F...... 203 265-9308
  Wallingford *(G-9340)*
Reliable Electric Motor Inc ....F...... 860 522-2257
  Hartford *(G-3676)*
Rite-Way Electric Motors Inc ....G...... 860 528-8890
  East Hartford *(G-2366)*
Tibbys Electric Motor Service ....G...... 203 748-4694
  Bethel *(G-353)*
Total Control Inc ....G...... 203 269-4749
  Wallingford *(G-9390)*
Traver Electric Motor Co Inc ....E...... 203 753-5103
  Waterbury *(G-9617)*

ELECTRIC SERVICES

Direct Energy Inc ....F...... 800 260-0300
  Stamford *(G-8186)*

ELECTRIC SVCS, NEC: Power Generation

Robran Industries Inc ....G...... 203 510-6292
  Waterbury *(G-9594)*

ELECTRIC TOOL REPAIR SVCS

Air Tool Sales & Service Co ....G...... 860 673-2714
  Unionville *(G-9110)*
Cnc Machine Tl Specialist LLC ....G...... 860 873-1816
  East Haddam *(G-2239)*

ELECTRICAL APPARATUS & EQPT WHOLESALERS

Ademco Inc ....G...... 860 257-3266
  Rocky Hill *(G-7218)*
Ademco Inc ....G...... 203 877-2702
  Milford *(G-4440)*
Asea Brown Boveri Inc ....G...... 203 750-2200
  Norwalk *(G-6076)*
Eastern Conectr Specialty Corp ....G...... 860 355-8100
  New Milford *(G-5530)*
EC Holdings Inc ....G...... 203 846-1651
  Norwalk *(G-6153)*
Hartford Fire Equipment ....E...... 860 747-2757
  Plainville *(G-6821)*
HI Temp Electric Company ....E...... 661 259-9225
  Andover *(G-9)*
Lighting Edge Inc ....G...... 860 767-8968
  Essex *(G-2724)*
On Line Building Systems LLC ....G...... 203 798-1194
  Danbury *(G-1899)*
Pathway Lighting Products Inc ....D...... 860 388-6881
  Old Saybrook *(G-6564)*
Precision Devices Inc ....F...... 203 265-9308
  Wallingford *(G-9340)*
Rexel ....G...... 203 969-6601
  Stamford *(G-8391)*
Thermal Fluidics ....G...... 860 740-4880
  Durham *(G-2159)*

ELECTRICAL APPLIANCES, TELEVISIONS & RADIOS WHOLESALERS

Conair Corporation ....D...... 800 492-7464
  Torrington *(G-8914)*

ELECTRICAL CURRENT CARRYING WIRING DEVICES

ABB Enterprise Software Inc ....A...... 860 747-7111
  Plainville *(G-6763)*

ELECTRICAL EQPT & SPLYS

Allied Controls Inc ....F...... 860 628-8443
  Stamford *(G-8072)*
American Specialty Pdts LLC ....G...... 860 871-2279
  Vernon *(G-9130)*
Bead Industries Inc ....E...... 203 301-0270
  Milford *(G-4466)*
Burndy LLC ....D...... 203 792-1115
  Bethel *(G-267)*
Dering-Ney Inc ....G...... 847 932-6782
  Bloomfield *(G-406)*
Dicon Connections Inc ....E...... 203 481-8080
  North Branford *(G-5835)*
Eaton Aerospace LLC ....E...... 203 796-6000
  Bethel *(G-292)*
Eaton Corporation ....G...... 203 796-6000
  Bethel *(G-293)*
Ek-Ris Cable Company Inc ....E...... 860 223-4327
  New Britain *(G-4980)*
Everlast Products LLC ....G...... 203 250-7111
  Cheshire *(G-1387)*
Faria Beede Instruments Inc ....C...... 860 848-9271
  North Stonington *(G-6024)*
Floodmaster LLC ....G...... 203 488-4477
  Branford *(G-595)*
Gordon Products Incorporated ....E...... 203 775-4501
  Brookfield *(G-1194)*
Hubbell Incorporated Delaware ....C...... 475 882-4800
  Shelton *(G-7469)*
Hubbell Incorporated Delaware ....D...... 475 882-4000
  Shelton *(G-7470)*
Hubbell Technical Ctr ....G...... 203 337-3333
  Bridgeport *(G-789)*
Hubbell Wiring Device ....F...... 203 882-4800
  Milford *(G-4549)*
Legrand Holding Inc ....E...... 860 233-6251
  West Hartford *(G-9828)*
Lex Products LLC ....C...... 203 363-3738
  Shelton *(G-7490)*
Old Cambridge Products Corp ....G...... 860 243-1761
  Bloomfield *(G-454)*
Old Ni Incorporated ....G...... 203 327-7300
  Stamford *(G-8338)*
On Line Building Systems LLC ....G...... 203 798-1194
  Danbury *(G-1899)*
Oslo Switch Inc ....E...... 203 272-2794
  Cheshire *(G-1425)*
Ripley Tools LLC ....E...... 860 635-2200
  Cromwell *(G-1715)*
Siemon Company ....E...... 860 945-4218
  Watertown *(G-9735)*
Spectrum Associates Inc ....F...... 203 878-4618
  Milford *(G-4651)*
Thomas Products Ltd ....G...... 860 621-9101
  Southington *(G-7987)*
Times Wire and Cable Company ....G...... 203 949-8400
  Wallingford *(G-9387)*
United Electric Controls Co ....D...... 203 877-2795
  Milford *(G-4668)*
Wiremold Company ....A...... 860 233-6251
  West Hartford *(G-9874)*
World Cord Sets Inc ....G...... 860 763-2100
  Enfield *(G-2708)*

ELECTRICAL DISCHARGE MACHINING, EDM

Arcade Technology LLC ....E...... 203 366-3871
  Bridgeport *(G-699)*
Cgl Inc ....F...... 860 945-6166
  Watertown *(G-9691)*
Michaud Tool Co Inc ....G...... 860 582-6785
  Terryville *(G-8765)*
Precision E D M Inc ....F...... 413 733-2813
  Windsor *(G-10423)*
Pw Precision Machine LLC ....G...... 203 889-8615
  Higganum *(G-3777)*
Quality Wire Edm Inc ....G...... 860 583-9867
  Bristol *(G-1101)*
To The tenth Inc ....G...... 203 248-9437
  Hamden *(G-3521)*
Wire Tech LLC ....G...... 860 945-9473
  Watertown *(G-9750)*

ELECTRICAL EQPT & SPLYS

Alent Inc ....D...... 203 575-5727
  Waterbury *(G-9425)*
Alent USA Holding Inc ....B...... 203 575-5727
  Waterbury *(G-9426)*
Arthur J Hurley Company ....G...... 860 257-5505
  East Hartford *(G-2293)*
Ascentech LLC ....G...... 860 526-8903
  Chester *(G-1463)*

ELECTRICAL EQPT & SPLYS

PRODUCT SECTION

Astrophonic Corp America .... G 203 853-9300
  Norwalk *(G-6079)*
B & G Industries LLC .... G 860 571-8873
  Wethersfield *(G-10182)*
Bam Electric LLC .... G 203 595-0008
  Stamford *(G-8107)*
Brookfield Industries Inc .... E 860 283-6211
  Thomaston *(G-8782)*
C & E Electric .... G 203 546-7255
  Brookfield *(G-1167)*
Carey Manufacturing Co Inc .... E 860 829-1803
  Cromwell *(G-1694)*
Carey Manufacturing Co Inc .... E 860 829-1803
  Cromwell *(G-1695)*
Circuit Breaker Sales Ne Inc .... G 203 888-7500
  Seymour *(G-7340)*
Clark Power Systems Inc .... G 203 775-8444
  Brookfield *(G-1172)*
Data Collection Dispersal Inc .... G 860 623-7364
  Broad Brook *(G-1146)*
DC & D Inc .... G 860 623-2941
  Broad Brook *(G-1147)*
E-J Electric T & D LLC .... D 203 626-9625
  Wallingford *(G-9256)*
Eagle Electric Service LLC .... F 860 868-9898
  Bethlehem *(G-369)*
Eastern Electric Cnstr Co .... G 860 485-1100
  Harwinton *(G-3726)*
Eastside Electric Inc .... F 860 485-0700
  Harwinton *(G-3727)*
Electro Mech Specialists LLC .... G 860 887-2613
  Bozrah *(G-524)*
Electrodes Incorporated .... E 203 878-7400
  Milford *(G-4528)*
Etron LLC .... G 860 673-0121
  Burlington *(G-1268)*
Evse Llc .... G 860 745-2433
  Enfield *(G-2644)*
Fuelcell Energy Inc .... E 860 496-1111
  Torrington *(G-8927)*
Guest Co .... G 203 235-4421
  Berlin *(G-185)*
Housatonic Mch & Prototype LLC ..... G 203 922-2714
  Shelton *(G-7467)*
Hubbell Incorporated .... D 475 882-4000
  Shelton *(G-7468)*
Iemct .... G 203 683-4382
  Milford *(G-4552)*
J Ro Grounding Systems Inc .... G 860 747-2106
  Plainville *(G-6827)*
Jamieson Laser LLC .... G 860 482-3375
  Litchfield *(G-3893)*
Jared Manufacturing Co Inc .... F 203 846-1732
  Norwalk *(G-6219)*
Newco Condenser Inc .... G 475 882-4000
  Shelton *(G-7510)*
Power Up Electric .... G 203 312-0601
  Danbury *(G-1910)*
Presco Incorporated .... F 203 397-8722
  Woodbridge *(G-10615)*
Rexel .... G 203 969-6601
  Stamford *(G-8391)*
Richter Electric Inc .... G 203 667-4644
  Darien *(G-2041)*
Sherric Group LLC .... G 860 673-3924
  Unionville *(G-9128)*
Stanley Black & Decker Inc .... C 860 677-2861
  Farmington *(G-2960)*
T J Russell Electric LLC .... G 203 791-8950
  Danbury *(G-1958)*
Thermal Fluidics .... G 860 740-4880
  Durham *(G-2159)*
Trine Access Technology Inc .... F 203 730-1756
  Bethel *(G-356)*
United Technologies Corp .... B 860 728-7000
  Farmington *(G-2972)*
Westfair Electric Contractors .... G 203 586-1760
  Southbury *(G-7885)*

ELECTRICAL EQPT FOR ENGINES

All Tech Auto/Truck Electric .... G 203 790-8990
  Danbury *(G-1736)*
Beede Electrical Instr Co Inc .... C 603 753-6362
  North Stonington *(G-6020)*

ELECTRICAL EQPT REPAIR & MAINTENANCE

Conair Corporation .... D 800 492-7464
  Torrington *(G-8914)*
Integrated Packg Systems Inc .... G 860 623-2623
  East Windsor *(G-2499)*
Talk N Fix CT Inc .... G 203 790-8905
  Danbury *(G-1959)*
William Linkovich .... G 860 824-0298
  East Canaan *(G-2184)*

ELECTRICAL EQPT REPAIR SVCS

Leppert/Nutmeg Inc .... E 860 243-1737
  Bloomfield *(G-441)*
On Line Building Systems LLC .... G 203 798-1194
  Danbury *(G-1899)*

ELECTRICAL EQPT: Automotive, NEC

E G Tech Solutions LLC .... G 203 200-7047
  Old Greenwich *(G-6471)*
West End Auto Parts .... G 203 453-9009
  North Branford *(G-5867)*

ELECTRICAL GOODS, WHOLESALE: Burglar Alarm Systems

Alarm One .... G 203 239-1714
  North Haven *(G-5898)*

ELECTRICAL GOODS, WHOLESALE: Cable Conduit

Underground Systems Inc .... E 203 792-3444
  Bethel *(G-357)*

ELECTRICAL GOODS, WHOLESALE: Connectors

Fct Electronics LP .... D 860 482-2800
  Torrington *(G-8923)*
Phoenix Company of Chicago Inc ..... D 630 595-2300
  Naugatuck *(G-4910)*

ELECTRICAL GOODS, WHOLESALE: Electronic Parts

Component Concepts Inc .... G 860 523-4066
  West Hartford *(G-9792)*
Cudzilo Enterprises Inc .... G 203 748-4694
  Bethel *(G-275)*
Eastern Conectr Specialty Corp .... G 860 355-8100
  New Milford *(G-5530)*
Midstate Electronics Co .... F 203 265-9900
  Wallingford *(G-9322)*
Mil-Con Inc .... D 630 595-2366
  Naugatuck *(G-4901)*
Park Distributories Inc .... F 203 366-7200
  Bridgeport *(G-865)*
Park Distributories Inc .... G 203 579-2140
  Bridgeport *(G-863)*
Servers Storage Networking LLC .... G 203 433-0808
  Norwalk *(G-6343)*
Wanho Manufacturing LLC .... G 203 759-3744
  Cheshire *(G-1457)*

ELECTRICAL GOODS, WHOLESALE: Flashlights

Sapphire Mltnational Group Inc .... G 860 693-1233
  Torrington *(G-8966)*

ELECTRICAL GOODS, WHOLESALE: Generators

Ac/DC Industrial Electric LLC .... G 860 886-2232
  Yantic *(G-10695)*

ELECTRICAL GOODS, WHOLESALE: Irons

Kostas Custom Ir Fabrications .... G 203 328-1308
  Stamford *(G-8279)*

ELECTRICAL GOODS, WHOLESALE: Lighting Fixtures, Comm & Indl

Point Lighting Corporation .... E 860 243-0600
  Bloomfield *(G-467)*

ELECTRICAL GOODS, WHOLESALE: Motor Ctrls, Starters & Relays

In-Motion LLC .... G 860 742-3612
  Coventry *(G-1656)*

ELECTRICAL GOODS, WHOLESALE: Motors

Aparos Electric Motor Service .... G 860 276-2044
  Southington *(G-7891)*
B & F Electric Motors LLC .... G 203 359-2626
  Stamford *(G-8103)*
Cudzilo Enterprises Inc .... G 203 748-4694
  Bethel *(G-275)*
Electric Enterprise Inc .... F 203 378-7311
  Stratford *(G-8607)*
Electrical Maintenance Svc Co .... G 203 333-6163
  Bridgeport *(G-761)*
Elinco International Inc .... G 203 275-8885
  Fairfield *(G-2780)*
Industrial Drives Contrls Inc .... F 203 753-5103
  Waterbury *(G-9504)*
Industrial Electric Motors .... G 203 743-9611
  Danbury *(G-1849)*
Magna-Wind Inc .... G 203 269-4749
  Wallingford *(G-9309)*
Palmers Elc Mtrs & Pumps Inc .... G 203 348-7378
  Norwalk *(G-6290)*
Piela Electric Inc .... F 860 889-8476
  Preston *(G-6987)*
Reliable Electric Motor Inc .... F 860 522-2257
  Hartford *(G-3676)*
Rite-Way Electric Motors Inc .... G 860 528-8890
  East Hartford *(G-2366)*
SEC Electrical Inc .... F 203 562-5811
  New Haven *(G-5390)*

ELECTRICAL GOODS, WHOLESALE: Security Control Eqpt & Systems

Grayfin Security LLC .... G 203 800-6760
  Madison *(G-3923)*

ELECTRICAL GOODS, WHOLESALE: Sound Eqpt

Vibrascience Inc .... G 203 483-6113
  Branford *(G-666)*

ELECTRICAL GOODS, WHOLESALE: Telephone Eqpt

Southern Neng Telecom Corp .... B 203 771-5200
  New Haven *(G-5401)*
Total Communications Inc .... E 203 882-0088
  Milford *(G-4666)*
Total Communications Inc .... D 860 282-9999
  East Hartford *(G-2386)*

ELECTRICAL GOODS, WHOLESALE: Transformer & Transmission Eqpt

Carlyle Johnson Machine Co LLC ...... E 860 643-1531
  Bolton *(G-508)*

ELECTRICAL GOODS, WHOLESALE: Wire & Cable

Autac Incorporated .... G 203 481-3444
  Branford *(G-550)*
Marmon Engnered Wire Cable LLC ... G 860 653-8300
  Hartford *(G-3635)*
Rel-Tech Electronics Inc .... D 203 877-8770
  Milford *(G-4624)*
Specialty Cable Corp .... G 203 265-7126
  Wallingford *(G-9372)*

ELECTRICAL GOODS, WHOLESALE: Wire & Cable, Ctrl & Sig

Protection Industries Corp .... G 203 375-9393
  Stratford *(G-8671)*

ELECTRICAL GOODS, WHOLESALE: Wire & Cable, Electronic

Advanced Product Solutions LLC ...... G 203 745-4225
  Hamden *(G-3412)*
Phoenix Company of Chicago Inc ..... D 630 595-2300
  Naugatuck *(G-4910)*
Times Wire and Cable Company .... G 203 949-8400
  Wallingford *(G-9387)*

PRODUCT SECTION — EMBROIDERING & ART NEEDLEWORK FOR THE TRADE

ELECTRICAL HOUSEHOLD APPLIANCE REPAIR
W H Preuss Sons Incorporated ....G....... 860 643-9492
Bolton (G-521)

ELECTRICAL INDL APPARATUS, NEC
90 River Street LLC ....G....... 203 772-4700
New Haven (G-5216)
Harby Power Solutions LLC ....G....... 203 265-0012
Wallingford (G-9278)

ELECTRICAL SPLYS
Circuit Breaker Sales Ne Inc ....E....... 203 888-7500
Seymour (G-7340)
Mil-Con Inc ....D....... 630 595-2366
Naugatuck (G-4901)
Traver Electric Motor Co Inc ....E....... 203 753-5103
Waterbury (G-9617)

ELECTRICAL SUPPLIES: Porcelain
Coorstek Inc ....E....... 860 653-8071
East Granby (G-2200)

ELECTRODES: Thermal & Electrolytic
Carbon Tools Inc ....G....... 860 228-9483
Amston (G-2)

ELECTROMEDICAL EQPT
Atlantic Inertial Systems Inc ....A....... 203 250-3500
Cheshire (G-1357)
Bio-Med Devices Inc ....D....... 203 458-0202
Guilford (G-3329)
Coolspine LLC ....G....... 203 263-6188
Woodbury (G-10631)
Coopersurgical Inc ....C....... 203 601-5200
Trumbull (G-9017)
Epicurean Feast Medtron O ....G....... 203 492-5000
North Haven (G-5937)
Hobbs Medical Inc ....E....... 860 684-5875
Stafford Springs (G-8031)
Philips Ultrasound Inc ....D....... 203 753-5215
Waterbury (G-9576)
Razzberry Operating Co Inc ....G....... 510 495-5366
Hamden (G-3503)
Respironics Novametrix LLC ....C....... 203 697-6475
Wallingford (G-9351)
Seclingua Inc ....G....... 203 922-4560
Stamford (G-8406)
Walker Magnetics Group Inc ....E....... 508 853-3232
Windsor (G-10461)

ELECTRON BEAM: Cutting, Forming, Welding
Integral Technologies Inc ....G....... 860 741-2281
Enfield (G-2652)

ELECTRON TUBES
Conklin-Sherman Company Incthe ...G....... 203 881-0190
Beacon Falls (G-133)
Connecticut Coining Inc ....D....... 203 743-3861
Bethel (G-273)
Whelen Engineering Company Inc ...B....... 860 526-9504
Chester (G-1485)

ELECTRONIC COMPONENTS
Defense Cmmnications Solutions ....G....... 203 947-6283
Danbury (G-1791)
Ens Microwave LLC ....G....... 203 241-1888
Danbury (G-1812)
Insys Micro Inc ....G....... 917 566-5045
Norwalk (G-6209)
Ja Electronics LLC ....G....... 860 921-7549
Waterbury (G-9508)
Preferred PDT & Mktg Group LLC ...G....... 203 567-0221
Shelton (G-7536)
Winstanley Inc ....G....... 203 238-6614
Meriden (G-4269)

ELECTRONIC DEVICES: Solid State, NEC
Delcom Products Inc ....G....... 914 934-5170
Danbury (G-1792)
Servers Storage Networking LLC ....G....... 203 433-0808
Norwalk (G-6343)

T&K Technical Services LLC ....G....... 860 235-5882
Quaker Hill (G-7085)

ELECTRONIC EQPT REPAIR SVCS
Arthur Rodgers ....G....... 860 967-4598
Ledyard (G-3867)
Doosan Fuel Cell America Inc ....C....... 860 727-2200
South Windsor (G-7739)
Modern Electronic Fax & Cmpt ....G....... 203 292-6520
Fairfield (G-2816)
Nct Inc ....F....... 860 666-8424
Newington (G-5684)
T-S Display Systems Inc ....G....... 203 964-0575
Stamford (G-8456)

ELECTRONIC LOADS & POWER SPLYS
Hartford Electric Sup Co Inc ....F....... 860 760-4887
Rocky Hill (G-7240)
Topex Inc ....F....... 203 748-5918
Danbury (G-1963)

ELECTRONIC PARTS & EQPT WHOLESALERS
Action Media Inc ....G....... 203 466-5535
East Haven (G-2407)
Cara C Andreoli ....G....... 860 888-6553
Glastonbury (G-3019)
Radio Frequency Systems Inc ....E....... 203 630-3311
Meriden (G-4227)
Systems and Tech Intl Inc ....G....... 860 871-0401
Tolland (G-8880)
UTC Fire SEC Americas Corp Inc ....G....... 941 739-4200
Farmington (G-2974)
Winstanley Inc ....G....... 203 238-6614
Meriden (G-4269)
Xiaohao Jia ....G....... 203 866-3120
Norwalk (G-6403)

ELECTRONIC SHOPPING
Bellable LLC ....G....... 800 212-2603
West Hartford (G-9778)
J J Lane Designs ....G....... 860 849-0815
Suffield (G-8722)
Loving Life LLC ....G....... 860 326-1459
Voluntown (G-9190)

ELECTROPLATING & PLATING SVC
Chromalloy Component Svcs Inc .....G....... 203 924-1666
Shelton (G-7418)
Gybenorth Industries LLC ....F....... 203 876-9876
Milford (G-4546)
Jarvis Precision Polishing ....F....... 860 589-5822
Bristol (G-1052)
M & Z Engineering Inc ....G....... 860 496-0282
Torrington (G-8945)
National Integrated Inds Inc ....C....... 860 677-7995
Farmington (G-2933)
Sifco Applied Srfc Cncepts LLC ......G....... 860 623-6006
East Windsor (G-2518)
Usc Technologies LLC ....G....... 203 378-9622
Stratford (G-8701)

ELEMENTARY & SECONDARY SCHOOLS, SPECIAL EDUCATION
Bushy Hill Nature Center ....G....... 860 767-2148
Ivoryton (G-3784)

ELEVATORS & EQPT
Ascend Elevator Inc ....C....... 215 703-0358
Bloomfield (G-391)
Bay State Elevator Company Inc .....F....... 860 243-9030
Bloomfield (G-393)
International Elevator Corp ....G....... 203 302-1023
Cos Cob (G-1634)
K-Tech International ....E....... 860 489-9399
Torrington (G-8941)
Netz New Haven Norton ....G....... 203 507-2108
New Haven (G-5340)
Otis Elevator Company ....B....... 860 674-3000
Farmington (G-2942)
Otis Elevator Company ....G....... 860 290-3318
Farmington (G-2943)
United Technologies Corp ....B....... 860 728-7000
Farmington (G-2972)

ELEVATORS WHOLESALERS
Otis Elevator Company ....B....... 860 242-3632
Bloomfield (G-456)

ELEVATORS: Installation & Conversion
Bay State Elevator Company Inc .....F....... 860 243-9030
Bloomfield (G-393)
Otis Elevator Company ....B....... 860 242-3632
Bloomfield (G-456)
Otis Elevator Company ....B....... 860 674-3000
Farmington (G-2942)
Stevenson Group Corporation ....G....... 860 689-0011
Harwinton (G-3740)

EMBLEMS: Embroidered
Connecticut Screen Print ....G....... 203 877-6655
Milford (G-4498)
Mead Monogramming ....G....... 203 618-0701
Cos Cob (G-1637)
Seems Inc ....F....... 203 284-0259
Ansonia (G-50)

EMBROIDERING & ART NEEDLEWORK FOR THE TRADE
A Dancing Thread ....G....... 860 669-9094
Clinton (G-1489)
A2z Embroidery ....G....... 860 747-9849
Plainville (G-6762)
Ad Embroidery LLC ....G....... 860 653-9553
East Granby (G-2187)
Ad Embroidery LLC ....G....... 860 651-4410
West Simsbury (G-9971)
All League Embroidery ....G....... 203 377-7215
Stratford (G-8567)
American Eagle Embroidery LLC ....G....... 203 239-7906
North Haven (G-5901)
American Stitch & Print Inc ....G....... 203 239-5383
North Haven (G-5902)
Artwork Embroidery ....G....... 860 620-0456
Southington (G-7892)
Bdg Embroidery ....G....... 203 258-0175
Fairfield (G-2751)
Cameo Embroidery ....G....... 860 301-3123
Durham (G-2140)
Cjs Embroidery LLC ....G....... 203 650-9066
Bridgeport (G-735)
Dr Stitch Seamstress To Stars ....G....... 706 631-0859
New Britain (G-4975)
Earth Loving Stitches ....G....... 405 833-9343
Bristol (G-1025)
Embroidery Wizard ....G....... 860 379-3294
Winsted (G-10519)
Embroidery World Inc ....G....... 203 281-7303
Hamden (G-3445)
Fernellie LLC ....G....... 860 799-7739
New Milford (G-5534)
Gem Embroidery ....G....... 860 326-0676
Ledyard (G-3873)
Grand Embroidery Inc ....F....... 203 888-7484
Oxford (G-6663)
Guidera Marketing Services ....E....... 860 599-8880
Pawcatuck (G-6713)
H J Hoffman Company ....G....... 203 853-7740
Norwalk (G-6189)
Hilversum Embroidery ....G....... 860 729-8532
Middletown (G-4351)
Initial Step Monogramming ....G....... 860 665-0542
West Hartford (G-9821)
Ink and Stitch Solutions LLC ....G....... 203 600-7161
Meriden (G-4174)
J & D Embroidering Co ....G....... 860 822-9777
Baltic (G-120)
JC Embroidery ....G....... 860 742-8686
Coventry (G-1657)
Kamelot Kreations LLC ....G....... 860 564-7399
Sterling (G-8511)
Keepsake Embroidery ....G....... 203 503-1725
Orange (G-6607)
Lee Lowe & Stitch LLC ....G....... 860 536-1392
Mystic (G-4825)
Lookers Embroidery ....G....... 203 468-7262
East Haven (G-2439)
Mad Sportswear LLC ....G....... 203 932-4868
West Haven (G-9929)
Modern Stitch Company ....G....... 860 927-5065
Kent (G-3824)
Monogram Mary LLC ....G....... 203 536-9526
Riverside (G-7197)

Employee Codes: A=Over 500 employees, B=251-500
C=101-250, D=51-100, E=20-50, F=10-19, G=1-9

EMBROIDERING & ART NEEDLEWORK FOR THE TRADE

New England Custom Built LLC .... G 203 828-6480
  Seymour *(G-7359)*
Nitch To Stitch LLC .... G 203 948-9921
  Brookfield *(G-1209)*
Personally Yours .... G 860 537-2248
  Colchester *(G-1564)*
Pink Fish Embroidery and D .... G 860 339-5083
  Old Saybrook *(G-6566)*
Pj Specialties .... F 860 429-7626
  Willington *(G-10254)*
R F H Company Inc .... F 203 853-2863
  Norwalk *(G-6313)*
Ridgefeld Scrnprinting EMB LLC .... G 203 438-1203
  Ridgefield *(G-7167)*
S&V Screenprinting & Embroider ...... G 203 468-7538
  East Haven *(G-2449)*
Scuttlebutt .... G 860 572-3999
  Mystic *(G-4843)*
Sharon M Stinson .... G 860 218-7282
  Middletown *(G-4411)*
Son of A Stitch LLC .... G 203 272-2548
  Cheshire *(G-1450)*
Stitch In Time EMB Svcs LLC .... G 860 496-0226
  Torrington *(G-8973)*
Stitchers Hideaway LLC .... G 860 268-4741
  Manchester *(G-4098)*
Stitches & Seams Usa LLC .... G 708 872-7326
  Terryville *(G-8772)*
Stitching On Maple Studio .... G 860 480-2793
  Norfolk *(G-5827)*
Straight Stitches .... G 203 804-0409
  Hamden *(G-3514)*
Town Pride .... G 860 664-0448
  Clinton *(G-1532)*
Tri State Embroidery LLC .... G 203 732-7636
  Ansonia *(G-53)*
Ulittlestitch .... G 860 857-4066
  East Lyme *(G-2477)*
Wild Bills Action Sports LLC .... G 860 536-6648
  Groton *(G-3319)*

EMBROIDERING SVC

Al-Lynn Sales LLC .... G 203 922-7840
  Shelton *(G-7390)*
American Embroidery .... G 860 829-8586
  Berlin *(G-156)*
ARC Services .... G 203 264-0866
  Southbury *(G-7844)*
Bruce Park Sports EMB LLC .... G 203 853-4488
  Norwalk *(G-6100)*
CK Imaging and Embroidery .... G 716 984-1957
  Burlington *(G-1264)*
Designs In Stitches Embroidery .... G 203 730-1013
  Danbury *(G-1793)*
Embroidery Works .... G 800 681-0805
  Berlin *(G-177)*
Expert Embroidery .... F 203 269-9675
  Wallingford *(G-9264)*
Forsa Team Sports LLC .... G 203 466-2890
  East Haven *(G-2429)*
Gg Sportswear Inc .... E 860 296-4441
  Hartford *(G-3599)*
James Kingsley .... G 203 458-6626
  Guilford *(G-3363)*
Jennifers Tailor Shop .... G 860 489-8968
  Torrington *(G-8938)*
Michael Violano .... G 203 934-3368
  West Haven *(G-9937)*
Monas Monograms .... G 860 463-9530
  Andover *(G-14)*
Monogramit LLC .... G 860 779-0694
  Brooklyn *(G-1249)*
Rainbow Graphics Inc .... G 860 646-8997
  Manchester *(G-4082)*
Rss Enterprises LLC .... G 203 736-6220
  Derby *(G-2124)*
S Tm Embroidery LLC .... G 860 376-4537
  Jewett City *(G-3800)*
Shirt Graphix .... G 203 294-1656
  Wallingford *(G-9365)*
Silkscreening Plus Inc .... G 203 622-6909
  Greenwich *(G-3234)*
Son of A Stitch .... G 203 527-3432
  Waterbury *(G-9604)*
Stitches By ME .... G 860 653-9701
  Granby *(G-3115)*
Terris Embroidery .... G 860 928-0552
  Putnam *(G-7074)*
TSS & A Inc .... F 800 633-3536
  Prospect *(G-7027)*

EMBROIDERY ADVERTISING SVCS

Macwear LLC .... G 203 579-4277
  Southport *(G-8006)*
Nomis Enterprises .... G 631 821-3120
  Wallingford *(G-9327)*
R & B Apparel Plus LLC .... G 860 333-1757
  Groton *(G-3311)*

EMERGENCY ALARMS

Ademco Inc .... G 860 257-3266
  Rocky Hill *(G-7218)*
Ademco Inc .... G 203 877-2702
  Milford *(G-4440)*
Care Connection LLC .... G 860 274-1251
  Watertown *(G-9690)*
Cord-Mate Inc .... G 203 272-8415
  Cheshire *(G-1375)*
Endoto Corp .... G 860 289-8033
  East Hartford *(G-2323)*
Lumentum Operations LLC .... F 408 546-5483
  Bloomfield *(G-444)*
Nutmeg Utility Products Inc .... E 203 250-8802
  Cheshire *(G-1423)*
United Technologies Corp .... B 860 728-7000
  Farmington *(G-2972)*

EMPLOYMENT AGENCY SVCS

ABB Enterprise Software Inc .... A 860 747-7111
  Plainville *(G-6763)*

EMPLOYMENT SVCS: Teachers' Registry

Bunting & Lyon Inc .... G 203 272-4623
  Cheshire *(G-1365)*

ENAMELING SVC: Metal Prdts, Including Porcelain

Hartford Industrial Finshg Co .... G 860 243-2040
  Bloomfield *(G-418)*

ENCODERS: Digital

Mango Dsp Inc .... E 203 857-4008
  Norwalk *(G-6245)*

ENCRYPTION EQPT & DEVICES

Video Messengercom Corp .... G 203 358-8842
  Stratford *(G-8702)*

ENERGY MEASUREMENT EQPT

General Electric Company .... D 518 385-7164
  Norwalk *(G-6177)*
Uses Mfg Inc .... G 860 443-8737
  Quaker Hill *(G-7086)*

ENGINE REBUILDING: Gas

Automotive Machine .... G 860 627-9244
  East Windsor *(G-2482)*
Pmr Performance .... G 860 828-8828
  Kensington *(G-3817)*
Terry Brick .... G 860 889-2232
  Norwich *(G-6436)*

ENGINEERING SVCS

American Specialty Pdts LLC .... G 860 871-2279
  Vernon *(G-9130)*
Apcompower Inc .... E 860 688-1911
  Windsor *(G-10362)*
Asea Brown Boveri Inc .... G 203 750-2200
  Norwalk *(G-6076)*
Ciaudelli Productions Inc .... G 860 848-0411
  Montville *(G-4769)*
Connecticut Analytical Corp .... F 203 393-9666
  Bethany *(G-239)*
Cummins Envirotech .... G 860 598-9564
  Old Lyme *(G-6500)*
DC & D Inc .... G 860 623-2941
  Broad Brook *(G-1147)*
Electric Boat Corporation .... D 860 433-3000
  Groton *(G-3286)*
Electric Boat Corporation .... A 860 433-3000
  Groton *(G-3287)*
Emhart Teknologies LLC .... F 800 783-6427
  New Britain *(G-4983)*
Engineered Fibers Tech LLC .... F 203 922-1810
  Shelton *(G-7440)*
Flexco .... G 860 583-0219
  Bristol *(G-1040)*
Gardner Denver Nash LLC .... D 203 459-3923
  Trumbull *(G-9028)*
GE Steam Power Inc .... G 860 688-1911
  Windsor *(G-10391)*
General Dynamics Info Tech Inc ...... D 203 441-2400
  Pawcatuck *(G-6712)*
Goldenrod Corporation .... E 203 723-4400
  Beacon Falls *(G-135)*
Henkel Loctite Corporation .... E 860 571-5100
  Rocky Hill *(G-7245)*
I3 Engineering Sciences LLC .... G 908 625-2347
  Hartford *(G-3616)*
Ja Electronics LLC .... G 860 921-7549
  Waterbury *(G-9508)*
John Zink Company LLC .... D 203 925-0380
  Shelton *(G-7481)*
Jonal Laboratories Inc .... D 203 634-4444
  Meriden *(G-4180)*
Lakeview Engineering & Mfg LLC ..... G 860 490-2760
  Higganum *(G-3767)*
Mike Sadlak .... G 860 742-0227
  Coventry *(G-1663)*
Pioneer Arspc Def Systems Corp ..... G 860 528-0092
  South Windsor *(G-7805)*
Simulations LLC .... G 860 978-0772
  East Granby *(G-2230)*
Vector Engineering Inc .... F 860 572-0422
  Mystic *(G-4851)*
Vertafore Inc .... A 860 602-6000
  Windsor *(G-10459)*

ENGINEERING SVCS: Acoustical

GE Steam Power Inc .... C 423 648-4161
  Windsor *(G-10389)*

ENGINEERING SVCS: Aviation Or Aeronautical

Goodrich Corporation .... B 505 345-9031
  Danbury *(G-1834)*
Kenzinc LLC .... G 203 307-5369
  Shelton *(G-7484)*

ENGINEERING SVCS: Building Construction

Arnitex LLC .... G 203 869-1406
  Cos Cob *(G-1624)*

ENGINEERING SVCS: Construction & Civil

Division X Specialties LLC .... G 860 402-7736
  Vernon *(G-9137)*

ENGINEERING SVCS: Electrical Or Electronic

AB Electronics Inc .... E 203 740-2793
  Brookfield *(G-1155)*
Aztech Engineering LLC .... G 860 659-8892
  Glastonbury *(G-3009)*
Dark Field Technologies Inc .... F 203 298-0731
  Shelton *(G-7428)*
Data Collection Dispersal Inc .... G 860 623-7364
  Broad Brook *(G-1146)*
Delcom Products Inc .... G 914 934-5170
  Danbury *(G-1792)*
High Voltage Outsourcing LLC .... G 203 456-3101
  Danbury *(G-1844)*
Silicon Integration Inc .... E 203 876-2844
  Milford *(G-4645)*
T&K Technical Services LLC .... G 860 235-5882
  Quaker Hill *(G-7085)*
Tornik Inc .... C 860 282-6081
  Rocky Hill *(G-7269)*
Vintage Performance LLC .... G 860 542-5753
  Norfolk *(G-5828)*

ENGINEERING SVCS: Energy conservation

Saigeworks LLC .... G 203 767-1035
  Trumbull *(G-9069)*

ENGINEERING SVCS: Heating & Ventilation

New Air Technologies Inc .... G 860 767-1542
  Ivoryton *(G-3787)*

PRODUCT SECTION

ENGINEERING SVCS: Industrial

Act Robots Inc .... G 860 314-1557
  Bristol (G-956)
Tenova Inc .... E 203 265-5684
  Wallingford (G-9380)

ENGINEERING SVCS: Machine Tool Design

Ceda Company Inc .... G 860 666-1593
  Newington (G-5638)
Johnson Gage Company .... E 860 242-5541
  Bloomfield (G-428)
Mc Clintock Manufacturing .... G 203 263-4743
  Woodbury (G-10642)
Prospect Machine Products Inc .... E 203 758-4448
  Prospect (G-7019)
T L S Design & Manufacturing .... G 860 439-1414
  New London (G-5492)

ENGINEERING SVCS: Marine

Docko Inc .... G 860 572-8939
  Mystic (G-4812)

ENGINEERING SVCS: Mechanical

109 Design LLC .... G 203 941-1812
  New Haven (G-5215)
Atp Industries LLC .... F 860 479-5007
  Plainville (G-6773)
Dufrane Nuclear Shielding Inc .... F 860 379-2318
  Winsted (G-10516)
Mannan 3d Innovations LLC .... G 860 306-4203
  Higganum (G-3768)
P & S Manufacturing LLC .... G 203 685-2256
  Bridgeport (G-858)
Quality Engineering Svcs Inc .... E 203 269-5054
  Wallingford (G-9345)

ENGINEERING SVCS: Professional

Alstom Power Co .... F 860 688-1911
  Windsor (G-10358)

ENGINES: Diesel & Semi-Diesel Or Duel Fuel

Jacobs Vehicle Systems Inc .... B 860 243-5222
  Bloomfield (G-425)
T/A Engines .... G 860 747-6713
  Plainville (G-6866)

ENGINES: Internal Combustion, NEC

Brash Engines Inc .... G 203 843-0757
  Branford (G-564)
Cummins - Allison Corp .... G 203 794-9200
  Cheshire (G-1377)
Cummins Enviro Tech Inc .... F 860 388-6377
  Old Lyme (G-6499)
Cummins Envirotech .... G 860 598-9564
  Old Lyme (G-6500)
Cummins Inc .... E 860 529-7474
  Rocky Hill (G-7230)
Ex Model Engines .... G 860 681-2451
  Southington (G-7919)
Liquidpiston Inc .... F 860 838-2677
  Bloomfield (G-443)
Smith Hill of Delaware Inc .... E 860 767-7502
  Essex (G-2733)

ENGINES: Jet Propulsion

CAM Group LLC .... F 860 646-2378
  Manchester (G-3989)
Kco Numet Inc .... F 203 375-4995
  Orange (G-6606)

ENGINES: Marine

Atlantic Outboard Inc .... G 860 399-6773
  Westbrook (G-9991)
Johnson Marine .... G 860 536-8026
  Mystic (G-4823)

ENGRAVING SVC, NEC

Baron Technology Inc .... E 203 452-0515
  Trumbull (G-9003)
Eccles-Lehman Inc .... G 203 268-0605
  Easton (G-2551)
Executive Graphic Systems LLC .... G 203 678-6432
  Wallingford (G-9261)

Leonard Dongweck .... G 860 388-0700
  Old Saybrook (G-6552)
Meco Precision Industries Inc .... G 860 210-1801
  Gaylordsville (G-2994)
Tex Elm Inc .... F 860 873-9715
  East Haddam (G-2249)

ENGRAVING SVC: Jewelry & Personal Goods

A & E Engraving Service .... G 860 582-6503
  Bristol (G-950)
Dexter & Co .... G 860 536-9506
  Mystic (G-4811)
F J Weidner Inc .... G 203 469-4202
  East Haven (G-2425)
Robert Audette .... G 203 872-3119
  Cheshire (G-1440)
Rodriguez Ruiz Rosa Margarita ..... G 860 840-0344
  Hartford (G-3681)
Silversmith Inc .... G 203 869-4244
  Greenwich (G-3235)

ENGRAVING SVCS

A D Perkins Company .... G 203 777-3456
  New Haven (G-5217)
Ann S Davis .... F 860 642-7228
  Lebanon (G-3846)
Biomerics LLC .... D 203 268-7238
  Monroe (G-4698)
Elite Engraving & Awards .... G 860 643-7459
  Manchester (G-4014)
Finest Engraving LLC .... G 860 742-7579
  Andover (G-7)
Meco Precision Industries Inc .... G 860 210-1801
  Gaylordsville (G-2994)
Robert Audette .... G 203 872-3119
  Cheshire (G-1440)
Rokap Inc .... G 203 265-6895
  Wallingford (G-9359)

ENGRAVINGS: Plastic

Recognition Inc .... G 860 659-8629
  Glastonbury (G-3079)

ENTERTAINERS & ENTERTAINMENT GROUPS

Cliffside Entertainment LLC .... G 203 290-7484
  Bridgeport (G-736)
Dizzy Fish Music LLC .... G 203 599-5700
  Milford (G-4512)
Madonna Black Buddist LLC .... G 203 589-9796
  Greenwich (G-3196)
Nollysource Entertainment LLC .... G 347 264-6655
  Bridgeport (G-853)

ENTERTAINMENT GROUP

World Wrestling Entrmt Inc .... C 203 352-8600
  Stamford (G-8502)

ENTERTAINMENT SVCS

Dlpublshers Mystryntrtnmentllc .... G 203 556-4893
  Bridgeport (G-755)
Yolanda Dubose Records and .... F 203 823-6699
  West Haven (G-9967)

ENVELOPES

Cenveo Inc .... D 203 595-3000
  Stamford (G-8138)
Cenveo Corporation .... E 303 790-8023
  Stamford (G-8139)
Cenveo Enterprises Inc .... G 203 595-3000
  Stamford (G-8140)
Cenveo Worldwide Limited .... F 203 595-3000
  Stamford (G-8141)
Cwl Enterprises Inc .... G 303 790-8023
  Stamford (G-8174)

ENVELOPES WHOLESALERS

Massachusetts Envelope Co Inc .... E 860 727-9100
  Hartford (G-3636)

ENVIRONMENTAL QUALITY PROGS ADMIN, GOVT: Recreational

Town of Vernon .... G 203 268-7200
  Easton (G-2567)

EPOXY RESINS

Hexcel Corporation .... E 203 969-0666
  Stamford (G-8233)

EQUIPMENT: Pedestrian Traffic Control

Onsite Services Inc .... F 860 669-3988
  Clinton (G-1517)
Preusser Research Group Inc .... E 203 459-8700
  Trumbull (G-9056)
Q-Lane Turnstiles LLC .... F 860 410-1801
  Sandy Hook (G-7327)

EQUIPMENT: Rental & Leasing, NEC

Able Scale & Equipment Corp .... G 860 646-6929
  Manchester (G-3975)
Hartford Aviation Group Inc .... G 860 549-0096
  Hartford (G-3606)
Pastanch LLC .... E 203 720-9478
  Naugatuck (G-4909)
Thomas Keegan & Sons Inc .... G 203 239-9248
  North Haven (G-5999)
Welder Repair & Rental Svc Inc ..... G 203 238-9284
  Durham (G-2161)

ERASERS: Rubber Or Rubber & Abrasive Combined

Acme United Corporation .... C 203 254-6060
  Fairfield (G-2743)

ETCHING & ENGRAVING SVC

Ad Comm Ink .... G 860 824-7565
  Canaan (G-1280)
Metamorphic Materials Inc .... F 860 738-8638
  Winsted (G-10529)
Pelegnos Stined GL Art Gallery ..... G 860 621-2900
  Plantsville (G-6907)
U-Marq Usa LLC .... G 860 799-7800
  New Milford (G-5603)

ETCHING SVC: Metal

Conard Corporation .... E 860 659-0591
  Glastonbury (G-3022)
Summit Corporation of America .... D 860 283-4391
  Thomaston (G-8811)

ETHYLENE-PROPYLENE RUBBERS: EPDM Polymers

Fluoropolymer Resources Inc .... G 860 291-9521
  East Hartford (G-2325)
Si Group USA (usaa) LLC .... C 203 702-6140
  Danbury (G-1946)
Specialty Polymers Inc .... G 203 575-5727
  Waterbury (G-9605)

EXCAVATING EQPT

Double Diamond Construction ...... G 203 357-7757
  Stamford (G-8188)

EXHAUST SYSTEMS: Eqpt & Parts

Autopart International Inc .... F 203 931-9189
  West Haven (G-9885)

EXPLOSIVES

Austin Powder Company .... E 860 564-5466
  Sterling (G-8507)
Ensign-Bickford Industries Inc ...... E 860 658-4411
  Simsbury (G-7622)
Independent Explosives .... G 860 243-0137
  Bloomfield (G-421)
Maxam Initiation Systems LLC ..... F 860 774-3507
  Sterling (G-8512)
Maxam North America Inc .... G 860 774-2333
  Sterling (G-8513)
Metal Finish Eqp & Sup Co Inc ..... E 860 668-1050
  Suffield (G-8726)
Precision Explosives Inc .... G 860 567-4952
  Bantam (G-127)

EXTRACTS, FLAVORING

America Extract Corporation .... F 860 267-4444
  East Hampton (G-2252)
Charles Boggini Company LLC ..... G 860 742-2652
  Coventry (G-1649)

Employee Codes: A=Over 500 employees, B=251-500
C=101-250, D=51-100, E=20-50, F=10-19, G=1-9

2020 Harris Connecticut
Manufacturers Directory

EYEGLASSES

Encore Optics .... F 860 282-0082
  South Windsor (G-7749)
L A Vision LLC .... G 860 523-0339
  Hartford (G-3624)
Lenses Only LLC .... F 860 769-2020
  Bloomfield (G-440)
Pilla Inc .... G 203 894-3265
  Ridgefield (G-7161)
Precision Optical Co .... E 860 289-6023
  East Hartford (G-2361)
University Optics LLC .... G 860 779-6123
  Dayville (G-2076)

EYEGLASSES: Sunglasses

Cashon .... G 786 325-4144
  Groton (G-3276)
Worldscreen Inc .... G 860 274-9218
  Watertown (G-9751)

EYELASHES, ARTIFICIAL

Eyelash Extensions and More .... F 860 951-9355
  West Hartford (G-9809)

FABRIC STORES

C & D Upholstery .... G 203 838-1050
  Norwalk (G-6104)
Jane Sterry .... G 860 342-4567
  Portland (G-6960)
R & M Associates Inc .... F 860 633-0721
  Glastonbury (G-3078)

FABRICATED METAL PRODUCTS, NEC

Action Steel LLC .... G 860 216-6595
  Hartford (G-3546)
Dangelo Family LLC .... G 203 235-1238
  Waterbury (G-9460)
Farmington Mtal Fbrication LLC .... G 860 402-5148
  Bristol (G-1035)
Independent Metalworx Inc .... G 203 520-4089
  Ansonia (G-39)
M&M Metal Fabrication LLC .... G 203 889-6468
  East Haven (G-2440)
Mak Metal Fab .... G 203 213-0269
  Wallingford (G-9311)
Metallon Inc .... G 203 437-8540
  Waterbury (G-9540)
Royal Welding LLC .... G 203 232-5255
  Hartford (G-3683)
Specialty Metals and Fab .... G 203 509-5028
  Naugatuck (G-4921)
Vintage Sheet Metal Fabg .... G 860 595-8423
  Berlin (G-230)

FABRICS & CLOTH: Quilted

Jane Sterry .... G 860 342-4567
  Portland (G-6960)
Kadomar Krafts .... G 860 346-2000
  Middletown (G-4359)
Memory Lane Quilters LLC .... G 203 272-1010
  Cheshire (G-1415)

FABRICS & YARN: Plastic Coated

Deitsch Plastic Company Inc .... D 203 934-6601
  West Haven (G-9896)

FABRICS: Alpacas, Mohair, Woven

Bella Alpacas .... G 860 946-3076
  New Milford (G-5510)
Brook Burgis Alpacas LLC .... G 203 605-0588
  Canterbury (G-1296)
Chakana Sky Alpacas .... G 860 204-1646
  Chester (G-1466)
Drunk Alpaca LLC .... G 646 415-4995
  Riverside (G-7193)
Flatland Alpacas .... G 860 376-4658
  Griswold (G-3264)
Hidden Meadow Alpaca .... G 203 262-1669
  Southbury (G-7856)
Quinnipiac Valley Alpacas .... G 203 271-0773
  Cheshire (G-1433)
Roaring Acres Alpacas LLC .... G 860 668-7075
  Suffield (G-8734)
Round Hill Alpacas LLC .... G 860 742-5195
  Coventry (G-1672)

FABRICS: Apparel & Outerwear, Cotton

Mytyme LLC .... G 860 327-2356
  Windsor (G-10411)

FABRICS: Apparel & Outerwear, From Manmade Fiber Or Silk

Sally Conant .... F 203 878-3005
  Orange (G-6628)

FABRICS: Blankets & Blanketing, Wool Or Similar Fibers

Apparel Solutions Incorporated .... G 203 226-8600
  Bridgeport (G-698)

FABRICS: Broadwoven, Synthetic Manmade Fiber & Silk

Challenge Sailcloth .... G 860 871-8030
  South Windsor (G-7728)
Deer Creek Fabrics Inc .... G 203 964-0922
  Stamford (G-8183)
Deitsch Plastic Company Inc .... D 203 934-6601
  West Haven (G-9896)
Dimension-Polyant Inc .... E 860 928-8300
  Putnam (G-7039)
G Thomas and Sons Inc .... G 860 935-5174
  North Grosvenordale (G-5886)
Nextec Applications Inc .... G 203 661-1484
  Greenwich (G-3209)
Second Lac Inc .... G 203 321-1221
  Norwalk (G-6341)
Swift Textile Metalizing LLC .... D 860 243-1122
  Bloomfield (G-490)

FABRICS: Canvas

Atlantic Sail & Canvas Co .... G 203 254-1315
  Stratford (G-8574)
Baremore Canvas LLC .... G 860 691-1402
  East Lyme (G-2463)
Ben Barrett Canvas Service LLC .... G 203 268-4315
  Monroe (G-4697)
Blank Canvas Interiors LLC .... G 203 226-5602
  Weston (G-10020)
Coastal Canvas .... G 203 270-7408
  Sandy Hook (G-7303)
Creative Canvas LLC .... G 860 559-8509
  Lebanon (G-3851)
Custom Marine Canvas LLC .... G 203 572-9547
  Groton (G-3281)
D&R Marine Upholstery & Canvas .... G 860 989-9646
  Rocky Hill (G-7232)
Donnas Canvas Creations .... G 860 276-0327
  Southington (G-7916)
Eastern Canvas Works .... G 860 245-9174
  Willimantic (G-10225)
Island Style Mar Canvas Repr .... G 707 338-8789
  Norwalk (G-6212)
Janes Custom Canvas LLC .... G 203 376-6778
  Griswold (G-3266)
Lucky Enough Canvas .... G 860 455-6994
  Hampton (G-3537)
Mago Point Canvas .... G 860 442-2111
  Waterford (G-9661)
Nautigirl Marine Canvas .... G 203 891-8558
  Orange (G-6615)
Offshore Canvas & Cushions LLC .... G 860 442-7803
  Waterford (G-9665)
Precision Canvas LLC .... G 860 693-2353
  Collinsville (G-1600)
Seafarer Canvas .... G 203 939-1872
  Norwalk (G-6338)
Serge & Friends LLC .... G 860 526-3882
  Cromwell (G-1718)
Simply Canvas LLC .... G 203 265-0659
  Wallingford (G-9368)

FABRICS: Card Roll, Cotton

Arnitex LLC .... G 203 869-1406
  Cos Cob (G-1624)

FABRICS: Coated Or Treated

Advanced Def Slutions Tech LLC .... G 860 243-1122
  Bloomfield (G-380)
American Metaseal of Conn .... G 203 787-0281
  Hamden (G-3414)
Nextec Applications Inc .... G 203 661-1484
  Greenwich (G-3209)
Second Lac Inc .... G 203 321-1221
  Norwalk (G-6341)

FABRICS: Denims

Dune Denim LLC .... G 203 241-5409
  Bethel (G-283)
Exclusive Denim .... G 203 549-9844
  Fairfield (G-2783)
My Denim Queen .... G 860 729-1142
  Columbia (G-1609)

FABRICS: Dress, From Manmade Fiber Or Silk

Scarlethread LLC .... G 860 528-0667
  East Hartford (G-2369)

FABRICS: Fiberglass, Broadwoven

Claremont Sales Corporation .... E 860 349-4499
  Durham (G-2143)

FABRICS: Filter Cloth, Cotton

Scapa North America Inc .... G 860 688-8000
  Windsor (G-10433)

FABRICS: Fur-Type, From Manmade Fiber

Furs By Prezioso Ltd .... G 203 230-2930
  Hamden (G-3449)

FABRICS: Glass & Fiberglass, Broadwoven

Noreaster Yachts Inc .... G 203 877-4339
  Milford (G-4593)

FABRICS: Jean

Marcia Jean Fabric and Cft LLC .... G 203 273-1665
  Old Greenwich (G-6479)

FABRICS: Laminated

Brookwood Laminating Inc .... D 860 774-5001
  Wauregan (G-9752)

FABRICS: Metallized

Swift Textile Metalizing LLC .... D 860 243-1122
  Bloomfield (G-490)

FABRICS: Nonwoven

Lydall Inc .... E 860 646-1233
  Manchester (G-4050)
Lydall Thermal Acoustical Inc .... G 860 646-1233
  Manchester (G-4051)
New England Nonwovens LLC .... F 203 891-0851
  West Haven (G-9939)
Suominen US Holding Inc .... F 860 386-8001
  East Windsor (G-2524)
Swift Textile Metalizing LLC .... D 860 243-1122
  Bloomfield (G-490)
Web Industries Inc .... G 860 779-3403
  Dayville (G-2079)
Windsor Locks Nonwovens Inc .... E 860 292-5600
  East Windsor (G-2533)
Xamax Industries Inc .... E 203 888-7200
  Seymour (G-7375)

FABRICS: Papermakers Felt, Woven, Wool, Mohair/Similar Fiber

Scapa North America Inc .... G 860 688-8000
  Windsor (G-10433)

FABRICS: Resin Or Plastic Coated

Au New Haven LLC .... C 203 468-0342
  New Haven (G-5238)
Defender Industries Inc .... C 860 701-3400
  Waterford (G-9652)
Emson Inc .... G 860 489-6249
  Torrington (G-8922)
Trelleborg Ctd Systems US Inc .... C 203 468-0342
  New Haven (G-5421)

FABRICS: Sail Cloth

Dimension-Polyant Inc .... E 860 928-8300
  Putnam (G-7039)

PRODUCT SECTION

FENCING: Chain Link

North Sails Group LLC ....D..... 203 874-7548
  Milford (G-4594)

FABRICS: Satin

Satin Style LLC ....G..... 203 287-5466
  Hamden (G-3507)

FABRICS: Slip Cover, Cotton

Tom Voytek ....G..... 203 367-3991
  Bridgeport (G-926)

FABRICS: Specialty Including Twisted Weaves, Broadwoven

Hartford Artisans Weaving Ctr ....G..... 860 727-5727
  Hartford (G-3605)

FABRICS: Stretch, Cotton

American Woolen Company Inc ....G..... 860 684-2766
  Stafford Springs (G-8017)

FABRICS: Trimmings

Advanced Graphics Inc ....E..... 203 378-0471
  Stratford (G-8564)
Allied Printing Services Inc ....B..... 860 643-1101
  Manchester (G-3980)
Art Screen ....G..... 203 744-1991
  Bethel (G-258)
C Libby Leonard ....G..... 203 375-6205
  Stratford (G-8591)
Concordia Ltd ....G..... 203 483-0221
  North Branford (G-5832)
Cook Print ....G..... 203 855-8785
  Norwalk (G-6129)
Hi-Tech Fabricating Inc ....E..... 203 284-0894
  Cheshire (G-1396)
Hot Tops LLC ....F..... 203 926-2067
  Shelton (G-7466)
Jornik Man Corp ....F..... 203 969-0500
  Stamford (G-8268)
Kinamor Incorporated ....E..... 203 269-0380
  Wallingford (G-9297)
Logod Softwear Inc ....E..... 203 272-4883
  Cheshire (G-1407)
Michael Zoppa ....G..... 860 289-5881
  South Windsor (G-7794)
Mytyme LLC ....G..... 860 327-2356
  Windsor (G-10411)
Project Graphics Inc ....F..... 802 488-8789
  Woodbury (G-10652)
Quality Name Plate Inc ....D..... 860 633-9495
  East Glastonbury (G-2185)
R F H Company Inc ....F..... 203 853-2863
  Norwalk (G-6313)
Second Lac Inc ....G..... 203 321-1221
  Norwalk (G-6341)
Systematic Automation Inc ....E..... 310 218-3361
  Farmington (G-2962)

FABRICS: Upholstery, Cotton

Dominics Decorating Inc ....G..... 203 838-1827
  Norwalk (G-6145)

FABRICS: Upholstery, Wool

Dominics Decorating Inc ....G..... 203 838-1827
  Norwalk (G-6145)

FABRICS: Warp Knit, Lace & Netting

Novelty Textile Mills LLC ....G..... 860 774-5000
  Waterford (G-9664)

FABRICS: Weft Or Circular Knit

Swift Textile Metalizing LLC ....D..... 860 243-1122
  Bloomfield (G-490)

FABRICS: Woven, Narrow Cotton, Wool, Silk

H-O Products Corporation ....E..... 860 379-9875
  Winsted (G-10523)

FACILITIES SUPPORT SVCS

Johnson Controls Inc ....G..... 860 887-7185
  Norwich (G-6419)
Johnson Controls Inc ....D..... 678 297-4040
  Meriden (G-4179)

Pitney Bowes Inc ....A..... 203 356-5000
  Stamford (G-8362)
Pitney Bowes Inc ....E..... 203 356-5000
  Shelton (G-7530)

FACSIMILE COMMUNICATION EQPT

Pitney Bowes Inc ....A..... 203 356-5000
  Stamford (G-8362)
Pitney Bowes Inc ....E..... 203 356-5000
  Shelton (G-7530)

FAMILY CLOTHING STORES

Bleshue LLC ....G..... 203 405-1034
  Woodbury (G-10627)
Fyc Apparel Group LLC ....D..... 203 481-2420
  Branford (G-599)

FANS, EXHAUST: Indl Or Commercial

Kennedy Gustafson and Cole Inc ....E..... 860 828-2594
  Berlin (G-191)

FARM & GARDEN MACHINERY WHOLESALERS

Stihl Incorporated ....E..... 203 929-8488
  Oxford (G-6695)

FARM PRDTS, RAW MATERIALS, WHOLESALE: Sugar

CSC Sugar LLC ....F..... 203 846-5610
  New Canaan (G-5100)

FARM SPLYS, WHOLESALE: Equestrian Eqpt

William Martin ....G..... 860 355-1919
  Gaylordsville (G-2997)

FARM SPLYS, WHOLESALE: Feed

Central Conn Cooperative Farme ....E..... 860 649-4523
  South Windsor (G-7727)
HJ Baker & Bro LLC ....E..... 203 682-9200
  Shelton (G-7465)

FARM SPLYS, WHOLESALE: Garden Splys

Inocraft Products Inc ....E..... 860 933-0485
  Tolland (G-8866)

FARM SPLYS, WHOLESALE: Insecticides

Nantucket Spider LLC ....G..... 203 423-3031
  Wilton (G-10315)
Pic20 Group LLC ....F..... 203 957-3555
  Norwalk (G-6299)

FARM SPLYS, WHOLESALE: Soil, Potting & Planting

Grillo Services LLC ....E..... 203 877-5070
  Milford (G-4544)

FASTENERS WHOLESALERS

East Coast Lightning Eqp Inc ....E..... 860 379-9072
  Winsted (G-10518)
Timber-Top Inc ....G..... 860 274-6706
  Watertown (G-9741)

FASTENERS: Brads, Alum, Brass/Other Nonferrous Metal/Wire

Kovacs Tamas ....G..... 860 738-8976
  Pine Meadow (G-6734)

FASTENERS: Metal

Timber-Top Inc ....G..... 860 274-6706
  Watertown (G-9741)

FASTENERS: Metal

Engineered Inserts & Systems ....F..... 203 301-3334
  Milford (G-4531)
Norse Inc ....G..... 860 482-1532
  Torrington (G-8952)
Specialized Marketing Intl Inc ....G..... 860 779-3264
  Dayville (G-2074)
Wtm Company ....G..... 860 283-5871
  Thomaston (G-8826)

FASTENERS: Notions, Hooks & Eyes

Metalform Acquisition LLC ....F..... 860 224-2630
  New Britain (G-5016)

FASTENERS: Notions, NEC

Bernies Tool & Fastener Svcs ....G..... 203 466-5252
  Orange (G-6585)
ITW Powertrain Fastening ....G..... 203 720-1676
  Naugatuck (G-4892)
Manchester TI & Design ADP LLC .....G..... 860 296-6541
  Hartford (G-3633)
Paneloc Corporation ....E..... 860 677-6711
  Farmington (G-2945)
Rome Fastener Corporation ....G..... 203 874-6719
  Milford (G-4631)
Rome Fastener Sales Corp ....F..... 203 874-6719
  Milford (G-4632)
Timber-Top Inc ....G..... 203 274-6706
  Watertown (G-9741)

FASTENERS: Notions, Snaps

Lord & Hodge Inc ....F..... 860 632-7006
  Middletown (G-4369)
Rings Wire Inc ....E..... 203 874-6719
  Milford (G-4629)

FASTENERS: Notions, Zippers

Bees Knees Zipper Wax LLC ....G..... 203 521-5727
  Berlin (G-162)

FATTY ACID ESTERS & AMINOS

Henkel of America Inc ....B..... 860 571-5100
  Rocky Hill (G-7246)
Waste Resource Recovery Inc ....G..... 860 287-3332
  Lebanon (G-3866)

FELT PARTS

H&H Engineered Solutions Inc ....G..... 860 575-0005
  Old Saybrook (G-6537)

FELT: Acoustic

Wilhelm Gdale Elzabeth Designs ....G..... 203 371-8787
  Bridgeport (G-937)

FENCES OR POSTS: Ornamental Iron Or Steel

Burdon Enterprises LLC ....G..... 860 345-4882
  Higganum (G-3762)
Edi Landscape LLC ....F..... 860 216-6871
  Hartford (G-3583)
US Barricades LLC ....G..... 203 883-8660
  Darien (G-2050)

FENCING DEALERS

Walpole Woodworkers Inc ....E..... 508 668-2800
  Ridgefield (G-7181)
Walpole Woodworkers Inc ....G..... 203 255-9010
  Westport (G-10173)

FENCING MADE IN WIREDRAWING PLANTS

Graham Whitehead & Manger Co ......G..... 978 887-0430
  Shelton (G-7452)

FENCING MATERIALS: Plastic

Wayside Fence Co ....G..... 860 594-1090
  Newington (G-5722)

FENCING MATERIALS: Wood

Pleasant Valley Fence Co Inc ....F..... 860 379-0088
  Pleasant Valley (G-6925)
Walpole Woodworkers Inc ....E..... 508 668-2800
  Ridgefield (G-7181)
Walpole Woodworkers Inc ....G..... 203 255-9010
  Westport (G-10173)

FENCING: Chain Link

Stephens Pipe & Steel LLC ....F..... 877 777-8721
  Manchester (G-4095)

FERTILIZER, AGRICULTURAL: Wholesalers

Clinton Nursery Products Inc .... C 860 399-3000
Westbrook *(G-9994)*

FERTILIZERS: NEC

Scotts Company LLC .... D 860 642-7591
Lebanon *(G-3862)*
Siteone Landscape Supply LLC .... G 860 673-6912
Avon *(G-113)*

FIBER & FIBER PRDTS: Organic, Noncellulose

Naturally Nutritous Vend LLC .... G 860 416-9848
Wolcott *(G-10577)*
Proteem LLC .... G 203 787-2221
North Haven *(G-5982)*
R L Pritchard & Co Inc .... G 203 393-0260
South Lyme *(G-7685)*

FIBER & FIBER PRDTS: Polyester

Fairfield Processing Corp .... C 203 744-2090
Danbury *(G-1823)*

FIBER & FIBER PRDTS: Vinyl

Age Plastics LLC .... G 860 502-0418
New Britain *(G-4940)*

FIBER OPTICS

Fluid Coating Technology Inc .... G 860 963-2505
Putnam *(G-7041)*
Nufern .... D 860 408-5000
East Granby *(G-2220)*
O E M Controls Inc .... C 203 929-8431
Shelton *(G-7517)*
Pioneer Optics Company Inc .... F 860 286-0071
Bloomfield *(G-465)*

FIBER PRDTS: Pressed, Wood Pulp, From Purchased Materials

Yumi Ecosolutions Inc .... G 203 803-1880
Westport *(G-10178)*

FIBERS: Carbon & Graphite

Hexcel Corporation .... E 203 969-0666
Stamford *(G-8233)*

FILM & SHEET: Unsuppported Plastic

American Polyfilm Inc .... G 203 483-9797
Branford *(G-543)*
Apogee Corporation .... D 860 963-1976
Putnam *(G-7030)*
Apogee Corporation .... D 860 632-3550
Cromwell *(G-1687)*
Berry Global Inc .... G 413 529-7602
East Hampton *(G-2256)*
Brushfoil LLC .... F 203 453-7403
Guilford *(G-3335)*
Filmx Technologies .... G 860 779-3403
Dayville *(G-2062)*
Flagship Converters Inc .... D 203 792-0034
Danbury *(G-1826)*
Spartech LLC .... C 203 327-6010
Stamford *(G-8432)*
Str Holdings Inc .... F 860 272-4235
Enfield *(G-2699)*
Vacumet Corp .... G 860 731-0860
East Hartford *(G-2399)*

FILM: Motion Picture

CT Films LLC .... G 203 734-8307
Seymour *(G-7343)*
Kitty Guerrilla Films .... G 203 259-8395
Fairfield *(G-2806)*

FILTERS

3M Purification Inc .... B 203 237-5541
Meriden *(G-4135)*
Connecticut Leaf Filter LLC .... G 203 857-0846
Norwalk *(G-6127)*
Dynamic Bldg Enrgy Sltions LLC .... G 860 571-8590
Rocky Hill *(G-7236)*
Gutter Filter New England LLC .... G 860 274-5943
Oakville *(G-6454)*
Isopur Fluid Technologies Inc .... F 860 599-1872
North Stonington *(G-6027)*
Locking Filter LLC .... G 203 691-1221
Hamden *(G-3476)*
Mott Corporation .... C 860 793-6333
Farmington *(G-2931)*
MSC Filtration Tech Inc .... F 860 745-7475
Enfield *(G-2664)*
US Filter Surface Preparatio .... G 203 284-7825
Wallingford *(G-9397)*

FILTERS & SOFTENERS: Water, Household

Core Filtration LLC .... G 860 904-6640
Hartford *(G-3571)*
Evoqua Water Technologies LLC ...... E 860 528-6512
South Windsor *(G-7754)*
Guardian Envmtl Tech Inc .... F 860 350-2200
New Milford *(G-5541)*
Safe Water .... G 203 732-4806
Seymour *(G-7366)*

FILTERS & STRAINERS: Pipeline

Triad Concepts Inc .... G 860 399-4045
Westbrook *(G-10012)*

FILTERS: Air

Guardian Envmtl Tech Inc .... F 860 350-2200
New Milford *(G-5541)*
Lydall Inc .... E 860 646-1233
Manchester *(G-4050)*
Microshield LLC .... G 800 553-1290
Stamford *(G-8308)*

FILTERS: Air Intake, Internal Combustion Engine, Exc Auto

Accutrol LLC .... E 203 445-9991
Danbury *(G-1730)*
Filter Fab Inc .... G 860 749-6381
Somers *(G-7658)*

FILTERS: General Line, Indl

Applied Porous Tech Inc .... F 860 408-9793
Tariffville *(G-8744)*
Elmar Filter Corporation .... G 203 624-1708
New Haven *(G-5276)*
Pallflex Products Company .... E 860 928-7761
Putnam *(G-7057)*
Stormwaterworkscom LLC .... G 203 324-0045
Stamford *(G-8445)*
Tinny Corporation .... E 860 854-6121
Middletown *(G-4427)*

FILTERS: Motor Vehicle

Lydall Inc .... E 860 646-1233
Manchester *(G-4050)*
Phillips Fuel Systems .... G 203 908-3323
Bridgeport *(G-871)*
Russell Speeders Car Wash LLC ...... G 203 925-0083
Shelton *(G-7547)*

FILTERS: Oil, Internal Combustion Engine, Exc Auto

Dynamic Bldg Enrgy Sltions LLC .... F 860 599-1872
North Stonington *(G-6022)*
Expressway Lube Centers .... G 203 744-2511
Danbury *(G-1820)*

FILTRATION DEVICES: Electronic

3M Purification Inc .... C 860 684-8628
Stafford Springs *(G-8015)*
Able Coil and Electronics Co .... E 860 646-5686
Bolton *(G-504)*
Aer Control Systems LLC .... G 203 772-4700
North Haven *(G-5897)*
JB Filtration LLC .... G 860 333-7962
Essex *(G-2721)*
New England Filter Company Inc ..... G 860 531-0500
Greenwich *(G-3208)*
Purfx Inc .... G 860 399-4045
Westbrook *(G-10005)*

FINANCIAL INVESTMENT ADVICE

Brynwood Partners V Ltd Partnr .... G 203 622-1790
Greenwich *(G-3138)*
Wexford Capital LP .... D 203 862-7000
Greenwich *(G-3258)*

FINDINGS & TRIMMINGS: Fabric

Byron Lord Inc .... G 203 287-9881
Old Lyme *(G-6493)*

FINISHING AGENTS

Unimetal Surface Finishing LLC .... E 860 283-0271
Thomaston *(G-8816)*

FINISHING SVCS

Dav-Co Finishing LLC .... G 860 828-5552
Berlin *(G-175)*

FIRE ARMS, SMALL: Guns Or Gun Parts, 30 mm & Below

Colts Manufacturing Co LLC .... C 860 236-6311
West Hartford *(G-9791)*
Grimes Firearms LLC .... G 203 843-2271
North Haven *(G-5944)*
Gunworks International L L C .... G 860 388-4591
Old Saybrook *(G-6536)*
J & E Hidalgo Enterprises LLC .... G 203 246-2252
Norwalk *(G-6214)*
Jkb Daira Inc .... G 203 642-4824
Norwalk *(G-6223)*
Kill Shot Precision LLC .... G 860 681-3162
Bristol *(G-1057)*
Kinetic Development Group LLC ...... G 203 888-4321
Seymour *(G-7353)*
Lionheart Militaria Llc .... G 203 800-5759
Guilford *(G-3369)*
M2 Tactical Solutions LLC .... G 203 247-3477
Norwalk *(G-6243)*
New Designz Inc .... F 860 384-1809
Cheshire *(G-1420)*

FIRE ARMS, SMALL: Machine Guns/Machine Gun Parts, 30mm/below

Colt Defense LLC .... B 860 232-4489
West Hartford *(G-9790)*
Continental Machine Tl Co Inc .... D 860 223-2896
New Britain *(G-4965)*
Xavier Marcus .... G 203 543-2032
Stratford *(G-8711)*

FIRE ARMS, SMALL: Pellet & BB guns

Scott Olson Enterprises LLC .... G 860 482-4391
Torrington *(G-8967)*

FIRE ARMS, SMALL: Pistols Or Pistol Parts, 30 mm & below

Sturm Ruger & Company Inc .... B 203 259-7843
Southport *(G-8010)*

FIRE ARMS, SMALL: Revolvers Or Revolver Parts, 30 mm & Below

US Firearms Manufacturing Co .... G 860 296-7441
Hartford *(G-3711)*

FIRE ARMS, SMALL: Rifles Or Rifle Parts, 30 mm & below

Mike Sadlak .... G 860 742-0227
Coventry *(G-1663)*
Stag Arms LLC .... G 860 229-9994
New Britain *(G-5058)*
Stag Arms LLC .... G 860 229-9994
New Britain *(G-5059)*
Wilson Arms Company .... F 203 488-7297
Branford *(G-675)*

FIRE ARMS, SMALL: Shotguns Or Shotgun Parts, 30 mm & Below

Dewey J Manufacturing Company .... G 203 264-3064
Oxford *(G-6655)*
Mossberg Corporation .... G 203 230-5300
North Haven *(G-5966)*
O F Mossberg & Sons Inc .... C 203 230-5300
North Haven *(G-5970)*

PRODUCT SECTION

FIRE DETECTION SYSTEMS
Protection Industries Corp..........G........ 203 375-9393
  Stratford (G-8671)
United Technologies Corp............B........ 954 485-6501
  Farmington (G-2973)

FIRE ESCAPES
S M Churyk Iron Works Inc..........G........ 860 355-1777
  New Milford (G-5588)

FIRE EXTINGUISHERS: Portable
Fire Prevention Services..............F........ 203 866-6357
  Norwalk (G-6167)

FIRE PROTECTION EQPT
AAA Fire and Safety Inc...............G........ 860 267-1965
  Bloomfield (G-379)

FIREARMS & AMMUNITION, EXC SPORTING, WHOLESALE
Barile Printers LLC.......................G........ 860 224-0127
  New Britain (G-4950)
Gems Sensors Inc..........................F........ 800 378-1600
  Plainville (G-6816)

FIREARMS: Large, Greater Than 30mm
G W Elliot Inc.................................G........ 860 528-6143
  East Hartford (G-2329)
Tek Arms Inc..................................G........ 860 748-6289
  Hebron (G-3757)

FIREARMS: Small, 30mm or Less
Colt Defense Emplye Pln..............G........ 860 232-4489
  West Hartford (G-9789)
Deburring House Inc.....................E........ 860 828-0889
  East Berlin (G-2165)
G W Elliot Inc.................................G........ 860 528-6143
  East Hartford (G-2329)
Maverick Arms Inc........................G........ 203 230-5300
  North Haven (G-5961)
Savage Arms Inc............................G........ 860 668-7049
  Suffield (G-8735)
United States Fire Arms Mfg Co....E........ 860 296-7441
  Hartford (G-3708)

FIREPLACE & CHIMNEY MATERIAL: Concrete
Snaplok Systems LLC...................G........ 888 570-5407
  Bloomfield (G-487)

FIREWOOD, WHOLESALE
Eylward Timber Co.......................G........ 203 265-4276
  Wallingford (G-9265)

FIREWORKS
Constitution Sparkler Sales...........G........ 203 324-5159
  Stamford (G-8158)
Sparklers..G........ 860 669-5110
  Clinton (G-1527)

FISH & SEAFOOD PROCESSORS: Canned Or Cured
Tri-Union Seafoods LLC................G........ 203 426-1266
  Newtown (G-5793)

FISH & SEAFOOD PROCESSORS: Fresh Or Frozen
Rich Products Corporation............C........ 609 589-3049
  New Britain (G-5045)

FISH & SEAFOOD WHOLESALERS
Tri-Union Seafoods LLC................G........ 203 426-1266
  Newtown (G-5793)

FISHING EQPT: Lures
B & D Lures...................................G........ 860 861-6530
  Ledyard (G-3868)
High Hook Lures LLC....................G........ 860 334-2324
  Old Lyme (G-6513)

FITTINGS & ASSEMBLIES: Hose & Tube, Hydraulic Or Pneumatic
Faxon Engineering Company Inc...F........ 860 236-4266
  Bloomfield (G-410)
Fluid Dynamics LLC.....................G........ 860 791-6325
  Manchester (G-4018)
Funkhouser Industrial Products.....G........ 860 653-1972
  East Granby (G-2205)
Ruby Fluid Power LLC..................E........ 860 243-7100
  Bloomfield (G-480)

FITTINGS & SPECIALTIES: Steam
Industrial Components CT LLC.....G........ 203 882-8201
  Milford (G-4555)

FITTINGS: Pipe
Crane Co..D........ 203 363-7300
  Stamford (G-8166)

FLAGS: Fabric
Bushy Hill Nature Center..............G........ 203 767-2148
  Ivoryton (G-3784)
Flagman of America LLP.............G........ 860 678-0275
  Avon (G-81)

FLARES
Russian Flare LLC........................G........ 860 404-1781
  Avon (G-107)

FLAT GLASS: Construction
Juanos Glass LLC........................G........ 203 449-5378
  Bridgeport (G-811)

FLAT GLASS: Laminated
Laminated Glass Solutions LLC...G........ 203 250-1025
  Cheshire (G-1404)

FLAT GLASS: Window, Clear & Colored
Onpoint Connections....................G........ 860 253-0489
  Enfield (G-2673)

FLAVORS OR FLAVORING MATERIALS: Synthetic
Bedoukian Research Inc...............E........ 203 830-4000
  Danbury (G-1750)

FLOOR COVERING STORES
Agw Clssic Hardwood Floors LLC..E........ 203 640-3106
  Westbrook (G-9989)
Prospect Flooring..........................G........ 203 758-4207
  Prospect (G-7017)

FLOOR COVERING STORES: Carpets
Carpet Products............................G........ 860 278-6160
  Hartford (G-3563)
Ethan Allen Retail Inc...................B........ 203 743-8000
  Danbury (G-1818)
Holland & Sherry Inc....................F........ 212 628-1950
  Norwalk (G-6201)
Lyons Upholstery Shop Inc..........G........ 203 269-3782
  Wallingford (G-9308)
Stanley Steemer Intl Inc...............E........ 860 274-5540
  Watertown (G-9738)

FLOOR COVERING STORES: Rugs
Rugsalecom LLC..........................G........ 860 756-0959
  West Hartford (G-9853)

FLOOR COVERINGS WHOLESALERS
Ascon Products Co.......................G........ 860 439-1305
  New London (G-5456)
Carpet Products............................G........ 860 278-6160
  Hartford (G-3563)

FLOOR COVERINGS: Art Squares, Textile Fiber
Graphic Memories By McKie........G........ 860 434-5222
  Old Lyme (G-6511)

FLOOR COVERINGS: Textile Fiber
Joseph Cohn Son Tile Trazo LLC..E........ 203 772-2420
  North Haven (G-5955)
Rugsalecom LLC..........................G........ 860 756-0959
  West Hartford (G-9853)

FLOOR COVERINGS: Twisted Paper, Grass, Reed, Coir, Etc
Aj Mfg..G........ 860 963-7622
  Thompson (G-8828)

FLOORING: Hard Surface
Conformis Inc................................C........ 203 793-7178
  Wallingford (G-9237)

FLOORING: Hardwood
Artistic Hardwood Floors CT........G........ 860 537-5334
  Colchester (G-1540)
Carpet Products............................G........ 860 278-6160
  Hartford (G-3563)
Conway Hardwood Products LLC..E........ 860 355-4030
  Gaylordsville (G-2991)
Diamond Hrdwd Flrs of Fairfld.....G........ 203 650-9192
  Bridgeport (G-751)
Jgf Hardwood Floor......................G........ 203 650-9192
  Bridgeport (G-805)
Stepping Stones Marble...............G........ 203 293-4796
  Westport (G-10160)
Tallon Lumber Inc.........................E........ 860 824-0733
  Canaan (G-1293)
Tg Floors.......................................G........ 860 355-5660
  New Milford (G-5595)
Ultimate Hardwood Floors...........G........ 203 746-9692
  New Fairfield (G-5181)
Wilson Woodworks Inc.................F........ 860 870-2500
  Windsor (G-10464)

FLOORING: Rubber
Ascon Products Co.......................G........ 860 439-1305
  New London (G-5456)

FLORAL ARRANGEMENT INSTRUCTION
Wilhelm Gdale Elzabeth Designs..G........ 203 371-8787
  Bridgeport (G-937)

FLORIST: Flowers, Fresh
Petal Prfctn & Confection LLC.....G........ 203 263-0353
  Woodbury (G-10649)
Rose To Occassion LLC...............G........ 860 628-6880
  Southington (G-7968)

FLORISTS
Interior Plantworks Inc.................G........ 860 289-9499
  South Windsor (G-7775)

FLORISTS' SPLYS, WHOLESALE
Raymond J Bykowski....................G........ 203 271-2385
  Cheshire (G-1438)

FLOWER ARRANGEMENTS: Artificial
Blumen Laden Artificial Flower...G........ 860 693-8600
  Collinsville (G-1589)

FLOWER POTS: Red Earthenware
Mc Cann Bros Inc.........................E........ 203 335-8630
  Monroe (G-4734)

FLOWERS, ARTIFICIAL, WHOLESALE
Mc Cann Bros Inc.........................E........ 203 335-8630
  Monroe (G-4734)

FLOWERS: Artificial & Preserved
Articrafts.......................................G........ 203 618-1715
  Greenwich (G-3123)
Countryside Crafts........................G........ 860 774-0446
  Dayville (G-2059)
Raymond J Bykowski....................G........ 203 271-2385
  Cheshire (G-1438)

FLUID METERS & COUNTING DEVICES

Eastern Utility Products LLC .... G 860 399-1724
  Westbrook *(G-9995)*
Gems Sensors Inc .... B 860 747-3000
  Plainville *(G-6815)*
Habco Industries LLC .... E 860 682-6800
  Glastonbury *(G-3045)*

FLUID POWER PUMPS & MOTORS

Fluid Solutions LLC .... G 203 245-0708
  Madison *(G-3921)*
Hamilton Sundstrand Corp .... A 860 654-6000
  Windsor Locks *(G-10491)*
Navtec Rigging Solutions Inc .... E 203 458-3163
  Clinton *(G-1515)*
Parker-Hannifin Corporation .... G 860 920-4231
  East Hartford *(G-2351)*

FLUID POWER VALVES & HOSE FITTINGS

Atp Industries LLC .... F 860 479-5007
  Plainville *(G-6773)*
Enfield Technologies LLC .... F 203 375-3100
  Shelton *(G-7439)*
Parker-Hannifin Corporation .... C 860 827-2300
  New Britain *(G-5030)*

FLUXES

Alent USA Holding Inc .... B 203 575-5727
  Waterbury *(G-9426)*
Inventec Prfmce Chem USA LLC .... E 860 526-8300
  Deep River *(G-2094)*

FOAM RUBBER

Latex Foam International LLC .... D 203 924-0700
  Shelton *(G-7487)*
New England Foam Products LLC .... E 860 524-0121
  Hartford *(G-3650)*
Reilly Foam Corp .... E 860 243-8200
  Bloomfield *(G-476)*

FOIL & LEAF: Metal

Dexmet Corporation .... D 203 294-4440
  Wallingford *(G-9249)*
Foilmark Inc .... F 860 243-0343
  Bloomfield *(G-414)*
PPG Industries Inc .... D 203 294-4440
  Wallingford *(G-9337)*

FOOD PRDTS, BREAKFAST: Cereal, Granola & Muesli

Granola Bar .... G 914 763-6320
  Greenwich *(G-3170)*

FOOD PRDTS, BREAKFAST: Cereal, Oatmeal

Garden of Light Inc .... D 860 895-6622
  East Hartford *(G-2330)*
Munk Pack Inc .... F 203 769-5005
  Greenwich *(G-3207)*

FOOD PRDTS, BREAKFAST: Cereal, Rye

Rivera Marina .... G 917 676-4100
  New Haven *(G-5381)*

FOOD PRDTS, CANNED OR FRESH PACK: Fruit Juices

Guida-Seibert Dairy Company .... C 860 224-2404
  New Britain *(G-4994)*

FOOD PRDTS, CANNED: Barbecue Sauce

Nantucket Blonde LLC .... G 203 415-1522
  Cheshire *(G-1417)*

FOOD PRDTS, CANNED: Ethnic

D & M Packing LLC .... E 203 591-8986
  Waterbury *(G-9458)*

FOOD PRDTS, CANNED: Fruit Juices, Fresh

Juice Press LLC .... G 212 777-0034
  Greenwich *(G-3185)*

FOOD PRDTS, CANNED: Fruits

Cosmos Food Products Inc .... E 800 942-6766
  West Haven *(G-9893)*
Country Pure Foods Inc .... C 330 753-2293
  Ellington *(G-2583)*
Fruitbud Juice LLC .... E 203 790-8200
  Danbury *(G-1830)*
James P Smith .... G 203 744-1031
  Danbury *(G-1857)*
Natural Country Farms Inc .... D 860 872-8346
  Ellington *(G-2597)*
Premier Foods Inc .... G 203 226-6577
  Westport *(G-10143)*

FOOD PRDTS, CANNED: Italian

A S Fine Foods .... D 203 322-3899
  Stamford *(G-8052)*
Sacla North America Inc .... G 203 855-1356
  Norwalk *(G-6335)*

FOOD PRDTS, CANNED: Jams, Jellies & Preserves

Conant Valley Jams .... G 203 403-3811
  Ridgefield *(G-7129)*
Herbs Farmstead & Goods .... G 860 876-3670
  Old Saybrook *(G-6540)*
Omnomnom Jams and Jellies LLC .... G 203 630-6557
  Meriden *(G-4213)*
Sweet Country Roads LLC .... G 860 537-0069
  Colchester *(G-1578)*

FOOD PRDTS, CANNED: Marmalade

Winding Drive Corporation .... G 203 263-6961
  Woodbury *(G-10655)*

FOOD PRDTS, CANNED: Mushrooms

Sabatino North America LLC .... E 718 328-4120
  West Haven *(G-9951)*

FOOD PRDTS, CANNED: Spaghetti & Other Pasta Sauce

Conopco Inc .... E 708 606-0540
  Trumbull *(G-9014)*
Onofrios Ultimate Foods Inc .... F 203 469-4014
  New Haven *(G-5355)*
Ragozzino Foods Inc .... F 203 238-2553
  Meriden *(G-4229)*
Thomas J Lipton Inc .... A 206 381-3500
  Trumbull *(G-9081)*

FOOD PRDTS, CANNED: Spanish

Louis Rodriguz .... G 203 777-6937
  New Haven *(G-5321)*

FOOD PRDTS, CONFECTIONERY, WHOLESALE: Candy

Deborah Anns Hmmade Chocolates ..... G 203 438-0065
  Ridgefield *(G-7135)*
Thompson Brands LLC .... D 203 235-2541
  Meriden *(G-4254)*

FOOD PRDTS, CONFECTIONERY, WHOLESALE: Snack Foods

Pepperidge Farm Incorporated .... A 203 846-7000
  Norwalk *(G-6298)*

FOOD PRDTS, DAIRY, WHOLESALE: Frozen Dairy Desserts

Rich Products Corporation .... B 860 827-8000
  New Britain *(G-5044)*

FOOD PRDTS, FISH & SEAFOOD, WHOLESALE: Seafood

Coastal Seafoods Inc .... F 203 431-0453
  Fairfield *(G-2765)*

FOOD PRDTS, FISH & SEAFOOD: Canned & Jarred, Etc

Greenport Foods LLC .... F 203 221-2673
  Westport *(G-10093)*

FOOD PRDTS, FISH & SEAFOOD: Chowders, Frozen

Seafood Gourmet Inc .... F 203 272-1544
  Wolcott *(G-10586)*

FOOD PRDTS, FISH & SEAFOOD: Crab cakes, Frozen

Coastal Seafoods Inc .... F 203 431-0453
  Fairfield *(G-2765)*
Saugatuck Kitchens LLC .... G 203 334-1099
  Stratford *(G-8675)*

FOOD PRDTS, FISH & SEAFOOD: Fish, Cured, NEC

Bottarga Brothers LLC .... G 203 355-1134
  Stamford *(G-8114)*

FOOD PRDTS, FISH & SEAFOOD: Oysters, Preserved & Cured

Golden Oyster Company .... G 203 929-3389
  Shelton *(G-7451)*

FOOD PRDTS, FROZEN: Breakfasts, Packaged

Just Breakfast & Things .... G 860 376-4040
  Lisbon *(G-3881)*

FOOD PRDTS, FROZEN: Fruit Juice, Concentrates

Quality Kitchen Corp Delaware .... G 203 744-2000
  Danbury *(G-1923)*

FOOD PRDTS, FROZEN: Fruits, Juices & Vegetables

Conopco Inc .... D 203 381-3557
  Trumbull *(G-9015)*
Fruitbud Juice LLC .... E 203 790-8200
  Danbury *(G-1830)*
Natureseal Inc .... E 203 454-1800
  Westport *(G-10127)*
Santorini Breeze LLC .... G 203 640-3431
  Branford *(G-646)*

FOOD PRDTS, FROZEN: NEC

Kohler Mix Specialties LLC .... C 860 666-1511
  Newington *(G-5670)*
Lucille Piccirillo .... G 203 366-2353
  Bridgeport *(G-826)*
Ragozzino Foods Inc .... F 203 238-2553
  Meriden *(G-4229)*
Villarina Pasta & Fine Foods .... G 203 917-4463
  Danbury *(G-1972)*

FOOD PRDTS, FROZEN: Snack Items

Orange Cheese Company .... G 917 603-4378
  Orange *(G-6619)*

FOOD PRDTS, FROZEN: Soups

Flemming LLC .... G 818 746-6495
  Bloomfield *(G-411)*

FOOD PRDTS, FRUITS & VEGETABLES, FRESH, WHOLESALE

Gracies Kitchens Inc .... F 203 773-0795
  New Haven *(G-5288)*

FOOD PRDTS, MEAT & MEAT PRDTS, WHOLESALE: Cured Or Smoked

Manchester Packing Company Inc .... D 860 646-5000
  Manchester *(G-4053)*

FOOD PRDTS, MEAT & MEAT PRDTS, WHOLESALE: Fresh

Baretta Provision Inc .... F 860 828-0802
  East Berlin *(G-2164)*
Noacks Meat Products .... G 203 235-7384
  Meriden *(G-4209)*

PRODUCT SECTION

FOOD PRDTS, WHOLESALE: Beverages, Exc Coffee & Tea

Als Holding Inc .... G 860 627-7003
  East Windsor (G-2481)

FOOD PRDTS, WHOLESALE: Chocolate

Hvc Lizard Chocolate LLC .... F 203 899-3075
  Norwalk (G-6203)
Nel Group LLC .... G 860 413-9042
  East Granby (G-2216)
Nel Group LLC .... F 860 683-0190
  Windsor (G-10412)

FOOD PRDTS, WHOLESALE: Cocoa

Cofco Americas Resources Corp .... B 203 252-5200
  Stamford (G-8151)

FOOD PRDTS, WHOLESALE: Condiments

Omar Coffee Company .... E 860 667-8889
  Newington (G-5689)

FOOD PRDTS, WHOLESALE: Flavorings & Fragrances

Saccuzzo Company Inc .... G 860 665-1101
  Newington (G-5702)

FOOD PRDTS, WHOLESALE: Food Gift Baskets

Copeland Latasha .... G 860 728-8289
  Hartford (G-3570)

FOOD PRDTS, WHOLESALE: Grains

Central Conn Cooperative Farme .... E 860 649-4523
  South Windsor (G-7727)
Louis Dreyfus Holding Company .... B 203 761-2000
  Wilton (G-10310)

FOOD PRDTS, WHOLESALE: Health

Advanced Golf Nutrition LLC .... G 203 554-9120
  Fairfield (G-2744)
Old Lyme Gourmet Company .... E 860 434-7347
  Deep River (G-2097)

FOOD PRDTS, WHOLESALE: Juices

Guida-Seibert Dairy Company .... C 860 224-2404
  New Britain (G-4994)

FOOD PRDTS, WHOLESALE: Organic & Diet

D & M Packing LLC .... E 203 591-8986
  Waterbury (G-9458)
Herbasway Laboratories LLC .... E 203 269-6991
  Wallingford (G-9280)

FOOD PRDTS, WHOLESALE: Pasta & Rice

Vita Pasta Inc .... G 860 395-1452
  Old Saybrook (G-6577)

FOOD PRDTS, WHOLESALE: Sauces

Gracies Kitchens Inc .... F 203 773-0795
  New Haven (G-5288)

FOOD PRDTS, WHOLESALE: Sugar, Refined

Imperial Sugar Company .... C 203 761-8474
  Wilton (G-10301)

FOOD PRDTS, WHOLESALE: Water, Mineral Or Spring, Bottled

Crystal Rock Spring Water Co .... B 860 945-0461
  Watertown (G-9698)

FOOD PRDTS, WHOLESALE: Wine Makers' Eqpt & Splys

Cocchia Norwalk Grape Co .... F 203 855-7911
  Norwalk (G-6119)
Huntington Capital MGT LLC .... G 203 339-2126
  Shelton (G-7471)

FOOD PRDTS: Bread Crumbs, Exc Made In Bakeries

Pepperidge Farm Incorporated .... C 860 286-6400
  Bloomfield (G-463)
Pepperidge Farm Incorporated .... A 203 846-7000
  Norwalk (G-6298)

FOOD PRDTS: Cereals

Kellogg Company .... A 860 665-9920
  Newington (G-5669)

FOOD PRDTS: Chocolate Liquor

Green Tomatillo LLC .... G 860 749-0172
  South Windsor (G-7765)

FOOD PRDTS: Cocoa, Instant

Cote DIvoire Imports .... G 203 243-4841
  Stratford (G-8600)

FOOD PRDTS: Cocoa, Powdered

CSC Cocoa LLC .... G 203 846-5611
  New Canaan (G-5099)

FOOD PRDTS: Coconut, Desiccated & Shredded

Local Traffic Fusion LLC .... G 203 938-8862
  Redding (G-7097)

FOOD PRDTS: Coffee

Als Beverage Company Inc .... E 860 627-7003
  East Windsor (G-2480)
Cote DIvoire Imports .... G 203 243-4841
  Stratford (G-8600)
Fjb America LLC .... G 203 682-2424
  Westport (G-10083)
Oasis Coffee Corp .... E 203 847-0554
  Norwalk (G-6283)

FOOD PRDTS: Coffee Roasting, Exc Wholesale Grocers

Ashlawn Farm Store .... G 860 434-3636
  Old Lyme (G-6490)
B & B Ventures Ltd Lblty Co .... E 203 481-1700
  Branford (G-554)
Omar Coffee Company .... E 860 667-8889
  Newington (G-5689)
Saccuzzo Company Inc .... G 860 665-1101
  Newington (G-5702)
Sacred Grunds Cof Roasters LLC ...... G 860 717-2871
  Sherman (G-7604)
Tm Ward Co of Connecticut LLC .... G 203 866-9203
  Norwalk (G-6371)

FOOD PRDTS: Cooking Oils, Refined Vegetable, Exc Corn

Lw Global LLC .... G 860 519-7134
  Simsbury (G-7632)

FOOD PRDTS: Cottonseed Oil, Deodorized

O-Liminator LLc .... G 800 608-9541
  Darien (G-2036)

FOOD PRDTS: Dips, Exc Cheese & Sour Cream Based

Guasa Salsa Vzla .... G 203 981-7011
  Norwalk (G-6187)
Salsa Fresca New Haven .... G 301 675-6226
  New Haven (G-5386)
Yumelish Food LLC .... G 203 522-6933
  Fairfield (G-2868)

FOOD PRDTS: Dough, Pizza, Prepared

Michele Schiano Di Cola Inc .... G 203 265-5301
  Wallingford (G-9318)
Zeneli Pizzeria .... G 203 745-4194
  New Haven (G-5453)

FOOD PRDTS: Dressings, Salad, Raw & Cooked Exc Dry Mixes

Da Silva Klanko Ltd .... G 203 756-4932
  Waterbury (G-9459)
Kerry R Wood .... G 203 221-7780
  Westport (G-10107)
Newmans Own Inc .... E 203 222-0136
  Westport (G-10128)
Thomas J Lipton Inc .... A 206 381-3500
  Trumbull (G-9081)

FOOD PRDTS: Eggs, Processed

Whispering Winds Animal .... G 860 796-8098
  Coventry (G-1682)

FOOD PRDTS: Flavored Ices, Frozen

Liberato Italian Ices Inc .... G 203 772-0381
  New Haven (G-5318)

FOOD PRDTS: Flour & Other Grain Mill Products

Archer-Daniels-Midland Company ..... G 203 966-4755
  New Canaan (G-5088)
Central Conn Cooperative Farme .... E 860 649-4523
  South Windsor (G-7727)
Channel Alloys .... G 203 975-1404
  Norwalk (G-6112)
Pelletier Millwrights LLC .... G 860 564-8936
  Danielson (G-2000)

FOOD PRDTS: Flour Mixes & Doughs

Watson LLC .... B 203 932-3000
  West Haven (G-9960)

FOOD PRDTS: Fresh Vegetables, Peeled Or Processed

Gracies Kitchens Inc .... F 203 773-0795
  New Haven (G-5288)

FOOD PRDTS: Fruit Juices

Fruta Juice Bar LLC .... G 203 690-9168
  Bridgeport (G-772)
Riverside Express .... G 203 326-1245
  Riverside (G-7201)

FOOD PRDTS: Fruits, Freeze-Dried

Zanni Ani Organic Snacks LLC .... G 203 214-2360
  Oxford (G-6702)

FOOD PRDTS: Granola & Energy Bars, Nonchocolate

Cavegrl LLC .... G 914 261-5801
  Stamford (G-8132)

FOOD PRDTS: Honey

Skaarship Apiaries LLC .... G 860 805-9398
  Greenwich (G-3238)

FOOD PRDTS: Ice, Cubes

Dee Zee Ice LLC .... F 860 276-3500
  Southington (G-7912)
Twenty Five Commerce Inc .... G 203 866-0540
  Norwalk (G-6379)

FOOD PRDTS: Instant Coffee

Riseandshine Corporation .... F 917 599-7541
  Stamford (G-8393)

FOOD PRDTS: Macaroni, Noodles, Spaghetti, Pasta, Etc

Carlas Pasta Inc .... C 860 436-4042
  South Windsor (G-7726)
Grotto Always Inc .... F 203 754-0295
  Waterbury (G-9491)
Oasis Coffee Corp .... E 203 847-0554
  Norwalk (G-6283)
Villarina Pasta & Fine Foods .... G 203 917-4463
  Danbury (G-1972)

FOOD PRDTS: Nuts & Seeds

Wizards Nuts Holdings LLC..............D....... 708 483-1315
　Greenwich *(G-3260)*

FOOD PRDTS: Oils & Fats, Animal

Darling International Inc..............G....... 203 597-0773
　Waterbury *(G-9462)*

FOOD PRDTS: Olive Oil

Devin David..............G....... 203 322-4000
　Stamford *(G-8184)*
Essex Olive Oil Company LLC..............G....... 860 526-2205
　Deep River *(G-2088)*
New Canaan Olive Oil LLC..............G....... 845 240-3294
　Stamford *(G-8322)*
Nsf Gourmet Products..............G....... 203 856-4995
　Westport *(G-10129)*
Olive Capizzano Oils & Vinegar..............G....... 860 495-2187
　Pawcatuck *(G-6721)*
Olive Chiappetta Oil LLC..............G....... 203 223-3655
　Stamford *(G-8339)*
Olive Nutmeg Oil..............G....... 860 354-7300
　New Milford *(G-5578)*
Olive Oil Factory LLC..............F....... 203 591-8986
　Waterbury *(G-9570)*
Olive Oils and Balsamics LLC..............G....... 860 563-0105
　Rocky Hill *(G-7260)*
Olive Sabor Oil Co..............G....... 860 922-7483
　Somers *(G-7666)*
Shoreline Vine..............G....... 203 779-5331
　Madison *(G-3957)*

FOOD PRDTS: Pasta, Rice/Potatoes, Uncooked, Pkgd

Nuovo Pasta Productions Ltd..............C....... 203 380-4090
　Stratford *(G-8659)*

FOOD PRDTS: Pasta, Uncooked, Packaged With Other Ingredients

Durantes Pasta Inc..............G....... 203 387-5560
　West Haven *(G-9902)*
Fine Food Services Inc..............E....... 860 445-5276
　Groton *(G-3288)*
Grana Pastificio LLC..............G....... 203 979-2828
　Norwalk *(G-6184)*
Mastriani Gourmet Food LLC..............G....... 203 368-9556
　Bridgeport *(G-833)*
Vita Pasta Inc..............G....... 860 395-1452
　Old Saybrook *(G-6577)*

FOOD PRDTS: Peanut Butter

Peanut Butter and Jelly..............G....... 203 504-2280
　Stamford *(G-8354)*

FOOD PRDTS: Potato & Corn Chips & Similar Prdts

Frito-Lay North America Inc..............A....... 860 412-1000
　Dayville *(G-2063)*
Mediterranean Snack Fd Co LLC..............F....... 973 402-2644
　Stamford *(G-8305)*
Smart Alex Foods LLC..............G....... 203 322-3368
　Stamford *(G-8425)*
U T Z..............G....... 860 383-4266
　North Franklin *(G-5879)*

FOOD PRDTS: Potato Chips & Other Potato-Based Snacks

Old Lyme Gourmet Company..............E....... 860 434-7347
　Deep River *(G-2097)*

FOOD PRDTS: Poultry Sausage, Lunch Meats/Other Poultry Prdts

Waybest Foods Inc..............G....... 860 289-7948
　South Windsor *(G-7839)*

FOOD PRDTS: Preparations

Amber Food Sales..............G....... 860 749-7272
　Enfield *(G-2614)*
Atlantic Street Capitl MGT LLC..............E....... 203 428-3150
　Stamford *(G-8098)*
Bonney-Gee Cuisines..............G....... 203 372-3385
　Bridgeport *(G-716)*
Chen-Man Foods LLC..............G....... 860 659-9549
　Glastonbury *(G-3020)*
Chowder Pot of Hartford LLC..............G....... 860 244-3311
　Hartford *(G-3566)*
Crave Foods LLC..............G....... 203 227-6868
　Westport *(G-10071)*
Dp Foods L L C..............G....... 203 271-6212
　Cheshire *(G-1382)*
Entrees Made Easy..............G....... 203 261-5777
　Monroe *(G-4716)*
Field Energy LLC..............G....... 860 817-2654
　West Hartford *(G-9810)*
First Chance Inc..............F....... 860 346-3663
　Middletown *(G-4345)*
Frescobene Foods LLC..............G....... 203 610-4688
　Fairfield *(G-2788)*
George Bailey..............G....... 860 423-2136
　Storrs *(G-8549)*
Global Palate Foods LLC..............G....... 203 543-3028
　Westport *(G-10090)*
Green Leaf Foods LLC..............G....... 860 657-4404
　Glastonbury *(G-3043)*
Harrison Farm..............G....... 203 488-7963
　North Branford *(G-5842)*
Hummel Bros Inc..............D....... 203 787-4113
　New Haven *(G-5298)*
Ikigai Foods LLC..............G....... 203 954-8083
　Shelton *(G-7473)*
Infinite Nutrition Inc..............G....... 203 940-1783
　Old Greenwich *(G-6477)*
Kohler Mix Specialties LLC..............C....... 860 666-1511
　Newington *(G-5670)*
Lawrence Mc Conney..............G....... 203 735-1133
　Derby *(G-2118)*
Lesser Evil..............G....... 203 529-3555
　Danbury *(G-1872)*
Malta Food Pantry Inc..............G....... 860 725-0944
　Hartford *(G-3632)*
Maple Craft Foods LLC..............G....... 203 913-7066
　Sandy Hook *(G-7321)*
Mozzicato Pastry & Bake Shop..............E....... 860 296-0426
　Hartford *(G-3646)*
National Institutional Sup LLC..............G....... 203 263-3455
　Woodbury *(G-10645)*
Nutmeg Food Brokers LLC..............G....... 860 289-9566
　South Windsor *(G-7797)*
Nutriventus Inc..............G....... 860 990-9324
　Cromwell *(G-1712)*
Old Castle Foods LLC..............G....... 203 426-1344
　Newtown *(G-5766)*
Olive Flavored..............G....... 203 641-2086
　Meriden *(G-4211)*
Paridise Foods LLC..............G....... 203 283-3903
　Milford *(G-4603)*
Podunk Popcorn..............G....... 860 648-9565
　South Windsor *(G-7808)*
Premiere Packg Partners LLC..............E....... 203 694-0003
　Waterbury *(G-9586)*
Sodexo Inc..............E....... 860 679-2803
　Farmington *(G-2958)*
Source Inc..............G....... 203 488-6400
　North Branford *(G-5858)*
Sovipe Food Distributors LLC..............G....... 203 648-2781
　Danbury *(G-1954)*
Supreme Storm Services LLC..............G....... 860 201-0642
　Southington *(G-7983)*
Swamp Yankee Products LLC..............G....... 203 720-1202
　Naugatuck *(G-4923)*
Whole G Food Intl Distrs LLC..............G....... 203 848-2136
　New Haven *(G-5431)*

FOOD PRDTS: Prepared Meat Sauces Exc Tomato & Dry

Muggers Marrow LLC..............G....... 203 548-9566
　Bridgeport *(G-845)*

FOOD PRDTS: Salads

Kerry R Wood..............G....... 203 221-7780
　Westport *(G-10107)*

FOOD PRDTS: Sandwiches

Burnside Supermarket LLC..............G....... 860 291-9965
　East Hartford *(G-2301)*
Parma 1901 Usa Inc..............G....... 203 855-1356
　Norwalk *(G-6291)*

FOOD PRDTS: Seasonings & Spices

Uncle Wileys Inc..............F....... 203 256-9313
　Fairfield *(G-2860)*

FOOD PRDTS: Soup Mixes

Conopco Inc..............E....... 708 606-0540
　Trumbull *(G-9014)*
Thomas J Lipton Inc..............A....... 206 381-3500
　Trumbull *(G-9081)*

FOOD PRDTS: Soy Sauce

Onofrios Ultimate Foods Inc..............F....... 203 469-4014
　New Haven *(G-5355)*

FOOD PRDTS: Spices, Including Ground

Amodios Inc..............F....... 203 573-1229
　Waterbury *(G-9430)*

FOOD PRDTS: Sugar

Cofco Americas Resources Corp..............B....... 203 252-5200
　Stamford *(G-8151)*
Dulcify LLC..............G....... 203 344-1671
　Riverside *(G-7194)*
Huntington Capital MGT LLC..............G....... 203 339-2126
　Shelton *(G-7471)*

FOOD PRDTS: Sugar, Cane

Jenkins Sugar Group Inc..............F....... 203 853-3000
　Norwalk *(G-6221)*

FOOD PRDTS: Sugar, Granulated Cane, Purchd Raw Sugar/Syrup

Imperial Sugar Company..............C....... 203 761-8474
　Wilton *(G-10301)*

FOOD PRDTS: Sugar, Liquid Sugar Beet

CSC Sugar LLC..............F....... 203 846-5610
　New Canaan *(G-5100)*

FOOD PRDTS: Sugar, Maple, Indl

Balsam Woods Farm..............G....... 860 265-1800
　Stafford Springs *(G-8018)*

FOOD PRDTS: Sugar, Refined Cane, Purchased Raw Sugar/Syrup

CSC Sugar LLC..............F....... 203 846-5610
　New Canaan *(G-5100)*

FOOD PRDTS: Syrup, Maple

Brothers & Sons Sugar House..............G....... 860 489-2719
　Torrington *(G-8907)*
Bureaus Sugar House..............G....... 860 434-5787
　Old Lyme *(G-6492)*
Fabyan Sugar Shack LLC..............G....... 860 935-9281
　North Grosvenordale *(G-5884)*
Papas Maple Syrup..............G....... 860 379-0117
　New Hartford *(G-5205)*
Richard Walker..............G....... 860 267-7117
　East Hampton *(G-2278)*
Rivers Edge Sugar House..............G....... 860 429-1510
　Ashford *(G-65)*

FOOD PRDTS: Syrups

Carriage House Companies Inc..............B....... 860 647-1909
　Manchester *(G-3992)*
Unilever Ascc AG..............B....... 203 381-2482
　Shelton *(G-7575)*

FOOD PRDTS: Tea

Conopco Inc..............E....... 708 606-0540
　Trumbull *(G-9014)*
Herbasway Laboratories LLC..............E....... 203 269-6991
　Wallingford *(G-9280)*
RC Bigelow Inc..............C....... 888 244-3569
　Fairfield *(G-2834)*
Thomas J Lipton Inc..............A....... 206 381-3500
　Trumbull *(G-9081)*

FOOD PRDTS: Tortilla Chips

Severance Foods Inc..............E....... 860 724-7063
　Hartford *(G-3684)*

PRODUCT SECTION

FUELS: Ethanol

FOOD PRDTS: Vegetables, Brined
TSty Brands Inc..............................G....... 203 609-4391
  Stamford *(G-8479)*

FOOD PRDTS: Vinegar
Vinegar Syndrome LLC ....G....... 212 722-9755
  Bridgeport *(G-934)*

FOOD PRODUCTS MACHINERY
A & I Concentrate LLC ....F....... 203 447-1938
  Shelton *(G-7385)*
Amt Micropure Inc ....G....... 203 226-7938
  Weston *(G-10017)*
Capricorn Investors III LP ....F....... 203 861-6600
  Greenwich *(G-3141)*
Conair Corporation ....D....... 800 492-7464
  Torrington *(G-8914)*
Penco Corporation ....C....... 860 347-7271
  Middletown *(G-4392)*
Treif USA Inc ....F....... 203 929-9930
  Shelton *(G-7569)*

FOOD STORES: Convenience, Chain
Mercury Fuel Service Inc ....D....... 203 756-7284
  Waterbury *(G-9539)*

FOOD STORES: Convenience, Independent
Spicer Plus Inc ....G....... 860 445-2436
  Groton *(G-3313)*

FOOD STORES: Supermarkets
Burnside Supermarket LLC ....G....... 860 291-9965
  East Hartford *(G-2301)*

FOOD WARMING EQPT: Commercial
Creative Mobile Systems Inc ....G....... 860 649-6272
  Manchester *(G-4000)*

FOOTWEAR, WHOLESALE: Boots
Dsw Inc ....F....... 860 644-6200
  Manchester *(G-4012)*
Dsw Inc ....F....... 203 985-8241
  North Haven *(G-5933)*

FOOTWEAR, WHOLESALE: Shoe Access
Crista Grasso LLC ....G....... 347 946-2533
  Tolland *(G-8856)*

FOOTWEAR: Cut Stock
Darlene Ann Miconi ....G....... 203 245-4127
  Madison *(G-3917)*
Pace Chiropractic Wellness Ctr ....G....... 203 281-9635
  Hamden *(G-3493)*

FOOTWEAR: Except Rubber, NEC
Buestan Usa LLC ....G....... 203 954-8889
  Ansonia *(G-25)*

FORGINGS
Bourdon Forge Co Inc ....C....... 860 632-2740
  Middletown *(G-4326)*
Bristol Instrument Gears Inc ....F....... 860 583-1395
  Bristol *(G-989)*
Carlton Forge Works ....E....... 860 873-9730
  Moodus *(G-4773)*
Cunningham Industries Inc ....G....... 203 324-2942
  Stamford *(G-8171)*
East Shore Wire Rope ....G....... 203 469-5204
  East Haven *(G-2422)*
Iron and Grain Co LLC ....G....... 860 840-2179
  West Hartford *(G-9823)*
J J Ryan Corporation ....C....... 860 628-0393
  Plantsville *(G-6897)*
OEM Sources LLC ....G....... 203 283-5415
  Milford *(G-4597)*
Paradigm Manchester Inc ....C....... 860 649-2888
  Manchester *(G-4069)*
Perry Technology Corporation ....D....... 860 738-2525
  New Hartford *(G-5206)*
Roller Bearing Co Amer Inc ....E....... 203 758-8272
  Middlebury *(G-4289)*
White Bronze LLC ....G....... 214 605-7352
  Bridgeport *(G-936)*

FORGINGS: Aircraft, Ferrous
Consoldted Inds Acqsition Corp ....D....... 203 272-5371
  Cheshire *(G-1374)*

FORGINGS: Iron & Steel
J J Ryan Corporation ....C....... 860 628-0393
  Plantsville *(G-6897)*

FORGINGS: Mechanical Power Transmission, Ferrous
J & H Mobile Mechanic LLC ....G....... 203 266-4748
  Woodbury *(G-10639)*

FORGINGS: Ordnance, Ferrous
Geneve Holdings Inc ....G....... 203 358-8000
  Stamford *(G-8216)*

FORMS HANDLING EQPT
Energy Saving Products and Sls ......E....... 860 675-6443
  Burlington *(G-1267)*

FOUNDRIES: Aluminum
Charles W Simmons ....G....... 203 254-3388
  Fairfield *(G-2759)*
JET Corporation ....F....... 203 334-3317
  Bridgeport *(G-804)*
Pyrotek Incorporated ....G....... 509 926-6212
  Killingworth *(G-3838)*

FOUNDRIES: Brass, Bronze & Copper
American Sleeve Bearing LLC ....E....... 860 684-8060
  Stafford Springs *(G-8016)*
Mystic River Foundry LLC ....G....... 860 536-7634
  Mystic *(G-4835)*
Spirol International Corp ....C....... 860 774-8571
  Danielson *(G-2003)*

FOUNDRIES: Nonferrous
Custom Metal Crafters Inc ....D....... 860 953-4210
  Newington *(G-5645)*
Doncasters Inc ....D....... 860 446-4803
  Groton *(G-3282)*
Elm City Pttern Fndry Wrks Inc ....G....... 203 481-2518
  Branford *(G-588)*
F M Associates ....G....... 860 693-2263
  Canton *(G-1314)*

FOUNDRIES: Steel
Polstal Corporation ....G....... 203 849-7788
  Wilton *(G-10320)*

FOUNDRIES: Steel Investment
Doncasters Inc ....D....... 860 446-4803
  Groton *(G-3282)*
Dundee Holding Inc ....G....... 860 677-1376
  Farmington *(G-2898)*
Integra-Cast Inc ....D....... 860 225-7600
  New Britain *(G-4999)*
Miller Castings Inc ....C....... 860 822-9991
  North Franklin *(G-5875)*
Tps Acquisition LLC ....G....... 860 589-5511
  Waterbury *(G-9616)*

FOUNDRY MACHINERY & EQPT
Gerber Technology LLC ....B....... 860 871-8082
  Tolland *(G-8865)*

FRACTIONATION PRDTS OF CRUDE PETROLEUM, HYDROCARBONS, NEC
Madonna Black Buddist LLC ....G....... 203 589-9796
  Greenwich *(G-3196)*

FRAMES: Handbag & Pocketbook
Boxtree Accessories Inc ....G....... 203 637-5794
  Old Greenwich *(G-6468)*

FRANCHISES, SELLING OR LICENSING
Congress Catering Inc ....E....... 860 291-8182
  East Hartford *(G-2309)*
Stanley Steemer Intl Inc ....E....... 860 274-5540
  Watertown *(G-9738)*

FREIGHT FORWARDING ARRANGEMENTS
Commandtech LLC ....G....... 860 857-8502
  Groton *(G-3278)*

FRICTION MATERIAL, MADE FROM POWDERED METAL
Tek-Motive Inc ....D....... 203 468-2224
  Branford *(G-662)*
Torqmaster Inc ....E....... 203 326-5945
  Stamford *(G-8471)*

FRUIT & VEGETABLE MARKETS
Herbs Farmstead & Goods ....G....... 860 876-3670
  Old Saybrook *(G-6540)*

FRUIT STANDS OR MARKETS
Lyman Farm Incorporated ....C....... 860 349-1793
  Middlefield *(G-4302)*

FRUITS & VEGETABLES WHOLESALERS: Fresh
Grand Fish Market LLC ....G....... 203 691-8904
  New Haven *(G-5289)*

FUEL ADDITIVES
Armored Autogroup Parent Inc ....G....... 203 205-2900
  Danbury *(G-1747)*

FUEL CELLS: Solid State
Doosan Fuel Cell America Inc ....C....... 860 727-2200
  South Windsor *(G-7739)*
Fuelcell Energy Inc ....E....... 860 496-1111
  Torrington *(G-8927)*

FUEL DEALERS: Wood
Hancock Logging & Forestry MGT ...G....... 860 289-5647
  South Windsor *(G-7767)*
Rainbow Forest Log & Firewd ....G....... 860 455-1023
  Hampton *(G-3539)*

FUEL OIL DEALERS
Devine Brothers Incorporated ....E....... 203 866-4421
  Norwalk *(G-6136)*
Mercury Fuel Service Inc ....D....... 203 756-7284
  Waterbury *(G-9539)*

FUELS: Diesel
App Polonia LLC ....G....... 860 747-3397
  Plainville *(G-6771)*

FUELS: Ethanol
Advanced Fuel Co LLC ....G....... 860 642-4817
  North Franklin *(G-5869)*
Alternative Fuel & Energy LLC ....G....... 860 537-5345
  Colchester *(G-1539)*
American Greenfuels LLC ....F....... 203 672-9028
  New Haven *(G-5227)*
Anthony s Fuel ....G....... 203 513-7400
  Shelton *(G-7396)*
Bestway Food and Fuel ....G....... 860 447-0729
  Waterford *(G-9643)*
Black Dog Fuel LLC ....G....... 860 489-0655
  New Milford *(G-5511)*
Cobal-USA Altrnative Fuels LLC ....G....... 203 751-1974
  Ansonia *(G-29)*
Crossroads Deli & Fuel LLC ....G....... 860 824-8474
  Falls Village *(G-2869)*
CTS Services LLC ....G....... 203 268-5865
  Shelton *(G-7424)*
Deep River Fuel Terminals LLC ....G....... 860 342-4619
  Portland *(G-6956)*
E&S Automotive Operations LLC .....G....... 203 332-4555
  Bridgeport *(G-759)*
Extra Fuel ....G....... 203 330-0613
  Bridgeport *(G-766)*
Falls Fuel LLC ....G....... 860 744-3835
  Bethel *(G-299)*
Firehouse Discount Oil LLC ....G....... 860 404-1827
  Unionville *(G-9115)*
Fuel First ....G....... 203 735-5097
  Ansonia *(G-35)*
Fuel For Humanity Inc ....G....... 203 255-5913
  Westport *(G-10086)*

Employee Codes: A=Over 500 employees, B=251-500
C=101-250, D=51-100, E=20-50, F=10-19, G=1-9

FUELS: Ethanol

Fuel Lab .... G 860 677-4987
  Farmington *(G-2911)*
Galaxy Fuel LLC .... G 203 878-8173
  Milford *(G-4539)*
Hitbro Realty LLC .... G 860 824-1370
  Canaan *(G-1286)*
Husky Fuel .... G 203 783-0783
  Oxford *(G-6665)*
Mercury Fuel Co .... G 860 793-6602
  Plainville *(G-6843)*
Mercury Fuel Service Inc .... G 203 291-0833
  Westport *(G-10119)*
Miller Fuel LLC .... G 860 675-6121
  Burlington *(G-1274)*
New England Fuels & Energy LLC ... G 860 585-5917
  Terryville *(G-8766)*
Power Fuels LLC .... G 203 699-0099
  Cheshire *(G-1431)*
Priced Right Fuel LLC .... G 203 856-7031
  Norwalk *(G-6305)*
Pucks Putters & Fuel LLC .... F 203 877-5457
  Milford *(G-4619)*
Pucks Putters & Fuel LLC .... G 203 494-3952
  Shelton *(G-7540)*
Superior Fuel Co .... G 203 337-1213
  Bridgeport *(G-917)*
Ultra Food and Fuel .... G 860 223-2005
  New Britain *(G-5077)*
Victory Fuel LLC .... G 860 585-0532
  Terryville *(G-8777)*
Waste To Green Fuel LLC .... G 203 536-5855
  Bridgeport *(G-935)*
Wildcat Fuel Systems Conn LLC ...... G 203 627-4310
  Hamden *(G-3530)*
XCEL Fuel .... G 203 481-4510
  Branford *(G-677)*

FUELS: Jet

Annies Oil Co .... G 203 237-9276
  Meriden *(G-4143)*

FUELS: Oil

Hart Technology LLC .... G 860 482-6160
  Torrington *(G-8932)*
Leclaire Fuel Oil LLC .... G 203 922-1512
  Shelton *(G-7489)*
STP Products Manufacturing Co ...... F 203 205-2900
  Danbury *(G-1957)*

FUNDRAISING SVCS

Olympia Sales Inc .... D 860 749-0751
  Enfield *(G-2672)*

FUNERAL HOMES & SVCS

Dignified Endings LLC .... D 860 291-0575
  East Hartford *(G-2314)*

FUR: Apparel

Varpro Inc .... E 203 227-6876
  Westport *(G-10171)*

FUR: Coats & Other Apparel

Sherwood Group Inc .... F 203 227-5288
  Westport *(G-10156)*

FURNACES & OVENS: Indl

American Catatech Inc .... G 203 483-6692
  Branford *(G-542)*
David Weisman LLC .... G 203 322-9978
  Stamford *(G-8182)*
Earth Engineered Systems .... G 203 231-4614
  Derby *(G-2112)*
Furnace Concepts .... G 203 264-7856
  Southbury *(G-7853)*
Furnace Source LLC .... F 860 582-4201
  Terryville *(G-8755)*
Hamworthy Peabody Combustn Inc .. E 203 922-1199
  Shelton *(G-7457)*
HI Heat Company Inc .... G 860 528-9315
  South Windsor *(G-7772)*
Jad LLC .... E 860 289-1551
  South Windsor *(G-7776)*
Modean Industries Inc .... G 203 371-6625
  Easton *(G-2559)*
Noble Fire Brick Company Inc .... G 860 623-9256
  East Windsor *(G-2513)*

Preferred Utilities Mfg Corp .... D 203 743-6741
  Danbury *(G-1918)*
Sandvik Wire and Htg Tech Corp ...... D 203 744-1440
  Bethel *(G-337)*
Tvu Gold Coating Services .... G 860 657-2666
  Glastonbury *(G-3092)*

FURNACES & OVENS: Vacuum

Envax Products Inc .... G 203 264-8181
  Oxford *(G-6657)*

FURNITURE & CABINET STORES: Cabinets, Custom Work

B H Davis Co .... G 860 923-2771
  Thompson *(G-8829)*
Design Shop Llc .... G 203 937-1651
  West Haven *(G-9897)*
Edward Tomkievich .... G 860 633-5811
  Glastonbury *(G-3032)*
Ian Ingersoll Cabinetmaker .... F 860 672-6334
  West Cornwall *(G-9764)*
Kitchenmax LLC .... G 203 330-5041
  Bridgeport *(G-819)*
Kitchens By Deane Inc .... E 203 327-7008
  Stamford *(G-8276)*
McMellon Associates LLC .... G 203 272-5859
  Cheshire *(G-1413)*
S J Pappas Inc .... G 203 237-7701
  Meriden *(G-4236)*

FURNITURE & CABINET STORES: Custom

Richards Creative Interiors .... G 203 484-0361
  Wallingford *(G-9355)*

FURNITURE & FIXTURES Factory

Brand Factory Agency .... G 203 984-6178
  Southport *(G-8000)*

FURNITURE COMPONENTS: Porcelain Enameled

Seward Group LLC .... G 203 357-1900
  Darien *(G-2044)*

FURNITURE REPAIR & MAINTENANCE SVCS

Joshua Friedman & Co LLC .... F 860 439-1637
  New London *(G-5475)*

FURNITURE STOCK & PARTS: Carvings, Wood

GA Mals Woodwoorking LLC .... G 860 747-4767
  Plainville *(G-6814)*

FURNITURE STOCK & PARTS: Turnings, Wood

JC Turn Mfg .... G 203 366-6164
  Bridgeport *(G-802)*
Juan Gallegos .... G 203 744-0575
  Danbury *(G-1866)*

FURNITURE STORES

Adirondack Wood Products LLC .... G 203 322-4518
  Stamford *(G-8062)*
Cerrito Furniture Inds Inc .... F 203 481-2580
  Branford *(G-573)*
Domino Media Group Inc .... E 877 223-7844
  Westport *(G-10074)*
Ducduc LLC .... G 860 482-1322
  Torrington *(G-8918)*
Ethan Allen Interiors Inc .... B 203 743-8000
  Danbury *(G-1817)*
Ethan Allen Retail Inc .... B 203 743-8000
  Danbury *(G-1818)*
Ethan Allen Retail Inc .... B 203 743-8600
  Danbury *(G-1819)*
Hitchcock Holding Company Inc .... G 860 738-0141
  New Hartford *(G-5193)*
Kensington Woodworking Co .... G 860 828-4972
  Kensington *(G-3812)*
Lovesac Company .... G 888 636-1223
  Stamford *(G-8290)*
Mommy & ME .... G 860 269-6226
  Unionville *(G-9121)*

Nap Brothers Parlor Frame Inc .... F 860 633-9998
  Glastonbury *(G-3062)*
Porta Door Co .... E 203 888-6191
  Seymour *(G-7362)*

FURNITURE STORES: Custom Made, Exc Cabinets

Craig Dascanio .... G 860 651-0466
  West Simsbury *(G-9975)*
Nec A Nec Woods Inc .... G 203 431-0621
  Redding *(G-7104)*
Salisbury Artisans .... G 860 435-0344
  Salisbury *(G-7297)*

FURNITURE STORES: Office

W B Mason Co Inc .... D 888 926-2766
  Meriden *(G-4265)*
W B Mason Co Inc .... E 888 926-2766
  Norwalk *(G-6392)*
W B Mason Co Inc .... D 888 926-2766
  Norwich *(G-6439)*
W B Mason Co Inc .... C 888 926-2766
  East Windsor *(G-2530)*

FURNITURE STORES: Outdoor & Garden

Connecticut Outdoor Wood Frncs ..... G 203 263-0625
  Woodbury *(G-10630)*
Walpole Woodworkers Inc .... E 508 668-2800
  Ridgefield *(G-7181)*
Walpole Woodworkers Inc .... G 203 255-9010
  Westport *(G-10173)*

FURNITURE UPHOLSTERY REPAIR SVCS

Little Joes Upholstery .... G 203 975-2871
  Stamford *(G-8286)*

FURNITURE WHOLESALERS

Donghia Inc .... D 800 366-4442
  Milford *(G-4514)*
Focal Metals .... G 203 743-4443
  Bethel *(G-300)*
Get Back Inc .... G 860 274-9991
  Oakville *(G-6453)*
Thule Inc .... G 203 881-9600
  Milford *(G-4664)*

FURNITURE, BARBER & BEAUTY SHOP

Formatron Ltd .... F 860 676-0227
  Farmington *(G-2908)*

FURNITURE, HOUSEHOLD: Wholesalers

CB Seating Etc LLC .... G 203 359-3880
  Norwalk *(G-6109)*
Ethan Allen Retail Inc .... B 203 743-8600
  Danbury *(G-1819)*

FURNITURE, OUTDOOR & LAWN: Wholesalers

Baldwin Lawn Furniture LLC .... F 860 347-1306
  Middletown *(G-4322)*

FURNITURE, WHOLESALE: Racks

Di-Cor Industries Inc .... F 860 585-5583
  Bristol *(G-1017)*
Thule Inc .... C 203 881-9600
  Seymour *(G-7368)*

FURNITURE: Assembly Hall

FM Industries LLC .... G 860 610-0340
  East Hartford *(G-2327)*

FURNITURE: Bean Bag Chairs

Lovesac Company .... G 888 636-1223
  Stamford *(G-8290)*

FURNITURE: Bedroom, Wood

Ethan Allen Interiors Inc .... B 203 743-8000
  Danbury *(G-1817)*

FURNITURE: Bookcases, Wood

Kensington Woodworking Co .... G 860 828-4972
  Kensington *(G-3812)*

PRODUCT SECTION

FURNITURE: Cabinets & Vanities, Medicine, Metal

Advanced Prototype Development .....G..... 203 267-1262
 Southbury *(G-7842)*

FURNITURE: Chairs, Household Wood

CB Seating Etc LLC .....G..... 203 359-3880
 Norwalk *(G-6109)*
Ian Ingersoll Cabinetmaker .....F..... 860 672-6334
 West Cornwall *(G-9764)*
Oomph LLC .....G..... 203 216-9848
 New Canaan *(G-5128)*

FURNITURE: End Tables, Wood

Christopoulos Designs Inc .....F..... 203 576-1110
 Bridgeport *(G-733)*

FURNITURE: Foundations & Platforms

Demattia Charitable Found .....G..... 203 254-1558
 Fairfield *(G-2773)*
J J Concrete Foundations .....G..... 203 798-8310
 Bethel *(G-315)*

FURNITURE: Household, Metal

Columbia Mat & Upholstering Co .....G..... 203 789-1213
 Hamden *(G-3429)*
Durham Manufacturing Company .....D..... 860 349-3427
 Durham *(G-2146)*
Get Back Inc .....G..... 860 274-9991
 Oakville *(G-6453)*
Modern Objects Inc .....G..... 203 378-5785
 Norwalk *(G-6264)*
Morris Woodworking .....G..... 860 346-7500
 Middletown *(G-4382)*
Salamander Designs Ltd .....E..... 860 761-9500
 Bloomfield *(G-484)*
Southern Almnum Intrmdte Hldin .....G..... 870 234-8660
 New Canaan *(G-5145)*

FURNITURE: Household, NEC

Accolade Furniture LLC .....G..... 203 265-0524
 Wallingford *(G-9196)*

FURNITURE: Household, Novelty, Metal

Bruce Kahn .....G..... 203 329-7441
 Stamford *(G-8121)*
Rj Kach Ltd .....G..... 203 457-1349
 Madison *(G-3951)*

FURNITURE: Household, Upholstered, Exc Wood Or Metal

Ducduc LLC .....G..... 860 482-1322
 Torrington *(G-8918)*

FURNITURE: Household, Wood

American Wood Products .....G..... 203 248-4433
 North Haven *(G-5903)*
Andre Furniture Industries .....G..... 860 528-8826
 South Windsor *(G-7709)*
Bolton Hill Industries Inc .....G..... 860 742-0311
 Coventry *(G-1647)*
Bonito Manufacturing Inc .....D..... 203 234-8786
 North Haven *(G-5915)*
Cherner Chair Company LLC .....G..... 203 894-4702
 Ridgefield *(G-7127)*
Connecticut Solid Surface LLC .....E..... 860 410-9800
 Plainville *(G-6791)*
Craig Dascanio .....G..... 860 651-0466
 West Simsbury *(G-9975)*
Custom Furniture & Design LLC .....F..... 860 567-3519
 Litchfield *(G-3887)*
Daniel Richardson .....G..... 860 774-3675
 Danielson *(G-1988)*
Designers Resource .....G..... 203 874-7431
 Milford *(G-4509)*
Edko Cabinets LLC .....G..... 203 463-8346
 Seymour *(G-7345)*
Finishing Touch Woodcraft .....G..... 860 916-2642
 Canton *(G-1315)*
G A Mals Woodworking .....G..... 860 828-8702
 Berlin *(G-183)*
Genie Shelf .....G..... 203 241-7523
 Brookfield *(G-1190)*

Get Back Inc .....G..... 860 274-9991
 Oakville *(G-6453)*
Hitchcock Chair Company Ltd .....G..... 860 738-0141
 Riverton *(G-7208)*
Hitchcock Holding Company Inc .....G..... 860 738-0141
 New Hartford *(G-5193)*
Industrial Wood Product Co .....G..... 203 735-2374
 Shelton *(G-7475)*
L & L Capital Partners LLC .....F..... 203 834-6222
 Wilton *(G-10307)*
Lookout Solutions LLC .....G..... 203 750-0307
 Norwalk *(G-6237)*
Madigan Millwork Inc .....G..... 860 673-7601
 Unionville *(G-9119)*
Moran Woodworking LLC .....G..... 203 438-0477
 Ridgefield *(G-7156)*
Morris Woodworking .....G..... 860 346-7500
 Middletown *(G-4382)*
Nap Brothers Parlor Frame Inc .....F..... 860 633-9998
 Glastonbury *(G-3062)*
Old House Woodcraft LLC .....G..... 860 228-2174
 Columbia *(G-1610)*
Paul Dringoli .....G..... 203 248-0281
 Hamden *(G-3496)*
Salamander Designs Ltd .....E..... 860 761-9500
 Bloomfield *(G-484)*
Springbrook Woodcrafters LLC .....G..... 860 870-7303
 Ellington *(G-2602)*
St Johns Bridge LLC .....G..... 860 927-3315
 Kent *(G-3826)*
Thomas Lord Cabinet Maker .....G..... 860 546-9283
 Canterbury *(G-1302)*
Tudor House Furniture Co Inc .....E..... 203 288-8451
 Hamden *(G-3524)*
USA Wood Incorporated .....G..... 203 238-4285
 Meriden *(G-4262)*
Walpole Woodworkers Inc .....G..... 203 255-9010
 Westport *(G-10173)*
Walpole Woodworkers Inc .....E..... 508 668-2800
 Ridgefield *(G-7181)*
Woodworkers Heaven Inc .....F..... 203 333-2778
 Bridgeport *(G-940)*
Woody Mosch Cabinet Makers .....G..... 203 266-7619
 Bethlehem *(G-377)*

FURNITURE: Institutional, Exc Wood

Air Cruisers Co .....G..... 732 681-3527
 South Windsor *(G-7703)*
Morris Woodworking .....G..... 860 346-7500
 Middletown *(G-4382)*

FURNITURE: Juvenile, Wood

Nec A Nec Woods Inc .....G..... 203 431-0621
 Redding *(G-7104)*

FURNITURE: Kitchen & Dining Room

Home Sweeter HM Kit & Bath LLC .....G..... 203 948-6482
 Bethel *(G-309)*

FURNITURE: Kitchen & Dining Room, Metal

Stonewall Kitchen LLC .....C..... 860 648-9215
 South Windsor *(G-7831)*

FURNITURE: Lawn, Wood

Adirondack Wood Products LLC .....G..... 203 322-4518
 Stamford *(G-8062)*
Baldwin Lawn Furniture LLC .....F..... 860 347-1306
 Middletown *(G-4322)*
Carefree Building Co Inc .....F..... 860 267-7600
 Colchester *(G-1544)*
Transportable LLC .....G..... 203 455-9208
 Chaplin *(G-1343)*

FURNITURE: Living Room, Upholstered On Wood Frames

Tudor House Furniture Co Inc .....E..... 203 288-8451
 Hamden *(G-3524)*
Weiss Sleep Shop Inc .....G..... 860 445-1219
 Groton *(G-3317)*

FURNITURE: Mattresses & Foundations

Symbol Mattress of New England .....B..... 860 779-3112
 Dayville *(G-2075)*
Water & Air Inc .....G..... 860 423-0234
 South Windham *(G-7693)*

FURNITURE: Mattresses, Box & Bedsprings

A&S Innersprings Usa LLC .....G..... 860 298-0401
 Windsor *(G-10351)*
Columbia Mat & Upholstering Co .....G..... 203 789-1213
 Hamden *(G-3429)*
Ramdial Parts and Services LLC .....G..... 860 296-5175
 Hartford *(G-3675)*
Saatva Inc .....E..... 877 672-2882
 Westport *(G-10153)*

FURNITURE: Mattresses, Innerspring Or Box Spring

Blue Bell Mattress Company LLC .....C..... 860 292-6372
 East Windsor *(G-2484)*
Restopedic Inc .....G..... 203 393-1520
 Bethany *(G-249)*
Subinas USA LLC .....G..... 860 298-0401
 Windsor *(G-10445)*

FURNITURE: NEC

Thames River Furniture LLC .....G..... 201 312-2050
 Uncasville *(G-9105)*

FURNITURE: Office Panel Systems, Wood

Knoll Inc .....E..... 860 395-2093
 Old Saybrook *(G-6550)*
Neiss Corp .....F..... 860 872-8528
 Vernon *(G-9148)*

FURNITURE: Office, Exc Wood

Bonito Manufacturing Inc .....D..... 203 234-8786
 North Haven *(G-5915)*
Conco Wood Working Inc .....G..... 203 934-9665
 West Haven *(G-9890)*
Durham Manufacturing Company .....D..... 860 349-3427
 Durham *(G-2146)*
One and Co Inc .....F..... 860 892-5180
 Norwich *(G-6427)*
Sabon Industries Inc .....G..... 203 255-8880
 Fairfield *(G-2840)*
Static Safe Products Company .....F..... 203 937-6391
 Cornwall Bridge *(G-1620)*

FURNITURE: Office, Wood

Atlantic Group Connecticut LLC .....G..... 203 847-0000
 Norwalk *(G-6080)*
Belmont Corporation .....E..... 860 589-5700
 Bristol *(G-980)*
Bergan Architectural Wdwkg Inc .....E..... 860 346-0869
 Middletown *(G-4324)*
Bloomfield Wood & Melamine Inc .....F..... 860 243-3226
 Bloomfield *(G-398)*
Bold Wood Interiors LLC .....F..... 203 907-4077
 New Haven *(G-5249)*
Bolton Hill Industries Inc .....G..... 860 742-0311
 Coventry *(G-1647)*
Conco Wood Working Inc .....G..... 203 934-9665
 West Haven *(G-9890)*
Cyr Woodworking Inc .....G..... 860 232-1991
 Newington *(G-5646)*
Innovant Inc .....G..... 203 594-7270
 New Canaan *(G-5111)*
Lesro Industries Inc .....D..... 800 275-7545
 Bloomfield *(G-442)*
Professional Trades Netwrk LLC .....G..... 860 567-0173
 Watertown *(G-9726)*
S J Pappas Inc .....G..... 203 237-7701
 Meriden *(G-4236)*
Salamander Designs Ltd .....E..... 860 761-9500
 Bloomfield *(G-484)*

FURNITURE: Outdoor, Wood

Parish Associates Inc .....G..... 203 335-4100
 Fairfield *(G-2826)*

FURNITURE: Picnic Tables Or Benches, Park

Town of Vernon .....G..... 203 268-7200
 Easton *(G-2567)*
Wepa Sports LLC .....G..... 203 971-9372
 New London *(G-5496)*

FURNITURE: Rattan

Dbo Home LLC .....G..... 860 364-6008
 Sharon *(G-7377)*

FURNITURE: Restaurant

General Seating Solutions LLC .... F 860 242-3307
  South Windsor (G-7757)

FURNITURE: Studio Couches

Vijon Studios Inc .... G 860 399-7440
  Old Saybrook (G-6575)

FURNITURE: Table Tops, Marble

Creative Stone LLC .... F 203 624-1882
  East Haven (G-2420)
Marble & Granite Creations LLC .... G 860 350-1306
  New Milford (G-5560)

FURNITURE: Television, Wood

Christopoulos Designs Inc .... F 203 576-1110
  Bridgeport (G-733)

FURNITURE: Unfinished, Wood

Western Conn Craftsmen LLC .... G 203 312-8167
  New Fairfield (G-5183)

FURNITURE: Upholstered

C & D Upholstery .... G 203 838-1050
  Norwalk (G-6104)
Cerrito Furniture Inds Inc .... F 203 481-2580
  Branford (G-573)
Clark Manner Marguarite .... G 860 444-7679
  New London (G-5463)
Craig Dascanio .... G 860 651-0466
  West Simsbury (G-9975)
Da Cunha Woodworks .... G 860 529-3889
  New Britain (G-4970)
Daniel Richardson .... G 860 774-3675
  Danielson (G-1988)
Ethan Allen Interiors Inc .... B 203 743-8000
  Danbury (G-1817)
Ethan Allen Retail Inc .... B 203 743-8600
  Danbury (G-1819)
J G Taglieri .... G 860 645-1060
  Manchester (G-4037)
Little Joes Upholstery .... G 203 975-2871
  Stamford (G-8286)
Reborn House .... G 203 216-9874
  Branford (G-640)
Reid Interiors .... G 860 569-1240
  East Hartford (G-2364)

FURNITURE: Wall Cases, Office, Exc Wood

Peristere LLC .... G 860 783-5301
  Manchester (G-4075)

FURRIERS

Sherwood Group Inc .... F 203 227-5288
  Westport (G-10156)

Furs

Flying Fur LLC .... G 860 623-0450
  Windsor Locks (G-10484)
Fur Side LLC .... G 203 403-3369
  Ridgefield (G-7143)
MA & PA Fur LLC .... G 860 659-7766
  Middletown (G-4373)

GAMES & TOYS: Automobiles & Trucks

Mwb Toy Company LLC .... G 212 598-4500
  Danbury (G-1890)

GAMES & TOYS: Baby Carriages & Restraint Seats

Toddler Teams LLC .... G 203 972-7713
  New Canaan (G-5153)

GAMES & TOYS: Blocks

Poof-Alex Holdings LLC .... G 203 930-7711
  Greenwich (G-3217)

GAMES & TOYS: Board Games, Children's & Adults'

Brainbeat Inc .... G 917 291-9747
  Stamford (G-8118)

GAMES & TOYS: Craft & Hobby Kits & Sets

Bear Market .... G 860 379-8943
  Winchester Center (G-10343)
Crafty Creations .... G 203 673-6225
  Avon (G-79)
Eco Pallet World LLC .... G 203 343-9089
  Milford (G-4525)
Essex Wood Products Inc .... E 860 537-3451
  Colchester (G-1550)
Nancy Dighello .... G 860 763-4294
  Enfield (G-2665)
New Beginnings Sea Glass .... G 203 329-7623
  Stamford (G-8321)
Rose To Occassion LLC .... G 860 628-6880
  Southington (G-7968)
Spera Cottage Crafters .... G 860 738-2391
  Colebrook (G-1587)
Spots and Ladybugs LLC .... G 203 378-8232
  Trumbull (G-9076)
Worms Eye .... G 203 888-0895
  Seymour (G-7374)

GAMES & TOYS: Darts & Dart Games

Pub Games Plus .... G 203 846-5991
  Norwalk (G-6310)

GAMES & TOYS: Dolls & Doll Clothing

Chantys Closet .... G 860 752-4512
  Windsor (G-10372)

GAMES & TOYS: Dolls, Exc Stuffed Toy Animals

Rags A Muffin .... G 203 377-7063
  Stratford (G-8672)

GAMES & TOYS: Electronic

Berwick Industries LLC .... G 475 228-5822
  Darien (G-2008)
Enterplay LLC .... F 203 458-1128
  Guilford (G-3351)
Most Excllent Cmics Cllctibles ...... G 860 741-0113
  Enfield (G-2662)
Puzzlesocial LLC .... G 917 515-1030
  Westport (G-10144)

GAMES & TOYS: Erector Sets

Lego Systems Inc .... A 860 749-2291
  Enfield (G-2655)

GAMES & TOYS: Game Machines, Exc Coin-Operated

Card Carrier Games LLC .... G 203 521-0291
  Milford (G-4483)

GAMES & TOYS: Marbles

Infinity Stone Inc .... F 203 575-9484
  Waterbury (G-9505)

GAMES & TOYS: Models, Railroad, Toy & Hobby

Tacdab LLC .... G 860 447-9023
  Waterford (G-9674)

GAMES & TOYS: Puzzles

A Piece of Pzzle Bhvral Intrve .... G 860 250-8054
  West Hartford (G-9769)
Bedard Puzzles .... G 860 657-3781
  Glastonbury (G-3013)
Mark Cappitellas Hnd-Cut Wden .. G 860 818-4334
  East Haddam (G-2244)
One Piece of Puzzle LLC .... G 860 919-6956
  Hartford (G-3659)
Pieces of Puzzle Daycare .... G 203 916-8332
  Bridgeport (G-873)
Puzzle Rings Creations LLC .... G 203 550-1591
  Stamford (G-8383)
S&A Puzzle LLC .... G 860 675-0477
  Avon (G-108)
Three Across LLC .... G 203 866-6688
  Norwalk (G-6367)

GAMES & TOYS: Rocking Horses

Rocking Horse Saloon .... G 860 247-2566
  Hartford (G-3680)

GAMES & TOYS: Structural Toy Sets

World Wide Games Inc .... G 860 537-3451
  Colchester (G-1583)

GAMES & TOYS: Trains & Eqpt, Electric & Mechanical

Ross Curtis Product Inc .... G 860 886-6800
  Norwich (G-6429)

GAMES & TOYS: Tricycles

Tricycle Granola LLC .... G 203 861-1740
  Greenwich (G-3249)
Tricycle Hill LLC .... G 203 895-2217
  Fairfield (G-2858)

GARAGES: Portable, Prefabricated Metal

Mdm Products LLC .... F 203 877-7070
  Milford (G-4576)

GARMENT: Pressing & cleaners' agents

Rite Way Cleaner .... G 203 789-9561
  New Haven (G-5380)
Sally Conant .... F 203 878-3005
  Orange (G-6628)

GAS & OIL FIELD EXPLORATION SVCS

Ace Energy LLC .... G 860 623-3308
  Broad Brook (G-1143)
Ammonite Corp .... G 203 972-1130
  New Canaan (G-5087)
Bedrock Oil LLC .... G 860 295-8230
  Marlborough (G-4121)
Brownstone Exploration .... G 860 866-0208
  Portland (G-6954)
Castleton Commodities .... G 203 564-8100
  Stamford (G-8131)
CCI East Texas Upstream LLC ...... G 203 564-8100
  Stamford (G-8135)
El Paso Prod Oil Gas Texas LP ..... F 860 293-1990
  Hartford (G-3584)
Ellignton Energy Inc .... G 860 872-9276
  Ellington (G-2588)
Equinor Shipping Inc .... G 203 978-6900
  Stamford (G-8197)
Equinor US Holdings Inc .... C 203 978-6900
  Stamford (G-8198)
Jager Prof Gas Svcs LLC .... G 860 388-3422
  Old Saybrook (G-6546)
Maine Power Express LLC .... G 203 661-0055
  Greenwich (G-3197)
RTS Corporation .... G 203 459-9835
  Trumbull (G-9065)
Vab Inc .... G 860 793-0246
  Plainville (G-6875)

GAS & OIL FIELD SVCS, NEC

Artic Oil .... G 860 693-6925
  Canton (G-1305)
J and R Shelter Rock Road LLC .... G 203 739-0697
  Danbury (G-1855)
Jonas Lieponis .... G 203 458-6912
  Guilford (G-3364)
Kc Servicing LLC .... G 860 822-9766
  Preston (G-6985)

GAS STATIONS

G H Berlin Oil Company .... G 800 426-7754
  Hartford (G-3594)

GASES: Helium

A Helium Plus Balloons LLC .... G 860 833-1761
  Wethersfield (G-10179)
Helium Plus Inc .... G 203 304-1880
  Newtown (G-5742)

GASES: Hydrogen

Haynes Hydrogen LLC .... G 203 605-2837
  Meriden (G-4172)

PRODUCT SECTION

GLASS & GLASS CERAMIC PRDTS, PRESSED OR BLOWN: Tableware

Hydrogen Highway LLC ....G...... 203 871-1000
  North Branford (G-5844)

GASES: Indl

Airgas Usa LLC ....G...... 203 729-2159
  Naugatuck (G-4856)
Airgas Usa LLC ....E...... 860 442-0363
  Waterford (G-9641)
Airgas Usa LLC ....C...... 203 792-1834
  Danbury (G-1733)
Aldlab Chemicals LLC ....G...... 203 589-4934
  North Haven (G-5899)
Praxair Inc ....E...... 203 793-1200
  Wallingford (G-9339)
Praxair Inc ....E...... 203 720-2477
  Naugatuck (G-4913)
Praxair Inc ....D...... 860 292-5400
  Suffield (G-8729)
Praxair Inc ....B...... 203 837-2000
  Danbury (G-1913)
Praxair Distribution Inc ....E...... 860 349-0305
  Durham (G-2154)
Praxair Distribution Inc ....F...... 203 837-2000
  Danbury (G-1914)
Praxair Distribution Inc ....F...... 203 837-2162
  Danbury (G-1915)
Tech Air Northern Cal LLC ....G...... 203 792-1834
  Danbury (G-1961)

GASES: Neon

Just Neon Company ....G...... 860 881-7446
  Vernon (G-9142)
New England Ortho Neuro LLC ....G...... 203 200-7228
  Hamden (G-3489)

GASES: Oxygen

Boost Oxygen LLC ....G...... 203 331-8100
  Milford (G-4476)
O2 Concepts LLC ....G...... 877 867-4008
  Middlebury (G-4286)

GASKET MATERIALS

Auburn Manufacturing Company ....E...... 860 346-6677
  Middletown (G-4319)

GASKETS

Chas W House & Sons Inc ....D...... 860 673-2518
  Unionville (G-9112)
Corru Seals Inc ....F...... 203 284-0319
  Wallingford (G-9241)
Lydall Inc ....E...... 860 646-1233
  Manchester (G-4050)
Parker-Hannifin Corporation ....D...... 203 239-3341
  North Haven (G-5974)
Rubber Supplies Company Inc ....G...... 203 736-9995
  Derby (G-2125)
Spirol International Corp ....C...... 860 774-8571
  Danielson (G-2003)
Standard Washer & Mat Inc ....E...... 860 643-5125
  Manchester (G-4094)
Sur-Seal Holding LLC ....G...... 203 625-0770
  Norwalk (G-6360)
Vanguard Products Corporation ....D...... 203 744-7265
  Danbury (G-1970)

GASKETS & SEALING DEVICES

American Seal and Engrg Co Inc ....E...... 203 789-8819
  Orange (G-6581)
Derby Cellular Products Inc ....C...... 203 735-4661
  Shelton (G-7430)
H-O Products Corporation ....E...... 860 379-9875
  Winsted (G-10523)
Kenneth Industrial Pdts Inc ....G...... 860 349-7454
  Durham (G-2150)
Linda Hoagland ....G...... 203 878-7188
  Milford (G-4568)
SKF USA Inc ....E...... 860 379-8511
  Winsted (G-10536)

GASOLINE FILLING STATIONS

Mercury Fuel Service Inc ....D...... 203 756-7284
  Waterbury (G-9539)
Spicer Plus Inc ....G...... 860 445-2436
  Groton (G-3313)

GASOLINE WHOLESALERS

Mercury Fuel Service Inc ....D...... 203 756-7284
  Waterbury (G-9539)

GASTROINTESTINAL OR GENITOURINARY SYSTEM DRUGS

Unicorn Pharmaceuticals Inc ....G...... 973 699-3843
  Greenwich (G-3251)

GATES: Ornamental Metal

Artistic Iron Works LLC ....G...... 203 838-9200
  Norwalk (G-6075)

GAUGES

All Five Tool Co Inc ....E...... 860 583-1693
  Berlin (G-154)
D & M Tool Company Inc ....G...... 860 236-6037
  West Hartford (G-9797)
E and S Gage Inc ....F...... 860 872-5917
  Tolland (G-8862)
Hartford Gauge Co ....G...... 860 233-9619
  West Hartford (G-9817)
Highland Manufacturing Inc ....E...... 860 646-5142
  Manchester (G-4028)
LLC Dow Gage ....E...... 860 828-5327
  Berlin (G-196)
Lyons Tool and Die Company ....E...... 203 238-2689
  Meriden (G-4190)
Meyer Gage Co Inc ....F...... 860 528-6526
  South Windsor (G-7792)
Moore Tool Company Inc ....D...... 203 366-3224
  Bridgeport (G-843)
North Haven Manufacturing Co ....G...... 203 284-8578
  Wallingford (G-9328)
Precision Punch + Tooling Corp ....G...... 860 225-4159
  Berlin (G-211)
Q Alpha Inc ....E...... 860 357-7340
  Colchester (G-1569)
Sirois Tool Company Inc ....D...... 860 828-5327
  Berlin (G-220)
Victor Tool Co Inc ....G...... 203 634-8113
  Meriden (G-4264)
Zero Check LLC ....G...... 860 283-5629
  Thomaston (G-8827)

GAUGES: Pressure

Ashcrft-Ngano Kiki Hldings Inc ....G...... 203 378-8281
  Stratford (G-8571)
Ashcroft Inc ....B...... 203 378-8281
  Stratford (G-8572)

GEARS

United Gear & Machine Co Inc ....F...... 860 623-6618
  Suffield (G-8737)

GEARS: Power Transmission, Exc Auto

Cunningham Industries Inc ....G...... 203 324-2942
  Stamford (G-8171)
JET Corporation ....F...... 203 334-3217
  Bridgeport (G-804)
Rexnord LLC ....G...... 860 355-0478
  New Milford (G-5584)

GENERATING APPARATUS & PARTS: Electrical

Afcon Products Inc ....F...... 203 393-9301
  Bethany (G-234)
Polaris Management Inc ....G...... 203 261-6399
  Easton (G-2561)

GENERATION EQPT: Electronic

Acceleron Inc ....E...... 860 651-9333
  East Granby (G-2186)
Advanced Sonics LLC ....G...... 203 266-4440
  Oxford (G-6639)
B S T Systems Inc ....D...... 860 564-4078
  Plainfield (G-6742)
Parmaco LLC ....G...... 860 573-7918
  Glastonbury (G-3067)

GENERATOR REPAIR SVCS

Afcon Products Inc ....F...... 203 393-9301
  Bethany (G-234)

GENERATORS SETS: Steam

American Wind Capital Co LLC ....G...... 860 767-1579
  Essex (G-2711)
Asea Brown Boveri Inc ....G...... 203 750-2200
  Norwalk (G-6076)

GENERATORS: Automotive & Aircraft

Merl Inc ....G...... 203 237-8811
  Meriden (G-4199)

GENERATORS: Electric

Ac/DC Industrial Electric LLC ....G...... 860 886-2232
  Yantic (G-10695)
Drs Naval Power Systems Inc ....B...... 203 366-5211
  Bridgeport (G-756)
Drs Naval Power Systems Inc ....E...... 203 366-5211
  Bridgeport (G-757)
Ward Leonard CT LLC ....D...... 860 283-2294
  Thomaston (G-8819)

GENERATORS: Ultrasonic

Rinco Ultrasonics USA Inc ....G...... 203 744-4500
  Danbury (G-1929)

GIFT SHOP

Bovano Industries Incorporated ....F...... 203 272-3208
  Cheshire (G-1361)
James Kingsley ....G...... 203 458-6626
  Guilford (G-3363)
Jane Sterry ....G...... 860 342-4567
  Portland (G-6960)
Nel Group LLC ....G...... 860 413-9042
  East Granby (G-2216)
Nel Group LLC ....F...... 860 683-0190
  Windsor (G-10412)
Taylors Luggage Inc ....G...... 203 966-9961
  New Canaan (G-5150)

GIFT, NOVELTY & SOUVENIR STORES: Artcraft & carvings

Company of Craftsmen ....G...... 860 536-4189
  Mystic (G-4808)
Eco Pallet World LLC ....G...... 203 343-9089
  Milford (G-4525)

GIFT, NOVELTY & SOUVENIR STORES: Gift Baskets

Rose To Occassion LLC ....G...... 860 628-6880
  Southington (G-7968)
Rosie Blakes Chocolates LLC ....G...... 732 604-3327
  New Britain (G-5048)

GIFT, NOVELTY & SOUVENIR STORES: Party Favors

Hudson Paper Company ....E...... 203 378-8759
  Stratford (G-8628)

GIFT, NOVELTY & SOUVENIR STORES: Trading Cards, Sports

Cliffside Entertainment LLC ....G...... 203 290-7484
  Bridgeport (G-736)

GIFTS & NOVELTIES: Wholesalers

Concord Industries Inc ....E...... 203 750-6060
  Norwalk (G-6124)
Executive Greetings Inc ....B...... 860 379-9911
  New Hartford (G-5190)
Nel Group LLC ....G...... 860 413-9042
  East Granby (G-2216)
Nel Group LLC ....F...... 860 683-0190
  Windsor (G-10412)
Recognition Inc ....G...... 860 659-8629
  Glastonbury (G-3079)
Sourcebooks Inc ....G...... 203 876-9790
  Milford (G-4648)

GLASS & GLASS CERAMIC PRDTS, PRESSED OR BLOWN: Tableware

Dbo Home LLC ....G...... 860 364-6008
  Sharon (G-7377)

Employee Codes: A=Over 500 employees, B=251-500
C=101-250, D=51-100, E=20-50, F=10-19, G=1-9

GLASS & GLASS CERAMIC PRDTS, PRESSED OR BLOWN: Tableware

Periodic Tableware LLC .... F 310 428-4250
  Shelton (G-7524)

GLASS FABRICATORS

Baron Technology Inc .... E 203 452-0515
  Trumbull (G-9003)
Connectcut Tmpred GL Dstrs LLC .... G 860 379-5670
  Winsted (G-10514)
Flabeg Technical Glass US Corp .... E 203 729-5227
  Naugatuck (G-4880)
Glass Master LLC .... G 860 658-0040
  Simsbury (G-7628)
Glassworks .... G 860 673-1250
  New Hartford (G-5192)
Legacy Corp .... G 860 236-6500
  West Hartford (G-9827)
Marilyn Gehring .... G 203 358-8700
  Stamford (G-8296)
Opera Glass Networks LLC .... G 203 919-2777
  Norwalk (G-6286)
U S Glass Distributors Inc .... E 860 741-3658
  Enfield (G-2703)

GLASS PRDTS, FROM PURCHASED GLASS: Art

Garden Glass LLC .... G 203 330-8789
  Fairfield (G-2789)

GLASS PRDTS, FROM PURCHASED GLASS: Enameled

Bovano Industries Incorporated .... F 203 272-3208
  Cheshire (G-1361)

GLASS PRDTS, FROM PURCHASED GLASS: Glassware

Advanced Glass Design LLC .... G 860 426-0401
  Plantsville (G-6882)
Glass Industries America LLC .... F 203 269-6700
  Wallingford (G-9276)

GLASS PRDTS, FROM PURCHASED GLASS: Mirrors, Framed

Ark Innovations LLC .... G 860 674-8800
  Farmington (G-2878)
National Picture Frame Inc .... G 860 774-5668
  Brooklyn (G-1251)

GLASS PRDTS, PRESSED OR BLOWN: Furnishings & Access

Magic Industries Inc .... F 860 949-8380
  Bozrah (G-527)
Whalley Glass Company .... D 203 735-9388
  Derby (G-2131)

GLASS PRDTS, PRESSED OR BLOWN: Glass Fibers, Textile

Fiberoptics Technology Inc .... D 860 928-0443
  Pomfret (G-6932)

GLASS PRDTS, PRESSED OR BLOWN: Glassware, Art Or Decorative

Zsiba & Smolover Ltd .... G 860 354-5221
  New Milford (G-5610)

GLASS PRDTS, PRESSED OR BLOWN: Lighting Eqpt Parts

Koninklijke Philips Elec NV .... F 860 886-2621
  Norwich (G-6421)

GLASS PRDTS, PRESSED OR BLOWN: Optical

Accuratus Optics Tech LLC .... G 213 344-9397
  Cheshire (G-1346)
Flabeg Technical Glass US Corp .... E 203 729-5227
  Naugatuck (G-4880)
Flabeg US Holding Inc .... G 203 729-5227
  Naugatuck (G-4881)
PQ Optics .... G 860 582-2636
  Bristol (G-1094)

Vogel Optics LLC .... G 203 925-9619
  Shelton (G-7582)

GLASS PRDTS, PRESSED OR BLOWN: Stationers Glassware

Incjet Inc .... F 860 823-3090
  Norwich (G-6417)

GLASS PRDTS, PRESSED OR BLOWN: Yarn, Fiberglass

Woolworks Ltd .... G 860 963-1228
  Putnam (G-7081)

GLASS PRDTS, PRESSED/BLOWN: Glassware, Art, Decor/Novelty

Artist and Craftsman .... G 203 330-0459
  Bridgeport (G-703)

GLASS STORE: Leaded Or Stained

Glass Source LLC .... G 203 924-4368
  Shelton (G-7449)
Marilyn Gehring .... G 203 358-8700
  Stamford (G-8296)
Paul Petrushonis Staind Glss .... G 203 878-0163
  Milford (G-4604)
Pelegnos Stined GL Art Gallery .... G 860 621-2900
  Plantsville (G-6907)
Vijon Studios Inc .... G 860 399-7440
  Old Saybrook (G-6576)

GLASS: Fiber

Fiberglass Repairs & .... G 860 628-4962
  Southington (G-7923)
Vitro Technology Ltd .... G 203 783-9566
  Milford (G-4676)

GLASS: Flat

Glass Design Studio .... G 860 651-4233
  Simsbury (G-7627)
Marilyn Gehring .... G 203 358-8700
  Stamford (G-8296)
Paul Petrushonis Staind Glss .... G 203 878-0163
  Milford (G-4604)

GLASS: Indl Prdts

Liberty Glass and Met Inds Inc .... E 860 923-3623
  North Grosvenordale (G-5888)

GLASS: Insulating

Insulpane Connecticut Inc .... D 800 922-3248
  Hamden (G-3465)

GLASS: Pressed & Blown, NEC

Bovano Industries Incorporated .... F 203 272-3208
  Cheshire (G-1361)
Bristow Studio Glass .... G 860 364-1670
  Sharon (G-7376)
C C D Center .... G 203 348-0052
  Stamford (G-8123)
Fair Haven Glass .... G 203 773-3040
  New Haven (G-5280)
G Schoeperinc .... F 203 250-7794
  Cheshire (G-1391)
Greenwood Glass .... G 860 738-9464
  Riverton (G-7207)
Greywall Inc .... G 860 267-6177
  East Hampton (G-2262)
Marilyn Gehring .... G 203 358-8700
  Stamford (G-8296)
Medelco Inc .... G 203 275-8070
  Bridgeport (G-836)
Schaeffler Aerospace USA Corp .... D 860 379-7558
  Winsted (G-10534)
Simon Pearce US Inc .... G 203 861-0780
  Greenwich (G-3236)
Tops Manufacturing Co Inc .... G 203 655-9367
  Darien (G-2047)
West Rock Art Glass Inc .... G 203 488-8225
  Branford (G-671)

GLASS: Stained

Glass Source LLC .... G 203 924-4368
  Shelton (G-7449)

Peleganos Stained Glass Studio .... G 203 272-8067
  Cheshire (G-1428)
Renaissance Studio Inc .... G 203 226-9674
  Westport (G-10148)
Vijon Studios Inc .... G 860 399-7440
  Old Saybrook (G-6576)

GLASSWARE STORES

Greenwood Glass .... G 860 738-9464
  Riverton (G-7207)

GLASSWARE WHOLESALERS

Whalley Glass Company .... D 203 735-9388
  Derby (G-2131)

GLASSWARE: Laboratory

Periodic Tableware LLC .... F 310 428-4250
  Shelton (G-7524)

GLOBAL POSITIONING SYSTEMS & EQPT

I Tech Services Inc .... G 800 559-8991
  Danbury (G-1847)
Wagz Inc .... G 203 553-9336
  Stamford (G-8487)

GLOVES: Fabric

Fabric Bty Inc .... G 203 845-7966
  Norwalk (G-6160)

GLOVES: Safety

Playtex Products LLC .... D 203 944-5500
  Shelton (G-7531)

GOLD STAMPING, EXC BOOKS

O Berk Company Neng LLC .... F 203 932-8000
  West Haven (G-9940)

GOLF CLUB & EQPT REPAIR SVCS

Demane Golf Inc .... G 203 531-9126
  Greenwich (G-3151)
S Hassel Golf Works .... G 860 274-4011
  Watertown (G-9732)

GOLF COURSES: Public

Lyman Farm Incorporated .... C 860 349-1793
  Middlefield (G-4302)

GOLF DRIVING RANGES

Burlington Golf Center Inc .... G 860 675-7320
  Burlington (G-1262)
Valley Golf Center CT LLC .... G 860 799-7605
  New Milford (G-5605)

GOLF EQPT

Brampton Technology Ltd .... G 860 667-7689
  Newington (G-5634)
Demane Golf Inc .... G 203 531-9126
  Greenwich (G-3151)
Golf Galaxy LLC .... G 203 855-0500
  Norwalk (G-6182)
Lure of Cripple Creek .... G 860 564-5799
  Moosup (G-4781)
Robert W Broska Enterprises .... G 203 846-0583
  Norwalk (G-6327)
Swing Rite Golf .... G 203 748-4985
  Bethel (G-351)
Wild Card Golf LLC .... G 860 296-1661
  Hartford (G-3715)

GOLF GOODS & EQPT

Demane Golf Inc .... G 203 531-9126
  Greenwich (G-3151)
Golf Galaxy LLC .... G 203 855-0500
  Norwalk (G-6182)
Lyman Farm Incorporated .... C 860 349-1793
  Middlefield (G-4302)

GOVERNMENT, LEGISLATIVE BODIES: Town Council

Town of Bridgewater .... F 860 354-5250
  Bridgewater (G-947)

PRODUCT SECTION

GRAIN & FIELD BEANS WHOLESALERS

Bridgwell Rsurces Holdings LLC .... G 203 622-9138
  Greenwich *(G-3137)*
Cofco Americas Resources Corp .... B 203 252-5200
  Stamford *(G-8151)*

GRANITE: Crushed & Broken

Mid-Island Aggregates/Distribu .... G 860 605-6753
  Sherman *(G-7598)*
Skyline Quarry .... E 860 875-3580
  Stafford Springs *(G-8038)*

GRANITE: Cut & Shaped

Granitech LLC .... G 860 620-1733
  Plantsville *(G-6895)*
Salem Stone Design Inc .... F 860 439-1234
  Waterford *(G-9668)*
Stone Workshop LLC .... G 203 362-1144
  Bridgeport *(G-914)*
Stoneage LLC .... G 203 926-1133
  Shelton *(G-7559)*
Surface Plate Co .... G 860 652-8905
  Glastonbury *(G-3084)*
Timeless Stone Inc .... G 860 242-3300
  Bloomfield *(G-492)*

GRANITE: Dimension

Armetta LLC .... E 860 788-2369
  Middletown *(G-4317)*
GS Ruff Stuff .... G 860 859-9355
  Salem *(G-7289)*
Stony Creek Quarry Corporation .... G 203 483-3904
  Branford *(G-659)*

GRANITE: Dimension

Academy Marble & Granite LLC .... G 203 791-2956
  Bethel *(G-256)*
Jf Granite & Marble .... G 860 355-4414
  New Milford *(G-5550)*
LH Gault & Son Incorporated .... D 203 227-5181
  Westport *(G-10112)*

GRAPHIC ARTS & RELATED DESIGN SVCS

A To A Studio Solutions Ltd .... F 203 388-9050
  Stamford *(G-8053)*
Alphacom Inc .... G 203 637-7006
  Greenwich *(G-3117)*
Aquastone Graphix LLC .... G 860 206-4935
  Hartford *(G-3552)*
Arteffects Incorporated .... E 860 242-0031
  Bloomfield *(G-390)*
Exhibitease LLC .... G 203 481-0792
  Branford *(G-592)*
Fastsigns .... G 203 239-9090
  North Haven *(G-5941)*
Graffeast Inc .... G 203 622-1622
  Greenwich *(G-3169)*
Image Processing .... E 203 488-3252
  Guilford *(G-3361)*
Kat Art Inc .... G 860 350-8016
  New Milford *(G-5554)*
Meredith Graphics & Design .... G 203 375-1039
  Stratford *(G-8650)*
Originals LLC .... G 203 421-4867
  Madison *(G-3944)*
P C I Group .... F 203 327-0410
  Stamford *(G-8349)*
Paper Mill Graphix Inc .... E 203 531-5904
  Greenwich *(G-3213)*
PB&j Design Inc .... G 203 332-4433
  Derby *(G-2121)*
Photo Arts Limited .... G 860 489-1170
  Torrington *(G-8957)*
Play-It Productions Inc .... F 212 695-6530
  Colchester *(G-1566)*
Print Shop of Wolcott LLC .... G 203 879-3353
  Wolcott *(G-10581)*
Pro Graphics Inc .... F 860 668-9067
  Suffield *(G-8731)*
Project Graphics Inc .... F 802 488-8789
  Woodbury *(G-10652)*
Quinn and Gellar Marketing LLC .... G 860 444-0448
  New London *(G-5485)*
R R Donnelley & Sons Company .... F 860 649-5570
  Manchester *(G-4078)*
Schwerdtle Stamp Company .... E 203 330-2750
  Bridgeport *(G-898)*
Shadow Graphics .... G 203 590-3533
  Trumbull *(G-9073)*
Spectrum Mktg Cmmnications Inc .... G 203 853-4585
  Norwalk *(G-6353)*
Tower Printing Inc .... G 203 757-1030
  Waterbury *(G-9615)*
Unlimited Signs Designs & Grap .... G 203 546-7267
  Brookfield *(G-1235)*
Villano J Sign Company LLC .... G 203 624-7550
  New Haven *(G-5427)*
Xtreme Designs LLC .... G 203 773-9303
  New Haven *(G-5437)*
Yush Sign Display Co Inc .... G 860 289-1819
  East Hartford *(G-2402)*

GRAPHIC LAYOUT SVCS: Printed Circuitry

Tri Star Graphics .... G 203 748-4792
  Bethel *(G-355)*

GRAVE MARKERS: Concrete

Mt Hope Cemetery Association .... G 860 643-4264
  Vernon *(G-9146)*

GREENHOUSES: Prefabricated Metal

Star Steel Structures Inc .... G 860 763-5681
  Somers *(G-7672)*

GREETING CARDS WHOLESALERS

Executive Greetings Inc .... B 860 379-9911
  New Hartford *(G-5190)*
Olympia Sales Inc .... D 860 749-0751
  Enfield *(G-2672)*
Raven Ad Specialties .... G 203 521-8687
  Stratford *(G-8673)*

GRILLS & GRILLWORK: Woven Wire, Made From Purchased Wire

Best In Backyards .... G 203 917-4381
  Danbury *(G-1756)*

GRINDING SVC: Precision, Commercial Or Indl

Advanced Machine Services LLC .... G 203 888-6600
  Waterbury *(G-9423)*
Nct Inc .... F 860 666-8424
  Newington *(G-5684)*
State Cutter Grinding Svc Inc .... G 203 888-8821
  Seymour *(G-7367)*
White Hills Tool .... G 203 590-3143
  Monroe *(G-4765)*

GRINDING SVCS: Ophthalmic Lens, Exc Prescription

New England Quartz Co .... G 203 846-9723
  Norwalk *(G-6273)*

GRITS: Crushed & Broken

Galasso Materials LLC .... C 860 527-1825
  East Granby *(G-2206)*
Joe Passarelli & Co .... G 203 877-1434
  Milford *(G-4560)*

GROCERIES WHOLESALERS, NEC

Durantes Pasta Inc .... G 203 387-5560
  West Haven *(G-9902)*
Jmf Group LLC .... D 860 627-7003
  East Windsor *(G-2500)*
Supreme Storm Services LLC .... G 860 201-0642
  Southington *(G-7983)*

GROMMETS: Rubber

Lord & Hodge Inc .... F 860 632-7006
  Middletown *(G-4369)*

GUARDRAILS

Atlas Industrial Services LLC .... E 203 315-4538
  Branford *(G-549)*
Highway Safety Corp .... D 860 659-4330
  Glastonbury *(G-3049)*

GUIDED MISSILES & SPACE VEHICLES

Capstone Manufacturing Inc .... G 413 636-6170
  South Windsor *(G-7723)*

GUN SIGHTS: Optical

Brightsight Llc .... G 860 208-0222
  Woodstock *(G-10658)*

GUN STOCKS: Wood

Custom Checkering .... G 860 747-8035
  Plainville *(G-6794)*

GUTTERS

Dfs In-Home Services .... G 845 405-6464
  Danbury *(G-1794)*
Hartford Seamless Gutters .... G 860 266-2516
  West Hartford *(G-9819)*
Savetime Corporation .... F 203 382-2991
  Bridgeport *(G-897)*

GUTTERS: Sheet Metal

A-1 Seamless Gutters .... G 860 432-9118
  Manchester *(G-3972)*
Hartford Seamless Gutters .... G 860 266-2516
  West Hartford *(G-9819)*
Toms Seamless Gutters Inc .... G 203 269-2296
  Wallingford *(G-9389)*
U-Sealusa LLC .... D 860 667-0911
  Newington *(G-5716)*
Yost Manufacturing & Supply .... F 860 447-9678
  Waterford *(G-9677)*

GYROSCOPES

Ais Global Holdings LLC .... A 203 250-3500
  Cheshire *(G-1349)*
Atlantic Inertial Systems Inc .... B 203 250-3500
  Cheshire *(G-1356)*
Atlantic Inertial Systems Inc .... A 203 250-3500
  Cheshire *(G-1357)*

HAIR & HAIR BASED PRDTS

Dash N Lash Extensions LLC .... G 203 726-2952
  Naugatuck *(G-4875)*
Tracy S Products .... G 203 787-2013
  New Haven *(G-5419)*

HAIR CARE PRDTS

Angela Cosmai Inc .... G 203 329-7403
  Stamford *(G-8085)*
Golden Sun Inc .... F 800 575-7960
  Stamford *(G-8217)*

HAIR DRESSING, FOR THE TRADE

Bunny Do LLC .... G 860 621-2365
  Plantsville *(G-6887)*
Sandra Mercier Procaccin .... G 203 929-6968
  Shelton *(G-7550)*

HAMPERS: Solid Fiber, Made From Purchased Materials

Westrock Rkt Company .... C 860 284-9820
  Farmington *(G-2978)*

HAND TOOLS, NEC: Wholesalers

Kell-Strom Tool Intl Inc .... E 860 529-6851
  Wethersfield *(G-10207)*

HANDBAG STORES

The Did Collection .... G 203 807-4305
  Stamford *(G-8464)*

HANDBAGS

Dooney & Bourke .... G 203 795-3131
  Orange *(G-6597)*
Leatherby .... G 860 658-6166
  Weatogue *(G-9757)*
Patricia Beavers .... G 860 233-4071
  Hartford *(G-3662)*

Employee Codes: A=Over 500 employees, B=251-500
C=101-250, D=51-100, E=20-50, F=10-19, G=1-9

HANDBAGS: Men's
Boccelli ....G...... 860 862-9300
  Uncasville *(G-9096)*

HANDBAGS: Women's
Coach Inc ....F 203 372-0208
  Trumbull *(G-9012)*
Dooney & Bourke Inc ....E 203 853-7515
  Norwalk *(G-6146)*
Its In Bag LLC ....G...... 860 229-6672
  New Britain *(G-5004)*

HANDYMAN SVCS
Rk Stucco LLC ....G...... 860 331-1791
  New Britain *(G-5046)*

HANGERS: Garment, Plastic
Calanca & Assoc LLC ....G...... 203 972-6344
  New Canaan *(G-5092)*

HARDWARE
Ador Inc ....G...... 860 583-2367
  Bristol *(G-958)*
Air-Lock Incorporated ....E 203 878-4691
  Milford *(G-4444)*
Bmr Associates ....G...... 203 453-1796
  Guilford *(G-3330)*
Brookfield Industries Inc ....E 860 283-6211
  Thomaston *(G-8782)*
Composite McHining Experts LLC ....G...... 203 624-0664
  North Haven *(G-5923)*
D & M Screw Machine Pdts LLC ....G...... 860 410-9781
  Plainville *(G-6795)*
Hicks and Otis Prints Inc ....E 203 846-2087
  Norwalk *(G-6200)*
Industrial Shipg Entps MGT LLC ....G...... 203 504-5800
  Stamford *(G-8247)*
J Ro Grounding Systems Inc ....G...... 860 747-2106
  Plainville *(G-6827)*
Land Sea Air Inc ....G...... 860 448-9004
  Groton *(G-3294)*
Lewmar Inc ....E 203 458-6200
  Guilford *(G-3367)*
Mc Kinney Products Company ....C 800 346-7707
  Berlin *(G-199)*
Michael J Macisco ....G...... 203 924-0013
  Shelton *(G-7499)*
Nations Rent ....G...... 860 665-1489
  Newington *(G-5683)*
Nielsen/Sessions ....G...... 860 522-8145
  Hartford *(G-3654)*
Oslo Switch Inc ....E 203 272-2794
  Cheshire *(G-1425)*
Outland Engineering Inc ....F 800 797-3709
  Milford *(G-4601)*
Paradigm Manchester Inc ....C 860 649-2888
  Manchester *(G-4069)*
Pemko Manufacturing Co ....G...... 901 365-2160
  New Haven *(G-5358)*
Perry Technology Corporation ....D...... 860 738-2525
  New Hartford *(G-5206)*
Roller Bearing Co Amer Inc ....E 203 758-8272
  Middlebury *(G-4289)*
Stanley Black & Decker Inc ....D...... 860 225-5111
  New Britain *(G-5062)*
Stanley Industrial & Auto LLC ....E 800 800-8005
  New Britain *(G-5066)*
Tiger Enterprises Inc ....E 860 621-9155
  Plantsville *(G-6914)*
Unger Industrial LLC ....G...... 203 336-3344
  Bridgeport *(G-931)*
Vector Engineering Inc ....F 860 572-0422
  Mystic *(G-4851)*
Wind Corporation ....E 203 778-1001
  Newtown *(G-5799)*

HARDWARE & BUILDING PRDTS: Plastic
AA & B Co ....G...... 203 933-9110
  West Haven *(G-9879)*
Division X Specialties LLC ....G...... 860 402-7736
  Vernon *(G-9137)*
Hosokawa Micron Intl Inc ....E 860 828-0541
  Berlin *(G-188)*
Spectrum Marking Materials LLC ....G...... 860 533-9533
  Glastonbury *(G-3083)*

HARDWARE STORES
F W Webb Company ....F 203 865-6124
  New Haven *(G-5279)*
Plastic and Met Components Co ....F 203 877-2723
  Milford *(G-4609)*

HARDWARE STORES: Pumps & Pumping Eqpt
Proflow Inc ....E 203 230-4700
  North Haven *(G-5980)*
Sulzer Pump Solutions US Inc ....E 203 238-2700
  Meriden *(G-4247)*
Thomas J Hunt Inc ....G...... 203 775-5050
  Brookfield *(G-1230)*

HARDWARE STORES: Tools
Alternate Inc ....G...... 203 938-4125
  Redding *(G-7088)*
Chapman Manufacturing Company .....F 860 349-9228
  Durham *(G-2141)*
Swanson Tool Manufacturing Inc ....E 860 953-1641
  West Hartford *(G-9863)*

HARDWARE STORES: Tools, Hand
Ttpockettools LLC ....G...... 860 642-6020
  Lebanon *(G-3865)*

HARDWARE WHOLESALERS
Michael J Macisco ....G...... 203 924-0013
  Shelton *(G-7499)*
Plastic and Met Components Co ....F 203 877-2723
  Milford *(G-4609)*
Steeltech Building Pdts Inc ....D...... 860 290-8930
  South Windsor *(G-7829)*
Viking Kitchen Cabinets LLC ....E 860 223-7101
  New Britain *(G-5080)*
Wenger Na Inc ....G...... 845 365-3500
  Monroe *(G-4764)*

HARDWARE, WHOLESALE: Builders', NEC
Prescott Cabinet Co ....G...... 860 495-0176
  Pawcatuck *(G-6723)*

HARDWARE, WHOLESALE: Chains
East Shre Wre Rpe/Rggng Spply ....F 203 469-5204
  North Haven *(G-5934)*

HARDWARE, WHOLESALE: Furniture, NEC
Bloomfield Wood & Melamine Inc ....F 860 243-3226
  Bloomfield *(G-398)*

HARDWARE, WHOLESALE: Power Tools & Access
Air Tool Sales & Service Co ....G...... 860 673-2714
  Unionville *(G-9110)*

HARDWARE, WHOLESALE: Security Devices, Locks
Loctec Corporation ....E 203 364-1000
  Newtown *(G-5755)*

HARDWARE: Aircraft
Compair Inc ....G...... 860 635-8811
  Middletown *(G-4331)*
D & B Tool Co LLC ....G...... 203 878-8026
  Milford *(G-4504)*
Hartford Aircraft Products ....E 860 242-8228
  Bloomfield *(G-417)*
James Ippolito & Co Conn Inc ....E 203 366-3840
  Bridgeport *(G-799)*
Kell-Strom Tool Co Inc ....E 860 529-6851
  Wethersfield *(G-10206)*
Kell-Strom Tool Intl Inc ....E 860 529-6851
  Wethersfield *(G-10207)*
Morning Star Tool LLC ....G...... 203 878-6026
  Milford *(G-4585)*
Paneloc Corporation ....E 860 677-6711
  Farmington *(G-2945)*

HARDWARE: Aircraft & Marine, Incl Pulleys & Similar Items
Dsd Distributor LLC ....G...... 860 378-4487
  Plainville *(G-6801)*

HARDWARE: Builders'
Colonial Bronze Company ....D...... 860 489-9233
  Torrington *(G-8912)*
Stanley Black & Decker Inc ....C 860 225-5111
  New Britain *(G-5061)*
Stanley Black & Decker Inc ....E 860 225-5111
  New Britain *(G-5064)*
Stanley Black & Decker Inc ....C 860 225-5111
  New Britain *(G-5063)*

HARDWARE: Cabinet
Halls Edge Inc ....G...... 203 653-2281
  Stamford *(G-8222)*
Horton Brasses Inc ....G...... 860 635-4400
  Cromwell *(G-1705)*

HARDWARE: Door Opening & Closing Devices, Exc Electrical
Connecticut Greenstar Inc ....G...... 203 368-1522
  Fairfield *(G-2766)*
Connecticut Trade Company Inc ....G...... 203 368-0398
  Fairfield *(G-2767)*

HARDWARE: Furniture, Builders' & Other Household
McMellon Associates LLC ....G...... 203 272-5859
  Cheshire *(G-1413)*
Panza Woodwork & Supply LLC ....G...... 203 934-3430
  West Haven *(G-9943)*
York Street Studio Inc ....G...... 203 266-9000
  New Milford *(G-5609)*

HARDWARE: Parachute
Bourdon Forge Co Inc ....C 860 632-2740
  Middletown *(G-4326)*
Crrc LLC ....D...... 860 635-2200
  Cromwell *(G-1697)*
Peregrine Technical Svcs LLC ....G...... 813 469-9355
  Colchester *(G-1563)*

HARDWARE: Plastic
Specialized Marketing Intl Inc ....G...... 860 779-3264
  Dayville *(G-2074)*

HARNESS ASSEMBLIES: Cable & Wire
Data Signal Corporation ....E 203 882-5393
  Milford *(G-4505)*
Electronic Connection Corp ....E 860 243-3356
  Waterbury *(G-9473)*
Lq Mechatronics Inc ....G...... 203 433-4430
  Branford *(G-619)*
Power Trans Co Inc ....G...... 203 881-0314
  Oxford *(G-6688)*
Precision Electronic Assembly ....F 203 452-1839
  Monroe *(G-4747)*
Rel-Tech Electronics Inc ....D...... 203 877-8770
  Milford *(G-4624)*
Robert Warren LLC ....E 203 247-3347
  Westport *(G-10150)*
Siemon Company ....A 860 945-4200
  Watertown *(G-9734)*
T&K Technical Services LLC ....G...... 860 235-5882
  Quaker Hill *(G-7085)*
Technical Manufacturing Corp ....E 860 349-1735
  Durham *(G-2158)*
Tornik Inc ....C 860 282-6081
  Rocky Hill *(G-7269)*

HARNESSES, HALTERS, SADDLERY & STRAPS
Equestrian Collection ....G...... 860 749-2964
  Somers *(G-7657)*
Fiddle Horse Farm LLC ....G...... 203 557-3285
  Westport *(G-10080)*
The Smith Worthington Sad Co ....G...... 860 527-9117
  Hartford *(G-3702)*

PRODUCT SECTION

HEALTH & ALLIED SERVICES, NEC
Eastern Conn Hlth Netwrk ....G...... 860 652-3182
  Glastonbury *(G-3030)*

HEALTH AIDS: Exercise Eqpt
Aqua Massage International Inc ....F...... 860 536-3735
  Mystic *(G-4799)*
Physical Fitness Consultants ....G...... 860 653-4655
  East Granby *(G-2225)*

HEALTH FOOD & SUPPLEMENT STORES
First Chance Inc ....F...... 860 346-3663
  Middletown *(G-4345)*

HEARING AID REPAIR SVCS
Zenith-Omni Hearing Center ....G...... 203 624-9857
  New Haven *(G-5454)*

HEARING AIDS
Advanced Hearing Solutions LLC ....F...... 860 674-8558
  Avon *(G-72)*
New England Ctr For Hring Rhab ....G...... 860 455-1404
  Hampton *(G-3538)*
Ooshears Inc ....G...... 415 230-0154
  Woodbridge *(G-10610)*
Zenith-Omni Hearing Center ....G...... 203 624-9857
  New Haven *(G-5454)*

HEAT EXCHANGERS: After Or Inter Coolers Or Condensers, Etc
American Indus Acqisition Corp ....G...... 203 952-9212
  Stamford *(G-8075)*
Mp Systems Inc ....F...... 860 687-3460
  East Granby *(G-2214)*

HEAT TREATING: Metal
A G C Incorporated ....C...... 203 235-3361
  Meriden *(G-4138)*
Advance Heat Treating Co ....G...... 203 380-8898
  Bridgeport *(G-684)*
American Heat Treating Inc ....E...... 203 268-1750
  Monroe *(G-4692)*
Amk Welding Inc ....E...... 860 289-5634
  South Windsor *(G-7707)*
Anderson Specialty Company ....G...... 860 953-6630
  West Hartford *(G-9774)*
Beehive Heat Treating Svcs Inc ....G...... 203 866-1635
  Fairfield *(G-2752)*
Bodycote Thermal Proc Inc ....E...... 860 225-7691
  Berlin *(G-164)*
Eastern Metal Treating Inc ....F...... 860 763-4311
  Enfield *(G-2638)*
General Heat Treating Co ....G...... 203 755-5441
  Waterbury *(G-9486)*
Johnstone Company Inc ....E...... 203 239-5834
  North Haven *(G-5954)*
Nelson Heat Treating Co Inc ....F...... 203 754-0670
  Waterbury *(G-9556)*
New Britain Heat Treating Corp ....F...... 860 223-0684
  Enfield *(G-2667)*
O W Heat Treat Inc ....G...... 860 430-6709
  South Glastonbury *(G-7681)*
Paradigm Manchester Inc ....C...... 860 649-2888
  Manchester *(G-4069)*
Sousa Corp ....F...... 860 523-9090
  Newington *(G-5706)*
Specialty Steel Treating Inc ....E...... 860 653-0061
  East Granby *(G-2231)*
Weld TEC LLC ....G...... 860 628-5750
  Plantsville *(G-6918)*

HEATERS: Space, Exc Electric
Dp2 LLC Head ....F...... 203 655-0747
  Darien *(G-2022)*

HEATERS: Swimming Pool, Oil Or Gas
Aquacomfort Solutions LLC ....G...... 203 265-0100
  Wallingford *(G-9210)*
Cheryl Aiudi & Son LLC ....G...... 860 575-8462
  Westbrook *(G-9993)*
Kerigans Fuel Inc ....G...... 203 334-3646
  Bridgeport *(G-815)*

HEATING & AIR CONDITIONING UNITS, COMBINATION
ACR Technical Services ....G...... 860 225-0572
  New Britain *(G-4935)*
All Phase Htg Coolg Contr LLC ....G...... 860 873-9680
  East Haddam *(G-2235)*
Comfortable Environments ....G...... 203 876-2140
  Milford *(G-4492)*
George Usaty Sons Heat ....G...... 860 350-2622
  New Milford *(G-5535)*

HEATING EQPT & SPLYS
American Radiant Technolo ....G...... 203 484-2888
  Middlefield *(G-4299)*
Carlin Combustion Tech Inc ....G...... 413 525-7700
  North Haven *(G-5918)*
CP Solar Thermal LLC ....G...... 860 877-2238
  Bristol *(G-1008)*
Fives N Amercn Combustn Inc ....G...... 860 739-3466
  East Lyme *(G-2465)*
Fives N Amercn Combustn Inc ....E...... 216 271-6000
  Southington *(G-7925)*
Jad LLC ....E...... 860 289-1551
  South Windsor *(G-7776)*
Lewis R Martino ....G...... 203 463-4430
  Oxford *(G-6673)*
Macristy Industries Inc ....C...... 860 225-4637
  Newington *(G-5674)*
Maxon Corporation ....G...... 860 571-6411
  Rocky Hill *(G-7256)*
McDowell Group Inc ....G...... 203 494-4120
  Guilford *(G-3373)*
McIntire Company ....F...... 860 585-8559
  Bristol *(G-1070)*
Omega Engineering Inc ....C...... 203 359-1660
  Norwalk *(G-6284)*
Red Barn Radiator Co ....G...... 860 829-2060
  Berlin *(G-215)*
Schindler Combustion LLC ....G...... 203 371-5068
  Fairfield *(G-2844)*
Shippee Solar and Cnstr LLC ....G...... 860 630-0322
  Putnam *(G-7064)*

HEATING EQPT: Complete
Alteris Renewables Inc ....G...... 860 535-3370
  Stonington *(G-8521)*
Ductworx Unlimited LLC ....G...... 203 535-1425
  Hamden *(G-3440)*
Novy International Inc ....G...... 203 743-7720
  Danbury *(G-1896)*

HEATING UNITS & DEVICES: Indl, Electric
Birk Manufacturing Inc ....D...... 800 531-2070
  East Lyme *(G-2464)*
Duralite Incorporated ....F...... 860 379-3113
  Riverton *(G-7206)*
Industrial Heater Corp ....D...... 203 250-0500
  Cheshire *(G-1400)*
Manufacturers Coml Fin LLC ....E...... 860 242-6287
  West Hartford *(G-9832)*
Sshc Inc ....F...... 860 399-5434
  Westbrook *(G-10010)*
Warmup Inc ....F...... 203 791-0072
  Danbury *(G-1975)*

HELICOPTERS
Kaman Aerospace Corporation ....E...... 860 242-4461
  Bloomfield *(G-431)*
Kaman Corporation ....D...... 860 243-7100
  Bloomfield *(G-434)*
Sikorsky Aircraft Corporation ....B...... 203 384-7532
  Bridgeport *(G-907)*
Sikorsky Aircraft Corporation ....A...... 203 386-7861
  Shelton *(G-7556)*
Sikorsky Aircraft Corporation ....A...... 203 386-4000
  Stratford *(G-8678)*
Sikorsky Aircraft Corporation ....E...... 610 644-4430
  Farmington *(G-2957)*
Sikorsky Export Corporation ....B...... 203 386-4000
  Stratford *(G-8679)*
Sikorsky International Product ....G...... 203 375-0095
  Stratford *(G-8680)*

HELMETS: Steel
Government Surplus Sales Inc ....G...... 860 247-7787
  Hartford *(G-3601)*

HIGHWAY SIGNALS: Electric
T-S Display Systems Inc ....G...... 203 964-0575
  Stamford *(G-8456)*

HOBBY & CRAFT SPLY STORES
Grannys Got It ....G...... 203 879-0042
  Wolcott *(G-10566)*

HOBBY, TOY & GAME STORES: Arts & Crafts & Splys
Artist and Craftsman ....G...... 203 330-0459
  Bridgeport *(G-703)*
Crafty Creations ....G...... 860 673-6225
  Avon *(G-79)*

HOBBY, TOY & GAME STORES: Children's Toys & Games, Exc Dolls
X44 LLC ....G...... 860 480-5560
  Torrington *(G-8993)*

HOLDERS, PAPER TOWEL, GROCERY BAG, ETC: Plastic
Orban Designs LLC ....G...... 860 605-7975
  Torrington *(G-8954)*

HOLDING COMPANIES: Investment, Exc Banks
Avara US Holdings LLC ....G...... 203 655-1333
  Norwalk *(G-6085)*
Brook & Whittle Holding Corp ....G...... 203 483-5602
  Guilford *(G-3333)*
Hitchcock Holding Company Inc ....G...... 860 738-0141
  New Hartford *(G-5193)*
Kco Numet Inc ....F...... 203 375-4995
  Orange *(G-6606)*
Legrand Holding Inc ....E...... 860 233-6251
  West Hartford *(G-9828)*
Polymedex Discovery Group Inc ....F...... 860 928-4102
  Putnam *(G-7059)*
Salin-Mpregilo US Holdings Inc ....G...... 203 439-2900
  Cheshire *(G-1441)*
Sur-Seal Holding LLC ....G...... 203 625-0770
  Norwalk *(G-6360)*
Video Messengercom Corp ....G...... 203 358-8842
  Stratford *(G-8702)*
Wizards Nuts Holdings LLC ....D...... 708 483-1315
  Greenwich *(G-3260)*
Xerox Holdings Corporation ....G...... 203 968-3000
  Norwalk *(G-6402)*

HOLDING COMPANIES: Personal, Exc Banks
Longview Holding Corporation ....G...... 203 869-6734
  Greenwich *(G-3192)*
Naiad Maritime Group Inc ....E...... 203 944-1932
  Shelton *(G-7507)*

HOME CENTER STORES
Thomas Bernhard Building Sys ....E...... 203 925-0414
  Southport *(G-8013)*

HOME ENTERTAINMENT EQPT: Electronic, NEC
Viola Audio Laboratories Inc ....G...... 203 772-0435
  New Haven *(G-5428)*

HOME FURNISHINGS WHOLESALERS
Ethan Allen Retail Inc ....B...... 203 743-8600
  Danbury *(G-1819)*
Viking Kitchen Cabinets LLC ....E...... 860 223-7101
  New Britain *(G-5080)*

HOME HEALTH CARE SVCS
Regenerative Medicine LLC ....G...... 203 629-1438
  Greenwich *(G-3223)*

HOME IMPROVEMENT & RENOVATION CONTRACTOR AGENCY
Beyond Home Improvement ....G...... 203 859-0113
  North Haven *(G-5914)*

HOME IMPROVEMENT & RENOVATION CONTRACTOR AGENCY

This Old House Ventures LLC ....E.... 475 209-8665
Stamford *(G-8465)*

HOMEBUILDERS & OTHER OPERATIVE BUILDERS

J&A Woodworking Co Inc ....G.... 203 287-1915
Hamden *(G-3466)*

HOMEFURNISHING STORE: Bedding, Sheet, Blanket, Spread/Pillow

Artemisia Inc ....G.... 917 797-7644
Old Lyme *(G-6489)*
Ethan Allen Retail Inc ....B.... 203 743-8000
Danbury *(G-1818)*
Sammi Sleeping Systems LLC ....G.... 203 684-3131
New Haven *(G-5388)*

HOMEFURNISHING STORES: Lighting Fixtures

Acme Sign Co ....F.... 203 324-2263
Stamford *(G-8059)*
Washington Copper Works Inc ....G.... 860 868-7637
Washington *(G-9415)*

HOMEFURNISHING STORES: Mirrors

Kensington Glass and Frmng Co ....G.... 860 828-9428
Berlin *(G-192)*
Mirror Polishing & Pltg Co Inc ....E.... 203 574-5400
Waterbury *(G-9544)*
New Haven GL & Mirror Co LLC ....G.... 203 469-2440
New Haven *(G-5344)*

HOMEFURNISHING STORES: Pictures & Mirrors

Picture This Hartford Inc ....G.... 860 528-1409
East Hartford *(G-2355)*

HOMEFURNISHING STORES: Pottery

Cornwall Bridge Pottery Inc ....G.... 860 672-6545
Warren *(G-9407)*

HOMEFURNISHING STORES: Venetian Blinds

Arrow Window Shade Mfg Co Mrdn ......F.... 860 563-4035
Wethersfield *(G-10181)*

HOMEFURNISHING STORES: Window Furnishings

Window Pdts Awngs Blind Shade ....G.... 203 481-9772
Branford *(G-676)*

HOMEFURNISHING STORES: Window Shades, NEC

Arrow Window Shade Mfg Co ....G.... 860 956-3570
Wethersfield *(G-10180)*

HOMEFURNISHINGS & SPLYS, WHOLESALE: Decorative

Modern Objects Inc ....G.... 203 378-5785
Norwalk *(G-6264)*

HOMEFURNISHINGS, WHOLESALE: Blinds, Vertical

Window Pdts Awngs Blind Shade ....G.... 203 481-9772
Branford *(G-676)*

HOMEFURNISHINGS, WHOLESALE: Carpets

Holland & Sherry Inc ....F.... 212 628-1950
Norwalk *(G-6201)*
Wool Solutions Inc ....G.... 203 845-0921
Norwalk *(G-6400)*

HOMEFURNISHINGS, WHOLESALE: Kitchenware

Glass Industries America LLC ....F.... 203 269-6700
Wallingford *(G-9276)*

HOMEFURNISHINGS, WHOLESALE: Mirrors/Pictures, Framed/Unframd

National Picture Frame Inc ....G.... 860 774-5668
Brooklyn *(G-1251)*

HOMEFURNISHINGS, WHOLESALE: Wood Flooring

Ben Barretts LLC ....G.... 860 928-9373
Thompson *(G-8830)*

HOMES FOR THE ELDERLY

Evangelical Christian Center ....G.... 860 429-0856
Ashford *(G-61)*

HOMES, MODULAR: Wooden

Giuliano Construction LLC ....G.... 203 230-3094
Hamden *(G-3451)*
Nu Vision Homes LLC ....G.... 860 209-8492
Middletown *(G-4388)*

HOMES: Log Cabins

Country Log Homes ....G.... 413 229-8084
Canaan *(G-1285)*
Country Log Homes Inc ....F.... 413 229-8084
Goshen *(G-3097)*
Design Ltd ....G.... 203 426-5539
Sandy Hook *(G-7309)*
Post & Beam Homes Inc ....G.... 860 267-2060
East Hampton *(G-2274)*

HONEYCOMB CORE & BOARD: Made From Purchased Materials

Pactiv Corporation ....E.... 203 288-7722
North Haven *(G-5972)*

HOODS: Range, Sheet Metal

Denlar Fire Protection LLC ....G.... 860 526-9846
Chester *(G-1469)*

HORSE & PET ACCESSORIES: Textile

Lathrop Stables LLC ....G.... 860 230-9949
Plainfield *(G-6746)*
Puppy Hugger ....G.... 203 661-4858
Greenwich *(G-3219)*

HORSE DRAWN VEHICLE REPAIR SVCS

Serafin Sulky Co ....G.... 860 684-2986
Stafford Springs *(G-8037)*

HORSESHOES

Red Oak Stable LLC ....G.... 860 642-4671
Lebanon *(G-3861)*
William Martin ....G.... 860 355-1919
Gaylordsville *(G-2997)*

HOSE: Flexible Metal

East Coast Metal Hose Inc ....G.... 203 723-7459
Naugatuck *(G-4877)*
Senior Operations LLC ....D.... 860 741-2546
Enfield *(G-2692)*

HOSE: Rubber

Rubco Products Company ....G.... 860 496-1178
Torrington *(G-8965)*

HOSES & BELTING: Rubber & Plastic

Kongsberg Actuation ....G.... 860 668-1285
Suffield *(G-8723)*
Ram Belting Company Inc ....G.... 860 438-7029
New Britain *(G-5040)*

HOSPITALS: Rehabilitation, Drug Addiction

Altasci LLC ....G.... 860 224-6668
New Britain *(G-4942)*

HOT AIR BALLOONS & EQPT DEALERS

Mooney Time Inc ....G.... 203 263-0167
Woodbury *(G-10644)*

HOT TUBS

Thermospas Hot Tub Products ....E.... 203 303-0005
Wallingford *(G-9381)*

HOUSEHOLD APPLIANCE STORES

T C Kitchens Inc ....G.... 203 375-4469
Stratford *(G-8693)*

HOUSEHOLD APPLIANCE STORES: Air Cond Rm Units, Self-Contnd

Thomas J Hunt Inc ....G.... 203 775-5050
Brookfield *(G-1230)*

HOUSEHOLD APPLIANCE STORES: Electric

W H Preuss Sons Incorporated ....G.... 860 643-9492
Bolton *(G-521)*

HOUSEHOLD APPLIANCE STORES: Electric Household, Major

Clarke Distribution Corp ....G.... 203 838-9385
Norwalk *(G-6116)*

HOUSEHOLD ARTICLES: Metal

Alvarez Industries LLC ....G.... 203 799-2356
Orange *(G-6580)*
Alvarez Industries LLC ....G.... 203 401-1152
New Haven *(G-5226)*
J OConnor LLC ....F.... 860 665-7702
Newington *(G-5666)*

HOUSEHOLD FURNISHINGS, NEC

Hills Point Industries LLC ....G.... 917 515-8650
Westport *(G-10095)*
Latex Foam International LLC ....D.... 203 924-0700
Shelton *(G-7487)*
Laura Spector Rustic Design ....G.... 203 254-3952
Fairfield *(G-2809)*
R L Fisher Inc ....D.... 860 951-8110
Hartford *(G-3674)*
Stephen Smith ....G.... 405 420-2226
Eastford *(G-2543)*

HOUSEKEEPING & MAID SVCS

Ether & Industries LLc ....G.... 475 224-0650
New Haven *(G-5277)*

HOUSEWARES, ELECTRIC: Appliances, Personal

Urban Antique Radio ....G.... 203 877-2409
Milford *(G-4671)*

HOUSEWARES, ELECTRIC: Blowers, Portable

Crrc LLC ....D.... 860 635-2200
Cromwell *(G-1697)*

HOUSEWARES, ELECTRIC: Bottle Warmers

Mayborn Usa Inc ....F.... 781 269-7490
Stamford *(G-8298)*

HOUSEWARES, ELECTRIC: Broilers

Bkmfg Corp ....E.... 860 738-2200
Winsted *(G-10510)*

HOUSEWARES, ELECTRIC: Cooking Appliances

Black & Decker (us) Inc ....G.... 860 225-5111
New Britain *(G-4951)*
Black & Decker (us) Inc ....G.... 860 225-5111
New Britain *(G-4952)*

HOUSEWARES, ELECTRIC: Fans, Exhaust & Ventilating

Betlan Corporation ....F.... 203 270-7898
Newtown *(G-5729)*

PRODUCT SECTION

HOUSEWARES: Dishes, Earthenware
Cornwall Bridge Pottery Inc .... G 860 672-6545
  Warren (G-9407)

HOUSEWARES: Pots & Pans, Glass
Weekend Kitchen .... G 860 767-1010
  Essex (G-2737)

HUB CAPS: Automobile, Stamped Metal
Distinctive Steering Wheels .... G 860 274-9087
  Watertown (G-9702)

HYDRAULIC EQPT REPAIR SVC
Dependable Repair Inc .... F 203 481-9706
  North Branford (G-5834)
Faxon Engineering Company Inc .... F 860 236-4266
  Bloomfield (G-410)
Power-Dyne LLC .... E 860 346-9283
  Middletown (G-4395)

HYDRAULIC FLUIDS: Synthetic Based
Ai Divestitures Inc .... G 203 575-5727
  Waterbury (G-9424)
Element Solutions Inc .... E 203 575-5850
  Waterbury (G-9475)
Houston Macdermid Inc .... G 203 575-5700
  Waterbury (G-9500)
Macdermid Anion Inc .... G 203 575-5700
  Waterbury (G-9527)
Macdermid Brazil Inc .... G 203 575-5700
  Waterbury (G-9528)
Macdermid South America Inc .... G 203 575-5700
  Waterbury (G-9531)
Macdermid South Atlantic Inc .... G 203 575-5700
  Waterbury (G-9532)

HYDROFLUORIC ACID COMPOUND: Etching Or Polishing Glass
Cytec Industries Inc .... C 203 284-4334
  Wallingford (G-9245)

HYDROPONIC EQPT
Liquid Sun .... G 860 254-5747
  East Windsor (G-2508)

Hard Rubber & Molded Rubber Prdts
Cooper Crouse-Hinds LLC .... D 860 683-4300
  Windsor (G-10377)
Rubberhouse .... G 860 646-3012
  Bolton (G-518)

ICE
Dynaxa LLC .... G 203 300-5237
  Bethel (G-290)
Grotto Always Inc .... F 203 754-0295
  Waterbury (G-9491)
Leonard F Brooks .... G 203 335-4934
  Bridgeport (G-824)
Olde Burnside Brewing Co LLC .... G 860 528-2200
  East Hartford (G-2349)
Vaporizer LLC .... E 860 564-7225
  Moosup (G-4784)

IDENTIFICATION TAGS, EXC PAPER
Ann S Davis .... F 860 642-7228
  Lebanon (G-3846)

IGNEOUS ROCK: Crushed & Broken
Nu-Stone Mfg & Distrg LLC .... G 860 564-6555
  Sterling (G-8514)

IGNITION SYSTEMS: High Frequency
Simmonds Precision Pdts Inc .... E 203 797-5000
  Danbury (G-1952)

INCENSE
Three Kings Products LLC .... G 860 945-5294
  Watertown (G-9740)

INDL & PERSONAL SVC PAPER, WHOL: Bags, Paper/Disp Plastic
Hudson Paper Company .... E 203 378-8759
  Stratford (G-8628)

INDL & PERSONAL SVC PAPER, WHOLESALE: Boxes & Containers
Fortis Solutions Group LLC .... E 860 872-6311
  Ellington (G-2590)

INDL & PERSONAL SVC PAPER, WHOLESALE: Disposable
Yumi Ecosolutions Inc .... G 203 803-1880
  Westport (G-10178)

INDL & PERSONAL SVC PAPER, WHOLESALE: Shipping Splys
American-Digital LLC .... G 203 838-0148
  Bridgeport (G-695)
Equinor Shipping Inc .... G 203 978-6900
  Stamford (G-8197)
IR Industries Inc .... F 203 790-8273
  Bethel (G-313)
Penmar Industries Inc .... F 203 853-4868
  Stratford (G-8663)

INDL EQPT SVCS
Afcon Products Inc .... F 203 393-9301
  Bethany (G-234)
Brian Arnio .... G 860 779-2983
  Sterling (G-8508)
Environmental Monitor Service .... G 203 935-0102
  Meriden (G-4169)
First Reserve Fund Viii LP .... G 203 661-6601
  Stamford (G-8205)
Hydro Service & Supplies Inc .... G 203 265-3995
  Middletown (G-4353)
Machine Builders Neng LLC .... F 203 922-9446
  Shelton (G-7493)
Nalco Wtr Prtrtment Sltons LLC .... G 860 224-4443
  New Britain (G-5019)
Nemtec Inc .... G 203 272-0788
  Cheshire (G-1418)
North Eastern Scale Corp .... G 203 634-7942
  Meriden (G-4210)

INDL GASES WHOLESALERS
Connecticut Analytical Corp .... F 203 393-9666
  Bethany (G-239)

INDL MACHINERY & EQPT WHOLESALERS
A & C Connection Inspection .... G 203 287-8504
  Hamden (G-3408)
A F M Engineering Corp .... G 860 774-7518
  Brooklyn (G-1244)
Anderson Technologies Inc .... G 860 663-2100
  Killingworth (G-3828)
Arthur I Platt Inc .... G 203 874-0091
  Milford (G-4459)
Beardsworth Group Inc .... G 860 283-4014
  Thomaston (G-8780)
Bernell Tool & Mfg Co .... F 203 756-4405
  Waterbury (G-9438)
Bjm Pumps LLC .... E 860 399-5937
  Old Saybrook (G-6524)
Bloomy Controls Inc .... E 860 298-9925
  Windsor (G-10368)
Bremser Technologies Inc .... F 203 378-8486
  Stratford (G-8585)
Cable Electronics Inc .... G 860 953-0300
  Hartford (G-3560)
Csg Automation LLC .... G 860 691-1885
  Niantic (G-5804)
Del-Tron Precision Inc .... E 203 778-2727
  Bethel (G-280)
Devar Inc .... E 203 368-6751
  Bridgeport (G-749)
Finishers Technology Corp .... F 860 829-1000
  East Berlin (G-2168)
Gems Sensors Inc .... B 860 747-3000
  Plainville (G-6815)
George Bullock & Sons Inc .... G 860 355-1243
  Roxbury (G-7277)

INDL PROCESS INSTRUMENTS: Digital Display, Process Variables

Hall Machine Systems Inc .... G 203 481-4275
  North Branford (G-5840)
Helander Products Inc .... F 860 669-7953
  Clinton (G-1507)
Interface Devices Incorporated .... G 203 878-4648
  Milford (G-4557)
Jimbpa Enterprises LLC .... G 203 755-9237
  Waterbury (G-9509)
Jovil Universal LLC .... E 203 792-6700
  Danbury (G-1864)
Kenneth Industrial Pdts Inc .... G 860 349-7454
  Durham (G-2150)
L M Gill Welding and Mfr LLC .... F 860 647-9931
  Manchester (G-4046)
Novo Precision LLC .... E 860 583-0517
  Bristol (G-1081)
Planit Manufacturing LLC .... G 203 641-6055
  Bristol (G-1092)
Record Products America Inc .... F 203 248-6371
  Hamden (G-3504)
Richard Dahlen .... G 203 584-8226
  Bristol (G-1108)
Royal Machine and Tool Corp .... E 860 828-6555
  Berlin (G-217)
Shuster-Mettler Corp .... E 203 562-3178
  Plainville (G-6861)
Tenova Inc .... E 203 265-5684
  Wallingford (G-9380)
Viking Tool Company .... E 203 929-1457
  Shelton (G-7579)
Wittmann Battenfeld Inc .... D 860 496-9603
  Torrington (G-8991)

INDL MACHINERY REPAIR & MAINTENANCE
Arico Engineering Inc .... G 860 642-7040
  North Franklin (G-5870)
Cnc Engineering Inc .... E 860 749-1780
  Enfield (G-2627)
H G Steinmetz Machine Works .... F 203 794-1880
  Bethel (G-307)
Haesche Machine Repair Service .... G 203 488-7271
  Branford (G-602)
OEM Design Services LLC .... G 203 467-5993
  East Haven (G-2445)
Planit Manufacturing LLC .... G 203 641-6055
  Bristol (G-1092)
Quick Machine Services LLC .... G 203 634-8822
  Meriden (G-4226)
Rydz Engineering .... G 203 878-5499
  Milford (G-4636)
Thomas La Ganga .... G 860 489-0920
  Torrington (G-8977)

INDL PROCESS INSTRUMENTS: Absorp Analyzers, Infrared, X-Ray
Buck Scientific Inc .... D 203 853-9444
  Norwalk (G-6101)
Kahn and Company Incorporated .... G 860 529-8643
  Wethersfield (G-10203)

INDL PROCESS INSTRUMENTS: Control
Bristol Inc .... B 860 945-2200
  Watertown (G-9686)
Gordon Engineering Corp .... F 203 775-4501
  Brookfield (G-1193)
Micromod Automation & Controls ...... F 585 321-9209
  Wallingford (G-9320)

INDL PROCESS INSTRUMENTS: Controllers, Process Variables
Louis Electric Co Inc .... G 203 879-5483
  Wolcott (G-10571)
Prime Technology LLC .... C 203 481-5721
  North Branford (G-5853)
Quad/Graphics Inc .... A 203 288-2468
  North Haven (G-5985)

INDL PROCESS INSTRUMENTS: Digital Display, Process Variables
Kapcom LLC .... G 203 891-5112
  East Haven (G-2436)

Employee Codes: A=Over 500 employees, B=251-500
C=101-250, D=51-100, E=20-50, F=10-19, G=1-9

INDL PROCESS INSTRUMENTS: Fluidic Devices, Circuit & Systems

PRODUCT SECTION

INDL PROCESS INSTRUMENTS: Fluidic Devices, Circuit & Systems

Diba Industries Inc .... C 203 744-0773
  Danbury *(G-1795)*
Lee Company .... A 860 399-6281
  Westbrook *(G-10000)*
Lee Company .... C 860 399-6281
  Essex *(G-2723)*

INDL PROCESS INSTRUMENTS: Indl Flow & Measuring

C F D Engineering Company .... F 203 754-2807
  Waterbury *(G-9445)*
Cidra Corporate Services Inc .... D 203 265-0035
  Wallingford *(G-9228)*
Cidra Corporation .... D 203 265-0035
  Wallingford *(G-9229)*
Proflow Inc .... E 203 230-4700
  North Haven *(G-5980)*

INDL PROCESS INSTRUMENTS: Moisture Meters

Kahn Instruments Incorporated .... G 860 529-8643
  Wethersfield *(G-10205)*
Laticrete Supercap LLC .... G 203 393-4558
  Bethany *(G-246)*

INDL PROCESS INSTRUMENTS: Temperature

Jad LLC .... E 860 289-1551
  South Windsor *(G-7776)*
Underground Systems Inc .... E 203 792-3444
  Bethel *(G-357)*

INDL PROCESS INSTRUMENTS: Water Quality Monitoring/Cntrl Sys

Danaher Tool Group .... F 203 284-7000
  Wallingford *(G-9246)*

INDL SPLYS WHOLESALERS

Automation Inc .... F 860 236-5991
  West Hartford *(G-9777)*
Barker Steel LLC .... E 860 282-1860
  South Windsor *(G-7717)*
Dayton Bag & Burlap Co .... G 860 653-8191
  East Granby *(G-2202)*
Dunbar Commercial Enterprises .... G 203 469-7575
  East Haven *(G-2421)*
Kell-Strom Tool Intl Inc .... E 860 529-6851
  Wethersfield *(G-10207)*
Lbi Inc .... F 860 446-8058
  Groton *(G-3296)*
New Britain Saw Tech .... G 860 410-1077
  Plainville *(G-6846)*
Ruby Automation LLC .... C 860 687-5000
  Bloomfield *(G-479)*
Ruby Industrial Tech LLC .... D 860 687-5000
  Bloomfield *(G-481)*
Spectrum Associates Inc .... F 203 878-4618
  Milford *(G-4651)*
Sperry Automatics Co Inc .... C 203 729-4589
  Naugatuck *(G-4922)*
Stanley Black & Decker Inc .... E 860 225-5111
  New Britain *(G-5064)*

INDL SPLYS, WHOL: Fasteners, Incl Nuts, Bolts, Screws, Etc

C-Tech Manufacturing Co LLC .... G 860 274-6879
  Watertown *(G-9689)*
Plastic and Met Components Co .... F 203 877-2723
  Milford *(G-4609)*
Spirol International Corp .... C 860 774-8571
  Danielson *(G-2003)*

INDL SPLYS, WHOLESALE: Abrasives

Associated Chemicals & Abr Inc .... G 203 481-7235
  Branford *(G-548)*

INDL SPLYS, WHOLESALE: Bearings

Bmr Associates .... G 203 453-1796
  Guilford *(G-3330)*

F K Bearings Inc .... F 860 621-4567
  Southington *(G-7922)*
Kaman Aerospace Corporation .... E 860 242-4461
  Bloomfield *(G-431)*
Kaman Corporation .... D 860 243-7100
  Bloomfield *(G-434)*

INDL SPLYS, WHOLESALE: Bottler Splys

O Berk Company Neng LLC .... F 203 932-8000
  West Haven *(G-9940)*

INDL SPLYS, WHOLESALE: Filters, Indl

MSC Filtration Tech Inc .... F 860 745-7475
  Enfield *(G-2664)*
Tinny Corporation .... G 860 854-6121
  Middletown *(G-4427)*

INDL SPLYS, WHOLESALE: Fittings

Burt Process Equipment Inc .... E 203 287-1985
  Hamden *(G-3420)*
Faxon Engineering Company Inc .... G 860 236-4266
  Bloomfield *(G-410)*

INDL SPLYS, WHOLESALE: Gears

Protek Ski Racing Inc .... G 860 628-9643
  Southington *(G-7962)*

INDL SPLYS, WHOLESALE: Power Transmission, Eqpt & Apparatus

Altra Industrial Motion Corp .... G 860 379-1673
  New Hartford *(G-5185)*

INDL SPLYS, WHOLESALE: Rubber Goods, Mechanical

Alltop Ltd .... G 203 746-1509
  New Fairfield *(G-5160)*
Applied Rubber & Plastics Inc .... F 860 987-9018
  Windsor *(G-10363)*
Gordon Rubber and Pkg Co Inc .... E 203 735-7441
  Derby *(G-2114)*

INDL SPLYS, WHOLESALE: Signmaker Eqpt & Splys

US Highway Products Inc .... F 203 336-0332
  Bridgeport *(G-932)*

INDL SPLYS, WHOLESALE: Springs

Lee Spring Company LLC .... E 860 584-0991
  Bristol *(G-1062)*

INDL SPLYS, WHOLESALE: Tools, NEC

Nelson Apostle Inc .... G 860 953-4633
  Hartford *(G-3649)*
Wadsworth Falls Mfg Co .... F 860 346-3644
  Rockfall *(G-7216)*
William Magenau & Company Inc .... G 860 423-7713
  Willimantic *(G-10238)*

INDL SPLYS, WHOLESALE: Valves & Fittings

Carlyle Johnson Machine Co LLC .... E 860 643-1531
  Bolton *(G-508)*
Royce Industries Inc .... F 860 674-2700
  Southington *(G-7969)*

INDL TOOL GRINDING SVCS

M & M Carbide Inc .... G 860 628-2002
  Southington *(G-7948)*

INDUCTORS

Henkel Loctite Corporation .... E 860 571-5100
  Rocky Hill *(G-7245)*

INDUSTRIAL & COMMERCIAL EQPT INSPECTION SVCS

Mystic River Mar Surveyors LLC .... G 860 857-1798
  Mystic *(G-4836)*

INFORMATION RETRIEVAL SERVICES

I Tech Services Inc .... G 800 559-8991
  Danbury *(G-1847)*

INFRARED OBJECT DETECTION EQPT

Brandstrom Instruments Inc .... E 203 544-9341
  Ridgefield *(G-7126)*
Sensor Switch Inc .... E 203 265-2842
  New Haven *(G-5392)*

INK OR WRITING FLUIDS

Chad Labs Corporation .... G 203 877-3891
  Milford *(G-4487)*
Eastern Tech LLC .... E 203 877-5386
  Milford *(G-4524)*
Pulse International Inc .... E 860 290-7878
  South Windsor *(G-7816)*

INK: Duplicating

Corporate Cartridge .... G 203 655-7197
  Darien *(G-2015)*

INK: Printing

Hubergroup Usa Inc .... F 860 687-1617
  Windsor *(G-10395)*
Superior Printing Ink Co Inc .... E 203 281-1921
  Hamden *(G-3515)*

INSECTICIDES

Chemtura Receivables LLC .... G 203 573-3327
  Waterbury *(G-9449)*

INSECTICIDES & PESTICIDES

Bedoukian Research Inc .... E 203 830-4000
  Danbury *(G-1750)*
Connecticut Tick Control LLC .... F 203 855-7849
  Norwalk *(G-6128)*
Mist Hill Property Maint LLC .... G 203 648-7434
  Brookfield *(G-1207)*
Nantucket Spider LLC .... G 203 423-3031
  Wilton *(G-10315)*
Pic20 Group LLC .... G 203 957-3555
  Norwalk *(G-6299)*
Tick Box Technology Corp .... G 203 852-7171
  Norwalk *(G-6368)*

INSPECTION & TESTING SVCS

Eastern Connecticut .... F 860 423-1972
  Willimantic *(G-10226)*

INSTRUMENTS & ACCESSORIES: Surveying

Data Technology Inc .... E 860 871-8082
  Tolland *(G-8860)*

INSTRUMENTS & METERS: Measuring, Electric

Altek Electronics Inc .... C 860 482-7626
  Torrington *(G-8892)*
Omega Engineering Inc .... D 714 540-4914
  Norwalk *(G-6285)*

INSTRUMENTS, LABORATORY: Analyzers, Elemental

Nats Inc .... F 860 635-6820
  Middletown *(G-4384)*

INSTRUMENTS, LABORATORY: Analyzers, Thermal

Hamilton Sndstrnd Space .... A 860 654-6000
  Windsor Locks *(G-10489)*

INSTRUMENTS, LABORATORY: Flame Photometers

G F E .... G 203 371-7334
  Easton *(G-2555)*

INSTRUMENTS, LABORATORY: Infrared Analytical

Cam2 Technologies LLC .... G 203 456-3025
  Danbury *(G-1761)*

PRODUCT SECTION

INSTRUMENTS, SURGICAL & MEDICAL: Plates & Screws, Bone

INSTRUMENTS, LABORATORY: Magnetic/Elec Properties Measuring
Madison Technology Intl .... G 860 245-0245
  Mystic *(G-4830)*

INSTRUMENTS, LABORATORY: Mass Spectroscopy
Czitek LLC .... G 888 326-8186
  Danbury *(G-1781)*
Real-Time Analyzers Inc .... G 860 635-9800
  Middletown *(G-4403)*

INSTRUMENTS, LABORATORY: Photometers
Hoffman Engineering LLC .... D 203 425-8900
  Stamford *(G-8240)*

INSTRUMENTS, LABORATORY: Ultraviolet Analytical
American Ultraviolet .... G 203 926-0140
  Shelton *(G-7394)*

INSTRUMENTS, MEASURING & CNTRL: Auto Turnstiles
Q-Lane Turnstiles LLC .... F 860 410-1801
  Sandy Hook *(G-7327)*

INSTRUMENTS, MEASURING & CNTRL: Geophysical & Meteorological
Pmd Scientific Inc .... G 860 242-8177
  Bloomfield *(G-466)*

INSTRUMENTS, MEASURING & CNTRL: Radiation & Testing, Nuclear
Independent Repair Service .... G 203 234-0218
  North Haven *(G-5947)*
Mirion Tech Canberra Inc .... B 203 238-2351
  Meriden *(G-4204)*

INSTRUMENTS, MEASURING & CNTRL: Tester, Acft Hydc Ctrl Test
American Design & Mfg Inc .... E 860 282-2719
  South Windsor *(G-7705)*

INSTRUMENTS, MEASURING & CNTRL: Testing, Abrasion, Etc
Electro-Methods Inc .... C 860 289-8661
  South Windsor *(G-7747)*
Radiation Safety Assoc Inc .... G 860 228-0721
  Hebron *(G-3754)*
Wesdyne International LLC .... G 860 731-1683
  Windsor *(G-10463)*

INSTRUMENTS, MEASURING & CNTRLG: Aircraft & Motor Vehicle
Bauer Inc .... D 860 583-9100
  Bristol *(G-978)*
Eastern Technology Corporation .... G 860 528-9821
  East Hartford *(G-2318)*
Harcosemco LLC .... C 203 483-3700
  Branford *(G-603)*
Simmonds Precision Pdts Inc .... E 203 797-5000
  Danbury *(G-1952)*

INSTRUMENTS, MEASURING & CNTRLG: Thermometers/Temp Sensors
Microtechnologies Inc .... G 860 517-8314
  Farmington *(G-2929)*
Mission Bmdical Scientific Inc .... G 860 941-8896
  East Lyme *(G-2468)*
Perrella Specialties .... G 203 264-1758
  Southbury *(G-7872)*
Semco Instruments Inc .... C 661 257-2000
  Branford *(G-650)*

INSTRUMENTS, MEASURING & CNTRLNG: Levels & Tapes, Surveying
Miracle Instruments Co .... F 860 642-7745
  Lebanon *(G-3858)*

INSTRUMENTS, MEASURING & CNTRLNG: Nuclear Instrument Modules
Judge Tool & Gage Inc .... G 800 214-5990
  Stratford *(G-8638)*

INSTRUMENTS, MEASURING & CONTROLLING: Breathalyzers
OXY Couture LLC .... G 860 257-8750
  Rocky Hill *(G-7261)*

INSTRUMENTS, MEASURING & CONTROLLING: Gas Detectors
Sperian Protectn Instrumentatn .... C 860 344-1079
  Middletown *(G-4422)*

INSTRUMENTS, MEASURING & CONTROLLING: Ultrasonic Testing
Boudreau Vasiliki .... G 203 734-6754
  Ansonia *(G-24)*
Technisonic Research Inc .... G 203 368-3600
  Fairfield *(G-2853)*
TLC Ultrasound Inc .... G 860 354-6333
  New Milford *(G-5599)*

INSTRUMENTS, MEASURING/CNTRL: Compasses, Magnetic, Portable
Connecticut Compass Service .... G 860 434-2019
  Lyme *(G-3903)*

INSTRUMENTS, MEASURING/CNTRL: Gauging, Ultrasonic Thickness
Power-Dyne LLC .... E 860 346-9283
  Middletown *(G-4395)*
Zactech Ultrasonics LLC .... G 860 438-0004
  Ridgefield *(G-7187)*

INSTRUMENTS, MEASURING/CNTRLG: Fire Detect Sys, Non-Electric
Bojak Company .... G 203 378-5086
  Milford *(G-4474)*

INSTRUMENTS, MEASURING/CNTRLNG: Med Diagnostic Sys, Nuclear
Daybreak Nuclear & Med Systems .... G 203 453-3299
  Guilford *(G-3343)*
Eastern Conn Hlth Netwrk .... G 860 652-3182
  Glastonbury *(G-3030)*
Interpace Diagnostics Corp .... G 855 776-6419
  New Haven *(G-5302)*
Onsite Mammography .... G 860 254-5097
  West Suffield *(G-9988)*

INSTRUMENTS, OPTICAL: Elements & Assemblies, Exc Ophthalmic
Adaptive Optics Associates Inc .... F 860 282-4401
  East Hartford *(G-2287)*
Nvizix Corp .... G 203 222-8723
  Westport *(G-10130)*

INSTRUMENTS, OPTICAL: Gratings, Diffraction
Ciaudelli Productions Inc .... G 860 848-0411
  Montville *(G-4769)*

INSTRUMENTS, OPTICAL: Lenses, All Types Exc Ophthalmic
Fedora Optical Inc .... G 860 646-3577
  Manchester *(G-4017)*
Optical Research Technologies .... G 203 762-9063
  Wilton *(G-10316)*
Orafol Americas Inc .... C 860 676-7100
  Avon *(G-98)*
Retina Systems Inc .... E 203 881-1311
  Seymour *(G-7365)*

INSTRUMENTS, OPTICAL: Magnifying, NEC
Scope Technology Inc .... F 860 963-1141
  Plainfield *(G-6752)*

INSTRUMENTS, OPTICAL: Mirrors
Flabeg Technical Glass US Corp .... E 203 729-5227
  Naugatuck *(G-4880)*

INSTRUMENTS, OPTICAL: Sighting & Fire Control
Bradley Gun Sight Co Inc .... G 860 589-0531
  Bristol *(G-986)*

INSTRUMENTS, OPTICAL: Test & Inspection
4 D Technology Corporation .... G 860 365-0420
  East Hampton *(G-2251)*
Abet Technologies Inc .... G 203 540-9990
  Milford *(G-4438)*

INSTRUMENTS, SURGICAL & MED: Needles & Syringes, Hypodermic
Becton Dickinson and Company .... B 860 824-5487
  Canaan *(G-1281)*
Connecticut Hypodermics Inc .... D 203 265-4881
  Wallingford *(G-9238)*

INSTRUMENTS, SURGICAL & MEDI: Knife Blades/Handles, Surgical
Microspecialities Inc .... F 203 874-1832
  Middletown *(G-4377)*

INSTRUMENTS, SURGICAL & MEDICAL: Biopsy
Lorad Corporation .... C 203 790-5544
  Danbury *(G-1876)*

INSTRUMENTS, SURGICAL & MEDICAL: Blood & Bone Work
E M M Inc .... E 203 245-0306
  Madison *(G-3918)*
Furnace Source LLC .... F 860 582-4201
  Terryville *(G-8755)*
Highland Medical Products Inc .... G 860 454-0625
  Ellington *(G-2592)*
Joseph L Gentile Entps LLC .... G 203 421-5144
  Madison *(G-3932)*
Newmark Medical Components Inc .... F 203 753-1158
  Waterbury *(G-9560)*
Seclingua Inc .... G 203 922-4560
  Stamford *(G-8406)*
Vivax Medical Corporation .... F 203 729-0514
  Naugatuck *(G-4929)*

INSTRUMENTS, SURGICAL & MEDICAL: Blood Pressure
Cas Medical Systems Inc .... G 203 315-6953
  Branford *(G-569)*

INSTRUMENTS, SURGICAL & MEDICAL: Blood Transfusion
Novatek Medical Inc .... G 203 356-0156
  Stamford *(G-8332)*

INSTRUMENTS, SURGICAL & MEDICAL: Catheters
Synectic Engineering Inc .... F 203 877-8488
  Milford *(G-4660)*

INSTRUMENTS, SURGICAL & MEDICAL: Inhalators
Convexity Scientific LLC .... G 949 637-1216
  Fairfield *(G-2768)*

INSTRUMENTS, SURGICAL & MEDICAL: Plates & Screws, Bone
Fusion Medical Corporation .... G 860 906-7856
  West Haven *(G-9910)*

Employee Codes: A=Over 500 employees, B=251-500
C=101-250, D=51-100, E=20-50, F=10-19, G=1-9

INSTRUMENTS, SURGICAL & MEDICAL: Stapling Devices, Surgical

Southington Tool & Mfg Corp .... E 860 276-0021
Plantsville *(G-6912)*

INSTRUMENTS, SURGICAL/MED: Bronchoscopes, Exc Electromedical

Lenses Only LLC .... F 860 769-2020
Bloomfield *(G-440)*

INSTRUMENTS: Airspeed

Mtu Aero Engines N Amer Inc .... G 860 258-9700
Rocky Hill *(G-7258)*

INSTRUMENTS: Analytical

Alpha 1c LLC .... G 860 354-7979
Sherman *(G-7590)*
Applied Biosystems LLC .... G 781 271-0045
Norwalk *(G-6071)*
Buck Scientific Inc .... D 203 853-9444
Norwalk *(G-6101)*
Carestream Health Molecular .... E 888 777-2072
New Haven *(G-5254)*
Connecticut Analytical Corp .... F 203 393-9666
Bethany *(G-239)*
Designs & Prototypes Ltd .... G 860 658-0458
Simsbury *(G-7615)*
Dimension Zero Ltd .... G 860 325-7073
Willimantic *(G-10224)*
Energy Beam Sciences Inc .... F 860 653-0411
East Granby *(G-2203)*
Idex Health & Science LLC .... C 860 314-2880
Bristol *(G-1050)*
Ihs Herold Inc .... D 203 857-0215
Norwalk *(G-6204)*
Industrial Analytics Corp .... G 203 245-0380
Madison *(G-3931)*
K A F Manufacturing Co Inc .... E 203 324-3012
Stamford *(G-8272)*
Max Analytical Tech Inc .... E 989 772-5088
East Windsor *(G-2510)*
Owlstone Inc .... G 203 908-4848
Westport *(G-10136)*
Perkinelmer Inc .... G 203 925-4600
Shelton *(G-7525)*
Perkinelmer Hlth Sciences Inc .... C 203 925-4600
Shelton *(G-7526)*
Precipio Inc .... G 203 907-2205
New Haven *(G-5370)*
Precipio Inc .... E 402 452-5400
New Haven *(G-5371)*
Spectral LLC .... G 860 928-7726
Putnam *(G-7069)*
Tomtec Inc .... D 203 281-6790
Hamden *(G-3522)*
Trajan Scientific Americas Inc .... G 203 830-4910
Bethel *(G-354)*
Wagner Instruments Inc .... G 203 869-9681
Cos Cob *(G-1643)*
Wentworth Laboratories Inc .... G 203 775-9311
Brookfield *(G-1240)*

INSTRUMENTS: Analyzers, Radio Apparatus, NEC

Gold Line Connector Inc .... E 203 938-2588
Redding *(G-7093)*

INSTRUMENTS: Colonoscopes, Electromedical

Door Step Prep LLC .... G 860 550-0460
West Hartford *(G-9801)*

INSTRUMENTS: Combustion Control, Indl

North Controls Company LLC .... G 860 584-8364
Bristol *(G-1079)*

INSTRUMENTS: Electrolytic Conductivity, Laboratory

Prospect Products Incorporated .... E 860 666-0323
Newington *(G-5698)*

INSTRUMENTS: Electron Test Tube

Fitzhugh Electrical Corp .... G 203 453-3171
Guilford *(G-3352)*

INSTRUMENTS: Electronic, Analog-Digital Converters

ARS Products LLC .... E 860 564-0208
Plainfield *(G-6739)*

INSTRUMENTS: Endoscopic Eqpt, Electromedical

American Dream Unlimited LLC .... G 860 742-5055
Andover *(G-6)*

INSTRUMENTS: Eye Examination

Opticare Health Systems Inc .... C 203 574-2020
Waterbury *(G-9571)*
United Ophthalmics LLC .... G 203 745-8399
Meriden *(G-4259)*

INSTRUMENTS: Flow, Indl Process

Cidra Chemical Management Inc ..... D 203 265-0035
Wallingford *(G-9227)*
Cidra Mineral Processing Inc .... D 203 265-0035
Wallingford *(G-9230)*

INSTRUMENTS: Humidity, Indl Process

WMW LLC .... G 203 227-4992
Weston *(G-10046)*

INSTRUMENTS: Indicating, Electric

Oslo Switch Inc .... E 203 272-2794
Cheshire *(G-1425)*

INSTRUMENTS: Indl Process Control

AKO Inc .... E 860 298-9765
Windsor *(G-10357)*
Alloy Engineering Co Inc .... E 203 366-5253
Bridgeport *(G-685)*
Ametek Inc .... C 203 265-6731
Wallingford *(G-9203)*
Appleton Grp LLC .... E 860 653-1603
East Granby *(G-2190)*
Bristol Babcock Employees Fede ..... G 860 945-2200
Watertown *(G-9687)*
Clinton Instrument Company .... E 860 669-7548
Clinton *(G-1494)*
Devar Inc .... G 203 368-6751
Bridgeport *(G-749)*
Differential Pressure Plus .... G 203 481-2545
Branford *(G-579)*
Emerson Electric Co .... G 203 891-1080
Orange *(G-6598)*
Faria Beede Instruments Inc .... C 860 848-9271
North Stonington *(G-6024)*
Fleet Management LLC .... G 800 722-6654
Enfield *(G-2647)*
GE Steam Power Inc .... G 860 688-1911
Windsor *(G-10391)*
H & B Tool & Engineering Co .... E 860 528-9341
South Windsor *(G-7766)*
Haydon Kerk Mtion Slutions Inc .... C 203 756-7441
Waterbury *(G-9497)*
Idex Health & Science LLC .... C 860 314-2880
Bristol *(G-1050)*
Innovative Components LLC .... G 860 621-7220
Plantsville *(G-6896)*
Johnson Gage Company .... E 860 242-5541
Bloomfield *(G-428)*
Kaman Aerospace Corporation .... C 860 632-1000
Middletown *(G-4360)*
Kde Instrumentation .... G 860 657-2744
Glastonbury *(G-3053)*
Lee Company .... E 860 399-6281
Westbrook *(G-10001)*
Lq Mechatronics Inc .... G 203 433-4430
Branford *(G-619)*
Minteq International Inc .... C 860 824-5435
Canaan *(G-1289)*
National Magnetic Sensors Inc .... G 860 621-6816
Plantsville *(G-6904)*
NDC Technologies Inc .... G 860 635-2100
Middletown *(G-4385)*
Omega Engineering Inc .... G 203 359-7922
Stamford *(G-8340)*
Omega International Corp .... G 203 359-1660
Stamford *(G-8341)*
Projects Inc .... C 860 633-4615
Glastonbury *(G-3075)*
RA Smythe LLC .... G 860 398-5764
Middletown *(G-4401)*
Sperian Protectn Instrumentatn .... C 860 344-1079
Middletown *(G-4422)*
Syba Systems LLC .... G 401 829-0822
Norwich *(G-6433)*
Tek-Air Systems Inc .... E 203 791-1400
Monroe *(G-4758)*
Veeder-Root Company .... D 860 651-2700
Weatogue *(G-9760)*
Vertiv Corporation .... E 203 294-6020
Wallingford *(G-9401)*
Wentworth Laboratories Inc .... G 203 775-9311
Brookfield *(G-1240)*

INSTRUMENTS: Infrared, Indl Process

Singularity Space Systems LLC .... G 860 713-3626
Granby *(G-3114)*

INSTRUMENTS: Laser, Scientific & Engineering

Albrayco Technologies Inc .... G 860 635-3369
Cromwell *(G-1686)*
Swift Scientific LLC .... G 860 498-8577
Coventry *(G-1680)*

INSTRUMENTS: Liquid Level, Indl Process

Floodmaster LLC .... G 203 488-4477
Branford *(G-595)*
Madison Company .... E 203 488-4477
Branford *(G-621)*

INSTRUMENTS: Measuring & Controlling

AC Tek Instruments .... G 203 431-0825
Ridgefield *(G-7114)*
Aftel Corp .... G 203 329-2273
Stamford *(G-8064)*
Ai-Tek Instruments LLC .... E 203 271-6927
Cheshire *(G-1348)*
Anchor Science LLC .... G 203 231-6181
Branford *(G-545)*
Array Systems LLC .... G 203 877-4625
Milford *(G-4457)*
Clinton Instrument Company .... E 860 669-7548
Clinton *(G-1494)*
CMI Time Management LLC .... G 800 722-6654
Enfield *(G-2626)*
Comet Technologies USA Inc .... E 203 447-3200
Shelton *(G-7421)*
Digysol LLC .... G 860 232-1614
West Hartford *(G-9800)*
Edmunds Manufacturing Company ... D 860 677-2813
Farmington *(G-2903)*
Gems Sensors Inc .... F 800 378-1600
Plainville *(G-6816)*
Gold Line Connector Inc .... E 203 938-2588
Redding *(G-7093)*
Habco Industries LLC .... E 860 682-6800
Glastonbury *(G-3045)*
Hitachi Aloka Medical Ltd .... D 203 269-5088
Wallingford *(G-9282)*
Hitachi Aloka Medical Amer Inc .... D 203 269-5088
Wallingford *(G-9283)*
Image Insight Inc .... G 860 528-9806
East Hartford *(G-2337)*
Jovian Technologies .... G 860 896-1539
Ellington *(G-2593)*
Jurman Metrics Inc .... F 203 261-9388
Monroe *(G-4723)*
Kahn and Company Incorporated ..... G 860 529-8643
Wethersfield *(G-10203)*
Lex Products LLC .... C 203 363-3738
Shelton *(G-7490)*
Luxpoint Inc .... G 860 982-9588
Rocky Hill *(G-7255)*
Megasonics Inc .... G 203 966-3404
New Canaan *(G-5120)*
Mistras Group Inc .... E 860 447-2474
Waterford *(G-9663)*
Owlstone Inc .... G 203 908-4848
Westport *(G-10136)*
Pratt Whtney Msurement Systems ... E 860 286-8181
Bloomfield *(G-469)*

PRODUCT SECTION

INSTRUMENTS: Pressure Measurement, Indl

Preferred Utilities Mfg Corp .... D 203 743-6741
  Danbury *(G-1918)*
Semco Instruments Inc .... G 661 362-6117
  Branford *(G-651)*
Soldream Inc .... E 860 871-6883
  Vernon Rockville *(G-9180)*
Specialist Sensor .... G 203 287-9699
  Hamden *(G-3511)*
Specialty Components Inc .... G 203 284-9112
  Wallingford *(G-9374)*
Strain Measurement Devices Inc .... E 203 294-5800
  Wallingford *(G-9377)*
Tek-Air Systems Inc .... E 203 791-1400
  Monroe *(G-4758)*
Trans-Tek Inc .... E 860 872-8351
  Ellington *(G-2608)*
Weigh & Test Systems Inc .... F 203 698-9681
  Riverside *(G-7205)*

INSTRUMENTS: Measuring Electricity

Ashcroft Inc .... E 203 378-8281
  Stratford *(G-8573)*
Bloomy Controls Inc .... E 860 298-9925
  Windsor *(G-10368)*
Bristol Babcock Employees Fede .... G 860 945-2200
  Watertown *(G-9687)*
Clinton Instrument Company .... E 860 669-7548
  Clinton *(G-1494)*
Dictaphone Corporation .... C 203 381-7000
  Stratford *(G-8606)*
Dyadic Innovations LLC .... G 630 738-4113
  Farmington *(G-2900)*
Faria Beede Instruments Inc .... C 860 848-9271
  North Stonington *(G-6024)*
Habco Industries LLC .... E 860 682-6800
  Glastonbury *(G-3045)*
Hoffman Engineering LLC .... D 203 425-8900
  Stamford *(G-8240)*
Image Graphics Inc .... E 203 926-0100
  Shelton *(G-7474)*
Information Security Assoc LLC .... G 203 736-9587
  Seymour *(G-7351)*
KLA Kemp LLC .... G 860 464-6746
  Gales Ferry *(G-2986)*
Nutmeg Utility Products Inc .... E 203 250-8802
  Cheshire *(G-1423)*
Tektronix .... G 203 730-2730
  Danbury *(G-1962)*
Wentworth Laboratories Inc .... G 203 775-0448
  Brookfield *(G-1239)*

INSTRUMENTS: Measuring, Electrical Power

Space Electronics LLC .... E 860 829-0001
  Berlin *(G-221)*

INSTRUMENTS: Medical & Surgical

109 Design LLC .... G 203 941-1812
  New Haven *(G-5215)*
Abbott Associates Inc .... F 203 878-2370
  Milford *(G-4437)*
Acme Monaco Corporation .... C 860 224-1349
  New Britain *(G-4934)*
All Cell Recovery LLC .... G 203 948-2566
  Brookfield *(G-1158)*
AMG Development LLC .... G 203 292-8444
  Westport *(G-10056)*
Ankleaid LLC .... G 860 305-5178
  Ellington *(G-2575)*
Arm Medical Devices Inc .... G 860 583-5165
  Bristol *(G-965)*
Auto Suture Company Australia .... G 203 845-1000
  Norwalk *(G-6081)*
Auto Suture Company UK .... B 203 845-1000
  Norwalk *(G-6082)*
Auto Suture Russia Inc .... G 203 845-1000
  Norwalk *(G-6083)*
Beekley Medical .... G 860 583-4700
  Bristol *(G-979)*
Bio-Med Devices Inc .... D 203 458-0202
  Guilford *(G-3329)*
Boston Endo-Surgical Tech LLC .... D 203 336-6479
  Bridgeport *(G-717)*
Boston Scientific Corporation .... B 860 673-2500
  Avon *(G-78)*
Bridge Innvations Ventures LLC .... G 203 520-8241
  Trumbull *(G-9007)*
Brown Larkin & Co LLC .... G 860 280-8858
  Burlington *(G-1261)*
Butterfly Network Inc .... E 855 296-6188
  Guilford *(G-3336)*
C & W Manufacturing Co Inc .... E 860 633-4631
  Glastonbury *(G-3017)*
C3 Manufacturing LLC .... G 914 943-6877
  New Fairfield *(G-5163)*
Calmare Therapeutics Inc .... G 203 368-6044
  Fairfield *(G-2756)*
Campo Enterprises .... G 203 776-0664
  Hamden *(G-3422)*
Carwild Corporation .... E 860 442-4914
  New London *(G-5461)*
Cas Medical Systems Inc .... G 203 488-1957
  Branford *(G-568)*
Cirtec Medical Corp .... C 860 814-3973
  Enfield *(G-2623)*
Clinical Dynamics Conn LLC .... G 203 269-0090
  Plantsville *(G-6888)*
Coopersurgical Inc .... C 203 601-5200
  Trumbull *(G-9017)*
Covidien Holding Inc .... G 203 492-5000
  North Haven *(G-5927)*
Covidien LP .... B 203 492-6332
  North Haven *(G-5928)*
Covidien LP .... B 781 839-1722
  New Haven *(G-5265)*
Covidien LP .... A 203 492-5000
  North Haven *(G-5929)*
Cygnus Medical LLC .... G 800 990-7489
  Branford *(G-578)*
Dcg-Pmi Inc .... E 203 743-5525
  Bethel *(G-279)*
Delfin Marketing Inc .... G 203 554-2707
  Greenwich *(G-3150)*
Elidah Inc .... G 978 435-4324
  Monroe *(G-4715)*
Eppendorf Manufacturing Corp .... C 860 253-3400
  Enfield *(G-2643)*
First Airway LLC .... G 860 679-9285
  Farmington *(G-2906)*
Frank Roth Co Inc .... D 203 377-2155
  Stratford *(G-8611)*
Gr Enterprises and Tech .... G 203 387-1430
  Woodbridge *(G-10601)*
Graphic Cntrls Acqisition Corp .... E 203 759-1020
  Wolcott *(G-10567)*
Gynion LLC .... G 203 520-8241
  Trumbull *(G-9032)*
Hitachi Aloka Medical Ltd .... D 203 269-5088
  Wallingford *(G-9282)*
Hitachi Aloka Medical Amer Inc .... D 203 269-5088
  Wallingford *(G-9283)*
Hobbs Medical Inc .... E 860 684-5875
  Stafford Springs *(G-8031)*
Hologic Inc .... C 203 790-1188
  Danbury *(G-1845)*
Home Diagnostics Corp .... C 203 445-1170
  Trumbull *(G-9035)*
Johnson & Johnson .... G 860 621-9111
  Southington *(G-7945)*
Kbc Electronics Inc .... F 203 298-9654
  Milford *(G-4563)*
Kenzinc LLC .... G 203 307-5369
  Shelton *(G-7484)*
Lambdavision Incorporated .... G 860 486-6593
  Farmington *(G-2923)*
Lee Company .... A 860 399-6281
  Westbrook *(G-10000)*
Liberty Products Inc .... G 860 829-2122
  Berlin *(G-194)*
Life Warmer Inc .... G 860 204-1711
  Canton *(G-1317)*
Lumendi LLC .... G 203 528-0316
  Westport *(G-10114)*
Marel Corporation .... F 203 934-8187
  West Haven *(G-9932)*
Medi Products .... G 203 324-3711
  Stamford *(G-8303)*
Medtronic Inc .... E 203 492-5764
  North Haven *(G-5962)*
Medtronic Xomed Inc .... E 860 572-9586
  Mystic *(G-4832)*
Memry Corporation .... C 203 739-1100
  Bethel *(G-326)*
Memry Corporation .... G 203 739-1146
  Bethel *(G-327)*
Monopol Corporation .... F 860 583-3852
  Danbury *(G-1073)*
Natural Polymer Devices Inc .... G 860 679-7894
  Farmington *(G-2934)*
New Wave Surgical Corp .... E 954 796-4126
  New Haven *(G-5349)*
Newmark Inc .... G 203 272-1158
  Cheshire *(G-1422)*
Oral Fluid Dynamics LLC .... G 860 561-5036
  Farmington *(G-2941)*
Orthozon Technologies LLC .... G 203 989-4937
  Stamford *(G-8346)*
Oxford Science Inc .... F 203 881-3115
  Oxford *(G-6685)*
Oxford Science Center LLC .... G 203 751-1912
  Oxford *(G-6686)*
Precision Engineered Pdts LLC .... G 203 336-6479
  Bridgeport *(G-878)*
Precision Metal Products Inc .... C 203 877-4258
  Milford *(G-4612)*
Respironics Novametrix LLC .... C 203 697-6475
  Wallingford *(G-9351)*
Retinographics Inc .... G 203 853-1735
  Norwalk *(G-6322)*
S-Y-M Products Company LLC .... F 203 329-2469
  Litchfield *(G-3899)*
Saar Corporation .... F 860 674-9440
  Farmington *(G-2955)*
SEI II Inc .... F 203 877-8488
  Milford *(G-4641)*
Sequel Special Products LLC .... E 203 759-1020
  Wolcott *(G-10589)*
Smiths Medical Asd Inc .... B 860 621-9111
  Southington *(G-7975)*
Soft Tissue Regeneration Inc .... G 973 879-6367
  New Haven *(G-5398)*
Spine Wave Inc .... D 203 944-9494
  Shelton *(G-7558)*
Stryker Corporation .... F 860 528-1111
  East Hartford *(G-2379)*
Summit Orthopedic Tech Inc .... E 203 693-2727
  Milford *(G-4655)*
Surgiquest Inc .... D 203 799-2400
  Milford *(G-4658)*
Tarry Medical Products Inc .... F 203 794-1438
  Danbury *(G-1960)*
Tomtec .... G 203 795-5030
  Orange *(G-6631)*
Tyco International MGT Co LLC .... G 203 492-5000
  North Haven *(G-6003)*
Ultimate Wireforms Inc .... D 860 582-9111
  Bristol *(G-1134)*
Utitec Inc .... D 860 945-0605
  Watertown *(G-9744)*
Utitec Holdings Inc .... G 860 945-0601
  Watertown *(G-9745)*
Wallach Surgical Devices Inc .... E 203 799-2000
  Trumbull *(G-9094)*
Wallach Surgical Devices Inc .... F 800 243-2463
  Trumbull *(G-9095)*
Winslow Automatics Inc .... D 860 225-6321
  New Britain *(G-5084)*

INSTRUMENTS: Meteorological

Airflo Instrument Company .... G 860 633-9455
  Glastonbury *(G-3005)*

INSTRUMENTS: Meters, Integrating Electricity

Nutmeg Energy Savers .... G 203 733-0147
  Bethel *(G-330)*

INSTRUMENTS: Nautical

Drs Naval Power Systems Inc .... B 203 798-3000
  Danbury *(G-1800)*

INSTRUMENTS: Photographic, Electronic

Macroscopic Solutions LLC .... G 410 870-5566
  Tolland *(G-8869)*

INSTRUMENTS: Power Measuring, Electrical

Solar Data Systems Inc .... F 203 702-7189
  Bethel *(G-345)*

INSTRUMENTS: Pressure Measurement, Indl

Orange Research Inc .... D 203 877-5657
  Milford *(G-4598)*
PMC Engineering LLC .... E 203 792-8686
  Danbury *(G-1909)*
Precision Sensors Inc .... E 203 877-2795
  Milford *(G-4613)*

Employee Codes: A=Over 500 employees, B=251-500
C=101-250, D=51-100, E=20-50, F=10-19, G=1-9

INSTRUMENTS: Pressure Measurement, Indl

United Electric Controls Co .... D 203 877-2795
  Milford *(G-4668)*

INSTRUMENTS: Radar Testing, Electric
Energy Tech LLC .... G 860 345-3993
  Haddam *(G-3404)*

INSTRUMENTS: Radio Frequency Measuring
AMS Strategic Management Inc .... G 845 500-5635
  Stamford *(G-8083)*
Ets-Lindgren Inc .... G 203 838-4555
  Norwalk *(G-6158)*

INSTRUMENTS: Temperature Measurement, Indl
Microtechnologies Inc .... G 860 517-8314
  Farmington *(G-2929)*
Moeller Instrument Company Inc .... E 800 243-9310
  Ivoryton *(G-3786)*
Omega Engineering Inc .... C 203 359-1660
  Norwalk *(G-6284)*

INSTRUMENTS: Test, Electrical, Engine
MB Systems LLC .... G 203 881-1583
  Seymour *(G-7356)*
Test Logic Inc .... F 860 347-8378
  Middletown *(G-4425)*

INSTRUMENTS: Test, Electronic & Electric Measurement
AKO Inc .... E 860 298-9765
  Windsor *(G-10357)*
All-Test Pro LLC .... F 860 399-4222
  Old Saybrook *(G-6522)*
International Contact Tech .... E 203 264-5757
  Southbury *(G-7862)*
International Instruments Div .... G 203 481-3450
  North Branford *(G-5845)*
Kahn and Company Incorporated .... G 860 529-8643
  Wethersfield *(G-10203)*
Madison Tstg Acqstion Svcs LLC .... G 203 421-9388
  Madison *(G-3938)*

INSTRUMENTS: Test, Electronic & Electrical Circuits
Microtools Inc .... G 860 651-6170
  Simsbury *(G-7635)*

INSTRUMENTS: Testing, Semiconductor
Wentworth Laboratories Inc .... G 203 775-9311
  Brookfield *(G-1240)*

INSTRUMENTS: Thermal Conductive, Indl
Solar Generations LLC .... G 203 453-3920
  Guilford *(G-3392)*

INSTRUMENTS: Transducers, Volts, Amperes, Watts, VARs & Freq
Trans-Tek Inc .... E 860 872-8351
  Ellington *(G-2608)*

INSTRUMENTS: Vibration
Unholtz-Dickie Corporation .... E 203 265-9875
  Wallingford *(G-9395)*

INSULATING COMPOUNDS
East Coast Insulation LLC .... G 302 685-3152
  Meriden *(G-4168)*
Lydall Inc .... E 860 646-1233
  Manchester *(G-4050)*

INSULATION & CUSHIONING FOAM: Polystyrene
Claremont Sales Corporation .... E 860 349-4499
  Durham *(G-2143)*
Extreme Foam Insulations LLC .... G 203 522-2207
  Bridgeport *(G-767)*
Foam Plastics New England Inc .... G 203 758-6651
  Waterbury *(G-9481)*
H-O Products Corporation .... E 860 379-9875
  Winsted *(G-10523)*

Sprayfoampolymerscom LLC .... G 800 853-1577
  Wilton *(G-10333)*
Vibrascience Inc .... G 203 483-6113
  Branford *(G-666)*

INSULATION MATERIALS WHOLESALERS
Vibrascience Inc .... G 203 483-6113
  Branford *(G-666)*

INSULATION: Fiberglass
Ecologic Energy Solutions LLC .... E 203 889-0505
  Stamford *(G-8192)*
Installed Building Pdts Inc .... G 203 889-0505
  Stamford *(G-8251)*
The E J Davis Company .... E 203 239-5391
  North Haven *(G-5998)*

INSULATORS, PORCELAIN: Electrical
Newco Condenser Inc .... G 475 882-4000
  Shelton *(G-7510)*

INSURANCE CARRIERS: Dental
Essel Dental .... G 860 254-6955
  East Windsor *(G-2492)*

INTEGRATED CIRCUITS, SEMICONDUCTOR NETWORKS, ETC
Alacrity Semiconductors Inc .... G 475 325-8435
  Branford *(G-540)*
Metis Microsystems LLC .... G 203 512-8453
  Newtown *(G-5760)*
Photronics Inc .... B 203 775-9000
  Brookfield *(G-1211)*

INTERCOMMUNICATIONS SYSTEMS: Electric
AMS Strategic Management Inc .... G 845 500-5635
  Stamford *(G-8083)*
Applied Physical Sciences Corp .... D 860 448-3253
  Groton *(G-3271)*
Datacomm Management Svcs LLC ...... G 203 858-9846
  Darien *(G-2020)*
Farmington River Holdings LLC .... G 203 777-2130
  Hamden *(G-3447)*
Voice Express Corp .... G 203 221-7799
  Fairfield *(G-2865)*

INTERIOR DECORATING SVCS
Custom Upholstery Workshop .... G 203 367-4231
  Fairfield *(G-2770)*

INTERIOR DESIGN SVCS, NEC
Creative Enhancement Inc .... E 860 833-8493
  West Hartford *(G-9795)*
Kilcourse Specialty Products .... G 860 210-2075
  New Milford *(G-5555)*

INVERTERS: Nonrotating Electrical
Sober Touch Sensoring LLC .... G 203 540-2486
  Ansonia *(G-51)*

INVESTMENT ADVISORY SVCS
Baxter Bros Inc .... G 203 637-4559
  Greenwich *(G-3130)*
Compass Group Management LLC ...... F 203 221-1703
  Westport *(G-10068)*
Eagle Investment Systems LLC .... F 860 561-4602
  West Hartford *(G-9803)*
Phraction Management LLC .... G 860 531-9590
  Colchester *(G-1565)*
Timer Digest Publishing Inc .... G 203 629-2589
  Greenwich *(G-3245)*

INVESTMENT BANKERS
Stamford Capital Group Inc .... A 800 977-7837
  Stamford *(G-8436)*

INVESTMENT COUNSELORS
Geneve Corporation .... E 203 358-8000
  Stamford *(G-8215)*

INVESTMENT FUNDS, NEC
L & L Capital Partners LLC .... F 203 834-6222
  Wilton *(G-10307)*

INVESTMENT FUNDS: Open-Ended
Eagle Investment Systems LLC .... F 860 561-4602
  West Hartford *(G-9803)*

INVESTMENT RESEARCH SVCS
Ihs Herold Inc .... D 203 857-0215
  Norwalk *(G-6204)*

INVESTORS, NEC
American Wind Capital Co LLC .... G 860 767-1579
  Essex *(G-2711)*
TD&s Acquisition LLC .... G 860 341-1001
  Middletown *(G-4424)*

IRON & STEEL PRDTS: Hot-Rolled
Ccr Products LLC .... E 860 953-0499
  West Hartford *(G-9786)*
Gerdau Ameristeel US Inc .... G 860 351-9029
  Plainville *(G-6817)*

IRON ORE PELLETIZING
Farrel Corporation .... D 203 736-5500
  Ansonia *(G-34)*

IRON ORES
Iron Oxen Network Comm .... G 203 228-2556
  Oxford *(G-6669)*

JACKETS: Indl, Metal Plate
Thermaxx LLC .... G 203 672-1021
  West Haven *(G-9959)*

JACKS: Hydraulic
Richard Dudgeon Inc .... G 203 336-4459
  Waterbury *(G-9593)*

JANITORIAL & CUSTODIAL SVCS
Front Line Apparel Group LLC .... C 860 859-3524
  Hebron *(G-3749)*

JANITORIAL EQPT & SPLYS WHOLESALERS
Edsan Chemical Company Inc .... C 203 624-3123
  New Haven *(G-5273)*

JARS: Plastic
Colts Plastics Company Inc .... C 860 774-2277
  Dayville *(G-2058)*

JEWELRY & PRECIOUS STONES WHOLESALERS
AG Jewelry Designs LLC .... G 800 643-0978
  Stamford *(G-8065)*
AG Jewelry Designs LLC .... G 800 643-0978
  Norwalk *(G-6063)*
Wenger Na Inc .... G 845 365-3500
  Monroe *(G-4764)*

JEWELRY APPAREL
Asha .... G 203 253-0146
  Greenwich *(G-3124)*
Gregmans Inc .... G 203 464-2530
  Milford *(G-4543)*
J J Lane Designs .... G 860 849-0815
  Suffield *(G-8722)*

JEWELRY FINDINGS & LAPIDARY WORK
Boxtree Accessories Inc .... G 203 637-5794
  Old Greenwich *(G-6468)*
Ncc .... G 203 966-8307
  Sandy Hook *(G-7323)*
Yankee Mineral & Gem Co .... G 860 267-0167
  East Hampton *(G-2284)*

JEWELRY REPAIR SVCS
Arpie Krisie Gems & Jewelry .... G 203 799-8927
  Orange *(G-6583)*

Dantes Jewelry & Repair .... G 860 346-4779
  Middletown (G-4335)
Goldworks .... G 203 743-9668
  Danbury (G-1833)
Johannes Sulek Jewelry .... G 203 968-1729
  Stamford (G-8267)
Joseph Hannoush Family Inc .... F 860 561-4651
  Farmington (G-2921)
N Karpel Studio LLC .... G 203 782-9108
  New Haven (G-5338)
Swedes Jewelers Inc .... G 860 623-3916
  East Windsor (G-2525)

JEWELRY STORES

Goldworks .... G 203 743-9668
  Danbury (G-1833)
J J Lane Designs .... G 860 849-0815
  Suffield (G-8722)
Joseph A Cnte Mfg Jewelers Inc .... G 203 248-9853
  Hamden (G-3469)
Nancy Dighello .... G 860 763-4294
  Enfield (G-2665)

JEWELRY STORES: Clocks

Taylors Luggage Inc .... G 203 966-9961
  New Canaan (G-5150)

JEWELRY STORES: Precious Stones & Precious Metals

A&D Schneider LLC .... G 203 870-9474
  Stratford (G-8563)
Buisson Jewelers Inc .... G 203 869-8895
  Greenwich (G-3139)
Dexter & Co .... G 860 536-9506
  Mystic (G-4811)
Elm City Mfg Jewelers Inc .... G 203 248-2195
  Hamden (G-3444)
Jewelry Designs Inc .... E 203 797-0389
  Danbury (G-1861)
Joseph Hannoush Family Inc .... F 860 561-4651
  Farmington (G-2921)
Kasson Jewelers of Southport .... G 203 319-0021
  Southport (G-8005)
Silver Little Shop Inc .... G 860 678-1976
  Avon (G-112)
Swedes Jewelers Inc .... G 860 623-3916
  East Windsor (G-2525)
Vincent Jewelers .... G 203 882-8900
  Milford (G-4674)

JEWELRY STORES: Silverware

Silversmith Inc .... G 203 869-4244
  Greenwich (G-3235)

JEWELRY, PRECIOUS METAL: Cases

Mrk Fine Arts LLC .... G 203 972-3115
  New Canaan (G-5122)

JEWELRY, PRECIOUS METAL: Pearl, Natural Or Cultured

Dawn Hill Enterprises LLC .... G 860 496-9188
  Torrington (G-8917)

JEWELRY, WHOLESALE

Dawn Hill Enterprises LLC .... G 860 496-9188
  Torrington (G-8917)
Elm City Mfg Jewelers Inc .... G 203 248-2195
  Hamden (G-3444)
Johannes Sulek Jewelry .... G 203 968-1729
  Stamford (G-8267)
M H Pierce & Co .... G 203 327-2970
  Stamford (G-8293)
Tommys Supplies LLC .... G 860 265-2199
  Somers (G-7674)

JEWELRY: Decorative, Fashion & Costume

Beadazzle .... G 860 747-5101
  Plainville (G-6776)
Buisson Jewelers Inc .... G 203 869-8895
  Greenwich (G-3139)
Crista Grasso LLC .... G 347 946-2533
  Tolland (G-8856)
Designs By Diana .... G 860 649-1812
  Manchester (G-4006)
Gabriel Inc .... G 860 824-1412
  Falls Village (G-2870)
Glitzy Lady .... G 203 924-5663
  Shelton (G-7450)
K2steam .... G 860 251-9824
  Avon (G-86)
Mix Box .... G 203 591-8887
  Waterbury (G-9546)
Potters Ink Inc .... G 860 896-5909
  Vernon Rockville (G-9176)
Smiling Dog .... G 860 344-0707
  Middletown (G-4419)
Swarovski North America Ltd .... G 203 462-3357
  Stamford (G-8453)
Swarovski North America Ltd .... G 203 372-0336
  Trumbull (G-9080)

JEWELRY: Precious Metal

A&D Schneider LLC .... G 203 870-9474
  Stratford (G-8563)
AG Jewelry Designs LLC .... G 800 643-0978
  Stamford (G-8065)
AG Jewelry Designs LLC .... G 800 643-0978
  Norwalk (G-6063)
Arpie Krisie Gems & Jewelry .... G 203 799-8927
  Orange (G-6583)
Beautybrain Bracelet LLC .... G 203 245-8913
  Madison (G-3910)
Brannkey Inc .... E 860 510-0501
  Old Saybrook (G-6525)
Carol Ackerman Designs .... G 860 693-1013
  Collinsville (G-1590)
Chainmail & More LLC .... G 860 741-2965
  Enfield (G-2622)
Dantes Jewelry & Repair .... G 860 346-4779
  Middletown (G-4335)
Elm City Mfg Jewelers Inc .... G 203 248-2195
  Hamden (G-3444)
Emilie Cohen .... G 860 693-9427
  Collinsville (G-1594)
Gabriel Inc .... G 860 824-1412
  Falls Village (G-2870)
Gemma Oro Inc .... G 203 227-0774
  Westport (G-10088)
George S Preisner Jewelers .... G 203 265-0057
  Wallingford (G-9275)
Goldworks .... G 203 743-9668
  Danbury (G-1833)
Herff Jones LLC .... F 203 368-9344
  Stratford (G-8624)
House of Bubba LLC .... G 860 429-4250
  Willington (G-10250)
Jewelry Designs Inc .... E 203 797-0389
  Danbury (G-1861)
Johannes Sulek Jewelry .... G 203 968-1729
  Stamford (G-8267)
Joseph A Cnte Mfg Jewelers Inc .... G 203 248-9853
  Hamden (G-3469)
Joseph Hannoush Family Inc .... F 860 561-4651
  Farmington (G-2921)
Karavas Fashions Ltd .... F 203 866-4000
  Norwalk (G-6228)
Kasson Jewelers of Southport .... G 203 319-0021
  Southport (G-8005)
Kenneth R Carson .... G 860 247-2707
  Manchester (G-4044)
Lfbw LLC .... G 203 966-8499
  New Canaan (G-5114)
N Karpel Studio LLC .... G 203 782-9108
  New Haven (G-5338)
O C Tanner Company .... G 203 944-5430
  Shelton (G-7516)
Odyssey Jewelry .... G 203 574-4956
  Waterbury (G-9568)
Russell Amy Kahn .... F 203 438-2133
  Ridgefield (G-7169)
Silver Little Shop Inc .... G 860 678-1976
  Avon (G-112)
Silversmith Inc .... G 203 869-4244
  Greenwich (G-3235)
Swedes Jewelers Inc .... G 860 623-3916
  East Windsor (G-2525)
Tabar Designs .... G 203 453-8868
  Guilford (G-3397)

JIGS & FIXTURES

Apex Machine Tool Company Inc .... D 860 677-2884
  Cheshire (G-1353)
Astro Industries Inc .... G 860 828-6304
  Berlin (G-161)
F J Weidner Inc .... G 203 469-4202
  East Haven (G-2425)
Gary Tool Company .... G 203 377-3077
  Stratford (G-8616)
Hartford Gauge Co .... G 860 233-9619
  West Hartford (G-9817)
M & R Manufacturing Inc .... G 860 666-5066
  Newington (G-5673)
Sirois Tool Company Inc .... D 860 828-5327
  Berlin (G-220)

JOB PRINTING & NEWSPAPER PUBLISHING COMBINED

Cromwell Chronicle .... G 860 257-8715
  Rocky Hill (G-7229)
Glastonbury Citizen Inc .... E 860 633-4691
  Glastonbury (G-3040)
Lakeville Journal Company LLC .... D 860 435-9873
  Lakeville (G-3845)
Middlbury Bee-Intelligencer-Ct .... G 203 577-6800
  Middlebury (G-4284)
Record-Journal Newspaper .... G 860 536-9577
  Mystic (G-4841)

JOB TRAINING & VOCATIONAL REHABILITATION SVCS

3 Ethos LLC .... G 860 415-9191
  Mystic (G-4794)

JOB TRAINING SVCS

Advanced Vacuum Technology Inc ...... G 860 653-4176
  Simsbury (G-7609)
Park Group Solutions LLC .... G 203 459-8784
  Newtown (G-5769)

KAOLIN & BALL CLAY MINING

Sandballz International LLC .... G 860 465-9628
  Storrs Mansfield (G-8560)

KEYBOARDS: Computer Or Office Machine

Precision Electronic Assembly .... F 203 452-1839
  Monroe (G-4747)

KITCHEN & COOKING ARTICLES: Pottery

Cornwall Bridge Pottery Inc .... G 860 672-6545
  Warren (G-9407)
Tonmar LLC .... G 860 974-3714
  Pomfret Center (G-6947)

KITCHEN ARTICLES: Semivitreous Earthenware

Express Cntertops Kit Flrg LLC .... G 203 283-4909
  Orange (G-6599)

KITCHEN CABINET STORES, EXC CUSTOM

East Hartford Lamination Co .... G 860 633-4637
  Glastonbury (G-3029)
Martin Cabinet Inc .... E 860 747-5769
  Plainville (G-6840)
Royal Woodcraft Inc .... F 203 847-3461
  Ansonia (G-49)

KITCHEN CABINETS WHOLESALERS

A -Line Custom Counter Top .... G 860 747-1917
  Plainville (G-6758)
A Matter of Style LLC .... G 203 272-1337
  Cheshire (G-1345)
Master Craft Kitchens .... G 203 366-1461
  Bridgeport (G-832)
Professional Trades Netwrk LLC .... G 860 567-0173
  Watertown (G-9726)
S J Pappas Inc .... G 203 237-7701
  Meriden (G-4236)
Viking Kitchen Cabinets LLC .... E 860 223-7101
  New Britain (G-5080)
Yankee Finishing .... G 203 910-0645
  Newington (G-5724)

KITCHEN TOOLS & UTENSILS WHOLESALERS

Airigan Solutions LLC .... G 203 594-7781
  Southport (G-7998)

KITCHEN UTENSILS: Market Baskets, Wood

Mc Cann Bros Inc....................E........ 203 335-8630
Monroe *(G-4734)*

KITCHENWARE: Plastic

Rapid Slicer LLC ....G........ 203 610-3673
Shelton *(G-7543)*
Tops Manufacturing Co Inc ......G........ 203 655-9367
Darien *(G-2047)*

KNIT GOODS, WHOLESALE

Baby Knits and More ....G........ 860 485-0146
Harwinton *(G-3721)*

LABELS: Cotton, Printed

Sterling Name Tape Company ....G........ 860 379-5142
Winsted *(G-10540)*

LABELS: Paper, Made From Purchased Materials

Biomerics LLC.........................D........ 203 268-7238
Monroe *(G-4698)*
Flexo Label Solutions LLC........G........ 860 243-9300
Deep River *(G-2089)*
Specialty Printing LLC..............D........ 860 623-8870
East Windsor *(G-2521)*

LABORATORIES, TESTING: Metallurgical

Pti Industries Inc......................E........ 800 318-8438
Enfield *(G-2683)*

LABORATORIES, TESTING: Pollution

Park City Packaging Inc............F........ 203 579-1965
Bridgeport *(G-862)*

LABORATORIES, TESTING: Product Testing

AKO Inc..................................E........ 860 298-9765
Windsor *(G-10357)*
F S P Research Inc..................G........ 203 874-3417
Milford *(G-4534)*
Sousa Corp............................F........ 860 523-9090
Newington *(G-5706)*

LABORATORIES, TESTING: Product Testing, Safety/Performance

Connecticut Breaker Co Inc......G........ 203 378-2240
Stratford *(G-8597)*

LABORATORIES, TESTING: Radiation

Nats Inc..................................F........ 860 635-6820
Middletown *(G-4384)*
Radiation Safety Assoc Inc......G........ 860 228-0721
Hebron *(G-3754)*

LABORATORIES, TESTING: Soil Analysis

Macroscopic Solutions LLC......G........ 410 870-5566
Tolland *(G-8869)*

LABORATORIES: Biological Research

Aptuit Global LLC ....G........ 203 660-6000
Greenwich *(G-3122)*
Brain Institute of America LLC ..G........ 860 967-5937
Groton *(G-3273)*
Precipio Inc.............................E........ 402 452-5400
New Haven *(G-5371)*

LABORATORIES: Biotechnology

Achillion Pharmaceuticals Inc....D........ 203 624-7000
New Haven *(G-5219)*
Arvinas Inc..............................F........ 203 535-1456
New Haven *(G-5234)*

LABORATORIES: Commercial Nonphysical Research

Dimension Zero Ltd ....G........ 860 325-7073
Willimantic *(G-10224)*

LABORATORIES: Dental

Mark D Tweedie DDS ....G........ 860 649-0436
Manchester *(G-4056)*

LABORATORIES: Electronic Research

Connecticut Analytical Corp......F........ 203 393-9666
Bethany *(G-239)*
Doltronics LLC ....E........ 203 488-8766
Branford *(G-580)*
Electronic Design Lab Inc........G........ 203 790-0500
Bethel *(G-296)*
GE Steam Power Inc...............C........ 423 648-4161
Windsor *(G-10389)*
Madison Technology Intl ....G........ 860 245-0245
Mystic *(G-4830)*

LABORATORIES: Noncommercial Research

Thoughtventions Unlimited LLC ....G........ 860 657-9014
Glastonbury *(G-3086)*

LABORATORIES: Physical Research, Commercial

Accustandard Inc.....................D........ 203 786-5290
New Haven *(G-5218)*
Cara Therapeutics Inc.............E........ 203 406-3700
Stamford *(G-8127)*
Charles River Laboratories Inc...........E........ 860 429-7261
Storrs *(G-8546)*
Cytec Industries Inc.................D........ 203 321-2200
Stamford *(G-8176)*
Hampford Research Inc..........E........ 203 375-1137
Stratford *(G-8622)*
Henkel Loctite Corporation......E........ 860 571-5100
Rocky Hill *(G-7245)*
Herbasway Laboratories LLC .....E........ 203 269-6991
Wallingford *(G-9280)*
Jet Process Corporation ....G........ 203 985-6000
North Haven *(G-5953)*
Pfizer Inc.................................E........ 860 441-4000
Groton *(G-3306)*
Spectrogram Corporation ....G........ 203 245-2433
Madison *(G-3960)*
Supercool Metals LLC ....G........ 203 823-9032
New Haven *(G-5404)*

LABORATORIES: Testing

Acuren Inspection Inc..............A........ 203 702-8740
Danbury *(G-1731)*

LABORATORIES: Testing

Enginuity Plm LLC...................F........ 203 218-7225
Milford *(G-4532)*
Greywall Inc............................G........ 860 267-6177
East Hampton *(G-2262)*
Hoffman Engineering LLC........D........ 203 425-8900
Stamford *(G-8240)*
Precipio Inc.............................E........ 402 452-5400
New Haven *(G-5371)*

LABORATORY APPARATUS & FURNITURE

Fmp Products..........................G........ 203 422-0686
Greenwich *(G-3164)*
Idex Health & Science LLC......C........ 860 314-2880
Bristol *(G-1050)*
Mark V Laboratory Inc.............G........ 860 653-7201
East Granby *(G-2211)*
Novatech................................G........ 860 871-4180
Tolland *(G-8874)*
Proteowise Inc........................G........ 203 430-4187
Branford *(G-638)*
Tomtec Inc..............................D........ 203 281-6790
Hamden *(G-3522)*

LABORATORY APPARATUS: Calibration Tapes, Phy Testing Mach

Environics Inc ....E........ 860 872-1111
Tolland *(G-8863)*

LABORATORY APPARATUS: Shakers & Stirrers

Eppendorf Holding Inc.............E........ 860 253-3417
Enfield *(G-2642)*

LABORATORY CHEMICALS: Organic

Dragonlab LLC........................G........ 860 436-9221
Rocky Hill *(G-7235)*
RT Vanderbilt Holding Co Inc...F........ 203 295-2141
Norwalk *(G-6331)*

Yale University ....G........ 203 432-3916
New Haven *(G-5447)*

LABORATORY EQPT: Balances

CFM Test & Balance Corp ....G........ 203 778-1900
Bethel *(G-269)*

LABORATORY EQPT: Centrifuges

Dragonlab LLC........................G........ 860 436-9221
Rocky Hill *(G-7235)*

LABORATORY EQPT: Chemical

Novamont North America Inc ...F........ 203 744-8801
Shelton *(G-7514)*

LABORATORY EQPT: Clinical Instruments Exc Medical

Bioclinica Inc...........................G........ 860 701-0082
New London *(G-5458)*

LABORATORY EQPT: Measuring

Ancera Inc..............................G........ 203 819-2322
Branford *(G-544)*

LABORATORY EQPT: Sterilizers

Mayborn Usa Inc.....................F........ 781 269-7490
Stamford *(G-8298)*

LACQUERING SVC: Metal Prdts

Baron & Young Co Inc.............G........ 860 589-3235
Bristol *(G-976)*

LADDERS: Permanent Installation, Metal

Jacobs Ladder........................G........ 203 833-2227
Naugatuck *(G-4894)*

LAMINATED PLASTICS: Plate, Sheet, Rod & Tubes

Beckson Manufacturing Inc .....E........ 203 366-3644
Bridgeport *(G-709)*
CT Composites & Marine Svc LLC ....G........ 860 282-0100
South Windsor *(G-7738)*
Cytec Industries Inc.................C........ 203 284-4334
Wallingford *(G-9245)*
Diba Industries Inc..................C........ 203 744-0773
Danbury *(G-1795)*
Panolam Industries Inc...........E........ 203 925-1556
Shelton *(G-7522)*
Pioneer Plastics Corporation...D........ 203 925-1556
Shelton *(G-7527)*
Polymedex Discovery Group Inc ....F........ 860 928-4102
Putnam *(G-7059)*
Quality Name Plate Inc............D........ 860 633-9495
East Glastonbury *(G-2185)*
The E J Davis Company ....E........ 203 239-5391
North Haven *(G-5998)*

LAMINATING SVCS

Flagship Converters Inc..........D........ 203 792-0034
Danbury *(G-1826)*
John L Prentis & Co Inc..........G........ 203 634-1266
Meriden *(G-4178)*
Technical Reproductions Inc ...F........ 203 849-9100
Norwalk *(G-6365)*
United Enterprises Inc.............G........ 860 225-9955
New Britain *(G-5078)*

LAMP & LIGHT BULBS & TUBES

Brian Cody..............................G........ 203 331-7382
Stratford *(G-8586)*
Electro-Lite Corporation ....F........ 203 743-4059
Bethel *(G-295)*
Grigerek Co............................G........ 860 677-2560
Farmington *(G-2914)*
Voltarc Technologies Inc.........G........ 203 753-6366
Waterbury *(G-9624)*
Whelen Engineering Company Inc.......B........ 860 526-9504
Chester *(G-1485)*

LAMP BULBS & TUBES, ELECTRIC: For Specialized Applications
Southern Neng Ultraviolet Inc .... G 203 483-5810
  Branford *(G-654)*

LAMP BULBS & TUBES, ELECTRIC: Light, Complete
Revolution Lighting .... G 203 504-1111
  Stamford *(G-8388)*
Revolution Lighting Tech Inc .... C 203 504-1111
  Stamford *(G-8389)*

LAMP BULBS & TUBES/PARTS, ELECTRIC: Generalized Applications
Lcd Lighting Inc .... C 203 799-7877
  Orange *(G-6610)*

LAMP FIXTURES: Ultraviolet
Incure Inc .... G 860 748-2979
  New Britain *(G-4998)*

LAMP SHADES: Metal
Bb Shades .... G 203 849-9345
  Westport *(G-10060)*

LAMP STORES
Keeling Company Inc .... G 860 349-0916
  Old Lyme *(G-6514)*
Vijon Studios Inc .... G 860 399-7440
  Old Saybrook *(G-6576)*

LAMPS: Ultraviolet
Light Sources Inc .... C 203 799-7877
  Orange *(G-6611)*
Triton Thalassic Tech Inc .... G 203 438-0633
  Ridgefield *(G-7177)*
Uv Inc .... G 203 333-1031
  Woodbridge *(G-10620)*

LAND SUBDIVISION & DEVELOPMENT
Richard Riggio and Sons Inc .... E 860 767-0812
  Ivoryton *(G-3789)*

LAPIDARY WORK: Contract Or Other
International Mines Outlet .... G 203 264-9207
  Southbury *(G-7863)*

LAPIDARY WORK: Jewel Cut, Drill, Polish, Recut/Setting
Opal Manning Company Inc .... G 203 292-6981
  Fairfield *(G-2825)*

LASER SYSTEMS & EQPT
Advanced Photonics Intl Inc .... G 203 259-0437
  Fairfield *(G-2745)*
Coherent-Deos LLC .... C 860 243-9557
  Bloomfield *(G-405)*
Hamar Laser Instruments Inc .... E 203 730-4600
  Danbury *(G-1841)*
Medical Laser Systems Inc .... G 203 481-2395
  Branford *(G-625)*
Quality Scanning Solution .... G 203 270-1833
  Newtown *(G-5771)*
Total Register Inc .... F 860 210-0465
  New Milford *(G-5600)*

LASERS: Welding, Drilling & Cutting Eqpt
Cadence Ct Inc .... D 860 370-9780
  Suffield *(G-8716)*
Epilog Lasers of New England .... G 203 405-1124
  Woodbury *(G-10635)*
Varnum Enterprises LLC .... F 203 743-4443
  Bethel *(G-362)*

LATEX: Foamed
Ktt Enterprises LLC .... G 203 288-7883
  Hamden *(G-3470)*
Latex Foam Intl Holdings Inc .... C 203 924-0700
  Shelton *(G-7488)*
Universal Foam Products LLC .... F 860 216-3015
  Bloomfield *(G-496)*

LATHES
Rbk Lathe LLC .... G 860 321-7243
  Farmington *(G-2953)*

LAUNDRY & GARMENT SVCS, NEC: Garment Alteration & Repair
Jennifers Tailor Shop .... G 860 489-8968
  Torrington *(G-8938)*

LAUNDRY EQPT: Commercial
Sea-Lion America Company .... G 860 316-5563
  Middletown *(G-4408)*
Sumal Enterprises LLC .... G 860 945-3337
  Watertown *(G-9739)*

LAUNDRY EQPT: Household
Instinctive Works LLC .... G 203 434-8094
  Westport *(G-10101)*

LAUNDRY SVCS: Indl
A & P Coat Apron & Lin Sup Inc .... D 914 840-3200
  Hartford *(G-3542)*

LAWN & GARDEN EQPT
Dirt Guy Topsoil .... G 860 303-0500
  Durham *(G-2145)*
Fortified Holdings Corp .... G 203 594-1686
  Norwalk *(G-6171)*
Greenscape of Clinton LLC .... G 860 669-1880
  Clinton *(G-1506)*
Woodland Power Products Inc .... E 888 531-7253
  West Haven *(G-9966)*

LAWN & GARDEN EQPT: Lawnmowers, Residential, Hand Or Power
Worth Properties LLC .... G 203 281-1792
  Hamden *(G-3531)*

LAWN MOWER REPAIR SHOP
Darien Lawn Mower Repair .... G 203 656-1869
  Darien *(G-2018)*
W H Preuss Sons Incorporated .... G 860 643-9492
  Bolton *(G-521)*

LEAD
Alent USA Holding Inc .... B 203 575-5727
  Waterbury *(G-9426)*

LEAD PENCILS & ART GOODS
Bic Corporation .... A 203 783-2000
  Shelton *(G-7407)*

LEAF TOBACCO WHOLESALERS
Nuway Tobacco Company .... D 860 289-6414
  South Windsor *(G-7798)*

LEASING & RENTAL SVCS: Oil Field Eqpt
P2 Science Inc .... G 203 821-7457
  Woodbridge *(G-10611)*

LEASING & RENTAL: Computers & Eqpt
International Systems Cons .... G 203 268-1045
  Trumbull *(G-9036)*

LEASING & RENTAL: Construction & Mining Eqpt
Richard Dudgeon Inc .... G 203 336-4459
  Waterbury *(G-9593)*

LEASING & RENTAL: Medical Machinery & Eqpt
Vivax Medical Corporation .... F 203 729-0514
  Naugatuck *(G-4929)*

LEASING & RENTAL: Trucks, Without Drivers
Standard Welding Company Inc .... G 860 528-9628
  East Hartford *(G-2377)*

LEASING: Shipping Container
Mobile Mini Inc .... E 860 668-1888
  Suffield *(G-8727)*

LEATHER GOODS: Belting & Strapping
Brockway Ferry Corporation .... G 860 767-8231
  Essex *(G-2713)*

LEATHER GOODS: Cigarette & Cigar Cases
Ecoflik LLC .... G 860 460-4419
  Old Lyme *(G-6507)*

LEATHER GOODS: Cosmetic Bags
Putu LLC .... G 203 594-9700
  New Canaan *(G-5136)*

LEATHER GOODS: Garments
A X M S Inc .... G 203 263-5046
  Woodbury *(G-10622)*
Triumph Consulting .... G 860 263-8335
  Hartford *(G-3706)*

LEATHER GOODS: Holsters
Left Handed Holsters .... G 203 488-9654
  Branford *(G-618)*

LEATHER GOODS: Mill Strapping, Textile Mills
Can Straps LLC .... G 203 281-7333
  Hamden *(G-3423)*

LEATHER GOODS: NEC
Leatherworks .... G 860 658-6178
  Weatogue *(G-9758)*
Mr Connecticut Leather Inc .... G 203 230-2166
  Hamden *(G-3485)*
Pauls Leather Co .... G 203 871-7238
  Branford *(G-632)*
VO Leather Inc .... G 203 345-8442
  Stratford *(G-8703)*

LEATHER GOODS: Personal
Brockway Ferry Corporation .... G 860 767-8231
  Essex *(G-2713)*
Dooney & Bourke Inc .... E 203 853-7515
  Norwalk *(G-6146)*
Mayan Corporation .... F 203 854-4711
  Norwalk *(G-6251)*
Waterbury Leatherworks Co .... F 203 755-7789
  Waterbury *(G-9627)*

LEATHER GOODS: Riding Crops
Grand View Stable LLC .... G 860 228-3791
  Columbia *(G-1605)*

LEATHER GOODS: Wallets
Leatherby .... G 860 658-6166
  Weatogue *(G-9757)*
Old Leather Wallet Company LLC .... G 860 350-9868
  Roxbury *(G-7280)*

LEATHER TANNING & FINISHING
Buestan Usa LLC .... G 203 954-8889
  Ansonia *(G-25)*
MGI usa Inc .... G 203 312-1200
  Danbury *(G-1883)*

LEATHER: Accessory Prdts
Patricia Poke .... G 860 354-4193
  New Milford *(G-5580)*

LEATHER: Bag
Veto Pro Pac LLC .... G 203 847-0297
  Norwalk *(G-6388)*

LEATHER: Bookbinders'
Cutter & Drill Parts LLC .... G 203 483-0876
  North Branford *(G-5833)*

LEATHER: Processed

LEATHER: Processed
Sean Christian Leather LLC ....G....... 787 690-7039
West Hartford *(G-9854)*

LEATHER: Shoe
Cuero Operating ....G....... 203 253-8651
Westport *(G-10073)*

LEGAL OFFICES & SVCS
Peter Kelsey Publishing Inc ....G....... 860 231-9300
West Hartford *(G-9843)*

LICENSE TAGS: Automobile, Stamped Metal
Conn Dept Motor Vehicles ....G....... 203 840-1993
Norwalk *(G-6126)*

LIFTS & TRUCKS: Bomb
Automar Ne LLC ....G....... 203 793-7630
Wallingford *(G-9215)*

LIGHT SENSITIVE DEVICES
Photronics Inc ....G....... 203 740-5669
Brookfield *(G-1212)*

LIGHTING EQPT: Locomotive & Railroad Car Lights
Ridge View Associates Inc ....D....... 203 878-8560
Milford *(G-4628)*

LIGHTING EQPT: Motor Vehicle, Dome Lights
Light Fantastic Realty Inc ....C....... 203 934-3441
West Haven *(G-9926)*

LIGHTING EQPT: Motor Vehicle, NEC
Whelen Engineering Company Inc .....B....... 860 526-9504
Chester *(G-1485)*

LIGHTING EQPT: Motor Vehicle, Parking Lights
Celb LLC ....G....... 203 739-0157
Danbury *(G-1765)*

LIGHTING EQPT: Outdoor
Architectural Outdoor Lighting ....G....... 860 659-5795
Glastonbury *(G-3007)*
Dave Ross ....G....... 203 775-4327
Brookfield *(G-1177)*
Pennsylvania Globe Gaslight Co .....E....... 203 484-7749
North Branford *(G-5851)*
Point Lighting Corporation ....E....... 860 243-0600
Bloomfield *(G-467)*

LIGHTING EQPT: Searchlights
Searchlight LLC ....G....... 203 577-4400
Middlebury *(G-4290)*

LIGHTING EQPT: Spotlights
Sapphire Mltnational Group Inc ....G....... 860 693-1233
Torrington *(G-8966)*

LIGHTING FIXTURES WHOLESALERS
Pennsylvania Globe Gaslight Co .....E....... 203 484-7749
North Branford *(G-5851)*
Washington Copper Works Inc ....G....... 860 868-7637
Washington *(G-9415)*

LIGHTING FIXTURES, NEC
American Metaseal of Conn ....G....... 203 787-0281
Hamden *(G-3414)*
American Solar & Alternative ....G....... 203 324-7186
Stamford *(G-8078)*
Astralite Inc ....G....... 203 775-0172
Brookfield *(G-1161)*
Elc Acquisition Corporation ....G....... 203 743-4059
Bethel *(G-294)*
Fidelux Lighting LLC ....F....... 860 436-5000
Hartford *(G-3589)*
Jon Minard Lighting ....G....... 860 228-9069
Amston *(G-3)*
Led Lighting Hub ....G....... 860 232-7141
West Hartford *(G-9826)*
M & I Industries Inc ....G....... 860 747-6421
Plainville *(G-6837)*
Macris Industries Inc ....G....... 860 514-7003
Mystic *(G-4829)*
Malco Inc ....F....... 860 584-0446
Terryville *(G-8764)*
Moonlighting LLC ....G....... 203 740-8964
Brookfield *(G-1208)*
Mv Lighting ....G....... 203 856-3564
Norwalk *(G-6266)*
Nova Electronics ....G....... 860 537-3471
Colchester *(G-1561)*
Pathway Lighting Products Inc ....D....... 860 388-6881
Old Saybrook *(G-6564)*
Pathway Lighting Source ....G....... 860 537-0600
Colchester *(G-1562)*
Reflex Ltg Group of CT LLC ....F....... 860 666-1548
Wethersfield *(G-10218)*
Robin Reed Ltd LLC ....G....... 203 481-6378
Branford *(G-642)*
Rsl Fiber Systems LLC ....F....... 860 282-4930
East Hartford *(G-2367)*
Sensor Switch Inc ....E....... 203 265-2842
New Haven *(G-5392)*
Snibbetts Inc ....G....... 860 526-5536
Deep River *(G-2101)*
Solais Lighting Inc ....F....... 203 683-6222
Stamford *(G-8427)*
Sorenson Lighted Controls Inc ....D....... 860 527-3092
West Hartford *(G-9858)*
Studio Steel Inc ....G....... 860 868-7305
New Preston *(G-5613)*
Whelen Engineering Company Inc .....B....... 860 526-9504
Chester *(G-1485)*
Whiting Lighting LLC ....G....... 860 626-0734
Torrington *(G-8989)*
York Street Studio Inc ....G....... 203 266-9000
New Milford *(G-5609)*
Yourlightingsource Co LLC ....G....... 917 439-6501
West Haven *(G-9968)*

LIGHTING FIXTURES: Airport
Airflo Instrument Company ....G....... 860 633-9455
Glastonbury *(G-3005)*
CBA Lighting and Controls Inc ....G....... 860 623-1924
Windsor Locks *(G-10477)*
Connecticut Valley Inds LLC ....G....... 860 388-0822
Old Saybrook *(G-6529)*
Cooper Crouse-Hinds LLC ....D....... 860 683-4300
Windsor *(G-10377)*
Eaton Electric Holdings LLC ....F....... 860 683-4300
Windsor *(G-10382)*
Integro LLC ....E....... 860 832-8960
New Britain *(G-5000)*

LIGHTING FIXTURES: Decorative Area
Electrix LLC ....D....... 203 776-5577
New Haven *(G-5274)*

LIGHTING FIXTURES: Fluorescent, Commercial
Newco Lighting Inc ....G....... 475 882-4000
Shelton *(G-7511)*

LIGHTING FIXTURES: Indl & Commercial
3t Lighting Inc ....G....... 203 775-1805
Brookfield *(G-1154)*
A&A Home Solutions ....G....... 203 993-1735
Shelton *(G-7386)*
Green Ray Led Intl LLC ....G....... 203 485-1435
Greenwich *(G-3172)*
Innovative ARC Tubes Corp ....E....... 203 333-1031
Bridgeport *(G-792)*
Lcd Lighting Inc ....C....... 203 799-7877
Orange *(G-6610)*
Led Lighting Solutions LLC ....G....... 860 770-6023
Berlin *(G-193)*
Lighting Edge Inc ....G....... 860 767-8968
Essex *(G-2724)*
Lumivisions Architectural Elem ......G....... 203 529-3232
Norwalk *(G-6240)*
Nutron Manufacturing Inc ....E....... 860 887-4550
Norwich *(G-6426)*
Pathway Lighting Products Inc ....D....... 860 388-6881
Old Saybrook *(G-6564)*
Pegasus Capital Advisors LP ....E....... 203 869-4400
Stamford *(G-8356)*
Prolume Inc ....G....... 203 268-7778
Monroe *(G-4749)*
Seesmart Inc ....E....... 203 504-1111
Stamford *(G-8407)*
Sylvan R Shemitz Designs LLC .....C....... 203 934-3441
West Haven *(G-9957)*
The L C Doane Company ....F....... 860 767-8295
Ivoryton *(G-3790)*
Top Priority Tool LLC ....G....... 860 665-1012
New Britain *(G-5076)*
Tri-State Led Inc ....F....... 203 813-3791
Greenwich *(G-3248)*
Whelen Engineering Company Inc .....F....... 860 526-9504
Chester *(G-1486)*
Whelen Engineering Company Inc .....B....... 860 526-9504
Chester *(G-1485)*

LIGHTING FIXTURES: Marine
Cornell-Carr Co Inc ....E....... 203 261-2529
Monroe *(G-4706)*
The L C Doane Company ....F....... 860 767-8295
Ivoryton *(G-3790)*
Water Transit Services LLC ....G....... 860 625-3625
Waterford *(G-9676)*

LIGHTING FIXTURES: Motor Vehicle
Naugatuck Emergency Eqp LLC ....G....... 203 228-7117
Oakville *(G-6457)*

LIGHTING FIXTURES: Residential
3t Lighting Inc ....G....... 203 775-1805
Brookfield *(G-1154)*
E-Lite Technologies Inc ....F....... 203 371-2070
Trumbull *(G-9022)*
Electri-Cable Assemblies Inc ....G....... 203 924-6617
Shelton *(G-7437)*
Keeling Company Inc ....G....... 860 349-0916
Old Lyme *(G-6514)*
Keelings ....G....... 860 399-4527
Westbrook *(G-9999)*
Light Fantastic Realty Inc ....C....... 203 934-3441
West Haven *(G-9926)*
Light Sources Inc ....C....... 203 799-7877
Milford *(G-4567)*
Lumivisions Architectural Elem ......G....... 203 529-3232
Norwalk *(G-6240)*
Premier Mfg Group Inc ....D....... 203 924-6617
Shelton *(G-7539)*
Seesmart Inc ....E....... 203 504-1111
Stamford *(G-8407)*
Siempre LLC ....G....... 203 873-0303
Bridgeport *(G-902)*
Washington Copper Works Inc ....G....... 860 868-7637
Washington *(G-9415)*

LIGHTING FIXTURES: Street
Pegasus Capital Advisors LP ....E....... 203 869-4400
Stamford *(G-8356)*
Smartcap Innovations LLC ....G....... 860 878-4688
West Hartford *(G-9856)*

LIGHTING FIXTURES: Swimming Pool
Aqua Comfort Technologies LLC ...G....... 203 265-0100
Wallingford *(G-9209)*
Aquacomfort Solutions LLC ....G....... 407 831-1941
Cheshire *(G-1355)*

LIGHTING MAINTENANCE SVC
Lumivisions Architectural Elem ......G....... 203 529-3232
Norwalk *(G-6240)*

LIME
Pink Lemon Blue Lime LLC ....G....... 203 521-2464
Norwalk *(G-6301)*

LIME ROCK: Ground
Lime Rock Resources GP III LP .....G....... 203 293-2750
Westport *(G-10113)*

LIMESTONE: Crushed & Broken
Specialty Minerals Inc ....C....... 860 824-5435
Canaan *(G-1292)*

PRODUCT SECTION

LUGGAGE & LEATHER GOODS STORES: Luggage, Exc Footlckr/Trunk

Trap Rock Quarry .... G 203 263-2195
   Southbury *(G-7881)*

LIMESTONE: Dimension

Coccomo Brothers Drilling LLC .... F 860 828-1632
   Berlin *(G-171)*

LINEN SPLY SVC: Uniform

A & P Coat Apron & Lin Sup Inc .... D 914 840-3200
   Hartford *(G-3542)*

LINENS: Table & Dresser Scarves, From Purchased Materials

Nesola Scarves LLC .... G 203 288-5058
   Cheshire *(G-1419)*

LINENS: Tablecloths, From Purchased Materials

Beautiful Tables LLC .... G 203 602-9969
   Stamford *(G-8108)*

LINERS & COVERS: Fabric

Commercial Sewing Inc .... C 860 482-5509
   Torrington *(G-8913)*
Custom Covers .... G 860 669-4169
   Clinton *(G-1499)*
Lubbert Supply Company LLC .... G 203 690-1105
   Milford *(G-4570)*

LININGS: Apparel, Made From Purchased Materials

Sam & Ty LLC .... G 212 840-1871
   Norwalk *(G-6337)*

LIP BALMS

Quanah Scents LLC .... G 888 849-2016
   Manchester *(G-4077)*

LOADS: Electronic

Extreme Tech Pros LLC .... G 203 903-3050
   Hamden *(G-3446)*

LOCKS

Assa Inc .... G 800 235-7482
   New Haven *(G-5236)*
Camlock Systems Inc .... G 860 378-0302
   Southington *(G-7902)*
Eastern Company .... E 203 729-2255
   Naugatuck *(G-4878)*
Fsb Inc .... F 203 404-4700
   Berlin *(G-182)*
Loctec Corporation .... E 203 364-1000
   Newtown *(G-5755)*
Pro-Lock USA LLC .... G 203 382-3428
   Monroe *(G-4748)*
Sargent Manufacturing Company .... C 203 562-2151
   New Haven *(G-5389)*
Specialty Products Mfg LLC .... G 860 621-6969
   Southington *(G-7979)*
Yale Security Inc .... B 865 986-7511
   Berlin *(G-233)*
Zephyr Lock LLC .... F 866 937-4971
   Newtown *(G-5800)*

LOCKSMITHS

West Hartford Lock Co LLC .... F 860 236-0671
   Hartford *(G-3714)*

LOGGING

B&B Logging LLC .... G 860 982-2425
   Higganum *(G-3760)*
Brad Kettle .... G 860 546-9929
   Canterbury *(G-1295)*
Brandy Hill Logging .... G 860 923-3175
   Thompson *(G-8831)*
Brian Reynolds .... G 860 267-2021
   East Hampton *(G-2259)*
Can-AM Trading & Logistics LLC .... G 860 961-9932
   Old Lyme *(G-6497)*
Clover Hill Forest LLC .... G 860 672-0394
   Cornwall *(G-1616)*
Cold River Logging LLC .... G 860 334-9506
   North Windham *(G-6036)*
Davis Tree & Logging LLC .... E 203 938-2153
   Danbury *(G-1789)*
Fair Weather Logging LLC .... G 860 394-8217
   Enfield *(G-2645)*
Industrial Forrest Products LL .... G 203 863-9486
   Greenwich *(G-3180)*
J and K Logging .... G 860 653-6165
   East Hartland *(G-2403)*
James Callahan .... G 914 641-2852
   Ridgefield *(G-7149)*
James M Munch .... G 802 353-3114
   Sherman *(G-7596)*
L & M Logging LLC .... G 860 208-9884
   Windham *(G-10349)*
Limb-It-Less Logging LLC .... G 860 227-0987
   Essex *(G-2725)*
Mud River Services .... G 860 767-0592
   Essex *(G-2727)*
Nichols Forestry & Logging LLC .... G 860 642-4292
   Lebanon *(G-3859)*
Northeast Logging Inc .... G 860 974-2959
   Eastford *(G-2538)*
R & M Logging .... G 860 429-6209
   Willington *(G-10255)*
Saugatuck Tree & Logging LLC .... G 203 470-9195
   Brookfield *(G-1221)*
Saugatuck Tree & Logging LLC .... G 203 304-1326
   Newtown *(G-5778)*
Sprague Logging LLC .... G 860 455-9768
   Chaplin *(G-1342)*
Stanley Burr .... G 860 345-3578
   Higganum *(G-3779)*
Trowbridge Forest Products LLC .... G 860 455-9931
   Hampton *(G-3540)*
Witkowsky John .... G 203 483-0152
   North Branford *(G-5868)*

LOGGING CAMPS & CONTRACTORS

Bryan Heavens Logging & Firewo ...... G 860 485-1712
   Harwinton *(G-3723)*
C & C Logging .... G 860 683-0071
   Windsor *(G-10370)*
Daves Logging .... G 860 684-6533
   Stafford Springs *(G-8025)*
Fowler D J Log Land Clearing .... G 860 742-5842
   Coventry *(G-1654)*
Guilford Logging .... G 203 453-5190
   Guilford *(G-3357)*
Hancock Logging & Forestry MGT ...... G 860 289-5647
   South Windsor *(G-7767)*
Luc-Tardiff Logging .... G 860 485-0693
   Harwinton *(G-3733)*
P&P Logging Co .... G 860 267-2176
   East Hampton *(G-2272)*
Perry S Sawyer .... G 860 572-9473
   Stonington *(G-8535)*
R&J Harvesting LLC .... G 860 974-1323
   Eastford *(G-2540)*
Rainbow Forest Log & Firewd .... G 860 455-1023
   Hampton *(G-3539)*
Ralph B Fletcher Logging & Lan .... G 860 668-5404
   Suffield *(G-8732)*
Riendeau & Sons Logging LLC .... G 860 429-7919
   Ashford *(G-64)*
Rm Landclearing & Logging LLC .... G 860 228-1499
   Columbia *(G-1611)*
Robert Downey Logging .... G 860 693-2914
   Collinsville *(G-1602)*
Thomas Carr III .... G 860 653-3431
   North Granby *(G-5882)*
Timberwolf Logging .... G 860 683-0071
   Windsor *(G-10451)*
Wayne Horn .... G 860 491-3315
   New Hartford *(G-5214)*

LOGGING: Stump Harvesting

Ibbitson Tree Service .... G 860 388-0624
   Old Saybrook *(G-6541)*

LOGGING: Timber, Cut At Logging Camp

Oxford Outdoor Services LLC .... G 860 800-6260
   Oxford *(G-6684)*
Tr Landworks LLC .... G 860 402-6177
   East Hartland *(G-2405)*
Worthington Logging .... G 860 684-9605
   Stafford Springs *(G-8047)*

LOGGING: Wooden Logs

Chadbourne Woodshop .... G 203 468-4715
   East Haven *(G-2415)*

LOOSELEAF BINDERS

American CT Rng Bnder Index & .... F 860 868-7900
   Washington *(G-9411)*

LOTIONS OR CREAMS: Face

Bara Essentials LLC .... G 203 428-1786
   Stratford *(G-8577)*
Beiersdorf Inc .... G 203 563-5800
   Wilton *(G-10271)*
Beiersdorf Inc .... B 203 854-8000
   Norwalk *(G-6088)*
Beiersdorf North America Inc .... F 203 563-5800
   Wilton *(G-10272)*
Bunsen Rush Laboratories Inc .... G 203 397-0820
   Woodbridge *(G-10596)*
Conopco Inc .... B 860 669-8601
   Clinton *(G-1498)*
Durol Laboratories LLC .... F 866 611-9694
   West Haven *(G-9903)*
Jolen Cream Bleach Corp .... F 203 259-8779
   Fairfield *(G-2803)*
Lady Anne Cosmetics Inc .... G 203 372-6972
   Trumbull *(G-9041)*
Raffaele Ruberto LLC .... G 860 573-4094
   Wethersfield *(G-10216)*
Skin & Co North America LLC .... G 888 444-9971
   West Haven *(G-9955)*

LOTIONS: SHAVING

Black Pltnum MNS Essntials LLC .... G 203 501-3768
   Danbury *(G-1757)*
Edgewell Per Care Brands LLC .... B 203 944-5500
   Shelton *(G-7435)*

LOUDSPEAKERS

Source Loudspeakers .... G 860 918-3088
   South Windsor *(G-7824)*

LOZENGES: Pharmaceutical

Henry Thayer Company .... G 203 226-0940
   Easton *(G-2556)*

LUBRICANTS: Corrosion Preventive

Rand Innovations LLC .... F 475 282-4643
   Bridgeport *(G-885)*

LUBRICATING EQPT: Indl

Automation Inc .... F 860 236-5991
   West Hartford *(G-9777)*

LUBRICATING OIL & GREASE WHOLESALERS

Artech Packaging LLC .... G 845 858-8558
   Bethel *(G-259)*
David H Johnson Inc .... G 860 677-5595
   West Hartford *(G-9798)*
Fuchs Lubricants Co .... E 203 469-2336
   East Haven *(G-2431)*

LUGGAGE & BRIEFCASES

Commercial Sewing Inc .... C 860 482-5509
   Torrington *(G-8913)*
Manup LLC .... G 203 588-9861
   Norwalk *(G-6246)*
Marc Johnson .... G 860 774-3315
   Danielson *(G-1998)*

LUGGAGE & LEATHER GOODS STORES

Leatherby .... G 860 658-6166
   Weatogue *(G-9757)*

LUGGAGE & LEATHER GOODS STORES: Luggage, Exc Footlckr/Trunk

Taylors Luggage Inc .... G 203 966-9961
   New Canaan *(G-5150)*

Employee Codes: A=Over 500 employees, B=251-500
C=101-250, D=51-100, E=20-50, F=10-19, G=1-9

LUGGAGE: Traveling Bags

Leader Management Corp .... G 860 643-4445
Bolton *(G-514)*

Prima Dona LLC 203 820-9327
Bridgeport *(G-879)*

LUMBER & BLDG MATLS DEALER, RET: Garage Doors, Sell/Install

A-1 Garage Door Co .... G 203 866-6620
Westport *(G-10049)*

LUMBER & BLDG MATRLS DEALERS, RET: Bath Fixtures, Eqpt/Sply

Kensco Inc .... F 203 734-8827
Ansonia *(G-44)*

LUMBER & BLDG MATRLS DEALERS, RETAIL: Doors, Wood/Metal

Williams Walter Ovrhd Door LLC 203 488-8620
Branford *(G-674)*

LUMBER & BLDG MTRLS DEALERS, RET: Doors, Storm, Wood/Metal

Cusson Sash Company .... G 860 659-0354
Glastonbury *(G-3025)*

LUMBER & BLDG MTRLS DEALERS, RET: Insultn & Energy Consrvtn

Viridian Energy LLC .... D 203 663-5089
Stamford *(G-8485)*

LUMBER & BLDG MTRLS DEALERS, RET: Planing Mill Prdts/Lumber

Iffland Lumber Company Inc .... E 860 489-9218
Torrington *(G-8935)*

South Norfolk Lumber Co .... G 860 542-5650
Norfolk *(G-5826)*

LUMBER & BUILDING MATERIALS DEALER, RET: Door & Window Prdts

Hatch and Bailey Company .... E 203 866-5515
Norwalk *(G-6193)*

Leek Building Products Inc .... E 203 853-3883
Norwalk *(G-6232)*

LUMBER & BUILDING MATERIALS DEALER, RET: Masonry Matls/Splys

Beard Concrete Co Derby Inc .... F 203 735-4641
Derby *(G-2109)*

Midwood Quarry and Cnstr Inc .... F 860 289-1414
East Hartford *(G-2345)*

LUMBER & BUILDING MATERIALS DEALERS, RETAIL: Brick

O & G Industries Inc .... E 203 323-1111
Stamford *(G-8336)*

LUMBER & BUILDING MATERIALS DEALERS, RETAIL: Countertops

A -Line Custom Counter Top .... G 860 747-1917
Plainville *(G-6758)*

Focal Metals .... G 203 743-4443
Bethel *(G-300)*

LUMBER & BUILDING MATERIALS DEALERS, RETAIL: Flooring, Wood

Ben Barretts LLC .... G 860 928-9373
Thompson *(G-8830)*

LUMBER & BUILDING MATERIALS DEALERS, RETAIL: Sand & Gravel

Desiato Sand & Gravel Corp .... E 860 429-6479
Storrs Mansfield *(G-8555)*

LH Gault & Son Incorporated .... D 203 227-5181
Westport *(G-10112)*

Powder Hill Sand & Gravel LLC .... G 860 741-7274
Enfield *(G-2679)*

Windham Materials LLC .... D 860 456-4111
Willimantic *(G-10241)*

LUMBER & BUILDING MATERIALS DEALERS, RETAIL: Tile, Ceramic

La Pietra Thinstone Veneer .... G 203 775-6162
Brookfield *(G-1201)*

LUMBER & BUILDING MATERIALS RET DEALERS: Millwork & Lumber

Bonito Manufacturing Inc .... D 203 234-8786
North Haven *(G-5915)*

Chapman Lumber Inc .... E 860 283-6213
Thomaston *(G-8785)*

Gary D Kryszat .... G 860 526-3145
Chester *(G-1473)*

Lingard Cabinet Co LLC .... G 860 647-9886
Manchester *(G-4048)*

LUMBER & BUILDING MATLS DEALERS, RET: Concrete/Cinder Block

Devine Brothers Incorporated .... E 203 866-4421
Norwalk *(G-6136)*

New Milford Block & Supply .... F 860 355-1101
New Milford *(G-5568)*

LUMBER: Box

Interstate + Lakeland Lbr Corp .... F 203 531-8050
Greenwich *(G-3182)*

LUMBER: Cut Stock, Softwood

Edmund Price .... G 860 658-1441
West Simsbury *(G-9979)*

LUMBER: Hardwood Dimension

Stake Company LLC .... G 860 623-2700
East Windsor *(G-2523)*

LUMBER: Hardwood Dimension & Flooring Mills

Ben Barretts LLC .... G 860 928-9373
Thompson *(G-8830)*

Caballros Hrdwood Flors Pntinc .... G 914 312-0695
Stamford *(G-8125)*

E R Hinman & Sons Inc .... G 860 673-9170
Burlington *(G-1266)*

Hull Forest Products Inc .... E 860 974-0127
Pomfret Center *(G-6939)*

Kellogg Hardwoods Inc .... G 203 797-1992
Bethel *(G-319)*

LUMBER: Piles, Foundation & Marine Construction, Treated

Techno Mtal Post Watertown LLC ...... G 203 755-6403
Waterbury *(G-9610)*

Winthrop Construction LLC .... G 860 322-4562
Deep River *(G-2106)*

LUMBER: Plywood, Hardwood

Bergan Architectural Wdwkg Inc .... E 860 346-0869
Middletown *(G-4324)*

Thomas Bernhard Building Sys .... E 203 925-0414
Southport *(G-8013)*

LUMBER: Plywood, Prefinished, Hardwood

Reis Floor Finishing .... G 203 367-1273
Shelton *(G-7546)*

MACHINE PARTS: Stamped Or Pressed Metal

Addamo Manufacturing Inc .... G 860 667-2601
Newington *(G-5619)*

Alfro Custom Manufacturing Co .... G 203 264-6246
Southbury *(G-7843)*

Astro Industries Inc .... G 860 828-6304
Berlin *(G-161)*

Bowden Engineering Co .... G 203 583-9585
Bristol *(G-985)*

Consulting Engrg Dev Svcs Inc .... D 203 828-6528
Oxford *(G-6653)*

Danco Manufacturing LLC .... G 860 870-1706
Vernon Rockville *(G-9167)*

Forrest Machine Inc .... D 860 563-1796
Berlin *(G-180)*

Guaranteed Quality Parts L L C .... G 860 450-0419
Willimantic *(G-10228)*

Hoyt Manufacturing Co Inc .... G 860 628-2050
Southington *(G-7936)*

J D Precision Machine Inc .... G 860 653-7787
East Granby *(G-2208)*

Joval Machine Co Inc .... E 203 284-0082
Yalesville *(G-10694)*

Leelynd Corp .... G 203 753-9137
Waterbury *(G-9517)*

Meriden Manufacturing Inc .... D 203 237-7481
Meriden *(G-4197)*

Midconn Precision Mfg LLC .... G 860 584-1340
Bristol *(G-1071)*

Paradigm Prcision Holdings LLC .... G 860 649-2888
Manchester *(G-4071)*

Performance Machine Inc .... G 860 974-3664
Woodstock *(G-10678)*

Pressure Blast Mfg Co Inc .... F 800 722-5278
South Windsor *(G-7811)*

Record Products America Inc .... F 203 248-6371
Hamden *(G-3504)*

Schaeffler Aerospace USA Corp .... B 203 744-2211
Danbury *(G-1936)*

Scott Metal Products .... G 860 928-4366
Woodstock *(G-10683)*

Somers Tool & Weld Shop .... G 860 314-1075
Bristol *(G-1120)*

Tyger Tool Inc .... F 203 375-4344
Stratford *(G-8699)*

MACHINE SHOPS

A & M Auto Machine Inc .... G 203 237-3502
Meriden *(G-4136)*

AJ Tuck Company .... E 203 775-1234
Brookfield *(G-1157)*

Altek Electronics Inc .... C 860 482-7626
Torrington *(G-8892)*

Bracone Metal Spinning Inc .... E 860 628-5927
Southington *(G-7897)*

Bristol Tool & Die Company .... E 860 582-2577
Bristol *(G-993)*

Budrad Engineering Co LLC .... G 203 452-7310
Monroe *(G-4702)*

Carnegie Tool Inc .... F 203 866-0744
Norwalk *(G-6108)*

Continuity Engine Inc .... G 203 907-4470
New Haven *(G-5262)*

El Mar Inc .... G 860 729-7232
West Hartford *(G-9806)*

Faille Precision Machining .... G 860 822-1964
Baltic *(G-119)*

Innovative Mechanics LLC .... G 203 530-6071
Milford *(G-4556)*

Integral Technologies Inc .... G 860 741-2281
Enfield *(G-2652)*

Interface Devices Incorporated .... G 203 878-4648
Milford *(G-4557)*

Jeff Manufacturing Co Inc .... F 860 482-8845
Torrington *(G-8937)*

Jem Special Tool Co LLC .... G 860 276-9767
Southington *(G-7942)*

Jlp Machine Company .... G 860 649-5730
Bolton *(G-512)*

Joseph Rembock .... G 860 738-3981
Pleasant Valley *(G-6923)*

MB Consulting LLC .... G 860 889-7941
Yantic *(G-10698)*

Michele Pavisic .... G 860 876-2509
Kensington *(G-3814)*

Mj Tool & Manufacturing Inc .... G 860 352-2688
Simsbury *(G-7636)*

Mrh Tool LLC .... G 203 878-3359
Milford *(G-4586)*

Naiad Dynamics Us Inc .... E 203 929-6355
Shelton *(G-7506)*

New England Traveling Wire LLC ..... G 860 223-6297
New Britain *(G-5023)*

S P Johnson Inc .... G 860 871-8664
Stafford Springs *(G-8036)*

Stacy B Goff .... G 860 623-2547
East Windsor *(G-2522)*

Straton Industries Inc .... G 203 375-4488
Stratford *(G-8687)*

Top Priority Tool LLC .... G 860 665-1012
New Britain *(G-5076)*

Voyteks Inc .... G 860 967-6558
East Windsor *(G-2529)*

Wallingford Industries Inc ....F 203 481-0359
  Branford *(G-668)*

MACHINE TOOL ACCESS: Balancing Machines

Sjm Properties Inc ....G 860 979-0060
  Ellington *(G-2600)*
Space Electronics LLC ....E 860 829-0001
  Berlin *(G-221)*

MACHINE TOOL ACCESS: Broaches

Center Broach & Machine Co ....G 203 235-6329
  Meriden *(G-4156)*
Eastern Broach Inc ....F 860 828-4800
  Plainville *(G-6802)*

MACHINE TOOL ACCESS: Cams

Haesche Machine Repair Service ....G 203 488-7271
  Branford *(G-602)*

MACHINE TOOL ACCESS: Cutting

Alden Corporation ....D 203 879-8830
  Wolcott *(G-10548)*
Alden Tool Company Inc ....E 860 828-3556
  Berlin *(G-153)*
Brass City Technologies LLC ....G 203 723-7021
  Naugatuck *(G-4863)*
Drill Rite Carbide Tool Co ....G 860 583-3200
  Terryville *(G-8751)*
Ewald Instruments Corp ....F 860 491-9042
  Bristol *(G-1032)*
Guhring Inc ....C 860 216-5948
  Bloomfield *(G-416)*
Juskhas Wp Co ....G 860 455-0502
  Hampton *(G-3536)*
Kinetic Tool Co Inc ....F 860 627-5882
  East Windsor *(G-2505)*
M & M Carbide Inc ....G 860 628-2002
  Southington *(G-7948)*
M & R Manufacturing Inc ....G 860 666-5066
  Newington *(G-5673)*
Marena Industries Inc ....F 860 528-9701
  East Hartford *(G-2343)*
Nelson Apostle Inc ....G 860 953-4633
  Hartford *(G-3649)*
Powerhold Inc ....E 860 349-1044
  Middlefield *(G-4304)*
Tool The Somma Company ....E 203 753-2114
  Waterbury *(G-9613)*
Universal Precision Mfg ....G 203 374-9809
  Trumbull *(G-9089)*

MACHINE TOOL ACCESS: Diamond Cutting, For Turning, Etc

M T S Tool LLC ....G 860 945-0875
  Oakville *(G-6456)*
R&R Tool & Die LLC ....G 860 627-9197
  East Windsor *(G-2515)*

MACHINE TOOL ACCESS: Pushers

Powder Pushers ....G 860 295-6406
  Marlborough *(G-4129)*

MACHINE TOOL ACCESS: Threading Tools

Swanson Tool Manufacturing Inc ....E 860 953-1641
  West Hartford *(G-9863)*

MACHINE TOOL ACCESS: Tool Holders

Arthur I Platt Inc ....G 203 874-0091
  Milford *(G-4459)*
Byron Lord Inc ....G 203 287-9881
  Old Lyme *(G-6493)*
Micro Insert Inc ....G 860 621-5789
  Milldale *(G-4685)*

MACHINE TOOL ACCESS: Tools & Access

Comex Machinery ....G 203 334-2196
  Bridgeport *(G-738)*
J F Tool Inc ....G 860 349-3063
  Rockfall *(G-7213)*
James J Scott LLC ....G 860 571-9200
  Rocky Hill *(G-7252)*
Meadow Manufacturing Inc ....F 860 357-3785
  Kensington *(G-3813)*

Pine Meadow Machine Co Inc ....G 860 623-4494
  Windsor Locks *(G-10493)*
Southwick & Meister Inc ....C 203 237-0000
  Meriden *(G-4244)*

MACHINE TOOL ATTACHMENTS & ACCESS

Accu-Rite Tool & Mfg Co ....F 860 688-4844
  Tolland *(G-8847)*
Advanced Vacuum Technology Inc ....G 860 653-4176
  Simsbury *(G-7609)*
Century Tool and Design Inc ....F 860 621-6748
  Milldale *(G-4683)*
Danjon Manufacturing Corp ....F 203 272-7258
  Cheshire *(G-1380)*
Edrive Actuators Inc ....G 860 953-0588
  Newington *(G-5650)*
Pmt Group Inc ....C 203 367-8675
  Bridgeport *(G-875)*
Total Machine Co ....G 203 481-8780
  Clinton *(G-1530)*
Walker Magnetics Group Inc ....E 508 853-3232
  Windsor *(G-10461)*

MACHINE TOOLS & ACCESS

Admill Machine Co ....G 860 667-3676
  Newington *(G-5620)*
Aircraft Forged Tool Company ....G 860 347-3778
  Rockfall *(G-7210)*
AKO Inc ....E 860 298-9765
  Windsor *(G-10357)*
American Grippers Inc ....E 203 459-8345
  Trumbull *(G-8997)*
Coastal Group Inc ....G 860 452-4148
  Killingworth *(G-3830)*
Command Tooling Systems ....G 203 284-9615
  Wallingford *(G-9234)*
Danco Manufacturing LLC ....G 860 870-1706
  Vernon Rockville *(G-9167)*
Durant Machine Inc ....G 860 572-8211
  Mystic *(G-4814)*
Edmunds Manufacturing Company ....D 860 677-2813
  Farmington *(G-2903)*
Fletcher-Terry Company LLC ....D 860 828-3400
  East Berlin *(G-2169)*
Goldenrod Corporation ....E 203 723-4400
  Beacon Falls *(G-135)*
H & B Tool & Engineering Co ....E 860 528-9341
  South Windsor *(G-7766)*
Hgh Industries LLC ....G 860 644-1150
  South Windsor *(G-7771)*
J J Industries Conn Inc ....F 860 628-4655
  Southington *(G-7941)*
Jet Tool & Cutter Mfg Inc ....E 860 621-5381
  Southington *(G-7943)*
Leeco Inc ....G 860 404-8876
  Avon *(G-88)*
MDN Assoc Inc ....G 203 758-6721
  Prospect *(G-7010)*
Mid-State Manufacturing Inc ....F 860 621-6855
  Milldale *(G-4686)*
Moon Cutter Co Inc ....E 203 288-9249
  Hamden *(G-3484)*
Paradigm Prcision Holdings LLC ....D 860 829-3663
  East Berlin *(G-2173)*
Perry Technology Corporation ....D 860 738-2525
  New Hartford *(G-5206)*
Preferred Utilities Mfg Corp ....D 860 743-6741
  Danbury *(G-1918)*
Producto Corporation ....F 203 366-3224
  Bridgeport *(G-882)*
Viking Tool Company ....E 203 929-1457
  Shelton *(G-7579)*
W J Savage Co Inc ....G 203 468-4100
  East Haven *(G-2459)*

MACHINE TOOLS, METAL CUTTING: Exotic, Including Explosive

B & L Tool and Machine Company ....G 860 747-2721
  Plainville *(G-6774)*
Connecticut Tool & Cutter Co ....E 860 314-1740
  Bristol *(G-1006)*
Gary Tool Company ....G 203 377-3077
  Stratford *(G-8616)*
Moore Tool Company Inc ....D 203 366-3224
  Bridgeport *(G-843)*
Pmt Group Inc ....C 203 367-8675
  Bridgeport *(G-875)*

MACHINE TOOLS, METAL CUTTING: Jig, Boring & Grinding

Ceda Company Inc ....G 860 666-1593
  Newington *(G-5638)*
Co-Op Jig Boring Jig Grinding ....G 860 828-9882
  Berlin *(G-170)*

MACHINE TOOLS, METAL CUTTING: Robot, Drilling, Cutting, Etc

North Haven Manufacturing Co ....G 203 284-8578
  Wallingford *(G-9328)*

MACHINE TOOLS, METAL CUTTING: Sawing & Cutoff

Hallden Shear Service of Amer ....G 860 283-4386
  Thomaston *(G-8791)*

MACHINE TOOLS, METAL CUTTING: Saws, Power

W J Savage Co Inc ....G 203 468-4100
  East Haven *(G-2459)*

MACHINE TOOLS, METAL CUTTING: Screw & Thread

Baldwin Thread Rolling ....G 860 283-4948
  Thomaston *(G-8779)*
L C M Tool Co ....G 203 757-1575
  Waterbury *(G-9516)*

MACHINE TOOLS, METAL CUTTING: Tool Replacement & Rpr Parts

American Automation ....G 203 556-7839
  Bridgeport *(G-690)*
Dennis Savela ....G 860 774-3963
  Danielson *(G-1989)*
Guiseppe Mazzettini ....G 203 597-9035
  Waterbury *(G-9492)*
Machine Repair Services LLC ....G 860 729-7410
  Middletown *(G-4374)*
Mark Machine Tool LLC ....G 203 910-5942
  Wolcott *(G-10574)*
Nemtec Inc ....G 203 272-0788
  Cheshire *(G-1418)*
Sadlak Industries LLC ....E 860 742-0227
  Coventry *(G-1673)*
Talk N Fix CT Inc ....G 203 790-8905
  Danbury *(G-1959)*

MACHINE TOOLS, METAL CUTTING: Ultrasonic

Sonitek Corporation ....E 203 878-9321
  Milford *(G-4647)*

MACHINE TOOLS, METAL CUTTING: Vertical Turning & Boring

Atp Industries LLC ....F 860 479-5007
  Plainville *(G-6773)*
Charter Oak Automation LLC ....G 203 562-0699
  Wallingford *(G-9226)*
Iamaw ....G 860 228-0049
  Hebron *(G-3750)*

MACHINE TOOLS, METAL FORMING: Bending

Accubend LLC ....G 860 378-0303
  Plantsville *(G-6881)*

MACHINE TOOLS, METAL FORMING: Container, Metal Incl Cans

Universal Storage Cntrs LLC ....G 203 966-3043
  New Canaan *(G-5156)*

MACHINE TOOLS, METAL FORMING: Die Casting & Extruding

Ace Finishing Co LLC ....G 860 582-4600
  Bristol *(G-955)*

MACHINE TOOLS, METAL FORMING: Forming, Metal Deposit

Proiron LLC .... G 203 934-7967
  West Haven *(G-9948)*

MACHINE TOOLS, METAL FORMING: Marking

A G Russell Company Inc .... G 860 247-9093
  Hartford *(G-3543)*

MACHINE TOOLS, METAL FORMING: Rebuilt

Fenn LLC .... E 860 259-6600
  East Berlin *(G-2167)*
L R Brown Manufacturing Co .... G 203 265-5639
  Wallingford *(G-9300)*

MACHINE TOOLS, METAL FORMING: Robots, Pressing, Extrudg, Etc

New England PLC Systems LLC .... G 860 793-2975
  Southington *(G-7956)*

MACHINE TOOLS, METAL FORMING: Spinning, Spline Rollg/Windg

Advanced Machine Services LLC .... G 203 888-6600
  Waterbury *(G-9423)*

MACHINE TOOLS, METAL FORMING: Spring Winding & Forming

L M Gill Welding and Mfr LLC .... F 860 647-9931
  Manchester *(G-4046)*

MACHINE TOOLS, METAL FORMING: Stretching

Vital Stretch LLC .... G 203 847-4477
  Norwalk *(G-6391)*

MACHINE TOOLS: Metal Cutting

83 Erna Avenue LLC .... G 203 243-7426
  Trumbull *(G-8996)*
AMR Machines LLC .... G 860 336-6208
  Putnam *(G-7029)*
Benetec Inc .... G 860 745-4455
  Enfield *(G-2617)*
Bernell Tool & Mfg Co .... G 203 756-4405
  Waterbury *(G-9438)*
Book Automation Inc .... G 860 354-7900
  New Milford *(G-5512)*
Branson Ultrasonics Corp .... B 203 796-0400
  Danbury *(G-1759)*
C V Tool Company Inc .... E 978 353-7901
  Southington *(G-7901)*
Center Mass LLC .... G 860 350-0239
  New Milford *(G-5518)*
Cnc Engineering Inc .... E 860 749-1780
  Enfield *(G-2627)*
CT Tool & Manufacturing LLC .... G 860 846-0800
  Farmington *(G-2895)*
D T Technologies Inc .... G 203 312-3527
  Ridgefield *(G-7134)*
Denco Counter-Bore LLC .... G 860 276-0782
  Southington *(G-7914)*
Edac Technologies LLC .... F 860 789-2511
  East Windsor *(G-2490)*
Edac Technologies LLC .... C 203 806-2090
  Cheshire *(G-1383)*
Emhart Teknologies LLC .... E 203 790-5000
  Danbury *(G-1807)*
Emhart Teknologies LLC .... F 800 783-6427
  New Britain *(G-4983)*
Engineering Components Pdts LLC .... G 860 747-6222
  Plainville *(G-6806)*
Farmington Machine Tools LLC .... G 860 676-7736
  Farmington *(G-2905)*
Fletcher-Terry Company LLC .... D 860 828-3400
  East Berlin *(G-2169)*
Gmn Usa LLC .... F 800 686-1679
  Bristol *(G-1046)*
Hata Hi-Tech Machining LLC .... E 203 333-9139
  Ansonia *(G-38)*
JL Lucas Machinery Co Inc .... F 203 597-1300
  Waterbury *(G-9510)*
Laser Tool Company Inc .... F 860 283-8284
  Thomaston *(G-8796)*

Lefferts Brothers Vintage Mach .... G 203 205-0500
  Bethel *(G-322)*
Max-Tek LLC .... F 860 372-4900
  Wallingford *(G-9315)*
Microbest Inc .... C 203 597-0355
  Waterbury *(G-9542)*
Mid-State Manufacturing Inc .... F 860 621-6855
  Milldale *(G-4686)*
Mikron Corp Monroe .... G 203 261-3100
  Monroe *(G-4737)*
Moon Cutter Co Inc .... E 203 288-9249
  Hamden *(G-3484)*
New England Plasma Dev Corp .... F 860 928-6561
  Putnam *(G-7053)*
New England Tooling Inc .... F 800 866-5105
  Killingworth *(G-3837)*
Nowak Products Inc .... G 860 666-9685
  Newington *(G-5687)*
Okamoto Corp .... G 860 219-1006
  Windsor *(G-10415)*
Producto Corporation .... F 203 366-3224
  Bridgeport *(G-882)*
Ramdy Corporation .... E 860 274-3713
  Oakville *(G-6460)*
Ready Tool Company .... E 860 524-7811
  West Hartford *(G-9849)*
Relx Inc .... G 860 219-0733
  Windsor *(G-10430)*
RWS Co Inc .... G 860 434-2961
  Old Lyme *(G-6518)*
Scott A Hebert .... G 860 990-0793
  Plainville *(G-6860)*
Secondary Operations Inc .... F 203 288-8241
  Hamden *(G-3509)*
Shuster-Mettler Corp .... E 203 562-3178
  Plainville *(G-6861)*
Sperry Automatics Co Inc .... E 203 729-4589
  Naugatuck *(G-4922)*
Syman Machine LLC .... G 860 747-8337
  Plainville *(G-6865)*
United Tool and Die Company .... C 860 246-6531
  West Hartford *(G-9871)*
Viking Tool Company .... E 203 929-1457
  Shelton *(G-7579)*

MACHINE TOOLS: Metal Forming

American Actuator Corporation .... F 203 324-6334
  Redding *(G-7089)*
Arrow Diversified Tooling Inc .... E 860 872-9072
  Ellington *(G-2576)*
Deringer-Ney Inc .... C 860 242-2281
  Bloomfield *(G-407)*
Grant Manufacturing & Mch Co .... E 203 366-4557
  Bridgeport *(G-779)*
Joshua LLC .... E 203 624-0080
  New Haven *(G-5304)*
Lou-Jan Tool & Die Inc .... F 203 272-3536
  Cheshire *(G-1408)*
Merritt Extruder Corp .... E 203 230-8100
  Hamden *(G-3481)*
Okay Industries Inc .... G 860 225-8707
  Berlin *(G-204)*
Oxford General Industries Inc .... F 203 758-4467
  Prospect *(G-7013)*
Peter Hoelzel .... G 860 749-4070
  Enfield *(G-2676)*
Raymon Tool LLC .... F 203 248-2199
  Hamden *(G-3501)*
Richard Dahlen .... G 860 584-8226
  Bristol *(G-1108)*
Riveting Systems USA LLC .... G 203 366-4557
  Bridgeport *(G-891)*
Sandviks Inc .... G 866 984-0188
  Danbury *(G-1933)*
Savage Products LLC .... G 203 440-1766
  Meriden *(G-4240)*
Sirois Tool Company Inc .... D 860 828-5327
  Berlin *(G-220)*
Stamptech Incorporated .... F 860 628-9090
  Southington *(G-7980)*

MACHINERY & EQPT FINANCE LEASING

Southern Neng Telecom Corp .... B 203 771-5200
  New Haven *(G-5401)*

MACHINERY & EQPT, AGRICULTURAL, WHOLESALE: Landscaping Eqpt

Mist Hill Property Maint LLC .... G 203 648-7434
  Brookfield *(G-1207)*

MACHINERY & EQPT, AGRICULTURAL, WHOLESALE: Poultry Eqpt

Engineering Services & Pdts Co .... D 860 528-1119
  South Windsor *(G-7750)*

MACHINERY & EQPT, INDL, WHOL: Brewery Prdts Mfg, Commercial

Cocchia Norwalk Grape Co .... F 203 855-7911
  Norwalk *(G-6119)*

MACHINERY & EQPT, INDL, WHOL: Controlling Instruments/Access

Jad LLC .... E 860 289-1551
  South Windsor *(G-7776)*
Kde Instrumentation .... G 860 657-2744
  Glastonbury *(G-3053)*
Raman Power Technologies LLC .... G 203 695-4885
  Wallingford *(G-9348)*

MACHINERY & EQPT, INDL, WHOLESALE: Cement Making

Das Distribution Inc .... G 860 844-3058
  East Granby *(G-2201)*

MACHINERY & EQPT, INDL, WHOLESALE: Cranes

CT Crane and Hoist Service LLC .... G 860 283-4320
  Plymouth *(G-6928)*

MACHINERY & EQPT, INDL, WHOLESALE: Engines, Gasoline

Cummins Inc .... E 860 529-7474
  Rocky Hill *(G-7230)*

MACHINERY & EQPT, INDL, WHOLESALE: Engs/Transportation Eqpt

Advanced Pwr Systems Intl Inc .... E 860 921-0009
  New Hartford *(G-5184)*

MACHINERY & EQPT, INDL, WHOLESALE: Fans

EBM-Papst Inc .... B 860 674-1515
  Farmington *(G-2902)*

MACHINERY & EQPT, INDL, WHOLESALE: Hydraulic Systems

Faxon Engineering Company Inc .... F 860 236-4266
  Bloomfield *(G-410)*
Spectrum Associates Inc .... F 203 878-4618
  Milford *(G-4651)*

MACHINERY & EQPT, INDL, WHOLESALE: Indl Machine Parts

American Precision Product LLC .... G 860 274-7301
  Watertown *(G-9680)*
F & W Rentals Inc .... F 203 795-0591
  Orange *(G-6600)*
Goldenrod Corporation .... E 203 723-4400
  Beacon Falls *(G-135)*
Seitz LLC .... E 860 489-0476
  Torrington *(G-8969)*

MACHINERY & EQPT, INDL, WHOLESALE: Instruments & Cntrl Eqpt

Kahn Instruments Incorporated .... G 860 529-8643
  Wethersfield *(G-10205)*

MACHINERY & EQPT, INDL, WHOLESALE: Machine Tools & Access

JL Lucas Machinery Co Inc .... F 203 597-1300
  Waterbury *(G-9510)*

MACHINERY & EQPT, INDL, WHOLESALE: Machine Tools & Metalwork

Bryce Gear Inc .... G 860 747-3341
  Plainville *(G-6779)*

PRODUCT SECTION

Mikro Industrial Finishing Co ....G....... 860 875-6357
Vernon *(G-9143)*

MACHINERY & EQPT, INDL, WHOLESALE: Measure/Test, Electric

Baumer Ltd ....F....... 860 621-2121
Southington *(G-7894)*
Hamar Laser Instruments Inc ....E....... 203 730-4600
Danbury *(G-1841)*
Madison Tstg Acqstion Svcs LLC ....G....... 203 421-9388
Madison *(G-3938)*

MACHINERY & EQPT, INDL, WHOLESALE: Packaging

Millwood Inc ....F....... 203 248-7902
North Haven *(G-5965)*

MACHINERY & EQPT, INDL, WHOLESALE: Petroleum Industry

Frc Founders Corporation ....E....... 203 661-6601
Stamford *(G-8209)*

MACHINERY & EQPT, INDL, WHOLESALE: Pneumatic Tools

Air Tool Sales & Service Co ....G....... 860 673-2714
Unionville *(G-9110)*

MACHINERY & EQPT, INDL, WHOLESALE: Processing & Packaging

Fortis Solutions Group LLC ....E....... 860 872-6311
Ellington *(G-2590)*

MACHINERY & EQPT, INDL, WHOLESALE: Safety Eqpt

East Coast Sign and Supply Inc ....G....... 203 791-8326
Bethel *(G-291)*

MACHINERY & EQPT, INDL, WHOLESALE: Sewing

Industrial Saws Inc ....G....... 860 496-7000
Torrington *(G-8936)*

MACHINERY & EQPT, INDL, WHOLESALE: Threading Tools

Swanson Tool Manufacturing Inc..........E....... 860 953-1641
West Hartford *(G-9863)*

MACHINERY & EQPT, INDL, WHOLESALE: Water Pumps

Rema Dri-Vac Corp ....F....... 203 847-2464
Norwalk *(G-6321)*

MACHINERY & EQPT, WHOLESALE: Construction, General

D P Engineering Inc ....G....... 203 421-7965
Madison *(G-3916)*
Erection & Welding Contrs LLC ....G....... 860 828-9353
Berlin *(G-178)*
Numa Tool Company ....D....... 860 923-9551
Thompson *(G-8841)*
Westfair Electric Contractors ....G....... 203 586-1760
Southbury *(G-7885)*

MACHINERY & EQPT: Farm

16 Case LLC ....G....... 860 995-0455
Farmington *(G-2873)*
Case Association ....G....... 860 989-6533
West Suffield *(G-9985)*
Comex Machinery ....G....... 203 334-2196
Bridgeport *(G-738)*
Connectcut Cswork Spclists LLC ....G....... 203 934-9665
West Haven *(G-9891)*
Hunter Industries ....G....... 860 961-9646
Deep River *(G-2092)*

MACHINERY & EQPT: Gas Producers, Generators/Other Rltd Eqpt

Hamilton Standard Space ....E....... 860 654-6000
Windsor Locks *(G-10490)*
Proton Energy Systems Inc ....D....... 203 678-2000
Wallingford *(G-9343)*

MACHINERY & EQPT: Liquid Automation

Alstom Power Co ....F....... 860 688-1911
Windsor *(G-10358)*
Environmantal Systems Cor ....F....... 860 953-5167
Hartford *(G-3585)*
Prospect Industries LLC ....G....... 203 758-3736
Prospect *(G-7018)*
Qsonica LLC ....G....... 203 426-0101
Newtown *(G-5770)*
Sonics & Materials Inc ....D....... 203 270-4600
Newtown *(G-5781)*

MACHINERY & EQPT: Metal Finishing, Plating Etc

Mikro Industrial Finishing Co ....G....... 860 875-6357
Vernon *(G-9143)*
PYC Deborring LLC F/K/A C & ....G....... 860 828-6806
Berlin *(G-213)*

MACHINERY BASES

Airpot Corporation ....E....... 800 848-7681
Norwalk *(G-6064)*
Center Mass LLC ....G....... 860 350-0239
New Milford *(G-5518)*
Dcg-Pmi Inc ....E....... 203 743-5525
Bethel *(G-279)*
Oxford General Industries Inc ....F....... 203 758-4467
Prospect *(G-7013)*

MACHINERY, COMMERCIAL LAUNDRY: Washing, Incl Coin-Operated

Edro Corporation ....E....... 860 828-0311
East Berlin *(G-2166)*

MACHINERY, EQPT & SUPPLIES: Parking Facility

Snapwire Innovations LLC ....G....... 203 806-4773
Cheshire *(G-1448)*

MACHINERY, FOOD PRDTS: Beverage

Cimbali Usa Inc ....G....... 203 254-6046
Fairfield *(G-2761)*

MACHINERY, FOOD PRDTS: Homogenizing, Dairy, Fruit/Vegetable

Pro Scientific Inc ....F....... 203 267-4600
Oxford *(G-6689)*

MACHINERY, FOOD PRDTS: Mills, Food

Sun Farm Corporation ....G....... 203 882-8000
Milford *(G-4657)*

MACHINERY, FOOD PRDTS: Mixers, Commercial

EMI Inc ....G....... 860 669-1199
Clinton *(G-1502)*

MACHINERY, FOOD PRDTS: Mixers, Feed, Exc Agricultural

Sonic Corp ....F....... 203 375-0063
Stratford *(G-8683)*

MACHINERY, FOOD PRDTS: Ovens, Bakery

Bakery Engineering/Winkler Inc ....F....... 203 929-8630
Shelton *(G-7400)*

MACHINERY, FOOD PRDTS: Roasting, Coffee, Peanut, Etc.

Ventures LLC DOT Com LLC ....G....... 203 930-8972
Vernon *(G-9157)*

MACHINERY, FOOD PRDTS: Slicers, Commercial

Newgate Designs Co ....G....... 860 653-6991
East Granby *(G-2217)*

MACHINERY, MAILING: Mailing

Agissar Corporation ....D....... 203 375-8662
Stratford *(G-8565)*
Hasler Inc ....G....... 203 301-3400
Shelton *(G-7461)*
Mailroom Finance Inc ....G....... 203 301-3400
Milford *(G-4574)*
Pitney Bowes Inc ....A....... 203 356-5000
Stamford *(G-8362)*
Pitney Bowes Inc ....E....... 203 792-1600
Shelton *(G-7528)*
Pitney Bowes Inc ....E....... 203 356-5000
Shelton *(G-7530)*

MACHINERY, MAILING: Postage Meters

Neopost USA Inc ....C....... 203 301-3400
Milford *(G-4588)*
Pitney Bowes Inc ....E....... 203 356-5000
Stamford *(G-8363)*
Pitney Bowes Inc ....G....... 860 285-7450
Windsor *(G-10420)*
Pitney Bowes Inc ....E....... 203 922-4000
Shelton *(G-7529)*

MACHINERY, METALWORKING: Assembly, Including Robotic

Adamczyk Enterprises Inc ....G....... 860 745-9830
Enfield *(G-2612)*
Clear Automation LLC ....E....... 860 621-2955
Southington *(G-7906)*
Force Automation Inc ....G....... 860 622-1618
New Britain *(G-4990)*
Nielsen Consulting Inc ....G....... 914 831-1681
New Milford *(G-5573)*
Te Connectivity Corporation ....C....... 860 684-8000
Stafford Springs *(G-8041)*
Vangor Engineering Corporation ....G....... 203 267-4377
Oxford *(G-6698)*
Wtp Machine Robotics ....G....... 860 716-7281
Southington *(G-7996)*

MACHINERY, METALWORKING: Coil Winding, For Springs

Jovil Universal LLC ....E....... 203 792-6700
Danbury *(G-1864)*

MACHINERY, METALWORKING: Coiling

P/A Industries Inc ....E....... 860 243-8306
Bloomfield *(G-459)*

MACHINERY, METALWORKING: Cutting & Slitting

Shuster-Mettler Corp ....E....... 203 562-3178
Plainville *(G-6861)*

MACHINERY, OFFICE: Dictating

Dictaphone Corporation ....C....... 203 381-7000
Stratford *(G-8606)*

MACHINERY, OFFICE: Duplicating

Bidwell Industrial Group Inc ....E....... 860 346-9283
Middletown *(G-4325)*

MACHINERY, OFFICE: Paper Handling

Bell and Howell LLC ....E....... 860 526-9561
Deep River *(G-2085)*
Xerox Corporation ....B....... 203 968-3000
Norwalk *(G-6401)*
Xerox Holdings Corporation ....G....... 203 968-3000
Norwalk *(G-6402)*

MACHINERY, OFFICE: Pencil Sharpeners

Acme United Corporation ....C....... 203 254-6060
Fairfield *(G-2743)*

MACHINERY, OFFICE: Stapling, Hand Or Power

Stanley Fastening Systems LP .... G 860 225-5111
New Britain *(G-5065)*

MACHINERY, OFFICE: Time Clocks & Time Recording Devices

Accu-Time Systems Inc .... E 860 870-5000
Ellington *(G-2570)*
Pyramid Time Systems LLC .... E 203 238-0550
Meriden *(G-4225)*

MACHINERY, OFFICE: Typing & Word Processing

A Westport Wordsmith .... G 203 354-7309
Norwalk *(G-6058)*

MACHINERY, PACKAGING: Packing & Wrapping

PDC International Corp .... D 203 853-1516
Norwalk *(G-6292)*
Staban Engineering Corp .... F 203 294-1997
Wallingford *(G-9375)*

MACHINERY, PAPER INDUSTRY: Coating & Finishing

Zatorski Coating Company Inc .... F 860 267-9889
East Hampton *(G-2285)*

MACHINERY, PAPER INDUSTRY: Converting, Die Cutting & Stampng

Bar-Plate Manufacturing Co .... F 203 397-0033
Hamden *(G-3417)*

MACHINERY, PRINTING TRADES: Lithographic Stones

Asml Us LLC .... A 203 761-4000
Wilton *(G-10270)*

MACHINERY, PRINTING TRADES: Plates

Verico Technology LLC .... E 800 492-7286
Enfield *(G-2704)*

MACHINERY, PRINTING TRADES: Printing Trade Parts & Attchts

Arico Engineering Inc .... G 860 642-7040
North Franklin *(G-5870)*

MACHINERY, SERVICING: Coin-Operated, Exc Dry Clean & Laundry

Elegant Drycleaning .... G 203 849-1000
Norwalk *(G-6156)*

MACHINERY, SEWING: Buttonhole/Eyelet Mach/Attachments, Indl

Edward Segal Inc .... E 860 283-5821
Thomaston *(G-8788)*

MACHINERY, SEWING: Sewing & Hat & Zipper Making

Bausch Advanced Tech Inc .... E 860 669-7380
Clinton *(G-1492)*

MACHINERY, TEXTILE: Embroidery

Ehriched Stitch LLC .... G 203 210-5107
Wilton *(G-10290)*
Monogram Studio Greenwich CT .... G 203 428-5700
Greenwich *(G-3206)*
Mp Impressions LLC .... G 860 873-1797
Moodus *(G-4774)*
Tri Star Graphics .... G 203 748-4792
Bethel *(G-355)*
Ultramatic West .... G 203 745-4688
Hamden *(G-3525)*

MACHINERY, TEXTILE: Printing

Image Star LLC .... G 888 632-5515
Middletown *(G-4355)*

MACHINERY, TEXTILE: Silk Screens

Screen-Tech Inc .... G 860 496-8016
Torrington *(G-8968)*
Systematic Automation Inc .... E 310 218-3361
Farmington *(G-2962)*

MACHINERY, WOODWORKING: Bandsaws

Cedar Accessories .... G 860 350-6969
New Milford *(G-5517)*

MACHINERY, WOODWORKING: Cabinet Makers'

Bender Showroom .... G 860 618-2944
Torrington *(G-8902)*
Carls Closets LLC .... G 203 457-9401
Guilford *(G-3338)*
Northeast Cabinetry LLC .... G 860 216-0781
Bloomfield *(G-452)*

MACHINERY, WOODWORKING: Jointers

Walsh Claim Services .... G 203 481-0680
North Branford *(G-5865)*

MACHINERY, WOODWORKING: Sanding, Exc Portable Floor Sanders

Cournoyer Flr Sanding Finshg .... G 860 963-7088
Thompson *(G-8833)*
Johns Floor Sanding .... G 860 423-3852
Windham *(G-10348)*

MACHINERY/EQPT, INDL, WHOL: Cleaning, High Press, Sand/Steam

Northeastern Metals Corp .... G 203 348-8088
Stamford *(G-8330)*

MACHINERY: Ammunition & Explosives Loading

Lyman Products Corporation .... D 860 632-2020
Middletown *(G-4370)*
Lyman Products Corporation .... E 860 632-2020
Middletown *(G-4371)*

MACHINERY: Assembly, Exc Metalworking

A F M Engineering Corp .... G 860 774-7518
Brooklyn *(G-1244)*
Arthur G Russell Company Inc .... D 860 583-4109
Bristol *(G-967)*
Brown Larkin & Co LLC .... G 860 280-8858
Burlington *(G-1261)*
Csg Automation LLC .... G 860 691-1885
Niantic *(G-5804)*
Mid State Assembly & Packg Inc .... G 203 634-8740
Meriden *(G-4202)*
Naiad Dynamics Us Inc .... E 203 929-6355
Shelton *(G-7506)*
New England Machine Co LLC .... G 860 526-7844
Deep River *(G-2096)*
Packard Inc .... E 203 758-6219
Prospect *(G-7014)*
Rondo America Incorporated .... C 203 723-5831
Naugatuck *(G-4917)*
RWS Co Inc .... G 860 434-2961
Old Lyme *(G-6518)*
Schaefer Machine Company Inc .... G 860 526-4000
Deep River *(G-2099)*

MACHINERY: Automotive Related

Center Mass LLC .... G 860 350-0239
New Milford *(G-5518)*
Day Machine Systems Inc .... F 860 229-3440
New Britain *(G-4971)*
Evans Cooling Systems Inc .... G 860 668-1114
Suffield *(G-8718)*
Freds Auto Machine .... G 203 744-2950
Bethel *(G-302)*
Windham Automated Machines Inc .... F 860 208-5297
South Windham *(G-7695)*

MACHINERY: Blasting, Electrical

Pressure Blast Mfg Co Inc .... F 800 722-5278
South Windsor *(G-7811)*

MACHINERY: Brewery & Malting

Diamond Brewing Service .... G 860 508-0013
Manchester *(G-4008)*

MACHINERY: Construction

Bagela Usa LLC .... G 203 944-0525
Shelton *(G-7398)*
Canterbury Machinery Rnd Llc .... G 860 546-5000
Canterbury *(G-1297)*
Conair Corporation .... D 800 492-7464
Torrington *(G-8914)*
Ezflow Limited Partnership .... E 860 577-7064
Old Saybrook *(G-6533)*
H Barber & Sons Inc .... E 203 729-9000
Naugatuck *(G-4886)*
North America Overland LLC .... G 203 658-3697
Monroe *(G-4744)*
Rawson Manufacturing Inc .... F 860 928-4458
Putnam *(G-7062)*
Rayginn Mfg LLC .... G 860 243-2257
Bloomfield *(G-473)*
Spray Foam Outlets LLC .... G 631 291-9355
Norwalk *(G-6354)*
Tbs Adjusting Inc .... G 203 274-5525
Stamford *(G-8459)*
Terex Utilities Inc .... G 860 436-3700
Hartford *(G-3701)*
Tinsley GROup-Ps&w Inc .... D 919 742-5832
Milford *(G-4665)*

MACHINERY: Cryogenic, Industrial

Saf Industries LLC .... E 203 729-4900
Meriden *(G-4237)*

MACHINERY: Custom

Darly Custom Technology Inc .... F 860 298-7966
Windsor *(G-10379)*
Dufrane Nuclear Shielding Inc .... F 860 379-2318
Winsted *(G-10516)*
Durstin Machine & Mfg .... G 860 485-1257
Harwinton *(G-3725)*
Flexco .... G 860 583-0219
Bristol *(G-1040)*
Fryer Corporation .... G 203 888-9944
Oxford *(G-6659)*
L R Brown Manufacturing Co .... G 203 265-5639
Wallingford *(G-9300)*
M & Z Engineering Inc .... G 860 496-0282
Torrington *(G-8945)*
Manchester TI & Design ADP LLC .... G 860 296-6541
Hartford *(G-3633)*
My Tool Company Inc .... G 203 755-2333
Waterbury *(G-9551)*
Pilot Machine Designers Inc .... G 203 866-2227
Norwalk *(G-6300)*
Swageco LLC .... G 860 331-3477
Coventry *(G-1679)*
T L S Design & Manufacturing .... G 860 439-1414
New London *(G-5492)*
Vortex Manufacturing .... G 860 749-9769
Somers *(G-7675)*

MACHINERY: Deburring

Deburring Laboratories Inc .... E 860 829-6300
New Britain *(G-4972)*
Precision Deburring Inc .... G 860 583-4662
Bristol *(G-1096)*

MACHINERY: Die Casting

OEM Sources LLC .... G 203 283-5415
Milford *(G-4597)*

MACHINERY: Electrical Discharge Erosion

New England Die Co Inc .... F 203 574-5140
Waterbury *(G-9558)*

MACHINERY: Electronic Component Making

Accurate Automation LLC .... G 203 988-9426
Wallingford *(G-9197)*
B & A Design Inc .... G 860 871-0134
Vernon Rockville *(G-9161)*

PRODUCT SECTION

MACHINERY: Semiconductor Manufacturing

Hitek Electronics LLC .... G 203 982-4574
Naugatuck *(G-4888)*
Omega Engineering Inc .... D 714 540-4914
Norwalk *(G-6285)*
Synergy Sales Ltd .... G 860 974-3288
Woodstock *(G-10689)*

MACHINERY: Electronic Teaching Aids

Don Pomaski .... G 860 693-4469
Collinsville *(G-1593)*
Technical Consulting .... G 203 268-8890
Monroe *(G-4757)*

MACHINERY: Fiber Optics Strand Coating

Merritt Extruder Corp .... E 203 230-8100
Hamden *(G-3481)*

MACHINERY: Gas Producers

Cold LLC .... G 203 543-6861
Milford *(G-4490)*
Praxair Inc .... B 203 837-2000
Danbury *(G-1913)*

MACHINERY: Gear Cutting & Finishing

Bryce Gear Inc .... G 860 747-3441
Plainville *(G-6779)*
Nortek Gear and Machine LLC .... G 860 355-5541
New Milford *(G-5574)*

MACHINERY: General, Industrial, NEC

American Kuhne .... G 401 326-6200
North Stonington *(G-6019)*
Andersen Laboratories Inc .... G 860 286-9090
Bloomfield *(G-385)*
GL and V .... G 203 876-5400
Milford *(G-4540)*
M P Robinson Production .... E 203 938-1336
Redding *(G-7099)*
North Haven Eqp & Lsg LLC .... G 203 795-9494
Orange *(G-6617)*
Parts Feeders Inc .... G 860 528-9579
East Hartford *(G-2352)*
Red Barn Innovations .... G 203 393-0778
Prospect *(G-7023)*

MACHINERY: Glassmaking

Emhart Glass Inc .... D 860 298-7340
Windsor *(G-10383)*
Quest Plastics Inc .... F 860 489-1404
Torrington *(G-8962)*

MACHINERY: Grinding

Dunbar Commercial Enterprises .... G 203 469-7575
East Haven *(G-2421)*
Finishers Technology Corp .... F 860 829-1000
East Berlin *(G-2168)*
Magcor Inc .... G 203 445-0302
Monroe *(G-4731)*
Marena Industries Inc .... F 860 528-9701
East Hartford *(G-2343)*
Tetco Inc .... F 860 747-1280
Plainville *(G-6869)*
US Avionics Inc / Superabr .... G 860 528-1114
South Windsor *(G-7837)*

MACHINERY: Ice Cream

Taylor Coml Foodservice Inc .... A 336 245-6400
Farmington *(G-2963)*

MACHINERY: Ice Making

Croteau Development Group Inc .... G 860 684-3605
Stafford Springs *(G-8022)*

MACHINERY: Industrial, NEC

Ace Industrial LLC .... G 203 272-7675
Cheshire *(G-1347)*
Acufab .... G 203 263-3490
Woodbury *(G-10623)*
American Metallizing .... G 860 289-1677
South Windsor *(G-7706)*
At Industries LLC .... G 860 739-6639
Niantic *(G-5801)*
Beck Industries LLC .... G 203 260-8864
Stratford *(G-8582)*

Broadstripes LLC .... G 203 350-9824
New Haven *(G-5251)*
Eastern Truck & Machine LLC .... G 860 528-0258
South Windsor *(G-7746)*
Gypsum Systems LLC .... G 860 470-3916
Burlington *(G-1269)*
In Da Cut Music .... G 860 895-9445
East Hartford *(G-2339)*
Irex Machine Inc .... G 860 870-1677
Vernon Rockville *(G-9170)*
Macton Oxford LLC .... G 203 267-1500
Oxford *(G-6675)*
Mail Corecron .... G 860 342-1055
Portland *(G-6964)*
Motherstar Online LLC .... G 860 896-1869
Tolland *(G-8871)*
Northeast Tool Dist LLC .... G 860 973-1455
Bristol *(G-1080)*
Precision Metals and Plas .... G 860 559-8843
Berlin *(G-208)*
Precision Products .... G 203 265-2061
Wallingford *(G-9342)*
Space Craft Mfg Inc .... G 860 583-1387
Meriden *(G-4245)*
Veeder-Root Co .... G 860 450-0895
Willimantic *(G-10237)*
Wdss Corporation .... F 203 854-5930
Norwalk *(G-6393)*
Wire Cutting Precision .... G 860 496-9302
Torrington *(G-8990)*

MACHINERY: Jack Screws

National Filter Media Corp .... E 203 741-2225
Wallingford *(G-9325)*

MACHINERY: Jewelers

Medelco Inc .... G 203 275-8070
Bridgeport *(G-836)*

MACHINERY: Labeling

James J Chasse .... G 860 572-0838
Stonington *(G-8531)*

MACHINERY: Marking, Metalworking

C & G Precisions Products Inc .... G 203 879-6989
Wolcott *(G-10551)*

MACHINERY: Metalworking

Alpha-Core Inc .... E 203 954-0050
Shelton *(G-7392)*
Charter Oak Automation LLC .... G 203 562-0699
Wallingford *(G-9226)*
Fletcher-Terry Company LLC .... D 860 828-3400
East Berlin *(G-2169)*
Foilmark Inc .... F 860 243-0343
Bloomfield *(G-414)*
Hall Machine Systems Inc .... G 203 481-4275
North Branford *(G-5840)*
Herrick & Cowell Company Inc .... G 203 288-2578
Hamden *(G-3463)*
L M Gill Welding and Mfr LLC .... F 860 647-9931
Manchester *(G-4046)*
Merritt Extruder Corp .... E 203 230-8100
Hamden *(G-3481)*
MGS Manufacturing Inc .... G 203 481-4275
North Branford *(G-5849)*
Obi Laser Products .... G 860 305-0038
Canton *(G-1322)*
Tmf Incorporated .... G 203 267-7364
Southbury *(G-7880)*
True Position Mfg LLC .... G 860 291-2987
South Windsor *(G-7835)*
Tyger Tool Inc .... F 203 375-4344
Stratford *(G-8699)*

MACHINERY: Milling

Machine Builders Neng LLC .... F 203 922-9446
Shelton *(G-7493)*
Turbine Controls Inc .... D 860 242-0448
Bloomfield *(G-495)*
Watertown Jig Bore Service Inc .... F 860 274-5898
Watertown *(G-9748)*

MACHINERY: Optical Lens

Berkshire Photonics LLC .... G 860 868-0412
Washington Depot *(G-9416)*

Bg Machinery Services LLC .... G 203 374-4732
Fairfield *(G-2754)*

MACHINERY: Packaging

B & B Equipment LLC .... G 860 342-5773
Portland *(G-6951)*
Beardsworth Group Inc .... G 860 283-4014
Thomaston *(G-8780)*
Gtrpet Smf LLC .... G 203 661-1229
Cos Cob *(G-1632)*
Integrated Packg Systems Inc .... G 860 623-2623
East Windsor *(G-2499)*
Millwood Inc .... F 203 248-7902
North Haven *(G-5965)*
OEM Sources LLC .... G 203 283-5415
Milford *(G-4597)*
Packard Inc .... E 203 758-6219
Prospect *(G-7014)*
RWS Co Inc .... G 860 434-2961
Old Lyme *(G-6518)*
Sanford Redmond Inc .... G 203 351-9800
Stamford *(G-8402)*
Standard-Knapp Inc .... D 860 342-1100
Portland *(G-6974)*

MACHINERY: Paper Industry Miscellaneous

Andritz Shw Inc .... E 860 496-8888
Torrington *(G-8896)*
Goldenrod Corporation .... E 203 723-4400
Beacon Falls *(G-135)*
Lakeview Engineering & Mfg LLC .... G 860 490-2760
Higganum *(G-3767)*
Sonic Corp .... F 203 375-0063
Stratford *(G-8683)*

MACHINERY: Pharmaciutical

Nicholas Precision Pdts LLC .... G 518 428-8109
Portland *(G-6966)*

MACHINERY: Photographic Reproduction

Nancy Tenenbaum Films .... G 203 221-6830
Weston *(G-10033)*

MACHINERY: Plastic Working

Davis-Standard Holdings Inc .... B 860 599-1010
Pawcatuck *(G-6708)*

MACHINERY: Printing Presses

Image Star LLC .... G 888 632-5515
Middletown *(G-4355)*

MACHINERY: Recycling

Startech Environmental Corp .... F 203 762-2499
Wilton *(G-10334)*

MACHINERY: Road Construction & Maintenance

Town of Ledyard .... G 860 464-9060
Gales Ferry *(G-2988)*

MACHINERY: Robots, Molding & Forming Plastics

Wittmann Battenfeld Inc .... D 860 496-9603
Torrington *(G-8991)*

MACHINERY: Rubber Working

Colmec Usa Inc .... G 203 502-8822
Trumbull *(G-9013)*
Farrel Corporation .... D 203 736-5500
Ansonia *(G-34)*
M I R Inc .... F 203 888-2541
Beacon Falls *(G-141)*

MACHINERY: Semiconductor Manufacturing

C&G Mfg .... G 860 274-9785
Watertown *(G-9688)*
Emhart Teknologies LLC .... G 877 364-2781
Danbury *(G-1806)*
Jet Process Corporation .... G 203 985-6000
North Haven *(G-5953)*
Prospect Products Incorporated .... E 860 666-0323
Newington *(G-5698)*

Employee Codes: A=Over 500 employees, B=251-500
C=101-250, D=51-100, E=20-50, F=10-19, G=1-9

2020 Harris Connecticut
Manufacturers Directory

MACHINERY: Semiconductor Manufacturing

Toppan Photomasks Inc .... E 203 775-9001
  Brookfield *(G-1231)*
Xavier Marcus .... G 203 543-2032
  Stratford *(G-8711)*

MACHINERY: Separation Eqpt, Magnetic

Walker Magnetics Group Inc .... E 508 853-3232
  Windsor *(G-10461)*

MACHINERY: Sheet Metal Working

Trumpf Inc .... B 860 255-6000
  Farmington *(G-2967)*
Trumpf Inc .... B 860 255-6000
  Plainville *(G-6872)*
Trumpf Inc .... B 860 255-6000
  Farmington *(G-2968)*

MACHINERY: Snow Making

Snowathome LLC .... G 860 584-2991
  Terryville *(G-8770)*

MACHINERY: Specialty

International Plating Tech LLC ..... G 860 589-2212
  Southington *(G-7940)*
Lynch Corp .... G 203 452-3007
  Greenwich *(G-3195)*

MACHINERY: Swaging

US Product Mechanization Co ...... G 860 450-1139
  Columbia *(G-1614)*

MACHINERY: Textile

France Voiles Co Inc .... G 203 364-9454
  Sandy Hook *(G-7311)*
Gros-Ite Precision Spindle .... G 860 679-7490
  Farmington *(G-2915)*
Reynolds Carbide Die Co Inc .... E 860 283-8246
  Thomaston *(G-8802)*
Sonic Corp .... F 203 375-0063
  Stratford *(G-8683)*

MACHINERY: Thread Rolling

Cole S Crew Machine Products .... E 203 723-1418
  North Haven *(G-5922)*

MACHINERY: Tobacco Prdts

Single Load LLC .... G 860 944-7507
  Bridgeport *(G-909)*

MACHINERY: Woodworking

Bakers Architectural Wdwkg LLC .. G 203 483-3173
  Branford *(G-555)*
Patriotic Spirit 704 239-4289
  Suffield *(G-8728)*
United Abrasives Inc .... B 860 456-7131
  North Windham *(G-6040)*

MACHINES: Forming, Sheet Metal

Rader Industries Inc .... G 203 334-6739
  Bridgeport *(G-884)*

MACHINISTS' TOOLS: Measuring, Precision

Hermann Schmidt Company Inc ... F 860 289-3347
  South Windsor *(G-7769)*
Vertech Inc .... G 203 876-1552
  Milford *(G-4673)*

MACHINISTS' TOOLS: Precision

Apex Machine Tool Company Inc .. D 860 677-2884
  Cheshire *(G-1353)*
Blue Chip Tool .... G 860 875-7999
  Tolland *(G-8852)*
FDM LLC .... G 860 684-7466
  Stafford Springs *(G-8029)*
Hart Tool & Engineering .... G 203 264-9776
  Oxford *(G-6664)*
Integral Industries Inc .... F 860 953-0686
  Newington *(G-5663)*
Jims Machine Shop Inc .... G 860 928-5151
  Putnam *(G-7050)*
Johnson Gage Company .... E 860 242-5541
  Bloomfield *(G-428)*

Mrh Tool LLC .... G 203 878-3359
  Milford *(G-4586)*
Preferred Tool & Die Inc .... E 203 925-8525
  Shelton *(G-7538)*
Ray Machine Corporation .... E 860 582-8202
  Terryville *(G-8769)*
Skico Manufacturing Co LLC .... G 203 230-1305
  Hamden *(G-3510)*
White Hills Tool .... G 203 590-3143
  Monroe *(G-4765)*

MAGNESIUM

Magnesium Interactive LLC .... G 917 609-1306
  Westport *(G-10115)*

MAGNETIC INK & OPTICAL SCANNING EQPT

Gerber Scientific LLC .... C 860 871-8082
  Tolland *(G-8864)*
Verico Technology LLC .... E 800 492-7286
  Enfield *(G-2704)*

MAIL-ORDER HOUSE, NEC

Defender Industries Inc .... C 860 701-3400
  Waterford *(G-9652)*
Olympia Sales Inc .... D 860 749-0751
  Enfield *(G-2672)*

MAIL-ORDER HOUSES: Arts & Crafts Eqpt & Splys

Color Craft Ltd .... F 800 509-6563
  East Granby *(G-2197)*

MAIL-ORDER HOUSES: Books, Exc Book Clubs

Scholastic Library Pubg Inc .... A 203 797-3500
  Danbury *(G-1939)*

MAIL-ORDER HOUSES: Clothing, Exc Women's

Del Arbour LLC .... F 203 882-8501
  Milford *(G-4506)*

MAIL-ORDER HOUSES: Collectibles & Antiques

Vijon Studios Inc .... G 860 399-7440
  Old Saybrook *(G-6576)*

MAIL-ORDER HOUSES: Computer Software

Cogz Systems LLC .... F 203 263-7882
  Woodbury *(G-10628)*

MAIL-ORDER HOUSES: Educational Splys & Eqpt

Geneve Corporation .... E 203 358-8000
  Stamford *(G-8215)*

MAIL-ORDER HOUSES: Novelty Merchandise

World Wide Games Inc .... G 860 537-3451
  Colchester *(G-1583)*

MAIL-ORDER HOUSES: Order Taking Office Only

Ngraver Company .... G 860 823-1533
  Bozrah *(G-530)*

MAILBOX RENTAL & RELATED SVCS

Norwich Printing Company Inc ..... F 860 887-7468
  Norwich *(G-6425)*
UPS Authorized Retailer .... G 203 256-9991
  Fairfield *(G-2862)*

MAILING LIST: Compilers

Action Letter Inc .... E 203 323-2466
  Stamford *(G-8061)*

MAILING SVCS, NEC

American Rubber Stamp Company .... G 203 755-1135
  Cheshire *(G-1351)*

Automated Mailing Services LLC .. G 203 439-2763
  Cheshire *(G-1358)*
Brescias Printing Services Inc ..... G 860 528-4254
  East Hartford *(G-2300)*
Fusion Cross-Media LLC .... G 860 647-8367
  Manchester *(G-4020)*
Oddo Print Shop Inc .... G 860 489-6585
  Torrington *(G-8953)*
Technique Printers Inc .... G 860 669-2516
  Clinton *(G-1529)*

MANAGEMENT CONSULTING SVCS: Automation & Robotics

Flexco .... G 860 583-0219
  Bristol *(G-1040)*
Nielsen Consulting Inc .... G 914 831-1681
  New Milford *(G-5573)*

MANAGEMENT CONSULTING SVCS: Business

Automotive Coop Couponing Inc .. G 203 227-2722
  Weston *(G-10018)*
Camarro Research .... G 203 254-1755
  Fairfield *(G-2757)*
Sail Spars Design LLC .... G 860 429-9866
  Storrs Mansfield *(G-8559)*
Symphonycs LLC .... G 860 884-2308
  Lisbon *(G-3883)*

MANAGEMENT CONSULTING SVCS: Business Planning & Organizing

Morthanoscom LLC .... G 203 378-2414
  Stratford *(G-8651)*

MANAGEMENT CONSULTING SVCS: Construction Project

Marks Construction Co LLC .... G 860 407-2391
  Portland *(G-6965)*

MANAGEMENT CONSULTING SVCS: Food & Beverage

Metabev Inc .... F 203 967-8502
  Stamford *(G-8307)*

MANAGEMENT CONSULTING SVCS: Hospital & Health

Functional Concepts LLC .... G 203 813-0157
  Stratford *(G-8614)*
Triumph Consulting .... G 860 263-8335
  Hartford *(G-3706)*
Vital Hlthcare Cmmncations LLC .. G 866 478-4825
  Milford *(G-4675)*

MANAGEMENT CONSULTING SVCS: Industrial

Energy USA Incorporated .... G 203 791-2222
  Danbury *(G-1811)*

MANAGEMENT CONSULTING SVCS: Industrial & Labor

Anderson David C & Assoc LLC .. F 860 749-7547
  Enfield *(G-2615)*

MANAGEMENT CONSULTING SVCS: Industry Specialist

F S P Research Inc .... G 203 874-3417
  Milford *(G-4534)*
Optical Energy Technologies .... G 203 357-0626
  Stamford *(G-8344)*
PRA Holdings Inc .... G 203 853-0123
  Stamford *(G-8370)*
Relocation Information Svc Inc .... E 203 855-1234
  Norwalk *(G-6319)*
Sfc Koenig LLC .... E 203 245-1100
  North Haven *(G-5992)*

MANAGEMENT CONSULTING SVCS: Training & Development

Clever Clover LLC .... G 860 501-2800
  Pawcatuck *(G-6706)*

PRODUCT SECTION

Reac Ready LLC ....G..... 860 760-8886
  Avon *(G-103)*

MANAGEMENT SERVICES

Brennan Realty LLC ....C..... 203 929-6314
  Shelton *(G-7409)*
Conair Corporation ....D..... 800 492-7464
  Torrington *(G-8914)*
Elot Inc ....G..... 203 388-1808
  Old Greenwich *(G-6472)*
General Dynamics Ordnance ....F..... 860 404-0162
  Avon *(G-82)*
Sleep Management Solutions LLC ....F..... 888 497-5337
  Hartford *(G-3690)*
SS&c Technologies Inc ....C..... 860 298-4500
  Windsor *(G-10438)*
Urban Exposition LLC ....E..... 203 242-8717
  Trumbull *(G-9090)*
Wexford Capital LP ....D..... 203 862-7000
  Greenwich *(G-3258)*

MANAGEMENT SVCS, FACILITIES SUPPORT: Environ Remediation

D R Charles Envmtl Cnstr LLC ....G..... 203 445-0412
  Monroe *(G-4709)*
Supreme Storm Services LLC ....G..... 860 201-0642
  Southington *(G-7983)*

MANAGEMENT SVCS: Business

AMS Strategic Management Inc ....G..... 845 500-5635
  Stamford *(G-8083)*

MANAGEMENT SVCS: Financial, Business

Frc Founders Corporation ....E..... 203 661-6601
  Stamford *(G-8209)*
Rain Cii Carbon LLC ....F..... 203 406-0535
  Stamford *(G-8385)*

MANAGEMENT SVCS: Hospital

Yale-New Haven Hlth Svcs Corp ....D..... 203 688-2100
  New Haven *(G-5452)*

MANDRELS

Mandrel ....G..... 410 507-7767
  Shelton *(G-7495)*

MANICURE PREPARATIONS

Crystal Nails and Spa of Sh ....G..... 203 323-0551
  Stamford *(G-8170)*
Kims Nail Corporation ....G..... 203 380-8608
  Stratford *(G-8640)*
Nina Nail Spa ....G..... 203 270-0777
  Newtown *(G-5765)*

MANIFOLDS: Pipe, Fabricated From Purchased Pipe

Vas Integrated LLC ....G..... 860 748-4058
  Berlin *(G-229)*

MANPOWER TRAINING

Sugar Run K9 LLC ....G..... 860 591-4193
  Voluntown *(G-9191)*

MANUFACTURING INDUSTRIES, NEC

210 Innovations ....G..... 860 445-0210
  Groton *(G-3269)*
283 Industries Inc ....G..... 203 276-8956
  Ridgefield *(G-7113)*
A C Manufacturing ....G..... 860 314-8225
  Bristol *(G-951)*
AA Industries LLC ....G..... 860 291-8929
  South Windsor *(G-7697)*
Aberdeen Mfg ....G..... 860 774-9679
  Danielson *(G-1986)*
Ace Wlding Fbrction Rstoration ....G..... 203 758-3550
  Prospect *(G-6992)*
Ack Industries LLC ....G..... 860 677-0056
  Farmington *(G-2875)*
Action Industries ....G..... 860 644-3020
  Manchester *(G-3978)*
Addison Industries LLC ....G..... 203 809-0254
  West Haven *(G-9881)*
Additive Experts LLC ....G..... 860 351-3324
  New Britain *(G-4937)*

Additive Manufacturing Neng ....G..... 860 316-5946
  Middletown *(G-4313)*
Advanced Specialist LLC ....G..... 860 945-9125
  Watertown *(G-9679)*
Aero Precision Mfg LLC ....G..... 203 675-7625
  Wallingford *(G-9198)*
AK Interactive USA LLC ....G..... 845 313-9380
  Branford *(G-539)*
ALC Manufacturing LLC ....G..... 860 496-0883
  Torrington *(G-8888)*
Alexis Aerospace Inds LLP ....G..... 860 673-6801
  Avon *(G-74)*
American Hydrogen Northeast ....E..... 203 449-4614
  Bridgeport *(G-692)*
American Industries ....G..... 860 381-5083
  Gales Ferry *(G-2980)*
American Prototype Hob ....G..... 203 323-6832
  Stamford *(G-8077)*
American Recreational Inds ....G..... 203 375-5900
  Stratford *(G-8568)*
Andher Mfg LLC ....G..... 860 874-8816
  East Hartford *(G-2291)*
Apiject Systems Corp ....G..... 203 461-7121
  Stamford *(G-8088)*
Apricus Inc ....G..... 203 889-2667
  North Haven *(G-5907)*
Arrow Lock Manufacturing Co ....G..... 203 603-5959
  New Haven *(G-5233)*
Art Metal Industries AMI ....G..... 860 799-5575
  New Milford *(G-5506)*
ASAP Mfg Co LLC ....G..... 860 738-4831
  Winsted *(G-10506)*
Atech Industries LLC ....G..... 203 887-4900
  Orange *(G-6584)*
B & M Fabrication LLC ....G..... 860 379-5444
  Winsted *(G-10508)*
B-E Industries ....G..... 203 357-8055
  Stamford *(G-8104)*
Bar Industries LLC ....G..... 203 729-4490
  Naugatuck *(G-4861)*
Barco Industries New England ....G..... 860 798-8258
  Glastonbury *(G-3012)*
Barn Beam Co of Neng LLC ....G..... 860 488-0317
  Northfield *(G-6042)*
Belle Industries LLC ....G..... 203 245-0382
  Madison *(G-3912)*
Biological Industries ....G..... 860 316-5197
  Cromwell *(G-1692)*
Biomass Industries Inc ....G..... 203 207-9958
  Bethel *(G-265)*
Bk Industries LLC ....G..... 832 744-3067
  Vernon *(G-9132)*
Blackbird Manufacturing and De ....G..... 860 331-3477
  Coventry *(G-1645)*
Bolt Custom & Mfg LLC ....G..... 203 685-1840
  Bridgeport *(G-715)*
Bomba Industries LLC ....G..... 203 304-9051
  Sandy Hook *(G-7300)*
Boss Industries ....G..... 860 819-1637
  Vernon Rockville *(G-9163)*
BR Industries LLC ....G..... 203 216-3576
  Norwalk *(G-6098)*
Bromley Industries ....G..... 860 370-9566
  Broad Brook *(G-1145)*
Btx Industries ....G..... 203 359-4870
  Stamford *(G-8122)*
Bullie Industries LLC ....G..... 203 393-9763
  Bethany *(G-236)*
C&G Mfg ....G..... 860 274-9785
  Watertown *(G-9688)*
C&S Collectibles ....G..... 860 872-6825
  Tolland *(G-8853)*
Cad/CAM Dntl Stdio Mil Ctr Inc ....G..... 203 733-3069
  Newtown *(G-5731)*
CAM Industries ....G..... 860 738-8338
  Colebrook *(G-1584)*
CAM Manufacturing Co LLC ....G..... 203 301-0153
  Milford *(G-4480)*
CAM Manufacturing LLC ....G..... 203 415-0411
  Milford *(G-4481)*
Canine Core Industries LLC ....G..... 203 459-1584
  Trumbull *(G-9009)*
Carin Industries Inc ....G..... 860 489-1122
  Torrington *(G-8909)*
Carl Rizzo & Associates ....G..... 860 644-5849
  South Windsor *(G-7725)*
Carlin Mfg Kitchens To Go ....G..... 413 519-2822
  Mystic *(G-4805)*
Cash Time Industries LLC ....G..... 860 770-7192
  New Britain *(G-4956)*

Castro Industries LLC ....G..... 203 249-9268
  Greenwich *(G-3142)*
Cavallo Manufacturing LLC ....G..... 203 596-8007
  Waterbury *(G-9447)*
Cavar Industries LLC ....G..... 860 684-0706
  Union *(G-9109)*
Charles Manufacturing Co ....G..... 860 747-3550
  Plainville *(G-6787)*
Chef Gretchen LLC ....G..... 203 252-8892
  Stamford *(G-8142)*
Cicchetti & Co LLC ....G..... 860 945-0424
  Watertown *(G-9692)*
Classic Tool & Mfg LLC ....G..... 203 755-6313
  Waterbury *(G-9451)*
Clean Tech Industries LLC ....G..... 860 447-1434
  New London *(G-5464)*
Cleansource Industries ....G..... 203 401-1535
  Madison *(G-3913)*
Coastal Industries LLC ....G..... 860 535-9043
  Stonington *(G-8526)*
Components For Mfg LLC ....G..... 860 245-5326
  Mystic *(G-4809)*
Concentric Tool Mfg Co ....G..... 203 723-8846
  Naugatuck *(G-4871)*
Connecticut Metal Industries ....G..... 203 736-0790
  Ansonia *(G-30)*
Connecticut Mfg Svcs LLC ....G..... 860 667-8712
  Newington *(G-5642)*
Controlled Interfaces LLC ....G..... 917 328-4471
  Ridgefield *(G-7130)*
Corco Mfg ....G..... 203 284-1831
  Wallingford *(G-9240)*
Corelli Industries LLC ....G..... 203 356-9058
  Stamford *(G-8160)*
CPS Millworks LLC ....G..... 860 283-4276
  Terryville *(G-8750)*
Creative Cupolas ....G..... 203 261-2178
  Trumbull *(G-9018)*
Croton Industries East Africa ....G..... 407 947-4481
  Wilton *(G-10285)*
CSS Industries LLC ....G..... 203 521-5246
  Stratford *(G-8601)*
CT Pyro Mfg LLC ....G..... 203 856-8313
  Sandy Hook *(G-7306)*
CT Sprayfoam Industries LLC ....G..... 203 232-0961
  Southbury *(G-7849)*
Custom Creations LLC ....G..... 203 522-2113
  Naugatuck *(G-4874)*
Customized Foods Mfg LLC ....G..... 203 759-1645
  Waterbury *(G-9457)*
Cyro Industries ....G..... 203 269-4481
  Orange *(G-6594)*
D & C Industries ....G..... 203 453-4424
  Guilford *(G-3342)*
Dangerous Industries Quality ....G..... 860 986-0879
  Waterbury *(G-9461)*
Dar More Mfg Co ....G..... 860 605-9164
  Harwinton *(G-3724)*
Ddk Industries LLC ....G..... 203 641-4218
  Shelton *(G-7429)*
Delcon Industries ....G..... 203 371-5711
  Trumbull *(G-9020)*
Delcon Industries ....G..... 203 540-5757
  Bridgeport *(G-744)*
Delcon Industries LLC ....G..... 203 331-9720
  Bridgeport *(G-745)*
Delta-Source LLC ....F..... 860 461-1600
  West Hartford *(G-9799)*
Dexon Tech LLC ....G..... 860 584-1442
  Bristol *(G-1015)*
Diversified Manufact ....G..... 203 734-0379
  Ansonia *(G-32)*
Dt Manufacturing LLC ....G..... 860 384-8449
  Bristol *(G-1021)*
Dythnam Industries LLC ....G..... 860 480-7980
  Glastonbury *(G-3028)*
E6s Industries LLC ....G..... 512 920-3671
  Colchester *(G-1548)*
East Coast Precision Mfg ....G..... 860 322-4624
  Chester *(G-1470)*
Elevation Sells Group LLC ....G..... 203 871-7172
  New Haven *(G-5275)*
Ellis Manufacturing LLC ....G..... 865 518-0531
  Plainville *(G-6805)*
Elmo Nash Industries ....G..... 203 459-3648
  Trumbull *(G-9025)*
Enaqua ....G..... 203 269-9890
  Wallingford *(G-9257)*
Ensign Bickford Industries ....F..... 203 843-2126
  Simsbury *(G-7619)*

Employee Codes: A=Over 500 employees, B=251-500
C=101-250, D=51-100, E=20-50, F=10-19, G=1-9

MANUFACTURING INDUSTRIES, NEC

Eye-Con Foods LLC .... G 203 752-7525
  Bethany *(G-240)*
Ezee Fabricators LLC .... G 860 429-5664
  Mansfield Center *(G-4113)*
Factor Industries LLC .... G 203 244-5429
  Ridgefield *(G-7140)*
Farace Industries LLC .... G 203 315-1293
  North Branford *(G-5838)*
Finn-Addict Manufacturing LLC .... G 860 464-2053
  Gales Ferry *(G-2983)*
Flowe Manufacturing .... G 860 859-1573
  Bozrah *(G-525)*
Four Twenty Industries LLC .... G 860 818-3334
  Berlin *(G-181)*
G A Industries .... G 860 261-5484
  Bristol *(G-1044)*
GA Remanufacturing LLC .... G 860 404-5186
  Farmington *(G-2912)*
Garbeck Airflow Industries .... G 860 301-5032
  Middletown *(G-4346)*
Garrett & Co Mfg LLC .... G 203 494-0935
  Ansonia *(G-36)*
Global Manufacturing .... G 860 315-5502
  Woodstock *(G-10666)*
Go Green Industries LLC .... G 914 772-0026
  New Milford *(G-5538)*
Gpk Mfg LLC .... G 860 536-2084
  Mystic *(G-4819)*
Greenway Industries Inc .... G 203 885-1059
  Brookfield *(G-1195)*
Greenwood Industries Inc .... G 203 234-2041
  North Haven *(G-5943)*
H & K Industries LLC .... G 857 237-3944
  Hartford *(G-3603)*
Hak Industries LLC .... G 860 572-7305
  Mystic *(G-4820)*
Harley Industries LLC .... G 860 951-5727
  Higganum *(G-3765)*
HI Industries LLC .... G 203 783-1084
  Milford *(G-4548)*
Hill Industries Llc .... G 860 747-6421
  Plainville *(G-6822)*
Hopewell Harmony LLC .... G 203 222-2268
  Newtown *(G-5745)*
Hpi Manufacturing Inc .... G 203 777-5395
  Hamden *(G-3464)*
Hps Industries LLC .... G 203 915-5627
  New Haven *(G-5297)*
Hub Industries .... G 203 803-8836
  Bridgeport *(G-788)*
Hxb Industries LLC .... G 203 348-5922
  Stamford *(G-8242)*
ICC Wire Harness Mfg LLC .... G 203 469-8481
  East Haven *(G-2435)*
Illicit Industries .... G 203 264-6293
  Southbury *(G-7859)*
Incord Ltd .... G 860 537-1414
  Oakdale *(G-6443)*
Ink Tank Industries LLC .... G 203 274-2717
  Stamford *(G-8250)*
Innovative Industries LLC .... G 860 225-0000
  Meriden *(G-4175)*
Innovative Mfg Systems LLC .... G 203 284-2605
  Wallingford *(G-9288)*
Interspace Industries LLC .... G 203 814-1879
  Brookfield *(G-1198)*
Ironhorse Industries LLC .... G 203 598-8720
  Watertown *(G-9712)*
Isaac Industries .... G 203 778-3239
  Danbury *(G-1852)*
J & S Industries LLC .... G 203 220-8970
  Monroe *(G-4722)*
J&P Mfg LLC .... G 860 747-4790
  Plainville *(G-6828)*
J&T Industries LLC .... G 203 375-8424
  Bridgeport *(G-798)*
Jak Industries LLC .... G 877 964-2725
  Stonington *(G-8530)*
Jam Industries LLC .... G 860 225-8862
  New Britain *(G-5006)*
Jaz Industries LLC .... G 860 243-9357
  Windsor *(G-10399)*
Jcm Industries .... G 203 748-1806
  Danbury *(G-1858)*
Jeff Osborne Industries .... G 203 794-0863
  Danbury *(G-1860)*
Jfn Manufacturing LLC .... G 860 621-0069
  Southington *(G-7944)*
Jfs Industries .... G 203 592-0754
  Thomaston *(G-8794)*

Jimbpa Enterprises LLC .... G 203 755-9237
  Waterbury *(G-9509)*
Jlc Industries .... G 315 761-8051
  West Haven *(G-9918)*
Joseph Manufacturing Co .... G 203 431-6400
  Ridgefield *(G-7151)*
Jra Industries LLC .... G 475 343-0262
  Meriden *(G-4183)*
JS Industries .... G 860 928-0786
  Thompson *(G-8835)*
Jungle Brew LLC .... G 860 335-4941
  Bloomfield *(G-429)*
K2 Manufacturing Inc .... G 413 636-6170
  South Windsor *(G-7781)*
K4 Industries LLC .... G 203 459-4992
  Easton *(G-2558)*
Katy Industries Inc .... G 314 656-4321
  Middlebury *(G-4281)*
Keith Reed Industries LLC .... G 860 677-7739
  Unionville *(G-9117)*
Kellog Splitters Inc .... G 860 738-4986
  New Hartford *(G-5200)*
Kh Industries LLC .... G 860 875-4779
  Tolland *(G-8867)*
Kimlar Industries LLC .... G 203 220-2200
  Trumbull *(G-9040)*
Koster Keunen Manufacturing .... G 860 693-1295
  Collinsville *(G-1596)*
Kpb Industries LLC .... G 203 687-7943
  Madison *(G-3935)*
La Care Industries LLC .... G 860 231-7772
  West Hartford *(G-9825)*
Lesco .... G 203 353-0061
  Stamford *(G-8282)*
Lily Force Industries .... G 860 729-2458
  Coventry *(G-1661)*
Lion Heart Industries LLC .... G 203 376-2212
  Guilford *(G-3368)*
Lombardo Industries LLC .... G 203 948-8562
  Sandy Hook *(G-7320)*
Long FA Inc .... G 203 270-3878
  Newtown *(G-5756)*
Lookingforsolutionscom LLC .... G 475 239-5773
  Shelton *(G-7492)*
Madd Fiusch Industries .... G 203 982-8306
  Madison *(G-3937)*
Magnum Industries .... G 860 490-9513
  Enfield *(G-2657)*
Mak Industries LLC .... G 860 623-4911
  East Windsor *(G-2509)*
Manufacturing Assists .... G 203 934-6574
  West Haven *(G-9931)*
Manufacturing Productivi .... G 860 916-8189
  Windsor *(G-10406)*
Manufctring Alnce Svc Corp Inc .... G 203 596-1900
  Waterbury *(G-9533)*
Martin Mfg Services LLC .... G 860 663-1465
  Killingworth *(G-3836)*
McGuire Manufacturing Co Inc .... G 203 301-0270
  Milford *(G-4575)*
McGurk Industries .... G 917 524-5132
  Trumbull *(G-9047)*
Metal Components Mfg .... G 203 267-5510
  Southbury *(G-7867)*
Mf Industries .... G 860 355-8188
  New Milford *(G-5562)*
Mfg Directions .... G 203 483-0797
  North Branford *(G-5848)*
Mfg Service Co .... G 860 749-8316
  Enfield *(G-2659)*
MHS Industries .... G 860 798-7981
  Windsor *(G-10410)*
Mikron Corp Stratford .... G 203 261-3100
  Monroe *(G-4738)*
Mindscape Industries .... G 860 574-9308
  New London *(G-5480)*
MJM Marga LLC .... G 203 597-9035
  Waterbury *(G-9547)*
Mk Millwork LLC .... G 860 567-0173
  Morris *(G-4790)*
ML Industries .... G 203 820-4922
  Bridgeport *(G-841)*
MLS Acq Inc .... F 860 386-6878
  East Windsor *(G-2512)*
Mondo Sauce LLC .... G 206 714-0390
  Stamford *(G-8313)*
Motive Industries LLC .... G 860 423-2064
  North Windham *(G-6039)*
Murphy Industries LLC .... G 203 426-1772
  Sandy Hook *(G-7322)*

Mylo Industries LLC .... G 860 228-1192
  Amston *(G-4)*
New York Transit Shoes .... G 203 968-6642
  Stamford *(G-8326)*
Njd Enterprises .... G 860 210-1113
  Litchfield *(G-3897)*
Oak Hill Industries Inc .... G 203 755-4400
  Waterbury *(G-9566)*
Oak Tree Moulding LLC .... G 860 455-3056
  Woodstock *(G-10674)*
OConnell Industries Inc .... G 860 508-7052
  Manchester *(G-4065)*
Original Materials Inds LLC .... G 203 535-1192
  Hamden *(G-3492)*
Outdoor Industries LLC .... G 203 350-2275
  Madison *(G-3945)*
Parva Industries Inc .... G 203 248-5553
  Hamden *(G-3495)*
Paul Maxx Industries LLC .... G 203 417-2446
  Southbury *(G-7871)*
Perfex Manufacturing .... G 203 739-0930
  Danbury *(G-1904)*
Perry Industries LLC .... G 203 505-5187
  Cos Cob *(G-1639)*
Petro-Tech Industries LLC .... G 860 881-5890
  Willington *(G-10253)*
Polar Bear Industries LLC .... G 203 858-4396
  Westport *(G-10141)*
Polster Industries LLC .... G 203 521-8517
  Fairfield *(G-2830)*
Precision Express Mfg LLC .... F 860 584-2627
  Bristol *(G-1097)*
Precision Fire Fabrication LLC .... G 203 706-0749
  Plantsville *(G-6908)*
Precision Interface .... G 203 235-2718
  Meriden *(G-4219)*
Precision Metal Manufacturing .... G 973 253-0500
  Simsbury *(G-7641)*
Privateer Divers LLC .... G 860 742-2699
  Coventry *(G-1670)*
Progress Manufacturing LLC .... G 860 563-6254
  Wethersfield *(G-10215)*
Purple Heart Industries LLC .... G 203 655-5039
  Darien *(G-2040)*
Qds LLC .... G 203 338-9668
  Shelton *(G-7541)*
Queenie Industries LLC .... G 917 848-4490
  Hamden *(G-3499)*
R and K Industries .... G 860 289-3879
  East Hartford *(G-2362)*
R S Industries LLC .... G 203 261-1146
  Trumbull *(G-9060)*
RC Fabrication and Off Rd LLC .... G 203 500-7071
  North Haven *(G-5986)*
Realizers Group LLC .... G 203 253-9510
  Westport *(G-10146)*
Red Door Industries .... G 860 243-1960
  Bloomfield *(G-475)*
Redco Industries LLC .... G 860 537-2664
  Colchester *(G-1572)*
Regional Industries LLC .... G 860 227-3627
  Clinton *(G-1520)*
Riopel Industries .... G 860 384-9610
  Bristol *(G-1109)*
Risdon Manufacturing Co .... G 860 283-2000
  Thomaston *(G-8803)*
Rockwood Manufacturing Co .... G 800 582-2424
  New Haven *(G-5382)*
Rolling Motion Industries .... G 860 846-0530
  Plainville *(G-6857)*
Ronaco Industries Inc .... G 203 979-7712
  Roxbury *(G-7281)*
Rooster Malt Company LLC .... G 203 364-7612
  Newtown *(G-5777)*
Ross Industries .... G 203 838-6180
  Norwalk *(G-6328)*
Ruch Industries LLC .... G 203 268-6514
  Trumbull *(G-9066)*
Ryan Industries LLC .... G 860 716-0226
  Broad Brook *(G-1152)*
Sabol Industries LLC .... G 203 430-6502
  Orange *(G-6627)*
Sadlak Manufacturing LLC .... E 860 742-0227
  Coventry *(G-1674)*
Sandy Brook Manufacturing LLC ...... G 860 205-4438
  Colebrook *(G-1586)*
Scrapeitrx LLC .... G 203 918-8323
  Fairfield *(G-2845)*
Seaboard Industries Inc .... G 973 427-8500
  Stratford *(G-8676)*

PRODUCT SECTION

MASTIC ROOFING COMPOSITION

Seasaw LLC .... G 203 815-9022
  Milford *(G-4640)*
Seawolfs Products Co .... G 203 225-0110
  Shelton *(G-7552)*
Sigma Engineering Tech LLC .... G 508 243-2888
  Durham *(G-2156)*
Simkins Industries .... G 203 787-7171
  East Haven *(G-2453)*
Siskin Agency .... G 860 561-2937
  Hartford *(G-3689)*
SJS Industries LLC .... G 203 552-3001
  Greenwich *(G-3237)*
Skyline Industries LLC .... G 860 209-8013
  East Hartford *(G-2372)*
Solon Manufacturing .... G 203 230-5300
  North Haven *(G-5996)*
Sparrow Industries .... G 203 598-0034
  Middlebury *(G-4294)*
Spartan Industries LLC .... G 203 464-8600
  North Haven *(G-5997)*
Specialty Paper Mfg LLC .... G 860 654-8044
  East Windsor *(G-2519)*
Spv Industries LLC .... G 860 953-5928
  West Hartford *(G-9861)*
Standard Manufacturing Co LLC .... G 860 225-6581
  New Britain *(G-5060)*
Stephen Mazzarelli .... G 860 482-8200
  Torrington *(G-8972)*
Sterling Industries LLC .... G 860 434-6239
  Old Lyme *(G-6519)*
Stm Industries LLC .... G 860 785-8419
  South Windsor *(G-7830)*
Suburban Industries Inc .... G 203 716-8085
  Stamford *(G-8448)*
Super Cell Industries Inc .... G 203 393-1335
  Bethany *(G-250)*
Swiss Tactics Industries LLC .... G 203 974-3427
  New Haven *(G-5408)*
Sylag Manufacturing LLC .... G 860 832-8772
  New Britain *(G-5071)*
T and A Industries LLC .... G 860 309-9211
  Torrington *(G-8975)*
Thermal Energy Resource Mfg & .... G 860 225-8792
  New Britain *(G-5073)*
Thomas Manufacturing LLC .... G 203 209-4568
  Stratford *(G-8695)*
Thommen Industries LLC .... G 203 332-7999
  Bridgeport *(G-925)*
Thorn Industries LLC .... G 845 531-7767
  Bethel *(G-352)*
Three Kings Products LLC .... G 860 945-5294
  Watertown *(G-9740)*
Tjl Industries LLC .... G 203 250-2187
  Cheshire *(G-1456)*
Torq Industries LLC .... G 860 537-8539
  Colchester *(G-1579)*
Total Industries LLC .... G 203 624-0426
  New Haven *(G-5416)*
Total Quality & Mfg Assoc .... G 203 261-3074
  Monroe *(G-4762)*
Trades Industries .... G 203 297-5648
  Danbury *(G-1965)*
Triangle Industries LLC .... G 203 297-6255
  Danbury *(G-1966)*
Triton Excimer Group LLC .... G 203 733-1063
  Ridgefield *(G-7176)*
UCI Sales Group LLC .... G 860 667-4766
  Newington *(G-5717)*
Ultra Mfg LLC .... G 203 888-1180
  Seymour *(G-7371)*
United-Bim Inc .... G 860 289-1100
  East Hartford *(G-2398)*
Valkyrie Industries .... G 860 518-5311
  Hartford *(G-3712)*
Vijay Manufacturing Co LLC .... G 860 627-4901
  Windsor Locks *(G-10501)*
VIP Associates LLC .... G 203 230-1878
  Old Lyme *(G-6521)*
Vr Industries LLC .... G 860 618-2772
  Torrington *(G-8987)*
Waterfalls .... G 203 377-1540
  Stratford *(G-8705)*
Watson Fabrication LLC .... G 860 912-8778
  Niantic *(G-5819)*
Web Industries .... G 860 779-3403
  Dayville *(G-2077)*
Wildside Fabrication LLC .... G 860 585-0514
  Bristol *(G-1140)*
Windsor Mfg .... G 860 688-6411
  Windsor *(G-10465)*

Wire Burn Industries LLC .... G 203 597-9424
  Waterbury *(G-9634)*
Wmb Industries LLC .... G 203 927-2822
  North Haven *(G-6015)*
Wmo Industries LLC .... G 203 246-2366
  Norwalk *(G-6397)*
Wraith Industries LLC .... G 860 454-4003
  Ashford *(G-70)*
Wtf Mfg Co LLC .... G 860 387-7472
  Cheshire *(G-1460)*
Yield Industries LLC .... G 860 307-8202
  Goshen *(G-3105)*
Z&Z Industries LLC .... G 203 230-9533
  Hamden *(G-3533)*
Zachman Industries LLC .... G 860 337-2234
  New Britain *(G-5085)*

MAPS

Frank Drago Custom Mapping .... G 203 483-7594
  Branford *(G-596)*
Harbor Publications Inc .... G 203 245-8009
  Madison *(G-3925)*

MARBLE BOARD

Central Marble & Granite LLC .... G 203 734-4644
  Ansonia *(G-28)*
Stepping Stones MBL & Gran LLC ..... G 203 854-0552
  Norwalk *(G-6357)*

MARBLE, BUILDING: Cut & Shaped

Eastern Marble & Granite LLC .... F 203 882-8221
  Milford *(G-4522)*
Hartford Stone Works Inc .... G 860 684-7995
  Willington *(G-10249)*
La Pietra Thinstone Veneer .... G 203 775-6162
  Brookfield *(G-1201)*
New England Stone Inc .... F 203 876-8606
  Milford *(G-4590)*
Pistritto Marble Imports Inc .... G 860 296-5263
  Hartford *(G-3664)*

MARBLE: Dimension

Infinity Stone Inc .... F 203 575-9484
  Waterbury *(G-9505)*

MARINAS

Brewer Yacht Yards Inc .... G 860 399-5128
  Old Saybrook *(G-6526)*

MARINE CARGO HANDLING SVCS

M Friedman Company .... G 860 447-9935
  Mystic *(G-4828)*

MARINE CARGO HANDLING SVCS: Marine Terminal

Stevens Industries Inc .... E 203 966-7555
  New Canaan *(G-5147)*

MARINE HARDWARE

Beckson Manufacturing Inc .... E 203 366-3644
  Bridgeport *(G-709)*
C Sherman Johnson Company .... F 860 873-8697
  East Haddam *(G-2237)*
Cornell-Carr Co Inc .... E 203 261-2529
  Monroe *(G-4706)*
Dwyer Aluminum Mast Company .... F 203 484-0419
  North Branford *(G-5836)*
Marine Fabricators .... G 203 488-7093
  Branford *(G-624)*
Walz & Krenzer Inc .... F 203 267-5712
  Oxford *(G-6699)*
Yacht Specialty Products .... G 203 565-5598
  Hamden *(G-3532)*

MARINE RELATED EQPT

Dp Marine LLC .... G 917 705-7435
  Riverside *(G-7192)*
Maretron LLP .... F 602 861-1707
  Plainville *(G-6838)*
Naiad Dynamics Us Inc .... E 203 929-6355
  Shelton *(G-7506)*
Naiad Maritime Group Inc .... E 203 944-1932
  Shelton *(G-7507)*

MARINE SPLY DEALERS

Defender Industries Inc .... C 860 701-3400
  Waterford *(G-9652)*
Seaport Marine Inc .... E 860 536-9651
  Mystic *(G-4844)*

MARINE SPLYS WHOLESALERS

Dawid Manufacturing Inc .... G 203 734-1800
  Ansonia *(G-31)*
Defender Industries Inc .... C 860 701-3400
  Waterford *(G-9652)*
Lbi Inc .... F 860 446-8058
  Groton *(G-3296)*

MARKING DEVICES

Allen of Ansonia Stamps .... G 203 736-2222
  Derby *(G-2108)*
American Sign Inc .... E 203 624-2991
  New Haven *(G-5229)*
First Place USA LLC .... G 203 777-5510
  Hamden *(G-3448)*
Hart Stamp & Seal LLC .... G 860 474-5382
  Bolton *(G-510)*
Schwerdtle Stamp Company .... E 203 330-2750
  Bridgeport *(G-898)*
Stampt By J .... G 860 995-3292
  East Hartford *(G-2376)*
United Stts Sgn & Fbrction .... E 203 601-1000
  Trumbull *(G-9088)*
William Korn Inc .... G 860 647-0284
  Manchester *(G-4107)*

MARKING DEVICES: Date Stamps, Hand, Rubber Or Metal

American Rubber Stamp Company ..... G 203 755-1135
  Cheshire *(G-1351)*

MARKING DEVICES: Embossing Seals & Hand Stamps

A D Perkins Company .... G 203 777-3456
  New Haven *(G-5217)*
Arlene Lewis .... G 860 887-4265
  Preston *(G-6981)*
D R S Desings .... G 203 744-2858
  Bethel *(G-276)*

MARKING DEVICES: Irons, Marking Or Branding

Van Deusen & Levitt Assoc Inc .... E 203 445-6244
  Weston *(G-10042)*

MARKING DEVICES: Pads, Inking & Stamping

Gutkin Enterprises LLC .... G 203 777-5510
  Hamden *(G-3454)*

MARKING DEVICES: Printing Dies, Marking Mach, Rubber/Plastic

A G Russell Company Inc .... G 860 247-9093
  Hartford *(G-3543)*

MARKING DEVICES: Textile Making Stamps, Hand, Rubber/Metal

Acme Sign Co .... F 203 324-2263
  Stamford *(G-8059)*

MASQUERADE OR THEATRICAL COSTUMES STORES

Lady and The Leopard .... G 413 531-4811
  West Suffield *(G-9987)*

MASSAGE THERAPIST

Naturally Relaxed LLC .... G 860 402-0613
  Milldale *(G-4687)*

MASTIC ROOFING COMPOSITION

Westfort Construction Corp .... G 860 833-7970
  Hamden *(G-3529)*

Employee Codes: A=Over 500 employees, B=251-500
C=101-250, D=51-100, E=20-50, F=10-19, G=1-9

MASTS: Cast Aluminum

Dwyer Aluminum Mast Company .....F 203 484-0419
  North Branford *(G-5836)*

MATERIAL GRINDING & PULVERIZING SVCS NEC

Grinding System Services LLC ....G..... 860 208-5196
  Storrs Mansfield *(G-8556)*
Hamden Grinding ....G..... 203 288-2906
  Hamden *(G-3455)*
K and R Precision Grinding ....G..... 860 505-8030
  New Britain *(G-5008)*

MATERIALS HANDLING EQPT WHOLESALERS

Conveyco Technologies Inc ....E..... 860 589-8215
  Bristol *(G-1007)*
Global Machine Movers LLC ....F..... 860 484-4449
  Watertown *(G-9709)*
Linvar LLC ....G..... 860 951-3818
  Rocky Hill *(G-7254)*
Metal Finish Eqp & Sup Co Inc ....E..... 860 668-1050
  Suffield *(G-8726)*

MATS OR MATTING, NEC: Rubber

Klean Air Supplies Inc ....G..... 860 583-1589
  Bristol *(G-1058)*

MATS, MATTING & PADS: Bathmats & Sets, Textile

American Veteran Textile LLC ....G..... 203 583-0576
  Ansonia *(G-19)*

MATTRESS STORES

Water & Air Inc ....G..... 860 423-0234
  South Windham *(G-7693)*
Weiss Sleep Shop Inc ....G..... 860 445-1219
  Groton *(G-3317)*

MEAT & FISH MARKETS: Fish

Beckley Inc ....G..... 203 488-1019
  Branford *(G-557)*
Grand Fish Market LLC ....G..... 203 691-8904
  New Haven *(G-5289)*

MEAT & FISH MARKETS: Food & Freezer Plans, Meat

Martin Rosols Inc ....E..... 860 223-2707
  New Britain *(G-5014)*

MEAT & MEAT PRDTS WHOLESALERS

App Polonia LLC ....G..... 860 747-3397
  Plainville *(G-6771)*

MEAT CUTTING & PACKING

E & J Andrychowski Farms ....G..... 860 423-4124
  Windham *(G-10345)*
Grote & Weigel Inc ....E..... 860 242-8528
  Bloomfield *(G-415)*
Manchester Packing Company Inc ....D..... 860 646-5000
  Manchester *(G-4053)*
Martin Rosols Inc ....E..... 860 223-2707
  New Britain *(G-5014)*
Maurices Country Meat Mkt LLC ....G..... 860 546-9588
  Canterbury *(G-1300)*
Noacks Meat Products ....G..... 203 235-7384
  Meriden *(G-4209)*
Teys (usa) Inc ....G..... 203 227-0481
  Westport *(G-10166)*

MEAT MARKETS

Manchester Packing Company Inc ....D..... 860 646-5000
  Manchester *(G-4053)*
Newington Meat Center ....F..... 860 666-3431
  Newington *(G-5686)*
Noacks Meat Products ....G..... 203 235-7384
  Meriden *(G-4209)*

MEAT PRDTS: Bologna, From Purchased Meat

Martin Rosols Inc ....E..... 860 223-2707
  New Britain *(G-5014)*

MEAT PRDTS: Prepared Beef Prdts From Purchased Beef

Custom Food Pdts Holdings LLC ....D..... 310 637-0900
  Greenwich *(G-3148)*

MEAT PRDTS: Sausages & Related Prdts, From Purchased Meat

Baretta Provision Inc ....F..... 860 828-0802
  East Berlin *(G-2164)*
Janik Sausage Co Inc ....G..... 860 749-4661
  Enfield *(G-2653)*

MEAT PRDTS: Sausages, From Purchased Meat

Hummel Bros Inc ....D..... 203 787-4113
  New Haven *(G-5298)*
Lamberti Packing Company ....G..... 203 562-0436
  New Haven *(G-5315)*

MEAT PRDTS: Snack Sticks, Incl Jerky, From Purchased Meat

Mister BS Jerky Co ....G..... 203 631-2758
  Meriden *(G-4206)*

MEAT PROCESSED FROM PURCHASED CARCASSES

Baltasar & Sons Inc ....G..... 203 723-0425
  Naugatuck *(G-4860)*
Capitol Sausage & Provs Inc ....G..... 860 527-5510
  Hartford *(G-3562)*
Cardoros Inc ....G..... 860 442-2907
  Waterford *(G-9644)*
Chris & Zack Gourmet Foods ....G..... 203 912-7805
  Orange *(G-6591)*
Deyulio Sausage Company LLC ....F..... 203 348-1863
  Bridgeport *(G-750)*
Grote & Weigel Inc ....E..... 860 242-8528
  Bloomfield *(G-415)*
Longhini LLC ....E..... 212 219-1230
  New Haven *(G-5320)*
Manchester Packing Company Inc ....D..... 860 646-5000
  Manchester *(G-4053)*
Maurices Country Meat Mkt LLC ....G..... 860 546-9588
  Canterbury *(G-1300)*
Newington Meat Center ....F..... 860 666-3431
  Newington *(G-5686)*

MECHANISMS: Coin-Operated Machines

Blackwold Inc ....D..... 860 526-0800
  Chester *(G-1464)*
Eastern Company ....D..... 860 526-0800
  Chester *(G-1471)*

MEDIA BUYING AGENCIES

Chief Executive Group LLC ....F..... 785 832-0303
  Stamford *(G-8143)*

MEDIA: Magnetic & Optical Recording

BEI Holdings Inc ....F..... 203 741-9300
  Wallingford *(G-9219)*
Dictaphone Corporation ....C..... 203 381-7000
  Stratford *(G-8606)*
Trod Nossel Prdctns & Rcrdng S ....G..... 203 269-4465
  Wallingford *(G-9391)*
Video Outlet ....G..... 860 568-7473
  East Hartford *(G-2400)*

MEDICAL & HOSPITAL EQPT WHOLESALERS

New England Quartz Co ....G..... 203 846-9723
  Norwalk *(G-6273)*
Tarry Medical Products Inc ....F..... 203 794-1438
  Danbury *(G-1960)*

MEDICAL & SURGICAL SPLYS: Bandages & Dressings

Beiersdorf Inc ....B..... 203 854-8000
  Norwalk *(G-6088)*
Beiersdorf North America Inc ....F..... 203 563-5800
  Wilton *(G-10272)*
Hermell Products Inc ....E..... 860 242-6550
  Bloomfield *(G-419)*

MEDICAL & SURGICAL SPLYS: Clothing, Fire Resistant & Protect

Ctl Corporation ....G..... 860 651-9173
  West Simsbury *(G-9976)*

MEDICAL & SURGICAL SPLYS: Cosmetic Restorations

Inka Inc 212 475-2180
  Greenwich *(G-3181)*

MEDICAL & SURGICAL SPLYS: Crutches & Walkers

Krutch Pack LLC ....G..... 860 836-1745
  Newington *(G-5671)*

MEDICAL & SURGICAL SPLYS: Dressings, Surgical

Dermapac Inc ....G..... 203 924-7148
  Shelton *(G-7431)*

MEDICAL & SURGICAL SPLYS: Ear Plugs

Johnson Meadows LLC ....G..... 860 642-0618
  Lebanon *(G-3856)*

MEDICAL & SURGICAL SPLYS: Grafts, Artificial

Comprhnsive Prsthetic Svcs LLC ....G..... 203 315-1400
  Branford *(G-575)*
Orteoponix LLC ....G..... 203 804-9775
  Storrs *(G-8550)*

MEDICAL & SURGICAL SPLYS: Gynecological Splys & Appliances

Coopersurgical Inc ....G..... 203 601-5200
  Trumbull *(G-9016)*
Coopersurgical Inc ....C..... 203 601-5200
  Trumbull *(G-9017)*

MEDICAL & SURGICAL SPLYS: Ligatures

Ethicon Inc ....B..... 860 621-9111
  Southington *(G-7918)*
Ethicon Inc ....G..... 860 658-7653
  Simsbury *(G-7625)*

MEDICAL & SURGICAL SPLYS: Limbs, Artificial

Biometrics Inc ....G..... 203 261-1162
  Trumbull *(G-9004)*
Connecticut Brace and Limb LLC ....G..... 860 740-2154
  Haddam *(G-3403)*
Nash Surgical Supply Co Inc ....G..... 203 828-6098
  Oxford *(G-6681)*
New England Orthotic & Prost ....F..... 203 634-7566
  Meriden *(G-4208)*
Out On A Limb ....G..... 203 315-8977
  Branford *(G-630)*
Prosthetic and Orthotic ....G..... 860 904-2419
  Bloomfield *(G-470)*
Stride Inc ....F..... 203 758-8307
  Middlebury *(G-4295)*

MEDICAL & SURGICAL SPLYS: Orthopedic Appliances

Ability Prsthtics Orthtics LLC ....G..... 860 571-8979
  Glastonbury *(G-3002)*
Adolf Gordon Corporation ....G..... 860 872-9037
  Vernon *(G-9129)*
Avitus Orthopaedics Inc ....F..... 860 637-9922
  Farmington *(G-2880)*
Cranial Technologies Inc ....F..... 203 318-8739
  Madison *(G-3915)*

MEDICAL, DENTAL & HOSPITAL EQPT, WHOLESALE: Orthopedic

GSC Orthotics Prosthetics LLC..............G...... 203 857-0887
  Norwalk *(G-6186)*
Kaufman Enterprises Inc..........................F...... 203 777-2396
  New Haven *(G-5307)*
Medical Industries America LLC..............G...... 203 254-8080
  Fairfield *(G-2813)*
Orchid Orthpd Solutions LLC....................G...... 203 922-0105
  Shelton *(G-7521)*
Wellinks Inc...G...... 650 704-0714
  New Haven *(G-5430)*
Westconn Orthopedic Laboratory...........G...... 203 743-4420
  Danbury *(G-1981)*

MEDICAL & SURGICAL SPLYS: Personal Safety Eqpt

Elvex Corporation...................................F...... 203 743-2488
  Shelton *(G-7438)*
Safety Dispatch Inc................................G...... 203 885-5722
  Ridgefield *(G-7171)*

MEDICAL & SURGICAL SPLYS: Prosthetic Appliances

Alternative Prosthetic Svcs....................G...... 203 367-1212
  Bridgeport *(G-688)*
Hanger Prsthetcs & Ortho Inc..................G...... 203 377-8820
  Stratford *(G-8623)*
Leona Corp..G...... 860 257-3840
  Wethersfield *(G-10209)*
New England Orthotic & Prost.................G...... 860 967-0877
  Hartford *(G-3651)*
Yale Comfort Shoe Center Inc.................G...... 203 338-8485
  Stratford *(G-8713)*

MEDICAL & SURGICAL SPLYS: Respiratory Protect Eqpt, Personal

Contemporary Products LLC..................E...... 860 346-9283
  Middletown *(G-4332)*
Praxair Inc...D...... 800 772-9247
  Danbury *(G-1912)*

MEDICAL & SURGICAL SPLYS: Stretchers

Dougherty Sons Fur Stretchers...............G...... 860 839-0096
  Suffield *(G-8717)*

MEDICAL & SURGICAL SPLYS: Tape, Adhesive, Non/Medicated

Ict Business..G...... 203 595-9452
  Stamford *(G-8243)*

MEDICAL & SURGICAL SPLYS: Technical Aids, Handicapped

Prospect Designs Inc.............................G...... 860 379-7858
  New Hartford *(G-5207)*

MEDICAL & SURGICAL SPLYS: Welders' Hoods

Fire & Iron...G...... 203 934-3756
  West Haven *(G-9909)*

MEDICAL EQPT: Cardiographs

Heart Health Inc....................................G...... 800 692-7753
  New Haven *(G-5295)*
Mobile Sense Technologies Inc..............G...... 203 914-5375
  Farmington *(G-2930)*

MEDICAL EQPT: Defibrillators

Defibtech LLC......................................D...... 866 333-4248
  Guilford *(G-3344)*

MEDICAL EQPT: Diagnostic

Biorasis Inc..G...... 860 429-3592
  Storrs *(G-8543)*
Cas Medical Systems Inc......................D...... 203 488-6056
  Branford *(G-570)*
Catachem Inc.......................................G...... 203 262-0330
  Oxford *(G-6649)*
Hamilton Sndstrnd Space......................A...... 860 654-6000
  Windsor Locks *(G-10489)*
M G M Instruments Inc..........................E...... 203 248-4008
  Hamden *(G-3478)*
Perosphere Technologies Inc.................G...... 475 218-4600
  Danbury *(G-1906)*

Radx Cloud...G...... 909 910-7434
  New Haven *(G-5376)*
Sekisui Diagnostics LLC........................G...... 203 602-7777
  Stamford *(G-8408)*
Sleep Management Solutions LLC..........F...... 888 497-5337
  Hartford *(G-3690)*
Supernova Diagnostics Inc....................G...... 301 792-4345
  New Canaan *(G-5149)*
Tangen Biosciences Inc.........................G...... 203 433-4045
  Branford *(G-660)*

MEDICAL EQPT: Electromedical Apparatus

Home Diagnostics Corp..........................C...... 203 445-1170
  Trumbull *(G-9035)*
Novatek Medical Inc..............................G...... 203 356-0156
  Stamford *(G-8332)*
Ram Technologies LLC..........................F...... 203 453-3916
  Guilford *(G-3385)*
Teclens LLC...G...... 919 824-5224
  Stamford *(G-8461)*
Tomtec Inc...D...... 203 281-6790
  Hamden *(G-3522)*
United States Surgical Corp....................A...... 203 845-1000
  New Haven *(G-5425)*
Vesselon Inc...G...... 203 989-0500
  Norwalk *(G-6387)*

MEDICAL EQPT: Electrotherapeutic Apparatus

Loon Medical Inc...................................G...... 860 373-0217
  Tolland *(G-8868)*

MEDICAL EQPT: Laser Systems

Abbey Aesthetics LLC...........................G...... 203 242-0497
  Avon *(G-71)*
Coherent Inc...E...... 860 243-9557
  Bloomfield *(G-404)*
Dynamic Lasers LLC..............................G...... 866 731-9610
  New Milford *(G-5528)*
Focus Medical LLC................................G...... 203 730-8885
  Bethel *(G-301)*
Jeffrey Gold..G...... 203 281-5737
  Hamden *(G-3467)*
Pioneer Optics Company Inc..................F...... 860 286-0071
  Bloomfield *(G-465)*
Respond Systems.................................F...... 203 481-2810
  Branford *(G-641)*
Safe Laser Therapy LLC........................G...... 203 261-4400
  Stamford *(G-8400)*
Star Tech Instruments Inc......................G...... 203 312-0767
  New Fairfield *(G-5176)*

MEDICAL EQPT: MRI/Magnetic Resonance Imaging Devs, Nuclear

Eclipse Systems Inc..............................G...... 203 483-0665
  Branford *(G-585)*

MEDICAL EQPT: Pacemakers

Charlies Ride..G...... 860 916-3637
  Windsor Locks *(G-10478)*

MEDICAL EQPT: Patient Monitoring

Intracranial Bioanalytics LLC..................G...... 914 490-1524
  Woodbridge *(G-10602)*
Ivy Biomedical Systems Inc...................E...... 203 481-4183
  Branford *(G-610)*
Kent Scientific Corporation....................F...... 860 626-1172
  Torrington *(G-8942)*
Vital Hlthcare Cmmncations LLC............G...... 866 478-4825
  Milford *(G-4675)*

MEDICAL EQPT: Ultrasonic Scanning Devices

Non-Invasive Med Systems LLC.............G...... 914 462-0701
  Stamford *(G-8329)*

MEDICAL EQPT: Ultrasonic, Exc Cleaning

Legnos Medical Inc...............................F...... 860 446-8058
  Groton *(G-3297)*

MEDICAL EQPT: X-Ray Apparatus & Tubes, Radiographic

High Energy X-Rays Intl Corp.................G...... 203 909-9777
  Wallingford *(G-9281)*
Lorad Corporation.................................C...... 203 790-5544
  Danbury *(G-1876)*

MEDICAL FIELD ASSOCIATION

C S M S-I P A.......................................G...... 203 562-7228
  North Haven *(G-5917)*

MEDICAL HELP SVCS

Igs-Med LLC...G...... 203 698-0396
  Old Greenwich *(G-6476)*

MEDICAL PHOTOGRAPHY & ART SVCS

Macroscopic Solutions LLC...................G...... 410 870-5566
  Tolland *(G-8869)*

MEDICAL SVCS ORGANIZATION

C S M S-I P A.......................................G...... 203 562-7228
  North Haven *(G-5917)*

MEDICAL X-RAY MACHINES & TUBES WHOLESALERS

Associated X-Ray Corp..........................F...... 203 466-2446
  East Haven *(G-2412)*

MEDICAL, DENTAL & HOSPITAL EQPT, WHOL: Hospital Eqpt & Splys

O Berk Company Neng LLC....................F...... 203 932-8000
  West Haven *(G-9940)*

MEDICAL, DENTAL & HOSPITAL EQPT, WHOL: Hosptl Eqpt/Furniture

Dermapac Inc.......................................G...... 203 924-7148
  Shelton *(G-7431)*
Hitachi Aloka Medical Ltd......................D...... 203 269-5088
  Wallingford *(G-9282)*
Hitachi Aloka Medical Amer Inc..............D...... 203 269-5088
  Wallingford *(G-9283)*
Marel Corporation.................................F...... 203 934-8187
  West Haven *(G-9932)*

MEDICAL, DENTAL & HOSPITAL EQPT, WHOL: Surgical Eqpt & Splys

Boston Endo-Surgical Tech LLC.............D...... 203 336-6479
  Bridgeport *(G-717)*
Precision Engineered Pdts LLC..............G...... 203 336-6479
  Bridgeport *(G-878)*

MEDICAL, DENTAL & HOSPITAL EQPT, WHOLESALE: Med Eqpt & Splys

Adolf Gordon Corporation.......................G...... 860 872-9037
  Vernon *(G-9129)*
Airgas Usa LLC.....................................G...... 860 442-0363
  Waterford *(G-9640)*
Contemporary Products LLC..................E...... 860 346-9283
  Middletown *(G-4332)*
Coopersurgical Inc................................G...... 203 601-5200
  Trumbull *(G-9016)*
Coopersurgical Inc................................C...... 203 601-5200
  Trumbull *(G-9017)*
S-Y-M Products Company LLC..............F...... 203 329-2469
  Litchfield *(G-3899)*
Z-Medica LLC.......................................D...... 203 294-0000
  Wallingford *(G-9405)*

MEDICAL, DENTAL & HOSPITAL EQPT, WHOLESALE: Medical Lab

Origio Midatlantic Devices Inc................E...... 856 762-2000
  Trumbull *(G-9053)*

MEDICAL, DENTAL & HOSPITAL EQPT, WHOLESALE: Orthopedic

Krutch Pack LLC...................................G...... 860 836-1745
  Newington *(G-5671)*

MEMBERSHIP ORGANIZATIONS, NEC: Charitable

MEMBERSHIP ORGANIZATIONS, NEC: Charitable

East Lyme Puppetry Project .... G 860 739-7225
  Niantic *(G-5805)*

MEMBERSHIP ORGANIZATIONS, PROFESSIONAL: Accounting Assoc

Financial Accnting Foundation .... C 203 847-0700
  Norwalk *(G-6165)*

MEMBERSHIP ORGANIZATIONS, REL: Churches, Temples & Shrines

A Guideposts Church Corp .... B 203 749-0203
  Danbury *(G-1726)*

MEMBERSHIP ORGANIZATIONS, RELIGIOUS: Assembly Of God Church

Evangelical Christian Center .... G 860 429-0856
  Ashford *(G-61)*

MEMBERSHIP ORGS, BUSINESS: Growers' Marketing Advisory Svc

Creative Stone Group Inc .... G 203 554-7773
  Stamford *(G-8169)*

MEMBERSHIP SPORTS & RECREATION CLUBS

Club Resource Inc .... G 317 225-6940
  Canton *(G-1310)*

MEMORIALS, MONUMENTS & MARKERS

Signature Pet Memorials .... G 860 455-0118
  Chaplin *(G-1341)*

MEN'S & BOYS' HATS STORES

32 Degrees LLC .... G 978 602-2007
  West Hartford *(G-9768)*

MEN'S & BOYS' SPORTSWEAR WHOLESALERS

Del Arbour LLC .... F 203 882-8501
  Milford *(G-4506)*
Gg Sportswear Inc .... E 860 296-4441
  Hartford *(G-3599)*
Michael Violano .... G 203 934-3368
  West Haven *(G-9937)*

MEN'S CLOTHING STORES: Everyday, Exc Suits & Sportswear

Montanas Board Sports .... G 860 537-2927
  Colchester *(G-1557)*

METAL COMPONENTS: Prefabricated

Brw Associates Inc .... G 203 426-3318
  Sandy Hook *(G-7301)*
Rwt Corporation .... E 203 245-2731
  Madison *(G-3953)*

METAL CUTTING SVCS

Emhart Teknologies LLC .... G 877 364-2781
  Danbury *(G-1808)*
Precision Cut-Off Service Inc .... G 860 582-7521
  Bristol *(G-1095)*

METAL DETECTORS

Colonial Metal Detectors .... G 860 317-1284
  Plainfield *(G-6745)*

METAL FABRICATORS: Architechtural

All Star Welding & Dem LLC .... G 203 948-0528
  Danbury *(G-1735)*
American Iron Works .... G 203 469-6117
  East Haven *(G-2409)*
ARC and Hammer .... G 860 605-0344
  Canton *(G-1304)*
Company of Craftsmen .... G 860 536-4189
  Mystic *(G-4808)*

Dyco Industries Inc .... E 860 289-4957
  South Windsor *(G-7741)*
East Windsor Metal Fabg Inc .... F 860 528-7107
  South Windsor *(G-7745)*
Eastern Metal Works Inc .... E 203 878-6995
  Milford *(G-4523)*
Engineered Building Pdts Inc .... E 860 243-1110
  Bloomfield *(G-409)*
F & L Iron Work Inc .... G 203 777-0751
  New Haven *(G-5278)*
Falling Hammer Productions LLC .... G 203 879-1786
  Wolcott *(G-10565)*
Ida International Inc .... E 203 736-9249
  Derby *(G-2116)*
International Pipe & Stl Corp .... F 203 481-7102
  North Branford *(G-5846)*
Jeffrey Mingollello Backhoe Sr .... G 203 735-5458
  Ansonia *(G-42)*
Jozef Custom Ironworks Inc .... F 203 384-6363
  Bridgeport *(G-810)*
Kammetal Inc .... E 718 722-9991
  Naugatuck *(G-4897)*
Ken Hastedt .... G 203 268-6563
  Monroe *(G-4725)*
Kenneth Lynch & Sons Inc .... G 203 762-8363
  Oxford *(G-6671)*
Leed - Himmel Industries Inc .... D 203 288-8484
  Hamden *(G-3472)*
Leek Building Products Inc .... G 203 853-3883
  Norwalk *(G-6232)*
Lpg Metal Crafts LLC .... G 860 982-3573
  Plainville *(G-6835)*
Luckey LLC .... F 203 285-3819
  New Haven *(G-5322)*
Magic Industries Inc .... F 860 949-8380
  Bozrah *(G-527)*
Musano Inc .... F 203 879-4651
  Wolcott *(G-10575)*
Richard Sadowski .... G 203 372-2151
  Fairfield *(G-2836)*
Ryall Rbert Archtctral Ir Wrks .... G 203 458-1356
  Guilford *(G-3387)*
Schiess John .... G 860 664-0336
  Clinton *(G-1522)*
Shepard Steel Co Inc .... D 860 525-4446
  Hartford *(G-3685)*
Shepard Steel Co Inc .... E 860 525-4446
  Newington *(G-5704)*
Stamford Forge & Metal Cft Inc .... G 203 348-8290
  Stamford *(G-8437)*
Steve S Custom Ironworks LLC .... G 203 229-0612
  Norwalk *(G-6358)*
Steven Rosenburg .... G 203 329-8798
  Stamford *(G-8443)*
Susan Martovich .... G 203 881-1848
  Oxford *(G-6696)*
United Metal Solutions .... G 860 610-4026
  East Hartford *(G-2388)*
Washington Concrete Products .... F 860 747-5242
  Plainville *(G-6876)*

METAL FABRICATORS: Plate

Apcompower Inc .... E 860 688-1911
  Windsor *(G-10362)*
Brian Arnio .... G 860 779-2983
  Sterling *(G-8508)*
Containment Solutions Inc .... C 860 651-4371
  Simsbury *(G-7614)*
CTI Industries Inc .... E 203 795-0070
  Orange *(G-6593)*
GE Steam Power Inc .... G 860 688-1911
  Windsor *(G-10391)*
Hi-Tech Fabricating Inc .... E 203 284-0894
  Cheshire *(G-1396)*
Johnstone Company Inc .... E 203 239-5834
  North Haven *(G-5954)*
Mitchell-Bate Company .... G 203 233-0862
  Waterbury *(G-9545)*
United Steel Inc .... C 860 289-2323
  East Hartford *(G-2389)*
Vulcan Industries Inc .... C 860 683-2005
  Windsor *(G-10460)*

METAL FABRICATORS: Sheet

A B & F Sheet Metal .... G 203 272-9340
  Cheshire *(G-1344)*
A G C Incorporated .... C 203 235-3361
  Meriden *(G-4138)*
Acier Fab LLC .... G 860 282-1211
  South Windsor *(G-7700)*

Advanced Sheetmetal Assoc LLC .... E 860 349-1644
  Middlefield *(G-4298)*
Advantage Sheet Metal Mfg LLC .... E 203 720-0929
  Naugatuck *(G-4854)*
Aerocor Inc .... F 203 281-9274
  East Windsor *(G-2479)*
Airtech of Stamford Inc .... E 203 323-3959
  Stamford *(G-8070)*
All Steel Fabricating Inc .... G 203 783-1860
  Milford *(G-4450)*
American Cladding Technologies .... G 860 413-3098
  East Granby *(G-2188)*
American Performance Pdts LLC .... G 203 269-4468
  Wallingford *(G-9201)*
Ansonia Stl Fabrication Co Inc .... E 203 888-4509
  Beacon Falls *(G-129)*
Atlantic Vent & Eqp Co Inc .... G 860 635-1300
  Cromwell *(G-1690)*
B L C Investments Inc .... G 203 877-1888
  Milford *(G-4464)*
Bantam Sheet Metal .... G 860 567-9690
  Bantam *(G-123)*
Barzetti Welding LLC .... G 203 748-3200
  Bethel *(G-261)*
Bull Metal Products Inc .... E 860 346-9691
  Middletown *(G-4329)*
C B S Contractors Inc .... F 203 734-8015
  Ansonia *(G-26)*
Carlson Sheet Metal .... G 860 354-4660
  New Milford *(G-5516)*
Clemson Sheet Metal LLC .... G 203 871-9369
  Vernon Rockville *(G-9164)*
Clemson Sheetmetal LLC .... G 860 721-7906
  Ellington *(G-2581)*
Complete Sheet Metal LLC .... G 860 310-5447
  Berlin *(G-172)*
Connecticut Fabricating Co Inc .... G 203 878-3465
  Milford *(G-4496)*
Copperworks Inc .... G 203 248-3516
  Hamden *(G-3432)*
Country Side Sheet Metal .... G 860 872-5729
  Ellington *(G-2584)*
Croteau Development Group Inc .... G 860 684-3605
  Stafford Springs *(G-8022)*
Custom & Precision Pdts Inc .... G 203 281-0818
  Hamden *(G-3436)*
Dasco Welded Products Inc .... F 203 754-9353
  Waterbury *(G-9463)*
DBA Ne Sheet Metal .... G 860 584-0362
  Bristol *(G-1013)*
Dyco Industries Inc .... E 860 289-4957
  South Windsor *(G-7741)*
East Coast Sheet Metal LLC .... F 860 283-1126
  Litchfield *(G-3888)*
Engineered Building Pdts Inc .... E 860 243-1110
  Bloomfield *(G-409)*
Erickson Metals Corporation .... E 203 272-2918
  Cheshire *(G-1386)*
Fonda Fabricating & Welding Co .... G 860 793-0601
  Plainville *(G-6812)*
G & R Welding .... G 860 526-3353
  Deep River *(G-2090)*
General Dynamics Info Tech Inc .... D 860 441-2400
  Pawcatuck *(G-6712)*
Gintys Welding Service Inc .... G 203 270-3399
  Sandy Hook *(G-7314)*
Hamden Sheet Metal Inc .... G 203 776-1472
  Hamden *(G-3459)*
Hasson Sheet Metal LLC .... G 860 698-6951
  Enfield *(G-2648)*
Hi-Tech Fabricating Inc .... E 203 284-0894
  Cheshire *(G-1396)*
Hollums Sheet Metal LLC .... G 860 640-4970
  West Haven *(G-9915)*
Illinois Tool Works Inc .... E 203 720-1676
  Naugatuck *(G-4890)*
J M Sheet Metal LLC .... G 860 747-5537
  Plainville *(G-6826)*
J OConnor LLC .... F 860 665-7702
  Newington *(G-5666)*
JV Sheet Metal .... G 203 540-0383
  Stamford *(G-8271)*
Ken Hastedt .... G 203 268-6563
  Monroe *(G-4725)*
Labco Welding Inc .... G 860 632-2625
  Middletown *(G-4367)*
Leek Building Products Inc .... E 203 853-3883
  Norwalk *(G-6232)*
Link Mechanical Services Inc .... E 860 826-5880
  New Britain *(G-5011)*

PRODUCT SECTION

METAL STAMPING, FOR THE TRADE

Lostocco Refuse Service LLC .... E 203 748-9296
  Danbury *(G-1877)*
Lyons Slitting Inc .... F 203 755-4564
  Waterbury *(G-9520)*
M Cubed Technologies Inc .... E 203 304-2940
  Newtown *(G-5757)*
M J Boller Company .... G 860 738-8073
  Pine Meadow *(G-6735)*
M J Williams Heating and AC .... G 860 923-6991
  Woodstock *(G-10670)*
Marine Fabricators .... G 203 488-7093
  Branford *(G-624)*
Marsco Sheetmetal LLC .... G 203 459-2698
  Monroe *(G-4733)*
McMullin Manufacturing Corp .... E 203 740-3360
  Brookfield *(G-1204)*
Microfab Company .... G 203 267-1000
  Oxford *(G-6677)*
Midget Louver Company Inc .... G 203 783-1444
  Milford *(G-4578)*
Mrnd LLC .... G 860 749-0256
  Enfield *(G-2663)*
Niklyn Corp .... G 860 440-6244
  New Haven *(G-5350)*
Northern Comfort Mech LLC .... G 203 456-5163
  Danbury *(G-1895)*
Panel Shop Inc .... G 203 377-6208
  Stratford *(G-8661)*
Phoenix Sheet Metal LLC .... G 860 478-4579
  Bloomfield *(G-464)*
Precision Shtmtl Fabrication .... G 860 388-4466
  Old Saybrook *(G-6567)*
Progressive Sheetmetal LLC .... E 860 436-9884
  South Windsor *(G-7814)*
Reliable Welding & Speed LLC .... G 860 749-3977
  Enfield *(G-2687)*
Richard Sadowski .... G 203 372-2151
  Fairfield *(G-2836)*
Rissolo Precision Sheet Metal .... G 860 355-1949
  New Milford *(G-5585)*
Saw Mill Sheet Metal LLC .... G 860 779-3194
  Sterling *(G-8516)*
Seconn Automation Solutions .... F 860 442-4325
  Waterford *(G-9669)*
Sheetmetal Systems Inc .... G 203 878-2633
  Milford *(G-4642)*
Shoreline Metal Services LLC .... G 203 466-7372
  East Haven *(G-2452)*
Sound Manufacturing Inc .... D 860 388-4466
  Old Saybrook *(G-6569)*
Stauffer Sheet Metal LLC .... G 860 623-0518
  Windsor *(G-10443)*
Suraci Corp .... D 203 624-1345
  New Haven *(G-5406)*
Target Custom Manufacturing Co .... G 860 388-5848
  Old Saybrook *(G-6573)*
Tech-Air Incorporated .... E 860 848-1287
  Uncasville *(G-9104)*
Thomas La Ganga .... G 860 489-0920
  Torrington *(G-8977)*
Thyssenkrupp Materials NA Inc .... E 203 265-1567
  Wallingford *(G-9382)*
Trumpf Photonics Inc .... G 860 255-6000
  Farmington *(G-2969)*
United Steel Inc .... C 860 289-2323
  East Hartford *(G-2389)*
United Stts Sgn & Fbrction .... E 203 601-1000
  Trumbull *(G-9088)*
Universal Metalworks LLC .... G 203 239-6349
  North Haven *(G-6009)*
Vernier Metal Fabricating Inc .... D 203 881-3133
  Seymour *(G-7372)*
Vulcan Industries Inc .... C 860 683-2005
  Windsor *(G-10460)*
Wendon Technologies Inc .... D 203 348-6271
  Stamford *(G-8491)*
Whitcraft LLC .... C 860 974-0786
  Eastford *(G-2544)*
Whitcraft Scrborough/Tempe LLC .... C 860 974-0786
  Eastford *(G-2545)*

METAL FABRICATORS: Structural, Ship

Berlin Steel Construction Co .... E 860 828-3531
  Kensington *(G-3806)*

METAL FINISHING SVCS

Accurate Burring Company .... F 860 747-8640
  Plainville *(G-6765)*
Allied Metal Finishing L L C .... G 860 290-8865
  South Windsor *(G-7704)*
Anodic Incorporated .... F 203 268-9966
  Stevenson *(G-8520)*
Connecticut Anodizing Finshg .... E 203 367-1765
  Bridgeport *(G-739)*
Deburr Co .... G 860 621-6634
  Plantsville *(G-6890)*
Ems International Inc .... G 860 526-2060
  Chester *(G-1472)*
Eyelet Crafters Inc .... D 203 757-9221
  Waterbury *(G-9476)*
Hubbard-Hall Inc .... C 203 756-5521
  Waterbury *(G-9501)*
J H Metal Finishing Inc .... G 860 223-6412
  New Britain *(G-5005)*
Lake Grinding Company .... G 203 336-3767
  Bridgeport *(G-822)*
Nemfi Pfs .... G 860 640-4600
  Windsor *(G-10413)*
Plainville Electro Plating Co .... G 860 525-5328
  Hartford *(G-3665)*
Quality Rolling Deburring Inc .... D 860 283-0271
  Thomaston *(G-8801)*
Reliable Plating & Polsg Co .... G 860 366-5261
  Bridgeport *(G-888)*
Scotts Metal Finishing LLC .... F 860 589-3778
  Bristol *(G-1116)*
Suraci Metal Finishing LLC .... E 203 624-1345
  New Haven *(G-5407)*
Technical Metal Finishing Inc .... E 203 284-7825
  Wallingford *(G-9379)*

METAL MINING SVCS

Amci Capital LP .... G 203 625-9200
  Greenwich *(G-3118)*
Imagin Minerals .... G 203 762-1249
  Wilton *(G-10300)*

METAL RESHAPING & REPLATING SVCS

Rader Industries Inc .... G 203 334-6739
  Bridgeport *(G-884)*

METAL SERVICE CENTERS & OFFICES

Alloy Specialties Incorporated .... E 860 646-4587
  Manchester *(G-3981)*
M Cubed Technologies Inc .... E 203 304-2940
  Newtown *(G-5757)*
Scotts Metal Finishing LLC .... F 860 589-3778
  Bristol *(G-1116)*
Smm New England Corporation .... F 203 777-7445
  New Haven *(G-5397)*
Stamptech Incorporated .... F 860 628-9090
  Southington *(G-7980)*
Titanium Metals Corporation .... F 860 627-7051
  East Windsor *(G-2527)*

METAL SLITTING & SHEARING

Goodyfab Llc .... G 203 927-3059
  North Branford *(G-5839)*
Lyons Slitting Inc .... F 203 755-4564
  Waterbury *(G-9520)*

METAL SPINNING FOR THE TRADE

American Standard Company .... E 860 628-9643
  Southington *(G-7889)*
Bracone Metal Spinning Inc .... E 860 628-5927
  Southington *(G-7897)*
Fries Spinning & Stampings .... G 203 265-1678
  Wallingford *(G-9271)*

METAL STAMPING, FOR THE TRADE

A & D Components Inc .... G 860 582-9541
  Bristol *(G-949)*
Acme Monaco Corporation .... C 860 224-1349
  New Britain *(G-4934)*
Alto Products Corp Al .... E 860 747-2736
  Plainville *(G-6769)*
Arcade Technology LLC .... E 203 366-3871
  Bridgeport *(G-699)*
Arrow Manufacturing Company .... E 860 589-3900
  Bristol *(G-966)*
Atlas Stamping & Mfg Corp .... E 860 757-3233
  Newington *(G-5629)*
Barlow Metal Stamping Inc .... E 860 583-1387
  Bristol *(G-972)*
Barnes Group Inc .... B 860 583-7070
  Bristol *(G-973)*
Bessette Holdings Inc .... E 860 289-6000
  East Hartford *(G-2298)*
Blase Manufacturing Company .... D 203 375-5646
  Stratford *(G-8584)*
Bml Tool & Mfg Corp .... D 203 880-9485
  Monroe *(G-4699)*
Bridgeport TI & Stamping Corp .... E 203 336-2501
  Bridgeport *(G-723)*
Bristol Tool & Die Company .... E 860 582-2577
  Bristol *(G-993)*
C F D Engineering Company .... E 203 758-4148
  Prospect *(G-6996)*
Companion Industries Inc .... D 860 628-0504
  Southington *(G-7907)*
Component Engineers Inc .... E 203 269-0557
  Wallingford *(G-9235)*
Connectcut Spring Stmping Corp .... B 860 677-1341
  Farmington *(G-2891)*
Cowles Stamping Inc .... E 203 865-3117
  North Haven *(G-5931)*
Eyelet Crafters Inc .... D 203 757-9221
  Waterbury *(G-9476)*
Eyelet Design Inc .... D 203 754-4141
  Waterbury *(G-9477)*
Eyelet Toolmakers Inc .... E 860 274-5423
  Watertown *(G-9705)*
Four Star Manufacturing Co .... E 860 583-1614
  Bristol *(G-1041)*
Gem Manufacturing Co Inc .... D 203 574-1466
  Waterbury *(G-9485)*
Gemco Manufacturing Co Inc .... E 860 628-5529
  Southington *(G-7926)*
Glen Manufacturing Co Inc .... G 860 589-0881
  Terryville *(G-8758)*
Globe Tool & Met Stampg Co Inc .... E 860 621-6807
  Southington *(G-7929)*
H&T Waterbury Inc .... C 203 574-2240
  Waterbury *(G-9494)*
Hob Industries Inc .... E 203 879-3028
  Wolcott *(G-10568)*
Hobson and Motzer Incorporated .... C 860 349-1756
  Durham *(G-2149)*
Howard Engineering LLC .... E 203 729-5213
  Naugatuck *(G-4889)*
J & J Precision Eyelet Inc .... D 203 283-8243
  Thomaston *(G-8793)*
J T Tool Co Inc .... G 203 874-1234
  Milford *(G-4558)*
Jo Vek Tool and Die Mfg Co .... G 203 755-1884
  Waterbury *(G-9511)*
Joma Incorporated .... E 203 759-0848
  Waterbury *(G-9513)*
Lawrence Holdings Inc .... F 203 949-1600
  Wallingford *(G-9301)*
Lyons Tool and Die Company .... E 203 238-2689
  Meriden *(G-4190)*
Marion Manufacturing Company .... E 203 272-5376
  Cheshire *(G-1411)*
Mastercraft Tool and Mch Co .... F 860 628-5551
  Southington *(G-7950)*
McM Stamping Corporation .... E 203 792-3080
  Danbury *(G-1881)*
McMullin Manufacturing Corp .... E 203 740-3360
  Brookfield *(G-1204)*
Metalform Acquisition LLC .... F 860 224-2630
  New Britain *(G-5016)*
Metallon Inc .... E 860 283-8265
  Thomaston *(G-8797)*
MJM Marga LLC .... G 203 729-0600
  Naugatuck *(G-4903)*
Mohawk Manufacturing Company .... G 860 632-2345
  Middletown *(G-4381)*
National Die Company .... G 203 879-1408
  Wolcott *(G-10576)*
National Spring & Stamping Inc .... E 860 283-0203
  Thomaston *(G-8798)*
Okay Industries Inc .... C 860 225-8707
  Berlin *(G-204)*
Oscar Jobs .... G 860 583-7834
  Bristol *(G-1083)*
Owen Tool and Mfg Co Inc .... G 860 628-6540
  Southington *(G-7961)*
P&G Metal Components Corp .... F 860 243-2220
  Bloomfield *(G-458)*
Patriot Manufacturing LLC .... G 860 506-2213
  Bristol *(G-1086)*
Precision Resource Inc .... C 203 925-0012
  Shelton *(G-7534)*
Precision Rsurce Intl Sls Corp .... G 203 925-0012
  Shelton *(G-7535)*

Employee Codes: A=Over 500 employees, B=251-500
C=101-250, D=51-100, E=20-50, F=10-19, G=1-9

METAL STAMPING, FOR THE TRADE

Preferred Tool & Die Inc .... D 203 925-8525
  Shelton *(G-7537)*
Preyco Mfg Co Inc .... G 203 574-4545
  Waterbury *(G-9587)*
Prospect Machine Products Inc .... E 203 758-4448
  Prospect *(G-7019)*
Richards Metal Products Inc .... F 203 879-2555
  Wolcott *(G-10583)*
RTC Mfg Co Inc .... G 800 888-3701
  Watertown *(G-9731)*
Satellite Aerospace Inc .... E 860 643-2771
  Manchester *(G-4085)*
Southington Tool & Mfg Corp .... E 860 276-0021
  Plantsville *(G-6912)*
Spirol International Corp .... C 860 774-8571
  Danielson *(G-2003)*
Spirol Intl Holdg Corp .... C 860 774-8571
  Danielson *(G-2004)*
Stewart Efi LLC .... C 860 283-8213
  Thomaston *(G-8807)*
Stewart Efi Texas LLC .... G 860 283-8213
  Thomaston *(G-8810)*
Taco Fasteners Inc .... F 860 747-5597
  Plainville *(G-6867)*
Target Custom Manufacturing Co .... G 860 388-5848
  Old Saybrook *(G-6573)*
Tiger Enterprises Inc .... E 860 621-9155
  Plantsville *(G-6914)*
Truelove & Maclean Inc .... C 860 274-9600
  Watertown *(G-9743)*
Truelove Maclean Inc .... G 203 574-2240
  Waterbury *(G-9619)*
Weimann Brothers Mfg Co .... F 203 735-3311
  Derby *(G-2130)*

METAL STAMPINGS: Perforated

Excel Spring & Stamping LLC .... G 860 585-1495
  Bristol *(G-1033)*
Hylie Products Incorporated .... F 203 439-8786
  Cheshire *(G-1397)*

METAL TREATING COMPOUNDS

United States Chemical Corp .... G 860 621-6831
  Plantsville *(G-6917)*

METALS SVC CENTERS & WHOL: Structural Shapes, Iron Or Steel

Logan Steel Inc .... E 203 235-0811
  Meriden *(G-4188)*

METALS SVC CENTERS & WHOLESALERS: Bars, Metal

Fox Steel Products LLC .... F 203 799-2356
  Orange *(G-6602)*
Fox Steel Services LLC .... G 203 799-2356
  Orange *(G-6603)*

METALS SVC CENTERS & WHOLESALERS: Cable, Wire

Guaranteed Quality Parts L L C .... G 860 450-0419
  Willimantic *(G-10228)*
Loos & Co Inc .... B 860 928-7981
  Pomfret *(G-6933)*
Tsmc Inc .... G 860 283-8265
  Torrington *(G-8985)*

METALS SVC CENTERS & WHOLESALERS: Nonferrous Sheets, Etc

Tico Titanium Inc .... E 248 446-0400
  Wallingford *(G-9384)*

METALS SVC CENTERS & WHOLESALERS: Pipe & Tubing, Steel

International Pipe & Stl Corp .... F 203 481-7102
  North Branford *(G-5846)*
Stephens Pipe & Steel LLC .... F 877 777-8721
  Manchester *(G-4095)*

METALS SVC CENTERS & WHOLESALERS: Reinforcement Mesh, Wire

Miller Rebar LLC .... G 203 717-6645
  New Haven *(G-5331)*

METALS SVC CENTERS & WHOLESALERS: Rope, Wire, Exc Insulated

East Shre Wre Rpe/Rggng Spply .... F 203 469-5204
  North Haven *(G-5934)*

METALS SVC CENTERS & WHOLESALERS: Sheets, Metal

Aerospace Alloys Inc .... D 860 882-0019
  Bloomfield *(G-382)*

METALS SVC CENTERS & WHOLESALERS: Stampings, Metal

Newhart Products Inc .... E 203 878-3546
  Milford *(G-4592)*

METALS SVC CENTERS & WHOLESALERS: Steel

American Metals Coal Intl Inc .... F 203 625-9200
  Greenwich *(G-3120)*
ATI Flat Rlled Pdts Hldngs LLC .... F 203 756-7414
  Waterbury *(G-9435)*
Bushwick Metals LLC .... G 203 630-2459
  Meriden *(G-4152)*
Contractors Steel Supply .... F 203 782-1221
  North Haven *(G-5926)*
Eastern Metal Works Inc .... E 203 878-6995
  Milford *(G-4523)*
Magna Steel Sales Inc .... F 203 888-0300
  Beacon Falls *(G-142)*
Nesci Enterprises Inc .... G 860 267-2588
  East Hampton *(G-2271)*
Pepin Steel and Iron Works LLC ...... G 860 582-1852
  Bristol *(G-1090)*
Superb Steel LLC .... G 860 518-7281
  New Britain *(G-5068)*

METALS SVC CENTERS & WHOLESALERS: Strip, Metal

Ulbrich Stainless Steels .... D 203 239-4481
  North Haven *(G-6008)*

METALS SVC CNTRS & WHOL: Metal Wires, Ties, Cables/Screening

MGS Manufacturing Inc .... G 203 484-9275
  North Branford *(G-5850)*

METALS SVC CTRS & WHOLESALERS: Aluminum Bars, Rods, Etc

Erickson Metals Corporation .... E 203 272-2918
  Cheshire *(G-1386)*
Yarde Metals Inc .... B 860 406-6061
  Southington *(G-7997)*

METALS: Honeycombed

Hexcel Corporation .... E 203 969-0666
  Stamford *(G-8233)*

METALS: Precious NEC

Amentos Gold Buyers and Secon .... G 203 691-1020
  North Haven *(G-5900)*
Bal International Inc .... E 203 359-6775
  Stamford *(G-8106)*
Elemetal Direct Usa LLC .... G 860 290-1701
  East Hartford *(G-2320)*
Judith E Goldstein Company .... G 860 644-4646
  South Windsor *(G-7780)*
Northeastern Metals Corp .... G 203 348-8088
  Stamford *(G-8330)*
R & A Precious Metals LLC .... G 203 220-8265
  Trumbull *(G-9059)*
Reliable Silver Corporation .... F 203 574-7732
  Naugatuck *(G-4916)*

METALS: Precious, Secondary

Viking Platinum LLC .... F 203 574-7979
  Waterbury *(G-9621)*

METALS: Primary Nonferrous, NEC

Aztec Industries LLC .... E 860 343-1960
  Middletown *(G-4321)*

Engelhard Surface Technologies ...... G 860 623-9901
  East Windsor *(G-2491)*
Ulbrich Stainless Steels .... C 203 269-2507
  Wallingford *(G-9393)*

METALWORK: Miscellaneous

Aerospace Alloys Inc .... D 860 882-0019
  Bloomfield *(G-382)*
C & S Engineering Inc .... E 203 235-5727
  Meriden *(G-4153)*
Cem Group LLC .... F 860 675-5000
  Burlington *(G-1263)*
Engineered Building Pdts Inc .... E 860 243-1110
  Bloomfield *(G-409)*
Graycon Defense Industries LLC ..... G 860 339-2505
  Chester *(G-1474)*
Helix Mooring Systems .... G 860 628-0933
  Southington *(G-7933)*
Met Tech Inc .... G 203 254-9319
  Fairfield *(G-2814)*
Michael Petruzzi .... G 860 621-7515
  Plantsville *(G-6902)*
Quality Engineering Svcs Inc .... E 203 269-5054
  Wallingford *(G-9345)*
Shamrock Sheet Metal .... G 860 537-4282
  Colchester *(G-1576)*
Simpson Strong-Tie Company Inc ... F 860 741-8923
  Enfield *(G-2697)*
Supercool Metals LLC .... G 203 823-9032
  New Haven *(G-5404)*
United Metal Solutions .... G 860 610-4026
  East Hartford *(G-2388)*

METALWORK: Ornamental

Art Metal Industries LLC .... G 203 733-3092
  New Milford *(G-5505)*
Connecticut Iron Works Inc .... G 203 869-0657
  Greenwich *(G-3144)*
Future Swiss .... G 860 283-4358
  Thomaston *(G-8790)*
Garden Iron LLC .... G 860 767-9917
  Westbrook *(G-9997)*
Goodyfab Llc .... G 203 927-3059
  North Branford *(G-5839)*
Pequonnock Ironworks Inc .... F 203 336-2178
  Bridgeport *(G-868)*
United Steel Inc .... G 860 289-2323
  East Hartford *(G-2389)*

METERING DEVICES: Measuring, Mechanical

Veeder-Root Company .... D 860 651-2700
  Weatogue *(G-9760)*

METERING DEVICES: Water Quality Monitoring & Control Systems

American Marine Inc .... G 914 763-5367
  Greenwich *(G-3119)*

METERS: Liquid

Jedcontrol Corp .... G 914 328-8593
  Danbury *(G-1859)*

METERS: Turbine Flow, Indl Process

Hamilton Sundstrand Corp .... A 860 654-6000
  Windsor Locks *(G-10491)*

MGMT CONSULTING SVCS: Matls, Incl Purch, Handle & Invntry

Management Hlth Solutions Inc .... E 888 647-4621
  Stratford *(G-8647)*

MICA PRDTS

Brico Inc .... G 203 693-0323
  Bloomfield *(G-400)*

MICROCIRCUITS, INTEGRATED: Semiconductor

Carten-Fujikin Incorporated .... G 203 699-2134
  Cheshire *(G-1367)*

MICROPHONES

Telefunken USA LLC .... F 860 882-5919
  South Windsor *(G-7832)*

PRODUCT SECTION

MICROPROCESSORS
Oracle America Inc ....D...... 203 703-3000
  Stamford (G-8345)

MICROSCOPES
Macroscopic Solutions LLC..................G...... 410 870-5566
  Tolland (G-8869)

MICROSCOPES: Electron & Proton
Macroscopic Solutions LLC..................G...... 410 870-5566
  Tolland (G-8869)

MICROWAVE COMPONENTS
Ens Microwave LLC..............................G...... 203 794-7940
  Danbury (G-1813)
Times Microwave Systems Inc ....B...... 203 949-8400
  Wallingford (G-9386)

MILITARY GOODS & REGALIA STORES
Recon Tactical LLC...............................G...... 860 677-8202
  Farmington (G-2954)

MILITARY INSIGNIA, TEXTILE
Airborne Industries Inc..........................F...... 203 315-0200
  Branford (G-538)

MILL PRDTS: Structural & Rail
Boudreaus Welding Co Inc ....E...... 860 774-2771
  Dayville (G-2055)

MILLING: Chemical
3d Solutions LLC..................................G...... 860 454-7302
  Tolland (G-8845)

MILLING: Corn Grits & Flakes, For Brewers' Use
Lake House Brewing Company LLC .....G...... 917 620-6636
  Goshen (G-3102)

MILLWORK
450 Woodworking LLC ....G...... 860 350-0525
  New Milford (G-5501)
542 Rustic Woodworks..........................G...... 860 387-8680
  Norfolk (G-5822)
AB Custom Woodwork LLC ....G...... 203 334-7882
  Fairfield (G-2742)
AGA Mill Work LLC................................G...... 860 426-9901
  Southington (G-7888)
Aj Wood Work LLC.................................G...... 203 826-9851
  Danbury (G-1734)
Alvarado Custom Cabinetry LLC...........F...... 203 831-0181
  Norwalk (G-6067)
American Custom Fine Woodwrkng .....G...... 860 871-8783
  Tolland (G-8848)
Anchor Woodworking LLC.....................G...... 860 376-0795
  Jewett City (G-3791)
Apex Cstm Cabinetry Wdwkg LLC........G...... 203 396-0496
  Bridgeport (G-697)
Apple Hill Woodworking LLC.................G...... 860 945-6102
  Watertown (G-9682)
Arbon Equipment Corporation ....G...... 410 796-5902
  Bloomfield (G-388)
Architectural Door Corp ....G...... 203 255-3033
  Fairfield (G-2748)
Atlantic Woodcraft Inc ....F...... 860 749-4887
  Enfield (G-2616)
Atlas Metal and Wood Works LLC.........G...... 805 450-7031
  West Hartford (G-9776)
Axels Custom Woodworking LLC..........G...... 203 869-1317
  Greenwich (G-3126)
AZ Woodworking LLC............................G...... 203 595-9063
  Stamford (G-8102)
Aztec Woodworking................................G...... 203 272-3814
  Cheshire (G-1359)
B Douglass Custom Mllwk LLC..............G...... 860 338-9305
  Glastonbury (G-3010)
B H Davis Co ....G...... 860 923-2771
  Thompson (G-8829)
Belo Woodworking LLC.........................G...... 727 249-8514
  West Simsbury (G-9972)
Bergan Architectural Wdwkg Inc............E...... 860 346-0869
  Middletown (G-4324)
Birkett Woodworking LLC.......................G...... 860 361-9142
  Morris (G-4787)

Blais Woodworks LLC...........................G...... 860 274-2906
  Watertown (G-9684)
Bonnieview Woodwork LLC...................G...... 860 767-3299
  Ivoryton (G-3783)
Bradley Woodworking LLC....................G...... 203 746-8357
  New Fairfield (G-5162)
Breakfast Woodworks Inc ....G...... 203 458-8888
  Guilford (G-3332)
Brian Daigle ....G...... 860 263-7831
  Hartford (G-3559)
Budget Woodworker LLC......................G...... 860 468-5551
  Niantic (G-5802)
Built To Last Fine Wdwkg LLC ....G...... 860 619-0119
  New Preston (G-5611)
Byrne Woodworking Inc ....G...... 203 953-3205
  Bridgeport (G-727)
C J Cushing Woodworking....................G...... 860 848-2746
  Old Lyme (G-6494)
C J S Millwork Inc..................................F...... 203 708-0080
  Stamford (G-8124)
C West Woodworks ....G...... 860 309-7362
  Torrington (G-8908)
Cabin Woodworks..................................G...... 203 410-1073
  Hamden (G-3421)
Cambrdge Fine Wdwkg Renovation......G...... 860 583-7561
  Bristol (G-998)
Candle Woodworks................................G...... 860 350-4390
  Sherman (G-7591)
Cavekraft Woodworking LLC.................G...... 860 230-4480
  North Stonington (G-6021)
Cedar Woodworking ....G...... 203 335-4108
  Bridgeport (G-732)
Century Woodworking Inc ....F...... 860 379-7538
  Pleasant Valley (G-6921)
Chandler Furniture & Wdwrk LLC ....G...... 203 895-6289
  Shelton (G-7416)
Chapman Lumber Inc ....E...... 860 283-6213
  Thomaston (G-8785)
Charles A Boucher Co Inc....................G...... 860 868-2881
  Washington (G-9412)
Charlys Custom Woodworking...............G...... 860 227-2155
  Killingworth (G-3829)
Chesnut Woodworking ....G...... 860 592-0383
  Kent (G-3821)
Chestnut Wdwkg & Antiq Flrg Co..........G...... 860 672-4300
  West Cornwall (G-9761)
Chris Dedura..G...... 203 257-7304
  Trumbull (G-9011)
Chris Krawczyk Woodwork LLC............G...... 203 895-5785
  Shelton (G-7417)
Christensen Woodworking ....G...... 860 712-6166
  Windsorville (G-10503)
Cko Woodworking..................................G...... 203 234-7156
  North Haven (G-5920)
Cko Woodworking LLC..........................G...... 203 815-3092
  Meriden (G-4158)
Clancy Woodworking LLC.....................G...... 860 355-3655
  Sherman (G-7592)
Colonial Wood Products Inc..................F...... 203 932-9003
  West Haven (G-9889)
Concept Woodworks LLC......................G...... 860 746-4271
  Enfield (G-2632)
Connecticut Carpentry LLC ....E...... 203 639-8585
  Meriden (G-4161)
Connecticut Custom Wdwrk LLC...........G...... 203 888-3948
  Seymour (G-7342)
Connecticut Custom Woodwork ....G...... 203 231-0097
  Milford (G-4494)
Connecticut Custom Woodworking.........G...... 860 741-8946
  Somers (G-7653)
Connecticut Millwork Inc.......................G...... 860 875-2860
  Vernon (G-9135)
Connecticut Woodworks LLC................G...... 860 367-7449
  Waterford (G-9648)
Corgyn Woodworks ....G...... 860 402-8273
  Manchester (G-3999)
Correia Wood Works LLC......................G...... 203 515-7670
  Fairfield (G-2769)
CT Fine Woodworking ....G...... 860 613-0856
  Cromwell (G-1698)
CT Woodworking LLC............................G...... 860 884-9586
  North Franklin (G-5872)
Curtiss Woodworking Inc ....F...... 203 527-9305
  Prospect (G-6998)
Custom Carpentry Unlimited ....G...... 860 742-8932
  Coventry (G-1650)
Custom Design Woodworks LLC ....G...... 860 434-0515
  Old Lyme (G-6502)
Custom Woodwork Etc..........................G...... 860 638-1006
  Middletown (G-4334)

MILLWORK

Custom Woodworking.............................G...... 860 868-0257
  Washington Depot (G-9417)
Custom Woodworking.............................G...... 860 456-4466
  Lebanon (G-3852)
Custom Woodworking By Norman ....G...... 860 663-3462
  Killingworth (G-3831)
Customized Woodworking LLC..............G...... 860 274-4025
  Watertown (G-9699)
Dalbergia LLC......................................G...... 860 870-2500
  Tolland (G-8858)
Dalvento LLC.......................................G...... 203 263-6497
  Woodbury (G-10632)
Danbury Stairs Corporation..................G...... 203 743-5567
  Bethel (G-278)
Danchak Woodworks LLC.....................G...... 860 346-6057
  Durham (G-2144)
Daniel F Crapa ....G...... 203 746-5706
  New Fairfield (G-5167)
Dante Ltd Liability Company ....G...... 860 376-0204
  Griswold (G-3263)
David W Lintz Company ....G...... 860 349-1392
  Middlefield (G-4301)
Defelice Woodworking Inc ....G...... 203 445-0199
  Trumbull (G-9019)
Depercio Woodworking LLC..................G...... 860 477-1051
  Ashford (G-59)
Dlz Architectural Mill Work....................G...... 860 883-7562
  Hartford (G-3578)
Dooney Woodworks LLC........................G...... 203 340-9770
  Cos Cob (G-1631)
Dooney Woodworks LLC........................G...... 203 869-5457
  Greenwich (G-3155)
Drb Woodworks....................................G...... 203 216-7071
  Monroe (G-4712)
Dream Construction & Wdwkg ....G...... 774 573-0495
  Eastford (G-2535)
Elite Woodworking LLC.........................G...... 860 655-7806
  Glastonbury (G-3033)
End Grain Woodworks LLC...................G...... 203 817-7154
  Wilton (G-10291)
Errichetti Woodworks LLC.....................G...... 203 528-3977
  Prospect (G-7003)
Esg Woodworking and Bldg LLC ....G...... 203 667-0811
  Newtown (G-5737)
Exterior Trim Specialities LLC ....G...... 860 261-5194
  Terryville (G-8754)
Fac Woodworking LLC..........................G...... 203 469-1900
  East Haven (G-2426)
Fairfield County Millwork ....F...... 203 393-9751
  Bethany (G-241)
Fairfield Wood Works ....G...... 203 838-6883
  Norwalk (G-6161)
Fairfield Woodworks LLC......................F...... 203 380-9842
  Stratford (G-8609)
Fine Lines Custom Cabinetry &............G...... 860 729-6526
  Plainville (G-6810)
Fine Woodworker.................................G...... 203 717-2444
  Norwalk (G-6166)
Fine Woodworking ....G...... 203 762-8197
  Wilton (G-10296)
Fineline Architechtural Wdwkg ....G...... 914 426-2648
  Danbury (G-1825)
First Class Custom Woodworking ....G...... 203 857-1000
  Norwalk (G-6168)
Freddie Nelson Woodworks..................G...... 203 378-2330
  Stratford (G-8612)
G M F Woodworking LLC......................G...... 203 788-8979
  Norwalk (G-6172)
G M Woodworking................................G...... 860 599-3781
  North Stonington (G-6026)
Gabriels Woodworking LLC..................G...... 860 263-7831
  Hartford (G-3597)
Gary D Kryszat....................................G...... 860 526-3145
  Chester (G-1473)
Gideon S Fleece Woodworkin ....G...... 860 663-2757
  Killingworth (G-3834)
GNB Woodworking LLC........................G...... 860 282-0595
  South Windsor (G-7761)
Gngwoodworking..................................G...... 203 996-5255
  West Haven (G-9913)
Good Earth Millwork LLC.....................G...... 203 226-7958
  Westport (G-10092)
Gordon Woodworking LLC....................G...... 860 489-5445
  Morris (G-4789)
Grdn Woodworks..................................G...... 203 814-6446
  Trumbull (G-9031)
Greenworks Woodworking ....G...... 203 886-8573
  Bethel (G-305)
Gregory Penta.....................................G...... 860 747-2681
  Plainville (G-6819)

Employee Codes: A=Over 500 employees, B=251-500
C=101-250, D=51-100, E=20-50, F=10-19, G=1-9

Griffin Green ....G.... 203 266-5727
Bethlehem *(G-371)*
H & S Woodworks L T D ....G.... 914 391-3926
New Milford *(G-5544)*
Hard Hill Woodworking LLC ....G.... 203 263-2820
Woodbury *(G-10638)*
Harris Enterprise Corp ....E.... 860 649-4663
Manchester *(G-4025)*
Harry & Hios Woodworking LLC ....G.... 860 267-1535
East Hampton *(G-2263)*
Head East Woodworking ....G.... 860 537-2072
Colchester *(G-1553)*
Highland Woodworks ....G.... 203 758-6625
Prospect *(G-7004)*
Hunt Architectural Wdwkg Inc ....G.... 203 947-1137
Danbury *(G-1846)*
Hurley Woodworking LLC ....G.... 818 643-5809
Sandy Hook *(G-7316)*
Indars Stairs LLC ....G.... 860 208-3826
Lebanon *(G-3854)*
Integrated Woodworks LLC ....G.... 860 563-4537
Wethersfield *(G-10199)*
Integrity Custom Wdwkg LLC ....G.... 860 302-3726
Southington *(G-7939)*
Iorfino Woodworking ....G.... 203 329-1075
Stamford *(G-8257)*
Island View Woodworks LLC ....G.... 203 494-1760
Killingworth *(G-3835)*
J G M Woodworks ....G.... 203 934-3726
West Haven *(G-9917)*
Ja Custom Woodwork ....G.... 203 540-5747
Stratford *(G-8635)*
Jacobsen Woodworking Co Inc ....G.... 203 531-9050
Greenwich *(G-3183)*
Jask Woodworking Inc ....G.... 954 766-7105
Bridgeport *(G-801)*
Jjk Woodworking LLC ....G.... 203 224-0139
Bridgeport *(G-806)*
Joe Salafia Woodworking LLC ....G.... 860 345-8657
Haddam *(G-3405)*
John M Kriskey Carpentry ....G.... 203 531-0194
Greenwich *(G-3184)*
Johnson Millwork Inc ....G.... 860 267-4693
East Hampton *(G-2267)*
Jordan Woodworks ....G.... 203 512-3581
Bethel *(G-317)*
Joshua Friedman & Co LLC ....F.... 860 439-1637
New London *(G-5475)*
K L S Custom Wood Working ....G.... 203 520-5193
Monroe *(G-4724)*
K Smith Custom Woodworking LLC ....G.... 203 981-4268
New Canaan *(G-5113)*
K&M Woodworking LLC ....G.... 203 406-0694
Stamford *(G-8273)*
Kariba Woodworks ....G.... 203 246-8917
Sandy Hook *(G-7318)*
Kenyon Woodworking ....G.... 860 432-4641
Manchester *(G-4045)*
Kerry D Hogan ....G.... 203 213-4624
Wallingford *(G-9296)*
Kitchens By Deane Inc ....E.... 203 327-7008
Stamford *(G-8276)*
Lagnese Woodworking ....G.... 203 426-6434
Newtown *(G-5753)*
Lee & Sons Woodworkers ....G.... 860 742-7707
Andover *(G-12)*
Legacy Woodworking LLC ....G.... 203 440-9710
Meriden *(G-4186)*
Legere Group Ltd ....C.... 860 674-0392
Avon *(G-89)*
Legno Bldrs & Fine Wdwkg LLC ....G.... 860 282-0091
Coventry *(G-1660)*
Level Woodworks ....G.... 203 266-7153
Bethlehem *(G-374)*
Lingard Cabinet Co LLC ....G.... 860 647-9886
Manchester *(G-4048)*
Loranctis Orgnal Woodworks LLC ....G.... 860 924-8810
Terryville *(G-8763)*
Lota Woodworking LLC ....G.... 203 978-0277
Norwalk *(G-6239)*
Luckey LLC ....F.... 203 285-3819
New Haven *(G-5322)*
M K M Woodworks LLC ....G.... 203 838-5605
Norwalk *(G-6242)*
M Squared Woodworking LLC ....G.... 860 673-6079
Unionville *(G-9118)*
Maclean Woodworking LLC ....G.... 203 452-8285
Monroe *(G-4730)*
Mars Architectural Millwork ....G.... 203 579-2632
Bridgeport *(G-831)*
Martel Woodworking Co ....G.... 860 564-1983
Plainfield *(G-6748)*
Matthew Ryan Woodworking LLC ....G.... 203 268-8469
Trumbull *(G-9046)*
Meadow Woodworking LLC ....G.... 203 213-3332
Cheshire *(G-1414)*
Mh Woodworking Inc ....G.... 860 871-7321
Tolland *(G-8870)*
Michaels Woodworking LLC ....G.... 203 470-0867
Southbury *(G-7868)*
Miliard Custom Woodworks LLC ....G.... 860 621-5131
Plantsville *(G-6903)*
Millwork Shop LLC ....G.... 860 489-8848
Torrington *(G-8948)*
Mise En Place Wood Works Inc ....G.... 860 921-0208
New Hartford *(G-5202)*
Mitchell Woodworking LLC ....G.... 203 878-4249
Milford *(G-4583)*
Mitered Edge Woodworking ....G.... 860 576-6657
South Windham *(G-7691)*
Modern Woodcrafts LLC ....D.... 860 677-7371
Plainville *(G-6845)*
Morgan Woodworks LLC ....G.... 203 913-2489
Milford *(G-4584)*
Morris Woodworking ....G.... 860 346-7500
Middletown *(G-4382)*
Morton Wood Works ....G.... 203 594-6678
West Haven *(G-9938)*
Mt Carmel Woodwork LLC ....G.... 203 230-8377
Hamden *(G-3486)*
Mt Lebanon Joinery ....G.... 860 974-0896
Eastford *(G-2537)*
Nancy R Marryat ....G.... 860 749-2632
Enfield *(G-2666)*
Nci Woodworking LLC LLC ....G.... 203 391-1614
Fairfield *(G-2822)*
Ne Wood Works LLC ....G.... 860 883-3106
Manchester *(G-4058)*
New England Cabinet Co Inc ....F.... 860 747-9995
New Britain *(G-5021)*
New England Fine Woodworking ....G.... 860 526-5799
Chester *(G-1475)*
New England Joinery Works Inc ....G.... 860 767-3377
Essex *(G-2728)*
New England Woodworking ....G.... 203 505-0830
Norwalk *(G-6274)*
New England Woodworking LLC ....G.... 203 984-5032
Norwalk *(G-6275)*
Nichols Woodworking LLC ....G.... 860 350-4223
Washington Depot *(G-9419)*
Nolan Woodworking LLC ....G.... 203 258-1538
Bridgeport *(G-852)*
Nolan Woodworking LLC ....G.... 860 283-6000
Thomaston *(G-8799)*
North Canton Custom Wdwkg ....G.... 508 451-5826
Canton *(G-1320)*
North Hill Woodworking LLC ....G.... 203 985-0200
North Haven *(G-5968)*
Northeast Stair Company LLC ....G.... 860 875-3358
Tolland *(G-8872)*
Nutmeg Woodworks LLC ....G.... 203 980-5700
Milford *(G-4596)*
Omondi Woodworking ....G.... 860 513-2292
Coventry *(G-1667)*
Orion Manufacturing LLC ....G.... 860 572-2921
Mystic *(G-4838)*
Owh LLC ....E.... 860 693-9464
Canton *(G-1323)*
Oxford Woodworking LLC ....G.... 203 482-0982
Oxford *(G-6687)*
Paco Assensio Woodworking LLC ....G.... 203 536-2608
Norwalk *(G-6288)*
Patalanos Woodworking LLC ....G.... 203 612-7537
Bridgeport *(G-866)*
Patriot Woodworking LLC ....G.... 860 653-4349
East Hartland *(G-2404)*
Petrunti Design & Wdwkg LLC ....G.... 860 953-5332
West Hartford *(G-9844)*
Pinkham Woodworking ....G.... 860 733-3903
Torrington *(G-8958)*
Porta Door Co ....E.... 203 888-6191
Seymour *(G-7362)*
Precision Mill LLC ....G.... 860 357-4729
Berlin *(G-209)*
Premiere Kitchens & Wdwkg LLC ....G.... 203 882-1745
Milford *(G-4615)*
Prescott Cabinet Co ....G.... 860 495-0176
Pawcatuck *(G-6723)*
Proctor Woodworks LLC ....G.... 860 767-9881
Essex *(G-2731)*
Qa Woodworking LLC ....G.... 203 720-1781
Naugatuck *(G-4914)*
R Botsford Custom Wdwkg LLC ....G.... 203 994-5302
Newtown *(G-5773)*
R D Woodwork LLC ....G.... 203 947-9550
Danbury *(G-1926)*
R E S Woodworking LLC ....G.... 860 664-9663
Clinton *(G-1519)*
R F Case ....G.... 203 956-6348
Norwalk *(G-6312)*
R Woodworking Larson Inc ....E.... 860 646-7904
Manchester *(G-4079)*
R&R Woodworking ....G.... 508 202-3543
Thompson *(G-8842)*
Radius Mill Work ....G.... 860 645-1036
Manchester *(G-4081)*
RG Woodworking LLC ....G.... 860 742-0397
Coventry *(G-1671)*
Rgb Woodworking ....G.... 203 537-1177
Meriden *(G-4232)*
Ribeiro Woodworking LLC ....G.... 203 942-5838
Bethel *(G-335)*
Richard Woodworking ....G.... 203 265-0887
Wallingford *(G-9354)*
Richmond Woodworks LLC ....G.... 860 974-9995
Woodstock *(G-10680)*
RMS Wood Works LLC ....G.... 203 405-3051
Woodbury *(G-10653)*
Roman Woodworking ....G.... 860 490-5989
New Britain *(G-5047)*
S G R Woodworks ....G.... 203 216-3327
Trumbull *(G-9068)*
Sainte-Anne Custom Woodwork ....G.... 203 961-9403
Stamford *(G-8401)*
Saxony Wood Products Inc ....G.... 203 869-3717
Greenwich *(G-3232)*
Schwank Archtctural Woodworker ....G.... 203 912-0109
Redding *(G-7107)*
Scott Wallace Woodworking ....G.... 860 867-7229
Mystic *(G-4842)*
Select Woodworking LLC ....G.... 203 743-1159
Danbury *(G-1943)*
Shelbrack Woodworking ....G.... 860 431-5028
Simsbury *(G-7644)*
Sheldon Woodworks ....G.... 203 260-2703
Fairfield *(G-2847)*
Silver Hill Woodworks LLC ....G.... 860 318-1887
Cornwall Bridge *(G-1619)*
Smg Woodworking ....G.... 203 804-1029
New Haven *(G-5396)*
Soja Woodworking LLC ....G.... 860 345-3909
Higganum *(G-3778)*
Sound Custom Woodworking & Des ....G.... 203 948-5594
Ridgefield *(G-7175)*
Splinters Woodworking LLC ....G.... 203 272-1314
Cheshire *(G-1453)*
Spruce It Up Woodworking LLC ....G.... 203 740-7975
Brookfield *(G-1226)*
St Johns Bridge LLC ....G.... 860 927-3315
Kent *(G-3826)*
St Peter Woodworks ....G.... 860 816-0455
Manchester *(G-4093)*
Stephen Wenning ....G.... 203 906-9273
Trumbull *(G-9077)*
Stillwater Architectural Wood ....G.... 860 923-2858
Woodstock *(G-10687)*
Stonington Woodworks LLC ....G.... 646 321-6412
Ledyard *(G-3880)*
Style Woodworking ....G.... 860 944-7179
Coventry *(G-1677)*
Summit Atelier ....G.... 646 284-0304
West Simsbury *(G-9983)*
Sutters Mill ....G.... 860 585-5333
Bristol *(G-1124)*
Swanhart Woodworking ....G.... 203 746-1184
New Fairfield *(G-5178)*
Szostek Custom Woodworking LLC ....G.... 203 891-9127
Orange *(G-6630)*
Thomas F Kyasky ....G.... 860 567-4077
Litchfield *(G-3902)*
Thomas Townsend Custom Marine ....G.... 860 536-9800
Mystic *(G-4849)*
Timbers Edge Woodworking ....G.... 860 836-7328
Bozrah *(G-533)*
Tl Woodworking ....G.... 203 787-9661
Hamden *(G-3519)*
Todd Lucien Mendes LLC ....G.... 203 228-3134
Waterbury *(G-9612)*
Tolland Architectural Wdwkg LLC ....G.... 860 875-9841
Tolland *(G-8882)*

PRODUCT SECTION

MOLDS: Indl

Tread Well Stair & Millwo ....G....... 203 488-2146
  North Branford *(G-5864)*
TS Whitman Custom Wdwkg LLC ....G....... 860 575-1923
  South Lyme *(G-7686)*
Ultimate Woodworking LLC ....G....... 203 243-3367
  Shelton *(G-7573)*
Unlimited Woodworking ....G....... 203 380-2340
  Stratford *(G-8700)*
V & V Woodworking LLC ....G....... 203 740-9494
  Bethel *(G-360)*
V B Woodworking LLC ....G....... 860 747-0228
  Plainville *(G-6874)*
Valley Woodworking LLC ....G....... 860 667-1241
  Newington *(G-5719)*
Vision Kitchens and Mllwk LLC ....G....... 203 775-0604
  Brookfield *(G-1238)*
W G Woodworking ....G....... 203 262-8308
  Southbury *(G-7883)*
Walker Woodworking LLC ....G....... 860 429-2644
  Ashford *(G-68)*
Walpole Woodworkers Inc ....G....... 203 595-9930
  Stamford *(G-8488)*
Walters Wood Working LLC ....G....... 860 683-8478
  Windsor *(G-10462)*
Warren Woodworking LLC ....G....... 860 408-0030
  West Simsbury *(G-9984)*
Wayne Woodworks ....G....... 203 362-8084
  Fairfield *(G-2866)*
Wezenski Woodworking ....G....... 203 488-3255
  Branford *(G-672)*
Wheeler Woodworking ....G....... 860 355-1638
  Kent *(G-3827)*
White Dog Woodworking LLC ....G....... 860 482-3776
  Torrington *(G-8988)*
White Dove Woodworking LLC ....G....... 860 268-4426
  Coventry *(G-1683)*
Willis Mills House LLC ....G....... 917 287-3260
  New Canaan *(G-5159)*
Willow Woodworking Inc ....G....... 203 426-8200
  Newtown *(G-5798)*
Winchester Woodworks LLC ....G....... 860 379-9875
  Winsted *(G-10547)*
Window Master Real WD Pdts LLC ....G....... 203 230-2638
  North Haven *(G-6014)*
Windsor Woodworks ....G....... 203 386-6975
  New Haven *(G-5434)*
Windsors & Woodwork LLC ....G....... 860 526-4092
  Chester *(G-1487)*
Wood Works By Aranda LLC ....G....... 203 908-3010
  Stamford *(G-8499)*
Woodmsters Mllwk Rstration LLC ....G....... 203 745-3165
  North Haven *(G-6016)*
Woodwork Specialties Inc ....G....... 860 583-4848
  Bristol *(G-1141)*
Woodworkers ....G....... 860 669-9113
  Clinton *(G-1535)*
Woodworkers Club LLC ....G....... 203 847-9663
  Norwalk *(G-6399)*
Woodworking ....G....... 860 354-6757
  New Milford *(G-5608)*
Woodworking Plus LLC ....G....... 203 393-1967
  Bethany *(G-253)*
Woodworks of Connecticut Ltd ....G....... 914 318-7970
  Monroe *(G-4767)*
Yankee Woodworks LLC ....G....... 860 933-9882
  Mansfield Center *(G-4116)*
Yes Fine Woodworking LLC ....G....... 203 255-6366
  Southport *(G-8014)*
York Millwork LLC ....G....... 203 698-3460
  Old Greenwich *(G-6485)*
Z & M Woodworking LLC ....G....... 860 378-0563
  Plantsville *(G-6919)*
Zander Wood Works LLC ....G....... 203 493-5066
  Ridgefield *(G-7188)*
Zavarella Woodworking Inc ....G....... 860 666-6969
  Newington *(G-5725)*

MINE & QUARRY SVCS: Nonmetallic Minerals

Veronica Matthews Minerals ....G....... 860 399-0063
  Westbrook *(G-10013)*

MINERAL WOOL

Leek Building Products Inc ....E....... 203 853-3883
  Norwalk *(G-6232)*
Zampell Refractories Inc ....F....... 860 564-2883
  Plainfield *(G-6757)*

MINERALS: Ground Or Otherwise Treated

Miyoshi America Inc ....F....... 860 779-3990
  Dayville *(G-2065)*
Miyoshi America Inc ....G....... 860 779-3990
  Dayville *(G-2066)*

MINERALS: Ground or Treated

Ultimate Growers LLC ....G....... 203 269-9027
  Wallingford *(G-9394)*

MINING EXPLORATION & DEVELOPMENT SVCS

East Delta Resources Corp ....G....... 860 434-7750
  Old Lyme *(G-6506)*

MINING MACHINES & EQPT: Sedimentation, Mineral

Tipping Pt Resources Group LLC ....G....... 800 603-8902
  New Haven *(G-5415)*

MINING SVCS, NEC: Bituminous

Buchanan Minerals LLC ....D....... 304 392-1000
  Wilton *(G-10277)*

MIXTURES & BLOCKS: Asphalt Paving

A-1 Asphalt Paving ....G....... 860 436-6085
  Rocky Hill *(G-7217)*
All States Asphalt Inc ....G....... 860 774-7550
  Dayville *(G-2053)*
Brico Inc ....G....... 203 693-0323
  Bloomfield *(G-400)*
Christopher Annelli ....G....... 860 537-4397
  Colchester *(G-1545)*
E B Asphalt & Landscaping LLC ....F....... 860 639-1921
  Norwich *(G-6412)*
Firestone Building Pdts Co LLC ....D....... 860 584-4516
  Bristol *(G-1039)*
O & G Industries Inc ....E....... 203 977-1618
  Stamford *(G-8335)*
O & G Industries Inc ....D....... 860 354-4438
  New Milford *(G-5576)*
O & G Industries Inc ....D....... 203 263-2195
  Southbury *(G-7870)*
O & G Industries Inc ....E....... 203 366-4586
  Bridgeport *(G-854)*
Tilcon Connecticut Inc ....D....... 860 224-6010
  New Britain *(G-5074)*
Tilcon Inc ....B....... 860 223-3651
  Newington *(G-5713)*

MOBILE COMMUNICATIONS EQPT

General Network Service Inc ....G....... 203 359-5735
  Stamford *(G-8213)*
Latino Multiservice LLC ....G....... 203 691-9715
  New Haven *(G-5316)*
Sonitor Technologies Inc ....G....... 727 466-4557
  Greenwich *(G-3239)*

MOBILE HOMES

Champion Enterprises Inc ....G....... 860 429-3537
  Storrs *(G-8545)*
Old Coach Home Sales ....E....... 860 774-1379
  Sterling *(G-8515)*

MOBILE HOMES: Indl Or Commercial Use

Rv Parts & Electric Inc ....G....... 203 754-5962
  Waterbury *(G-9595)*

MODELS

Fx Models LLC ....G....... 860 589-5279
  Terryville *(G-8756)*

MODELS: Airplane, Exc Toy

Richard Batchelder ....G....... 860 526-1614
  Chester *(G-1481)*

MODELS: General, Exc Toy

Case Patterns Inc ....G....... 860 445-6722
  Groton *(G-3275)*
Modelvision Inc ....G....... 860 355-3884
  New Milford *(G-5563)*

Stevenson Prototype ....G....... 203 245-0278
  Guilford *(G-3394)*

MODULES: Solid State

Viavi Solutions Inc ....G....... 860 243-6600
  Bloomfield *(G-498)*

MOLDED RUBBER PRDTS

Anchor Rubber Products LLC ....G....... 860 667-2628
  Newington *(G-5627)*
Gordon Rubber and Pkg Co Inc ....E....... 203 735-7441
  Derby *(G-2114)*
Hutchinson Precision Ss Inc ....C....... 860 779-0300
  Danielson *(G-1993)*
Sur-Seal Holding LLC ....G....... 203 625-0770
  Norwalk *(G-6360)*

MOLDING COMPOUNDS

JCB Plastics LLC ....G....... 203 315-8154
  North Branford *(G-5847)*
Precision Dip Coating LLC ....G....... 203 805-4564
  Waterbury *(G-9584)*

MOLDINGS & TRIM: Metal, Exc Automobile

CT Moldings Inc ....G....... 203 612-4922
  Bridgeport *(G-740)*

MOLDINGS & TRIM: Wood

CT Moldings Inc ....G....... 203 612-4922
  Bridgeport *(G-740)*
Jakes Jr Lawrence ....E....... 860 974-3744
  Pomfret Center *(G-6940)*

MOLDINGS OR TRIM: Automobile, Stamped Metal

C Cowles & Company ....D....... 203 865-3117
  North Haven *(G-5916)*
CT Moldings Inc ....G....... 203 612-4922
  Bridgeport *(G-740)*
Edison Atlas LLC ....G....... 860 335-6455
  Rocky Hill *(G-7237)*

MOLDINGS, ARCHITECTURAL: Plaster Of Paris

CT Moldings Inc ....G....... 203 612-4922
  Bridgeport *(G-740)*

MOLDINGS: Picture Frame

Church Hill Classics Ltd ....D....... 800 477-9005
  Monroe *(G-4703)*
Thomas Delspina Fine Frames ....G....... 203 256-8628
  Bridgeport *(G-924)*

MOLDS: Indl

Advance Mold & Mfg Inc ....C....... 860 432-5887
  Manchester *(G-3979)*
American Molded Products Inc ....F....... 203 333-0183
  Bridgeport *(G-694)*
American Precision Mold Inc ....G....... 860 267-1356
  East Hampton *(G-2255)*
B & D Machine Inc ....F....... 860 871-9226
  Tolland *(G-8850)*
Betz Tool Company Inc ....G....... 203 878-1187
  Milford *(G-4468)*
Ferron Mold and Tool LLC ....G....... 860 774-5555
  Dayville *(G-2061)*
J & L Tool Company Inc ....E....... 203 265-6237
  Wallingford *(G-9291)*
Moldvision LLC ....G....... 860 315-1025
  Thompson *(G-8840)*
Omni Mold Systems LLC ....G....... 888 666-4755
  Lisbon *(G-3882)*
Precision Mold and Polsg LLC ....G....... 860 489-6249
  Torrington *(G-8959)*
R&R Tool & Die LLC ....G....... 860 627-9197
  East Windsor *(G-2515)*
Savoir Consulting & Mfg Co LLC ....G....... 860 933-7614
  Willington *(G-10257)*
Scan Tool & Mold Inc ....E....... 203 459-4950
  Trumbull *(G-9070)*
South Windsor Quality Black MO ....G....... 860 385-2740
  South Windsor *(G-7827)*
Superior Mold Corp ....G....... 860 225-7654
  New Britain *(G-5069)*

Employee Codes: A=Over 500 employees, B=251-500
C=101-250, D=51-100, E=20-50, F=10-19, G=1-9

2020 Harris Connecticut
Manufacturers Directory

MOLDS: Indl

Upper Valley Mold LLC .... G 860 489-8282
  Torrington (G-8986)
Watertown Plastics Inc .... E 860 274-7535
  Watertown (G-9749)

MOLDS: Plastic Working & Foundry

Heise Industries Inc .... D 860 828-6538
  East Berlin (G-2170)
Mohawk Tool and Die Mfg Co Inc .... F 203 367-2181
  Bridgeport (G-842)
Mold Threads Inc .... G 203 483-1420
  Branford (G-627)
Plastic Design Intl Inc .... E 860 632-2001
  Middletown (G-4393)
Somerset Plastics Company .... E 860 635-1601
  Middletown (G-4421)

MONUMENTS & GRAVE MARKERS, EXC TERRAZZO

Artista Studio Monument .... G 203 333-9224
  Bridgeport (G-704)

MORTAR: High Temperature, Nonclay

HI Temp Electric Company .... E 661 259-9225
  Andover (G-9)

MOTION PICTURE & VIDEO PRODUCTION SVCS

Bff Holdings Inc .... C 860 510-0100
  Old Saybrook (G-6523)
Blue Sky Studios Inc .... C 203 992-6000
  Greenwich (G-3135)
Kapcom LLC .... G 203 891-5112
  East Haven (G-2436)
Trod Nossel Prdctns & Rcrdng S .... G 203 269-4465
  Wallingford (G-9391)

MOTION PICTURE & VIDEO PRODUCTION SVCS: Indl

Fx Models LLC .... G 860 589-5279
  Terryville (G-8756)

MOTION PICTURE EQPT

Rosco Holdings Inc .... D 203 708-8900
  Stamford (G-8398)
Rosco Laboratories Inc .... E 203 708-8900
  Stamford (G-8399)

MOTOR HOMES

GM Home Solutions .... G 305 608-9721
  Waterbury (G-9490)

MOTOR REBUILDING SVCS, EXC AUTOMOTIVE

Andys Automotive Machine .... G 860 793-2455
  Plainville (G-6770)
Bemat TEC LLC .... G 860 632-0049
  Cromwell (G-1691)

MOTOR REPAIR SVCS

Servotech Inc .... G 860 632-0164
  Middletown (G-4410)

MOTOR VEHICLE ASSEMBLY, COMPLETE: Autos, Incl Specialty

Abair Manufacturing Company .... F 203 757-0112
  Waterbury (G-9422)
C B Fabrication .... G 860 889-8030
  Taftville (G-8740)
Markow Race Cars .... G 860 610-0776
  South Windsor (G-7790)
Motor Connections .... G 860 583-3407
  Bristol (G-1075)
Rustic Rstrtions Race Cars LLC .... G 203 929-4813
  Shelton (G-7548)
Sharp Racing Enterprises .... G 203 699-1191
  Cheshire (G-1444)

MOTOR VEHICLE ASSEMBLY, COMPLETE: Buses, All Types

American Vehicles Sales LLC .... G 860 886-0327
  Yantic (G-10696)
M & J Bus Co Inc .... G 203 624-0836
  North Haven (G-5960)
M & J Bus Co Inc .... G 860 437-3721
  Waterford (G-9660)
M & J Bus Inc .... G 860 668-6526
  Suffield (G-8724)

MOTOR VEHICLE ASSEMBLY, COMPLETE: Cars, Armored

Raceworks Inc .... G 860 829-1312
  Berlin (G-214)

MOTOR VEHICLE ASSEMBLY, COMPLETE: Fire Department Vehicles

Bloomfield Center Voluntee .... G 860 242-1779
  Bloomfield (G-397)
Glastonbury Fire Training Ctr .... G 860 633-3429
  Glastonbury (G-3041)
Meriden Fire Marshals Office .... G 203 630-4010
  Meriden (G-4196)

MOTOR VEHICLE ASSEMBLY, COMPLETE: Military Motor Vehicle

AMS Strategic Management Inc .... G 845 500-5635
  Stamford (G-8083)

MOTOR VEHICLE ASSEMBLY, COMPLETE: Patrol Wagons

Mhq Inc .... F 888 242-1118
  Middletown (G-4376)

MOTOR VEHICLE ASSEMBLY, COMPLETE: Road Oilers

Triple D Transportation Inc .... G 860 243-5057
  Bloomfield (G-493)

MOTOR VEHICLE ASSEMBLY, COMPLETE: Snow Plows

Condon LLC .... D 860 883-5416
  Old Saybrook (G-6528)
Structured Solutions II LLC .... G 203 972-5717
  New Canaan (G-5148)
Universal Body & Eqp Co LLC .... F 860 274-7541
  Oakville (G-6466)

MOTOR VEHICLE DEALERS: Automobiles, New & Used

Scap Motors Inc .... C 203 384-0005
  Fairfield (G-2843)

MOTOR VEHICLE PARTS & ACCESS: Bearings

Alinabal Holdings Corporation .... B 203 877-3241
  Milford (G-4449)

MOTOR VEHICLE PARTS & ACCESS: Body Components & Frames

Johnson Controls Inc .... G 860 887-7185
  Norwich (G-6419)
Johnson Controls Inc .... D 678 297-4040
  Meriden (G-4179)

MOTOR VEHICLE PARTS & ACCESS: Electrical Eqpt

All Tech Auto/Truck Electric .... G 203 790-8990
  Danbury (G-1736)
Casco Products Corporation .... F 203 922-3200
  Bridgeport (G-731)

MOTOR VEHICLE PARTS & ACCESS: Engines & Parts

Callaway Cars Inc .... F 860 434-9002
  Old Lyme (G-6495)
Callaway Companies Inc .... F 860 434-9002
  Old Lyme (G-6496)
Moroso Performance Pdts Inc .... C 203 453-6571
  Guilford (G-3376)

MOTOR VEHICLE PARTS & ACCESS: Engs & Trans, Factory, Rebuilt

Anh Refractories .... G 203 795-0597
  Orange (G-6582)

MOTOR VEHICLE PARTS & ACCESS: Fifth Wheels

Tru Hitch Inc .... F 860 379-7772
  Pleasant Valley (G-6927)

MOTOR VEHICLE PARTS & ACCESS: Fuel Pumps

Stanadyne LLC .... A 860 525-0821
  Windsor (G-10441)
Stanadyne Parent Holdings Inc .... G 860 525-0821
  Windsor (G-10442)

MOTOR VEHICLE PARTS & ACCESS: Fuel Systems & Parts

Clarcor Eng MBL Solutions LLC .... D 860 920-4200
  East Hartford (G-2306)
Stanadyne Intrmdate Hldngs LLC .... C 860 525-0821
  Windsor (G-10440)

MOTOR VEHICLE PARTS & ACCESS: Horns

Nathan Airchime Inc .... G 860 423-4575
  South Windham (G-7692)

MOTOR VEHICLE PARTS & ACCESS: Lifting Mechanisms, Dump Truck

Lac Landscaping LLC .... F 203 807-1067
  Milford (G-4566)

MOTOR VEHICLE PARTS & ACCESS: Lubrication Systems & Parts

Franks Performance .... G 860 426-0439
  Plantsville (G-6893)

MOTOR VEHICLE PARTS & ACCESS: Oil Strainers

JPsexton LLC .... G 860 748-2048
  Windsor (G-10401)

MOTOR VEHICLE PARTS & ACCESS: Tie Rods

Alinabal Inc .... C 203 877-3241
  Milford (G-4448)

MOTOR VEHICLE PARTS & ACCESS: Tops

Thule Inc .... C 203 881-9600
  Seymour (G-7368)
Thule Holding Inc .... F 203 881-9600
  Seymour (G-7370)

MOTOR VEHICLE PARTS & ACCESS: Transmission Housings Or Parts

Defeo Manufacturing Inc .... E 203 775-0254
  Brookfield (G-1181)

MOTOR VEHICLE PARTS & ACCESS: Transmissions

Dynamic Racing Transm LLC .... G 203 315-0138
  North Branford (G-5837)

MOTOR VEHICLE SPLYS & PARTS WHOLESALERS: New

Cadentia LLC .... G 860 995-0173
  Bristol (G-997)

MOTOR VEHICLE: Hardware

Pierce-Correll Corporation .... G 203 799-1208
  Orange (G-6624)

MOTOR VEHICLES & CAR BODIES

Airflow Truck Company .... G 860 666-1977
  Newington *(G-5623)*
CD Racing Products .... G 203 264-7822
  Oxford *(G-6650)*
Oshkosh Corporation .... F 860 653-5548
  East Granby *(G-2221)*
Puritan Lane LLC .... G 203 602-5555
  Stamford *(G-8382)*
Rock Hard Offroad LLC .... G 860 919-3118
  Wallingford *(G-9357)*
Special Vhcl Developments Inc .... G 203 272-7928
  Cheshire *(G-1451)*

MOTOR VEHICLES, WHOLESALE: Commercial

American Vehicles Sales LLC .... G 860 886-0327
  Yantic *(G-10696)*

MOTOR VEHICLES, WHOLESALE: Motorized Cycles

MH Rhodes Cramer LLC .... G 860 291-8402
  South Windsor *(G-7793)*

MOTOR VEHICLES, WHOLESALE: Truck bodies

Composite Truck Body LLC .... G 800 735-1668
  Sherman *(G-7593)*

MOTORCYCLE ACCESS

Cat LLC .... G 860 953-1807
  Hartford *(G-3564)*

MOTORCYCLE DEALERS

Danbury Powersports Inc .... F 203 791-1310
  Danbury *(G-1786)*

MOTORCYCLE DEALERS

Ems International Inc .... G 860 526-2060
  Chester *(G-1472)*

MOTORCYCLE PARTS & ACCESS DEALERS

Government Surplus Sales Inc .... G 860 247-7787
  Hartford *(G-3601)*

MOTORCYCLE REPAIR SHOPS

Ems International Inc .... G 860 526-2060
  Chester *(G-1472)*

MOTORCYCLES & RELATED PARTS

Daads LLC .... G 860 274-1589
  Watertown *(G-9700)*
Fusion One Industries Inc .... G 860 992-4377
  Cromwell *(G-1701)*
Grasschoppers LLC .... G 860 294-1620
  Terryville *(G-8760)*
Kobuta Choppers LLC .... G 203 234-6047
  North Haven *(G-5958)*
Tri State Choppers LLC .... G 860 210-1854
  New Milford *(G-5601)*

MOTORS: Electric

Tritex Corporation .... C 203 756-7441
  Waterbury *(G-9618)*
Ward Leonard CT LLC .... C 860 283-5801
  Thomaston *(G-8818)*

MOTORS: Generators

Carter Inv Holdings Corp .... G 860 283-5801
  Thomaston *(G-8783)*
Cramer Company .... G 860 291-8402
  South Windsor *(G-7737)*
Elinco International Inc .... G 203 275-8885
  Fairfield *(G-2780)*
Fuelcell Energy Inc .... E 860 496-1111
  Torrington *(G-8927)*
GE Steam Power Inc .... G 860 688-1911
  Windsor *(G-10391)*
Generators On Demand LLC .... F 860 662-4090
  Old Lyme *(G-6510)*
Hydrotec Inc .... G 203 264-6700
  Oxford *(G-6666)*

Ktcr Holding .... G 203 227-4115
  Westport *(G-10110)*
Libby Power Systems LLC .... G 203 393-1239
  Bethany *(G-247)*
Power Strategies LLC .... G 203 254-9926
  Fairfield *(G-2831)*
Rowley Spring & Stamping Corp .... C 860 582-8175
  Bristol *(G-1113)*
Sandvik Wire and Htg Tech Corp .... D 203 744-1440
  Bethel *(G-337)*
Technipower Systems Inc .... G 203 748-7001
  Brookfield *(G-1229)*
Thomson Arpax Mechatronics LLC .... G 516 883-8000
  Cheshire *(G-1455)*
Ward Leonard Holdings LLC .... G 860 283-5801
  Thomaston *(G-8820)*
Ward Leonard Inv Holdings LLC .... G 860 283-5801
  Thomaston *(G-8821)*
Ward Leonard Operating LLC .... G 860 283-5801
  Thomaston *(G-8822)*
Ward Lonard Houma Holdings LLC .... G 860 283-5801
  Thomaston *(G-8823)*
Wl Intermediate Holdings LLC .... G 860 283-5801
  Thomaston *(G-8825)*

MOTORS: Pneumatic

Sfc Koenig LLC .... E 203 245-1100
  North Haven *(G-5992)*

MOTORS: Torque

AKO Inc .... E 860 298-9765
  Windsor *(G-10357)*

MOUNTING SVC: Map

Sinish Works .... G 860 693-0073
  Collinsville *(G-1603)*

MOUTHPIECES, PIPE & CIGARETTE HOLDERS: Rubber

Bite Tech Inc .... E 203 987-6898
  Norwalk *(G-6093)*

MOVING SVC: Local

United Enterprises Inc .... G 860 225-9955
  New Britain *(G-5078)*

MULTIPLEXERS: Telephone & Telegraph

General Datacomm Inds Inc .... E 203 729-0271
  Oxford *(G-6662)*

MUSIC ARRANGING & COMPOSING SVCS

Madonna Black Buddist LLC .... G 203 589-9796
  Greenwich *(G-3196)*

MUSIC DISTRIBUTION APPARATUS

Nollysource Entertainment LLC .... G 347 264-6655
  Bridgeport *(G-853)*

MUSIC RECORDING PRODUCER

American Melody Records .... G 203 457-0881
  Guilford *(G-3325)*

MUSIC SCHOOLS

Music Together Fairfield Child .... G 203 256-1656
  Fairfield *(G-2821)*

MUSIC VIDEO PRODUCTION SVCS

Nollysource Entertainment LLC .... G 347 264-6655
  Bridgeport *(G-853)*

MUSICAL INSTRUMENT PARTS & ACCESS, WHOLESALE

Nollysource Entertainment LLC .... G 347 264-6655
  Bridgeport *(G-853)*

MUSICAL INSTRUMENTS & ACCESS: NEC

Big City String Co .... G 203 371-8117
  Bridgeport *(G-712)*
Fender Musical Instrs Corp .... G 860 379-7575
  New Hartford *(G-5191)*
Mary Jeans Musical Instrs LLC .... G 860 887-0633
  Salem *(G-7290)*

Nollysource Entertainment LLC .... G 347 264-6655
  Bridgeport *(G-853)*
Sharps & Flats .... G 203 438-3300
  Redding *(G-7108)*
Ute Brinkmann Geigenbaumeister .... G 203 265-7456
  Wallingford *(G-9398)*
Vision Musical Instruments .... G 203 416-6359
  Norwalk *(G-6390)*

MUSICAL INSTRUMENTS & ACCESS: Pipe Organs

Broome & Company LLC .... G 860 623-0254
  Windsor Locks *(G-10474)*

MUSICAL INSTRUMENTS & SPLYS STORES

Sweetheart Flute Company LLC .... G 860 749-8514
  Enfield *(G-2700)*

MUSICAL INSTRUMENTS & SPLYS STORES: String instruments

Acoustic Music .... G 203 458-2525
  Guilford *(G-3321)*

MUSICAL INSTRUMENTS: Flutes & Parts

Sweetheart Flute Company LLC .... G 860 749-8514
  Enfield *(G-2700)*

MUSICAL INSTRUMENTS: Guitars & Parts, Electric & Acoustic

Acoustic Music .... G 203 458-2525
  Guilford *(G-3321)*
Jerry Freeman Pennywhistles .... G 860 498-0014
  Coventry *(G-1658)*
Jobo Enterprizes LLC .... G 203 367-7517
  Bridgeport *(G-807)*
Strings By Aurora LLC .... G 203 583-9929
  Stratford *(G-8688)*

MUSICAL INSTRUMENTS: Harmonicas

Two Bsses & A Hrmonca Prdctns .... G 203 259-5916
  Easton *(G-2568)*

MUSICAL INSTRUMENTS: Harpsichords

Zuckerman Hrpsichords Intl LLC .... G 860 535-1715
  Stonington *(G-8542)*

MUSICAL INSTRUMENTS: Ocarinas

Mountain Ocarinas .... G 860 242-6626
  Bloomfield *(G-448)*

MUSICAL INSTRUMENTS: Organs

Austin Organs Incorporated .... E 860 522-8293
  Hartford *(G-3554)*
Broome & Co LLC .... G 860 653-2106
  East Granby *(G-2193)*

MUSICAL INSTRUMENTS: Recorders, Musical

Blu & Grae Music .... G 857 204-3095
  Stamford *(G-8113)*
Dizzy Fish Music LLC .... G 203 599-5700
  Milford *(G-4512)*

MUSICAL INSTRUMENTS: Trombones & Parts

Viz-Pro LLC .... G 860 379-0055
  Winsted *(G-10542)*

MUSICAL INSTRUMENTS: Violins & Parts

Alexander Tulchinsky Violins .... G 203 698-7844
  Riverside *(G-7189)*
Violin Performance Co .... G 860 836-8647
  South Windsor *(G-7838)*

MUTUAL ACCIDENT & HEALTH ASSOCIATIONS

Cliffside Entertainment LLC .... G 203 290-7484
  Bridgeport *(G-736)*

NAILS: Steel, Wire Or Cut

Tsmc Inc..................................G....... 860 283-8265
  Torrington (G-8985)

NAME PLATES: Engraved Or Etched

American Rubber Stamp Company.......G....... 203 755-1135
  Cheshire (G-1351)
Ann S Davis................................F....... 860 642-7228
  Lebanon (G-3846)
Biomerics LLC..............................D....... 203 268-7238
  Monroe (G-4698)
Identification Products Corp..................G....... 203 331-0931
  Bridgeport (G-790)
Identification Products Corp..................F....... 203 334-5969
  Bridgeport (G-791)

NAMEPLATES

Executive Graphic Systems LLC..........G....... 203 678-6432
  Wallingford (G-9261)
Precision Graphics Inc......................E....... 860 828-6561
  East Berlin (G-2174)

NATURAL GAS LIQUIDS PRODUCTION

Impact Nutraceuticals LLC..................G....... 203 493-4268
  Greenwich (G-3179)

NATURAL GAS PRODUCTION

Direct Energy Inc..........................F....... 800 260-0300
  Stamford (G-8186)
Fpr Pinedale LLC...........................G....... 203 542-6000
  Stamford (G-8206)
Louis Dreyfus Holding Company..........B....... 203 761-2000
  Wilton (G-10310)
South Bend Ethanol LLC....................G....... 203 326-8132
  Stamford (G-8430)
Viridian Energy LLC........................D....... 203 663-5089
  Stamford (G-8485)

NATURAL GAS TRANSMISSION & DISTRIBUTION

Castleton Commodities.....................G....... 203 564-8100
  Stamford (G-8131)
CCI East Texas Upstream LLC.............G....... 203 564-8100
  Stamford (G-8135)

NATURAL PROPANE PRODUCTION

Servco Oil Inc..............................G....... 203 762-7994
  Wilton (G-10328)
Spicer Plus Inc.............................G....... 860 445-2436
  Groton (G-3313)

NATURAL RESOURCE PRESERVATION SVCS

Connecticut Forest & Park Assn...........F....... 860 346-2372
  Rockfall (G-7211)
Renewable Energy Natural RES...........G....... 860 923-1091
  Thompson (G-8843)

NAUTICAL REPAIR SVCS

Farrar Sails Inc.............................G....... 860 447-0382
  New London (G-5471)

NAVIGATIONAL SYSTEMS & INSTRUMENTS

Airflo Instrument Company.................G....... 860 633-9455
  Glastonbury (G-3005)

NEEDLES

588 Smainst LLC..........................G....... 860 482-1625
  Torrington (G-8884)
Connectcut Prcsion Cmpnnts LLC........G....... 860 489-8621
  Torrington (G-8915)

NETTING: Cargo

International Cordage East Ltd.............D....... 860 873-5000
  Colchester (G-1555)

NETTING: Plastic

Pucuda Inc.................................F....... 860 526-8004
  Madison (G-3949)

NICKEL ALLOY

Norilsk Nickel USA Inc......................G....... 203 730-0676
  Ridgefield (G-7157)

NIPPLES: Rubber

Playtex Products LLC......................D....... 203 944-5500
  Shelton (G-7531)

NONCURRENT CARRYING WIRING DEVICES

Chase Corporation.........................F....... 203 285-1244
  Woodbridge (G-10597)
Wiremold Company.........................F....... 860 263-3115
  West Hartford (G-9875)
Wiremold Legrand Co Centerex..........E....... 877 295-3472
  West Hartford (G-9876)

NONDURABLE GOODS WHOLESALERS, NEC

Chef Gretchen LLC........................G....... 203 252-8892
  Stamford (G-8142)

NONFERROUS: Rolling & Drawing, NEC

Doncasters Inc............................D....... 860 446-4803
  Groton (G-3282)
Tico Titanium Inc..........................E....... 248 446-0400
  Wallingford (G-9384)
Titanium Metals Corporation..............F....... 860 627-7051
  East Windsor (G-2527)
Ulbrich Stainless Steels...................C....... 203 269-2507
  Wallingford (G-9393)
United Stts Sgn & Fbrction................E....... 203 601-1000
  Trumbull (G-9088)

NONMETALLIC MINERALS: Support Activities, Exc Fuels

Fred Rein..................................G....... 860 460-8086
  Mystic (G-4818)
Haynes Aggregates - Deep River.........G....... 203 888-8100
  Seymour (G-7349)

NOVELTIES

PB&j Design Inc...........................G....... 203 332-2433
  Derby (G-2121)

NOVELTIES, DURABLE, WHOLESALE

Online River LLC..........................F....... 203 801-5900
  Westport (G-10134)

NOVELTIES: Plastic

United Plastics Technologies..............F....... 860 224-1110
  New Britain (G-5079)

NOVELTY SHOPS

Ciaudelli Productions Inc..................G....... 860 848-0411
  Montville (G-4769)

NOZZLES & SPRINKLERS Lawn Hose

Butler Irrigation...........................G....... 203 877-2248
  Orange (G-6587)

NUCLEAR REACTORS: Military Or Indl

Recon Tactical LLC........................G....... 860 677-8202
  Farmington (G-2954)

NURSERIES & LAWN & GARDEN SPLY STORES, RETAIL: Top Soil

Grillo Services LLC........................E....... 203 877-5070
  Milford (G-4544)

NURSERIES & LAWN/GARDEN SPLY STORE, RET: Lawnmowers/Tractors

Darien Lawn Mower Repair................G....... 203 656-1869
  Darien (G-2018)
W H Preuss Sons Incorporated...........G....... 860 643-9492
  Bolton (G-521)

NURSERIES & LAWN/GARDEN SPLY STORES, RET: Garden Splys/Tools

American Standard Company.............E....... 860 628-9643
  Southington (G-7889)

NURSERY & GARDEN CENTERS

Bobbex Inc................................G....... 800 792-4449
  Monroe (G-4700)
Midwood Quarry and Cnstr Inc............F....... 860 289-1414
  East Hartford (G-2345)

NURSERY STOCK, WHOLESALE

Clinton Nursery Products Inc..............C....... 860 399-3000
  Westbrook (G-9994)

NUTS: Metal

Metalform Acquisition LLC.................F....... 860 224-2630
  New Britain (G-5016)

NYLON FIBERS

Atco Wire Rope and Indus Sup...........G....... 203 239-1632
  North Haven (G-5911)

OFFICE EQPT WHOLESALERS

Agissar Corporation.......................D....... 203 375-8662
  Stratford (G-8565)

OFFICE FIXTURES: Wood

Premier Mfg Group Inc....................D....... 203 924-6617
  Shelton (G-7539)

OFFICE HELP SPLY SVCS

Corporate Express CT.....................G....... 203 455-2500
  Stratford (G-8599)

OFFICE MACHINES, NEC

Its New England Inc.......................G....... 203 265-8100
  Wallingford (G-9290)

OFFICE SPLY & STATIONERY STORES

AMG Development LLC...................G....... 203 292-8444
  Westport (G-10056)
Eccles-Lehman Inc........................G....... 203 268-0605
  Easton (G-2551)
Fedex Office & Print Svcs Inc.............F....... 203 799-2679
  Orange (G-6601)
Mc Hugh Business Forms.................G....... 203 268-3500
  Monroe (G-4735)

OFFICE SPLY & STATIONERY STORES: Office Forms & Splys

Adkins Printing Company.................E....... 800 228-9745
  New Britain (G-4938)
Copy Stop Inc.............................G....... 203 288-6401
  Hamden (G-3433)
Hartford Business Supply Inc..............E....... 860 233-2138
  Hartford (G-3607)
Jyl LLP....................................G....... 860 767-7733
  Essex (G-2722)
Ross Copy & Print LLC...................G....... 203 933-8732
  West Haven (G-9950)
W B Mason Co Inc.......................D....... 888 926-2766
  Meriden (G-4265)
W B Mason Co Inc.......................G....... 888 926-2766
  Norwalk (G-6392)
W B Mason Co Inc.......................D....... 888 926-2766
  Norwich (G-6439)
W B Mason Co Inc.......................C....... 888 926-2766
  East Windsor (G-2530)

OFFICE SPLYS, NEC, WHOLESALE

Adkins Printing Company.................E....... 800 228-9745
  New Britain (G-4938)
AMG Development LLC...................G....... 203 292-8444
  Westport (G-10056)

OFFICES & CLINICS OF DENTISTS: Dental Clinic

Essel Dental..............................G....... 860 254-6955
  East Windsor (G-2492)

OFFICES & CLINICS OF DENTISTS: Dental Clinics & Offices

Bridgeport Dental LLC .... G 203 384-2261
  Bridgeport (G-720)

OFFICES & CLINICS OF DOCTORS OF MEDICINE: Ophthalmologist

Jeffrey Gold .... G 203 281-5737
  Hamden (G-3467)

OFFICES & CLINICS OF DOCTORS OF MEDICINE: Pediatrician

Childrens Medical Group .... E 860 242-8330
  Bloomfield (G-402)

OFFICES & CLINICS OF DOCTORS OF MEDICINE: Radiologist

Branford Open Mri & Diagnostic .... G 203 481-7800
  Branford (G-563)
Eastern Conn Hlth Netwrk .... G 860 652-3182
  Glastonbury (G-3030)

OFFICES & CLINICS OF DRS OF MED: Clinic, Op by Physicians

Yale-New Haven Hlth Svcs Corp .... D 203 688-2100
  New Haven (G-5452)

OFFICES & CLINICS OF HEALTH PRACTITIONERS: Physical Therapy

Clever Clover LLC .... G 860 501-2800
  Pawcatuck (G-6706)

OIL & GAS FIELD MACHINERY

First Reserve Fund Viii LP .... G 203 661-6601
  Stamford (G-8205)
Numa Tool Company .... D 860 923-9551
  Thompson (G-8841)

OIL FIELD MACHINERY & EQPT

Oil Purification Systems Inc .... F 203 346-1800
  Waterbury (G-9569)

OIL FIELD SVCS, NEC

Cameron International Corp .... F 860 633-0277
  Glastonbury (G-3018)
Cedar Ridge Oil Co .... G 860 435-9398
  Salisbury (G-7295)
Dimauro Oil Co LLC .... G 860 342-2969
  Portland (G-6958)
East Mountain Oil Co LLC .... G 203 757-7774
  Prospect (G-7001)
Franklin-Howard LLC .... G 860 923-3343
  Woodstock (G-10665)
Frc Founders Corporation .... E 203 661-6601
  Stamford (G-8209)
P J S Services .... G 860 345-4896
  Higganum (G-3774)
R&M Service .... G 860 645-7771
  Manchester (G-4080)
Santa Energy Corporation .... G 800 937-2682
  Bridgeport (G-895)
Sigma Tankers Inc .... F 203 662-2600
  Norwalk (G-6347)
Weatherford International LLC .... E 203 294-0190
  Wallingford (G-9402)
Williams Oil Company .... G 860 664-9587
  Clinton (G-1534)

OILS & GREASES: Lubricating

Artech Packaging LLC .... G 845 858-8558
  Bethel (G-259)
Axel Plastics RES Labs Inc .... E 718 672-8300
  Monroe (G-4694)
Castrol Industrial N Amer Inc .... G 860 928-5100
  Putnam (G-7032)
CCL Industries Corporation .... D 203 926-1253
  Shelton (G-7412)
Interflon of New England .... G 860 305-8976
  Wethersfield (G-10200)
Permatex Inc .... E 860 543-7500
  Hartford (G-3663)

Safe Harbour Products Inc .... G 203 295-8377
  Norwalk (G-6336)

OILS: Cutting

Chessco Industries Inc .... E 203 255-2804
  Westport (G-10064)
Fuchs Lubricants Co .... E 203 469-2336
  East Haven (G-2431)

OILS: Lubricating

Chessco Industries Inc .... E 203 255-2804
  Westport (G-10064)
Du-Lite Corporation .... G 860 347-2505
  Middletown (G-4337)

OILS: Lubricating

Macdermid Incorporated .... C 203 575-5700
  Waterbury (G-9522)
Sheldon Automotive Enterprises .... F 203 372-4948
  Fairfield (G-2846)

OPERATOR: Nonresidential Buildings

Fletcher-Terry Company LLC .... D 860 828-3400
  East Berlin (G-2169)
Macristy Industries Inc .... C 860 225-4637
  Newington (G-5674)
Stevens Industries Inc .... E 203 966-7555
  New Canaan (G-5147)

OPHTHALMIC GOODS

Central Optical .... G 860 236-2329
  West Hartford (G-9787)
Coburn Technologies Inc .... C 860 648-6600
  South Windsor (G-7731)
Gerber Coburn Optical Inc .... C 800 843-1479
  South Windsor (G-7758)
Hoya Corporation .... B 860 289-5379
  South Windsor (G-7773)
Lens .... G 203 426-8833
  Newtown (G-5754)
Lenses Only .... G 860 278-2020
  Hartford (G-3627)
McLeod Optical Company Inc .... G 203 754-2187
  Waterbury (G-9538)

OPHTHALMIC GOODS WHOLESALERS

Precision Optical Co .... E 860 289-6023
  East Hartford (G-2361)

OPHTHALMIC GOODS, NEC, WHOLESALE: Contact Lenses

Doctors of Optometry .... G 203 743-9897
  Danbury (G-1798)

OPHTHALMIC GOODS: Lenses, Intraocular

Mager & Gougelman Inc .... G 203 773-1753
  New Haven (G-5324)

OPHTHALMIC GOODS: Lenses, Ophthalmic

Gerber Scientific LLC .... C 860 871-8082
  Tolland (G-8864)

OPHTHALMIC GOODS: Protectors, Eye

Shari M Roth MD .... G 860 676-2525
  Avon (G-111)

OPTICAL GOODS STORES

Opticare Health Systems Inc .... C 203 574-2020
  Waterbury (G-9571)

OPTICAL GOODS STORES: Contact Lenses, Prescription

Opticare Eye Health & Vision .... G 203 261-2619
  Trumbull (G-9052)

OPTICAL GOODS STORES: Opticians

Central Optical .... G 860 236-2329
  West Hartford (G-9787)
Fedora Optical Inc .... G 860 646-3577
  Manchester (G-4017)

OPTICAL INSTRUMENT REPAIR SVCS

Coburn Technologies Intl Inc .... G 860 648-6600
  South Windsor (G-7732)
Coburn Tecnologies Canada .... D 860 648-6710
  South Windsor (G-7733)

OPTICAL INSTRUMENTS & APPARATUS

Conoptics Inc .... F 203 743-3349
  Danbury (G-1773)

OPTICAL INSTRUMENTS & LENSES

Advanced Photonics Intl Inc .... G 203 259-0437
  Fairfield (G-2745)
Aecc/Pearlman Buying Group LLC .... F 203 598-3200
  Middlebury (G-4272)
Aperture Optical Sciences Inc .... G 860 301-2589
  Higganum (G-3759)
Aperture Optical Sciences Inc .... G 860 301-2372
  Meriden (G-4144)
Argyle Optics LLC .... G 203 451-3320
  Milford (G-4456)
Coating Design Group Inc .... E 203 878-3663
  Stratford (G-8596)
Coburn Technologies .... G 800 262-8761
  South Windsor (G-7730)
Coburn Technologies Inc .... C 860 648-6600
  South Windsor (G-7731)
Coburn Technologies Intl Inc .... G 860 648-6600
  South Windsor (G-7732)
Coburn Tecnologies Canada .... D 860 648-6710
  South Windsor (G-7733)
CT Fiberoptics Inc .... F 860 763-4341
  Somers (G-7654)
Data Technology Inc .... E 860 871-8082
  Tolland (G-8860)
Doctors of Optometry .... G 203 743-9897
  Danbury (G-1798)
Gerber Coburn Optical Inc .... C 800 843-1479
  South Windsor (G-7758)
Karl Stetson Associates LLC .... G 860 742-8414
  Coventry (G-1659)
Mev Technologies LLC .... G 203 227-4723
  Westport (G-10120)
Nntechnology Moore Systems LLC .... G 203 366-3224
  Bridgeport (G-851)
Odis Inc .... G 860 450-8407
  Storrs Mansfield (G-8557)
Optical Design Associates .... G 203 249-6408
  Stamford (G-8343)
Paramount Glassworks LLC .... G 860 315-7624
  Woodstock (G-10675)
Sparrow Woods Co LLC .... G 203 215-5200
  Woodbridge (G-10618)
Spectral Optics Inc .... G 978 682-1302
  Putnam (G-7070)
UTC Fire SEC Americas Corp Inc .... C 203 426-1180
  Newtown (G-5796)
Zygo Corporation .... G 860 347-8506
  Middlefield (G-4310)

OPTICAL SCANNING SVCS

Ebeam Film LLC .... F 203 926-0100
  Shelton (G-7434)

OPTOMETRISTS' OFFICES

Doctors of Optometry .... G 203 743-9897
  Danbury (G-1798)
Opticare Health Systems Inc .... C 203 574-2020
  Waterbury (G-9571)

ORAL PREPARATIONS

Connectcut Crnial Fcial Imgery .... G 860 643-2940
  Manchester (G-3998)

ORDNANCE

Capstone Manufacturing Inc .... G 413 636-6170
  South Windsor (G-7723)
Ensign-Bickford Industries Inc .... E 860 658-4411
  Simsbury (G-7622)
Fenrir Industries Inc .... F 203 977-0671
  Stamford (G-8203)
Kaman Aerospace Corporation .... C 860 632-1000
  Middletown (G-4360)

ORDNANCE: Flame Throwers
Simulations LLC .... G 860 978-0772
East Granby *(G-2230)*

ORGANIZATIONS: Biotechnical Research, Noncommercial
Sibtech Inc .... G 203 775-5677
Brookfield *(G-1223)*

ORGANIZATIONS: Medical Research
Alexion Pharma LLC .... E 203 272-2596
New Haven *(G-5221)*
Butterfly Network Inc .... E 855 296-6188
Guilford *(G-3336)*
Protein Sciences Corporation .... D 203 686-0800
Meriden *(G-4224)*

ORGANIZATIONS: Physical Research, Noncommercial
Rand Innovations LLC .... F 475 282-4643
Bridgeport *(G-885)*

ORGANIZATIONS: Professional
Wire Association Intl Inc .... E 203 453-2777
Madison *(G-3968)*

ORGANIZATIONS: Religious
NRG Connecticut LLC .... E 860 231-2424
Hartford *(G-3657)*

ORGANIZERS, CLOSET & DRAWER Plastic
Bidwell Industrial Group Inc .... E 860 346-9283
Middletown *(G-4325)*
CT Organizer LLC .... G 203 858-5824
Westport *(G-10072)*

ORNAMENTS: Christmas Tree, Exc Electrical & Glass
Interior Plantworks Inc .... G 860 289-9499
South Windsor *(G-7775)*
Roland A Parent .... G 860 928-9158
Woodstock *(G-10682)*

OUTBOARD MOTOR DEALERS
Ace Marine Service Inc .... G 860 489-5960
Torrington *(G-8886)*

OUTBOARD MOTORS: Electric
Coherent Inc .... E 860 243-9557
Bloomfield *(G-404)*

OUTREACH PROGRAM
Barclay-Davis Enterprises LLC .... G 860 578-9563
Hartford *(G-3555)*

PACKAGE DESIGN SVCS
Defined Design Creative Art .... G 203 378-2571
Stratford *(G-8604)*

PACKAGING & LABELING SVCS
East Coast Packaging LLC .... G 860 675-8500
Farmington *(G-2901)*
Jyl LLP .... G 860 767-7733
Essex *(G-2722)*
Mid State Assembly & Packg Inc .... G 203 634-8740
Meriden *(G-4202)*
Midstate Printing Group LLC .... G 203 998-7575
Stamford *(G-8309)*
Olive Oil Factory LLC .... F 203 591-8986
Waterbury *(G-9570)*

PACKAGING MATERIALS, WHOLESALE
Hudson Paper Company .... E 203 378-8759
Stratford *(G-8628)*
Pactiv Corporation .... E 203 288-7722
North Haven *(G-5972)*
Park City Packaging Inc .... E 203 378-7384
Stratford *(G-8662)*
Park City Packaging Inc .... F 203 579-1965
Bridgeport *(G-862)*
Penmar Industries Inc .... F 203 853-4868
Stratford *(G-8663)*

PACKAGING MATERIALS: Paper
Agi-Shorewood Group Us LLC .... A 203 324-4839
Stamford *(G-8067)*
Ansel Label and Packaging Corp .... E 203 452-0311
Trumbull *(G-8999)*
Atlas Agi Holdings LLC .... A 203 622-9138
Greenwich *(G-3125)*
Biomerics LLC .... D 203 268-7238
Monroe *(G-4698)*
CCL Label Inc .... C 203 926-1253
Shelton *(G-7413)*
Flagship Converters Inc .... D 203 792-0034
Danbury *(G-1826)*
Fluted Partition Inc .... C 203 368-2548
Bridgeport *(G-770)*
Fortis Solutions Group LLC .... E 860 872-6311
Ellington *(G-2590)*
Identification Products Corp .... G 203 331-0931
Bridgeport *(G-790)*
Identification Products Corp .... F 203 334-5969
Bridgeport *(G-791)*
Knox Enterprises Inc .... G 203 226-6408
Westport *(G-10108)*
Mid State Assembly & Packg Inc .... G 203 634-8740
Meriden *(G-4202)*
Packaging and Crating Tech LLC .... G 203 759-1799
Waterbury *(G-9572)*
Paxxus Inc .... E 860 242-0663
Bloomfield *(G-461)*
Penmar Industries Inc .... F 203 853-4868
Stratford *(G-8663)*
Polymer Films Inc .... E 203 932-3000
West Haven *(G-9946)*
Quality Name Plate Inc .... D 860 633-9495
East Glastonbury *(G-2185)*
Rol-Vac Limited Partnership .... F 860 928-9929
Dayville *(G-2072)*
Sealed Air Corporation .... C 203 791-3648
Danbury *(G-1942)*
Sonoco Prtective Solutions Inc .... E 860 928-7795
Putnam *(G-7068)*
Stora Enso N Amercn Sls Inc .... G 203 541-5178
Stamford *(G-8444)*
Tht Inc .... G 203 226-6408
Westport *(G-10167)*
Windham Container Corporation .... E 860 928-7934
Putnam *(G-7079)*

PACKAGING MATERIALS: Paper, Coated Or Laminated
Amgraph Packaging Inc .... C 203 822-2000
Baltic *(G-118)*
Miami Wabash Paper LLC .... E 203 847-8500
Norwalk *(G-6257)*

PACKAGING MATERIALS: Plastic Film, Coated Or Laminated
Bollore Inc .... D 860 774-2930
Dayville *(G-2054)*
General Packaging Products Inc .... G 203 846-1340
Norwalk *(G-6178)*
Polymeric Converting LLC .... E 860 623-1335
Enfield *(G-2678)*

PACKAGING MATERIALS: Polystyrene Foam
Covit America Inc .... B 860 274-6791
Watertown *(G-9696)*
Fc Meyer Packaging LLC .... D 860 847-8500
Norwalk *(G-6162)*
General Packaging Products Inc .... G 203 846-1340
Norwalk *(G-6178)*
Paxxus Inc .... E 860 242-0663
Bloomfield *(G-461)*
Sealed Air Corporation .... C 203 791-3648
Danbury *(G-1942)*
Sonoco Prtective Solutions Inc .... E 860 928-7795
Putnam *(G-7068)*
Universal Foam Products LLC .... F 860 216-3015
Bloomfield *(G-496)*

PACKAGING: Blister Or Bubble Formed, Plastic
Packaging and Crating Tech LLC .... G 203 759-1799
Waterbury *(G-9572)*
Southpack LLC .... E 860 224-2242
New Britain *(G-5057)*

PACKING MATERIALS: Mechanical
EMR Global Inc .... G 203 452-8166
East Hartford *(G-2322)*

PACKING SVCS: Shipping
American-Digital LLC .... G 203 838-0148
Bridgeport *(G-695)*
Park City Packaging Inc .... E 203 378-7384
Stratford *(G-8662)*
Park City Packaging Inc .... F 203 579-1965
Bridgeport *(G-862)*

PAINT & PAINTING SPLYS STORE
Artist and Craftsman .... G 203 330-0459
Bridgeport *(G-703)*

PAINT STORE
Color Craft Ltd .... F 800 509-6563
East Granby *(G-2197)*
ICI Dulux Paints .... G 860 621-8661
Southington *(G-7937)*
Merrifield Paint Company Inc .... G 860 529-1583
Rocky Hill *(G-7257)*

PAINTING SVC: Metal Prdts
Advanced Graphics Inc .... E 203 378-0471
Stratford *(G-8564)*
American Bus Tele & Tech LLC .... G 860 643-2200
Manchester *(G-3982)*
Farrell Prcsion Mtalcraft Corp .... E 860 355-2651
New Milford *(G-5532)*
Fonda Fabricating & Welding Co .... G 860 793-0601
Plainville *(G-6812)*
Halco Inc .... D 860 575-9450
Waterbury *(G-9495)*
High Grade Finishing Co LLC .... G 860 749-8883
Enfield *(G-2649)*
Imperial Metal Finishing Inc .... F 203 377-1229
Stratford *(G-8631)*
Jonmandy Corporation .... G 860 482-2354
Torrington *(G-8940)*
Pauway Corp .... F 203 265-3939
Wallingford *(G-9333)*

PAINTING: Hand, Textiles
Painted Tiles Co .... G 860 658-7218
Simsbury *(G-7638)*

PAINTS & ADDITIVES
FMI Paint & Chemical Inc .... F 860 218-2210
East Hartford *(G-2328)*
Merrifield Paint Company Inc .... G 860 529-1583
Rocky Hill *(G-7257)*

PAINTS & ALLIED PRODUCTS
A G C Incorporated .... C 203 235-3361
Meriden *(G-4138)*
Air Born Coatings .... G 860 684-6762
East Hartford *(G-2289)*
Albert Kemperle Inc .... F 860 727-0933
Hartford *(G-3550)*
Chromalloy Component Svcs Inc .... C 860 688-7798
Windsor *(G-10373)*
Colonial Coatings Inc .... E 203 783-9933
Milford *(G-4491)*
Dumond Chemicals Inc .... D 609 655-7700
Milford *(G-4517)*
Dumond Chemicals Inc .... D 609 655-7700
Milford *(G-4518)*
Five Star Products Inc .... E 203 336-7900
Shelton *(G-7444)*
Fougera Pharmaceuticals Inc .... F 203 265-2086
Wallingford *(G-9269)*
Greenmaker Industries Conn LLC ...... F 860 761-2830
West Hartford *(G-9814)*
ICI Dulux Paints .... G 860 621-8661
Southington *(G-7937)*

PRODUCT SECTION

Impermia Coatings Llc ....G...... 413 356-0077
  East Hartford *(G-2338)*
J + J Branford Inc ....G...... 203 488-5637
  Branford *(G-611)*
Jet Process Corporation ....G...... 203 985-6000
  North Haven *(G-5953)*
Mantrose-Haeuser Co Inc.........................E...... 203 454-1800
  Westport *(G-10117)*
Minteq International Inc ....G...... 860 824-5435
  Canaan *(G-1289)*
PPG Industries Inc ....G...... 203 750-9553
  Norwalk *(G-6304)*
PPG Industries Inc ....G...... 860 627-7401
  Windsor Locks *(G-10494)*
PPG Industries Inc ....G...... 203 562-5173
  New Haven *(G-5369)*
PPG Industries Inc ....G...... 203 744-4977
  Danbury *(G-1911)*
PPG Industries Inc ....G...... 860 522-9544
  Hartford *(G-3668)*
PPG Industries Inc ....G...... 860 953-1153
  West Hartford *(G-9846)*

PAINTS, VARNISHES & SPLYS, WHOLESALE: Paints

Color Craft Ltd ....F...... 800 509-6563
  East Granby *(G-2197)*
Grafted Coatings Inc ....F...... 203 377-9979
  Stratford *(G-8620)*
ICI Dulux Paints ....G...... 860 621-8661
  Southington *(G-7937)*

PAINTS: Lead-In-Oil

Brico LLC ....G...... 860 242-7068
  Bloomfield *(G-399)*

PAINTS: Waterproof

M & D Coatings LLC ....G...... 203 380-9466
  Stratford *(G-8644)*

PALLETS

Better Pallets Inc ....G...... 203 230-9549
  Branford *(G-558)*
Global Pallet Solutions LLC ....G...... 860 826-5000
  New Britain *(G-4992)*
Pallet Guys LLC ....G...... 203 691-6716
  North Haven *(G-5973)*
Pallet Inc LLC ....G...... 203 227-8148
  Westport *(G-10137)*
Toy Pallet ....G...... 860 803-9838
  Ellington *(G-2607)*

PALLETS & SKIDS: Wood

Acm Warehouse & Distribution ....G...... 203 239-9557
  North Haven *(G-5895)*
FCA LLC ....G...... 203 857-0825
  Norwalk *(G-6163)*
Guy Ravenelle ....G...... 860 564-3200
  Central Village *(G-1337)*

PALLETS: Wooden

Burn Time Enterprises LLC ....G...... 860 410-0747
  Plainville *(G-6780)*
Central Pallet & Box ....F...... 860 224-4416
  New Britain *(G-4959)*
Coastal Pallet Corporation ....E...... 203 333-1892
  Bridgeport *(G-737)*
HI-Tech Packaging Inc ....E...... 203 378-2700
  Stratford *(G-8626)*
Industrial Pallet LLC ....E...... 860 974-0093
  Eastford *(G-2536)*
J J Box Co Inc ....G...... 203 367-1211
  Bridgeport *(G-796)*
M & M Pallet Inc ....G...... 203 754-2606
  Waterbury *(G-9521)*
R & R Pallet Corp ....F...... 203 272-2784
  Cheshire *(G-1434)*
Southern Conn Pallet Co Inc ....G...... 203 265-1313
  Wallingford *(G-9371)*
St Pierre Box and Lumber Co ....G...... 860 413-9813
  Canton *(G-1326)*
Talmadge & Valentine Co Inc ....G...... 860 350-3534
  New Milford *(G-5592)*
Vermont Pallet & Skid Shop ....G...... 860 822-6949
  Norwich *(G-6437)*
Westwood Products Inc ....F...... 860 379-9401
  Winsted *(G-10543)*

PANELS: Building, Plastic, NEC

Nevamar Company LLC ....B...... 203 925-1556
  Shelton *(G-7508)*
Panolam Industries Inc ....E...... 203 925-1556
  Shelton *(G-7522)*
Panolam Industries Intl Inc ....E...... 203 925-1556
  Shelton *(G-7523)*

PANELS: Electric Metering

Reactel Inc ....G...... 203 773-0135
  New Haven *(G-5377)*

PAPER & BOARD: Die-cut

American CT Rng Bnder Index & ....F...... 860 868-7900
  Washington *(G-9411)*
B-P Products Inc ....E...... 203 288-0200
  Hamden *(G-3416)*
Kiss-U Corps LLC ....G...... 203 226-7730
  Weston *(G-10031)*
Makino Inc ....F...... 860 223-0236
  New Britain *(G-5012)*
Walker Products Incorporated ....F...... 860 659-3781
  Glastonbury *(G-3094)*

PAPER CONVERTING

B-P Products Inc ....E...... 203 288-0200
  Hamden *(G-3416)*
Dietzgen Corporation ....G...... 813 849-4334
  West Haven *(G-9899)*
Esten McGee Inc ....G...... 203 544-2000
  West Redding *(G-9969)*
Knox Industries Inc ....C...... 203 226-6408
  Westport *(G-10109)*
Mercantile Development Inc ....E...... 203 922-8880
  Shelton *(G-7497)*
Stafford Paper Company ....G...... 860 749-0787
  Somers *(G-7671)*
Tudor Converted Products Inc ....E...... 203 304-1875
  Newtown *(G-5795)*

PAPER MANUFACTURERS: Exc Newsprint

Ahlstrom Windsor Locks LLC ....F...... 860 654-8629
  Windsor Locks *(G-10468)*
Brant Industries Inc ....F...... 203 661-3344
  Greenwich *(G-3136)*
Bristol Bliss LLC ....G...... 203 704-0952
  Bristol *(G-988)*
Coveris Advanced Coatings ....G...... 413 244-9685
  West Haven *(G-9894)*
Finch Paper Holdings LLC ....G...... 203 622-9138
  Greenwich *(G-3159)*
First Papermill LLC ....G...... 203 740-1991
  Brookfield *(G-1188)*
International Paper - 16 Inc ....G...... 203 329-8544
  Stamford *(G-8254)*
International Paper Company ....C...... 860 928-7901
  Putnam *(G-7047)*
Kimberly-Clark Corporation ....C...... 973 986-8454
  Stratford *(G-8639)*
Kiss-U Corps LLC ....G...... 203 226-7730
  Weston *(G-10031)*
Mafcote International Inc ....F...... 203 644-1200
  Norwalk *(G-6244)*
McMullan Wall Coverings ....G...... 860 569-6260
  East Hartford *(G-2344)*
Norton Paper Mill LLC ....G...... 860 861-9701
  Colchester *(G-1560)*
Sre Bristol 322 Park St LLC ....G...... 860 348-0198
  East Berlin *(G-2177)*
Web Industries Inc ....G...... 860 779-3403
  Dayville *(G-2079)*

PAPER PRDTS

Over Moon ....G...... 203 853-2498
  Norwalk *(G-6287)*

PAPER PRDTS: Feminine Hygiene Prdts

W2w Partners LLC ....G...... 781 424-7824
  Greenwich *(G-3255)*

PAPER PRDTS: Infant & Baby Prdts

Alfa Nobel LLC ....G...... 203 876-2823
  Milford *(G-4447)*
Kimberly-Clark Corporation ....A...... 860 210-1602
  New Milford *(G-5556)*

PAPER: Coated & Laminated, NEC

Kimberly-Clark Corporation ....C...... 973 986-8454
  Stratford *(G-8639)*

PAPER PRDTS: Sanitary

Dunn Paper LLC ....D...... 860 466-4141
  East Hartford *(G-2317)*
Georgia-Pacific LLC ....G...... 203 866-9774
  Norwalk *(G-6180)*
Soundview Paper Mills LLC ....G...... 201 796-4000
  Greenwich *(G-3240)*

PAPER PRDTS: Sanitary Tissue Paper

Kimberly-Clark Corporation ....A...... 860 210-1602
  New Milford *(G-5556)*

PAPER PRDTS: Tampons, Sanitary, Made From Purchased Material

Edgewell Per Care Brands LLC ....B...... 203 944-5500
  Shelton *(G-7435)*
Playtex Products LLC ....D...... 203 944-5500
  Shelton *(G-7531)*

PAPER PRDTS: Towels, Napkins/Tissue Paper, From Purchd Mtrls

Aci Industries Converting Ltd ....G...... 740 368-4166
  Stamford *(G-8058)*

PAPER PRDTS: Wrappers, Blank, Made From Purchased Materials

Eagle Tissue LLC ....F...... 860 282-2535
  South Windsor *(G-7742)*

PAPER: Adhesive

Design Label Manufacturing Inc ....E...... 860 739-6266
  Old Lyme *(G-6505)*
H-O Products Corporation ....E...... 860 379-9875
  Winsted *(G-10523)*
Illinois Tool Works Inc ....C...... 860 646-8153
  Manchester *(G-4031)*
Neato Products LLC ....G...... 203 466-5170
  Milford *(G-4587)*

PAPER: Bristols

Bristol Adult Resource Ctr Inc ....E...... 860 583-8721
  Bristol *(G-987)*
Bristol Nitro Softball Corp ....G...... 860 940-1924
  Bristol *(G-990)*
Bristol Plaza ....G...... 617 553-1820
  Bristol *(G-991)*
Cifc Early Lrng Programs/Wic ....G...... 203 206-6341
  Danbury *(G-1768)*
Community Acpncture Brstol LLC ....G...... 860 833-9330
  Bristol *(G-1004)*
Doubletree ....F...... 860 589-7766
  Bristol *(G-1018)*
LP Hometown Pizza LLC ....G...... 860 589-1208
  Bristol *(G-1064)*
Magnificat Mother of Div Mrcy ....G...... 860 584-8803
  Bristol *(G-1067)*
Smart Foods of Bristol ....G...... 860 582-8882
  Bristol *(G-1118)*
State of Connecticut Educ ....G...... 860 584-8433
  Bristol *(G-1123)*

PAPER: Building, Insulating & Packaging

B 9 Air Quality Services LLC ....G...... 203 387-1709
  Wallingford *(G-9217)*
Honey Cell Inc ....G...... 203 925-1818
  Bridgeport *(G-785)*

PAPER: Card

American Banknote Corporation ....G...... 203 941-4090
  Stamford *(G-8074)*

PAPER: Cigarette

UST LLC ....G...... 203 817-3000
  Stamford *(G-8483)*

PAPER: Coated & Laminated, NEC

Alsip Acquisition LLC ....G...... 203 202-7777
  Westport *(G-10053)*

PAPER: Coated & Laminated, NEC

Copy Cats Inc ....F 860 442-8424
New London (G-5465)
Lgl Group Inc ....G 407 298-2000
Greenwich (G-3191)
Markal Finishing Co Inc ....E 203 384-8219
Bridgeport (G-830)
Scapa Holdings Inc ....B 860 688-8000
Windsor (G-10432)
Scapa North America Inc 860 688-8000
Windsor (G-10433)
Specialty Printing LLC ....D 860 623-8870
East Windsor (G-2521)
The E J Davis Company ....E 203 239-5391
North Haven (G-5998)

PAPER: Corrugated

Park City Packaging Inc ....E 203 378-7384
Stratford (G-8662)
Valley Container Inc ....E 203 368-6546
Bridgeport (G-933)

PAPER: Cover

Yourcover LLC ....G 203 563-9233
Wilton (G-10342)

PAPER: Greeting Card

Up With Paper ....G 203 453-3300
Guilford (G-3400)

PAPER: Insulation Siding

Xamax Industries Inc ....E 203 888-7200
Seymour (G-7375)

PAPER: Kraft

American Kraft Paper Inds LLC ....G 203 323-1916
Stamford (G-8076)

PAPER: Newsprint

Resolute FP US Inc ....B 203 292-6560
Southport (G-8008)

PAPER: Packaging

Arrow Marketing Inc ....G 203 375-7541
Stratford (G-8570)
Graphics Services Corporation ....G 203 270-7578
Newtown (G-5740)

PAPER: Poster & Art

DAmbruoso Studios LLC ....G 203 758-9660
Middlebury (G-4276)

PAPER: Printer

Dynamic Printing ....G 203 459-8762
Monroe (G-4714)
Norcell Inc ....F 203 254-5292
Shelton (G-7513)

PAPER: Specialty

Steven Rosendahl Inc ....G 860 928-3136
Woodstock (G-10685)

PAPER: Specialty Or Chemically Treated

Ahlstrom-Munksjo USA Inc ....F 860 654-8300
Windsor Locks (G-10470)

PAPER: Wallpaper

JM Shea LLC ....G 203 431-4435
Ridgefield (G-7150)

PAPER: Writing

Vanilla Politics LLC ....G 203 221-0895
Weston (G-10043)

PAPERBOARD

Connecticut Container Corp ....C 203 248-2161
North Haven (G-5924)
Fluted Partition Inc ....C 203 368-2548
Bridgeport (G-770)
Graphic Packaging Intl LLC ....G 860 567-4196
Litchfield (G-3890)
Metsa Board Americas Corp ....D 203 229-0037
Norwalk (G-6256)
Rice Packaging Inc ....D 860 870-7057
Ellington (G-2598)
Russell Partition Co Inc ....G 203 239-5749
North Haven (G-5988)
Schrafel Paperboard Converting ....E 203 931-1700
West Haven (G-9953)
Sonoco ....G 860 928-7795
Putnam (G-7067)

PAPERBOARD CONVERTING

Meadwestvaco Packg Systems LLC .....G 409 276-3137
Stamford (G-8301)
Rand-Whitney Recycling LLC ....D 860 848-1900
Montville (G-4770)
Schrafel Paperboard Converting ....E 203 931-1700
West Haven (G-9953)

PAPERBOARD PRDTS: Automobile Board

Lydall Inc ....E 860 646-1233
Manchester (G-4050)

PAPERBOARD PRDTS: Container Board

Paper Alliance LLC ....G 203 315-3116
Branford (G-631)
Westrock Rkt Company ....C 860 284-9820
Farmington (G-2978)

PAPERBOARD PRDTS: Folding Boxboard

Millen Industries Inc ....G 203 847-8500
Norwalk (G-6259)

PAPERBOARD PRDTS: Packaging Board

Pact Inc ....F 203 759-1799
Waterbury (G-9573)

PAPERBOARD: Boxboard

Action Packaging Systems Inc ....G 860 222-9510
Ellington (G-2571)
B-P Products Inc ....E 203 288-0200
Hamden (G-3416)

PAPERBOARD: Corrugated

Westrock Cp LLC ....C 860 848-1500
Uncasville (G-9108)

PARACHUTES

Cap-Tech Products Inc ....F 860 490-5078
Wethersfield (G-10185)
Pioneer Arspc Def Systems Corp ....G 860 528-0092
South Windsor (G-7805)

PARTICLEBOARD

Biofibers Capital Group LLC ....G 203 561-6133
Ashford (G-57)
Panolam Industries Intl Inc ....E 203 925-1556
Shelton (G-7523)
Robran Industries Inc ....G 203 510-6292
Waterbury (G-9594)

PARTITIONS & FIXTURES: Except Wood

Displaycraft Inc ....E 860 747-9110
Plainville (G-6799)
Durham Manufacturing Company ....D 860 349-3427
Durham (G-2146)

PARTITIONS WHOLESALERS

Steeltech Building Pdts Inc ....D 860 290-8930
South Windsor (G-7829)

PARTITIONS: Metal, Ornamental

Stephen Hawrylik ....G 860 688-8651
Windsor (G-10444)

PARTITIONS: Nonwood, Floor Attached

Musano Inc ....F 203 879-4651
Wolcott (G-10575)

PARTITIONS: Wood & Fixtures

Absolute Countertops LLC ....G 203 395-8259
Derby (G-2107)
BP Countertop Design Co LLC ....G 203 732-1620
Derby (G-2110)
C Mather Company Inc ....G 860 528-5667
South Windsor (G-7721)
Creative Dimensions Inc ....E 203 250-6500
Cheshire (G-1376)
Edko Cabinets LLC ....G 203 463-8346
Seymour (G-7345)
Edward Tomkievich ....G 860 633-5811
Glastonbury (G-3032)
John M Kriskey Carpentry ....G 203 531-0194
Greenwich (G-3184)
Modern Woodcrafts LLC ....D 860 677-7371
Plainville (G-6845)
Morris Woodworking ....G 860 346-7500
Middletown (G-4382)
Mr Shower Door Inc ....G 203 838-3667
Norwalk (G-6265)
One and Co Inc ....F 860 892-5180
Norwich (G-6427)
Robert L Lovallo ....G 203 324-6655
Stamford (G-8396)
St Johns Bridge LLC ....G 860 927-3315
Kent (G-3826)
Stevenson Group Corporation ....F 860 689-0011
Harwinton (G-3740)
Viking Kitchen Cabinets LLC ....G 860 223-7101
New Britain (G-5080)

PARTS: Metal

Mimforms LLC ....G 800 445-1245
Norwalk (G-6260)
Planit Manufacturing LLC ....G 203 641-6055
Bristol (G-1092)
SMR Metal Technology ....G 860 291-8259
South Windsor (G-7823)

PARTY & SPECIAL EVENT PLANNING SVCS

Urban Exposition LLC ....E 203 242-8717
Trumbull (G-9090)

PATENT OWNERS & LESSORS

Capricorn Investors II LP ....A 203 861-6600
Greenwich (G-3140)
Capricorn Investors III LP ....F 203 861-6600
Greenwich (G-3141)

PATIENT MONITORING EQPT WHOLESALERS

Vital Hlthcare Cmmncations LLC ....G 866 478-4825
Milford (G-4675)

PATTERNS: Indl

Arrow Diversified Tooling Inc ....E 860 872-9072
Ellington (G-2576)
Case Patterns Inc ....G 860 445-6722
Groton (G-3275)
Equipment Designs Associate ....G 860 217-1573
Simsbury (G-7624)
Pamelas Patterns ....G 610 534-4182
Vernon Rockville (G-9173)
Pattern Genomics LLC ....G 203 779-5470
Madison (G-3947)
Paw Patterns LLC ....G 401 338-4723
Amston (G-5)
Pony Patterns LLC ....G 203 535-0347
New Haven (G-5368)
Post Pattern ....G 860 774-7911
Brooklyn (G-1252)
Progressive Pattern ....G 860 748-0088
Windsor (G-10426)

PAVERS

Calvin Brown ....G 860 536-6178
Gales Ferry (G-2982)
Daves Paving and Construction ....G 203 753-4992
Prospect (G-7000)
LH Gault & Son Incorporated ....D 203 227-5181
Westport (G-10112)
Pavers of New England Inc ....G 860 289-7778
South Windsor (G-7804)
Robran Industries Inc ....G 203 510-6292
Waterbury (G-9594)

PRODUCT SECTION

PAVING MATERIALS: Prefabricated, Concrete

Dalton Enterprises Inc .... D 203 272-3221
  Cheshire (G-1379)

PENCILS & PENS WHOLESALERS

Mega Sound and Light LLC .... G 203 743-4200
  Danbury (G-1882)

PENS & PARTS: Ball Point

Bic Consumer Pdts Mfg Co Inc .... G 203 783-2000
  Shelton (G-7406)
Bic Consumer Products Mfg Co .... C 203 783-2000
  Milford (G-4469)
Bic Corporation .... A 203 783-2000
  Shelton (G-7407)
Bic Corporation .... G 203 538-5028
  Milford (G-4470)
Bic USA Inc .... C 203 783-2000
  Shelton (G-7408)

PENS & PENCILS: Mechanical, NEC

Gillette Company .... G 203 796-4000
  Bethel (G-303)
Mega Sound and Light LLC .... G 203 743-4200
  Danbury (G-1882)

PENS: Meter

Carla Way .... G 203 351-7815
  Stamford (G-8128)

PERFORMANCE RIGHTS, PUBLISHING & LICENSING

EPic Publishing Services LLC .... G 860 204-7450
  East Haddam (G-2241)

PERFUME: Concentrated

Bedoukian Research Inc .... E 203 830-4000
  Danbury (G-1750)

PERFUME: Perfumes, Natural Or Synthetic

Chemessence Inc .... G 860 355-4108
  New Milford (G-5519)
Parfums De Coeur Ltd .... E 203 655-8807
  Stamford (G-8350)

PERFUMES

American Distilling Inc .... G 860 267-4444
  Marlborough (G-4119)
American Distilling Inc .... D 860 267-4444
  East Hampton (G-2253)

PERSONAL DOCUMENT & INFORMATION SVCS

Creative Stone Group Inc .... G 203 554-7773
  Stamford (G-8169)

PEST CONTROL IN STRUCTURES SVCS

Connecticut Tick Control LLC .... F 203 855-7849
  Norwalk (G-6128)

PET COLLARS, LEASHES, MUZZLES & HARNESSES: Leather

Tillys Natural Blend LLC .... G 203 270-8406
  Newtown (G-5792)

PET FOOD WHOLESALERS

Blue Buffalo Company Ltd .... B 203 762-9751
  Wilton (G-10274)

PET SPLYS

A L C Inovators Inc .... G 203 877-8526
  Milford (G-4436)
Foxrun Danes .... G 860 685-8784
  Higganum (G-3763)
Leaps & Bones LLC .... G 860 648-9708
  South Windsor (G-7787)
Nano Pet Products LLC .... G 203 345-1330
  Norwalk (G-6268)

Peaks Parrots .... G 860 316-2788
  Middletown (G-4391)
Pleasant Valley Fence Co Inc .... F 860 379-0088
  Pleasant Valley (G-6925)
Posh Pups LLC .... G 860 454-4055
  Vernon Rockville (G-9175)
Pups In A Tub .... G 203 879-2947
  Wolcott (G-10582)
Raf Industries LLC .... G 203 228-4290
  Southbury (G-7873)
Stephanie Lauren LLC .... G 203 938-0364
  Redding (G-7110)
Valore Inc .... G 203 854-4799
  Norwalk (G-6381)
Wings N Things .... G 860 859-9514
  Salem (G-7293)

PETROLEUM & PETROLEUM PRDTS, WHOLESALE Crude Oil

Equinor Shipping Inc .... G 203 978-6900
  Stamford (G-8197)
Equinor US Holdings Inc .... C 203 978-6900
  Stamford (G-8198)

PETROLEUM & PETROLEUM PRDTS, WHOLESALE Fuel Oil

Armor All/STP Products Company .... G 203 205-2900
  Danbury (G-1744)

PETROLEUM & PETROLEUM PRDTS, WHOLESALE: Bulk Stations

Lexa International Corporation .... F 203 326-5200
  Stamford (G-8284)

PEWTER WARE

George S Preisner Jewelers .... G 203 265-0057
  Wallingford (G-9275)
Woodbury Pewterers Inc .... E 203 263-2668
  Woodbury (G-10656)

PHARMACEUTICAL PREPARATIONS: Druggists' Preparations

Achillion Pharmaceuticals Inc .... D 203 624-7000
  New Haven (G-5219)
Avara US Holdings LLC .... G 203 655-1333
  Norwalk (G-6085)
Boehringer Ingelheim Roxane Inc .... E 203 798-5555
  Ridgefield (G-7123)
Brookfeld Mdcl/Srgical Sup Inc .... F 203 775-0862
  Brookfield (G-1165)
Cardioxyl Pharmaceuticals Inc .... G 919 869-8586
  Wallingford (G-9225)
Carogen Corporation .... G 203 606-8796
  Hamden (G-3425)
Condomdepot Co .... G 860 747-1338
  Plainville (G-6789)
Cytogel Pharma LLC .... G 203 662-6617
  Darien (G-2016)
Mitchell Wods Phrmcuticals LLC .... G 203 258-1305
  Shelton (G-7504)
Pre -Clinical Safety Inc .... G 860 739-9797
  East Lyme (G-2471)
Quality Care Drg/Cntrbrook LLC .... G 860 767-0206
  Centerbrook (G-1332)

PHARMACEUTICAL PREPARATIONS: Medicines, Capsule Or Ampule

Boehringer Ingelheim Corp .... A 203 798-9988
  Ridgefield (G-7120)
Boehringer Ingelheim USA Corp .... C 203 798-9988
  Ridgefield (G-7122)
New Haven Naturopathic Center .... G 203 387-8661
  New Haven (G-5345)

PHARMACEUTICAL PREPARATIONS: Pills

Cisen Usa Inc .... G 203 706-9536
  Middlebury (G-4275)
Purdue Pharma Inc .... G 203 588-8000
  Stamford (G-8377)

PHARMACEUTICALS

PHARMACEUTICAL PREPARATIONS: Powders

Aptuit Global LLC .... G 203 660-6000
  Greenwich (G-3122)

PHARMACEUTICAL PREPARATIONS: Proprietary Drug PRDTS

Lipid Genomics Inc .... G 443 465-3495
  Farmington (G-2925)
New Leaf Pharmaceutical .... F 203 270-4167
  Newtown (G-5763)

PHARMACEUTICAL PREPARATIONS: Solutions

Arkalon Chemical Tech LLC .... G 352 505-8098
  Meriden (G-4146)
Intensity Therapeutics Inc .... G 203 682-2434
  Westport (G-10103)
Sca Pharmaceuticals LLC .... G 501 312-2800
  Windsor (G-10431)

PHARMACEUTICAL PREPARATIONS: Tablets

Foster Delivery Science Inc .... F 860 630-4515
  Putnam (G-7044)

PHARMACEUTICALS

A & S Pharmaceutical Corp .... E 203 368-2538
  Bridgeport (G-679)
Actimus Inc .... D 617 438-9968
  Cromwell (G-1685)
Aeromics Inc .... G 216 772-1004
  Branford (G-537)
Alexion Pharma LLC .... E 203 272-2596
  New Haven (G-5221)
Arvinas Inc .... F 203 535-1456
  New Haven (G-5234)
Avara Pharmaceutical Svcs Inc .... E 203 918-1659
  Norwalk (G-6084)
Avrio Health LP .... A 888 827-0624
  Stamford (G-8101)
Beta Pharma Inc .... F 203 315-5062
  Shelton (G-7403)
Biohaven Pharmaceuticals Inc .... D 203 404-0410
  New Haven (G-5245)
Biomed Health Inc .... F 860 657-2258
  Glastonbury (G-3014)
Bioxcel Therapeutics Inc .... F 475 238-6837
  New Haven (G-5247)
Cara Therapeutics Inc .... E 203 406-3700
  Stamford (G-8127)
Cardinal Health 414 LLC .... G 860 291-9135
  East Hartford (G-2302)
Carigent Therapeutics Inc .... G 203 887-2873
  New Haven (G-5255)
Celldex Therapeutics Inc .... G 203 864-5771
  Branford (G-572)
Chemin Pharma LLC .... G 203 208-2811
  Woodbridge (G-10598)
Enw Pharma Writing LLC .... G 860 663-0263
  Killingworth (G-3833)
Evotec (us) Inc .... E 650 228-1400
  Branford (G-591)
Foster Delivery Science Inc .... F 860 928-4102
  Putnam (G-7043)
Frederick Purdue Company Inc .... B 203 588-8000
  Stamford (G-8210)
Frequency Therapeutics Inc .... E 978 436-0704
  Farmington (G-2910)
Gaia Chemical Corporation .... G 860 355-2730
  Gaylordsville (G-2992)
Glaxosmithkline LLC .... E 203 232-5145
  Southbury (G-7855)
Hoffmann-La Roche Inc .... A 203 871-2303
  Branford (G-605)
Innoteq Inc .... E 203 659-4444
  Stratford (G-8633)
Iterum Therapeutics Inc .... G 860 391-8349
  Old Saybrook (G-6545)
J & J Precision Eyelet Inc .... D 860 283-8243
  Thomaston (G-8793)
Kasten Inc .... G 702 860-2407
  Bridgeport (G-813)
Kolltan Pharmaceuticals Inc .... E 203 773-3000
  New Haven (G-5311)
Koster Keunen LLC .... F 860 945-3333
  Watertown (G-9715)

Employee Codes: A=Over 500 employees, B=251-500
C=101-250, D=51-100, E=20-50, F=10-19, G=1-9

2020 Harris Connecticut
Manufacturers Directory

PHARMACEUTICALS

Loxo Oncology Inc .... E 203 653-3880
  Stamford (G-8291)
Mannkind Corporation .... G 203 798-8000
  Danbury (G-1879)
Marinus Pharmaceuticals Inc .... G 484 801-4670
  New Haven (G-5325)
MD Solarsciences Corporation .... F 203 857-0095
  Stamford (G-8300)
Medinstill LLC .... G 860 350-1900
  New Milford (G-5561)
Melinta Subsidiary Corp .... E 203 624-5606
  New Haven (G-5329)
Melinta Therapeutics Inc .... G 908 617-1309
  New Haven (G-5330)
Micro Source Discovery Systems .... G 860 350-8078
  Gaylordsville (G-2995)
New England Bphrmcuticals Corp .... G 917 992-4250
  Darien (G-2033)
Northstar Biosciences LLC .... G 203 689-5399
  Guilford (G-3380)
Novo Nordisk Pharmaceuticals .... G 860 779-2668
  Danielson (G-1999)
Novogen Inc .... F 203 972-5901
  New Canaan (G-5126)
Oncoarendi Therapeutics LLC 609 571-0306
  Madison (G-3943)
Perosphere Inc .... F 203 885-1111
  Danbury (G-1905)
PF Laboratories Inc .... C 973 256-3100
  Stamford (G-8359)
Pfizer Inc .... G 860 389-7509
  Groton (G-3307)
Pfizer Inc .... G 860 441-4568
  Trumbull (G-9055)
Pfizer Inc .... G 203 401-0100
  New Haven (G-5361)
Pfizer Inc .... C 860 441-4100
  Groton (G-3308)
Pfizer Inc .... G 860 441-4000
  Groton (G-3306)
Pqxhealthholding Inc .... C 203 786-3400
  New Haven (G-5362)
Pharmaceutical Discovery Corp .... G 203 796-3425
  Danbury (G-1907)
Pharmaceutical RES Assoc Inc .... G 203 588-8000
  Stamford (G-8360)
Pointpharma LLC .... G 203 668-8543
  Ridgefield (G-7164)
PRA Holdings Inc .... G 203 853-0123
  Stamford (G-8370)
Protein Sciences Corporation .... D 203 686-0800
  Meriden (G-4224)
Purdue Pharma LP .... B 203 588-8000
  Stamford (G-8378)
Purdue Pharmaceutical Pdts LP .... G 203 588-5000
  Stamford (G-8380)
Purdue Pharmaceuticals LP .... F 252 265-1900
  Stamford (G-8381)
Renetx Bio Inc .... G 203 444-6642
  New Haven (G-5378)
Rx Analytic Inc .... G 203 733-0837
  Ridgefield (G-7170)
Sheffield Pharmaceuticals LLC .... F 860 442-4451
  Norwich (G-6431)
Shire Rgenerative Medicine Inc .... G 877 422-4463
  Westport (G-10157)
Shore Therapeutics Inc 646 562-1243
  Stamford (G-8413)
Sinol Usa Inc .... F 203 470-7404
  Newtown (G-5780)
Systamedic Inc .... G 860 912-6101
  Groton (G-3314)
Syzygy Halthcare Solutions LLC .... G 203 226-4449
  Wilton (G-10336)
Theracour Pharma Inc .... G 203 937-6137
  West Haven (G-9958)
Tower Laboratories Ltd .... E 860 669-7078
  Clinton (G-1531)
Trevi Therapeutics Inc .... F 203 304-2499
  New Haven (G-5422)

PHARMACEUTICALS: Medicinal & Botanical Prdts

Botanica Chachitas .... G 860 247-5103
  Hartford (G-3558)
Candlewood Stars Inc .... G 203 994-8826
  Danbury (G-1762)
Henkel of America Inc .... B 860 571-5100
  Rocky Hill (G-7246)
Henkel US Operations Corp .... B 860 571-5100
  Rocky Hill (G-7247)
Mantrose-Haeuser Co Inc .... E 203 454-1800
  Westport (G-10117)
Modern Nutrition & Biotech .... G 203 244-5830
  Ridgefield (G-7155)
Pfizer Inc .... G 860 441-4000
  Groton (G-3306)
Yale University .... G 203 432-6320
  New Haven (G-5449)

PHONOGRAPH RECORDS: Prerecorded

Mosaic Records Inc .... G 203 327-7111
  Stamford (G-8314)

PHOTOCOPY MACHINES

Freedom Grafix LLC .... G 815 900-6189
  Fairfield (G-2787)
Reliance Business Systems Inc .... G 203 281-4407
  North Haven (G-5987)
Xerox Corporation .... B 203 968-3000
  Norwalk (G-6401)
Xerox Holdings Corporation .... G 203 968-3000
  Norwalk (G-6402)

PHOTOCOPYING & DUPLICATING SVCS

Action Letter Inc .... E 203 323-2466
  Stamford (G-8061)
Agjo Printing Service .... G 860 599-3143
  Pawcatuck (G-6703)
Alexander Hussey .... G 860 354-0118
  New Milford (G-5503)
Alliance Graphics Inc .... F 860 666-7992
  Newington (G-5624)
Audubon Copy Shppe of Firfield .... G 203 259-4311
  Bridgeport (G-705)
Baker Graphics Corporation .... E 203 226-6928
  Westport (G-10059)
Biz Wiz Print & Copy Ctr LLC .... G 860 633-7446
  Glastonbury (G-3015)
Brescias Printing Services Inc .... G 860 528-4254
  East Hartford (G-2300)
Commercial Service .... G 203 755-0166
  Waterbury (G-9454)
Copy Cats Inc .... F 860 442-8424
  New London (G-5465)
Curry Printing & Copy Ctr LLC .... G 203 878-5767
  Milford (G-4502)
Custom Printing & Copy Inc .... F 860 290-6890
  Enfield (G-2637)
Derosa Printing Company Inc .... F 860 646-1698
  Manchester (G-4005)
Digital Copy LLC .... G 203 540-5181
  Bridgeport (G-753)
East Longmeadow Business Svcs .... G 413 525-6111
  Enfield (G-2637)
Economy Printing & Copy Center .... G 203 792-5610
  Danbury (G-1803)
Economy Printing & Copy Center .... G 203 438-7401
  Ridgefield (G-7137)
Fedex Office & Print Svcs Inc .... F 860 233-8245
  Hartford (G-3588)
Fedex Office & Print Svcs Inc .... F 203 799-2679
  Orange (G-6601)
G & R Enterprises Incorporated .... G 203 549-6120
  Hartford (G-3593)
Glenn Curtis .... G 860 349-8679
  Durham (G-2147)
Hedges & Hedges Ltd .... G 860 257-3170
  Wethersfield (G-10196)
Jerrys Printing & Graphics LLC .... G 203 384-0015
  Bridgeport (G-803)
Jyl LLP .... G 860 767-7733
  Essex (G-2722)
Oddo Print Shop Inc .... G 860 489-6585
  Torrington (G-8953)
Pancoast Associates Inc .... G 203 377-6571
  Trumbull (G-9054)
Paper Mill Graphix Inc .... E 203 531-5904
  Greenwich (G-3213)
Printers of Connecticut Inc .... G 203 852-0070
  Norwalk (G-6306)
Quinn and Gellar Marketing LLC .... G 860 444-0448
  New London (G-5485)
Sazacks Inc .... G 860 647-8367
  Manchester (G-4086)
Tech-Repro Inc .... F 203 348-8884
  Stamford (G-8460)
Two Ems Inc .... G 203 245-8211
  Madison (G-3965)
Tyco Printing & Copying .... G 203 562-2679
  New Haven (G-5424)

PHOTOFINISHING LABORATORIES

Cine Magnetics Inc .... C 914 273-7600
  Stamford (G-8147)
Yankee Plak Co Inc .... E 203 333-3168
  Bridgeport (G-942)

PHOTOGRAPH DEVELOPING & RETOUCHING SVCS

Cls Design Group .... G 860 307-2810
  Torrington (G-8911)

PHOTOGRAPH ENLARGING SVCS

John L Prentis & Co Inc .... G 203 634-1266
  Meriden (G-4178)

PHOTOGRAPHIC EQPT & SPLYS

Bidwell Industrial Group Inc .... E 860 346-9283
  Middletown (G-4325)
Bpi Reprographics .... F 203 866-5600
  Norwalk (G-6097)
Dan Chichester .... G 203 722-4619
  Stamford (G-8178)
Fujifilm Elctrnic Mtls USA Inc .... G 203 363-3360
  Stamford (G-8211)
John Pecora .... G 860 677-9323
  Farmington (G-2920)
Kenyon Laboratories LLC .... G 860 345-2097
  Higganum (G-3766)
Mid State ARC Inc .... E 203 238-9001
  Meriden (G-4201)
River Valley Photographic LLC .... G 860 368-0882
  South Glastonbury (G-7682)
Xerox Services .... G 860 883-8377
  Cromwell (G-1725)

PHOTOGRAPHIC EQPT & SPLYS WHOLESALERS

Ciaudelli Productions Inc .... G 860 848-0411
  Montville (G-4769)
Fujifilm Elctrnic Mtls USA Inc .... G 203 363-3360
  Stamford (G-8211)

PHOTOGRAPHIC EQPT & SPLYS, WHOLESALE: Printing Apparatus

Garrett Printing & Graphics .... G 860 589-6710
  Bristol (G-1045)

PHOTOGRAPHIC EQPT & SPLYS: Cameras, Aerial

Aerial Imaging Solutions LLC .... G 860 434-3637
  Old Lyme (G-6488)

PHOTOGRAPHIC EQPT & SPLYS: Enlargers

Cag Imaging LLC .... G 860 887-0836
  Norwich (G-6408)

PHOTOGRAPHIC EQPT & SPLYS: Graphic Arts Plates, Sensitized

Verico Technology LLC .... E 800 492-7286
  Enfield (G-2704)

PHOTOGRAPHIC EQPT & SPLYS: Lantern Slide Plates, Sensitized

Image In Motion .... G 203 264-6784
  Southbury (G-7860)

PHOTOGRAPHIC EQPT & SPLYS: Stands, Camera & Projector

Industrial Sensor Vision Inter .... G 203 592-8723
  Oxford (G-6667)

PHOTOGRAPHIC EQPT & SPLYS: Toners, Prprd, Not Chem Plnts

Laserman of Connecticut .... G 203 972-2887
  Norwalk (G-6231)

PRODUCT SECTION

PHOTOGRAPHIC EQPT & SPLYS: X-Ray Film
Flexxray LLC ....G....... 203 689-5435
  Guilford *(G-3353)*
Medical Imaging Group Inc ....G....... 203 588-1921
  Stamford *(G-8304)*

PHOTOGRAPHIC PEOCESSING CHEMICALS
Cine Magnetics Inc ....C....... 914 273-7600
  Stamford *(G-8147)*
Recycle 4 Vets LLC ....G....... 203 222-7300
  Westport *(G-10147)*

PHOTOGRAPHY SVCS: Commercial
River Valley Photographic LLC.................G....... 860 368-0882
  South Glastonbury *(G-7682)*

PHOTOGRAPHY SVCS: Home
River Valley Photographic LLC.................G....... 860 368-0882
  South Glastonbury *(G-7682)*

PHOTOGRAPHY SVCS: Still Or Video
Cine Magnetics Inc ....C....... 914 273-7600
  Stamford *(G-8147)*
Glenn Curtis ....G....... 860 349-8679
  Durham *(G-2147)*
John Pecora ....G....... 860 677-9323
  Farmington *(G-2920)*

PHOTOGRAPHY: Aerial
Ebeam Film LLC..F....... 203 926-0100
  Shelton *(G-7434)*

PHOTOTYPESETTING SVC
A&V Typographics ....G....... 860 276-9060
  Plantsville *(G-6880)*
Childrens Press..G....... 203 972-9404
  New Canaan *(G-5094)*

PHOTOVOLTAIC Solid State
Opel Connecticut Solar LLC ....E....... 203 612-2366
  Shelton *(G-7519)*

PICTURE FRAMES: Metal
Artful Framer LLC..G....... 860 678-1321
  Avon *(G-76)*
M & B Enterprise LLC ....F....... 203 298-9781
  Derby *(G-2119)*
National Picture Frame Inc ....G....... 860 774-5668
  Brooklyn *(G-1251)*
Steven Rosendahl Inc................................G....... 860 928-3136
  Woodstock *(G-10685)*
Victoria Art & Frame ....G....... 860 274-8222
  Watertown *(G-9746)*

PICTURE FRAMES: Wood
Alpine Management Group LLC ....G....... 954 531-1692
  Westport *(G-10052)*
Artful Framer LLC..G....... 860 678-1321
  Avon *(G-76)*
Classic Framers ....G....... 401 596-6820
  Stonington *(G-8525)*
Ebk Picture Framing & Gallery ....G....... 860 523-9384
  Hartford *(G-3581)*
Kensington Glass and Frmng Co ....G....... 860 828-9428
  Berlin *(G-192)*
Michael Shortell ....G....... 860 236-4787
  Hartford *(G-3642)*
Paul Dringoli ....G....... 203 248-0281
  Hamden *(G-3496)*
Petrini Art & Frame LLC ....G....... 860 677-2747
  Avon *(G-99)*
Rockwell Art & Framing LLC ....G....... 203 762-8311
  Wilton *(G-10325)*
Steven Rosendahl Inc................................G....... 860 928-3136
  Woodstock *(G-10685)*

PICTURE FRAMING SVCS, CUSTOM
Church Hill Classics Ltd............................D....... 800 477-9005
  Monroe *(G-4703)*
Classic Framers ....G....... 401 596-6820
  Stonington *(G-8525)*

PIECE GOODS, NOTIONS & DRY GOODS, WHOLESALE: Sewing Access
Tri State Embroidery LLC..........................G....... 203 732-7636
  Ansonia *(G-53)*

PIECE GOODS, NOTIONS & OTHER DRY GOODS, WHOL: Flags/Banners
Soapstone Media Inc ....G....... 860 749-0455
  Somers *(G-7669)*

PIECE GOODS, NOTIONS & OTHER DRY GOODS, WHOLESALE: Fabrics
Challenge Sailcloth ....G....... 860 871-8030
  South Windsor *(G-7728)*
Donghia Inc ....D....... 800 366-4442
  Milford *(G-4514)*
Reid Interiors...G....... 860 569-1240
  East Hartford *(G-2364)*

PIECE GOODS, NOTIONS/DRY GOODS, WHOL: Fabrics, Synthetic
Thomas W Raftery Inc...............................E....... 860 278-9870
  Hartford *(G-3703)*

PIECE GOODS, NOTIONS/DRY GOODS, WHOL: Linen Piece, Woven
Patricia Spratt For Home LLC..................F....... 860 434-9291
  Old Lyme *(G-6517)*

PINS
Spirol International Corp ....C....... 860 774-8571
  Danielson *(G-2003)*
Spirol Intl Holdg Corp................................C....... 860 774-8571
  Danielson *(G-2004)*
Wire Solutions LLC ....G....... 860 836-0787
  Plainville *(G-6878)*

PINS: Dowel
Horberg Industries Inc..............................F....... 203 334-9444
  Bridgeport *(G-787)*
Rbc Prcision Pdts - Bremen Inc ....E....... 203 267-7001
  Oxford *(G-6692)*

PIPE & FITTING: Fabrication
Carli Farm & Equipment LLC ....G....... 860 908-3227
  Salem *(G-7287)*
Clear Water Manufacturing Corp ....G....... 860 372-4907
  Wethersfield *(G-10188)*
Diba Industries Inc ....C....... 203 744-0773
  Danbury *(G-1795)*
Farmington Mtal Fbrication LLC ....G....... 860 404-7415
  Bristol *(G-1036)*
Frank Porto ....G....... 203 596-0811
  Watertown *(G-9707)*
Long Island Pipe Supply Inc ....G....... 860 688-1780
  Windsor *(G-10405)*

PIPE & FITTINGS: Cast Iron
Bingham & Taylor Corp ....G....... 540 825-8334
  Rocky Hill *(G-7223)*
Virginia Industries Inc ....G....... 860 571-3600
  Rocky Hill *(G-7271)*

PIPE CLEANERS
Hydro-Flex Inc ....G....... 203 269-5599
  Stratford *(G-8629)*
UST LLC ....G....... 203 817-3000
  Stamford *(G-8483)*

PIPE FITTINGS: Plastic
F F Screw Products Inc ....E....... 860 621-4567
  Southington *(G-7921)*
Monarch Plastic LLC ....F....... 860 653-2000
  Granby *(G-3112)*

PIPE: Concrete
Advanced Drainage Systems Inc ....E....... 860 529-8188
  Rocky Hill *(G-7219)*

PIPE: Plastic
Advanced Drainage Systems Inc ....E....... 860 529-8188
  Rocky Hill *(G-7219)*
Monarch Plastic LLC ....F....... 860 653-2000
  Granby *(G-3112)*
Virginia Industries Inc ....G....... 860 571-3600
  Rocky Hill *(G-7271)*

PIPE: Sheet Metal
Ovl Manufacturing Inc LLC ....G....... 860 829-0271
  Berlin *(G-205)*

PIPES & TUBES: Steel
Gordon Corporation ....D....... 860 628-4775
  Southington *(G-7931)*
Piper..G....... 860 405-1495
  Groton *(G-3309)*

PISTONS & PISTON RINGS
Schwing Bioset Technologies ....E....... 203 744-2100
  Danbury *(G-1941)*

PLANT HORMONES
Andrews Arboriculture LLC ....G....... 203 565-8570
  Naugatuck *(G-4857)*

PLAQUES: Picture, Laminated
Gutkin Enterprises LLC.............................G....... 203 777-5510
  Hamden *(G-3454)*

PLASMAS
Cold Plasma Neck.......................................G....... 203 935-0300
  Meriden *(G-4160)*
Plasma Coatings Inc..................................G....... 203 598-3100
  Waterbury *(G-9578)*
Plasma Technology Incorporated ....E....... 860 282-0659
  South Windsor *(G-7807)*

PLASTER WORK: Ornamental & Architectural
John Canning & Co Ltd ....E....... 203 272-9868
  Cheshire *(G-1401)*

PLASTER, ACOUSTICAL: Gypsum
Proudfoot Company Inc ....F....... 203 459-0031
  Monroe *(G-4750)*

PLASTIC COLORING & FINISHING
Coating Design Group Inc.......................E....... 203 878-3663
  Stratford *(G-8596)*
Lisern Enterprises Inc ....G....... 203 426-9079
  Sandy Hook *(G-7319)*

PLASTIC PRDTS
Connecticut Valley Packg LLC ....G....... 860 693-0776
  Collinsville *(G-1592)*
Nelcote Inc..G....... 203 509-5247
  Waterbury *(G-9555)*
Predcision Plastics Inc ....G....... 203 775-7047
  Brookfield *(G-1216)*
Saltwater Usa LLC ....G....... 860 899-9240
  Bloomfield *(G-485)*
Selectives LLC ....G....... 860 585-1956
  Thomaston *(G-8805)*
Trinity Polymers LLC ....G....... 860 321-7209
  Farmington *(G-2966)*
Vivan Trucking LLC ....G....... 573 486-2811
  Hartford *(G-3713)*

PLASTICIZERS, ORGANIC: Cyclic & Acyclic
RSA Corp ....E....... 203 790-8100
  Danbury *(G-1931)*

PLASTICS FILM & SHEET
Atlas Metallizing Inc..................................F....... 860 827-9777
  New Britain *(G-4946)*
Clopay Corporation ....C....... 203 230-9116
  North Haven *(G-5921)*
Plastic Factory LLC ....G....... 203 908-3468
  Bridgeport *(G-874)*
Polymer Films Inc ....E....... 203 932-3000
  West Haven *(G-9946)*

Rowland Technologies Inc....................D....... 203 269-9500
Wallingford *(G-9361)*
Superior Plas Extrusion Co Inc............G....... 860 234-1864
Cromwell *(G-1720)*
Superior Plas Extrusion Co Inc............E....... 860 963-1976
Putnam *(G-7071)*

PLASTICS FILM & SHEET: Polyethylene

Engineering Services & Pdts Co...........D....... 860 528-1119
South Windsor *(G-7750)*

PLASTICS FILM & SHEET: Vinyl

Grimco Inc...............................G....... 800 542-9941
New Britain *(G-4993)*
Orafol Americas Inc.........................C....... 860 676-7100
Avon *(G-98)*

PLASTICS FINISHED PRDTS: Laminated

Alcat Incorporated...........................E....... 203 878-0648
Milford *(G-4446)*
Aptar Inc..................................G....... 860 489-6249
Torrington *(G-8897)*
Hicks and Otis Prints Inc......................E....... 203 846-2087
Norwalk *(G-6200)*

PLASTICS FOAM, WHOLESALE

Sprayfoampolymerscom LLC..............G....... 800 853-1577
Wilton *(G-10333)*

PLASTICS MATERIAL & RESINS

Allnex USA Inc..............................D....... 203 269-4481
Wallingford *(G-9199)*
Allread Products Co LLC....................F....... 860 589-3566
Terryville *(G-8747)*
Anapo Plastics Corp.........................G....... 860 874-8174
Farmington *(G-2877)*
Axel Plastics RES Labs Inc...................E....... 718 672-8300
Monroe *(G-4694)*
Bakelite N Sumitomo Amer Inc...............D....... 860 645-3851
Manchester *(G-3985)*
C Mather Company Inc.......................G....... 860 528-5667
South Windsor *(G-7721)*
Chessco Industries Inc.......................E....... 203 255-2804
Westport *(G-10064)*
Cytec Industries Inc..........................C....... 203 284-4334
Wallingford *(G-9245)*
Ditriorichard................................G....... 203 531-0625
Greenwich *(G-3153)*
Enflo Corporation...........................E....... 860 589-0014
Bristol *(G-1029)*
Engineered Polymers Inds Inc................G....... 203 272-2233
Cheshire *(G-1385)*
Fimor North America Inc.....................E....... 203 272-3219
Cheshire *(G-1389)*
Fimor North America Inc.....................G....... 941 921-5138
Cheshire *(G-1390)*
Henkel of America Inc.......................B....... 860 571-5100
Rocky Hill *(G-7246)*
Henkel US Operations Corp...................B....... 860 571-5100
Rocky Hill *(G-7247)*
Hexcel Corporation..........................G....... 203 969-0666
Stamford *(G-8234)*
Lanxess Solutions US Inc.....................E....... 203 573-2000
Shelton *(G-7486)*
Line X of Western Connecticut................G....... 860 355-6997
Bridgewater *(G-946)*
Osterman & Company Inc....................D....... 203 272-2233
Cheshire *(G-1426)*
Oxford Performance Mtls Inc..................E....... 860 698-9300
South Windsor *(G-7801)*
Plastics Color Corp Inc.......................G....... 800 922-9936
Dayville *(G-2070)*
Polymer Resources Ltd.......................D....... 203 324-3737
Farmington *(G-2949)*
Polyone Corporation.........................G....... 203 327-6010
Stamford *(G-8368)*
Presidium USA Inc..........................G....... 203 674-9374
Stamford *(G-8372)*
Ravago Americas LLC........................E....... 203 855-6000
Wilton *(G-10324)*
Roehm America LLC.........................E....... 203 269-4481
Wallingford *(G-9358)*
Seaview Plastic Recycling Inc.................G....... 203 367-0070
Bridgeport *(G-899)*
SMS Machine Inc............................G....... 860 829-0813
East Berlin *(G-2176)*
Sonoco Prtective Solutions Inc.................E....... 860 928-7795
Putnam *(G-7068)*
Spartech LLC...............................C....... 203 327-6010
Stamford *(G-8432)*
Summit Plastics LLC.........................G....... 860 740-4482
Portland *(G-6975)*
Total Ptrchemicals Ref USA Inc...............E....... 203 375-0668
Stratford *(G-8698)*
Trinseo LLC................................E....... 860 447-7298
Gales Ferry *(G-2989)*
Tyne Plastics LLC...........................G....... 860 673-7100
Burlington *(G-1277)*

PLASTICS MATERIALS, BASIC FORMS & SHAPES WHOLESALERS

Nevamar Company LLC......................B....... 203 925-1556
Shelton *(G-7508)*
Preferred Foam Products Inc..................G....... 860 669-3626
Clinton *(G-1518)*

PLASTICS PROCESSING

Anderson David C & Assoc LLC...............F....... 860 749-7547
Enfield *(G-2615)*
Ensign-Bickford Industries Inc................E....... 860 658-4411
Simsbury *(G-7622)*
Entegris Inc................................B....... 800 766-2681
Danbury *(G-1814)*
Fiberglass Engr & Design Co.................G....... 203 265-1644
Wallingford *(G-9266)*
Idex Health & Science LLC...................C....... 860 314-2880
Bristol *(G-1050)*
Lingol Corporation..........................F....... 203 265-3608
Wallingford *(G-9303)*
Pel Associates LLC..........................G....... 860 446-9921
Groton *(G-3305)*
Precision Engineered Pdts LLC...............E....... 203 265-3299
Wallingford *(G-9341)*
Precision Plastic Fab.........................G....... 203 775-7047
Brookfield *(G-1215)*
Sound View Plastics LLC.....................G....... 860 322-4139
Deep River *(G-2102)*
Spartech LLC...............................C....... 203 327-6010
Stamford *(G-8432)*

PLASTICS: Blow Molded

Plastic Forming Company Inc................E....... 203 397-1338
Woodbridge *(G-10613)*

PLASTICS: Extruded

Cowles Products Company Inc...............D....... 203 865-3110
North Haven *(G-5930)*
Davis-Standard LLC.........................B....... 860 599-1010
Pawcatuck *(G-6707)*
Farrel Corporation..........................D....... 203 736-5500
Ansonia *(G-34)*
Merritt Extruder Corp.......................E....... 203 230-8100
Hamden *(G-3481)*

PLASTICS: Finished Injection Molded

Accumold Technologies Inc..................G....... 203 384-9256
Bridgeport *(G-681)*
Apex Machine Tool Company Inc..............D....... 860 677-2884
Cheshire *(G-1353)*
Brighton & Hove Mold Ltd....................G....... 203 264-3013
Oxford *(G-6647)*
Celeste Industries Corporation................G....... 860 278-9800
Hartford *(G-3565)*
Create A Castle LLC.........................G....... 203 648-3553
New Milford *(G-5524)*
Doss Corporation...........................G....... 860 721-7384
Wethersfield *(G-10191)*
GP Industries Ltd LLC.......................G....... 860 350-5400
New Milford *(G-5540)*
Injectech Engineering LLC...................G....... 860 379-9781
New Hartford *(G-5199)*
Marlborough Plastics Inc.....................G....... 860 295-9124
Marlborough *(G-4125)*
Mbsw Inc..................................D....... 860 243-0303
West Hartford *(G-9835)*
Molding Technologies LLC...................G....... 860 395-3230
Old Saybrook *(G-6558)*
New Star Mold Inc..........................G....... 860 567-7760
Bantam *(G-125)*
RES-Tech Corporation.......................D....... 860 828-1504
Berlin *(G-216)*
Rogers Manufacturing Company..............D....... 860 346-8648
Rockfall *(G-7215)*
Romano Construction LLC....................G....... 203 223-3136
Southbury *(G-7877)*
Schaeffler Aerospace USA Corp...............B....... 203 744-2211
Danbury *(G-1936)*
Seitz LLC..................................E....... 860 489-0476
Torrington *(G-8969)*

PLASTICS: Injection Molded

Aba-PGT Employee Medical Trust..............G....... 860 649-4591
Manchester *(G-3973)*
Aba-PGT Inc...............................C....... 860 649-4591
Manchester *(G-3974)*
Aba-PGT Inc...............................G....... 860 872-2058
Vernon Rockville *(G-9158)*
Able Coil and Electronics Co.................E....... 860 646-5686
Bolton *(G-504)*
Accurate Mold Company Inc..................G....... 860 301-1988
Cromwell *(G-1684)*
Ace Technical Plastics Inc....................G....... 860 278-2444
Hartford *(G-3545)*
Advance Mold & Mfg Inc.....................C....... 860 432-5887
Manchester *(G-3979)*
Aero-Med Molding Technologies...............F....... 203 735-2331
Ansonia *(G-17)*
American Molded Products Inc................F....... 203 333-0183
Bridgeport *(G-694)*
American Plastic Products Inc.................C....... 203 596-2410
Waterbury *(G-9428)*
Better Molded Products Inc...................C....... 860 589-0066
Bristol *(G-982)*
Betz Tool Company Inc.......................G....... 203 878-1187
Milford *(G-4468)*
Burteck LLC................................F....... 860 206-8872
Windsor *(G-10369)*
C Cowles & Company........................D....... 203 865-3117
North Haven *(G-5916)*
Carpin Manufacturing Inc.....................D....... 203 574-2556
Waterbury *(G-9446)*
Connecticut Tool Co Inc......................E....... 860 928-0565
Putnam *(G-7035)*
Dymotek Corporation........................G....... 800 788-1984
Somers *(G-7656)*
Dymotek Corporation........................E....... 860 875-2868
Ellington *(G-2587)*
East Branch Engrg & Mfg Inc.................F....... 860 355-9661
New Milford *(G-5529)*
Edco Industries Inc..........................F....... 203 333-8982
Bridgeport *(G-760)*
Empire Tool LLC............................G....... 203 735-7467
Derby *(G-2113)*
Ensinger Prcsion Cmponents Inc..............D....... 860 928-7911
Putnam *(G-7040)*
Fimor North America Inc.....................E....... 203 272-3219
Cheshire *(G-1389)*
Fimor North America Inc.....................G....... 941 921-5138
Cheshire *(G-1390)*
Fluoropolymer Resources LLC................G....... 860 423-7622
East Hartford *(G-2326)*
Fsm Plasticoid Mfg Inc......................F....... 860 623-1361
East Windsor *(G-2493)*
Ginter Hill Corporation......................G....... 203 293-4301
Westport *(G-10089)*
Hawk Integrated Plastics LLC.................F....... 860 337-0310
Columbia *(G-1606)*
Heck D Tool LLC............................G....... 860 935-9274
Thompson *(G-8834)*
Illinois Tool Works Inc.......................E....... 860 435-2574
Lakeville *(G-3844)*
Inline Plastics Corp.........................C....... 203 924-5933
Shelton *(G-7479)*
Joseph Organek.............................G....... 860 342-1906
Portland *(G-6962)*
K-Tec LLC.................................G....... 860 283-8875
Thomaston *(G-8795)*
Kinamor Incorporated.......................E....... 203 269-0380
Wallingford *(G-9297)*
Lacey Manufacturing Co LLC..................B....... 203 336-7427
Bridgeport *(G-821)*
Lorex Plastics Co Inc........................G....... 203 286-0020
Norwalk *(G-6238)*
Manchester Molding and Mfg Co..............E....... 860 643-2141
Manchester *(G-4052)*
Meriden Precision Plastics LLC...............G....... 203 235-3261
Meriden *(G-4198)*
Mohawk Tool and Die Mfg Co Inc..............F....... 203 367-2181
Bridgeport *(G-842)*
Mold Threads Inc...........................G....... 203 483-1420
Branford *(G-627)*
Orbit Design LLC...........................F....... 203 393-0171
Meriden *(G-4214)*
Paragon Products Inc........................G....... 860 388-1363
Old Saybrook *(G-6563)*

PRODUCT SECTION — PLATING SVC: Gold

Pastanch LLC .... E 203 720-9478
  Naugatuck *(G-4909)*
Phillips-Moldex Company .... E 860 928-0401
  Putnam *(G-7058)*
Plasco LLC .... G 860 217-1187
  Simsbury *(G-7640)*
Plastic Design Intl Inc .... E 860 632-2001
  Middletown *(G-4393)*
Plastic Molding Technology .... G 203 881-1811
  Seymour *(G-7361)*
Plastic Solutions LLC .... G 203 266-5675
  Bethlehem *(G-375)*
Plasticoid Manufacturing Inc .... E 860 623-1361
  East Windsor *(G-2514)*
Plastics and Concepts Conn Inc .... F 860 657-9655
  Glastonbury *(G-3072)*
Polymer Engineered Pdts Inc .... D 203 324-3737
  Stamford *(G-8367)*
Polymold Corp .... F 203 272-2622
  Cheshire *(G-1430)*
Polytronics Corporation .... G 860 683-2442
  Windsor *(G-10421)*
Precision Plastic Products Inc .... F 860 342-2233
  Portland *(G-6969)*
Prospect Products Incorporated .... E 860 666-0323
  Newington *(G-5698)*
Prototype Plastic Mold Co Inc .... E 860 632-2800
  Middletown *(G-4398)*
Quest Plastics Inc .... F 860 489-1404
  Torrington *(G-8962)*
Reblee Inc .... G 203 372-3338
  Trumbull *(G-9063)*
Scan Tool & Mold Inc .... E 203 459-4950
  Trumbull *(G-9070)*
Somerset Plastics Company .... E 860 635-1601
  Middletown *(G-4421)*
Stelray Plastic Products Inc .... E 203 735-2331
  Ansonia *(G-52)*
Swpc Plastics LLC .... C 860 526-3200
  Deep River *(G-2103)*
Technical Industries Inc .... D 860 489-2160
  Torrington *(G-8976)*
Technology Plastics LLC .... F 806 583-1590
  Terryville *(G-8774)*
Trento Group LLC .... G 860 623-1361
  East Windsor *(G-2528)*
TWC Trans World Consulting .... G 860 668-5108
  Windsor Locks *(G-10499)*
Vanguard Plastics Corporation .... E 860 628-4736
  Southington *(G-7992)*
Vision Technical Molding .... G 860 783-5050
  Manchester *(G-4105)*
Watertown Plastics Inc .... E 860 274-7535
  Watertown *(G-9749)*
Wepco Plastics Inc .... E 860 349-3407
  Middlefield *(G-4309)*
Wilkinson Tool & Die Co .... G 860 599-5821
  North Stonington *(G-6032)*

PLASTICS: Molded

Advance Mold Mfg Inc .... G 860 783-5024
  Ellington *(G-2572)*
Atlas Hobbing and Tool Co Inc .... F 860 870-9226
  Vernon Rockville *(G-9160)*
Awm LLC .... D 860 386-1000
  Windsor Locks *(G-10473)*
Balfor Industries Inc .... F 203 828-6473
  Oxford *(G-6645)*
Bennice Molding Co .... G 203 440-2543
  Meriden *(G-4149)*
Bey-Low Molds .... G 860 482-6561
  Torrington *(G-8904)*
Canevari Plastics Inc .... G 203 878-4319
  Milford *(G-4482)*
Crown Molding Etc LLC .... G 203 287-9424
  Hamden *(G-3434)*
Fred Radford .... G 203 377-6189
  Trumbull *(G-9027)*
Homar Molds & Models Co .... G 203 753-9017
  Waterbury *(G-9498)*
J POMfret& Assoc Inc .... G 860 691-2149
  East Lyme *(G-2467)*
J&L Plastic Molding LLC .... G 203 265-6237
  Wallingford *(G-9292)*
Little Bits Manufacturing Inc .... G 860 923-2770
  North Grosvenordale *(G-5889)*
MPS Plastics Incorporated .... E 860 295-1161
  Marlborough *(G-4127)*
Plastics Techniques .... G 203 335-8048
  Fairfield *(G-2829)*

Quatum Inc .... G 860 666-3464
  Hartford *(G-3673)*
Shaeffer Plastic Mfg Corp .... G 860 537-5524
  Colchester *(G-1575)*
Summit Plastics LLC .... G 860 832-9730
  New Britain *(G-5067)*
Super Seal Corp .... F 203 378-5015
  Stratford *(G-8690)*

PLASTICS: Polystyrene Foam

Ansonia Plastics LLC .... D 203 736-5200
  Ansonia *(G-20)*
Duz Manufacturing Inc .... G 203 874-1032
  Milford *(G-4519)*
Gilman Corporation .... E 860 887-7080
  Gilman *(G-3000)*
Hhc LLC .... E 860 456-0677
  Manchester *(G-4027)*
Hopp Companies Inc .... F 800 889-8425
  Newtown *(G-5746)*
Hydrofera LLC .... G 860 456-0677
  Manchester *(G-4030)*
Madison Polymeric Engrg Inc .... E 203 488-4554
  Branford *(G-622)*
Merrill Industries Inc .... E 860 871-1888
  Ellington *(G-2595)*
New England Foam Products LLC .... E 860 524-0121
  Hartford *(G-3650)*
Plastic Forming Company Inc .... E 203 397-1338
  Woodbridge *(G-10613)*
Preferred Foam Products Inc .... G 860 669-3626
  Clinton *(G-1518)*
Reilly Foam Corp .... E 860 243-8200
  Bloomfield *(G-476)*

PLASTICS: Thermoformed

Lehvoss North America LLC .... F 860 495-2046
  Pawcatuck *(G-6718)*
Newhart Plastics Inc .... G 203 877-5367
  Milford *(G-4591)*
Siemon Company .... A 860 945-4200
  Watertown *(G-9734)*

PLATEMAKING SVC: Color Separations, For The Printing Trade

Endo Graphics Inc .... G 203 778-1557
  Danbury *(G-1810)*
Four Color Ink LLC .... G 860 395-5471
  Old Saybrook *(G-6534)*
Gateway Digital Inc .... F 203 853-4929
  Norwalk *(G-6175)*
Ghp Media Inc .... C 203 479-7500
  West Haven *(G-9912)*

PLATEMAKING SVC: Gravure, Plates Or Cylinders

Schrader Bellows .... E 860 749-2215
  Enfield *(G-2689)*

PLATES

Baron Technology Inc .... E 203 452-0515
  Trumbull *(G-9003)*
Cag Imaging .... G 203 632-5799
  Naugatuck *(G-4866)*
Eccles-Lehman Inc .... G 203 268-0605
  Easton *(G-2551)*
Exceptional Scratch Games LLC .... G 203 526-8696
  Bridgeport *(G-764)*
Paul Dewitt .... F 203 792-5610
  Danbury *(G-1902)*
Quinn and Gellar Marketing LLC .... G 860 444-0448
  New London *(G-5485)*
Success Printing & Mailing Inc .... F 203 847-1112
  Norwalk *(G-6359)*

PLATFORMS: Cargo

Wet Crow Internet Inc .... G 860 919-0164
  Middletown *(G-4431)*

PLATING & FINISHING SVC: Decorative, Formed Prdts

Country Creations By Carol .... G 860 848-0276
  Uncasville *(G-9097)*
Mike Fineran .... G 860 974-3276
  Pomfret Center *(G-6942)*

PLATING & POLISHING SVC

A & A Products and Services .... G 860 683-0879
  Windsor *(G-10350)*
C & S Engineering Inc .... E 203 235-5727
  Meriden *(G-4153)*
Chicks Sandblasting .... G 203 334-0059
  Preston *(G-6982)*
Colonial Coatings Inc .... E 203 783-9933
  Milford *(G-4491)*
Color Ite Refinishing Co .... G 203 393-0240
  Bethany *(G-238)*
Deburring Laboratories Inc .... E 860 829-6300
  New Britain *(G-4972)*
P&G Metal Components Corp .... F 860 243-2220
  Bloomfield *(G-458)*
Plasma Technology Incorporated .... E 860 282-0659
  South Windsor *(G-7807)*
Sousa Corp .... F 860 523-9090
  Newington *(G-5706)*
United States Fire Arms Mfg Co .... E 860 296-7441
  Hartford *(G-3708)*

PLATING COMPOUNDS

Macdermid Incorporated .... E 203 575-5700
  Waterbury *(G-9524)*
Macdermid Incorporated .... C 203 575-5700
  Waterbury *(G-9522)*

PLATING SVC: Chromium, Metals Or Formed Prdts

CRC Chrome Corporation .... F 203 630-1008
  Meriden *(G-4163)*
Custom Chrome Plating .... G 203 265-5667
  Wallingford *(G-9244)*
Mirror Polishing & Pltg Co Inc .... E 203 574-5400
  Waterbury *(G-9544)*
National Chromium Company Inc .... F 860 928-7965
  Putnam *(G-7052)*
New England Chrome Plating .... G 203 528-7176
  East Hartford *(G-2346)*
Rader Industries Inc .... G 203 334-6739
  Bridgeport *(G-884)*
Rollcorp LLC .... G 860 347-5227
  Middletown *(G-4406)*

PLATING SVC: Electro

American Electro Products Inc .... C 203 756-7051
  Waterbury *(G-9427)*
Bar Plating Inc .... G 203 630-1046
  Meriden *(G-4148)*
Bass Plating Company .... E 860 243-2557
  Bloomfield *(G-392)*
Clear & Colored Coatings LLC .... G 203 879-1379
  Wolcott *(G-10554)*
Danbury Metal Finishing Inc .... G 203 748-5044
  Danbury *(G-1784)*
Gar Electro Forming .... G 203 885-1105
  Danbury *(G-1832)*
Halco Inc .... D 203 575-9450
  Waterbury *(G-9495)*
National Integrated Inds Inc .... D 203 756-7051
  Waterbury *(G-9553)*
Nylo Metal Finishing LLC .... G 203 574-5477
  Waterbury *(G-9565)*
Rayco Metal Finishing Inc .... F 860 347-7434
  Middletown *(G-4402)*
Seaboard Metal Finishing Co .... E 203 933-1603
  New Britain *(G-5053)*
Seidel Inc .... D 203 757-7349
  Waterbury *(G-9601)*
Spec Plating Inc .... F 203 366-3638
  Bridgeport *(G-911)*
Summit Corporation of America .... D 860 283-4391
  Thomaston *(G-8811)*
Superior Plating Company .... D 203 255-1501
  Southport *(G-8011)*
Superior Technology Corp .... C 203 255-1501
  Southport *(G-8012)*
Unimetal Surface Finishing LLC .... E 203 729-8244
  Naugatuck *(G-4924)*

PLATING SVC: Gold

Vincent Jewelers .... G 203 882-8900
  Milford *(G-4674)*

Employee Codes: A=Over 500 employees, B=251-500
C=101-250, D=51-100, E=20-50, F=10-19, G=1-9

PLATING SVC: NEC

A&R Plating Services LLC ....G..... 860 274-9562
Oakville *(G-6448)*
A-1 Chrome and Polishing Corp.........F..... 860 666-4593
Newington *(G-5616)*
Alpha Plating and Finishing Co.........F..... 860 747-5002
Plainville *(G-6768)*
B & P Plating Equipment LLC..........F..... 860 589-5799
Bristol *(G-969)*
Component Technologies Inc............E..... 860 667-1065
Newington *(G-5641)*
Concept Team Associates LLC..........G..... 203 269-5152
Wallingford *(G-9236)*
Dav-Co Finishing LLC.................G..... 860 828-5552
Berlin *(G-175)*
Har-Conn Chrome Company..............D..... 860 236-6801
West Hartford *(G-9815)*
Hitech Chrome Pltg & Polsg Lc.........G..... 860 456-8070
North Windham *(G-6038)*
K & K Black Oxide LLC................G..... 860 223-1805
New Britain *(G-5007)*
Marsam Metal Finishing Co............E..... 860 826-5489
New Britain *(G-5013)*
Plainville Plating Company Inc.........D..... 860 747-1624
Plainville *(G-6852)*
Praxair Inc...........................B..... 203 837-2000
Danbury *(G-1913)*
Precision Finishing Svcs Inc..........E..... 860 882-1073
Windsor *(G-10424)*
Prestige Metal Finishing LLC..........G..... 860 974-1999
Woodstock Valley *(G-10693)*
Whyco Finishing Tech LLC.............E..... 860 283-5826
Thomaston *(G-8824)*

PLAYGROUND EQPT

Creative Playthings Ltd...............G..... 203 748-7206
Brookfield *(G-1175)*
Jammar Mfg Co Inc....................G..... 866 848-1113
Niantic *(G-5811)*
Trassig Corp.........................G..... 203 659-0456
Georgetown *(G-2999)*

PLEATING & STITCHING FOR THE TRADE: Appliqueing

Baa Creations........................G..... 860 464-1339
Ledyard *(G-3869)*

PLEATING & STITCHING FOR THE TRADE: Decorative & Novelty

K&P Weaver LLC......................G..... 203 795-9024
Orange *(G-6605)*

PLEATING & STITCHING FOR THE TRADE: Eyelets

Eyelets For Industry Inc..............G..... 203 754-6502
Waterbury *(G-9478)*

PLEATING & STITCHING FOR THE TRADE: Lace, Burnt-Out

NCM Embroidery & Sportswear.........G..... 860 223-1589
New Britain *(G-5020)*

PLEATING & STITCHING SVC

All American Embroidery..............G..... 203 906-9656
Monroe *(G-4691)*
Cook Print...........................G..... 203 855-8785
Norwalk *(G-6129)*
Hot Tops LLC.........................F..... 203 926-2067
Shelton *(G-7466)*
Jeffrey Morgan.......................G..... 860 583-2567
Bristol *(G-1054)*
Logod Softwear Inc...................E..... 203 272-4883
Cheshire *(G-1407)*
Robert Audette.......................G..... 203 872-3119
Cheshire *(G-1440)*
Zuse Inc.............................F..... 203 458-3295
Guilford *(G-3402)*

PLUGS: Drain, Magnetic, Metal

Farmington Engineering Inc............G..... 800 428-7584
North Haven *(G-5940)*

PLUMBING & HEATING EQPT & SPLY, WHOL: Htg Eqpt/Panels, Solar

5n Plus Corp.........................F..... 608 846-1357
Trumbull *(G-8994)*
American Solar & Alternative.........G..... 203 324-7186
Stamford *(G-8078)*

PLUMBING & HEATING EQPT & SPLYS WHOLESALERS

Granite Group Wholesalers LLC........G..... 860 537-7600
Colchester *(G-1552)*
Kensco Inc...........................F..... 203 734-8827
Ansonia *(G-44)*
Pequot...............................G..... 800 620-1492
Bridgeport *(G-869)*
Superior Products Distrs Inc..........F..... 203 250-6700
Cheshire *(G-1454)*
Tinny Corporation....................E..... 860 854-6121
Middletown *(G-4427)*
Viking Supply Co.....................G..... 860 886-0220
Norwich *(G-6438)*

PLUMBING & HEATING EQPT & SPLYS, WHOL: Pipe/Fitting, Plastic

Jolley Precast Inc....................E..... 860 774-9066
Danielson *(G-1995)*

PLUMBING & HEATING EQPT & SPLYS, WHOL: Plumbing Fitting/Sply

F W Webb Company....................F..... 203 865-6124
New Haven *(G-5279)*
New Resources Group Inc..............G..... 203 366-1000
Bridgeport *(G-850)*
The Keeney Manufacturing Co..........C..... 603 239-6371
Newington *(G-5711)*
Thomas J Hunt Inc....................G..... 203 775-5050
Brookfield *(G-1230)*

PLUMBING & HEATING EQPT & SPLYS, WHOL: Water Purif Eqpt

Dpc Quality Pump Service.............G..... 203 874-6877
Milford *(G-4515)*

PLUMBING & HEATING EQPT & SPLYS, WHOLESALE: Brass/Fittings

Neoperl Inc..........................D..... 203 756-8891
Waterbury *(G-9557)*

PLUMBING & HEATING EQPT & SPLYS, WHOLESALE: Oil Burners

John Zink Company LLC................D..... 203 925-0380
Shelton *(G-7481)*

PLUMBING & HEATING EQPT & SPLYS, WHOLESALE: Pwr Indl Boiler

Eastern Utility Products LLC..........G..... 860 399-1724
Westbrook *(G-9995)*

PLUMBING FIXTURES

Bead Industries Inc..................E..... 203 301-0270
Milford *(G-4466)*
Burt Process Equipment Inc...........E..... 203 287-1985
Hamden *(G-3420)*
Butler Property Svc..................G..... 203 530-4554
Orange *(G-6588)*
Colonial Bronze Company..............D..... 860 489-9233
Torrington *(G-8912)*
F W Webb Company....................F..... 203 865-6124
New Haven *(G-5279)*
Fitzgerald & Wood Inc................G..... 203 488-2553
Branford *(G-594)*
Granite Group Wholesalers LLC........G..... 860 537-7600
Colchester *(G-1552)*
Macristy Industries Inc..............C..... 860 225-4637
Newington *(G-5674)*
Mc Guire Manufacturing Co Inc........D..... 860 699-1801
Cheshire *(G-1412)*
Thomas J Hunt Inc....................G..... 203 775-5050
Brookfield *(G-1230)*
Viking Supply Co.....................G..... 860 886-0220
Norwich *(G-6438)*

PLUMBING FIXTURES: Brass, Incl Drain Cocks, Faucets/Spigots

Neoperl Inc..........................D..... 203 756-8891
Waterbury *(G-9557)*
The Keeney Manufacturing Co..........C..... 603 239-6371
Newington *(G-5711)*

PLUMBING FIXTURES: Plastic

Neoperl Inc..........................D..... 203 756-8891
Waterbury *(G-9557)*
New Resources Group Inc..............G..... 203 366-1000
Bridgeport *(G-850)*
World Link Imports-Exports...........G..... 203 792-0281
Danbury *(G-1983)*

POINT OF SALE DEVICES

Hopp Companies Inc...................F..... 800 889-8425
Newtown *(G-5746)*
Positive Ventures LLC................G..... 860 499-0599
Bloomfield *(G-468)*
Worldwide Products Inc...............G..... 855 972-2867
Roxbury *(G-7286)*

POLES & POSTS: Concrete

Techno Mtal Post Watertown LLC.......G..... 203 755-6403
Waterbury *(G-9610)*

POLISHING SVC: Metals Or Formed Prdts

EDS Perfect Polishing................G..... 203 259-5187
Fairfield *(G-2779)*
Etherington Brothers Inc..............G..... 860 585-5624
Bristol *(G-1031)*
Rayco Inc............................G..... 860.357-4693
New Britain *(G-5041)*
Seidel Inc............................D..... 203 757-7349
Waterbury *(G-9600)*
Silversmith Inc......................G..... 203 869-4244
Greenwich *(G-3235)*
Smart Polishing......................G..... 203 559-1541
Stamford *(G-8426)*

POLYCARBONATE RESINS

Lumivisions Architectural Elem.......G..... 203 529-3232
Norwalk *(G-6240)*
Osterman & Company Inc...............E..... 203 272-2233
Cheshire *(G-1427)*

POLYETHYLENE RESINS

Thornton and Company Inc.............F..... 860 628-6771
Southington *(G-7988)*

POLYSTYRENE RESINS

Polar Industries Inc..................E..... 203 758-6651
Prospect *(G-7016)*

POLYVINYL CHLORIDE RESINS

Galata Chemicals LLC.................F..... 203 236-9000
Southbury *(G-7854)*

PORCELAIN ENAMELED PRDTS & UTENSILS

Minh Long Fine Porcelain.............G..... 860 586-8755
Hartford *(G-3643)*

POTTERY

CJ Ceramics and More LLC.............G..... 203 246-2798
Darien *(G-2013)*
David Christian Ceramics LLC.........G..... 203 758-1532
Middlebury *(G-4278)*
Griffith & Parrott...................G..... 203 245-7837
Madison *(G-3924)*
Jessica Howard Ceramics..............G..... 646 295-4778
Fairfield *(G-2801)*
Lilywork Ceramic Ornament LLC........G..... 215 859-8753
Pawcatuck *(G-6719)*
Visionage............................G..... 203 787-0037
New Haven *(G-5429)*

POTTING SOILS

Clinton Nursery Products Inc.........C..... 860 399-3000
Westbrook *(G-9994)*

PRINTING & ENGRAVING: Card, Exc Greeting

Grillo Services LLC .... E 203 877-5070
  Milford *(G-4544)*

POULTRY & SMALL GAME SLAUGHTERING & PROCESSING

Chris & Zack LLC .... G 203 298-0742
  Orange *(G-6592)*
Moark LLC .... E 951 332-3300
  North Franklin *(G-5876)*
Phoenix Poultry Corporation .... E 413 732-1433
  Enfield *(G-2677)*

POWDER: Iron

Ametek Inc .... C 203 265-6731
  Wallingford *(G-9203)*

POWDER: Metal

Allied Sinterings Incorporated .... E 203 743-7502
  Danbury *(G-1737)*
Allread Products Co LLC .... F 860 589-3566
  Terryville *(G-8747)*
Conn Engineering Assoc Corp .... F 203 426-4733
  Sandy Hook *(G-7305)*
Norwalk Powdered Metals Inc .... D 203 338-8000
  Stratford *(G-8657)*

POWER GENERATORS

A-1 Machining Co .... D 860 223-6420
  New Britain *(G-4931)*
Alstom Renewable US LLC .... G 860 688-1911
  Windsor *(G-10359)*
NGS Power LLC .... G 860 873-0100
  Moodus *(G-4775)*

POWER SPLY CONVERTERS: Static, Electronic Applications

71 Pickett District Road LLC .... G 860 350-5964
  New Milford *(G-5502)*
Neeltran Inc .... C 860 350-5964
  New Milford *(G-5564)*
Raman Power Technologies LLC .... G 203 695-4885
  Wallingford *(G-9348)*
Validus DC Systems LLC .... F 203 448-3600
  Brookfield *(G-1236)*

POWER SUPPLIES: All Types, Static

Dsaencore LLC .... D 203 740-4200
  Brookfield *(G-1185)*
Power Controls Inc .... F 203 284-0235
  Wallingford *(G-9336)*
Prime Technology LLC .... C 203 481-5721
  North Branford *(G-5853)*
Transformer Technology Inc .... F 860 349-1061
  Durham *(G-2160)*
Tri Source Inc .... F 203 924-7030
  Shelton *(G-7570)*

POWER TOOL REPAIR SVCS

Air Tool Sales & Service Co .... G 860 673-2714
  Unionville *(G-9110)*

POWER TOOLS, HAND: Cartridge-Activated

Amro Tool Co .... G 860 274-9766
  Watertown *(G-9681)*

POWER TOOLS, HAND: Drill Attachments, Portable

Alden Corporation .... D 203 879-8830
  Wolcott *(G-10548)*

POWER TOOLS, HAND: Drills & Drilling Tools

Ridge View Associates Inc .... D 203 878-8560
  Milford *(G-4628)*

POWER TRANSMISSION EQPT: Mechanical

Altra Industrial Motion Corp .... G 860 379-1673
  New Hartford *(G-5185)*
Bead Industries Inc .... E 203 301-0270
  Milford *(G-4466)*
Converter Consultants LLC .... G 203 729-1031
  Naugatuck *(G-4873)*
Del-Tron Precision Inc .... E 203 778-2727
  Bethel *(G-280)*
F K Bearings Inc .... F 860 621-4567
  Southington *(G-7922)*
Gwilliam Company Inc .... F 860 354-2884
  New Milford *(G-5543)*
Kasheta Power Equipment .... G 860 528-8421
  South Windsor *(G-7782)*
Kevin G Barry .... G 203 263-4948
  Woodbury *(G-10640)*
Perry Technology Corporation .... D 860 738-2525
  New Hartford *(G-5206)*
Roller Bearing Co Amer Inc .... G 203 758-8272
  Middlebury *(G-4289)*

POWER TRANSMISSION EQPT: Vehicle

Southington Transm Auto Repr .... G 860 329-0381
  Southington *(G-7978)*

PRECAST TERRAZZO OR CONCRETE PRDTS

Coreslab Structures Conn Inc .... D 860 283-8281
  Thomaston *(G-8786)*

PRECIOUS METALS WHOLESALERS

Northeastern Metals Corp .... G 203 348-8088
  Stamford *(G-8330)*

PRECIOUS STONES WHOLESALERS

Opal Manning Company Inc .... G 203 292-6981
  Fairfield *(G-2825)*

PRECISION INSTRUMENT REPAIR SVCS

Kde Instrumentation .... G 860 657-2744
  Glastonbury *(G-3053)*
Projects Inc .... C 860 633-4615
  Glastonbury *(G-3075)*

PREFABRICATED BUILDING DEALERS

Giuliano Construction LLC .... G 203 230-3094
  Hamden *(G-3451)*

PRESSURE COOKERS: Stamped Or Drawn Metal

Utitec Inc .... D 860 945-0605
  Watertown *(G-9744)*
Utitec Holdings Inc .... G 860 945-0601
  Watertown *(G-9745)*

PRESTRESSED CONCRETE PRDTS

Blakeslee Prestress Inc .... B 203 315-7090
  Branford *(G-561)*

PRIMARY METAL PRODUCTS

Defabrications LLC .... G 203 791-1407
  Danbury *(G-1790)*
Lisa Lee Creations Inc .... G 203 479-4462
  New Haven *(G-5319)*
Wade R Moore .... G 203 767-6146
  Milford *(G-4678)*

PRINT CARTRIDGES: Laser & Other Computer Printers

Sandri Products .... G 860 824-0001
  Canaan *(G-1291)*

PRINTED CIRCUIT BOARDS

AB Electronics Inc .... E 203 740-2793
  Brookfield *(G-1155)*
Accutron Inc .... C 860 683-8300
  Windsor *(G-10354)*
Advanced Product Solutions LLC .... G 203 745-4225
  Hamden *(G-3412)*
Altek Electronics Inc .... C 860 482-7626
  Torrington *(G-8892)*
American Backplane Inc .... E 860 567-2360
  Morris *(G-4785)*
Apct-Ct Inc .... G 203 284-1215
  Wallingford *(G-9207)*
Carlton Industries Corp .... E 203 288-5605
  Hamden *(G-3424)*
Custom Design Service Corp .... G 203 748-1105
  Danbury *(G-1780)*
Cyclone Microsystems Inc .... E 203 786-5536
  Hamden *(G-3437)*
Eastern Company .... E 860 669-2233
  Clinton *(G-1501)*
Electronic Design Lab Inc .... G 203 790-0500
  Bethel *(G-296)*
Electronic Spc Conn Inc .... E 203 288-1707
  Hamden *(G-3442)*
Enhanced Mfg Solutions LLC .... F 203 488-5796
  Branford *(G-589)*
Midstate Electronics Co .... F 203 265-9900
  Wallingford *(G-9322)*
Norfield Data Products Inc .... F 203 849-0292
  Norwalk *(G-6280)*
Northeast Circuit Tech LLC .... G 860 633-1967
  Glastonbury *(G-3065)*
Te Connectivity Corporation .... C 860 684-8000
  Stafford Springs *(G-8041)*
Technical Manufacturing Corp .... E 860 349-1735
  Durham *(G-2158)*
Tek Industries Inc .... E 860 870-0001
  Vernon *(G-9154)*
Ttm Printed Circuit Group Inc .... C 860 684-8000
  Stafford Springs *(G-8043)*
Ttm Technologies Inc .... B 860 684-5881
  Stafford Springs *(G-8044)*
Ttm Technologies Inc .... D 860 684-8000
  Stafford Springs *(G-8045)*

PRINTERS & PLOTTERS

Macdermid Incorporated .... C 203 575-5700
  Waterbury *(G-9522)*
Prolaser Prolaser .... G 203 939-1750
  Norwalk *(G-6308)*
Red Rocket Site 2 .... G 860 581-8019
  Centerbrook *(G-1333)*
Transact Technologies Inc .... C 203 859-6800
  Hamden *(G-3523)*

PRINTERS' SVCS: Folding, Collating, Etc

Chapin Packaging LLC .... G 203 202-2747
  Darien *(G-2011)*
Xijet Corp .... F 203 397-2800
  New Haven *(G-5436)*

PRINTERS: Computer

Alinabal Holdings Corporation .... B 203 877-3241
  Milford *(G-4449)*
Flo-Tech LLC .... D 860 613-3333
  New Haven *(G-5283)*
Fremco LLC .... F 203 857-0522
  Ridgefield *(G-7142)*
Magnetec Corporation .... D 203 949-9933
  Wallingford *(G-9310)*
Omega Engineering Inc .... C 203 359-1660
  Norwalk *(G-6284)*
Xijet Corp .... F 203 397-2800
  New Haven *(G-5436)*

PRINTERS: Magnetic Ink, Bar Code

Interntnl Bar Code Systms .... G 860 659-9660
  Glastonbury *(G-3051)*
Yellowfin Holdings Inc .... E 866 341-0979
  Ellington *(G-2609)*

PRINTING & BINDING: Books

Ppc Books Ltd .... G 203 226-6644
  Westport *(G-10142)*
R R Donnelley & Sons Company .... F 860 649-5570
  Manchester *(G-4078)*

PRINTING & BINDING: Textbooks

Wesleyan University .... G 860 685-7727
  Middletown *(G-4429)*

PRINTING & ENGRAVING: Card, Exc Greeting

Cannelli Printing Co Inc .... G 203 932-1719
  West Haven *(G-9886)*

Employee Codes: A=Over 500 employees, B=251-500
C=101-250, D=51-100, E=20-50, F=10-19, G=1-9

PRINTING & ENGRAVING: Financial Notes & Certificates

PRINTING & ENGRAVING: Financial Notes & Certificates

Hampton Associates LLC ....G....... 203 817-0161
  Stamford (G-8223)

PRINTING & ENGRAVING: Invitation & Stationery

Ideas Inc...G....... 203 878-9686
  Milford (G-4551)
Master Engrv & Printery Inc ....G....... 203 723-2779
  Waterbury (G-9535)
Scribbling Scribe ....G....... 203 329-7140
  Stamford (G-8405)

PRINTING & ENGRAVING: Poster & Decal

East Coast Name Plates Inc ....G....... 203 261-4347
  Easton (G-2549)
Popcorn Movie Poster Co LLC ....F....... 860 610-0000
  East Hartford (G-2356)

PRINTING & STAMPING: Fabric Articles

Ace Finishing Co LLC......................G....... 860 582-4600
  Bristol (G-955)
Bennettsville Holdings LLC ....D....... 860 444-9400
  Hebron (G-3745)
Rainbow Graphics Inc ....G....... 860 646-8997
  Manchester (G-4082)

PRINTING & WRITING PAPER WHOLESALERS

Hartford Toner & Cartridge Inc ....G....... 860 292-1280
  Broad Brook (G-1150)
Mega Sound and Light LLC ....G....... 203 743-4200
  Danbury (G-1882)
Wallingford Prtg Bus Forms Inc ......F....... 203 481-1911
  Branford (G-669)

PRINTING INKS WHOLESALERS

Hartford Toner & Cartridge Inc ....G....... 860 292-1280
  Broad Brook (G-1150)

PRINTING MACHINERY

A & E Engraving Service ....G....... 860 582-6503
  Bristol (G-950)
Baldwin Graphic Systems Inc ....G....... 203 925-1100
  Shelton (G-7401)
Davinci Technologies Inc ....G....... 860 265-3388
  Enfield (G-2636)
I Q Technology LLC ....F....... 860 749-7255
  Enfield (G-2651)
Interpro LLC ....F....... 860 526-5869
  Deep River (G-2093)
J-Teck Usa Inc ....G....... 203 791-2121
  Danbury (G-1856)
Santec Corporation ....F....... 203 878-1379
  Milford (G-4638)
Systematic Automation Inc ....E....... 310 218-3361
  Farmington (G-2962)

PRINTING MACHINERY, EQPT & SPLYS: Wholesalers

Colors Ink ....G....... 203 269-4000
  Wallingford (G-9233)
New England Graphics Mtls LLC ....F....... 860 210-2180
  New Milford (G-5566)

PRINTING, COMMERCIAL: Business Forms, NEC

Encore Sales Corp ....G....... 203 301-4949
  Milford (G-4530)
Micro Printing LLC ....G....... 203 265-5578
  Wallingford (G-9319)
Mlk Business Forms Inc ....F....... 203 624-6304
  New Haven (G-5335)
New Fairfield Press Inc ....F....... 203 746-2700
  New Fairfield (G-5172)

PRINTING, COMMERCIAL: Cards, Souvenir, NEC

Snoogs & Wilde LLC ....G....... 860 824-9865
  Falls Village (G-2872)

PRINTING, COMMERCIAL: Cards, Visiting, Incl Business, NEC

Action Printing ....G....... 203 366-4413
  Shelton (G-7388)

PRINTING, COMMERCIAL: Envelopes, NEC

Envelopes & More Inc ....F....... 860 286-7570
  Newington (G-5651)
Patriot Envelope LLC ....G....... 860 529-1553
  Wethersfield (G-10214)
Wadsworth Press 860 623-3820
  East Windsor (G-2531)

PRINTING, COMMERCIAL: Imprinting

L P Macadams Company Inc ....D....... 203 366-3647
  Bridgeport (G-820)

PRINTING, COMMERCIAL: Invitations, NEC

Beyond Invite ....G....... 203 219-9434
  Shelton (G-7405)
Paper Station ....G....... 860 667-9087
  Newington (G-5692)
Parkway Printers Inc ....G....... 203 281-6773
  Hamden (G-3494)
Pushing Envelope LLC ....G....... 203 745-0988
  Hamden (G-3498)

PRINTING, COMMERCIAL: Labels & Seals, NEC

Ad Label Inc ....G....... 860 779-0513
  Brooklyn (G-1245)
Ansel Label and Packaging Corp ....E....... 203 452-0311
  Trumbull (G-8999)
CCL Label (delaware) Inc ....G....... 203 926-1253
  Shelton (G-7414)
Cenveo Corporation ....E....... 303 790-8023
  Stamford (G-8139)
Design Label Manufacturing Inc ....E....... 860 739-6266
  Old Lyme (G-6505)
George Schmitt & Co Inc ....G....... 203 453-4334
  Guilford (G-3356)
Specialty Printing LLC ....D....... 860 623-8870
  East Windsor (G-2521)
Surys Inc ....C....... 203 333-5503
  Trumbull (G-9078)

PRINTING, COMMERCIAL: Letterpress & Screen

Up Top Screen Printing ....G....... 860 412-9798
  Danielson (G-2005)

PRINTING, COMMERCIAL: Literature, Advertising, NEC

Clicroi LLC ....G....... 203 599-1237
  Danbury (G-1769)
R R Donnelley & Sons Company ...E....... 860 773-6140
  Avon (G-102)

PRINTING, COMMERCIAL: Magazines, NEC

Lrp Conferences LLC ....E....... 203 663-0100
  Trumbull (G-9044)

PRINTING, COMMERCIAL: Periodicals, NEC

Omega Engineering Inc ....C....... 203 359-1660
  Norwalk (G-6284)

PRINTING, COMMERCIAL: Promotional

Barbara Garelick Enterprises ....G....... 203 855-9897
  Norwalk (G-6086)
Digital Chameleon LLC ....G....... 203 354-4111
  Bridgeport (G-752)
Kramer Printing Company Inc ....F....... 203 933-5416
  West Haven (G-9924)
Prime Resources Corp ....B....... 203 331-9100
  Bridgeport (G-880)

PRINTING, COMMERCIAL: Publications

Aquastone Graphix LLC ....G....... 860 206-4935
  Hartford (G-3552)
Bayard Inc ....E....... 860 437-3012
  New London (G-5457)

Digital Copy LLC ....G....... 203 540-5181
  Bridgeport (G-753)
Laser Engraved Services ....G....... 203 779-5116
  Madison (G-3936)
Ledgewood Publications ....G....... 860 693-9055
  Collinsville (G-1597)
Paragon Publications 860 875-4366
  Vernon (G-9149)
Phocuswright Inc ....E....... 860 350-4084
  Sherman (G-7601)
Speedi Sign ....G....... 203 431-0836
  Bethel (G-346)
Wm Corvo Consultants Inc ....G....... 860 346-6500
  Middletown (G-4432)

PRINTING, COMMERCIAL: Screen

101 Business Solutions LLC ....G....... 860 774-6904
  Brooklyn (G-1243)
A 2 Z Screen Printing LLC ....G....... 860 526-9684
  Ivoryton (G-3782)
A 2 Z Screen Printing LLC ....G....... 860 526-9684
  Deep River (G-2081)
Accent Screenprinting ....G....... 203 284-8601
  Wallingford (G-9195)
Advanced Graphics Inc ....E....... 203 378-0471
  Stratford (G-8564)
Affordable Sign Co ....G....... 203 874-0875
  Milford (G-4443)
American Silk Screening LLC ....G....... 860 828-5486
  Berlin (G-157)
American Stitch & Print Inc ....G....... 203 239-5383
  North Haven (G-5902)
ARM Screen Printing ....G....... 860 649-6295
  Manchester (G-3984)
Arnow Silk Screening LLC ....G....... 203 964-1963
  Stamford (G-8093)
Art Screen ....G....... 203 744-1991
  Bethel (G-258)
B T S Graphics LLC ....G....... 860 274-6422
  Oakville (G-6449)
Basement Screen Printing ....G....... 860 462-9103
  Broad Brook (G-1144)
Been Printed LLC ....G....... 860 618-3600
  Torrington (G-8901)
BI Printing Shop ....G....... 203 334-7779
  Bridgeport (G-713)
Blue Moon Printing LLC ....G....... 860 245-0827
  Mystic (G-4801)
Britelite Promotions ....G....... 203 481-5755
  Branford (G-565)
C J Macsata LLC ....G....... 860 623-6755
  Enfield (G-2619)
C Libby Leonard ....G....... 203 375-6205
  Stratford (G-8591)
Collinsville Screen Printing ....G....... 860 693-2601
  Collinsville (G-1591)
Collinsville Screen/Embroidery ......G....... 860 693-2601
  Canton (G-1311)
Colorgraphix LLC ....G....... 203 264-5212
  Oxford (G-6652)
Colour TS LLC ....G....... 860 298-0594
  Windsor (G-10375)
Concordia Ltd ....G....... 203 483-0221
  North Branford (G-5832)
Custom Tees Plus ....E....... 203 752-1071
  New Haven (G-5266)
Custom TS n More LLC ....G....... 203 438-1592
  Ridgefield (G-7133)
Cutting Edge Sgns Graphics LLC ...G....... 203 758-7776
  Prospect (G-6999)
Depaul Industries ....G....... 203 882-1331
  Milford (G-4508)
ECI Screen Print Inc ....F....... 860 283-9849
  Watertown (G-9703)
Emulsion Apparel ....G....... 860 495-5792
  Pawcatuck (G-6710)
Ever Ready Press ....G....... 203 734-5157
  Ansonia (G-33)
Falcon Press ....G....... 860 763-2293
  Enfield (G-2646)
Fit To A Tee Cstm Screen Prtg ....G....... 860 828-6632
  Kensington (G-3810)
Forsa Team Sports LLC ....G....... 203 466-2890
  East Haven (G-2429)
Fresh Ink LLC ....G....... 860 656-7013
  West Hartford (G-9812)
Frontline Screen Printing & Em .....G....... 860 749-0232
  Somers (G-7660)
Images Unlimited ....G....... 860 350-6608
  New Milford (G-5545)

PRINTING: Commercial, NEC

Ink 13 LLC .... G 860 921-6910
  Burlington (G-1270)
Integrated Print Solutions Inc .... F 203 330-0200
  Bridgeport (G-793)
Iovino Bros Sporting Goods .... G 203 790-5966
  Danbury (G-1851)
Jb Muze Enterprises .... G 860 355-5949
  New Milford (G-5549)
Jeffrey Morgan .... G 860 583-2567
  Bristol (G-1054)
Jump 4 Tees .... G 860 228-4813
  Hebron (G-3752)
Kaibry Screen Printing .... G 860 774-0234
  Danielson (G-1996)
Keno Graphic Services Inc .... E 203 925-7722
  Shelton (G-7483)
Korzon Screen Printing LLC .... G 203 729-1090
  Beacon Falls (G-138)
Korzon Silk Screening .... G 203 888-3273
  Beacon Falls (G-139)
Liberty Screen Print Co LLC .... F 203 632-5449
  Beacon Falls (G-140)
Living Word Imprints LLC .... G 860 882-1679
  Hartford (G-3629)
Logo Sportswear Inc .... G 203 678-4700
  Wallingford (G-9306)
Logod Softwear Inc .... E 203 272-4883
  Cheshire (G-1407)
Lorenco Industries Inc .... F 203 743-6962
  Bethel (G-323)
Macwear LLC .... G 203 579-4277
  Southport (G-8006)
Mad Sportswear LLC .... G 203 932-4868
  West Haven (G-9929)
Multiprints Inc .... F 203 235-4409
  Meriden (G-4207)
Novel Tees Screen Prtg EMB LLC .... F 860 643-6008
  Manchester (G-4062)
Novel-Tees Unlimited LLC .... G 860 643-6008
  Manchester (G-4063)
O Berk Company Neng LLC .... F 203 932-8000
  West Haven (G-9940)
On Time Screen Printing & Embr .... F 203 874-4581
  Derby (G-2120)
Picture Perfect Printing Inc .... G 203 386-9696
  Stratford (G-8665)
Pio Tee Gio LLC .... G 860 280-7073
  Vernon Rockville (G-9174)
Production Decorating Co Inc .... E 203 574-2975
  Waterbury (G-9589)
Quality Name Plate Inc .... D 860 633-9495
  East Glastonbury (G-2185)
R & B Apparel Plus LLC .... G 860 333-1757
  Groton (G-3311)
Rosemarie Querns .... G 860 349-3315
  Durham (G-2155)
Royaltees LLC .... G 203 767-2808
  Bridgeport (G-893)
S & V Screen Printing .... G 203 208-3112
  Branford (G-645)
Screen Designs .... G 203 797-9806
  Bethel (G-340)
Shirt Graphix .... G 203 294-1656
  Wallingford (G-9365)
Shirt Shark .... G 860 552-4197
  Clinton (G-1524)
Signs Now LLC .... G 860 667-8339
  Newington (G-5705)
Silkscreen Plus LLC .... G 203 879-0345
  Wolcott (G-10590)
Sirocco Screenprints Inc .... G 203 288-3565
  North Haven (G-5994)
Special Events Screen Prtg LLC .... G 203 468-5453
  East Haven (G-2454)
Sportees LLC .... G 860 440-3922
  Waterford (G-9673)
Tee Squares .... G 844 669-8437
  Bridgeport (G-922)
Tees Plus .... F 800 782-8337
  Bridgeport (G-923)
Town Pride .... G 860 664-0448
  Clinton (G-1532)
Unique Graphics .... G 203 634-1932
  Meriden (G-4258)
Varsity Imprints .... G 203 354-4371
  Milford (G-4672)
Vios Sports Plus .... G 203 234-7231
  North Haven (G-6013)
Vision Designs LLC .... F 203 778-9898
  Brookfield (G-1237)

Work n Gear LLC .... G 203 795-8998
  Orange (G-6636)
Work n Gear LLC .... G 203 467-1156
  East Haven (G-2460)
Xtreme Designs LLC .... G 203 773-9303
  New Haven (G-5437)
Yankee Screen Printing .... G 203 924-9926
  Derby (G-2133)
Yush Sign Display Co Inc .... G 860 289-1819
  East Hartford (G-2402)

PRINTING, COMMERCIAL: Tags, NEC

Online River LLC .... F 203 801-5900
  Westport (G-10134)

PRINTING, COMMERCIAL: Wrappers, NEC

Vrd Customs Ltd .... G 475 329-5184
  Danbury (G-1974)

PRINTING, LITHOGRAPHIC: Calendars

Ziga Media LLC .... G 203 656-0076
  Darien (G-2052)

PRINTING, LITHOGRAPHIC: Calendars & Cards

Ready4 Print LLC .... G 203 345-0376
  Bridgeport (G-887)

PRINTING, LITHOGRAPHIC: Forms, Business

Inform Inc .... G 203 924-9929
  Shelton (G-7477)
Tower Printing Inc .... G 203 757-1030
  Waterbury (G-9615)

PRINTING, LITHOGRAPHIC: Offset & photolithographic printing

Macdermid Incorporated .... C 203 575-5700
  Waterbury (G-9522)

PRINTING, LITHOGRAPHIC: Promotional

Automated Mailing Services LLC .... G 203 439-2763
  Cheshire (G-1358)

PRINTING, LITHOGRAPHIC: Publications

Arcat Inc .... G 203 929-9444
  Fairfield (G-2747)

PRINTING: Book Music

M Baron Company .... G 860 536-1594
  Mystic (G-4827)

PRINTING: Books

Bq Business Solutions .... G 203 268-3500
  Monroe (G-4701)
Cagno Enterprises LLC .... G 203 729-3883
  Naugatuck (G-4867)

PRINTING: Commercial, NEC

5 Star Printing .... G 203 975-1000
  Stamford (G-8050)
Acme Typesetting Service Co .... G 860 953-1470
  West Hartford (G-9772)
Alexander Hussey .... G 860 354-0118
  New Milford (G-5503)
Allied Printing Services Inc .... B 860 643-1101
  Manchester (G-3980)
American Banknote Corporation .... G 203 941-4090
  Stamford (G-8074)
American Solution For Business .... G 860 413-9415
  East Granby (G-2189)
Amgraph Packaging Inc .... C 860 822-2000
  Baltic (G-118)
Anything Printed LLC .... G 860 429-1244
  Willington (G-10245)
Autobond Eastern .... G 860 383-8982
  Pleasant Valley (G-6920)
Automated Graphic Systems Inc .... G 860 659-1076
  South Glastonbury (G-7679)
AZ Copy Center Inc .... G 860 621-7325
  Southington (G-7893)

B-P Products Inc .... E 203 288-0200
  Hamden (G-3416)
Bardell Printing Corp .... G 203 469-2441
  East Haven (G-2413)
Benettieris Studio .... G 860 568-3590
  East Hartford (G-2297)
Biz Wiz Print & Copy Ctr LLC .... G 860 721-0040
  Rocky Hill (G-7224)
Biz Wiz Print & Copy Ctr LLC .... G 860 633-7446
  Glastonbury (G-3015)
Bread and Wine Publishing LLC .... G 860 649-3109
  Manchester (G-3988)
C C and P .... G 203 222-8260
  Westport (G-10062)
Christopher Condors .... G 203 852-8181
  Norwalk (G-6114)
Classic Label Inc .... G 203 389-3535
  Woodbridge (G-10599)
Copy Cats Inc .... F 860 442-8424
  New London (G-5465)
Core Studios .... G 203 364-9594
  Newtown (G-5734)
Creative Envelope Inc .... G 860 963-1231
  Putnam (G-7038)
Crystal Labels Co .... G 860 870-8627
  Ellington (G-2585)
Custom TS .... G 860 644-1514
  Manchester (G-4002)
D Cello Enterprises LLC .... G 860 659-0844
  Glastonbury (G-3027)
Desai Mukesh .... G 860 529-4141
  Rocky Hill (G-7234)
Diversified Printing Solutions .... G 203 826-7198
  Danbury (G-1796)
Doctor Stuff LLC .... G 203 785-8475
  Wallingford (G-9252)
Eastwood Printing Inc .... F 860 529-6673
  Wethersfield (G-10192)
Elm Press Incorporated .... E 860 583-3600
  Terryville (G-8752)
Epic Printing Compny Inc .... G 203 469-3988
  East Haven (G-2424)
Executive Greetings Inc .... B 860 379-9911
  New Hartford (G-5190)
Executive Office Services Inc .... E 203 373-1333
  Bridgeport (G-765)
Exhibitease LLC .... G 203 481-0792
  Branford (G-592)
Fairfield Marketing Group Inc .... F 203 261-0884
  Easton (G-2552)
Fedex Office & Print Svcs Inc .... F 860 233-8245
  Hartford (G-3588)
Four Color Inc .... G 860 691-1782
  Niantic (G-5806)
G & R Enterprises Incorporated .... G 203 549-6120
  Hartford (G-3593)
Gateway Digital Inc .... F 203 853-4929
  Norwalk (G-6175)
George Schmitt & Co Inc .... D 203 453-4334
  Guilford (G-3355)
Glenn Curtis .... G 860 349-8679
  Durham (G-2147)
Hat Trick Graphics LLC .... G 203 748-1128
  Danbury (G-1842)
Hunt Printing Co .... G 203 891-5778
  Middletown (G-4352)
Hw Graphics .... G 860 278-2338
  Windsor (G-10396)
Image One Prtg & Graphics Inc .... G 203 459-1880
  Monroe (G-4720)
Imperial Grphic Cmmnctions Inc .... E 203 650-3478
  Milford (G-4553)
International Comm Svcs Inc .... G 401 580-8888
  Guilford (G-3362)
International Printing Access .... G 860 599-8005
  Pawcatuck (G-6717)
J & J Printing Co .... G 860 355-9535
  New Milford (G-5548)
Jeanann Stagnita .... G 860 516-4655
  Bristol (G-1053)
JMS Graphics Inc .... G 203 598-7555
  Middlebury (G-4280)
Joyce Printers Inc .... G 203 389-4452
  Woodbridge (G-10603)
Kool Ink LLC .... F 860 242-0303
  Bloomfield (G-439)
L R K Communications Inc .... G 203 372-1456
  Fairfield (G-2808)
Larkin Litho .... G 860 535-0116
  Stonington (G-8534)

Employee Codes: A=Over 500 employees, B=251-500
C=101-250, D=51-100, E=20-50, F=10-19, G=1-9

2020 Harris Connecticut
Manufacturers Directory

PRINTING: Commercial, NEC

Linda Case Writing Graphic .... G 860 563-5713
  Wethersfield (G-10210)
Mailourinvitationscom .... G 203 758-1860
  Middlebury (G-4283)
Mallace Industries Corp .... G 800 521-0194
  Clinton (G-1514)
McLodesignscom .... G 203 296-1400
  Bridgeport (G-835)
McWeeney Marketing Group Inc .... G 203 891-8100
  Orange (G-6613)
Mediagraphicscom Inc .... F 203 404-7233
  Durham (G-2153)
Merrill Corporation .... D 860 249-7220
  Hartford (G-3638)
Mickey Herbst .... G 203 993-5879
  Fairfield (G-2815)
Moonlight Media LLC .... G 860 345-3595
  Haddam (G-3407)
Muir Envelope Plus Inc .... F 860 953-6847
  Newington (G-5681)
New England Printing LLC .... G 860 745-3600
  Enfield (G-2669)
Nice T-Shirt .... G 860 349-0727
  Middletown (G-4386)
Norwalk Rutledge Printing Off .... G 203 956-5967
  Norwalk (G-6281)
Olde Tyme Graphics .... G 203 748-3360
  Danbury (G-1898)
Omniprint LLC .... G 203 881-9013
  Oxford (G-6683)
P M Hill .... G 860 242-2915
  Bloomfield (G-457)
Paul Dewitt .... F 203 792-5610
  Danbury (G-1902)
Planes Road Assoc LLC .... G 860 469-3200
  Essex (G-2730)
Platt Brothers Realty II LLC .... G 203 562-5112
  New Haven (G-5367)
Print & Post Services .... G 203 336-0055
  Bridgeport (G-881)
Print Producers LLC .... G 203 761-9877
  Wilton (G-10321)
Print Shop of Wolcott LLC .... G 203 879-3353
  Wolcott (G-10581)
Print Source Ltd .... G 203 876-1822
  Milford (G-4617)
Printing House The Inc .... G 203 869-1767
  Greenwich (G-3218)
Psd Inc .... G 860 305-6346
  East Haven (G-2448)
Quinn and Gellar Marketing LLC .... G 860 444-0448
  New London (G-5485)
R R Donnelley & Sons Company .... F 860 649-5570
  Manchester (G-4078)
Rainbow Graphics Inc .... G 860 646-8997
  Manchester (G-4082)
Robert Audette .... G 203 872-3119
  Cheshire (G-1440)
Roto-Die Company Inc .... F 860 292-7030
  East Windsor (G-2516)
Saint Vincent De Paul Place .... G 860 889-7374
  Norwich (G-6430)
Saybrook Press Incorporated .... F 203 458-3637
  Guilford (G-3388)
Shadow Graphics .... G 203 590-3533
  Trumbull (G-9073)
Sheila P Patrick .... G 203 575-1716
  Waterbury (G-9602)
Sibtech Inc .... G 203 775-5677
  Brookfield (G-1223)
Sigmawear .... G 860 924-2908
  Berlin (G-219)
Spectrum Mktg Cmmnications Inc .... G 203 853-4585
  Norwalk (G-6353)
Speed Printing & Graphics Inc .... G 203 324-4000
  Stamford (G-8433)
Speedy Printing LLC .... G 860 445-8252
  Mystic (G-4846)
STS Motorsports Graphics .... G 860 698-6697
  Somers (G-7673)
Tef LLC .... G 203 878-9740
  Milford (G-4662)
True Inspiration LLC .... G 860 635-7941
  Cromwell (G-1722)
Tyco Printing & Copying .... G 203 562-2679
  New Haven (G-5424)
UPS Authorized Retailer .... G 203 256-9991
  Fairfield (G-2862)
Visual Impact LLC .... G 203 790-9650
  Danbury (G-1973)

Vp Printing .... G 203 736-1756
  Ansonia (G-56)
Wallingford Prtg Bus Forms Inc .... F 203 481-1911
  Branford (G-669)
Warren Press Inc .... G 203 431-0011
  Ridgefield (G-7182)
Wink Ink LLC .... G 860 202-8709
  Somers (G-7677)
Wolfe Promotional Services LLC .... G 203 452-7692
  Monroe (G-4766)
Yale University .... E 203 737-1244
  New Haven (G-5446)

PRINTING: Engraving & Plate

Urg Graphics Inc .... E 860 928-0835
  Stafford Springs (G-8046)

PRINTING: Flexographic

CCL Industries Corporation .... D 203 926-1253
  Shelton (G-7412)
CCL Label Inc .... C 203 926-1253
  Shelton (G-7413)
Identification Products Corp .... G 203 331-0931
  Bridgeport (G-790)
Identification Products Corp .... F 203 334-5969
  Bridgeport (G-791)
Privateer Ltd .... F 860 526-1837
  Old Saybrook (G-6568)

PRINTING: Gravure, Announcements

Michael Lazorchak .... G 203 775-0608
  Brookfield (G-1205)

PRINTING: Gravure, Cards, Exc Greeting

Ideas Inc .... G 203 878-9686
  Milford (G-4551)

PRINTING: Gravure, Catalogs, No Publishing On-Site

R R Donnelley & Sons Company .... F 860 649-5570
  Manchester (G-4078)

PRINTING: Gravure, Forms, Business

Sterling Forms and Cmpt Sups .... G 203 876-7337
  Milford (G-4653)

PRINTING: Gravure, Invitations

Simcha Designs .... G 203 273-1593
  Stamford (G-8422)

PRINTING: Gravure, Labels

Rubber Labels USA LLC .... G 203 713-8059
  Milford (G-4635)
Trade Labels Inc .... G 860 535-4828
  Mystic (G-4850)

PRINTING: Gravure, Rotogravure

Brook & Whittle Limited .... C 203 483-5602
  Guilford (G-3334)
Jean Marie Papery LLC .... G 203 877-4299
  Milford (G-4559)
Massachusetts Envelope Co Inc .... E 860 727-9100
  Hartford (G-3636)
Mc Hugh Business Forms .... G 203 268-3500
  Monroe (G-4735)
Naugatuck Vly Photo Engrv Inc .... G 203 756-7345
  Waterbury (G-9554)
Quad/Graphics Inc .... A 203 288-2468
  North Haven (G-5985)

PRINTING: Gravure, Stationery & Invitation

A Flood of Paper .... G 203 529-3030
  Wilton (G-10265)
Aquastone Graphix LLC .... G 860 206-4935
  Hartford (G-3552)
ECR Enterprises LLC .... G 860 426-3098
  Southington (G-7917)
Montambault Riva .... G 203 758-4981
  Prospect (G-7011)
Roseville Designs LLC .... G 203 858-5744
  Darien (G-2042)
Sugarplums .... G 860 426-9945
  Middlebury (G-4296)

Tulaloo .... G 860 417-2587
  Oakville (G-6465)

PRINTING: Laser

A To A Studio Solutions Ltd .... F 203 388-9050
  Stamford (G-8053)
Dst Output East LLC .... E 816 221-1234
  South Windsor (G-7740)
Hartford Toner & Cartridge Inc .... G 860 292-1280
  Broad Brook (G-1150)

PRINTING: Letterpress

Amity Printing & Copy Ctr LLC .... G 860 828-0202
  Berlin (G-158)
Clanol Systems Inc .... G 203 637-9909
  Old Greenwich (G-6469)
Colonial Printers of Windsor .... G 860 627-5433
  Windsor Locks (G-10480)
Frank Printing Co R .... G 203 265-6152
  Wallingford (G-9270)
Hawkeye Press Inc .... G 203 855-8580
  Norwalk (G-6194)
Ideal Printing Co Inc .... G 203 777-7626
  New Haven (G-5299)
Majestic Press .... G 860 673-2064
  Unionville (G-9120)
Matthews Printing Co .... F 203 265-0363
  Wallingford (G-9314)
Silvermine Press Inc .... G 203 847-4368
  Norwalk (G-6350)

PRINTING: Lithographic

1 Way Custom Print .... G 860 712-0027
  Manchester (G-3970)
24 Hours Design & Print .... G 347 350-4484
  Bridgeport (G-678)
5 Star Printing .... G 203 975-1000
  Stamford (G-8050)
A Grey Soiree LLC .... G 203 530-0277
  Branford (G-534)
Action Letter Inc .... E 203 323-2466
  Stamford (G-8061)
Action Printing .... G 203 366-4413
  Shelton (G-7388)
Advance Images LLC .... G 860 749-1166
  Enfield (G-2613)
Advanced Screen Printing LLC .... G 860 845-8337
  Bristol (G-959)
Alexander and Mason .... G 860 349-0496
  Durham (G-2136)
Alexander Hussey .... G 860 354-0118
  New Milford (G-5503)
AlphaGraphics LLC .... G 203 230-0018
  Hamden (G-3413)
American-Republican Inc .... D 203 574-3636
  Waterbury (G-9429)
Amgraph Packaging Inc .... C 860 822-2000
  Baltic (G-118)
Anderson Publishing LLC .... G 860 621-2192
  Southington (G-7890)
Anray Lithographers .... G 203 877-1000
  Milford (G-4453)
Apb Associates LLC .... G 203 740-9792
  Brookfield (G-1159)
Apps Screen Printing LLC .... G 860 938-7596
  Waterbury (G-9432)
AR Robinson Printing .... G 203 961-1787
  Stamford (G-8089)
Arch Parent Inc .... G 860 336-4856
  Willimantic (G-10221)
Arrowhead Group LLC .... G 954 771-5115
  Windsor (G-10365)
Bam Custom Printing .... G 888 583-6690
  Shelton (G-7402)
Barron Print .... G 860 355-9535
  New Milford (G-5509)
BCT Reporting LLC .... G 860 302-1876
  Plainville (G-6775)
BCT-042 LLC .... G 203 331-0008
  Bridgeport (G-708)
Benenson Family Realty LLC .... G 919 544-7839
  Weston (G-10019)
Bizcard Xpress LLC .... G 860 324-6840
  Higganum (G-3761)
Blue Print .... G 203 948-3883
  Danbury (G-1758)
Boltprintingcom .... G 203 885-0571
  Brookfield (G-1163)

Brass City Custom ....G 860 995-9321
Waterbury *(G-9441)*
Brian Berlepsch ....G 203 484-9799
North Branford *(G-5830)*
Business Cards Tomorrow Inc ....G 203 723-5858
Naugatuck *(G-4864)*
Byrne Group Inc ....G 203 573-0100
Waterbury *(G-9444)*
Cadmus ....G 203 595-3000
Stamford *(G-8126)*
Capitol Printing Co Inc ....G 860 522-1547
Hartford *(G-3561)*
Ceci Printer LLC ....G 203 994-6314
Danbury *(G-1764)*
Cenveo Corporation ....E 303 790-8023
Stamford *(G-8139)*
Child Evngelism Fellowship Inc ....E 203 879-2154
Wolcott *(G-10553)*
Classic Ink ....G 860 225-3652
New Britain *(G-4961)*
Coastline Printing ....G 203 481-2744
Branford *(G-574)*
Concord Litho ....G 203 866-9394
Norwalk *(G-6125)*
Corporate Forms Printing ....G 800 840-9945
New Britain *(G-4967)*
Creative Printed Products LLC ....G 203 268-8980
Monroe *(G-4707)*
Critical Scrn Printg & EMB ....G 860 443-4327
Waterford *(G-9649)*
CT Prints ....G 203 281-6996
Hamden *(G-3435)*
CT Prints & More LLC ....G 860 604-5694
Hartford *(G-3573)*
Custom Tee ....G 718 450-1210
Stamford *(G-8173)*
D & D Printing & Advertising ....G 860 871-7774
Vernon Rockville *(G-9166)*
D Cello Enterprises LLC ....G 860 659-0844
Glastonbury *(G-3027)*
Dane Millette ....G 860 635-6383
Cromwell *(G-1699)*
Das State of CT ....G 860 566-4718
Hartford *(G-3576)*
Data Management Inc ....G 800 243-1969
Farmington *(G-2896)*
Data-Graphics Inc ....D 860 667-0435
Newington *(G-5647)*
Design & Print Interests LLC ....G 203 494-9072
Orange *(G-6596)*
Digital Imagining & Packaging ....G 203 458-3509
Guilford *(G-3345)*
Digitaldruker Inc ....G 203 888-6001
Oxford *(G-6656)*
Dmjc Printing LLC ....G 860 502-4882
Hartford *(G-3579)*
Eagle Printing Co ....G 860 953-2152
West Hartford *(G-9804)*
East Coast Name Plates Inc ....G 203 261-4347
Easton *(G-2549)*
Easy Graphics Inc ....G 203 622-0001
Greenwich *(G-3156)*
Edge Printing ....G 609 707-4555
Norwalk *(G-6155)*
Emulsion LLC ....G 860 440-8685
Stonington *(G-8527)*
Enfield Printing Company ....G 860 745-3600
Enfield *(G-2639)*
Entersport Management Inc ....G 203 972-9090
New Canaan *(G-5103)*
Evergreen Printing ....G 203 323-4717
Stamford *(G-8201)*
Executive Office Services Inc ....E 203 373-1333
Bridgeport *(G-765)*
Fairfield Marketing Group Inc ....F 203 261-0884
Easton *(G-2552)*
Falcon Press ....G 860 763-2293
Enfield *(G-2646)*
Financial Prtg Solutions LLC ....G 860 886-9931
Preston *(G-6983)*
Fine Print New England Inc ....G 860 953-0660
Newington *(G-5652)*
Fleetprinters LLC ....G 860 684-2352
Stafford Springs *(G-8030)*
Framing and Printing Solu ....G 860 664-9679
Clinton *(G-1504)*
Frank Obuchowski ....G 860 535-4739
Stonington *(G-8528)*
Franklin Print Shoppe Inc ....G 860 496-9516
Torrington *(G-8926)*
Fresh Prints of CT LLC ....G 860 398-4893
Rockfall *(G-7212)*
FSNB Enterprises Inc ....G 203 254-1947
Monroe *(G-4718)*
Fulcrum Promotions & Printing ....G 203 909-6362
Bridgeport *(G-773)*
Fusion Cross-Media LLC ....G 860 647-8367
Manchester *(G-4020)*
G & R Enterprises Incorporated ....G 860 549-6120
Hartford *(G-3593)*
Gateway Digital Inc ....F 203 853-4929
Norwalk *(G-6175)*
Grafik Print Shopp ....G 203 335-0777
Bridgeport *(G-778)*
Gravelines Amercn Martial Arts ....G 860 753-1402
Brooklyn *(G-1247)*
Hartford Prints LLC ....G 860 578-8447
Hartford *(G-3613)*
Herff Jones LLC ....G 203 266-7170
Bethlehem *(G-372)*
III Ink Graphic & Prtg Svcs ....G 203 748-0711
Danbury *(G-1848)*
Image Ink Inc ....G 860 665-9792
Newington *(G-5661)*
Images Fine Print ....G 203 482-1695
Brookfield *(G-1196)*
Ink Well T-Shirts LLC ....G 860 355-3065
New Milford *(G-5546)*
Inkbyte LLC ....G 203 939-1140
Shelton *(G-7478)*
Inkwell ....G 860 666-8312
Newington *(G-5662)*
Ins Sreen Printing & Air ....G 860 779-0566
Danielson *(G-1994)*
Instant Replay ....G 203 264-1177
Oxford *(G-6668)*
Instant Style Home Staging ....G 203 417-0131
Weston *(G-10029)*
Instant Win Innovations ....G 203 648-4499
Newtown *(G-5750)*
Interctive Print Solutions LLC ....G 860 217-0412
Simsbury *(G-7630)*
J & T Printing LLC ....G 860 529-4628
Wethersfield *(G-10201)*
Jornik Screen Printing ....G 203 969-0500
Stamford *(G-8269)*
K&D Print LLC ....G 203 483-1199
Branford *(G-615)*
Katahdin Printing ....G 860 461-7037
Bloomfield *(G-437)*
Kathy Pooler ....G 860 889-2893
Norwich *(G-6420)*
Kenny Kalipershad ....G 917 345-5038
Greenwich *(G-3188)*
Kingsley Printing Assoc LLC ....G 203 345-6046
Stratford *(G-8641)*
Kool Ink LLC ....F 860 242-0303
Bloomfield *(G-439)*
Kris Squires Printing & P ....G 860 582-0782
Bristol *(G-1059)*
L P Macadams Company Inc ....D 203 366-3647
Bridgeport *(G-820)*
Leading Edge Printers LLC ....G 203 592-4477
Prospect *(G-7007)*
Liberty Screen Print Co LLC ....F 203 632-5449
Beacon Falls *(G-140)*
Lighthouse Printing LLC ....G 860 388-2677
Old Saybrook *(G-6554)*
Liturgical Publications Inc ....G 860 635-9560
Cromwell *(G-1706)*
Lone Wolfe Printing LLC ....G 203 444-5131
Hamden *(G-3477)*
Lowbrow ....G 203 518-4189
Bethel *(G-324)*
M Design & Printing Svcs LLC ....G 860 344-8289
Middletown *(G-4372)*
Mainely Custom Carving ....G 203 426-8375
Newtown *(G-5759)*
Maple Print Services Inc ....G 860 381-5470
Jewett City *(G-3799)*
Mark Ramponi Printing ....G 860 673-5507
Burlington *(G-1272)*
Massachusetts Envelope Co Inc ....E 860 727-9100
Hartford *(G-3636)*
Master Engrv & Printery Inc ....G 203 723-2779
Waterbury *(G-9535)*
Material Promotions Inc ....G 203 757-8900
Waterbury *(G-9536)*
Max Productions LLC ....G 203 838-2795
Norwalk *(G-6250)*
Melega Inc ....G 203 961-8703
Stamford *(G-8306)*
Middletown Printing Co Inc ....F 860 347-5700
Middletown *(G-4379)*
Midnight Printing LLC ....G 203 257-3307
Monroe *(G-4736)*
Midstate Printing Group LLC ....G 203 998-7575
Stamford *(G-8309)*
Milestone Graphics ....G 203 218-4528
Bridgeport *(G-838)*
Minute Man Press ....G 203 891-6251
Hamden *(G-3483)*
Minuteman Press ....G 973 748-7160
Danbury *(G-1885)*
Minuteman Press ....G 203 445-6971
Shelton *(G-7502)*
Minuteman Press ....G 860 646-0601
Manchester *(G-4057)*
Minuteman Press ....G 860 646-0601
Hartford *(G-3644)*
Minuteman Press ....G 203 261-8318
Trumbull *(G-9049)*
Minuteman Press ....G 860 266-4154
Glastonbury *(G-3059)*
Minuteman Press ....G 860 529-4628
Wethersfield *(G-10212)*
Minuteman Press ....G 860 496-7525
Torrington *(G-8949)*
Minuteman Press ....G 203 261-9569
Newtown *(G-5761)*
Minuteman Press ....G 860 674-8700
Avon *(G-93)*
Minuteman Press LLC ....G 203 922-9228
Shelton *(G-7503)*
Minuteman Press of Bristol ....G 860 589-1100
Bristol *(G-1072)*
Minuteman Press of Danbury ....G 203 743-6755
Danbury *(G-1886)*
Misfit Prints LLC ....G 203 306-6322
Meriden *(G-4205)*
Mk & T Design & Print LLC ....G 203 295-8211
Norwalk *(G-6262)*
Muir Envelope Plus Inc ....F 860 953-6847
Newington *(G-5681)*
Murphy Boyz Printing Mark ....G 860 836-0829
Litchfield *(G-3896)*
Murphy Boyz Prtg & Mktg LLC ....G 860 485-0607
Harwinton *(G-3734)*
Naugatuck Vly Photo Engrv Inc ....G 203 756-7345
Waterbury *(G-9554)*
New Fairfield Press Inc ....F 203 746-2700
New Fairfield *(G-5172)*
New Haven Register LLC ....A 203 789-5200
New Haven *(G-5346)*
New Haven Rgster Fresh Air Fnd ....G 800 925-2509
New Haven *(G-5347)*
New London Printing Co LLC ....G 860 701-9171
New London *(G-5481)*
Nielsen Company ....G 203 586-1819
Woodbury *(G-10647)*
Norwich Printing Co Inc ....G 860 745-3600
Enfield *(G-2671)*
Omniprint LLC ....G 203 881-9013
Oxford *(G-6683)*
Optamark CT LLC ....G 203 325-1180
Stamford *(G-8342)*
P & M Investments LLC ....G 860 745-3600
Enfield *(G-2674)*
P & S Printing LLC ....G 203 327-9818
Stamford *(G-8348)*
Pancoast Associates Inc ....G 203 377-6571
Trumbull *(G-9054)*
Paw Print Pantry LLC ....G 860 447-8442
East Lyme *(G-2470)*
Paw Print Pantry LLC ....G 860 447-8442
Niantic *(G-5815)*
Peach Printing Solutions ....G 203 793-7381
Wallingford *(G-9334)*
Peaches Prints ....G 860 856-3525
Windsor *(G-10417)*
Pequot Printing LLC ....G 860 381-5193
Ledyard *(G-3879)*
Petes Print Shop ....G 860 581-8043
Essex *(G-2729)*
Phoenix Memorial Printing LLC ....G 203 364-9617
Sandy Hook *(G-7326)*
Pinpoint Promotions & Prtg LLC ....F 203 301-4273
West Haven *(G-9944)*
Play-It Productions Inc ....F 212 695-6530
Colchester *(G-1566)*

PRINTING: Lithographic

Pointer Press .... G 650 269-3492
  New Canaan (G-5131)
Pony Express Print Co .... G 203 592-7095
  Waterbury (G-9581)
Prinertechs .... G 203 249-6646
  Stamford (G-8373)
Print B2b LLC .... G 203 744-5435
  Bethel (G-333)
Print House LLC .... G 860 652-0803
  Glastonbury (G-3074)
Print Hub .... G 860 580-7907
  Windsor (G-10425)
Print Lab LLC .... G 860 410-6624
  New Britain (G-5037)
Print MGT & Consulting LLC .... G 860 521-7444
  West Hartford (G-9847)
Print Promotions Inc .... G 203 778-2672
  Bethel (G-334)
Printer Source Inc .... G 800 788-5101
  Trumbull (G-9057)
Printer Techs LLC .... G 203 322-1160
  Stamford (G-8374)
Printing Solutions & Resources ...... G 203 965-0090
  Stamford (G-8375)
Project Graphics Inc .... F 802 488-8789
  Woodbury (G-10652)
Promos & Printing .... G 860 481-9212
  Pomfret Center (G-6946)
Qmdi Press Services LLC .... G 860 942-8822
  Willimantic (G-10235)
Quebecor World (usa) Inc .... G 203 532-4200
  Greenwich (G-3220)
Quiet Corner Printing LLC .... G 860 753-0420
  Brooklyn (G-1253)
R R Donnelley & Sons Company .... E 860 773-6140
  Avon (G-102)
Rd Printing LLC .... G 860 841-1397
  Windsor (G-10429)
Reliable Printing LLC .... G 203 261-8867
  Trumbull (G-9064)
Retail Print Solutions .... G 203 438-5457
  Ridgefield (G-7166)
Rf Printing LLC .... G 203 265-9939
  Wallingford (G-9352)
RKP Printing Services LLC .... G 860 242-0131
  Bloomfield (G-477)
Ross Type .... G 203 227-2007
  Westport (G-10152)
Ruiz Impress Scrn Printg & .... G 203 750-0050
  Norwalk (G-6333)
Ruiz Impressions Screen Prntg ...... G 203 559-4865
  Norwalk (G-6334)
S and Z Graphics LLC .... G 203 783-9675
  Milford (G-4637)
Sabar Graphics LLC .... G 203 467-3016
  East Haven (G-2450)
Sarah May Block21prints .... G 860 604-4004
  Unionville (G-9127)
Savin Rock Printing .... G 203 500-1577
  West Haven (G-9952)
Savour Instant LLC .... G 203 374-4599
  Easton (G-2565)
Screen Tek Printing Co Inc .... G 203 248-6248
  Hamden (G-3508)
Scripture Research & Pubg Co .... G 203 272-1780
  Cheshire (G-1443)
Seven Stitches Screen Prntng .... G 860 749-1166
  Enfield (G-2693)
Signature 22 Painting .... G 914 450-9780
  Danbury (G-1951)
Sir Speedy Printing .... E 203 346-0716
  Middlebury (G-4292)
Sir Speedy Prntng Ctr of N Bri .... G 860 826-1798
  New Britain (G-5054)
Smoke & Print Universe .... G 203 540-5151
  Bridgeport (G-910)
Specialty Printing LLC .... F 860 654-1850
  East Windsor (G-2520)
Spectrum Press .... F 203 878-9090
  Milford (G-4652)
Step Saver Inc .... E 860 621-6751
  Southington (G-7982)
Stevens Printing .... G 203 245-3267
  Madison (G-3962)
Summit Promotional Printing LL ..... G 860 666-1605
  Newington (G-5707)
Swipe Ink Screen Printing LLC .... G 203 783-0468
  Milford (G-4659)
Tashua Litho .... G 203 268-5561
  Monroe (G-4756)

Team Destination Inc .... G 203 235-6000
  Meriden (G-4251)
Testing Technologies Inc .... G 212 835-3617
  Wilton (G-10337)
Tfac LLC .... G 203 776-6000
  New Haven (G-5414)
Thelemic Printshop .... G 860 383-4014
  Plainfield (G-6754)
Three D Print LLC .... G 203 590-3463
  Monroe (G-4760)
Toto LLC .... F 203 776-6000
  New Haven (G-5417)
Transmonde USa Inc .... D 203 484-1528
  North Branford (G-5863)
Tri-State EMB Screen Prtg LLC ..... G 203 732-7636
  Ansonia (G-54)
Turnstone Inc .... F 203 625-0000
  Greenwich (G-3250)
Typeisright .... G 860 564-0537
  Moosup (G-4783)
US Games Systems Inc .... E 203 353-8400
  Stamford (G-8481)
Vernon Printing Co Inc .... G 860 872-1826
  Vernon Rockville (G-9186)
Versa Prints .... G 203 256-2342
  Fairfield (G-2864)
Versifi LLC .... G 860 890-1982
  Meriden (G-4263)
W B Mason Co Inc .... G 888 926-2766
  Meriden (G-4265)
W B Mason Co Inc .... E 888 926-2766
  Norwalk (G-6392)
W B Mason Co Inc .... D 888 926-2766
  Norwich (G-6439)
W B Mason Co Inc .... C 888 926-2766
  East Windsor (G-2530)
Walsh Prints .... G 860 829-5566
  Kensington (G-3820)
Warren Press Inc .... G 860 431-0011
  Ridgefield (G-7182)
Westrock Commercial LLC .... G 203 595-3130
  Stamford (G-8492)
Whhs B Wing Elevator .... G 203 288-5949
  West Haven (G-9965)
Wiki Community LLC .... G 860 582-3489
  Bristol (G-1139)
Wild Rver Cstm Screen Prtg LLC ... G 203 426-1500
  Newtown (G-5797)
Williams Printing LLC .... G 860 813-1717
  Manchester (G-4108)
Wing STC Revision Project .... G 203 432-1753
  New Haven (G-5435)
Yale-New Haven Hlth Svcs Corp .... D 203 688-2100
  New Haven (G-5452)
Yankee Screen Printing .... G 203 924-9926
  Derby (G-2133)

PRINTING: Manmade Fiber & Silk, Broadwoven Fabric

Smyth Ink .... G 203 801-4335
  New Canaan (G-5143)

PRINTING: Offset

A B C Printing Inc .... F 203 468-1245
  East Haven (G-2406)
A1 Commercial Printing Co LLC .... G 203 975-1000
  Stamford (G-8054)
Abbey Printing .... G 860 745-0122
  Enfield (G-2611)
Abbott Printing Company Inc .... G 203 562-5562
  Hamden (G-3410)
Academy Printing Service .... G 860 828-5549
  Kensington (G-3803)
Acme Press Inc .... G 203 334-8221
  Milford (G-4439)
Acme Press Printers LLC .... G 203 237-2702
  Meriden (G-4140)
Adkins Printing Company .... E 800 228-9745
  New Britain (G-4938)
Agjo Printing Service .... G 203 599-3143
  Pawcatuck (G-6703)
Alliance Graphics Inc .... F 860 666-7992
  Newington (G-5624)
Allied Printing Services Inc .... B 860 643-1101
  Manchester (G-3980)
Amity Printing & Copy Ctr LLC ...... G 860 828-0202
  Berlin (G-158)
Ampco Publishing & Prtg Corp ...... G 203 325-1509
  Stamford (G-8080)

Arrow Printers Inc .... G 203 734-7272
  Ansonia (G-21)
Audubon Copy Shppe of Firfield .... G 203 259-4311
  Bridgeport (G-705)
Back Country Graphics .... G 203 531-5878
  Greenwich (G-3128)
Baker Graphics Corporation .... E 203 226-6928
  Westport (G-10059)
Barile Printers LLC .... G 860 224-0127
  New Britain (G-4950)
Bethel Printing & Graphics .... G 203 748-7034
  Bethel (G-263)
Brescias Printing Services Inc .... G 860 528-4254
  East Hartford (G-2300)
Briarwood Printing Company Inc ... F 860 747-6805
  Plainville (G-6778)
Brody Printing Company Inc .... F 203 384-9313
  Bridgeport (G-724)
Caco Print Productions LLC .... G 860 583-1223
  Bristol (G-996)
Cannelli Printing Co Inc .... G 203 932-1719
  West Haven (G-9886)
Chase Graphics Inc .... F 860 315-9006
  Putnam (G-7034)
Clanol Systems Inc .... G 203 637-9909
  Old Greenwich (G-6469)
Colonial Printers of Windsor .... G 860 627-5433
  Windsor Locks (G-10480)
Commercial Service .... G 203 755-0166
  Waterbury (G-9454)
Compumail Corp .... G 860 583-1906
  Bristol (G-1005)
Connecticut Valley Litho Club .... G 203 234-0536
  North Haven (G-5925)
Conner Printing .... G 203 929-2070
  Shelton (G-7423)
Copy Stop Inc .... G 203 288-6401
  Hamden (G-3433)
Copy-Rite Inc .... G 203 272-6923
  Plantsville (G-6889)
Craftsmen Printing Group Inc .... G 203 327-2817
  Stamford (G-8163)
Cricket Press Inc .... G 860 521-9279
  West Hartford (G-9796)
Curry Printing & Copy Ctr LLC .... G 203 878-5767
  Milford (G-4502)
Custom Printing & Copy Inc .... F 860 290-6890
  Enfield (G-2634)
D&D Printing Enterprises .... G 860 684-2023
  Stafford Springs (G-8023)
Data Management Incorporated .... E 860 677-8586
  Unionville (G-9113)
Del Printing LLC .... G 860 342-2959
  Portland (G-6957)
Derosa Printing Company Inc .... F 860 646-1698
  Manchester (G-4005)
Design Idea Printing .... G 860 896-0103
  Ellington (G-2586)
Dlorio Printing Service .... G 203 656-0557
  Darien (G-2021)
Docuprint & Imaging Inc .... G 203 776-6000
  New Haven (G-5267)
E R Hitchcock Company .... E 860 229-2024
  New Britain (G-4977)
East Coast Packaging LLC .... G 860 675-8500
  Farmington (G-2901)
East Longmeadow Business Svcs . G 413 525-6111
  Enfield (G-2637)
Eccles-Lehman Inc .... G 203 268-0605
  Easton (G-2551)
Economy Printing & Copy Center .. G 203 792-5610
  Danbury (G-1803)
Economy Printing & Copy Center .. G 203 438-7401
  Ridgefield (G-7137)
Ellington Printery Inc .... G 860 875-3310
  Ellington (G-2589)
Elm Press Incorporated .... E 860 583-3600
  Terryville (G-8752)
Empire Printing Systems LLC .... G 860 633-3333
  Glastonbury (G-3034)
Executive Press Inc .... G 860 793-0060
  Plainville (G-6807)
Executive Printing Darien LLC .... G 203 655-4691
  Darien (G-2023)
Fairfield Minuteman .... G 203 752-2711
  New Haven (G-5282)
Flow Resources Inc .... E 860 666-1200
  Newington (G-5653)
Fox Print .... G 860 485-0429
  Harwinton (G-3729)

Garcia Printing Inc .... G 203 378-6200
Stratford (G-8615)
Garrett Printing & Graphics .... G 860 589-6710
Bristol (G-1045)
George Bullock & Sons Inc .... G 860 355-1243
Roxbury (G-7277)
Ghp Media Inc .... C 203 479-7500
West Haven (G-9912)
Goodcopy Printing Center Inc .... E 203 624-0194
New Haven (G-5287)
Goulet Enterprises Inc .... F 860 379-0793
Pleasant Valley (G-6922)
Graphic Image Inc .... E 203 877-8787
Milford (G-4542)
Graphic Plus .... G 203 723-8387
Naugatuck (G-4885)
Guilford Printing Inc .... G 203 453-5585
Guilford (G-3358)
Gulemo Inc .... G 860 456-1151
Willimantic (G-10229)
Hartford Business Supply Inc .... E 860 233-2138
Hartford (G-3607)
Harty Press Inc .... D 203 562-5112
New Haven (G-5293)
Hat Trick Graphics LLC .... G 203 748-1128
Danbury (G-1842)
High Ridge Copy Inc .... F 203 329-1889
Stamford (G-8237)
Holly Press Inc .... G 203 846-1720
Norwalk (G-6202)
Ideal Printing Co Inc .... G 203 777-7626
New Haven (G-5299)
Imperial Grphic Cmmnctions Inc .... E 203 650-3478
Milford (G-4553)
Impression Point Inc .... F 203 353-8800
Stamford (G-8246)
Imprint Printing .... G 203 794-1092
Bethel (G-310)
Integrity Graphics Inc .... D 800 343-1248
Simsbury (G-7629)
Jerrys Printing & Graphics LLC .... G 203 384-0015
Bridgeport (G-803)
JMS Graphics Inc .... G 203 598-7555
Middlebury (G-4280)
John L Prentis & Co Inc .... G 203 634-1266
Meriden (G-4178)
Joseph Merritt & Company Inc .... G 203 743-6734
Danbury (G-1863)
Joseph Merritt & Company Inc .... E 860 296-2500
Hartford (G-3620)
JS McCarthy Co Inc .... E 203 355-7600
Stamford (G-8270)
Jupiter Communications LLC .... F 475 238-7082
West Haven (G-9920)
K & G Graphics .... G 203 481-4884
Branford (G-614)
Kramer Printing Company Inc .... F 203 933-5416
West Haven (G-9924)
Late Nite Printing Co .... G 203 374-9287
Bridgeport (G-823)
Lithographics Inc .... D 860 678-1660
Farmington (G-2926)
Magnani Press Incorporated .... G 860 236-2802
Hartford (G-3631)
Majestic Press .... G 860 673-2064
Unionville (G-9120)
Maple Print Services Inc .... G 860 381-5470
Griswold (G-3267)
Marketing Sltons Unlimited LLC .... E 860 523-0670
West Hartford (G-9834)
Matthews Printing Co .... F 203 265-0363
Wallingford (G-9314)
Minit Print Inc .... G 203 776-6000
New Haven (G-5333)
Minuteman Arms LLC .... G 203 268-4853
Trumbull (G-9048)
Minuteman Land Services Inc .... G 203 854-4949
Norwalk (G-6261)
Napp Printing Plate Dist Inc .... G 203 575-5727
Waterbury (G-9552)
New England Info Districts .... G 860 446-1906
Groton (G-3300)
New Milford Print Works Inc .... G 860 799-0530
New Milford (G-5572)
Northeast Printing Networ .... G 860 788-3572
Cromwell (G-1710)
Oddo Print Shop Inc .... G 860 489-6585
Torrington (G-8953)
One Source Print and Promo LLC .... G 860 635-3257
Cromwell (G-1713)

P C I Group .... F 203 327-0410
Stamford (G-8349)
Paladin Commercial Prtrs LLC .... E 860 953-4900
Newington (G-5691)
Palmisano Printing LLC .... G 860 582-6883
Bristol (G-1085)
Paper Mill Graphix Inc .... E 203 531-5904
Greenwich (G-3213)
Parkway Printers Inc .... G 203 281-6773
Hamden (G-3494)
Paul Dewitt .... F 203 792-5610
Danbury (G-1902)
Phoenix Press Inc .... E 203 865-5555
New Haven (G-5363)
Photo Arts Limited .... G 860 489-1170
Torrington (G-8957)
Precision Press LLC .... G 203 359-0211
Stamford (G-8371)
Prentis Printing Solutions Inc .... G 203 634-1266
Meriden (G-4220)
Print Indie LLC .... G 860 986-9446
Plainville (G-6854)
Print Master LLC .... G 860 482-8152
Torrington (G-8960)
Print Shop of Wolcott LLC .... G 203 879-3353
Wolcott (G-10581)
Printers of Connecticut Inc .... G 203 852-0070
Norwalk (G-6306)
Printing Services Inc .... G 860 584-9598
Bristol (G-1098)
Printing Solutions LLC .... G 203 965-0090
Riverside (G-7200)
Printing Solutions Group LLC .... G 860 647-0317
Hebron (G-3753)
Pro Graphics Inc .... F 860 668-9067
Suffield (G-8731)
Professional Graphics Inc .... F 203 846-4291
Norwalk (G-6307)
Professional Print Graphics .... G 203 686-0151
Meriden (G-4222)
Pronto Printer of Newington .... G 860 666-2245
Newington (G-5697)
Prospect Printing LLC .... F 203 758-6007
Prospect (G-7021)
Prosperous Printing LLC .... G 203 834-1962
Wilton (G-10322)
Protopac Inc .... G 860 274-6796
Watertown (G-9727)
Pyne-Davidson Company .... E 860 522-9106
Hartford (G-3670)
Qg Printing II Corp .... A 860 741-0150
Enfield (G-2685)
Quad/Graphics Inc .... A 203 288-2468
North Haven (G-5985)
Quality Printers Inc .... G 860 443-2800
New London (G-5484)
Quick Print .... G 860 425-5580
Colchester (G-1570)
R R Donnelley & Sons Company .... F 860 649-5570
Manchester (G-4078)
Rare Reminder Incorporated .... E 860 563-9386
Rocky Hill (G-7264)
Record-Journal Newspaper .... C 203 235-1661
Meriden (G-4230)
River Dog Prints LLC .... G 860 276-1578
Avon (G-105)
Rm Printing .... G 860 621-0498
Plantsville (G-6909)
Rmi Inc .... C 860 875-3366
Vernon Rockville (G-9177)
Rollins Printing Incorporated .... G 203 248-3200
Hamden (G-3506)
Romark Printing Service .... G 860 691-0626
East Lyme (G-2474)
Ronald Bottino .... G 860 585-9505
Bristol (G-1111)
Ross Copy & Print LLC .... G 203 933-8732
West Haven (G-9950)
Sazacks Inc .... G 860 647-8367
Manchester (G-4086)
Sister Act Printing .... G 203 481-7171
North Branford (G-5856)
Southbury Printing Centre Inc .... G 203 264-0102
Southbury (G-7878)
Speed Printing & Graphics Inc .... G 203 324-4000
Stamford (G-8433)
Speedy Printing LLC .... G 860 445-8252
Mystic (G-4846)
Streamline Press .... G 203 484-9799
North Branford (G-5859)

Streamline Press LLC .... G 203 484-9799
North Branford (G-5860)
Success Printing & Mailing Inc .... F 203 847-1112
Norwalk (G-6359)
System Intgrtion Cnsulting LLC .... G 203 926-9599
Shelton (G-7562)
Tech-Repro Inc .... F 203 348-8884
Stamford (G-8460)
Technical Reproductions Inc .... F 203 849-9100
Norwalk (G-6365)
Technique Printers Inc .... G 860 669-2516
Clinton (G-1529)
Tektronix Graphics Printing .... G 203 359-8003
Stamford (G-8463)
Trend Offset Printing Svcs Inc .... G 860 773-6140
Avon (G-117)
Trumbull Printing Inc .... C 203 261-2548
Trumbull (G-9082)
Valley Press New Area Prtg Co .... G 860 526-5696
Deep River (G-2105)
Value Print Incorporated .... F 203 265-1371
Wallingford (G-9399)
Wethersfield Offset Inc .... G 860 721-8236
Rocky Hill (G-7273)
Wethersfield Printing Co Inc .... F 860 721-8236
Rocky Hill (G-7274)
Williams Printing Group LLC .... G 860 423-8779
North Windham (G-6041)
Woodway Print Inc .... G 203 323-6423
Stamford (G-8500)
Youngs Communications Inc .... F 860 347-8567
Middletown (G-4434)

PRINTING: Photo-Offset

Cag Imaging LLC .... G 860 887-0836
Norwich (G-6408)
Hamden Press Inc .... G 203 624-0554
Hamden (G-3458)

PRINTING: Screen, Broadwoven Fabrics, Cotton

Bushy Hill Nature Center .... G 860 767-2148
Ivoryton (G-3784)
To Give Is Better .... G 860 261-5443
Bristol (G-1129)
Ultimate Ink LLC .... G 203 762-0602
Wilton (G-10339)

PRINTING: Screen, Fabric

3rd Half Productions .... G 860 828-6929
Kensington (G-3802)
Connecticut Screen Print .... G 203 877-6655
Milford (G-4498)
Fat City Screen Printers .... G 860 354-4650
New Milford (G-5533)
Images Unlimited .... G 860 350-6608
New Milford (G-5545)
J & D Embroidering Co .... G 860 822-9777
Baltic (G-120)
Michael Violano .... G 203 934-3368
West Haven (G-9937)
Pro Form Printed Bus Solutions .... G 203 266-5302
Bethlehem (G-376)
Screen Designs .... G 203 797-9806
Bethel (G-340)
Seems Inc .... F 203 284-0259
Ansonia (G-50)
Tshirts Etc Inc .... G 860 657-3551
Glastonbury (G-3090)
Zuse Inc .... F 203 458-3295
Guilford (G-3402)

PRINTING: Screen, Manmade Fiber & Silk, Broadwoven Fabric

Lmj Designs Inc .... G 845 363-1120
Norwalk (G-6235)
Tees & More LLC .... G 860 244-2224
Hartford (G-3700)

PRINTING: Thermography

CT Thermography LLC .... G 860 415-1150
Farmington (G-2894)
CT Thermography LLC .... G 860 690-9202
Newington (G-5644)
E & A Enterprises Inc .... E 203 250-8050
Wallingford (G-9255)

Employee Codes: A=Over 500 employees, B=251-500
C=101-250, D=51-100, E=20-50, F=10-19, G=1-9
2020 Harris Connecticut
Manufacturers Directory
733

PRINTING: Thermography

Pinpoint Thermography LLC ....G....... 203 546-8906
New Fairfield *(G-5174)*
Practical Automation Inc ....D....... 203 882-5640
Milford *(G-4611)*
Therma-Scan Inc ....G....... 860 872-9770
Vernon Rockville *(G-9181)*

PROFESSIONAL EQPT & SPLYS, WHOLESALE: Engineers', NEC

John L Prentis & Co Inc ....G....... 203 634-1266
Meriden *(G-4178)*
Joseph Merritt & Company Inc ....G....... 203 743-6734
Danbury *(G-1863)*
Technical Reproductions Inc ....F....... 203 849-9100
Norwalk *(G-6365)*

PROFESSIONAL EQPT & SPLYS, WHOLESALE: Optical Goods

Coburn Technologies Intl Inc ....G....... 860 648-6600
South Windsor *(G-7732)*
Coburn Tecnologies Canada ....D....... 860 648-6710
South Windsor *(G-7733)*
Electro-Lite Corporation ....F....... 203 743-4059
Bethel *(G-295)*
Globenix Inc ....G....... 203 740-7070
Norwalk *(G-6181)*
Hoya Corporation ....B....... 860 289-5379
South Windsor *(G-7773)*
Sign In Soft Inc ....G....... 203 216-3046
Shelton *(G-7555)*

PROFESSIONAL EQPT & SPLYS, WHOLESALE: Scientific & Engineerg

Tower Optical Company Inc ....G....... 203 866-4535
Norwalk *(G-6376)*

PROFESSIONAL INSTRUMENT REPAIR SVCS

Jakes Repair LLC ....G....... 203 627-8603
Old Saybrook *(G-6547)*

PROFILE SHAPES: Unsupported Plastics

Web Industries Hartford Inc ....E....... 860 779-3197
Dayville *(G-2078)*

PROMOTION SVCS

Wolfe Promotional Services LLC ....G....... 203 452-7692
Monroe *(G-4766)*
Wrenfield Group Inc ....E....... 203 438-0090
Ridgefield *(G-7186)*

PROPELLERS: Boat & Ship, Cast

Propeller LLC ....G....... 203 831-0877
Norwalk *(G-6309)*

PROPULSION UNITS: Guided Missiles & Space Vehicles

Atk Golf Services ....G....... 203 615-2099
Trumbull *(G-9000)*

PROTECTION EQPT: Lightning

East Coast Lightning Eqp Inc ....E....... 860 379-9072
Winsted *(G-10518)*
Northast Lghtning Prtction LLC ....F....... 860 243-0010
Bloomfield *(G-451)*
Woods Lightning Protection ....G....... 203 929-1868
Shelton *(G-7588)*

PUBLIC LIBRARY

Godfrey Memorial Library ....G....... 860 346-4375
Middletown *(G-4347)*

PUBLIC RELATIONS SVCS

Two Ems Inc ....G....... 203 245-8211
Madison *(G-3965)*

PUBLISHERS: Art Copy

Historical Art Prints ....G....... 203 262-6680
Southbury *(G-7858)*

PUBLISHERS: Art Copy & Poster

American Art Heritage Pubg ....G....... 203 973-0564
Stamford *(G-8073)*

PUBLISHERS: Book

African Link ....G....... 203 925-1632
Shelton *(G-7389)*
Andree Brooks ....G....... 203 226-9834
Westport *(G-10057)*
Bay Tact Corporation ....E....... 860 315-7372
Woodstock Valley *(G-10691)*
Belvoir Publications Inc ....G....... 203 857-3100
Norwalk *(G-6090)*
Bff Holdings Inc ....C....... 860 510-0100
Old Saybrook *(G-6523)*
Biennix Corp ....G....... 203 254-1727
Fairfield *(G-2755)*
Birdtrack Press ....G....... 203 389-7789
New Haven *(G-5248)*
Blauner Books ....G....... 203 222-6042
Greenwich *(G-3134)*
Carala Ventures Ltd ....E....... 800 483-6449
Stratford *(G-8592)*
Career Concepts ....G....... 203 378-9943
Stratford *(G-8594)*
Charles Alain Publishing Ltd ....G....... 203 226-2882
Westport *(G-10063)*
Clever Clover LLC ....G....... 860 501-2800
Pawcatuck *(G-6706)*
Connectcut Acdemy Arts Scences ....G....... 203 432-3113
New Haven *(G-5259)*
Connecticut Bass Guide ....G....... 860 827-0787
New Britain *(G-4962)*
Connecticut Law Book Co Inc ....F....... 203 458-8000
Guilford *(G-3340)*
Connecticut Parent Magazine ....F....... 203 483-1700
Branford *(G-576)*
Creative Media Applications ....F....... 203 226-0544
Weston *(G-10023)*
Early Advantage LLC ....F....... 203 259-6480
Fairfield *(G-2778)*
Editorial Directions Inc ....G....... 203 245-2011
Madison *(G-3919)*
Erinco Marketing ....G....... 203 545-4550
Danbury *(G-1816)*
Eye Ear It LLC ....F....... 203 487-8949
Woodbury *(G-10636)*
Five Ponds Press Books Inc ....G....... 877 833-0603
Windsor *(G-10386)*
Forecast International Inc ....D....... 203 426-0800
Newtown *(G-5739)*
Fredercks Jnne Literarary Agcy ....G....... 203 972-3011
New Canaan *(G-5105)*
Gamut Publishing ....E....... 860 296-6128
Hartford *(G-3598)*
Glacier Publishing ....G....... 860 621-7644
Southington *(G-7928)*
Godfrey Memorial Library ....G....... 860 346-4375
Middletown *(G-4347)*
Graduate Group ....G....... 860 233-2330
West Hartford *(G-9813)*
Greenwich Workshop Inc ....E....... 203 881-3336
Seymour *(G-7348)*
Information Today Inc ....F....... 203 761-1466
Wilton *(G-10302)*
Inside Track ....G....... 203 431-4540
Ridgefield *(G-7147)*
Island Nation Press LLC ....G....... 203 852-0028
Norwalk *(G-6211)*
Kieffer Associates Inc ....G....... 203 323-3437
Stamford *(G-8275)*
Konecky & Konecky LLC ....G....... 860 388-0878
Old Saybrook *(G-6551)*
Lindsay Graphics ....G....... 860 355-8744
Sherman *(G-7597)*
Little Blue Book ....G....... 860 409-7000
Avon *(G-90)*
Little Blue Insite LLC ....G....... 203 202-7690
Darien *(G-2032)*
Mobius Press ....G....... 860 767-0880
Essex *(G-2726)*
Octavo Editions LLC ....G....... 860 388-5772
Old Saybrook *(G-6562)*
Omicronworld Entertainment LLC ....G....... 203 453-5700
Guilford *(G-3381)*
Orchard Press ....G....... 860 672-4273
Cornwall Bridge *(G-1618)*
Paul D Wolff ....G....... 203 319-7242
Easton *(G-2560)*
Peter James Associates Inc ....G....... 203 972-1070
New Canaan *(G-5130)*
Ppc Books Ltd ....G....... 203 226-6644
Westport *(G-10142)*
S Karger Publishers Inc ....G....... 860 675-7834
Unionville *(G-9126)*
Sasc LLC ....G....... 203 846-2274
Greenwich *(G-3231)*
Scholastic Inc ....G....... 212 343-6100
Danbury *(G-1938)*
Scholastic Library Pubg Inc ....F....... 573 632-1762
Danbury *(G-1940)*
Scripture Research & Pubg Co ....G....... 203 272-1780
Cheshire *(G-1443)*
Society For Exprmntal McHanics ....G....... 203 790-6373
Bethel *(G-343)*
Society Plastics Engineers Inc ....E....... 203 740-5422
Bethel *(G-344)*
Stamler Publishing Company ....G....... 203 488-9808
Branford *(G-655)*
Stoneslide Media LLC ....G....... 203 464-3471
Guilford *(G-3395)*
Summer Camp Stories LLC ....G....... 203 705-1600
Stamford *(G-8449)*
Summer Street Press LLC ....F....... 203 978-0098
Stamford *(G-8450)*
Toni Leland ....G....... 860 892-8890
Uncasville *(G-9106)*
Ubm LLC ....G....... 203 662-6501
Darien *(G-2048)*
Weddles LLC ....G....... 203 964-1888
Stamford *(G-8489)*
Wesleyan University ....G....... 860 685-2980
Middletown *(G-4430)*
Wild Leaf Press Inc ....G....... 203 415-5309
Bethany *(G-252)*
Windcheck LLC ....G....... 203 332-7639
Bridgeport *(G-938)*
Writers Press LLC ....G....... 860 242-9271
Bloomfield *(G-502)*
Writestuff Creative Services L ....G....... 860 343-1919
Middletown *(G-4433)*
Yale University ....E....... 203 432-2550
New Haven *(G-5443)*
Yale University ....D....... 203 764-4333
New Haven *(G-5444)*
Zp Couture LLC ....G....... 888 697-7239
North Haven *(G-6017)*

PUBLISHERS: Book Clubs, No Printing

EPic Publishing Services LLC ....G....... 860 204-7450
East Haddam *(G-2241)*

PUBLISHERS: Books, No Printing

A Guideposts Church Corp ....B....... 203 749-0203
Danbury *(G-1726)*
AJK Publishing ....G....... 203 259-8026
Fairfield *(G-2746)*
Artchrist Com Inc ....G....... 203 245-2246
Madison *(G-3907)*
Begell House Inc ....F....... 203 456-6161
Danbury *(G-1751)*
Bick Publishing House ....G....... 203 208-5253
Branford *(G-559)*
Bosphorus Books ....G....... 860 536-2540
Groton *(G-3272)*
Bunting & Lyon Inc ....G....... 203 272-4623
Cheshire *(G-1365)*
Burns Walton ....G....... 203 422-5222
Branford *(G-566)*
Charles McDougal ....G....... 860 739-9952
Niantic *(G-5803)*
Chicory Blue Press Inc ....G....... 860 491-2271
Goshen *(G-3096)*
Clear & Simple Inc ....G....... 860 658-1204
West Simsbury *(G-9974)*
Commandtech LLC ....G....... 860 857-8502
Groton *(G-3278)*
Cortina Learning Intl Inc ....F....... 800 245-2145
Wilton *(G-10283)*
Crown House Publishing Co LLC ....G....... 203 778-1300
Bethel *(G-274)*
Graphics Press LLC ....G....... 203 272-9187
Cheshire *(G-1394)*
Green Editorial ....G....... 860 364-5100
Sharon *(G-7379)*
Grolier Overseas Incorporated ....G....... 203 797-3500
Danbury *(G-1838)*
Industrial Press Inc ....F....... 212 889-6330
Norwalk *(G-6206)*

Kendall Svengalis	G	860 535-0362	Guilford *(G-3365)*
Life Study Fllwship Foundation	E	203 655-1436	Darien *(G-2031)*
McBooks Press Inc	G	607 272-2114	Guilford *(G-3372)*
Midnight Reader	G	860 643-4220	Bolton *(G-516)*
Millbrook Press Inc	E	203 740-2220	Brookfield *(G-1206)*
New England Publishing Assoc	G	860 345-7323	Higganum *(G-3771)*
Next Door Creations LLC	G	860 933-0366	Glastonbury *(G-3064)*
Peninsula Publishing	G	203 292-5621	Westport *(G-10138)*
R G L Inc	E	860 653-7254	East Granby *(G-2226)*
Rothstein Associates Inc	G	203 740-7400	Brookfield *(G-1219)*
Sanguinaria Publishing Inc	G	203 576-9168	Bridgeport *(G-894)*
Scholastic Library Pubg Inc	A	203 797-3500	Danbury *(G-1939)*
Sourcebooks Inc	G	203 876-9790	Milford *(G-4648)*
Symphonycs LLC	G	860 884-2308	Lisbon *(G-3883)*
Tantor Media Incorporated	C	860 395-1155	Old Saybrook *(G-6572)*
Taunton Inc	A	203 426-8171	Newtown *(G-5785)*
Taunton Interactive Inc	G	203 426-8171	Newtown *(G-5786)*
Vital Health Publishing Inc	G	203 438-3229	Ridgefield *(G-7180)*
Vocalis Limited	G	203 753-5244	Waterbury *(G-9623)*
Windhover Information Inc	E	203 838-4401	Norwalk *(G-6396)*
Wood Pond Press	G	860 521-0389	West Hartford *(G-9877)*
Ziga Media LLC	G	203 656-0076	Darien *(G-2052)*

PUBLISHERS: Comic Books, No Printing

Comicana Inc	G	203 968-0748	Stamford *(G-8153)*

PUBLISHERS: Directories, NEC

Campus Yellow Pages LLC	G	860 523-9909	West Hartford *(G-9783)*
Relocation Information Svc Inc	E	203 855-1234	Norwalk *(G-6319)*

PUBLISHERS: Guides

Shoppers-Turnpike Corporation	F	860 928-3040	Putnam *(G-7065)*
Stamford Capital Group Inc	A	800 977-7837	Stamford *(G-8436)*

PUBLISHERS: Magazines, No Printing

A Guideposts Church Corp	B	203 749-0203	Danbury *(G-1726)*
Accent Magazine	G	203 853-6015	Norwalk *(G-6061)*
Active Interest Media Inc	G	860 767-3200	Essex *(G-2710)*
Air Age Inc	E	203 431-9000	Wilton *(G-10267)*
American Library Association	E	860 347-6933	Middletown *(G-4315)*
Belvoir Media Group LLC	G	203 857-3128	Norwalk *(G-6089)*
Beverage Publications Inc	G	203 288-3375	Hamden *(G-3418)*
Bottom Line Inc	D	203 973-5900	Stamford *(G-8115)*
Charting Economy	G	860 667-9909	Newington *(G-5640)*
Chief Executive Group LLC	F	785 832-0303	Stamford *(G-8143)*
Chief Executive Group LP	E	203 930-2700	Stamford *(G-8144)*
Circuit Cellar Inc	F	860 289-0800	East Hartford *(G-2305)*
Corporate Connecticut Mag LLC	G	860 257-0500	Wethersfield *(G-10189)*
Domino Media Group Inc	E	877 223-7844	Westport *(G-10074)*
Donnin Publishing Inc	G	203 453-8866	Guilford *(G-3347)*
Douglas Moss	G	203 854-5559	Norwalk *(G-6149)*
Evangelical Christian Center	G	860 429-0856	Ashford *(G-62)*
Fairfield County Look	G	203 869-0077	Greenwich *(G-3158)*
Fed Russell LLC	G	203 934-2501	West Haven *(G-9908)*
Granta USA Ltd	F	440 207-6051	Danbury *(G-1837)*
Informa Media Inc	G	203 885-1045	Danbury *(G-1850)*
Information Today Inc	F	203 761-1466	Wilton *(G-10302)*
Interstate Tax Corporation	G	203 854-0704	Norwalk *(G-6210)*
Joseph Malavenda	G	203 746-4160	New Fairfield *(G-5170)*
L M T Communications Inc	F	203 426-4568	Newtown *(G-5752)*
Lighthouse Maps	G	203 981-1090	Brookfield *(G-1203)*
Mason Medical Communications	G	203 227-9252	Westport *(G-10118)*
Moffly Publications Inc	F	203 222-0600	Westport *(G-10123)*
Moffly Publications Inc	E	203 222-0600	Westport *(G-10124)*
Morthanoscom LLC	G	203 378-2414	Stratford *(G-8651)*
Naffa Inc	G	203 562-3159	New Haven *(G-5339)*
National Shooting Sports Found	E	203 426-1320	Newtown *(G-5762)*
Penny Marketing Ltd Partnr	E	203 866-6688	Norwalk *(G-6295)*
Penny Press Inc	C	203 866-6688	Norwalk *(G-6296)*
Penny Press Inc	E	203 866-6688	Milford *(G-4605)*
Relocation Information Svc Inc	E	203 855-1234	Norwalk *(G-6319)*
Scholastic Library Pubg Inc	A	203 797-3500	Danbury *(G-1939)*
Seasons Media LLC	G	860 413-2022	West Simsbury *(G-9982)*
Sixfurlongs LLC	G	203 255-8553	Fairfield *(G-2848)*
Soundings Publications LLC	E	860 767-8227	Essex *(G-2735)*
Strategic Insights Inc	G	203 595-3200	Stamford *(G-8446)*
Sumner Communications Inc	E	203 748-2050	Bethel *(G-349)*
Tam Communications Inc	E	203 425-8777	Norwalk *(G-6362)*
Taunton Inc	A	203 426-8171	Newtown *(G-5785)*
Taunton Press Inc	B	203 426-8171	Newtown *(G-5787)*
Tauton Press	G	203 304-3000	Newtown *(G-5788)*
This Old House Ventures LLC	E	475 209-8665	Stamford *(G-8465)*
Timer Digest Publishing Inc	G	203 629-2589	Greenwich *(G-3245)*
Toastmasters International	F	203 847-5667	Norwalk *(G-6372)*
Venu Magazine LLC	G	203 259-2075	Fairfield *(G-2863)*
Wicks Business Information LLC	F	203 334-2002	Shelton *(G-7586)*
Windhover Information Inc	E	203 838-4401	Norwalk *(G-6396)*
Wire Association Intl Inc	E	203 453-2777	Madison *(G-3968)*
Wire Journal Inc	E	203 453-2777	Madison *(G-3969)*
World Wrestling Entrmt Inc	C	203 352-8600	Stamford *(G-8502)*
Yale Alumni Publications Inc	G	203 432-0645	New Haven *(G-5439)*

PUBLISHERS: Maps

Floating World Editions	G	860 868-0890	Warren *(G-9408)*

PUBLISHERS: Miscellaneous

12 Paws Publishing LLC	G	203 232-4534	Seymour *(G-7334)*
3 Ethos LLC	G	860 415-9191	Mystic *(G-4794)*
Accession Media	G	203 702-4951	Brookfield *(G-1156)*
Action Media Inc	G	203 466-5535	East Haven *(G-2407)*
Afroasia Publication LLC	G	917 692-3937	Stamford *(G-8063)*
Alexander Street Press	G	203 389-6881	New Haven *(G-5220)*
Algonquian Free Press LLC	G	860 572-4811	Groton *(G-3270)*
Altare Publishing Inc	G	860 490-6144	Avon *(G-75)*
American Trade Fairs Org	G	203 221-0114	Westport *(G-10055)*
Antrim House	G	860 217-0023	Simsbury *(G-7611)*
Apple Publications	G	860 392-8348	Tolland *(G-8849)*
Arcat Inc	G	203 929-9444	Fairfield *(G-2747)*
Arp Publishing Inc	G	888 503-6617	Middletown *(G-4318)*
Ashkaar Publishers LLC	G	203 248-4804	North Haven *(G-5910)*
Audubon Copy Shppe of Firfield	G	203 259-4311	Bridgeport *(G-705)*
Bay Tact Corporation	E	860 315-7372	Woodstock Valley *(G-10691)*
Beardsley Publishing Corp	G	203 263-0888	Woodbury *(G-10626)*
Beautiful Publications	G	347 508-2798	Stratford *(G-8581)*
Belle Impression Pubg Inc	G	203 826-5426	Danbury *(G-1755)*
Belvoir Publications	G	203 422-7300	Greenwich *(G-3132)*
Bench Press 3 LLC	G	203 848-5545	Fairfield *(G-2753)*
Bff Holdings Inc	C	860 510-0100	Old Saybrook *(G-6523)*
Biographical Publishing Co	G	203 758-3661	Prospect *(G-6995)*
Black Crow Press LLC	G	203 281-1034	Hamden *(G-3419)*
Bm Publishing LLC	G	860 778-1583	Bristol *(G-984)*
BMHs Press Box	G	203 810-4380	Norwalk *(G-6095)*
BNE Publishing Inc	G	860 498-0032	Coventry *(G-1646)*
Brandon Nicholas Eza Pubg	G	860 498-0032	Coventry *(G-1648)*
Btac Publications	G	203 560-7742	Southbury *(G-7846)*
Burns Walton	G	203 422-5222	Branford *(G-566)*
Business Marketing & Pubg Inc	G	203 834-9959	Wilton *(G-10279)*
Butterfly Press LLC	G	860 621-2883	Southington *(G-7899)*
Butterfly Wings Pubg Co LLC	G	203 642-4481	Norwalk *(G-6103)*
Bvc Publishing	G	860 202-0704	Bristol *(G-995)*
Bwd Publishing LLC	G	860 651-1966	West Simsbury *(G-9973)*
C Q Publishing	G	860 292-1566	Windsor Locks *(G-10476)*
Calhoun Press Inc	G	860 202-0998	Lebanon *(G-3849)*
Campbell Publicity LLC	G	646 532-1512	Middlebury *(G-4274)*
Captive Global LLC	G	860 302-6706	Southington *(G-7903)*
Cara C Andreoli	G	860 888-6553	Glastonbury *(G-3019)*
Caribe House Press LLC	G	812 320-5303	Guilford *(G-3337)*
Carlos Lee Publishing	G	860 536-8450	Mystic *(G-4806)*
Cat Tales Press Inc	G	203 268-3505	Easton *(G-2548)*
Cema Publishing LLC	G	585 317-3724	Stamford *(G-8137)*

Employee Codes: A=Over 500 employees, B=251-500
C=101-250, D=51-100, E=20-50, F=10-19, G=1-9

2020 Harris Connecticut
Manufacturers Directory

735

Charmed Press LLC G 203 877-3777
Milford *(G-4489)*

Chiara Publications G 203 797-1905
Bethel *(G-270)*

Chicken Soup For Soul LLC E 203 861-4000
Cos Cob *(G-1626)*

Chicken Soup For Soul Entrmt I G 855 398-0443
Cos Cob *(G-1627)*

Chicken Soup For Soul Pubg LLC G 203 861-4000
Cos Cob *(G-1628)*

Chicken Soup For The Soul G 855 398-0443
Cos Cob *(G-1629)*

Childrens Health Market Inc G 203 762-2938
Wilton *(G-10280)*

Christian Science Committee On G 203 866-1200
Norwalk *(G-6113)*

Cimarron Music Press G 860 536-2185
Ledyard *(G-3870)*

Cimarron Music Press LLC G 860 859-3705
New London *(G-5462)*

Cisse Publications LLC G 203 685-4189
Shelton *(G-7420)*

Complimentary Healing G 203 622-1697
Cos Cob *(G-1630)*

Computer Xpress LLC G 203 469-6107
East Haven *(G-2419)*

Connecticut Digital Post Inc G 203 268-4554
Monroe *(G-4704)*

Connecticut Press G 203 257-6020
Cheshire *(G-1372)*

Connelly 3 Pubg Group Inc G 860 664-4988
Clinton *(G-1497)*

Corporate Express CT G 203 455-2500
Stratford *(G-8599)*

Cotton Press LLC G 203 257-7958
Wilton *(G-10284)*

Coupon Magazine Publishers Inc G 561 676-6498
Danbury *(G-1777)*

Cygnal Publishing Co G 860 983-4757
Mystic *(G-4810)*

Db Press LLC G 203 699-9510
Cheshire *(G-1381)*

Debrasong Publishing LLC G 413 204-4682
Lyme *(G-3904)*

Directory Assistants Inc E 860 633-0122
Wethersfield *(G-10190)*

Dlpublshers Mystryntrtnmentllc G 203 556-4893
Bridgeport *(G-755)*

Dmb Publishing LLC G 203 798-9231
Bethel *(G-281)*

Dogwood Publishing LLC G 203 292-3815
Fairfield *(G-2775)*

Dollar Express LLC G 203 495-9209
New Haven *(G-5268)*

Down Home Publishing G 860 521-6177
Newington *(G-5648)*

Duneland Press G 860 535-0362
Guilford *(G-3348)*

Dunnottar Publishing LLC G 203 488-0350
Branford *(G-581)*

Ecua Express G 860 344-1144
Middletown *(G-4340)*

Educational Reference Publishi G 203 797-1517
Danbury *(G-1804)*

Edwin Publishing Company G 203 228-9396
Waterbury *(G-9471)*

Ef Lee Publishing LLC G 203 546-7148
Brookfield *(G-1187)*

Ek Publishing LLC G 203 246-9683
Westport *(G-10077)*

Erielle Media LLC G 203 563-9159
Wilton *(G-10293)*

Essex Publishing Co G 314 627-0300
Branford *(G-590)*

Evertide Games Inc G 203 701-9145
New Canaan *(G-5104)*

Executive Greetings Inc B 860 379-9911
New Hartford *(G-5190)*

Experience Publishing Inc G 203 637-2324
Riverside *(G-7195)*

Exponent Publishing Co G 203 264-1130
Southbury *(G-7852)*

Express Lab Service G 860 571-0355
Hartford *(G-3586)*

Express Lane Foods G 860 889-2266
North Franklin *(G-5873)*

Fayerweather Press LLC G 203 367-1601
Bridgeport *(G-768)*

Felk Publishing LLC G 203 421-3714
Madison *(G-3920)*

Flat Hammock Press G 860 572-2722
Mystic *(G-4816)*

Floral Greens G 860 995-8772
Bloomfield *(G-412)*

Flying Aces Press LLC G 203 791-1172
Danbury *(G-1827)*

For Children With Love Public G 860 940-9878
Farmington *(G-2907)*

Frank Alexander Weems Pubg LLC G 203 898-4654
Stamford *(G-8207)*

Freedom Press G 860 599-5390
Pawcatuck *(G-6711)*

Frog Prints Publishing LLC G 610 425-0090
Shelton *(G-7447)*

Galassia Press LLC G 203 846-9075
Norwalk *(G-6174)*

Gale Thomson G 203 397-2600
Woodbridge *(G-10600)*

Gallagher Katie Publishers Rep G 203 221-7140
Westport *(G-10087)*

Gcooper Legacy Publishing LLC G 203 357-1483
Stamford *(G-8212)*

Get Go It Publishing G 203 772-9877
New Haven *(G-5286)*

Gettysburg Publishing LLC G 203 268-7111
Trumbull *(G-9029)*

Girl Cop Publishing LLC G 860 529-3424
Wethersfield *(G-10193)*

Global American Publishers LLC G 860 432-7589
Manchester *(G-4022)*

Global Publications & Mktg LLC G 860 676-9109
Farmington *(G-2913)*

Glorian Publishing Inc G 844 945-6742
Clinton *(G-1505)*

Gmq Publishing G 203 558-6142
Beacon Falls *(G-134)*

Goldpoint Publishing LLC G 860 432-8934
South Windsor *(G-7762)*

Grand Publications LLC G 203 288-5721
Hamden *(G-3453)*

Great American Publishing Soc G 203 531-9300
Greenwich *(G-3171)*

Greenwich Free Press LLC G 203 622-1731
Greenwich *(G-3174)*

Grey House Publishing Inc G 860 364-1444
Sharon *(G-7380)*

Greycourt Publishing LLC G 203 894-1535
Ridgefield *(G-7144)*

Halurgite Publishing LLC G 860 563-0372
Wethersfield *(G-10195)*

Harvard Business School Pubg G 203 318-1234
New Haven *(G-5294)*

Hawkline Press G 203 248-4615
Hamden *(G-3461)*

Hawks Nest Publishing LLC G 860 536-5868
Madison *(G-3926)*

HB Publishing & Marketing G 203 852-9200
Norwalk *(G-6196)*

HB Publishing & Marketing Co G 203 852-1324
Norwalk *(G-6197)*

Healing Arts Press LLC G 203 374-2084
Fairfield *(G-2793)*

Hearst Corporation E 203 438-6544
New Canaan *(G-5109)*

Heartland Publications LLC G 860 388-3470
Old Saybrook *(G-6539)*

Helen Grace G 203 661-1927
Cos Cob *(G-1633)*

Hersam Publishing Company B 203 966-9541
New Canaan *(G-5110)*

Hew Publishing LLC G 860 514-2045
Cromwell *(G-1704)*

Higher Consciousness LLC G 310 977-7541
Avon *(G-84)*

Hill House Press LLC G 203 405-1158
Southbury *(G-7857)*

Hilltop Publishing LLC G 203 426-8834
Newtown *(G-5743)*

Hiram Rock Publishing LLC G 203 453-0440
Guilford *(G-3360)*

HMS Publications Inc G 860 739-3187
Niantic *(G-5810)*

Hollow Frost Publishers G 860 974-2081
Woodstock *(G-10667)*

Hotchkiss Publishing G 203 430-6289
Branford *(G-606)*

Industrial Press G 203 838-4080
Norwalk *(G-6205)*

Ink LLC G 860 581-0026
East Haddam *(G-2243)*

Ink Publishing LLC G 860 581-0026
Old Saybrook *(G-6542)*

Intangible Matter LLC G 203 219-9619
Stamford *(G-8252)*

Iona Press G 860 841-5006
West Hartford *(G-9822)*

J C Publishing LLC G 860 525-7226
Hartford *(G-3619)*

Jacoby G 203 227-2220
Weston *(G-10030)*

Jim Press Home Improvement G 860 416-4494
Manchester *(G-4039)*

JRC Publishing LLC G 203 942-2726
Ridgefield *(G-7152)*

Jsan Publishing LLC G 203 210-5495
Wilton *(G-10306)*

Juice Publishing LLC G 203 226-5715
Westport *(G-10106)*

Kathleen Parker OBeirne G 860 536-7179
Mystic *(G-4824)*

Kathy Pooler G 860 889-2893
Norwich *(G-6420)*

Kc Publishing G 203 318-8544
Madison *(G-3933)*

Keeper Press LLC G 860 810-9626
Glastonbury *(G-3054)*

Keiterbennett Publishers LLC G 860 308-2666
East Hartford *(G-2342)*

Kiera Publishing Inc G 203 838-5485
Norwalk *(G-6229)*

Kimberly Bon Publishing LLC G 203 258-9829
Trumbull *(G-9039)*

Kingsnake Publishing LLC G 860 865-0307
Groton *(G-3292)*

Kiwi Publishing Inc G 203 389-6220
Woodbridge *(G-10604)*

Labrador Press LLC G 860 887-0567
Bozrah *(G-526)*

Labrador Publishing LLC G 860 552-2564
Clinton *(G-1512)*

Langner Press LLC G 203 226-7752
Weston *(G-10032)*

Lasting Legacy Publishers LLC G 860 917-3545
Ledyard *(G-3876)*

Lda Publishers G 203 438-1484
Westport *(G-10111)*

Learners Dimension G 860 228-1236
Columbia *(G-1607)*

Lefora Publishing LLC G 860 845-8445
Bristol *(G-1063)*

Life Study Fllwship Foundation E 203 655-1436
Darien *(G-2031)*

Lindqist Historical Guides Inc G 203 335-8568
Bridgeport *(G-825)*

Little King Press G 203 981-2324
Fairfield *(G-2811)*

Liturgical Publications Inc F 203 966-6470
New Canaan *(G-5115)*

Lowencorp Publishing LLC G 203 966-3474
New Canaan *(G-5116)*

Lucky Duck Press G 347 703-3984
Winsted *(G-10527)*

Malachite Publishing LLC G 860 495-5484
Pawcatuck *(G-6720)*

Mandel Vilar Press G 806 790-4731
Simsbury *(G-7633)*

Manuscritos Publishing LLC G 860 432-9519
Manchester *(G-4055)*

Mary Carroll G 860 543-0750
Andover *(G-13)*

Maryjanesfarm Publishing Group G 203 857-4880
Norwalk *(G-6249)*

Mason Press Inc G 860 625-3707
Waterford *(G-9662)*

Masters Publishing G 860 295-8454
Marlborough *(G-4126)*

Mathword Press LLC G 203 288-8114
Hamden *(G-3479)*

Mc Mahon Publishing Co G 203 544-8389
Redding *(G-7100)*

Medhumor Med Publications LLC G 203 550-9041
Stamford *(G-8302)*

Media Ventures Inc E 203 852-6570
Norwalk *(G-6253)*

Metro Neighbors Publishing LLC G 203 494-3600
Madison *(G-3940)*

MI Gente Express G 860 447-2525
New London *(G-5478)*

Militarylife Publishing LLC G 203 402-7234
Shelton *(G-7501)*

Millerwalk Publishing LLC ......G 203 397-8926
New Haven *(G-5332)*
Minuteman Press ......G 203 261-8318
Trumbull *(G-9049)*
Misfit Publishing Co LLC ......G 860 444-6796
Quaker Hill *(G-7083)*
Mlj Publishing Record Co LLC ......G 203 752-9021
New Haven *(G-5334)*
Mme Publishing LLC ......G 860 228-1369
Columbia *(G-1608)*
More Than Asleep Pubg LLC ......G 860 872-5757
Vernon *(G-9145)*
Moriartys Desktop Publishing ......G 860 345-8063
Higganum *(G-3769)*
Move Books LLC ......G 203 709-0490
Beacon Falls *(G-144)*
Municipal Stadium ......G 203 755-4019
Waterbury *(G-9548)*
Music Together Fairfield Child ......G 203 256-1656
Fairfield *(G-2821)*
Musica Russica Inc ......G 203 458-3225
Guilford *(G-3378)*
MWK Publishing LLC ......G 860 675-6067
Hartford *(G-3647)*
Nancy Larson Publishers Inc ......E 860 434-0800
Old Lyme *(G-6515)*
Nancy Larson Publishers Hq ......G 860 598-9783
Old Lyme *(G-6516)*
National Shooting Sports Found ......E 203 426-1320
Newtown *(G-5762)*
Nelson & Miller Associates ......G 203 356-9694
Stamford *(G-8319)*
Nelson Publishing ......G 860 404-5292
Burlington *(G-1275)*
New Amrcan Political Press Inc ......G 860 747-2037
New Haven *(G-5341)*
New England Press Parts LLC ......G 203 623-7533
Cheshire *(G-1421)*
Newsbank Inc ......G 203 966-1100
New Canaan *(G-5125)*
Next Level Publishing LLC ......G 860 282-2428
East Hartford *(G-2347)*
Ninety-Nine Cent Pubg LLC ......G 203 922-9917
Shelton *(G-7512)*
Noroton Publishing Co ......G 203 655-1436
Darien *(G-2034)*
North Shore Publishing LLC ......G 860 561-8768
West Hartford *(G-9838)*
Northast Tnnis Pblications LLC ......G 203 984-1088
Weston *(G-10034)*
Northeast Publications LLC ......G 860 399-4801
Old Saybrook *(G-6560)*
Northern Wolf Press LLC ......G 860 227-0135
Middletown *(G-4387)*
Novanglus Publishing LLC ......G 203 885-7476
Greenwich *(G-3211)*
Office Insight ......G 203 966-5008
New Canaan *(G-5127)*
Open Science Publishing LLC ......G 860 568-4675
East Hartford *(G-2350)*
Organizational & Diversity Con ......G 203 777-3324
New Haven *(G-5356)*
Outer Office ......G 203 329-8600
Stamford *(G-8347)*
Owl King Publishing LLC ......G 203 530-6846
Orange *(G-6621)*
Pagani Publishing ......G 860 614-0303
Enfield *(G-2675)*
Palm Canyon Pictures ......G 203 853-1808
Norwalk *(G-6289)*
Paper and Prose Publishing LLC ......G 203 775-8228
Brookfield *(G-1210)*
Parkhill Publishing LLC ......G 203 938-9199
West Redding *(G-9970)*
Partner In Publishing LLC ......G 860 430-9440
Glastonbury *(G-3068)*
Passport Publications of ......G 631 736-6691
Middletown *(G-4390)*
Patrick Barrett DBA Lucky Duck ......G 347 703-3984
Canaan *(G-1290)*
Pattagansett Publishing Inc ......G 860 693-6156
Canton *(G-1324)*
Paw To Press ......G 303 709-2807
Groton *(G-3303)*
Pelican Island Publishing ......G 908 227-0991
Stamford *(G-8357)*
Pemberton Press Inc ......G 203 761-1466
Wilton *(G-10318)*
Penny Publications LLC ......E 203 866-6688
Milford *(G-4606)*
Pennycorner Press ......G 860 873-3545
East Haddam *(G-2247)*
Permanent Press LLC ......G 860 788-6001
Portland *(G-6967)*
Perry Heights Press LLC ......G 203 767-6509
Wilton *(G-10319)*
Pigeonhole Press LLC ......G 203 629-5754
Greenwich *(G-3215)*
Pine Bush Publishing LLC ......G 203 570-3523
Danbury *(G-1908)*
PINke&brown Publishing LLP ......G 860 798-9858
Avon *(G-100)*
Pinnacle Press LLC ......G 203 254-1947
Fairfield *(G-2828)*
Pinnacle Training and Publ ......G 203 691-6221
New Haven *(G-5365)*
Pixels 2 Press LLC ......G 203 642-3740
Norwalk *(G-6302)*
Pocket Parks Publishing LLC ......G 203 499-7416
West Haven *(G-9945)*
Podskoch Press ......G 860 267-2442
Colchester *(G-1567)*
Pointer Press ......G 203 355-0677
Stamford *(G-8366)*
Portfolio Arts Group Ltd ......F 203 661-2400
Norwalk *(G-6303)*
Premiere ......G 203 756-0178
Waterbury *(G-9585)*
Press Hartford ......G 860 216-6538
Hartford *(G-3669)*
Press On Sandwich Crafters ......G 860 694-9882
Groton *(G-3310)*
Press On Sandwich Crafters LLC ......G 860 415-9906
North Stonington *(G-6031)*
Primo Press LLC ......G 203 527-7904
Waterbury *(G-9588)*
Prison Publications Inc ......G 860 928-4055
Putnam *(G-7060)*
Proquest Inc ......G 860 644-2392
South Windsor *(G-7815)*
Prs Air Elite ......G 203 327-3500
New Canaan *(G-5135)*
Prs Mobile LLC ......G 203 909-5249
Prospect *(G-7022)*
Prs Woods LLC ......G 860 364-5173
Sharon *(G-7382)*
Publishing Dimensions LLC ......G 203 856-7716
Weston *(G-10037)*
Publishing Directions LLC ......G 860 673-7650
Avon *(G-101)*
Puddingstone Publishing LLC ......G 203 454-3939
Weston *(G-10038)*
Puppet Press ......G 203 838-3665
Norwalk *(G-6311)*
Pushpin Press ......G 203 797-8691
Danbury *(G-1922)*
Qmdi Press ......G 860 642-8074
North Franklin *(G-5878)*
Quantum Health Press ......G 203 396-0222
Trumbull *(G-9058)*
Quick & Dirty Press ......G 860 817-0912
Tolland *(G-8876)*
Quixpress Car Wash ......G 203 364-9777
Newtown *(G-5772)*
R and R Publishing LLC ......G 860 944-2085
Storrs Mansfield *(G-8558)*
Rambling Dog Publications LLC ......G 203 254-9230
Easton *(G-2563)*
Rand Media Co LLC ......G 203 226-8727
Westport *(G-10145)*
Rcsi Publishing ......G 203 917-4223
Danbury *(G-1927)*
Red Beard Publishing LLC ......G 203 847-1655
Norwalk *(G-6317)*
Red Mat Media Inc ......G 203 283-5290
Milford *(G-4623)*
Register For Publications ......G 860 302-6706
Southington *(G-7966)*
Registrant James Trippe ......G 203 517-7567
Greenwich *(G-3224)*
Remesas Express ......G 203 330-1444
Bridgeport *(G-889)*
Richmond Press ......G 860 649-0552
South Windsor *(G-7819)*
Ricia Mainhardt Agency ......G 718 434-1893
Meriden *(G-4234)*
Ridgetop Publishing LLC ......G 860 489-9555
New Hartford *(G-5210)*
Rotounderworld LLC ......G 202 236-7103
Fairfield *(G-2839)*
Rowayton Press LLC ......G 203 866-6646
Norwalk *(G-6329)*
Ruckus Media Group Inc ......G 203 939-1409
Norwalk *(G-6332)*
Saltbox Press LLC ......G 203 762-9731
Wilton *(G-10327)*
Sandvik Pubg Interactive Inc ......F 203 205-0188
Danbury *(G-1932)*
Savant Publishing LLC ......G 203 740-9850
Brookfield *(G-1222)*
Scene 1 Arts LLC ......G 203 748-0899
Bethel *(G-339)*
Scholastic Inc ......G 212 343-6100
Danbury *(G-1938)*
Scott American LLC ......G 203 733-5512
Trumbull *(G-9071)*
Scriptural RES & Pubg Co Inc ......G 860 609-5138
Southington *(G-7972)*
Scripture Research & Pubg Co ......G 203 272-1780
Cheshire *(G-1443)*
Sea House Press LLC ......G 860 552-4141
Clinton *(G-1523)*
Senior Network Inc ......E 203 969-2700
Stamford *(G-8409)*
Senior Resource Publishing LLC ......G 203 295-3477
Stamford *(G-8410)*
Shiller and Company Inc ......D 203 210-5208
Wilton *(G-10330)*
Smantics ......G 860 238-7714
Winsted *(G-10537)*
Solana Publishing LLC ......G 203 380-2851
Trumbull *(G-9075)*
Solution Publishing ......G 203 758-9137
Middlebury *(G-4293)*
Somers Music Publications ......G 860 763-0366
Somers *(G-7670)*
Sound of Fury Publishing LLC ......G 860 803-0651
Coventry *(G-1675)*
South End Express 2 ......G 203 720-2085
Naugatuck *(G-4920)*
South Wind Music Pubg LLC ......G 860 644-2357
South Windsor *(G-7825)*
Stamler Publishing Company ......G 203 488-9808
Branford *(G-655)*
Starstatus Publishing ......G 877 453-9532
Derby *(G-2127)*
Stonington Publications Inc ......G 860 599-2019
Pawcatuck *(G-6725)*
Summer Street Content LLC ......G 203 536-9895
Westport *(G-10162)*
Summit Ridge Publishing LLC ......G 860 689-3463
Harwinton *(G-3741)*
Sunny Publishing Company LLC ......G 203 619-3831
Vernon *(G-9153)*
Symmetry Press LLC ......G 203 988-2329
New Haven *(G-5409)*
Tab Brown Publishing LLC ......G 860 985-9621
Hartford *(G-3697)*
Tall Trees Press ......G 860 233-7024
West Hartford *(G-9864)*
Tam Communications Inc ......E 203 425-8777
Norwalk *(G-6362)*
Teed Off Publishing Inc ......G 561 266-0872
Greenwich *(G-3243)*
Tell ME Press LLC ......G 203 562-4215
New Haven *(G-5413)*
Think Big Publications LLC ......G 203 685-4957
Fairfield *(G-2855)*
Thirdshift Publishing ......G 860 521-6613
West Hartford *(G-9866)*
Thomson Reuters Corporation ......F 203 466-5055
East Haven *(G-2456)*
Three Poets Publishing Co LLC ......G 203 248-0200
Hamden *(G-3518)*
Thursdays Child Publishing LLC ......G 203 929-5080
Shelton *(G-7567)*
Tiffany Press Inc ......G 914 806-2245
Stamford *(G-8469)*
Times Publishing LLC ......G 860 349-8532
Middlefield *(G-4308)*
Tom Santos Publishing ......G 860 599-5067
Pawcatuck *(G-6729)*
Topaz Enterprise Sand Pubg ......G 203 449-1903
Norwalk *(G-6374)*
Topaz Enterprises & Pubg LLC ......G 203 993-9051
Norwalk *(G-6375)*
Treble Clef Music Press ......G 919 932-5455
Niantic *(G-5818)*
Trusource Publications LLC ......G 860 350-6477
New Milford *(G-5602)*

Employee Codes: A=Over 500 employees, B=251-500
C=101-250, D=51-100, E=20-50, F=10-19, G=1-9

2020 Harris Connecticut
Manufacturers Directory

737

PUBLISHERS: Miscellaneous

Turkey Tail Publishing LLC .... G 860 671-0800
  Washington (G-9414)
Twisko Press LLC .... G 203 938-3466
  Redding (G-7111)
Ubm LLC .... G 203 662-6501
  Darien (G-2048)
Unicorn Press LLC .... G 203 938-7405
  Redding (G-7112)
Universe Publishing Co LLC .... G 203 283-5201
  Milford (G-4669)
University Hlth Pubg Group LLC .... G 203 791-0101
  Bethel (G-359)
US Games Systems Inc .... E 203 353-8400
  Stamford (G-8481)
Valley Press Inc .... E 860 651-4700
  Simsbury (G-7650)
Van Cott Rowe & Smith .... G 860 242-0707
  Bloomfield (G-497)
Ventureout Publications LLC .... G 203 668-9162
  Wallingford (G-9400)
Versimedia .... G 203 604-8094
  Norwalk (G-6386)
Vitis Press .... G 860 921-8570
  Watertown (G-9747)
Vocalis Limited .... G 203 753-5244
  Waterbury (G-9623)
Wake Publishing .... G 860 559-2787
  Monroe (G-4763)
Webwrite Publishing LLC .... G 203 544-9728
  Weston (G-10045)
Weidner Publication Group .... G 203 272-2463
  Cheshire (G-1458)
Wine Capp Inc .... G 860 355-0521
  Sherman (G-7607)
Winespeak Press LLC .... G 203 968-8882
  Stamford (G-8496)
Wizard Too LLC .... G 203 984-7180
  Westport (G-10177)
Woodhall Press LLP .... G 203 428-1876
  Norwalk (G-6398)
Word For Words LLC .... G 203 894-1908
  Ridgefield (G-7185)
Wyndemere Publishing LLC .... G 860 868-1490
  Warren (G-9410)
Yale Printing and Pubg Svcs .... G 203 432-6560
  New Haven (G-5442)
Yankee Delivery System .... G 860 243-1056
  Bloomfield (G-503)
Yellow Girl Press LLC .... G 860 819-0260
  Marlborough (G-4131)
Ziga Media LLC .... G 203 656-0076
  Darien (G-2052)
Zossima Press .... G 203 687-9385
  Cheshire (G-1461)

PUBLISHERS: Music Book

Flea Market Music Inc .... G 860 664-1669
  Clinton (G-1503)
Yale Daily News Publishing Co .... G 203 432-2400
  New Haven (G-5440)

PUBLISHERS: Music Book & Sheet Music

Hendrickson Group .... G 203 426-9266
  Sandy Hook (G-7315)
Lead Dog Production .... G 203 732-4566
  Oxford (G-6672)

PUBLISHERS: Music, Sheet

S & L Systems .... G 203 757-6159
  Waterbury (G-9596)

PUBLISHERS: Newsletter

Four Winds Inc .... G 203 445-0733
  Easton (G-2554)
James P King .... G 203 834-0050
  Wilton (G-10304)
Odyssey Interactive LLC .... G 860 799-6088
  New Milford (G-5577)
Rockefeller Treasury Services .... G 203 264-8404
  Southbury (G-7875)

PUBLISHERS: Newspaper

200 Mill Plain Road LLC .... G 203 254-0113
  Fairfield (G-2740)
Alm Media LLC .... E 860 527-7900
  Hartford (G-3551)
Barbara Jones .... G 203 596-9219
  Waterbury (G-9437)
Bargain News Free Classified A .... D 203 377-3000
  Stratford (G-8578)
Brian and Brenda Basinger .... G 203 972-9407
  New Canaan (G-5089)
Cantata Media LLC .... F 203 951-9885
  Norwalk (G-6106)
Chromatic Press US Inc .... G 860 796-7667
  West Hartford (G-9788)
Circle Publishing LLC .... G 516 459-5016
  Fairfield (G-2762)
Coffee News .... G 860 613-0796
  Cromwell (G-1696)
Efitzgerald Publishing LLC .... G 860 904-7250
  West Hartford (G-9805)
Foothills Trader Classified .... G 860 489-3121
  Torrington (G-8925)
Four County Catholic Newspaper ...... G 860 886-1281
  Norwich (G-6413)
Freemans News Service .... G 860 485-1000
  Harwinton (G-3731)
Freshiana LLC .... G 800 301-8071
  Greenwich (G-3165)
Gamut Publishing .... E 860 296-6128
  Hartford (G-3598)
Hartford Monthly Meeting .... G 860 232-3631
  West Hartford (G-9818)
Hearst Communications Inc .... G 203 964-2200
  Stamford (G-8231)
Hearst Corporation .... G 203 926-2080
  Shelton (G-7463)
Jewish Leader Newspaper .... G 860 442-7395
  New London (G-5474)
Journal Register East .... G 203 401-4004
  New Haven (G-5305)
Judy Low .... G 860 491-9101
  Goshen (G-3099)
Los Angles Tmes Cmmnctions LLC ... C 203 965-6434
  Stamford (G-8289)
M&G Berman Inc .... G 203 834-8754
  Wilton (G-10311)
Mkrs Corporation .... G 203 762-2662
  Wilton (G-10312)
Morris Communications Co LLC .... D 203 458-4500
  Guilford (G-3377)
Natural Spring Ventures LLC .... G 203 556-2420
  Woodbury (G-10646)
New England Theatre Conference ..... G 203 288-8680
  Hamden (G-3490)
Newspaper Space Buyers .... G 203 967-6452
  Norwalk (G-6277)
Newtown Sports Group .... G 508 341-1238
  Newtown (G-5764)
Old Farmers Almanac .... G 860 862-9100
  Uncasville (G-9101)
Pages of Yesteryear .... G 203 426-0864
  Newtown (G-5767)
Pollinate News .... G 203 801-9623
  New Canaan (G-5132)
Quinnipiac Valley Times .... G 203 675-9483
  Hamden (G-3500)
Reminder Broadcaster .... D 860 875-3366
  Vernon (G-9151)
Silver Arrow Publisher LLC .... G 203 265-4653
  Wallingford (G-9367)
Sin Frntras Hspnic Newsppr LLC ...... G 203 691-5986
  New Haven (G-5395)
Sports Department LLC .... G 860 872-0873
  Ellington (G-2601)
Stella Press LLC .... G 203 661-2735
  Greenwich (G-3241)
The Around The Worlds Around .... G 860 871-7241
  Ellington (G-2606)
Toms News .... G 860 535-1276
  Stonington (G-8541)
Town of Bridgewater .... F 860 354-5250
  Bridgewater (G-947)
Town Tribune LLC .... G 203 648-6085
  New Fairfield (G-5179)
Track180 LLC .... G 203 605-3540
  New Haven (G-5418)
Tradewinds .... G 203 723-6966
  Beacon Falls (G-148)
Tradewinds .... G 203 324-2994
  Stamford (G-8472)
Weekly Retail Service LLC .... G 203 244-5150
  Ridgefield (G-7183)

PUBLISHERS: Newspapers, No Printing

21st Century Fox America Inc .... G 203 563-6600
  Wilton (G-10263)
Advisor .... F 203 239-4121
  North Haven (G-5896)
Car Buyers Market .... E 516 482-0292
  Trumbull (G-9010)
Catholic Transcript Inc .... F 860 286-2828
  Bloomfield (G-401)
CCC Media LLC .... G 860 225-4601
  New Britain (G-4957)
Chase Media Group .... F 914 962-3871
  Newtown (G-5733)
Citizen News .... G 203 746-4669
  New Fairfield (G-5166)
EPic Publishing Services LLC .... G 203 204-7450
  East Haddam (G-2241)
Hamlethub LLC .... G 203 431-6400
  Ridgefield (G-7145)
Hartford Courant Company .... G 860 678-1330
  Avon (G-83)
Hartford Courant Company LLC .... G 860 525-5555
  Hartford (G-3609)
Hispanic Communications LLC .... G 203 624-8007
  New Haven (G-5296)
Life Publications .... E 860 953-0444
  West Hartford (G-9831)
Local Media Group Inc .... G 860 354-2273
  New Milford (G-5558)
Minuteman Newspaper .... E 203 226-8877
  Westport (G-10121)
Northend Agents LLC .... G 860 244-2445
  Hartford (G-3656)
Penfield Communications Inc .... G 203 387-0354
  New Haven (G-5359)
Prime Publishers Inc .... G 860 274-6721
  Watertown (G-9724)
Second Wind Media Limited .... F 203 781-3480
  New Haven (G-5391)
Swedish News Inc .... G 203 299-0380
  Norwalk (G-6361)
The Bee Publishing Company .... G 203 426-0178
  Newtown (G-5790)
Tribuna Newspaper LLC .... G 203 730-0457
  Danbury (G-1967)
True Publishing Company .... F 203 272-5316
  Wallingford (G-9392)
Valley Publishing Company Inc .... F 203 735-6696
  Derby (G-2129)
Wicks Business Information LLC ...... F 203 334-2002
  Shelton (G-7586)

PUBLISHERS: Pamphlets, No Printing

De Villiers Incorporated .... G 203 966-9645
  New Canaan (G-5101)
Sunday Paper .... G 203 624-2520
  New Haven (G-5403)

PUBLISHERS: Periodical, With Printing

Aapi .... G 203 268-2450
  Monroe (G-4690)
Aquastone Graphix LLC .... G 860 206-4935
  Hartford (G-3552)
Creative Stone Group Inc .... G 203 554-7773
  Stamford (G-8169)
Evangelical Christian Center .... G 860 429-0856
  Ashford (G-61)
Premier Graphics LLC .... D 800 414-1624
  Stratford (G-8668)

PUBLISHERS: Periodicals, Magazines

Access Intelligence .... G 203 854-6730
  Norwalk (G-6062)
Aquatic Mammals Journal Nfp .... G 860 514-4704
  Stonington (G-8522)
Artes Magazine LLC .... G 203 530-9811
  Branford (G-547)
Bargain News Free Classified A .... D 203 377-3000
  Stratford (G-8578)
Bay Tact Corporation .... E 860 315-7372
  Woodstock Valley (G-10691)
Bff Holdings Inc .... C 860 510-0100
  Old Saybrook (G-6523)
Connecticut Forest & Park Assn .... F 860 346-2372
  Rockfall (G-7211)
Editors Only .... G 860 881-2300
  New Britain (G-4979)
Gamut Publishing .... E 860 296-6128
  Hartford (G-3598)
Hartford Marathon Foundation .... G 860 652-8866
  Glastonbury (G-3048)

PRODUCT SECTION

PUBLISHING & PRINTING: Magazines: publishing & printing

Imani Magazine/Fmi .... G 203 809-2565
  West Haven (G-9916)
Informa Business Media Inc .... C 203 358-9900
  Stamford (G-8249)
Karger S Publishers Inc .... G 860 675-7834
  Unionville (G-9116)
Legal Affairs Inc .... G 203 865-2520
  Hamden (G-3473)
Liturgical Publications Inc .... F 203 966-6470
  New Canaan (G-5115)
Liturgical Publications Inc .... G 860 635-9560
  Cromwell (G-1706)
Living Magazine .... G 203 283-5290
  Milford (G-4569)
Matchbox USA .... G 860 349-1655
  Durham (G-2152)
Media Ventures Inc .... E 203 852-6570
  Norwalk (G-6253)
Merlin Associates Inc .... G 860 567-1620
  Litchfield (G-3895)
Motorcyclists Post .... G 203 929-9409
  Shelton (G-7505)
Ppc Books Ltd .... G 203 226-6644
  Westport (G-10142)
Relx Inc .... A 203 840-4800
  Norwalk (G-6320)
Reserved Magazine .... G 860 560-9120
  Hartford (G-3678)
S Karger Publishers Inc .... G 860 675-7834
  Unionville (G-9126)
Sage Magazine .... G 347 452-3752
  New Haven (G-5384)
Scripture Research & Pubg Co .... G 203 272-1780
  Cheshire (G-1443)
Snreview .... G 203 366-5991
  Fairfield (G-2849)
Suzanne Ramljak .... G 203 792-5599
  Bethel (G-350)
Ubm LLC .... G 203 662-6501
  Darien (G-2048)
Val Scansaroli Magazine Cnsltn .... G 203 229-0256
  Norwalk (G-6380)
Westchester Forge Inc .... G 914 584-2429
  New Canaan (G-5158)
Woolworks International Ltd .... G 203 661-7076
  Stamford (G-8501)
Yale Law Journal Co Inc .... G 203 432-1666
  New Haven (G-5441)

PUBLISHERS: Periodicals, No Printing

Baxter Bros Inc .... G 203 637-4559
  Greenwich (G-3130)
Financial Accnting Foundation .... C 203 847-0700
  Norwalk (G-6165)
Ibnr LLC .... G 860 676-8600
  Farmington (G-2916)
Overseas Ministries Study Ctr .... F 203 624-6672
  New Haven (G-5357)
R G L Inc .... E 860 653-7254
  East Granby (G-2226)
Steed Read Horsemans Classifie .... G 860 859-0770
  Salem (G-7292)

PUBLISHERS: Racing Forms & Programs

R G L Inc .... E 860 653-7254
  East Granby (G-2226)

PUBLISHERS: Sheet Music

Hog River Music .... G 860 523-1820
  Hartford (G-3614)
Mr Boltons Music Inc .... G 646 578-8081
  Westport (G-10125)
Tune Door Inc .... G 914 713-0257
  New Fairfield (G-5180)

PUBLISHERS: Technical Manuals

Business Journals Inc .... D 203 853-6015
  Norwalk (G-6102)
Real Data Inc .... G 203 255-2732
  Southport (G-8007)

PUBLISHERS: Technical Manuals & Papers

I3 Engineering Sciences LLC .... G 908 625-2347
  Hartford (G-3616)
Intechs LLC .... G 203 260-8109
  Monroe (G-4721)
Tax Tracker LLC .... G 860 296-8143
  Hartford (G-3698)

PUBLISHERS: Telephone & Other Directory

Administrative Publications In .... G 860 747-6768
  Plainville (G-6766)
Connectcut Hspnic Yellow Pages .... F 860 560-8713
  Hartford (G-3569)
Hometown Publishing LLC .... G 203 426-5252
  Newtown (G-5744)

PUBLISHERS: Textbooks, No Printing

Educational Resources Network .... G 203 866-9973
  Ridgefield (G-7138)
Edward Fleur Fncl Educatn Corp .... G 203 629-9333
  Greenwich (G-3157)
K C K Publishing .... G 203 924-1147
  Shelton (G-7482)
Kirchoff Wohlberg Inc .... F 212 644-2020
  Madison (G-3934)
Originals LLC .... G 203 421-4867
  Madison (G-3944)
Pass Perfect LLC .... G 203 629-9333
  Greenwich (G-3214)
Real Sltons Edctl Cnslting Inc .... G 203 220-2279
  Trumbull (G-9062)

PUBLISHERS: Trade journals, No Printing

Airtime Publishing Inc .... E 203 454-4773
  Westport (G-10051)
Business Journals Inc .... D 203 853-6015
  Norwalk (G-6102)
Camarro Research .... G 203 254-1755
  Fairfield (G-2757)
Ida Publishing Co Inc .... G 203 661-9090
  Greenwich (G-3178)
International Mktg Strategies .... F 203 406-0106
  Stamford (G-8253)
Society For Exprmntal McHanics .... G 203 790-6373
  Bethel (G-343)
Society Plastics Engineers Inc .... E 203 740-5422
  Bethel (G-344)
Yale University .... G 203 432-0499
  New Haven (G-5450)
Zackin Publications Inc .... E 203 262-4670
  Oxford (G-6701)

PUBLISHING & BROADCASTING: Internet Only

AAR Results LLC .... G 203 627-2193
  Branford (G-535)
Axol Media Inc .... G 650 315-1743
  South Windsor (G-7715)
Bagogames LLC .... G 860 801-7462
  Torrington (G-8900)
Bellable LLC .... G 800 212-2603
  West Hartford (G-9778)
Betx LLC .... G 860 459-1681
  New Hartford (G-5186)
Brain Institute of America LLC .... G 860 967-5937
  Groton (G-3273)
Broadcastmed Inc .... E 860 953-2900
  Farmington (G-2886)
Doors To Explore Inc .... G 978 761-7210
  Sandy Hook (G-7310)
Functional Concepts LLC .... G 203 813-0157
  Stratford (G-8614)
Gcn Publishing Inc .... F 203 665-6211
  Norwalk (G-6176)
Integer-Comfab Enterprises LLC .... G 646 620-9112
  Westport (G-10102)
Leasefish LLC .... G 203 293-3603
  Wilton (G-10309)
Luxury Brand Network LLC .... G 203 930-2703
  Greenwich (G-3194)
Mowmedia LLC .... G 203 240-6416
  Stamford (G-8315)
Web Savvy Marketers LLC .... G 860 432-8756
  East Hartford (G-2401)

PUBLISHING & PRINTING: Art Copy

Mongillo Press .... G 203 467-1371
  New Haven (G-5336)

PUBLISHING & PRINTING: Book Music

Bryan Doughty .... G 860 536-2185
  New London (G-5459)
Nollysource Entertainment LLC .... G 347 264-6655
  Bridgeport (G-853)

Robison Music Media & Pubg LLC .... G 203 858-8106
  Wallingford (G-9356)

PUBLISHING & PRINTING: Books

Air Age Inc .... E 203 431-9000
  Wilton (G-10267)
Bigs Publishing LLC .... G 203 249-1059
  Greenwich (G-3133)
Bradt Enterprises LLC .... G 203 323-8501
  Stamford (G-8116)
Comicana Inc .... G 203 968-0748
  Stamford (G-8153)
Pocket Parks Publishing LLC .... G 203 499-7416
  West Haven (G-9945)
Rocket Books Inc .... G 203 372-1818
  Easton (G-2564)
Two Ems Inc .... G 203 245-8211
  Madison (G-3965)

PUBLISHING & PRINTING: Catalogs

Barker Advg Specialty Co Inc .... D 203 272-2222
  Cheshire (G-1360)
Brook & Whittle Holding Corp .... G 203 483-5602
  Guilford (G-3333)
Julie Wakely Enterprises LLC .... G 860 376-4515
  Jewett City (G-3797)
Yale University .... E 203 432-2550
  New Haven (G-5443)
Yale University .... D 203 764-4333
  New Haven (G-5444)

PUBLISHING & PRINTING: Comic Books

Most Excllent Cmics Cllctibles .... G 860 741-0113
  Enfield (G-2662)

PUBLISHING & PRINTING: Directories, NEC

Tots411 LLP .... G 203 558-5369
  Westport (G-10168)

PUBLISHING & PRINTING: Directories, Telephone

Media Metrix LLC .... G 203 386-0228
  Stratford (G-8649)
Southern Neng Telecom Corp .... B 203 771-5200
  New Haven (G-5401)

PUBLISHING & PRINTING: Guides

Bertram Sirkin .... G 860 656-7446
  West Hartford (G-9779)

PUBLISHING & PRINTING: Magazines: publishing & printing

Clemons Productions Inc .... G 203 316-9394
  Stamford (G-8150)
Commerce Connect Media Inc .... A 800 547-7377
  Westport (G-10066)
Dulce Domum LLC .... E 203 227-1400
  Norwalk (G-6151)
Edible Nutmeg .... G 818 383-4603
  Washington (G-9413)
Informa Business Media Inc .... D 203 358-9900
  Stamford (G-8248)
Little India Publications Inc .... F 212 560-0608
  Torrington (G-8943)
Maplegate Media Group Inc .... E 203 826-7557
  Danbury (G-1880)
Natural Nutmeg LLC .... G 860 206-9500
  Avon (G-95)
Park Group Solutions LLC .... G 203 459-8784
  Newtown (G-5769)
Penny Publications LLC .... D 203 866-6688
  Norwalk (G-6297)
Quad/Graphics Inc .... A 203 288-2468
  North Haven (G-5985)
Racing Times .... E 203 298-2899
  Wallingford (G-9347)
Red 7 Media LLC .... E 203 853-2474
  Norwalk (G-6316)
Show Management Associates LLC .... G 203 939-9901
  Norwalk (G-6345)
Urban Exposition LLC .... E 203 242-8717
  Trumbull (G-9090)
Yale University .... E 203 432-2550
  New Haven (G-5443)

Employee Codes: A=Over 500 employees, B=251-500
C=101-250, D=51-100, E=20-50, F=10-19, G=1-9

PUBLISHING & PRINTING: Magazines: publishing & printing

Yale University .... D 203 764-4333
  New Haven *(G-5444)*

PUBLISHING & PRINTING: Newsletters, Business Svc

Chief Executive Group LLC .... F 785 832-0303
  Stamford *(G-8143)*
Crossfield Concepts Inc .... G 203 938-5667
  Redding *(G-7091)*
Custom Publishing Design Group .... F 860 513-1213
  Rocky Hill *(G-7231)*
Shop Smart Central Inc .... G 914 962-3871
  Newtown *(G-5779)*
The Merrill Anderson Co Inc .... F 203 377-4996
  Stratford *(G-8694)*
Wakeen Gallery .... G 860 763-4565
  Somers *(G-7676)*

PUBLISHING & PRINTING: Newspapers

8 Times LLC .... G 203 227-7575
  Westport *(G-10048)*
Amandas Daily Ideas LLC .... G 203 761-8599
  Wilton *(G-10269)*
American-Republican Inc .... D 203 574-3636
  Waterbury *(G-9429)*
American-Republican Inc .... C 860 496-9301
  Torrington *(G-8894)*
Browser Daily .... G 860 469-5534
  Winsted *(G-10511)*
C S M S-I P A .... G 203 562-7228
  North Haven *(G-5917)*
Capital Cities Communications .... G 203 784-8800
  New Haven *(G-5253)*
Central Conn Cmmunications LLC ...... D 860 225-4601
  New Britain *(G-4958)*
Comunidade News .... G 203 730-0175
  Danbury *(G-1772)*
Conn Daily Campus .... G 860 486-3407
  Storrs Mansfield *(G-8553)*
Connecticut Newspapers Inc .... G 203 964-2200
  Stamford *(G-8157)*
Courant Specialty Products Inc .... E 860 241-3795
  Hartford *(G-3572)*
Daily Fare LLC .... G 203 743-7300
  Bethel *(G-277)*
Daily Impressions LLC .... G 203 508-5305
  Hamden *(G-3439)*
Daily Mart .... G 860 529-5210
  Rocky Hill *(G-7233)*
Day Trust .... G 860 442-2200
  New London *(G-5467)*
Disco Chick .... G 860 788-6203
  Middletown *(G-4336)*
Fairfield County Gazette .... G 203 929-1405
  Shelton *(G-7442)*
Footnote Journal LLC .... G 203 924-0391
  Shelton *(G-7446)*
Gatehouse Media LLC .... C 860 886-0106
  Norwich *(G-6414)*
Greenwich Gofer .... G 203 637-8425
  Old Greenwich *(G-6473)*
Greenwich Sentinel .... G 203 883-1430
  Greenwich *(G-3175)*
Greenwich Time .... G 203 253-2922
  Stamford *(G-8221)*
Hamden Journal LLC .... G 203 668-6307
  Hamden *(G-3456)*
Hamiltonbookcom LLC .... G 860 824-0275
  Falls Village *(G-2871)*
Hartford Courant Company .... F 860 560-3747
  West Hartford *(G-9816)*
Hartford Courant Company LLC .... A 860 241-6200
  Hartford *(G-3608)*
Hearst Corporation .... E 203 438-6544
  New Canaan *(G-5109)*
Hearst Corporation .... E 203 625-4445
  Norwalk *(G-6199)*
Hersam Acorn Cmnty Pubg LLC .... F 203 261-2548
  Trumbull *(G-9034)*
Hersam Acorn Cmnty Pubg LLC .... F 203 438-6544
  Ridgefield *(G-7146)*
Hispanic Communications LLC .... G 203 674-6793
  Stamford *(G-8239)*
India Weekly Co .... G 203 699-8419
  Cheshire *(G-1399)*
Inquiring News .... G 860 983-7587
  Bloomfield *(G-422)*
Jj Portland News LLC .... G 860 342-1432
  Middletown *(G-4358)*

Journal of Experimntal Scndary .... G 203 630-6508
  Meriden *(G-4182)*
Journal Publishing Company Inc ...... A 860 646-0500
  Manchester *(G-4040)*
Meade Daily Group LLC .... G 860 399-7342
  Westbrook *(G-10004)*
Medianews Group Inc .... F 203 333-0161
  Norwalk *(G-6254)*
Miller Tina-Attorney .... G 203 938-8507
  Redding *(G-7103)*
My Citizens News .... G 203 729-2228
  Waterbury *(G-9550)*
New Mass Media Inc .... E 860 241-3617
  Hartford *(G-3653)*
News 12 Connecticut .... E 203 849-1321
  Norwalk *(G-6276)*
News Times .... G 203 744-5100
  Danbury *(G-1892)*
Northeast Minority News Inc .... G 860 249-6065
  Hartford *(G-3655)*
Northwest News Service .... G 860 567-4150
  Bantam *(G-126)*
NRG Connecticut LLC .... E 860 231-2424
  Hartford *(G-3657)*
Online Journalism Project Inc .... G 203 668-5790
  New Haven *(G-5354)*
Orange Democrat .... G 203 298-4575
  Orange *(G-6620)*
Our Town Crier .... G 203 400-5000
  Westport *(G-10135)*
Peaceful Daily Inc .... G 203 909-2961
  Guilford *(G-3383)*
Post Publishing Company .... G 203 333-0161
  Bridgeport *(G-877)*
Prospect Pages LLC .... G 203 758-6934
  Prospect *(G-7020)*
Rhode Island Beverage Journal ..... G 203 288-3375
  Hamden *(G-3505)*
Ritch Herald & Linda .... G 203 661-8634
  Greenwich *(G-3227)*
Rmi Inc .... C 860 875-3366
  Vernon Rockville *(G-9177)*
Southington Citizen .... G 860 620-5960
  Meriden *(G-4243)*
Suburban Voices Publishing LLC ... G 203 934-6397
  West Haven *(G-9956)*
Ten 22 Inc .... G 860 963-1050
  Putnam *(G-7072)*
Thomson Reuters Risk MGT Inc .... G 203 539-8000
  Stamford *(G-8467)*
Thomson Reuters US LLC .... E 203 539-8000
  Stamford *(G-8468)*
Times Community News Group ..... G 860 437-1150
  New London *(G-5494)*
TLC Media LLC .... G 203 980-1361
  Hamden *(G-3520)*
Trumbull Transfer LLC .... G 203 377-2487
  Shelton *(G-7571)*
Twice Baked Twins LLC .... G 203 368-8841
  Trumbull *(G-9083)*
Unger Publishing LLC .... G 203 588-1363
  Stamford *(G-8480)*
Valley Independent Sentinel .... G 203 446-2335
  Ansonia *(G-55)*
Westerly Sun .... G 401 348-1000
  Pawcatuck *(G-6732)*
Woodbridge Town News .... G 203 298-4399
  Orange *(G-6635)*
Yale Daily News Publishing Co ..... G 203 432-2400
  New Haven *(G-5440)*
Yale Law Journal Co Inc .... G 203 432-1666
  New Haven *(G-5441)*
Yale University .... G 203 432-2880
  New Haven *(G-5445)*
Yankee Delivery System .... G 860 243-1056
  Bloomfield *(G-503)*
Yankee Pennysaver Inc .... E 203 775-9122
  Brookfield *(G-1242)*

PUBLISHING & PRINTING: Pamphlets

Marlin Company .... D 203 294-9800
  Wallingford *(G-9312)*

PUBLISHING & PRINTING: Patterns, Paper

Kanine Knits .... G 203 272-8548
  Cheshire *(G-1402)*

PUBLISHING & PRINTING: Shopping News

Rare Reminder Incorporated .... E 860 563-9386
  Rocky Hill *(G-7264)*
Step Saver Inc .... E 860 621-6751
  Southington *(G-7982)*

PUBLISHING & PRINTING: Technical Papers

Insight Media LLC .... G 203 831-8464
  Norwalk *(G-6208)*
Technical Brief .... G 203 432-8188
  New Haven *(G-5411)*

PUBLISHING & PRINTING: Textbooks

Calculator Training .... G 860 355-8255
  New Milford *(G-5513)*
Peter Kelsey Publishing Inc .... G 860 231-9300
  West Hartford *(G-9843)*

PUBLISHING & PRINTING: Trade Journals

Advantage Communications LLC ... E 203 966-8390
  New Canaan *(G-5086)*

PULP MILLS

Cellmark Pulp & Paper Inc .... F 203 299-5050
  Norwalk *(G-6111)*
Eldorado Usa Inc .... G 203 208-2282
  Branford *(G-587)*
International Paper - 16 Inc .... G 203 329-8544
  Stamford *(G-8254)*
Willimantic Waste Paper Co Inc ... C 860 423-4527
  Willimantic *(G-10240)*

PUMPS

A V I International Inc .... G 860 482-8345
  Torrington *(G-8885)*
Beckson Manufacturing Inc .... E 203 366-3644
  Bridgeport *(G-709)*
Flowserve Corporation .... E 203 877-4252
  Milford *(G-4537)*
Foleys Pump Service Inc .... E 203 792-2236
  Danbury *(G-1828)*
Gardner Denver Nash LLC .... D 203 459-3923
  Trumbull *(G-9028)*
Hamworthy Peabody Combustn Inc ... E 203 922-1199
  Shelton *(G-7457)*
Harrier Technologies Inc .... G 203 625-9700
  Greenwich *(G-3176)*
Hisco Pump Incorporated .... E 860 243-2705
  Bloomfield *(G-420)*
Ingersoll-Rand Company .... D 860 616-6600
  Rocky Hill *(G-7250)*
ITT Water & Wastewater USA Inc ... D 262 548-8181
  Shelton *(G-7480)*
McVac Environmental Svcs Inc ... E 203 497-1960
  New Haven *(G-5327)*
MSC Filtration Tech Inc .... F 860 745-7475
  Enfield *(G-2664)*
Omega Engineering Inc .... D 714 540-4914
  Norwalk *(G-6285)*
Phillips Pump LLC .... F 203 576-6688
  Bridgeport *(G-872)*
Proflow Inc .... E 203 230-4700
  North Haven *(G-5980)*
Sfc Koenig LLC .... E 203 245-1100
  North Haven *(G-5992)*
Sonic Corp .... F 203 375-0063
  Stratford *(G-8683)*
Talcott Mountain Engineering ... F 860 651-3141
  Simsbury *(G-7649)*
Xylem Inc .... G 203 521-4934
  Milford *(G-4682)*
Xylem Water Solutions USA Inc ... E 203 450-3715
  Shelton *(G-7589)*

PUMPS & PARTS: Indl

Bjm Pumps LLC .... E 860 399-5937
  Old Saybrook *(G-6524)*
Idex Health & Science LLC .... G 203 774-4422
  Wallingford *(G-9286)*
Preferred Utilities Mfg Corp ...... D 203 743-6741
  Danbury *(G-1918)*
Stancor LP .... E 203 268-7513
  Monroe *(G-4753)*
Sulzer Pump Solutions US Inc ... E 203 238-2700
  Meriden *(G-4247)*

PRODUCT SECTION

PUMPS & PUMPING EQPT REPAIR SVCS
A V I International Inc ....G....... 860 482-8345
  Torrington *(G-8885)*
Hisco Pump Incorporated ....E....... 860 243-2705
  Bloomfield *(G-420)*

PUMPS & PUMPING EQPT WHOLESALERS
Dpc Quality Pump Service ....G....... 203 874-6877
  Milford *(G-4515)*
Hisco Pump Incorporated ....E....... 860 243-2705
  Bloomfield *(G-420)*
MSC Filtration Tech Inc ....F....... 860 745-7475
  Enfield *(G-2664)*
Proflow Inc..E....... 203 230-4700
  North Haven *(G-5980)*
Pump Technology Incorporated ....E....... 203 736-8890
  Ansonia *(G-47)*
Stancor LP ....E....... 203 268-7513
  Monroe *(G-4753)*
Sulzer Pump Solutions US Inc ....E....... 203 238-2700
  Meriden *(G-4247)*

PUMPS: Domestic, Water Or Sump
Dpc Quality Pump Service ....G....... 203 874-6877
  Milford *(G-4515)*
Marsars Water Rescue Systems..........G....... 203 924-7315
  Shelton *(G-7496)*
Pump Technology Incorporated ....E....... 203 736-8890
  Ansonia *(G-47)*

PUMPS: Hydraulic Power Transfer
Crane Co ....D....... 203 363-7300
  Stamford *(G-8166)*

PUMPS: Measuring & Dispensing
Innovationcooperative3d LLC ....G....... 860 540-4172
  Farmington *(G-2918)*
Proflow Inc..E....... 203 230-4700
  North Haven *(G-5980)*

PUMPS: Vacuum, Exc Laboratory
Comvac Systems Inc ....G....... 860 265-3658
  Enfield *(G-2631)*

PUNCHES: Forming & Stamping
Precision Punch + Tooling Corp..........D....... 860 229-9902
  Berlin *(G-210)*

PUPPETS & MARIONETTES
East Lyme Puppetry Project ....G....... 860 739-7225
  Niantic *(G-5805)*
M P Robinson Production ....E....... 203 938-1336
  Redding *(G-7099)*

QUILTING SVC & SPLYS, FOR THE TRADE
Quilted Lizard..G....... 860 927-4296
  Kent *(G-3825)*

QUILTING: Individuals
Jane Sterry ....G....... 860 342-4567
  Portland *(G-6960)*

RACEWAYS
Family Raceway LLC ....G....... 860 896-0171
  Vernon *(G-9138)*
Rhode Island Raceway LLC ....G....... 860 701-0192
  Quaker Hill *(G-7084)*
Roaming Raceway and RR LLC...........G....... 413 531-3390
  Suffield *(G-8733)*
Stamford RPM Raceway LLC................G....... 203 323-7223
  Stamford *(G-8440)*
Wiremold Company ....A....... 860 233-6251
  West Hartford *(G-9874)*

RACKS: Bicycle, Automotive
Thule Canada Holding LLC ....G....... 203 881-4919
  Seymour *(G-7369)*

RACKS: Display
Di-Cor Industries Inc............................F....... 860 585-5583
  Bristol *(G-1017)*

Mitchell-Bate Company ....E....... 203 233-0862
  Waterbury *(G-9545)*

RADIATORS, EXC ELECTRIC
Enterex America LLC............................G....... 860 661-4635
  Westbrook *(G-9996)*

RADIO & TELEVISION COMMUNICATIONS EQUIPMENT
Commscope Technologies LLC ....F....... 203 699-4100
  Prospect *(G-6997)*
Comsat Inc..F....... 203 264-4091
  Southbury *(G-7848)*
Cuescript Inc ....G....... 203 763-4030
  Stratford *(G-8602)*
Fenton Corp ....F....... 203 221-2788
  Westport *(G-10079)*
Frontier Vision Tech Inc ....E....... 860 953-0240
  Rocky Hill *(G-7238)*
Lf Engineering Co Inc...........................G....... 860 526-4759
  East Haven *(G-2438)*
Matrixx Productions ....G....... 860 218-5565
  Hartford *(G-3637)*
Merl Inc ....G....... 203 237-8811
  Meriden *(G-4199)*
Microtech Inc..D....... 203 272-3234
  Cheshire *(G-1416)*
Peak Antennas LLC ....G....... 203 268-3688
  Monroe *(G-4746)*

RADIO & TELEVISION REPAIR
Cable Electronics Inc............................G....... 860 953-0300
  Hartford *(G-3560)*

RADIO BROADCASTING & COMMUNICATIONS EQPT
Connecticut Radio Inc..........................G....... 860 563-4867
  Rocky Hill *(G-7228)*
Fisher Electronics ....G....... 860 646-7779
  Vernon Rockville *(G-9168)*
Northastern Communications Inc ....F....... 203 381-9008
  Stratford *(G-8654)*
Tactical Communications Inc ....F....... 203 453-2389
  Guilford *(G-3398)*
Titus Technological Labs ....G....... 860 633-5472
  Glastonbury *(G-3088)*

RADIO BROADCASTING STATIONS
Clemons Productions Inc....................G....... 203 316-9394
  Stamford *(G-8150)*
Evangelical Christian Center ....G....... 860 429-0856
  Ashford *(G-61)*

RADIO EQPT: Citizens Band
Gold Line Connector Inc ....E....... 203 938-2588
  Redding *(G-7093)*

RADIO REPAIR & INSTALLATION SVCS
Fisher Electronics ....G....... 860 646-7779
  Vernon Rockville *(G-9168)*

RADIO REPAIR SHOP, NEC
Sean Mecesery ....G....... 203 869-2277
  Cos Cob *(G-1641)*
Tactical Communications Inc ....F....... 203 453-2389
  Guilford *(G-3398)*

RADIO, TELEVISION & CONSUMER ELECTRONICS STORES: Antennas
Peak Antennas LLC ....G....... 203 268-3688
  Monroe *(G-4746)*

RADIO, TELEVISION & CONSUMER ELECTRONICS STORES: Eqpt, NEC
Ultimate Interfaces Corp ....G....... 203 230-8184
  Milford *(G-4667)*

RADIO, TV/CONSUMER ELEC STORES: Antennas, Satellite Dish
Peak Antennas ....G....... 203 268-3688
  Monroe *(G-4745)*

REAL ESTATE APPRAISERS

RAILINGS: Prefabricated, Metal
American Iron Works ....G....... 203 624-7360
  New Haven *(G-5228)*
Mono Crete Step Co of CT LLC ....F....... 203 748-8419
  Bethel *(G-328)*

RAILROAD CARGO LOADING & UNLOADING SVCS
Composite Panel Tech Co ....G....... 203 729-2255
  Naugatuck *(G-4869)*

RAILROAD EQPT
James L Howard and Company Inc .....E....... 860 242-3581
  Bloomfield *(G-427)*
Winchester Industries Inc ....G....... 860 379-5336
  Winsted *(G-10544)*

RAILROAD EQPT & SPLYS WHOLESALERS
A & K Railroad Materials Inc ....G....... 203 495-8790
  Hamden *(G-3409)*

RAILROAD EQPT: Brakes, Air & Vacuum
Winslow Automatics Inc........................D....... 860 225-6321
  New Britain *(G-5084)*

RAILROAD EQPT: Cars & Eqpt, Dining
Hammer Transport LLC ....G....... 860 338-0667
  Chaplin *(G-1340)*

RAILROAD EQPT: Cars & Eqpt, Interurban
Transit Systems Inc ....G....... 860 747-3669
  Plainville *(G-6871)*

RAILROAD EQPT: Cars & Eqpt, Train, Freight Or Passenger
L T A Group Inc ....E....... 860 291-9911
  South Windsor *(G-7785)*

RAILROAD RELATED EQPT: Ballast Distributors
K&L Enterprises.....................................G....... 860 645-7257
  Manchester *(G-4042)*

RAILROAD RELATED EQPT: Laying Eqpt, Rail
A & K Railroad Materials Inc ....G....... 203 495-8790
  Hamden *(G-3409)*

RAILROAD TIES: Wood
Tronox Incorporated ....C....... 203 705-3800
  Stamford *(G-8476)*

RAILS: Steel Or Iron
Arnio Welding LLC ....F....... 860 564-7696
  Central Village *(G-1335)*

RAZORS, RAZOR BLADES
Bic Corporation......................................A....... 203 783-2000
  Shelton *(G-7407)*
Bic USA Inc...C....... 203 783-2000
  Shelton *(G-7408)*
Edgewell Per Care Brands LLC ....D....... 203 882-2300
  Milford *(G-4526)*
Edgewell Per Care Brands LLC ....B....... 203 944-5500
  Shelton *(G-7435)*
Edgewell Personal Care Company.......E....... 203 882-2308
  Milford *(G-4527)*
Gillette Company ....G....... 203 796-4000
  Bethel *(G-303)*
Schick Manufacturing Inc ....D....... 203 882-2100
  Milford *(G-4639)*

REAL ESTATE AGENTS & MANAGERS
Condon LLC ....D....... 860 883-5416
  Old Saybrook *(G-6528)*

REAL ESTATE APPRAISERS
Naffa Inc..G....... 203 562-3159
  New Haven *(G-5339)*

Employee Codes: A=Over 500 employees, B=251-500
C=101-250, D=51-100, E=20-50, F=10-19, G=1-9

REAL ESTATE OPERATORS, EXC DEVELOPERS: Commercial/Indl Bldg

American Metals Coal Intl Inc ....F 203 625-9200
  Greenwich *(G-3120)*
Louis Dreyfus Holding Company ....B 203 761-2000
  Wilton *(G-10310)*

REAL ESTATE OPERATORS, EXC DEVELOPERS: Property, Retail

EPic Publishing Services LLC ....G 860 204-7450
  East Haddam *(G-2241)*

RECLAIMED RUBBER: Reworked By Manufacturing Process

Tellus Technology Inc ....G 646 265-7960
  Darien *(G-2046)*

RECORDERS: Sound

Omnicron Electronics ....G 860 928-0377
  Putnam *(G-7055)*

RECORDERS: Tape, Computer Data

Clg Enterprises Inc ....F 203 741-9300
  Wallingford *(G-9232)*

RECORDS & TAPES: Prerecorded

Bff Holdings Inc ....C 860 510-0100
  Old Saybrook *(G-6523)*
Trod Nossel Prdctns & Rcrdng S ....G 203 269-4465
  Wallingford *(G-9391)*

RECORDS OR TAPES: Masters

American Melody Records ....G 203 457-0881
  Guilford *(G-3325)*

RECOVERY SVC: Iron Ore, From Open Hearth Slag

Centritec Seals LLC ....G 860 594-7183
  East Hartford *(G-2304)*

RECREATIONAL CAMPS

Evangelical Christian Center ....G 860 429-0856
  Ashford *(G-61)*

RECREATIONAL VEHICLE PARTS & ACCESS STORES

Rv Parts & Electric Inc ....G 203 754-5962
  Waterbury *(G-9595)*
Tri-County Mold & Machine ....G 860 642-7033
  Lebanon *(G-3864)*

RECREATIONAL VEHICLE REPAIRS

Rv Parts & Electric Inc ....G 203 754-5962
  Waterbury *(G-9595)*

RECTIFIERS: Electronic, Exc Semiconductor

Edal Industries Inc ....E 203 467-2591
  East Haven *(G-2423)*

RECYCLING: Paper

Heritage Newsprint LLC ....G 203 393-0567
  Bethany *(G-244)*

REFINERS & SMELTERS: Copper

Ametek Inc ....C 203 265-6731
  Wallingford *(G-9203)*

REFINERS & SMELTERS: Gold

Specialty Metls Smlters & Rfne ....G 203 366-2500
  Fairfield *(G-2850)*

REFINERS & SMELTERS: Lead, Secondary

Alent USA Holding Inc ....B 203 575-5727
  Waterbury *(G-9426)*
Surf Metal Co Inc ....G 203 375-2211
  Stratford *(G-8692)*

REFINERS & SMELTERS: Nonferrous Metal

5n Plus Wisconsin Inc ....F 203 384-0331
  Trumbull *(G-8995)*
Lajoies Auto Wrecking Co Inc ....E 203 870-0641
  Norwalk *(G-6230)*
MJ Metal Inc ....E 203 334-3484
  Bridgeport *(G-840)*
Paradigm Manchester Inc ....C 860 649-2888
  Manchester *(G-4069)*
Smm New England Corporation ....F 203 777-7445
  New Haven *(G-5397)*
Thyssenkrupp Materials NA Inc ....E 610 586-1800
  Wallingford *(G-9383)*
Ulbrich Stainless Steels ....D 203 239-4481
  North Haven *(G-6008)*
Willimantic Waste Paper Co Inc ....C 860 423-4527
  Willimantic *(G-10240)*

REFINERS & SMELTERS: Platinum Group Metals, Secondary

Utitec Inc ....D 860 945-0605
  Watertown *(G-9744)*

REFINING LUBRICATING OILS & GREASES, NEC

Price-Driscoll Corporation ....G 860 442-3575
  Waterford *(G-9666)*

REFINING: Petroleum

CCI Corpus Christi LLC ....G 203 564-8100
  Stamford *(G-8133)*
G H Berlin Oil Company ....G 800 426-7754
  Hartford *(G-3594)*
Mercury Fuel Service Inc ....D 203 756-7284
  Waterbury *(G-9539)*

REFRACTORIES: Brick

Redland Brick Inc ....C 860 528-1311
  South Windsor *(G-7818)*

REFRACTORIES: Clay

Bonsal American Inc ....E 860 824-7733
  Canaan *(G-1283)*
Harbisonwalker Intl Inc ....G 203 934-7960
  West Haven *(G-9914)*
Zampell Refractories Inc ....F 860 564-2883
  Plainfield *(G-6757)*

REFRACTORIES: Nonclay

Joshua LLC ....E 203 624-0080
  New Haven *(G-5304)*
Specialty Minerals Inc ....C 860 824-5435
  Canaan *(G-1292)*

REFRIGERATION & HEATING EQUIPMENT

Air Solutions East LLC ....G 860 883-4700
  Avon *(G-73)*
AMS Strategic Management Inc ....G 845 500-5635
  Stamford *(G-8083)*
Latin American Holding Inc ....G 860 674-3000
  Farmington *(G-2924)*
Lenox Strategies LLC ....E 203 927-0871
  East Haven *(G-2437)*
Lenox34 LLC ....G 203 869-6909
  Greenwich *(G-3190)*
Mechanical Engnered Systems LLC ....G 203 400-4658
  New Canaan *(G-5119)*
Tld Ace Corporation ....B 860 602-3300
  Windsor *(G-10452)*
Trane Inc ....D 860 437-6208
  New Haven *(G-5420)*
Trane US Inc ....G 203 295-2170
  Stamford *(G-8473)*
Trane US Inc ....G 800 544-1642
  Stamford *(G-8474)*
Trane US Inc ....D 860 437-6208
  New London *(G-5495)*
Trane US Inc ....D 860 470-3901
  Farmington *(G-2965)*
Trane US Inc ....G 860 541-1721
  Hartford *(G-3705)*
Ulitsch Mechanical Svcs LLC ....G 860 623-4223
  Windsor Locks *(G-10500)*
United Tech Advnced Prjcts Inc ....G 860 610-7159
  East Hartford *(G-2390)*
United Technologies Corp ....C 860 565-7622
  East Hartford *(G-2392)*
United Technologies Corp ....B 860 767-9592
  Essex *(G-2736)*
United Technologies Corp ....B 860 728-7000
  Farmington *(G-2972)*
Vector Controls LLC ....F 203 749-0883
  Bethel *(G-363)*

REFRIGERATION EQPT & SPLYS WHOLESALERS

David H Johnson Inc ....G 860 677-5595
  West Hartford *(G-9798)*

REFRIGERATION EQPT & SPLYS, WHOLESALE: Beverage Coolers

Mp Systems Inc ....F 860 687-3460
  East Granby *(G-2214)*

REFRIGERATION EQPT & SPLYS, WHOLESALE: Beverage Dispensers

Als Holding Inc ....G 860 627-7003
  East Windsor *(G-2481)*

REFRIGERATION EQPT: Complete

Demartino Fixture Co Inc ....E 203 269-3971
  Wallingford *(G-9248)*
Wine Well Chiller Comp Inc ....G 203 878-2465
  Milford *(G-4681)*

REFUSE SYSTEMS

MJ Metal Inc ....E 203 334-3484
  Bridgeport *(G-840)*
Tipping Pt Resources Group LLC ....G 800 603-8902
  New Haven *(G-5415)*

REGULATORS: Line Voltage

71 Pickett District Road LLC ....G 860 350-5964
  New Milford *(G-5502)*
Neeltran Inc ....C 860 350-5964
  New Milford *(G-5564)*
Neeltran International Inc ....G 860 350-5964
  New Milford *(G-5565)*

REHABILITATION CENTER, OUTPATIENT TREATMENT

Functional Concepts LLC ....G 203 813-0157
  Stratford *(G-8614)*

RELAYS: Electronic Usage

Allied Controls Inc ....F 860 628-8443
  Stamford *(G-8072)*
Component Concepts Inc ....G 860 523-4066
  West Hartford *(G-9792)*
Computer Components Inc ....F 860 653-9909
  East Granby *(G-2199)*
General Electro Components ....G 860 659-3573
  Glastonbury *(G-3039)*

REMOVERS & CLEANERS

Clean Up Group ....G 203 668-8323
  Meriden *(G-4159)*
Handyscape LLC ....G 860 318-1067
  Southington *(G-7932)*

RENTAL SVCS: Aircraft

Aircastle Advisor LLC ....D 203 504-1020
  Stamford *(G-8069)*

RENTAL SVCS: Beach & Water Sports Eqpt

Wild Bills Action Sports LLC ....G 860 536-6648
  Groton *(G-3319)*

RENTAL SVCS: Business Machine & Electronic Eqpt

Neopost USA Inc ....C 203 301-3400
  Milford *(G-4588)*
Pitney Bowes Inc ....A 203 356-5000
  Stamford *(G-8362)*
Pitney Bowes Inc ....E 203 356-5000
  Stamford *(G-8363)*

PRODUCT SECTION

Pitney Bowes Inc .... E 203 922-4000
  Shelton *(G-7529)*
Pitney Bowes Inc .... E 203 356-5000
  Shelton *(G-7530)*

RENTAL SVCS: Home Cleaning & Maintenance Eqpt

Prospect Flooring .... G 203 758-4207
  Prospect *(G-7017)*

RENTAL SVCS: Recreational Vehicle

M & J Bus Co .... G 203 624-0836
  North Haven *(G-5960)*
M & J Bus Co Inc .... G 860 437-3721
  Waterford *(G-9660)*
M & J Bus Inc .... G 860 668-6526
  Suffield *(G-8724)*

RENTAL SVCS: Saddle Horse

Lathrop Stables LLC .... G 860 230-9949
  Plainfield *(G-6746)*

RENTAL SVCS: Tent & Tarpaulin

3333 LLC .... G 860 643-1384
  Manchester *(G-3971)*

RENTAL SVCS: Video Disk/Tape, To The General Public

Video Outlet .... G 860 568-7473
  East Hartford *(G-2400)*

RENTAL: Video Tape & Disc

Botanica Chachitas .... G 860 247-5103
  Hartford *(G-3558)*

REPRODUCTION SVCS: Video Tape Or Disk

Cine Magnetics Inc .... C 914 273-7600
  Stamford *(G-8147)*
Joseph Malavenda .... G 203 746-4160
  New Fairfield *(G-5170)*
Play-It Productions Inc .... F 212 695-6530
  Colchester *(G-1566)*

RESEARCH, DEVELOPMENT & TEST SVCS, COMM: Business Analysis

Litigation Analytics Inc .... F 203 431-0300
  Ridgefield *(G-7154)*

RESEARCH, DEVELOPMENT & TEST SVCS, COMM: Cmptr Hardware Dev

Newmack Inc .... G 203 568-0443
  Middlebury *(G-4285)*
Ventus Technologies LLC .... F 203 642-2800
  Norwalk *(G-6385)*

RESEARCH, DEVELOPMENT & TEST SVCS, COMM: Research, Exc Lab

Callaway Companies Inc .... F 860 434-9002
  Old Lyme *(G-6496)*
Chad Labs Corporation .... G 203 877-3891
  Milford *(G-4487)*
Composites Inc .... G 860 646-1698
  Manchester *(G-3997)*
Freethink Technologies Inc .... F 860 237-5800
  Branford *(G-597)*
Healthy Harvest Inc .... G 203 245-3786
  Madison *(G-3927)*
Innophase Corp .... G 860 399-2269
  Westbrook *(G-9998)*

RESEARCH, DEVELOPMENT & TESTING SVCS, COMM: Research Lab

F S P Research Inc .... G 203 874-3417
  Milford *(G-4534)*

RESEARCH, DEVELOPMENT & TESTING SVCS, COMMERCIAL: Business

Marlin Company .... D 203 294-9800
  Wallingford *(G-9312)*

Sonalysts Inc .... B 860 442-4355
  Waterford *(G-9672)*
Vitek Research Corporation .... F 203 735-1813
  Naugatuck *(G-4928)*

RESEARCH, DEVELOPMENT & TESTING SVCS, COMMERCIAL: Education

Benedict M Lai .... G 425 698-7267
  Manchester *(G-3986)*

RESEARCH, DEVELOPMENT & TESTING SVCS, COMMERCIAL: Energy

Alacrity Semiconductors Inc .... G 475 325-8435
  Branford *(G-540)*
Ebeam Film LLC .... F 203 926-0100
  Shelton *(G-7434)*
Frc Founders Corporation .... E 203 661-6601
  Stamford *(G-8209)*
Maine Power Express LLC .... G 203 661-0055
  Greenwich *(G-3197)*

RESEARCH, DEVELOPMENT & TESTING SVCS, COMMERCIAL: Medical

Home Diagnostics Corp .... C 203 445-1170
  Trumbull *(G-9035)*

RESEARCH, DEVELOPMENT & TESTING SVCS, COMMERCIAL: Physical

Beta Pharma Inc .... F 203 315-5062
  Shelton *(G-7403)*

RESEARCH, DEVELOPMENT SVCS, COMMERCIAL: Indl Lab

Integral Technologies Inc .... G 860 741-2281
  Enfield *(G-2652)*

RESEARCH, DVLPT & TEST SVCS, COMM: Mkt Analysis or Research

Information Resources Inc .... D 203 845-6400
  Norwalk *(G-6207)*
Tri Source Inc .... F 203 924-7030
  Shelton *(G-7570)*

RESIDENTIAL REMODELERS

Jim N I LLC .... G 860 646-5155
  Andover *(G-10)*

RESIDUES

Lanxess Solutions US Inc .... E 203 573-2000
  Shelton *(G-7486)*

RESINS: Custom Compound Purchased

Electric Cable Compounds Inc .... D 203 723-2590
  Naugatuck *(G-4879)*
Foster Corporation .... D 860 928-4102
  Putnam *(G-7042)*
Neu Spclty Engineered Mtls LLC .... F 203 239-9629
  North Haven *(G-5967)*
New Polymer Systems .... G 203 594-7774
  New Canaan *(G-5124)*
Performance Compounding Inc .... G 860 599-5616
  Pawcatuck *(G-6722)*
Pioneer Plastics Corporation .... D 203 925-1556
  Shelton *(G-7527)*
Visual Polymer Tech LLC .... G 603 488-5263
  Canton *(G-1328)*

RESISTORS

Able Coil and Electronics Co .... E 860 646-5686
  Bolton *(G-504)*
Prime Technology LLC .... C 203 481-5721
  North Branford *(G-5853)*
Vishay Americas Inc .... B 203 452-5648
  Shelton *(G-7580)*

RESPIRATORY SYSTEM DRUGS

Infirst Healthcare Inc .... G 203 222-1300
  Westport *(G-10100)*

RETAIL BAKERY: Cakes

RESTAURANT EQPT: Carts

JJ Greco Carting LLC .... G 203 661-4947
  Cos Cob *(G-1635)*

RESTAURANT EQPT: Food Wagons

Copeland Latasha .... G 860 728-8289
  Hartford *(G-3570)*
DJS Campus Kitchen LLC .... G 860 439-1572
  New London *(G-5469)*

RESTAURANTS: Delicatessen

Bagelman III Inc .... F 203 792-0030
  Danbury *(G-1749)*
Beckley Inc .... G 203 488-1019
  Branford *(G-557)*

RESTAURANTS: Full Svc, American

Congress Catering Inc .... E 860 291-8182
  East Hartford *(G-2309)*
Krystal Inc LLC .... G 860 844-1267
  Granby *(G-3110)*

RESTAURANTS: Full Svc, Chinese

Lu Lu Holdings LLC .... E 203 861-1988
  Greenwich *(G-3193)*

RESTAURANTS: Full Svc, Ethnic Food

Chef J R ME Rest Group Corp .... G 860 940-8038
  New Britain *(G-4960)*

RESTAURANTS: Full Svc, Family

Vazzanos Catering LLC .... F 203 378-3331
  Trumbull *(G-9091)*

RESTAURANTS: Full Svc, Italian

Grotto Always Inc .... F 203 754-0295
  Waterbury *(G-9491)*
Libbys Italian Pastry Shop .... G 203 234-2530
  North Haven *(G-5959)*

RESTAURANTS: Limited Svc, Coffee Shop

Daybrake Donuts Inc .... E 203 368-4962
  Bridgeport *(G-742)*
What A Life LLC .... G 860 632-1962
  Cromwell *(G-1724)*
Whole Donut .... F 860 745-3041
  Enfield *(G-2706)*

RESTAURANTS: Limited Svc, Ice Cream Stands Or Dairy Bars

Big Dipper Ice Cream Fctry Inc .... E 203 758-3200
  Prospect *(G-6994)*
Cold Stone Creamery .... G 860 669-7025
  Clinton *(G-1495)*
J Foster Ice Cream .... G 860 651-1499
  Simsbury *(G-7631)*
Jaksy 2 LLC .... G 203 371-4111
  Fairfield *(G-2799)*
Michaels Dairy Inc .... F 860 443-7617
  New London *(G-5479)*

RESTAURANTS: Ltd Svc, Ice Cream, Soft Drink/Fountain Stands

Smoothie King .... G 860 574-9382
  Waterford *(G-9671)*

RETAIL BAKERY: Bread

Amoun Pita & Distribution LLC .... E 866 239-9990
  South Windsor *(G-7708)*
Apicellas Bakery Inc .... E 203 865-6204
  New Haven *(G-5232)*
Oasis Coffee Corp .... E 203 847-0554
  Norwalk *(G-6283)*

RETAIL BAKERY: Cakes

Modern Pastry Shop Inc .... E 860 296-7628
  Hartford *(G-3645)*
Mozzicato Pastry & Bake Shop .... E 860 296-0426
  Hartford *(G-3646)*
Rafael Cakes & Sugar LLC .... G 203 642-4840
  Norwalk *(G-6314)*

RETAIL BAKERY: Doughnuts

DAndrea Corporation .... F 203 932-6000
  West Haven *(G-9895)*
Darien Doughnut LLC .... G 203 656-2805
  Darien *(G-2017)*
Donut Stop .... G 203 924-7133
  Shelton *(G-7433)*
Pops Donuts .... G 203 876-1210
  Milford *(G-4610)*
Realejo Donuts Inc .... F 860 342-5120
  Portland *(G-6971)*
Spencer Street Inc .... G 860 647-2955
  Manchester *(G-4092)*
Whole Donut .... F 860 745-3041
  Enfield *(G-2706)*

RETAIL LUMBER YARDS

A & K Railroad Materials Inc .... G 203 495-8790
  Hamden *(G-3409)*
Board Silly Custom Sawmill LLC . G 203 438-3631
  Ridgefield *(G-7119)*
Conway Hardwood Products LLC E 860 355-4030
  Gaylordsville *(G-2991)*
Distributors of Standard Tile .... G 860 439-0627
  New London *(G-5468)*
Harris Enterprise Corp .... E 860 649-4663
  Manchester *(G-4025)*
St Pierre Box and Lumber Co ..... G 860 413-9813
  Canton *(G-1326)*

RETAIL STORES, NEC

Amentos Gold Buyers and Secon G 203 691-1020
  North Haven *(G-5900)*

RETAIL STORES: Architectural Splys

Technical Reproductions Inc .... F 203 849-9100
  Norwalk *(G-6365)*
West Hartford Lock Co LLC .... F 860 236-0671
  Hartford *(G-3714)*

RETAIL STORES: Audio-Visual Eqpt & Splys

John Samuel Group .... G 860 806-5734
  Torrington *(G-8939)*

RETAIL STORES: Awnings

Awnings Plus LLC .... G 860 496-7996
  Torrington *(G-8899)*
Meriden Awning & Decorating Co G 203 634-0067
  Meriden *(G-4194)*
Window Pdts Awngs Blind Shade G 203 481-9772
  Branford *(G-676)*

RETAIL STORES: Banners

Young Flan LLC .... G 203 878-0084
  Derby *(G-2134)*

RETAIL STORES: Canvas Prdts

Econony Canvas Co .... G 860 289-5281
  Hartford *(G-3582)*

RETAIL STORES: Concrete Prdts, Precast

Washington Concrete Products ... F 860 747-5242
  Plainville *(G-6876)*

RETAIL STORES: Cosmetics

Revive Beauty and Wellness LLC G 860 921-4952
  Brookfield *(G-1218)*

RETAIL STORES: Educational Aids & Electronic Training Mat

Hotseat Chassis Inc .... G 860 582-5031
  Waterbury *(G-9499)*
Sugar Run K9 LLC .... G 860 591-4193
  Voluntown *(G-9191)*

RETAIL STORES: Electronic Parts & Eqpt

Koninklijke Philips Elec NV .... F 860 886-2621
  Norwich *(G-6421)*

RETAIL STORES: Flags

Flagman of America LLP .... G 860 678-0275
  Avon *(G-81)*

RETAIL STORES: Hearing Aids

Zenith-Omni Hearing Center .... G 203 624-9857
  New Haven *(G-5454)*

RETAIL STORES: Insecticides

Pic20 Group LLC .... F 203 957-3555
  Norwalk *(G-6299)*

RETAIL STORES: Mobile Telephones & Eqpt

American Bus Tele & Tech LLC .. G 860 643-2200
  Manchester *(G-3982)*

RETAIL STORES: Monuments, Finished To Custom Order

Artista Studio Monument .... G 203 333-9224
  Bridgeport *(G-704)*

RETAIL STORES: Motors, Electric

Aparos Electric Motor Service ..... G 860 276-2044
  Southington *(G-7891)*
Central Electric Motor .... G 860 642-7421
  Lebanon *(G-3850)*
Industrial Electric Motors .... G 203 743-9611
  Danbury *(G-1849)*
Nicholas Melfi Jr .... G 203 853-7235
  Norwalk *(G-6278)*
Palmers Elc Mtrs & Pumps Inc ... G 203 348-7378
  Norwalk *(G-6290)*
Power Quality and Drives LLC ... G 203 217-2353
  Woodbury *(G-10651)*

RETAIL STORES: Orthopedic & Prosthesis Applications

Kaufman Enterprises Inc .... F 203 777-2396
  New Haven *(G-5307)*

RETAIL STORES: Plumbing & Heating Splys

Granite Group Wholesalers LLC . G 860 537-7600
  Colchester *(G-1552)*
Kensco Inc .... F 203 734-8827
  Ansonia *(G-44)*

RETAIL STORES: Police Splys

Fenrir Industries Inc .... F 203 977-0671
  Stamford *(G-8203)*
Mhq Inc .... F 888 242-1118
  Middletown *(G-4376)*

RETAIL STORES: Rubber Stamps

Academy Printing Service .... G 860 828-5549
  Kensington *(G-3803)*
Acme Sign Co .... F 203 324-2263
  Stamford *(G-8059)*
Arlene Lewis .... G 860 887-4265
  Preston *(G-6981)*

RETAIL STORES: Safety Splys & Eqpt

Stormwaterworkscom LLC .... G 203 324-0045
  Stamford *(G-8445)*

RETAIL STORES: Telephone & Communication Eqpt

Northastern Communications Inc F 203 381-9008
  Stratford *(G-8654)*

RETAIL STORES: Training Materials, Electronic

T&K Technical Services LLC ...... G 860 235-5882
  Quaker Hill *(G-7085)*

RETAIL STORES: Water Purification Eqpt

Clearwater Treatment Systems L G 860 799-0303
  New Milford *(G-5520)*

RETAIL STORES: Welding Splys

Praxair Distribution Inc .... F 203 837-2000
  Danbury *(G-1914)*

RETREADING MATERIALS: Tire

Major Tire Co LLC .... G 203 543-0334
  Stratford *(G-8645)*

REUPHOLSTERY & FURNITURE REPAIR

Bonito Manufacturing Inc .... D 203 234-8786
  North Haven *(G-5915)*
High Grade Finishing Co LLC ..... G 860 749-8883
  Enfield *(G-2649)*

REUPHOLSTERY SVCS

Ben Baena & Son .... G 203 334-8568
  Bridgeport *(G-710)*
C & D Upholstery .... G 203 838-1050
  Norwalk *(G-6104)*
Custom Upholstery Workshop .... G 203 367-4231
  Fairfield *(G-2770)*
General Seating Solutions LLC .. F 860 242-3307
  South Windsor *(G-7757)*
Lyons Upholstery Shop Inc .... G 203 269-3782
  Wallingford *(G-9308)*
Tassels .... G 203 231-0973
  Derby *(G-2128)*

RIBBONS & BOWS

Charles Clay Ltd .... G 203 662-0125
  New Canaan *(G-5093)*

RIBBONS, NEC

National Ribbon LLC .... G 860 742-6966
  Coventry *(G-1664)*

RIDING APPAREL STORES

Fiddle Horse Farm LLC .... G 203 557-3285
  Westport *(G-10080)*

RIVETS: Metal

Edson Manufacturing Inc .... F 203 879-1411
  Wolcott *(G-10563)*
Howard Engineering LLC .... E 203 729-5213
  Naugatuck *(G-4889)*
Nucap US Inc .... E 203 879-1423
  Wolcott *(G-10578)*

ROBOTS: Assembly Line

Act Robots Inc .... G 860 314-1557
  Bristol *(G-956)*

RODS: Plastic

East Coast Precision Mfg LLC .... G 978 887-5920
  Killingworth *(G-3832)*

RODS: Steel & Iron, Made In Steel Mills

CMI Specialty Products Inc .... F 860 585-0409
  Bristol *(G-1003)*
Nucor Steel Connecticut Inc .... C 203 265-0615
  Wallingford *(G-9330)*

RODS: Welding

Weldingrodscom LLC .... G 888 935-3703
  Suffield *(G-8738)*

ROLLERS: Wooden

American Metaseal of Conn .... G 203 787-0281
  Hamden *(G-3414)*

ROLLING MILL EQPT: Rod Mills

Technology In Controls Inc .... G 860 283-8405
  Plymouth *(G-6929)*

ROLLING MILL MACHINERY

Adam Z Golas .... G 860 224-7178
  New Britain *(G-4936)*
Compass Group Management LLC F 203 221-1703
  Westport *(G-10068)*
Ulbrich Stainless Steels .... C 203 269-2507
  Wallingford *(G-9393)*

ROLLING MILL ROLLS: Cast Steel

Tenova Inc .... E 203 265-5684
  Wallingford *(G-9380)*

ROLLS & ROLL COVERINGS: Rubber

American Roller Company LLC ....F...... 203 598-3100
  Middlebury (G-4273)
Scapa North America Inc ....G...... 860 688-8000
  Windsor (G-10433)

ROLLS: Rubber, Solid Or Covered

Nauta Roll Corporation ....G...... 860 267-2027
  East Hampton (G-2270)

ROOF DECKS

Jhs Restoration Inc ....F...... 860 757-3870
  South Windsor (G-7777)

ROOFING MATERIALS: Asphalt

Epdm Coatings ....G...... 203 225-0104
  Shelton (G-7441)
Qba Inc ....G...... 860 963-9438
  Woodstock (G-10679)
Roofing Solutions ....G...... 860 444-0486
  New London (G-5487)

ROOFING MATERIALS: Sheet Metal

Northeast Panel Co LLC ....G...... 860 678-9078
  Farmington (G-2940)
Nt Lawn Service ....G...... 203 573-0285
  Waterbury (G-9563)

ROOFING MEMBRANE: Rubber

Courtman Enterprises LLC ....G...... 860 322-2837
  Windsor (G-10378)

RUBBER PRDTS

Apache Mill ....G...... 401 597-5580
  Branford (G-546)
Buestan Usa LLC ....G...... 203 954-8889
  Ansonia (G-25)
HI Tech Profiles Inc ....G...... 401 377-2040
  Pawcatuck (G-6714)
Ross Enterprises ....G...... 860 308-2238
  Hartford (G-3682)
Warco of Ne LLC ....G...... 203 393-1691
  Woodbridge (G-10621)

RUBBER PRDTS: Mechanical

Acmt Inc ....D...... 860 645-0592
  Manchester (G-3977)
Applied Rubber & Plastics Inc ....F...... 860 987-9018
  Windsor (G-10363)
Buestan Usa LLC ....G...... 203 954-8889
  Ansonia (G-25)
Jem Manufacturing Inc ....G...... 203 250-9404
  Wallingford (G-9294)
Vanguard Products Corporation ...D...... 203 744-7265
  Danbury (G-1970)

RUBBER PRDTS: Reclaimed

Meridian Operations LLC ....F...... 860 564-8811
  Plainfield (G-6749)
Rogers Corporation ....C...... 860 928-3622
  Woodstock (G-10681)

RUBBER PRDTS: Silicone

FMI Chemical Inc ....F...... 860 243-3222
  Bloomfield (G-413)
Heaters Inc ....G...... 860 739-5477
  Niantic (G-5809)

RUBBER PRDTS: Sponge

Griswold LLC ....D...... 860 564-3321
  Moosup (G-4779)

RUBBER STAMP, WHOLESALE

First Place USA LLC ....G...... 203 777-7510
  Hamden (G-3448)

RUGS : Hand & Machine Made

Srirret America ....G...... 203 988-1852
  Madison (G-3961)

RULES: Slide

Slide Rule Group LLC ....G...... 860 317-1624
  Moosup (G-4782)

SADDLERY STORES

Fiddle Horse Farm LLC ....G...... 203 557-3285
  Westport (G-10080)

SAFE DEPOSIT BOXES

Yarde Metals Inc ....B...... 860 406-6061
  Southington (G-7997)

SAFETY EQPT & SPLYS WHOLESALERS

Elvex Corporation ....F...... 203 743-2488
  Shelton (G-7438)

SAILBOAT BUILDING & REPAIR

McClave Philbrick & Giblin ....G...... 860 572-7710
  Mystic (G-4831)

SAILS

Ace Sailmakers ....G...... 860 739-5999
  East Lyme (G-2462)
Fairclough Sailmakers Inc ....G...... 203 787-2322
  New Haven (G-5281)
Farrar Sails Inc ....G...... 860 447-0382
  New London (G-5471)
Kappa Sails LLC ....G...... 860 399-8899
  Gales Ferry (G-2985)
Liberty Services LLC ....G...... 860 399-0077
  Westbrook (G-10002)
Mbm Sales ....F...... 203 866-3674
  Norwalk (G-6252)
North Sails Group LLC ....D...... 203 874-7548
  Milford (G-4594)
Sail Spars Design LLC ....G...... 860 429-9866
  Storrs Mansfield (G-8559)

SALES PROMOTION SVCS

Ark Innovations LLC ....G...... 860 674-8800
  Farmington (G-2878)
Educational Resources Network ...G...... 203 866-9973
  Ridgefield (G-7138)
Fairfield Marketing Group Inc ....F...... 203 261-0884
  Easton (G-2552)

SALT

Eastern Salt Company ....G...... 203 466-6761
  New Haven (G-5272)

SAND & GRAVEL

Adelman Sand & Gravel Inc ....E...... 860 889-3394
  Bozrah (G-522)
Almond Sand Elephants ....G...... 860 232-4888
  West Hartford (G-9773)
B & C Sand & Gravel Company ...G...... 203 335-6640
  Bridgeport (G-706)
Bethel Sand & Gravel Co ....G...... 203 743-4469
  Bethel (G-264)
Brooklyn Sand & Gravel LLC ....G...... 860 779-3980
  Danielson (G-1987)
Dan Beard Inc ....F...... 203 924-4346
  Shelton (G-7427)
Dens Sand & Gravel ....G...... 860 642-6478
  Lebanon (G-3853)
Desiato Sand & Gravel ....G...... 860 742-7573
  Coventry (G-1652)
Desiato Sand & Gravel Corp ....E...... 860 429-6479
  Storrs Mansfield (G-8555)
Doug Hartin ....G...... 860 377-4283
  Woodstock (G-10663)
Freedom Properties ....G...... 860 508-3349
  West Hartford (G-9811)
Galasso Materials LLC ....C...... 860 527-1825
  East Granby (G-2206)
Hathaway Sand & Gravel LLC ......G...... 860 647-7772
  Bolton (G-511)
Jn Construction LLC ....G...... 914 483-2998
  Stamford (G-8264)
John Hychko ....G...... 203 757-3458
  Waterbury (G-9512)
Midwood Quarry and Cnstr Inc .....F...... 860 289-1414
  East Hartford (G-2345)
O & G Industries Inc ....E...... 203 323-1111
  Stamford (G-8336)
Palumbo Sand & Gravel ....G...... 860 350-5322
  Sherman (G-7600)
Pine Ridge Gravel LLC ....G...... 860 873-2500
  East Haddam (G-2248)
Powder Hill Sand & Gravel LLC ....G...... 860 741-7274
  Enfield (G-2679)
Skyline Quarry ....E...... 860 875-3580
  Stafford Springs (G-8038)
Sterling Sand and Gravel LLC ......G...... 860 774-3985
  Sterling (G-8518)
Thomas Keegan & Sons Inc ....G...... 203 239-9248
  North Haven (G-5999)
Turning Stone Sand & Grav LLC ..G...... 413 519-1560
  Enfield (G-2702)
Valley Sand & Gravel Corp ....E...... 203 562-3192
  North Haven (G-6010)
West Hartford Stone Mulch LLC ...G...... 860 461-7616
  West Hartford (G-9872)
Woodview Construction Svcs LLC ..G..... 860 402-9032
  Windsor (G-10466)

SAND MINING

Brennan Realty LLC ....C...... 203 929-6314
  Shelton (G-7409)
Geer Construction Co Inc ....G...... 860 376-5321
  Jewett City (G-3795)
Judith Bennett ....G...... 203 729-6548
  Naugatuck (G-4895)
Judith Bennett ....G...... 203 255-6363
  Fairfield (G-2804)
Tilcon Connecticut Inc ....G...... 860 756-8016
  Newington (G-5712)
Tronox LLC ....E...... 203 705-3800
  Stamford (G-8478)
Wfs Earth Materialsi LLC ....G...... 203 488-2055
  Branford (G-673)

SAND: Hygrade

Unimin Lime Corporation ....F...... 203 966-8880
  New Canaan (G-5155)

SANDBLASTING EQPT

Bobs Sandbox ....G...... 860 267-4530
  Colchester (G-1543)

SANITARY SVCS: Dumps, Operation Of

Grillo Services LLC ....E...... 203 877-5070
  Milford (G-4544)

SANITARY SVCS: Environmental Cleanup

Cloverdale Inc ....G...... 860 672-0216
  West Cornwall (G-9762)
McVac Environmental Svcs Inc ....E...... 203 497-1960
  New Haven (G-5327)

SANITARY SVCS: Rubbish Collection & Disposal

Lostocco Refuse Service LLC ....E...... 203 748-9296
  Danbury (G-1877)

SANITARY SVCS: Waste Materials, Recycling

G & G Beverage Distributors ....D...... 203 949-6220
  Wallingford (G-9273)
Good Earth Tree Care Inc ....G...... 203 375-7962
  Stratford (G-8619)
Seaview Plastic Recycling Inc ....G...... 203 367-0070
  Bridgeport (G-899)

SANITATION CHEMICALS & CLEANING AGENTS

Citra Solv LLC ....G...... 203 778-0881
  Ridgefield (G-7128)
Edsan Chemical Company Inc .....C...... 203 624-3123
  New Haven (G-5273)
Global Shield Solutions LLC ....G...... 860 983-3566
  Brookfield (G-1192)
Griffith Company ....G...... 203 333-5557
  Bridgeport (G-780)
Hubbard-Hall Inc ....C...... 203 756-5521
  Waterbury (G-9501)
NC Brands LP ....D...... 203 295-2300
  Norwalk (G-6269)
Nci Holdings Inc ....E...... 203 295-2300
  Norwalk (G-6270)

SASHES: Door Or Window, Metal

Liberty Glass and Met Inds Inc .... E 860 923-3623
North Grosvenordale *(G-5888)*

SATCHELS

Leatherby .... G 860 658-6166
Weatogue *(G-9757)*

SATELLITE COMMUNICATIONS EQPT

Directv .... G 203 445-2876
Trumbull *(G-9021)*

SATELLITES: Communications

Newtec America Inc .... F 203 323-0042
Stamford *(G-8327)*

SAW BLADES

DArcy Saw LLC .... G 800 569-1264
Windsor Locks *(G-10481)*
Elka Precision .... G 860 526-1674
New Britain *(G-4981)*
Nesci Enterprises Inc .... G 860 267-2588
East Hampton *(G-2271)*

SAWDUST & SHAVINGS

Autumn Colors .... G 860 822-6568
Norwich *(G-6407)*

SAWING & PLANING MILLS

A&D Enterprises .... G 860 779-9025
Danielson *(G-1985)*
Board Silly Custom Sawmill LLC .... G 203 438-3631
Ridgefield *(G-7119)*
Burell Bros Inc .... G 860 455-9681
Hampton *(G-3534)*
Cedar Swamp Log & Lumber .... G 860 974-2344
Woodstock *(G-10661)*
Charles Pike & Sons .... G 860 455-9968
Hampton *(G-3535)*
Dalla Corte Lumber .... G 860 875-9480
Stafford Springs *(G-8024)*
Davis Sawmill .... G 860 354-6008
New Milford *(G-5527)*
Eylward Timber Co .... G 203 265-4276
Wallingford *(G-9265)*
Gebhardts Sawmill .... G 860 423-0123
Windham *(G-10346)*
Gregorys Sawmill LLC .... G 203 762-8298
Wilton *(G-10298)*
Hardwood Lumber Manufacturing .... E 860 423-2447
Scotland *(G-7332)*
Hedden Forest Products .... G 860 672-6023
West Cornwall *(G-9763)*
Henry W Zuwalick & Sons Inc .... G 203 488-3821
Branford *(G-604)*
Hull Forest Products Inc .... E 860 974-0127
Pomfret Center *(G-6939)*
John J Pawloski Lumber Inc .... G 203 794-0737
Bethel *(G-316)*
Jordan Saw Mill L L C .... F 860 774-0247
Sterling *(G-8510)*
Mallery Lumber Inc .... G 860 632-3505
Cromwell *(G-1707)*
Moores Sawmill Inc .... G 860 242-3003
Bloomfield *(G-446)*
New England Forest Products .... G 203 457-0314
Guilford *(G-3379)*
Parker Septic Service .... F 860 749-8220
Somers *(G-7667)*
Saw Mill Capital LLC .... G 203 662-0573
Darien *(G-2043)*
Saw Miners Mill .... G 860 599-5012
Pawcatuck *(G-6724)*
Sigfridson Wood Products LLC .... G 860 774-2075
Brooklyn *(G-1254)*
South Norfolk Lumber Co .... G 860 542-5650
Norfolk *(G-5826)*
Walker Industries LLC .... G 860 455-3554
Ashford *(G-67)*

SAWING & PLANING MILLS: Custom

Jim N I LLC .... G 860 646-5155
Andover *(G-10)*

SAWS & SAWING EQPT

Darien Lawn Mower Repair .... G 203 656-1869
Darien *(G-2018)*
Kucko Chain Saw Supplies .... G 860 684-3887
Willington *(G-10251)*

SCAFFOLDS: Mobile Or Stationary, Metal

Bhs .... G 860 585-0125
Bristol *(G-983)*

SCALE REPAIR SVCS

Able Scale & Equipment Corp .... G 860 646-6929
Manchester *(G-3975)*

SCALES & BALANCES, EXC LABORATORY

Able Scale & Equipment Corp .... G 860 646-6929
Manchester *(G-3975)*
Action Scale Service .... G 203 577-6420
Middlebury *(G-4271)*
Kenneth Allevo .... G 860 745-0740
Enfield *(G-2654)*
Reliable Scales & Systems LLC .... G 860 380-0600
Bristol *(G-1105)*
Rice Lake Weighing Systems Inc .... G 203 270-6012
Newtown *(G-5775)*

SCALES: Indl

Compuweigh Corporation .... E 203 262-9400
Woodbury *(G-10629)*
North Eastern Scale Corp .... G 203 634-7942
Meriden *(G-4210)*

SCANNING DEVICES: Optical

Dark Field Technologies Inc .... F 203 298-0731
Shelton *(G-7428)*
Eye Ear It LLC .... F 203 487-8949
Woodbury *(G-10636)*
Iwco Direct .... G 203 557-4303
Westport *(G-10105)*
Mannan 3d Innovations LLC .... G 860 306-4203
Higganum *(G-3768)*
Scan-Optics LLC .... D 860 645-7878
Manchester *(G-4087)*

SCHOOL SPLYS, EXC BOOKS: Wholesalers

S & S Worldwide Inc .... C 860 537-3451
Colchester *(G-1574)*

SCIENTIFIC EQPT REPAIR SVCS

Independent Repair Service .... G 203 234-0218
North Haven *(G-5947)*

SCISSORS: Hand

Acme United Corporation .... C 203 254-6060
Fairfield *(G-2743)*

SCRAP & WASTE MATERIALS, WHOLESALE: Auto Wrecking For Scrap

Lajoies Auto Wrecking Co Inc .... E 203 870-0641
Norwalk *(G-6230)*

SCRAP & WASTE MATERIALS, WHOLESALE: Ferrous Metal

MJ Metal Inc .... E 203 334-3484
Bridgeport *(G-840)*
Surf Metal Co Inc .... G 203 375-2211
Stratford *(G-8692)*

SCRAP & WASTE MATERIALS, WHOLESALE: Metal

All Star Welding & Dem LLC .... G 203 948-0528
Danbury *(G-1735)*

SCRAP & WASTE MATERIALS, WHOLESALE: Paper

Willimantic Waste Paper Co Inc .... C 860 423-4527
Willimantic *(G-10240)*

SCRAP STEEL CUTTING

Reliant Services LLC .... G 860 346-6107
Middletown *(G-4404)*

SCREW MACHINE PRDTS

Alinabal Inc .... F 860 828-9933
Kensington *(G-3805)*
Atp Industries LLC .... F 860 479-5007
Plainville *(G-6773)*
Automatic Machine Products .... G 860 346-7064
Middletown *(G-4320)*
B&T Screw Machine Co Inc .... F 860 314-4410
Bristol *(G-971)*
Bar Work Manufacturing Co Inc .... F 203 753-4103
Waterbury *(G-9436)*
Biedermann Mfg Inds Inc .... G 860 283-8268
Thomaston *(G-8781)*
Bobken Automatics Inc .... G 203 757-5525
Waterbury *(G-9439)*
Brass City Technologies LLC .... G 203 723-7021
Naugatuck *(G-4863)*
Bristol Tool Works LLC .... G 860 585-7302
Bristol *(G-994)*
Brophy Metal Products Inc .... G 860 621-3636
Southington *(G-7898)*
C & A Machine Co Inc .... E 860 667-0605
Newington *(G-5636)*
C C Precision Products Co Inc .... G 860 628-4403
Southington *(G-7900)*
C-Tech Manufacturing Co LLC .... G 860 274-6879
Watertown *(G-9689)*
Cadcom Inc .... F 203 877-0640
Milford *(G-4479)*
Caine Machining Inc .... G 860 738-1619
Winsted *(G-10513)*
Cole S Crew Machine Products .... E 203 723-1418
North Haven *(G-5922)*
Creed-Monarch Inc .... B 860 225-7884
New Britain *(G-4968)*
Curtis Products LLC .... F 203 754-4155
Bristol *(G-1010)*
D & M Screw Machine Pdts LLC .... G 860 410-9781
Plainville *(G-6795)*
Dacruz Manufacturing Inc .... G 860 584-5315
Bristol *(G-1011)*
David Derewianka .... G 860 649-1983
Manchester *(G-4003)*
Day Fred A Co LLC .... G 860 589-0531
Bristol *(G-1012)*
Day Machine Systems Inc .... F 860 229-3440
New Britain *(G-4971)*
Deco Products Inc .... G 860 528-4304
East Hartford *(G-2312)*
Devon Precision Industries Inc .... D 203 879-1437
Wolcott *(G-10560)*
Don S Screw Machine Pdts LLC .... G 860 283-6448
Thomaston *(G-8787)*
Duda and Goodwin Inc .... F 203 263-4353
Woodbury *(G-10634)*
Durco Manufacturing Co Inc .... G 203 575-0446
Waterbury *(G-9467)*
E P M Co Inc .... G 860 589-3233
Bristol *(G-1024)*
Electro-Tech Inc .... E 203 271-1976
Cheshire *(G-1384)*
F F Screw Products Inc .... E 860 621-4567
Southington *(G-7921)*
Fleetwood Industries Inc .... G 860 747-6750
Plainville *(G-6811)*
Forestville Machine Co Inc .... G 860 747-6000
Plainville *(G-6813)*
G M T Manufacturing Co Inc .... G 860 628-6757
Plantsville *(G-6894)*
Garmac Screw Machine Inc .... F 203 723-6911
Naugatuck *(G-4883)*
Horst Engrg De Mexico LLC .... E 860 289-8209
East Hartford *(G-2334)*
J & R Projects .... G 203 879-2347
Waterbury *(G-9507)*
J J Ryan Corporation .... C 860 628-0393
Plantsville *(G-6897)*
James Wright Precision Pdts .... F 860 928-7756
Putnam *(G-7049)*
Jay Sons Screw Mch Pdts Inc .... F 860 621-0141
Milldale *(G-4684)*
Jeskey LLC .... E 203 772-6675
North Haven *(G-5952)*
Kamatics Corporation .... E 860 243-9704
Bloomfield *(G-435)*

PRODUCT SECTION — SECURITY PROTECTIVE DEVICES MAINTENANCE & MONITORING SVCS

Kemby Manufacturing ....G....... 860 582-2850
  Terryville *(G-8761)*
Leipold Inc ....E....... 860 298-9791
  Windsor *(G-10404)*
Mackson Mfg Co Inc ....F....... 860 589-4035
  Bristol *(G-1065)*
Mailly Manufacturing Company ....G....... 203 879-1445
  Wolcott *(G-10573)*
Manufacturers Associates Inc ....E....... 203 931-4344
  West Haven *(G-9930)*
Mario Precision Products ....G....... 203 758-3101
  Prospect *(G-7009)*
Matthew Warren Inc ....G....... 203 888-2133
  Seymour *(G-7355)*
Microbest Inc ....C....... 203 597-0355
  Waterbury *(G-9542)*
Mitchell Machine Screw Company ....G....... 860 633-7713
  Glastonbury *(G-3061)*
Multi-Metal Manufacturing Inc ....E....... 203 723-8887
  Naugatuck *(G-4904)*
OEM Sources LLC ....G....... 203 283-5415
  Milford *(G-4597)*
Olson Brothers Company ....F....... 860 747-6844
  Plainville *(G-6850)*
Palladin Precision Pdts Inc ....E....... 203 574-0246
  Waterbury *(G-9574)*
Petron Automation Inc ....E....... 860 274-9091
  Watertown *(G-9722)*
Precision Methods Incorporated ....F....... 203 879-1429
  Wolcott *(G-10580)*
Prime Engneered Components Inc ....G....... 860 274-6773
  Watertown *(G-9723)*
Prime Screw Machine Pdts Inc ....D....... 860 274-6773
  Watertown *(G-9725)*
Pro-Manufactured Products Inc ....G....... 203 564-2197
  Plainfield *(G-6750)*
Quality Automatics Inc ....E....... 860 945-4795
  Oakville *(G-6459)*
Raypax Manufacturing Co Inc ....G....... 203 758-7416
  Waterbury *(G-9592)*
Rgd Technologies Corp ....D....... 860 589-0756
  Bristol *(G-1107)*
Royal Screw Machine Pdts Co ....E....... 860 845-8920
  Bristol *(G-1114)*
S & M Swiss Products Inc ....G....... 860 283-4020
  Thomaston *(G-8804)*
Selectcom Mfg Co Inc ....G....... 203 879-9900
  Wolcott *(G-10588)*
Sga Components Group LLC ....G....... 203 758-3702
  Prospect *(G-7024)*
Sheldon Precision LLC ....G....... 203 758-4441
  Waterbury *(G-9603)*
Sheldon Precision LLC ....G....... 203 758-4441
  Prospect *(G-7025)*
Space Swiss Manufacturing Inc ....F....... 860 567-4341
  Litchfield *(G-3900)*
Specialty Products Mfg LLC ....G....... 860 621-6969
  Southington *(G-7979)*
Sperry Automatics Co Inc ....E....... 203 729-4589
  Naugatuck *(G-4922)*
Sun Corp ....G....... 860 567-0817
  Morris *(G-4792)*
Supreme-Lake Mfg Inc ....D....... 860 621-8911
  Plantsville *(G-6913)*
T & J Screw Machine Pdts LLC ....G....... 860 417-3801
  Oakville *(G-6463)*
Thomastn-Mdtown Screw Mch Pdts ....F....... 860 283-9796
  Thomaston *(G-8812)*
Thomaston Industries Inc ....F....... 860 283-4358
  Thomaston *(G-8813)*
Tomz Corporation ....C....... 860 829-0670
  Berlin *(G-226)*
Tri-Star Industries Inc ....E....... 860 828-7570
  Berlin *(G-227)*
Tryon Manufacturing Company ....G....... 203 929-0464
  Shelton *(G-7572)*
Tyler Automatics Incorporated ....E....... 860 283-5878
  Thomaston *(G-8815)*
Ville Swiss Automatics Inc ....F....... 203 756-2825
  Waterbury *(G-9622)*
Waterbury Screw Machine ....G....... 203 756-8084
  Waterbury *(G-9629)*
Waterbury Screw Mch Pdts Co ....E....... 203 756-8084
  Waterbury *(G-9630)*
Waterbury Swiss Automatics ....G....... 203 573-8584
  Waterbury *(G-9631)*
Whiteledge Inc ....G....... 860 647-1883
  Manchester *(G-4106)*
Winslow Manufacturing Inc ....F....... 203 269-1977
  Wallingford *(G-9403)*
Wold Tool Engineering Inc ....G....... 860 564-8338
  Brooklyn *(G-1259)*

SCREW MACHINES
Tornos Technologies US Corp ....G....... 203 775-4319
  Brookfield *(G-1232)*

SCREWS: Metal
Aerotech Fasteners Inc ....F....... 860 928-6300
  Putnam *(G-7028)*
Crescent Mnfacturing Operating ....E....... 860 673-1921
  Burlington *(G-1265)*
L & M Manufacturing Co Inc ....E....... 203 379-2751
  New Hartford *(G-5201)*
Narragansett Screw Co ....F....... 203 379-4059
  Winsted *(G-10531)*
North East Fasteners Corp ....E....... 860 589-3242
  Terryville *(G-8767)*
Thread Rolling Inc ....F....... 860 528-1515
  East Hartford *(G-2385)*
Triem Industries LLC ....E....... 203 888-1212
  Terryville *(G-8775)*
Universal Thread Grinding Co ....F....... 203 336-1849
  Fairfield *(G-2861)*

SCREWS: Wood
John C Green ....G....... 203 878-3781
  Milford *(G-4561)*

SEALANTS
Grafted Coatings Inc ....F....... 203 377-9979
  Stratford *(G-8620)*
Sealpro LLC ....G....... 860 289-0804
  East Hartford *(G-2370)*
Smarter Sealants LLC ....G....... 860 218-2210
  East Hartford *(G-2374)*

SEALS: Hermetic
Northeast Electronics Corp ....D....... 203 878-3511
  Milford *(G-4595)*

SEARCH & DETECTION SYSTEMS, EXC RADAR
Exocetus Autonomous Systems ....G....... 860 512-7260
  Wallingford *(G-9263)*

SEARCH & NAVIGATION SYSTEMS
Beacon Group Inc ....C....... 860 594-5200
  Newington *(G-5631)*
Boeing Company ....G....... 860 627-9393
  East Windsor *(G-2485)*
Carrier Corp ....G....... 860 728-7000
  Rocky Hill *(G-7225)*
Chromalloy Component Svcs Inc ....C....... 860 688-7798
  Windsor *(G-10373)*
Cloud Cap Technology Inc ....G....... 541 308-1089
  Danbury *(G-1770)*
Connecticut Analytical Corp ....F....... 203 393-9666
  Bethany *(G-239)*
Drs Leonardo Inc ....E....... 203 798-3172
  Danbury *(G-1799)*
Edac Nd Inc ....D....... 860 633-9474
  Glastonbury *(G-3031)*
Electro-Methods Inc ....C....... 860 289-8661
  South Windsor *(G-7747)*
Gems Sensors Inc ....B....... 860 747-3000
  Plainville *(G-6815)*
Hartford Aircraft Products ....E....... 860 242-8228
  Bloomfield *(G-417)*
Lee Company ....A....... 860 399-6281
  Westbrook *(G-10000)*
Lockheed Martin Corporation ....G....... 860 447-8553
  New London *(G-5477)*
Meriden Manufacturing Inc ....D....... 203 237-7481
  Meriden *(G-4197)*
Northrop Grumman Corporation ....D....... 860 282-4461
  East Hartford *(G-2348)*
Passur Aerospace Inc ....E....... 203 622-4086
  Stamford *(G-8351)*
Polar Corporation ....E....... 860 223-7891
  New Britain *(G-5035)*
Raytheon Company ....E....... 860 446-4900
  Mystic *(G-4840)*
Spectrogram Corporation ....G....... 203 245-2433
  Madison *(G-3960)*
Sperian Protectn Instrumentatn ....C....... 860 344-1079
  Middletown *(G-4422)*

SEATING: Chairs, Table & Arm
Halls Rental Service LLC ....G....... 203 488-0383
  North Branford *(G-5841)*

SECRETARIAL & COURT REPORTING
A&V Typographics ....G....... 860 276-9060
  Plantsville *(G-6880)*
Graduate Group ....G....... 860 233-2330
  West Hartford *(G-9813)*
Kat Art Inc ....G....... 860 350-8016
  New Milford *(G-5554)*
Warren Press Inc ....G....... 203 431-0011
  Ridgefield *(G-7182)*

SECRETARIAL SVCS
Outer Office ....G....... 203 329-8600
  Stamford *(G-8347)*

SECURE STORAGE SVC: Document
CD Solutions Inc ....E....... 203 481-5895
  Branford *(G-571)*

SECURITY CONTROL EQPT & SYSTEMS
Assa Inc ....B....... 203 624-5225
  New Haven *(G-5235)*
Command Corporation ....F....... 800 851-6012
  East Granby *(G-2198)*
Donali Systems Integration Inc ....G....... 860 715-5432
  Guilford *(G-3346)*
Morse Watchmans Inc ....E....... 203 264-1108
  Oxford *(G-6679)*
New Line USA Inc ....G....... 860 498-0347
  Coventry *(G-1666)*
Security Systems Inc ....G....... 800 833-3211
  Middletown *(G-4409)*
SOS Security Incorporated ....G....... 860 563-2121
  Rocky Hill *(G-7265)*
Thomas Meade ....G....... 203 209-7591
  Shelton *(G-7565)*

SECURITY DEVICES
Aeroturn LLC ....G....... 203 262-8309
  Oxford *(G-6640)*
Check It Darien LLC ....G....... 203 655-2036
  Darien *(G-2012)*
Insight Plus Technology LLC ....G....... 860 930-4763
  Bristol *(G-1051)*
Isupportws Inc ....F....... 203 569-7600
  Stamford *(G-8260)*
Lighthouse Communications ....G....... 203 445-9733
  Monroe *(G-4728)*
R K S Security LLC ....G....... 860 749-4106
  Enfield *(G-2686)*
Stanley Black & Decker Inc ....C....... 860 225-5111
  New Britain *(G-5063)*
Stanley Black & Decker Inc ....C....... 860 225-5111
  New Britain *(G-5061)*
United Technologies Corp ....B....... 954 485-6501
  Farmington *(G-2973)*
United Technologies Corp ....B....... 860 610-7000
  East Hartford *(G-2395)*

SECURITY DISTRIBUTORS
Isupportws Inc ....F....... 203 569-7600
  Stamford *(G-8260)*

SECURITY EQPT STORES
Barile Printers LLC ....G....... 860 224-0127
  New Britain *(G-4950)*
Clg Enterprises Inc ....F....... 203 741-9300
  Wallingford *(G-9232)*

SECURITY PROTECTIVE DEVICES MAINTENANCE & MONITORING SVCS
Clg Enterprises Inc ....F....... 203 741-9300
  Wallingford *(G-9232)*
I Tech Services Inc ....G....... 800 559-8991
  Danbury *(G-1847)*
Insight Plus Technology LLC ....G....... 860 930-4763
  Bristol *(G-1051)*
Pequot ....G....... 800 620-1492
  Bridgeport *(G-869)*

Employee Codes: A=Over 500 employees, B=251-500
C=101-250, D=51-100, E=20-50, F=10-19, G=1-9

SECURITY PROTECTIVE DEVICES MAINTENANCE & MONITORING SVCS

Q-Lane Turnstiles LLC .... F 860 410-1801
  Sandy Hook *(G-7327)*

SECURITY SYSTEMS SERVICES

Isupportws Inc .... F 203 569-7600
  Stamford *(G-8260)*
Manup LLC .... G 203 588-9861
  Norwalk *(G-6246)*

SEMICONDUCTOR CIRCUIT NETWORKS

Fiber Mountain Inc .... E 203 806-4040
  Cheshire *(G-1388)*

SEMICONDUCTOR DEVICES: Wafers

Saphlux Inc .... G 475 221-8981
  Branford *(G-647)*

SEMICONDUCTORS & RELATED DEVICES

Advanced Semiconductor .... G 860 349-1121
  Durham *(G-2135)*
Advanced Technology Mtls Inc .... G 203 794-1100
  Danbury *(G-1732)*
AG Semiconductor Services LLC .... E 203 322-5300
  Stamford *(G-8066)*
Asct LLC .... G 860 349-1121
  Durham *(G-2139)*
Branbroks Dntl Stffing Sltions .... G 704 784-1056
  Stamford *(G-8119)*
Convergent Solutions LLC .... G 203 293-3534
  Westport *(G-10069)*
Edal Industries Inc .... E 203 467-2591
  East Haven *(G-2423)*
Emosyn America Inc .... E 203 794-1100
  Danbury *(G-1809)*
Gordon Products Incorporated .... E 203 775-4501
  Brookfield *(G-1194)*
Hoffman Engineering LLC .... D 203 425-8900
  Stamford *(G-8240)*
Micro-Probe Incorporated .... G 203 267-6446
  Southbury *(G-7869)*
Microphase Corporation .... E 203 866-8000
  Shelton *(G-7500)*
Newco Condenser Inc .... G 475 882-4000
  Shelton *(G-7510)*
Paul Gaffney .... G 203 221-1249
  Weston *(G-10035)*
Pequot .... G 800 620-1492
  Bridgeport *(G-869)*
Photronics Texas Inc .... G 203 546-3039
  Brookfield *(G-1213)*
Photronics Texas I LLC .... G 203 775-9000
  Brookfield *(G-1214)*
Rmi Corporation .... G 860 680-7368
  Avon *(G-106)*
Silicon Catalyst LLC .... G 203 240-0499
  Ridgefield *(G-7173)*
Soluthin Inc .... G 860 424-1228
  Madison *(G-3958)*
Trianja Technologies Inc .... G 203 775-9000
  Brookfield *(G-1233)*
United Electric Controls Co .... D 203 877-2795
  Milford *(G-4668)*
Vishay Americas Inc .... B 203 452-5648
  Shelton *(G-7580)*

SENSORS: Radiation

Radeco of Ct Inc .... F 860 564-1220
  Plainfield *(G-6751)*

SENSORS: Temperature, Exc Indl Process

Omega Engineering Inc .... D 714 540-4914
  Norwalk *(G-6285)*

SEPTIC TANK CLEANING SVCS

Coastline Environmental LLC .... G 203 483-6898
  North Branford *(G-5831)*
Parker Septic Service .... F 860 749-8220
  Somers *(G-7667)*

SEPTIC TANKS: Concrete

Arrow Concrete Products Inc .... E 860 653-5063
  Granby *(G-3106)*
Connecticut Precast Corp .... E 203 268-8688
  Monroe *(G-4705)*
David Shuck .... G 860 434-8562
  Old Lyme *(G-6503)*

Jolley Precast Inc .... E 860 774-9066
  Danielson *(G-1995)*
M & M Precast Corp .... F 203 743-5559
  Danbury *(G-1878)*
Rogers Septic Tanks Inc .... F 203 259-9947
  Westport *(G-10151)*
Superior Concrete Products LLC ..... G 860 342-0186
  Portland *(G-6976)*

SEWAGE & WATER TREATMENT EQPT

Ecosystem Consulting Svc Inc .... G 860 742-0744
  Coventry *(G-1653)*
New Milford Commission .... F 860 354-3758
  New Milford *(G-5569)*
Shaws Pump Company Inc .... G 860 872-6891
  Ellington *(G-2599)*
Town of Vernon .... G 860 870-3699
  Vernon Rockville *(G-9183)*

SEWER CLEANING & RODDING SVC

A & C Connection Inspection .... G 203 287-8504
  Hamden *(G-3408)*

SEWING CONTRACTORS

DS Sewing Inc .... F 203 773-1344
  New Haven *(G-5270)*

SEWING MACHINE REPAIR SHOP

Industrial Saws Inc .... G 860 496-7000
  Torrington *(G-8936)*

SEWING MACHINES & PARTS: Indl

E S Williams Co .... G 203 888-0093
  Seymour *(G-7344)*
Industrial Saws Inc .... G 860 496-7000
  Torrington *(G-8936)*
Media One LLC .... E 203 745-5825
  Hamden *(G-3480)*
Puritan Industries Inc .... E 860 693-0791
  Collinsville *(G-1601)*

SEWING, NEEDLEWORK & PIECE GOODS STORE: Needlework Gds/Sply

James Kingsley .... G 203 458-6626
  Guilford *(G-3363)*

SEWING, NEEDLEWORK & PIECE GOODS STORES

Kanine Knits .... G 203 272-8548
  Cheshire *(G-1402)*

SEWING, NEEDLEWORK & PIECE GOODS STORES: Knitting Splys

Baby Knits and More .... G 860 485-0146
  Harwinton *(G-3721)*

SEXTANTS

Sextant Btsllc .... G 203 500-3245
  Killingworth *(G-3839)*

SHADES: Window

Arrow Window Shade Mfg Co .... G 860 956-3570
  Wethersfield *(G-10180)*
Debbie Pileika Interiors .... G 860 668-6324
  West Suffield *(G-9986)*

SHAFTS: Shaft Collars

American Collars Couplings Inc .... F 860 379-7043
  Winsted *(G-10504)*

SHAPES & PILINGS, STRUCTURAL: Steel

DRM Associates LLC .... G 860 583-7744
  Bristol *(G-1020)*
Industrial Flame Cutting Inc .... G 203 723-4897
  Beacon Falls *(G-136)*
McCann Sales Inc .... G 860 614-0992
  West Simsbury *(G-9980)*
Pequonnock Ironworks Inc .... F 203 336-2178
  Bridgeport *(G-868)*

PRODUCT SECTION

SHEET METAL SPECIALTIES, EXC STAMPED

Anco Engineering Inc .... D 203 925-9235
  Shelton *(G-7395)*
Axis Laser .... G 203 284-9455
  Wallingford *(G-9216)*
Brittany Company Inc .... G 203 269-7859
  Wallingford *(G-9222)*
Chapco Inc .... D 860 526-9535
  Chester *(G-1467)*
Ductco LLC .... E 860 243-0350
  Bloomfield *(G-408)*
Farrell Prcsion Mtalcraft Corp .... E 860 355-2651
  New Milford *(G-5532)*
Hispanic Enterprises Inc .... E 203 588-9334
  Bridgeport *(G-784)*
Jared Manufacturing Co Inc .... F 203 846-1732
  Norwalk *(G-6219)*
Jgs Properties LLC .... E 203 378-7508
  Stratford *(G-8636)*
Jones Metal Products Co Inc .... G 860 289-8023
  South Windsor *(G-7779)*
Lyon Manufacturing LLC .... G 203 876-7386
  Milford *(G-4571)*
M & W Sheet Metal LLC .... G 860 642-7748
  North Franklin *(G-5874)*
Milford Fabricating Co Inc .... D 203 878-2476
  Milford *(G-4579)*
Paradigm Manchester Inc .... D 860 646-4048
  Manchester *(G-4066)*
Paradigm Manchester Inc .... C 860 646-4048
  Manchester *(G-4067)*
Paradigm Manchester Inc .... C 860 649-2888
  Manchester *(G-4069)*
Paradigm Manchester Inc .... G 860 646-4048
  Manchester *(G-4070)*
Pro Forming Sheet Metal LLC .... G 860 886-9900
  Norwich *(G-6428)*
Quality Sheet Metal Inc .... F 203 729-2244
  Naugatuck *(G-4915)*
R & D Precision Inc .... F 203 284-3396
  Wallingford *(G-9346)*
R W E Inc .... E 860 974-1101
  Putnam *(G-7061)*
R-D Mfg Inc .... F 860 739-3986
  East Lyme *(G-2473)*
Seconn Fabrication LLC .... D 860 443-0000
  Waterford *(G-9670)*
Statewide Sheet Metal LLC .... G 203 315-1159
  Branford *(G-656)*

SHEETS & STRIPS: Aluminum

CMI Specialty Products Inc .... F 860 585-0409
  Bristol *(G-1003)*
Panel Pro Technology .... G 203 333-0083
  Bridgeport *(G-861)*

SHELLAC

Materials Proc Dev Group LLC .... G 203 269-6617
  Wallingford *(G-9313)*

SHIMS: Metal

Beta Shim Co .... E 203 926-1150
  Shelton *(G-7404)*
Spirol International Corp .... C 860 774-8571
  Danielson *(G-2003)*
Spirol Intl Holdg Corp .... C 860 774-8571
  Danielson *(G-2004)*

SHIP BLDG/RPRG: Submersible Marine Robots, Manned/Unmanned

Exocetus Atonomous Systems LLC ..... G 860 512-7260
  Wallingford *(G-9262)*
Exocetus Autonomous Systems ..... G 860 512-7260
  Wallingford *(G-9263)*
Globenix Inc .... G 203 740-7070
  Norwalk *(G-6181)*

SHIP BUILDING & REPAIRING: Cargo Vessels

Connecticut Diesel and Marine .... G 203 481-1010
  Milford *(G-4495)*
Igs-Med LLC .... G 203 698-0396
  Old Greenwich *(G-6476)*

PRODUCT SECTION

SHIP BUILDING & REPAIRING: Cargo, Commercial
LM Gill Welding & Mfg LLC .... E 860 647-9931
 Manchester *(G-4049)*
Magnuss Services Inc .... G 347 703-0750
 Westport *(G-10116)*

SHIP BUILDING & REPAIRING: Ferryboats
NGS Power LLC .... G 860 873-0100
 East Haddam *(G-2246)*

SHIP BUILDING & REPAIRING: Military
Naiad Dynamics Us Inc .... E 203 929-6355
 Shelton *(G-7506)*

SHIP BUILDING & REPAIRING: Rigging, Marine
Navtec Rigging Solutions Inc .... E 203 458-3163
 Clinton *(G-1515)*
Ocean Rigging LLC .... G 800 624-2101
 Bridgeport *(G-855)*

SHIP BUILDING & REPAIRING: Trawlers
Timbercraft LLC .... G 860 355-5538
 New Milford *(G-5597)*

SHIPBUILDING & REPAIR
Brewer Yacht Yards Inc .... G 860 399-5128
 Old Saybrook *(G-6526)*
Bridgeport Boatwork Inc .... G 860 536-9651
 Bridgeport *(G-719)*
Bridgeport Boatwork Inc .... G 860 536-9651
 Groton *(G-3274)*
Dorado Tankers Pool Inc .... E 203 662-2600
 Norwalk *(G-6147)*
M Friedman Company .... G 860 447-9935
 Mystic *(G-4828)*
Naiad Maritime Group Inc .... E 203 944-1932
 Shelton *(G-7507)*
Thames Shipyard & Repair Co .... D 860 442-5349
 New London *(G-5493)*

SHOCK ABSORBERS: Indl
Jpo Solutions Inc .... G 203 502-8609
 Trumbull *(G-9038)*

SHOE MATERIALS: Counters
Bean Counters .... G 860 404-2930
 Farmington *(G-2883)*
Catskill Gran Countertops Inc .... F 860 667-1555
 Newington *(G-5637)*
Top Source Inc .... G 203 753-6490
 Waterbury *(G-9614)*

SHOE MATERIALS: Quarters
687 State Street Assoc LLC .... G 203 915-8469
 North Haven *(G-5893)*
Little T Qarter Midget CLB Inc .... G 860 823-7258
 Thompson *(G-8839)*
Little T Quarter Midget Club .... G 860 885-1376
 Oakdale *(G-6444)*
Middle Quarter Animal Hospital .... G 203 263-4772
 Woodbury *(G-10643)*
Quarter Mile .... G 203 438-9718
 Ridgefield *(G-7165)*
Wbcb Ventures LLC .... G 860 383-4203
 Preston *(G-6991)*

SHOE MATERIALS: Rands
Rand Newco LLC .... G 203 699-9125
 Cheshire *(G-1436)*
Rand Whitney .... G 860 354-6063
 New Milford *(G-5583)*

SHOE STORES
Cuero Operating .... G 203 253-8651
 Westport *(G-10073)*

SHOE STORES: Children's
Dsw Inc .... F 203 985-8241
 North Haven *(G-5933)*

SHOE STORES: Custom & Orthopedic
Dsw Inc .... F 860 644-6200
 Manchester *(G-4012)*

SHOES: Athletic, Exc Rubber Or Plastic
Dsw Inc .... F 860 644-6200
 Manchester *(G-4012)*
Dsw Inc .... F 203 985-8241
 North Haven *(G-5933)*

SHOES: Men's
B H Shoe Holdings Inc .... E 203 661-2424
 Greenwich *(G-3127)*
Buestan Usa LLC .... G 203 954-8889
 Ansonia *(G-25)*
Fisher Footwear LLC .... F 203 302-2800
 Greenwich *(G-3161)*
Mbf Holdings LLC .... F 203 302-2812
 Greenwich *(G-3200)*

SHOES: Men's, Dress
Vcs Group LLC .... G 203 413-6500
 Greenwich *(G-3253)*

SHOES: Men's, Work
HH Brown Shoe Company Inc .... E 203 661-2424
 Greenwich *(G-3177)*

SHOES: Orthopedic, Children's
Kaufman Enterprises Inc .... F 203 777-2396
 New Haven *(G-5307)*

SHOES: Orthopedic, Men's
Kaufman Enterprises Inc .... F 203 777-2396
 New Haven *(G-5307)*

SHOES: Orthopedic, Women's
Kaufman Enterprises Inc .... F 203 777-2396
 New Haven *(G-5307)*

SHOES: Plastic Or Rubber
Inocraft Products Inc .... E 860 933-0485
 Tolland *(G-8866)*
Moda LLC .... G 203 302-2800
 Greenwich *(G-3204)*

SHOES: Women's
Buestan Usa LLC .... G 203 954-8889
 Ansonia *(G-25)*
Dooney & Bourke Inc .... E 203 853-7515
 Norwalk *(G-6146)*
Fisher Footwear LLC .... F 203 302-2800
 Greenwich *(G-3161)*
Fisher Sigerson Morrison LLC .... E 203 302-2800
 Greenwich *(G-3162)*
HH Brown Shoe Company Inc .... E 203 661-2424
 Greenwich *(G-3177)*
Moda LLC .... G 203 302-2800
 Greenwich *(G-3204)*

SHOES: Women's, Dress
Aj Casey LLC .... G 203 226-5961
 Norwalk *(G-6065)*

SHOT PEENING SVC
Aqua Blasting Corp .... F 860 242-8855
 Bloomfield *(G-387)*
Blasting Techniques Inc .... G 860 528-4717
 South Windsor *(G-7718)*
Hydro Honing Laboratories Inc .... E 860 289-4328
 East Hartford *(G-2335)*
Metal Improvement Company LLC .... E 860 635-9994
 Middletown *(G-4375)*
Metal Improvement Company LLC .... E 860 224-9148
 New Britain *(G-5015)*
Metal Improvement Company LLC .... E 860 688-6201
 Windsor *(G-10409)*
Metal Improvement Company LLC .... D 860 523-9901
 East Windsor *(G-2511)*
P&G Metal Components Corp .... F 860 243-2220
 Bloomfield *(G-458)*
Peening Technologies Eqp LLC .... E 860 289-4328
 East Hartford *(G-2353)*

SIGNS & ADVERTISING SPECIALTIES

SHOWER STALLS: Plastic & Fiberglass
Trumbull Recreation Supply Co .... G 860 429-6604
 Willington *(G-10260)*

SHUTTERS, DOOR & WINDOW: Metal
Green Shutter Inc .... G 203 359-3863
 Stamford *(G-8220)*
Shutters & Sails LLC .... G 860 331-1510
 Mystic *(G-4845)*

SIDING & STRUCTURAL MATERIALS: Wood
Decks R US .... G 860 505-0726
 New Britain *(G-4973)*
Ppk Inc .... G 203 376-9180
 Branford *(G-636)*
Reusable Greenworks .... G 203 745-3695
 New Haven *(G-5379)*

SIGN LETTERING & PAINTING SVCS
Graphics Unlimited .... G 860 928-1407
 Putnam *(G-7045)*

SIGN PAINTING & LETTERING SHOP
Agjo Printing Service .... G 860 599-3143
 Pawcatuck *(G-6703)*
American Sign Inc .... E 203 624-2991
 New Haven *(G-5229)*
Archer Sign Service LLC .... G 203 377-5362
 Milford *(G-4455)*
Century Sign LLC .... G 203 230-9000
 Hamden *(G-3427)*
Douglas M Gagnon .... G 860 779-2255
 Danielson *(G-1990)*
Landino Signs LLC .... G 203 248-5437
 Hamden *(G-3471)*
Nu Line Design LLC .... G 203 949-0726
 Wallingford *(G-9329)*
Signs Unlimited Inc .... G 203 734-7446
 Derby *(G-2126)*
Villano J Sign Company LLC .... G 203 624-7550
 New Haven *(G-5427)*
Yush Sign Display Co Inc .... G 860 289-1819
 East Hartford *(G-2402)*

SIGNALING APPARATUS: Electric
Trans-Tek Inc .... E 860 872-8351
 Ellington *(G-2608)*

SIGNALS: Traffic Control, Electric
M-Systems Inc .... G 203 270-8926
 Newtown *(G-5758)*

SIGNALS: Transportation
Gac Inc .... G 860 633-1768
 Glastonbury *(G-3038)*

SIGNS & ADVERTISING SPECIALTIES
27 West Main Street LLC .... G 860 799-6494
 New Milford *(G-5499)*
Acme Sign Co .... F 203 324-2263
 Stamford *(G-8059)*
Action Signs .... G 860 496-1232
 Torrington *(G-8887)*
Agjo Printing Service .... G 860 599-3143
 Pawcatuck *(G-6703)*
AIM Vinyl Signs .... G 203 868-1413
 Windsor *(G-10356)*
Albert Gramesty and Dawn Grame .... G 203 924-7947
 Shelton *(G-7391)*
All Tech Sign & Crane Service .... G 203 272-2207
 Cheshire *(G-1350)*
American Pront and Sign .... G 203 400-2155
 Trumbull *(G-8998)*
American Sign Inc .... E 203 624-2991
 New Haven *(G-5229)*
Archer Sign Service LLC .... G 203 377-5362
 Milford *(G-4455)*
Arrow Engraving & Sign LLC .... G 860 349-1788
 Durham *(G-2138)*
Art Craft Signs .... G 203 212-3980
 Bridgeport *(G-702)*
Asi Sign Systems Inc .... G 860 828-3331
 East Berlin *(G-2162)*
Automotive Coop Couponing Inc .... G 203 227-2722
 Weston *(G-10018)*

SIGNS & ADVERTISING SPECIALTIES — PRODUCT SECTION

Company	Sec	Phone
Barneys Sign Service Inc, Stratford (G-8579)	G	203 878-3763
Baytek Sign Co, Tolland (G-8851)	G	860 872-9279
Belmeade Group LLC, West Granby (G-9766)	G	860 413-3569
Better Letters Signs, Enfield (G-2618)	G	860 749-7235
Big Prints LLC, East Haven (G-2414)	G	203 469-1100
Brass City Signs LLC, Cheshire (G-1362)	G	860 628-2046
Bristol Signart Inc, Bristol (G-992)	G	860 582-2577
Brushline Design, Old Lyme (G-6491)		860 434-5055
City Sign, Hartford (G-3567)	G	860 232-4803
Classic Sign & Graphics, Wilton (G-10281)	G	203 834-1145
Concord Industries Inc, Norwalk (G-6124)	E	203 750-6060
Connectcut Dgital Graphics LLC, Seymour (G-7341)	G	203 888-6509
Connecticut Carved Sign Co LLC, Watertown (G-9695)	G	860 274-2039
Connecticut Container Corp, North Haven (G-5924)	C	203 248-2161
Connecticut Sign Factory, Southington (G-7908)	G	860 833-5689
Connecticut Sign Service LLC, Old Lyme (G-6498)	G	860 391-9614
Connecticut Sign Service LLC, Essex (G-2714)	G	860 767-7446
Copy Signs LLC, Plainville (G-6793)	G	860 747-1985
Creative Edge Solutions L, Torrington (G-8916)	G	860 626-0007
Critical Signs Graphics &, Waterford (G-9650)	G	860 443-7446
Critical Signs & Graphics, Waterford (G-9651)	G	860 443-7446
CRS I Group Inc, Southington (G-7909)	G	860 593-4886
CT Sign Service LLC, Deep River (G-2087)	G	860 322-3954
Custom Art Sgns LLC, Danbury (G-1779)	G	203 837-7674
Cutting Edge Sgns Graphics LLC, Prospect (G-6999)	G	203 758-7776
David R Wttrwrth Son Signs LLC, Waterbury (G-9464)	G	860 753-3666
Defined Design Creative Art, Stratford (G-8604)	G	203 378-2571
Digit-X Inc, Southington (G-7915)	G	860 620-1221
Dundorf Designs USA Inc, Salem (G-7288)	G	860 859-2955
Eagle Signs LLC, Essex (G-2716)	G	860 227-1959
East Coast Name Plates Inc, Easton (G-2549)	G	203 261-4347
Elite Engraving & Awards, Manchester (G-4014)	G	203 643-7459
Exhibitease LLC, Branford (G-592)	G	203 481-0792
Fast Sign, Stamford (G-8202)	G	203 348-0222
Fastsigns, Milford (G-4535)	G	203 298-4075
Fastsigns, Waterford (G-9653)	G	860 437-7446
Fastsigns, Hartford (G-3587)	G	860 969-3030
Fastsigns, Avon (G-80)	G	860 470-7936
Fastsigns, Middletown (G-4343)	G	860 347-8569
Fastsigns, Middletown (G-4344)	G	860 347-8569
Fastsigns, Bristol (G-1037)	G	860 583-8000
Fastsigns, North Haven (G-5941)	G	203 239-9090
Fastsigns of Hartford, Manchester (G-4016)	G	860 644-5700
Ferrucci Signs, East Haven (G-2428)	G	203 469-0043
Fit To A Tee Cstm Screen Prtg, Kensington (G-3810)	G	860 828-6632
Flag Store, Meriden (G-4170)	G	203 237-8791
Focus Sign Awning, Hartford (G-3591)	G	860 890-6577
Fs Signs LLC, Stratford (G-8613)	G	203 612-4447
Gerber Scientific LLC, Tolland (G-8864)	C	860 871-8082
Ghezzi Enterprises Inc, South Windsor (G-7759)	G	860 787-5338
Gjg Signs Digital Signs, East Windsor (G-2494)	G	413 627-1852
Gorilla Signs & Wraps, Cheshire (G-1393)	G	203 439-8838
Granata Signs LLC, Stamford (G-8219)	G	203 358-0780
Grand Slam Signs, Ledyard (G-3874)	G	972 874-3658
Graphic Identity LLC, Glastonbury (G-3042)	G	860 657-9755
Graphica Sign Studios, East Haven (G-2433)	G	203 619-2255
Graphics Unlimited, Putnam (G-7045)	G	860 928-1407
Harry Tutunjian, Shelton (G-7460)	G	203 944-9444
Horizons Unlimited Inc, Willimantic (G-10230)	F	860 423-1931
Hot Tops LLC, Shelton (G-7466)	F	203 926-2067
I Level Sign and Graphics, Shelton (G-7472)	G	203 256-9486
I95 Signs LLC, Stratford (G-8630)	G	203 296-2141
Ignatowski John, Monroe (G-4719)	G	203 452-9601
Image 360, Newington (G-5660)	G	860 667-8339
Image Works Sign & Graph, Coventry (G-1655)	G	860 569-7446
Image360, Wallingford (G-9287)	F	203 949-0726
Innovative Signs LLC, Vernon (G-9140)	G	860 870-7446
J&R Signs, Bridgeport (G-797)	G	203 551-0781
Jaime M Camacho, Norwalk (G-6216)	G	203 846-8221
James Woznick, Sandy Hook (G-7317)	G	203 426-5585
Jason Kurtzman Signs, Norwalk (G-6220)	G	203 847-4397
Jk Sign & Stamp LLC, Oakville (G-6455)	G	860 729-3860
Jk Sign Company, Norwalk (G-6222)	G	203 544-7373
Jornik Man Corp, Stamford (G-8268)	F	203 969-0500
Kyle C Niles, Plantsville (G-6900)	G	860 637-7625
Lamar Advertising Company, Windsor (G-10403)	E	860 246-6546
Landino Signs LLC, Hamden (G-3471)	G	203 248-5437
Landmark Sign Service, South Windsor (G-7786)	G	860 474-5305
Landmark Sign Service LLC, Hartford (G-3625)	G	860 206-0643
Lewtan Industries Corporation, West Hartford (G-9830)	D	860 278-9800
Logod Softwear Inc, Cheshire (G-1407)	E	203 272-4883
Lorence Sign Works LLC, Berlin (G-198)	G	860 829-9999
Magic Signs, Danielson (G-1997)	G	860 457-8940
Margaret Witham, Westbrook (G-10003)	G	860 399-6403
McFigs Beyond Signs LLC, Bethel (G-325)	G	203 792-4057
McIntire Company, Bristol (G-1070)	F	860 585-8559
Melvin Mayo, Enfield (G-2658)	G	802 698-7635
Metro Signs LLC, West Haven (G-9936)	G	203 933-0333
Michael Zoppa, South Windsor (G-7794)	G	860 289-5881
Mikes Sign Maintenance LLC, Middletown (G-4380)	G	860 347-1462
Millennium Shade & Sign LLC, Stamford (G-8310)	G	203 968-5080
Mkr Sign Company, Enfield (G-2661)	G	860 265-7996
Mr Skylight LLC, New Canaan (G-5121)	G	203 966-6005
Murdoch and Co, Westport (G-10126)	G	203 226-2800
Murray Signs & Designs Bob, Stratford (G-8652)	G	203 375-7351
Neonworks, Bridgeport (G-846)	G	203 335-6366
New England Post A Sign, Waterbury (G-9559)	G	203 635-3171
New England Signal LLC, New Milford (G-5567)	G	860 350-3212
New Haven Sign Co, Hamden (G-3491)	G	203 891-5710
New Haven Sign Company, Northford (G-6051)	G	203 484-2777
Ninas Signs, Morris (G-4791)	G	315 963-2531
Nomis Enterprises, Wallingford (G-9327)	G	631 821-3120
Norwalk Sign Company Inc, Norwalk (G-6282)	G	203 838-1942
Nu Line Design LLC, Wallingford (G-9329)	G	203 949-0726
Ogs Technologies Inc, Cheshire (G-1424)	E	203 271-9055
Paper Mill Graphix Inc, Greenwich (G-3213)	E	203 531-5904
Pariot Sign Company Llc, Newtown (G-5768)	G	203 364-9009
Parking Lt Strpng & Asphlt Sgn, Danbury (G-1900)	G	203 648-6323
Point View Displays LLC, East Haven (G-2447)	G	203 468-0887
Pop Graphics Inc, Meriden (G-4218)	G	203 639-1441
Prime Resources Corp, Bridgeport (G-880)	B	203 331-9100
Project Graphics Inc, Woodbury (G-10652)	F	802 488-8789
Prokop Sign Co, Taftville (G-8742)	G	860 889-6265
Quality Signs of Watertown, Watertown (G-9728)	G	860 274-4828
Quinn and Gellar Marketing LLC, New London (G-5485)	G	860 444-0448
R Way Signs LLC, Oxford (G-6690)	G	203 888-9709
Ram Arts Signs, Watertown (G-9729)	G	860 274-6833
Revolution Lighting, Stamford (G-8388)	G	203 504-1111
Revolution Lighting Tech Inc, Stamford (G-8390)	F	203 504-1111
Revolution Lighting Tech Inc, Stamford (G-8389)	C	203 504-1111
Rich Signs & Designs, Willington (G-10256)	G	860 429-2165
Rising Sign Company Inc, Norwalk (G-6325)	G	203 853-4155
Rossi Pter Signs Lettering LLC, Stafford Springs (G-8035)	G	860 684-9229
Rykam LLC, East Hartford (G-2368)	G	860 721-1411
Sam Augeri & Sons Signs, Middletown (G-4407)	G	860 346-1261
Say It With Signs, Plantsville (G-6910)	G	860 621-6535
Semiotics LLC, Manchester (G-4088)	G	860 644-5700
Siam Valee, Wallingford (G-9366)	G	203 269-6888
Sign A Rama, Vernon Rockville (G-9178)	G	860 870-7446
Sign A Rama, Enfield (G-2694)	G	860 265-7996
Sign A Rama, New London (G-5489)	G	860 443-9744
Sign A Rama, Orange (G-6629)	G	203 795-5450
Sign A Rama, Danbury (G-1949)	G	203 792-4091
Sign A Rama Inc, Stamford (G-8415)	G	203 674-8900
Sign and Wonders LLC, Watertown (G-9736)	G	860 274-8526

PRODUCT SECTION

SIGNS, EXC ELECTRIC, WHOLESALE

Company	Code	Phone
Sign By Greubel	G	860 632-2573
Cromwell (G-1719)		
Sign Center Ltd Liability Co	G	203 549-9820
Bridgeport (G-903)		
Sign Connection Inc	G	860 870-8855
Vernon Rockville (G-9179)		
Sign Craft LLC	G	860 739-2863
Niantic (G-5817)		
Sign Factory	F	860 763-1085
Enfield (G-2695)		
Sign Fast	G	203 549-8500
Bridgeport (G-904)		
Sign In Soft Inc	G	203 216-3046
Shelton (G-7555)		
Sign of Flying Turtle LLC	G	860 830-3132
West Hartford (G-9855)		
Sign Smarts LLC	G	203 854-0808
Norwalk (G-6348)		
Sign Solutions Inc	G	860 583-8000
Bristol (G-1117)		
Sign Wiz LLC	G	860 351-5368
Plainville (G-6862)		
Sign Wizard	G	860 525-7729
Hartford (G-3687)		
Sign-It LLC	G	203 377-8831
Trumbull (G-9074)		
Signature Signs	G	860 704-0397
Middletown (G-4412)		
Signature Signworks LLC	G	860 646-4598
Bolton (G-519)		
Signcenter LLC	G	800 269-2130
Milford (G-4644)		
Signman Signs LLC	G	203 296-2846
Bridgeport (G-906)		
Signmart LLC	G	860 347-7446
Middletown (G-4413)		
Signs By Anthony Inc	G	203 866-1744
Norwalk (G-6349)		
Signs By Flach	G	203 881-0272
Beacon Falls (G-147)		
Signs By MB	G	203 710-9948
Cheshire (G-1446)		
Signs By Scavotto	G	860 745-5629
Enfield (G-2696)		
Signs Direct Inc	G	860 658-9589
Simsbury (G-7646)		
Signs Now LLC	G	860 667-8339
Newington (G-5705)		
Signs of America	G	860 412-0054
Brooklyn (G-1255)		
Signs of Success Inc	G	203 329-3374
Stamford (G-8417)		
Signs On Demand	G	860 346-1720
Middletown (G-4414)		
Signs Unlimited Inc	G	203 734-7446
Derby (G-2126)		
Signworks Studios LLC	G	203 268-3993
Monroe (G-4752)		
Simply Signs	G	203 595-0123
Stamford (G-8423)		
Smart Signs LLC	G	860 656-5257
East Hartford (G-2373)		
Smart Signs Pro LLC	G	203 684-9839
Milford (G-4646)		
Sons of Un Vtrans of Civil War	G	816 241-5353
Avon (G-114)		
Sound Marketing Concepts	G	860 257-9367
Rocky Hill (G-7266)		
South Paint and Sign Co	G	203 245-7591
Madison (G-3959)		
Specialty Sign Services LLC	G	860 391-3291
Clinton (G-1528)		
Spooky Signs and Holiday Creat	G	860 742-2805
Coventry (G-1676)		
Spot-On Sign Solutions Inc	G	860 584-9008
Berlin (G-222)		
Stavola Signs	G	860 395-0897
Old Saybrook (G-6570)		
Sundance Signs LLC	G	860 432-5760
Manchester (G-4099)		
Swahn Engraving LLC	G	860 657-4709
Glastonbury (G-3085)		
Thirty Two Signs	G	860 822-1132
Baltic (G-122)		
Thirty Two Signs LLC	G	860 564-0532
Plainfield (G-6755)		
Tims Sign & Lighting Service	G	203 634-8840
Meriden (G-4256)		
Trophy Shop	G	860 871-0867
Vernon Rockville (G-9184)		
United Stts Sgn & Fbrction	E	203 601-1000
Trumbull (G-9088)		
US Highway Products Inc	F	203 336-0332
Bridgeport (G-932)		
Visual Impact Signs	G	860 621-7446
Southington (G-7994)		
Vital Signs & Graphic LLC	G	860 829-7446
Berlin (G-232)		
Vital Signs LLC	G	860 365-0897
Colchester (G-1580)		
Vital Signs Medical LLC	G	860 563-4969
Rocky Hill (G-7272)		
Wesport Signs	G	203 557-3668
Westport (G-10174)		
Wesport Signs	G	203 286-7710
Norwalk (G-6394)		
Whats Your Sign LLC	G	814 823-7807
Stratford (G-8708)		
Wilburt Signs	G	203 313-4950
Danbury (G-1982)		
Window Tinting & Signs Inc	G	203 336-5539
Bridgefield (G-939)		
Write Way Signs & Design Inc	G	860 482-8893
Torrington (G-8992)		
X L Color Corp	G	860 653-9705
East Granby (G-2234)		
Yankee Plak Co Inc	E	203 333-3168
Bridgeport (G-942)		
Young Flan LLC	G	203 878-0084
Derby (G-2134)		
Yush Sign Display Co Inc	G	860 289-1819
East Hartford (G-2402)		

SIGNS & ADVERTISING SPECIALTIES: Artwork, Advertising

Company	Code	Phone
Archambault Group LLC	G	860 635-4006
Cromwell (G-1688)		
Artwork By Nora LLC	G	860 963-0723
Pomfret Center (G-6937)		
Graffeast Inc	G	203 622-1622
Greenwich (G-3169)		
Jvcart LLC	G	917 497-8791
Darien (G-2030)		
Peter Ortali & Associates LLC	G	203 571-8023
Sandy Hook (G-7325)		
Picture This Hartford Inc	G	860 528-1409
East Hartford (G-2355)		

SIGNS & ADVERTISING SPECIALTIES: Displays, Paint Process

Company	Code	Phone
Leichsenring Studios LLC	G	203 452-7710
Trumbull (G-9043)		

SIGNS & ADVERTISING SPECIALTIES: Letters For Signs, Metal

Company	Code	Phone
Lifetime Acrylic Signs Inc	G	203 255-6751
Fairfield (G-2810)		

SIGNS & ADVERTISING SPECIALTIES: Novelties

Company	Code	Phone
A D Perkins Company	G	203 777-3456
New Haven (G-5217)		
Jyl LLP	G	860 767-7733
Essex (G-2722)		

SIGNS & ADVERTISING SPECIALTIES: Signs

Company	Code	Phone
A To Z Signs	G	203 840-0644
Norwalk (G-6057)		
ABC Sign Corporation	E	203 513-8110
Shelton (G-7387)		
Accent Signs LLC	G	203 975-8688
Stamford (G-8056)		
Affordable Sign Co	G	203 874-0875
Milford (G-4443)		
Art Signs	G	860 871-8361
Ellington (G-2577)		
Arteffects Incorporated	E	860 242-0031
Bloomfield (G-390)		
Artistic Sign Language LLC	G	203 245-8213
Madison (G-3909)		
Benoit Signs & Graphics	G	860 870-8300
Stafford Springs (G-8019)		
Cameron Bortz	G	860 599-0477
Pawcatuck (G-6704)		
Compu-Signs LLC	G	860 747-1985
Plainville (G-6788)		
Computer Sgns Old Saybrook LLC	G	860 388-9773
Old Saybrook (G-6527)		
Custom Sign Solutions LLC	G	203 975-8344
Stamford (G-8172)		
Davids Legal Signs	G	203 268-8943
Monroe (G-4710)		
Derrick Mason	G	413 527-4282
Norwich (G-6410)		
Douglas M Gagnon	G	860 779-2255
Danielson (G-1990)		
East Coast Sign and Supply Inc	G	203 791-8326
Bethel (G-291)		
J G Kurtzman	G	203 838-7791
Norwalk (G-6215)		
Jill Ghi	G	860 824-7123
Canaan (G-1288)		
Joseph Garrity	G	860 693-2134
Canton (G-1316)		
Merritt Sign	G	860 233-3557
Hartford (G-3639)		
New England Sign Carvers	G	860 349-1669
Middlefield (G-4303)		
Post Sign Specialists	G	203 723-8448
Naugatuck (G-4912)		
Reflected Image	G	203 484-0760
Northford (G-6052)		
Rokap Inc	G	203 265-6895
Wallingford (G-9359)		
Sign Creations	G	203 259-8330
Southport (G-8009)		
Sign of Our Times	G	860 669-4318
Clinton (G-1526)		
Sign Pro Inc	F	860 229-1812
Plantsville (G-6911)		
Sign Professionals	G	860 823-1122
Norwich (G-6432)		
Sign Stop Inc	G	860 721-1411
East Hartford (G-2371)		
Signcrafters Inc	G	203 353-9535
Stamford (G-8416)		
Signs By Autografix	G	203 481-6502
Branford (G-652)		
Signs of All Kinds	G	860 649-1989
Manchester (G-4089)		
Signs Plus Inc	G	860 653-0547
East Granby (G-2229)		
Signs Plus LLC	G	860 423-3048
Willimantic (G-10236)		
Signs Pro LLC	G	203 323-9994
Stamford (G-8418)		
Sinsigalli Signs & Designs	G	860 627-8712
Windsor Locks (G-10496)		
Speedi Sign LLC	G	203 775-0700
Brookfield (G-1225)		
Wad Inc	E	860 828-3331
East Berlin (G-2179)		
Yankee Signs	G	860 623-8651
Windsor Locks (G-10502)		

SIGNS & ADVERTSG SPECIALTIES: Displays/Cutouts Window/Lobby

Company	Code	Phone
Corr/Dis Incorporated	G	203 838-6075
Norwalk (G-6130)		
Displaycraft Inc	E	860 747-9110
Plainville (G-6799)		
Farmington Displays Inc	E	860 677-2497
Farmington (G-2904)		
John Oldham Studios Inc	E	860 529-3331
Wethersfield (G-10202)		
S D & D Inc	F	860 357-2603
East Berlin (G-2175)		
Sonalysts Inc	B	860 442-4355
Waterford (G-9672)		

SIGNS, ELECTRICAL: Wholesalers

Company	Code	Phone
Derrick Mason	G	413 527-4282
Norwich (G-6410)		
Lorence Sign Works LLC	G	860 829-9999
Berlin (G-198)		
Yush Sign Display Co Inc	G	860 289-1819
East Hartford (G-2402)		

SIGNS, EXC ELECTRIC, WHOLESALE

Company	Code	Phone
Acme Sign Co	F	203 324-2263
Stamford (G-8059)		
Biz Wiz Print & Copy Ctr LLC	G	860 633-7446
Glastonbury (G-3015)		
Signature Signworks LLC	G	860 646-4598
Bolton (G-519)		

Employee Codes: A=Over 500 employees, B=251-500
C=101-250, D=51-100, E=20-50, F=10-19, G=1-9

SIGNS, EXC ELECTRIC, WHOLESALE

Trophy Shop .... G 860 871-0867
 Vernon Rockville (G-9184)
Vision Designs LLC .... F 203 778-9898
 Brookfield (G-1237)

SIGNS: Electrical

420 Sign Design Inc .... G 203 852-1255
 Norwalk (G-6056)
Adamsahern Sign Solutions Inc .... F 860 523-8835
 Hartford (G-3547)
Applied Advertising Inc .... F 860 640-0800
 Danbury (G-1741)
Archer Sign Service LLC .... G 203 882-8484
 Milford (G-4454)
Arnco Sign Company .... E 203 238-1224
 Wallingford (G-9211)
Art Q Tech Signs .... G 203 874-6504
 Milford (G-4458)
Camaro Signs Inc .... G 860 886-1553
 Yantic (G-10697)
Century Sign LLC .... G 203 230-9000
 Hamden (G-3427)
Connecticut Sign Craft Inc .... G 203 729-0706
 Naugatuck (G-4872)
Creative Dimensions Inc .... E 203 250-6500
 Cheshire (G-1376)
Crossroads Signs .... G 203 894-5938
 Ridgefield (G-7131)
Designs & Signs .... G 203 775-0152
 Brookfield (G-1182)
John Rawlinson John Leary .... G 203 882-8484
 Milford (G-4562)
Kedo Koncepts LLC .... G 860 315-7392
 Thompson (G-8836)
Lauretano Sign Group Inc .... E 860 582-0233
 Terryville (G-8762)
One Look Sign Company .... G 860 581-8574
 Centerbrook (G-1331)
Pattison Sign Group Inc .... G 860 583-3000
 Bristol (G-1087)
Shiner Signs Inc .... E 203 634-4331
 Meriden (G-4241)
Sign Language LLC .... G 203 778-2250
 Danbury (G-1950)
Unlimited Signs Designs & Grap .... G 203 546-7267
 Brookfield (G-1235)
Villano J Sign Company LLC .... G 203 624-7550
 New Haven (G-5427)

SIGNS: Neon

Knight Lite Neon .... G 203 238-4423
 Meriden (G-4184)
Sign Maintenance Service Co .... G 203 336-1051
 Bridgeport (G-905)

SILICONE RESINS

Age Plastics LLC .... G 860 502-0418
 New Britain (G-4940)

SILICONES

Blue Barn Works LLC .... G 203 389-0923
 Woodbridge (G-10594)
Midsun Group Inc .... G 860 378-0100
 Southington (G-7954)

SILK SCREEN DESIGN SVCS

Barker Advg Specialty Co Inc .... D 203 272-2222
 Cheshire (G-1360)
Cook Print .... G 203 855-8785
 Norwalk (G-6129)
Embroidery World Inc .... G 203 281-7303
 Hamden (G-3445)
H J Hoffman Company .... G 203 853-7740
 Norwalk (G-6189)
Hot Tops LLC .... F 203 926-2067
 Shelton (G-7466)
Michael Zoppa .... G 860 289-5881
 South Windsor (G-7794)
Pj Specialties .... F 860 429-7626
 Willington (G-10254)
Silkscreening Plus Inc .... G 203 622-6909
 Greenwich (G-3234)
TSS & A Inc .... F 800 633-3536
 Prospect (G-7027)

SILVERSMITHS

House of Bubba LLC .... G 860 429-4250
 Willington (G-10250)

SILVERWARE

Boardman Silversmiths Inc .... F 203 265-9978
 Wallingford (G-9220)

SILVERWARE & PLATED WARE

Silversmith Inc .... G 203 869-4244
 Greenwich (G-3235)

SILVERWARE, STERLING SILVER

Silver Touch .... G 203 778-1778
 Bethel (G-342)

SINK TOPS, PLASTIC LAMINATED

East Hartford Lamination Co .... G 860 633-4637
 Glastonbury (G-3029)

SINKS: Vitreous China

Painted Tiles Co .... G 860 658-7218
 Simsbury (G-7638)
Syn-Mar Products Inc .... F 860 872-8505
 Ellington (G-2604)

SIRENS: Vehicle, Marine, Indl & Warning

Aquatic Sensor Netwrk Tech LLC .... F 860 429-4303
 Storrs Mansfield (G-8552)

SKIN CARE PRDTS: Suntan Lotions & Oils

Browne Hansen LLC .... G 203 269-0557
 Wallingford (G-9224)
Playtex Products LLC .... D 203 944-5500
 Shelton (G-7531)

SKYLIGHTS

E-Skylight Inc .... G 203 208-1351
 Branford (G-584)

SLAB & TILE, ROOFING: Concrete

Traditional Bath and Tile .... G 347 539-2088
 Bridgeport (G-929)

SLAUGHTERING & MEAT PACKING

Frank Demartino and Sons .... G 203 734-1074
 Seymour (G-7346)

SLINGS: Lifting, Made From Purchased Wire

Pauls Wire Rope & Sling Inc .... F 203 481-3469
 Branford (G-633)

SLINGS: Rope

East Shre Wre Rpe/Rggng Spply .... F 203 469-5204
 North Haven (G-5934)

SLIPCOVERS & PADS

Dominics Decorating Inc .... G 203 838-1827
 Norwalk (G-6145)

SNOW PLOWING SVCS

Central CT Snow LLC .... G 860 467-3107
 East Hampton (G-2260)
Hayes Services LLC .... G 860 739-2273
 East Lyme (G-2466)
Svl LLC .... G 860 819-9929
 Avon (G-116)

SNOW REMOVAL EQPT: Residential

Maltese Services LLC .... G 203 805-7669
 Monroe (G-4732)
Mikes Plowing & Maintenance .... G 860 868-1413
 Washington Depot (G-9418)

SOAPS & DETERGENTS

Country Soap Samplers .... G 203 881-1986
 Oxford (G-6654)
Goat Boy Soap .... G 860 350-0676
 New Milford (G-5539)
Henkel Consumer Goods Inc .... A 475 210-0230
 Stamford (G-8232)
Henkel Corporation .... G 860 571-5100
 Rocky Hill (G-7244)
Pharmacal Research Labs Inc .... E 203 755-4908
 Waterbury (G-9575)
Robert Chang .... G 203 737-2264
 Stamford (G-8395)
Robert Dinucci .... G 860 561-3730
 Hartford (G-3679)
Simply Soap .... G 860 347-4174
 Middletown (G-4416)
Unilever Ascc AG .... B 203 381-2482
 Shelton (G-7575)
Unilever Home and Per Care NA .... D 203 502-0086
 Trumbull (G-9085)

SOAPS & DETERGENTS: Textile

Bara Essentials LLC .... G 203 428-1786
 Stratford (G-8577)

SOAPSTONE MINING

Soapstone Landing LLC .... G 860 875-6200
 Stafford Springs (G-8039)

SOCIAL SVCS CENTER

Saint Vincent De Paul Place .... G 860 889-7374
 Norwich (G-6430)

SOCIAL SVCS, HANDICAPPED

Mid State ARC Inc .... E 203 238-9001
 Meriden (G-4201)

SOCIAL SVCS: Individual & Family

Triumph Consulting .... G 860 263-8335
 Hartford (G-3706)

SOCKETS: Electronic Tube

Surface Mount Devices LLC .... G 203 322-8290
 Stamford (G-8452)

SODA ASH MINING: Natural

American Natural Soda Ash Corp .... E 203 226-9056
 Westport (G-10054)

SODIUM CHLORIDE: Refined

Kuehne New Haven LLC .... E 203 508-6703
 New Haven (G-5312)

SOFT DRINKS WHOLESALERS

G & G Beverage Distributors .... D 203 949-6220
 Wallingford (G-9273)
Pepsi-Cola Metro Btlg Co Inc .... C 203 234-9014
 North Haven (G-5975)

SOFTWARE PUBLISHERS: Application

Actualmeds Corporation .... G 888 838-9053
 East Hartford (G-2286)
Advanced Decisions Inc .... F 203 402-0603
 Orange (G-6579)
Afficiency Inc .... G 718 496-9071
 Westport (G-10050)
Allexcel Inc .... G 203 764-2036
 West Haven (G-9882)
Beverage Boss LLC .... G 203 865-2240
 New Haven (G-5244)
Blue Crystal Enterprises LLC .... G 203 856-5397
 Trumbull (G-9006)
Bottomline Technologies De Inc .... G 203 431-9787
 Ridgefield (G-7124)
Breach Intelligence Inc .... E 844 312-7001
 Farmington (G-2885)
Cadentia LLC .... G 860 995-0173
 Bristol (G-997)
Calumma Technologies LLC .... G 914 557-4562
 Norwalk (G-6105)
Cita LLC .... G 203 545-7035
 Stamford (G-8148)
Clg Solutions LLC .... G 203 507-1105
 West Haven (G-9887)
Club Resource Inc .... G 317 225-6940
 Canton (G-1310)
Computer Tech Express LLC .... G 203 810-4932
 Norwalk (G-6123)

PRODUCT SECTION

SOFTWARE PUBLISHERS: Education

Cya Technologies Inc .... E 203 513-3111
  Shelton (G-7425)
David Smith .... G 860 877-3232
  Southington (G-7911)
Drug Imprment Dtction Svcs LLC ...... G 203 616-3735
  Danbury (G-1802)
Enginuity Plm LLC .... F 203 218-7225
  Milford (G-4532)
Fergtech Inc .... G 203 656-1139
  Darien (G-2024)
Financial Navigator Inc .... G 800 468-3636
  Stamford (G-8204)
Flexiinternational Sftwr Inc .... E 203 925-3040
  Shelton (G-7445)
Gamers That Lift LLC .... G 203 988-9211
  Orange (G-6604)
Golf Research Associates .... G 203 968-1608
  Stamford (G-8218)
Grey Wall Software LLC .... F 203 782-5944
  New Haven (G-5291)
Healthper Inc .... G 203 506-0957
  Hamden (G-3462)
Hexplora LLC .... G 860 760-7601
  Rocky Hill (G-7248)
Imprimi Fotos Ya LLC .... G 860 628-1787
  New Haven (G-5300)
Innovaticx LLC .... G 203 836-3501
  New Haven (G-5301)
Kando Apps LLC .... G 203 722-4359
  Norwalk (G-6227)
Keypoint Forensics LLC .... G 860 877-6586
  Naugatuck (G-4898)
Lablite LLC .... F 860 355-8817
  New Milford (G-5557)
Locallive Networks Inc .... G 877 355-6225
  Stamford (G-8287)
Loving Life LLC .... G 860 326-1459
  Voluntown (G-9190)
Lu Lu Holdings LLC .... E 203 861-1988
  Greenwich (G-3193)
Mannan 3d Innovations LLC .... G 860 306-4203
  Higganum (G-3768)
Mental Canvas LLC .... G 475 329-0515
  Madison (G-3939)
Microsoft Corporation .... E 860 678-3100
  Farmington (G-2928)
Mind2mind Exchange LLC .... G 203 856-0981
  Stamford (G-8311)
Mindtrainr LLC .... G 914 799-1515
  Stamford (G-8312)
Mt Calvary Holy Church .... G 203 785-1253
  New Haven (G-5337)
New England Computer Svcs Inc .... E 475 221-8200
  Branford (G-629)
Nohtbook Inc .... G 203 493-1633
  Norwalk (G-6279)
Only Queens LLC .... G 860 888-4413
  Bloomfield (G-455)
Open Water Development LLC .... G 646 883-2062
  Old Greenwich (G-6481)
Parent Engagement Tracker LLC .... G 860 209-5522
  Hartford (G-3661)
Pawtrait Inc .... G 848 992-4599
  Stamford (G-8353)
Pergenex Software LLC .... G 860 274-7318
  Watertown (G-9721)
Phraction Management LLC .... G 860 531-9590
  Colchester (G-1565)
Pmoys LLC .... G 203 541-0995
  Stamford (G-8365)
Qscend Technologies Inc .... E 203 757-6000
  Waterbury (G-9591)
Racemyface LLC .... G 203 285-8090
  Wilton (G-10323)
Reynolds and Reynolds Company .... G 203 323-3748
  Stamford (G-8392)
Rindle LLC .... G 551 482-2037
  Norwalk (G-6324)
Sas Institute Inc .... E 860 633-4119
  Glastonbury (G-3081)
Satori Audio LLC .... G 203 571-6050
  Westport (G-10154)
Sepdx .... G 803 479-6332
  New Haven (G-5393)
Sepsisdx .... G 856 359-5309
  New Haven (G-5394)
Servco Oil Inc .... G 203 762-7994
  Wilton (G-10328)
Servicetune Inc .... G 860 284-4445
  Avon (G-110)

Sobrio LLC .... G 860 880-1990
  Storrs (G-8551)
Softstorms LLC .... G 860 578-8515
  West Hartford (G-9857)
Still River Software Co LLC .... G 860 263-0396
  Woodstock (G-10686)
Stony Creek Liquor LLC .... G 203 488-3318
  Branford (G-658)
Student Employment Sftwr LLC .... G 203 485-9417
  Greenwich (G-3242)
Swing By Swing Golf Inc .... G 310 922-8023
  Hartford (G-3695)
Syrver LLC .... G 203 598-5810
  Fairfield (G-2852)
Tangoe Us Inc .... C 973 257-0300
  Shelton (G-7564)
Telenity Inc .... C 203 445-2000
  Monroe (G-4759)
Ultra Golden Software LLC .... G 203 227-4009
  Westport (G-10169)
Unimelon Inc .... G 201 774-2786
  Ridgefield (G-7179)

SOFTWARE PUBLISHERS: Business & Professional

Accessware .... G 860 235-2982
  Mystic (G-4795)
Advance Software LLC .... G 860 429-3721
  Willington (G-10244)
Aristo Data Systems .... G 203 322-1113
  Stamford (G-8092)
Arrochar Software LLC .... G 203 987-5412
  Newtown (G-5728)
Avalon It Systems .... G 203 323-7000
  Stamford (G-8099)
Blackrock Media Inc .... G 203 374-0369
  Easton (G-2547)
Bottomline Technologies De Inc .... G 203 761-1289
  Wilton (G-10276)
Ca Inc .... E 800 225-5224
  East Windsor (G-2487)
Channel Sources LLC .... F 203 775-6464
  Brookfield (G-1169)
Cietrade Systems Inc .... G 203 323-0074
  Stamford (G-8146)
Coastalogix LLC .... G 203 521-4770
  Westport (G-10065)
Criterion Inc .... E 203 703-9000
  Norwalk (G-6133)
Cuprak Enterprises LLC .... G 203 376-8789
  Cheshire (G-1378)
Deep River LLC .... G 860 388-9442
  Old Lyme (G-6504)
Desrosier of Greenwich Inc .... F 203 661-2334
  Greenwich (G-3152)
Eagle Investment Systems LLC .... F 860 561-4602
  West Hartford (G-9803)
Earnix Inc .... F 203 557-8077
  Westport (G-10076)
Eatzy LLC .... G 303 720-7532
  Old Saybrook (G-6532)
Epath Learning Inc .... E 860 444-7900
  New London (G-5470)
Express Software Production .... G 860 844-0085
  East Granby (G-2204)
Fergtech Inc .... G 203 656-1139
  Darien (G-2025)
Fieldstone Cnsulting Group LLC .... G 203 610-5592
  Easton (G-2553)
Flagpole Software LLC .... G 203 426-5166
  Newtown (G-5738)
Frevvo Inc .... F 203 208-3117
  Branford (G-598)
Grayfin Security LLC .... G 203 800-6760
  Madison (G-3923)
Handhold Adaptive LLC .... G 203 526-6313
  Shelton (G-7458)
Harpoon Acquisition Corp .... A 860 815-5736
  Glastonbury (G-3047)
Healthprize Technologies LLC .... G 203 957-3400
  Norwalk (G-6198)
Heckman Consulting LLC .... G 860 434-5877
  Old Lyme (G-6512)
Honeypotz Inc .... G 203 542-7891
  Old Greenwich (G-6475)
Hypack Inc .... F 860 635-1500
  Middletown (G-4354)
Innovation Group .... E 860 674-2900
  Farmington (G-2917)

It Helps LLC .... G 860 799-8321
  New Milford (G-5547)
Jmp Software .... G 203 984-4096
  Norwalk (G-6224)
Jpg Consulting Inc .... G 203 247-2730
  Wilton (G-10305)
Kol LLC .... E 203 393-2924
  Woodbridge (G-10605)
Letout & Bliss LLC .... G 203 775-3548
  Brookfield (G-1202)
Link Systems Inc .... F 203 274-9702
  Stamford (G-8285)
Management Hlth Solutions Inc .... E 888 647-4621
  Stratford (G-8647)
Management Software Inc .... G 860 536-5177
  Ledyard (G-3877)
Market76 Inc .... G 866 808-5491
  Guilford (G-3370)
Mbsiinet Inc .... F 888 466-2744
  Southbury (G-7866)
Me2health LLC .... G 203 208-8927
  Guilford (G-3374)
Newman Information Systems .... G 860 286-0540
  Bloomfield (G-449)
Nexvue Information Systems Inc .... F 203 327-0800
  Stamford (G-8328)
Open Solutions LLC .... C 860 815-5000
  Glastonbury (G-3066)
Oracle Corporation .... B 860 632-8329
  Middletown (G-4389)
Polymath Software .... G 860 423-5823
  Willimantic (G-10234)
Pricing Excellence LLC .... G 866 557-8102
  Suffield (G-8730)
Proserv Software & Support LLC .... G 866 833-8999
  Meriden (G-4223)
Qdiscovery LLC .... E 860 271-7080
  New London (G-5483)
Results-Based Outsourcing Inc .... G 203 635-7600
  Fairfield (G-2835)
Scry Health Inc .... F 203 936-8244
  Woodbridge (G-10616)
Shibumicom Inc .... F 855 744-2864
  Norwalk (G-6344)
Siggpay Inc .... G 203 957-8261
  Norwalk (G-6346)
Software By Design LLC .... G 203 271-1061
  Cheshire (G-1449)
Stamford Risk Analytics LLC .... F 203 559-0883
  Stamford (G-8439)
Tagetik North America LLC .... G 203 391-7520
  Stamford (G-8457)
Technosoft Solutions Inc .... E 203 676-8299
  Branford (G-661)
Ticket Software LLC .... G 860 644-0422
  South Windsor (G-7833)
Voice Glance LLC .... F 800 260-3025
  Mystic (G-4852)

SOFTWARE PUBLISHERS: Computer Utilities

API Wizard LLC .... G 914 764-5726
  Ridgefield (G-7117)

SOFTWARE PUBLISHERS: Education

Active Internet Tech LLC .... C 800 592-2469
  Glastonbury (G-3003)
Becaid LLC .... G 203 915-6914
  New Haven (G-5241)
Benedict M Lai .... G 425 698-7267
  Manchester (G-3986)
Business & Prof Microcompter .... G 860 231-7302
  West Hartford (G-9780)
Careerpath Mobile LLC .... G 203 512-2379
  New Milford (G-5515)
Connecticut Computer Svc Inc .... G 860 276-1285
  Milford (G-4493)
Hanna RES & Consulting LLC .... G 860 443-0443
  Quaker Hill (G-7082)
Hotseat Chassis Inc .... G 860 582-5031
  Waterbury (G-9499)
Micro Training Associates Inc .... F 860 693-7740
  Canton (G-1318)
National Educ Suppt Trust US .... G 860 420-8008
  Branford (G-628)
Prolink Inc .... G 860 659-5928
  Glastonbury (G-3076)
Soundview Horizons Dgtl Ldrshp .... G 203 292-0880
  Weston (G-10040)

Thebeamer LLC.....F..... 860 212-5071
East Hartford (G-2383)
Urise LLC.....G..... 860 833-3009
Hartford (G-3710)
Zillion Group Inc.....F..... 203 810-5400
Norwalk (G-6404)

SOFTWARE PUBLISHERS: Home Entertainment

Cliffside Entertainment LLC.....G..... 203 290-7484
Bridgeport (G-736)
Dataprep Inc.....E..... 203 795-2095
Orange (G-6595)
Loden Software.....G..... 203 949-9416
Wallingford (G-9304)

SOFTWARE PUBLISHERS: NEC

2394 Berlin Turnpike Assoc LLC.....G..... 860 347-1624
Middletown (G-4311)
3 Story Software LLC.....G..... 203 530-3224
New Milford (G-5500)
360alumni Inc.....G..... 203 253-5860
Weston (G-10016)
Advanced Reasoning.....G..... 860 437-0508
Waterford (G-9639)
Agile Computer Systems.....G..... 860 633-7807
Glastonbury (G-3004)
Aicas Inc.....G..... 203 359-5705
Stamford (G-8068)
Al Huppenthal.....G..... 203 364-1028
Sandy Hook (G-7299)
Alva Health Inc.....G..... 832 515-8235
New Haven (G-5225)
Andeco Software LLC.....G..... 225 229-2491
Danbury (G-1740)
Aniyaq LLC.....G..... 860 531-2835
Marlborough (G-4120)
Applied Software.....G..... 860 289-9153
South Windsor (G-7710)
Appstract Ideas.....G..... 860 857-1123
Bristol (G-964)
Arbot Software.....G..... 860 209-8460
West Hartford (G-9775)
Array Technologies Inc.....G..... 860 657-8086
Glastonbury (G-3008)
Art of Wellbeing LLC.....G..... 917 453-3009
Stamford (G-8095)
Asset Vantage Inc.....G..... 475 218-2639
Stamford (G-8097)
Auras Oracle.....G..... 860 308-0893
Coventry (G-1644)
Automatech Inc.....F..... 860 673-5940
Unionville (G-9111)
Blue Sky Studios Inc.....C..... 203 992-6000
Greenwich (G-3135)
Brass City Gamers Tournament.....G..... 203 584-3359
Waterbury (G-9442)
C P I Computer Center Inc.....G..... 203 483-8505
Branford (G-567)
Capstone Software LLC.....G..... 617 413-4444
Mystic (G-4804)
CD Solutions Inc.....E..... 203 481-5895
Branford (G-571)
Center Road Software LLC.....G..... 860 402-2767
East Haddam (G-2238)
Century Software Systems.....G..... 203 888-5233
Seymour (G-7339)
Cerberus Enterprise Sftwr LLC.....G..... 860 432-3861
Manchester (G-3993)
Channel Sources Dist Co LLC.....G..... 203 775-6464
Brookfield (G-1170)
Cobra Green LLC.....A..... 203 354-5000
Norwalk (G-6118)
Codebridge Software Inc.....G..... 203 535-0517
West Haven (G-9888)
Community Brands Holdings LLC.....F..... 203 227-1255
Westport (G-10067)
Compart North America Inc.....F..... 860 799-5612
New Milford (G-5522)
Computer Prgrm & Systems Inc.....G..... 203 324-9203
Stamford (G-8155)
Computer Software Educ SE.....G..... 860 677-4527
Farmington (G-2890)
Computer Support People LLC.....G..... 203 653-4643
Norwalk (G-6122)
Computer Technologies Corp.....G..... 860 683-4030
Windsor (G-10376)
Continuity Control.....G..... 203 459-0155
New Haven (G-5261)
Coss Systems Inc.....G..... 800 961-0288
Greenwich (G-3145)
Coss Systems Inc (not Inc).....G..... 732 447-7724
Old Greenwich (G-6470)
Couponz Direct LLC.....G..... 212 655-9615
Greenwich (G-3146)
Coyote Software.....G..... 203 227-6510
Westport (G-10070)
CPC Software LLC.....G..... 203 348-9684
Stamford (G-8162)
Craig Keating.....G..... 203 852-0571
Norwalk (G-6132)
Custom Computer Systems.....G..... 203 264-7808
Southbury (G-7850)
Darien Technology Foundation I.....G..... 203 655-5099
Darien (G-2019)
Dayspring Communications LLC.....G..... 336 775-2059
Fairfield (G-2771)
Dell Software Inc.....G..... 203 259-0326
Southport (G-8003)
Device42 Inc.....F..... 203 409-7242
West Haven (G-9898)
Dmt Solutions Global Corp.....A..... 203 233-6231
Danbury (G-1797)
Document Dynamics LLC.....G..... 860 376-2944
Jewett City (G-3794)
Dreamer Software LLC.....G..... 860 645-1240
Manchester (G-4011)
Eagle Consulting LLC.....G..... 203 445-1740
Trumbull (G-9023)
Expansion Software LLC.....G..... 860 274-0338
Watertown (G-9704)
Fiduciaryai Inc.....G..... 203 724-7571
Norwalk (G-6164)
First Light Software Inc.....G..... 860 217-0673
Simsbury (G-7626)
Freethink Technologies Inc.....F..... 860 237-5800
Branford (G-597)
Gerber Scientific LLC.....C..... 860 871-8082
Tolland (G-8864)
Graybark Enterprises LLC.....G..... 203 255-4503
Fairfield (G-2792)
Habanero Software Incorporated.....G..... 203 453-5458
Guilford (G-3359)
Higgins Sftwr Consulting LLC.....G..... 203 468-2350
East Haven (G-2434)
Horizon Software Inc.....G..... 860 633-2090
Glastonbury (G-3050)
I-Logic Software.....G..... 860 875-7760
Vernon Rockville (G-9169)
Illume Health LLC.....G..... 203 242-7801
Westport (G-10096)
Imagine Software LLC.....G..... 203 271-0252
Cheshire (G-1398)
Information Builders Inc.....F..... 860 249-7229
Hartford (G-3617)
Information Resources Inc.....D..... 203 845-6400
Norwalk (G-6207)
Information Tech Intl Corp.....G..... 860 648-2570
Manchester (G-4033)
Inner Office Inc.....G..... 860 564-6777
Moosup (G-4780)
Innovative Software.....G..... 203 264-1564
Southbury (G-7861)
Innovative Software LLC.....G..... 860 228-4144
Hebron (G-3751)
Insight Enterprises Inc.....G..... 860 647-0848
Vernon (G-9141)
Insight Enterprises Inc.....G..... 203 374-2013
Easton (G-2557)
Intelium Software LLC.....G..... 860 667-4300
Newington (G-5665)
Intellgent Clearing Netwrk Inc.....G..... 203 972-0861
North Haven (G-5948)
International Systems Cons.....G..... 203 268-1045
Trumbull (G-9036)
Inverse Media LLC.....G..... 203 255-9620
Westport (G-10104)
J H R Software.....G..... 203 723-4091
Naugatuck (G-4893)
J Squared Software.....G..... 203 325-0275
Stamford (G-8261)
Jcascio Software Inc.....G..... 860 535-2864
Stonington (G-8533)
Jenkins Software Assoc LLC.....G..... 203 483-8386
Branford (G-612)
Jmjp LLC.....G..... 888 737-7577
Brooklyn (G-1248)
Jonathan David Humpherys.....G..... 415 847-3032
Weatogue (G-9756)
Kaya Software LLC.....G..... 203 267-7817
Southbury (G-7865)
Komputation Computer Services.....G..... 203 744-3652
Danbury (G-1871)
Lab Software Associates.....G..... 203 762-1342
Wilton (G-10308)
Langlais Computer Cons LLC.....G..... 860 589-0093
Bristol (G-1061)
Lateral Thinking Software Sys.....G..... 203 452-9713
Trumbull (G-9042)
Light Speed LLC.....G..... 203 248-8550
Hamden (G-3475)
Litigation Analytics Inc.....F..... 203 431-0300
Ridgefield (G-7154)
Littlefingers Software.....G..... 203 938-2684
Redding (G-7096)
Lost Code Software LLC.....G..... 203 626-9133
Wallingford (G-9307)
MB Software Development.....G..... 203 928-0436
West Haven (G-9934)
Mc Keon Computer Services.....G..... 860 496-7171
Torrington (G-8947)
Medpipes.....G..... 860 658-7300
West Simsbury (G-9981)
Medpricercom Inc.....G..... 203 453-4554
Guilford (G-3375)
Mission Critical Software.....G..... 860 748-6946
Glastonbury (G-3060)
Montage Software Systems Inc.....G..... 203 834-1144
Wilton (G-10313)
Mpi Systems Inc.....G..... 203 762-2260
Wilton (G-10314)
National Instruments Corp.....G..... 203 661-6795
Riverside (G-7198)
Navtech Systems Inc.....G..... 203 661-7800
Old Greenwich (G-6480)
Neasi-Weber International.....G..... 203 857-4404
Norwalk (G-6271)
Network Expert Sftwr Systems.....G..... 860 829-1427
Kensington (G-3815)
Norfield Data Products Inc.....F..... 203 849-0292
Norwalk (G-6280)
North Star Computing Svcs LLC.....G..... 860 635-7117
Cromwell (G-1709)
Nuance Communications Inc.....G..... 781 565-5000
Stratford (G-8658)
Nupal LLC.....G..... 860 227-7964
Chester (G-1476)
Nxtid Inc.....F..... 203 266-2103
Oxford (G-6682)
O/D Dominion Software LLC.....G..... 860 904-9261
Bloomfield (G-453)
Old Road Software Inc.....G..... 914 755-1329
Ridgefield (G-7159)
Openiam Software LLC.....G..... 203 202-7186
Redding (G-7105)
Orisha Oracle Inc.....G..... 203 612-8989
Bridgeport (G-857)
Packrat Software.....G..... 860 774-1538
Dayville (G-2068)
Paladin Software Inc.....G..... 203 966-0548
New Canaan (G-5129)
Pallasian Software LLC.....G..... 203 758-5868
Prospect (G-7015)
Peartree Point Software LLC.....G..... 203 940-1069
Darien (G-2037)
Peerless Systems Corporation.....F..... 203 350-0040
Stamford (G-8355)
Penney Software Services.....G..... 860 870-3443
Tolland (G-8875)
People Meeting LLC.....G..... 860 933-0366
Glastonbury (G-3069)
Peter Hannan.....G..... 203 226-4335
Westport (G-10140)
Pilot Software Inc.....G..... 203 252-2463
Stamford (G-8361)
Pitney Bowes Inc.....A..... 203 356-5000
Stamford (G-8362)
Pitney Bowes Software Inc.....G..... 603 595-2060
Stamford (G-8364)
Prime Business Services.....G..... 203 453-1627
Guilford (G-3384)
Private Communications Corp.....F..... 860 355-2718
Sherman (G-7602)
Protegrity Usa Inc.....E..... 203 326-7200
Stamford (G-8376)
Protoshield.....G..... 203 527-0321
Middlebury (G-4288)
Psj Software LLC.....G..... 203 315-1523
Branford (G-639)

PRODUCT SECTION

Qualedi Inc .... G 203 538-5320
  Shelton (G-7542)
Qualedi Inc .... G 203 874-4334
  Milford (G-4621)
Ramco Systems Corporation .... G 860 496-0099
  New Hartford (G-5209)
Reel Time LLC .... G 203 326-0664
  New Canaan (G-5138)
Regenerative Medicine LLC .... G 203 629-1438
  Greenwich (G-3223)
Relational Data Solutions LLC .... G 860 231-7682
  West Hartford (G-9851)
Relprog LLC .... G 203 734-7000
  Derby (G-2123)
Republic Systems Inc .... G 860 291-8832
  East Hartford (G-2365)
Richard Breault .... G 203 876-2707
  Milford (G-4626)
Robust Software LLC .... G 860 231-9880
  West Hartford (G-9852)
S-Frame Software LLC .... G 203 421-8527
  Madison (G-3954)
Saleschain LLC .... F 203 262-1611
  Waterbury (G-9597)
Savin Rock Software LLC .... G 203 272-5039
  Cheshire (G-1442)
Schulz Consulting LLC .... G 860 657-4497
  Glastonbury (G-3082)
Securities Software & Con .... G 860 242-7887
  Bloomfield (G-486)
Securities Software & Consulti ...... G 860 298-4500
  Windsor (G-10435)
Shagmeisters Enterprises .... G 203 937-5584
  West Haven (G-9954)
Shiloh Software Inc .... G 203 272-8456
  Cheshire (G-1445)
Sigmund Software LLC .... F 800 448-6975
  Danbury (G-1948)
Skythink Inc .... G 203 324-1108
  Stamford (G-8424)
Slv Consulting Inc .... G 917 892-4034
  Wilton (G-10332)
Smartpay Solutions .... G 860 986-7659
  Southington (G-7974)
Snowdog Software LLC .... G 203 265-7116
  Wallingford (G-9370)
Software Cnslting Rsources Inc .... G 860 491-2689
  Goshen (G-3104)
Software Establishment LLC .... G 860 426-2700
  Southington (G-7976)
Software Gallery Inc .... G 203 775-0520
  Brookfield (G-1224)
Software Matters .... G 860 354-8804
  Roxbury (G-7285)
Software Studios LLC .... G 203 288-3997
  North Haven (G-5995)
Software Systems & Support LLC .... G 203 470-8482
  Middletown (G-4420)
SS&c Technologies Inc .... G 860 930-5882
  Windsor (G-10437)
SS&c Technologies Inc .... C 860 298-4500
  Windsor (G-10438)
SS&c Technologies Holdings Inc ..... D 860 298-4500
  Windsor (G-10439)
Success App .... G 203 218-6264
  Stratford (G-8689)
Synergy Solutions LLC .... G 203 762-1153
  Wilton (G-10335)
Tangoe Us Inc .... B 203 859-9300
  Shelton (G-7563)
Tavisca LLC .... G 203 956-1000
  Stamford (G-8458)
Technology Group LLC .... G 860 524-4400
  Hartford (G-3699)
Technolutions Inc .... E 203 404-4835
  New Haven (G-5412)
Telemark Systems Inc .... G 860 355-8001
  New Milford (G-5594)
Tenzingbrook Software LLC .... G 203 918-4500
  New Canaan (G-5151)
Think Ahead Software LLC .... G 860 463-9786
  West Hartford (G-9865)
Tiny B Code LLC .... G 617 308-9635
  West Hartford (G-9867)
Torrington Ig Partners LLC .... G 860 482-7868
  Torrington (G-8982)
Travers & Co LLC .... G 860 633-8586
  Glastonbury (G-3089)
Traxx Software LLC .... G 860 632-8712
  Cromwell (G-1721)

Trinity Mobile Networks Inc .... G 301 332-6401
  New Haven (G-5423)
Trycycle Data Systems US Inc .... G 860 558-1148
  Farmington (G-2970)
Turnkey Software LLC .... G 860 604-0837
  East Hampton (G-2282)
Tutors & Computers Inc .... G 203 393-3006
  Bethany (G-251)
Ultimate Interfaces Corp .... G 203 230-8184
  Milford (G-4667)
Vertafore Inc .... A 860 602-6000
  Windsor (G-10459)
Villa Ridge LLC .... G 303 330-9183
  Norwalk (G-6389)
Visual Software Systems LLC .... G 860 829-1223
  Berlin (G-231)
Warren Computer Services .... G 203 929-5725
  Shelton (G-7583)
Wdl Software Llc .... G 203 366-8640
  Fairfield (G-2867)
Web Charity LLC .... G 203 481-7600
  Branford (G-670)
Wipl-D (usa) LLC .... G 860 570-0678
  West Hartford (G-9873)
X Over Y Systems .... G 860 885-0034
  New London (G-5497)
Xolvi LLC .... G 339 222-3616
  Simsbury (G-7652)
Yourmembershipcom Inc .... G 860 271-7241
  Groton (G-3320)

SOFTWARE PUBLISHERS: Operating Systems

Agencyport Software Corp .... G 860 674-6135
  Farmington (G-2876)
DSar Company .... G 203 324-6456
  Stamford (G-8189)
Mvp Systems Software Inc .... F 860 269-3112
  Unionville (G-9122)
Oracle America Inc .... D 203 703-3000
  Stamford (G-8345)

SOFTWARE PUBLISHERS: Publisher's

Dirtcircle Media LLC .... G 860 532-0674
  Milford (G-4511)
Genesis D T P .... G 860 350-2827
  Gaylordsville (G-2993)
Kenneth Finn .... G 914 764-4938
  Greenwich (G-3187)
Living Abroad LLC .... G 203 221-1997
  Norwalk (G-6234)
Radical Computing Corporation ...... G 860 953-0240
  Newington (G-5699)
Uniworld Bus Publications Inc .... G 201 384-4900
  Darien (G-2049)

SOFTWARE TRAINING, COMPUTER

American-Digital LLC .... G 203 838-0148
  Bridgeport (G-695)
Compart North America Inc .... F 860 799-5612
  New Milford (G-5522)

SOLAR CELLS

Fidelux Lighting LLC .... F 860 436-5000
  Hartford (G-3589)

SOLAR HEATING EQPT

Allgreenit LLC .... G 860 516-4948
  Bristol (G-961)
Flabeg US Holding Inc .... G 203 729-5227
  Naugatuck (G-4881)
Optical Energy Technologies .... G 203 357-0626
  Stamford (G-8344)

SOLDERING EQPT: Electrical, Exc Handheld

Air-Vac Engineering Co Inc .... E 203 888-9900
  Seymour (G-7335)
Systems and Tech Intl Inc .... G 860 871-0401
  Tolland (G-8880)

SOLDERS

Alent USA Holding Inc .... B 203 575-5727
  Waterbury (G-9426)
Torrey S Crane Company .... E 860 628-4778
  Plantsville (G-6915)

SPECIALTY FOOD STORES: Soft Drinks

SOLENOIDS

Able Coil and Electronics Co .... E 860 646-5686
  Bolton (G-504)
Bicron Electronics Company .... D 860 482-2524
  Torrington (G-8905)

SOLVENTS

Purification Technologies LLC .... F 860 526-7801
  Chester (G-1480)
US Chemicals Inc .... G 203 655-8878
  New Canaan (G-5157)

SONAR SYSTEMS & EQPT

Thayermahan Inc .... F 860 785-9994
  Groton (G-3315)

SOUND RECORDING STUDIOS

Trod Nossel Prdctns & Rcrdng S ..... G 203 269-4465
  Wallingford (G-9391)

SPACE FLIGHT OPERATIONS, EXC GOVERNMENT

Singularity Space Systems LLC .... G 860 713-3626
  Granby (G-3114)

SPACE SUITS

Hamilton Standard Space .... E 860 654-6000
  Windsor Locks (G-10490)

SPACE VEHICLE EQPT

Accupaulo Holding Corporation ...... E 860 666-5621
  Newington (G-5617)
Aerocess Inc .... F 860 357-2451
  Berlin (G-151)
Braxton Manufacturing Co Inc .... C 860 274-6781
  Watertown (G-9685)
Edac Technologies LLC .... F 860 789-2511
  East Windsor (G-2490)
Edac Technologies LLC .... C 203 806-2090
  Cheshire (G-1383)
Kaman Aerospace Group Inc .... F 860 243-7100
  Bloomfield (G-433)
Meriden Manufacturing Inc .... D 203 237-7481
  Meriden (G-4197)
Ramar-Hall Inc .... E 860 349-1081
  Middlefield (G-4306)
Spartan Aerospace LLC .... D 860 533-7500
  Manchester (G-4090)
Sterling Engineering Corp .... C 860 379-3366
  Pleasant Valley (G-6926)
United Tool and Die Company .... C 860 246-6531
  West Hartford (G-9871)

SPACE VEHICLES

Singularity Space Systems LLC .... G 860 713-3626
  Granby (G-3114)

SPAS

Bella Nail & Spa LLC .... G 860 436-3119
  Rocky Hill (G-7222)

SPEAKER SYSTEMS

Marathon Wood Work .... G 203 847-2800
  Norwalk (G-6247)

SPECIAL EVENTS DECORATION SVCS

Zp Couture LLC .... G 888 697-7239
  North Haven (G-6017)

SPECIALTY FOOD STORES: Coffee

Sacred Grunds Cof Roasters LLC ..... G 860 717-2871
  Sherman (G-7604)

SPECIALTY FOOD STORES: Food Gift Baskets

Grotto Always Inc .... F 203 754-0295
  Waterbury (G-9491)

SPECIALTY FOOD STORES: Soft Drinks

Harvest Hill Holdings LLC .... F 203 914-1620
  Stamford (G-8230)

Employee Codes: A=Over 500 employees, B=251-500
C=101-250, D=51-100, E=20-50, F=10-19, G=1-9

SPECIALTY FOOD STORES: Soft Drinks

Hosmer Mountain Btlg Co Inc...............G....... 860 643-6923
  Manchester (G-4029)

SPEED CHANGERS

Carlyle Johnson Machine Co LLC.........E....... 860 643-1531
  Bolton (G-508)

SPINDLES: Textile

Advanced Machine Services LLC...........G....... 203 888-6600
  Waterbury (G-9423)
Advanced Machine Services LLC...........G....... 203 888-6600
  Oxford (G-6638)

SPONGES: Plastic

Mdm Products LLC................................F....... 203 877-7070
  Milford (G-4576)

SPORTING & ATHLETIC GOODS: Arrows, Archery

Archers Only LLC ....G....... 860 689-0594
  Harwinton (G-3720)
Wasp Archery Products Inc ....G....... 860 283-0246
  Plymouth (G-6930)

SPORTING & ATHLETIC GOODS: Bobsleds

Bo-Dyn Bobsled Project Inc....................G....... 860 526-9504
  Chester (G-1465)

SPORTING & ATHLETIC GOODS: Boomerangs

Boomerang Consignment ....G....... 203 788-9002
  South Kent (G-7683)
Boomerang Studio ....G....... 203 689-5155
  Guilford (G-3331)

SPORTING & ATHLETIC GOODS: Bowling Balls

Brandmark Studios LLC..........................G....... 203 438-9400
  Ridgefield (G-7125)

SPORTING & ATHLETIC GOODS: Driving Ranges, Golf, Electronic

Bonenfants Drv Your Auto Svc...............G....... 203 222-2239
  Westport (G-10061)
Valley Golf Center CT LLC ....G....... 860 799-7605
  New Milford (G-5605)

SPORTING & ATHLETIC GOODS: Dumbbells & Other Weight Eqpt

Yakka LLC...G....... 617 877-7553
  New Haven (G-5438)

SPORTING & ATHLETIC GOODS: Fencing Eqpt

International Soccer & Rugby.................G....... 203 254-1979
  Southport (G-8004)

SPORTING & ATHLETIC GOODS: Fishing Eqpt

Compleat Angler ....G....... 203 655-9400
  Darien (G-2014)
Edgewater International LLC ....F....... 860 851-9014
  Stafford Springs (G-8028)

SPORTING & ATHLETIC GOODS: Gymnasium Eqpt

Sports Center ....G....... 860 768-4650
  West Hartford (G-9860)

SPORTING & ATHLETIC GOODS: Hockey Eqpt & Splys, NEC

East Coast Hockey Depot LLC ....G....... 203 247-3476
  Stamford (G-8191)

SPORTING & ATHLETIC GOODS: Pools, Swimming, Exc Plastic

Fairfield Pool & Equipment Co ....G....... 203 334-3600
  Fairfield (G-2785)
Group Works ....G....... 203 834-7905
  Wilton (G-10299)

SPORTING & ATHLETIC GOODS: Rods & Rod Parts, Fishing

JW Gallas Rod Co ....G....... 203 790-4188
  Danbury (G-1867)
K & D Business Ventures LLC ....G....... 860 237-1458
  Jewett City (G-3798)

SPORTING & ATHLETIC GOODS: Shafts, Golf Club

Gary Morris Clubmaker ....G....... 860 482-5929
  Torrington (G-8929)
Paul Ramee LLC....................................G....... 860 927-7135
  South Kent (G-7684)
S Hassel Golf Works ....G....... 860 274-4011
  Watertown (G-9732)

SPORTING & ATHLETIC GOODS: Shooting Eqpt & Splys, General

Robert Louis Company Inc ....G....... 203 270-1400
  Newtown (G-5776)

SPORTING & ATHLETIC GOODS: Skateboards

Coma Skateboards ....G....... 860 933-4830
  Storrs (G-8547)
Hoodlum Skateboard Company LLC ....G....... 860 690-6201
  East Hartford (G-2333)
Impaled Longboards LLC ....G....... 860 379-1101
  New Hartford (G-5195)
Rampage LLC ....F....... 203 930-1022
  Trumbull (G-9061)
Ransom Skateboards and App ....G....... 860 538-5577
  Unionville (G-9125)
Zombie Gang Skateboards LLC ....G....... 860 367-2650
  New London (G-5498)

SPORTING & ATHLETIC GOODS: Snow Skiing Eqpt & Sply, Exc Skis

Mike Sadlak ....G....... 860 742-0227
  Coventry (G-1663)

SPORTING & ATHLETIC GOODS: Snow Skis

Frostbite LLC ....G....... 203 240-3449
  Wilton (G-10297)

SPORTING & ATHLETIC GOODS: Snowshoes

Toms Taz Lures ....G....... 860 429-0307
  Willington (G-10259)

SPORTING & ATHLETIC GOODS: Soccer Eqpt & Splys

Soccer N More ....G....... 860 282-0224
  East Hartford (G-2375)

SPORTING & ATHLETIC GOODS: Targets, Archery & Rifle Shooting

Sadlak Industries LLC ....E....... 860 742-0227
  Coventry (G-1673)

SPORTING & ATHLETIC GOODS: Team Sports Eqpt

MB Sports Training LLC ....G....... 203 269-1410
  Northford (G-6050)

SPORTING & ATHLETIC GOODS: Tennis Eqpt & Splys

Danbury Grassroots Tennis Inc.............G....... 203 797-0500
  Danbury (G-1782)

SPORTING & ATHLETIC GOODS: Track & Field Athletic Eqpt

Wepa Sports LLC...................................G....... 203 971-9372
  New London (G-5496)

SPORTING & ATHLETIC GOODS: Treadmills

Samsara Fitness LLC ....F....... 860 895-8533
  Chester (G-1483)

SPORTING & ATHLETIC GOODS: Water Sports Eqpt

Uniboard Corp ....G....... 860 428-5979
  Putnam (G-7075)

SPORTING & ATHLETIC GOODS: Winter Sports

X44 LLC ....G....... 860 480-5560
  Torrington (G-8993)

SPORTING & REC GOODS, WHOLESALE: Camping Eqpt & Splys

Shelterlogic Corp ....C....... 860 945-6442
  Watertown (G-9733)
Slogic Holding Corp ....G....... 203 966-2800
  New Canaan (G-5142)

SPORTING & RECREATIONAL GOODS & SPLYS WHOLESALERS

Jacob Sportz LLC ....G....... 860 450-1073
  Willimantic (G-10231)
Jaypro Sports LLC ....E....... 860 447-3001
  Waterford (G-9656)
Wenger Na Inc ....G....... 845 365-3500
  Monroe (G-4764)

SPORTING & RECREATIONAL GOODS, WHOLESALE: Fishing Tackle

Compleat Angler ....G....... 203 655-9400
  Darien (G-2014)

SPORTING & RECREATIONAL GOODS, WHOLESALE: Fitness

Yakka LLC..G....... 617 877-7553
  New Haven (G-5438)

SPORTING & RECREATIONAL GOODS, WHOLESALE: Golf

Golf Galaxy LLC ....G....... 203 855-0500
  Norwalk (G-6182)
Wild Card Golf LLC ....G....... 860 296-1661
  Hartford (G-3715)
Wild Card Golf LLC ....G....... 860 296-1661
  Hartford (G-3716)

SPORTING & RECREATIONAL GOODS, WHOLESALE: Watersports

Bic Corporation ....A....... 203 783-2000
  Shelton (G-7407)

SPORTING GOODS

Ammunition Stor Components LLC......G....... 860 225-3548
  New Britain (G-4945)
Batrolling4u LLC ....G....... 860 439-1994
  Waterford (G-9642)
Beckley Inc ....G....... 203 488-1019
  Branford (G-557)
Bob Vess Building LLC ....G....... 860 729-2536
  Cromwell (G-1693)
Chromations LLC..................................G....... 203 929-8007
  Shelton (G-7419)
CT Amateur Jai Alai LLC ....G....... 860 357-2544
  Berlin (G-174)
Dewey J Manufacturing Company ....G....... 203 264-3064
  Oxford (G-6655)
Ernest Ferraro ....G....... 914 921-4376
  Weston (G-10025)
Europa Sports Products Inc ....G....... 860 688-1110
  Windsor (G-10385)
Facet Skis ....G....... 203 529-3681
  Wilton (G-10294)

PRODUCT SECTION

STAGE LIGHTING SYSTEMS

Fishing Innovations LLC .... G 860 434-3974
  Old Lyme (G-6509)
Gilman Corporation .... E 860 887-7080
  Gilman (G-3000)
Glovewhisperer Inc .... G 203 487-8997
  Greenwich (G-3167)
Hamden Sports Center Inc .... G 203 248-9898
  Hamden (G-3460)
Homeland Fundraising .... G 860 386-6698
  East Windsor (G-2498)
Intersec LLC .... G 860 985-3158
  Rocky Hill (G-7251)
Jacob Sportz LLC .... G 860 450-1073
  Willimantic (G-10231)
Jaypro Sports LLC .... E 860 447-3001
  Waterford (G-9656)
Marty Gilman Incorporated .... D 860 889-7334
  Gilman (G-3001)
Marty Gilman Incorporated .... G 860 889-7334
  Bozrah (G-528)
Montanas Board Sports .... G 860 537-2927
  Colchester (G-1557)
NES Sports LLC .... G 765 532-2178
  Bridgeport (G-847)
Recreational Equipment Inc .... G 860 313-0128
  West Hartford (G-9850)
Road-Fit Enterprises LLC .... G 860 371-5137
  Plainville (G-6856)
Sfn LLC .... G 203 314-8436
  Guilford (G-3389)
Stone Innovations .... G 203 347-8536
  Torrington (G-8974)
Swivel Machine Works Inc .... G 203 270-6343
  Newtown (G-5783)
Tater Bats LLC .... G 203 510-4054
  Waterbury (G-9609)
Warren Trading Company .... G 860 868-7848
  Warren (G-9409)
We String It .... G 203 512-4513
  Danbury (G-1977)
Wiffle Ball Incorporated .... F 203 924-4643
  Shelton (G-7587)
Wild Card Golf LLC .... G 860 296-1661
  Hartford (G-3716)

SPORTING GOODS STORES, NEC

Avalanche Downhill Racing Inc .... G 860 537-4306
  Colchester (G-1541)
Forsa Team Sports LLC .... G 203 466-2890
  East Haven (G-2429)
Gunworks International L L C .... G 203 388-4591
  Old Saybrook (G-6536)
Iovino Bros Sporting Goods .... G 203 790-5966
  Danbury (G-1851)
Macwear LLC .... G 203 579-4277
  Southport (G-8006)
Probatter Sports LLC .... G 203 874-2500
  Milford (G-4618)
Seems Inc .... F 203 284-0259
  Ansonia (G-50)
Swivel Machine Works Inc .... G 203 270-6343
  Newtown (G-5783)

SPORTING GOODS STORES: Archery Splys

New Technologies Mfg Inc .... G 860 872-7605
  Vernon Rockville (G-9171)

SPORTING GOODS STORES: Bait & Tackle

Beckley Inc .... G 203 488-1019
  Branford (G-557)
Wild Bills Action Sports LLC .... G 860 536-6648
  Groton (G-3319)

SPORTING GOODS STORES: Baseball Eqpt

Tucci Lumber Co LLC .... G 203 956-6181
  Norwalk (G-6378)

SPORTING GOODS STORES: Firearms

G W Elliot Inc .... G 860 528-6143
  East Hartford (G-2329)
M2 Tactical Solutions LLC .... G 203 247-3477
  Norwalk (G-6243)
Warren Trading Company .... G 860 868-7848
  Warren (G-9409)

SPORTING GOODS STORES: Skating Eqpt

Del Arbour LLC .... F 203 882-8501
  Milford (G-4506)

SPORTING GOODS STORES: Skiing Eqpt

Frostbite LLC .... G 203 240-3449
  Wilton (G-10297)

SPORTING GOODS STORES: Specialty Sport Splys, NEC

Manup LLC .... G 203 588-9861
  Norwalk (G-6246)
Pilla Inc .... G 203 894-3265
  Ridgefield (G-7161)

SPORTING GOODS STORES: Team sports Eqpt

X44 LLC .... G 860 480-5560
  Torrington (G-8993)

SPORTING GOODS: Archery

New Technologies Mfg Inc .... G 860 872-7605
  Vernon Rockville (G-9171)

SPORTING GOODS: Fishing Nets

Hooked On Fishing Charters .... G 203 257-3431
  Fairfield (G-2794)
Judith Lynn Charters LLC .... G 203 246-6662
  Norwalk (G-6225)

SPORTS APPAREL STORES

Michael Violano .... G 203 934-3368
  West Haven (G-9937)
Wild Bills Action Sports LLC .... G 860 536-6648
  Groton (G-3319)

SPORTS PROMOTION SVCS

Entersport Management Inc .... G 203 972-9090
  New Canaan (G-5103)
Video Messengercom Corp .... G 203 358-8842
  Stratford (G-8702)

SPRAYS: Artificial & Preserved

Jenray Products Inc .... E 914 375-5596
  Brookfield (G-1199)
Wide Horizons Co Inc .... G 203 661-9252
  Greenwich (G-3259)

SPRINGS: Clock, Precision

U S Hairspring LLC .... G 860 747-9526
  Plainville (G-6873)

SPRINGS: Coiled Flat

Dynamic Manufacturing Company ...... G 860 589-2751
  Bristol (G-1023)
Excel Spring & Stamping LLC .... G 860 585-1495
  Bristol (G-1033)

SPRINGS: Instrument, Precision

Plymouth Spring Company Inc .... D 860 584-0594
  Bristol (G-1093)

SPRINGS: Mechanical, Precision

A & A Manufacturing Co Inc .... E 262 786-1500
  North Haven (G-5894)
Century Spring Mfg Co Inc .... E 860 582-3344
  Bristol (G-1000)
DR Templeman Company .... F 860 747-2709
  Plainville (G-6800)
Lee Spring Company LLC .... E 860 584-0991
  Bristol (G-1062)
Rowley Spring & Stamping Corp .... C 860 582-8175
  Bristol (G-1113)
Thomas Spring Co of Connenicut ...... G 203 874-7030
  Milford (G-4663)

SPRINGS: Precision

Barnes Group Inc .... B 860 583-7070
  Bristol (G-973)
Dayon Manufacturing Inc .... E 860 677-8561
  Farmington (G-2897)

Excel Spring & Stamping LLC .... G 860 585-1495
  Bristol (G-1033)
Matthew Warren Inc .... D 860 621-7358
  Southington (G-7952)
Ulbrich of Georgia Inc .... G 203 239-4481
  North Haven (G-6005)

SPRINGS: Steel

Acme Monaco Corporation .... C 860 224-1349
  New Britain (G-4934)
American Specialty Co Inc .... F 203 929-5324
  Shelton (G-7393)
Arrow Manufacturing Company .... G 860 589-3900
  Bristol (G-966)
Century Spring Mfg Co Inc .... E 860 582-3344
  Bristol (G-1000)
Connectcut Spring Stmping Corp ...... B 860 677-1341
  Farmington (G-2891)
Dayon Manufacturing Inc .... E 860 677-8561
  Farmington (G-2897)
Hurley Manufacturing Company .... E 860 379-8506
  New Hartford (G-5194)
Lee Spring Company LLC .... E 860 584-0991
  Bristol (G-1062)
Mark Nicoletti .... G 860 582-5645
  Bristol (G-1068)
Matthew Warren Inc .... D 860 621-7358
  Southington (G-7952)
Newcomb Spring Corp .... E 860 621-0111
  Southington (G-7957)
Oscar Jobs .... G 860 583-7834
  Bristol (G-1083)
Rowley Spring & Stamping Corp .... C 860 582-8175
  Bristol (G-1113)
Spring Computerized Inds LLC .... G 860 605-9206
  Harwinton (G-3739)
Tollman Spring Company Inc .... E 860 583-4856
  Bristol (G-1130)
Triple A Spring Ltd Partnr .... E 860 589-3231
  Bristol (G-1132)

SPRINGS: Wire

Atlantic Precision Spring Inc .... E 860 583-1864
  Bristol (G-968)
Barnes Group Inc .... G 860 298-7740
  Farmington (G-2882)
Barnes Group Inc .... D 860 582-9581
  Bristol (G-974)
Connectcut Spring Stmping Corp ...... B 860 677-1341
  Farmington (G-2891)
Deka Enterprises .... G 860 582-6976
  Bristol (G-1014)
Fourslide Spring Stamping Inc .... E 860 583-1688
  Bristol (G-1042)
Gemco Manufacturing Co Inc .... E 860 628-5529
  Southington (G-7926)
Mark Nicoletti .... G 860 582-5645
  Bristol (G-1068)
National Spring & Stamping Inc .... E 860 283-0203
  Thomaston (G-8798)
Newcomb Spring Corp .... E 860 621-0111
  Southington (G-7957)
Newcomb Springs Connecticut .... E 860 621-0111
  Southington (G-7958)
Oscar Jobs .... G 860 583-7834
  Bristol (G-1083)
Southington Tool & Mfg Corp .... E 860 276-0021
  Plantsville (G-6912)
Spring Computerized Inds LLC .... G 860 605-9206
  Harwinton (G-3739)
Springfield Spring Corporation .... F 860 584-6560
  Bristol (G-1121)
Utica Spring Company Inc .... G 860 628-6165
  Southington (G-7991)

SPRINKLING SYSTEMS: Fire Control

Fire Technology Inc .... G 860 276-2181
  Southington (G-7924)
Jones Fire Sprinkler Co LLC .... G 860 464-7284
  Gales Ferry (G-2984)

STACKS: Smoke

Connectcut Boiler Repr Mfg Inc .... E 860 953-9117
  West Hartford (G-9793)

STAGE LIGHTING SYSTEMS

Contemprary Lights Staging LLC .... G 203 359-8200
  Stamford (G-8159)

STAINLESS STEEL

- **90 Arch St LLC** ... G ... 860 881-2063 — Hartford *(G-3541)*
- **ATI Flat Rlled Pdts Hldngs LLC** ... F ... 203 756-7414 — Waterbury *(G-9435)*
- **ATI New England** ... G ... 860 358-9698 — Cromwell *(G-1689)*
- **Brookfield Stainless LLC** ... G ... 203 987-6773 — Brookfield *(G-1166)*
- **Dufrane Nuclear Shielding Inc** ... F ... 860 379-2318 — Winsted *(G-10516)*
- **Portland Slitting Co Inc** ... G ... 860 342-1500 — Portland *(G-6968)*
- **Yankee Steel Service LLC** ... G ... 203 879-5707 — Wolcott *(G-10593)*

STAINLESS STEEL WARE

- **Ulbrich Solar Wire LLC** ... F ... 203 239-4481 — North Haven *(G-6007)*

STAIRCASES & STAIRS, WOOD

- **B & R Stair** ... G ... 860 582-6584 — Bristol *(G-970)*
- **Best Built Custom Stair Buildi** ... G ... 203 488-8031 — North Branford *(G-5829)*
- **Colonial Woodworking Inc** ... F ... 203 866-5844 — Norwalk *(G-6120)*
- **East Coast Stairs Co Inc** ... G ... 860 528-7096 — South Windsor *(G-7744)*
- **KB Custom Stair Builders Inc** ... G ... 203 234-0836 — North Haven *(G-5957)*
- **Leos Kitchen & Stair Corp** ... G ... 860 225-7363 — New Britain *(G-5010)*
- **Naugatuck Stair Company Inc** ... F ... 203 729-7134 — Naugatuck *(G-4907)*
- **New England Stair Company Inc** ... E ... 203 924-0606 — Shelton *(G-7509)*
- **Quality Stairs Inc** ... E ... 203 367-8390 — Bridgeport *(G-883)*
- **Robert L Lovallo** ... G ... 203 324-6655 — Stamford *(G-8396)*
- **Stately Stair Co Inc** ... E ... 203 575-1966 — Waterbury *(G-9607)*
- **Steven Vandermaelen LLC** ... G ... 203 457-0143 — Guilford *(G-3393)*
- **Summit Stair Co Inc** ... F ... 203 778-2251 — Bethel *(G-348)*
- **Walston Inc** ... G ... 203 453-5929 — Guilford *(G-3401)*
- **Wesconn Stairs Inc** ... G ... 203 792-7367 — Danbury *(G-1978)*
- **West Hrtford Stirs Cbinets Inc** ... D ... 860 953-9151 — Newington *(G-5723)*

STAMPINGS: Automotive

- **3M Company** ... D ... 203 237-5541 — Meriden *(G-4134)*
- **Progressive Stamping Co De Inc** ... E ... 248 299-7100 — Farmington *(G-2951)*

STAMPINGS: Metal

- **A G Russell Company Inc** ... G ... 860 247-9093 — Hartford *(G-3543)*
- **Alinabal Inc** ... C ... 203 877-3241 — Milford *(G-4448)*
- **Alinabal Holdings Corporation** ... B ... 203 877-3241 — Milford *(G-4449)*
- **American Precision Product LLC** ... G ... 860 274-7301 — Watertown *(G-9680)*
- **Anderson Manufacturing Company** ... G ... 203 263-2318 — Woodbury *(G-10624)*
- **Atlantic Precision Spring Inc** ... E ... 860 583-1864 — Bristol *(G-968)*
- **B & G Forming Technology Inc** ... G ... 203 235-2169 — Meriden *(G-4147)*
- **Barnes Group Inc** ... D ... 860 582-9581 — Bristol *(G-974)*
- **Barnes Group Inc** ... G ... 860 298-7740 — Farmington *(G-2882)*
- **Ben Art Manufacturing Co Inc** ... G ... 203 758-4435 — Prospect *(G-6993)*
- **Beta Shim Co** ... E ... 203 926-1150 — Shelton *(G-7404)*
- **Birotech Inc** ... G ... 203 968-5080 — Stamford *(G-8112)*
- **Carpin Manufacturing Inc** ... D ... 203 574-2556 — Waterbury *(G-9446)*
- **Century Spring Mfg Co Inc** ... E ... 860 582-3344 — Bristol *(G-1000)*
- **Cgl Inc** ... F ... 860 945-6166 — Watertown *(G-9691)*
- **Cheshire Manufacturing Co Inc** ... G ... 203 272-3586 — Cheshire *(G-1369)*
- **Cly-Del Manufacturing Company** ... C ... 203 574-2100 — Waterbury *(G-9452)*
- **Connecticut Fine Blanking** ... G ... 203 925-0012 — Shelton *(G-7422)*
- **Demsey Manufacturing Co Inc** ... E ... 860 274-6209 — Watertown *(G-9701)*
- **Deringer-Ney Inc** ... C ... 860 242-2281 — Bloomfield *(G-407)*
- **Di-El Tool & Manufacturing** ... G ... 203 235-2169 — Meriden *(G-4166)*
- **Dynamic Manufacturing Company** ... G ... 860 589-2751 — Bristol *(G-1023)*
- **Empire Industries Inc** ... E ... 860 647-1431 — Manchester *(G-4015)*
- **Eyelet Tech LLC** ... E ... 203 879-5306 — Wolcott *(G-10564)*
- **Fabor Fourslide Inc** ... G ... 203 753-4380 — Waterbury *(G-9479)*
- **Ferre Form Metal Products** ... F ... 860 274-3280 — Oakville *(G-6452)*
- **Finest Engraving LLC** ... G ... 860 742-7579 — Andover *(G-7)*
- **Fourslide Spring Stamping Inc** ... E ... 860 583-1688 — Bristol *(G-1042)*
- **Hessel Industries Inc** ... G ... 203 736-2317 — Derby *(G-2115)*
- **Hi-Tech Fabricating Inc** ... E ... 203 284-0894 — Cheshire *(G-1396)*
- **Hurley Manufacturing Company** ... E ... 860 379-8506 — New Hartford *(G-5194)*
- **Illinois Tool Works Inc** ... E ... 203 720-1676 — Naugatuck *(G-4890)*
- **Illinois Tool Works Inc** ... C ... 203 574-2119 — Waterbury *(G-9503)*
- **ITW Drawform Inc** ... E ... 203 574-3200 — Waterbury *(G-9506)*
- **Jennings Associates Inc** ... G ... 860 749-4281 — Somers *(G-7662)*
- **M & I Industries Inc** ... G ... 860 747-6421 — Plainville *(G-6837)*
- **Mark Nicoletti** ... G ... 860 582-5645 — Bristol *(G-1068)*
- **New Hartford Industrial Park** ... E ... 860 379-8506 — New Hartford *(G-5203)*
- **Nucap US Inc** ... E ... 203 879-1423 — Wolcott *(G-10578)*
- **OEM Sources LLC** ... G ... 203 283-5415 — Milford *(G-4597)*
- **Platt Brothers & Company** ... D ... 203 753-4194 — Waterbury *(G-9580)*
- **Pr-Mx Holdings Company LLC** ... F ... 203 925-0012 — Shelton *(G-7532)*
- **Pratt-Read Corporation** ... F ... 860 625-3620 — Branford *(G-637)*
- **R A Tool Co** ... G ... 203 877-2998 — Milford *(G-4622)*
- **Rowley Spring & Stamping Corp** ... C ... 860 582-8175 — Bristol *(G-1113)*
- **Semco Tool Manufacturing Co** ... G ... 203 723-7411 — Naugatuck *(G-4918)*
- **Siemon Company** ... A ... 860 945-4200 — Watertown *(G-9734)*
- **Solla Eyelet Products Inc** ... E ... 860 274-5729 — Watertown *(G-9737)*
- **Sonchief Electrics Inc** ... G ... 860 379-2741 — Winsted *(G-10538)*
- **Spartan Aerospace LLC** ... D ... 860 533-7500 — Manchester *(G-4090)*
- **Stevens Company Incorporated** ... D ... 860 283-8201 — Thomaston *(G-8806)*
- **Stewart Efi LLC** ... E ... 860 283-2523 — Thomaston *(G-8808)*
- **Stewart Efi Connecticut LLC** ... C ... 860 283-8213 — Thomaston *(G-8809)*
- **Telke Tool & Die Mfg Co** ... G ... 860 828-9955 — Kensington *(G-3819)*
- **Tops Manufacturing Co Inc** ... G ... 203 655-9367 — Darien *(G-2047)*
- **Washer Tech Inc** ... G ... 203 886-0054 — Meriden *(G-4266)*
- **Wces Inc** ... F ... 203 573-1325 — Waterbury *(G-9632)*
- **West Shore Metals LLC** ... G ... 860 749-8013 — Enfield *(G-2705)*
- **Whitebeck John** ... G ... 860 567-1398 — Bantam *(G-128)*

STATIONERY & OFFICE SPLYS WHOLESALERS

- **Recycle 4 Vets LLC** ... G ... 203 222-7300 — Westport *(G-10147)*

STATIONERY PRDTS

- **American CT Rng Bnder Index &** ... F ... 860 868-7900 — Washington *(G-9411)*
- **Classic Images Inc** ... G ... 860 243-8365 — Bloomfield *(G-403)*
- **Forgetful Gentleman LLC** ... G ... 203 431-2486 — Ridgefield *(G-7141)*
- **Harpers Invitations** ... G ... 860 257-4615 — Glastonbury *(G-3046)*
- **Professional Mktg Svcs Inc** ... F ... 203 610-6222 — Stratford *(G-8669)*
- **Pulp Paper Products Inc** ... G ... 860 806-0143 — Torrington *(G-8961)*

STATORS REWINDING SVCS

- **Piela Electric Inc** ... F ... 860 889-8476 — Preston *(G-6987)*
- **SEC Electrical Inc** ... F ... 203 562-5811 — New Haven *(G-5390)*

STEAM HEATING SYSTEMS SPLY SVCS

- **Saigeworks LLC** ... G ... 203 767-1035 — Trumbull *(G-9069)*

STEAM, HEAT & AIR CONDITIONING DISTRIBUTION SVC

- **P&G Metal Components Corp** ... F ... 860 243-2220 — Bloomfield *(G-458)*

STEEL & ALLOYS: Tool & Die

- **Mark Tool Co** ... G ... 860 673-5039 — Avon *(G-92)*
- **Mott Corporation** ... C ... 800 289-6688 — Farmington *(G-2932)*
- **National Integrated Inds Inc** ... C ... 860 677-7995 — Farmington *(G-2933)*
- **Rcd LLC** ... G ... 203 712-1900 — Shelton *(G-7544)*

STEEL FABRICATORS

- **Accutron Inc** ... C ... 860 683-8300 — Windsor *(G-10354)*
- **Acquisitions Controlled Svcs** ... G ... 203 327-6364 — Stamford *(G-8060)*
- **All Panel Systems LLC** ... D ... 203 208-3142 — Branford *(G-541)*
- **All Star Welding & Dem LLC** ... G ... 203 948-0528 — Danbury *(G-1735)*
- **Alloy Welding & Mfg Co Inc** ... F ... 860 582-3638 — Bristol *(G-962)*
- **Anco Engineering Inc** ... D ... 203 925-9235 — Shelton *(G-7395)*
- **Andert Inc** ... G ... 860 974-3893 — Eastford *(G-2534)*
- **Ansonia Stl Fabrication Co Inc** ... E ... 203 888-4509 — Beacon Falls *(G-129)*
- **Applied Laser Solutions Inc** ... G ... 203 739-0179 — Danbury *(G-1742)*
- **ARC Dynamics Inc** ... G ... 860 563-1006 — Rocky Hill *(G-7221)*
- **Atlantic Eqp Installers Inc** ... E ... 203 284-0402 — Wallingford *(G-9213)*
- **Atlantic Fabricating Co Inc** ... F ... 860 291-9882 — South Windsor *(G-7712)*
- **Atlas Metal Works LLC** ... F ... 860 282-1030 — South Windsor *(G-7713)*
- **Barzetti Welding LLC** ... G ... 203 748-3200 — Bethel *(G-261)*
- **Bri Metal Works Inc** ... G ... 203 368-1649 — Bridgeport *(G-718)*
- **Capstan Inc** ... G ... 508 384-3100 — Weston *(G-10021)*
- **Carpin Manufacturing Inc** ... D ... 203 574-2556 — Waterbury *(G-9446)*
- **Center Mass LLC** ... G ... 860 350-0239 — New Milford *(G-5518)*

PRODUCT SECTION

STONE: Dimension, NEC

Central Construction Inds LLC .... E 860 963-8902
  Putnam *(G-7033)*
Cirillo Manufacturing Group .... G 203 484-5010
  East Haven *(G-2416)*
Coastal Steel Corporation .... E 860 443-4073
  Waterford *(G-9646)*
Colonial Iron Shop Inc .... G 860 763-0659
  Enfield *(G-2629)*
Connecticut Iron Works Inc .... G 203 869-0657
  Greenwich *(G-3144)*
Contractors Steel Supply .... F 203 782-1221
  North Haven *(G-5926)*
Delany & Long Ltd .... G 203 532-0010
  Greenwich *(G-3149)*
Di-Cor Industries Inc .... F 860 585-5583
  Bristol *(G-1017)*
Division 5 LLC .... G 860 752-4127
  Stafford Springs *(G-8027)*
Eagle Manufacturing Co Inc .... F 860 537-3759
  Colchester *(G-1549)*
East Windsor Metal Fabg Inc .... F 860 528-7107
  South Windsor *(G-7745)*
Eastern Inc .... G 203 563-9535
  New Canaan *(G-5102)*
Engineered Building Pdts Inc .... E 860 243-1110
  Bloomfield *(G-409)*
Enginering Components Pdts LLC .... G 860 747-6222
  Plainville *(G-6806)*
Equipment Works .... G 860 585-9686
  Bristol *(G-1030)*
ES Metal Fabrications Inc .... F 860 585-6067
  Terryville *(G-8753)*
Flashback Welding .... G 860 738-1122
  Winsted *(G-10521)*
Fox Steel Products LLC .... F 203 799-2356
  Orange *(G-6602)*
Fox Steel Services LLC .... G 203 799-2356
  Orange *(G-6603)*
Frank Porto .... G 203 596-0811
  Watertown *(G-9707)*
Fwt4 LLC .... G 203 775-7087
  Brookfield *(G-1189)*
George H Olson Steel Co Inc .... E 203 375-5656
  Stratford *(G-8617)*
Grover D & Sons LLC .... G 860 429-9420
  Willington *(G-10248)*
Gulf Manufacturing Inc .... E 860 529-8601
  Rocky Hill *(G-7239)*
HRF Fastener Systems Inc .... E 860 589-0750
  Bristol *(G-1049)*
Iron Craft Fabricating LLC .... G 860 923-9869
  North Grosvenordale *(G-5887)*
Jwc Steel Co LLC .... E 860 296-6517
  Hartford *(G-3621)*
K J Welding .... G 860 345-8743
  Haddam *(G-3406)*
Kinamor Incorporated .... E 203 269-0380
  Wallingford *(G-9297)*
Kostas Custom Ir Fabrications .... G 203 328-1308
  Stamford *(G-8279)*
Lemac Iron Works Inc .... G 860 232-7380
  West Hartford *(G-9829)*
LH Gault & Son Incorporated .... D 203 227-5181
  Westport *(G-10112)*
Logan Steel Inc .... E 203 235-0811
  Meriden *(G-4188)*
Magna Steel Sales Inc .... F 203 888-0300
  Beacon Falls *(G-142)*
Mayarc Industries Inc .... G 860 871-1872
  Ellington *(G-2594)*
Metalpuck Co LLC .... G 860 561-5936
  West Hartford *(G-9836)*
Mobile Mini Inc .... E 860 668-1888
  Suffield *(G-8727)*
Mtj Manufacturing Inc .... G 203 334-4939
  Bridgeport *(G-844)*
Mystic Stainless & Alum Inc .... G 860 536-2236
  Mystic *(G-4837)*
Nesci Enterprises Inc .... G 860 267-2588
  East Hampton *(G-2271)*
Northern Fabrication .... G 860 693-0635
  Canton *(G-1321)*
Nutmeg Welding Company Inc .... G 203 756-7458
  Waterbury *(G-9564)*
Ovl Manufacturing Inc LLC .... G 860 829-0271
  Berlin *(G-205)*
Passion Engineering LLC .... G 203 204-3090
  Guilford *(G-3382)*
Pcx Aerostructures LLC .... E 860 666-2471
  Newington *(G-5694)*

Pepin Steel and Iron Works LLC .... G 860 582-1852
  Bristol *(G-1090)*
Platt & Labonia Company LLC .... E 800 505-9099
  North Haven *(G-5976)*
Putnam Welding & Eqp Repr Inc .... G 860 974-0292
  Eastford *(G-2539)*
Quality Erectors LLC .... G 860 548-0248
  Hartford *(G-3672)*
Reliable Welding & Speed LLC .... E 860 749-3977
  Enfield *(G-2687)*
Romco Contractors Inc .... F 860 243-8872
  Bloomfield *(G-478)*
Rwt Corporation .... E 203 245-2731
  Madison *(G-3953)*
Shepard Steel Co Inc .... E 860 525-4446
  Newington *(G-5704)*
Stamford Iron & Stl Works Inc .... F 203 324-6751
  Stamford *(G-8438)*
Steeltech Building Pdts Inc .... D 860 290-8930
  South Windsor *(G-7829)*
Steven Rosenburg .... G 203 329-8798
  Stamford *(G-8443)*
Stratford Steel LLC .... E 203 612-7350
  Stratford *(G-8686)*
Swift Innovations LLC .... G 860 572-8322
  Mystic *(G-4847)*
Swift Innovations LLC .... G 860 710-2725
  Preston *(G-6990)*
Thomas La Ganga .... G 860 489-0920
  Torrington *(G-8977)*
Tico Titanium Inc .... E 248 446-0400
  Wallingford *(G-9384)*
Tiger Fabrication LLC .... G 860 460-7600
  Pawcatuck *(G-6728)*
Tinsley GROup-Ps&w Inc .... D 919 742-5832
  Milford *(G-4665)*
Total Fab LLC .... F 475 238-8176
  East Haven *(G-2457)*
United Metal Solutions .... G 860 610-4026
  East Hartford *(G-2388)*
United Steel Inc .... C 860 289-2323
  East Hartford *(G-2389)*
Valley Welding Co Inc .... G 203 283-5768
  Thomaston *(G-8817)*
Varnum Enterprises LLC .... F 203 743-4443
  Bethel *(G-362)*
Vernier Metal Fabricating Inc .... D 203 881-3133
  Seymour *(G-7372)*
Viking Enterprises Inc .... G 860 440-0728
  Waterford *(G-9675)*
Web Industries Inc .... G 860 779-3403
  Dayville *(G-2079)*
Yankee Metals LLC .... G 203 612-7470
  Bridgeport *(G-941)*

STEEL MILLS

Ball & Roller Bearing Co LLC .... F 860 355-4161
  New Milford *(G-5508)*
H&A Detail On Wheels .... G 203 354-8845
  Norwalk *(G-6191)*
Mills On Wheels .... G 860 705-2903
  Norwich *(G-6423)*
Program Dynamix Inc .... G 860 282-0695
  South Windsor *(G-7813)*
Thermo Conductor Services Inc .... G 203 758-6611
  Prospect *(G-7026)*
Tms International LLC .... G 203 629-8383
  Greenwich *(G-3246)*
Ulbrich Stainless Steels .... D 203 239-4481
  North Haven *(G-6008)*
Ulbrich Stainless Steels .... C 203 269-2507
  Wallingford *(G-9393)*
Waterbury Rolling Mills Inc .... D 203 597-5000
  Waterbury *(G-9628)*
Wheels of Hope Inc .... G 203 305-5762
  Shelton *(G-7585)*

STEEL, COLD-ROLLED: Sheet Or Strip, From Own Hot-Rolled

Bushwick Metals LLC .... G 203 630-2459
  Meriden *(G-4152)*
Kimchuk Incorporated .... F 203 790-7800
  Danbury *(G-1868)*
Redifoils LLC .... F 860 342-1500
  Portland *(G-6972)*

STEEL, COLD-ROLLED: Strip NEC, From Purchased Hot-Rolled

Ulbrich Stainless Steels .... D 203 239-4481
  North Haven *(G-6008)*

STEEL, COLD-ROLLED: Strip Or Wire

Feroleto Steel Company Inc .... D 203 366-3263
  Bridgeport *(G-769)*

STEEL: Cold-Rolled

Deringer-Ney Inc .... C 860 242-2281
  Bloomfield *(G-407)*
Eastern Company .... E 203 729-2255
  Naugatuck *(G-4878)*
North East Fasteners Corp .... E 860 589-3242
  Terryville *(G-8767)*
Paradigm Manchester Inc .... C 860 649-2888
  Manchester *(G-4069)*
Sandvik Wire and Htg Tech Corp .... D 203 744-1440
  Bethel *(G-338)*
Sandvik Wire and Htg Tech Corp .... D 203 744-1440
  Bethel *(G-337)*
Shepard Steel Co Inc .... E 860 525-4446
  Newington *(G-5704)*
Telling Industries LLC .... G 860 731-7975
  Windsor *(G-10449)*
Theis Precision Steel USA Inc .... C 860 589-5511
  Bristol *(G-1127)*
Ulbrich Stainless Steels .... C 203 269-2507
  Wallingford *(G-9393)*

STEEL: Laminated

Alinabal Inc .... C 203 877-3241
  Milford *(G-4448)*
Alinabal Holdings Corporation .... B 203 877-3241
  Milford *(G-4449)*

STEERING SYSTEMS & COMPONENTS

Global Steering Systems LLC .... C 860 945-5400
  Watertown *(G-9710)*
Lewmar Inc .... E 203 458-6200
  Guilford *(G-3367)*

STENCILS

Biomerics LLC .... D 203 268-7238
  Monroe *(G-4698)*
Liftline Capital LLC .... F 860 395-0150
  Old Saybrook *(G-6553)*
Mbsw Inc .... D 860 243-0303
  West Hartford *(G-9835)*

STENCILS & LETTERING MATERIALS: Die-Cut

Liftline Capital LLC .... F 860 395-0150
  Old Saybrook *(G-6553)*

STITCHING SVCS

Cook Print .... G 203 855-8785
  Norwalk *(G-6129)*

STITCHING SVCS: Custom

Tshirts Etc Inc .... G 860 657-3551
  Glastonbury *(G-3090)*

STONE: Cast Concrete

Signature Pet Memorials .... G 860 455-0118
  Chaplin *(G-1341)*

STONE: Dimension, NEC

Arts of Stone LLC .... G 860 355-9468
  New Milford *(G-5507)*
Connecticut Stone Supplies Inc .... D 203 882-1000
  Milford *(G-4499)*
Exquisite Surfaces Inc .... G 203 866-9100
  Norwalk *(G-6159)*
Midwood Quarry and Cnstr Inc .... F 860 289-1414
  East Hartford *(G-2345)*
West Hartford Stone Mulch LLC .... G 860 461-7616
  West Hartford *(G-9872)*

Employee Codes: A=Over 500 employees, B=251-500
C=101-250, D=51-100, E=20-50, F=10-19, G=1-9

STONE: Quarrying & Processing, Own Stone Prdts

French River Mtls Thompson LLC	G	860 450-9574
North Grosvenordale *(G-5885)*		
Kenneth Lynch & Sons Inc	G	203 762-8363
Oxford *(G-6671)*		
New England Materials LLC	G	203 261-5500
Monroe *(G-4743)*		
O & G Industries Inc	F	203 729-4529
Beacon Falls *(G-146)*		
Paul H Gesswein & Company Inc	G	860 388-0652
Old Saybrook *(G-6565)*		
Skyline Quarry	E	860 875-3580
Stafford Springs *(G-8038)*		

STONES, SYNTHETIC: Gem Stone & Indl Use

Lexo Group	G	203 847-8293
Norwalk *(G-6233)*		
Opal Manning Company Inc	G	203 292-6981
Fairfield *(G-2825)*		

STONEWARE PRDTS: Pottery

One Pair of Hands	G	860 364-0027
Sharon *(G-7381)*		

STORE FIXTURES: Exc Wood

In Store Experience Inc	E	203 221-4777
Westport *(G-10097)*		

STORE FIXTURES: Wood

Phone Booth Inc	G	203 859-5389
New Haven *(G-5364)*		

STORES: Auto & Home Supply

International Automobile Entps	F	860 224-0253
New Britain *(G-5001)*		
M & B Automotive Machine Shop	G	203 348-6134
Stamford *(G-8292)*		
Major Tire Co LLC	G	203 543-0334
Stratford *(G-8645)*		

STORES: Drapery & Upholstery

Tassels	G	203 231-0973
Derby *(G-2128)*		

STOVES: Wood & Coal Burning

Hot Spot Stoves & Mech LLC	G	860 829-7283
Berlin *(G-189)*		

STRAIN GAGES: Solid State

LLC Dow Gage	E	860 828-5327
Berlin *(G-197)*		
Strain Measurement Devices Inc	E	203 294-5800
Wallingford *(G-9377)*		

STRAINERS: Line, Piping Systems

Ctv Piping and Structural	G	860 257-3027
Hartford *(G-3574)*		

STRAPPING

H G Steinmetz Machine Works	F	203 794-1880
Bethel *(G-307)*		
Tides Black Group LLC	G	203 244-8433
Monroe *(G-4761)*		

STRAPS: Beltings, Woven or Braided

Brockway Ferry Corporation	G	860 767-8231
Essex *(G-2713)*		

STRIPS: Copper & Copper Alloy

Miller Company	E	203 235-4474
Meriden *(G-4203)*		

STRUCTURAL SUPPORT & BUILDING MATERIAL: Concrete

WJ Kettleworks LLC	G	203 377-5000
Stratford *(G-8710)*		

STUCCO

AK Stucco LLC	G	860 832-9589
New Britain *(G-4941)*		
Assoc Stucco	G	860 221-5791
Burlington *(G-1260)*		
Connecticut Stucco LLC	G	203 237-9500
Hamden *(G-3431)*		
Evolution Stucco LLC	G	203 507-3639
Wallingford *(G-9260)*		
Kelby Stucco LLC	G	203 527-9501
Prospect *(G-7005)*		
Northeast Stucco LLC	G	860 770-9473
New Britain *(G-5024)*		
S & J Stucco LLC	G	203 260-1457
Monroe *(G-4751)*		
Stucco Depot LLC	G	203 430-9186
Wallingford *(G-9378)*		
U S Stucco LLC	G	860 667-1935
Newington *(G-5715)*		
Vincent Masonry	G	860 836-5916
New Britain *(G-5081)*		

STUDIOS: Artist

DAmbruoso Studios LLC	G	203 758-9660
Middlebury *(G-4276)*		
Dawn Hill Enterprises LLC	G	860 496-9188
Torrington *(G-8917)*		
Steve Cryan Studio	G	860 388-5010
Old Saybrook *(G-6571)*		
Vanilla Politics LLC	G	203 221-0895
Weston *(G-10043)*		

SUBMARINE BUILDING & REPAIR

Electric Boat Corporation	D	860 433-0503
Groton *(G-3285)*		
Electric Boat Corporation	D	860 433-3000
Groton *(G-3286)*		
Electric Boat Corporation	A	860 433-3000
Groton *(G-3287)*		
Mystic River Mar Surveyors LLC	G	860 857-1798
Mystic *(G-4836)*		

SUBSCRIPTION FULFILLMENT SVCS: Magazine, Newspaper, Etc

Barker Advg Specialty Co Inc	D	203 272-2222
Cheshire *(G-1360)*		

SUITCASES

Dooney & Bourke Inc	E	203 853-7515
Norwalk *(G-6146)*		

SUNROOMS: Prefabricated Metal

LLC Glass House	G	860 974-1665
Pomfret Center *(G-6941)*		
Niantic Awning Company	G	860 739-0161
Niantic *(G-5813)*		

SUPERMARKETS & OTHER GROCERY STORES

Cco Llc	G	860 757-3434
Rocky Hill *(G-7226)*		
CFM Test & Balance Corp	G	203 778-1900
Bethel *(G-269)*		
Wizards Nuts Holdings LLC	D	708 483-1315
Greenwich *(G-3260)*		

SURFACE ACTIVE AGENTS

Henkel of America Inc	B	860 571-5100
Rocky Hill *(G-7246)*		
Henkel US Operations Corp	B	860 571-5100
Rocky Hill *(G-7247)*		
Lanxess Solutions US Inc	E	203 573-2000
Shelton *(G-7486)*		

SURFACE ACTIVE AGENTS: Oils & Greases

Solidification Pdts Intl Inc	G	203 484-9494
Northford *(G-6053)*		

SURFACE ACTIVE AGENTS: Processing Assistants

Alternative Choice LLC	G	860 875-7529
Vernon Rockville *(G-9159)*		

SURFACE ACTIVE AGENTS: Textile Processing Assistants

Chemloid Chemicals Inc	G	203 255-7495
Fairfield *(G-2760)*		

SURGICAL & MEDICAL INSTRUMENTS WHOLESALERS

Meditech LLC	G	203 219-3688
Norwalk *(G-6255)*		

SURGICAL APPLIANCES & SPLYS

Bio Med Packaging Systems Inc	E	203 846-1923
Norwalk *(G-6092)*		
Brymill Corporation	F	860 875-2460
Ellington *(G-2579)*		
K W Griffen Company	E	203 846-1923
Norwalk *(G-6226)*		
Schaeffler Aerospace USA Corp	B	203 744-2211
Danbury *(G-1936)*		

SURGICAL APPLIANCES & SPLYS

Auto Suture Company Australia	G	203 845-1000
Norwalk *(G-6081)*		
Auto Suture Company UK	B	203 845-1000
Norwalk *(G-6082)*		
Becton Dickinson and Company	B	860 824-5487
Canaan *(G-1281)*		
Cardiopulmonary Corp	E	203 877-1999
Milford *(G-4484)*		
Carwild Corporation	E	860 442-4914
New London *(G-5461)*		
Danbury Medi-Car Service Inc	G	203 748-3433
Danbury *(G-1783)*		
Danbury Ortho	G	203 797-1500
Danbury *(G-1785)*		
Gordon Engineering Corp	F	203 775-4501
Brookfield *(G-1193)*		
Hanger Prsthetcs & Ortho Inc	G	860 482-5611
Torrington *(G-8931)*		
Hanger Prsthetcs & Ortho Inc	G	203 230-0667
North Haven *(G-5945)*		
Hanger Prsthetcs & Ortho Inc	G	860 667-5300
Cromwell *(G-1703)*		
Hanger Prsthetcs & Ortho Inc	F	860 545-9050
Hartford *(G-3604)*		
Hanger Prsthetcs & Ortho Inc	G	860 667-5370
Newington *(G-5658)*		
Hanger Prsthetcs & Ortho Inc	G	860 871-0905
Vernon *(G-9139)*		
Kbc Electronics Inc	F	203 298-9654
Milford *(G-4563)*		
Kelyniam Global Inc	F	800 280-8192
Collinsville *(G-1595)*		
Limbkeepers LLC	G	860 304-3250
Lyme *(G-3905)*		
Lynne Marshall	G	860 245-3645
Groton *(G-3299)*		
McIntire Company	F	860 585-8559
Bristol *(G-1070)*		
McNeil Healthcare Inc	G	203 934-8187
West Haven *(G-9935)*		
Meditech LLC	G	203 219-3688
Norwalk *(G-6255)*		
New England Shoulder Elbow Soc	G	860 679-6600
Farmington *(G-2937)*		
Respironics Inc	G	203 697-6490
Wallingford *(G-9350)*		
Scapa Tapes North America LLC	C	860 688-8000
Windsor *(G-10434)*		
Teleflex Incorporated	E	860 742-8821
Coventry *(G-1681)*		
Tyco International MGT Co LLC	G	203 492-5000
North Haven *(G-6003)*		
United States Surgical Corp	A	203 845-1000
New Haven *(G-5425)*		

SURGICAL EQPT: See Also Instruments

Aplicare Products LLC	C	203 630-0500
Meriden *(G-4145)*		
Blairden Precision Instrs Inc	G	203 799-2000
Trumbull *(G-9005)*		
Ipsogen	G	203 504-8583
Stamford *(G-8258)*		
Lacey Manufacturing Co LLC	B	203 336-7427
Bridgeport *(G-821)*		
Oerlikon AM Medical Inc	D	203 712-1030
Shelton *(G-7518)*		

PRODUCT SECTION

United States Surgical Corp ....A....... 203 845-1000
New Haven *(G-5425)*

SURGICAL IMPLANTS

Dental Implant Services LLC ....G....... 203 720-1873
Naugatuck *(G-4876)*

SVC ESTABLISHMENT EQPT & SPLYS WHOLESALERS

Ace Beauty Supply Inc ....G....... 203 488-2416
Branford *(G-536)*

SVC ESTABLISHMENT EQPT, WHOL: Cleaning & Maint Eqpt & Splys

Griffith Company ....G....... 203 333-5557
Bridgeport *(G-780)*

SVC ESTABLISHMENT EQPT, WHOLESALE: Beauty Parlor Eqpt & Sply

Tracy S Products ....G....... 203 787-2013
New Haven *(G-5419)*

SVC ESTABLISHMENT EQPT, WHOLESALE: Shredders, Indl & Comm

Cummins - Allison Corp ....G....... 203 794-9200
Cheshire *(G-1377)*

SWAGE BLOCKS

US Product Mechanization Co ....G....... 860 450-1139
Columbia *(G-1614)*

SWITCHBOARDS & PARTS: Power

Lex Products LLC ....C....... 203 363-3738
Shelton *(G-7490)*

SWITCHES

Amphenol Corporation ....D....... 203 327-7300
Stamford *(G-8081)*
Carling Technologies Inc ....C....... 860 793-9281
Plainville *(G-6785)*

SWITCHES: Electric Power

Ashcrft-Ngano Kiki Hldings Inc ....G....... 203 378-8281
Stratford *(G-8571)*
Ashcroft Inc ....B....... 203 378-8281
Stratford *(G-8572)*
Baumer Ltd ....F....... 860 621-2121
Southington *(G-7894)*
Linemaster Switch Corporation ....C....... 860 630-4920
Woodstock *(G-10669)*
Noank Controls LLC ....G....... 860 449-6776
Groton *(G-3301)*
Pepperl + Fuchs Inc ....G....... 860 923-2703
Woodstock *(G-10677)*

SWITCHES: Electric Power, Exc Snap, Push Button, Etc

ABB Enterprise Software Inc ....A....... 860 747-7111
Plainville *(G-6763)*
Control Concepts Inc ....F....... 860 928-6551
Putnam *(G-7037)*
Oslo Switch Inc ....E....... 203 272-2794
Cheshire *(G-1425)*

SWITCHES: Electronic

Bloomy Controls Inc ....E....... 860 298-9925
Windsor *(G-10368)*
Component Concepts Inc ....G....... 860 523-4066
West Hartford *(G-9792)*
Eaton Aerospace LLC ....E....... 203 796-6000
Bethel *(G-292)*
Linemaster Switch Corporation ....G....... 860 564-7713
Plainfield *(G-6747)*
Royce Industries Inc ....F....... 860 674-2700
Southington *(G-7969)*

SWITCHES: Electronic Applications

Cogstate Inc ....G....... 203 773-5010
New Haven *(G-5258)*
Control Concepts Inc ....F....... 860 928-6551
Putnam *(G-7037)*

Kc Crafts LLC ....G....... 860 426-9797
Plantsville *(G-6898)*

SWITCHES: Flow Actuated, Electrical

Airflo Instrument Company ....G....... 860 633-9455
Glastonbury *(G-3005)*
Thomas Products Ltd ....E....... 860 621-9101
Southington *(G-7987)*

SWITCHES: Stepping

Tritex Corporation ....C....... 203 756-7441
Waterbury *(G-9618)*

SWITCHES: Time, Electrical Switchgear Apparatus

MH Rhodes Cramer LLC ....G....... 860 291-8402
South Windsor *(G-7793)*

SWITCHGEAR & SWITCHBOARD APPARATUS

ABB Finance (usa) Inc ....G....... 919 856-2360
Norwalk *(G-6059)*
Allied Controls Inc ....F....... 860 628-8443
Stamford *(G-8072)*
Asea Brown Boveri Inc ....G....... 203 750-2200
Norwalk *(G-6076)*
Ensign-Bickford Industries Inc ....E....... 860 658-4411
Simsbury *(G-7622)*
Faria Beede Instruments Inc ....C....... 860 848-9271
North Stonington *(G-6024)*
Gems Sensors Inc ....B....... 860 747-3000
Plainville *(G-6815)*
General Electro Components ....G....... 860 659-3573
Glastonbury *(G-3039)*
J Ro Grounding Systems Inc ....G....... 860 747-2106
Plainville *(G-6827)*
John Olsen ....G....... 203 624-5544
Trumbull *(G-9037)*
Kilo Ampere Switch Corporation ....G....... 860 877-5994
Milford *(G-4565)*
Madison Company ....E....... 203 488-4477
Branford *(G-621)*
Mil-Con Inc. ....D....... 630 595-2366
Naugatuck *(G-4901)*
Newco Condenser Inc ....G....... 475 882-4000
Shelton *(G-7510)*
Omega Engineering Inc ....D....... 714 540-4914
Norwalk *(G-6285)*
Quality Name Plate Inc ....D....... 860 633-9495
East Glastonbury *(G-2185)*
Satin American Corporation ....E....... 203 929-6363
Shelton *(G-7551)*
Siemon Company ....A....... 860 945-4200
Watertown *(G-9734)*
Wiles Charles Preston M D ....G....... 203 562-7550
New Haven *(G-5433)*

SWITCHGEAR & SWITCHGEAR ACCESS, NEC

Capitol Electronics Inc ....F....... 203 744-3300
Bethel *(G-268)*

SYRUPS, DRINK

Nobby Beverages Inc ....G....... 860 747-3888
Plainville *(G-6848)*

SYSTEMS ENGINEERING: Computer Related

Sonalysts Inc ....B....... 860 442-4355
Waterford *(G-9672)*

SYSTEMS INTEGRATION SVCS

Amsys Inc ....E....... 203 431-8814
Ridgefield *(G-7116)*
Frontier Vision Tech Inc ....E....... 860 953-0240
Rocky Hill *(G-7238)*
Harpoon Acquisition Corp ....A....... 860 815-5736
Glastonbury *(G-3047)*
Modern Electronic Fax & Cmpt ....G....... 203 292-6520
Fairfield *(G-2816)*
Nielsen Consulting Inc ....G....... 914 831-1681
New Milford *(G-5573)*
Open Solutions LLC ....C....... 860 815-5000
Glastonbury *(G-3066)*

Oracle America Inc ....D....... 203 703-3000
Stamford *(G-8345)*
Process Automtn Solutions Inc ....E....... 203 207-9917
Danbury *(G-1920)*
Visionpoint LLC ....E....... 860 436-9673
Newington *(G-5720)*

SYSTEMS INTEGRATION SVCS: Local Area Network

Interactive Marketing Corp ....G....... 203 248-5324
North Haven *(G-5949)*
Opera Glass Networks LLC ....G....... 203 919-2777
Norwalk *(G-6286)*

SYSTEMS INTEGRATION SVCS: Office Computer Automation

Management Software Inc ....G....... 860 536-5177
Ledyard *(G-3877)*
Mannan 3d Innovations LLC ....G....... 860 306-4203
Higganum *(G-3768)*
Universal Building Contrls Inc ....F....... 203 235-1530
Meriden *(G-4260)*

SYSTEMS SOFTWARE DEVELOPMENT SVCS

Aicas Inc ....G....... 203 359-5705
Stamford *(G-8068)*
Desrosier of Greenwich Inc ....F....... 203 661-2334
Greenwich *(G-3152)*
Enginuity Plm LLC ....F....... 203 218-7225
Milford *(G-4532)*
Norfield Data Products Inc ....F....... 203 849-0292
Norwalk *(G-6280)*

TABLE OR COUNTERTOPS, PLASTIC LAMINATED

A S J Specialties LLC ....G....... 203 284-8650
Wallingford *(G-9194)*
Ace Cabinet Company ....G....... 860 225-6111
New Britain *(G-4933)*
Leos Kitchen & Stair Corp ....G....... 860 225-7363
New Britain *(G-5010)*

TABLECLOTHS & SETTINGS

Patricia Spratt For Home LLC ....F....... 860 434-9291
Old Lyme *(G-6517)*

TABLETS & PADS: Book & Writing, Made From Purchased Material

Gleason Group Incorporated ....G....... 203 312-0683
New Fairfield *(G-5168)*
Panagrafix Inc ....E....... 203 691-5529
West Haven *(G-9942)*

TACKS: Nonferrous Metal Or Wire

Ccr Products LLC ....E....... 860 953-0499
West Hartford *(G-9786)*

TAGS & LABELS: Paper

Cenveo Inc ....D....... 203 595-3000
Stamford *(G-8138)*
Cenveo Enterprises Inc ....G....... 203 595-3000
Stamford *(G-8140)*
Cenveo Worldwide Limited ....F....... 203 595-3000
Stamford *(G-8141)*
Cwl Enterprises Inc ....G....... 303 790-8023
Stamford *(G-8174)*
Royal Consumer Products LLC ....E....... 203 847-8500
Norwalk *(G-6330)*
Surys Inc ....C....... 203 333-5503
Trumbull *(G-9078)*

TAILORS: Custom

Ida Dean ....G....... 860 482-3589
Torrington *(G-8934)*

TALC MINING

RT Vanderbilt Holding Co Inc ....F....... 203 295-2141
Norwalk *(G-6331)*

Employee Codes: A=Over 500 employees, B=251-500
C=101-250, D=51-100, E=20-50, F=10-19, G=1-9

TANKS & OTHER TRACKED VEHICLE CMPNTS

New England Airfoil Pdts Inc .... E 860 677-1376
Farmington *(G-2936)*

Shawnee Chemical .... G 203 938-3003
Redding *(G-7109)*

TANKS: Concrete

J B Concrete Products Inc .... G 860 928-9365
Putnam *(G-7048)*

Nteco Inc .... E 203 656-1154
Darien *(G-2035)*

TANKS: Fuel, Including Oil & Gas, Metal Plate

Angel Fuel LLC .... G 203 597-8759
Waterbury *(G-9431)*

Matias Importing & Distrg Corp .... G 860 666-5544
Newington *(G-5675)*

Quality Tank Service LP .... G 203 792-9373
Danbury *(G-1924)*

Safe-T-Tank Corp .... G 203 237-6320
Meriden *(G-4239)*

TANKS: Standard Or Custom Fabricated, Metal Plate

Tesco Resources Inc .... G 203 754-3900
Waterbury *(G-9611)*

TANKS: Water, Metal Plate

Walz & Krenzer Inc .... G 203 267-5712
Oxford *(G-6700)*

TAPE MEASURES

Acme United Corporation .... C 203 254-6060
Fairfield *(G-2743)*

TAPE: Rubber

Midsun Specialty Products Inc .... E 860 378-0111
Berlin *(G-200)*

TAPES, ADHESIVE: MedicaL

First Aid Bandage Co Inc .... F 860 443-8499
New London *(G-5472)*

TAPES: Plastic Coated

Composites Inc .... G 860 646-1698
Manchester *(G-3997)*

TAPES: Pressure Sensitive

Beiersdorf Inc .... B 203 854-8000
Norwalk *(G-6088)*

Beiersdorf North America Inc .... F 203 563-5800
Wilton *(G-10272)*

Ipg (us) Holdings Inc .... G 813 621-8410
Ansonia *(G-40)*

TAPES: Pressure Sensitive, Rubber

IR Industries Inc .... F 203 790-8273
Bethel *(G-313)*

TAR

TAR LLC .... G 203 449-4520
Bridgeport *(G-920)*

TAX RETURN PREPARATION SVCS

Hampton Associates LLC .... G 203 817-0161
Stamford *(G-8223)*

Inner Office Inc .... G 860 564-6777
Moosup *(G-4780)*

TELECOMMUNICATION EQPT REPAIR SVCS, EXC TELEPHONES

General Datacomm Inc .... E 203 729-0271
Oxford *(G-6661)*

TELECOMMUNICATION SYSTEMS & EQPT

Arris Technology Inc .... F 678 473-8493
Wallingford *(G-9212)*

Avaya Inc .... G 203 234-9300
North Haven *(G-5912)*

Carrier Access - Trin Networks .... G 203 778-8222
Brookfield *(G-1168)*

Freedom Technologies LLC .... G 860 633-0452
Glastonbury *(G-3037)*

Gdc Federal Systems Inc .... G 203 729-0271
Naugatuck *(G-4884)*

Hubbell Premise Wiring Inc .... F 860 535-8326
Mystic *(G-4821)*

IPC Systems Inc .... F 203 339-7000
Old Saybrook *(G-6543)*

IPC Systems Inc .... C 860 271-4100
Fairfield *(G-2797)*

K-Tech International .... E 860 489-9399
Torrington *(G-8941)*

Microphase Corporation .... E 203 866-8000
Shelton *(G-7500)*

Nutmeg Utility Products Inc .... E 203 250-8802
Cheshire *(G-1423)*

Radio Frequency Systems Inc .... E 203 630-3311
Meriden *(G-4227)*

Total Communications Inc .... D 860 282-9999
East Hartford *(G-2386)*

Total Communications Inc .... E 203 882-0088
Milford *(G-4666)*

TELECOMMUNICATIONS CARRIERS & SVCS: Wired

Ahead Communications Systems .... D 203 720-0227
Naugatuck *(G-4855)*

TELECOMMUNICATIONS CARRIERS & SVCS: Wireless

Ahead Communications Systems .... D 203 720-0227
Naugatuck *(G-4855)*

TELEPHONE EQPT: Modems

Canoga Perkins Corporation .... G 203 888-7914
Seymour *(G-7337)*

Tango Modem LLC .... G 203 421-2245
Madison *(G-3963)*

TELEPHONE EQPT: NEC

Ahead Communications Systems .... D 203 720-0227
Naugatuck *(G-4855)*

Dac Systems Inc .... F 203 924-7000
Shelton *(G-7426)*

Elot Inc .... G 203 388-1808
Old Greenwich *(G-6472)*

General Datacomm Inc .... E 203 729-0271
Oxford *(G-6661)*

Pamela D Siemon Lcsw LLC .... G 203 232-8009
Watertown *(G-9719)*

Siemens AG .... G 860 651-1399
Simsbury *(G-7645)*

Sigmavoip Llc .... G 203 541-5450
Westport *(G-10159)*

Sound Control Technologies .... G 203 854-5701
Norwalk *(G-6352)*

TELEPHONE EQPT: PBX, Manual & Automatic

Synectix LLC .... G 203 283-0701
Milford *(G-4661)*

TELEPHONE SET REPAIR SVCS

Total Communications Inc .... E 203 882-0088
Milford *(G-4666)*

Total Communications Inc .... D 860 282-9999
East Hartford *(G-2386)*

TELEPHONE SVCS

American Bus Tele & Tech LLC .... G 860 643-2200
Manchester *(G-3982)*

Sound Marketing Concepts .... G 860 257-9367
Rocky Hill *(G-7266)*

TELEPHONE: Fiber Optic Systems

Amphenol Corporation .... D 203 265-8900
Wallingford *(G-9204)*

Cardiophotonics LLC .... G 203 645-6077
Bethany *(G-237)*

Communication Networks LLC .... E 203 796-5300
Danbury *(G-1771)*

Daniel K Rogers .... G 860 455-0530
Chaplin *(G-1338)*

Fibre Optic Plus Inc .... G 860 646-3581
South Windsor *(G-7756)*

Opticonx Inc .... E 888 748-6855
Putnam *(G-7056)*

Photon Partners LLC .... G 203 807-3623
Darien *(G-2039)*

Ruckus Wireless Inc .... E 203 303-6400
Wallingford *(G-9362)*

United Photonics LLC .... G 617 752-2073
Vernon Rockville *(G-9185)*

TELEVISION BROADCASTING & COMMUNICATIONS EQPT

Axerra Networks Inc .... G 203 906-3570
Woodbury *(G-10625)*

Media Links Inc .... F 860 206-9163
Windsor *(G-10408)*

Video Technologies Group LLC .... G 203 341-0474
Westport *(G-10172)*

Xintekidel Inc .... G 203 348-9229
Stamford *(G-8503)*

TELEVISION FILM PRODUCTION SVCS

World Wrestling Entrmt Inc .... C 203 352-8600
Stamford *(G-8502)*

TENTS: All Materials

Shelterlogic Corp .... C 860 945-6442
Watertown *(G-9733)*

Slogic Holding Corp .... G 203 966-2800
New Canaan *(G-5142)*

TERRAZZO PRECAST PRDTS

Platt Brothers & Company .... D 203 753-4194
Waterbury *(G-9580)*

TEST BORING SVCS: Nonmetallic Minerals

New England Boring Contractors .... F 860 633-4649
Glastonbury *(G-3063)*

TEST KITS: Pregnancy

Cabea LLC .... G 860 738-0819
Winsted *(G-10512)*

TESTERS: Battery

Digatron Power Electronics Inc .... E 203 446-8000
Shelton *(G-7432)*

TESTERS: Environmental

A Douglas Thibodeau LLC .... G 860 295-9189
Marlborough *(G-4118)*

Omega Engineering Inc .... C 203 359-1660
Norwalk *(G-6284)*

Scots Landing .... G 860 923-0437
Fabyan *(G-2739)*

Spectrogram Corporation .... G 203 245-2433
Madison *(G-3960)*

TESTERS: Gas, Exc Indl Process

Kahn and Company Incorporated .... G 860 529-8643
Wethersfield *(G-10203)*

TESTERS: Spark Plug

Forte Rts Inc .... G 860 464-5221
Ledyard *(G-3872)*

TEXTILE DESIGNERS

American Woolen Company Inc .... G 860 684-2766
Stafford Springs *(G-8017)*

TEXTILE FABRICATORS

Cuvee 59 .... G 707 259-0559
Coventry *(G-1651)*

James Stenqvist .... G 203 339-6418
North Haven *(G-5950)*

John Demarchi .... G 860 649-9685
Willimantic *(G-10232)*

Kohinoor USA .... G 203 388-1850
Stamford *(G-8277)*

PRODUCT SECTION

TEXTILE FINISHING: Chem Coat/Treat, Man, Broadwoven, Cotton
- Nextec Applications Inc ....G....... 203 661-1484
  Greenwich *(G-3209)*

TEXTILE FINISHING: Dyeing, Finishing & Printng, Linen Fabric
- Gorilla Graphics Inc ....F....... 860 704-8208
  Middletown *(G-4348)*

TEXTILE PRDTS: Hand Woven & Crocheted
- A Kick In Crochet ....G....... 413 210-7890
  Enfield *(G-2610)*
- Crochet Away 203 ....G....... 203 690-7904
  Weston *(G-10024)*
- Crocheted By Bianca ....G....... 860 916-2925
  Manchester *(G-4001)*
- Off The Hookhandmadecrochetllc ....G....... 203 912-1638
  Sandy Hook *(G-7324)*

TEXTILE: Finishing, Raw Stock NEC
- Brookwood Laminating Inc ....D....... 860 774-5001
  Wauregan *(G-9752)*
- Grand Embroidery Inc ....F....... 203 888-7484
  Oxford *(G-6663)*

TEXTILES
- Cap-Tech Products Inc ....F....... 860 490-5078
  Wethersfield *(G-10185)*

TEXTILES: Crash, Linen
- Advanced Linen Group ....F....... 203 877-3896
  Milford *(G-4441)*

TEXTILES: Fibers, Textile, Rcvrd From Mill Waste/Rags
- A Al Harding ....G....... 203 238-1993
  Meriden *(G-4137)*

TEXTILES: Flock
- Engineered Fibers Tech LLC ....F....... 203 922-1810
  Shelton *(G-7440)*

TEXTILES: Jute & Flax Prdts
- J & S Fashion ....G....... 203 572-0154
  Bridgeport *(G-795)*

TEXTILES: Mill Waste & Remnant
- A & P Coat Apron & Lin Sup Inc ....D....... 914 840-3200
  Hartford *(G-3542)*

THEATRICAL PRODUCERS & SVCS
- Mosaic Records Inc ....G....... 203 327-7111
  Stamford *(G-8314)*

THEATRICAL SCENERY
- Global Scenic Services Inc ....E....... 203 334-2130
  Bridgeport *(G-776)*
- Show Motion Inc ....E....... 203 866-1866
  Milford *(G-4643)*

THERMOCOUPLES
- Atlantic Sensors & Contrls LLC ....G....... 203 878-8118
  Milford *(G-4461)*
- Projects Inc ....C....... 860 633-4615
  Glastonbury *(G-3075)*

THERMOCOUPLES: Indl Process
- Kulas Systems Inc ....G....... 860 749-6645
  Somers *(G-7664)*

THERMOMETERS: Medical, Digital
- Cooper-Atkins Corporation ....C....... 860 349-3473
  Middlefield *(G-4300)*

THERMOPLASTIC MATERIALS
- Dow Chemical Company ....G....... 203 740-7510
  Brookfield *(G-1184)*

- Forum Plastics LLC ....E....... 203 754-0777
  Waterbury *(G-9482)*
- Mc Clintock Manufacturing ....G....... 203 263-4743
  Woodbury *(G-10642)*
- Neu Spclty Engineered Mtls LLC ....F....... 203 239-9629
  North Haven *(G-5967)*
- Oxford Industries Conn Inc ....E....... 860 225-3700
  New Britain *(G-5027)*
- Oxpekk Performance Mtls Inc ....F....... 860 698-9300
  South Windsor *(G-7802)*
- W S Polymers ....G....... 203 268-1557
  Trumbull *(G-9093)*

THERMOSETTING MATERIALS
- Resinall Corp ....F....... 203 329-7100
  Stamford *(G-8387)*

THIN FILM CIRCUITS
- Entegris Prof Solutions Inc ....C....... 203 794-1100
  Danbury *(G-1815)*

THREAD: All Fibers
- Thread Mill Partners LLC ....G....... 860 495-5319
  Pawcatuck *(G-6727)*

THREAD: Embroidery
- J Arnold Mittleman ....E....... 860 346-6562
  Middletown *(G-4356)*
- Terris Affordable Embroidery ....G....... 860 928-0552
  Putnam *(G-7073)*

TIES, FORM: Metal
- M-Fab LLC ....G....... 860 496-0055
  Torrington *(G-8946)*

TILE: Brick & Structural, Clay
- Protiviti Inc ....G....... 203 371-5542
  Fairfield *(G-2832)*
- Redland Brick Inc ....C....... 860 528-1311
  South Windsor *(G-7818)*

TILE: Clay, Drain & Structural
- Eljen Corporation ....E....... 860 610-0426
  East Hartford *(G-2321)*

TILE: Fireproofing, Clay
- K & G Corp ....F....... 860 643-1133
  Manchester *(G-4041)*

TILE: Precast Terrazzo, Floor
- Carpet Products ....G....... 860 278-6160
  Hartford *(G-3563)*

TILE: Stamped Metal, Floor Or Wall
- Keberg LLC ....G....... 860 255-8135
  Plainville *(G-6829)*

TILE: Terrazzo Or Concrete, Precast
- Pauls Marble Depot LLC ....F....... 203 978-0669
  Stamford *(G-8352)*

TILE: Wall & Floor, Ceramic
- Aspecta ....G....... 855 400-7732
  Norwalk *(G-6077)*
- Painted Tiles Co ....G....... 860 658-7218
  Simsbury *(G-7638)*

TIMERS: Indl, Clockwork Mechanism Only
- Lantern LLC ....G....... 866 203-5715
  Woodstock *(G-10668)*
- Marhall Browing Intl Corp ....G....... 203 264-2702
  Oxford *(G-6676)*

TIMING DEVICES: Cycle & Program Controllers
- Food Atmtn - Svc Tchniques Inc ....C....... 203 377-4414
  Stratford *(G-8610)*

TIMING DEVICES: Electronic
- (fast) International Inc ....G....... 203 380-3489
  Stratford *(G-8562)*

TOBACCO & TOBACCO PRDTS WHOLESALERS

- HI Tek Racing LLC ....G....... 203 378-5210
  Stratford *(G-8625)*
- Idevices LLC ....E....... 860 352-5252
  Avon *(G-85)*

TINPLATE
- Tinplex Corporation ....G....... 203 335-8217
  Fairfield *(G-2857)*

TIRE & INNER TUBE MATERIALS & RELATED PRDTS
- Town Fair Tire Centers Inc ....F....... 860 646-2807
  Manchester *(G-4103)*

TIRE CORD & FABRIC
- United Abrasives Inc ....B....... 860 456-7131
  North Windham *(G-6040)*

TIRE DEALERS
- Firestone Building Pdts Co LLC ....D....... 860 584-4516
  Bristol *(G-1039)*
- Toce Brothers Incorporated ......E....... 860 496-2080
  Torrington *(G-8978)*

TIRE RECAPPING & RETREADING
- Firestone Building Pdts Co LLC ....D....... 860 584-4516
  Bristol *(G-1039)*

TIRES & INNER TUBES
- BF Enterprises LLC ....G....... 860 693-8953
  Collinsville *(G-1588)*
- BF Services LLC ....G....... 860 289-6929
  East Hartford *(G-2299)*
- Edwards & Schmidt LLC ....G....... 203 393-5666
  Prospect *(G-7002)*
- Toce Brothers Incorporated ......E....... 860 496-2080
  Torrington *(G-8978)*

TIRES & TUBES WHOLESALERS
- Firestone Building Pdts Co LLC ....D....... 860 584-4516
  Bristol *(G-1039)*
- Toce Brothers Incorporated ......E....... 860 496-2080
  Torrington *(G-8978)*

TIRES: Auto
- Ace Tire & Auto Center Inc ....F....... 203 438-4042
  Ridgefield *(G-7115)*

TITANIUM MILL PRDTS
- Aerospace Metals Inc ....C....... 860 522-3123
  Hartford *(G-3548)*
- Doncasters Inc ....D....... 860 449-1603
  Groton *(G-3283)*
- Precision Powders LLC ....G....... 203 748-7879
  Danbury *(G-1917)*
- Titanium Electric LLC ....G....... 203 810-4050
  Norwalk *(G-6370)*
- Titanium Industries Inc ....G....... 860 870-3939
  Tolland *(G-8881)*

TITANIUM ORE MINING
- Tronox Limited ....G....... 203 705-3800
  Stamford *(G-8477)*

TOBACCO & PRDTS, WHOLESALE: Cigarettes
- Foundation Cigar Company LLC ....F....... 203 738-9377
  Windsor *(G-10387)*

TOBACCO & PRDTS, WHOLESALE: Smoking
- Smokey Mountain Chew Inc .....G....... 203 304-9200
  Sandy Hook *(G-7330)*

TOBACCO & TOBACCO PRDTS WHOLESALERS
- Hay Island Holding Corporation ....C....... 203 656-8000
  Darien *(G-2027)*
- Polep Distribution Services J ....G....... 203 378-2193
  Stratford *(G-8666)*

Employee Codes: A=Over 500 employees, B=251-500
C=101-250, D=51-100, E=20-50, F=10-19, G=1-9

TOBACCO LEAF PROCESSING

Markowski Farm.................................G........ 860 668-5033
Suffield *(G-8725)*

UST..F........ 203 661-1100
Greenwich *(G-3252)*

TOBACCO: Chewing

Hay Island Holding Corporation........C........ 203 656-8000
Darien *(G-2027)*

TOBACCO: Chewing & Snuff

Nordic American Smokeless Inc........F........ 203 207-9977
Danbury *(G-1893)*
Nuway Tobacco Company................D........ 860 289-6414
South Windsor *(G-7798)*
Smokey Mountain Chew Inc.............G........ 203 656-1088
Darien *(G-2045)*
US Smokeless Tobacco Co LLC........D........ 203 661-1100
Stamford *(G-8482)*
UST LLC...G........ 203 817-3000
Stamford *(G-8483)*

TOBACCO: Cigarettes

Polep Distribution Services J............G........ 203 378-2193
Stratford *(G-8666)*
Smokey Mountain Chew Inc.............G........ 203 304-9200
Sandy Hook *(G-7330)*

TOBACCO: Cigars

F D Grave & Son Inc........................G........ 203 239-9394
North Haven *(G-5939)*
Foundation Cigar Company LLC.......F........ 203 738-9377
Windsor *(G-10387)*
What A Life LLC..............................G........ 860 632-1962
Cromwell *(G-1724)*

TOBACCO: Smoking

Bomboo LLC....................................G........ 475 731-0865
Norwalk *(G-6096)*

TOILET PREPARATIONS

Gillette Company............................G........ 203 796-4000
Bethel *(G-303)*

TOILETRIES, COSMETICS & PERFUME STORES

Lady Anne Cosmetics Inc.................G........ 203 372-6972
Trumbull *(G-9041)*
Tommys Supplies LLC.....................G........ 860 265-2199
Somers *(G-7674)*

TOILETRIES, WHOLESALE: Toilet Soap

Crabtree & Evelyn Ltd....................C........ 800 272-2873
Woodstock *(G-10662)*

TOILETRIES, WHOLESALE: Toiletries

T N Dickinson Company...................F........ 860 267-2279
East Hampton *(G-2281)*

TOILETS: Portable Chemical, Plastics

Coastline Environmental LLC...........G........ 203 483-6898
North Branford *(G-5831)*

TOOL & DIE STEEL

American Standard Company...........E........ 860 628-9643
Southington *(G-7889)*
Jo Vek Tool and Die Mfg Co.............G........ 203 755-1884
Waterbury *(G-9511)*
Ultra Mfg LLC..................................G........ 203 888-1180
Seymour *(G-7371)*
Washburn Design LLC.....................G........ 860 675-3215
Burlington *(G-1279)*

TOOL REPAIR SVCS

Eastern Broach Inc..........................F........ 860 828-4800
Plainville *(G-6802)*
Hallden Shear Service of Amer.........G........ 860 283-4386
Thomaston *(G-8791)*

TOOLS: Carpenters', Including Levels & Chisels, Exc Saws

Classic Trim LLC.............................G........ 860 543-9102
Bristol *(G-1002)*

TOOLS: Hand

A Line Design Inc............................G........ 203 294-0080
Wallingford *(G-9193)*
Ampol Tool Inc................................G........ 203 932-3161
West Haven *(G-9884)*
Changesurfer Consulting.................G........ 312 702-3742
Willington *(G-10247)*
Crrc LLC...D........ 860 635-2200
Cromwell *(G-1697)*
E-Z Tools Inc...................................G........ 203 838-2102
Norwalk *(G-6152)*
Edge Tool LLC.................................G........ 860 747-1820
Plainville *(G-6803)*
Fletcher-Terry Company LLC...........D........ 860 828-3400
East Berlin *(G-2169)*
Integrity Manufacturing LLC............G........ 860 678-1599
Farmington *(G-2919)*
Ipt Technology................................G........ 860 395-1083
Old Saybrook *(G-6544)*
Irwin Industrial Tool Company.........G........ 860 438-3460
New Britain *(G-5003)*
Kell-Strom Tool Co Inc....................E........ 860 529-6851
Wethersfield *(G-10206)*
Kell-Strom Tool Intl Inc...................E........ 860 529-6851
Wethersfield *(G-10207)*
Online River LLC.............................F........ 203 801-5900
Westport *(G-10134)*
Rostra Tool Company......................E........ 203 488-8665
Branford *(G-644)*
Southwire Company LLC..................F........ 203 324-0067
Stamford *(G-8431)*
Stanley Black & Decker Inc.............F........ 860 225-5111
Farmington *(G-2959)*
Stanley Black & Decker Inc.............C........ 860 225-5111
New Britain *(G-5061)*
Stanley Black & Decker Inc.............E........ 860 225-5111
New Britain *(G-5064)*
Stephen A Besade...........................G........ 860 443-6033
New London *(G-5490)*
Tiger Enterprises Inc......................E........ 860 621-9155
Plantsville *(G-6914)*
Tool 2000.......................................G........ 860 620-0020
Southington *(G-7989)*
Toolmax Designing Tooling Inc........G........ 860 871-7265
Tolland *(G-8883)*
Trumpf Inc......................................B........ 860 255-6000
Farmington *(G-2967)*
Trumpf Inc......................................B........ 860 255-6000
Farmington *(G-2968)*
Trumpf Inc......................................B........ 860 255-6000
Plainville *(G-6872)*
Ttpockettools LLC...........................G........ 860 642-6020
Lebanon *(G-3865)*
Unger Enterprises LLC....................C........ 203 366-4884
Bridgeport *(G-930)*
V Cannelli Co LLC............................G........ 203 421-4697
Madison *(G-3966)*
Wadsworth Falls Mfg Co..................F........ 860 346-3644
Rockfall *(G-7216)*

TOOLS: Hand, Engravers'

Ngraver Company............................G........ 860 823-1533
Bozrah *(G-530)*

TOOLS: Hand, Ironworkers'

Conquip Systems LLC......................G........ 860 526-7883
Chester *(G-1468)*

TOOLS: Hand, Jewelers'

Eds Jewelry LLC..............................G........ 203 757-0018
Waterbury *(G-9470)*
Present Time Visions......................G........ 860 435-4997
Salisbury *(G-7296)*
Signature Gold................................G........ 860 523-0385
Hartford *(G-3688)*
Sterling Jewelers Inc......................G........ 860 644-7207
Manchester *(G-4096)*

TOOLS: Hand, Mechanics

An Designs Inc................................G........ 860 618-0183
Torrington *(G-8895)*

Cambridge Specialty Co Inc.............D........ 860 828-3579
Berlin *(G-168)*
J J Ryan Corporation......................C........ 860 628-0393
Plantsville *(G-6897)*
Ullman Devices Corporation............D........ 203 438-6577
Ridgefield *(G-7178)*

TOOLS: Hand, Plumbers'

M G Solutions..................................G........ 203 945-9615
Norwalk *(G-6241)*

TOOLS: Hand, Power

Air Tool Sales & Service Co.............G........ 860 673-2714
Unionville *(G-9110)*
Apex Machine Tool Company Inc......D........ 860 677-2884
Cheshire *(G-1353)*
Black & Decker (us) Inc...................G........ 860 563-5800
Wethersfield *(G-10184)*
Black & Decker (us) Inc...................G........ 860 225-5111
New Britain *(G-4951)*
Black & Decker (us) Inc...................G........ 860 225-5111
New Britain *(G-4952)*
Blackstone Industries LLC...............D........ 203 792-8622
Bethel *(G-266)*
DArcy Saw LLC................................G........ 800 569-1264
Windsor Locks *(G-10481)*
Frasal Tool Co Inc...........................F........ 860 666-3524
Newington *(G-5654)*
HRF Fastener Systems Inc...............E........ 860 589-0750
Bristol *(G-1049)*
Slater Hill Tool LLC.........................G........ 860 963-0415
Putnam *(G-7066)*
Stanley Black & Decker Inc.............G........ 860 460-9122
Southington *(G-7981)*
Stanley Black & Decker Inc.............C........ 860 225-5111
New Britain *(G-5061)*
Stanley Black & Decker Inc.............E........ 860 225-5111
New Britain *(G-5064)*
Stihl Incorporated...........................E........ 203 929-8488
Oxford *(G-6695)*
Trumpf Inc......................................B........ 860 255-6000
Plainville *(G-6872)*
Trumpf Inc......................................B........ 860 255-6000
Farmington *(G-2967)*
Trumpf Inc......................................B........ 860 255-6000
Farmington *(G-2968)*
Universal Precision Mfg...................G........ 203 374-9809
Trumbull *(G-9089)*
W J Savage Co Inc...........................G........ 203 468-4100
East Haven *(G-2459)*

TOOLS: Hand, Stonecutters'

W J Savage Co Inc...........................G........ 203 468-4100
East Haven *(G-2459)*

TOOLS: Soldering

Uniprise International Inc................E........ 860 589-7262
Terryville *(G-8776)*

TOOTHPASTES, GELS & TOOTHPOWDERS

Sheffield Pharmaceuticals LLC.........C........ 860 442-4451
New London *(G-5488)*

TOUR OPERATORS

DAmbruoso Studios LLC..................G........ 203 758-9660
Middlebury *(G-4276)*

TOWERS, SECTIONS: Transmission, Radio & Television

Com Tower......................................G........ 203 879-6568
Wolcott *(G-10557)*
Remote Site Service LLC.................G........ 860 691-1911
Niantic *(G-5816)*

TOYS

Anjar Co...G........ 203 321-1023
Stamford *(G-8086)*
Col-Lar Enterprises Inc....................G........ 860 799-6970
Brookfield *(G-1173)*
Col-Lar Enterprises Inc....................F........ 203 798-1786
New Milford *(G-5521)*
Game On LLC..................................G........ 860 608-8931
East Haddam *(G-2242)*
Imagine 8 LLC.................................G........ 203 421-0905
Madison *(G-3928)*

Mark G Cappitella .... G 860 873-3093
  East Haddam (G-2245)
Roto-Die Company Inc .... F 860 292-7030
  East Windsor (G-2516)
S & S Worldwide Inc .... C 860 537-3451
  Colchester (G-1574)
Team Walbern .... G 860 667-7627
  Newington (G-5710)
US Games Systems Inc .... E 203 353-8400
  Stamford (G-8481)
Westport Model Works .... G 203 226-2798
  Westport (G-10175)
X44 LLC .... G 860 480-5560
  Torrington (G-8993)

TOYS & HOBBY GOODS & SPLYS, WHOLESALE: Model Kits

AAA Distributors .... G 860 346-0230
  Middletown (G-4312)

TOYS & HOBBY GOODS & SPLYS, WHOLESALE: Playing Cards

US Games Systems Inc .... E 203 353-8400
  Stamford (G-8481)

TOYS & HOBBY GOODS & SPLYS, WHOLESALE: Toys & Games

Leisure Learning Products Inc .... F 203 325-2800
  Stamford (G-8281)

TOYS & HOBBY GOODS & SPLYS, WHOLESALE: Video Games

Card Carrier Games LLC .... G 203 521-0291
  Milford (G-4483)

TOYS, HOBBY GOODS & SPLYS WHOLESALERS

Lego Systems Inc .... A 860 749-2291
  Enfield (G-2655)

TOYS: Dolls, Stuffed Animals & Parts

Anjar Co .... G 203 321-1023
  Stamford (G-8086)
New England Toy LLC .... G 860 655-6089
  Simsbury (G-7637)
Tiny Woodshop .... G 203 866-6725
  Norwalk (G-6369)

TOYS: Electronic

Walts Trooper Factory LLC .... G 203 871-9254
  North Branford (G-5866)

TOYS: Kites

Keyes On Kites Tattoo Gallery .... G 203 387-5397
  New Haven (G-5309)
Kite Business Solutions LLC .... G 860 302-0682
  Plantsville (G-6899)
Skydog Kites LLC .... G 860 365-0600
  Colchester (G-1577)

TRADE SHOW ARRANGEMENT SVCS

L M T Communications Inc .... F 203 426-4568
  Newtown (G-5752)
Show Management Associates LLC ... G 203 939-9901
  Norwalk (G-6345)

TRADERS: Commodity, Contracts

Boehringer Ingelheim Corp .... A 203 798-9988
  Ridgefield (G-7120)
Louis Dreyfus Holding Company .... B 203 761-2000
  Wilton (G-10310)

TRAILERS & PARTS: Truck & Semi's

All Star Welding & Dem LLC .... G 203 948-0528
  Danbury (G-1735)
Kensington Welding & Trlr Co .... G 860 828-3564
  Kensington (G-3811)
Mark Karotkin .... G 860 202-7821
  Hartford (G-3634)
Miller Professional Trans Svc .... G 860 871-6818
  Vernon (G-9144)

Webbers Truck Service Inc .... F 860 623-4554
  East Windsor (G-2532)

TRANSDUCERS: Electrical Properties

Ashcrft-Ngano Kiki Hldings Inc .... G 203 378-8281
  Stratford (G-8571)
Ashcroft Inc .... B 203 378-8281
  Stratford (G-8572)

TRANSDUCERS: Pressure

Eaton Aerospace LLC .... E 203 796-6000
  Bethel (G-292)
Sens All Inc .... G 860 628-8379
  Southington (G-7973)

TRANSFORMERS: Coupling

Macneill Altrntive Cncepts LLC .... G 860 877-3968
  Bristol (G-1066)
Omnicron Electronics .... G 860 928-0377
  Putnam (G-7055)

TRANSFORMERS: Electric

Bicron Electronics Company .... D 860 482-2524
  Torrington (G-8905)
Bridgeport Magnetics Group Inc .... E 203 954-0050
  Shelton (G-7410)
Power Trans Co Inc .... G 203 881-0314
  Oxford (G-6688)
Transformer Technology Inc .... F 860 349-1061
  Durham (G-2160)

TRANSFORMERS: Electronic

71 Pickett District Road LLC .... G 860 350-5964
  New Milford (G-5502)
Alpha Magnetics & Coils Inc .... G 860 496-0122
  Torrington (G-8890)
Neeltran Inc .... C 860 350-5964
  New Milford (G-5564)

TRANSFORMERS: Fluorescent Lighting

Lighticians Inc .... G 203 494-2542
  Clinton (G-1513)

TRANSFORMERS: Power Related

ABB Enterprise Software Inc .... D 203 790-8588
  Danbury (G-1728)
ABB Enterprise Software Inc .... D 860 285-0183
  Windsor (G-10353)
ABB Enterprise Software Inc .... F 203 329-8771
  Stamford (G-8055)
Able Coil and Electronics Co .... E 860 646-5686
  Bolton (G-504)
Alpha-Core Corp .... G 203 335-6805
  Bridgeport (G-687)
Alpha-Core Inc .... E 203 954-0050
  Shelton (G-7392)
Asea Brown Boveri Inc .... G 203 750-2200
  Norwalk (G-6076)
Carling Technologies Inc .... C 203 793-9281
  Plainville (G-6785)
Diagnostic Devices Inc .... G 203 651-6583
  Simsbury (G-7616)
Diagnostic Devices Inc .... G 860 651-6583
  Simsbury (G-7617)
Emsc LLC .... G 203 268-5101
  Stamford (G-8195)
Pw Power Systems LLC .... E 860 368-5900
  Glastonbury (G-3077)
Superior Elc Holdg Group LLC .... E 860 582-9561
  Plainville (G-6864)

TRANSFORMERS: Specialty

K & D Precision Manufacturing .... G 203 931-9550
  West Haven (G-9922)
Universal Voltronics Corp .... E 203 740-8555
  Brookfield (G-1234)

TRANSPORTATION EPQT & SPLYS, WHOL: Aircraft Engs/Eng Parts

Turbine Support Services Inc .... G 860 688-4800
  Windsor (G-10456)

TRANSPORTATION EPQT & SPLYS, WHOLESALE: Helicopter Parts

American Unmanned Systems LLC .... G 203 406-7611
  Stamford (G-8079)
Helicopter Support Inc .... B 203 416-4000
  Trumbull (G-9033)

TRANSPORTATION EPQT & SPLYS, WHOLESALE: Marine Crafts/Splys

Aerocess Inc .... F 860 357-2451
  Berlin (G-151)

TRANSPORTATION EQPT & SPLYS WHOLESALERS, NEC

AMS Strategic Management Inc .... G 845 500-5635
  Stamford (G-8083)
Columbia Manufacturing Inc .... D 860 228-2259
  Columbia (G-1604)

TRANSPORTATION EQUIPMENT, NEC

Hoffman Towing & Transport .... G 860 627-0405
  East Windsor (G-2497)
New England Crrage Imports LLC ...... G 860 889-6467
  Bozrah (G-529)

TRANSPORTATION PROGRAMS REGULATION & ADMINISTRATION SVCS

Transportation Conn Dept .... G 860 342-5996
  Portland (G-6979)

TRANSPORTATION SVCS, WATER: Surveyors, Marine

Mystic River Mar Surveyors LLC .... G 860 857-1798
  Mystic (G-4836)

TRAP ROCK: Crushed & Broken

York Hill Trap Rock Quarry Co .... F 203 237-8421
  Meriden (G-4270)

TRAVEL TRAILERS & CAMPERS

Fiberglass Engr & Design Co .... G 203 265-1644
  Wallingford (G-9266)
Keystone Rv Company .... C 203 367-9847
  Bridgeport (G-816)
Thule Holding Inc .... F 203 881-9600
  Seymour (G-7370)

TRAVELER ACCOMMODATIONS, NEC

Lighthouse Maps .... G 203 981-1090
  Brookfield (G-1203)

TRAYS: Cable, Metal Plate

Wanho Manufacturing LLC .... E 203 759-3744
  Cheshire (G-1457)

TRAYS: Greenhouse Flats, Wood

Duhamels .... G 860 928-4101
  Woodstock (G-10664)
Eddinger Assoc LLC .... G 860 344-0508
  Middletown (G-4341)

TRAYS: Plastic

Form-All Plastics Corporation .... G 203 634-1137
  Meriden (G-4171)

TROPHIES: Metal, Exc Silver

Greco Industries Inc .... G 203 798-7804
  Bethel (G-304)

TROPHY & PLAQUE STORES

A & E Engraving Service .... G 860 582-6503
  Bristol (G-950)
Dragon Hollow Design LLC .... G 860 861-6200
  Norwich (G-6411)
Elite Engraving & Awards .... G 860 643-7459
  Manchester (G-4014)
Swahn Engraving LLC .... G 860 657-4709
  Glastonbury (G-3085)

TROPHY & PLAQUE STORES

Trophy Shop .... G 860 871-0867
   Vernon Rockville *(G-9184)*

TRUCK & BUS BODIES: Automobile Wrecker Truck

Robert Kenneth Andrade LLC .... G 203 937-8697
   West Haven *(G-9949)*

TRUCK & BUS BODIES: Garbage Or Refuse Truck

Lo Stocco Motors .... G 203 797-9618
   Danbury *(G-1875)*
Sidney Dobson .... G 203 255-5545
   Westport *(G-10158)*

TRUCK & BUS BODIES: Truck Cabs, Motor Vehicles

Composite Panel Tech Co .... G 203 729-2255
   Naugatuck *(G-4869)*
Sure Industries Inc .... G 860 289-2522
   East Hartford *(G-2381)*

TRUCK & BUS BODIES: Truck, Motor Vehicle

Alton Enterprises Inc .... G 203 469-9719
   East Haven *(G-2408)*
Schwartz Body Company LLC .... G 203 234-6046
   North Haven *(G-5991)*
Universal Body & Eqp Co LLC .... F 860 274-7541
   Oakville *(G-6466)*

TRUCK & BUS BODIES: Utility Truck

Composite Truck Body LLC .... G 800 735-1668
   Sherman *(G-7593)*

TRUCK GENERAL REPAIR SVC

Rapid Truck Service Inc .... G 860 482-5500
   Torrington *(G-8963)*
Torrington Diesel Corporation .... G 860 496-9948
   Torrington *(G-8980)*

TRUCK PAINTING & LETTERING SVCS

Fastsigns .... G 203 239-9090
   North Haven *(G-5941)*
Ferrucci Signs .... G 203 469-0043
   East Haven *(G-2428)*
Rokap Inc .... G 203 265-6895
   Wallingford *(G-9359)*

TRUCK PARTS & ACCESSORIES: Wholesalers

WH Rose Inc .... E 860 228-8258
   Columbia *(G-1615)*

TRUCKING & HAULING SVCS: Contract Basis

Grillo Services LLC .... E 203 877-5070
   Milford *(G-4544)*

TRUCKING & HAULING SVCS: Furniture, Local W/out Storage

Berlin Industries LLC .... G 860 819-9997
   Berlin *(G-163)*

TRUCKING & HAULING SVCS: Heavy, NEC

GS Ruff Stuff .... G 860 859-9355
   Salem *(G-7289)*

TRUCKING & HAULING SVCS: Lumber & Log, Local

Hancock Logging & Forestry MGT .... G 860 289-5647
   South Windsor *(G-7767)*

TRUCKING, AUTOMOBILE CARRIER

Laydon Industries LLC .... D 203 562-7283
   New Haven *(G-5317)*

TRUCKING, DUMP

Judith Bennett .... G 203 255-6363
   Fairfield *(G-2804)*

TRUCKING: Local, Without Storage

Coastline Fuel Inc .... G 203 846-3601
   Norwalk *(G-6117)*
Thomas Keegan & Sons Inc .... G 203 239-9248
   North Haven *(G-5999)*
Yankee Delivery System .... G 860 243-1056
   Bloomfield *(G-503)*

TRUCKS & TRACTORS: Industrial

Dri-Air Industries Inc .... E 860 627-5110
   East Windsor *(G-2489)*
Macton Corporation .... D 203 267-1500
   Oxford *(G-6674)*
New Haven Companies Inc .... F 203 469-6421
   East Haven *(G-2444)*
Pierce-Correll Corporation .... G 203 799-1208
   Orange *(G-6624)*
Terex Corporation .... F 203 222-7170
   Westport *(G-10163)*

TRUCKS: Forklift

L G Associates .... G 860 677-7167
   Avon *(G-87)*

TRUNKS

2 Girl A Trunk .... G 203 762-0360
   Wilton *(G-10262)*
Tack Trunk .... G 203 880-9972
   Monroe *(G-4754)*

TRUSSES: Wood, Floor

Universal Component Corp .... E 203 481-8787
   East Haven *(G-2458)*

TRUSSES: Wood, Roof

Thomas Bernhard Building Sys .... E 203 925-0414
   Southport *(G-8013)*
Truss Manufacturing Inc .... F 860 665-0000
   Newington *(G-5714)*

TUB CONTAINERS: Plastic

Kensco Inc .... F 203 734-8827
   Ansonia *(G-44)*

TUBE & TUBING FABRICATORS

Creative Rack Solutions Inc .... G 203 755-2102
   Waterbury *(G-9455)*
EA Patten Co LLC .... D 860 649-2851
   Manchester *(G-4013)*
Harry Thommen Company .... G 203 333-3637
   Bridgeport *(G-782)*
L&P Aerospace Acquisition LLC .... D 860 635-8811
   Middletown *(G-4366)*
Macristy Industries Inc .... C 860 225-4637
   Newington *(G-5674)*
Plastics and Concepts Conn Inc .... F 860 657-9655
   Glastonbury *(G-3072)*
Scantube Inc .... G 203 743-0908
   Danbury *(G-1935)*
Spencer Turbine Company .... C 860 688-8361
   Windsor *(G-10436)*

TUBES: Generator, Electron Beam, Beta Ray

Stmicroelectronics Inc .... G 860 928-7700
   Woodstock *(G-10688)*

TUBING: Flexible, Metallic

Uniprise International Inc .... E 860 589-7262
   Terryville *(G-8776)*

TUBING: Plastic

Cebal Americas .... G 203 845-6356
   Norwalk *(G-6110)*
Plastic Factory LLC .... G 203 908-3468
   Bridgeport *(G-874)*
Polymedex Discovery Group Inc .... F 860 928-4102
   Putnam *(G-7059)*
Putnam Plastics Corporation .... C 203 774-1559
   Dayville *(G-2071)*

TUMBLING

HI-Tech Polishing Inc .... F 860 665-1399
   Newington *(G-5659)*

Precision Deburring Inc .... G 860 583-4662
   Bristol *(G-1096)*

TURBINES & TURBINE GENERATOR SET UNITS, COMPLETE

Gas Turbine Supply and Svc LLC .... G 860 254-5651
   Suffield *(G-8719)*

TURBINES & TURBINE GENERATOR SETS

American Metal Masters LLC .... G 860 621-6911
   Plantsville *(G-6884)*
Becon Incorporated .... D 860 243-1428
   Bloomfield *(G-394)*
GE Transportation Parts LLC .... G 816 650-6171
   Fairfield *(G-2791)*
International Turbine Systems .... G 860 761-0358
   Bloomfield *(G-423)*
Northeast Wind Energy .... G 860 779-2179
   East Killingly *(G-2461)*
Pequot 800 620-1492
   Bridgeport *(G-869)*
R&D Dynamics Corporation .... E 860 726-1204
   Bloomfield *(G-472)*

TURBINES & TURBINE GENERATOR SETS & PARTS

Blastech Overhaul & Repair .... F 860 243-8811
   Bloomfield *(G-396)*
Doncasters Inc .... D 860 449-1603
   Groton *(G-3283)*
Winsol Clean Energy LLC .... G 203 216-1972
   Stamford *(G-8497)*
Winsol Economic Dev Corp .... G 203 216-1972
   Stamford *(G-8498)*

TURNKEY VENDORS: Computer Systems

Tek Industries Inc .... E 860 870-0001
   Vernon *(G-9154)*

TURNSTILES

Hayward Turnstiles Inc .... G 203 877-7096
   Milford *(G-4547)*
Online River LLC .... F 203 801-5900
   Westport *(G-10134)*
Perey Turnstiles Inc .... G 203 333-9400
   Bridgeport *(G-870)*

TWINE

Brownell & Company Inc .... F 860 873-8625
   Moodus *(G-4771)*

TYPESETTING SVC

Acme Typesetting Service Co .... G 860 953-1470
   West Hartford *(G-9772)*
Action Letter Inc .... E 203 323-2466
   Stamford *(G-8061)*
Action Printing .... G 203 366-4413
   Shelton *(G-7388)*
Allied Printing Services Inc .... B 860 643-1101
   Manchester *(G-3980)*
Alphacom Inc .... G 203 637-7006
   Greenwich *(G-3117)*
Arkettype .... G 860 350-4007
   New Milford *(G-5504)*
Birdtrack Press .... G 203 389-7789
   New Haven *(G-5248)*
Brenda Jubin .... G 203 393-2366
   Bethany *(G-235)*
Brescias Printing Services Inc .... G 860 528-4254
   East Hartford *(G-2300)*
Conner Printing .... G 203 929-2070
   Shelton *(G-7423)*
Copy Stop Inc .... G 203 288-6401
   Hamden *(G-3433)*
Criscola Design LLC .... G 203 248-4285
   North Haven *(G-5932)*
Desai Mukesh .... G 860 529-4141
   Rocky Hill *(G-7234)*
E R Hitchcock Company .... G 860 229-2024
   New Britain *(G-4977)*
Eccles-Lehman Inc .... G 203 268-0605
   Easton *(G-2551)*
Elm Press Incorporated .... E 860 583-3600
   Terryville *(G-8752)*

PRODUCT SECTION

VALVES: Aircraft

Executive Office Services Inc .... E 203 373-1333
  Bridgeport (G-765)
Fairfield Marketing Group Inc .... F 203 261-0884
  Easton (G-2552)
Four Color Inc .... G 860 691-1782
  Niantic (G-5806)
Franklin Print Shoppe Inc .... G 860 496-9516
  Torrington (G-8926)
G & R Enterprises Incorporated .... G 860 549-6120
  Hartford (G-3593)
Gateway Digital Inc .... F 203 853-4929
  Norwalk (G-6175)
Guy Lindsay .... G 860 646-7865
  Manchester (G-4024)
Hedges & Hedges Ltd .... G 860 257-3170
  Wethersfield (G-10196)
IM Your Type LLC .... G 203 967-4063
  Stamford (G-8244)
Image Processing .... E 203 488-3252
  Guilford (G-3361)
Jerrys Printing & Graphics LLC .... G 203 384-0015
  Bridgeport (G-803)
John Pecora .... G 860 677-9323
  Farmington (G-2920)
Kat Art Inc .... G 860 350-8016
  New Milford (G-5554)
Kool Ink LLC .... F 860 242-0303
  Bloomfield (G-439)
Lettering Inc of New York .... E 203 329-7759
  Stamford (G-8283)
Magnani Press Incorporated .... G 860 236-2802
  Hartford (G-3631)
Master Engrv & Printery Inc .... G 203 723-2779
  Waterbury (G-9535)
Meredith Graphics & Design .... G 203 375-1039
  Stratford (G-8650)
Oddo Print Shop Inc .... G 860 489-6585
  Torrington (G-8953)
Palmisano Printing LLC .... G 860 582-6883
  Bristol (G-1085)
Pancoast Associates Inc .... G 203 377-6571
  Trumbull (G-9054)
Paper Mill Graphix Inc .... E 203 531-5904
  Greenwich (G-3213)
Paul Dewitt .... F 203 792-5610
  Danbury (G-1902)
Phoenix Press Inc .... E 203 865-5555
  New Haven (G-5363)
Professional Graphics Inc .... F 203 846-4291
  Norwalk (G-6307)
Prosperous Printing LLC .... G 203 834-1962
  Wilton (G-10322)
Quinn and Gellar Marketing LLC .... G 860 444-0448
  New London (G-5485)
Saybrook Press Incorporated .... F 203 458-3637
  Guilford (G-3388)
Speedy Printing LLC .... G 860 445-8252
  Mystic (G-4846)
Step Saver Inc .... E 860 621-6746
  Southington (G-7982)
Supertype Inc .... G 216 816-8119
  New Haven (G-5405)
Tech-Repro Inc .... F 203 348-8884
  Stamford (G-8460)
Vernon Printing Co Inc .... G 860 872-1826
  Vernon Rockville (G-9186)
Westchster Bk/Rnsford Type Inc .... C 203 791-0080
  Danbury (G-1980)

TYPESETTING SVC: Computer

Jupiter Communications LLC .... F 475 238-7082
  West Haven (G-9920)
Kiagraphics .... G 203 261-4328
  Monroe (G-4726)

TYPESETTING SVC: Hand Composition

Westchester Pubg Svcs LLC .... G 203 791-0080
  Danbury (G-1979)

TYPOGRAPHY

A To A Studio Solutions Ltd .... F 203 388-9050
  Stamford (G-8053)
Sk Systems .... G 860 691-0366
  East Lyme (G-2475)

ULTRASONIC EQPT: Cleaning, Exc Med & Dental

Ultra Clean Equipment Inc .... G 860 669-1354
  Clinton (G-1533)

UMBRELLAS: Garden Or Wagon

Bug Umbrella Gazebo LLC .... G 860 651-0030
  East Granby (G-2194)

UNDERCOATINGS: Paint

Element 119 LLC .... F 860 358-0119
  Thomaston (G-8789)

UNIFORM STORES

Al-Lynn Sales LLC .... G 203 922-7840
  Shelton (G-7390)
Work n Gear LLC .... G 203 795-8998
  Orange (G-6636)
Work n Gear LLC .... G 203 467-1156
  East Haven (G-2460)

UNIVERSITY

Wesleyan University .... G 860 685-7727
  Middletown (G-4429)
Wesleyan University .... G 860 685-2980
  Middletown (G-4430)
Yale University .... E 203 432-2550
  New Haven (G-5443)
Yale University .... D 203 764-4333
  New Haven (G-5444)
Yale University .... E 203 737-1244
  New Haven (G-5446)
Yale University .... G 203 432-0499
  New Haven (G-5450)
Yale University .... G 203 432-2880
  New Haven (G-5445)
Yale University .... G 203 432-3916
  New Haven (G-5447)
Yale University .... G 203 432-2424
  New Haven (G-5448)
Yale University .... G 203 432-6320
  New Haven (G-5449)
Yale University .... G 203 432-7494
  New Haven (G-5451)

UPHOLSTERY MATERIAL

Reid Interiors .... G 860 569-1240
  East Hartford (G-2364)

UPHOLSTERY WORK SVCS

Columbia Mat & Upholstering Co .... G 203 789-1213
  Hamden (G-3429)
J G Taglieri .... G 860 645-1060
  Manchester (G-4037)
Richards Creative Interiors .... G 203 484-0361
  Wallingford (G-9355)

USED CAR DEALERS

Car Buyers Market .... E 516 482-0292
  Trumbull (G-9010)
Ems International Inc .... G 860 526-2060
  Chester (G-1472)
New Age Motorsports LLC .... G 203 268-1999
  Monroe (G-4741)

USED MERCHANDISE STORES: Art Objects, Antique

Michael Shortell .... G 860 236-4787
  Hartford (G-3642)
Riccio Artifacts .... G 860 267-6023
  East Hampton (G-2277)

USED MERCHANDISE STORES: Rare Books

Townsend John .... G 860 526-3896
  Deep River (G-2104)

UTENSILS: Household, Cooking & Kitchen, Metal

Cee Orange LLC .... G 203 799-2665
  Orange (G-6590)

VACUUM CLEANER STORES

Brian Cheney .... G 203 734-4793
  Seymour (G-7336)

VACUUM CLEANERS: Household

A A Gentle House Washing .... G 860 243-8800
  Bloomfield (G-378)
Matsutek Enterprises LLC .... G 860 276-2464
  Southington (G-7951)
Stanley Steemer Intl Inc .... E 860 274-5540
  Watertown (G-9738)
Traumaway LLC .... G 860 628-0706
  Plantsville (G-6916)

VACUUM CLEANERS: Indl Type

Spencer Turbine Company .... C 860 688-8361
  Windsor (G-10436)

VALUE-ADDED RESELLERS: Computer Systems

Connecticut Computer Svc Inc .... G 860 276-1285
  Milford (G-4493)
Document Dynamics LLC .... G 860 376-2944
  Jewett City (G-3794)
Grayfin Security LLC .... G 203 800-6760
  Madison (G-3923)

VALVES

Air Valves LLC .... G 203 266-7175
  Bethlehem (G-366)
Carten Controls Inc .... F 203 699-2100
  Cheshire (G-1366)
James J Scott LLC .... G 860 571-9200
  Rocky Hill (G-7252)
Pearse Bertram LLC .... G 860 612-9060
  New Britain (G-5031)
Skinner Valve Division .... G 860 827-2300
  New Britain (G-5055)

VALVES & PIPE FITTINGS

Carten Controls Inc .... F 203 699-2100
  Cheshire (G-1366)
Dancar Corporation .... G 203 598-0205
  Middlebury (G-4277)
Enfield Technologies LLC .... F 203 375-3100
  Shelton (G-7439)
Fisher Controls Intl LLC .... C 860 599-1140
  North Stonington (G-6025)
Genalco Inc .... G 203 932-5991
  West Haven (G-9911)
Houston Weber Systems Inc .... G 203 481-0115
  Branford (G-607)
Hydrolevel Company .... F 203 776-0473
  North Haven (G-5946)
Idex Health & Science LLC .... C 860 314-2880
  Bristol (G-1050)

VALVES & REGULATORS: Pressure, Indl

First Reserve Fund Viii LP .... G 203 661-6601
  Stamford (G-8205)

VALVES Solenoid

Kip Inc .... C 860 677-0272
  Farmington (G-2922)
Parker-Hannifin Corporation .... C 860 827-2300
  New Britain (G-5030)
Peter Paul Electronics Co Inc .... C 860 229-4884
  New Britain (G-5032)

VALVES: Aerosol, Metal

Aptargroup Inc .... B 203 377-8100
  Stratford (G-8569)
Metalcraft LLC .... G 860 361-6767
  Bantam (G-124)

VALVES: Aircraft

Nutek Aerospace Corp .... G 860 355-3169
  New Milford (G-5575)
Saf Industries LLC .... E 203 729-4900
  Meriden (G-4237)

Employee Codes: A=Over 500 employees, B=251-500
C=101-250, D=51-100, E=20-50, F=10-19, G=1-9

VALVES: Aircraft, Control, Hydraulic & Pneumatic

American Metal Masters LLC .... G 860 621-6911
Plantsville *(G-6884)*

VALVES: Aircraft, Fluid Power

Saf Industries LLC .... E 203 729-4900
Meriden *(G-4237)*

VALVES: Control, Automatic

Cr-TEC Engineering Inc .... G 203 318-9500
Madison *(G-3914)*
Fisher Controls Intl LLC .... C 860 599-1140
North Stonington *(G-6025)*

VALVES: Fluid Power, Control, Hydraulic & pneumatic

Clarcor Eng MBL Solutions LLC .... D 860 920-4200
East Hartford *(G-2306)*
Crane Aerospace Inc .... G 203 363-7300
Stamford *(G-8165)*
Crane Co .... D 203 363-7300
Stamford *(G-8166)*
Crane Controls Inc .... G 203 363-7300
Stamford *(G-8167)*
Crane Intl Holdings Inc .... G 203 363-7300
Stamford *(G-8168)*
Navtec Rigging Solutions Inc .... E 203 458-3163
Clinton *(G-1515)*
Norgren Inc .... C 860 677-0272
Farmington *(G-2938)*
Stanadyne Intrmdate Hldngs LLC .... C 860 525-0821
Windsor *(G-10440)*

VALVES: Indl

BNL Industries Inc .... E 860 870-6222
Vernon *(G-9133)*
Contemporary Products LLC .... E 860 346-9283
Middletown *(G-4332)*
Conval Inc .... C 860 749-0761
Enfield *(G-2633)*
Haltech Manufacturing Svcs LLC .... G 860 625-0189
New London *(G-5473)*
Noank Controls LLC .... G 860 449-6776
Groton *(G-3301)*
Rostra Vernatherm LLC .... G 860 582-6776
Bristol *(G-1112)*
Ruby Automation LLC .... C 860 687-5000
Bloomfield *(G-479)*
Ruby Industrial Tech LLC .... C 860 687-5000
Bloomfield *(G-481)*
Watts .... G 203 230-8582
Hamden *(G-3528)*

VALVES: Plumbing & Heating

Hytek Plumbing and Heating LLC .... G 860 389-1122
Preston *(G-6984)*

VALVES: Regulating & Control, Automatic

Logic Seal LLC .... G 203 598-3400
Plainville *(G-6834)*
Universal Building Contrls Inc .... F 203 235-1530
Meriden *(G-4260)*

VALVES: Regulating, Process Control

Oventrop Corp .... E 860 413-9173
East Granby *(G-2222)*
Saf Industries LLC .... E 203 729-4900
Meriden *(G-4237)*

VALVES: Water Works

Northeast Pipeline Service LLC .... G 860 621-6921
Southington *(G-7960)*

VEHICLES: All Terrain

Danbury Powersports Inc .... F 203 791-1310
Danbury *(G-1786)*

VENDING MACHINES & PARTS

Bobs Vending .... G 860 426-1232
Southington *(G-7896)*
Kk Manufacturing LLC .... G 860 644-5330
South Windsor *(G-7784)*
Smile Exchange LLC .... G 860 342-0333
Middletown *(G-4418)*
Waterside Vending LLC .... G 860 399-6039
Westbrook *(G-10014)*

VENETIAN BLINDS & SHADES

Arrow Window Shade Mfg Co Mrdn .... F 860 563-4035
Wethersfield *(G-10181)*

VENTILATING EQPT: Metal

Bills Sheet Metal .... G 860 859-2821
Oakdale *(G-6441)*

VENTURE CAPITAL COMPANIES

Atlantic Street Capitl MGT LLC .... E 203 428-3150
Stamford *(G-8098)*
Cobra Green LLC .... A 203 354-5000
Norwalk *(G-6118)*
Med Opportunity Partners LLC .... G 203 622-1333
Greenwich *(G-3201)*

VETERINARY PHARMACEUTICAL PREPARATIONS

Skyline Vet Pharma Inc .... G 860 625-0424
Groton *(G-3312)*

VIDEO & AUDIO EQPT, WHOLESALE

Video Outlet .... G 860 568-7473
East Hartford *(G-2400)*

VIDEO EQPT

Harman International Inds Inc .... C 203 328-3500
Stamford *(G-8228)*

VIDEO PRODUCTION SVCS

Fed Russell LLC .... E 203 934-2501
West Haven *(G-9908)*

VIDEO TAPE PRODUCTION SVCS

Taunton Inc .... A 203 426-8171
Newtown *(G-5785)*

VISES: Machine

Advanced Torque Products LLC .... G 860 828-1523
Newington *(G-5622)*
Lord & Hodge Inc .... F 860 632-7006
Middletown *(G-4369)*

VISUAL COMMUNICATIONS SYSTEMS

Essential Trading Systems Corp .... F 860 295-8100
Marlborough *(G-4123)*
Victor F Leandri .... G 860 345-8705
Higganum *(G-3781)*
Visionpoint LLC .... E 860 436-9673
Newington *(G-5720)*

VITAMINS: Natural Or Synthetic, Uncompounded, Bulk

Biomed Health Inc .... F 860 657-2258
Glastonbury *(G-3014)*
Effihealth LLC .... G 888 435-3108
Stamford *(G-8193)*
Optima Specialty Chemical .... G 203 929-2031
Shelton *(G-7520)*
Watson LLC .... B 203 932-3000
West Haven *(G-9960)*

VITAMINS: Pharmaceutical Preparations

Humphreys Pharmacal Inc .... F 860 267-8710
East Hampton *(G-2264)*
Pharmavite Corp .... G 860 651-1885
Simsbury *(G-7639)*
SDA Laboratories Inc .... G 203 861-0005
Greenwich *(G-3233)*

WALL COVERINGS WHOLESALERS

Donghia Inc .... D 800 366-4442
Milford *(G-4514)*

WALLPAPER & WALL COVERINGS

Ambiance Painting LLC .... F 203 354-8689
Norwalk *(G-6068)*
Flat Vernacular .... G 347 457-6227
Norwalk *(G-6170)*

WALLPAPER STORE

Ethan Allen Retail Inc .... B 203 743-8000
Danbury *(G-1818)*
Reid Interiors .... G 860 569-1240
East Hartford *(G-2364)*

WAREHOUSE CLUBS STORES

Astrophonic Corp America .... G 203 853-9300
Norwalk *(G-6079)*

WAREHOUSING & STORAGE FACILITIES, NEC

American Bus Tele & Tech LLC .... G 860 643-2200
Manchester *(G-3982)*
Macristy Industries Inc .... C 860 225-4637
Newington *(G-5674)*

WAREHOUSING & STORAGE, REFRIGERATED: Cold Storage Or Refrig

Natural Country Farms Inc .... D 860 872-8346
Ellington *(G-2597)*
Supreme Storm Services LLC .... G 860 201-0642
Southington *(G-7983)*

WAREHOUSING & STORAGE: General

L P Macadams Company Inc .... D 203 366-3647
Bridgeport *(G-820)*

WAREHOUSING & STORAGE: Refrigerated

M S B International Ltd .... G 203 466-6525
Branford *(G-620)*

WARM AIR HEATING/AC EQPT/SPLY, WHOL Humidifier, Exc Portable

Belimo Aircontrols (usa) Inc .... C 800 543-9038
Danbury *(G-1752)*
Belimo Customization USA Inc .... G 203 791-9915
Danbury *(G-1754)*

WARM AIR HEATING/AC EQPT/SPLYS, WHOL Warm Air Htg Eqpt/Splys

Buckley Associates Inc .... G 203 380-2405
Stratford *(G-8590)*
Electrical Maintenance Svc Co .... G 203 333-6163
Bridgeport *(G-761)*

WARP KNIT FABRIC FINISHING

Lisas Clover Hill Quilts LLC .... G 860 828-9325
Berlin *(G-195)*

WASHERS

Luis Pressure Washer .... G 203 706-7399
Waterbury *(G-9518)*

WASHERS: Plastic

Cultec Inc .... F 203 775-4416
Brookfield *(G-1176)*
Standard Washer & Mat Inc .... E 860 643-5125
Manchester *(G-4094)*

WASHERS: Rubber

Auburn Manufacturing Company .... E 860 346-6677
Middletown *(G-4319)*
Standard Washer & Mat Inc .... E 860 643-5125
Manchester *(G-4094)*

WASHING MACHINES: Household

Brian & Son Powerwashing LLC .... G 860 963-1243
Woodstock *(G-10657)*

WATCHES

Morristown Star Struck LLC .... E 203 778-4925
Bethel *(G-329)*

PRODUCT SECTION

Timex Group Usa Inc .... C 203 346-5000
  Middlebury *(G-4297)*

WATER HEATERS

Eemax Inc .... D 203 267-7890
  Waterbury *(G-9472)*

WATER PURIFICATION EQPT: Household

3M Purification Inc .... B 203 237-5541
  Meriden *(G-4135)*
Kx Technologies LLC .... F 203 799-9000
  West Haven *(G-9925)*
Northeast Fluid Technology .... G 860 620-0393
  Plantsville *(G-6906)*
Renewable Energy Natural RES .... G 860 923-1091
  Thompson *(G-8843)*

WATER PURIFICATION PRDTS: Chlorination Tablets & Kits

Purdue Pharma Manufacturing LP .... E 252 265-1924
  Stamford *(G-8379)*
Pure Cycle Environmental LLC .... G 203 230-3631
  North Haven *(G-5983)*

WATER SOFTENER SVCS

Clearwater Treatment Systems L .... G 860 799-0303
  New Milford *(G-5520)*

WATER TREATMENT EQPT: Indl

Affordable Water Trtmnt .... G 860 423-3147
  Mansfield Center *(G-4111)*
Alliance Water Treatment Co .... G 203 323-9968
  Stamford *(G-8071)*
Aqualogic Inc .... E 203 248-8959
  North Haven *(G-5909)*
Atlas Filtri North America LLC .... F 203 284-0080
  Wallingford *(G-9214)*
Best Management Products Inc .... G 860 434-0277
  East Haddam *(G-2236)*
Brasco Technologies LLC .... G 203 484-4291
  Northford *(G-6043)*
Clearwater Treatment Systems L .... G 860 799-0303
  New Milford *(G-5520)*
Crane Co .... D 203 363-7300
  Stamford *(G-8166)*
Ecochlor Inc .... G 203 915-4593
  North Haven *(G-5935)*
Fractal Water LLC .... G 888 897-6968
  Harwinton *(G-3730)*
H Krevit and Company Inc .... E 203 772-3350
  New Haven *(G-5292)*
Hydro Service & Supplies Inc .... G 203 265-3995
  Middletown *(G-4353)*
Meurer Industries .... G 303 279-8373
  Meriden *(G-4200)*
Nalco Wtr Prtrtment Sltons LLC .... G 860 224-4443
  New Britain *(G-5019)*
Suez Wts Services Usa Inc .... E 860 291-9660
  East Hartford *(G-2380)*
Town of Montville .... F 860 848-3830
  Uncasville *(G-9107)*
Town of Vernon .... F 860 870-3545
  Vernon *(G-9156)*

WATER: Distilled

Perfect Infinity Inc .... G 203 906-0442
  Milford *(G-4608)*
Perricone Hydrogen Wtr Co LLC .... G 844 341-5941
  Meriden *(G-4217)*

WATER: Mineral, Carbonated, Canned & Bottled, Etc

Crystal Rock Holdings Inc .... E 860 945-0661
  Watertown *(G-9697)*

WATER: Pasteurized & Mineral, Bottled & Canned

Danone Holdings Inc .... A 203 229-7000
  Stamford *(G-8179)*

WATER: Pasteurized, Canned & Bottled, Etc

Drinking Water Div .... G 860 509-7333
  Hartford *(G-3580)*

Hosmer Mountain Btlg Co Inc .... G 860 643-6923
  Manchester *(G-4029)*

WATERPROOFING COMPOUNDS

Caap Co Inc .... E 203 877-0375
  Milford *(G-4478)*

WAVEGUIDES & FITTINGS

Microtech Inc .... D 203 272-3234
  Cheshire *(G-1416)*

WAXES: Mineral, Natural

Koster Keunen Inc .... G 860 945-3333
  Watertown *(G-9714)*
Koster Keunen Mfg Inc .... D 860 945-3333
  Watertown *(G-9716)*

WAXES: Petroleum, Not Produced In Petroleum Refineries

Koster Keunen LLC .... F 860 945-3333
  Watertown *(G-9715)*

WEATHER STRIP: Sponge Rubber

H-O Products Corporation .... E 860 379-9875
  Winsted *(G-10523)*
Jay Tee Corp .... G 203 732-5215
  Ansonia *(G-41)*

WEATHER VANES

Carob Designs LLC .... G 203 630-9171
  Meriden *(G-4155)*

WELDING & CUTTING APPARATUS & ACCESS, NEC

Advanced Vacuum Technology Inc ...... G 860 653-4176
  Simsbury *(G-7609)*
New Hope Wldg Fabrication LLC .... G 203 357-0080
  Stamford *(G-8324)*

WELDING EQPT

Airgas Usa LLC .... G 860 442-0363
  Waterford *(G-9640)*
Branson Ultrasonics Corp .... B 203 796-0400
  Danbury *(G-1759)*
Industrial Prssure Washers LLC .... G 860 608-6153
  Wethersfield *(G-10197)*
L & P Gate Company Inc .... G 860 296-8009
  Hartford *(G-3623)*
Magnatech LLC .... D 860 653-2573
  East Granby *(G-2210)*
Nelson Stud Welding Inc .... G 800 635-9353
  Farmington *(G-2935)*
Quality Welding Service LLC .... G 860 342-7202
  Portland *(G-6970)*
Sonics & Materials Inc .... D 203 270-4600
  Newtown *(G-5781)*
Sonitek Corporation .... E 203 878-9321
  Milford *(G-4647)*
Thermatool Mill Syst .... G 203 468-4178
  Farmington *(G-2964)*
Tim Welder LLC .... G 860 646-1356
  Manchester *(G-4101)*

WELDING EQPT & SPLYS WHOLESALERS

Airgas Usa LLC .... C 203 792-1834
  Danbury *(G-1733)*
Airgas Usa LLC .... E 860 442-0363
  Waterford *(G-9641)*
Nesci Enterprises Inc .... G 860 267-2588
  East Hampton *(G-2271)*
Praxair Distribution Inc .... F 203 837-2000
  Danbury *(G-1914)*
Thavenet Machine Company Inc .... G 860 599-4495
  Pawcatuck *(G-6726)*

WELDING EQPT & SPLYS: Arc Welders, Transformer-Rectifier

Eastern Conectr Specialty Corp .... G 860 355-8100
  New Milford *(G-5530)*

WELDING EQPT & SPLYS: Electrode Holders, Electric Welding

Cadi Co Inc .... E 203 729-1111
  Naugatuck *(G-4865)*

WELDING EQPT REPAIR SVCS

A & L Welding Service .... G 860 664-1700
  Clinton *(G-1488)*
Advanced Vacuum Technology Inc ...... G 860 653-4176
  Simsbury *(G-7609)*
Ewald Instruments Corp .... F 860 491-9042
  Bristol *(G-1032)*
Ives Welding Service .... G 860 423-6139
  South Windham *(G-7688)*

WELDING EQPT: Electric

Praxair Surface Tech Inc .... D 860 646-0700
  Manchester *(G-4076)*

WELDING EQPT: Electrical

Magnatech LLC .... D 860 653-2573
  East Granby *(G-2210)*

WELDING MACHINES & EQPT: Ultrasonic

Branson Ultrasonics Corp .... B 203 796-0400
  Danbury *(G-1759)*

WELDING REPAIR SVC

A & A Welding LLC .... G 860 933-1284
  Moosup *(G-4777)*
A Z Welding .... G 860 872-1301
  Tolland *(G-8846)*
AC Skips Welding Inc .... G 203 838-2089
  Norwalk *(G-6060)*
Accurate Welding Services LLC .... F 860 623-9500
  Windsor Locks *(G-10467)*
Ack Precision Machine Co .... G 860 664-0789
  Clinton *(G-1490)*
Advanced Welding & Repair Inc .... G 860 242-0400
  Bloomfield *(G-381)*
Aerotek Welding Co Inc .... G 860 653-0120
  North Granby *(G-5880)*
Alloy Welding .... G 203 737-5609
  New Haven *(G-5224)*
American Steel Fabricators Inc .... G 860 243-5005
  Bloomfield *(G-384)*
American Welding Service .... G 860 935-5314
  North Grosvenordale *(G-5883)*
American Wldg Fabrication LLC .... G 860 918-2094
  New Britain *(G-4944)*
Amk Welding Inc .... E 860 289-5634
  South Windsor *(G-7707)*
Anderson Tool Company Inc .... G 203 777-4153
  New Haven *(G-5231)*
Ansonia Stl Fabrication Co Inc .... E 203 888-4509
  Beacon Falls *(G-129)*
Anthony Da RE Welding .... G 860 526-2659
  Deep River *(G-2083)*
Apex Machine Tool Company Inc .... G 203 806-2090
  Cheshire *(G-1354)*
Arp Welding & Repair LLC .... G 203 924-6811
  Shelton *(G-7397)*
Astro Welding Inc .... G 860 289-6272
  East Hartford *(G-2294)*
B & F Machine Co Inc .... D 860 225-6349
  New Britain *(G-4949)*
B T Welding .... G 860 537-6197
  Colchester *(G-1542)*
Bahres Welding .... G 860 693-4950
  Canton *(G-1306)*
Barzetti Welding LLC .... G 203 748-3200
  Bethel *(G-261)*
Bethany Welding .... G 203 393-0002
  New Haven *(G-5243)*
Bob Worden .... G 860 567-4722
  Lakeside *(G-3841)*
Bonati Brothers Welding & Fabr .... G 860 582-5000
  Plainville *(G-6777)*
C and B Welding LLC .... G 860 423-9047
  Lebanon *(G-3848)*
C V Tool Company Inc .... E 978 353-7901
  Southington *(G-7901)*
Carlos Welding and Fab LLC .... G 860 647-8592
  Manchester *(G-3991)*
Carlson Welding & Fabrication .... G 860 788-3569
  Moodus *(G-4772)*

Employee Codes: A=Over 500 employees, B=251-500
C=101-250, D=51-100, E=20-50, F=10-19, G=1-9

Carlucci Welding & Fabrication............G....... 203 588-0746
Norwalk *(G-6107)*
Carrano Railings....................................G....... 203 248-7245
Hamden *(G-3426)*
Cheshire Manufacturing Co Inc............G....... 203 272-3586
Cheshire *(G-1369)*
Chiappettas Welding..............................G....... 203 637-1522
Riverside *(G-7190)*
City Welding..G....... 860 951-4714
Hartford *(G-3568)*
Ckg Welding Fabrication LLC................G....... 860 628-7129
Southington *(G-7905)*
Crewelding..G....... 855 204-7352
Middletown *(G-4333)*
Ctr Welding..G....... 704 473-1587
Danbury *(G-1778)*
D and L Welding LLC..............................G....... 860 429-8259
Storrs Mansfield *(G-8554)*
Daigles Diversfd Wldg Svc LLC............G....... 860 265-3024
Somers *(G-7655)*
Danbury Welding LLC............................G....... 203 482-9306
Danbury *(G-1788)*
Dark Moon Metals LLC..........................G....... 203 858-3015
Norwalk *(G-6134)*
Davco Systems..G....... 860 546-9681
Canterbury *(G-1298)*
Doctor Weld LLC....................................G....... 203 877-3433
Milford *(G-4513)*
Durant Machine Inc................................G....... 860 536-7698
Mystic *(G-4813)*
Duros Welding Services........................G....... 203 982-6978
Waterbury *(G-9468)*
Dyco Industries Inc................................E....... 860 289-4957
South Windsor *(G-7741)*
East Windsor Metal Fabg Inc................F....... 860 528-7107
South Windsor *(G-7745)*
Erection & Welding Contrs LLC............G....... 860 828-9353
Berlin *(G-178)*
Eric Nordlund Welding............................G....... 203 544-8293
Wilton *(G-10292)*
EZ Welding LLC......................................G....... 860 707-3099
New Britain *(G-4987)*
EZ Welding LLC......................................G....... 860 707-3100
New Britain *(G-4988)*
F & W Rentals Inc....................................F....... 203 795-0591
Orange *(G-6600)*
Fabtron Incorporated..............................G....... 860 410-1801
Plainville *(G-6808)*
Farrell Prcsion Mtalcraft Corp................E....... 860 355-2651
New Milford *(G-5532)*
Fonda Fabricating & Welding Co............G....... 860 793-0601
Plainville *(G-6812)*
Fowlers Steel & Welding........................G....... 860 647-7641
Manchester *(G-4019)*
Frank Porto..G....... 203 596-0811
Watertown *(G-9707)*
Frys Welding LLC....................................G....... 860 944-2547
Winsted *(G-10522)*
Gabbro Forge and Welding LLC..............G....... 617 699-0031
Hamden *(G-3450)*
Gaida Welding Co & Mar Repr................G....... 203 924-4868
Shelton *(G-7448)*
Gardner Welding LLC..............................G....... 203 265-1036
Wallingford *(G-9274)*
Gavin Welding LLC..................................G....... 203 393-9707
Bethany *(G-243)*
General Welding Company Inc................G....... 203 753-6988
Waterbury *(G-9487)*
General Wldg & Fabrication Inc..............F....... 860 274-9668
Watertown *(G-9708)*
Gintys Welding Service Inc......................G....... 203 270-3399
Sandy Hook *(G-7314)*
Goodyfab Llc..G....... 203 927-3059
North Branford *(G-5839)*
Guy Montanari..G....... 203 791-0642
Danbury *(G-1840)*
H G Steinmetz Machine Works................F....... 203 794-1880
Bethel *(G-307)*
Harry Thommen Company........................G....... 203 333-3637
Bridgeport *(G-782)*
Hs Welding LLC..G....... 860 599-0372
Pawcatuck *(G-6716)*
Hutch Welding Company..........................G....... 860 496-9082
Torrington *(G-8933)*
Independent Welding & Fabg..................G....... 860 605-4712
New Hartford *(G-5196)*
Innovative Fusion Inc................................E....... 203 729-3873
Naugatuck *(G-4891)*
Ironman Welding L L C............................G....... 203 979-4063
Stamford *(G-8259)*
Ives Welding Service................................G....... 860 423-6139
South Windham *(G-7688)*
J T Fantozzi Co Inc..................................G....... 203 238-7018
Meriden *(G-4177)*
Jacquier Welding......................................G....... 860 824-4182
Canaan *(G-1287)*
Jakes Repair LLC......................................G....... 203 627-8603
Old Saybrook *(G-6547)*
James A Blazys..G....... 860 274-3857
Watertown *(G-9713)*
Jeff Manufacturing Co Inc........................F....... 860 482-8845
Torrington *(G-8937)*
Jim Murray Wldg & Fabrication..............G....... 860 889-7777
North Stonington *(G-6028)*
Jims Welding Service LLC........................G....... 203 744-2982
Danbury *(G-1862)*
Jnt Welding Services LLC........................G....... 860 350-3957
New Milford *(G-5551)*
Joe & Son Wldg Fabrication LLC............G....... 203 380-2072
Stratford *(G-8637)*
Joining Technologies Inc..........................D....... 860 653-0111
East Granby *(G-2209)*
Joseph Rembock..G....... 860 738-3981
Pleasant Valley *(G-6923)*
K & L Welding LLC..................................G....... 860 970-2390
Hartford *(G-3622)*
K J Welding..G....... 860 345-8743
Haddam *(G-3406)*
K L & P Welding..G....... 860 986-2518
East Windsor *(G-2502)*
K T I Turbo-Tech Inc................................F....... 860 623-2511
East Windsor *(G-2503)*
Kell-Strom Tool Intl Inc............................E....... 860 529-6851
Wethersfield *(G-10207)*
Ken Hastedt..G....... 203 268-6563
Monroe *(G-4725)*
Kensington Welding & Trlr Co................G....... 860 828-3564
Kensington *(G-3811)*
Kin-Therm Inc..F....... 860 623-2511
East Windsor *(G-2504)*
Kordys Welding Inc....................................G....... 860 621-2271
Southington *(G-7946)*
Kostas Cstm Ir Fbrications LLC..............G....... 203 667-0881
Stamford *(G-8278)*
KTI Bi-Metallix Inc....................................F....... 860 623-2511
East Windsor *(G-2506)*
KTI Inc..F....... 860 623-2511
East Windsor *(G-2507)*
L M Gill Welding and Mfr LLC..................E....... 860 647-9931
Manchester *(G-4047)*
Labco Welding Inc......................................G....... 860 632-2625
Middletown *(G-4367)*
Lemac Iron Works Inc................................G....... 860 232-7380
West Hartford *(G-9829)*
LM Gill Welding & Mfg LLC......................E....... 860 647-9931
Manchester *(G-4049)*
Lostocco Refuse Service LLC....................E....... 203 748-9296
Danbury *(G-1877)*
Louie S Welding..G....... 203 634-0873
Meriden *(G-4189)*
Lynn Welding Co Inc..................................F....... 860 667-4400
Newington *(G-5672)*
M D Welding & Fabricating LLC................G....... 860 643-2448
Bolton *(G-515)*
M L Guerrera Welding................................G....... 203 879-6823
Wolcott *(G-10572)*
Mackenzie Mch & Mar Works Inc..............G....... 203 777-3479
East Haven *(G-2441)*
Mainville Welding Co Inc............................G....... 203 237-3103
Meriden *(G-4191)*
Marc Bouley..G....... 860 450-1713
Willimantic *(G-10233)*
Marks Construction Co LLC......................G....... 860 407-2391
Portland *(G-6965)*
Matias Importing & Distrg Corp................G....... 860 666-5544
Newington *(G-5675)*
Metal Industries Inc....................................G....... 860 296-6228
Hartford *(G-3640)*
Metals Edge Welding LLC..........................G....... 203 500-5644
Shelton *(G-7498)*
Mikes Welding..G....... 203 855-9631
Norwalk *(G-6258)*
Mobile Welding Repair................................G....... 203 459-2744
Monroe *(G-4739)*
Modified Welding LLC................................G....... 860 428-3599
North Grosvenordale *(G-5891)*
Msr Welding Service..................................G....... 860 234-9949
Brooklyn *(G-1250)*
Murphy & Sons Welding & Repair............G....... 203 635-3372
Stamford *(G-8316)*
National Welding LLC................................G....... 860 818-1240
Middletown *(G-4383)*
Nct Inc..F....... 860 666-8424
Newington *(G-5684)*
New Canaan Forge LLC..............................G....... 203 966-3858
New Canaan *(G-5123)*
New England Welding Svcs LLC................G....... 860 406-4030
Plantsville *(G-6905)*
New Milford Foundry & Mch Co................G....... 860 354-5561
New Milford *(G-5571)*
Nutmeg Welding Company Inc..................G....... 203 756-7458
Waterbury *(G-9564)*
On-Site Welding LLC..................................G....... 860 662-6332
Collinsville *(G-1598)*
Optimum Welding Solutions LLC..............G....... 203 598-8489
Prospect *(G-7012)*
P & M Welding Co LLC..............................G....... 860 528-2077
South Windsor *(G-7803)*
Palladino Welding......................................G....... 203 729-7542
Naugatuck *(G-4908)*
Paul Welding Company Inc........................F....... 860 229-9945
Newington *(G-5693)*
Pelchs Welding & Repair............................G....... 860 693-6328
Collinsville *(G-1599)*
Perez Welding Services LLC......................G....... 203 876-1066
Milford *(G-4607)*
Phils Welding..G....... 860 685-1713
Higganum *(G-3775)*
Phoenix Machine Inc..................................G....... 203 888-1135
Seymour *(G-7360)*
Phoenix Welding..G....... 860 657-9481
Glastonbury *(G-3070)*
Polish Welding LLC....................................G....... 860 347-0368
Middletown *(G-4394)*
Pop Moody Welding Services....................G....... 860 749-9537
Somers *(G-7668)*
Precision Welding..G....... 860 423-7772
Mansfield Center *(G-4115)*
Precision Welding Services LLC................G....... 860 268-0580
Coventry *(G-1668)*
Quality Welding LLC..................................G....... 860 585-1121
Bristol *(G-1100)*
Quality Welding Service LLC......................G....... 860 342-7202
Portland *(G-6970)*
R & F Welding Co..G....... 203 393-2851
New Haven *(G-5374)*
R Lange Welding-Fabrication....................G....... 203 994-5516
Brookfield *(G-1217)*
Rapid Truck Service Inc..............................G....... 860 482-5500
Torrington *(G-8963)*
Recor Welding Center Inc..........................G....... 860 573-1942
Southington *(G-7965)*
Reliable Welding & Speed LLC..................G....... 860 749-3977
Enfield *(G-2687)*
Reliant Services LLC..................................G....... 860 346-6107
Middletown *(G-4404)*
Reno Machine Company Inc......................D....... 860 666-5641
Newington *(G-5700)*
Reyes Welding Svcs....................................G....... 203 505-1111
Norwalk *(G-6323)*
Robert Schwartz..G....... 203 515-8162
Gaylordsville *(G-2996)*
Rodney Tulba Welding & Fabg....................G....... 860 442-9840
Waterford *(G-9667)*
Ronald R Eschner..G....... 860 485-9373
Harwinton *(G-3738)*
Rossitto Welding Inc....................................G....... 860 223-1598
New Britain *(G-5049)*
Rozelle Specialty Processes......................G....... 860 793-9400
Plainville *(G-6859)*
S S Fabrications Inc....................................G....... 860 974-1910
Eastford *(G-2541)*
Safin Wldg & Fabrication LLC....................G....... 860 974-3831
Eastford *(G-2542)*
Sandy Hook Welding & Fabg......................G....... 203 731-9844
Sandy Hook *(G-7329)*
Saucier Welding Services............................G....... 860 747-4577
Southington *(G-7970)*
Sauciers Misc Metal Works LLC..................G....... 860 747-4577
Southington *(G-7971)*
Serena Granbery Welding............................G....... 860 435-2322
Salisbury *(G-7298)*
Shm Welding and Repair LLC......................G....... 860 267-4012
East Hampton *(G-2279)*
Shoreline Boiler & Welding LLC..................G....... 860 575-0944
Westbrook *(G-10008)*
Singers Welding Works................................G....... 203 743-9353
Danbury *(G-1953)*
Solutions With Innovation LLC....................G....... 203 729-3873
Naugatuck *(G-4919)*

PRODUCT SECTION — WIRE & WIRE PRDTS

Somers Manufacturing Inc ....G...... 860 314-1075
  Bristol *(G-1119)*
Sonic Welding Co ....G...... 203 348-8021
  Stamford *(G-8429)*
Sorge Industries Inc ....G...... 203 924-8900
  Shelton *(G-7557)*
Spiers Welding Service ....G...... 203 322-1004
  Stamford *(G-8434)*
Spot Welders Inc ....G...... 203 386-8938
  Stratford *(G-8684)*
Standard Welding Company Inc ....G...... 860 528-9628
  East Hartford *(G-2377)*
State Welding & Fabg Inc ....G...... 203 294-4071
  Wallingford *(G-9376)*
State Wide Welding Service ....G...... 860 489-2465
  New Hartford *(G-5213)*
Sterzingers Welding LLC ....G...... 203 685-1575
  Danbury *(G-1956)*
Steven Sabo ....G...... 860 642-6031
  Lebanon *(G-3863)*
Sunnyside Fab & Welding Inc ....G...... 203 378-9515
  Bridgeport *(G-916)*
Superb Steel LLC ....G...... 860 518-7281
  New Britain *(G-5068)*
Superior Welding ....G...... 860 584-2632
  Terryville *(G-8773)*
Swistro Welding ....G...... 860 978-3238
  New Britain *(G-5070)*
Sylvia Engineering Wldg & Eqp ....G...... 860 859-1791
  Norwich *(G-6434)*
Teck Welding & Fabrication LLC ....G...... 203 584-1264
  Bristol *(G-1126)*
Ted Boccuzzi ....G...... 860 354-3799
  New Milford *(G-5593)*
Thomas La Ganga ....G...... 860 489-0920
  Torrington *(G-8977)*
Tim Welding ....G...... 203 488-3486
  North Branford *(G-5862)*
Tinsley GROup-Ps&w Inc ....D...... 919 742-5832
  Milford *(G-4665)*
Tito Welding LLC ....G...... 860 354-1536
  New Milford *(G-5598)*
Torrington Diesel Corporation ....G...... 860 496-9948
  Torrington *(G-8980)*
Total Fab LLC ....F....... 475 238-8176
  East Haven *(G-2457)*
Trap Rock Ridge Welding LLC ....G...... 203 213-7578
  Meriden *(G-4257)*
Trico Welding Company LLC ....G...... 203 720-3782
  Beacon Falls *(G-149)*
Uneeda Welder ....G...... 203 929-4507
  Shelton *(G-7574)*
United Steel Inc ....C...... 860 289-2323
  East Hartford *(G-2389)*
Upscale Welding & Fabrica ....G...... 203 265-0800
  Wallingford *(G-9396)*
Valley Welding Co Inc ....G...... 860 283-5768
  Thomaston *(G-8817)*
Wally-B Welding ....G...... 203 264-3853
  Southbury *(G-7884)*
Watchdog Welding LLC ....G...... 860 355-9549
  Bridgewater *(G-948)*
Weld TEC LLC ....G...... 860 628-5750
  Plantsville *(G-6918)*
Weld-All Inc ....F....... 860 621-3156
  Southington *(G-7995)*
Welder Repair & Rental Svc Inc ....G...... 203 238-9284
  Durham *(G-2161)*
Welding On Wheels Services LLC ......G...... 203 449-6273
  Stratford *(G-8706)*
Whatever Welding LLC ....G...... 860 779-7703
  Dayville *(G-2080)*
White Welding Company Inc ....G...... 203 753-1197
  Waterbury *(G-9633)*
William Clark Welding Inc ....G...... 860 537-0122
  Colchester *(G-1582)*
William Linkovich ....G...... 860 824-0298
  East Canaan *(G-2184)*
Willies Welding Inc ....G...... 203 237-6235
  Meriden *(G-4268)*
WS Welding LLC ....G...... 860 262-0214
  Portland *(G-6980)*
Yard Welding and Repair LLC ....G...... 860 402-4921
  Bristol *(G-1142)*

WELDING SPLYS, EXC GASES: Wholesalers

Airgas Usa LLC ....C...... 203 792-1834
  Danbury *(G-1733)*

WELDING TIPS: Heat Resistant, Metal

Bob Worden ....G...... 860 567-4722
  Lakeside *(G-3841)*
Performance Connection Systems ......G...... 203 868-5517
  Meriden *(G-4216)*
Sunnyside Fab & Welding Inc ....G...... 203 348-5040
  Stamford *(G-8451)*

WELDMENTS

Jacob David Poppel ....G...... 860 904-3749
  Burlington *(G-1271)*
Vitta Corporation ....E....... 203 790-8155
  Bethel *(G-364)*
Whitcraft LLC ....C...... 860 974-0786
  Eastford *(G-2544)*
Whitcraft Scrborough/Tempe LLC ....C...... 860 974-0786
  Eastford *(G-2545)*

WELL CURBING: Concrete

Stephanie Mark ....G...... 203 329-7562
  Stamford *(G-8441)*

WHEELCHAIRS

210 Innovation LLC ....G...... 860 444-1986
  Waterford *(G-9638)*
Enduro Wheelchair Company ....G...... 860 289-0374
  East Hartford *(G-2324)*
Kinetic Innvtive Sting Sys LLC ....G...... 203 488-1758
  Branford *(G-617)*
Motiv Technology Inc ....G...... 203 371-7011
  Fairfield *(G-2820)*
United Seating & Mobility LLC ....G...... 860 761-0700
  Rocky Hill *(G-7270)*

WHEELS

Everything 2 Wheels LLC ....G...... 860 225-2453
  New Britain *(G-4986)*
Wheels 45 ....G...... 203 762-8684
  Wilton *(G-10341)*

WHEELS: Abrasive

Avery Abrasives Inc ....E....... 203 372-3513
  Trumbull *(G-9001)*
Magcor Inc ....G...... 203 445-0302
  Monroe *(G-4731)*

WINCHES

Show Motion Inc ....E....... 203 866-1866
  Milford *(G-4643)*

WINDINGS: Coil, Electronic

Classic Coil Company Inc ....D...... 860 583-7600
  Bristol *(G-1001)*
Quality Coils Incorporated ....C...... 860 584-0927
  Bristol *(G-1099)*

WINDMILLS: Electric Power Generation

Gamma Ventures Inc ....G...... 860 653-2613
  Granby *(G-3107)*

WINDOW & DOOR FRAMES

Advanced Window Systems LLC ....F....... 800 841-6544
  Berlin *(G-150)*
Ckh Industries Inc ....D...... 860 563-2999
  Wethersfield *(G-10187)*
Lee Brown Co LLC ....F....... 860 379-4706
  Riverton *(G-7209)*

WINDOW BLIND REPAIR SVCS

Arrow Window Shade Mfg Co ....G...... 860 956-3570
  Wethersfield *(G-10180)*

WINDOW FRAMES & SASHES: Plastic

All-Time Manufacturing Co Inc ....F....... 860 848-9258
  Montville *(G-4768)*

WINDOWS: Frames, Wood

Winters Group ....G...... 860 749-3317
  Enfield *(G-2707)*

WINDOWS: Louver, Glass, Wood Framed

New Haven GL & Mirror Co LLC ....G...... 203 469-2440
  New Haven *(G-5344)*

WINDOWS: Wood

Schuco USA LIIp ....D...... 860 666-0505
  Newington *(G-5703)*

WINDSHIELD WIPER SYSTEMS

G W P Inc ....G...... 860 953-1153
  Hartford *(G-3595)*

WINE CELLARS, BONDED: Wine, Blended

Horse Ridge Cellars LLC ....G...... 860 763-5380
  Somers *(G-7661)*

WIRE

Accel Intl Holdings Inc ....E....... 203 237-2700
  Meriden *(G-4139)*
Atco Wire Rope and Indus Sup ....G...... 203 239-1632
  North Haven *(G-5911)*
Lee Spring Company LLC ....E....... 860 584-0991
  Bristol *(G-1062)*
Siri Manufacturing Company ....E....... 860 236-5901
  Danielson *(G-2002)*
UNI Machine & Mfg LLC ....G...... 860 485-0643
  Harwinton *(G-3742)*
Wiretek Inc ....F....... 860 242-9473
  Bloomfield *(G-501)*

WIRE & CABLE: Aluminum

Omerin Usa Inc ....E....... 475 343-3450
  Meriden *(G-4212)*

WIRE & CABLE: Nonferrous, Aircraft

American Imex Corporation ....G...... 203 261-5200
  Monroe *(G-4693)*

WIRE & CABLE: Nonferrous, Automotive, Exc Ignition Sets

Autac Incorporated ....G...... 203 481-3444
  Branford *(G-550)*

WIRE & CABLE: Nonferrous, Building

Hamden Metal Service Company ....F....... 203 281-1522
  Hamden *(G-3457)*

WIRE & WIRE PRDTS

Acme Monaco Corporation ....C...... 860 224-1349
  New Britain *(G-4934)*
Acme Wire Products Co Inc ....E....... 860 572-0511
  Mystic *(G-4796)*
Apco Products ....E....... 860 767-2108
  Centerbrook *(G-1329)*
Arrow Manufacturing Company ....E....... 860 589-3900
  Bristol *(G-966)*
Bes Cu Inc ....G...... 860 582-8660
  Bristol *(G-981)*
Bridgeport Insulated Wire Co ....E....... 203 333-3191
  Bridgeport *(G-721)*
Bridgeport Insulated Wire Co ....E....... 203 375-9579
  Stratford *(G-8589)*
C R Springs Inc ....G...... 203 879-3357
  Wolcott *(G-10552)*
East Shre Wre Rpe/Rggng Spply ....F....... 203 469-5204
  North Haven *(G-5934)*
ERA Wire Inc ....F....... 203 933-0480
  West Haven *(G-9906)*
General Cable Industries Inc ....C...... 860 456-8000
  Willimantic *(G-10227)*
Habasit America Inc ....D...... 860 632-2211
  Middletown *(G-4350)*
Hessel Industries Inc ....G...... 203 736-2317
  Derby *(G-2115)*
International Pipe & Stl Corp ....F....... 203 481-7102
  North Branford *(G-5846)*
John P Smith Co ....G...... 203 488-7226
  Branford *(G-613)*
Knox Enterprises Inc ....G...... 203 226-6408
  Westport *(G-10108)*
Loos and Co Inc ....G...... 304 445-7820
  Pomfret *(G-6935)*
Meyer Wire & Cable Company LLC ....E....... 203 281-0817
  Hamden *(G-3482)*

Employee Codes: A=Over 500 employees, B=251-500
C=101-250, D=51-100, E=20-50, F=10-19, G=1-9

WIRE & WIRE PRDTS

Netsource Inc .... G 860 282-8994
  South Windsor (G-7795)
Netsource Inc .... D 860 649-6000
  Manchester (G-4059)
Novo Precision LLC .... E 860 583-0517
  Bristol (G-1081)
Performance Fabrication .... G 860 678-8070
  Farmington (G-2948)
Radcliff Wire Inc .... E 312 876-1754
  Bristol (G-1103)
Rowley Spring & Stamping Corp .... C 860 582-8175
  Bristol (G-1113)
Tiger Enterprises Inc .... E 860 621-9155
  Plantsville (G-6914)
U-Tech Wire Rope & Supply LLC .... G 203 865-8885
  North Haven (G-6004)
Ultimate Wireforms Inc .... D 860 582-9111
  Bristol (G-1134)
Wire Design Originals .... G 203 795-3783
  Orange (G-6634)
Wire Solutions LLC .... G 860 836-0787
  Plainville (G-6878)
Wiremold Company .... A 860 233-6251
  West Hartford (G-9874)

WIRE FABRIC: Welded Steel

Tool Logistics II .... F 203 855-9754
  Norwalk (G-6373)

WIRE MATERIALS: Copper

Specialty Wire & Cord Sets .... F 203 498-2932
  Hamden (G-3512)

WIRE MATERIALS: Steel

Ametek Inc .... C 203 265-6731
  Wallingford (G-9203)
Bridgeport Insulated Wire Co .... E 203 333-3191
  Bridgeport (G-721)
City Data Cable Co .... G 203 327-7917
  Stamford (G-8149)
International Pipe & Stl Corp .... F 203 481-7102
  North Branford (G-5846)
Polstal Corporation .... G 203 849-7788
  Wilton (G-10320)
Sandvik Wire and Htg Tech Corp .... D 203 744-1440
  Bethel (G-337)
Shuster-Mettler Corp .... E 203 562-3178
  Plainville (G-6861)
Ulbrich Solar Technologies Inc .... G 203 239-4481
  North Haven (G-6006)
Wiremold Company .... A 860 233-6251
  West Hartford (G-9874)

WIRE PRDTS: Ferrous Or Iron, Made In Wiredrawing Plants

Housatonic Wire Co .... F 203 888-9670
  Seymour (G-7350)
Nutmeg Wire .... F 860 822-8616
  Baltic (G-121)

WIRE PRDTS: Steel & Iron

Microdyne Technologies .... G 860 747-9473
  Plainville (G-6844)
Sandvik Wire and Htg Tech Corp .... D 203 744-1440
  Bethel (G-337)

WIRE WINDING OF PURCHASED WIRE

Protopac Inc .... G 860 274-6796
  Watertown (G-9727)

WIRE: Communication

DNE Systems Inc .... G 203 265-7151
  Wallingford (G-9251)
General Cable Industries Inc .... G 860 456-8000
  Willimantic (G-10227)
Ortronics Inc .... D 860 445-3900
  New London (G-5482)
Ortronics Inc .... G 877 295-3472
  West Hartford (G-9841)

WIRE: Magnet

American Wire Corporation .... F 203 426-3133
  Newtown (G-5727)
Bridgeport Magnetics Group Inc .... E 203 954-0050
  Shelton (G-7410)

Luvata Waterbury Inc .... D 203 753-5215
  Waterbury (G-9519)

WIRE: Mesh

Nucor Steel Connecticut Inc .... C 203 265-0615
  Wallingford (G-9330)

WIRE: Nonferrous

Algonquin Industries Inc .... D 203 453-4348
  Guilford (G-3324)
Alpha-Core Inc .... E 203 954-0050
  Shelton (G-7392)
Altek Electronics Inc .... C 860 482-7626
  Torrington (G-8892)
American Alloy Wire Corp .... G 203 426-3133
  Newtown (G-5726)
Bridgeport Insulated Wire Co .... E 203 333-3191
  Bridgeport (G-721)
Bridgeport Insulated Wire Co .... E 203 375-9579
  Stratford (G-8589)
Cable Technology Inc .... C 860 429-7889
  Willington (G-10246)
Fiberoptics Technology Inc .... C 860 928-0443
  Pomfret (G-6931)
Insulated Wire Inc .... F 203 791-1999
  Bethel (G-311)
Loos & Co Inc .... B 860 928-7981
  Pomfret (G-6933)
Marmon Utility LLC .... E 203 881-5358
  Seymour (G-7354)
Multi-Cable Corp .... F 860 589-9035
  Bristol (G-1076)
Norfield Data Products Inc .... F 203 849-0292
  Norwalk (G-6280)
Ofs Companies .... G 860 678-6574
  Bristol (G-1082)
Ofs Fitel LLC .... B 860 678-0371
  Avon (G-96)
Platt Brothers & Company .... D 203 753-4194
  Waterbury (G-9580)
Radcliff Wire Inc .... E 312 876-1754
  Bristol (G-1103)
REA Magnet Wire Company Inc .... D 203 738-6100
  Guilford (G-3386)
Rscc Wire & Cable LLC .... B 860 653-8300
  East Granby (G-2228)
Sandvik Wire and Htg Tech Corp .... D 203 744-1440
  Bethel (G-337)
Sandvik Wire and Htg Tech Corp .... D 203 744-1440
  Bethel (G-338)
Siemon Company .... A 860 945-4200
  Watertown (G-9734)
Specialty Cable Corp .... D 203 265-7126
  Wallingford (G-9372)
Times Microwave Systems Inc .... B 203 949-8400
  Wallingford (G-9386)
Wiretek Inc .... F 860 242-9473
  Bloomfield (G-501)

WIRE: Steel, Insulated Or Armored

Marmon Utility LLC .... E 203 881-5358
  Seymour (G-7354)
S A Candelora Enterprises .... F 203 484-2863
  North Branford (G-5854)

WIRE: Wire, Ferrous Or Iron

Hamden Metal Service Company .... F 203 281-1522
  Hamden (G-3457)
Loos & Co Inc .... F 860 928-6681
  Pomfret (G-6934)
Loos & Co Inc .... B 860 928-7981
  Pomfret (G-6933)
Radcliff Wire Inc .... E 312 876-1754
  Bristol (G-1103)

WIRING DEVICES WHOLESALERS

Ripley Tools LLC .... E 860 635-2200
  Cromwell (G-1715)

WOMEN'S & CHILDREN'S CLOTHING WHOLESALERS, NEC

Flemming LLC .... G 818 746-6495
  Bloomfield (G-411)
Mandee .... G 860 644-2128
  Manchester (G-4054)
My Fair Lady .... G 860 322-4542
  Deep River (G-2095)

PRODUCT SECTION

WOMEN'S & GIRLS' SPORTSWEAR WHOLESALERS

Del Arbour LLC .... F 203 882-8501
  Milford (G-4506)
Gg Sportswear Inc .... E 860 296-4441
  Hartford (G-3599)
Michael Violano .... G 203 934-3368
  West Haven (G-9937)

WOMEN'S CLOTHING STORES

April Rose Designs .... G 203 453-1797
  Guilford (G-3326)
Mandee .... G 860 644-2128
  Manchester (G-4054)

WOMEN'S CLOTHING STORES: Ready-To-Wear

Mangladesh LLC .... G 203 299-0697
  Fairfield (G-2812)

WOMEN'S KNITWEAR STORES

Kielo America Inc .... G 203 431-3999
  Ridgefield (G-7153)

WOOD CHIPS, PRODUCED AT THE MILL

Biomass Energy LLC .... E 540 872-3300
  Weatogue (G-9755)
Ensign-Bickford Renewable Ener .... E 860 843-2000
  Simsbury (G-7623)

WOOD EXTRACT PRDTS

Sychron Inc .... G 860 953-8157
  Newington (G-5708)

WOOD PRDTS

111 Brentwood LLC .... G 203 284-5065
  Wallingford (G-9192)
170 Mountainwood Road LLC .... G 203 252-4284
  Stamford (G-8048)
227 Greenwood LLC .... G 203 798-9716
  Bethel (G-254)
26 Beechwood Avenue LLC .... G 203 713-6425
  Milford (G-4435)
29 Wychwood Road LLC .... G 860 434-8078
  Old Lyme (G-6486)
6 Brookwood Drive LLC .... G 860 945-3456
  Watertown (G-9678)
Candlewood Boat Restoration .... G 203 223-7893
  New Fairfield (G-5165)
Creative Woodworking LLC .... G 203 518-0336
  Waterbury (G-9456)
DAngelo Woodcraft LLC .... G 860 402-7175
  Enfield (G-2635)
Devellis Woodworks LLC .... G 203 610-4762
  Kensington (G-3809)
Eastwoods Arms LLC .... G 203 615-3476
  Guilford (G-3350)
Edgewood Prospect LLC .... G 860 255-7799
  Unionville (G-9114)
Greenwood Sub LLC .... G 860 291-8833
  East Hartford (G-2332)
Jdm-Greenwood LLC .... G 203 358-4816
  Stamford (G-8262)
LLC Wolff Woods .... G 860 415-9089
  Mystic (G-4826)
Luther Fence Inc .... G 860 445-5660
  Groton (G-3298)
N A B Fine Woodworking LLC .... G 203 667-3922
  Stamford (G-8317)
Nantz Woodcraft .... G 860 267-8853
  Colchester (G-1558)
Northeast Wood Sales .... G 860 621-9613
  Marion (G-4117)
Renaissance Craftsmen LLC .... G 860 916-3583
  Hartford (G-3677)
Sherwood Equine LLC .... G 860 653-3599
  Granby (G-3113)
Vitale Woodworks LLC .... G 203 387-3565
  Orange (G-6633)

WOOD PRDTS: Applicators

Wood-N-Tap .... G 203 265-9663
  Wallingford (G-9404)

WOOD PRDTS: Barrels & Barrel Parts

Bonito Manufacturing Inc..................D....... 203 234-8786
  North Haven (G-5915)

WOOD PRDTS: Baskets, Fruit & Veg, Round Stave, Till, Etc

Indulge By Mersene LLC.................G....... 203 644-6172
  Westport (G-10098)

WOOD PRDTS: Beekeeping Splys

North Forty Pest Ctrl Co LLC................G....... 203 263-4551
  Woodbury (G-10648)

WOOD PRDTS: Engraved

Saint Josephs Wood Pdts LLC..............G....... 203 787-5746
  New Haven (G-5385)

WOOD PRDTS: Moldings, Unfinished & Prefinished

Conway Hardwood Products LLC........E....... 860 355-4030
  Gaylordsville (G-2991)
Pagoda Timber Frames ....G....... 860 526-3077
  Chester (G-1477)

WOOD PRDTS: Mulch Or Sawdust

Mulch Ferris Products LLC ....G....... 203 790-1155
  Danbury (G-1889)
Sweet Peet North America Inc ....G....... 860 361-6444
  Litchfield (G-3901)

WOOD PRDTS: Mulch, Wood & Bark

D R Charles Envmtl Cnstr LLC ....G....... 203 445-0412
  Monroe (G-4709)
Freezer Hill Mulch Company LLC.........G....... 203 758-3725
  Bethany (G-242)

WOOD PRDTS: Novelties, Fiber

Essex Wood Products Inc ....E....... 860 537-3451
  Colchester (G-1550)
Purvins Woodcraft ....G....... 860 456-1933
  Lebanon (G-3860)

WOOD PRDTS: Outdoor, Structural

Connecticut Outdoor Wood Frncs ....G....... 203 263-0625
  Woodbury (G-10630)

WOOD PRDTS: Panel Work

Dante Ltd ....G....... 860 376-0204
  Jewett City (G-3793)
Rogers Woodsiding.............................G....... 203 879-9747
  Wolcott (G-10584)

WOOD PRDTS: Plugs

W R Hartigan & Son Inc ....G....... 860 673-9203
  Burlington (G-1278)

WOOD PRDTS: Rulers & Rules

Acme United Corporation ....C....... 203 254-6060
  Fairfield (G-2743)

WOOD PRDTS: Saddle Trees

E & F Wood LLC..................................G....... 860 377-0601
  Woodstock Valley (G-10692)

WOOD PRDTS: Signboards

Connecticut Sign Service LLC..............G....... 860 767-7446
  Essex (G-2714)

WOOD PRDTS: Stepladders

Regional Stairs LLC............................G....... 860 290-1242
  East Hartford (G-2363)

WOOD PRDTS: Trim

Yoguez Woodworking LLC...................G....... 203 943-6950
  Bridgeport (G-944)

WOOD PRDTS: Trophy Bases

Diy Awards LLC...................................G....... 800 810-1216
  Stamford (G-8187)
Nohha Inc ....G....... 203 687-6741
  Orange (G-6616)

WOOD PRODUCTS: Reconstituted

Harris Wood Products Inc....................G....... 860 649-7936
  Manchester (G-4026)
Mohegan Wood Pellets LLC.................G....... 860 862-6100
  Uncasville (G-9099)

WOOD SHAVINGS BALES, MULCH TYPE, WHOLESALE

Good Earth Tree Care Inc....................G....... 203 375-7962
  Stratford (G-8619)

WOOD TREATING: Millwork

Amerifix LLC.......................................G....... 203 931-7290
  West Haven (G-9883)

WOOD TREATING: Wood Prdts, Creosoted

Bridgwell Rsources Holdings LLC ....G....... 203 622-9138
  Greenwich (G-3137)

WOODWORK & TRIM: Exterior & Ornamental

Gilbert G Fitch ....G....... 860 824-5832
  Lakeville (G-3843)

WOODWORK & TRIM: Interior & Ornamental

Phoenix Woodworking ....G....... 203 512-3521
  New Fairfield (G-5173)
Precision Woodcraft Inc......................G....... 860 693-3641
  Canton (G-1325)

WOODWORK: Carved & Turned

Dundorf Designs USA Inc ....G....... 860 859-2955
  Salem (G-7288)
Fagan Design & Fabrication ....G....... 203 937-1874
  West Haven (G-9907)
Jim Kephart Woodturning ....G....... 860 643-9431
  Manchester (G-4038)
Juan Gallegos ....G....... 203 744-0575
  Danbury (G-1866)

WOODWORK: Interior & Ornamental, NEC

77 Mattatuck Heights LLC ....E....... 203 597-9338
  Waterbury (G-9420)
Di Venere Co.......................................G....... 860 582-0208
  Bristol (G-1016)
Ferraro Custom Woodwork LLC...........G....... 203 876-1280
  Milford (G-4536)
Gothers & Martin Wdwkg LLC ....G....... 860 982-4193
  Wethersfield (G-10194)
James H Quinn ....G....... 203 809-6046
  Wallingford (G-9293)
James J Licari ....G....... 203 333-5000
  Bridgeport (G-800)
Maddog LLC..G....... 203 878-0147
  Milford (G-4572)
Madigan Millwork Inc..........................G....... 860 673-7601
  Unionville (G-9119)
Maurer & Shepherd Joyners ....F....... 860 633-2383
  Glastonbury (G-3057)
Peter Arch Woodworking LLC ....G....... 203 374-9977
  Fairfield (G-2827)
Winchester Woodworking LLC.............G....... 860 485-0742
  Harwinton (G-3743)

WOODWORK: Ornamental, Cornices, Mantels, Etc.

Fagan Design & Fabrication ....G....... 203 937-1874
  West Haven (G-9907)
Industrial Wood Product Co ....G....... 203 735-2374
  Shelton (G-7475)

WORD PROCESSING SVCS

Commercial Service............................G....... 203 755-0166
  Waterbury (G-9454)

WOVEN WIRE PRDTS, NEC

Amtec Corporation ....E....... 860 230-0006
  Plainfield (G-6737)
C O Jelliff Corporation........................D....... 203 259-1615
  Southport (G-8001)
Gemco Manufacturing Co Inc ....E....... 860 628-5529
  Southington (G-7926)

WREATHS: Artificial

Heatherwreath Partners LP.................G....... 203 662-1084
  Darien (G-2028)
RR Design ....G....... 203 792-3419
  Bethel (G-336)
Sidel & McElwreath LLC ....G....... 203 834-2946
  Wilton (G-10331)

WRENCHES

Brimatco Corporation ....G....... 203 272-0044
  Cheshire (G-1364)
H&H Tool LLC.....................................G....... 203 879-4519
  Waterbury (G-9493)
Power-Dyne LLC................................E....... 860 346-9283
  Middletown (G-4395)
Skillcraft Machine Tool Co ....F....... 860 953-1246
  South Windsor (G-7822)

WRITING FOR PUBLICATION SVCS

Gleason Group Incorporated ....G....... 203 312-0683
  New Fairfield (G-5168)
Kathleen Parker OBeirne ....G....... 860 536-7179
  Mystic (G-4824)

X-RAY EQPT & TUBES

5w LLC ....G....... 860 751-9209
  Farmington (G-2874)
Associated X-Ray Corp ....F....... 203 466-2446
  East Haven (G-2412)
Bidwell Industrial Group Inc ....E....... 860 346-9283
  Middletown (G-4325)
Biowave Innovations LLC ....C....... 203 982-8157
  Wilton (G-10273)
Comet Technologies USA Inc ....E....... 203 447-3200
  Shelton (G-7421)
Hologic Inc..C....... 203 790-1188
  Danbury (G-1845)
Kub Technologies Inc ....E....... 203 364-8544
  Stratford (G-8643)
Parker Medical Inc ....G....... 860 350-3446
  New Milford (G-5579)
Precision X-Ray Inc ....F....... 203 484-2011
  North Branford (G-5852)
Remote Technologies Inc ....G....... 203 661-2798
  Greenwich (G-3225)
Topex Inc ....F....... 203 748-5918
  Danbury (G-1963)

YARN MILLS: Texturizing, Throwing & Twisting

Altenergy LLC....................................G....... 203 299-1400
  Norwalk (G-6066)

YARN, ORGANIC SYNTHETIC

Scapa North America Inc ....G....... 860 688-8000
  Windsor (G-10433)

YARN: Specialty & Novelty

Heidi M Greene Inc.............................G....... 203 938-4132
  Redding (G-7094)

YARN: Weaving, Spun

Buffalo Industrial Fabrics Inc ....G....... 203 553-9400
  Wilton (G-10278)